WILDHAGEN
ENGLISH–GERMAN
GERMAN–ENGLISH
DICTIONARY

ENGLISCH-DEUTSCHES DEUTSCH-ENGLISCHES WÖRTERBUCH

IN ZWEI BÄNDEN

*

Enzyklopädische streng wissenschaftliche Darstellung des Wortschatzes der Neuzeit und der Gegenwart, mit besonderer Berücksichtigung der Syntax, des Stils und idiomatischen Brauches

von

DR. KARL WILDHAGEN

weiland ord. Professor der Englischen Philologie an der Universität Kiel

neu bearbeitet und erweitert
von

DR. WILL HÉRAUCOURT

vormals ord. Professor der Englischen Philologie an der Universität Königsberg (Pr)

*

BAND II

Deutsch-Englisch

Zweite, vollkommen überarbeitete und erweiterte Auflage

1972

BRANDSTETTER VERLAG · WIESBADEN

GEORGE ALLEN & UNWIN LTD · LONDON

ENGLISH-GERMAN
GERMAN-ENGLISH
DICTIONARY

IN TWO VOLUMES

*

An encyclopaedic and strictly scientific representation of the vocabulary of the modern and present-day languages, with special regard to syntax, style, and idiomatic usage

by

DR. KARL WILDHAGEN

late Professor of English Philology in the University of Kiel

revised and enlarged by

DR. WILL HÉRAUCOURT

formerly Professor of English Philology in the University of Königsberg (Pr)

*

VOLUME II

German-English

Second edition completely revised and enlarged

1972

BRANDSTETTER VERLAG · WIESBADEN

GEORGE ALLEN & UNWIN LTD · LONDON

In diesem Wörterbuch werden, wie in allgemeinen Nachschlagwerken üblich, etwa bestehende Patente, Gebrauchsmuster oder Warenzeichen nicht erwähnt. Wenn ein solcher Hinweis fehlt, heißt das also nicht, daß eine Ware oder ein Warennamen frei ist.

In this dictionary as in general reference works existing patents, registered patterns, trade marks etc. are not mentioned. If such a reference is absent, it does not mean that a commodity or tradename is "free".

2. vollkommen überarbeitete und erheblich erweiterte Auflage 1972

Gesamtherstellung: Oscar Brandstetter Druckerei KG, Wiesbaden

Library of Congress Catalogue Card Number Af 28088

ISBN 3-87097-047-2

Printed in Germany

Der Völkerverständigung
gewidmet

To the growth of international
understanding

Inhaltsverzeichnis

Table of Contents

Vorwort

Professor Dr. Karl Wildhagen wurde am 7. August 1945, nach einem langen erfolgreichen der Forschung und Lehre gewidmeten Leben, mitten aus der Arbeit an dem II. Bande des vorliegenden Werkes durch einen plötzlichen Tod dahingerafft. *Sein Andenken lebt in der Erinnerung jedes Anglisten.*

Als die *Tauchnitz-Edition* einige Zeit darauf mit der Bitte an mich herantrat, das Wildhagensche Werk zu vollenden, war ich mir der Größe dieser *verpflichtenden Aufgabe* aber auch ihrer Dankbarkeit bewußt, denn der I. Band galt und gilt dank seiner wissenschaftlichen Gründlichkeit bei uns wie im Auslande als ein Standardwerk auf seinem Gebiete.

Die *Straffung der Form* (des Wildhagenschen Manuskripts, das bis zum Worte Installation vorlag,) gab die Möglichkeit der *Ausführlichkeit im Inhalt.* Es wurde Wert darauf gelegt, den Wortschatz und Sprachgebrauch des *modernen und modernsten Deutsch* (19. und 20. Jahrhundert) in der ganzen Mannigfaltigkeit seiner sozialen und individuellen Struktur darzustellen: den Standard (als Grundlage), die gehobene Sprache, die gebildete Umgangssprache, die familiäre Sprache, die literarische und dichterische Sprache, die Amts- und Zeitungssprache, die Mundarten, das Burschikose und Vulgäre, die Gauner- und Teenagersprache.

Auf eine eingehende Behandlung des Wortschatzes der früheren Jahrhunderte und auf ausführlichere etymologische Angaben bei den einzelnen Stichwörtern ist mit Absicht verzichtet worden, um Raum zu gewinnen. Die *Etymologie* ist gebührend berücksichtigt worden, wo sie von wirklich praktischem Nutzen ist, insbesondere durch Zusammenfassung von Zusammengehörigem in jeweils *einem* Artikel (aber Trennung von zwar Gleichlautendem aber nicht Zusammengehörigem).

Das Wörterbuch ist nicht nur auf *Schule* und *Universität* ausgerichtet, sondern auch auf die moderne *Wissenschaft* und *Industrie*, auf *Handel* und *Gewerbe*, aber auch auf den „*Mann von der Straße*", auf den Leser der großen Literatur wie auf den der illustrierten Wochenzeitungen, auf Männer unter sich und auf Frauen unter sich. Es geht immer von dem Grundsatz aus „*Proper words in proper places*" und, wie einer meiner englischen Kollegen sich ausdrückte: „*I call a spade a spade; some call it a b–y shovel*". – „*Man muß die Mutter im Hause, die Kinder auf der Gassen, den gemeinen Mann auf dem Markt drumb fragen und denselbigen auf das Maul sehen, wie sie reden, und darnach dolmetschen*" (Martin Luther, 8. 9. 1530). Hierzu siehe z. B. *A-a, Baba, Heia, Piepvogel, Wauwau* etc.; – *prima, knorke*, ⟨iron⟩ *edel*; – *Mords-, Pfunds-, Heiden-, Scheiß-* etc. Es ist ein Unterschied, ob der Bauer oder die Bäuerin *Holz vor der Hütt'n* hat, genauso, wie ob er oder sie *die Hosen anhat**.

Unter allen einfachen Stichwörtern, die das *Technische* und die *Industrie* betreffen (Rad, Zange, Klammer, Scheibe, Schlüssel, Schraube etc.) sind die Abarten dieser Dinge aufgeführt. Für *Handel, Bank* und *Gewerbe* finden sich Anrede, Briefanfang und -schluß, Angebot, Bestellung, Rechnungs- und Reklamewesen. Die neuesten *Erfindungen* vom Kugelschreiber über das Fernsehen zur Atomforschung und Raumforschung sind erfaßt. Der *Mediziner, Physiker, Chemiker, Zoologe, Botaniker, Architekt, Forstmann, Musiker* usw. findet hier, was er sucht.

Dieses Buch stellt auch einen ersten Versuch dar, nicht nur im Kommerziellen über das isolierte Wort hinausgehend die heute noch immer stiefmütterlich behandelte *Syntax* und den *Stil* systematisch in das Wortmaterial einzubauen. Die Artikel

---

* „Les audaces de langage, la conviction que tout doit se dire, qu'il y a des mots abominables nécessaires comme des fers rouges, qu'une langue sort enrichie de ces bains de force."

(Emile Zola [Zusatz des Verf. zum Neusatz.])

sind daher oft nach syntaktischen bzw. stilistischen Gesichtspunkten eingerichtet, um die charakteristischen – syntaktischen wie idiomatischen – Eigenheiten des betreffenden Wortes plastisch in Erscheinung treten zu lassen und den Benutzer zu befähigen, die im Gebrauch auftretenden Schwierigkeiten sofort zu erkennen und das Wort richtig zu handhaben. Es sei nur stichprobenartig auf einige Artikel verwiesen:

Präpositionen wie: an, auf... zu; siehe dazu auch Band I;

Hauptwörter wie: Auge, Bau, Berg, Betrieb, Bild, Blatt, Bruch... Dienst, Dose, Fenster, Gabel, Griff... Riemen, Ring, Scheibe, Schwemme,... Waage, Wagen, Wille, Wind, Winkel, Wort, Wunder, Zeit;

Zeitwörter wie: abgehen, abhalten, ankommen, annehmen, bitten, bleiben, bringen, denken,... wirken, wissen, wollen, ziehen;

Adjektiva wie: hoch, klein,... wahr, wirklich, wohl;

Burschikoses wie: °Anhalter, °Animus, °Armleuchter,... °Papierkrieg, °Sardelle, °Schlamassel, °Schnäpser, °(Regiments-)Spieß, °Trauerkloß, °Wonnekloß.

Dem *Engländer* und *Amerikaner* wird hier wohl zum erstenmal in einem zweisprachigen Wörterbuch die deutsche Sprache in ihren Höhen und in ihren Tiefen nahegebracht. Das Deutsche hat auch seinen Slang; er ist nicht weniger reichhaltig und blühend als der amerikanische und englische. Nur haben wir keinen Partridge, der ihn gesammelt hätte*. Hier ist ein erster Versuch gemacht, nicht nur „das Ei des Kolumbus", sondern auch das „Gemsenei" zu finden. Und der deutsch- wie der englisch-sprechende Gebraucher des Wörterbuches findet zu allermeist nicht nur eine blasse Erklärung, sondern eine möglichst treffende Übertragung.

All dies stellte die Forderung der sauberen Klärung der grammatischen Konstruktion und syntaktischen Verbindung des Wortes mit den übrigen Gliedern des Satzes durch Anführung *vieler und verschiedener Beispiele*, die dem Benutzer gerade bei komplizierten Sachverhalten und Idiomen vor falscher Anwendung oder Konstruktion bewahren wird...

Marburg, am 8. Mai 1953 *Will Héraucourt*

---

* Heute aber haben wir den ausgezeichneten Küpper!: Heinz Küpper, Wörterbuch der deutschen Umgangssprache („a. A. d. W."), 6 Bände, Hamburg 1963ff. und H. Küpper: dtv-Wörterbuch der deutschen Alltagssprache, München 1971.

Preface

Professor Karl Wildhagen died on August 7th 1945 after a life devoted to successful research and scholarship. But amongst students of the English language he will never be forgotten. His sudden passing interrupted his work on this dictionary which was left uncompleted by his death.

When, soon thereafter, the *Tauchnitz Edition* approached me with the request that I should complete the work I was fully sensible not only of the responsibility but also of the honour of such an undertaking, for the first volume, thanks to the erudition upon which it was based, was and will remain here and abroad a standard reference work of its kind.

In laying aside other work in order to accept this far from simple task I was conscious above all of the necessity for completing an undertaking which rested upon so broad a foundation. On the other hand I welcomed the opportunity this would afford for incorporating the results of many years of research of my own, carried out in connection with other reference works, and I believed that my hitherto unused files of neologisms, Americanisms and idioms could make their modest contribution to the final edition. That the completion of the dictionary required a period of seven years and the extent of the completed second volume far exceeded that of the first volume can constitute no real cause for surprise. As work on the dictionary had been begun in the early twenties the amount of material collected even for the unfinished part was very considerable. So thorough had been the work upon the letters already treated in draft that it would be a slight to the memory of Professor Wildhagen to endeavour, by cutting, to reduce the second volume to uniformity with the first.

Only in a very few connections did I feel entitled to be more concise.

1) Proverbs, proverbial sayings and idiomatic expressions occur, in general, only once and are given under the first substantive, e.g. "*Man soll den Tag nicht vor dem Abend loben*" . . . under "Tag".

2) I feel, furthermore, that it was quite in accordance with the principles of Professor Wildhagen that I decided to supplement his list of some 120 with a further score of readily understandable abbreviations, e.g. ⟨*artill*⟩, ⟨*gyn*⟩, ⟨*pap*⟩, ⟨*swim*⟩, ⟨*tan*⟩, etc. In particular must be mentioned abbreviations already established in the first volume as grammatical symbols e.g. *h* = *haben*, *s* = *sein* which I have utilised throughout the text. To these I have added *k* = *kommen*, *m* = *machen*, *w* = *werden*.

3) The parts of the verb are given only for the *simple* and not the compound verb, e.g. for *schlafen* [*schlief*/*ge*~] but not e.g. for *ein-*, *verschlafen*. In the declension of nouns the following signs denote that no plural form exists – e.g. *Redlichkeit* ~/. Under "*Würde*": the signs ~/~*n* represent "*der Würde*" [gen sg]/ *die Würden* [nom pl], under "*Kalb*": ~/(*e*)*s*/≃*er* represent "*des Kalb*(*e*)*s* [gen sg]/*die Kälber* [nom pl]" with *umlaut*. The inflected forms of nouns are given only for the simple and not for the compound noun, e.g. not for *Mondkalb*. *Schmiß -isses*/*-isse* is used to avoid the necessity for repetition of the whole word. (List of abbrevations on page XXXV.)

In order to ensure for the 2nd volume an even more enthusiastic reception than that which had been accorded to the first volume in English-speaking countries *German script* was discarded. This introduced the necessity of placing the abbreviations in brackets, afforded, on the other hand, a welcome means of differentiating between grammatical and other references, e.g. [ell] = *elliptical* (as to the construction of the sentence); ⟨el⟩ = *electricity;* [inf] = *infinitive;* ⟨ins⟩ = *insurance;* [rel] = *relative;* ⟨rel⟩ = *religion*, etc.

Conciseness in form has permitted comprehensiveness in content.

The object of this book is to represent, in the whole diversity of its social and individual structure, the vocabulary and usage of present-day German, i. e. of the 19th cent. and 20th cent., including standard speech (as basis), the conversational language of the educated classes, colloquial speech ⟨*fam*⟩, the poetical language, dialect, slang, and teenager-slang ⟨*teens*⟩.

In order to provide space for the living language we have deliberately refrained from dealing fully with the vocabulary of earlier centuries and from giving detailed etymological data. *Etymology* has received due treatment where it is of eminently practical value. This has been achieved especially by the grouping under one heading of etymologically connected catchwords and by referring from one catchword to the other.

Thanks to the closeness of spelling and pronunciation in German it was possible to restrict *phonetic transcription* to a minimum (see p. XXXIII).

The dictionary is not intended exclusively for school and university nor even for science, industry, and commerce but also for the "man in the street". It will serve alike those who read the classics and those who read the illustrated weeklies. Where the rule is "gentlemen only" it will serve its purpose just as well as amongst "ladies only". The guiding principle has always been "Proper words in proper places"; as an English colleague remarked "I call a spade a spade; some call it a b. .y shovel". Consult in this connection e.g. *A-a*, *Baba*, *Heia*, *Piepvogel*, *Wauwau*, *etc.* – *prima*, *knorke*, *edel*; – *Mords-*, *Pfunds-*, *Heiden-*, *Scheiß-*, *etc.* It makes a world of difference whether he or she wears the trousers. The "unmentionables" of the 19th century have their place in this dictionary just like all forms and varieties of the word *Hose*, from the substantial *Arbeitshose* to the flimsy *scanties* (honni soit qui mal y pense!→ Knigge). Equally under the simple forms of technical and industrial terms are given the various derivatives (Rad, Zange, Klammer, Scheibe, Schlüssel, Schraube, etc.). The latest scientific and technical advances from ballpoint-pens to television sets and from atomic research to synthesis of vitamins are represented. The physician, the physicist, the chemist, the zoologist, the botanist, the architect, the forester, the musician, etc. all find here what they need.

This book also represents the first systematic attempt at bringing *syntax* and *style*, which have hitherto always suffered neglect, within the framework of the word-material. The articles have, therefore, often been arranged purely from the standpoint of syntax and idiom, in order to throw into relief the characteristic peculiarities – syntactic as well as idiomatic – of the word in question and to enable the reader to recognize at once such difficulties as may arise in use of the word and to apply it correctly. In passing we may cite briefly one or two instances:

prepositions: an, auf... zu;
nouns: Auge, Bau, Berg, Betrieb, Bild, Blatt, Bruch... Dienst, Dose, Fenster, Gabel, Griff... Riemen, Ring, Scheibe, Schwemme... Waage, Wagen, Wille, Wind, Winkel, Wort, Wunder, Zeit;
verbs: abgehen, abhalten, ankommen, annehmen, bitten, bleiben, bringen, denken... wirken, wissen, wollen, ziehen;
adjectives: hoch, klein... wahr, wirklich, wohl;
slang expressions: °Anhalter, °Animus, °Armleuchter... °Papierkrieg, °Sardellen, °Schlamassel, °Schnäpser, °(Regiments-)Spieß, °Trauerkloß, °Wonnekloß.

For the first time the German language in its most refined and unrefined forms is laid open to all who speak English and American. German slang is in no sense less picturesque than the English and the American but there has been no Partridge to collate it*. Our dictionary includes not only "das Ei des Kolumbus" but also the "Gemsenei", and the English speaker who consults it will find not only a simple explanation but also the most appropriate equivalent.

The putting into practice of all these principles made it necessary to distinguish carefully between grammatical construction, syntactic connections, and idiomatic usage of the words in question by illustrating the case with several different examples, in order to guard the reader against applying or construing a word wrongly.

Marburg, May 8th 1953 *Will Héraucourt*

* The last decade presented us with the excellent *Küpper*: Heinz Küpper, Wörterbuch der deutschen Umgangssprache, 6 Bände, Hamburg 1963 ff. and with his dtv-Wörterbuch der deutschen Alltagssprache, München 1971. (The compiler's remark to this new edition of our dictionary.)

Verlagsvorwort

Nach dem Ableben von Professor Dr. Karl Wildhagen, dem Verfasser des englisch-deutschen Teiles dieses Wörterbuches, entstand für den Verlag das Problem, wem die Vollendung des deutsch-englischen Lexikonteiles, der im Rohmanuskript erst zum geringeren Teile vorlag, anvertraut werden konnte. Nach längeren Verhandlungen fiel die Wahl auf Professor Dr. Will Héraucourt, vormals Ordinarius für Anglistik an der Universität Königsberg (Pr). Die Gründe hierfür waren vornehmlich die, daß Prof. Dr. Héraucourt nicht nur bereits über langjährige Erfahrung auf dem Gebiet der Lexikographie verfügte, sondern selbst ein ähnliches Wörterbuch plante. Für dieses Werk hatte er schon umfangreiches Material der modernen englischen und amerikanischen Sprache zusammengetragen, daß insbesondere dadurch wertvoll war, daß nicht oft nur Erklärungen der Wörter und Ausdrücke gegeben wurden, sondern *mutatis mutandis* ein möglichst genaues Äquivalent als „*le mot juste*" in der lebendigen englischen und amerikanischen Sprache angestrebt war.

Durch sein Aufgewachsensein in beiden Sprachen, sein langjähriges Studium des Deutschen, Englischen und Amerikanischen besonders auch in ihren geographischen, stilistischen und sozialen Verhältnissen und durch seine Aufzeichnungen in zwei Weltkriegen erschien Prof. Héraucourt als überaus geeigneter Sachverwalter des wissenschaftlichen Nachlasses von Prof. Wildhagen.

Es ist dem Verlag eine besondere Ehre, anläßlich des Erscheinens des deutsch-englischen Teiles des Wildhagen-Lexikons, das Konzeption und Entwurf noch Prof. Wildhagen verdankt, mit der Herausgabe dieser ebenbürtigen Vollendung seines Werkes die Tradition eines großen Rufes aufrecht zu erhalten und fortzuführen, die im In- und Auslande uneingeschränkte Anerkennung gefunden hat.

Wiesbaden, im Mai 1953. *Der Verlag*

Publishers' Foreword

With the passing of Professor Wildhagen, the compiler of the English-German part of this dictionary, the publishers were faced with the problem of finding someone to complete the German-English part of which the rough draft of only a section had been made. After lengthy negotiations the task was entrusted to Professor Héraucourt former Head of the Department of English in the University of Königsberg (now Russian). The reasons for this choice were not only the long lexicographical experience of Professor Héraucourt but also the fact that he himself was planning a similar work. For his projected work he had already gathered together much material (including Americanisms) which was of particular value due to the fact that words and expressions were not merely explained but that every endeavour was made to give an equivalent as "*le mot juste*" in modern English and American.

Thanks to his bilingual upbringing and his many years' scholarship in the fields of German, English and American, with particular reference to geographical and social conditions and problems of style, and to the notes assiduously collected by him in the course of two World Wars, Professor H. seemed the ideal person to carry out the task upon which Professor Wildhagen had made a beginning. It is a great honour to the publishers, upon the occasion of the appearance of this German-English part of the dictionary, conceived and sketched out by Professor W., to be able to add to the English-German part a fitting and worthy complement and therewith uphold and carry on the tradition of a work which has enjoyed so high a reputation at home and abroad.

Wiesbaden, May 18th 1953. *The Publishers*

Vorwort

zum Mono-photo-type-Neusatz der durchgesehenen und stark erweiterten zweiten Auflage

Meine Überarbeitung und Erweiterung des I. Bandes des in der ganzen Welt in hohem Ansehen stehenden „Wildhagen" hat fast neidlos begeisterte Aufnahme und auch im Rundfunk besondere Anerkennung gefunden. Dies gab mir den Mut, ja machte es mir zur Pflicht, nun auch den 1953 erstmals erschienenen II. Band ganz neu herauszubringen. „*La vieillesse n'est pas un temps perdu. Au contraire, elle permet de rattraper le temps perdu!*" ist der Leitspruch der Zeitschrift *La Vie Montente.*

Bereits in der Erstausgabe hatte ich als Ergebnis langjähriger Sammlungen bereits in gewissem Maße eigenes Material beitragen können. Dieser eigene Beitrag wurde nunmehr von ausschlaggebender Notwendigkeit und Bedeutung, obwohl ich an dem Wildhagen-Plan, wo immer möglich, festgehalten habe.

Die Entwicklung der Welt auf wissenschaftlichen und technischen Gebieten aller denkbaren Bereiche machte eine Neubearbeitung und Erweiterung und damit einen Neusatz erforderlich, der noch mit meinem hochverehrten, leider allzufrüh aus dem Leben gegangenen Verleger Wolfgang Brandstetter eingehend besprochen werden konnte.

Mittlerweile hatten sich so viele sachkundige Mitarbeiter der verschiedensten Interessensphären angeboten*, daß mir die verantwortungsvolle Arbeit wesentlich erleichtert wurde: *il n'est guère de tâche plus ingrate que la confection d'un dictionnaire* sagt die *Académie Française* sehr eindringlich.

Hierbei galt mir, wie bei der Erweiterung des I. Bandes, der leitende Gedanke, das Wörterbuch im Sinne Wildhagens als eine *enzyklopädische, streng wissenschaftliche Darstellung* des deutschen Wortschatzes der Neuzeit und Gegenwart mit besonderer Berücksichtigung der *Syntax,* des *Stils* und des *idiomatischen Brauchs* zu erweitern, wobei das *österreichische* und das *schweizerische Wortgut* nicht wie bisher vernachlässigt werden sollten (s. u.). Die Mundarten wurden durch Hinweise spezifiziert. Die Aufnahme dargestellter Stilebenen wurden um *Amts- und Zeitungssprache* sowie um *Teenager-Slang* erweitert.

Die moderne Sprachentwicklung wurde bewußt verfolgt (z. B. Stahlbeton neben Eisenbeton, Schraubendreher neben Schraubenzieher, Oxid neben Oxyd).

In großem Umfang wurden weitere Sachgebiete *in extenso* aufgenommen: z. B.

Aerodynamik, Akustik, Astronautik, Ballistik, Bankwesen, Bevölkerungswissenschaft, Bilanzwesen, Billard, Biochemie, Brauwesen, Bühnentechnik, Computer, Dekorationswesen, Demographie, Destillation, Elektronik, Ethologie, Feuerbestattung, Filmtechnik, Finanzwesen, Flugwesen, Formgießerei, Funktechnik, Funkwesen, Hygiene, Kartographie, Keramik, Kosmetik, Krematorium, Kybernetik, Linguistik, Logarithmik, Logistik, Maniküre, Maurerhandwerk, Metallguß, Mühlenwerke, Nachrichtenwesen, Näherei, Numismatik, Okkultismus, Pädagogik, Privatrecht, Raketentechnik, Raumfahrt, Rechenmaschinen, Reprographie, Schulwesen, Sex, Statistik, Steuerwesen, Strafrecht, Taktik, Textilwesen, Theologie, Tonaufnahme und -wiedergabe, Turbinenwesen, Umschulung, Verhaltensforschung, Vertragsrecht, Wirtschaftswesen, Zivilrecht, Zollwesen.

Darüber hinaus sei auf neuere Erfindungen hingewiesen wie z. B. Luftkissenboot, Tragflächenboot, Wasserski, Wellenreiten, PCM-Verfahren usw.

Die weitgespannte Zielsetzung brachte anlagetechnische Probleme mit sich, besonders den ständigen Zwang, eine möglichst gedrängte typographische Gestaltung

---

* Hierzu siehe die Seite XXII

zu erreichen, um den Band nicht unnötig anschwellen zu lassen. Besonders in längeren Artikeln wurden deshalb immer wiederkehrende Hauptwörter (eindeutig erkennbar) abgekürzt, zumal dies Verfahren auch visuell seine Vorteile hat.

Aus dem gleichen Grunde wurde, um unnötige Wiederholungen zu vermeiden z. B. in bezug auf Tier- und Pflanzenarten auf das entsprechende übergeordnete englische Stichwort im I. Band (durch →...) verwiesen, wo diese sehr eingehend zweisprachig behandelt wurden.

Mit Bezug auf die große Mannigfaltigkeit der von mir im I. Band angeführten Satzbeispiele schrieb ein Rezensent: Das Wörterbuch liest sich fast wie ein Roman. Die Satzbeispiele habe ich im II. Band noch beträchtlich vermehrt, denn was nützen dem Gebraucher die *Wörter*, wenn er sie nicht zu *Worten* zusammenfügen kann. Ein sachkundiger Rezensent* hob lobend hervor, daß ich dem gegen Wildhagen früher gelegentlich gemachten Vorwurf, er habe „in allzuvielen Fällen eher eine Übersetzung der Definition des Concise Oxford Dictionary als eine wirkliche Entsprechung gegeben", entgegengearbeitet habe, indem ich immer, *le mot juste* (Flaubert) zu finden, bestrebt war. Diese Bestrebung habe ich mir auch im vorliegenden Band zur besonderen Aufgabe gemacht.

Neben Anhang X. lag mir die Einarbeitung der *Grammatik* ins eigentliche Wörterbuch durch Anführen vieler typischer Beispiele am Herzen, vor allem auch die Anwendung des regierenden bzw. regierten Kasus. Das rückbezügliche Fürwort [(pron) refl] „sich" bereitet dem Ausländer hinsichtlich des Kasus oft Schwierigkeit: deshalb habe ich den Dativ (im Gegensatz zum Akkusativ) durch [dat] kenntlich gemacht; z. B. verschließen: Tür hinter sich [dat] ∼; etwas in sich [dat] ∼; aber ⟨fig⟩ verschossen in [acc]. Ebenso ist bei z. B. *einer Sache* [gen] bzw. [dat] angegeben.

Die *etymologische* Zusammengehörigkeit von Wörtern habe ich dadurch gekennzeichnet, daß ich sie i. a. und wo dies möglich war ohne Absatz aufeinander folgen lasse (z. B. Zwie- [→ Zwei]: zwiefach usw., Zwiesel, Zwille, Zwillich, Zwilling; oder durch Verweis (→..) z. B. Verschalung (→ Schale); andererseits Trennung von nichtverwandten Wörtern wie Katechu gegenüber katechisieren-Katechumen oder von Paradies/Parasit usw./Parapluie-Parasol.

Anglizismen und *Amerikanismen*, die in die deutsche Sprache Eingang gefunden haben und als solche noch empfunden werden, findet man im I. Band. Englische Wörter aus dem Deutschen ins Englische zurückzuübersetzen (etwa *image*, *publicity*, *understatement*) wurde i. a. vermieden, es sei denn, daß im Deutschen ein abweichender Plural gebildet wird. Sich nicht deckende *Idiomatik* wurde durch ⟨m. m.⟩ kenntlich gemacht, nicht jedoch, wenn der Unterschied ganz sinnfällig ist, wie z. B. in „sich die Hände waschen" ⟨übtr⟩ "*to powder one's nose*".

Die *Satz- und Wortbetonung* in der englischen Übersetzung wurde in besonderen Fällen durch einen hochgesetzten Punkt vor dem zu betonenden Vokal gekennzeichnet (z. B. „Was machen wir bloß?" – "What ·are we to do?" oder: pr·esent/to pres·ent).

Bei aller verwendeten Mühe und Sorgfalt: „Ein Wörterbuch wird nie fertig." Für Anregungen und konstruktive Kritik bin ich immer dankbar, denn « un dictionnaire, on ne saurait trop le redire, n'est jamais une œuvre parfaite» (Académie Française). "Dictionaries are like watches, the worst is better than none, and the best cannot be expected to go quite true." Aber noch gilt Dr. Samuel Johnsons berühmt gewordene Formulierung: "Every other author may aspire to praise; the lexicographer can only hope to escape reproach."

Ich halte mich lieber an optimistischere Aussagen wie diese: Hat man ein hohes Ziel, ist schon das Wollen von Wert.

Marburg, 27. März 1971 *Will Héraucourt*

---

* Wolf Friederich

Preface

to the revised and greatly enlarged 2th edition in mono-photo-type setting

Almost ungrudgingly enthusiastic reception was accorded my revised and enlarged edition of the English-German part of our dictionary, which stands in high esteem all over the world and which also met with unanimous approval over the radio. These expressions of acceptance gave me the courage, even made it my obligation, to bring out in entirely new form the German-English part too which made its first appearance in 1953. *La vieillesse n'est pas un temps perdu. Au contraire, elle permet de rattraper le temps perdu!* (La Vie Montente).

If I was able to contribute in the first edition to a great measure my own material as a result of many years' collections this addition now became a quite decisive factor as to need and importance. The development of the world in scientific and technical fields of every conceivable province made a revision and enlargement indispensable and consequently also a complete reset which could yet be the subject of thorough discussion with my highly esteemed publisher Wolfgang Brandstetter, who unfortunately met with an untimely end.

Meanwhile so many expert contributors of very varied spheres of interest had offered their services that my responsible work was substantially lightened: *il n'est guère de tâche plus ingrate que la confection d'un dictionnaire* (Académie Française).

At this work I was guided by the idea, as I had been when enlarging the first volume, to expand the dictionary to Wildhagen's intentions also corresponding to modern linguistic development, so that the dictionary will serve as an *encyclopaedic, strictly scientific representation* of the modern and present-day German vocabulary (e. g. *Stahlbeton* besides *Eisenbeton*, *Schraubendreher* besides *Schraubenzeiher*, *Oxid* besides *Oxyd*). Particular consideration was given the *syntax*, *style* and *idiomatic usage*. Special regard was accorded to German as spoken in *Austria* as well as in *Switzerland*.

To a large extent additional subject matters were included *in extenso*, in particular the following ones:

acoustics, accounting machines, aerodynamics, aeronautics, astronautics, balance sheet, ballistics, banking, biochemistry, brewery, cartography, casting, ceramics, civil law, customs, cybernetics, decoration, demography, distillation, economics, education, electronics, ethology, filming, finance, founding, linguistics, logarithms, logistics, manicure, mills, numismatics, occultism, pedagogy, private law, radio, recording, (occupational) rehabilitation, reprography, rockets, sewing, sex*, statistics, taxes, textiles, turbines.

Attention may be drawn, moreover, to recent inventions as e. g. *Luftkissenboot*, *Tragflächenboot*, *Wasserski*, *Wellenreiten*, *PCM-Verfahren*, etc.

On the other hand to avoid unnecessary repetitions (e. g. in respect to species of animals and plants) cross-reference was made (by →. .) to the analogous superordinate catchword as contained in the first volume, in which the species were treated in a very thorough manner.

With regard to the great variety of illustrative phrases quoted by me in the first volume a reviewer wrote "*This dictionary reads almost as a novel*". The sentence examples in the second volume have now been even considerably increased, for

---

* *Certissimamente, Amore è una bestial novella* (a tricky business) says Aretino; but: ⟨Gr⟩ *me taumázein!* (There's nothing new under the sun).

what is the use of single detached words to the user who cannot find them syntactically construed to connected words. A really expert reviewer* commended highly that by my steady endeavour to find *le mot juste* (Flaubert) I have counteracted the reproach formerly laid occasionally on Wildhagen that he had "in too many instances provided rather a translation of the definitions found in the Concise Oxford Dictionary than an actual equivalent." I have made a point of adhering to my principle. Besides appendage Deutsche Grammatik I set my heart upon incorporating *grammar* into the dictionary proper by citing a great number of typical examples, above all those concerning the use of the governing and governed case respectively. The reflexive pronoun *sich* often causes the foreigner particular difficulty as to the case: I have therefore marked the dative (as contrasted with the accusative) by [dat] e.g. *verschließen: die Tür hinter sich* [dat] ~; but ⟨fig⟩ *verschossen in* [acc]. For the same reason at e.g. *Sache: einer* ~ [gen] or [dat] has been inserted.

Words that belong together etymologically I have characterized by having them in general and wherever possible run on (e.g. *zwie-* [↦*zwei*]: ~*fach* etc.; *Zwiesel, Zwille, Zwillich, Zwilling*); or by reference [↦...] (e.g. *Verschalung* [↦*Schale*] or respectively seperating not related words as *Katechu* opposite *katechisieren-Katechumen* or of *Paradies*/*Parasit* etc./*Parapluie-Parasol.*

Anglicisms and *Americanisms* which have found their way into the German language and are yet felt as such are to be found in the first volume. It was therefore generally avoided to retranslate English words from German into English (e. g. image, publicity, understatement) unless a different plural is formed in German.

Not identical idiomatic expressions are marked by ⟨m. m.⟩ = *mutatis mutandis*, not however if the difference is quite obvious, as e.g. in „*sich die Hände waschen*" ⟨übtr⟩ "*to powder one's nose*".

In the English translation the stress in sentences and in words was characterized in particular cases by a dot above the line put before the letter to be stressed (e.g. „*Was machen wir bloß?*" "*What ˙are we to do?*" or *pr˙esent*/*to pres˙ent*).

Despite every labour and care spent: „*Ein Wörterbuch wird nie fertig*". I shall be thankful for suggestions and constructive criticism, for «*un dictionnaire, on ne saurait trop le redire, n'est jamais une œuvre parfaite*» (Académie Française) or "*Dictionaries are like watches, the worst is better than none, and the best cannot be expected to go quite true*". Though I don't want to see the Italian proverb *traduttore – traditore* generalized, yet Dr. Samuel Johnson's wording which has become famous holds true: "*Every other author may aspire to praise, the lexicographer can only hope to escape reproach*". – I prefer adhering to more optimistic sayings like these: *in magnis et voluisse sat est* (Sext. Aur. Propertius). *Hat man ein hohes Ziel*/*Ist schon das Wollen von Wert.*

Marburg, 27. März 1971 *Will Héraucourt*

Mein Dank gilt auch bei dieser Auflage in besonderem Maße den Tastern (Setzern) der Druckerei Brandstetter, die mit verständigem Einfühlungsvermögen und viel Geduld nach der durchweg handgeschriebenen Vorlage hervorragende Arbeit geleistet haben. *W. H.*

I feel greatly indebted again for the present volume to the mono-photo-typesetters of the *Brandstetter Druckerei* who had to work from a handwritten text. They did this with great empathy as to my German as well as to my Latin characters. *W. H.*

---

* The well-known interpreter *Wolf Friederich.*

Verlagsvorwort

Nahezu ein Vierteljahrhundert dem Wildhagenschen Werk verbunden, legt Professor Héraucourt hiermit die vollkommen überarbeitete und erweiterte Fassung des deutsch-englischen Bandes vor. Der Verlag hofft, daß diese Neuauflage allen alten Freunden wiederum eine zuverlässige und treue Hilfe sein und zugleich den Kreis der Benutzer dieses weithin bekannten Wörterbuches noch wesentlich erweitern möge.

Herrn Professor Héraucourt sei für die umfangreiche und langjährige Arbeit, die Einsatz, Zeit und Kraft eines Menschen bis aufs äußerste in Anspruch genommen hat, aufrichtig gedankt. Die Resonanz dieses Buches, das deutlich die Auffassung seines Bearbeiters zeigt, wird sichtbare Anerkennung für alle Mühe und Arbeit sein.

Wiesbaden, im Herbst 1971 *Der Verlag*

Publishers' Foreword

Devoted to Professor Wildhagen's works for nearly 25 years, Professor Héraucourt is now presenting the completely revised and updated German-English part of this well-known dictionary. We are confident that the new edition, as a reliable source of information, will be of great assistance to a steadily increasing number of users.

We are greatly indebted to Professor Héraucourt for his invaluable efforts, enthusiasm and encouragement in compiling the dictionary. The approval this new volume will meet with is a perceptible reward for all his efforts.

Wiesbaden, Autumn 1971 *The Publishers*

Anerkennung

Für Mitarbeit, Anregungen, bereitwilligst erteilte Auskünfte und das Lesen der Korrektur sei hier nochmals allen beteiligten Personen gedankt:

C. F. Adams-London; General der Artillerie a. D. Bader-Emmendingen; Jesuitenpater Professor Dr. Barlogh-Rom; Frederick Bass, M. D.-New York; Dr. med. Bayer-Marburg; Dr. Günther Beckers-Kairo; Dipl.-Ing. H. Bitting-Warendorf (Westf.); Dorothee Boschen (WDR)-Baden-Baden; Dr. h. c. Hans Brockhaus-Wiesbaden; A. Bscher-Mannheim; Lecturer Norman F. Budgey, M. A.-Oxford; Bundesministerium für Wissenschaft und Forschung-Bonn; Patricia Cameron-Whitley Bay, Northumberland; R. E. Clark-Frankfurt-M.; Minati Das-Madras; † Professor Dr. Max Deutschbein-Marburg; Professor Dr. Patricia I. Diffené-London; Dr. Martin Dolch-Kaiserslautern; Professor Dr. Walter Döpp-Marburg; Gertrude Eckhard, MTA-Mainz; Professor Dr. med. Ehrhardt-Marburg; Joseph M. Ember-Omaha, Nebr., USA; Oberstleutnant a. D. Fritz Eschricht-Berlin-Charlottenburg; Pfarrer Theo Fehn-Tiefenthal-Pfalz; Diplom-Dolmetscher Wolf Friederich-München; Kommodore Freiherr Hans-Carl von Friesen-Rheine (Westf.); Führungsakademie der Bundeswehr-Hamburg; Sidney F. Fuller am Rückerstattungsgericht für Berlin; Forstassessor W. Grandjot-Brügge (Westf.); Assessor B. Hafemann-Berlin; † Professor Dr. Richard Hamann-Marburg; J. C. Hansen-Hamburg; Studienrat R. Hauff-Eßlingen; † Blanchefleur Héraucourt-Wiesbaden; Oberstleutnant a. D. Ferry A. Héraucourt-Hamburg; Professor Dr. Otto Hietsch, M. Litt.-Regensburg; Dr. Richard Hoff-Ottawa, Canada; Bergassessor W. Huber-Goslar; Diana Hughes-Rhosneiger, Wales; Professor Dr. H. Jacob-Marburg; Dipl.-Ing. Robert Kersting-Ettlingen; Dr. Werner Kleinsteuber-Konstanz; Friedrich Krollmann-Bonn; Dr. med. Heinrich Lamm, M. D., F. A. C. S.-Harlingen, Texas; Oberbahnarzt i. R. Dr. med. Carl Lazar-Marburg; Tom C. Lethbridge, F. S. A.-Cambridge; Kriminalmeister W. Lötje-Hamburg; Dr. Erich Mann-Bonn; Redakteur Fritz Mannhardt-Innsbruck; Karl-Marx-Universität-Leipzig; Studienrat Rudolf Meldau-Frankfurt a. M.; Dr. Ing. Karl Münnich-Siegen; Sgt/Maj Francis Murphy-Princeton, N. J., USA; Bernhard G. Newton-Huddersfield, Yorksh.; Oxford English Dictionary Supplement-Oxford; Professor Dr. Ronald Peacock-Manchester; Dr. Hans Pfannkuch-Wiesbaden; Max-Planck-Institut für Internationales Privatrecht-Hamburg; Andrea Podestà, Kosmetikerin (Revlon)-Wiesbaden; Fritz Preuss-Berlin-Charlottenburg; Dr. P. Putzig-Hamburg; Dr. H. F. Reich-Rheydt (Westf.); Hermann Reiss-Eberhardt-Neustadt (Weinstraße); Dr. L. Ritter-Leimen bei Heidelberg; Professor Norman B. Roberg, M. D.-Illinois; Dr. Eugen Rost-Marburg; Professor Dr. Kurt Scharlau-Marburg; † Blanchefleur Schlott-Héraucourt-Wiesbaden; Charles H. Scoles-Northwood, Middlesex; Studienrat Dr. Helmut Singer-München; T. W. Smith-Nachrodt in Westfalen; Forstmeister Erich Siebert-Reichensachsen (Kr. Eschwege); Dr. W. B. Spatz (Max-Planck-Institut für Hirnforschung)-Frankfurt/M.; R. A. Dr. Gerd Spreen-Hamburg; Gisela Spreen-Héraucourt-Hamburg; Oberstudienrat Dr. Leo Stahl-Frankfurt/M.; Lektorin Edith Steckner-Köln; Dr. jur. Joseph Stirnberg-Yokohama; Professor Dr. H. Stutte-Marburg; Fa. Friedrich Tanck, Export-Hamburg; Charles F. Tebutt Eynesbury-St. Neots, Hunts.; Theatherwissenschaftliches Institut der Universität-Köln-Wahn; Lecturer Paul Turner-London; Studienrat K. Uhde-Schöningen (Braunschweig); Regierungsrat Zollinspektor K. Voigt-Ludwigshafen; Oberstudienrat Dr. F. Wallberg-Windhoek und Hamburg; Lecturer Robert Worsley-White, M. A.-Oxford und Marburg; Margret Zuber-Bonn.

Will Héraucourt

Acknowledgements

Thanks are due to all those who have assisted with the work in any way, through practical help, correspondence, useful suggestion and a readiness to supply information at any time:

C. F. ADAMS-London; General der Artillerie a. D. BADER-Emmendingen; Jesuitenpater Professor Dr. BARLOGH-Rom; Frederick BASS, M. D.-New York; Dr. med. BAYER-Marburg; Dr. Günther BECKERS-Kairo; Dipl.-Ing. H. BITTING-Warendorf (Westf.); Dorothee BOSCHEN (WDR)-Baden-Baden; Dr. h. c. Hans BROCKHAUS-Wiesbaden; A. BSCHER-Mannheim; Lecturer Norman F. BUDGEY, M. A.-Oxford; BUNDESMINISTERIUM für Wissenschaft und Forschung-Bonn; Patricia CAMERON-Whitley Bay, Northumberland; R. E. CLARK-Frankfurt-M.; Minati DAS-Madras; † Professor Dr. Max DEUTSCHBEIN-Marburg; Professor Dr. Patricia I. DIFFENÉ-London; Dr. Martin DOLCH-Kaiserslautern; Professor Dr. Walter DÖPP-Marburg; Gertrude ECKHARD, MTA-Mainz; Professor Dr. med. EHRHARDT-Marburg; Joseph M. EMBER-Omaha, Nebr., USA; Oberstleutnant a. D. Fritz ESCHRICHT-Berlin-Charlottenburg; Pfarrer Theo FEHN-Tiefenthal-Pfalz; Diplom-Dolmetscher Wolf FRIEDERICH-München; Kommodore Freiherr Hans-Carl VON FRIESEN-Rheine (Westf.); FÜHRUNGSAKADEMIE DER BUNDESWEHR-Hamburg; Sidney F. FULLER am Rückerstattungsgericht für Berlin; Forstassessor W. GRANDJOT-Brügge (Westf.); Assessor B. HAFEMANN-Berlin; † Professor Dr. Richard HAMANN-Marburg; J. C. HANSEN-Hamburg; Studienrat R. HAUFF-Eßlingen; † Blanchefleur HÉRAUCOURT-Wiesbaden; Oberstleutnant a. D. Ferry A. HÉRAUCOURT-Hamburg; Professor Dr. Otto HIETSCH, M. Litt.-Regensburg; Dr. Richard HOFF-Ottawa, Canada; Bergassessor W. HUBER-Goslar; Diana HUGHES-Rhosneiger, Wales; Professor Dr. H. JACOB-Marburg; Dipl.-Ing. Robert KERSTING-Ettlingen; Dr. Werner KLEINSTEUBER-Konstanz; Friedrich KROLLMANN Bonn; Dr. med. Heinrich LAMM, M. D., F. A. C. S.-Harlingen, Texas; Oberbahnarzt i. R. Dr. med. Carl LAZAR-Marburg; Tom C. LETHBRIDGE, F. S. A.-Cambridge; Kriminalmeister W. LÖTJE-Hamburg; Dr. Erich MANN-Bonn; Redakteur Fritz MANNHARDT-Innsbruck; KARL-MARX-UNIVERSITÄT-Leipzig; Studienrat Rudolf MELDAU-Frankfurt a. M.; Dr. Ing. Karl MÜNNICH-Siegen; Sgt/Maj Francis MURPHY-Princeton, N. J., USA; Bernhard G. NEWTON-Huddersfield, Yorksh.; OXFORD ENGLISH DICTIONARY SUPPLEMENT-Oxford; Professor Dr. Ronald PEACOCK-Manchester; Dr. Hans PFANNKUCH-Wiesbaden; Max-PLANCK-Institut für Internationales Privatrecht-Hamburg; Andrea PODESTÀ, Kosmetikerin (Revlon)-Wiesbaden; Fritz PREUSS-Berlin-Charlottenburg; Dr. P. PUTZIG-Hamburg; Dr. H. F. REICH-Rheydt (Westf.); Hermann REISS-EBERHARDT-Neustadt (Weinstraße); Dr. L. RITTER-Leimen bei Heidelberg; Professor Norman B. ROBERG, M. D.-Illinois; Dr. Eugen ROST-Marburg; Professor Dr. Kurt SCHARLAU-Marburg; † Blanchefleur SCHLOTT-HÉRAUCOURT-Wiesbaden; Charles H. SCOLES-Northwood, Middlesex; Studienrat Dr. Helmut SINGER-München; T. W. SMITH-Nachrodt in Westfalen; Forstmeister Erich SIEBERT-Reichensachsen (Kr. Eschwege); Dr. W. B. SPATZ (Max-Planck-Institut für Hirnforschung)-Frankfurt/M.; R. A. Dr. Gerd SPREEN-Hamburg; Gisela SPREEN-HÉRAUCOURT-Hamburg; Oberstudienrat Dr. Leo STAHL-Frankfurt/M.; Lektorin Edith STECKNER-Köln; Dr. jur. Joseph STIRNBERG-Yokohama; Professor Dr. H. STUTTE-Marburg; Fa. Friedrich TANCK, Export-Hamburg; Charles F. TEBUTT Eynesbury-St. Neots, Hunts.; THEATHERWISSENSCHAFTLICHES INSTITUT der Universität-Köln-Wahn; Lecturer Paul TURNER-London; Studienrat K. UHDE-Schöningen (Braunschweig); Regierungsrat K. VOIGT-Ludwigshafen (Zollinspektor); Oberstudienrat Dr. E. WALLBERG-Windhoek and Hamburg; Lecturer Robert WORSLEY-WHITE, M. A.-Oxford and Marburg; Margret ZUBER-Bonn.

Will Héraucourt

Einrichtung des Buches und Richtlinien für seine Benutzung

Arrangement of the Dictionary and Directions for its Use

I. Wortschatz

1. Das Wortmaterial umfaßt über den gewöhnlichen Rahmen hinaus:

a) Die wichtigsten Ausdrücke für Sachen, Einrichtungen und Fakten des gesamten kulturellen Lebens Deutschlands unter Hinweis auf Entsprechendes oder Ähnliches in Amerika, England und (in Auswahl) in Schottland, Irland sowie den Kolonien.

b) Die grundlegende Terminologie der Künste und wissenschaftlichen Disziplinen.

c) Die wichtigsten im heutigen Deutschland gebräuchlichen Fremdwörter.

d) Die wichtigsten Sprichwörter, sprichwörtlichen Redensarten und idiomatischen Ausdrücke aller Schichten.

2. a) Die Präfixe sind systematisch behandelt, bei Verben besonders hinsichtlich ihrer Trennbarkeit oder Untrennbarkeit:
d·urch|dringen — durchdr·ingen
und ihres Partizipiums der Vergangenheit (pp):
d·urchgedrungen — durchdr·ungen.

b) Auch die Suffixe sind besonders behandelt worden:
-haft, -heit, -nis etc.

3. a) Bei Substantiven ist die Flexion angegeben:
gen sg/nom pl: **Ball** ~(e)s/~̈lle
~̈ ist das Zeichen des jeweiligen Umlauts; ~̈e steht hier also für Bälle.

b) Endet ein Substantiv auf ein *-ß* oder *-s* (in gotischer Schrift Rund-ꞩ), so ist durch Wiederholung der Endung angedeutet, daß bei der Verdoppelung des s in gotischer Schrift zwei lange s (ſſ) zu schreiben sind. Statt der Tilde ist dann der Bindestrich verwendet worden:
Ergebnis: -nisses/-nisse;
Genuß: -nusses/-nüsse.

4. a) Bei starken (unregelmäßigen) Verben sind *pret* und *pp* angegeben:
geben: [gab/gegeben].

b) Bei Zusammensetzungen mit trennbaren Präfixen ist die Flexion unter dem Simplex zu finden:
für **ab|geben** unter **geben.**

5. Eigennamen im engeren Sinne sind im Prinzip in einer besonderen Liste am Schluß zusammengefaßt. Doch sind Gattungsnamen wie *Röntgenstrahlen* und Namen in Verbindung mit Redensarten wie „*das Ei des Kolumbus*" im eigentlichen Wörterbuch aufgeführt.

II. Anordnung der Stichwörter

1. Die Stichwörter sind alphabetisch angeordnet, wobei die Komposita — zur Andeutung ihrer etymologischen Zusammengehörigkeit — unter dem dazugehörigen Simplex oder dessen Stamm zu finden sind (wie Brautjungfer unter Braut, Brauhaus unter Brau-). Die Einfügung unter dem Grundwort geschieht mit Hilfe der Tilde (~).

I. Vocabulary

1. The vocabulary contains over and above the general scheme of a dictionary:

a) The most important terms for things, institutions, and facts bearing on the whole cultural life of Germany with reference to corresponding or similar notions in America and England and, in a limited measure, also in Scotland and Ireland as well as in the colonies.

b) The chief terminology of the arts and sciences.

c) The main foreign words as used in German today.

d) The chief proverbs, proverbial phrases, and idiomatic expressions of all classes.

2. a) Prefixes have been treated systematically, those of verbs especially as to the possibility or impossibility of being separated from these verbs:
d·urch|dringen — durchdr·ingen
and as to their past participle:
d·urchgedrungen — durchdr·ungen.

b) Suffixes have been treated separately as well
e.g. -haft, -heit, nis, etc.

3. a) The flexion of substantives has been added as e. g.:
gen sg/nom pl: **Ball** (e)s/~̈e
~̈ is the sign for the *umlaut*-form of a, o, u; ~̈e here means Bälle.

b) The flexion of substantives ending in -ß or -s (-ꞩ in black-letter) requires two ss (ſſ in black-letter); therefore, in order to repeat the whole ending, the hyphen has been used instead of the tilde-mark (~):
Ergebnis: -nisses/-nisse;
Genuß: -nusses/-nüsse.

4. a) To the irregular ("strong") verbs the preterite and past participle (separated by an oblique bar) have been added in [] brackets:
geben: [gab/gegeben].

b) For compound verbs with separable prefix the flexion will be found under the simple verb; thus for
ab|geben under **geben.**

5. As a rule proper names in the narrower sense have been collected in a special list at the end, with the exception of those cases in which they are used in compound words like *Röntgenstrahlen* or in phrases like "*das Ei des Kolumbus*".

II. Arrangement of Catchwords

1. The catchwords are arranged in alphabetical order. Compounds, however, will be found under the simple noun to which they etymologically belong (e. g. Brautjungfer under Braut, Brauhaus under Brau-). Such groupings under the root-word have been made with the aid of the tilde-mark (~).

2. Abgeleitete Wörter (wie *glaubhaft*, *glaubwürdig*) stehen i. a. an ihrer richtigen Stelle im Alphabet, wobei ihre Zugehörigkeit zu *Glaube*, *glauben* durch die örtlich unmittelbare Nähe zu diesen Wörtern ins Auge springt. Wo nötig ist aber auf die Zugehörigkeit hingewiesen.

3. Verbalkomposita (wie: *ich nehme an*) finden sich unter dem Infinitiv (*an|nehmen*).

III. Das Stichwort

1. Wortklassen verschiedener Art (Substantiv, Adjektiv, Adverb, Verb etc.) aber derselben Form, sind meist — unter besonderen Nummern — unter einem Stichwort zusammengefaßt.

2. Dem Stichwort als Grundwort sind im allgemeinen die von ihm mit Sicherheit abgeleiteten Wörter — und nur diese — in Fettdruck angefügt. Die Anfügung erfolgt durch die Tilde (~):

   ·Achsel- ~band... ~drüse.

   Unter den fettgedruckten abgeleiteten Stichwörtern bezieht sich diese Tilde also stets nur auf das an der Spitze stehende Grundwort; vgl. III. 4.

3. Beginnt das abgeleitete Wort im Gegensatz zu dem Grundwort mit einem großen Buchstaben oder umgekehrt, so wird dies durch Schrägkreuz über der Tilde gekennzeichnet (≚):

   glaubwürdig... ≚keit (= Glaubwürdigkeit).

4. Jede Tilde innerhalb eines Artikels (d. h. zwischen zwei fettgedruckten Stichwörtern) bezieht sich stets auf das vorhergehende fettgedruckte Stichwort, auch wenn dieses abgeleitet ist:

   gleich- ...≚berechtigung..; politische ~ (= politische Gleichberechtigung); vgl. III. 2.

IV. Die Aussprache

1. Der Aussprachebezeichnung (nach dem Stichwort in eckiger [ ] Klammer) ist die Umschrift der allgemein anerkannten *International Phonetic Association* zugrunde gelegt.

2. Die Betonung ist durch einen hochgestellten Punkt (·) vor dem zu betonenden Vokal des Stichworts gekennzeichnet. Auch bei einsilbigen Wörtern ist dieser Betonungspunkt gesetzt, wenn von dem Stichwort Komposita vorhanden sind; dies bedeutet, daß auch bei den Kompositen der Ton auf der ersten Silbe bleibt. Ausnahmen sind besonders vermerkt:

   ·Acht- ~eck, aber: **~m·onatskind.**

   Betonungsbezeichnungen in abgeleiteten oder zusammengesetzten Wörtern heben die Betonungsbezeichnung des Stammwortes auf.

V. Die Wortklassen

1. Gleich hinter dem Stichwort (wenn erforderlich hinter dem phonetischen Hinweis) steht die Bezeichnung der Wortkategorie:

   a = Adjektiv, adv = Adverb etc. → Liste der Abkürzungen auf S. XXXV f.

2. Derivatives (such as *glaubhaft*, *glaubwürdig*) are generally to be found in their proper places in the alphabet. It is evident that they belong to *Glaube*, *glauben* which they follow almost immediately. In all cases where doubts may arise reference has been made from one word to the other.

3. Separated compound verbs (such as *ich nehme an*) will be found under the infinitive (*an|nehmen*)

III. The Catchword

1. Words identical in form but constituting different parts of speech (noun, adjective, adverb, etc.) are generally recorded — in specially numbered sub-headings — under one catchword.

2. To the catchword in its function as root-word are generally added (in thick-faced type) words that may safely be claimed to be derivations — and these only. Such addition is indicated by the tilde-mark (~):

   ·Achsel- ~band ...~drüse.

   The tilde-mark when used in derivative catchwords printed in heavy type always refers exclusively to the root-word heading the article; cf. III. 4.

3. When, in contrast to the root-word the derivative begins with a capital letter or vice versa, this is indicated by an x-shaped cross put over the tilde-mark (≚:)

   glaubwürdig... ≚keit (= Glaubwürdigkeit).

4. Please note that every tilde-mark within an article (i. e. between two catchwords in heavy type) always refers to the preceding catchword in heavy type, even when this is a derivative:

   gleich- ... ≚berechtigung..; politische ~ (= politische Gleichberechtigung); cf. III. 2.

IV. The Pronunciation

1. The phonetic transcription (in [ ] brackets behind the catchword) here used is that of the universally recognized *International Phonetic Association* (cf. p. XXXIII f.).

2. The stress is marked by a dot above the line (·) before the stressed vowel of every catchword. Monosyllables followed by derivatives or compounds are marked thus too in order to indicate that the stress remains on the first syllable. Exceptions are marked specially:

   ·Acht- ~eck, ... but **~m·onatskind.**

   Stresses marked in derivatives and compounds are meant to cancel the stresses indicated in the root-words.

V. The Parts of Speech

1. The catchword (or its phonetic transcription when there is one added) is followed by an indication of the part of speech to which the catchword belongs:

   a = adjective, adv = adverb, etc. → list of abbreviations on p. XXXV f.

2. Substantiva sind durch großen Anfangsbuchstaben hinreichend als solche gekennzeichnet. Hinter den Substantiven ist das Geschlecht bezeichnet (m, f, n) → Liste der Abkürzungen S. XXXVf. Wo möglich gilt die Geschlechtsbezeichnung für mehrere Stichwörter der gleichen Bedeutung.

   m pl = Maskulin Plural.

   Wenn zur gehörigen Hervorhebung erforderlich, sind die grammatikalischen Hinweise in eckiger Klammer [ ] gegeben.

3. Verbum (v):

   a) Verben, die transitiv und zugleich intransitiv vorkommen, tragen die Bezeichnung vt/i oder vi/t.

   b) Verbalflexion → I. 4. b).

2. German substantives, being characterized sufficiently by their capitals, are followed immediately by an indication of their gender (m, f, n); → list of abbreviations on p. XXXVf.

   When two or more catchwords of the same meaning and gender follow each other only one designation of their gender is added.

   m pl = masculine plural.

   Sometimes, for clearness' sake, these designations are put into brackets: [m pl].

3. The verb (v):

   a) Verbs used transitively and intransitively are indicated by vt/i or vi/t.

   b) For the flexion of verbs → I. 4. b).

VI. Anordnung der Artikel

Die englische Wiedergabe und Erläuterung

Klare Gliederung der Artikel und übersichtliche Anordnung der Bedeutungen und der idiomatischen Verwendung waren hier oberstes Prinzip.

A. Bedeutungen und erklärende Beispiele

1. Die verschiedenen Bedeutungen sind meist durch römische Ziffern, große Buchstaben (A., B. etc.), arabische Ziffern, kleine Buchstaben (a., b. etc.), einen Balken (|) oder zwei Striche (||), die abstufend verwandt werden, auseinandergehalten:

   → **Bruch, brüllen,** etc.

2. Die grammatischen Beziehungen des Stichworts zu den anderen Wortklassen sind in längeren Artikeln durch Ziffern getrennt und meist alphabetisch geordnet, so daß ein schnelles Auffinden erleichtert wird. Demselben Zwecke dient auch die Hervorhebung durch gelegentlichen Fettdruck innerhalb der langen Artikel.

3. In den erläuternden Beispielen, die fast ausschließlich den Sammlungen der beiden Autoren entstammen, erfolgt die Wiederholung des fettgedruckten Stichworts durch die Tilde ~ (bei verändertem Anfangsbuchstaben ≈) — wohlgemerkt des Stichworts!

4. Sachgebiete und Stilebenen sind in Rasurklammer gesetzt; z. B.: ⟨min⟩ = Bergbau, ⟨vulg⟩ = vulgär.

B. Der deutsche und der englische Text

1. a) Im deutschen Text sind eine Reihe von Abkürzungen verwandt worden; → Abkürzungsverzeichnis S. XXXVf.:

   h, s, m, k, gek, l, zus, e-a, e-e, e-n, etc.

   b) Oft ist der Abkürzungsstrich (-) für die Vor- oder Schlußsilbe des vorhergehenden Wortes gebraucht worden.
   Bei Flexionsangaben wiederholt der Strich (-) nur einen Teil des Stichwortes (nicht das ganze Stichwort); vgl. I. 3. b).

   Ergebnis: ...-nisses/-nisse.

   c) Unter zusammengesetzten trennbaren Verb-Stichwörtern steht *-ge-* für das *pp*:

   an|geben: ...-ge- (= angegeben).

VI. Arrangement of the Articles

Rendering and Illustrative Examples in English

It has been here our guiding principle to arrange the articles in clear-cut subdivisions and to group the meanings and the usage in such a way as to facilitate a rapid survey.

A. Meanings and illustrative examples

1. The various meanings are kept apart largely by Roman numbers, capital letters (A., B., etc.), Arabic numbers, small letters (a., b., etc.), vertical bars (|) or (||) by way of sub-heading:

   → **Bruch, brüllen,** etc.

2. In articles of some length the grammatical combinations of the catchword with other parts of speech are subdivided by numbers and put into alphabetic order. Within the longest articles the reading is also facilitated by heavy type.

3. In the illustrative examples, which are almost exclusively based on collections of our own, the catchword, which is printed in heavy type, is repeated by the tilde-mark (~); (the notation ≈ being used to indicate a change of the initial letter into the capital or vice versa).

4. The various departments of knowledge, and spheres of style have been put in ⟨ ⟩-shaped brackets, e. g. ⟨minr⟩ = mineralogy; ⟨fam⟩ = *familiär*; → list of abbreviations on p. XXXVf.

B. The German and the English Text

1. a) In the German text ample use has been made of abbreviations (→ p. XXXVf.):

   h, s, k, gek, l, zus, e-a, e-e, e-n, etc.

   b) We frequently use the sign (-) by way of abbreviation. This symbol stands for the prefix or suffix of the preceding word.
   In references concerning the flexion it repeats part of the catchword instead of the whole of it (→ I. 3. b).

   Ergebnis: ... -nisses/-nisse.

   c) Under separable compound verbs *-ge-* stands for the *pp*:

   an|geben: -ge- (= angegeben).

2. Im deutschen wie im englischen Text wird ein Wort (meist Substantiv) bei Wiederholungen durch den oder die Anfangsbuchstaben abgekürzt.

3. Fremdwörter sind, wo es irgend möglich war oder geboten erschien, durch entsprechende Verdeutschungen erklärend ergänzt. Ebenso ist seltenen, dem Laien unbekannten Ausdrücken meistens eine erklärende Bedeutung zugefügt.

4. Wörter und Redensarten, die dem Jargon oder der vulgären Sprache angehören, sind durch ein davorgesetztes Kreischen (°) gekennzeichnet.

5. Dialektausdrücke sind als Stichwörter mit einem davorgesetzten Schrägkreuzchen (×) versehen, im Text meist durch ⟨dial⟩ gekennzeichnet.

6. Die Wortverbindungen und Komposita bieten im Englischen ein verwirrendes Bild und schwer lösbares Problem. Die Tatsache, daß in dieser Sprache nichts durch Regeln festgelegt und durch das Leben in ihr in einem sich ständig verändernden Fluß begriffen ist — eine Erscheinung, die ja auf allen Gebieten, nicht nur dem der Sprache festzustellen ist und daher jede systematische Behandlung ungemein erschwert —, macht sich gerade bei den Kompositen recht deutlich und unangenehm bemerkbar. Ein und dieselbe Zusammensetzung erscheint in der Literatur und in den verschiedenen Wörterbüchern bald in einem Wort, bald in zwei Wörtern gedruckt (woodcraft — wood-craft). Und die Gruppe, die im allgemeinen getrennt auftritt, erscheint bald mit Bindestrich, bald ohne Bindestrich.
Es wurde hier im allgemeinen die Praxis des N. E. D. zugrundegelegt.

2. In both the German and the English texts a word (mostly of the substantive kind) when repeated is often abbreviated by the initial.

3. Foreign words have been given an additional explanation in German whenever this was possible or seemed necessary.
An explanatary note has likewise been added to uncommon technical terms unknown to the layman.

4. Words and idioms belonging to jargon or vulgar speech have a circle above the line (°) prefixed to them.

5. Dialectal catchwords are marked by an x-shaped cross above the line (×) prefixed to them. Within the articles English dialect is marked ⟨dial⟩.

6. The combinations of words and compounds in English present a chaotic picture and an almost insoluble problem. Nothing in the language is fixed by rules, and its life is in a state of continuous flux. This fact, which is not restricted to language alone but traceable in all spheres, and which renders any systematic treatment extremely difficult, is clearly noticeable, and unpleasantly so, when dealing with English compounds. One and the same compound appears, in literature and in various dictionaries, now as one word, now as two words (woodcraft — wood-craft), the group of compounds which is generally separated appearing sometimes with a hyphen, sometimes without. We have, on the whole, followed the practice established by the N. E. D.

Allgemeine Bemerkungen über
I. Geographische Namen

1. In den englisch-sprechenden Ländern werden nicht-britische oder nicht-amerikanische geographische Namen in weiterem Umfang, als das im Deutschen der Fall ist, „unübersetzt", also in der jeweiligen Landessprache belassen; z. B. ⟨Ger⟩ Lüneburger Heide, Elbsandsteingebirge, Frisches Haff, Kurische Nehrung, Fränkische Schweiz, Oberharz, Unterharz, Thüringer Wald, Frankenwald, Fichtelgebirge (oder es wird nur der Oberbegriff übersetzt:

Weser Canal, etc.
⟨Schwed⟩ *Lake Vetter* (*Lake Véner*).

Weitere Beispiele:

⟨Span⟩ *Sierra Nevada*, *Cape Peñas*
⟨Fr⟩ *Cévennes*, *Le Puy*
Chan Bak San (in Korea)
Nienchen Tangla (im Himalaya)
Sinkian (im Tarim-Becken)
Cape São Roque (in Brasilien)
Minas Geraes (in Brasilien).

2. Wenn die englische Bezeichnung nicht angegeben ist, so schreibt sie sich wie im Deutschen; oft sind nähere Hinweise bezüglich der Lage und des Begriffes gegeben.

3. Im Gegensatz zur Erstausgabe des Deutsch-Englisch-Bandes dieses Wörterbuchs wurden die geographischen Namen in das eigentliche Wörterbuch eingearbeitet, um dem Benutzer das Nachschlagen zu erleichtern.

II. Raketen- und Raumforschung

Da die Raumfahrt im I. Band noch nicht genügend berücksichtigt werden konnte, sind in dem vorliegenden Band auch die englischen bzw. amerikanischen einschlägigen Ausdrücke und Wendungen sowohl im eigentlichen Wörterbuch als auch im Abkürzungsverzeichnis aufgenommen worden, da im deutschen Schrifttum oft nur die englischen Ausdrücke gebraucht werden.

III. Französismen

Französische und aus dem Französischen abgeleitete Ausdrücke, wie sie noch um die Jahrhundertwende Mode waren und die im vorliegenden Wörterbuch nicht aufgeführt sind, schlage man in einem guten französischen Wörterbuch nach, etwa im *Petit Larousse*. Gemeint sind Ausdrücke wie Pli [m] ⟨fig⟩ (z. B. Garde∼ ⟨mil⟩); ambieren (auf etw) (vgl. franz. ambition); medisant; hors concours.

Benutzte Literatur
Books Consulted

I

A New **English** Dictionary on Historical Principles by Sir James A. H. Murray. Oxford 1884–1921 (N.E.D.).

A New English Dictionary: Supplement. Oxford 1933ff.

The Oxford English Dictionary, XXII vols., Oxford 1933.

Chamber's 20th Century Dictionary, London 1952.

Webster's New International Dictionary of the English Language, 2 vols. Second Edition Unabridged. London 1934.

The Universal Dictionary of the English Language by H. C. Wyld. London 1932.

The American College Dictionary ed. by Clarence L. Barnhart, New York 1948.

Webster's New World Dictionary of the American Language, Encyclopedic Edition, Cleveland & New York 1951.

Webster's Students' Dictionary ed. by A. Merriam-Webster, New York 1938.

The New Century Dictionary ed. by H. G. Emery & K.G. Brewster, New York 1942.

A. Merriam Webster, Webster's New Collegiate Dictionary, Springfield, Mass. 1953.

Webster's Seventh New Collegiate Dictionary, Springfield, Mass. 1967.

The Winston Dictionary, Philadelphia, Toronto 1947.

Webster's Third New International Dictionary, A Merriam-Webster, Springfield, Mass. 1961.

The Westminster Dictionary ed. by J. M. Parrish & John R. Crossland, London n. d.

Words, The New Dictionary ed. by Charles P. Chadsey, etc., New York 1951.

Thorndike-Barnhart, Comprehensive Desk Dictionary, New York 1951.

Standard Dictionary of the English Language, International Edition, New York 1965.

Harrap's Standard **German and English**, London 1963–.

Allgemeines Englisch-Deutsches und Deutsch-Englisches Wörterbuch von Dr. Felix Flügel. 3 Bde. Braunschweig 1908.

The Concise Oxford Dictionary of Current English by H. W. Fowler and F. G. Fowler, 3. Edition. Oxford 1934.

Cassel's German and English Dictionary by Karl Breul, 3rd ed., London 1942/1959.

Deutsch-englisches Satzlexikon von H. Rabe, Stuttgart, o. J.

Schöffler-Weis, Taschenwörterbuch der englischen und deutschen Sprache, Stuttgart 1949, 1955.

Heinz Küpper, Wörterbuch der deutschen **Umgangssprache** I–VI, Hamburg 1963ff.

Paul Berg, A Dictionary of **New Words** in English. London 1953.

Otto Hietsch, Moderner Wortschatz des Englischen, Wien 1957.

Otto Hietsch, Englische Neologismen, in Moderna Språk 1956/4.

E. Leisi, Das heutige Englisch, Heidelberg 1955.

Eric Partridge, John W. Clark, British and American English since 1900, London 1951.

Mary Reifer, A Dictionary of New Words, New York 1955.

L. Pound, "Then and Now", PMLA, März 1956.

S. V. Baum, From Awol to Veep: The Growth and Specialization of the Acronym, in American Speech, Mai 1955, S. 103–110.

New Words: Oxford English Dictionary Supplement, in Supplement to The Periodical.

The English **Dialect** Dictionary by Joseph Wright. London 1898–1905.

A Dictionary of Slang and Unconventional English by Eric Partridge. London 1961.

William Freeman, A Concise Dictionary of English Slang. London 1955.

Slang, Phrase and **Idiom** in Colloquial English and their Use by Thomas R. G. Lyell. Tokyo 1931.

English Idioms by James Main Dixon, London. n d.

Logan Pearsall Smith, Words and Idioms, London 1943.

Collins, A Book of English Idioms, Longmans and Green 1956.

Alfons Weber, Idioms and Phrases, Bonn 1951.

K. Engeroff-Cicely Lovelace-Käufer, An English-German Dictionary of Idioms, 2. Aufl., München 1969.

A Dictionary of English **Style** by A. Reum, Leipzig 1931.

Eric Partridge, A Dictionary of Clichés, New York 1940.

H. W. Fowler, A Dictionary of Modern English Usage, Oxford 1926, 2. Aufl. 1965.

An A. B. C. of English Usage by H. A. Treble and G. H. Vallins, Oxford 1936.

A Dictionary of Modern **American** Usage by H. W. Horwill. Oxford 1935, 1952.

A Dictionary of American English, 4 vols., London 1938–.

The American Everyday Dictionary ed. by Jess Stein. New York 1949.

Mitford M. Mathews, A Dictionary of Americanisms, OUP 1951, Chicago 1951, 1956.

A Glossary of Americanisms compiled by H. Mutschmann, Tartu-Dorpat 1931.

Noah J. Jacobs, Amerikanische Umgangssprache, Berlin 1949.

American Variations by H. W. Horwill (S.P.E. Tract XLV), Oxford 1936.

The Study of American English by W.A. Craigie (S.P.E. Tract XXVII), Oxford 1927.

American Slang by Fred Newton Scott (S.P.E. Tract XXIV), Oxford 1926.

Dictionary of American Slang, Webster' Giant Illustrated Dictionary, edited by Joseph Devlin. The World Publishing Company, 1943.

The American Thesaurus of Slang by Lester V. Berrey & Melvin van den Bark, New York 1952.
John Baker Opdycke, Mark My Words, New York 1949.

The Oxford Dictionary of English **Proverbs,** Oxford 1948.
Burton Stevenson, The Homebook of Proverbs, Maxims, and Familiar Phrases, New York 1948.

Author's and **Printers'** Dictionary by F.H. Collins. 7. Edition. London 1933.
Säuberlich-Würfel, Buchgewerblich-graphisches Taschenlexikon. Wiesbaden 1957.
Rules for Compositors and Readers by H. Hart. 29. Edition. London 1930.
Begriffe der Reprographie, Concepts of Reprography, Hrsg. Dr. E. Ühlen, Frankfurt/M. o. J.
Elsevier's Dictionary of Printing and Allied Industries, Wijnekus 1967.

An English **Pronouncing** Dictionary by Daniel Jones. London 1967.
Broadcast English I. 3rd Ed. London 1935 (B.B.C.).
Broadcast English II. by A. Lloyd James. London 1930.
Broadcast English III. by A. Lloyd James. London 1932.
Pronunciation. A Practical Guide to American Standards by Th. Larsen and F. C. Walker. Oxford 1930.
The American Pronouncing Dictionary ed. by Frank O. Colby, New York 1950.

II

C. V. Good, Dictionary of **Education.** New York 1945.
Joseph T. Shipley, Dictionary of World Literature. New York 1953.
Dictionary of **World Literature,** ed. by Joseph T. Shipley, New York 1955.
Höfer u. Rahner (Hrsg.) Lexikon für **Theologie** u. Kirche, Freiburg 1957.
H. Brunotte u. O. Weber (Hrsg.) Kirchlich-theologisches Handwörterbuch, Göttingen 1956.
Pharos, London 1934 ff., **Cremation** Movement
H. Schmidt, **Philosophisches** Wörterbuch, Stuttgart 1955.
Wörterbuch der Philosophischen Begriffe, Hrsg. J. Hoffmeister, Hamburg 1955.
K. H. Pfeffer, Handwörterbuch der **Politik,** Darmstadt 1956.
Günther Haensch, Wörterbuch der internationalen Beziehungen u. Politik, München 1965.
Taschenbuch für den Gemeinsamen Markt, Frankfurt/M. 1957.
Europäische u. Internationale Zusammenschlüsse (Europa-Taschenbuch), Bonn 1959.

German-English Science Dictionary by Louis de Vries. New York & London 1946.
A Dictionary of **Scientific** Terms by I. F. Henderson and W. D. Henderson. Edinburgh and London 1929 & 1953.
A German-English Technical and Scientific Dictionary (Botanical Section) by A. Webel. London 1930 & 1953.
Franke, Lexikon der Physik, Stuttgart 1969.
ABC Technik u. Naturwissenschaften (Harri Deutsch), Frankfurt/M. 1969.
ABC Chemie (Harri Deutsch), Frankfurt/M. 1969.
German-English **Geological** Terminology by Dr. A. Cissarz and W. R. Jones. London 1931.
Geological and Allied Sciences by Walther Huebner, New York 1939.
Taschenbuch der Geologie, Die Entwicklungsgeschichte der Erde, Hanau u. Leipzig 1962.
S. A. Cooper, Concise International Dictionary of **Mechanics** and Geology. London 1949.
G. Haensch, Internationale Terminologie. Stuttgart 1956.

Wörterbuch für **Recht, Wirtschaft u. Politik** mit erläuternden und rechtsvergleichenden Kommentaren, E-D ⟨Am⟩ von Prof. Dr. jur. Gerhard Erdsiek, Dr. jur. Clara-Erika Dietl, Anneliese A. Weil, B. A., Solicitor u. a., Schloß Bleckede b. Hamburg 1966–68
Wörterbuch des Englischen Rechts von Dr. Karl Wertheim. Berlin 1899.
A Dictionary of English Law by W. J. Byrne. London 1923.
F. Weißenstein, Anglo-amerikanisches Rechtswörterbuch, Zürich 1950.
Hanns P. Kniepkamp, Rechtswörterbuch (E–D, D–E)[4] Berlin u. New York 1968.
K. H. Basedow, Dictionary of Legal Terms, Hamburg 1947.
Law Dictionary by L. D. Egbert, New York 1949.
Volkswirtschaftliches Wörterbuch von Dr. H. Price. Berlin 1926.
Taschenbuch des öffentlichen Lebens, Bonn 1967 ff.
Spezialwörterbuch für **Handel u. Wirtschaft,** hrsg. R. v. Eichhorn, Stuttgart 1947.
R. v. Eichborn, Wirtschaftswörterbuch, Englisch-Deutsch, Düsseldorf 1969.
F. Schönpflug, Betriebswirtschaftslehre, Stuttgart 1954.
A. Lehmbruck, Lexikon der Wirtschaft, Frankfurt/M. 1955.
Dr. Gablers Wirtschaftslexikon, Kurzausgabe 1969, Frankfurt und Wiesbaden.
H. Niklisch, Handwörterbuch der Betriebswirtschaft, Stuttgart 1956.
Deutsch-Englisches Glossarium finanzieller u. wirtschaftlicher Fachausdrücke, Frankfurt/M. 1958.
Klein, Einführung in die **DIN**-Normen, Stuttgart 1970.
H. K. Leistritz, **Außenhandelslexikon.** Frankfurt/M. 1955.
Deutsche Wirtschaftsdienst G.m.b.H., Köln, Die definierten Lieferungsklauseln des internationalen Warenhandels, [3]1953.
V. H. Frank, Company Accounts. London 1952.
G. O. May, **Financial** Accounting. New York 1946.
Siegfried Heinze, Fachwörterbuch des **Versicherungswesens** (D–E), Wiesbaden 1961.
Gebräuchliche Fachausdrücke in Handel & **Werbung** von Internationale Handelskammer, Basel o. J.
Norbert Wiener, Kybernetik, [2]1963 Econ Verlag.
W. Ross, An Introduction to Cybernetics, London 1957.
English, French & German **Banking** Terms ... by H. Scott. London 1931.
Hoppenstedt, Vademecum der Investmentfonds, Darmstadt 1967 ff.

P. Beck, Fachausdrücke der **Presse,** Vocabulary of the Press, Frankfurt/M. 1950.
W. Meyer-Eppler, Grundlagen u. Anwendung der Informationstheorie, Springer 1959.
Colin Cherry, Kommunikationsforschung, S. Fischer o. J.

Fachwörterbuch für **Forst-** & Holzwirtschaft, hrsg. v. d. Bayr. Landesforstverwaltung. München 1946.

H. Bading, Wörterbuch der **Landwirtschaft,** Park-Verlag 1947.

A. Kaestner, Lehrbuch der speziellen **Zoologie,** Stuttgart 1954 f.

J. Graf, Tierbestimmungsbuch, München 1961.

Matthew L. Harrison, British Mammals, London 1952.

A Field Guide to the **Birds** of Britain and Europe by R. T. Peterson, Guy Mountfort, P. A. D. Hollom. London 1954.

Dieselben, Die Vögel Europas, Hamburg 1954.

G. Niethammer, Handbuch der deutschen Vogelkunde, Leipzig 1937–42.

A Field to the Birds by R. T. Peterson. Cambridge (Mass.) 1947.

N. Tinbergen, The Study of Instinct. Oxford n. d.

Prof. Dr. N. Tinbergen, Instinktlehre, Berlin u. Hamburg 1952.

Konrad Lorenz, Das sogenannte Böse, Wien 1963.

Konrad Lorenz, On Aggression, London 1967.

Konrad Lorenz, Paul Leyhausen, Antriebe tierischen u. menschlichen Verhaltens, München 1968.

C. E. Hare, The Language of **Field Sports.** London & New York 1949.

E. B. Ford, **Butterflies,** London 1945.

Schröter/Schmid, **Flora** des Südens, 2. Aufl., Zürich 1956.

Botanical Section → ⟨a.⟩ II *sub* Scientific

Oleg Polunin and Anthony Huxley, Flowers of the Mediterranean, London 1965.

Louis Réau, Lexique polyglotte des termes **d'art** et d'archéologie, Ms. Wien, o. J.

Time-Life International, Ancient Egypt, Time Inc. 1965.

Time-Life International, Classical Greece, Time Inc. 1964.

Time-Life International, Imperial Rome, Time Inc. 1965; etc.

The Radio Times Dictionary of **Musical** Terms. Oxford 1930.

An International Vocabulary of Technical **Theatre** Terms, ed. by Kenneth Rae and Richard Southern, Bruxelles 1959.

Vocabulaire du **Cinéma,** Service d'informations des Pays-Bas, Service Cinematographique, Lattaye s. d.

Hoyer-Kreuter, **Technological** Dictionary. 6. Edition by Dr. A. Schlomann. Vol. I and Vol. II. Berlin 1932.

Illustrierte Technische Wörterbücher hrsg. von A. Schlomann. Bd. 10: Motorfahrzeuge. 2. Aufl. Berlin 1910. Bd. 17: Luftfahrt. Berlin 1932.

Dictionary of Technological Terms Used in Electrical Communication by O. Sattelberg. Part First. Berlin 1925.

Richard Ernst, Technisches Wörterbuch. Wiesbaden 1971.

Richard Ernst, Dictionary of Industrial Technics, 11th edition, Wiesbaden 1965.

Louis de Vries, English-German Technical and Engineering Dictionary, Wiesbaden 1954; 1965 ed. Theo. M. Herrmann.

H. G. Freeman, Das Englische Fachwort. Essen 1955.

H. G. Freeman, Elektrotechnisches Englisch. Essen 1956.

H. F. Schwenkhagen, Fachwörterbuch der Elektrotechnik (engl. u. dt.) Essen ^{2}1967.

W. Goedecke, Wörterbuch der Elektrotechnik, Fernmeldetechnik u. Elektronik, Wiesbaden 1964.

Elsevier's Electrotechnical Dictionary, London, New York 1965.

H. G. Freeman, Deutsch-englisches Spezialwörterbuch für das **Maschinenwesen** etc, 5. Aufl., Essen o. J.

Karl Steinbuch, Automat u. Mensch, ^{2}1963 Springer

Glossary of Terms used in Automatic **Data Processing,** London 1960.

Volker Hauff, Wörterbuch der Datenverarbeitung, Stuttgart 1966.

Carl Schneider, Taschenlexikon der Datenverarbeitung, Stuttgart 1967.

Fachausdrücke der Datenverarbeitung, IBM System-Literatur, o. J.

Wörterverzeichnis der Internationalen Büromaschinen-Gesellschaft, o. J.

Television Encyclopedia by Stanley Kempner. New York 1943–46.

W. E. Clason, Elsevier's Fachwörterbuch für Fernsehen, Funkortung u. Antennen. München 1955.

W. E. Miller, Television Explained. London 1953.

H. Thali, Technical Dictionary of the Terms Used in Electrical Engineering, Radio, Television, etc. Luzern 1954–55.

Coyne, Electrical School, Technical Dictionary of... Television, Radio, etc. Chicago 1955.

M. Polanyi, Dictionary of **Textile** Terms. London & New York 1956.

Louis de Vries, Wörterbuch der Textilindustrie, Bd. I, (D–E), Wiesbaden 1959, Nachtrag 1963.

Derrick O. Nicholson, Fachwörterbuch Textil, Frankfurt/M. 1967.

M. K. King, **Photographic** Dictionary (E–G). Düsseldorf 1956.

Elsevier's Dictionary of Photography, New York 1965.

Ernst Schulz, Wörterbuch der Optik u. Feinmechanik, Wiesbaden 1960.

F.-W. Meyer-Jenin, D–E & E–D, Taschenwörterbuch für den **Straßenverkehr.** Berlin 1948.

Fachwörterbuch des Kraftfahrzeugwesens etc., Wiesbaden 1957.

B. V.-Aral A.G., „Gute Reise". Berlin o. J. ⟨mot⟩.

Elsevier's Dictionary of **Detergents,** Glossary by Carrière, New York 1960.

Elsevier's Dictionary of **High Vacuum** Science and Technology, F. Weber, New York 1968.

Dictionary of Water and Sewage Engineering, compiled by Meinck and Möhle, (Elsevier) München 1963.

K. H. Eitzen, Deutsch-Englisches, Englisch-Deutsches **Militär**-Wörterbuch, 3. Aufl., Berlin 1943.

The Military Eitzen. Bonn 1957.

War Department, German Military Dictionary. Washington 1944.

Elbridge Colby, **Army Talk.** Princeton 1942.

Luftwaffen-Fachwörterbuch, hrsg. v. W. Voigtländer-H. Zuerl, Braunschweig 1940.

R. Cescotti, Luftfahrtwörterbuch (E–D, D–E). München 1954.

Marinewörterbuch/Fünfsprachig hrsg. v. Obkdo. d. Kriegsmarine. Berlin o. J.

Langenscheidts Fachwörterbuch, Wehrwesen Englisch, Berlin 1957.

Handbook of **Astronautical** Engineering, H. H. Koelle, Editor-in-Chief McGraw-Hill Book Company, Inc. 1961.

Outer Space, Prospects for Man and Society, The American Assembly, Columbia University, 1962.

Astronautik, Erfolge der Gegenwart – Projekte der Zukunft von Kenneth W. Gatland, Mainz 1963.

Eugen Sänger, Raumfahrt etc, Econ-Verlag 1963.

Fourth National Conference on the Peaceful Uses of Space, Boston Mass., 1964, National Aeronautics and Space Administration, Washington D.C., 1964, NASA SP–51.

H. H. Koelle, Theorie u. Technik der Raumfahrzeuge, Stuttgart 1964.

Elsevier's Dictionary of Aeronautics, New York 1964.

Dictionary of Technical Terms for Aerospace Use, NASA SP–7, 1965.

Weltraum-ABC, hrsg. v. Dipl.-Ing. H. Gartmann, Econ-Verlag.

Apollo 14: Science at Fra Mauro by Walter Froehlich, Produced by the Office of Public Affairs, National Aeronautics and Space Administration, Washington, D. C. 1971.

Architectural and Building Trades Dictionary by A. E. Burcke, etc, Chicago 1950.

F. Gaynor, Pocket Encyclopedia of **Atomic** Energy. New York 1950.

Rau, Wörterbuch der Kernphysik und der Kernchemie (D–E, E–D). Wiesbaden 1964.

E. Veillon, **Medizinisches** Wörterbuch, Medical Dictionary. Bern 1950.

L. De Vries, German-English Medical Dictionary. New York & London 1952.

F. Lejeune & W. E. Bunjes, Englisch-Deutsches Wörterbuch für Ärzte. Stuttgart 1953.

Wörterbuch der Medizin, hrsg. v. Prof. Dr. Maxim Zetkin & Dr. Herbert Schaldach, Berlin 1956.

Klinisches Wörterbuch von Willibald Pschyrembel, Berlin 1969.

A **Psychiatric** Glossary published by the American Psychiatric Association, Hartford, Con. 1957.

Psychische Hygiene, Hrsg. Brezina, Stransky, Wien/Bonn 1955.

Psychiatrie u. Gesellschaft, Hrsg. Ehrhardt, Ploog, Stutte, Stuttgart 1958.

Beigel: Dictionary of **Psychology** and Related Fields, New York 1971, German-English.

Bundesinstitut für **Arbeitsschutz,** 1. Arbeitsraum für Schwerbeschädigte. Soest o. J. 2. Hilfe fürs Leben, Versorgung der Körperbehinderten etc. Soest o. J.

Federal Security Agency, Vocational Rehabilitation. Washington 1947.

Elsevier's **Pharmaceutical** Technology, New York 1968.

Fünfsprachige Zusammenstellung der wichtigsten pharmazeutischen Fachausdrücke, Stuttgart 1968

Heinz Schwenk, Wörterbuch **demographischer** Grundbegriffe, Statistisches Bundesamt, Wiesbaden 1960.

The Master Dictionary of **Food** and Cookery by Henry Smith, F. H. C. T., London 1950.

Erich Lück, Fachwörterbuch des Lebensmittelwesens, Wiesbaden 1963.

III

The Encyclopaedia Britannica. 14. Edition. London 1929.

Routledge's Universal Encyclopaedia. London 1934.

Whitaker's Almanach. London 1938.

The Dictionary of National Biography. London 1885 ff.

Meyers Lexikon. 7. Aufl. 15 Bde. Leipzig 1924 bis 1933.

Der Neue **Brockhaus.** In 4 Bdn. 2. Aufl. Leipzig 1943.

Der Große Duden, Rechtschreibung, 11. Aufl. Leipzig 1934; 16. Aufl. 1968.

Der Sprach-Brockhaus. 4. Aufl. Leipzig 1944, 1955.

Herders Volkslexikon. Freiburg 1955.

Der Große Brockhaus. Wiesbaden 1952–57.

Das aktuelle Lexikon, Gütersloh 1955.

Lutz Mackensen, Neues Wörterbuch der deutschen Sprache, Darmstadt 1963.

Gerhard Wahrig, Deutsches Wörterbuch, Gütersloh 1968.

IV

Von den **Fachzeitschriften** wurden vor allem benutzt:

Sprachenkurier, Herausgeber O. Monien, Hamburg.

Die Fremdsprache, Herausgeber Deutscher Dolmetscher-Bund e. V., München.

Lebende Sprachen, Berlin 1956 ff.

idioma (Zeitschrift für Idiomatik der lebenden Sprachen), München 1961 ff. bis 1969.

Bild der **Wissenschaft,** Stuttgart 1966 ff.

H. L. Mencken, The **American Language.** New York 1943–47.

Deutsche **Hotel-Nachrichten** (international) 1959 ff.

Kunstnachrichten, Zeitschrift für internationale Kunst, Herausgeber: Kunstkreis Luzern/Freudenstadt/Wien 1964 ff.

V

Current **Abbreviations** ed. by G. E. Shankle, New York 1940.

Spillner-Göttling, Buch der Abkürzungen, Bamberg 1952.

Stephenson Abbrevs. (A Dictionary of Abbreviations), New York 1952.

Handbuch der **NATO**-Abkürzungen, Koblenz 1958.

Erklärung der phonetischen Umschrift

Die phonetische Umschrift in diesem Wörterbuch ist die der *International Phonetic Association*, die D. Jones in seinem *English Pronouncing Dictionary, eleventh Edition, Revised and Enlarged*, London 1960, zugrunde gelegt hat.
: bezeichnet die Länge des vorhergehenden Lautes [iː].
. unter einem Konsonanten bezeichnet, daß der Laut silbisch ist [ˈpænl̩].
Der Hauptton wird bezeichnet durch ˈ vor der betreffenden Silbe [ˈæktiv] [inˈæktiv].
Nebenton wird bezeichnet durch ˌ vor der Silbe [ˌinəˈtentiv].

Die Zeichen und ihre phonetischen Werte

I. Vokale

1. Englische Laute

ɑː wie in *ar*m, h*al*f, gl*a*ss, p*a*th, f*a*ther, d*a*nce
æ h*a*t
æː b*a*d
ʌ b*u*t, s*o*n, fl*oo*d, c*ou*ple
e b*e*t; h*ea*d
i b*i*t, h*y*mn; harml*e*ss, obstin*a*te, speci*me*n, circ*ui*t; *e*nhance, d*e*scend
iː b*e*, s*ee*, b*ea*t; bel*ie*f, mar*i*ne
ɔ n*o*t, l*o*ng, w*a*nt
ɔː s*aw*, *a*ll, b*o*rn, b*ough*t, y*our*, t*augh*t
o m*o*lest, *o*bey, el*o*quence
ə ide*a*, bett*er*, speci*a*l, nerv*ou*s; *a*bout, p*a*rticular, p*er*haps, c*o*nstruct, s*u*bsist; suff*o*cate
əː h*er*, b*ir*d, w*or*d, t*ur*n; *ear*n, j*our*ney
u p*u*t, l*oo*k; c*ou*ld
uː d*o*, f*oo*d; l*u*bricate, r*ue*
ẙ p*hew* (stimmloses y → 2.)

2. Nicht-englische Laute

y wie in Fr men*u*
ø Fr p*eu*
œ Fr p*eu*r
ɑ̃ Fr t*an*te
ɛ̃ Fr v*in*
ɔ̃ Fr b*on*
œ̃ Fr br*un*

II. Diphthonge und Triphthonge

ai wie in l*i*fe, l*igh*t, n*igh*t, dr*y*
aiə *fire*, *liar*, *tyre*
au h*ou*se, h*ow*
auə *our*, *hour*
ɔi b*oy*, m*oi*st
ɔiə *joyous*
ɛə h*air*, *heir*; b*are*, th*ere*
iə h*ere*, h*ear*, f*ie*rce; infer*ior*
uə p*oor*, s*ure*
ei d*ay*, n*a*me; r*eig*n, th*ey*
ou g*o*, l*ow*, c*oa*t, J*oa*n
ouə l*ower*

III. Konsonanten

1. Englische Laute

p wie in *p*ast
b *b*ed
f *f*at, tou*gh*
v *v*ain, o*f*; ⟨Ger⟩ *w*ir, *W*elt; ⟨Ind⟩ *bh*akti
t *t*ear, wish*ed*
d *d*ay, sinn*ed*
θ *th*in, me*th*od, pa*th*
ð fa*th*er, *th*at; pa*th*s

Key to the Phonetic Transcription

The phonetic notation used in this dictionary is that of the *International Phonetic Association* adopted by D. Jones in his *English Pronouncing Dictionary, eleventh Edition, Revised and Enlarged*, 1960 London.
: indicates that the preceding sound is long [iː].
. placed below a consonant indicates that the consonant is syllabic [ˈpænl̩].
The stress accent is marked by the sign ˈ before the syllable [ˈæktiv] [inˈæktiv].
Secondary stress is indicated by the sign ˌ before the syllable [ˌinəˈtentiv].

The Symbols and their Phonetic Values

I. Vowels

1. English Sounds

ɑː as in *ar*m, h*al*f, gl*a*ss, p*a*th, f*a*ther, d*a*nce
æ h*a*t
æː b*a*d
ʌ b*u*t, s*o*n, fl*oo*d, c*ou*ple
e b*e*t; h*ea*d
i b*i*t, h*y*mn; harml*e*ss, obstin*a*te, speci*me*n, circ*ui*t; *e*nhance, d*e*scend
iː b*e*, s*ee*, b*ea*t; bel*ie*f, mar*i*ne
ɔ n*o*t, l*o*ng, w*a*nt
ɔː s*aw*, *a*ll, b*o*rn, b*ough*t, y*our*, t*augh*t
o m*o*lest, *o*bey, el*o*quence
ə ide*a*, bett*er*, speci*a*l, nerv*ou*s; *a*bout, p*a*rticular, p*er*haps, c*o*nstruct, s*u*bsist; suff*o*cate
əː h*er*, b*ir*d, w*or*d, t*ur*n; *ear*n, j*our*ney
u p*u*t, l*oo*k; c*ou*ld
uː d*o*, f*oo*d; l*u*bricate, r*ue*
ẙ p*hew* (voiceless y → 2.)

2. Non-English Sounds

y as in Fr men*u*
ø Fr p*eu*
œ Fr p*eu*r
ɑ Fr t*an*te
ɛ̃ Fr v*in*
ɔ̃ Fr b*on*
œ̃ Fr br*un*

II. Diphthongs and Triphthongs

ai as in l*i*fe, l*igh*t, n*igh*t, dr*y*
aiə *fire*, *liar*, *tyre*
au h*ou*se, h*ow*
auə *our*, *hour*
ɔi b*oy*, m*oi*st
ɔiə *joyous*
ɛə h*air*, *heir*; b*are*, th*ere*
iə h*ere*, h*ear*, f*ie*rce; infer*ior*
uə p*oor*, s*ure*
ei d*ay*, n*a*me; r*eig*n, th*ey*
ou g*o*, l*ow*, c*oa*t, J*oa*n
ouə l*ower*

III. Consonants

1. English Sounds

p as in *p*ast
b *b*ed
f *f*at, tou*gh*
v *v*ain, o*f*; *w*ir, *W*elt; ⟨Ind⟩ *bh*akti
t *t*ear, wish*ed*
d *d*ay, sinn*ed*
θ *th*in, me*th*od, pa*th*
ð fa*th*er, *th*at; pa*th*s

s wie in *s*ee, de*c*ide, *sc*ene; hat*s*
z *z*eal, ri*se*, hi*s*; bed*s*, base*s*
ʃ *sh*ow; ma*ch*ine; mo*t*ion, spe*c*ial, mi*ss*ion
tʃ *ch*in, ri*ch*, pic*t*ure
ʒ vi*s*ion, mea*s*ure; gara*ge*
dʒ *g*erm, *j*ust, *J*ordan, bri*dge*
k *c*at, mo*ck*; s*ch*ool; *k*ey; *qu*ay
g *g*ive, ba*g*
h *h*ang; *h*ospital; *wh*ole
n *n*ever; *kn*ee, *gn*at
n̩ cott*on*y
m *m*uch; la*mb*, colu*mn*
ŋ ri*ng*, so*ng*, si*ng*er; fi*n*ger, li*n*k
r *r*iver, glo*r*y; *wr*ong
l *l*ook, *l*i*l*y
l̩ origin*al*
j *y*es, *y*oung; mill*i*on
w *w*in, *wh*ich; pers*u*ade, q*u*aint

2. Nicht-englische Laute

ç wie in Ger i*ch*
x Scot, Ir lo*ch*, lou*gh*, pibro*ch*; Ger do*ch*
ɲ Fr Colo*gn*e

IV. Verbindungen von Konsonanten und Vokalen oder Diphthongen

ju: wie in d*u*ty, n*ew*, d*eu*ce, s*ui*t
juə p*ure*, c*u*rious

s as in *s*ee, de*c*ide, *sc*ene; hat*s*
z *z*eal, ri*se*, hi*s*; bed*s*, base*s*
ʃ *sh*ow; ma*ch*ine; mo*t*ion, spe*c*ial, mi*ss*ion
tʃ *ch*in, ri*ch*, pic*t*ure
ʒ vi*s*ion, mea*s*ure; gara*ge*
dʒ *g*erm, *j*ust, *J*ordan, bri*dge*
k *c*at, mo*ck*; s*ch*ool; *k*ey; *qu*ay
g *g*ive, ba*g*
h *h*ang; *h*ospital; *wh*ole
n *n*ever; *kn*ee, *gn*at
n̩ cott*on*y
m *m*uch; la*mb*, colu*mn*
ŋ ri*ng*, so*ng*, si*ng*er; fi*n*ger, li*n*k
r *r*iver, glo*r*y; *wr*ong
l *l*ook, *l*i*l*y
l̩ origin*al*
j *y*es, *y*oung; mill*i*on
w *w*in, *wh*ich; pers*u*ade, q*u*aint

2. Non-English Sounds

ç as in Ger i*ch*
x Scot, Ir lo*ch*, lou*gh*, pibro*ch*; Ger do*ch*
ɲ Fr Colo*gn*e

IV. Combinations of Consonants and Vowels or Diphthongs

ju: as in d*u*ty, n*ew*, d*eu*ce, s*ui*t
juə p*ure*, c*u*rious

In diesem Wörterbuch verwandte Abkürzungen

Abbreviations used in this dictionary

~ (fett)	Wiederholung des Stichworts z. B. **Auftrag: ~geber** = Auftraggeber
≈	Wiederholung des Stichworts mit kl (statt gr) bzw. mit gr (statt kl) Anfangsbuchstaben z. B. **auseinander: ≈setzung** = Auseinandersetzung **achtbar: ≈keit** = Achtbarkeit
~ (mager)	(im Text) Wiederholung des Stichworts bzw. Unterstichworts z. B. **auseinander: ≈setzung:** ~en = Auseinandersetzungen
~̈	Wiederholung des Stichworts mit Umlaut: z. B. Abhang: ~̈e = Abhänge Land: ~̈er = Länder Baum: ~̈e = Bäume
–	mst ⟨tech⟩ = bis: 6–8 cm; hängt das Folgende an e–n Buchstaben des Stichworts sinnvoll an: bezeichnen: –net = bezeichnet
·	steht vor dem zu betonenden Vokal od Diphthong z. B. ·Amme, ·Auge; aber auch in einsilbigen Wörtern, von denen Flexion oder Ableitungen angegeben sind
~(e)s/~̈er	z. B. Wald ~(e)s/~̈er, wobei ~(e)s den [gen sg] u ~̈er den [nom pl] bedeuten
/	stellt bei unregelmäßigen Verben das pret und das pp nebeneinander z. B. kommen [kam/gekommen]
|	das zus-gesetzte Verb ist trennbar: z. B. ab|fangen, auf|fangen: ich fange ab, auf; pp: ab–, aufgefangen; → –ge–, –zu–; betr. Konjugation → das Simplex: z. B. fangen
„ .. "	bildlich, *figurative(ly)*
→	siehe (a. im anderen Band)
→ d.	siehe dort
→ o.	siehe oben
→ u.	siehe unten
×	mundartlich, *dialect*
*	selten
°	burschikos, Jargon, vulgär
†	ausgestorben, archaisch
[ ]	betr. Grammati(kali)sches, Herkunft, Aussprache [etc.
( )	betr. Ergänzungen, Erklärungen
⟨ ⟩	betr. Sachgebiete & Stil
&	und, *and*
(P)	auf Personen bezüglich (*of persons*)
(S)	auf Sachen bezüglich (*of things*)
(T)	auf Tiere bezüglich (*of animals*)

a (nach dem Stichwort)	*adjective*
a. ⟨a.⟩	auch, *also*
[abbr]	*abbreviated*, Abkürzung
[abs]	absolut gebraucht
[abstr]	abstrakt
⟨ac⟩	*acoustics*
[acc]	*accusative*
⟨acc mach⟩	*accounting machine*, Buchungsmaschine
[act]	*active voice*, Aktiv
A. D.	*Anno Domini* nach Christi Geburt
⟨ad⟩	*advertising*, Reklame
adj	*adjective*
adv	*adverb*
⟨a-engl⟩	außerenglisch, nicht in englischer Kultur, *not English*
⟨aero⟩	*aeronautics*, Flugwesen
⟨aerodyn⟩	*aerodynamics*
⟨æsth⟩	*æsthetics*
⟨agr⟩	*agriculture*, Landwirtschaft
ags	angelsächsisch, *Anglo-Saxon*
⟨AInd⟩	*Anglo-Indian*
⟨AIr⟩	*Anglo-Irish*
(allg)	allgemein(e, –er, –es)
⟨allg⟩	im allgemeinen Sinne
⟨Am⟩	*America*(*nism*), (urspr) amerikanisch
⟨a–n⟩	*astronautic*(*al*), Raumfahrt
⟨anat⟩	*anatomy*
⟨ant⟩	*antiquity*, Altertum
⟨anthr⟩	*anthropology*
a p	*a person*
[Arab]	Arabien, arabisch
⟨arch⟩	*architecture*
⟨archa⟩	*archaic*
⟨archæol⟩	*archæology*
⟨arith⟩	*arithmetic*
[art, Art]	*article*, Artikel
⟨artill⟩	*artillery*
⟨arts⟩	*fine arts*, Kunst
Ass	*Association*
⟨astr⟩	*astronomy*
⟨astrol⟩	*astrology*
⟨astronaut⟩	*astronautic*(*al*), Raumfahrt
⟨A. T.⟩	Altes Testament
⟨at⟩	*atom*(*ic*)
⟨athl⟩	*athletics*
[attr]	attributiv
⟨Aust⟩	*Australia*(*nism*)
[Austria]	österreichisch, *Austrian*
[aux]	*auxiliary*, Hilfs–
⟨bact⟩	*bacteriology*
⟨bak⟩	*baking*, Bäckerei
⟨bal⟩	*balance sheet*, Bilanz
⟨ball⟩	*ballistics*
⟨bank⟩	*banking*, Bankwesen
⟨bay⟩	bayerisch, *Bavarian*
B. C.	*Before Christ*
Bdtg	Bedeutung, *meaning*
bek	bekommen

bes	besonders, besondere
best	bestimmt(–e, –es etc)
betr	betreffend, betreffs
⟨bib⟩	*biblical*
⟨bill⟩	*billards*
⟨biochem⟩	Biochemie
⟨biol⟩	*biology*
⟨bookb⟩	*bookbinding*
⟨bot⟩	*botany*
⟨box⟩	*boxing*
⟨BR⟩	Bundesrepublik
⟨brew⟩	*brewery*, Brauwesen
⟨brit⟩	britisch
bzw	beziehungsweise
c	*century*, Jahrhundert
⟨call⟩	*calligraphy*
⟨Cambr⟩	*Cambridge*
⟨Can⟩	*Canada, Canadian*
⟨carp⟩	*carpentry*, Zimmererarbeit
⟨cart⟩	*cartography*
⟨cast⟩	*casting*, Metallguß
⟨cav⟩	*cavalry*, Kavallerie
⟨C. E.⟩	*Church of England*
⟨Celt⟩	Celtic
⟨ceram⟩	*ceramics*, Keramik
⟨chem⟩	*chemistry*
⟨chron⟩	*chronology*
⟨civ l⟩	*civil law*
⟨Col⟩	*Colonies*
⟨com⟩	commercial
⟨comm⟩	*communications*, Nachrichtenwesen
[comp]	compound(s), zus-gesetzt (Wort)
⟨comp⟩	*computer & tabulator*, Rechenmaschinen
[compr]	*comparative*
[conj]	*conjunction*
⟨cont⟩	contemptuously, verächtlich
⟨contr⟩	*contract*, Vertrag
⟨cosm⟩	*cosmetics*
⟨crem⟩	*cremation*, Feuerbestattung
⟨crick⟩	*cricket*
⟨crim l⟩	*criminal law*
⟨cryst⟩	*crystallography*
⟨cul⟩	*culinary*, Küche, Kochen
⟨cust⟩	*customs*, Zollwesen
⟨cyb⟩	*cybernetics*, Kybernetik
⟨cycl⟩	*cycling*, Radfahren
d.	dort
[dat]	dative
⟨DBR⟩	Deutsche Bundesrepublik, → GFR
⟨decor⟩	*decoration*
⟨DDR⟩	Deutsche Demokratische Republik
d–e(r, –n etc)	deine(r), deinen etc
[def]	*definite*
⟨demog⟩	*demography*, Bevölkerungswissenschaft
⟨dent⟩	*dentistry*, Zahnheilkunde
⟨dero⟩	*derogatory*, abfällig
desgl.	desgleichen, *as well*
⟨dial⟩	*dialect(al)*, mundartlich
[dim]	*diminutive*, verkleinernd
⟨dipl⟩	*diplomacy*
⟨distil⟩	*distillation*
dtsch	deutsch, im dtsch Kulturleben
(–) e–a (–)	einander
ebd	ebenda
⟨ec⟩	*ecclesiastical*, kirchlich
⟨eco⟩	*economics*, Wirtschaftswesen
⟨educ⟩	*education*, Schulwesen
⟨Eg⟩	*Egyptian*, ägyptisch
⟨eig⟩	im eigentlichen Sinne
⟨el⟩	*electricity*
⟨electro⟩	*electronic (device)*
[ell]	*elliptisch*

⟨embr⟩	*embroidery*, Stickerei
⟨emph⟩	emphatisch
⟨engin⟩	*engineering*, Ingenieurwesen
Engl	England
⟨engl⟩	englisch, in England, im englischen Kulturleben
⟨engr⟩	*engraving*, Gravieren, Radierung
⟨ent⟩	*entomology*, Insektenkunde
e–s, e–r etc	eines, einer *etc*
etc	*et cetera* L und so weiter
⟨eth⟩	*ethology*, Verhaltensforschung
⟨ethn⟩	*ethnology*, Völkerkunde
etw	etwas
⟨euph⟩	*euphemistic*
⟨exch⟩	*stock exchange*, Börsenwesen
f	für, *for*
f (nach e–m Hauptwort)	*feminine* (*gender*), weiblich
⟨fam⟩	familiär, *colloquial*
⟨fenc⟩	*fencing*, Fechtkunst
⟨fig⟩	*figurative(ly)*, bildlich
⟨film⟩	Film, *film*
⟨fin⟩	*finance*, Finanzwesen
Fn.	Familienname
folg	folgende(r, –s), folgendes Stichwort
⟨for⟩	*forestry*, Forstwesen
⟨fort⟩	*fortification*, Befestigungswesen
⟨found⟩	*founding*, (Form-)Gießerei
[Fr], Fr	*French*
⟨ftb⟩	*football*, Fußball
Galsw	*Galsworthy*
⟨gard⟩	*gardening*, Gärtnerei
–ge–	z. B. an|ge|geben, v an|geben
geg∼	z. B. geg|essen, v essen
⟨geh. Spr.⟩	gehobene Sprache
gek	gekommen, *come*
[gen]	*genitive*
⟨geneal⟩	*genealogy*
⟨geog⟩	*geography*
⟨geol⟩	*geology*
⟨geom⟩	*geometry*
⟨Ger⟩	*German*
geschr	geschrieben
gespr	gesprochen
gest	gestiftet
⟨GFR⟩	*German Federal Republic*
ggr	gegründet, *founded*
Ggs	Gegensatz, *opposite*
⟨glass⟩	*glassmaking*
[Gr], (Gr)	*Greek*, griechisch
gr	große(r, –s etc)
⟨gram⟩	*grammar*, Grammatik
gw	gewesen
⟨gym⟩	*gymnastics*, Turnen
⟨gyn⟩	*gynaecology*
h	haben, (*to*) *have*
[h]	mit haben konstruiert
[h & s]	mit haben & sein konstruiert
H. C.	*House of Commons*
H. L.	*House of Lords*
⟨hebr⟩	hebräisch, *Hebrew*
⟨her⟩	*heraldry*, Heraldik
⟨hist⟩	*history*, Geschichte
⟨hock⟩	*hockey*
[holl]	holländisch
⟨hors⟩	*horsemanship*, Reitkunst
⟨hort⟩	*horticulture*, Gartenbau(kunst)
⟨hot⟩	*hotel*, *restaurant*
h.s.	*himself*, *herself*
⟨hum⟩	*humorously*
⟨hunt⟩	*hunting*, Jagd
⟨hyg⟩	*hygiene*
i. a.	im allgemeinen

⟨ich⟩	*ichthyology*, Fischkunde
[imp]	*imperative mood*, Befehlsform
[imps]	*impersonal*, unpersönlich
[in comp]	*in compound(s)*, in Zus–setzung(en)
⟨Ind⟩	*Indian*
⟨ind⟩	*industry*
[indef]	*indefinite*, unbestimmt
[inf]	*infinitive*
⟨ins⟩	*insurance*, Versicherungswesen
[insep]	*inseparable*, nicht trennbar
[interr]	*interrogative*, Frageform
[intj]	*interjection*, Ausruf
[invar]	invariabel, nicht flektiert
[Ir]	*Irish*
⟨iron⟩	*ironically*
[irr]	*irregular*, unregelmäßig
[It], It	*Italian*, italienisch
⟨Jap⟩	*Japan(ese)*
jd(s, –m, –n)	jemand(es, –em, –en)
Jh(s)	Jahrhundert(s)
⟨journ⟩	*journalese*, Zeitungssprache
⟨jur⟩	*jurisprudence*
k	kommen ([⟨a.⟩ *in comp*])
[kaus]	*kausativ*
kl	kleine(r, –s *etc*)
k–n (–m, –s)	keinen, keinem, keines
[koll]	kollektiv
[konkr]	konkret
Kons.	Konsonant
[konstr]	konstruiert
kz	kurz(er, –es *etc*)
l	lassen
[L]	*Latin*, Latein
⟨lex⟩	*lexicography*
⟨ling⟩	*linguistics*
⟨Lit⟩	Literatur
⟨liter⟩	literarisch
⟨loc⟩	*local*
⟨log⟩	*logic*
⟨logar⟩	*logarithmic*
⟨logist⟩	*logistics*, Logistik
⟨luth⟩	lutherisch
m (nach e–m Hauptwort)	*masculine (gender)*, männlich
m	machen ([⟨a⟩ *in comp*] ausm *etc*)
⟨mach⟩	*machinery*, Maschinenbau
⟨man⟩	*manicure*
⟨mar⟩	*marine*
⟨mas⟩	*masonry*, Maurerhandwerk
⟨math⟩	*mathematics*
⟨md⟩	mitteldeutsch
⟨mech⟩	*mechanics*
⟨med⟩	*medicine*
m–e, –r, –n	meine, –r, –n
⟨met⟩	*metallurgy*
⟨meteor⟩	*meteorology*
⟨micro⟩	*microscope*, Mikroskop
⟨mil⟩	*military*
⟨min⟩	*mining*, Bergwerkswesen
⟨minr⟩	*mineralogy*
⟨m. m.⟩	*mutatis mutandis* → Abkürzungsverzeichnis (Anhang)
⟨mod⟩	*modern*
⟨Moham⟩	*Mohammedan*
⟨mot⟩	*motoring*, Kraftfahrwesen
⟨mount⟩	*mountaineering*, Bergsteigen
m.s.	*myself*
Ms(s)	*manuscript(s)*
m–s, –r etc	meines, meiner *etc*
mst	meist, *mostly*
⟨mus⟩	*music(al)*
⟨myth⟩	*mythology*
N	NATO

n	*neuter (gender)*, sächlich
⟨naut⟩	*nautical*, nautisch
⟨nav⟩	*navy*, die Flotte betreffend
⟨nazi⟩	*National Socialistic*
[neg]	*negativ*, in negativen Sätzen
[neol]	*neologism*
niedd	niederdeutsch
[nom]	*nominative*
nod	nordostdeutsch
nordd	norddeutsch
npr	*nomen proprium*, Eigenname
⟨N. T.⟩	Neues Testament
⟨num⟩	*numismatics*, Münzenkunde
nwd	nordwestdeutsch
→ o.	siehe oben
o. ä.	oder ähnliches
obb	oberbayerisch
obd	oberdeutsch
[obs]	*obsolete*, veraltet
⟨occ⟩	*occultism*
od	oder
⟨off⟩	*officialese*, *office*, Amt(ssprache)
omd	ostmitteldeutsch
ond	ostniederdeutsch
⟨opt⟩	*optics*
[opt]	*optative*, Wunschform
⟨orn⟩	*ornithology*, Vogelkunde
o.s.	*oneself*
österr	österreichisch, *Austrian*
⟨Oxf⟩	*Oxford*
P	Person(en)
(P)	auf Personen bezüglich, *of persons*
p, *p*	*person*
⟨paint⟩	*painting*, Malerei
⟨pal⟩	*palæontology*
⟨pap⟩	*paper manufacturing*
⟨parl⟩	*parliamentary*
⟨Parl⟩	*Parlament*
[part]	*participle*
[pass]	*passive voice*, Passiv
⟨path⟩	*pathology*
⟨ped⟩	*pedagogy*, Pädagogik
⟨pharm⟩	*pharmacology*
⟨phil⟩	*philology*
⟨philos⟩	*philosophy*
⟨phon⟩	*phonetics*
⟨phot⟩	*photography*
⟨phys⟩	*physics*
⟨physiol⟩	*physiology*
[pl]	*plural*
[pl konstr]	pluralisch konstruiert
⟨poet⟩	*poetry*, *poetical*
⟨pol⟩	*politics*, *political*
⟨pop⟩	*popular*, volkstümlich
[Port]	*Portuguese*
[pp]	*past participle*
⟨praeh⟩	prähistorisch
[pred]	*predicative*
[pref]	*prefix*
[prep]	*preposition*
[pres]	*present*, Gegenwart
⟨Presb⟩	*Presbyterian*
[pret]	*preterite*, Vergangenheit
⟨print⟩	*printing*, Druckwesen
⟨priv l⟩	*private law*
⟨prob⟩	*probability*, Wahrscheinlichkeit
[pron]	*pronoun*, Fürwort
[pron dem]	*demonstrative pronoun*
[pron interr]	*interrogative pronoun*
[pron pers]	*personal pronoun*
[pron poss]	*possessive pronoun*
[pron rel]	*relative pronoun*
⟨pros⟩	*prosody*
⟨prov⟩	*proverb*, Sprichwort
[prs]	*present*
[prs p]	*present participle*

[psych]	*psychology*
[qual]	*qualitative*, *quality*
[quant]	*quantitative*, *quantity*
⟨rad⟩	*radio*, Funk
⟨rail⟩	*railway*, *railroad*, Eisenbahn
⟨R. C.⟩	*Roman-Catholic*
rd	rund, *about*
⟨rec⟩	*recording*, (Ton-)Aufnahme
[recip]	*reciprocal*
[refl]	*reflexive*, rückbezüglich
[reg]	*regular*, regelmäßig
⟨rehab⟩	(*occupational*) *rehabilitation*
⟨rel⟩	*religion*
[rel]	*relative*
⟨rep⟩	*reprography*
⟨rhein⟩	rheinisch
⟨rhet⟩	*rhetorical*
⟨Rug⟩	*Rugby*
[Russ]	*Russian*, russisch
S	Sache
(S)	auf Sachen bezüglich, *of things*
s (nach e–m Hauptwort)	*substantive*
s	sein [vb]
[s]	mit sein konstruiert
[s & h]	mit sein & haben konstruiert
s.	siehe
⟨SAfr⟩	*South Africa*(*n*)
s.b.	*somebody*, jemand
⟨SBZ⟩	Sowjetisch Besetzte Zone, → DDR
sc	*scilicet*, nämlich
schw	schweizerisch
⟨scient⟩	*scientific*, wissenschaftlich
⟨Scot⟩	*Scottish*, *Scotland*
⟨sculp⟩	*sculpture*, Bildhauerei
sd	süddeutsch
s. d.	siehe dort
s–e(r, –n, –m)	seine(r, –n, –m)
[sep]	*separable*, trennbar
⟨sew⟩	*sewing*, Näherei
⟨sex⟩	*sex*
[sg]	*singular*
[sg konstr]	singularisch konstruiert
Shak	*Shakespeare*
⟨ski⟩	*ski-ing*, Skilauf
⟨sl⟩	*slang*, der Slang
⟨soc⟩	*sociology*
sod	südostdeutsch
[Span]	*Spanish*
⟨spin⟩	*spinning*, Spinnerei
⟨sport⟩	Sport
Spr	Sprache, *speech*
s–s, s–r etc	seines, seiner *etc*
⟨stat⟩	*statistics*
Std.	Stunde(n), *hour*(*s*)
⟨st exch⟩	*stock exchange*, Börsenwesen
sth	*something*, etwas
⟨stud⟩	*students'*
s. u.	siehe unten
[subj]	*subjunctive*, Konjunktiv
[subst]	*substantive*(*s*)
[subst a]	substantiviertes Adjektiv
südd	süddeutsch
[suff]	*suffix*
[sup]	*superlative*
⟨surg⟩	*surgery*, Chirurgie
⟨surv⟩	*surveying*, Vermessungswesen
s. vor.	siehe voriges Stichwort
svw	soviel wie

Sw	*Swiss*, schweizerisch
swd	südwestdeutsch
⟨swim⟩	*swimming*
(T)	Tier, auf Tiere bezüglich, *of animals*
⟨tact⟩	*tactics*, *tactical*
⟨tail⟩	*tailoring*, Schneiderei
⟨tan⟩	*tanning*, Gerberei
⟨tax⟩	*tax*, Steuer
⟨tech⟩	*technical*
⟨teens⟩	*Teenager Slang*
⟨telg⟩	*telegraphy*
⟨telph⟩	*telephony*
⟨telv⟩	*television*, Fernsehen
⟨ten⟩	*lawn tennis*, (Rasen-)Tennis
⟨tex⟩	*textile* (*fabrics*)
th, *ths*	*thing*(*s*), Ding(e)
Thack	*Thackeray*
⟨theat⟩	*theatre*, *theatrical*
⟨theol⟩	*theology*
⟨turbo⟩	Turbinen–
⟨typ⟩	*typography*
⟨typewr⟩	*typewriter*, Schreibmaschine
u	und
→ u.	siehe unten
u.	unten
u. a.	unter anderem
u ä	und ähnliches
übl	übliche(r, –s *etc*)
übs	übersetzt
⟨übtr⟩	in übertragenem Sinne
⟨univ sl⟩	*university slang*
urspr	ursprünglich(e, –er *etc*)
USA	*United States of America*
v (nach dem Stichwort)	*verb*, Zeitwort
v	von, vom
[v aux]	*auxiliary verb*, Hilfszeitwort
vb	*verb*, Zeitwort
versch	verschieden(e, –en *etc*)
⟨vet⟩	*veterinary*, Tierheilkunde
vgl	vergleiche
[vi]	*verb intransitive*
[vi/t]	*verb intransitive and transitive*
Vn.	Vorname
[voc]	*vocative*
Vok	Vokal, *vowel*
→ vor.	siehe voriges Stichwort
[vrefl]	*verb reflexive*, rückbezügliches Zeitwort
[vt]	*verb transitive*
[vt/i]	*verb transitive and intransitive*
⟨vulg⟩	*vulgar*
w	werden
⟨weav⟩	*weaving*, Weberei
⟨wir⟩	*wireless*, Funkwesen
⟨wrest⟩	*wrestling*, Ringkampf
WWI	*World War I*
y.s.	*yourself*, *-lves*
z	zu, zum, zur
⟨zoo⟩	*zoology*
–zu–	z. B.: an|zu|geben, v an|geben
zus–	zusammen–
zw	zwischen
Zw–	Zwischen–

DAS WÖRTERBUCH

A

A, a n ~/~ *A, a* | (ich bin) das A und O (*I am*) *Alpha and Omega* ‖ von A bis Z *from beginning to end*, (Buch) *from cover to cover* ‖ Wer A sagt, muß auch B sagen *he who calls the tune must pay the piper*; *in for a penny, in for a pound* **⁓-Kohle** f ⟨pharm⟩ *activated carbon*

A, a n ~/~ ⟨mus⟩ *A, a*; geben Sie mal ~ *give me an A* ‖ A(-dur) *A* (*major*); a(-moll) *a* (*minor*) ‖ ~-Saite *A-string*

à [Fr] ⟨com⟩ *at*; *each* ‖ 3 Pfd ~ 3 M *3 lbs at 3 marks a pound*; vgl 9 Bde ~ 2,50 M *9 vols each 2/6* (od *2/6 each*)

a [It] ⟨com⟩ ~ Konto *on account*; → Akontozahlung

a- pref (in Fremdwörtern) (nicht–, un–, –los) *a–* (→ amoralisch) ‖ → an–

Ä, ä n (auch ae geschrieben) der Umlaut des a

A-a! n ⟨Kindersprache⟩ *ha-ha*! ‖ mach' ~! *make a motion*!, *do number two*!

Aa, Aach, Ach f ~/~en *river, brook*

·Aachen n *Aachen, Aix-la-Chapelle* [Fr]

Aal m ~(e)s/~e ⟨ich⟩ *eel*; M·eer≈ *conger, conger eel*; junger, unreifer ~ *elver*; ~ in Gelee *jellied eel* | glatt wie ein ~ = ≈glatt | sich winden wie ein ~ *to wriggle like an eel* ⟨a. fig⟩ **≈artig** a *eel-like*; **~fang** m *eel-fishing, catching of eels*; **≈förmig** a *eel-shaped*; **~gabel** f *eel-spear*; **·≈gl·att** a *slippery as an eel* ⟨a. fig⟩; ⟨Am fig sl⟩ *slick*; **⁓molch** m ⟨zoo⟩ *eel-like amphibian*; *Congo snake*; **⁓quappe, ⁓raupe** f *eel-pout, burbot*

·aalen vrefl [h] sich ~ *to laze, lounge*; *to be idle* (od *lazy*); ⟨Am fam⟩ *to feel like a million dollars*

Aar m ~s/~e ⟨poet⟩ *eagle*

Aar, ·Aare f (Fluß in der Schweiz) *Aar*

·Aargau m (Schweiz. Kanton) *Aargau, Argovia*

·Aargauer m, **·aargauisch** a *Argovian*

·Aarhus n (dän. Stadt)

·Aas n ~es/~e & Äser **1.** *carrion* ‖ (Kadaver) *carcass*; ⟨bib⟩ wo ~ ist, da sammeln sich die Raben *wheresoever the carcass is, there will the eagles be gathered together* **2.** (Köder) *bait, lure* **3.** ⟨fig⟩ (Schimpfwort) *beast*; *louse*; *rascal*; *bitch* ‖ ein ~ *a sharp fellow* (so ein ~! *that's a sh. f.*); *a slyboots* ‖ °kein ~ (= niemand) *not a blooming soul* ⟨sl⟩ **4. ⁓fliege** f *carrion–, dung-fly* **⁓fresser** m ⟨bes ent⟩ *scavenger* **⁓geier** m (→ Schmutzgeier) *Egyptian vulture*, → Milan; ⟨fig⟩ *vulture* **⁓käfer** m *carrion-beetle* (*silphidae* pl) **⁓krähe** f *carrion-crow*

·aasen (a. aaßen) vi/t [h] **1.** vi (*of deer*) *to browse, graze, pasture* ‖ ⟨fig⟩ ~ mit etw *to squander* od *waste a th*; *to lavish a th* **2.** vt (abschaben) *to flesh* (*hides*) | *to bait* (*the hook*) **·aasig 1.** a *cadaverous, foul*; *filthy, rotten* ‖ ⟨fig⟩ *disgusting*; *dirty, ugly* ‖ *enormous*; *beastly* (*hunger*) **2.** adv *disgustingly* ‖ ⟨fam⟩ *jolly* (*cold*); *beastly*

ab I. adv **1.** (räumlich) **a.** *off* ‖ ⟨vulg⟩ *garn*! ‖ von hier ~ *from here*; weit ~ von *far off from*; vom Wege ~ *out of the way* | Hut ~! *off with your hat*! *hats off*! ‖ Gewehr ~! *order arms*! der Knopf ist ~ *the b. is off* → 4. **b.** ⟨theat⟩ *exit* L (Hamlet ~ *exit H.*), pl *exeunt* **c.** auf u ~ *up and down, to and fro* **2.** (zeitlich) von . . ~ *from*; v heute ~ *from today*; *to take over the Division as from Monday week*; v jetzt ~ *henceforth, in the future* ‖ vom 1. April ~ *from April 1* (*onwards*) | ~ u an, ~ u zu *off and on*; *now and again, now and then*; *sometimes*; *occasionally*; . . . einmal *once in a way* **3.** ⟨math⟩ v sechs drei ~ *from six take three* **4.** ⟨übtr & fig⟩ ganz ~ s *to be quite exhausted* (od *worn out, done up*) ‖ kurz ~ *abruptly* (*he answered a.*); *shortly* ‖ ~ nach Kassel! *be off*! *clear off*! *away with you*! **II.** prep **1.** (zeitlich) ~ heute *from to-day*; ~ 1. Oktober *from Oct. 1* (*onwards*) **2.** ⟨com⟩ *ex*; ~ Bergwerk *ex mine*; ~ Lager *ex store* od *stock*, etc. ‖ ⟨ind, com⟩ ~ Werk *ex works*; ~ Kai *ex quay* ~ Hamburg (*goods*) *to be delivered at H.* ‖ ~ dort *freight to be paid by buyer* ‖ frei ~ hier *free on wag(g)on*, etc.; *free loco* | (abzüglich) *less, deducting, deducted*; ~ Skonto *less discount*; ~ Spesen *less charges, deducting charges*; *charges* (*to be*) *deducted*

ab- pref [stets betont] **I.** [untrennbar vor nicht v Verben abgeleiteten Subst., desgl. vor Adj. u Adv.]: ·Abdankung; ·abwegig **II.** [trennbar vor Verben]: ·ab|nehmen — ich nehme ·ab; pp ·abgenommen **1.** (weg) *off, away* (*to break off, to sail away*) | (hinab) *down* (*to drift down* ·ab|treiben) ‖ (beiseite) *aside* (*to step aside*) **2.** jdm etw ·ab|borgen *to borrow a th from a p* ‖ °jdm etw ab|lotsen *to wangle a th out of a p* **3.** (zu Ende) *out* ‖ sich ab|arbeiten *to drudge, toil*

ab- pref [unbetont, untrennbar] in Fremdwörtern (in festen alten Zus-setzungen): absolvieren *to absolve* etc.

-ab suff *down*; bergab *downhill*

Abak·afaser f ⟨tex⟩ *Manila hemp, abaca fibre*

·Abakus m ~/~ ⟨arch⟩ *abacus* L

·abänderlich a *alterable, variable* ‖ ⟨gram⟩ *declinable, variable*; **≈keit** f *variability*

·ab|ändern 1. vt [h] (etw) *to alter, change, vary* ‖ *to correct, modify, rectify* ‖ ⟨parl⟩ (Vorlage) *to amend* ‖ ⟨jur⟩ (Urteil) *to commute* (in *to*) ‖ ⟨gram⟩ *to decline, to inflect* **2.** ≈ n = **·Abänderung** f ~/~en *alteration, variation*; *change* (e–r S *of a th*) ‖ *modification* ‖ ⟨jur⟩ *amendment* ‖ ⟨gram⟩ *inflection, declension* **⁓s- ⁓antrag** m *amendment* **≈fähig** a = abänderlich

·ab|angeln vt [h] (Fluß) ~ *to fish, whip*

·ab|ängstigen vrefl [h] sich ~ *to be in great anxiety* (um *for*); *to worry o.s. out with fretting*

·ab|arbeiten [h] **1.** vt (Schuld) *to pay off by work*; ⟨Am⟩ *to work out* ‖ (Tier) *to wear out, to overtire* ‖ (Fett) *to work off* ‖ → abgearbeitet **2.** vrefl **sich ⁓** *to drudge*; *to toil* od *work hard*; *to wear the flesh off one's bones*; sich ~ f jdn *to work o.s.* od *one's fingers to the bone for a p*

·ab|ärgern vrefl [h] sich ~ *to fret o.s. to death*

·Abart f ~/~en *modification* ‖ ⟨bot, etc.⟩ *variety* ‖ ⟨fig⟩ *version* **·ab|arten** vi [h] *to degenerate* **·abartig** a *degenerate* **·Abartung** f *degeneration* ‖ *variation*

***·ab|äschern** vrefl [h] sich ~ *to toil and moil*

·ab|ästen vt [h] (Baum) *to poll, lop, prune*

·ab|ätzen vt [h] *to corrode*; *to remove by caustics*

·ab|äugen vt [h] ⟨hunt⟩ *to beat up* (nach *for*)

·ab|backen vt/i [h] [→ backen] **1.** vt *to bake too much*; das Brot ist abgebacken *the crust comes off the bread* **2.** vi *to finish baking*

·ab|baken vt [h] ⟨mar⟩ *to buoy*; *to mark with beacons* **·ab|balgen** [h] **1.** vt *to skin, flay* **2.** vrefl ° sich ~ *to* (*have a*) *tussle*

·ab|bangen vrefl [h] sich ~ = sich abängstigen

·Abbau m ~s/ **1.** *gradual abolition, removal*; *withdrawal* (in *of*); *retrenchment*; (Behörden≈) *the axe* ⟨fig⟩, *decontrol* ‖ *reduction* (*of wages*, *barriers*) | *dismissal* (*of a p*) ⟨demog⟩ (Entvölkerung) *decongestion* **2.** ⟨med⟩ *decomposition* **3.** ⟨min⟩ *mining, working*; *exploitation, exhaustion* **4.** ⟨agr⟩ (v z.B. Kartoffelsorten) *degeneration* **5.** ⟨tech⟩ *dismantling* **6.** ⟨chem⟩ *degradation* **~feld, ~gebiet** n *sett* **~meißel** m *drilling bit* **~produkt** n *decomposition product* **~würdig** a ⟨min⟩ *payable, workable*; ~es Erztrum *pay-streak*

·ab|bauen vt/i [h] **A.** vt **1.** (Gebäude) *to pull* od *take down*; (Maschine) *to take to pieces* **2.** (Einrichtungen) *to demolish*; *abolish, remove*; (Opposition) *to clear the field of o.*; (Zwangswirtschaft) *to decontrol* ‖ (Stellen) *to axe* ‖ (Personal) *to reduce* | (Löhne) *to reduce* | (Ausgaben) *to retrench, axe* **3.** ⟨min⟩ (Grube) *to work, exploit*; *to work out, to exhaust* | (Minerale) *to win, work* **4.** ⟨physiol⟩ *to destroy, decompose, digest, disintegrate* **5.** ⟨theat⟩ [a. abs] *to strike* **B.** vi *to slacken from exhaustion*; *to flag* ‖ *to decamp*

·ab|bäumen vt [h] ⟨weav⟩ *to take from the loom*

Abbaz·ia n → Opatija

·ab|beeren vt [h] (Strauch) *to strip of berries*

***·ab|befehlen** vt [h] *to countermand*; (jdn) *to call back* °**·ab|behalten** vt [h] *to keep off*; den Hut ~ *to remain uncovered* **·ab|beißen** vt/i [h] **1.** vt *to bite off*; sich die Nägel ~ *to bite one's nails* ‖ (etw) *to bite* (v etw *off a th*) ‖ (Zahn) *to break off* **2.** vi laß mich mal ~ *give me a bite*

·ab|beizen vt [h] *to remove by caustics*; *to pickle* ‖ (Häute) *to taw* **Abbeizmittel** n ~s/~ *caustic*; *paint remover*

·ab|bekommen vt [→ kommen] [h] **1.** (lösen) (Schmutz etc) *to get off* ‖ (Gegenstand) *to get loose* **2.** (erhalten) etw ~ *to get a share of a th*, s–n Teil ~ v etw *to get one's share of a th*; *to come in for a th* | °hast du was ~? *did you get hurt, wounded*, ⟨fig⟩ . . *a scolding*?

·ab|berufen vt [→ rufen] [h] *to call away* od *home*; (Botschafter) *to recall*; (jdn) *to relieve, remove* (*a p*) (vom Amt *from his office*) ‖ Gott hat ihn ~ *he was gathered to his fathers*; er ist ~ ⟨mil fam⟩ *he's cashed-in* **·Abberufung** f ~/~en *recall* ‖ *decease, death* **~s- ~order** f, **~schreiben** n *letters* pl *of recall*

·ab|bestellen vt [h] (etw) *to countermand, cancel*; *to withdraw*; (Zeitung) *to discontinue*; ich bestellte die Zeitung ab *I stopped my subscription* | (jdn) *to put* (*a p*) *off* **·Abbestellung** f *countermand*; *cancellation*; *withdrawal*

·ab|beten vt [h] *to atone for* (*one's sins*) *by prayers*; *to tell* (*one's beads*) | *to recite monotonously* **·ab|betteln** vt [h] jdm etw ~ *to wheedle a th out of a p*

·ab|bezahlen vt [h] (Schuld) *to pay off, to discharge* ‖ (etw) in Raten ~ *to pay* (*a th*) *by instalments* **·ab|biegen** vt/i **1.** vt [h] ⟨eig⟩ *to bend off* ‖ ⟨tech⟩ (Blech) *to fold* ‖ (Gefahr) *to ward off, to prevent* ‖ (Gespräch) *to turn off* ‖ (Tatsache, Gesetz) *to wrest*; *to pervert*; *distort*; *to turn* (in *into*) **2.** vi [s] *to turn aside* od *off*; von der Hauptstraße ~ *to turn off the main street*; vom Wege ~ *to turn off on a road* ‖ ⟨mot⟩ *to turn* ‖ (of roads) *to branch* od *turn off* ‖ *to edge away* (v *from*) ‖ . . nach *to bear off to* **3.** ~ n: beim ~ *when turning* **A–gung** f (*of a road*) → Abzweigung

·Abbild n ~(e)s/~er *copy, duplicate* ‖ (Ebenbild) *image* ‖ (Bildnis) *effigy, portrait, likeness* **·ab|bilden** vt [h] (jdn) *to portray*; *draw*; *paint*; *represent* (*a p*); *to take a likeness of* (*a p*); *to picture* (*Mr. N.* ~*d below*) | (etw) *to represent*; *to copy*; ⟨surv⟩ *to map*

·Abbildung f **1.** [abstr] *representation*; *copy* **2.** [konkr] (Bild) *representation* ‖ *picture, illustration, engraving* (*in a book*); (Buch) mit ~en versehen *to illustrate* **~s- ~fehler** m (Verzeichnung) ⟨phot⟩ *aberration* **~maßstab** m *image* od *reproduction ratio* od *scale* **~tiefe** f ⟨phot⟩ *depth of definition*

·ab|binden 1. vt [h] (losbinden) *to unbind, untie* | (einschnüren) (Ader) *to ligate*; (Warze) *to remove by ligature* | (entwöhnen) *to wean* (*a calf*) ‖ ⟨spin⟩ (Garn) *to skein* **2.** ~ n *ligature, ligation* (*of a vein*) (⟨surg⟩ *to place a ligature under the artery*; *preparatory to ligating the vessel*); ⟨bes Am fam⟩ *tie* (*to place a tie around a v.*) ‖ ⟨tech⟩ (Festwerden) *setting, hardening*; (Leim) *curing, setting*

·Abbitte f *apology*; *recantation*; *deprecation* ‖ ~ leisten or tun *to apologize* (bei *to*); *to eat humble-pie*; öffentlich ~ tun *to make a public apology*; *to recant* (für etw *a th*) **·ab|bitten** vt [h] etw ~ *to apologize for a th*; (öffentlich) *to recant* ‖ jdm etw ~ → abbetteln | **~d** a *apologetic*

·ab|blasen vt/i [h] **1.** vt (wegpusten) *to blow off* ‖ ⟨tech⟩ (mit Sand) *to sandblast* | (beenden) (Streik) *to call off* ‖ ⟨mil⟩ *to break off*; Übung ~! *practice finished*! **2.** vi ⟨mil⟩ *to sound the retreat*

·ab|blassen vi [s] *to fade*; *to lose colour*

·ab|blättern vt/i **1.** vt [h] *to strip* (*a plant*) *of its leaves*; *to flake* (*a plant*) | **sich ~** = **2.** vi [s] *to exfoliate, to flake off*; *to scale*; (*of bark*) *to peel, to peel off*; *to shred away* ‖ die Pflanze blättert ab *the plant loses* od *sheds its leaves*; **sich ~ v** *to peel from* (*the door*) ‖ (of bones) *to exfoliate*

·Abblätterung f *exfoliation* ‖ (Losschälen) *flaking*; *peeling, leafing*

·ab|bleichen vt/i **1.** vt [h] *to bleach* **2.** vi [s] *to fade*; *to lose colour*

·ab|blenden vt/i [h] **1.** vt (Licht) *to dim, screen* ‖ ⟨mot⟩ *to dip* (*headlights*) ‖ ⟨phot⟩ *to stop down* ‖ ⟨film⟩ (Bild) *to dissolve* ‖ ⟨wir⟩ *to fade down* od *out* ‖ (Schiff) *to darken* **2.** vi ⟨mot⟩ *to turn down* (od *to dim, dip*) *the headlights*; *to switch the dim lights on*; ⟨mar⟩ abgeblendet fahren *to cruise without lights* **·Abblend- ~licht** n ⟨mot⟩ *dimmed light* **~schalter** m ⟨mot⟩ *dipper switch*; ⟨wir⟩ *fader* **~ung** f *dim-out* ‖ ⟨mot⟩ *dipping the headlights* ‖ etc **~vorrichtung** f ⟨tech⟩ *dimmer*

·ab|blitzen vi [s] ⟨fig⟩ *to be snubbed, to meet with a rebuff* od *a snub* ‖ (of lover) ⟨sl⟩ *to get the mitten*; er ist abgeblitzt ⟨Am fam⟩ *he couldn't make her*; jdn ~ l ⟨sl⟩ *to give a p the mitten*

·ab|blühen vi [s & h] *to cease blooming*; die Rosen haben (sind) abgeblüht *the roses are over* ‖ ⟨fig⟩ *to fade* **·ab|borgen** vt [h] jdm etw ~ *to borrow a th from a p* **·ab|böschen** vt [h] ⟨mil⟩ (Wall etc) *to* (*e*)*scarp*

·Abbrand m ~(e)s/~e ⟨met⟩ *fire waste of metals* ‖ *scaling loss*; *calcination* ‖ ⟨at⟩ *burn-up*

·ab|brauchen vt [h] *to wear off* od *out*

·ab|bräunen vt [h] (Mehl) *to brown*

·ab|brausen 1. vi [s] *to steam off* od *out* **2.** vt (jdn) *to douche* | **sich ~** *to douche, shower*

·ab|brechen vt/i **I.** vt [h] **1. a.** (Haus etc.) *to demolish*; *to break up*; *to break* (od *pull, take*) *down* | (Lager) *to break* (*up*), *to move*; (Zelte) *to strike* ‖ alle Brücken hinter sich ~ *to burn one's boats* **b.** (ein Stück) *to break* (v *from*); *to pluck* ‖ (Zweig) *to snap off* **c.** ⟨typ⟩ (Wort) *to divide* ‖ die Zeile ~ *to break the line* **2.** (Vorgang, Beziehung) *to break off*; *to cut, discontinue, drop, stop* (*a th*); (Belagerung) *to raise* ‖ (Urlaub) *to cut short* ‖ (Spiel) ⟨sport⟩ *to abandon* ‖ ⟨aero⟩ *to break off, to stop*, ⟨sl⟩ *to abort* ‖ das Gefecht ~ *to cease combat* **II.** vi **1.** [s] (sich lösen) *to come off* **2.** [h] (aufhören) *to cease, pause, stop*; *to break* od *leave off*; plötzlich ~ *to stop dead* od *short* ‖ die Geschichte bricht gerade hier ab *the story leaves off just at this point*; wir wollen hier(von) ~ *let us drop the subject* **III.** ~ [n] des Gefechts *withdrawal from action* **Abbrechfehler** m ⟨a. comp⟩ *truncation error*

·ab|bremsen 1. vt [h] ⟨aero⟩ (Flugzeug) *to brake*; *to run* od *race up* ‖ (Kernspaltung) ⟨at⟩ *to moderate* ‖ den Motor e–r Maschine ~ *to test an engine* ‖ ⟨übtr⟩ (etw) *to scotch, stifle* **2.** ≈ n *slowing down* ‖ ⟨at⟩ *moderation*

·ab|brennen A. vt [h] **1.** (Haus) *to burn down* (bis auf den Grund *to the ground*); *to destroy by fire* **2.** (Feuerwerk) *to let off* **3.** ⟨met⟩ *to refine*; (Stahl) *to temper* **B.** vi [s] **1.** *to burn down*; *to be destroyed by fire* **2.** (P) *to be ruined by fire*

Abbrennstumpfschweißung f *flash butt welding*

Abbreviat·ur f ~/~en *abbreviation*

·ab|bringen vt [h] jdn ~ v . . *to dissuade a p from* (*a purpose*); *to argue* od *reason a p out of* (*an opinion*) ‖ jdn davon ~ z tun *to prevail on a p* (od *to induce a p*) *not to do, to put a p off doing*; sich nicht ~ l v etw *to cling* od *stick to a th*; davon lasse ich mich nicht ~ *I won't be argued out of that* ‖ jdn v e–m Thema ~ *to lead a p away from a subject* ‖ jdn vom Wege ~ *to lead a p astray* | (befreien) jdn v etw ~ *to disabuse a p of a th* (*of an illusion*)

·ab|bröckeln vi [s] *to crumble* (*away*) ‖ ⟨übtr⟩ *to decline*; ⟨com⟩ (*of rates, etc.*) *to drop off*; *to ease off* **·Abbröckelung** f ~/~en ⟨com⟩ *decline*

·Abbruch m ~(e)s/≈e **1.** ⟨eig⟩ *breaking-down*; *pulling-down*; *demolition* (*of a house*); ein Haus auf ~ verkaufen *to sell a house as old material* **2.** ⟨übtr⟩ *breaking-off*; *discontinuance, rupture* (*of relations*); *break-down* (*of negotiations*); ⟨pol⟩ *breach* (*of relations with . .*) **3.** ⟨fig⟩ (Schaden) nur in: e–r S ~ tun *to damage, impair, prejudice a th*; *to derogate, detract from a th*; *to be detrimental, prejudicial to a th*; *to interfere with a th* **~gebiet** n (~stelle [f]) ⟨geog⟩ *large* (*small*) *parent ledge*; *source area*; (*head of a*) *landslide* **~höhe** f (⟨aero⟩ Lande≈, Mindest≈) *breaking-off height* **≈reif** a *ripe for demolition, abolition* **~s- ~gesellschaft** f *wrecking company*

·ab|brühen vt [h] ⟨cul⟩ *to scald*; *to parboil*

°**·ab|brummen** vt [h] s–e Strafe ~ (= absitzen) *to serve time*, ⟨sl⟩ *to do* (*one's*) *time*; 3 Jahre ~ *to serve 3 years*

·ab|buchen vt [h] ⟨com⟩ (Summe) *to deduct* (v *from*); (Verlust) *to cut* ‖ (absetzen) *to write off* ‖ ⟨bes mil⟩ *to voucher off* **·Abbuchung** f ~/~en *deduction* ‖ (Absetzen) *write-off*

·ab|bürsten vt [h] (Staub) *to brush* (v *from*); *to brush away* od *off* (v *from*) ‖ (jdn, e–n Rock) *to give . . a brush* ‖ ⟨typ⟩ → abklopfen

·ab|büßen vt [h] *to expiate*; *to atone for* ‖ s–e Strafe ~ *to serve time*

·Abbüßung f ~/~en *expiation, atonement*

Abc, Abec·e n ~/~ *ABC, alphabet*; nach dem ~ *alphabetically* ‖ ⟨fig⟩ *the elements*, (*the first*) *rudiments* pl (*of a th*) **~-Buch** n *primer, spelling-book* **~-Kampfmittel** pl *ABC-munitions* **~-Meldezentrale** f *radiological center* **~-Schüler, ~-Schütze** m *ABC-learner*; *tiro, tyro* **~-Staaten** m pl (Argentinien, Brasilien, Chile) *ABC-powers* pl **~-Waffen** f pl (= **a**tomare, **b**akteriologische & **c**hemische) *ABC-weapons*

·ab|dachen vt [h] (abschrägen) *to slant, slope* (*a th*); *to give a slope to* (*a th*) ‖ **sich ~** *to slope*

·Abdachung f ~/~en *slope, declivity*; ⟨fort⟩ *escarp*(*ment*); ⟨geol⟩ *escarpment*

·ab|dämmen vt [h] *to dam up*; *to embank*; (Bohrloch) mit Lehm etc. ~ *to tamp* ‖ (Erz) *to bank up* ‖ ⟨übtr a⟩ *to insulate*

·Abdämmung f *damming-up, embankment, etc*

·Abdampf m ~(e)s/≈e *exhaust–, waste-steam*; *dead steam* **~apparat** m *evaporating apparatus* **~entöler** m *oil extractor* **~kessel** m *ev. boiler* od *vessel* **~rückstand** m *evaporation residue* **~turbine** f *waste-steam turbine* **~verwertung** f *exhaust-steam utilization* **~vorrichtung** f *evaporator*

·ab|dampfen 1. vt [h] (verdunsten l) *to evaporate* **2.** vi [s] *to steam off* od *out* ‖ (P) *to be* (⟨sl⟩ *beetle*) *off* (nach *for*); ⟨sl⟩ *to beat it*

·ab|dämpfen vt [h] → dämpfen

·Abdampfung f *evaporation*

·ab|danken vt/i [h] **1.** vt (jdn) *to dismiss, discharge*; (Offizier) *to cashier*; *to put on half-pay* | (Schiff) *to lay up* **2.** vi *to resign, retire*; abgedankter Offizier *retired officer* ‖ (Monarch etc.) *to abdicate* (*the throne*) **·Abdankung** f ~/~en **1.** (Entlassung) *dismissal, discharge* **2.** (Rücktritt) *resignation, retirement* ‖ (Monarch) *abdication*; **~s- ~urkunde** f *instrument of abdication*

·ab|darben vrefl [h] sich etw ~ → absparen

·Abdeck- ~blech n *cover sheet* **~haube** f ⟨typewr⟩ *top cover* **~plane** f *tarpaulin* **~rahmen** m ⟨phot⟩ *printing mask* **~schirm** m (filament) *screen* **·ab|decken** vt/i [h] **A.** vt **1.** *to uncover*; *to clear* (*the table*) | (Dach) *to unroof, untile* **2.** ⟨tech⟩ *to cover* ‖ ⟨theat⟩ *to mask* **3.** (Tier) *to skin, flay* **4.** (Schuld) *to pay back, to repay* **5.** ⟨etching⟩ *to stop out* **B.** vi *to clear the table*; *to remove the things* **·Abdeckung** f ~/~en ⟨theat⟩ *masking piece* **·Abdecker** m ~s/~ *knacker, flayer* **~·ei** f *knackery*

·ab|deichen vt [h] *to dike, dyke*; *to dam up*

·Abdicht- ~klappe f *shutter* **~mittel** n *packing means, sealing compound*

·ab|dichten vt [h] *to isolate*; ⟨tech⟩ *to pack* ‖ ⟨mar⟩ *to caulk* **·Abdichtung** f *obturation*, ⟨tech⟩ [abstr] *tightening, jointing*; *packing, leak-proofing, sealing*; ⟨bes mar⟩ *caulking* ‖ [konkr] *sealing, packing, stuffing*

·ab|dienen vt [h] (Schuld etc.) *to work off by service* ‖ ⟨mil⟩ *to serve* (*one's year, one's time*), *to complete* (*one's term of service*)

·ab|dingen vt [h] **1.** (Lehrling) *to dismiss* **2.** jdm etw ~ *to bargain a p out of a th* **·ab|disputieren** vt [pp abdisputiert] [h] jdm etw ~ *to argue with a p about a th* **·ab|docken** vt [h] ⟨tex⟩ *to unwind* ‖ *to take the bobbins from the twiner* **·ab|dorren 1.** vi [s] *to dry up* **2.** vt/i [h/s] *to wither* **·ab|drängen** vt [h] *to push off* od *aside* ‖ ⟨mot⟩ ([seitlich] beim Überholen) *to side-swipe*

·Abdrehdiamant m *abrasive* od *dressing diamond*

·ab|drehen vt/i [h] **1.** vt *to twist off*; e–m Tier den Hals ~ *to wring the neck of an animal* ‖ (Gas) *to turn off* ‖ ⟨el⟩ (Licht) *to switch off, to turn out* **2.** vi ⟨mar⟩ *to turn away*; ⟨aero⟩ *to turn* od *veer away* od *off* [⟨a⟩ vt] ‖ *to change one's course* ‖ ⟨aero⟩ (aus dem Pulk) *to break away*, ⟨fam⟩ *to peel off*

·ab|dreschen vt [h] → verdr., abgedroschen

·Abdrift f ⟨mar, etc.⟩ *drift*; ~messer [m] *drift indicator*

·ab|dringen vt [h] → abnötigen

·ab|drosseln vt [h] ⟨tech⟩ *to throttle* (*back*); (Motor) *to stall*

·Abdruck m **1.** ~(e)s/~e ⟨typ⟩ (*off*)*print* (aus *from*); *striking-off*; → Abzug ‖ *impression*; *copy, reproduction* ‖ (Abguß) *cast*; ⟨engr⟩ (Probe≈) *proof* ‖ ⟨phot⟩ *print* ‖ ⟨tex⟩ *impression, print* **2.** pl ~e, ≈e *impress, imprint*; *print*, Finger≈ *finger-print* ‖ (of a seal) *stamp, seal*; *mark* ‖ ⟨dent⟩ *mould*: e–n ~ m *to take a m.* ‖ ~ auf Wachs *squeeze*; e–n ~ auf W. nehmen *to squeeze*

·ab|drucken vt [h] ⟨typ⟩ *to print*; neu *or* wieder ~ *to reprint* ‖ *to impress* (in Wachs *on wax*) ‖ (Muster) *to print*

·ab|drücken vt [h] **1.** (nachbilden) *to mould* **2.** *to pull* (*the trigger*); (Gewehr) *to discharge*; *to fire* (*off*) ‖ (Pfeil) *to let fly, to shoot* **3.** (jdn) *to give* (*a p*) *a hearty squeeze*; *to clasp, press* (*a p*) *to one's breast*; *to hug* **4.** jdm das Herz ~ *to break a p's heart*

Abdukti·on f ~/~en ⟨med⟩ *abduction*

·ab|dunkeln vt [h] *to darken, to make darker* ‖ (Farben) *to deepen* | vt/i [h] (Zimmer) *to black out*

·**ab|dunsten** vt [h] *to evaporate* ·**Abdunstung** f ~/~en *evaporation*

·**ab|duschen** vrefl; sich ~ *to have a wash down; to take a shower*

·**ab|ebben 1.** vi ⟨mst fig⟩ *to ebb (away); to ooze away; to decline* **2.** ≗ n: im ~ sein *to ebb*

Abec·e n ~/~ → ABC

·**ab|eifern** vrefl; sich ~ *to exhaust o.s. with zeal; to wear o.s. out* (z tun *doing*)

Ab·ele f ~/~n ⟨bot⟩ (Silberpappel) *abele*

·**Abelmoschus** m ~/~se ⟨bot⟩ *gumbo*

·**Abend** m ~s/~e **A. 1.** (→ gesellig) *evening; night*; am ~ des 15. Oktober *on the evening* od *night of Oct. 15th* || ⟨poet⟩ *eve* | ⟨mus & theat⟩ *night*; am ersten ~ *on the first night*; ein Wagner≗ *a night of Wagner* | geselliger ~ *evening*; Empfangs≗, literarischer ~ *conversazione*; (Lieder≗ etc) *recital*; ein vergnügter ~ ⟨sl⟩ *a binge* **2.** ⟨poet⟩ (Westen) *the West, the Occident* **B.** ~ des Lebens → Lebens≗ | e–s ~s *one evening*, ⟨liter & dial⟩ *of an evening*; des ~s (spät), (spät) **am** ~ (late) *in the evening* → abends || am Heiligen ~ *on Christmas Eve* || am vorhergehenden ~ *on the night before* | **alle** ~e *every evening* | gestern ~ *last night* || guten ~! *good evening*! || heute ~ [mst] *tonight; this evening* || morgen ~ *tomorrow night* | es **wird** ~ *evening is drawing near; it is getting dark* || e–n ~ ausspannen *to have a night out* od *off* || ⟨prov⟩ → Tag || zu ~ essen *to sup* || sich e–n vergnügten ~ m *to go on the loose, racket, spree*; ⟨sl⟩ *to go on the bend* (od *bust, randan, razzle-dazzle*) **~andacht** f *ev. prayer(s* [pl]) **~anzug** m *ev. dress* od *clothes* **~besuch** m *ev. visit* **~ausgabe** f, **~blatt** n *ev. paper* **~brot** n *supper* **~dämmerung** f *dusk, twilight, nightfall* **~essen** n *supper*; ⟨engl⟩ *dinner*; ⟨univ⟩ (im Saal) *Hall (after H.)*; spätes leichtes ~ *supper*; nach dem ~ *after dinner, supper*; das ~ einnehmen *to have d., s.* **~farbe** f ⟨tail⟩ *evening shade* ≗**füllend** a *filling up* od *taking up the ev.* || *full-length* (film) **~gebet** n *ev. prayer* **~geläut(e)** n *vesper-bell* **~gesang** m *evensong* **~gesellschaft** f *evening party, dinner party; soirée* Fr; ⟨fam⟩ *rout* **~glocke** f *ev.–, vesper-bell, angelus; curfew* **~gottesdienst** m *ev. service* od *prayer; vespers* pl **~imbiß** m *supper* **~kasse** f ⟨theat⟩ *box-office* **~kleid** n *ev. dress* **~kühle** f *the cool of the ev., ev. breeze* **~land** n das ~ *the West, the Occident* **~länder** m *inhabitant of a western country, westerner* ≗**ländisch** a *western, occidental* || **~luft** f *ev. air* **~mahl** n *supper* | ⟨ec⟩ *Communion*, das Heilige ~ *the Holy C., the Lord's Supper, the Sacrament*; ⟨C.E.⟩ *the Eucharist* || zum ~ gehen *to go to C.*; das ~ empfangen *to receive the Sacr.* od *Eucharist* || das ~ nehmen *to take the Sacr.; to communicate; to partake of the Lord's Supper* || das ~ reichen *to administer the Sacr.* (jdm *to a p*); ~sbrot n *host; consecrated bread; eucharist*; ~sfeier f *communion-service, celebration*; ~sgast m *communicant*; ~skelch m *communion-cup, chalice*; ~stisch m *altar; communion-table*; ~swein m *consecrated wine* **~mahlzeit** f *supper* **~mantel** m *ev. coat* **~mette** f *vespers* pl **~musik** f *serenade* **~pfauenauge** n ⟨ent⟩ *eyed hawk-moth* **~punkt** m ⟨astr⟩ *the true west* **~rot** n, (**~röte**) f *afterglow, ev. glow, sunset sky* od *glow*; ~ Gutwetterbot' *a red night is the shepherd's delight* **~schoppen** m *ev. glass, night cap* **~kurs** m, **~schule** f *ev.* (⟨Am⟩ *night*) *school* **~segen** m *ev. prayer* **~seite** f *west side* **~sonne** f *setting sun* **~ständchen** n *serenade* **~stern** m *ev. star; Hesperus* (= Venus) **~stille** f *ev. calm* **~stunde** f: in den ~n *in the ev.s* **~tau** m *night-dew* **~tisch** m *supper(-table)* **~trunk** m = ~schoppen **~unterhaltung** f *ev. entertainment, ev. party; soirée; conversazione* **~völker** n pl *western nations* pl **~wind** m *ev. breeze* **~zeit** f *ev.; night-time*; ⟨poet⟩ *eventide* **~zeitung** f *ev. paper* **~zirkel** m *ev. party; soirée*

·**abendlich** a *evening* || (–che Stille *ev. calm*)

·**abends** adv (spät) ~ *(late) in the evening, (late) at night*

·**Abenteuer** n ~s/~ *adventure* || ⟨übtr⟩ *strange* od *unusual happening* | galantes ~ *love affair*; ~ mit Weibern *adventures with women* || auf ~ ausgehen, –ziehen *to go adventuring, to go in quest of adventures, to seek adventures* || ein ~ bestehen *to go through an adventure* **~geschichte** f *a. story* **~lust** f *love of a.* ≗**lustig** a *a. hungry* **~roman** m *picaresque novel*

·**abenteuerlich 1.** a *adventurous* || ⟨fig⟩ *odd, strange; quixotic, fantastic; wild (plan); wild-cat (scheme)* **2.** adv *fantastically* ≗**keit** f ~/~en *adventurousness* || ⟨übtr⟩ *strangeness, oddity; quixotism* || *strange occurrence* od *th*

·**abenteuern** vi [h] *to lead an adventurous life* | **~d** a *adventurous*; ~der Ritter m *knight-errant*

·**Abenteurer(in** f ~/~nen) m ~s/~ *adventurer* (f *adventuress*) || *knight-errant* | ⟨derog⟩ *desperado; sharper; swindler*; ⟨Am sl⟩ *sooner* **~leben** n ein ~ führen *to lead an adventurous life*; ⟨fig⟩ *to live by one's wits* **~politik** f *risky politics* pl

·**aber I.** adv *again*; hundert u ~hundert *hundreds upon hundreds* || ~ u abermals, *over and over again, again and again* **II.** conj **1.** *but, however* || ~ ander(er)seits *but then*; ~ doch *but yet* || nun ~ *but now, now however* || oder ~, sonst ~ *or, otherwise; or else* **2.** *though* [am Satzende]: ~ ich wünschte, du hättest es mir gesagt *I wish you had told me, though* **3.** als intj; ~ Betty (tröstend, gereizt) *Betty, dear*! ~ Mutter! *I say mother*! Nun ~! *I say*! || ~ ~! *come, come! now, now! there now*! || *indeed; of course* | [unbetont] ⟨mst dial⟩ ~ j·a! *certainly, absolutely*! || ~ freilich! *rather*!; ~ schnell! *quickly please*!; ~ natürlich! *but there*!; ~ tüchtig! *with a vengeance*! || (..~..): ich hab' ~ 'nen Durst! *I h·ave a thirst*!; sehen d·ie ~ merkwürdig aus! *d·on't they look strange*? siehst d·u ~ gut aus! *you d·o look well*!

·**Aber** n ~s/~ *but; objection* | → Wenn || er hat immer ein ~ *he will always have objections* || die Sache hat ein ~ *there is a but in the question* || bitte kein ~! *but me no buts*! || wenn das ~ nicht wär... *if there were no ifs and ans*

·**Aberacht** f *strict ban*; Acht und ~ *repeated excommunication, double-ban*

·**Aberglaube** m *superstition* || *superstitiousness*

·**abergläubisch** a *superstitious*; ~es Verhalten *superstition, superstitiousness*

·**ab|erkennen** vt [h] (Ersatz) *to disallow* || jdm etw ~ *to deny a p a th*; ⟨jur⟩ *to deprive a p of a th (by judicial decree), to dispossess a p of a th*

·**Aberkennung** f ~/~en ⟨jur⟩ *abjudication; dispossession* (e–r S *from a th*); ~ bürgerlicher Ehrenrechte *civil degradation, loss of civil rights*; ⟨jur⟩ *deprivation of c. r.* || ~ der Dienstzeit ⟨mil⟩ *forfeiture of service*

·**abermalig** a *repeated; renewed; another (change)*

·**abermals** adv *again, anew, once more*

·**ab|ernten** vt [h] (Feld) *to harvest, reap*; (Flachs) *to pull*

·**Aber- ~raute** f ~/~n ⟨bot⟩ = Eberraute **~witz** m *craziness, madness; folly* ≗**witzig** a *crazy; foolish; absurd*

·**ab|essen** vt/i [h] **1.** vt *to pick (a bone)* || *to clear (a plate)* || e–e lange Speisenfolge ~ *to sit out a long dinner* **2.** vi *to finish eating* || –geg– h *to have done eating*

Abess·inier m ~s/~; **~in** f ~/~nen *Abyssinian* **abess·inisch** a *Abyssinian*

·**ab|fädeln** vt [h] (Perlen etc.) *to unstring* || (Bohnen) *to string*

·**ab|fahren** vi/t **A.** vi [s] **1. a.** *to depart, start, sail; to set out* (v *from*; nach *for*) ‖ fahr ab! *begone!* ⟨sl⟩ *clear off!* ‖ (a. of carriages) *to drive* (⟨sl⟩ *push*) *off* **b.** (of trains) *to leave; to go* od *move out* ‖ (of ships) *to leave; to steam away; to put out to sea; to set sail, to sail, clear* **c.** (sterben) *to die* **2.** (ausgleiten) (Messer etc.) *to slip off* **3.** (hinabfahren) ⟨mount⟩ *to glissade;* ⟨ski⟩ *to race downhill* → Schlitten **4.** ⟨fig⟩ *to be snubbed, to meet with a snub* ‖ mit jdm ~, jdn ~ l *to be short with, to wipe the ground with a p; to snub a p* **B.** vt [h] **1.** (Last) *to carry* od *cart away* od *off* **2.** (Glied) *to cut* od *tear off by driving over;* ihm wurde ein Bein abgefahren *he lost a leg (in a motor-accident)* **3.** (abnutzen) *to wear out* od *away, use up by driving* **4.** (Strecke) *to cover,* ⟨fam⟩ *to do;* ganz Bayern ~ *to do the whole of B.*

·**Abfahrt** f ~/~en **1.** *departure, setting-out, start(ing);* ⟨mar⟩ *sailing;* ⟨sport⟩ start ‖ bei ~ des Zuges *on the train leaving;* noch eine Minute bis zur ~ *still a minute to go* **2.** ⟨mount⟩ *glissade;* ⟨ski⟩ *down race* **~s- ~bahnhof** m *departure station* **~bahnsteig** m, **~halle** f *starting-platform;* (in London) *down-platform;* **~schuß** m ⟨mar⟩ *sailing gun* ‖ ⟨ski⟩ = Abfahrt **~signal** n ⟨rail⟩ *starting signal;* (in London) *down signal* **~tag** m ⟨mar⟩ *day of sailing* **~wimpel** m = blauer Peter, → blau I. A. 2. **~zeit** f *time of departure*

·**Abfall** m ~(e)s/~̈e **A.** ⟨abstr⟩ [mst sg] **1.** *fall(ing off)* **2.** *declivity, steepness, slope; descent* **3.** ⟨fig⟩ **a.** *apostasy; secession, defection* (v *from*); *desertion;* ⟨Am⟩ *bolt* ‖ *Revolt (of the Netherlands)* **b.** (Sinken) *decrease; deterioration* | *loss of weight, under-weight* **c.** (Gegensatz) *contrast, difference* | (Ungunst) *disfavour* **B.** ⟨konkr⟩ [oft pl] *refuse,* (Baumwoll~̈e) *trash; wastage, waste;* (bes Fleisch) *offal;* (Getreide) *tailings* pl ‖ ⟨tail⟩ *cuttings* ‖ *pickings, scrapings, scraps* pl; ⟨Am⟩ *discards* pl ‖ ⟨sl⟩ *junk* ‖ (Küchen~̈e) *garbage, parings, trimmings, peelings; refuse* | ⟨tech⟩ (Späne, Bruch) *chips, clippings, cuttings, parings, shavings, shreds* pl **~ausscheidung** f *separation of waste* **~baumwolle** f *cotton strip* **~beseitigung** f *disposal of ..,* ⟨at⟩ *fall-out d.* **~eimer, ~Kübel** m *dustbin,* → Mülleimer, -kübel **~energie** f *waste energy* **~haufen** m *junk heap* **~holz** n ⟨for⟩ *slashings* **~papier** *waste-paper* **~prahm** m *refuse lighter* **~produkt** n *waste product* **~stoffe** m pl *wastes* **~verwertung** f *utilization of waste; salvage* **~ware** f *waste*

·**ab|fallen** vi [s] **A.** ⟨eig⟩ *to fall off; to fall, drop* (v from); *to come down* ‖ ⟨typ⟩ (*of letters*) *to drop* (od *fall*) *out* | ⟨übtr⟩ etw wird dabei für ihn ~ *he'll profit by it; he'll not come off a loser* **B.** ⟨übtr & fig⟩ **1.** (sich abschrägen) *to slope;* (*of ground*) *to fall away, to slope* ‖ (*of coast*) *to shelve* **2.** ⟨mar⟩ (abgetrieben w) *to fall off; to fall to leeward; to veer* **3.** (abnehmen) *to fall off; to decrease, diminish* ‖ (P) *to lose flesh* ‖ ⟨theat⟩ *to decline in interest, to fall off; to lose* **4.** *to be inferior* (gegen jdn *to a p*) **5.** (untreu w) *to apostatize; backslide; revolt; to fall off* (v *from*), *to revolt* (*against*); *to desert, forsake* (*a p*) **6.** (scheitern) *to fail; to meet with a rebuff;* ~ bei jdm *to be snubbed by a p;* jdn ~ l *to snub a p; to give a p the cold shoulder* ·**abfallend** a ⟨tech⟩ *decreasing* od *dropping* (Drehzahl *speed*)

·**abfällig I.** a **1.** *sloping* (*surface*) | ⟨for⟩ *declining, taper* a (Baumspitze), *conical* **2.** † *disloyal;* ~ w *to revolt* **3.** ⟨fig⟩ *disapproving, depreciatory, detractive; derogatory* (*remark*); *severe* **II.** adv etw ~ beurteilen, ~ urteilen über etw *to detract* (od *derogate*) *from a th; to criticize a th unfavourably; to depreciate, disparage a th;* jdn ~ beurteilen *to speak slightingly of a p; to run a p down*

·**ab|fangen** vt [h] **1.** (etw) *to snatch* | (Wasser, Strahlen; Truppen; Brief) *to intercept* ‖ Telegramme ~ *to tap, milk telegraph wires;* → mithören ‖ ⟨mar⟩ e–m Schiff den Wind ~ *to take the wind out of a ship's sails* **2.** (jdn) *to catch* ‖ (Kunden) *to take away* **3.** (Wild) *to kill* **4.** ⟨sport⟩ *to overtake* (*a p*); *to catch* (*a p*) *up; to pull up to* od *with a p* **5.** ⟨aero⟩ *to right* (*an aeroplane*), *to pull out of a dive, to flatten out;* (vor dem Aufsetzen) *to hold off* **6.** ⟨tech⟩ (stützen) *to prop, support*

·**Abfangtaktik** f ~/ ⟨bes aero⟩ *interception tactics* pl

·**ab|färben** vi [h] *to lose colour; to stain;* das Tuch hat rot abgefärbt *the cloth has come off red* | ⟨übtr⟩ ~ (*or* sich ~) auf jdn *to affect* od *influence a p;* unangenehm ~ auf jdn *to tell on a p* ‖ (of taints) *to contaminate a p*

·**ab|fasern** vi/refl [h] ~, sich ~ *to lose fibres; to fray*

·**ab|fassen** vt [h] **1.** (jdn) *to get hold of* (*a p*); *to catch;* auf frischer Tat ~ *to catch in the* (*very*) *act;* → ertappen ‖ *to seize, to arrest* **2.** (etw) *to compose, write; to draw up,* (Gesuch) *to formulate* ‖ *to pen; to put* od *set down* ‖ *to word*

·**Abfassung** f ~/~en **1.** *seizure; arrest* **2.** *composition; drawing up; writing* ‖ *wording; tenor;* (e–s Textes) *styling* ‖ Kunst der ~ *craftsmanship*

·**abfasen** vt [h] ⟨tech⟩ *to chamfer* ·**A-sung** f ~/~en *chamfer*

·**ab|faulen** vi [s] *to rot* (*off*), *disintegrate*

·**ab|federn** vt [h] *to pluck* ‖ ⟨hunt⟩ *to kill* ‖ ⟨tech⟩ *to spring, cushion* ·**A-rung** f ~/~en ⟨tech⟩ *shock-absorption;* ⟨mot a.⟩ *suspension*

·**ab|fegen** vt [h] *to sweep off* (v *from*); *to whisk* (*off*); den Staub ~ v etw *to dust a th* ‖ (Fläche) *to give* (*a th*) *a sweep*

·**ab|feilen** vt [h] *to file* (off) ‖ (Münzen) *to clip* | ⟨übtr⟩ *to smooth, polish; elaborate*

·**Abfeilicht** n ~(e)s/ *filings* pl

·**ab|feilschen** vt [h] → abhandeln

·**ab|feimen** vt [h] *to skim* ‖ → abgefeimt

·**ab|fertigen I.** vt [h] **1.** (Geschäfte) *to dispatch, expedite* ‖ ⟨off⟩ *to clear* (⟨a. cust, aero, etc⟩ Einfuhr ~) ‖ ⟨rail⟩ (e–n Zug) *to dispatch* **2.** (jdn) *to attend to; to serve* ‖ *to dismiss* ‖ beim Zoll abgefertigt w *to pass the customs;* → bevorzugen | ⟨übtr⟩ *to settle a p's hash; to send a p about his business* ‖ jdn ~ mit *to put a p off with* | jdn kurz ~ *to snub a p, to give a snub,* kz abgefertigt w *to meet with short shrift* **II.** ~̈ n =

·**Abfertigung** f ~/~en **1.** schnelle ~ *dispatch expedition* ‖ ⟨cust, aero, etc⟩ *clearance* **2.** (Kunden~̈) *attendance* **3.** (Abweisung) *rebuff, refusal;* derbe ~ *snub, set-down;* ⟨fam⟩ *settler;* **~sschein** m (*customs*) *declaration; permit* **~sstelle** f ⟨rail⟩ *goods-platform* ‖ ⟨com⟩ *dispatching office; office of dispatch*

·**ab|fetten** vt [h] *to skim off the fat*

·**ab|feuern 1.** vt [h] *to fire* (*off*), *discharge, shoot, to let off* **2.** ~̈ n *firing* (*off*); *discharge*

·**Abfeuervorrichtung** f *firing device* ‖ ⟨artill & phot⟩ *release mechanism*

·**ab|finden** vt [h] **1.** (jdn) *to satisfy, content; to pay off* ‖ (Fürsten) *to compensate, indemnify* ‖ (Gläubiger) *to compound with;* abgefunden w dadurch, daß man tut *to compound by doing* ‖ (Teilhaber) *to buy out* **2. sich ~ mit** *to compound* od *settle with* (*a p*); *to settle matters* (od *to come to terms*) *with* (*a p*); *to square* (*a p*) ‖ ⟨jur⟩ *to make a compromise with* (*a p*) | *to tolerate* (*a th*); *to put up with* (*a th*); *to reconcile o.s., to be reconciled with* (*a th*); *to resign o.s. to* od *to make the best of* (*a fact*); *to settle down in* (*one's job*), *for* (*a th*) ‖ sich damit ~ z tun *to resign o.s. to doing* ‖ sich mit s–m Gewissen ~ *to compound with* (od *to silence*) *one's conscience;* sich mit den Tatsachen *or* damit ~ *to face facts;* ⟨Am fam⟩ *to take one's medicine* ·**Abfindung** f ~/~en **1.** *satisfaction; agreement, settlement* ‖

composition (mit *with*) ‖ (Schadloshaltung) *indemnification, compensation* **2.** [konkr] *allowance, portion*; (des Arbeitnehmers) *severance pay*; endgültige ~ *full and final payment* ‖ ⟨ins⟩ *lump-sum* od *accommodation settlement* **~sgeld** n, **~ssumme** f *indemnity, compensation* **~svertrag** m ⟨jur⟩ *deed of composition*; *transaction* (*with the creditors*) ‖ ⟨ins⟩ *lump sum, sum payable on settlement*

·ab|fischen vt [h] (Teich) *to fish out* | ⟨übtr⟩ das Beste ~ von *to take the cream of* (*a th*) ‖ jdm etw ~ *to cheat a p out of a th*

·ab|fitzen vt [h] ⟨spin⟩ *to skein*

·ab|flachen vt/i [h] **1.** vt *to level, flatten, slope* | **sich ~** = **2.** vi *to slope down, to flatten*; *to subside into a plain* ‖ (of water) *to* (*become*) *shallow* **·Abflachung** f ~/~en *flattening, slope*

·ab|flauen 1. vi [s] (Wind) *to abate, decrease, drop*; *to subside*; *to* (*be on the*) *wane*; *to calm, die* (*down*) ‖ ⟨mil⟩ (Geschützfeuer etc) *to ease* (*off*) vi | ⟨übtr: com⟩ *to slacken*; *to grow dull* ‖ (of interest) *to fall off*; *to flag* **2.** ~ n: im ~ s = abflauen

·Abfleischmesser n ⟨tech, tex, archæol⟩ *scraper*

·ab|fliegen 1. vi [s] *to fly off*; ⟨aero⟩ *to depart, start*; *to take off*; *to take the air* **2.** vt [h] ein Gelände ~ *to patrol an area*

·ab|fließen vi [s] (Wasser) *to flow* od *run off* od *down* (nach *to*); *to drain* (*off*); *to fall* (in *into*) ‖ (Geld) *to flow* od *stream* | (etw) ~ l *to run* (*a th*) *off* (v *from*)

·Abflug m ~(e)s/~̈e ⟨aero⟩ *departure, start*; *taking-off*; *going flight*; im ~ gemeldet *reported air-borne* **~deck** n *flight-deck* **~ort** m *point of departure*, ⟨fam⟩ *jump-off point* **~schneise** f *departure corridor* **~station** f ⟨a–n⟩ *jumping-off point*

·Abfluß m –usses/–üsse **1.** *flowing off*; *issue, outlet, outfall* ‖ (Gas~) *escape*; (Blut~) *issue*; (Eiter~) *discharge*; (Bad~) *waste* (Wasser); ⟨geog⟩ *discharge, runoff* | [konkr] *gutter, sink*; (Rohr) *outlet*; ⟨geog⟩ *outlet* **2.** ⟨übtr⟩ (Geld~) *efflux, outflow, drain*, ~ nach dem Auslande *foreign drain* **~anlage** f *drains* pl; *drainage* **~gebiet** n ⟨geog⟩ *drainage area* **~graben** m *drain* **~kanal** m *spillway* **~leitung** f, **~rohr** n, **~röhre** f *outlet, discharge pipe, drain-pipe*; (am Klosett) *soil-pipe* ‖ ⟨tech⟩ *escape-, waste-pipe* ‖ ⟨mar⟩ → Speigatt **~ventil** n *escape-valve*

·Abfolge f ~/~n *succession* (*in rapid s.*) ‖ (Reihenfolge) *sequence*

·ab|fordern vt [h] jdm etw ~ *to demand a th of* od *from a p*; er forderte mir 3 Mark ab *he charged me 3 marks* **·Abforderung** f *demand*

·ab|formen vt [h] (etw) *to mould, model*; *to form from* (od *to cast in*) *a mould*; *to take a cast of* (*a th*) ‖ *to copy, imitate*

·ab|forsten vt [h] *to clear of trees* ‖ *to disforest*

·Abfrage- [in comp] ⟨el⟩ *answering* (*cord, equipment, etc*) **~gerät** n *interrogator-responsor*; ⟨comp⟩ *interrogating tapewriter* **~möglichkeit** f ⟨comp⟩ *information retrieval* **~station** f ⟨comp⟩ *agent set*; *inquiry station* **~steuerung** f ⟨comp⟩ *interrogating tapewriter control*

·ab|fragen vt [h]: ich fragte ihm s–e Aufgabe ab *I heard him his lesson*

·ab|fressen vt [h] (of cattle, etc.) *to browse, crop*; *to nibble off* ‖ → auffressen

·ab|frieren vi [s] *to be bitten by cold*

·Abfühl- [in comp] **~einheit** f ⟨comp⟩ *reading unit* **~station** f ⟨comp⟩ *sensing station* **·ab|fühlen 1.** vt [h] ⟨comp⟩ *to sense, extract* **2.** ~ [n] der eingegebenen Lochkarten *extraction of the original data* **·Abfühlung** f ~/~en ⟨comp⟩ (beim Ordnen) *sensing*

·Abfuhr f ~/~en **1.** *transport, conveyance*; *carriage, cartage*; *removal*; *carrying off*; ⟨for⟩ (Holz~) *haulage* **2.** ⟨fenc⟩ *disabling*; ⟨univ⟩ *serious wound received in fencing* ‖ ⟨fig, sport⟩ e–e ~ erhalten *to be beaten* **3.** (Abweisung) *rebuff*; *snub, set-down*; *brush-off, turn-down* ⟨fam⟩ *settler*, ⟨sl⟩ *snorter* ‖ jdm e–e ~ erteilen *to give a p a snub, to snub a p, to give a p a b.-off, to turn a p down*; e–e ~ bek *to meet with a snub* od *rebuff*

·Abführ- [in comp] *purgative*

·ab|führen I. vt/i [h] **A.** vt **1.** (P) **a.** *to carry* od *march* (*a p*) *off* (ins Gefängnis *to prison*); als Gefangener abgeführt w *to be marched off captive*; v (d. Polizei) –ge–rt w *to be lead away by* .. ‖ ⟨jur⟩ *to remove*, abgeführt w ⟨vulg⟩ *to be walked off* | ⟨fenc⟩ *to disable* **b.** jdn vom rechten Wege ~ *to lead a p astray*; *to take a p out of his way*; *to mislead a p* **c.** ⟨übtr⟩ jdn ~ *to give a p a snub*; jdn tüchtig ~ *to wipe the floor with a p* **2.** (T) *to lead off* **3.** (Waren) *to dispatch*; *to send off* ‖ (Schuld etc) *to pay* (*off*), *to discharge* | e–e Summe ~ an jdn *to credit a p with a sum, to pass a sum to a p's credit*; (Steuern) *to deduct* **B.** vi ⟨med⟩ *to loosen* od *relieve the bowels*; *to purge*; *to be aperient* od *aperitive* **II.** ~ n ~s/ ⟨med⟩ *purgation, evacuation* **·abführend** a ⟨med⟩ *aperient, aperitive, evacuant, laxative, purgative* ‖ ~es Brausepulver ⟨pharm⟩ *Seidlitz powder* ‖ ~ wirken *to be aperitive*

·Abführmittel n ⟨med⟩ *aperient, evacuant, laxative, purgative* ‖ jdm ein ~ geben *to purge a p*

·Abführung f **1.** *dispatch*; *removal*; *carriage*; *carrying away* ‖ (e–r Schuld) *payment* **2.** (e–r P) *carrying-off*; *removal* (*to prison*) **3.** ⟨med⟩ *evacuation, purgation*; → abführen

·Abfüll- ~apparat m (f Bier) *racker* **~betrieb** m *bottling factory* **~maschine** f *filling machine* **~vorrichtung** f *emptying contrivance*

·ab|füllen vt [h] *to fill out* ‖ (Wein) *to bottle* (Bier etc.) *to draw* od *rack off* ‖ (Faß) *to empty*

·ab|füttern vt [h] **1.** *to feed* | (Kleid) *to line*

·Abfütterung f **1.** *feeding*; ⟨fam⟩ *spread*; ⟨Am sl⟩ *feed* **2.** (Kleid~) *lining*

·Abgabe f ~/~n **A. 1.** (Auslieferung) *delivery* (bei ~ *on d.*) ‖ *surrender* (*of a ticket*) | ⟨com⟩ *sale*; *surrender* **2.** (Stimmen~) *vote* **B. 1.** (Steuer) *duty, impost*; *assessment*; (Staats~) *tax*; (Kommunal~) *rate*; (~ auf Einfuhr) *customs* pl; Natural~ *payment in kind* | (Schul~n) *fees* pl ‖ → Tribut **2.** ⟨com⟩ (gezogener Wechsel) *draft, bill* **C.** [konkr] *cloak-* (⟨Am⟩ *check*) *room* (Gepäck~) **~frei** a *duty-free*; *tax--free*; nicht ~ ⟨cust⟩ *not free of duties and taxes*; *exemptions from d. & t. not granted* **~freiheit** f *immunity*; *exemption from duty* **~nbefreiung** f ⟨cust⟩ *tax exemption* **~ndurchschnittsätze** m pl *average rates of taxes* **~nvergütung** f *tax reimbursement* **~pflicht** f *taxability* **~pflichtig** a *taxable*; *dutiable*, ~e Waren *d. goods*; *liable to duty* od *tax* **~schlauch** m *delivery hose* **~spindel** f *creel spindle* **~wesen** n *taxation*; *taxes in general*

·Abgang m ~(e)s/~̈e **1.** *departure*; *start* ‖ Schul~ *school leaving*; Zeit des Schul~s *leaving time* ‖ (Zug) *departure* ‖ (Schiff) *sailing* | (Beamter etc.) *retirement*; *resignation*; *dismissal* | ⟨theat⟩ *exit*; (eindrucksvolle ~sworte bei Szenenschluß, oft reimender Zweizeiler) *tag*; [attr] *tag rhyme* **2.** ⟨med⟩ (Abfluß) *flux*; *discharge*; *loss*; ~̈e [pl] *losses*, ⟨bal⟩ *retirements* **3.** ⟨com⟩ (Verlust) *deficiency, loss*; *wastage, waste*; (of liquids) *leakage, ullage*; ⟨a.⟩ (*magnetic*) *leak* **4.** (Abfall) *waste*; *offal, refuse*; *waste-paper*; ~̈e [pl] ⟨bes tex⟩ *dirt, discard, refuse* **5.** ⟨com⟩ (Verkauf) *outlet, sale*; *market* ‖ ~ finden *to find an outlet* (f *for*); k–n (schlechten) ~ finden *to find no sale* (*to sell badly*); schnellen (schweren) ~ finden *to meet with a ready market* od *sale* (*to be a drug in the market*)

·abgängig a **1.** (*easily*) *sal*(*e*)*able*; *marketable* **2.** *decrepit* ⟨a. for⟩

·**Abgangs-** ~**alter** n, (Schul≗) *school leaving age* ~**dampf** m *exhaust-steam* ~**entschädigung** f ⟨ins⟩ *sum allowed on withdrawal* ~**fehler** m (des Gewehrs etc beim Schuß) *angle jump* ~**geschwindigkeit** f *initial velocity* ~**hafen** m *port of clearance* od *sailing* ~**karte** f ⟨comp, com⟩ *issue card* ~**ordnung** [f] der Ledigen ⟨demog⟩ *net nuptiality table* ~**prüfung** f *leaving* od *final examination* ~**winkel** m ⟨ball⟩ (*quadrant*) *angle of departure* ~**zeugnis** n *leaving certificate*, ⟨Am⟩ *credit*

·**Abgas** n *exhaust-gas*; *waste-gas* ~**kanal** m *exhaust passage* ~**temperatur** f *exhaust-gas t.* ~**turbolader** m *exhaust-driven turbo-supercharger* ~**umleitung** f *gas exhaust-pipe* ~**verwertung** f *utilization of waste-gas*

·**ab|gaunern** vt [h] jdm etw ~ *to fleece a p of a th*; *to trick a p out of a th*; *to cheat* (od *swindle*, ⟨fam⟩ *do*) *a p out of a th*

·**abgearbeitet** a *jaded* (*man*); *stale* (v *with*); *toil-worn*; *overwrought*; [pred] *run down*

·**ab|geben** vt/i [h] **I.** vt **A. 1.** (verzichten auf) *to give up*; *to renounce*; *to dispense with*; *to do without* (*a th*) || *to dispose of*; *to cede* bzw. *sell* (*a th*) || jdm (v) etw ~ *to let a p share in a th*; *to share a th with a p*; gib ihm etw davon ab *give him some of it* **2.** (übergeben) *to deliver*; *to hand over* (bei jdm *to a p*); (Billet) *to surrender* || (Hut) *to resign* || (ausgeben) *to dispense* || abzugeben bei *care of* (abbr c/o [*c/o Mr. N.*]) || (e–n Fall) *to depute* (an *to*) | (hinterlassen) *to leave*; s–e Karten ~ bei jdm *to leave one's cards with a p*; dies ist für Sie –ge– *this has been left for you* || (zur Aufbewahrung) *to deposit* **3.** (liefern) (Ernte) *to yield*; *to supply*; (Erzeugnisse) *to surrender*; (herstellen) *to do* (*we do the article at* 3/6 = zu ..); wir können es z diesem Preise nicht ~ *we cannot supply it on these terms* || ([gespeicherte] Energie) *to release*, ⟨el⟩ *to yield*; (Wärme) *to transfer* (an *to*) | (P) ⟨mil⟩ *to detach* **4.** (v sich geben) e–e Stimme ~ *to cast a vote*; s–e St. ~ *to poll, vote* (f *for*) | e–n Schuß ~ *to fire a shot*; *to fire* | (äußern) *to make* (*a declaration*); *to give* (*an opinion*); ein Urteil ~ *to pass* od *pronounce judgement*, sein U. ~ *to pass one's verdict* (über etw *on a th*); ⟨jur⟩ das Urteil ~ *to give* od *deliver judgement* (gegen *against*; z Gunsten v *for*); → Urteil **5.** ⟨com⟩ e–n Wechsel ~ auf jdn *to draw on a p* **6.** ⟨übtr⟩ jdm etw ~ *to hit a p a rap* od *blow*; *to give a p a thrashing* | es wird noch Regen ~ *we'll have some rain still* || das gibt aber was ab *now you* od *we are in for it* **B.** (sich eignen als) *to act* od *serve as*; *to be fit for*; e–n Narren ~ *to play the fool*; er hätte e–n guten Minister –ge– *he would have made a good m.* **C. sich ~ mit etw** *to concern* od *occupy o.s. with a th*; *to take to a th*; (aus Liebhaberei) *to dabble in a th*; sich ungern ~ mit *to take unkindly to* (*a th*); sich viel ~ mit etw *to spend much time on a th*; geben Sie sich damit nicht ab *keep clear of it* || **sich ~ mit jdm** *to have to do with a p*; *to associate o.s.* (od *to traffic*) *with a p*; *to frequent a p's company*; mit ihm gebe ich mich nicht ab *I won't have anything to do with him* **II.** vi ⟨cards⟩ *to deal for the last time*

·**abge-** ~**blüht** a ⟨bot⟩ *deflorate* || ⟨fig⟩ *faded*; [pred] *passée* (*woman*) ~**brannt** [pp v abbrennen] a ⟨fig⟩ *out of cash*; *penniless*; ⟨sl⟩ *stony*(*-broke*), *broke*, *cut up*; ~ s ⟨fam a.⟩ *to be down on one's uppers* ~**brochen** [pp v abbrechen] a ⟨fig⟩ *abrupt*, *disjointed*, *chopped* (*sentences*) ⟨mil etc⟩ *abortive* (Auftrag *mission*) ≗**heit** f ~/ *abruptness* ~**brüht** a (*case-*)*hardened*; ⟨fig⟩ *callous* (gegen *to*); *inured* (*to*) ~**drechselt** a ⟨fig⟩ *rounded-off*; *polished* ~**droschen** [pp v abdreschen] a ⟨fig⟩ *commonplace*, *trivial*; *trite*; *hackneyed*, *threadbare* (*subject*); ~e Wendung *outworn*, *well-worn*, *banal expression*; *cliché*; *jaded* (*sense*) ~**fahren** a (Reifen) ⟨mot⟩ *worn smooth* ≗**fallene[r]** m ⟨ec⟩ *apostate* ~**feimt** a ⟨fig⟩ *cunning*, *artful*, *crafty*; *knowing* || ~er Schurke *utter* (od *arch-*)*rogue*; *arrant knave*; *thorough-paced* (od *out and out*) *rascal* ~**froren** [pp v abfrieren] a → erfroren ~**glichen** a *balanced* (*aerial*, *modulation*) ~**griffen** [pp v abgreifen] a *worn-out*; (*well-*)*thumbed* (*book*) || ⟨fig⟩ *hackneyed*, *debased* (*word*); *well-worn*; ~e Wendung *cliché* Fr ~**hackt** a ⟨fig⟩ = abgebrochen ~**hangen** a (→ abhängen) (⟨a⟩ gut ~) *hung* (Wild) ~**härmt** a *care-worn*; *pinched*; *pinch-faced*; ⟨fam⟩ *peaked*, *peaky* ~**härtet** a *hardy*, *weather-beaten* (p); ⟨tech⟩ (*case-*)*hardened*

·**ab|gehen I.** vi [s] **A.** ⟨eig⟩ **1.** (fortgehen) *to go* od *walk away* od *off*, *to start* || (Zug) *to go off* od *out*; *to depart*, *to leave*; (Schiff) *to sail* || vom Wege ~ *to go astray* | (Beamte) *to retire*, *resign*; °er ist abgegangen worden *he has got the sack* || v der Schule ~ *to leave school*, *to get away* (*without sufficient training*) || ⟨theat⟩ *to make one's exit* | ~, mit dem Tode ~ *to depart this life*; *to make one's exit* od *bow*; *to pass away* od *out*; zu der gr Armee ~ *to join the majority* **2.** (Waren) *to be delivered*, *dispatched*, *sent* (vgl C. 4.) || (Post) *to leave* (*when does the mail leave?*); *to got out* | ~ l *to forward*, *to send off*; *to dispatch*, *expedite* **3.** (abfließen) *to come out*; ⟨med⟩ *to be discharged* od *lost*; ihm ging viel Blut etc. ab *he lost much blood*, *he passed* (*worms*), *he voided* (*a stone*) || ⟨fig⟩ kein Mahl ging ohne Tränen ab *there were tears at every meal* **B.** ⟨übtr⟩ **1.** (abweichen v) *to depart* (od *to make a departure*) (v *from*) || ~ **von ..** *to change* (*one's mind* od *opinion*), *to swerve from* (*a purpose*); *to deviate from* (*truth*); vom Thema ~ *to digress*; v s–m Vorhaben nicht ~ *to persist in* (od *to stick to*) *one's plan*; davon kann ich nicht ~ *I must insist on that* **2.** (abzweigen) (of roads) *to branch off*; *to turn* **3.** (sich lockern) *to come* od *wear off*; *to come* od *get loose* (*the button came off*) || (Farbe) *to come off* **C.** ⟨fig⟩ **1.** (verlaufen) *to pass off*; *to turn out* || gut ~ *to pass off well*, *to succeed*, *to be a success*; schlecht ~ *to turn out badly*, *to fail* **2.** (→ A. 3.) jdm ~ *to be wanting*, es geht ihm der Mut ab *he lacks* od *wants courage*, *he is lacking* od *wanting in c.* || es geht ihm nichts ab *he has got all he wants* | sich etw ~ l *to stint* od *pinch o.s. in* od *for a th*; *to deny o.s. a th*; er ließ sich nichts ~ *he did not stint himself for anything*; laß ihm nichts ~ *let him want for nothing* **3.** ⟨com⟩ *to be abated*, *deducted* od *reduced*; geht nichts vom Preise ab? *is there no reduction?*, *is this your lowest* (od *bottom*) *price?*; (auf Rechnungen) hiervon geht ab .. *less* od *deduct ..*; *discount ..* **4.** ⟨com⟩ (Ware) *to sell* (zum Preise v *at*) (vgl A. 2.); *to go off*; gut ~ *to meet with a good sale*, *to be in great demand*; reißend ~ *to take on rapidly*; nicht ~ *to find no sale* **D.** [gleichsam transitiv] (Strecke, Raum) *to walk*; die ganze Front (des Hauses) ~ *to walk along the whole front* (..) **II.** ≗ n ⟨übtr⟩ *departure* (v *from*) | ~ der Front *walking along the front*

·**abgehend** a *outgoing* (*mail*) || (ausscheidend) *outgoing* (*tenant*)

·**ab|geizen** vt [h] sich etw ~ *to stint o.s. in a th*

·**abge-** ~**kämpft** a *worn out*, *exhausted*, *spent*; *weak and weary* || ~**kartet** a e–e ~e S *a put-up job*; ⟨Am⟩ *a frame-up*; ⟨fam⟩ (*it's all*) *cut and dried* ≗**kehrtheit** f *detachment* ~**klappert** a ⟨fig⟩ *decrepit*; *fragile*; *shaky* || alles ~ h *to have searched everything* ~**klärt** ⟨fig⟩ *detached* (*mind*); *balanced* (*judgment*) || ⟨mus⟩ *mellow* || *mellow* (*age*) || (P) *dispassionate*, *mature*, *wise*, *serene*; (jdn, den Geist) ~ m *to mellow* ≗**klärtheit** f *detachment*, *balance*; *poise*; *serenity* ~**lagert** a *matured* (*wine*) || *well-seasoned* (*cigar*) || ~e Massen pl ⟨geol⟩ *deposits* pl ~**laufen** → ablaufen

~lebt a ⟨fig⟩ *worn out* (*with age*); *decrepit, effete, decayed* **≃lebtheit** f *decrepitude* **~legen** [pp v abliegen] a (entfernt) *remote, distant*; ⟨Am⟩ *out-of-the-way* (*town*) ‖ *obscure* (Ort) ‖ (abgeschieden, einsam) *retired, secluded; devious, sequestered* **≃legenheit** *distance, remoteness* ‖ *seclusion* **~legt** a *left off, cast-off, discarded* (*clothing*) **~leiert** a ⟨fig⟩ *well-worn, hackneyed, trite* **~leitet** a: die ≃e ⟨math⟩ *the derivate*

·**ab|gelten** vt [h] *to discharge, satisfy; pay* ‖ ·**Abgeltung** f *composition, compromise; compensation delivery; reimbursement; repayment*

·**abge- ~macht** a ~! *agreed! all right! settled! that's a bargain!*; ~ ist ~! *a bargain is a b.!*; (ist es) ~? *is it a go?* ‖ ⟨Am fam⟩ *it's a deal!*; ⟨sl⟩ *put it there* ‖ (erledigt) *done* ‖ e–e ~e S *a cut-and-dried affair* **~magert** a *emaciated; shrunken* **~messen** a *measured* ‖ (genau ~) *exact* | ⟨fig⟩ *regular; rhythmical* **≃messenheit** f *exactness*; ⟨fig⟩ *regularity* **~neigt** a e–r S ~ *disinclined for* od *to a th; averse to a th*; dem Dorfleben ~ *alien to village life* ‖ ~ z tun *loath, reluctant, disinclined to do* ‖ nicht ~ s gegen etw *to be equal to a th* (*I am e. to a glass of wine*) ‖ nicht ~ s z tun *to be prepared to do; to feel like doing*; ich bin durchaus nicht ~ *I am nothing loath*, ⟨fam⟩ *I don't care if I do* | jdm ~ *unfavourably disposed, ill-disposed to* od *towards a p* **≃neigtheit** f ~ gegen etw, ~ zu tun *disinclination, reluctance, indisposition to a th, to do* ‖ ~ gegen jdn *antipathy against* od *to a p; aversion to* od *from a p; dislike to* od *of, for a p* **≃nutzt** a *worn-out; used-up*; → abgetragen; *timeworn* ⟨a. fig⟩ **≃nutztheit** f *threadbareness*

·**Abgeordnete**([**r**] m –ten/–ten) f –ten/–ten *deputy, delegate, representative* | ⟨parl⟩ *elected member of a legislative assembly*; ⟨engl⟩ *Member of Parliament* (abbr M. P.); der ~ f. N. *the honourable Member for N.* ‖ ⟨Am⟩ die ~n e–s Staates pl *the delegation* ‖ ⟨Ger⟩ *deputy*, m–e Herren ~n! *Members* pl *of the German Bundestag!* **~nhaus** n ⟨Ger hist & West-Berlin⟩ *The* (*Prussian*) *Chamber of Deputies*, → Unterhaus **~nmandat** n *mandate*; ⟨engl⟩ *seat* **~nwahl** f *election of deputies*

·**abge- ~packt** a *prepack* (Ware); (*vegetables*) *sold in prepacks*; ~e Menge f *package* **~paßt** a ⟨tex⟩ *shaped* (*garment length*), *bordered* (*design*) **~rissen** [pp v abreißen] a (Kleider, P etc) *torn, ragged, shabby* | ⟨fig⟩ *abrupt, disjointed* (*style*) ‖ *incoherent; disconnected* (*sentences*) **~rundet** a ⟨fig⟩ *rotund, well-rounded* (*style*); *balanced* ‖ in ~en Zahlen *in round numbers* **~sagt** a *cancelled* (*performance*) ‖ *declared* od *sworn* (*enemy*), ⟨poet⟩ *open* (*foe*) **≃sandte**([**r**] m ~ten/~ten) f ~ten/~ten *messenger*; (geheimer) ~r *emissary* ‖ ⟨pol⟩ *ambassador; delegate* ‖ päpstlicher ~r *nuncio* It **≃sang** m ~(e)s/≃e ⟨Ger hist pros⟩ (Ggs Aufgesang) *concluding part of a stanza* **~schabt** a *threadbare, shabby* (*coat*) **~schieden** [pp v abscheiden] a *secluded, retired* ‖ (verstorben) *deceased, defunct* **≃schiedenheit** f *retirement, seclusion* **~schliffen** [pp v abschleifen] a ⟨fig⟩ *polished; elegant; refined* **≃schliffenheit** f ⟨fig⟩ *elegance; refinement* **~schlossen** [pp v abschließen] a ⟨fig⟩ *isolated; secluded*, ~ leben *to live in seclusion* ‖ *exclusive* ‖ in sich ~ [pred] *complete in itself*; [attr] *detached, self-contained* (*house*); *independent* | (abgemacht) *settled* **≃schlossenheit** f *seclusion; privacy* ‖ (Zurückhaltung) *reserve, exclusiveness* **~schmackt** a *absurd, insipid, preposterous; inept*, ~e Bemerkung *ineptitude* ‖ *extravagant, mawkish, tasteless* ‖ *flat, dull, namby-pamby* (*conversation*) **≃schmacktheit** f ~/~en *insipidity, ineptitude; absurdity; extravagance, –cy* ‖ *inanity, fatuity, dullness* **~schrägt** a → ~stumpft **~sehen:** ~ von, von .. ~ *apart* (⟨Am⟩ *aside*) *from, without regard to; except for; not allowing for, barring* (*a th*); ~ v den Mitgliedern *without counting the m.* ‖ ~ davon [abs] *in addition*; ~ davon, daß .. *save that; let alone that* **~sessen** a *dismounted*; ~! *dismount!* **~setzt** a → absetzen ‖ ~e Welle *stepped shaft* **~sondert** a *separate* (v *from*) ‖ *secluded, retired*; ~ leben *to live in seclusion, to seclude o.s.* ‖ ⟨philos⟩ ~ betrachten *to abstract* **~spannt** a ⟨fig⟩ *unstrung* (*nerves*) ‖ [mst pred] *done up* (von, vor *with*); *exhausted, fatigued, wearied, tired* (*out*); ⟨med⟩ *debilitated* ‖ [pred] *knocked up; run down* **≃spanntheit** f *exhaustion, tiredness* **~standen** [pp v abstehen] a *stale, flat, vapid; stony* **~stellt** a (→ ausgefallen) *dead* (*engine*) **~steppt** a ⟨tex⟩ rechts ~ *top--stitched* **~storben** [pp v absterben] a *torpid; dry, dead* (*plant*) | (gefühllos) *numb* (*limb*) ‖ (P) *indifferent, insusceptible* (für *to*) **~stumpft** [pp v abstumpfen] a → abgeschrägt; *canted* (Ecke *angle*); *blunt, dull* (*razor*) ‖ ⟨übtr⟩ *blunt*(*ed*), *dull; obtuse, stuporous* | ⟨fig⟩ *blasé; indifferent* (gegen *to*); *insensible, insusceptible* (gegen *of, to*) | ≃heit [f] ⟨fig⟩ (geistige ~) *dullness, obtuseness*; ⟨Am⟩ *sog* ‖ *indifference, insensibility* (gegen *to*) **~takelt** a *unrigged, dismantled* ‖ ⟨fig⟩ *has-been* (*p*) **~tan** [pp v abtun] a (erledigt) *settled*; das ist alles ~ *that's all finished with*; (*of ideas*) *gone* | (unschädlich gemacht) *done for; ruined; killed* **~tragen** a *threadbare, shabby* (*coat*); [pred] *the worse for wear* **~treten** a (Absatz) *run-down* **~trieben** [pp v abtreiben] a *worn out, spent* (*animal*) **≃wandheit** f *aloofness*

·**ab|gewinnen** vt [h] **1.** jdm etw (Land etc.) ~ *to win a th from a p* ‖ *to wring a th from a p* ‖ jdm den Vorsprung ~ *to pull up to* od *with a p, to get the start of a p, to gain on a p*; ⟨fig⟩ *to steal a march upon a p*; jdm Vorteil ~ *to get* od *have the better* od *wind of a p* | e–m Schiff den Wind ~ *to get* od *have the wind of a ship* **2.** ⟨übtr⟩ e–r S etw ~; e–r S Geschmack ~ *to acquire a taste for a th* ‖ jdm G. ~ ⟨theat⟩ *to appeal to a p* ‖ e–r S Genuß ~ *to derive* od *gain pleasure from a th* ‖ dem Meere Land ~ *to reclaim land from the sea* ‖ dem Boden Früchte ~ *to wrest fruits from the soil* ·**Abgewinnung** f (Land≃) *reclamation* (*from the sea*)

·**Abgewogenheit** f (u Behutsamkeit) e–s Urteils *considered* (*and careful*) *judgment*

·**ab|gewöhnen** vt [h] jdm etw ~ *to wean a p from a th, to break a p of a th; to disaccustom a p to a th* | sich etw ~ *to break o.s. of a th* (*of a habit*); *to discontinue a th*; ich kann es mir nicht ~ *I can't break m.s. of it; I cannot get out of the habit of it*; sich das Spielen ~ *to leave off* (od *to give up*) *gambling*

·**abge- ~zehrt** a *wasted, emaciated* **~zirkelt** a ⟨fig⟩ *elaborate* (*thoughts*) ‖ *ceremonious*

·**ab|gieren** vi [h] ⟨mar⟩ *to sheer off*

·**ab|gießen** vt [h] *to pour off* ‖ vorsichtig ~ ⟨chem⟩ *to decant* | ⟨tech⟩ *to make a cast of; to cast*

·**Abglanz** m ~es/ *resplendence; reflected splendour; reflection* ‖ ⟨fig⟩ nur ein (schwacher) ~ *only an imperfect image; only a shadow; a mere shadow*; er ist nur ein schwacher ~ s–s Bruders ⟨fam⟩ *he is only a weak edition of his brother*

·**ab|glänzen** vt [h] ⟨tex⟩ *to polish*

·**ab|glätten** vt [h] *to smooth, to polish*

·**Abgleich-** ⟨tech⟩ **~fehler** m *balance error* **~frequenz** f *balancing frequency* **~kondensator** m *trimming capacitor* **~spule** f *alignment coil* **~wicklung** f *adjusting winding*

·**ab|gleichen** vt [h] **1.** *to equalize; to make even*; ⟨carp⟩ *to even, to level*; ⟨tech⟩ *to adjust; to balance*; ⟨opt⟩ *to equalize* **2.** ⟨übtr⟩ (Rechnungen) *to square* ‖ (Konto) *to balance* ·**Abgleichung** f ~/~en *equalization; balance; levelling*

·**ab|gleiten** vi [s] *to slip* (*he slipped*); *to lose one's footing*; sein Fuß glitt ab *his foot slipped* ‖ (S) *to glide off, to slip off*; (Rad) *to skid*; ~ an etw *to glance off a th* ‖ (hinabgleiten) *to slip down* | ⟨fig⟩ alle Ermahnungen gleiten an ihm ab *he is deaf to* (od *makes light of*) *all exhortations*; *all exh. go off him like water off a duck's back*

·**Abgott** m ~(e)s/⁼er *idol* ‖ ⟨übtr⟩ jdn zum ~ m., als ~ verehren *to adore, to idolize a p* ‖ **~schlange** f ⟨zoo⟩ *boa constrictor* ·**Abgötter·ei** f ~/~en *idolatry*; ~ treiben, *to worship idols* ‖ ⟨übtr⟩ ~ treiben mit jdm *to idolize a p* ·**abgöttisch** **1.** a *idolatrous* ‖ ⟨übtr⟩ *immoderate, excessive* **2.** adv ⟨übtr⟩ *excessively*; jdn ~ verehren *to worship a p with idolatry*

·**ab|graben** vt [h] *to dig off* ‖ (Wasserweg) *to drain*; *to draw off*; ⟨fig⟩ jdm das Wasser ~ *to knock the bottom out of a p's resources, to strip a p of all his resources*

·**ab|grämen** vrfl [h] sich ~ *to pine away* (über *for*)

·**ab|grasen** vt [h] (of cattle) (Weide) *to graze* ‖ ⟨fig⟩ alles ~ nach *to search for a th all over*

·**Abgratpresse** f ⟨tech⟩ *trimming press*

·**ab|greifen** vt [h] *to wear out* (*by constant handling*) ‖ (Buch) *to thumb* ‖ → abgegriffen ‖ (Entfernung) *to measure* .. (*from a map* [*with compasses, etc*])

·**ab|grenzen** vt [h] (etw) *to demarcate, to mark off* (gegen, von *from*); ⟨a. übtr⟩ ‖ (festlegen) *to delimit* (*the frontiers of a country*) ·**Abgrenzung** f ~/~en *demarcation, delimitation* (*of a frontier*)

·**Abgrund** m ~(e)s/⁼e **1.** (grundlos) *abyss*; *gulf*; (steil) *precipice* ‖ (Meer) *depth* **2.** ⟨fig⟩ *gulf, abyss*; ⟨fig⟩ dicht am ~ entlanggehen *to be sailing exceedingly close to the wind*; Politik am Rande des ~s *brinkmanship* **⁼tief** **1.** a *abysmal, unfathomable* ⟨a. fig⟩; ⟨fig⟩ *profound* (Zynismus), **2.** adv *abysmally*

·**ab|gucken** vt [h] → absehen

·**Abgunst** f ~/ = Mißgunst

·**ab|gürten** vt [h] (Schwert) *to ungird*

·**Abguß** m –gusses/–güsse **1.** (Abgießen) *pouring off*; *decanting, decantation* | ⟨met⟩ (Gießen) *founding, casting* **2.** (das Gegossene) ⟨bes sculp⟩ *cast*; *copy*

·**ab|haaren** vi/t [h] **1.** vi *to lose hair*; der Pelz haart ab *the hair of the fur comes off* **2.** vt *to strip* (*a th*) *of hair*; *to scrape the hair from* (*a th*); *to unhair* (*a th*)

·**ab|haben** vt [h] **1.** den Hut (etc.) ~ *to have one's hat* (etc.) *off* **2.** etwas ~ v e–r S *to have a part of a th* ‖ etw ~ wollen *to want a share of a th*; ⟨iron⟩ dafür sollst du was ~ *you'll be punished for it*! ⟨fam⟩ *you'll get it* (*for it*)!

·**ab|hacken** vt [h] *to cut* od *chop off* ‖ (Baum) *to chop down*; → –ge–kt

·**ab|hageln** vrefl [h] es hat sich abgehagelt *it has stopped hailing*

·**ab|häkeln** vt [h] *to copy in crochetwork*

·**ab|haken** vt [h] **1.** *to unhook* **2.** ~ *to check off*

·**ab|halftern** vt [h] **1.** *to unhalter* **2.** ⟨fig⟩ (jdn) *to dismiss, discharge* ‖ ⟨mil⟩ *to cashier* | ⟨fam⟩ *to give* (*a p*) *the sack* | *to snub* (*a p*)

·**ab|halten** vt/i [h] **I.** vt **A.** jdn *or* ein Tier ~ **1.** (fernhalten) *to keep off*; *to hold off* (*hold the dog off*!) **2.** (aufhalten) *to detain*; –ge– w. durch *to be detained by* **3.** (zurückhalten, hindern) *to deter, restrain* (v *from*) ‖ (Feind) *to check*; *to head off* ‖ jdn davon ~ z tun *to hinder* od *prevent a p* (*to fend a p* [*off*]) *from doing*; → hindern | sich nicht ~ l durch etw *to be unmindful of a th*; l Sie sich nicht ~ durch .. *don't be deterred by* .. **4.** (Kind) *to hold out* **B.** etw ~ **1.** (fernhalten) (Regen etc.) *to keep out* ‖ (Licht) *to keep away* (v *from*) **2.** (Schlag) *to ward off*; *to parry* **3.** (veranstalten) (Fest) *to celebrate*; *observe*; *hold, keep*; Gesellschaften ~ *to have parties* ‖ (Gottesdienst, Prüfung, Sitzung, Wahl) *to hold* | (Schule) *to keep*; (Stunden) *to give* ‖ ⟨univ⟩ (Vorlesungen) *to deliver* od *give* | ⟨theat⟩ Proben ~ *to take rehearsals* **4.** (ertragen) *to bear, stand* **II.** vi vom Lande ~ *to bear off* ‖ (of ships) vom Winde ~ *to bear up*

·**Abhaltung** f ~/~en **1.** (Hindernis) *detention, hindrance*; ~en h *to be detained* (durch *by*); *to be otherwise engaged* **2.** *celebration*; *observation* (*of a feast*) | *holding* (*of a meeting* od *procession*)

·**ab|handeln** vt [h] **1.** (erörtern) *to discuss*; *to debate on*; *to treat*; *to treat of* ‖ *to negotiate, settle* **2. a.** (abkaufen) jdm etw ~ *to buy* od *purchase a th of a p by bargaining* **b.** Geld ~ von etw, etw vom Preise e–r S ~ *to beat* od *bring down the price of a th*; ich handelte ihm 3 Mark ab *I obtained 3 marks by bargaining, I got a reduction of 3 m. by b.*; er läßt sich nichts ~ *there is no beating him down, he will not take off a farthing*

abh·anden adv: ~ k *to get lost, to be mislaid* ‖ ~ gek *missing*; ~ gek s *to be missing*; das Messer ist mir ~ gek *I have lost the knife*

·**Abhandlung** f ~/~en *essay*; wissenschaftliche ~ *dissertation, paper, treatise, tractate, sketch, monograph* ‖ (mündliche) *discussion* ‖ ~en [pl] *proceedings, transactions* pl (*of a learned society*)

·**Abhang** m ~(e)s/⁼e *declivity, incline, slope*; an e–m ~ gelegen *tilted* ‖ → Gefälle

·**ab|hangen** vi [h] [heute mst: abhängen] **1.** (herabhängen) *to hang*; *to be suspended*; *to hang down* (v *from*) ‖ *hanging* **2.** ⟨fig⟩ → ·**abhängen** **I.** vt/i (h) **1.** vt (etw) *to unhang*; *to take off* od *down*; *to detach* ‖ ⟨tech⟩ *to disconnect* (v *from*); *to uncouple* ‖ ⟨fig⟩ (Freund[in]) °~ *to shoot down* ⟨sl⟩ **2.** vi [f älteres abhangen, s. d.] ⟨fig⟩ **a.** (S) [abs] das Wild hängt ab, hing ab, ist abgehangen .. *hung*; wir häng(t)en d. W. ab, wir h d. W. ⁼ l *the game is hung* ‖ ~ v etw *to depend, to be dependent* od *contingent on a th*; *to hang on, to turn on* (*the answer turns on how* ..); *to be conditioned by a th*; ⟨fam⟩ [ell] das hängt davon ab *that depends* | ~ von jdm *to depend on a p*; es hängt nur von dir ab *it depends only on you, it lies* od *rests only with you* **b.** (P) (angewiesen s) ~ von jdm *to be dependent, to depend on a p* (*he depends entirely on his parents*) **c.** ⟨telph⟩ [ell] *to ring off* **II.** ⁼ n (v Fleisch) *conditioning*

·**abhängig** a **1.** (geneigt) *sloping*; sehr ~ *declivitous* **2.** ⟨fig⟩ *dependent*; *ancillary* (*industries*); ⟨pol⟩ ~es Gebiet *a dependency* ‖ jdn in e–e ~e Lage bringen v jdm *to make a p dependent on a p* | [pred] ~ v etw (*to be*) *dependent on* (*circumstances*), *contingent on* (*time*), *subject to* (*conditions*), *conditioned by* | ~ v jdm *dependent on a p* (→ **un~**); *to be at the mercy of a p*; v einander ~ *interdependent* ‖ Shakespeare ist ~ v Plutarch *Sh. has borrowed from* (od *made use of*) *Pl.* | ⟨gram⟩ *indirect, oblique* (*speech, case*)

·**Abhängige[r]** m *dependant, –ent*; ⟨übtr⟩ *vassal*

·**Abhängigkeit** f ~/~en ⟨fig⟩ *dependence, –cy* (v *on, upon*); gegenseitige ~ *interdependence* ‖ ⟨übtr⟩ *vassalage* (v *to*) **~sverhältnis** n *state of dependence*; *dependent relation* ‖ (of languages etc.) *filiation*

·**ab|härmen** vrefl [h] sich ~ *to grieve* (über *at, for*); *to pine* (*away*) (über, vor *with*); *to languish* ‖ *to eat one's heart out*; → abgehärmt

·**ab|härten** vt [h] (jdn) *to harden* | ⟨fig⟩ *to harden, strengthen*; *inure, season* (gegen *to*); abgehärtet s gegen *to be inured to* (*cold*) | **sich ~** *to harden, steel, season o.s.* (*against*) ‖ → abgehärtet

·**Abhärtung** f ~/~en *hardening*; *strengthening*; *inurement* (gegen *to*)

·**ab|haspeln** vt [h] **1.** ⟨weav⟩ *to reel off* **2.** ⟨fig⟩ *to deliver* (*a th*) *mechanically*; *to rattle off*; *to jabber* | **sich ~** *to bustle* (*about*)

·**ab|hasten** vrefl → sich abhetzen, abplagen

·ab|hauen vt/i **1.** vt [h] *to cut* od *chop off* ‖ (Kopf) *to cut off*; (Baum) *to cut down, to fell*; –ge–er Baum *log, trunk* ‖ (Getreide) *to cut, mow* **2.** ° vi [s] ⟨fig⟩ *to be off; to bolt, decamp, slope; to stump it; to sling* od *buzz off; to scamper; to make a bolt for it; to hook* od *hop it; to kick out; to skedaddle* ⟨a. mil fliehen⟩; °hau ab! *be off!, scram!, scat(ter)!; to push* (od ⟨bes mil vulg⟩ *fuck*) *off*; hau ab damit! *make away with it!* ‖ ich hau ab! *my name's Walker!; it's time to toddle* ‖ mit Vollgas ~ *to go through the gate* ‖ ⟨aero⟩ *to take off*

·ab|häuten vt [h] *to skin* ‖ (Tier) *to flay*

·Abhebe- ~geschwindigkeit f ⟨aero⟩ *taking-off* od *rising* (od ⟨fam⟩ *get-away* od *unstick*) *speed*

·ab|heben vt/i [h] **I.** vt **1.** (Deckel etc.) *to lift (off)*; ⟨telph, etc.⟩ *to take off* | (Karten) *to cut* **2.** ⟨aero⟩ (Flugzeug) ⟨sl⟩ *to hoi(c)k off*; → II. 2. **3.** ⟨com⟩ (Geld) *to draw (out), to withdraw. to take out* (v der Bank *from the b.*); bares G. ~ *to draw cash* ‖ (Dividende) *to collect* **3.** (hervorheben) etw (deutlich) ~ *to bring, place, throw a th into* (od *in*) *(full, strong) relief*; etw ~ gegen *or* von *to relieve* (od *to set off*) *a th against* (*a background*) | **sich ~** gegen *to contrast with*; sich deutlich ~ *to stand out in relief, to relieve, to stand out* (gegen .. *against a cloudless sky*); *to stand out boldly from* (*a background*); sich scharf ~d gegen *in relief against* **II.** vi **1.** ⟨cards⟩ *to cut* **2.** ⟨aero⟩ *to break ground, to rise*, ⟨fam⟩ *to unstick*; → I. 2. **III.** ≗ n ⟨aero⟩ *rising, etc; get--away* [s] ‖ ⟨a–n⟩ *lift-off*

·Abhebung f ~/~en (Geld≗) *withdrawal of money (from a bank)* ‖ [konkr] ~en [pl] *drawings* pl **~sformular** n *withdrawal-form*

·ab|heften vt [h] *to file (letters)*

·ab|heilen vi [h & s] *to heal (up)* **·Abheilung** f ~/~en, *healing; healing-up*

·ab|helfen vi [h] (Schmerzen [dat]) *to ease* ‖ (e–m Mangel) *to meet; to supply* ‖ (e–m Mißstande) *to remedy, redress, remove* ‖ (e–m Fehler) *to correct, rectify* ‖ (Schwierigkeiten) *to remove* ‖ (Beschwerden) *to meet, redress* | dem ist nicht abzuhelfen *that is past remedy, it cannot be helped*

·ab|herzen vt [h] (jdn) *to hug and kiss; to kiss heartily*

·ab|hetzen vt [h] (Pferd) *to overdrive* | (jdn) *to overwork, harass, tire, fatigue (a p)* ‖ **sich ~** *to tire* od *wear o.s. out*

·Abhilfe f ~/ **1.** *remedy, redress, relief, corrective*; Maßnahmen zur ~ *remedial measures* pl | dafür gibt es k–e ~ *there is no help for it* ‖ hier muß man ~ schaffen *this must be remedied* ‖ das Übel verlangt sofortige ~ *the evil calls for immediate redress* **2.** [in comp] (e–m Übel) ~ schaffend *remedial (measures)* **~maßnahmen** f pl *remedial measures, m. to remedy the situation* ‖ ~ ergreifen, treffen *to take corrective action* od *measures*

·Abhitze f ~/ *waste heat* **~kessel** m *wasteheat boiler*

·ab|hobeln vt [h] *to plane (off); to smooth*; (Kanten) *to shoot*

·abhold a; jdm ~ *unfavourably disposed* od *ill-disposed towards a p; unfriendly to a p* ‖ e–r S ~ *alien, averse to a th (not averse to a glass of wine); opposed to a th* ‖ → abgeneigt

·ab|holen vt [h] **1.** (P) *to fetch; to call for*, ich werde Sie ~ *I shall call for you* ‖ *to come to meet* ‖ (mit dem Wagen) *to come for (a p), to pick (a p) up* (v Haus *at his house*); wann soll ich Sie ~? *when shall I come and pick you up?* ‖ *to go to meet, to go for*, ich werde ihn abholen *I shall go for him*; Sie werden abgeholt w v .. *you will be met by (my sister)* ‖ jdn vom Bahnhof ~ *to meet a p at the station* **2.** (S) *to call for*; abzuholen *to be called for* ‖ *to go* od *come for* ‖ (Güter) *to collect* ‖ (bestelltes Billett) *to claim*; ⟨rail⟩ (Gepäck) wieder ~ *to reclaim* ‖ ⟨mil⟩ *to pick up (supplies)* | [als vi] (= den Briefkasten leeren) *to collect (the) letters* **3.** ~ lassen *to send for*

·Abhol- ~fach n *post-office box* **~gebühr** f *official fee for fetching a parcel* (etc.) **~ung** f ~/~en *fetching; calling for* ‖ *collection (of goods)* ‖ (Briefkastenleerung) *collection*, die Zeit der ~ *the time of c.*

·Abholz n ~es/ *dead* od *waste wood* ‖ *chips* pl

·ab|holzen vt [h] (bewaldete Gegend) *to deforest, disforest; to clear (a wood) of trees*

·abholzig a ⟨for⟩ *very conical; tapered*

·Abholzung f ~/~en *clearance; clearing*

·Abhör- ~apparat m ⟨telph⟩ *wire tapping device*; ⟨mar⟩ *overhearing plant* **~box** f ⟨Tonfilm⟩ *mixing desk* **~dienst** m ⟨mil⟩ *interception service*; ⟨rad⟩ *monitoring s.* **~stelle** f *interception station* **~verstärker** m *monitoring amplifier*

·ab|horchen I. vt [h] ⟨med⟩ *to sound, auscultate*; ⟨tech⟩ *to monitor* **II.** ≗n ⟨med⟩ *auscultation*

·Abhorcher m ⟨telph⟩ *wire-tapper*

·ab|hören vt [h] **1.** jdn ~ (jdm etw ~); ich hörte ihn ab (*or* ich h. ihm die Aufgaben ab) *I heard (him) his lesson(s), he recited his l. to me* **2.** ⟨med⟩ = abhorchen **3.** ⟨telph⟩ *to listen to illicitly; to overhear*; ⟨wir⟩ *to intercept*; ⟨tech⟩ *to monitor*; ⟨a. mil⟩ Gespräche ~ *to tap the telephone wire*; → auffangen ‖ Funksprüche ~ *to intercept wireless* **4.** ⟨com⟩ (Rechnungen) *to audit*

·Abhub m ~(e)s/ *offal; leavings, remains; fragments* ‖ (P) (Auswurf) *sweepings* pl

·ab|hülsen vt [h] *to shell, hull, husk* ‖ (Mandeln) *to blanch*

·ab|hungern vrefl [h] sich ~ *to starve (o.s.)*

·Abi n ~s/~s = Abitur(ientenexamen) *leaving examination*; ⟨sl⟩ *Highers*; *vgl G.C.E.* = *General Certificate of Education "A" level*

·ab|impfen vt [h] ⟨med⟩ *to inoculate* (auf *on*)

·ab|irren vi [s] *to lose one's way; to go astray; to stray* (v *from*) | ⟨fig⟩ *to deviate* (v *from*); *to err, stray* **·Abirrung** f ~/~en *deviation* ‖ ⟨phys⟩ *aberration, deviation*

Abit·ur n ~s/~e ⟨Ger⟩ → Abi

Abituri·ent m ~en/~en ⟨Ger⟩ *candidate for the leaving examination* ‖ ⟨engl⟩ *boy of the upper 6th form of a secondary school applying for his higher school certificate* ‖ ⟨Am⟩ *graduate* **~enexamen** n, **~enprüfung** f ⟨Ger⟩ *final* od *leaving examination* ‖ ⟨engl⟩ *higher school certificate examination* ‖ **~enzeugnis** n ⟨Ger⟩ *certificate that the final examination has been passed*

·ab|jagen vt [h] **1.** (Pferd) *to overdrive*; (durch Reiten) *to founder, jade, override* **2.** jdm etw ~ *to rescue, recover, retrieve a th from a p* ‖ ⟨fam⟩ *to do a p out of a th* **3.** ⟨hunt⟩ ein Feld ~ *to shoot over a field* **4. sich ~** *to tire, wear o.s. out by running; to overexert* od *overdo o.s.*

·ab|kämmen vt [h] *to comb (off)*; (Wolle) *to card*

·ab|kanten vt [h] (Rand) *to edge; to round off*; (Fläche) schräg ~ *to bevel; to chamfer* ‖ (Steine) *to square* **·Abkantpresse** f ⟨tech⟩ *folding press*

·ab|kanzeln vt [h] (jdn) *to read a p off, to read* od *give a lecture to a p, to rebuke; lecture, reprimand, to take (a p) to task*; ⟨fam⟩ *to jaw; to bawl (a p) out; to haul (a p) up*; ⟨sl⟩ *to (bally)rag, wig, slate; to tick (a p) off* ‖ jdn tüchtig ~ *to dress* (⟨Am⟩ *to salt*) *a p down; to haul a p over the coals*; ⟨sl⟩ *to give a p a sound wigging* ‖ abgekanzelt w ⟨sl⟩ *to get a wigging, to receive a flea in one's ear*

·ab|kappen vt [h] ⟨hort⟩ *to lop off* ‖ ⟨mar⟩ *to cut (off)*

·ab|karten vt [h] *to concoct, fabricate (a th), to trump (a th) up*; sie hatten es zwischen sich abgekartet *they had fixed it up between them* || etw mit jdm ~ *to concert, plot, pre-arrange; to get up a th with a p* || vorher abgekartet *pre-concerted* || → abgekartet

·**ab|kauen** vt [h] sich ~ (Pferd) *to champ (the bit)* || sich [dat] die Nägel ~ *to bite one's nails*

·**ab|kaufen** vt [h] *to buy* od *purchase a th of* od *from* || jdm alles ~ ⟨sl⟩ *to buy up the whole lot*

·**Abkehr** f ~/ ⟨übtr⟩ (Abwendung) *turning away* (v *from*) || (Verzicht) *renunciation* (v *of*) || ⟨min⟩ (Entlassung) *dismissal* || ⟨übtr⟩ völlige ~ *about-face*

·**ab|kehren**[1] vt/i [h] **1.** vt (abwenden) *to turn off* **2. sich ~** *to turn away* (v *from*); *to turn one's back* (v jdm *on a p*) **3.** vi ⟨min⟩ *to leave off work*

·**ab|kehren**[2] vt [h] = abfegen, s. d. || ein abgekehrter Besen *a broom worn to the stump*

·**ab|ketten** vt [h] *to unchain*

·**ab|kippen** vi [s] *to tip, tilt, topple* || ⟨aero⟩ (über den Flügel) *to fall off, to bank away*; (aus dem Verband) *to pitch out*, ⟨fam⟩ *to peel off*

·**Abkippgeschwindigkeit** f ⟨aero⟩ *stalling speed*

°·**ab|klabastern** vrefl sich ~ *to toil hard*

·**ab|klappern** vt [h] *to do (the museums)*; (Bettler) *to tramp, call (I called the whole street)*

·**ab|klären** vt [h] **1.** *to clear*; (Flüssigkeit) *to clarify; to fine (down)* || ⟨chem⟩ *to filter, decant* **2. sich ~** *to clarify; to fine (down)* | ⟨fig⟩ (of the mind) *to become detached*; → abgeklärt

·**Abklärung** f, ~/~en *clarification (of liquids)* || ⟨chem⟩ *decantation*

·**Abklatsch** m ~es/~e **1.** (Abdruck) *impression; counter-proof; copy, duplicate; cast*; ⟨engr⟩ *rubbing; cliché* Fr; ⟨typ⟩ *stereotype* (abbr *stereo*), *stereotypeplate* || (Korrekturabzug) *proof(-sheet)* **2.** (Ebenbild) *image; he's the very model (spit) of his father* **3.** ⟨fig⟩ *edition, version; weak* od *feeble imitation*

·**ab|klatschen** vt [h] **1.** ⟨engr⟩ *to rub* || *to dab* || ⟨typ⟩ *to strike off; to stereotype* || *to copy* **2.** (jdn) *to flip a p with wet towels; to clap one's hands asking for the rest of a dance with a p's partner*, ⟨Am⟩ *to cut in* [adv]

·**ab|klettern** vi [s] = hinab–, hinunterklettern

·**ab|klingeln** vi [h] ⟨telph⟩ *to ring off*

·**ab|klingen 1.** vi [s] [nur 3. sg u pl] *to die away* | ⟨übtr⟩ *to abate; to fade (away* a. Krankheit); (of pain) *to pass off* || (of hope) *to evaporate* **2.** ≗ n (e–r Krankheit) *remission*

·**ab|klopfen** vt/i [h] **1.** vt *to beat* od *knock off*; (Teppich) *to beat*; den Staub ~ *to beat out the dust* || (Kesselstein) *to scale* | ⟨med⟩ = beklopfen | (Metall mit dem Hammer) *to burr over*, ⟨Am⟩ *to peen (down)* **2.** vi (of a bandmaster) *to cut off* || ⟨typ⟩ (e–n Bürstenabzug m.) *to strike off a proof with the beating brush*

·**ab|knabbern** vt [h] (of rabbits, etc.) *to nibble* || (Knochen) *to pick; to gnaw off*; → abnagen

·**ab|knallen** vi/t [s & h] **1.** vi *to explode; to go off* **2.** vt *to fire (off)*

·**ab|knappen,** ·**ab|knapsen** vt [h] **1.** ⟨hort⟩ *to lop off* **2.** jdm etw ~ *to stint a p of a th; to withhold a th from a p* || jdm etw am Lohne ~ *to screw down* (od *to curtail*) *a p's wage(s)* | **sich** [dat] etw ~ *to stint o.s. in a th*

·**ab|kneifen** vt [h] *to pinch* od *nip off*

·**ab|knicken** vt [h] *to break* od *snap off*

·**ab|knöpfen** vt [h] *to unbutton*; (den Kragen) *to undo* || jdm etw ~ ⟨fam⟩ *to do a p out of a th; to coax* od *wheedle a th out of a p*

·**ab|knüpfen** vt [h] *to untie, unbind, undo*

·**ab|knutschen** vt [h] *to smother with caresses*

·**ab|kochen** vt/i [h] *to boil* || ⟨chem⟩ *to decoct* || (Obst) *to stew*, (Milch) *to scald* | vi [h] ⟨mil, etc.⟩ *to cook a meal (in camp*, etc.) ·**Abkochung** f ~/~en *boiling*, ⟨chem⟩ *decoction*

·**Abkomm-** ⟨mil⟩ **~kanone** f *sub-calibre gun* **~lauf** m *Morris tube* **~punkt** m *marking-point; point of aim* **~schießen** n *sub-calibre practice*

·**ab|kommandieren** vt [h] ⟨mil⟩ (jdn) *to detach, detail; depute; to tell* od *order off* (zu, für *for*; z tun *to do*); *to assign* (zu *to*); ins Ausland ~ *to order abroad*; abkommandierte Abteilung *detail*; → Kommando || e–n Offizier zum Stabe ~ *to second an officer for service on the staff* ·**A–dierung** f ~/~en *detachment, assignment, etc; detached duty* od *service*

·**Abkomme** m ~n/~n *descendant; scion* || ~n pl *descendants* pl; *offspring, progeny, issue* || ohne männliche(n) ~n *without male issue* **~nschaft** f ~/ = Abkommen pl

·**ab|kommen** vi [s] **A.** (wegkommen) **1.** *to come* od *get away* || ich kann nicht ~ *I can't get away*; können Sie einige Minuten ~? *can you spare me a few minutes?* er kann gut ~ *we can do without him quite well* **2. ~ von** *to get away from* || von der Fährte ~ *to get off the scent* || vom Wege ~ *to lose one's way; to (go a)stray* || || ⟨übtr⟩ v etw ~ *to abandon, to give up a th*; v e–r Ansicht ~ *to alter an opinion*; v e–m Gegenstande ~ *to drop a subject*; v Thema ~ *to digress*; v der Wahrheit ~ *to deviate from truth*; v rechten Wege ~ *to leave the path of rectitude; to err* || ich bin ganz davon –ge– *I have given it up entirely* || billig davon ~ *to come off cheaply* **3.** ⟨aero⟩ *to deviate; to wander off course*; ⟨mar⟩ *to sheer* || v Winde ~ *to fall to leeward* **4.** ⟨sport⟩ *to start successfully* **5.** ⟨mil⟩ (beim Schießen) *to aim* od *lay a gun; to lay mark*; ⟨fig sex vulg⟩ *to get off* **B.** (abstammen) *to come of; to be descended from* **C.** (ungebräuchlich w.) *to come out of use, to fall into desuetude* od *disuse; to go out of fashion; to become obsolete*; (Mode) *to go out*

·**Abkommen** n ~s/~ **1.** = Abkunft **2.** (Finanz–, Währungs–, Wirtschafts≗ *economic, financial, monetary) agreement, settlement*; gütliches ~ *amicable arrangement*; durch mündliches ~ *by (an) oral agreement* || *deal*, Flotten≗ *naval deal* || ~ über die Nichtweitergabe von Kernwaffen *nuclear non-proliferation agreement*; ein ~ treffen *to come to an agreement, to make an arrangement* od *deal* **3.** (Aufhören) *falling into disuse; desuetude* **4.** ⟨sport⟩ *successful start* **5.** ⟨mil⟩ (Haltepunkt) *point of aim* **~genauigkeit** f ⟨mil⟩ *accuracy of aim*

·**Abkommin** f ~/~nen pl = Abkomme

·**abkömmlich** a *not engaged; to be spared* || nicht ~ *engaged*

·**Abkömmling** m ~s/~e = Abkomme || ⟨chem⟩ *derivative*

·**ab|konterfeien** vt [h] *to portray; to take (a p's) likeness*

·**ab|koppeln** vt [h] *to uncouple*

·**ab|kören** vt [h] (Hengst) *to reject (as unfit)*

·**Abkratz- ~eisen** n ⟨tech⟩ *scraper*

·**ab|kratzen** vt/i **1.** vt [h] (Oberfläche) *to scrape; to rasp* || den Schmutz von den Stiefeln ~ *to scrape the dirt off* [prep] *one's boots*; sich [dat] die Stiefel ~ *to scrape one's boots* || (Kesselstein) ~ → abklopfen **2.** °vi [s] (sterben) ⟨sl⟩ *to kick (the bucket* od *it); to pip, peg* od *kick out; to kick up one's heels, to turn up one's toes, to hop the twig, to go off (°the hooks)*, ⟨Am⟩ *to cash in*

·**ab|kriegen** vt [h] = abbekommen; krieg ich was ab? ⟨fam⟩ *am I to be in on this?*

·**Abkühl-** [in comp] *cooling* || **~apparat** m *cooler; refrigerator*

·**ab|kühlen** vt [h] *to throw* od *cast a chill upon a th; to cool (down); to refrigerate* || (Metall) *to anneal*; (Gas) *to quench* || ⟨fig⟩ *to cool, moderate, appease* | sich ~ *to cool down, to get cool*

·**Abkühlung** f ~/~en *cooling; refrigeration* || ⟨fig⟩ *damper, wet blanket* | **~s- ~geschwindigkeit** f *cooling rate* **~mittel** n ⟨a. med⟩ *refrigerant* **~pause** f *cooling-off period* **~raum** m *refrigerating chamber* **~wärme** f ⟨phys⟩ *heat of cooling*

·**Abkunft** f ~/≗e **1.** (P) *descent, birth; extraction; lineage; origin* ‖ von edler *or* hoher ~ *nobly descended, of noble birth*; ein Mann v hoher ~ *a man of birth* ‖ v guter ~ *of good family, of gentle birth* ‖ v niedriger ~ *low-born, of low* (od *obscure, humble*) *birth* **2.** (T) *breed; pedigree*

·**ab|kürzen** vt [h] *to shorten* ‖ (Buch, Inhalt etc) *to abridge; to condense* ‖ (Rede, Geschichte, Wort) *to abbreviate* ‖ ⟨math⟩ *to reduce* ‖ mit –ge–zter Bezeichnung *alphabetic* (*agency*)

·**Abkürzung** f ~/~en *shortening* ‖ (Inhalts≗) *abridgment* ‖ (Wort≗) *abbreviation* ‖ ⟨math⟩ *reduction* **~sverzeichnis** n *list of abbreviations* **~szeichen** n (*sign of*) *abbreviation, abbreviature*

·**ab|küssen** vt [h] (P) *to smother with kisses* ‖ (Tränen) *to kiss away*

·**Ablade-** ⟨com⟩ **~gebühr** f *discharging-fee; landing charge* **~gewicht** n *shipping-weight* **~platz** m *port of discharge* **~schein** m *discharging-, landing-certificate* **~stelle** f *dumping-ground, -place; shoot, dump* ⟨a fig⟩

·**ab|laden** vt [→ laden] [h] (Schiff) *to unload, to discharge* ‖ (etw) *to unlade* (v *from*) ‖ (Schutt) *to dump, tip, deposit*; (Abfall) *to shoot* (auf *on to*); hier kann Schutt abgeladen w *rubbish may be shot here* ‖ °Geld, Asche ~ *to plank down one's money* ·**Ablader** m ~s/~ *discharger; unloader*; (Kohlen≗) *heaver* ‖ ⟨mar⟩ *freighter, lighterman, shipper* ·**Abladung** f ~/~en *discharge; unloading*

·**Ablage** f ~/~n (Ort) *place of deposit; depot* ‖ (Kleider≗) *cloak-room*, ⟨Am⟩ *checkroom; coat-rack* | Sw = Agentur | **~fach** n ⟨comp⟩ *pocket*

·**ab|lagern** vt/i [h] **1.** vt (ablegen) ⟨chem⟩ *to deposit* ‖ (Bier) *to store, age* (⟨a.⟩ ~ l) | **sich ~** = **2.** vi **a.** (sich absetzen) (in liquids) *to settle*; (an Güte zunehmen) *to season*; (Wein) *to grow mellow, to mature* ‖ (Zigarre) *to get well-seasoned* ‖ (Bier) *to store, age* **b.** ~ l (sich setzen l) (Kaffee) *to settle* | (reifen l) *to season, to improve* (*a th*) *by storage* ‖ → abgelagert ·**Ablagerung** f ~/~en **1.** [abstr] ⟨geol, med⟩ *deposition* ‖ *seasoning; maturing* **2.** [konkr] (Abgelagertes) *deposit*; ~ im Urin *sabulous matter*

Ablaktati·on [*ts*] f ~/~en **1.** (Entwöhnung) *ablactation* **2.** ⟨hort⟩ *inarching* **ab|lakt·ieren** vt [pp ablaktiert] [h] (entwöhnen) *to wean* ‖ ⟨hort⟩ (veredeln) *to inarch*

·**ablandig, -ä-** a ⟨mar⟩ *offshore* (*wind*)

·**Ablaß** m Ablasses/Ablässe **1.** R.C. *indulgence, pardon* **2.** ⟨com⟩ *deduction, rebate; reduction* **3.** (Abfluß) *outlet; pipe, drain* **4.** † ohne ~ *incessantly* **5.** [in comp] ⟨tech⟩ *delivery, waste* **~brief** m ⟨ec⟩ *letter of indulgence* **~graben** m *ditch, drain* **~hahn** m ⟨tech⟩ *discharge-, drain-, delivery-cock* **~handel** m ⟨ec⟩ *the selling of indulgences* **~krämer** m ⟨ec⟩ *seller of indulgences* **~prediger** m *preacher* od *seller of indulgences* **~stopfen** m *vent plug* **~tage** m pl ⟨ec⟩ *days of grace* **~ventil** n ⟨tech⟩ *delivery-valve, outlet* od *drain* od *dump valve* **~woche** f *Corpus Christi week*

·**ab|lassen** **I.** vt/i [h] **A.** vt **1.** (ablaufen l) **a.** (Wasser etc) *to let off; to run off* (v *from*); *to run* (aus *out of*); *to drain* ‖ Blut ~ *to let blood* ‖ (Wein) *to draw off* ‖ (Dampf) *to blow off* ‖ (Luft) *to exhaust* **b.** (leeren) (Faß) *to broach* ‖ (Teich) *to drain, sluice* **2.** ⟨übtr⟩ (in Bewegung setzen) *to start* ‖ (Ballon) *to start* ‖ (Zug) *to run* ‖ (Telegramm) *to send* (*off*) **3.** (überlassen) jdm etw ~ *to let a p have a th; to spare a p a th: could you spare me a copy?* ‖ ⟨jur⟩ *to cede a th to a p* | ⟨com⟩ (Waren) *to sell* (zum Selbstkostenpreis *at cost-price*) **4.** (etw) vom Preise ~ *to deduct; to take off*: er ließ 2 Mark ab *he deducted 2 marks, reduced the price by 2 marks*; ich kann nichts ~ *I can't allow any reduction* **B.** vi **von etw ~** *to desist from, to leave off, to stop, discontinue a th*; laß davon ab! *leave it alone! give it up!* ‖ davon ~ z tun *to leave off* (od *to discontinue, stop*) *doing* **II.** ≗ n *letting-off* etc ‖ ⟨mot⟩ ~ v Abgasen *scavenging*

Ablati·on [*ts*] f ~/~en ⟨a. geog⟩ *ablation*

·**Ablativ** m ~s/~e ⟨gram⟩ *ablative; a. case*

°·**ab|latschen** vt [h] (Schuhe) *to wear down*

°·**ab|lauern** vt [h] etw ~ *to spy a th out; to lie in wait for a th* ‖ *to watch for* (*an opportunity*)

·**Ablauf** m ~(e)s/≗e **A.** [abstr] **1.** *running off; drainage* ‖ *issue* ‖ ⟨mar⟩ (Stapellauf) *launch* ‖ ⟨sport⟩ *start* **2.** ⟨übtr⟩ (of events) *course; round* (*the daily round*) ‖ nicht ordnungsgemäßer ~ ⟨mach⟩ *malfunction* ‖ den ~ (e–s Vorgangs) festlegen *to phase* | (of time) *lapse* (*a l. of 5 years*) ‖ *the passing* (*of a year*) | (Beendigung) *result* (e–r S *of a th*); *issue, completion; end; expiration, expiry* (*of a set term*); bei ~ v *on expiration of*; mit ~ des 1. Mai *with the passing of May 1st*; nach ~ des Jahres *at the end of the year* ‖ *maturity* (*of a bill*) **B.** [konkr] **1.** (Abfluß) *outlet; escape-, waste-pipe; sewer, sink* **2.** ⟨arch⟩ (*e*)*scape; apophyge* **~bahn** f (f Segelflugzeuge) *slip-way* **~linie** ⟨tact⟩ *line of departure* **~punkt** m ⟨tech, mil, tact⟩ *initial point* **~rinne** f *drain, gutter* **~rohr** n (f Kondenswasser) *drip-pipe* **~röhre** f *escape--pipe; sink* **~(s)frist** f ⟨com⟩ *date of expiration*

·**ab|laufen** vi/t **A.** vi [s] **1.** (abfließen) *to run* od *go off* | (etw) ~ l *to let* (*a th*) *off; to run* (*a liquid*) *off* (in *into*) **2.** (abgehen) ⟨mar⟩ *to sail; to put* (*out*) *to sea* | ⟨mar⟩ *to be launched*; ~ l *to launch* | ⟨sport⟩ *to start* **3.** ⟨übtr⟩ ~ an jdm *to leave a p cold; to make no impression on a p* | jdn ~ l *to send a p on his business; to give a p a set-down; to rebuff* od *snub a p*; → abfahren A. 4. **4.** ⟨übtr⟩ (vor sich gehen) *to come* od *pass off* (*well, badly*); *to turn out* (für jdn *to a p*); es lief glänzend für mich ab *I came off splendidly*; nicht gut ~ *to cause trouble*; wie wird das ~? *what will be the end* od *result of this?* **5.** (ein Ende erreichen) (Uhr[werk]) *to run down* | ⟨übtr⟩ s–e Stunde ist abgelaufen *his hour is come* | ⟨com⟩ *to come to an end* od *close*; (Frist) *to end, expire, terminate*; (Wechsel) *to become* od *fall due*; (of a lease) *to fall in*; (of contract) *to run out*; –ge– s *to be out* **B.** vt [h] (Strecke) *to run off*; die ganze Stadt ~ *to run through the whole town* | (die Hacken) *to wear away* | jdm den Rang ~ *to cut a p out; to outdo, to outstrip a p; to get the start* (od *the upper hand*) *of a p* | **sich** die Beine *or* Hacken ~ *to do* (od *run*) *one's utmost* (*to get a th*); *to run o.s. off one's legs*; sich die Hörner ~ *to sow one's wild oats*; das habe ich mir an den Schuhen abgelaufen *I have known it a long time*

·**Ablaufsform** f ⟨gram⟩ *progressive form*

·**Ablauge** f ~/~n *waste* (⟨pap⟩ *spent*) *liquor*

·**ab|lauschen** vt [h] e–r S etw ~ *to get behind a th, to feel one's way into a th*; der Natur die Geheimnisse ~ *to pry* (od *gain an insight*) *into the secrets of nature* ‖ dem Leben abgelauscht *true to nature, to life* | jdm etw ~ *to get behind a p's ways; to imitate a p successfully*

·**Ablaut** m ~(e)s/~e ⟨gram⟩ (*vowel*) *gradation; ablaut* ⟨Ger⟩ ·**ab|lauten** vi [h] (of verbs) *to change its radical vowel*; das Verb lautet ab *the verb is subject to gradation*

·**ab|läuten** vi/t [h] ⟨rail⟩ *to give the signal for starting* | vt ⟨sport⟩ (Rennen) *to call off*

·**ab|läutern** vt [h] ⟨brew⟩ *to clarify, drain, draw, strain* ·**A–rungsbatterie** f ⟨brew⟩ *drawing apparatus*

·**ab|leben** **I.** vi → abgelebt **II.** ≗ n ~s/ (P) *death*; ⟨bes jur⟩ *demise, decease* **≗sversicherung** f *life assurance* (*sum payable at death*)

·**ab|lecken** vt [h] *to lick* (*off*)

·**Ablege-** **~fach** n *pigeon-hole*; ⟨comp⟩ *stacker*

·**ab|legen** vt/i [h] **I.** vt **A.** **1.** ⟨eig⟩ (niederlegen) *to lay* od *put down* | (beiseitelegen) *to lay* od *put aside*; (ausscheiden) *to discard, to leave off; to file* (*letters*); abgelegt *discarded* od *left-off* (*garments*); (Garantieakt) als gegenstandslos ~

to close the files in respect of (*a guarantee*) | (v sich legen) *to put* od *take* od *pull off*; (schnell) *to throw off*; alle Kleider ~ *to undress* || die Maske ~ *to take the mask off*, ⟨fig⟩ *to unmask, to throw off all disguise* | ⟨typ⟩ *to distribute* || ⟨comp⟩ (Lochkarten) *to stack* | ⟨hort⟩ *to layer* **2.** ⟨übtr⟩ (Gewohnheit etc) *to get rid of*; *to give up*; *to live down, to outgrow*; *to shed*; *to discard*; *to throw off*; *to break* || die Kinderschuhe ~ *to be one's age* **B.** ⟨übtr⟩ (leisten) ein Bekenntnis ~ *to make a confession*; *to confess* (getan z h *to doing*) || *to take* (*an oath*) (auf jdn *to a p*; z tun *to do*) || *to make* od *take* (*a vow*) (jdm *to a p*) || *to pass* od *take* (*an examination*) || Rechenschaft ~ *to give an account* (über *of*); *to account* (über *for*) || Rechnung ~ *to render an account*; ⟨fig⟩ *to give an a.* || Zeugnis ~ *to bear witness* (v *of, to*), *to give evidence* (v *of*); ⟨jur⟩ *to give evidence* (*against*; *for*) || ° **es darauf** ~ → absehen **C.** ⟨min⟩ (Grube) *to shut down* || (Arbeiter) *to dismiss* **D.** ° jdn ~ *to let a p down*; *to leave a p in the lurch* **II.** vi **1.** Legen Sie ab, bitte ⟨fam⟩ *take off your things, please*; wollen Sie ~? *will you leave your overcoat*?; wo kann ich ~? *where can I leave my things*? **2.** ⟨cont⟩ = gebären

·**Ableger** m ~s/~ ⟨hort⟩ *layer, offset, offshoot*; *slip, scion*; e–n ~ v e–r Pflanze m *to slip a plant* || ⟨übtr⟩ *scion, slip*; *offset* | ⟨typ⟩ *distributor* || ~schwarm [m] (of bees) *new swarm*, ·**Ablegesatz** m ⟨typ⟩ *dead matter*

Ab·legung f ~/~en **1.** *laying down* od *aside* etc. **2.** *the making* (*of a vow*) || *the taking* (*of an oath*) || *the passing* (*of an examination*) || etc

·**ab|lehnen** vt [h] (**etw** verweigern) *to decline, refuse* (*a th*); ~ z tun *to decline doing, to refuse to do*; ⟨com⟩ ich muß es ~ z tun *I must be excused from doing* || [abs] dankend *or* höflich ~ *to decline with thanks* || (Antrag) *to reject*; *to negative*; ⟨Am⟩ *to throw* od *turn down* || ⟨parl⟩ *to throw out* (*a bill*); *to disclaim* (*all responsibility*) | (**etw** nicht anerkennen) *to dismiss* (*a th*); *to object to* (*a th*); *to make an objection* od *to take exception* (*to a th*); ⟨jur⟩ (Berufung) *to dismiss* || abgelehnt w (of plans) *to come to grief* | **jdn** ~ *to criticize a p adversely*; *to dismiss a p*; (Geschworene etc.) *to challenge* ·**ablehnend** a *deprecatory*; schroff ~ *intransigent* || (zurückhaltend) *passive* || ~es Verhalten *passiveness, passivity* || bloß ~ *destructive* (Kritik) || sich ~ verhalten *to be passive*; *to refuse*

·**Ablehnung** f ~/~en *declining, refusal, rejection* || ⟨Am⟩ *declination* (*of a p*; *to do*), *turn-down* (e–s Anspruchs *of a claim*) || ⟨jur⟩ *challenge* (*of witnesses*, etc.) || ~! *thumbs down*!

·**ab|leiern** vt [h] *to deliver mechanically, to drawl*

·**ab|leisten** vt (Eid) *to take* || (Dienst) *to fulfil*; *to perform*; den Militärdienst ~ *to serve one's time* ·**Ableistung** f ~/~en *fulfilment*; ~ der Militärzeit *serving one's time*

·**ableitbar** a *derivable* || ⟨log⟩ *deducible*

·**ab|leiten** vt [h] **1.** (ablenken) jdn vom rechten Wege ~ *to mislead*; *to seduce a p* | (Flüssigkeit) *to drain* (*off*) || (Flußstrom) *to divert* || ⟨el⟩ (Strom) *to lead away, to shunt off* || ⟨übtr⟩ (Aufmerksamkeit, Gedanken) *to divert*; *to draw off*; *to distract* (v *from*) **2.** (Ursprung) *to derive, deduce, trace* (v *from*); *to trace back* (v *to*); s–e Herkunft ~ von (P) *to be descended from, to trace one's descent back to*; (S) *to derive its origin from* | ⟨gram & math⟩ (Wort) *to derive* (v *from*); (Methode, Schluß etc.) *to deduce* (v *from*) **3. sich** ~ v (P) = s–e Herkunft ~ | (S) *to derive*

·**Ableiter** m ~s/~ ⟨el⟩ *conductor* ~**stange** f ⟨typ⟩ *conducting bar*

·**Ableitung** f ~/~en **1.** (of water, etc.) *turning aside*; *diversion* || ⟨el⟩ *shunt conduction* || (of attention) *distraction* **2.** ⟨gram, math⟩ *derivation*

·**Ableitungs-** ~**graben** m *drain*; *sewer* ~**kanal** m *drain* ~**rohr** n *drain-pipe* ~**silbe** f *derivative affix*; *suffix* ~**wort** n *derivative*

·**Ablenk-** ~**barkeit** f *possibility of averting, etc* → folg. || *distractability* ~**feld** n (Radar) *deflection field*

·**ab|lenken** vt/i [h] **I.** vt (**etw**) *to turn aside* (od *away, off*) || (Fluß, Magnetnadel) *to deflect* || ⟨opt⟩ *to diffract* || (Augen) *to avert* (v *from*) | (Gefahr, Schlag) *to avert*; *to ward off* | (Aufmerksamkeit etc.) *to draw off, to divert, distract* (v *from*); *to stray away* (in *into*) || (Verdacht) *to avert* | (**jdn**) *to divert* (v *from*); *to side-track* (don't *s.-t. me*!) || *to throw* (*a p*) *off the scent* || *to distract* | **sich** ~ *to relax* (in *in* [*festivals*]); *to be taken out of o.s.* (*in the cinema*) **II.** vi *to take another direction*; ⟨mar⟩ *to sheer off* || ~ von *to turn away* (od *off*) *from* | vom Thema ~ (S) *to digress* ·**A–kung** f ~/~en *turning off* || (der Magnetnadel) *deviation, deflection* || ~ durch Wind *wind deflection* || ⟨übtr bes mil⟩ *diversion* || (Zerstreuung) *distraction*; ~ suchen in *to relax in* (*festivals*); nicht genug ~en h *not to have enough distractions* || ~**smanöver** n ⟨mil⟩ *diversion*; *diversionary attack, operation, etc* || ⟨fig⟩ *red herring*; ein ~ betreiben *to draw a r. h. across the path* od *trail*

·**ab|lernen** vt [h] (jdm) etw ~ *to learn a th from*

·**ablesbar** a *legible* || ⟨comp⟩ ~ m *to provide visual indication*

·**Ablese-** ~**fehler** m *reading* od *index error* ~**fenster** n *indicator* od *inspection window* ~**fernrohr** n *reading telescope* ~**marke** f *index mark*

·**ab|lesen** vt/i [h] **I.** vt **1.** (Text) *to read off* | (Thermometer etc.) *to read* (*off*) **2.** (absuchen) (Raupen) *to pick* || *to clear* (*a th*) *of* **3.** ⟨übtr⟩ jdm etw vom Auge, Gesicht ~ *to read a th in a p's eyes, face*; er liest ihr jeden Wunsch v. d. A. ab *he anticipates her every wish* || (herleiten) *to derive, infer* (v *from*) **4.** ⟨school⟩ *to crib* **5.** ⟨comp⟩ *to read out*; (das ≈ gestatten *to provide visual indication*) **II.** vi (of preacher, etc.) *to read*

·**Ableser** m ~s/~ (*gas-meter*) *reader*

·**ab|leugnen** vt [h] *to deny, disavow* || ⟨jur⟩ (Behauptung) *to traverse* ·**Ableugnung** f ~/~en *denial, disavowal* || ⟨jur⟩ *traverse, disclaimer* || ⟨pol⟩ *dementi* Fr

·**Ablichtung** f ~/~en [neol] ⟨phot⟩ *copy*

·**ab|liefern** vt [h] *to deliver*; *to hand over* (jdm, an jdn *to a p*) || (Waffen) *to surrender* ·**Ablieferung** f ~/~en *delivery*; bei ~, gegen ~ ⟨com⟩ *on delivery* (→ Lieferung); nach erfolgter ~ *when delivered*; verspätete ~ *delay in delivery*

·**Ablieferungs-** ~**frist** f ⟨st exch⟩ *period fixed for delivery* ~**gewicht** n *weight delivered* ~**schein** m *delivery-order* ~**soll** n *delivery obligations* [pl] od *quota* ~**tag,** ~**termin** m *date fixed for delivery*; ⟨st exch⟩ *settling-, settlement-day* ~**zeit** f = –frist

·**ab|liegen** vi [s] [nur 3. sg & pl] **1.** von einem Orte ~ *to lie at a distance from a place*; weit ~ *to be far away* (v *from*) || → abgelegen **2.** (reif w) *to lie until mellow*; *to get seasoned*: (Wein) *to mature*; (Obst) *to ripen through lying*

·**ab|listen** vt [h] jdm etw ~ *to trick a p out of a th*; *to coax* (od *wangle, wheedle*) *a th out of a p*

·**ab|locken** vt [h] jdm etw ~ *to get a th out of a p*; (schmeichelnd) *to coax* od *wheedle a th out of a p*

·**ab|lohnen,** ·**ab|löhnen** vt [h] (Lohn zahlen u. entlassen) *to pay* (*a p*) *off*; *to discharge* (*a p*)

·**Ablohnung** f ~/~en *paging off*; *discharge*

·**ablösbar** a ⟨com⟩ *redeemable* | ⟨jur⟩ durch Geld ~ *commutable* (*offence*)

·**ab|löschen** vt [h] (abkühlen) *to chill, quench*; (Stahl) *to temper*; (Kalk) *to slake*; (Tinte) *to dry up*

·**ab|lösen** vt [h] **1.** (Schicht, Stein) *to take off, to detach* (v *from*) | (lockern) *to loose*(*n*); *to unloose*; (Rinde) *to peel off* **2.** ⟨fig⟩ (**etw**) (Schuld

loose(n) | **sich** ~ *to come off, to come* (od *get*) etc.) *to discharge, redeem* | (Strafe etc.; durch Geld etc.) (abkaufen) *to commute a th for* od *into a th* | (ersetzen) *to exchange* od *substitute a th for a th; to alternate a th with a th* | **sich** ~ (S) *to alternate* (*joy and grief alternate*) **3.** **(jdn)** *to replace* od *supersede; to take (a p's) place, to take over from,* (in der Arbeit)* *to spell* || ⟨mil⟩ *to relieve* || die Wache ~ *to relieve guard* | **sich ~, einander ~** *to relieve one another;* ⟨Am⟩ *to spell each other* || sich als Torwart ~ *to take turns at being goal-keeper*

·**ablöslich** a *separable* | ⟨com⟩ → ablösbar

·**Ablösung** f ~/~en **1.** *the detaching (of a th)* || *the loosening* || (of debts, etc.) *discharge; redemption* || ~ der 1. (Raketen-)Stufe *separation of first stage* **2.** (durch Geld) *commutation;* → frei **3.** (Ersatz) [abstr] *supersession* (durch *by*); *quid pro quo* (L) (e–r S *for a th*) || ⟨mil⟩ *the changing of the guard* || ⟨post etc⟩ Frei durch ~ ⟨hist⟩ (portofrei) ⟨m.m.⟩ *Official Paid,* ⟨Am⟩ *official business* | [konkr] ⟨mil⟩ *relief; relieving guard; relay* || ~ vor! *sentry, on!* | (of workmen) *shift* **~sanleihe** f ⟨com⟩ *redemption-loan* **~ssystem** n *relay-system*

°·**ab|lotsen** vt [h] jem etw ~ *to wangle a th out of a p*

°·**ab|luchsen** vt [h] jdm etw ~ **1.** *to learn a th from a p by stealthily watching him* **2.** *to trick* od *cheat a p out of a th; to wangle a th out of a p*

·**Abluft** f ~/ ⟨tech⟩ *used air*

·**ab|lügen** vt [h] *to deny (a th) by lying*

·**ab|machen I.** vt [h] **1.** (losmachen) (Kragen) *to undo; to untie* || *to detach, loosen* **2.** (erledigen) *to arrange, settle; to agree upon (a th)* || (ein Geschäft) *to settle; to wind up;* (Vertrag) *to stipulate, to conclude* || → abgemacht **3.** [abs] **mit jdm ~** *to agree, arrange, to make an agreement* od *arrangement with a p;* sie machten unter sich ab, daß .. *they agreed that* ..; .. z tun *they agreed upon doing* **II.** ⁓ n es ist ·ein ~ → Aufwaschen

Abmachung f ~/~en *agreement, arrangement; contract, settlement;* e–e ~ treffen *to make an agreement* od *arrangement* (mit *with*); ist das e–e ~? *is it a go?* || durch ~en mit .. *by arrangement with* .. || vertragliche ~ *stipulation*

·**ab|magern** vi [s] *to get thin, to grow lean, to lose flesh* ·**Abmagerung** f ~/~en *emaciation;* ⟨med⟩ *atrophy* **~skur** f *slimming-cure, -diet* || e–e ~ m *to slim* (*she is slimming, she is on a reducing diet*) || (jdn) e–e ~ m l *to reduce*

·**ab|mähen** vt [h] *to mow off* od *down*

·**ab|mahnen** vi [h] jdm ~ = abraten

·**ab|maischen** vt [h] ⟨brew⟩ [abs] *to finish mashing* ·**Abmaischtemperatur** f *final mashing t.*

·**ab|malen** vt [h] *to paint;* (jdn) *to portray* || (Gemaltes) *to copy* || nach dem Leben ~ *to draw* od *paint from life;* **sich ~** l *to have one's portrait taken* || °du kannst dich ~ l! *you do look a sight!* bzw. *says who?* (*don't be silly*)

·**ab|marachen** vrfl [h] sich ~ = sich abrackern

·**Abmarsch** m ~(s)s/⁓e **1.** [abstr] *marching off; departure; start;* ~! *skedaddle! get along with you! get away!;* ⟨vulg⟩ *fuck off* || zum ~ blasen ⟨mil⟩ *to sound the march* **2.** [konkr] ⟨mil⟩ *squad* **⁓bereit** a *ready to march (off)* od *to start* **~punkt** m ⟨bes mil⟩ *marching-off* od *initial point* **~zeit** f *start time*

·**ab|marschieren** vi [s] *to march off; to start* || (aufbrechen) *to decamp; to march out of camp* || ⟨mil⟩ (einer hinter dem anderen) *to file off* od *away:* rechts abmarschiert! *right file, march!*

·**ab|martern** vrefl [h] **sich ~** *to pine away* || *to toil hard, to drudge*

·**Abmaß** m ~es/~e *dimension, measure*

·**ab|matten** vt [h] (Tier) *to fatigue, weary* || *to tire (out)* ganz abgemattet *knocked out* od *up*

·**Abmattung** f ~/~en *exhaustion; weariness, fatigue*

·**Abmeierung** f ~/~en ⟨Ger jur⟩ *dispossession of a farmer from the farm* || *withdrawal of the interest in a farm*

·**ab|meißeln** vt [h] ⟨med⟩ *to chisel off;* ⟨sculp⟩ *to knock off*

·**ab|melden** vt [h] jdn bei der Polizei ~ *to give notice to the police of the departure* (od *removal*) *of a p* || e–n Schüler ~ *to give notice that a pupil will leave the school* | **sich ~** ⟨univ⟩ *to take one's name off;* ⟨mil⟩ *to report for leave;* ⟨club, etc⟩ *to withdraw* (in *from*); ⟨hotel, etc⟩ *to give notice for departure,* ⟨Am⟩ *to check out* | ⟨fig⟩ ° der ist bei mir –ge–det ⟨fam⟩ *I am finished* od *through with him* ·**Abmeldeschein, ~zettel** m *formal written notice to the police of the departure of a p; form of notice of departure* ·**Abmeldung** f ~/~en *withdrawal;* (Polizei) *formal notice of departure*

Abmelker·ei f ~/~en ⟨bes Am⟩ *milking parlo(u)r*

·**ab|mergeln** vt [h] *to emaciate, waste; wear out*

·**ab|merken** vt [h] jem etw ~ = ablauschen

·**ab|messen** vt [h] **1.** *to measure (off);* ⟨surv⟩ *to survey;* ⟨tech⟩ (genau ~) *to gauge* || ⟨pros⟩ (Verse) *to scan* **2.** ⟨übtr⟩ *to measure;* –ge– *measured (movements)* || (im richtigen Verhältnis ~) *to proportion* || (abwägen) *to weigh,* → abwägen; s–e Worte sorgsam ~ *to weigh one's words* | (beurteilen) *to judge* (nach *by*) ·**Abmessung** f ~/~en *measurement, size* || *survey* || ⟨pros⟩ *scansion* | (oft pl ~en) *proportion; dimension;* ~en *dimensions* pl; *proportionment;* ⟨mach a.⟩ *physical details*

·**ab|mieten** vt [h] jdm etw ~ *to hire a th from a p;* jdm ein Haus ~ *to rent a house from a p*

·**Abmieter** m ~s/~ *tenant, lessee*

·**ab|montieren** vt [h] *to take to pieces* od *down* || ⟨mot⟩ *to disassemble* || (Schiff) *to dismantle* || (Geschütz) *to dismount*

°·**ab|mucken** vt [h] (jdn) *to snub, silence, settle*

·**ab|mühen** vrefl [h] sich ~ *to exert, tire o.s.; to slave; to toil and moil* || *to labour* (an *or* mit e–r S *at a th;* für, um .. *for a th*) || sich mit etw ~ *to struggle with a th*

°·**ab|murksen** vt [h] *to kill (off), to polish off* || ⟨Am sl⟩ *to bump (a p) off; to give a p the works; to do (a man's) job for him; to work a p over*

·**ab|mustern** vt [h] ⟨mar⟩ *to pay off; discharge*

·**ab|nagen** vt [h] (T) *to gnaw (off); to gnaw ([at] a bone)* || (P) (Knochen) *to pick*

·**ab|nähen** vt [h] *to seam up;* (Falte) *to sew (a fold) wedgewise (so as to make a skirt [etc.] close-fitting)*

·**Abnäher** m ~s/~ *wedge-like fold (in a skirt)*

·**Abnahme** f ~/~n **1.** (Ab–, Wegnahme) *taking away* od *down* od *off; removal* || ⟨med⟩ *amputation, removal* || ⟨bib⟩ *the Descent (from the Cross)* **2.** (Entgegennahme) **a.** ⟨mst com⟩ *taking delivery, taking over* || *purchase;* bei ~ v 100 Exemplaren .. *for an order of 100 copies* ..; sich zur ~ v 100 E. verpflichten *to engage (o.s.) to take 100 copies* **b.** die ~ e–s Eides *the administering* od *tendering of an oath* **3.** (Revision) ⟨com⟩ *examination; audit* | ⟨tech, mil⟩ *official test* od *acceptance;* ⟨mil⟩ (e–r Baulichkeit) beim Einzug *marching-in inspection;* ⟨bes for⟩ *approval* (e–s Schlages); ⟨bes mot, racing⟩ *weighing-in* **4.** (Verminderung) *diminution; decline* (e–r S *of* od *in a th*) || ~ der Flut *ebb* || *wane (of the moon)* || *the shortening (of the days); decrease, shrinkage* (e–r S *in a th*); ~ der Geschwindigkeit *deceleration; loss (in weight); the falling-off (in the numbers);* (Umfang⁓ e–s Stammes gegen den Gipfel) ⟨for⟩ *taper* || (Gewicht⁓) *reduction (of 5 pounds)* || ⟨com⟩ *dropping-off, loss (of customers)* **5.** (Übernahme bei der ~prüfung) *acceptance*

·**Abnahme-** **~beamter** m *quality inspector* **~beschuß** m ⟨mil⟩ *proof-firing test* **~flug** m ⟨aero⟩ *test flight* **~lehre** f *inspection gauge* **~probefahrt** f *acceptance trial trip* **~prüfung** f (*official*) *acceptance* od *inspection test* **~schein** m *receipt* **~stelle** f *acceptance centre* **~wesen** n *quality inspection*

·**abnehmbar** a *removable* (*cape*); *detachable, demountable*

·**Abnehme-** **~spiel** n (Bindfaden-~) *string game, cat's cradle*

·**ab|nehmen** **I.** vt/i [h] **A.** vt **1.** (wegnehmen) **a.** *to take away* (od *down, off*); *to remove*; jdm den Überzieher ~ *to relieve a p of his overcoat* ‖ nimm's mir ab! *take it off my hands* ‖ (Früchte) *to gather, pick* ‖ (Bart) *to shave off* ‖ (Maschen) *to cast off* ‖ ⟨typ⟩ e–n Rahmen ~ *to strip a form* | ⟨arith⟩ nimm 4 v 8 ab *take 4 from 8* **b.** ⟨med⟩ (Bein) *to amputate*: *to cut off* **c.** sich ~ l (of lids, etc.) *to take off* ‖ sich den Bart ~ l *to get shaved* **2. jdm etw ~** ⟨eig⟩ *to take a th from a p*; *to relieve a p of a th*; *to deprive* od *rob a p of a th*; jdm sein Amt ~ *to relieve a p of his office* ‖ jdm ein Bein ~ *to amputate a p's leg* | ⟨übtr⟩ (Aufgabe, Mühe, etc.) *to take* (*a th*) *off a p's hands*; jdm die Mühe ~ *to save a p the trouble* (z tun *of doing*); *to relieve a p of* (*the responsibility*); jdm ein Versprechen ~ *to make a p give a promise, to make a p promise* (*a th*) ‖ jdm e–n Eid ~ *to administer* od *tender an* (od *the*) *oath to a p* | ⟨übtr⟩ das nehme ich dir nicht ab *I don't believe a word of it,* (*you may*) *tell that to the horse-marines*! **3.** ⟨mst com⟩ (entgegennehmen) (Waren) *to take* (*off a p's hands*); *to take delivery of* (*goods*) ‖ *to purchase, to buy* **4.** (prüfen) **a.** ⟨com⟩ (Bücher) *to audit* **b.** etw behördlich ~ *to test a th, to take responsibility for a th* **c.** ⟨mil⟩ die Parade ~ *to take the salute at a* (od *the*) *parade*; den Vorbeimarsch ~ *to take the salute at the march past* **5.** jdn ~ *to paint, to portray*; *to photograph a p* | sich ~ l *to have one's portrait* (od *photograph, likeness*) *taken* **B.** vi **1.** (sinken; schwinden) **a.** (Wasser) *to sink* ‖ (Flut) *to recede* ‖ (Wind) *to abate, subside*; (Mond) *to* (*be on the*) *wane*; bei ~dem Mond *in the wane of the moon* | ⟨med⟩ (Schwellung) *to go down* **b.** (P) *to lose flesh*; *to grow thin, to get worse*; er nahm zusehends ab *he was visibly wasting away* **c.** ⟨übtr⟩ (of produce, strength, trade) *to decline, decrease, diminish, lessen*; *to fall off* od *away*; *to* (*be on the*) *wane*; *to recede*; *to shrink*; *to progress downward* ‖ an Geschwindigkeit ~ *to decelerate, slacken* ‖ (of sensations, etc.) *to pass off* ‖ (of interest) *to flag, to fall off* **2.** (Tisch abdecken) *to take away* od *off* **3.** (Maschen abnehmen) *to narrow* **4.** ⟨cards⟩ *to cut* **II.** ⩪ n → Abnahme ‖ im ~ begriffen s (Mond) *to be on the wane* ⟨a. übtr⟩ | (Kinderspiel) → Abnahmespiel, Faden⩪

·**Abnehmer** m ~s/~ *buyer, purchaser, customer*; keine ~ [pl] *no market* (f *for*), *no buyers* ‖ (keine) ~ finden *to find a* (*no*) *market*; die englischen ~ *the English market*; wir w ~ des Artikels s *we shall be in the market for this article* ‖ der Artikel findet in Deutschland keine ~ *there is no market for this a. in G.* ‖ wenig ~ f (of papers) *to have few subscribers* od *readers* **~kamm** m ⟨tex⟩ *doffer comb* **~land** n *buying country*

·**Abneigung** f ~/~en **1.** (gegen [**etw**]) *disinclination, reluctance, indisposition* (*to a th*; z tun *to do*); *distaste* (*for a th*); *impatience* (*for*); *unwillingness* (*to do*); ~ zeigen *to be disinclined* (*for, to a th*; z tun *to do*) **2.** natürliche ~ *antipathy* (gegen **jdn** *against, to a p*) **3.** (gegen [**etw** od **jdn**]) *dislike* (*of, to, for*) **starke** ~ *aversion* (*to, from a th*; *to, for a p*); *repugnance* (*to, against a th*; *for a p*) ‖ e–e ~ fassen gegen *to take* (od *conceive*) *a dislike* od *an aversion to* **4.** (oft: krankhafte) *idiosyncrasy*

abn·orm a *anomalous, irregular*; ⟨a. med⟩ *abnormal* | ⟨übtr⟩ *abnormal, unusual, exceptional* (*situation*); *exorbitant* **Abnormit·ät** f ~/~en *abnorm*(*al*)*ity*; *monstrosity*

·**ab|nötigen** vt [h] jdm etw ~ *to force a th out of a p, to force a p to do a th*; *to extort* (od *wring*) *a th from a p* ‖ jdm Bewunderung ~ *to command* od *challenge* od *compel a p's admiration*

·**ab|nutzen,** ·**ab|nützen** vt [h] *to use up*; *to wear out by use*; *to wear thin*; (Kragen) *to fray*; ⟨tech⟩ *to gall* | **sich ~** *to wear* (*off* od *out*) ‖ *to fray* ‖ → abgenutzt

·**Abnutzung** f ~/~en (natürliche) *wear and tear*, die ~ durch die Zeit *the w. and t. of time* ‖ ⟨typ⟩ *wearing-out* ‖ (Verschleiß) *abrasion* ‖ (Wert⩪) *depreciation* **~sprozeß** m *wearing process* **~staktik** f ⟨aero⟩ *exhausting-tactics* pl

Abonnem·ent [abɔnəˈmɑ̃:] n (Fr) ~s/~s *subscription* (auf *to*) ‖ im ~ *by subscription*; das ~ läuft am 1. April ab *the s. will expire on April 1st* ‖ ⟨rail, etc⟩ ein ~ h *to have a season-ticket*

Abonnem·ents- **~karte** f *subscription-ticket*; ⟨a. rail⟩ *season-ticket, contract-ticket* **~konzert** n *subscription concert* **~liste** f *list of subscribers* **~preis** m *subscription-rate*

Abonn·ent m ~en/~en *subscriber* (auf *to*); ~enkreis [m] ⟨fam⟩ *constituency*; ~ensammler [m] *canvasser* **Abonn·entin** f ~/~nen = Abonnent

abonn·ieren vi [h] **1.** *to subscribe* (auf *to*); [als vt] (Zeitschrift) ~ *to take out a subscription to* **2.** abonniert s *or* h *to have subscribed* (auf *to*); *to be a subscriber* (*to*); *to have a season ticket*; auf e–e Zeitung abonniert s *to take a paper in*

·**ab|ordnen** vt [h] *to depute, to delegate* (nach *to*) ‖ ⟨mil⟩ *to draft* ·**Abordnung** f ~/~en **1.** [abstr] *delegation, deputation* **2.** [konkr] *delegation*; *delegates* pl ‖ ⟨mil⟩ *draft*; *detachment*; *contingent*

·**Abort**[1] m ~(e)s/~e *toilet, privy*; *water-closet* (abbr *W.C.*), *closet*; *lavatory* ‖ ⟨mil, etc.⟩ *latrine*

Ab·ort[2] m ~(e)s/~e ⟨med⟩ *abortion, miscarriage* ⩪**ieren** vi [h] *to abort* ⩪**tiv** a ⟨med & bot⟩ *abortive* **A–tiv-Kur** f ⟨med⟩ *abortive treatment*

·**ab|pachten** vt [h] (jdm) etw ~ *to rent a th from*

·**ab|packen** **1.** vt/i [h] *to unlade, unload, unpack* ‖ ⟨com⟩ *to package* **2.** ⩪ n *packaging*

·**ab|passen** vt [h] **1.** *to measure*; → abmessen **2.** ⟨übtr⟩ **etw ~** *to look out* (od *watch, wait*) *for a th* ‖ *to time a th*; etw genau ~ *to cut it fine*; gut abgepaßt! *well timed*! ‖ die (*or* e–e gute) Gelegenheit ~ *to wait one's chance* od *opportunity*; *to watch one's time* ‖ s–e Zeit, den rechten Augenblick ~ *to bide one's time* | **jdn ~** *to look out* (od *watch*) *for a p* ‖ *to waylay a p* ‖ ⟨Am fam⟩ *to head a p off*

·**ab|patrouillieren** vt [h] *to patrol*; (Gegenden) *to beat up*

·**ab|pausen** vt [h] to *trace*, → Pauspapier

·**ab|pellen** vt [h] *to peel* (*off*)

·**Abperl-** **~effekt** m, **~erscheinung** f *water-repellent effect*

·**ab|pfählen** vt [h] *to enclose with palings*

·**ab|pfeifen** vt [h] ⟨sport⟩ *to give the signal for stopping, the stopping signal* ‖ ⟨film⟩ *to interrupt*

·**ab|pflöcken** vt [h] *to peg* (*out*); *to mark off with pegs*

·**ab|pflücken** vt [h] *to pluck*; *pick off*; *gather*

·**ab|placken,** ·**ab|plagen** vrefl [h] sich ~ *to toil* (*and moil*); *to drudge, slave, fag*; *to tire* od *knock o.s. out*; *to sweat one's guts out*

·**ab|plaggen** vt [h] (→ Plagge) *to sod*

·**ab|platten** vt [h] *to flat*(*ten*) ‖ abgeplattet ⟨astr⟩ *oblate* | **sich ~** *to flatten*; *to become flat*

·**Abplattung** f ~/~en *flattening* ‖ ⟨astr⟩ *oblateness*

·**ab|platzen** v [s] (nur 3. sg & pl) *to become detached, to come* od *get loose, to c.* od *split off*

·**ab|prägen** vt [h] *to stamp, mint, coin* | **sich ~** ⟨fig⟩ *to leave an impress* (auf *on*); *to make an impression* (*on*)

·**Abprall** m ~(e)s/~e *rebound, recoil* ‖ (Geschoß) *ricochet* ‖ (Abgleiten) *glance*

·**ab|prallen 1.** vi [s] *to rebound, recoil* (v *from*); *to spring* od *fly back* ‖ (Waffe etc.) *to glance* (v *from*); *to glance off* ‖ (Geschoß) *to ricochet* ‖ (Licht, Schall) *to reverberate* | ⟨fig⟩ alles prallt v ihm ab *it all leaves him cold*; *it all runs off him like water off a duck's back*; *he is impervious to satire* **2.** ≗ → Abprall

·**Abpraller** m ~s/~ *ricochet shot* **~-Bombenwurf** m *skip bombing* **~schießen** n *ricochet fire*

·**ab|pressen** vt [h] jdm etw ~ *to extort a th from a p*; *to press a p for a th*; → abringen

·**ab|protzen 1.** vt [h] ⟨mil⟩ (Geschütz) *to unlimber* **2.** ° vi [h] ⟨vulg hum⟩ *to do number two*

·**ab|pumpen** vt [h] jdm etw ~ *to borrow a th from a p, to get a th out of a p*; *to touch a p for a th*

·**Abputz** m ~es/~e *recoating* (*of a house*) ‖ *rough-cast*

·**ab|putzen** vt [h] **1.** *to clean, cleanse*; *polish* ‖ *to scour*; *to wipe* (*off*) ‖ (Kabel) *to scrape* ‖ (Gemüse) *to pick* | (Pferd) *to rub down* **2.** (bewerfen) (Mauer) *to plaster, coat*; roh ~ *to rough-cast*; ein Haus ~ *to plaster the walls of a house* **3.** ⟨fig⟩ ° **jdn ~** *to give a p a set-down*; *to snub a p* ·**Abputzer** m *snub*

·**ab|quadern** vt [h] ⟨arch⟩ *to rusticate*

·**ab|quälen** vrefl [h] sich ~ → abplacken ‖ *to labour* (an, mit e–r S *at a th*) ‖ *to worry o.s.*

·**ab|quetschen** vt [h] *to squeeze* od *crush off*

°**ab|rabazzen,** ·**ab|rackern,** ·**ab|racksen** vrefl [h] ⟨vulg⟩ → abplacken

·**ab|radieren** vt [h] *to scratch out, to erase*

·**ab|rahmen** vt [h] *to skim* ‖ abgerahmte Milch *skimmed milk*, ⟨Am⟩ *skim-milk*

·**Abraham** ~s/~e ⟨fig⟩ in ~s Schoß sitzen *to be in Abraham's bosom*

Abrakad·abra n ~s (Gefasel) *drivel(ling talk)*

Abrasi·on f ~/~en (of the sea) *abrasion*

·**ab|raten** vt/i [h] **I.** vt (etw) mit jdm ~ *to arrange .. with a p* **II.** vi **1.** jdm v etw ~ *to dissuade a p from a th*; *to warn a p against a th* **2.** ~ v *to advise against* (*a plan*); ich möchte ~ *I would advise against it* **III.** ≗ n ~s/ *dissuasion*

·**Abraum** m ~(e)s/ *rubbish, trash* ‖ ⟨min⟩ *spoil*; *barren rocks* pl | ~halde [f] *waste-dump*; ~salze [n pl] *potassium-magnesium salts* pl

·**ab|räumen** vt [h] *to clear, remove*; (den Tisch) ~ *to clear away* (*the table, tea things,* etc.) ‖ ⟨min⟩ *to discard* ‖ ⟨theat mst vi⟩ *to remove*; *to clear* (*the stage*)

·**ab|reagieren 1.** vt [h] [pp abreagiert] ⟨psych⟩ (Ärger etc.) *to abreact, to work off* **2.** ≗ n *abreaction* (⟨a.⟩ ·Abreaktion ⟨psych⟩; ⟨eth⟩ ~ am Ersatzobjekt *discharging* (*some instinct*) *at a substitute object*, ⟨Am⟩ *abreaction*; reinigendes ~ *catharsis*

·**ab|rechnen** vt/i [h] **1.** vt (abziehen) **a.** ⟨math⟩ *to subtract, to take* (v *from*) **b.** ⟨com⟩ *to deduct* (v *from*); jdm 3 Schilling pro Pfd ~ *to allow a p 3 shillings in the pound* **c.** abgerechnet von *except*; *except for*; *apart from*; *with the exception of*; diese Seiten abgerechnet, ist das Buch .. *these pages excepted the book is ..* ‖ → ausgenommen **2.** vi **mit jdm ~** *to settle* (*up*) od *to balance accounts with a p*; *to make a settlement*; *to settle* (od *square*) *with a p* | ⟨fig⟩ *to get even with a p*; ich rechne noch ab mit dir *I've still an account to settle with you*

·**Abrechnung** f ~/~en **1.** ⟨com⟩ *liquidation* od *settlement* (*of accounts*) ‖ auf ~ *on account*; laut ~ *per account rendered*; ~ halten *to balance* od *settle accounts* | ⟨übtr⟩ *retribution, requital*; der Tag der ~ *the day of reckoning*; mit jdm ~ halten *to get even with a p* ‖ ⟨fig⟩ ~ mit etw *grappling with, attack on a th* **2.** ⟨com⟩ *clearing* **3.** ⟨com⟩ *deduction*; nach ~ der Spesen *after deducting expenses*; in ~ bringen *or* stellen *to deduct* **~s- ~haus, ~kontor** n *clearing-house* **~kurs** m *rate of settlement* **~scheck** m *clearing cheque* **~stelle** f = Abrechnungshaus **~tag** m *settling day* **~verkehr** m *clearing* **~zeitraum** m ⟨com⟩ *period under account, accounting period*

·**Abrechte** f ~/~en (of cloth) *the wrong side*

·**Abrede** f ~/~n **1.** *denial* ‖ etw (entschieden) in ~ stellen *to deny a th* (*positively*); *to disavow, dispute, challenge a th*; *to give a denial to a th*; (Tatsache) *to get away from*; (Verhalten) *to disclaim* **2.** *understanding*; *agreement*; (vertragliche) *stipulation* | laut ~ *as agreed upon, according to agreement*; ⟨com⟩ *as per agreement* ‖ es bleibt bei unserer ~ *we abide by our agreement* ‖ e–e ~ treffen *to make an agreement*; *to agree* (daß *that*)

·**ab|reden** vi/t [h] **1.** [vi] jdm v etw ~ *to dissuade a p from a th*, ⟨fam⟩ *to talk a p out of a th* ‖ ich will weder ~ noch zureden *I will not say anything either against or for it* **2.** [vt] etw mit jdm ~ *to arrange a th with a p*

·**ab|regnen 1.** vt [h] (Gas etc) *to spray* | (Wolken) z ≗ bringen *to seed* **2.** vrefl [h] sich ~ *to leave off* (od *to stop*) *raining*

·**ab|reiben I.** vt [h] **1.** (Schmutz etc.) *to rub off* | (Pferd) *to rub down* ‖ (Fläche etc.) *to rasp*; *to rub* (mit *with*); *to give* (*a th*) *a rub* ‖ (Fußboden) *to rub up* ‖ (Schiffsboden) *to hog* | (Silber) *to polish*; mit Bimsstein ~ *to pumice* | (Tier) *to rub down* ‖ (jdn) *to rub down, to towel*; **sich ~** *to have a rub-down, to rub o.s.* (*down*) | °jdn ~ *to thrash a p* **2.** (abnutzen) *to wear down* (od *out*) *by friction*; (die Haut etc.) *to chafe*; **sich ~** (Tuch) *to wear down* (od *out*) (*by friction*); (Haut) *to chafe*; *to get chafed* **II.** ≗ n = ·**Abreibung** f ~/~en **1.** *rub*(*bing off*) **2.** ⟨med⟩ *rub-down, towelling* | ~ *thrashing*; *set-down* **3.** *wearing down*; ⟨geol⟩ *detrition* **4.** ⟨fig⟩ jdm e–e ~ geben *to haul a p over the coals*

·**Abreise** f ~/~n *departure, setting out* (nach *for*); bei meiner ~ *on my departure*

·**ab|reisen** vi [s] (vom Hause) *to set out* (nach *for*); *to depart, leave, start* (nach *for*)

·**Abreiß- ~band** n ⟨typ⟩ *breaking-band* **~block** m *memorandum block, tear-off block* **~feder** f ⟨telg⟩ *antagonistic spring* **~hebel** m ⟨mot⟩ *interrupter touch* **~kalender** m *block-date-calendar, tear-off c.*; ⟨Am a.⟩ *daily* od *pad c.* **~schnur** f (Fallschirm) *breaking cord* **~zünder** m *rip-cord igniter* **~zündung** f ⟨mot⟩ *make and break ignition*

·**ab|reißen** vt/i **I.** vt [h] **1.** (lösen) *to strip* (v *from, off*), *to tear* od *wrench* od *break off* ‖ (Plakat) *to tear down* ‖ (Blumen) *to pluck* (*off*) ‖ (entfernen) *to clear away* ‖ (abspalten) *to sliver* **2.** (niederreißen) (Brücke, Gebäude) *to pull* od *take down*; *to demolish* ‖ (Wand) *to break down* **3.** (abnutzen) *to wear out* **4.** *to draw in outline*; *to sketch* **II.** vi [s] **1.** *to come off violently*; *to break* (*off*) ‖ → reißen vi **2.** ⟨übtr⟩ *to cease*; die Arbeit reißt nicht ab *there's never a let-up in my work*; m–e Geduld riß ab *my patience was at an end, I lost all patience*; das Gespräch riß ab *the conversation came to a dead stop* od *stopped dead* od *short* ‖ das reißt gar nicht ab *there is no end to it* ‖ → abgerissen

·**ab|reiten** vi/t **I.** vi [s] **1.** *to ride away* **2.** ⟨hunt⟩ (of wild-fowl) *to fly up* od *away* **II.** vt [h] **1.** (Strecke, Gebiet) *to ride*; *to cover* od *traverse on horseback*; e–n Ort ~ *to ride over a place* **2.** die Front ~ *to ride along* od *down the front*; die

F. e–s Regiments ~ *to inspect a regiment* (*on horseback*) **3.** ⟨mar⟩ (Sturm) *to ride out, to weather* **4.** (Pferd) *to ride down, to override*

·**ab|rennen** vi/t **1.** vi [s] *to start* (*running*) **2.** vt [h] **a.** die ganze Stadt ~ *to run all over the town* **b. sich ~** *to exhaust o.s. with running*; sich [dat] die Beine ~ ⟨fig⟩ *to run o.s. off one's legs*

·**ab|richten** vt [h] **1.** ⟨tech⟩ (gerade, richtig m) *to dress, adjust*; *to level, true, plane* || ⟨mas⟩ (Stein) *to clear off* **2. a.** (Hund etc.) *to train*; (junge Hunde auf d. Fuchs) *to enter* || (Pferde) *to break in* **b.** jdn ~ zu etw (od zu tun) *to drill, train a p for* od *in, to a th* (*to do a th*) ·**Abrichter** m ~s/~ *trainer* || ⟨tech⟩ *dressing tool* ·**Abrichtung** f ~/~en *training*; *breaking-in*

·**Abrieb** m ~s/ ⟨tech⟩ *abrasion*

·**ab|riegeln** vt [h] (Tür) to bolt, bar || (Straße) *to block*; (of police) *to cordon off* || ⟨tact⟩ *to block* ·**Abriegelungs- ~feuer** n ⟨mil⟩ *box* od *defensive barrage* **~front** f ⟨tact⟩ *bolt position*

·**ab|rinden** vt [h] *to* (*strip* [*a tree*] *of*) *bark*; *to peel*; ⟨liter⟩ *to decorticate* (*a tree*)

·**ab|ringen** vt [h] jdm etw ~ *to extort, wrest, wring a th from a p*; *to strain* (*a smile*) *from a p to make o.s. smile*; *to get* (*a promise*) *out of a p*

·**ab|rinnen** vi [nur 3. sg pl] [s] *to flow down*; *to run off* od *down*

·**Abriß** m –sses/–sse **1.** (Abreißen) *pulling-down*; *demolition* **2.** *draft, design*; *sketch* **3.** kurzer ~ *summary, abstract, epitome*; *short extract*; (in Buchform) *compendium* L

·**Abroll- ~spule** f ⟨film⟩ *revolving* od *rolling bobbin* ·**ab|rollen I.** vt/i **A.** vt [h] **1.** (Seil) *to uncoil, unroll* || *to unreel*; ⟨phot⟩ *to unwind* **2.** (expedieren) *to cart, forward, convey* **3. sich ~** *to unroll*; *to unreel* || (Ereignis) *to pass off*; *to develop* || ⟨übtr⟩ (Veranstaltung) *to display* od *unfold itself*; ⟨theat⟩ *to be enacted* **B.** vi [s] || *to roll away* || (Wasser) *to roll* || ⟨aero⟩ *to taxi* | ~ l *to let go*; (Kabel) *to pay out*; *to slip* **II.** ≈ ⟨fig⟩ (Zeit) *devolution* ·**Abroller** m ⟨typ⟩ *roller*

·**ab|rubbeln** vt [h] (jdn mit Tuch) *to rub .. down*

·**ab|rücken I.** vt/i **1.** vt [h] (Stuhl) *to* (*re*)*move* (v *from*) **2.** vi [s] *to* (*re*)*move*; ⟨mil⟩ *to march off* || (fortgehen) *to toddle* | ⟨fig⟩ **v. etw ~** *to dissociate o. s. from a th*; *to go back on, to cry off from, to disavow a th*; **v jdm ~** *to draw away* od *back from*, ⟨übtr⟩ *to break with, go back on, abandon* od *drop a p* **II.** ≈ n ~s/ ⟨mil⟩ *departure, marching-off*

·**ab|rudern I.** vi **1.** [s] *to row off* **2.** [h] *to close the rowing season* **II.** ≈ n *close of the r. s.*

·**Abruf** m ~(e)s/~e ⟨com⟩ *recall*; auf ~ *on call*; Vertrag auf ~ (der Lieferung) *call contract* || (sich) auf ~ (bereithalten) *at short notice* || ⟨comp⟩ ≈ v Informationen *information retrieval*

·**ab|rufen** vt [h] **1. jdn ~**; *to call away* || *to call back, to recall* || der Tod hat ihn –ge– *death has carried him off* || jdn ~ l *to send for a p* **2. etw ~** (Waren) *to recall*; (geliehenes Geld) *to call in*; ⟨st exch⟩ *to call* || ⟨Ger rail⟩ e–n Zug ~ *to call out the time of departure*

·**ab|rüffeln** vt [h] *to reprimand severely*; *to give* (*a p*) *a set-down*; ⟨sl⟩ *to blow up*

·**ab|runden** vt [h] **1.** (Ecken) *to round off*; (Zahlen) *to round off*; nach unten ~ *to level down, to eliminate odd amounts* **2.** ⟨übtr⟩ (Satz) *to round* (*off*) (mit *with*); *to finish off*; *to polish* ·**Abrundung** f ~/~en *rounding off* || ⟨fig⟩ *roundness, rounding*; (Stil≈) *finish* **~sbogen** m (e–s Säulenschaftes) ⟨arch⟩ *escape fillet* **~sfehler** m ⟨comp⟩ *truncation error*

·**ab|rupfen** vt [h] *to pluck* (*off*) || (Wolle etc) *to pull*

abr·upt 1. a *abrupt, sudden, unexpected* | *abrupt, disconnected* | *steep* **2.** adv *abruptly*, etc.

·**ab|rüsten I.** vt/i [h] **1.** vt (Gerüst) *to take down* **2.** vi ⟨mil⟩ *to disarm* || ~des Jahr *dying year* **II.** ≈n = ·**Abrüstung** f ~/~en ⟨mil⟩ *disarmament*

·**Abrutsch** m ~es/~e ⟨mount⟩ *downhill glide*; *glissade* ·**ab|rutschen** vi [s] **1.** *to glide down*; *to slip* || ⟨aero⟩ *to slide, slip*; seitlich ~ *to side-slip* (in der Kurve *in the turn*); über den Schwanz ~ *to tail-slide* **2.** °⟨fig⟩ (sterben) ⟨sl⟩ *to go pop, to pop off* od *out*; *to hop the twig*

Abr·uzzen, die ~ pl *the Abruzzi* pl

Abs n ⟨fam⟩ südd = Absolut·orium → Abi

·**ab|säbeln** vt [h] jdm den Kopf ~ *to chop a p's head off* || ein Stück Brot ~ *to cut off a piece of bread*

·**Absack- ~waage** f *sack gross* (*net*) *weigher*; *bagging and weighing machine*

·**ab|sacken** vt [h] *to put in sack*; → folg.

·**ab|sacken** vi [s] *to subside, sink, sag* || ⟨aero⟩ *to pancake* || ⟨übtr⟩ *to be reduced* (auf *to*) || (sterben) ⟨mar fam⟩ *to go out with the ebb*

·**Absage** f ~/~n *cancellation, countermand* | *denial*; *refusal*; *rebuff* (an to) | (Kampf) ~ an *challenge to* **~brief** m *letter of renunciation*; (Fehdebrief) *challenge*

·**ab|sagen** vt/i [h] **A.** vt **1.** (widerrufen) *to recall*; *to call off*; (Verabredung) *to withdraw*; *to cry off from* (*a bargain*) || (Vortrag etc.) *to cancel* || ⟨com⟩ *to countermand* **2.** (abschlagen) *to refuse, decline* **B.** vi **1.** e–r S ~ *to break with, to break away from, to renounce* od *drop a th* **2.** (schriftlich) ~ *to send a* (*written*) *refusal*; *to cancel the appointment* || jdm ~ *to put a p off* || ~ l *to send an excuse, to beg to be excused*; sie ließ mir, ihm ~ *she sent word she couldn't come*

·**ab|sägen** vt [h] **1.** (etw) *to saw off* **2.** °⟨fig⟩ jdn ~ *to ax(e) a p*; *to give a p the sack*

·**ab|satteln** vt [h] (Pferd) *to unsaddle*

·**Absatz** m ~es/≈e **A. 1.** (Unterbrechung) *break*; *pause*; *stop* || in ≈en *at intervals, in* od *by snatches, by fits and starts, intermittently*; in ≈en erfolgend *snatchy* || ohne ~ *without a break*; (*to empty*) *at a* od *one draught* **2.** ⟨typ⟩ (Zeileneinrückung) *indentation*; e–n ~ m *to indent a line* || (Abschnitt) *paragraph* ⟨a jur⟩ **B. 1.** (abgesetzte Fläche) Mauer≈ *offset*; ⟨gothic arch⟩ *cusp* || Treppen≈ *landing*; Fels≈ *shelf*; (an e–m Abhang) *terrace*; → Sims **2.** (am Schuh) *heel* || mit hohen ≈en *high-heeled*; mit schiefen ≈en *down at heels*; ohne ≈e *heelless*, → Hausschuh || mit ≈en versehen *to heel*; auf dem ~ (kurz) kehrt m *to turn on one's heels* **C.** (Abgesetztes) *sediment*; ⟨chem⟩ *deposit* **D.** ⟨com⟩ (Verkauf) *sale*; *market*; *outlet*; (of papers) *circulation* || ~ finden *to be sold*; *to move*; schnellen, reißenden ~ finden *to meet with* (od *to find, have*) *a ready, rapid sale*; *to have a great run*; k–n ~ finden *to find no sale* || ein Buch, das den besten *or* sehr guten ~ hat ⟨sl⟩ *a best-seller* **~becken** n (f Abwässer) *sludge pit* **~bedingungen** f pl ⟨com⟩ *conditions of marketing goods* **≈fähig** a *marketable* **~fleck** m *heel-piece*; *heel-tap* **~gebiet** n *market*(*-area*) **~genossenschaft** f *co-operative marketing society* **~kanäle** m pl = –wege **~markt** m *outlet* **~methoden** f pl *selling methods, marketing techniques* **~möglichkeit** f *outlet*; *opening for a good sale* **~organisation** f *market organization* **~politik** f (systematische) *marketing* **~quelle** f *market* **~raum** m (f Luftlandetruppen) *landing area* **~stockung** f *stagnant market*; *slump* **~wege** m pl *channels of distribution* **≈weise** [adv] *at intervals* **~zeichen** n ⟨typ⟩ *paragraph-mark*

·**ab|saugen** vt [h] *to suck off*; *to extract, exhaust*

·**Absaug- ~pumpe** f *scavenge pump* ⟨a. mot⟩

·**ab|saugen** vt [h] ⟨tech⟩ *to suction, evacuate*

·**ab|säugeln,** ·**ab|säugen** vt [h] ⟨hort⟩ (Pflanze) *to inarch* ·**Absaugungsanlage** f *exhaust plant*

·**abschaben** vt [h] *to shave* od *scrape off* || (beschneiden) *to edge off*

·Abschabsel n ∼s/∼ *shavings, parings; scrapings* pl

°**·ab|schachern** vt [h] jdm etw ∼ *to get* od *buy a th from a p by bargaining* od *haggling*

·ab|schaffen vt [h] **1.** etw ∼, (Einrichtungen) *to abolish; to do away with; to phase out;* die Opposition ∼ *to clear the field of opp.*; (Gesetz) *to annul, rescind; to repeal; to abrogate; to invalidate* ‖ (Mißbrauch) *to redress; to remove* | (Gegenstand) *to get rid of; to dispose of;* (ausrangieren) *to put on the shelf* **2.** **(Tier)** *to part with; to give up keeping (a dog)* **3.** **(jdn)** *to discharge, to dismiss; to send away*

·Abschaffung f ∼/∼en **1.** *abolition, abolishment* (of institutions) ‖ ∼ der Sklaverei ⟨Am⟩ *abolition*; Anhänger der ∼ der Sk. *abolitionist* | *abrogation; repeal; annulment (of laws,* etc); *removal; reform, redress (of abuses)* **2.** (v P) *discharge, dismissal*

·ab|schälen vt [h] **1.** (Früchte) *to peel (off); to pare* ‖ (Baum) *to bark* ‖ (Mandeln) *to blanch* ‖ (Eier) *to shell* **2.** (die Haut) *to excoriate* **3.** **sich ∼** *to peel off; to come off in peels; to scale off* ‖ (Baum) *to lose the bark* **·Abschälung** f ∼/∼en *peeling, paring* ‖ *barking (of a tree)*

·Abschalt- ∼temperatur f *cut-off t.* **∼ventil** n *shut-off valve*

·ab|schalten vt [h] *to switch* od *turn off; to disconnect*

·ab|schatt(ier)en vt [h] (abhebend) *to adumbrate* | (abtönend) *to shade, tint, tone* ‖ abschatten *to shade off* **·Abschattung** f ∼/∼en **1.** *screen* **2.** *adumbration* | *shade, shading; tint, tone* **3.** ⟨opt⟩ *the fading of the picture towards the margin of the field of vision*

·abschätzbar a *estimable*

·ab|schätzen vt [h] ⟨com⟩ (Wert) *to estimate, value* (auf *at*); (durch Sachverständigen) *to appraise, evaluate;* nicht abzuschätzend *inestimable* ‖ (Steuer- etc. Betrag) *to assess* ‖ (Inhalt) *to inventory* | ⟨übtr⟩ *to estimate, to form an estimate of (a th); to gauge* (nach *by*); *to place* ‖ ⟨Am fam⟩ *to size (a p) up* **·Abschätzer** m ∼s/∼ *appraiser, (professional) valuer* **·abschätzig** a & adv = abfällig

·Abschätzung f ∼/∼en *estimate; estimation, valuation*; nach ungefährer ∼ *at a rough estimate*; e–e ∼ vornehmen *to make an estimate* ‖ ⟨übtr⟩ *estimate, estimation* ‖ (e–s Betrages) *assessment* **∼skommission** f *commission for the assessment of taxes; Assessment Committee*

·Abschaum m ∼(e)s/ *scum, dross; scrapings, scourings* pl | ⟨fig⟩ *dregs, offscourings* pl, *offscum*; der ∼ der Gesellschaft *the dregs* od *scum of society; the rabble, rag-tag, riff-raff* **·ab|schäumen** vt [h] *to scum, skim* **·Abschäum- ∼löffel** m *skimming ladle*

·ab|scheiden **I.** vt/i **1.** vt [h] *to separate* (v *from*) ‖ (Metalle) *to refine* ‖ ⟨chem⟩ *to disengage* **sich ∼** [h] ⟨chem⟩ *to be precipitated* **2.** vi [s] *to die; to depart (this life)* ‖ ⟨chem⟩ *to disengage* **II.** ∸ n **1.** *decease, death* **2.** auch: ·Abscheidung f *separation* ‖ ⟨chem⟩ *precipitation* **·Abscheider** m ∼s/∼ ⟨tech⟩ *trap*

·ab|scheren vt/i [h] **1.** vt (Schaf, Tuch) *to shear (off)* ‖ (Bart) *to shave off* ‖ (Haare) *to cut (off); to crop* ‖ ⟨tech⟩ *to shear off* (⟨a.⟩ durch Beanspruchung) **2.** vi ⟨rowing⟩ *to feather the oars*

·Abscheu m ∼(e)s/ **1.** [abstr] *abhorrence, horror* (vor, gegen *of*); *aversion* (vor, gegen etw *to, from a th*; vor jdm *to, for a p*) ‖ *execration; abomination* (mit ∼ *with a.*); *loathing*; jdn mit ∼ erfüllen, jdm ∼ einflößen *to fill a p with loathing*; ∼ h *or* empfinden vor *to abhor, detest, loathe (a p, a th)* ‖ → Abneigung **2.** [konkr] *abomination*; → zuwider | (P & S) er (es) ist mir ein ∼ *he (it) is my aversion* **∸erregend** a *nauseating, revolting; disgusting*

·ab|scheuern vt [h] **1.** *to scour* od *scrub off* **2.** (Kragen) *to fray* **3.** (Haut) *to chafe; to grind*; sich [dat] das Knie ∼ *to skin one's knee* **4.** **sich ∼** (Tuch) *to fray; to wear off* od *out, to fret*

absch·eulich **1.** [a] *abominable, detestable, odious* (:*he is o.*); *revolting; horrid, horrible (story); atrocious, execrable, heinous (crime)*; ∼e Tat *atrocity* | ∼ *awful, dreadful, nasty (weather)*; ⟨fam⟩ *vile (pen); infernal*; ⟨sl⟩ *beastly, blasted* | es war ∼ v ihm *it was nasty, horrid, rude of him* **2.** [adv] *abominably (slaughtered)* | ∼ *awfully; execrably* (:*he sang e.*); ⟨sl⟩ *beastly*

Absch·eulichkeit f ∼/∼en *abomination, abominableness; detestableness; atrociousness* ‖ (Handlung, Tat) *atrocity, atrociousness*

·ab|schicken vt [h] (etw) *to send off; to dispatch, forward* | (Boten) *to send, depute* ‖ → absenden **·Abschickung** f ∼/∼en *sending, dispatch, dispatching, forwarding*

·ab|schieben vt/i **I.** vt [h] **1.** (Stuhl) *to push, to (re)move* (v *from*) **2.** ⟨übtr⟩ (e–e S) *to try to get rid of (a th)* ‖ (Arbeit etc.) ∼ auf jdn *to devolve (work) on a p*; (Last) *to throw .. on a p; to shove .. off* (auf jdn *on a p*); ⟨Am⟩ *to side-track .. on a p* ‖ etw v sich ∼ *to withdraw from a th; to back out of a th*; (Beschuldigung) *to clear o.s. of (a charge)* **3.** (jdn) *to try to get rid of (a p)* ‖ (Ausländer) *to deport* (in gr Massen *en masse*) **II.** °vi [s] ∼ *to go, leave; to make away* od *off; to sheer* od *shuffle off*; ⟨sl⟩ *to beetle off*; ⟨Am sl⟩ *to biff off* ‖ schieb ∼! *get away with you!, push off!* **·Abschiebung** f ∼/∼en (polizeiliche ∼) *deportation*, → abschieben I. 3., Abschub

·Abschied m ∼(e)s/∼e **1.** (Weggang) *departure* ‖ von der Welt ∼ nehmen *to depart this life* **2.** *separation, parting* (beim ∼ *at p.*); *leave (-taking)* | ∼ nehmen *to take one's l.*, ∼ nehmen von jdm *to take l. of a p, to bid a p farewell* (od *farewell to a p*); weggehen, ohne ∼ zu nehmen *to take French leave*; vom Alten Jahre ∼ nehmen *to ring out the Old Year* **3.** (Entlassung) *dismissal*, jdm den ∼ geben *or* erteilen *to discharge, dismiss a p*; ⟨fam⟩ *to give a p the sack; to sack a p* ‖ *to place a p on the retired list*; (e–m Offizier) *to cashier* ‖ ⟨bes mil⟩ schlichter ∼ *dishonourable discharge*; ehrenvoller ∼ *"white" discharge*; jdm den schl. ∼ geben ⟨mil⟩ *to cashier* ‖ s–n ∼ erhalten *to be discharged* od *dismissed*, ⟨fam⟩ *to get the sack*; (v Beamten) um s–n ∼ einkommen, s–n ∼ einreichen *to tender one's resignation; to hand* od *send in* (od *to give*) *one's resignation*; s–n ∼ nehmen *to resign*; ⟨a. mil⟩ *to quit the service, to retire, to be retired, to go on half-pay* **4.** ⟨Ger parl⟩ *the last* od *final resolution (of the former Reichstag)*; ⟨jur⟩ *sentence*

·Abschieds- ∼ansprache f → -rede, ⟨Am⟩ *valedictory* **∼audienz** f *farewell audience* **∼ besuch** m *farewell visit, take-leave call* **∼brief** m *farewell letter* **∼feier** f ⟨engl⟩ *farewell dinner* **∼gabe** f, **∼geschenk** n *farewell presentation; parting gift* od *present* **∼gesuch** n *(tender of) resignation*; sein ∼ einreichen *to tender one's resignation* **∼kuß** m *parting kiss, kissing (a p) good-bye* **∼rede** f *valedictory address* od *speech*; ⟨Am⟩ *valedictory* **∼schmaus** m *farewell dinner* od *banquet* **∼schmerz** m *wrench* **∼ständchen** n *send-off* (bringen *to give*) **∼stunde** f *parting hour* **∼trunk** m *parting-cup*; (of a rider) *stirrup-cup* **∼worte** n pl *parting words* pl; *valediction* **∼zeugnis** n *certificate of leave; leaving certificate*

·ab|schießen vt/i **I.** vt [h] **1.** (Gewehr etc.) *to discharge; to fire* od *shoot (off)*; ⟨fam⟩ *to pop*; Revolverschüsse auf jdn ∼ *to fire revolver shots at a p* ‖ (Pfeil) *to shoot, wing; to let fly* ‖ *to sink (a mine) (by rifle [gun] fire)* ‖ (Flugzeug, Torpedo, Fernlenkkörper, Rakete, Raumschiff) *to launch*; → Katapult, katapultieren **2.** (Wild) *to kill; to shoot (off), to pick off* ‖ (Vogel) *to bring* *down, to drop*; ⟨fig⟩ den Vogel ~ *to bear* od *carry away the bell*; *to get away with it*; ‖ (Flugzeug) *to bring* od *shoot down*, ⟨fam⟩ *to down* (brennend *in flames*); abgeschossen *shot-down* (*plane*) **3.** ein Feld ~ *to shoot* (*over*) *a field* **4.** (ein Glied) *to shoot off*; ihm wurde ein Bein abgeschossen *he had a leg shot off* (*by* ..) **II.** vi [s] (Farbe) = verschießen

·ab|schinden vt [h] **1.** *to skin, flay* **2.** °**sich ~** *to work o.s. to death*; *to fag* (*o.s.*), *to toil and moil*; sich ~ mit e–r S *to labour at a th*

·Abschirmdienst m ⟨Ger mil⟩ *counter-in-telligence* **·ab|schirmen** vt [h] ⟨tech⟩ *to screen, to shield* (*shielded antenna*) ‖ ⟨mil⟩ (mit Feuer) *to cover*; (durch Nebel) *to blanket* **·Abschirmung** f ~/~en *screening, guarding*; ⟨tech⟩ *shield*(*ing*) ‖ ⟨aero-tact⟩ *umbrella*

·ab|schirren vt [h] *to unharness*

·ab|schlachten vt [h] (Vieh; Menschen) *to slaughter, butcher* **·Abschlachtung** f ~/~en **1.** ⟨übtr⟩ (*of men*) *slaughter, butchery*; *massacre* (*of opponents*); *murder* **2.** = Schlachten

·Abschlag m ~(e)s/~̈e **A.** ⟨eig⟩ **1.** (of trees) *cutting-down, felling* **2.** ⟨sport⟩ *rebound* ‖ ⟨hock⟩ *bully* ‖ ⟨golf⟩ (Ausgangspunkt) *tee-shot* **3.** (Prägung) *impress*(*ion*); *cast*; e–n ~ herstellen v *to strike off* (*a coin*) ‖ *matrice* **4.** (Vorschlag) *partition* **5.** ⟨hunt⟩ (of birds) *pairing-time*; → Balz **B.** ⟨übtr⟩ **1.** (Ablehnung) *decline, refusal* **2.** (Abnahme) *abatement, diminution*; *fall*; *reduction* (e–r S *in a th*; der Löhne *in wages*) ‖ ⟨com⟩ *allowance, discount*; *deduction*; mit e–m ~ verkaufen *to sell at a discount* = Disagio **3.** (Teilzahlung) auf ~ *in part-payment*, auf ~ zahlen *to pay on account* od *by instalments* **~kamm** m ⟨spin⟩ *stripping comb* **~schiene** f ⟨tech⟩ *knocking-over bar* **~sdividende** f *interim dividend* **~szahlung** f *instalment, payment on account, part-payment*

·ab|schlagen vt/i **I.** vt [h] **A.** ⟨eig⟩ **1.** (Zweige) *to cut off*; *to cut away* (v *from*) ‖ (Baum) *to fell*; *to cut* od *hew down* ‖ (etw) *to knock off* (v *from*) ‖ jdm das Haupt ~ *to cut* od *strike off a p's head* **2.** (Zelt) *to strike* ‖ (Gerüst, Bettstelle) *to take down* ‖ (Segel) *to unbend* **3.** ⟨sport⟩ (Ball) *to send* (*off*); ⟨golf⟩ den Ball ~ *to tee off* **4.** (Feind) *to repel, repulse*; (Angriff) *to beat off, to repel, repulse*; (Stoß) *to parry*; *to ward off* **5.** (abklatschen) ⟨typ⟩ *to take an impression of* (*a th*); *to strike off* (*a coin*); *to cast* **6.** (ableiten) *das* Wasser ~ *to make* od *pass water* **B.** ⟨übtr⟩ (ablehnen) (Bitte etc.) *to decline, refuse, reject*; ein Anerbieten rundweg ~ *to refuse an offer point--blank*; jdm etw ~ *to deny a p a th*; Sie dürfen es mir nicht ~ *I won't be refused*; *I will take no refusal*; jdm etw rundweg ~ *to give a p a flat refusal*; er schlug es ab *he said nay* **II.** vi [s] **1.** *to abate*; *to decline*; (Preis) *to fall off* **2.** (Ball) *to rebound* **3.** (of players) ⟨hock⟩ *to bully*

·abschlägig **1.** [a] *negative* (*answer*); *implying a refusal, refusing*; [pred] *in the negative* ‖ ~e Antwort *refusal, denial, rebuff*; e–e ~e Antwort erhalten *to meet with a refusal* od *rebuff*; keine ~e Antwort annehmen *to take no refusal* **2.** [adv] jdn ~ bescheiden *to refuse a p, to answer a p in the negative*; jdm e–e Bitte ~ bescheiden *to refuse a request* **·abschläglich** [a] *on account*

·ab|schlämmen vt [h] ⟨tech⟩ *to levigate, wash* (*by gravity*)

·ab|schleifen vt [h] **1.** (Messer etc.) *to grind, whet, sharpen* ‖ (Glas, Steine) *to smooth, polish*; (Edelstein) *to cut* | ⟨übtr⟩ (Manieren; Stil) *to polish*; *refine*; *to make elegant*; *to give polish to* (*a th*) **2.** sich ~ *to smooth* (*down*); *to become smooth*; (P) *to improve one's manners, to improve in manners*; *to refine*

·ab|schleißen vt [h] *to wear off* od *out*

·Abschlepp- ~dienst m *recovery organization*; ⟨bes mot⟩ *wrecker service* **~kran** m *salvage* (⟨Am⟩ *wrecking*) *crane* **~seil** n *towing rope* **~vorrichtung** f *towing attachment* **~wagen** m ⟨mot⟩ *break-down vehicle* od *lorry*, ⟨Am⟩ *wrecking car*, ⟨fam⟩ *wrecker* **·ab|schleppen** **1.** vt [h] *to drag away*; *to tow* (*off*), *to take in tow*; **sich ~** mit etw *to tire o.s. with carrying a th* **2.** ~̈ n *recovery, etc*

·ab|schließen vt/i [h] **I.** vt **1.** (verschließen) (Tür) *to lock* (*up*) ‖ (Haus, Zimmer) *to shut up* ‖ (Röhre etc.) *to occlude*, ⟨a. übtr⟩ (Straße) **2.** (fernhalten) (etw, jdn) *to seclude, to shut off, to separate*, ⟨Am⟩ *to close off* (v *from*); **sich ~** *to shut o.s. in* od *up*; *to shut o.s. off* (v *from*); sich v der Welt ~ *to seclude* (od *immure*) *o.s.* **3.** (beenden) (e–n Vorgang) *to close, settle*; (Rede etc.) *to wind up* (mit *by, with*); ⟨com⟩ (Bücher) *to balance*; (Rechnung) *to close, settle* | (Handel) *to strike*; (Verkauf) *to effect*; ⟨ins⟩ e–e Versicherung ~ *to effect* (od *take out*) *a policy* ‖ (Abkommen) *to arrive at*; e–n Vertrag ~ ⟨pol⟩ *to conclude, sign a treaty*; ⟨jur & com⟩ *to enter into a contract* ‖ ⟨jur⟩ die Beweisaufnahme ~ *to rest the case* **II.** vi **1.** **~ mit** jdm *to come to an understanding* od *arrangement with a p* **2.** ~ mit etw **a.** (enden) *to wind up with*; er schloß ab mit den Worten .. *he wound up by saying*; den Abend ~ mit *to round off the evening with* **b.** ⟨übtr⟩ *to settle accounts with* (*life*); *to have done with* (*a th*); er hat mit der Welt abgeschlossen *he has renounced the world* **·abschließend** a *definitive*; *conclusive, final* (*verdict*) **·Abschließung** f **1.** *locking*(*-up*); *shutting-up* **2.** *separation* (v, gegen *from*) ‖ *segregation*; *seclusion*

·Abschluß m –sses/–~̈sse → Schluß– **1.** (Trennung) → Abschließung 1. & 2. **2.** (Ende) *closing, close*; *winding-up*; (of a quarrel) *settlement*; den Tag zum ~ bringen mit *to round off the day with* (*a dance*); (of plan, etc) zum ~ k *to be realised*; *to materialize* | ⟨com⟩ *the balancing* (*of one's books, of an account*) ‖ Knoten~̈ *balance*; → Jahres~̈ | ⟨theat & fig⟩ (Ausklang) *curtain* (*a clever c.*) ‖ ein passender ~ *a fitting crown* (für *to*) **3.** (Abmachung) *settlement* ‖ *conclusion* (of a treaty) : zum ~ bringen *to bring to a c.* | (Kaufvertrag) *sale, transaction, business*, wenige Abschlüsse wurden getätigt *few sales were done* od *effected, took place* **4.** e–e Gesetzesvorlage z ~ bringen *to take final action on a bill* **5.** ⟨arch etc⟩ *end-ornament, crowning* **~bogen** m *balance--sheet* **~kosten** pl ⟨ins⟩ *acquisition costs* **~note** f *note of sale* **~prüfung** f *passing-out examination* **~rechnung** f *final account* **~schraube** f *screw plug* **~ventil** n *stop-valve* **~vergütung** f ⟨ins⟩ *bonus for acquisitions* **~vertreter** m ⟨ins, etc⟩ *under-writing agent* **~zahlung** f *final payment* **~zeugnis** n *terminal* od *final report*

°**·abschmatzen** **I.** vt [h] *to smother with kisses* **II.** ~̈n *slobberation*

·ab|schmecken vt [h] ⟨cul⟩ *to taste*; *to judge by its flavour*; *to season*

·ab|schmeicheln vt [h] jdm etw ~ *to coax* od *wheedle a th out of a p*

°**·ab|schmeißen** vt [h] (v Pferde) *to throw off*

·Abschmelzdraht m ⟨el⟩ *fusible wire* **·ab|-schmelzen** vt/i **1.** vt [h] (Metall) *to fuse* ‖ (Erz) *to smelt*; *to separate by smelting* | (Schnee) *to melt* (*off*); *to dissolve* **2.** vi [s] (of snow) *to dissolve, melt* ‖ ⟨tech⟩ *to fuse* **·Abschmelz-sicherung** f ⟨el⟩ *safety fuse* od *cut-out*

·Abschmier- ~dienst m, **~stelle** f ⟨mot⟩ (*Esso–, Mobil-* ®) *lubrication service, greasing station*

·ab|schmieren vt/i **1.** vt [h] ⟨mot⟩ *to lubricate*; l Sie den Wagen (gründlich) ~ *see to* (*all*) *lubrication* | ⟨typ⟩ (Farbe) *to slur* | ° ⟨fig⟩ (Brief) *to scribble off* ‖ (unerlaubt) *to crib* (v *from*) **2.** vi [s] ⟨aero⟩ *to crash*; *to nose-dive*; (P) → abblitzen

·**ab|schminken** vt [h] (jdn, sich ~) *to take off a p's, one's make-up, to remove make-up*

·**ab|schmutzen** vi [h] *to soil*; ⟨typ⟩ *to blot*

·**ab|schnallen** vt [h] *to unbuckle*; (Schwert) *to unbelt* | ⟨aero⟩ ≃ *release from the parachute harness*

·**ab|schnappen** vi [s] *to break off suddenly, to stop short* ‖ °(sterben) *to peg, pop* od *pip out*, ⟨Am sl⟩ *to cash in* ‖ = abrutschen 2.

·**ab|schneiden** vt/i [h] **I.** vt **1.** ⟨eig⟩ *to cut (off)*; jdm die Kehle ~ *to cut a p's throat* | (Baumspitzen) *to poll*; (Zweige) *to lop off*; *to prune (off)*; (Hecke) *to trim* | (die Haare kurz ~) *to crop*; (den Bart) *to clip*; sich die Nägel ~ *to cut* od *pare one's nails* | (die Flügel) *to clip*; (Wolle) *to clip* (v *from* [*a sheep*]) ‖ (den Schwanz, die Ohren [e–s Tieres]) *to crop*; (den Schwanz [e–s Pferdes]) *to dock* | (Zinsscheine) *to detach* **2.** ⟨übtr⟩ (den Weg) *to (short-)cut* ‖ (Rückzug, Zufuhr, Feind) *to cut off*; jdm den Weg ~ *to bar a p's passage*, ⟨mil⟩ *to intercept* ⟨a. tact⟩ | ⟨fig⟩ den Weg zu e–r S ~ *to bang the door on a th* | ⟨wir⟩ (Verbindung) *to jam* | jdm jede Ausflucht, Möglichkeit ~ *to leave a p not a hole to creep out at* ‖ jdm die Ehre ~ *to defame, revile, vilify, backbite a p*; jdm alle Hoffnungen ~ *to blight* od *blast a p's hopes*; jdm den guten Leumund ~ *to blast* od *injure a p's reputation* | jdm das Wort ~ *to cut a p short, to snap a p up* **II.** vi (P) *to come* (od *get*) *off*; wie hast du abgeschnitten beim Tennis? *how have you done in tennis?* ‖ gut ~ *to come off well; to do well* (*in an examination*); am besten ~ *to have the best of it, to make the running*, ⟨a. fig⟩ schlecht ~ *to come off badly*; nicht zu schl. ~ *to do not too badly*; sie schnitten bei Besichtigungen gut ab ⟨mil⟩ *they turned out well for inspections*

·**Abschneider** m ~s/~ (Schneidewerkzeug) *cutter*; Zigarren≃ *cigar-cutter*

·**ab|schnellen** vt/i **1.** vt [h] *to let fly with a jerk; to flip, jerk, fillip; to flick away* **2.** vi [s] *to fly off with a jerk, to flip, fillip*

·**ab|schnippen** vt [h] (Zigarettenasche) *to flick off*

·**Abschnitt** m ~(e)s/~e **1.** (Abschneiden) *cut(ting)* ‖ ⟨med⟩ *section* **2.** (Abgeschnittenes) *cutting* ⟨a. tex⟩; *section; piece cut off; shred*; ⟨for⟩ *billet*; ⟨carp⟩ *cut-off beam-head* ‖ Muster≃ *pattern* | ablösbarer Papier≃ *coupon; counterfoil*, ⟨Am⟩ *stub* (*of admission ticket*) | ⟨typ⟩ *chapter, paragraph*; ⟨jur typ⟩ *section, paragraph*; ⟨com⟩ Kontroll≃ *counterfoil* | (am Zinsbogen) *dividend-warrant, coupon; bill of exchange* **3.** (Teilstück) *part, section; portion*; (Kapitel) *chapter; paragraph; part*; ⟨mil⟩ Gelände≃ *sector*; (Kampf≃) (*battle*) *section* | (Zeit≃) *period* (*in this p. of his life*); *phase* (*of development*); *epoch* (*of history*) | ⟨math & scient⟩ *segment* (*the s. of a circle; of a worm*) in 3 ~e fallen *to fall into 3 sections* (etc.) ≃**schnitt(s)weise** a/adv *in stages* ‖ ⟨tech⟩ *by sectors* ‖ *successive(ly)* ‖ ~s Vorgehen ⟨tact⟩ *advancing by successive increments of the total distance*

·**Abschnittling** m ~s/~e ·**Abschnitz** m ~es/~e ·**Abschnitzel** n ~s/~ [mst pl] *shreds, chips, clippings, shavings* [pl] ·**ab|schnitzeln,** ·**ab|schnitzen** vt [h] *to cut* od *chip off*

·**ab|schnüren** vt [h] **1.** (Gebiet) *to separate, to cut off* (v *from*) **2.** ⟨med⟩ *to tie up*; (Ader) *to ligature, strangulate* **3.** ⟨surv⟩ *to measure with a string* od *line* ·**Abschnürung** f ⟨med⟩ *ligature, strangulation*

·**ab|schnurren** vt [h] *to rattle off*

·**ab|schöpfen** vt [h] *to skim (off), to scum*; v ~ e–r S den Rahm *or* das Fett ~ ⟨fig⟩ *to skim* od *take the cream off a th*

·**ab|schrägen** vt [h] *to slope, slant* ‖ ⟨carp⟩ (Kante) *to bevel, chamfer; to splay* ‖ (Oberfläche) *to weather* ·**Abschrägung** f *bevelling; splay*

·**ab|schrauben** vt [h] *to screw off; unscrew* (a.: sich ~ l) | °⟨fig hum⟩ (S) *to pinch*, (⟨a⟩ P) (*a girl* jdm *from a p*)

·**ab|schrecken** vt [h] **1.** (jdn) *to intimidate, frighten*; jdn v etw ~ *to deter, discourage a p from a th*; jdn davon ~ z tun *to discourage a p from doing, to frighten a p out of doing*; er läßt sich leicht ~ *he is easily discouraged* **2.** ⟨met⟩ *to chill* (a.: Eier ~); *to quench, harden*

·**abschreckend 1.** a *deterrent; exemplary* (*severity*); ~es Beispiel *warning* | (abstoßend) *shocking, repulsive; forbidding* (*appearance*); *frightful* **2.** adv *horribly, frightfully*; ~ häßlich *shockingly ugly; frightful* (*house*)

·**Abschreckung** f ~/~en *deterrence; intimidation*; als ~ *exemplary* **~smittel** n *deterrent; determent; disincentive*; als ~ für jdn *for the determent of a p* **~swaffe** f *deterrent weapon* (z. B. Kernwaffen)

·**Abschreibe- ~fehler** m *error in copying* **~gebühr** f *copying-fee*

·**ab|schreiben I.** vt/i [h] **A.** vt **1.** (etw) *to transcribe, copy; to write out* ‖ ⟨jur⟩ (Urkunde korrekt ~) *to engross* **2.** (unerlaubt) *to plagiarize*; ⟨fam⟩ *to crib* (v, aus *from*) **3.** (abbestellen) *to cancel; to countermand* **4.** (Schuld) *to write* od *wipe off*; (Summe) *to deduct* | (gutschreiben) *to carry* (*a th*) *to* (*a p's*) *credit, to credit* od *transfer* (*a th to a p*) **5.** (abnutzen) (Feder) *to wear off* od *out* (a. **sich ~**); *to use up; to blunt* ‖ sich die Finger ~ *to wear out one's fingers with writing* **6.** (Patienten) ⟨med, sl⟩ *to slate*; °er ist abgeschrieben ⟨Am, fam⟩ *his goose is cooked* **7.** ⟨aero, mil, sl⟩ (Flugzeug etc.) *to write off* **B.** vi **1.** (unerlaubt) *to crib* (aus *from, out of*) **2.** jdm ~ *to put a p off* **II.** ≃ *copying; transcription*

·**Abschreiber** m ~s/~ *copyist, transcriber* ‖ (widerrechtlicher) *plagiarist*; ⟨sl⟩ *cribber*

·**Abschreibung** f ~/~en **1.** (Widerruf) *cancellation* **2.** (im Rechnungswesen etc.) *depreciation*; ~en [pl] f Verluste etc. *deductions made for losses*; ⟨bal⟩ *write-off*; (Gesamtsumme der) ~en ⟨bal⟩ (*accumulated*) *depreciation* **~sreserven** f pl *depreciation reserves*

·**ab|schreien** vrefl [h] sich ~ *to scream o.s. hoarse* (nach *after, for*)

·**ab|schreiten** vt [h] (Raum) *to pace* ‖ → Front

·**Abschrift** f ~/~en (*written*) *copy, transcript; transcription*; (mit der Schreibmaschine) *type-written copy* ‖ ⟨com & jur⟩ *duplicate* | beglaubigte ~ *attested copy*; getreue ~ *true copy*; handschriftliche ~ *manuscript copy* ‖ e–e ~ nehmen *to take a copy* (v *from*) ·**abschriftlich 1.** a *copied* (*out*) **2.** adv *as a copy; by way of a copy; in duplicate*

·**Abschrot** m ~(e)s/~e (Amboßeinsatz) *chisel*

·**Abschub** m ~(e)s/ = Abschiebung; *evacuation* (*of casualties*) **~kapazität** f *clearance capacity* **~rampe** f *launching pad*

°·**ab|schuften** vrefl [h] sich ~ *to work o.s. to death; to drudge; to toil*

·**ab|schultern** vt [h] ⟨mil⟩ (Gewehr) *to take* (*the gun*) *from the shoulder*

·**ab|schuppen** vt [h] (Fisch) *to scale* ‖ (Haut) *to desquamate* | **sich ~** *to scale off; to flake off; to come off in scales* ‖ (Haut) *to desquamate*

·**Abschuppung** f *scaling; desquamation*

·**ab|schürfen** vt [h] (Haut) *to excoriate*; sich [dat] die Haut ~ *to excoriate, abrade, graze, chafe one's skin; to bark* (*one's elbows*) ‖ ⟨agr⟩ *to drill* | **sich ~** (Haut) *to chafe; to become sore*

·**Abschürfung** f ~/~en *excoriation; abrasion* (*of the skin*)

·**Abschuß** m -sses/≃sse **1.** [abstr] *discharge, firing* | ⟨hunt⟩ *killing* (*of game*) ‖ *bringing-down* (*of a plane*) ‖ *tank-busting* ‖ ⟨aero⟩ (Katapultstart) *launch(ing)* **2.** [konkr] ⟨hunt⟩ *kill* **~basis** f *launching site* **~geschwindigkeit** f *launching speed* **~gestell** n (f Fernlenkkörper) *l. rack* **~kontrollraum** m *firing control room* **~kraft** f *l. power* **~liste** f *drop dead list* **~plattform** f (f Raketen) *pad* **~vorrichtung** f (f Raketen) *launching device*

·**abschüssig** a *declivitous, sloping*; *steep, precipitous*; ~ s *to slope* ‖ ⟨zoo⟩ *declivous (profile)* **≈keit** f ~/~en *declivity, steepness*

·**ab|schütteln** vt [h] *to shake* od *cast off*; den Staub von den Füßen ~ *to shake off the dust from one's feet* ‖ ⟨cul⟩ (abtropfen l) *to drain* ‖ etw von sich ~ ⟨fig⟩ *to shake off, to get rid of a th* ‖ jdn ~ *to fling* od *shake a p off*; *to break with a p*; *to send a p to Coventry*

·**ab|schütten** vt [h] (etw) *to pour off* (in *into*)

·**ab|schwächen** vt [h] **1.** (Wirkung etc.) *to weaken, diminish*; *reduce* | (Eigenschaft, Ausdruck) *to qualify* ‖ (Vergehen) *to extenuate* | (Färbung) *to tone down* ‖ (Ton) *to soften down*; (Schmerz) *to deaden* ‖ ⟨phot⟩ *to reduce* **2. sich ~** *to become weaker, to fall off*; *to decline, decrease*; *soften* ·**Abschwächer** m ~s/~ ⟨phot⟩ *reducer* **A–chung** f ~/~en *weakening* ‖ *decrease*; *decline*

·**ab|schwatzen** vt [h] jdm etw ~ *to talk* od *inveigle a p out of a th*; *to wheedle a th out of a p*

·**ab|schweifen** vi [s] **1.** ⟨eig⟩ *to swerve, to turn aside*; *to digress*; *to diverge* (v *from* [*a path*]) **2.** ⟨übtr & fig⟩ *to deviate, to swerve*; *to wander* (v *from* [*the point*]); vom Thema *or* in s–n Gedanken ~ *to digress, divagate, excurse*; *to ramble* (in *into*) ·**abschweifend** a ⟨fig⟩ *digressive* ·**Abschweifung** f ~/~en ⟨fig⟩ *digression, divagation* (v *from*); *excursion*

·**Abschwellung** f ⟨med⟩ *detumescence*

·**ab|schwemmen** vt (Schmutz) *to wash away* od *off* (v *from*) ‖ *to ride* (*a horse*) *into the water*

·**ab|schwenken** vt/i **1.** vt [h] (Schmutz) *to shake off* (v *from*) **2.** vi [s] *to turn aside*; *to swerve* (in *into*); *to cut away* (nach links *to the left*) ‖ ⟨mil⟩ in Kolonnen ~ *to file off in columns*

·**ab|schwindeln** vt [h] jdm etw ~ *to swindle a th out of a p*; *to cheat, trick a p out of a th*

°·**ab|schwirren** vi [s] *to be off, to decamp, to get out*; *to disappear*; ⟨sl⟩ *to beetle off* ‖ (sterben) ⟨sl⟩ *to pop off*

·**ab|schwören** vt [h] **1.** (unter Eid verzichten auf) (Gefolgschaft etc.) *to abjure, forswear*; *to recant* od *renounce by oath* **2.** (ableugnen) (Schuld) *to deny by oath* **3.** (e–e & e–r S) ~ *to swear off (drinking)* ·**Abschwörung** f *abjuration*

·**Abschwung** m ~(e)s/≈e ⟨gym⟩ *swing down* ‖ ⟨aero⟩ *split S, bunt* | (der Konjunktur) *decline*

·**ab|segeln I.** vi **1.** [s] *to sail* (nach *for*); *to set sail, to sail away* **2.** [h] *to close the sailing* od *yachting season* **II.** ≈ n **1.** *sailing* (nach *for*) **2.** *close of the sailing season*

·**absehbar** a ⟨eig⟩ *within sight*; *visible*; *measurable* | ⟨mst übtr⟩ *recognizable*; *imaginable, conceivable*; nicht ~ *hard to foresee* od *conceive*; *inconceivable*; in ~er Zeit *within a measurable time, before long, within reasonable time, within the foreseeable future*

·**ab|sehen I.** vt/i [h] **A.** vt **1.** etw jdm ~ *to learn the knack* od *trick of a th from a p*; *to learn a th by looking at a p* ‖ jdm etw von den Augen ~ *to read a th in a p's eyes*; e–n Wunsch .. *to anticipate a p's wishes* | ⟨school⟩ etw von jdm ~ *to copy a th from a p* **2.** (erkennen) *to perceive, foresee, foretell*; *to conceive*; man kann das Ende nicht ~ *you cannot foresee the end*; die Folgen sind nicht –zu– *or* lassen sich nicht ~ *the c.s are not to be foreseen*; da ist kein Ende –zu– *there is no prospect of an end* ‖ → hinaus **3.** ist **es** darauf –ge–? *is it that you are driving at*? **es** –ge– h auf jdn, etw *to aim at a p*; *to drive at a th*; *to have a th in view*; (Bittsteller) *to set one's cap at a p*; *to be on a p's track*; *to have designs* (od *one's eyes*) *on* .. ‖ **es** auf jds Verderben –ge– h *to scheme a p's ruin* ‖ **es** darauf ~ z tun *to study to do* ‖ die Feinde h **es** auf ihn –ge– *his enemies have marked him out for a target*; **es** war auf mich –ge– *it was directed against me* od *meant for me* **B.** vi **von etw ~** *to leave a th out of account*; *to take no account of a th*; *to disregard* od *drop a th*; davon ~ (etw z tun) *to desist from a th (from doing ..)* **II.** ≈ n ~s/~ **1.** (Visier am Gewehr etc.) *sight* **2.** ⟨fig⟩ *design, intention*; sein ~ richten *or* h auf .. *to have .. in view, to aim at..*

·**ab|seifen** vt [h] *to (clean .. with) soap*

·**ab|seihen** vt [h] (Flüssigkeit) *to strain, filter*

·**ab|seilen 1.** vrefl [h] sich ~ ⟨mount⟩ *to rope down, to abseil, to rappel* **2.** ≈ n *rappel*

·**ab|sein** vi [s] **1.** (entfernt s) weit ~ *to be at a great distance* **2.** (abgetrennt s) *to be (broken) off* **3.** ⟨fig⟩ ich bin ganz ab *I am done (up)* od *worn out*

·**Abseite** f ~/~n **1.** (Rückseite) *reverse* **2.** (Verschlag) *partition*; (e–r Dachkammer) *side-loft* **3.** ⟨arch, ec⟩ *apse* **4.** ⟨ftb, etc⟩ *off side* ·**abseitig** a *distant*; *remote*

·**abseits** adv *aside, astray, apart, aloof* (v *from*); ⟨sport⟩ *offside* ‖ ein wenig ~ stehen *to stay a little way off*, → u. ⟨fig⟩; ~ vom Wege *out of the way* ‖ ~ von Bondstreet *off B.* ‖ ~ der breiten Straße ⟨fig⟩ *off the beaten track* ‖ weit ~ *(a)far off, at a great distance*; *a long way off* ‖ ⟨fig⟩ ~ stehen, sich ~ halten *to stand off*; *to keep out of the way, aloof* (v *from*) **≈ball**, **≈flug** m ⟨golf⟩ hook

·**ab|senden A.** vt [h] **1.** (Waren) *to dispatch, forward, address*; *to send off*; (durch Schiff) *to consign* ‖ (Brief) *to dispatch, post* ‖ (Geld) *to send, to remit* (*to*) **2.** (P) (Abgeordnete) *to depute* ‖ ⟨mil⟩ *to detach* **B.** ≈ n *sending, forwarding*; → Absendung ·**Absender** m ~s/~ (v *or* auf Briefen) *sender*; Adresse des ~s *return address*; ⟨post⟩ ~: N.N. *from N.N.* ‖ ⟨bes mil⟩ *originator* ‖ ⟨com⟩ *forwarder*; *consignor*; ⟨Am⟩ *shipper* ·**A–dung** f ~/~en *sending, dispatching*; *consignment, shipping, shipment, posting* | (P) *delegation* **~sort** m, **~sstation** f *place of dispatch, forwarding-station*

·**ab|sengen** vt [h] (Geflügel) *to singe (off)*

·**ab|senken** vt [h] ⟨min⟩ *to sink* | ⟨hort⟩ *to layer* ·**Absenker** m ~s/~ ⟨hort⟩ *layer, shoot*; *sprout* | *descendant*

abs·ent a *absent*; *not present* | **≈**enliste [f] *list of absentees* **absent·ieren** vrefl: sich ~ *to absent o.s.* **Absent·ismus** m ⟨engl⟩ (Wohnen v Großgrundbesitzern fern vom Gute) *absenteeism* **Abs·enz** f ~/~en *absence*

·**absetzbar** a (P) *removable*; *subject to removal* od *dismissal* | ⟨com⟩ (Waren) *salable*; *marketable* **≈keit** f *removability* ‖ *salability*

·**Absetz- ~gelände** n ⟨aero⟩ *dropping area* **~maschine** f ⟨aero⟩ *paratroop dropper*

·**ab|setzen** vt/i [h] **I.** vt **A.** ⟨eig⟩ **1.** (Hut etc.) *to take off, to doff* | den Becher ~ *to take the cup off one's lips* **2.** (entwöhnen) (Kind, Tier) *to wean* **3.** ⟨typ⟩ *to set (up in type)*; abgesetzt *in type* **4.** ⟨chem & geol⟩ *to deposit* ‖ ⟨aero⟩ (mit Fallschirm) *to paradrop* ‖ ⟨übtr⟩ v der Verpflegung ~ ⟨mil⟩ *to put out of rations* | (Last) *to put* od *set down* | (Boot) *to shove off* | (P) (v Wagen) *to set (a p) down, to deposit, to drop*, ⟨Am⟩ *leave*; ⟨rail⟩ *to detrain (a p)* | **sich** ~ (S) *to settle* ‖ sich (v Feinde) ~ ⟨mil⟩ *to disengage o.s., to break away (from)* **B.** ⟨übtr⟩ **1.** (Beamte) *to discharge, dismiss*; *to remove, unstick*; (Herrscher) *to depose, dethrone* **2.** ⟨theat⟩ (Stück) *to take off the repertoire*; abgesetzt w *to come off* **3.** (unterbrechen) e–e Zeile ~ (beim Schreiben) *to begin a new line* | (Verhandlungen) *to break off, to interrupt* **4.** (abheben) *to contrast* (gegen *with*); *to set off* (auf e–m Hintergrund *against a background*) || (Farben) gegeneinander ~ *to gradate* | **sich ~** *to* (*form a*) *contrast* (gegen *with*); *to show up* (*against*) **5.** ⟨com⟩ (abschreiben) *to write off*; *to deduct* | (Waren) *to sell, to market*; *to dispose of*; v dem Buch sind 1 000 000 Exemplare abgesetzt *the book has sold a million copies*; schwer (leicht) –zu–(d) *difficult* (*easy*) *to sell* **6.** [imps] **es** wird was ~! → setzen [imps] **II.** vi **1.** (aufhören) *to break off*; *to stop, pause, rest* || ohne –zu– *uninterruptedly*; *without a break*; (beim Trinken) *at a draught* **2.** ⟨mar⟩ *to shove off* **·Absetzen** n ~s/ (→ absetzen) **1.** *taking-off* (*of the hat*) || *weaning* || ⟨typ⟩ *setting-up* || *putting-down, setting-down* **2.** *pause* || → Absetzung; Absatz **·Absetzer** m ~s/~ ⟨aero⟩ (P) *jumpmaster*; ⟨fam⟩ *dispatch sergeant, dispatcher* **·Absetzung** f ~/~en *removal, dismissal* (*of officials*) || *deposition, dethronement* (*of rulers*) | *deduction* || → Absatz, Absetzen

·Absicherung f ~/ ⟨mil⟩ *security screen*

·Absicht f ~/~en **A.** (*specific*) *intent, intention* (z tun *to do, of doing*) || (Vorsatz) *purpose, design*; *plan* || (bösliche) ⟨jur⟩ *malice* || (geheime) *game* || ~en (z Heiraten) *intentions* || ⟨tact⟩ eigene ~ *own plan* **B.** (Wendungen) **1. in** welcher ~? *for what purpose*? in der ~ z betrügen *with intent to defraud*; **in** *or* **mit** der ~ z tun *with the intention, purpose, view of doing*; *with a view to doing*; *on purpose* od *in order to do* **2. mit ~** *deliberately*; *on purpose*; ob durch Zufall oder mit ~ *whether by accident or by design* || ohne ~ *unintentionally* **3. in** der **besten ~,** mit den b. ~en *with the best intentions* || **feste ~** *fixed purpose*; *determination*; mit der festen ~ *with the determination* (*to do*) || in **guter ~** *with a good intention* || mit **voller ~** *of set purpose, on purpose* **4.** s–e ~ **erreichen** *to carry one's point, to gain one's end* || ich **habe** die ~ *my intention is, it is my i., I intend* (*to do*); ich habe nicht die ~, mehr z zahlen *I'm not going to pay more* || (feindliche) ~en h auf *to have designs on* || es **lag** nicht in m–r ~ *it was not my intention, I did not intend* (*to do*)

·absichtlich 1. a *intentional, intended* || (bewußt) *deliberate*; *wilful* (*murder*) **2.** adv *purposely*; ich tue es ~ *I do it on purpose, I am on set purpose doing it* || *of set purpose*; *deliberately, wilfully* **≁keit** f (Zielstrebigkeit) *purposiveness* **·absichtslos** a *unintentional* **·Absichtssatz** m ⟨gram⟩ *final clause, clause of purpose*

·ab|sieden vt [h] *to decoct, boil* || e–n Trank ~ *to make a decoction*

·ab|singen 1. vt [h] *to sing* od *to chant* (*a song*) (*to the end*) **2.** ≁ n *singing*; ≁ v Psalmen *psalmody*; nach ≁ der Hymne *after singing the hymn*; unter ≁ v Liedern *singing songs* **·Absingung** f ~/ = Absingen

·ab|sinken 1. vi [s] (of water) *to sink in level, to subside*; *to run off* || ⟨übtr⟩ *to deteriorate* **2.** ≁ n *subsidence* || *dropping* (*of voltage*) || ⟨übtr⟩ *deterioration*

Abs·inth m ~(c)s/~e **1.** ⟨bot⟩ *wormwood* **2.** (Branntwein) *absinth*(*e*)

·ab|sitzen vi/t **I.** vi [h] *to sit away* (v *from*) | [s] ⟨hors⟩ *to dismount, alight*; ~! *dismount*! **II.** vt [h] **1.** s–e Strafe ~ *to serve one's sentence* || (Strafzeit) ⟨sl⟩ *to do time*; 9 Monate ~ *to serve one's 9 months* || ⟨engl⟩ e–e Schuld ~ *to pay off a debt by undergoing imprisonment* **2.** die Schulzeit ~ *to pass through a school*

absol·ut I. a **1.** (unbedingt) *absolute* (*fact*); *unconditional* (*proof*) | (unumschränkt) *absolute* (*monarch*) | ~e Mehrheit *absolute majority* (*of votes*) **2.** (rein) ⟨chem⟩ *absolute* (*alcohol*) | (vollendet) *absolute, perfect* (*beauty*) | *absolute, thorough* (*fool*); ⟨fam⟩ *pure, sheer, perfect, arrant* (*nonsense*) **II.** adv *absolutely*; ~ genommen *or* betrachtet *considered in the absolute* || *perfectly, purely* (*accidental*) || ~ nicht *not a bit*; es ist ~ nicht nötig *there is no reason in the world*; er konnte es ~ nicht finden *for the life of him he could not find it*; ~ nichts *not a trace, not an iota*; ~ nichts Wahres daran *not a bit* od *particle of truth in it* || ~ kein ⟨fam⟩ *not a blessed* .. || ~ k–n Ehrgeiz h *to have no ambition whatever* od *no a. at all* || wenn du ~ ein Engel s willst *if you* a r e *going to be an angel* **≁fahrtmesser** m ⟨aero⟩ *true airspeed indicator*

Absol·ute n ~en/~en; das ~ *the absolute*

Absoluti·on f ~/~en *absolution*; ~ v Sünden erhalten *to be shriven of sins*

Absolut·ismus m ~/ *absolutism* **absolut·istisch 1.** a *absolutist, absolute*; *despotic* **2.** adv *absolutely*; *despotically*

Absolut·orium n ~s/–rien → Abi, Abs

absolv·ieren vt [h] **1.** ⟨ec⟩ (jdn) *to absolve* || *to acquit* **2.** e–e Schule ~ *to pass through a school*; ⟨Am⟩ *to graduate from a school*; e–e Sch. absolviert h ⟨Am⟩ *to be a graduate of a school* || (Studien) *to complete, to finish* (*up*); ⟨engl⟩ s–e Studienzeit an den Inns of Court ~ *to eat one's dinners* || (Prüfung) *to pass* **Absolv·ierung** f *graduation* (*of a school*) || *completion* (*of studies*)

abs·onderlich 1. a *peculiar*; *singular, strange* || *eccentric*; *funny*; *odd* (*people*); *queer, quaint* (*dress*); ⟨sl⟩ *rum, rummy* **2.** adv *peculiarly* || → sonderlich **≁keit** f ~/~en *peculiarity*; *singularity, oddity* || *trick* (*of a p*), [oft pl] ~en *tricks*

·ab|sondern vt [h] **1.** *to separate, divide*; ⟨mil⟩ *to detach* (v *from*) | (isolieren) *to segregate*; *isolate*; (abschließen) *to seclude* (gegen, v *from*) | **sich ~** *to seclude o.s.* || *to separate* (v *from*); *to cut o.s. adrift* (v *from*) || ein abgesondertes Leben führen *to keep to o.s.* **2.** ⟨physiol⟩ (of glands) *to secrete*; ~d *secretive* || (Schleim) *to excrete* || (Eiter) *to discharge*

·Absonderung f ~/~en *separation* (v *from*) || ~ v Pfandrechten v der Konkursmasse ⟨jur⟩ *seclusion of property* || (Abschließung) *retirement, seclusion*; soziale ~ *social segregation* | ⟨physiol⟩ *secretion*; *excretion*; (Eiter≁) *discharge* **·Absonderungs-** [in comp] *secretive*; *secretory* **≁berechtigt** a ⟨jur⟩ *secured* (*creditor*) **~drüse** f *secretory gland*

absorb·ieren vt [h] ⟨chem⟩ *to absorb*; *to occlude*; wieder ~ *to resorb* || ⟨übtr⟩ (jds Aufmerksamkeit) *to absorb, engross, occupy* **absorb·ierend** a *absorbent*; ~es Mittel *absorbent*

·ab|sorgen vrefl [h] sich ~ *to fret* (*one's life away*); *to pine* (*away*)

Absorpti·on f ~/~en ⟨phys⟩ *absorption*; erneute ~ *resorption*; (v Gasen) *occlusion* | **~s-** [in comp] *absorption* [*attr*] (*a. modulation, a. wavemeter*) **≁fähig** a *absorptive* **~streifen** m *absorption band* **~vermögen** n *power of absorption*

·ab|spalten vt [h] (etw) *to sliver*; *to split off* (v *from*); ⟨a. übtr⟩ | **sich ~** *to split off* (v *from*); ⟨übtr⟩ *to separate* (v *from*) **·Abspaltung** f ~/~en *separation* (v *from*)

·ab|spänen, ·ab|spanen vt (Ferkel) *to wean*

·ab|spannen vt [h] **1.** (Bogen) *to unbend* **2.** (Pferd) *to unharness, to unyoke* || (Gewehrhahn etc.) *to uncock* | ⟨fig⟩ *to relax*; *to tire* **3.** ⟨arch⟩ *to secure* od *support* (*by ropes*) || → abgespannt

·Abspannung f ~/~en **1.** *unbending* | ⟨fig⟩ *lassitude*; *relaxation* **2.** *unharnessing* **3.** ⟨arch⟩ *supporting device by ropes*

·ab|sparen vt [h] sich [dat] etw (am *or* vom Munde) ~ *to stint* od *pinch o.s.* (*in food*) *for a th* (*to stint o.s. of a th*)

·ab|speisen vi/t [h] **1.** vi *to finish dinner* od *supper* **2.** vt *to feed* | jdn ~ mit *to put* od *cut a p off with* (:*with fair words*), mit einigen Brocken, mit leeren Versprechungen *to fob a p off with some bits, with empty promises* || er läßt sich nicht ~ ⟨fig⟩ *he won't take 'no' for an answer*

·abspenstig a; jdn e–r P *or* S ~ m *to alienate* od *estrange a p from a p, from a th* | sich [dat] jdn ~ m *to alienate a p*; (Kunden) ~ m *to entice away* | ~ w *to desert*; jdm, e–r S ~ w *to abandon a p, to break with a p*; *to desert a th* ‖ jdm etw ~ m *to coax a p out of a th*

·ab|sperren vt [h] **1.** (Raum) *to shut up*; (Straße etc.) *to block, barricade*, (durch Polizei) *to cordon off* **2.** (Wasser, Dampf, Gas) *to shut* od *turn off* **3.** (Verkehr) *to obstruct, stop* **4.** (jdn) *to separate* (v *from*), *to isolate*

·Absperrhahn m ~(e)s/~̈e *stop-cock*

·Absperrung f ~/~en **1.** *shutting-up* | (Straßen~̈) *blocking, barricading*; *barricade* **2.** (Wasser etc.) *shutting off, turning-off* **3.** (Verkehr) *obstruction, stoppage* **4.** *stoppage* (*of a pipe*) *by a valve* (etc.) **5.** (P) *separation* (v *from*), *isolation* **~ssystem** n → Prohibitivsystem

·Absperrventil n *stop-valve*; *shut-off* (*valve*)

·Absperrvorrichtung f *shut-off* (*device*)

·ab|spiegeln vt [h] *to mirror, reflect* ‖ **sich ~** *to be mirrored* od *reflected* (in *in*) **·Abspiegelung** f ~/~en *reflection*

·ab|spielen vt [h] **1.** ⟨mus⟩ (Stück) *to play*; *to play to satiety* ‖ (Band, Platte) *to play back* **2.** (vom Blatte) *to play at sight* **3.** (abnutzen) *to wear out by playing* **4.** ⟨fig⟩ sich ~ *to come off*; *to happen*; *to take place*; *to pass* (*on*); *to come to pass*; ⟨Lit⟩ *to take place, to be laid* (*in the country*); ⟨theat⟩ *to be enacted*

·ab|spinnen vt [h] *to spin off*

·Absplìß m –sses/ *thread of a rope*

·ab|splitten vt [h] (→ Splitt) ⟨tech⟩ *to cover* (*road*) *with gravel, to gravel* (*a road*) ‖ ⟨arch⟩ *to blind with chippings*

·ab|splittern vt/i **1.** vt [h] *to splinter off* ‖ **sich ~** = **2.** vi [s] *to come off in splinters*; *to chip off*

·Absprache f *agreement, arrangement, appointment* **~̈gemäß** a, adv *as agreed upon*

·ab|sprechen vt/i [h] **1.** jdm etw ~ *to deny* od *refuse a p a th*; ⟨jur⟩ *to refuse a th to a p by judicial decree* ‖ jdm alle Hoffnung ~ *to take all hope from a p* ‖ jdm das Leben ~ *to condemn a p to death*; ⟨med⟩ *to give a p up* **2.** vi; ~ über etw, jdn *to cavil at a th*; *to find fault with a p*; *to give a peremptory opinion of a th* **·absprechend 1.** a *adverse, dogmatic, peremptory*, (anmaßend) *overbearing*; ⟨fam⟩ *sniffy* **2.** adv *dogmatically*; *peremptorily* ‖ *overbearingly*

·ab|sprengen vt/i **1.** vt [h] *to chip* (v *from*); *to chip off* ‖ (mit Pulver etc.) *to blow off* | (besprengen) *to sprinkle* **2.** vi [s] *to gallop off*

·ab|springen I. vi [s] **1.** **(P)** (vom Wagen) *to jump* (od *leap*) *down* od *off* ‖ ⟨sport⟩ *to jump* od *take off*; mit Fallschirm ~ *to parachute*, ⟨sl⟩ *to bail out* ‖ ⟨hors⟩ *to alight* | ⟨übtr⟩ plötzlich vom Gegenstande ~ *to digress, excurse, to go off at a tangent*; *to ramble*; spring nicht ab *keep to the point* ‖ v e–r Partei ~ *to break away, to secede from a party*; → abrücken ‖ v e–m Geschäft ~ *to back out of a bargain* **2.** **(S)** (Ball:) *to rebound*; (aus der urspr. Richtung ~) *to twist* | *to chip*; *to crack off* | (Knopf) *to come* od *get loose*; *to come off* **II.** ~̈ n *jumping down* od *off* ‖ (zum Entweichen) *doubling* | (vom Thema) *digression, excursion*; → Absprung

·ab|spritzen vt [h] ⟨mot⟩ *to run the hose over* (*the body of a car*) **·ab|sprühen** vt [h] (Flüssigkeit) *to spray* ‖ (Gegenstand) *to spray*

·Absprung m ~(e)s/~̈e *jump*(*ing-off*); *take-off*; Stelle des ~s *take-off* ‖ (ins Wasser) *dive* ‖ (Fallschirm~̈) *parachuting* **~flugplatz** m ⟨tact⟩ *jump-off base* **~gebiet** n ⟨aero⟩ *descent area* **~punkt** m *j.-o. point*; → abspringen

·ab|spulen vt [h] *to unwind from the spool*; *to wind* (*yarn*) *off a reel* **·A–ler** m *reel handle*

·ab|spülen vt [h] (etw) *to wash* (v *from*); *to wash off*; (Wäsche etc) *to rinse* (in fließendem Wasser *under running water*) ‖ (Geschirr) *to wash up* ‖ (Oberfläche, Gesicht) *to swill*; (Straße, Kanal) *to flush* ‖ (Wunde etc) *to wash, bathe* | (etw) gründlich ~ *to wash down* | (fortspülen) (Unrat) *to wash .. away* **·Abspülicht** m ~(e)s/~e **1.** *used dishes*, etc [pl] **2.** *dish-water*

·Abspülung f ~/~en *washing* (*off*); *rinsing* ‖ *washing-up, etc*

·Abstamm m ~(e)s/ = Abkommenschaft

·ab|stammen vi [s] ~ v *to be descended from* ‖ (of words, etc.) *to be derived from*

·Abstämmling m ~(e)s/~e *descendant*

·Abstammung f ~/~en *descent, extraction*; *birth*; *blood* ‖ ein Kennzeichen südländischer ~ *a note of southern extraction*; → Geburt ‖ ⟨übtr⟩ *derivation* (v *from*); *origin* **~slehre** f *theory of descent*

·Abstand m ~(e)s/~̈e **1. a.** (räumlich) *distance* (zwischen *between*; von .. bis *from .. to*) ‖ *interval* (in Abständen *at intervals*) ‖ wie groß ist der ~ ..? *what is the distance ..?* ‖ in e–m ~ v 3 Metern *at a distance of 3 metres*, in gleichem ~ *at an equal distance*, in gleichem ~ liegen *to lie equidistant* (*between*) ‖ (Zeilen~̈) ⟨typ⟩ *spacing* (*to type in* od *with double spacing*) ‖ Streifen in ~̈en v .. *stripes at 2″ spacings* ‖ ⟨mot⟩ *distance* (*between two vehicles*); Sicherheits~̈ (beim Überholen etc) *safe gap*; ~ halten ⟨bes mil⟩ *to maintain a suitable interval*; ⟨mot⟩ *not to drive nose to tail* ‖ ⟨mil⟩ Marschkolonne mit festem ~̈en *fixed distance column* | (Entfernung) *distance* (in weitem ~ v *at a d. from*) **b. Zeit~̈** *distance of time*; *interval* ‖ in Abständen *at intervals, intermittently, –ttingly*; *periodically*; *every now and then*; in Abständen erfolgend *periodical* (*revision*) **2.** ⟨übtr⟩ *difference*; *contrast*; *discrepancy* ‖ ⟨st exch & sport⟩ *margin*; er siegte mit e–m ~ v 4 Sekunden *he won by a margin of 4 seconds*; jdn mit ~ hinter sich l *to distance a p* ‖ ⟨fam⟩ mit ~ besser etc. *far better, etc.* **3.** ⟨jur⟩ *renunciation of a right*; *recession*; → ~sgeld **4.** ⟨fig⟩ ~ halten *to keep the* (od *one's*) *distance*; *to keep aloof* (v *from*) ‖ ~ nehmen v etw *to desist from a th*; *to renounce a th*; davon ~ nehmen z tun *to desist* od *refrain from doing* | **~s- ~feuer** n ⟨aero⟩ *marker light* **~geld** n, **~summe** f *recession-, forfeit-money*; *compensation*; (f Wohnung) *key money* **~̈getreu, ~̈gleich** a *equidistant* **~zahlung** f *premium money*; (f Wohnung) *key m.* **~zünder** m (Raketen~̈) *variable time fuse*

·ab|statten vt [h] *to make, render, give*; → Bericht, Besuch, Dank

·Abstaub- [in comp] *dusting*; ~maschine *dusting machine* **·ab|stauben,** ~̈ vt [h] *to dust*; e–n Tisch leicht ~ *to give a table a flick with the duster*; den Treppenabsatz ~ *to do some dusting on the l.* | ⟨fig⟩ ° bei jdm etw ~ *to get* (*a bottle of wine*) *out of a p*, ⟨sl⟩ *to touch a p for a th*, → stibitzen **·Abstäuber** m ~s/~ *duster, featherbroom*

·ab|stechen vt/i **A.** vt [h] **1.** (T) *to stab, pierce*; (Schwein) *to stick* | ⟨übtr⟩ (P) (im Turnier) *to beat, defeat, unhorse* ‖ ⟨cards⟩ (jdn) *to* (*over-*) *trump* **2.** (abtrennen) (Stück) *to cut off* ‖ *to cut* (*sods*); *to drain* **3.** (abgrenzen) (Fläche etc.) *to mark off* od *out*; (Plan) *to trace out*; *to edge* (*the lawn*) **4.** (stechend nachbilden) (Muster) *to prick* (*out*) **5.** (ableiten) (Teich) *to drain* ‖ ⟨tech⟩ (abfließen l) *to run off*; den Hochofen ~ *to tap the furnace* **B.** vi **1.** [s] † *to turn aside, to swerve* | ⟨mar⟩ *to push* od *sheer off* **2.** [h] ~ von [dat], gegen [acc] *to contrast with* (*a p, a th*); *to stand out against* od *from a th* **·Abstecher** m ~s/~ *excursion, trip*; *outing*; e–n ~ m *to take* (*to go on*) *a trip*; *to make an excursion* ‖ e–n kl ~ zu jdm m *to look a p up on one's way*

·Absteck- (→ abstecken) **~fähnchen** n *surveyor's flag* **~leine** f *tracing cord* **~pfahl** m *picket*; *tracing-picket*; *stake* **~pflock** m *peg*

·ab|stecken vt [h] **1.** (Nadeln abnehmen) (Haar etc.) *to unpin, undo* **2.** (abgrenzen) *to mark off* od *out*; (Linien) *to set out* ‖ (Gebiet mit Pflöcken) *to peg out*; (mit Pfählen) *to stake off* od *out* ‖ (Lager, Vermessung) *to lay out, to trace (out)* ‖ (Minenfeld etc) *to tape off* | (Kleid) *to (make) fit*

·ab|stehen I. vi/t [h] **A.** vi **1.** (entfernt stehen) *to stand far* (v *from*); das Haus steht 5 Meter ab v .. *the house is* od *stands at a distance of 5 metres from (the other)* **2.** ⟨hunt⟩ (of wild fowl) *to fly off* **3.** (vorstehen) *to project, protrude*; *to jut, stick, stand out* (v *from*) **4.** [s] (durch Stehen etc. ~) (of food) *to get stale*; *to decay* ‖ (of fish) *to perish* ‖ (of tea) *to get stony*; → abgestanden **5.** ⟨übtr⟩ ~ v etw *to stand off* (od *to desist*) *from a th*; *to give up, renounce, forgo a th*; v e–m Rechte ~ *to waive a right* **B.** vt **1.** † etw ~ *to cede, surrender a th* (jdm *to a p*) **2.** sich die Beine ~ *to get tired with standing* **II.** ≈ n **1.** *projection, protrusion*; *sticking-out* **2.** *getting stale*; *decay* **3.** *desistance* (v *from*); *renunciation* (v *of*) **·abstehend** a *distant*; gleich weit ~ *equidistant* ‖ ⟨bot⟩ *spreading* | *protrusive, projecting, sticking--out, protruding (ears)*; ‖ *away-from-the-neck (collar)*

·ab|stehlen vt [h] jdm etw ~ *to steal a th from a p* | dem lieben Gott die Tage ~ ⟨fig⟩ *to idle away* od *to waste one's time*

·ab|steifen vt [h] (Mauer etc.) *to support, prop*

·ab|steigen vi [s] *to descend, alight*; *to get down*; v Pferde ~ *to alight, dismount* (v *from*) ‖ ⟨math⟩ ~de Reihe *descending series* | in e–m Gasthof ~ *to stop at, to put up at an inn*; bei jdm ~ *to stay with a p* **·Absteigequartier** n ~(e)s/~e *accommodation, lodging*; *quarters* pl; ⟨übtr⟩ *pull-up* (f *for*)

·Abstell- **~bahnhof** m *switchyard* **~box** f ⟨aero⟩ *revetment* **~druckknopf** m *stop button* **~gleis** n ⟨rail⟩ *siding, side-track, dead end* **~hahn** m *shut-off valve* **~platz** m ⟨mot⟩ *parking area*; ⟨aero⟩ *dispersal bay* ‖ ⟨mil allg⟩ *dispersal area* **~raum** m *storage room*; ⟨theat⟩ *dock*

·ab|stellen vt [h] **1.** (abrücken) (Möbel) *to (re)move* (v der Wand *from the wall*) ‖ (Soldaten) *to post* ‖ **sich ~** (P) *to stand away* (v *from* [*the wall*]) **2.** (niederstellen) (Last) *to put* od *set down* ‖ (Wagen etc.) *to park* ‖ *to dump*; → abladen **3.** (anhalten) ⟨übtr⟩ (Dampf, Wasser etc.) *to shut* od *turn off* ‖ (Licht) *to switch off* ‖ (Maschine) *to stop, to ungear*; sich ~ *to be switched off, to stop* ‖ ⟨typ⟩ (Walzen) *to throw off* ‖ (Telephon etc.) *to disconnect*; ⟨bes Am⟩ *to cut off* ‖ mit –ge–lltem Motor ⟨aero⟩ *with power off* ‖ das Radio ~ *to turn off the wireless* ‖ ⟨fig⟩ (Mißstand) *to correct, rectify, redress, remedy*; ⟨jur⟩ *to abate*; *to abolish*; (Gewohnheit) *to cut off* **4.** ⟨fig⟩ (P) ⟨mil, mar⟩ *to detach* | (S) *to stop*; ⟨fam⟩ *to put a stopper on a th* **abgestellt** s auf *to be tuned to*; → zugeschnitten **Abstellung** f ~/~en ⟨fig⟩ *redress*; *abolition* ‖ (e–s Offiziers) *secondment*

·ab|stempeln vt [h] *to stamp*; (Fahrkarte) → lochen ‖ ⟨cust⟩ *to affix the official stamp on .. (e. g. an import certificate)* | ⟨übtr⟩ jdn ~ *to stamp* od *mark a p* (als *as*) **·Abstempelung** f *stamping*

·ab|steppen vt [h] *to quilt*

·Absterbe- **~ordnung** f ⟨ins⟩ *life table*

·ab|sterben I. vi [s] **1.** (Familie, Rasse) *to die off* od *out* **2.** ⟨übtr⟩ (Pflanzen) *to die down*; *to wither*; *to dry up*; *to fade* | ⟨path⟩ (Gewebe) *to mortify*; (Sinne) *to atrophy* **3.** ⟨fig⟩ (Glieder) *to get numb*; *to become insensible* | (verschwinden) *to die* od *fade away*; (Zeit, Feuer) *to die down*; (Gebräuche) *to die out* | (P) *to become dead* od *indifferent* (gegen *to*); e–r S (:der Welt) ~ *to be deadened to a th* ‖ → abgestorben **4.** ⟨mach⟩ *to peter out* **II.** ≈ n *death*; *extinction*; → Brand, Tod

absterg·ierend a ⟨med⟩ (reinigend) *abstergent, abstersive*; ~es Mittel *abstergent* **Abstersi·on** f ~/~en ⟨med⟩ *abstersion*

·Abstich m ~(e)s/~e **1.** *stabbing*; *sticking (of pigs)* **2.** *cutting-off*; *the cutting (of pieces)* **3.** (of liquids) *tap(ping)* **4.** ⟨found⟩ *tapping* **5.** *separation of wine from lees* **~rinne** f ⟨found⟩ *runner*

·ab|sticken vt [h] *to copy in embroidery*

·Abstieg m ~(e)s/~e *descent* (in den Brunnen *of the well*) | ⟨fig⟩ *downward career*; ⟨soc⟩ *comedown*, im ~ *on the way down*; ⟨demog⟩ *downward social mobility* ‖ ⟨com⟩ *decline* ‖ moralischer ~ *moral decay* od *declension*

·ab|stielen vt [h] (Früchte) *to pick*

·Abstimm- **~kreis** m ⟨wir⟩ *tuned circuit* **~spule** f ⟨wir⟩ *tuning coil* **~visier** n ⟨opt⟩ *collimating sight* **~vorrichtung** f ⟨wir⟩ *tuner*

·ab|stimmen I. vt/i [h] **A.** vt **1.** (Instrument) *to tune* (auf *to*) ‖ (Apparat) *to adjust*; ⟨wir⟩ *to set*; *to tune in*; *to syntonize* (auf *to*); den Apparat ~ *to tune in* (auf *to*) | ⟨übtr⟩ (Sinn) *to (at)tune* (auf *to*) ‖ ⟨fig⟩ *to harmonize, reconcile* **2.** ⟨com⟩ (prüfen) *to balance, to check off, to control* **3.** ⟨rail etc⟩ (Fahrpläne) zeitlich ~ *to synchronize* ‖ muß –ge–mt w mit *must be integrated with* **B.** vi *to vote* (nach der Kopfzahl *by head*) (f. *for*; über *on*); *to take a vote*; es wurde abgestimmt *a vote was taken* (über *on*); über etw ~ l *to put a th to the vote* ‖ geheim ~ *to ballot* (über jdn *for a p*) | ⟨parl⟩ *to divide, to go into division*; das Haus ~ l *to divide the House* (über *on*) **II.** ≈ n → Abstimmung **·Abstimmung** f ~/~en **1.** *tuning* | ⟨wir⟩ *syntonization, syntony, tuning-in* **2.** *checking, control* **3.** | *vote, voting* (durch Zuruf *by acclamation*, durch Heben der Hände *by show of hands*) | etw durch ~ beseitigen *to vote a th away*; jdn durch ~ v e–r Liste beseitigen *to vote a p off a list* ‖ e–e Summe durch ~ bewilligen *to vote a sum* ‖ etw zur ~ bringen *to put a th to the vote* ‖ etw durch ~ feststellen, e–e ~ vornehmen über etw *to take a vote on a th* ‖ jdn durch ~ wählen *to vote a p* (in *into*); (jdn) durch ~ suspendieren *to vote to suspend* | **geheime ~** *(secret) ballot*, die ~ ist geheim, erfolgt in geheimer Wahl *voting is by ballot* | ⟨parl⟩ **namentliche ~** *division*; nach ~ *upon a division*; zur ~! *divide*! zur ~ schreiten *to take a division*; *to divide*; *to go into division* **4.** Volks≈ *plebiscite*; e–e ~ abhalten *to hold* od *take a plebiscite* | **~s- ~gebiet** n ⟨pol⟩ *plebiscitary district* **~zeichen** n ⟨wir⟩ *test signal*

abstin·ent a *abstinent, teetotal* **Abstin·enz** f ~/ *abstinence* (völlige ~ *total a.*) **Abstin·enzler** m ~s/~ **Abstin·enzlerin** f ~/~nen *(total) abstainer, teetotaller*; ⟨fam⟩ *blue-ribboner, -ribbonite*; wie ein ~ *teetotally* **Abstin·enzprinzip** n *teetotalism*

·ab|stoppen vt/i → stoppen

·Abstoß m ~es/≈e *shot*; ⟨ftb⟩ *goal kick*

·ab|stoßen vt/i [h] **I.** vt **A.** (Ggs anziehen) **1.** ⟨phys⟩ (Kraft) *to repel*; e–a (*or* sich gegenseitig) ~ *to repel each other* **2.** (of actions etc.) jdn ~ *to repel, disgust, revolt (a p)*; → II. 1. ‖ → abstoßend **B.** (entfernen) **1.** (Stücke etc.) *to knock* od *scrape off* (v *from*) ‖ (Geweih, Zähne) *to shed*; (of trees) (Blätter) *to shed, drop* | sich die Hörner ~ *to sow one's wild oats* **2.** (wegstoßen) *to push off* **3.** ⟨übtr com⟩ (Waren) *to get rid of, to sell*; *to dispose of* ‖ (Aktien etc.) *to unload* ‖ (Bücherrestbestände) billig ~ *to remainder* ‖ (Schuld) *to pay off, to discharge* | ⟨med⟩ *to eliminate* **C.** (abnutzen) *to wear away by use*; *to grind*; *to rub off* ‖ (Kragen etc.) *to fray* (a. **sich ~**) **D.** ⟨gym⟩ **sich ~** *to push off with a* *swing* **II.** vi **1.** (abstoßend s) *to repel*, er stößt ab *he repels* **2.** *to shove off* ‖ (of ships) *to push off* (v *from*) **·Abstoßen** n **1.** *knocking-off* ‖ *shedding* **2.** ⟨com⟩ *sale* ‖ *discharge* ‖ → Abstoß **·abstoßend 1.** a *repulsive, revolting, forbidding, disgusting*; sich gegenseitig ∼e Charaktere *antipathetic characters*; ∼es Wesen *repulsiveness* **2.** adv *disgustingly* **·Abstoßung** f ⟨phys⟩ *repulsion* ‖ ∼ e–s verpflanzten Organs *rejection* **~skräfte** f pl ⟨phys⟩ *repulsive forces*

·ab|strafen vt [h] (jdn) *to punish*

abstrah·ieren vt [h] *to abstract* ‖ ⟨übtr⟩ [abs] v etw ∼ *to leave a th out of consideration*

abstr·akt 1. a (Ggs konkret) *abstract*; im ∼en Sinne *in the abstract*; das ∼̈e *the abstract* ‖ ⟨übtr⟩ *metaphysical* (*language*) | ∼e Gemälde [pl] *abstractions*; ∼e Malerei *abstractionism*; ∼e Kunst *abstractionism, non-objective* od *non--representational art* ‖ ∼er Künstler *abstractionist* **2.** adv *in the abstract* **Abstrakti·on** f ∼/∼en, *abstraction*

Abstr·aktum L n ∼s/–kta ⟨gram⟩ *abstract noun*

·Abstrebung f ∼/∼en ⟨arch⟩ *strutting*

·Abstreich m ∼(e)s/∼e ⟨com⟩ (Zuschlag auf Mindergebot) *Dutch auction*

·ab|streichen vt/i **I.** vt [h] **1.** (entfernen) (Schaum) *to skim* ‖ ⟨tech⟩ (Schlacken) *to scum*; ⟨typ⟩ die Walze ∼ *to scrape up the roll* | (Kornmaß) *to strike* (*off*); *to make level*; *to sweep off* | (abwischen) *to wipe off*; *to scrape*; sich die Füße ∼ *to scrape the dirt off one's shoes* | (Messer) *to strop, whet* **2.** ⟨com⟩ (abziehen) *to deduct*; *to take off*; (Kosten) *to strike out, to cancel* **3.** (absuchen) (Gelände, Horizont) *to sweep*; (Gebiet) *to beat* (nach *for*) **II.** vi [s] ⟨hunt⟩ (of wild-fowl) *to fly away* od *off*: *the pheasant rocketed over the wood*

·Abstreicher m ∼s/∼ **1.** = Abstreichholz **2.** (Fuß–) *scraper* **·Abstreichholz** n (f Korn etc.) *strike, strickle* **·Abstreichmaß** n *strike-measure*

·Abstreif- ~ring m ⟨tech⟩ *scraper ring*

·ab|streifen vt/i [h] **I.** vt **1.** (ablegen) (Fesseln) *to cast off* ‖ (Kleid etc.) *to pull* od *take off*; schnell ∼ *to slip* od *throw off*; die Kleider ∼ *to strip, undress*; (Füße, Schuhe) *to wipe one's feet* (*on a mat*) | ⟨bot⟩ (Blätter) *to shed* ‖ ⟨zoo⟩ (Haut etc.) *to cast, to shed, to slough*; (Geweih) *to cast* | ⟨übtr & fig⟩ *to get rid of, to lay aside*; *to put off*; *to divest o.s. of* (*a th*); (Gewohnheit, Charakter) *to shed* **2.** (das Meer etc.) *to patrol, traverse* **II.** vi **1.** ⟨hunt⟩ der Hirsch streift ab *the stag casts off* od *sheds its antlers* **2.** [s] (of missiles) *to glance off* **3.** [s] *to turn aside, to swerve* ‖ ⟨fig⟩ *to digress*

·ab|streiten vt [h] (Schuld) *to deny* ‖ (Tatsache) *to argue down* ‖ (Behauptung) *to contradict*; *to get away from a th*; (Möglichkeit) *to deny, to gainsay*; ∼, daß *to deny* od *gainsay that* ‖ jdm etw ∼ *to deny a th*, er stritt es mir rundweg ab *he flatly denied it*; das lasse ich mir nicht ∼ *I won't be argued out of that* ‖ jdm etw (Titel etc.) ∼ *to dispute a th to a p*; jdm das Recht ∼ *to contest, dispute a p's right* (z *to*; z tun *to do*)

·ab|streuen vt [h] ⟨mil⟩ Gelände ∼ *to stray* od *sweep the ground with fire*

·Abstrich m ∼(e)s/∼e **1.** (beim Schreiben) *downward stroke, down-stroke* **2.** ⟨bact & med⟩ *swab* (a. **~bausch**); ⟨Am⟩ *smear*; e–n ∼ m *to take a specimen with a swab* **3.** ⟨com⟩ *deduction, cut* (e–r S *in a th* [*cut in pay*]); ∼e [pl] *economies* (e–r S *in a th*), ∼e m *to economize*; *to make cuts*

·ab|stricken vt [h] (Nadel) *to knit off* ‖ (Muster) *to copy*

·ab|strömen vi [s] *to be carried off* od *away*; *to flow* od *run off rapidly* | ⟨fig⟩ *to disperse, scatter*

abstr·us a *abstruse, recondite*

·ab|stufen vt [h] **1.** *to form into steps, to arrange in steps* (etc.) ‖ *to mark out in portions* od *degrees* (etc.); *to graduate* | ⟨übtr⟩ *to arrange in gradations*; (Steuer; Erziehung) *to grade* ‖ (Farbtöne etc.) *to gradate, tone*; *to shade* (*off*); ⟨mus⟩ (Ton) *to modulate* (nach *to*) **2. sich ~** *to graduate, to be arranged in steps* ‖ (of colours) *to gradate*; *to shade off*

·Abstufung f ∼/∼en *arranging in steps* od *in degrees*; *graduation* | (of colours) *gradation*; *shade* ‖ ⟨mus⟩ *modulation* | (of meaning) *nuance*

·ab|stumpfen vt [h] **1.** *to blunt* | abgestumpft *truncated* (*cone*) **2.** ⟨übtr⟩ *to blunt*; (Geist) *to dull, hebetate* ‖ *to take the edge off* (*one's appetite*); (Gefühl) *to deaden, to dull* (gegen *to*); (Wirkung) *to flatten* | (jdn) *to stupefy*; *to make* (*a p*) *indifferent* (gegen *to*) od *insusceptible* (gegen *of*) **3.** ⟨chem⟩ *to neutralize* **4. sich ~** *to become blunted* od *dull* | ⟨fig⟩ *to become blunted* od *indifferent* (gegen *to*) **5.** [abs nur prs & pret] ⟨fig⟩ (= abgestumpft w.) man stumpft ab *one is getting indifferent* ‖ es stumpft ab (P) *it leads to apathy* ‖ → abgestumpft **·Abstumpfung** f ∼/ *dullness*; *deadening, deadness*; *indifference*

·Absturz m ∼es/∼̈e **1.** (*violent* od *sudden*) *fall*; (in e–n Abgrund) *engulfment*; → Sturz ‖ ⟨aero & mot⟩ *crash*; *drop*; zum → bringen *to crash* (*an aeroplane*); z ∼ ins Meer br. *to send .. crashing into the sea* **2.** (Abhang) *precipice, steep* **·ab|stürzen** vi [s] **1.** *to fall down* ‖ ⟨mount⟩ *to fall down a precipice*; *to plummet*; → stürzen ‖ ⟨aero⟩ *to crash* (brennend *in flames*) **2.** (abschüssig s) *to descend steeply* od *perpendicularly*

·ab|stutzen vt [h] *to cut off, to cut short* ‖ (Baum) *to lop, prune, pollard*; (Hecke) *to trim* ‖ (Flügel) *to clip* etc. → abschneiden

·ab|stützen vt [h] *to shore* (*up*); → stützen

·ab|suchen vt [h] **1.** (Ungeziefer) *to pick* (v e–m Baum *off a tree*) **2.** (Gebiet) *to scour* (nach *for*); ⟨hunt⟩ *to beat up* (nach *for*); ⟨mil⟩ *to reconnoitre, explore*; *to search, to make a search in* (*a room*) (*for*) ‖ (of police) (Distrikt) *to comb* ‖ (Horizont, Gebiet) mit den Augen ∼ *to rake, search, sweep .. with the eye* ‖ (Radar) *to scan*

·Absud m ∼(e)s/∼e ⟨chem⟩ *decoction*

abs·urd a *absurd, preposterous, foolish, ridiculous* **Absurdit·ät** f ∼/∼en, *absurdity*

·ab|süßen vt [h] ⟨tech⟩ (waschen, wässern) *to dulcify*

Absz·eß m –szesses/–szesse ⟨path⟩ *abscess*; (Lungen∼̈) *vomica* (L)

Absz·isse f ∼/∼n ⟨math⟩ *abscissa* **~n-Achse** f *x-axis*

Abt m ∼(e)s/Äbte *abbot*; Amt *or* Würde e–s ∼es *abbotship*, Gerichtsbarkeit e–s ∼es *abbacy* ‖ ∼ mit der Bischofswürde bekleidet *mitred abbot*; gefürsteter ∼ *Lord Abbot*

·ab|takeln vt [h] (Schiff) *to unrig, dismantle* ‖ (Mast) *to strip* ‖ (Schiff außer Dienst stellen) *to lay up* ‖ ° (jdn) ∼ = abbauen **·Abtakelung** f *unrigging, dismantling, laying-up, etc.*

·ab|tanzen vt [h] (Tanz) *to dance* | sich die Beine ∼ *to wear out one's legs with dancing*

·Abtast- ~einrichtung f ⟨a. Radar⟩ *scanning device* **~höhenmesser** m ⟨aero⟩ (f Höhe über Grund) *absolute altimeter* **~muster** n (Radar) *scanning pattern* **~scheibe** f ⟨telv⟩ *scanner, hunting disk* **~strahl** m *scanning beam* **~verstärker** m ⟨wir⟩ (*scanning*) *pre-amplifier*

·ab|tasten I. vt [h] ⟨med⟩ *to palpate* ‖ etw nach e–r S ∼ *to feel a th for a th* ‖ ⟨phot⟩ (mit Licht) *to scan* ‖ ⟨comp⟩ *to scan, sense* **II.** ∼̈ n (e–r Zeitfunktion) ⟨commun⟩ *sampling* | **~d** a: ∼er Elektronenstrahl *scanning beam*

·ab|tauen vi/t [s/h] *to thaw* (*off*)

Abt·ei f ∼/∼en *abbey*; zur ∼ gehörig *abbatial* ‖ ∼kirche [f] *abbey-church*

·Abteil n ∼(e)s/∼e ⟨rail⟩ *compartment*; ∼ erster Klasse *first-class c.*; ∼ f (Nicht-)Raucher (*non-*)*smoking c.* ‖ ⟨Am⟩ (Schlafwagen∼̈) *section*

·**ab|teilen** vt [h] *to divide* || (durch Verschlag etc.) *to partition off* || ⟨mil⟩ in Sektionen ~ *to form into sections*; → einteilen

·**Abteilung** f ~/~en **1.** [abstr] *division; detachment, separation* **2.** [konkr] (Verschlag) *partition* || (Fach) *compartment, partition* || (Abschnitt) *section* | (P) *cohort* || (Gesellschaftsklasse) *class* | (of administration, etc.) *department* || ⟨com⟩ *department, branch* || (of a school) *division* || (of a prison, hospital, etc.) *ward* | ⟨mil⟩ *detachment, division, section, group* || [·–] ⟨artill⟩ *battalion* → Gruppe, Trupp, Zug || ~ marsch! ⟨mil⟩ *quick march!*; → Nachrichten-ᷢ **~schef, ~sdirektor, ~sdirigent, ~sleiter** m *head* od *superintendent of a department; department(al) manager*; ⟨com⟩ *departmental* (od *branch*) *manager, shopwalker*, ⟨Am⟩ *floorwalker* **~skommandeur** m *battalion commander* **~sschießen** n *fire of a brigade* **~sunterricht** m *simultaneous instruction of children of all ages* (etc.) **~svorsteher** m = Abteilungschef

·**ab|telegraphieren** vi [h] *to decline* od *refuse by wire, to wire refusal* || jdm ~ *to put a p off by wire*; etw ~ *to cancel* od *countermand a th by w.*

·**Abteufpumpe** f ⟨min⟩ *submersible sinking pump*

·**ab|teufen** **1.** vt [h] ⟨min⟩ (Schacht) *to sink*; (Öl) *to drill* **2.** ᷢ n *sinking* || (e–r Bohrung) ⟨oil⟩ *drilling of a well*

·**ab|tippen** vt [h] ⟨typewr⟩ *to copy*

Äbt·issin f ~/~nen *abbess*

·**ab|tönen** vt [h] ⟨paint⟩ (Farben) *to tone, shade, tint* | ⟨übtr⟩ *to weigh, balance*; abgetönt *measured, balanced* ·**Abtönung** f *shade, tone, tint* || ⟨paint⟩ *tonality, shade*

·**ab|töten** vt [h] **1.** *to kill*; (Bakterien etc.) *to destroy* **2.** ⟨fig⟩ (das Fleisch etc.) *to mortify* || *to macerate*, sich ~ *to macerate o.s.* (durch Fasten *with fasting*) || (Gefühl etc.) *to stifle, deaden* ·**Abtötung** f ~/~en *kill, killing; destruction* || *mortification* (*of the flesh*); *maceration*

·**ab|traben** vi [s] *to trot off* | vt [h] *trot out*

·**Abtrag** m ~(e)s/ᷢe **1.** *instalment, payment* **2.** jdm ~ (Schaden) tun *to injure a p*; → Abbruch

·**ab|tragen** vt [h] **A.** ⟨eig⟩ **1.** (Erdhügel) *to* (*reduce to a*) *level, to lay low* **2.** (Gebäude) *to take* od *pull down*; *to raze* **3.** (Speisen) *to clear away, to remove*; die Tafel ~ *to clear the table, to clear away*, → abdecken **4.** ⟨surg⟩ *to remove, excise* **5.** ⟨hunt⟩ (Habicht) = dressieren **B.** ⟨übtr⟩ **1.** (Schuld) *to pay off* od *up*; *to wipe off* || jdm Dank ~ *to return* od *render thanks to a p* **2.** *to wear away*; (Kleider) *to wear out* | **sich ~** *to wear* (*off* od *out*) **C.** (abzeichnen) (Linie etc) *to convey, draw, transfer* (auf *on*)

·**abträglich** a *detrimental, harmful, injurious, prejudicial* (e–r S *to a th*); e–r S ~ s *to detract from a th*; *to be damaging to a th* (a. *to a p*)

·**Abtragung** f ~/~en **1.** ⟨geol⟩ *denudation* || (Auswaschung) *erosion* **2.** (of buildings) *pulling--down, demolition* **3.** *removal* **4.** (of a debt) *payment, liquidation* | *returning* (*of thanks*) **5.** → Abnutzung

·**Abtransport** m *dispatch; conveyance; transport* ||*evacuation* (*of casualties, etc*) ·**ab|transportieren** vt [h] *to dispatch; convey; remove, transport* (nach *to*)

·**ab|treiben** vt/i **I.** vt [h] **A.** ⟨eig⟩ **1.** *to drive away* od *off* || (Dämpfe) *to expel* **2.** *to drive* (*a ship*) *from the right course*; abgetrieben w *to be crabbed off* **3.** (Bandwurm etc.) *to expel, remove* **4.** ein Kind ~ ⟨jur⟩ *to commit, procure, produce abortion* **B.** (ein Tier) *to overdrive*; (jdn) *to overwork* **C. 1.** (abholzen) *to cut down, to clear* **2.** (abweiden l) *to graze* **3.** ⟨met⟩ (reinigen) (Silber) *to refine by cupellation* **II.** vi [s] ⟨mar⟩ *to be driven* (od *to drift*) *off*; *to drive* od *fall to leeward, to go adrift*; *to make leeway* || ⟨aero⟩ *to be drifted out of one's course*; ⟨a–n⟩ *to fall away*; *to yaw* ·**abtreibend** a ⟨jur⟩ *abortifacient* (a. ~es Mittel)

·**Abtreibung** f ~/~en **1.** *driving off* **2.** *expulsion* (*of worms*) **3.** ⟨jur⟩ *abortion, foeticide* **~smittel** n *abortifacient*

·**Abtrennpolice** f ⟨ins⟩ *ticket* od *coupon policy*

·**abtrennbar** a *separable*

·**ab|trennen** vt [h] **1.** *to separate, detach* (v *from*); (Glied) *to sever* (v *from*) || (durch e–n Zaun etc.) *to fence off*; (durch Verschlag [Mauer]) *to partition* [*wall*] *off* (v *from*) **2.** (Genähtes) *to unpick, unstitch*; *to rip off* **3. sich ~** *to separate* (v *from*) | *to come unstitched* od *off* || ·**Abtrennung** f ~/~en *separation*; *severance* (v *from*) | (Naht) *unpicking, unstitching*

·**abtretbar** a *transferable* (an jdn *to a p*)

·**ab|treten** **I.** vt/i **A.** vt [h] **1.** *to wear off* || (Treppe etc.) *to wear away* od *down* || (die Hacken) *to wear down* | **sich ~** (of steps, etc.) *to wear off* **2.** (entfernen) den Schmutz v den Schuhen ~ *to scrape the dirt* od *mud off one's shoes*; *to wipe one's feet* | **sich ~** *to wipe one's feet* **3.** (Gebiet etc.) *to relinquish, resign, cede*; (Festung etc.) *to surrender, to yield* (jdm *to a p*); ⟨jur⟩ (Recht, Anspruch) *to assign, to surrender* (jdm *to a p*) || jdm etw ~, etw an jdn ~ *to cede, resign, transfer* (*to hand* od *make over*) *a th to a p* **B.** vi [s] **1.** *to step aside, to withdraw*; *to stand down* od *off*; *to exit* (:*he exited*); *to make one's exit* || ⟨mil⟩ ~! *dismiss!* **2.** ⟨theat⟩ [nur 3. sg & pl prs] → ab I. 1. b. **3.** ⟨übtr⟩ (sich zurückziehen v e–m Amt etc.) *to resign, retire*; vom Schauplatz ~ *to retire from the scene* || jdn ~ l *to dismiss, retire a p* | ° (sterben) *to quit the scene, to make one's bow, to* (*make one's*) *exit, to go West* od *off* **II.** ᷢ n *wearing-away, -down, -off* || *wiping-off*; *cleaning* || ⟨theat⟩ *curtain*; → Abtretung ·**abtretend** a (P) *outgoing*

·**Abtreter** m ~s/~ *scraper, doorscraper; doormat* | ⟨jur⟩ *ceder; assignor; transferrer*

·**Abtretung** f ~/~en **1.** ⟨jur⟩ → Zession, *assignment* (*of rights*, etc.); *conveyance, transfer* (*of property*); *cession* (*of a territory*) (an *to*) **2.** (Abtreten) *withdrawal* || *retirement, resignation* || → Abgang, Abtreten, Abtritt **~sgebiet** n *ceded territory* **~surkunde** f *transfer*; (*deed* od *instrument of*) *conveyance*; *deed of assignment* od *cession*

·**Abtrieb** m ~(e)s/~e **1.** *clearance*, → Kahlhieb **2.** *driving-down* (*of the cattle*) *from the alp* **~alter** n ⟨for⟩ *final age*

·**Abtrift** f ~/~en **1.** ⟨mar, etc⟩ *leeway, drift* **2.** = Abtrieb 2; Abdrift

·**ab|trinken** vt [h] *to drink from* od *off* (*a liquid*), trink die Blume ab! *take the top off it!*

·**Abtritt** m ~(e)s/~e **1.** *withdrawal* || ⟨theat⟩ *exit* **2.** *retirement, resignation*; → Abgang, Abtreten, Abtretung **3.** = Abort

·**ab|trocknen** vt/i **1.** vt [h] *to dry* (am Feuer *by the fire*); *to wipe dry* || **sich** [dat] die Hände (Tränen) ~ *to dry one's hands* (*eyes*; *to wipe one's tears away*) | **sich ~** *to dry o.s.* **2.** vi [s] *to get dry* || *to dry up* || *to wither* || ⟨med⟩ *to shrivel*

·**Abtropf- ~bank** f, **~gestell** n, **~ständer** m *drainer, draining rack* ·**ab|tropfen** vi [s] (allmählich) *to drop away* od *off*; ⟨cul⟩ *to drain*

·**ab|trotzen** vt [h] jdm etw ~ *to get a th out of a p by pertinacity* (od *in the teeth of opposition*); *to bully a th out of a p*

·**ab|trudeln** vi [s] ⟨aero⟩ *to go into* (od *come down in*) *a spin*; *to* (*side-*)*slip*; *to tail-spin* → trudeln; *to auger*

·**ab|trumpfen** vt [h] *to trump* || jdn ~ ⟨fig⟩ *to give a p a set-down, to snub a p*

·**abtrünnig** a *faithless, unfaithful, disloyal* || e–e ~e Provinz etc *a break-away province* etc || ⟨ec⟩ *apostate* | falls jd ~ w sollte *in case of defection* || e–r S ~ w *to desert a th* (*a party, a* *cause*, etc.); jdm ~ w *to prove faithless to a p*; *to revolt against a p* ‖ s–m Glauben ~ w *to abandon one's faith, to apostatize*; *to backslide* | ≗e(r m) f ~n/~n *deserter, renegade* ‖ *diviationist* ‖ ⟨ec⟩ *apostate, backslider* ≗**keit** f ~/ *defection, desertion* ‖ (Empörung) *revolt* ‖ ⟨ec⟩ *apostasy*

·**ab|tun** vt [h] **1.** (Kleider) *to take* od *put off*; *to doff* **2.** (beiseite schieben) *to put aside* ‖ *to abolish, to get rid of, to dispose of, to do away with* (*a th*) ‖ schnell ~ *to polish off* ‖ jdn ~ *to dismiss a p* (als nutzlos *as useless*) ‖ etw verächtlich ~ *to treat a th with contempt, to pooh-pooh a th* (*as* ..); etw mit e–r verächtlichen Handbewegung ~ *to dismiss a th with a contemptuous wave of one's hand*, mit e–m Achselzucken ~ *to shrug off* ‖ *to skate over a th* **3.** (erledigen) *to dispose of*; *to settle*; etw in Eile ~ *to dash a th off, to dispatch a th*; gütlich ~ *to arrange*; kurz ~ *to dismiss*: *Goethe is dismissed in a couple of pages*; *to make short work of* od *with a th* ‖ damit ist die S nicht abgetan *that doesn't settle the matter, the matter cannot rest there*; er ist f mich abgetan *I have done with him* ‖ → abgetan **4. a.** (T) *to kill, slaughter* **b.** (P) *to execute, dispatch* | *to do for, to ruin*; ⟨fam⟩ *to settle a p's hash, to dish a p* **5.** ⟨hunt⟩ **sich ~** (of game) *to separate from the herd*

·**ab|tupfen 1.** vt [h] *to dab* (mit *with*); *to dry by dabbing* **2.** ≗ n *dab*

Abuk·ir *Ab*(*o*)*ukir*; die Schlacht bei ~ *the Battle of the Nile* (1798)

·**ab|urteilen** vt/i [h] **A.** vt (S) *to decide* (*a case*) *finally by judicial sentence*; *to adjudicate* (*a th*) ‖ (P) *to give a verdict against* (*a p*); *to bring* (*a p*) *to trial* | ⟨übtr⟩ im voraus ~ *to prejudge* (*a th, a p*) **B.** vi; ~ über etw, jdn **1.** → A. (etw, jdn ~) **2.** ⟨übtr⟩ *to pronounce against a th, a p, to criticize a th, a p severely* ‖ *to condemn a p hastily* ·**Aburteilung** f ~/~en *adjudication* ‖ *trial*; jdn zur ~ bringen *to bring a p to trial*; jdn dem Gericht zur ~ übergeben *to commit a p for trial* | ⟨übtr⟩ *harsh criticism*; *hasty condemnation*

·**ab|verdienen** vt [h] (Schuld) *to pay off* (*a debt*) *by labour*; *to work out* (*a debt*); ⟨mar⟩ die Überfahrt ~ *to work one's passage*

·**ab|verlangen** vt [h] jdm etw ~ *to demand a th of* od *from a p*; *to ask a p for a th*

·**ab|vermieten** vt [h] *to sublet, underlet*

·**ab|vieren** vt [h] ⟨carp⟩ *to square*

·**ab|wägen** vt [h] **1.** = abwiegen **2.** ⟨fig⟩ *to weigh* (gegen *with, against*); s–e Worte ~ *to weigh one's words*; s–e Worte nicht ~ *not to mince one's words*; e–e S gegen e–e andere ~ *to balance one thing against another*; → erwägen

·**Abwägung** f ~/~en ⟨fig⟩ *weighing, balancing* ‖ bei ~ aller Umstände *on balance* (*it was a good thing*); bei genauer ~ *on close examination*

·**ab|wählen** vt [h] *to vote to suspend* (*a p*)

·**ab|wälzen** vt [h] **1.** (hinabrollen) *to roll down* **2.** ⟨mst fig⟩ (Arbeit etc.) *to devolve, to throw* (auf jdn *on a p*) ‖ (Verantwortung) *to shift* (auf *on, to*); etw von sich ~ *to shift a th off*; *to shift a th from one's shoulders* od *from o.s.* (auf *on, to*) ‖ die Schuld von sich ~ *to clear* od *exonerate o.s. from a charge, to exculpate o.s.* **3.** (Steuer) *to transform* ‖ (Kosten) *to pass on* (auf *to*)

·**Abwälzung** f ~/~en (of duties, etc.) *devolution*; *shifting* ‖ (of a tax) *transformation*

·**ab|wandeln** vt **1.** ⟨gram⟩ → beugen **2.** ⟨übtr⟩ (Thema) *to vary* ·**abwandelbar** a → beugbar

·**ab|wandern 1.** vi [s] *to wander away, to migrate* (aus *from*, nach *to*) **2.** ≗ n = ·**Abwanderung** f ~/~en *migration* (vom Lande in die Städte *from the land to the towns*); → Landflucht ‖ ~ des Kapitals *exodus of capital* ‖ ⟨übtr⟩ *outward drift* (aus *from* [*the centres*]) ‖ ⟨arts⟩ *transfer* **~süberschuß** m ⟨demog⟩ *net emigration*

·**Abwandlung** f ~/~en ⟨gram⟩ → Beugung ‖ ⟨übtr⟩ in amerikanischer ~ *with an American twist* ‖ *transformation*

·**Abwärme** f ~/ ⟨tech⟩ *waste heat*

·**ab|warten I.** vt/i [h] **1.** vt; etw ~ *to wait for a th*; jds Kommen ~ *to wait for a p to come*; jds Rückkehr ~ *to wait a p's return, to wait for a p to return* | die Gelegenheit ~ *to wait* od *watch one's opportunity* ‖ die Zeit ~ *to bide* od *watch one's time*; *to temporize* ‖ das Abendessen ~ *to stay for dinner*, ⟨fam⟩ *to stay dinner* | das Ende e–r S ~ *to stay to the end of a th*; den Regen ~ *to wait till it has ceased raining* ‖ wir wollen es ruhig ~ *we'll wait and see*; ich kann es ~ *I can bide my time*; wartet's nur ab *just wait till you see* | Anweisungen (etc.) ~ *to await instructions* | * (P & T) = pflegen **2.** vi *to wait and see*; wir müssen ~ *we must wait and see*; ⟨Am⟩ *to straddle* ‖ ~ bis *to wait till* od *until*; *to mark time until*; *to sit on the fence until* ‖ es bleibt –zu– *it remains to be seen* (ob *whether*) ‖ ~ und Tee trinken! *patience!, wait and see!* **II.** ≗ n *waiting* (*for*) ·**abwartend** a *temporizing* ‖ die ~e Haltung *the temporizing*; e–e ~e H. einnehmen, sich ~ verhalten *to temporize*; *to take up a wait-and-see* od *a waiting attitude* ‖ ⟨med⟩ *expectant* (*method*)

·**abwärts** adv **I.** *down, downward, downwards* ‖ den Fluß ~ *down the river*, (berg~) *downhill* | ~ gerichtet *downward* (*movement*); *down* (*look*) ‖ eine Tendenz nach ~ *a downward tendency* ‖ ~ fahren ⟨mar⟩ *to go downstream* ‖ ⟨fig⟩ mit ihm geht es ~ *he is going downhill* (od *down in the world*) **II.** [in comp] **1.** → berg~ etc. ‖ strom~ *downstream, downward*(*s*) **2.** ≗- *downward* ≗**bewegung** f *downward movement* ≗**gang** m ⟨tech⟩ *downward stroke* ≗**hub** m ⟨mot⟩ *inward stroke*

*·**Abwartung** f ~/~en (P & T) = Pflege

·**Abwasch** m ~es/ **1.** *used dishes* (etc.) *pl* **2.** *washing-up* (*of dishes* etc.) **~becken** n (in der Küche) *sink* **~faß** n *washing-tub* **~magd** f *scullerymaid* **~lappen** m *dish-cloth* **~wasser** n *dish-water*; *wash*; *washings* pl ‖ (f Schweine) *hog-wash*

·**abwaschbar** a *washable*

·**ab|waschen I.** vt [h] **1.** (etw) *to wash* (v *from*); *to give* (*a th*) *a wash*; jdm den Schmutz v den Händen ~ *to wash the dirt off a p's hands* | (jdn im Bad) *to bathe*; (Kind) *to rinse*, ⟨fam⟩ *to sluice* (mit *with*) ‖ gründlich ~ *to wash down*; jdn v oben bis unten ~ *to sponge down* | (Geschirr) *to wash* (*up*) **2.** (of the sea) (Boden) *to wash away* **3. sich ~** *to have a wash*; *to wash o.s.*, *to have a sponge*; ⟨rel⟩ *to perform one's ablution* **II.** ≗ n ~s/ ⟨fig⟩ das ist ein ~ *that is killing two birds with one stone* ‖ → ·**Abwaschung** f ~/~en *ablution*; ⟨rel⟩ [pl] *a.s* ‖ ⟨chem⟩ *bath*

·**Abwasser** n ~s/≗ [oft pl] *waste* od *back water*; *sullage*; städtische ≗ ⟨hyg⟩ *sewage* (dünn *weak*, dick *strong*) **~klärung** f *waste water clarification* **~klär-**, **~reinigungsanlage** f *w.w. purifying plant*, → Kläranlage ·**abwassern** vi [h] ⟨aero⟩ *to take off on water* ·**abwässern** vt [h] **1.** (Heringe) *to water, soak* **2.** (entwässern) (Feld) *to drain*

·**ab|wechseln** vi/t [h] **I.** vi **1.** (wechseln) *to vary*; *to take place alternately* od *by turns* ‖ Freude u Leid wechseln ab *joy and grief alternate*, → 2. u 4. ‖ regelmäßig ~ *to rotate*, → 2. u 4. **2. ~ mit** etw *to alternate with a th*; Freude wechselt ab mit Leid (*or*: Freude u Leid wechseln [sich] ab → 1. u 4.) *joy alternates with grief* | etw ~ l *to alternate a th* (mit etw *with a th*); regelmäßig ~ l *to rotate a th* **3. ~ in** etw *to vary a th* (*one's meals, a motif*) **4. sich ~,** (mit) einander ~ *to alternate* (*joy and grief alternate,* → 1. u 2.); sich regelmäßig ~ *to rotate* (→ 1. u 2.) | (P) *to take turns* (*we shall t. t.*); *to relieve one another by turns*; miteinander in etw ~ *to do, perform, take a th by turns* **II.** vt; etw ~ mit = etw ~ l → I. 2.

·abwechselnd 1. a *changeable*; *variable*; mit ~em Erfolg *with varying success* | mit e–a ~ *alternate, alternating*; *occurring by turns*; ~ Tag u Nacht (*or* T. u N. ~) *alternate day and night*; rote Farben mit blauen ~ *red colours alternate with blue ones*; Steinschichten mit Holzschichten ~ *alternate layers of stone and timber* **2.** adv *alternately, by turns, by turn and turn about*; ~ abbeißen *to bite about*; ~ östlich u westlich laufen *to run alternately east and west* ‖ ~ amtieren *to hold office by* od *in rotation*

·Abwechslung f ~/~en **1.** *change*; der ~ wegen, zur ~ *for a change*; *by way of a change* od *of variety* | ⟨übtr⟩ (Buntheit) *variety*, zwecks ~ *for the sake of variety*; ~ in etw (hinein)-bringen *to diversify, to variegate a th* ‖ angenehme ~ *relief* (fürs Auge *to the eye*) ‖ (im Stil) *elegant variation* **2.** (regelmäßige) *alternation* (*alternations of* [zwischen, von] *affection and dislike*) ‖ *turn* ‖ *rotation* (*of crops*) **·abwechslungsreich, -voll 1.** a *diversified*; *variegated*; *varied* (*life*); *chequered* (*lot*) **2.** adv; (Rede) ~ gestalten *to diversify*

·ab|wedeln vt [h] ⟨phot⟩ (Abzug etc z Hellerlassen) *to dodge*; (z Dunkler–w–l) *to burn in*

·Abweg m ~(e)s/~e **1.** † ⟨eig⟩ *by-way, detour, side-path* **2.** ⟨übtr⟩ *wrong way*; auf dem ~ *on the wrong w.* ‖ ~e [pl] *devious paths* pl ‖ auf ~e geraten *to go astray* od *wrong* ‖ ⟨übtr⟩ *to err* ‖ ⟨fig⟩ *to take the wrong path*

·abwegig a **1.** (irrig) *devious* ‖ (abschweifend) *digressive*; *stray* (*thoughts*) **2.** (unpassend) *inapt* (*remark*) ‖ [pred] *out of the way, out of place, not to the point* **·abwegs** adv *out of the way*; *some distance off*

·Abwehr f ~/ **1.** *warding-, keeping-off*; ⟨fenc⟩ *parrying* ‖ ⟨mil⟩ (Spionage≈) *counter-intelligence* | ~ gegen *defence against*; *protection from* od *against*; als ~, zur ~ *in defence* (*against*) ‖ ⟨übtr⟩ *buffer, check* (*against*) **2.** [in comp] *defensive*; *precautionary*, *protective* **~aktion** f *defensive* od *precautionary action* (od *activity*) **~bereitschaft** f ⟨bes mil⟩ *state of preparedness* **~bügel** m ⟨rail⟩ *cow-catcher* | (Spionage- u) **~dienst** m *Secret Service*; *intelligence service* **~ferment** n ⟨med⟩ *protective ferment* **~geschoß** n *anti-missile* **~geschütz** n, **~kanone** f (→ Flak) *anti-aircraft gun* **~jäger** m ⟨aero⟩ *defensive fighter* **~krieg** m *defensive war*(*fare*) **~maßnahme** f *defensive* od *precautionary measure*; ~n [pl] gegen Luftangriff *air-raid precautions* [pl] (abbr. *A. R. P.*) **~mittel** n *preventive, prophylactic* **~rakete** f *interceptor missile* | vorderer Rand des **~raumes** m *forward edge of the battle area*, → Verteidigung **~schlacht** f *defensive battle* **~stelle** f *military security control service* **~streik** m *defensive strike* **~waffe** f *defensive weapon* (*against*) **~zauber** m → Amulett; *apotropaion* Gr

·ab|wehren I. vt [h] **1.** (jdn) *to keep down*; *to head* od *stave off* **2.** etw ~ (Stoß, Hieb) *to ward* od *fend off, to parry*; ~der Stoß *parry* ‖ (Ball) *to intercept* ‖ (fernhalten) *to keep* od *hold off*; (Fliegen etc) *to drive* od *frighten away* | ⟨übtr⟩ (Gefahr) *to avert*; *to fight* od *ward off*; *to prevent*; (Ruin) *to stave off*; (Vorschlag etc) *to demur to* | etw v jdm ~ *to keep a th away from a p*; *to protect a p from a th* **II.** ≈ = Abwehr **·abwehrend 1.** a *defensive* **2.** adv *defensively*; ~ sagen *to protest*

·ab|weichen I. vi [s] **A.** (abgehen) **1.** ⟨eig⟩ *to alter one's course, to depart* (v *from*); *to deflect* (v e–m Wege *from a course*; nach rechts *to one's right*); *to turn aside* (in *into*); vom richtigen Wege ~ *to go astray*; ⟨aero⟩ v Flugauftrag ~ *to abort* ⟨sl⟩ **2.** ⟨übtr⟩ *to digress, diverge, swerve, veer, shift, turn* ‖ *to depart, to deviate, to make a departure* (v *from*); v s–n Grundsätzen, e–r Regel ~ *to depart* od *deviate from one's principles, from a rule*; v e–m Grundsatz ~ *to compromise a principle*; v e–m Ideal ~ *to deflect from an ideal*; v e–m Vorhaben ~ *to swerve from a purpose*; v der Wahrheit ~ *to deviate from the truth*; vom rechten Wege ~ *to leave the path of rectitude*; *to err* **B.** (sich unterscheiden) **1.** ~ von *to differ, vary* od *diverge from*; *to be different* od *divergent from*; m–e Meinung weicht sehr von der s–n ab *my opinion differs widely from his*; v jds Folgerungen ~ *to join issue with a p's conclusions* **2.** ~, v e–a ~ *to differ, to vary* (in etw *in a th*); sie weichen sehr von e–a ab *they differ, vary widely* **II.** ≈ *turning-aside*; *deflexion* (v *from*) | ⟨übtr⟩ *deviation*; → Abweichung **·abweichend** a ⟨übtr⟩ *different* (v *from, to*); *divergent* (v *from*); [pred] (*to be*) *at variance* (v *with*) | ⟨gram⟩ *anomalous, irregular* ‖ v der Norm ~ *heterodox* **·Abweichlertum** n *deviationism*

·Abweichung f ~/~en **1.** (→ abweichen) *deflexion* (v e–m Wege *from a course*) | ⟨phys⟩ *deflexion*; *deviation* (v *from*) ‖ (der Nordnadel v wahren N.) *true bearing*; *declination*; *variation*; *deviation* ‖ ⟨astr⟩ (Winkelabstand vom Äquator) *declination* | ⟨übtr⟩ *departure* (v *from*); *deviation* (v der Wahrheit *from the truth*); *lapse* (*from virtue*) ‖ ⟨a. gram⟩ *exception* (*to the rule*); ~ v e–r allgemeinen Regel *anomaly* ‖ ~en [pl] *variation* **2.** (Verschiedenheit) *difference, discrepancy* (*between*); *divergence* (*of opinions, etc*) **~sgröße** f *amount of aberration, etc*

·ab|weiden vt [h] *to graze* od *pasture* (*a meadow*); *to graze* od *feed* (*on a meadow*); (Wiese) ~ l *to feed down* od *off* ‖ (Sprossen) *to browse, crop*

·Abweis m ~es/~e → Abweisung, Ablehnung

·ab|weisen vt [h] **1.** (S) *to decline, to refuse*; (Bitte) *to repel*; (Antrag, Vorschlag) *to reject, repel*; ⟨sl⟩ *to turn down*; ⟨jur⟩ (Berufung) *to dismiss* (kostenpflichtig *with costs*) ‖ ⟨com⟩ (Wechsel) *to dishonour* | (Angriff) *to beat back* od *off*; *to repulse, repel* ‖ etw v sich ~ *to disapprove, to discountenance a th*; es v sich ~ z tun *to refuse to do* **2.** (P) *to refuse admittance* (od *entrance*) *to* (*a p*); *to turn* (*a p*) *away* (v der Tür *from the door*) ‖ (jdn) kurz ~ *to snub* (*a p*), *to give* (*a p*) *a snub*; *to send* (*a p*) *about his business*; abgewiesen w *to meet with a snub* (od *rebuff*) | jdn ~ *to repulse a p*; (Kandidaten, Bewerber) *to refuse* ‖ ich lasse mich nicht ~ *I will take no refusal* (od *denial*), *I won't be refused* | ⟨jur⟩ (Kläger) *to nonsuit* **·abweisend** a *unfriendly* (gegen *to*); jdn ~ behandeln, ~ s gegen jdn, mit jdm *to snub a p, to give a p a snub* **·Abweiser** m ~s/~ **1.** *kerbstone, kerb* **2.** (Buhne) *groyne, breakwater* **3.** (Schutzvorrichtung) (*arm-*)*guard*; (Prellstein) *guard stone* **·Abweisung** f ~/~en **1.** *refusal*; grobe ~ *snub, rebuff, repulse* ‖ (of a claim) *rejection* ‖ ⟨jur⟩ (of a case) *dismissal*; (of a suit) *nonsuit* ‖ (of a charge, a statement) *disclaimer, denial* ‖ ⟨com⟩ (of a bill) *non-acceptance* | (of an attack) *repulse* **2.** (P) *turning away*; jdm e–e ~ erteilen *to give a p the brush-off* | (of an enemy) *repulse* **~sbescheid** m, **~surteil** n ⟨jur⟩ *nonsuit*

·abwendbar a *preventable, avertible*

·ab|wenden vt [h] **1.** (etw) **a.** (das Gesicht etc) *to turn away*; die Augen ~ *to avert one's eyes*; die Augen v jdm ~ *to take one's eyes off a p*; s–e Hand v jdm ~ *to withdraw* od *withhold one's support from a p*; *to break with a p* ‖ → abwendig **b.** e–n Hieb v sich ~ *to parry a thrust* |

(Gefahr) *to avert, to ward off*; *to prevent*; (Krise, Unheil) *to stave off* **c.** etw ~ v jdm *to save a p from a th*; *to protect a p from* od *against a th*; er verstand es, die Schande von ihm abzuwenden *he knew how to save him from the disgrace* **2.** **sich ~** *to turn aside* od *away*; sich ~ v etw *to turn away from a th* ‖ sich v jdm ~ *to abandon a p*; *to give a p the cold shoulder, to break with a p* ‖ **·abwendig** a; jdn, (etw) jdm ~ m *to alienate, to estrange a p, (a th) from a p*; sich [dat] jdn ~ m *to alienate a p*; jdm die Kunden ~ m *to take* (od *entice*) *a p's customers away* **·Abwendung** f ~/~en *averting* (of a danger etc); *prevention*

·ab|werben vt [h] (Arbeiter etc) *to entice .. away from his job, etc*; *to take .. away*; ⟨jur⟩ (als unlauterer Wettbewerb) *to commit deprivation of services* ‖ ⟨ec⟩ *to win over*; *to convert, to proselytize* **·Abwerbung** f ~/~en *enticing away* ([gen] *an employee*); *enticement*; ⟨jur⟩ *deprivation of services* ‖ ⟨ec, sport⟩ *proselytizing*; rücksichtslose ~ *cut-throat competition* (*among churches, sporting organizations, etc*)

·abwerfbar a ⟨aero⟩ *jettisonable* (Kanister etc)

·ab|werfen vt/i [h] **I.** vt **A.** ⟨eig⟩ **1.** (Last, Rock) *to throw* od *pull off*; (schnell ~) *to slip off*; *to slough* (*one's knapsack*) **2.** (aus der Höhe ~) *to drop*; (Ballast) *to discharge, to throw out, to heave* ‖ ⟨aero⟩ *to jettison*; Bomben ~ *to drop, release, lighten bombs* (auf *on*); .. ~ auf e–e Stadt *to bomb a town* ‖ (Flugblätter) *to drop, to scatter from the air* **3.** (jdn) (of a horse) *to throw off* **4.** ⟨bot & zoo⟩ (Blätter) *to shed* ‖ (Haut) *to cast, to shed, to slough*; (Geweih) *to shed* **5.** (Schlacken) *to remove* **6.** Karten ~ *to discard cards, to discard* **B.** ⟨übtr⟩ **1.** (Fesseln etc) *to cast off*; (Joch) *to shake off* ‖ die Maske ~ → ablegen I. A. l. c. ‖ (äußere Hüllen) *to slough* **2.** Gewinn ~ *to bring in, to yield, return a profit*; *to pay* (*well*); Gewinn ~ f jdn *to pay a p*; das Geschäft wirft nichts ab *the business does not pay*; nichts ~ ⟨com⟩ *to be unprofitable* ‖ gewinn~d [a] *lucrative, paying* (*concern*); *remunerative* (*position*) **II.** vi ⟨hunt⟩ der Hirsch wirft ab *the stag casts off its antlers* **·Abwerfen** n ~s/ *throwing-off* ‖ ~ v Bomben *the dropping of bombs*, od *bomb-dropping*; *the bombing*; ~ des Ballastes *discharge of the ballast* ‖ *shedding* | *casting-off, shaking-off* ‖ → Abwurf

·ab|werten vt [h] (Geld) *to devaluate, to devalue*; *to depreciate* ⟨a. übtr⟩ **·Abwertung** f ~/~en *devaluation*; *depreciation*; → Aufwertung

·abwesend a *absent*; *not present* ‖ *absent* (od *away*) *from home*, ⟨fam⟩ *not in* | (zerstreut) *absent-minded, distracted, abstracted* **~e(r** m) f ~en/~en *absentee* ⟨a. school⟩

·Abwesenheit f ~/ *absence* (in jds ~ *in the a. of a p*) ‖ ⟨jur⟩ *non-attendance, non-appearance* ‖ → Absentismus | ⟨fig⟩ (Geistes≈) *absence of mind, absent-mindedness, abstractedness, distraction* **~s-** **~liste** f *absentee list* **~spfleger** m *curator absentis* L

·abwickelbar a ⟨math⟩ (of a curve) *capable of unfolding* **·Abwickel-** **~haspel** f *wind-off reel* **~spule** f *feed* od *delivery spool* od *reel*; ⟨film⟩ *supply spool*

·ab|wickeln vt [h] **1.** (etw) *to wind* (v *from, off* [*a reel*]); *to reel* od *wind* (*a th*) *off*; *to unroll, to unwind*; *to open out* **2.** ⟨com⟩ *to arrange, to manage, to settle, to wind up, to liquidate* ‖ (Verkehr) *to deal with*; Geschäfte ~ *to transact business* (mit *with*); (Verkehr) *to handle* **3.** **sich ~** *to unwind, to come unwound*; *to unroll, to unreel* | ⟨übtr⟩ *to pass* (od *go*) *off*; *to develop*; sich gut ~ ⟨com⟩ *to go off well, to turn out well*; → abrollen I. A. 3 **·Abwick(e)lung** f ~/~en **1.** *unwinding* **2.** ⟨übtr com⟩ *arrangement, management, settlement*; *transaction, winding up*; *liquidation* ‖ die ~ e–r S *the disposal of a th, the dealing with a th*; schnelle ~ *dispatch*; → reibungslos **3.** ⟨math⟩ (of curves) *evolution* **4.** ⟨fig⟩ *unfolding, development* ⟨a. ins⟩ **5.** des Verkehrs *regulation of the traffic* **~sbehörde** f *Liquidation Department*

·ab|wiegeln vt [h] ⟨liter⟩ (Ggs aufwiegeln) *to appease*; *to calm*

·Abwiege- **~maschine** f *dosing machine* **·ab|wiegen** vt [h] (Ware) *to weigh out* ‖ → abwägen

°**·ab|wimmeln** vt [h] **1.** (S & P) *to ward off* ‖ (jdn) *to keep* (*a p*) *aloof*; *to rid oneself of, to get rid of* (*a p*); *to fling* (*a p*) *off* **2.** ⟨cards⟩ (Karten) *to discard*

·Abwind m ~es/~e ⟨aero⟩ *downward current*

·ab|winden vt [h] (etw) *to wind* (v *from, off* [*a reel*]); *to wind* od *reel* (*a th*) *off*; *to unwind* | sich ~ *to unwind*

·ab|winken vi [h] jdm ~ *to wave a p away*; e–r S ~ *to wave a th aside* (od *away*) ‖ [abs] ~ *to signify disapproval*; *to give a sign of refusal* ‖ ich habe °abgewunken [statt: abgewinkt] *I* (*have*) *declined*

·ab|winkeln vt [h] *to square off*; ⟨sport⟩ *to flex*

·ab|wirtschaften vt/i [h] (Land etc) *to ruin* od *to wreck by mismanagement* | vi *to get ruined by mismanagement* ‖ er hat abgewirtschaftet ⟨fig⟩ *he is done for* od *played out*

·ab|wischen vt [h] **1.** (Oberfläche, Möbel etc) *to wipe* (*a th*) *off* (mit *with*); *to give* (*a th*) *a wipe* ‖ **sich** [dat] das Gesicht, den Mund ~ *to wipe one's face, one's mouth* ‖ (mit e–m Tuch) *to mop*; sich die Stirn ~ *to mop one's forehead* (*with*); (mit e–m Schwamm) *to sponge* **2.** (wegwischen) (etw) *to wipe* (v *from*); den Staub v etw ~ *to dust a th* (: *furniture* etc) ‖ den Schweiß ~ *to wipe off the perspiration* ‖ **sich** [dat] die Tränen ~ *to dry one's tears, to wipe one's tears away*

·Abwischlappen m, **·Abwischtuch** n *duster* ‖ (f Geschirr) *dish-cloth*

·ab|wohnen vt [h] (abnutzen) *to wear out*

·ab|wracken vt [h] (Schiff) *to break up*

·Abwurf m ~(e)s/≈e **1.** = Abwerfen → d.; ⟨aero⟩ airdrop **2.** ⟨com⟩ *yield*; *profit* **3.** ⟨Ger sport⟩ (im Handball) *shot by the goal-keeper* **4.** = ~sendung **~bahn** f ⟨aero⟩ *air-to-ground trajectory* **~behälter** m ⟨aero⟩ *slip* od *drop* od *jettisonable tank*; (mit Fallschirm) *paracrate*; *parachute container* **~meldung** f ⟨aero⟩ *dropped message* **~platz** m (Versorgung) ⟨aero⟩ *dropping station* **~raketengeschoß** n *rocket projectile* **~rechengerät** n *bombing calculator* **~sendung** f ⟨aero⟩ *dropped mail-bag* **~trommel** f ⟨tech⟩ *delivery cage* **~verfahren** n *jettison procedure* **~vorrichtung** f ⟨mar⟩ *chute* (*for depth charges*)

·ab|würgen vt [h] *to strangle, to throttle*; ⟨übtr⟩ *to ruin*; ⟨mot, etc fam⟩ *to kill*; ⟨aero⟩ *to stall*

ab·yssisch a *abyssal* (*more than 300 fathoms below sea surface*) ‖ *abysmal* (⟨bes fig⟩ *a.mal ignorance*)

·abzahlbar a in Raten ~ *payable by instalments*

·Abzähl- **~vers** m (Spiel) *counting-out rhyme*

·abzählbar a ⟨math⟩ *enumerable* (*aggregate*)

·ab|zahlen vt [h] (Schuld, Summe) *to pay off, to clear off, to discharge* ‖ in Raten ~ *to pay by the instalment system*; (etw) in Raten *or* nach u nach ~ *to pay* (*a th*) *by instalments* ‖ → Abschlag

·ab|zählen vt [h] *to count*; *to tell* od *number off*; zu dreien ~ *to tell* od *count off by threes*; ⟨mil⟩ (Abschuß etc) *to count down*; (P) ~! *count off*!; → nachzählen ‖ (einzelne Dinge) an den Fingern ~ *to tick off on one's fingers*; die Namen an den F. ~ *to check the names on one's fingers*; ⟨fig⟩ das können Sie sich an den Fingern ~ *that is clear as daylight* | (abziehen) *to deduct*

·Abzahlung f ~/~en **1.** (Tilgung) *paying off, payment in full, discharge*; *liquidation* **2.** **a.** (Abschlagszahlung) *payment on account* **b.** (Teilzahlung) *part-payment, instalment*; Kauf auf ~ *hire-purchase*; auf ~ kaufen *to purchase on the instalment plan* **~sgeschäft** n **1.** [konkr] *tally-shop, shop on the instalment system* **2.** [abstr] = Abzahlungskauf **~skauf** m *hire-purchase* ‖ = Abzahlungssystem **~ssystem** n *instalment system* od *plan*; *hire-purchase system*; **tally-system* **~svertrag** m *hire-purchase agreement* **~swesen** n *instalment system*

·Abzählung f ~/~en *counting off* (od *over*) ‖ → Aufzählung

·ab|zapfen vt [h] **1.** (Flüssigkeit, Bier etc) *to tap, to draw* (*off*); *to broach* ‖ jdm Blut ~ *to bleed a p* ‖ (Eiter etc) *to drain* **2.** (Gefäß, Faß) *to tap, to broach*; *to draw the liquid from* (*a cask*) **3.** ⟨fig⟩ jdm etw (Geld etc) ~ *to tap a p for a th*; *to fleece a p of a th*; e–m Lande die Schätze ~ *to drain a country of its treasures* **·Abzapfung** f ~/~en *tapping* ‖ *bleeding*

·ab|zäumen vt [h] *to unbridle* ‖ **·Abzäumung** f ~/~en *unbridling*

·ab|zäunen vt [h] *to fence in* od *off*; *to mark off by a hedge* ‖ **·Abzäunung** f ~/~en *fencing* | (Zaun) *fence, fencing*; *enclosure*

·ab|zehren vt/i [h] **1.** vt (jdn) *to waste, to emaciate* | **sich ~** *to consume* od *pine away* (vor *with*) **2.** vi [s] *to waste away, to fall off* ‖ **·abzehrend** a *consumptive, wasting* (*disease*) ‖ **·Abzehrung** f ~/~en **1.** *wasting*; *emaciation, tabes*; *atrophy* **2.** *consumption*; ⟨med⟩ (*pulmonary*) *phthisis* [Gr]

·Abzeichen n ~s/~ **1.** (Merkmal) *mark, sign* **2.** (Unterscheidungszeichen) mst ⟨mil⟩ *badge*; *distinguishing mark* (od *badge*); → Armbinde, Streifen, Tressenwinkel ‖ Dienstgrad~ *distinguishing mark* (*of a corporal*) ‖ Rang~ *badge of rank* | ⟨Ger mil, etc⟩ Hoheits~, National~ *nationality mark*; Uniform~ *uniform badge* ‖ Partei~ *party badge* ‖ ⟨hist⟩ Reichssport~ *Reich Sport Badge* **3.** *decoration*, ~ [pl] *insignia* L [pl] ‖ Verwundeten~ ⟨Ger⟩ *war-wounded decoration* (engl = *the gold stripe*; ⟨Am⟩ *the Purple Heart*) **4.** (T) *white patch* (*on skin* etc)

·ab|zeichnen vt [h] **1.** *to sketch, to draw*; *to delineate* ‖ (v e–r Vorlage) *to copy* ‖ (Schriftstück mit Namenzeichen) *to initial* **2.** (abgrenzen) *to mark off*; (mit Kreide) *to chalk* (*off*) **3.** **sich ~** (S) *to limn o.s.* (auf e–m Hintergrund *against a background*); → sich abheben ‖ ⟨übtr⟩ *to loom* (*up*), *impend*; *to be imminent, to be indications* (*of* od *that*) ‖ (*new developments*) *are noticeable, can be observed* ‖ es zeichnet sich (klar) ab, daß (*all*) *indications are that* ..; e–e Verstimmung über die Wirtschaftslage zeichnet sich ab *there is economic discontent stirring* **Abzeichnung** f ~/~en *sketch, drawing, delineation* ‖ *copy* ‖ *contour*; *outlines* [pl]

·Abzieh- ~apparat m (f Wein etc) *racker* ‖ ⟨typ⟩ *proof-press* ‖ *proof-roller* **~bild** n *decal-(comania)* ⟨abbr fam⟩; *transfer-picture*; ⟨typ⟩ *metachromatype, –chromot–* **~bilderdruck** m ⟨typ⟩ [abstr] *transfer-printing* **~bogen** m ⟨typ⟩ *tympan-sheet* **~bürste** f ⟨typ⟩ *beating brush, letter-brush* **~feile** f *smoothing-file* **~muskel** m ⟨anat⟩ *abductor* **~papier** n *proof-paper, transfer type* (*stripping*) *paper* **~presse** f *proof-press* **~riemen** m *razor-strop* **~stein** m (Wetzstein) *sharpening stone* **~zahl** f *subtrahend*

·abziehbar a *deductible*

·ab|ziehen vt/i **I.** vt [h] **A.** ⟨eig⟩ **1.** *to pull* (od *take*) *off*; (die Handschuhe) *to draw* (od *pull, strip*) *off*; den Hut ~ *to pull* (od *take*) *off one's hat* (vor jdm *to a p*); den Ring vom Finger ~ *to pull* od *slip the ring off* od *from one's finger* ‖ den Schlüssel ~ *to take out* (od *to remove*) *the key* **2.** e–m Tier das Fell ~ *to strip the hide from an animal*; *to skin* od *flay an animal* **3.** ein Bett ~ *to strip a bed* | (Bohnen) *to string* **4.** v e–m Instrument die Saiten ~ *to unstring an instrument* **B.** ⟨übtr⟩ **1.** jds Aufmerksamkeit, Sinn etc ~ *to draw* (od *draw off*; *to divert*; *to distract*) *a p's attention, mind* (v etw) *from a th* ‖ s–e Hand v jdm ~ *to withdraw one's support from a p* | jdn ~ v *to draw* (od *to divert*) *a p* (od *a p's mind*) *from* (*his work*); *to draw a p away from* **2.** (Flüssigkeit) *to draw* (*off*), (Gift) *to milk out* ‖ (Wein v der Hefe) *to rack off* ‖ (auf Flaschen) *to bottle* | (destillieren) *to distil* | Suppe mit e–m Ei ~ *to beat up soup with an egg* **3.** (Rasiermesser) *to hone, strop, strap*; (Messer) *to grind, sharpen, stone* **4.** (losschießen) (Waffe) *to discharge* **C.** **1.** ⟨math⟩ *to subtract* (*four from eight*); → bleiben, wenig **2.** ⟨com⟩ (Betrag) *to deduct*; e–e Summe vom Preise ~ *to take a sum off the price*; jdm e–e Summe vom Lohne ~ *to take* od *knock off a sum from a p's wages* **3.** ⟨philos⟩ *to abstract* **D.** ⟨tech, typ, print⟩ (Druckbogen etc) *to pull*; *to strike off*; → abklatschen; (Matrize) *to run off*; ein Blatt ~ *to pull a page* ‖ *to transfer* (*a painting*) (auf *to*) ‖ überschüssige Farbe von der Walze ~ *to sheet the roller* ‖ ⟨phot⟩ *to print* **II.** vi **1.** (P) *to depart, to go away*; ⟨fam⟩ *to be off, to toddle off, to trot off* ‖ ⟨mil⟩ *to march off*; v der Wache ~ *to come off guard* | mit langer Nase ~ *to meet with a rebuff, to come away with a flea in one's ear*; mit leeren Händen ~, unverrichteter S ~ *to come away* (od *go off*) *disappointed*; *to be balked of one's purpose*; mit Schimpf u Schande ~ *to leave with* od *in disgrace* **2.** (of smoke etc) *to escape*; *to pass* (durch *through*) **·Abziehen** n ~s/ **1.** *pulling-off, taking-off* (v *from*) ‖ *skinning* **2.** ⟨übtr⟩ *diversion* ‖ *drawing*(*-off*) ‖ *stropping*; *grinding* | ⟨math⟩ *subtraction* (v *from*) ‖ ⟨com⟩ *deduction* ‖ ⟨philos⟩ *abstraction* **3.** ⟨typ⟩ *pulling* **4.** *departure* | (of smoke) *escape* ‖ → Abzug

·Abzieher m ⟨print⟩ *puller* ‖ = Abziehmuskel

·ab|zielen vi [h] ⟨übtr⟩ auf etw ~ *to aim* od *drive at a th, to tend to a th*; *to plot a th, to have a th in view*; *to be out for a th*; ⟨Am⟩ *to squint at a th* ‖ darauf ~ z tun *to aim at doing* (⟨Am⟩ *to a. to do*); *to be out to do* | ~ auf jdn; es war auf dich abgezielt *it was meant* od *intended for you, it was directed against you*

·ab|zirkeln vt [h] *to measure* (*a th*) *with the compasses* ‖ ⟨fig⟩ etw (Betragen etc) ~ *to be scrupulous, exact, subtle in* (od *about*) *a th*; → abwägen 2 ‖ **·Abzirk(e)lung** f ~/~en *measurement with the compasses*; *exact measurement* ‖ ⟨fig⟩ *formality, exactitude*

·Abzug m ~(e)s/~e **I.** (zu abziehen vt) **1.** (Geld~) *deduction*; *reduction*; *discount, allowance*; *rebate*; → Rabatt; Diskont ‖ ~ vom Lohn, Lohn~ *deduction from the wages, stoppage* ‖ Zins~ *discount* ‖ ~ vom Gewicht *tare* | ohne ~ *clear*; nach ~ der Kosten *all charges* od *expenses deducted*; nach ~ der Schulden *clear after debts paid* ‖ etw in ~ bringen *to deduct a th* **2.** ⟨typ⟩ *pull, proof, proof-sheet*, (korrigiert) *clean proof*; Fahnen~ *slip, galley-proof, slip-proof* ‖ ⟨engr etc⟩ *impression, copy*; ~ vor der Schrift *proof before letters* | ⟨phot⟩ *print, copy*; e–n ~ m v *to print .. off* **3.** (Gewehr~) *trigger* **4.** ⟨spin⟩ *the total of full spools* **II.** (zu abziehen vi) **1.** *departure*; *withdrawal* ‖ *migration*; → Abwanderung ‖ ⟨mil⟩ *retreat*; zum ~ blasen *to sound the retreat* **2.** (of smoke etc) *escape*; (of water etc) *outlet, issue*; *outflow*; *drain* ‖ [konkr] *conduit, channel*; *funnel*; → ~sgraben etc., Abziehen **·abzüglich** adv *less*, ~ der Spesen *less charges, charges deducted* **·Abzugpapier** n *duplicating paper* ‖ ⟨phot⟩ *printing-out paper* (abbr *P.O.P.*) **~rohr** n → Abzugsrohr

·Abzugs- ~bogen m ⟨typ⟩ *proof-sheet* **~bügel** m (Gewehr~) *trigger-guard*; → Abzug I. 3.

~̽**fähig** a *deductible* (⟨tax⟩ *expenses*) (*expenses* [*for tax purposes*]) **~film** m *stripping film* **~graben** m *drain* **~kanal** m *sewer* **~öffnung** f ⟨tech⟩ *discharge opening* **~papier** n → Abzugpapier **~rohr** n *drain*(*-pipe*), *exhaust* od *vent pipe*, *waste-pipe*, (Haus) mit ~en versehen *to drain*; (Boden) mit ~en versehen *to sewage* **~röhre** f = ~rohr **~schnur** f, **~vorrichtung** (am Schloß e–r Feuerwaffe) f *sere, sear*, ⟨artill⟩ *trigger mechanism*

·**ab**|**zupfen** vt [h] *to pluck, pick*

°·**ab**|**zwacken** vt [h] jdm etw ~ *to squeeze a th from* (od *out of*) *a p*; *to extort* od *extract a th from a p* | *to stint a p of a th*; jdm etw am Lohne (etc) ~ *to cut down a p's wages* etc ‖ **sich** [dat] etw am Munde ~ → absparen

·**Abzweig- ~brett** n ⟨theat-el⟩ *special effects board*, ⟨Am⟩ *auxiliary switchboard* **~dose** f ⟨el⟩ *connector-box, junction box* **~leitung** f ⟨el⟩ *branch* (*line* od *circuit*) **~schalter** m *tapping switch* **~stecker** m *distribution plug* **~stelle** f *branch point* ⟨a. el⟩

·**ab**|**zweigen** vt/i **1.** vt [h] *to detach, to separate*; *to branch off* | **sich ~** = **2.** vi [s] *to branch off*; *to fork, to bifurcate* ‖ ~ von (of a street) *to be a turning off* (*Oxford Street*)

·**Abzweigung** f ~/~en **1.** [abstr] *detachment, separation*; *bifurcation* **2.** [konkr] (Zweig) *branch, offshoot*; *turning* (of a street); ⟨Am⟩ *branching off* (*how far from here is the b. o.*?; *are there any b.s o.* [pl]?); *bifurcation* (of a river); ⟨rail⟩ *branch line* | ⟨übtr⟩ *offshoot*; ~en *offshoots, ramifications* (of a school)

·**ab**|**zwicken** vt [h] *to nip* od *pinch off*

·**ab**|**zwingen** vt [h] jdm etw ~ *to force a th* (: *facts*) *out of a p*; *to wrest* od *wring a th* (: *an answer, promise*, etc) *from a p*; *to extort a th* (: *money, a confession*) *from a p*

Acajou [aka'ʒu:] m = **~baum** m ⟨bot⟩ *cashew tree* **~holz** n *mahogany* **~nuß** f *acajou nut* **~öl** n *cashew-nut oil*

A-capp·ella-Musik f *vocal music*

ach intj **1.** ~! *ah!, o!, oh!, alas!* | ~ ja! ~ G·ott! (*o*) *dear!, my!, o my!, my eye!* ‖ (stärker) *dear, dear!* (*o*) *dear me! good heavens!* | ~ daß er hier wäre! ~ wäre er doch hier! *Oh that he were here!, would* (od *I wish*) *he were here!* ‖ ~ daß ich ein Pferd hätte! *Oh for a horse!* | ~ u weh schreien *to cry aloud* od *pitifully* | ~ welche Überraschung! *Oh, what a surprise!* ‖ ~ wie schön *oh, how beautiful!* **2.** [abgeblaßt] ~ j·a! *o yes! o indeed! yes indeed!*; ~ n·ein! *o no!* ‖ ~ g·ar!, ~ w·as!, ~ w·o! *nonsense! certainly not! not a bit* (*of it*)!; ⟨Am fam⟩ *oh nuts!* ‖ ~ so! *Oh! I see!* | ~ Sie sind es! *oh, it is you!* ‖ ~, was Sie sagen! *Oh, is that so?, you don't say so!* | ~, da fällt mir ein (..) *by the way it just occurs to me* (*that* ...) ‖ ~ sagen Sie mal *please tell me*

Ach n ~s/ *lament, lamentation* (kein ~ *no l.*); *wail, wailing* ‖ das ewige ~ u Weh (od Weh u ~) *the endless grief* od *sorrow* ‖ mit ~ u Krach *only with the greatest difficulty*; *with a close* od *narrow shave*; *by the skin of one's teeth*

Ach f ~/~e = Aa

Ach·äer m ~s/~ ⟨ant⟩ *Achæan*; die ~ *the Achæans, Achæi* (L) pl **ach·äisch** a *Achæan*

† **Ach·aia** (antike Gr. Landschaft)

Ach·at m ~(e)s/~e **1.** ⟨minr⟩ *agate* **2.** [in comp] *agate* ~̽**farben** *agate-coloured*

·**Ache** f ~/~n = Aa

·**Achel** f ~/~n ⟨bot⟩ (of flax) *awn*

°·**acheln** vi [h] (Gaunerspr.) *to eat*

·**Achensee** m (Alpensee in Nordtirol)

·**Acheron** m ~s ⟨ant⟩ *Acheron* †

Ach·ill m ~(e)s = **Ach·illes** m ~/ *Achilles* **~ferse** f ⟨fig⟩ *Achilles heel* (*weak point* od *side, soft spot* [*of a p*]) **~sehne** f ⟨anat⟩ *Achilles tendon*

Achol·ie f ⟨med⟩ *acholia*

Achromas·ie f ⟨phys⟩ *achromasia* **achrom·a·tisch** a ⟨phys⟩ *achromatic* ‖ ~ m *to achromatize*

·**Achs-** (→ Achse) **~abstand** m *wheel base* (weit *long*, eng *short*); *centre distance* **~antrieb** m *final drive* ‖ ~slager n ⟨mot⟩ federndes ~ *elastic axle box* ‖ ~smotor m *direct-drive engine* **~drehung** f *rotation* **~druck** m *axle weight* **~eisen** n *axle-tree* **~kilom·eter** n *amount of kilometres in a given time per car* **~lager** n *axle-bearing* **~nagel** m *linchpin* ~̽**recht** a *axial* **~schenkel** m ⟨mot⟩ *steering knuckle*; *spindle*; *stub axle* **~schere** f *shaft-bar*; *futchel*(*l*) **~stand** m *wheel-base* **~strebe** f *axle strut* **~verwindung** f *axle torque*

·**Achse** f ~/~n **1.** (Mittellinie) ⟨arch⟩ *axis* ‖ (gedachte) ⟨geom, cryst etc⟩ *axis* (*of a cone*, etc.); durchgehende *passing axis* **2.** (Drehlinie) *axis*; die Erde dreht sich um ihre eigene ~ *the earth rotates about its own axis* | ⟨pol⟩ die ~ Berlin-Rom *the Berlin-Rome axis*; die ~nmächte [pl] *the Axis Powers* pl **3.** ⟨math⟩ (Gerade) Koordinaten~̽ *the axes of coordinates*; die waagerechte ~ im Koordinatensystem *absciss*(*e*), *abscissa* **4.** (Stange etc) (Rad-) *axle-tree*; *axle* ‖ **auf** (der) ~ *on the track* od *road*; °(= unterwegs) ⟨fam⟩ *in the pipe-line*, (Zirkus) *on the scent*; auf e–r ~ *without change of wag*(*g*)*on* **per ~** *by wag*(*g*)*on*, per ~ (Ggs per Schiff) befördern *to convey by road* (od *by land*[*-carriage*]) ‖ Fahrrad~̽ *spindle* | ⟨mech⟩ *arbor, shaft* **5.** ⟨bot⟩ *central stem* (*of a plant*)

·**Achsel** f ~/~n *shoulder* → Schulter | die ~n (*or* mit den ~n) zucken *to shrug one's shoulders*; *to give a shrug* ‖ etw auf die leichte ~ nehmen ⟨fig⟩ *to make light of a th, to treat a th with levity*, auf die leichte ~ nehmend *easy-going* ‖ auf beiden ~n tragen ⟨fig⟩ *to serve two masters, to stand* od *sit on the fence*, → Achselträger ‖ etw auf s–e ~ nehmen ⟨fig⟩ *to take the responsibility for a th* ‖ jdn über die ~ ansehen ⟨fig⟩ *to look down upon a p*; *to give a p the cold shoulder* ‖ gleichgültig mit den ~n zucken *to shrug an indifferent shoulder*

·**Achsel-** [in comp] *shoulder*; ⟨anat⟩ *axillary* **~band** n ⟨mil⟩ *aiguillette* [Fr] **~drüse** f ⟨anat⟩ *axillary gland* **~grube, ~höhle** f *arm-pit* **~klappe** f ⟨mil⟩ (f Unteroffiziere) *shoulder-strap* **~schnur, ~schnüre** f ⟨mil⟩ *aiguillette* [Fr]; *lanyard* **~stück** n ⟨mil⟩ (f Offiziere) *shoulder-piece, shoulder-strap* ‖ ⟨mar⟩ *epaulette* [Fr] **~träger** m ⟨fig⟩ *ambidexter, turncoat* (*opportunist, time-server*); ⟨pol⟩ *trimmer*; ⟨Am⟩ *pussyfooter* **~träger·ei** f ⟨fig⟩ *opportunism, time-serving*; *hypocrisy, duplicity* ~̽**trägerisch** a *time-serving* **~tuch** n (des Meßpriesters) R. C. *amice* **~zucken** n *shrug*

·**Achsen-** (→ Achs-) **~antrieb** m *final drive* ~̽**förmig** a *axial* **~mächte** f/pl ⟨pol⟩ *Axis Powers* **~verschiebung** f ⟨arch⟩ *deflection* **~winkel** m *optic angle*

Acht[1] f nur in best. Verbindungen (mst acht) **a.** (Gesundheit etc) **in** ~̽ nehmen *to be careful of, to take care of*; *to look after* (*a th*); etw nicht in ~̽ nehmen *to neglect* od *ignore a th* | **sich in** ~̽ nehmen *to take care*; *to have a care*; [nur imp u inf] *to beware* (vor *of*; daß .. nicht *lest* [od *that .. not*]); *to take care* (nicht z tun *not to do*); nimm dich in ~̽! *take care! look out! be careful* od *cautious!* ⟨sl⟩ *mind your eye!* nimm dich vor den Stufen, dem Hunde in ~̽ *mind the steps, mind* (od *beware of*) *the dog* ‖ sich sehr in ~̽ nehmen *to mind one's P's and Q's*; → Hut | **außer** ~̽ l *to overlook*; *to neglect, to ignore, to disregard*; *to leave out of account* | → achtgeben, achthaben

Acht[2] f ~/ **1.** ⟨hist⟩ *outlawry, proscription* ‖ ⟨ec⟩ *ban, excommunication* ‖ ⟨ant⟩ *ostracism* | in ~ *under the ban* ‖ jdn in die ~ erklären, in ~ u Bann tun, die ~ über jdn aussprechen *to lay*

a p under the ban, to outlaw, to proscribe a p; ⟨cc⟩ *to excommunicate a p* || in die ~ verfallen *to become an outlaw* **2.** ⟨übtr⟩ *ban*; (*social, political*) *ostracism*, in ~ u Bann stehen *to suffer ostracism* || → Verruf

acht ⟨fam a. ~e⟩ **1.** a *eight* [Kleinschreibung: es, wir sind (unser) ~ *we are eight*; v achten; wir gehen zu ~; es ist (schlägt) ~ *it is eight o'clock*]; [Großschreibung: → 2.] ~unddreißig *thirty-eight*, **eight and thirty* || Vers *or* Wort v ~ Silben *octosyllable*; Stanze v ~ zehnsilbigen Versen *ottava rima* || ~ mal zwei (8×2) ist [nicht sind!] 16 *eight times two is 16* | **~ Tage** *a week* || **auf** ~ Tage *for a week* | **binnen** *or* **in** ~ Tagen *within a week* || Montag in ~ T. *Monday week* || morgen in ~ Tagen *to-morrow week* | **nach** ~ Tagen *a week afterwards* | **über** ~ Tage *a week hence, this day* (od *to-day*) *week*, ⟨Am⟩ *a week from to-day* | **vor** ~ Tagen *a week ago*; heute vor ~ Tagen *to-day week* | mit ~en **fahren** *to drive a carriage and eight* || wir **sind zu** ~(en) *we'll be eight* **2.** ~̂ f, e–e ~ *a figure of eight*; mit der (Linie) ~̂ fahren *to take the eight* **3.** [in comp] *eight* ..

·Acht- **~eck** n ⟨geom⟩ *octagon* **~̂eckig** a *octagonal* **~̂einhalb** a *eight and a half* (→ achte) **~ender** m *a stag with eight antlers*, → Achter 2. **~̂fach, ~̂fältig** a *eightfold, octuple*; ~ multiplizieren *to octuple* **~flach** n, **~flächner** m ⟨math⟩ *octahedron* **~füßer** m ⟨zoo⟩ *octopod* **~hundertjahrfeier** f *octocentenary* **~̂jährig** a *eight years old*; ein ~es Kind *an eight-year old child*; ein ~jähriger *an eight-year-old* ([pl] ... *olds*) **~̂mal** adv *eight times* **~̂malig** a (*done*) *for the eighth time* **~m·onatskind** n *eight months' child* **~̂seitig** a ⟨math⟩ *octagonal* **~̂silbig** a ⟨pros⟩ *octosyllable* [attr]; ~er Vers *octosyllable* (in franz. Romanzen, *Chaucer's Romaunt of the Rose*) **~spänner** m *coach* od *carriage and eight* **~̂spännig** a *eight-horse* (*coach*); ~ fahren *to drive eight in hand* **~st·undentag** m *eight hours' day* **~̂stündig** a *lasting eight hours*; der ~e Arbeitstag *the eight-hours' day* **~̂tägig** a *eight-day*; *lasting a week, weekly*; ~e Feier f ⟨ec⟩ *octave* **~zehn** → bes Artikel **~̂zeilig** a *of eight lines*; *eight-line* ..; ~e Strophe f *octave* (⟨bes⟩ *ottava rima* It) **~zylindermotor** m *eight-cylinder-engine*

·achtbar a *respectable* (*man*), *reputable* (*character*) || e–e ~e P *a respectable*; die ~en Leute *the respectables* [pl] | **~̂keit** f *respectability*

·achte a **1.** ⟨fam⟩ f. acht **2.** der, die, das ~ ... *the eight*; [Kleinschreibung: der ~ (der Reihe nach) Großschreibung der ~̂ (der Leistung nach; der ~̂ des Monats); Heinrich der ~̂ *or* VIII. *Henry VIII*]; am ~n Juli (*on*) *the eighth of July, on July the eighth*, (*on*) *July 8th* || ~r Tag nach e–m Feste ⟨ec⟩ *octave* || ~halb *seven and a half*

·Achtel n (⟨Sw⟩ m) ~s/~ *the eighth part, the eighth*; ein ~ v *an eighth of* | ~̂ [a] ein ~̂ Pfund *an eighth of a pound* **~kreis** m *octant* **~meile** f ⟨engl⟩ → Meile **~note** f ⟨mus⟩ *quaver* **~pause** f ⟨mus⟩ *quaver rest* **~schlag** m ⟨math⟩ *the half of a right angle* **~takt** m ⟨mus⟩ *quaver time*

·achten vt/i [h] **I.** vt **1.** (erachten) *to deem, esteem, judge, think* || es f richtig ~ *to deem it right, to think fit* od *proper* (z tun *to do*); es f s–e Pflicht ~ *to deem* od *think it* (*to be*) *one's duty* es f e–e Schande ~ *to consider it* (*to be*) *a disgrace* **2.** (beachten) die Gesetze (etc) *to observe*; (Rechte) *to respect* || etw gering (*or* nicht) ~ *to think lightly of a th*; (Mahnung) nicht ~ *to set at nought, to disregard* || sein Leben nicht ~ *to be ready to risk* od *sacrifice one's life* | (berücksichtigen) (jds Gefühle etc) *to consider*; *to respect*; *to pay regard to* (*a th*); nicht ~ *to have no regard for* od *to a th* **3.** (schätzen) (jdn) *to esteem*; *to hold* (*a p*) *in esteem*; *to respect*; jdn hoch~ *to hold a p in high esteem* (od *regard*); bei jdm hoch geachtet sein *to stand high in the estimation* od *regard of a p*; allgemein hoch geachtet w *to be held high in general esteem* **II.** vi **~ auf** *to attend to*; *to pay attention to*; *to listen to* (*a p* od *a th*) (: *to a p's words*) || achte ja auf m–e Worte *mark* od *mind my words* | *to take care of, to have an eye to, to attend to, to look after a p* od *a th* (: *one's own business, the children*); er achtet auf alles *he has his eyes about him* || darauf ~ daß .. *to see to it that* ...; sorgsam ~ auf *to be careful of*; wohl *or* sehr ~ auf *to attach a great importance to* (*the price*) || nicht ~ auf *to be careless of*; *to be unmindful* od *oblivious of*

·ächten vt [h] *to proscribe, outlaw* | ⟨übtr⟩ *to boycott*; *to ostracize* (aus der Gesellschaft *from society*); *to send a p to Coventry*

·achtens adv *eightly, in the eighth place*

·achtenswert, -würdig a *estimable, respectable*; *worthy of esteem*

·achter ⟨mar⟩ **1.** *⟨außer mar⟩ [prep] *after, behind* || ⟨mar⟩ *abaft* **2.** [adv] ⟨mar⟩ (hinten im Schiff) *aft, abaft*; *astern* || nach ~ zu *abaft, aft, astern*

·Achter m ~s/~ **1.** (Boot mit 8 Riemen) *eight-oar*; (Boot f 8 Ruderer) *eight* (*the Oxford eight*); → Ruderwettkampf **2.** ⟨hunt⟩ *eight-pointer*; ungerader ~ *seven-pointer*, → Achtender

·achteraus adv *abaft, aft, astern* **·Achterdeck** n ⟨mar⟩ *quarter-deck* **·Achterkante** f ⟨mar⟩ *trailing edge* **·achterlastig** a ⟨mar⟩ (*down*) *by the stern*; ⟨aero⟩ *tail-heavy* **·achterlei** a *of eight different kinds* od *sorts*

·Achter- **~mannschaft** f *eight* **~rennen** n ⟨Oxf & Cambr⟩ das ~ *the Eights* pl **~riemen** m (Boot mit 8 Riemen) *eight-oar*

·achtern adv ⟨mar⟩ = achter 2.

·Achter- **~schiff** n *stern* **~sitz** m, ~e pl *stern-sheets* pl **~steven** m ⟨mar⟩ *stern-post*

·acht|geben, ·acht|haben vi [h] **1.** *to heed* (: *he did not heed*), *to pay attention*; *to watch* || gib (*or* hab) acht *take care, look out*; *be careful* (*to do*); ⟨Am⟩ *take care of yourself* || gib (hab) acht: Auto, Stufe! *mind the car, the step!* | gib (hab) acht, daß .. (nicht) *take care that* .. (*not*); *look* (od *see*) *to it that* .. (*not*); .. daß .. nicht *beware lest* (od *that* .. *not*) **2. ~ auf a.** *to attend* od *look to, to pay attention to* || *to watch* (*a development*) || gib (hab) acht auf meine Worte *mark my words*; .. auf meine Warnung *heed my warning* **b.** (sich kümmern um) *to attend to, to take care of, to look after* (*a th, a p*); gib (hab) acht auf die Kinder *look after the children*

·achtlos **1.** a *heedless, negligent, unmindful, careless* (gegen, gegenüber etw *of a th*); *inattentive* (*to a th*) **2.** adv ~ vorübergehen an etw *to ignore, to disregard a th* **·Achtlosigkeit** f ~/~en *carelessness, negligence, unmindfulness, disregard* (gegenüber e–r S *of a th*); *inattention*

·achtsam a *heedful, careful, mindful* (auf *of*); *attentive* (auf *to*) **~̂keit** f ~/~en *carefulness, heedfulness, attentiveness, attention*

·achtundvierziger **1.** a ⟨typ⟩ in ~ Format *in 48mo* **2.** ~̂ m ⟨Ger⟩ *adherent of the 1848 German revolution*

·Achtung f ~/ **1.** (Achtgeben) *attention* || (Rücksicht) *regard* | ~! *take care! look out!*; ~, Stufen! *mind the steps* || ⟨mil⟩ *attention!* ⟨fam⟩ *'shun* || ~! *caution!* || ⟨a–n⟩ *stand by!* | → achtgeben auf **2.** (Hoch~̂) *deference, esteem, respect, regard* (**vor** *for*) || die ~ vor sich selbst *self-esteem* **A. an** ~ verlieren, verloren h *to be deprecated*; **aus** ~ vor *or* gegen *out of respect* od *regard for, in deference to*; **bei** aller ~ **vor** *with all due deference to* || alle ~ vor Ihrem Urteil! *I compliment you on your judgement!* || v ~ vor dem Gesetz erfüllt *law-abiding* **B.** jdm s–e ~ **bezeigen** (erweisen) *to pay respect to a p* ‖ jdm ~ einflößen *to inspire a p with respect* ‖ sich allgemeiner ~ erfreuen *to be held in general esteem*; sich allgemeine ~ erwerben *to gain universal esteem*; sich jds ~ erwerben *to win a p's estimation* ‖ ~ gebieten *to command respect* ‖ (gr) ~ **genießen** *to be highly esteemed* od *respected*; ... bei jdm *to enjoy the esteem* od *estimation of a p*; jds ~ g. *to stand high in a p's esteem* ‖ keine gr ~ genießen *to enjoy but little esteem*; (S) *to be at a discount* ‖ vor jdm die größte ~ **h** *or* **hegen** *to entertain* od *have a high regard for a p, to hold a p in the highest esteem* od *regard* ‖ in hoher ~ **stehen** *to be highly esteemed; to be (held) in high respect* od *esteem* (unter *amongst*); ... bei jdm *to stand high in the estimation* (od *regard*) *of a p* ‖ in jds ~ steigen *to rise in the estimation of a p* ‖ sich ~ z verschaffen wissen *to make o.s. respected*

·Ächtung f ~/~en *proscription, outlawry* ‖ ⟨übtr⟩ *ostracizing*; *ostracism, ban* (jds *on a p*)

·achtunggebietend n *commanding* (*position*; *power of ..*); *imposing*

·Achtungs- ~**bezeigung** f *mark of respect* (od *esteem*); *tribute* (f *to*) ~**erfolg** m *moral success*; ⟨Lit⟩ *succès d' estime* (Fr) ≃**los** a (*a p*) *without respect* ≃**voll** 1. a *respectful* 2. adv *respectfully*

·achtzehn a *eighteen*; ⟨Ger⟩ ~ Uhr *six o'clock p. m.*; ⟨mil & Am⟩ *eighten hours* ‖ ⟨typ⟩ in ~er Format *in 18mo* (= *eighteenmo* aus L *octodecimo*) ~**jährig** a *eighteen years old*; ein ≃er *an eighteen--year-old* [pl *--olds*]

·achtzehnte a (ein ~r) *eighteenth* **·Achtzehntel** n *eighteenth*

·achtzig 1. a *eighty*; **fourscore* ‖ zweiund~ *eighty-two*, **two and eighty* ‖ °er ist auf ~ (sc. km/h ⟨mot⟩) ⟨fam⟩ *his irritation has reached explosion point* 2. ≃ f *eighty* ‖ in den ≃ern *in the eighties* ‖ er ist Mitte ~ *or* Mitte der ≃er *he is half-way between eighty and ninety*

·Achtziger 1. m ~s/~; ein ~ *an octogenarian, a man of eighty* od *in the eighties* | die ~ (*or* ~jahre) [pl] *the eighties* [pl] (: *to be in the e.*); ein Mann in den ~n (~jahren) *a man on the wrong side of 80*; .. hoch in den ~n .. *on the right side of ninety* 2. ≃ a. die ~ Jahre des 19. Jhs. *the eighties* [pl] *of the 19th century*

·achtzigjährig a *octogenarian*; *eighty years old, eighty-year old* (*p*) ≃**e(r** m) f *octogenarian*

·Achtzigste a (ein ~r) *eightieth* ‖ **·Achtzigstel** n ~s/~ *the eightieth*

Achyl·ie f ⟨med⟩ (Fehlen e–s Verdauungssaftes) *achylia*

·ächzen vi [h] *to groan* (unter *under*; vor *with*); *to puff* ‖ ⟨übtr⟩ (Räder) *to groan, creak*

·Acker m ~s/≃ 1. *soil, arable land*; *field, ground, land* ‖ fetter ~ *rich soil* ‖ den ~ bestellen *to cultivate* od *till the land* od *ground* ‖ ≃ pl *ploughlands, arable lands, fields* ‖ ⟨fig⟩ das ist nicht auf s–m eigenen ~ gewachsen *that is not his own product* 2. (Feldmaß, 22–65 Ar) *acre* 3. [in comp] *agricultural, land .., farm ..* ‖ ~**bau** m *agriculture*; *farming, husbandry* ‖ *tillage, cultivation of the land* ~**bauausstellung** f *agricultural show* ~**bauer** m *tiller* (*of the soil*), *husbandman* ~**baugesellschaft** f *agricultural society* ~**baukunde,** ~**baulehre** f *agronomy*; Student der ~ (stud. agr.) *agronomist* ~**bauminister** m ⟨engl⟩ *Minister of Agriculture* ~**bauschule** f *agricultural school* (od *college*) ≃**bautreibend** a *agricultural* ~**bestellung** f *tillage*; *cultivation of the land* ~**boden** m *arable soil, farm land* ‖ ~art [f] *agrotype* ~**bürger** m *farming townsman* ~**distel** f ⟨bot⟩ *creeping thistle* ~**erde** f ⟨agr⟩ *upper* (od *surface*) *soil*; *mould* ~**eule** ⟨ent⟩ *winter-moth* ~**feld** n *arable field* ~**frucht** f *fruit of the soil* ~**furche** f *furrow* ~**gaul** m *plough-horse, farm-horse* ~**gerät** n *agricultural implement(s* [pl]); *farming utensil(s* [pl]) ~**gesetz** n *agrarian law* ~**kamille** f ⟨bot⟩ *corn-camomile* ~**knecht** m *farmer's man, ploughman, ploughboy* ~**krume** f ⟨agr⟩ *topsoil* ~**kult** m *cult of the soil* ~**kultur** f *agriculture*; *cultivation of the land* ~**land** n *arable*; *arable land*; *tilled* (od *ploughed* od *farm*) *land*; *tillage* ~**mennig** m ⟨bot⟩ *agrimony* ~**minze** f ⟨bot⟩ *corn-mint* ~**mohn** m ⟨bot⟩ *field-poppy, corn-poppy* ~**nuß** f ⟨bot⟩ *meadow vetchling* ~**pacht** f = Ackerzins ~**pflug** m *plough* ~**röte** f ⟨bot⟩ *field madder* ~**schlepper** m *farm tractor* ~**schnecke** f ⟨zoo⟩ *limax* [L]; *slug* ~**scholle** f *clod* ~**senf** m ⟨bot⟩ *charlock* ~**smann** m *ploughman, husbandman, tiller* ~**vieh** n *farm--stock* ~**winde** f ⟨bot⟩ *lesser* (od *small*) *bindweed*; *cornwind* ~**wirtschaft** f = Ackerbau ~**zins** m *farm-rent*

·ackern I. vt/i [h] 1. vt *to plough*; *to till* ‖ **sich** ~ = 2. vi ⟨übtr⟩ *to plough, to plod* (durch *through*) II. ≃ n *tillage, tilth, tilling*

à condition [Fr] ⟨com⟩ (zur Ansicht, nicht fest) *on approval, on commission*

a conto [It] ⟨com⟩ *on account*

Acquit [a'ki:] m ~s/~s ⟨com⟩ *receipt* ‖ per ~ *paid, received*

Actinomyk·ose f ⟨med⟩ (Strahlenpilzkrankheit) *actinomycosis*

ad (L) [prep] etw ~ absurdum führen *to show up the absurdity* (od *inconsistency*) *of a th*; *to ridicule a the*; *to reduce to absurdity*; *to stultify* (*a thesis*) ‖ ~ acta legen *to put* (*a th*) *on the shelf*

·ada-·ada! intj ⟨Kinderspr⟩ *ta-ta*! *bye-bye*! ‖ ~ gehen *to go for a ta-ta*

ad·agio (It) adv *adagio* **Ad·agio** n ~s/~s ⟨mus⟩ *adagio*

·Adam m ~s/ 1. *Adam* ‖ den alten ~ ausziehen ⟨fig⟩ *to shake off the old Adam* ⟨a. m sex⟩, *to turn over a new leaf* 2. nach ~ Riese *according to Cocker* ~**sapfel** m 1. ⟨bot⟩ *Adam's apple* 2. ⟨anat⟩ *Adam's apple*; *thyroid cartilage* ‖ ~**skostüm** n ⟨hum⟩ *the altogether*; im ~ *in buff, stripped to the buff, in the altogether*

Adam·it m ⟨ec⟩ ~en pl *the Adamites* pl

Adans·onie f ⟨bot⟩ → Affenbrotbaum

Adaptation f [–ts–] ~/~en *adaptation* | ~sfähigkeit [f] *adaptive ability*

adäqu·at 1. a *adequate*; ~e Beschaffenheit *adequacy*; in ~er Weise *adequately* 2. adv *adequately*

Add·enda (L pl = Zusätze) *addenda* [pl]

add·ieren 1. vt/i [h]; vt *to add*; *to sum up*; ⟨fam⟩ *to tot* (*up*) ‖ alles zus-~ *to total* (*up*), *to take the sum total* | vi ⟨school fam⟩ *to do tots* 2. ≃ n *adding*; ⟨fam⟩ *tot* **Add·ier-** ~**einrichtingung** f ⟨comp⟩ *adder* ~**maschine** f *adding machine*, ⟨comp & fam⟩ *adder* → Rechenmaschine ~**werk** n ⟨tech⟩ *adder*

·Addis ·Abeba n *Addis Ababa* (Abessinien)

Addit·ion f ~/~en *addition*; *summing up* ~**sfehler** m *mistake in adding* ~**smaschine** f *adding machine* ~**sstufe** f ⟨telv⟩ *adder* **addit·iv** [–f] a *additive* ⟨a. telv⟩ ≃**kreis** m ⟨telv⟩ *adder*

Add·uktor m ⟨anat⟩ (Anziehmuskel) *adductor*

ad·e! intj *adieu*! *farewell*! *good-bye*! ⟨fam⟩ *bye-bye*! *ta-ta*! ‖ jdm ~ sagen *to bid a p farewell*

·Adebar m ~s/~e ⟨niedd⟩ („Glücksbringer“) ⟨orn⟩ *stork*, → Storch

·Adel m ~s/ 1. (erblicher ~) *noble birth*, vom ~ sein *to be of noble birth*; v altem ~ *of ancient stock*; echter ~ *blue-blood* 2. [koll] *the aristocracy* | ⟨engl⟩ der höhere ~ *the nobility*; *the peerage* (: *duke, marquis, earl, viscount, baron*); Angehöriger des höheren ~s *peer*; (jdn) in den ~ erheben *to raise* (*a p*) *to the peerage*, *to create* (*a p*) *a peer* ‖ der niedere ~ *the gentry* (: *baronet, knight*) 3. ⟨fig⟩ [abstr] *nobility*; *nobleness* ‖ Seelen≃ *nobility of mind*

Adela·ide n (Stadt in Australien) *Adelaide*

·adeln vt [h] **1.** ⟨engl⟩ (jdn) *to ennoble; to raise (a p) to the peerage* (od *to the rank of a noble*); *to create (a p) a peer* **2.** ⟨fig⟩ (jdn, etw) *to ennoble; to elevate, to exalt; to dignify*

·Adels- [in comp] *nobiliary* **~brief** m *patent of nobility* **~buch** n ⟨allg⟩ *Gothaer Almanach* ‖ ⟨engl⟩ *the Peerage; Debrett's* (*Peerage, Baronetage*, etc.) **~diplom** n = Adelsbrief **~genossenschaft** f *society of nobles* **~herrschaft** f *aristocracy* **~kalender** m = Adelsbuch **~krone** f *coronet* **~partikel** f, **~prädikat** n, **~titel** m *nobiliary prefix*

·Adelstand m (Rang) *nobility* ‖ [koll] *the nobility, the nobles* [pl]; in den ~ erheben *to ennoble, to raise (a p) to the peerage; to create* od *make (a p) a peer* **·Adelstolz** m *pride of birth; aristocratic pride* **·adelstolz** a *proud of one's noble birth* **·Adelstitel** m *title* **·Adelung** f ~/~en *exaltation*

·Aden n (Hafenstadt in Südjemen), Golf v ~ *Gulf of Aden*

Ad·ept m ~en/~en *adept*; → Meister

·Ader f ~/~n **1.** ⟨anat⟩ *blood-vessel; vein*; → Schlag∸, Krampf∸ ‖ die goldene ~ *haemorrhoidal vein* | → abbinden, abschnüren ‖ jdm die ~ öffnen, jdn zur ~ l *to bleed a p*, ⟨med⟩ *to phlebotomize a p*; er wurde zur ~ gelassen *he was bled*, † *he was let blood* **2.** ⟨geol⟩ (Gang) *vein, lode; dike, dyke* | (im Gestein) *flaser* **3.** (im Blatt) *vein, nerve, rib* ‖ (im Holz etc) *grain, vein, streak, stripe* **4.** ⟨el⟩ *core* (*of a cable*) **5.** ⟨fig⟩ e–e komische ~ *a streak* (od *vein*) *of humour*; mathematische ~ *arithmetical turn of mind* (: *he had not a calculating turn*); sarkastische ~ *a vein of sarcasm*; es ist keine gute ~ an ihm *there is no good in him* **~bruch** m → Krampfaderbruch

·Äderchen n ~s/~ *veinlet, venule*

·Adergeschwulst f ⟨med⟩ *angioma* [L]

·Aderhaut f *choroid* (*of the eye*) **·aderig, ·äderig** a → adrig, ädrig **·Aderlaß** m, –lasses/–lässe *bleeding, blood-letting*; ⟨med⟩ *phlebotomy, venesection*, ⟨path⟩ *haemorrhage* ⟨a. fig⟩ ‖ e–n ~ m bei (*or* an) jdm *to bleed, phlebotomize a p*

·adern, ·ädern vt [h] *to streak, to vein*; ⟨paint⟩ *to grain* ‖ → geädert, gemasert **·Aderöffnung** f → Pulsaderöffnung **·Aderpresse** f ⟨surg⟩ *torcular, tourniquet* **·aderreich** a *veined, veiny*

·Aderung f ⟨bot⟩ *nervation* **·Aderverkalkung** f → Arterienverkalkung

adhär·ieren vi [h] ⟨phys⟩ *to adhere* (an *to*)

Adhäsi·on f ~/~en ⟨phys⟩ *adhesion*

adi·eu [ɑ'djø] intj → ad·e

·ad hoc (L) *ad hoc* (L), *designed for this purpose, for the occasion*

Adiab·ate f ⟨phys⟩ *adiabatic line* od *curve* adiab·atisch a *adiabatic* (*cooling*)

ad infinitum (L) *for ever, ad infinitum* (L)

·Adjektiv n ~s/~e → Eigenschaftswort **·adjektivisch** a *adjectival, adjective*; in ~er Form *adjectively, adjectivally*

Adj·unkt m ~en/~en *assistant, adjunct*

°**adj·üs** intj = ade; → tjüs

Adjust·ier- [in comp] *gauging* ‖ *adjusting* (*screw*) **adjust·ieren** vt [h] (Maße etc) *to adjust*; (Gewichte) *to gauge*; (Münzen) *to test* | (richtig einstellen) (Fernrohr) *to adjust* ‖ (Kleidung) *to arrange properly* od *officially* **Adjust·ierung** f ~/~en *adjustment* ‖ *arrangement in proper order; official form of dress*

Adjut·ant m ~en/~en ⟨mil⟩ *adjutant; aide-de-camp* (abbr. *A. D. C.*); [pl] *aides-de-camp* (*of a general*) ‖ *lieutenant* (*of a minister*) ‖ *equerry* (*of a king*)

·Adler m ~s/~ **1.** ⟨orn⟩ *eagle*; junger ~ *eaglet*; → See–, Steinadler **2.** ⟨mil & her⟩ (Wappen) *eagle*, Doppel∸ *double-headed eagle*; ⟨Ger⟩ ~ mit ausgebreiteten Flügeln *spreadeagle* **3.** (Auszeichnung) *the eagle*; → ~orden **4.** ⟨astr⟩ (Sternbild) *eagle* **5.** (goldenes Zehndollarstück) ⟨Am⟩ *eagle* **6.** (Bummelstreik) ⟨rail⟩ *working to rule*

·Adler- [in comp] *eagle* ... ‖ **~baum** m ⟨bot⟩ *eagle-wood tree* **~blick** m ⟨fig⟩ mit e–m ~ *eagle-eyed, keen-sighted* **~farn** m ⟨bot⟩ *brake, bracken* **~holz** n *eagle-wood* **~horst** m *aerie, aery* **~nase** f *aquiline nose* **~orden** m ⟨Ger⟩ Deutscher ~ mit dem Stern *the Order of the German Eagle with star*; ⟨hist⟩ roter (schwarzer) ~ *the Red* (*Black*) *Eagle* **~pult** n ⟨ec⟩ *lectern* **~schild** m ⟨Ger⟩ *the Shield of the German Eagle* **~stein** m ⟨geol⟩ *geode* (Fr) **~träger** m ⟨mil⟩ *standard bearer* **~vögel** m pl → Bd. I *eagle*

ad libitum (L) *ad libitum* (L), *at pleasure, to any extent*

·adlig a *noble, titled* (: *a titled family*); v ~em Blut *blue-blooded*; die ~en Grundbesitzer [pl] *the territorial nobility* **∸e 1.** der ~e (ein ~er) m ~en/~en *nobleman; noble; peer* ‖ die ~n [pl] *the noblemen, nobles; the nobility*, ⟨bes a-engl⟩ *the noblesse* **2.** die ∸e (e–e ~e) f ~n/~n *noblewoman; peeress*

Administrati·on f ~/~en *administration* **administrat·iv** n *administrative* **Administr·ator** m ~s/–·oren *administrator, trustee; agent; steward*

administr·ieren vt [h] *to administer, to manage*

Admir·al m ~(e)s/~e *admiral*; Flotten∸, General∸ *Admiral of the Fleet*, → Groß∸, Konter∸, Vize∸ | ⟨ent⟩ *red-admiral; vanessa*

Admiralit·ät f ~/~en *the admiralty*; ⟨engl parl⟩ Parlamentssekretär bei der ~ *Parliamentary Secretary to the Admiralty*

Admiralit·äts- [in comp] **~anker** m *stocked anchor* **~gericht** n *the Admiralty Court* od *Court of Admiralty* **~inseln** f [pl] *Admiralty Islands* [pl] (in Melan·esien) **~jacht** f *admiralty yacht*

Admir·alsflagge f *admiral flag* **Admir·alsschiff** n *admiral's ship, flagship*

Admir·alstab m *the naval staff*; ⟨engl⟩ der Chef des ~es *the First Sea Lord and Chief of the Naval Staff* **Admir·alswürde** f *admiralship*

ad n·otam [L] etw ~ nehmen *to bear a th in mind; to take notice of a th* **ad ·oculos** [L] etw ~ demonstrieren *to demonstrate a th; to make a th evident by demonstration; to describe a th vividly*

Ad·onis m *Adonis* **~röschen** n ⟨bot⟩ *Adonis, pheasant's eye* **ad·onisch** a *Adonic*; ~er Vers *Adonic, Adonic verse*

adopt·ieren vt [h] *to adopt* **Adopt·ierte(r** m) f *adoptee* **Adopti·on** f ~/~en *adoption* **Adopt·iv-** [in comp] *adoptive, adopted* **~bruder** m *adoptive brother, br. by adoption* **~sohn** m *adoptive son*

Adorati·on f ⟨ec⟩ *worship, adoration*

adouc·ieren vt (Metall) *to anneal; to temper* | (Farben) *to wash*

Adr·emagerät® n → Adressiermaschine

Adr·eß- **~buch** n *directory; guide* **~büro** n *register* (od *registry*)-*office; inquiry-office* **~kalender** m = Adreßbuch **~karte** f *business-card* **~kontor** n = Adreßbüro **~modifikation** f ~/~en ⟨comp⟩ *conditional transfer* **~zettel** m *label, ticket*

Adress·ant m ~en/~en (of letters) *addresser, sender* ‖ (of goods) *consignor* ‖ (of a bill) *drawer*

Adress·at m ~en/~en (of letters) *adressee* ‖ (of goods) *consignee* ‖ (of a bill) *drawee; payee*

Adr·esse (abbr Adr.) f ~/~n (P) *address*; (on letters) *direction* ‖ die falsche ~ *the wrong address*; an Ihre ~ *to your address, to you*; per ~ (*or* unter der ~ v) *care of* (abbr *c/o*) | ⟨übtr⟩ die richtige ~ *the proper quarter* ‖ an die falsche ~ k ⟨fam⟩ *to come to the wrong shop*, ⟨Am fam⟩ *to bark up the wrong tree*

Adr·essen- **~nachweis** m *inquiry-office; register* (od *registry*)-*office* **~selektion** f ~/~en ⟨comp⟩ *channel* od *track selection, automatic self-indexing* **Adress·ier-** **~maschine** f *addressograph, addressing machine* **adress·ieren** vt [h] *to address,* *to direct* || (Waren) *to consign* || (Brief) falsch ~ *to misdirect*; schlecht adressierter Brief *blind letter* **Adress·ierung** f ~/~en *addressing* || ~ nach Zeichen ⟨comp⟩ *a.g by character position*

adr·ett a *neat, pretty*; *properly* od *tastefully dressed*

·Adria f **1.** *the Adriatic, the Adriatic Sea* **2.** (Stadt) *Adria* **adri·atisch** a *Adriatic*, das ~e Meer *the Adriatic*

Adrian·opel n *Adrianople*; (Türk.) *Edirne*

·adrig a *veiny* (*hands*); *veined*, fein~ *finely veined*; ⟨übtr⟩ *veined* (*structure*)

·Adschmir n (Stadt u Bezirk in Vorder-Indien) *Ajmer*

adsorb·ieren vt ⟨bes chem & tech⟩ *to adsorb*

Adsorpt·ion f ⟨tech⟩ *adsorption* (*of gases*, etc)

adstring·ierend a ⟨med⟩ *astringent*; ~es Mittel *astringent*

Adv·ent m ~(e)s/~e ⟨ec⟩ *Advent* **Advent·ist** m ⟨ec⟩ (Angehöriger der Sekte) *adventist* **advent·iv** a ⟨bot⟩ *adventive*

Adv·ents- [in comp] *Advent* **~brauch** m *Advent custom* **~zeit** f *Advent, Advent season*

Adv·erb n ~(e)s/~ien ⟨gram⟩ *adverb*; durch ein ~, in Form e–s ~s *adverbially* **adverbi·al** **1.** a *adverbial*; ~e Bestimmung *adverbial qualification*; *adverb-equivalent, adverb phrase* (z B: *with difficulty*) **2.** [adv] *adverbially* **Adverbi·alsatz** m *adverb clause* **Adv·erbium** n = Adverb

Advoc·atus Di·aboli L ~/ *the Devil's advocate*

Advok·at m ~en/~en **1.** → Anwalt, Rechtsanwalt, Verteidiger **2.** *egg-liqueur*

Advok·aten- **~gebühr** f *lawyer's fee* **~kniff,** **~streich** m *legal quibble, lawyer's trick* **~schreiber** m *attorney's* (od *solicitor's*) *clerk*

Advokat·ur f ~/~en → Rechtsanwaltschaft

Aer·obier m ~s/~, **Aerobi·ont** m ~en/~en (Ggs Anaerobiont) ⟨biol⟩ *aerobe* **Aerodyn·amik** f ~ *aerodynamics* pl **Aerol·ith** m ~en/~en ⟨min⟩ *aerolite* **Aeromech·anik** f *aeromechanics* pl **Aeron·aut** m *aeronaut* **Aeron·autik** f *aeronautics* **aeron·autisch** a *aeronautic*(*al*) **Aeroph·on** n ~(e)s/~e *aerophone* **Aeropl·an** m ~(e)s/~e *aeroplane*, ⟨Am⟩ *airplane*

Aeros·ol n ~s/ *aerosol*

Aerost·at m ~(e)s/~e *aerostat* **Aerost·atik** f ~/ *aerostatics* pl

Aff·äre f ~/~n *affair, business, job*; *matter* || e–e böse ~ *a bad business*; sich aus der ~ ziehen *to back out*; *to retreat out of a difficulty*

·Äffchen n ~s/~ *little monkey*; Seiden~ *marmoset*

·Affe m ~n/~n *ape, monkey* **1.** ⟨zoo⟩ **a.** (schwanzloser ~) *ape*, Menschen~ *anthropoid ape*; → Gorilla, Schimpanse, Orang-Utan || → Pavian **b.** (geschwänzter ~) *monkey* **2.** °⟨fig⟩ **a.** (Geck) *ape, fool*; *jackanapes* || °dieser ~! *this silly ass* od *donkey* **3.** °⟨mil⟩ (Tornister) *knapsack, pack, kit-bag* **4.** Wendungen: °wie'n ~ auf'm Schleifstein *like a monkey on a gridiron* || °nicht f e–n Wald v ~n *not for the life of me, not for the world* || vom blauen ~n gebissen s *to have cut a folly tooth* || °e–n ~n an jdm gefressen h *to be infatuated* (od *smitten*) *with a p* || °ich glaub', mich laust der ~! *well, I'll be hanged!, well, I never!* || °lehr 'nen alten ~n Grimassen schneiden! *teach your grandmother to suck eggs!* || °e–n ~n (Rausch) h *to be tipsy* (od *drunk*) || °sich e–n ~n kaufen *to get drunk* **5.** [in comp] → Affen–

Aff·ekt m ~(e)s/~e ⟨psych⟩ *affect*, ~e [pl] *emotional factors* || *strong emotion*; *passion*; im ~ *under the urge of passion*; *on an impulse, in a burst of feeling*; (*to act*) *under the influence of emotions* **~leben** n *emotional life*

affekt·iert a *affected*; *conceited, pompous, sententious* (*style*) || ~es Wesen = ~**heit** f ~/~en *affectation, affectedness* || *pomposity, sententiousness*

·Affen- ~**artig** a *apish, ape-like*; *monkeyish, monkey-like*; *simian* (*arms*); mit ~er Geschwindigkeit *like old boots* od *gooseberry, like blazes* od *hell* (*with incredible speed*; *in no time*; *with the agility of a monkey*), → Deibel **~brotbaum** m ⟨bot⟩ *baobab* °**~fahrt** f ~/ ⟨mot sl⟩ *hell-for--leather drive* od *driving*, ⟨aero sl⟩ *h.-f.-l. flying* **~geschlecht** n (*the order of*) *quadrumana* L [pl] **~komödie** f ⟨fig⟩ *foolery, foolishness* °**~landung** f ⟨aero sl⟩ *hooshing* **~liebe** f ⟨fig⟩ *foolish fondness*; *doting love* ~**mäßig** a = affenartig **~mensch** m ⟨anthr⟩ *the missing link in Darwinism* || *pithecanthropus* | *microcephalous person* **~nase** f *flat nose* **~pinscher** m ⟨zoo⟩ *pug* e–e °**~schande** f *a wicked* (od *an awful*) *shame, an absolute scandal*; ⟨sl⟩ *a beastly mess* od *nuisance* **~schwanz** m *tail of a monkey* | °⟨fig⟩ (P) *jackanapes*; *coxcomb, fob* **~spektakel** m ein ~ *a hell of a row* **~theater** n ⟨fig⟩ = ~komödie **~weibchen** n *she-ape, female ape*; *she-* od *female monkey*

·äffen vt [h] (jdn) *to mock*; *to ape, to banter, to chaff, to hoax* || *to deceive*

Äffer·ei f *apishness* || (Neckerei) *mockery, banter*

Affid·avit (L) n (eidesstattl. Versicherung) ⟨com⟩ *affidavit*

·affig a ⟨fig⟩ *apish, foolish, silly, foppish*, → albern

·Äffin f ~/~nen = Affenweibchen

affin·ieren vt [h] ⟨chem⟩ *to refine* **Affinit·ät** f ~/~en affinity

·äffisch a = affenartig

Aff·ix n ~es/~e ⟨gram⟩ *affix* **affiz·ierbar** a *sensitive, susceptible, impressionable* **affiz·ieren** vt [h] *to affect, to excite*; *to work on* (*feelings*)

Affod·ill m ~(e)s/~e ⟨bot⟩ *asphodel*

Affrik·ate f ~/~n ⟨phon⟩ *affricate* (: pf)

Affr·ont [aˈfrɔ̃] m ~s/~s *affront* ~**iert** a ⟨arts⟩ *confronted*

Afgh·ane m *Afghan*; → Pakistan **afgh·anisch** a *Afghan*

·Afrika n *Africa*, **Afrik·aner(in** f) m, **afrikanisch** a *African*

Afrik·aans n ~/ (offizielle holländ. Sprache in Südafrika) *Afrikaans* (das ~ ist .. *A. is* ..)

Afrik·ander m ~s/~ *Afrikander* **Afrik·aner** m ~s/~; ~in f ~/~innen *African* **afrik·anisch** a *African*

·After m ~s/~ ⟨anat⟩ *anus*; (of birds, etc) *vent*

·after- pref **1.** (nach hinten) *back*(*ward*) **2.** (aus zweiter Hand) *at second hand* → Aftermieter **3.** (minderwertig) *false, sham*; *pseudo–*

·After- **~beredsamkeit** f *false eloquence* **~gelehrsamkeit** *sham learning* (od *erudition*) **~klauen** pl ⟨zoo⟩ *dew-claws* pl **~kristall** n ⟨minr⟩ *pseudomorph* **~kritiker** *would-be critic* **~lehen,** **~lehn** *mesne-fief* **~lehnsherr** *mesne lord* **~miete** *sublease, subtenancy*; in ~ wohnen *to live in furnished lodgings*; ... wohnen bei jdm *to be a p's subtenant, underletter* **~mieter** *lodger, undertenant, subtenant, underletter* **~pacht** *sublease, subtenancy* **~rede** *backbiting, calumny, slander* **~reden** vi [ich afterrede; pp aftergeredet] [h] *to backbite*; ~ v jdm *to speak ill of a p, to backbite a p* **~vermietung** f *subletting* **~weisheit** f *sham wisdom* **~zins** m *compound interest*

·Agadir n (Hafenstadt in Marokko)

Äg·adische Inseln f pl (westl. v Sizilien) *Ægadean Islands*, ⟨ant⟩ *Ægates* pl

ägä·isch a die ~e Kultur *Aegean civilization*; das ~e Meer *the Aegean Sea*

ag·am a (geschlechtslos) ⟨biol & bot⟩ *agamic, agamous*

Ag·ama f ⟨zoo⟩ (Eidechsenart) *agama*; *agamoid ground-lizard*

·Agar-·Agar m ~s/ (Gallertsubstanz) *agar--agar*

Ag·ave f ~/~n ⟨bot⟩ *agave* ‖ gegorenes Getränk aus der ~ *pulque* **~faser** f *sisal hemp, henequen*

Ag·ende f ~/~n **1.** ⟨ec⟩ (Gottesdienstordnung) *liturgy*; *ritual* ‖ (liturg. Buch) *ritual*; ⟨C. E.⟩ ~ der anglik. Kirche *Book of Common Prayer* **2.** (Merkbuch) *agenda, minute-book, memorandum book* (⟨a.⟩ Agenda)

·Agens (L) n ~/Ag·enzien ⟨chem⟩ *agent*

Ag·ent m ~en/~en *agent*; *representative* ‖ ⟨ins, etc⟩ *field-worker* ‖ ⟨com⟩ *agent, factor*; ⟨Am⟩ (Geschäfts≗) *solicitor* ‖ (geheimer) *emissary* **~engebühr, ~enkommission** f *commission*

agent provocateur (Fr) [a'ʒɑ̃ prɔvɔka'tø:] m (Lockspitzel) *agent provocateur* (Fr)

Ag·entschaft, Agent·ur f ~/~en *agency* ‖ (Büro) *agency, agent's office* ‖ ⟨ins etc⟩ *field--office*

·Agfa (abbr. f. Aktien-Gesellschaft f. Anilinfabrikation) f *Agfa*

Agglomer·at n ~(e)s/~e ⟨geol⟩ *agglomerate* ‖ ⟨übtr⟩ *agglomeration* **Agglomerati·on** f ~/~en ⟨demog⟩ *population aggregate* od *cluster, aggregation, conglomeration*

Agglutinati·on f ~/~en ⟨med & gram⟩ *agglutination* **agglutin·ieren** vt/i *to agglutinate*; ~d *agglutinate*; *agglutinative* (*languages*)

Aggreg·at n ~(e)s/~e *aggregate* ‖ ⟨mach⟩ (einzelnes) ~ (*compact*) *unit*; *mill, machine*; *set* **~zustand** m ⟨phys⟩ *state of aggregation*; *condition* od *physical state of matter*

aggress·iv [–f] a *aggressive*; ~es Verhalten *aggressiveness*; ~w *to assume* (od *take*) *the aggressive* ‖ *enterprising, pushing, up-and--coming, ambitious*; *venturesome, hustling*; (⟨Am hum⟩ *as aggressive as a 200-lb gnat*)

Aggressivit·ät f *aggression, etc* ‖ *ambitiousness*

Äg·ide f ~/~n ⟨fig⟩ *aegis, protection*; unter der ~ v *under the aegis of* (*a p*)

ag·ieren vi/t [h] **1.** vi *to act, to operate* | *to gesticulate* **2.** vt ⟨theat⟩ (Rolle) *to enact*; *to act*

ag·il a *agile*, → flink, beweglich

·Agio ['ɑ:ʒio] n ~s/~s ⟨com⟩ *agio, premium* **~gewinn** m *premium, agio* **~konto** n, **~rechnung** f *agio* (od *premium*)*-account* **~tage** [ɑ:ʒio'tɑ:ʒə] f (Fr) ~ *agiotage, stock-jobbing*; ⟨sl⟩ *premium--hunting* **Agioteur** [–'tør] m (Fr) *stock-jobber*, (mit Eintrittskarten) *ticket scalper* **agiot·ieren** vi [h] *to do in stock-jobbing*

·Ägis f ⟨ant myth⟩ *aegis*

Agitati·on f ~/~en *agitation*; *public excitement* ‖ (Werbung) *canvassing*; *propaganda*

Agit·ator m ~s/~en **1.** *agitator* ‖ *propagandist* **2.** ⟨chem⟩ (Apparat) *agitator* **agitat·orisch** a *agitating, agitatorial*; *propagandistic* ‖ ~e Tätigkeit *agitation, propagandism* **agit·ieren** vi [h] *to agitate* (f. *for*); *to stir up political* (etc.) *unrest* ‖ (werben) *to canvass*

·Aglei f ~/ ⟨bot⟩ → Akelei

Agn·at m ~en/~en ⟨jur⟩ *agnate*; → Schwertmage **Agnati·on** f *agnation*

Agn·ostiker m ~s/~ ⟨ant⟩ *agnostic* **Agnostiz·ismus** m ~/ *agnosticism*

Ag·one f ~/~n ⟨phys⟩ *agonic line*

Agon·ie f ~/~n *agony*; *death throes*

Agoraphob·ie f ⟨med⟩ *agoraphobia*

Agr·affe f ~/~n *agraffe, fibula*; *clasp*; *brooch*; *slide* ‖ ⟨med⟩ (Wundklammer) *agraffe*

·Agram n (Stadt in Jugoslawien) *Zagreb*

Agr·ar- [in comp] *agrarian, agricultural*; *farming* **~gemeinschaft** f *farming community* **~geschichte** f *history of agriculture* **~krise** f *agricultural crisis* **~markt** m *agricultural market* **~politik** f *agrarian policy* **~reform** f *land-reform* **~staat** m *agrarian state* **~verbrechen** n *agrarian crime* **~verfassung** f *agricultural system* **~zoll** m *agricultural* od *agrarian duty*

Agr·arier m ~s/~ (*big*) *landowner, landed proprietor*; *squire* ‖ die ~ [pl] ⟨pol⟩ *the country party* **Agr·ariertum** n *the big landowners* pl

Agr·eement [ə'gri:mənt] n [engl] *agreement*; Gentlemen's ~ *gentleman agreement*

agrément [agre'mɑ̃:] n (Fr) ~s/~s ⟨dipl⟩ *agrément*

Agrikult·ur f ~/~en *agriculture*

Agron·om m ~en/~en *agronomist* **Agronom·ie** f ~/~n *agronomy*

Agr·ume f ~/~n *tropical fruit, fruit from the south* (*citrus fruit* etc)

Ag·uti m & n ~s/~s ⟨zoo⟩ *agouti*

Ägy·pten n *Egypt*

Äg·ypter m ~s/~ *Egyptian* **Äg·ypterin** f ~/~nen *Egyptian woman*; *Egyptian* **äg·yptisch** a **1.** *Egyptian*; ~e Altertumskunde *Egyptology*; ~es Pfund *Egyptian pound* (abbr *£E*) **2.** [in comp] ~-abessinisch *Egypto-Abyssinian* (*front*)

Ägyptol·og m ~en/~en *Egyptologist* **Ägyptolog·ie** f ~/ *Egyptology*

ah intj ~! *ah*! *ha*! | ~ ja! *o yes*! ‖ ~, nun verstehe ich *oh, I understand now*; → ach 2.

äh! intj *yah*! **äh-äh-Ton** m ⟨Ger⟩ *Jerry officers' twang*

ah·a! intj *aha*! *there you see*! ‖ *ah*! *ha*!, *ha ha*! | ≗**moment** [m] ⟨eth⟩ *aha-moment*

·Ahlbeere f ~/~n *black currant*

·Ahle f ~/~n *awl, pricker* ‖ ⟨typ⟩ *point, bodkin*

·Ahlkirsche f ~/~n ⟨bot⟩ **1.** = Traubenkirsche **2.** *fly-honeysuckle*

·Ahming, ·Ahmung f ~/~e ⟨mar⟩ (Tiefseemesser) *draught-marks* pl

·Ahn m ~s/~en *ancestor, forbear, forefather* ‖ ° = Großvater | ~en pl *ancestors* pl; *ancestry*; *forefathers* pl ‖ ° = Großeltern

·ahnden vt [h] (Verbrechen, Unrecht) *to avenge, to punish* ‖ etw ~ an jdm *to revenge* (*a th*) *on a p*; Sünden (etc) ~ an jdm *to visit sins on a p*; geahndet w mit *to be visited with* **·Ahndung** f ~/~en *retribution, punishment, revenge*

·Ahne 1. m ~n/~n = Ahn **2.** f ~/~n *ancestor*; *grandmother, grandparent* ‖ → Atavismus

·ähneln vi [h] jdm ~ *to resemble a p*; *to have* (od *bear*) *a resemblance to a p*; *to be similar to a p* (od *a th*) ‖ **sich** ~ *to resemble one another*

·ahnen vt [h] **1.** (vorempfinden) *to have a presentiment of* (*a th*), *to be presentient of* (*a th*), *to divine*; *to presage* (*a th*); instinktiv ~ *to sense* (*a th*; *that*) ‖ (voraussehen) *to anticipate, to foresee* ‖ (Böses) *to forebode*; *to have a foreboding of* (*a th*) ‖ (etw) ~ l *to foreshadow, suggest* (*a th*) | (vermuten) *to surmise, to suspect*; nicht ~ *to be unaware* (od *unconscious, unsuspecting*) *of* (*a th*); nicht ~, daß .. *to be unaware that* ..; nichts ~d adv *unsuspectingly*, → ahnungslos | ohne z ~ *without dreaming* (*that*); → ungeahnt ‖ du ahnst es nicht! *fancy, now*! *good*(*ness*) *gracious*! *what a surprise*! **2.** mir ahnt so, es ahnt mir, daß *I have a presentiment that* ‖ mir ahnte (*or* es ahnte mir) nichts Gutes *my mind misgave me, I was tortured by* (*various*) *apprehensions and misgivings, I had a foreboding* (*that*) (betreffs *about*; daß *that*)

·Ahnen- [in comp] *ancestral* .. **~bild** n, **~figur** f *figure* od *representation of an ancestor* **~forschung** f *ancestry* od *genealogical research* **~kult** m *ancestor-worship* **~paß** m ⟨Ger⟩ *genealogical tree*; *pedigree* **~probe** f *proof of nobility* **~reihe** f *line of ancestors* **~stolz** m *pride of ancestry* **~tafel** f *genealogical tree*; *pedigree* **~verehrung** f = Ahnenkult

·Ahnfrau f ~/~en *ancestress* **·Ahnherr** m ~en/~en *or* ~n/~n *ancestor*

·ähnlich I. a **1.** [attr] *resembling* (*structure*), *resemblant* (*features*); ein sprechend ~es Bild *a lifelike* od *speaking portrait* | *similar* (*objects, facts*), *like* (*subjects*); ein ~er Angriff wie der, welcher ... *a similar attack to the one that* ...; ~e Dinge *similar things, similars* [pl]; v ~en Leidenschaften wie *of like passions with* ‖ in ~er Weise wie *similarly to* .., *in parallel with* .., ⟨math⟩ *similar* ‖ (entsprechend) *corresponding; parallel, analogous* **2.** [pred] **a.** jdm ~ s *or* sehen *to resemble a p, to have* (od *bear*) *resemblance to a p, to be* (od *look*) *like a p*; ⟨fam⟩ *to favour a p*; die beiden sind e–a sehr ~ *the two are very like each other*; jdm sehr (*or* auffallend) ~ sehen *to resemble a p closely*, ⟨Am sl⟩ *to be a dead ringer for a p*; er sieht s–m Vater sprechend ~ *he is the very image of his father* ‖ jdm ~ w *to take after a p* ‖ das sieht ihm (so recht) ~ *that is just like him*, ⟨fam⟩ *that's* (*e. g. James*) *all over*; es sah ihm ~ *it was like him* (*to do*) ‖ sie sagte das – es sah ihr ~ *she was saying so – she would*! ‖ e–r S wenig ~ sehen *to bear little resemblance to a th* ‖ **b.** *like*; das Bild ist nicht ~ *the picture is not like*; eine Stimme ~ e–r Posaune *a voice like a trumpet*; ~ wie ein Ei dem andern *as like as two peas* ‖ *similar* (e–r S *to a th*) ‖ .. oder so ~ *or sth like that* **II.** ≃es, das ≃e *the similar*; ich habe nie etw ≃es gesehen *I never saw anything like it, I've never seen the like* (*of it*); u ≃es *and things like that*; °oder so was ≃es ⟨fam⟩ (*sheets*) *or that* **III.** adv ~ gelagert *similarly circumstanced*; ich empfand ~ *I felt that way also* ‖ jdn z Sprechen ~ treffen ⟨paint, etc⟩ *to get a p to the life* **IV.** –~ [suff] *para*(–) (*para-medical, paramilitary*; *–type* (*adding machine-type*)

·**Ähnlichkeit** f ~/~en *likeness* (zwischen *between*; mit *to*) *resemblance, similarity* (mit *to*) ‖ ⟨math⟩ *similarity* ‖ e–e frappante ~ *a striking likeness* ‖ ~ h mit jdm *to bear resemblance to a p, to resemble a p* ‖ er hat k–rlei ~ mit *he bears no likeness whatever to* (*his brother*) | ⟨übtr⟩ *correspondence, analogy*; ~ zeigen mit etw *to be like a th, to bear analogy to a th*

·**Ahnung** f ~/~en **1.** (Vorgefühl) *presentiment*; (oft: böse) *foreboding, premonition* (*of a disaster*); e–e ~, daß .. *a hunch that* .. ‖ böse ~ *misgiving* ‖ (Vorhersehen) *prevision*; *prescience* (*of* ..) ‖ (Argwohn) *suspicion* **2.** (Vorstellung) *idea, notion*, ich hatte keine ~ *I had no notion*; wenig ~ h *to have little idea* (wie *how*); keine blasse (*or* nicht die geringste, leiseste) ~ *not the slightest* (od *vaguest*) *notion* ‖ dunkle ~ *inkling* ‖ keine ~! *not a glimmer*; *not the gl. of an idea*! *not a bit of it*!; *I haven't the faintest idea*; ⟨fam⟩ *I haven't the ghost of an idea*!; ⟨Am sl⟩ *search me*! ‖ → wissen ≃slos **1.** a *unconscious, unsuspecting* (*people*) **2.** adv *unsuspectingly*; *without misgiving* ‖ **~svermögen** n *flair* (Fr) **~svoll** a *presentient*; *full of presentiments, forebodings, misgivings*

ah·oi! intj ⟨mar⟩ *ahoy*; Boot ~! *boat ahoy*!

·**Ahorn** m ~(e)s/~e ⟨bot⟩ **1.** *maple*; Berg≃ *great m.*; ⟨Am⟩ *sycamore maple* Spitz≃ *Norway m.* **2.** [in comp] *maple* **~blatt** n *maple-leaf*

·**ahornen** a *maple*

Ahr f (Nebenfluß des Rheins) *the Ahr*

·**Ährchen** n ~s/~ ⟨bot⟩ *spiculet, spikelet*; mit ~ bedeckt *spiculate* ≃**förmig** a *spicular, spikewise*

·**Ähre** f ~/~n ⟨bot⟩ (Korn≃) *ear*; (Blumen≃) *spike*; *spica* (L); mit ~n versehen [a] *eared* ‖ ~n bilden *to come into ear*; ⟨Am⟩ *to ear* ‖ ~n lesen *to glean* | **~n- ~bildung** f *coming into ear*, (*the*) *forming* (*of*) *ears* **~feld** n *corn-field in ear* **~fischchen** n pl ⟨Am⟩ *Silversides* pl ≃**förmig** a ⟨bot⟩ *spicate* **~lese** f *gleaning* **~leser(in)** m (f) *gleaner* **~lilie** f ⟨bot⟩ *bog asphodel*

·**ährig** a *eared*; *spiked* ‖ voll~ *full-eared*

·**Ahrgau,** der ⟨Ger⟩ *the Ahr district*

·**Ai, Aï** n ~s/~s ⟨zoo⟩ *ai, sloth*

Aide [æːd] m (Fr) ~/~s *partner*; *play-fellow* | ~ de camp [æːddəˈkɑ̃] m (Fr) → Adjutant

Aigr·ette [æːˈgret] f (Fr) ~/~n *aigrette* (Fr)

Air [ˈɛør] n (Fr) ~s/~s **1.** ⟨mus⟩ *air* **2.** (Aussehen) *air*; sich ein ~ geben *to give o.s. airs*

Airedaleterrier [ˈɛədeilteriə] m ~s/~ *Airedale-terrier*; *Airedale*

Aïs n ~/~ ⟨mus⟩ *A sharp*

Aj·accio [–tʃo] n (Stadt auf Korsika)

à jour [aˈʒur] (Fr) *transparent* **Ajourarbeit** f *à jour-work*; *fret*; *fret-work*

ajust·ieren vt [h] *to adjust*

Akadem·ie f ~/~n *academy*; die Königl. ~ der Künste *the Royal Academy of Arts, the Academy*; Mitglied e–r ~ *academician* ‖ *university*; ⟨fam⟩ *college* **Akad·emiker** m ~s/~ ⟨allg⟩ *academician* ‖ *university man* **akad·emisch** **1.** a **a.** ⟨allg⟩ *academic* ‖ (abstrakt, theoretisch) *academic* **b.** ⟨univ⟩ *collegiate* (*career*), *academic* (*rank*); mst *academical* (*costume, life, year*); in ~er Hinsicht *academically* ‖ ~e Bildung *university education* ‖ ~er Bürger *university resident* ‖ ~er Grad, ~e Würde *degree*; jd, der e–n ~en Grad erworben hat *graduate*; jdm e–n ~en G. verleihen *to confer a degree* (*up*)*on a p* ‖ ~e Tracht f *gown*; (volle) *academicals* pl ‖ ~es Viertel n *quarter of an hour allowed before a lecture* (etc) **2.** adv; ~ gebildet *university-bred*; ~ Gebildeter *university man*

Ak·adien n (Gebiet Kanadas) *Acadia*; jetzt *Nova Scotia*

Akajou → Acajou

Ak·anthus m ~/~ **1.** ⟨bot⟩ *acanthus* **2.** ⟨arch⟩ (Zierform) *acanthus*

akatal·ektisch a ⟨pros⟩ *acatalectic* (*verse*)

Ak·azie f ~/~n ⟨bot⟩ *acacia*; Blaublättrige ~ *Blue-leaved Wattle*; Langblättrige ~ *Sydney Golden Wattle*; Persische ~ *Umbrella Acacia* ‖ ⟨engl⟩ falsche *or* unechte ~ *acacia, locust-tree*; → Robinie ‖ es ist um auf die ~n zu klettern (etwa:) *it gets my dander up*

Akel·ei f ~/~en ⟨bot⟩ *columbine, aquilegia* (L)

·**Akka,** ·**Akkon** (Stadt in Israel) n *Acre*

Akklamati·on f ~/~en (Beifall) *acclamation* ‖ (bei Wahl) (Zuruf) (durch ~ *by a.*) **akklam·ieren** vt [h] *to acclaim*

Akklimatisati·on f ~/~en *acclimatization*; ⟨Am⟩ *acclimation* **akklimatis·ieren** vt [h] *to acclimatize*, ⟨Am⟩ *to acclimate* | **sich ~** *to acclimatize o.s.* (an *to*); ⟨Am⟩ *to acclimate*

Akklimatis·ierung f ~/~en *acclimatization*

Akkol·ade f ~/~n (Klammer) ⟨mus⟩ *accolade* ‖ ⟨typ⟩ *brace* (}{)

Akkommodati·on f ~/~en (Anpassung) *accommodation*; *adaptation* **akkommod·ieren** vt [h] *to accommodate*; *to adapt*

Akkompagnement [akɔmpanjəˈmɑ̃ː] n (Fr) ⟨mus⟩ *accompaniment* (zu *to*)

Akk·ord m ~(e)s/~e **1.** ⟨mus⟩ *chord*; e–n ~ greifen *to reach a ch.* **2.** ⟨jur⟩ (Vergleich) *composition*; *settlement* **3.** ⟨com⟩ *contract, compact*; *agreement*; ⟨min⟩ *tut* | auf ~ *by contract*; ⟨min⟩ *upon tut* ‖ in ~ *by the job* (: *to pay a p by the job*) ‖ im ~ arbeiten *to do piece-work* ‖ in ~ geben *to let* (*a th*) *by contract* **4.** (~lohn) *piece-wages* **~arbeit** f *job-work, piece-work*; ⟨min⟩ *tut-work, task-work* **~arbeiter** m *piece-worker*; *jobber* **~berechnung** f *rate fixing* **~lohn** m *piece-wages* **~preis** m *contract-price* **~satz** m *rate of composition* **~system** n *competitive wage system* **~zulage** f *line allowance*

Akk·ordeon n ~s/~s ⟨mus⟩ *accordion*

akkord·ieren vt/i [h] **1.** vt mit jdm etw ~ *to arrange a th with a p*; *to agree with a p upon a th* **2.** vi mit jdm ~ *to come to an agreement, to make a contract with a p* ‖ *to compound with a p* (über, wegen *for*); *to compromise with a p* (über *on*), *to arrange with a p* (über *about*)

Akk·ordion n ~s/~s ⟨mus⟩ *accordion*

akkredit·ieren vt [h] jdn bei jdm ~ **1.** ⟨dipl⟩ *to accredit*, bei jdm *to a p* (*a king* etc.); (bei Hofe *at court*); [mst pass] *he was accredited* **2.** ⟨com⟩ *to open a credit with a p* (od *at a bank*) *in favour of a p* **Akkredit·iv** n ~(e)s/~e ⟨com⟩ *letter of credit*; ⟨dipl⟩ *credentials* [pl]

Akkresz·enz f ⟨jur⟩ *accretion*; → Anwachsung

Akkulturati·on [–ts–] f ~/~en (junger Staaten) *acculturation*

Akkumulati·on f ~/~en *accumulation*

Akkumul·ator m ~s/–lat·oren, [abbr] **·Akku** m ~s/~s ⟨el & tech⟩ *accumulator* ‖ ~enbatterie f *accumulator*; *storage battery* **~(en)kasten** m *accumulator tank*

akkumul·ieren vi/t [h] *to accumulate*

akkur·at a *accurate, exact* **Akkurat·esse** f ~/ *accuracy, exactness, exactitude*; *minuteness*

·Akkusat·iv m ~(e)s/~e ⟨gram⟩ *accusative*

·Akme f ~/ (Höhepunkt) *acme, height*; ⟨med⟩ *crisis*

·Akne f ~/~n ⟨med⟩ (Pickel) *acne*

Akol·uth m ~(e)s/~en ⟨ec⟩ *acolyte*

Akon·it n ~(e)s/~e ⟨bot⟩ *aconite*, → Eisenhut

Ak·ontozahlung f *payment on account*; *instalment*

Akquisit·eur [akwizi'tør] m (Fr), ~s/~e ⟨com⟩ *canvasser*; ⟨ins⟩ *insurance-broker* **Akquisiti·on** f ~/~en ~*acquisition*; *canvassing*

ˣ**akr·at** a = akkurat

Akrib·ie f ~/ *scrupulous exactitude*

·akro- pref *acro–* **Akrob·at** m ~en/~en *acrobat* **Akrob·atik** f ~/~en *acrobatics* [pl] **Akrob·atin** f ~/~nen = Akrobat **akrob·atisch** a *acrobatic* **Akromegal·ie** f ⟨path⟩ *acromegaly*; –meg·alisch a *–megalic* **Akron·ym** n ~s/~e *acronym* (→ d. Bd. I) (*e.g.* Care-Paket)

·Akron n (Stadt in Ohio, U.S.A.)

Akr·opolis f ~/Akrop·olen *acropolis*

Akr·ostichon n ~s/–stichen *acrostic*

°**äks** intj ~! *fie!*, → pfui

·Akt m ~(e)s/~e **1.** *act*, ein feierlicher ~ *a solemn act*, ein ~ der Gerechtigkeit *an act of justice* ‖ *action, deed*; ein ~ der Verzweiflung *a desperate deed* ‖ *act, performance* **2.** ⟨theat & Lit⟩ *act*; ein Stück von 3 ~en *a three-act play* ‖ (Varieté⩪, Zirkus⩪) *act, turn* **3.** = Akte **4.** ⟨arts⟩ (Nacktdarstellung) *nude* **5.** ⟨med⟩ *coitus* (L) **~modell** n *life-model* ‖ jdm ~ sitzen *to pose to a p for the altogether* **~schluß** m *the end of an act* **~studie** f *study from the nude*

·Akte f ~/~n *deed*; (*official*) *document*; [mst pl] ~n *deeds, documents* [pl]; die im Briefordner befindlichen Brief⩪n *the file*, unter den ~n *on the file* ‖ die über e–e S *or* P gesammelten ~n *the dossier* (Fr); sind das die ~n? *is that the dossier?* | e–n Bericht zu den ~n legen *to file a report*; ⟨übtr⟩ → (ad acta) *to put* (*a th*) *on the shelf*; *to pigeonhole*; *to shelve* ‖ etw in die ~n eintragen *to make an entry of a th*; *to register a th* ‖ f Ihre ~n ⟨off⟩ *for your retention*

·Akten- ~bündel n *file* **~deckel** m *folder*; *dossier–*, *file-cover* **~heft** n = Aktenbündel **~hefter** m *document-file* **~klammer** f *clip* **⩪kundig** a *on record* [pred] **~mappe** f (im Büro) *file*; → Aktentasche **⩪mäßig** a *documentary* **~mensch** m *red-tapist*; *bureaucrat*; (wichtigtuender) *jack-in-office* **~ordner** m (S) *file*, → Registrator **~papier** n *foolscap* **~schluß** m *the stopping of legal proceedings* **~schnur** f *red-tape* **~schrank** m *shelves, pigeonholes* [pl]; *filing cabinet* **~schreiber** m *clerk* **~schwanz** m *marker* **~seite** f *foolscap page* **~stück** n *official document, deed* **~tasche** (lederne ~) *portfolio*; *document-, briefcase* ‖ → Aktenmappe **~vermerk** m *file-mark* **~vernichter** m, **~vernichtungsmaschine** f *paper shredding machine* **~zeichen** n *reference-mark*

·Aktie f ~/~n, ⟨com⟩ *share*; ~n [pl] *shares, stocks*; ⟨Am⟩ *stock*; (firmeneigen *treasury*; kaduziert *forfeited*; [nicht] stimmberechtigt [*non*] *voting*; Gründer– *founders'* od *promotors'* ..; Inhaber– *bearer* ..; Namens– *registered* ..) Stamm⩪ *original* od *ordinary share*, (bevorzugte .. = Vorzugs⩪ *preferred sh.*; → Interims⩪ | ~n ausgeben *to issue shares* ‖ ~n besitzen *to hold shares* (*in a company*) ‖ in ~n spekulieren *to gamble in shares* ‖ die ~n stehen gut *the shares are* (od *stand*) *at a premium* ‖ ⟨übtr⟩ s–e ~n stehen gut (schlecht) *his prospects are good* (*poor*); wie stehen die ~n? *how are you getting on? how are things?*

·Aktien- ~abschnitt m *coupon, dividend-warrant* **~ausgabe** f *share-issue* **~ausgabenüberwacher** m *registrar* **~bank** f *joint-stock bank* **~besitz** m *holdings* [pl] (in *in*) **~börse** f *Stock Exchange* **~brauerei** f *joint-stock brewery* **~buch** n *stockholders' ledger* **~fonds** m *share-capital*, ⟨Am⟩ *capital stock* **~gesellschaft** (abbr AG) f *joint-stock company*; (mit beschränkter Haftbarkeit) *limited* (*liability*) *company* **~handel** m *dealing in shares, stock-jobbing* **~händler** m *stock-broker, stock-jobber* **~inhaber** m *share-holder*; ⟨Am⟩ *stock-holder* **~kapital** n = Aktienfonds **~kommanditgesellschaft** f *combination of limited liability company and special partnership* **~konto** n *share-holder's account* **~kurs** m *share-quotation* **~makler** m *stock-broker* **~markt** m *share* (od *stock*)*-market* **~schein** m *share-* od *stock-certificate* **~schiebung** f ⟨Am⟩ *stock-jobbing* **~spekulant** m *speculator*; → Baissier, Haussier **~spekulation** f *speculation in stocks* | Buch f **~umschreibungen** f pl .. *transfer journal* **~unternehmen** n *joint-stock undertaking* (od *venture*) **~zeichnung** f *subscription of* .. **~zertifik·at** n *share-certificate*

Akt·inie f ~/~n ⟨zoo⟩ *sea-anemone*; *actinia* (L)

akt·inisch a ⟨med⟩ *actinic* (disease) **Akt·inium** n ~s/ ⟨chem⟩ *actinium* (L)

Akt·ino- (Strahlen–) [in comp] *rayed* **~mykose** f ~/ *actinomycosis* (L)

Akti·on [*ts*] f ~/~en *action*; gemeinsame ~ *joint action*; ~en [pl] *activity, activities* ‖ ⟨mil⟩ *action*; *warfare* | in ~ *in action* ‖ in ~ setzen *to bring into action* ‖ in ~ treten *to enter into action*; *to take action*; ⟨mil & übtr⟩ *to take the field* | **~s- ~art** f ⟨engl gram⟩ z. B.: *continuous tense* (*I am going*) ‖ *aspect* **~komitee** n *council of action*, ⟨SBZ⟩ *action* od *executive group* od *committee* **~malerei** f (vitale ~) *action painting* **~radius** m *radius of action*, ⟨mot⟩ *cruising range* **~strom** m *action current* **~turbine** f *impulse turbine*

Aktion·är [*ts*] m ~s/~e ⟨com⟩ *shareholder*, ⟨Am⟩ *stock-holder* ‖ ~ e–r Gesellschaft sein *to hold shares in a company*

akt·iv I. a **1.** (tätig) *active*; ~er Teilhaber *active partner* ‖ ⟨mil⟩ *active* (→ Heer); *regular* (Truppe, Offizier, Soldat [Ggs *wartime soldier*]); (einsatzbereit) ~e Truppen [pl] *effectives* [pl] ‖ im ~en Dienst *on active service* ‖ ⟨mil hum⟩ *tailor–* (= *machine-*)*made* (*cigarette*) ‖ ⟨Ger univ⟩ ~ w bei e–r Verbindung *to join* (od *to become a menber of*) *a students' club* **2.** ⟨gram⟩ *active* (*verb, voice*) **3.** ⟨chem⟩ *effective*; *reactive* **4.** ⟨com⟩ *active, favourable*; ~e Handelsbilanz *favourable balance of trade* **5.** kulturell ~ *culturally prolific* od *productive* **II.** adv *actively*

·Aktiv n ~s/ ⟨gram⟩ *active voice*

Aktiv- ⟨com⟩ **~außenstände** m pl *active* (od *outstanding*) *debts* **~bestand** m *assets* pl ‖ ⟨mil⟩ *actual* (od *effective*) *strength* **~geschäft** n *active business* **~handel** m *export-trade* **~kohle** f ⟨chem⟩ *activated carbon* **~legitimation** f ⟨jur⟩ *capacity of sue* **~masse** f *a bankrupt's assets* pl **~posten** m *asset*; *credit*; *item* **~saldo** m *credit balance* **~schuld** f *active* (od *outstandig*) *debt* **~vermögen** n *assets* pl

Akt·iva L pl v Aktivum

·Aktive f ~n/~n ⟨mil hum⟩ *tailor- (= machine-)made cigarette*

aktiv·ieren vt [h] ⟨bal⟩ *to post on the assets*

Aktiv·ismus m ⟨philos⟩ *activism* **aktiv·ieren** vt [h] *to make active* od *effective*; *to put into action*; (jdn) *to actuate*; *to act upon* **Aktiv·ist** m ~(e)s/~en ⟨bes SBZ⟩ *activist* **Aktivit·ät** f ~/ *activity*; ~bedürfnis [n] *urge for activity*

Akt·ivum n ~s **1.** ⟨gram⟩ *active voice* **2.** ⟨com⟩ *asset*; [mst pl] Aktiva (*floating*) *assets* [pl]; Aktiva u. Passiva *assets and liabilities*

Aktualit·ät f ~/~en *topical interest, topicality*

Aktu·ar m ~(e)s/~e *actuary, registrar*

aktu·ell a (zeitgemäß) *current*; *topical*; *immediate* (*interest*); ~e Bedeutung *topicality* ‖ (*problems*) *of the day*; ~es Interesse h *to be of topical interest* ‖ *burning* (*question*) ‖ *present day* (*conditions*), *up-to-date* (*information*); (*problems*) *of the day* | [pred] die Frage wurde ~ *the qu. was brought to a point* ‖ ⟨med⟩ wieder ~ w (*of disease*) *to act up*

·Aktus m ~/Akti *act* (: *a solemn act*); (in der Schule) *speech-day*

·Aküsprache f = Abkürzungssprache

Ak·ustik f ~/~en **1.** ⟨phys⟩ *acoustics* [sg konstr] **2.** ⟨übtr⟩ (*of a room*) *acoustics* [pl konstr], *acoustic properties* **ak·ustisch** a *acoustic* ‖ *audible* (Signal)

ak·ut a ⟨med⟩ *acute* | ⟨übtr⟩ *pressing, urgent*; ~ w (of questions) *to arise*; e–e Frage wieder ~ w l *to reopen a question*

Ak·ut m ~s/~e ⟨gram⟩ *acute accent*

akzed·ieren vi/t [h] **1.** [vi] *to accede, to agree* **2.** [vt] etw ~ *to accede* (od *agree*) *to a th*

Akz·ent m ~s/~e **1.** ⟨gram & pros⟩ *accent*; *stress* (auf *on*); schwebender ~ *hovering accent*, → Betonung; der ~ liegt auf .. *the stress is on* ..; den ~ legen auf .. *to put the accent on* ..; (Wort) mit e–m ~ versehen *to accent* **2.** (Aussprache) *accent* (*a good a.*), *pronunciation*; sein Englisch hat e–n reinen ~ *his English has no foreign accent*; irischer ~ *brogue* **3.** ⟨übtr⟩ *accent, emphasis, stress*; den ~ legen auf etw *to stress a th* **akzentu·ieren** vt [h] *to accent, to accentuate*

Akz·ept n ~(e)s/~e ⟨com⟩ *acceptance*, mangels ~s *for want of acceptance*; das ~ einholen *to obtain acceptance*; zum ~ vorzeigen *to present* (*a bill*) *for acceptance*; ein ~ zurückgehen l *to dishonour a bill*; → Annahme ‖ *accepted bill*; *bill* (*of exchange*) **~geschäft** n *acceptance-business* **~kredit** m *acceptance-credit*; *blank credit* **~provision** f *accepting provision*

akzept·abel a *acceptable* (für *to*)

Akzept·ant m ~en/~en ⟨com⟩ *acceptor, drawee* **Akzeptati·on** f ~/en ⟨com⟩ *acceptance* **akzept·ieren** vt [h] *to accept* ‖ (Wechsel) *to accept, to take up, to honour*; nicht ~ *to dishonour* **Akz·eptor** m ~s/–·oren *acceptor*

Akzess·it n ~(s)/~(s) *second prize* ‖ (auf Akten) *date* (od *day*) *of entry* **akzess·orisch** a *accessory* **Akzess·orium** n ~s/–rien → Beiwerk; Nebensache, –anspruch

·akzidens a ⟨philos⟩ *accidental* **·Akzidens** n **1.** (unwesentl. Eigenschaft) *accident*; *accidental*; pl Akzidenzien (Begleiterscheinungen) *accessories* pl **2.** ⟨jur⟩ *accidental*; pl Akzidentalien *accidentals* pl

Akzid·enz f **1.** /~ien (Nebeneinnahme); [mst pl] ~ien *perquisites*; *emoluments* [pl] **2.** [pl ~en] ⟨typ⟩ **a.** = ~druck **b.** ~en pl *display-work*; *job-work* **c.** [in comp] *job*; *jobbing* **~druck** m ⟨typ⟩ (Gelegenheitsdruck) *job-printing, jobbing work* **~drucker** m *job-printer* **~presse** f *job-press*; *jobbing-machine* **~schrift** f ⟨print⟩ *display face*

Akz·ise f ~/~n *excise* (*duty*) | **~n-** **~amt** n *the Board of Customs and Excise* **~beamte** m, der ~ (ein ~r), **~einnehmer** m *exciseman*; *commissioner of excise*

akzisepflichtig a *excisable*

à la [Fr] *à la, after*; *after the manner of*; *in the style of*; ⟨cul⟩ .. *–style*

Alab·ama n (Staat der U.S.A.) **~-Fluß** m *Alabama River*

Alab·aster m ~s/ ⟨minr⟩ *alabaster* **≗weiß** a *brilliant white* (*paper*) **alab·astern** a *alabaster, made of a.* ‖ *like a.*; *white*

à la carte [a lɑˈkɑ:t] [Fr] *à la carte* **à la mode** [Fr] adv *à la mode* **Alamode**– *alamode* ..

·Ala Dagh m (Gebirgszüge in Kleinasien)

·Aland m ~s/~e ⟨ich⟩ *white-fish*; *dace* ‖ = **·Alant** m ~s/~e ⟨bot⟩ *elecampagne*

·Alandinseln f pl (finn. Inselgruppe) *Aland Islands* pl

†**Al·anen** pl ⟨ant⟩ (skyth. Volksstamm) *Alans, Alani* pl

Al·arm m ~(e)s/~e **1. a.** ⟨mil⟩ *alarm*; ~! ⟨mil⟩ *fall in at the double*; blinder ~ *false alarm*; stiller ~ *still alarm*; ~ blasen, ~ schlagen *to sound the alarm* ‖ den ~(zustand) aufheben *to give* (*the*) *stand-down* (⟨anti-aero⟩ *the all clear*) ‖ ⟨aero⟩ Flieger≗ *air raid warning*; *alert* (: *alert was given when* ..) **b.** (Warnung) *alarm* **2.** (Lärm) *tumult, disturbance* **~·abstellplatz** m ⟨aero⟩ *alert platform* **≗bereit** a ⟨mil⟩ *in constant readiness*; *on the alert* **~bereitschaft** f *alert*; ⟨mil⟩ *stand-by* s; ⟨aero⟩ *preparedness for an air-raid*; *ground alert*; in ~ *in constant readiness*; *on the alert* (od *look-out*); in ~ setzen *to alert* (*troops*) **~glocke** f *alarum, tocsin* **~ruf** m *alarm* **~start** m ⟨mil aero⟩ *scramble* **~stellung** f ⟨mil⟩ *action station* **~stufe** f *stage of alarm* **~übung** f *practice alarm* **~unterkunft** f *close billets* pl **~signal** n, **~zeichen** n *alarm*, das ~ geben *to give* od *raise the alarm*; ⟨aero⟩ (bei Luftangriff) *to sound the air raid warning* **~zustand** m → Alarm-(bereitschaft), *stand-to* s

alarm·ieren vt/i [h] **1.** [vt] *to alarm*; (jdn) *to call out, to alert* ‖ (Polizei, Feuerwehr) ⟨mst⟩ *to call* **2.** [vi] *to give* (od *raise*) *the alarm*

Al·aska n *Alaska* (NW-Amerika)

Al·aun m ~s/~e ⟨chem⟩ *alum* **≗artig** a *aluminous* **~bad** n ⟨chem⟩ *alum bath* **~erde** f *alum earth* **≗haltig** a *aluminous* **~gerber** m *tawer* **~gerberei** f *tawery* ‖ [abstr] *tawing* **~leder** n *white leather* **~schiefer** m *alum-shale* **~stein** m *stone alum* **~werk** a *alum-works* [pl]

Alb m ~(e)s/~e **1.** *elf* **2.** (Alp) *nightmare*

Alb f ~/~en = Alm | **Alb** f ~/ ⟨Ger⟩ (Gebirge); die rauhe ~ *the Suabian Alb*

Alb·aner m ~s/~, **Alban·ese** m ~n/~n *Albanian* **Alb·aner Gebirge** n ⟨It⟩ *Monti Albani*, ⟨a.⟩ *Alban Mount* **Alb·aner See** m ⟨It⟩ *Lago di Albano* **alb·anisch** *Albanian*

Albar·ello m ~s/~s *chemist's vessel*

·Albatros m ~/–trosse ⟨orn⟩ *albatross*

·Albe f ~/~n ⟨R. C. & C. E.⟩ (weißes Priestergewand) *alb*

Alber·ei f ~/~en = Albernheit

·albern I. a **1.** (mst v P) (dumm) *childish, foolish, simple*; *fatuous*; *silly* ⟨fam⟩ *namby-pamby* **2.** (mst v S) (fade) *inane, inept*; *absurd*; *footling* (*play*) **3.** ~e Bemerkung f *ineptitude* ‖ °~e Gans *silly goose* ‖ ~er Mensch m *simpleton, fool* ‖ ~es Geschwätz n *inanities* [pl] ‖ ~es Zeug n *nonsense* **II.** adv *childishly, foolishly* ‖ sich ~ benehmen *to be silly* **III.** vi [h] *to behave childishly* od *foolishly*; *to be silly, to play the fool*

·Albernheit f ~/~en *childishness, silliness*; *tomfoolery*; *nonsense* ‖ e–e ~ *a piece of folly*; *an inanity* ‖ ~en [pl] *foolish things*

Albig·enser m ~s/~ ⟨ec⟩ die ~ [pl] *Albigenses*

Albin·ismus m ~/ ⟨med⟩ *albinism* **Alb·ino** m ~s/~s *albino*

·Albion n ~s/ *Albion, England*

·Album n, ~(e)s/Alben *album*; (zum Einkleben) *scrap-book*
Album·in n ~s/~e ⟨chem⟩ *albumin*; ~papier n ⟨phot⟩ *albuminpaper*
·Albus f ~/~ (= automatische Löschung bei unrichtigen Salden) ⟨comp⟩ *Arib* (= *automatic rejection of incorrect balances*)
Alcalde m ~n/~n → Alkalde
Alchem·ie f ~/ *alchemy*
·Älchen n ~s/~ ⟨zoo⟩ *threadworm*
Alchim·ie f ~/ *alchemy* **Alchim·ist** m ~en/~en *alchemist* **alchim·istisch** a *a.stic(al), alchemic(al)*
alcy·onisch a → friedlich (~e Tage)
Aldeh·yd m ~(e)s/~e ⟨chem⟩ *aldehyde*
Alderman [ˈɔːldəmən] m ~s/-men ⟨engl⟩ (Stadtrat) *alderman*
·Aldusblätter n pl ⟨print⟩ *florets, flowers*
Ale [eil] n ~s/ ⟨engl⟩ *ale* (helles Bier)
Alem·anne m ~n/~n *Alemannian*; *Alemannian German* **alem·annisch** a *Alemannic (dialect)*; *Alemannian*
Al·eppo n jetzt Haleb → d.
Aless·andria n (Stadt u Prov. in Oberitalien)
Aletschgletscher m (in den Berner Alpen)
·Aleuron n ~s/-r·one (Eiweiß) *aleuron(e)*
Ale·uten, Ale·utische Inseln f pl *Aleutian Islands* pl; (Bewohner) *Aleut*; **Ale·utischer Graben** m ⟨mar⟩ *Aleutian Trough* od *Trench*
·Alex m = Alexanderplatz (Berlin) (am .. *in*)
Alexandr·ia, Alex·andrien n [Eg] *Alexandria*
Alexandr·iner m ~s/~ **1.** (P) ⟨philos⟩ *Alexandrian* **2.** ⟨pros⟩ *the Alexandrine*; *Alexandrine verse* (v 12 Silben) **alexandr·inisch** a *Alexandrian, Alexandrine*
·Alfa f, ~gras n *alfa*; *esparto (grass)*
°**Alfanzer·ei** f ~/~en *(tom)foolery* ‖ ~ treiben *to play the fool*
·Alföld (die niederungarische Tiefebene)
·Algäu m → Allgäu
·Alge f ~/~n ⟨bot⟩ *alga* [pl -*gae*] L; *seaweed*; Rot≃ *dulse* ‖ am Meeresstrand ausgeworfene ~nmassen [pl] *wrack*
·Algebra f ~/ *algebra* **Algebr·aiker** m ~s/~ *algebraist* **algebr·aisch** a ⟨scient⟩ *algebraic (equation)* | *algebraical (signs, treatise)*
Algec·iras n (spanische Hafenstadt) *Algeciras*
·Algen- [in comp] *algal (cell, element)*
Alg·erien n *Algeria* **alg·erisch** a *Algerian* **·Algier** n *Algiers* **Alg·ierer** m, **~in** f *Algerine, Algerian*
Alg·onkin pl (Indianer Nordamerikas) *Algonquin* [pl]
Algor·ithmus m ~/ [Arab-Gr] *algorithm*
·alias [L] *alias*; *otherwise (called)*
·Alibi n ~s/~s ⟨jur⟩ *alibi*; sein ~ beweisen *or* erbringen *to establish* (od *prove*) *one's a., to set up an a.* ‖ vorgetäuschtes ~ *false a.*; ⟨Am⟩ *stall*
Alic·ante n ⟨span⟩ (Stadt u Provinz)
align·ieren [-nji-] vt [h] ⟨print⟩ *to straighten lines*
aliment·är a *alimentary* **Alimentati·on** [ts] f ~/~en *alimony* **Alim·ente** n pl *legal payments of a father for the support of his illegitimate child*; ⟨m.m.⟩ *alimony* **aliment·ieren** vt [h] jdn ~ *to pay alimony to a p*
a limine [L] jdn ~ abweisen *to give a p a snub*
Al·inea n [L] ~/~e *new paragraph*; *break*
aliph·atisch a ⟨chem⟩ *aliphatic*
aliqu·ant a ⟨math⟩ *aliquant* **aliqu·ot** a (*5 is an*) *aliquot (part of 15)*
Alizar·in n ~s/ ⟨chem⟩ (Krapprot) *alizarin*
Alk m ~(e)s/~e ⟨orn⟩ *auk*; gr ~ *garefowl*
Alk·alde m ~n/~n *alcalde, magistrate*
Alk·ali n ~s/~en ⟨chem⟩ *alkali*; in ein ~ verwandeln *to alkalify* **~t·ät** f ~/ *alkalescence*
alk·alisch a *alkaline* **·Alkaloid** n ⟨chem⟩ *alkaloid*
Alk·anna f ~/ ⟨bot⟩ *alkanet*
Alk·ide m ⟨ant⟩ *Heracles*
·Alkohol m ~s/~e ⟨chem⟩ *alcohol* ‖ ⟨Am⟩ *rum*, ⟨sl⟩ *hooch*; → alkoholisch ‖ absoluter ~ *absolute alcohol*; mit ~ sättigen *to alcoholize*
·Alkohol- [in comp] *alcoholic* **~ausschank** m unerlaubter ~ (Laden) ⟨Am sl⟩ *speak-easy* **≃frei** a *non-alcoholic*; ⟨fam⟩ *soft (drinks)* **~gegner** m *prohibitionist, dry* [pl *drys*]; ⟨Am⟩ *pussyfoot* **~gehalt** m *alcoholic strength* **≃haltig** a *alcoholic* **~kraftstoff** m ⟨mot⟩ *alcohol-blended fuel* **≃löslich** a *spirit-soluble* **~monopol** n *monopoly of* (od *in*) *brandy* **~schmuggel** m *liquor-smuggling* ⟨Am sl⟩ *bootlegging* **~schmuggler** m *liquor-smuggler*; ⟨Am⟩ *rum-runner* ‖ ⟨sl⟩ *bootlegger* **~verbot** n *Prohibition*; unter ~ stehend ⟨Am⟩ *dry*; das ~ einführen *to go dry* **~vergiftung** f *alcoholism*
Alkoh·oliker m ~s/~ *alcoholic, alcoholist*
alkoh·olisch a *alcoholic (drink)*; stark ~ *hard (drink)*; ~es Getränk [n] ⟨Am sl⟩ *tanglefoot* ‖ ~e Getränke n [pl] *alcoholic drinks*; *spirituous liquors*; *spirits* [pl]; ⟨Am fam⟩ *wet goods*
alkoholis·ieren vt [h] ⟨chem⟩ *to alcoholize*
Alkohol·ismus m ~/ *alcoholism*
Alkoholom·eter n ~s/~ *alcoholometer* **Alkoholometr·ie** f ~/ *alcoholometry*
Alkor·an m ~s/ der ~ *the Koran*
Alk·oven m ~s/~ *alcove, recess*
Alk·ydharz n *alkyd resin*
alky·onisch a (friedlich) → **alcyonisch**
all 1. a [in geh. Spr. unflektiert vor pron poss & dem] ~ sein Gut *all his goods*; er verlor ~ seine Habe *he lost his all* ‖ ~ s-e Kraft *all his* (od *his whole*) *energy*; trotz ~ m-r Anstrengungen *in spite of all my efforts* ‖ → alle **2.** [abs] ~ und jeder *all and every, all and sundry*; *each and every* **3.** [adv] † *very, quite* **4.** [in comp] *all* ..
·All n ~s/ *the universe*; *the world* ‖ Rufe aus dem ~ *voices from the outer space*
·all- ~·abendlich adv *every evening, every night* **~bek·annt** a *well-known (writer)* ‖ *notorious (fact)*; es ist ~, daß *it is notorious* (od *common knowledge*) *that* | ⟨aero⟩ *notorious (plagiator)* **~ber·eits** adv = bereits **≃buch** n *encyclop(a)edia* **~deutsch** a *Pan-German (League)* **≃f·arbenempfindlich** a *panchromatic* ‖ ≃keit f ~/ *panchromatism*; *sensivity to all colo(u)rs* **≃g·egenwart** f *omnipresence, ubiquity* **~gegenw·ärtig** a *omnipresent, ubiquitous* **~gem·ach** adv = allmählich **~gem·ein** → dort **≃gewalt** f *omnipotence* **~gew·altig** a *omnipotent, almighty* **~g·ütig** a *all-bountiful, infinitely good* **≃h·eilmittel** n *universal remedy*; *panacea (against)* **~j·ährig** a *yearly* **~j·ährlich 1.** a *yearly, annual* **2.** adv *annually, yearly*; *every year* **≃macht** f *omnipotence* **~m·ächtig** a *almighty, all-powerful, omnipotent* der ≃e *the Almighty, Almighty God* **~m·ählich** → dort **≃m·ende, ·Almeinde** f *common land, common*; *common pasture*; *common forest* **~m·onatlich 1.** a *monthly* **2.** adv *every month*; *once a month* **≃radlenkung** f *all-wheel steering* **≃seitenbühne** f ⟨theat⟩ *theatre in the round*; *central* od *circular acting aera* **~seitig 1.** a *universal* ‖ *all-round* (Bildung) **2.** adv *universally*; ~ betrachten *to consider from every angle* **≃seitigkeit** f *universality* **≃sichtkabine** f *full view cabin* **≃stahl-** *unisteel* .. **≃strom** m ⟨el⟩ *universal current* **≃stromempfangsgerät** n ⟨wir⟩ *all-mains receiver, ac–dc set* **≃synchrongetriebe** n ⟨mot⟩ *all-synchromesh gear box* **≃tag, ~täglich, ~tags** → dort **·≃über·all** adv *everywhere*; *all round* **~umf·assend** a *all-embracing*; *universal (mind)*; *general (education)*; *sweeping (measures, reform, etc)*; *across-the-board (tax cut)*; *encyclop(a)edic(al) (knowledge)* **·≃vater** m *Woden, Father of all* **~ver·ehrt** a *universally revered* **≃wellenempfänger** m ⟨wir⟩ *all-wave receiver* **≃wetter-** *all-weather (outfit)* ‖ ~flugzeug [n] *a.-w. aircraft* ‖ ~verdeck [n] ⟨mot⟩ *weatherproof fabric top* **~w·issend** a *all-knowing*,

omniscient **≗w·issenheit** f *omniscience* **~w·ö-chentlich 1.** a *weekly, hebdomadal, hebdomadary* **2.** adv *every week* **·~zeit** adv → allezeit **·~zu** etc → dort **≗zweck-** *all-duty* (*tractor*), *carry-all-* (*truck*) || ~fahrzeug [n] *general purpose vehicle*

·Allah, All·ah (arabisch) *Allah*

Allahab·ad n (ind. Stadt)

alld·a adv *there; at the same place* **·alldieweil** † conj *because* || ⟨jur⟩ *whereas*

·alle I. a [stets stark flektiert] (→ alles) **A.** [sg] **1.** [attr] **a.** (ganz) *all*; (jeder) *every*; *any* || ~ Welt *all the world, everybody* || ~s Geld *all the money*; ~s Gute *everything good*; ~s denkbar Gute *all the good in the world*; ~s Mögliche *all sorts of things* || ~n Kontakt verlieren *to lose all contact* (od *any contact whatever*) || ~ Parteien umfassend *all-party* [attr] **b. auf ~** mögliche Art *in every possible way* || → Ding II. A. 3. b. || **ohne** ~n Grund *without any reason*; ohne ~ Ursache *without any reason*; ohne ~n Zweifel *beyond all doubt* **c.** [verstärkend] **mit** ~r Eile *with all speed*; mit ~r Macht *with might and main* || **in** ~r Frühe *first thing in the morning* || in ~r Nacht *at dead of night* || wer, was, warum, wie in ~r Welt ..? *who, what, why, how on earth* (od *in the world*) ..? **2.** [pred]° **a. (S) ~ s:** *to be at an end*; *to be* (*all*) *gone* (:*the veal's all gone*); (*the soap*) *is used up*; (*our money*) *is spent* || etw **~m** *to finish up* || **~w:** *to run out* (:*our supplies have run out*; .. sind ~ (geworden) *we have run out of s.s*) || ⟨Kinderspr.⟩ ~ ~! *all gone*! **b. (P)** es ist ~ mit ihm *he is done for* ⟨Am⟩ *all-in*; *it is all up with him*; ich bin ganz ~ *I am done up*; → ab I. 4. || die Dummen werden nicht ~ *there is no end of fools*; → abreißen || jdn ~ m *to exhaust, finish a p* **B.** [pl] **1. ~ Bewerber** *all* (*the*) *candidates*; ~ Schulen *all schools* || sie suchten alle kl Reste auf, die sie nur finden konnten *they picked up what trifles they might find* || ~ anderen *all the others*; ~ Beide *both of them* | ~ Menschen *everybody* || ~ s–e Blicke *his every look*; ~ nur denkbaren Schandtaten *every imaginable outrage*; ~ nur möglichen Maßnahmen *any measures whatever* || ~ möglichen Dinge *all sorts of things* **2.** Wendungen **a. ~ Tage** *every day, daily*; ~ zwei Tage *every other* (od *second*) *day*; ~ (*or* aller) drei Tage *every third day, every three days*; alle acht Tage *once a week*; alle (*or* aller) zehn Tage *every ten days* **b.** [nach prep] **auf ~** Fälle *at all events, in any case, at any rate* || auf ~n vieren *on all fours* || **aus** ~r Herren Ländern *from all over the world, from all the corners of the earth* || ein f ~mal *once and for all; for good and all* || **nach** ~n Richtungen *in all directions* || **unter** ~n Umständen *under any circumstances* || **vor** ~n anderen *of all others* || vor ~n Dingen *above* (od *before, of*) *all things*, → alles **II.** [abs] **A.** [pl] (→ all 2.) **1.** ~ *all*; *everyone* || fast ~ *most all* || ~, **die ..** *all who .., whoever*; ~, die etwas bedeuten *everybody who is anybody* || ~ sind sich einig *all are agreed*; die Herren wurden ~ eingeladen *the gentlemen were all invited*; sie sahen sich ~ um *everyone looked about them*; schicke sie ~ fort *send them away, everyone* | ~ außer e–r beschränkten Anzahl *all but a limited number* || ~ zus– *one and all* | **wir ~** *all of us*; **sie ~** *all of them* **2.** in der Stadt **in ~r Munde** sein *to be much talked of in the town, to be the talk of a town* || **vor ~r Augen** *openly, publicly*; *unblushingly*; → aller– **B. ~s 1. (S** etc) **a.** *all* || (~s einzelne) *everything*; (~s Beliebige *or* Mögliche) *anything* || ~s, was ... *all that .., everything that ...* || was auch ~s *whatever* || z ~m fähig *capable of anything* || **b.** (Wendungen:) **ist das ~s**? *is that all* ⟨fam⟩ *is that the lot*?, ⟨iron⟩ *a fat lot*! || das ist ~s u. nichts weiter *that is all there is to it* || das ist noch nicht ~s *there is more to it than this* || ~s ist verloren (*or* aus) *all is lost*; *the game is up* || ~s (ist) in Ordnung! *all right*! || ~s andere, nur nicht .., ~s andere als .. *anything but* || es ist mir ~s eins (*or* gleich) *it is all one* (od *all the same*) *to me* || ~s zugleich *all in one* || ~s oder nichts *neck or nothing*, (*all or nothing at all*) || das ist ~s ganz schön, aber .. *that is all very fine* (od *well*) *but* .. || er ist bemüht ~ z sein *he endeavours to be the whole th* (od *show*) || ~s Irische *things* [pl] *Irish*; ~s Weibliche *things* [pl] *feminine* || Ende gut ~s gut *all's well that ends well* || er ist mein ~s *he is my all* | [nach prep] Mädchen **für ~s** *general servant, maid-of-all-work*; ⟨fam⟩ *the general* || sich **in ~s** fügen *to submit to everything* || **in ~m** *in all* (:*£ 50 in all*); ~s in ~m *all in all*; (*up*)*on the whole*; *by and large*; *first and last*; → u. || **nach ~m** *after all* || **trotz ~m** *after all* || **über ~s** gehen (of things) *to stand supreme* || Du giltst (*or* gehst) ihm über ~s *you are everything* (od *you are all in all*; *you are all the world*) *to him* || **vor ~m** *above all, first of all*; zu jener Zeit vor ~m *at that time of all times*; → I. B. 2. b. || **~s aufbieten** *to do one's utmost, to make every effort* (*to do*) || ~ tun, was .. *not to leave anything undone that* .. || ~s mit sich reißend *carrying all before him* (*he* ..) || [oft vor prs p] ~s durchdringend *all-pervading* (*truth*); ~s übertreffend *all-surpassing* || **~s in ~m genommen,** ~s zus–genommen *taken all round, taken all in all*; *after all is said and done*; *taking one th with another* (→ o.) **2. (P) ~s lacht** *everyone is laughing* || ~s lief dahin *all* (*the*) *people flocked there* **3. (als Verstärkung) a. ~s das, das ~s** *all that, all this* || es hat ~s k–n Zweck *it is no use whatever* || was soll das ~s? *what is the use of all that*? || wer weiß, was ~s besprochen wurde *goodness knows what was discussed* || wer weiß, wer ~s dort war *goodness knows who were there* (od *present*) || nicht um ~s in der Welt *not for the world* **b. bei ~dem, trotz ~dem** *after all*

All·ee f ~/~n [–e:ən] *avenue, walk* (*tree lined*) || (Park ≗) *alley* (*yew alley*), ⟨Am⟩ *parkway*

Allegh·eny m (Quellfluß des Ohio) **Allegh·eny-gebirge** n *Alleg*(*h*)*eny* (*Mountains*)

Allegor·ie f ~/~n *allegory* **alleg·orisch 1.** a *allegoric*(*al*); in ~em Sinn = ~ adv **2.** adv *allegorically* **allegorisieren** vt [h] *to allegorize*

allegr·etto 1. adv ⟨mus⟩ *allegretto* **2.** ≗ n ~s/~s *allegretto* **all·egro 1.** [adv] ⟨mus⟩ *allegro* **2.** ≗ n ~s/~s *allegro* [pl *allegros*]

all·ein 1. a [nur pred] **a.** (ohne Begleitung) *alone* (: *to be, travel alone*); (f sich) ~ s *to be by o.s.* || *solitary, single* (: *to live single*) || ein Mann ~ im Boot *a man by himself in the boat* | ganz ~ *all alone*; nicht ~ *not alone, not by o.s.* || für dich ~ *for your very own* || ein Haus für sich ~ *a self-contained house* || zu zweit ~ **fahren** etc ⟨sl⟩ *to solo it*; ~ **fliegen** ⟨aero⟩ *to solo* || jdm ganz ~ **gehören** *to be one's very own* || die Tatsache ~ genügt *the very fact suffices* || **laß** mich ~ *leave* od *let me alone* || ich konnte ihn nicht ~ **sprechen** *I could not speak to him privately* || Sie **stehen** nicht ~ mit dieser Ansicht *you are not alone in that opinion* **b.** (ohne Hilfe) *alone, of oneself*; das Kind **läuft** schon ~ *the child walks already of itself*; ~ **stehen,** ~ kämpfen *to play a lone hand* (*in a war*) || er kann es ~ **tun** *he can do it alone*; **c.** (bloß) er ~ *he alone* (*came*); *only he* || die Tatsache ~ genügt *the fact alone suffices* || der Gedanke ~, schon ~ der Gedanke *the very thought, the mere* (od *bare*) *thought* || ihr Blick ~ *their very look* **2.** [adv] (nur) *alone, only*; ~ der Vater *only the father, the f. alone*; nicht ~ .. sondern auch *not alone* od *not only .. but also* **3.** [conj] *but, however*

all·ein- [in comp] *sole*; *exclusive* **~berechtigt** a *possessing all rights* **≗berechtigung** f *exclusive* *right* **≃besitz** m *sole, absolute* od *exclusive possession* **≃flug** m ⟨aero⟩ *solo (-flight)* **≃gespräch** n *soliloquy, monologue* **≃handel** m *monopoly*; ~ treiben mit *to monopolize* **≃händler** m *monopolist*; *sole agent* **≃herrschaft** f *monarchy* || *autocratic rule, autocracy* || *dominion* **≃herrscher** m *monarch*; ~ sein in *to reign supreme in* (*a region*) || *autocrat* **≃hersteller** m *monopolist* **≃inhaber** m *sole owner* **≃sein** n *loneliness, solitariness*; *isolation* || (Unverheiratetsein) (*blessed*) *singleness* || Zeiten des ~s *times of loneliness* **~seligmachend** a ⟨ec⟩ *only saving* (*faith*) **~stehend** a *alone*; *solitary*; ~er Herr, ≃er *single man*, (a) *man by himself*; ~ s *to live alone* || (of buildings) *detached*; *standing apart*; ~es Doppelhaus *two semi-detached houses* **≃verkauf** m ⟨com⟩ *monopoly*; *sole agency*; *exclusive right(s) of sale* **≃vertreter** m *sole agent* **≃vertrieb** m: den ~ h *to be the sole distributors* [pl] (*of a th*), *the sole agents* [pl] (*for a p*)

all·einig a *only, sole* (*owner*), *exclusive* (*agent*); *unique* || der ~e Gott *the one God* || Schriftstellern war s–e ~e Beschäftigung *writing was his one occupation* | [pred] *alone*; dies war das ~e Ziel *this alone was the aim*

·Allel n ~s/ ⟨biol⟩ *allele*

allemal adv **1.** *always, every time*; ein f ~ *once and for all* || ~ wenn *whenever* .. **2.** *in any case*; *without question* || *of course*

·allenfalls adv *if need be*; *if necessary* || (höchstens) *at the most* || (vielleicht) *perhaps, possibly*

allenth·alben adv *everywhere*; → überall

·aller- **~art** a [nicht flektierbar] = allerhand **~·äußerst** a (*the*) *utmost* (*ends*); (*the*) *uttermost* (*parts*) || ~er Preis *the bottom price* **~b·est** a *best of all, the very best*; das ≃e *the very best thing*; ⟨fam⟩ *the best of the bunch* **~chr·istlichst** a ⟨a-engl⟩ Seine ~e Majestät *His Most Christian Majesty* **~d·ings** adv → bes Artikel **~dr·inglichst** a (*the*) *most urgent* **~·einzigst** a (*my*) *one and only* **~·erst 1.** [a] *the first and foremost*; *first--ever* || die ~e Sorge *the number one concern* **2.** [adv] ~, zu ~ *first of all*; *first and foremost* **~ger·ingst** a *the very lowest*; nicht im ~en *not in the very least* **~gn·ädigst** a *most gracious* **~gr·ößt** a: mit ~er Eile *with the utmost speed* **~hand** a → dort **≃h·eiligen** n *All-Hallows*; *All Saints' Day* (1. Nov.) **~h·eiligst** a *the most holy* || das ≃e (Hochaltarstätte) *the sanctuary*; (im jüdischen Tempel) *the Holy of Holies* **~höchst** a *the highest of all*; der ≃e (= Gott) *the Holy, One the Most High* .. || ≃derselbe *His Majesty*; ≃dieselben *His Royal Highness*; auf ≃en Befehl *by order of His Majesty*; Aufführung auf ≃en B. *command performance* **~h·öchstens** adv *at the very most* **~l·etzt 1.** [a] *the very last, the last of all*; das ~e versuchen *to try the utterest, to grab at straws*, → Möglichkeit || die ~en *the latest* (*novelties*) **2.** [adv] ~, zu ~ *last of all*; *in the end* || bis zu ~ *to the very end*; daran denkt man zu ~ *that is the last place in a p's thought*, → denken **~l·iebst** a *lovely, most delightful*; *adorable*; *charming*; was für e–e (*or* e–e ganz) ~e Kette! *what a love of chain*! ganz (*or* welch) ~e Tassen *what loves of cups*; ein (ganz) ~er Wagen *a peach of a car* || (der, die) ≃e *sweetheart* || am ~en möchte ich gehen *I should like best* (*of all*) *to leave* | ⟨iron⟩ ~! *you don't say so*!, *that is bad*! **≃mannsh·arnisch** m ⟨bot⟩ *wild mandrake, serpent's garlic* **~m·eist** a *most*; der ~e Teil *most part* (*of the year*); *the* (*by far*) *greater part* (*of them*) || am ~en *most*; *most of all*; *for the most part* **~n·ächst** a *the very next* **~n·eust** a *the very newest*; *the latest, up-to-the minute* (*fashion*) **~niedrigst** a ⟨fam⟩ *rock-bottom* (*price*) | das ≃notwendigste *the barest necessities* **~orten, ~orts** adv *everywhere*; *allover the world* **~schl·immst** a *the worst of all*; aufs ≃e *in the worst way possible* **~s·eelen** n ⟨ec⟩ *All Souls' Day* (2. Nov.) **~seits** adv → dort **~·untertänigst** a *most humble* **~wärts, ~wegen** adv *everywhere*; *all round* **≃w·eltsfreund** m *everybody's friend* **≃w·eltskerl** m: ein ~ *a devil of a fellow*; → Mordskerl **~w·erteste** m *backside, posterior*; ⟨fam⟩ *the b.t.m.* (= *bottom*)

allerd·ings adv **1.** [unbetont] *it is true*; *indeed* (: *the servants were indeed few*); *one must remember* od *not forget* (*that the man is an artist*); *I admit* od *confess*; ~ ist er ein Künstler (*it is*) *true, he is an artist*; *he is an a., it is true*; ich mag ~ Unrecht h *I may, indeed, be wrong* **2.** [betont & in Antworten] *decidedly, certainly, doubtless, of course, to be sure*; (*he is an artist*) *indeed*; ⟨Am⟩ *sure* || ~ glaube ich das *I do think so* || → freilich

Allerg·ie f ~/ ⟨physiol⟩ (Überempfindlichkeit) *allergy* **–gol·oge** m ~n/~n *allergologue*

·allerhand a [nicht flektierbar] *diverse, sundry*; ~ Sachen *all sorts of things*; *things of all kinds* (od *sorts*) | ~ Geld *a pretty penny* | °allerh·and *a good deal*; ⟨sl⟩ (*he knows*) *a th or two* || das ist allerh·and f e–n Jungen v deiner Größe *that's not bad* (od *that's well enough*) *for a kid of your size* || das ist allerh·and! *that's too much of a good thing*!, *that is bad*! || *that's putting it strong*

·allerlei 1. a [nicht flektierbar] = allerhand **2.** ≃ n: ein ~ v *a variety of*..; *a medley of* (*things*) || ⟨cul⟩ (Mischgemüse) *mixed vegetables* || ⟨übtr Lit & mus⟩ *medley, miscellany*

allers·eits adv *from* (od *on*) *all sides, on* (od *from*) *every side* (→ Seite); *from all parts*: *all--round*; *everywhere* || Guten Abend ~ *good night everybody*; ich empfehle mich ~ *my compliments to you all*

Allerw·elts- **~kerl** m *devil of a fellow*

·alles → alle II. B. || was sahen wir nicht ~! *what didn't we see*? || ~ in allem .. *taking all things together, all things considered*; *generally speaking* || ~, nur nicht .. *all* od *everything but* od *except* ..; ~ übrige, ~ weitere *everything else, the rest* **≃brenner** m *all-fuel fire* **≃kleber** m *all-purpose adhesive* **≃könner** m *all-round man* od ⟨fam⟩ *fellow* **≃wisser** m: die ~ [pl] *the know--alls* **·allesamt** adv *all together* **allew·eil(e), allw·eil** adv *always* || *just now*; *only just* **allez·eit, allz·eit** adv *always*; (*at*) *any time*

·Allgäu, ·Algäu n ⟨Ger⟩ (Landschaft in Oberbayern, Württemberg u Vorarlberg)

Allgäuer Alpen pl *Algau Alps* pl

allgem·ein I. [a] **1. a.** *universal, general, common*; *public* || *all-round* (*reduction*); *across-the--board* (*tax cut*); ⟨bes Am⟩ *over-all* (*shortages*); *global* (*research*) | ⟨übtr⟩ *broad* (*outline* etc); e–e zu ~e Behauptung *a sweeping assertion* **b.** ~e Anwendung *universality* || ~e Äußerung *generality* || das ~e Beste *the general good, the common weal* || ~e Bildung *general knowledge* || ~er Charakter *generality, universality*; e–r S ~en Ch. verleihen *to universalize a th* || auf e–e ~e Formel bringen *to generalize* || zu ~em Gebrauch *for general use* || zur ~en Kenntnis bringen *to bring to public notice* || sich in ~en Redensarten bewegen *to generalize*; *to talk in general* || ~e Schlüsse ziehen *to generalize* (aus *from*) || ~e Verbreitung *universality* || ~es Wahlrecht *universal suffrage* || ~e Wehrpflicht *compulsory service, conscription* || mit ~er Zustimmung *by common consent* **c.** ~ m *to generalize* **2.** [abs] **das ≃e** *the universal, the general, the common*; *the generality*; das ≃e e–r S betonen *to generalize a th* || zum ~en aufsteigen *to ascend to generals* | im ~en *in* (*the*) *general*; *generally* (*speaking*); *commonly, altogether*; ⟨Am fam⟩ *by and large*; im ~en sprechen *to generalize* | das tat ich im ~en nicht *I usen't to*

II. adv *generally, commonly* | ~ anerkannt *received* (*text*); *generally accepted* ‖ ~ bekannt *widely known*; ~ bekannt m *to make public*; ~ bekannt s *to be public property* ‖ ~ bindend *universal* (*rules*); ⟨Am⟩ *blanket* (*law*); ~ bindend m *to universalize* ‖ ~ durchgeführt (*or* gebräuchlich) *general, universal* ‖ ~ gebraucht w *to obtain, to prevail* ‖ ~ gesprochen *generally speaking* ‖ ~ verbreiten (*or* verwenden) *to universalize*; ~ verbreitet *widespread*; ~ verbreitet s *to be universal* (unter *among*) ≃**begriff** m *general idea*; *concept*; *universal* ≃**bildung** f *general knowledge*; gr ~ *wide culture* ~**gültig** a *universal* (*rules*); *all-round* ‖ das ≃e dargestellt am Einzelfall ⟨Lit⟩ *concrete universal* ≃**gültigkeit** f *universality* ≃**gut** n ⟨übtr⟩ *common knowledge* (~ geworden s *to be c. k.*); *public property* ~**verständlich** a *intelligible to the general* (od *to all*) ≃**wohl** n *common welfare*

Allgem·einheit f [abstr] *universality, generality* ‖ (Volk) *the general* (: *caviare to the g.*); *the public*

·Allheit f *totality* ‖ *universality*

allh·ier adv *here*; *in this* (*very*) *place*

Alli·anz f ~/~en *alliance* (*Holy A.*); *league*

Allig·ator m ~s/–gat·oren ⟨zoo⟩ *alligator*

alli·ieren vt [h]: sich ~ *to ally oneself* (mit *to, with*); alliiert *allied* (mit *to, with*) **Alli·ierte** m [der ~ (ein ~r)] ~n/~n *ally*; die ~n [pl] *the allies* pl

Alliterati·on f ~/~en *alliteration* **alliter·ieren** vi [h] *to alliterate*; ~d a *alliterative*

allm·ählich **1.** a *gradual* **2.** adv *gradually*; *by degrees*; *by little and little*; *little by little*; ~ aufsteigend *progressive*; sie wurden ~ reich *they grew wealthy*; er wurde ~ bekannt *he came to be known by slow degrees*

Allm·ende, ⟨Sw⟩ **Allm·end** f ~/~(e)n *common* (*pasture land*)

·allo- [in comp] ⟨mst med⟩ *allo–*

·Allod n ~s/~e *al(l)odium* [late L] **allodi·al** a *al(l)odial*; ≃gut n *al(l)odial estate*; *estate in fee simple*; *freehold*

Allogam·ie f ~/ ⟨bot⟩ (Fremdbestäubung) *allogamy* **allog·en** a ⟨geol⟩ (Ggs autogen) *allogeneous*

Allokuti·on [ts] f ⟨R. C.⟩ *allocution*

All·onge [aˈlɔ̃ʒə] f [Fr] ⟨com⟩ (am Wechsel) *allonge, rider* ‖ (im Buche) *fly-leaf* ~**perücke** f *full-bottomed wig*

Allop·ath m ~en/~en *allopath, allopathist*

Allopath·ie f ~/ *allopathy* **allop·athisch** a *allopathic* **Alloph·on** n ~s/~e ⟨phon⟩ (Variation e–s Phonems z.B. in Koch u Küche) *allophone* **allothig·en** a ⟨geol⟩ *allogeneous*

All·otria [Gr] n *stuff and nonsense tomfoolery* ‖ ~ treiben *to do a bit of skylarking*

Allotrop·ie f ~/ ⟨chem⟩ *allotropy* **allotr·opisch** a *allotropic*(*al*)

·Alltag m *workday, working-day, week-day* ‖ ⟨übtr⟩ *monotony* (grauer ~ *sad m.*) ‖ *daily life*; Lust u Leid des ~s *joys and sorrows of everyday life*; der literarische ~ *popular literature*

allt·äglich **1.** a *daily, everyday* (*occurrence*) ‖ ⟨fig⟩ *workaday* (*clothes*); *common*(*place*); *trite, trivial* ‖ das ≃e *the commonplace*; es ist nichts ≃es *it is not every day* (daß *that* ..) ‖ etw (nicht) ≃es *something* (*out*) *of the ordinary* **2.** adv *on week-days*; *every day* | ≃**keit** f ⟨fig⟩ *commonplaceness*; *commonness*; *triviality, triteness*

·alltags adv *on workdays* od *week-days*

·Alltags- [in comp] *everyday, workday* (*clothes, dress, suit*) ‖ ⟨fig⟩ *commonplace, workaday* ~**kost** f *ordinary fare*; *pot-luck* ~**leben** n *everyday life* (: *he showed them their e. lives*); *workaday life* ~**mensch** m *ordinary man* ~**welt** f *workaday world* ~**wort** n *household word*

All·üre f (Fr) ~/~n **1.** ⟨hors⟩ *gait, pace* **2.** [pl] ~n *bearing, carriage*; *ways* [pl]; gute ~n *manners* [pl]; vornehme ~n *airs* [pl]

alluvi·al a *alluvial* **Alluvi·alland** n *alluvial flat*; ⟨Scot⟩ *haugh* **Alluvi·on** f ~/~en *alluvion*, → Anlandung, Anschwemmung **All·uvium** n ~s/ ⟨geol⟩ *alluvium* → –zän, Holozän

allw·eil adv = alleweile **allw·o** adv *where*

·allzu adv *too* **·allzumal, allzus·ammen** adv *all together* **·allzusehr** adv *overmuch* **·allzuviel** adv *too much, overmuch* ‖ ~ ist ungesund *enough is as good as a feast*

Alm f ~/~en *summer mountain pasture, Alpine meadow* od *pasture*; alp ‖ ~abfahrt *driving of cattle from the Alpine pasture*; ~fahrt *the driving of cattle to the A. pasture*

Almag·est m ~s/ *almagest*

·Alma m·ater (L) f ~/ *alma mater, university*; *college*

·Almanach m ~(e)s/~e *almanac*

Almand·in m ~s/~e ⟨minr⟩ *almandine*

·Almenrausch m ~es/ ⟨bot⟩ → Almrausch

·Almer, ·Älmler m ~s/~ *inhabitant of an alp*

·Almosen n ~s/~ alms; charity | jdn um ein ~ bitten *to ask* (od *beg*) *alms of a p* ‖ ~ empfangen, von ~ leben, auf ~ angewiesen s *to live on alms* (od *charity*); ⟨fam⟩ *to be* (od *go*) *on the dole* ‖ jdm ein ~ geben *to give a p alms*; *to bestow alms* (*up*)*on a p* ~**amt** n *almonry* ~**büchse** f *alms* (od *poor*)*-box* ~**empfänger** m *pauper, almsman*; ~in f *almswoman* ~**geben** n, ~**pflege** f *alms--giving*; *charitable relief of the poor* ~**pfleger** m *almoner* ~**spende** f *eleemosynary gift* ~**stock** m *poor-box*

·Almrausch m ~(e)s/ ⟨bot⟩ *rhododendron, Alpine rose*

·Aloe f ~/~n ⟨bot⟩ **1.** *aloe*; hundertjährige ~ = Agave **2.** [in com] *aloetic* ~**hanf** m *Mexican fibre* ~**tinktur** f *aloes* pl

aloof (engl) [adv] *aloof* ‖ ⟨mar⟩ *windward*

Alp m ~(e)s/~e **1.** *goblin, elf* **2.** *fool* **3.** (~drücken im Traum) *nightmare*; *incubus* (L) ‖ ⟨übtr⟩ *nightmare*; vom ~ gedrückt w *to be oppressed by a n.*; es lag ihm wie ein ~ auf der Brust *it haunted him like a n.*; *it was a regular n. to him* ‖ an ~drücken leidend *hagridden* (*p*)

Alp f ~/~en = Alm ‖ ~wirtschaft → Alpen–

Alp·aka n ~s/~s **1.** ⟨zool⟩ *alpaca* **2.** ~wolle f Gewebe *or* Stoff aus ~wolle *alpaca*

Alp·aka n ~s/ (Neusilbermischung) *German silver*

al pari (It) ⟨com⟩ *at par*

·Alpdrücken n ~s/ → Alp m 3.

·Alpe f ~/~n = Alm **·Alpen** [pl] die ~ *the Alps* [pl]; dieseits (sc nach Italien zu) der ~ gelegen *cisalpine*; jenseits der ~ gelegen *transalpine* (→ ultramontan) ≃**artig** a *Alpine* ~**bahn** f *Alpine railway* ~**bewohner** m *inhabitant of the Alps* ~**führer** m *guide* (od *guidebook*) *to the Alps* ‖ (P) *guide* ~**glühen** n *Alpine glow* ~**jäger** m [pl] ⟨Ger mil⟩ *Alpine rifles* [pl] ~**klub** m = Alpenverein ~**landschaft** f *Alpine scenery* ~**lattich** m ⟨bot⟩ *purple-flowered lettuce* ~**paß** m *Alpine pass* ~**pflanze** f *alpine plant, alpine* ~**rose** f = Almrausch ~**stock** m *alpenstock* [Ger] ~**veilchen** n ⟨bot⟩ (*wild*) *cyclamen*, Europäisches ~ *sowbread* ~**verein** m *Alpine mountaineering* (od *climbing*) *club* ~**vorland** n *foothills of the Alps*; *Alpine plateau* ~**wirtschaft** f *Alpine farming*

·Alpha n ~s/~s (Gr) *alpha* ~**b·et** n ~(e)s/~e *alphabet* | ⟨demog⟩ m ~en/~en (Ggs An≃) *literate* | ≃**b·etisch** **1.** a *alphabetical* (*order*) **2.** adv *alphabetically* ‖ ~ ordnen *to arrange a.lly, to alphabetize* ≃**merisch** a *alphameric*(*al*) ≃**numerisch** a ⟨a. comp⟩ *alphanumeric*(*al*) (Arbeiten *data handling*) ~**strahlen** m pl *alpha rays*

alp·in a *Alpine* **Alpin·ismus** m ~ *Alpinism*

Alpin·ist m *Alpinist* **Alp·inum** n ~s/–nen

rockgarden **·Älpler(in** f) m *inhabitant of* od *cowherd in the Alps*

Alr·aun m ~(e)s/~e, **~e** f ~/~n ⟨bot⟩ *mandrake, mandragora* (L)

als I. [adv] **1.** *as*; **~ Dichter** (war er ..) *as a poet* (*he was* ..); Will ~ reicher oder armer Mann *Will poor or Will rich*; ~ ehrlicher Mann *as an honest man* ‖ s–e Erfahrung ~ öffentlicher Redner *his experience as a public speaker*; die Stellung ~ Lehrer *the position as master* | **~ Freund** *in the character of a friend*; mit Herrn N. ~ Partner *with Mr. N. for a partner*; ~, in der Eigenschaft ~ *in the capacity of*; *qua* (L); in s–r E. ~ *in his capacity as*; *qua* (: *qua chairman*) ‖ ~ Soldat (mußte er ..) *being a soldier* (*he had to* ..) ‖ ein Fremder ist willkommen ~ solcher *a stranger is welcome as such* ‖ ⟨theat⟩ ~ Lear auftreten *to appear in the character of Lear, to play the part of L.* **2.** (Ziel, Zweck) *by way of*; **~ Einleitung** *by way of introduction*; ~ Entschuldigung (*to say* ..) *by way of excuse*; ~ E. f *in excuse of*; ~ Antwort auf *in reply to* **3.** [bei Verben] **a.** [mst unübersetzt] sie **starb ~** Witwe *she died a widow*; er kehrte ~ Sieger heim *he returned a victor*; er wurde ~ Christ erzogen *he was reared a Christian*; die Beiden fuhren zurück ~ die besten Freunde *the two drove back the b. of f.s*; er endete sein Leben ~ Gefangener *he ended his life a prisoner* **b.** jdn **anerkennen, zulassen ~** .. *to acknowledge, to admit a p as* ..; jdn ~ s–n Freund betrachten *to look upon a p, to regard a p as one's friend* (od *to be one's f.*), *to consider a p one's friend*; er wird ~ reicher Mann betrachtet *he is considered* (*to be*) *a rich man*; (etw) ~ wertlos betrachten *to count* (*a th*) *as worthless* ‖ er wurde ~ König ausgerufen (gekrönt, gewählt) *he was proclaimed* (*crowned, chosen*) *king* ‖ bekannt s ~ *to be known as* ‖ gelten ~ *to pass for* od *as*; (jdn) fälschlich ausgeben ~ *to pass off for* od *as*; irrtümlich verfolgen ~ *to pursue* (*a p*) *for* .. | [vor adj] sich ~ **(un)schuldig** bekennen *to plead* (*not*) *guilty*; sich ~ wahr erweisen *to prove true* **4.** (zeitlich) **schon ~** Kind pflegte er .. *when* (*only*) *a child he used to* .. **II.** [conj] **A.** [beiordnend u vergleichend] **1.** (→ wie) **a. sowohl .. ~ auch**; *both* .. *and* [mit folg. pl]; sowohl in Frankreich ~ auch in England *in France as well as in England*; sie sowohl ~ ich wurden ruiniert *they as well as I were ruined*, sowohl ich ~ sie wurden ruiniert *I as well as they was ruined* ‖ sowohl f. Feinde ~ auch f. Freunde *to enemies and friends alike* **b.** [nach neg *or* fragend] *but*: **niemand ~** *none* od *nobody but*; kein anderer ~ er *nobody else but he* ‖ **nichts ~** *nothing but*; nichts weiter bleibt übrig ~ zu danken *nothing more remains but to thank*; was bleibt ihm übrig ~ nachzugeben? *what can he do but yield*, es bleibt nichts übrig ~ z tun *there is nothing for it but to do* **2.** [nach compr] *than* **größer** ~ du *taller than you*; sie wollten lieber sterben ~ sich ergeben *they would rather die than surrender*; .. mehr ~ es ihre Gewohnheit war .. *more than was their habit* ‖ (sie verstehen mich besser) ~ du (..) *than you do*; (..) ~ dich (..) *than they do you* ‖ größer ~, höher(stehend) ~ *superior to*; tiefer(stehend) ~ *inferior to*; → älter ‖ doppelt so viel ~ (statt wie) *twice as much as* **3.** [vor Konjunktionen] **a. ~ ob, ~ wenn** *as if, as though*; er sieht aus, ~ wenn er krank wäre (*or* ~ wäre er krank) *he looks as if he were* (⟨fam⟩ *was*) *ill*; (...) ~ wenn er andeuten wollte (*he smiled*) *as though to suggest* ‖ es sieht so aus, ~ wollte es regnen *it looks as if it were* (⟨fam⟩ *was*) *going to rain* ‖ ⟨Am fam⟩ *like* (: *she acts l. we're six*, .. *l. she had a headache*) ‖ [abs] so tun, als ob *to pretend*, ⟨sl⟩ *to go through the motions* **b. ~ daß:** zu schwer, ~ daß es schwimmen könnte *too heavy to float*; es war zu schwierig, ~ daß sie es verstehen konnten *it was too difficult for them to understand it*; ich bin noch kein .., ~ daß es mich nicht getroffen hätte *I'm still not enough of a criminal not to have had this affect me* **4.** [relativisch] die üblichen Übungen, **~ da sind** Reiten (*or* ~ Reiten), Jagen .. *the usual excercises such as riding, hunting* .. **B.** [unterordnend u zeitlich] **1.** während *as, while*; **~ ich las** *as* od *while I was reading* (*I* ..); er grinste, ~ er vorüberging *he grinned when* od *while passing*; ~ er e–n Brief schrieb, hörte er .. *writing a letter he heard* .. ‖ er ging dorthin, ~ er jung war *he went there young*; ~ er noch ein kl Junge war *when* (*that*) *he was a l. b.* ‖ → wie **2.** (gerade wie) *when* ‖ **die Zeit ~** *the time when*; zu der Zeit ~ *when* ‖ **sobald ~** *as soon as*; *when*; ~ **er** zurück war *when back* (*he* ..) | **~ er** zurückgekehrt war, (schrieb **er** ..) *having returned* (*he wrote* ..) ‖ er wurde begrüßt, ~ er sich erhob *he was cheered on rising* ‖ **~ dieses** getan war, gingen **sie** heim *this done they went home*; ~ er zugelassen war (...) *on his being admitted* (*they* ..)

alsb·ald adv *presently*; *immediately, directly*

alsd·ann adv *then*; *upon that, thereupon* ‖ u ~ *when, whereupon*

·Alse f ~/~n ⟨ich⟩ *shad*

·also 1. † [adv] *thus, so, in this manner* **2.** [conj] *so, consequently, therefore* ‖ nun ~ *now then*; na (nun) ~! *well then!*; *here we* od *you are!*

·Alt m ~(e)s/~stimmen ⟨mus⟩ *contralto, alto* **~geige** f = Bratsche **~schlüssel** m *alto-clef* **~solo** n *contralto solo* **~stimme** f *contralto voice*

alt a **I.** (P & T) **A.** [mst pred] **1.** *old*; ⟨sl⟩ *a bit long in the teeth* | 3 Jahre ~ *3 years old, 3 years of age, aged three*; ein 6 J. ~er Knabe *a boy of 6 years* (*old*), *a boy 6 years of age, a six-year-old* (*boy*) ‖ unter (über) 40 J. ~ *on the right* od *sunny side* (*on the wrong* od *shady side*) *of 40* | **wie ~** bist du? *how old are you? what is your age?* ‖ für wie ~ halten Sie mich? *what age do you give me?* ‖ wie ~ w sie (sc Vögel)? *to what age do they live?* | er ist **so ~ wie** ich, wie Georg *he is my, George's age*; er sieht nicht so ~ aus wie er ist *he does not look his age* ‖ als ich so ~ war .. *in my day* (*I* ..) ‖ in e–m J. wirst du **zu ~** *in another year you will be over age* (*for it*); **~ aussehen** *to look old* ‖ **~ w, ~ m** *to age* **2.** (Pferd = über 6 J. ~) *aged* **3.** (bejahrt) *old*; *advanced* od *stricken in years* (⟨a.⟩ ~ u grau) **B.** [mst attr] **1.** (bejahrt) *old, aged*; der ~e Wolsey *Old W.*, *the aged W.* ‖ **ziemlich ~** *elderly, oldish* **2.** (uralt) ⟨liter → II. 1.⟩ *ancient*; die ~en Germanen *the ancient Teutons, the old Teutonic tribes* ‖ (früher, Ggs modern) die ~en Meister ⟨arts⟩ *the Old Masters* **3.** ⟨übtr⟩ (ehemalig) *old, late*, ein ~er Krieger, Soldat *an old soldier*; ein ~er Schüler (e–r Schule etc) *an old boy*; ⟨Am⟩ *a graduate* ‖ ⟨Ger univ⟩ ein Alter Herr *an old member* (*of a club*) ‖ der ~e Lord Mayor *the late L. M.* **4.** ein ~er Seebär *an old sailor*, ein ~er Freund *a fr. of old*; ~e Freunde *old friends*; ein ~er Bekannter *an old fr.*; → Schrot ‖ ein ~er „Kämpfer", Verbrecher *an old fighter, offender* **5.** ⟨fam⟩ der ~e Herr (= Vater) *the Old Man*; mein lieber ~er Freund *my old man*; ~es Haus *old bean*; der ~e Adam *the Old Adam* | ein ~er Knabe *an oldster* | °ein ~er Knacker ⟨sl⟩ *an old bloke*; ein ~er Tropf *a stupid old thing* ‖ ein ~es Waschweib *an old woman* **6.** ⟨übtr⟩ das ~e liebe Oxford *good old O.* **II.** (S) **1.** (altertümlich, ehemalig) *old, ancient* (→ ant·ik); das ~e England *Old England* ‖ ⟨arts⟩ die Bilder der ≃en Meister *the Old Masters* ‖ ⟨bes ant⟩ *ancient* (*statue*); die ≃e Geschichte *Ancient History* ‖ in ~en Zeiten (*in days*) *of yore*; *in olden times*; *in* ~en Tagen *in former days*; seit ≃esten Zeiten *from the earliest times* **2.** (Ggs neu) *the Old Testament* ‖ *the Old World* (Europa u Asien) ‖

the Old Style | (lange bestehend) *an old family*; e–e ~e Narbe *a scar of long standing*; ein ~er Wunsch *a long-standing wish* ‖ das ~e Lied ⟨fig⟩ *the old story* | (abgenutzt) *old* (*clothes*); *second-hand* (*books*); (etw) ~ **kaufen** *to buy second-hand* | (abgestanden) *stale* (*bread*); *flat* (*beer*) **3.** (unverändert) *old, unchanged*; ein ~er Glaube *an old belief* ‖ → Liebe **III.** [abs] ~ u jung *old and young* | er ist nicht mehr der ~e *he is no longer the same* (*man*); er ist wieder ganz der ~e *he is quite himself again* ‖ etw ~es *something old, an old thing*; das ist etw ~es *that's an old story* ‖ es bleibt beim ~en *things remain as they were* ‖ → Alte

·alt- **~·adelig** a *of old nobility* **~backen** a *stale* (*bread*); ⟨a. übtr⟩ **≗bau** m *old* (*part of a*) *building* ‖ ~wohnung [f] *dwelling in an old building* (⟨Ger soc⟩ bis 20. 6. 1948) **~bek·annt** a *well known, known of old* **≗besitz** m *old holding* ‖ *property since 1. July 1920 in the same hands* **~bewährt** a *time-tested, –tried*; [pred] *of long standing* **~deutsch** a *old German*; *medi(a)eval* **~·ehrwürdig** a *venerable, time-honoured* **~·eingesessen** a *old-established* (*family*) **≗eisen** n *scrap iron* ‖ ~händler [m] *dealer in scrap iron* **~englisch** a *old English* **~fränkisch** a = altmodisch **~gedient** a *veteran* **≗gedinge** n = Altenteil **≗geldguthaben** n *old currency credit balance* **≗gesell** m *foreman*; *old man*; *experienced journeyman* **~gewohnt** a *long-accustomed* **~gläubig** a *orthodox* **≗handel** m *second-hand trade* **≗händler** m *second-hand dealer* **~h·ergebracht, ~herkömmlich** a *traditional, customary*; *ancient* (*rights*); *standard* [attr a] **~hochdeutsch** a *old-high G.* **≗jahrtag** m [österr] *New Year's Eve* **~j·üngferlich** a *old-maidish* **≗j·ungferntum** n *spinsterhood* **≗katholik** m *Old Catholic* **≗kl·eiderhändler** *old clothes man* **~klug** a *precocious* **≗klugheit** f *precocity* **≗knecht** m ⟨agr⟩ *head labourer* **≗kunstsammler** m *antiquary* **≗mannsbart** m ⟨bot⟩ *Old Man's Beard* **≗material** n *salvage, junk* **≗meister** m *pastmaster* ‖ ⟨übtr⟩ ⟨arts, sport, scient⟩ *outstanding representative*; *master of a guild, etc.*; ⟨arts⟩ *master*; ⟨sport⟩ *champion*; der ~ (..) *the patriarch* (*of Literature*) **≗metall** n *scrap metal* **~modisch** a *antiquated, out of date*; *antique, frumpish, frumpy, old-**champion*; der ~ (..) *the patriarch* (*of Literature*) *-fashioned, old-fangled*; *demoded*; *outmoded*; *motheaten*; *old-school* [attr]; (P) (rückständig) ⟨fam⟩ *slow*; *antediluvian*; ~er Mensch *antediluvian, old-timer*; *backnumber*; ⟨bes Am⟩ *mossback* ‖ [pred] *behind the times* **≗öl** n *used oil* **≗papier** n *waste paper* ‖ ~sammlung [f] *w.-p. drive* **≗philolog(e)** m *classical scholar*; *student of the classics* **≗schrift** f ⟨typ⟩ *the Roman type* **≗silber** a *artificially darkened silver* **≗sitz** m = Altenteil **≗stadt** f *centre* od *old part of a city* od *town*; die Londoner ~ *the City* **~testamentlich** a *Old Testament* (*God*) **≗tier** n ⟨hunt⟩ *hind with calf* **≗vater** m *patriarch* **~v·äterlich** a *patriarchal*; *ancestral*; *grandfatherly*; *old-fashioned* **~vertraut** a *long-familiar* **≗vordere** m *ancestor, forbear* **≗waren** f [pl] *junk*; ~händler m *second-hand shopkeeper* **≗wasser** n (toter Flußarm) *dead channel, ox-bow* **~w·eibermäßig** a *anile* °**≗w·eibergewäsch** n *old women's chatter, old wives' talk* **≗w·eibersommer** m *Indian summer*; (Sommerfäden) *gossamer*; (Zeit) *St. Martin's summer* **≗zeit** f : die ~ der Erde *the palaeozoic age* od *period*

Alt·ai m, **Alt·aigebirge** n (in Sibirien) *Altai* **alt·aisch** a *Altaian, Altaic*

Alt·an m ~(e)s/~e, **Alt·ane** f ~/~n *platform, terrace*; **perron*; *gallery* ‖ *balcony*

Alt·ar m ~(e)s/≗e *altar* (a. Opferstein & ⟨ec arch⟩); jdn zum ~ führen *to lead a p to the altar* ‖ *Communion Table* ‖ zus. vor den ~ treten (als Paar) *to walk down the aisle* **~bekleidung** f → Antependium **~bild** n *altar-piece* **~decke** f *altar-cloth* **~flügel** m *wing-panel* **~gemälde** n *altar-piece* **~platz** m *chancel* **~raum** m *sanctuary* **~rückwand** f ⟨bes engl⟩ *reredos* **~schelle** f *mass-bell* **~schiff** n *altar-aisle* **~tuch** n *communion-cloth* **~umhang** m *parament*

Altbayern n ⟨Ger⟩ *Upper and Nether Bavaria*

·Alte m : der ~ (ein ~r) ~n/~n *the old man*; ⟨fam⟩ *the old chap*; mein guter ~r (*my*) *old man*; der liebe ~ ⟨fam⟩ *the dear old thing* ‖ °der ~ (Vater, Vorgesetzter etc) *the old man, the governor*; mein ~r *my g.* ‖ °mein ~r *my husband*, ⟨fam⟩ *my hub, hubby* ‖ → alt III.

·Alte f ~n/~n *old woman*; m–e liebe ~ (*my*) *old woman* ‖ °m–e ~ *my old lady* od *Dutch* **·Alte** n ~n/ das ~ *the customary*; am ~n hängen *to cling to tradition*; → alt III. **·Alten** [pl] /~ die ~ *the old* ‖ °m–e ~ *my parents*; wie die ~ sungen (= sangen), so zwitschern auch die Jungen ⟨prov⟩ *as the old cock crows the young ones learn*; *like father, like son* | die ~ (Griechen u Römer) *the ancients* [pl]

·Altenteil n *old man's part* (*share of property reserved by a farmer for himself in old age*) **·Altenteiler** m *retired farmer living on his* 'Altenteil'

·älter a [compr v alt] **I.** [attr] **1.** (nur P) *elder*: *my elder brother* | *the elder Spencer* **2.** *older* **a.** *the older sons* (*of the families*) ‖ die ~en Leute *the older people* **b.** *older*, das ~e Haus *the older house* **3.** ~e Leute als ich *my elders* ‖ die ~e P *the elder* **4.** (kein [compr] dem Sinne nach) **a.** (ältlich) *elderly* (*inhabitants*) **b.** *experienced*: *wanted an e. housemaid* **II.** [pred] *older* **a.** er ist ~ als ich *he is older than I*; er ist 3 Jahre ~ als ich *he is three years senior to me, he is my senior by 3 years* (od *3 years my s.*); etw ~ als .. *a little the senior of ..* **b.** dies Haus ist ~ *this house is older* **c.** man wird ~ *the shadows lengthen* **III.** [abs] der ≗e v ihnen *the elder of them* ‖ Schmidt der ≗e *Smith the elder, Smith senior* | die ≗en [pl] *the elders* ‖ → ältest

·Alter n ~s/~ **1.** (Lebenszeit) *age* | im frühen ~ *at an early age*; im zarten ~ *in early childhood, of tender age* ‖ mittleres ~ *middle age* ‖ reiferen ~s (*a* [*wo*]*man*) *past middle age* ‖ geistiges ~ *mental age* ‖ gesetzliches ~ *lawful age* ‖ zunehmendes (*or* vorgeschrittenes) ~ *anno domini* (: *a. d. also tells on me*); **im ~ v** 50 Jahren *at the age of fifty, at 50 years of age*; ⟨engl⟩ *all men of 50 or over*, ⟨Am⟩ *all men 50 or over* ‖ sie sind um 5 Jahre im ~ unterschieden *they are separated in age by five years* ‖ (sie sahen nie) Jungen ihres ~s (*they never saw*) *boys their own age* ‖ → Heirats≗, Kindes≗, Mannes≗ ‖ unmündiges ~ *minority, nonage*; ~ der Mündigkeit *majority* | er ist über das erforderliche ~ hinweg *he is over age* ‖ man sieht ihm sein ~ nicht an *he does not look his age* **2. hohes ~** *old age* (: *the infirmities of age*); sein sehr hohes ~ *his great age* ‖ im ~ *in old age*; bis ins hohe ~ *to a great age* ‖ ~ schützt vor Torheit nicht *it is not a logical necessity that we grow wiser as we grow older*; *there is no fool like an old fool* **3.** (S) hohes ~ *antiquity*, Münzen v hohem ~ *coins of great antiquity* **4.** (Zeitalter) age; → Zeitalter; Bronzezeit, Eiszeit etc

Alterati·on f ~/~en *alteration* (an to) | ⟨fig⟩ *violent emotion*; *excitement*; *anger* **alter·ieren** vt [h] sich ~ *to be vexed, annoyed, irritated* (über *at*); *to put o.s. out, to be put out* (über *about*)

·altern 1. vi [h & s] *to grow old*; *to age*; *to get on in years*; ~d *senescent* **2.** vt ⟨met⟩ *to fatigue, age* ‖ → veralten **3.** ≗ n *senescence*

Altern·anz, Alternati·on [*ts*] f ~/~en *alternation* **alternat·iv** a *alternate*; ⟨bot⟩ ~ stehend *alternate* ‖ (abwechselnd) *alternative*; [adv] *alter-*

nately **Alternat·ive** f ~/~en *alternative* **altern·ieren** vi [h] *to alternate* (mit *with*) ‖ ~der Strom → Wechselstrom; ~der Vers → Wechsel

·alters adv vor ~ *of old, in times of old,* (*in days*) *of yore*; seit ~, v *or* seit ~ her *from of old, from ancient time*

·Alters- ~aufbau m *arrangement of population according to age, classification of population by age-groups*; ⟨demog⟩ *age group structure*; (stabiler) ~ (*stable*) *age distribution* **~bild** n *picture* (*of a p*) *painted in his* (*her*) *old age* **~blödsinn** m *senile dementia* **~fürsorge** f ⟨off⟩ *old age relief*; ärztliche ~ *medical care for the aged,* ⟨Am⟩ *medicare* **~genosse** m *contemporary*; sein(e) ~(n) *his equal(s) in age* **~grenze** f *age-limit*; die ~ erreicht h *to be due to retire*; infolge Erreichung der ~ in den Ruhestand treten *to retire under the age-limit*; → entpflichten **~gruppe** f *age-group* **~heim** n *home for old* (od *aged*) *people, home for the aged* **~hilfe** f *old-age benefits* **~jahr** n ⟨Sw⟩ = Lebensjahr **~klasse** f *age-group* **~pension** f *old-age pension* **~präsident** m *chairman by seniority* **~pyramide** f ⟨demog⟩ *population pyramid* **~rente** f = Alterspension **~rentner(in** f) m *insurance pensioner* **≗schwach** a *decrepit, infirm, anile*; *senile*; ⟨fam⟩ *doddering*; [pred] *on one's last legs* ‖ → gebrechlich ‖ ⟨übtr⟩ *effete* **~schwäche** f *decrepitude*; *senile decay, senility*; *weakness of old age* **~sichtigkeit** f *long-sightedness of old age* **~stufe** f *age, stage of life*; *age-class* **~unterschied** m *disparity of age* **~veränderung** f ⟨biol⟩ *senile change* **~versicherung** f *old-age insurance,* ⟨Am⟩ medizinische ~ *medicare* **~versorgung** f *old age pension* (*scheme*), ⟨com etc⟩ *pension trust*; ~skasse f *provident fund* **~zulage** f *bonus* (od *extra pay*) *for age* (od *seniority*)

·Altertum n ~(e)s/ **1.** das (klassische) *antiquity* (: *a history of a.*) ‖ im grauen ~ *in ancient days* **2.** (Frühzeit) *the early history* (*of a people*) ‖ **·Altertümer** n [pl] *antiquities, ancient relics* [pl] **·altertümeln** vi *to dabble in antiquities* **·altertümlich** a *antiquarian*; *ancient, antique* ‖ *antique, antiquated, old-fashioned* | **≗keit** [f] *antiquity*

·Altertums- ~forscher m *antiquary, antiquarian*; *archaeologist* **~forschung, ~kunde, ~wissenschaft** f *archaeology* **~stück** n *antique*

·Alterung f ~/ *ag(e)ing* ⟨met⟩ (Vergütung) *precipitation hardening* **≗sbeständig** a *non-ag(e)ing*

·älteste a [sup v alt] (→ älter) **1.** [attr] (P) *eldest*: *my eldest brother* **b.** (S) *oldest*: *the oldest house* **2.** [pred] *oldest*, er (dieses Haus) ist der (das) ~ (an Aussehen) *he* (*this house*) *is the oldest* **3.** [abs] der ~ v ihnen *the oldest of them*; mein ≗r *my eldest son,* m-e ≗ *my eldest daughter* | (Kirchen≗r) *the elder,* die ~n [pl] *the elders* [pl]

Alt·ist m ~en/~en, **Alt·istin** f ~/~nen *contralto(-singer)*; *alto(-singer)* **·ältlich** a *elderly, oldish* (*widow*) ‖ ~ aussehend *elderly-looking*

·Altmark f ⟨Ger⟩ (v Brandenburg) *Old March*

·Altona n (Stadtteil Hamburgs an der Elbe)

Altru·ismus m *altruism, unselfishness*

Altru·ist m ~en/~en *altruist* **altru·istisch** a *altruistic, unselfish*; in ~er Weise *altruistically*

·Altvatergebirge n (Sudetenzug in Mähren)

Alum·inium n ⟨chem⟩ *aluminium*; ⟨Am⟩ *aluminum* **~oxid, ~oxyd** n *alumina*

Alumn·at n ~(e)s/~e *boarding-school*; ~schule f ⟨engl⟩ *Public School* **A.·umne** m ~n/~n *alumnus* (L)

alveol·ar a *alveolar* **Alve·ole** f ~/~n ⟨anat⟩ *alveolus* (L)

am prep (aus: an dem) **1.** (in bes Wendungen) ~ Anfang *in the beginning,* ~ Ende *after all,* → Ende; (etw) ~ Schnürchen h *to have at one's fingers' ends* | Frankfurt ~ Main *Frankfort on the Main* | ~ Abend, Morgen *in the evening, morning*; ~ Montag *on Monday*; ~ 1. Mai *on the first of May* **2.** [vor subst inf] ~ Schreiben s *to be writing*; ~ Schlagen s ⟨sport⟩ *to be in* **3.** [vor abs sup] ~ besten *best*; ~ besten s, sich ~ besten zeigen *to be at one's best*; (Eigenschaften) ~ klarsten zeigen *to show qualities at their clearest*; ich täte ~ besten, nicht z gehen *I had best not go* ‖ ~ größten *greatest, at the greatest*

Amalg·am n ~s/~e ⟨chem⟩ *amalgam* **amalgam·ieren** vt [h] *to amalgamate* ‖ ⟨fig⟩ *amalgamate, to fuse* **Amalgam·ierung** f ~/~en *amalgamation*

Amanu·ensis (L) m ~/–nuenses *amanuensis* (L)

Amar·ant m ~s/~e **1.** ⟨bot⟩ *amaranth* **2.** ⟨orn⟩ *weaver-finch* **Amor·elle** f ~/~n ⟨bot⟩ *morel*

Amar·yllis f ~/–ryllen ⟨bot⟩ *amaryllis*

Amat·eur [ama'tør] m (Fr) ~s/~e *amateur* ‖ ⟨sport⟩ *non-professional*; ~e [pl] *Gentlemen* [pl] (*versus Professionals*) **~photograph** m *amateur photographer* **~rennwagen** n ⟨bes Am⟩ *hot-rod*

Am·ause f ~/~n ⟨minr⟩ *imitated jewel*

Amaz·onas 1. n (Staat Brasiliens) **2.** m = **Amaz·onenstrom,** der *the Amazon* (*-River*)

Amaz·one f ~/~n *Amazon* ‖ ⟨fig⟩ *virago* **≗nhaft** a *amazonian*; *horsey* **~strom** m = Amazonas

·Amber m = Ambra

ambi-, (ambo-) ~dexter a *ambidextrous* **≗guität** f ~/~en *ambiguity*

·Ambitus m ~/~ ⟨ec arch⟩ *ambulatory*; *processional path*; *periapsidal aisle*;

·Amboß m –sses/–sse **1.** *anvil* **2.** ⟨anat⟩ (im Ohr) *anvil(-bone), incus* (L) **3.** (an der Patrone) *detonator cap* **~bahn** f *anvil plate* **~einsatz** m *anvil tool* **~horn** n *beak* **~stöckel** m *inset stake*

·Ambra f ~s/ (Riechmittel) *ambergris*

Ambr·osia f ~/ *ambrosia* ⟨a. fig⟩ **ambr·osisch** a *ambrosial*

ambul·ant 1. a ⟨med⟩ *ambulant, outpatient* (*treatment*) **2.** adv ~ behandelter Kranker *outpatient* **Ambul·anz** f **1.** (Krankenwagen) *ambulance* **2.** (Poliklinik) *outpatients* (od *outdoor patients*) *department* **ambulat·orisch** a *ambulatory* **Ambulatorium** n ~s/–rien *out-patients' department*

·Ameise f ~/~n ⟨ent⟩ *ant*; Arbeiter≗ *ergates* (L), *worker ant* ‖ Weiße ~ → Termite

·Ameisen- ~bär m ⟨zoo⟩ *anteater* **~ei** n (Larve) *ant-worm* **~fresser** m ⟨zoo⟩ *ant-eater* **~haufen** m *ant-hill*; *formicary*; ⟨fig⟩ → ~laufen **~igel** m ⟨zoo⟩ *echidna* ‖ ⟨ent⟩ *spiny ant* **~jungfer** f ⟨ent⟩ *myrmeleon* **~laufen** n ⟨med⟩ *formication*; *pins and needles* [pl] **~löwe** m *ant--lion* **~nest** n *ants' nest* **~säure** f ⟨chem⟩ *formic acid*

Amelioration f ~/~en (Boden–) *amelioriation*

·Amelkorn n ⟨bot⟩ = Spelz **·Amelmehl** n *starch*

†**·Amelungen** m pl (Ostgotenstamm) *Amelungs*

·Amen n ~s/~ *amen* ‖ Ja u ~ sagen zu etw *to say amen to a th, to consent to a th*; so sicher wie ein ~ in der Kirche *sure as a gun* od *as death*

Amenorrh·oe [–'rø] f *amenorrhoea*

Am·erika *America* ‖ Mittel≗ *Central A.*; Nord≗ *North A.*; ‖ die Vereinigten Staaten [pl] v Nord≗ *the United States of America*; ⟨fam⟩ *Uncle Sam* ‖ Eingeborener v Nord–, Mittel–, Süd≗ *Amerindian* **≗freundlich** a *pro-American* **~haus** n ⟨Am⟩ *Information Center*

Amerik·aner m ~s/~ (Nord–) *American*; ⟨fam⟩ *Yankee*; ⟨cont⟩ *gringo* ‖ der typische ~, die ~ [pl] *Uncle Sam, Brother Jonathan, Yankeedom* **amerik·anisch 1.** a *American*; *Yankee* ‖ die ~e Nationalflagge *the star--spangled banner, stars and stripes* [pl]; ~es Nationallied *star-spangled banner*; ⟨hist⟩ *Yankee doodle*; ~e Sprache *American*; *A. language* **2.** ≗, das ≗ n *American* (auf ≗ *in A.*), *Unitedstatish* **amerikanis·ieren** vt [h] *to americanize* **Amerikanis·ierung** f *americanization* **Amerika-**

n·ismus m *Americanism, American idiom* || *American outlook* od *spirit*

Ameth·yst m ~(e)s/~e ⟨minr⟩ *amethyst* **≗-artig, ≗farben** a *a.ine, a.-coloured*

Ameublem·ent [amøblə'mɑ̃] n (Fr) ~s/~s [abstr] *furnishing* || [konkr] *furniture; furnishings*

°**·Ami** m ~s/~s ⟨Ger fam⟩ *gum(–)chum*

Am·id n ~s/~e ⟨chem⟩ *amide*

Ami·ens (a'miɛ̃] n (Stadt in Nord-Frankreich)

Am·ikt n ~(e)s/~e (Humerale) *amice*

Am·ino- ~Ende n (der Peptidkette) ⟨bio-chem⟩ *N-terminal* **~säure** f *amino acid*

·Amme f ~/~n *nurse, wet-nurse,* (jdn) als ~ nähren *to wet-nurse* || ⟨fig⟩ *nurse* **~nmärchen** n *nursery tale, old wives' tale;* ⟨übtr⟩ *cock-and--bull story*

·Ammer f ~/~n & m ~s/~ **~ling** m ~s/~e ⟨orn⟩ *bunting,* → *bundting* (Bd. I)

Amm·on n ~s/ = Ammonium **Ammon·al** n (Sprengstoff) *ammonal* **Ammoni·ak** n ~s/ ⟨chem⟩ *ammonia;* ~wasser n *liquid ammoniac* **Ammon·it** m ~en/~en ⟨zoo⟩ *ammonite* **Am-m·onium** n ~s ⟨chem⟩ *ammonium* **·Ammonshorn** n = Ammonit

Amnes·ie f ~/~n ⟨med⟩ *amnesia*

Amnest·ie f ~/~n, *amnesty, general pardon; indemnity Act* || (erlassen *to issue*) *a general pardon*

amnest·ieren vt [h] *to amnesty*

·Amnion n ~s/Amni·onen ⟨anat⟩ *caul*

Am·öbe f ~/~n (Wechseltierchen) *amoeba*

·Amok m ~s/ *amuck, amok;* ~ laufen *to run a.*

am·ön a → anmutig

·Amor (L) m ~s/Am·oren ⟨myth⟩ *Cupid*

·amoralisch n *amoral, non-moral*

Amor·ette f ~/~n *amoretto* [pl *amoretti*]

am·orph a ⟨minr⟩ *amorphous* || (formlos) *amorphous, shapeless*

Amortisati·on f ~/~en *amortization, redemption* (*of National Debt*) || *extinction; liquidation* (*of a debt*) **~sfonds** m, **~skasse** f *sinking-fund* **~sschein** m *bill of amortization* **amortis·ierbar** a *amortizable; redeemable* **amortis·ieren** vt [h] *to amortize;* (Schuld) *to pay off;* (Nationalschuld) *to redeem, sink* || (Wechsel) *to cancel*

Amour·ettengras n ⟨bot⟩ = Zittergras

amour·ös a → liebreizend || → verliebt

·Ampel f ~/~n **1.** *hanging* od *swinging lamp, pendant-lamp* **2.** *hanging flower-pot* **3.** Verkehrs≗ *traffic sign* [pl] **4.** = Ampulle

Amp·ere [ɑ̃'pæːr] (abbr. A., Amp.) n ⟨el⟩ *ampere* **~meter** n *ammeter, aperemeter* **~sekunde** f *ampere second; coulomb* **~stunde** (abbr Ah) f *ampere hour*

·Ampfer m ~s/~ ⟨bot⟩ *sorrel, dock*

·amphi- (Gr) [in comp] *amphi–*

Amph·ibie f ~/~n *amphibian; amphibious animal;* ~n [pl] *Amphibia* (L); ~nfahrzeug [n] *amphibian vehicle* **amph·ibisch** a *amphibian, amphibious* (a. ⟨mil⟩ *operation*); ⟨mil⟩ ~ ausgebildet u organisiert *amphibious* (*corps*)

Amphibol·ie f ~/~n (Zweideutigkeit) *amphibology* **Amphi·oxus** m ~/~ (Lanzettfisch) *lancelett* **Amph·itheater** n ~s/s *amphitheatre*

Amph·ora f ~/–ren ⟨archæol⟩ *amphora*

Amplit·ude f ~/~n ⟨phys⟩ *amplitude* **~n- ~-frequenzkurve** f *amp. frequency characteristic* **~frequenzverlauf** m *amp. fr. response* **~modulation** f *amp. modulation* **~sieb** n *amp. separator*

Amp·ulle f ~/~en *ampulla* (L) || ⟨med⟩ *phial*

Amputati·on f ~/~en *amputation;* Ober–, Unterschenkel≗ *amp. above, below knee* **amput·ieren** vt [h] *to amputate* **Amput·ierte(r** m) f *amputee;* Doppelt-(Bein-)~ *double a.;* Arm- u Bein≗, Voll≗ *quadruple a.*

·Amsel f ~/~n ⟨orn⟩ *blackbird* **~feld** n ⟨hist⟩ (Schlacht bei Kossowo, 1389) *plain of the black--birds*

·Amt n ~(e)s/≗er **A.** (Dienstleistung) **1. a.** (Stellung) *employment; position; post;* ein ~ bekleiden *to hold a position;* das ~ e–s Organisten *the post of an organist* **b.** ⟨übtr⟩ (Funktion) *function; office;* das ~ des Wirtes *the office of host;* s–s ~es walten *to perform one's functions;* → amtieren || *province, place;* es ist nicht m–s ~es *it is not my place, it is beyond my province* (z tun *to do*) **2.** (öffentl. staatliche Dienststellung) *appointment; office;* das ~ e–s Schatzmeisters *the office of treasurer;* v ~s wegen *ex officio* (L), *by virtue of office; by right(s);* (*member*) *as of right* || das ~ antreten *to enter upon office, to take office;* das ~ ausüben als *to function as;* ein (öffentl.) ~ bekleiden *to hold an appointment; to be in office; to hold office;* im ~e bleiben *to succeed o.s.;* in ein ~ einführen *to install* (*a p*) *in an office;* (jdn) s–s ~s entsetzen *to deprive* (*a p*) *of his office;* wem Gott ein ~ gibt, dem gibt er auch Verstand *where God bestows an office he provides brains to fill it;* jds ~ übernehmen *to step into a p's shoes;* vom ~ zurücktreten *to resign office* || Ämterhandel *traffic in offices* | geistliches ~ *ministry* || einträgliches, müheloses ~ *sinecure* || in ~ u Würden *holding an office, in a lucrative position* **3.** ⟨R.C.⟩ *mass,* Hoch≗ *high mass* **B.** (Behörde, Dienststelle) **1.** (obrigkeitl. ~) *magistracy* || *administration; board; department;* ⟨Am⟩ *bureau* || *the authorities* [pl] || ⟨jur⟩ *jurisdiction; court of law* || ⟨pol⟩ das Auswärtige ~ *The Foreign Office,* das Kolonial-≗ *the Colonial Office* || ⟨Ger⟩ *section;* Jugend≗ *Youth Section;* Presse≗ *Press Section;* || ⟨telph⟩ *exchange,* ⟨Am⟩ *central;* das ~ bitte (vom Nebenanschluß aus) *give me the exchange* (od *a line*), *please* **2.** (amtl. Gebäude) *Office;* zum ~ gehen *to go to the office* || Post≗ *the Post Office, the Post* || das Auswärtige ~ → B. 1. **C.** (Bezirk) *administrative district; township* **D.** [in comp]

·Amt- ~haus n *office* **~mann** m ⟨Ger⟩ *head* (od *chief*) *of a district* od *township* || *magistrate* || *agent* (*of an estate*); ⟨hist⟩ *bailiff;* ⟨jur m.m.⟩ *magistrate* (*at petty*) *sessions;* Justiz≗, Regierungs≗ *Principal Clerk* **amt·ieren** (a. **·amten**) vi [h] *to be in office, to hold office* || ⟨ec⟩ *to officiate;* ~der Geistlicher *officiant* || ⟨übtr⟩ *to officiate, to act* (als *as*) **amtlich 1.** a *official; officiary* (*title*); *ex officio* (*member*); die ~en Kreise *the official circles; officialdom;* nicht ~ *inofficial;* → halb~; voll~ **2.** adv *officially; ex officio* || nicht ~ gesprochen *off the record*

·Amts- ~adel m *official nobility* **~alter** n *seniority in office* **~anmaßung** f *usurpation of office; overstepping of official powers* **~antritt** m *entering upon office* || ⟨Am⟩ (des Präsidenten) *inauguration;* Tag des ~s *Inauguration Day* **~anwalt** m ⟨m.m.⟩ *circuit attorney* **~arzt** m *public health commissioner* **~befugnis** f *authority, competence* **~bereich** m *jurisdiction;* ohne ~ ⟨pol⟩ (*minister*) *without portfolio* **~bewerber** m *applicant* (od *candidate*) *for an office,* ⟨Am⟩ *office-seeker* **~bezeichnung** f *position* **~bezirk** m (local administration) *district, extent of jurisdiction; venue* **~blatt** n *gazette;* in e–m ~ bekannt m *to g.* **~bruder** m *colleague;* → Kollege; *brother negotiator* **~dauer** f *term* (od *duration, tenure*) *of office* **~diener** m *beadle, usher, bailiff* **~eid** m *oath of office;* den ~ ablegen *to take the oath of office; to be sworn in o.* **~einkünfte** f *emoluments* **~enthebung** f *dismissal* **~führung** f *administration* **~geheimnis** n *secrecy* **~gehilfe** m *colleague, adjunct* **~gericht** n ⟨Ger⟩ *the lowest civil and criminal court;* ⟨engl⟩ *county court;* ⟨Am⟩ *district court* **~geschäfte** n [pl] *official duties* [pl] **~gewalt** f *official power* **~handlung** f *function* (: *the first* ~ *of the king*) **~hauptmann** m ⟨Ger⟩ *prefect, provost* **~hauptmannschaft** f ⟨Ger⟩ *prefecture* **~hilfe** f *official assistance* **~inhaber** m *incumbent*

~jäger m *officehunter* **~kette** f ⟨univ, etc⟩ *chain of office*; ⟨engl⟩ ~ des Lord Chief Justice v England *the Collar of Esses* **~kleidung** f *robes* [pl], *official dress* **~leiter** m ⟨Ger⟩ *office-bearer* **~lokal** n *office premises* pl **~miene** f ⟨übtr⟩ *grave, solemn air* **~mißbrauch** m *abuse of official position* **~müde** a *weary of office* **~niederlegung** f *laying down of office* **~pflicht** f *official duty* ‖ s–e ~ verletzen *to infringe one's offocial duties* **~richter** m ⟨Ger⟩ *judge in an* Amtsgericht (→ d.) **~schimmel** m ⟨übtr⟩ *red-tape, red-tapism*; wiehernder ~ *paper* (od *red-tape*) *curtain*; Wiehern [n] des ~s *gobbledygook* **~schreiber** m *bailiff's clerk* **~siegel** n *seal of office* **~stube** f *office* **~tätigkeit** f = Amtshandlung **~tracht** f = Amtskleidung **~träger** m *office-bearer* **~übung** f ~en [pl] ⟨ec⟩ *ministrations* [pl] **~vergehen** n *malpractice* **~verschwiegenheit** f *secrecy*, zur ~ verpflichtet w *to be sworn to s.* **~verwalter, ~verweser** m *administrator of an office*; *deputy*; *steward* **~vormund** m *public guardian* od *trustee* **~vorsteher** m ⟨Ger⟩ *chief official of a district, sheriff* **~walter** m *functionary* **~wechsel** m *rotation in office* **~wohnung** f *official residence* **~zeichen** n ⟨telph⟩ *dial tone* **~zeit** f *term of office*

·Amu Darj·a m (Fluß in Turkestan) *Amu-Darya*

Amul·ett n ~(e)s/~e *amulet, talisman, charm*

Amur, der (Strom in Ostasien) *the Amoor, the Amur*

amüs·ant a *amusing* ‖ er ist sehr ~ *he is great fun* ‖ *readable* (*book, etc.*) (*in a gossipy sort of way*) **Amüsem·ent** [amyzəm'ɑ̃:] n (Fr) ~s/~s *amusement* (zum ~ *for a.*); ⟨hum & dial⟩ viel ~! *have fun*! *I hope you'll enjoy yourself*! *have a good time*!

Amüs·ier- ~mädchen n *prostitute, playmate*

amüs·ieren vt [h] **1.** (jdn) *to amuse, to delight* **2. sich** ~ *to amuse* od *enjoy o.s.*; *to take pleasure*; *to have a good time*; ⟨fam⟩ *to go on the loose*; *to have one's fling, to spree, to be* (od *go*) *on the spree*; ⟨sl⟩ *to be out on the tiles*; ⟨Am⟩ *to go places, to make whoopee*; → Bummel 2. ‖ sich ~ über *to delight* (od *to take delight*) *in* (*a th*); *to be amused by* (*a joke*) ‖ .. über jdn *to make fun of a p*

an prep (→ am, ans) **I. (Ruhe** [doch engl oft verschiedene Auffassung, vgl 3.], mit dat) **A.** ⟨eig⟩ **1.** (~ e–r Fläche) *on, upon*; *on the wall* ‖ ~ Bord *on board*; *on the coast*; *on a river*; *the ring on her finger*; *with a lady on his arm*; *to end on the gallows*; *to go about on crutches*; hochangehäuft ~ den Türen (*snow*) *high piled about the doors* ‖ am Horizont *on the horizon*; → Himmel **2.** (~ e–m **Punkte)** *at*; ~ der Tür *at the door*; ~ der Ecke *at* (⟨Am⟩ *on*) *the corner*; (er saß) am Tisch (..) *at the table*; ~ den Ellbogen zerrissen *out at elbows*; → Seite ‖ nagen ~ *to gnaw at* ‖ *take* od *hold baby by the hand*!; *take the cup by the handle*! ‖ *she trembled in every limb* (an allen Gliedern) ‖ *in many places* ‖ *in the first place* (= erstens) ‖ *the Battle of the Nile* ‖ ⟨fig⟩ *a place in the sun* | ~ e–r Schule *at a school*; Professor ~ der Universität Berlin *Professor in the University of Berlin* (od *at Berlin U.*) ‖ (wir waren) ~ der See (..) *at the seaside* | *at the altar*; *at the beginning*; *at the bottom of the glass*; *at the window*; *at the front*, (aber:) *on the Eastern front* ‖ *to sit by the window, by the fireside* ‖ ~ **vorbei:** *the car rushed by* od *past us* → Stelle **3.** (bei bestimmten Verben der **Richtung)** *to* (→ II. A. 3.); **befestigen** ~ *to attach, to fasten to*; ⟨übtr⟩ festhalten ~ *to cling, stick to* ‖ Rükken ~ Rücken *back to back* | *repairs to a building*; *an operation to her neck*; *he is ambassador to the Court of* ..; *he suffered an injury to his hand* **4.** *by*; vorübergehen ~ *to pass by*; ~ e–m Bande hängen *to be suspended by a ribbon*; ⟨übtr⟩ ~ e–m Faden hängen *to hang by a thread*; → hängen ‖ *to lead a p by the nose*; am Wege *by the way* **5.** am Ufer **entlang** *along the shore* **6. nahe** ~ *near to, near* (*the house*) **B.** ⟨übtr⟩ **1.** ~ der Arbeit *at work*; arbeiten ~ *to work at, to work on* **2.** (gefunden w etc) ~ jdm *in* od *about a p*; er hatte e–n gewissen Reiz, e–e komische Art ~ **sich** *had a charm about him, a strange way with him*; ⟨übtr⟩ der Ton hatte etw ~ sich v.. *the tone had a ring of* .. *about it* **3. Wendungen:** die Schuld liegt ~ dir *the fault is* od *lies with you* ‖ es liegt (nicht) ~ mir .. *it is* (*not*) *for me to do it* ‖ soviel ~ mir liegt *as far as lies in my power*; *as for me* ‖ es ist ~ dir *it is for you, it is up to you* (*to do*) | ~ **sich** (S) *in itself*; *properly speaking*; *to be precise*; *actually*; *as a matter of fact* ‖ ~ sich wertvolle Meinungen *opinions valuable in themselves*; ~ **u für sich** *properly speaking*; ~ u für sich betrachtet *in the abstract* ‖ es ist nichts ~ der S *there is nothing in it, it is untrue* ‖ es ist ~ **d·em** *it is really so, it is the fact* (*that*); es ist nicht ~ d·em *it is untrue* **C. (Zeit)** am Abend *in the evening*; am Tage *by day, in the daytime*; spät am Tage *late in the day* ‖ am Abend des 6. Mai *on the evening of May 6.*; ~ e–m schönen Morgen *on a fine morning, on weekdays, on a given day* ‖ *at Easter, etc.*; *at the very beginning* od *outset*; *in the end* (= schließlich) ‖ es ist ~ der Zeit *it is* (*high, about*) *time* **D. (Grad, Maß)** *in*; ~ Größe *in size*; 6 ~ (der) Zahl *6 in number*; (jdm gleich) ~ Stärke (*a p's equal*) *in strength* | Mangel ~ *want of, lack of*; → fehlen ‖ reich ~ *rich in*, → arm | ~ 50 Mark *about* (od *nearly*) *50 marks* ‖ *to diminish in weight* ‖ *the wind abates in fury* ‖ ⟨com⟩ ~ Waren *to goods* **E.** (in Verbindung mit **Verben)** → teilnehmen, hindern; handeln; rächen; erkennen; zweifeln, verzweifeln; leiden; sterben **II. (Richtung** [doch engl andere Auffassung in 2.], mit acc) **A.** ⟨eig⟩ **1.** (etw) ~ die Wand hängen *to hang on the wall*; (Hut etc) ~ e–n Haken hängen *to hang* (*a hat*) *on a peg*; (→ hängen); *he stuck a flower in his hat* ‖ *the car ran into a lamp-post* ‖ *I'll see* (begleiten) *you to the station*; steck den Ring ~ den Finger *slip the ring on to your finger*; *the curtain was frozen to the window*; → werfen **2.** ~ die Tür klopfen *to knock at the door* [engl: Ruhe → I.A.2.] ‖ etw, jdn ~ die Wand stellen *to stand a th, a p against the wall*; *lean against me*; *the rain beats against the window* **3.** binden ~ *to tie to* **4.** ~ die See gehen *to go to the seaside*; → Land **5.** bis ~ *up to*; v .. bis ~ *from* .. *to* **B.** ⟨übtr⟩ ~ die Arbeit gehen *to go* od *set to work* ‖ ~ jdn schreiben *to write to a p*; (Brief) richten ~ *to address* (*a letter*) *to* ‖ → denken; erinnern; glauben ‖ → Glocke; Haken; Hals; Herz; Licht; Nagel; Reihe; Tag; Wand

an adv **1.** (räumlich) *on*, (er trat ein) mit dem Mantel ~ (..) *with his coat on* **2.** (zeitlich) v .. ~ *from*, v heute ~ *from today*; v jetzt ~ *henceforth, from this time forth*, v der Zeit ~ *ever since* ‖ ab u ~ → ab I. 1. **3.** ⟨übtr⟩ *the gas is on*

an- pref [stets betont] **1.** [untrennbar vor mst v Verben abgeleiteten Subst., dsgl. vor Adj u Adv] Annahme; angängig **2. a.** [trennbar vor Grundverben] ·annehmen: ich nehme ·an — ·angenommen; in den Bedeutungen der [prep] an **b.** [trennbar *or* untrennbar vor zus-gesetzten Verben] anberaumen: ich beraume an, anberaume; anerkennen: erkenne an, anerkenne)

an- (Gr) pref [untrennbar, in Fremdwörtern] *an–* (→ organisch)

-an suff *up*; berg~ *up hill*; → himmel~; neben~

ana- (Gr) pref [untrennbar, in Fremdwörtern] *ana–*

Anachor·et m ~en/~en *anchorite, anchoret*

Anachron·ismus m ~/–men *anachronism*

Anadol·u n ⟨türk.⟩ → Anatolien

Anaer·obier m ∼s/∼, **Anaerobi·ont** m ∼en/∼en ⟨biol⟩ (Ggs Aerobier, –biont) *anaerobe*

Anagr·amm n ∼(e)s/∼e *anagram*

Anakol·uth n ∼s/∼e *anacoluthon* [pl *–tha*]

Anak·onda f ∼/∼s ⟨zoo⟩ *anaconda*

anakre·ontisch a *anacreontic*

Anal·ekten f [pl] *analecta* (L)

anal·eptisch a ⟨med⟩ (stärkend) *analeptic*; ∼es Mittel *analeptic*

anal·og I. a **1.** [mst pred] *analogous* (e–r S *to a th*); *similar* (*to*) **2.** [attr] *analogic* (*form*), *analogical*; *corresponding* **II.** adv: ∼ schließen *to argue from analogy* **Analog·ie** f ∼/∼n *analogy* (zu *to*, *with*); gebildet nach ∼ v, als ∼ nach *formed on the analogy of*; nach ∼ schließen *to argue from analogy* ‖ ∼bildung, ∼form f *analogic form* ‖ ∼rechengerät [n] *analogy computer* **anal·ogisch 1.** a *analogic*(*al*) **2.** adv ∼ gebildet nach *formed on the analogy of* od *by analogy with* **-gisieren** vi [h] *to analogize*

An·alogon (Gr) n ∼s/–ga *analogue* (: *no* ∼ *in*)

Anal·ogrechner m *analogue computer*

Analphab·et m ∼en/∼en *illiterate* **Analpha-b·etentum** n ∼s/ *illiteracy*

Analys·ator m ⟨phys⟩ *analyser* (*–lyzer*)

Anal·yse f ∼/∼n ⟨a. chem⟩ *analysis*; durch ∼ *analytically*; e–e ∼ vornehmen *to make an analysis*; *breakdown* ‖ ∼n über Löhne *wages analyses* pl **analys·ieren** vt [h] *to analyse* ‖ ⟨gram⟩ (Satz) *to analyse*, *to parse* ‖ *to examine point by point* **An·alysis** f ∼/ ⟨math⟩ *analysis* **Anal·ytiker** m ∼s/∼ *analyst* **anal·ytisch** a *analytic*(*al*); nach ∼er Methode *analytically*

Anäm·ie f ∼/∼n ⟨med⟩ *anæmia* **an·ämisch** a *anæmic*

Anamn·ese f ∼/∼n ⟨med⟩ (Vorgeschichte e–r Krankheit) *anamnesis*; *case history*

·Ananas f ∼/–sse ⟨bot⟩ *pineapple*; Treibhaus f ∼ *pinery* **∼erdbeere** f ⟨bot⟩ *pineapple strawberry* **∼essenz** f *pineapple essence*

Anap·äst m ∼(e)s/∼e *anapaest* **anap·ästisch** a ⟨pros⟩ *anapaestic*

An·apher f ∼/∼n ⟨rhet⟩ *anaphora*

Anarch·ie f ∼/∼n *anarchy* **an·archisch** a *anarchic*(*al*) **Anarch·ismus** m *anarchism* **Anar-ch·ist** m ∼en/∼en *anarchist* **anarch·istisch** a *anarchic*(*al*), *anarchist*

anast·atisch a ⟨typ⟩ ∼er Druck *anastatic printing* (*process*)

Anästhes·ie f ∼/∼n ⟨med⟩ *anaesthesia* **anästhes·ieren** vt [h] *anaesthetize* **anästh·etisch** a *anaesthetic*; lokal∼es Mittel n *local anaesthetic*; *stovaine* **-sist** m ∼en *anaesthetist*

Anastigm·at m ∼s/∼e ⟨opt⟩ *anastigmat*

Anath·em n ∼(e)s/∼e, **An·athema** n ∼s/∼s ⟨R.C.⟩ *anathema* **≗atis·ieren** vt [h] *to anathematize*

Anat·olien n *Anatolia* **Anat·olier** m, **∼in** f *Anatolian* **anat·olisch** a *Anatolian*, *Anatolic*

Anat·om m ∼en/∼en *anatomist* **Anatom·ie** f ∼/∼n **1.** (Wissenschaft) *anatomy*; vergleichende ∼ *comparative a.* **2.** (Anstalt) *anatomical theatre*; *dissecting room* **anat·omisch** a *anatomical*; in ∼er Hinsicht *anatomically*

·an|backen vt/i **1.** vt [h] *to bake gently* **2.** vi [s] (festkleben) ∼ an etw *to stick to a th*

·an|backen vt [h] (Gewehr) → anlegen

·an|bahnen vt [h] *to start*; *lead to*; *to enter* od *embark upon*, *to enter into* (*a th*); *to pave the way*, *to work for* (*a th*), *to prepare the ground for* (*a th*) ‖ neue Handelsbeziehungen ∼ *to open up new markets* | vrfl **sich** ∼ *to be developing*; welche Änderungen h sich angebahnt? *what changes have shown, have been noticeable?*

·Anbahnung f *preparation*; *beginning*, *opening*

°**·an|bändeln** vi [h] ∼ mit jdm **1.** *to make up to a p*; *to scrape acquaintance with a p* ‖ mit e–m Mädchen ∼ *to carry on* (od *flirt*, *get off*, *take on*) *with a girl* **2.** *to pick a quarrel with a p*

·Anbau m ∼(e)s/∼e *cultivation* **1.** [abstr] (Anbauen) *cultivation* (*of grain*, *etc.*); *growing*, *growth* (*of fruit*); ∼ v Nahrungs– u Futterpflanzen *food-growing* ‖ (Bebauen) *cultivation*, *tillage* (*of the land*) **2.** ∼(e)s/–bauten (Nebengebäude) *outbuilding*, *side-building*, *lean-to*; *annex*, *addition* od *extension* (an *to*); *outwork* **3.** ⟨tech⟩ *attachment* **∼fläche** f *area sown* od *planted* ‖ ∼- (u Weide)fläche *acreage* **∼möbel** [n pl] *add-on* od *unit* od *sectional furniture* **·an|bauen 1.** vt [h] **a.** (Getreide) *to cultivate*; (Pflanzen) *to grow*, *to raise*; *to rear* ‖ (Land) *to start cultivating* od *tilling* | **sich** ∼ to *settle* **b.** (Haus, Flügel) *to add*; (an ein Haus *to a building*) ‖ –gebaut *lean-to* (*shed*) **2.** ≗ n *cultivation*; *growing* **·Anbauer** m ∼s/∼ *cultivator*; *grower*; *planter* ‖ (Ansiedler) *colonist*, *settler*; ⟨Am a.⟩ *squatter*

·an|befehlen vt [h] jdm ∼ *to command*, *enjoin*, *order a p* (z tun *to do*)

·Anbeginn m ∼(e)s/ ⟨bib⟩ = Beginn; v ∼ *from the beginning*, *since time began* ‖ *inception*, v ∼ dieser Bekanntschaft *from the i. of ..*

·an|behalten vt [→ halten] [h] (den Rock) *to keep* (*one's coat*) *on*

anb·ei adv ⟨bes com⟩ *herewith*; *enclosed*, *attached*, *annexed*; ∼ Faktura *invoice enclosed*

·an|beißen I. vi/t **1.** vi [h] (of fish) *to bite*, *to nibble*; *to take* ‖ ⟨fig⟩ *to bite*; *to rise at* (od *to*) *a bait*, *to rise to it*, *to swallow the bait*; er wollte nicht ∼ *he would not bite*; er biß sofort an *he took to it like a duck to water* | → abbeißen **2.** vt (etw) *to bite at*, *to nibble* **II.** ≗ n *bite*; *nibble* ‖ zum ∼ *enticingly sweet*; ⟨sl⟩ (*she's*) *good eating*

·an|belangen vt [nur 3. sg] was mich anbelangt *as far as I am concerned*, *for my part*, *I for one*; *as to* (od *as for*) *me* ‖ was –gt ⟨a.⟩ *in terms of*

·an|bellen vt [h] (jdn) *to bark at* (*a p*)

·an|bequemen vt [h] (etw) *to accommodate*, *adapt* (e–r S *to a th*) ‖ **sich** ∼ *to accommodate* (od *adapt*, *conform*) *o.s.*, *to submit* (e–r S *to a th*); *to put up* (e–r S *with a th*); sich den Wünschen jds ∼ *to comply with a p's wishes*

·an|beraumen vt [h] ⟨jur⟩ (Termin etc) *to appoint*, *to fix* ‖ (Sitzung) *to call* (auf M. *for Monday*); *the session is scheduled on M.* **·An-beraumung** f ∼/∼en ⟨jur⟩ *appointment* (*of a term*); ohne ∼ e–s Termins *sine die* L

·an|beten vt [h] *to adore*, *to worship*; die Angebetete *the adored one*, *the idol* ‖ → vergöttern

·Anbeter m ∼s/∼ *adorer*, *worshipper* ‖ e–r Dame *adorer*; *ardent admirer*; *lover*, [obs] *beau*

·Anbetracht m: in ∼ e–r S *in view of a th*, *in consideration* od *on account of a th*; in ∼ der Umstände *considering the circumstances* ‖ in ∼ dessen, daß *seeing that*; ⟨jur⟩ *whereas* **·anbetreffs** [prep] = in Anbetreff **·Anbetreff** m: in ∼ des Hauses *regarding*, *respecting the house* **·anbe-treffen** vt [nur 3. sg prs & pret] = anbelangen

·an|betteln vt [h] (jdn) *to solicit alms of* (*a p*), *to importune* (*a p*) *by begging*

·Anbetung f ∼/∼en *adoration*, *worship*(*ping*) **≗swert**, **≗swürdig** a *adorable*

·an|biedern vrefl [h] sich ∼ *to make o.s. at home*; sich ∼ bei *or* mit jdm *to hobnob with a p*; *to chum up*, *pal up with a p*; *to intrude* (od *obtrude*) *o.s.*; *to intrude*, *obtrude upon a p*, *to insinuate* od *worm o.s. into a p's favour* ‖ sie h sich bald angebiedert *they soon made friends with each other*

·Anbiederung f *intrusion*

·an|biegen vt [h] (etw) *to bend* (an *to*)

·an|bieten vt/i [h] **1.** vt (etw) *to offer*, *tender*; zum Verkauf angeboten *on offer* ‖ jdm etw ∼ *to offer* (⟨liter⟩ *to proffer*; ⟨Am⟩ *to tender*) *a p a th* od *a th to a p*; *to hold a th out to a p*; jdm etw wiederholt ∼ *to ply a p with a th*; e–r Dame die Hand ∼ (zur Heirat) *to offer one's hand to a lady* | **sich** ∼ *to offer o.s.* (*to a p*); *to offer one's* *services; to volunteer (to do)* | es bietet sich an *it has much to recommend it* **2.** vi (bei Auktionen) *to start bidding; to start a price*

·**an|binden** vt/i [h] **1.** vt (T, S) *to tie, to bind* (an *to*); (T) mit e–m Seil ~ *to tether* (an *to*); (Schiff) *to moor* || ⟨fig⟩ °e–n Bären ~ *to run up debts* **2.** vi ⟨fig⟩ mit jdm ~ *to pick a quarrel with a p* || → angebunden

·**Anbiß** m –bisses/–sse *the first bite* || (Köder) *bait, lure*

·**an|blasen** vt [h] **1.** (Glas, Thermometer etc) *to blow (one's breath) upon (a th)*; das Feuer ~ *to blow (up) the fire*; (Hochofen) *to blow in* || wie angeblasen *suddenly* **2.** die Jagd ~ *to sound* od *blow the (bugle-)horn* **3.** *to blow one's breath on a p*; ⟨übtr⟩ (anschreien) *to blow a p up; to snub a p*

*·**an|blecken** vt [h] (jdn) *to mock* || = °anfahren

·**an|bleien** vt [h] ⟨hunt⟩ = anschießen

·**Anblick** m ~(e)s/~e **1.** (Anblicken) *look, view, sight*; bei s–m ~ (= als ich ihn anblickte) *at the sight of him*; beim ersten ~ *at first sight; at the first blush* || versunken in den ~ *absorbed in the sight (of ..)* **2.** (das Angeblickte) *sight; view; (the) looks* pl *(of the place)*; ein lieblicher ~ ⟨a.⟩ *a vision of loveliness*; ein großartiger ~ *a grand show*; ein freudiger ~ *a sight for sore eyes*; ein prächtiger ~ *a sight to see*; ein ~ f Götter *a sight for the gods*; e–n seltsamen, traurigen ~ darbieten *to be* od *look a sight* ·**an|blikken** vt [h] jdn *or* etw ~ *to look at a p* od *a th*; → ansehen || jdn düster *or* finster, unwillig ~ *to frown* (od *scowl*) *at a p*; jdn flüchtig ~ *to glance at a p*; jdn prüfend ~ *to view a p*; jdn scharf ~ *to look a p squarely in the eyes*; jdn starr ~ *to glare* od *stare at a p*

·**an|blinze(l)n** vt [h] *to wink at (a p)*

·**an|blocken** vt [h] (Getriebe an Motor) *to unitize*

·**an|blöken** vt [h] (of sheep) (jdn) *to bleat at*, (of cattle) *to bellow at (a p)* || °⟨übtr⟩ = anschnauzen

·**an|bohren** **1.** vt [h] *to cut holes in; to bore, to pierce* || (ein Faß) *to broach, tap* || (Schiff) *to scuttle* | ⟨fig⟩ ° jdn ~, bei jdm ~ *to tap a p, to borrow money of* od *from a p* **2.** ≈ n (Schiff) durch ~ versenken *to scuttle (a ship)* ·**Anbohrung** f ~/~en ⟨tech⟩ [konkr] *centre hole*; [abstr] *tapping, boring*

·**an|borgen** vt [h] (jdn) *to borrow of* od *from*

·**an|braten** vt [h] (Fleisch) *to (begin to) roast*

·**an|brechen** **I.** vt/i **1.** vt [h] (Kuchen etc) *to break, cut* | Vorräte ~ *to break into stores* || (Kiste Zigarren) *to open*; noch nicht angebrochen *unopened* || *to start* || e–e neue Packung ~ *to open ..* || ⟨med⟩ **sich** [dat] e–n Knochen ~ *to suffer an incomplete fracture of a bone; to fracture a bone incompletely*; angebrochen *(partly) fractured (bone)* **2.** vi [s] (of the day, etc.) *to break, to dawn* (: *the dawn had just broken*) || (anfangen) *to begin* || die Nacht bricht an *the night is coming on* od *drawing near* || → angebrochen **II.** ≈ n *break*, bei ~ des Tages *at break of day, at day break*

·**an|brennen** vt/i **1.** vt [h] (anzünden) (ein Licht, Feuer) *to light; to kindle* || (Haus) *to set fire to; to set on fire* **2.** vi [s] *to begin to burn; to catch* od *take fire* || ⟨cul⟩ *to burn*; ~ l *to burn*; es riecht angebrannt *it smells of burning*; angebr. schmecken *to have a burnt taste*; → Rauch

·**Anbrennholz** n *kindling, kindling wood*

·**an|bringen** vt [h] **1.** (herbeischaffen) *to bring* || *(of dog) to retrieve, fetch* | ⟨übtr⟩ (Gründe) *to adduce; to bring forward* **2.** (an e–n passenden Ort bringen) **a.** *to place, to posit* || falsch ~ *to misplace* **b.** (Gerüst) *to erect, to build*; (Plakat) *to put up*; (etw) ~ an *to fix to*; ~ auf *to adjust* (od *fix*) *on* || (in richtige Lage bringen) *to fix in position* **c.** (unterbringen) (jdn) *to establish, to place* (in *in*); *to settle* **d.** (Bemerkung etc) *to put in* || (das Kind) bringt (alles) bei der Mutter an .. *tells* od *sneaks about .. to its m.* || .. ~ wollen *to want to impart a piece of news* **e.** ⟨jur⟩ (Klage) *to lodge* (gegen *against*) || → angebracht **3.** (Geld) *to spend* || ⟨com⟩ (Waren) *to get rid of; to dispose of, to market, to sell* || *to marry off (one's daughter)*

·**Anbringung** f ~/~en *the placing (of a nail)*; ⟨tech⟩ *fixing; attachment*; (Montage) *assembly* || *the putting-up (of a notice)* || → Art

·**Anbruch** m ~(e)s/≈e **1.** *opening(-up)*; ⟨min⟩ *the opening(-up) of a mine* | ⟨min⟩ *open lode* **2.** *rotten wood* **3.** ⟨übtr⟩ (Anfang) *break*; bei ~ des Tages *at break of day*, → Tages≈; bei ~ der Nacht *at nightfall* ·**anbrüchig** a *putrescent; decaying* || *decayed, rotten (wood); putrid; tainted (wine)*

·**an|brüllen** vt [h] jdn ~ *to bawl* (od *bellow, roar*) *at a p* || sich *or* e–a ~ *to roar at each other*

·**anbrummen** vt [h] jdn ~ *to grumble at a p*

°·**an|buffen** [h] ⟨sex⟩ *to punch* || sie hat sich ~ l *she's been playing tricks*

Anch·ovis f = Anschovis

Anciennit·ät f ~/~en *seniority*; nach der ~ *by seniority*; → Dienstalter

Ancien Régime [ɑ̃ː'sjɛ̃ː reː'ʒiːm] n (Fr) *ancien régime, the time before the French revolution*

·**Andacht** f ~/~en *devotion*; mit ~ *devoutly*; der ~ dienend *devotional* || (kz Gottesdienst) *devotions* [pl]; seine ~ verrichten *to be at one's devotions, to say one's prayers* ·**andächteln** vi *to affect devotion* ·**andächtig** **1.** a *devout, pious, religious* || die ≈en [pl] *the worshippers* | ⟨fig⟩ *attentive* **2.** adv *devoutly* | *attentively*

·**Andacht(s)-** *devotional* **~buch** n *manual of devotion; devotional guide* **≈los** a *undevout, irreverent* **~stunde** f *hour of devotion* (od *prayer*) **~übung** f *devotional exercise* **≈voll** a *devout*

Andal·usien n ⟨Span⟩ (Landschaft) *Andalusia*

Andal·usier m, **~in** f, **andal·usisch** a *Andalusian*

Andam·anen(inseln) f pl (ostind. Inselgruppe) *Andamans, Andaman Islands* pl

and·ante (It) adv ⟨mus⟩ *andante* || ≈ n ~s/~s *andante*

·**an|dauern** vi [h] *to go on* || (of weather) *to last* (: *too good to l.*); *to continue; to hold*; der Regen dauerte noch an *the rain still held, it kept on raining* || *to endure, to persist* || die Freundschaft dauert noch an *the friendship still holds* ·**andauernd** **1.** a *lasting, continuous; protracted; constant, perpetual, unceasing* || ~e Periode *spell* (: *a spell of good weather*); ~es Unglück *a run of bad luck* **2.** adv ~ tun *to keep doing*

·**Anden,** die [pl] *the Andes* pl, → ⟨a.⟩ Kordilleren

·**Anden-** *Andean (region)* **~rose** f ⟨bot⟩ *Andean mountain-rose*

·**Andenken** n ~s/ **1.** [abstr] *remembrance, memory* | z ~ an *in memory* od *remembrance of (a p)*; seligen ~s *of blessed memory* || im ~ behalten *to bear in mind* || jdm ein freundliches ~ bewahren *to keep a p in kind remembrance* || das ~ feiern an .. *to commemorate (a th, a p)* || bei allen noch in frischem ~ s *to be yet fresh in the minds of all men* **2.** [konkr] [pl ~] (Geschenk) *keepsake, souvenir* Fr, *memento* L; *token; relic* (an *of*)

·**andere, andre** **I.** a **A.** [sg] der (die, das) ~ **1.** (nicht derselbe; der nicht erwähnte etc v zweien etc) *the other ..*; auf der ~n Seite *on the other side (of the street)* || das ~ Geschlecht *the other sex* || ⟨parl⟩ das ~ Haus *another place* || ein ~r *another*; die beiden ~n *the other two*, → II. 1. manch ~(r) *many another (poet)* || ein um das ~ Mal *time and again*; e–n Tag um den ~n, e–n um den ~n T. *on alternate days, on each alternate day, every other* (od *second*) *day* ||

am ~n Morgen (*on*) *the next* od *following morning* **2.** (neu, weitere) *other*; irgendein ~r Teil *any other part*; e–e Zeile nach der ~n s–r Reden zeigt .. *line after line of his speeches shows* .. || *fresh* **3.** (verschieden) *other* (als *than, from*); *different* (als *from; to, than*); ~e Leute *a different kind of people*; e–e ganz ~ Welt als unsere *a world quite different* (od *a quite different w.*) *from ours* | ich bin ganz ~r Meinung als du *I am of an entirely different opinion from you* || er wurde ein ~r Mensch *he became another man*; aus jdm e–n ~n Mann m *to make a new man of a p* || ~n Sinnes w *to change one's mind* || e–r S e–e ~e Farbe geben *to change the colo(u)r of a th* **B.** [pl] ~, die ~n .. *the other* ..; die ~n Beiden *the other two*; viele ~ Dinge *many other things* || in ~n Umständen s *to be in an interesting condition* || mit ~n Worten *in other words* || ihre Ziele waren ganz ~e *her objects were quite other* | (die übrigen) *the other books* (*will follow*) **II.** [abs] **1.** der (die, das) ~ *the other*; mst: der eine .. der ~ *the one .. the other*; e–r folgte dem ~n *one followed the other*; e–r nach dem ~n *one after another* (od *the other*) || der e–e od ~ *one or other* (*of us*) || (diese Tinte ist schlecht) hast du (etw) ~? (..) *have you any other*? || ein Wort gab das ~ *one word led to another* || gib mir ein ~s *give me another* (*book*) **2.** [pl] ~, die ~n (*the*) *others*, ~ s–r Dramen *others of his plays*; die beiden ~n *the two others* || es gibt noch ~ wie er *he is not the only pebble on the beach*; unter ~n *among others*; vor allen ~n *of all others* **III.** s **1. a.** der (die) ~ *the other person, the other one* || **ein** ~r *another man* || er war ein ~r geworden *he had become another man* || **kein** ~r als *no one else than, no* († *none*) *other than* **b.** [pl] ~ *others, other persons* [pl] **2. ~s, das ~; etw ~s** *something else*; etw ~s? *anything else*?; alles ~ *everything else*; alles ~ s als angenehm *to be anything but pleasant, to be the reverse of p.* || nichts ~s als *nothing else than* | *another thing*; das ist etw ~s *that's another thing* das ist etw ganz *or* völlig ~s *that's quite another* (od *a different*) *th* od *story*; ⟨fam⟩ *that's an apple of another tree, a horse of a different colo(u)r, a bird of another feather* || es ist etw ~s, erstens z wissen u zweitens z glauben *to know is one th, to believe is another* || u vieles ~ *and many other things*; unter ~m *among other things* **c.** *other*; es ist unmöglich ~s z tun als .. *it is impossible to do other than* ..; er konnte nichts ~s tun als .. *he could do no other but* (od *than*) .. **d. Wendungen:** ~s vorhaben *to be otherwise engaged* || ich habe mich e–s ~n besonnen *I have changed my mind* || eins ins ~ gerechnet *one with the other, one with another* || eins kommt zum ~n *one thing leads to another*; u ~s mehr *and the like*; → II. 1.

·anderenfalls, ·anderenteils = andernfalls, –teils **·andererseits** = anderseits

·andermal adv ein ~ *another time* od *day*; *on some other occasion*

·ändern vt [h] **A. 1.** *to alter* (zu *into*) || das ändert die S *that alters the case*; *that makes a difference* || das ändert nichts an .. *that does not make any difference to* .. || es ändert nichts an der Tatsache *it does not alter the fact* (*that*); was ändert das an den T.n? *what's the odds*? | (abändern) *to modify*; ~ Sie nichts daran *make no alteration to it* **2.** (wechseln) *to change*, s–e Meinung ~ *to change one's opinion*; den Ton ~ *to ch. one's tone* | die Lage ~ *to shift* || e–n Plan ~ *to depart from a plan* || s–n Standpunkt ~ *to shift one's ground* **3.** (abhelfen) ich kann es nicht ~ *I cannot help it*; Sie können das nicht ~ *you cannot help it*; daran ist nichts z ~, es ist nicht z ~ *it cannot be helped*; was sich nicht läßt ~, muß man l schlendern *what cannot be cured must be endured*; geschehene Dinge sind nicht zu ~ *it is no use crying over spilt milk* **B. sich** ~ *to alter* || *to change* || sich vollkommen (v Grund aus) ~ *to change completely*; das Wetter ändert sich *the weather is changing* || *to shift* || (of prices) *to vary* | das läßt sich nicht ~ *it cannot be helped; there is no help for it*

·andernfalls adv *otherwise, else; failing this*

·andern·orts adv *elsewhere, somewhere else*

·andernteils adv *on the other hand*

·anders adv **1.** (auf andere Art) [bei Verben] *different, else, differently, otherwise*, es steht ~ mit ihm *it is otherwise with him*; ~ w *to change*; er ist ganz ~ geworden *he has changed greatly* od *turned out quite differently*; es konnte nicht ~ s *it was inevitable*; dies muß ganz ~ gemacht w *this must be done quite otherwise* || *differently*; ~ beschaffen s (P) *to be made differently*, (S) *to be of a different kind* || ihm erging es nicht ~ *he did not fare differently* | **~ als** *otherwise than, other than; in a different way than, differently from*; er war ganz ~ als irgend jemand *he was unlike anyone*; er konnte nicht ~ als zurücktreten *he couldn't do other than resign*; sein Ausdruck ist ~ (als zuvor) *his expression has changed*; ich bin ganz ~ als er *I am quite different to* (⟨Am⟩ *from*) *him*; er denkt ~ als du *he thinks differently from you* | **Wendungen:** aber das ist nun mal nicht ~ *that's the way it is, but there it is* || etw ~ auffassen *to place a different construction on a th* || ~ aussehen *to look different*; ganz ~ aussehen *to look a different man* || sich ~ besinnen *to change one's mind* || ich kann nicht ~ *I cannot help myself*; ich kann nicht ~, ich muß es ablehnen *I cannot help declining it*; *I cannot but decline it*; *I have no other course left but to decline it* || es wird noch (ganz) ~ kommen *things will be getting worse* || die S verhält sich so u nicht ~ *that is just how it* (od *the situation*) *is* || er macht es nun mal nicht ~ *that is his way* (*of doing it*) || es ist doch ganz ~ geworden *it has turned out quite differently* || das Wetter ist ~ geworden *the weather has changed* || er ist ~ geworden *he has become another man* || ° mir wird ganz ~ *I am not feeling well, I am feeling unwell* **2.** (sonst, außerdem) [bei pron] **jemand** ~ *somebody else* **niemand** ~ *nobody else* (als *but*); **wer** ~? *who else* (als *but*)? || **wo~**? *where else*?; irgendwo ~ *somewhere else*; nirgendwo ~ *nowhere else* **3.** [nach *if* etc] **wenn** ~, wofern ~ *if indeed, if in fact, if really, if .. at all*; *provided that*; wenn ~ .. nicht *unless* || wenn es nicht ~ s kann *if there is no other way*

·anders- ~artig a *different*; [pred] *of a different kind* || *alien* (als *from*) **~denkend** a *dissenting; dissident* **~geschlechtlich** a *heterosexual* **~gesinnt** a *otherwise-minded* **~gläubig** a *heterodox, heretical* | ≗e(r [m]) [f] *I'm belonging to a denomination other than the one mentioned*; ⟨engl⟩ *dissenter* **~wie** adv *in some other way* **~wo** adv *elsewhere; somewhere else* **~woher** adv *from elsewhere* **~wohin** adv *to another place; elsewhere*; ⟨Am⟩ (*to go*) *someplace else*

·anderseits adv *on the other hand*; → erstens

·anderthalb a *one and a half*; ~ Pfund *one and a half pounds, a pound and a half*; ~ Jahre *eighteen months* | [in comp] *sesqui–*, ~mal soviel *sesquialter(al)* ≗**decker** m ⟨aero⟩ *sesquiplane*

·Änderung f ~/~en *change* (e–r S *in a th*); *alteration*; e–e ~ des Wetters *a change in the weather* → Veränderung || (Abänderung) *modification* (an *to*) || *fluctuation, variation* (*of prices*) | e–e ~ erfahren *to undergo a change* || e–e ~ treffen *to make an alteration; to make some modification* (an etw *to a th*) **~santrag** m ⟨parl⟩ *amendment* **~sgesetz** n *amending law, act amendatory* od *supplementary*

·**anderwärts** adv *elsewhere, in another place*

·**anderweit** adv *elsewhere; otherwise* ·**anderweitig 1.** a *other, further; ulterior (aims)* **2.** adv *elsewhere; otherwise*

·**an|deuten** vt [h] **1.** (kz erörtern) *to indicate (a th); to hint at (a th);* angedeutet *sketched;* es kann hier nur angedeutet w *it can only be indicated here* ‖ *to allude to* | (hindeuten auf) *to hint at (: the colour hinted at the coming spring)* **2.** (z verstehen geben) etw ~ *to indicate; to intimate; to suggest, to hint a th;* ohne etw anzudeuten *without a hint of a th* ‖ im geheimen ~ *to insinuate a th* | (durchblicken l) *to imply;* (sie sagte nicht, daß ..,) aber sie deutete es an (..) *but she implied it; she outlined (a gesture of invitation)* | ~ **daß** .. *to hint, intimate, suggest, imply; insinuate that ..;* **jdm ~ daß** .. *to intimate (od motion, suggest) to a p that ..* (od *to do*); *to give a p to understand that ..* | **nur ~d erwähnen** *to mention only allusively;* etw ~d erwähnen *to allude to a th*

·**Andeutung** f ~/~en **(Anzeichen)** *indication, suggestion, trace (v of)* **ohne jede** ~ v Stärke *without any suggestion of strength* | (Anhauch) *suspicion, trace, touch, shade* | **(Wink)** *hint* (über *as to,* v *of*); jdm e–e ~ m *to give a p a hint;* ~en m *to throw out hints* ‖ ~en m über *to give indications of* ‖ *intimation; suggestion (that);* e–e ~ m *to suggest* ‖ (feine Anspielung) *insinuation;* **bloße** ~ *allusiveness;* **geheime** ~ *innuendo,* geheime ~en m *to make innuendos, to innuendo;* versteckte ~ ⟨bes Am⟩ *dark hint* ≈**sweise** adv *allusively; by way of innuendo; indirectly*

·**an|dichten** vt [h] **1.** jdm etw ~ *to attribute* (od *impute*) *a th falsely to a p; to credit a p with a th* **2.** s–e Geliebte ~ *to make "(woeful) ballads to one's mistress' eyebrow"*

·**an|dienen** vt [h] ⟨com⟩ (gewählt f: anbieten) jdm etw ~ *to tender a p a th* od *a th to a p* ·**Andienung** f ~/~en ⟨st exch⟩ *notification of the delivery of goods*

·**an|donnern** vi/t [h] **1.** vi (heftig schlagen) *to knock violently* (an *at*) **2.** vt °jdn ~ *to thunder* od *roar at a p* ‖ wie angedonnert dastehen *to stand thunder-struck*

And·orra n *Andorra* (in den Ost-Pyrenäen); Bewohner(in) v ~ *Andorran, Andorrese*

·**Andrang** m ~(e)s/ *throng, press; heavy traffic* ‖ *run* (zu e–m Gebäude *on a building*); *rush* (nach Waren *for goods*); → Ansturm, Nachfrage ‖ ~ des Blutes *congestion* ·**an|drängen** vrefl [h] sich ~ an jdn *to curry favour with a p, to obtrude o.s. upon a p*

·**andre** → andere

Andr·easkreuz n *St. Andrew's Cross* (×)

·**an|drehen** vt [h] **1.** (Gas, Licht; Radio) *to turn on, to put on* ‖ → anknipsen; wählen **2.** ° etw ~ *to manage,* ich weiß nicht, wie ich es ~ soll *I do not know how to m. it* **3.** °jdm etw ~ *to plant a th on a p; to work,* ⟨Am⟩ *palm a th off on a p* ·**Andrehkurbel** f ~/~n ⟨mot⟩ *starting–* od *starter crank* (od *handle*)

·**an|dringen** vi [s] *to press forward; to draw near;* ~gegen jdn *to make a rush on a p*

·**an|drohen** vt [h] (Strafe) *to threaten, to menace;* jdm etw ~ *to threaten a p with a th;* ihm wurde Strafe angedroht *he was threatened with punishment* ·**Androhung** f ~/~en *threat, menace* ‖ unter ~ e–r S *under the threat of a th*

Andr·omeda f ~/~s ⟨bot⟩ *marsh andromeda; wild rosemary;* Japanische ~ *Japanese Pieris*

·**Andruck** m ~(e)s/~e ⟨typ⟩ *proof* ·**an|drucken** vt [h] ⟨typ⟩ *to pull*

·**an|drücken** vt/i [h] **1.** vt etw ~ an etw *to press a th close to* od *against a th;* die Tür fest ~ *to shut the door closely* (⟨a.⟩ [abs]) ⟨aero⟩ *to nose down, to depress the nose* **2.** vi ⟨aero⟩ *to put on speed*

°·**an|dudeln** vt [h] sich e–n ~ = sich betrinken

°·**an|ecken** vt/i [h] **1.** vt ⟨fig⟩ jdn ~ *to push* od *knock against a p* **2.** vi *to cause annoyance;* bei jdm ~ *to give offence to a p, to hurt a p; to incur the displeasure of a p;* → Anstoß

·**an|eifern** vt [h] *to animate (a p)*

·**an|eignen** vt [h] sich [dat] etw (gewaltsam) ~ *to seize* od *commandeer a th; to appropriate a th (to o.s.);* ⟨sl⟩ *to collar, to mop a th;* → annektieren, besetzen ‖ sich etw (Thron, Macht etc) widerrechtlich ~ *to usurp a th,* ⟨jur⟩ *to convert;* sich (Geld) .. ~ *to misappropriate* | ⟨übtr⟩ *to acquire (abilities, knowledge, etc.); to contract* od *acquire (a habit)* ‖ *to adopt (the opinion of a p)* ‖ *to learn (a language)*

·**Aneignung** f ~/~en *appropriation; occupancy; conversion to one's own use* ‖ unrechtmäßige ~ *usurpation, assumption;* ⟨jur⟩ *conversion*

anein·ander adv *together;* → zusammen **~binden** vt [h] *to bind* od *tie together* **~fügen** vt [h] *to join together;* ⟨übtr⟩ *to weld* **~geraten** vi [s] *to come to blows;* ⟨übtr⟩ *to quarrel; to fall out* (mit *with*) **~grenzen** vi (of houses, etc) *to be contiguous* od *adjacent; to adjoin, to join* **~grenzend** a *contiguous, adjacent, adjoining* **~kleben** vt/i [h & s] *to stick together* **~kommen** vi [s] *to touch* ‖ = aneinandergeraten **~prallen 1.** vi [s] *to collide, to come into violent contact* **2.** ≈ n *collision, impact* **~reihen** vt [h] (Perlen) *to string; to arrange in a row;* ⟨übtr⟩ (Teile) *to connect, to join* ‖ sich ~ *to be strung together* ≈**reihung** f ⟨demog⟩ ~en [pl] *series* **~schmieden, ~schweißen** vt [h] *to weld* **~stoßen** vi = ~grenzen | **~ vorbeireden** vi [h] *to talk at cross purposes* **~wachsen** vi [s] *to grow together;* (of bones) *to coalesce*

Anekd·ote f ~/~n *anecdote; story;* ⟨fam⟩ *yarn* **anekd·otenh·aft** a *anecdotal, anecdotic(al)*

·**an|ekeln** vt [h] **1.** (S) [act] [nur 3. sg & pl] jdn ~ (S) *to disgust, revolt, sicken a p; to pall on a p; to give a p a pain in the neck;* sein Benehmen ekelt mich an *his conduct disgusts* od *sickens me, makes me sick; I detest* od *loathe his c.* ‖ es ekelt mich an *I am sick of it; it disgusts me, I loathe* (z tun *to do*); → ekelhaft; ekeln | [pass] angeekelt w *or* s *to be disgusted* (od *fed up*) (durch; von *with*); sich angeekelt fühlen *to feel disgusted* **2.** (P) °jdn ~ *to annoy* (od *irritate*) *a p disgustingly*

Anemom·eter n ~s/~ (Windmesser) *anemometer; windage scale* **Anem·one** f ~/~n ⟨bot⟩ *anemone; windflower;* Brocken≈ *pulsatilla;* → Buschwindröschen

·**anempfehlen** vt [ich empfehle an, *or* ich anempfehle] [h] jdm ~ *to recommend* od *advise a p* (z tun *to do*); (dringend) *to urge a p (to do);* mir wurde anempfohlen *I was recommended (to do)* ‖ jdm etw ~ *to recommend a p a th* od *a th to a p* ·**Anempfehlung** f ~/~n *recommendation;* → Rat

·**anempfunden** a nur ~ *imitated, not genuine*

·**Anerbe** m ~n/~n *principal heir (to a farm)* **~ngericht** n *hereditary farm court* **~nrecht** n *right of succession to undivided farm estate*

·**Anerbieten** n ~s/~ *tender, offer, proposal* (m *to make*) ·**an|erbieten** vt/vrfl → bieten *to tender, etc* ‖ sich ~ *to propose, suggest o.s. (to do)*

·**anerkannt** [pp v anerkennen] **1.** a *acknowledged; admitted; recognized (fact, truth); accepted (authority)* (auf dem Gebiete v *on*) ‖ allg ~, als gültig ~ *received (pronunciation);* ~e Bedeutung *acception (of a word)* ‖ staatlich ~ *certificated (teacher)* ‖ ⟨jur⟩ (nicht) ~ *(dis)allowed (claim)* **2.** adv *admittedly (excellent quality)* (= *acknowledged excellence*) **~erm·aßen** adv *confessedly; admittedly;* ⟨Am⟩ *concededly*

·**aner- ~kennen** vt [erk·enne ·an, ·anerkenne] [h] **1.** (gesetzlich ~) (jdn, etw) *to acknowledge* (als *as*); man erkannte ihn als König an *they ac-*

knowledged him as (od *to be*) *king, he was acknowledged as* (*to be*) *k.* ‖ *to recognize* (als *as*); jdn als s–n Erben ~ *to recognize a p as one's heir* | (jds Oberhoheit; Vaterschaft) *to own*; nicht ~ *to disavow*; *to disown*; (Verantwortung) nicht ~ *to disclaim* | (Ansprüche) *to recognize, allow*; nicht ~ *to disallow*; (Staatsschuld) 〈bes Am〉 nicht ~ *to repudiate*; s–e Unterschrift nicht ~ *to refuse to recognize one's signature*; (Wechsel) *to honour, accept*; nicht ~ *to dishonour* | (zugeben) *to admit, to allow, to recognize, to own* (*a th*; *that*..) 〈Am〉 *to concede* | jdm etw ~ *to credit a p with a th* **2.** (lobend ~) (jds Verdienste etc) *to recognize, to approve, to appreciate*; *to do justice to* **-kennend** a *approving, appreciative, appreciatory*; in ~er Weise *approvingly* **-kennenswert** a *commendable* (*restrain*); *praiseworthy, creditable*; *deserving of recognition, worthy of appreciation* **·Anerkenntnis** n –nisses/–nisse 〈jur〉 (bes Schuld–) *recognizance* | ~urteil [n] *judgment by confession*

·Anerkennung f ~/~en **1.** (**Billigung**) *acknowledgment, acceptance* (*of a th*) ‖ *recognition* (jds als *of a p as*; durch jdn *by a p*); amtliche ~ e–s ausländ. Konsuls durch die Landesregierung *exequatur* L (: *to receive one's e.*); 〈engl〉 die ~ des Königs (bei der Krönung) durch das Volk *the Recognition* ‖ (Schuld–) *recognizance* ‖ *acceptance* (*of a bill*) ‖ 〈pol〉 *recognition* ‖ 〈agr〉 Saaten~̈ *seed recogn.* **2.** (**lobende ~**) *acknowledg(e)ment* (für *of*) ‖ *recognition*, als ~ f *in recognition of*; um ~ ringen *to struggle for r.* ‖ *appreciation*; *approval*, ~ finden *to meet with approval*; *to win recognition, to come to be recognized* (bei *with*), lobende ~ finden *to get credit* (f *for*); hohe ~ gewinnen *to win golden opinions* (seitens *from*) **~sschreiben** n *letter of acknowledg(e)ment* **~sspalte** f (e–r Zeitung) *credit column* **~szahlung** f *token payment*

Anero·id n, ~s/~e *aneroid (barometer)*

·an|erziehen vt [h] jdm etw ~ *to accustom a p to a th by education*; *to inculcate a th* (*up*)*on* (od *in*) *a p*; *to instil(l) a th into a p's mind* (*by education*) ‖ jdm anerzogen s (of qualities) *to have been acquired by education*

·an|fachen vt [h] *to blow into a flame, to make burn* | 〈fig〉 (Gefühle) *to inflame*; *to kindle*, (Leidenschaften) *to rouse, stir*; (Haß) *to foment*

·Anfahr- ~beschleunigung f 〈mot, etc〉 *acceleration from rest* (od *dead stop*) **~moment** n 〈mach〉 *starting moment* **~strecke** f *starter distance* **~zugkraft** f 〈mot fam〉 *zip*

·an|fahren vi/t **I.** vi [s] **1.** *to come along* (od *advance, arrive*) *in a carriage*, etc, *on a bicycle*; er kam (im Wagen) angefahren *he came driving along, he came along* (od *he drove up*) *in his car* **2.** (of vehicles) *to come* od *move off*; *to start*; der Wagen fährt weich an *the car starts smoothly* **3.** 〈min〉 *to descend* (*into*) *the shaft* **II.** vt [h] **1.** (jdn, etw) 〈mot〉 *to hit*; jdn *to run into a p*; e–n Pfahl, Stein ~ *to drive* (od *strike*) *against a post* ‖ 〈mar〉 (Schiff) *to foul* ‖ 〈min〉 (Gang) *to meet* **2.** (anlaufen) e–n Hafen ~ *to call* (od *touch*) *at a port* **3.** (herbeifahren) (Steine, Heu) *to carry* (od *bring, cart, convey*) *by wag(g)on* (etc) ‖ 〈übtr〉 *to bring* (*up*) **4.** 〈fig〉 °jdn ~ *to snap at a p*; *to fly in a p's face*; *to snap a p's head* (od *nose*) *off*; *to fly out* (od *to let fly*) *at a p, to jump* (od *round*) *on a p* ‖ er fuhr mich an (wer sind Sie?) *he asked me gruffly* (*who* ..) ‖ (of dogs) die Leute ~ *to rush at people*

·Anfahrt f ~/~en **1.** (Ankommen) *arrival*; *approach* ‖ 〈min〉 *descent* (*down the shaft*) **2.** (Herbeischaffen) *conveyance, transport* **3.** (Zufahrtsweg) *avenue, drive* ‖ 〈mar〉 *landing-place, quay* **~straße** f *approach*

·Anfall m ~(e)s/~̈e **1.** (Angriff) *attack, assault*; → Angriff **2.** 〈med〉 *attack, onset* (*of an illness*); (Schub) *attack* (*of jaundice*, 〈fam〉 *spell* (: *she had one of her spells*; 〈fam〉 *a go* (*of measles*); *seizure*; (periodischer Anfall) *fit*; *paroxysm*; epileptischer ~ *fit of epilepsy*; → Ohnmachts~̈, Schlag~̈ ‖ leichter ~ *touch*, ein ~ v Gicht *a t. of gout*; Husten~̈ *fit of coughing* | 〈übtr〉 *fit, paroxysm* ‖ Lach~̈ *paroxysm of laughter*; Wut~̈ *paroxysm of rage*, 〈Am〉 *conniption fit* ‖ sie hatte hysterische ~̈e *she went into hysterics* ‖ → Krampf | 〈fig〉 *spasm*; ein ~ v Furcht *a s. of fear*; Anfälle v Melancholie *accesses of melancholy* **3.** 〈jur〉 *accession to an inheritance*; *inheritance* **4.** 〈com, etc〉 *rate* (v *of*) **5.** 〈min〉 (Stützung) *prop, stay*

·an|fallen vt/i **1.** vt [h] (jdn) *to assail, to assault, attack*; *to fall* (od *be*) *upon* (*a p*); → angreifen; herfallen ‖ (of an illness) (jdn) *to attack* | (anpöbeln) *to mob* ‖ 〈fig〉 jdn hinterrücks ~ *to stab a p in the back* **2.** vi [s] jdm ~ *to fall to a p*; *to devolve on a p* ‖ 〈chem〉 *to be disengaged* od *developed* **·anfallend** a *about to be disengaged* ‖ *casual, occasional*; (entstehend) *available* **·anfällig** a (kränklich) *crank(y), shaky*; *wonky*; *weak* (Lunge *chest*); *susceptible* (*constitution*) (f *to*); [pred] *in poor health*

·Anfalls- ~recht n 〈jur〉 bedingtes ~ *contingent remainder*, rechtwirksames ~ *vested r.* **~steuer** f *inheritance tax*

·Anfang m ~(e)s/~̈e **1.** (Zeit) *beginning*; *outset*; *push-off*; (gewählt:) *commencement*; → Beginn **2.** (of institutions, etc.) der ~, die ersten Anfänge *the beginnings* (*of drama*); *inception, origin* (*of life*); *source* | (Grundlage) *the elements, rudiments* [pl] **3.** (S) *beginning*; *opening* (*of a letter*); *exordium* (*of a treatise*); *introduction* **4. Wendungen: am** ~ s–r Laufbahn *at the outset of his career*; am ~ des 19. Jhds *at the beginning of the 19th c.*; am ~ war der Roman interessant *at the b. the novel was interesting* | **f den** ~ 〈Am〉 *as* (od *for*) *a starter*; ganz gut f den ~ *quite good as* (od *for*) *a beginning* | **im** ~ *in the beginning* | **v ~ an** *from the first, from the beginning*, 〈fam〉 *from scratch* → gleich; **v ~ bis** z Ende *from beginning to end, from start to finish*; (Buch) *from cover to cover* | z ~ *at first*; → gleich; ein **neuer** ~ *a new beginning* ‖ ein schwacher (*or* erster) ~ *the thin end of the wedge* ‖ der ~ vom Ende *the beginning of the end* | der ~ des 19. Jhds *the early 19th c.*; ~ **Mai** *early in May*; ~ dieser Woche *early this week*; er ist ~ **dreißig,** ~ der Dreißiger *he is* (*in the*) *early thirties* | **den ~ m** *to begin* (: *you b.*); *to fire away* ‖ den ~ m mit e–r S (= zuerst beginnen mit) *to make a beginning with, to begin* (od *start*) *with a th* ‖ e–n guten ~ m mit *to have a good start with*; mach endlich den ~ mit der S *begin the matter at last* ‖ s–n ~ **nehmen** *to commence, to begin*; *to start* (v *from*) ‖ wir **stehen** erst noch am ~ hiermit *it's in its early stages*, 〈Am〉 *its infancy* | **aller** ~ ist schwer *nothing so hard as the beginning, the first step is all the difficulty*

·an|fangen vt/i [h] **I.** vt **1.** *to begin*, e–n Streit ~ *to begin* (od *pick*) *a quarrel* (*with*); die Arbeit ~ *to start work* ‖ (gewählt:) *to commence*; e–n Prozeß ~ *to commence a lawsuit* | ein Geschäft ~ *to set up* (od *to open*) *a business* (od *shop*); *to start in business*; e–e Unterhaltung ~ *to enter upon a conversation* ‖ du mußt es anders ~ *you must set about it differently* ‖ zuviel(erlei) ~ *to have too many irons in the fire* ‖ → wieder ~ **2.** (verblaßt: tun) was sollen wir ~? *what are we to do*? was hast du die ganze Zeit –ge–? *what have you been doing with yourself all the time*?; was h Sie heute –ge–? *what have you done with y.s. to-day*? ‖ ich weiß nicht, was ich damit ~ soll *I do not know what to do with it*; er konnte damit nichts ~ *he could make nothing of it* ‖ mit ihm ist nichts –zu– (z m) *there is no dealing* *with him* **II.** vi **1.** *to begin, to make a beginning* od *start; to commence* || ⟨theat⟩ Achtung! ~! *beginners please!*, ⟨Am⟩ *places!*; (Kino) ⟨fam⟩ *to go on* || (f sich) ~ *to begin the world* || mit nichts ~ *to start from scratch*; v vorn ~ ⟨fig⟩ *to make a new start* (od *departure*) || es fing an zu schneien *it came on to snow* || wieder v vorn ~ *to begin over again* || da fängst du schon wieder an *there you go again*; → wieder ~ **2.** ~ z tun *to begin to do*; * *to commence to do* || z reden ~ *to begin*; eifrig z sprechen ~ *to burst into speech* | *to begin* (od *commence, start*) *doing* **3.** ~ **an** e–r Stelle *to begin at a place* | ~ **mit** etw *to begin* (od *commence*), *to make a beginning with a th*; das Alphabet fängt mit A an *the alphabet begins with A* || damit ~ z tun *to begin by doing* | immer wieder **von** etw ~ *to keep on repeating a th*

·Anfänger m ~s/~ *beginner, learner, novice, tyro, tiro* (in etw *in a th*); Lesebuch f ~ *junior* (od *first*) *reader*; ⟨fig⟩ *Johnny Raw, fledgeling*; °blutiger ~ *greenhorn*, ⟨Am fam⟩ *rookie*, ⟨Am sport⟩ *duffer*; **~flugzeug** n *training aircraft* **~rolle** f ⟨theat⟩ *utility*

·anfänglich 1. a *initial, incipient, first, early* **2.** adv = **·anfangs** adv *in the beginning*; *at first* || *to begin with* (*and then* ..) || ~ Mai *early in May* || → gleich

·Anfangs- *initial* .. **~buchstabe** m ⟨typ⟩ *initial letter, initial* || großer ~ *capital*; kleiner ~ *small initial* || mit den ~en unterzeichnen *to initial* **~druck** m ⟨tech⟩ *admission pressure* **~gehalt** n, **~lohn** m *beginning wages* **~geschwindigkeit** f *initial speed*, ⟨phys⟩ *initial velocity*; (of a projectile) *muzzle velocity* **~gründe** m [pl] *the* (*first*) *elements* od *principles*; *rudiments* [pl]; ~ der Arithmetik *elementary arithmetic*; jdn in den ~n e–r S unterrichten *to ground a p in a th* **~kolumne** f ⟨typ⟩ *head-page* **~kurs** m *junior course* || ⟨com⟩ *the opening price* **~punkt** m *starting-point* **~spannung** f ⟨el⟩ *initial tension* **~sperre** f ⟨rail⟩ *incoming block* **~stadium** n *incipience*; *early* (od *initial, rudimentary*) *stage*; *the beginnings* od *origins* (*of a th*) [pl]; *germ* **~unterricht** m *grounding* (in *in*); *elementary instruction*; *the junior school* **~zeile** f ⟨typ⟩ *initial line, head-line* **~zustand** m *initial state*

·an|färben vt [h] *to colour, to paint*; *to tinge*

·Anfärbung f ⟨typ⟩ *first inking*

·an|fassen vt/i [h] **I.** vt **1.** ⟨eig⟩ **jdn** ~ *to catch* (od *lay, seize*) *hold of a p, to seize a p* (am Arm *by the arm*) || (schlagen) *to touch* (: *I did not touch him*) | **sich** ~, **e-a** ~ *to hold* (od *join*) *hands* | **(etw)** *to touch* (: *he never touched a card*) || *to handle* || etw mit beiden Händen ~ *to get both hands to a th* | **sich** kalt (etc) ~ = sich anfühlen → d. **2.** ⟨übtr⟩ (behandeln) *to handle*; jdn grob ~ *to handle a p without mittens* || (Aufgabe) *to approach*; *to set about* (*a th*); etw richtig ~ *to have got the right end of the stick*; etw verkehrt ~ *to put the cart before the horse, to go to work the wrong way* || → angreifen, anpacken | (jdn) *to treat, handle*, jdn grob ~ *to handle a p roughly, to rough-house a p*; jdn mit Handschuhen (*or* sanft) ~ *to treat a p gently* **II.** vi fest ~ *to tighten one's grip* || mit ~, ~ helfen *to bear* od *lend a hand* (bei *in, at*); *to play one's part*; *to help*

·Anfassen n *seizing, touching* || ⟨übtr⟩ *handling*; *treatment* **·Anfasser** m *pot-holder*

·an|fauchen vt [h] (of cats) *to spit at* || ⟨übtr⟩ = anfahren

·an|faulen vi [s] *to begin to rot*; *to putrefy*

·anfechtbar a *contestable, impugnable*; *debatable*; *rescindable*; *controversial* (*evidence*); *pregnable* (*idea*); [pred] *open to criticism*

·an|fechten vt [h] **1.** *to call in question*; (Meinung) *to attack, assail*; *to impugn*; (Behauptung, Recht etc) *to challenge, contest, dispute*; (Testament) *to contest* || ⟨jur⟩ e–e Entscheidung ~ *to appeal against a decision*; (Zeugen, Geschworene) *to challenge* || (Behauptung) durch Deutelei ~ *to quibble at* **2.** (of evils, feelings) (jdn) *to disturb, to trouble*; was ficht dich an? *what ails you? what's the matter with you?* was ficht mich das an? *what is that to me?*; laß dich das nicht ~! *never mind that!*, *take it easy* || Zweifel ficht ihn an *doubt assails him* || (in Versuchung führen) *to tempt*

·Anfechtung f ~/~en **1.** (Beanstandung) *contestation*; *impugnment*; ⟨jur⟩ *appeal* (e–r Entscheidung *from a decision*); *challenge* (*of a juror*) **2.** *temptation*

·an|feilen vt [h] *to file slightly*

·an|feinden vt [h] jdn ~ *to bear malice to a p*; *to feel ill-will, to cherish hostile* od *revengeful feelings towards a p*; *to persecute a p* || *to criticize a p* **·Anfeindung** f ~/~en *malice, ill-will, spite*; *persecution* || *criticism*, starke ~ *strong c.* (seitens *from*)

·an|fertigen vt [h] *to make*; (Anzug) *to build, to tailor*; (Aufsatz) *to write*; (e–e Liste) *to draw up* || ⟨tech⟩ *to manufacture*; *to produce*; *to prepare* || (schaffen) (Stück) *to produce* | etw ~ l *to have a th done* **·Anfertiger** m *maker* || *manufacturer*

·Anfertigung f ~/~en *making*; *drawing-up*; (of bills) *preparation* || ⟨tech⟩ *manufacture*; *production*; ~skosten [pl] *production costs* [pl]

·an|fetten vt [h] *to grease*

·an|feuchten vt [h] *to moisten*; *to wet, to damp* || ° (sich) die Kehle ~ *to wet one's whistle*

·Anfeucht- ~maschine f *spray damper* **~pinsel** m *wetting brush*

·Anfeuer- ~holz n *kindling wood*

·an|feuern vt [h] **1.** (Ofen) *to heat* **2.** ⟨fig⟩ *to inflame, incite, key up*; *kindle*, (zu *to*); ⟨Am sl⟩ *to pep* || *to encourage, to animate* || ~d *stimulating, etc* **·Anfeuerung** f ~/~en ⟨fig⟩ *encouragement*; *incitement* (zu *to*)

·an|finden vt [h] → antreffen || sich ~ *to be found*

·an|flehen vt [h] (jdn) *to implore, to supplicate* (*a p*), *to cry to* (*a p*); *to beseech* (um *for*; z tun *to do*); *to entreat* (*to do*)

·an|flicken vt [h] (etw) *to put a patch on* (*a th*); *to sew* od *stitch* (an etw *on to a th*) || ⟨fig⟩ (hinzufügen) *to tag* (an *to*)

·an|fliegen vi/t **1.** vi [s] angeflogen k. *to come flying along* | ⟨übtr⟩ (of seed) *to be scattered* (od *sown*) *by the wind* | ⟨fig⟩ eine Krankheit flog ihn an *an illness befell him* (od *came upon him*) *all of a sudden, he was seized with an illness*; wie angeflogen (*it came upon him*) *like a bolt from the blue* || es fliegt mir nur so an *I learn it easily, I acquire it without effort*; der Sieg flog ihm nur so an *he won hands down* **2.** vt [h] ⟨aero⟩ e–n Flughafen ~ *to make a pass at* (od *to approach*) *an airport*; (Ziel) *to run up*

·Anflug m ~(e)s/⸚e **1.** *approach* (*of flying birds*); (Auffliegen) *soaring* | ⟨aero⟩ *approach, coming-on flight, arrival* **im** ~ *in-bound*; *coming* (⟨fam⟩ *to town*); im ~ gemeldet *reported airborne* **2.** ⟨übtr⟩ *plants sprung from winged seeds* [pl] **3.** (schwacher Beschlag) ⟨bot⟩ (Flaum) *bloom*; *down* || ⟨minr⟩ *efflorescence* || *down* (of beard) **4.** ⟨fig⟩ (Anzeichen) *indication, suggestion* (v *of*); *trace*; ein ~ v Bart *a suspicion of a beard*, .. grauen Haares *a touch of grey in a p's hair*, mit e–m ~ v Grau (P) *with a streak of grey*, .. v Korpulenz .. *suspicion of corpulence*; .. v Lächeln *a ghost of a smile*; in e–m ~ v Großzügigkeit *in a fit of generosity* || *fragrance, flavour, savour*; ein ~ v Bosheit *a spice* (od *whiff*) *of malice* || *touch, tinge, tincture*; ein ~ v Röte *a slight blush* (od *flush*) || → Anstrich, Beigeschmack, Spur, Zug | (Anwandlung) *fit*

(: *a fit of* ..); *strain* (*of melancholy, insanity*); *qualm*; *spasm* (*of fear*) || e–n ∼ v Genie h *to be touched with genius* | ∼- ⟨aero⟩ *approach* [attr] **∼beginn** m *initial a.* **∼freigabe** f *a. clearance* **∼kurs** m *a. path* **∼leuchtfeuer** n *a. beacon* **∼schneise** f *gate* od *lane of a.* **∼weg** m *a. path* **∼winkel** m *a. angle*

·**an|fluten** vi [s] (of waves) *to approach* || ⟨übtr⟩ *to arrive*; *to flow in*

·**an|fordern** vt [h] *to claim, to demand* (v *from*); *to ask* od *call for* (*a th*) || ⟨mil⟩ *to requisition a th, to make requisition for* (*a th*); etw ∼ v (*or* bei) jdm *to indent upon a p for a th* ·**Anforderung** f ∼/∼en *demand*; → Anspruch || *request* || *requirement* || ⟨school⟩ (*educational*) *standard*(*s*); den ∼en genügen *to be up to the mark*; übermäßige ∼(en) *exaction*; zu gr ∼en stellen an *to overwork* (*a th, a p*) || ⟨mil⟩ *requisition* (*of horses*) | allen ∼en genügen *to meet all requirements, to be up to date* || gr ∼en stellen an jdn *to put a p through his paces*; gr ∼en stellen an jdn (of things) *to make great demands* (*up*)*on a p*; .. an etw *to put a great strain on a th*

·**Anfrage** f ∼/∼n *inquiry*, auf ∼ *on i.*, durch ∼ *by i.* || ⟨parl⟩ *question, interpellation* || e–e ∼ richten an jdn *to put a p a question* od *a question to a p, to ask a p* || ⟨comp⟩ *interrogation*

·**an|fragen** vi [h] ∼ wegen *or* über etw *to inquire about a th*; bei jdm ∼ wegen etw *to ask a p about a th, to inquire of a p about a th*; ∼ ob *to inquire if* ..

·**an|fressen** vt [h] *to gnaw*; *to gnaw at* (*a th*); → Motte | ⟨übtr⟩ *to attack* || (of acids, etc) *to corrode*; *to eat away* || ⟨fig⟩ *to canker*; angefressen v *infected with, poisoned by*

·**an|freunden** v [refl] [h] sich ∼ *to become friends*; sich ∼ mit jdm *to chum* od *pal up with, to make friends with a p*

·**an|frieren** vi [s] *to freeze* (an *to*)

·**an|frischen** vt [h] *to freshen*; *to refresh* || → frischen; auffrischen

·**an|fügen** vt [h] *to join, to attach* (an *to*) || *to add, to annex* (an *to*); (Unterschrift etc) *to affix* (an *to*) || *to enclose* ·**Anfügung** f ∼/∼en *addition, attachment* (an *to*); unter ∼ der Briefmarken *enclosing the stamps* (*I* ..)

·**an|fühlen** vt [h] *to feel, to touch, to handle* || man fühlt es ihm an, daß .. *one feels that* .. | **sich** ∼ *to feel*; Samt fühlt sich weich an *velvet feels soft, velvet is soft to the touch*; es fühlt sich gut an (*of cloth, etc*) *it has a good feeling*, .. sich heiß an *it is hot to the touch*

·**Anfuhr** f ∼/∼en (Anfahren) *carriage, cartage, conveyance, transport* || (Zufuhr) *supply*

·**anführbar** a *adducible*

·**an|führen** vt [h] **1.** ⟨eig⟩ *to lead*; den Tanz ∼ *to lead the dance* || ⟨mil⟩ (Heer) *to lead, command*; (Feldzug etc) *to conduct, to lead*; (als Stoßtrupp) ∼ *to spearshead* **2.** (**vorbringen**) *to allege*; (Grund) *to adduce, give, quote* (als *as*); (Beispiel) *to advance*; (Argument) *to bring forward*; e–e Entschuldigung ∼ *to offer an apology*; *to advance an excuse*; (etw) als Entschuldigung ∼ *to allege*; *to plead* (*a th*) *as an excuse*; als Grund ∼, daß .. *to allege that* ..; s–e Unwissenheit als E. anführen *to plead one's ignorance*; was können Sie zu Ihrer Rechtfertigung ∼? *what have you to say for yourself?* | (**zitieren**) (jdn, etw) als Beispiel *to instance, to cite, to quote* (*a p, a th*); *to adduce* (*a p, a th*) *as an example* || jds Worte ∼ *to quote a p*; (etw einzeln) ∼ *to particularize*; falsch ∼ *to misquote* **3.** (täuschen) *to dupe, fool*; *cheat, deceive, gull*; *to take in* || sich ∼ l v *to be the dupe of* (*a p*); sich leicht ∼ l *to be easily taken in* (od *imposed upon*) || leicht –zu– *gullible*

·**Anführer** m ∼s/∼ *chief, chieftain*; *leader*; ∼ s *to lead* || ⟨mil⟩ *commander*; ∼ s *to be in command* || ⟨sport & fig⟩ *captain* || (Rädelsführer) *ringleader*

·**Anführung** f ∼/∼en **1.** → Führung **2.** (Vorbringen) *adduction* (*of a proof*) || *reference* (v Sachverständigen *to experts*) | *quotation, citation* **∼szeichen** n, **∼sstriche** m pl *inverted commas*, ⟨Am⟩ *quotation marks* pl; einfache ∼ ⟨fam⟩ *semiquotes* pl ('..') || ∼ zu! (im Diktat) *unquote*!

·**an|füllen** vt [h] *to fill* (*up*); *to cram*; *to stock* (mit *with*) || angefüllt s mit *to be full of, to abound in*; die Straßen waren mit Menschen angefüllt *the streets were crowded with people* || wieder ∼ *to replenish* (mit *with*) || → anhäufen

·**Anfüllung** f *filling*; Wieder∼ *replenishment*

·**Angabe** f ∼/∼n **1.** (**Erklärung**) *statement* (nach s–r ∼ *according to his s.*); nach ∼n verfertigt *made to specifications*; *declaration*; *assertion* || *representation, description*; falsche ∼n *false representations*, ⟨jur⟩ *false pretenses* || (Zoll–) *declaration, entry* || z geringe *or* ungenügende ∼ *understatement* **2.** (**Mitteilung**) *information* (über *about*); bestimmte ∼n *particular information*; nähere ∼n [pl] *particulars* [pl]; ohne nähere ∼n ⟨off⟩ *not stated*; ohne ∼ v Gründen *without giving the reasons* || (Unterlagen) ∼n [pl] *data* L [pl] || ⟨comp⟩ alphab·etische u num·erische ∼n *alphabetical and numerical data* || e–e genaue ∼ m f etw *to give chapter and verse for a th* || soweit notwendig sind ∼n über alle weiteren wesentlichen Tatsachen beizufügen *attach hereto schedules of any additional material information* **3.** (**Anweisung**) *direction*(*s*); *instructions, orders* [pl]; nach den ∼n *on the instructions*; nach jds ∼ *under a p's direction*(*s*) **4.** ⟨ten⟩ *service* **5.** °∼ = Aufschneiderei **6.** ×∼ = Handgeld || ∼**pflichtig** a *subject to declaration*

·**an|gaffen** vt [h] jdn ∼ *to gape* (od *gaze, stare*) *at a p*

·**an|gähnen** vt [h] jdn ∼ *to yawn at a p, to yawn in a p's face*

·**angängig** a (möglich) *possible*; *feasible* || (zulässig) *admissible, permissible*

·**angebaut** a ⟨arch⟩ *built on* od *added* (an *on to* [a house]), ⟨mach⟩ *integral* (an *with*); → anbauen

·**an|geben** vt/i [h] **I.** vt **1.** (als Anzahlung geben) *to give* (*a th*) *in part payment* **2.** ⟨ten⟩ (Ball) *to serve* **3.** (**bestimmen**) *to assign*; (Tag) *to appoint*; *to fix* || den Takt ∼ *to beat time*; ⟨fig⟩ *to lead, set* (*the fashion*); *to set* (*the tone*) (z *of*); → Ton, Melodie **4.** (**erklären**) (Waren bei Verzollung) *to declare, enter* || *to declare* (*the value of a parcel*) | (**mitteilen**) *to state* (ob *whether*); z hoch ∼ *to overstate*; z niedrig ∼ *to understate*; falsch ∼ *to misstate* || *to mention*; *to refer to* || (Adresse, Namen) *to give, to state*; (Datum) *to name*; *to give* (*the reason for*) (= *to account for a th*); näher ∼ *to particularize*; (Gründe) *to specify*; = anführen → d. 2 | ⟨com⟩ (Preis) *to quote* || amtlich ∼ *to return*, e–n Soldaten als getötet ∼ *to return a soldier as killed* || (aussagen) (S) *to tell* (über *about*) | **sich** ∼ als = sich ausgeben als, → d. | (**anzeigen**) *to inform against, to denounce* (*a p*); ⟨sl⟩ *to split on a p*; e–n ∼ ⟨Am sl⟩ *to snitch* **5.** × *to do*, was sollen wir ∼? *what are we to do*? → anfangen I. 2. || Unsinn ∼ *to play tricks, to be up to mischief.* **II.** vi **1.** ⟨cards⟩ *to deal first* **2.** °∼ (**sich dick tun**) *to bounce, swagger*; *to put on airs*; *to show off*; ⟨mil sl⟩ *to breeze*; ⟨sl⟩ *to have side*; ⟨Am⟩ *to put on side* od *the dog* || gib nicht so an *draw it mild* || ∼ wie ein Sack voller Mücken usw. *to come the nob* od *heavy*; *to make a pretentions display* (mit *of*); wer angibt, hat mehr v Leben, .. hat's nötig! ⟨m. m.⟩ *he's* (od *don't be*) *an awful show-off* ⟨bes Am⟩; *bouncers are lucky devils, they lack intelligence*; → aufschneiden vi

·**Angeber** m ~s/~ *informer*; berufsmäßiger ~ *common informer*; ⟨sl⟩ *squeaker* | ⟨school⟩ *sneak*; *talebearer, taleteller*; ⟨sl⟩ *snout* || (Urheber) *author* || (Prahler) *swaggerer, bouncer, puss-in-boots*, ⟨Am fam⟩ *show-off* **~stöckchen** n ⟨mil⟩ *swagger* **Angeber·ei** f ~/~en *denunciation* || *talebearing, taletelling* ·**angeberisch** a *denunciatory*; *informing* || (prahlend) *swagger*; ⟨Am fam⟩ *showing off, ritzy*

Angeb·etete f ~n/~n *lady love* || ~! *dearest!, adorable!*

·**Angebinde** n ~s/~ (Geburtstags-etc) *present, gift*

·**angeblich** 1. a (vermutlich) *alleged* (*assault*); *supposed, reputed* || (vorgeblich) *putative*; *pretended*; *ostensible* (*demand*); *so-called* (*poet*) **2.** adv *supposedly*; *reputedly*; *allegedly*; er stammt ~ aus Indien *he is supposed* (od *reported, said*) *to come from India* || *ostensibly*; *professedly*

·**ange-** **~bissen** a *partly eaten* ([*piece of*] *chocolate, etc*) **~boren** a *born, inborn, innate, inherent* (jdm *in a p*); *connate* (jdm *with a p*); *native, natural, connatural* (jdm *to a p*); jdm ~ s *to be inherent* od *innate in a p*; *to be native* od *natural to a p*; der jdm ~e Zustand *inherence, -cy* | [nur attr] *inbred* (*qualities*); *congenital* (*defect*) || ⟨übtr⟩ *natural* **≃bot** n ~(e)s/~e **1.** ⟨mst com⟩ *offer* || (bei Auktionen) *bid* || ⟨com⟩ Lieferungs≃ etc *tender* (auf *for*); ein ~ m auf *to tender for* | (formelles) *overture* **2.** (Angebotenes zum Kauf) *supply*, laufendes ~ *floating supply*; ~ u Nachfrage *supply and demand*; das ~ war stärker als die Nachfrage *there were less buyers than sellers* || Abgabe e-s schriftlichen ~s *drawing up of a tender* || jd, der ein ~ macht *tenderer* | angebotene Menge *pitch* **~bracht** a [pp v anbringen] *well-timed, timely, apt, seasonable*; *opportune*; [mst pred] *expedient*; [pred] *in place*, ⟨Am⟩ *in order*; ~ s *to be called for*, ⟨Am⟩ *to be in order* (z tun *to do*; daß jd tut *for a p to do*); es würde ~ s *it would be as well* (z tun *to do*; daß jd tut *for a p to do*) | falsch ~ *misplaced* (*confidence*); schlecht ~ *ill-timed* || nicht ~ *impertinent*; *out of place*; *not tactful*, → un~; nicht ~ s *to be misplaced*; bei jdm nicht ~ s *to be lost upon a p*; das ist bei mir nicht ~ *that won't do with me*; deine Kniffe sind bei mir nicht ~! *none of your tricks!* **~brochen** a [pp v anbrechen] ein ~er Abend *a half-lost* (od *half-spoiled*) *evening* || *open* (od *fraction* [attr]) (*box*) || ⟨med⟩ *slightly broken, fractured* (*bone*) °**~bufft** a ⟨sex vulg⟩ (schwanger gemacht) *lumpy, kidded* **~bunden** [pp v anbinden] **1.** [a] kz ~ ⟨fig⟩ *abrupt, blunt, offhand*; [mst pred] kz ~ s (*to be rudely*) *curt*; *snappish, short* (mit jdm *with a p*) **2.** [adv] *abruptly*; *shortly* (: *to answer a p sh.*) **~deihen** vi [nur inf in Verbindung mit lassen] jdm etw ~ l *to give* (od *grant*) *a th to a p* od *to give a p a th*; *to bestow a th upon a p*; er hat ihm Schutz ~ l *he has favoured him with* (*his*) *protection* || jdm Unterstützung ~ l *to give* (od *lend*) *countenance to a p* **≃denken** n, → Andenken; m-e Tante seligen ~s *my aunt of blessed memory* || verblaßten ~s (P & S) *faded from memory* **≃fälle** n ~s/~ **1.** *inheritance* **2.** ⟨arch⟩ *abutment* **~fault** a ⟨bes for⟩ *partially decayed* **~flogen** a ⟨for, hort⟩ *self-sown* **~führt** a: der (die) ≃e *the dupe*; → dumm, anführen, düpieren, Gimpel **~gangen** [pp v angehen] *unsound* (*fish*; *fruit*; *timber*); *high* (*game*); leicht ~es Fleisch *tainted meat*, (mit Wildgeruch) *gam(e)y* **~gossen** a [pp v angießen] *cast-on* (*flange*) || ⟨fig⟩ wie ~ sitzen (of clothes) *to fit like a glove*; es sitzt ihr wie ~ *it fits her to a T* **~graut** a (P) *with a streak of grey* (*in one's hair*) **~griffen** a [pp v angreifen] ⟨fig⟩ *bad* (*leg*); *affected* (*eyes*), (*his heart was*) *affected* || *unstrung* (*nerves*); *shaken* (*health*) | ~ aussehen *to look ill* (od *poorly, seedy*; *tired, exhausted*) || sich ~ fühlen, ~ s *to feel bad* (od *weak*; *tired*), *to be in a poor state of health* | ≃heit [f] ~/ *exhaustion*; *poor state of health* **≃hänge** n ~s/~ (Schmuck) *pendant* **~heiratet** a *by marriage*, ein ~er Vetter *a cousin by m.* **~heitert** a *elevated, animated*; *mellowed* (*by alcohol*); *squiffy*; *tipsy*; *jolly, merry*; ⟨sl⟩ *moony*; | [pred] *half-seas-over*; *a little high*; *far gone*; *lit*; *bright in the eye*

·**an|gehen** vi/t **I.** vi [s] **1.** ~ gegen jdn *to rush upon* od *against a p*, *to attack* (od *butt*) *a p*; ⟨Am⟩ *to buck against a p* || ⟨übtr⟩ ~ gegen etw *to combat* od *fight against*; *to take measures against a th* || mutig dagegen ~ *to make a fight of it* **2.** (of roads, etc.) *to ascend, to rise*; es geht steil an hier *the road ascends* (od *is steep*) *here* **3.** (of shoes, clothes) *to admit of being put on*; leicht ~ *to go on easily*; nicht ~ *to refuse to go on* **4.** (**beginnen**) *to begin, commence, start* || *church has begun already* || *when is the movie on?* || die Schule geht am 1. April an *school will begin* od *open on April 1.* || nicht ~ (of engines) *to refuse to go* (od *run, start, work*) | (of ⟨el⟩ light) *to come on*; (of fire) *to begin to burn, to burn*; nicht ~ *to refuse to burn* || (of plants) *to take*; *to take root, to strike* | es sachte ~ l ⟨fam⟩ *to take it easy* **5.** [nur 3. sg] **es geht an** *it will do, it's not so bad after all*; das geht nicht an *that won't do*; es mag noch ~, es geht gerade noch an *it may pass*; mit der Hitze ging es noch an in diesem Jahre *the heat was tolerable* (od *endurable, passable*) *this year* **6.** (of food, etc.) *to grow stale* (od *putrid*); *to taint* || → angegangen **II.** vt [h] **1.** (P) etw ~ (sich in etw versuchen) *to have a go at a th* || ⟨hunt⟩ (of stags) *to attack*; *to rush at* **2.** (bitten) (jdn) *to approach* (*a p*); jdn um etw ~ *to apply to a p for a th, to solicit* (od *ask*) *a p for a th* **3.** (betreffen) [nur 3. sg & pl] *to concern*; *to regard*; es geht m-e Ehre an *my honour is concerned*; ⟨jur⟩ an alle, die es angeht *to whom it may concern*; was ihn angeht, (so ..) *regarding him .., as regards him .., as for* (od *to*) *him ..* || das geht ihn an *that regards him*; *that is meant for him* || das geht Sie nichts an *that's none of your business* od *no business of yours, mind your own b.*; ⟨sl⟩ *none of your funeral* || es geht niemand etw an *it is nobody's business* || das geht mich nichts an *that is no concern of mine*; *that has nothing to do with me*; *that is all one to me*; das geht mich e-n °Dreck an *I could(n't) care less*; was geht es dich an? *what has that to do with you?* | er geht uns nichts an *he has nothing to do with us, he is nothing to us* ·**angehend** a *beginning, incipient*; *dawning* (*moustache*) || *young*; *inexperienced* || (*an artist, a gentleman*) *in the bud, in the making*; *rising* (*doctor, etc*); ⟨fam⟩ *sucking* (*lawyer*) || *budding* (*artist*); *expectant* (*father*) || ~er Neunziger *a man going on for ninety, a man of about ninety* || er ist ein ~er Arzt etc *he is going to become a doctor* (etc)

·**an|gehören** vi [h] **1.** (gehören zu) (e-r Klasse, Periode etc) *to belong* (od *pertain, appertain*) *to* (*a class, etc*); e-r Gesellschaft ~ *to be a member of a society* || (eigentümlich s) *to belong to, to pertain to* (*a disease*) || gr Leidenschaft -rt der Vergangenheit an *gr p. is a th of the past* || (zustehen) *to appertain to, to belong to* (*the bishop*) **2.** (als Eigentum ~) *to belong to* (*a state*, etc)

·**ange-** **~hörig** a: e-r Zeit ~ *belonging to, related to a period* **≃hörige:** der ~ (ein ~r) ~n/~n; die ~ f ~n/~n **1.** ~r e-s Staates (etc) s *to belong to a state*; .. e-r Gesellschaft .. *to be a member of a society* **2.** (Verwandter) *relation, relative*; m-e ~n *my family, my people, my relations*; viele Grüße an dich u d-e ~en *kind regards to you and yours*; ohne jede ~n *without kith and kin* || ⟨bes demog⟩ ~ ohne Hauptberuf *dependent* **≃klagte:** der ~ (ein ~r)

~n/~n; die ~ f ~n/~n ⟨jur⟩ *the accused, the prisoner at the bar* ‖ (Vergehens) *the defendant*; (Ehescheidung) *respondent* **~klatscht** a *slicked down* (*hair*) **~kränkelt** a *sickly, ailing* | ⟨fig⟩ *morbid*; *sicklied* (*sentiment*); *unwholesome* ‖ ~ s *to be sicklied over* (v *with*)

·Angel f ~/~n **1.** (Haken) (*fish-*)*hook* ‖ (Gerät) *fishing-gear, -tackle* ‖ die ~ auswerfen *to angle* od *fish* (nach *for*); *to whip the stream* | Schwimm≗ *pulley* **2.** (Tür≗) *hinge* ‖ (Drehzapfen) *pin, pivot* ‖ aus den ~n ⟨fig⟩ *off the hinges* ‖ aus den ~n heben (Tür) *to unhinge*; ⟨fig⟩ *to unhinge, unsettle* ‖ zw Tür u ~(n) *in passing*; *by the way*; zw Tür u ~ s ⟨fig⟩ *to be between two fires* ‖ (Tür) mit ~n versehen *to hinge* **3.** (Griffzapfen an Werkzeugen) *tang*; *pin*; *spike* ‖ → Fuß≗ **~fischerei** f *angling*; *fishing with line and hook* **~fliege** f *fishing-fly*; (f Forellen) *trout-fly*, (etc.) **~gerät** n *fishing-tackle* **~haken** m *fish-hook* **~karte** f *fishing licence* **~leine** f *fishing-line* **~platz** m *fishing-nook, fishing-water* **~punkt** m ⟨astr⟩ *pole* | ⟨fig⟩ *hinge, pivot, central* (od *pivotal*) *point*; *hub*; das ist der ~ *that is the cardinal point, that is the pivot on which everything turns*; als ~ dienend *pivotal* **~rute** f *fishing-rod* **~schnur** f *fishing-line* **~sport** m *sport of fishing*; *the gentle sport* **~stern** m *pole-star* **≗weit** adv: ~ offen stehen *to be wide open*

·an|gelangen vi [s] *to arrive*

·angelaufen a (beschlagen, S) *misted* (*glasses*)

·Angeld n *earnest(-money)* (auf *of*) ‖ *first instal(l)ment, first part-payment*

ange- ~legen a [pp v anliegen] er hatte nichts ≗eres z tun *nothing was more important to him to do* (als *than*) ‖ es sich [dat] ~ s l z tun *to be concerned, to care to do*; *to make a point* (od *feature*) *of doing*; *to take to doing*; *to make it one's business to do, to make a b. of doing*; sich e–e S ~ s l *to care* (od *be concerned*) *to do a th*; *to make a* (*special*) *point of doing a th*; *to make a th one's business to do*; ich will mir die S ~ s l *I will take care of* (od *look after*) *the matter* **≗legenheit** f ~/~n *affair, concern*; *business, matter*; ⟨Am⟩ *proposition*; ⟨sl⟩ *show* ‖ jds ~ s *to be a p's concern* ‖ sich um s e eigenen ~en kümmern *to mind one's own business* ‖ sich in jds (*or* fremde) ~en mischen *to meddle* od *interfere with other people's business* ‖ s–e eigenen ~en verrichten *to go about one's business* | ~en des Staates *affairs of* (*the*) *state* ‖ auswärtige ~en *foreign affairs*; Minister der Ausw. ~en ⟨engl⟩ *Secretary of State for Foreign Affairs* ‖ innere ~en *domestic* od *home affairs* **~legentlich 1.** adv *earnestly, urgently*; (*to beg*) *particularly* ‖ sich ~ bemühen *to do one's utmost* (*to do*); sich jdm ~ empfehlen *to send a p one's kindest regards*; empfiehl mich Deiner Mutter ~ *give my k. r. to your mother* **2.** a *earnest, insistent*; *pressing, urgent* (*request*) ‖ ~e Grüße *kindest regards* ‖ aufs ~ste empfehlen *to recommend strongly* **~lehnt** adv ⟨arch⟩ *addorsed* ‖ (Tür) [pred] *ajar*; *adjacent* (*troops*), beiderseits ~ *with friendly units on both flanks* **~lernt** a *taught* (*trick*); nur ~ *mechanical* ‖ *semi-skilled, partly instructed* (*workman*) ‖ nicht ~ *untaught*

·Angeles, Los n → Los Angeles

Ang·elika f ⟨bot⟩ *angelica*

·Angeln 1. n *Anglia* **2.** [pl] *the Angles*

·angeln I. vi/t [h] **1.** vi *to angle, to fish* (*with*); *to have a fish* ‖ ~ **nach** *to angle* od *fish for*; (mit der Schleppangel, dem Köder *or* auf Rolle laufender Schnur ~) *to troll for* ‖ in dem Fluß angelt es sich gut *the river is fishing well* ‖ mit künstlichen Fliegen ~ *to fly-fish* | ⟨übtr⟩ *to snaggle* (aus *out of*) ‖ ⟨fig⟩ ~ **nach** (etw, jdm) *to angle* (od *to fish*) *for* (*a th, a p*); (of women) *to set one's cap at* (*a p*); ⟨Am⟩ *to set one's bag for* (*an office*); *to fish* (*for compliments*) **2.** vt (Fische) *to angle* (od *fish*) *for* (*fish*); → fangen | ⟨fig⟩ jdn ~ *to angle for a p*; *to hook a p*; jdn zu ~ suchen *to set one's cap at a p* **II.** ≗ n *angling*

·an|geloben vt [h] jdm etw ~ *to vow a th to a p*; *to promise a p a th* (od *a th to a p*) *solemnly*

·Angelöbnis n –nisses/–nisse **·Angelobung** f ~/~en *vow*; *solemn promise*

·Angelsachse m ~n/~n *Anglo-Saxon* **·angelsächsisch** a *Anglo-Saxon* ‖ **das** ≗**e** n *Anglo-Saxon, Old English*

·Angelus- ~gebet n ⟨R. C.⟩ *angelus* L **~läuten** n *a. bell*

·angemessen 1. a (passend, entsprechend) *apt* (*words*); *adequate* (*amount*), *appropriate*; *proper* (*distribution*); *reasonable* (*price*); *fair* (*standard of living*); *suitable* (*climate*) ‖ **jdm ~, f. jdn ~** *fit for a p, adequate to a p* ‖ e–r S ~, f e–e S ~ *suitable to* (od *for*) *a th, adequate* (od *conformable, proper*) *to a th, compatible with a th*; dem Klima ~e Kleidung *clothes suitable to the climate*; der Jahreszeit ~ *seasonable*; e–e dem Gewicht ~e Geschwindigkeit *a speed proportionate to the weight*; → Einklang, Übereinstimmung | ~e **Belohnung** *worthy reward* ‖ sein Verhalten war s–m hohen Amte ~ *his conduct was worthy of his high office* ‖ ~er Preis *reasonable* (od *acceptable*) *price*; ~e Kleidung *proper dress* | **es ist ~, daß ..** *it is fit that* ‖ **es f. ~ halten** *to think fit* (od *proper*) (*to do*) **2.** adv *comfortably, suitably*; *in conformity with*; *conforming to* | **≗heit** f ~/ *appropriateness*; *aptness, aptitude*; *suitability, suitableness, adequacy, fitness* ‖ *propriety* (*of conduct*, etc.)

·angenehm I. a **1.** (beliebt) ⟨bes bib⟩ (mst P) *agreeable* (*man*) ‖ [pred] jdm ~, für jdn ~ *agreeable to a p*; sich ~ m bei jdm *to make o.s. agreeable to a p, to ingratiate o.s. with a p*; tun Sie was Ihnen ~ ist *do as you please* od *like* ‖ (Gast) *welcome*; du bist mir stets ~ *you are always welcome* | ⟨com⟩ (begehrt) *in demand* **2.** (gefällig, erfreulich) (mst S) *pleasurable, delightful*; *congenial* ‖ *pleasant* (*companion*; *face*; *journey*; *time*, etc.); *pleasing* (*manners, prospects, thought*, etc.); *welcome* (*relief*); *acceptable* (*offer*); ⟨sl⟩ *cushy* (*job*); → behaglich ‖ etw ~ m *to sweeten a th* | ~ v Geschmack *pleasant to the taste*; *palatable*; ~ für's Ohr *grateful to the ear*; es ist mir sehr ~ *I am very pleased* (z hören *to hear*) ‖ ⟨vulg⟩ Sehr ~! (beim Vorstellen) *very pleased to meet* od *see you*! **II.** adv *agreeably* (*surprised*); ~ aussehend *pleasant*(*est*)*-looking*

·angenommen a [pp v annehmen] *available* (*Ms.*) ‖ ~ daß *granted that*; *say that*; ⟨fam⟩ *given that* ‖ *suppose* (od *supposing*) (*that*) ‖ ~ dies wäre wahr *granting* (*let us assume*) *this to be true*; ~ er wäre in England geboren *suppose* od *supposing him born in England*

·Anger m ~s/~ *meadow*, auf dem ~ *in the m.*; *grassplot, pasture* ‖ Dorf≗ *common*; *village green* (*on* ..) ‖ *~ = Rain ‖ → Schind≗

·ange- ~raucht a *partly smoked* (*cigar*) **~regt** a [pp v anregen] *lively* (*talk*); *buoyant* (*spirits*) ‖ *interesting* ‖ (P) ~ v *having drawn inspiration from* **~säuert** a *acidulated* (*water*) °**~säuselt** a = angeheitert *tipsy*; [pred] *half-gone* **~schlagen** a ⟨mil⟩ *weakened*; *badly shaken* **~schlossen** a [pp v anschließen] ⟨wir⟩ *connected* (an *to*); *linked-up* (Sender *stations*) ~ (sind, waren) alle amerik. etc Sender ⟨Am fam⟩ *on a national hook-up* ‖ an öffentl. Netz (Gas etc) ~es Grundstück *serviced lot* ‖ ~er Verband *affiliate* s **~schossen** a [pp v an|schießen] ⟨hunt⟩ *pricked* (*bird*) **~schrieben** a [pp v anschreiben] bei jdm gut ~ s *to be* (od *stand*) *high in a p's favour*; *to be in a p's good books*, bei jdm schlecht ~ s *to be in a p's bad books* ‖ bei s–r Frau schlecht ~s ⟨Am fam⟩ *to be in the doghouse* **~schuldigt**

a: der ≗e → beschuldigt **~schwemmt** a [pp v anschwemmen] *alluvial* **~schwollen** a *swelled* (*belly*); mst *swollen* (*veins*); *risen* (*rivers*) **~sehen** a *notable, respectable* (*man*; *firm*); *prestigious, influential, important*; *distinguished, esteemed, respected* (*officer*); ~e Persönlichkeit *notability, worthy* ‖ ~ s *to be respected* **~sessen** a [pp v ansitzen] *settled, resident* **~setzt** a → ansetzen ≗**sicht** n ~(e)s/~e(r) **1.** [abstr] (Anblinken) im ~ Gottes *in the sight of God* ‖ im ~ (od ≗s) der Heimatstadt *at* (od *in*, *within*) *sight of my native town* ‖ ≗s der Tatsache *in view of the fact, considering the fact*; ≗s der Gefahr *in the presence of the danger, faced with the danger* **2.** [konkr] (Antlitz) *face, countenance* ‖ ⟨bib⟩ im Schweiße des ~s *by* (od *in*) *the sweat of one's brow* ‖ ⟨bib⟩ von ~ zu ~ *face to face* ‖ dem Tode ins ~ schauen *to look death in the face* **~sichts** adv → Angesicht **~spannt** a aufs höchste ~ s (of the senses) *to be on the strain* ‖ [attr] *strained* (*nerves*); *close* (*attention*); *intense* (*life*); *intensive* (*study*); *zealous* ‖ (spannungsreich) *stressful* **~spült** a [pp v anspülen] *alluvial* ‖ ~es Land *alluvion* **~stammt** a *ancestral, hereditary* ≗**stellte**; der ~ (ein ~r) ~n/~n; die ~ (e–e ~) ~n/~n (*salaried*) *employee*; *office worker*; *clerk*; Post≗(r) *postal servant*; Haus≗(r) *domestic servant* | ⟨demog⟩ *clerical* od *office worker* ‖ –te [pl] *people*; *office staff*; –te des öffentl. Dienstes *government employees*; → Beamte u –te d. öff. D.s *civil servants* ‖ leitende –te *managerial staff*, ⟨com⟩ *senior management* ‖ te in einfacher Stellung *foremen, supervisors*; –te in gehobener St. *executive staff* ‖ –tenmangel m (Ggs *unemployment*) *overemployment*; –tenversicherung f *insurance for office* (etc) *workers* °**~stiefelt** a: ~ kommen *to come* (*striding* od *stalking*) *along*; *to turn up*; *to appear* **~stochen** a **1.** ⟨eig⟩ *stuck*: wie ein ~es Kalb *like a stuck pig* **2.** = betrunken **3.** ≠ verrückt **~strengt** [pp v anstrengen] **1.** a *intense*; *intensive, close* (*attention*); *strenuous* (*efforts*) ‖ nicht bei ~ester Arbeit der Einbildungskraft *not .. by any stretch of imagination* **2.** adv *strenuously*; *hard* **~tan** a [pp v antun] **1.** beschaffen, geeignet; die Lage ist ganz danach ~, uns Schwierigkeiten z m *in all probability* od *likelihood the situation will get us into trouble, the situation is likely* od *apt to get us into t.*; weniger ~ z tun (*a question*) *less calculated to do*; → geeignet **2.** ~ s v *to be fond of* (od *pleased with*); *to have a liking for* (*a p, a th*); *to take to*; er war dem Gedanken nicht ~ *he did not take to the idea, the idea did not appeal to him* ‖ v sich ~ s *to be conceited, to have a high opinion of o.s.* ‖ → eingenommen; vernarrt **~trunken** a [pp v antrinken] (leicht ~) *tipsy*; schon etw ~ s *to be the worse for liquor* ‖ *drunk*(*en*); *intoxicated, boozy*; stark ~ *advanced in liquor* ≗**trunkenheit** f *tipsiness* ‖ *drunkenness, inebriation* **~wandt** a [pp v anwenden] *applied* (*sciences*); *economic* (*botany*); → Experimental **~wiesen** a [pp v anweisen] *dependent* (auf *on*); ~ s auf *to be dependent on, to depend on, to be at the mercy of of* (*a p*); *to be thrown* (*back*) *upon* (*a p, a th*); auf sich selbst ~ s *to be thrown upon o.s.*; *to be thrown upon* (od *to be left to*) *one's own resources*

·**an|gewöhnen** vt [h] jdm etw ~ *to accustom* (od *habituate, inure*) *a p to a th*; sich etw ~ *to get accustomed to a th, to accustom oneself to a th*; sich das Rauchen ~ *to contract* (od *take on*) *the habit of smoking* ·**Angewohnheit** f ~/~en *habit* ‖ *quirk* ‖ aus ~ *from habit*; *habitually* ‖ e–e üble ~ z tun *a trick of doing*; die schlechte ~ haben z tun *to be guilty of doing* ·**Angewöhnung** f ~/~en *habituation* (e–r S *to a th*)

·**angezogen** [pp v ·an|ziehen] gut ~ *well-dressed, –groomed*

·**an|gießen** vt [h] *to pour on* od *over* ‖ (Pflanzen) *to water*; *to sprinkle with water* ‖ → angegossen

Ang·ina L f ~/–nen ⟨med⟩ *angina* L; *sore throat* ‖ ~ pectoris L *angina pectoris, breastpang*

Angiosp·erme f ~/~n ⟨bot⟩ (bedecktsamige Pflanze; Ggs Gymnosperme) *angiosperm*

·**an|gleichen** vt [h] *to assimilate, to bring up* (an *to*) ‖ angeglichen w *to assimilate* (an *to*)

·**Angleichung** f ~/~en *assimilation* (an *to*)

·**Angler** m ~s/~ *angler* **~fisch** m ⟨ich⟩ *angler*

·**an|gliedern** vt [h] (Körperschaft etc) *to affilate* (an *to*); *to incorporate* (an *in*) ‖ sich e–r Körperschaft ~, e–r K. angegliedert w *or* s *to be affiliated to a body* ‖ (etw) *to annex, to append, to attach, to join* (an *to*) **sich** ~ *to be annexed*; *to become attached* (an *to*)

Anglik·aner m ~s/~, **~in** f ~/~nen ⟨engl ec⟩ *Anglican* **anglik·anisch** a *Anglican*; die ~e Kirche *the Anglican Church, the Church of England* **Anglikan·ismus** m ~ *Anglicanism*

anglis·ieren vt [pp anglisiert] [h] *to Anglicize*

Angl·ist m ~en/~en, **~in** f ~/~nen ⟨Ger⟩ *student of English philology*; *English scholar* **Angl·istik** f ~/ ⟨Ger⟩ *anglistics* [sg konstr], *English philology* **Angliz·ismus** m ~/–men *Anglicism, Briticism*

Anglo- (= englisch) *Anglo–* **~amerik·aner** m *Anglo-American* ≗**franz·ösisch** a *Anglo-French* **~inder** m *Anglo-Indian* **~kathol·ik** m ⟨engl⟩ *Anglo-Catholic, ritualist* **~katholiz·ismus** m *Anglo-Catholicism, ritualism* **~man·ie** f *anglomania* **~norm·anne** m *Anglo-Norman*

·**an|glotzen** vt [h] jdn ~ *to gape* (od *glower, goggle*) *at a p*; → anstarren, –stieren

Ang·ola n (West-Afrika) *Angola*

Ang·ora- (= Ankara) **~katze** f ⟨zoo⟩ *Angora cat* **~wolle** f *mohair*; Stoff aus ~ *angola, angora, mohair* **~ziege** f ⟨zoo⟩ *Angora goat*

Angost·ura- der **~bittere** m *Angostura bitters* [pl] **~rinde** f *angostura bark*

†·**Angra Pequ·ena** n (alter Name für ⟨†Ger⟩ Lüderitzbucht) *Angra Pequena* (SW-Afrika)

·**angreifbar** a *assailable*; ⟨fig⟩ *pregnable* (*idea*)

·**an|greifen** vt/i [h] **I.** vt **A.** ⟨eig⟩ **1.** (mst dafür: anfassen, → d.) *to seize*; *to get* od *seize hold of* (*a th*) ‖ *to handle*; *to touch*; wer Pech angreift, besudelt sich *who touches pitch will be defiled* | **sich** weich ~ → sich anfühlen **2.** (unerwünscht, –erlaubt anfassen) Vorräte ~ → anbrechen; Reserven ~ *to trench on reserves* ‖ *to touch* (*the capital*); (fremde Gelder) *to embezzle*; die Kasse ~ *to rob the desk* ‖ → plündern **B.** ⟨übtr⟩ **1.** (unternehmen) *to begin*; *to set about* (*a th*); *to undertake, to take in hand*; *to put one's hand to* (*a th*); *to enter upon* (*one's task*) → anfassen ‖ (Schwierigkeit) *to tackle* → anpacken **2.** (feindlich ~) ⟨bes mil⟩ *to charge* (mit *with*); *to attack*; (heftig) *to assail*; (plötzlich) *to assault* (*a p*); *to fall* (od *be, set, turn*) (*up*)*on* (*a p*); *to lash* (od *set*) *at* (*a p*); *to let into* (*a p*) ‖ ⟨sport, ftb⟩ (Gegner im Besitz des Balles) *to tackle* | ⟨fig⟩ (mit Worten etc) *to attack, to assail* (wegen *for*) jdn bei der Ehre ~ *to hurt a p's honour* ‖ *to criticize, to call* (*a p*) *over the coals* (wegen *for*); etw scharf ~ *to take out ferociously against a th* **3.** (nachteilig beeinflussen) ⟨chem⟩ (Metall etc) *to attack*; *to corrode*; *to eat away* | (Augen, Nerven etc) *to affect, to try*; *to strain, to put a great strain on, to be detrimental to* (*an organ*); *to attack* (*the vocal cords*) | ⟨tech⟩ *to act upon* | (jdn) *to subject* (*a p*) *to a severe strain, to try*; die Reise hat ihn ziemlich angegriffen *the journey has tried him a good deal* ‖ *to exhaust, to fatigue*; *to weaken*; → angegriffen | °**sich** ~ *to do one's utmost, to exert o.s.*; → sich anstrengen **II.** vi **1.** (selbst) mit ~ = anfassen II. **2.** ⟨mil⟩ *to charge*; *to come on*; *to make an attack*; sofort ~! *engage at once* **3.** ⟨übtr⟩ so etw greift an *that takes a lot out of you* ·**Angreifen** n **1.** *seizing, touching* **2.** ⟨Ass ftb⟩ *tackle* **3.** ⟨chem⟩ *attack; corrosion, eating-away* | *strain, exhaustion, weakening* ‖ → Angriff **angreifend** a ⟨mil⟩ *aggressive, offensive*; der ~e Staat *the aggressor state*, der ~e Teil *the aggressor* | *trying (journey)*; *fatiguing, tiring, exhausting* ·**Angreifer** m ~s/~ **1.** *aggressor; assailant* **2.** (Griff) *grip* ·**angreiferisch** a *aggressive; provocative*

·**an|grenzen** vi [h] ~ an → grenzen ·**angrenzend** a *adjacent, contiguous* (an *to*); *adjoining (room)* ‖ an die Straße ~ *adjoining the road* ·**Angrenzer** m *next-door neighbour*

·**Angriff** m ~(e)s/~e **1.** → Angreifen **2.** (feindlicher) **a.** ⟨mil allg⟩ *attack* (auf *on*); Flanken⍨ *flank attack*, Frontal⍨ *frontal attack*, rollender ~ *relay attack*; ~ in mehreren Wellen *successive attack*; ~ v hinten *tail attack*; → Umfassung ‖ (Vorstoß) *advance* ‖ heftiger ~ *brunt*; plötzlicher ~, Sturm⍨ *charge; assault* ‖ ein Flugzeug im ~ *a plane attacking*; ~ vorbei! *raiders passed*! ‖ Signal zum ~ *charge* ‖ e–n ~ abschlagen *to repel* (od *beat off*) *an attack*); zum ~ blasen *to sound the charge* (od *attack*); zum ~ über–, vorgehen *to launch an attack; to make a charge, to charge*; der Wucht des ~s standhalten *to bear the brunt*; e–n ~ vortragen *to advance an attack*; (Beginn e–r Feindseligkeit) *aggression* **b.** *attack, assault* (auf jdn *on, upon a p*; v Seiten jds *from a p*) ‖ (in Worten) *attack* (auf *on*); (heftiger) *onslaught* (auf *on*); tätlicher ~ (verbunden mit Körperverletzung) ⟨jur⟩ *assault and battery* **3.** ⟨übtr⟩ etw in ~ nehmen *to move in a matter, to get down to a th, to set about (doing)*; (Plan) *to embark (up)on; to set about, to put one's hand to (a th); to take (a th) in hand* ‖ (schwieriges Problem) *to attack, tackle (a th); to cope* od *grapple with (a th)* ‖ e–n bescheidenen ~ m auf *to make a timid stab at*

·**Angriffs-** ~**bereitstellung** f *assembly for attack* ~**bewegung** f *offensive movement, offensive* ~**breite** f *front in attack* ~**flächen** f pl: bieten *to be open* ([dat] *to criticism*) ~**geist** m *aggressiveness, militancy* ~**höhe** f ⟨aero⟩ *bombing altitude* ~**krieg** m *offensive war* ~**lust** f ⟨bes eth⟩ *aggressiveness* ⍨**lustig** a *aggressive (mood)* ~**punkt** m *point of attack* ‖ ⟨übtr⟩ günstiger ~ *purchase, point of advantage* (für *for*); *advantage* (für to) ‖ ⟨tech⟩ *working* od *straining point* ~**truppen** f pl *assault troops* ~**waffen** f pl *offensive arms* ~**weise** f *manner of attack* ⍨**weise** adv *by way of attack; offensively*; ~ verfahren ⟨fig⟩ *to act on* (od *to take*) *the offensive* ~**welle** f ⟨tact⟩ *echelon* ~**ziel** n *objective* (erstes *immediate*) ~**zwischenziel** n *intermediate objective*

·**an|grinsen** vt [h] jdn ~ *to grin* (od *leer*) *at a p*

°·**an|grunzen** vt [h] jdn ~ *to grunt at a p*

Angst f ~/⍨e **1.** (Furcht) *fear* (vor *of*) ‖ gr ~ *fright, terror*; ⟨sl⟩ *funk* (vor *of*), ⟨Am sl⟩ *jitters* [pl]; ständige gr ~ ⟨sl⟩ *stew* ‖ °Mords⍨ ⟨sl⟩ *blue funk*; Todes⍨, gr ~ *deadly fear* **2.** (Schmerz, Sorge) *fear, anxiety* (für, um *for*), *alarm* (über *at*); in gr ~ *in great anxiety* ‖ *anguish, pang*; Seelen⍨ *anguish of mind* **3.** **Wendungen:** keine ~! *no fear*!, *never fear*! ‖ ~ bek *to take alarm*; gr ~ (*or* ° es mit der ~) bek *to get into a panic, to be seized with p.*, ⟨sl⟩ *to get into funk, to get the wind up* ‖ in gr ~ geraten *to take alarm* (über *at*); ⟨sl⟩ *to funk* (bei, über *at*) ‖ ~ h *to be in fear* (vor jdm *of a p*); ⟨fam⟩ *to have cold feet, to shake in one's shoes*; *to fear* (um *for*); ~ h z tun *to fear to do*, ⟨sl⟩ *to funk doing*; er hat ~ z fallen *he fears falling*; → fürchten ‖ er hatte gr ~ *his heart was in his boots* ‖ in ständiger Todes⍨ leben *to go in fear of one's life* ‖ jdm ~ m → einschüchtern, *to put the wind up a p; to give a p cold feet* ‖ in tausend Ängsten (*or* fürchterlicher ~) schweben *or* s *to be in deadly* (od *in an agony of*) *fear*, ⟨sl⟩ *in a blue funk, in a stew* ‖ vor ~ bebend *tremulous* **angst** a [nur in best. Wendungen]: mir ist ~ um deine Gesundheit *I am very anxious about your health* ‖ es ist mir ~ u bange *I am in great* (od *deadly*) *fear* (vor *of*) ‖ es wird mir ~ u bange, es wird mir himmel~ *I am getting greatly alarmed*; ⟨sl⟩ *I am getting into funk* ‖ jdm ⍨ u bange m *to put a p in fear; to frighten* (od *alarm*) *a p*

·**Angst-** ⍨**erfüllt** a *fearful, full of fear* ~**gefühl** n *sinking at the* (od *one's*) *heart; uneasiness; trepidation, flutter* ~**geschrei** n *cries* [pl] *of alarm* (od *distress*) °~**hase** m *coward, panicmonger*; ⟨sl⟩ *funk, funker*; ⟨Am sl⟩ *jitter-bug* ~**käufe** m pl ⟨com⟩ *scare-buying* ~**klausel** f *proviso containing the words 'without prejudice'* (od *'without liability'*) °~**meier** m = Angsthase °~**röhre** f *(top-hat)*; ⟨fam⟩ *chimney-pot; tile; topper*; ⟨Am⟩ *stove-pipe (hat), shiner* ~**ruf**, ~**schrei** m *cry of alarm* ~**schweiß** m *cold sweat* ⍨**voll** a *fearful* ~**zustand** m *anxiety state*

·**ängsten**, ·**ängstigen** vt [h] (jdn) *to alarm, to frighten* (z Tode *to death*) ‖ (quälen) *to torment; to distress* ‖ jdn wahnsinnig ~ *to frighten a p out of his senses* | sich ~ [h] *to be frightened* (z Tode *to death*), *to be afraid* (vor *of*); *to be alarmed* (über, um *about*), *to feel uneasy, to have misgivings, to fret (about)* ‖ sich über, um etw ~ *to worry about a th*

·**Angster** m ~s/~ *glass vessel of a bizarre shape* (seit 1462 bezeugt)

·**ängstlich** a **1. a.** [pred] *anxious, uneasy* (um *about*); *nervous, upset; tremulous*; ⟨Am⟩ *rattled* ‖ nur nicht ~! *never fear*! *never say die*! ‖ die S ist nicht ~ *there is no need for alarm* **b.** (schüchtern) *timid, shy*; ~er Natur s *to be timid by nature* **2.** (überpeinlich) *scrupulous, precise, exact* | ⍨**keit** f ~/~en *anxiety, anxiousness* ‖ (Schüchternheit) *timidity, shyness* ‖ (Peinlichkeit) *scrupulousness, conciseness, exactness*

·**Ångströmeinheit** f (nach dem Schweden Ångstrøm 1814–74) ⟨phys⟩ *Angstrøm* (⟨Am⟩ *anstrom*) *unit* (abbr *A.U.*)

·**an|gucken** vt [h] jdn ~ *to look* (od *peep*) *at a p*

·**Anguß** m gusses/–güsse *feeding head* ‖ ⟨typ⟩ *break, jet (of a letter)* | ~**masse** [f] (für keramische Erzeugnisse) *engobe*

·**an|haben** vt [h] **1.** (Rock etc) *to have (a coat) on; to wear (a coat)*; wir hatten das Feuer nicht an *we didn't have the fire on* **2.** ⟨fig⟩ jdm etw ~ wollen *to have designs on* (od *against*) *a p; to try to harm* (od *prejudice*) *a p* od *to find fault with a p* ‖ jdm nichts ~ können *to have no effect on a p, to be unable (to get at* od) *to get the better of a p*; er kann mir nichts ~ *he has not got a handle against me*; (= gleichkommen) *he can't touch me*; das kann mir nichts ~ *that cannot do me any harm; that's nothing to me*

·**an|haften** vi [h] jdm ~ *to cling to a p; to be peculiar to a p*; (v Natur) *to be inherent in a p* ‖ *to attach to*; der menschlichen Natur ~ *to be incident to human nature* ‖ ~**d** a *inherent* (jdm *in a p*), die ihm ~e Güte *the kindness inherent in him*

·**an|häkeln** vt [h] (etw) *to crochet* (an etw *on to a th*)

·**an|haken** vt [h] *to hitch* (an *to*); *to hook* (an *on to, to*) ‖ (Schiff mit Enterhaken ~) *to grapple* | (Wort) *to tick (off); to mark off*

·**an|halftern** vt [h] (Pferd) *to (fasten by a) halter*

†·**Anhalt** n ⟨Ger⟩ (†Land) *Anhalt*

·**Anhalt** m ~(e)s/~e **1.** (Stütze) *hold, prop, support* **2.** (Anhaltepunkt) *stopping-place* **3.** ⟨fig⟩ (Anhaltpunkt) *clue* (für *to*), e–n ~ gewähren *to give a clue* (für *to*)

·**Anhalte-** ~**lager** n (P) *detention camp*

·**an|halten** vt/i [h] **I.** vt **1.** (e–n Gegenstand) *to hold up* (an *to*) ‖ → festhalten **2.** (aufhalten) (Maschine, Schiff) *to stop*; (Pferd) *to pull up*; ⟨mot⟩ (den Wagen) *to halt*; (zu) plötzlich ~ *to pull up* (*might cause an accident*) ‖ (Taxi) *to flag* ‖ (Waren) *to put a stop on* ‖ (Verkehr) *to block*; ⟨crick⟩ (Ball mit dem Schlagholz) *to block* ‖ den Atem ~ *to hold one's breath* ‖ ⟨jur⟩ (Verfahren) *to arrest* | ⟨mus⟩ (Ton) *to hold* **3.** *to detain*; *to accost* ‖ (belästigen) *to importune*; *to keep at* (*a p*) **4.** jdn ~ um etw *to apply to a p for a th* | jdn ~ z etw: jdn zur Arbeit ~ *to keep a p working* (od *a p at his job*); jdn zu schwerer Arbeit ~ *to work a p terribly hard*; jdn zum Gehorsam ~ *to get a p to obey*; jdn ~ z tun *to bring, to exhort, to get, to urge a p to do* **II.** vi **1.** (halten) *to stand still, to be at* (od *come to*) *a standstill*; *to stop*; (of a car) *to draw up* (vor *at, before*); (of rider, etc.) *to pull up*; mit dem Wagen ~ *to halt the car* (*at the gate*) ‖ ⟨mar⟩ ~ an *to call* od *touch at* (*a port*) **2.** (andauern) *to continue, to last, to hold,* der Frost hielt noch an *the frost still held* **3.** ~ um etw *to apply for a th* ‖ *to ask for a th* | ~ um die Hand e–s Mädchens *to ask a woman in marriage, to propose for* (*the hand of*) *a woman, to ask a p to marry him, to propose to a woman* ·**Anhalten** n **1.** *stop, stopping* (*of a ship*), *stoppage* **2.** *application* (um *for*) **3.** (Dauer) *continuity, continuance* (*of a quarrel*) ‖ → Heiratsantrag

·**anhaltend** a *constant, continuous* (→ häufig); *ceaseless, uninterrupted*; *continued*; *persistent* (*demand*); *persevering, unwearying* (*charm*); *steady* ‖ ~er Beifall *prolonged cheers* pl; ~er Fleiß *assiduity*; ~er Angriff *sustained attack*

·**Anhalter** m, **~in** f ⟨Ger⟩ *inhabitant of Anhalt*

°·**Anhalter** m ~s/~ (P) ⟨mot⟩ *hitch-hiker* ‖ auf *or* per ~ fahren *to travel on thumb, to lorry-hop* (*it*) ‖ ⟨sl⟩ *to hitch-hike*, ⟨Am⟩ *to bum a ride* ‖ um ~ bitten *to thumb a lift* **~fahrt** f *pick-up* **~zeichen** geben *to thumb*

·**Anhaltspunkt** m *clue* (für *to*); *indication* (über *about*); *guide, guiding principle*; *lead, line* (v *from*); e–n ~ gewinnen *to get a lead* od *line* (über *on*); e–n kl ~ finden *to get a bit of a lead*; jdn e–n ~ geben *to give a p s.th. to go on* od *by*; k–n ~ h *to have nothing to go by*

·**Anhang** m ~(e)s/≃e **1.** (Zugabe) *appendage* (zu *to*) ‖ (Zusatz) *addition* (zu *to*); ⟨jur⟩ *rider, appendix*; (Ergänzung) *supplement* (*to a book*); *addendum* ‖ ⟨com⟩ → Allonge **2.** (P) *following, adherents* pl, *followers* pl; ~ gewinnen *to find adherents* ‖ *party, faction* (→ clique) **3.** *family*; *friends* pl; e–e Witwe ohne ~ *a widow without children and other relations*

·**Anhänge-** **~etikett** n (*tie-on*) *label* od *tag* **~last** f ⟨mot⟩ *towed load* **~schloß** n *padlock* **~vorrichtung** f ⟨mot tech⟩ *hitch*(*ing mechanism*) **~wagen** m → ~r 4. **~zettel** m → ~etikett ‖ mit e–m ~ versehen *to tag*

·**an|hängen** vt/i [h] **I.** vt **1. a.** (Mantel, Hut) *to hang* (*a hat*) *up* ‖ ⟨telph⟩ (Hörer) *to hang up* ‖ → hängen **b.** (Perlen, Schmuck) *to put on* **2.** (befestigen) (etw) *to annex, to attach, to affix*; *to fasten, to join* (an *to*); *to make* (*a th*) *adhere* (an *to*) ‖ ⟨übtr⟩ *to add* (an *to*); *to tag* (an *to*); *to tack* (an *to, onto*); ein angehängter Zettel *a tag, label* **3.** ⟨fig⟩ **jdm etw** ~ *to cast an imputation* (od *aspersions*) *on a p*; *to place suspicion on a p* ‖ jdm Waren ~ *to palm* (*off*) *goods on a p*, → anschmieren **4. sich ~ an** etw, jdn → hängen | sich ~ ⟨mar⟩ *to form astern* **II.** vi **1.** [urspr anhangen; → hängen] ⟨übtr⟩ jdm ~ *to cleave, to cling to a p*; *to be attached* (od *devoted*), *to attach o.s. to a p* (od *to a cause* etc.) **2.** ⟨telph⟩ (= den Hörer ~) *to hang up*; *to ring off*; im Gespräch ~ *to hang up on a p*

·**Anhänger** m ~s/~ **1.** *adherent* (*of a p*), *follower* (*of a party*), *supporter* (*of the monarchy*); *dependant*; *hanger-on*; die ~ [pl] *the following* (*of a p*; *of a theory*) ‖ ⟨pol⟩ *partisan*; politischer ~ *henchman* ‖ ⟨Lit & arts⟩ *disciple* ‖ (Verfechter e–r S) *advocate*; *votary* (*of sports*) **2.** Uhr≃ *trinket* ‖ (Schmuck) *pendant* **3.** ⟨hort⟩ (Pfropfreis) *scion, graft* **4.** (Wagen) ⟨mot & el⟩ *trailer* **5.** = Anhängezettel, (Aktenfahne) *tab* **~kupplung** f ⟨mot⟩ *trailer coupling* | **~schaft** f *the following*; *followers* [pl] ·**anhängig** a ⟨jur⟩ *pending* ‖ ~ w (of a case) *to be initiated* ‖ e–n Prozeß ~ m *to commence a suit*, gegen jdn *to bring an action against a p* ‖ ⟨übtr⟩ e–e S ~ m *to raise a matter* (bei *with*)

·**anhänglich** a *devoted* (*husband*); *faithful* (*friend*) ‖ [pred] *attached, devoted* (an *to*) **≃keit** f ~ *adherence, attachment*; *devotion* (an *to*) ·**Anhängsel** n ~s/~ **1.** *appendage* ‖ *appendix* L; *attachment* (zu *to*); → Anhang 1. **2.** (Schmuck) *pendant* **3.** ⟨fig⟩ (Schmarotzer) *hanger-on*

·**an|hassen** vt [h] ⟨orn⟩ (Eule ~) *to mob*

·**Anhauch** m ~(e)s/ **1.** *breath, breathing* **2.** ⟨übtr⟩ = Anflug 4. ‖ *inspiration* ‖ ·**an|hauchen** vt [h] **1.** etw ~ *to breathe upon a th* | ⟨übtr⟩ rosig –ge–cht *rose-coloured, roseate* (*cheeks*) ‖ künstlerisch –ge–cht s *to be fond of art*; –ge–cht v *impressed* (od *inspired*) by **2.** °jdn ~ *to blow* (*a p*) *up*

·**an|hauen** vt [h] (Revier) *to begin to cut* (od *hew*) *down* | jdn ~ *to accost*, ⟨fam⟩ *tackle a p*; → anpumpen

·**an|häufeln** vt [h] = anhäufen ‖ Erde ~ *to earth up* ·**an|häufen** **1.** vt [h] *to accumulate*; *to heap* (od *pile*) *up*; (Geld) *to amass* ‖ (einlagern, horten) *to stockpile* ‖ ⟨übtr⟩ → anfüllen | sich ~ *to accumulate* **2.** ≃ n *piling-up, heaping-up*; *stockpiling*; → Anhäufung ·**Anhäufung** f ~/~en *heaping-up, piling-up*; *accumulation, congestion* ‖ (Masse) *conglomeration*

·**an|heben** **1.** vt [h] (etw) *to heave, to lift*; *to tip* (*the platter*) ‖ *to give* (*a th*) *a lift* | ⟨fig⟩ (anfangen) *to begin, commence* [a. abs] **2.** ≃ n *lift*(*ing*)

·**an|heften** **1.** vt [h] *to attach, affix, fasten, tack* (an *to*; *on to*); → anhängen ‖ *to pin*, (annähen) *to stitch, sew* (an *to*) ‖ ⟨übtr⟩ → heften **2.** ≃ n *attachment* (an *to*)

·**an|heilen** **1.** vt/i **a.** vt [h] (Knochen) *to join by healing* **b.** vi [s] *to heal up* od *together* **2.** ≃ n *healing-up*

anh·eim- [adv] **~fallen** vi [s] jdm ~ *to fall to, to devolve on a p*; die Krone fiel s–m Sohne anheim *the crown devolved on his son* **~geben** vt [h] **~stellen** vt [h] jdm ~ z tun *to leave* (*it*) *to a p to do*; ich stelle es Ihnen anheim *I leave* od *put it to you* (*to do*); ich stelle Ihnen die S anheim *I leave it in your hands*; es ist Ihnen anheimgestellt *it rests with you* (*to do*) | (zur Erwägung geben) jdm ~ *to submit to a p* (*that*); ich stelle anheim *I submit* (*that*)

·**an|heimeln** vt [h] (jdn) *to remind a p of home*; *to make a p feel homy* (od *at home*) ·**anheimelnd** a *homelike, homely*; *cosy, snug*, ⟨fam⟩ *homy*, ⟨Am⟩ *homey*

·**Anheirat** f ~/~en *relationship by marriage*

·**an|heiraten** vt → angeheiratet

·**anheischig** a sich ~ m *to undertake* (z tun *to do*); *to pledge* od *oblige o.s., to offer* (*to do*)

·**Anheiz-** **~zeit** f *heating time* ·**an|heizen** vt/i [h] **1.** *to kindle a fire* **2.** *to heat up* vi

·**an|helfen** vt [h] jdm den Rock ~ *to help a p on with the* od *his coat*

·**an|herrschen** vt [h] jdn ~: → anfahren II. 4.

·**an|heuern** vt [h] (Matrosen) *to hire* ‖ sich ~ l *to sign the article*

·**an|hexen** vt [h] → anfliegen ‖ wie angehext *like a bolt from the blue*

·**Anhieb** m ~(e)s/ ⟨fenc⟩ *first stroke* od *blow* ‖ auf ~, auf den ersten ~ *at the first go-off*, ⟨Am⟩

right off the bat | ⟨fig⟩ jdn auf ~ erkennen *to recognize a p at first sight* od *at once*

·an|himmeln vt [h] °jdn ~ *to enthuse* (od *be enthusiastic*) *about a p*; *to gush about* (*a th*)

anh·in adv ⟨Sw⟩ = bis jetzt

·Anhöhe f ~/~n *rising ground*; *eminence, elevation*; *hill*; *rise*

·an|holen vt [h] (Tau) *to haul*; *to pull*

·an|hören I. vt [h] **1. etw** ~ *to listen to a th* ‖ *to attend to a th* ‖ ⟨wir⟩ *to listen in to a th* ‖ es ist nicht anzuhören *it is unbearable* od *unendurable* ‖ ganz ~ *to sit through* (*a lecture*) | **jdn** ~ *to hear a p* (: *let us h. him*); *to give a p a hearing*; *to listen to a p*; → Gehör ‖ jdn ganz ~ *to hear a p out* (od *to the end*); angehört w *to gain a hearing* ‖ jdn nicht ~ (wollen) *to refuse to hear a p*; *not even to listen to a p* **2. man hört ihm** die Erkältung nicht an *you don't hear, you wouldn't think that he has got a cold*; man hört ihm den Schotten an *you can hear* (od *tell*) *by his accent that he is a Scotchman*; man hört ihm den Ausländer kaum an *he has scarcely any foreign accent* **3. sich** ~ *to sound*; sich gut ~ *to sound well*; so hörte es sich an *that's what it sounded like* **II.** ≈ n ~s/ ⟨a. jur⟩ *the hearing* (*of witnesses*)

·an|husten vt [h] jdn ~ *to cough at a p*

Anhydr·id n ~s/~e ⟨chem⟩ *anhydride*

Anhydr·it m ~s/~e ⟨minr⟩ *anhydrite*

Anil·in n ~s/~e *aniline* **~blau** n *aniline blue* **~fabrik** f *aniline works* [pl] **~farbe** f *aniline dye* **~rot** n *aniline red*

anim·alisch a *animal* (*instinct*) | adv ~ geleimt *tub-sized* (*paper*) **Animal·ismus** m ~/ *animalism*

anim·ieren vt [h] (jdn) *to animate*; *to incite, to instigate, to stimulate, to urge* (*on*) (zu *to*; z tun *to do*) **Anim·ier- ~dame** f ⟨fam⟩ *come-on girl, bar-vamp*, ⟨Am⟩ *B-girl* **~kneipe** f *amusement bar*; ⟨fam⟩ *shady pub*

Anim·ismus m ~/ *animism*

Animosit·ät f ~/~en *animosity* (gegen *against*)

°**·Animus** [L] m *mind*; *vague notion* (od *feeling*)

An·is m –ses/–se ⟨bot⟩ *anise* ‖ (~samen) *aniseed* **~likör** m = Anisette **~öl** n *aniseed-oil*

Anis·ette f ~/~n *anisette*

·anjagen vi [s] angejagt k *to come galloping* od *rushing along at a gallop* od *impetuously*

°**anjebufft** a ⟨dial⟩ = angebufft; sie ist ~ ⟨vulg⟩ *she caught*; *she's up the pole*

·an|jochen vt [h] (Tier) *to yoke*

†**·Anjou** [ã'ʒuː] n (ehem. frz. Provinz) *Anjou*; aus ~, Einwohner(in) v ~ *Angevine*

·an|kämpfen vi [h] ~ gegen jdn *to battle against* od *with a p*; *to struggle with a p* | ~ gegen etw *to battle, buck, struggle, wrestle against a th*; *to fight a th back*; *to fight against* (*tears*); *to buck* od *stem a th* ‖ gegen die Flut ~ ⟨mar⟩, ⟨übtr⟩ gegen den Strom ~ *to stem the tide* ‖ dagegen ~ *to fight one's way, to show fight, to make a fight of it, to stem the tide*; er hatte gegen vieles –zu– *he had amny ths against him*

·Ankara n ⟨Türk.⟩ (Hauptstadt)

·Ankauf m ~(e)s/≈e [abstr] *purchase, buying*; [konkr] *acquisition* **·an|kaufen** vt [h] *to purchase, buy*; (Wechsel) *to discount* ‖ **sich** ~ *to buy land* od *property*; *to settle*

·ankehrig a Sw = anstellig

°**·an|keilen** vt [h] = (jdn) ansprechen, aufsuchen

·Anker m ~s/~ **1.** ⟨mar & aero⟩ *anchor*; Patent≈ *patent a.* ‖ → Dragge; Bug≈, Nor≈, Warp≈ | den ~ auswerfen *to cast* od *drop anchor* ‖ den ~ kippen u fest m *to fish the anchor* ‖ den ~ lichten *to weigh anchor* | **vor** ~ *at anchor* ‖ vor ~ gehen, sich vor ~ legen *to come to anchor*; *to* (*drop*) *anchor*; *to moor* ‖ vor ~ liegen *to lie* od *ride at anchor*; *to be moored*; Licht am Schiff, das vor ~ liegt *riding light* od *lamp*; der für ein vor ~ liegendes Schiff erforderliche Raum *berth* ‖ vor ~ treiben *to drag the anchor* | ⟨fig⟩ (Rettungs≈) *anchor, sheet-anchor* **2.** ⟨übtr arch etc⟩ *iron bar as a device for fastening*; *brace*; *stay* | ⟨phys & el⟩ *armature* (*of a dynamo*, etc.) | (an Uhr) *lever* **3.** ⟨el⟩ *armature*; *keeper* **4.** † (Hohlmaß) *anker* **~balken** m ⟨arch⟩ *tie-beam* **~boje** f *anchor-buoy* **~flügel** m *fluke* **~gang** m (Uhr≈) *escapement* **~geld** n anchorage **~grund** m *anchor-ground*; *anchorage* **~hand** f = Ankerflügel **~hemmung** f (Uhr≈) *lever escapement* **~kern** m *armature*, → Anker 2. **~kette** f *anchor-chain*; *chain-cable* **~klüse** f *hawse* **~laterne** f *riding light* **~mast** m *mooring-mast*; (f Luftschiff) *anchor tower* **~möglichkeit** f *riding* **~pfahl** m *stay block* **~pflock** m *deadman* **~pflug** m *fluke* (od *palm*) *of the anchor* **~platz** m *anchorage*; *moorings* [pl] **~schaft** m *shaft of the anchor* **~seil** n *cable*; ⟨aero⟩ *guide-rope* **~spill** n *capstan* **~stelle** f *anchorage* **~tau** n *cable*; *mooring-rope* **~uhr** f (*patent*) *lever-watch*; *lever* **~vorrichtung** f *mooring-device* (od *mechanism*) **~wicklung** f *armature* **~winde** f *capstan*; *windlass*; (etw) mit e–r ~ heben *to windlass*

·ankern I. vi/t [h] **1.** vi ⟨mar⟩ *to* (*cast*) *anchor*; *to moor* **2.** vt ⟨aero⟩ (Flugzeug auf fliegendem Luftschiff) ~ *to anchor* **II.** ≈ n *anchoring*; Möglichkeit z ~ *riding*

·an|ketten vt [h] (Hund etc) *to chain* (*an to*)

·an|kitten vt [h] *to cement* (an *to*); *to join with putty, to putty together*

·an|kläffen vt [h] jdn ~ *to yelp* od *bark at a p*

·anklagbar a *accusable, impeachable* (p) ‖ (strafbar) *actionable*; *indictable* (*crime*)

·Anklage f ~/~n **1.** ⟨jur⟩ *accusation, arraignment, charge*; *trial* (wegen Diebstahls *for theft*) ‖ (vor der Grand Jury vorgebrachte) ~ *indictment* (gegen *against*) | ~ **erheben** gegen jdn *to bring an accusation against a p*; *to charge a p* (wegen *with*; getan z h *with doing*) ‖ **unter** ~ stehen wegen .. *to be on* (*one's*) *trial, to stand trial for*; *to be under an accusation for* ..; *to be charged with* .. ‖ jdn unter ~ stellen *to arraign a p*; .. stellen *to put .. in the block*; unter ~ gestellt w *to undergo a trial* (wegen *for*) ‖ die ~ **vertreten** *to prosecute*; Herr N., der Vertreter der ~ (*or* Herr N., der die ~ vertrat) sagte .. *Mr. N. prosecuting said* .. ‖ e–e ~ **vorbringen** *to bring* (od *prefer*) *a charge* (*against*) **2.** ⟨übtr⟩ (Beschuldigung) *accusation, imputation* (wegen Unehrlichkeit *of dishonesty*) **~akte** f ⟨jur⟩ *bill of indictment* **~bank** f *dock*; auf der ~ sitzen *to be in the dock* **~erhebung** f (öffentlich) *true bill* **~jury** f *Grand Jury* **~punkt** m count **~schrift** f (*bill of*) *indictment*; (Anklage) *charge* **~zustand** m: jdn in ~ versetzen *to bring a p to trial*

·an|klagen vt [h] (jdn) *to accuse* (wegen *of*; e–r S *of a th*; bei *before, to*; getan z h *of doing*); *to arraign* (wegen *for*); *to inform against, to impeach* (e–r S *of a th*) ‖ (öffentlich ~) *to denounce* (als *as*) | ⟨jur⟩ *to arraign*; *to charge* (e–s Verbrechens *with a crime*; getan z h *with doing*); *to indict, to prosecute* (wegen *for*); des Mordes an jdm angeklagt w *to be indicted for the murder of a p* | **~d** a *accusing*(*ly* adv)

·Ankläger m ~s/~ Anklägerin f ~/~nen *accuser*; *informer* | ⟨jur⟩ öffentl. ~ (im Strafprozeß) *Public Prosecutor* ‖ (Kläger) *plaintiff*

·an|klammern vt [h] *to fasten with cramps* | **sich** ~ *to cling* (an *to a th, a p*) *to clasp* (*a th*); *to take hold of* (*a th*) ‖ ⟨fig⟩ sich ~ an *to cling* (*to a p, a th*); *to attach o.s. to a p*; *to hang on a p*

·Anklammerung f *attachment, adherence* (an *to*)

·Anklang m ~(e)s/≈e **1.** (Erinnerung) *reminiscence, suggestion* (an *of*) ‖ ≈e an *components reminiscent of* **2.** (freundl. Aufnahme) *appeal, approval*; *applause*; → Anziehungskraft ~ **finden** *to catch* (od *take*) *on*; *to go down well*; *to be approved of*; *to be well received*; *to meet with approbation, approval, favour*; *to be popular*;

⟨com⟩ *to take* ‖ ∼ f. bei jdm *to appeal to, to make an appeal to a p; to gain upon a p; to go down with a p*; (of novels, etc.) *to take with a p* ‖ k–n ∼ f. *to fall flat* (bei *with*)

·**an|kleben** vt/i [h] **1.** vt (etw) *to stick* (an *on*); (Plakat) *to stick up*; *to post* (an *at*) ‖ mit Kleister ∼ *to paste up* (*a notice*) ‖ *to fasten with gum* ‖ → anleimen; kleben **2.** vi ⟨fig⟩ → kleben ‖ **sich** ∼ an jdn *to attach o.s. to, to hang on* od *about a p*

·**Anklebezettel** m *sticker*

·**an|kleiden 1.** vt [h] (jdn) *to dress, to attire* ‖ feierlich ∼ *to robe* (*a p*) **sich** ∼ [h] *to dress o.s.*; *to dress* (zum Abendessen *for dinner*) **2.** ≃ n *dressing*; *toilet* ·**Ankleideraum** m, **-zimmer** n *dressing-room* ⟨a. theat⟩; ⟨Am a.⟩ *wardrobe, closet* –**der(in** f) m ⟨theat⟩ *dresser*

·**an|kleistern** vt [h] → ankleben

·**an|klingeln** vt [h] ⟨telph⟩ (jdn) *to ring* (*a p*) *up*; *to give* (*a p*) *a ring*; ⟨fam⟩ *to phone* (*a p*) ‖ [abs] ich werde ∼ *I'll ring you up*

·**an|klingen** vi [h] **1.** † = anstoßen **2.** ⟨fig⟩ ∼ an *to be a reminder of*; *to be suggestive of* (*a th*); *to bear resemblance to* (*a th*); diese Dichtung klingt an Shakespeare an *there is a reminiscence of Sh. in this poetry* ‖ Erinnerungen ∼ l *to arouse recollections*

·**an|klopfen 1.** vt [h] an die Tür ∼ *to knock* od *rap at the door*; *to give a knock*; ⟨engl⟩ zweimal ∼ *to give a double knock* | ⟨fig⟩ bei jdm ∼ *to sound a p* (wegen *about*) **2.** ≃ n *knock, rap* (an *at*)

·**an|knipsen** vt [h] (el. Licht) *to switch, click, turn on*; (Schalter) *to flick, flip*

·**an|knöpfen** vt [h] *to button* (an *to*); *to fasten* (*a th*) *by buttoning* ‖ **sich** ∼ l *to button* ·**Anknöpfkragen** m *button-on collar*

·**an|knüpfen** vt/i [h] **1.** vt *to fasten, tie* (an *to*); (durch Knoten) *to knot* | ⟨übtr⟩ *to connect, to join* (an *to*) ‖ ⟨fig⟩ e–e Bekanntschaft ∼ (mit jdm) *to make* (*a p's*) *acquaintance* ‖ Beziehungen ∼ *to enter into relations*, enge B. ∼ *to knit up close relations* (*with*) ‖ e–n Briefwechsel ∼ *to enter into correspondence, to open a c.* (*with*) ‖ Geschäftsverbindungen ∼ *to form business connexions* (*with*) ‖ ein Gespräch ∼ mit jdm *to engage a p in a conversation*; ein G. wieder ∼ *to resume a c.* **2.** vi ⟨fig⟩ ∼ an *to refer to*; ∼ an den Faden e–r Geschichte *to resume the thread of a story* ‖ wieder ∼ an *to hark back to, to revert to*

·**Anknüpfung** f ∼/∼en *fastening* (an *to*) | ⟨übtr⟩ *connexion* ‖ die ∼ e–r Bekanntschaft *the making* od *starting of an acquaintance* | = **∼spunkt** m ⟨fig⟩ (*point of*) *contact* (*between persons*); *connexion*; *connecting link*

·**an|knurren** vt [h] jdn ∼ *to snarl, growl at a p*

·**an|kochen** vt [h] *to boil partially, to parboil*

·**an|kommen** vi/t **I.** vi [s] **1.** °(**nahe k**) *to come along*, °mag er nur ∼! *let him come along!*; ∼ mit etw *to come along with a th* ‖ ∼ an jdn, *or* etw; jdm, *or* e–r S ∼ *to get at a p, a th*; *to approach a p*; *to reach a th*; °komm mir nur nicht an mit deinen Kniffen *none of your tricks*; ich konnte an den Zweig nicht ∼ *I could not get at the branch* | ⟨übtr⟩ mit ist ein Ekel –ge–: → Ekel: e–n E. bek **2.** (**eintreffen**) *to arrive* (an e–m Ort *at a place*; auf dem Bahnhof *at the station*; trocken ∼ *to arrive in the dry* ‖ ∼de Personen, Züge, Schiffe *arrivals*; in e–r Stadt (bes London) ∼der Zug *up-train* ‖ ⟨mar⟩ *to reach port* | (Zug) ∼ in *to get to* (*London at 5*) ‖ (S) *to arrive*; *to come to hand* | (**erscheinen**) *to appear, to make one's appearance* **3.** ⟨übtr⟩ ∼ bei jdm *to be engaged by a p*; ∼ bei e–m Buchhändler *to get employment at a bookseller's* | ⟨fig⟩ gut (schlecht) bei jdm ∼ *to fare well* (*ill*) *with a p, to be well* (*ill*) *received by a p* ‖ du wirst bei ihm schön ∼ *you will meet with a nice reception*; mit d–r Bitte wirst du übel ∼ *your request will be ill received* ‖ damit kannst du bei mir nicht (*or* schlecht) ∼ *I am up to your little game* ‖ ⟨theat⟩ (beim Publikum) (*his gags*) *come across* **4. gegen jdn (etw)** ∼ *to cope* (od *deal successfully*) *with a p* (*a th*); dagegen ist nicht –zu– *that beats all*; er konnte gegen ihn nicht ∼ *he came off second best* **5.** [imps] **es kommt auf jdn, etw an** *it depends on a p, a th* .. nur auf dich an *it depends entirely on you*; .. auf die Umstände an .. *on the circumstances*; ich sah worauf es ankam *I saw the point*; es kommt auf jeden einzelnen an *it is everybody that matters*; jeder, auf den es –mt *everybody who counts* ‖ es kommt auf e–n Versuch an *let's have a try* od *go*; es k. auf jeden einzelnen an *it depends on everyone*; es k. darauf an z tun *it is essential to do*; es k. mir auf jeden einzelnen an *I can't do without any one of them* ‖ es kommt mir nicht an auf .. *I do not mind* ..; *I am not particular about* ..; es kommt mir nicht auf ein paar Mark an *I don't mind a few marks, a few m. won't matter* | **es kommt darauf an** *that* od *it* (*all*) *depends*, ⟨fam⟩ *that's according* ‖ ..an, ob *the question is whether* ‖ darauf kommt es (nicht) an *that is* (*not*) *the point* (*of the question*); *that's what matters* ‖ worauf es ankommt (..) (*he doesn't see*) *what the point of the question is, what matters* ‖ es kommt mir viel darauf an *it is of great consequence to me* (*to know*) ‖ darauf soll es mir nicht ∼ *I don't mind risking that* | **ich lasse es** auf Sie, auf Ihre Entscheidung ∼ *I'll let it depend on you* (od *on your decision*); *I'll leave it to you* (od *to your decision*) ‖ es darauf ∼ l *to take* od *stand one's chances, to see what happens* ‖ ‖ ich würde es nicht auf e–n Prozeß ∼ l *I should not go to law on that* ‖ ich lasse es aufs Äußerste ∼ *I'll go to extremities* | es darauf ∼ l *to take* od *stand chance*; *to let the matter take its course*; *to wait and see* ‖ ich lasse es drauf ∼! *as well be hanged for a sheep as a lamb!* ‖ wollen Sie es darauf ∼ l? *will you take the risk of that?* | **wenn's drauf ankam** *on the proper occasion*; *if it came down to brass tacks*, ⟨Am⟩ *when it came to the pinch* od *to a show-down* (*he held the cards*) **II.** vt [s] [nur 3. sg & pl] jdn ∼ (of feelings, etc.) *to befall a p*; *to fall upon a p*; *to come over* od *upon a p* ‖ es kam ihn die Lust, eine Furcht (etc) an *he was seized with a desire, a fear* (*to do*) ‖ der Schlaf kam ihn an *sleep came upon him* ‖ es kommt ihn hart an *it is hard on him* (*to do*) mich (⟨a.⟩ mir) kommt ein Ekel an → Ekel

·**Ankömmling** m ∼s/∼n (neuer ∼) *new-comer*; *arrival*; *stranger*

·**an|koppeln** vt [h] (T) *to couple* (an *to*); ⟨hunt⟩ (Hunde) *to leash* ‖ ⟨a–n⟩ (Kapseln) *to dock*

·**an|kränkeln** vt [h] ⟨mst fig⟩ *to make* (*a p*) *effeminate*; → angekränkelt

·**an|kreiden** vt [h] *to chalk, to mark* (*off*) *with chalk* ‖ (mit Kreide schreiben) *to chalk up* | ⟨fig⟩ (Schuld) *to chalk up*; jdm e–e Summe ∼ *to score a sum against a p* ‖ ∼ l *to buy* od *take on credit* (⟨fam⟩ *on tick*) ‖ das werde ich ihm ∼ ⟨iron⟩ *I won't forget it*

·**Ankreis** m (äußerer Tangentialkreis) ⟨math⟩ *escribed circle*

·**an|kreuzen** vt [h] (Namen auf e–r Liste) *to check, tick, mark off*

·**an|kündigen** vt [h] (jdn, etw) *to announce*; *to signal* ‖ (inserieren) (Waren) *to advertise* ‖ (öffentlich) *to proclaim, to publish* ‖ (feierlich ∼) *to herald*; (den Frühling) *to usher in* ‖ die gr –ge–digte Rede *the much heralded speach* | jdm etw ∼ *to notify a th to a p* (od *a p of a th*)

·**Ankündigung** f ∼/∼en *announcement* ‖ (amtliche) *notification* ‖ (Inserat) *advertisement* ‖ fentliche) *proclamation*; kz ∼ *notice* ‖ mit kurzfristiger ∼ *at short notice* **∼sbefehl** m ⟨mil⟩ *warning order*; (Drill) = **∼skommando** n *preparatory command* **∼ssignal** n *warning signal*

·**Ankunft** f ~/⸛e *arrival, coming* ‖ bei (der) ~ *on arrival*; nach der ~ (..) *on arriving* (*he wrote*..) ·**Ankunfts- ~bahnsteig** m ⟨rail⟩ *arrival--platform*; (e–r gr Stadt, bes Londons) *up-platform* **~buch** n *arrival book* **~gleis** n *up-line* **~hafen** m *port of arrival* **~ort** m *place of arrival* **~zeit** f *time of arrival*

·**an|kuppeln** vt [h] *to couple* (an *to*)

·**an|kurbeln** vt/i [h] **1.** vt (Maschine) *to turn on*; (Motor) *to crank*, mst *to crank up*; (Auto) *to start* (*up*) (vi) | ⟨fig⟩ *to speed up*; (Handel) *to enliven*; (Wirtschaft) ⟨sl⟩ *to pep up, to boost* **2.** vi *to crank up*; ⟨fam⟩ *to start, to take the wheel* ·**Ankurbeln** n ·**Ankurbelung** f ⟨mot⟩ *cranking-up* ‖ ⟨fig⟩ *enlivening*; ⟨Am, com, pol⟩ *pump priming* **~skommission** f (Wirtschaft 1945: Arbeitgeber, –nehmer u Unparteiischer) *working party*

·**an|lächeln** vt [h] jdn ~ *to smile at a p*; *to give a p a smile*; jdn dumm ~ *to smile a silly smile at a p*; → zulächeln ·**anlachen** vt [h] jdn ~ *to smile at a p*; *to laugh in a p's face*; jdn strahlend ~ *to beam upon a p*

·**Anlage** f ~/~n **A. 1.** [abstr] (**Anlegung**) *arrangement* ‖ *building*; *construction* ‖ (e–r Druckseite *etc*) *lay-out*; *laying-out* (*of a garden*); → ~plan ‖ *configuration* (*of a room*) ‖ *structure* (*of a novel*) | (**Fertigstellung**) *establishment*; *completion*; *foundation* | (**Kapital**⸛) *investment* **2.** (**Plan**) *conception, plan*; *design, outline* (*of a building*) **3.** (**Angelegtes**) **a.** ⟨hort⟩ (Garten⸛[n]) *park*; *gardens*, (*pleasure-*)*grounds* [pl]; (Wandel⸛) *promenade*; (Grün⸛n) *gardens, parks, lawns*; städtische ~n *municipal gardens, parks* | mechanische ~ *device* (für *for*) | (Fabrik⸛) *plant*; *factory*; ⟨mach⟩ *unit*; elektrische Kraft⸛ *electric plant, generating plant*; elektr. ~ (im Hause) *electric fittings* [pl]; (Gas⸛ etc) *installation*; Heißwasser⸛ *hot water connexions* [pl] ‖ Bergwerks⸛, Gruben⸛ *workings* [pl] ‖ Entwässerungs⸛ *drainage* ‖ Sprung⸛ (im Schwimmbad) *diving platform* ‖ [pl] *installations*; *system* (*heating s.*); *facilities* (*sanitary f., production f., recreational f.*) | (~kapital) *investment*; *invested money* **B.** (**Beilage**) *annex* (*to a deed*) ‖ ⟨jur⟩ *rider* ‖ *enclosure* (*in a letter*); ⟨com⟩ laut ~ *as annexed*; aus der ~ ersehen Sie *from the annexed you will see*; in der ~ übersenden wir .. *enclosed* (od *herewith*) *we send*.. **C.** ⟨übtr⟩ **1.** ⟨bot & zoo⟩ (**Keim**) *germ, rudimentary form* ‖ vererbbare ~n ⟨biol⟩ *inheritable characters* **2.** (**Neigung**) ⟨mst med⟩ *inclination, tendency* (zur Korpulenz *to corpulence*); *predisposition* (zur Tuberkulose *to tuberculosis*) | natürliche ~, Gemüts⸛ *temperamental adaptation* (f *for*), *disposition*; *natural tendency* (zu *to*); e–e heitere Gemüts⸛ *a cheerful disposition*; charakterliche ~ *strain* (z *of*) ‖ Geistes⸛ *cast of mind*; *vein* (z Humor *of humour*) **3.** (**Begabung**) gift, talent (z *for*), s–e dichterische ~ *his talent as a poet*; ~n [pl] *abilities, aptitudes* [pl]; keine ~ besitzen z *to be inapt for*..; dazu hat er keine ~n *his talents do not lie that way* **D.** ⟨mil⟩ (*angle of*) *inclination of an escarp* **~kapital** n *invested capital* **~kosten** pl *prime* od *initial cost, cost of installation* **~kredit** m *long-term credit* (*for building*, etc.) **~markt** m *investment market* **~papier** n *investment paper* **~plan** m: ~ der Gebäude in e–r Fabrik *lay-out plan of a factory* **~vermögen** n *fixed* od *capital assets*

·**Anlände** f ~/~n *landing-place* ·**an|landen** **1.** vi [s] *to land, to disembark, to come to shore* **2.** ⸛ [n] (a. Anlandung) *landing, disembarcation*

Anl·andgehen n → Land 6. ‖ ⟨tact⟩ *ship-to--shore movement*

·**Anlandung** f ~/~en = Anschwemmung ·**an|langen** vi/t **1.** vi [s] *to arrive* → gelangen **2.** vt [nur 3. sg pres & pret] = anbelangen

·**Anlaß** m, –sses/Anlässe **1.** ⟨mot⟩ *start*; leichter ~ *easy st.* **2.** (**Ursache**) *cause* (z *for*; z tun *to do*); *occasion* (*for*; *to do, of doing*); *ground, reason* (*for*; *to do, for doing*) ‖ *motive* (*for*; *for doing*); *inducement* (z *to*) ‖ dringender ~ *need* (z *for*; *to do*) | **Wendungen:** aus diesem ~ *for this reason*, aus verschiedenen Anlässen *for several reasons* ‖ auf jds ~ *at a p's instigation, suggestion, request*; auf ~ der Regierung *by order of the Government* ‖ ohne jeden ~ *without any reason*; *without the slightest provocation* | kein ~ zu .. *no ground for* (*pessimism*), *no occasion for* (*anger*), .. zum Lachen *no occasion to laugh* | **~ geben** zu etw *to give rise* od *occasion to a th, to cause a th, to be the occasion of* (od *for*) *a th* ‖ jdm ~ geben z tun *to make a p do* ‖ allen ~ h *to have every reason* (*for doing*); k–n ~ *to have no occasion* (*to do*) ‖ es liegt durchaus kein ~ zur Beunruhigung vor *there is no need* od *reason for alarm* **3.** (**Gelegenheit**) aus ~ des Jahrestages *on the occasion of the anniversary*; **~ nehmen** z tun *to take occasion* (od *to seize the opportunity*) *to do* ‖ etw z ~ nehmen *to avail o.s. of a th* ‖ ein Ereignis z ~ e–r Untersuchung nehmen *to make an event the occasion of an examination* ‖ (Feiern) und andere Anlässe (..) *and other occasions* (od *events*)

·**Anlaß-** ⟨tech⟩ *starting*.. **~druckknopf** m *self--starter button* **~hebel** m, **~kurbel** f *starting--handle* **~kolben** m *trigger* **~kraftstoff** m *starting fuel*; *priming*; ~ einspritzen *to prime an engine* ‖ ~leitung [f] *starting manifold* **~magnet** m *starting magneto* ‖ ~zünder [m] ⟨aero⟩ *booster magneto* **~motor** m *starting* od *starter motor*, ⟨aero⟩ *booster* **~schalter** m *starting switch* **~ventil** n *discharge* (od *outlet*) *valve* **~vorrichtung** f *st.g device* **~widerstand** m *st.g resistance*

·**an|lassen I.** vt [h] **A.** → anbehalten ‖ laß das Licht an *leave the light on* **B.** (in Gang setzen) **1.** (Maschine) *to start*; *to set* (*a th*) *going* ‖ ⟨mot⟩ (Motor) *to start, to crank* (*up*) ‖ (Dampf, Wasser) *to turn* (od *to put*) *on* | *to let loose*; ⟨hunt⟩ Hunde ~ *to slip hounds* (auf *on*) **2.** (Metalle) *to temper* **3.** jdn hart, übel ~ *to address, receive a p with harsh words*; *to rebuke* od *to snub a p* **C. sich ~** [heute mst nur 3. sg & pl] *to appear, seem, sound* (als ob *as if*) ‖ sich gut ~ (P) *to promise well*; *to make good progress, to be doing well* od *nicely*; ein junger Mann, der sich gut anläßt *a promising lad*; er ließ sich prächtig an *he took to it like a duck to water* ‖ (S) *to bid fair*; *to be successful*; die S läßt sich gut an *things are shaping up well*; .. läßt sich (nicht) schlecht an *things are* (*not*) *going* (*too*) *badly* **II.** ⸛ [n] ~s/ ⟨mot⟩ *ignition*

·**Anlasser** m ~s/~ ⟨el⟩ *starting device*; ⟨mot & wir⟩ *starter*; (Motor) *cranking motor*; selbsttätiger ~ *self-starter* **~knopf** m *starter-button* **~ritzel** n *starter pinion*

·**anläßlich** [prep] ~ e–r S *on the occasion of a th*; ~ der Jahrestagsfeier *on the occasion of the celebration of the anniversary*

·**an|lasten** vt [h] österr = aufbürden; beschuldigen

·**Anlauf** m ~(e)s/Anläufe **1.** (Angriff) *charge*; *onset*, im ersten ~ *at the first onset* **2.** ⟨gym⟩ ~ (zum Sprung) *starting run* (→ Sprung) ‖ ⟨übtr⟩ *start* ‖ e–n **~ nehmen** *to take off* (zu *for*); e–n gr, kz ~ nehmen *to take a long, short run*; ⟨fig⟩ e–n guten ~ nehmen *to make a good start* | *skiing approach* **3.** ⟨arch⟩ *apophyge, escape, scape*; (e–s Bogens etc) *spring* **4.** = **~farbe** f *annealing colo*(*u*)*r* **~hafen** m *port of call* **~strecke** f ⟨gym⟩ *starting run* **~zeit** f *initial period*; ⟨el, tech⟩ *response time, rise t., settling t.*; ⟨logist, tech, com⟩ *lead time* | (bei Arbeitsbeginn) *start--up time*

·**an|laufen** vi/t **I.** vi [s] **A.** (P & T) **1.** angelaufen k *to come runing along* ‖ ⟨hunt⟩ (v

Wild) 1.) *to come within shot*; 2.) *to rush upon* (*the spear*) **2. ~ gegen** *to run against, to rush upon* (*a p*); *to strike against* (*a th*); → (an)rennen | ⟨übtr⟩ → ankämpfen **3.** (**beginnen**) *to start*; (Maschine) ∼ l *to set going, to start* **4.** °**übel, schön ~** = ankommen I. 3. **5.** °**blau ~** *to blush, flush,* → B. 2. **B.** (S) **1.** (anschwellen) dick ∼ *to swell* (v *with*) ‖ *to increase*; *to rise*; (of interest, etc.) *to run up, to accumulate*; Rechnung ∼ l *to run up a bill* **2.** sich trüben (of metal) *to tarnish*; (of glass) *to* (*grow*) *dim* ‖ Stahl blau ∼ l *to blue steel* ‖ (Glas) schwarz ∼ l *to darken, to smoke* **II.** vt [h] **1.** ⟨hunt⟩ (Jäger) *to rush upon, to attack* **2.** ⟨mar⟩ e–n Hafen ∼ *to call* (od *touch*) *at a port, to make port*

·**Anlaufen** n *tarnish* (*of metal*)

·**Anlaut** m ∼(e)s/∼e ⟨gram⟩ *initial sound*; *anlaut* [Ger] ‖ im ∼ *initially*; h im ∼ *h initially, initial h* ·**an|lauten** vi [h] ∼ mit *to begin with* (*a consonant*); ein ∼der Vokal *an initial vowel*

·**an|läuten** vt [h] ⟨telph⟩ *to ring up a p*

·**Anlege-** (→ anlegen) **~apparat** m *feeder*; ⟨typ⟩ *feeding apparatus* **~gebühren** f [pl] *anchorage* **~hafen** m → Anlauf- **~kante** f *fitting* od *adjusting edge* **~platz** m = ∼stelle **~punkt** m ⟨surv⟩ *reference point* **~schloß** n *padlock* **~stelle** f ⟨mar⟩ *landing-place*; *quay, pier*

·**an|legen** vt/i [h] **I.** vt **1.** (**legen**) (Verband etc) *to apply* (an *to*) ‖ *to lay, put* (an *to, against*), (Holz etc) *to put* (*wood*) *on the fire* ‖ → Axt; Feuer; Leiter ‖ den Hund ∼ (sc an die Kette) *to chain up the dog*, (z Fährte) ⟨hunt⟩ *to lift* ‖ → Boot | **sich ~** *to lean* (an *against*) ‖ sich mit jdm ∼ *to pick a quarrel with a p* | e–m Fasse Reifen ∼ *to hoop a barrel* ‖ e–m Pferd den Zaum ∼ *to bridle a horse, to put the bridle on a horse* ‖ jdm ein Kleid ∼ *to dress a p*; jdm Fesseln ∼ *to put a p in irons, to fetter up* ‖ jdm Zügel ∼ *to curb a p, to keep a p in check, to keep a tight hand on a p* | **Hand ~** an etw *to take a th in hand, to set about a th*; mit Hand ∼ *to lend a hand,* → anfassen ‖ die letzte Hand ∼ *to give* (od *put*) *the finishing touches* (od *a final touch*) *to a th* ‖ → Maßstab | → legen **2.** (**anziehen**) (Kleider) *to put* (od *get*) *on*; *to don*; den Sonntagsstaat ∼ ⟨fam⟩ *to put on one's Sunday best* ‖ Trauer ∼ *to go into mourning* (um *for*) **3.** ⟨übtr⟩ (**Plan** etc) *to lay out*; *to sketch* (*out*); *to plan* ‖ (Buch) *to open*, (Album, Kartei, Sammlung) *to start* | (etw) *to design* (nach e–m Plan *on a plan*) ‖ (Garten) *to lay out* (od *down*); (Siedlung) *to plant* ‖ (Straße) *to lay down* ‖ (Eisenbahn) *to build* ‖ (Stadt) *to found*; (Gebäude) *to build, to construct*; (Geschäft) *to establish* ‖ elektrische Leitung in e–m Zimmer ∼ *to wire a room*; (Gas; Telephon) *to install* **4.** ⟨com⟩ (**Geld**) *to invest* (zu 5% *at 5%*; in *in*); gut ∼ *to invest* (*money*) *to advantage, to turn* (*money*) *to good account*; Geld fest ∼ *to lock up one's money*; Geld auf Zinsen ∼ *to put out money at interest* ‖ ein Konto ∼ *to open an account* | (lose:) Geld ∼ für etw *to pay for, to spend on a th*; ich kann nur einige Mark ∼ *I can spend only a few marks* **5.** das **Gewehr ~** (zielend) *to level* od *present the rifle* (auf jdn *at a p*); ⟨mil⟩ legt ∼! Feuer! *present! fire!* | ⟨übtr⟩ **es ~ auf** etw *to aim at a th*; *to plan*; *to contrive, to plot a th*; es darauf ∼ z tun *to make it one's object to do*; alles war darauf angelegt (..) *everything was deliberately designed* (od *calculated*) (*to ruin him*) **II.** vi **1.** ⟨mar⟩ *to land*; *to moor*; *to put in*; *to dock*; → ankern, anlaufen **2.** (= Holz etc ∼) *to put fuel* (etc) *on the fire* **3.** auf jdn ∼ *to aim* (od *take aim*) *at a p*; ⟨Am⟩ *to pull a pistol on a p*; ⟨mil⟩ legt an! *aim!* ·**Anlegen** n *application* (an *to*) ‖ *putting-on* (*of clothes*) ‖ *laying-out* (*of streets*); *lay-out*

·**Anleger** m (P) ⟨typ⟩ *feeder*; *layer-on*

·**Anlegung** f ∼/∼en **1.** → Anlegen **2.** → Anlage I. 1. **3.** *investment* (*of money*)

·**an|lehnen** vt [h] **1.** (etw) *to lean* (an *against*) **2.** ⟨übtr⟩ (Truppen zum Schutz) *to make* (*the troops*) *lean* (an e–n Wald *on a wood*) **3.** die Tür ∼ *to leave the door ajar* **4. sich ~** *to lean, rest* (an die Wand *against the wall*); sich mit dem Rücken an die Wand ∼ *to lean one's back against the wall* | ⟨übtr⟩ (of troops) *to lean on* (*a wood*) | ⟨fig bes pol⟩ *to lean on*; *to cling to a p*; *to go with a p, to act in accordance with a p*; anschließen ‖ ⟨Lit & scient⟩ *to take* (*a p*) *as a guide*; *to lean to* (od *to espouse*) *the opinion of a p*; *to depend on a p* (od *a th*); *to follow a p* (*a th*); *to borrow from a p* (*a th*) ‖ ⟨arts⟩ *to imitate* (*a style*)

·**Anlehnen** n *leaning* (an *against*); → Anlehnung ·**Anlehnung** f ∼/∼en **1.** ⟨übtr⟩ ∼ und Unterstützung *protection and support* **2.** ⟨fig⟩ *dependence* (an jdn *on a p*); *borrowing* (an *from*) ‖ *imitation* | **in ~ an** *in connexion with*; *in accordance* (od *compliance*) *with* ‖ *in imitation of, on the model of* ‖ **ohne ~ an** *dispensing with* ‖ ⟨mil⟩ ohne ∼ *without flank contact*; unter ∼ an *maintaining fl. c. with*

·**Anleihe** f ∼/∼n **1.** *loan* (auf *on*; an *to*) ‖ öffentliche ∼ *Government* (od *Public, State*) *Loan*; Kommunal≈ *municipal bond*; Staats≈ *government bond* ‖ e–e ∼ m. *or* aufnehmen *to raise a loan, to take up a loan* **2.** bei jdm e–e ∼ m. *to borrow money of* (od *from*) *a p* | ⟨fig⟩ *to borrow from a p*; *to imitate a p* **~ablösung** f *loan-liquidation* **~kapital** n *loan-capital* **~papier** n *Government-stock* **~zinsen** m pl *interest on loans*

·**an|leimen** vt [h] (etw) *to fasten with glue*; *to glue* (an *to*); ⟨übtr⟩ wie angeleimt an *as if glued to* (*a th*)

·**an|leiten** vt [h] (unterweisen) *to train* (z *to*; *to do*) ‖ *to instruct, to initiate, to school* (in *in*)

·**Anleiter** m ∼s/∼ *guide*; *instructor* ·**Anleitung** f ∼/∼en *guidance, direction*; unter s–r ∼ *under his d.* ‖ *training* (z *to, towards*); *instruction, initiation, schooling* (in *in*) | (Lehrbuch) *small text-book*; *manual, guide*

·**an|lernen** vt [h] jdn ∼ *to give initial training to a p, to instruct a p in the elements of a trade*, etc. ‖ (T) *to enter* ‖ ⟨übtr⟩ *to teach, to instruct, to school a p* (in *in*) ‖ ⟨bes sport⟩ *to train* ‖ → angelernt

·**an|lesen** vt [h] ein Buch ∼ *to read only the beginning of a book* ‖ sich (etw) ∼ *to acquire* (*a th*) *by reading*

·**an|leuchten** vt [h] (mit Scheinwerfer) *to pick up*

·**an|liegen** vi [h] **1.** (of clothes) *to sit close, to fit well*; das Jackett liegt gut (schlecht) an *the jacket is a good* (*bad*) *fit* **2.** (**angrenzen**) ∼ an *to lie close* (od *near*) *to*; *to border on*; *to be adjacent to*; e–a *to be adjacent to each other*; → ∼d 1. **3.** ⟨com⟩ (**beiliegen**) heute nur: ∼d (= in der Anlage) *herewith, enclosed* (*we send*); → ∼d 3. **4.** ⟨mar⟩ (**steuern**) e–n Ort ∼ *to bear up* (od *to stand*) *for a place* **5.** jdm (od jdn) ∼ (= mit Bitten bedrängen) *to entreat* od *solicit a p*; *to importune, worry a p with urgent requests* ‖ → angelegen; angelegentlich ·**Anliegen** n ∼s/∼ **1.** (Passen) *fit* (*of a garment*) **2.** (Anteil, Sorge) *concern* **3.** (Bitte) *application, petition*; *request* ‖ *wish, desire* ‖ ich habe ein ∼ an Sie *I want to ask a favour of you* ‖ was ist Ihr ∼? *what is your request?* ‖ ein ∼ vorbringen *to express, to utter a wish*

·**anliegend** a **1.** *adjacent* (*angles*); (angrenzend) *adjoining, contiguous* **2.** *fitting*; eng ∼ *clinging*; fest ∼ *tight* (*coat*) **3.** *enclosed, annexed* (*letter*); → anliegen 3. ·**Anlieger** m ∼s/∼ **1.** *neighbour*; ∼siedlung [f] *settlement adjacent to a factory, etc*; ∼staaten [pl] *neighbouring states* [pl] **2.** *abut-*

ting property owner || nur für ~, ~ frei! ⟨mot⟩ *for residents only, open to residents* | ~staat [m] *border state*

·an|locken 1. vt [h] (Vögel etc) *to decoy*; (Wild) *to flag, bait* || ⟨übtr⟩ *to allure, bait, entice, attract* **2.** ≗ n = **·Anlockung** f ~/~en *allurement, bait, enticement*

·an|löten vt [h] *to fasten* od *join with solder*; *to solder* (an *to*)

·an|lügen vt [h] *to lie to a p*; *to tell a p a lie*

·an|luven vi [h] ⟨mar⟩ *to luff, to bring a ship nearer the wind*

·an|machen I. vt [h] **1.** (befestigen) *to attach, fix, fasten* (an *to*) **2.** (zubereiten) *to prepare*; (Salat) *to dress, mix*; → würzen | (Farben) *to temper*; → löschen **3.** Feuer → *to light* od *kindle a fire* || °Licht ~ *to light the lamp*; ⟨el⟩ *to switch on the light* **4. sich** an jdn ~ → heranmachen **II.** ≗ n *fastening* (an *to*) || *mixing* || *lighting*

·Anmachholz n → Anfeuerholz

·an|mahnen vt [h] *to hasten* (*a reply, voucher, return*); (Betrag) bei jdm ~ *to remind a p of* .. **·Anmahnung** f ~/~en *hastener*

·an|malen vt [h] *to paint*; die Tür blau ~ *to p. the door blue*

·Anmarsch m ~(e)s/≗e *marching on*; *advance*; im ~ s *to be advancing* || ~ u Entfaltung ⟨mil⟩ *developing approach* **~weg** m *route of approach* (z Arbeit *to the shop*) **·an|marschieren** vi [s] *to march on, to advance*

·an|maßen [vrefl] [h] **1.** sich (unberechtigt) etw ~ (Rechte, Thron) *to usurp a th*; *to arrogate* (**to assume*) *a th to oneself* **2.** (sich herausnehmen) *to pretend to a th*, ich maße mir keine Gelehrsamkeit an *I do not p. to learning* | sich ~ z s *to pretend* (od *profess*; *set up*) *to be* (:*I do not p. to be a scholar*) **3.** (wagen) sich ~ z tun *to presume, pretend to do*; ich maße mir kein Urteil an *I dare not pretend to give an opinion*

·anmaßend, †·anmaßlich a (dünkelhaft) *pretentious, presumptuous, overweening*; (herrisch) *haughty, uppish, overbearing, high and mighty*; *high-handed*; *arrogant, truculent, insolent*; ⟨Am fam⟩ *fresh* || in ~er Weise *encroachingly*; ~es Wesen → Anmaßung 2.; f s–e Stellung zu ~ w *to grow to big for one's boots* | (z zuversichtlich) *presumptuous* (*it is p. to think*) **·Anmaßung** f ~/~en **1.** (unrechtmäßige Aneignung) → Aneignung **2.** (Dünkel) *presumption, presumptuousness* (: *without p.*); *side*; *pretension, pretentiousness*; *haughtiness, overbearance, overbearing, arrogance, truculence, insolence, effrontery* || (gr Selbstsicherheit) *presumptuousness* || e–e Portion ~ ⟨Am sl⟩ *a fat nerve*

·Anmelde- ~frist f *time* od *period for application* **~gebühr** f *registration-fee* **~pflicht** f *duty of reporting* (*one's address*, etc. *to the police*) **~schein** m *entry-form* || *statistical declaration* **~stelle** f *registrar's office* **~zeit** f ⟨telph⟩ *request time*

·an|melden vt [h] **1.** (jds Ankunft **mitteilen**) (jdn) *to announce*; *to usher in*; wollen Sie mich bitte ~? *will you take in my card, please*? || Sind Sie angemeldet (sc bei dem Arzt)? *have you an appointment*? || jdn telephonisch ~ bei jdm *to put a p through to a p* | **sich ~** *to announce o.s.* || ich hätte mich ~ sollen *I ought to have made an appointment* || sich ~ l *to send in one's card* || sich z Dauerwelle ~ *to book a perm* || sich ~ bei *to make an appointment with* (Arzt etc) **2. (amtlich ~)** (etw) *to register, notify*; *to give notice of* (*a th* od *an event*); jdn ~, jds Adresse (Ankunft) bei der Polizei ~ *to report* (*to*) od *register a p's address* (*arrival*) *to* (*with*) *the police*; **sich ~** *to report o.s., to give formal notice of one's address* (*arrival*) **3. (aufnehmen l) a.** (jdn) *to enrol*; *to nominate*; Kind zur Schule ~ *to enroll a child in school*; jdn z Rennen ~ *to enter a p for a race*; sich z R. ~ *to enter for a race*; **sich ~** *to register o.s., to give formal notice of one's arrival, to enter one's name* (bei e–m Klub *as a member of a club*); **b.** (Waren beim Zoll) *to declare* || (Gespräch) *to book* (*a call*); *to put* od *place* (*a call* nach .. *to Paris* || ein Patent ~ *to apply for* (od *to take out*) *a patent* || den Konkurs ~ *to file one's petition in bankruptcy* **·Anmeldung** f ~/~en *announcement*; nur bei vorheriger ~ *only by appointment* || ohne ~ *without warning* || (amtliche) *notification, notice*; (Geburts–, Schul–) *registration* || (Zoll–) *entry, declaration* || Patent≗ *application for a patent* || Konkurs≗ *petition in bankruptcy* **~sformular** *entry-form*; *form of application*

·an|merken vt [h] **1.** (äußern) *to remark* (daß *that*) **2.** (an–, bezeichnen) (etw) *to note*; *to put* (od *write*) *down*; sich etw ~ *to make* (od *take*) *a note of a th*; *to mark a th* || sich jdn ~ *to mark out a p* (*for*) **3.** jdm etw ~ *to notice, observe, to remark a th in a p*; man merkte ihm die Müdigkeit an *you could see that he was tired* || dem Buche merkt man die Flüchtigkeit an *the book shows signs of sloppiness* | **sich** .. (nicht) ~ l *to give* (*no*) *sign of* (*surprise, irritation, etc*); er ließ sich nichts ~ *he did not betray his feelings*; laß dir nichts ~! ⟨Am fam⟩ *don't let on*!

·Anmerkung f ~/~en **1.** (Bemerkung) *short observation* od *remark* (z etw *on a th*), *comment* (z *on*) **2.** (kritische ~ im Buch) *comment*; *annotation note*; (Fußnote) *foot-note* || mit ~en versehen 1. vt *to annotate* (*a book*) 2. a *annotated*

·an|messen vt [h] jdm e–n Rock (etc) ~ *to take a p's measure for a coat, to measure a p for a coat*; sich e–n Anzug ~ l *to get measured for* ..

·an|mustern vt [h] ⟨mil & mar⟩ *to enrol*; *to sign on*; sich ~ l *to be enrolled, to sign on*

·Anmut f ~/ (P) *grace*; *comeliness, attractiveness*; in *or* mit ~ altern *to age gracefully*; (Liebreiz) *charm, sweetness*; [dat] ~ verleihen *to lend grace to, to give a charm to* (*a p, a th*) || (Ort etc) *amenity*, oft *amenities* [pl] || (*of style*) *elegance*

·anmuten vt [h] **1.** jdn ~ *to please a p*; [mst 3. sg] es mutet mich an *it pleases me* **2.** jdn fremd ~ *to seem strange* (od *curious*) *to a p*; es mutet mich an *it sounds to me* (als wenn *as if*) || ~d *in appearance*; altertümlich ~de Fenster [pl] *windows somewhat antique in appearance*

·anmutig, ·anmutsvoll a *graceful*; *charming, comely, sweet*; *debonair*

·an|nageln vt [h] *to fasten with a nail* (od *with nails*); *to nail* (an *to*) || wie angenagelt ⟨fig⟩ *as if nailed* od *glued to the wall* (etc)

·an|nähen 1. vt [h] e–n Knopf (etc) ~ *to sew a button* (etc) *on* **2.** ≗ n *the sewing on* (*of a b.*)

·an|nähern vt [h] etw e–r S ~ *to bring* od *get a th near a th* (od *close, near to a th*) || (verschiedene Dinge) *to approximate* | **sich** e–r S ~ ⟨übtr⟩ (S) *to approximate to a th* (: *to a. to a theory*); *to approach a th*; → nähern

·annähernd 1. a *approximate, approximative*; *rough* (*estimate*); *fairly exact* **2.** adv *approximately* (*equal*); *about* || nicht ~ *not nearly*; nicht ~ 200 Leute *nowhere near 200 people*; es ist nicht ~ so billig wie.. *it is nothing* (od *it is not anything*) *like as cheap as*..; e–r S nicht ~ gerecht w *not to do anything like justice to a th* || nicht (auch nur) ~ alles *not anything like all*

·Annäherung f ~/~en **1.** ⟨eig⟩ *approach* (an jdn *to a p*); bei s–r ~ *on his a.* || ~ der Nacht *a. of night* | ⟨übtr⟩ ~en *approaches, advances*; Friedens≗en *overtures of peace* (an *to*) || e–e ~ zustandebringen zwischen Gegnern *to bring about an understanding* (od *personal relations*) *between opponents, to bring opponents in contact* (od *touch*) *with one another* **2. ~ an** etw *approximation* (od *approach*) *to a th* (: *an approximation to the truth*) **~sgraben** ⟨mil⟩ *approach*(*-trench*) **~sversuch** m [mst pl] ~e *approaches, advances*

[pl]; ~e m bei jdm *to make advances to a p* **~sweg** m ⟨mil⟩ *approach* **≃sweise** adv *approximately, nearly* **~szünder** m (elektronischer) *radar proximity fuse*

·**Annahme** f ~/~n **1.** (Entgegennahme) *acceptance* (*of goods, an offer* etc); bedingte ~ *qualified acceptance*; → Aufnahme; Empfang ‖ *acceptance* (*of a bill of exchange*); mangels ~ *for want of acceptance*; wegen nicht erfolgter ~ *for non-acceptance* ‖ die ~ verweigern *to refuse acceptance* ⟨a. post⟩; die ~ e–s Wechsels verweigern *to dishonour a bill* | ~ an Erfüllungs Statt *compensation delivery* ‖ ~ an Kindes Statt *adoption* **2.** (Zustimmung) *acceptance, adoption* (*of a plan, a doctrine* etc) ‖ *agreement* (e–r S *to a th*); ⟨parl⟩ e–r Vorlage *the passing of a bill* ‖ ~ finden *to wash* (: *that doctrine won't wash*); ~ finden bei jdm *to go down with a p* **3.** (Vermutung) *assumption, supposition*; in der ~, daß *on the assumption* od *supposition that*; unter der sicheren (*or* stillschweigenden) ~, daß *on the understanding that* ‖ (Hypothese) *hypothesis* **4.** [in comp] **~erklärung** f ⟨bes contr⟩ *acceptance* **~stelle** f *filing* od *receiving-office* **~verweigerung** f *non-acceptance* **~verzug** m ⟨jur⟩ *n.-a. of a discharge*

Ann·alen [pl] *annals* [pl]; die ~ der Vergangenheit *the records of the past* ‖ in den ~ der Geschichte verzeichnet sein *to be* (*up*)*on record that* **Annal·ist** m ~en/~en *annalist*

†·**An(n)am** n *An(n)am*, → Vietnam **An(n)am·ite** m *An(namese, An(n)amite*

·**annehmbar** a **1.** *acceptable* (für jdn *to a p*) ‖ (Preis) *reasonable*, [pred] *within reason*; (ohne Risiko) *sporting* (*offer*) ‖ (als beweiskräftig) *admissible* ‖ *plausible* (*argument*) ‖ **2.** (**leidlich**) *passable*; *colourable* (*imitation*) ‖ *reasonable* (*price*) **3.** (**angenehm**) *agreeable*; ⟨fam⟩ *decent* (*cigar*) ‖ (passend) *eligible* (*young man*) **4.** *supposable*; *conceivable* | **≃keit** f *acceptability*

·**an|nehmen** vt/i [h] **I.** vt **A. 1.** (Brief; Geschenk; Einladung) *to accept*; dankend ~ *to a. with thanks* ‖ ich bitte Sie, das Geschenk anzunehmen *I request your kind acceptance of the present, do me the favour of accepting the p.* ‖ (Angebot) *to close with, to accept*; freudig ~ *to jump at* (*a th*) ‖ (e–e Stelle) *to take*; (Arbeit) *to take on* ‖ jds Forderung ~ ⟨Am fam⟩ *to take a p on* ‖ ⟨com⟩ (Wechsel) *to accept, to honour*; nicht ~ *to dishonour* | (**jdn**) *to receive*; Besuch ~ *to receive visitors*; *to be at home*; k–n B. ~ *not to be at home* (*on Sundays*) ‖ jdn an Kindes Statt ~ *to adopt a p* ‖ (Arbeiter etc) *to engage*; *to hire*; *to take on* | (Aufträge) *to undertake* **2.** (**zustimmend**) *to accept*; (Bitte etc) *to accede to*; e–n Vorschlag ~ *to close with, to subscribe to a proposal* ‖ e–n Antrag ~ *to agree to a motion*; .. nicht ~ *to reject* ‖ Entschließung (etc) ~ *to carry a resolution*; einstimmig angenommen w *to be carried unanimously* ‖ ⟨parl⟩ Gesetzentwurf ~ *to pass a bill* ‖ ⟨jur⟩ e–e Anklage ~ *to find a true bill* | die Herausforderung ~ *to pick* (od *take*) *up the gauntlet*; (Wette) *to take* (*on*) | (zulassen) *to admit* ‖ ⟨univ⟩ (Dissertation) *to approve* **3.** ⟨übtr⟩ (**P**) (sich zu eigen m) *to adopt*; nicht ~ *to refuse* ‖ (Titel, Namen etc) *to adopt* ‖ (Gewohnheit etc) *to contract, to acquire, to pick up* ‖ (Religion etc) *to embrace* | e–n Rat ~ von jdm *to take a p's advice* ‖ Vernunft ~ *to listen to reason* | sich [dat] etw ~ *to take a th to heart* | (**S**) der Magen nimmt feste Nahrung nicht an *the stomach refuses solid food* ‖ der Stoff nimmt leicht Schmutz an *the fabric soils easily* od *quickly* ‖ (Farbe, Glanz etc) *to take, to absorb*; das Tuch nimmt die Farbe gut an *the cloth dyes well* **4.** (**vorübergehend**) [vgl. anlegen] (Aussehen, Charakter, Gestalt, Miene) *to put on, to take on, to assume* ‖ (Haltung) *to take up, to assume* **B.** ([Worte, Tatsachen] **hinnehmen, voraussetzen, verstehen**) *to accept* (*as true, etc*) ‖ *to assume* (*a th*; daß etw ist *a th to be*; *that*); *to take* (*a th*) *for granted* ‖ wie wir ~ *as we take it* ‖ selbstverständlich (*or* sicher) ~ *to understand* (*that*) ‖ ich nehme es mit Bestimmtheit an! ⟨Am⟩ *I guess!*; ich nahm an, er sagte .. *I understood him to say*; man nahm an, daß er sagen wollte *he was understood to imply* ‖ man kann mit Sicherheit ~ *it can be safely assumed*; das Beste f e–n ~ *to give a p the benefit of the doubt* | **als möglich ~** *to suppose*; ⟨jur⟩ ich wage als m. anzunehmen *I suggest* (*that*) ‖ angenommen, daß *put the case that* ‖ nehmen wir an .., angenommen .. *suppose* (od *supposing*) ..; angenommen wir gingen *suppose* (*–sing*) *we went*, .. er wäre hier geboren *suppose* (*–sing*) *him born here* ‖ (willkürlich) angenommen *assumptive* | (**vermuten**) *to suppose* (*that*); daß jd, etw ist *a th, a p to be*); ich nehme an, daß er Künstler ist *I suppose him* (*to be*) *an artist*; man nimmt an, daß er abreist *he is supposed to leave* **C.** ⟨hunt⟩ **1.** e–n Hund ~ *to attach a hound to the leash* **2.** (of dogs) die Spur ~ *to take up the scent* **3.** (*of game*) jdn ~ *to charge*; *turn on a p* **D. sich jds, e-r S ~** *to take care of a p, a th*; *to look after a p*; ⟨übtr⟩ *to accept action on a matter* ‖ sich e–r S ~ *to take a th up*; *to attend to a th*; sich e–r guten S ~ *to espouse* (od *to stand up for*) *a good cause* **II.** vi [ell] *to accept the invitation* ‖ (bei Tisch) *to help o.s.*

·**annehmenswert** a = annehmbar 1. 2. 3.

·**Annehmer** m ~s/~ *accepter, receiver*; ⟨com⟩ = Akzeptant ·**annehmlich** a = annehmbar 1. 2. 3. ·**Annehmlichkeit** f ~/~en *convenience*; *agreeableness*; die idealen ~en (e–s Grundstückes etc) *the amenities* [pl]; die ~en des Lebens (etc) *the comforts* od *sweets of life*

annekt·ieren vt [h] *to annex* **Annektierung** f ~/~en *annexation* **Ann·ex** m **1.** (Beilage) *annex* (zu *to*); *enclosure*; *accessories* [pl] **2.** (Anbau) *annex* **Annexi·on** f *annexation*

·**an|niesen** vt [h] jdn ~ *to sneeze in a p's face* ‖ °jdn ~ → anhauchen 2. °·**Annieser** m ~s/~ *snotting*; ⟨school sl⟩ *snubber*; ⟨mil euph⟩ → Anschiß

annihil·ieren vt [h] *to annihilate*

·**anno** (L) adv *in the year* .. ‖ °~ dazumal *of yore* ‖ °v ~ dazumal *time out of mind, from time immemorial*; [attr] *as old as the hills*; Bräuche v ~ dazumal, °v ~ Tobak *customs of old time*; *ancient customs*

Ann·once [a'nõsə] f (Fr) ~/~n *advertisement*; ⟨Am⟩ *ad* **Ann·oncen- ~büro** n, **~expedition** f *advertising-office* **~wesen** n *publicity*

Annonc·eur [–'sœr] m ~s/~e ⟨hotel⟩ *kitchen-clerk* **annonc·ieren** vt [h] *to advertise*

Annuit·ät f ~/~en *annuity*

annull·ierbar a *rescindable, etc* **annull·ieren** vt [h] ⟨jur⟩ *to annul, to cancel, to void, to nullify*; *to revoke*; (Urteil) *to quash* **Annull·ierung** f *annulment, nullification, cancellation*; *revocation*

An·ode f ~/~n ⟨el⟩ (Ggs Kathode) *anode, positive electrode*; ⟨Am⟩ *plate*

An·oden- ⟨wir, etc⟩ **~batterie** f *anode battery* **~gleichrichter** m *anode bend detector* **~kennlinie** f *anode bend* **~kreis** m *plate-circuit* **~schutznetz** n *anode screening-grid* **~spannung** f *anode potential* **an·odisch** a *anodal*

°·**an|öden** vt [h] jdn ~ *to bore* (od *tire out*) *a p* (mit *with*) ‖ to annoy *od* irritate a p

anom·al a *anomalous* ‖ *abnormal, irregular, unusual* **Anomal·ie** f ~/~n **1.** *anomaly*; *irregularity, abnormity* **2.** ⟨astr⟩ (Winkelabstand) *anomaly*

An·one f ~/~n ⟨bot⟩ *sweet-sop*

anon·ym 1. a *anonymous* (*writer*; *letter*); ~e P *anonym* **2.** adv *anonymously* **Anonymit·ät** f ~/ *anonymity* **An·onymus** m ~/–mi *anonym, anonymous person* (od *outhor, writer*)

An·opheles f ∼/∼ ⟨ent⟩ *anopheles*

·Anorak m ∼s/∼s *anorak*

·an|ordnen vt [h] **1.** *to arrange*; sich in Reihen ∼ (S) *to arrange o.s. in lines* ‖ *to order, to regulate* ‖ (etw) reihen–, schichtenweise ∼ *to tier*; richtig ∼ *to adjust* | (Truppen) *to dispose, array*; *to put in order*; *to marshal* ‖ *to order, regulate* **2.** (Sorge tragen) ich werde ∼, daß er dort ist *I shall arrange for him to be there* | (befehlen) *to decree*; (Vormarsch) *to order* ‖ ∼ daß etw geschieht *to order a th to be done*; ihm wurde Ruhe angeordnet *he was ordered rest* **·Anordner** m ∼s/∼ *arranger*; *organiser* **·Anordnung** f ∼/∼en **1.** *arrangement, disposal, disposition* (*of troops*) ‖ ⟨Lit & arts⟩ *grouping*; *structure* **2.** (Vorkehrung) ∼en treffen *to make arrangements* od *dispositions* | (Befehl) *direction, order*; [mst pl] ∼en *directions, instructions, orders* [pl]; ∼en treffen *to give directions, instructions, orders* (daß etw geschieht *for a th to be done*; *that .. should*)

·anorganisch a ⟨chem⟩ *inorganic*; *mineral*

·anormal a *abnormal*; *anomalous*; → anomal

·an|packen I. vt [h] **1.** jdn ∼ *to catch* (od *lay, seize*) *hold of a p*; *to grip a p tightly, to seize a p firmly* (am Arm *by the arm*); ⟨fam⟩ *to tackle a p* ‖ jdn beim Kragen ∼ *to collar a p* ‖ jdn rauh ∼ ⟨sl⟩ *to man-handle a p* | etw krampfhaft *or* gierig ∼ *to clutch* od *grasp a th* **2.** ⟨übtr⟩ (Aufgabe etc) *to assail, attack*; *to set about a th*; *to take a th on*; pack an! ⟨fam⟩ *pull up your socks*! (Problem) *to tackle*; *to grapple* (od *cope*) *with*; die Schwierigkeit ∼ *to grasp the nettle* ‖ er packte es fest an *he put his shoulder to the wheel* ‖ ein Übel an der Wurzel ∼ *to strike at the root of an evil* ‖ die S am rechten (falschen) Ende ∼, richtig (falsch) ∼ *to have* od *get the right* (*wrong*) *end of the stick* **II.** ≈ n *seizing*; *grip* ‖ *tackling*

·an|passen I. vt [h] **1.** (Kleider) *to fit on* ‖ (anprobieren) *to try on* **2.** (Benehmen, Worte) *to adapt, to accommodate, to adjust*; *to frame*; *to suit* ‖ (e–r S *to a th*); jdm *to a p*); ‖ der Gelegenheit angepaßt s *to fit the occasion* ‖ speziellen Anforderungen (der Kunden) –ge–ßt w können *to meet individual requirements* ⟨a. comp⟩ ‖ an etw –ge–ßt (S) *made to fit into a th* | **sich** e–r S ∼ *to adapt* (od *conform*) *o.s., to conform to a th*; *to humour a th*; sich der Gelegenheit ∼ *to suit the occasion*; sich den Verhältnissen ∼ *to adapt o.s. to circumstances* ‖ ⟨pol⟩ sich ∼ *to trim*; sich den Zeiten ∼ *to trim with the times*; sich vorläufig ∼ *to temporize* | sich jdm ∼ *to humour a p.* ⟨Am⟩ *to fall in with a p's way of living* **II.** ≈ n *fitting*; *trying-on* ‖ → Anpassung

·Anpaßraum m *fitting-room*

·Anpassung f ∼/∼en *adaptation, accommodation, adjustment* (an *to*); *conformity* (an etw *with* od *to a th*); ∼en durchführen *to make adjustments*, (kulturelle) *acculturation*; die Wissenschaft v den ∼en bei Tier u Pflanze *oecology, ecology* **≈sfähig** a *accomodating, adaptive* (an *to*) ‖ *flexible, elastic* (*language*) **~sfähigkeit** f, **~svermögen** n *adaptiveness, adaptability* (an *to*) ‖ *flexibility* **~smensch** m *oppurtunist* **~spolitik** f *opportunism* **~swert** m ⟨eth⟩ *adaptive value*

·an|peilen vt [h] *to aim at, to head toward* (*a th*); e–n Stern ∼ ⟨mar aero⟩ *to bear to a star*

°·an|petzen vt (jdn) (→ angeben) ⟨sl⟩ *to tell* od *squeal on a p*

·Anpfahl m ⟨min⟩ = Anfall 4.

°·an|pfeffern vt [h] *to pep up*

·anpfeifen vi/t [h] ‖ angepfiffen kommen *to come whistling along* | vt °jdn ∼ *to blow a p up*

°·Anpfiff m *snub, rebuke*; ⟨mil sl⟩ *rep, raspberry* ‖ jdm e–n ∼ verpassen *to give a p a reading off*

·an|pflanzen 1. vt [h] (Bäume) *to plant*; *to cultivate* | **sich** ∼ [h] ⟨fig⟩ *to settle, to colonize* **2.** ≈ n *planting*; *plantation* ‖ *settling* **·Anpflanzer** m ∼s/∼ planter; *cultivator* ‖ *settler* **·Anpflanzung** f ∼/∼en **1.** → Anpflanzen **2.** *plantation*; *settlement*; *colony*

°·an|pflaumen I. vt [h] *to poke fun at, to pull* (*a p's*) *leg* **II.** ≈ n *leg-pull* ‖ l Sie doch das ewige ∼! ⟨Am fam⟩ *quit your kidding*

·an|pflocken vt [h] (T) *to peg* (an *to*)

·an|picken vt [h] etw ∼ *to peck at a th*

·an|pinseln vt [h] *to daub over*; → anmalen

°·an|plärren vt [h] = anbrüllen

°·an|pöbeln vt jdn ∼ *to mob a p* **·Anpöbelung** f *mobbing*

·an|pochen vi [h] *to knock* (an *at*)

·Anprall m ∼(e)s/∼e *collision*; *impingement, impact* (auf *on*; gegen *against*); unter dem ∼ e–r S *under the impact of a th* ‖ ⟨mil⟩ *shock*; die Wucht des ersten ∼s aushalten *to bear the brunt of fighting* ‖ ⟨fig⟩ *shock* **·an|prallen** vi [s] *to bound* (od *dash*) (gegen *against*)

·an|prangern vt [h] (jdn) *to pillory* (als *as*); *to gibbet a p, expose a p to public ridicule*

·Anprangerung f *denunciation*

·an|preisen vt [h] ⟨mst com⟩ (jdn; Waren durch Reklame) *to puff, boom*; ⟨sl⟩ *to boost*, ⟨Am sl⟩ *to ballyhoo* ‖ ⟨fig⟩ *to plug* **·Anpreisung** f ∼/∼en *fulsome recommendation* od *praise* (*of a p, a th*); ⟨mst com⟩ (durch Reklame) *puff, puffing*; *boom*, ⟨sl⟩ *boost*, ⟨Am sl⟩ *ballyhoo*

·Anprobe f *fitting*; letzte ∼ *final f.*; sie kam zur ∼ *she came to be fitted, went for a f.g* **~raum** m ⟨tail⟩ *f.g room* **·an|probieren** vt [h] *to try on, to fit on*; *to see the clothes on*

·an|pumpen vt [h] *to tap*, ⟨sl⟩ *to touch a p* (um *for*), ⟨sl⟩ *to hit* (*a p*) *for a touch*

·an|pusten vt [h] etw *to breathe upon a th*

·Anputz m ∼es/ *gaudy dress*; *showy finery*; *frills, furbelows* [pl] **·an|putzen** vt [h] (jdn) *to trick* (od *deck*) out; *to spruce up* ‖ (Gegenstand) *to decorate* | **sich** ∼ *to dress up*; *to bedizen* (od *prink, titivate*) *o.s.*; *to put on* (*one's*) *frills*

°·an|qualmen vt [h] jdn ∼ (beim Rauchen) *to blow the smoke in a p's face*

·Anrainer m ∼s/∼ = Anlieger, ⟨agr⟩ *neighbour*

°·an|ranzen vt [h] = °anfahren, anschnauzen

·an|raten 1. vt [h] jdm etw ∼ *to advise* od *recommend a p to do a th* ‖ jdm dringend ∼ *to urge a p* (*to do*) **2.** ≈ n *counsel, advice*; auf sein ∼ *on* od *by his advice*

·an|rauchen vt [h] (Zigarre) *to begin to smoke, to light* ‖ (Pfeife) *to colour*; *to season* | jdn ∼ *to puff the smoke in a p's face*

·an|räuchern vt [h] (etw) *to smoke slightly*; *to fumigate* **·Anräucherung** f *fumigation*

·anrechenbar a → anrechnungsfähig

·an|rechnen vt [h] **1.** (**berechnen**) jdm Geld ∼ *to charge a p* (für *for*); wieviel rechnen Sie mir dafür an? *how much do you charge me for it*? jdm zuviel ∼ *to overcharge a p* (*for*) ‖ (belasten) jdm (e–n Betrag) ∼ *to put down* (*a sum*) *to a p's account* (od *debit*); *to debit a p with* (*a sum*) | ⟨übtr⟩ jdm etw ∼ *to lay a th to a p's charge*; etw der Schuld jds ∼ *to impute a th to the fault of a p*; ich will's dir diesmal nicht ∼ *I'll pass it over this once* **2.** (**gutschreiben**) jdm e–n Betrag ∼ *to enter* (od *place, put*) *a sum to a p's credit, to allow a p a sum, to credit a sum to a p*; jdm etw auf ein altes Auto ∼ *to make a p an allowance on an old car*; (Darlehn) *to set off* (auf *against*) ‖ | ⟨übtr⟩ *to take into account*; nicht ∼ *to disregard* ‖ (Dienstzeit) *to reckon*; jdm etw ∼ *to credit a p with*, ihm wurden 3 Jahre angerechnet *he was credited with 3 years' service* ‖ jdm etw **hoch** (od als Verdienst, zur Ehre) ∼ *to give a p credit for a th* ‖ ich rechne ihm s–e Verdienste hoch an *I value his services greatly* | **es sich zur Ehre ~** *to deem it an honour* (*to do*) **·Anrechnung** f ∼/ **1.** *the charging*; *putting to a p's account* | ⟨übtr⟩ jdm etw in ∼ bringen *to lay a th to a p's charge* **2.** *putting to a p's credit* ‖ ⟨übtr⟩ etw in ∼

bringen *to make allowance for a th*; sie brachten ihm s–e Jugend in ~ *they made allowance for his youth* ‖ es wurden ihm 3 Jahre in ~ gebracht *they allowed him 3 years service in fixing his salary* ≂**sfähige** Dienstjahre *reckonable service*

·**Anrecht** n ~(e)s/~e *right, claim, title* (auf etw *to a th*); erstes ~ *first refusal* (auf *of*) ‖ ein ~ h (od besitzen) auf etw *to be entitled to a th*; ⟨übtr⟩ .. auf jds Hilfe *to have a claim on a p's help*

·**Anrede** f ~/~n **1.** *address* ‖ (feierliche *harangue*) (des Papstes) *allocution* ‖ ⟨rhet⟩ (lebhafte) *apostrophe* ‖ e–e ~ richten an jdn *to give an address to a p*; *to address a p* **2.** (~form) *form* (od *formula, mode*) *of address*; die ~ des Erzbischofs ist 'Your Grace' *the archbishop is addressed as Your Grace*; ~ im Brief → ergeben, geehrt, lieb **~fall** m *vocative* (*case*)

·**an|reden** vt [h] **1.** (jdn) *to address, to talk* (od *speak*) *to* (*a p*) ‖ jdn deutsch ~ *to speak to a p in* (⟨fig⟩ *plain*) *German* ‖ (feierlich) *to harangue*; (lebhaft) *to apostrophize* | (ansprechen) *to accost* ‖ *to approach* **2.** (jdn) ~ als .. *to address a p as ..*; jdn mit Sir ~ *to call .. Sir*

·**an|regen** vt/i [h] **I.** vt **1.** (**jdn**) *to animate, stimulate, excite*; *to galvanize* (*into action*); *to inspire, interest* | jdn ~ z etw *to incite, invite a p to a th*; ..z tun *to incite, bring, get a p to do* | **sich** durch Alkoholgenuß ~ ⟨fam⟩ *to stimulate* | (**Geist,** Neugierde, Tätigkeit) *to animate, to stimulate*; (Mut) *to raise*; (Nerven, Organ, Haut) *to stimulate*; den Appetit ~ *to give an edge to the appetite* ‖ → angeregt, anregend **2.** (**zur Sprache bringen**) *to suggest* (*a th*; z tun *doing*; *that .. should*); *to propose* (*a th*); ich will das mal ~ *I'll suggest it* ‖ (Frage) *to raise, start* **II.** vi **1.** ~ **zu** *to add to*; *to increase, animate*; es wird zur Unterhaltung ~ *it will animate the conversation* **2.** Kaffee regt an *coffee is stimulating* od *acts as a stimulant* ·**anregend** a *animating*; *interesting* (*p*) | *challenging, stimulating*; *suggestive* (*article*); *fruity* (*language*) ‖ ⟨med⟩ *stimulating, stimulant, stimulative*; ~es Mittel *stimulant* ‖ *suggestive* (*question*), (→ Suggestivfrage)

·**Anreger** m ~s/~ *proposer*; *mover* (*of a proposal*)

·**Anregung** f ~/~en **1.** *stimulation, animation*; *incitation, stimulation*; *impulse, incitement, stimulus* (zu etw *to a th*) **2.** *suggestion, hint*; *intimation*; auf ~ jds *at the suggestion of a p* ‖ die ~ geben, man solle .. *to move that ..* **~smittel** n *energizer* ⟨fam⟩ *stay-awake pill, etc*; → Erregungs– ⟨bes *el*⟩

·**an|reiben** vt [h] (Farben) *to grind and prepare*

·**an|reichern** vt [h] (Erze; Brot; Uran; Kraftstoff/Luftgemisch, etc) *to enrich* ‖ (Getränk) mit Alkohol ~ *to needle*

·**Anreicherung** f *the turning of ore to better account*; *raising of the yield* od *productivity of ore*

·**an|reihen** vt [h] (Perlen) *to string* ‖ (durch lange Stiche) *to tack* ‖ ⟨übtr⟩ *to add, join* (an *to*); **sich** an e–a ~ *to form in a row* ‖ sich würdig ~ *to be a worthy successor of* od *to* (*a p, a th*) ·**Anreihung** f ⟨übtr⟩ *sequence, succession* (*of events*)

·**Anreim** m ~s/~e *alliteration*

·**Anreiß- ~vorrichtung** f *marking device*

·**an|reißen** vt/i [h] **1.** vt (Papier) *to begin to tear* | Vorräte, Kiste Zigarren etc ~ → anbrechen **2.** vi (= Kunden werben) *to tout*

·**Anreißer** m ~s/~ ⟨com⟩ *tout*

·**an|reiten** vi/t **1.** vi [s] er kam angeritten *he came riding along, he came along on horseback*; *he rode up* **2.** vt [h] jdn ~ *to ride against a p*

·**Anreiz** m ~es/~e *incitation, incitement, impulse, stimulus, incentive* (zu *to*; z tun *to doing*); *inducement* (zur Ehe) | *fillip, stimulus* (f *to*)

·**an|reizen** vt [h] (jdn) *to incite, to instigate, prompt, stimulate* (z *to*; z tun *to do*) ‖ (verlocken) *to tempt* (z *to*; z tun *to do*) | [abs] der Lohn reizt an *the reward is tempting* ·**anreizend** a *interesting* (*conversation*) ·**Anreizung** f ~/~en = Anreiz

°·**an|rempeln 1.** vt [h] jdn ~ *to push against a p*; *to jostle a p* ‖ ⟨ftb⟩ *to charge* ‖ ⟨übtr⟩ *to pester a p* **2.** ≂ n ·**Anrempelung** f *jostle*; *elbowing* ‖ ⟨ftb⟩ *charge* ‖ ⟨übtr⟩ *pestering*

·**an|rennen** vi/t **1.** vi [s] angerannt k *to come running along* | ~ gegen (jdn, etw) *to rush upon*; *to run up, to run full tilt against* ‖ ⟨übtr⟩ *to battle* (od *butt*, ⟨Am⟩ *buck*; *struggle*) *against a th*; *to buck* od *stem a th* **2.** vt [h] jdn ~ *to jostle a p*; *to cannon against a p*; mit dem Arm ~ *to elbow a p* ‖ (Schiff) *to foul*

·**Anrichte** f ~/~n ⟨cul⟩ *dresser, sideboard*; (Raum) *servery* ·**an|richten** vt [h] **1.** (das Essen) *to serve up, to dish up* ‖ (Salat) *to dress* ‖ es ist angerichtet *dinner is ready* od *served* **2.** ⟨fig⟩ *to cause, to occasion*; *to bring about* ‖ Schaden, Unheil ~ *to do damage, to do* od *work mischief*; gr Sch. wurde angerichtet *great mischief was wrought* (von, durch *by*); Verwüstung ~ *to cause havoc*; .. *the storm worked* od *wrought great ruin* (Schaden); °etw Schönes ~ *to get into mischief*; *to make sad work of it*; ° da hast du was Schönes angerichtet! *there now, you've made a pretty muddle* (od *fine mess of it*)!, *you put your foot in it right up to the knee*! ·**Anrichter** m ~s/~ ⟨met⟩ *assayer*

·**an|riechen** vt [h] etw ~ *to* (*take a*) *smell at* (⟨Am⟩ *of*) *a th* ‖ man roch es ihm an, daß er getrunken hatte *he smelt of drink*

·**an|rollen** vi [s] ⟨aero⟩ *to taxi*

·**anrüchig** a *disreputable, notorious, shady* (*p*); *shady, fishy, smelly, cloudy, hole-and-corner* (*transactions*) ‖ *foul* (*language*) ·**Anrüchigkeit** f ~/~en *disrepute, ill repute*; *notoriety* ‖ *shadiness, fishiness, cloudiness*

·**Anrück- ~sperre** f ⟨rail⟩ *approach lock*

·**an|rücken I.** vt/i **1.** vt [h] (Stuhl etc) *to bring* od *move near* (an die Wand *the wall* od *to the w.*) **2.** vi [s] *to draw near, to approach* ‖ ⟨mil⟩ *to advance* (gegen *against, on*) **II.** ≂ n *approach* ‖ ⟨mil⟩ *advance*

·**an|rudern I.** vi [h] angerudert k *to come rowing along* ‖ *to open the rowing season* **II.** ~ n ⟨fam a.⟩ *pipe-opener*

·**Anruf** m ~(e)s/~e *call*; *hail* ‖ ⟨mil⟩ (des Postens) *challenge* | ⟨telph⟩ (*telephone*) call | **~er** m ~s/~ *hailer, etc*

·**an|rufen I.** vt [h] **1.** jdn ~ *to call to a p*; (laut) *to shout to a p* ‖ ⟨mil⟩ (of sentry) *to challenge* | (Schiff) *to hail* **2.** (anflehen) *to invoke, implore* (*a p*) ‖ jds Hilfe ~ *to evoke the assistance of a p*; jdn um Hilfe (etc) ~ *to call on a p* (od *appeal to a p*) *for help* | ⟨jur⟩ jdn zum Zeugen ~ *to call a p to* (od *as a*) *witness* ‖ e–e höhere Instanz ~ *to appeal to a higher court* **3.** ⟨telph⟩ (jdn) *to* (*tele*)*phone* (*a p*), *to call* od *ring* (*a p*) *up*; rufe mich an *give me a call* od *ring*, ⟨fam⟩ *'phone me*; Sie wurden heute –ge– *there was a call for you today*; Sie wurden viermal –ge– *you had four calls, Sir* **II.** ≂ n *calling* (jds *to a p*); ⟨bes mar⟩ *hail*(*ing*)

·**Anrufung** f ~/~en **1.** *invocation*; (jds *to* od *of a p*) ⟨a. übtr⟩ **2.** ⟨jur⟩ *appeal* (e–r höheren Instanz *to a higher court*)

·**an|rühren 1.** vt [h] (etw, jdn) *to touch*; *handle* ‖ (aufrühren) *to stir*; *to mix* (*with*) ‖ rühr es nicht an *don't meddle with it*; rühre nicht daran *leave it alone, let it rest* | ⟨cul⟩ (Speisen) ich konnte nichts ~ *I couldn't touch anything*; ich rühre k–n Schnaps mehr an *I'm off gin for good* **2.** ≂ n *touch*; *handling*

ans = an das; bis ~ Ende *to the last*

·**Ansage** f ~/~n **1.** *announcement* ‖ *notification, intimation* ‖ → Kampf ≂ **2.** [in comp] *announcing* (*microphone, room*) ·**an|sagen** vt [h]

1. *to announce* ⟨a. wir⟩ ‖ **sich** z Besuch ~ *to announce one's visit* (bei jdm *to a p*) | ⟨cards⟩ die Trumpffarbe ~ *to declare the trump(-suit)*; Sie sagen an *it's your call* **2.** (Sitzung) *to notify, intimate* (jdm *to a p*) ‖ (öffentlich) *to make public, to proclaim, to publish* ‖ der Beginn des Festes ist auf 11 Uhr angesagt *the festivity is timed to begin at 11 o'clock* | ⟨übtr⟩ jdm (e–r S) den Kampf ~ *to challenge a p; to throw* (od *fling*) *down the gauntlet to a p* (*a th*) **·Ansager** m ~s/~ ⟨wir, theat⟩ *announcer*; *conferencier* (Fr); ⟨Am⟩ *Master of Ceremony*, ⟨fam⟩ *M. C.*, *emcee* ‖ ⟨rad telv⟩ *compère* [Fr]; (Nachrichten≃) *newscaster* ‖ ⟨mil⟩ (bei Scharfschießen) *spotter*

·an|sammeln vt [h] *to collect, to gather* ‖ (anhäufen) *to accumulate*; *to amass* ‖ (Zorn) *to battle up* | **sich** ~ *to collect, to gather* ‖ *to accumulate* ‖ (of forces) *to converge* (auf *on*) **·Ansammlung** f ~/~en (Häufung, Menge) *collection* (*of facts*; *of dust*) *accumulation* (*of rubbish*); *hoarding* (*of treasures*) ‖ *congestion* (*of population*); gr ~en v Menschen [pl] *crowds* [pl]

·ansässig s (ständig wohnhaft) *resident*; ⟨ec⟩ *residentiary*; nicht ~ *non-resident* ‖ [pred] *domiciled* (in *in*) ‖ ~ s *to reside*; ⟨übtr⟩ *to be domiciled* (*in*) | (Ggs *nomadic*) *settled*; sich ~ m, ~ w *to settle* (in *in*) **·Ansässige**: der ~ (ein ~r), die ~ *the resident*; der Nicht≃ *the non-resident* **·Ansässigkeit** f ~/ *residence*

·Ansatz m ~es/≃e **I.** [abstr] **1.** → Ansetzen ‖ in den ≃en stecken bleiben *to get stuck at the very outset* ‖ ⟨biol & fig⟩ *rudimentary stage*, | ⟨übtr⟩ (f die Lösung e–r Frage) *starting point* ‖ ⟨mil⟩ beim ~ des Angriffs *at the outset of* ..; *commitment* (*of forces*); ~ v Aufklärung *conduct of reconnaissance* **2.** (Anrechnung) *account*, jdm etw in ~ bringen *to put to a p's account* ‖ *charge*; *fee* (*in a bill*) | (Abschätzung) *valuation, quotation, rate* ‖ *estimate* **3.** ⟨math⟩ *statement*; *arrangement* (*of a sum*) **II.** ⟨gym⟩ (Anlauf → d.) *run* | ⟨übtr⟩ *start*; e–n ~ m z etw *to make a start on a th, to start a th* ‖ ~ zu e–r Lösung *an approach to a solution* | ⟨mus⟩ (Einsatz) *attack* | ⟨zoo⟩ *rudiment* (zu *of*) ‖ → Anflug 3. **III.** (Angesetztes) (in e–m Gefäß etc) *coating, deposit, fur, sediment*; *crust* (*of wine*) **IV.** (angesetztes Stück) *extension* (an *to*); *lengthening-piece* ‖ ⟨arch⟩ (e–s Bogens) *spring* ‖ ⟨mus⟩ *mouthpiece* (*of a wind-instrument*) ‖ ⟨tech⟩ Rohr≃ *socket*; mit e–m ~ versehen *to socket* **~feile** f *hand-file* **~rohr** n *additional pipe*; *lengthening tube* | ⟨phon⟩ *passages* [pl] *above the glottis* **~stück** n *lengthening-piece* (od *bar*) **~stutzen** m *adapter piece* **~teil** m → Brause

·an|säuern vt [h] *to* (*mix with*) *leaven*

°**·an|saufen** vt [h] sich e–n ~ *to drink one's fill*; *to get drunk*

·an|saugen 1. vt [h] *to prime* (*a pump*) ‖ **sich** ~ *to become attached by suction* ‖ der Blutegel hat sich angesogen *the leech has taken* **2.** ≃ n *suction*

·Ansaug- ~leitung f ⟨mot⟩ *intake* **~luft** f *induced air* **~rohr** n *induction manifold* **~schacht** m *air duct* **~stutzen** m *air-scoop* **~volumen** n *inspired volume* **~vorrichtung** f ⟨typ⟩ *sucker apparatus*

·an|säuseln vt [h] (of the wind) etw ~ *to blow* od *breathe gently upon a th*; *to fan a th*

·Ansbach n (Stadt in Mittelfranken)

·an|schaffen vt [h] **1.** (etw) *to procure* → beschaffen, liefern | jdm etw ~ *to buy, get, procure a p a th* od *a th for a p*; sich etw ~ *to buy, purchase, acquire a th*; *to get* od *buy o.s. a th* od *a th for o.s.* **2.** ⟨com⟩ (überweisen) *to remit* **3.** vi [abs] das schafft an! ⟨teens⟩ *there is money in it*!

·Anschaffung f ~/~en **1.** *procuring, procurement*; → Lieferung ‖ *acquisition, purchase*; ~en m *to make purchases*, wir können durchaus k–e ~en m *we can't afford to buy anything*
2. ⟨com⟩ *remittance* **~skosten** [pl], **~spreis** m *prime cost, purchase-cost, cost-price*; *cost of acquisition*; *capital cost* **~swert** m *purchase-value*; *acquisition value*

·an|schäften vt [h] (Stiefel) *to top*; *to put tops to* (*a boot*) | (Beil etc) *to helve* ‖ (Gewehr) *to stock*

·an|schauen vt [h] (jdn) *to look at* (*a p*); *to view a p* ‖ (geistig) *to contemplate*; ⟨philos⟩ (durch Intuition) *to envisage*

·anschaulich 1. a (konkret) *concrete, plastic* (*illustration*); ~e Darstellung *demonstration, illustration*; *vivid* (*picture*), ~es Bild *illustration* ‖ etw ~ m *to demonstrate, elucidate, illustrate a th* (durch *by*); (S) *to be illustrative of a th* ‖ *clear*; *plain*; jdm etw ~ m *to make a th clear to a p, to give a p a clear idea of a th, to explain a th to a p* | (lebhaft) *descriptive, graphic* (*narrative*); *picturesque, vivid* (*description*) **2.** adv *plastically* ‖ *descriptively, graphically, vividly* ‖ ~ empfindend *eidetic* ‖ ~ erläutern *to be illustrative of* | **≃keit** f ~/~en *plasticity* ‖ *clearness, distinctness* ‖ *descriptiveness, graphicness, vividness*

·Anschauung f ~/~en **1.** (sinnliche) *sight, view*; der ~ dienend ⟨aero⟩ *demonstration* (*flight*) | (Betrachten) *contemplation* **2.** (Vorstellung) *perception, notion*; *idea* ‖ etw zur ~ bringen *to elucidate, illustrate a th* | (Meinung) *view, opinion* (über *of*), was ist Ihre ~ darüber? *what are your views on this matter*; nach dieser ~ *from this point of view* ‖ Art der ~ *approach* **3.** ⟨philos⟩ *perception* ‖ *cognition* | (intuitive) *intuition* ‖ *outlook*; → Weltanschauung

·Anschauungs- ~bild n ⟨psych⟩ sinnlich empfundenes ~ *eidetic image*; in ~ern (*to see*) *eidetically* **~material** n n *visual aids* [pl], *illustrative material* **~stunde** f *object lesson* **~unterricht** m *object teaching*; *object-lessons* [pl] **~vermögen** n *intuitive power* **~weise** f *mentality, mode of thinking*; die konventionelle ~ e–r Zeit *the conventions* [pl] *of a period*

·Anschein m ~(e)s/ *appearance, semblance* (: *the semblance of completeness*) | dem ~ **nach** *in appearance* ‖ allem ~ nach *to all appearance(s)*; dem äußeren ~ nach *to outward view*; → Wahrscheinlichkeit | **es hat, erweckt** den ~ *it appears* od *seems to me* (als wenn *as if*); es hat ganz den ~ *there is every appearance* (daß *that*; als ob *as if*; als ob sich das Wetter besserte *of the weather improving*) | (P) den ~ **erwecken** *to have the* (od *wear an*) *appearance* (z s *of being*) ‖ er gibt sich den ~ *he assumes an appearance* (z s *of being*); *he makes believe* (*to do, to be*); → tun

·anscheinend 1. a *apparent* ‖ [statt: scheinbar] *seeming* **2.** adv *apparently* ‖ [statt: scheinbar] *in appearance*; *seemingly*

·an|scheren vt [h] ⟨weav & mar⟩ *to warp*

·an|schicken vrefl [h] sich ~ z etw *to prepare for*; *he set to work* od *about his work* ‖ sich ~ z tun *to compose* (od *prepare, set, set out, set to*; ⟨Am⟩ *fix*) *to do* (od *doing*); *to dispose o.s. to do*; *to set about doing*

·an|schieben vt/i [h] **1.** vt (Wagen etc) *to give* (*a th*) *a swing, to set* (*a th*) *going* **2.** vi (im Kegelspiel) *to bowl first*

·an|schienen vt [h] ⟨surg⟩ (Bein) *to splint* ‖ ⟨tech⟩ *to fix* od *join with iron bands*

·an|schießen vt/i [h] **I.** vt **1.** jdn ~ *to shoot at a p* (: *he was shot at by* ..) ‖ *to feather*, (im Flügel) *to wing* (*a bird*) **2.** (Gewehr) *to test, try* **3.** ⟨typ⟩ (Bogen) *to supplement, add* **II.** vi **1.** ⟨übtr⟩ angeschossen k *to come rushing* od *shooting along* **2.** (bei Festen etc) *to shoot first* **3.** ⟨minr⟩ *to crystallize* **III.** ≃ n ⟨mil⟩ *gun trials* [pl], ⟨tech⟩ *trial* od *proof firing* ‖ ⟨minr⟩ *crystallization* ‖ → Anschuß

·an|schimmeln vi [s] *to begin to get mouldy*

·**an|schirren** vt/i [h] **1.** vt (Pferd) *to harness; to get in;* **2.** vi *to harness the horse(s)*

°·**Anschiß** m -sses/-sse ⟨mil⟩ *rep; blowing up; H.E.* (= *high explosive*) ‖ → Anpfiff, Annieser

·**Anschlag** m ~(e)s/∸e **A. 1.** → Anschlagen **2.** *striking* (an, gegen *at, against*); der ~ der Wellen ans Ufer *the breaking of the waves against* od *on the shore* ‖ *stroke* (*of a bell, clock*) ‖ Versteckspiel mit ~ *hide-and-seek* **3.** ⟨übtr mus⟩ *touch* (*of a pianist*, etc; weich *soft*, hart *heavy*) **4.** (of dogs) *challenge, bark* **5.** (beim Stricken etc) *the taking-up of the first stitch* **B.** (Angeschlagenes) *poster, placard, bill;* e–n ~ m *to post up a notice;* (etw) durch ~ bekannt m *to placard* (*a th*); ∸e an e–r Mauer m *to post a wall with notices* **C. 1.** ⟨mil⟩ (schußfertige Haltung) *aiming* od *firing position;* ~ sitzend *sitting p.*, stehend *standing p;* ~ kniend! *present* [pri'zent] *kneeling!* ‖ im ~ *at the present, taking aim;* in ~ gehen, im ~ liegen od s *to take aim at;* ein Gewehr im ~ h *to level a gun* (auf *at*) ‖ der ~ liegend (etc) aufgelegt *the present lying, with rest,* der ~ liegend freihändig *the p. l., without support* | (Gewehrkolben) *butt(-end)* **2.** ⟨übtr⟩ ~ auf jdn (*or* jds Leben) *attempt upon a p's life,* e–n ~ auf jdn m *to attempt a p's life* ‖ hinterlistiger ~ *design* (gegen jdn *against a p*); *plot, scheme, machination;* ⟨Am sl⟩ *frame-up* ‖ Anschläge m *to conspire, plot* (*against*) ‖ der ~ schlug fehl *the plot miscarried* (od *failed*); (Plan) *project, plan* **D.** ⟨übtr⟩ (Abschätzung) *estimate* (→ Voranschlag); *valuation, rate; calculation, computation;* nach oberflächlichem ~ *at a rough estimate* ‖ in ~ bringen *to take into account* od *consideration; to allow for, to make allowance for a th* **E.** ⟨tech⟩ *head, stock* (*of a T-square*) ‖ (Hemmvorrichtung) *stop;* ⟨telph⟩ *finger-stop* **~brett** n *notice* od *display* od ⟨bes Am⟩ *bulletin board* **~geschwindigkeit** f (Rakete) *impact velocity* **~kolben** m (am Gewehr) *extension stock* **~platte** f *stop plate* **~sarten** f [pl] *firing positions* [pl] ‖ (Klavier∸) *touch nuances* **~säule** f *advertising* (od *poster*) *pillar; hoardings* [pl] **~stange** f *stop-rod* **~tafel** f = ~brett **~- u Zielübungen** f pl *dry firing* **~winkel** m *square* **~zettel** m *bill, poster, placard*

·**an|schlagen** vt/i **I.** vt **A. 1.** den Rand e–r Tasse ~ *to chip the edge of a cup;* die Tassen sind -ge- *there is a chip out of the cups, the cups have got a chip on the edge;* der Spiegel war -ge- *the mirror was slivered;* → anspringen **2.** (Glokke) *to sound;* (Taste, Akkord) *to strike;* (Klavier, Saite) *to touch* ‖ (of bells) (Zeit) *to toll* | ⟨fig⟩ den Ton ~ *to call the tune; to set the tone of;* e–n Ton ~ *to adopt a tone;* e–n anderen Ton ~ *to change one's tune, to sing another tune* ‖ immer dasselbe Thema ~ *to recur constantly to* (od ⟨fam⟩ *to harp on*) *the same subject* **3.** ⟨min⟩ e–e Ader ~ *to strike a vein* ‖ Faß ~: → anstechen **B.** (befestigen) *to (af)fix, fasten* (an *to*); (mit Nägeln) *to nail* (an *to*) ‖ (Plakat) *to post* (an *at*); *to post, put, stick up;* (Bekanntmachung) *to placard* (an, auf *on*) ‖ (Haus zwecks Versteigerung) *to put up for sale* | (mit langen Stichen anheften) *to tack* **C.** ⟨mil⟩ (Flinte) *to level* (auf *at*) **D.** ⟨übtr⟩ (abschätzen) (Kosten etc) *to estimate, to value, to calculate;* → schätzen ‖ z hoch ~ (Haus) *to overestimate;* (Fähigkeiten) *to overrate;* der Wert der S kann nicht z hoch -ge- w *the value of the matter cannot be placed too high* ‖ z gering *or* niedrig ~ *to underestimate; to underrate, to understate* **II.** vi **A. 1.** *to knock* od *strike* (an *against, on*); mit dem Kopfe ~ *to knock* od *strike one's head* (*against*) ‖ (of waves) *to be thrown* (an *on*) **2.** (beim Spiel) *to strike first, to strike the first blow* **3.** ⟨übtr⟩ (of bells) *to toll* **4.** (of dogs) *to give tongue, to bark* **B.** ⟨mil⟩ ~ auf jdn *to take aim at a p* **C.** ⟨übtr⟩ **1.** (of plants) *to take root* **2.** (wirken) *to act; to catch on;* (of medicines) *to take, operate;* das schlägt nicht an *that does not take* ‖ stark ~ bei jdm *to operate powerfully on a p* ‖ unangenehm ~ bei jdm *to tell on a p;* bei ihm schlägt nichts mehr an *he is past hope* ‖ die Kur schlägt an *the cure agrees with me* ‖ → wirken

·**Anschlagen** n **1.** *affixing; nailing* (an *to*) **2.** *posting-up* **3.** *sounding, striking; tolling* ‖ → Anschlag ·**Anschläger** m l. (P) ⟨min⟩ *striker, onsetter* 2. (an Gegenständen) *jack* ·**anschlägig** a **1.** *handy, skilful, useful, efficient* (*p*) ‖ → schlau, pfiffig **2.** = bekömmlich

·**an|schleichen** **1.** vi [s] & vrfl [h] a.: angeschlichen k *to approach stealthily, to come slinking* (od *sneaking*) *along* **2.** vt [h] (Wild) ~ *to stalk; to creep up* (*upon*)

·**an|schleifen** vt [h] **1.** (etw) *to put an edge on a th* ‖ e–e Spitze ~ (sc an ein Messer) *to grind* (*a knife*) *to a point* **2.** °jdn, etw angeschleift bingen *to drag a p, to trail a th along the ground; to bring* od *drag a p along with one*

·**anschließbar** a ⟨tech⟩ ist, sind ~ *may be fitted*

·**an|schließen** vt/i [h] **I.** vt **A. 1.** (etw) *to fasten* (*a th*) *with a padlock;* (jdn, etw) mit Ketten ~ *to chain* (an *to*) **2.** ⟨übtr⟩ (hinzufügen) *to add, annex, join* (an *to*) | (beilegen) *to enclose* | (angliedern) (Körperschaft) *to affiliate* (an *to*) | ~ an *to join, attach to; fasten to* od *on* ‖ ⟨tech & el⟩ (Maschine etc) *to connect* (*up*), *to rig* (an *to*); ⟨tech⟩ *to fit* ⟨a. comp⟩; angeschlossen ⟨comp etc⟩ *employed* (*unit*); an (x) ist (y) angeschlossen (*x*) *is connected to* (*y*); → angeschlossen **B. sich ~ 1.** (P) sich jdm (*or* an jdn) ~ *to come a p's way, to accompany a p, to join a p* (*in a walk*), ⟨Am⟩ *to tie to a p; to tie up to* (od *with*) *a p* ‖ sich ~ (sc e–m Zuge) *to catch on;* er schloß sich ihnen an *he made one of them* | ⟨übtr⟩ *to attach o.s. to, to make friends with a p;* sich leicht jdm ~ *to take readily to a p* ‖ *to side* (od *take sides*) *with, to take up with a p* ‖ sich e–r Partei ~ *to join* (od *accede to*) *a party* | sich e–r **Ansicht ~** *to subscribe to a view* ‖ sie schlossen sich seinem Beispiel an *they followed suit;* .. der Meinung an *they concurred* ‖ sich e–m Schreiben ~ *to associate o.s. with a letter* ‖ sich e–m Urteil ~ *to concur in a verdict;* sich e–m Vorschlag etc ~ *to accede to a proposal* ‖ → entsprechen | ⟨mil⟩ rechts angeschlossen! *close to the right!* **2.** (S) das Kleid schließt **sich** eng an *the dress fits closely* od *is a tight fit* | **(örtlich)** sich ~ an *to be adjacent to, to border on; to be near* (od *close to*) *a th;* an das Haus schließt sich ein Park an *close to the house there is a park* ·**anschließend** a [attr] *subsequent* | [als adv] **~ an** den Vortrag fand ein Essen statt, an den Vortrag schloß sich ein Essen an *the lecture was followed by a dinner, following the lecture a dinner took place* ‖ die sich ~den Folgen *the attendant consequences* **II.** vi das Kleid schließt fest an → I. B. 2. ‖ → Anschluß ·**Anschließen** n *fastening; chaining* | (of dress) *fit* | (P) *the joining* (*up*)

·**Anschluß** m –usses/–üsse **A.** [abstr] **1.** → Anschließen **2.** *adding, addition* (an *to*) | (of a body) *affiliation* (an *to*) | ⟨pol⟩ *union* (an *with*); der ~ Österreichs an das Reich *the "Anschluß"* [Ger] | (P) *accession* (an e–e Partei *to a party*) ‖ (Anhänglichkeit) *attachment, adhesion* (an *to*) **3.** ⟨rail⟩ *connexion* (*of trains*); ~ h (P) *to get one's connexion* ‖ ~ h an (of trains) *to run in connexion with* (*a steamer*), *to connect with;* k–n ~ h *to have no connexion* ‖ den ~ erreichen *to achieve c.* ‖ den ~ verpassen *to miss one's connexion;* ⟨fig sl⟩ *to miss the bus* ⟨fig⟩; *to be put on the shelf;* (of women) *to be on the shelf* | ⟨telph⟩ ~ h *to be on the phone;* Neben∸ *line;* 4 Anschlüsse *4 lines;* ~ bek. *to get through, to* *be put through*; ~ herstellen mit *to get on to* | ⟨wir⟩ *connexion*; ~ an verschied. Sender ⟨Am⟩ *hook-up* **4.** ⟨übtr⟩ | *acquaintance*, ~ finden *to meet company, to pick up new friends*; er findet leicht ~ *he is very sociable* od *companionable, he takes readily to other people* ‖ ⟨com⟩ *connection*; *contact* (an *with*) | **durch** ~ an ⟨mach⟩ *linked to* (*e.g. a tabulator*) | **im** ~ **an** *following*; *subsequent to* (*the interview we had..*); im ~ an den Vortrag fand ein Essen statt *following the lecture a dinner took place*; → anschließend an | im ~ an mein Schreiben *in connexion with, in pursuance of, referring to my letter* **B.** [konkr] **1.** (Beilage) *enclosure* (*in a letter*) **2.** Heißwasser≗ *hot water connexions* [pl]; Wasser≗ → Hydrant; → Anlage ⟨telph⟩ *substation* ‖ ⟨phot⟩ (f Blitz) *nipple* **~bahn** f ⟨rail⟩ *branch-line* **~bereich** m ⟨telph⟩ *service area* **~blatt** n ⟨cart⟩ *adjacent sheet*; ≗er [pl] (in Briefen etc) *continuation sheets* **~dose** f ⟨el⟩ *wall-socket* **~gleis** n *private* od *own siding* **~klemme** f ⟨el⟩ *connexion terminal* **~leitung** f (f Wasser etc) *service pipe line* **~möglichkeit** f ⟨tech⟩ *connexion* **~rohr** n *connecting* od *service-pipe* **~station** f ⟨rail⟩ *connecting train stop*; *junction* **~stecker** m *attaching plug* **~stelle** f ⟨mot⟩ *turn-out* **~zug** m *connexion, connecting-train*

·**an**|**schmeicheln** vrefl [h] sich ~ bei jdm *to ingratiate o.s.* (od *to curry favour*) *with a p*; *to fawn* (*up*)*on a p*; *to insinuate o.s. into a p's favour*

·**an**|**schmieden** vt [h] *to fasten* od *join by forging*; *to forge* (an *on to*) ‖ (Verbrecher) *to chain up, to put* (*a p*) *in irons*

·**an**|**schmiegen** vt **1.** den Kopf ~ *to nestle one's head* (an *against*) **2. sich** ~ an jdn *to snuggle* (*up*) *to a p, to nestle against* od *to a p* | ⟨übtr⟩ *to cling to*; (of clothes) *to sit closely* ‖ ⟨fig⟩ sich e–r Form ~ *to follow a form* ·**anschmiegsam** a *pliant, pliable* (*voice*); *supple* ‖ *amenable, complaisant, obliging* (*p*)

°·**an**|**schmieren** vt [h] **1.** (jdn) *to cheat*; *to take in* ‖ ⟨sl⟩ *to pot*; *to have* (: *you have been had*) ‖ ⟨Am sl⟩ *to sell a p a gold-brick*; angeschmiert w ⟨sl⟩ *to be sold* ‖ jdn ~ mit etw, jdm etw ~ *to fob* od *palm a th off on a p, to foist* od *plant a th on a p*; ⟨sl⟩ *to stick a p with a th* **2. sich bei jdm** ~ = sich bei jdm anschmeicheln

·**an**|**schnallen** vt [h] (etw) *to buckle* (*a th*) *on* ‖ Bitte ~! ⟨aero⟩ *Fasten Seat Belt*!

·**Anschnall- ~gurt** m ~(e)s/~e *seat* od *safety-belt* ⟨a. aero⟩ | ~vorrichtung [f] *s.-b. assembly*

·**an**|**schnauben,** ·**an**|**schnauzen** vt [h] (jdn) *to snarl at* (*a p*); *to haul* (*a p*) *over the coals*; *to snub*, ⟨sl⟩ *to pi-jaw* (*a p*); ⟨Am⟩ *to bawl* (*a p*) *out*; ⟨sl⟩ *to blow* (*a p*) *up, to tell* (*a p*) *off* ‖ → anfahren

°·**Anschnauzer** m ~s/~ *rep*(*rimand*), *scolding, rating*, ⟨sl⟩ *blowing up* ‖ e–n ~ bek *to be reprimanded*, ⟨sl⟩ *to be blown up*

·**Anschneidemesser** n ~s/~ *carving-knife*

·**an**|**schneiden** vt [h] *to cut* (*a loaf*); *to begin to cut* od *carve*; *to give the first cut to* (*a th*) | ⟨fig⟩ *to broach, to embark* (od *enter*) *upon*; *to raise, ventilate* (*a question*, etc); *to broach* (*a subject*); ein anderes Thema ~ *to change to another subject* ‖ (Unangenehmes) immer wieder ~ *to rip up* ·**Anschnitt** m ~(e)s/~e *cut*; *first cut* od *slice* ‖ im ~ verkaufen *to sell by retail* ‖ ⟨found⟩ *gate*

·**Anschoppung** f ~/~en ⟨med⟩ *engorgement, congestion*

Ansch·ovis f ~/~ ⟨ich⟩ *anchovy*

·**an**|**schrauben** vt [h] *to screw on*; *to screw* (an *to, on to*)

·**Anschreibebuch** n *household book*; *note-book* ‖ ⟨sport⟩ *score-book*

·**an**|**schreiben I.** vt [h] **A. 1.** (etw) *to write* (an die Tafel *on the blackboard*); ⟨comp⟩ to print ‖ (Spielstand; Zeche an die Tafel) *to chalk up*; *to score up* **2.** ⟨übtr⟩ (jdm auf Rechnung setzen) etw ~ f jdn *to place* (od *put*) *a th to a p's account, to charge* od *debit a p with a th*; etw ~ l *to buy* od *take a th on credit* (⟨fam⟩ *on tick*); ⟨fam⟩ ~! *tick it up*!; ⟨Am⟩ *put it on the cuff* **3.** ⟨fig⟩ → angeschrieben **B.** (e–e Feder) *to use* (*a pen*) *for the first time* **II.** ≗ n *writing-down* ‖ *booking*

·**an**|**schreien** vt [h] jdn ~ *to shout* od *roar at a p*; *to hail* od *whoop a p*

·**Anschrift** f ~/~en *address*; (on letters) *direction* ‖ die richtige ~ (bei hohen P) *the proper style* (*of the archbishop*) ‖ ⟨comp⟩ *printing, listing*

·**Anschub** m ~(e)s/≗e (im Kegelspiel) *first shove* od *throw*

·**an**|**schuhen** vt [h] = vorschuhen

·**an**|**schuldigen** vt [h] jdn e–r S ~ *to accuse a p of a th, to charge a p with a th* ‖ → beschuldigt

·**Anschuldigung** f ~/~en *accusation, charge*; *recrimination* (betreffs *about*); e–e ~ gegen jdn erheben *to bring* od *prefer a charge against a p*

·**an**|**schüren** vt [h] → schüren

·**Anschuß** m –usses/–üsse **1.** → Anschießen **2.** *first shot*, den ~ h *to shoot first* **3.** ⟨hunt⟩ *place where the game was shot*

·**an**|**schütten** vt [h] *to bank* od *fill up* | ≗ n = ·**Anschüttung** f ~/~en *fill*(*ing-up*) ‖ ⟨geol⟩ *deposition* (*of sand, pebbles, etc*)

·**an**|**schwänzeln** vi [s] angeschwänzelt k (of dogs) *to come along wagging the tail* ‖ ⟨übtr⟩ *to come wriggling along* od *up*

·**an**|**schwärzen** vt [h] **1.** ⟨eig⟩ (das Gesicht) *to blacken* **2.** ⟨fig⟩ jdn ~ *to blacken a p* od *a p's character*; *to cast aspersions upon a p*; ⟨bes pol⟩ *to smear*; → verleumden ·**Anschwärzer** m ~s/~ ⟨fig⟩ *backbiter, calumniator, slanderer*

·**Anschwärzung** f ~/~en ⟨fig⟩ *aspersion, backbiting, calumny* ‖ ~en [pl] ⟨bes pol⟩ *smears*

·**an**|**schweben I.** vi [s] ⟨aero⟩ *to glide for a landing* **II.** ≗ n ~s/ *final descent*

·**an**|**schweißen** vt [h] (Metallstück) *to weld*

·**an**|**schwellen I.** vi/t **1.** vi [s] **a.** (Fluß) *to swell* (*out* od *up*); *to rise* (bis z e–r Höhe *to a height*) **b.** (Glieder) *to swell* (*out* od *up*); *his hand is swollen* ‖ → angeschwollen **c.** (Segel) *to swell, bag* **d.** ⟨übtr⟩ (Ton) *to swell*; (Preis) *to swell, to rise*; *to increase* ‖ ~ l *to swell* ‖ an– u abschwellend *rhythmic*(*al*) **2.** vt [h] (Fluß) *to swell* ‖ *to increase*: der Regen hat den Fluß –ge–llt .. *has increased* .. **II.** ≗-n *swelling*; ⟨mus⟩ *swell* ‖ An- u Abschwellen *rhythm* (of a movement) ‖ z ~ bringen *to swell* ‖ → ·**Anschwellung** f ~/~en **1.** [abstr] *swelling* ‖ ⟨übtr⟩ *rise* **2.** [konkr] ⟨med⟩ *swelling, tumour, intumescence*; kl ~ *rising*

·**an**|**schwemmen** vt [h] *to wash* (*a th*) *ashore* ‖ angeschwemmtes Land *alluvion* ·**Anschwemmung** f ~/~en *alluvial deposit*; *alluvium* ‖ Landverbreiterung durch ~ *alluvion* **~sebene** f ⟨geol⟩ *piedmont alluvial plain*

°·**an**|**schwindeln** vt [h] (jdn) *to swindle, cheat*

·**an**|**segeln** vi/t **1.** vi [s] angesegelt k *to come up* (od *approach*) *sailing* | *to open the* (*yachting*) *season* **2.** vt [h] e–n Hafen ~ *to put into port*; (Land) *to make for* | ein Schiff ~ *to foul a ship*; *to fall* (od *run*) *foul of a ship* ·**Ansegelungstonne** f ⟨mar⟩ leading buoy

·**an**|**sehen** vt/i [h] **I.** vt **A.** (sinnlich) **1. a.** (gewählt) *to regard* (*a p, a th*); (mst) *to* (*have a*) *look at* (*a p, a th*) ‖ es war prächtig –zu- *it was a sight to see* ‖ sieh nur einer den Schlingel an! *look at that rascal now*! sieh doch das nur einer an! *look at that now*! sieh mal einer an! *well, I'm blessed*!, *well, I never*! **b.** jdn ängstlich ~ *to look at a p with apprehension*; jdn direkt ~ *to face a p*; jdn gut (aus der Nähe) ~ *to take a* *close look at a p*; jdn scharf ~ *to look hard at a p, to direct a sharp glance at a p*; jdn vorwurfsvoll ~ *to turn complaining eyes on a p*; jdn z letzten Male ~ *to look one's last at a p* ‖ jdn einladend ~ ⟨sl⟩ *to give a p the glad eye*; finster, unwillig ~ *to frown at*; gerade ~ *to look straight at*; giftig ~ *to look daggers at a p*; groß *or* erstaunt ~ *to stare at a p in surprise*; scheel ~ *to look askance at*; ⟨fig⟩ → Schulter; starr ~ *to glare* od *stare at a p*; verliebt ~ *to make eyes at*; verstohlen ~ *to cast a furtive glance at a p* **c.** flüchtig ~ *to glance* (od *cast a glance*) *at* (*a p, a th*), *to give a p a fleeting glance* ‖ näher ~ *to have a look at, to look closely at, to take a close look at a p* ‖ prüfend ~ *to look a p over, to eye, regard, view a p*; jdn v oben bis unten ~ *to eye a p from top to toe* (od *up and down*) → angesehen **2. jdm etw ~:** man sieht ihm sein Alter, s–e 70 Jahre nicht an *he does not look his age, his 70 years* ‖ man sieht ihm an, daß er müde ist *you can tell by his face that he is tired*; *he looks tired*; → anmerken ‖ (s–e Arbeit ist besser), als man ihm ~ würde (..) *than you'd think from the look of him* **3. etw mit ~** *to witness a th, to be* (*eye-*)*witness of a th, to be present at a th* ‖ wir sahen es nur (*or* stillschweigend) mit an *we merely looked on, we were mere lookers-on* | [neg & interr] wer kann das mit ~? *who can permit* (od *tolerate, endure*) *it*? ich kann es nicht länger mit ~ *I can't endure it any longer* **4.** [neg] ⟨übtr⟩ **(nicht beachten)** ⟨bib⟩ die P nicht ~ *to be no respecter of persons*; er sieht das Geld nicht an *he doesn't care a pin about money* **5. sich** [dat] etw ~ = etw betrachten; sich die Sehenswürdigkeiten, Gegend ~ *to sightsee* **B. (geistig) a.** (betrachten, beurteilen) etw anders, mit anderen Augen ~ *to see* od *view a th with other eyes* (od *in a different light*), *to take a different view of a th*; etw ernst ~ *to view a th in a grave light, to take a grave* (od *serious*) *view of a th*; etw in günstigem Lichte ~ *to take a bright view of a th*, etw v der falschen Seite ~ *to see a th in the wrong light*; → auffassen, betrachten ‖ wie ich die S ansehe *to my view*; *in my opinion, to my* (*way of*) *thinking*; wie man es auch ~ mag *in whatever light you may look at it* **b. (halten f)** jdn ~ *to look upon a p, to regard a p* **(als, für** *as*), *to consider* ..; ich habe ihn f. s–n Freund –ge– *I have looked upon him as his fr., I have considered him* (*to be*) *his fr.*, man sieht ihn f. s–n F. an *he is considered* (*to be*) *his fr.* (od *looked upon as his fr.*) | **wofür** siehst du mich an? *what do you take me for*? ‖ jdn **(irrtümlich)** ~ für *to* (*mis*)*take a p for* (: *I took him for her brother*) **II.** vi: sieh mal einer an! *look at that now*! *just fancy*! *to be sure*! *well, I never*!

·**Ansehen** n ~s/ **1.** *looking-at*; nicht des ~s wert *not worth looking at* ‖ jdn v ~ kennen *to know a p by sight* ‖ → Blick ‖ ~ kostet nichts *examining costs nothing*; *people are welcome to walk round* **2. (Aussehen)** *appearance, look*; *sight*; *aspect*; die Dinge h ein widerwärtiges ~ bek *affairs* od *things have taken on an ugly look* od *aspect*; e–m Vorfall ein ganz anderes ~ geben *to put a very different complexion on an incident* | sich ein vornehmes ~ geben *to give o.s.* (od *put on*) *airs* **3. (Rücksicht)** ohne ~ der P *without respect of persons*; Gott kennt kein ~ der P *God is no respecter of persons* **4. (Achtung)** *credit*; *repute, reputation* (*of a p*); *prestige, standing*; Männer v ~ *men of reputation*; ein Mann v hohem ~ *a man of high standing*; in hohem ~ *in high repute* ‖ hohes ~ genießen *to enjoy a high reputation* (als Schriftsteller *as a writer*); in hohem ~ stehen *to be well* (od *highly*) *reputed, to be held in high estimation*; jdm ~ verschaffen *to add to a p's reputation*; sein ~ verlieren *to lose face*; → Einfluß ‖ ⟨bes pol⟩ *prestige, standing* (*of a country*); das ~ des Landes ist in Ihrer Hut *the prestige of the country is in your keeping*; geschwundenes ~ *lost prestige*

·**ansehnlich** a **1.** *sightly*; *shapely* (*book*); *presentable* (*gift*) ‖ *good-looking, comely* (*p*); ⟨liter⟩ *personable*; → stattlich **2.** ⟨übtr⟩ (beträchtlich) *considerable, respectable* (*income, number*); v ~er Größe *fair-sized* (*town, etc*) **≈keit** f *comeliness* | *considerableness*

·**Ansehung** f ~/~en **1. in** ~ e–r S *in* od *with regard to, in respect of, with respect to a th*; *considering a th, in consideration of a th* **2. ohne** ~ der P → Ansehen 3.

·**an|seilen 1.** vt [h] ⟨mount⟩ (jdn) *to rope*; angeseilt *on the rope* **2. ≈** n *roping*

·**an|sengen** vt [h] *to singe* od *burn slightly*

·**an|setzen** vt/i [h] **I.** vt **A. 1.** ⟨eig⟩ (etw) *to put, to move* (an *near, to*) ‖ (Knopf) *to sew on*; *to sew* (an *to*) ‖ (Stück) *to add, to join* (an *to*) | den Becher ~ *to put the cup to the lips*; die Flöte ~ *to put the flute to one's mouth* ‖ Blutegel ~ *to apply leeches* (an *to*) | die Feder ~ *to take up the pen, to put* od *set pen to paper*; *to begin to write*; den Pinsel ~ *to take up the brush*; *to begin to paint* ‖ das Messer (den Spaten) ~ *to begin to cut* (*dig*) ‖ (Truppen) ~ *to commit*, (z Angriff) *to launch* **2.** Fleisch z Kochen ~ *to put meat on to boil* | (Getränk) *to prepare, make, mix, brew* **3.** ⟨bot⟩ Knospen ~ *to put forth buds, to bud*; Blätter ~ *to* (*come into*) *leaf* | Schimmel ~ *to mould, to grow mouldy* | Rost ~ *to rust*; Kesselstein ~ *to scale*; Rahm ~ *to cream* | (P) Fleisch (etc) ~ *to put* od *take flesh on*; Fett, Fleisch ~ *to put on weight* **4.** ⟨übtr: theat⟩ (Stück) *to put on* ‖ (Waren) zum Verkauf ~ *to put up for sale* ‖ (e–n Hund) *to set on*; (z Fährte) ⟨hunt⟩ *to lift* **B.** ⟨math⟩ *to put up* (*an equation*) **C.** ⟨übtr⟩ **1.** ⟨com⟩ **(berechnen)** (etw) *to charge*; das Buch ist Ihnen mit 6 sh angesetzt *the book is charged to you at 6/*; → anrechnen 1. ‖ **(abschätzen)** *to assess, estimate, rate* (auf *at*); *to tax*; (Preis) *to fix, quote* **2. (Zeit)** *to set aside* (f. *for*); (Tag etc) *to appoint, fix, allocate* (f. *for*); (Ereignis) zeitlich ~ *to place*; *date* ⟨a. arts⟩ ‖ (nach Plan **Zeitpunkt** ~ f) *to schedule* (⟨theat⟩ *a play*; *a train, a ship*) (: *the ship is scheduled to start on May 27*) *to time* (*a race*); (Sitzung) ~ f. *to schedule for* (*Monday*); angesetzt s (of meetings, etc.) *to be down* (für *or* auf Montag *for Monday*) ‖ angesetzte Veranstaltung (etc) *fixture* **D. sich ~** [nur 3. sg & pl; vgl etw ~ A. 3.] **1.** es setzen sich schon Knospen an *buds are coming forth* (*already*) **2.** es hat sich Rost an das Eisen angesetzt (= das Eisen hat Rost angesetzt) *the iron has rusted* (od *has become rusty*) **II.** vi **1.** ⟨bot⟩ *to strike root*; *to put forth fruit buds*; gut ~ *to be doing* well | (P) *to grow fat* (od *stout*) **2.** ~ zu tun *to begin* od *set to do, to start doing* od *to do*; er setzte z Sprung an *he prepared* (od *got ready*) *for a jump* ‖ ⟨aero⟩ z Gleitflug ~ *to pass* od *go into a glide* ‖ z Angriff ~ ⟨mil⟩ *to start the attack*; z Landung ~ ⟨aero, mar⟩ *to come in for a landing* ‖ er setzte noch einmal an *he had another try, he made a fresh start* ‖ angesetzt k *to come rushing* od *sweeping along*

·**Ansetzen** n **1.** *application* (an *to*); ~ an den Mund *the putting* (*of an instrument*) *to the mouth* ‖ *taking-up* (*of the pen*) | *making*; *mixing* | ⟨typ⟩ *following up* **2.** *budding*; *formation* (*of fruit*) ‖ ~ v Fett *accumulation of fat* **3.** (zeitlich) *appointment* (*of a term*); *dating* ‖ → Ansatz

·**Ansetzer** m ~s/~ ⟨artill⟩ *rammer* (*of a gun*)

·**Ansetzung** f = Ansetzen

·**Ansicht** f ~/~en **A.** (sinnlich) **1. (Ansehen)** Bücher etc zur ~ senden *to send books on approval* od *approbation*; auf 10 Tage kostenlos z ~ *for ten days' free examination*; → Beobachtung; Besichtigung, Durchsicht; Sicht **2. (Blick**

auf . .) *view*; Front∼ *front-view*, Seiten∼ *side-view*; Rund∼ *panorama* ‖ *sight*; → Sehenswürdigkeit ‖ *aspect* → Ausblick, Blick **3.** [konkr] **(Bild)** ⟨bes phot & arts⟩ *view*, (ich kaufte) ∼en v Berlin *views of Berlin*; ∼ v unten ⟨tech⟩ *inverted plan view* **B. (geistig) 1.** *view, opinion* (über *of*); s–e ∼ über Carlyle *his view of C.*; ∼en *views*, s–e ∼en über *his view of, about, on* **2. Wendungen:** e–e weitverbreitete ∼ *a widely held opinion* ‖ m–e ∼ über diese Frage *my side of this question* ‖ **nach der ∼** des Herrn N. *in the opinion, view of Mr. N.*; nach m–r ∼, m–r ∼ nach (m.A.n.) *in my opinion, view*, ⟨fam⟩ *to my thinking* | **es ist** die allgemeine ∼ *it is common ground* (*that*) ‖ das ist m–e ∼ *I mean it* ‖ was ist Ihre ∼ ? *what are your views* (*on* ..)? | **ich bin der ∼** *I am of* (*the*) *opinion* (*that*) ‖ ich bin vollständig Ihrer ∼ *I am entirely of your opinion* ‖ ich bin anderer ∼ als Sie *I differ from you* ‖ ich habe e–e neue ∼ über . . *I have a new line on . .* ‖ über viele Punkte sind die ∼en geteilt *on many points opinion is divided* | s–e ∼ **ändern** *to change one's view* od *opinion* ‖ sich [acc] (schließlich doch) jds ∼ anschließen *to come around to a p's view* sich [dat] e–e ∼ **bilden** *to form a view* (*of*) ‖ ich bleibe der ∼ *I remain of the opinion* (*that*) ‖ e–e ∼ **haben** *to hold* od *take a view* (*of a th*); eigene ∼en haben *to have views of one's own* ‖ zu der ∼ k *to reach a view* ‖ ich neige zu der ∼ *I incline to the opinion* ‖ die ∼ **vertreten** *to hold* od *take the view, to take the line* (*that*); s–e ∼ (laut) vertreten *to voice one's opinion* ‖ mit s–r ∼ zurückhalten *to withhold one's opinion* **∼sexemplar** n (Buch) *forward copy, copy for inspection*; (f den Lehrer) *specimen copy* **∼skarte** f *picture postcard*; ⟨Am⟩ *postcard* **∼skopien** f pl ⟨film⟩ *rushes* **∼ssache** f *matter of opinion* **∼ssendung** f *delivery* (od *parcel sent*) *on approval* **∼sskizze** f *panoramic sketch*

·ansichtig a: jds, e–r S ∼ w *to get a sight of, to catch sight of a p, a th*

·an|siedeln vt [h] **1.** (jdn) *to plant, settle, colonize* **2. sich ∼** *to plant o.s.*; *to settle, colonize* (in *in*); ⟨Am⟩ *to locate* (in *at*) ‖ sich in e–m Lande ∼ *to settle a country* ‖ sich ohne Rechtstitel ∼ ⟨Am⟩ *to squat* ‖ ⟨übtr⟩ sich ∼ *to establish o.s.*

·Ansiedler m ∼s/∼ *settler, colonist* ‖ ∼ ohne Rechtstitel ⟨Am⟩ *squatter* **·Ansiedlung** f ∼/∼en *settlement*; ⟨Am⟩ *location* (*of a p*) ‖ *colonization*

·an|sinnen I. vt [h] jdm etw ∼ *demand a th of* od *from a p*; jdm ∼ z tun *to require of a p to do*; das kann ich ihm nicht ∼ *I cannot expect it of him, I cannot suggest it to him* ‖ → zumuten **II.** ∼ n *immoderate* od *unreasonable demand* od *request*; *unfair suggestion*; jdm ein ∼ stellen = jdm etw ansinnen, → d. ‖ → Zumutung

·Ansitz m ⟨hunt⟩ *hide*; (*screened, concealed*) *shooting-stand*; *sitting-up* **·an|sitzen** vi [h] ⟨hunt⟩ *to lie in concealment*

ans·onsten adv = sonst ‖ ⟨Sw, bay, österr⟩ = andernfalls

·an|spannen I. vt [h] **1.** ⟨eig⟩ Bogen, Sehne ∼ → spannen | ⟨übtr⟩ (Kredit) *to strain, stretch*; die Lage ist angespannt *the situation is strained* | ⟨fig⟩ (Geduld) *to tax*; (Nerven etc) *to string, tauten* ‖ aufs äußerste ∼ *to force*; aufs höchste ∼ *to strain to breaking-point*; aufs höchste angespannt *on the strain* ‖ alle s–e Kräfte ∼ *to brace one's energies, to strain every nerve*; **sich ∼** *to brace o.s.* ‖ → angespannt **2. a.** (Pferd) *to inspan*; *to harness* (an *to*) | die Pferde, den Wagen ∼ *to put the horses to*; ist angespannt? *are the horses put to?* ‖ laß ∼! *order the carriage!* | ⟨fig⟩ jdn ∼ *to inspan a p*; .. z etw, z tun *to put* od *urge a p to a th, to do* **II.** ∼ n *harnessing, yoking*; *inspanning*; → Anspannung

·Anspänner m *small farmer*

·Anspannung f ∼/∼en *strain* (*of a rope*) | ⟨übtr⟩ *strain, tension*, e–e ∼ des Kredits *a strain on credit*; ∼ m–r Hilfsmittel *a strain on my resources* ‖ ⟨fig⟩ *strain, exertion*; *stress* (*of dayly life*) ‖ e–e hohe ∼ der Geduld jds *a tax on a p's patience* ‖ immer in ∼ s *to be perpetually on the strain*; mit äußerster ∼ *with the utmost exertion, at full strain*

·an|speien vt [h] jdn ∼ *to spit at* od *upon a p*

·an|speile(r)n vt [h] (etw) *to fasten with skewers*

·an|spielen I. vt/i [h] **1.** vt ⟨mus⟩ (Instrument) *to use for the first time*; *to try* ‖ (Stück) *to begin to play* | ⟨cards⟩ (eine Karte, Farbe) to lead; e–e Farbe ∼ *to lead a suit* ‖ (Billardball) *to put on* **2.** vi ⟨mus⟩ *to begin to play* ‖ ⟨cards⟩ *to* (*have the*) *lead* ‖ ⟨sport⟩ *to lead off* | ⟨fig⟩ ∼ auf etw *to allude* (od *make an allusion*) *to, to hint at a th*; *to insinuate a th*; **II.** ∼ n ⟨cards⟩ *lead* **·anspielend** a ⟨fig⟩ *allusive* (*remark*) ‖ ∼ auf *in allusion to* **·Anspielung** f ∼/∼en ⟨fig⟩ *allusion, hint*; ∼ auf ⟨a.⟩ *reference* (auf *to*); verächtliche ∼en *contemptuous reference* ‖ mit ∼ auf *in allusion to, alluding to* ‖ feine ∼ *insinuation*; versteckte ∼ *innuendo* ‖ e–e ∼ hören, verstehen *to hear sth behind the words*

·an|spinnen vt [h] **1.** (Faden) *to join by spinning* | ⟨fig⟩ den Faden e–r Erzählung ∼ *to join the thread of a narrative* (an *to*); den Faden wieder ∼ *to resume, to take up the thread* **2.** (eine Unterhaltung etc) *to embark upon, to enter into* | **sich ∼** *to begin*; *to arise*; *to spring up*; *to come into existence*

·an|spitzen vt [h] (Bleistift etc) *to point, sharpen*; *to put an edge on . .*

·Ansporn m ∼(e)s/ *spur, stimulus* (für jdn *to a p*; z etw *to a th*); *fillip, encouragement, incitement, incentive* (z etw *to a th*; z tun *to do, to doing*) **·an|spornen** vt [h] (Pferd) *to spur*; *to set* od *put spurs to* (*a horse*) ‖ ⟨hunt⟩ (Hunde) *to halloo* | ⟨fig⟩ (jdn) *to spur, incite, stimulate*; *rouse, encourage* (zu *to*; z tun *to do*); *to prod* (z *into*) ‖ (Appetit) *to give an edge to*; (Gedächtnis) *to prod*

·Ansprache f ∼/∼n *address*; *speech* (v jdm *by a p*) ‖ feierliche ∼ *harangue*; formelle ∼ *allocution* | e–e ∼ halten *to give an address, to make a speech*; *to harangue* ‖ er fand k–e ∼ *they took no notice of him* **·ansprechbar** a: ∼ s f etw *to be susceptible to a th* **∼kelt** f, **Ansprechempfindlichkeit** f *responsiveness, susceptibility* **·an|sprechen** vt/i [h] **I.** vt **1.** jdn ∼ *to address, accost*; (belästigend) (of women) *to solicit a p* ‖ ∼ u (am Rockaufschlag oder Arm) festhalten *to buttonhole* (*a p*), ich habe ihn daraufhin angesprochen *I have spoken to him about it* ‖ (Schiff) *to hail* ‖ ⟨mil⟩ (Ziel) *to designate* | jdn **um etwas ∼** *to ask a p for a th, to apply to a p for a th, to beg a th of a p* | ⟨golf⟩ (Ball) *to address* **2. (beanspruchen)** etw als sein Eigentum ∼ *to claim a th for o.s.*; *to lay claim to a th, to assert a th as one's own* ‖ → Anspruch **3.** ⟨übtr⟩ **(halten für)** jdn irrtümlich **∼ für** *to* (*mis*)*take a p for* | etw (jdn) ∼ **als** *to consider, declare, pronounce a th* (*to be . .*); *to class* od *assume a th as*; das Stück wird als unecht angesprochen *the play is considered* (*to be*) *spurious* (od . . *is looked upon as sp.*); das Bild wurde als Fälschung angesprochen *the picture was pronounced to be a forgery* **4. (gefallen)** jdn ∼ (S) *to please a p, to be pleasing to a p*; *to appeal to a p, to interest a p* (mst [intr] → II. 2.) **II.** vi **1.** ⟨mus⟩ (of instruments) *to* (*give* od *emit a*) *sound*; leicht ∼ *to respond well, to play easily*; schlecht ∼ *to sound off*; das Klavier spricht leicht an *the piano has a light* (od *an easy*) *touch*; der Ton spricht nicht an *the tone does not sound pure* ‖ ⟨tech, mach⟩ *to act* **2.** (*of qualities*) *to be pleasing*; *to meet with approval* ‖ ⟨Lit⟩ (*of plays*) *to take, to take on*; das Stück spricht sehr an *the play is a good draw*

3. ⟨psych⟩ ~ **auf** *to react to*; *to be susceptible to* (*a th*) **III.** ≗ n *responsiveness*; (e–s Zieles) *identification* ‖ ⟨el⟩ ein Relais z ~ bringen *to cause . . to respond* **·ansprechend** a *appealing, pleasing*; *engaging, winning, taking a p's fancy*; sie hat sehr viel ≗es in ihrem Wesen *her ways are very winning, she has very winning ways* ‖ ~e Formgebung ⟨com⟩ *attractive design*

·an|sprengen vi/t **1.** vi [s] *to come galloping along* od *up, to come up at a gallop* **2.** vt [h] (Blumen) *to sprinkle, to water*

·an|springen vi/t **I.** vi [s] **1.** angesprungen k *to come jumping* od *skipping along*; **2.** ⟨sport⟩ *to spring first* **3.** ⟨übtr⟩ ⟨mot⟩ (of cars) *to start* (*up*) ‖ ⟨aero⟩ (of motor) *to pick up*; (Flugzeug) ~ l *to zoom* **4.** die Tasse ist angesprungen *the cup is cracked* **II.** vt [h] jdn ~ (of dogs) *to jump up against a p*

·an|spritzen vt [h] (Pflanzen) *to syringe, to* (*be*)*sprinkle*; (of mud) (Kleid) *to splash, bespatter* ‖ ⟨mot⟩ (Vergaser etc) *to prime*

·Anspruch m, ~(e)s/≗e **A. 1.** ⟨jur⟩ (Rechts-) *claim, title* (auf *to*; z tun *to do*) ‖ Besitz≗ *tenure* | ⟨übtr⟩ *claim* (auf *to* [*completeness*]); *title* (auf *to* [*a place*]); *pretension* (auf *to*; z sein *to be*) **2.** ⟨jur⟩ (Forderung) *demand* (an jdn *upon a p*) ‖ ~ auf Schadenersatz *claim for compensation* | ⟨übtr⟩ →: **B. Wendungen 1.** Ansprüche befriedigen *to satisfy claims* ‖ ~ erheben auf etw *to enter* (od *put in*) *a claim for a th*; k–n ~ erh. auf *to make no pretence to* ‖ den ≗en genügen *to fill the bill* | ~ h **auf** etw *to have a title to, to be entitled to a th*; ~ auf Rückzahlung h ⟨contr⟩ *to have claim to recover payment*; ~ h auf jdn, auf jds Hilfe *to have a claim on a p*(*'s* help) | s–e ≗e herabsetzen, zurückschrauben *to reduce, moderate one's claims*; ~ m auf etw *to lay claim to a th, to claim a th*; *to pretend to a th*; (. . *to be*) ‖ gr ≗e m *to be fastidious, to be hard to please* ‖ e–n ~ nach-, erweisen *to substantiate a claim* ‖ gr Ansprüche stellen an jdn *to make great* od *big demands on a p* **2. in ~ nehmen** = ~ m auf ~ B. 1. | ⟨mil⟩ (Stadt etc) *to requisition* (f *for*) | jds Aufmerksamkeit, Mitleid etc . . *to engage a p's attention, compassion* ‖ jds Dienste . . *to avail o.s. of a p's services*; jds Hilfe . . *to call in a p's help*; *to enlist a p's help* (f *for*); jdn, etw in ~ n. *to indent upon a p* od *a th* (f *for a th*) ‖ (all)zu sehr . . *to overtax* (*one's strength*) ‖ völlig . . *to task all faculties of a p*; *to claim a p's full attention* od *time* ‖ ⟨com⟩ *to implement* (*a guarantee*) ‖ e–n Anwalt in ~ n. *to brief a counsel* (*for*) ‖ ein Werk, e–n Autor in ~ n. *to draw upon a work, an author* | **über Gebühr** in ~ n.: jds Geduld *to tax a p's patience*; jds Güte *to encroach* (*up*)*on a p's kindness*; (Kraft, Zeit) *to draw on a p's energy, time*; jds Zeit *to engross a p's time*; *to encroach* (od *trespass*) (*up*)*on a p's time*; jds Mittel, Kräfte *to tax a p's resources, a p's strength* | **(S)** *to subject to strain* (od *stress*); **es nimmt** s–n Geldbeutel sehr in ~ *it is a great drain on his purse* ‖ Zeit in ~ n. *to take time*, viel Zeit in ~ n. *to take* (*up*) *a long time* (z tun *to do, in doing*); ihre Reise nahm 3 Wochen in ~ *their journey occupied* (od *took*) *3 weeks* ‖ jdn in ~ n. *to take a p* (*to do*): es wird dich 2 Stunden in ~ n. *it will take you 2 hours* (*to do*) ‖ [mst pass] in ~ genommen s od w von etw *to be absorbed in a th, engaged in* (od *on*) *a th*; *to be wrapped* (od *bound*) *up in a th*; *to be taken up* (od *occupied*) *with a th*; nicht in ~ gen. w von etw *to have no concern with a th*; ich bin sehr in ~ gen. *I have got my hands full* (*with . .*); *I am fully occupied* (od *very busy*)

·anspruchs- ~berechtigt a *having a claim* ‖ ≗e(r m) f *beneficiary* **~los** a *unassuming* (*p*); *unexacting*; ⟨for, bot⟩ *little exacting*; *unambitious* (*class*) ‖ *unpresuming* (*title*); *unostentatious* (*habits*) ‖ *unpretentious* (*story*) ‖ *unpretending* (*house*); *frugal* (*life*); *plain* (*dinner*), *moderate* ‖ *contented, easily satisfied* **≗losigkeit** f *unassumingness*; *unpretendingness, unpretentiousness* **~voll** *a pretentious, demanding, exacting* (*in*) ‖ (wählerisch) *fastidious, discerning, discriminating*; *hard to please* ‖ *up-to-date* ‖ ~es Wesen *pretentiousness* ‖ ⟨arts⟩ (*a play*) *with* (*literary*) *pretensions*

·an|spucken vt [h] jdn ~ *to spit at* (od *upon*) *a p*

·an|spülen vt [h] (of the sea) (etw) *to wash ashore* ‖ angespültes Land *alluvial soil* **·Anspülung** f ~/~en = Anschwemmung

·an|stacheln vt [h] ⟨fig⟩ *to goad* (z *to*; z Wut *to fury*; z tun *to do*; *into doing*); *to prod* (mit *with*; z Handeln *into action*); → anreizen

·Anstalt f ~/~en **1.** [abstr] (**Vorkehrung**) ~en m *to get ready, to prepare* (z tun *to do*); ~ m z Aufbruch *to stir*; → anschicken ‖ ~en treffen *to make arrangements, preparations, provision* (f *for*; gegen *against*) | (**Einrichtung**) *institution*; (Erziehungs≗ *educational i.*); *establishment* ‖ (öffentlichrechtliche) *corporation* (Rundfunk≗ *broadcasting c.*) **2.** [kontr] (**Gebäude**) *institution, institute, establishment*; *asylum, home*, Kranken≗ *hospital*; Straf≗ *prison* | (**Heilstätte**) *home*; *hospital* (*mental h.*); jdn in e–r ~ unterbringen *to find a place for a p in a home* **~serziehung** f *the upbringing of orphans* etc *in a charitable institution* **~shaushalt** m ⟨demog⟩ *non-family household* **~kranke(r** m) f *in patient*

·Anstand m, ~(e)s/≗e **1.** ⟨hunt⟩ *lying-in--wait*; → Ansitz; bester ~ ⟨sl⟩ *the warm corner*; schlechtester ~ ⟨sl⟩ *the worst corner*; auf den ~ gehen *to lie in wait* | = Ansitz **2.** (**Bedenken** [urspr Stillestehen]) *hesitation*; *doubt*; *objection* ‖ k–n ~ nehmen *not to hesitate* (z tun *to do*); ~ n. *to scruple* (*to do*); ohne ~ zahlen *to pay without any objection* (od *without more ado*) **3.** (**Benehmen** [urspr Passen]) *manners* [pl]: jdn ~ lehren *to teach a p m.* ‖ *polite* (od) *pleasing manners* [pl]; *good grace*; mit ~ *gracefully*, (*to take a defeat*) *with good grace* ‖ *address, tact* | (**Sittsamkeit**) *decorum, decency*; (gesellschaftlicher) *propriety, respectability*; den ~ wahren *to keep up decorum*; den ~ verletzen *to offend against decency* (od *decorum*)

·anständig I. a **1.** *respectable* (*man, girl, family*); ~ aussehen *to have an air of respectability about one* ‖ *gentlemanly* od *gentlemanlike* (*behaviour*); *reputable* (*life*) ‖ *decorous* (*clothes*) ‖ es ist nicht ~ v jdm *it is not becoming in a p* (*to do*); das ist nicht ~ *that's not proper, that's not the correct thing, not decent, not fair* ‖ sehr ~ v ihm *sporting of him*; ⟨sl⟩ *that's bully of you* ‖ *decent*, (*story*, etc); *proper* (*look*) ‖ ~er Kerl ⟨sl⟩ *good egg*; ein ~es Mädchen ⟨sl⟩ *a square bit* od *piece* **2.** °~ (nett) *decent* (*fellow*) ‖ (annehmbar) *decent* (*wages*; *cigar*) ‖ (beträchtlich) *considerable, respectable, handsome, tidy* (*income*; *fortune*) **II.** adv (*to behave*) *decently*; *properly* (*dressed*); *square* (:*to do a th sq. and proper*); jdn ~ behandeln *to give a p a square deal* ‖ ~ handeln *to act straight*; → ehrlich adv | °es regnet ganz ~ *it's raining nicely* (od *pretty heavily*) | ≗**keit** f ~/~en, *becomingness decency, decorum*; (anerkannte gesellschaftliche) *propriety, respectability*

·Anstands- ~besuch m *formal call* **~dame** f *chaperon*; die ~ spielen *to play gooseberry*; jdn als ~ begleiten *to chaperon a p* **~formen** f [pl] *manners*; *the proprieties* [pl] **~gefühl** n *sense of decency* (od *propriety*); *delicacy, tact* **~geschenk** n *formal gift* ≗**halber** adv *for decency's sake, for the sake of decency* ≗**los 1.** a *unhesitating* **2.** adv *unhesitatingly, without hesitation* (od *objection*); *readily, willingly* **~regeln** f [pl] (*rules of*) *etiquette* °**~wauwau** m *chaperon* [Fr], ⟨Am univ sl⟩ *fire-extinguisher* **≈widrig** *a indecorous, indecent; improper; unseemly*

·an|starren vt [h] jdn ~ *to stare, gaze, glare at a p*; → anglotzen, -stieren

anst·att 1. prep [gen]; ~ e–r S, jds *instead of, in the place of, in lieu of a th, a p*; ~ dessen *in lieu thereof* **2.** conj; ~ z arbeiten, ~ daß er arbeitet *instead of working* (*he . .*)

·an|staunen vt [h] jdn ~ *to stare, gaze at a p in wonder* (od *in surprise*)

·an|stechen vt [h] (Stück Fleisch) *to spit*; *to put* (*meat*) *on a spit*; (ein Faß) *to broach, tap*

·Ansteck- ~artikel m [pl] *favours* [pl] **~sträußchen** n *corsage* (*of orchids*) **·an|stecken I.** vt/i [h] **A.** vt **1.** (Schleife, Blume, mit Nadel) *to fasten with a pin* (od *with pins*); *to pin* (an *to*) ‖ (Ring) *to put on, to slip* (an den Finger *on to one's finger*) ‖ ⟨fig⟩ das kannst du dir ~! *put that in your pipe and smoke it*! **2.** (Feuer, Licht, Pfeife, Zigarre) *to light*; stecken Sie sich eine Zigarre an *have a cigar* od *a smoke* ‖ (Haus etc) *to set fire to, to set on fire* **3.** ⟨übtr⟩ (aus 2.) **a.** (P) *to infect*; er hat mich mit s–r Erkältung angesteckt *he has given me his cold* ‖ angesteckt w, **sich ~** *to become* od *get infected* (durch *by*; mit *with*); *to catch the infection* **b.** ⟨fig⟩ *to infect* (mit e–r Gewohnheit *with a habit*); angesteckt w *to be bitten* (v e–r Mode *by* od *with a fashion*); v der Furcht der anderen –ge–kt w *to catch the fear of the others*; s–e Unruhe hat auch sie –ge–kt *his restlessness has affected her too*; sie wurden v der Begeisterung angesteckt *they caught the enthusiasm* **c.** (moralisch vergiften) *to contaminate, canker, taint, corrupt* **4.** = anstechen **B.** vi ⟨fig⟩ (of diseases) ⟨ & fig⟩ *to be catching* (od *contagious, infectious*) **II.** ≈ n *fastening*; *putting on* | *lighting*; *setting on fire* ‖ → Ansteckung

·ansteckend a *contagious, infectious, taking* (*disease*) ‖ [mst pred] (*to be*) *catching* | ⟨übtr⟩ *infectious, contagious* (*laughter*)

·Ansteckung f ~/~en **1.** → Anstecken **2.** ⟨med⟩ (jeder Art, mst innere) *infection*; (nur durch Berührung) *contagion*; durch ~ *by contagion, contagiously* | ⟨übtr⟩ *contagion* (*of a bad example*); *infection* (*of an error*); (Stimmungsübertragung) *sympathetic induction* **~sgefahr** f *danger of infection* **~sherd** m ⟨med⟩ *fomes* [pl *fomites*] **~skraft** f *virulence* **~sstoff** m *infectious matter*; ⟨med⟩ → -herd; (giftiger) *virus* (*of smallpox*) **~sträger** m (S) ⟨med⟩ → -herd

·an|stehen vi [h & s] **A. 1. a.** *(= stehen an) der Schrank steht (z nah) an der Wand an *the wardrobe stands* (*too*) *close to the wall* **b.** ⟨hunt⟩ = ansitzen **c.** ⟨geol⟩ *to appear on the surface*; ~d ⟨min⟩ *unworked* (Kohle); ~des Gestein *bed rock* **2.** (of time) der Termin steht an *the term is fixed* **B.** jdm ~ **1.** (*of clothes*) *to fit a p* **2.** ⟨übtr⟩ *to become a p, to sit* (*up*)*on a p*; es steht ihm besser an *it is more fitting for him* (z tun *to do*); . . schlecht an *it is unbecoming in him*; *it ill becomes him* (*to do*) **3.** (zusagen) *to please, to suit* **C. 1.** (sich anstellen) *to queue* (*up*), *to take one's place* (od *to wait*) *in a queue*, ⟨Am⟩ *to line up* **2.** (of things) **a.** (verschoben w) *to be delayed* (od *put off*); (etw) ~ l *to delay, postpone, suspend* (*a th*); e–e Schuld ~ l *to defer the payment of a debt* **b.** (dauern) es stand nicht lange an, so fand er .. *it was not long before he found* .. **3.** [neg] **nicht ~ z tun** *not to hesitate, mind, scruple to do* (*I don't mind telling you*)

·an|steigen I. vi [s] **1.** (of a path, etc) *to ascend* ‖ ⟨übtr⟩ (of the voice) *to rise*; (of prices) *to increase, mount*, (schnell) *to zoom*; (of debts) *to mount up* **2.** (P) **to ascend* ‖ ⟨übtr⟩ angestiegen k *to come strutting* (od *stalking*) *along* **II.** ≈ n = Anstieg ‖ ⟨theat, etc⟩ (des Zuschauerraumes) *rake*

·an|stellen I. vt [h] **A. 1.** ⟨eig⟩ (etw) *to place; to stand* (an *against*); → stellen **2.** ⟨übtr⟩ jdn ~ *to put a p on, to appoint a p* (in etw, f etw *in a th*; z tun *to do*); (⟨Am fam⟩ *the right to hire and fire* –zu– und zu entlassen) | (einstellen) *to take on* (*to do*); *to engage*; (Besatzung) *to sign on*; → ernennen ‖ *to employ*; wieder ~ *to re-employ* ‖ angestellt s bei ⟨com⟩ *to be with* (*a firm*) ‖ jdn fest ~ *to give a p a permanent position* (od *post*); fest angestellt *permanently appointed* **3.** (in Gang setzen) **a.** (Maschine, Wasser, Heizung, Radio) *to turn on*; das Wasser ~ *to turn on taps*; (elektr. Strom) *to switch on*, (⟨wir & el⟩ *she flipped the switch*) **b.** ⟨übtr⟩ (machen) *to arrange*; *to manage, to contrive, to bring about*; wie soll ich das ~? *how am I to manage it*? *how should I go about*?; wie stellt man es an? *how does one go to work*? ‖ etw klug ~ *to manage a th cleverly*; was ich auch ~ mochte *whatever I did* (*I . .*) ‖ was hast du die ganze Zeit angestellt? *what have you been doing with yourself all the time*?; was hast du da bloß angestellt! ⟨fam⟩ *what have you been up to*? ‖ etw ~ *to get into mischief* ‖ → anfangen I. 2.; anfassen I. 2.; anrichten 2. ‖ (begehen) *to commit*; *to cause, to do*; was hast du mit m–m H. angestellt? *what have you done to my hat*? ‖ stelle nur nicht wieder etw an ⟨sl⟩ *you mustn't ask for trouble again* | *to make*; Betrachtungen ~ *to indulge* (*o.s.*) *in speculations*; . . über *to reflect on* ‖ e–e Untersuchung ~ *to make* (od *institute*) *an inquiry* (über etw *into a th*) ‖ e–n Vergleich ~ *to draw a parallel* ‖ e–n Versuch ~ *to make a trial* **4.** ⟨com⟩ (Waren) *to offer* **B. sich ~ 1.** ⟨eig⟩ *to queue on*; sich in e–r Reihe ~ *to line up* (od *take one's place*) *in a queue*; ⟨Am⟩ *to line up* **2.** ⟨übtr⟩ **a.** *to behave*; sich klug ~ *to go* (od *set*) *to work cleverly* ‖ *to make* (*as if* . .); *to put it on*; er stellt sich nur so an *he is putting it on*; stell dich nicht so an *don't make such a fuss* (wegen *about*); er stellte sich jämmerlich an *he cut a miserable figure* **II.** ≈ n *placing* ‖ *appointing* ‖ *turning-on* (*of a machine*) | (P) (Sich-) ~ Farbiger vor Kino- [etc Kasse] f Weiße ⟨Am⟩ *stand-in* [pl ~s] **·anstellig** a *able, skilful, handy, clever* | ≈keit [f] ~/ *ability, aptitude, skill*

·Anstellung f ~/~en **1.** [abstr] *appointment*; ⟨Am⟩ *assignment* ‖ *tenure* (Sicherheit der ~ *security of t.*); ~s- *tenurial* ‖ → Anstellen **2.** (Stellung) *place, post, situation*; feste ~ *permanent place* | ~sbedingungen [f pl] → Beschäftigungs- **·Anstellwinkel** m ⟨aero⟩ *angle of incidence* (od *attack*); *pitch attitude*

·an|stemmen vt [h] (Rücken etc) *to press* (an *against*) ‖ **sich ~** gegen etw *to stem a th*

·an|steuern vt [h] ⟨aero⟩ → anfliegen

Ansteuerung f *approach*

·Anstich m ~(e)s/~e *piercing, broaching* ‖ ein frischer ~ *a fresh tap* | *first cut*; ⟨fenc⟩ *first stab* od *thrust*

·an|sticken vt (etw) *to embroider* (an *on to*)

·Anstieg m ~(e)s/~e *ascending*; *ascent*; (mühsamer) *pull* | ⟨übtr⟩ *rise* (der Preise *in* od *of prices*) ‖ *improvement*; im ~ *on the increase*

·an|stieren vt [h] *to glower at* (*a p, a th*)

·an|stiften I. vt [h] **1.** (Verwirrung etc) *to cause, to occasion, to bring about* ‖ (Unheil etc) *to brew*; *to do*; → anrichten ‖ (Aufruhr) *to instigate, to foment*; *to promote*; (Verbrechen) *to abet* **2.** (P) *to instigate, to egg* od *set on*; *to stir up*; *to induce* (z etw *to a th*; *to do*) ‖ → antreiben **II.** ≈ n *instigation*; auf ~ jds *at the instigation of a p* ‖ → Anstiftung

·Anstifter m ~s/~, Anstifterin f ~/~nen *instigator, plotter*; (Urheber) *author* ‖ ⟨jur⟩ *accessary before the fact*; *abetter, -tor* **·Anstiftung** f ~/~en *causing, contriving*; *brewing* ‖ *fomentation, instigation* (auf ~ jds *at the i. of a p*); *incitement* (z *to*)

·an|stimmen I. vt/i [h] **1.** vt **a.** ⟨mus⟩ den Grundton ~ *to give the key note* **b.** (Lied) *to strike up*; *to lead off into* (*a song*) || ⟨bes ec⟩ *to intone, to intonate* || ein Klagelied ~ *to break into lamentations* | ⟨fig⟩ e–n Ton ~ → anschlagen I. A. 2. **2.** vi *to strike up*; stimm an *strike up* **II.** ≈ n, a. **Anstimmung** *striking up*; *intonation*

·Anstoß m ~es/≈e **A. 1. a.** ⟨eig⟩ (Stoß) *impact* (gegen *against*); leichter ~ *jog, nudge* **b.** (Hemmung) ohne ~ (*to recite*) *without stopping* (od *interruptions*), *fluently*; (*to answer without hesitation* **2.** ⟨übtr⟩ (Ärgernis) *offence*, (⟨Am⟩ *offense*); *scandal, umbrage* || ~ erregen *to cause offence*; . . bei jdm *to give offence* (od *umbrage*) *to a p, to scandalize a p*; k–n ~ erregen *to give no trouble*; ohne ~ z erregen *without offence* || ~ erregend *invidious*; = anstößig || ~ nehmen an etw *to take offence* (od *umbrage*) *at, to be scandalized at, to stumble at a th, to disapprove* (*of*) *a th*; → beleidigt s durch | Stein des ~es *stumbling block*; *rock of offence* **B. 1.** ⟨eig⟩ dem Pendel e–n ~ geben *to give the pendulum a push* **2.** (der erste Stoß) *the first thrust* (etc) || ⟨ftb⟩ *kick-off*; den ~ haben *to kick off* **3.** ⟨übtr⟩ (Anregung) *impulse, inducement* (z *to*); *initiative*; den ersten ~ geben z etw *to suggest, to initiate a th, to take the initiative* (od *the first step*) *in a th* || den ~ geben z etw *to produce, to originate a th*; *to give rise to a th* || den ~ dazu geben *to start it off, to set it going* **C.** * = Grenze **~flugpreis** m (v e–r Linie z anderen) *proportionable fare*

·an|stoßen vt/i [h] **I.** vt **1.** jdn (tüchtig) ~ *to give a p a* (*good*) *push*; jdn leicht mit dem Ellenbogen ~ *to jog, to nudge a p, to give a p a jog*; jdn (mit dem Fuße) ~ *to give a p a kick*; am Ellenbogen ~ *to jog a p's ellow* **2.** die Gläser ~ → II. 2. **3.** ⟨min⟩ (Feuer) = anzünden **II.** vi **A. 1.** ~ an = stoßen an → stoßen vi **2.** *to chink* (:~!); mit den Gläsern ~ (= die Gläser ~) *to click* (*the*) *glasses*; (mit jdm) ~ *to clink* od *touch glasses* (*with a p*); auf jdn, jds Gesundheit (*or* Wohl) ~ *to drink the health* od *toast of a p, to drink to a p* **3.** mit der Zunge ~ *to lisp* || im Reden ~ *to speak interruptedly* (od *with interruptions*); ohne anzustoßen *without interruptions, fluently* **4.** (Anstoß erregen) ~ mit etw *to cause offence by a th*; ~ bei jdm *to give offence to a p*, → Anstoß A. 2. **B.** (*of buildings, etc*) ~ an etw *to adjoin a th, to be contiguous to, to abut* (od *border*) *on a th* | **~d** a *contiguous* (an *to*); *adjoining* (*room*); *contiguous* (*house*)

·Anstößer m ⟨bes Sw⟩ (*next*) *neighbour*

·anstößig 1. a (sehr ~) *shocking, scandalous* (*conduct*) || *objectionable, obnoxious, offensive* (*manners, words*) **2.** adv (*to behave*) *shockingly* | ≈keit [f] ~/~en *offensiveness*; *scandalousness*

·an|strahlen vt [h] (etw, jdn) *to shed radiance on, to shine on* || (etw durch Scheinwerfer) *to* (*high-*)*light* | ⟨fig⟩ jdn (lächelnd) ~ *to beam* (od *smile*) *upon* od *at a p*

·an|strängen vt [h] die Pferde ~ *to put the horses to*

·an|streben vt/i [h] **1.** vt; etw ~ *to aspire to* (od *after*); *to strive for* (od *after*) *a th*; *to make great efforts to reach a th* || es ist -zu-, es z tun ⟨a.⟩ *it is desirable* od *preferable to do it* **2.** vi → ankämpfen gegen

·an|streichen I. vt [h] **1. a.** (Haus etc) *to paint*; die Tür blau ~ *to p. the door blue*; *to colour* || schlecht u grob ~ *to daub* | (tünchen) *to whitewash*; → Kalktünche || → Firnis, Teer **b.** ⟨übtr⟩ mit Blei ~ *to pencil*; *to mark, to underline*; (anhaken) *to mark* (od *tick*) *off* | ⟨fig⟩ °jdm etw ~ f *to pay a p out for a th, to make a p pay for a th* **2.** (Streichholz) *to strike* **II.** ≈ n *painting* || *whitewashing* | *marking*

·Anstreicher m ~s/~ *house-painter*; *whitewasher*; ⟨hum⟩ (Maler) *brother of the brush*

·an|strengen (→ ansträngen) vt [h] **1.** ⟨jur⟩ e–e Klage, e–n Prozeß ~ gegen jdn *to bring an action against a p* **2. a.** (geistige Kräfte etc) *to bring into operation* (od *play*), *to bring to bear* | sehr ~ (über~) *to strain, to tax*; die Augen sehr ~ (of print) *to be trying for the eyes* || → anspannen I. 1.; Anspruch B. 2. | (ermüden) (jdn) *to exhaust, to fatigue* **b. sich ~** *to pull o.s. together*; *to exert o.s., to do one's utmost*; *to make an effort* ⟨a. fig⟩ | (keine Kosten scheuen) *to loosen the purse-strings, to come down handsomely* || → angestrengt

·anstrengend a *hard, arduous*; *exacting* (*piece of work*); *trying* (f *to*); *exhausting* (*day*) **·Anstrengung** f ~/~en *exertion* (f jdn *to a p*); *effort* (f jdn *for a p*; *to do*); gr ~ *strain* (f jdn *on a p*; *to do*) || die größten ~en m *to make the greatest efforts* od *exertions*; des tägl Lebens → Anspannung; mit äußerster ~ *with a last supreme effort*; alle ~en m *to put one's shoulder to the wheel*; . . etw z erlangen *to make a strong bid for* || ohne ~ gewinnen *to win hands down*; trotz unserer Anstrengungen *do what we could* (*we* . .) || mit gr ~ konnte man es sehen *if you concentrated you could see it* → Anspannung

·Anstrich m ~(e)s/~e **A. 1.** → Anstreichen **2.** [konkr] *paint*(*coat*); ⟨her⟩ *tincture*; der erste ~ *the first coat of paint, the priming coat of p.*; → Grundierung; ein neuer ~ *a fresh coat of p.*; → Firnis **3.** ⟨übtr⟩ äußerer ~ *varnish, veneer*; *colour*; *tinge, tincture*; → Anflug || ein (äußerer) ~ v Wissen *a sprinkling* od *smattering of knowledge* || e–r S e–n ~ geben *to colour, varnish, veneer a th* (*with*); *to impart a varnish to a th*; sich e–n gelehrten ~ geben *to assume a learned air*: sich e–n vornehmen ~ geben *to give o.s. airs, to put on airs* || e–n ~ v etw h *to be tinctured* od *tinged with a th*; *to savour* (od *to be redolent*) *of a th* **B.** ⟨mus⟩ *the first stroke* od *touch of the bow* **~farbe** f *paint*

·an|stricken vt [h] (etw) *to knit* (an *on to*) || (e–n Strumpf) *to foot*

·an|strömen vi [s] angeströmt k *to come rushing* (od *sweeping*) *along*; → strömen

·an|stückeln, an|stücken vt [h] (etw) *to patch, to piece* (an *on to*)

·Ansturm m ~(e)s/≈e **1.** *attack, charge, onset, assault, onslaught* (auf *on*) | ⟨übtr⟩ *onrush* (*of water*) **2.** (Andrang) *influx* (*of visitors*) || *run* (auf e–e Bank *on a bank*); ⟨com⟩ *rush* (auf *on*)

·an|stürmen vi [s] **1.** angestürmt k *to come dashing* (od *rushing*) *along* **2.** ~ gegen (od auf) *to storm against, to rush upon* || (of waves) *to dash against* || ⟨mil⟩ *to assault, to charge* (*the enemy*) | ⟨übtr⟩ *to battle* (od *buck, struggle, surge*) *against* (*fate, a movement*); → ankämpfen

·an|stürzen vi [s] = anstürmen 1.

***·an|suchen 1.** vi [h] bei jdm um etw ~ *to apply to a p for a th*; *to ask* (od *petition, solicit*) *a p for a th*; → angehen, ersuchen, nachsuchen **2.** ≈ n ~s/~ *application*; *petition, request, solicitation*; auf das ~ jds *on the application, at the request of a p, at a p's request*

Antagon·ismus m ~/-men *antagonism* (gegen *to*) **Antagon·ist** m ~en/~en *antagonist, adversary* **antagon·istisch** *a antagonistic*(*al*)

°**·an|tanzen** vi [s] *to come along*; *to arrive*; *to appear, to make one's appearance*

Ant·arktis f ~/ *the Antarctic* **ant·arktisch** a *antarctic, south-polar*; → Südliches Eismeer

·an|tasten vt [h] **1.** *to touch*; *to handle* || das Kapital ~ *to touch the capital* **2.** ⟨übtr⟩ **a.** (jdn, jds Ruf etc) *to attack*; *offend*; *hurt, injure* **b.** (jds Rechte) *to encroach* (od *infringe*) (*up*)*on*; *to call in question, to impugn*

antedat·ieren vt [h] (Brief etc) *to antedate*

antediluvi·anisch a (vorsintflutlich) *antediluvian*; ~es Wesen *antediluvian*

Anteflexi·on f ~/~en ⟨med⟩ *anteflexion*

·**Anteil** m ~(e)s/~e **1.** (der e–m zukommende Teil) **a.** *share* (von, an *of*); *part*; verhältnismäßiger ~ *quota*; *proportion* ⟨a. demog⟩ (an *of*) ‖ ⟨demog⟩ ~ der Sterbefälle (nach Ursachen) *deathratio*; ~ der unehelich Geborenen *illegitimacy ratio* ‖ (Land⁓) *allotment* ‖ ⟨jur⟩ (Erbteil) *portion* (an *of*) ‖ (Pflicht⁓) *contingent* | ⟨com⟩ (Aktie) *share* **b.** ⟨übtr fam⟩ *whack*, s–n ~ bek *to get one's w.* (von *at*) **2.** (Beteiligung) **a.** ⟨mst com⟩ *share* (an *in*); ~ am Gewinn *share in profits* ‖ *interest* (an *in*); *percentage* (an *of*) e–n ~ h an *to have an interest, a share in* (*a business, a mine*) **b.** ⟨übtr⟩ *share, part* (an *in*); sein ~ an der Aufgabe *his part in the task* ‖ ~ gewähren *to impart*; er hatte gr ~ an dem Mißerfolge *he had a large share in bringing about the failure*; aktiven ~ nehmen an *to take an active part in*; regen ~ nehmen an *to be strong on*; → Interesse; teilhaben; teilnehmen **3.** (innere Teilnahme) *sympathy* (an etw *in a th*); ~ nehmen an etw *to feel sympathy for* (od *with*) *a th, to sympathize with a th*

·**Anteil-** [in comp] *share-* . .; *quota-* . . ~**haber** m *partner, partaker* ‖ *shareholder* ⁓**mäßig** a = anteilig ‖ adv ~ verteilen *to pro-rate* ~**nahme** f *sympathy*; *concern* (*with deep c.*); innere ~ *inner campassion*; z Tode (jds) spreche ich Ihnen m–e aufrichtige ~ aus *I offer you my sincere sympathy on the death of* .. ~**schein** m *share--certificate*

·**anteilig** a *sharing* (*terms*); *proportional*; *pro rata* (Stromgebühr . . *electricity charge*)

·**an|telephonieren** vt [h] jdn ~ *to* (*tele*)*phone a p*; *to ring a p up* (*on the phone*); *to give a p a ring* ‖ ein Herr hat Sie antelephoniert *there's been a gentleman on the telephone to you* | [abs] ich werde ~ *I'll ring you up*; es wurde antelephoniert *there was a call*

Ant·enne f ~/~n **1.** ⟨zoo⟩ *antenna* L **2.** ⟨wir⟩ *aerial, antenna*; ⟨Am sl⟩ *stak* ‖ Boden⁓ *ground aerial*, Draht⁓ *aerial wire*; Drehrahmen⁓ *loop-antenna*; Empfangs⁓ *receiving aerial*; Hoch⁓ *roof* od *overhead* od *outdoor aerial*; Netz⁓ *main aerial*; Peil⁓ *direction finding antenna*; Rahmen⁓ *frame aerial*; Richtstrahl⁓ *beam aerial*; Rundstrahl⁓ *omnidirectional ant.*; Schirm⁓ *umbrella aerial*; Schlepp⁓ ⟨aero⟩ *trailing aerial*; Sende⁓ *emitting aerial*; *transmitting aerial* Zimmer⁓ *indoor aerial* **3.** [in comp] ~**n**-; ~**ableitung** f *down-lead* ~**abstimmung** f *aerial tuning* ~**anlage** f *radiating system* ~**draht** m (-Litze *standard*) *aerial wire* ~**ei** n (der Schlepp⁓) *antenna weight* ~**kreis** m *ant. circuit* ~**leistung** f *ant. energy* od *power* ~**leitung** f *aerial lead* ~**mast** m *aerial mast* od *pole* ~**nahbereich** m *ant. proximity zone* ~**turm** m *radio tower* ~**zuleitung** f *lead-in*

·**Antep·endium** (L) n ~s/-dien ⟨ec arch⟩ *antependium*

Antezed·ens n (L) ~/-denzien *antecedent* ‖ [mst pl] *antecedents*; *foundations* [pl]

Anth·elien [pl] ⟨astr⟩ *anthelia* L [pl]

Anth·emion n ~s/-mien ⟨archeol⟩ *floral ornament, palmette*

Anth·ere f ~/~n ⟨bot⟩ *anther*

Antholog·ie f ~/~n *anthology*

Anthoz·oen [pl] ⟨zoo⟩ *anthozoa* L [pl]

Anthraz·en n ~s/ *anthracene* ‖ **Anthraz·it** m ~(e)s/ ⟨min⟩ *anthracite* (*coal*); ⟨Am a.⟩ *hard coal*

Anthropo-~**gen·ie** f ⟨biol⟩ *anthropogeny* ~**geograph·ie** f *anthropogeography* ~**·ide** m: der ~ *the anthropoid ape* ~**l·og** m ~en/~en *anthropologist* ‖ ~**log·ie** f ~/ *anthropology* ⁓**l·ogisch** a *anthropological* ~**metr·ie** f ~/ *anthropometry* ~**m·orphe** m: der ~ = Anthropoide ~**morph·ismus** m *anthropomorphism* ~**phag·ie** f *anthropophagy* ~**soph·ie** f *anthroposophy* ⁓**zentrisch** a *anthropocentric*

Anth·urium n ~s/-rien ⟨bot⟩ (Schwanzblume) *anthurium*

anti-.. [pref] *anti-*

Anti·ar m ~s/~e = Upasbaum

·**Anti-** ~**babypille** f *contraceptive pill*, ⟨fam⟩ (*the*) *Pill* ~**bi·otikum** n ~s/-ka, ⁓**bi·otisch** a *antibiotic* [s & a] ⁓**chambr·ieren** vi [h] *to stay* (*long*) *in the antechamber* ‖ *to dance attendance* (*up*)*on a p* ‖ ⟨parl Am⟩ *to lobby* ~**chapeaut·isten** m [pl] *the hatless brigade* ~**christ** m ~(e)s/ *Antichrist*

·**an|ticken** vt [h] *to push* (od *touch*) *lightly*

·**Anti-** ~**fa** m ~s/~s = ~faschist [m] ~en/~en "*anti-fascist*" ~**fa-** [in comp] "*anti-fascistic*" ~**frikti·ons-** *antifriction* (*metal*) ~**g·en** n ~s/~e ⟨physiol⟩ *antigen* [mst pl] ~**idr·otikum** n ~s/-ka *anti-perspirant* ~**g·en** n ~s/~e ⟨physiol⟩ *antigen* [mst pl]

ant·ik a **1.** (griech.-röm.) *ancient* (*art*), *antique* (*world*); ~es Kunstwerk *antique* ‖ ⟨Lit⟩ *classical* (*drama, literature*) **2.** (alt) *antique*; *archaic*; *old-fashioned* ⁓**druckpapier** n *art cardboard*

Ant·ike f ~/ **1.** die ~ [abstr] ⟨lit etc⟩ *antiquity* **2.** (Kunstwerk) [pl ~n] *antique*(*s*), *antiquities* [pl] ~**ngrün** n *verd-antique* ~**nhändler** m *antique dealer* **antikis·ierend** a *in the style* (od *after the manner*) *of antiquity*

·**Anti-** ⁓**klerikal** a *anti-clerical* ~**klin·ale** f ~/~n ⟨geol⟩ *anticline* ~**klopfmittel** n ⟨mot⟩ *de--pinker*; *anti-knock dope* ~**materie** f *antimatter* ~**oxidans** n *antioxidant* ⁓**konzeption·ell** a = empfängnisverhütend ~**körper** m (Schutzstoff) *antibody* ~**krit·ik** f ~/~en *anticritism*

·**Antil·ibanon** m (Gebirge in Syrien) (*Mount*) *Anti-Lebanon*

Ant·illen, die [pl] (Westind. Inselgruppe) *the Antilles* pl; kleine ~ *Lesser Antilles* od *Caribbees*; über (unter) dem Winde *the Windward* (*Leeward*) *Islands* pl; ~**meer,** das *the Caribbean Sea*

Antil·ope f ~/~n ⟨zoo⟩ *antelope*; gr quergestreifte ~ *koodoo, kudu*; Rappen⁓ *sable antelope*; Steppen⁓ *saiga*; → Hartebeest, Kama

Antimak·assar m ~s/~e (Schutzdecke) *antimacassar*

Antim·on n ~s/ ⟨chem⟩ *antimony*; *stibium* L ~**blei** n *antimony* (od *antimonial*) *lead* ~**blende** f *red antimony, antimony blende* ~**blüte** f *antimony bloom*; *valentinite* ~**glanz** m *antimony glance*; *gray antimony ore*; *antimonite*

antimon·archisch a *antimonarchical*

Antimon·it m ~s/ = Antimonglanz

·**Anti-** ~**nom·ie** f ~/~n ⟨jur & log⟩ *antimony*

Antioch·ia, Anti·ochien n (Stadt in Syrien) *Antioch* **antioch·enisch** a *Antiochian*

Anti- ~**path·ie** f ~/~n *antipathy* (gegen *against, to*) ~**perist·altik** f ⟨med⟩ *antiperistalsis* ~**ph·on** f ~/~en ⟨ec⟩ *antiphon* ~**p·ode** m ~n/~n **1.** (Gegenfüßler) die ~n [pl] *the antipodes* [pl] **2.** ⟨übtr⟩ *antipode* ‖ er war sein ~ *he was the very antipode* (od *antipodes*) *to himself*

·**an|tippen** vt [h] (etw) *to touch lightly* (od *with the finger-tips*); *to tap* | ⟨übtr⟩ *to touch upon* (*a subject*)

·**Anti-** ~**pyr·in** n ~s/ ⟨chem⟩ *antipyrin*(*e*), *antipyretic* s

Ant·iqua f ~/~ ⟨typ⟩ (Ggs Fraktur) *the Roman type* (abbr rom.), *Roman*; ältere ~ (Kursiv) *old face* (*italic*), jüngere ~ *modern face*, jüngere ~ Kursiv *modern italic*; fette ~ *fat face*; ~-Versalien [f pl] *Roman capitals*; ~-Gemeine [f] *Roman lower case* ~**buchstaben** pl, ~**schrift** f *Roman letters* (od *characters*); *Romans* pl

Antiqu·ar m (e)s/~e *antiquary*; *antiquarian*;

antique dealer || (Buchhändler) *second-hand bookseller*

Antiquari·at n ~(e)s/~e **~sbuchhandlung** f *second-hand bookshop* (od *bookstall*) **antiqu·arisch 1.** a *second-hand*; ⟨Am⟩ *used* (*book*) **2.** adv (*to buy*) *second-hand* **antiqu·iert** a *antiquated*; *out of date* || *old-fashioned*

Antiquit·ät f ~/~en *antique relic*; [mst pl]; *antiquities, ancient relics* pl | **~en- ~händler** m *dealer in antiques* (od *antiquities, curios, curiosities*; *articles of virtu*) **~laden** m *antique shop*; (*old*) *curiosity shop* **~sammler** m *antiquary, antiquarian*; *collector of antiquities* (od *curios*); (~ u Kenner) *virtuoso*

·antirevolution·är a *antirevolutionary*

Anti- ~rakete f *anti-missile* **~resistenzbehandlung** f (bei Herzverpflanzung) *immunosuppressive treatment* **~semit** m ~en/~en *anti-Semite* **≈-sem·itisch** a *anti-Semitic* **~semit·ismus** m *anti-Semitism* **~s·epsis** f ⟨med⟩ (Ggs Asepsis) *antisepsis* Gr **≈s·eptisch** a ⟨med⟩ *antiseptic*; ~es Mittel ⟨engl⟩ *eau de Javelle* Fr; *Dakin's solution*; → Eusol **≈sozi·al** a *antisocial* **~str·ophe** f ~/~en *antistrophe* **~teilchen** n *antiparticle* **~th·ese** f ~/~n *antithesis* Gr (von, zu *of, to*) **~tox·in** n ~s/~e ⟨biol⟩ *antitoxin* **~-Virus-Mittel** n *anti-virus agent* **≈zip·ando** adv (L) ⟨com⟩ *in anticipation, in advance* **~zip·ation** f ~/~en *anticipation*; ⟨com⟩ *advance* (*of payment*) **≈zip·ieren** vt [h] *to anticipate*; *to pay before maturity* **~zykl·one** f *anticyclone*

·Antlitz n ~es/~e ⟨bib, poet & liter⟩ = Angesicht; Gesicht

Ant·öken m pl (Gegenwohner) *Antoeci* L; *Antecians* pl

Ant·oniuskreuz n *the Cross of St. Anthony* (T)

·Antonskraut n ⟨bot⟩ *willow-herb*

Antonym n ~s/~e *antonym* (*good and bad are antonyms*)

an|traben vi [s] *to begin* (od *start*) *trotting* || angetrabt k *to come trotting* od *running along*

·Antrag m ~(e)s/≈e **1.** (Vorschlag) **a.** *proposal* (→ 2.); *application* (v Seiten jds *from a p*); e–n ~ stellen *to make a proposal* **b.** ⟨parl⟩ *motion* (auf *for*; auf Vertagung *to adjourn*) || (Gesetzes-≈) *bill*; ~ e–s Abgeordneten *private* (⟨Am *special*) *bill* | auf jds ~ *on the motion of a p*; ein v jdm schriftlich eingebrachter (od gestellter) ~ *a m. standing in a p's name* | → ablehnen 1. || über e–n ~ abstimmen *to take a vote on a motion* || e–n ~ annehmen *to agree to a m.*; der ~ wurde angenommen *the m. was agreed to* || e–n ~ durchbringen *to carry a m.* || den ~ e–r S einbringen *to move a th* || e–n Abänderungs≈ einbringen zu .. *to move an amendment to* .. || e–m ~ stattgeben *to grant a motion* || e–n ~ stellen auf . . *to bring forward a motion for, to move for* . .; den ~ auf Ablehnung e–r Vorlage st. *to move the rejection of a bill* || f e–n ~ stimmen *to vote for a motion* || e–n ~ unterstützen *to second a motion* **2.** (Heirats≈) *proposal*; *offer* od *overture of marriage* || e–n ~ erhalten *to have a proposal* || jdm e–n ~ m *to make an offer of marriage to a p, to propose to a p*; e–n ~ stellen, vorlegen (⟨Am⟩ verschieben) *to table a motion* **~sdelikt** n *offence prosecuted* (*only*) *on application of the injured party, minor criminal delict* **~sformular** n *application form* **~steller** m *proposer*; *claiment, applicant, appellant, enrollee* || ⟨parl⟩ *mover* (*of a bill*) || ⟨jur⟩ *petitioner*

·an|tragen vt/i [h] **1.** vt **a.** (etw) *to bring* (*along*); *to carry*; → apportieren **b.** ⟨übtr⟩ jdm etw ~ *to offer* od *tender a p a th* od *a th to a p*; *to propose a th to a p*, ihm wurde e–e Stelle angetragen *he was offered a post* || er trug ihr s–e Hand an *he proposed to her* **2.** vi † auf etw ~ *make a motion, to move for a th*; *to propose, to suggest a th*; darauf ~, daß . . *to suggest that*

·an|trauen vt [h] ein Mädchen jdm ~ *to marry* od *wed a woman to a p*; *to give a woman in marriage to a p* || angetraut *wedded* (: *my wedded wife*)

·an|treffen vt [h] (jdn) *to find, to meet*; ich traf ihn nicht an *I did not find him at home* od *in*; ich traf ihn zufällig an *I met him* (sc *at home*) *by chance*; ich hoffe, diese Zeilen treffen dich gut an *I trust this finds you well* → treffen | *to come across, to meet with, to find* (: *where do you find cabs nowadays*?)

·an|treiben vt/i **I.** vt [h] **1.** (*of the sea*) (etw) *to carry along*; Eisschollen wurden angetrieben *blocks of ice were washed ashore* || (Schneemassen) *to drift*; → treiben **2.** (T) *to goad, to drive*; *to push* (*to do*) || die Pferde ~ *to touch up the, one's horses* || ⟨hunt⟩ Hunde ~ *to tally-ho* | (jdn) *to urge on*; *to goad* (z tun *into doing*); *to impel, actuate, urge* (zu *to*; *to do*) || wir l uns nicht ~ *we won't be rushed* || (anreizen) (jdn) *to egg* od *set on, to incite, to instigate* (z *to*; *to do*); *to motivate*; → anspornen | jdn zur letzten Anstrengung ~ *to put a p to his trumps* | (Boot) *to propel* || (Gedächtnis) *to fillip* || (Maschine) *to propel*; *to drive* [mst pass]; (Kran) *to work* || (Düsenflugzeug) *to power* **3.** (befestigen) Reifen am Faß ~ *to hoop a cask* **II.** vi [s] ans Land ~ *to drift, to be washed ashore*; → treiben

·Antreiben n drift || *driving, pushing* || → Antrieb **·Antreiber** m ~s/~ ⟨übtr⟩ *impeller*; *inciter, instigator*

·an|treten vi/t **I.** vi [s] **1.** *to take one's place*; *to line up* (z *for*), zum Marsch ~ *to line up* (od *get ready*) *for the march*; z Angriff ~ *to start the attack*; in e–r Linie ~ *to toe the line* || ⟨mil⟩ *to fall in* (z Dienst *for service*); angetreten! *fall in*!; ~ müssen *to be ordered to parade*; → Appell || im Kampfe ~ mit jdm *to do battle with a p* || ⟨sport⟩ z Rennen (etc) ~ *to toe the line* **2.** mit dem falschen Fuß ~ *to set out with the wrong foot* **3.** (Arbeitsstelle, Pacht etc ~) *to clock in* **4.** tüchtig mit ~ *to play one's part*, → anfassen II. || da kannst du nicht mit ~ *you can't beat that*! **II.** vt [h] **1.** (Motorrad) *to start up* **2. a.** e–e Reise (etc) ~ *to start on, to set out* (od *forth*) *on a journey*; e–e Tour ~ *to leave on* (od *for*) *a tour* (*through*) || das 10. Jahr ~ *to enter one's tenth year* **b.** e–n Beruf ~ *to enter a profession* || e–e Stelle ~ *to take up a post* || ein Amt ~ *to enter upon, to accede to an office*; jds Amt ~ *to succeed to the office of a p*; die Macht ~ *to come into power*; die Regierung ~ *to come to the throne* **c.** e–e Erbschaft ~ *to enter upon an inheritance*; den Besitz e–s Gutes (etc) ~ *to succeed to an estate* || s–e Strafe ~ *to serve time* **d.** ⟨jur⟩ e–n Beweis ~ *to produce evidence*; den B. ~ f. etw *to prove a th* **2.** † ⟨bibl⟩ jdn ~ = herantreten an jdn → herantreten **·Antreten** n *taking one's place*; *lining-up* (*for*) || *falling-in*; → Antritt

·Antrieb m ~s/~e **1.** ⟨eig⟩ *impulse* ⟨a. mech⟩ || *impulsion* ⟨a. psych⟩ (unter dem ~ *under the i.*); *impetus*; *stimulus, motive* || ⟨phys⟩ *thrust, propulsion* (*jet pr.*) || ⟨tech mot⟩ *drive* ⟨a. biol⟩; Ketten≈ *chain drive*; ~ mit e–r Kette *single chain drive*; Einzel≈ *separate d.*, Gruppen≈ *group d.* || elektrischer ~ *electric drive*; Maschine mit elektr. ~ *machine worked by electricity* || Fahrrad≈ *cycle driving gear* || mit Diesel-, Pedal≈ *Diesel, pedal driven* || ⟨sport⟩ *drive* || ⟨aero⟩ & Raketen≈ ⟨a–n⟩ *propulsion* **2.** ⟨übtr⟩ (innerer ~) *motion*; *urge* (: *religious u.*) | e–n ~ auslösen ⟨psych⟩ *to motivate an action* || aus eigenem ~ *of one's own volition* (od *will*); *spontaneously, unprompted*, ich tat es aus eig. ~ *I did it on my own* || aus freiem ~ *of one's own accord* || aus natürlichem ~ *instinctively* || (Neigung) *inclination*, nicht der geringste ~ *not the slightest i.* (*to do*) | (Ansporn) *encourage-*

ment, fillip (für jdn, etw *to a p, a th*) ‖ (Anreiz) *impulse, incentive, inducement, encouragement* (zu *to*; *to do*); e–r S e–n frischen ~ geben *to give a fresh impetus to a th* **~sdynamo** m *driving dynamo* **~shebel** m *driving lever* **~skette** f *driving chain* **~skraft** f ⟨mech⟩ *propulsive power*; (P) *driving need* **~smaschine** f *motor, engine* **~smittel** n ⟨mot⟩ *working fluid* **~smöglichkeiten** f pl *types of possible driving* **~motor** m *driving motor* **~s-phase** f beim Start ⟨a–n⟩ *initial driving phase* **~rad** n ⟨mot⟩ *d.g gear* **~srakete** f (Startrakete) *booster rocket* **~sriemen** m *d.g belt* **~svorrichtung** f *driving gear*; *motor* **~swelle** f *driving shaft*

·an|trinken vt/i [h] **1.** vt (ein Glas) *to begin to drink off* (*a glass*) **|** °sich [dat] e–n ~ *to drink one's fill*; *to drink o.s. drunk*; *to get tipsy* ‖ sich Mut ~ *to fire one's courage by a drink* ‖ sich e–e Krankheit ~ *to drink o.s. into an illness* ‖ → angetrunken **2.** vi *to drink first*

·Antritt m ~(e)s/~e **1.** → Antreten **2.** ⟨cycl racing⟩ *acceleration* **3.** ⟨arch⟩ *the first step* (*of a staircase*) **4.** ⟨übtr⟩ *setting out, start*; ~ e–r Reise *starting on a journey* ‖ ~ e–s Amtes (etc) *entrance into* (od *upon*) *an office* **|** *accession* (e–r S *to a th*); ~ der Regierung *a. to the throne* ‖ ~ e–r Erbschaft *accession to an inheritance* **~saudienz** f *the first audience* **~sbesuch** m *the first visit* (bei *to*) **~srede** f *inaugural*; *inaugural address* **~svorlesung** f ⟨Ger⟩ *inaugural lecture*

·Antrunk m ~(e)s/ *the first drink*; den ~ h *to drink first*

·an|tun vt [h] **1.** °(Kleid etc) ~ = anziehen, -legen → d. ‖ → angetan **2.** ⟨übtr⟩ (zufügen) **a.** jdm Gutes etc ~ *to confer benefits upon a p, to do good to a p*; jdm Ehre ~ *to do honour to a p* ‖ s–n Feinden etw ~ *to inflict a th upon . .* ‖ jdm Unrecht ~ *to do* od *commit wrong on a p* ‖ jdm Böses ~ *to do a p harm*; *to harm* od *injure a p*; → Schande, Schimpf; tu mir dies **nicht** an *spare me this humiliation* (etc) **|** jdm, e–r S **Gewalt** ~ *to do violence to a p, to a th*; e–r Frau G. ~ *to violate* od *ravish a woman*; ⟨übtr⟩ dem Sinne e–s Worts (etc) G. ~ *to strain* (od *force*) *the sense of a word*; *to twist a word* **b.** sich [dat] **Zwang** ~ *to force o.s.* (*to do*); *to act under compulsion, to put o.s. under constraint*; *to do with reluctance*; tun Sie sich keinen Zwang an *do just as you like, be quite at your ease, take your ease* **| sich** [dat] **etw** ~ *to lay hands upon o.s.*; er könnte sich etwas *or* ein Leid(s) ~ *he might lay hands on himself, he might do something to h.s.* **c. es jdm** ~ *to bewitch, to enchant, to fascinate, to impress a p*; sie hat es ihm angetan *he is smitten by her*

·an|tupfen vt [h] *to dab* (mit *with*)

·Antwort f ~/~en **1.** *answer, reply, response* (auf *to*); deutliche ~ *plain answer* ‖ scharfe ~ (*neat*) *retort*; sie erhielt die ~, daß .. *she received answer that* .. ‖ kz scharfe ~ *short answer*; abschlägige ~ *refusal, rebuff*; schlagfertige ~ *repartee, witty retort*; treffende ~ *clincher*; umgehende ~ *reply by return of post* **2.** ⟨übtr⟩ (Reaktion) *answer, reaction, response* (auf *to*) **3. Wendungen: a** als ~ *for answer*; *in reply* (*he said*) ‖ als ~ auf *in answer* (od *reply, response*) *to* ‖ k–e ~ ist auch e–e ~ *silence gives consent* **b.** um ~ wird gebeten (abbr u.A.w.g.) *the favour of an answer is requested* (abbr *R.S.V.P.* = *répondez s'il vous plaît*); *an answer will oblige*; sie blieb ihm k–e ~ schuldig *she was a match for him* ‖ e–e ~ erhalten *to be answered*; man erhielt k–e ~ am Telephon *the telephone was not answered* ‖ er erhob sich zur ~ *he rose to reply* (vi) ‖ e–e ~ geben *to give* (od *make, return*) *an answer, to make a reply*; zur ~ geben *to answer, to reply* ‖ gleich mit der ~ bei der Hand s *to be quick* (od *good*) *at repartee* ‖ die ~ kannst du dir schenken! *the answer is a lemon!* ‖ um k–e ~ verlegen s *to be never at a loss for an answer* ‖ → Rede **~bereitschaft** f ⟨eth⟩ *responsivenes* **~gerät** n (Radar≈) *responser* **~(post)karte** f (⟨com⟩ *business*) *reply card* **~schein** m *reply coupon* **~schreiben** n (*written*) *answer, reply*

·antworten I. vt/i [h] **A.** vt (etw) *to say in reply, to answer, to reply* (: *he replied nothing*) ‖ ich erinnere mich nicht, was er ihnen antwortete (. .) *what he answered them* (od *replied to them*) **B.** vi **1. a.** *to answer, to reply* (an Stelle jds *for a p*); *to return an answer, to make a reply*; → ja, nein ‖ frech ~ *to answer back* ‖ hastig ~ *to snap out* ‖ schriftlich ~ *to reply by letter*, umgehend ~ *to r. by return of post* ‖ ~d *in reply* (*he pointed out*) ‖ ⟨ec⟩ *to respond* **b.** ~ auf etw *to answer a th* (: *he answered her letter*); *to reply to a th*; auf jds Frage ~ *to answer to a p's question*; auf s–e Frage antwortete sie *in reply to his question she said* (*that*) **c.** jdm ~ *to answer a p, to reply to a p*; jdm ~ auf etw *to answer a p to a th*, jdm auf s–e Frage ~ *to answer a p his question*; *to answer to a p's qu., to give an answer to a p's qu.*; jdm ~ daß . . *to answer* (*to*) *a p that..* **2.** ⟨übtr⟩ (reagieren) *to answer, to respond*; *to make a response* (auf *to*) ‖ *to answer, to respond* (mit *with*); *to reply* (mit *by*) **II.** ≈ n *answering*; schnell im ~ *quick in repartee*

·antwortlich adv [prep] ~ Ihres Schreibens *in answer* od *reply to your letter*

·An- u ·Ausschalter m ⟨bes rec⟩ *on-off switch*

Anur·ie f ~/ ⟨med⟩ *anury, anuria*

·Anus m ⟨med⟩ *anus* (L)

·an|vertrauen vt [h] **1.** jdm etw ~ *to* (*en*)*trust a th to a p, to consign a th to a p* (od *to a p's care*); *to put a th under a p's charge*; s–e Seele Gott ~ *to commit one's soul to God* ‖ sein Kind jdm ~ *to entrust* (*the care of*) *one's child to a p* ‖ jdm e–e Aufgabe ~ *to charge* (od *entrust*) *a p with a task* **|** sich der Nachsicht jds ~ *to throw o.s. upon the indulgence of a p* **2.** (mitteilen) jdm etw ~ *to confide a th to a p* **|** sich jdm ~ *to confide o.s. to a p, to fling o.s. on a p, to unbosom o.s. to a p*; *to put o.s. in a p's hands* od *care*; *to entrust o.s. to, to confide in, to open one's heart to a p* **·Anvertrauen** n *entrusting*; *consignment, commitment* (*to a p*) ‖ *confiding*; *trust*

·anverwandt a jdm ~ *related to a p* **·Anverwandte 1.** m: der ~ (ein ~r) ~n/~n ⟨allg⟩ *relation, relative* ‖ (männlicher) *kinsman* **2.** die ~ f ~n/~n *kinswoman* **3.** ~, die ~n [pl] *kinsfolk* [pl konstr] ‖ (des Ehemannes, der Ehefrau) *in-laws* [pl]; Verwandte u ~ *kith and kin*

·an|visieren vt [h] *to sight* (*out*); ⟨artill, etc⟩ *to align* od *aline* (*the*) *sight*(*s*) *on*

·Anwachs m Anwachses → Anwachsung

·an|wachsen I. vi [s] **1.** (festwachsen) *to grow* (an *to*); *to grow together* ‖ (of plants) *to take root* **|** ⟨übtr⟩ *to adhere, to become firmly united* od *attached, tied* (an *to*) ‖ die Zunge war ihm wie -ge- *he was tongue-tied* od *speechless* **2.** (zunehmen) *to accumulate*; *increase, augment*; *swell* (zu *into, to*) ‖ (of rivers) *to rise, swell* **II.** ≈ n *increase* (e–r S *in a th*); *rise*; im ~ *on the increase* (od *rise*) ‖ *swell*; z ~ bringen *to swell*

·Anwachsung f ~/~en *growth, increment*; *accretion* **|** [konkr] (Zuwachs) *accretion* ‖ ⟨jur⟩ *accession*; (Erb-) *accretion* ‖ → Anwachsen

·Anwalt m ~(e)s/≈e **1.** ⟨jur⟩ *lawyer* ‖ = Rechtsanwalt → d. ‖ als ~ auftreten f *to hold a brief for* (*a p*) **|** → Kron≈ **2.** ⟨pol⟩ (bevollmächtigter Vertreter) *attorney*; *agent, proxy* **3.** ⟨übtr⟩ (Verfechter) *advocate* (e–r S *of a th*) **~sgebühren** pl *barrister's, solicitor's fee* **~skammer** f ⟨Ger⟩ *representative body of German barristers*; ⟨bes Can⟩ *Bar Association* **~vorschuß** m *advance payment of costs*; (pauschal) *retainer*

·Anwaltschaft f ~/~en **1.** [abstr] *agency*,

attorneyship **2.** ⟨jur⟩ (Genossenschaft) *the Bar*

·an|wandeln vi/t **1.** vi [s] angewandelt k *to approach slowly* **2.** vt [h] [nur 3. sg & pl] ⟨fig⟩ jdn ~ (of feelings, illness) *to befall a p; to come upon a p*; e–e Krankheit wandelte ihn an *he was seized with an illness* ‖ was wandelt dich an? *what on earth do you mean?, what is the matter with you?* **·Anwandlung** f ~/~en (Anfall) *slight attack, fit*; e–e ~ v Furcht *a spasm of fear*; → Anfall **|** = Anflug 4 b.

·an|wärmen vt [h] (etw) *to warm gently; to preheat*; Getränk leicht ~ *to take the chill off a liquid*

·Anwärter m ~s/~ *expectant* (auf *of*); *claimant* (auf *to*); Thron≗ *expectant of the throne, claimant to the throne* ‖ ⟨jur⟩ *reversioner* ‖ *non--permanent official* **~(probe)zeit, ·Anwartszeit** f *qualifying period*

·Anwartschaft f ~/~en *expectancy; prospect* (auf *of*); ~ habend *expectant* (auf *of*) ‖ *entitlement; candidature* ‖ ⟨jur⟩ *remainder; reversion* (of *of*) ‖ die ~ (auf Arbeitslosenunterstützung) erfüllen *to establish a benefit period* ‖ ~srecht [n] *revisionary interest*; (des Entdeckers, Souveräns) *inchoate title* **·anwartschaftlich** a ⟨jur⟩ *reversionary*

·an|wassern vi [s] ⟨aero⟩ *to alight on the water*

·an|wehen vi/t **1.** vi [s] *to drift*, Blätter sind angeweht *leaves have drifted* **2.** vt [h] *to drift*, der Wind hat Massen v Schnee angeweht *the wind has drifted a mass of snow* **|** jdn ~ *to blow upon* (od *towards*) *a p* ‖ das Haus weht mich heimatlich an *the house makes me feel homy* (od *at home*); angeweht = angeflogen → unfliegen 1 b.

·an|weisen vt [h] **1.** jdn ~ *to instruct, direct, order a p* (*to do*); die Angestellten sind angewiesen (→ d.) *the staff have instructions* (*to do*) **2.** (zuweisen) jdm etw (Zimmer, Platz, Stellung) ~ *to assign* od *allot a th to a p*; im Speisesaal (etc) jdm e–n Platz ~ *to show a p to a seat* ‖ jdm e–n bestimmten Teil ~ *to allowance a p a definite amount* **3.** (Geld) *to assign, to remit* (jdm *to a p*); e–e Summe auf e–e Bank ~ *to make a sum payable at a bank*; → Wechsel

·Anweiser m ~s/~ *instructor* (*in*); *adviser*

·an|weißen vt [h] = weißen

·Anweisung f ~/~en **1.** (Anleitung) *instruction; guidance; advice* ‖ (Befehl) *order, direction*; auf ~ v *by order* od *direction of; at a word from* (*a p*); ~ erteilen *to enjoin* (daß *that*) **|** ~en [pl] *directions, instructions*, nach den ~en *on the instructions* (*of a p*); → Angaben ‖ Gebrauchs≗en *directions; instructions for use* ‖ ~en erhalten *to receive orders* (*to do*) ‖ ~en geben *to give directions* od *instructions*; jdm ~en g. *to instruct a p* ‖ ⟨aero wir⟩ werde ~(en) befolgen *will comply* (WILCO) **2.** (Zuteilung) *assignation, assignment* (an *to*) **3.** (Geld≗) *assignment of money, remittance*; (Zahlungs≗) *cheque* (auf 5 Pfd *for* £ *5*); → Post≗; Wechsel **4.** ⟨comp⟩ *statement*

·anwendbar a *practicable; available* ‖ *applicable* (auf *to*) ‖ *employable* (für, zu *for*) ‖ allgemein ~ *of universal application* ‖ ~ s *to apply* (auf *to*); vielseitig ~ s *to be widely employed in many applications*; dies ist nicht ~ auf gegenwärtige Umstände *this has no application to present circumstances* **≗keit** f ~ *applicability* (auf *to*); *availability*

·an|wenden vt [h] **1.** (gebrauchen) **a.** (etw) *to make use of; to employ* (in, bei *in, on*; für, zu *for*); (Fleiß, Sorgfalt, Vorsicht) *to use* ‖ (Druck) *to bring to bear; to bring into play*; Gewalt ~ *to use violence, to resort to force* ‖ ohne Gewalt –zu– *without resort to force* ‖ alle Kräfte ~ *to strain every nerve* ‖ neue Methoden ~ *to resort to new methods* ‖ → Mühe **|** (etw) gut ~ *to make good use of* (*a th*); schlecht ~ *to make a bad use of*; falsch etc ~ *to misapply, to abuse* (*a th*) ‖ nützlich ~ *tu put* (*a th*) *to use* **b.** (sein Geld) nützlicher ~ *to put one's money to better uses*; ich kann nicht mehr ~ *I can't spend* (od *afford*) *more* **2.** etw ~ auf *to apply a th to* (*a th, a p*); *to bring a th to bear upon* **| sich ~ l** (auf) *to apply* (*to*); *to be applicable* (*to*) **3.** angewandt s bei jdm → angebracht **·Anwender** m ~s/~ ⟨agr⟩ *neighbour* **·Anwendung** f ~/~en **1.** *employment, use* (: *the u. of arms*); ~ v Gewalt *resort to aggression* **2.** (Beziehung) *application* (auf, für *to*); falsche ~ *misapplication* **3. Wendungen:** in ~ bringen *to apply* (f *to*); *to employ, to use* (*for*); (Einfluß) *to exert*; (e–e Idee) .. f etw *to bring* (*an idea*) *to bear upon a th* ‖ ~ finden *to be used, to apply* vi; dies findet k–e ~ auf .. *this has* (od *finds*) *no application to, this does not apply to ..* ‖ zur ~ k f *to be used; to be brought to bear upon* **~sbereich** m *range of application*, (e–s Abkommens) *scope*, e–s Gesetzes *scope of the law*

·an|werben vt [h] ⟨mil⟩ *to enlist, to recruit*; Rekruten ~ *to recruit* ‖ **sich ~ l** ⟨mil⟩ *to enlist*

·Anwerbung f ~/~en ⟨mil, mar & aero⟩ *enlistment; recruitment*

·Anwerf- ~drehzahl *cranking speed* **~moment** n *cr. torque* **·an|werfen** vi/t [h] **1.** vi *to throw first, to have the first throw* **2.** vt **a.** (etw) *to throw* od *fling* (an *against, on*) → verputzen; Putz **b.** ⟨mot & aero⟩ (Motor etc) *to start up*

·Anwesen n ~s/~ *estate, property; premises* pl

·anwesend a **1.** [pred] *present*; ~ s ⟨univ⟩ *to be up*; ~ s bei etw *to be present at a th, to attend a th* **2.** [attr] die ~en Mitglieder *the members present, present company*; tatsächlich ~e Schüler *pupils in attendance*; ~e P ⟨demog⟩ *permanent resident*, vorübergehend ~er Ausländer ⟨stat⟩ *alien visitor, visiting alien* **·Anwesende:** der ~ (ein ~r) m ~n/~n jeder ~ *every one present*; die ~n *those* (od *the persons*) *present*; die ~n stets ausgenommen *present company always excepted, to* (um . . zu) *injure no present susceptibilities*

·Anwesenheit f ~/ *presence*; in jds ~ *in* (*the*) *p. of a p, in a p's p.* ‖ *attendance* (bei *at*) **|** [in comp] **~s- appell** m ⟩mil⟩ *roll call* **~dauer** f ⟨bes demog⟩ *duration of stay* **~liste** f *attendance list* **~unterlagen** f pl *att. records*

·an|widern vt [h] = anekeln l.; er fühlte sich –ge–rt *his gorge rose* ‖ → widerwärtig, zuwider

·Anwohner m ~s/~ *neighbour* ‖ [pl] der Küste *dwellers* [pl] *by the sea coast, coastal residents*; ~ des Flusses *d. by the riverside*

·Anwuchs m -wuchses/-wüchse *growth* ‖ junger ~ *copse* **|** ⟨übtr⟩ (Anwachsen) *increase*

·Anwunsch m *good wish* **·anwünschen** vt jdm etw ~ → wünschen; *to wish a the on a p* **·Anwünschung** f ~/~en ‖ *adoption* (*of a child*)

·Anwurf m ~(e)s/≗e **1.** ⟨sport⟩ *first throw* (od *cast*); den ~ h *to throw first* ‖ ⟨mot⟩ *starting-up* **2.** [konkr] ⟨arch⟩ *plaster*; (roher) *roughcast* **3.** (Vorwurf) *reproach; invective; slander*; (Verleumdung) *aspersion* (auf *on*)

·an|wurzeln vi [s] *to take* od *strike root* ‖ wie angewurzelt ⟨fig⟩ *as if rooted to the ground*

·Anzahl f ~/ *number, quantity* ‖ e–e ~ Bücher (*or* v Büchern) *a number of books*; e–e gr (ziemliche) ~ *a great* (*good*) *many* [pl konstr] e–e gr (ziemliche) ~ war anwesend *a great* (*good*) *many were present*; e–e gr ~ der Bücher ist .. *a great many books* (od *of the b.*) *are ..*; e–e ganze ~ *ever so many*; .. Beispiele *a good many examples*; die sehr geringe ~ *the extreme paucity* **·an|zahlen** vt [h] *to pay* (*a th*) *on account; to deposit* **·Anzahlung** f ~/~en *first instalment; payment on account; part-payment; deposit*; e–e ~ leisten *to make* (od *pay*) *a d.*

(auf *on*) || *earnest* (auf *of*), *earnest* od *token money*

·**Anzapf-** *bleeder* [attr] (*current*) **~ventil** n *bl.* od *extraction valve*

·**an|zapfen** vt [h] **1.** (Faß) *to tap, to broach* || (Baum) *to box* | (sich widerrechtlich zugängig m) (Kabelleitung) *to tap*, ⟨fam⟩ *to milk* | ⟨übtr⟩ (etw) *to broach* **2.** ⟨fig⟩ °jdn ~ **a.** (aushorchen) *to pump; to draw* (über *on*) **b.** (anpumpen) *to tap*, ⟨sl⟩ *to touch* (um *for*) **c.** (reizen) *to irritate, to annoy; to tease*

·**Anzapfung** f ⟨geol⟩ *stream capture*

·**an|zaubern** vt [h] jdm etw (Krankheit) ~ *to inflict a th on a p by a magic spell* || wie angezaubert *spell-bound*

·**Anzeichen** n ~s/~ *indication, sign* (für *of*; daß *that*), ⟨a. med⟩ *symptom* (für, v *of*) (deutlich *clear, plain*), ⟨med⟩ *syndrome*: hirnorganisches ~ *brain syndrome* || ein ~ für die gehobene Stimmung *an indication of the high spirits*; es sind bestimmte ~ da, daß .. *the signs are that*; wenn nicht alle ~ trügen *if appearances are not deceptive, unless I am greatly deceived* || (Kennzeichen) *mark* (f frühe Zeit *of early date*) | warnendes ~ *warning* (für of) || schlimmes ~ *portent* (: *the portents of war*) || (böse Vorbedeutung) *omen* (für *for*), *augury, presage, foreboding* **~beweis** m *circumstantial evidence*

·**an|zeichnen** vt [h] (bezeichnen) *to mark, to note* || → zeichnen

·**Anzeige** f ~/~en **1.** (Ankündigung) **a.** *announcement, intimation, notification* || (schriftliche) *notice*; ⟨univ⟩ Schwarzes Brett f ~en *noticeboard*; ⟨theat⟩ *poster* || ⟨com⟩ (Mitteilung) *advice*, ~en *advices* **b.** (Rezension) *review* (*of a book*); kz ~ *notice* **c.** (Inserat) *advertisement*; kleine (Zeitungs-)~en *classified advertisements* || e–e ~ aufgeben *to insert an a.* (in *in*) || kz ~ *notice*; Todes≈ *obituary n.*; Verlobungs≈ *notice of an engagement* || → Annonce **2.** ⟨jur⟩ *information*, ~en [pl] *informations*; jdn zur ~ bringen, ~ m *or* erstatten gegen *to lodge* (od *lay an*) *information* (od *to inform*) *against a p* || *denunciation* || (amtliche) → Fehl≈, Straf≈ **3.** ⟨med⟩ *indication* **~bereich** m *indication range* **~gerät** n *indicator* **~lampe** *telltale lamps* | etc → dort

·**an|zeigen** vt [h] **1.** (ein Anzeichen sein v. für) *to indicate* (*a th*; *that*); *to give indication of*; *to be indicative* (od *significant, symptomatic*) *of* (*a th*); *to denote*; *to signify*; düstere Wolken zeigen Regen an *louring clouds indicate* (od *signify*) *rain*; ein schneller Puls zeigt Fieber an *a quick pulse denotes fever* | (Schlimmes) *to augur, portend, presage, forebode* (*a storm*) **2.** (zeigen, andeuten) **a.** *to indicate* (*a th*; *that*) || das Thermometer zeigt 2 Grad unter Null an *the thermometer indicates* (od *reads*) *2 degrees below freezing-point* **b.** ⟨med⟩ angezeigt s *to be indicated*; (Behandlung) angezeigt erscheinen l *to indicate* | ⟨übtr⟩ angezeigt s *to be advisable* od *expedient* (*to do*); es f angezeigt halten *to think fit* (*to do*); → angebracht **c. sich ~** *to show* **3.** (kundtun, ankündigen) **a.** (Anfang, Entschluß, Resultat etc) *to announce*; *intimate* || ⟨mech⟩ *to signal* || (öffentlich) *to publish, proclaim*; den Empfang e–r S ~ *to acknowledge the receipt of a th*; ⟨com⟩ (Tratte) *to advise* || jdm etw ~ *to notify a th to a p* (od *a p of a th*); *to inform* (od *apprise*) *a p of a th*; ⟨com⟩ *to advise a p of a th* | (jdn amtlich) *to report* **b.** (besprechen) (Buch) *to notice* **c.** (in Zeitung ~) *to advertise* **4.** ⟨jur⟩ jdn ~ *to denounce a p, to inform against, to lay an information, to bring a charge against a p*; ⟨fam⟩ *to tell on a p*; jdn ~ wegen etw *to charge a p with a th*, .. getan z h .. *with doing* || ⟨übtr⟩ *to denunciate a p*; ⟨sl⟩ *to split on a p*; = anpetzen → d.

·**Anzeigen-** **~akquisiteur** [akwizitøə], **~fachmann** m *advertising* (⟨fam⟩ *ad-*) *man* **~preis** m *ad.-rate* **~teil** m *advertising columns* **~mittler** m, **~vermittlung** f *advertising agency* **~schluß** m *closing* od *press date* **~steuer** f *ad.-tax* **~teil** m (e–r Zeitung) *advertising columns* pl

·**Anzeigepflicht** f ⟨jur Ger⟩ *the duty incumbent upon a p to denounce certain crimes* | **≈ig** a *notifiable* (*disease*)

·**Anzeiger** m ~s/~ **1.** (P) *indicator* || *spotter, marker* ⟨a. mil⟩ || → Ansager || *informer* (*of crimes*); ⟨school⟩ *telltale*, ⟨sl⟩ *sneak* **2.** (Zeitung etc) *advertiser*; Bundes≈ *Federal Herald* **3.** ⟨tech⟩; (Brennstoffvorrats≈) ⟨mot⟩ *liquidometer* **~deckung** f (cf. 1.) *marker's gallery* od *pit* | → Scheiben≈kommando

·**an|zetteln** vt [h] (Aufstand etc) *to plot, originate, brew*; (Verschwörung) *to hatch, to contrive*; *to trump up* || er hat das Ganze angezettelt *it's all his doing* ·**Anzettlung** f ~/~en *hatching* od *contrivance of a plot*; *scheme, intrigue* ·**Anzettler** m ~s/~ *plotter, contriver, schemer*

·**anziehbar** a (durch Magneten) *attractable*

·**an|ziehen** vt/i [h] **I.** vt **A.** etw ~ **1.** (straffen) *to strain*; *to stretch*; (loses Band) *to pull tight*; fest ~ *to keep pull on, to give a tug to* (*a th*) || (Zügel) *to draw*; *to tighten*; die Zügel straffer ~ bei jdm *to make a p tighten his belt* || Tau kräftig ~ *to haul a rope* (od *at a r.*) **2.** (ziehen) (den Wagen) *to draw, pull* || Tür fest ~ *to draw the door to* || (Schraube) *to put on*; *to tighten*; *to drive home*; die Steuerschraube ~ *to screw* (od *raise*) *the taxes* || (Bremse) *to put on* **3.** ⟨phys⟩ *to attract* | (Feuchtigkeit) *to absorb, to soak in, to imbibe* || den Geruch e–r S ~ *to become impregnated with the smell of a th* **4.** (Kleid etc) *to don, to put on*; (Strümpfe) *to pull on*; schnell ~ *to throw on* || (Handschuhe) *to draw on* || jdm den Mantel ~ helfen *to help a p with the coat*; → umziehen || den bunten Rock ~ *to enlist*, ⟨fam⟩ *to go for a soldier* || e–n neuen Menschen ~ *to turn over a new leaf* **5.** (Beispiel, Quelle etc) *to quote, cite*; *to refer to* || (Ereignis) *to instance* (*for*); → anführen **B.** jdn ~ **1.** (ankleiden) *to dress*; schmuck ~ *to smarten, to spruce*; schwarz angezogen *clad in black* | **sich** (geschmackvoll, -los) ~ *to dress* (*well, badly*); sich schmuck ~ *to dress up, to smarten* **2.** ⟨übtr⟩ (fesseln) *to attract*; *to interest*; (Kunden) *to draw* **3.** † Tiere ~ → aufziezen **II.** vi **1.** (of horses) *to begin to pull* **2.** ⟨chess⟩ *to move first, to make first move* **3.** Salz zieht an *salt is liable* od *subject to getting damp* **4. a.** ⟨tech⟩ *to take effect, to begin to act* (od *operate*); *to work effectively, to take* || (of glue) *to stick* **b.** ⟨übtr⟩ (of prices) *to advance, harden, rise, stiffen*; (of the market) *to improve*; ⟨fam⟩ *to look up* **5.** angezogen k *to come marching along* ·**Anziehen** n *the drawing*; *tightening* || *pull* | *the putting-on, pulling-on* (*of clothes*) | *the dressing* | *the rising, hardening* (*of prices*) ·**anziehend** a ⟨com⟩ *rising* (*prices*); *improving* (*market*) | ⟨fig⟩ *attractive, engaging* (*story*); *interesting*; *inviting* (*prospects*); ⟨Am⟩ *cute* || nicht ~ *not prepossessing*; *unattractive, uninteresting*; *uninviting* || ~e S, ~er Gegenstand *attraction*; ~es Wesen *attractiveness*

·**Anziehung** f ~/~en **1.** → Anziehen **2.** ⟨phys⟩ *attraction* (: *magnetic a.*); Massen≈ *gravitation* **3.** *quotation* (*of an author*) **4.** ⟨fig⟩ *attraction* **~skraft** f **1.** ⟨phys⟩ *attractive power* (od *force*) || *attraction of gravity* | *gravitational pull*; *pull* (*of the moon*) **2.** ⟨fig⟩ *attraction*; *eye appeal* || ⟨sl⟩ *draw*, ⟨theat, film⟩ *box-office value* || ~ ausüben *to exert attraction* (auf *on*); ⟨sl⟩ *to be a draw* (: *he is a big d.*); ~ h *or* ausüben auf .. *to exercise fascination over, to attract* (*a p*), *to have attraction for* (*a p*) | → Anzugs- **~spunkt** m ⟨phys⟩ *centre of gravity* || ⟨übtr⟩ *centre of* *attraction*; *attraction* (: *the chief a. of the evening was* . .); *clou* (Fr); (gewählt:) *cynosure*

·**Anzucht** f ∼/ ⟨hort⟩ *cultivation*; *nursery*, *plantation* ‖ ⟨min⟩ *dresshole* **∼garten** m *nursery-garden*

·**Anzug** m ∼(e)s/∼̈e **1.** (Herankommen) ⟨a. mil⟩ *approach*, *advance* ‖ im ∼e s *to draw near*, *to approach*, *to be imminent*; der Feind ist im ∼e *the enemy is approaching*; ⟨übtr⟩ (of storm) *to brew*, *to gather*; (of danger) *to brew*, *to threaten*, *to be in the offing*; ein Gewitter, Unheil ist im ∼e *a storm*, *mischief is brewing* ‖ ⟨fig⟩ es ist etw im ∼e *there's something in the wind* **2.** (Zuzug) *settlement*; *residence*, *establishment* **3.** ⟨chess⟩ *first move* **4.** (Kleidung f Männer, sonst †) *suit of clothes*, *suit*; ∼ aus e–m Stoff *dittos* pl, *a ditto suit*, *a suit of dittos* ‖ → Kleidung **5.** (∼s-kraft) ⟨mot⟩ *acceleration* ‖ → Anziehungs-**∼stoff** m *suiting*, ⟨Am a.⟩ *pattern* **∼svermögen** n → dort

·**anzüglich** a *personal* (*remarks*), *pointed*; *offensive*; ∼ w *to become personal*; ∼e Bemerkungen [pl] *personalities* [pl] ‖ (schlüpfrig) *obscene*, *nasty* ·**Anzüglichkeit** f ∼/∼en *personal remark*, *personality*, *offensiveness*; *innuendo*

·**Anzugsvermögen** n ⟨mot⟩ (V_0) (rasant *quick*) *get-away* (of *a car*) ‖ ⟨mot⟩ ($V_1 > V_n$) *vivid acceleration*

·**an|zünden I.** vt [h] **1.** (Feuer, Licht) *to light*, *to kindle*; *to ignite* ‖ angezündet *alight*; ich zündete mir e–e Zigarette an *I lit a cigarette*; ich zündete ihm ein Streichholz an *I struck a match for him* | (Haus etc) *to burn*, *to fire*, *inflame* **II.** ∼̈ n → Anzündung ·**Anzünder** m ∼s/∼ **1.** (P) *lighter*; **kindler*; Laternen∼̈ *lamplighter* ‖ °⟨aero⟩ (Beleuchtungsverband) (P) *marker force* **2.** (Gerät; Holz etc als ∼) *lighter* ·**Anzündung** f ∼/ *kindling*, *lighting*, *ignition* ‖ *burning*, *firing* (*of a house*)

·**an|zweifeln** vt [h] (Aussage etc) *to doubt*; *to question*, *to call in question*; (Recht etc) *to dispute*; *to contest* ‖ → anfechten ·**Anzweiflung** f ∼/∼en *doubting*, *questioning*

† **Ä·olier**, ·**Äoler** m pl *Aeolians* pl **ä·olisch** a *Aeolian*, *Aeolic* **Ä·olische Inseln** f pl → Liparische Inseln ·**Äolsharfe** f ∼/∼n *Aeolian harp*

Ä·onen pl *aeons*, *eons* pl

Aor·ist m ∼(e)s/∼e ⟨gram⟩ *aorist*

A·orta f ∼/∼ten ⟨anat⟩ *aorta*

Ap·ache [a'paʃə, a'patʃə] m ∼n/∼n (Indianerstamm u Pariser Gauner) *Apache*

Apan·age [apa'na:ʒə] f ∼/∼n *appanage*

ap·art 1. adv *apart*; etw ∼ legen *put a th aside* **2.** a *special* | ⟨fig⟩ *out of the common*; *attractive*; *superior* **Ap·arte** f ∼/∼n ⟨theat⟩ (beiseite gesprochene Worte) *aside*

Apath·ie f ∼/ *apathy*, *listlessness*; *indifference* (gegen *to*) **ap·athisch** a *apathetic*, *listless*; *indifferent* (gegen *to*) ‖ ∼es Elend ⟨path⟩ *apathetic misery*

Apat·it m ∼s/∼e ⟨minr⟩ *apatite*

Apen(n)·in, der; die Apen(n)·inen [pl] ⟨It⟩ (Gebirgskette) *the Apennines* pl **∼halbinsel** f *Apennines Peninsula*

·**aper** a ⟨österr⟩ (= schneefrei) *open*

Aperçu [apɛr'sy] n (Fr) ∼s/∼s *aperçu*, *summary* | *brain-wave*, *sally*

aperi·odisch a *aperiodic* (*instrument*) ‖ ⟨el⟩ ∼ gedämpft, im ∼en Grenzzustand *critically damped*

Aperit·if m (Fr) ∼s/∼s *aperitive*, *appetizer*

Apert·ur f ∼/∼en **1.** *aperture* | ⟨opt⟩ → Linse **2.** ⟨jur⟩ = Heimfall

apet·al a ⟨bot⟩ (blumenblattlos) *apetalous*

·**Apex** m (L) ∼/Apices **1.** (Scheitel) *apex* **2.** ⟨astr⟩ *apex* (*of the sun*) **3.** ⟨gram⟩ *long mark* (ā); ⟨mus⟩ *accent*

·**Apfel** n ∼s/∼̈ **1.** ⟨bot⟩ *apple*; ∼ im Schlafrock ⟨cul⟩ *dumpling* ‖ wilder ∼ *crab* (*-apple*) **2.** ⟨übtr⟩ → Aug∼̈; ∼ des Paris, ∼ der Zwietracht *apple of discord* **3. Wendungen:** in den sauren ∼ beißen müssen *to swallow the bitter pill*, *to take one's medicine* ‖ der ∼ fällt nicht weit vom Stamm *like father*, *like son* ‖ es konnte kein ∼ zur Erde fallen *there wasn't room enough to swing a cat* (*in*) ‖ °für'n ∼ u 'n Ei losschlagen *to knock down for a song* **4.** [in comp] *apple*; ⟨chem⟩ *malic* **∼äther** m *malic ether* **∼bäckchen** n pl *cheeks lik apples* **∼baum** m *apple-tree* **∼blütenstecher** m ⟨ent⟩ *apple-blossom weevil* **∼diät** f *apple-diet* **∼frucht** f → Kernobstfrucht **∼gehäuse** n *apple-core* **∼kern** m *pip* **∼kloß** m *apple-dumpling* **∼kompott** n *stewed apples* pl **∼kuchen** m *apple-tart* **∼most** m *new cider* **∼mus** n *apple-sauce*, ⟨Am a.⟩ *apple-butter* **∼pastete** f *apple-pie* **∼säure** f *malic acid* **∼schale** f ∼n [pl] *apple-parings* [pl] **∼schimmel** m ⟨zoo⟩ *dapple-grey horse* **∼schnittchen** n [pl] *apple-fritters* [pl] **∼stecher** m ⟨cul⟩ *apple-corer* **∼torte** f *apple-tart*, *apple-puff* **∼wein** m *cider*

·**apfelig** a *dotted*

Apfels·ine f ∼/∼n *orange* **∼nbaum** m *orange-tree* **∼nsaft** m *orange juice* **∼nschale** f *orange peel*

Aphär·ese f ∼/ ⟨gram⟩ *aphaeresis*

Aphas·ie f ∼/ ⟨med⟩ *aphasia*

Aph·el n (Ggs Perihel) *aphelion*

Aphon·ie f ∼/ ⟨med⟩ *aphonia*

Aphor·ismus m ∼/-men *aphorism* **aphor·istisch 1.** a *aphoristic* **2.** adv *aphoristically*

Aphrodis·iakum n ∼s/-siaka ⟨med⟩ *aphrodisiac*

·**Aphthe** f ∼/∼n ⟨med⟩ ∼n [pl] *aphthae* (L) **∼nseuche** f = Maul- u Klauenseuche

Aph·ylle f ∼/∼n ⟨bot⟩ *aphyllous plant*

Apikult·ur f ∼/ = Bienenzucht

Api·ol n ∼s/ *apiol*; *parsley-camphor*

·**Apis** m ⟨ant⟩ *Egyptian Apis*

Aplan·at m ∼s/∼e ⟨phot⟩ (Linsensatz → Linse) *aplanat*

Apl·it m ∼s/ ⟨geol⟩ *aplite*; *aplitic dyke rock*

Apl·omb (Fr) m ∼s/ *aplomb* (: *with great a.*); *self-possession*; *assurance*

·**apo-** [Gr pref] *apo-* **∼d·iktisch 1.** a *apodictic*, *apodeictic* **2.** adv *apodictically* ∼̈**g·äum** n ∼s/ ⟨astr⟩ (Erdferne) *apogee* (Ggs Perigäum) ∼̈**kal·ypse** f ∼/ *apocalypse* **∼kal·yptisch** a *apocalyptic*; die ∼en Reiter [pl] *the a. horse* [pl], *the four horsemen* **Ap·okope** f ∼/ ⟨gram⟩ *apocope* **apo-kr·yph** a *apocryphal* **Apokr·yphen** n pl ⟨bib⟩ *Apocrypha* pl

Apollin·aris f **∼brunnen** m ⟨Ger⟩ *Apollinaris*, *A. water*, (*table-water from Neuenahr*) **apollinisch** a *Apollonian*; *serene and majestic* **Apollo** m ∼s/∼ ⟨ent⟩ *Apollo butterfly*

·**apo-** ∼̈**l·og** m ∼s/∼e (Fabel) *apologue* ∼̈**-log·etik** f ∼/ ⟨theol⟩ *apologetics* pl **∼log·etisch** a *apologetic* ∼̈**log·ie** f ∼/∼n *apology* ∼̈**-phth·egma** n ∼s/∼ta (Sinnspruch) *apophthegm* ∼̈**ph·yse** f ∼/∼n ⟨zoo & bot⟩ *apophysis* ∼̈**pl·ektiker** m ∼s/∼ *person suffering*, *tending to*, *apoplexy* **∼pl·ektisch** a *apoplectic* ∼̈**plex·ie** f ∼/∼n *apoplexy* ∼̈**r·ie** f ∼/∼n ⟨log⟩ *aporia* ∼̈**stas·ie** f ∼/∼n ⟨ec⟩ *apostasy* ∼̈**st·at** m ∼en/∼en ⟨ec⟩ *apostate*; z ∼en w *to apostatize* **Ap·ostel** m ∼s/∼ *apostle*; nach Art der ∼, durch die ∼ *apostolically* ‖ Taten der ∼ *Deeds of the Apostles* ⟨a. arts⟩ **∼amt** n *apostolate*, *apostleship* **∼balken** m *rood-beam* **∼geschichte** f ⟨bib⟩ *Acts* [pl] *of the Apostles* **∼würde** f = Apostelamt

a posteri·ori adv [L] *a posteriori* **aposteriorisch** a ⟨philos⟩ (Ggs apriorisch) *a posteriori* L

Apostol·at n ∼s/∼e = Apostelamt **Apost·olikum** n [L] / *Apostles' Creed* **apost·olisch** a *apostolic*; ∼es Glaubensbekenntnis n = Apostolikum ‖ (päpstlich) *Apostolic* (*See*, *Succession*); *papal* ‖ ∼̈e Majestät *title of the kings of Hungary*; Apostel

Apostr·oph m ~(e)s/~e *apostrophe* (') **Ap·o-strophe** f ~/~n (Anrede) *apostrophe* **apostro-ph·ieren** vt [h] *to apostrophize*

Apoth·eke f ~/~n *chemist's shop, dispensary* ‖ ⟨fig fam⟩ *clip joint* ‖ in der ~ *at the chemist's*

Apoth·eker m ~s/~ *dispensing* (od *pharmaceutical*) *chemist, dispenser, pharmacist*; ⟨Am⟩ *druggist* **~gewicht** n *apothecary's weight* **~rech-nung** f ⟨fig⟩ *clip joint bill* **~waren** f [pl] *medicinal drugs*

Apothe·ose f ~/~n **1.** *apotheosis, deification* **2.** ⟨übtr⟩ *apotheosis, glorification, exaltation* **3.** *curtain* (*effective picture at the end of a show*)

Appal·achen pl (Gebirge in N.-O.-Amerika) *Appalachian Mountains* pl

Appar·at m ~(e)s/~e **1.** (Gerät) *apparatus* ‖ [koll] ~e [pl] *apparatus* (: *a large number of a.*); ein feinerer ~ *a more delicate piece of apparatus* ‖ (Vorrichtung) *contrivance, device, gadget* | ⟨phot⟩ *camera* ‖ ⟨wir⟩ *set*, Radio≗ *wireless set* ‖ ⟨telph⟩ *telephone, instrument*; bleiben Sie, bitte, am ~ *hold the line, hold on please*; (bin, ist selbst) am ~ *speaking* **2.** ⟨übtr⟩ Verdauungs≗ *digestive apparatus* ‖ *the structure*; *workings* [pl] (*of a system*) **3.** (Ausrüstung) *equipment, utensils* [pl] **4.** kritischer ~ *critical apparatus* **5.** (Aufwand) *expenditure*; *expense*; mit gr ~ *on a large scale* **6.** °⟨fig hum⟩ *hefty, buxom wench*

Appartement [apartəˈmãː] n (Fr) ~s/~s *apartment* ‖ *apartments, chambers* [pl] ‖ ⟨hotel⟩ *suite of rooms*

*·**Appel** m ~s/≗ (= Apfel) (etw) für'n ~ un 'n Ei (bek, jdm zuschlagen *to get, to knock down*) *for a song* **~kahn** m *clumsy boat* ‖ ⟨hum⟩ *bed* ‖ [mst pl] ≗e ⟨hum⟩ *large shoes* [pl]

App·ell m ~(e)s/~e **1.** (Aufforderung) *appeal* (an *to*); e–n ~ richten an *to make an a. to* | *resort*; ~ an die Waffen *r. to arms* **2.** ⟨mil⟩ *roll-call*; e–n ~ abhalten *to hold a roll-call*; angetreten z ~! *fall in for calling the roll*!; Fuß≗ *inspection of boots* ‖ *rally*; *congress* **3.** ⟨fenc⟩ *dodge* **4.** ⟨hunt⟩ der Hund hat k–n ~ *the dog is badly broken in*

Appellati·on f ~/~en ⟨jur⟩ *appeal* (gegen *from*; bei *to*) **~sgericht** n, **~shof** m *Court of Appeal*, ⟨Am⟩ *Apellate Court* **~srat** m ⟨Ger⟩ *Judge of a Superior Court* ‖ → Berufung

Appellat·iv n ~s/~e, **Appellat·ivum** n ~s/-tiva ⟨gram⟩ *appellative*

appell·ieren vi [h] ~ an *to appeal* (od *to make an appeal*) *to*; ~ an jdn ⟨a.⟩ *to invoke a p*

App·endix m ~/-dizes *appendix* L ‖ ⟨anat⟩ = Wurmfortsatz —**diz·itis** f ⟨med⟩ *appendicitis*

apperzip·ieren vt ⟨psych⟩ *to apperceive*

Apperzepti·on [-tsiɔːn] f ~/~en *apperception*

Appet·enz- [in comp] ⟨eth, biol⟩ *appetitive* (*behaviour*) **Appet·it** m ~(e)s/ *appetite* (auf, nach *for*); ⟨a. übtr⟩ ‖ mit ~ (*to eat*) *with an app.* | den ~ anregen *to stimulate the app.* ‖ den ~ anregend *appetizing*; ⟨fam⟩ *mouth-watering*; den ~ anregendes Mittel *appetizer*, (alkoh. Getränk) *aperitif*; ~ bek *to get an app.* ‖ ~ h *to have an app.*; ich hätte ~ auf . . *I am equal to* . . ‖ k–n (rechten) ~ h *to be off one's feed* ‖ der ~ kommt beim Essen *app. comes with eating* ‖ (jdm) ~ m *to give* (*a p*) *an app.* ‖ jdm den ~ nehmen (*or* verderben) *to take away* (od *spoil*) *a p's app.*; es verging ihm der ~ *he dropped his fork for good*, °⟨fig⟩ *he lost all appetite* (f *for*) ‖ guten ~! *I hope you'll enjoy your meal*! ≗**lich** **1.** a *appetizing, dainty, tasty* ‖ *savoury*; *pleasant* (*place*); *agreeable*; nicht gerade ~ *unsavoury, not savoury* **2.** adv *appetizingly* **~losigkeit** f *lack of appetite*; *inappetence* **~shäppchen** n [mst pl] *cocktail canapé*(*s*) (*-pe*[*s*]); *sandwich*(*es*), *appetizer*(*s*)

†·**Appische Str·aße,** die (v Rom nach Capua) *the Appian Way*

applaud·ieren vi [h] jdm ~ *to applaud* (od *cheer, clap*) *a p*; [a. abs] (*to cheer loudly*) **applaud·ierend** a *applauding, applausive* **Appl·aus** m -ses/-se *applause*; *clap* ‖ rasenden ~ h *to bring the house down*; starker, gr ~ ⟨bes Am fam⟩ *big hand*; mit dem ~ kargen *to sit on one's hands* → Beifall

Applikati·onsstickerei f ~/~en *appliqué*; *appliqué work* **Applikat·ur** f ~/~en ⟨mus⟩ *fingering*

appliz·ieren vt [h] *to apply* ‖ (Farben) *to lay on* | °⟨übtr⟩ → Ohrfeige; verabreichen

Appoint [apˈwɛ̃ː] m (Fr) ~s/~s ⟨com⟩ = Ausgleichswechsel ‖ per ~ *per appoint*

app·ort [Fr] ~! *go fetch*! **App·ort** [aˈpɔrt] m ~s/~s ⟨com⟩ = Sacheinlage

apport·ieren vt/i [h] **1.** vt (of dogs) (Wild) *to retrieve* **2.** vi *to fetch and carry*

Appositi·on f ~/~en ⟨gram⟩ *apposition*; → Beisatz

appret·ieren vt [h] ⟨tech⟩ (Tuch) *to dress, finish* **Appret·ur** f ~/~en ⟨tech⟩ **1.** [abstr] *dressing, finishing* **2.** [konkr] (Flüssigkeit) *finish*; *sizing boards*

Approbati·on f ~/~en **1.** *license for a doctor or dispensing chemist to practise* **2.** ⟨R. C. a.⟩ **Approb·atur** (L) *the imprimatur of the bishop* **approb·ieren** vt [h] *to approve* ‖ staatlich approbiert *certified*; *certificated* (*doctor, teacher*, etc)

approximat·iv a *approximative*; ⟨math⟩ *approximate*

Après-Sch·i- **~-Kleidung** f *after-ski clothers* pl **~-Schuhe** m pl *zip-up* od *chukka boots*

Aprik·ose f ~/~n ⟨bot⟩ *apricot* (⟨österr⟩ Marille) **~nbaum** m *apricot-tree*

Apr·il m ~s/~e *April* | der erste ~ ⟨fig⟩ *All Fool's Day, April-Fool-day*; ~! ~! *April-fool*! ‖ jdn in den ~ schicken *to send a p on a fool's errand, to make an April-fool of a p* **~narr** m *April-fool* **~scherz** m *April fish* (*trick played upon a p on April 1st*) **~wetter** n ⟨fam⟩ *devil's smiles*

a pri·ori (L) adv ⟨philos⟩ *a priori* **apri·orisch** a ⟨philos⟩ *a priori*

apropos [aprɔˈpoː] adv *by the way, by the bye*; *apropos*

Aps·ide f ~/~n ⟨astr⟩ *apsis* ·**Apsis** f ~/-siden ⟨arch⟩ *apse*

Apteryg·oten pl ⟨ent⟩ *apterygotous* (od *thysanurous*) *insects* [pl]; *Apterygota* L [pl]

Ap·ulien n ⟨It⟩ (Landschaft) *Apulia*, (jetzt) *Puglia* [It] **ap·ulisch** a *Apulian*

Aquäd·ukt m ~(e)s/~e *aqueduct*

Aquamar·in m ~s/~e ⟨minr⟩ *aquamarine*

Aquar·ell n ~(e)s/~e (Bild) *water-colour*; *aquarelle*, ⟨a.⟩ *drawing* ‖ ~e [pl] ⟨fam⟩ *waters* [pl] **~druck** m *water-colour printing* **~farbe** f *water-colour* (: *to paint in water-colours*) **~gemälde** n *water-colour, aquarelle* **~maler** m *aquarellist, water-colourist* **~malerei** f *water-colours* pl **~-Pinzelzeichnung** f *water-colour drawing* **~-Skizze** f *w.-c. sketch*

Aquat·inta f ~/–ten (~verfahren) *aquatint* ‖ (~abdrucke) *aquatint*

Aqu·arium [L] n ~s/–rien *aquarium, vivarium* L

Äqu·ator m ~s/~en *equator*; *the line* | **~taufe** [f] *ducking on "crossing the line"* ‖ **Äquatori·al-, äquatori·al** a *equatorial* (*telescope*)

Aquav·it m ~s/~e *aqua-vitae*

äquilibr·ieren vt/i [h] *to equilibrate* **Äquili-br·ist** m ~en/~en *equilibrist*

äquinokti·al a *equinoctial* ≗**gegenden** f [pl] *the tropics* [pl] ≗**sturm** m *equinoctial gale* **Äquin·oktium** n ~s/–tien *equinox*

Äquipotenti·al- [in comp] ⟨phys⟩ *equipotential* (*lines, surfaces*)

†**Aquit·anien** n (Prov. des alten Galliens) *Aquitania, Aquitain(e)*

Äquival·ent 1. n ~s/~e *equivalent* (für *of*) 2. a *equivalent*; ~e Eigengeschwindigkeit ⟨aero⟩ *e. airspeed* **äquiv·ok** a *equivocal*

Ar n ~s/~e (Flächenmaß = 100 qm) *are*

·**Ara** m & f ~s/~s ⟨orn⟩ (Sittich) *ara*

·**Ära** f. ~/Ären *era*, Viktorianische ~ *the Victorian Era*; e–e neue ~ beginnen *to inaugurate a new e.*

·**Araber** m ~s/~ *Arab* (a. Pferd), *Arabian*; **~einfall** m *Arab raid* **Arab·eske** f. ~/~n ⟨arch⟩ *arabesque* ⟨a. typ⟩ **Ar·abien** n *Arabia*, ⟨poet⟩ *Araby* **ar·abisch** a *Arabian* **Ar·abische Meerbusen**, der *the Gulf of Arabia, the Arabian Sea* **ar·abisch** 1. a *Arabian* (*desert, fauna, flora*); *Arab* (*chief, horse, sheikh*) | die ~e Sprache *Arabic* ‖ ~e Ziffern *Arabic numerals* [pl] 2. ~̽, das ~̽e (= ~e Sprache) *Arabic*, auf ~̽ *in A.*

Arab·ist m *arabist*

Arag·onier m ~s/~ *Aragonese*, die ~ [pl] *the A.* **arag·onisch** a *Aragonese*

·**Aragon, Arag·onien** n *Aragon* **Arag·onier** m, **~in** f **arag·onisch** a *Aragonese*

Aragon·it m ~s/ ⟨minr⟩ *aragonite*

Ar·alie f ~/~n ⟨bot⟩ *aralia*; → Angelika

·**Aralsee** m (Asien) *Aral Sea, Sea of Aral*

†**Aram·äa** n (⟨ant⟩ etwa Syrien u Mesopotamien) *Aramæa*

aram·äisch a *Aramaean*

Aräom·eter n ~s/~ (Senkwaage z Bestimmung des spez. Gewichts) *areometer*; *hydrometer*; (f. Öle) *elaeometer*

Är·ar n ~s/~e (in Österreich) *Exchequer, Treasury* ‖ *national property* **Är·arium** n ~s/ –rien 1. ⟨ant⟩ *fisc* 2. ⟨mod⟩ *Exchequer, Treasury*

·**Ararat** m (Gebirgsmassiv südl. v Kaukasus)

Arauk·aner pl (Indianerstamm in Chile) *Araucanians* pl

Arauk·arie f ~/~n ⟨bot⟩ (Nadelbaum) *araucaria*; Brasili·anische ~ *Brazil Pine*; Chil·enische ~ *Chile Pine*, ⟨fam⟩ *Monkey-Puzzle*

·**Arbe** f ~/~n ⟨bot⟩ = Zirbelkiefer

·**Arbeit** f. ~/~en A. (Mühe, Plage) *toil, labour*; *sweat*; *trouble*; ~ m *or* verursachen *to make work*; es macht k–e ~ *it is no trouble* (*to do*) B. (zweckbewußte menschl. Anstrengung) 1. ⟨allg⟩ *work, labour*; menschliche ~ *human labour* ‖ *business* (bei dieser ~ *at this b.*); ⟨sl⟩ *dinkum* ‖ bei *or* an der ~ *on the job* (a. vulg sex) | schwere ~ *hard work*; *donkey-work*; *labour*; *slog*; e–e ungeheuere ~ *an awful sweat* ‖ leichte ~ *easy meat* ‖ jdm ~ geben *to give work to a p*, ⟨Am fam⟩ *to put a p to work* ‖ erst die ~ dann 's Vergnügen *business before pleasure* ‖ die ~ geht ihm leicht v der Hand *he is a quick worker* ‖ ⟨fig⟩ gründliche ~ m *to make a clean shave* ‖ ~en aus|führen, durch|führen *to handle work* ‖ ~ leisten *to do work* ‖ ~ schaffen, beschaffen *to provide work* (für *for*) ‖ ~ sparen *to save labour* ‖ halbe ~ verrichten *to mess about* | der ~ aus dem Wege gehen *to shirk work, to loaf* ‖ die ~ einstellen *to stop work, to strike* | [nach prep] (Arbeiter) **an** der ~ hindern *to ratten* ‖ an die ~ gehen, sich an die ~ m *to go* (od *set*) *to work*; *to get on* (od *down*) *to business*; eifrig an die ~ gehen *to buckle to* (adv) ‖ tüchtig **bei** der ~ *hard at work*; bei der ~ s *to be at work* (an *on*); *to busy o.s.*; wir sehen ihn bei der ~ *we see him busying h.s.* (an .. *with a th*) ‖ **in** ~ geben *to put* (*an order*) *in work* ‖ jdn **zur** ~ anhalten → anhalten I. 4. b. | die Überfahrt durch ~ an Bord bezahlen *to work one's passage* ‖ ~ macht das Leben süß *no sweet without sweat* | durch Tod mitten aus der ~ gerissen w *to die in harness* ‖ (T) z ~ verwenden *to work an animal* 2. (die einzelne ~) e–e ~ *a piece of work, a job*; *chore*; *a task*; Gelegenheits~̽en [pl] *odd jobs* [pl] ‖ e–e verflucht schwere ~ *a devil of a job*; es war e–e ziemliche ~ *it was rather a job* (*to do*) ‖ ~en annehmen *to take jobs*; jdm e–e ~ aufgeben *to set a p a task* ‖ belehrende ~ *instruction*; erzieherische ~ *training* ‖ ich habe e–e ~ f Sie ⟨Am⟩ *I have a labo(u)r for you* ‖ ein Stück ~ leisten *or* verrichten *to do a job of work* ‖ er hat s–e bestimmte ~ *his work is cut out for him* ‖ er ist f diese ~ wie geschaffen *he is cut out for this work* 3. (Berufs~̽) *employment* ‖ ohne ~ *out of employment, without work*; → Stellung ‖ die täglichen ~en *the day's routine*; s–e laufenden regelmäßigen ~en *his routine work* ‖ (feste) ~ h *to be in* (*good*) *work*, k–e ~ h *to be unemployed* (od *out of work*); jd, der ~ hat *in-work*; jd, der k–e ~ hat *out-of-work* (: *the in-works and out-of-works*) ‖ jdn in ~ nehmen → anstellen I. A. 2. ‖ ~ nehmen *to take employment* 4. ⟨tech & arch⟩ (größere ~) [mst pl] ~en *operations* [pl] ‖ öffentl. bauliche ~en *works* [pl]; staatliche ~en *public works* [pl]; ⟨engl⟩ Behörde f öffentl. ~en *Office of Works* ‖ Aufräumungs~̽en [pl] *clearing-up operations* [pl] 5. (~ in Volkswirtschaft) *labour*; Kapital u ~ *Capital and Labour*; ~ u Wirtschaft *Labour and Industry* C. (v S) 1. (Arbeiten) *working* (*of the brain*); *functioning* (*of a motor*); 2. (Be-, Verarbeitung) in ~ *in the making*; *in preparation* ‖ etw in ~ geben *to put a th in hand, to get work started on a th* ‖ in ~ nehmen *to start on a th, to take a th in hand* ‖ in ~ s *to be in hand, to be* (*in*) *making* D. (Qualität der ~) *workmanship* ‖ ⟨com⟩ *make* E. ⟨phys⟩ (Ergebnis aus Kraft mal Weg) *work* F. (Ergebnis der ~) *work, workmanship* (: *this is my w.*), *handiwork*; e–e ~ *a piece of work* ‖ ⟨arts, etc⟩ *handicraft, making* → Leistung; eigene ~ *independent work* | ⟨school⟩ schriftliche ~ *paper, composition*; ⟨univ⟩ schr. ~en *essays* [pl] ‖ ⟨scient⟩ *treatise*, (Vortrag) *paper* ‖ → durchbrochen; eingelegt; erhaben etc; Hand-, Nadelarbeit etc G. [in comp] → Arbeit-, Arbeits-

·**Arbeit- ~geber** m *employer, master*; [pl] ⟨a.⟩ *management, business* ‖ ⟨Am sl⟩ *boss*; ~verband, *Employer's Association* **~nehmer** m *employee*; *man, hand*; [pl] *labo(u)r*; ~verband [m] *trades union* **~̽sparend** a *labo(u)r-saving* **~suchende**: der ~ (ein ~r) *person in search of work*; ⟨demog m. m.⟩ "*seeking work*"; erstmalig ~ *inexperieneed* od *new worker*; ~, der bereits e–e Stellung hatte *experieneed worker*

·**arbeiten** vi/t [h] I. vi 1. (P) *to work* (a. ⟨fig⟩ = stehlen) (f *for*); *to be active*; *to labour*; ⟨Am a.⟩ *to operate* (in *in*) ‖ angestrengt ~ *to work double-tides*; *to hammer* (an *at*) ‖ (P) ~ wie ein Pferd *to work like a horse*, ⟨fam⟩ *to horse it* ‖ schwer ~ *to toil* (an *at*); schwer ~ müssen *to keep one's nose to the grindstone* ‖ mit Hochdruck ~ *to work at high pressure* ‖ billig u dabei gut ~, gut u billig ~ *to keep one's prices down and one's work up* ‖ jdn schwer ~ l *to work a p terribly hard* ‖ ~ nur um Geld z verdienen ⟨sl⟩ *to pot-boil* | er hat k–n Handschlag gearbeitet *he has not done a stroke of work* ‖ nicht mehr ~ können *to be past work* | auf eigene Faust, für sich ~ *to play a lone hand* ‖ auf Tagelohn ~ *to work by the day* | in Akkord ~ *to work by the job* ‖ jdm in die Hände ~ *to play into a p's hands* (sich in die H. ~ *to p. into each other's h.*) | mit Händen u Füßen ~ *to make a desperate struggle* ‖ mit den Kinnbacken ~ *to work the jaws* | ~ **an** etw *to work at a th* ‖ an e–m Stück ~ *to* (*be at*) *work on a play* ‖ ~ an jdm *to work* (*upon*) *a p*; an sich selbst ~ *to seek to improve o.s.* ‖ ~ an e–m Hund → abrichten 2. a. | ~ l: bei welchem Schneider l Sie ~? *who tailors you?* ‖ jdn (*or* ein

Tier) ~ l *to work a p* || (Maschine, Betrieb) ~ l ⟨Am⟩ *to operate* **2. a.** (of ships) (bei Seegang) *to labour* || (of organs) *to function, to operate* || (of the face) krampfhaft ~ *to work* | (of machines, etc) *to function, to work; to go; to be at work; to operate, to be operated; to act;* gut ~ *to behave well* | (of capital) *to bear* (od *yield*) *interest* **b.** (etw) ~ l *to work* (⟨Am⟩ *to operate*) *a th* || die Gesellschaft arbeitet mit 60 Schiffen *the company operates 60 vessels* **3.** ⟨com⟩ ~ in etw *to deal* (od *do business*) *in a th* | ~ mit jdm *to deal* (od *do, transact business*) *with a p* **4.** (Stellung haben) ~ in e–r Firma *to be employed in a firm;* ~ bei jdm *to be in the employ of a p* **5.** (gären) (of must) *to ferment* || (of *dough*) *to rise* || (of volcanoes) *to be active* **6.** (of timber) *to warp* **II.** vt **1.** *to work* (*a shawl*); *to work at* od *to embroider* (*a table-cloth*); [mst pass & pp] gearbeitet *wrought* (*in marble*); ⟨übtr⟩ fein gearbeitet *finely wrouht* (*character*) || → bearbeiten **2. a.** (jdn, ein T) müde ~ *to tire .. out* **b. sich** ~ *to work o.s.* (in *into*), *to work one's way; to plough* (durch *through*); *to extricate o.s.* (aus *from*); sich frei ~ *to shake o.s. free;* sich tot *or* z Tode ~ *to work o.s. to death* **3. es** arbeitet **sich** heute schlecht, es läßt sich heute schlecht ~ *work progresses badly to-day;* e–e Basis, auf (Theorie, mit) der sich ~ läßt *a working basis* (*theory*) **·Arbeiten** n *the working* (: *the w. of the brain, of his mind;* im Laufe des ~s *in the course of working* | das mühsame ~ *the labouring* (*of the heart*); das laute ~ *the thrash* (*of the screw*)

·arbeitend a *working, labouring* (*classes, population*); ständig ~ *continuous-working*

·Arbeiter m~s/~ **1.** (Hand~) (Ggs *employer*) *workman, working-man; worker* (in *in*); [pl] *workmen;* (*manual*) *labourer; hand; operative* || (un)gelernter ~ (*un*)*skilled workman;* ungelernte ~ [pl] *unskilled labour;* ungelernte ~ einstellen *to dilute labour* || → Lohn~; Arbeitnehmer **2.** ⟨allg⟩ *worker* (an *at; a hard w.*); *workman* (: *he is a slow w.*); geistiger ~ *brain-worker* || manueller ~, ~ der Faust *blue-collar worker* || städtischer ~ *labo(u)ring townsman* **~angebot** n *labour supply* **~ausschließung** f *lock-out* **~ausschuß** m *workers committee* **~ausstand** m (*worker's*) *strike* **~bevölkerung** f *working population* od *classes* **~bewegung** f *Labour Movement* **~biene** f ⟨ent⟩ *worker-bee* **~bildung** f *workers' education* **~b·ildungsverein** m *Workers' Educational Association* | gewerkschaftliche **~einstellungspraktiken** f pl *featherbedding practices* **~fahrkarte** f ⟨Ger⟩ auf ~ reisen *to travel at a reduced fare* **~frage** f *labour question* **~führer** m ⟨engl⟩ *Labour leader* **~gruppe** f *panel* | verbilligte **~(rück)fahrkarte** f ⟨rail, etc⟩ *workman's ticket* **~klasse** f *working--class* **~kolonie** f *labour colony* **~kons·umverein** m *Work(ing)men's Cooperative Society* **~-Kontroll-Nr.** *clock No.* (a. comp⟩ **~mangel** m *shortage of labour* **~nebenkosten** pl *accessory expenses for workmen* **~organisation** f *labour organisation* **~partei** f ⟨engl⟩ *Labour Party* **~-priester** m Fr *priest-worker* **~rat** m ⟨Ger⟩ *Workers' Council* **~schaft** f *workmen* [pl]; *working--class; labo(u)r;* (Belegschaft) *worker staff* **~-schutz** m *protection of labour* **~schutzgesetzgebung** f *protective labour legislation* **~sekretär** m ⟨engl⟩ *Trades Union Secretary* **~siedlung** f *workers' housing estate* **~sperre** f *lock-out* **~stand** m *Labour, working-class(es)* **~verband, ~verein** m *trades-union* **~versicherung** f *industrial insurance* **~viertel** n *working-quarter* **~wohnhausbau** m *building accommodation for workers' families* **~wohnung** f *workman's dwelling* | auf **~-Zeitkarte** fahren ⟨bes Am⟩ *to commute,* → ~(rück)fahrkarte

·Arbeiterin f ~/~nen **1.** *workwoman, working girl* od *woman; woman* od *female worker;* ~nen [pl] *woman-* od *women-workers* [pl] | ⟨allg⟩ *worker* (: *a hard w.*) **2.** ⟨ant⟩ *worker-bee, working-bee*

·Arbeits- [in comp mst] *working ..* **~ablauf** m *work-flow;* ⟨tech⟩ *sequence of operations;* ⟨comp⟩ *posting* **~amt** n *Labour Office* **~anfall** m *work-load;* starker ~ *heavy commitments* pl **~anfang** m → registrieren **~anleitung** f *instruction, training;* (Buch) *guide,* ⟨univ, etc⟩ *study guide,* → –ausbildung **~anzug** m *ouverall(s* pl); ⟨mil⟩ *working uniform, fatigue dress,* ⟨fam⟩ *fatigues;* → Arbeitskittel | aktiver **~arm** m ⟨rehab⟩ *standard hook* **~art** f (*kind of*) *job* **~-aufwand** m *employment of labo(u)r* | an der Stelle vorgenommene **~ausbildung** *on-the-job training* (→ –anleitung) **~ausschuß** m ⟨Ger⟩ *Local Labour Committee,* **~basis** f *working basis* **~bedingungen** f pl ⟨allg⟩ *working conditions,* ⟨off⟩ *terms of employment,* ⟨Am a.⟩ *labor contract* Anpassung der ~ an den Menschen *human engineering* **~bereich** m → Bereich 2. a., ⟨mach⟩ *working capacity* **~beschaffung** f *provision of work* **~beschaffungs-** *remploy* (z. B. –Fabrik) **~-besuch** m ⟨pol⟩ *working visit* **~beutel** m (f Nadelarbeit) *work-bag; reticule* **~bewertung** f *job evaluation* **~bewilligung** f *labo(u)r permit* **~biene** f ⟨ent⟩ *working* od *worker bee* **~börse** f *labour exchange* **~buch** n ⟨Ger⟩ *employment-book* **~dienst** m ⟨engl mil⟩ *fatigue* (*-duty*) || ⟨Ger⟩ → Reichs~ || ~pflicht [f] *Labour Conscription* **~direktor** m *plant-manager; manager* od (als Beamter) *officer in charge of personnel* od *of labo(u)r relations; personnel* od *welfare officer* **~eifer** m, (–wut [f] *great*) *eargerness in work* **~einkommen** n *earned income* **~einsatz** m *employment of labo(u)r,* ⟨Ger hist⟩ *planned distribution of labour* **~einstellung** f *stoppage of work; strike;* ⟨Am⟩ *tie-up* **~entgelt** n *remuneration* **~ergebnis** n *final result(s)* ⟨a. comp⟩ **~ersparend** a *labour-saving* **~ersparnis** f *labour-saving* **~essen** n ⟨pol⟩ *working dinner* **~fähig** a *capable of work; ablebodied* || ⟨parl⟩ ~e Mehrheit *working majority* **~fähigkeit** f *ability to work, capability for work* || ⟨phys⟩ *energy* **~feld** n *sphere of action* (od *work*); *department* °**~fimmel** m: e–n ~ h ⟨Am⟩ *to be a whale for work* **~flugzeug** n ⟨aero⟩ *army cooperation aeroplane* **~frau** f *workwoman, working woman* **~freude, ~freudigkeit** f *joy* od *pleasure in one's work* **~front** f ⟨Ger hist⟩ die Deutsche ~ *the German Labour Front* **~galerie** f ⟨theat⟩ *fly-floor* | ~geländer [n] *fly-rail* **~gang** m *practice; sequence* (*of operation*); *working feed; process; operation* ⟨a. comp, etc⟩; ⟨mach⟩ *machine cycle* ⟨a. comp⟩ || in e–m einfachen ~ *in one efficient operation* **~gemeinschaft** f *working community* od *team* od *partnership; combine;* ⟨Ger school, univ⟩ (S) *team-work class;* (P) *class-team, study group;* ⟨tech⟩ (P) *work-shop group* (a. übtr. f. Wissenschaftler); ⟨Am univ⟩ seminar; || ~ Abu Simbel *Joint Venture Abu Simbel* | e–e ~ bilden mit ⟨bes Am⟩ *to team up with* **~gerät** n *implements, tools* [pl] **~gericht** n *Industrial Court,* ⟨Ger⟩ *Labour Court* **~gerichtsbarkeit** f ⟨Ger⟩ *Industrial Jurisdiction* **~geschwindigkeit** f *machine speed* **~gruppe** f *team* **~haus** n *workhouse* || ⟨Ger⟩ (Besserungsanstalt) *house of correction* **~hose** f *slacks,* ⟨Am⟩ *jeans* [pl] **~kampf** m *labo(u)r* (od *industrial*) *dispute* **~karte** f ⟨Ger⟩ *card for child-workers under 13 years* **~kasten** m, **~kästchen** n *tool-box* || (für Damen) *work-box* **~kittel** m *smock, working-clothes* [pl]; *overall,* ⟨Am⟩ *overalls* [pl] **~kommando** n ⟨mil⟩ *fatigue-detail* od *party* **~konflikt** m *labo(u)r conflict* **~kopie** f ⟨film⟩ *studio reel* **~korb** m *work-basket* **~kraft** f *working-power;* mit höchster Anspannung aller

~ *to full capacity* | (P) e–e tüchtige ~ *a good worker* || –kräfte [pl] *workmen* [pl]; *workers, manpower*; gelernte ~ *skilled labo(u)r*; ≗e (e–s Landes) *labour force, working population* **~lager** n ⟨Ger⟩ *labour-* od *work-camp* **~leben** n *industrial life*; in das ~ treten *to enter occupational life, to start gainful employment* **~lehre** f (S) *shop gauge* **~leistung** f *efficiency of labour* **~leute** [pl] *operatives*; *hands*; *work-people* [pl] **~lohn** m *wages, earnings* [pl]; *wage, pay* **≗los** a → d. **~mann** m *labouring man, labourer*; ⟨Am⟩ *hired man* || ⟨Ger⟩ *labour conscript* **~mantel** m *smock* **~markt** m *labour-market*; → –einsatz **~material** n ⟨übtr⟩ *stock-in-trade* (: *a scholar's stock-in-trade*) **~medizin** f *occupational* (⟨Am⟩ *industrial*) *medicine* **~minister** m ⟨engl⟩ *Minister of Labour* **~ministerium** n ⟨engl⟩ *Ministry of Labour*; ⟨Am⟩ *Department of Labor* **~möglichkeiten** f pl *job opportunities* **~nachweis** m *Labour Exchange*; *employment exchange, unemployment bureau*; *registry-office* **~norm** f *work quota*; *individual production quota* **~not** f *scarcity of work* **~ordnung** f ⟨Ger⟩ *Organization of National Labour*; → Ordnung **~pause** f *pause* od *break in work*; ⟨Am⟩ *lay-off* **~pensum** n *work-load*; *particular task, piece of work*; *lesson* **~pferd** n *working-horse* || ⟨übtr⟩ (P) *slog-horse* **~pflicht** f *moral duty incumbent upon a member of a community to work* **~physiologie** f *physiology of effort* **~plan** m *production* od *manufacturing plan* od *schedule*; ⟨theat⟩ *time book* (⟨Am⟩ *sheet*) **~planung** f *production scheduling* **≗platz** m ⟨allg⟩ *position, job* || (~ der P) *place of work*; *bench*; *office chair*; leere ≗e [pl] *vacancies*, k–e ≗e frei! *no vacancies*! || jds ~einnehmen *to step into a p's place of employment* (⟨fam⟩ .. *shoes*) **~preis** m *price of labour* **~programm** n *business* od *agenda* (*of a conference*) **~prozeß** m *process of work* **~punkt** m (e–s Systems) ⟨commun⟩ *system point* **~raum** m *work-room* || Einrichtung e–s ~s [abstr] *site preparation*, [konkr] *environmental conditions* **~recht** n *labo(u)r legislation*, ⟨Ger hist⟩ *National Labour Law* **≗reich** a *laborious, strenuous* (*life*) **~reserve** f *labo(u)r pool* **~saal** m *work-room* **~scheu** f *work-shyness* **≗scheu** a *work-shy*; *unwilling to work*; die ≗en *the work-shy* **~schicht** f (bei Schichtarbeit) ⟨ind⟩ *shift* **~schlichtungsausschuß** m *labo(u)r relations board* **~schluß** m: ~ registrieren *to clock out* od *off* || ~pfiff m ⟨fam⟩ *knocking-off whistle* **~schule** f *platoon-school* **~schutz** m *protection of labour*; ⟨pol⟩ *industrial protection* **~sperre** f *lock-out* **~statistik** f *labour statistics* [pl] **~stätte** f *place of work*; *workshop* **~stelle** f *job*; neue ~en schaffen *to create new jobs* (*for*) **~streckung** f *decrease in working hours* **~stube** f *work-room*; *study* **~studie** f *work* od *job study* **~stufe** f *stage in a process of work* **~stunde** f *man-hour*; ~n [pl] *working hours* [pl] **~tag** m *working-day, workday* **~teilung** f *division of labour*; *work specialization* **~therapie** f *occupational therapy* **~teufel** m, **~tier** n (P) ⟨fig⟩ *demon for work* **~tisch** m *working table* od *bench*, ⟨comp⟩ *console*; (Schreibtisch) *desk* **~tür** f ⟨met⟩ *charging door* **≗unfähig** a *incapable of work*; *unfit for work*; ~ w *to be laid aside* || ·A–ge(r m) f ⟨demog⟩ *unemployable* **~unfähigkeit** f *disablement* **~unfallversicherung** f *industrial injury insurance* **~unterricht** m *method of the platoon-school* **~urlaub** m *occupational leave* **~vereinigung** f ⟨Ger⟩ *coordination of labour* **~verfahren** n *working method*; (tooling) *process, procedure* **~verhältnis** n *working condition* **~vermittlung** f ⟨Ger⟩ *Labour Exchange* | mutwillige **~versäumnis** f *absenteeism* **~verschleppung** f *go-slow-tactics* **~vertrag** m *contract of employment* **≗verwendungsfähig** a ⟨Ger mil⟩ *fit for service at home* **≗voll** a *strenuous* (*life*) **~vorgang** m *process of manufacture* **~wanderung** f *labo(u)r migration* **~weise** f *working method*; *behaviour* (*of machines*); ⟨tech⟩ *procedure*; *function*; ⟨mach, comp⟩ *operating cycle* **~welle** f ⟨wir⟩ *transmitting* od *signal wave* | ~ (Wärme-)**wert** m *mechanical equivalent* **~wille** m *will to work* **~wissenschaft** f *science of labour* **≗wissenschaftlich** a ⟨Ger⟩ ~es Institut *Labour Research Institute* **~zeit** f *working time* (od *hours*); ⟨off⟩ *clerical time*; ⟨tech⟩ (Stückzeit) *production time*; tägliche ~ *working-day*; → registrieren **~zeug** n *tools* [pl]; *working rig* **~zimmer** n *work-room, study*

·**arbeitsam** a *laborious, industrious*; *hard-working*; *painstaking*; *studious* ·**Arbeitsamkeit** f *laboriusness, industry*; *diligence*; *painstaking*

·**arbeitslos** a *out of work*; *workless, unemployed*; vorübergehend ~ ⟨Am fam⟩ *laid off*; ~ m *to throw* (*a p*) *out of work*; ~ w *to be thrown out of work* (od *employment*)

·**Arbeitslose** m: der ~ (ein ~r) *the out-of-work*; die ~n [pl] *the unemployed, the workless, the out-of-works*, ⟨demog⟩ *unemployed persons* || ~nquote [f] *level of unemployment, unemployment as a percentage of the labo(u)r force* **~nunterstützung** f, *unemployment-benefit* (od *relief*); *the dole*; ~ beziehen *to be* (od *go*) *on the dole*; *to draw unemployment-benefit* **~nversicherung** f ⟨Ger⟩ *unemployment insurance*

·**Arbeitslosigkeit** f *unemployment*

Arbitr·age [arbi'tra:ʒə] f ~/~n ⟨com⟩ *arbitrage* **~rechnung** f *arbitration of exchange*

Arbitrag·eur [arbitra'ʒør] m (Fr) *dealer in arbitrage* **arbitr·ieren** vi *to arbitrate, to deal in exchange*

Arch·aikum n ⟨goel⟩ *archaean period* **arch·aisch** a *archaic* **arch·äisch** a ⟨geol⟩ *archaean*

·**archais·ieren** vt/i *to archaize* **Archa·ismus** m ~/~men *archaism* **archa·istisch** a *archaistic*

Archäol·og(e) m –gen/–gen *archaeologist*

Archäolog·ie f ~/ *archaelogy* **archäol·ogisch** a *archaeological*

·**Arche** f ~/~n **1.** (Kiste) *chest, receptacle*; *trunk* || → Bundeslade **2.** (Boot) *ark* **3.** (a. Spielzeug) *Noah's ark* **4.** (Buhne) *groyne*

·**Archetyp** m ~s/~en *archetype* || ⟨Lit⟩ *pattern* || *basic blueprint*

Archidiak·on m ~s/~e *archdeacon* **Archidiakon·at** n ~(e)s/~e *archdeacony* **Archidi·akonus** (L) m = Archidiakon

Archimandr·it m ~en/~en *archimandrite* (morgenländ. Titel)

Archip·el m ~s/~e *archipelago*

Archiphon·em n ~s/~e *archiphoneme* (*e. g. d/t*: Wald [-t]/Wälder [-d-]

Archit·ekt m ~en/~en *architect* **Architekt·onik** f ~/ *architectonics* [pl] **architekt·onisch** a *architectonic, architectural*; in ~er Hinsicht *architecturally* **Architekt·ur** f ~/~en *architecture* || Architektur– *architectural*

Architr·av m ~s/~e ⟨arch⟩ *architrave, epistyle*

Arch·iv n ~(e)s/~e *archives* [pl]; *Record office* (*of an office*); ⟨engl⟩ Staats≗ *Record Office* **~beamter** m *registrar*

Archiv·ar m ~(e)s/~e *archivist*; *registrar*; ⟨Am⟩ *register* || *keeper of public records*; ⟨engl⟩ Staats≗ *Clerk of the Records*

Archiv·olte f ~/~n ⟨arch⟩ *archivolt*

Arch·ont m ~en/~en ⟨ant⟩ *archon*

Ard·ennen pl, **Ard·enner Wald** m *Ardennes* pl

·**Are** f ~/~n Sw = Ar [n]

Are·al n ~s/~e *area*; *superficial extent*; *region, tract*; *scope, range*

·**Arelat** n, das Arel·atische Reich *Arelatum* → *Arles*

Ar·ena [L] f ~/–nen ⟨ant⟩ *arena* (L) || ⟨mod⟩ (Zirkus–) *ring* (*in the r.*); (Stierkampf≗) *bull*

ring; um die ~ herum *at the ring-side* || ⟨fig⟩ *arena* (*of politics*)

·**Arengpalme** f ⟨bot⟩ *gomuti*

Areop·ag m ~(e)s/~e *Areopagus*

arg I. a **1. a.** *bad, evil* || *mischievous, wicked* (*scoffer*); *hopeless* (*sinner*); *hard* (*drinker*); *inveterate* (*smoker*) || *severe* (*winter*) || ein ~er Geselle *a bad egg*; ein ~er Schelm ⟨hum⟩ *a sad rogue* || das ist ~ *that's bad*; das ist z ~ *that's the limit, that's going too far*, → Höhe | **ärger** *worse*; immer ä. w *to grow worse and worse*; (etw) noch ä. m *to aggravate*; *to render worse* || sein **ärgster** Feind *his worst enemy*; im ärgsten Falle *if the worst comes to the worst* || die ärgste Sonne *the worst of the sun* **b.** [abs subst] ~**es** denken v jdm *to think ill of a p*; nichts ~es im Sinn h, an nichts ~es denken *to have no malicious intent* (od *no designs*); *to be without guile*; ich dachte mir nichts ~es dabei *I meant no harm* (*by it*); noch sehr im ~en liegen *to be in a bad way, to be in a sad* od *desperate state* | **das Ärgste** daran ist .. *the worst of it is* ..; das Ärgste kommt noch nach *the worst is yet to come* || **am ärgsten** *worst*; das Feuer war am ä. in .. *the fire was at its worst in* .. **2.** °(stark, groß) ein ~er Narr *a desperate fool* || e–e ~e Erkältung *a bad cold*; e–e ~e Nachlässigkeit *a gross carelessness*; e–e ~e Verwirrung *a fearful* od *an awful mess*; → riesig, ungeheuer **II.** adv (sehr) *badly* (*beaten*; *used*); ~ jung *very young* || es geht ihm ~ schlecht *he is badly off*; jdm ~ mitspielen *to treat a p harshly*; es zu ~ treiben *to go too far* **III.** ~ n ~s/ (→ I. 1. b.) *malice, guile*; ohne ~ *without malice, guileless, undesigning*; er ist ohne ~; es ist kein ~ an ihm *he is a guileless fellow*

·**arg-** ~**list** f, ~**listigkeit** f ~/ *malice, craftiness, cunning, deceit* ~**listeinrede** f ⟨jur⟩ *estop* ~**listig** a *malicious, crafty, cunning, deceitful*; *wilful* (*deceit*) || ~e Täuschung ⟨jur⟩ *fraud*; *active concealment* | adv *in bad faith* ~**los** a *guileless* || (naiv) *harmless*; *artless, innocent, simple-hearted* (od *-minded*); *unsophisticated* || (ahnungslos) *unsuspecting* ~**losigkeit** f *guilelessness* || *harmlessness*; *innocence*

Arg·ali m ⟨zoo⟩ (wildes Schaf) *argali*

Argent·inien n *the Argentine* **Argent·inier** m ~s/~ *Argentine* **argent·inisch** a *Argentine, Argentinian*; **Argent·inisches Becken** n ⟨mar⟩ *Argentine Basin*; die Argentinische Republik *the Argentine, the A. Republic*

·**Ärger** m ~s/ **1.** (Zorn) *anger, spite*; *indignation, irritation* (über *at, over*); *chagrin* (Fr); ⟨fam⟩ *aggravation, wax* || s–n ~ auslassen *to give vent to one's anger, to vent one's indignation* (an jdm *on, upon a p*); → Entrüstung, Zorn **2.** (Verdruß) *chagrin, vexation* (z m–m gr ~ *to my great v.*); *worry, annoyance*; jdm ~ m *or* verursachen *to give a p trouble*

·**ärgerlich I.** a **1.** (P) *angry* (über etw *at, about a th*; über, auf jdn *with a p*); vexed (über etw *at a th*; auf jdn *with a p*); *irritated* (über *at, by*); *petulant*; ⟨sl⟩ *peeved, ratty* (über *about*) || jdn ~ m *to anger, to exasperate, to irritate a p*; *to get a p's back up*; ~ aussehen *to look dangerous*; ~ w ⟨sl⟩ *to lose one's wool* od *hair* **2.** (unangenehm) *vexatious* (*situation*), *annoying, aggravating, troublesome* (*cough*); *vexing* (*cares*); es ist ~ *it is vexatious* od *tiresome*; *it is a bore* (*that*); wie ~! *what a bore*! || ~! *bother*! *botheration*! **II.** adv (*to say*) *irritably* || *annoyingly* ·**Ärgerlichkeit** f ~/~en *irascribility, bad temper* | *fret*; ~en [pl] *troubles, vexations* [pl] ·**ärgern I.** vt [h] **1.** (jdn) *to make angry*; *to anger, exasperate, irritate*; *to put* (*a p*) *out*; ⟨fam⟩ *to aggravate, to plague* || ⟨sl⟩ *to peeve*; ⟨Am⟩ *to get* od *peeve* (*a p*) || *to annoy, vex, worry, harass, irk*; ⟨fam⟩ *to get a p's goat* || es ärgert die anderen *it angers the others* (*that*); es ärgert mich *it frets me*, ⟨fam⟩ *it gets my goat* (*to know*; *that*) || jdn tot, zu Tode ~ *to worry a p out of his life, to plague a p's life out* | **sich** ~ *to worry* (über *about*); *to chafe* (*at*); *to be annoyed* od *offended*; *to be vexed* od *worried* (über etw *at a th*; über jdn *with a p*); *to fret* (od *worry*) *o.s.* || sich die Schwindsucht an den Hals ~ *to fret* (od *worry*) *o.s. to death* || sich wütend ~ *to fret and fume*; *to burst with anger* **2.** ⟨† & bib⟩ (Anstoß geben) *to scandalize* | **sich** ~ **an** *to be scandalized at* **II.** ~ n *annoying, vexing, worrying*

·**Ärgernis** n –nisses/–nisse **1.** = Anstoß A. 2. **2.** (Verletzung des sittl. Gefühls) ein öffentl. ~ *a public nuisance*; ein ständiges ~ *an open sore*; ein ~ beseitigen *to abate a nuisance* **3.** † f ~/ = Ärger ~**erregung** f *scandalizing public morals*

†**Arg·iver** m pl ⟨Gr⟩ *Argives* **arg·ivisch** a *Argive*

Argon·aute m ~n/~n ⟨ant⟩ *Argonaut*

Arg·onnen pl, **Arg·onner Wald** m *Argonne region*

Argot [ar'go:] n (Fr) ~s/~s *argot*

ärgst, ·Ärgste → arg I. a 1. a. & b.

Argum·ent n ~(e)s/~e *argument*; *fact* (od *reason*) *advanced* (*against, for*); ein durchschlagendes ~ *a sweeping argument case, contention*, sein Haupt~ ist *his case is* (*that*); die ~e [pl] sind nicht stichhaltig *the reasons given do not hold water* || **Argumentati·on** f ~/~en *argumentation* **argument·ieren** vi [h] *to argue* (über *about*); mit (*with a p*); *to reason* (*with a p*)

·**Argus** m ⟨ant⟩ ⟨fig⟩ (Wächter) *Argus* ~**augen** n [pl] *Argus-eyes* [pl], *extreme vigilances* || mit ~ *vigilantly*; ~ h *to be argus-eyed*

·**Argwohn** m ~s/ *suspicion* (gegen *of a p, a th*); → Mißtrauen || ~ erregen *to arouse suspicion* || ~ hegen *to entertain, have a s.*; ~ hegen gegen jdn *to suspect a p* || sie h den ~, daß .. *they suspect that* .. ·**argwohnen, -wöhnen** vt (etw) *to suspect*; *to mistrust, to be suspicious of* (*a th*)

·**argwöhnisch 1.** a *suspicious*; *shy, jealous* (gegen *of*) **2.** adv *suspiciously*

Ari·adnefaden m *Ariadne's clue*

Ari·aner m ~s/~ ⟨ec⟩, **ari·anisch** a *Arian*

·**Arie** f ~/~n ⟨mus⟩ *aria* || *air, song* **Ari·ette** f ⟨mus⟩ *ariette*

·**Arier** m *Aryan*; ⟨Ger hist⟩ ~paragraph *collective term for legal decrees bearing on the Aryanization of the German people* ·**arisch** a *Aryan*; ~e Sprache *Aryan* **aris·ieren** vt *to make Aryan, to aryanize* **Aris·ierung** f ~/ *aryanization*

·**Aries** (L) m ~/ ⟨astr⟩ *Aries*

Aristokr·at m ~en/~en *aristocrat*; ⟨a. übtr⟩

Aristokrat·ie f ~/~n *aristocracy* || ⟨übtr⟩ *aristocracy, cream* (*of sfudents*) **aristokr·atisch** a *aristocratic*

Arist·oteleshirsch m (= Rusahirsch) *sambur*

aristot·elisch a *Aristotelian*

Arithmet·ik f ~/ *arithmetic* **Arithm·etiker** m ~s/~ *arithmetician* **arithm·etisch** a *arithmetical*; in ~er Hinsicht *arithmetically*

Ariz·ona n (Staat der U.S.A.)

Ark·ade f ~/~n *arcade*

Ark·adien ⟨fig⟩ *Arcadia* **Ark·adier** m *Arcadian*

ark·adisch a *Arcadian, idyllic*

Ark·ansas 1. m (Nbfl. des Mississippi) **2.** n (Staat der U.S.A.)

Arkeb·use f ~/~n (*h*)*arquebus* **Arkeb·usier** m ~s/~e (*h*)*arquebusier*

·**Arktis** f ~/ *the arctic circle* (od *regions*)

·**arktisch** a ⟨geog⟩ *arctic*; → nördl. Eismeer

Arkt·urus m ~/ ⟨astr⟩ *Arcturus*

Arles [*arl*] n ⟨Fr⟩ (Stadt), → Arelat

arm a **A.** (P) **1.** *poor, indigent*; *poverty--stricken*, → mittellos | ~ an *poor in, lacking in*; *destitute* od *void of* || ~er s um etw ⟨Am⟩ *to be shy* (*of*) *a th* || er war jetzt um e–e Hoffnung ~er *he was now one hope the poorer*; ich war um £ 20 ∼̈er *I was down £ 20, I was £ 20 out* || ∼ m *to pauperize* **2.** (gefühlsbetont) **a.** (bedauernswert) *poor, miserable*; ∼es Kind *poor child*; mein ∼er (verstorbener) Vater *my poor father*; ein ∼er Kerl *a wretched fellow* || das ∼e Ding! *poor little thing*!; ich ∼̈er! *poor me*!; der Ärmste! (*the*) *poor dear*!, *poor fellow*! **b.** ⟨cont⟩ (kläglich) *despicable, poor* (*creature*) **c.** ⟨fig cul⟩ ∼e Ritter [pl] *fritters* [pl] **B.** (S) *poor* (*soil*); *barren* || *low-grade* (*ore*); (Erz, Gas) *lean*; (Gemisch) ⟨mot⟩ *weak* **C.** [abs, subst] **1.** ein ∼̈er *a poor p*; der ∼̈e (= Almosenempfänger) *the pauper* **2.** die ∼̈en *the poor, paupers* [pl]; *pauperdom* || die englischen ∼̈en *the English poor*; die verschämten ∼̈en *the respectable poor* **3.** → A. 2. a.

Arm m ∼(e)s/∼e **1.** ⟨anat⟩ *arm*; Unter∼̈ *forearm*, Ober∼̈ *upperarm* || ich hab auch nur einen rechten ∼ ⟨hum m. m.⟩ *my name is Simpson, not Samson* || auf ∼es Länge *at arm's length* || der längere ∼ ⟨fig m. m.⟩ *the inside track* | .. mit s–r Frau am ∼ *with his wife on his arm* || ∼ in ∼ *arm in arm* || ∼ in ∼ gehen ⟨sl⟩ *to crooky* || mit offenen ∼en *with open arms* | jdm in den ∼ fallen *to seize a p by the arm*; ⟨fig⟩ *to hinder* od *prevent a p* || jdm die ∼e entgegenstrecken *to hold out one's arms to a p* || jdn unter die ∼e fassen *to give a p a lift* ⟨a. fig⟩ || jdn am ∼ führen *to lead a p by the arm* || jdm den ∼ geben *to give a p one's arm* || jdm unter die ∼e greifen ⟨fig⟩ *to hold out a helping hand to a p, give a p a lift* || die ∼e kreuzen *to fold one's arms* || den ∼ gerne krumm m (= trinken) *to lift the elbow too often* || ⟨fig⟩ jdm in die ∼ laufen *to run into a p's arms*, ⟨übtr⟩ *to run across a p* || ein Kind auf die ∼e nehmen *to take a child in one's arms, to pick up a ch.* || ⟨fig⟩ jdn auf den ∼ nehmen *to lead a p up the garden-path*; du kannst mich nicht auf den ∼ nehmen! *you can't take a rise out of me*! || die Beine unter die ∼e nehmen *to stir one's stumps* || sich in die ∼e nehmen *to embrace* || jdn in die ∼e schließen *to take a p in one's arms, to embrace a p* || ⟨gym⟩ stell dich auf m–e ∼e *get on my arms* || sich e–r S in die ∼e werfen *to give o.s. up to a th* (*a passion*, etc) || die ∼e voll v .. *with armloads of* (*flowers*) **2.** ⟨übtr⟩ (Fluß-, Meeres-) *arm*, ⟨Am⟩ *branch* || kl ∼ *armlet* || (of a tree) *big branch*; *arm* | (Stuhl-) *arm* | ⟨tech⟩ *handle, boom*; (Anker-, Signal-, etc) *arm*; Wand∼̈ *bracket*; Deichsel∼̈ *shaft-bar*; → Schaft || ∼ (an e–r Welle) *tappet* **3.** ⟨übtr⟩ (Arbeitskraft) der beste ∼ *the best worker* **4.** ⟨fig⟩ (Macht) *arm, authority*; der ∼ des Gesetzes *the arm of the law*

Arm- ∼band n *bangle, bracelet, wristband, wristlet*; ∼̈er [pl] "*bracelets*" (*handcuffs*); ∼uhr [f] *wrist-watch* || ∼wecker [m] *wrist alarm, alarm wrist-watch* **∼beuge** f *bend of the arms* || ⟨gym⟩ *the bending of arms* **∼binde** f ⟨med⟩ *arm-sling* || (Abzeichen) ⟨Ger⟩ *armlet* (: *party armlets*); *armband* **∼bruch** m *fracture of an arm* **∼brust** f *cross-bow*; ∼schießen *archery*; ∼schütz(e) m *cross-bowman* **∼̈dick** a *as thick as one's arm* **∼füßer** m ∼s/∼ ⟨zoo⟩ *brachiopod*; (vorweltlich) Gattung der ∼ *terebratula* **∼geige** f ⟨mus⟩ *viola* **∼kachel** f *elbow-piece* (*of coat of mail*) **∼länge** f *arm's length* (auf ∼ *at* ..) **∼lehne** f *arm*; *elbow-piece, elbow-rest*; (bes e–s Chorstuhls) *prop* **∼leuchter** m *chandelier, branched candle-stick* || °⟨euphem⟩ = °Arschloch *shit* (P) **∼muskel** m (zweiköpfiger) *biceps* (L) **∼reif(en)**, **∼ring** m *bangle* **∼schiene** f **1.** *vambrace, arm-guard* (*of coat of mail*) **2.** *splint* **∼schild** m *small shield*; *buckler* **∼schlagader** f ⟨anat⟩ *brachial artery* **∼sessel** m *armchair, easy-chair* **∼spange** f *bangle, bracelet*; *armlet* (f Oberarm) **∼stuhl** m = Armsessel **∼stulp** m ⟨fenc⟩ *gauntlet* **∼stumpf** m *stump of an arm* **∼- u Beinamputierter** m *basket case* **∼voll** m: ein ∼ .. *an armful* (*of* ..), zwei Arme voll *two armsful* od *armfuls* **∼zeug** n = Armschiene 1.

Arm·ada f ∼/–den *armada* (⟨bes⟩ 1588)

Armad·ill m ∼s/∼e ⟨zool⟩ *armadillo*

Armat·ur f ∼/∼en ⟨tech⟩ *armature*, [mst pl] ∼en *armatures, fittings, mountings* [pl] **∼beleuchtung** f = –leuchte **∼enbrett** n ⟨mot⟩ *dashboard*; *instrument-board* od *-panel* od *layout* **∼leuchte** f *dashboard light*, ⟨mot⟩ *panel lighting*

·Ärmchen n ∼s/∼ *little arm*

Arm·ee f ∼/∼n *army* || zur gr ∼ abgerufen od versammelt w *to be gathered to one's fathers*, ⟨fam⟩ *to join the majority* **∼befehl** m *army-order* **∼bericht** m *army-bulletin* **∼hauptquartier** n *army headquaters* pl **∼korps** n *army-corps* **∼lieferant** m *army-contractor* **∼oberkommando** n *Commander-in-Chief and his staff*

·Ärmel m ∼s/∼ *sleeve, arm* (*of a jacket*) | mit ∼n versehen *to sleeve*; mit ∼n *sleeved* || ohne ∼ *sleeveless* || jdn am ∼ festhalten *to buttonhole a p* || sich die ∼ aufkrempeln *to tuck, turn, roll up one's sleeves*; °krempele man die ∼ auf! → anpacken || aus dem ∼ schütteln ⟨fig⟩ *to toss .. off, to do* (*a th*) *off-hand*; *to improvise* **∼abzeichen** n *sleeve badge* **∼aufschlag** m *cuff* || ⟨mil⟩ *cuff, facings* [pl] **∼halter** m [pl] (f Hemd) *sleeve-suspenders* [pl] **∼kanal** m *the* (*English*) *Channel* **∼schoner** m *sleeve-protector* **∼streifen** m *stripe*, → Tresse **∼weste** f ⟨Am⟩ *lumber-jack*

Armel·euteviertel n *slums* [pl], *poor-district*

-ärmelig a *-sleeved*, kurz∼ *short-sleeved*

·Armen- *poor-* .. **∼anstalt** f = Armenhaus **∼anwalt** m *solicitor* od *counsel for the poor* **∼arzt** m *parish-doctor* **∼asyl** n *pauper asylum* **∼aufseher** m *overseer of the poor* **∼behörde** f jetzt: *Local Government Board* (früher: *Poor Law Board*) **∼bezirk** m *relieving-district* **∼büchse** f *poor-box* **∼fürsorge** f *poor relief*, ⟨Am⟩ *relief and care of the poor* **∼geld** n *alms* [pl] **∼gesetz** n *the Poor-Law* **∼haus** n ⟨engl⟩ *Poor Law* (od *Public Assistance*) *Institution*; † *workhouse* || *poorhouse*; (f Alte) *alms-house*; ⟨Am⟩ *town farm* **∼kasse** f *relief-fund* **∼kommissar** m = Armenpfleger **∼krankenhaus** n ⟨engl⟩ *Poor Law Hospital* **∼liste** f *list of the paupers* **∼pflege** f *poor relief*; ⟨engl oft⟩ *Family Welfare Association* **∼pfleger** m ⟨engl⟩ *relieving-officer, overseer of the poor*; ⟨Am⟩ *poormaster* || *almoner*; *guardian of the poor* **∼rat** m *parish-council* **∼recht** n (*Poor Law*) *legal aid to poor persons*; auf ∼ klagen ⟨jur⟩ *to sue in forma pauperis*; Kläger *or* Beklagter im ∼ *pauper*; (jdm) das ∼ entziehen *to dispauper*(*ize*) **∼schule** f *charity-school* **∼steuer** f *poor-rate* **∼unterstützung** f (*civil*) *parish*; ∼ empfangen *to go on the parish* || ∼sausschuß [m] *parish-council* **∼viertel** n *poor-district*; (in London) *slums* [pl] **∼vogt**, **∼vorsteher** m = Armenpfleger **∼wesen** n *System of Poor Relief*

Arm·enien n *Armenia* **Arm·enier** m *Armenian* **arm·enisch** a *Armenian*

Armes·ünder m *condemned criminal* od *delinquent* **∼glocke** f *knell rung for an execution* **∼hemd** n ⟨hist⟩ (der v der Inquisition Verurteilten) *sanbenito* **∼miene** f *hang-dog look*

arm·ieren vt [h] (Festung etc) *to fit out* od *to equip with arms*; *to arm*; das Schiff ist mit 9 Geschützen armiert *the ship mounts* (od *is mounted with*) *9 guns* || (Beton) *to armour, to reinforce* || ⟨phys⟩ (Magnet) *to arm* || ⟨el⟩ –rt *armoured* (*cable*) **Arm·ierung** f ∼/∼en **1.** [abstr] *armament, equipment* **2.** [konkr] ⟨bes mar⟩ (Geschütze etc) *armament*; das Schiff hat e–e ∼ v 9 Geschützen *the ship mounts 9 guns*

-·armig a *–armed*, lang∼ *long-armed*

Armill·arsphäre f ∼/ ⟨astr⟩ *armillary sphere*

·ärmlich a **1.** *poor, miserable, wretched* (*man*) ||

humble (*birth*; *dwelling*); *dingy* (*dwelling*); ~e Verhältnisse [pl] *poverty*; aus ä. V.n zu .. *from p. to* ‖ *shabby* (*street*) **2.** (unzureichend) *poor* (*breakfast*); *scanty* (*income*) **3.** (kläglich) *pitiful*; *trivial*; *paltry*; *thin* (*content*); *beggarly* **4.** → armselig **·Ärmlichkeit** f ~/~en *poorness, wretchedness* ‖ *scantiness* ‖ *paltriness*

·armselig a = ärmlich ‖ ~e Anstellung *two--penny-halfpenny job* **≈keit** f = Ärmlichkeit

·Ärmling m ~s/~e **1.** *oversleeve* **2.** *poor p*

Armori·al n ~s/~e (Wappenbuch) *armorial*

armorik·anisch a (= bretonisch) *Armoric(an)*

·Armut f ~/ **1.** *poverty, penury, indigence*; (Not) *destitution*; *necessity* (*compelled him to steal*); verschämte ~ *respectable poverty* ‖ dauernde ~, Massen≈ *pauperism, pauperdom* | durch ~ heruntergekommen *poverty-stricken* ‖ in ~ geraten *to be reduced to penury* ‖ ~ tut weh *poverty is a sharp sting* **2.** (Mangel) *poorness, poverty, destitution* (an *of*) | geistige ~ *intellectual thinness* **~szeugnis** n *certificate of poverty* ‖ ⟨übtr⟩ (geistiges) *proof of spiritual poverty*; *showing a lack of knowledge* ‖ sich [dat] ein (geistiges) ~ ausstellen ⟨fig⟩ *to show one's own incapacity, to compromise* od *commit o.s.*

·Arnika f ~/~s ⟨bot⟩ *arnica* **~tinktur** f (*tincture of*) *arnica*

·Arno m (Fluß in Mittelitalien)

Ar·om n ~s/~e ⟨mst poet⟩ = **Ar·oma** n ~s/–men *aroma*; *flavour* (*of wine*); *fragrance* **arom·atisch** a *aromatic*; *fragrant, flavorous*

·Aron m = **~stab** m ⟨bot⟩ Gefleckter ~ *cuckoo-pint, arum* **~wurz** f = Aronstab

Arp·eggio [arˈpedʒoː] [It] n ~s/-gien ⟨mus⟩ *arpeggio*

·Arrak m ~s/~e *arrack*

Arrangem·ent [arɑ̃ːʒəˈmɑ̃ː] n (Fr) ~s/~s **1.** (Anordnung) *arrangement* **2.** (Vorbereitung) [mst pl] ~s *arrangements*, ~s treffen *to make a.* **3.** *agreement, arrangement* ‖ *composition* (*with*) **4.** ⟨mus & Lit⟩ *adaptation, arrangement*

Arrang·eur [arɑ̃ːˈʒør] m [Fr] ~s/~e *arranger, manager* **arrang·ieren** [arɑ̃ːˈʒiːrən] vt [h] *to arrange*; *to organize*; *to manage* ‖ (veranstalten) *to get up* vt ‖ **sich** mit s–n Gläubigern ~ *to compound, settle* (od *make a composition*) *with one's creditors*

Arr·est m ~s/~e **1.** (Haft) *arrest, attachment* | ⟨mil⟩ *arrest*; *detention*; ⟨mar⟩ *cells* [pl] **2.** (Beschlagnahme) *attachment, seizure*; ⟨bes mar⟩ *embargo* (e–r S *on a th*) **3.** ⟨school⟩ *detention* **4. Wendungen:** ⟨mil⟩ leichter (strenger) *open* (*close*) *arrest* | (Waren etc) mit ~ belegen *to seize*; *to lay an embargo on* (*a ship*) ‖ ~ bek h ⟨mil⟩ *to be put under arrest*; ⟨school⟩ *to be kept in* ‖ jdn mit ~ bestrafen, jdm ~ geben ⟨mil⟩ *to put a p under arrest*; ⟨school⟩ *to keep a p in, to detain a p* **~befehl** m ⟨priv l⟩ *order of attachment* (S), *of detention* (P) **~lokal** n ⟨mil⟩ *confinement facility, detention room*; ⟨mar⟩ *cells* pl **~strafe** f ⟨m. m.⟩ *sentence of confinement*

Arrest·ant m ~en/~en *prisoner*

arret·ieren vt [h] *to arrest, capture* ‖ (anhalten) (etw) *to arrest, check, stop* **Arret·ierung** f ~/~en *arrest, capture*

Arret·ier- ~klinke f *arresting lath*; *stop*

Arriereg·arde [arˈjær-] f (Fr) ~/~n ⟨mil⟩ = Nachhut

arrog·ant a *arrogant*; → anmaßend **Arrog·anz** f ~/~en *arrogance*; → Anmaßung

arrond·ieren vt [h] (Grundstücke) *to consolidate, concentrate* **Arrondissement** n ~s/~s [arɔ̃ːdisˈmɑ̃] (Fr) *arondissement*

°**·Arsch** m ~es/≈e ⟨vulg⟩ *arse*; ⟨fig⟩ du kannst mich .. *I'll see you further first* ‖ am ~e des Propheten ⟨m. m.⟩ *all at hell* ‖ v e–m traurigen ~ kann man k–n fröhlichen Furz erwarten (Martin Luther) etwa: *get a fart of a dead man*! ‖ ihm geht der ~ mit Grundeis *he's in a blue funk* **~backe** f *butt* **≈kriechen** ⟨Am mil⟩ *to brown-nose* **~kriecher** m *arse-crawler* (*his nose is always brown*) **~kriecher·ei** f *arse-crawling, bum-sucking* **~lecker** m ⟨fig⟩ *bum-sucker*, **~leder** n *breech--leather* **~loch** n *arse-hole* ‖ (als Schimpfwort) *arse-holes* (*to you*)! **~pauker** m *kid-walloper*, ⟨m.m.⟩ *gerund grinder*

Ars·en n ~s/ ⟨chem⟩ (Grundstoff) *arsenic* [abbr As] **~blende** f gelbe ~ *orpiment*; rote ~ *realgar* **≈haltig** a *arsenic(al)* **~kies** m *arsenical pyrites* **~silber** n ⟨minr⟩ *huntilite* **~trioxid** n = Arsenik **~vergiftung** f *arsenical poisoning*

Arsen·al n ~(e)s/~e *arsenal*; *Ordnance Department*; *naval store depot*

ars·enig a ⟨min⟩ *arsenious*

Ars·enik n ~s/ ⟨chem⟩ (Zus-setzung) *arsenic*, ⟨scient⟩ *trioxide of a.* **~esser** m *arsenic addict* **~mehl** n *flowers* [pl] *of arsenic*

·Art f ~/~en **A.** †(**Abkunft**) *birth, descent*; *origin* **B. 1.** (angeborene Natur) *nature*; *kind*; *natural disposition, character* ‖ es liegt nicht in s–r ~ *it is not in his nature* (*to do*) ‖ ~ läßt nicht v ~ *what is bred in the bone will come out in the flesh*; *like father, like son* ‖ aus der ~ schlagen *to degenerate*; ⟨übtr⟩ *to be an exception* (*to the others*, etc); jd, der aus der ~ geschlagen ist *a runt* **2. a.** (**Eigentümlichkeit, Gewohnheit** → d.) *manner, way(s)*; in s–r ~ *in his way* ‖ einzig in s–r ~ *unique*; *unique of its kind* ‖ gut in ihrer ~ *good in their way* ‖ s–e ~ z tun *his way of doing*; das ist so s–e ~ *that is his way*; es ist nicht s–e ~ *it is not his way* (*to do*); er hat e–e gewisse ~ *he has a way* (*of speaking*); er hat e–e furchtbare ~ an sich *he has a terrible way with him* ‖ die englische ~ *the English way* (*of thinking*); nach englischer ~ *in the E. taste* ‖ e–e üble ~ *a trick* (z tun *of doing*) **b.** die ~ **u Weise** der Ausführung *the style of the execution*; → B. 4. ‖ stelle dir die ~ u W. vor, in der (*or* wie) .. *imagine the way that* ‖ die ~, wie Sie es behandeln *your method of dealing with it* | **auf** die (diese) ~ (u Weise) *in that* (*this*) *way*; auf die ~ *like that*; auf die e–e od andere ~ *some way or other*; auf jede ~ u Weise *in every possible way*; auf irgendeine ~ *anihow, somehow* | **in** e–r (gewissen) ~ *in a way* | **nach** der ~ v *after the manner of, in the way of, in the nature of*; nach der ~ des Hauses ⟨cul⟩ .. *specialty of the house*; es ist nach ~ v .. *it is in the line of* ..; geschrieben nach ~ v *written on the lines of* ..; in dieser ~ denken *to think on these lines* ‖ nach ~ der Anbringung der Pflöcke *according to the way in which the pegs are fixed*; nach ~ der Fortbewegung .. *according to the way it is* (od *they are*) *propelled* .. ‖ [⟨engl⟩ oft durch adv]: nach ~ e–r Fuge *fugally* **3.** (**Benehmen**) *manner*; Lebens≈ *manners* [pl] ‖ das ist k–e ~ *that won't do*; das ist k–e ~ z tun *that is not a nice thing* (od *not the way*) *to do* | daß es e–e ~ hat *hammer and tongs, with a vengeance, thoroughly*; daß es nur so e–e ~ hat! *like a thousand* (*of*) *bricks*! *with knobs on*! **4.** ⟨arts⟩ (Ausführung) *handling*; ⟨paint⟩ (Manier) *brush--work* **C. 1.** (**Gattung**) **a.** *kind, sort*; *class, species*; *category, type*; *breed*; *kidney*; ⟨Am⟩ *stripe* ‖ Denker derselben ~ *thinkers of the same breed* ‖ die altmodische ~ v Dienstmädchen *the old--fashioned type of servant*; die wesentlichen Züge e–r ~ aufweisend *true to type* ‖ ein Gentleman v Georgs ~ *a gentleman of George's kidney* ‖ ein Tyrann der schlimmsten ~ *a tyrant of the worst description* | e–e ~ Kompliment *a c. of sorts*, → C. 2. ‖ e–e neue ~ v Reifen *a new sort of tire* ‖ eine andere ~ Verbrechen als .. *a different nature of crime from* ..; → Ding **b.** ⟨zoo & bot⟩ *species* (z. B. ⟨zoo⟩ [Wildkatze] → Gattung [Katzen], → Familie [Katzen], → Ordnung [Raubtiere], → Klasse [Säugetiere], → Unterstamm [Wirbeltiere], → Stamm [Chordatiere]) || ~ läßt nicht v ~ *birds of a feather flock together*, → B. 1. || Fortpflanzung der ~en *propagation of species* || *breed* **2. (verblaßt)** *sort, kind, variety*, e–e ~ v *a kind* od *sort of*; welche ~ (von) Buch? *what kind of book*? etw, nichts der ~ *something, nothing of the sort* || er ist nicht die ~ v Mensch, er ist nicht ein M. der ~ *he is not the sort of man* (*who* . .) | so e–e ~ Friede *a sort of a peace* || so e–e ~ Dichter *a bit of a poet, a poet of sorts* || e–e seltsame ~ v Mensch *a strange sort of man* | diese ~ Buch, ein B. dieser ~ *this kind* od *sort of book, a book of this kind, sort* || diese ~ Leute, L. dieser ~ *these sort* od *kind of men* (*are* . .) | derselben ~ ⟨Scot⟩ *of that ilk* || er war v derselben ~ *he was tarred with the same brush* || alle v derselben ~ wie *all of a kind with* . . | alle ~en Bücher, B. aller ~ *all kinds* od *sorts of books, books of all kinds* || aller ~en *of all kinds* od *sorts* **~aufspaltung** f ⟨biol⟩ *speciation* **≗erhaltend** a ⟨biol⟩ *survival* [attr] (Wert) **≗gemäß** a *true to type* [pred] **~genosse** m, -ssin f *man of the same race*; ⟨zoo⟩ *congener* | Arten- etc

Artef·akt n ~s/~en *artefact, artifact*

·arteigen a *specific* (*forms*) || *native*; *racy*

Artem·isie f ~/~n ⟨bot⟩ *artemisia* [L], → Absinth, Beifuß, Eberraute

·arten vi [s] ~ nach jdm *to resemble a p, to take after a p* || → geartet, beschaffen

·Arten- ~gruppe f *closely related species* pl **~trennung** f ⟨biol⟩ *speciation* **~wandel** m ⟨biol⟩ *mutation*

Art·erie f ~/~n *artery* | **~n-** *arterial*; *artery* **~abbinder** m *artery underbinder* **~verkalkung** f *sclerosis of the arteries* **art·erioskler·otisch** a *arteriosclerotic*

art·esisch a *Artesian*, ~er Brunnen *a. well*

·artfremd a *alien to the race* || *not native, not genuine*; *exotic, foreign*

·artig I. a **1.** *good, well-bred, well-behaved* (*children*); sehr ~ *as good as gold* || sei ~ *be good*; seid recht ~, Kinder! *behave yourselves, dears*! *mind you are very good children*! das ist mal ein ~er Junge! *there's a good boy*! || *nice, pretty, pleasing, gainly*; *polite, civil*; *urbane* **2.** [in comp] **a.** → bös~, gut~ **b.** *-form, -like*; fluß~ *river-like*; hunde~ *dog-like* **II.** adv: sich recht ~ benehmen *to be on one's best behaviour*

..artig a-suffix .. *like* (*snail-like*); → artig I. 2.

·Artigkeit f ~/~en *good behaviour* || *politeness, courtesy, civility* || **(Anmut)** *prettiness, neatness* || [mst pl] *compliments, civilities* [pl]

Art·ikel m ~s/~ **1.** (Abschnitt) **a.** *article*; *clause*; → Glaubens≗, Kriegs≗; ⟨engl ec⟩ die 39 ~ (Glaubensbekenntnis der C. E.) *the Thirty-Nine Articles* | kz ~ *paragraph* **b.** (Aufsatz) *article, paper* **c.** ⟨com⟩ (Eintragung) *item, entry* **2.** ⟨gram⟩ → Geschlechtswort **3.** ⟨com⟩ (Warengattung) *article, item, commodity, line* (: *a useful l.*); ~ [pl] *goods, wares*, e–n ~ führen *to keep an article* || ~ [pl], die eingehen *moribund lines* **~karte** f ⟨comp⟩ *detail card* **≗los** a ⟨gram⟩ *without the article*, ⟨scient⟩ *anarthrous* **~nummer** f ⟨com⟩ *item number* **~schreiber** m *paragraphist, columnist*

Artikulati·on f ~/~en **1.** ⟨gram⟩ *articulation*; *enunciation* **2.** ⟨anat⟩ (Gelenk) *joint, articulation* **artikul·ieren** vt [h] **1.** ⟨anat⟩ (gliedern) *to articulate* **2.** ⟨gram⟩ (etw) *to articulate* || artikuliert sprechen *to a.*

·Artillerie f ~/~n ⟨mil⟩ (Waffengattung) *artillery*; ⟨engl⟩ *Royal A.* || (Geschütze) *a., ordnance* || leichte ~ *light a.*; schwere ~ *heavy a.* od *ordnance*; *heavy guns* [pl] || reitende ~ *horse a.*; ⟨engl⟩ *Royal Horse A.* || ⟨engl⟩ Feld≗ *the Royal Field A.* [abbr *R.F.A.*] **~·ausbildungs·unteroffizier** m *sergeant-major instructor in gunnery* (⟨fam⟩ *smig*) **~beobachter** m *spotter* **~be·obachtungsflugzeug** n *artillery spotting plane* **~einschlag** m *shell hit* **~feuer** n *cannonade*; *bombardment* **~kommandeur** m *corps* od *division artillery commander* **~leitstand** m ⟨mar⟩ *gun control tower* **~leitung** f ⟨mar⟩ *gun control* **~offizier** m ⟨mar⟩ *artillery-officer* **~park** m *a. park* **~stellung** f *gun area* **~techniker** m *artificer* **~vorbereitung** f *preparation bombardment* od *fire* **~werkstatt** f *ordnance factory* **~zentrale** f ⟨mar⟩ *transmitting room*

·Artillerist m ~en/~en *artilleryman, gunner* **a-·istisch** a: ~er Punkt *artillery reference point*

Artisch·ocke f ~/~n ⟨bot⟩ *artichoke*; Erd≗ *Jerusalem a.*; ⟨cul⟩ *globe* od *French a.*; wilde ~ *cardoon* **~nboden** m ⟨cul⟩ *chard*

Art·ist m ~en/~en; **~in** f ~/~nen *artist, acrobat*, ⟨fam⟩ *stuntman* **≗isch** a *of an acrobat* | *referring to the skills* (od *in the manner*) *of an artist* || ⟨arts, etc⟩ (verfeinert) *refined*; (gekünstelt) *artificial, affected*

·artverwandt a *naturally related* (mit *to*)

·Arve f = Arbe

Arzn·ei f ~/~en **1.** *medicine*; ⟨fam⟩ *physic* **2.** [in comp] *medicinal* **~buch** n amtliches ~ *pharmacopoeia* **~fex** m *drug addict*; *drug fiend* **~fläschchen** n *phial* **~kapsel** f *capsule* **~kunde** f *pharmacology* **≗kundlich** a *pharmaceutical* **~mittel** n *medicine, medicament*; *preparation* **~mittellehre** f *pharmacology* **~pflanze** f *medicinal plant* **~trank** m *potion, draught* **~ware** f *drug* **~wissenschaft** f *pharmaceutics* [pl], *pharmacy*

Arzt m ~es/≗e (nicht operierend) *physician*; || (Chirurg) *surgeon*; ⟨mil⟩ *medical officer* || praktischer ~ *general practitioner, doctor* (⟨Am⟩ [abbr *G.P.*]; *medical practitioner, practising physician*), *visiting doctor* || Fach≗ *consultant doctor*, f innere Krankheiten *internist* | ⟨fam⟩ *doctor*; ⟨Am⟩ *physician* || Kassen≗ *panel-doctor*, als Kassen≗ zugelassen *on the panel* || Land≗ *country doctor* **~helferin** f *doctor's assistant* **~praxis** f ~/–xen *general practice*

·Ärzte- ~jargon m *medicalese* **~kammer** f *Chamber of Physicians* **~rat** m ⟨engl⟩ (Reichs–) *the General Medical Council* **~schaft** f *body of physicians*; *medical profession*

·Ärztin f ~/~nen *lady* od *woman doctor*, ~nen [pl] *lady-doctors, women* (od *woman*)*-doctors*

·ärztlich 1. a *medical*; ~e Bemühungen [pl] *medical attention* od *services*; ~e Hilfe in Anspruch nehmen *to call in a doctor* || ⟨engl⟩ die ~e Fachwelt *Harley Street* **2.** adv: jdn ~ behandeln *to doctor a p* **~erseits** adv *medically*

As n Asses/Asse ⟨cards⟩ *ace*; Karo≗ *ace of diamonds* (etc); blankes ~ *bare ace* **~flöte** f *royal flush*

As n ~/~ ⟨mus⟩ *A flat*; ~-Dur (≗-Moll) *A flat major* (*minor*)

As·ant m ~s/ (Gummiharz) *asafoetida* (L)

Asb·est m ~(e)s/~e *asbestos*; → Bergholz || [in comp] *asbestine* **asb·estartig, -haltig** a *asbestine*

Asch m ~(e)s/≗e (Napf) *basin, bowl* || *pot* **~kuchen** m *pound-cake*, → Napfkuchen

Asch·anti 1. m pl (Negerstamm in W.-Afrika) *Ashanti* **2.** n Königreich *Ashanti*

·Asch- ~becher m *ash-stand, ash-tray* **≗bleich** a = aschfahl **≗blond** a *ash-blond(e)* **≗fahl** a *ashy(-pale), grey-pale* (*complexion, face*) **~farbe** f *ash-colour* **≗farben** a *ashen, ash-coloured*; *ashy* **≗grau** a *ash-grey, ashen-white*; *ashy*; das geht ins ≗e *that goes too far, that's a stunner* **~huhn** n ⟨orn⟩ = Ralle **~kraut** n ~s/ ⟨bot⟩ *cineraria* **~wurz** f ⟨bot⟩ → Diptam

·Asche f ~/~n **1.** ⟨chem⟩ (of coal, etc) *ash, cinders* [pl]; viel ~ *a great deal of ash*, vulkanische ~ *volcanic ash* || Zigarren≗ *cigar ash* || glimmende ~ *embers* [pl] **2.** (of a body) *ashes*; *dust*; Staub u ~ *dust and ashes*; Friede s–r ~!

peace to his ashes; in Sack u ~ trauern *to mourn in sack and ashes* **3.** ⟨übtr⟩ (etw) in ~ verwandeln *to burn* od *reduce* (*a th*) *to ashes, to lay* (*a th*) *in ashes* **4.** ⟨fig⟩ °~ (Geld) ⟨sl⟩ *dust* ‖ *ungebrannte ~ *a thrashing*

·Äsche f ~/~n ⟨ich⟩ *grayling*

·Äschel m ~s/~ ⟨minr⟩ *the ash of cobalt-ores*

·Aschen- ~aufzug m ⟨mar⟩ *ash-hoist* **~bahn** f ⟨sport⟩ *cinder–, dirt-track*; Motorrennen auf der ~ *dirt-track racing* **~becher** m = Aschbecher **~brödel** n ~s/ **1.** (Märchengestalt) *Cinderella* **2.** ⟨übtr⟩ *drudge*, das ~ s *to be the d.* (*in*) ‖ *ugly duckling* **~ejektor** m ⟨mar⟩ *ash-ejector* **~garten** m (Gedächtnis-) ⟨crem⟩ *garden of remembrance* **~grube** f *ash-pit, dust-hole* **~haufen** m *dust-heap* **~kasten** m *dust-bin, ash-box* **~krug** m → –urne, ⟨praeh⟩ *funeral urn* od *cist* **~mühle** f (Knochenmühle) ⟨crem⟩ *cremulator* **~prahm** m *ash boat* **~pulverisierer** m ⟨crem⟩ *cremulator®* **~pulverisierung** f ⟨crem⟩ *cremulation* **~puttel** n = Aschenbrödel **~raum** m ⟨mar⟩ *ashpit* **~regen** m *rain of ashes* **~reste** m pl ⟨crem⟩ *cremated ashes* od *remains* pl **~urne** f *cinerary* od *sepulchral urn* **~vulkan** m *cinder cone* **~salz** n † = Pottasche

·Ascher m ~s/~ **1.** = Aschbecher **2.** =

·Äscher m ~s/~ *mixture* od *lye of ash and slaked lime*

Ascherm·ittwoch m ~s/~e *Ash-Wednesday*

·äschern vt **1.** (Häute) *to treat with lye* **2.** = einäschern **3.** (Weg) *to strew with ashes*

·aschig a *ashy, covered with ashes*

·Asen m [pl] ⟨myth⟩ *Ases, Aesir* [pl]

·äsen vi [h] *to browse, graze, feed*; → aasen

As·epsis, As·eptik f ~ ⟨med⟩ *asepsis* **as·eptisch** a *aseptic*

·Äser m ~s/~ ⟨mil⟩ = Brotbeutel **·Äser** [pl] v Aas

Asi·at m ~en/~en; **~in** f ~/~nen; **asi·atisch** a *Asian* (*influenza*); *Asiatic* **·Asien** n *Asia*

Ask·anier m ⟨Ger hist⟩ (Dynastie) *Ascanian*

Ask·ari m ~s/~s (eingeborener Soldat in Ostafrika) *Askari*; ~s [pl] *Askari*(*s*)

Ask·ese f *ascesis, asceticism* ‖ ⟨übtr⟩ *abstinence*

Ask·et m ~en/~en *ascetic* **ask·etisch 1.** a *ascetic*(*al*) ‖ *abstinent* **2.** adv (*to live*) *ascetically*

Äskul·ap- ~natter f ~/~n *a non-poisonous snake* **~schlange** f, **~stab** m *Aesculapian rod* od *staff*; ⟨Am⟩ *caduceous*

As·owsche Meer, das (Seitenbecken des Schwarzen Meers) *the Sea of Azov*

·asozial a *asocial*; *antisocial*; *unsocial*

·Aspe f = Espe

Asp·ekt m **1.** ⟨astr⟩ *aspect* **2.** (Gesichtspunkt) *aspect* **3.** ⟨phil⟩ = Aktionsart

Asperg·ill n ⟨R.C.⟩ *aspergill*(*um*) [L] **Aspersi·on** f ⟨R.C.⟩ *aspersion*

Asph·alt m ~(e)s/~e **1.** *asphalt*; *tarmac*(*adam*) ‖ ~ treten *to beat the streets* **2.** [in comp] *asphalt*; *asphaltic* **~arbeiter, ~leger** m *asphalter* **~guß** m *masticic asphalt* **~lack** m *black japan* °**~pflanze** f *town-bred girl*; *prostitute* **~pflaster** n *asphalt pavement* **~presse** f *newspapers* [pl] *in large towns with enormous circulation* **~splitt** m *bituminized chippings* pl °**~spucker** m *loafer, corner-boy*

asphalt·ieren vt [h] *to asphalt*

Asph·odelos, -d·ill m ~s/ ⟨bot⟩ = Affodill

Asphyx·ie ~/~n *asphyxia* (L)

Asp·ik m, n ~s/~e *aspic, aspic jelly, galantine*

Aspir·ant m ~en/~en *aspirant*

Aspir·ata f ~/–ten ⟨gram⟩ *aspirate* **Aspirati·on** f ~/~en ⟨gram & tech⟩ *aspiration* **Aspir·ator** m ⟨tech⟩ *aspirator* **aspir·ieren** vt ⟨gram⟩ *to aspirate*

Aspir·in n ~s/ ⟨chem⟩ *aspirin*

aß, ·aßest, ·aßen pret v essen

·Assam n (Vorderind. Prov.) *Assam* ‖ **~·it** m ~**·itisch** a; die Assamiten pl *the Assamese*

Assekur·ant m ~en/~en *insurer* ‖ (ship's) *underwriter* **Assekur·anz** f ~/~en *insurance*; ~brief [m] *insurance-policy* ‖ *underwriting* (*of ships*) ‖ → Versicherung **Assekur·at** m ~en/~en *insuree*; *insured p* **assekur·ieren** vt [h] *to insure*

·Assel f ~/~n ⟨zoo⟩ *isopod*; (Bohr~) *wood-louse*, → d. Bd. I. ‖ (Tausendfüßer) *centipede*

Ass·embler- ~-Syst·em n ⟨comp⟩ *assembly system*

Ass·essor m ~s/–ess·oren ⟨jur⟩ *assessor*; *assistant judge* | ⟨Ger⟩ *candidate*

Assign·ant m ~en/~en ⟨com⟩ *drawer* (*of a bill*) **Assign·at** m ~en/~en ⟨com⟩ *drawee* **Assignat·ar** m ~s/~e *assignee* **Assign·ate** f (Fr) ~/~n ⟨hist⟩ *assignat, papermoney* (*of the first French republic*) **assign·ieren** vt [h] *to assign*; (Scheck) *to draw*

Assimilati·on f ~/~en ⟨a. gram⟩ *assimilation*; ~sprozeß *assimilative process* **assimil·ieren** vt [h] (etw) *to assimilate* (e–r S *to a th*) | **sich** ~ *to assimilate* **Assimil·ierung** f *assimilation*; ~sprozeß m *assimilative process*

Ass·ise f ~/~n ⟨jur⟩ *sitting, session* ‖ ~n [pl] (Schwurgericht) ⟨engl⟩ *assizes* [pl]

Assist·ent m ~en/~en *assistant, adjunct*; **~in** f ~/–innen: medizinisch-technische ~ *medical technician*; technische ~ ⟨med⟩ *instrument sister* → Assistenzarzt

Assist·enz f ~/~en *assistance* ‖ *attendance, presence* **~arzt** m *doctor's* od *medical assistant*; *assistant-surgeon, dresser*; (im Krankenhaus wohnender) ⟨Am⟩ *intern*(*e*)

assist·ieren vi; jdm ~ *to assist a p* ‖ *to attend*

Associé [asɔ'sje:] m ~s/~s ⟨com⟩ → Teilhaber **Assozi·ierung** f ~/~en *association*

Asson·anz f ~/~en ⟨pros⟩ *assonance* **asson·ierend** a *assonant*; ~es Wort *assonant*

assort·ieren vt [h] *to assort*; assortiertes Lager *assortment* **Assortim·ent** n ~(e)s/~e *assortment*

Assoziati·on [–tsio:n] f ~/~en ⟨psych⟩ *association*; Ideen~ *a. of ideas* ‖ ⟨com⟩ *association, partnership* | **~s-** ⟨psych⟩ *associational* **~szentren** [pl] *association centres* **assozi·ieren** vt [h] (Gedanken) *to associate* | ⟨com⟩ **sich** ~ mit jdm *to enter into partnership with a p*

Assu·an n (Stadt in Oberägypten) *Aswân*

†Ass·yrien n *Assyria* **Ass·yrier** m ~s/~, **ass·yrisch** a die ~e Sprache *Assyrian*

·Ast m ~es/~e **1.** *bough, branch*; kl ~ *branchlet*; Äste [pl] ⟨oft übtr⟩ *branches* [pl], *ramification*(*s*); (f. Zellstoff) *rejects*; (of veins, etc) sich in ~en ausbreiten *to ramify* (über *over*) ‖ den ~ absägen, auf dem man sitzt *to kill the goose with the golden eggs* **2.** (~ansatz) *knot, knob* **3.** ⟨übtr⟩ (Höcker) *hunch, hump*; °sich e–n ~ lachen *to split* od *crack one's sides* **~frei** a ⟨for⟩ *clear, limbless* (Holz) **~loch** n *knot-hole* **~los** a *without knots* od *knobs* **~rein** a ⟨for⟩ *clear of branches*; *free of knots* **~reinheit** f ⟨for⟩ *clearness* **~reisig** n *loppings* pl **~werk** n *branches, boughs* [pl]

ast·atisch a ⟨phys⟩ *astatic* (*needle*)

·Ästchen n ~s/~ *branchlet, twig, sprig*

·Aster f ~/~n ⟨bot⟩ *aster*; Sommer~ *China aster*

Aster·iskus m ~/–ken *asterisk* (*) **Astero·id** m ~s/~en ⟨astr⟩ *asteroid* ‖ ⟨zoo⟩ *starfish*

Asthen·ie f ~/ ⟨med⟩ *asthenia* **Asth·eniker** m *asthenic person*

Ästh·et m ~en/~en *aesthete*

Ästh·etik f **1.** ~/ *aesthetics* pl [sg konstr] **2.** ⟨philos⟩ (Lehre v der Sinneserkenntnis) *aesthesis* **Ästh·etiker** m ~s/~ *aesthete* **ästh·etisch 1.** a *aesthetic*; in ~er Hinsicht *aesthetically* **2.** adv *aesthetically* **Ästhetiz·ismus** m *aestheticism*

·Asthma n ~s/ *asthma* ‖ ~kranker *asthmatic*

patient **Asthm·atiker** m ~s/~ *asthmatic* **asthm·a-tisch** a *asthmatic*

·astig, ·ästig a *branchy* (*tree*); ⟨übtr⟩ *ramified, ramose* | *knotty, knobby, gnarled, gnarly* (*wood*)

Astigmat·ismus m ⟨med⟩ *astigmatism*

ästim·ieren vt [h] (jdn) *estimate, to hold in estimation*

·Astrachan, Astrach·an n ⟨Russ⟩ (Gebiet u Stadt) *Astrac(h)an, Astrakhan* ‖ m ~s/ (Lammfell) *astrakhan* ‖ (Plüschgewebe) *astrakhan*

Astrag·al m ~s/~e ⟨arch⟩ (an Säule) *astragal*

astr·al a *astral* **≗geister** m [pl] *astral spirits* [pl] **≗lampe** f *astral lamp* **≗leib** m *astral body*

Astrobiolog·ie f ~/ *astrobiology*

Astrol·abium n ~s/–bien ⟨astr⟩ *astrolabe*

Astrol·og m ~en/~en *astrologer* **Astrolog·ie** f ~/ *astrology* **astrol·ogisch** a *astrologic(al)*

Astron·aut m ~en/~en *astronaut* **a-n·autisch** a *astronautic(al)* **-navigation** f ~/ *astronomical* od *celestial navigation* ‖ ~skuppel [f] ⟨aero⟩ *astrodome*

Astron·om m ~en/~en *astronomer* **Astrono-m·ie** f ~/ *astronomy*; mit Hilfe der ~ *astronomically*

astron·omisch a *astronomic(al)* ‖ ⟨aero⟩ *celestial* (Kurssteuerung *guidance*) ‖ ~er Ort *astronomical position*; ~e Zeichen [pl] *astronomical signs* [pl]

Astrophys·ik f *astrophysics* [pl; sg konstr]

Ästu·arium n ~s/–rien *estuary*

·Ästung f ~/ ⟨for⟩ *pruning*

Ast·urien n ⟨Span⟩ (Provinz) *Asturias, Asturia*

Ast·urier m, **~in** f **ast·urisch** a *Asturian*

·Äsung f ~/ ⟨hunt⟩ *grazing, browsing* ‖ (Futter) *food*

As·yl n ~(e)s/~e **1.** (Freistätte) *asylum, sanctuary, place of refuge* **2.** (Heim) *asylum*; ~ f Obdachlose *casual ward* **~recht** n *right of a.*

Asymmetr·ie f ~/~en *asymmetry*

Asympt·ote f ~/~n ⟨math⟩ *asymptote*

·asynchr·on a *non-synchronous, asynchronous*; ⟨film mst⟩ *non-sync*

As·yndeton n ~s/–ta ⟨gram⟩ *asyndeton*

Aszend·ent m ~en/~en *ascendant*; ⟨demog⟩ *progenitor*

Asz·ese f etc → Askese

Asz·idie f ~/~n ⟨zoo⟩ *ascidian*

Atak·ania-Graben m → Peru-Chile-Graben

Atav·ismus m ~/–men ⟨biol⟩ *atavism, reversion*

atav·istisch a *atavistic, reversionary*

Ateli·er [atel'je:] n ~s/~s (Künstler–) *atelier, studio* ‖ ⟨film⟩ (Aufnahme–) *studio*

·Atem m ~s/ **A. 1.** (Luft f die Lunge) *breath, breathing, respiration*; übelriechender ~ ⟨med⟩ *halitosis* ‖ *wind*; kz ~ (of horses) *broken wind* **2.** (Atemzug) *breath, respiration* **3.** ⟨übtr⟩ (Hauch) *spirit* (*of freedom*); *life* ‖ (Duft) *breath, fragrance* (*of spring*) **B. Wendungen**: **1. außer ~** *out of breath*; *breathless, puffed, winded* ‖ **in** e–m *or* demselben ~ ⟨fig⟩ *in one* (od *the same*) *breath*; *in one go*; (..) nicht in e–m ~ z nennen mit .. *not to be named in the same day with* (*his cousin*) ‖ **mit** verhaltenem ~ *with bated breath* ‖ kaum **zu** ~ k *hardly to regain breath*, ⟨fig⟩ *to get hardly any time for o.s.* **2.** den ~ **anhalten** *to hold* od *catch one's breath* | **es ging** ihm der ~ aus *he lost his wind* ‖ ~ **holen** *or* schöpfen *to draw breath, to fetch a b., to get one's b.* od *wind*; (ausruhen) *to take b.* (od *a breather*), *to pause for b.*; tief ~ holen *to draw a deep* od *long b.*; frischen ~ holen *to get one's second wind* ‖ jdm den ~ **nehmen** *to take a p's breath away* ‖ jdm den ~ **rauben** *or* versetzen *to knock a p's breath out of him* | den ~ **verlieren** *to lose one's wind* **3. außer ~ kommen** *to lose one's wind, to be breathed* od *winded* (*by running*); leicht außer ~ k. *to have a bad wind, to be short-winded*; nicht leicht außer ~ k. *to have a long* (od *good*) *wind, to be long-winded* | jdn **in ~ halten** *to keep a p busy*; *to keep a p in suspense* | ich bin bis jetzt vor Arbeit nicht z ~ gek. *I have not had a minute's leisure as yet*; lassen Sie mich erst z ~ k. *give me time to breathe*; → verschnaufen ‖ **wieder z ~ k.** *to breathe again*, ⟨fig⟩ *to recover* ‖ Wieder-zu-~-k. [n] *second wind*

·Atem- ~beklemmung f, **~beschwerde** f *shortness of breath, difficulty in breathing* **≗beraubend** a = atemberaubend **~gerät** n *oxygen apparatus*; (Unterwasser≗) ⟨bes Am⟩ *self-contained underwater breathing apparatus*, [mst abbr] *scuba*, ([a. attr] *scuba diver*). **~geräusch** n (in Lungen) (vesikuläres ~ *vesicular*) *murmur* **~gymnastik** f *deep breathing* **~holen** n *breathing, respiration* **~kanal** m, **~loch** n ⟨ent⟩ *spiracle* **≗los** a *breathless*; –lose Stille *dead silence* ‖ noch fast ~ *yet too breathless* ⟨a.fig⟩ **~losigkeit** f *breathlessness*; ⟨med⟩ *apnoea* **~maske** f *oxygen mask* **~not** f ⟨med⟩ *dyspnoea*; *shortness of b.* → Asthma **~pause** f *breathing-space* (od *time*); ⟨übtr⟩ *reprieve*, jdm e–e ~ gewähren *to reprieve a p*; e–e ~ m *to pause for a breath* **≗raubend** a *breath-taking* ⟨a. Am ad⟩ (*e.g. laces*); ⟨übtr⟩ *flabbergasting* **~schlauch** m *oxygen tube*; ⟨mst⟩ *hose* **~schutzgerät** n (1. Filter- 2. Frischluft- 3. Sauerstoffschutzgerät 4. Preßluftatmer) = –gerät **~übung** f (im Freien) *breather, breathing* **~zug** m *breath, respiration*; *gasp* | bis zum letzten ~ *to the last breath* od *gasp* ‖ in den letzten –zügen *at one's* od *the last gasp* ‖ in einem ~ *in one* (od *the same*) *breath* ‖ den letzten ~ tun *to breathe one's last*

·atembar a *respirable* (*air*)

athanasi·anisch a ⟨ec⟩ *Athanasian* (*Creed*)

Athe·ismus m ~/ *atheism* **Athe·ist** m ~en/~en *atheist* **athe·istisch** a *atheistic(al)*

Ath·en n (Stadt) *Athens* (~ ist .. *A. is* ..) ‖ Eulen nach ~ tragen *to carry coals to Newcastle* **~er(in** f) m; **ath·enisch, atheni·ensisch** a *Athenian*

·Äther m ~s/ ⟨phys & chem⟩ *ether* ‖ ⟨übtr wir⟩ *ether* ‖ ~wellen [pl] *ether waves* [pl]; ⟨wir⟩ (starke) *atmospherics* **äth·erisch** a **1.** ⟨phys⟩ *etheric, etheral* **2.** (himmlisch; zart) *ethereal, aerial* ‖ ~ m *to etherealize* **3.** ⟨chem⟩ (flüchtig) ~e Öle *volatile* od *essential oils*

Äthi·opien n *Ethiopia* **Äthi·opier** m ~s/~, **~in** f ~/~nen *Ethiopian* **äthi·opisch** a *Ethiopian, Ethiopic*; die ~e Sprache *Ethiopic*

Athl·et m –en/~en *athlete* ⟨a. übtr⟩ | *p engaging in heavy athletics* ‖ ⟨fig⟩ *robust man*; ⟨hum⟩ *devil of a fellow* **Athl·etik** f ~/ *athletics* pl [pl konstr]; Leicht≗ *athletic sports* [pl], "*track and field*" **athl·etisch** a *athletic*

Äth·yl m ~s/ ⟨chem⟩ *ethyl*; ~alkohol m *ethyl alcohol*; ~äther *ethylic ether* **Äthyl·en** n ~s/~e ⟨chem⟩ *ethylene* **Ätiolog·ie** f ~/ *aetiology*

Atl·ant m ~en/~en ⟨arch⟩ *atlas*, [mst pl] *atlantes*; *telamon*

Atl·anta n (Hauptstadt v Georgia, U.S.A.)

Atl·antik m *the Atlantic* | ~charta [f] *A.-Charter*; ~pakt [m] → NATO **Atl·antis** f ~/ *Atlantis*

atl·antisch a *Atlantic*; der ≗e Ozean *the Atlantic Ocean, the Atlantic* | ≗e Schwelle f ⟨mar⟩ *the Atlantic Ridge*

·Atlas[1] m **1.** ⟨Gr myth⟩ ~/ *Atlas* | ~-Gebirge *the Atlas* (*Mountains*) **2.** ⟨anat⟩ –lasses/–lasse (oberster Halswirbel) *atlas*

·Atlas[2] m –lasses/–sse & –l·anten *atlas* **~format** n ⟨typ⟩ *atlas folio*; *large square folio*

·Atlas[3] m –lasses/–lasse (Stoff) *satin*; Halb≗ *satinet(te)* **≗ähnlich, ≗artig** a *satin*; *satin-like*; *satiny* **~band** n *satin ribbon* **~barchent** m *satin-top* **~glanz** m *satin-lustre* **~papier** n *satin-paper*

·atmen I. vi/t [h] **1.** vi *to breathe, respire*; *to draw breath*, wieder frei ~ ⟨fig⟩ *to breathe again* od *freely*; mühsam ~ *to breathe hard* (od *with difficulty*); *to heave*; schwer ~ *to gasp*; tief ~ *to draw a deep breath* (od *deep breaths*) ‖ **es** atmet sich leichter dort *breathing is easier there* | ⟨fig⟩ *to live*: *as long as I live* **2.** vt (Luft etc) *to breathe, respire* | ⟨fig⟩ (e–n Geist, Jugend, Einfachheit etc) *to breathe*; *to be redolent* od *reminiscent of, to be impregnated with* (*a th*); *to exhale, exude* (*a th*) **II.** ≈ n *breathing*; ⟨bot⟩ *respiration*; schweres ~ *gasp* ‖ → Atmung

Atmom·eter n ~s/~ (Verdunstungsmesser) *atmometer*

Atmosph·äre f ~/~n **1.** *atmosphere*; → Stratosphäre, Troposphäre **2.** ⟨phys⟩ *atmosphere* (: *under a pressure of 500 atmospheres*) **3.** ⟨übtr⟩ (Umgebung) *atmosphere* (: *an a. of confidence*) *surrounding element, environment* | ~nüberdruck m → atü **atmosph·ärisch** a *atmospheric*(*al*) ‖ ~e Maschine *atmospheric engine* ‖ ~e Störungen [pl] ⟨wir⟩ *atmospheric noise*; *atmospherics, statics, strays* [pl]

·Atmung f ~/~en *breathing, respiration* **~sapparat** m *respirator* **~sorgane** n pl = –werkzeuge ‖ Erkrankung der ~ *respiratory disease* **~stätigkeit** f *respiratory activities* [pl] **~swerkzeuge** n [pl] *respiratory organs* [pl] **~szahl** f *respiration rate*

·Ätna m (*Mount*) *Etna, Ætna*

†Ät·olien n ⟨Gr ant⟩ (Landschaft) *Ætolia*

At·oll n ~s/~e (ringförm. Koralleninsel) *atoll*

At·om n ~s/~e ⟨phys⟩ *atom* ‖ in ~e auflösen *to atomize* | ⟨übtr⟩ (bißchen) *atom, particle, jot, shred* (*no shred of evidence*) *bit*, nicht ein ~ Wahrheit *not an atom of truth*; nicht ein ~ älter *not one a. older* ‖ markiertes ~ (Leitisotop) *labelled atom* **~abstand** m *interatomic distance* **~batterie** f → Isotopenbatterie **~bau** m *atomic structure* **~bindung** f *atomic bond* **~bombe** f *atom*(*ic*) *bomb, A-bomb* ‖ ~nverseucht [a] *radio-activated* (Gebiet) **~brenner** m → Kernreaktor **~bunker** m *atomic bomb shelter* **~energie** f → Kernenergie ‖ friedliche Verwendung der ~ *application of atomic energy to peaceful pursuits* | ~-Behörde [f] (*International*) *Atomic Energy Agency* **~gefechtskopf** m *atomic warhead* **~gewicht** n *atomic weight* **~gitter** n *atomic lattice* **~kern** m *atomic nucleus* **~kraftwerk** n *nuclear* od *atomic power plant* od *station* **~modell** n *atom*(*ic*) *modell* **~müll** m *radioactive waste* **~physik** f *atom physics* [sg konstr] **~pilz** m *atomic mushroom* **~reaktor** m → Kernreaktor **~-Sperrvertrag** m → Abkommen über die Nichtweitergabe von Kernwaffen **~streitmacht** f *atomic power* **~-U-Boot** n *atomic* od *nuclear* od *atom-powered submarine* **~versuch** m *nuclear test* **~volumen** n *atomic volume* **~waffen** f pl → Kernwaffen | ≈frei [a] *denuclearized* (*zone*) **~wärme** f *atomic heat* **~zeitalter** n *atomic age* **~zertrümmerung** f → Kernspaltung → Bd. I. *atom*(*ic*)

atom·ar a *atomic* **Atom·ismus** m *atomism*

aton·al a ⟨mus⟩ *atonal*

Aton·ie f ~/ ⟨path⟩ *atony*

Ato·ut [a'tu:] [Fr] n ~s/~s ⟨cards⟩ *trump*

·Atrium (L) n ~s/–rien ⟨ant & anat⟩ *atrium*

·atro a ⟨tech⟩ (Abk. f. absolut trocken) *absolute dry*

Atroph·ie f ~/~n [–i:ən] ⟨med⟩ *atrophy*

Atrop·in n ~s/~e *atropine*

°**ätsch** intj ~! *there*! *serves you right*! °**·ätschen** vt [h] (jdn) *to scorn, ridicule*

Attaché [ata'ʃe:] (Fr) m *attaché* (Fr) (: *naval a.*) **attach·ieren** [ata'ʃi:rən] vt (jdn) *to attach* (jdm *to a p*) ‖ ⟨cul⟩ → anbraten

Att·acke f ~/~n ⟨mil⟩ *cavalry charge* (auf *on*) ‖ ⟨med & übtr⟩ *attack* **attack·ieren** vt [h] *to charge* ‖ *to attack*

Attent·at n ~s/~e (*attempted*) *assassination* (*of a p*), *criminal attack* (auf *on*); ein ~ auf jdn *an attempt on a p's life*; ein ~ auf jdn begehen, versuchen *to attempt a p's life* ‖ *outrage*; Tränengasbomben≈ *tear-gas bomb outrage* **~(s)versuch** m *assasination attempt* **Attent·äter** m ~s/~ *one who attemps another's life*; *assassinator*; *criminal culprit*; *perpetrator* ⟨a. übtr⟩

Att·est n ~es/~e *attestation*; *certificate* (für *to a p*); *testimonial* ‖ ärztliches ~ *doctor's c.*; Gesundheits≈ *health c.* ‖ jdm ein ~ ausstellen *to give a p a c., to write a c. for a p* | Führungs≈ *testimonial to a p's character* **attest·ieren** vt [h] (etw) *to attest, certify*

·Attich m ~s/~e ⟨bot⟩ *dwarf-elder*

·Attika n (Landschaft in Mittel-Griechenland) *Attica* **·Attika** f ~/–ken ⟨arch⟩ *attic*

·attisch a ⟨ant⟩ *Attic* ‖ ~er Ausdruck, Stil *atticism*; ~er Witz, ~es Salz *Attic wit* od *salt*

Attrakti·on f ~/~en ⟨theat, etc⟩ *attraction*; ⟨sl⟩ *draw*; ~ ausüben *to draw* | [konkr] *attraction, turn* (*in a music-hall*); Haupt≈ *star-turn* | effektvolle ~skunst [f] *showmanship* **attrakt·iv** [-f] a *attractive*

Attr·appe f ~/~n **1.** *dummy*; *sham package*; ⟨com⟩ *display specimen*; *show piece* ‖ ⟨mil & aero⟩ *mock-up* | ⟨fig⟩ *duffer*; *nincompoop* **2.** (Falle) *trap* | als ~ ⟨mil⟩ *in token*

Attrib·ut n ~(e)s/~e **1.** *attribute* **2.** ⟨gram⟩ *attributive, attribute* ‖ ~enraum m ⟨commun⟩ *attribute space* **attribut·iv** a ⟨gram⟩ *attributive*

Attriti·on f ~/~en ⟨R.C.⟩ *attrition*

at·ü m (**Atmosphärenüberdruck**) 5 ~ = 71 p.s.i. (*p*ounds per *s*quare *i*nch); *lbf/in*²

Ätz m ~es/ = Ätzung

·Ätz- ~grund m ⟨typ⟩ *etching-ground* **~kali** n ⟨chem⟩ *caustic potash* **~kunst** f ⟨typ⟩ *art of etching* **~lauge** f ⟨chem⟩ *caustic lye*; ⟨typ⟩ *etching-lye* **~maschine** f ⟨typ⟩ *etching-machine* **~mittel** n *corrosive*; ⟨med⟩ *caustic, cautery* **~nadel** f ⟨typ⟩ *etching-needle* **~natron** n ⟨chem⟩ *caustic soda* **~stift** m ⟨typ⟩ *burin* **~sublimat** n ⟨chem⟩ *corrosive sublimate* **~verfahren** n *caustic process*; → Aquatinta **~wasser** n *aqua-fortis, strong water*

·Atzel f ~/~n **1.** ⟨orn⟩ *magpie* **2.** *black-white wig, toupee, toupet* Fr

·atzen, ·ätzen vt [h] (T) (Junge) *to feed*

·ätzen 1. vt [h] ⟨chem⟩ *to corrode* (mit *with*) ‖ ⟨med⟩ *to cauterize*; *to sear* ‖ ⟨typ⟩ *to etch* **2.** ≈ n ⟨typ⟩ *etching* **·ätzend** a ⟨chem⟩ *corrosive, caustic* **·Ätzung** f ~/~en *corrosion* ‖ ⟨med⟩ *cauterization*; *cautery* ‖ ⟨typ⟩ (Verfahren) *photo-engraving* ‖ (Druckstock) *process-block*

·Atzung f ~/~en *feeding* ‖ *food*

au intj ~! *ow*; ⟨liter⟩ *ouch*; *oh, o dear*! ‖ ⟨hum⟩ *did you ever*?, *well, I never*!, *Well*!

Au, ·Aue f ~/~(e)n *river* (od *water*)-*meadow*; ⟨poet⟩ *lea, mead*

Aubergine [ober'ʒi:n] f ~/~n ⟨bot⟩ *aubergine* (Fr), *fruit of eggplant*; ⟨cul⟩ *aubergine*

auch conj **1.** **(ebenfalls) [betont]** *also*; ⟨engl⟩ (nie am Anfang des Satzes; stets nach dem Zusatzwort:) *too* ‖ *likewise, as well* ‖ ~ ein Denker! *a near-thinker* ‖ ~ mein Freund, mein F. ~ *also my friend* od *my f. also*; *my f. too*; wir ~, ~ wir *we also, we too*; ~ wir finden *we also find*; ich werde ~ unterzeichnen *I shall sign too*; er wurde ruiniert u sie ~ (..) *and they likewise* (od *as well*) ‖ ‚Ich ging heim'. ‚Wir ~' *I went home. So did we* | das kann ich ~, so grob kann ich ~ s *two can play at that game* ‖ du bist ein Lügner! (als Antwort:) Du ~! *You are a liar. You are another*! | ich ~ nicht *nor I either* od *neither* ‖ ich kann nicht schwimmen u mein Bruder ~ nicht *I cannot swim, neither can my brother* (od *nor my b. either*); wenn du nicht zeichnest, so zeichne ich ~ nicht *if you do not sign I shall not* (*sign*) *either* | (als Antwort) .. ich, mir (etc) ~! ⟨fam⟩ *same here*!; du auch *same there*!; .. ich (dir) ~! *same here*! | nicht nur ..

sondern ~ *not only .. but also* || sowohl .. als ~ → als II. A. 1. a. | **[unbetont]** Du siehst müde aus. (Antwort:) Das bin ich ~. *You look tired. So I am* || ~ hatte niemand gesehen *nor had anybody see* (*that*) **2.** **(sogar)** **[unbetont]** *even*; ~ (nicht) das geringste Geräusch (*not*) *even the least noise* || ~ nicht einer *never a one*, ~ nicht ein Wort *never a word* || ohne ~ nur z fragen *without so much as asking* | (in Einräumungssätzen) ~ **wenn**, wenn ~, **ob** ~ *even if, even though; although*; wäre er ~ **noch** so reich *were he* (od *let him be*) (*n*)*ever so rich*; mag er ~ noch so bemüht s *try he ever so much* (*he will find* ..); so ungern er sie ~ hat *much as he may dislike them* (*he* ..) | **wer ~ immer** *whoever*; was ~ immer *what*(*so*)*ever*; was f. Gründe du ~ haben magst *whatever reasons you have*; → wann, wo **3.** **[verblaßt, unbetont]** **(wirklich)** willst du es ~ tun? *are you sure to do it? and you will really do it?* ist es ~ wahr? *is it really true?* das wußte er doch ~ *surely, he must have known it* | ⟨iron⟩ das wäre ~ an der Zeit *it would be the highest time* || das fehlte ~ noch! *that's the limit! that settles it!*

·**Aucklandsinseln** f pl (z Neu-Seeland) *Auckland Islands*

Audi·enz f ~/~en *audience* (bei jdm *of, with a p*); *hearing* | jdn in ~ empfangen *to receive* (*a p*) *in audience*; jdm e–e ~ erteilen *or* gewähren *to give* od *grant a p an audience* od *a hearing* || ~ erhalten bei jdm *to be admitted to an audience by a p* **~saal** m, **~zimmer** n *presence-chamber*

A·udion n ~s/~s ⟨wir⟩ *audion* **~empfänger** m *audion receiver*

·**Audio- ~-Animatr·onik** f ~/ (*Walt Disney's*) *audio-animatronics* pl **~-visu·ell** a *audio-visual*

Auditeur [audiˈtør] m ~s/~e ⟨Ger⟩ (bis 1900) ⟨mil⟩ *judicial official, regimental judge*

audit·iv a *auditive*

Aud·itor (L) m ~s/–dit·oren ⟨R.C.⟩ *member of the papal Audience Court* **Audit·orium** (L) n ~s/–rien (Hörsaal) *auditorium, autitory* || (Zuhörerschaft) *audience, auditory*

·**Aue** f → Au

·**Auer** m ~s/~ = Auerochs **~hahn** m ~s/–hähne ⟨orn⟩ *capercailye, –cailzie, mountain-cock, cock of the woods*; die Balz des ~s *the display of the cock in the mating season* **~henne** f ~/~n *mountain-hen* **~huhn** n ⟨orn⟩ *capercailye, –cailzie*; *wood-grouse* **~ochse** m ~n/~n ⟨zoo⟩ *aurochs*; *urus* [L]

auf prep **I.** **(Ruhe**, mit dat) **A.** ⟨eig⟩ **1.** *on, upon*; ~ dem Dach, Stuhl *on the roof, chair*; → Seite || ~ der 'Europa' *on the Europe* || aber: *he's a sailor in the Europe* || *in* (od *on*) *an island*; aber: *in Cyprus* || ~ dem Klavier *on the piano* || *a ring on one's finger* || ~ dieser Welt *in this world*, ~ Erden *on earth*; auf der Welt *in the world* | *to carry a child in one's arms* || ~ allen Vieren *on all fours*; früh ~ den Beinen s *to be up and doing*, immer ~ den B. *never off one's legs* || *a scene in a picture* || (*there are but few apples*) *in the tree* || *in the same parallel* (Breitengrad) || *in the meadow* || *he is in his room* | ~ dieser **Seite** des Flusses *on this side the river*; ~ der rechten S. *on the right side, to the right*; z Vieren ~ jeder S. sitzen *to sit four a side* || ich hatte es ~ der Zunge *I had it on the tip of my tongue* || *to ride on a horse*; *I bought it on the market*; *to play on the piano, etc.* || ~ der Stelle *on the spot*; *to live on a farm* || → Boden | mitten ~ *in the midst* (od *middle*) *of* || oben ~ *on* (*the*) *top of* **2.** *in*; ~ der Straße, dem Hofe, Markte, dem Lande etc *in* (⟨Am⟩ *on*) *the street* (od *road*), *court-yard, market, country, etc.*; ~.. entlang *along* (*the street*) || ~ s–m Zimmer *in one's room* || ~ offenem Meer *in the open, in mid-ocean* **B.** ⟨übtr⟩ **1.** mst *on*: ~ der **Reise** *on the journey*; **~ Besuch** bei *on a visit to* .. || **~ See** *at sea*; ⟨geog⟩ ~ der Höhe v *off* (*the Isle of Wight*) | er ist schon ~ dem **Wege** *he is on his way*; → Weg || ~ dem Wege über .. *by the way of* ..; geh ~ dem Wege zurück, auf dem du kamst *go back by the way you came*; ~ dem Seewege *by sea*; so: *by land, by air* (*to go by air*) | ~ jds Seite (Partei) *on a p's side* || ~ allen Seiten *on* (od *from*) *all sides* (od *every side*); *at page ten* | *at zero, at boiling-point* | *blind of* od *in one eye, lame of* od *in one leg* || → Seite || → Stufe **2.** **(beschäftigt)** *at*; ~ dem Bahnhof etc *at the station*; *at his castle*; *at the post-office*; *at the university* || *at a funeral* || *at the banquet, dinner*; *at a ball* || *at a fair* || *at a congress, meeting* || *cook is at* (*the*) *market* **C.** ⟨fig⟩ (Zustand, Umstand) ~ frischer Tat *in the very act* || ~ der Höhe s *to be up to the mark* || ~ dem Wege der Besserung *in the way of recovery*; ~ dem üblichen geschäftlichen Wege *in the way of business* **D.** es hat viel ~ **sich** *it is of great importance* (od *consequence*); es hat nichts ~ sich *it is of no consequence, it does not matter* **II.** **(Richtung**, mit acc) **A.** ⟨eig⟩ **1.** **a.** *on, on to*; setz es ~ den Tisch *place it on the table*; ~ den Boden (*throw it*) *on the floor*; er trat ~ den Balkon *he stepped on to the balcony*; → Seite **b.** *to*; ~ die Füße springen *to spring to one's feet*; ~ den Boden geworfen w *to be thrown to the ground* | er kam **auf mich zu** *he came up to me*; so: *the ship drove towards the cliff* **2.** ~ die Straße (*to run out*) *into the street*; das Fenster geht ~ die St. *the window looks on* od *into the street*, (*has a view*) *of the river*; ~s Land *into the country*, ~ sein Zimmer (*he went*) *to his room*; ~ e–n Balkon klettern *to climb to a balcony*; ~ e–n Baum klettern *to climb* (*up*) *a tree* | ~ .. hinauf *up*, ~ den Hügel h. *up the hill* **B.** ⟨übtr⟩ **1.** ein Marsch, Angriff ~ *a march, an attack on* (*a town*, etc) || sich stürzen *or* werfen ~ *to rush on* (*a p*) || ~ jdn, etw zugehen *to walk towards a p, a th* || ~ ihn mit Gebrüll! *up and at him!* | ~ die Jagd gehen *to go hunting* || ~ Wache ziehen *to mount guard* **2.** *to*; ~ den B., die P., den Markt etc gehen *to go to the station, to the post-office, to market*; *take this letter to the post!*; (Brief) ~ die Post geben *to post*; ~ die Universität gehen (zum Studium) *to go up to the university* | (Stück) ~ die Bühne bringen *to bring on* (od *to*) *the stage* **3.** (Maß, Entfernung etc) ein Schilling ~s Pfd *a shilling in the pound*; drei ~s Dutzend *three to the dozen*; *12 inches go to the foot*; 3 Schilling ~ den Kopf (*or* die P) *3 shillings per head*; *take a spoonful to a glass of water* || bis ~ den letzten Mann *to a man*; (bis) ~ 2% genau *within 2% of accuracy* → bis | ~ Armlänge *at arm's length* || ~ ein Haar *to a hair's breadth*; *to a T, a nicety* | ~ die Minute *to a minute* || *bis* ~ → bis I. A. **C.** **(Zeit)** ~ 50 Jahre *for 50 years*; e–e Versammlung einberufen ~ morgen, den 15. Mai *to call a meeting for to-morrow, for May 15th*; die Sitzung auf 14 Tage vertagen *to adjourn the sitting till that day fortnight* || es geht ~ 5 Uhr *it is getting for* (od *on to*) *5 o'clock*; ~ ewig *for ever* || ein Viertel ~ eins *a quarter to one* | Schlag ~ Schlag *blow upon blow* || Gruppe ~ Gruppe *group after group* (*left him*) || ~ einmal *at once* || zwei ~ einmal *two at a time* (*entered*) || bis ~ → bis I. A. **D.** ⟨fig⟩ (Zustand, Umstand) **1.** **a.** ~ den Blick *at a glance*; ~ den ersten B. *at first sight* || ~ e–n Zug *at a draught* **b.** ~ mein Wort, m–e Ehre *upon my word, my honour* || ~ Ihr Wohl! *here's to you!* | ~ e–n Augenblick *for a moment*; ~ immer u ewig *for ever, for good* || e–e S ~ Tod u Leben *a matter of life and death*; ~ eigene Gefahr *at your own risk* **c.** (Art u Weise) ~ Halbsold *on half-pay* || ~ diese Weise *in this way, after this fashion* || ~s beste *in the best possible way* || ~ jeden Fall *in any case*, ~ alle Fälle *at all events, at any rate, by all means* |

~ deutsch *in German* **d.** ~ Grund v *on; by reason of* || ~ dein Versprechen hin *on the strength of your promise* **2.** ⟨mst com⟩ ~ Anfrage *on application, on inquiry* || ~ Befehl v *by order of* || ~ Bestellung v *on the order(s) of* || ~ Ihre Bitte *at your request* || ~ m–e Kosten *at my expense*, ~ Kosten der Gesundheit *at the cost of health* || ~ Kredit *on crdit* || ~ Rechnung *on account* || ~ Sicht *at sight* **3.** bis ~ → bis I. A. E. in Verbindung **1.** mit Verben → anstoßen; antworten; bauen; beharren; (sich) belaufen, bestehen; hoffen; richten; schätzen; trinken; (sich) verlassen; zielen ~ **2.** mit Subst. → Aussicht; Einfluß; Hoffnung; Wirkung ~ **3.** mit Adj. → eifersüchtig; gefaßt; neidisch; stolz ~

auf adv **I.** (**Richtung**) **1. a.** (in die Höhe, Luft; aufrecht) in Verbindung mit Verben → auf- .. | **~ u ab** *up and down; to and fro; seesaw;* ~ u abgehend *seesaw (way)*; die ~ u abgehende Bewegung *the up and down motion*; die Straße ~ u ab gehen *to walk the street*; einige Male im Garten ~ u ab gehen *to take a couple of turns up and down the garden*; im Zimmer ~ u ab schreiten *to pace* od *traverse the room* | ⟨fig⟩ ~ u ab gehen (of feelings) *to ebb and flow*; **das** ≗ u Ab *the seesaw (of fashion)*; das ≗ u Ab im Leben *the ups and downs of life, the vicissitudes of life*; ein ≗ u Ab *a systole and diastole (of life)* || **~ u nieder** *up and down* || **~u davon** *off and away* **b.** (**zeitlich**) v Jugend ~ *from a child* **c.** [als intj] ~! *up! get up!* ~ mit dir! *up with you* **2.** (**offen**) *undone* (: *is it*) [*the dress*] *u.*?); → auf- .. **II.** (**Ruhe**) mit dem Hut ~ *with his hat on* | ~ s *to be up*; sie ist wieder ~ *she is out of bed again* **III. ~ daß** *in order that*; ~ daß nicht *lest; that not*

auf- pref [stets betont] **1.** [untrennbar vor mst v Verben abgeleiteten Subst., desgl. vor Adj. u Adv.]: Aufstieg *uprise*; Aufhören *breakup*; → Aufnahme; auffällig **2.** [trennbar vor Verben] mst *up*: aufnehmen (ich nehme auf — aufgenommen) *to take up*; aufpolstern *to upholster* **a.** (in die Höhe, Luft) → aufblicken, –fliegen || (auf die Beine) → aufstehen **b.** (offen) → aufreißen **c.** (los) → aufbrechen **d.** (oben auf) → auftragen, –schreiben **e.** (in Ordnung; zu Ende) → aufkehren, –arbeiten **f.** (v neuem) → aufwärmen

-auf suff *up*; berg~ *uphill*

·auf|achten vi [h] *to attend, mark; mind*

·auf|arbeiten vt [h] **1.** (auffrischen) *to work* od *furbish up; to recondition* ⟨fam⟩ *to do up* || *to mend, repair* || *to re-pulp (paper)* **2.** (erledigen) *to work* od *clear off* || (vollenden) *to complete*, sein Tagewerk ~ *to get through one's day's work* **3.** (verbrauchen) (Vorräte) *to use up* | sich [dat] die Hände ~ *to blister one's hands, to work one's hands raw*

·Aufartung f *race-improvement*

·auf|atmen vi [h] (tief) ~ *to draw a (long* od *easy* od *deep) breath; to fetch* od *heave a (deep) sigh*; erleichtert ~ *to heave a sigh of relief, to sigh with relief* | ⟨fig⟩ *to respire*; befreit ~, wieder (frei) ~ *to breathe again* od *freely; to recover*

·auf|bahren vt [h] *to put upon the bier*; ⟨Am⟩ *to lay out* || (Sarg) *to place in the chapel* od *church*

·Aufbahrung f: feierliche ~ *lying-in-state*

·auf|bänken vt [h] (Fluß) *to bank up* || ⟨mar⟩ (die Feuer) *to bank up*

·Aufbau m ~(e)s/~ten **1.** (Aufbauen) *erection, building up; construction* || ~ neuer Städte *new towns development*; Körperschaften f den ~ n. St. *n. t. d. corporations* | ⟨übtr⟩ *building (of a story); upbuilding (of the navy)* || ⟨geol⟩ *formation* (e–s Gebirges) || *(social) uplift* **2.** (Anordnung) ⟨arch⟩ *structure, composition* | ⟨übtr⟩ *constitution; organization*, ⟨Am fam⟩ *set-up (of traffic)* || ⟨Lit⟩ *structure, composition*; → Gefüge **3.** ⟨arch⟩ (Überbau) *superstructure* || Schiffs≗ *island*; ⟨mot⟩ *body*; [pl] ~ten ⟨mar⟩ *superstructure* **4.** ⟨chem⟩ *synthesis* **5.** [in comp] *building; constructive* || *structural* **~arbeit** f *constructive work*; soziale ~ *social uplift* **~möbel** n pl *unit furniture* **~methode** f *synthetic method* **~programm** n *development programme, constructive scheme* **~prozeß** m ⟨chem⟩ *synthetic process* **~schule** f ⟨Ger⟩ *a higher grade school following on the 'Mittel-' or 'Volksschule' with a shortened curriculum for gifted pupils where they can qualify for university entrance after 6 years*

·auf|bauen vt [h] **1.** *to erect, construct; to build up*; || ⟨übtr⟩ *to establish; organize* | schnell u leicht ~ *to run up* || neu ~ *to rebuild*; ⟨übtr⟩ *to reorganize* **2.** ⟨arch⟩ *to build* (auf *on*); ⟨theat⟩ *to set* | ⟨übtr⟩ *to found, base* (auf *on*) || **sich ~**, aufgebaut s *to be based* (auf *on*) **3.** ⟨chem⟩ *to synthesize* **·aufbauend** a ⟨übtr⟩ *constitutive (forces); constructive (politics)*

·auf|baumen vi [h] ⟨hunt⟩ (auf e–n Baum klettern etc) *to tree* **·auf|bäumen** vrefl [h] **sich ~** (of horses) *to rear (up), to prance* || ⟨fig⟩ *to rebel, to revolt* (gegen *against*)

·auf|bauschen vt [h] **1.** (Segel etc) *to puff out, to swell out, up* | **sich ~** *to bulge, bag* **2.** ⟨fig⟩ *to exaggerate; to overstate* [a. abs] || ⟨Am fam⟩ *to play up (a th)*

·auf|begehren 1. vi [h] *to effervesce, to flare up*; ~ gegen jdn *to snap* od *(fly out) at a p*; ~ gegen etw *to protest, remonstrate, revolt against a th* **2.** ≗ n *protest; revolt*

°**·auf|behalten** vt [→ halten] (den Hut) *to keep on* | (Augen) *to keep open*

°**·auf|bekommen** vt [→ kommen] [h] **1.** *to get (a door) open; to get (a knot) undone* **2.** (verzehren) *to consume, to eat up; to finish* **3.** er hat e e Aufgabe ~ *he has (got) a task set to him*

·auf|bereiten vt [h] ⟨min⟩ (Erze) *to dress, prepare; wash*; ⟨at⟩ *to process (spent fuel)* || ⟨übtr⟩ (darbieten) *to present*

·Aufbereitung f ⟨min⟩ *(ore-)dressing* od *washing* || *winning and renewing (of a stuff)* || ⟨at⟩ *processing (of spent fuel)*; ⟨comp⟩ ~ des Zahlenmaterials *data pr. system* || → Zeilen ≗ || ⟨demog⟩ statistische ~ *collation, compilation* || ⟨tech⟩ z ~ geeignet *fertile (residues)* ⟨a. at⟩ **~sanlage** f *(waste paper, etc) dressing plant* ⟨a. min⟩; ⟨at⟩ *processing plant* **~smaschine** f *preparation machinery* **~sverfahren** n *conditioning* od *treating process*

·auf|bessern vt [h] *to ameliorate, improve* || (Gehalt) *to raise, increase* | (Möbel etc) *to vamp (up); to furbish* od *do up; to renew*; neu ~ ⟨sl⟩ *to duff*; → auffrischen **·Aufbesserung** f ~/~en *amelioration, improvement* || *rise* (der Löhne *of wages*, etc); *increase* (des Gehalts *of salary*; der Löhne *in wages*) || (Beihilfe) *allowance* | *vamping-up*

·auf|bewahren vt [h] (behalten) *to keep, preserve*; jdm etw ~ *to keep a th for a p* || (aufspeichern) *to store up*; ⟨übtr⟩ *to set aside* (f. *for*); etw aufbewahrt haben f. jdn ⟨übtr⟩ *to have a th in store for a p*; etw f. später ~ *to postpone a th* | (verwahren) ⟨rail⟩ (Gepäck) *to take charge of*; (Gold) im Auftrage jds ~ *to hold (gold) to the order of a p* || (Dokument) *to file* **·Aufbewahrung** f ~/~en *preservation* || *the taking charge of* || *safe custody (of securities)* | ~sgebühr [f] *safe custody fee*; ~sort, ~sraum [m] *depository, repository* (f *for*), *storehouse* || ⟨rail⟩ (f Gepäck) *cloak-room*

·auf|bieten vt [h] **1.** (zus-rufen) **a.** *to call up* (od *in*); *to summon* || (Truppen) *to muster, levy, raise; to call up* **b.** ⟨fig⟩ (zus-nehmen) (Kraft) *to gather; to put forth; to sum up (courage, strenght)*

alle Energie ~ *to summon all one's energy*; alle Kräfte ~ *to muster all one's strength* (od *powers*); alles Geschick, das er ~ konnte *all the skill which he could command* || alles ~ *to exert o.s. to the* (od *to do one's*) *utmost, to leave no stone unturned* | s–n Einfluß ~ *to bring one's influence to bear* (f. *or* in bezug auf *upon*) || s–e Reize ~ *to display one's charms* **2.** ⟨ec⟩ (Verlobte) *to publish* (od *put up*) *the banns of* (*two persons*); sie wurden gestern z ersten Male aufgeboten, sie h sich gestern .. ~ l *they had their banns published yesterday for the first time* ·**Aufbietung** f ~/~en *summons*; *mustering* | ⟨fig⟩ *display*; mit (*or* unter) ~ aller Kräfte *using every effort* od *exertion*; *with the utmost exertion* → Aufgebot

·**auf|binden** vt [h] **1.** (hochbinden) (Pflanzen etc) *to tie up* || ⟨fig⟩ sich e–e Rute ~ *to make a rod for one's own back* **2.** (auflösen) (Knoten etc) *to undo*; *unfasten, unbind, untie, loosen* **3.** ⟨fig⟩ jdm etw (*or* eins) ~, jdm e–n Bären ~ *to put a th* (od *it*) *over on a p, to hoax a p*; *to impose upon a p*; *to practise on a p's credulity* || sich (leicht) etw ~ l *to be* (*easily*) *imposed upon* (od *taken in*)

·**auf|blähen** vt [h] (etw) *to puff out* (od *up*), *to swell*; *to inflate* | ⟨fig⟩ (jdn) *to inflate*; aufgebläht v *inflated* (od *swollen*) *with* || sich ~ *to be inflated* (od *puffed up*) (vor Stolz *with pride*); *to peacock o.s.* ·**Aufblähung** f ~/~en *puffing-out*; *inflation* || ⟨fig⟩ *inflation*

·**auf|blasen** vt [h] (Schlauch) *to blow up*; *to inflate*, (Ballon) *to distend*; (die Backen) *to puff out* | ⟨fig⟩ → aufgeblasen || **sich ~** *to be puffed up* od *inflated* (vor *with*)

·**auf|blättern** vt [h] (Buch etc) *to open*; *to turn over the leaves of* (*a book*) | **sich ~** (of flowers) *to open*

·**auf|bleiben** vi [s] (P) *to stay, stop, sit up*; die ganze Nacht ~ *to be up all nicht* **2.** (door, etc) *to remain* (od *to be left*) *open*

·**auf|blenden** vt/i [h] ⟨mot⟩ *to turn the headlights on*

·**Aufblick** m ~(e)s/~e *upward look* od *glance*

·**auf|blicken 1.** vi [h] *to look* od *glance up* (vom Buche *from the book*; z etw *or* jdm *at a th, a p*) || erstaunt ~ *to open one's eyes in astonishment* (über *at*); entrüstet ~ *to raise* od *lift one's eyebrows* || z Gott ~ *to lift* (*up*) *one's eyes to God* || ⟨übtr⟩ z jdm ~ *to look up to a p* (als *as* [*one's leader*]) **2.** ≃ n *lift of the eyebrow*, entrüstetes ~ *eyebrow raising*

·**auf|blitzen** vi [s & h] *to flash* (*up*); *to sparkle* || *to give a wink* | ⟨fig⟩ *to flash* (von, vor *with*)

·**auf|blocken** vi [h] (of birds of prey) *to perch* (auf *on*)

·**auf|blühen 1.** vi [s] *to burst into bloom, to* (*come into*) *flower*; *to flourish, unfold, open*; ~d [a] *efflorescent* | ⟨fig⟩ *to come into bloom*; *to bloom*; *to flourish*; *to get going*; *to bud* (zu *into*); *to thrive, prosper*; (of economy) *to expand* || das Geschäft blüht auf *business is picking up* || wieder ~ *to revive* **2.** ≃ n ⟨fig⟩ *flowering, efflorescence*

·**auf|bocken** vt [h] ⟨mot⟩ *to lay* od *jack up* (*a car*)

·**auf|braten** vt [h] (etw) *to roast over again*

·**auf|brauchen** vt [h] *to use up, to consume*; *to run away with* (: *the rates would r. away with the profits*) || (Kräfte) *to waste, to wear out*

·**auf|brausen 1.** vi [h & s] (of the sea) *to roar*; *to surge*; → (auf)schäumen | ⟨mst fig⟩ *to flare* od *fire up*; *to fly* od *get into a rage* od *passion* **2.** ≃ n *flare-up* ·**aufbrausend** a ⟨fig⟩ *irascible, irritable, quick-tempered*

·**auf|brechen** vt/i **I.** vt [h] **1.** (Land) *to hoe*; *to plough up* **2.** (mit Gewalt öffnen) *to break* od *force open*; (Tür, Schloß) *to prize* od *prise up* od *open* || ⟨hunt⟩ (Wild) *to cut open, to rip up, to gralloch*, → Aufbruch **II.** vi [s] **1.** *to break*; *to burst open*; (of wounds) wieder ~ *to recrudesce* || (of flowers) *to open* **2.** (fortgehen) *to rise to go*; *to depart, to start*; *to set out* (nach *for*; z tun *to do*); früh ~ *to make an early start*; z e–r Wanderung ~ *to start off on a hike* || es ist Zeit aufzubrechen *it is time to make a move* || ⟨mil⟩ aus dem Lager ~ *to decamp* || jdn ~ l *to start a p on the way* | –gebrochen ⟨meteor⟩ *broken* (Bewölkung *clouds*) ·**Aufbrechen** n *breaking open* || *bursting*; → Aufbruch

·**auf|brennen** vt [h] **1.** (etw) *to burn* (*up*), jdm ein Mal ~ *to brand a p, to mark a p with a brand* | °jdm e–e Kugel ~ *to fire* od *have a shot at a p* || °jdm e–e Strafe ~ *to inflict a punishment on a p*

·**Aufbrief** m ⟨mar⟩ *bill of tonnage*

·**auf|bringen I.** vt [h] **1.** (Schiff) *to capture, intercept* **2.** (zus–bringen) **a.** (Truppen) *to raise, collect, levy* | (Zeugen) *to produce* **b.** ⟨übtr⟩ *to procure*; *to supply*; (Mittel) *to find*; (Geld) *to raise, afford*; *to defray* (*the expenses*); (Geld) durch Beiträge ~ *to subscribe* (z *to*) **c.** ⟨übtr⟩ (Grazie) *to achieve*; (Kraft etc) *to gather*; *to summon up*; *to bring into play*; *to put forth*; *to muster* || soviel Mut, Interesse, (wie) sie ~ konnte *as much courage, interest as she could command* **3.** (öffnen) **a.** (Tür etc) *to force open*; *to open, undo, unlock* **b.** ⟨übtr⟩ (Sitte, Mode) *to start*; (Gegenstand) *to introduce* || (Gerücht) *to spread* **4.** jdn ~ **a.** → aufziehen **b.** ⟨fig⟩ *to exasperate, exacerbate, irritate*; ⟨fam⟩ *to rile*; *to get* od *put a p's back up*; Pn gegen–e–a ~ *to set persons against each other* || → aufgebracht **II.** ≃ n *breaking up* od *open* || *raising* (*of money*); (durch Beiträge) *subscription*

·**Aufbringung** f ⟨mar⟩ *capture* (*of a ship*)

·**Aufbruch** m ~(e)s/≃e ⟨übtr⟩ *start*; *setting-out, departure* (nach *for*) || ⟨mil⟩ *decampment* | ⟨fig⟩ *sudden appearance*; *burst* || ⟨pol⟩ (*up*)*rising*; *new start*; *change in* (*one's*) *attitude towards life* || ⟨hunt⟩ (v Wild) *gralloch* **~hammer** m *heavy breaker* **~signal** n *starting signal*

·**auf|brühen** vt [h] *to scald*

°·**auf|brummen** vt [h] jdm e–e Strafe ~ → aufbrennen 2.

°·**auf|buckeln** vt [h] = aufbürden

·**auf|bügeln** vt [h] *to iron* || (Hut) *to do up*

°·**auf|bumsen** vt *to thump* (auf *on*)

·**auf|bürden** vt [h] jdm e–e Aufgabe etc ~ *to burden* (od *saddle*) *a p with a task, to impose a t. on a p*; jdm viel ~ *to lay a heavy burden on a p* || (zuschreiben) jdm etw ~ *to impute a th to a p*; *to charge a p with a th*; *to lay a th to a p's charge*; → Schuld ·**Aufbürdung** f ~/~en *imposition* (*of taxes*) | *charge*

·**auf|bürsten** vt [h] *to brush up*

·**auf|dämmern** vi [s] *to dawn* | ⟨fig⟩ e–e Ahnung dämmerte (in) ihm auf *it dawned upon him* (*that*)

·**Aufdeck- ~arbeit** f (im Steinbruch) *uncaping*

·**auf|decken** vt/i [h] **I.** vt **1.** das Tischtuch ~ *to lay* od *spread the cloth* **2. a.** ein Bett ~ *to turn down a bed*; sich ~ *to uncover o.s.* **b.** ⟨fig⟩ *to disclose, to lay open* od *bare, to uncover, to reveal*; (Lüge, Komplott) *to expose*; (Plan) *to unveil*; alle Einzelheiten e–r S ~ *to rout out all the details of a th* || *to exhibit*; (Ursache) *to determine* **II.** vi *to lay the cloth* ·**Aufdeckung** f ~/~en *unvovering, disclosure, exposure* (*of a plot*)

°·**auf|donnern** vrefl [h] **sich ~** *to rig o.s. out, to dress* od *doll o.s. up, to smarten* od *spruce o.s.* → aufgedonnert

·**auf|dornen** vt [h] ⟨mech⟩ (weiten) (Loch etc) *to drift, enlarge*; *expand*

·**auf|drängen** vt [h] **1.** jdm etw ~ (Geschenk etc) *to force, to press a th upon a p*; (s–e Meinung) *to intrude* od *obtrude a th upon a p*; *to ply a p with a th*; jdm Vertraulichkeiten ~ *to throw confidences upon a p* **2. sich** jdm ~ (of persons, thoughts) *to force, intrude, obtrude o.s. upon a p*; *to intrude* od *obtrude upon a p*; es drängte sich ihr der Gedanke auf *it was borne in upon her, it came forcibly into her mind* (*that*) | (of thoughts) sich ~ *to force* (od *obtrude*) *o.s., to suggest o.s.*; zwei Fragen drängen sich auf *two questions suggest themselves* ‖ sich jdm ~ *to crowd in on a p's mind* ‖ es drängte sich m–r Aufmerksamkeit *or* Beobachtung auf *it was forced upon my attention* ‖ sich jds Bekanntschaft [dat] ~ *to impose* od *force one's acquaintance upon a p*; *to importune a p with one's acq.*

·auf|drehen I. vt/i [h] **A.** vt **1.** (öffnen) ⟨tech⟩ (Hahn) *to turn on*; (Schraube) *to unscrew* | → aufflechten **2.** (hochwinden) *to wind up* **3.** (festschrauben) *to screw down* **B.** vi ⟨mar⟩ *to haul the wind*, → Kurs **II.** ≃ n *turning-on*; *unscrewing*

†**·auf|dringen** vt [h] = aufdrängen

·aufdringlich a *obtrusive, officious, pressing*; *importunate*; ~ w *to presume* | ⟨übtr⟩ (auffällig) *blatant, noisy* (*music*); *showy, gaudy* (*colours*); *flaring, glaring* **·Aufdringlichkeit** f ~/~en *obtrusion, importunity*; *gaudiness, showiness*

·auf|dröseln vt [h] = aufflechten

·Aufdruck m ~(e)s/~e ⟨typ⟩ *printing, print*; *overprint(ing)*; *imprint* | (neuer ~ auf Marken) *surcharge* **·auf|drucken** vt [h] (etw) *to imprint, to print* (auf *on*)

·auf|drücken vt/i [h] **I.** vt **1.** (Stempel etc) *to impress*; *to stamp* (auf *on, upon*); (Siegel) *to put* (auf *upon*) ‖ ⟨übtr⟩ e–r S s–n Stempel ~ *to set one's stamp upon a th* **2.** (öffnen) *to open by pressing, to press open* **II.** vi (beim Schreiben) *to press*

aufein·ander 1. adv *one after another* (od *each other*); *one upon another* (od *the other*); *inter-* **2.** [in comp] [**bei Verben** betontes, trennbares] pref: ≃**folge** f *succession*; ⟨bes demog⟩ ~ v Geburten *birth timing* **~|folgen** vi [s] *to succeed* (one *another*) **~folgend** a *successive, consecutive* (*5 c. days*) **~|legen** vt [h] 3 Laken ~ *to superimpose 3 sheets one on the other* **~|platzen, ~|prallen 1.** vi [s] *to clash, to collide* **2.** ≃ n *clash* (*of wills*); *impact*; *collision* ≃**prall,** ≃**stoß** m *clash*; *collision*; *impact* **~|sitzen** vi [h] *to sit on the top of each other* **~|stoßen** vi [s] = aufeinanderprallen **~|wirken** vi [h] *to interact*

·auf|eisen vt [h] e–n Teich *to break the ice on a pond*; e–e Straße ~ *to clear a street of ice*

·Aufenthalt m ~(e)s/~e **1.** (Verweilen) *sojourn, stay* (in e–m Ort *at a place*, bei jdm *with a p*); bei m–m ~ *during my stay*; e–n ~ nehmen *to make a stay*; *to stay* | ⟨rail⟩ *stop*; (*of trains*) (k–n) ~ h (*not*) *to stop* ‖ wie lange h wir ~? *how long do we stop here*? ‖ ohne ~ *without stop(ping)*; ein Zug ohne ~ *a non-stop train* **2.** (Verzögerung) *delay, hindrance, stoppage* **3.** (Wohnort) (*place of*) *residence*; festen ~ h *to be stationary* (in *at*); sein zeitweiliger ~ war unbekannt *his whereabouts was unknown* **4.** *board and residence* | **~s- ~dauer** f ⟨rail⟩ *stop* **~erlaubnis** f *permit of residence* **~karte** f *domiciliary permit*; *permit of residence* **~ort** m *abode*, (ständiger) (*place of*) *residence*; *domicile*; (zeitweiliger) (*place where a p stays at a given time*) *temporary abode, whereabouts*, s ~ ist unbekannt *his whereabouts is unknown* **~raum** m *day–, rest–-room* ⟨bes school⟩; *recreation room* ‖ ⟨a–n⟩ *living space*, ≃e [pl] *l.g-quarters* **~veränderung(en** pl) f *movement(s)* **~verbot** n *residence ban*

·auf|erlegen vt [h] **1.** jdm etw ~ *to put* od *enjoin a th on a p*; (zwangsmäßig) *to enforce* od *thrust a th* (*up*)*on a p*; jdm e–e Aufgabe, Steuer (etc) ~ *to impose a task, tax*, etc (*up*)*on a p*; das Schicksal hatte ihm e–e gr Verantwortung auferlegt *fate had brought a great responsibility to him*; jdm Verpflichtungen ~ *to lay obligations on a p*; jdm die Pflicht ~ *to make it incumbent on a p* (*to do*) ‖ jdm e–e Strafe ~ *to inflict* od *lay a punishment* (*up*)*on a p*; jdm e–e Geldstrafe ~ *to mulct a p* | wir wollen uns keinen Zwang ~ *we will have no ceremony* **2.** (**befehlen**) jdm (etw) ~ *to dictate a th to a p* ‖ jdm Gehorsam, Stillschweigen ~ *to enjoin* (od *impose*) *obedience, silence upon a p* **·auferlegt** a *enforced* (*silence*, etc.)

·auferstanden a der ~e Herr Christus *the risen Christ* **·auferstehen** vi [s]; [mst nur inf & pp] ⟨ec⟩ v den Toten ~ *to rise from the dead* ‖ wieder ~ *to resurrect*

·Auferstehung f ~/ ⟨ec⟩ *resurrection*, die ~ Christi *the Resurrection*; das Fest der ~ = ~s-fest ‖ → Wieder≃ **~sfest** n *Resurrection, Easter* **~stag** m *Resurrection-Day, Easter-Day*

·auferwecken vt [mst nur inf & pp] [h] ⟨bib⟩ (jdn) *to raise* (*a p*) *from the dead*; → wieder~

·Auferweckung f ~/~en *raising from the dead*; ⟨bib arts⟩ *Raising* (des Lazarus); → Wieder~; Erweckung

·auf|erziehen vt [h] = aufziehen, erziehen

·auf|essen vt [h] *to eat up, to consume*; *to dispose of* (*a meal*); ⟨fam⟩ *to demolish* ‖ schnell ~ *to dispatch, despatch*

·auf|fädeln vt [h] (Perlen etc) *to thread* (auf *on*), *to string*

·auf|fahren vi/t **I.** vi [s] **A. 1.** (hochsteigen) *to go up*; *to mount*; *to rise*; gen Himmel ~ *to ascend to heaven* **2.** (aufspringen, erschrecken) *to jump, to give a jump*; *to bounce, to pounce*; *to jump up* (vom Stuhl *from the chair*); *to start up suddenly*; *to be startled* **3.** (zornig w) *to flare up, to fly out, to get into a passion*; zornig ~ *to bristle* **B. 1.** *to drive up* (vor e–m Hause *to a house*) **2.** ~ auf etw *to drive* (od *run*) *against a th* ‖ ⟨mot⟩ [abs] (bei Stauung) *to jump the queue* ‖ ⟨mar⟩ *to run on a th*; auf e–n Felsen *to strike* (*on*) *a rock*; auf dem Grund ~ *to run aground, to ground* **II.** vt [h] **1.** (Wagen) ~, ~ l *to bring together, to bring into line* od *position*; *to array* ‖ (Geschütz) *to mount*; Flugzeuge ~ *to range up aircraft*; ⟨fig⟩ schweres Geschütz ~ *to bring one's heavy artillery into play* (od *to b. one's a. to bear*); *to adduce* (od *array*) *convincing evidence* (od *arguments*) (f *for*, gegen *against*); (Speisen, Getränke) *to dish up* **2.** (Weg, Boden) *to make loose and soft by driving*; *to churn up, to cut up*; *to poach* **3.** → beschottern **4.** ⟨min⟩ (Stollen) *to drive* **III.** ≃ n *start, etc*

·auffahrend a *irritable, passionate, vehement*

·Auffahrt f ~/~en **1.** *ascension, rising, ascent*; → Aufstieg **2.** *progress*, k–e ~ des Hofes *no royal p.* **3.** (Reihe) *range, array* (*of cars*, etc); ⟨a. übtr⟩ **4.** (Fahrweg) *approach*, (*carriage*) *drive, avenue*; schräge ~ *ascent, ramp*; gebogene ~ *sweep, carriage-sweep* ‖ (Zufahrt) ⟨bes mot⟩ *access*; (Autobahn≃) ⟨bes Am⟩ *Merging Traffic*!, *Merge*! **5.** ⟨südd⟩ = Himmelfahrt

·auf|fallen vi/t **I.** vi [s] **1.** der Stein fiel auf *the stone fell down* ‖ ⟨hunt⟩ (of birds) *to alight suddenly, to sweep down* **2.** ⟨fig⟩ *to be evident* (od *in evidence*); *to be* (od *make o.s.*) *conspicuous*, man fällt hier nicht auf *one is not c. here* ‖ *to stick out* ⟨a. mil⟩ fällt in der Menge gar nicht auf *may, might, will, would pass in a crowd*; nicht (weiter) ~ *to pass unnoticed* ‖ es fiel allgemein auf *it was generally noticed* ‖ dem Auge ~ *to catch the eye* ‖ (P & S) unangenehm ~ *to make a bad impression*, (of impressions) *to be blatant*; (P) *to drop a brick*, ⟨mil sl⟩ *to d. the clangour*; nur nicht ~! ⟨mil, mar⟩ *mind your S's*! er ist -ge- ⟨mil sl⟩ *he's had it* ‖ es fällt verdammt auf *it sticks* od *stands out like a sore thumb* ‖ weniger ~ *to be less noticeable* | **jdm ~** *to strike a p* (daß *that*); fiel dir nicht auf, daß ..? *did it not strike you that* ..? dem Auge *to strike the eye*

II. vt [h] sich [dat] den Kopf (etc) ~ *to break one's head by a fall*

·**auffallend 1.** a. *cospicuous; spectacular* (*celebrity*) || *striking* || (S) *viewy, ostentatious,* (Kleidung) *gaudy* | unangenehm ~ *glaring, "loud"; showy, garish,* ⟨fam⟩ *flashy;* ~es Aussehen, Benehmen *showiness* **2.** adv ~ gekleidet *showily dressed* || = auffällig adv

·**auffällig 1.** a ⟨mst dero⟩ *peculiar, strange; eccentric* || *obtrusive; ostentatious, gaudy, showy;* ~es Aussehen *gaudiness, showiness* **2.** adv *showily, loudly* (*dressed*) || sich ~ benehmen *to be* (od *make o.s.*) *conspicuous; to make an exhibition of o.s.* **Auffälligkeit** f *peculiarity; eccentricity* || *showiness*

·**Auffang- ~gebiet** n (bei Evakuierung) *reception area* **~schale** f *drip cup; oil collector* **~stelle** f ⟨bes mil⟩ *staging* od *collecting point* od *station* (P & S) **~stellung** f ⟨tact⟩ *reserve* od *prepared position* (*in the rear*) **~trichter** m ⟨tech⟩ *receiving hopper*

·**auf|fangen** vt [h] **a.** (Ball) *to catch* (*up*) || (Regenwasser etc) *to collect* || (of dogs) (etw) *to snap up* || jdn im Fallen ~ *to break a p's fall* **b.** (Neuigkeiten; Töne, Zeichen) *to pick up;* (Blick) *to intercept;* jds Blick ~ *to catch a p's eye* || (e–n Hieb, Angriff) *to parry, to ward off* || (Strahlen; Briefe, Funksprüche) *to intercept* **c.** (widerrechtlich ~) ⟨telg⟩ → abfangen 1.

·**auf|färben** vt [h] *to dye afresh, to re-dye*

·**auf|fassen** vt [h] (begreifen) *to comprehend, conceive; view;* wie ich es auffasse .. *as I take it* (*the* ..) || schnell (schwer) ~ *to be quick* (*dull*) *of apprehension* od *unterstanding* || e–e Frage ähnlich ~ *to place a similar construction on a question;* etw im besten Sinne ~ *to put the best construction upon a th;* die S läßt sich verschieden ~ *the matter admits of several constructions* || ⟨theat⟩ e–e Rolle gut ~ *to interpret a part correctly* | wie ist das -zu- *how is this to be taken to mean?* wie sollen wir s–e Rede ~? *how are we to understand his speech?* || falsch ~ *to misconceive;* etwas völlig falsch aufgefaßt h *to have got hold of the wrong end of the stick*

·**Auffassung** f ~/~en **1.** (~sgabe) *conception, apprehension* **2.** (das Aufgefaßte) *conception* (v *of*); falsche ~ *misconception* || moralische ~ *moral outlook* | (Deutung) *conception* (e–r Rolle *of a part*), *interpretation* (*of a text*), *reading* (e–r Rolle *of a part;* e–r Lage *of a situation*), *view* (*of a situation*); *version* (*of an evidence*); falsche ~ *misinterpretation* | (Meinung) *view, point of view; opinion* (über *of*) || nach m–r ~ *in my view, to my way of thinking; as I take it* || sich e–e ~ bilden über *to form a view of* || e–e ~ h v *to hold* (od *take*) *a view of* || v etw e–e ganz andere ~ h *to have an entirely different view of a matter, to see a m. in quite a d. light* || das Gericht trat der ~ des Klägers bei *the Court accepted the argument of the plaintiff* || z der ~ k *to reach a view* (*that*) || die ~ vertreten, der ~ Ausdruck geben *to take the view* (od *line*) (*that*) || **~sgabe** f *conception, apprehension; perceptive faculty, perceptivity; powers* [pl] *of conception;* schnelle ~ *intelligence* **~skraft** f, **~svermögen** n = Auffassungsgabe

·**Auffavorit** m ⟨racing⟩ *odds-on favourite*

·**auf|fegen** vt [h] *to sweep* (*a th*) *up*

·**auffindbar** a *discoverable, traceable* ·**auf|finden** vt [h] (Wild) *to retrieve* || (etw) *to ferret out, to find* (*out*); *to retrieve; to trace; to discover*

·**Auffindung** f ~/~en *discovery, finding* || ⟨ec⟩ ~ des Kreuzes *Invention of the Cross*

·**auf|fischen** vt [h] (jdn, etw) *to fish up* || ⟨fig⟩ *to pick up* ·**auf|flackern** vi [s] *to flicker up; to flare up;* ⟨a übtr⟩

·**auf|flammen 1.** vi [s] *to flame up, to burst into flame* | ⟨fig⟩ (of passion etc) *to blaze up; to flame out, to leap into flame, to flare up* || (of civil war) *to flare up* **2.** ≗ n *flare up* || ⟨fig⟩ *flare up, outbreak;* kz ~ *spurt; flash*

·**auf|flattern** vi [s] *to rise* (od *mount*) *fluttering into the air*

·**auf|flechten** vt [h] *to untwine, to untwist;* (Tau) *to unlay;* (Haare) *to unbraid*

·**auf|fliegen I.** vi [s] **1. a.** (of birds) *to take wing; to fly* (od *mount*) *upwards;* → aufsteigen **b.** ⟨übtr⟩ (of mines, etc.) *to blow up, to explode:* (Schiff) ~ l *to blow up, to explode* **c.** ⟨fig⟩ *der* Klub flog auf *the club was dissolved* | (of undertakings, etc.) *to fail; to meet with* (od *end in*) *failure* **2.** (of doors, etc.) *to fly open* **II.** ≗n *blowing up;* zum ~ bringen *to blow up, to explode*

·**Aufflug** m, ~(e)s/≗e **1.** [abstr] *flying-up; soaring-up* || → Aufstieg **2.** [konkr] (flügge Brut), *flight, flock of fledgelings*

·**auf|fordern** vt [h] **1.** (jdn) *to call* (*up*)*on, to ask* (z etw *for a th;* z tun *to do*); *to invite, to challenge* (z *to;* z tun *to do*); *to enjoin* (*to do*); man forderte ihn auf zu antworten *they bade him answer;* sie wurden zum Verlassen des Raumes aufgefordert *they were called upon to leave the room* | (jdn) dringend ~ *to press* (z etw *for a th; to do*); *to summon* (*to do*) | ⟨parl⟩ jdn ~, die Sitzung z verlassen *to name a p* **2.** (**einladen**) (jdn) *to beg, ask, request, invite* (z tun *to do*); er wurde z Essen aufgefordert *he was invited to dinner;* z e–r Rede .. *he was called upon for a speech;* jdn z Tanz ~ *to ask a p for a dance* (: *he asked her for the next d.*)

·**Aufforderung** f ~/~en *call, invitation* (z etw *to a th;* z tun *to do*) || e–e ~ an jdn *a call on a p* (*to do*); *an invitation; a challenge, a summons* (*to a p*); e–e ~ richten an jdn *to make a call* (*up*)*on a p, to call* (*up*)*on a p;* auf erste ~ (hin) zahlen *to pay on first demand;* → Forderung, Herausforderung || ⟨jur⟩ schriftl. ~ *writ* (z *for*) || (Einladung) *invitation* (*to;* an *to*) | *instigation* (*to*)

·**auf|forsten** vt [h] *to afforest; to re-afforest*

·**Aufforstung** f ~/~en *afforestation*

·**auf|fressen** vt [h] *to eat* (*up*), *to devour;* er wurde v e–m Tiger -gefressen *he got eaten by a tiger* || ⟨fig⟩ jdn ~ *to bite a p's nose off*

·**auf|frieren** vi [s] (of plants) *to freeze out; to be uprooted by frost*

·**auf|frischen** vt/i [h] **1.** vt (Gemälde) *to retouch, to touch up;* (Möbel etc) *to varnish, to renew; to furbish* (od *vamp, do*) *up* | (Gedächtnis) *to refresh, to rub up;* (Geist) *to recreate;* (Kenntnisse) *to brush* (od *rub*) *up* || (e–e Unterhaltung) wieder ~ *to revive* **2.** vi (of wind) *to freshen up*

·**Auffrischung** f ~/~en *varnishing* || *refreshment; brush-up* || (v Truppen im Ruheraum) *rehabilitation*

·**aufführbar** a *performable*

·**auf|führen** vt [h] **1.** (Mauer) *to erect;* (Gebäude) *to build, to construct; to raise;* (Gerüst) *to put up* **2. a.** (Gefangene) im Triumph ~ *to lead in triumph* || (Zeugen) *to produce* **b.** ⟨com⟩ *to book, enter; to include* (unter *among*); (Posten) einzeln ~ *to specify* | = anführen 2. b. **3.** ⟨theat⟩ (Stück) *to bring on* od *to the stage; to put up; to stage; perform, represent, give;* (*en*)*act;* das Stück wurde 40 Abende hinter e–a aufgeführt *the play had a run of 40 nights; to do* (*we hear it every time it's done*) ⟨a. mus⟩ || ⟨mus⟩ (etw) *to give, play* **4. sich ~** *to behave; to conduct o.s.* || sich anständig ~ (z Kindern gespr.) *to behave o.s.* ·**Aufführung** f ~/~en **1.** (Bauen) *erection, building* **2.** *production* (*of witnesses*) | ⟨com⟩ *entry;* nach Stück erfolgte ~ *specification* **3.** ⟨theat⟩ *performance, production, representation;* z ~ bringen *to put up; to perform, give* || ⟨mus⟩ *performance,* z ~ bringen *to perform, give* **4.** (Benehmen) *conduct, behaviour* (*good, bad*) **~srecht** n ⟨theat⟩ *stage-right;* ~e [pl] *acting* *rights* [pl] **~sserie** f ⟨theat⟩ *run* (: *a r. of 50 nights*)

·**auffüllbar** a *refillable*

·**auf|füllen** vt [h] *to fill up*; *to supplement* ‖ (Lager) wieder ~ *to replenish, restock*; *refill* ‖ (Wein) *to bottle* ·**Auffüllung** f ~/~en ⟨com⟩ ~ des Lagerbestandes *replacement of inventories*

·**auf|füttern** vt [h] *to bring up by careful feeding*; *to feed up*; *to rear* ·**Auffütterung** f ~/~en *artificial feeding*

·**Aufgabe** f ~/~en **A. 1. (Übergabe)** *posting* (*of a letter*); *dispatch, handing-in* (*of a telegram*); *booking* (*of luggage*) **2.** ⟨com⟩ **a. (Angabe)** *quotation* (*of price*) **b. (Mitteilung)** *advice*; [mst pl] *instruction, direction*; laut ~ *as per advice, as advised* **B. (Amt, Pflicht) 1. a.** *task, business*; *mission*; *responsibility*; *work*; ⟨fam⟩ *job* ‖ ⟨Am⟩ *assignment* (*of a reporter*) ‖ (a. v S) *office*; *function* (*of a law*) | s–e ~n **beherrschen** *to be proficient in one's duties* ‖ **es ist s-e ~** *it is his task, office, business, it is up to him* (*to do*); das ist nicht d–e ~ *you are not supposed to do this*; es ist nicht m–e ~ *it is not my province* (*to do*) ‖ ihm fiel die ~ zu *to him fell the task* (z tun *of doing*) ‖ er hatte die ~ z tun *he was by way of doing* ‖ **es sich zur ~ m** *to make it one's business* od *object, to set o.s.* (*to do*); *to make a point* (*of doing*) ‖ jdm (sich) e–e ~ stellen *to set a p* (*o.s.*) *a task, to task a p*; ‖ s–r ~ gewachsen s *to be equal* (od *up*) *to one's work, to understand one's business* **b. schwierige ~** ⟨bes math⟩ *problem*, e–e ~ lösen *to solve a problem*; e–e ~ stellen *to set a problem*; vor e–e ~ gestellt w *to be brought up against a problem* **c.** (S) *business, matter*; ⟨Am sl⟩ *proposition* (: *an easy p.*) **2. (Schul≗)** *task, lesson, exercise*; s–e ~ m *to do one's lessons*; ⟨Am⟩ *assignment* ‖ (Schieß–, Übungs≗) ⟨bes mil⟩ *requirement* **C. 1. (Aufgeben)** ~ des Geschäfts *retirement from business*; ~ des Amtes *resignation of an office* ‖ ~ e–s Planes (etc) *giving up, abandonment of a plan*; .. e–r Gewohnheit *discontinuance of a habit*; .. e–s Rechtes *renunciation of a right*; *surrender* (*of a p's will*) ‖ *surrender* (*of a fortress*) **2.** ⟨racing⟩ *abandonment* (*of a race*); *retirement, dropping out* **D.** ⟨tech⟩ *blast furnace mouth* ‖ (Mahlgut) [abstr] *feed* **~apparat** m ⟨tech⟩ *feeder* **~gut** n ⟨mill⟩ (raw) *material* ([*which is fed*] *for grinding*) **~gerinne** n ⟨mill⟩ *chute* **~körnung** f feed size **~schein** m *receipt*; *acknowledgement of delivery* **~schnecke** f *screw conveyor* **~station** f *sending station* **~stempel** m *stamp* **~stücke** n pl ⟨mill⟩ *feed* **~vorrichtung** f ⟨met⟩ *feeding apparatus* **~zeit** f *time of dispatch*

·**auf|gabeln** vt [h] *to take up a fork* ‖ °(jdn) ~ *to pick, fish, hook up*

·**Aufgaben- ~bereich** m *sphere of duties, range of functions* **~buch, ~heft** n *exercise-book*; *note-book* **~kreis** m *responsibility* **~sammlung** f *collection of problems*

·**Aufgallop** m *trial gallop* ‖ ⟨racing⟩ *parade past the stands*

·**Aufgang** m ~(e)s/≗e **1. a. (Aufsteigen)** → Aufstieg ‖ ~ der Sonne *the rising of the sun, sunrise*; ⟨a. übtr⟩ | ⟨tech⟩ *up-stroke* (*of a piston*) **b.** ⟨hunt⟩ *opening* (*of the season*) **2. (Weg)** *ascent* (z *to*); (Treppe) *flight of steps*; *stairs, staircase*

·**auf|geben** vt/i [h] **I.** vt **A. 1.** (Essen) *to serve*; *to dish* **2.** ⟨ten⟩ *to serve* **3.** ⟨met⟩ am Ofen die Beschickung ~ *to charge, to feed, to fill the furnace* ‖ ⟨mill⟩ wenn (das Mahlgut) gleichmäßig –ge– wird *with evenly fed material* **4. a. (z Beförderung)** (Brief) *to post*; (Telegramm) *to hand in, to dispatch* (*des*–); (Gepäck) *to book, register* ‖ ein Inserat ~ *to put an advertisement in a paper* | ⟨com⟩ e–e Bestellung ~ *to give an order* **b.** den Geist ~ *to give up the ghost* **c.** → angeben I. 4. **5. (auferlegen) a.** jdm (e–e Arbeit) ~ *to impose a task on a p, to set a p a task* ‖ wie weit habe ich euch –ge–? *how far did I set you?* **b.** (befehlen) jdm ~ z tun *to order a p to do* **c.** ein Problem (etc) ~ *to give up, to propound a problem* ‖ ein Rätsel ~ *to give up, to propose, to set a riddle* **d.** (v S) Schwierigkeiten, Rätsel ~ *to offer difficulties, riddles* **B. 1. (verzichten auf) a.** (etw [Absicht, Gewohnheit, Plan etc]) *to abandon, discontinue*; (Plan) *to discard* ‖ *to give up* (*a th*; z tun *doing*); das Rauchen ~ *to leave off smoking*; –ge– w *to go* (: *the declaration must go*) ‖ (Arbeit, Dienst) *to leave, quit*; (Amt) *to resign*; das Geschäft ~ *to retire from business, to go out of b.*; (Stellung) *to throw up*; ⟨sl⟩ *to chuck* | (Freiheit; Recht etc) *to surrender*; *to relinquish* ‖ (Anspruch) *to give up, to resign, to waive*; (Vorteil) *to forgo* ‖ (Rang, Namen) *to sink*; (Stolz) *to give over* **b.** jdn, jds Bekanntschaft ~ *to drop a p*; ⟨sl⟩ *to chuck, to unstick a p*; *to have done* (od *to break*) *with a p* **2.** (als hoffnungslos ~) (Kampf etc) *to abandon*; *to resign*; den Kampf ~ *to throw in one's hands* ‖ ⟨cards⟩ das Spiel ~ *to throw up the cards* ‖ (jdn, e–n Kranken) *to give up*; (of a physician) *to condemn a p*) **II.** vi ⟨sport⟩ *to drop out, to retire*; ⟨sl⟩ *to chuck it* ·**Aufgeber** m ~s/~ *sender* (*of letters*) ‖ *consignor* (*of goods*)

·**aufge- ~blasen** a **1.** ~e Backen *blown cheeks* **2.** ⟨fig⟩ *inflated, puffed-up* (von, vor *with*); *hightoned*; *arrogant, conceited, snobby, supercilious, vainglorious, bumptious*; ⟨fam⟩ *swell-headed, stuckup* (p) ‖ ~es Wesen *bumptiousness, arrogance*; ~ s *to suffer from swelled head* ‖ ~ tun *to peacock o.s.* | ≗heit [f] ~/ *inflation, swelled head*; *arrogance, bumptiousness*; *snobbery, snobbism* **~blondet** a *blondined* ≗**bot** n ~(e)s/~e **A. 1.** ⟨jur⟩ **a.** *public notice* od *proclamation to report claims* od *rights before a certain date* **b.** ⟨ec⟩ (kirchliches ~) *banns* [pl], *publication of banns*, letztes ~ *last p.*; beim dritten ~ *at the third time of asking* **2.** ⟨mil⟩ *levy*; allgemeines ~ *levy en masse* **3.** ⟨übtr⟩ = Aufbietung **B.** [konkr] (P) ~ v Polizei *posse* od *body of constables*, ⟨Am⟩ *platoon of police*; Extra≗ *extra-posse* ‖ *strong force* ‖ *galaxy* (*of great men*) (Menge) *array* (*of troops*) **~bracht** a [pp v aufbringen] **1.** ⟨mar⟩ *captured* (*ship*) **2.** ⟨fig⟩ (zornig) *angry* (über etw *at, about a th*; über jdn *with a p*); *exasperated* (über *at, by*); *dangerous*; *snorty*; leicht ~ *irascible* ‖ ~ s *to fume*; *to be offended* (über *at a th*); *to be sick* (über jdn *with a p*) ‖ er wurde ~ *he got angry* (od *into a passion*) ‖ → wütend **~braucht** a *exhausted*, → aufbrauchen °**~donnert** a [pp v aufdonnern] *bedizened, spruce, dolled* od *dressed up to the nines* od *to kill*; *prettified*; *flash, swell* ‖ *gaudy* (*dress*) ‖ ⟨vulg⟩ [pred] *tarted up* **~dreht** a (P) ⟨fam⟩ = aufgekratzt **~dunsen** a [pp v †aufdinsen] *bloated, bloated* (*face*) *sodden* (*complexion*), *puffed up, swelled* (v *with*)

·**auf|gehen** vi/t **I.** vi [s] **A. 1.** (aufsteigen, hochgehen) **a.** (of the sun, stars) *to rise*, der Mond ist aufgegangen *the moon has risen* (od *is up*) ‖ (of smoke; the curtain) *to rise* **b.** (of dough) *to rise, swell*; ~ l *to leaven* ⟨übtr⟩ aufgegangen = aufgedunsen **c.** (of plants, etc) *to take*; (of seed) *to come forth*; *to sprout* ‖ wie Kressensamen ~: *the intimacy between them sprang up like Jack's Bean-stalk* **d.** ⟨fig⟩ **es ging mir ein Licht,** °Seifensieder, °Talglicht auf *it dawned* (od *it was borne in*) *upon me* (*that*), *I got it, I saw the point*, ⟨sl⟩ *I tumbled to it* ‖ die Bedeutung des Satzes ging ihm plötzlich auf *he suddenly grasped the meaning of the sentence, the m. of the s. became clear to him*; die Wahrheit ging mir auf *the truth flashed upon me* (od *into my mind*) **2.** ⟨übtr⟩ **in Flammen ~** *to go up in flames*; *to be consumed by the flames*; in Rauch ~ *to end in smoke*; ⟨fam⟩ *to go up in a puff of smoke*; *to* *flower into pillars of smoke* ‖ in Asche ~ *to be reduced to ashes* **3.** ⟨math⟩ 5 geht in 15 ohne Rest auf, 5 geht in 15 auf *5 divides 15*; *5 goes into 15 without (leaving) a remainder*, 2, 3, 4, 6 gehen alle in 12 auf *2, 3, 4, 6 are all measures of 12* **4.** ⟨übtr⟩ (*of groups, countries*, etc) ~ in (ein Teil w v) *to be merged* od *incorporated in*, Hessen ging in Preußen auf *Hesse was merged in Prussia*; (*of foreign elements*) *to infiltrate into* (*national life*); ~ l in *to merge* (*a part*) *in* **5.** ⟨fig⟩ (P) ~ in etw, jdm *to be absorbed* (od *bound up, wrapped up*) *in, to be taken up with a th, a p*; *to humour a p* ‖ ~ für etw, jdn *to live for a th, a p* **B. (sich öffnen) 1.** (of a door, bottle; flower) *to open*; das Fenster geht nicht auf *the window won't open* ‖ (of a knot) *to come* od *get loose* od *untied*; (of a string) *to come undone* ‖ *to untwist*; *to give way* ‖ (of an ulcer) *to break* | ⟨fig⟩ ihm gingen die Augen auf *his eyes were opened* (f. etw *to a th*), *he began to see clearly* (*that*) ‖ ihm ging das Herz auf *his heart leapt* **II.** vt [h] sich [dat] die Füße ~ *to walk one's feet sore* **·Aufgehen** n **1.** *rising*; ⟨theat⟩ *rise* (*of curtain*), *curtain rise* | *dawn*(*ing*) **2.** *mergence* (in *in*); *merging* (in *in, into*) **3.** *absorption* (in *in*) **4.** *opening*

·aufge- ~klärt a *enlightened*; *cultivated, civilized* ‖ ⟨pol⟩ *liberal* | ≃heit [f] *enlightenment*; *civilization* °**~knöpft** a *communicative*; → aufgeschlossen ‖ [pred] *in an unbuttoned frame of mind* °**~kratzt** a ⟨fig⟩ *bucked-up, pepped-up* **~laufen** a *accrued* (*interest*)

·Aufgeld n ~(e)s/~er *premium*; *agio* ‖ (Draufgeld) *earnest*(*-money*) ‖ (Zuschlag) *surcharge, extra-charge* ‖ (Anzahlung) *payment on account* ‖ Ihr Wagen wird gegen ein ~ umgetauscht *your old car is taken in part exchange*

·aufge- ~legt a ⟨fig⟩ **1.** *disposed, inclined* (z *to*); zum Scherzen (etc) ~ *in a jesting* (*etc*) *mood* ‖ *game* (z for; z tun *to do*); ~ s *to be in the vein* od *humour* (z *for*; z tun *for doing*); gut (schlecht) ~ *in good* (*bad*) *humour*; nicht ~ s *to be in no mood* (zur Arbeit *for work*; z tun *to do*); ich bin nicht ~ *I don't feel like it* **2.** [attr] ~er Schwindel *downright swindle* **~löst** a *melted* (*sugar*) **~nordet** a *blondined* **~paßt**! intj *look here*! *mind your p's and q's*! **~pumpt** a *inflated*; nicht genügend ~ *underinflated* **~räumt** a (P) ⟨fig⟩ *merry, cheerful, good humo*(*u*)*red*, → heiter ‖ [pred] *in good humour*; *in high spirits* | ≃heit [f] *cheerfulness*; *good humour*; *high spirits* [pl] **~regt** a *agog* (über *over*); *excited, flurried, fussy*; *flustered*; *nervous*; ~ s *to be on the fret*, ⟨bes Am fam⟩ *in a lather, het up*; sehr (*or* bes) ~ s *to be high-strung*; ⟨sl⟩ *to be in a great way* ‖ (reizbar) *excitable, irritable, nervous* ‖ → zornig | ≃heit [f] *nervousness* **~richtet** a *standing* (Stein)

·Aufgesang m ~(e)s/≃e ⟨Ger hist pros⟩ (Ggs Abgesang) *the first two parts of a tripartite stanza*

·aufge- ~schlagen a [pp v aufschlagen] *upcast* (*eyes*); *open*(*ed*) (*book*) **~schlossen** a [pp v aufschließen] ⟨tech⟩ *converted* ‖ ~e Marschkolonne *close column, close-order march formation* ‖ ⟨fig⟩ *communicative* (*p*); *open-minded, -hearted*; *broad-minded, liberal, receptive*; *open*; *responsive, susceptible* (f *to*); frei u ~ *free-minded*; ~ w *to expand, to unbend*; ⟨Am sl⟩ *to loosen up* | ≃heit [f] *openness* (f *to*); *open-mindedness* **~schmissen** a [pp v aufschmeißen] ⟨fig⟩ [pred] *helpless, lost* (ganz ~ *quite lost*); *up a gum-tree*; *at sea* (ganz ~ *all at s.*); ~ s *to be done for, to be on one's beam-ends, to be at the end of one's tether* **~schossen** a [pp v aufschießen] ⟨fig⟩ hoch~, lang~ *lanky* (*lad*), *overgrown* **~schürzt** a [pp v aufschürzen] *tucked-up* (*skirt*) **~schwemmt** a ⟨fig⟩ = *aufgedunsen* ‖ *flabby* **~sessen** [pp v → aufsitzen] **~stülpt** a (Stupsnase) *tiptilted* | ≃sein *tiptilt*; → aufgeworfen **~takelt** a ⟨mar⟩ *rigged* ‖ ⟨fig⟩ = aufgedonnert **~tragen** a ⟨fig⟩ dick ~ *smeared on thickly* **~wärmt** a *cooked* (od *warmed*) *up* (*dish*) ‖ ⟨fig⟩ *rehashed*; ~er Brei *rehash*; (*story*) *twice-told* | ≃es [n] ⟨cul fam⟩ *bubble and squeak* **~weckt** a ⟨fig⟩ *deft*; *bright, clever, intelligent* (*child*) | ≃heit [f] *deftness*; *brightness*; *cleverness* **~worfen** a [pp v aufwerfen] ⟨fig⟩ *pouting* od *protruding* (*lips*) ‖ *turned up, snub* (*nose*); ~e Nase *snub*

·auf|gießen vt [h] (etw) *to pour* (auf [*up*]*on*) ‖ (Tee) *to make, infuse*; (Kaffee) *to make*

·auf|gipfeln vi [s] *to form a pyramid*

·Aufglasurmalerei f *on-glaze decoration*

·auf|gleisen vt [h] ⟨rail⟩ *to rerail*

·Aufgleitwolke f *rising cloud*

·aufgliederbar a *classifiable* → **·auf|gliedern** vt [h] *to analyse*; *to arrange* (*in groups, etc*) ‖ *to break down, to subdivide*; *to split up* ‖ (Produktion etc) *to phase* → **·Aufgliederung** f *analysis*; (in Sparten) *breakdown* ‖ ~ v *details of*; → gliedern, Gliederung

·auf|glimmen vi [s] *to flicker up*

·auf|graben vt [h] (Straße) *to break*; *to dig* (od *pick*) *up*; *to rout up*; → ⟨a.⟩ ausheben

·auf|greifen vt [h] (jdn) *to catch*; *to seize* ‖ (etw) *to snatch up*; *to snatch at* (*a th*) | ⟨übtr⟩ (Vorschlag) *to take up*; e–n Gedanken sofort ~ *to catch up an idea, to catch* (od *jump*) *at an idea*; e–e Anregung (etc) ~ *to seize on a suggestion*

°**·auf|gucken** vi [h] *to look up*

·Aufguß m –sses/≃sse *infusion* ‖ °es ist nur ~ *that is mere wash* **~tierchen** n ⟨zoo⟩ → Infusorium, –rien

·auf|haben vt [h] **1.** e–n Hut ~ *to wear a hat*; den H. ~ *to have one's hat on* **2.** (of shops) *to keep open* **3.** ⟨school⟩ *to have* (*lessons*) *to do*; viel ~ *to have* (*got*) *much home work*

·auf|hacken vt [h] (Boden) *to hoe up*; *to peck* (od *pick*) *up*

·auf|haken vt [h] (Kleid) *to unhook*; *unclasp*

·auf|halsen vt **1.** (aufhängen) jdm etw ~ *to fob off a th on a p*; *to foist a th on a p* **2.** (aufbürden) jdm etw ~ *to let a p in for a th*; jdm die Verantwortung für etw ~ *to saddle a p with the responsibility for a th* | sich etw ~ *to let o.s. in for a th*; *to saddle o.s. with a th* ‖ sich Schulden ~ *to incur debts*

·Aufhalt m ~(e)s/~e *stoppage, stopping, checking*; *pulling-up* (*of a horse*) **·auf|halten** vt [h] **1. a.** (Pferd, Schlag) *to stop* ‖ *to hold up*; das Auto wurde unterwegs –ge– *the car was held up on the way* (durch *by*) ‖ ⟨Am⟩ *to halt* ‖ (Feind) *to keep off* **b.** (Verkehr) *to stay, obstruct*; ⟨Am⟩ *to hold up* **c.** (Krankheit) *to stay*; (Ereignisse; Verfahren) *to arrest, to stay*; ⟨Am⟩ *to halt*; den Fall des Franken ~ *to stay the fall of the franc* ‖ (auffangen) *to intercept* **d. 1.** (jdn) *to retard, to delay, detain* (*a p*); jdn nicht länger ~ *not to take up any more of a p's time*; ich möchte Sie nicht länger ~ *don't let me keep you any longer*; halten Sie ihn etw auf *keep him hanging about* **2.** (offen halten) (die Augen) *to keep open* **3. sich ~** *to be* (: *to be in London for 3 days*); *to stop* (bei *with a p*) ‖ *to live, reside, stay* (in .. *at a place* od *a p's house*; bei *with a p*) | ⟨übtr⟩ sich ~ bei etw *to dwell on a th*; sich lange ~ *to linger* (bei e–m Gegenstand *over* od *upon a subject*) ‖ *to occupy o.s. with a th*; sich bei Kleinigkeiten ~ *to waste one's time on trifles* | sich ~ **über** etw, jdn *to find fault with, to criticize a th, a p* ‖ *to scoff at, to make game of, to ridicule a th, a p* ‖ sich über die Zeit –ge– h *to be behind schedule* **·Aufhalten** n *stoppage, stopping*; *stay*; *hindrance*; *obstruction* ‖ → Aufhaltung **·Aufhalter** m ⟨tech⟩ *device for stopping* od *staying*; *brake*; *brake-shoe* **·Aufhaltung** f *detention, delay*; ~en h *to be delayed* od *detained* (durch *by*)

·**Aufhänge- ~boden** m *drying-loft* **~haken** m *suspension-hook* **~kreuz** n ⟨typ⟩ *printer's peel* **~seil** n ⟨theat⟩ *line* **~verdopplung** f ⟨theat⟩ *bridle*

·**auf|hängen** vt [h] **1.** (etw) *to hang* (an *from*); *to suspend* (an der Decke *from the ceiling*); (Hut) *to hang up, to hang* (auf *on*); Wäsche zum Trocknen ~ *to hang out the washing* **2.** jdn ~ *to hang a p* (*by the neck*); ⟨sl⟩ *to scrag a p* ‖ aufgehängt w *to hang*, → hängen | **sich ~** *to hang o.s.* ‖ wo hänge ich mich auf? *where do I hang up my things?* **3.** ⟨übtr⟩ jdm etw ~ (°anschmieren) *to fob* (od *palm*) *off a th on a p, to foist a th on a p*; jdm e–e Lüge ~ *to tell a p a fib* ‖ (aufbürden) jdm e–n Prozeß ~ *to involve a p in a lawsuit*; → aufbürden, aufhalsen ·**Aufhängen** n *suspension*; (v Bildern) *hanging* ·**Aufhänger** m (P) *hanger* ‖ = → ·**Aufhängsel** n (of a coat) *tab* ·**Aufhängung** f *suspension*; (v Bildern) *hanging*; → kardanisch ‖ Vorderrad-~ *front wheel susp.*

·**auf|hauen** vt [h] *to hew open, to cut open* ‖ → hauen ·**Aufhauer** m = Meißel

·**auf|häufeln** vt [h] *to form into small heaps* ‖ (Pflanzen, Kartoffeln) *to hill* ·**auf|häufen** vt [h] *to accumulate*; *to heap* od *pile up*; (Reichtümer) *to amass* | **sich ~** *to accumulate* ·**Aufhäufung** f ~/~en *accumulation*; *amassment*

·**auf|heben 1.** (Stein etc vom Boden) *to lift* (*up*); *to pick up*; → hochheben, (er)heben ‖ die Augen ~ *to lift* (*up*) od *to raise one's eyes* ‖ den Fehdehandschuh ~ *to pick* (od *take*) *up the gauntlet, to accept the challenge* **2. (aufbewahren)** *to keep, to preserve*; *to lay up, to pigeon-hole, to reserve, to save* (für *for*); (Geld) *to earmark* (*for*) ‖ gut aufgehoben s *to be well looked after* (od *taken care of*); *to be in good hands* (bei *with*); Sie sind in dem Hotel gut a. *they will do you well at that hotel* **3.** ⟨übtr⟩ **a. (überrumpeln)** (Bande) *to surprise, to overcome by surprise* ‖ *to seize, arrest* ‖ *to clean up* **b.** ⟨min⟩ *to clear up* **c. (auflösen)** → Tafel; (Versammlung etc) *to dissolve* ‖ (Belagerung) *to raise* **d. (streichen,** rückgängig m) *to cancel*; *to abolish, to do away with* (*a th*); *to set aside* ‖ (Entfernung) *to annihilate* ‖ (Beschränkungen) *to lift*; (Bräuche) *to abolish*; *to abrogate* ‖ (Gesetz etc) *to annul, to repeal, to rescind*; *to* (*make null and*) *void*; ⟨Am⟩ *to nullify* ‖ ⟨jur⟩ (Urteil) *to quash* ‖ ein Verbot ~ *to cancel* (od *remove*) *a prohibition, to lift* (od *raise*) *a ban* (e–r Zeitung *on a paper*); (Verlobung) *to break off*; (Vertrag) *to cancel, to denounce* | aufgeschoben ist nicht aufgehoben *postponement is not abandonment*; besser aufgeschoben als aufgehoben *better late than never* **4.** ⟨übtr⟩ ⟨fig⟩ **(ausgleichen)** *to cancel, to neutralize* ‖ *to counterbalance*; *to compensate*; (Vorteile) *to offset* ‖ → heben | **sich ~, e-a ~** *to neutralize each other* ‖ (of numbers) *to cancel out*; *to cancel each other* ·**Aufheben** n **1.** *lift, lifting* **2.** *keeping* **3.** ⟨übtr⟩ *ado, fuss, to-do*; *pother*; viel ~s, gr ~ m *to make a to-do* (od *fuss*), *to fuss* (über, von *about*) ·**Aufheber** m (Zapfen) ⟨tech⟩ *thumb* ·**Aufhebung** f ~/~en **1.** → Aufheben **2.** ⟨übtr⟩ *seizure, arrest* **3.** ~ der Tafel *conclusion of the meal* | *raising* (*of a siege*) **4.** *dissolution* (*of a meeting*) ‖ *abolition* (*of a custom*); *suppression* (*of a convent*) ‖ *repeal* (*of a law*; *decree*; *embargo, etc*); *abrogation, annulment, cancellation, denunciation* (*of a treaty*); teilweise ~ *derogation*; ~ der diplomatischen Anerkennung *derecognition*

·**auf|heitern** vt [h] **1.** (jdn) *to cheer* (*up*); *to exhilarate*; *to brighten up, to gladden*; *to inspire* (*a p*) *with joy* ‖ *to encourage* **2. sich ~ a.** *to relax one's mind* (mit etw *with a th*) **b.** (Wetter) *to clear up*, (Himmel) *to brighten*; (Gesicht) *to brighten, to become bright* od *cheerful*

·**Aufheiterung** f ~/~en (P) *cheering-up* ‖ (Wetter) *clearing up*, (Himmel) *brightening*

·**auf|helfen** vi [h] jdm ~ *to help a p up, to give a p a hand up* od *a lift*

·**auf|hellen** vt [h] **1.** (heller m) *to clarify, to render pellucid* ‖ ⟨theat⟩ *to fade in* ‖ ⟨paint⟩ *enlighten* | (Himmel) *to clear, brighten* **2.** ⟨fig⟩ (Frage; Zus–hang etc) *to clear up*; *to elucidate*; *illuminate*; *clarify* **3. sich ~** (Wetter) *to clear* (*up*); (Himmel) *to brighten* (*up*) | (Gesicht) ⟨fig⟩ *to clarify* ‖ *to brighten* (*up*) ·**Aufheller** m ~s/~ (in Waschmitteln) *brightener* ·**Aufhellung** f ~/~en *clearing up* ‖ *elucidation*

·**auf|hetzen** vt [h] (Hund) *to set on* (auf *to*; *to do*) ‖ (P) *to incite, instigate* (z *to*); → aufreizen; Leute gegen e–a ~ *to set persons by the ears*

·**Aufhetzer** m ~s/~ *instigator*; *fire-brand* ·**Aufhetzung** f ~/~en *incitement, instigation* (z *to*) ‖ ⟨pol⟩ *agitation, violent propaganda*

·**auf|hissen** vt [h] → hissen

·**auf|hocken 1.** vi [h & s] ⟨orn hunt⟩ *to sit* | ⟨gym⟩ *to squat* | Sw *to get onto a cart, etc* **2.** vt [h] *to put, wear, carry .. on one's back* | ⟨agr⟩ *to put* (*sheaves*) *together*

·**auf|holen** vt/i **1.** vt **a.** (hissen) *to pull up, to hoist* **b.** (of trains) Zeit ~ *to make time*; (Verspätung) ~ *to make up lost time*; Versäumtes ~ *to make up* (*the*) *leeway* **2.** vi ⟨sport⟩ *to draw up*; *to pull up, to catch up*

·**auf|horchen** vi [h] *to listen attentively* (auf *to*); *to prick up one's ears, to listen with both ears*; ⟨Am⟩ *to sit up and take notice*

·**auf|hören** vi [h] **1. (zu Ende gehen)** *to end*; *to cease*; *to come to an end*; (allmählich) *to peter out* ‖ die Bäume hörten hier auf *here the trees came to an end*; die Firma hörte auf *the firm gave up* ‖ in Geldsachen hört die Gemütlichkeit auf *business is business* ‖ da hört doch alles auf, da hört (sich) doch die Gemütlichkeit (*or* verschiedenes, alles) auf! *that's the limit* (od *top*)!, *that is beyond everything*; *that's a bit too thick!* | **(schließen)** ~ bei *to finish with* (: *he finished with Queen Elizabeth*); nicht ~ etw z tun *to continue doing a th*; er hörte beim 3. Kapitel auf *he left off at the third chapter* ‖ ~ mit *to end with* (: *it ended with a talk*) | **(schwinden)** (of customs, etc) *to die* (*out*) ‖ (of wind) *to calm down* **2. (ablassen) a.** *to give up*; ⟨Am⟩ *to quit* **b. ~ mit** (ablassen v) e–m Brauch etc *to discontinue, to give up a custom*; → aufgeben **c. ~, mit** etw ~ *to desist from doing a th*, mit der Arbeit ~ *to knock off*; *to cease* (od *finish, leave off, stop, knock off*) *work*; mit der Zahlung ~ = z zahlen → d. ‖ du mußt uns versprechen, damit aufzuhören *you must give us your word to have done with that* ‖ hör damit auf ⟨Am⟩ *let up on that*; nicht ~, bis *not to let up until*; mit Arbeiten (*etc*) ~ (= ~ z arbeiten) *to cease* (od *stop, leave off*) *working* **d. ~ z tun** *to cease to do* od *doing, to stop* (od *leave off, finish, knock off*) *doing*; ⟨Am⟩ *to quit doing*; nicht ~ z tun *to keep doing, to continue doing* (*a th*) ‖ ~ z lärmen *or* reden *to hold one's noise*; ~ z sprechen *to dry up*; ~ z zahlen *to cease* (od *suspend*) *payment* **e.** plötzlich ~ *to stop short* (od *dead*) ‖ hör auf! *shut up!, have done!* ‖ ⟨parl⟩ ~! *withdraw!*

°·**Aufhupferl** n ~s/~ ⟨vulg⟩ *mount* ‖ ein ~ m *to bounce, to hop on, to do a leap*

·**Aufhütte** f ~/~n ⟨hunt⟩ *hut used in crow--killing*

·**auf|jagen** vt [h] (Wild) *to rouse, to startle, to start* ‖ (Fuchs) *to unearth* ‖ (Vögel) *to flush* (Rebhühner etc) *to spring* | (P) *to scare, to startle*; jdn aus dem Bett ~ *to rout a p out* (aus dem Schlaf *from sleep*)

·**auf|jauchzen** vi [h] *to shout* (*with delight* od *joy*)

·**Aufkauf** m ~(e)s/⸚e *buying up* (*of lands*, etc); *wholesale buying* ·**auf|kaufen** vt [h] *to buy up*;

etw billig ~ *to pick a th up cheap*; schnell ~ *to snap up*; den Markt ~ *to corner* (⟨engl hist⟩ *forestall*) *the market* ‖ → ankaufen

·**Aufkäufer** m ~s/~ *wholesale buyer, cornerer* ‖ †⟨engl hist⟩ *forestaller*

·**auf|keilen** vt [h] *to wedge on*

·**auf|keimen** vi [s] *to germinate, sprout; bud* (z *to*); ~ l *to sprout, germinate*; ⟨a. fig⟩

·**auf|keschern** vt [h] (P) ⟨bes Am⟩ *to jazz up*

·**Aufkimmung** f ~/ *slope of a ship's bottom*

·**auf|klaftern** vt [h] (Holz) *to stack, to cord*

·**Aufklang** m ~(e)s/⁓̈e = Auftakt

·**aufklappbar** a *hinged* (*lid*); ⟨mot⟩ *folding* (*top*) ·**auf|klappen** vt [h] (Hutrand etc) *to turn up* | (Messer) *to open, to unclasp*

·**auf|klaren** vi/t [h] **1.** vi (nur 3. sg) ⟨mar⟩ (Wetter) *to clear up* **2.** vt (aufräumen) ⟨mar⟩ *to clear up, to clear decks* ⟨a. fig: Tisch⟩; ⟨mar sl⟩ *to dig up* ·**Aufklarer** m ~s/~ ⟨mar⟩ *peggy*; ~ s, spielen *to stand one's peggy*

·**auf|klären** vt [h] **1.** (den **Himmel**) *to clear up, to brighten* | ⟨übtr⟩ (dunkle Stellen) *to clear up; to illuminate, elucidate; clarify; to make clear, to explain; to shed light on*; (Ursache e–r S) *to determine* ‖ gründlich ~ *to thrash out* **2.** (**Unwissende,** Heiden) *to enlighten*; jdn ~ *to enlarge a p's mind* ‖ jdn ~ *to enlighten* (über *on, as to*), *to let a p in* (über *on*), *to inform* (über *of, about*); *to put a p right* (über *on*); *to make a p aware* (*of*); ⟨Am⟩ *to sell* (*on*); jdn über e–n Irrtum ~ *to undeceive* (od *disillusion*) *a p* ‖ ~der Umstand *eye-opener* ‖ → aufgeklärt **3.** ⟨mil⟩ *to reconnoitre*; **4. sich ~** (Wetter) *to clear up, to brighten* | ⟨übtr⟩ *to brighten*; sein Antlitz klärte sich auf *he brightened up* | (of mysteries) *to be explained*

·**Aufklärer** m ~s/~ → Aufklärungs- **1.** *enlightener, instructor* **2.** ⟨mil⟩ (P) *scout*; ⟨aero⟩ (Flugzeug, Schiff) *scout* **3.** ⟨philos⟩ *representative* od *adherent of Enlightenment* ‖ *rationalist, intellectual* ‖ *liberal* ·**aufklärerisch** a *enlightened* ‖ *rationalistic; intellectual* ‖ *liberal* ·**Aufkläricht** m ~s/ *pseudoenlightenment; purely rationalistic outlook*

·**Aufklärung** f ~/~en **1.** *clearing up; elucidation* (*of a mystery*); *explanation* ‖ (S) *message* (: *to give a m.*) **2.** ⟨mil⟩ *reconnaissance* **3.** (P) *instruction, enlightenment*; sexuelle ~ *sex education* **4.** ⟨philos⟩ das Zeitalter der ~ *the Age of Enlightenment* ‖ → Propaganda ‖ ⟨jur⟩ *briefing*

·**Aufklärungs-** ⟨mil, mar & aero⟩ *reconnoitring* (*troops*); *scouting* (*vessels*); *reconnaissance* (*party*) **~beamter** m ⟨pol, etc⟩ *public relations officer* **~dienst** m ⟨mil & aero⟩ *reconnaissance duty*; ⟨mar⟩ *reconnoitring duty* **~elemente** n pl *information collecting elements* (a. mil⟩ **~ergebnis** n *r.e intelligence* **~fahrt** f ⟨mar⟩ *r.e cruise* **~fahrzeug** n *scout vehicle*, ⟨mar⟩ *scout vessel* **~feldzug** m *enlightenment campaign* **~flieger** m, **~flugzeug** n ⟨aero⟩ *scout airplane* od *aircraft; reconnaissance plane*; (*speed-*) *scout*; ⟨Am fam⟩ *look-see* ‖ Nah-~ *observation aircraft* **~jäger** m ⟨aero⟩ *reconnaissance fighter* **~kreuzer** m ⟨mar⟩ *scout* **~satellit** m *reconnaissance* od *spy satellite* **~truppe** f *reconnaissance* **~zeitalter** → Aufklärung 4.

·**auf|klauben** vt [h] *to pick up*

·**aufklebbar** a *adhesive* ·**auf|kleben** vt [h] (etw) *to paste, stick; to fasten with paste* (auf *on, on to*); (Briefmarke) *to affix* (auf e–n Brief, ein Paket *to a letter, to a parcel*) ·**Aufkleber** m ~s/~ *filer*; → Etikett

·**auf|klinken** vt [h] (Tür) *to unlatch*

·**auf|klopfen** vt [h] *to knock open*

·**auf|knacken** vt [h] (Nüsse) *to crack*; → Nuß

·**auf|knöpfen** vt [h] (Rock) *to unbutton; undo*; (Manschette) *to unlink* | °(Augen) *to* (*keep*) *open* ‖ (Ohren) *to pin back* ‖ → aufgeknöpft ‖ die Tasche, den Geldbeutel ~ ⟨fig⟩ *to open one's pocket*

·**auf|knoten** vt [h] (Paket) *to untie, to undo*

·**auf|knüpfen** vt [h] *to untie, undo* | °jdn ~ *to hang a p; to string a p up*

·**auf|kochen I.** vt/i [h] **1.** vt *to boil* (*up*); *to boil again* **2.** vi *to boil up* ‖ nur ~ l *to parboil* **II.** ⁓ *ebullience*

·**Aufkohlung** f ⟨tech⟩ *carburization*

·**auf|kommen** vi [s] **A. 1.** (aufstehen) *to get up, to rise* **2.** ⟨mar⟩ (of a ship) *to approach; to gain* | ⟨sport⟩ *to gain on* (od *come up with; catch up on* od *to*) *one's opponents* **3.** ⟨übtr⟩ **a.** (**gesunden**) *to recover; to come round* ‖ (**wachsen**) *to grow; to prosper, thrive*; jdn nicht ~ l *to give a p no chance* | (Pflanze) *to come up*; (T) *to grow up* **b. ~ gegen** jdn *to prevail against a p*; nicht ~ können gegen *to be unable to cope with* (od *to make head against*) *a p*; k–e Firma konnte gegen den Wettbewerb ~ *no firm could survive against the competition*; er läßt niemend gegen (*or* neben) sich ~ *he admits no rival* **c. ~ f. etw** *to answer, to be* (od *make o.s.*) *responsible, to take the responsibility for a th; to pay* od *provide for a th; to guarantee a th*; für die Unkosten ~ *to defray the expenses* | f jdn, sich selbst ~ *to provide for a p, for o.s.* **B.** ⟨fig⟩ (S) **1.** (Wind) *to spring up, to rise* **2.** *to arise, to spring up* ‖ (Sitte etc) *to arise, to come in, to come into use* (od *fashion, vogue*) ‖ (Gedanken etc) *to suggest o.s.* ‖ Zweifel ~ l *to give rise to doubts, to allow doubts to rise*; k–e Z. ~ l *to prevent the rise of d., to admit of no d.* **3.** *to come in*; aus der Zeichnung ist wenig -ge- *the subscription has had a bad result*

·**Aufkommen** n ~s/ **1.** *recovery from illness*; man zweifelt an s–m ~ *his recovery is despaired of* **2.** *incidence* (*of the wind*) **3.** (Entstehen) *rise, origin* ‖ ~ neuer Mittel *introduction of new material* ·**aufkommend** a *arising* ‖ ⟨fig⟩ *nascent*

·**auf|kratzen** vt [h] *to scratch up* ‖ (Wolle) *to card* | ⟨fig⟩ jdn ~ *to cheer a p up* → aufgekratzt

·**auf|kräuseln** vt [h] *to curl* (*up*)

·**auf|kreischen** vi [h] *to shriek* od *scream out*

·**auf|krempeln** vt [h] (Hose) *to roll up, to turn up* ‖ (Ärmel) *to tuck up* ·**auf|krempen** vt [h] (Hutrand) *to turn up*

·**auf|kreuzen** vt/i **1.** vt [h] ⟨bot⟩ *to improve by crossing*; ⟨zoo⟩ . . *by cross-breeding* **2.** vi [s] ⟨mar⟩ *to cruise up, to heave in sight* ⟨a. fig⟩; ⟨fig⟩ (P) *to turn* od *show up*

°·**auf|kriegen** vt [h] = aufbekommen

·**auf|kündigen** vt [h] (etw) = kündigen ‖ jdm die Freundschaft ~ *to break with a p, to renounce a p's friendship* ‖ jdm den Gehorsam ~ *to refuse a p one's obedience* ‖ ·**Aufkündigung** f ~/~en = Kündigung

·**Aufkunft** f ~/⁓̈e = Aufkommen

·**auf|lachen** vi [h] *to give a laugh; to burst out laughing*; laut ~ *to give a loud laugh, to give a shout of laughter; to laugh outright*

·**Aufladegebühr** f *loading* (od *lading*)*-charges* [pl] ·**Aufladekosten** [pl] *loading-costs* [pl]

·**auf|laden I.** vt [h] **1.** (Holz, Heu) *to lade, to load* **2.** jdm etw ~ *to burden a p with a th* | ⟨übtr⟩ *to burden* (od *charge, saddle*) *a p with a th, to saddle a th* (*up*)*on a p* | ⟨el⟩ *to charge* (*a battery*) | sich [dat] etw ~ *to saddle o.s. with a th*; ich kann mir nicht mehr Verpflichtungen ~ *I can't be saddled with more obligations* **II.** vi [h] (das Schiff) ladet auf [abs] *is taking in cargo* **III.** ⁓ n ⟨aero⟩ (mit Bomben) *bombing up*

·**Auflader** m ~s/~ *loader; packer; porter*

·**Aufladung** f ~/~en **1.** *raising of a dike by sand-bags* **2.** ⟨mot⟩ hohe ~ *high degree of boost*

·**Auflage** f ~/~n **1.** [abstr] ⟨jur⟩ *condition obligatory on donee; testamentary burden*

2. †(Steuer) *impost, tax* **3.** *edition* (*of a book*); *impression*; verbesserte u vermehrte ~ *revised and enlarged edition* ‖ wie stark ist die erste ~? *what size* (od *how big*) *is the first edition*? das Buch hat 6 ~n erlebt *the book has gone through six editions* ‖ die ~ wird wahrscheinlich rasch vergriffen s *the edition is likely to be taken up* (od *out of print*) *rapidly* | *circulation* (*of a newspaper*) | ⟨fig⟩ *edition*, (: *he is only a weak e. of* ..); *version* **4.** ⟨cul⟩ *cold meats* [pl] **5.** ˣ*g*(*u*)*ild-meeting* **6.** ⟨arch & tech⟩ (Stütze) *rest*; Arm≗ *elbow rest*; Fuß≗ ⟨ski-ing⟩ *footplate* | **~nhöhe** f *circulation* (bes v Zeitungen etc)

·**Auflager** n ~s/~ ⟨arch⟩ *support*; (of a bridge, dike) *bearing*; *impost* (of an arch), → Kämpfer ·**Auflagerung** f ~/~en ⟨geol⟩ übergreifende ~ *transgression*

·**auflandig** a (*wind*) *blowing from the sea*; ~er Wind *sea-breeze*

·**Auflandung** f ~/~en = Anschwemmung

·**auf|lassen** vt [h] **I.** (Ruhe) **1.** °(Tür) *to leave open*, → offen **2.** °(Hut) → aufbehalten **II.** (Bewegung) **3.** ⟨min, ind⟩ (Grube, Werk) *to shut down* ‖ (Geschäft liquidieren) *to close* (*business, shop, etc*) **4.** ⟨jur Ger⟩ ein Haus ~ *to convey a house formally to another* **5.** ⟨aero⟩ *to start* (*a plane*) ·**auflässig** a ⟨min⟩ *shut down* ·**Auflassung** f ~/~en **1.** ⟨min⟩ *shutting-down* **2.** ⟨jur Ger⟩ *formal conveyance* (*of property*, etc); (v Grundstücken) *surrender*

·**Auflau(e)rer** m ~s/~ *waylayer, lurker, spy*

·**auf|lauern** vi [h] jdm ~ *to lie in wait for a p, to waylay a p*

·**Auflauf** m ~(e)s/≗e **1.** *accumulation* (*of money*); ~ der Zinsen *increase of interest* **2.** *rush, crowd* ‖ *tumult*; (Volks≗) *uproar, riot*; e-n ~ verursachen *to kick up a row*; *to row*; ⟨jur⟩ *unlawful assembly* **3.** ⟨cul⟩ *soufflé, trifle*; Apfel≗ *flapjack* ‖ ~form [f] ⟨cul⟩ *Pyrex dish* (*trade mark*) ·**auf|laufen** vi/t **I.** vi [s] **1.** *to rise, to swell*; (Saat) *to spring up* **2.** (anwachsen) *to accumulate, to accrue*; *to increase*; *to run up* (z *to*); die Rückstände ~ l *to let the arrears run on*; -ge-e Zinsen [pl] *accrued interest* **3.** (of a ship) *to run aground* **4.** ⟨mil⟩ *to mass* **II.** vt [h] sich die Füße ~ *to walk one's feet sore* ‖ ⟨mil⟩ ~ (nachfolgender Kräfte) *jamming up of* .. | **~bremse** f *overrun*(*ning*) *brake*

·**Aufläufer** m ~s/~ ⟨mar⟩ *ordinary sailor* ‖ ⟨met⟩ *charger, feeder*

·**auf|leben** **1.** vi [s] (wieder ~) *to revive, to recover* **2.** ≗ n *revival, uprising* (*of a new spirit*)

·**auf|lecken** vt [h] *to lick up*; *to lap up*

·**auf|legen** vt [h] **1. a.** (etw) ⟨allg⟩ *to fit on*; *to lay, to put* (auf *on*); (Ziegel) *to put on*; (Tischtuch) *to lay*; noch ein Gedeck ~ *to lay another cover* ‖ ⟨tech⟩ (Riemen) *to ship*; (Schallplatte) *to put on*; ⟨telph⟩ (Hörer) *to replace* ‖ (ein Pflaster) *to apply*; (Farben) *to lay on*; (Schminke) *to put* od *lay on* ‖ e-m Pferd den Sattel ~ *to put the saddle on* (*to*) *a horse, to saddle a horse* ‖ den Ellbogen auf den Tisch ~, sich mit dem E. auf den Tisch ~ *to lean* od *rest one's elbow on the table* **b.** (ein Schiff) *to lay up* **c.** (Steuer) *to impose* (jdm *on a p*); (Strafe) *to inflict* (jdm *on a p*); → auferlegen **d.** ein Faß Bier ~ *to stand* (*o.s.*) (od *to have*) *a barrel of beer* **e.** ⟨cards⟩ die Karten ~ *to show one's hand* **2.** (öffentlich ~) (Zeitschriften) *to lay out* ‖ zum Verkauf ~ *to expose for sale* ‖ (e-e Anleihe) *to float*; e-e Liste zur Zeichnung ~ f. etw *to invite subscription to a th* **3.** (Buch) *to publish, print*; neu ~ *to reprint* ‖ → aufgelegt ·**Aufleger** m ~s/~ ⟨met⟩ *feeder* ·**Auflegung** f ~/~en *the laying on* (*of hands*) ‖ *application* (*of a plaster*) ‖ *the laying-up* (*of a ship*) | *imposition* (*of a tax*) ‖ *infliction* (*of a punishment*)

·**auf|lehnen** vt [h] **1.** (Ellbogen, Kopf) *to lean* od *rest* (auf *on*) **2. sich ~ a.** *to lean* od *rest* (auf *on*) **b.** (revoltieren) *to resist, to rebel* (gegen *against*); *to mutiny*; sich offen ~ *to go into open rebellion* (*against*) ‖ ⟨übtr⟩ (widersprechen) *to chafe, to kick*; *to surge* (gegen *against*); *to be opposed* (gegen jdn, etw *to a p, to a th*)

·**Auflehnung** f ~/~en *resistance, rebellion* (gegen *against*)

·**auf|leimen** vt [h] *to glue, stick* (auf *on, on to*)

·**auf|lesen** vt [h] *to pick up, to gather* ‖ (Ähren) *to glean* ‖ *to collect* | ⟨übtr⟩ (Krankheit) *to catch*; (jdn) *to pick up*

·**auf|leuchten** vi [h] *to flash* (*up*); (*of eyes*) *to light up*; Lichter leuchteten auf *lights flashed* od *sprang up* ‖ ⟨mot⟩ (*red*; *etc*) *to show, appear* ‖ jdn, jds Antlitz, Augen, Gesicht ~ l *to brighten a p's eyes, to light up a p's face*

·**Auflicht** n *incident light*; → Licht

·**auf|liegen** **I.** vi [h] **1.** (of a ship) *to lie up* (of periodicals, etc) *to be kept* od *taken in*; *to be available*; *to be laid out* ‖ zum Verkauf ~ (of books) *to be exposed for sale*; (Zeichnungsliste) *to be opened* **3.** jdm ~ → obliegen **4. sich ~** *to get sore from lying* **II.** ≗ n ⟨med⟩ *bed-sore*

·**auf|lockern** vt [h] *to loosen*; (Boden) *to scarify* ‖ (Fasern der Baumwolle etc) *to willow* ‖ (Gewebe) *to disaggregate* ‖ (Truppen) *to disperse* ·**Auflockerung** f *loosening* ‖ *disaggregation* | *abatement, flagging*; *beginning of dissolution* ‖ ⟨tact⟩ *dispersal* | ⟨übtr allg⟩ *easing*

·**auf|lodern** **1.** vi [s] *to blaze* od *flare up*; *to spring into a blaze, to burst into flames*; *to leap* (v *with*) **2.** ≗ n *blaze* (*of passion*)

·**auflösbar** a *dissoluble* (*marriage*); *solvable* (*problem*); nicht ~ *insoluble* (*substance*; *mystery*)

·**auf|lösen** **I.** vt [h] **A.** (**Knoten** etc) *to loose, unknit, unknot*; (Strickerei) *to unknit* ‖ *to undo, untie* | aufgelöst [a] *dishevelled* (*hair*) **B. 1.** (etw **in Flüssigkeit**) *to dissolve*; *to melt*; aufgelöst ⟨chem⟩ (*salts*) *in solution* ‖ in Tränen aufgelöst *dissolved in tears* **2.** ⟨chem & math⟩ *to resolve* (in *into*); etw in s-e Bestandteile ~ *to resolve a th into its component parts* ‖ ⟨mus⟩ (Dissonanz) *to resolve* | (**zerlegen**) *to break up* (in *into*); *to disintegrate, decompose*; ⟨a. gram⟩ *to analyse* ‖ ⟨rail⟩ (Zug) *to split up* **3.** (**Rätsel**) *to solve*, → erraten ‖ (Geheimnis) *to clear up* ‖ ⟨math⟩ Bruch *to reduce*, (Gleichung) *to solve*; **4. a.** ⟨übtr⟩ (Truppen, Organisation) *to disband*; ⟨aero⟩ (Verband) *to peal off* ‖ (Verlobung) *to break* (*off*) ‖ (Ehe) → lösen ‖ das Parlament ~ *to dissolve Parliament, to appeal* (od *go*) *to the country* ‖ (Versammlung) *to break up*; *to dissolve* ‖ ⟨bank⟩ (Konto) *to close*; ⟨com⟩ (Gesellschaft) *to wind up*; (Vertrag etc) *to cancel, annul*; (Landbesitz) *to split* od *break up* **b.** ⟨fig⟩ *to dissolve*; *to be disruptive* (od *subversive*) *of*; ~d wirken auf .. *to act as a dissolvent* (*up*)*on* **C. sich ~ 1.** *to dissolve, melt* (: *sugar melts in tea*) ‖ sich in Tränen ~ *to melt in*(*to*) *tears* **2.** (ein Ganzes) *to divide* (in *into*) ‖ ⟨chem⟩ *to disintegrate*; *decompose* **3.** das Problem löst sich auf in .. *the problem resolves itself into* .. **4.** ⟨übtr⟩ (of a meeting) *to dissolve, to break up*; *to split up*; (of a crowd) *to disperse*; (auf d. Flucht) *to scatter*; (of institutions) *to disintegrate* (z *to*); (schwinden) *to melt, to melt away* (in *into*); (v Nebel) *to dissipate*; sich in Wohlgefallen ~ *to smooth down, to end peacefully*; *to come to nothing* ‖ *to die* **II.** ≗ n *unknitting, unknotting*; *untying* ‖ ⟨rail⟩ *splitting-up* (*of trains*)

·**auflöslich** a = auflösbar ·**Auflösung** f ~/~en **1.** → Auflösen **2.** *breaking, dissolution* (*of a pact*) ‖ *disintegration, decomposition*; *desubstantiation* ‖ der ~ verfallen *to break up*; *collapse* ⟨a. fig⟩ ‖ ⟨chem, math & mus⟩ *resolution* (z *to*; in *into*) | ⟨chem⟩ (Lösung) *solution* **3.** ⟨math⟩ *solution* (*of an equation*); *reduction* (*of fractions*) ‖ *solu-*

tion (of a riddle) 4. ⟨übtr⟩ disbandment (of troops), ~ des Heeres demobilization ‖ dissolution (of Parliament) ‖ winding-up (of a company) ‖ cancellation (of a contract) 5. ⟨fig⟩ disintegration (of a state etc); inactivation; disruption | ⟨Lit⟩ dénouement | death, decease **~smittel** n dissolvent **~svermögen** n dissolving (⟨opt⟩ resolving) power **~szeichen** n ⟨mus⟩ natural

·auf|löten vt [h] to solder (auf on to)

·auf|machen I. vt [h] **1. (öffnen) a.** (Paket etc) to undo, to open; to unfasten ‖ (Knoten etc) untie, undo; (Korsett) unlace ‖ (Flasche) uncork; (Nuß) to crack ‖ die Augen ~ to open one's eyes, to keep one's eyes open; die Ohren ~ to listen with all one's ears, → spitzen **b.** [abs] ich werde ~ (sc die Tür) I shall open (od answer) the door od answer the bell; jdm ~ to open to a p **2. (anbringen)** (Vorhänge etc) to put up; (Schirm) to put up **3. (zurechtmachen)** ⟨mst com⟩ to arrange; (Bücher) to make up; (Saldo) to state; to calculate; (Rechnung) to make out; (Konto) to open ‖ die Havariekosten ~ to adjust the average ‖ Dampf ~ to get up steam | e–n Prozeß tendenziös ~ to cook a trial; to get up a trial tendentiously; °mach k–n Laden auf! don't make a fuss about it ‖ (Ereignis) filmdramatisch ~ to feature **4. sich ~ a.** to prepare to start; to set out (nach for; z tun to do), to make for (N.); sich auf u davon m to decamp, → ausreißen **b.** (of the wind) to rise, to spring up **c.** ⟨cosm⟩ to make up **II.** ≈ n **1.** undoing, opening **2.** putting-up (of an umbrella)

·Aufmachung f ~/~en **1.** → Aufmachen **2.** ⟨com⟩ making-up (of books); statement (of account) ‖ adjustment (of average) **3.** ⟨com⟩ finish, form, package, -ging; (attractive) get-up ‖ (Kleidung) get-up ‖ ⟨Am⟩ build-up; Wert der ~ display value **4.** ⟨theat⟩ (of actors) make up ‖ get-up, staging; ⟨theat⟩ hohle sentimentale ~ ⟨sl⟩ hokum | ⟨übtr⟩ display; show; window-dressing; ⟨Am sl⟩ stunt ‖ etw mit gr ~ wiedergeben to make much play with a th; to give great prominence to a th; (of newspapers) in gr ~ berichten to report in flaring headlines (about)

·Aufmarsch m ~(e)s/≈e ⟨mil⟩ build-up, draw-up; march past, march; parade ‖ ~ in Linien deploy, deployment ‖ (im Kriege) the drawing up of the forces in battle array ‖ ⟨tact⟩ concentration | ⟨übtr⟩ parade; stattlicher ~ array **~gebiet** n ⟨tact⟩ deployment zone; assembly od concentration area **~raum** m ⟨tact⟩ marshalling area **·auf|marschieren** vi [s] **1.** ⟨mil⟩ to march (in procession); to form into line ‖ aus geschlossener Kolonne) to deploy; in Parade ~ to line up on parade; to parade | ⟨übtr⟩ to come forward (to do); to line up (z for) **2.** (Truppen) ~ l ⟨mil⟩ to array; to draw up; to deploy; in Parade ~ l to parade; ~ & ~ l to assemble in concentration area | ⟨übtr⟩ to bring to bear, to bring into play; to display; Kräfte ~ l to array forces (against a p)

·Aufmaß- ~buch n ⟨for⟩ tally book

·auf|merken vi [h] to spring to attention; to attend, mark, mind; ⟨Am⟩ to sit up and take notice

·aufmerksam 1. a attentive (auf to); mindful, thoughtful, observant (auf of); alert; wide-awake ‖ ich wurde plötzlich ~ I became all attention; plötzlich ~ w ⟨Am⟩ to sit up and take notice ‖ jdn ~ m auf to call a p's attention to (a th); er wurde durch ihn ~ he got his lead from him | **(höflich)** attentive, civil; kind, obliging **2.** adv attentively; ~ zuhören to be all ears, to listen with all one's ears **≈keit** f ~/~en attention, attentiveness (auf to) ‖ gespannte ~ fierce attention ‖ ~ erregen to attract attention ‖ jds ~ fesseln to arrest (od hold, rivet) a p's a., to engage a p's mind ‖ die (jds) ~ lenken auf to draw od call (a p's) attention to (a th) ‖ s–e ~ richten auf to focus one's attention on a th ‖ e–r S ~ schenken to pay (od give) attention to a th ‖ jds ~ verlangen to challenge od claim a p's att. ‖ e–r S die sorgsamste ~ zuwenden to give a th one's very careful consideration | (Höflichkeit) attention

°**·auf|möbeln** vt [h] jdn ~ to cheer a p up

°**·auf|mucken** vi [h] to kick, chafe; revolt (gegen against)

·Aufmunterer m ~s/~ encourager **·auf|muntern** vt [h] (jdn) to cheer (up); to encourage, to animate; to buck up ‖ (ermuntern) to rally (mit with); to pat a p on the back; to rouse (zu to) **·Aufmunterung** f ~/~en encouragement (zu to) ‖ impulse; incitement (zu to)

°**·auf|mutzen** vt [h] jdm etw ~ to reproach a p with a th, to find fault with a p od to rebuke a p for a th

·auf|nageln vt [h] to nail (auf on, upon)

·Aufnäharbeit f (Stickerei) appliqué; appliqué-work; embroidery on a groundwork **·auf|nähen** vt [h] **1.** to sew (auf on) **2.** (kürzer m) (Kleid) to tuck **3.** (Zwirn) to use up in sewing **·Aufnäher** m ~s/~ (Falte am Kleid) tuck

·Aufnahme f ~/~n **A. (Aufnehmen)** lift, lifting ‖ ⟨el⟩ absorption **B. 1.** reception (of air, food) ‖ the taking in (of goods); ⟨Scot⟩ intake ‖ z ~ v Gerät to carry equipment **2. (Empfang)** reception (of a p, of a th); freundliche ~ welcome (e–s Buches to a book) ‖ günstige ~ e–s Gesuches favourable consideration of an application ‖ jdm e–e freundliche ~ bereiten to receive a p kindly; e–m Wechsel ~ bereiten to pay due honour to a bill ‖ gute (schlechte, geteilte) ~ finden to meet with (od to have) a good (bad, mixed) reception (bei jdm from a p) **3.** ~ jds **in e-n Klub** the admission of a p into (od to) a club; enrolment; entering ‖ ~ finden to be admitted (in to, into) **4.** ⟨biol⟩ assimilation **C.** ⟨übtr⟩ **1.** start, beginning (of a work); ~ e–s Inventars the making of an inventory; Bestands≈ stock-taking ‖ the drawing-up (of a report, etc) **2.** the taking-up (of capital); the taking-up od raising of a loan **3.** ⟨surv⟩ mapping-out; survey (of land) ‖ sketch **4.** ⟨phot⟩ the taking (of a photograph); exposure ‖ (Bild) photograph, ⟨fam⟩ photo; e–e ~ m to take a photograph ‖ Moment≈ snapshot ‖ ⟨film⟩ shot; ⟨arts⟩ view ‖ Luft≈ aerial view; ~n m von to take views of | ⟨film⟩ [abstr] shoot; ~! shoot! ‖ (Bild) shot; Groß≈, intime ~ close-up ‖ ~ m to shoot **5.** ⟨wir, etc⟩ the making (of a record); recording (of a song, etc) ‖ ⟨telv⟩ telerecording; der Hörbericht wurde als ~ gesendet the eye-witness account was relayed from a recording **D. (geistige ~)** apprehension, comprehension **E. (Gedeihen)** (etw) in ~ bringen to bring a th into vogue od fashion; to launch a th ‖ in ~ k to come into vogue (od fashion) ‖ in ~ s to be in vogue

·Aufnahme-, ~atelier n ⟨film⟩ studio **≈fähig** a admissible, eligible ‖ ⟨com⟩ (of the market) capable of absorption | receptive (f of, to), sensible (f to); nicht ~ unreceptive ‖ capacious (mind) **~fähigkeit** f ⟨com⟩ capacity for absorption | receptiveness, receptivity (f to) | absorptivity, absorbing power, → –vermögen ⟨comp⟩ amount (of data) that can be recorded **~flug** m ⟨aero fam⟩ smile-please run | rasche **~folge** f rapid sequence of photographs **~gebiet** n reception area (f Evakuierte) **~gebühr** f entrance (od admission; ⟨Am⟩ initiation) fee **~gerät** n ⟨phot & film⟩ camera | phonograph-recorder ‖ ⟨telph, wir⟩ recording equipment, ⟨fam⟩ telecord **~knopf** m recording button **~leistung** f ⟨el⟩ input **~leiter** m ⟨film⟩ director **~material** n ⟨phot⟩ negative material **~prüfung** f entrance examination; matriculation(-examination) **~raum** m ⟨wir⟩

(*radio*) *studio* **~schein** m ⟨univ⟩ *certificate of matriculation* **~stab** m *film unit* **~stelle** f *filing office* **~stellung** f ⟨mil⟩ *rallying position* **~-Übertragungswagen** m ⟨wir⟩ *television mobile unit* **~vermögen** n *storage capacity*; ⟨comp⟩ → -fähigkeit; **~willigkeit** f ⟨com⟩ *consumer acceptance*

·**auf|nehmen** vt/i [h] **I.** vt **A.** (**aufheben**) **1.** *to lift*; *to pick up*; *to collect*; (Hingeworfenes) *to recover* ‖ (jdn) *to gather up* (*in one's arms*) ‖ ⟨ten⟩ (Ball) (überm Boden zurückschlagen) *to whip up* ‖ Maschen ~ *to take up stitches*; die ersten Maschen ~ *to cast on stitches* | ([Schmutz vom] **Fußboden**) *to mop*; (Zimmer) *to dust*, *to do* **2.** (**Waffen**) *to take up*; den Handschuh ~ *to take* (od *pick*) *up the gauntlet*; den Kampf ~ *to take up the cudgels* (f *for*) | ⟨übtr⟩ **es ~ mit** jdm *to cope* od *to vie with*, *to try a fall with a p to challenge a p pretty closely*; *to be a match for a p*, *to match* od *rival a p* ‖ .. mit etw *to manage a th*, *to cope with a th* **B.** ⟨übtr⟩ **1.** (**etw**) **a.** *to take in*; *to include* (in *in*) ‖ (of a ship) (Wasser) *to ship* | *to raise* (*loans*) | e–e Karte kann Angaben ~ *information can be got on to a card* ⟨a. comp⟩ | (in sich ~) *to absorb*; *to assimilate*; *to imbibe* (*a th*); (**Eindrücke**) *to receive*; *to inventory*; (Gedanken) *to assimilate*; *to incorporate*; *to appropriate*; nach Gehör ~ *to pick up by ear* ‖ ⟨tech⟩ *to absorb* (*forces*) ‖ ⟨biol⟩ vollständig ~ *to resorb* **b.** (**annehmen**) *to receive* (mit Grausen *with horror*); mit Enttäuschung ~ *to greet* (*a th*) *with disappointment*; beifällig ~ *to approve of* (*a play*); gut (schlecht) aufgenommen w *to meet with a good* (*bad*) *reception*; mit gemischten Gefühlen aufgen. w (*of statements*) *to have a mixed press*; die Rede wurde kritisch aufgen. *the speech was accorded a critical reception* **c.** (**auffassen**) *to take in*; (etw) gut (übel) ~ *to take well* (*ill*); etw als Scherz ~ *to take a th as a joke* **2. a.** (jdn als **Gast**) *to receive* (*at a house*; in *into*; unter *among*); *to take in*; *to entertain*, *accommodate* ‖ (Flüchtlinge etc) *to absorb*, *take* **b.** (jdn als **Mitglied**) *to accept as member*, *to affiliate*; *to admit* (in *into*, *to*); *to enrol* (*in a society*) ‖ wieder in die Reihen e–s Regiments aufgen. w *to rejoin the ranks of a regiment*; sich ~ l in e–e Gesellschaft *to join a society*, *to become a member of a society* ‖ (Schüler) *to enter*; ~ l *to enter* (*at a school*) **C.** (**beginnen**) **1.** (Arbeit, Gespräch) wieder ~ *to resume*, *to take up* ‖ (Verhandlungen etc) *to enter into*, *to embark upon*; (Verbindung, Beziehungen) *to establish* (mit *with*) ‖ ⟨hunt⟩ die Fährte ~ *to find* (od *recover*) **2.** (**schriftlich**) in eine Liste ~ *to catalogue*; Bericht, Protokoll etc) *to draw up the scent* ‖ ⟨fam⟩ *to pick up* (*a message by phone*) ‖ (Telegramm, Diktat) *to take down* **3.** ⟨com⟩ (Geld) *to borrow* (bei jdm *of*, *from a p*); (Anleihe) *to raise*; (Kredit) *to contract* ‖ ein Inventar ~ *to draw up an inventory*; Bestand ~ *to take stock* **4.** ⟨surv⟩ (Gegend) *to map out*; *to survey* **5.** ⟨phot⟩ (jdn, etw) *to photograph* (*a p*, *a th*); *to take a picture of* (*a th*); *to take* (*a p*); sich gut ~ l *to take well* | ⟨film⟩ (Landschaft etc) *to shoot* | (Schallplatte) *to make* (*a record*); (Stimme, Lied) in e–n Phonographen ~ *to record* (*a voice*, *a song*); sich gut phonographisch ~ l *to record well* | ⟨tech⟩ → indizieren **II.** vi **1.** (T) *to become big with young* **2.** (of beast of prey) *to take to its food*

·**Aufnehmer** m *mop* ‖ ⟨tech⟩ (~ e–r Verbundmaschine) *receiver* ‖ (Putzlappen) *floor-cloth* **~presse** f ⟨agr⟩ *pick-up baler*

·**auf|nieten** vt [h] *to rivet* (auf *on*, *upon*)

·**auf|nötigen** vt [h] jdm etw ~ *to force a th upon a p* ‖ *to press* (*one's views*) *upon a p* ·**Aufnötigung** f *forcing*, *enforcement*

·**auf|notieren** vt [h] (etw) *to note*; *to note down*

·**auf|oktroyieren** → oktroyieren

·**auf|opfern** vt [h] sich ~ *to sacrifice o.s.* (f *for*)

·**aufopfernd 1.** a *devoted*; *loyal* **2.** adv *devotedly*

·**Aufopferung** f ~/~en *sacrifice*; Selbst≗ *self-sacrifice* ‖ *devotedness*, *faithfulness*

·**auf|packen** vt [h] jdm etw ~ = aufladen

·**auf|päppeln** vt [h] *to cosset up*

·**auf|passen** vi/t [h] **1.** vi *to attend*; *to be attentive*, *to pay attention*; *to mind* ‖ paß(t) auf! aufgepaßt! ~! *attend*! *attention*! *now listen*!; *take care*! *look out*!; paß mal ~ *look here*; passen Sie auf, es kommt e–e Stufe *mind the step*, *please*; passen Sie auf! (*you*) *mark my words*!; *mind this*!, *look here*! ‖ auf jdn ~ *to take care of*, *to look after a p* (: *mind the baby*!) ‖ gut, genau ~ *to look sharp*; wie ein Schießhund ~ *to watch like a hawk* (*to be on the alert*) | †jdm ~ = auflauern **2.** vt (e–n Hut) *to try on*; jdm e–n Hut ~ *to fit a hat on a p* (od *on a p's head*)

·**Aufpasser** m ~s/~ *watcher*; → Aufseher ‖ ⟨school⟩ *prefect*, *monitor* | *spy*

·**auf|peitschen** vt [h] (Wasser, Wellen) *to churn up*; *to agitate* ‖ ⟨übtr⟩ jds Blut ~ *to stir a p's blood*; (Nerven) *to stimulate* ‖ (Gefühle) *to work up*; (Leidenschaft) *to rouse*; *to whip up*

·**auf|pflanzen** vt [h] *to set up*; (Seitengewehr) *to fix* (: *fix bayonets*!) | °**sich ~** vor jdn *to plant o.s. in front of a p*

·**auf|pfropfen** vt [h] ⟨hort⟩ (Zweig) *to graft* (auf *on*) ·**auf|picken** vt [h] (of birds) *to pick*

·**auf|plätten** vt [h] *to iron out* ·**auf|platzen** vi [s] *to burst open*, *to burst*; *to crack*; *to split*

°·**auf|plumpsen** vi [s] *to fall heavily*, *to bump* (auf *on*)

·**auf|plustern** vt & vrefl [h] das Gefieder ~, sich ~ (of birds) *to ruffle one's feathers* ‖ (Haar) *to fluff* | ⟨fig⟩ = sich aufblähen

·**auf|pochen** vt/i [h] **1.** vt (etw) *to open by knocking* **2.** vi ⟨fig⟩ *to protest*

·**auf|polieren** vt [h] *to repolish*, *to polish up*, *to refurbish*

·**auf|polstern** vt [h] *to upholster*

·**auf|prägen** vt [h] (etw) *to imprint*, *to impress* (auf *on*) | ⟨fig⟩ e–r S den Stempel s–s Geistes ~ *to set one's stamp upon a th*

·**Aufprall** m ~s/ *collision*, *clash*, *impact*; *smash*, *crack-up* **~fläche** f ⟨phys⟩ *target area*

·**auf|prallen 1.** vi [s] (of balls) *to bounce*; *to bound* (auf *against*); *to rebound* ‖ ~ l *to bounce* (*a ball*) ‖ (of light) *to impinge* (auf [up]on) **2.** ≗ n *bounce*, *bound*; *rebound*, beim ~ *on the bound*; (Ball) beim ~ schlagen *to take* (*a ball*) *on the bound*; → Aufprall

·**auf|probieren** vt [h] (Hut) *to try on*

·**auf|protzen** vt [h] ⟨mil⟩ (Geschütz) *to limber* (*up*), *to mount*

·**auf|pumpen** vt [h] (Reifen) *to pump up*, *to inflate*, ein aufgepumpter Reifen *a pumped-up tyre*

·**Aufputsch- ~mittel** n ⟨sport⟩ *dope* **~pille** f *pep pill* ·**auf|putschen** vt [h] (Leute) *to stir* (*up*), *incite*, *instigate* ‖ ⟨sl⟩ (Nerven, jdn) *to pep up* ‖ ⟨sport⟩ *to dope*

·**Aufputz** m *finery*; *attire* ‖ ⟨übtr⟩ *get-up*, *make-up* ‖ ·**auf|putzen** vt [h] (jdn) *to bedizen*; *to dress up*; (Hut) *to trim* ‖ (Bild) ⟨Am⟩ *to slick up* | **sich ~** *to bedizen o.s.*, *to get o.s. up*, *to deck o.s. out*, *to array o.s.*

·**auf|quellen** vi/t **1.** vi [s] (of water etc) *to well* od *spring up* ‖ (of grain etc) *to rise*, *swell* **2.** vt ⟨cul⟩ (Trockengemüse) *to soak*

·**auf|raffen** vt [h] **1.** (etw) *to rake* od *snatch up*; *to pick up* | **sich ~** *to struggle to one's feet* ‖ ⟨fig⟩ *to rouse o.s.*; *to nerve o.s.*, *to brace* (od *screw*) *o.s. up* (z *to*; z tun *to do*); *to brace one's energies*; *to take heart*, *to pluck up courage*; *to pull o.s. together* (*for*); *to bestir o.s.* ‖ sich zu etw ~ *to exert o.s. to do a th*

·**auf|ragen** vi [h] *to rise*, *to tower*; *to jut*, *to*

stand out || drohend (*or* gewaltig) ~ *to loom large* ⟨a. übtr⟩ | (hoch) **~d** a *lofty, towering*

·**auf|rappeln** [vrefl] [h] sich ~ *to recover* || *to shake one's wits together* || sich v Boden ~ *to scramble to one's feet*

·**auf|rauchen** vt [h] *to finish (a cigar)*

·**auf|rauhen** vt [h] (Oberfläche) *to roughen* || (Tuch) *to nap*

·**auf|räumen I.** vt/i [h] **A.** vt **1.** (wegschaffen) *to remove, to clear* od *take away* **2.** (ordnen) *to put in order*; *to straighten*; *to clear* od *clean up*; (Zimmer) *to tidy (up)*; *to do (up)*; → einräumen **II.** vi **1.** ⟨übtr⟩ ~ unter der Bevölkerung (of diseases, etc) *to play havoc among the population*; *to decimate the population* **2.** mit etw (Ware etc) ~ ⟨com⟩ *to dispose of, to sell off a th* || ⟨übtr⟩ *to make* od *do away with a th*; *to make a clean sweep of a th*; mit e–m (herrschenden) Brauch ~ *to do away with* (od *to put an end to*) *a custom*, (*to break a precedent*) || → aufgeräumt **II.** ≗ n = ·**Aufräumung** f ~/en *removing*; *clearing-up*; ~sarbeiten [pl] *clearing-up operations* [pl] ·**Aufräumer** m ⟨met tech⟩ *reamer*

·**auf|rechnen** vt/i [h] **1.** vt (ausgleichen) *to set off* (gegen *against*) || (aufzählen) *to reckon* od *count up*; (Beträge) ⟨Am⟩ *to offset*; → anrechnen **2.** vi *to settle* (od *balance*) *accounts*

·**Aufrechnung** f ~/~en *compensation, set-off* | *balancing* (od *settlement*) *of accounts*

·**aufrecht** a **1.** ⟨eig⟩ [pred] *upright, erect* || ~ gehen *to walk upright*; ~ sitzen *to sit upright*; (etw) ~ hinstellen *to put (a th) on its end* || sich ~ setzen *to sit up*; sich ~ (hin)stellen *to stand up* || (jdn) ~ halten *to hold (a p) up, to uphold (a p)*; sich ~ halten *to hold o.s. up* || (of things) (etw) *to sustain* || sich ~ haltend *upright* || ~ stehend *upright* od *erect (figure)*; *vertical* **2.** ⟨übtr⟩ *upright, straight (fellow)* **~|erhalten** vt (Ordnung, Brauch etc) *to uphold*; *to maintain*; *to sustain*; *to support*; (Angebot) *to hold open* od *firm* || e–e Ansicht ~ *to stick* (od *adhere*) *to an opinion* || (jdn) *to hold up, to uphold, to support*; *to sustain* (: *hope sustained her*); jdn (durch Hoffnung etc) ~ *to buoy a p (by hope)* | **sich ~** *to hold up one's head, to keep up* **≗erhaltung** f ~/ *maintenance (of security)*; *support*

·**aufregbar** a *excitable* ·**auf|regen** vt [h] (Gefühle) *to stir up, to rouse* || (jdn) *to upset, to excite*; *to fluster, to flutter, to fret, to ruffle, to worry*, → ärgern || aufgeregt s *to be excited*; *to fume*; *to be on the fret*; ganz –ge–gt ⟨bes Am⟩ in a lather | **sich ~** = sich ärgern, *to get excited, to get worked up*; *to be upset, to fret o.s.*; *to fuss, to get fussed* (über *about*); *to chafe* (über *at*); *to care* (über *about*); (seelisch) *to worry (o.s.)* || ⟨sl⟩ *to get into* (od *to be in*) *a stew, to take on* || sich nicht ~ *not to bother (to do)*; reg dich nicht unnötig *or* vorher auf *never trouble, trouble till trouble troubles you* || °**tun** Sie sich nicht ~! ⟨fam⟩ *keep your shirt on!, don't fash yourself*

·**aufregend** a *stirring (times)* || *exciting*; *thrilling*; nicht gerade °~ *not really exciting* (Buch etc); ~er Moment *or* Vorgang *thrill* (: a *game full of thrills*); *hair-raising (trick)*

·**Aufregung** f ~/~en *agitation*; *excitement, flutter, fluster*; *racket*; ⟨Am a.⟩ *gale* || die ~ um das Gold *the gold racket* || *thrill (of a lover)* || *bustle*; *commotion, fussation, hurly-burly*; *discomposure, disconcertment*; *worry* (über *about*) || ⟨sl⟩ (gr ~) *stew* || aber d·arum (nur) k–e ~! *but don't let's get intense about it!* || in ~ s *to be put about*; in gr ~ s *to be in great agitation*; *to be in a great way* || ~en des Lebens *life's upsets*, (od *irritabilities, annoyances*), *the fret and fume of life* || jdn in ~ versetzen *to agitate* (od *to excite, fluster, flutter*) *a p*; *to put a p about* || vor ~ schwitzend ⟨bes Am⟩ *in a lather*

·**auf|reiben** vt [h] **1.** (Haut) *to rub sore, to gall* **2.** ⟨tech⟩ (Nietlöcher) *to ream*; *to open out* **3.** ⟨übtr⟩ (jdn) **a.** ⟨mil⟩ (Heer) *to decimate, to cut up* || (vertilgen) *to extirpate, destroy, ruin, kill* **b.** ⟨fig⟩ *to wear a p out, to exhaust a p* | **sich ~** *to wear o.s. out*; (vor Gram) *to fret one's life away, to worry o.s. to death* || sich gegenseitig ~ *to wear each other out*; *to ruin one another*

·**aufreibend** a ⟨fig⟩ *wearing (life), trying (job, time)*; *exhausting*; *sapping*; ~ f jdn *wearing to a p* || *harrassing, worrying*; ein ~er Tag *a gruelling day* ·**Aufreiber** m ⟨tech⟩ *broachrimer*

·**auf|reihen** vt [h] (Perlen) *to string, thread* || (Papiere) *to file* || (Stoff) *to gather*

·**auf|reißen** vt/i **I.** vt [h] **1.** *to tear*; (Paket etc) *to tear* (od *rip*) *open* | (Oberfläche) *to break*; (Straße) *to take up*; *to pull* od *tear up* | (of frost) (Hände) *to chap* || sich [dat] die Hände ~ *to tear one's hands* || unsere Stiefel waren aufgerissen vom Marsch *our boots were broken with the march* **2. a. (Tür)** *to throw* (od *fling*) *open* **b.** °die Augen ~ *to open one's eyes wide*; *to stare*; °Mund u Nase ~ *to gape* || °das Maul ~ *to open one's mouth wide*; *to swagger, to talk big*; ⟨sl⟩ *to buck* **3. (zeichnen)** *to sketch*; *to draw* **II.** vi [s] (of seam) *to burst*; (of wood) *to crack, to split*; *to give way*; → reißen vi

·**auf|reizen** vt [h] (jdn) *to exasperate*, → reizen || *to incite, instigate, rouse* (z *to*; *to do*); ⟨fam⟩ *to egg (a p) on* ·**aufreizend** a *provocative*; *inflammatory (speech)* || *hot (music)* ·**Aufreizung** f ~/~en *provocation*; *instigation, incitement* (z *to*)

·**auf|ribbeln** vt [h] (Strumpf) *to unravel*

·**auf|richten** vt [h] **1.** (Stein) *to set upright*; *to right*; *to set on end* || (Pfahl) *to erect*; *to plant* | (jdn) *to raise (a p from his knees)*; *to help* (od *lift*) *up* || (etw) wieder ~ *to right*; (Monarchie) *to restore* | → aufführen 1., aufstellen **2.** (einrichten) *to establish, to found* **3.** ⟨übtr⟩ (trösten) (jdn) *to comfort, to console*; *to encourage, to cheer up* **4. sich** ~ *to erect* (od *straighten*) *o.s.*; *to straighten*; (of ship) *to right* || sich in voller Höhe ~ *to draw o.s. up to one's full height*; sich wieder ~ *to right o.s.* || (im Sitzen) *to sit up*, sich im Bette ~ *to sit up in bed*; → kerzengerade | sich an jds Worten ~ *to take heart from a p's words*

·**aufrichtig** **1.** a *sincere (friend)*; *candid, ingenuous, open, outspoken*; *upright (fellow)* || *single (heart)*; *frank (look)*; *sincere (devotion), genuine (respect)*; *whole-hearted (support)* || um ~ gegen Sie zu s *to be frank with you* **2.** adv *sincerely*, Ihr ~ ergebener .. *Yours sincerely* .. || ~ gesagt *speaking frankly*; ≗**keit** f *sincerity, uprightness*; *genuineness, cando(u)r, candidness*; *frankness*; *singleness (of heart)*

·**Aufrichtung** f ~/~en *erection* || *establishment, foundation* | (innere) *comfort*; ⟨Am⟩ *uplift*

·**auf|riegeln** vt [h] (Tür) *to unbar, to unbolt*

·**Aufriß** m –risses/–risse ⟨arch⟩ *front, elevation*; *orthography* ⟨a tech⟩; *vertical section* || im ~ *in plan* || ⟨übtr⟩ *sketch, lay-out*; *graph (of a plot)*

·**auf|ritzen** vt [h] *to rip open*; (Haut) *to excoriate*; sich die Hand ~ *to scratch one's hand* || *to slit*

·**auf|rollen** vt [s] **1.** (zus–rollen) *to roll up* || *to clew up*; (Segel, Fahne) *to furl* || **sich ~** *to roll o.s.* **2.** ⟨mil⟩ den Gegner ~ *to roll up, to turn the enemy flank* **3.** (entfalten) *to unroll*; aufgerollt w *to unroll* **4.** (Gegenstand) *to broach*; (Frage) *to bring up, to raise*; *to open*; aufgerollt w (of subjects) *to come up* || → anschneiden, anzapfen

·**auf|rücken** vi [s] **1.** = aufmarschieren **2.** (vorrücken) *to advance*; *to close up* **3.** ⟨übtr⟩ er rückte zum Oberst auf *he was promoted (to be) colonel* od *to the rank of colonel*, .. z Vorsitzenden auf *he rose to be chairman* || in e–e höhere Stufe ~ *to move up to a higher grade* **4.** †jdm etw ~ = vorwerfen

·**Aufruf** m ~(e)s/~e **1.** (Aufschrei) *outcry, scream, shriek*; *shout* **2.** (öffentl. Aufforderung) **a.** *call* (zur Einheit *to unity*) ‖ *challenge, summons* (an jdn *to a p*); e–n ~ ergehen l an jdn *to call up, to summon a p*; *proclamation*; ~ an das Volk ⟨engl⟩ *appeal to the country* **b.** ⟨mil⟩ ~ des Jahrgangs 1913 *calling-up of the 1913 class* **3.** ⟨com⟩ (Ungültigkeitserklärung) *calling-in, invalidation* (*of bank-notes*) ‖ ⟨comp⟩ ~ in der Programmfolge *call-in* ·**auf|rufen** vt [h] **1.** e–n Schüler ~ *to call a boy's name*; *to call upon* (*to do*); *to ask*; einzeln beim Namen ~ *to call over by name* **2.** (behördlich) *to summon*; z Zeugen ~ *to summon* (*a p*) *as a witness* ‖ das Volk ~ ⟨engl⟩ *to appeal to the country* ‖ (Militär) *to call out* ‖ ⟨mil⟩ den Jahrgang 1913 ~ *to call up the 1913 class* (*for military service*) ‖ (Kräfte) *to call forth* **3.** ⟨com⟩ (Banknoten) *to call in*

·**Aufruhr** m ~(e)s/~e **1.** *agitation, commotion* (*of the waves*), *excitement* (*of feelings*) ‖ *convulsion, cataclysm* ‖ *turbulence, disturbance, unrest*; *tumult, uproar*, e–n ~ verursachen *to cause a disturbance* **2.** ⟨pol⟩ *trouble*; *commotion*, → Tumult; *upheaval*; *revolt* (in ~ *in r.*); *sedition*, (*up*)*rising, insurrection*; (Volks–) *riot, rebellion*; ⟨mil & nav⟩ *mutiny* ‖ in vollem ~ *up in arms* ‖ e–n ~ erregen *to raise a rebellion*; in ~ geraten *to riot, to revolt*; (Land) in ~ versetzen *to rouse* (*a country*) *to rebellion, to excite* (*a country*) *to revolt* **~akte** f, **~gesetz** n ⟨engl⟩ *the Riot Act* (*1719*) ‖ → Strafgesetzgebung **~stifter** m *instigator, agitator* ‖ → Aufrührer

·**auf|rühren** vt [h] **1.** (Bodensatz etc) *to stir* (*up*); *to agitate* ‖ (Gefühle etc) *to rouse up*; (Skandal) *to rake* od *rip up* | (Volk) *to agitate, to rouse to rebellion* **2.** ⟨übtr⟩ (e–e alte Geschichte) *to rake up*; (Erinnerungen) *to revive* ‖ (Unangenehmes) immer wieder ~ *to rip up* ·**Aufrührer** m ~s/~ *rebel, insurgent, resurgent*; *mutineer* ·**aufrührerisch** a *seditious, mutinous, rebellious*; [nur attr] *rebel* (*chief*) ‖ *turbulent* (*crowd*) ‖ ~er Geist *spirit of sedition*; → aufreizend ‖ ~ w *to revolt, to rebel*

·**auf|runden** vt [h] (Zahl) *to round off*; (Betrag) *to level* od *even up*, → abrunden

·**Aufrüst- ~position** f ⟨aero⟩ → Aufrüstungs– **~zeit** f (bei Arbeitsbeginn) *start-up time*

·**auf|rüsten** vt/i [h] **1.** vt (Flugzeug) *to rig* **2.** vi ⟨mil⟩ *to rearm* ‖ (Land wieder ~) *to remilitarize* ·**Aufrüstung** f ~/~en *scaffolding* | ⟨mil⟩ (*re*)*armament*; ~sprogramm *r. programme* **~sposition** f ⟨aero⟩ *rigging position*

·**auf|rütteln** vt [h] (jdn) aus dem Schlafe (etc) *to rouse* (*a p*) *from sleep*; *to make* (*a p*) *sit up* | ⟨übtr⟩ (jdn) *to arouse, to stir* (*up*), *to shake up*; *to rally*; *to waken* (z *to, into*); *to startle* (aus *out of*) ‖ jds Gedächtnis ~ *to jog a p's memory*; (Gewissen) *to stir* | **sich ~** *to shake off one's lethargy*; *to rouse one's timbers*; *to bestir* (od *rouse*) *o.s.*; sich zur Arbeit ~ *to shake o.s. into action* ·**Aufrütt(e)lung** f (geistige) *stir*

°**aufs** = auf das ‖ ~ beste *best*; *in the best possible way* ‖ ~ Geratewohl *at random*

·**auf|sacken** vt [h] (etw) *to take upon one's shoulders* ‖ °jdm etw ~ → aufbürden, auferlegen

·**Aufsage** f *notice, warning* ‖ *refusal* ‖ → Kampfansage

·**auf|sagen I.** vt [h] **1.** *to recite*; (Aufgaben) *to say, to repeat*; → hersagen **2.** (kündigen) jdm den Dienst ~ (of employees) *to give a p notice* (od *warning*) ‖ jdm den Gehorsam ~ *to refuse a p one's obedience* ‖ jdm die Freundschaft ~ *to break with a p, to cease friendly relations with a p* ‖ (Vertrag) *to abrogate* **II.** ≃ n *repetition*; *recital, recitation* ·**Aufsagung** f = Aufsage

·**auf|sammeln** vt [h] *to gather up, to pick up*; *to collect*

·**aufsässig** a *hostile, inimical* ‖ *obstinate, rebellious, refractory*; ~ w *to become restive, to rebel, to revolt* ‖ (jdm) ~ s ⟨fam⟩ *to sit on* (*a p*), *to nag at* (od *be on*) **≃keit** f *hostility* ‖ *obstinacy, restiveness*

·**Aufsatz** m ~es/≃e **A.** (**Gegenstand**) **1.** (Aufbau) *top, head-piece* (*of a mirror*, etc) ‖ (auf dem Tische) *centre-piece* ‖ Tafel≃ *epergne* [Fr] ‖ → Service **2.** (Orgelpfeife) *reed-pipe* **3.** ⟨mil⟩ (am Geschütz) *tangent-sight* (od *scale*); *telescopic sight*; ~ mit Rundblickfernrohr *gun sight* **4.** (am Pferde) *part between neck and trunk, withers* **B.** (**Abhandlung**) (Schularbeit) (*free*) *composition*; *essay*; ⟨Am a.⟩ *theme* | ⟨Lit⟩ (in der Zeitung) *article* ‖ (literarisch) *essay* ‖ vermischte ≃e [pl] *miscellanies* [pl] **~brett** n (e–r Kegelbahn) *starting-board* **~fernrohr** n *telescopic* (*etc*) *sight* **~höhe** f ⟨mil⟩ *elevation* **~platte** f ⟨mil⟩ *scale-plate* **~stange** f ⟨mil⟩ *bar of the tangent-scale, sight-bar* **~teilung** f range scale **~thema** n (in Schulen) *essay-subject, subject for a composition* **~trommel** f *elevation drum* **~winkel** m *tangent* od *quadrant elevation*

·**aufsätzig** a → aufsässig

·**auf|saugen** vt [h] *to suck up*; ⟨chem⟩ *to absorb*; ⟨biol⟩ *to resorb* ·**aufsaugend** a *absorbent*; *resorbent* ‖ ~er Stoff, ~es Mittel *absorbent*

·**Aufsaugung** f ~/ *absorption* ‖ ⟨biol⟩ *resorption*; erneute ~ *resorbence*

·**auf|scharren** vt [h] (Boden) *to scratch up*

·**auf|schauen** vi [h] *to look up* (v *from* [*a book*]; z jdm *to a p*); z Himmel ~ *to look up to heaven*

·**auf|schaufeln** vt [h] *to shovel up*

·**auf|schäumen 1.** vi [s] *to bubble, effervesce* ⟨a. übtr⟩ **2.** ≃ n *effervescence*

·**auf|scheuchen** vt [h] (Wild) *to startle, scare*

·**auf|scheuern** vt [h] sich [dat] die Haut ~ → aufreiben 1

·**auf|schichten** vt [h] *to pile up*; (Holz etc) *to stack*; → schichten

·**aufschiebbar** a *postponable, defer*(*r*)*able*; *admitting of delay* od *postponement*

·**auf|schieben** vt [h] **1.** (Tür) *to push* (od *shove*) *open* ‖ (Riegel) *to unbar, to unbolt* **2.** ⟨fig⟩ (Entscheidung etc) *to postpone, procrastinate*; *adjourn* ‖ *to delay, defer*; *to put off* (*a th*; auf [acc], bis *till*; z tun *doing*); (Zahlung) *to defer* (*payment*); **es läßt sich nicht** länger ~ *it admits of no delay* ‖ aufgeschoben ist nicht aufgehoben → aufheben 3. ·**aufschiebend** a *dilatory, etc*

·**Aufschiebung** f **1.** = Aufschub **2.** ⟨geol⟩ *stratified layer*

·**auf|schießen** vi/t **1.** vi [s] (of plants) *to shoot up, to spring* (*up*); *to sprout* ‖ (of flames) *to leap*; *to shoot up*; *to flare* od *blaze up* ‖ (of institutions, etc.) *to rise*; *to spring up* ‖ → aufgeschossen **2.** vt ⟨mar⟩ (Tau) *to coil*

·**Aufschlag** m ~(e)s/≃e **1. a.** *striking* (auf *on, upon*) ‖ (of water) *dash*; *lap* (gegen *against*) ‖ (of a bullet) *impact, ricochet* ‖ *fall* (*of shot*) ‖ ⟨crick⟩ (~stelle) *pitch* **b.** ⟨ten⟩ *service*; Art des ~s *serve*; ~ v unten *underarm service*; den ~ h *to serve* ‖ Spieler, der den ~ hat *server* **2.** (Öffnen) *opening* (*of the eyes*), *raising* **3.** (an Kleidung) *revers*; Ärmel≃ *cuff*; Rock≃ *lapel* ‖ ⟨mil⟩ [mst pl] ≃e *facings* [pl] ≃e auf e–n Rock setzen *to face a coat* **4.** ⟨com⟩ (Preis≃) *rise in price, advance* (auf *on*); *additional charge, surcharge*; *excess* (od *extra*) *charge*; ⟨Am a.⟩ *mark-up* ‖ ein ~ v 3 Schilling an *additional 3 shillings* ‖ Steuer≃ *additional duty* (auf *on*); *surtax* **5.** ⟨hort⟩ *young growth*; *seedlings* [pl] **~beobachtung** f *burst spotting* **~detonation** f *graze burst* **~feld** n ⟨ten⟩ *service-court* **~geschwindigkeit** f (a. Rakete) *impact velocity* **~linie** f ⟨ten⟩ *service-line* **~schießen** n *impact fire*

~zünder m (Az) ⟨mil⟩ *percussion* od *contact fuse, direct action fuse*; empfindlicher ~ *graze fuse*; ~ mit Verzögerung (m. V.) *delay(ed) f.*
·**auf|schlagen** vt/i **I.** vt [h] **A. 1.** *(Kiste) *to break open* ‖ (Ei) *to break (in a glass)*; (Nuß) *to crack* | jdm den Kopf ~ *to break a p's head*; sich den K. ~ *to bash one's head* ‖ ⟨tech⟩ (Halbzeug mahlen) *to break* **2.** (Buch) *to open*; *to unfold*; (Seite) *to turn up*, ich schlug S 30 auf *I opened at page 30*; (Stelle, Wort) *to look up* **3.** ⟨fig⟩ eine Lache ~ *to give a laugh, to burst out laughing* **B. 1.** (Ärmel, Hose) *to turn* od *tuck up* ‖ (Augen) *to turn up*; *to raise, open*; (Karte) *to turn up* **2.** (Gerüst, Bude, Bett) *to put up* ‖ (Zelt) *to erect, pitch* ‖ sein Quartier ~ *to take up one's quarters* **II.** vi **1.** [s] *to bump, strike, thump* (auf *on*); dumpf ~ *to thud (on)* ‖ (of water) *to dash* (auf *on*) ‖ (of bullet) wiederholt ~ *to ricochet*; (of balls) *to bounce, pitch* | ⟨ten⟩ *to serve* | ⟨aero⟩ *to hit ground* **2.** [s] (of doors) *to open* (nach außen *outwards*) | ich schlug auf [sc] (das Buch) *I opened* **3.** [s] ⟨übtr⟩ (of flames) → aufschießen **4.** [h] ⟨com⟩ er schlägt (mit dem Preise) auf *he raises the price* ‖ der Preis des Tabaks schlägt auf *tobacco rises in price*
·**Aufschlagen** n *opening* | *looking up* | *putting up* | ⟨ten⟩ *serve*
·**Aufschlämmung** f ~/~en = Auflandung
·**Aufschlepphelling** f ⟨mar⟩ *hauling-up slip*
·**auf|schließen** vt/i [h] **I.** vt **1.** (öffnen) (Tür etc) *to unlock, open*; das Haus (die Tür) selbst ~ *to let o.s. in (with one's key)* **2.** ⟨übtr⟩ **a.** (Grube, Land) *to develop, to open up*; ⟨min⟩ *to open (by blasting)*; (neuen Markt) *to open up* **b.** *to disintegrate*; ⟨chem⟩ *to render soluble* ‖ (Nahrung) *to break up*; *to render useful* **3.** ⟨fig⟩ *to reveal, to disclose, to unfold*; (Herz etc) *to unlock, open*; **sich ~** *to unfold, to open*; sich jdm ~ *to open one's heart, to unbosom o.s. to a p* ‖ → aufgeschlossen **II.** vi ⟨mil⟩ (aufrücken) *to close ranks, to close up* ·**Aufschließen** n *unlocking, opening* | *opening-up* ‖ → Aufschluß
·**auf|schlitzen** vt [h] *to slit (open), to rip open* od *up*; *to unrip*; (Gewand) *to slash (open)* ‖ (den Bauch) *to rip* (od *slit*) *open*; jds Bauch ~ *to disembowel a p*; jds Kehle ~ *to slit a p's throat*
·**auf|schluchzen** vi [h] *to give a loud sob, to sob loud*
·**Aufschluß** m, –schlusses/–schlüsse **1.** → Aufschließen **2.** ⟨geol⟩ [abstr] *exposure*; ⟨min⟩ [konkr] *open lode* **3.** ⟨fig⟩ *disclosure, explanation*; *elucidation* (über *of*); ~, –schlüsse *information* (über *about, on*); lichtvolle –schlüsse [pl] *sidelights* (über *on*); → Auskunft ‖ ~ geben über etw *to explain a th*; *to give information about a th*; –schlüsse geben (v S) *to give messages*; dies gibt ~ über s–n Charakter *this gives a clue to his ch.* ‖ sich [dat] ~ verschaffen über etw *to inform o.s. of* (od *about*) *a th* **~arbeiten** f pl ⟨min⟩ *prospecting* **≈reich** a *instructive, informatory, informative*; *informing (paper, writer)*; *revealing*; *illuminating* (: *it is i. to read*) ‖ [pred] *telling one much*
·**auf|schlüsseln** vt [h] *to break down, to arrange (in groups, etc)* ·**Aufschlüsselung** f ~/~en *breakdown*
·**auf|schmeißen** vt → aufgeschmissen
·**auf|schmieren** vt [h] (Butter) *to smear, spread* (auf *on*) ‖ (Brot) *to butter* ‖ → hinschmieren
·**auf|schnallen** vt [h] **1.** (etw) *to buckle* (auf *on to*); (Koffer) *to buckle on* **2.** (abschnallen) *to unbuckle, unstrap*
·**auf|schnappen** vt [h] **1.** (of dogs) etw *to catch*; *to snap up* | ⟨übtr⟩ e–e Nachricht ~ *to pick up a piece of news* **2.** die Tür ist aufgeschnappt *the door has flown open*
·**Aufschneidemaschine** f (f Fleisch) *(meat-) cutting-machine*; *slicer*; → –schnitt–
·**auf|schneiden** **I.** vt/i [h] **1.** vt **a.** (etw) *to cut open*; (Haut) ⟨Am⟩ *to snip open* ‖ jdm die Kehle ~ *to slit a p's throat* ‖ ⟨med⟩ jds Leib ~ *to cut a p open* | (Knoten) *to cut*; *to slash* ‖ (Brief) *to slit open* ‖ ein Buch ~ *to cut the leaves of a book* **b.** (zum Essen ~): (Fleisch) *to carve*; Braten ~ *to cut* od *slice up a joint* ‖ *to split* (scones) **2.** vi *exaggerate*; *to bounce, brag, rodomontade, swagger*, ⟨sl⟩ *swank*; *to talk big, to buck*; *to come it strong*; stark (⟨hum⟩ gelinde) ~ *to pitch it too strong*; (flunkern) *to draw the long bow, to long-bow*; das ist gewaltig aufgeschnitten! ⟨sl⟩ *what a stretcher*! er schneidet nicht auf *he has no side* **II.** ≈ n *cutting (open)* = Aufschneiderei
·**Aufschneider** m ~s/~ ⟨fig⟩ *bouncer, boaster, braggart, braggadocio*; *swaggerer* ‖ *humbug*
·**Aufschneider·ei** f ~/~en ⟨fig⟩ *bounce, bouncer, brag, boast, swagger, rodomontade* ‖ *blague* (Fr); *bombast*; *claptrap*; *yarn* ‖ ⟨sl⟩ *stretcher, swank*; ⟨Am fam⟩ *splurge* → angeben II. 2.
·**auf|schnellen** vi [s] *to flip*; ~ l *to flip* ‖ (of doors) *to fly open*
·**Aufschnitt** m ~(e)s/~e n **1.** *cut, slit* ‖ (an Orgelpfeife) *mouth* **2.** (Aufgeschnittenes) kalter ~ *slices* [pl] *of mixed cold meat*; *cold cut* **~maschine** f *slicer*; → –schneide–
·**auf|schnüren** vt [h] **1.** *to fasten with a cord* (auf *on to*); (Koffer) *to cord up* **2.** (lösen); (Schuhe) *to unlace*; *to untie*
·**auf|schobern** vt [h] ⟨agr⟩ (Korn) *to pile* (od *put*) *up in stacks* od *cocks, to stack*; (Heu) *to cock*
·**auf|schöpfen** vt [h] *to scoop up*; *to ladle*
·**auf|schottern** vt [h] *to coat (a road) with broken stones* ·**Aufschotterung** ~/~en *coating* ..
·**auf|schrauben** vt [h] **1.** (etw) *to screw on*; *to screw* (auf *on to*) ‖ (hochschrauben) *to screw up* **2.** (losschrauben) *to unscrew* ‖ **sich** ~ l *to unscrew*
·**auf|schrecken** vi/t **1.** vi [s] *to start* (bei *at*); *to be startled* **2.** vt [h] (jdn) *to rouse* (aus dem Bett *from his bed*); → aufjagen ‖ *to frighten up, to startle*; *to scare*; ⟨Am⟩ *to throw a scare into (a p)* ‖ (Wild) *to start*; → schrecken
·**Aufschrei** m, ~(e)s/~e *outcry*; (gellender) *scream, screech, shriek, yell* ‖ ⟨übtr⟩ ~ der Entrüstung *outcry* (gegen *against*)
·**auf|schreiben** vt [h] **1. (etw)** *to write, take*, ⟨Am fam⟩ *put .. down to note (down), to make* od *take a note of (a th)* | ×(in Rechnung stellen) *to put to a p's account* **2. (jdn) a.** (vormerken) *to book, to enter* **b.** jdn ~ (of policeman) *to take a p's name* ‖ ⟨mil⟩ ~! *take his name*! **3. (Tinte)** *to use up*
·**auf|schreien** vi [h] *to give a cry, to cry loud*; *to scream to shriek*; fast ~d *with almost a shriek*
·**Aufschrift** f ~/~en (auf Denkmälern etc) *inscription*; *epigraph*; (auf Gräbern) *epitaph* ‖ die ~ tragen *to be inscribed*; (Brief≈ etc) *address, direction*; → Adresse | (Überschrift) *heading, title* | (Etikett) *label, ticket*
·**Aufschub** m ~(e)s/ *deferring, delay*; *postponement*; *procrastination*; ⟨parl⟩ *adjournment* ‖ die S leidet *or* duldet k–n ~ *the matter brooks* (od *admits of*) *no delay*; ohne ~ *without delay* | ⟨jur⟩ (Straf≈, Vollstreckungs≈) *reprieve* | ⟨com⟩ (Frist) *respite*
·**auf|schürzen** vt [h] (Kleid) *to tuck up*; (Rock) *to kilt up* ‖ **sich ~** *to tuck up one's clothes*
·**auf|schütteln** vt [h] (Bett etc) *to shake up* ‖ → aufrütteln
·**auf|schütten** vt [h] *to pour, to throw* (auf *on, upon*) ‖ (aufspeichern) *to heap up, to store up* ‖ (Erde) *to fill up*; (Damm) *to raise, to construct* ‖ Kies ~ auf e–n Weg *to gravel a path*; → beschottern ·**Aufschüttung** f ⟨geol⟩ *deposit-*

(*ion*), *sediment* || (Speicherung) *piling-up*; *storing* || (*road*) *raising*; (Makadam≗) *macadamizing*

·**auf|schwänzen** vt ⟨com⟩ (aufkaufen) *to corner*

·**auf|schwatzen** vt [h] jdm etw ∼ *to coax* (od *talk*) *a p into buying* (od *taking*) *a th*; *to palm off, to foist a th on a p*; → anschmieren, aufhängen || → weismachen

·**aufschweißbar** a *weldable* ·**auf|schweißen** vt [h] ⟨tech⟩ *to weld* (auf *on, on to*)

·**auf|schwellen** vi/t **1.** vi [s] *to swell* (*up*); *to tumefy* || (of river) *to rise, to swell* || (of sail) *to draw out, to swell* || ⟨übtr⟩ *to increase*; *to surge up* **2.** vt [h] (etw) *to* (*cause to*) *swell*; *to distend*; (Früchte) *to plump* || (Segel) *to bag*; *to puff out* || ⟨übtr⟩ *to enlarge*

·**auf|schwemmen** vt [h] (den Leib) *to swell, bloat* || (Backen) *to plump* || → aufgeschwemmt || ⟨phys⟩ *to suspend* (*solid particles in a fluid medium*) || ·**Aufschwemmung** f ⟨phys⟩ *suspension* || ⟨geol⟩ *deposition*

·**auf|schwingen** [vrefl] [h] **sich** ∼ *to soar*; *to rise* || ⟨übtr⟩ *to soar* (z *to, into* [*the heights of*]); *to make one's way*; *to rise* (*to*) || ⟨fig⟩ sich ∼ zu etw *to brace o.s. up to a th*; *to work up to a th*; sich dazu ∼ z tun *to screw o.s. up to doing*; ich kann mich nicht ∼ *I cannot feel it in me* (*to do*) | ∼**d** a ⟨arch⟩ ∼er Bogen *upsweep*

·**Aufschwung** m ∼(e)s **1.** [pl ≗e] ⟨gym⟩ *upward circle* (am Reck *at the bar*) **2.** ⟨übtr⟩ *upward surge*; *recovery, revival*; *impetus*; *upswing* (des Handels *in the trade*); ⟨com⟩ wirtschaftlicher ∼ *economic expansion*; plötzlicher ∼ *boom, boost*; e–r S ∼ geben *to give a new stimulus* od *impulse to a th*; e–n ∼ nehmen *to receive an impetus, to advance*; *to boom*; *to take a turn for the better*; im ∼ begriffen *flourishing* **3.** ⟨fig⟩ (geistiger ∼) *rise, rising*; *flight* (*of fancy*); *enthusiasm*

·**auf|sehen 1.** vi [h] *to look up* (v *from*); *to turn up one's eyes* **2.** ≗ n *looking-up*

·**Aufsehen** n ∼s/ ⟨übtr & fig⟩ *fussation, stir, to-do, sensation*; *surprise* | ∼ **erregen** *to cut a dash*; *to make a to-do* od *stir*; gr ∼ err. *to make a furore, to cause* (od *create*) *a* (*great*) *sensation* || (*of novels* etc) *to make a noise* (*in the world*); *to make a splash* (*in society*); ihr Tanz erregte ∼ *her dance was a great success* || öffentliches ∼ err. *to create a public uproar*; peinliches ∼ err. *to cause embarrassment*; ∼ erregend → auffallen, ≗erregend || ∼ m = ∼ erregen; m Sie kein ∼! *don't make a fuss*! || um ∼ zu vermeiden *to avoid notice* ≗**erregend** a *sensational*; *stirring, thrilling* || *extraordinary, challenging* (*novel*) || ∼e Unternehmung *stunt*; ∼es Ereignis *sensation*

·**Aufseher** m ∼s/∼ *overseer, surveyor, supervisor*; *inspector, superintendent* || (Haus≗) *care-taker* || ⟨school⟩ (Schüler) *prefect, monitor* || (Arbeiter–) *gaffer*; *ganger*; *foreman* || jdn als ∼ h über Leute *to have a p over people* ∼**amt** n, ∼**stelle** f *inspectorship, surveyorship*

·**auf|seilen** ⟨mount⟩ *to rope up* vt/refl

·**auf|sein** vi [s] **1.** *to be up, to be out of bed*; sind Sie auf? *are you up*?; die ganze Nacht ∼ *to be up all nicht* **2.** (offen s) *to be open*

·**auf|setzen** vt/i [h] **I.** vt **A. 1.** (Stein etc) *to put* (od *set*) *up*; (Kegel) *to set up*; (Holz) ⟨for⟩ *to cord, stack* || (Stückgüter) *to palletize* **2.** (den Fuß) *to plant*; *to put down* **3.** (Hut etc) *to put on, to pop on, to don*; den Hut keck, schief ∼ *to cock one's hat* || (Brille) *to put on*; wieder ∼ *to resettle* || (Ring) *to pull on, to slip on* || (Flicken) *to put on* || (Wasser etc) *to put on* (*to boil*) || (Segel) *to hoist* || ein Stockwerk ∼ *to add another storey* | (Schiff) *to run aground* **4. sich** ∼ (im Bett) *to sit up* **B.** ⟨übtr⟩ **1. a.** jdm Hörner ∼ *to make a cuckold of a p* || e–r S die Krone ∼ *to crown a th*; allem die K. ∼d schrieb er .. *to crown all he wrote* ..; das setzt allem die K. auf! ⟨fam⟩ *that settles it, that's the limit, that takes the cake* || e–n Kopf ∼ *to be obstinate, to have one's own way* **b.** ⟨paint⟩ Lichter ∼ *to insert light places* **c.** (Miene) *to put on, to assume* **2.** (abfassen) (Brief etc) *to draw up*; (Kontrakt, Telegramm, Testament) *to draft* (*out*); *to compose*; (Rechnung) *to make out* (od *up*) **II.** vi **1.** ⟨aero⟩ (of aeroplanes) *to touch* (wassern) *splash down*; hart ∼ *to come down hard, to land with a bump* **2.** (of deer) *to get* od *grow new antlers* **3.** ⟨vet⟩ das Pferd setzt auf *the horse is a crib-biter* (od *is addicted to crib-biting*)

·**Aufsetzen** n *the putting-up, setting-up* | *putting-on* | *composition*; *drawing-up* (*of a letter*)

·**Aufsicht** f ∼/ *inspection, superintendence* (über *over*); *supervision* (über *of*) *control* (*of, over*) || *inspectorship*, Staats≗ *State inspectorship* (*of*) || (Bewachung) *surveillance*; unter ständiger ∼ *under surveillance* || die ∼ h *to be in charge* (über *of*); unter s–r ∼ h *to have under one's watchful eye* || die ∼ führen (*or* h) (bei schriftlichen Prüfungen) *to invigilate* || die ∼ führen (*or* h) über etw *to control, to superintend, to be in care* (od *control*) *of* (od *to*) *a th*; *to supervise a th*; .. über jdn *to have the care of a p* || unter polizeilicher ∼ stehen *to be under police supervision* ∼**sucher** m ⟨phot⟩ *reflector view finder*

·**Aufsichts-** ∼**beamte** m: der ∼ (ein ∼r) *controlling officer, inspector, supervisor, superintendent* || ⟨engl univ⟩ *Proctor*, ⟨sl⟩ *Prog*, Gehilfen [pl] des ∼n *Bull Dogs* [pl] ∼**behörde** f *controlling body, supervising authority, board of control* ∼**führende** m: der ∼ (bei schriftl. Prüfungen) *invigilator* || ≗er Herr, ≗e Dame (in Läden) *shop walker* ∼**führung** f *invigilation* ∼**personal** n *inspectoral staff* ∼**pflicht** f *care*; Vernachlässigung der ∼ ⟨jur⟩ *neglect of tutelage* ∼**rat** m ⟨com⟩ *supervisory board*; *Board of Trustees* (*supervising the directors* [Vorstand] *of a stock company*); Mitglied des ∼s *member of the B. of T.*

·**Aufsitz-** ∼**block,** ∼**(prell)stein** m *horse* od *mounting-stone* ∼**stange** f (f Vögel) *perch roost*

·**auf|sitzen I.** vi [h & s] **1.** (aufbleiben) *to sit up* **2.** (sich aufsetzen) *to sit up* (*in bed*) **3.** (aufsteigen) *to mount*; ⟨mil⟩ aufgesessen! *mount*! || jdn ∼ l *to give a p a hoist* (od *lift*) || (auf Lkw) *to entruck* **4.** (festsitzen) das Schiff sitzt auf *the ship has run aground* || (of birds) *to perch, to roost* **5.** jdn ∼ l *to deceive* (od *fool*) *a p, to take a p in*; *to leave a p in the lurch* **6.** ⟨mil⟩ das Ziel ∼ l *to aim low* (*down on the target*) (*to put the foresight below the object aimed at*) **7.** aufgesessen [adv] geführt *mounted* (*attack*) **II.** ≗ n *sitting-up* | *mounting*

·**auf|spalten** vt/i **1.** vt [h] *to split up* (in *into*), *to cleave* || (Menschheit) *to break up* **2.** vi [s] *to slpit, cleave*; *burst* || ⟨biol⟩ → Merkmal ·**Aufspaltung** f ⟨biol⟩ *segregation*

·**Aufspann-** ∼**dorn** m ⟨tech⟩ *mandrel, arbor* ∼**vorrichtung** f *holding device*; *mounting device*

·**auf|spannen** vt [h] (Werkstück) *to mount* (auf *on*); *to strain* (über *over*) || (Karte etc) *to mount* || ⟨Saite⟩ → aufziehen B. | (Zelt) *to pitch* || (Segel) *to spread*; mehr Segel ∼ *to clap on more canvas* || (Fächer) *to unfurl*; (Schirm) *to put up* || (un)–ge–nte Leinwand ⟨paint⟩ (*un*)*stretched canvas*

·**auf|sparen** vt [h] *to save, reserve*; *to lay up* (od *aside, by*), *to set aside* (f *for*)

·**auf|speichern** vt [h] (Getreide) *to store up*; (Waren) *to warehouse* || (Reichtümer) *to amass, accumulate*; *to hoard* od *treasure up* | (Energie, Wärme) *to store*; (Zorn) *to bottle up* || → (an)-sammeln ·**Aufspeicherung** f ∼/∼en *storing, storage* || *accumulation, hoarding* (*of riches*)

·**auf|speisen** vt [h] = aufessen

·**auf|sperren** vt [h] *to open wide*; (Fenster),

to throw open | °das Maul, den Mund ~ *to gape*; ⟨fig⟩ °Mund u Nase ~ *to be struck dumb* (*with*)
·**auf|spielen** vt/i [h] **1.** vt **a.** (Lied) *to strike up* **b. sich ~** *to give o.s. airs*; *to put on side* od *airs*; *to put on a show*; sich ~ mit s–n Kärften *to air one's powers* || sich ~ als .. *to set up for* ..; sich als gr Künstler ~ *to play the great artist* (vor jdm *in the eyes of a p*) || .. z s *to be* .. **2.** vi zum Tanz ~ *to play for a dance*; spiel auf! *strike up*!
·**auf|spießen** vt [h] (Fleisch zum Rösten) *to spit* || (Braten) *to skewer* || (Heu etc) *to fork* | (jdn) *to spit, pierce* (mit *with*); (Kopf) *to impale*
·**Aufsplitterung** f ~/~en *dissolution, splitting*
·**auf|sprengen** vt [h] **1.** (Tür) *to burst* (od *blast, throw*) *open* || *to burst* **2.** (Wasser) *to sprinkle* (auf *on*) || → sprengen
·**auf|sprießen** vi [s] *to germinate, shoot, sprout*; *to spring up* || ⟨fig⟩ *to arise*; *to develop*
·**auf|springen I.** vi [s] **1.** (hochspringen) *to spring* (od *jump, leap,* ⟨fam⟩ *bob*) *up*; *to spring* od *jump to one's feet* || (of a ball) *to bounce, bound* | auf e–n Omnibus ~ *to jump on to a bus* **2.** (sich öffnen) (of doors) *to fly* (od *burst, spring*) *open* || (of buds) *to burst* || aufgesprungene Hände *chapped hands* | (zerspringen) *to break, crack* **II.** ≗ n *bounce, bound* (*of a ball*) || *chapping* (*of hands*)
·**auf|sprossen 1.** vi [s] = aufsprießen **2.** ≗ n → Sprossen
·**auf|sprudeln** vi [s] *to rise in bubbles, to buble up*
·**auf|spulen** vt [h] ⟨tech⟩ *to wind up*; *to spool, reel*; (Garn) *to wind on to a reel*
·**auf|spüren** vt [h] ⟨hunt⟩ (Wild) *to hunt* od *nose out, to track* || (P) *to find out*; *to spot, track, trace* || (S) *to hunt up*; *to spot, trace*; *to nose* od *ferret out* || (Feind) ⟨mil⟩ *to locate*
·**auf|stacheln** vt [h] (Stier) *to goad* | ⟨fig⟩ (P) *to egg on*; *to goad*; *incite*; *stimulate* (z *to*; *to do*) || (Gefühle) *to rouse*; *to work up*
·**auf|stallen** vt [h] *to stall* (*cattle*)
·**auf|stampfen** vi [h] mit dem Fuß ~ *to stamp*; *to stamp* (*with*) *one's foot* (vor Wut *with rage*); wütend mit dem Fuß ~ *to stamp an angry foot* || (of horses) mit dem Huf ~ *to paw the ground*
·**Aufstand** m ~(e)s/≗e **1.** = Aufruhr 2. **2.** ⟨min⟩ *statement* **3.** (of a column) *base, pedestal*
·**aufständisch** a *insurrectionary, rebellious, seditious*; [pred] *in revolt*
·**Aufständische:** der ~ (ein ~r) ~n/~n *rebel, insurgent, resurgent*
·**auf|stapeln** vt [h] *to pile up*; (Holz) *to stack* || ⟨com⟩ *to store* (*up*); → aufspeichern ·**A-lung** f ~/~en *storage, hoarding*; *accumulation*
·**auf|stauen** vt [h] (Wasser) *to dam* od *stem up* || (Waren) *to pile up*; → verstauen | ⟨psych⟩ (Erregung) *to accumulate* | **sich ~** (of traffic) *to gather, concentrate*
·**auf|stechen** vt [h] **1.** *to pierce* od *prick open*; *to puncture* || (Geschwür) *to lance* || (Land) *to break* | (entdecken) *to spot, detect* **2.** (befestigen) (Kupferplatte) *to fix*
·**Aufsteck- ~dorn** m → -spanndorn **~filter** m, n ⟨phot⟩ *push-on filter* **~kamm** m *dressing-comb* **~schlüssel** m *box wrench*; *socket spanner* **~schuh** m ⟨phot⟩ *accessory shoe* ·**auf|stecken** vt [h] **1.** (hochstecken) (Haar etc) *to put up* | ⟨übtr⟩ jdm ein Licht ~ *to enlighten a p*, .. über etw *to bring* od *drive a th home to a p*; → aufklären | ⟨übtr⟩ (Miene) *to assume*; e–e neue Miene ~ *to put on a new face*; e–e Amtsmiene ~ *to put on a solemn air, to look as grave as a judge* **2.** °(aufgeben) *to give up*; die S ~ ⟨fam⟩ *to throw up the sponge* ·**Aufstecker** m (→ aufstecken 2.) ⟨racing⟩ *casual racer*
·**auf|stehen** vi **A.** [s] (sich erheben) **1.** *to get up, to rise*; (vom Sitz) *to rise to one's feet* || vom Tische ~ *to rise* || aus dem Bett ~ *to turn out of bed, to get up*; ~! *get up, rouse up*!; aufgestanden s *to be up*; mit dem linken Fuß zuerst ~ *to get out of bed the wrong side* **2.** (of a prophet) *to appear, to make one's appearance* **3.** ⟨übtr⟩ *to revolt, to mutiny* || ~ gegen *to make a stand against* || *to take up arms, to rise* (*against*); das Volk steht auf *the nation rises* **4.** (of rocks, etc.) *to rise, tower* **5.** (of birds) *to fly up, to rise* **B.** [h] (offen stehen) (of doors) *to be* od *stand open* **C.** [h] dieser Fuß des Tisches steht nicht auf *this foot is too short*; der Stuhl steht nur mit 3 Beinen auf *the chair has only 3 legs touching the ground* ·**Aufsteher** m *getter-up*
·**auf|steigen I.** vi [s] **1.** (zu Pferd steigen) *to mount* || (auf e–n Wagen etc) *to jump up* || ~ auf (. .) *to mount* (*a horse*); → (be)steigen **2.** (emporsteigen) *to ascend, to go up* (*to heaven*) || (of the sun etc) *to rise*; am Himmel ~ (of the moon) *to climb into the sky* || (of smoke; roads, etc) *to ascend, rise* || (of mist) *to lift* || (of aeroplane) *to take the air*; *to take off* (v *from*) || wärst (du) nicht aufgestiegen (⟨dial⟩ aufigstiagen), wärst nicht abgerutscht (⟨dial⟩ abigrutscht) *blessed are they that expect nothing, for they shall not be disappointed* | ⟨übtr⟩ ein Gewitter steigt auf *a storm is coming on* od *up* || eine glückliche Zeit stieg auf *a glad day downed* || (of events) *to emerge*; *to crop up*; drohend ~ *to loom* | e–e Röte stieg in ihrem Antlitz auf *her cheeks mantled with blushes*; *the blood flushed in her face*; die Tränen stiegen ihr auf *tears welled up to* od *in her eyes* || mir steigt ein Gedanke auf *an idea occurs to* (od *strikes*) *me*; *an idea crosses* (od *rushes into*) *my mind*; mir stieg ein Verdacht auf *I had a suspicion* (in bezug auf *of*; daß . . *that* . .) | (aufragen) *to rise, to tower* **3.** ⟨fig⟩ *to rise*; *to mount* (zur Macht *to power*); (aufrücken) *to advance, to graduate* (v . . z *from* . . *to*); → aufrücken 3. **II.** ≗ n *ascent, ascension* || ⟨fig⟩ *ascendant, upgrade*; im ~ begriffen s *to be in the ascendant* od *on the upgrade* ·**aufsteigend** a *rising* (*ground*); *ascending* (*branch*; *scale*) || ⟨astr⟩ *ascendant* | *approaching, coming* (*tears*) || nach u nach ~ *progressive* || Verwandter in ~er Linie *ascendant* | ⟨übtr⟩ auf dem ~en Ast s *to be on the upgrade*
·**auf|stellen** vt [h] **1.** (S) (aufrichten) (Denkmal) *to erect* || *to set* || (Tisch, Bett) *to set* (od *draw, put*) *up* || (Stühle) *to arrange*; der Reihe nach ~ *to range* || (Wagen auf Parkplatz) *to park* ⟨mot, a. mil⟩ | ⟨tech⟩ (montieren) *to install* (Gerät) *to erect, pitch*; (Maschine) *to mount*; (Apparat) *to fit up*; zum Notbehelf ~ *to rig* || (Falle) *to set* | zum Verkauf ~ *to expose for sale*; (Pflanzen bei Ausstellung) *to stage* **2. a.** (P) *to marshal* || (heimlich) *to plant* || ⟨mil⟩ (Einheit) *to organize*; (in Reihen) *to range* || (Soldaten, Wache) *to station, post*; (Truppen) *to activate, to muster*; *to array* || (Schulkinder) *to muster*; *to line up* || aufgestellt w gegen e–a *to be ranged against one another* **b. sich ~** *to take one's stand*; *to station o.s.*; *to range o.s.* (an . . entlang *along* [*a road*]); *to form up* (um *around*) || ⟨mil⟩ *to form* (*up*) (in e–r Linie *into a line*); sich in breiter Front ~ *to deploy* || ⟨a. sport⟩ *to line up* (: *he lined up beside me*) **3.** ⟨übtr⟩ (einrichten) **a.** (Heer) *to establish* **b.** (Übersicht) *to draw up*; (Liste, Rechnung) *to make out* (od *up*); die Bilanz ~ *to strike the balance* || (Lehrplan) *to plan* || (Richtlinien, Voranschlag) *to formulate*; *to work out* (*a plan*); *to draw up* (*a prospectus*) || (Programm) *to work out*; *to formulate* || *to specify* **c.** (Gesetze, Regeln, Grundsatz) *to lay down*; (Hypothese) *to erect, to establish*; (Lehre, Theorie) *to enunciate, to set up*; e–e Behauptung ~ *to make an assertion* || (Rekord) *to establish, to create* || (Kräfte etc) *to marshal* **4.** (Kandidaten) *to put* (od *set*) *up*; *to put forward*; jdn zur Wahl ~ *to nominate a p* (*for*) || ⟨Am⟩ *to slate*

(f, z *for*) || jdn als Spieler ~ *to field a p* | **sich** ~ l *to offer o.s. as a candidate* **5.** °~ *to undertake*; mit ihm ist nichts –zu– *there is no dealing with him*, → anfangen

·**Aufstellung** f ~/~en **1.** *erection*; *setting-up*, *putting-up* || *arrangement* || *mounting* (*of a machine*); *fitting-up* || *display* (*of goods*) **2.** *disposition*, *drawing-up* (*of troops*); *mustering*; *formation*; *line-up* || ~ nehmen = aufstellen 2. b. **3.** *establishment* || *drawing-up*; *working-out* || ⟨com⟩ *statement*; (genaue) *specification*; *return* (*of stocks*) **4.** ~ als Kandidat *candidature* || (~ f. die Wahl) *nomination* **~sbefehl** m ⟨mil⟩ *initial organization order* **~skosten** [pl] *cost of mounting* (od *fitting-up*) **~sort** m *site*

·**auf|stemmen** vt [h] **1.** (Kiste) *to force* (od *prize*, *prise*) *open*; *to open with a chisel* (od *crowbar*) **2.** den Ellbogen ~, **sich** mit dem E. ~ *to support o.s. on one's elbow*; . . ~ auf *to lean* (od *rest*) *one's elbow upon*

·**Aufstieg** m ~(e)s|~e **1.** (Aufsteigen) *ascent*, *climb* (*of a p*) || *ascent*, *climb* (*of a balloon*); ⟨Am⟩ *ascension*; *der* ~ auf den Berg *the climb up the mountain* | ⟨fig⟩ der ~ jds *the rise* (⟨Am⟩ *ascension*) *of a p* (zur Macht *to power*) || *upspring* (*of the trade*); im ~ begriffen s *to be on the upgrade*, ⟨fam⟩ *on the way up*; → Aufschwung || *improvement*, *advance*(*ment*) || ⟨demog⟩ *upward social mobility* **2.** (Steigung) *ascent*, *slope* (*of the road*) **3.** (Weg aufwärts) *ascent*; *steps* [pl] **~klasse** f ~/~n (für begabte Schüler) *class with rising facility* (*for talented boys*) **~sbahn** f ⟨rocket, a–n⟩ *path of ascent*; *climb* od *ascent path* **~smeßgerät** n ⟨aero⟩ *climb indicator* **~smöglichkeit** f ~/~en *rising facility* || *advancement opportunity* **~sstufe** f ⟨a–n⟩ *ascend stage*

°·**auf|stippen** vt [h] (Tunke) *to sop up* (*with bread*)

·**auf|stöbern** vt [h] (Wild) *to put up*, *to rouse*; *to start* || (P, S) *to discover*, *to find* od *ferret out*; *to dig up*, *to trace*; *to unearth*; *to rout* (*a p*) *out*

·**auf|stocken** vt [h] ⟨arch⟩ *to raise the height* (*of a building*); *to add a stor*(*e*)*y to* (*a house*) | ⟨übtr⟩ *to supplement*, *replenish* ⟨bes ins⟩; ⟨com⟩ *to raise*

·**auf|stöhnen** vi [h] laut ~ *to fetch* od *give a groan*

·**auf|stören** vt [h] (jdn) *to stir*, *disturb*; *to rouse up* || → aufschrecken, –jagen

·**Aufstoß** m ~es/~̈e **1.** (Aufprall) *impact* **2.** ⟨hunt⟩ *bait*, *lure*

·**auf|stoßen** **I.** vt/i **A.** vt [h] (Tür) *to push* od *kick* od *fling open*; *to push* | [abs] (°rülpsen) *to eruct*(*ate*); *belch* (*forth*) **B.** vi [s] **1.** (of ships) *to strike* (*on*) *a rock*; *to run aground* || ⟨übtr⟩ auf den Boden ~ *to touch the ground* **2.** Sekt stößt auf, nach Sekt stößt e–m auf *champagne produces flatus*, *proves flatulent* **3.** ⟨fig⟩ (of scruple) *to arise* | jdm .. *to meet with*, *to light on*, *to come across*, es sind mir mehrere Beispiele –ge– *I have come across* (od *noticed*) *several instances* **II.** ~̈ n *eructation*; *belching*, *belch*

·**auf|streben** vi [h] (of buildings) *to rise*, *to tower up* | ⟨fig⟩ *to aspire* (z *to*) ·**aufstrebend** a *towering* | ⟨fig⟩ *go-ahead*; *aspiring* (*classes*)

·**Aufstreich** m (bei Auktionen) = Zuschlag

·**auf|streichen** vt [h] (Farbe etc) *to lay on* || (Butter) *to spread* (auf *on*); dick ~ *to spread thick*

·**auf|streifen** vt [h] (Ärmel) *to turn* od *tuck up*

·**Aufstrich** m **1.** (beim Schreiben) *upstroke* || (bei der Geige) *up-bow* **2.** (auf Brot) *butter*, *jam*, etc *spread on bread*; (v Fleischpaste) *spread*, *paste*

·**Aufstrom** m ~(e)s/~̈e (Luft, Wasser) *upward current*, *up-current*

·**auf|stülpen** vt [h] **1.** (Ärmel) *to tuck* od *turn up* || aufgestülpte Nase *turned-up nose*, *snub nose* **2.** (Hut) *to pop on*; *to clap* (auf *on*)

·**auf|stützen** **1.** vt [h] die Arme ~, sich mit den Armen ~ *to lean* (od *support*, *rest*) *one's arms on the table* (etc) || (jdn) *to prop up* (*in bed*) **2.** ~̈ n *support* (*of the elbow*)

·**auf|suchen** **1.** vt [h] (P) *to seek* od *search out* || *to go* od *come to see* (*a p*); *to see*, *to call on* (*a p*); *to see* (*one's principal*); ⟨fam⟩ *to look* (*a p*) *up* || (Arzt) *to see*, *consult* | (S) *to seek* od *search out* || (Land, Ort etc) *to visit*; *to resort to* (*a place*) || (Buchstelle, Werk) *to look up* || (das Hospital) *to enter* **2.** ~̈ n *seeing*; *looking-up* || *consultation* (*of a doctor*) | *looking-up* (*of a word*); *visit* (e–s Ortes *to a place*) ·**Aufsuchung** f = Aufsuchen

·**auf|summen** vrefl [h] sich ~ *to accumulate*; *to run up*, ⟨fam⟩ *to tot up* (z *to*)

·**auf|tafeln** vt [h] *to dish up*

·**auf|takeln** **1.** vt [h] ⟨mar⟩ (Schiff) *to rig* | ⟨übtr⟩ (jdn) *to rig*, *to bedizen*, *to get up*, *to trick out* (od *up*) || **sich** ~ *to rig up*; *to bedizen o.s.* **2.** ~̈ n ⟨übtr⟩ *get-up*, ⟨fam⟩ *rig*

·**Auftakt** m ~es/~e ⟨mus & pros⟩ *pick-up*, *anacrusis* **2.** ⟨übtr⟩ *beginning* (z *of*); *prelude*, *prologue*, *preamble* (z *to*); *initial phase*; *curtain-raiser* (z *to*); den ~ bilden z etw *to be* od *form the prologue to a th* || als ~ *as a starter* od *curtain-raiser* ⟨a. fig⟩

·**auf|tanken** vt/i [h] ⟨mot, aero⟩ *to refuel*

·**auf|tauchen** **I.** vi [s] **1.** (of fish) (aus der Tiefe) *to rise*; (U-Boot) *to surface*; wieder ~ *to re-surface* **2.** ⟨übtr⟩ (v P) *to emerge* (aus *from*); *to come along*; (plötzlich) ⟨fam⟩ *to bob up*, *to pop up* od *in*; ⟨Am a.⟩ *to show up*; → aufkreuzen || (of events) *to turn up*, *to appear*, *to crop up*; (of feelings) *to arise* || aus dem Dunkel (drohend) ~ *to loom up* **II.** ~̈ n *emergence*; *appearance* || plötzliches ~ *burst* (*of landscape*)

·**auf|tauen** **I.** vi/t **1.** vi [s] **a.** *to thaw*; ~ l *to thaw* **b.** ⟨fig⟩ (v P) *to melt*, *thaw*; *expand*, *unbend*; *to become affable*, *to come out of one's shell*; ⟨Am sl⟩ *to loosen up*; sein Herz taute auf *his heart melted* **2.** vt [h] **a.** (Eis) *to thaw*; *to melt* || (Leitung) *to thaw* **b.** ⟨fig⟩ (jdn) *to thaw*, *melt*; *soften* **II.** ~̈ n *thaw*; *zum* ~ bringen *to thaw*, *melt* ·**Auftauvorrichtung** f *defroster*

·**auf|teilen** vt [h] *to divide*, *parcel*; *apportion* (in *into*); (Gebiet) *to partition* (zwischen *between*); (Gut) *to break up* || neu ~ *to repartition* || (Wohnung) *to convert*; e–e (in kl Wohnungen) aufgeteilte Villa *a converted villa* || (Zeit etc) *to map out* ·**Aufteilung** *partition* (*of a country*); *break-up* (*of a big estate*) **~skoeffizient** m ⟨demog⟩ *separation factor*

·**auf|tischen** vt/i [h] **1.** vt (Speise) *to dish* od *serve up*; jdm ein Mahl ~ *to serve a meal to a p*, *to treat a p to a meal* | ⟨übtr⟩ (Geschichte) *to dish up*; v neuem ~ *to rehash*, *to warm up* || *jdm* etw ~ *to entertain a p with a th* **2.** vi jdm reichlich ~ *to entertain* (od *feast*, *treat*) *a p lavishly*, *to do a p well* (od *grand*)

·**Auftrag** m ~(e)s/~̈e **1.** → Auftragen **2.** (Befehl, zugeteilte Aufgabe) **a.** *charge*, *command*, *commission*, *order*; *instruction* || Zahlungs~̈ *order* (an *to*) **b.** (Sendung) *task*; *mission* ⟨a. mil-aero⟩, ~ ausgeführt! *mission accomplished* **c.** (Botengang) *errand*, ~̈e besorgen *to go on* (od *to run*) *errands* **d.** **im** ~e jds *by order of a p*; *on behalf of a p*, *in a p's name*; für u im ~e v *for and on behalf of*; im ~e der Regierung *on behalf of the Government*; im ~e m–s Vaters teile ich Ihnen mit *my father has directed me to tell you* (*that* ..) **e.** e–n ~ **ausführen** *to discharge* (od *carry out*, *execute*) *a commission*, *to acquit o.s. of a task* || jdn mit e–m ~ betreuen *to charge a p with a mission* || den ~ erhalten od h *to be commanded*, *commissioned*, *directed*, *ordered* (*to do*) || ich habe vom Könige den ~ *I have it in command from the king* (*to do*) || e–n ~ erteilen *to give an order* (*for*) ⟨a. com⟩; e–n ~ nicht erteilen *to withhold an order*; jdm den ~ erteilen od *geben to commission* (od *to direct*) *a p* (*to do*) ‖ Bau e–s Schiffes (etc) in ~ geben *to give an order for* (*the building of*) *a ship* **3.** ⟨jur⟩ *mandate*; ⟨pol⟩ völkerrechtlicher ~ *mandate* ‖ ⟨jur⟩ *brief*; e–m Barrister den ~ erteilen *to brief a barrister* (*for*) **4.** ⟨com⟩ *order* (auf *for*); *indent*; → 2. e. | **im** ~e u f Rechnung *by order and for account*; **laut** ~ as *ordered*; auswärtige ~̈e *foreign orders* ‖ jdn mit –trägen beehren *to favour a p with orders* ‖ e–n ~ erteilen *to give an order*, ..über etw *to place an order for a th* (bei jdm *with a p*) ‖ e–n ~ hereinholen, werben *to canvass an order*, widerrufen *to countermand an order* **~bürste** f *smearing brush* **~geber** m *employer, principal* ‖ *customer, consignor*; *client, patron* **~nehmer** m *party receiving order*; *consignee, mandatary*; ⟨pol⟩ *mandatory* **~(s)-Nr.** f ⟨comp⟩ *jot No.* **~sbesatzungskosten** pl *mandatory expenditure* ‖ ~haushalt [m] *mand. budget* **~sbuch** n *order--book* **~serteilung** f *the placing of orders* ⟨bes com⟩; *assignment of a mission* od *task* ⟨bes mil⟩ **~̈sgemäß** adv *as ordered* **~svergabe** f ⟨com⟩ = ~serteilung **~walze** f ⟨typ⟩ *inking-roller*

·**auf|tragen I.** vt/i [h] **A.** vt **1. a.** (Speisen) *to serve up*; es ist aufgetragen *dinner* (etc) *is served* ‖ (Butter) *to spread* (auf *on*) **b.** (Farben) *to apply, to lay on*; dick ~ *to impaste*; (auf Palette) *to load*; ⟨typ⟩ (Buchdruckfarbe) *to distribute*; Farbe auf die Form ~ *to roll the form, to take ink* **2.** jdm etw ~ *to charge a p with a th*; jdm e–e Arbeit ~ *to set a p a task*; er trug mir Grüße an dich auf *he asked me to give you his regards* (od *to remember him to you*) ‖ jdm ~ z tun *to commission* (od *direct, order*) *a p to do* **3.** (Kleid etc) *to wear out* **B.** vi **1.** stark ~ ⟨übtr⟩ *to lay* od *spread it on thick, to lay it on with a trowel*; *to come it strong* ‖ ⟨Am⟩ *to put on thick* **2.** [nur 3. sg & pl] (of clothes) das Futter trägt auf *the lining makes the suit bulky* **II.** ~̈ n *serving-up* ‖ *laying-on* (*of colours*); dickes ~ der Farbe *impasto* [It] ‖ → Auftrag ·**auftragend** a *bulky* (*paper*)

·**Auftreff- ~geschwindigkeit** f *impact velocity* **~punkt** m ⟨mil⟩ *point of impact* **~winkel** m *angle of impact* **~wucht** f *ram effect*

·**auf|treffen** vi [s] → aufprallen

·**auf|treiben** vt/i **I.** vt [h] **1.** (Reifen) *to fasten* (auf *on upon* [*a cask*]) **2.** (hochtreiben) (of the wind) (Staub) *to whirl up*; *to send up whirling*; *to fling up* | (Wild) *to rouse, start* ‖ jdn aus dem Bett ~ *to rout a p out* **3.** (weiten) **a.** ⟨tech⟩ (Rohr etc) *to expand* ‖ (Ballon) *to distend*; *to inflate*; *to blow up, to puff out* **b.** (Teig) *to cause ..to rise* ‖ (Leib) *to* (*cause to*) *swell*; aufgetriebener Leib *inflated abdomen* **4.** ⟨fig⟩ (finden) (etw, jdn) *to find out, to trace*; *to hunt up*; *to get hold of, to pick up, to obtain* ‖ etw f sich ~ *to find a th*; Geld ~ ⟨sl⟩ *to rustle up money, to dig up the* (*necessary*) *funds, to raise the wind*; schwer -zu- *hard to get hold of* **II.** vi [s] (of ship) *to run aground*

·**auf|trennen** vt [h] (Naht) *to rip* (*up*), *unpick, unstitch*; *to take out stitches*; (Stiche) *to unrip*; (Strickarbeit) *to undo* ‖ (Knäuel, Gewebe) *to unravel* | **sich** ~ *to come undone*

·**auf|treten I.** vt/i **A.** vt/[h] (Tür mit dem Fuß) *to kick* (*a door*) *open* **B.** vi [s] **1. a.** (den Fuß setzen) *to tread, step*; *walk*; kräftig ~ *to stamp*; leise ~ *to walk gently*; mit der ganzen Sohle ~ *to walk on the whole sole* **b.** ⟨übtr⟩ *to proceed* ‖ *to behave, act* ‖ *to come up* (gegen *against*); energisch, fest ~ *to put one's foot down* (*against*), *to assert o.s.*; *to take drastic measures* (*against*); *to stand up* (f *for*) **2.** ⟨übtr⟩ **a.** ⟨theat⟩ als Schauspieler ~ *to tread the boards* ‖ (of actors) *to enter*; *to arrive on the scene*; *to appear* (*on the stage*); *to act, perform*: (*the actress performed yesterday*) ‖ Hamlet tritt auf *enter H.*; zum ersten Mal ~ *to make one's début* (od *first appearance*) **b.** öffentlich ~ *to appear in public*; *to perform* (vor *before*) **c.** *to appear, to come forward*; *to make one's appearance, to appear on the scene*; (of *features*, etc) *to peep out* ‖ anmaßend ~ *to be overbearing* → Name ‖ ~ als *to pose* (od *figure, posture*) *as*; als Zeuge ~ *to appear as a witness*; als Kläger ~ gegen jdn *to appear as plaintiff* ‖ *to happen* (: *the British genius happens in contrasted pairs*) **d.** *to come* (: *mildew came in great spots on* ..); (of institutions) *to come into being* ‖ (of events) *to occur, happen*; *emerge*; (of motifs) *to figure* ‖ häufig ~, oft ~ *to be frequent, to be of frequent occurrence*; wiederholt ~ *to be repeated*; verheerend ~ *to ravage, to play havoc* (*among, in*) **II.** ~̈ n **1.** *procedure* | *bearing, demeanour, behaviour*; sicheres ~ *aplomb* [Fr], *self-possession, assurance*; würdiges ~ *dignified presence* **2.** ⟨theat⟩ *appearance*; erstes ~ *début* [Fr], *first appearance*; neues ~ *come-back* ‖ *performance* | *occurrence*; wiederholtes ~ *repetition* ‖ → Auftritt

·**Auftrieb** m ~(e)s/~e **1.** = Almfahrt, → Alm ‖ *the driving of cattle to the market*; *number* od *supply of animals at the market*; der ~ an Rindvieh war gering *cattle were scarce* **2.** ⟨mech⟩ (~skraft) *buoyancy* ‖ ⟨aero⟩ *lift*; *air bump* **3.** ⟨übtr⟩ *encouragement, stimulus, impetus* (z *to*); *lift*; *uplift*; e–r S neuen ~ geben *to give a fresh impetus to a th*; → erhalten B. 1.; Antrieb ‖ *aspiration*; *ambition* (*of a p*) ‖ ⟨com⟩ *business-activity, improvement of the market*; *upward surge*; *boom*; e–r S e–n ~ geben *to boom a th* **~skraft** f ⟨mech⟩ = Auftrieb 2. **~swind** m (anabatischer Wind) *anabatic wind*

·**Auftritt** m ~(e)s/~e **1.** *step, tread* (*of stairs*); *door-step* ‖ ⟨mil⟩ (f Schützen) *banquette, fire step* ‖ → Stufenbreite **2. a.** ⟨theat⟩ *scene*, der ~ beginnt in e–m Zimmer *the sc. opens in a room* ‖ *entrance* (*of actors*) **b.** ⟨übtr⟩ *incident*; (erregter ~) *scene*; e–n ~ m *to make a scene*, → Szene ‖ → Auftreten

·**auf|trocknen** vi/t **1.** vi [s] *to dry up* **2.** vt [h] (etw) *to dry up*; *to mop up* (mit *with*)

·**auf|trumpfen 1.** vi [h] ⟨fig⟩ *to put one's foot down*; *to protest* ‖ *to be self-assertive*; *to be overbearing*; ~ gegen jdn *to give a p a piece of one's mind* **2.** ~̈ n *self-assertion*; *overbearing*

·**auf|tun** vt [h] **1.** (öffnen) *to open*, den Mund ~ *to open one's mouth*; (laut sprechen) *to speak up*; tu die Augen auf! *open your eyes*! *look about you*! *look out*! **2.** (eröffnen) *to establish, to constitute*; ein Geschäft ~ *to start in business, to start a b.* **3.** °~ = (etw) aufsetzen, auflegen ‖ e–n Decke ~ *to cover the table* **4. sich ~ a.** (of door) *to open, to swing open*; (of flowers) *to expand* ‖ (of an *abyss*) sich weit ~ *to yawn* **b.** *to show*; (of chances) *to offer* ‖ (drohend) *to loom* **c.** (sich bilden) *to form* ‖ (Wind) *to spring up* ‖ sie taten sich als Klub auf *they constituted themselves a club* ‖ *to set up* (als *as* [*a hairdresser*])

·**auf|türmen** vt [h] *to pile* od *heap up* | **sich** ~ *to tower up* ‖ (sich häufen) *to accumulate*; *to mount up*; in s–m Leben türmten sich Gefahren auf *his life was beset with dangers*

auf und ab → auf adv I. 1. a.

·**auf|wachen** vi [s] *to awake, to wake* (*up*) ‖ ⟨fig⟩ wach auf! ⟨sl⟩ *snap out of it*!

·**Aufwachs** m = Aufwuchs

·**auf|wachsen** vi [s] *to adolesce*; *to grow up*; *to be brought up* (*mit with*); sie wuchsen z gesunden Jünglingen auf *they grew up healthy youths* ‖ -ge- s in *to be nurtured in* (*the spirit of* ..) ‖ wild ~ (P) *to run wild*; (of plants) *to grow up*; üppig ~ *to sprout*

·**auf|wägen** vt [h] *to counterbalance*; *to compensate for*; → aufwiegen

·**auf|wallen I.** vi [s] **1.** *to boil, bubble* ‖ *effer-*

vesce; *to froth up* **2.** ⟨übtr⟩ (of the sea) *to boil*; *churn*; *rage*, *surge* **|** ⟨fig⟩ (of emotions) *to boil*, *simmer* (vor *with*); *to surge up* **II.** ≈ n → Aufwallung **·aufwallend** a ⟨fig⟩ *ebullient*; *exuberant*

·Aufwallung f ~/~en (*act of*) *boiling*; *bubbling*; *ebullition*; *effervescence* ‖ (of the sea) *surge* **|** ⟨fig⟩ *vehement emotion*; *ebullience*, *-cy*, *ebullition*, *transport*; *exuberance*

·auf|walzen vt [h] ⟨tech⟩ (Flansch) *to roll*

·Aufwand m ~(e)s/≈e **1.** *expense* (an *of*); *expenditure* (an .. *of money*, *time*, *energy*); (v Kapital) *investment* ‖ ⟨jur⟩ *expenses* ‖ mit e–m ~ v *at an expense of*; mit e–m ~ an etw geschehen *to be at an expense of a th*; mit gr ~ verbunden *exertion*; *amount* (an Gelehrsamkeit *of learning*); → Aufbietung, Aufgebot **2.** (Prunk) *display*, *show*; *ostentatious splendour*; *sumptuousness*, *sumptuosity*; *luxury*; *extravagance of expenditure*; (Verschwendung) *waste* ‖ gr ~ m *to make a great display* **|** ⟨übtr⟩ *great display*; *extravagance*; *exuberance*; gr ~ an Worten *volubility*, *wordiness* **~sentschädigung** f ⟨Ger⟩ *allowance for official expenses*, *expense* od *representation allowance* (a. Dienst≈) **~sertrag** m ⟨com⟩ fallender ~ *diminishing return* **~steuer** f *tax on consumption*

·auf|wärmen 1. vt [h] *to cook* od *warm up* ‖ ⟨fig⟩ *to renew*, *revive*; *rehash*; (Skandal) *to rip* od *rake up*; → aufgewärmt **| sich** ~ *to warm* **2.** ≈ n ⟨fig⟩ *rehash*

·Aufwartefrau f ~/~en *charwoman*

·auf|warten vi [h] **1.** bei Tisch ~ *to wait at table* ‖ jdm ~ *to wait* od *attend* (*up*)*on a p*, *to be in attendance on a p*; (bei) jdm ~ (= Besuch m) *to call on a p* **2.** ~ mit etw *to oblige with a th*; *to come forward with a th*; *to offer a th*; jdm ~ mit etw *to treat a p to a th*; *to present a p with a th*, *to offer a p* (*good wine*) ‖ ⟨übtr⟩ *to hold a th in store for a p*; ⟨hum⟩ *to have* (*all sorts of tricks*) *up one's sleeve for a p* ‖ damit kann ich ~ *you may have it from me*; womit kann ich Ihnen ~? *what can I do for you*? ‖ (Sind Sie der Wirt?) Aufzuwarten! (..?) *At your service*!

·Aufwärter m ~s/~ (Diener) *attendant*; *servant* (*of a p*) **|** (Kellner) *waiter* ‖ (auf Schiffen) *steward* ‖ ⟨univ⟩ *scout* **·Aufwärterin** f ~/~nen (Dienerin) *attendant*; *servant* (*of a p*); *waiting-girl*, *-maid* **|** (Kellnerin) *waitress* ‖ (auf Schiffen) *stewardess* ‖ ⟨univ⟩ *scout*

·aufwärts adv **1.** *upwards*; ~? (*lift*:) *going up*?; ⟨mst poet⟩ *upward*; ~ sehen *to look upwards*; sich ~ bewegen *to move upwards* ‖ ⟨mot⟩ ~ schalten *to change into higher gear*, *to change up* ‖ vom 14. Jh. an ~ *from the 14th c upwards* ‖ v den niedrigsten Tieren ~ *from the lowest animals upward* ‖ es geht mit ihm ~ *he is getting on*; *he* (*the patient*) *is on the improve* **|** strom~ *upstream*; strom~ gelegen *upward* (*village*) ‖ ~ gerichtet, *upward* (*move*) **2.** [in comp] *upward* **≈bewegung** f *upward movement* (der Steuern *in rates*); *rise* (der Preise *in prices*) ‖ *upward trend*; *upswing* (*des* Handels *in the trade*) **≈geschwindigkeit** f *ascensional velocity* **≈haken** m ⟨box⟩ *upper-cut*

·Aufwartung f ~/~en **1.** (Bedienung) *waiting*, *attendance* (jds *upon a p*); ~ bei Hofe h *to be in waiting* **|** *odd job*; *char*(*e*), ⟨Am⟩ *chore* **2.** (Besuch) *formal call* od *visit* ‖ jdm s–e ~ m *to pay one's respects to*, *to wait upon*, *to call upon a p* **3.** = Aufwartefrau

·Aufwasch m ~es/ (das Aufwaschen) *washing-up* (*of dishes*) **2.** (gebrauchtes Geschirr) *dirty plates*, *dishes* (etc) [pl] ‖ ⟨fig⟩ alles in e–m ~ *all together*; es ist ein ~ *it is best done together with the whole lot*, *let us do the whole lot at one go*

·Aufwasch- ~becken n *wash-up sink* **~küche** f *scullery* **~wasser** n *dish-water* ⟨a. fig⟩

·auf|waschen I. vt/i **1.** vt [h] (Zimmer) *to wash down*; *to scour*, *clean* ‖ (Geschirr) *to wash up* ‖ (Schmutz) *to wash away* od *off* **2.** vi *to wash up*, *to do the dishes* **II.** ≈ n *washing-up*, *wash-up* **|** das ist ein ~ → Aufwasch

·auf|wecken vt [h] *to wake* (*up*); *to rouse from sleep*; → wecken ‖ → aufgeweckt

·auf|weichen vt/i **1.** vt [h] *to soften*; (of cattle) (Boden) *to poach* ‖ (etw in Wasser etc ~) *to soak*; → einweichen ‖ (of rain) (den Boden) *to sodden*; –geweicht *sodden* (v *with*) **2.** vi [s] *to grow soft* ‖ *to soak* ‖ (of metal) *to temper*

·aufweisbar a *producible* **·auf|weisen** vt [h] *to show*, *to exhibit*; (Spuren) *to bear* ‖ (Fähigkeit) *to command*; etw -zu- h *to boast a th*; etw nicht -zu- h *to be void of a th* **|** ⟨film⟩ (jdn) in der Hauptrolle ~ *to feature* (*a p*)

·auf|weiten vt [h] (Handschuhe) *to stretch*, *widen* ‖ (Stiefel) *to ease*, *stretch*, *tree* **|** ⟨tech⟩ (Rohr) *to expand*

·auf|wenden vt [h] (Geld, Zeit) *to spend* (f *on*); (Mühe, Zeit) *to expend* (f *on*, *in doing*), viel Mühe ~ *to go to great pains* (*to do*); (etw) unnütz, umsonst ~ *to waste* ‖ alles ~ *to make every effort*, *to strain every nerve* (*to do*) **·Aufwendung** f ~/~en *disbursement* (*of money*); *expenditure* (*of energy*, *money*, *pains*, etc); → Aufwand ‖ ~en [pl] *expenses* [pl] ⟨a. jur⟩, *expenditure* (f *for*) ‖ tatsächliche ~en *actual out-of-pocket expenses* ‖ → Aufbietung

·auf|werfen I. vt [h] **A.** (aufhäufen) (Wall etc) *to throw up*; (Damm) *to throw*; *to construct* ‖ (Graben) *to dig* ‖ Feuerung, Kohlen ~ *to mend* (od *make up*) *the fire* **B.** (in die Höhe werfen) **1.** (Karten) *to throw up*; Blasen ~ *to bubble* ‖ (Wellen) *to set up* ‖ den Kopf ~ *to toss one's head*; die Lippen ~ *to pout* (od *curl*) *one's lips*; die Nase ~ *to turn up one's nose*; → aufgeworfen **|** ⟨fig⟩ Staub ~ *to make* (od *kick up*, *raise*) *a dust*, *to make a stir* **2.** ⟨übtr⟩ eine Frage ~ *to raise* (od *pose*, *start*) *a question*; es wurde die Frage aufgeworfen *the question arose* (od *came up*) (*whether*) ‖ → anschneiden, aufrollen **3. sich** ~ z *to set up for*; sich ~ zum Führer, Richter *to put o.s. forward*, *to set o.s. up as a leader*, *a judge* **C.** (öffnen) (Tür) (of the wind) *to force* od *fling open* **|** (ausweiden) *to eviscerate* **II.** ≈ n *throwing-up* **|** *curl* (*of the lip*) ‖ *raising* (*of a question*)

·auf|werten vt/i [h] **1.** vt *to revalorize*, *revalue*, *reassess* **2.** vi: in Höhe v 5% ~ *to offer a revalwation of 5 per cent*

·Aufwertung f ~/~en *revalorization*, *revaluation* **~ssteuer** f ⟨Ger⟩ (bes Hauszinssteuer) *rents tax*

·Aufwickel- ⟨z. B. rec⟩ *take-up* [*attr*]

·auf|wickeln vt [h] **1.** (zus-rollen) *to wind up*; *to coil* ‖ (Knäuel) *to clew up* ‖ (Haar) *to put up in curl-papers* **2.** (loswickeln) **a.** *to unroll*; *untwist*; *unwind*; (Paket) *to undo*, *unwrap* ‖ (Haar) *to loosen*, *to let down* **b. sich** ~ *to unroll*; *untwist*; *unwind*

Aufwiegel·ei f ~/~en *stirring-up*; *instigation*; *incitement* (z *to*) **·auf|wiegeln** vt [h] *to stir up*, *to incite*, *to work up* (z *to*) **·Aufwiegelung** f = Aufwiegelei

·auf|wiegen vt [h] (S) *to outweigh*, *to counterbalance*, *to counterpoise*; *to countervail*; *to compensate for*; *to be equivalent to* (*a th*) ‖ (Nachteile) *to make up for*, *to make amends for* (*a th*) ‖ nicht mit Gold –zu– *worth one's weight in gold* ‖ (P) *to offset* (*one th with another*)

·Aufwiegler m ~s/~ *agitator* ‖ *incendiary*, *instigator*; *rabble-rouser* **·aufwieglerisch** a *agitating*; *inflammatory* (*speech*)

·Aufwind m ⟨aero⟩ *upward* (od *ascending*, *rising*) *current*, *up-current*; thermischer ~ *up-c. due to hot air* ‖ (Hangwind) *upslope wind* ‖ ⟨meteor a.⟩ *upwash*, *upwind* **~bö** f ⟨aero⟩ *bump*

·**auf|winden** vt [h] (Last) *to hoist*; *to wind up* ‖ den Anker ~ → lichten

·**auf|wirbeln** vi/t [h] **1.** vi *to whirl* (od *fly*) *up* **2.** (Staub) *to whirl up* | ⟨fig⟩ viel Staub ~ *to make* (od *kick up*, *raise*) *a dust*, *to make a stir*

·**auf|wischen** vt [h] (Deck etc) *to swab* (*down*); *to clean* | (Wasser etc) *to mop up* (mit *with*); *to swab up* ·**Aufwischlappen** m ~s/~ *mop*, *swab* ‖ *dishcloth*

·**Aufwuchs** m ~es/ *young growth* (*of trees*) ‖ *offspring*

·**auf|wühlen** vt [h] **1.** (Erde) *to dig* od *turn up* ‖ (of pigs) (Boden) mit der Schnauze ~ *to rout up*; mit den Hufen ~ *to poach* ‖ (of waves) (das Meer) *to agitate*, *to churn* (*up*) **2.** ⟨fig⟩ (Inneres) *to thrill*; *excite*; (of sights, etc) *to make the very bones shake in a p's body* ‖ (Leidenschaften) *to rouse*; *to work up*, → aufpeitschen ·**aufwühlend** a ⟨fig⟩ *exciting*; *hot*, *wild* (*music*)

·**auf|zählen** vt [h] (Geld) *to lay* od *pay down* | *to enumerate*, *detail*; die Namen an den Fingern ~ *to check the names on the fingers* ‖ (schriftlich) *to list* | 20 mit der Rute aufgezählt bek. *to get 20 strokes of the birch*

·**Aufzählung** f ~/~en *enumeration* ‖ ⟨jur⟩ *specification* (z. B. *of errors*)

·**auf|zäumen** vt [h] *to bridle* | ⟨fig⟩ das Pferd beim Schwanze ~ *to put the cart before the horse*

·**auf|zehren** vt [h] **1.** *to consume*, *to eat up*; → aufsaugen **2.** ⟨übtr⟩ (Vermögen) *to consume*; *to spend*; (Kräfte) *to waste*; *to sap* | **sich** ~ *to spend o.s.* (z tun *in doing*); *to be consumed* (vor *with*)

·**auf|zeichnen** vt [h] *to draw* (auf *upon*), *to draw*, *design*, *sketch* ‖ ⟨surv⟩ *to plot* (auf *on*) ‖ (genau) *to map out* | (niederschreiben) *to write* od *note down* ‖ (amtlich) *to enrol*, *register*, *record*; nicht aufgezeichnet *unrecorded* ‖ → buchen

·**Aufzeichnung** f ~/~en (Zeichnung) *sketch*, *design* | (schriftliche) *note*, *record*; ⟨comp⟩ *recording* ‖ *enumeration*; ⟨com⟩ die einzelne ~ *item*; kz ~ v einzelnen Punkten *memorandum* (L) ‖ ~en [pl] (Briefschaften etc) *papers* [pl] (*of the late Mr. N.*) **~sbuch** n ⟨surv⟩ *field book*; → Notizbuch

·**auf|zeigen** vt [h] (etw) *to show*, *produce*, *exhibit*; (Fehler) *to point out*; *to point* (*a moral*, etc)

·**Aufzieh- ~leine** f (Fallschirm) *rip cord* **~werk** n *winding-up mechanism* ·**auf|ziehen** vt/i **I.** vt [h] **A. 1.** (öffnen) (Schublade) *to* (*pull*) *open* ‖ (Gardine) *to draw* ‖ (Flasche) *to uncork* ‖ (Schleife) *to undo* **2.** (in die Höhe ziehen) (Vorhang) *to draw up* ‖ (Zugbrücke) *to draw* od *pull up*; *to raise* ‖ (Schleuse) *to open* ‖ (Fahne) *to hoist* **3.** ⟨übtr⟩ (Pflanze) *to cultivate*, *grow*, *rear*, *raise*; (T) *to breed*, *rear*, *raise* ‖ (Kind) *to bring up*; *to breed*, *educate*, *rear*; ⟨Am⟩ *to raise* ‖ er war als Christ aufgezogen *he had been reared a Christian* ‖ (Menschentyp) *to raise* ‖ → erziehen **4.** (Miene) → aufsetzen **B. (spannen) 1.** (Uhr) *to wind* (*up*); wieder ~ *to rewind*; nicht aufgezogen *unwound* (*watch*) ‖ (Saite) *to put on*; ⟨fig⟩ andere (gelindere) Saiten ~ *to adopt a different* (*milder*) *tone* | ⟨weav⟩ (Kettenfäden) *to warp* ‖ ⟨tech⟩ (Luftreifen) *to fit on* ‖ ⟨typ⟩ (Bogen) *to dress* | °(P) *to cheer up*, *enliven* ‖ → 5. ‖ er ist wie aufgezogen → aufgekratzt **2.** (strecken) (Metall) *to draw* **3.** (aufkleben) *to mount* **4.** °**etw** ~ *to make* (od *get*) *a th up*; *to make a display of a th*; e–e Bewegung ~ *to organize a movement*; (Vorgang, Fest) *to stage*; (Unternehmen) neu ~ *to harness*; etw großartig ~ *to make* (*a*) *great display of a th*, *to feature a th*; etw falsch (richtig) ~ *to get hold of the wrong* (*right*) *end of the stick*; etw politisch ~ *to make a political question of a th* **5.** °**jdn** ~ *to chaff*, *rally*, *flout*, *mock*, *hoax*, *green*, *ridicule*, *tease*, *banter*; ⟨Am a.⟩ *needle*, ⟨sl⟩ *to roast a p*, *to play on a p*, *to pull a p's leg* **II.** vi [s] **1.** *to approach*, *to draw on*; ein Gewitter zieht auf *a storm is coming on* od *up*, ..*is brewing* **2.** ⟨mil⟩ *to march*; *to form up into line*; in Parade ~ *to line up on parade*; *to parade* ‖ die Wache zieht auf (*the guard is mounted*) | ~ l *to draw up*; *to deploy*; in Parade ~ l *to parade* **3.** e–e Pflanze zieht auf *a plant is uprooted by frost* ·**Aufziehen** n *opening*; *drawing-up* ‖ *hoist* | *upbringing* (*of children*) | ⟨mil⟩ *the mounting of the guard* ‖ → Aufzieherei; Aufzucht; Aufzug ·**Aufzieherei** f ~/~en *hoax*, *chaff*; *teasing*

·**Aufzucht** f ~/ *breeding*, *rearing* ‖ *young brood*; → Nachwuchs

·**auf|zucken** vi [h] *to jerk*, *wince*, *start*; *to give a start* od *a wince* ‖ (of light) *to flash*; ⟨übtr⟩ (of eyes) *to flash* (v *with*)

·**Aufzug** m ~(e)s/~̈e **A.** (Aufziehen → d.) ⟨gym⟩ *pull-up*; e–n Rücken~̈ m *to skin the cat* **B.** (Aufgezogenes) **1. a.** (Hebezeug) *hoist*; Schräg~̈ *inclined hoist*; → Flaschenzug **b.** *lift*; ⟨Am⟩ *elevator*; (f. Speisen) ⟨Am⟩ *dumb-waiter* ‖ Paternoster~̈ *paternoster-wheel* **2.** ⟨weav⟩ *warp* **3.** ⟨theat⟩ *act*, ein Stück v 3 Aufzügen *a three act play* **4.** (Aufmarsch) *procession* ‖ (historischer) *pageant*; großartiger ~ *pageantry* ‖ ⟨mil⟩ *parade* **5.** (Kleidung) *attire*; *get-up*, *make-up*; stattlicher ~ *array*, *pomp*; *trappings* [pl] ‖ → Aufziehen; Aufzucht **~führer** m *lift-boy* **~kübel** m *lifting bucket* **~ritzel** n ⟨phot⟩ *cocking lever* **~sschacht** m *liftshaft* **~svorrichtung** f *hoisting-device* ‖ *winding-up device* (f Uhren)

·**auf|zwängen** vt [h] (Tür) *to force open*

·**auf|zwingen** vt [h] jdm etw ~ *to force a th on a p*; *to obtrude a th on a p*

·**Aug- ~apfel** m *eye-ball* ‖ ⟨übtr⟩ *apple of the eye*, jds ~ s *to be the apple of a p's eye* (od *to be a p's darling*) **~bolzen** m *eye-bolt* **~sproß** m (Geweih~̈) ⟨hunt⟩ *brow*

·**Auge** n ~s/~n **A.** (Sehwerkzeug) *eye*; [oft pl] die ~n *the eyes* (geübt, trainiert *educated*); dem ungeschulten ~ *to the casual eye*; mit den ~n *ocularly*; ohne ~n *eyeless*; mit eigenen ~n sehen *to witness* (*a th*); als mein ~ ihn erblickte *when I caught sight of him* ‖ Glas~̈ *glass-eye*; (des Pferdes) *wall-eye* ‖ Glotz~̈n *eyes like saucers*, → Glotzauge ‖ Stiel~̈ ⟨zoo⟩ *stalked eye* | ⟨übtr⟩ das ~ des Tages = Sonne) *the eye of day* od *heaven* ‖ das ~ des Feindes *the eye of the enemy* | ⟨fig⟩ magisches ~ ⟨wir⟩ *electric* od *electron-ray tube* | ⟨bib⟩ ~ um ~ *an eye for an eye* **B.** (Fähigkeit z sehen) *eye*; *sight*; *eyesight* ‖ ~n wie ein Luchs, Luchs~̈n *eyes like a hawk* ‖ das ~ des Gelehrten *the eye of the scholar* ‖ das ~ der Vernunft *the eyes of reason* ‖ das ~ des Gesetzes *the eye of the law* | sein geistiges ~ *his mind's eye*, *his mental gaze*; etw mit s–m geistigen ~ sehen *to see a th with the eye of one's mind*, *to visualize a th* ‖ es bedeutet mehr als das ~ sehen kann *there is more in it than meets the eye* **C.** ⟨übtr⟩ **1.** ⟨bot⟩ *eye*, *bud*, *bud-eye*; (im Holz) *knot* ‖ (Kartoffel~̈) *eye* **2.** (Punkt) ⟨cards⟩ *pip*; *point* ‖ (auf Suppe) *spot of grease* **3.** (Loch, Öffnung (im Käse) *hole* ‖ ⟨tech⟩ *eye*; *eyelet*; *lug*; *hole*; *ear* ‖ (Schleife) *eye*, *eyelet*, *loop* **4.** ⟨typ⟩ *face* **D.** [in comp] → ~n– **E. Wendungen: 1. blaues** ~ *black eye*; → 3. ‖ künstliches ~ *artificial eye* ‖ das rechte (linke) ~ (e–s Pferdes) *the off* (*near*) *eye* | ganz ~ s *to be all eyes*; → Ohr ‖ s–e ~n sind größer als der Mund *his eyes are bigger than his belly* | ⟨mil⟩ ~n gerade aus! *eyes front*! (die) ~n rechts (links)! *eyes right* (*left*)! die ~n v jdm **abwenden** *or* l *to take one's eyes off a p* ‖ die ~n **aufmachen** → aufmachen 1. a.; → aufreißen ‖ das ~ beleidigen *to offend the eye* ‖ das ~ erfreuen *to relieve the eye* | die ~n halb geschlossen **haben,** halb schließen *to squint* ‖ ich müßte 4 ~n h *I should require eyes in the back of my head* ‖ nur ~n h f *to notice nothing but* (*a* *p, a th*); die ~n überall h *to have one's eyes about one* ‖ ein ~ h auf *to give an eye to, to watch* (*a p, a th*) ‖ ein ~ h f *to have an eye for* (*colour*, etc) ‖ ein offenes ~ h f *to have an eye* (od *a good eye*) *for* ‖ ein wachsames ~ h auf *to keep a close eye on* | → Krähe ‖ die ~n offen halten *to keep one's eyes skinned* (f etw .. *peeled for a th*); (gr) ~n **machen** *to be all eyes*; *to stare in surprise, to open one's eyes wide* (od *in surprise*) ‖ er machte gr ~n *his eyes widened* ‖ ~n m wie ein gestochenes Kalb *to stare like a stuck pig*; jdm ~n m *to make a p open his eyes*; (kokettieren) *to give a p the glad eye, to make eyes at a p* ; ⟨fam⟩ jdm verliebte ~n m *to cast sheep's eyes at a p*; sie machte ihm verl. ~n *she made the soft eye at him* ‖ jdm die ~n **öffnen** *to open a p's eyes* (f etw *to a th*), *to undeceive a p* ‖ s–e ~n richten auf jdn *to direct one's eyes at* (od *towards*) *a p* ‖ vier ~n sehen mehr als zwei *two heads are better than one*; sehenden ~s *with one's eyes open* ‖ die ~n fest schließen *to shut one's eyes tightly, to screw the eyes shut* ‖ die ~n gingen ihm über ⟨fig⟩ *he gushed* (*with pleasure*), *his heart leapt* (*with joy*); *he was struck dumb* (*with surprise*) ‖ was sehen m–e entzündeten (⟨hum⟩ f entzückten) ~n! *my eyes! a sight for sore eyes!* ‖ s–e ~n gehen **spazieren** (er schielt) *he looks two ways to find Sunday*; ich traute m–n ~n nicht *I could not believe my eyes* ‖ sich die ~n verderben *to ruin one's sight, to strain one's eyes* ‖ (bigott) die ~n verdrehen *to turn up the white of one's eyes* ‖ ein ~ verlieren *to lose an eye*, beide ~n v. *to lose one's sight* ‖ die ~n verschließen gegen *to shut one's eyes to* (*a th*) ‖ s–e ~n weiden an *to feast one's eyes on*; ..weiden l ⟨fam⟩ *to get one's eyeful* ‖ sich [dat] die ~ aus dem Kopfe **weinen** *to cry one's eyes* od *heart out* ein ~ werfen auf *to cast an eye on*; *to squint at* (*a p*) ‖ er hat ein ~ auf sie geworfen *he is sweet upon her*; ein ~ zudrücken ⟨fig⟩ *to wink the other eye*; *to stretch a point*; beide ~n zudr. *to turn a blind eye to it*; ..bei etw *to connive* (od *wink*) *at a th, to make allowances to* (*a p*), *for* (*a th*) ‖ die ~n zus-kneifen *to narrow one's eyes* ‖ ich habe die Nacht kein ~ zugetan *I have not had a wink of sleep, I could not sleep a wink all night, I never batted an eyelid* ‖ jdm weit geöffnete ~n zuwenden *to gaze wide-eyed at a p* **3.** jdm etw **an** den ~n absehen → absehen I. A. 1. ‖ man sah es ihm an den ~n an *you could see* (od *tell*) *by his face* (*that ..*) | das paßt wie die Faust **aufs** ~ *that's like a square peg in a round hole*; *that's as like as chalk and cheese* ‖ das Geschlecht steht auf zwei ~n *the family is represented by one man* | **aus** den ~n, aus dem Sinn *out of sight, out of mind* ‖ geh mir aus den ~n *get out of my sight* ‖ aus den ~n k *to be lost to sight* ‖ (nicht) aus den ~n l (*to watch closely*), (*not*) *to lose sight of* (*a th, a p*); *to let a th out of one's sight*; etw nicht aus den ~n l können *not to be able to take one's eyes off a th* ‖ er ist s–m Vater wie aus den ~n geschnitten *he resembles his father to a T, he is the very image* (od *spit*) *of his father* ‖ der Schalk sieht ihm aus den ~n *he looks a perfect rogue, he has a roguish look in his eye* ‖ aus den ~n verlieren ⟨eig & fig⟩ *to lose sight of* (*a p*); man verlor ihn aus den ~n *he was lost to sight*; er durfte es nicht aus den ~n verlieren *he could not afford to ignore it* | **im** ~ behalten *to keep* (*a th*) *in sight* (od *mind, view*); *to keep an eye on a th* ‖ im ~ h *to intend, mean, purpose a th*; *to have* (*a th*) *in mind* (od *view*); *to contemplate, consider* (*a th*; z tun *doing*) ‖ ein Ziel im ~ h *to have an end in view* ‖ jdm ein Dorn im ~ s *to be a thorn in a p's side* | **in** jds ~en *in the eyes of a p*; in m–n ~n *in my opinion* (od *view*), *to me*; in den ~n der Franzosen *in the French eyes* (od *view*) ‖ ~ in ~ *face to face* ‖ jdm in die ~n sehen *to look at a p's eyes*; sieh mir in die ~n *look me in the face* ‖ in die ~n springen = ins ~ springen ‖ in die ~n stechen = ins ~ fallen; es stach mir in die ~n *it took my fancy* od *my eye* ‖ jdm Sand in die ~n streuen *to throw dust in a p's eyes* ‖ ~ in ~ *eye to eye* | **ins** ~, in die ~n fallen *to strike* (od *catch*) *the eye*; *to be conspicuous* (od *obvious, evident*); ins ~ fallend *conspicuous, spectacular, striking* ‖ jdm ins ~ fallen (of objects) *to catch a p's eye*; das erste, das ihm ins ~ fiel *the first thing that caught his eye*; mir fiel ein Bild ins ~ *my eye was caught by a picture*; es fiel mir sofort ins ~ *it caught my eye at once* ‖ (jdn) ins ~ fassen *to eye* (*a p*); (etw) *to envisage*; *to contemplate, consider* (*a th*; z tun *doing*); ⟨Am⟩ *to figure* (z tun *on doing*) ‖ s–e Interessen ins ~ fassen *to consult* (od *pay regard to*) *one's interests* ‖ Schlag ins ~ ⟨fam⟩ *blinkers* ‖ jdn ins ~ schlagen, treffen *to hit a p in the eye* ‖ e–r S (Gefahr) ins ~ sehen *to envisage a th, to face up to a th* (*life, realities*); den Dingen ins ~ sehen *to square up to difficulties*; *to tackle* (*a problem*) ‖ ins ~ springen *to leap to the eye, to spring to the eyes*; *to stand out* (: *he stands out like a sore thumb*) | **mit** anderen ~n *with other eyes*; .. ansehen *to take a different view of* ‖ mit einem ~ auf etw *with an eye to a th* ‖ mit feuchten ~n *wet-eyed* ‖ mit weit aufgerissenen ~n starren *to stare wide-eyed, ..with all one's eyes*; mit den ~n blinzeln (zwinkern) *to wink* (*one's eyes*) ‖ mit e–m blauen ~ davon k *to get* (od *come*) *off lightly*; *to have a hairbreadth* (od *narrow*) *escape*; das hieß, er ist mit e–m blauen ~ davongek *that was a close* od *narrow shave* ‖ mit bloßem ~ *with a naked* od *an unaided eye* ‖ etw mit einem *or* halbem ~ sehen *to see a th with half an eye* ‖ mit scheelen ~n *with an evil eye* ‖ mit geschlossenen ~n *with one's eyes shut* ‖ jdn mit gr ~n anblicken *to raise the eyelids at a p* ‖ mit halbem ~ blicken *to squint* ‖ jdn mit unverwandten ~n ansehen *to look fixedly at a p, to fix a p with a stony stare* | ~ **um** ~ → A. | **unter** vier ~n *in private, privately, confidentially, face to face, tête-a-tête* [Fr]; *between ourselves, between you and me* (*and the bedpost* od *gate-post*) ‖ jdm unter die ~ k *to face a p* | **vor** jds ~n *in the sight* (od *view*) *of a p*, direkt vor jds ~n *in full view of a p*; vor den ~n der Öffentlichkeit *in the limelight of publicity*, vor aller ~n *openly, in public, in full view* ‖ jdm etw vor ~n führen *to make a th clear to a p*; ..lebhaft .. *to bring a th vividly before a p* ‖ der Welt anschaulich vor ~n führen *to demonstrate to the world* (*a th*; *that*), jdm etw (überzeugend) vor ~n führen *to impress* od *urge a th upon a p* ‖ (etw) vor ~n h *to have* (*a th*) *before one* ‖ jdm etw vor ~n halten *to bring a th home to a p, to call a th to a p's attention* ‖ sich vor ~n halten *to realise, to bear in mind, to remember* (*a th*; *that*) ‖ komm mir nicht wieder vor die ~n *don't let me see your face again, I hope I've seen the last of you* ‖ sich [dat] das Bild v.. vor ~n rufen *to call up the image of ..* ‖ etw vor s–m geistigen ~ sehen → B., *to have a mental picture of a th* ‖ alles schwamm ihm vor den ~n *everything swam before his eyes* ‖ es wurde mir (grün u) schwarz vor den ~n *my head was swimming, a rather sinking sensation occurred within me*

Äugel·ei f ~/~en *wink*(*ing*) **·äugeln** vi/t [h] **1.** vi ~ auf jdn *to eye a p, to make eyes at a p* ‖ ~ mit jdm *to wink at, to ogle with a p* **2.** vt ⟨hort⟩ *to inoculate, graft*

·Augen- [im comp] eye ..; ⟨scient⟩ *ocular*; *oculo-* **~abstand** m *interpupillary distance* **~arzt** m *oculist, ophthalmologist* **~aufschlag** m *the lifting* od *raising of the eyes*; *lift of the eyebrows*; *upward look* **~bad** n *eye-bath* od *-douche* **~balsam** m *eye-ointment* **~befund** m ⟨med⟩ *status of the eye* **~bewegung** f *ocular motion*

~binde f *bandage for the eye, (eye-)bandage* **~blick** → d **~braue** f *eyebrow*, mit buschigen ~n *beetle-browed* **~brauenstift** m ⟨cosm⟩ *eyebrow pencil* ×°**~butter** f ⟨fam⟩ *sleepy-seeds* (*mucus forming about the eyes in sleep*) **~diagnose** f *iridiagnosis* [L] **~diener** m *eye-servant, eye-server* **~dienerei** f *eye-service* **~entzündung** f *inflammation of the eye(s); ophthalmia* [L], *ophthalmitis* [L] ⁓**fällig** a *conspicuous; obvious, evident; spectacular* **~falter** m ⟨ent⟩ *satyr*; Gattung der ~ *Satyridae* [pl] [L] **~fehler** m ⟨med⟩ *visual error* **~fleck** m ⟨zoo⟩ *eye-spot* (*of caterpillars*, etc) **~flimmern** n *twitching of the eye* **~glas** n *eyeglass* → Brille, Linse ‖ ⟨opt⟩ *eye-piece* (*of a telescope, mask*) **~haut** f ⟨orn⟩ *orbit* **~heilkunde** f *ophthalmology* **~höhe** f: in ~ halten .. *level with one's eyes* **~höhle** f *eye-hole, eye-socket; orbit* **~hornhautfleck** m (Leukoma) ⟨m. m.⟩ *wall-eye* **~klappe** f (P) *eye-shade*; ⟨med⟩ *patch*; ⟨hors⟩ = Augenleder **~klinik** f *ophthalmic hospital, eye hospital* ⁓**krank** a *ophthalmic* **~krankheit** → Augenleiden **~leder** n (Scheuklappe) *blinker* **~leiden** n *eye-complaint*; nervöses ~ *affection of the eyes* **~licht** n *eyesight* **~lid** n *eyelid* **~maß** n (*sense of*) *proportion* ‖ ein gutes ~ *a just* (od *sure*) *eye* (f *for*) ‖ nach dem ~ *as judged by the eye* ‖ ihm fehlt jedes ~ *he lacks all sense of proportion* **~merk** n *attention* ‖ sein ~ auf etw richten *to consider, contemplate a th; to give* od *turn one's mind to a th* **~mittel** n *ophthalmic remedy*; ⟨cosm⟩ *eye-lotion* **~muschel** f *eye-cup* **~muskel** m *eye muscle* **~nerv** m *optic nerve* **~optiker** m (staatl. geprüft) *ophthalmic optician* **~pulver** n (Arznei) *a medicine for the eyes* | (kl Druck) *very small print* (etc); das reinste ~ s (of script) *to be trying for the eyes* **~punkt** m *point of sight, visual point*; ⟨astr⟩ *vanishingpoint* **~reim** m ⟨pros⟩ *eye rhyme* (z. B. *move/love, watch/catch, misery/eye*) **~ring** m ⟨tech⟩ *grommet*; ~e pl *bags under the eyes* **~salbe** f *eye-ointment* **~schein** m **1.** *inspection; observation, examination* ‖ ~snahme f ⟨jur⟩ *ocular* od *eye inspection* ‖ etw in ~ nehmen *to take a view of a th, to inspect, examine a th* ‖ sich durch den ~ überzeugen *to make sure by inspection* **2.** (Anschein) *appearance*, dem ~ nach *to all appearance(s)*; der ~ trügt *appearances are deceptive* ⁓**scheinlich** a *evident, apparent, obvious*; ~ m *to evidence* **~scheinlichkeit** f *evidence, obviousness*; (*she was defrauded*), *and no mistake* **~schirm** m *shade for the eyes, eye-shade* **~schmerz** m, ~en [pl] *pain in the eyes* ~schminke f (Wimperntusche) *mascara* **~schwäche** f *weakness of sight* od *eyes*; ⟨med⟩ *asthenopia* **~spiegel** m ⟨med⟩ *ophthalmoscope* **~spinner** m ⟨ent⟩ *Saturnian; Saturniid moth* **~sprache** f *language of the eyes, eye-parley* **~sprosse** f (unterste Sprosse des Geweihs) *brow-antler* (od *tine*) **~stein** m ⟨minr⟩ *white sulphate of zinc* **~stern** m *pupil* ‖ ⟨fig⟩ → Augapfel **~täuschung** f *optical illusion* **~triefen** n *running of the eyes* **~tropfen** m [pl], **~wasser** n *eye-water, ~-lotion* **~trost** m ⟨bot⟩ *eyebright, euphrasy* **~weide** f ⟨fig⟩ *a sight for sore eyes; feast*; (sie ist) e–e wahre ~ ⟨sex⟩ .. *eye-filling girl* **~wimper** f *eyelash* **~winkel** m *corner* od *tail of the eye* **~zahl** f (Kartenspiel) *number of pips* od *points* **~zahn** m *eye-tooth; canine tooth* **~zeuge** m *eyewitness*, (zufälliger) *bystander*; ~ e–r S s *to (eye-)witness a th* ‖ ~nbericht [m] *eye-witness report* **~zeugnis** n *ocular testimony* od *proof* **~zittern** n ⟨med⟩ *nystagmus*

·äugen vi [h] nach jdm = äugeln auf jdn

·Augenblick m *moment, instant*; ⟨fam⟩ *shake* (*wait a sh.*), *snatch, wink* | **entscheidender ~** *push* ‖ glückliche ~e [pl] *happy snatches* [pl] ‖ ein günstiger ~ *a good opportunity, an occasion* (für, zu *for*) ‖ kritischer ~ *crisis juncture* (: *at this j.*) ‖ lichter ~ ⟨med⟩ *lucid interval*; ⟨übtr⟩ er hat s–e lichten ~e *he has his moments* ‖ der richtige ~ *the psychological moment* | **alle** ~e *every now and then* ‖ (warte) **e-n ~** *half a moment* od ⟨fam⟩ *mo; wait a moment* od *minute; let me think* ‖ °~, gleich sind Sie rasiert ⟨fam⟩ *now we shan't be long* ‖ **jeden ~** *any minute; momently*; sie wollte jeden ~ in Tränen ausbrechen *she was on the point of breaking into tears* | **k-n** ~ Ruhe *not a moment's peace* ‖ wir h es k–n ~ erwartet *we didn't expect it for a minute* | sich **an** den ~ verlieren *to be lost in the moment* | **auf** e–n ~ *for a moment* | für den ~ *for the moment* (od *present*); *for the time being; momentarily* | **für** den ~ *at this moment* | **im ~** (= augenblicklich) *at* od *for the moment, at present* ‖ (= im Nu) *in a trice, in a wink, in a twinkling* (od *twinkle*), *in the twinkling of an eye* ‖ (= gerade jetzt) *just now* ‖ im ersten ~ *at first; at first sight*; ⟨Am⟩ *first off* ‖ im letzten ~ *at the last moment; just in time*; gerade im letzten ~ *in the very nick of time*; im richtigen ~ *at the psychological moment; in the nick of time; just in time* ‖ **in** dem ~ *at that instant* (od *moment*) ‖ in dem ~, als ich ihn sah .. *the instant I saw him* (*he* ..); .. ~, als er eintrat *directly he entered* (*he saw* ..) ‖ in diesem ~ *at this moment; just now*; (= sofort) (come) *this instant* ‖ in e–m ~ *in a moment* ‖ sie liebte ihn **vom** ersten ~ an, als sie ihn sah *she loved him from the moment of seeing him* **·augenblicklich 1.** a *instantaneous, momentary; immediate* **2.** adv *at the moment, at present*

·Augenblicks- [in comp] *current* (*life table* ⟨demog⟩); *instantaneous* (*rate*) **~aufnahme** f ⟨phot⟩ *instantaneous photograph*, ⟨mst⟩ *snapshot* **~dauer** f *instantaneousness* **~erfolg** m *short-lived success* **~wert** m *present* od *momentary value* **~ziel** n ⟨mil⟩ *fleeting* od *transient target* **~zünder** m *instantaneous* od *quick* (od *high sensitive*) *fuse*

Aug·iasstall m ~s/~n *Augean stable* ‖ ⟨fig⟩ den ~ ausmisten *to cleanse the A. st.*

-äugig a [in comp] *eyed*, blau~ *blue-eyed*

Aug·it m ~s/~e ⟨min⟩ *augite*

·Äuglein n ~s/~ *little eye* ‖ ⟨bot⟩ *bud* **·Äugler** m ~s/~ **1.** *ogler* **2.** = Augendiener **3.** = Augenfalter **·Augling** m = Augenfalter

Augm·ent n ~s/~e ⟨gram⟩ *augment* **Augmentat·ion** [-ts-] f ~/~en ⟨mus⟩ *augmentation*

·Augsburg n ⟨Ger⟩ (Stadt) *Augsburg* **·Augsburger** m, **~in** f *inhabitant of Augsburg* **·Augsburgisch** a *Augsburgian* **·Augsburgische Konfession** f ⟨Ger⟩ *the Confession of Augsburg, the Augustan Confession*

Aug·ur m ~s & ~(e)n/~(e)n *augur* **~enlächeln** n *augur's laugh* **Aug·urium** n ~s/–rien *augury*

·August m ~s/~e ⟨übtr⟩ der dumme ~ *clown*

Aug·ust m ~(e)s/~e (Monat) *August* (im ~ *in A.*); **~krebs** m *the second half of A.*

August·iner m ~s/~ ⟨R. C.⟩ die ~ [pl] (Orden) *the Augustinians, the Black Canons* [pl] **~eremiten** m [pl] *Augustinian Hermits* [pl] **~kloster** n *Augustinian monastery* **~mönch** m *Augustinian; Augustinian monk* **~orden** m *the Order of Canons Regular of St. Augustine*

Aukt·ion f ~/~en *auction; open* od *public sale*; ⟨Scot⟩ *roup* ‖ ~ e–s Händlerverbandes *trade-sale* ‖ ~ mit Senkung des Preises, bis sich ein Käufer findet (Veiling) *Dutch auction* ‖ in die ~ geben *to auction, to sell by auction, to put up for auction* ‖ zur ~ k *to be sold by auction* **Auktion·ator** m ~s/–at·oren *auctioneer* **auktion·ieren** vt [h] *to sell by auction* **Aukt·ions- ~lokal** n *auction-room* **~preis** m *auction-price*

·Aula f ~/–len & ~s ⟨school & univ⟩ *great hall, assembly-hall* (*of a college*, etc.); ⟨Oxf⟩ *the Sheldonian*; ⟨Am⟩ *auditorium* [L]

***·Aulner** m = Töpfer

au pair [o:ˈpɛ:r] [Fr] adv *au pair*, [attr (*au pair terms*)]; → Austausch

·**Aura** f ~/ [L] v ⟨med⟩ *aura*

Aur·at n ⟨chem⟩ *aurate*

Aure·ole f ~/~n (Heiligenschein) *aureola, aureole*; ⟨a. astr⟩ (Mond–, Sonnenhof) || mit e–r ~ umgeben *to aureole* || ⟨min⟩ *gaseous cloud forming in safety-lamps as a warning*

Aurichalz·it m ~s/~e ⟨minr⟩ *aurichalcite*

Aurignaci·en [o:rinjaˈsjɛ̃:] n ~s/ ⟨praeh⟩ *Aurignacian era* (od *period*) **Aurignac-Rasse** [o:rinˈjak] f ⟨anthr⟩ *Aurignac-race*

Aur·ikel f ~/~n ⟨bot⟩ *auricula, bear's ear*

aurikul·ar a *auricular*

Auripigm·ent n ~(e)s/ ⟨minr⟩ *orpiment*

Aur·ora n ~s/ *aurora* [L]; → Nordlicht

aus adv **I. (Richtung) 1.** (hervor, heraus) **a.** → her~, hin~ || bes in Verbindung mit Verben → aus– | v da aus *thence, from there*; v wo aus *from where* || v Berlin ~ *from Berlin* || v Grund ~ *thoroughly, radically*; ein Schurke v Grund aus *a scoundrel out-and-out*; ein v Grund ~ guter Mensch *a good man at bottom* || v Haus ~ *by birth*; *by nature*; v Haus ~ war er arm *he came of poor parents* || v Natur ~ *by nature, naturally* || v diesem Standpunkt ~ *from this point of view* **b.** ~- u eingehen *to be in and out, to come and go*; im Zimmer ein– u ~g. *to be in and out of the room*; es gingen viele ~ u ein *there were many comings and goings* || bei jdm ~- u eingehen *to be a frequent visitor to a p's house, to frequent a p's h.* || jahr~, jahrein *year in year out, from year's end to year's end* | ⟨übtr⟩ er wußte nicht ~ noch ein *he was at the end of his tether* (od *at his wit's end*); *he was all adrift* **2.** ⟨übtr⟩ **(Ziel)** auf etw ~ s ⟨fam⟩ *to be out for a th*, auf s–n Vorteil ~ s *to consult one's interests*; darauf ~ s z tun *to be out to do*; *to intend to do* (od *doing*), *to contemplate doing* || (jdn) ~m ⟨crick⟩ *to bowl out* **II. (Ruhe) 1.** (außerhalb) ⟨sport⟩ der Ball ist ~ *the ball is out* **2.** (weg) er ist ~ *he is out* **3.** ⟨übtr⟩ ~! *enough!, over!*; ~ sein *to be at an end*; es würde ~ s mit .. *there would be an end to ..* || das Feuer ist ~ *the fire is* (od *has burnt*) *out* || die Schule ist ~ *school is up* (od *out, over*); der Krieg ist ~ *the war is over*; die Verhandlungen sind ~ *the negotiations are off* || trink es ~ *drink it off* (od *up*), *finish it* || Licht ~! *put that light out!* || ⟨aero mot⟩ (Zündkerzen) ~! *switch off!* || ich habe das Buch ~ *I have finished the book*; er hat das Glas ~ *he has emptied his glass* | es ist alles ~ *this, that is the end*; *it is all up, the game is up*, ⟨sl⟩ *the jig is up*; es ist ~ mit ihm *it is all up* od *over with him*

aus prep [mit dat] **I. (aus .. heraus)** *out of, from*; ⟨Am a.⟩ *out* (: *out the window*) **1. (örtlich) a.** ~ dem Lande *out of* (od *from*) *the country*; ~ aller Herren Ländern *from all over the world* ~ dem Hause, Zimmer *out of the house, room*; ~ dem Innern des Hauses *from within* (*the house*) || ~ dem Fenster fallen *to fall from* (od *out of* ⟨Am a.⟩ *out*) *the window*; .. sehen *to look out of the w.* || ~ der Höhe *from on high* || *he came from school, church, a concert* || ~ e–m Glase trinken *to drink out of a glass* **b.** ~ Osten *from the east* || direkt ~ Berlin (*straight*) *from Berlin*; ~ England *from England* **c.** ~ unserer Mitte *from our midst, from among*(*st*) *us*; ~ den Reihen des Adels *from within the nobility* || → austreten, –streichen || ein Herr ~ der Menge *a gentleman out of the crowd*; ein Auftritt ~ dem Stücke *a scene out of the play* || das ist ~ Goethe *that is out of Goethe* || *a passage* od *quotation from Milton* **d.** ~ dem Wege *out of the way*; → Weg, Licht, Auge, **e.** würden Sie mir das ~ der Hand nehmen? *would you take that off my hands?* **2. (Abstammung)** ~ ärmlichem Hause (*he came*) *from a poor home*; ~ guter Familie *of good family* od *stock*; er ist ein Kind ~ dem Volke *he has sprung from the people*; ~ niedrigem Stande s *to be of low condition*; er stammt (*or* ist gebürtig) ~ England *he comes* od *is from E., he is a native of E.* || *on her father's side, Queen Victoria was of the House of Hanover* || viele Kinder ~ dieser Ehe *many children by this marriage* || gezüchtet ~ *out of* **3. (zeitlich)** ein Werk ~ dem 18. Jh. *a work of the 18th c.* || .. ~ der Bronzezeit (*remains*) *from the bronze-age* || ~ der Zeit Friedrichs des Großen *from the time of Frederick the Great*; ~ der Zeit vor der Revolution *from before the revolution* **4.** ⟨übtr⟩ **a.** ~ den Zeitungen sehen *to see from the newspapers* || ~ Ihrem Schreiben ersehe ich *I see from* od *by your letter* || etw ~ jds Hand empfangen *to receive a th at the hands of a p*; ~ erster Hand *at first hand*; ~ guter Quelle *on good authority* **b.** ~ dem Gedächtnis (*to speak*) *from memory*; ~ eigener Kraft *by o.s.* || ~ eigenem Antrieb, ~ freien Stücken *of one's own accord, of one's own free will*; ~ Neid *out of envy*; etw ~ dem Grunde verstehen *to have the knack of a th* || ~ vollem Halse schreien *to scream at the top of one's voice* **c.** was wurde ~ der S? *what became of the matter?* was wird ~ ihm w? *what will become of him?* **d.** → folgern, schließen ~ **5.** ~ der **Art** schlagen *to degenerate* || ~ der **Form** *out of shape* || ~ den **Fugen** *out of joint* || jdn ~ dem **Konzept** bringen *to put a p out* || geh mir ~ dem **Licht** *get out of the light* || ~ der **Mode** *out of fashion*, diese Hüte sind ~ der Mode *these hats have gone out* || ~ dem **Takt** *out of time* **II. (Stoff)** *of*; gemacht, zus–gesetzt ~ *made, composed of*; → bestehen || ein Kleid ~ Seide *a silk dress, dress* (*made*) *of silk*; ein Kranz ~ Blumen *a wreath of flowers*; ~ Holz (etc) *of wood*; *wooden*; ein Kuchen ~ Weizenmehl *a cake of wheaten flour* || ~ e–m Guß ⟨fig⟩ *cast in one and the same mould*; *all of a piece* || → nichts **III.** ⟨fig⟩ **(Grund, Ursache)** *for*; *out of, from* || ~ demselben Grunde *for* od *on the same reason* || ~ den höchsten Motiven handeln *to act from the highest motives*; ~ eigenem Antrieb *of one's own accord*; ~ Gehorsam gegen *out of obedience to*; ~ Liebe *out of love, for l.*; ~ Mitleid *out of compassion*; ~ Notwendigkeit *out of necessity*; ~ Gründen der Religion *on religious grounds*; ~ dem Wunsche heraus *from the desire* (*to do*) || ~ Furcht *out of fear*; ~ Furcht vor *for fear of*; *from fear of punishment*; *out of envy*; *out of spite*; ~ Liebe zu *for the love of* || ~ Spaß *for fun* || ~ Mangel an *for* (od *from*) *want of* || ~ eigener Erfahrung *from* od *by one's own experience*; ich weiß ~ E. *I know by experience* || ~ Versehen getan *done by mistake* | **(seelisch-körperliche Ursache)** *of*: *to die of grief* | **(aus e–m augenblicklichem Gemützustand)** *through*: *through ambition, shame, carelessness, forgetfulness*, etc

Aus n [invar] ⟨sport⟩ ein ~ *a foul*; der Ball ging ins ~ .. *went out of play* od *bounds*

aus- [pref] [stets betont, aber: ~ein·ander etc] **1.** [trennbar vor Verben] mst *out*: ·ausgehen (ich gehe aus — ausgegangen) *to go out*; ·ausgeben *to outlay* **a.** heraus, hinaus; → austreten **b.** (weg) → ausgehen || (Richtung) → aussenden **c.** [mit Umsprung des Objekts] → (Glas) austrinken; (jdn) ausfragen **d.** ⟨übtr⟩ (z Ende) → auslernen || → ausbauen **2.** [untrennbar vor mst v Verben abgeleiteten Substantiven, desgl. Adj. u Adv.] ·Ausbruch *outbreak*; *breaking-out* | → Ausgang; ausgiebig || Ausleerung | → ausgelernt || → Ausbau

-aus [suff] *out*, jahr~ *year out*

†·**aus|antworten** vt ⟨jur⟩ *to surrender*

·**Ausapern** n ~s/ *melting-away of glacial snow*

·**aus|arbeiten I.** vt [h] **1.** *to work out*; *to hollow out*; (Schnitzerei) *to carve* ‖ *to rough-hew*; *mould, fashion* (aus *from*) ‖ (Ochsen) *to flay, skin* **2.** ⟨übtr⟩ (Gegenstand) *to work*, (Plan etc) *to work out*; *to amplify*; *to finish off, to perfect* ‖ *to work up* (z *to, into*) ‖ (Methode, Theorie) *to develop* ‖ (schriftlich) *to write, to compose*; ⟨arts⟩ *to make out* ‖ (Plan) *to draw up, to lay out*; (Einzelheiten) *to hammer* od *work out* ‖ im einzelnen, sorgfältig ~ *to work out in detail, to elaborate*, sorgsam ausgearbeitet *elaborate* (*design*) **3.** sich (körperlich) ~ *to take exercise*; *to take* (od *indulge in*) *bodily* od *physical exercise*, sich sehr ~ *to take plenty of exercise* **II.** ≗ n *working-out*; → ·**Ausarbeitung** f ~/~en **1.** (Ausarbeiten) *working-out, elaboration*; sorgfältige ~ *elaborateness, perfection* **2.** [konkr] (schriftliche) *treatise, composition*; *essay*

·**aus|arten** vi [s] *to degenerate* (in *into*) ‖ ⟨übtr⟩ *to degenerate, to develop* (z *into*); ~ in *to run to* (*exaggeration*) ·**Ausartung** f ~/~en *degeneration* ‖ (Zustand) *degeneracy* ‖ ⟨übtr⟩ *development*

·**aus|ästen**, ⟨for mst⟩ ·aus|asten vt [h] (Baum) *to prune*; *to rid of branches*; *to clear, trim*

·**Ausatemventil** n (an Gasmaske) *outlet valve*

·**aus|atmen** vt/i [h] vi/t *to breathe out, to exhale*; (sterben) ⟨a.⟩ die Seele ~ *to breathe one's last, to expire* ·**Ausatmung** f ~/~en *exhalation, expiration*; ~sbewegung *expiratory movement*

·**aus|baden** vt [h] ⟨fig⟩ (etw) *to face out*; *to suffer for, to pay for* (*a th*) ‖ die S ~ *to face the music*; *to face it out* ‖ es (*or* die S) ~ müssen *to be in for it*, ⟨bes Am fam⟩ *to be left holding the bag*; ich will sie die ganze S nicht ~ l *I won't have the whole thing visited on her*

·**aus|baggern** vt [h] (Teich) *to drag, dredge*

·**Ausbaggerung** f ~/~en *dragging, dredging*

°·**aus|baldowern** vt [h] *to find out, to discover*

·**aus|ballotieren** vt [h] (jdn) *to blackball*

·**Ausbau** m ~(e)s/e **1.** ⟨arch⟩ *finishing*; *completion* (*of a house*) ‖ *extension* | *construction* (*of fortifications*); *consolidation* (*of a position*) **2.** ⟨übtr⟩ *development, expansion, extension, enlargement* (*of an institution*) ‖ *improvement* **3.** [konkr] ⟨arch⟩ (Vorbau) *projecting part of a building* ‖ (Anbau) *extension* (an *to*) ≗**fähig** a ⟨com etc⟩ *progressive* (Stellung)

·**aus|bauchen** vt [h] *to belly* ‖ **sich** ~ *to swell out* (z *into*); *to belly, bulge*; ⟨bes mas⟩ *to sag*

·**Ausbauchung** f ~/~en *bulge, bulging*; *swelling* | [konkr] *swelling, protrusion, protuberance*; *convexity*

·**aus|bauen** vt [h] **1.** ⟨arch⟩ (Gebäude) *to complete, finish* ‖ (ein Stockwerk) *to add to*; *to enlarge* | (Grube) *to exhaust* ‖ (Schacht) *to timber* ‖ ⟨mil⟩ (Stellung) *to consolidate* **2.** ⟨übtr⟩ (Theorie) *to construct* | (Einrichtung, Plan) *to develop, extend, expand, enlarge* ‖ (Beziehungen) *to cultivate*; (Lage) *to improve* **3.** (Teile her~) *to remove, demount* **4.** ⟨tech⟩ *to dismantle*

·**aus|bauschen** vt [h] → ausbauchen

·**aus|bedingen** vt [→ dingen] [h] etw ~, sich etw ~ *to stipulate for a th*; ~, daß *to stipulate, to condition that*; etw bes ~, als wesentlich ~ *to stipulate a th*; ⟨jur⟩ *to reserve a th* ‖ → vorbehalten

·**aus|beinen** vt [h] ⟨cul⟩ *to bone*

·**aus|beißen** [h] vt/i **I.** vt **1.** e–n Zahn ~, sich [dat] e–n Zahn ~ *to break a tooth* **2.** ⟨übtr⟩ †(jdn) *to cut* (*a p*) *out*; *to oust, supplant* (*a p*) **3.** sich die Zähne an etw ~ *to be unable to cope with a th* **II.** vi ⟨geol⟩ *to crop out*

·**aus|beizen** vt [h] *to remove by corrosives*

·**Ausbesserer** m *mender*; *patcher*; (Schuh–) *cobbler* ·**aus|bessern** v/t [h] (Haus, Straße etc) *to repair*; *to mend*; ausgebessert w *to be under repair* | (Kleid) *to mend*; (Schuhe) *to vamp* (*up*); (flicken) *to patch up* ‖ (Strümpfe) *to darn* | (Schiff) *to refit* ‖ (Kunstwerk etc) *to restore*

·**Ausbesserung** f ~/~en *mend*(*ing*); *repair* ‖ *darn* | *refit*(*ment*) (*of a ship*) ‖ *restoration* (*of a church*, etc.)

·**aus|beulen** vt [h] *to fair* ·**Ausbeulung** f ~/~en ⟨tact⟩ *bulge*

·**Ausbeute** f ~/ *yield* ‖ (Gewinn) *gain, profit*; *spoil* ~**zeche** f *copious mine*

·**aus|beuteln** vt [h] (Mehl) *to sift*; † *to bolt* ‖ †° jdn ~ *to fleece a p*

·**aus|beuten** vt [h] **1.** (erfolgreich verwerten) (etw) *to turn* (*a th*) *to* (*good*) *account*; *to utilize, exploit*; (Grube) *to work, develop* **2.** (jdn unmäßig ~) *to take advantage of* (*a p*); *to exploit* ‖ (Arbeiter) *to sweat* ‖ jds Werke ~ *to draw upon a p's works* ·**Ausbeuter** m ~s/~ *exploiter* ‖ *sweater* (*of workmen*) ·**Ausbeutung** f ~/~en **1.** *exploitation, utilization*; *development*; *working* (*of a mine*) **2.** *exploitation* (*of a p*); *sweating* ~**sbetrieb** m *sweat-shop* ~**ssystem** n *sweating-system*

·**aus|bezahlen** vt [h] = auszahlen; → a. bezahlen

·**aus|biegen** vt/i **1.** vt [h] *to bend*; *to bend* (od *to bow*) *outwards* **2.** vi [s] *to make way*; jdm, e–r S ~ → ausweichen ‖ ⟨mot⟩ *to swerve*

·**aus|bieten** vt [h] *to offer* (od *put up*) *for sale*; ⟨fig⟩ etw wie saures Bier ~ *not to be able to get rid of a th* ‖ (in d Zeitung) *to advertise*

·**aus|bilden** vt [h] **1.** (jdn) *to teach, instruct*; er wurde in Eton (als Jurist) ausgebildet *he received his education at Eton* (*he was bred a lawyer*) ‖ (Schwestern; s–e Stimme) *to train*; *drill* (in *in*); als Lehrling ausgebildet w v jdm *to be apprenticed to a p* | ⟨mil & mar⟩ (Truppen) *to train, drill*; v neuem ~ *to retrain*; ausgebildet w *to drill* **2.** ⟨übtr⟩ (den Geist; Inneres) *to cultivate*; *form, mould* ‖ (Fähigkeiten) *to develop, perfect*; *cultivate, improve* **3. sich** ~ **a.** *to train* (als *as*; z *for*) **b.** *to perfect o.s.* (in *in*); *to improve one's knowledge* (in *in*) ‖ (beruflich) *to qualify o.s.* (f *for*), *to qualify* (als *as*); sich im Gesang ~ *to train to be a singer* ‖ sich bes ~ *to specialize* (f *for*; in *in*) ·**Ausbilder** m ~s/~ ⟨bes mil⟩ *instructor*; ⟨mil⟩ *drill sergeant*, (*NCO*) *instructor, trainer* ·**Ausbildung** f ~/~en **1.** *education, instruction* ‖ (berufliche) *education* (:*technical e.*), *training* (*of a p*); gründliche ~ *thorough grounding* (in *in*); ~ erfahren, erhalten *to undergo one's training* ‖ körperliche ~ *physical training* ‖ strenge ~ *drill*; vielseitige ~ *accomplishments, attainments* [pl]; ~ des Bedienenden *operator training*; mit ungenügender ~ (P) *of substandard qualifications* | ⟨mil⟩ *drill*; jdn e–r neuen ~ unterziehen *to retrain a p* ‖ ~ zum Flieger *training as an aviator* ‖ ⟨mil⟩ geschlossene ~ *unit training* **2.** *cultivation, improvement* (*of the mind*, etc) **3.** (genossene) ~ (Schulbildung etc) *educational background*

·**Ausbildungs-** ~**bataillon** n *training battalion* ~**beihilfe** f *tr. subsidy, educational grant* ~**hilfsmittel** n pl *tr. aids* ~**jahr** n ⟨Ger⟩ praktisches ~ (f Lehrer) *a year's training, training-year* ~**kursus** m *course of instruction* ~**lager** n *tr. camp* ⟨a. pol⟩ ~**richtlinien** f pl *tr. project outline*(*s*) ~**stelle** f *tr. centre* (⟨Am⟩ *center*) ~**unteroffizier** m ⟨artill⟩ *sergeant-major instructor on gunnery*, ⟨fam⟩ *smig*; → Ausbilder ~**vorschrift** f ⟨mil⟩ *tr. manual* ~**weg** m (bisheriger) *educational background* ~**zeit** f *period of instruction*

·**Ausbiß** m ⟨geol⟩ (an die Oberfläche tretende Lagerstätte) *outcrop*

·**aus|bitten** vt [h] **1.** sich etw ~ *to ask* od *beg for a th*; *to request* od *beg a th*; sich e–e Gunst ~ v jdm *to ask a p a favour, to ask a favour of a p* ‖ darf ich mir den Zucker ~? *would you* *pass the sugar, please; may I trouble you for the sugar?* | ich bitte mir Ruhe aus! *silence, please!* ich bitte mir aus, hier zu bleiben! *I must insist on your remaining!* ‖ das bitte ich mir aus! das will *or* möchte ich mir ausgebeten haben! *I insist upon it!* (drohend) ich bitte mir aus! *here, you!* **2.** jdn ~: wir sind heute abend ausgebeten *we are asked out to-night*

·**aus|blasen** vt [h] **1.** (Rauch) *to puff* (in e–r Wolke *in a cloud*) **2.** (Ei) *to blow* ‖ (Licht) *to blow* od *put out* ‖ (Hochofen) *to blow out* ‖ ⟨fig⟩ jdm das Lebenslicht ~ *to do for* (od *kill*) *a p*; (durch Schuß) *to blow a p's brains out* ·**Ausbläser** m *defective* (*non-exploding*) *shrapnel*; ⟨sl⟩ *dud* ·**Ausblashahn** m ⟨tech⟩ *blow-off cock*

·**aus|bleiben I.** vi [s] (P) *to stay away*; *to stay* od *stop out* ‖ lange ~ *to be long in coming*; er war ausgeblieben *he had not come* **2.** (S) *to fail to appear* od *arrive* ‖ die Post ist heute ausgeblieben *the mail has not come in to-day* ‖ der Regen ist ausgebl. *the rain has held off* | der Atem blieb ihm aus *he stopped breathing*; *his breath failed him* | die Strafe wird für sie nicht ~ *they won't escape punishment* ‖ es konnte nicht ~ *it was inevitable*, es konnte nicht ~ ihn z beeinflussen *it could not fail to influence him*; es konnte nicht ~, daß *it could not be helped that ..* **II.** ≃ n *staying-away* (od *out*) ‖ *absence*; unerlaubtes ~ *absence without leave* ⟨a. jur⟩; ⟨jur⟩ *non-appearance* ‖ *failure*; im Falle des ~s e–r S *failing a th* (: *failing an answer to .. I shall ..*)

·**aus|bleichen** vi/t **1.** vi [s] *to grow pale*; *to fade* **2.** vt [h] *to bleach*; ⟨übtr⟩ *to efface*

·**Ausblick** m ~s/~e *outlook* (über *over*), (offener, freier *open*) *view* (auf die Berge *of the mountains*, in den Hafen *of the port*); *peep* (auf die See *of the sea*); *prospect* (auf *of*; nach *to*; über *over*); weiter ~ *vista* (auf, über *of*); ⟨for⟩ (Lichtung) *opening* ‖ ein Zimmer mit ~ auf die Straße *a room overlooking* (od *giving on*, *facing*) *the street*; e–n ~ gewähren *or* h auf *to overlook* (: *the window overlooks the valley*) | ⟨übtr⟩ *outlook* (auf *on*; in die Zukunft *on the future*); *vista* (in *into*); neue ~e [pl] *new vistas* [pl]

·**ausblühen** vi [h] *to cease blooming* (od *flowering*); *to fade*; ausgeblüht h *to be finished* od *over* | (of rocks) *to effloresce* | ⟨fig⟩ *to fade*; *to decay* ·**Ausblühung** f ~/~en ⟨chem⟩ *efflorescence*

·**aus|bluten** vi [h] *to bleed*, laß es ~ *let it bleed* ‖ die Wunde hat ausgeblutet *the wound has ceased bleeding* ‖ (zu Tode) *to bleed to death*

·**aus|bohren** vt [h] *to drill*

·**aus|bojen** vt [h] *to mark by buoys*

·**aus|booten** vt [h] (jdn) *to bring* od *convey* (*a p*) *ashore in a boat* | ⟨übtr⟩ °jdn ~ *to dismiss a p* (*from office*); *to expel* (*from a club, etc*) ⟨fam⟩ *to give a p the sack*; ⟨sl⟩ *to sack a p*, *to kick* od *chuck a p out*, *to get a p chucked out* ·**Ausbootung** f *conveyance in boats* | *being dismissed* od ⟨sl⟩ *sacked*

·**aus|borgen** vt [h] (Geld) *to lend* (*out*)

·**aus|bracken** vt [h] (Vieh) = ausmerzen

·**aus|braten** vi/t **1.** vi [h & s] *to roast thoroughly* od *sufficiently* **2.** vt [h] (Fleisch) *to roast* ‖ (Schmalz, Fett) *to render*; *to melt down*

·**aus|brausen** vi [h] ~, sich ~ *to cease blustering* od *roaring*; *to calm down*

·**aus|brechen** vt/i **I.** vt [h] **1.** (Steine) *to quarry* (*out*); *to break* (aus *out of* [*the wall*]); (Erz) *to break* (*out of*) **2.** (Speise) *to throw up*; *to vomit*; *to nauseate*; (of the stomach) *to reject* **3.** ⟨hort⟩ Äste in e–m Baum ~ *to lop off branches from a tree*, *to lop* od *prune a tree* **II.** vi [s] **A. 1.** ein Brett bricht aus *a board comes* (od *gets*) *loose* **2.** (T) *to break loose* ‖ ⟨racing⟩ *to break course* ‖ ⟨aero⟩ (beim Start) *to swerve* (*in taking off*) **3.** (P) **a.** (of prisoners) *to break loose* **b.** ⟨mil⟩ *to make a sally* od *sortie* **B.** ⟨übtr⟩ *to break*, *burst out* od *forth*; *to burst* **1.** (Sturm) *to break* (*out*); (Vulkan) *to erupt* | (Seuche etc) *to break out* ‖ ~ über *to break on* (*the heads of ..*); die Krise ist ausgebrochen über .. *the crisis has arisen over ..* ‖ wieder ~ *to recrudesce* **2. in Beifall ~** *to break into applause* ‖ in Entzücken ~ *to go into raptures* (*over*) ‖ in e–n Ruf ~ *to raise* od *give a shout*; *to give vent to a hail* ‖ in Gelächter, Lachen ~ *to burst out laughing*, *to explode with laughter*, *raptures* ‖ in Schluchzen ~ *to break into sobs* ‖ in Schweiß ~ *to break into a sweat* ‖ in Tränen ~ *to burst into tears*; *to burst out crying* ‖ in Wut ~ *to explode with fury* ·**Ausbrechen** n **1.** *breaking*(*-out*) ‖ → Erbrechen **2.** *breaking loose* ‖ → Ausbruch

·**aus|breiten** vt [h] **A. 1.** (Tuch) *to spread*; *to pass* (über *over*); *to sprawl* (über *across*) ‖ (Teppich) *to spread out*, *to unroll* ‖ (Arme, Flügel) *to spread*; *to expand*; *to open* (*out*), *to splay* (*out*); *to throw* (*one's arms*) *aside* | (entfalten) *to unfold*, *display*, *exhibit* (vor jdm *before a p*) | (Licht, Wärme) *to diffuse* **2.** (Geschäft) *to extend* ‖ (Einfluß, Macht) *to extend* (über *over*); *to increase*, *strengthen* ‖ (Lehre etc) → verbreiten **B. sich ~ 1.** (S) *to sprawl* (über *over*) ‖ *to branch out* ‖ *to be in the increase* ‖ (of a plain) *to stretch* (meilenweit *for miles*); *to extend*; *to spread* (vor uns *before us*) | ⟨übtr⟩ (P) sich ~ über e–n Gegenstand *to enlarge* (od *expatiate*, *dilate*) *on a subject* **2. a.** (Raum gewinnen) *to gain ground*; (of diseases) *to spread*; (of fire) *to mushroom* ‖ (T) *to propagate* ‖ (of the sea) sich ~ über *to gain upon* (*the land*) **b.** *to* (*make*) *progress*; sich immer weiter ~ *to make great headway* ·**Ausbreitung** f ~/~en **1.** (Ausbreiten) *spreading*; *expansion* ‖ *diffusion* (*of light*, etc.); *dispersion* | *unfolding*, *display* **2.** (Vergrößerung) *extension* (*of influence*) ‖ *spread* (*of a disease*) ‖ *increase*; *progress* ‖ → Verbreitung **3.** (~sgebiet) ⟨geog⟩ *range*

·**aus|brennen** vt/i **I.** vt [h] **1.** (Haus) *to burn out*, *to gut*; vollkommen ausgebrannt *completely gutted by fire* **2.** ⟨med⟩ (Wunde) *to cauterize* **3.** (of the sun) (Boden) *to scorch*, *parch*; *to dry up* | mir ist die Kehle wie ausgebrannt *I am parched* (*with thirst*) **II.** vi [s] **1.** (of fire) *to burn out*, das Feuer ~ l *to let the fire burn* od *go out* ‖ ausgebrannter Krater *extinct volcano* **2.** das Haus brannte aus *the house was gutted* (od *burnt out*) **III.** ≃ n (Rakete) *burnout*

·**aus|bringen I.** vt [h] **1.** (Boote) *to bring out*, *to get out* | (Kücken) *to hatch*; *to produce*; (Junge) *to bear* **2.** ⟨typ⟩ (Zeile) *to drive out* **3.** ein dreifaches Hoch (drei Hurrarufe) ~ *to give three cheers* (*three hurrahs*) ‖ e–n Trinkspruch ~ auf jdn *to toast* od *drink to a p*, *to drink* od *propose a p's health*; *to give* (od *propose*, *submit*) *the toast of a p* ‖ viele Trinksprüche wurden ausgebracht *many toasts were proposed*, *many healths were drunk*; s–e Gesundheit wurde ausgebracht *his health was drunk* **4.** ⟨ind⟩ *to produce* **II.** ≃ n (Leistung) ⟨ind⟩ *production capacity*

·**Ausbruch** m ~(e)s/≃e **1.** → Ausbrechen **2.** *the breaking out* (*of a prisoner*) **3.** *eruption*, *outbreak* (*of a volcano*) ‖ *outbreak* (*of a fire*); *disease*; Kriegs≃ *outbreak of war*; ~ der Feindseligkeiten *commencement of hostilities*; frischer (neuer) ~ *recrudescence* (*of hostilities*) | (Gefühls≃) *outburst*; *eruption*, *explosion* (*of anger*, *laughter*); *burst* (*of applause*, *laughter*); *transport*, *thrill* (*of joy*); *blaze* (*of passion*) | zum ~ k *to break out*; (of critical events) *to come to a head*; nicht z ~ k (of storm) *to hold off*; die Dinge z ~ k l *to bring matters to a head*; nicht z ~ k l *to suppress*, *to nip in the bud* **4.** (of wine) = Auslese ≃**-ssicher** a *escape-proof* (*jail*)

·**aus|brüllen** vrefl [h] sich ~ *to roar* od *cry to one's heart's content*

·**aus|brüten I.** vt [h] **1.** (Eier) *to hatch, incubate*; (Junge) *to hatch* ‖ Junge ~ (of birds) *to hatch out*; (of eggs) ausgebrütet w *to hatch out* **2.** ⟨fig⟩ (Plan) *to hatch*; *contrive*; *devise*; (Unheil) *to plot* ‖ °~ = ·ausfressen **II.** ≗ n *hatching*; *incubation* (*of eggs*) ‖ ⟨fig⟩ *hatching, contrivance*; *plotting* ·**Ausbrütung** f = Ausbrüten

·**aus|buchen** vt [h] (Betrag wieder) ~ *to cancel* (*an entry*)

·**aus|buchsen** vt [h] ⟨tech⟩ *to bush*

°·**aus|büchsen** vi [s] *to skedaddle* (⟨a. mil⟩ fliehen) → abhauen 2.

·**aus|buchten** vt/i [h] **1.** vt *to bend* (od *bow, curve*) *convexly* od *outwards*; *to bulge out*; ausgebuchtet s, sich ~ *to be convex* | (Küste) *to indent*; ausgebuchtete Küste *indented coast-line* **2.** vi *to spread* od *splay out* (in *into*) ·**Ausbuchtung** f ~/~en *bulging* ‖ *convex bend* od *curve*; ⟨bot⟩ *sinus* | *indentation* (*of a coast*)

°·**aus|buddeln** vt [h] *to dig out*

·**aus|bügeln** vt [h] *to iron* ‖ ⟨fig⟩ das wird sich schon wieder ~ *things will dry straight*

·**Ausbund** m ~(e)s/≗e (P) *pattern, paragon* (der Tugend *of virtue*); ⟨a. iron⟩ ‖ ein ~ v Gelehrsamkeit (*he is*) *a prodigy of learning*; (*the work is*) *a marvel of l.* | ~ v Frechheit *the limit of insolence*; er ist ein ~ v Schurke *he is an arrant rogue, an arch-knave, a regular rascal* ‖ er ist ein wahrer ~ *he is a wanton* ·**ausbündig** a *excellent, exemplary* | *downright, regular*

·**aus|bürgern** vt [h] jdn *expatriate* ·**Ausbürgerung** f ~/~en *expatriation*

·**aus|bürsten** vt [h] *to brush, dust*; etw (tüchtig) ~ *to give a th a* (*thorough*) *brushing* ‖ ⟨mot⟩ die Polster ~ *to brush the cushions and seats*

·**Ausdauer** f ~/ *perseverance, persistence, persistency, pertinacity* (: *with great p.*); *staying-power, stay*; *steadfastness, steadiness* ‖ (Geduld) *endurance* ·**aus|dauern** vi/t [h] **1.** vi *to hold out*; *to persist, persevere* (in *in*) **2.** vt (etw) *to endure*

·**ausdauernd** a **1.** *persistent, persevering, tenacious, steadfast*; *steady*; *dogged* ‖ (fleißig) *assiduous*; ~er Fleiß *assiduity* ‖ (geduldig) *patient* **2.** ⟨bot⟩ *perennial* (*plants*)

·**ausdehnbar** a *expansible, expansile*; *dilatable* (*metal*) ‖ (v innen) *distensible*; *distensile* ‖ ⟨zoo⟩ *protractile* (*organ*) | *prolongable* (*meeting*) ·**Ausdehnbarkeit** f ~/ *extensibility, expansibility* ‖ *dilatibility* (*of metal*) ‖ *distensibility*

·**aus|dehnen** vt [h] **A. 1.** (Metall; die Brust) *to expand* ‖ (Organ) *to dilate*; *to distend* ‖ (Grenzen) *to extend* ‖ gewaltsam ~ *to stretch* ‖ *to spread* (*one's shoes, gloves*) **2.** (Zeit, Vorgang) *to extent*; *prolong*; (Debatte) *protract* ‖ (Besuch) *extend* **3.** ⟨übtr⟩ (Geschäft) *to extend, enlarge*; (Macht etc) *extend* (über *over*; auf *to*) ‖ (s–e Interessen etc) *to widen*; *spread* (über *over*) **B. sich ~ 1.** ⟨phys⟩ (of water, etc.) *to expand* (durch Hitze *with heat*); *to dilate* **2.** (of a flood) *to spread* (über *over*); *to widen* **3.** (of areas) *to extend o.s.*; *to extend, stretch, range* (an .. entlang *along* ..; nach Osten *east*; v .. bis *from* .. *to*; über *across, over*); *to sweep* (*away*) (nach Norden *north*); sich meilenweit ~ *to stretch* od *extend for miles* ‖ (of time) *to spread* (*over 5 years*); die Sitzung dehnte sich bis in die frühen Morgenstunden aus *the meeting lasted into the small hours* **4.** (of subjects) *to widen*; (of influence) *to increase* ‖ → ausgedehnt

·**Ausdehnung** f ~/~en **1.** ⟨phys⟩ *expansion* (*of steam*); Wärme≗ *heat e.* ‖ ~ in der Länge *linear e.* ‖ ⟨med⟩ *dilatation* (*of organs*), *dilation* **2.** *distension* ‖ *spread*; *extension* (über *over*) **3.** ⟨übtr⟩ *extension, enlargement* (*of a business*) | (of influence, etc.) *extension* (auf *to*); *increase* ‖ *widening* (*of relations with*) **4.** (Umfang) *extent, spread, stretch, range* (: *a wide r.*); *sweep*; *dimensions* [pl] (v gr ~ *of great d.*); → Umfang ‖ an ~ gewinnen *to extend*; *to increase*

·**Ausdehnungs-** ~**behälter** m *surge tank* ~**drang** m *tendency to expand* ≗**fähig** a *expansive* ~**fähigkeit** f *expansibility* ~**gebiet** n *range* (*of animals*, etc.) ~**gefäß** n *expansion tank* ~**koeffizient** m (kubischer, linearer) ~ *coefficient of* (*cubic, linear*) *expansion* ~**kraft** f *expansive force* ~**stoß** m, ~**stück** n *expansion joint* ~**vermögen** n *ability to expand* od *extend*; *expansive force*; *power of dilatation* ~**zahl** f *coefficient of expansion*

·**ausdenkbar** a *imaginable, conceivable*

·**aus|denken** vt [h] **1.** (z Ende denken) *to think out* ‖ die Folgen sind nicht –zu– *the consequences are unimaginable, inconceivable* (od *hard to conceive*), *do not bear thinking about* **2.** (ersinnen) *to think out* (⟨Am⟩ *up*); *to excogitate*; (Plan etc) *to devise*; *concoct, contrive*; *hatch, to invent, fabricate* (*a story*); *to plan* (*a th*); *to invent* (*a th*) | sich etw ~ *to imagine a th*; *to think of a th*; *to contrive a th*; sich ~ z tun *to contrive to do*; *to fancy a th for o.s.*; das hast du dir bloß ausgedacht *that is merely a concoction of yours* ‖ das läßt sich gar nicht ~ *that is beyond conception*

·**aus|deuten** vt [h] *to interpret, expound, explain* ‖ → auslegen ·**Ausdeutung** f ~/~en *interpretation, explanation*

·**aus|dienen** vi [h] *to serve one's time* ‖ ausgedient h (of garments, etc.) *to be worn out*; der Hut hat ausgedient *the hat has had its day* ‖ → ausgedient

·**aus|dorren** vi [s] *to dry up*; *to wither*; ⟨a. übtr⟩

·**aus|dörren** vt [h] *to dry up, to wither*; (of the sun) (Land) *to parch, scorch*; die Kehle ~ *to parch one's throat* ·**ausgedörrt** a *parched* (*land*); *dry, arid, sapless*

·**aus|drehen** vt [h] (das Gas) *to turn off*; (elektr. Licht) *to switch off*

·**aus|dreschen** vt [h] *to thresh*

·**Ausdruck** m ~(e)s/≗e **1.** (sprachlicher) *expression, term, word* ‖ (~sweise) *expression*; *diction, style, terms* [pl]; *wording*; *enunciation*; *utterance*; gekünstelte ~sweise *affected style* od *speech*; bilderreiche ~sweise *pictorial style* | bildlicher ~ *figurative expression*; euphemistischer ~ *euphemism*; falscher ~ *solecism*; floskelhafter ~ *flowery expression*; gemeiner ~ *vulgarism*; gewählter ~ *elegant expression*; idiomatischer ~ *idiom, phrase*; schiefer ~ *inexact expression*; veralteter ~ *archaism* ‖ Fach≗ (*technical*) *term*; Gewähltheit im ~ *elegance* **2.** (äußeres Zeichen f. innere Vorgänge) **a.** *expression* (*of feelings, thoughts*, etc.); Gesichts≗ *facial expression*; *cast of countenance* **b.** (Äußerung) *expression, enunciation*; *utterance*; *voice* ‖ *indicator* (*of e.g. economic growth* **3.** ⟨arts & mus⟩ *expression*, mit ~ *with expression*, ⟨mus⟩ *espressivo* **4.** Wendungen: s–e Meinung zum ~ bringen *to express* od *voice one's opinion*; s–n Protest zum ~ bringen *to record one's protest*; den deutschen Standpunkt zum ~ b. *to put the German point of view*; etw deutlich zum ~ bringen (of feelings) *to be eloquent* (od *expressive*) *of a th* | ~ finden in *to find expression* (od *voice*) *in* | e–m Gefühl etc ~ geben *or* verleihen *to give expression, voice, utterance to a feeling, to express* (od *to voice, to be expressive of*) *a feeling*; s–r Begeisterung ~ g. *to display one's enthusiasm*; s–r Entrüstung ~ geben *to express one's indignation*; s–r Genugtuung ~ g. *to demonstrate* od *express one's satisfaction*; der Überzeugung ~ g. *to record one's conviction* (*that*) | e–r S deutlichen ~ verleihen (of feelings) *to be eloquent* od *expressive of a th* | mit dem ~ größter, vorzüglichster Hochachtung (Briefschluß) "*with the expression of the deepest respect*" **5.** [in comp] → Ausdrucks- & Ausdruck 1. (~sweise)

·**ausdrückbar** a *expressible*

·**aus|drucken** vt [h] (ein Wort) *to print in full* ‖ *to print out*; ausgedruckter Satz ⟨typ⟩ *printed--out form*

·**aus|drücken** vt [h] **1.** (Schwamm) *to squeeze* ‖ (Saft) *to squeeze out* ‖ (Frucht) *to press* **2.** ⟨übtr⟩ (wiedergeben) **a.** *to express* ‖ (of the face) (Gefühl) *to be expressive of*; *to register* (*her face registered disapproval*) ⟨a. film⟩ ‖ nicht ~ *to be inexpressive of* ‖ ⟨arts & mus⟩ (Inneres, Charakter) *to represent, depict*; *reveal* | **sich ~** *to express o.s.* (: *beauty expresses itself in* ..) **b.** (in Worten) *to express*; *word*; *utter, voice*; *enunciate, to be enunciative of*; *to enounce*; in bes Art ~ *to put* ‖ s–e Meinung ~ *to express* (od *voice*; *give expression to*) *one's opinion*; die Meinung ~ daß .. *to express the view that* ..; → Beileid, Bedauern ‖ ich möchte es so ~ *I prefer to put it this way*; um es gelinde -zu- *to put it mildly*; ich weiß nicht, wie ich es ~ soll *I do not know how to put it* | **sich ~** *to express o.s.*; wie man sich gewöhnlich ausdrückt *in common parlance* ‖ wie soll ich mich ~? *how shall I put it*? ‖ sich derb (gemein) ~ *to use strong* (*bad*) *language* ‖ sich kurz ~ *to be brief* ‖ sich fließend, geläufig ~ *to be a fluent speaker* ‖ sich gewählt ~ *to be fastidious in one's expressions*

·**ausdrücklich 1.** a *definite, express* (*command*); *explicit* (*promise*); *categorical* **2.** adv *expressly, explicitly*; *categorically*; jdn ~ bitten *to beg a p particularly*; natürlich sagte er es nicht ~ *of course he didn't say so in so many words*

·**Ausdrucks- ~bewegung** f *expressive movement, gesture* (~ des Gesichts *facial g.*) **≗fähig** a *expressionable* **~form** f *expression-form* **~gymnastik** f *expressive* od *gestural gymnastics* [pl] **~kraft** f *expressiveness*; *significance, significancy* ‖ *enunciative power* **~kunst** f *expressionism* **≗los** a *expressionless, inexpressive*; *blank, vacant* (*look*); *vacuous* (*face*) **~losigkeit** f *inexpressiveness*; *blankness*; *vacuosity* (*of the face*) **~mittel** n [pl] *means* [pl] *of expression* **≗voll** a *expressive*; *eloquent* (*look, eyes*); *emphatic*; das ≗e *the expressiveness* **~weise** f → Ausdruck 1.; *phraseology*; → deutlich, Deutlichkeit

·**Ausdrusch** m *threshing* ‖ (Ausgedroschenes) *threshing, yield of threshing*

·**aus|duften** vt [h] (Wohlgeruch) *to send out*; *to transpire*

·**aus|dulden** vt/i [h] *to endure* od *suffer to the end*

·**ausdünstbar** a *perspirable* (*matter*)

·**aus|dunsten,** ·**aus|dünsten** vt/i [h] **1.** vt (Feuchtigkeit) *evaporate, to vaporize*; *to exhale*; *to transpire* ‖ (ausschwitzen) *to transpire, to perspire*; *to sweat* (*out*); ausgedünstet w *to transpire* **2.** vi *to evaporate, to exhale* ‖ *to transpire*

·**Ausdünstung** f ~/~en *evaporation, exhalation*; (schädliche) *effluvium* L ‖ (Haut≗) *transpiration*; *perspiration* | *vapour*; → Dunst

ausein·ander adv *apart*; *separated*; *asunder*; weit ~ *wide asunder*; die Verlobung ist ~ *the engagement is off* ‖ sie sind fast 8 Jahre ~ *there are nearly eight years between them* ‖ wollt ihr ~! *keep away from each other*! ~|**brechen** vt [h] & vi [s] *to break asunder* **~|breiten** vt [h] *to unfold*; *to spread out*; → ausbreiten **~|bringen** vt [h] *to separate, to sever* ‖ (Freunde) *to set at variance* **~|fallen** vi [s] *to fall asunder*; *to collapse* ⟨a. fig⟩ ‖ ⟨mil⟩ (P) *to be incapacitated*, (S) *to become inoperative* **~|falten** vt [h] *to unfold* **~|fliegen** vi [s] *to fly asunder, to scatter* **~gebracht** [pp v –|bringen] a *torn* (*asunder*), *divided, disunited* (*by strife, etc*) **~|gehen** vi [s] **1.** (P) *to separate*; *to part*; (Verlobte) *to part*; *to break off engagement, to come to an end with each other*; als Freunde ~ *to part friends* | (of a party, etc.) *to disperse*; *to scatter* ‖ die Verlobung ist auseinandergegangen *the engagement is off* **2.** (of roads, rays) *to diverge* | ⟨übtr⟩ (of reports, etc.) *to diverge, differ*; weit ~ *to vary widely* **3.** (of a chair) *to break*; *to come apart*; in Stücke ~ *to come asunder* **4.** (P) °~ *to grow stout, to put on flesh*; *to spread* **~gehend** a *divergent* (*rays*); *conflicting* (*views*); *different* **~|halten** vt [h] *to keep* (*things*) *apart* (od *asunder, separated*) ‖ ⟨übtr⟩ *to discriminate, distinguish one th from the other*; ich kann sie nicht ~ *I can't tell them apart, I don't know* (od *see*), *I can't tell which is which* ‖ zwei P ~ *to tell two persons apart* **~|jagen** vt [h] (e–e Menge) *to break up, to scatter, to disperse* **~|kommen** vi [s] *to become separated*; *to drift apart* ‖ im Gedränge ~k *to lose sight of each other in the crowd* ‖ mit jdm ~ *to fall out with a p* **~|laufen** vi [s] (P) *to separate* | (of roads) *to diverge* ‖ (of dough) *to run*; *to refuse to take form* **~|leben** vrfl [h] sich ~ *to lose all interest in each other*; *to come to hate living together* **~|legen** vt [h] **1.** *to spread out*; *to unfold* ‖ (Maschinen) *to take to pieces* **2.** (erklären) *to explain* **~|liegen** vi [s] *to lie apart*; weit ~ *to lie* (od *be*) *far asunder* °**~|machen** vt [h] (Paket) *to undo* ‖ *to separate* ‖ die Beine ~ *to open out one's legs* **~nehmbar** a *disconnectable* **~|nehmen** vt [s] *to take to pieces* (od *asunder*) ‖ *to strip*; *to knock down* ‖ (Maschinen) *to dismount*; (Schiff etc) *to dismantle* **~|reißen** vt [h] *to tear*; *disrupt* (*a group*) **~|sein** vi [s] *to be* (*at*) *outs* **~|rücken 1.** vi [s] *to move apart* **2.** ≗ n ⟨mil-pol⟩ *disengagement* **~|setzen** vt [h] **1.** (P) *to separate* ‖ (P & S) *to put* od *place* .. *apart* od *asunder* **2.** ⟨übtr⟩ **a.** *to explain*; *to point out* (jdm *to a p*); (Standpunkt) *to expound*; (Lage) *to elucidate* (jdm *to a p*) ‖ (darlegen) (Frage) *to argue*; (Gründe) *to set forth* od *out*; *to state* **b. sich ~ mit etw** *to argue a th* (: *to a. the advisability of* ..); *to expound*; (of statements) *to set out a th* ‖ (im Kampfe etc) *to cope with, to cross swords with, to come to grips with, to come up against a th*, sich mit dem Leben ~ *to face* (od *bring o.s. into contact with*) *the realities of life, to make up one's mind about life* | **sich ~ mit jdm** *to argue with, to join issue with a p* ‖ *to have it out with, to pick a bone with, to come to grips with a p* ‖ (gütlich) *to come to an understanding* (od *to terms*) *with*; ⟨com⟩ *to compound with* (*one's creditors*); *to settle with a p* **≗setzung** f **1.** *explanation, exposition*; *statement* ‖ (Debatte) *discussion*; offene ~ *heart-to-heart talk* **2. a.** *quarrel, contest, dispute, controversy, altercation, difference, disagreement* (mit *with*); *coming-to-grips* (*with*) ‖ sie hatten e–e erregte ~ *they had high words* (über *about*); stürmische ~en *stormy passages* (*with a p*) **b.** (gütliche) *arrangement* (*with*); ⟨com⟩ *composition* (*with one's creditors*); *settling of accounts* **3.** ⟨jur⟩ *partition* (*of an inheritance*) ‖ sich auf e–e ~ einlassen *to take issue* (mit *with*) **~|sprengen** vt/i **1.** vt [h] (Gebäude) *to blow up* ‖ (Feind) *to disperse* **2.** vi [s] *to gallop* od *run off in all directions* **~|stehen** vi [h] weit ~ *to be far apart*; ~d a *distant* (*teeth*) **~|stellen** vt [h] (P & S) *to separate* **~|treiben** vt [h] (Menge) *to break up, to disperse, scatter* **~|treten** vi [s] ~! *break it up*! **≗- u Zus-ziehen** n (e–r Fahrzeugkolonne) *accordion effect* **~|ziehen 1.** vt [h] *to draw asunder*; *to spread* ‖ ⟨mil⟩ *to remove into different quarters*; ⟨tact⟩ *to deploy* **2.** ≗ n ⟨tact⟩ *deployment, extension, dispersal*

·**auserkoren** a = auserlesen a

·**auserlesen** vt [nur im pp]: ich habe ihn ~ *I have chosen him* ·**auserlesen** a *selected* (*society*; *wines*; *taste*); *exquisite, excellent, choice* (*fruit*);

picked (*craftsmen*) ‖ mit ~em Geschmack *choicely, daintily*

·**ausersehen** vt [h] [nur in pp]: ich habe ihn ~ *I have chosen* od *selected him* (*for*) ‖ ~ s *to be designed* (od *marked out*) (f, z *for*; zum Juristen .. *to be a lawyer*; z tun *to do*); *to be designated* (z *to, for*); (of funds) *to be earmarked* (z *for*)

·**auserwählen** vt [nur in pp auserwählt]: er wurde od war auserwählt *he was chosen* (od *singled out*) (f. *for*); ⟨theol⟩ *elected, predestined*

·**auserwählt** a **1.** *selected*; *select* (*audience*); *choice* (*equipment*); → auserlesen ‖ ⟨theol⟩ *predestinate*; das ~e Volk *the chosen people* **2.** die ≗e *the girl of one's choice, one's bride-elect*; m–e ≗e *my love, my financée*; der ≗e *the bridegroom-elect*; mein ~er *my fiancé* **|** ⟨theol⟩ der (die) ≗e *the elect*; der v Gott ≗e *God's elect*; [mst pl] die ≗en *the elect, the chosen*; (Seligen) *The Saved* pl

·**aus|essen** vt [h] **1.** (Suppe) *to eat up*; (Schüssel) *to clear* **2.** ⟨fig⟩ *to pay for* ‖ was du dir eingebrockt hast, das mußt du ~ *as you have made your bed, so you must lie in it* ‖ wir müssen es jetzt ~ *we are in for it now*; *we must take the consequences*

·**aus|fädeln** vt [h] (Nadel) *to unthread*

·**Ausfahrbahn** f *guide-rail*; → u.: Ausfahr-

·**aus|fahren** vi/t **I.** vi [s] **1.** *to drive out, to go for a drive, to take a drive* **2.** (of trains) *to steam out*; (of ships) *to leave port*; (of the fleet) *to put* (*out*) *to sea* **|** ⟨min⟩ (aus dem Schacht ~) *to ascend*; *to leave the pit* **3.** ⟨path⟩ (ausschlagen) *to be covered with pimples* **4.** das Messer fuhr ihm aus *his knife slipped* (od *glanced off*) **II.** vt [h] **1.** (jdn) *to drive out, to take* (*a p*) *for a drive* **2.** (e–n Weg) *to rut*, [mst pp] -ge- *rutted, marked with ruts, rutty* (*road*); ⟨fig⟩ -ge–es Geleise *beaten track* **3.** e–e Kurve ~ *to make a wide sweep round a corner* **4.** ⟨aero⟩ (Fahrgestell) *to extend*

·**Ausfahr- ~katze** f ⟨aero⟩ *guide trolley* **~schacht** m *ascending shaft* **~signal** n *departure--signal*

·**Ausfahrt** f ~/~en **1.** *going-out*; *putting-out to sea*; *starting*; *departure* (aus *from*; nach *for*) **|** ⟨min⟩ *ascent* **2.** (Spazierfahrt) *drive*, e–e ~ m *to take a drive, to go for a drive*; ⟨bes hors⟩ *turn--out* **3.** (Torweg) *gateway*; *doorway* **4.** ⟨mot⟩ (*point of*) *exit*; *Exit*; ⟨bes mot⟩ (*Way*) *Out* **5.** [in comp] **~(straße, -bahn)** ⟨mot⟩ *sliproad*; Nördliche ~ *Northbound*

·**Ausfall** m ~(e)s/≗e **A. 1.** ⟨mil⟩ *sally, sortie*, e–n ~ m *to make a sortie, to sally* **2.** ⟨fenc⟩ *pass, thrust, lunge* (im ~ *in the l.*); e–n ~ m *to make a l., to lunge* (auf *at*) ‖ ⟨gym⟩ *lunge* (*with one's arms stretched upwards*) **3.** ⟨übtr⟩ *attack* (gegen *against*; heftiger ~ *invective* (*against*) **B.** (Verlust) **1.** *loss*; Haar≗ *loss of hair* **|** ⟨übtr⟩ *falling--off, shortage*; ~ am Gewicht *loss in weight, short weight, underweight*; (Fehlbetrag) *loss, deficit, deficiency* ‖ ⟨mach⟩ *break-down* ‖ ⟨mil⟩ (an Gerät etc) *outage* **C.** (Ergebnis) *issue, outcome*, (*of election*, etc); *result* (*of examination*) ‖ (an Gerät etc) *outage* **2.** *leaving-out, omission* (*of a word*); *annulment, cancelling, cancellation* (*of a meeting*) **3.** ⟨chem⟩ *precipitate*; ⟨at⟩ *fall-out* **C.** (Ergebnis) *issue, outcome* (*of election*, etc); *result* (*of examination*) ‖ ⟨ind, etc⟩ *output, yield* **~bürgschaft** f *guarantee against loss, collateral security* **~jahr** n ⟨agr⟩ *fail-year* **~pforte** f ⟨mil⟩ *sally-port* **~schwung** m → Telemark **~serscheinung** f ⟨med⟩ *organic deficiency*; ~en [pl] *deficiency symptoms* **~stellung** f ⟨fenc⟩ *lunge* (in ~ *in the l.*) **~straße** f *main road leading out of a city*; *main outlet*; ⟨mot⟩ *arterial road* **~tor** n *sally-port* **~winkel** m ⟨phys⟩ *angle of reflection* **~zeit** f ⟨tech, ind⟩ *down time*

·**aus|fallen** vi/t **I.** vi [s] **A. 1.** (of hair, etc) *to come out*; das Haar fällt ihm aus *he is losing his hair* **2.** ⟨übtr⟩ (wegfallen) *to be omitted*; *to go*; (of words, etc.) *to be struck out*; *to be removed* ‖ *to fail to take place* (od *to come off*); *to be cancelled* ‖ die Schule (etc) fällt heute aus *there is no school today*; e–e Stunde fällt aus *there is one lesson less*; die Sitzung fiel aus *the meeting was cancelled* (od *did not take place*) ‖ ein Spieler fällt aus *there is one player short* ‖ e–e Sitzung ~ l *to drop a conference* ‖ ⟨mil & tech⟩ (Geschütz, Maschine etc) *to be put out of action, to become inoperative*; (P) *to be incapacitated*; –ge– *dead* (*engine*) **B. 1.** ⟨mil⟩ *to sally* (*out*), *to make a sortie* **|** ⟨fenc⟩ *to make a lunge*; *to thrust* **2.** ⟨übtr⟩ ~d w → ausfallend **C.** ⟨fig⟩ (geraten) gut (schlecht) ~ *to answer, to fall out, to come off, to eventuate, to turn out well* (*badly*); (of goods) *to sample out*; ungleich ~ ⟨tech⟩ *to differ* ‖ anders ~ *to prove otherwise*; ungünstig ~ f. jdn *to go against a p*; die Aufführung ist sehr gut –ge– *the performance was a success*; → Verlauf **II.** vt; sich [dat] e–n Zahn ~ *to break a tooth by falling*; sich e–n Arm ~ *to dislocate an arm by f.* ‖ → ausgefallen

·**ausfallend** a *abusive*; *coarse, rude, insulting* (*remarks*); ~ w *to become abusive, insolent, personal, provocative*; ~ w gegen jdn *to offend, provoke, abuse, insult a p* ·**Ausfällung** f ~/~en ⟨chem⟩ *precipitate, precipitation*

·**aus|fasern** vt/i [h] **1.** vt (Gewebe) *to unravel, to ravel out*; *to frazzle* ‖ ausgefasertes Ende *ravel* **|** sich am Rande ~ *to fray, frazzle, ravel* **2.** vi *to fray, frazzle*; *to fuzz* (*out*)

·**aus|fechten** vt [h] e–n Kampf ~ *to fight a war, to resort to arms* **|** ⟨übtr⟩ etw ~ *to fight for a th*; *to face a th* ‖ die S ~ *to face* (od *fight*) *the matter out* ‖ ⟨jur⟩ e–n Streit unter sich ~ *to interplead* [vi] ‖ ⟨eig & übtr⟩ es ~ *to fight it out*

·**aus|fegen 1.** vt [h] (Zimmer) *to sweep* (*out*); *to give* (*a room*) *a sweep* ‖ (Schmutz) *to sweep away* (od *up*) **2.** ≗ n *sweep*(*ing*) ·**Ausfeger** m **1.** *broom* **2.** ⟨übtr⟩ = Kehraus

·**aus|feilen** vt [h] *to file*; *to smooth with a file* **|** ⟨übtr⟩ (Sätze etc) *to file, polish*

·**Ausfeld** n ⟨crick⟩ *out-field*

·**aus|fertigen** vt [h] (Schriftstück) *to write* (*out*); *to draw up*; *to draft* ‖ (Rechnung) *to make out* (od *up*) ‖ (Paß) *to issue*; (Wechsel) *to issue*; (Scheck) *to make* (od *write*) *out* ‖ ⟨jur⟩ (Urkunde) *to execute*; *to make out*; (Abschrift) *to make*; (etw) doppelt ~ *to* (*make out in*) *duplicate*

·**Ausfertigung** f ~/~en *drawing-up*; *making--out* ‖ *issue* (*of a bill*) **|** ⟨jur⟩ *execution* (*of a deed*) ‖ erste ~ *original, script*, (Abschrift) *copy* ‖ in doppelter ~ *in duplicate*, in dreifacher ~ *in triplicate*, in vierfacher ~ *in quadruplicate* **~sgebühr** f *fee for the execution of a deed* **~stag** m *date of issue*

·**aus|finden** vt [h] = herausfinden ·**ausfindig** a (jdn, etw) ~ m *to find* od *make* od *search out, to discover*; *spot, trace*; *to run to earth*; (Flüchtling) *to locate*; jdn durch e–e P ~ m l *to send* od *order a p to find a p* ‖ die Wahrheit ~ m *to search out the truth*; (Flüchtling) *to ferret out*

·**aus|fischen** vt [h] (Teich) *to fish out*

·**aus|flaggen** vt [h] ⟨sport⟩ (Kurs) *to flag*

·**aus|flicken** vt [h] *to mend, repair*; *patch*; (Schuhe) *to cobble*

·**aus|fliegen** vi [s] *to fly away* od *out*; ⟨fig⟩ der Vogel ist ausgeflogen *the bird is flown* **|** ⟨übtr⟩ (e–n Ausflug m) *to make an excursion, to go on a trip*; alles war ausgeflogen *everybody was away* (*on trips*)

·**aus|fließen** vi [s] *to flow out*; *to issue* (v *from*) ‖ ~ auf *to drain out onto* ‖ ⟨übtr⟩ (ausgehen) *to flow, emanate, issue* (v *from*)

·**aus|flocken** vt/i [h/s] *to flocculate*

·**Ausflucht** f ~/~≗e **1.** † → Schlupfloch **2.** ⟨übtr⟩ (Ausrede) *excuse, come-off*; *evasion*, *prevarication, shift; shuffle; subterfuge; equivocation, quibble, sophistry*; lügenhafte ~̈e *mere yarns*; → Finte 2. || ~̈e m *or* gebrauchen *to equivocate, prevaricate, quibble, shuffle, temporize; tergiversate; hedge*; k–e ~̈e! *no beating about the bush*! **3.** (Flugloch am Bienenstock) *entrance*

·**Ausflug** m ~(e)s/~̈e **1. a.** [abstr] *the flying-out* (*of birds*) **b.** [konkr] (*bee-hive*) *entrance* **2.** ⟨übtr⟩ (P) (kl Landpartie) *trip, excursion, outing*; ⟨liter⟩ *jaunt* || e–n ~ m *to make an excursion, to have an outing, to go on a trip* **~s(rückfahr)karte** f ⟨rail⟩ *excursion ticket* **~sverkehr** m *excursion-traffic* **~swagen** m *sight-seeing car* ·**Ausflügler** m ~s/~ *excursionist, tripper, tourist*; Fahrkarte f ~ *excursion* (od *tourist*)*-ticket* **~verkehr** m *traffic of excursionists* **~zug** m ⟨rail⟩ *beauty-spot train*

·**Ausfluß** m –usses/–üsse **1.** (Ausfließen) *flowing* (od *pouring*)*-out, effluence, outflow*; ⟨med⟩ *discharge* (*of matter*) | ⟨übtr⟩ *emanation, efflux*; *effusion* (*of feeling*) **2.** (Ausgeflossenes) *issue, efflux*; *effluent* || ⟨med⟩ (Eiter) *discharge* | ⟨fig⟩ (Ergebnis) *issue, outcome, result* (*of his energy*) **3.** (~stelle) *issue, outfall* (*for the bath*); *outlet*, ⟨a. übtr⟩ (f. *for*); *mouth* **~geschwindigkeit** f *velocity of outflow* (od *discharge*) **~rohr** n *adjutage*; (Wasser~̈) *water pipe*; *spout*

†·**aus|folgen** vt [h] jdm etw ~ (*or* ~ l) *to deliver, to hand over a th to a p*, → verabfolgen

·**aus|forschen** vt [h] (jdn) *to pump, sound* (in bezug auf *as to*) ·**Ausforschung** f ~/~en *investigation*; *sounding* || *pumping* (*of a p*)

·**Ausfracht** f ⟨com⟩ *outward freight*; Aus- u Rückfracht *freight out and home*

·**aus|fragen** vt [h] (jdn) *to catechize, question, interrogate*; ⟨jur⟩ *to examine* || ⟨Am⟩ *to quiz* | (aushorchen) *to sound, to suck out, to pump* (in bezug auf *as to*) || so fragt man die Leute aus! ⟨fam⟩ *stop pumping me* || → interviewen | peinlich ~d *inquisitional* ·**Ausfrager** m ~s/~ *interrogator* **Ausfrager·ei** f ~/ *questioning, pumping*

·**aus|fransen** vt/i [h] **1.** vt *to fray*; *to frazzle*; ein ausgefranster Kragen *a frayed collar* | sich ~ *to fray, frazzle*; *ravel* **2.** vi *to become frayed*; = sich ~

·**aus|fräsen** vt [h] (Loch) *to mill*

·**aus|fressen** vt [h] **1.** (T) (etw) *to eat up* || (Schüssel) *to clear, to empty* **2.** ⟨übtr⟩ (aushöhlen, zerstören) (of disease, grief, etc.) *to eat away, to corrode*; *to sap, to undermine, to waste* **3.** ⟨fig⟩ °(etw) *to perpetrate*; *to be up to mischief*; du hast sicher wieder etw –ge– *you've been up to some* (*of your*) *tricks again, I'm sure*; was hat er –ge–? *what has he done*? || → ausessen

·**aus|frieren** vi [s] (of soil) *to get loose, to loosen by frost* || (of plants) = auffrieren || (of a pond) *to freeze to the bottom*

·**aus|fugen** vt [h] *to point*; *to fill with mortar*

·**Ausfuhr** f ~/~en ⟨com⟩ **1.** [abstr] *exportation, export* **2.** [konkr] (Ausgeführtes) *export*, [mst] *exports* **~abgabe** f *export duty* **~artikel** m *export article*; ~ [pl] *exports* [pl] **~bewilligung** f *export licence* **~erlaubnis** f *permit* (*for exportation*) **~güter** n [pl] *exports, exported goods* [pl] **~hafen** m *shipping-port, port of exportation* **~handel** m *export-trade* **~händler** m *exporter* **~haus** n *export-house* **~land** n *exporting country* **~prämie** f *bounty on exports*; (Ausfuhrvergütung) *draw-back* **~schein** m = Ausfuhrerlaubnis **~sperre** f = Ausfuhrverbot **~steigerung** f *increase in exports* **~tarif** m ⟨rail⟩ *reduced tariff for exports* **~verbot** n *prohibition of* (od *embargo on*) *exports* **~vergütung** → Ausfuhrprämie **~waren** f [pl] *exports* [pl] **~zoll** m *export-duty* ~̈**zollpflichtig** a *liable to export-duty*

·**ausführbar** a *achievable, doable, feasible, practicable, workable*; nicht ~ *unfeasible, impracticable*; schwer ~ *difficult of execution* | ⟨com⟩ *exportable* ~̈**keit** f ~/ *practicability, feasibility, workability* || ⟨com⟩ *exportability*

·**aus|führen** vt [h] **1.** (jdn) *to take* (*a p*) *out* (*to dinner, etc*) || die Hunde ~ *to take the dogs for a run* **2.** (in Wirklichkeit umsetzen) (Aufgabe, Plan) *to carry out*; *to bring to effect*; *to carry into effect* (–geführt w *to go into e.*); *to execute*; *to perfect*; *to put into execution* (od *practice*); *to realize*; (Auftrag) ⟨Am⟩ *to fill* || *to bring about*; *to effect, effectuate*; *manage*; glücklich ~ *to put* (*a th*) *over* (od *across*) °Auftrag ausgeführt! ⟨fam⟩ *delivered the goods* || (Arbeit) *to make*; *accomplish, perform*; *complete, finish*; ⟨comp⟩ *to handle* || führe die S gut aus *make a smart job of it* || schnell ~ *to expedite* || (unter Schwierigkeiten ~) *to effect* || ⟨com⟩ –ge–rt w ⟨a.⟩ *to receive attention* || e–n Schlag ~ *to strike a blow* || (Verbrechen) *to perpetrate* | ⟨arts, mus & Lit⟩ *to work* (*out*); *to execute, to perform*; ⟨theat⟩ *to play, to act* **3.** (in Worten ~) *to point out, to set forth* || *to argue*, er führte folgendes aus .. *he said* (od *pointed out*) ..; etw weiter ~ *to amplify*; (Plan) näher ~ *to detail, to explain*, näher ~, daß .. *to comment that* ..; eingehend ~, daß .. *to labour the point that* .. || [a. abs] wie er ausführte *as he pointed out* **4.** °etw ~ (wegnehmen) *to filch, pinch, pilfer*; jdm etw ~ *to take a th from a p*, er hat mir m–n Bleistift ausgeführt *he has pinched my pencil*

·**ausführlich** **1.** a *detailed, full, ample*; (umständlich) *circumstantial, particular*; *prolix*; ~(er) w *to come down* (*more*) *to detail, to go into* (*greater*) *detail*(*s*) **2.** adv *in detail, fully, minutely*; *at length*; ~er *in greater detail*; sehr ~ *in great detail, at great length* || etw ~ behandeln, sich ~ auslassen über etw *to dwell at great length, to expatiate* (od *enlarge, dilate*) *on a th*; ~ erzählen *to detail* ~̈**keit** f ~/~en *completness, fulness* || (bis ins einzelne) *detail*; *minuteness* || (Weitschweifigkeit) *prolixity*

·**Ausführung** f ~/~en **1.** *exportation* (*of goods*) **2.** ⟨übtr⟩ (Verwirklichung) **a.** *carrying-out*; *execution, performance* (*of a work, an order*, etc.); *realization* (*of a plan*); zur ~ bringen *to carry into effect* od *execution*; *to bring to effect*; *to put into practice*; → ausführen || *accomplishment*; *completion*; *fulfilment* (*of a contract*) || *perpetration* (*of a crime*) || ⟨theat⟩ *performance* || in doppelter ~ → Ausfertigung **b.** (Machart) *make*; *decoration*, feine ~ *finish*, gute ~ *workmanship*, in geschmackvoller ~ *beautifully designed, etc*; ⟨tech⟩ *arrangement, model* || ⟨a. arts⟩ *workmanship*; *quality*; *style* **3.** (in Worten) *pointing-out, setting-forth*; *explanation, exposition* (über *of*); *statement*; *comment* (über *on*); ~en [pl] *arguments, remarks*; *discussions, speeches* [pl]; *exposition*; weitere ~(en) ⟨rhet⟩ *amplification*; lange ~en m *to embark upon circumstantial details, to go into details* (über *about*) **~sbefehl** m, **~skommando** n *command of execution* **~sbestimmungen** f [pl] ⟨Ger⟩ *regulations* [pl] (*of a law*); *regulatory statutes*; ~ zu .. *regulations under* (*the Food and Drugs Act*), *reg. issued under authority of* (*the Income Tax Act*); *provisions of* (*the National Defence Act*) *and regulations made thereunder* **~sgesetze** n pl *carry-out laws*

·**aus|füllen** vt [h] **1.** (Kleider) *to fill out* || → ausschmieren **2.** ⟨übtr⟩ (Lücke) *to fill*; (Hintergrund) *to supply* || ⟨typ⟩ *to space out* || (e–n Posten, Vakanz etc) *to fill*, → Platz || s–e Stelle (würdig) ~ *to fill one's post* (*worthily*); jds Stelle ~ *to supply a p's place* || die Zeit ~ *to employ one's time*, die Zeit (zw Morgen u Abend) ~ *to pass* .. || jds Seele (etc) ganz ~ (of thoughts) *to absorb, to engross a p* | (Formular) *to fill in* (od *up*; ⟨Am⟩ *out*); (Bestellkarte) ⟨bes Am⟩ *to complete*

·**Ausfüll- ~streifen** m ⟨mech⟩ (aus Holz etc) *shim* ‖ **~stücke** n [pl] ⟨arch⟩ *fill-in pieces* [pl]

·**Ausfüllung** f ~/~en *filling* (*of a post*) ‖ *filling-out* ‖ *filling-in, filling-up* (*of a form*)

·**aus|füttern** vt [h] (Kleidung) *to line* ‖ (Kasten) *to paper* ·**Ausfütterung** f ~/~en *lining* ‖ ⟨mech⟩ *liner*

·**Ausgabe** f ~/~en **A.** (Aushändigung, Verteilung) **1.** *delivery* (an *to*) **2.** *distribution* (v Karten *of tickets*); (v Lebensmitteln) *issue*; (v Munition) *distribution* **3.** Bücher≈ *lending department*; ⟨rail⟩ Fahrkarten≈ *booking-office* **4.** *issue* (*of banknotes, shares*); *emission* ‖ *issue* (*of an order*, etc); ⟨Am⟩ *issuance* ‖ → Veröffentlichung **5.** ⟨comp⟩ *out(-)put* **B.** (Geld≈) **a.** *disbursement, expenditure* **b.** (verausgabter Betrag) ~n *expenditure* (f *on*), *outlay* (f *on*); *expenses*, ⟨fam⟩ *exes* [pl]; ~en des allg. Geschäfts *expenses from non-* (z. B. ⟨ins⟩ *insurance*) *business* ‖ viele ~n h *to have many expenses*; besondere ~n *extras* [pl]; laufende ~n *oncost, current* (od *overhead*) *expenses*; unvorhergesehene ~n *incidental expenses* ‖ in ~ bringen *to spend, disburse* ‖ die ~n stimmen mit den Einnahmen überein *the expenses balance the receipts* ‖ sich der ~n f e–e S unterziehen *to go to the expense of buying a th* **C.** (Buch≈) *edition*; durchgesehene, überarbeitete ~ *revised edition*; *re-write*; → Abdruck ‖ Jubiläums≈ *jubilee edition*, Pracht≈ *edition de luxe*; Volks≈ *popular edition* | *issue, edition* (*of a paper*), Extra≈ *extra edition*; Spät≈ *extra special edition* ≈**beschränkt** a ⟨bes mil⟩ *regulated* (Artikel *item*) **~buch** n *cash-book* **~budget** n, **~etat** m *Supply* **~gerät** n ⟨comp⟩ *output unit* **~kurs** m ⟨st exch⟩ *issue par* od *quotation* **~nbuch** n *cash-book* **~posten** m *item of expenses* **~schein** m *issue slip* **~stelle** f *issuing office*, ⟨mil⟩ *supply point*

·**Ausgang** m ~(e)s/≈e **A. 1.** ⟨eig⟩ *egress*; *going-out, walk*(*ing out*), *out*; e–n ~ m *to take* (od *go for*) *a walk* ‖ → Weggang **2.** ⟨übtr⟩ (Ende) **a.** *end, ending* (*of a word*, etc.); → Reim ‖ ⟨typ⟩ → Absatz **b.** *end* (*of supplies*); *conclusion, close, termination*; ein Stück mit glücklichem ~ *a play with a happy end*(*ing*), ein Unfall mit tödlichem ~ *a fatal accident, an accident which proves fatal* ‖ am ~ des 15. Jhs *at the end, in the closing days* (od *years*) *of the 15th c.* | (Tod) *end*(*ing*), *exit* **c.** (Ergebnis) *event, issue, result*; *upshot* (*of a business*) ‖ glücklicher ~ *success*; zu e–m glücklichen ~ bringen *to bring to a successful issue*; e–n glücklichen (*or* guten) ~ nehmen *to turn out well, to come out all right* **B.** (das Hinausgehende) *export* ‖ (Geld) *expenditure, outgo* ‖ die –gänge [pl] *the outgoing mail* **C.** (Öffnung, Tür) *egress* (*of a church*); *exit*; *way-out* (aus *from*); *outlet* | *opening* (aufs Meer *to the sea*) | ⟨aero rail⟩ *gate* → Ausweg ‖ → Ausgehen **D.** (Ausgehtag etc) *day out*, s–n ~ haben *to have one's day out*; *evening out* (etc)

·**Ausgangs- ~beschränkung** f ⟨mil⟩ *confinement to barracks*; ⟨pol⟩ *curfew* **~gewicht** n der Tara *original tare weight* **~hafen** m *shipping-port*; (P) *port of embarkation* **~höhe** f ⟨aero⟩ *datum level* **~information** f ⟨comp⟩ *out(-)put* **~lage** f *original position* **~linie** f ⟨tact⟩ *jump*(*ing*)*-off line* **~marschordnung** f ⟨bes mil⟩ *root column* **~masse** f ⟨demog⟩ *radix, root* **~material** n → –stoff **~periode** f *base period* **~pfahl** m ⟨surv⟩ *datum peg* **~preis** m *export-price* **~produkt** n *commencing pr.* **~punkt** m *starting-point* (für *of*); *point of departure* (für *for*) **~sprache** f (Leit– bei Übersetzung & Wörterbuch) *source language*; → Zielsprache **~stellung** f ⟨tech & drill⟩ *normal position*, ⟨tech a.⟩ *intial* od *home pos.* ‖ ⟨tact⟩ *jump*(*ing*)*-off* od *initial pos.* **~stoff** m ⟨tech⟩ *source*; *s.* od *starting* od *initial material* od *substance* ‖ ⟨at⟩ *original mat.* **~straße** f *exit* **~tür** f *exit, way out* **~werkstoff** m *basic* od *raw material* **~werte** m pl ⟨artill, etc⟩ *transmitted data* **~zoll** m *export-duty* **~zustand** m *initial* od *parent state*

·**aus|geben** vt/i [h] **I.** vt **1.** (austeilen) (Waren etc) *to deliver* (an *to*); (Lebensmittel) *to give out, to distribute* (an *to*); (Bücher) *to pass out*; (Fahrkarten) *to issue* ‖ ⟨cards⟩ *to deal* | (Tau) *to pay away* (od *out*) **2. a.** ⟨com⟩ (Münzen, Banknoten etc) *to issue*; *to emit* ‖ e–e Anleihe ~ *to float a loan* **b.** (Befehle) *to give*; die Losung (*or* Parole) ~ *to give the word* **3. a.** (Geld) *to give out, to spend*; *to disburse, to lay out*; Geld schnell ~ *to make the money fly*; sein Einkommen nicht ~ *to live within one's income* ‖ –ge– w *to go* (für Zigarren *in* od *on cigars*) | °etw ~ für jdn *to treat a p to a th*; °e–n ~ für jdn *to stand a p a drink*; e–n ~, e–e Runde ~ *to stand a round of drinks* **b. sich ~** *to expend o.s., to run out of cash* | ⟨übtr⟩ (sich anstrengen) *to extend o.s.*; *to exhaust o.s.* **4.** jdn fälschlich ~ als, für *to give a p out as, to pass a p off as* (od *for*) | **sich ~ als, für** *to pass o.s. off as* (od *for*); *to give one's name as, to give o.s. out as*; *to set up for*; *to give o.s. out to be* ..; er gab sich aus als der Beamte des .. *he impersonated the officer of* .. **II.** vi (ausgiebig (sein) ~, gut ~ *to yield much*; nicht ~ *to fall short* ·**Ausgeber** m ~s/~ *distributor* ‖ (in großem Haushalt) *steward*; ~in f *stewardess* | ⟨com⟩ *drawer* (*of a bill*); *issuer*

·**ausge-** [mst in pp] **~baucht** a *swelling* **~baut** a *elaborate* (*road system, etc*) ‖ ⟨übtr⟩ (Wein) *ripe* **~beult** a [pp v ausbeulen] am Knie *baggy* (*trousers*) **~bildet** a [pp v ausbilden] *trained, skilled* ‖ *instructed* (*eye*) ‖ nicht ~ *unskilled*; *uninstructed* (*eye*); *untutored* (*palate*) ≈**bot** n ~(e)s/~e ⟨com⟩ *offer*; *setting up for sale* ‖ (bei Auktionen) *first bid* **~brannt** a → ausbrennen ‖ ⟨tech⟩ *depleted* (*fuel*); ⟨at⟩ *spent* (*element*) **~breitet** a [pp v ausbreiten] *extensive* ≈**burt** f ~/~en *monstrous production, monstrosity* ‖ e–e ~ von Schlechtigkeit *a monster of wickedness* ‖ ⟨übtr⟩ *product* **~gedehnt** a [pp v ausdehnen] *expansive* ‖ *extensive* (*fields*); *spacious*; *wide-range* [attr]; ein ~er Park *a sweep of park* | ⟨übtr⟩ *extensive* (*inquiries*, etc) ‖ *lengthy*; *wide-ranging* (*debate*); in ~em Maße *largely* ‖ → Wirkungskreis **~dient** a [pp v ausdienen] *retired, superannuated* (*official*) ‖ ~er Soldat *time-expired soldier, veteran* | ⟨übtr⟩ *used up*; *worn out* (*hat*) ≈**dinge** n = Altenteil **~fahren** a → ausfahren ‖ *bad* (Straße *road* [*surface*]), *worn-down* (*road*) **~fallen** a *inoperative, dead* (*engine* ⟨a. el⟩) ‖ (P) *incapacitated* (*soldier*); *immobilized* (*vehicle*) ‖ ⟨übtr⟩ *odd, queer strange*; *curious, funny*; *rare, unusual*; *oldfashioned*; *exceptional* (Lage); [pred] *out of the way* **~feimt** a *thorough-paced, out-and-out, arrant*; *artful, shifty* **~glichen** a [pp v ausgleichen] ⟨print⟩ (*optically*) *letter-spaced*; nicht ~ *no letter spacing*; ⟨fig⟩ *balanced, elegant* (*style*); *well-balanced, steady, level-headed* (*personality*) ‖ ≈heit [f] *roundness, concinnity* (*of style*) ‖ innere ~ *poise*; *mental balance* ‖ ⟨psych⟩ *ataraxy* °≈**grabener** m ⟨fam⟩ *dug-out* (*officer*), ⟨mar⟩ *vet*

·**Ausgeh-** (→ ausgehen) [in comp] **~abend** m mein ~ *my evening out* **~anzug** m *outdoor* (od *walking-out*) *dress*; ⟨mar⟩ *shore kit* **~tag** m: mein ~ *my day out* **~uniform** f *dress uniform* **~verbot** n ⟨mil⟩ *confinement to barracks*, ⟨fam⟩ *C. B.* ‖ ⟨pol⟩ ~ zwischen Abenddämmerung u Morgengrauen *curfew*; ein ~ erlassen *to impose a curfew*

·**aus|gehen** vi [s] (P & T) **I. 1.** ⟨eig⟩ *to go out*; *to take a walk, to go for a walk* (mit *with*); m–e Eltern sind ausgegangen *my parents are out* (od *not at home*) | ⟨übtr⟩ *to go out* (*for amusement*); abends ~ *to have an evening out* || viel ~ *to keep much company* || wollen wir nicht ~ ⟨Am⟩ *let's go places* **2. bei** jdm ein- u ~ → aus [adv] I. 1. b. **mit** (jdm) ~ → I. 1.; ⟨sl⟩ *to trot out* (*a judy*) **3.** frei ~ *to go unpunished, to get off scot--free* || leer ~ *to come away empty-handed* **4.** ~ v *to start* (od *set out*) *from* || ⟨übtr⟩ *to proceed, start from*; laßt uns v dort ~ *let us make our starting-point there*; v e–m Grundsatz, v den Erwägungen ~ *to start from a principle, to set out from the considerations* || er ging davon aus, daß .. *he started from the idea* (od *fact*) (*that* ..) **5. ~ auf;** → Abenteuer || auf Beute, Raub ~ *to go marauding* od *plundering*; (T) *to prowl after one's prey* | ⟨übtr⟩ ~ auf etw *to aim at; to be out for a th, to be up to a th; to have a th in view; to intend, contemplate a th*; auf Betrug ~ *to be out for* (od *bent on*) *fraud* || darauf ~ z tun *to be out to do, to intend to do* (od *doing*), *to contemplate, to consider doing* **II.** (S) **1.** → ~d **2.** die Strümpfe gehen leicht (schwer) aus *the stockings pull off easily* (*with difficulty*) **3.** (of hair) *to come out*, ihm geht das Haar aus *he is losing his hair* || (of colour) *to fade, disappear* || (of fire) *to go out, to expire* || er lief, bis ihm der Atem ausging *he ran till he was out of breath* **4.** ⟨geol⟩ *to outcrop, to crop up* **5.** (enden) *to end*; das Stück geht traurig aus *the play has a sad ending* || wie wird die S ~? *how will this matter end*? || (verlaufen) *to come off* (⟨Am⟩ *out*); gut (schlecht) ~ *to answer* (od *to fall out, come off, turn out*) *well* (*badly*); *to come to a good* (*bad*) *end* || ungünstig ~ f jdn *to go against a p* **6. ~ auf** (of words) *to end* (od *terminate*) *in* | **in** e–e Spitze ~ *to taper* (*off*) *to* (od *to end in*) *a point* **7. ~ von** *to start from*; v dem Platze gehen mehrere Straßen aus *several streets lead off from the square* || ⟨übtr⟩ ~ v *to issue, to proceed from; to derive, originate, result from* (*a source*) || (of results) *to flow from*; (of feelings) *to emanate from* || die Anregung ging v ihm aus *the suggestion originated with* (od *came from*) *him* **8.** ⟨übtr⟩ (of money, supplies) *to give out, to run short*; ihm waren die Zigarren ausgegangen *he had run out of cigars, his cigars had run short* || der Mut ging ihm aus *his courage failed him* ·**Ausgehen** n *starting, start* (v *from*) | *coming-out, loss* (*of hair*); *fading* (*of colour*) || *giving-out, running short* (*of supplies*) → Ausgang ·**ausgehend** a *outward bound, outbound* (*ship*) || *outgoing* (*mail*) || *outward* (*freight*)

·**ausge-** [mst in pp] **~hungert** a [pp v aushungern] *starved* (*-out*); *starveling, emaciated; famine-stricken* || ~e P *starveling* **~klügelt** a → ausklügeln; *sophisticated* **~kocht** a [pp v auskochen] ⟨fig⟩ *dyed in the wool*; *utter* (*rogue*); → ab–, ausgefeimt **~kragt** a ⟨arch, etc⟩ *protruding, corbelled* **~lassen** a [pp v auslassen] ⟨fig⟩ *frisky, frolicsome; jolly, merry, rollicking; boisterous; wanton*; ~ s *to be in high spirits* || ~es Mädchen *tomboy* | ~heit [f] ~/~en *great fun*; *friskiness, frolicsomeness; exuberant spirits* **~lastet** a: ~ s *to work to capacity* **~laufen** a ⟨tech⟩ (*the bearing has*) *run down* od *out* **~leiert** a [pp v ausleiern] ⟨fig⟩ *hackneyed, stereotyped, trite*; → abgedroschen **~macht** a [pp v ausmachen] **1.** *decided, determined on, settled* **2.** (gewiß) *certain, established; positive* (*fact*); e–e ~e S *a settled matter, a matter of course, a foregone conclusion, an understood thing*; als ~ annehmen *to take for granted*; wir nehmen das als ~ an *we'll let that be understood* | *confirmed, downright, inveterate* (*bachelor, atheist* etc.); *thorough-going* (*socialist*) || *perfect, out and out, thorough* (*scoundrel*) || er ist ein ~er Lügner *he is no better than a liar* **~mergelt** a [pp v ausmergeln] ⟨fig⟩ *effete* (*race*); *enervate, sapless; emaciated* (*country*)

~nommen [pp v ausnehmen] **1. a.** (befreit) *exempt* (v *from*); → Hering **b.** *excepted; except for* ..; ⟨bes contr⟩ *other than*; Anwesende ~ *present company excepted*; niemand ~ *bar none* || [nach *always, not, nothing, without*]: *excepting*, die 5. Klasse nicht ~ *not excepting the fifth form* **2.** (außer) *but, except, with the exception of, barring; save, saving*; wir waren alle da, ~ er (*or* ihn ~) *we were all there except* (od *but*) *him* || ~ hier *except here* || → abgesehen **3.** adv ~ daß [conj] *except; saving that* || ~ daß, ~ wenn *unless* **~nörgelt** a [pp v ausnörgeln] = ausgemergelt **~picht** a [pp v auspichen] ⟨fig⟩, ~e Kehle *hardened throat* || *seasoned* (*hunter*); ⟨sl⟩ *salted* (*trader*) || = abgefeimt **~prägt** a [pp v ausprägen] ⟨fig⟩ *distinct, distinctive, marked; pronounced* **~pumpt** a [pp v auspumpen] ⟨fig⟩ *exhausted, worn-out; stale, wizened* **~rechnet** a [pp v ausrechnen] ~ er *he of all people*; → fehlen || ~ Italien *Italy of all nations*; ~ um Mitternacht *at midnight of all times*; ~ heute *to-day of all days* || ~ das *this of all things* || ~ jetzt *now of all things* od *times*; ~ dies Gesetz (*it was*) *this law* || er mußte ~ abreisen *he had to leave, of all things; he must needs leave* || (*that his*) *of all others* (*should have been the hands to rescue her*) **~richtet** a: nicht *or* falsch ~ *misaligned* **~schaltet** a ⟨el⟩ *dead* (Leitung) **~schlossen** [pp v ausschließen] *out of the question*; ~! ⟨fam⟩ *nothing doing*! || das ist nicht ganz ~ ⟨fam⟩ *it's on the cards* **~schnitten** a [pp v ausschneiden] tief ~ *low* (*dress, shoe*); *décolleté, low-necked* (*dress*) **~schrieben** a [pp v ausschreiben] ~e Adresse *address in full* **≈siedelte(er** m) f *evacuee* **~sprochen** [pp v aussprechen] **1.** a *pronounced; distinct*(*ive*); *flat* (*failure*); ~e Ansichten h über etw *to feel very strongly on a th* || *determined* (*foes*); *declared* (*favourites*); *utter, out-and-out; outright, downright, positive* (*atheist*) **2.** adv ~ liberal *pronouncedly liberal*; ~ Shakespearisch *markedly Shakespearian* || ~ nein! *emphatically not*! **~stalten** vt [h] *to work out* od *up* (z *into*) **≈staltung** f ~/~en *shaping, arrangement* || *development* (*of talents*) || *organization* (*of a trip*) || ⟨com⟩ *fashioning* **~stattet** a wohl ~ *well appointed* (*hotel*) **~steuert** a **1.** *with a dowry* **2.** ⟨ins⟩ *without claim to insurance benefit*; die A.O.K. hat ihn ~ *his claims to panel assistance have expired* **~storben** a (T) *extinct* → aussterben; hier sind die Straßen um 21 Uhr wie ~ *in this town they roll up the sidewalks at 9 p. m.* **~sucht** [pp v aussuchen] **1.** a *choice, first-rate, exquisite* || *special* (*politeness*); *studied* (*indifference*) **2.** adv *specially* (*polite*); *unusually* **~treten** a *rutty* (*road*); *well-worn* (*path*) **~trocknet** a ⟨fig⟩ *desiccated, wizened* (*p*) **~wachsen** a *fullgrown* **~wählt** a *select, selected, chosen* (*letters*); sorgfältig ~ *choice* || (auserlesen) *exquisite, choice* **~wogen** a *balanced*; → –glichen ⟨fig⟩ *well-b.* | ~heit [f] ~/ *equilibrium* **~zackt** a → auszacken **~zahnt** a → denteliert **~zeichnet** a *labelled* (*goods*) || *honoured; decorated* (*officer*) || **~zeichnet** [bes pred & adv], **-z:eichnet** [pp v auszeichnen] **1.** a *excellent, prime, firstrate, high, superior* (*quality*); ~e Leistung *distinction* || *bright* (*prospects*); *beautiful* (*preacher*) || ⟨fam⟩ *famous* (*dinner*); ⟨Am⟩ *big* | *great, eminent, distinguished* (*scholar*) || ~! *splendid*! *fine*! **2.** adv (das paßt) ~! *that will do nicely* (od *fine, famously*); (*suits me*) *down to the ground* || (mir geht es) ~ (*I am*) *fine*, ⟨Am⟩ *just fine*; *I feel prime* || (*spoke*) *excellent* (*English*)

·**ausgiebig 1.** a *prolific, abundant; plenteous, plentiful, copious*; ~en Gebrauch m v etw *to make full* (od *good*) *use of a th, to use a th lavishly* || (ergiebig) *fertile* (*soil*); *productive* (*mine, soil*); *rich*; ~ s *to yield much* **2.** adv *copiously, plentifully* **≈keit** f ~/ *plenty, plenteousness* ‖ *productiveness, fertility*

·aus|gießen vt [h] **1. a.** (Flüssigkeit) *to pour* (in *into*; aus *out of*; auf *on, upon*); *to pour out*; (verschütten) *to spill* | **b.** (Eimer) *to empty* **c.** ⟨übtr⟩ (of the sun, etc.) (Licht, Wärme) *to diffuse, irradiate, shed*; *to send out*; (Strahlen) *to pour forth* | (Liebe, Güte, Frieden) *to irradiate, to pour out*; *to shed, shower* (auf *on, upon*) **2.** (auslöschen) (Feuer) *to extinguish, quench* **3.** ⟨tech⟩ (Fugen etc) mit Blei ~ *to fill with lead* **4.** (Modell) *to cast, mould*

·Ausgießung f ~/~en *pouring-out, outpouring* ‖ ⟨übtr⟩ *effusion, outpouring*, die ~ des Heiligen Geistes *the effusion of the Holy Spirit*; ⟨arts⟩ *Descent of the Holy Ghost* ‖ → Erguß

·aus|gipsen vt [h] (Loch) *to fill with plaster*

·aus|glätten vt [h] *to smooth (out)*

·Ausgleich m ~s/~e **1.** *equalization, equilibrating, neutralization* (*of distances, conflicting forces, tendencies*, etc.); *levelling(-up)* ‖ sozialer ~ *approach to social equality* | ⟨com⟩ *balancing* (*of expenses and receipts*); *equation* (*of demand and supply*, etc) ‖ (P) ⟨fig⟩ *balance wheel*; ~ persönlicher Mängel *personal equation* **2.** ⟨com⟩ (Begleichung) *clearance*; *adjustment*; *settlement* (*of an account*); z ~ Ihres Kontos *in settlement* (od *payment*) *of your account*; z (vollen) ~ unseres Kontos *in full discharge of our account* **3.** ⟨com⟩ *compensation, offset, set-off* (gegen *against, to*) ‖ ⟨übtr⟩ *counterbalance* (gegen *to*) **4.** (Abkommen) *agreement, arrangement*; *settlement, composition* (*with*); österreichisch-ungarischer ~ *the Austro-Hungarian Agreement* (*1867*); Finanz≈ *financial agreement* ‖ *settlement* (*of a quarrel*) ‖ = ~sverfahren **5.** ⟨el⟩ *balance* **6.** **~sport** m *compensatory sport activity* **~stein** m ⟨mar⟩ *levelling stone* **~steuer** f *equalization tax* (⟨a.⟩ Zoll); → Ausgleichs–

·aus|gleichen vt [h] **A. 1.** (Unebenheiten) *to remove, smooth* ‖ ⟨typ⟩ (Zeile) *to space equally* **2.** (Distanzen etc) *to equalize*; (Beiträge) *to clear*, ⟨Am⟩ *to offset*; (Unterschiede) *to adjust, to level (up)*; ⟨Am⟩ *to iron out* ‖ nach oben (unten) ~ *to level up (down)* ‖ (Gegenwirkung) *to neutralize* ‖ ~de Gerechtigkeit *social justice* | ⟨com⟩ (Etat etc) *to balance*; *to even up* **2.** *to compensate*; (Mangel) *to compensate for*; *to make good* (durch *by*); (Fehler) *to redeem*; *to offset*; *to set off* (gegen *against*); *to counterbalance* ‖ ⟨mech⟩ gegeneinander ~ *to compensate*; ~d *compensating* **3.** (begleichen) (Rechnung) *to balance, to settle, to square*; (Konto) *to clear* ‖ wir wären Ihnen dankbar, wenn Sie Ihr Debet ~ wollten *we should appreciate your forwarding to us a remittance to put your account in funds* **4.** ⟨übtr⟩ (Schwierigkeiten) *to adjust*; (Streit) *to arrange, to compose, to make up, to reconcile, to settle* **B. sich ~** *to balance* ‖ *to even up*; *to offset one another* | sich ~ mit jdm *to compound, to settle with a p* **·Ausgleicher** m *rectifier*

·Ausgleichs- [in comp] *equalizing* (*influence*); *neutralizing* (*clause, force*); *levelling* ‖ *balancing* ‖ *clearing* (*agreement, fund*) **~batterie** f ⟨el⟩ *compensating battery* **~betrag** m *balance* **~fläche** f ⟨aero⟩ Höhenruder mit ~ *compensated elevator* **~fonds** m *compensation fund* **~forderungen** f pl ⟨bank⟩ *equalization claims* **~getriebe** n ⟨mot⟩ *differential gear* **~gymnastik** f *gymnastics* [pl] *for correction of bodily defects* **~küste** f ⟨geog⟩ *mature shore line* **~leitung** f *compensation line* **~maßnahmen** f pl *arrangements for compensation, etc*; ⟨bal⟩ *arr. for carry-forward* **~rennen** n *handicap(-race)* **~stück** n ⟨typ⟩ *levelling-piece* **~tor** n ⟨ftb⟩ *equalizer* **~verfahren** n *clearing operations* [pl]; *composition with one's creditors* **~vorräte** m pl *buffer stocks* **~vorrichtung** f *compensating contrivance* **~wechsel** m *settlement per appoint*; durch ~ erledigen *to settle per appoint* **~zoll** m *countervailing duty*

·Ausgleichung f ~/~en = Ausgleich 1. 2. 3. ‖ ⟨stat⟩ *graduation, smoothing*; analytische ~ *curve fitting*

·aus|gleiten 1. vi [s] *to lose one's footing*; *to slide, slip*; ⟨fam⟩ *to slither* ‖ (*of wheels*) *to skid* (auf *on*); → abrutschen **2.** ≈ n *slip*; ⟨fam⟩ *slither* ‖ *skid*

·Ausgliederung f ~/ ⟨philos⟩ *part of an organic whole*

°**·ausglitschen** vi [s] = ausgleiten

·aus|glühen vt/i [h] **1.** vi *to heat thoroughly* ‖ (Metalle) *to anneal* **2.** vi *to cease glowing*; *to cool (down)*

·aus|graben vt [h] **1.** (etw) *to dig* (aus *from*); (Kartoffeln; Scherben etc) *to dig up* ‖ (Maulwurf etc) *to dig out*; (Schatz) *to unearth* | (Leichnam) *to disinter, exhume* **2.** (ein Loch) *to dig out*; *to excavate*; *to sink* **3.** ⟨archaeol⟩ (Ruinen) *to excavate*; *to unearth* **4.** ⟨übtr⟩ (P & S) *to unearth*; (alte Bestimmungen) *to grub up* ‖ **-ge-** ⟨fam⟩ *dug-out* (*officer*) **·Ausgrabung** f ~/~en *digging-up* ‖ *exhumation* (*of corpses*) ‖ ⟨archaeol⟩ *excavation* (*of ruins*), ⟨fam⟩ *dig* | [konkr] *excavation*; ~en [pl] *excavations* [pl]

·aus|gräten vt [h] (Fisch) *to bone*

·aus|greifen vi [h] (of horses) *to step out* ‖ ein Pferd ~ l *to give a horse his head* **·ausgreifend** a *wide-ranging* (*policy*)

·aus|grübeln vt [h] (etw) *to puzzle out*

·Ausguck m ~s/~e **1.** *look-out, outlook*; ~ halten, auf dem ~ stehen *to be on the look-out* (nach *for*), *to keep a good outlook* od *look-out* ‖ *peep* (auf das Meer *of the sea*) **2.** (Ort) *look-out*; ⟨mar⟩ (~ am Mast) *crow's nest* **·aus|gucken** vi [h] *to look, to be on the look-out* (nach *for*), *to keep an outlook*; sich die Augen ~ nach *to crane one's neck for* (*a p, a th*)

·Ausgucker m ~s/~ ⟨mar⟩ *look-out man*

·Ausguß m, –gusses/–güsse **1.** (~becken) *sink*; eingebauter Küchen≈ *sink unit*; ~eimer m *slop-pail* **2.** (Tülle) *nozzle, spout* **~reiniger** m (Gummistampfer) *plunger*

·aus|hacken vt [h] *to hack*; *to hew out* ‖ (v Vögeln) (Augen) *to pick out*

·aus|haken vt/i [h] **1.** vt (Fenster etc) *to unhook, to remove from the hook* ‖ (Kleid) *to unhook* | **sich ~** *to come unhooked* **2.** vi °jetzt hakt's aber aus *that's the limit*

·aus|halten vt/i [h] **I.** vt **1. a.** (ertragen) (Schmerz) *to bear, to endure* ‖ (Angriff, Belagerung, Stoß etc) *to sustain, to stand*; (Hitze) *to stand* ‖ e–n Vergleich ~ *to bear, stand, sustain comparison* (*with*) ‖ s–e Zeit ~ *to serve one's time* ‖ es länger ~ als, es ebenso lange ~ wie jd *to last a p out* ‖ → überstehen **b.** Wendungen: er kann viel ~ *he can stand a lot* ‖ ich halte es nicht länger aus *I can't stand it any longer* ‖ er hält es nirgends lange aus *he never sticks to a job long* ‖ der Stoff hält etwas aus *the cloth is good wear*; (*these shoes*) *can take punishment* ‖ wir müssen es ~ *we must put up with it* ‖ es ist nicht mehr –zu–, es ist nicht zum ≈ *it is beyond all bearing* (od *endurance*), *it is unbearable, unendurable, intolerable* ‖ können Sie denn das ~? *are you equal to this*? **2.** (unterhalten) (P) *to keep*; *to maintain* ‖ *to support* (*a p*); sie läßt sich ~ *she is a kept woman* **3.** ⟨mus⟩ (Ton) *to sustain* **II.** vi (P) *to continue* (auf e–m Posten *at a post*); *to persevere*; *to persist*; *to bear up, to hold out* (gegen *against*); *to last*; *to endure*; bis z Ende *to the end* ‖ wie lange habt Ihr gestern abend noch ausgehalten? *how long did you keep it up last night*? **·Aushalten** n *endurance, bearing* ‖ → Ausdauer

·Aushaltezeichen n ⟨mus⟩ *fermata* (It)

·**aus|hämmern** vt [h] (Gefäß) *to beat out*

·**aus|händigen** vt [h] jdm etw ~, etw ~ an jdn *to deliver up, to hand over a th to a p* ‖ (zurückgeben) *to turn in* ·**Aushändigung** f ~/~en *delivery, handing-over*; *surrender* (an jdn *to a p*)

·**Aushang** m ~(e)s/⁓e (Anschlag) *notice, placard, poster*

·**Aushänge-** ~**bogen** m ⟨typ⟩ *advance copy, adv. sheet* ~**kasten** m (f Zeitung) *display-box* ~**schild** n *sign(-board)*; ⟨Am⟩ *shingle* | ⟨fig⟩ *ostentation, show, display* ‖ *pretence*, jdn als ~ dienen *to serve a p as a pretence* ~**zeitung** f *wall-newspaper*

†·**aushangen** vi → hangen [h] = aushängen

·**aus|hängen** vt/i [h] **I.** vt **1.** (Tür etc) *to unhinge* ‖ ⟨mar⟩ (Riemen) *to unship* **2.** (Zeichen, Fahne) *to hang* od *put out* | ⟨übtr⟩ (Waren) *to display, to exhibit for sale* **3. sich** ~ (of clothes) *to smooth (out)* **II.** vi *to be hung out*; *to be exhibited*; *to be announced, published*; ⟨fam⟩ sie sind ausgehängt *their banns have been published*

·**aus|harren** vt [h] *to endure* (bis z Ende *to the end*); *to hold out, to persevere* ‖ auf dem Platze ~ *to stick to one's place*

·**aushärtend** a (hitzehärtbar) *thermosetting* (Plastik) ·**Aushärtung** f ~/ ⟨met⟩ *age-hardening* ‖ (v Kleb- & Kunststoffen) *curing*; *setting up*

·**Aushau** m ~(e)s/~e *clearing, glade* ‖ ⟨min⟩ = Abbau

·**aus/hauchen** vt [h] *to breathe out, exhale, expire* ‖ den Geist ~ *to breathe one's last, to give up one's ghost*

·**aus|hauen** vt [h] **1.** (Wald) *to clear, thin*; (Zweige etc) *to thin (out)*; *to lop* **2.** (Kohlen) *to hew*; (Steine) *to hew* (aus *out of*) | (behauen) (Steine) *to hew* (f *for*); *to carve* ‖ ⟨arts⟩ *to hew out*; *to sculpture* **3.** [abs] °es haut nicht aus *it won't do*

·**aus|hausen** vi [h] *to have wasted one's goods and chattels* ·**Aushäuser** m ~s/~ *squanderer, waster, wastrel* ·**aushäusig** a *pleasure-loving* ‖ ~e Erziehung = Anstaltserziehung

·**aus|häuten** vt [h] (T) *to flay, skin*

·**aus|heben** vt/i [h] **I.** vt **1.** *to lift* (aus *out of*), → heben ‖ (Tür) *to unhinge* ‖ ⟨typ⟩ (Form) *to lift out*; (Winkelhaken) *to empty* | (jdn) ⟨wrestling⟩ *to lift (a p) off his feet* **2.** (Pflanzen etc) *to take up, to uproot* **3.** (Nest) *to take*; *to rob*; Nester *to nest, to go bird's nesting* od *bird--nesting*, (Verbrechernest) *to take (by surprise)*, *to clear out* **4.** ⟨mil⟩ (*Soldaten*) *to levy, raise*; zwangsweise ~ *to conscript* **5.** sich die Schulter ~ *to dislocate* (od *sprain*) *one's shoulder* **II.** vi die Uhr hebt aus *the clock is about to strike*

·**Ausheber** m ~s/~ ⟨hort⟩ *trowel*

·**aus|hebern** vt [h] (Magen) *to siphon*

·**Aushebung** f ~/~en ⟨mil⟩ *levy(ing)*; *enlistment of soldiers*; (zwangsweise) *conscription*, ⟨Am a.⟩ *draft* ~**sbezirk** m ⟨mil⟩ *enlistment* (od *recruiting*) *district*

·**aus|hecken** vt [h] *to hatch out* ‖ ⟨mst fig⟩ *to hatch*; *brew, contrive, devise*; *concoct*; *forge*; ⟨Am⟩ *to think .. up*

·**aus|heilen** vi/t [h] **1.** vi *to heal perfectly*; *to heal up* **2.** vt *to heal completely* ·**Ausheilung** f *healing-up*; *complete healing*

·**ausheimisch** a *foreign* ‖ *exotic*

·**aus|helfen** vi [h] *to help*; *to lend a helping hand* (bei *with*; in *in*), *to play one's part* **2.** jdm ~ *to help a p out* ‖ jdm ~ mit *to supply* (od *accommodate a p with* (*a th*) ‖ → anziehen, ausziehen

·**Aushieb** m ~(e)s/~e **1.** ⟨fenc⟩ (beim Ausfall) *straight thrust* **2.** ⟨min⟩ assay **3.** = Auszugshieb ‖ ⟨for⟩ *extraction*

·**Aushilfe** f ~/~n **1.** *help, aid, assistance* ‖ (mit Geld) *accommodation* **2.** (Notbehelf) *makeshift*; *temporary expedient*; *shift*; als ~ *as* (od *by way of*) *a makeshift, as a pis aller* [Fr] **3.** [konkr] **a.** (P & S) *stop-gap, makeweight* **b.** *part-time girl*

·**aushilflich** a *makeweight jobbing*; *part-time (worker)* ·**Aushilfling** m = Aushilfe **3**

·**Aushilfs-** [in comp] *temporary*; *emergency, jobbing (gardener)* ~**arbeit** f *temporary work* ~**arbeiter** m *casual labourer, part-time worker, odd-job man* ~**gärtner** m *jobbing gardener* ~**kraft** f (P) *emergency-man* ~**lehrer** m *supply teacher*; *temporary assistant master* ~**mädchen** n *tweeny, t. maid, between-maid*; *part-time girl* ~**personal** n *temporary staff* ~**schauspieler** m *understudy* ⁓**weise** adv *as a makeshift, temporarily* ~**wohnung** f *alternative dwelling, etc*

·**aus|höhlen** vt [h] *to hollow* od *scoop out*; *to excavate, carve, gouge* ‖ (auskehlen) *to groove* ‖ (of water) (Felsen) *to undermine, to wear away* | ⟨fig⟩ (Staatsgewalt) *to undermine*; *to sap* ·**Aushöhlung** f ~/~en *hollow, excavation* ‖ *depression* ‖ ⟨fig⟩ *undermining*

·**aus|holen** vi/t [h] **I.** vi **1.** *to strike out* (nach *at*); mit dem Arm *to heave one's arm*; mit der Hand ~ *to lift one's hand*; mit der Peitsche ~ *to swing the whip* ‖ z e–m Schlage ~ *to draw back one's fist for a blow* (nach *at*); z Sprunge ~ *to prepare for a jump* **2.** ⟨sport⟩ *to draw out* ‖ ⟨mot⟩ *to swing out* **3.** ⟨übtr⟩ weit ~ *to range wide*; weit ~d *wide-ranging* ‖ *to go far back (in one's narration)*; *to be circumstantial* **II.** vt (P) *to pump, sound* (über *as to*); → ausfragen; *to draw .. out* (über *about*)

·**aus|holzen** vt [h] = abholzen

·**aus|horchen** vt [h] (jdn) *to draw* (über *on*); *to pump*; *to sound* (über *as to*) ·**Aushorcher** m *sounder*

·**Aushub** m ⟨tech⟩ (Erd⁓) *spoil*; *excavation* ‖ †⟨mil⟩ = Aufgebot

·**aus|hülsen** vt [h] (Erbsen etc) *to husk, hull, shell*

·**aus|hungern** vt [h] *to starve* ‖ (Festung) *to starve into submission* od *surrender* ‖ (Flugzeug vor dem Aufsetzen) *to flare out* ‖ → ausgehungert ·**Aushungerung** f *starvation* ‖ ⟨übtr⟩ *starving into submission*

·**aus|husten** vt/i [h] **1.** vt *to bring up by coughing, to expectorate* **2.** vi *to finish coughing*

·**aus|jagen** vt [h] *to chase out, to drive off*

·**aus|jäten** vt [h] *to weed out*

·**aus|kämmen** vt [h] (Haar etc) *to comb (out)* ⟨a. fig⟩ ‖ ⟨tech⟩ (Wolle) *to comb, card* ‖ ⟨übtr mil⟩ *to comb out*

·**aus|kämpfen** vi/t [h] **1.** vi *to fight it out, to fight to a finish* ‖ ausgekämpft h ⟨fig⟩ *to be at the end of one's struggles* **2.** vt (etw) *to fight (out)*

·**aus|kauen** vt/i [h] **1.** vt (etw) *to chew thoroughly*; *to extract* (aus *from*) ‖ ⟨übtr⟩ e–e S ~ *to enlarge (up)on a matter* **2.** vi *to finish chewing*

·**Auskauf** m *buying off* od *out* od *up*

·**aus|kaufen** vt [h] (jdn durch Kauf ausschließen) *to buy off (a p)*; ⟨mil⟩ (durch K. befreien) *to buy (a p) off* od *out* ‖ ⟨jur⟩ (jdn durch K. ablösen) *to buy out (a p)* | ⟨com⟩ (Waren) *to buy up*; ⟨hist⟩ † *to forestall, to regrate* ‖ ⟨com⟩ (jdn im K. ausstechen) *to outbid (a p)*

·**aus|kegeln** vt [h] (etw) *to play at skittles for*

·**Auskehle** f = Hohlkehle ·**aus/kehlen** vt [h] ⟨arch⟩ *to chamfer, channel, flute*; ⟨carp⟩ *to groove, gutter* ·**Auskehlung** f ~/~en *channelling*; *fluting groove, grooving*; → Hohlkehle

·**aus|kehren** vt [h] (Raum) *to sweep (out)* ‖ (Schmutz) *to sweep away* ·**Auskehricht** m = Kehricht

·**aus|keilen** vi [h] **1.** (of horses) *to kick*; *to lash out* **2.** ~, sich ~ ⟨min⟩ (of a layer) *to thin out*

·**aus|kennen** [vrefl] [h] sich ~ an e–m Ort *to know one's way about* (od *to find one's way in*)

a place ‖ sich ~ *to know the ropes*; sich ~ in etw *to be versed* (od *well up, quite at home*) *in a th* ‖ wir kennen uns nicht mehr aus *we are at the end of our tether* (od *at our wits' end*) ‖ man kennt sich bei solchen Leuten nie aus *you never know* (*where you are*) *with such people*

·**aus|kerben** vt [h] = einkerben

·**aus|kernen** vt [h] (Obst) *to stone* ‖ (Nüsse) *to shell*

·**aus|kitten** vt [h] *to cement, to fill with cement*; *to putty*

·**aus|klagen** vt/i [h] **1.** vt **a.** ⟨jur⟩ etw ~ *to sue for a th*; (Anspruch) *to prosecute to the end* **b. sich** ~ *to give full vent to one's grievances* **2.** vi *to cease lamenting*

·**Ausklang** m ~(e)s/≃e ⟨mus⟩ *the final notes* (od *beats*) [pl]; *end* (*of a composition*) | ⟨übtr⟩ *end*; *finish*; *curtain*; *sunset* (*of life*)

·**ausklappbar** a ⟨bookb⟩ *folding* (*leaf*)

·**aus|klarieren** vt [h] ⟨mar⟩ ein Schiff ~ *to clear* (*out*) ‖ ·**Ausklarierung** f *clearance*

°·**ausklatschen** vt [h] (ausplaudern) *to blab* (*a th out*)

·**aus|klauben** vt [h] *to pick out* ‖ ⟨fig⟩ *to devise*; *hatch*

·**aus|kleben** vt [h] (Kasten etc innen) *to line* (*with* ..) ‖ (Loch) *to fill up* (*with*)

·**Auskleide- ~kabine** f, **~raum** m ⟨bes Am⟩ *walk-in closet*

·**aus|kleiden I.** vt [h] **1.** (jdn) *to undress* ‖ **sich** ~ *to undress, strip* **2.** (Haus) *to face* (*with marble*) (Zimmer) *to cover* (*with carpets*) ‖ (Wand) mit Holz ~ *to wainscot* ‖ (Schrank) *to face* (*with a veneer*) ‖ (Dach) mit Holz ~ *to timber* ‖ (Brunnen) mit Planken ~ *to plank* ‖ (Schacht) *to line* (*with brickwork*) ‖ → auslegen **II.** ≃ n *undressing* → ·**Auskleidung** f ~/ *facing*; ⟨tech⟩ *lining*

·**aus|klingeln** vt [h] (bekanntmachen) *to announce by bell-ringing*

·**aus|klingen** vi [h] *to die away* | ~ in *to end in*; in ein Hoch ~ *to end in cheers* ‖ eine Rede ~ l in *to wind up a speech by* (*a warning*) ‖ → ausgehen, -laufen ‖ harmonisch ~ *to end harmonious*(*ly*)

·**aus|klinken** vt (Tür) *to unlatch* ‖ ⟨typ⟩ (Buchstaben) *to mortise* ‖ ⟨aero⟩ (Bomben, Segelflugzeug), ⟨tech⟩ (Sperrgetriebe, etc) *to release*

·**aus|klopfen** vt [h] **1.** (Rock etc) *to beat, dust* ‖ (P) ⟨fig⟩ *to dust a p's jacket* ‖ die Pfeife ~ *to knock the ashes out of one's pipe* **2.** (Kesselstein) *to scale* **3.** (bossieren) *to deboss* ·**Ausklopfer** m ~s/~, (Teppich-) *carpet-beater*

·**aus|klügeln** vt [h] (herausbringen) *to puzzle out* ‖ (ersinnen) *to subtilize*; (Plan) *to hatch*

°·**aus|kneifen** vi [s] *to decamp*, ⟨fam⟩ *to cut and run, to skedaddle*

·**aus|knipsen** vt [h] ⟨el⟩ (Licht) *to switch* od *snap off*

°·**aus|knobeln** vt [h] (entscheiden) *to settle by dicing* ‖ ein Glas Bier ~ *to play* (*at dice*) *for a glass of beer* | ⟨übtr⟩ = austüfteln

·**aus|kochen** vt/i [h] **1.** vt **a.** (Saft) *to decoct*; *to extract by boiling* (aus *from*) | (Fleisch) *to boil* (od *cook*) *thoroughly*; ausgekochtes Fleisch *meat which has lost all its goodness* **b.** (Wäsche) *to boil* **c.** (Geräte, Gefäße) *to scald out* **2.** vi *to cease boiling* ‖ → ausgekocht

·**aus|koffern** vt [h] (Straße) *to dig out a bed for a road*

·**Auskolkung** f ~/~en *erosion* (*of a river-bed*) ⟨a. tech⟩

·**aus|kommen** vi [s] **A.** (P) **1.** → heraus-, hinauskommen ‖ ich bin heute noch nicht -ge- *I have not been out to-day* **2.** ⟨übtr⟩ ~ mit etw *to do with, to get along with, to make-do with, to manage with a th*; ich werde schon damit ~ *I'll make it do* ‖ mit s-n Mitteln ~ *to make both ends meet*; er kommt mit s-m Einkommen gerade aus *he just manages on his income*; er kann mit wenig Büchern ~ *he can do with few books*; mit wenigem ~ *to cut and contrive* | ~ ohne etw *to do* (od *go, manage*) *without a th*; man kann ohne es nicht mehr ~ *it can no more be dispensed with* **3.** ~ mit jdm *to get on* (od *agree, mix*) *with a p*; (gut) ~ mit jdm *to hit it off* (*well*) *with a p*; mit jdm einigermaßen ~ ⟨fam⟩ *to knock along with a p*; es ist leicht mit ihm -zu- *he is easy to live with*; mit jdm leicht ~ *to have a way with a p*; es ist nicht mit ihm -zu- *there is no dealing with him* ‖ ohne jdn ~ *to get along without a p* **B.** (S) **1.** (*of eggs*) *to hatch, to produce young* | (of fire) *to break out* **2.** (bekannt w) (of secrets) *to take wind*; *to become public* od *known*; (of news) *to leak* od *ooze out*; (of crimes) *to be discovered* (od *found out*)

·**Auskommen** n ~s/ **1.** ~ mit jdm *dealing, peaceable intercourse with a p*; es ist kein ~ mit ihm *there is no dealing with him* **2.** *livelihood, subsistence, sufficient means of living*; *competence, -cy* ‖ ein bescheidenes ~ *a modest competence*; genügendes ~ *independence*; sein ~ h *to earn* (od *make*) *a* (od *one's*) *livelihood* (od *living*); sein gutes ~ h *to be well off*; eben sein ~ h *to have just enough to live on* **3.** *leakage, leaking-out*; *dispersion, dispersing* (*of news*)

·**auskömmlich** a **1.** *sufficient*; *adequate, competent* (*knowledge*) **2.** *peaceable, obliging*; ein ~er Mensch *a p easy to get on* (od *deal*) *with*

·**Auskopierpapier** n ⟨phot⟩ *daylight-loading paper*

·**aus|kosten** vt [h] *to taste* (od *enjoy, experience*) *thoroughly* ‖ (Trunk) bis zur Neige ~ *to drink to the dregs* | (Würze e-s Weins; Feinheiten) *to savour* ‖ (Vergnügungen) *to exhaust*

·**aus|kragen** vi/t [h] **1.** vi (of stones) *to project*; *to jut out* **2.** vt *to make* (*a stone*) *project* (od *jut out*); *to set off* ·**Auskragung** f *projection*

·**aus|kramen** vt [h] **1.** (Schrank etc) *to rummage out* (od *up*) **2.** (Waren) *to expose for sale* | ⟨übtr⟩ (Neuigkeiten etc) *to exhibit, display*; *to show off*; sein Wissen ~ *to parade one's knowledge*

·**aus|kratzen** vt/i **1.** vt [h] ⟨surg⟩ *to scratch* (od *scrape*) *out*; *to curette* ‖ *to erase* | sich gegenseitig die Augen ~ *to scratch each other's eyes out* **2.** vi °~ *to bolt, to make a bolt for it, to hook it, to sling* od *take one's hook*; ⟨Am sl⟩ *to vamo*(*o*)*se* ·**Auskratzung** f ⟨surg⟩ *erasion*; *curettage*

·**aus|kriechen** vi [s] *to creep* (aus *out of*) ‖ *to come forth, to emerge*; (of young birds) *to hatch out*

°·**aus|kriegen** vt [h] ich kann die Stiefel nicht ~ *I can't get my boots off*

·**aus|kugeln** vt [h] sich [dat] den Arm ~ *to dislocate one's arm*

Auskultati·on f ~/~en ⟨med⟩ *auscultation, stethoscopy* †**Auskult·ator** m ⟨Ger jur (bis 1869)⟩ = Referendar **auskult·ieren** vt [h] ⟨med⟩ *to auscultate, to stethoscope*

·**aus|kundschaften** vt [h] (Land) *to explore, to spy out* ‖ ⟨mil⟩ *to reconnoitre*; → erkunden, kundschaften ‖ ⟨übtr⟩ *to search out, to reconnoitre*; (Geheimnisse) *to ferret out* ·**Auskundschafter** m ~s/~ *scout, spy* ·**Auskundschaftung** f ~/~en *exploration* ‖ ⟨mil⟩ → Rekognoszierung

·**Auskunft** f ~/≃e **1.** *information* (über *about, on*); *intelligence*; ≃e [pl] *information* ‖ bündige ~ ⟨Am fam⟩ *the lowdown*; falsche ~ *misinformation*; nähere ~ *details* [pl] (über *of, about*), *particulars* [pl] (über *of*); nähere ~ hierselbst *for particulars inquire within* | jdn um ~ bitten *to ask a p* (über *about*); ~ einholen *to seek information* (bei *with*); ~ geben *to anwer inquiries on demand* ⟨a. comp⟩; ~ geben *or* erteilen über etw, jdn *to give* od *supply information about* (od *on*) *a th, a p* | ⟨phys⟩ *message*, jdm ~ geben *to give a p a message* (od *messages*) ‖ ~suchend *rogatory* **2.** = ~sbüro

·**Auskunfts- beamter** m *inquiry clerk* od *official*; ⟨telph⟩ *information operator* **≃berechtigt** a *entitled to obtain inf.* **~büro** n *information-bureau, inquiry-office*; ⟨Am⟩ *bureau of information* ‖ (über P etc) *intelligence-office* **~ersuchen** n *request for information* **~mittel** n *expedient*; *shift*; *resort*; → Ausweg **~person** f *informant*; *reference* **~pflicht** f ⟨Ger⟩ *obligation incumbent on banks of supplying information about a p's stock*, etc **~platz** m, **~tisch** m ⟨telph, etc⟩ *monitor desk* **~quelle** f *source of information* **~stelle** f = Auskunftsbüro

Auskunft·ei f ~/~en *inquiry agency* od *office*

·**aus|kuppeln** vt [h] ⟨tech⟩ *to disconnect*; *uncouple, ungear*; ⟨mot⟩ *to declutch*

°·**aus|kurieren** vt [h] = ausheilen

·**aus|lachen** vt [h] jdn ~ *to laugh at a p*; *to laugh a p in the face*; jdn tüchtig ~ *to have a good laugh at a p*; lach mich nicht noch aus *none of your chaff, please!* ‖ jdn ~ können *to have the laugh of a p* ‖ laß dich nicht ~! *don't make a fool of yourself!* | **sich** ~ *to laugh one's fill, to have one's laugh out*

·**Auslad** m ~s/ Sw = ~ung

·**Auslade- ~bahnhof** m *goods unloading station*; *railhead* ‖ ⟨mil⟩ *detraining point* **~bahnsteig** m *unloading platform* **~gebiet** n ⟨mot⟩ *detrucking area* **~gebühren** f [pl], **~kosten** [pl] *unloading fees* od *costs*; ⟨mar⟩ *landing costs* [pl] **~hafen** m *port of discharge* **~kopf** m ⟨mot⟩ *truck-head* **~kran** m *unloading crane* **~platz** m, **~stelle** f *place of discharge, unloading-place*; *discharging point* ‖ ⟨mar⟩ *landing-place, wharf, quay*

·**aus|laden** vt/i **I.** vt [h] **1.** (Güter) *to unload, discharge, unlade* (aus *from*); ⟨mar⟩ *to land, unship*; → löschen | (Truppen etc) *to disembark, to unship* ‖ ⟨rail⟩ *to detrain*; –ge– w *to detrain* | (Schiff) *to unload, unlade, discharge*; → leichtern **2.** °jdn ~ *to put a p off, to revoke the invitation to a p* **II.** vi **1.** [h] *to unload* **2.** [s] ⟨arch⟩ = auskragen 1. ·**ausladend** a *projecting* (*roof*); breit ~ *full-bottomed* (*boat*) ‖ ⟨übtr⟩ weit ~ *wide-ranging* (*policy*)

·**Auslader** m ~s/~ *unloader, discharger*; ⟨mar⟩ *stevedore, longshoreman, docker* ·**Ausladung** f ~/~en **1.** *discharge, unloading* (*of cargo*; *of a ship*); *landing* (*of goods*) **2.** °~ *cancellation of an invitation* **3.** ⟨arch⟩ *projection*; (Risalit) *set-off* | ⟨tech⟩ *overhang, sally* ‖ *length of jib*; *radius* (*of a crane*)

·**Auslage** f ~/~n **A. 1.** *laying-out* (*of lists*, etc.) **2.** ⟨com⟩ *display, exhibition*; *show* (*of goods*) *in a shop-window*; Fenster mit ~ *show-window* **3.** (Geld≃) *outlay, disbursement, expenditure*; ~n [pl] *outlay, expenditure* ‖ die ~n (= verausgabte Beträge) *the cash outlay*; kl Extra≃n *sundries* [pl], *petty* (od *out of pocket*) *expenses*; bare ~n *outlay in cash* ‖ die ~n bestreiten (zurückerstatten) *to defray* (*refund*) *the expenses*; jdm die ~n zurück– *to reimburse a p for his expenses* **B. 1.** ⟨fenc⟩ *prime* **2.** ⟨hunt⟩ *span* (*of antlers*) **3.** (am Deich) *projection* **~scheibe** f (zu A. 1.) (gebogene *concave*) *window*

·**Auslagerung** f ~/ *stockpiling*

·**Ausland** n ~(e)s/ **1.** *foreign parts* (od *countries, lands*); *foreign nations* od *states*; „~" ⟨aero⟩ "*International Transit*", → Inland; (P) *foreigners* [pl] im ~ leben *to live abroad*; im ~ geboren *foreign-born* ‖ ins ~ gehen, reisen *to go, travel abroad*; fürs ~ *for abroad* ‖ im In- u ~ *at home and abroad* ‖ ⟨com⟩ ins ~ gehend *outward-bound* (*ship*) **2.** [in comp] → Auslands-

·**Ausländer** m ~s/~; **~in** f ~/~nen *foreigner* ‖ ⟨jur⟩ (in England etc lebender) *alien*; lästiger ~ *undesirable alien*; ⟨engl⟩ Gesetz v 1905 betr Einwanderung v ~n *Aliens Act* ‖ teilweise eingebürgerter ~ *denizen* **Ausländer·ei** f ~/ *partiality* od *predilection for things foreign*; *affectation of foreign ways* ·**ausländisch** a *foreign*; ein ~er Besucher *a visitor from abroad* ‖ ⟨jur⟩ *alien* | ⟨bot & zoo⟩ *exotic* (*plant*) ‖ ⟨übtr⟩ ~es Gewächs *or* Wort *exotic*; ~es Idiom *exoticism* | ~ aussehend, fremdartig) *outlandish, strange* (*appearance*) | ~er Wechselkurs, ~verkehr, ~e Zahlungsmittel n pl *foreign exchange* sg

·**Auslands- ~anleihe** f *foreign loan* **~aufenthalt** m *stay abroad* **~bank** f *foreign* (od *overseas*) *bank* **~behörde(n** pl) f ⟨pol⟩ *representatives* **~brief** m *foreign letter* **~debatte** f ⟨engl parl⟩ *foreign affairs debate* **~erzeugnis** n *for. product* **~deutscher** m *German living abroad* **~deutschtum** n *Germans* (*living*) *abroad* **~funk** m *external broadcasting services* **~geschäft** n *foreign transaction* **~handel** m *for. commerce* **~hilfeprogramm** n *for. aid program* **~institut** n ⟨Ger⟩ das deutsche ~ *the German Foreign Institute* **~korrespondent(in** f) m (Zeitung) *for. correspondent*; ⟨com⟩ *for. correspondence clerk* **~kredit** m *for. credit* **~kunde** f *knowledge of foreign countries* **~markt** m *for. market* **~nachrichten** f pl *for. news* **~organisation** f ⟨Ger hist⟩ (Reichs≃) *Foreign Section* **~papiere** n pl *external bonds* **~paß** m *foreign passport* **~patent** n *for. patent* **~porto** n *foreign postage* **~propagandaabteilung** f ⟨engl⟩ ~ des Außenministeriums *the Foreign Publicity Department of the Foreign Office* **~recht** n *foreign law* **~reise** f *foreign travel, trip abroad* **~stimme** f ~n [pl] *voices* [pl] *from abroad* **~verkehr** m *for. travel* **~vermögen** n *foreign assets*

·**aus|langen** vi [h] **1.** ~ nach *to reach for* **2.** *to suffice, to be sufficient*; *to do* (: *that will do*) ‖ ich werde mit dem Gelde nicht ~ *I'll not have enough money* ‖ → auskommen

·**Auslaß** m -lasses/-lässe *outlet*; *bow-off*; ⟨mill⟩ *discharging slot* **~hahn** m ⟨tech⟩ *blow-off cock* **~nocken** m *exhaust cam* **~rohr** n, **~röhre** f *discharge-pipe* **~ventil** n *escape-valve, exhaust-valve*

·**aus|lassen I.** vt [h] **A.** (herauslassen) **1.** (Wasser etc) *to let* (aus *out of*); *to let out* ‖ (Dampf) *to let off* **2.** (Gefühl etc) *to give vent* (od *free play*) *to* (*a feeling*); s–e Gefühle an jdm ~ *to work off one's feelings on a p*; s–n Ärger, Zorn ~ *to vent* (od *let out*) *one's anger, one's wrath*; *to visit one's displeasure* (an *on*); s–e Rache ~ *to wreak one's spite* od *one's vengeance* (an jdm *on a p*); s–e Wut ~ an jdm *to take it out of a p* **3. a. sich ~ über** *to say one's say, to speak one's mind, to express o.s. about* ‖ *to enlarge, expatiate, to dilate* (*up*)*on* (*a th, a p*) ‖ sich über jds Charakter ~ *to speak to a p's character* **b.** (of feelings) *to spend o.s.* (an *on a p*) **B. 1.** (Saum, Kleid) *to ease, to let out* **2.** (Honig) *to strain* (*off*); (Fett) *to melt* (*down*); –ge–e Butter *melted* od *run butter* **C.** (überg·ehen) *to leave* od *miss out*; *to omit* ‖ ⟨typ⟩ –ge–er Buchstabe *out* **II.** ≃ n *letting-out*; → ·**Auslassung** f ~/~en **1.** → Auslassen **2.** (Ausdruck) *expression, utterance* **3.** (Weglassung) *omission*; *word omitted*; ⟨typ⟩ *out* **~szeichen** n ⟨gram⟩ *apostrophe* ‖ ⟨typ⟩ *caret* (‸)

·**Auslauf** m ~(e)s/≃e **1.** *sailing* (*of a ship*) **2.** ⟨aero⟩ *landing distance*; ⟨ski-ing⟩ *outrun* | ⟨übtr⟩ *end, finish* **3.** (Stelle des Auslaufens) *mouth* (*of a river*); *outlet*; ⟨tech⟩ *outlet spout* ‖ ⟨aero⟩ *landing run* ‖ (Hühner≃) *run* ‖ → Auslaufen **~band** n ⟨film⟩ *run-out leader* **~geschwindigkeit** f ⟨aero⟩ *speed on having touched ground* **~raum** m ⟨tech⟩ *volute chamber*

·**aus|laufen** vi/refl **I.** vi [s] **A. 1.** (of ships) *to put out to sea*; *to leave* (od *clear a*) *port*; *to* (*set*) *sail* (nach *for*); *to tide* **2. a.** (of liquids) *to run* od *flow out*; *to leak out*; (of a candle) *to gutter-out*

b. (of casks, etc.) *to run out, to leak* **c.** (of colours & ink) *to run* **3.** (of lines, streets, etc) *to go, run* || (of a pier) *to run out* (*into the sea*); das Tal läuft in e–e Bucht aus *the valley opens down* od *out into a bay* | ⟨arch⟩ *to project* **4.** (endigen) *to end* (*in*); in e–e Spitze ~ *to end in* (od *taper to*) *a point* | ⟨übtr⟩ *to turn out; to result* (in *in*); → ausgehen II. 4. **5.** ⟨tech⟩ (Lager) *to run down* od *out* **B.** ⟨hort⟩ **1.** Erbsen laufen aus *peas are washed out of the pod* (*by rain*) **2.** ein Baum läuft aus *a tree puts out runners* (od *new shoots*) **II.** vrefl [h] **1.** (P) **sich** ~ *to exercise the body by running, to have a long walk*; ⟨fam⟩ *to go for a tramp* **2.** (S) ⟨tech⟩ *to wear out* (*by friction*) ·**Auslaufen** n *sailing* (*of a ship*); ⟨mil-mar⟩ *sortie* (*to make a s.*) Befehl zum ~ *sailing orders* | *leakage* (*of liquids*) ·**auslaufend** a → ausgehend

·**Ausläufer** m ~s/~ **1.** *errand-boy, runner* **2.** ⟨bot & hort⟩ *runner, stolon*; *offshoot*; ~bildung f *the growing of runners* **3.** *spur* (*of a mountain*) || ~ [pl] *foot-hills* [pl] **4.** ⟨übtr⟩ (Nachkomme) *offset* (v *from*)

·**aus|laugen** vt [h] (Erde etc) *to lixiviate* || *to macerate* || ⟨geol⟩ *to leach* || ⟨min⟩ (Erze) *to wash, to buddle* **A.gung** f *lixiviation*; *wet extraction*

·**Auslaut** m ~(e)s/~e ⟨gram⟩ *final* (od *terminal*) *sound* || im ~ *finally, when final* ·**aus|lauten** vi [h] ⟨gram⟩ *to end, terminate* (in *in*) **~d** a *final*

·**aus|läuten** vt/i [h] **1.** vt (etw) *to proclaim by ringing a bell* || (das alte Jahr etc ~) *to ring out* **2.** vi *to cease ringing* || es hat ausgeläutet *the bells have stopped*

·**aus|leben** vi/refl/vt [h] **1.** vi *to cease living* **2.** vrefl **sich** ~ *to live one's life to the full*; *to sow one's wild oats* **3.** (Instinkte etc) *to gratify*

·**aus|lecken** vt [h] (Schüssel) *to empty by licking*; *to lick clean* od *out*

·**aus|leeren** vt/i [h] **1.** vt (Gefäß) *to empty, drain*; bis auf den Grund ~ *to drain* od *drink to the dregs* || (Briefkasten) *to clear* || (Darm) *to deplete, evacuate, relieve* | (Schutt) *to shoot* (auf *on to*) || (Stuhl, Kot) *to void* **2.** vi *to evacuate the bowels, to defecate* **Ausleerung** f ~/~en *emptying, clearing* || *defecation, evacuation* (*of the bowels*)

·**auslegbar** a *explainable*; *interpretable*

·**aus|legen** vt/i [h] **I.** vt **A.** ⟨eig⟩ **1.** (Zeitungen etc) *to lay out* || ⟨com⟩ (Waren) zum Verkauf ~ *to expose for sale; to display, to exhibit* || ⟨typ⟩ (Bogen) *to take off* **2.** (zurechtlegen) (Ruder, Mast) *to ship* || (Leichnam) *to lay out* **3.** (Zimmer) mit Teppichen ~ *to cover with carpets* || (Graben) mit Zement ~ *to line with cement*; → auskleiden || (Tischplatte etc) mit Elfenbein (etc) ~ *to inlay* (*encrust, incrust*) *with ivory* || ⟨cul⟩ *to line* (*a paste in a tin*) **B.** ⟨übtr⟩ **1.** (Geldbeträge) *to pay provisionally* (f jdn *for a p*); ich werde es ~ *I'll pay for the time being* **2.** (erklären) *to explain, to expound*; (Träume, Texte etc) *to interpret*; *to be interpretative of* (*a th*) || (Äußerung) *to construe* (als *as*); etw ähnlich ~ *to place a similar construction on a th*; etw dahingehend ~, daß *to construe a th as meaning*; falsch ~ *to misinterpret*; gut (schlecht) *to put a good* (*bad*) *construction on a th* || im besten (schlechtesten) Sinne ~ *to put the best* (*worst*) *construction on a th* || etw als Nachlässigkeit ~ *to put a the down to negligence*; jdm etw als Stolz ~ *to put* od *set a th down to a p's pride* || → entziffern || man legte es zu s–n Gunsten aus ⟨jur⟩ *they gave him the benefit of the doubt* **C. sich** ~ ⟨fenc⟩ *to put o.s. into a position of guard in carte* **II.** vi °~ *to grow fat* (od *stout*) ·**Auslegen** n *laying-out; display, exhibition* | *lining* (*with*) || → Auslage, Auslegung ·**auslegend** a *interpretative* (*power*); ⟨ec⟩ *exegetic*(*al*); *hermeneutic* ·**Ausleger** m ~s/~ **1.** (P) *expositor, expounder*; *interpreter* || ⟨typ⟩ *taker-off*; *fly* **2.** (S) **a.** ⟨arch & engin⟩ *cantilever*; (am Kran) *boom, jib, jib-arm* **b.** (am Boot) *boom; outrigger* **c.** ⟨typ⟩ (automatischer) *flyer, fly* **d.** = Auslieger **~boot** n *outrigger* **~brücke** f *cantilever-bridge* **~kran** m *jib* (od *cantilever*)-*crane*

·**Auslege-** **~schrift** f *published patent application* (*laid out for public inspection*) **~tisch** ⟨typ⟩ *delivery table*

·**Auslegung** f ~/~en **1.** → Auslagen, Auslage **2.** ⟨arts & tech⟩ *layout*; *inlaying* **3.** *explanation, exposition*; *interpretation*; falsche ~ *misinterpretation, misconstruction* || ⟨ec⟩ *exegesis*; Kunst der ~ *hermeneutics* [pl] | *construction*; e–r S die beste ~ geben *to put the best construction on a th*; zwei ~en zulassen *to admit of two constructions* || Fehler *or* Irrtümer in der ~ *interpretative mistakes*; *misinterpretations*

·**aus|leiden** vt/i [h] **1.** vt *to suffer to the end* **2.** vi *to cease suffering*; er hat ausgelitten *his sufferings are over*

·**aus|leiern** vt [h] (Schraube) *to wear out by friction* || → ausgeleiert

·**Ausleihbibliothek** f *lending library* ·**Ausleihe** f *lending department* od *desk* (*of a library*)

·**aus|leihen** vt [h] (Geld) *to lend* (*out*) (an jdn *to a p*); Geld auf Zinsen ~ *to put out* (od *lend*) *money at interest* (~ zu 5% .. *at 5 per cent*) || (Bücher etc) *to lend out*; (Wagen etc) *to lend on hire*; *to let out for hire* ·**Ausleiher** m ~s/~ *lender, money-lender* || *letter* (*of books*, etc)

·**aus|lernen** vi [h] *to finish learning* || er hat ausgelernt *he has finished* od *served his apprenticeship, he has taken up* (od *is out of*) *his indentures* || man lernt nie aus *we are never too old to learn, there are always new experiences turning up* || diese Kunst lernt sich nie aus *there is always something new to learn in this art*

·**Auslese** f ~/~n **1.** ⟨biol & übtr⟩ *selection*; natürliche ~ *natural selection*; durch ~ züchten, entwickeln *to weed out* (*race-horses*, etc.) **2.** (Ausgelesenes) *selection* (aus *from*) || *the best, the choice, the pick* (*of a th*) || Johannisberger ~ *Superior* od *Choice Johannisberger* || die ~ der Gesellschaft *the cream* od *élite of society* **3.** [in comp] *select* (⟨demog⟩ *select* [*life table*]) **~druck** m ⟨biol⟩ ~ der arterhaltenden Leistung *selection pressure exerted by the survival value* **~prüfung** f *selection examination* **~wert** m *s. value*

·**aus|lesen** vt [h] (wählen) *to choose, to select* (aus, von *from*; f. *for*); *to pick out* **2.** (zu Ende lesen) (Buch) *to read* (*a book*) *through*; *to finish* (*a book*)

·**Ausleuchtung** f ~/ ⟨phot⟩ *adequate illumination*, ⟨film⟩ *lighting*

·**aus|lichten** vt [h] (Wald) *to thin out*

·**auslieferbar** a *extraditable* (*criminal*)

·**aus|liefern** vt [h] **1.** (etw) *to deliver, to hand over, to surrender, to turn over* (jdm, an jdn *to a p*) || (Bücher) *to hand* od *pass out*; *to distribute* | (P) *to pass* (*a p*) *over* (jdm *or* an jdn *to a p*); ⟨jur⟩ (Täter) *to deliver up* (*to justice*) || (flüchtigen ausländischen Verbrecher) *to extradite* **2.** ⟨übtr⟩ die Bühne wurde den Musikern ausgeliefert *the stage was given up to the musicians* || jdn den Wölfen ~ *to throw a p to the wolves* || jdn der Erwerbslosenunterstützung ~ *to throw a p on the dole* || jdn der Verzweiflung ~ *to bring* od *reduce a p to despair* || jdm, e–r S ganz –ge–rt s *to be at the mercy of a p, a th*, .. hilflos .. *to be helpless in a p's hands* | **sich e–r S** ~ *to throw o.s.* (*up*)*on a th*

·**Auslieferung** f ~/~en **1.** *delivery* (an *to*); *distribution* ⟨a. com⟩ | ⟨book-trade⟩ *wholesale distributing agency* | *surrender* (*of combatants*) (an *to*) || *extradition* (*of a foreign criminal*) **2.** ⟨übtr⟩ *surrender* (an den Materialismus *to materialism*) **~sbefehl** m ⟨engl jur⟩ *writ of delivery* (e–r vorenthaltenen S) **~sprovision** f *agent's commission for delivery* **~sschein** m *bill of delivery* **~svertrag** m ⟨com⟩ *contract for delivery* ‖ ⟨pol⟩ (über Kriegsgefangene) *cartel* ‖ (über Verbrecher) *extradition-treaty*

·aus|liegen vi [h] **1.** (of goods) *to be exposed for sale*; *to be displayed* ‖ (of newspapers, etc.) *to be kept*; die "Times" liegt dort aus *they keep the Times there* **2.** ⟨fenc⟩ *to be in a position of guard* **·Auslieger** m ~s/~ ⟨mar⟩ *coast guard vessel*

·aus|loben vt [h] ⟨jur⟩ die Ermittlung e–s Täters ~ *to fix a public reward for the tracing of a perpetrator* **·Auslobung** f ~/~en *tender of a public reward for a successful entry in a competition*

·aus|löffeln vt [h] (Teller) *to empty with a spoon* ‖ (Suppe) *to spoon up* od *out* | ⟨fig⟩ etw ~ = ausessen 2.

·aus|logieren vt [h] (jdn) *to accommodate a p outside* (*the house*)

·auslösbar a *redeemable* (*treasury bonds*)

·auslöschbar a *extinguishable*; *quenchable*

·aus|löschen vt [h] **1.** (Feuer) *to extinguish*, ⟨poet⟩ *to quench* ‖ (Kerze etc) *to put* od *snuff out*; *to extinguish, douse* ‖ (Zigarette) *to stab out* **2.** (Geschriebenes) *to delete, efface*; *to blot out, to obliterate* **3.** ⟨übtr⟩ (Gefühle etc) *to obliterate, to wipe out* | (Schwierigkeit) *to sponge out* ‖ *to pass the sponge over* (*a th*); → tilgen, ausrotten **·Auslöscher** m ~s/~ *extinguisher* **·auslöschlich** a = auslöschbar

·Auslöse- [in comp] ⟨bes tech⟩ *release* **~hebel** m *release lever* ‖ ~feder [f] *trigger return spring* **~knopf** m *release knob* od *button*; ⟨phot⟩ *shutter release* (⟨a.⟩ –sung f) **~magnet** m *trip magnet* **~vorrichtung** f *releasing device*

·aus|losen vt [h] (etw) *to draw by lot, to draw lots for*; *to raffle, to raffle for*; *to toss up for* (*a th*) | (Schuldscheine) *to draw*; (Schatzanweisungen) *to redeem*

·aus|lösen vt [h] **1.** (Gefangene) *to redeem, ransom* ‖ (Pfand) *to redeem, recover*; *to take* (*a th*) *out of pawn* **2. a.** ⟨tech⟩ (Uhrwerk etc) *to release, uncog*; *to set free, to let go*; (Störung, etc) *to touch off*; ⟨el⟩ *to trigger*; *to actuate* ⟨a. übtr⟩; *to start* (*a chain reaction*) ⟨a. fig⟩ ‖ (Knochen aus dem Fleisch) *to separate* **b.** ⟨übtr⟩ (Gelächter) *to elicit, to bring*; *to arouse* (*interest, indignation, laughter, mirth*); starke Kritik ~ *to stir up, cause strong criticism* (Handlung) *to call forth, to evoke*; (Gefühl) *to elicit, evoke*; *inspire* (in jdm *in a p*); (Leidenschaften) *to unchain, unleash* ‖ (Krieg etc) *to trigger, provoke, start, spark* **·Auslöser** m ~s/~ *switch* ‖ ⟨phot⟩ *release, trigger*; Selbst≈ *self-timer* ‖ ⟨biol⟩ *releaser*

·Auslosung f ~/~en **1.** *draw* (f. *for*) (*to win a prize at a draw*, → Ziehung) ‖ ⟨com⟩ *drawing* ‖ ⟨sport⟩ *draw*; die ~ nach dem Setzprinzip vornehmen *to seed the draw* ‖ ⟨demog, etc⟩ *sampling* **2.** *redemption* (*of bonds*)

·Auslösung f ~/~en **1.** *redemption, ransom* (*of prisoners*) ‖ *redemption* (*of things in pawns*) **2. a.** *detent, ratch* ‖ ⟨phot, etc⟩ → Auslöse-; *release*; Feder der ~ *r. spring* ‖ ~ des eisernen Vorhangs ⟨theat⟩ *release of fire curtain* **b.** ⟨übtr⟩ *calling-forth* (*of actions*), *eliciting*; *evocation* (*of feelings*) **~sknopf** m *push-button* **~smechanismus** m *trigger mechanism*

·aus|lotsen vt [h] ⟨mar⟩ (Schiff) *to pilot* (od *take out*) *to sea*

·aus|lüften vt [h] *to air, ventilate* **·Auslüftung** f ~/~en *airing, ventilation*

·aus|machen vt [h] **A.** °~ **1.** (ausgraben) (Kartoffeln) *to dig* od *take up* ‖ (aushülsen) (Erbsen etc) *to husk, shell* **2.** (ausweiden) (Fisch) *to gut* ‖ (Geflügel) *to draw* ‖ (Austern) *to open* **3.** (Flecke) *to take out, to remove* **4.** (Falten) *to smooth* od *iron out* **5.** (Feuer) *to put out, to extinguish*; (elektr. Licht) *to turn out* **6.** ⟨sport⟩ (jdn) *to put out*; ⟨crick⟩ (Schläger durch Fangen des Balls) *to catch out* **B. 1.** (vereinbaren) *to arrange*; *to agree upon*; e–n Treffpunkt ~ *to fix a meeting-place* **2.** (bedingen) *to condition* ‖ sich etw ~ *to stipulate for a th*; ~, daß *to stipulate that*, → ausbedingen, abreden 2. ‖ ~, wie hoch gespielt wird *to fix the stakes* **3.** (entscheiden) *to settle*; *to decide on* (*a th*); sie mögen es mit e–a ~ *let them settle it between them*; was ist ausgemacht worden? *what has been decided on?* ‖ *to make up* ‖ mit jdm etw –zu– h *to have a bone to pick with a p* ‖ etw vor Gericht ~ *to settle a th in court* **C. 1.** (bilden) (of parts) *to compose, constitute, to be constitutive* od *constituent of, to make up*; *to form*; *to go to the making of* (*a th*); (of sums) *to amount* (od *come, run*) *to*; (wenn man 10 M monatlich spart,) so macht das 120 M im Jahre aus (..) *that will come to 120 marks a year*; wieviel macht die Rechnung aus? *what does the bill run to?* **2.** (bedeuten) *to represent* (*more than half of a th*); er hat viel, was .. ausmacht *he has much of the making of a fine gentleman* ‖ was macht das aus? *what's the odds?* was kann das schon ~? *what of that?* ‖ das macht etw aus *that makes a difference* (f.. *to a p*); es wird kaum etw ~ *it will hardly matter at all* ‖ das macht nichts aus *that makes no difference, that is of no consequence, it does not matter* ‖ (Erfolg): *that hardly adds up to a great success* ‖ das macht viel aus *that matters a great deal*; es macht nicht viel aus *it doesn't make much odds* ‖ macht es Ihnen etw aus, wenn ich rauche? *would you mind my* (od *me*) *smoking? .. mind, if I smoke?*; macht es Ihnen viel aus? *would you mind very much?* ‖ würde es Ihnen etw ~, wenn ..? *would it make any difference to you if ..?* ‖ es macht mir nichts aus *I don't care*; es macht ihm nicht das geringste aus, ..°verdammt nichts aus *he does not care a twopenny damn* ‖ er sagte, es mache ihm nichts aus *he said it made no odds to him* **D.** (ausfindig m, besorgen) jdm ein Quartier ~ *to find a p quarters* (od *quarters for a p*); jdm e–e Stelle ~ *to procure a p a position* (od *a position for a p*) | (e–n Dampfer auf See ~) *to sight, to make out* | ⟨hunt⟩ (of dogs) (Wild) *to scent, track*; *discover* ‖ → ausgemacht **·Ausmachung** f ~/~en **1.** *arrangement, agreement* ‖ *stipulation* ‖ *settlement* **2.** *trimming* (*of a dress*)

·aus|mahlen vt [h] (Korn) *to grind* (*thoroughly*)

·Ausmahlprodukt n ⟨tech⟩ *attrition product*

·aus|malen vt [h] **1.** (Zimmer) *to paint*; (Bild farbig) *to colour* ‖ (Schild) kunstgerecht ~ *to* (*em*)*blazon*; (Initialen etc) *to decorate, to illuminate* **2.** ⟨fig⟩ (in Worten ~) *to describe, depict, delineate, paint, picture*; bis ins einzelnste ~ *to depict* od *detail minutely* ‖ jdm etw ~ *to picture a th to* od *for a p* | sich [dat] etw im Geiste ~ *to picture a th* (*to o.s.* od *in one's mind's eye*); *to imagine, fancy, realize a th*; *to envisage, visualize a th*; sich jdn ~ *to picture a p* (als *as*)

·Ausmarsch m ~es/≈e *marching-out* ‖ (zum Kriege) *departure* **·aus|marschieren** vi [s] *to march out*

·Ausmaß n ~es/~e *measurement*; *spaciousness*; *extent, dimension, size*; *amount* ‖ ⟨tech⟩ *over-all length*; *amplitude* ⟨a. übtr⟩; ~e [pl] (*overall*) *dimensions*; *proportions* [pl]; *scope*; (Größenordnung) *scale*; gr ~ *magnitude* (*of a disaster*) ‖ geistiges ~ *stature*; *intellectual range*; *sweep* (*of a p's intellect*) | v großem ~ *of great dimensions*; Pläne v gr ~ *plans of vast scope* ‖ in gr ~ *in* (*a*) *great measure, to a great extent*; *on a large scale*; in hohem ~ *to a high degree* ‖ ein so gr ~ annehmen (daß ..) *to loom so large* (*that ..*); in größerem ~ erfolgen als früher *to be on a larger scale than before*

·aus|mauern vt [h] (innen ~) *to line with masonry* (od *stonework*) **·Ausmauerung** f *lining with masonry*

·**aus|meißeln** vt [h] *to chisel; to cut* od *carve with a chisel* ‖ *to cut out; to gouge out* ‖ ⟨tech⟩ *to chase* ‖ ⟨fig⟩ fein ausgemeißelt *well-cut*

·**aus|mergeln** vt [h] (Boden) *to exhaust*; (Land) *to impoverish* ‖ (jdn) *to enervate*; [bes pp] *to emaciate; emasculate; weaken* ‖ → ausgemergelt

·**Ausmerze** f ~/ ⟨biol⟩ = –merzung

·**aus|merzen** vt [h] **1.** (Vieh etc) *to cull; to sort out; to weed out* (aus, von *from*) ‖ (schlechte Pflanzen) *to extirpate; to reject* **2.** (Fehler) *to expunge; to remove* ‖ *to wipe out; to wash out*; (Übel) *to eradicate; to extirpate* ‖ *to clear away* (*objectionable matter from a book*); Anstößiges aus e–m Buch ~ *to expurgate a book* | (jdn) *to exclude* (aus *from*) ·**Ausmerzung** f *weeding-out* | *expunction* (*of words*) ‖ *eradication, extirpation* (*of evils*) ‖ *exclusion* (*of a p*)

·**aus|messen** vt [h] *to measure* ‖ (Dosis) *to measure out* ‖ (Land) *to survey* ‖ (Gefäß, Schiff) *to gauge* ·**Ausmesser** m ~s/~ *measurer* ‖ → Landmesser ·**Ausmessung** f ~/~en *measuring; measurement* ‖ *gauging* ‖ ⟨geog & math⟩ *surveying; survey*; → Landesvermessung ‖ → Ausmaß

·**aus|mieten** vt [h] (etw) *to hire out; to let out* ‖ (jdn) *to oust* od *dislodge* (*a p*) *by offering a higher rent*

·**aus|mieten** vt [h] **1.** *to take* (*potatoes*) *out of the clamp* **2.** Sw = vermieten

·**aus|misten** vt [h] (Stall) *to clear out; to clear of dung; to sweep out* ‖ ⟨übtr⟩ *to clean, to cleanse*; → Augiasstall

†·**aus|mitteln** vt [h] *to ascertain; to find out, to discover*

·**aus|möblieren** vt [h] *to provide with furniture, to furnish, to fit up*

·**aus|münden** vi [h] (of a river, etc.) *to fall, flow; to discharge itself, to empty* (in *into*) ‖ (of flats, roads) *to open* (in *into*; auf *on to*) ‖ ⟨fig⟩ *to issue* (*in*)

·**Ausmündung** f ~/~en *mouth* (*of a river*); *estuary*

·**aus|münzen** vt [h] (Metall) *to coin; to mint* | ⟨fig⟩ *to utilize* (f. *for*); *to put* (*a th*) *to use* ‖ *to make capital out of* (*a th*)

·**aus|mustern** vt [h] (etw) *to discard, reject, eliminate, scrap* ‖ ⟨mil & mar⟩ (jdn) *to discharge, exempt; to reject* (*as unfit*) ·**Ausmusterung** f ⟨Ger mil⟩ *discharge, exemption from military service*

·**Ausnahme** f ~/~n **1.** *exception* ‖ ohne ~ *without exception*; alle .. *all without e.* ‖ mit ~ Montag *with the exception of Monday, Monday excepted, except Monday*; mit ~ s–r Angehörigen *with the e. of his relatives*; → ausgenommen I.b.2. ‖ k–e ~ dulden *or* erleiden (S) *to admit of no exception*; k–e ~ zulassend *unexceptional* ‖ e–e ~ m *to make an exception, to draw a line* (: *only Mr. N. drew a line*); *to stretch a point*, ⟨sl⟩ *to make a burst*; k–e ~n m *to make no exceptions* ‖ e–e ~ m bei (*or* mit) jdm *to make an exception of a p. to except a p* **2.** (Ausgenommenes) (das ist) e–e ~ v der Regel (*that is*) *an exception to the rule* ‖ er macht *or* bildet e–e ~ v der Regel *he is an exception to the rule* ‖ die ~ bestätigt die Regel *the exception proves the rule*

·**Ausnahme-** [in comp] *exceptional; exceptive* **~fall** m *exceptional case* **~gebiet** n *protected area* **~gericht** n ⟨Ger⟩ *special court* **~gesetz** n *exceptional law* **~klausel** f *escape clause* **~preis** m ⟨com⟩ *special price* **~stellung** f *exceptional position* **~tarif** m → Staffeltarif **~zustand** m *state of emergency* ‖ ⟨Ger⟩ *state of martial law*; den ~ verhängen *to establish* od *proclaim m. l.*; in ~ versetzen *to place* (*a town*) *under m. l.*; den ~ verhängen über e–n Ort *to proclaim a place*; die Stadt befindet sich im ~ *the town is proclaimed*; im ~ befindlich *proclaimed* (*town*)

·**ausnahmslos 1.** a *unexceptional; admitting of no exception* **2.** adv *without exception* ·**ausnahmsweise** adv *exceptionally; by way of exception; for once*, (*for*) *once in a way*

·**aus|nehmen** vt [h] **A.** ⟨eig⟩ **1.** → herausnehmen ‖ Nest, Nester ~ → ausheben I. 3. **2.** (T) (ausweiden) *to eviscerate, disembowel*; (Fisch) *to gut*; (Geflügel) *to draw* **3.** (jdn beim Spiel etc) ⟨sl⟩ *to clean* (*out*); *to rob*; ⟨sl⟩ *to skin* (*a p*) | ich bin wie ausgenommen *my brain is tired*; ⟨fam⟩ *I've got brain-fag* **4.** (Kartoffeln) *to lift; to take up* **B.** (ausschließen) *to except* (aus, von *from, out of*); *to exempt* (v *from*); *to exclude* (v *from*) ‖ ⟨a. Am⟩ (jdn) *to count out* ‖ ausdrücklich ~ *to except explicitly*; k–n ~ *to make no exceptions* ‖ ich nicht ausgenommen *not excluding myself*, → ausgenommen | **sich** ~ *to except* (od *exclude*) *o.s.* ‖ sich ~ v *to contract o.s. out of* (*an arrangement*); *to contract out* **C.** ⟨übtr⟩ **sich** ~ (aussehen) *to look, show*; sich gut (schlecht) ~ *to look well* (*bad*) ‖ er nahm sich imposant (armselig) aus *he made an imposing figure* (*he cut a poor figure*)

·**Ausnehmen** n *evisceration* (*of animals*); *gutting* (*of fish*) ·**ausnehmend 1.** a *uncommon, exceptional; extraordinary*; (vorzüglich) *excellent* **2.** adv *exceptionally; exceedingly*; ~ höflich *elaborately polite*

·**aus|nutzen,** ·**aus|nützen** vt [h] **1.** (etw) (Gelegenheit) *to take advantage of*; (gut) *to turn to* (*good*) *account* (od *use*); *to utilize*; erfolgreich ~ *to exploit*; etw nach Kräften ~ *to make the best of a th*; die Zeit aufs beste ~ *to make the most of one's time* ‖ e–n Sieg (etc) voll ~ *to follow up one's victory* **2.** (mißbrauchen) jds Güte ~ *to trade upon a p's tender heart*, jds ungünstige Lage ~ *to take a p at a disadvantage*; jds Schwächen ~ *to practise on a p's weaknesses*; jds Unwissenheit ~ *to play on a p's ignorance* | jdn ~ *to take advantage of a p; to make a convenience of a p; to exploit a p* ⟨a. com⟩

·**Ausnutzung,** ·**Ausnützung** f ~/~en *profitable management; utilization; exploitation* (*of mines*, etc.) ‖ volle ~ *maximum utilization* | (Mißbrauch) ~ der Güte jds *trading upon a p's kindness* ‖ *exploitation* (*of a p*)

·**aus|packen I.** vt/i [h] **1.** vt (Koffer, Sachen) *to unpack* **2.** vi **a.** *to unpack*; ich habe wochenlang nicht ~ können *I have been living in my trunks for weeks* **b.** ⟨fig⟩ *to begin to tell*; (sich aussprechen) *to open out; to say one's say*; tüchtig ~ *to speak one's mind, to give vent to one's feelings* **II.** ≈ n *unpacking* ·**Auspacker** m ~s/~ *unpacker*

·**aus|pauken** vt/i [h] (of students) ⟨fenc⟩ *to fight to the end*

·**aus|peilen** vt [h] ⟨mar⟩ die Richtung ~ *to take one's bearings, to fix one's course*

·**aus|peitschen** vt [h] *to whip, flog, rawhide, scourge* ·**Auspeitschung** f *whipping, etc*

°·**aus|pellen** vt [h] → schälen ‖ °sich ~ *to take one's clothes off, to undress*; ⟨Am fam⟩ *to peel off*

·**aus|pfänden** vt [h] jdn ~ *to distrain* (*up*)*on a p* od (*up*)*on a p's goods*

·**Auspfändung** f ~/~en *distraint*; → Pfändung

·**Auspfarrung** f *transfer to another parish*

·**aus|pfeifen** vt [h] ⟨theat⟩ (Schauspieler, Stück) *to hiss, hoot*; ⟨sl⟩ *to boo; to give* (*an actor, a play*) *the bird*

·**aus|pflanzen** vt [h] *to bed out*

·**aus|pflastern** vt [h] (Straße) *to cover with pavement, to pave*

·**aus|pichen** vt [h] (Faß etc) *to pitch*; → ausgepicht

Ausp·izien [pl] *omen; prognostic* ‖ *prospects, auspices* [pl] ‖ (Schutz) *patronage, auspices* [pl]

·**aus|plappern** vt [h] *to blab* od *blurt out*

·**aus|plätten** vt [h] *to iron*; (falten) *to smooth out* (aus *from*)

·**aus|plaudern** vt/i [h] **1.** vt *to blab* od *let out*; *to divulge* || *to spread*; → Geheimnis **2.** vi *to finish chatt(er)ing*

·**aus|plündern** vt [h] (Land etc) *to sack, plunder, pillage*; (in bezug auf Lebensmittel) *to forage* || die Ladenkasse ~ *to rob the till* | jdn ~ *to rob* od *bleed a p*; ⟨sl⟩ *to clean* (*out*), *to skin a p* ·**Ausplünderung** f ~/~en *sack, plundering, pillaging* || *spoliation*; *robbery* (: *sheer r.*)

·**aus|polstern** vt [h] *to stuff, pad* || (Kleidungsstück) *to line with wadding, to wad*

·**aus|posaunen** vt [h] ⟨fig⟩ (etw) *to trumpet forth* od *abroad*; *to blaze* od *blazon abroad, to emblazon*; in alle Welt ~ *to blazon out to the world* || du brauchst es nicht –zu– *you don't have to shout it from the housetops*

·**aus|powern** vt [h] (Land) *to impoverish, drain* || (jdn) *to impoverish*; *exploit*, → ausplündern ·**Auspowerung** f *impoverishment* || *exploitation*

·**ausprägbar** a *coinable*

·**aus|prägen** vt [h] **1.** *to coin, stamp* **2. sich** ~ ⟨fig⟩ (*of quality*) *to express itself*; *to reveal* (od *show*) *itself*; *to find its expression* (in *in*) || → ausgeprägt ·**Ausprägung** f ~/~en *mark* || bes ~ *special accent* od *expression*; e–e bes ~ erfahren *to find a sp. expr.* (*in a th through a th*)

·**aus|pressen** vt [h] **1.** (Wasser) *to wring* (aus *from, out of*); (Saft), *to squeeze out*; *to press, to squeeze* (aus *from, out of*) | (Frucht) *to squeeze*; (Trauben) *to crush* **2.** ⟨fig⟩ (jdm etw) ~ *to squeeze a th from* (od *out of*) *a p* || → erpressen

·**aus|probieren I.** vt [h] *to try out* || (Wein) *to taste* **II.** ≚ n *Trial and Error*

·**Auspuff** m ~(e)s/~e **1.** ⟨mot⟩ *exhaust* **2.** [in comp] *exhaust* .. (⟨bes mot⟩ –schlitz [m] *e. port*, –takt [m] *e. stroke*) **~dampf** m *escape steam* **~flammendämpfer** m *exhaust-flame damper* **~gas** n *burnt gas* **~klappe** f *exhaust cut-out* (od *exhaust valve*) **~rohr** n *exhaust pipe* **~schalldämpfer, ~topf** m *silencer, muffler* °**~zahn** m ⟨teens fam mot⟩ *pillion girl*; → Zahn ⟨teens⟩

·**aus|puffen 1.** vi [s] ⟨mot⟩ *to scavenge, escape, exhaust* **2.** ≚ n *scavenging* ·**aus|pumpen** vt [h] **1.** (Wasser) *to pump out* (aus *from*) || (Luft) *to exhaust* | (Gefäß) *to exhaust*; e–n Brunnen ~ *to exhaust* (*the water in*) *a well* **2.** ⟨fig⟩ jdn ~ *to draw a p* (über *on*); *to draw* (od *suck*) *a p out*; *to pump a p*; die Reichen ~ *to soak the rich*; → ausgepumpt

·**aus|punkten** vt [h] ⟨box⟩ *to outpoint, to beat on points*

°·**aus|pusten** vt [h] (Licht) *to blow out*; *to put out*

·**Ausputz** m ~es/ *adornment*; *trimmings* [pl]; *finery* ·**aus|putzen** vt [h] **1.** (reinigen) (Ofen etc) *to clean, to cleanse* || (Licht) *to snuff out* || ⟨hort⟩ (Baum) *to prune* **2.** † (schmücken) *to decorate, adorn, attire, trim* **3.** °jdn ~ *to rebuke a p* ·**ausputzmaschine** f (f Schuhe) *finishing machine*

·**aus|quartieren** vt [h] (jdn) *to accommodate* (*a p*) *outside* (*the house*) || *to dislodge*

·**aus|quetschen** vt [h] **1.** (Zitrone) *to squeeze dry* **2.** °jdn ~ *to suck out* **3.** °**sich** ~ = sich aussprechen

·**aus|radeln** vi [s] *to go for a bicycle ride*

·**aus|radieren** vt [h] *to rub* od *scratch out*; *to erase, delete, efface, obliterate*

·**aus|rangieren** vt [h] (Sachen) *to sort out, to discard*; (Schiffe) *to scrap* || (Beamte etc) *to shelve, dismiss*; *to shunt*; ausrangiert s *to be on the shelf*

·**aus|rauben** vt [h] (Haus) *to rob*; die Ladenkasse ~ *to pinch the till* || ⟨min⟩ *to clear*

·**aus|rauchen** vt/i [h] **1.** vt (Zigarre) *to finish* **2.** vi *to finish one's smoke*

·**aus|räuchern** vt [h] (Zimmer) *to fumigate*; *to smoke out* || (durch Rauch vertreiben) *to smoke out* ·**Ausräucherung** f *fumigation*

·**aus|raufen** vt [h] (Unkraut etc) *to pluck* (od *pull, tear*) *out*; *to extirpate* || sich die Haare ~ ⟨mst fig⟩ *to tear one's hair*

·**aus|räumen I.** vt [h] **1.** (Gebiet, Kanal) *to clear* (*out*); *to evacuate*; (Zimmer, Schrank) *to turn out, to empty*; (Haus) durch Feuer ~ *to gut* **2.** (Sachen) *to clear away*; *to remove* || ⟨theat⟩ *to get* (⟨Am⟩ *take*) *out* **3.** ⟨geol⟩ *to excavate*; → beseitigen, wegräumen, –schaffen **II.** ≚ n ⟨theat⟩ *scenery get-out* (⟨Am⟩ .. *take-out*) ·**Ausräumer** m **1.** (P) *cleaner*; *navvy* **2.** (S) *scraping-iron* ·**Ausräumung** f ~/~en, *clearing, clearance* | *clearing away* (*of things*); → Wegschaffung

·**aus|rechnen** vt [h] *to cast* (⟨Am⟩ figure) *up*, *to calculate*; *to reckon up, to compute*; ein Exempel ~ *to do a sum*; E. ~ *to do sums*; falsch ~ *to miscalculate* || sich [dat] etw ~ *to calculate a th* | ⟨übtr⟩ *to calculate*; ⟨Am⟩ *to figure* (daß *that*) || → ausgerechnet ·**Ausrechnung** f ~/~en *calculation, computation*

·**aus|recken** vt [h] den Hals ~ *to crane*; sich [dat] den Hals ~ *to crane* (od *stretch*) *one's neck* (nach *for*; *to do*)

·**Ausrede** f ~/~n *subterfuge, evasion, excuse*; k–e ~n! *no excuse, sir!*; → Vorwand (: *a mere e.*) || e–e faule ~ *a fib, a poor* (od *lame*) *excuse*; faule ~n gebrauchen *to make lame excuses*, ⟨Am sl⟩ *to stall*; etw als ~ gebr. *to make a th an exc.* || e–e ~ findet sich immer *you can always find an excuse* || er hat immer e–e ~, er ist um e–e ~ nie verlegen *he is never at a loss for an excuse*

·**aus|reden** vi/t [h] **1.** vi *to finish speaking* || jdn ~ l *to hear a p out, to let a p have his say* **2.** vt **a. sich** ~ *to say one's say*; sich offen ~ *to speak out*; sich gründlich ~ *to be expatiatory* **b. sich** ~ *to find* (od *make*) *excuses*; *to excuse o.s.* **c.** jdm etw ~ *to talk a p out of a th, to talk a th out of a p's head*; *to dissuade a p from a th*; *to argue a p out of a th*; sich etw (ein Gefühl) ~ *to argue o.s. out of a th*; das lasse ich mir nicht ~ *I won't be argued out of that, I insist on it*

·**aus|regnen** vi [h] ~, sich ~ *to leave off raining*; es hat (sich) –ge–net *it has rained itself out*

·**aus|reiben** vt [h] *to rub out* || *to scrub*

·**aus|reichen** vi [h] *to be sufficient, to suffice, to do*; das wird kaum ~ *that will hardly do*; ich reiche mit der Summe aus *I can manage on the sum*; mein Geld wird dafür nicht ~ *my money will not run to that* || lange ~ *to go a long way*, nicht ~ *to go a short way* (z tun *to doing*) || f jdn *to last a p* (: *it will last me a week*) ·**ausreichend 1.** a *sufficient*; *ample, abundant*; *adequate* ⟨a. tech⟩; *working* (*knowledge*) **2.** adv *sufficiently*

·**aus|reifen** vi [h & s] *to ripen*; *mature*; *to come to maturity* | ⟨übtr⟩ *to mature* (zu *into*); (Plan) ~ l *to mature* || ausgereift *mature* (*age, thoughts*)

·**Ausreise** f *departure*; *sailing, exit* || *voyage out*; *way out*, auf der ~ *on my way out I* .. || *outward voyage* (*of a ship*); auf der ~ *outward(s)*, *outward bound*

·**aus|reißen** vt/i **1.** vt [h] **a.** (Unkraut) *to tear* (od *pull, pluck*) *out*; *to extirpate*; (Baum) mit den Wurzeln ~ *to uproot*; *to tear up by the roots*; → ausraufen, –ziehen || das Knopfloch ist ausgerissen *the buttonhole is torn* **b.** ⟨fig⟩ °sich ein Bein (*or* die Beine) ~ [oft neg] *to overstrain* od *overexert o.s.*; ⟨sl⟩ *to kill o.s.* (*with overwork*); → Baum 1. c; Bein II. 3. **2.** vi °~, wie Schafleder ~ *to decamp, escapade*; *to make a bolt for it*; *to run*; *to turn tail*; ⟨fam⟩ *to cut and run, to skedaddle* || ⟨sl⟩ *to guy*; *to hare* (od *hook, leg*) *it*; *to do a bunk*; *to scoot*; ⟨Am sl⟩ *to vamo(o)se* || s–e Frau ist ausgerissen *his wife has bolted* (*with Fred*) || *to make off* (*with the jewels*, etc.); → °ausrücken; °durchbrennen ·**Ausreißer** m ~s/~ *runaway, fugitive, deserter* || (Geschoß) *wild shot, stray bullet* || ⟨ind, tech⟩ *outlier*

·**aus|reiten** vi/t **1.** vi [s] *to go for a ride, to take a ride; to ride out* **2.** vt [h] ein Pferd ~ *to take a horse out*

·**aus|renken** vt [h] (Glied) *to disjoint, dislocate, splay;* sich [dat] den Fuß ~ *to sprain one's foot* ‖ sich den Hals ~ *to crane one's neck* (nach *for*)

·**Ausrenkung** f ~/~en *dislocation; sprain*

·**aus|reuten** vt [h] = ausroden

·**aus|richten** vt [h] **1.** (gerade richten) **a.** (einpassen) *to adjust;* ⟨tech⟩ ein Lager ~ *to true a bearing* ‖ *to straighten; to make straight* **b.** (in e–r Linie ~) *to align* ‖ ⟨mil⟩ sich ~ *to dress* (*the*) *ranks;* sich nach rechts ~ *to dress by the right* **c.** ⟨übtr⟩ (Geist, Menschen) *to discipline* (f *for*), *to organize, order, orientate, rule;* neu ~ *to rebuild, reorganize, reorientate* ‖ sich ~ *to organize o.s.* (nach .. hin *to*) **2. a.** (vollführen) (etw) *to accomplish, do, perform; to attend to* ‖ *to carry out, to execute; to effect(uate)* **b.** (erreichen) *to obtain; to attain;* mit Geld kann man viel ~ bei ihm ⟨fam⟩ *money has a great pull on* (od *with*) *him,* ⟨fam⟩ *money will do a lot with him;* damit w wir nichts ~ *that will get us nowhere;* er konnte nichts gegen sie ~ *he could not prevail against them* ‖ auch er richtete nichts aus *he also failed;* was h Sie ausgerichtet? *how did you fare?;* damit ist nichts ausgerichtet *nothing is effected by this* **c.** (Fest etc) *to give; to arrange; to get up* **d.** e–e Botschaft ~ *to deliver a message, to go on an errand* (od *a message*); ich will es ihm ~ *I'll give him the m., I'll tell him;* das sollte ich ihm v ihr ~ *she told me to tell him that;* ⟨telph⟩ jdm etw ~ *to give a p a message;* kann ich etw ~? *can I take a message?* ‖ Grüße v jdm ~ *to present a p's compliments;* richte ihm e–n schönen Gruß aus *give him my kind regards* **3.** ⟨min⟩ (Gang) *to discover; explore* ·**Ausrichtung** f ~/~en **1.** *adjustment* ‖ *alignment* ‖ *organizing; ordering* (*of a society*); *orientation* (nach *towards*) ‖ ⟨agr, com, etc⟩ *orientation* ‖ (Bauflucht) *alignment, alinement;* → Einstellung **2.** *execution* ‖ (Mitteilung) *communication*

·**aus|ringen** vt/i [h] **1.** vt (Wäsche) *to wring* (*out*) **2.** vi er hat ausgerungen ⟨fig⟩ *his struggles are over*

·**aus|rinnen** vi [s] *to run* od *trickle out, to leak*

·**Ausritt** m ~(e)s/~e *riding out; ride*

·**aus|roden** vt [h] (Bäume) *to root out* od *up, to stub* (*up*); *to unroot;* (Wald) *to clear; to grub out* (*root-stocks*) ·**Ausrodung** f ~/~en *clearing, clearance*

·**aus|rollen I.** vt/i [h] **1.** vt (Teig) *to roll* (*out*) **2.** vi ⟨aero⟩ (of aeroplanes) *to taxi to a standstill* **II.** ~ n ⟨aero⟩ *landing run*

·**ausrottbar** a *eradicable*

·**aus|rotten** vt [h] (Unkraut) *to eradicate, unroot, uproot* | ⟨fig⟩ *to eradicate, to outroot, to root out, to exterminate, to extirpate; to destroy;* (Rasse) *to wipe out* ‖ mit Stumpf u Stiel ~ *to destroy root and branch;* nicht auszurotten(d) *not eradicable* ·**Ausrottung** f ~/~en *eradication, extirpation, extermination*

·**aus|rücken** vi/t **1.** vi [s] ⟨mil⟩ *to march out* ‖ (ins Feld ~) *to take the field* | °~ = ausreißen 2. **2.** vt ⟨mech⟩ (Riemen etc) *to disengage, disconnect; ungear;* (Rad) *uncouple* ‖ ⟨typ⟩ *to stop*

·**ausrückbar** a *disconnectable* (*coupling*) ·**Ausrück-** ~**bolzen** m *release pin* ~**gabel** f *strap* od *disengaging fork* ~**hebel** m *disengaging lever* ~**vorrichtung** f *shifting device* ‖ (*belt*) *shifter; tripping gear*

·**Ausrückung** f ⟨tech⟩ *disengagement, disconnection* ·**Ausrückvorrichtung** f *disengaging gear*

·**Ausruf** m ~(e)s/~e *cry, outcry, exclamation; ejaculation* (*of sorrow, of surprise*) ‖ (öffentlicher) *proclamation*

·**aus|rufen** vt/i [h] **1.** vt *to publish, proclaim;* ⟨sl⟩ *to blaze* ‖ jdn zum König ~ *to proclaim a p king* ‖ etw ~ l *to have a th proclaimed by the town-crier* ‖ ⟨com⟩ s–e Waren ~ *to cry one's wares* **2.** vi *to cry* (*out*); *to exclaim* ·**Ausrufer** m ~s/~ (öffentlicher ~ *public crier, town-crier; bellman* ‖ ⟨com⟩ (vor Buden) *tout;* ⟨Am⟩ *barker* ‖ (Herold) *proclaimer, herald* ‖ (Straßenhändler) *hawker* ‖ (Auktionator) *auctioneer*

·**Ausrufewort** n ⟨gram⟩ *interjection*

·**Ausrufung** f ~/~en *exclamation; proclamation;* ~ zum Könige *p. as King* ~**zeichen** n ⟨gram⟩ *note* (od *mark, point*) *of exclamation, exclamation mark;* ⟨Am⟩ *exclamation point*

·**aus|ruhen** vi/t [h] **1.** vi *to rest* (v *from*); *to repose* (auf *on*); *to take a rest* | ⟨übtr⟩ *to recover* (v *from*) ‖ → Lorbeeren **2.** vt (ein Glied etc) *to rest;* die Augen ~ *to give one's eyes a rest;* bist du ganz ausgeruht? *are you quite rested?* | sich ~ *to rest o.s.; to repose* (auf *on*)

·**aus|rupfen** vt [h] (Federn etc) *to pull* od *pluck out*

·**aus|rüsten** vt [h] ⟨mil⟩ *to equip* ‖ (Schiff) *to fit out, to make ready for sea;* (mit Mannschaft) *to man* ‖ Häuser ausgerüstet mit .. *houses appointed with ..* | ⟨übtr⟩ (jdn) *to equip, to furnish, to fit out, to prime* (mit .. *with information*); → rüsten

·**Ausrüstung** f ~/~en **1.** [abstr] *equipment, finishing; fitting out* **2.** [konkr] (~sgegenstände) *attachment(s);* ⟨mil⟩ *equipment, equipage, kit;* ⟨tech, bookb⟩ *finishing* ‖ (Schiffs≗) *furniture;* ~ mit Geschützen *armament* (*of a ship*) ‖ ⟨zoo & bot⟩ Schutz≗ *armature* ‖ (Reise≗) *outfit; set-out* ~**sgegenstände** m [pl] *equipments* [pl], → Ausrüstung 2. ‖ ⟨tech⟩ *fittings* [pl] ~**skosten** [pl] *cost of outfit* ~**sstück** n *piece of equipment,* (Möbel) *p. of furniture*

·**Aussaat** f ~/~en **1.** [abstr] *sowing;* natürliche ~ *natural sowing* **2.** [konkr] *the seed sown; sowing; seed-corn* ·**aus|säen** vt [h] (Samen) *to sow* | ⟨fig⟩ *to disseminate; spread*

·**aussagbar** a *predicable* (v *of*)

·**Aussage** f ~/~n **1.** (v P) *assertion, declaration, statement;* e–e ~ m *to make a declaration* od *statement* ‖ (v S) ~n m *to give out messages* (über *about*) | ⟨jur⟩ (Zeugen≗) *deposition, evidence* (auf Grund der ~ *on the e. of ..;* .. Ihrer eigenen ~ *on your own showing*), mündliche ~ *parol evidence; testimony;* ~ vor Gericht *evidence in court;* s–e ~ m *to give evidence* ‖ ~n [pl] der Prozeßparteien *pleadings* [pl] **2.** ⟨gram⟩ (Satz≗) *predicate* ‖ ⟨log⟩ *proposition, predication* **3.** ⟨arts⟩ *statement* ~**logik** f *propositional logic* ~**satz** m ⟨gram⟩ *declarative statement* ~**weise** f ⟨gram⟩ *mood*

·**aus|sagen** vt/i [h] **1.** vt (etw) *to declare, state* ‖ ⟨log & gram⟩ (etw) *to predicate* (v *of*); ausgesagt w können v jdm *to be predicable of a p* ‖ (v S) Neues ~ *to give out fresh messages* | ⟨jur⟩ etw eidlich ~ *to depose* (*to*) *a th;* ~, daß .. *to depose that,* ~ getan z h *to depose to having done;* es wurde ausgesagt *it was given in evidence* (*that ..*) **2.** vi ~ v *to be predicative of* | ⟨jur⟩ ~ gegen, für *to depose, to give evidence against, for; to testify against* (*a p*); (bei Begnadigung) gegen s–e Mitschuldigen ~ *to turn king's evidence*

·**aussagend** a *predicative* (v *of*)

·**aus|sägen** vt [h] *to saw out*

·**Aussatz** m ~es/≗e ⟨med⟩ *leprosy* ‖ Mailändischer ~ *pellagra* ·**aussätzig** a *leprous*

·**Aussätzige** der ~ (ein ~r) m ~n/~n *leper* ~**nspital** n *lepers' hospital*

·**aus|säuern** vi [s] e–e Pflanze säuert aus *a plant dies* od *wilts in stagnant water from want of air*

·**aus|saufen** vt [h] *to quaff, to drink up;* ⟨sl⟩ *to swig*

·**aus|saugen I.** vt [h] **1.** (Flüssigkeit) *to suck out; to suck* (aus *from, out of*); jdm das Blut ~ *to suck the blood out of a p* | (Frucht) *to suck* ‖

(Wunde) *to suck* **2.** (Land) *to exhaust, drain* **3.** (jdn) *to suck, bleed; fleece; sweat;* jdn bis aufs Blut ~ ⟨fig⟩ *to suck the very blood out of a p,* → ausbeuten **II.** ≈ n *sucking, suction* | *exhaustion* | *bleeding, fleecing (of a p)* ·**Aussauger** m ~s/~ ⟨fig⟩ *blood-sucker, extortioner*

·**aus|schaben** vt [h] ⟨surg⟩ → auskratzen

·**Ausschabung** f → Auskratzung

·**aus|schachten** vt [h] (Graben) *to excavate, sink; deepen*

·**aus|schälen** vt [h] (Erbsen etc) *to peel, shell*

·**aus|schalten** vt [h] **1.** (Fehler etc) *to eliminate;* (e–e S) *to set aside; to rule out* ‖ (jdn) *to crowd* od *rule out; to suspend;* [abs] er schaltet beim Wettbewerb aus *he is ineligible for the competition* ‖ ⟨tact⟩ *to interdict* **2.** ⟨el⟩ *to disconnect;* (Strom) *to break; to put out of circuit;* (Licht) *to switch off* ‖ (Maschine) *to stop* ‖ ⟨mot⟩ (Richtungsanzeiger) *to cancel;* (Kupplung) *to throw out, to disengage* ‖ ⟨wir⟩ (Geräusche, Sender) *to cut* od *tune out* ·**Ausschalter** m ~s/~ ⟨el⟩ *cut-out, switch, circuit-breaker*

·**Ausschalttaste** f ⟨comp⟩ *cancel key* ·**Ausschaltung** f ~/~en *elimination; ruling-out, setting aside; removal, exclusion, suspension (of a p)* ‖ ⟨el⟩ *circuit-breaking, disconnexion (–ction);* ⟨wir⟩ *cutting-out*

·**Ausschank** m ~(e)s/≈e **1.** *retail of liquor* **2.** °(Kneipe) *public-house, bar;* ⟨fam⟩ *pub* ‖ → Wein ‖ ⟨übtr fam⟩ *digs* [pl]; ein kümmerlicher ~ *a miserable hole, a poor show* ‖ unerlaubter ~ ⟨Am⟩ *blind pig* od *tiger* ~**(-Genehmigung** f) *retail-licence*

·**aus|scharren** vt [h] ⟨zoo, orn⟩ *to dig up, to scratch out*

·**Ausschau** f ~/ ~ halten nach *to look (out) for (a p, a th)* ·**aus|schauen** vi [h] **1.** *to look (out), to watch* (nach *for*); nach jdm ~ *to peer out for a p* **2.** (aussehen) *to look,* er schaut blaß aus *he looks pale;* wie schaut's aus? *how are things?*

·**aus|schaufeln** vt [h] (etw) *to shovel out*

·**aus|scheiden I.** vi/t **1.** vi [s] *to resign; to retire* (aus *from* [an *office*]); aus e–m Klub ~ *to leave a club* ‖ *to stand down; to drop out; not to take part* ‖ ⟨sport⟩ *to be knocked out* (od *eliminated*) **2.** vt [h] *to eliminate; to separate* (v *from*) ‖ ⟨med⟩ (Säfte) *to secrete; excrete* ‖ (Stein) *to void* ‖ ⟨chem⟩ (Stoff) *to evolve; to extract* (aus *from*); (sich ~ l) *to precipitate* | (ausschließen) *to rule out;* (jdn) *to throw out, to exclude;* (e–n Gedanken) *to dispose of* ‖ daß er uns begleitet, scheidet aus *his accompanying us is out of the question* **II.** ≈ n *retirement, withdrawal* (aus *from*); → Ausscheidung ·**ausscheidend** a *retiring (minister); outgoing (tenant)*

·**Ausscheidung** f ~/~en **1.** → Ausscheiden **2. a.** [abstr] *separation* ‖ ⟨med⟩ *secretion* ‖ ⟨chem⟩ *elimination* ‖ *expurgation (of members)* ‖ ⟨sport⟩ *elimination;* durch e–n ~sprozeß *by a process of elimination* **b.** [konkr] *secretion, excretion* ‖ ⟨ind⟩ *by-product* ~**sorgan** n ⟨med⟩ *excretory organ* ~**skampf** m ~**srunde** f *heat, round;* die letzte ~ *the final (heat, round)* ~**sspiel** n ~ im Turnier *tie;* (zur Ermittlung e–r Auswahlmannschaft) *trial match;* Pokal [m] bei ~en *challenge-cup* ~**sturnier** n *knock-out* (⟨Am⟩ *elimination) tournament* ~**sverzögerung** f ⟨path⟩ *delay of the secretion*

·**aus|schelten** vt [h] *to chide, scold (a p);* jdn tüchtig ~ *to give a p a good scolding*

·**aus|schenken** vt [h] (Getränk) *to pour out* ‖ (als Schankwirt) *to dispense; to sell retail, to retail*

·**aus|scheren** vt/i [h] **1.** vt (den Nacken ~ *to crop* (od *shave*) *the hair in the neck* **2.** vi ⟨mar⟩ (of ships) *to break line, to haul out of the line* ‖ ⟨aero mst⟩ *to peel off* ‖ ⟨mot⟩ *to swerve, to fall out of line*

·**aus|scheuern** vt [h] (Kessel) *to scour (out)* ‖ (Zimmer) *to scrub*

·**aus|schicken** vt [h] *to send on an errand; to send out* (nach *for*); (Boten) *to dispatch, despatch*

·**aus|schießen** vt/i **I.** vt [h] **A. 1.** jdm ein Auge ~ *to shoot a p's eye out;* ihm ist im Krieg ein Auge ausgeschossen *he lost an eye in the war.* **2.** ⟨hunt⟩ der Distrikt ist ausgeschossen *the district is shot out* **3.** e–n Preis ~ *to shoot for a prize* **B. 1.** ⟨com⟩ (schlechte Ware) *to eliminate; scrap* **2.** (Brot) aus dem Ofen ~ *to take* od *draw out of the oven* **3.** ⟨typ⟩ (Kolumnen) *to impose* **II.** vi [s] (of plants, etc.) *to shoot, sprout*

·**aus|schiffen** vi/t **1.** *vi [s] *to set sail* ‖ *to disembark* **2.** vt [h] (P) *to disembark, unship; land* ‖ (S) *to discharge, unload* | **sich** ~ *to disembark, land*

·**Ausschiffung** f ~/~en *disembarking, disembarkation; landing* ~**shafen** m *port of debarkation* ~**soffizier** m *deb. officer* ~**splatz** m *landing-place, wharf*

·**aus|schimpfen** vt [h] jdn ~ *to scold,* ⟨fam⟩ *to slang a p; to call a p names, to swear at a p;* → beschimpfen, schmähen

·**aus|schlachten** vt [h] **1.** (Hammel etc) *to cut up for sale* ‖ ⟨übtr⟩ *to cannibalize (a motorcar); to gut (a book)* **2.** ⟨typ⟩ die Form ~ *to pull the form to pieces* **3.** ⟨fig⟩ (ein literarisches Werk) *to draw upon;* etw politisch ~ *to make political capital of* (od *out of*) *a th* ‖ °(Gelegenheit) *to make the most of, to employ to the best advantage* ‖ (etw) allzusehr ~ *to press too hard* ‖ → ausbeuten, –nutzen ·**Ausschlachtung** f ⟨mot⟩ *cannibalization*

·**aus|schlafen** vi/t **1.** vi [s & h], *to have one's sleep out; to sleep one's fill;* ich bin nicht recht –ge– *I have not had enough sleep* **2.** vt [h] etw ~ *to sleep a th off;* s–n Rausch ~ *to sleep off one's intoxiation, to sleep o.s. sober* | **sich** ~ = ~ vi

·**Ausschlag** m ~(e)s/≈e **A.** (Ab-, Ausweichen) **1.** *deflection (of the magnetic needle); amplitude (of a pendulum)* ‖ ~ des Zünglein an der Waage *turn of the scale(s);* der W. den ~ geben *to weigh down the scale* ‖ ⟨mot⟩ ~ der Vorderräder *steering lock* ‖ ≈e [pl] ⟨eth⟩ *swings* (in *of*) **2.** ⟨übtr⟩ *decision* ‖ den ~ geben *to decide (between); to tip the scale* od *balance; to make all the difference;* e–n gr (etc) ~ dagegen geben *to weigh heavily against it;* das gab den ~ *that turned the scale;* s–e Stimme gibt den ~ *his vote is decisive;* den ~ gebend → ≈gebend; das was den ~ gibt *the makeweight* **B. 1.** (Beschlag) *efflorescence;* (feuchter) *exudation* **2.** ⟨med⟩ *efflorescence, eruption, rash; exanthem(a);* v ~ begleitet *eruptive, exanthematous* **3.** (am Rock etc) *border, trimming* ‖ → Ausschlagen ≈**artig** a ⟨med⟩ *eruptive, exanthematic, exanthematous* ~**eisen** n *punch* ~**fieber** n *eruptive fever* ≈**gebend** a *decisive (battle),* ~ für *decisive for;* ~ s in *to be the last word in ..* ‖ ~e Stimme *casting-vote* ‖ *paramount, vital (importance); overriding (necessity, requirements);* nicht ~ ⟨a.⟩ *unconclusive* ‖ bei jdm ~ s *to weigh with a p* ~**punze** f = Ausschlageisen ~**winkel** m *angle of deflection*

·**aus|schlagen** vt/i **I.** vt **A. 1.** (Feuer) *to beat out, to extinguish by thrashing* **2.** (herausschlagen) *to knock out* ‖ (Bäume) *to fell* ‖ jdm ein Auge ~ *to knock a p's eye out* ‖ dem Faß den Boden ~ *to stave a cask;* ⟨fig⟩ das schlägt dem Faß den Boden aus *that's the limit, that settles it* **3.** (hämmern) *to beat* od *hammer out;* (Metall) *to flatten out* **B.** (verkleiden) (Zimmer etc) *to hang, to line (with); to face (with)* **C.** ⟨fig⟩ (Anerbieten etc) *to decline, refuse, reject;* ⟨Am⟩ *to pass up* ‖ ich würde e–e Tasse Tee nicht ~ *I won't say no to a cup of tea* **II.** vi **A. 1.** (of horses) *to kick; to lash out;* ein Pferd, das ausschlägt *a kicker* **2.** laß die Uhr ~ *let the clock strike* od *finish striking* **3.** (of plants) *to bud, shoot, sprout*; (of trees) *to come into leaf, to burst into leaves* | ⟨fig⟩ in Flammen ~ *to burst into flames* **4.** ⟨fig⟩ *to result* (in *in*); → ausgehen, –laufen ‖ z jds Verderben ~ *to result in a p's ruin*; z jds Vorteil ~ *to turn to a p's gain* **B.** (beschlagen) *to effloresce*; (of walls) *to grow moist* **C.** (*of a needle* etc) *to deflect*; (*of the tongue of a balance*) *to turn*

·**Ausschlagen** n **1.** *knocking-out* (*of an eye*) ‖ *beating-out* (*of metall*) ‖ *lashing-out* (*of a horse*) **2.** *lining* **3.** *refusal* **4.** *budding* (*of plants*) ‖ → Ausschlag

·**aus|schlämmen** vt [h] (Kanal) *to clear of mud*

·**aus|schleifen** vt [h] (glätten) *to grind, burnish* ‖ (Messer) *to grind down*

·**aus|schleppen** vt [h] (Schiff) *to tow* (*out of the harbour*)

·**aus|schließen** vt [h] **1.** ⟨eig⟩ (jdn) *to shut out, to lock out* (*a p*), *to shut the door on* (*a p*) ‖ man hatte ihn (*or* er war) ausgeschlossen *he had got the key of the street* **2.** ⟨übtr⟩ (verweisen) (jdn) *to expel*, er wurde v der Schule ausgeschlossen *he was expelled* (*from*) *the school* ‖ ⟨univ⟩ (jdn) f e–e Zeit ~ *to rusticate, to send down* ‖ (aus e–r Gesellschaft) *to blackball* ‖ ⟨mil⟩ *to cashier* ‖ ⟨parl⟩ jdn v der Sitzung ~ *to name a p* ‖ jdn v dem Verkehr ~ ⟨sl⟩ *to send a p to Coventry*; jdn aus der Gesellschaft ~ *to ostracize a p from society*; **3.** (ausnehmen, –scheiden) **a.** (P) *to cut off; to eliminate, except, exclude* (v *from*); ich nicht ausgeschlossen *not excluding myself*; mich ~d *exclusive of me* ‖ *to bar, to debar* (v *from*); er ist v der Krone ausgeschlossen *he is debarred the crown* ‖ ⟨Am⟩ *to freeze out* ‖ ⟨sport⟩ *to disqualify* **b.** (S) *to exclude; to be exclusive of; to preclude; to rule out*; das eine schließt das andere nicht aus *the one does not exclude the other* ‖ das ist ausgeschlossen *that is impossible* (od *out of the question*); es ist nicht ausgeschlossen *it is possible* (*that*); ausgeschlossen! *impossible! out of the question!* **4.** ⟨typ⟩ *to justify* **5. sich ~ a.** (P) *to exclude o.s.*; *to exclude* (od *dissociate*) *o.s.*; sich vom Spiel ~ *to stand down* **b.** (S) *to exclude o.s.*; die beiden Standpunkte schließen sich gegenseitig aus *the two standpoints are mutually exclusive* | ⟨med⟩ *to definitely deny*

·**ausschließlich 1.** a *exclusive; sole* **2.** adv *uniquely; exclusively; simply and solely; only* ‖ bis S. 50 ~ *up to exclusive of page 50* **3.** [prep] *exclusive of*, ~ der Kosten *exclusive of costs* **≈keit** f *exclusiveness*

·**Ausschließung** f ~/~en *shutting-out* ‖ ⟨univ⟩ zeitweise ~ *rustication* | *expurgation* (*of members*), *suspension, elimination, exclusion* (v *from*); *preclusion* (*of a magistrate*, etc. *from sitting on the bench*); → Aussperrung ‖ ⟨sport⟩ *disqualification* ‖ ⟨jur⟩ *foreclosure* | ⟨typ⟩ *justification* ‖ → Ausschluß

·**aus|schlüpfen** vi [s] (of young birds) *to emerge from the egg, to hatch* ‖ ⟨übtr⟩ *to come* od *slip out*

·**Ausschluß** m –schlusses/–schlüsse **1.** → Ausschließung **2.** *exclusion*; mit ~ v *exclusive of*; unter ~ v Luft *to the e. of air* ‖ ⟨jur⟩ unter ~ der Öffentlichkeit *in camera* **3.** ⟨typ⟩ *spaces* [pl]; → Quadrat **~frist** f *time of preclusion, preclusive period* **~kasten** m ⟨typ⟩ *space-case* **~stück** n → Spatium

·**aus|schmelzen** vt/i **1.** vt [h] (Metall) *to fuse; to melt; to smelt* ‖ (Talg) *to try*; ⟨tech⟩ (Fett) *to render* **2.** vi [s] *to fuse; to melt*

·**aus|schmieden** vt [h] *to beat* (od *hammer*) *out*

·**aus|schmieren** vt [h] *to smear* (mit *with*); etw mit Pech ~ *to pitch a th*, mit Teer ~ *to tar a th* ‖ die Fugen ~ *to fill* od *point the joints* ‖ → einschmieren

·**aus|schmücken** vt [h] *to adorn, decorate; to deck out* (mit *with*) ‖ (Kleider) *to trim* | (e–e Geschichte) *to embroider, to embellish; to interlard* (*with*); *to touch up* ·**Ausschmückung** f ~/~en [abstr & konkr] *ornamentation, adornment, decoration* | *embellishment; embroidering* (*of a story*)

·**aus|schnauben** vi/t [h] **1.** vi = ausschnaufen **2.** vt die Nase ~, sich ~ *to blow one's nose*

·**aus|schnaufen** vi [h] *to recover one's wind*

·**Ausschneide- ~eisen** n *punch* **~kunst** f *art of silhouetting*

·**aus|schneiden I.** vt [h] **1.** (Äste etc) *to cut out*; (Baum) *to prune, to lop* ‖ ⟨med⟩ *to extirpate* **2.** ⟨com⟩ (Stoff) *to sell retail, to sell by the yard* ‖ (Aufsätze in e–r Zeitung) *to cut* (*out*); *to excise*; ⟨Am⟩ *to clip* ‖ anstößige Stellen e–s Buches ~ *to bowdlerize, to expurgate a book* **3.** (schneidend formen) (Papier) *to cut* od *scissor*; (Holz) *to cut, to carve*; (Figuren) *to cut out*; aus schwarzem Papier ~ *to cut out of black paper*; ausgeschnittene Figur *cut-out* ‖ (Rand) bogenförmig ~ *to scallop*; (Leder) künstlich ~ *to pink* ‖ (Metall) *to stamp out* **4.** (Ärmel) bogenförmig ~ *to slope out* ‖ tief ausgeschnittenes Kleid *décolleté* (od *low*) *dress, low-necked dress*; tief ausgeschnitten gehen *to wear a low dress, to go in a low dress* (*to a ball*) **II.** ≈ n *cutting-out* ‖ *excision* ‖ ⟨a. med⟩ *extirpation* ‖ → Ausschnitt

·**Ausschnitt** m ~(e)s/~e **1.** (Kürzung) *cut* (*of a play*) **2.** (Teil) *cut-out*; ⟨paint⟩ *part* (*of a picture*); ⟨phot⟩ *part* (*of a negative*) ‖ (Kreis≈) *sector* ‖ (Zeitungs≈) *cutting; clipping; scrap* ‖ (literarischer ~) *extract* ‖ ⟨com⟩ im ~ verkaufen *to sell retail* | ⟨übtr⟩ *part, section* (*of German life*); im ~ *in part, in sections* **3.** (~ am Kleid) *neck, decolletage*, tiefer ~ *low neck* (*of a dress*); viereckiger ~ *square neck* ‖ *slope* (*of a sleeve*) ‖ bogenförmiger ~ (am Rande) *scallop* **~handel** m *retail trade* **~händler** m *retailer, retail dealer*; (v Meterwaren) *draper; mercer*; (v Kurzwaren) *haberdasher* **~handlung** f **~geschäft** n *retail shop* **~stickerei** f *Richelieu work* **~waren** f [pl] *retail goods*; (Meterwaren) *dry goods* [pl]; *drapery; mercery; haberdashery*

·**aus|schnitzen** vt [h] *to cut out, to carve*

·**aus|schöpfen** vt [h] (Wasser) *to ladle* (*out*); *to draw, scoop* (aus *out of*) ‖ (Gefäß) *to exhaust, empty* | ⟨übtr⟩ (e–n Gegenstand) *to exhaust; to treat fully*; (Hilfsquellen) *to exhaust*; alle Möglichkeiten ~ *to explore all possible avenues*

·**aus|schrägen** vt [h] (Fenster) *to flue; to splay* ‖ ausgeschrägt s *to flue* ·**Ausschrägung** f *splay*

·**aus|schrauben** vt [h] = losschrauben

·**aus|schreiben I.** vt [h] **1.** (Kurzschrift) *to write out* ‖ (Abkürzungen) voll ~ *to expand* ‖ (Namen) ganz ~ *to write down in full* ‖ e–e ausgeschriebene Hand *a fully developed hand* **2.** (beenden) (Brief) *to write to the end, to finish*; (Heft) *to fill; to use up* **3.** (Buchstellen) *to extract, to copy* (aus *from*) ‖ (unerlaubt) *to crib* (aus *from*); (Werk) *to plagiarize* **4.** (Rollen, Stimmen) *to write out; to transcribe* | ⟨com⟩ (Rechnung) *to make out*; (Wechsel) *to draw; to make out* **5.** (öffentlich bekannt geben) *to announce, to publish* ‖ (f Auftragsvergabe) *to invite tenders* ‖ (Landtag etc) *to convene, to convoke* ‖ (neue Steuern) *to impose* ‖ e–e Wahl ~ *to issue the writ for an election* ‖ Lieferungen ~ *to invite tenders*; öffentl. Arbeiten ~ *to order the calling of fresh tenders*; e–n Preis, Wettbewerb ~ *to invite entries for a competition, to set a c.* ‖ (Stelle) *to invite applications for* (*a post*), *to advertise* (*a post*); *to throw open* (*for competition*); e–e ausgeschriebene Stelle *an advertised post* **6. sich ~** *to write o.s. out, to exhaust o.s. in writing* **II.** ≈ n *writing-out; expanding* | *copy*(*ing*) (aus *from*); *extraction* ‖ *transcription* |

making-out (*of a bill*) || Preis–, Wettbewerbs≗ (*prize-*)*competition* || → **·Ausschreibung** f ~/~en **1.** → Ausschreiben **2.** *convocation* (*of a diet*) || *imposition* (*of new taxes*) || *advertisement* (*of a vacancy*) || (~ öffentlicher Arbeiten) *contract, tender*; *invitation, call* (*to submit tenders*); im Wege der (öffentlichen) ~ *by* (*public*) *tender* || ⟨sport⟩ *invitation to a competition* **~sbedingungen** f pl *terms of a tender*

·aus|schreien vt [h] (Waren) *to cry*; *to proclaim* | sich ~ *to cry to one's heart's content*

·Ausschreier m *crier*; *showman*; → Ausrufer

·aus|schreiten vi/t **1.** vi [s] *to step out*; tüchtig ~ *to step it out*; *to stride out, to take long strides*; *to strike out*; *to put one's best foot* (od *leg*) *forward* **2.** [h] (Raum) *to pace*; *to step out*

·Ausschreitung f ~/~en *excess, riot, outrage*, [mst pl] ~en *riots* [pl], *rioting*

·ausschulen vt [h] *to remove from a school*

·Ausschulung f *removal* (*of a boy*, etc.) *from a school* || (vorzeitige) *drop-out*

·Ausschuß m –schusses/–schüsse **1.** *refuse, shut-out, offal, rubbish, trash, trumpery*; *waste, broke*; *rejections* pl; ⟨pap⟩ *retree, broke*; ⟨com⟩ *waster, wastrel, rummage* **2.** (P) *committee, commission*; *delegation*; *delegates* [pl]; *board*; *panel* || engerer ~ *select committee*; beratender ~ *advisory panel*; ausführender ~ ⟨Am⟩ *steering committee*; leitender ~ *executive board*; ständiger ~ *standing committee* || ⟨parl⟩ *commission* || e–m ~ angehören *to be on a committee*; e–m ~ überweisen *to refer to a c.* **3.** *exit of a bullet* **4.** [in comp] ⟨oft⟩ *waste* **~material** n *scrap* **~mitglied** n *member of a committee* **~papier** n *refuse-paper, broke, shavings* **~sitzung** f *committee-meeting, board-meeting* **~ware** f *refuse, rubbish, offal, trash, waster, wastrel*; ~n [pl] *rummage, damaged* (od *defective* od *inferior*) *goods* [pl] **~wolle** f *waste wool* **~(wunde** f) *wound of exit* **~zigarre** f *defective cigar*

·aus|schütteln vt [h] *to shake out*

·aus|schütten I. vt [h] **1. a.** (Wasser etc) *to dash*; *to pour out*; *to pour* (aus *from, out of*; auf *on*); *to shower* (auf *on*) || (Abfall) *to shoot*; *to dump*; *to tip out* (od *off*) **b.** (Eimer etc) *to empty*; (Wagen) *to tip* **c.** ⟨übtr⟩ (Gefühle etc) *to pour out*; *to shed, to shower* (auf *on*); sein Leid ~ *to pour out one's woes* || sein Herz ~ *to open* (od *unburden*) *one's heart, to unbosom o.s.* (jdm *to a p*) **d.** → Kind **2.** ⟨com⟩ (Dividende) *to distribute, to pay*; (Konkursmasse) *to divide, distribute* **3. sich ~** vor Lachen *to shake one's sides with laughing, to be convulsed* (od *to roar*) *with laughter* **II.** ≗ n *pouring-out* || *shooting*

·Ausschüttung f ~/~en ⟨com⟩ *payment, distribution* (*of dividend*); *division, distribution* (*of bankrupt's estate*) | ⟨at⟩ *fall-out*

·aus|schwärmen vi [s] **1.** (of bees) *to swarm* **2.** ⟨mil⟩ *to extend*; ~l *to extend*; ausgeschwärmte Schützenlinie *extended order*

·aus|schwatzen vt [h] *to blab out* | jdm etw ~ *to talk a p out of a th*

·aus|schweben vi [s] ⟨aero⟩ *to flatten out*

·aus|schwefeln 1. vt [h] (Faß) *to sulphur, to fumigate with burning sulphur* **2.** ≗ n *matching*

·Ausschwefelung f *sulphuration* || *gassing with sulphuretted hydrogen*

·aus|schweifen vt/i [h] **1.** vt *to scallop*; *to cut out in a slope*; *to curve* || *to channel* **2.** vi *to digress* || → abschweifen || → ausschweifend

·ausschweifend a *excessive*; *extravagant, eccentric* (*imagination*) || (moralisch ~) *debauched, dissolute, licentious, gay* (*life*), *wild*; ~ leben, ein ~es Leben führen *to indulge in licentious courses, to lead a dissolute* od *gay life*; *to sow one's wild oats* **·Ausschweifung** f ~/~en **1.** *scallop*; *slope*; *curve* || → Abschweifung **2.** (Zügellosigkeit) *extravagance* || *dissipation, dissoluteness*; *debauch*(*ery*); *wildness* (*of youth*); *excess, orgy*; *sexual irregularity*

·aus|schweigen [vrefl] [h] sich ~ *to be* (od *keep*) *perfectly silent* (über *on*); *to be reticent* (über *about*); *to persist in silence* || *to say nothing*; *to be poor in words*; *to have nothing to say for o.s.* || ⟨Am pol⟩ *to pussyfoot* (über *on*)

·aus|schwemmen vt [h] (Graben) *to scour*; (ausspülen) *to flush*; ⟨fam⟩ *to sluice*

·aus|schwenken vt [h] (Glas) *to rinse*; *to wash out*

·Ausschwimmen n ~s/ (v Pigmenten) *floating, flooding*

·aus|schwingen vt/i [h] **1.** vt (Boot) *to swing* (*out*) **2.** vi (of a pendulum etc) *to cease swinging* || *to swing to the end* **·Ausschwingung** f ~/~en ⟨arch⟩ (*gothic*) *bend*

·aus|schwitzen vi/t [h] **1.** vi (of juice etc) *to exude*; *to sweat out*; *to transpire* **2.** vt (Feuchtigkeit) *to exude*; *to sweat out, to transpire* || (Krankheit) *to sweat out* **·Ausschwitzung** f ~/~en ⟨med⟩ *exudation, transpiration*

·aus|segeln vi/t **1.** vi [s] *to set sail, to sail out, to put to sea* **2.** vt [h] e–n Preis ~ *to compete for a prize in a sailing-match*

·aus|segnen vt [h] jdn ~ *to give a p the blessing*

·aus|sehen vi/t [h] **A.** vi **1.** ⟨eig⟩ ~ nach *to look* (*out*) *for* (*a p, a th*) **2. a.** (P) *to look*; er sieht blaß aus *he looks pale*; blaß ~d *white about the gills*; frisch ~d *rosy about the gills* || gut, wohl ~ *to look well*; gut, hübsch (übel) ~ *to be good-looking* (*bad-looking*); jd, der gut aussieht ⟨Am⟩ *a looker*; er sieht f sein Alter gut aus *he carries his age well* || um 10 Jahre jünger (älter) ~ *to look 10 years less* (*more*) *than one's age* || halbverhungert ~ *to have the appearance of being half-starved* || gut ~ *to have looks, to be a good-looker* || nicht sonderlich ~ ⟨Am⟩ *not to be much of a looker* || prächtig (ärmlich) ~ *to make a fine* (*poor*) *show* (od *appearance*) || toll ~ *to look a sight* || vorteilhafter ~ als *to be better looking than*; ⟨iron⟩ er sah schön aus *a nice object he looked*; seh ich so (dumm) aus? ⟨fam⟩ *do you see any green in my eye?*; so siehst du aus! *that's just like you!, says who?, you don't say!* (*you are mistaken!*); ⟨Am fam⟩ *you've got another guess coming!* | (S) die Lage sieht schlecht aus *things look badly* || so sieht es, die S aus *that's the state of affairs, nature of things, way it goes*, ⟨fam⟩ *size of it* || es sieht °faul (*or* windig) aus f ihn *things look bad for him* **b.** ~ **wie:** ganz so ~ wie *to have every appearance* od *sign of*; er sieht wie ein Narr aus *he looks a fool* || er sieht aus wie ein ehrlicher Mensch *he has the looks of an honest man* || *to wear a look of*; *to look* od *be like*; *to resemble* || etw (*or* ein wenig) ~ wie *to look something like*; er sieht nicht so alt aus wie er ist *he does not look his age* || wie sieht er aus? *what does he look like? what is he like?* || wie sieht es aus mit ..? *wat are the prospects for ..?* || wie sieht es aus mit Ihnen? *how goes the world with you?* || wie siehst du nur aus! *what a sight you are!* **c.** ~ **als ob** (wenn) *to look as if, as though*; er sah aus, als wäre er .. *he looked to be ..*; es sieht aus, als wollte es schneien *it looks like snow*; er sah so aus, als ob er wartete *he had the air* (od *gave the impression*) *of waiting* **d.** ~ **nach:** es sieht nach Regen aus *it looks like rain* | nach etw Besonderem ~ *to look something special*; nach nichts ~ *to cut a poor figure*; er sieht ganz danach aus *he quite looks it*; ⟨iron⟩ er sieht mir gerade danach aus *he doesn't look up to it* || es sieht nach etw (vornehm) aus *it makes a great show*; *he has airs* od *an air*; ⟨fam⟩ *this looks something like*; es soll nach etw ~ *it is meant to attract* (od *draw*); es sieht danach aus als ob .. *it looks as if ..*; ⟨iron⟩ es sieht auch danach aus *it* *looks like it* **II.** vt sich [dat] die Augen ~ nach *to crane* (od *stretch*) *one's neck for*

·**Aussehen** n ~s/ *exterior*; (Kleidung) *rig, cut of a p's jib* ‖ *appearance, look*; *aspect* (: *of charming aspect*); auffälliges ~ *sight* ‖ ⟨übtr⟩ *complexion* (*of a government*) | dem ~ nach *to outward view*; *in appearance* (*he* ..) ‖ nach s–m ~ *by the look of him* ‖ nach dem ~ gehen *to go by looks*; nach dem ~ urteilen *to judge by appearances* ‖ ein ~ annehmen *to assume* (od *take on*) *an appearance* (od *a look*); e–r S ein gefälliges ~ geben *to veneer* (od *varnish*) *a th*

·**aus|seigern** vt [h] *to liquate*

·**aus|sein** vi [s] → aus [adv] II. 3.

·**außen** adv [Ggs innen] *outside*; *without*; ~ auf dem Omnibus *on the outside of the bus*; ~ u innen weiß *white inside and out* ‖ ~ bleiben *to stay out, to keep outside*; ~ l *to leave outside* ‖ ~ befindlich *outer, outward, external, exterior* | nach ~ (hin) *outward(s), outwardly*; nach ~ k *to come outside* ‖ nach ~ kenntlich m *to exteriorize* ‖ die Füße nach ~setzen *to turn out one's toes*; stark nach ~ .. *to be splay-footed* ‖ von ~ *from outside* (od *without*); der zweite Ring v ~ *the last ring but one* ‖ v ~ öffnen *to open from the outside* ‖ v ~ kommend *outside* (*help*) ‖ nach ~ hin *or* v ~ her fröhlich erscheinen *to give an appearance of gaiety* ‖ → draußen

·**außen-** [in comp] *external*; *outside*; *outer*; *outward* **≗amt** n *Ministry of Foreign Affairs* **≗ansicht** f *exterior* **≗antenne** f ⟨wir⟩ *external* od *outside* od *outdoor aerial* **≗aufnahme** f ⟨phot⟩ *outd. ph.* ⟨film⟩ *outd. shot*; *exterior shooting*; *exterior*; auf ~ *on location* **≗backenbremse** f *external cheek brake* **≗bahn** ⟨sport⟩ *outside course* **≗bahnhof** m *outer station* **~beamter** m *outdoor* od *field official* **≗beleuchtung** f *outd. lighting* **≗beschaffenheit** f ⟨tech⟩ *surface condition* **≗bezirk** m *outlying district*; *outskirts* [pl] **≗bord** m *outboard*; ~farbe f *side-paint*; ~motor m *outboard-motor* **~bords** adv ⟨mar⟩ *outboard*; *outside the ship* **≗deich** m *fore-dike* **≗dienst** m *outdoor work* ‖ ⟨mil⟩ *duties outside barracks* ‖ Vertreter im ~ *agent in the field* ‖ ⟨pol⟩ Versetzung auf e–n Posten im ~ *transfer into the field* ‖ ⟨ins⟩ *field work*; (P) *f. staff* ‖ *outside job of a crime* | ~personal [n] *field-workers* ‖ ~stelle [f] *field office* **≗druckkörper** m *bulge* **≗drüse** f *external gland* **≗durchmesser** m *outside diameter* **≗feld** n = Ausfeld **≗fläche** f *surface, face* **≗fort** n ⟨fort⟩ *detached fort* **≗getriebe** n *external gearing* **≗gewässer** n *exterritorial waters* **≗gewinde** n *external* (od *male*) *screw* **≗graben** m ⟨fort⟩ *advanced* od *outer moat* **≗hafen** m *outport*; *outer harbour* **≗handel** m ⟨com⟩ *foreign* (od *external*) *trade*; *export trade*; *imports and exports* ‖ ~sabteilung f ⟨engl⟩ *Department of Overseas Trade* ‖ ~sbilanz [f] *b. of* (*foreign*) *trade* ‖ ~sförderung [f] *exp. promotion* ‖ ~skontrolle f *control of exports* ‖ ~smonopol n *monopoly of foreign trade* ‖ ~s-stelle f *export control office* **≗haut** f *outer skin* (*of a ship*); *outside* (od *skin*) *plating* ‖ ⟨anat⟩ *epidermis* ‖ ⟨aero⟩ *shell plating* **≗hülle** f *outside cover* **≗institut** n ⟨univ agr⟩ *experimental farm* (od *station*) **≗kante** f *outside edge* **≗lager** n ⟨tech⟩ *outer bearing*; *outside box* **≗landung** f ⟨aero⟩ *outside landing*; = Notlandung **≗leitung** f ⟨el⟩ *outdoor line* **~liegend** a *outlying* **≗luft** f *surrounding* od *ambient air* **≗maße** n pl *outside measures* **≗mauer** f *outer wall* **≗minister** m ⟨engl⟩ *Secretary of State for Foreign Affairs*; *F.n S.y*; ⟨Am⟩ *S.y of State* ‖ ⟨a-engl⟩ *the Foreign Minister* **≗ministerium** n ⟨engl⟩ *the Foreign Office*; ⟨Am⟩ *State Department* ‖ ⟨a-engl⟩ *Ministry of Foreign Affairs* **≗passagier** m *outside passenger* **≗politik** f *foreign affairs* [pl]; *foreign policy* **~politisch 1.** a *of* (od *referring to*) *foreign affairs*; ~e Lage *international situation* **2.** adv *with regard to foreign policy* **≗posten** m ⟨mil⟩ *outpost* **≗schicht** f *outer layer* **≗seite** f *the outside*; *the exterior*; *the surface*; *exteriority* (: *a man with a good e.*) ‖ (des Bürgersteigs) *kerbside* ‖ ⟨übtr⟩ e–e rauhe ~ *a rough outside*; ein Mensch v rauher ~ *a rough diamond* **≗seiter** m *outsider*; *non-conformist*; (gesellschaftlich) *deviant*; ⟨sport & fig⟩ *dark horse*; ⟨sport Am sl⟩ *mucker* **≗sitz** m *outside seat* **≗spieler** m ⟨ftb⟩ → Außenstürmer **≗stände** m [pl] ⟨com⟩ *outstanding* od *active debts* [pl], *outstandings* [pl]; ⟨bal⟩ *accounts receivable, receivables*; sichere ~ *good claims*; schlechte ~ *bad debts* [pl] **≗stehende**: der ≗ (ein ≗r) *the outsider* ‖ *looker-on* **≗stelle** f *detachment*; *branch office*; ⟨wir⟩ *outside-station* **≗stürmer** m ⟨ftb⟩ *wingman, winger*; (linker) *outside-left*, (rechter) *outside-right* **≗temperatur** f *outdoor, outside, external temperature* **≗versicherung** f ⟨ins⟩ *extra-mural insurance* **≗wache** f ⟨mil⟩ *outlying picket* **≗wand** f *outer wall* **≗welt** f *the external* od *outer world*; *the outside* (: *from the outside*) **≗werk** n ⟨fort⟩ *outwork*; *advanced work* **≗wert** m (of money) *extrinsic value* ‖ (of a currency) *foreign value* **≗winkel** m ⟨math⟩ *external angle* **≗wirtschaft** f *foreign trade*

·**aus|senden** vt [h] **1.** (jdn) *to send out* od *forth*; *to dispatch, des–* ‖ (Truppen) *to throw out*; (f. bes Dienst) *to detach* **2.** (Befehl etc) *to issue* **3.** (Zweige) *to shoot* od *throw out* ‖ (Strahlen) *to shoot out* ‖ (Licht, Wärme, Gase etc) *to send out, to emit*; *to give off*; *to shed*; *to throw off* ·**Aussendung** f ~/~en *sending out* ‖ *issue* (*of an order*); *emission* (*of light*, etc.)

·**außer I.** prep **A.** (örtlich) **1.** [mit gen] [nur in:] ~ Landes s, gehen etc *to be, go abroad* **2.** [mit dat] ~ dem Hause *out-of-doors, without doors*; ~ dem Hause essen *to dine out* ‖ wieder ~ Bett s *to be out of bed* (od *to be up*) *again* **B.** ⟨übtr⟩ [mit dat] **1.** ~ Betrieb *out of gear* od *action*; *shut down* ‖ ~ B.! (*lift*) *out of service* ‖ ~ Dienst *off duty*; *retired*; → Dienst ‖ ~ Gefahr *out of danger, past danger*; *safe* ‖ ~ Gefecht setzen *to put out of action* ‖ ~ Kraft setzen *to annul* ‖ ~ Kurs *out of circulation*, → Kurs ‖ ~ jds Reichweite *above, beyond, out of a p's reach* ‖ ~ der Reihe *out of one's turn*; niemand ~ der Reihe *in due order* ‖ ~ Übung *out of training* ‖ ~ der Zeit *out of season*; *untimely* **2. ~ acht** lassen *to leave out of account*; *to neglect* ‖ ~ **Atem** *out of breath* ‖ ~ **Fassung** *disconcerted, beside o.s.* ‖ ~ **Frage** *out of the* (od *without*) *question* ‖ ~ **Schußweite** ⟨mil⟩ *out of range* ‖ ~ **Zweifel** *beyond* (od *without*) *doubt*; ~ allem Z. *beyond dispute* **3.** ~ **sich** s *to be beside o.s., to be distracted* od *upset* (über *at*; vor *with*) ‖ jdn ~ sich bringen *to disconcert a p*; (vor Wut) ~ sich geraten ⟨fam⟩ *to get past o.s.* **C. 1. (ausgenommen)** [mst nach *all, only* & [neg], [interr]] *but, except, save, saving*; *apart* (⟨Am⟩ *aside*) *from*; *as distinct from* ‖ alle ~ ihm *all except* (od *but, save*) *him*; das Haus war leer ~ ihm *the house was empty but* od *except for himself* **2. (neben)** *besides*; *in addition to*; ~ ihm nahmen noch 20 teil *besides him there were 20 participants* ‖ *two other boys, besides me, were saved* **II.** [conj] *except, but, save, saving*; ~ **auf** dem Lande *except in the country*; ~ **daß** *but, except* (: *except it were lost*); *saving that*; ~ **wenn** *unless*; nichts bleibt noch übrig ~ **zu** danken *nothing more remains but ..*

·**außer- ~achsig** a ⟨tech⟩ *abaxial* **~amtlich** a *non-official, unofficial, private* **~artlich** a ⟨bot, zoo⟩ *extraspecific* (*colour, etc*) **~dienstlich** a *private, unofficial* **≗dienststellung** f (S) *inactivation* ‖ (P) *putting out of commission* **~ehelich** a *illegitimate* (*child*); *extra-marital, –matrimonial*; [*pred*] (*child*) *born out of wedlook* ‖ ~er Geschlechtsverkehr *sexual intercourse* od *relations outside marriage* **~etatsmäßig** a *extra-budgetary* **~fahrplanmäßig** a *not as scheduled, not in accordance with the time table*; ⟨bes aero⟩ *unscheduled* **~gerichtlich 1.** a *extra-judicial*; ~e Regelung [f] *settlement out of court*; ~e S *non-litigious matter* **2.** adv sich ~ einigen *to settle out of court*; (jdn) ~ u gerichtlich vertreten *to represent in judicial proceedings and in all other affairs* **~geschäftlich** a *private* **~gewöhnlich 1.** a *exceptional, uncommon, unusual; extraordinary, remarkable, singular*; ~er Zustand *or* Charakter *exceptionality* (*of his position*); ~e Fälle [pl] *exceptionalities* [pl]; nichts ~es *nothing out of the way* od *ordinary* **2.** adv *exceptionally; unusually; extremely* **≃kurssetzung** f *demonetization; withdrawal from circulation* **~mittig** a ⟨tech⟩ *eccentrical, off centre* **~ordentlich 1.** a *extraordinary*; [mst attr] *exceeding* → außergewöhnlich; → gewaltig, ungeheuer || ~e Ausgaben [f pl] ⟨parl⟩ *extra-budgetary expenditure*; ~e Einnahmen [f pl] *non-recurring income* || ~es Gericht n *special court* || ~er Professor *reader*; ⟨Am⟩ *assistant professor* **2.** adv *extraordinarily; exceedingly* (*pretty*); *eminently* (*suitable*); *extremely* (*doubtful*); (etw) ~ bedauern *to be exceedingly sorry for* .. || ⟨fam⟩ (*it's*) *no end* (*good of you*) **~planmäßig** a *supernumerary* (*official*); ⟨engl⟩ *senior* (Professor *lecturer*); ⟨Am⟩ *associate* (*professor*); → -fahr- **~sinnlich** a *extra-sensory* **~st·ande** adv ~ s *to be unable* (*to do*), *incapable* (*of doing*) || jdn ~ setzen *to put it out of a p's power* (*to do*) **~weltlich** a *other-worldly, metaphysical*

·**außerdem** adv *besides, moreover; furthermore* || *in addition; as well; also; too*; u ~ mein Bruder *and my brother as well*

·**äußere A.** a **1.** *exterior, outer* (*wall*), *external* (*husk*); *outside* (*diameter*) || *outward* (*appearance, conditions*); *external* (*events, evidence, world*); ~ Wahrnehmung *external evidence* || ~s Benehmen *exterior*; ~ Eigenschaft *externality* || e-r S ~ Form geben *to externalize, exteriorize* | (v außen wirkend) *extrinsic* (*reasons*); *extraneous* (*forces, light*); *outside* (*help, influence*) **2.** (Auslands-) *external* (*relations*); *foreign* (*affairs, mission*); *exterior* (*policy*) **B. das** ≃ **1.** *the exterior, outside* (*of a house*, etc.); *surface* | ⟨übtr⟩ *facade* (*of an institution*) **2.** (P) *appearance, look*; auf sein ≃s halten *to attend to one's appearance* | (Außenseite) *outside, exterior* || nach dem ≃n urteilen *or* gehen *to judge by the outside* od *by appearances*; Kunst (etc) des gepflegten ≃n *groomsmanship* **3.** Minister etc des ≃n → Außenminister etc

·**außerhalb 1.** adv *outside* (*of*) *the city* (od *town*); (Waren) nach ~ liefern *to send* (*goods*) *to outside customers* || (im Ausland) *abroad* **2.** prep [mit gen] *outside, outside of*; 3 Meilen ~ Londons *3 miles out of L.*; ~ der City *outside* (*of*) *the city* || *outside the gates* | ⟨übtr⟩ ~ e-r S *exterior* od *external to a th*; ein Punkt ~ der Kurve *a point exterior to the curve*; ~ m-s Bereichs *beyond my reach*; ~ des Christentums (*people*) *external to Christianity* || ~ der Geschäftszeit *out of office hours*

·**äußerlich 1.** a **a.** *external, outward* || für ~en Gebrauch *for external* od *outward application* od *use* **b.** (oberflächlich) *superficial; hollow, showy* || *formal* **2.** adv *externally, outwardly* || ~ betrachtet *on the surface, on the face of it* ·**Äußerlichkeit** f ~/~en *external appearance, externality* || ⟨übtr⟩ *outwardness* (*of a p*); ~en [pl] *formalities*; *externals*; Neigung z ~en *externalism* || sie hängt an ~en ⟨fam⟩ *she's a stickler for form*

·**außerm** = außer dem

·**äußern** vt [h] **1.** *to utter, express; to give utterance to* (*a th*); *to throw out*; ~, daß .. *to give out that* ..; die Bemerkung, die v ihm geäußert wurde .. *the remark that fell from him* .. || (Gedanken, Warnung) *to sound*; Zweifel ~ *to voice one's doubts* || (Gefühle etc) *to voice* || → zeigen **2. sich** ~ **a.** (P) *to express o.s.; to pronounce* (über *on*); sich ~ über etw *to speak to a th*; sich ausführlicher ~ über *to be more specific on* (*a th*) || es ist s-e S sich zu ~ ⟨fam⟩ *it's for him to say*; wollen Sie sich hierzu bitte ~ *will you please put forward your comments on it*; sich ~ über *to comment on*; .. günstig .. *to express one's satisfaction* (über *with*) **b.** (S) *to manifest* (od *show*) *itself*

·**äußerst 1.** a **a.** (örtlich) *the utmost* (*limits*); *the outermost, most remote, uttermost* (*parts of the world*); der ~e Norden *the farthest north* (*of the British Isles*) || ⟨fam⟩ *rock-bottom* (*price*); das ~e Ende, die ~e Grenze *the extreme end, the extremity* **b.** (zeitlich) *last; final, closing* (*date*) **c.** ⟨übtr⟩ ~e Bedingungen *the lowest* (od *minimum*) *conditions*, der ~e Preis *the bedrock* (od *lowest* od *best*) *price*; → höchst | (höchst) *extreme, utmost*; ~er Grad, ~e Maßnahme *extremity* || ~es Alter *extreme old age* || im ~en Falle *in case of need* (od *necessity*); *at the worst* || mit ~er Genauigkeit *with the utmost accuracy* || in ~er Not (*to be*) *reduced to extremities* || in ~er Verlegenheit *in a dire extremity* || v ~er Wichtigkeit *of the utmost* od *last importance* **2. das** ≃**e** n; das ≃e wagen *to risk all* || sein ≃es tun *to do one's best* od *one's utmost*; *to strain one's* (*every*) *nerve; to try one's hardest* (*to do*); **aufs ~e** *to the utmost*; **bis zum ~en** *to the last extremity; to the bitter end; to the utmost* od *uttermost* (*of one's power*); ⟨Am⟩ *to the limit* || bis zum ≃en gehen *or* schreiten *to go to extremes* od *extremities, to run to an extreme; to go to desperate lengths*; **zum** ≃**en** entschlossen s *to be resolved to risk all*; jdn zum ≃en treiben *to drive a p to extremes, to put a p to his trumps* **3.** adv *extremely, exceedingly; utterly; unusually* (*pretty*); *vitally* (*important*); (*fascinating*) *to the uttermost*; ~ groß *stark* (*despair*) || ⟨fam⟩ *mighty* (*little*; *easy*); *jolly, precious* (*good*) || *bitter, beastly* (*cold*) **~enfalls** adv *if the worst comes to the worst*

·**außerst·ande** adv ~ s *to be unable* (od *not in a position*) (*to do*); *to be incapable* (z tun *of doing*); *to be inapt* (*to do*)

·**Äußerung** f ~/~en **1.** (in Worten) *enouncement, pronouncement, utterance, expression; assertion, statement, views* pl (über *about*) || *observation, remark* (über *on*; v jdm *by a p*); ~en m über *to remark on, to make remarks on* (zu jdm *to a p*) **2.** (zeigen) *manifestation, demonstration* (*of feelings*)

·**aus|setzen** vt/i [h] **I.** vt **A. 1.** (Kind) *to abandon, expose* || (Bäume) *to plant out* **2.** (Boot) *to hoist out, to launch, to lower* || (Passagiere etc) *to land; to disembark; to unship* **3.** ⟨com⟩ e-n Posten ~ *to set out an entry* || ⟨ec⟩ (zur Schau) *to display, to expose* **4.** ⟨mus⟩ (Stimmen) *to copy* (aus der Partitur *from the score*) || ⟨typ⟩ (Wort) *to write in full*; (Werk) *finish the composing of* (*a work*) **5.** ⟨arch⟩ (Fachwerk) *to fill* (*with*) **6.** (das Herz) setzt e-n Schlag aus .. *misses* od *skips a beat* **B.** ⟨übtr⟩ **1.** (Belohnung) *to hold out* (od *forth*) (jdm *to a p*); *to offer, to promise*; (Pension) *to settle* (jdm *on a p, to a p*); (Pokal etc) als Preis ~ *to present* (*a cup*) *for competition*; (Summe) *to settle* (jdm *on a p, to a p*); *to allocate, to fix*; *to earmark* (f. *for*) || (etw) testamentarisch ~ *to bequeath* (jdm *to a p*); jdm ein Vermächtnis ~ *to make a settlement on a p* **2.** (P, S) e-r S ~ *to expose, subject* .. *to a th*; jdn dem Gelächter ~ *to hold a p up to ridicule* || jdn e-r gr(ößeren) Belastung ~ ⟨fig⟩ *to put a great strain on a p* || **sich** e-r S ~ *to expose* od *subject o.s. to a th*;

sich der Gefahr ~ *to run* od *take risks* od *the risk, a risk* (z tun *of doing*); sich e–r Gefahr (etc) ~ *to incur a danger*; sich (nicht) den Gefahren e–r S ~ *to take* (*no*) *chances with a th* **3.** ausgesetzt s *to be exposed* (od *liable, subject*) (e–r S *to a th*); e–r S ausgesetzt s ⟨a.⟩ *to be open to a th*; e–r heftigen Kritik .. *to come* od *be under fire*; es ist darauf zurückzuführen, daß es der Luft ausgesetzt war *it is due to its exposure to the air*; er starb dadurch, daß er den Unbilden der Natur ausgesetzt war *he died of exposure* **C. 1.** (Tätigkeit etc) *to discontinue, interrupt, intermit, stop, suspend*; (Kur) *to interrupt*; (Zahlung) *to suspend* || (Urteil) *to suspend; postpone; defer*; (Verfahren) *to stay* || e–n Tag ~ *to take a day off* **2. etw ~ an** *to take exception to, to object to*; *to cavil at* (*a th*); *to find fault with* (*a th, a p*); *to pick holes in* (*a th*); -zu- h an *to quarrel with* (*a th*); nichts -zu- h an *to have no quarrel with* (*a th*); er hätte an ihm nichts ~ können *he could not but have approved of him*; ich habe an ihm nichts -zu- *I have no fault to find with him*; was ist daran -zu-? *what's wrong with that*? ~d [a] *fault-finding* || → ausstellen, tadeln **II.** vi **1.** (of pulse, etc.) *to intermit*; ~d *intermittent* (*pulse*) **2.** (of motor) *to cut out*; (of engines) *to conk* (*out*); (of strength) *to give out* **3.** (P) *to set out, to pause, to make a pause, to stop* || ~ mit etw *to discontinue a th*; *to suspend a th*; damit ~ z tun *to discontinue* (od *cease*; *leave off*) *doing* ·**Aussetzen** n [→ aussetzen vi] *intermittence* (*of the pulse*); kz regelmäßige ~ (e–r Bewegung) *dwell* || *cutting-out* od *failure* (*of a motor*); *conking*(*-out*) (*of an engine*) || *pause, stop* ·**Aussetzung** f ~/~en **I.** → Aussetzen **II.** [→ aussetzen vt] **A. 1.** *exposure* (*of children*) **2.** *launching, hoisting-out* || *landing, disembarkation* **3.** ⟨ec⟩ *exposure* (*of the Host*) **4.** (gegenüber schädl. Einflüssen) *exposure* ⟨a. at⟩ **B.** ⟨übtr⟩ **1.** *offer, promise* (*of a reward*) || *settlement* (*of a pension*) **2.** → aussetzen I. B. 2. **C. 1.** (Unterbrechung) *discontinuance* (*of an action*); *intermittence, intermission*; *interruption*; *suspension* (*of a verdict*) || *stoppage* || *postponement* **2.** (Tadel) *blame*; *censure, criticism* (an *of*); *objection* (an *to*); ~en m an *to cavil at* (*a th*), *to find fault with* (*a p, a th*); *to object to* (*a th*)

·**Aussicht** f ~/~en **A.** *look-out, outlook* (über *over*); *view* (auf das Meer *of the sea*); *prospect* (auf *of*; nach *to*; über *over*); freie ~ *open view*; weite ~ *vista* (auf *of*) || ein Zimmer **mit** ~ auf den See *a room overlooking the lake, a r. commanding a view of the l.* || von hier hat man e–e herrliche ~ auf das Gebirge *from here you have a splendid view of the mountains* || das Fenster gewährt (*or* bietet, hat) e–e ~ auf das Tal *the window overlooks the valley* || jdm die ~ nehmen *to obstruct a p's view* **B.** ⟨übtr⟩ **1.** *chance, prospect* (auf *of*, z tun *of doing*; f. *for*); *promise* (auf *of*); *outlook* (f. *for*); [oft pl] *prospects, chances* [pl]; ohne ~ auf etw *without nothing to look forward to* **2.** Wendungen: **a.** e–e **günstige** ~ *an opening* (f. *for*) || ~en [pl] (*Canada is a land of*) *opportunities* || günstige ~en ⟨com, etc⟩ *bright prospects* || nicht die geringste ~ *not a cat's* od *dog's* (⟨Am⟩ *Chinaman's*) *chance, not a cat-in--hell's chance* || ebensoviel ~ wie k–e *an even chance* (z erhalten *of getting*) || die ~en sind gleich ⟨Am fam⟩ *it's a tossup* || schlechte ~en! *not a leg to stand on*! **b.** es **besteht** die ~, daß *chances are that*; es bestehen geringere ~en *there is less likelihood* || ~en **bieten** (of conditions) *to hold out prospects* (auf dauernden Frieden *of an enduring peace*); gute ~en bieten *to bid* (od *promise*) *fair*; e–e trübe ~ bieten *to present a gloomy outlook* (*for*) | ~en **haben** *to be in the running*; ⟨Am⟩ *to be in line* (auf *for*); wir h nur geringe, wenig ~ *prospects are rather remote*; k–e ~en h *to be out of the running* || gute ~en (auf Erfolg) h *to be in a fair way*; sehr gute ~en h *to have a very fair chance* (z erhalten *of getting*); sie hatten bessere (*or* größere) ~ *they stood a greater chance* (*of getting*) | es gibt, **verschafft,** verspricht gute ~en (z bek) *it bids fair* || gute (schlechte) ~en verkünden *to augur well* (*to bode ill*) (f *for*) || sich [dat] s–e (k–e) ~en **versperren** *to shut the* (*no*) *doors on life* | k–e ~ versprechen *to hold out no prospect* (*of granting*) | es ist ~ vorhanden *there is a prospect* (daß *that*); *there is a chance* (*of getting*) **c. in ~ haben** *to have* (*a th*) *in prospect* | (etw) in ~ nehmen *to arrange for, to propose* (*a th*); *to contemplate, to consider* (*a th*; z tun *doing*); *to intend* (*a th*; *to do, doing*); Ferien in ~ nehmen *to promise o.s. a holiday*; es ist in ~ genommen *it is contemplated* (*that*); *it is proposed* (*to do*) | (jdn) f Vergebung e–s Auftrags in ~ nehmen *to contemplate placing an order with* | in ~ stehen (*or* sein) *to be in prospect* | jdm etw in ~ stellen *to hold out a prospect of a th to a p*; *to make a p look forward to a th*; *to promise a p a th* (od *a th to a p*); ⟨Am⟩ *to place a p in line for* (*a th*) || Hoffnungen in ~ stellen *to hold forth hopes* (auf *of*) || in ~ stellen, daß .. *to announce, to intimate, to undertake that*

·**Aussichts- ~deck** n ⟨rail⟩ *vista dome* **~fenster** n *picture window* **≃los** a ⟨übtr⟩ *unpromising*; *hopeless*; [pred] *without prospects* || ~! ⟨fam⟩ *no*(*t an*) *earthly*! **~losigkeit** f *hopelessness* **~punkt** m (ins Land) *view-point* || ⟨mil⟩ *vantage point* **≃reich** a *promising* **~turm** m *observation* od *look-out tower* (od *station*), *look-out*; *belvedere* **~wagen** m ⟨rail⟩ *observation-car*; ⟨mot⟩ *view-mobile*; *excursion vehicle*

·**aus|sieben** vt [h] ⟨übtr⟩ *to sift out*; *to eliminate*

·**aus|siedeln** vt [h] *to evacuate* ·Aussied(e)lung f ~/~en *evacuation*

·**aus|sieden** vt [h] = auskochen

·**aus|singen** vi/t [h] **1.** vi *to sing to the end, to finish singing* **2.** vt die Stimme ist ausgesungen *the voice is worn out* (od *spoiled*) *by singing*

·**aus|sinnen** vt [h] *to think out, to excogitate*; (Plan etc) *to concoct, to contrive, devise, invent*; *frame*; *to design, lay* (*plans*), *to plot out*

·**aus|söhnen** vt [h] (jdn) *to conciliate, to win* od *gain over*; *to reconcile* (mit jdm *with a p*; mit den Tatsachen *to the facts*); → abfinden | **sich ~ mit** jdm *to reconcile o.s., to make one's peace with a p* || sie h sich -ge-hnt ⟨fam⟩ *they made it up with each other* || sich ~ mit etw *to be* (od *become*) *reconciled, to reconcile o.s. to a th* (: mit dem Schicksal *to one's fate*); *to put up with a th*

·**Aussöhnung** f ~/~en *reconciliation* (mit jdm *with a p*; mit e–r S *to a th*)

·**aus|sondern** vt [h] **1.** *to eliminate, exclude*; *to sort* od *weed out* || ⟨comp⟩ *to extract* **2.** (absondern) (Säfte) *to secrete, excrete* ·**Aussonderung** f ~/~en *elimination, exclusion* || ⟨med⟩ *secretion* || ⟨comp⟩ ~ v Gruppen *group selection*

·**aus|sortieren** vt [h] *to sort out*; → aussondern

·**aus|spähen I.** vt/i [h] **1.** vt *to spy out* **2.** vi ~ nach *to spy* (od *look out, watch*) *for* **II.** ≃ n *spying-out* ·**Ausspäher** m ~s/~ *spy, scout* || ⟨mar⟩ *look-out* [pl *look-outs*] ·**Ausspähung** f ⟨pol⟩ *espionage*

·**Ausspann** m ~(e)s/~e (Einkehrstätte) *pull--up*; *baiting-, halting-place*; *inn* || ⟨†hist⟩ (Ort des Pferdewechsels) *relay, stage*

·**aus|spannen** vt/i [h] **A.** vt **1.** (Seil etc) *to stretch* || (die Flügel) *to spread* **2. a.** (Zugtiere) *to unharness, unyoke* **b.** (Stickerei) *to take out of the frame*; (Werkstück) *to unclamp* **c.** °etw ~ *to purloin, pilfer*; *steal* (jdm *from a p*); *to get hold of*, ⟨sl⟩ *to collar a th, a p* **B.** vi **1.** *to pull* od *put up* (*at an inn*); *the farmers put up there*; *his carriage and horses always put up there* **2.** ⟨übtr⟩ *to* (*take a*) *rest*; *to recreate o.s., to take recreation* od *relaxation; to leave off work;* ⟨Am⟩ *to lay off* || e–n Abend ~ *to take an evening off, to have an e. out;* 8 Tage ~ *to take a week's holiday* **·ausspannend** a ⟨übtr⟩ *recreative* (*work*) **·Ausspannung** f ~/~en **1.** (S) *extension;* → Ausdehnung **2.** (T) *unharnessing* **3.** (P) *repose, rest; recreation, relaxation; distraction, diversion*

·aus|sparen vt [h] (Raum) *to leave open* (od *vacant*) **·Aussparung** f ~/~en *space left empty* od *blank* || ⟨tech⟩ *channel, recess, cutout, opening* || ⟨tact⟩ *safety limits* || ⟨mot⟩ *passage* (*for the plug*)

·aus|speien I. vt/i [h] **1.** vt (Schleim etc) *to spit out; to expectorate, to vomit* (*out* od *forth*) || (of whale) *to disgorge* || Lava ~ *to spout lava, to vomit* **2.** vi ⟨cont⟩ = ausspucken **II.** ~̈ n *expectoration; vomit(ing)*

·aus|sperren vt [h] *to shut out* || (Arbeiter) *to lock out* || ⟨typ⟩ *to lead, to lead* (od *space*) *out;* → durchschießen **·Aussperrung** f ~/~en *lock-out* (*of workers*); ~en [pl] *lock-outs* [pl]

·aus|spielen vt/i [h] **I.** vt **1.** (zu Ende spielen) (etw) *to play out* (od *to the end*) || ⟨übtr⟩ er hat s–e Rolle ausgespielt *he is played out; his time is up* **2.** (Karte) *to lead* || ⟨fig⟩ s–n letzten Trumpf ~ *to play one's trump-card* (*against a p*) **3.** (etw als Preis) *to play for* (*a th* [: *a goose*]) **4.** ⟨fig⟩ jdn ~ gegen *to pit a p, to play a p off against;* P.en gegeneinander ~ *to play persons off one against the other* || etw ~ *to back a th* (gegen etw *against a th*) **II.** vi ⟨cards⟩ *to lead;* der, welcher ausspielt *the elder* (od *eldest*) *hand; the leader;* wer spielt aus? *whose lead is it? who is the elder hand? who leads?* | ⟨übtr⟩ er hat ausgespielt *he is played out;* ⟨Am fam⟩ *he has swung;* jd, der ausgespielt hat *a has-been*

·aus|spinnen vt [h] **1.** (Faden) *to spin to the end* **2.** ⟨fig⟩ *to spin out* || (Gedanken) *to elaborate; to pursue* || (ersinnen) *to devise, plot*

·aus|spionieren vt [h] (Land) *to spy out* || jdn ~ *to be a spy on a p*

·aus|spotten vt [h] = verspotten

·Aussprache f ~/~n **1.** ⟨phon⟩ *pronunciation* || (Art der ~) *accent;* er hat e–e gute (reine) ~ *he speaks with a good* (*pure*) *accent, his pronunciation is without any foreign accent* || (Sprechweise) klare ~ *elocution;* ⟨Am⟩ *diction* **2.** *consultation* (mit *with;* über *on*); *discussion;* durch ~ *by d.;* heftige ~ *heated discussion;* ruhige ~ *quiet* od *friendly d., reasonable d.* || e–e offene ~ *a heart-to-heart talk* **3.** ⟨parl, etc⟩ *question period* || ⟨pol⟩ *discussion, talks* pl

·aussprechbar a *pronounceable, speakable* || *utterable*

·aus|sprechen vt/i [h] **I.** vt **1.** ⟨phon⟩ (Wort) *to pronounce; enounce* || (deutlich sprechen) *to articulate; to enunciate* | er spricht sich (*or* s–n Namen) [ˈrɔːli] aus *he pronounces* [ˈrɔːli] || sich ~ l (of words) *to be pronounceable* **2.** ⟨übtr⟩ → äußern **a.** (Gedanken etc) *to enounce, utter, express;* (jdm) s–n Dank ~ *to tender* (*a p*) *one's thanks* || (öffentlich ~) (Urteil etc) *to deliver, pronounce, return;* **b. sich** ~ → sich äußern; *to express o.s., to pronounce* (über *on*); *to declare, pronounce* (f. *for,* gegen *against*) | *to open o.s., to open out, to say one's say, to speak one's mind* (über *about*); sprich dich aus *speak your mind;* sich ~ mit jdm über etw *to discuss a matter, to talk a m. over with a p* || sich ~ gegenüber jdm *to confess o.s. to a p;* sich frei *or* offen ~ *to speak out* (gegenüber jdm *to a p*) || sich für (e–e S) ~ *to favo(u)r, support, advocate, champion; to espouse* (*a cause*) || → ausgesprochen **II.** vi *to finish* od *cease speaking; to speak to the end;* laß ihn ~ *let him finish, let him have his say*

·aus|spreizen vt [h] *to spread* od *stretch out;* die Beine ~ → spreizen || mit ausgespreizten Beinen *astraddle, astride,* mit a. B. sitzen *to sit straddle-legged* (auf *on*)

·aus|sprengen vt [h] **1.** (mit Sprengstoff) (Stück) *to blast* (*out of the rock*) **2.** (Wasser etc) *to sprinkle* **3.** ⟨fig⟩ (Gerücht etc) *to circulate, disseminate; to spread* (*abroad*)

·aus|springen vi/t **1.** vi [s] aus dem Glas ist ein Stück ausgesprungen *there's a chip out of the glass, the glass has got a chip on the edge* || → herausspringen **2.** vt [h] sich [dat] den Fuß ~ *to dislocate* od *sprain one's foot* **·ausspringend** a [Ggs einspringend] *salient* (*angle*)

·aus|spritzen vt [h] **1.** (T) (Flüssigkeit) *to squirt out; to spout; spirt, spurt* **2.** (die Ohren) *to syringe;* (e–e Wunde) *to inject* (mit *with*); *to wash out* **3.** (Feuer) *to extinguish*

·Ausspritzung f ~/~en *injection* (*of a wound*) || *syringing* (*of the ears*)

·Ausspruch m ~(e)s/~̈e *pronouncement, utterance;* → Äußerung || *saying; dictum* [L pl *dicta*], *maxim* || ⟨jur⟩ → Spruch

·aus|sprühen vt [h] *to spark* ⟨a. fig⟩, *to spray*

·aus|spucken vt/i [h] **1.** vt *to spit out;* ⟨Am⟩ *to expectorate* || ⟨fig⟩ *to cough up* (*money*) **2.** vi *to spit;* vor jdm ~ *to spit in a p's presence* (*in contempt*), ⟨fig⟩ *to spit upon a p; to belch forth* ⟨a. fig⟩

·aus|spülen vt [h] (Gefäß) *to rinse; to rinse* od *wash out* || (Mund) *to gargle* (mit *with*), *to rinse;* sich [dat] den Mund ~ *to rinse* (*out*) *one's mouth* || ⟨med⟩ (Organ etc) *to inject, insufflate* (mit *with*) || ⟨mot⟩ (Zylinder mit Luft) *to scavenge* || (of river) (Ufer etc) *to wash away* (od *out*) **·Ausspülicht** n & m = Spülwasser **A.lung** f ~/~en *rinse, rinsing; washing-out*

·aus|spüren vt [h] **1.** ⟨hunt⟩ → aufspüren **2.** ⟨übtr⟩ (etw) *to ferret* od *search out; to discover, explore; to spy out; to bring to light*

·aus|staffieren vt [h] (versehen) (jdn) *to furnish, provide, equip,* ⟨fam⟩ *to rig out* (mit *with*) || *to furnish* (*a room*) | (schmücken, putzen) (jdn) *to bedizen, to dress up;* ⟨fam⟩ *to doll* (*up*) || ⟨theat⟩ *to make up* || (Hut etc) *to trim, garnish;* **sich** ~ *to bedizen o.s.* **·Ausstaffierung** f ~/~en *equipment* (*with*) || (Ausputz) *make-up; trimming*

·Ausstand m ~(e)s/~̈e **1.** ⟨com⟩ [pl] Ausstände = Außenstände **2.** (Streik) *strike;* im ~ *on strike;* in den ~ treten *to come out* (od *to go*) *on strike* || **3.** *(Frist) delay, respite **·ausständig** a **1.** = ausstehend **2.** *on strike; striking*

·aus|stänkern vt [h] (T) *to stink out*

·aus|stanzen vt [h] *to stamp out*

·aus|statten vt [h] **1. a.** (P) *to fit out, to equip, furnish, prime, supply* (mit *with*); *to find* (*in*) : sie statteten ihn mit Nahrung u Wohnung aus *they found him in food and lodging* || ⟨übtr⟩ jdn mit Rechten ~ *to vest a p with rights;* [mst pass] ausgestattet s mit *to be vested with* .. | ⟨übtr⟩ (jdn begaben) *to endow, dower* (*with talents*) || mit den neuesten Nachrichten ausgestattet *primed with the latest news* | (die Tochter) *to portion; to dower* → aussetzen **b.** ⟨übtr⟩ Schule mit Lehrern ~ *to staff a school,* ein Krankenhaus ausgestattet mit Ärzten *a hospital staffed by doctors* || (Schule etc mit einem Legat ~) *to endow* (*a school*) **2.** (S) *to fit up* (*with*); (Zimmer) *to upholster* || (Bücher) *to get up* || ⟨theat⟩ (Stück) *to mount, stage*

·Ausstattung f ~/~en **1.** *outfit, equipment* (mit *with*); *fitment, attachments* pl || *furniture, fusnishings* [pl] (*of a room*); *set-out* (*of a p*); Sport~̈ *sports kit* **2.** (Heirats~̈) *dowry, dower; trousseau,* → Aussteuer **3.** *get-up* (*of a book*) **4.** ⟨theat⟩ (Bühnen~̈) *scenery, setting; decor; fitments* **5.** ⟨comp⟩ *configuration* **~sband** n *decorative ribbon* **~skarton** m ⟨pap⟩ *fancy carton* **~̈smäßig** adv *as to the outfit, etc* || ~ alles u mehr bietend *with all the usual features and many extra conveniences* **~spapier** n **~sstück** ⟨tech⟩

fitment (a. Möbel) || ⟨theat, film, telv⟩ *spectacular* od *lavish show*; *revue*; ⟨Am a.⟩ *spectacular*

·**aus|stauben** ≗ vt [h] (Zimmer) *to dust*

·**aus|stäupen** vt [h] jdn ~ *to whip*; *to flog a p*, *to give a p a flog(ging)*

·**aus|stechen** vt [h] **A. 1.** jdm die Augen ~ *to put* od *job out a p's eyes* **2.** (Graben) *to dig (out)*; (Rasen etc) *to cut out* **3.** (Muster) *to prick out* **4.** ⟨übtr⟩ °e–e Flasche Wein ~ *to crack a bottle of wine* **B.** ⟨fig⟩ (jdn) *to trump*; *cap, outblaze, outdistance, outdo, outshine*; *excel, surpass*; *to cut .. out*; *to score .. off*; *to supplant*; *to get the better of a p*; ⟨fam⟩ *to put a p's nose out of joint* || sich nicht (*or* v niemandem) ~ l *to keep up with the Joneses* || jdn bei jdm ~ *to cut a p out in a p's affections* od *favour* ·**Ausstech-** ~**form** f ⟨cul⟩ cutter ~**meißel** m *plugging chisel*

·**aus|stehen** vi/t [h] **1.** vi (of debts) *to be unpaid, to be owing* (od *outstanding* ⟨a.⟩ *of reply*) || es steht noch ein Betrag v 3 Pfd aus *there is still an amount of £ 3 outstanding* || ~ h *to have (money) owing to one* | die Antwort steht noch aus *the answer has not come to hand*; das Urteil steht noch aus *the verdict is still open* **2.** vt (Angst, Hunger etc) *to endure, suffer, bear*; *to undergo, to go* od *pass through* | jdn nicht ~ können *to have a down on a p, to hate the very sight of a p*; ich kann ihn nicht ~ *I cannot bear* (od *endure, stand,* ⟨sl⟩ *stick*) *him* ·**ausstehend** a *outstanding* (*debts*; *questions*); *open* (*verdict*)

·**aus|steigen 1.** vi [s] *to get out*; ⟨rail⟩ *to detrain, to alight* (aus *from*) || *to debus* || ⟨mar⟩ *to disembark* || ⟨aero fam⟩ (abspringen) *to bail out, to jump out of the window(s)* || → Ausstieg **2.** ≗ n *disembarkation* ⟨a. aero⟩, *etc*

·**Aussteigmanöver** n ⟨a–n⟩ *extravehicular activity* (EVA)

·**aus|steinen** vt [h] (Früchte) *to stone*

·**ausstellen** vt/i [h] **I.** vt **1.** (Wache) *to post, to set* **2.** ⟨com⟩ (Waren) *to lay* od *set out*; *to expose, display*; *to have a th showing* || (Produkte, Gemälde etc) *to exhibit, show* || *to put (specimens) on public view* || (Hunde etc) *to show,* ⟨a.⟩ *to bench* || ausgestellt w *to come on exhibition*; ausgestellt s *to be on view*; ausgestellter Gegenstand *exhibit* **3.** ⟨com⟩ (Urkunde) *to draw up, to make out*; (Rechnung) *to make out, to render*; (Paß) *to make out*, (Bescheinigung) *to issue*; (Quittung) *to give*; ein Billet auf den Namen N. ~ *to make out a ticket in the name of N.* || (Police) *to issue* || (Wechsel) *to draw, issue, write*; *to make out* (auf jds Namen *in a p's name*; über 3 Pfd *for £ 3*) || jdm ein Zeugnis ~ *to give a p a character*; .. *a testimonial* (über *on*) **4.** etw an jdm *or* e–r S ~ *to find fault with a p, a th*; → aussetzen I. C. 2. **II.** vi *to exhibit* ·**Ausstellen** n *posting* (*of a sentry*) ·**Aussteller** m ~s/~ *exhibitor* || *drawer* (*of a bill*) || (Messe≗) *exhibiting firm* ·**Ausstellung** f ~/~en **1.** → Ausstellen **2.** *display, set-out* || (stattliche ~) *array* (*of shoes*) | [a. konkr] *exhibition, show* (auf der ~ *at the sh.*); *fair*; *rally* (*British Motor Car R.*); ⟨Am⟩ *exposition* || ⟨arts, phot, etc⟩ *show, salon*; Blumen≗ *flower show*, Hunde≗ *dog show* (etc.); Welt≗ *the World Fair* **3.** ⟨com⟩ *drawing-up* (*of a document*); *making-out* (*of an account*, etc.) || *drawing* (*of a bill of exchange*) **4.** ⟨übtr⟩ *faultfinding* (an *with*); *censure, criticism* (an *of*); *objection* (*to*); ~en m an, gegen *to find fault with* (*a p, a th*); → aussetzen I. C. 2., Aussetzung C. 2.; tadeln ·**Ausstellungs-** ~**bauten** [pl] *exhibition buildings* [pl] ~**datum** n *date* (*of a bill of exchange*) ~**gebäude** n *exhibition building* ~**gegenstand** m *exhibit* ~**gestaltung** f *design in exhibitions* ~**graphiker** m *exhibit designer* ~**halle** f *exhibitions pavilion* od *hall* ~**modell** n *showroom pattern* ~**raum** m, ~**saal** m, ~**zimmer** n *exhibitionroom, showroom* ~**stand** m *display booth* ~**tag** m ⟨com⟩ *date*

·**aus|stemmen** vt [h] ⟨tech⟩ *to chisel, hollow out*

Austen·it n ~s/ ⟨met⟩ *austenite*

·**Aussterbeetat** m ~s/ (etw) auf den ~ setzen *to give up, to drop*; *to put on the shelf, to put out of use*; auf dem ~ stehen *to be dying out*; *to be destined to pass away, to be ripe for abolition*

·**aus|sterben I.** vi [s] **1.** ⟨zoo, bot⟩ *to die out*; (Familie) *to become extinct* || ⟨übtr⟩ *to die out*; (of superstitions, etc.) schwer ~ *to die hard* || längst ausgestorben s *to be as dead as mutton* **2.** (veröden) *to become deserted* od *desolate*; wie ausgestorben *deserted*; die Stadt ist wie a. *the town is as quiet as a churchyard* **II.** ≗ n *extinction, extinguishment* ·**Aussterbestand** m *impending* (*state of*) *extinction*

·**Aussteuer** f ~/~n *portion, dowry*; *dower*; *marriage outfit*; (an Kleidung, Wäsche, Schmuck) *trousseau*; ohne ~ *dowerless* | ~versicherung [f] *children's endowment assurance* | ~**fach** n ⟨com⟩ *reject* ·**aus|steuern** vt [h] *to portion* || er war ausgesteuert *his claims to insurance* od *assistance had expired* || (Karten) ⟨comp⟩ *to pull* ·**Aussteuerung** f *expiration of a p's claims to insurance* od *assistance* || ⟨comp⟩ *rejection*

·**Ausstich** m ~(e)s/ *the best produce, the choice* (*of a vintage*)

·**aus|sticken** vt [h] *to embroider*

·**Ausstieg** m ⟨rail⟩ *place* od *side of alighting*

·**aus|stöbern** vt [h] (ausfindig m) *to rummage* od *search out*; → aufstöbern

·**aus|stochern** vt [h] sich [dat] die Zähne ~ *to pick one's teeth*

·**aus|stopfen 1.** vt [h] (totes Tier) *to stuff* || (Kleidung) *to pad, wad*; *to line with wadding* **2.** ≗ n *stuffing*; (T) *taxidermy* || *padding*; Material z ~ *padding, wadding* ·**Ausstopfer** m ~s/~ (T) *stuffer*; *taxidermist, naturalist*

·**Ausstoß** m ~es/≗e **1.** *the tapping* (*of a cask*) **2.** (~rohr) *ejector-tube*; *torpedo-tube* || ⟨aero⟩ *tail pipe* **3.** ⟨min, ind, etc⟩ *output*

·**Ausstoß-** ~**hebel** m ⟨typ⟩ *pushing lever* ~**hobel** m *grooving-plane* ~**rohr** n *ejecting tube* → Ausstoß 2. ~**ventil** n *firing valve* ~**vorrichtung** f *launching apparatus* od *device*

·**aus|stoßen** vt/i [h] **I.** vt **1.** jdm ein Auge ~ *to gouge out a p's eye* || (Faß) *to stave in* || (Bier) *to tap* | ⟨tech⟩ (aushöhlen) *to groove* **2.** (P) *to thrust out*; *to turn* (aus *out of*); *to eject, expel* (aus *from*); (aus der Kirche) *to excommunicate* || ⟨mil⟩ (Offizier) *to cashier*; jdn aus der Gesellschaft ~ *to ostracize a p from society* || → ausschließen **3.** (Flüssigkeit, Rauch) *to ejaculate*; *eject*; *vomit*; *emit* **4.** (Worte) *to ejaculate, to shoot out, to sputter*; (Laut, Drohung, Seufzer) *to utter*, (Flüche) *to rap out*; e–n Schrei ~ *to scream, shriek* **II.** vi ⟨fenc⟩ *to make a pass* (nach *at*) || *to thrust first* ·**Ausstoßen** n *ejection, ejaculation* (*of smoke*, etc.) || *ejaculation* (*of words*) || → Ausstoßung ·**Ausstoßung** f ~/~en **1.** → Ausstoßen **2.** *thrusting-out*; *expulsion* (aus *from*); *suspension*; ⟨ec⟩ *excommunication* || ⟨mil⟩ *dishonourable discharge*

·**aus|strahlen** vt/i [h] **1.** vt (Licht) *to radiate, to emit*; (Dampf) *to give off* | ⟨übtr⟩ (Glück) *to radiate*; *to irradiate*; (innere Wärme) *to exude* **2.** vi (of light) *to radiate*; *to stream away* (*in all directions*); (of vapour) *to be given off* | ⟨übtr⟩ *to branch out, to radiate*; *to spread* (*abroad* ⟨a. arts hist⟩ [of style]) || *to emanate* (v *from*) ·**Ausstrahlung** f ~/~en *(ir)radiation* || ⟨übtr, a. psych⟩ *irradiation*

·**aus|strecken I.** vt [h] **1. a.** die Beine ~ *to stretch* (od *fling, shoot, stick*) *out one's legs*; er streckte die B. von sich aus *he stretched his legs in front of him* || die Hand ~ *to hold* (od *put, reach*) *out one's hand* (nach *for*); *to reach* (nach *for*); mit beiden Händen ausgestreckt *with both* *hands out* || → herausstrecken || e–n Fühler ~ *to throw out a feeler* | (of trees) (Zweige) *to reach out* (nach *towards*) **b. sich ~** *to stretch o.s.* || sein Arm streckte sich aus *his arm came out* || → ausdehnen **2.** lang ausgestreckt daliegen *to lie sprawled* (*on one's face*); *to sprawl*; ausgestreckte Lage *sprawl* **II.** ≗ n *stretching-out* || *holding-out, putting-out*; → Ausdehnung

·aus|streichen I. vt [h] **1.** (Wort) *to strike* od *cross out, to delete*; (Namen) *to strike* od *cross off* || ⟨com⟩ (Posten) *to cancel* **2.** (Falten) *to smooth out, to remove* (aus *from*); *to stroke* **3.** (Mörtel) *to spread* (auf *on*) || (Farbe) *to distribute* || (Fugen) *to flush, fill*; (abdichten) *to stop* **II.** ≗ n ⟨geol⟩ *cropping up* **·Ausstreichung** f *striking-out*; *cancellation*

·aus|streuen vt [h] (Samen) *to scatter*; (Dung) *to spread out* (über *over*) | (Gerücht) *to circulate*; *sow, spread*; → aussprengen **·Ausstreuung** f ~/~en *scattering* | *dissemination*; *spread*; ~ falscher Gerüchte *circulation of false reports*

·Ausstrich m ~(e)s/~e ⟨geol⟩ *outcrop*; *smear* (microscope)

·aus|strömen vi/t **1.** vi [s] (of water) *to flow* od *stream forth*; *to gush, jet* (aus *from, out of*); *to spring* || (of light) *to stream away* (v *from*) || (of gas, etc.) *to escape*; *to pass out* || (Wasser) durch e–e Schleuse ~ l *to sluice*; (Gas) ~ l *to let escape* | ⟨übtr⟩ (of influence, etc.) *to emanate, flow, issue* (v *from*) **2.** vt [h] (of wounds) (Blut) *to stream*; *discharge* || (Wärme etc) *to emit, radiate*; (Dampf etc) *to give off* od *out* || ⟨übtr⟩ (Kraft) *to give out*; *to distribute, spread*; (Einfachheit) *to breathe, exhale*; (Tugend) *to exude*

·Ausström- ~gas n *exhaust* (*of rocket*) **~hub** m *exh. stroke* **~öffnung** f *outlet opening* **~raum** m *diffuser* **·A.mung** f ~/~en *discharge*; *efflux* || *escape* (*of gas*) || *emission* (*of heat*); *emanation* (*of vapour*) | ⟨übtr⟩ *emanation*; *distribution, spread*

·aus|studieren vi/t [h] [pp ausstudiert] **1.** vi *to finish one's studies* **2.** vt *to find out* || (Buch) *to finish*

·aus|suchen vt [h] (jdn, etw) *to select, choose*; *to pick out* || (jdn) *to cull* (v *from*), *to single out* (f. *for*; *to do*); (Jury etc) ⟨Am⟩ *to hand-pick*; → ausgesucht || sich etw ~ *to choose* (od *pick out*) *a th* || → durchsuchen

ˣ**Aust** f ~/~en *harvest*

·aus|tapezieren vt [h] → tapezieren

·Austausch m ~(e)s/~e **1.** *exchange* (*of goods, etc*); *interchange* (*of commodities, ideas*); *substitution* (gegen *for*) || ⟨fam⟩ *swap* || Gefangenen≗ *exchange of prisoners*; Gedanken≗, Meinungs≗ *exchange of views*; freier gegenseitiger ~ *free interchange* **2.** (Aufenthalt im Ausland auf Gegenseitigkeit) *exchange visit*; auf dem Wege des ~s *au pair*; Ferien≗ *holiday interchange* **~anlage** f *conversion plant* **≗bar** a *exchangeable* (gegen *for*) || *interchangeable* (*parts*) **~bau** m ⟨tech⟩ *interchangeable construction*; (*the principle of*) *the interchangeability of parts*; *selection assembly* **~dienst** m ⟨Ger⟩ *Exchange Service* **~korrektur** f ⟨el⟩ *exchange correction* **~professor** m ⟨univ⟩ *exchange professor* **~schüler** m *exchange scholar* **~stahl** m *substitute steel* **~stück** n *spare part* **~student** m *exchange student* **~wechselwirkung** f ⟨el⟩ *exchange interaction* **~werkstoff** m *substitute*

·aus|tauschen vt [h] (Waren etc) *to exchange, barter, swap, swop, truck* (gegen *for*; mit *with a p*) || (Blicke; Gruß; Meinungen etc) *to exchange, interchange* (mit *with*) || unter e–a ~ *to interchange*; er tauschte die Flaschen aus *he substituted the bottles one for the other* || → auswechseln **·Austauscher** m *exchanger*

·aus|teilen vt [h] (Waren, Geld) *to distribute, spend* (an *to*; unter *among*); *to share out, to divide* (an *to*); gleichmäßig ~ *to apportion* || (Nahrung etc) *to serve out*; (das Sakrament) *to dispense*; (Abendmahl) *to administer* || den Segen ~ *to impart the blessing* || (Schläge) *to deal out*; *to plant* | (Befehle) *to issue, to give* **·austeilend** a *distributive* **·Austeilung** f ~/~en *distribution* (an *to*, unter *among*); gleichmäßige ~ *apportionment* || *administration* (*of the Lord's Supper*)

·Auster f ~/~n *oyster*; ~n aufbrechen *to open oysters* | °(Auswurf) *gob, oyster* ⟨fig⟩

·Auster(n)- ~bank f *oyster-bed* **~brecher** m *oyster-knife* **~dieb** m ⟨orn⟩ *oyster-catcher* **~fang** m *oyster-dredging* **~fischer** m **1.** *oyster-dredger* **2.** ⟨orn⟩ = Austerndieb **~fischerei** f *oyster--dredging* **~monate** m [pl] (Sept.–April) ⟨fam⟩ *pig months* **~park** m künstlicher ~ *oyster-farm* **~pastete** f *oyster-patty* **~schale** f *oyster-shell*

·aus|tiefen vt [h] (Graben) *to deepen*

·aus|tilgen vt [h] *to efface*; *obliterate* || (Rasse; Tiere) *to exterminate*; (Rasse; Übel) *to extirpate*

·Austilgung f ~/~en *effacement* || *extirpation*; *extermination*

·aus|toben vi/t [h] **1.** vi *to cease raging* **2.** vt s–e Wut ~, **sich ~** *to give vent to* (od *to let loose*) *one's fury* | **sich** (im Leben) ~ (P) *to sow one's wild oats*; *to have one's fling*; *to be on the rampage*; *to run riot*; *we had a bit of rough and tumble*; (of diseases) *to rage*; (of rage) *to exhaust itself* || (of storm) *to spend itself*

·aus|tollen vrefl [h] sich ~ (of children) *to frolic, wanton, romp to one's heart's content*

·aus|tonnen vt [h] ⟨mar⟩ *to mark by buoys*

·aus|tosen vrefl [h] sich ~ (of storm) *to exhaust itself*

·Austrag m ~(e)s/≗e **1.** (Schlichtung, Entscheidung) *arrangement, settlement*; *decision*; *decisive issue* || bis zum ~ der S *while the matter is pending*; *pending the settlement of the matter* || zum ~ bringen *to bring to a head*; *to determine, to decide*; *to settle*; vor Gericht zum ~ bringen *to settle* (*a th*) *in court* || zum ~ k *to come to a head, to* (*come to*) *be decided* (od *settled*) **2.** schiedsrichterlicher ~ *arbitration* **3.** = Altenteil

·aus|tragen I. vt [h] **1.** (Briefe etc) *to deliver* | (Geheimnisse) *to divulge*; *to blab out*; *to retail* || † (jdn) *to slander* **2.** (Streit) *to settle*; *to thrash out*; vor Gericht ~ *to settle* (*a th*) *in court* || (Kampf) *to decide, to bring to a head* (od *a decisive issue*) || ⟨sport⟩ (Spiel) *to play* (*off*); (Wettrennen) *to run*; *to race for*; (Meisterschaft) *to hold* **3.** (Kind) *to bear to maturity* || (Rock) *to wear out* **4.** das trägt nicht viel aus *that doesn't amount to much* **II.** ≗ n *delivery* (*of letters*) **·Austräger** m ~s/~ *errand-boy, carrier*; *deliverer*; (v Milch, Brötchen etc) *roundsman* || *letter-carrier, postman* || *newspaper-boy* | (Ausplauderer) *blabber, tell-tale* **·Austrägler** m = Altenteiler **·austräglich** a = einträglich **·Austragsgut** n *discharged goods* [pl] od *material* **·Austragung** f ~/~en **1.** → Austragen **2.** → Austrag **3.** (v Fertiggut) *discharge* (*of finished product*)

austr·al a *austral, southern, southerly* **austr·alasiatisch** a *Australasiatic* **Austr·alasien** n *Australasia* **austr·alasisch** a *Australasian, Austral*

Austr·algolf m (südl. v Austr.) *Great Australian Bight*

Austral·iden [pl] *members* [pl] *of the Australian race* **Austr·alien** n *Australia* || (~ mit Neu-Seeland etc) *Australasia*, **Austr·alier** m ~s/~, **~in** f ~/~nen *Australian*; ⟨fam⟩ *Aussie* **Austr·alinseln** f pl → Tubuainseln, → †Neuh·olland n (alter Name f Australien) **austr·alisch** a *Australian* **Austr·asien** n ⟨hist⟩ *Austrasia*

·austrauern vi [h] *to cease mourning*; *to mourn the due time*

·aus|träumen vi [h] *to cease dreaming*; ⟨übtr⟩ *to be awakened to realities*

·aus|treiben vt [h] **1.** (Vieh) *to drive out*; *to drive* (aus *out of*; nach *to*) **2.** (vertreiben) (jdn) *to expel; to eject; to turn out* (aus *from*) ‖ (Geister) *to exorcize* (aus *from, out of*); → Beelzebub, Teufel **3.** ⟨übtr⟩ jdm etw ~ *to flog* (od *take, whip*; ⟨sl⟩ *lick*) *a th out of a p*; jdm den Hochmut ~ *to knock* od *let the sawdust out of a p*; das werde ich dir ~! *I'll cure you of that*! **4.** ⟨tech⟩ *to beat out*; (Keil) *to drive out* **·Austreibung** f ~/~en *driving-out* ‖ *expulsion* (*of a p*); *exorcism* (*of an evil spirit*)

·aus|treten I. vt/i **A.** vt [h] **1.** (Feuer) *to tread* od *trample out* **2.** (Schuhe) *to break-in* | (Stufen etc) *to wear down* ‖ –ge–er Weg *beaten track* ⟨a. fig⟩ **B.** vi [s] **1.** ⟨mil⟩ (wegtreten) *to fall out* ‖ *to withdraw; to go somewhere; to want to see a man about a dog; to make* od *pass water, to ease o.s.*; ⟨vulg⟩ *to go to the bogs* ‖ → hinaustreten **2.** (of fluids) aus den Gefäßen ~ *to extravasate*; → Extravasat ‖ (of hernia) *to protrude* **3.** der Fluß ist ausgetreten *the river is flooded; the r. has overflowed its banks* **4.** ~ **aus** *to retire, to withdraw from, to leave* (*a club*); *to secede from* (*a church*); aus e–r Gesellschaft ~ *to resign membership of a society, to take one's name off the books of a s.* ‖ aus e–r Partei ~ ⟨Am⟩ *to bolt a party*; aus e–r Schule ~ *to leave a school* | [abs] ~ *to secede* **II.** ≃ n *withdrawal*; → Austritt ‖ (neuer Schuhe) *break-in*

·aus|tr·immen vt [h] (Flugzeug etc) *to trim*

·aus|trinken vt/i [h] **1.** vt (Glas) *to empty* (*one's glass*); (Bier etc) *to drink off* (od *up*); *to finish; to dispose of* **2.** vi *to finish one's glass*

·Austritt m ~(e)s/~e **1.** → Austreten; Heraustreten **2.** *retiring, retirement, withdrawal* (aus *from* [*a society*]), *secession* (*from a church*); sein ~ aus der Schule *his leaving the school* | *protrusion* (*of hernia*) **3.** [konkr] *balcony* | = Abort **~sarbeit** f ⟨electro⟩ *work function; electron affinity* **~sdurchmesser** m *effective diameter* **~sdüse** f *outlet nozzle* **~sgeschwindigkeit** f ⟨tech⟩ *exhaust speed*; (*of guns*) *muzzle velocity* **~söffnung** f ⟨tech⟩ *port*

·aus|trocknen vt/i **1.** vt [h] *to dry up, to desiccate, to make dry*; (Land) *to parch* ‖ (Brunnen) *to exsiccate*; (Teich) *to drain* ‖ (Korn etc) *to weather*; (Holz) *to season* | (die Kehle) *to parch* **2.** vi [s] *to dry up, to become* od *run dry* | (of the throat) *to be parched* **·austrocknend** a *desiccating, desiccative* **·Austrocknung** f ~/~en *desiccation, drying-up*

·aus|trommeln vt [h] (etw) *to announce* od *publish by beat of drum* ‖ ⟨fig⟩ = austrompeten

·aus|trompeten vt [h] **1.** (etw) *to publish by trumpet* **2.** ⟨fig⟩ *to trumpet forth*

·aus|tüfteln vt [h] *to excogitate; concoct, hatch; devise, invent*; → ausdenken

·aus|tummeln vrefl [h] sich ~ = sich austollen

°**·aus|tun** vt [h] **1.** (Licht) *to put out* ‖ (Kleid) *to put off* | ⟨com⟩ (Posten) *to cancel* ‖ (Wort) *to strike out, to erase* **2.** (jdn) *to board* (*a p*) *out*

·aus|tuschen vt [h] *to touch up with* (*Indian*) *ink*

·aus|üben vt [h] **1.** (Beruf etc) *to practise; to pursue*; (Gewerbe) *to carry on*; (Kunst) *to practise* ‖ ein Amt ~ *to fill* (od *hold*) *an office* | (Pflicht) *to carry out, to perform*; (Pflichten e–s Amts) *to serve* (z. B. als Geschworener) ‖ (ein Recht) *to exercise* **2.** (Scherz, Streich) *to perpetrate* ‖ (Verbrechen) *to commit, to perpetrate* ‖ Rache ~ *to take revenge* (an jdm *on a p*) **3.** ⟨übtr⟩ (Macht, Einfluß) *to exercise, exert, have* (auf *on*); Druck ~ auf jdn *to put pressure on, to bring pressure to bear upon a p; to press a p* (*to do*); (schwer liegen auf) *to press upon a p* ‖ Anziehungskraft ~ (of plays) *to draw*; ein Stück, das starke A. ausübt *a draw*

·ausübend a *practising, practical*; → praktizieren ‖ ⟨bes mus⟩ ein ~er Künstler, ein ≃er *an executant* | ⟨pol⟩ *executive*; die ~e Gewalt (im Staat) *the executive* [Ggs *legislature*]

·Ausübung f ~/~en *exercise* (*of rights*); *exertion*; in ~ der Vollmacht *in the exercise of one's powers*; praktische ~ *practice* ‖ *performance* (*of duties*)

Auv·ergne [o'verɲ] f (zentralfranz. Landschaft) *Auvergne*

·Ausverkauf m ~(e)s/≃e ⟨com⟩ *sales; selling-off* (od *-out*); (*clearance-*)*sale* **·aus|verkaufen** vt [h] ⟨com⟩ *to sell off* (od *out*) ‖ (räumen) *to clear*; der Artikel ist ausverkauft *the article has run out, we have run out of this article*; → ausgehen ‖ ⟨theat⟩ das Haus ist ausverkauft *the house is sold out, booked up; the h. is full* (od *is filled*) *to capacity, all the seats are taken* ‖ ~es Haus ⟨theat fam bes Am⟩ *sell-out*; vor ausverkauftem Hause spielen *to play to capacity* (od *a full h.*)

°**ausverschämt** a = unverschämt

·aus|wachsen I. vi/t **A.** vi [s] **1.** (P) *to reach full growth* (: *he has reached full g.*); → ausgewachsen **2.** (of corn etc) *to grow* (*out*), *to chit, to sprout* ‖ ~ zu → 5. **3.** (of the spine) *to become curved*; er ist –ge– *he is humpbacked* od *hunchbacked* **4.** ich bin fast –ge– vor Langerweile *I felt bored to death* → ≃ **5. sich ~ a.** (P) *to grow up* ‖ er wird sich z e–m gesunden Jungen ~ *he will grow up a healthy youth* **b.** (of boughs) sich ~ zu *to grow* od *develop into*; die Zweige h sich z e–r Krone –ge– *the boughs have developed a crown* **c.** ⟨übtr⟩ sich ~ zu *to develop* od *grow into* (*a quarrel*) **d.** *to disappear in the process of growth*; der Fehler wird sich noch ~ *the fault will disappear in course of time* **B.** vt [h] s–e Kleider ~ *to grow out of* (od *to outgrow*) *one's clothes* **II.** °≃ n: es war zum ~ *it was terribly boring, it was unbearable*; langweilig zum ~! *what a bore*!; z ~ langweilig *as dull as ditch-water, as dry as dust*

·Auswahl f ~/~en **1.** *choice; selection* ⟨a. comp⟩; e–e ~ treffen *to make* (od *take*) *one's* (od *a*) *choice, to make a selection* (aus *from*); selbst die ~ treffen *to make one's own selection* **2.** (Möglichkeit zum Auswählen) *choice* ‖ ohne ~ *without choice, indiscriminately* ‖ zur ~ *for selection*; viele Dinge zur ~ h *to have many things to choose from* **3.** [konkr] (Ausgewähltes) *choice, selection* (an *of*; aus *from*; v *of*), ⟨oft⟩ *selections* [pl] (: *selections from the Victorian-Poets*) ‖ ⟨com⟩ *assortment*; e–e gr ~ h *to have a large a.* (an, v *of*) | (gr Menge) *variety*; e–e gr ~ h *to have a great v. to choose from*; Waren in reicher ~ *a great v. of goods* **~grundlage** f ⟨demog⟩ *sampling frame* **~lehrgang** m *selection course* **~liste** f (aus größerer Liste) *short-list* **~mannschaft** f ⟨sport⟩ *select team* **~prinzip** n *selection principle* **~sendung** f ⟨com⟩ *books* od *goods* (*sent*) *on approval; assortment*

·aus|wählen vt [h] jdn, etw ~, sich [dat] jdn, etw ~ *to choose, to select a p, a th*; (sorgsam) *to pick a th out* (aus *from, from among*); (jdn) *to single out* (f *for*); (Leute) *to cull* (aus *from* [*a country*]) ‖ wähl dir das Beste davon aus *take the pick of it*; das B. ~ können *to have the pick of ..*

·aus|walzen vt [h] ⟨met⟩ *to roll out*

·Auswanderer m ~s/~ *emigrant*; ~schiff n *emigrant-ship* **·aus|wandern 1.** vi [s] *to emigrate*; ~d *emigrant* ‖ *to migrate* (nach *to*); *to transmigrate* (a. ⟨übtr⟩ & [abs]) **2.** ≃ n jdn beim ~ helfen *to emigrate a p*

·Auswanderung f ~/~en *emigration* ‖ *migration, transmigration* (nach *to*) **~ssteuer** f *e.-tax*

·auswärtig a **1.** *out-of-town* (*customer*); ⟨univ⟩ ~es Mitglied *non-resident member; non-resident* ‖ ⟨parl⟩ Mitglieder des Hauses u ~e Personen *members of this House and persons outside it* **2.** *foreign* (*affairs*); ~er Beobachter *observer from without*; ~er Besucher *visitor from abroad* ‖

das °~e Amt, Ministerium des °~en; ⟨Ger⟩ *the Foreign Ministry*; ⟨engl⟩ *the Foreign Office*

·**auswärts** adv **1.** (Richtung) *outward(s)*; nach ~ gehen *to leave the place, to remove to another place* ‖ die Füße ~ setzen *to turn out one's toes* **2.** (Ruhe) **a.** *outside (of) the city* od *town*; *in the country*; von ~ k *to come from outside (the town)* **b.** *out of doors*; *away from home* ‖ ~ essen, schlafen, *to eat out, sleep out*; ~ wohnen *to live out*; ⟨univ⟩ *to be non-resident*; jd, der ~ wohnt *non-resident* °~**spiel** n ⟨sport⟩ *away fixture* (od *game, match*)

·**aus|waschen** vt [h] **1. a.** (Schmutz etc) *to wash out*; *to wash* (aus *out of*) ‖ sich ~ l *to wash out* **b.** (Kessel, Topf) *to scour* ‖ (Gefäße) *to sluice (out)*; *to rinse* | (Röhre, Kanal) *to flush* **c.** (Tuch, Wolle) *to scour, to wash*; *to clean* ‖ (Kleid) *to wash*; *to sponge (up)* **d.** (Augen, Wunde) *to bathe, sponge, wash* (mit *with*) **e.** (Sand nach Gold) *to pan out* **f.** ⟨chem⟩ *to wash*; *lixiviate* **2.** (of river, etc) (Ufer) *to wash away* od *out*; (Felsen) *to erode* ‖ –ge– w *to wash out* **3.** (Farbe) *to wash out*; die Farbe ist –ge– *the colour has come out in the wash*; das Kleid ist –ge– (= hat die Farbe verloren) *the dress is washed out* ·**Auswaschung** f ~/~en *wash(ing)*; *washing-out* ‖ ⟨chem⟩ *lixiviation* ‖ ⟨geol⟩ *erosion, wash-out (of the soil)*

·**aus|wässern** vt [h] *to (put in) water* ‖ ⟨chem⟩ *to edulcorate* ·**Auswässerung** f ~/ *watering* ‖ *edulcoration*

·**auswechselbar** a *interchangeable* ‖ *replaceable* (gegen *by*) °~**keit** f *interchangeability* ·**auswechseln** vt [h] (Blicke, Grüße) *to exchange, interchange* (mit jdm *with a p*); einige Worte ~ *to have a few words (with)* ‖ etw ~ gegen etw *to exchange* od *substitute a th for a th, to replace a th by a th*; (Batterie) *to change*; *to replace*; morsche Balken ~ *to replace rotten beams* (gegen *by* [*new ones*]) | (P) er ist wie –ge–lt *his manner has completely changed* ·**Auswechslung** f ~/~en *exchange, interchange* (gegen *for*; mit *with*); ⟨com⟩ *commutation* ‖ *replacement* (gegen *by*); *substitution* (gegen *for*); die ~ e–r S gegen etw *the substitution of a th for another* ‖ *changing*

·**Ausweg** m –(e)s/~e **1.** *exit, outlet, passage out, way out*; *way* (aus *out of*) **2.** ⟨übtr⟩ *way out of the difficulty*; *loophole, outlet* (f *for*); *expedient*; *issue* (*we could see no other i. than ..*) ‖ der beste ~ *the best way out*; e–n ~ finden *to hit upon an expedient*; *to find (a) vent* (f *for*); e–n ~ sehen *to see a way out* | letzter ~ *last resort*; als letzter ~ *in the last resort, as a last resource* ‖ ich weiß k–n ~ mehr *I am at the end of my tether* ‖ nie um e–n ~ verlegen s *to be never at a loss* ‖ → Ausflucht °~**slos** a *without a way out* ~**slosigkeit** f *impasse*; *lack of a solution, an answer, escape*; *no way out of a difficulty*

·**Ausweich-** ~**betrieb** m ⟨mil tech⟩ *shadow factory* → Tarnbetrieb ~**bewegung** f ⟨mil, aero⟩ *evasive action* ~**flughafen** m *alternate airfield* ~**frequenz** f *alternative frequency* ~**gleis** n ⟨rail⟩ *siding* ~**landeplatz** m ⟨aero⟩ *dispersal landing field* ~**möglichkeit** f *possibility of* (od *opportunity for*) *evasion, avoidance, avoiding* ‖ *detour* ~**stelle** f (in e–m Kanal etc) *passing-place, siding* ‖ ⟨rail⟩ *turn-out* ‖ ⟨mot⟩ *passing-place*, (z Parken) *lay-by* ‖ ⟨wir⟩ *alternative frequency* ‖ ⟨com⟩ *emergency depot* od *branch*; *temporary branch* ~**straße** f *by-pass* ~**vorrichtung** f *siding* ~**ziel** n ⟨mil⟩ *secondary objective*; *alternative target*

·**Ausweiche** f (Weg zum Ausweichen) ⟨rail & übtr⟩ *turn-out*

·**aus|weichen I.** vi [s] **1.** *to go aside, to go to one side*; *to side-step, to move* (od *keep*) *out of the way* ‖ jdm ~, vor jdm ~ *to make way for a p*; (im Wagen) *to pull aside for ..*; e–m Auto ~ *to get out of the way of a car*; *to make way for a car* ‖ rechts ~ *to pass on the right, to keep to the r.*; (*of tram-car*) *to go on a loop-line* ‖ ⟨mil⟩ [abs] *to avoid contact* **2.** (e–m Stoß) *to evade*; ⟨fenc⟩ *to parry* **3.** ⟨übtr⟩ (P) (Verfolgern etc) *to elude, evade*; *to give (a p) the slip*; jds Blicken ~ *to blink a p's eyes* ‖ (e–r Frage) *to evade, dodge, side-step* ‖ (e–r Gefahr) *to dodge, elude* ‖ (meiden) (jdm ~) *to avoid, dodge (a p)*; *to fight shy of (a p)*; *to shun, to evade (a p)*; ⟨Am⟩ *to duck (a p)* ‖ (e–r Pflicht) *to shirk, avoid, evade*; *to fight shy of* ‖ e–r S ~ *to steer clear of a th, to steer around a th*; *to go back on a th*; der Entscheidung ~ *to side-step the issue*; dem wahren Sachverhalt ~ *to beg the question*; der Wahrheit (absichtlich) ~ *to blink the truth* ‖ [abs] *to dodge*; *to draw in*; *to hedge*; *to shirk*; weich nicht aus *don't hedge* **II.** °~ n *going aside, moving out of the way* ‖ *evasion* (vor e–r Pflicht *of a duty*), *avoidance* (vor jdm *of a p*) ‖ → Ausweichung

·**ausweichend** a *evasive (answer)*; *shuffling*; *non-committal* ‖ sich ~ verhalten *to temporize*

·**Ausweichung** f ~/~en ⟨mus⟩ *modulation*

·**aus|weiden** vt [h] (T) *to viscerate, (dis)-embowel*; (Fisch) *to gut*; (Geflügel) *to draw*

·**aus|weinen** vi/t [h] **1.** vi *to cease crying* od *weeping*; *to have one's cry out* **2.** vt: s–n Schmerz ~ *to relieve one's distress by weeping* ‖ sich [dat] die Augen ~ *to cry one's eyes* od *heart out* | **sich** ordentlich ~ *to have a good cry*

·**Ausweis** m, –ses/–se **1.** ⟨com⟩ (amtl. Beweisstück) *statement, return*; nach ~ e–r S *as proved by a th, according to the result of a th* **2.** (amtl. Papier) *papers* [pl]; ⟨jur⟩ *warrant* ‖ ⟨com⟩ *voucher* ‖ (Legitimation) *proof of a p's identity*; *identification*; *credentials* [pl]; → Paß ‖ ⟨a. mil⟩ *pass*; Sonder°~ *special pass* | ⟨übtr⟩ (Empfehlung) *passport* (f *to*) ‖ → Ausweisung **3.** [in comp] *qualifying (examination)* ~**karte** f *pass*; *permit* ‖ *identification-card, identity-card (for)* ‖ *warrant-card (of a constable)*; ⟨Am⟩ *shield* ~**papier** n *identity paper*

·**aus|weisen** vt [h] **1.** (vertreiben) (jdn) *to turn out, to expel* (aus *from*); (verbannen) *to exile, to banish* (aus *from*); er wurde aus dem Lande ausgewiesen *he was banished* od *expelled (from) the country* ‖ (Schüler) *to remove* (aus e–r Schule *from a school*) **2.** (beweisen, kundtun) *to demonstrate*; *to prove, show* ‖ die Zeit wird es ~ *time will show* ‖ das wird sich ~ *we shall see* **3.** (jdn) *to identify* (z s *as being*) **4. sich** ~ (P) **a.** *to prove one's identity* **b.** (s–e Befähigung nachweisen) *to qualify* (als Doktor *as a doctor*)

·**Ausweisung** f ~/~en (~ aus e–m Lande) *deportation (of a foreigner)* ‖ *expulsion* (aus *from* [*a country*]) ‖ (Verbannung) *exile, banishment* ‖ → Ausweis ~**sbefehl** m *expulsion order*

·**aus|weiten** vt [h] **1.** (Graben etc) *to widen* ‖ (Handschuh, Schuh) *to stretch* ‖ (Rohr) *to extend* ‖ (Kredit etc) *to extend* ‖ ⟨übtr⟩ *to widen, enlarge*; den Erfolg ~ *to enlarge upon one's success* **2. sich** ~ *to stretch* ‖ ⟨übtr⟩ *to extend* ·**A–tung** f *stretch* ‖ *enlargement*; *extension* ‖ ⟨übtr⟩ *increase, growth, amplification*; *gain*; (des Krieges bes im Gebrauch v nuklearen Waffen) *escalation*

·**auswendig 1.** *a *outer, exterior, outward, outside* **2.** adv **a.** *(außenseitig) *outwardly* **b.** ⟨übtr⟩ *by heart, by rote*; *without book*; ~ können (*or* wissen) *to know by heart, to have (a th) at one's fingers' ends*; ~ lernen *to learn by heart* (od *by rote*); ~ spielen *to play from memory* | e–e S in– u ~ kennen *to know the ins and outs of a matter*

·**aus|werfen** vt/i [h] **I.** vt **1.** jdm ein Auge ~ *to knock a p's eye out by a throw* **2.** (Angel) *to cast*; (Netz) *to throw*; den Anker ~ *to cast anchor* **3.** (Graben) *to dig* **4.** ⟨übtr⟩ (v sich geben) (Blut, Schleim) *to expectorate*; (of volcano) (Steine, Asche etc) *to discharge, emit, eject, jet*; → ausspeien **5.** ⟨fig⟩ (Summe) *to allow, grant; earmark* (f *for*); *to appoint; offer; settle* (jdm *on, to a p*); → aussetzen ‖ (Gehalt) *to fix, to settle* ‖ ⟨com⟩ (Posten) *to put* od *place to account* **II.** vi (of horses) *to place the hoofs outwards* ·**Auswerfen** n *throw* (*of a net*) ‖ *ejection; emission* ‖ *grant* (*of a sum*) ‖ → Auswurf ·**Auswerfer** m *ejector*, ⟨artill⟩ *extractor* ‖ Gewehr mit ~ *ejector gun*

·**Auswerte- ~lineal** n *plotting scale*; → Auswertungs-

·**aus|werten** vt [h] *to make full use of* (*a th*); *to exploit, utilize*; (Befunde etc) *to evaluate*; ⟨aero phot⟩ *to evaluate, compute, interpret*; (Flugmeldungen) *to filter* ‖ ⟨mil⟩ (Nachrichten) *to collate, etc*; → ausnutzen ‖ ⟨comp⟩ *to scan*

·**Auswerter** m (Rechner) ⟨mil⟩ *plotter*

·**Auswertung** f *exploitation, utilization*; ⟨aero phot⟩ *evaluation, computing, interpreting*; (v Flugmeldungen) *filtering* ‖ ⟨mil⟩ *plotting* **~sstelle** f ⟨mil⟩ *computing centre* (*flash spotting, sound ranging*) ‖ ⟨aero-phot⟩ *computing station, interpretation post*

·**aus|wetzen** vt [h] (Scharte) *to remove* (*a notch*); Scharten im Messer ~ *to grind down* | ⟨fig⟩ *to revenge*; (Fehler) *to wipe out*; e–e Scharte ~ *to wipe out a defeat* (od *blow; injury*)

·**aus|wickeln** vt [h] *to unwrap; unfold* ‖ (ein Kind) *to unswathe*; ⟨mst⟩ *change*

·**aus|wiegen** vt [h] *to weigh out* (*for*; jdm *to a p*)

·**aus|wintern** vt/i **1.** vt [h] (etw) *to subject to wintry conditions* ‖ (of frost) (Pflanzen) *to throw out of the ground* | *to winter* (in *in*) **2.** vi **a.** [s] (of seed) *to perish with cold* ‖ (of fish etc) *to be choked from lack of oxygen in winter* **b.** [h] es hat ausgewintert *the winter is over* ·**Auswinterung(sschaden** m) f ⟨agr⟩ *winter damage* (*to crops*)

·**aus|wirken** vt [h] **1.** (ausnehmen) (Wild) *to eviscerate, disembowel* **2.** (bearbeiten) (Teig) *to knead* | (e–n Huf) *to pare* **3.** ⟨übtr⟩ **a.** (be–, erwirken) *to effect; to bring about; to work out* ‖ jdm etw ~ *to procure a th for* (od *to*) *a p; to obtain a th for a p* ‖ → erwirken **b. sich** ~ (of plans) *to work; to operate*; (of events, etc.) *to work out*; (of a tendency) *to work o.s. out; to work one's way* (z *into*); der Fehler wirkte sich nicht zum Nachteil aus *the fault was on the right side* ‖ sich schwer ~ *to have serious consequences*; sich unangenehm ~ *to work out awkwardly*; sich verderblich ~ gegen *to tell against* (*a p*) ‖ sich ~ auf etw *to operate* od *tell on a th, to affect a th* ·**Auswirkung** f ~/~en *the working* (*of a test*) ‖ *consequence, outcome, outgrowth, result; effect* ‖ ⟨comp⟩ *impact*

·**aus|wischen** vt/i **I.** vt [h] **1.** (Gefäß) *to wipe out* ‖ (Zimmer) *to give* (*a room*) *a wipe; to dust* ‖ (Pinsel) *to clean* | sich die Augen ~ *to wipe one's eyes* **2.** (entfernen) (Staub) *to remove* (aus *from*) ‖ (Geschriebenes etc) *to wipe* (od *rub*) *out; to efface; to sponge* (v der Tafel *off the slate*) ‖ (verwischen) *to blot* od *smear out* ‖ ⟨übtr⟩ *to wipe out, to efface* **3.** ⟨fig⟩ °jdm eins ~ *to play a p a trick; to play a trick* od *prank* (*up*)*on a p*; ⟨sl⟩ *to sock a p one, to strafe a p* (*for*) ‖ °jdm e–e ~ *to give a p a box on the ear* **II.** vi [s] (entwischen) jdm ~ *to escape a p*

·**aus|wittern** **I.** vi/t **1.** vi [s] (of ore, etc.) *to effloresce* ‖ *to decompose, decay* ‖ (of wood) *to season* **2.** vt [h] **a.** *to cause* (*ore*) *to effloresce* ‖ (Holz) *to season* **b.** = ausspüren **II.** ≚ n *efflorescence* (*of ore* etc)

·**aus|wringen** vt [h] (Wäsche) *to wring* (*out*)

·**Auswuchs** m –wuchses/wüchse **1.** *excrescence* (an *on*); *excrescent growth; outgrowth* (an e–m Baum *on a tree*) | ⟨med⟩ *excrescence; protuberance, swelling*; e–n ~ bildend *excrescent*; → Höcker **2.** ⟨übtr⟩ *excrescence* (e–r Erzählung *on a tale*) **3.** ⟨fig⟩ *extravagance, excess, exaggeration* (*of a morbid mind*), [oft pl] –wüchse *extravagances*, etc.) *abuse, nuisance*; –wüchse *corrupt conditions* [pl]

·**aus|wuchten** vt [h] ⟨tech⟩ *to* (*counter*)*balance*

·**Auswucht- ~gewicht** n ⟨tech⟩ *balance weight* **~maschine** f *balancing machine* **~stück** n *balance piece* **Auswuchtung** f *balancing; balance* **~sverhältnis** n *mechanical balance*

·**aus|wühlen** vt [h] *to root up* ‖ *to undermine*

·**Auswurf** m ~(e)s/≚e **1.** → Auswerfen **2.** [konkr] (Ausgeworfenes) **a.** *expectoration, recrement*, ⟨med⟩ *sputum* [L]; *discharge* ‖ (Kot) *excrement* → Lava **b.** ⟨fig⟩ *dross, refuse, rubbish* ‖ der ~ der Menschheit *the dregs* [pl] od *scum, riff-raff of humanity* **~gestein** n ⟨geol⟩ *eruptive rocks* [pl] **~stoff** m (Kot) *excreta* [L]

·**aus|würfeln** vt [h] etw ~ *to cast dice for ..*

·**Auswürfling** m ~(e)s/~n ⟨geol⟩ *eruptive rock*

·**aus|wüten** vi [h] *to cease raging*; → –toben

·**aus|zacken** vt [h] (Rand etc) *to indent, jag; notch*; künstlich ~ *to pink*; ↔ ausschneiden ‖ ausgezackt *serrate; denticulate*; ⟨bot⟩ *crenate*

·**Auszackung** f *indentation, denticulation; serration*; ⟨bot⟩ *crenation, crenature*

·**auszahlbar** a *payable*

·**aus|zahlen** vt [h] **1.** (Geld) *to pay, to pay away* (od *out*); (Lohn) *to pay* (*out*); alles ~ *to pay in full* ‖ (Scheck) *to cash*; sich e–n Scheck v e–m Konto ~ l *to draw a cheque upon an account* ‖ jdm etw ~ *to pay a p a th* (od *a th to a p*); ihm wurde sein Gehalt ausgezahlt *he was paid his salary* ‖ (etw) bar ~ *to pay down* (*in cash*) **2.** (jdn) *to pay* (*a p*) *off* **3.** ⟨übtr⟩ sich ~ (= lohnen) *to* (*re*)*pay*

·**aus|zählen** **I.** vt [h] **1.** (Stimmen) *to count; to count to the end* ‖ (durchzählen) *to count one by one; to count over* ‖ (Münzen) *to count out* ‖ (Sekunden, bis null *or* x) ⟨tech⟩ *to count down* **2.** ⟨box⟩ (jdn) *to count out*; [oft pass] ausgezählt w *to be knocked out of time, to be counted out, to take the count* **3.** ⟨demog⟩ *to tabulate* **II.** ≚ n ⟨tech⟩ *count-down* ‖ ⟨box⟩ (in e–r Frist v 10 Sekunden) *count* ·**Auszählung** f ~/~en ⟨stat, demog⟩ *tabulation* ·**Auszählvorrichtung** f *counter*

·**Auszahlung** f ~/~en *payment; disbursement* ‖ (Anweisung in fremder Währung) *transfer*, Kabel≚ *cable transfer* ‖ *paying-off* (*of workers*) **~sbescheinigung** f *permit for receiving payment* **~sstelle** f *pay-office* **~stag** m *pay-day*

·**aus|zanken** vt/i [h] **1.** vt (jdn) *to scold; to rate* (*a p*); *to rate at* (*a p*) **2.** vi *to cease scolding*

·**aus|zehren** vt/i **1.** vt [h] (Kräfte) *to waste*; (Land) *to exhaust; to impoverish* ‖ **sich** ~ *to be consumed* (vor *with*) **2.** vi [h] *to consume* (od *pine, waste*) *away* (vor *with*) ·**auszehrend** a *consumptive* ·**Auszehrung** f ~/ *consumption*; → Schwindsucht

·**aus|zeichnen** vt [h] **1.** ⟨com⟩ (Waren) *to mark, tag, ticket, label, to sale-price* **2.** ⟨übtr⟩ **a.** (jdn) *to distinguish*; ~de Eigenschaft *distinction* ‖ (ehren) *to honour, favour* (mit *with*); *decorate* (*with*); jdn ~ mit etw *to award a th to a p*; → verleihen ‖ ausgezeichnet w ⟨univ sport⟩ *to get one's cap*, ⟨Am⟩ *to win one's letter* **b.** (kennzeichnen) etw (e–e Periode etc) *to mark* **3. sich** ~ **a.** (P) *to make a* (od *one's*) *mark* (*in the world*); *to distinguish o.s.* (durch *by*; in *in*); *to be distinguished* (durch *by*); *to make o.s. conspicuous* (od *prominent*), *to make o.s. a name; to stand out* (als *as*); *to excel* (als *as*; in e–r S *in* od *at a th*; im Rezitieren *in reciting*) **b.** (S) sich ~ durch *to be distinguished* od *marked by ..* (: *the era was distinguished by ..*) ·**Auszeichnung** f ~/~en **1.** ⟨com⟩ *marking* (*of goods*), *labelling* **2.** ⟨fig⟩ *distinction* ‖ *honour* (f *to*); e–e ~ f jdn *a feather* *in a p's cap* || ⟨univ⟩ *honours* [pl]; in Latein mit ~ bestehen *to get first-class honours in Latin, to take a First in L.*; ⟨school⟩ *to pass with distinction in L.* || er hat mit ~ bestanden ⟨univ⟩ *he is Senior Wrangler* od *First Class*; *he took high places in the honours* | [konkr] *award, prize* || *mark of honour*; (Ordens≃) *decoration, order* **3.** ⟨com⟩ [konkr] *tag*; *label, ticket*

Auszieh- ~fallschirm m *auxiliary parachute* **~flügel** m ⟨aero⟩ *telescopic span wing* **~platte** f, **~rohr** n *telescopic tube* **~sicherung** f ⟨el⟩ *push-in fuse* **~stück** n (Tisch≃) *leaf* **~tisch** m *pull-out* od *extension table* **~tusche** f *drawing* od *Indian ink* **·ausziehbar** a *extractable*; *pull-out* (*table*); *telescopic, extensible*; *removable, shiftable*

·aus|ziehen vt/i **I.** vt [h] **1. a.** (Kork etc) *to extract, pull* (aus *from, out of*) || (Zahn) *to draw, extract*; sich e–n Zahn ~ l *to have a tooth drawn* || Nägel aus e–r Kiste ~ *to unnail a box* **b.** (Flüssigkeit) *to extract* (aus *from*) **c.** (Beispiele, Zitate) *to excerpt, extract*; *to take out* (aus *from*) || (e–e Schrift, e–n Schriftsteller) *to make extracts from, to draw on* (*a writer* etc) | ⟨com⟩ (Posten) *to take out*; (Rechnung) *to make out, to draw up* **d.** ⟨math⟩ die Wurzel ~ (aus e–r Zahl) *to extract the root of a number* **2. a.** (Kleid etc) *to take* (od *slip*) *off*; ⟨fam⟩ *to peel off*; *to divest o.s. of* (*a coat*); jdm den Rock ~ helfen *to help a p off with his coat* | die Kinderschuhe ~ *to break away from the leading-strings, to be no longer in leading-strings* || die Uniform ~ *to tender one's resignation* || → Adam **b.** (jdn) *to undress*; ausgezogen s *to have one's clothes off* || **sich** (ganz) ~ *to undress*; *to strip* (*naked*), ⟨fam⟩ *to peel off*; *to buff it* **c.** ⟨übtr⟩ (plündern) (jdn) *to fleece, to pillage, rob* **3.** (Draht) *to draw, stretch, extend* | (Tisch etc) *to pull out* **4.** (Zeichnung) mit Tusche ~ *to ink in* od *over* || (punktierte Linie) *to extend*; ausgezogene Linie *full* od *unbroken line* **II.** vi **1.** ⟨mil⟩ *to march out*; in den Kampf ~ *to take the field* **2.** *to move out*; *to remove*; *to leave one's house*; ⟨fam⟩ *to clear out*; ⟨Am⟩ (aus e–m Hotel) *to check out* || ~ müssen *to have notice to quit* || *to emigrate* **·Ausziehen** n **1.** *pulling-out, extraction* (*of teeth*, etc.) || *extraction* (*of juice*) || *excerption* (*of quotations*) **2.** *taking-off* (*of a coat*) || → Auszug

·aus|zieren vt [h] = ausschmücken

·aus|zimmern vt [h] (Schacht) *to line with wood, to timber*

·aus|zirkeln vt [h] (etw) *to measure with compasses* || ⟨übtr⟩ = austüfteln

·aus|zischen vt [h] ⟨theat⟩ → auspfeifen

·Auszug m ~(e)s/~̈e **1.** [→ ausziehen II. vi] **a.** *departure*; *emigration*; ⟨bib⟩ ~ der Kinder Israels *Exodus* [L] || ⟨übtr⟩ *exodus* (aus *from*) **b.** ⟨mil⟩ *marching out* **c.** (~ aus e–r Wohnung) *removal* **d.** = Altenteil **2.** [→ ausziehen I. vt] [konkr] (Ausgezogenes) **a.** ⟨a. chem⟩ *extract*; *essence*, → Extrakt **b.** *excerpt, extract* (aus *from* [*a book*]); *epitome, summary, abstract* || im ~ *in extracts*; *by way of epitome, in the form of an extract*; etw nur im ~ mitteilen *to give a résumé of a th* **c.** ⟨com⟩ *abstract*, ⟨bank⟩ *statement*; Rechnungs≃ *statement of account* || ⟨stat⟩ *extraction* **d.** ⟨mus⟩ (Bearbeitung) *arrangement, adaptation*; Klavier≃ *pianoforte arrangement* **e.** (Schublade) *drawer* || → Ausziehen **~brett** n, **~platte** f *leaf* (*of a table*) **~(s)hieb** m *removal of old trees from a young plantation* **~mehl** n *superfine flour* **≃sweise** adv *in extracts*

·aus|zupfen vt [h] (Gewebe) *to unravel*

aut·ark a *self-supporting* (*state*), *autarchic*(*al*) **Autark·ie** f *autarky, self-sufficiency* **~politiker** m *isolationist*

authentifiz·ieren vt [h] *to authenticate*

auth·entisch 1. a *authentic, genuine* (*text*); *reliable* (*news*); v ~er Seite, aus ~er Quelle *on good authority, from an authentic source*; (etw) als ~ erweisen *to authenticate* || ⟨mus⟩ *authentic*; ~er Schluß *a. cadence* **2.** adv *authentically* (*interpreted*) **authentis·ieren** vt [h] *to authenticate* **Authent·ie** f *authenticity* **Authentizit·ät** f ~/ *authenticity*; *genuineness*; die ~ e–r S erweisen *to authenticate a th*

authig·en a ⟨geol⟩ (am Fundort entstanden; [Ggs allothig·en]) *authigenic*

Aut·ismus m ⟨philos⟩ *autism*

·Auto n [kz f ~mobil] ~s/~s → Kraftwagen || *motor-car*, ⟨Am mst⟩ *automobile* || ⟨fam⟩ *car*, ⟨Am⟩ *auto*; ⟨sl⟩ *bus*; billiges ~ ⟨Am sl⟩ *flivver* || Miet≃ *taxi*; mit *or* in e–m M. fahren *to* (*go by*) *taxi* || Last≃ *lorry, motorvan*; ⟨Am⟩ *truck* | mit dem ~ (*to go, travel*) *by car*; *by road* || ~ fahren *to go motoring* (: *we went m. for a short time*); im ~ fahren *to motor*; (jdn) im ~ befördern *to motor* || fahren Sie ~? *do you drive*? || → Automobil **~antenne** f *auto radio antenna* **~ausflug** m *motor-car trip* **~ausstellung** f *motor-show* **~bahn** f (E = Expreß) *motorway* (*M*), ⟨Am⟩ *express way, parkway* (*Cross Country PK WY*), *turnpike*, (Westen) *freeway super-* od *auto-highway*; ⟨Can⟩ *Queen's, King's Highway* | ~ f schnelle Wagen ⟨Am⟩ *speedway* || ⟨Ger hist⟩ Reichs≃en [pl] *national motorroads* [pl] || ~gebühr [f] ⟨Am⟩ *turnpike toll* || ~(dauer)geschwindigkeit [f] *cruising speed* || ~prolet [m] *road-hog* **~bandit** m *motor-bandit* **~basar** m *used car mar*(*ke*)*t* || ~inhaber [m] *used car dealer* **~benzin** n *automobile petrol*, ⟨Am⟩ .. *gas*(*oline*) **~bereifung** f *tyres* (⟨Am⟩ *tires*) *for motor-cars* **~bus** m *motor-bus*; *omnibus*; ⟨fam⟩ *bus*; ⟨Am⟩ *motor coach, auto-bus*; ein–, zweistöckiger ~ *single–, double-deck bus*; ~ mit billiger Taxe ⟨Am sl⟩ *jitney* || Gesellschafts≃ *char-a-banc* || mit dem ~ *by bus*; mit dem ~ fahren ⟨sl⟩ *to bus it* || ~fahrt [f] *busride* || ~haltestelle [f] *bus-stop* **~car** m Sw *hired* (*touring*) *bus, excursion vehicle* **~droschke** f *taxi-*(*cab*); *cab* **~empfänger** m ⟨wir⟩ *car radio receiver, auto radio* **~fahren** n *motoring* **≃fahrend** a *motoring*; ⟨Am⟩ *automobiling* **~fahrer** m *motorist*; ⟨Am⟩ *autoist*; (Herrenfahrer) *owner-driver*; (bezahlter) *driver* **~fahrschule** f *motor–* (od *driving-*)*school* **~fahrt** f *motor-drive*; e–n ~ m *to go motoring* **~falle** f *car-trap*; ⟨off⟩ *hidden speed check-point, h. traffic control-p.*; ⟨fam⟩ *speed cop* **~flugzeug** n *road-going aircraft, air-car* **~friedhof** m *scrap yard, junk pile* **~führer** m *chauffeur*; *taxi driver* || ~schein [m] *driving* od *drivers' licence* **~garage** f (*motor*)*-garage* **~halteplatz** m, **~haltestelle** f *cab* (od *taxi*)*-rank* **~händler** m *motor-car* (⟨Am⟩ *auto*) *dealer* **~hotel** n *motel* **~heber** m *jack* **~hupe** f *horn* **~industrie** f *motor-industry* **~kappe** f *driving helmet* **~karte** f *road* od *motoring map* **~kino** n *drive-in cinema* **~koffer** m *motor-car trunk* **~kolonne** f *motor vehicle column*; ⟨Am⟩ *motorcade* **~konzession** (*motor-*)*car licence* **~mobil** n *automobile, car* || ~- [in comp] → auto– [in comp], → Automobil– **~nummernschild** n *number* od *licence plate* **~park** m *fleet of cars* **~parkplatz** m *car park*, ⟨Am⟩ *parking lot* **~reiseführer** m (Buch) *road-book* **~reisezug** m *car-sleeper* (*express*), *car-carrier*, ⟨Am fam⟩ "*piggy back*" *train* **~rennbahn** f *racing track* **~rennen** n *motor race* **~reparaturwerkstatt** f *repair shop* **~ruf** m ⟨telph⟩ *taxicab call* **~schlepp** m ⟨mot⟩ *towing*, ⟨aero⟩ *catapulting of gliders by motor-car cable* **~schlosser** m *car mechanic* **~schnellbahn** f ⟨Am⟩ *turnpike*, → Autobahn; die alle anderen überkreuzt *skyway* **~scooter** m (Jahrmarkt≃) *dodgem* **~sport** m *motoring* **~start** m *auto-towed take-off* **~straße** f *motor-road, motor-way*; Haupt≃ *trunk road* **~unfall** m *motor accident*; e–n ~ h *to be in a mot. acc.* **~vermietung** f *hiring of cars*; „~!" "*Rent a* *car!"* ^~**wandern** vi [s] *to hitch-hike* **~wesen** n *motoring* **~zus-stoß** m (*motor*)*car-collision*; → Automobil

auto- [in comp] *auto-* ^~**biographie** f *autobiography* **~biographisch** a *autobiographic*(*al*) ^~**chrom** n ⟨typ⟩ (Bild) *autochrome*; ~platte f *a. plate*; ~verfahren *a. process* **~chth·on** a *autochthonal, -thonous*; die ^~en [pl] *the autochthon*(*e*)*s* ^~**dafé** n, ~s/~s (Ketzergericht) *autodafé* [pl *autos-da-fé*] ^~**did·akt** m ~en/~en *autodidact*; ~– [in comp] *self taught* ^~**gam·ie** f ⟨bot⟩ *autogamy* **~g·en** a *autogenous* (*training*) ‖ ^~apparat [m] *autogenous welding apparatus* ‖ ^~schweißen [n] *autogenous welding* ^~**g·iro** n ~s/~s ⟨aero⟩ *autogiro, -gyro* ^~**gr·amm** n ~s/~e *autograph* ^~**gr·aph** n ~s/~en *autograph* ^~**graph·ie** f *autography* **~graphieren** vt [h] *to autograph* **~graphisch** a *autographic* ^~**grav·üre** f ⟨typ⟩ *autogravure* ^~**katal·yse** f *autocatalysis* [pl *-ses*] **~katal·ytisch** a *autocatalytic* ^~**kl·av** m ~s/~en ⟨chem⟩ *autoclave* ^~**kr·at** m ~en/~en *autocrat* ^~**krat·ie** [*-ti:*] f ~/~n [-ti:ən] *autocracy* **~kr·atisch 1.** a *autocratic* **2.** adv *autocratically* ^~**m·at** m ~en/~en **1.** ⟨mus⟩ *automaton* ‖ *mechanical clock-work toy* od *figure* ‖ ⟨el⟩ (Sicherung) *automatic cut-out* **2.** (Verkaufsautomat) *slot-machine*; (f Getränke) *automatic drink depresser* ‖ ~enmittagessen [n] *buffet lunch* ‖ ~enrestaurant [n] *automatic restaurant*; *snack-bar*; ⟨Am⟩ *automat, cafeteria* ‖ ~enzähler [m] *prepayment counter* ^~**matik** f ⟨wir⟩ *automatic tuning means* **~m·atisch** a *automatic*; *press-button* [attr] (Steuerung, Kriegsführung); ~ [adv] senkrecht ausrichtend *self-squaring* ‖ völlig ~er Betrieb [m], ~e Produktion [f] *automa*(*tiza*)*tion* ‖ ~e Einrichtungen [f pl] *automatic features* ‖ ⟨comp⟩ ~e Funktionen des Buchungsvorgangs *accounting automaticity* ‖ ~e Schaltung *a.c gear change* ‖ ⟨comp⟩ ~e Vorrangssteuerung [f] *simultaneous mode control*; → Telephon **~matisieren** vt [h] *to automate* ^~**matisierung** f ~/~en, **~mation** f ~/ *automation* ^~**mat·ismus** m ⟨a. psych⟩ *automatism* ^~**mob·il** n ~(e)s/~e (*motor-*)*car*; ⟨Am⟩ *automobile*; ~ausstellung [f] *motor-show*; ~bau [m] *motor* (⟨Am⟩ *automotive*) *industry*; ~motor [m] *automobile engine*; ~papiere [n pl] (nur einzeln:) *driver's licence + car registration + insurance papers*; ~reisezugverkehr [m] *car-carrying rail service*; ~rennen [n] *motor-race*; *motor-racing*; ~sport m, ~wesen n *motoring* ‖ ~technik [f] *automobile engineering* ‖ ~verleih [m] *car hire firm*; ~vermietung [f] *car hiring*, (f Selbstfahrer) *drive-yourself service* ‖ ~zubehör [n] *spares and accessories* ^~**mobil·ismus** m *automobilism, motoring* ^~**mobil·ist** m *motorist* **~n·om** a *autonomous, independent, self-governing* (*state*); nicht ~es Gebiet *non-self-governing territory* ^~**nom·ie** f *autonomy*, (*right of*) *self-government*; *home rule* ^~**pl·astik** f ⟨surg⟩ *autoplasty* ^~**ps·ie** f *autopsy, personal inspection* ‖ *autopsy, postmortem examination* **~semantisch** a ⟨phil⟩ *autosemantic* ^~**suggesti·on** f *auto* (od *self*)*-suggestion*; ~ nach Coué [Fr] *Couéism* ^~**typ·ie** f ⟨typ⟩ (= Netzätzung) *autotype*; *half-tone engraving* (od *etching*) ‖ (Bild) *autotype*

·**Autor** m ~s/Aut·oren *author, writer* ‖ der Autor .. *this present writer* ..

Aut·oren- ~honorar n *author's fee*

autoris·ieren vt [h] (jdn) *to authorize* (*to do*); autorisiert *authorized* (*translation*)

Autorisat·ion f *authorization* **autorit·är** a ⟨pol⟩ *authoritarian* (*state*) **Autorit·ät** f **1.** [abstr] ~/ *authority*; aus eigener ~ *on one's own a.* ‖ ~s-zeichen → Hoheitszeichen | ⟨übtr⟩ *discipline*, die ~ wahren *to keep d.* **2.** (P) ~/~en *authority*, e–e ~ s auf dem Gebiete der Biologie *to be an a. on biology*; ärztliche ~ *consultant*; ~ in Geschmacksdingen *arbiter elegantiarum* L ‖ ~s-verletzung [f] *defiance of authority* **autoritat·iv** a *authoritative*

·**Autorschaft** f ~ *authorship*

autsch intj *ouch*

·**Auwald** m *lowland forest*

auxili·ar a *auxiliary*; ^~bischof = Weihbischof

Av·al [a'val] m [Fr] ~s/~e ⟨com a-engl⟩ *aval, guarantee for payment of a bill by a third party*; ~ geben *to stand surety* ‖ ~bürge [m] *surety*; als ~bürge *per aval*

aval·ieren, avalis·ieren vi [h] *to stand surety*

Av·ance [a'vɑ̃:sə] f [Fr] ~/~n *advantage*; *profit* ‖ ⟨com⟩ = Vorschuß ‖ ⟨sex⟩ jdm ~n m *to make a pass at a p*

Avancem·ent [avɑ̃:s'mɑ̃:] n [Fr] ~s/~s ⟨mil⟩ *advancement*; *promotion* (z *to*) **avanc·ieren** [avɑ̃:'si:rən] vi [s] *to advance, proceed* ‖ *to advance, to be promoted*

†**Avantag·eur** [avɑ̃:ta'ʒœr] m [Fr] ~s/~e ⟨Ger mil⟩ (bis 1899) *gentleman-cadet*; *ensign*

Av·antgarde [a'vɑ̃:gardə] f [Fr] ~/~n † = Vorhut ‖ ⟨pol⟩ *vanguard* ⟨a. arts⟩ **—d·ist** m *pioneer*; ⟨pol⟩ *champion*; ⟨arts⟩ *vanguardist* **a—d·istisch** a ⟨arts⟩ *vanguardist* [attr]

·**ave** [L] **1.** [intj] *ave* **2.** ^~ n ~s/~s *Ave* ‖ ^~ Maria [n] ~s/~s *Ave Maria*

°**Av·ek** m [Fr] *go, pluck*; ⟨fam⟩ *fizz, snap, vim* ‖ mit (e–m) ~ *with a snap*; *in the company of a girl* ‖ sie hat ein gewisses ~ *she has a way with her* od *something about her* ‖ mit e–m gewissen ~ *with a certain something*

Avent·in m ~s/ *the Aventine, the A. Hill* (*in Rome*)

Aventur·in m ~s/ ⟨minr⟩ *aventurine, avan–*

Av·erbo n ~ sagen *to give the principal parts of a verb*

Av·ers m ~es/~e [Ggs Revers] *observe, face, head* (*of a coin*)

Aversi·on f ~/~en = Abneigung

Av·ersum n [L], ~s/–sen ⟨com⟩ *indemnity, acquittance*

Avi·atik f, ~/ *aviation*

Avign·on ['aviɲɔ̃] n ⟨Fr⟩ (Stadt) *Avignon*

Av·is m & n ~es/~e ⟨com⟩ *advice* [pl *advices*]; *information, intelligence* ‖ laut ~ *as per advice, as advised* **~brief** m *letter of advice* **~klausel** f *words* 'laut Avis' *on a bill of exchange*

avis·ieren vt [h] ⟨com⟩ *to advise, inform, notify*

Av·iso m ~s/~s ⟨mar⟩ *aviso, advice-boat*

a vista [It] ⟨com⟩ *a vista, at sight*

Avitamin·ose f ⟨med⟩ *avitaminosis*

aviv·ieren vt [h] ⟨tech⟩ (Farbe e–s Stoffes) *to brighten*

Avos·ette f ~/~n ⟨orn⟩ *avocet, avoset*

·**Avus** f ([abbr] = **Automobil-Verkehrs- und Übungs-Straße** [bei Berlin]) *the Avus* (*motor-road*

Aw·aren [pl] ⟨hist⟩ *the Avars* [pl]

Aw·esta n *Avesta*

axi·al a *axial*; ^~druck, ^~-Längsdruck [m] *end thrust*; ^~straße [f] *axial route* **axill·ar** a *axillary*

Axiolog·ie f = Wertwissenschaft

Axi·om n ~s/~e *axiom* **Axiom·atik** f *axiomatical* (*treatment of a*) *theory* **axiom·atisch** a *axiomatic*(*al*), → gewiß, zweifellos [a & adv]

Axol·otl n ~s/~ ⟨zoo⟩ (Wassermolch) *axolotl*

Axt f ~/^~e *axe*; Zimmermanns^~ *carpenter's axe*; → Beil ‖ ⟨a. fig⟩ die ~ legen an etw *to lay the axe to a th, to axe a th* **~gesicht** n (lange Nase, langes Kinn) *hatchet-face* ·**~helm** ·**~stiel** m *handle of an axe*

·**Aya** f [Span] (Kinderfrau) *ayah*

Aye-Aye m ~/~ ⟨zoo⟩ (Fingertier) *aye-aye*

Azal·ee, Az·alie f ~/~n ⟨bot⟩ *azalea*

Azar·ole f ~/~n ⟨bot⟩ *azarole*
azeph·alisch a ⟨anthr⟩ *acephalous*
Azetanil·id n ~s/ ⟨chem⟩ *acetanilide*
Azet·at n ~s/~e ⟨chem⟩ *acetate*; ~seide f (Faserstoff) *acetate rayon* od *silk*
Azet·on n ~s/~e ⟨chem⟩ *acetone*
Azetyl·en n ~s/ ⟨chem⟩ *acetylene* **Azidimetr·ie** f *acidimetry* **Azid·ose** f ~/ *acidosis*; → Säure
Az·ilien [azi'ljɛ̃:] n ~s/ ⟨praeh⟩ (3. Zeitstufe der mittl. Steinzeit) *Azilian*
Azim·ut m & n ~s/~e ⟨astr⟩ *azimuth* **azimu·t·al** a *azimuthal*
·Azo- ⟨chem⟩ [in comp] = stickstoffhaltig **~benz·ol** n *azo-benzol* **~farbstoffe** m [pl] *azodyes* [pl] **~verbindung** f *azo-compound*
Az·oikum n ~s/ ⟨geol⟩ *Azoic age* **az·oisch** a *azoic*
Az·oren [pl] ⟨geog⟩ (Atlantik-Inseln) *Azores*
Azt·eken m [pl] (Indianerstamm Mexikos) *Aztecs* **azt·ekisch** a *Aztec(an)*
Az·ur m ~s/~e *azure* **~blau** n *azure*
az·urn a *azure*
Azyg·ie f ⟨biol⟩ *azygous condition* **az·ygisch** a *azygous*
az·yklisch a ⟨a. chem⟩ *acyclic*
·Azymon n *azymous* od *unleavened bread*

B

B, b [be:] n ~/~ *B, b* || → A | **b** ~/~ ⟨mus⟩ **1.** (Ton) *B flat* **2.** (Vorzeichen) *flat* || B-dur *B flat major*; b-moll *b flat minor* **b-Ader** f ⟨telph⟩ *R-(= ring) wire* **B-Produkte** n pl ⟨com⟩ *light steel products* **B-Stelle** f ⟨mil⟩ = Beobachtungs-*orange pip* (= *observation post*) **·B-Wolle** f (⟨hum⟩ f Baumwolle) *Manchester silk*
Baal m ~s/~e *Baal*; dem ~ dienen *to worship B.* (od *false gods*) **~sdiener, ~spriester** m *worshipper of Baal* **~sdienst** m *Baal-worship* **~spfaffe** m *false priest*
ˣ**Baas** m ~es/~e *boss*; (Meister, Aufseher, Vermittler)
Bab ⟨Arab⟩ *door, gate*
B·aba f **1.** *grandma, grannie* **2.** = Napfkuchen
°**B·aba** f (Kindersprache) *bye-bye* || in die ~ gehn! (*go to*) *beddy-* od *bye-byes!*, *beddy go-sy!*
°**babbeln** vi/t *to babble*; *prattle*
°**B·abbser** m ⟨mil⟩ = Zivilist
B·abel n ⟨übtr a.⟩ Sünden~ *sink of iniquity*
Babir·ussa m ⟨zoo⟩ (ind Schwein) *babir(o)ussa*
Bab·ismus m (Lehre e–r moham. Sekte) *babiism*
B·abuin m ~s/~e ⟨zoo⟩ *kind of baboon*
B·abul m, **~baum** m ⟨bot⟩ *babul, babool*
Bab·usche f (orient. Hausschuh) *babouche*, (*heelless*) *Turkish slipper*
Baby ['beibi] (engl) n *baby* **~sitter** m *baby-sitter*; ~ spielen *to sit in*
Babyl·onier m ~s/~ *Babylonian* **Babyl·onisch** a *Babylonian* (*Captivity*); ~er Turm *the Tower of Babel*; ~e Verwirrung [f] *babel*
Bacchan·al n ~s/~ien [mst pl] *bachanalia* [L] [pl], *wild orgies* [pl] **bacchanalisch** a *bacchanal*
Bacch·ant m ~en/~en *bacchant* || *bacchanal, reveller*; → Bachant **Bacch·antin** f ~/~nen *bacchante* **bacch·antisch** a *bacchanal, bacchanalian* **b·acchisch** a *bacchic*
B·ach m ~(e)s/~e *brook, rivulet*; (kl ~) *beck, rill* **~bunge** f ⟨bot⟩ *brooklime* **~forelle** f ⟨ich⟩ *river-trout* **~krebs** m ⟨zoo⟩ *crayfish* **~stelze** f ⟨orn⟩ (*water-*)*wagtail*, → *wagtail* Bd. II
Bach·ant m *travelling scholar*
B·ache f ~/~n ⟨zoo⟩ *wild sow* → *boar* || (Dächsin) *sow* **B·acher** m ~s/~ ⟨zoo⟩ (*2 year old*) *wild boar*
B·ächlein n ~s/~ *brooklet, beck, rill* || ein ~ m ⟨fam⟩ *to do a sweet-pea*
B·ack f ~/~en ⟨mar⟩ **1.** *forecastle, fo'c's'le*; *the bows* [pl] **2. a.** (Napf) *tin-bowl* **b.** ~, ~schaft (= Tischkameradschaft) *mess*; Mitglied e–r ~ *messmate*
B·ack- (→ backen) [in comp mst] *baking* . . **~apfel** m *baking-apple* **~blech** n *baking-tin* **~butter** f *frying-butter, margarine* **~fett** n *shortening, deep fat* **~fisch** m **1.** *small fish for frying* **2.** ⟨fig⟩ *flapper*; *girl in her teens, teenager*, → *teens*; *half-grown girl*; *miss*; ⟨Am sl⟩ *bobby-soxer*; (vor dem 1. Ball) *subdeb(utante)* || ~-Aquarium [n] *teenager managery* **~form** f *cake-tin, pastry-mould* **~hähnchen, ~huhn** n *roast chicken*; *chicken for roasting* ˣ**~hendl** n ~s/~ [österr] ⟨cul⟩ *fryer*, ⟨bes Am⟩ *frier* **~haus** n *bake-house* **~kohle** f *baking-coal* **~margarine** f *pastry margarine* **~obst** n *dried fruit* **~ofen** m (*baking-*) *oven* **~pflaume** f *prune* **~pulver** n *baking-powder, bake* **~röhre** f *baking oven* **~schaufel** f *peel* **~schüssel** f *baking-dish* (od *basin*) **~stein** m *brick*; ein Stück ~ *a brickbat*; ~bau [m] *brick architecture*; ~gotik [f] *Brick Gothic* **~stube** f *bakery* **~trog** m *kneading-trough* **~waren** f [pl] *bakery-goods, baker's wares* [pl]; (feine) *pastry* **~werk** n *pastry*; *confectionery*; leichtes ~ *puff*
B·ackbord m & n ⟨mar⟩ (Ggs Steuerbord) *port*, [obs] *larboard*; ~ voraus *off the port bow* **~licht** n (rot) ⟨mar, aero⟩ *port light* **~wache** f *port-watch*
B·acke f ~/~n, **B·acken** m ~s/~ **1.** *cheek*; *jowl*; → Hinter~, Kinn~ || ~ an ~ *cheek to cheek*; ⟨fam⟩ *cheek by jowl*; auf der ~ *in the cheek* || dicke *or* geschwollene ~ *swollen cheek*; eingefallene ~n *hollow cheeks, lantern-jaws* [pl]; mit vollen ~n *with blown cheeks*, mit v. ~n kauen *to eat lustily* || die ~n voll nehmen ⟨fam⟩ *to blow off steam* **2.** ⟨übtr⟩ **a.** (am Gewehr, Lehnstuhl etc) *cheek* **b.** ⟨mech & tech⟩ ~n [pl] *cheeks, side-pieces, side-beams* [pl] (*of a press*); *jaws* [pl] (*of a vice*); *clamps* [pl] | ⟨skiing⟩ *toe-irons* [pl] **3.** °au ~! *oh my!*
b·acke-b·acke K·uchen ⟨Kinderspr.⟩ *pat-a-cake*
B·acken- **~bart** m (*side*)-*whiskers* [pl]; ⟨Am⟩ *side-burns* [pl] **~bindung** f ⟨ski⟩ *toe-binding* **~brecher** m ⟨mech⟩ *jaw-breaker*; *stone-crusher* **~bremse** f *block* (od *shoe*) *brake* **~futter** n (Werkzeug) *jaw-chuck* **~grübchen** n *dimple* (*in the cheek*) **~klee** m (krautiger) *grass-like clover* **~knochen** m *cheek-bone*; *maxillary* **~streich** m *box on the ear, slap in the face*; jdm e–n ~ geben *to slap* (od *smack*) *a p's face* **~stück** n (am Geschirr) *cheek-piece* **~tasche** f (bei Tieren) *cheek-pouch* **~zahn** = Backzahn
b·acken I. vt/i [h] **A.** vt **1.** (Brot) *to bake*, (e–n Kuchen) *to make* **2.** (in schwimmendem Fett, in der Pfanne ~) *to fry* **3.** (Ziegel etc) *to burn, to fire* **4.** (Obst) *to dry* **B.** vi **1.** *to bake*; ich backe selbst *I do my own baking* **2.** (kleben) (of snow, etc.) *to stick* (an *to*); zus ~ *to stick together* **II.** ~ n *baking*; → Back-
B·äcker m ~s/~ *baker* || beim ~ *at the baker's* (*shop*); geh zum ~ *go to the baker's* **~beine** n [pl] = X-Beine **~brot** n *baker's bread* **~bursche, ~junge** m *baker's boy* **~geselle** m *journeyman baker* **~handwerk** n *baker's trade* **~innung, ~zunft** f *baker's guild* **~laden** m *baker's* (od *confectioner's*) *shop*; *bakery*

Bäcker·ei f *bakery* || *baker's shop* || ~en [pl] ⟨bes österr⟩ = Klein-Backwerk *pastry*

b·ackig a (klebrig) *sticky*

-backig [in comp] *cheeked*; rot~ *red-cheeked*

°**B·ackpfeife** f *slap in the face* ⟨a. übtr⟩; *box on the ear*

B·acksgast m (→ Back) *forecastle-man*

B·ackspier(e) f ⟨mar⟩ *swinging-boom*; die ~ ausbringen *to get out the boom*; die ~ beiklappen *to get aft the boom* **B·ackstag** n ~s/~e(n) *guy*

B·ackzahn m ~s/≃e *grinder, molar*; *back* od *molar tooth*; → Lückzahn, Prämolaren | ⟨fig⟩ ≃e, °**~er·ie** f (= Infanterie) ⟨fam⟩ *grinders*

Bad n ~(e)s/≃er **1. a.** (Wannen≃) ⟨a. med⟩ *bath*; Fuß≃ *foot-b.*; Luft≃ *air-b.*; Heißluft≃ *hot air-b.*; Schwitz≃ *sweating* od *sudatory b.*; Sitz≃ *sitz b.*; Sonnen≃ *sun-b.*; ⟨med⟩ elektrisches ~ *electric b.*; Moor≃ *mud b.*; → Bestrahlung, Höhensonne || (das Wasser f) ein heißes ~ anstellen *to turn on a hot bath, to draw one's tub* ein ~ nehmen *to have* od *take a b.* || → Kind **b.** (~ im Freien) *bathe, swim*; (rasch) ein ~ nehmen *to have a (quick) bathe* od *swim* **2.** ⟨chem & tech⟩ *bath*; Öl≃ *oil-bath*; galvanisches ~ *electrolytic bath*; Fixier≃ *hypo bath* **3.** (~eort) (mit Heilquellen) *spa*; *health-resort*; *watering-place*; ein ~ aufsuchen *to visit a watering-place* || (See≃) *watering-place, seaside-resort*; ins ~ reisen *to go to a watering-place* (od *to the seaside*)

B·ade- [in comp] *bathing* .., *bath* .. **~anstalt** f *bathing-establishment*; ⟨meist⟩ *baths* [pl] Schwimm ≃ *swimming baths* **~anzug** m *bathing-suit* → Badekostüm **~arzt** m *physician at a spa* (od *watering-place*) °**~buchse** f ⟨fam⟩ *bumbags*; → ~hose **~einrichtung** f *bath plant* **~frau** f *baths attendant* **~gast** m *visitor to a watering-place* **~haube** f *bathing cap* **~haus** n *baths* [pl], *hydropathic* [s] **~hose** f *bathing-drawers, slips, swimming trunks* [pl]; e–e ~ *a pair of* .. **~kabine** f *dressing-cabin* **~karren** m ⟨engl⟩ *bathing-machine* **~kostüm** n (f Damen) *bathing costume* (u Hose *and slips* [pl]). **~kur** f ⟨med⟩ *use* (od *course*) *of mineral waters*; e–e ~ m *to drink* od *take the waters* **~laken** n *bath(ing) towel* **~mantel** m *bathing-wrap*; *towel-robe* **~meister** m *bath attendant*; (Lehrer) *swimming-master* **~mütze** f *bathing-cap* **~ofen** m *bath stove*; (Gas-) *geyser* **~ort** m *watering-place* || (mit Heilquellen) *spa*; → Bad 3. **~reise** f *visit to a watering place* **~schönheit** f ⟨sl⟩ *aquabelle* **~schuh** m *bathing shoe* **~schwamm** m *bath-sponge* **~strand** m *beach* **~stube** f *bath-room* **~teppich** m *bath-mat* **~tuch** n *bath-towel* **~wanne** f *bath tub* **~wärter** m *baths attendant* **~wasser** n *bath-water*; das ~ auslassen *to empty the bath*, → Bad 1. a. **~zeit** f *bath-time* || (Saison) *(bathing-)season* **~zelle** f ⟨med⟩ *bath-cabin* **~zelt** n *bathing-tent* **~zimmer** n *bath-room*, ⟨Am a.⟩ *toilet*

b·aden I. vi/t [h] **1.** vi **a.** (in e–r Wanne) *to have* od *take a bath*; ⟨fam⟩ *to tub*; heiß ~ *to take a hot bath* **b.** (im Freien) *to bathe, to have a bathe* (od *swim*); ~ gehen *to go for a bathe* **2.** vt (Kind in der Wanne) *to bath*; ⟨fam fig⟩ als Kind zu heiß ge–t worden s *to have got a knock in the cradle*; (Glied) *to bathe*; *to imbrue* (in *in*); (in heißem Wasser) *to foment* | ⟨fig⟩ die Hände in Blut ~ *to bathe one's hands in blood* || in Schweiß gebadet *covered with sweat*; in Tränen g. *drenched* od *drowned in tears* **II.** ≃ n *bathing*; *bathe*; Todesfall beim ~ *bathing-fatality*

B·aden n ⟨Ger⟩ (Land) *Baden* || ~-~ [n] (bad. Badeort) *Baden-Baden* **B·adener** m, **Bad·enser** m, **~in** f *inhabitant of Baden* **b·adisch** a *of Baden*

B·adende [der ~, ein ~r, [pl] die ~en] (im Freien) *bather*

B·ader m ~s/~ (Barbier) *barber*

B·äderkunde f *balneology*, → Balneologie

Bädervereinigung f *Spas Federation*

baff 1. [intj] = paff **2.** °[a] *all of a heap, on one's back* || ~ m *to flummox, flabbergast*; *that knocks me* || ~ s *to be dumbfounded* od *taken aback*

B·äffchen n ~s/~ [falsch f] Beffchen

b·äffen vi *to (give a sharp) bark*

Bag·age [ba'gɑːʒə] [Fr] f ~/~n **1.** ⟨mil⟩ (sonst †, → Gepäck) *baggage* **2.** °⟨fig⟩ *lot*, ⟨sl⟩ *caboodle* (:*the whole c.*) **~pferd** n ⟨mil⟩ *bathorse* **~wagen** m ⟨mil⟩ *baggage-lorry*

Bag·asse f (ausgepreßte Stengel des Zuckerrohres) *bagasse, megass*

Bagat·elle f ~/~n *bagatelle* [Fr], *trifle* || *but that's a (mere) detail* || ⟨Am fam⟩ *chicken feed* **bagatellis·ieren** vt [h] (etw) *to minimize*; *understate, underrate*; *to play down*; ⟨fam⟩ *to pooh-pooh* **Bagat·ellsachen** f [pl] ⟨jur⟩ *petty causes* od *cases* [pl] **Bagatellschaden** m ⟨ins⟩ *petty case* (*of damage*); *trivial damage*; *petty* od *minor loss*

B·agdadbahn f *Bagdad Railway* (*begun 1903*)

B·agger m ~s/~ *dredge*; ⟨mar⟩ *dredger, dredging-machine*; Eimerketten≃ *bucket-ladder dredger*; Löffel≃ *excavator*, Tieflöffel≃ *backhoe*; Trocken≃ *navvy*; Saug≃ *suction dredger*; (etw) durch ~ entfernen *to dredge away* **~führer** m *dredgerman* **~gut** n *excavated material, spoil* od *rubbish* **~maschine** f *dredging machine*

b·aggern vt/i [h] *to dredge*; → aus~

bah [intj] ~! *bah!*

Bah·amainseln, Bah·amas f pl (Westind. Inselgruppe) *Bahama Islands, Bahamas* pl **Bah·amakanal** m *Bahama channel*

Bah·awalpur n (ind. Staat)

b·ähen vt [h] (erhitzen, baden) ⟨med⟩ *to foment*; *to poultice*; (Brot) ~ [österr] *to toast* **B·ähmittel** n → Foment

Bah·ia n (Stadt in Brasilien) *Bahia*

Bahn f ~/~en **1.** (ebene Fläche) *plane*; schiefe ~ *inclined p.*, abschüssige ~ *declivitous* od *downward slope*; *chute* || Gleit~ *slide, slide-way*; Rodel≃ *toboggan-slide* (od *shoot*) || ⟨fig⟩ auf e–e schiefe *or* abschüssige ~ geraten *to go downhill, to be on the down-grade* **2.** (Straße) **a.** *road, way*; *path* || freie ~ *free road*, ⟨fam⟩ *green light* ⟨a. übtr⟩; ~ frei [dat] *all clear for*; f etw freie ~ erhalten *to get the go-ahead on a th*; freie ~ dem Tüchtigen *full facilities for the efficient* **b.** ⟨sport, racing⟩ *track*, (Lauf–, Renn≃) *course, race-course*; *lane*; ⟨cycl⟩ *path*; in die gerade ~ einbiegen *to come round into the straight* || (Boden) *going* (:*the g. was good*) || → Aschen≃ || ⟨golf⟩ die kz geschnittene ~ *fairway, pretty* || (Kampf≃) *arena, stadium* || → Eis≃ **c.** ⟨übtr⟩ *path, road, walk*; *channel*; *line*; (Bereich) *orbit* || Lauf≃, Lebens≃ *career, course*; *path* od *walk of life* **d.** Wendungen: e–e neue ~ einschlagen *to strike out in a new direction*; *to make a new departure* || die ~ frei m für etw *to pave* od *prepare the way for a th* || in die richtigen ~en lenken *to direct into the right channels* || in andere ~en übergehen *to pass into other channels* || in jds ~en wandeln *to walk in the path of a p* | sich [dat] ~ brechen *to make* (od *force, push*) *one's way*; → sich durchsetzen; Blut (= Erbmasse) bricht sich ~ *blood will out* || sich in ähnlichen ~en bewegen (*or* vollziehen) wie .. *to be on similar lines to* .. || das Gespräch in ernstere ~en lenken *to strike a more serious note*, .. wieder .. *to bring the conversation back to seriousness*; (Geschoß) aus der ~ werfen *to diguide* **3.** ⟨astr, math, phys⟩ *orbit* (*of a planet*); *path* (*of a comet*); die scheinbare ~ der Sonne *the ecliptic* || Flug≃ *trajectory* (*of a projectile*) || ⟨mil⟩ Schieß≃ *range* **4.** ⟨mech & tech⟩ *face* (*of a hammer, plane*) || *groove* || ⟨comp⟩ *track, channel* **5.** (kz f Eisen≃) **a.** *railway, rail*; ⟨Am⟩ *railroad*; zweigleisige ~ *double-line railway* || *lines, rails* [pl] (*for tram-cars*) || → Drahtseil≃, Eisen≃, Hoch≃, Ring≃,

Schwebe≃, Straßen≃, Zahnrad≃ | **an** der ~ *at the station* ‖ **in** der ~ (*I met him*) *on the train* ‖ **mit** der ~ (*to travel, to send*) *by rail, by train* | frei ~ *free on rail* | jdn an die ~ begleiten (*or* bringen) *to see a p off* (*at the station*); (etw) mit der ~ befördern *to rail* ‖ zur ~ gehen *to go to the station* **6.** ⟨com⟩ (Stück v best. Breite) *breadth, width* (*of cloth*, etc) | ⟨pap, weav⟩ *web* **7.** [in comp] → Bahn-; Eisenbahn-

Bahn- [in comp] mst *railway* **≃amtlich** a *authorized by the railway companies*; *official*; *by rail* **~anlage** f *railway*; **~n** [pl] *r. sites* [pl] → Bahnkörper **~arbeiter** m *plate-layer*; *navvy*, ⟨Am⟩ *construction-laborer* **~aufseher** m *overseer of the line* **~bau** m [pl ~ten] *railway construction* **~beamte** der ~ (ein ~er) m *railway official* **~berechnung** f ⟨a-n⟩ *flight path computation*; *tracking*; (Korrekturbestimmung) *correction reading* **≃brechend** **1.** a ⟨fig⟩ *pioneering*; *epoch-making*; ⟨bes Am⟩ *pathbreaking, trailblazing*; ~e Arbeit *pioneer work* **2.** adv ~ wirken *to pioneer, to act as a pioneer, to blaze a trail* **~brecher** m *pioneer, trail-blazer*; als ~ fungieren bei *or* in e–r S *to pioneer a th*; *to be a pioneer in a th* **~damm** m *railway embankment* **~fahrt** f *railway journey* **≃frei** a *free station* **~geleise, ~gleis** n *railway track*; *line* **~häuschen** n *line-keeper's lodge*; *signal box* **~hof** m (*railway-*) *station* (der ~ N. *the st. of N.*); ⟨Am⟩ *depot*; er holte uns am ~ ab *he met our train*; ° ich verstehe (höre) immer nur ~ *it's all Greek to me*; auf dem ~ *at the station* . . ‖ Güter≃ *goods station*, Personen≃ *passenger station* ‖ (Endstation) *terminus* | „gr ~" (feierlicher Empfang) *red carpet treatment* | ~sgaststätte [f] → -wirtschaft; ~sgebäude [n] *station*; ~shalle [f] *stationhall*; ⟨Am⟩ *concourse*; ~shotel [n] *st. hotel*; ⟨Am⟩ *depot hotel*; ~skommandant [m] ⟨mil⟩ *railway* (⟨Am⟩ *railroad*) *transport officer* (abbr R. T. O.); ~sperre [f] ⟨bes Ger⟩ *platform barrier*; ~svorsteher [m] *station-master*; ~srestaurant [n], ~swirtschaft [f] *station restaurant, refreshment-room*; ⟨Am⟩ *railroad eating house* **~körper** m ⟨rail⟩ *substructure* **~kreuzung** f *level-crossing* **≃lagernd** a (of luggage) *to be called for, to be collected at the station* **~lenksystem** n ⟨a–n⟩ *flight path guidance system* **~linie** f (*railway*) *line*; ~ nach e–r Stadt (bes London) *up-line*, ~ v e–r St. *down-line* **~meister** m *inspector of the permanent way*; ~wagen [m] *troll(e)y* **~netz** n *railway* (⟨Am⟩ *railroad*) *system* od *network* **~personal** n *railway-staff* **~polizei** f *railway-police* **~post** f *railway-post* **~räumer** m (an der Lokomotive) *cow-catcher*; *fender* **~richter** m ⟨sport⟩ *track judge* **~schutz** m *protection of the permanent way* **~schwelle** f *sleeper* **~steig** m *platform*; ⟨engl⟩ Abfahrts≃ *down p.*, Ankunfts≃ *up p.* ~ nach London *up p.*; ~karte f *platform ticket* ~kartenautomat m *slot-machine for platform tickets*; ~schaffner m ⟨engl⟩ *ticket collector*, ⟨Am⟩ *gate keeper*; ~sperre f *platform-barrier*; ~unterführung f *platform underpass* **~strecke** f *line*, → Bahnlinie **~transport** m *railway* (⟨Am⟩ *railroad*) *transportation* **~übergang** m ([un]beschrankter, schienengleicher) ([*un*]*guarded*) *level* (⟨Am⟩ *grade*) *crossing*; *barrier l. c.*, ["*c. no gates*"] **~verkehr** m *railway-traffic* **~wärter** m *line-keeper*; *flag-* od *signal-man*; *gate-keeper* | ~haus n *line-keeper's cottage*; *signalman's cabin*

b·ahnen vt [h] **1.** (ebnen) (Weg) *to make passable* **2.** (bereiten) (Weg) *to prepare, to pave*; gebahnt *beaten* (*track*) **3.** sich den Weg ~ *to elbow one's way*; ⟨übtr⟩ e–n (neuen) Weg ~ *to clear* (od *prepare*; *open up*) *a way as a pioneer* (f *for*); *to pioneer a way* (f *for*); *to break a new path*; den W. ~ *to pioneer, to act as a pioneer* (f *for*); e–r S den W. ~ *to pave the way for a th*; *to facilitate the advance of a th* | jdm e–n Weg ~ *to open up a way to* (od *for*) *a p*; *to prepare a way for a p*; *to put a p on the way, to lead a p* (z *to*) ‖ sich [dat] e–n Weg ~ *to make* (od *force*) *one's way* ‖ → anbahnen

B·ahre f ~/~n *barrow* ‖ (für Kranke) *litter, stretcher* ‖ (Toten≃) *bier* ‖ v der Wiege bis zur ~ *throughout one's life* **B·ahrgericht** n ⟨hist⟩ *bier-right* **B·ahrtuch** n *pall*

B·ahreininseln, B·ahreïninseln f pl (Inselgruppe im pers. Meerbusen) *Bahrein Islands* pl

B·ähung f ~/~en *fomentation, poulticing*

Bai f ~/~en *bay*; → Bucht

Bai n ~s/~s (auf den Palauinseln) *richly decorated house for men*

B·aikalsee m (in Sibirien) *Lake Baikal*

Baiser [bɛ'ze:] n [Fr] ~s/~s ⟨cul⟩ *meringue* Fr; Eis≃ *ice-cream m.*; Sahne≃ *m. Chantilly*

Baisse [b'ɛ:sə] f [Fr] ~/~n ⟨st exch⟩ (Ggs Hausse) *decline* (od *fall, drop*) *in quotations or prices* ‖ (plötzliche) ⟨sl⟩ *slump* ‖ auf ~ (od *à la baisse*) spekulieren *to sell short*; *to* (*act as a*) *bear, to speculate for the fall* ‖ e–n **~angriff** m *to hammer the market* **~klausel** f *slump clause* **~spekulant** m = Baissier **~spekulation** f ⟨exch⟩ *dealing for a fall*; *bearing* **~stimmung, ~tendenz** f *downward tendency*; ~ aufweisen *or* zeigen *to be bearish* **Baissier** [bɛ'sje:) m [Fr] ~s/~s ⟨st exch⟩ *bear*

Bajad·ere f ~/~n (ind. Tänzerin) *bayadere*

Baj·azzo m [It] ~s/~s *clown, buffoon*

Bajon·ett n ~s/~e ⟨mil⟩ *bayonet* ‖ das ~ aufpflanzen *to fix the b.*; ~ ab! *unfix bayonets*! ‖ mit gefälltem ~ *with the b. at the charge*; *at the point of the b.* | mit dem ~ angreifen *to charge with the bayonet* ‖ mit dem ~ forttreiben *or* töten *to bayonet* ‖ mit dem ~ nehmen *to carry at the point of the b.*; ~ pflanzt auf! (an Ort!) (*un*)*fix b.s*! **~angriff** m *bayonet charge* **~fassung** f *b. socket* **~fechten** n *bayonet drill* **~stecker** m *b. plug* **~verschluß** m *b.-catch, b. joint* od *clutch*

°**Bajuw·are** m ~n/~n [= Bayer] *Bavarian*; † ~n [pl] (germ. Völkerbund) *Bavarians* **bajuw·arisch** *a Bavarian*

B·ake f ~/~n ⟨mar⟩ *beacon*; *boom*; → Boje ‖ *landmark*; *traffic signal*; ⟨aero⟩ *beacon* ‖ ⟨surv⟩ *marking-pole*

°**B·akel** m ~s/~ *stick, cudgel*

Bakel·it n ~s/~e ⟨chem⟩ *bakelite*

B·akengeld n *beaconage*

Bakkalaure·at n ~(e)s/ ⟨univ⟩ (niedrigster akad. Grad) *baccalaureate, bachelorship*

Bakkal·aureus m [L], ~/-rei ⟨univ⟩ *Bachelor*; ~ der philos. Fakultät *Bachelor of Arts* (*B. A.*)

B·akkarat n ~s/ ⟨cards⟩ *baccarat*

B·akschisch n ~s/~e (Trinkgeld) *baksheesh*

Bakt·erie f [L] ~/~n **1.** *bacterium*, [mst pl] ~n *bacteria* [pl] ‖ ⟨Am a.⟩ *bug* ‖ durch ~n vergiftet *bacterially infected* (*food*) **2.** [in comp] ~nfilter [m] *bacterial filter* ‖ ~nforschung [f] *microbiology* ‖ ≃nhaltig [a] *containing bacteria* ‖ ~nkrieg [m] *germ* od *bacteriological warfare* ‖ ≃ntötendes Mittel [n] *bactericide* **Bakteriol·oge** m *bacteriologist* **Bakteriologie** f *bacteriology* **bakteriologisch** *a bacteriological* (*warfare*) **bakterizid** *a bactericidal* (Wirkung *action*)

†**B·aktrer(in** f) m, **b·aktrisch** a *Bactrian* †**B·aktrien** n (⟨ant⟩ Gebiet um Hindukusch) *Bactria*

B·aku n (Hafenstadt am Kaspischen Meer) *Baku, Bakoo*

Balal·aika f ~/~s ⟨mus⟩ *balalaika*

Bal·ance [ba'lɑ̃:sə] f [Fr] *balance, equilibrium, equipoise* ‖ die ~ halten (verlieren) *to keep* od *preserve* (*to lose*) *one's b.*; → Gleichgewicht ‖ → Bilanz **~akt** m *balancing performance* od *feat* **~ruder** n ⟨mar⟩ *balance-rudder*

Balancier [balɑ̃:'sje:] m ~s/~s ⟨mach⟩ *beam, working beam* (*of a steam-engine*)

balanc·ieren [balɑ̃'si:ren] vt/i [h] **1.** vt **a.** (Stange) *to balance*, (Korb) *to poise* (*on one's* *head*) **b.** ⟨com⟩ *to balance, to settle, to square* **2.** vi *to balance* (*o.s.*) (auf *on*) **Balanc·ierstange** f *balancing-pole*

B·alata f ~/ (getrockneter Baumsaft) *balata*

bald adv (zeitlich) **1.** (in kz Zeit) *soon, shortly; before long; in a short time; at an early date; presently; directly; early;* nicht so ~ *not soon* ‖ (*he will*) *not* (*do it again*) *for some time* ‖ sie w ihn ~ erwischen *it won't be long before they get hold of him* ‖ er wird es so ~ nicht wieder tun *he won't do that in a hurry* ‖ möglichst ~ *as soon as possible;* sehr ~ quickly ‖ ~ genug *soon enough;* ~ darauf, ~ nachher *soon after*(*wards*), *shortly after; presently;* → sobald **2.** (beinahe) *nearly, almost;* seit ~ 5 Wochen *for nearly 5 weeks* **3.** ~ .. ~ .. *sometimes .. sometimes .., at times .. at times, now .. now ..;* ~ so, ~ so *now one way now another* od *the other*

B·aldachin m ~(e)s/~e *baldachin, canopy, tester* ‖ ⟨arch⟩ *canopy*

B·älde f [nur in:] in ~ (= bald) **b·aldig** a *quick, speedy; early* (*answer*) ‖ auf ~es Wiedersehn! *good-bye! so long!* **b·aldigst, bal·dmöglichst** adv *as soon as possible, at one's earliest convenience*

Bald·ower m = Gauner ‖ → ausbaldowern

B·aldr, B·aldur ⟨myth⟩ *Baldr, Baldur*

B·aldrian m ~s/~e ⟨bot & pharm⟩ *valerian* **~äther** m *valerianic ether* **~tee** m *valerian tea* **~tropfen** [pl] *valerian drops* **~wurzel** f *valerian root* ‖ → Valeriansäure

Bale·aren [pl] ⟨geog⟩ *the Balearic Islands*

Balg m ~(e)s/~̈e **1.** (Haut) *skin, hide* ‖ *slough* (*of a snake*) ‖ e–m T den ~ abziehen *to flay* od *skin an animal;* ⟨übtr⟩ jdm .. *to skin a p* **2.** ⟨übtr⟩ (Hülle) *case, shell; husk; capsula, cyst* **3.** *stuffed body of a doll* **4.** *bellows* [pl] (*of a camera*) ‖ Bälge [pl] (= Blasebalg) *bellows* [pl] (*of an organ,* etc.): die B. treten *to blow the b.*

Balg m & n ~s/~̈er ⟨oft cont⟩ *bantling, brat, urchin;* ein süßer ~ ⟨sl⟩ *a peach;* liebe kl Bälger *little dears* [pl]; wilder ~ *romp*

B·algdrüse f ⟨anat⟩ *follicular gland*

B·alge f ~/~n (Kufe) *tub* ‖ (Abzugsgraben) *drain* ‖ = kl Bucht

b·algen vt [h] **1.** → abbalgen **2.** sich ~ **a.** (sich tollen) *to romp* **b.** (sich raufen) *to scramble* (um *for*); *scuffle, tussle* (mit jdm um etw *with a p for a th*), *to have a scuffle* od *tussle* **B·algen** n, **Balger·ei** f *scramble* (um *for*): *scuffle, tussle*

B·älgetreter m ~s/~ *organ-blower*

B·algfrucht f ⟨bot⟩ *follicle* **B·algeschwulst** f ⟨med⟩ *cyst* ‖ (Grützbeutel) *atheroma, sebaceous cyst*

balhornis·ieren (nach J. Balhorn, † 1603) vt [h] *to spoil* (*a text*) *by wanting to improve it;* → ballhornisieren

B·ali n (e–e Sundainsel)

Bal·illa f ~/ *the Italian Fascist youth organization* (*of boys aged 5–12*)

B·alkan m ⟨geog⟩ **1.** (~gebirge) *the Balkans* [pl] **2.** (~staaten) der ~ *the Balkans* [pl], auf dem ~ *in the Balkans* **~halbinsel** f *the Balkan Peninsula* **~krieg** m *the Balkan War* **~länder** n pl **~staaten** m pl *the Balkans*

Bälkchen n ~s/ ⟨anat⟩ *trabecula*

B·alken m ~s/~ **1.** ⟨arch⟩ **a.** *beam;* Haupt~ *ba*(*u*)*lk;* aus ~n gebaut *trabeated;* armierter ~ *armed beam;* verzahnter ~ *indented built beam* ‖ Binde~ *binder, girder* ‖ Quer~ (f Decke etc) *joist;* (an Tür, Fenster) *transom;* mit Quer~ belegen *to joist* ‖ schräger Dach~ *rafter;* Trag~ *girder* ‖ Anker~ *tie-beam;* Deck~ ⟨mar⟩ *beam;* Stich~ *dragon-piece* ‖ Brücken~ *bridge-beam;* Rödel~ ⟨mar⟩ *ribband;* Waage~ *beam;* (an Zugbrücken) *bascule* **b.** Wendungen: der ~ in dem eigenen Auge *the beam in one's own eye* ‖ .., daß sich die ~ biegen .. *with a vengeance;* lügen, .. *to come it too strong,* fluchen, .. *to make the air blue* **2.** ⟨anat⟩ (Teil des Gehirns) *corpus callosum cerebri* [L] **3.** ⟨her⟩ (horizontaler Quer~) *fesse* **4.** *earth thrown up by the plough* **~bauart** f *trabeation* **~brücke** f *girder-bridge* **~decke** f *trabeated ceiling, wooden roof* **~gerüst** n (z Stützen v Brücken) *trestle* **~kopf** m *beam-head; abutment* **~lage** f *system of binders and joists* **~rost** m (f Schiffe im Dock) *gridiron* **~träger** m *corbel* (*of a roof*) **~überschrift** f (Zeitung) *banner, screamer* **~waage** f *beam balance* **~werk** n *framework*

Balkon [bal'kɔ̃ŋ, bal'koːn] m, ~s/~e **1.** *balcony* ⟨a. *theat*⟩ (*in auditorium* & *scenery*) ‖ ~tür [f] *French window* **2.** ⟨theat⟩ (1. Rang Mitte) *dress-circle*

Ball m ~s/~̈e (Kugel) **a.** *ball;* Erd~ *ball;* → Schnee~ ‖ Hohl~ *hollow b.;* Voll~ *solid b.* ‖ z e–m ~ zus-pressen *to ball;* sich z e–m ~ formen *to ball* **b.** (Spiel~) *ball;* → Fuß~, Golf~, Hand~, Tennis~, Wasser~ ‖ ⟨crick⟩ *catch* (:*to miss one's c.*) ‖ ein gut gespielter ~ *a good b.;* ⟨ten⟩ ein falsch gegebener ~ *a fault;* ein leichter ~ ⟨sl⟩ *a sitter;* ein schneller ~ ⟨crick⟩ *a fizzer* | ~ spielen *to play with a ball; to have a game of ball* ‖ ⟨ftb⟩ den ~ vor sich hertreiben *to dribble* ‖ ⟨billiards⟩ e–n ~ m *to score a point* ‖ ⟨crick⟩ ohne daß der ~ erst den Boden berührt *full-pitch* ‖ ⟨übtr⟩ wie ein ~ herumgeworfen w *to be tossed about like a ball;* ‖ ⟨fig⟩ am ~ bleiben *to keep the ball rolling* ‖ e–a die ~̈e zuwerfen ⟨pol⟩ *to roll each other's log* ~förmig a *ball-shaped* **~hammer** m *fuller* | *der* Schwur im **~haus** n *the Oath of the Tennis Court* **~holz** n ⟨crick⟩ *bat* **~hupe** f ⟨mot⟩ *bulb-horn* **~junge** m ⟨ten⟩ *ball-boy* **~spiel** n *ball-game, game of ball* **~wechsel** m ⟨ten⟩ *rally*

Ball m ~s/~̈e *ball, dance;* auf e–m ~ *at a ball* od *dance;* → Masken~ ‖ Schul~, Klassen~ ⟨Am⟩ *promenade,* ⟨fam⟩ *prom* ‖ e–n ~ geben *to give a ball;* auf den ~ gehen *to go to the b.;* den ~ eröffnen *to open the b.* **~dame** f (*lady*) *partner* **~fähig w** *to come out* **~handschuhe** m [pl] *dress-gloves* [pl] **~haus** n *ball-room; dance-hall* **~hausplatz** m ⟨hist⟩ *Foreign Office of the late Austro-Hungarian Empire* **~kleid** n *ball-dress* **~lokal** n *ballroom, dance-hall* **~mäßig** a *fit for a ball* **~mutter** f *chaperon* **~saal** = Ballokal **~schuhe** m [pl] *dancing-shoes* (od *slippers*), *pumps* [pl]

Ball·ade f *ballad* ‖ Volks~ *popular ballad;* ⟨engl Lit⟩ *broadside ballad* ‖ Geschichts~ *historical b.* ‖ ~nartig a *ballad-like* ‖ ~ndichtung f *ballad poetry* ‖ ~nsänger m *ballad-monger*

B·allast m ~(e)s/~e *ballast;* ⟨cul⟩ *roughage* ‖ ⟨fig⟩ *drag;* ohne ~ *unballasted;* ~ ab-, auswerfen *to discharge* (od *heave*) *ballast;* ⟨aero⟩ *to weigh off;* (Schiff) v ~ befreien *to unballast;* mit ~ beladen, versehen *to ballast;* ~ einnehmen *to take in b.,* nur mit ~ beladen [a] *in b.* | ⟨übtr⟩ *encumbrance, burden* **~eisen** n ⟨mar⟩ *kentledge* **~ladung** f *dead-freight* **~material** n *inert material* **~schiff** n *ballast-lighter* **~stoffe** m pl ⟨cul⟩ *roughage; bulkage*

B·ällchen n ~s/~ *small ball*

B·allen m ~s/~ **1.** ⟨anat⟩ *ball;* Fuß~ *ball of the foot;* Daumen~ *ball of the thumb, thenar* **~entzündung** f *bunion* **2.** ⟨com⟩ **a.** *bale; package, large bundle;* Stoff~ *bale of cloth* ‖ in ~ verpacken *to bale,* aus dem ~ packen *to unbale* **b.** (Maß) (= 10 Neuries Papier) *ten reams* (*of paper*) [pl]; → Sack **3.** ⟨typ⟩ *ball* **~binder** m ⟨com⟩ *packer* **~blume** f ⟨engl hist arch⟩ *ball-flower* **~gut** n, **~waren** f [pl] ⟨com⟩ *bale-goods* [pl] **~lohn** m *package* **~presse** f *baling press; baler* **~schnur** f *pack-thread* **~weise** adv *by the bale, in bales*

b·allen vt/i [h] **1.** vt **1. a.** (Schnee) *to form into a ball, to conglobate;* geballt [a] *conglobate* **b.** die

Faust ~ *clench* od *double one's fist*; geballte F. *balled fist* **c.** ⟨übtr⟩ geballt [a] *concise, terse* (*style*) **2. sich** ~ (of snow) *to form into a ball, to ball* ‖ (of clouds) *to gather* | s–e Faust ballte sich *his fist clenched itself* **II.** vi *to play with a ball*

Baller·ina f ~/-rinen *ballerina*

°**b·allern 1.** vi [h] (of a door) *to bang*; (of a gun) *to bang*; *to pop*; *to go off with a bang* **2.** ≃n *bang*

Ball·ett a ~s/~e *ballet*; Vortänzerin im ~ *coryphée* **~korps** n *corps de ballet* **~kunst** f *dancing* **~meister** m *ballet-master*; *choreagrapher* **~röckchen, ~kleidchen** n *tutu* **~schülerin** f *ballet-girl* **~su·ite** f *ballet-suite* **~tänzer(in)** m (f) *ballet-dancer*

Balletteuse [bɑle'tøzə] f [Fr] ~/~n *ballet--dancer*

ballhornis·ieren → balhor–

b·allig a *ball-shaped* ‖ *slightly curved* | ≃werden [n] *caking*

Ball·istik f ~/ *ballistics* [pl] [sg konstr]

ball·istisch a *ballistic*

Ball·on [bɑ'lɔ̃:, bɑ'lɔŋ] m [Fr] ~s/~s **1.** ⟨aero⟩ *balloon*; Drachen≃, *kite-balloon*; Fessel≃ *captive balloon*, ⟨sl⟩ *sausage*; Frei≃ *free balloon*; Pilot≃, Registrier≃ *pilot balloon* ‖ im ~ aufsteigen *to balloon* ‖ → Luftballon | ⟨übtr⟩ Versuchs≃ *ballon d'essai* [Fr] **2.** ⟨chem⟩ (gr Korbflasche) *carboy*; *demijohn* **3.** → Gummiballon **4.** ⟨übtr⟩ °(Kopf) ⟨sl⟩ *block, pannikin, nut*; ⟨Am⟩ *bean* **~fahren** n *ballooning* **~fahrt** f *balloon ascent* **~fahrzeug** n *balloon ship* **~führer** m *balloon-pilot* **~hülle** f *balloon-envelope* **~korb** m *nacelle* [Fr] **~netz** n *balloon net* **~reifen** m ⟨cycl⟩ *balloon tyre*, ⟨bes Am⟩ *b. tire* **~schiffahrtskunde** f ⟨scient⟩ *aerostation* **~sperre** f *balloon barrage* **~stoff** m *balloon fabric*

Ballot [bɑ'lo:] m [Fr] ~s/~s ⟨com⟩ (kl Ballen) *ballot*

Ballot·age [balɔ'tɑ:ʒə] f [Fr], ~/~n ⟨engl⟩ (geheime Wahl) *ballot(ing)* **ballot·ieren** vi [h] ⟨engl⟩ *to* (*vote by*) *ballot*

B·allung f ~/~en (Massierung) *concentration* ⟨a. mil⟩ **~sgebiet** n, **~sraum** m *concentrations* (*of population*), ⟨demog⟩ *conurbation* **~szentrum** n *overcrowded region*

Balneolog·ie f (Baderkunde) *balneology*

B·alsabaum m, **B·alsaholz** n *balsa*

B·alsam m ~s/~e (Harz) *balm, balsam*, ⟨a. übtr⟩ (*f for, to*) ‖ ~ in die Wunde gießen *to pour balm into a p's wounds* **~apfel** m *balsam-apple* **~duft, ~geruch** m *balmy odour*; *fragrance* **~kraut** n ⟨bot⟩ *costmary* **~tanne** f *balsam-fir*

balsam·ieren vt [h] *to embalm*

Balsam·ierung f *embalmment, embalming*

Balsam·ine f ~/~n ⟨bot⟩ *balsam* **bals·amisch** a *balsamic, balmy*; *fragrant* ‖ ⟨übtr⟩ *soothing*

B·alte m ~n/~n ⟨Ger⟩ *the Baltic German* ‖ *inhabitant of the old Baltic provinces* **B·altikum** n *the Baltic countries* [pl] **b·altisch** a *Baltic*; ~es Meer *the Baltic* (*Sea*)

Baltimorvogel m ⟨orn⟩ *Baltimore oriole*

Balustr·ade f ~/~n ⟨arch⟩ *balustrade*

Balz f ~/~en & m ~es/~e ⟨orn⟩ *pairing--time*; *courtship*; *mating season* | ~platz [m] (bes des Birkhahns) *lek* **b·alzen 1.** vi [h] (of wild fowl) *to pair* ‖ (locken) *to display*; *to indulge in curious love-songs and antics* **2.** ≃ n *display*

B·alzhandlung f e–e ~ ausführen *to display*

B·ambus m -busses/-busse ⟨bot⟩ *bamboo* **~bär** m *panda*; *bear cat* **~rohr** n *bamboo* ‖ *bamboo-cane* **~vorhang** m ⟨Asia pol⟩ *B. Curtain*

°**Bammel** m e–n mächtigen ~ h ⟨sl⟩ *to be in a blue funk*; e–n ~ bek *to get the wind up* °**b·ammeln** vi [h] *to dangle*; *swing*; *hang* (*down*)

Bams m → Pams

Ban m ~s/~e (in Südslawien) *chief of a* Banschaft ‖ Ban·at [n] ⟨†ungar.⟩ → Banschaft

ban·al a *banal, hackneyed, commonplace, trite*

Banalit·ät f ~/~en *banality, triteness*; *trite* od *commonplace saying*; *triviality*

Ban·ane f ~/~n ⟨bot⟩ *banana* ‖ überbackene ~ ⟨cul⟩ *b. fritters* pl | ~nfaser [f] → Manilahanf; ~nstecker [m] ⟨el⟩ *split* [pp] od *b. plug*

Ban·ause m ~n/~n *philistine, narrow-minded person*; *low-brow* ‖ ~ntum [n] *philistinism* **ban·ausisch** a *philistine, narrow-minded*; *low-brow*

Band m ~(e)s/¨~e (Buch) *volume* (abbr vol.); ein Roman in 3 Bänden *a three-volume novel*; ~nummer *number of the volume* (*of a series*) ‖ dicker ~ *tome* ‖ Noten≃ *book of music* | ⟨fig⟩ das spricht Bände *that speaks volumes*; darüber ließen sich Bände reden *that would fill volumes* ≃**weise** adv *in* (*single*)*volumes*

Band [bænd] f ~/~s ⟨mus⟩ (Kapelle) *band*

Band n **I.** ~es/¨~er **A. 1. a.** *band* (*of a hat*, etc.); *string, streamer* (*of a bonnet*) ‖ (Seiden≃) *ribbon, riband*; Ordens≃ *ribbon, order band*; ⟨sport⟩ das Blaue ~ *the Blue Riband*; mit Bändern versehen [a] *ribboned* ‖ (ec) goldgesticktes ~ auf geistl. Gewand *orphrey* ‖ fliegendes ~ (= Wimpel) *streamer* ‖ Farb≃ *ribbon* ‖ → Bindfaden **b.** festes schmales Baumwoll≃, Seiden≃ *ferret*; Zwirn≃ *tape*; mit e–m ~ versehen *to tape* ‖ Schnür≃ *lace* ‖ Stirn≃, Haar≃ *fillet*; Gurt≃ *webbing* ‖ Gummi≃ *elastic band* ‖ (Leder≃) *strap*; Bruch≃ *truss* ‖ → Arm≃; Hals≃ **c.** ⟨tech⟩ (Holz≃, Eisen≃) *band, hoop* ‖ laufendes, endloses ~ *endless belt*; *conveyer, conveyor, band* (od *belt*)-*conveyer*; Förder≃ *conveyer-belt*; System am laufenden ~ *conveyer--system* ‖ Führungs≃ *driving-band* **d.** ⟨phys⟩ farbiges ~ *spectrum* [L] **e.** ⟨rec⟩ (einzelnes) *reel* **2.** ⟨anat⟩ *band*; (Sehne) *cord, ligament*; Zungen≃ *string of the tongue*; Stimmbänder [pl] *vocal cords* [pl] **B. 1.** ⟨arch⟩ *band*; *bond*; *tie*; (aus Stein, Holz) *fascia* [L] ‖ (Stütz≃, Trag≃) *brace* **2.** ⟨met⟩ (Beschlag) (Gelenk≃) *hinge* **3.** (gangbare Felskante) *ledge* **4.** [in comp] → Band- **II.** ~es/~e ⟨übtr⟩ **1.** [oft pl] *bond*, Freundschafts≃ *bond of friendship*; die ~e des Blutes *the ties of blood*; die ~e der Freundschaft *the ties of friendship*; ~ der Ehe *conjugal ties* [pl] ‖ *link* (*of confidence*) | → Rand **2.** [nur pl] (= Fesseln) *bonds, shackles, fetters, trammels* [pl]; in ~en u Ketten *in chains* **~achat** m ⟨min⟩ *onyx* ≃**ähnlich** a *ribbonlike* ‖ ⟨anat⟩ *ligamentous* **~alge** f ⟨bot⟩ *desmid*; Gattung der ~n *Desmidiaceae* [L pl] ≃**artig** a = bandähnlich ≃**aufnahme** ⟨wir⟩ *tape recording*; ~ löschen *to wipe clean a t. r.* | ~ dienst [m] ⟨rad⟩ *transcription service* ‖ ~gerät [n] *magnetic* od *tape recorder* **~balken** m ⟨arch⟩ *brace* | selbständige **~berichtigung** f ⟨comp⟩ *automatic error* (*detection and*) *correction in the magnetic tape system* **~bibliothek** f ⟨wir⟩ *tape library* **~breite** f ⟨commun, rec⟩ *bandwidth* **~bremse** f *band-brake* **~drucker** m (S) ⟨comp⟩ *tape to print* **~einheit** f ⟨rec, comp⟩ (*magnetic*) *tape deck* od *unit* **~einstellung** f ⟨wir⟩ *band selection* **~eisen** n ⟨tech⟩ *hoop-iron* ‖ *steal strapping* (*for inforcing boxes, etc*) **~feder** f *flat spring* **~förderer** m *belt conveyor* **~förderung** f ⟨tech⟩ *belt-conveyance* **~gesims** n ⟨arch⟩ *head band* **~gras** n ⟨bot⟩ *ribbon-grass* **~haken** m *hasp* **~keramik** f *curvilinearly decorated ceramics* [pl] **~länge** f ⟨rec⟩ *recording time*; ⟨comp⟩ *reel* (0,3048 m ‖ 365,76 m = *120 reels*, 731,52 m = *2400 reels*) **~leitung** f ⟨typ⟩ *travelling bands* (od *tapes*) [pl] **~macher** m *ribbon-manufacturer, lacemaker* **~maß** n *tape-measure* **~nudeln** f [pl] *ribbon macaroni* **~papier** n *tape paper* **~rolle** f ⟨typ⟩ *tape-pulley* ‖ ⟨arts⟩ (Spruchband) *streamer* **~säge** f *band-saw* **~scheibenvorfall** m ⟨path⟩ *slipped disc* **~schleife** f farbige ~ *favour* **~speicher** m ⟨wir, telv, etc⟩ *tape store* **~spieler** m (Gerät) *sound reproducer* **~spitzen** f [pl] *pointlace* **~stahl** m *strip (-steel)* **~- u Schallplattenmusik** f *recorded music* **~walzen** f [pl] ⟨typ⟩ *tape-rollers* [pl] **~waren** f [pl] *ribbons* [pl] **~weber** m *ribbon--weaver* **~wiedergabe** f *transcription* od *recorded broadcast* **~wurm** m ⟨zoo⟩ *tapeworm*; *taenia* [L]; → Finne 2. c.; hast du e–n ~ (, daß du so viel ißt)? *you've got a tapeworm*! **~zähler** m ⟨rec⟩ *(indexing) place finder* **~zug(schreib)feder** f *oblique nib* (Warenmarke *relief nib*)

Band·age [ban'dɑːʒə] f ~/~n *band(age)* **bandagieren** [bandɑ'ʒiːrən] **1.** vt [h] *to bandage* **2.** ≗ n *bandaging* **Bandag·ist** [bandɑ'ʒist] m ~en/~en *bandagist* ‖ *truss-maker*

B·andainseln f pl (Molukken-Inselgruppe)

B·ändchen n ~s/~ (Stoff≗) *small narrow ribbon*; *lace*; *tape* **~stickerei** f *point lace*

B·ändchen n ~s/~ (kl Buch) *small volume*

B·ande f ~/~n (Rand) *border*; *edge*; *boards* [pl] ‖ (am Billard) *resilient sides* (od *cushions*) [pl]; ~nstoß m *bricole* ‖ *side* (*of a ship*)

B·ande f ~/~n *(Schar) *band*, *company*; e–e ~ bilden *to gang up*; ⟨hum⟩ die ganze ~ *the whole crowd* (*of children*) | ⟨cont⟩ *clique*, *crew*, *crowd*, *posse*, *set*; *pack*; Räuber≗ *band of robbers*; Verbrecher≗ *gang of criminals* ‖ °die ganze ~ *the whole lot*, ⟨sl⟩ *the whole caboodle*; °diese ~! eine tolle ~! (*what*) *an awful crowd*!

Bandeau [bɑ̃ː'doː] n [Fr] ~s/~s (Stirnband) *bandeau*, *fillet*

B·ändel n ~s/~ jdn am ~ h *to have a p under one's control*, *to have a hold on a p*; *she has two men on the string*

Bandel·ier n ~(e)s/~e ⟨mil⟩ *bandoleer*, *–lier*; *shoulder-belt*; ⟨hist⟩ *belt*

Banden-~diebstahl [m] *gang-robbery*; ~führer [m] *leader of a gang*; ≗gefährdet [a] *guerilla-* od *partisan-infested* (*area*); ~spektrum [n] *band spectrum*

B·ander m ⟨zoo⟩ → Rhesusaffe

b·ändereich a *voluminous*

B·änderspektrum n *band spectrum*

Bander·illa [bande'riljɑ] f [Span] ~/~s (Speer) *banderilla*

Bander·ole f ~/~n ⟨Ger⟩ *revenue-stamp* | ⟨arts⟩ (Spruchband) *banderole*

-bändig a [in comp] *volumed*, drei~ *three-volumed* (*novel*)

b·ändigen vt [h] **1.** (Löwen) *to tame* ‖ Pferd etc *to break* (*in*) ‖ das Feuer war bis 12 Uhr gebändigt *the fire was under control by 12 o'clock* **2.** ⟨übtr⟩ (Leidenschaft) *to curb*, *to master*, *to subdue*, *to restrain* | (jdn) *to check*, *restrain*; *to keep in check* od *control* ‖ nicht z ~ s *to run wild* ‖ **sich** ~ *to hold o.s. in hand*; *to restrain o.s.* **B·ändiger** m ~s/~ *tamer* **B·ändigung** f ~/~en *taming*; *breaking* ‖ ⟨übtr⟩ *checking*, *control*, *restraint*; *subduing*

B·andikut m ~s/~s ⟨zoo⟩ **1.** (Ratte) *bandicoot rat* **2.** (Beuteldachs) *rabbit bandicoot*

Band·it m ~en/~en *bandit*, [pl *bandits*, *banditti*]; *vagabond*; *outlaw*; *desperado*; *gangster*; ⟨Am⟩ *bad man* **~entum**, **~enwesen** n *banditry*

Band·ola f ~/~s ⟨mus⟩ (Mandoline) *bandola*

Band·onion n ~s/~s ⟨mus⟩ *bandonion*

B·ändsel n ~s/~ ⟨mar⟩ *seizing* | ~leine [f] *seizing line*

·bang a → bange **1.** ≗**büx(e)**, ≗**buxe** f ~/–xen → Bangebüchse

b·ange a **1.** [pred] ~, *bang **a.** (ängstlich) *afraid*, *alarmed*; → ängstlich, furchtsam ‖ nur nicht ~! *don't be alarmed*!; *never fear*! ‖ ich bin ~, mir ist ~ vor *I am afraid* od *in fear*, ⟨fam⟩ *frightened of* (*a p*); . . ~ davor z tun *I am afraid of doing* ‖ mir wird ~, angst u ~ *I'm getting alarmed*, *I'm filled with misgivings*; mir wird immer bänger *my fears increase more and more* ‖ jdn ~ m *to alarm*, *intimidate*, *frighten a p*; ⟨sl⟩ *to put the wind up a p*, *to give a p the jitters*; *to make a p sit up* ‖ ~ m gilt nicht! *you won't frighten me*! ⟨fam⟩ *are we downhearted*?; ⟨Am⟩ *I should worry*! ‖ °du bist ja gar nicht ~e! *you would have the nerve* (*to do it*)! **b.** (besorgt) *anxious*, *uneasy* (um *about*); *concerned* (um *for*); ~ s um *to fear* (*a p*; *a p's health*) **2.** [attr] *anxious* (*looks*); ~ Ahnung *misgiving*; ~ Stunden *hours full of anxiety*

B·ange f *fear*; *alarm* ‖ *anxiety* ‖ nur k–e ~! h Sie k–e ~! *don't be afraid*! *no fear*! *never fear*

°**B·angebüchse** f ⟨sl⟩ *funk*, *jitterbug* **B·angemachen** n *alarming*; *intimidation* ‖ ⟨pol⟩ *bluff*; → gelten **B·angemacher** m *alarmist*; *panicmonger* ‖ *bluffer*

b·angen **I.** vi/refl [h] **1.** vi **a.** **mir** bangt *I am afraid* (vor *of*), es bangt mir nicht vor ihm *I don't fear him* **b.** ich bange **um** *I am anxious about*, *I fear* (od *tremble*) *for* (*a p*, *a p's health*); man bangt um ihre Sicherheit *grave fears are entertained for their safety* **c.** †~ **nach** *to long* (od *yearn*) *for* **2. sich** ~ *to be anxious*, etc. → 1. b. **II.** ≗ n *anxiety* → hangen

B·angigkeit f ~/~en = Bange **b·änglich** a *somewhat alarmed*; *anxious*; → ängstlich

B·angkok n (Hauptstadt v Thailand [†Siam])

B·angsche Kr·ankheit f (Rinderabort) *epizootic* od *infectious abortion*

Bani·ane f ~/~n ⟨bot⟩ *banian*, *banyan*(*-tree*)

B·anjo n ~s/~s ⟨mus⟩ *banjo*

B·ank[1] f ~/≗e **A. 1.** (Sitzbank) *bench*; *seat*; Stein≗ *stone bench*, Holz≗ *wooden b.* | (Schul≗) *form*; auf der ersten ~ *in the first row* ‖ → Fenster≗, Fuß≗ **2.** ⟨jur⟩ Gerichts≗, Richter≗ *bench* ‖ Anklage≗ *dock* **3.** ⟨mar⟩ (Ruder≗ in Galeeren) *bank*, **4.** ⟨com⟩ Markt≗, Verkaufs≗ *stall*, *stand*; *booth* ‖ Schlacht≗ *shambles* [pl] **5.** (Werk≗) *bench*; Hobel≗ *carpenter's b.*; Dreh≗ *lathe* | optische ~ *optical bench* (od *bank*) **6.** Wendungen: durch die ~ *throughout*; *all round*, *indiscriminately*, *without distinction*; ⟨sl⟩ *the whole blooming lot* → durchweg ‖ auf die lange ~ schieben *to put* (*a th*) *on the shelf*, *to shelve* (*a th*), auf die l. ~ geschoben s *to be on the shelf* ‖ vor leeren Bänken reden *to speak to empty benches* **B. 1.** (Erd≗) *bank*, Austern≗ *oyster b.* ‖ Sand≗ *sand-bank*, *shoal* ‖ ⟨mar geog⟩ *bank* (*Great Bahama B.*) ⟨mil⟩ *mound of earth serving as parapet* ‖ ⟨fort⟩ Geschütz≗ *barbette* ‖ Wolken≗ *bank of clouds* **2.** ⟨geol⟩ *layer*, *bed* ‖ ⟨min⟩ *measure* **~eisen** n (f Holz) *crampiron*; (an der Hobelbank) *holdfast* **~haken** m *holdfast* **~hammer** m *bench-hammer* **~lehne** f *back of a seat* **~reihe** f *bench*

B·ank[2] f ~/~en **1.** ⟨com⟩ *bank*(*ing*)*-house* | ~ deutscher Länder, Bundes≗ ⟨Ger⟩ *Federal Central Bank* Aktien≗ *joint-stock b.*; Depositen≗ *deposit-b.*; Filial≗ *branch-b.*; Noten≗ *b. of issue*; Spar≗ *savings-b.*; → Giro≗ | auf der ~ *at the b.* ‖ Zahlungsauftrag an die ~ *banker's order* ‖ Geld auf der ~ (stehen) h *to have money in* od *at the b.* ‖ Geld in der ~ deponieren *to deposit money in* (od *at*) *the b.*; *to bank money* ‖ e–n Auftrag an die ~ geben, *or* die ~ anweisen *to give a banker's order* (*to pay* . .) ‖ (Betrag) durch die ~ überweisen *to pay* (od *remit*) *through the bank*; *to pay by bank* od *by banker's order*; **2.** (Summe bei Spielen) (*gambling-*)*bank* ‖ die ~ halten (*or* auflegen, machen) *to keep the b.* ‖ ~ setzen ⟨cards⟩ *to go* (*the*) *b.* ‖ die ~ sprengen *to break the b.* **3.** [in comp] *bank*(*ing*) **~akte** f ⟨engl⟩ *Bank Charter Act* (*1844*) **~aktie** f *bank--share* **~akzept** n *b.-acceptance* **~angestellte**: der ~ (ein ~r) m ~n/~n *b.-clerk* **~ausweis** m *b. returns* [pl]; (*weekly*) *statement* **~beamte**: der ~ (ein ~r) m ~n/~n *bank-clerk* od *official* †**~bruch** m *bankruptcy* **~buch** n *bankbook* **~direktor** m *bank-manager* **~diskont** m *bank-*

-*rate* **~fach** n [abstr] *banking(-line)* || [konkr] *safe* **≗fähig** a *bankable, negotiable* **~feiertag** m ⟨engl⟩ *Bank Holiday*; ⟨Ger⟩ *Saturday before principal holidays* **~filiale** f *branch(-bank)* **~gebäude** n *bank(-premises)* **~geheimnis** n *banker's discretion* **~geschäft** n [konkr] *bank(ing-house)* | ~e [pl] [abstr] *banking* sg **~guthaben** n *bank-balance* **~halter** m (beim Spielen) *banker, croupier* **~haus** n *bank, bankinghouse* **~kapital** n *bank-capital* **~konto** n *bank(ing)- account*; ~buch n *pass-book* **~krach** m *collapse of a bank* **~kreise** m [pl] die ~ *the banking interest* **~kunde** m *depositor* **≗mäßig** a *bankable* (Sicherheit) **~nebenstelle** f *sub-office of a bank* **~note** f *bank-note*; ⟨Am⟩ *(bank-)bill*; ~nfälscher [m] *slusher*; ~ntasche [f] *note-case* **~papier** n *bank-paper* **~postpapier** n *banks* [pl] **~sparbuch** m *savings bank pass book* **~überweisung** f *(bank-)transfer* **~verein** m *Bankers' Association* **~verkehr** m *banking* **~wechsel** m *bankbill* **~welt** f *the banking world* **~wesen** n *banking*; *the banks*

B·anka n (Sundainsel)

B·änkel- ~kind n = Bankert **~lied** n *ballad* **~sänger** *ballad-monger*; ⟨übtr⟩ *rhymester*

b·anken vi *to land on a bank* || ⟨aero⟩ *to bank*

B·ankert m ~s/~e *illegitimate child, bastard*

Bank·ett n ~s/~e *banquet*; auf, bei dem ~ *at the b.* || Teilnehmer an e–m ~ *banqueter* **~saal** m *banqueting-hall* od *room*

Bank·ett n ~s/~e *raised verge* od *(foot) way*; *(highway) shoulder*; *haunch*; ⟨mot⟩ (befahrbar) *hard shoulder*, (nicht befahrbar) *verge* || ⟨rail⟩ *side space (from outer rail on)* || ⟨arch⟩ *footing (of foundation)* || ⟨mil⟩ (Auftritt) *banquette*

bankett·ieren 1. vi [h] *to banquet* **2.** ≗ n *banqueting*

Bankier [baŋ'kje:] m ~s/~s *banker*; beim ~ *at the banker's, with one's banker* || (beim Spiel) *banker* || ⟨übtr⟩ *financier*

banko ['baŋko] a *banco*; Mark ~ *banco mark, mark banco*

Bankr·ott m ~s/~e ⟨com⟩ *bankruptcy, insolvency, failure*; betrügerischer (einfacher) ~ *fraudulent (simple) bankruptcy* || den ~ anmelden, ansagen *to file* od *present a petition in bankruptcy* || ~ m *to become* od *go bankrupt*; *to fail*; ⟨übtr⟩ *to be ruined* | ⟨übtr⟩ *bankruptcy*; *failure, wreck, ruin*; geistiger (politischer) ~ *intellectual (political) bankruptcy* **bankr·ott** a *bankrupt, insolvent* || ~ w *to become* od *go bankrupt* || (Bank) ~ m ⟨Am sl⟩ *to bust*; jdn ~ m *to bankrupt, to break a p*; ⟨übtr⟩ *to ruin a p* | ⟨übtr⟩ (abgebrannt) *stony(-broke)* || *broken (man)*; *bankrupt*; moralisch ~ *morally bankrupt* **Bankrotteur** [baŋkrɔ'tør] m ~s/~e = *bankrupt*

B·anksie f ~/~n ⟨bot⟩ *banksia*

B·ankul m ~s/ ⟨bot⟩ *candleberry-tree*

B·ann m ~(e)s/ **A. 1. a.** ⟨hist⟩ (Gerichtsbarkeit) *jurisdiction (of a king*, etc.) | (Befehl) *ban* || (Verbot) *interdict* **b.** ⟨übtr rel⟩ *taboo* **2.** (Strafe) **a.** ⟨hist⟩ *ban, outlawry, proscription* || ⟨ec⟩ *ban, excommunication* **b.** ⟨übtr⟩ *ban* (über jdn *on a p*); *banishment* || → Acht **c.** Wendungen: im ~ s *to be under the ban* || jdn in den ~ tun, jdn mit dem ~ belegen *to lay* (od *put*) *a p under a ban*; *to ban, to banish, to outlaw a p*; ⟨ec⟩ *to excommunicate a p*; ⟨com⟩ *to boycott*; (Buch) mit dem ~ belegen *to ban* **3.** ⟨fig⟩ (Zauber) *charm, spell (of a th)* || (Gewalt) *domination, power, sway*; *influence (of a p)* | im ~e e–r S *under the spell of a th, in obedience to a th*; ganz im ~e v *hypnotized by*; im ~e der Instinkte *under the sway of instincts*; im ~e e–r Idee s *to be in the grip of an idea* || im ~e jds *under the sway of a p* | jdn im ~e h *to have a p in tow* || jdn im ~e halten *to hold a p spell-bound* || jdn in s–n ~ schlagen *to cast a spell* od *glamo(u)r over a p*; . . in den ~ ziehen *to draw a p into the magic circle*; jdn in s–n ~ zwingen *to get a hold on a p*; (Zuhörer) *to enthral(l), to captivate (the audience)* || unter den ~ jds geraten *to fall unter a p's sway* **B. 1.** ⟨hist⟩ (Gebiet) *territory under a jurisdiction* **2.** *precinct (of an area*, etc.) **C. 1.** ⟨hist⟩ (Heerbann) *ban*; *body of vassals* (: *to convoke the ban*) **2.** ⟨Ger hist⟩ *unit of Hitler Youth* **~bruch** m *breach of the ban* **~bulle** f ⟨ec⟩ *bull of excommunication* **~fluch** m *anathema, ban, curse* **~forst** m *hunting district under a ban* **~meile** f **1.** ⟨hist⟩ *precinct of a jurisdiction*; *space within a mile's distance round a town*; *restricted area* **2.** ⟨übtr⟩ *precinct*; *space within the boundaries of a government building, in which meetings*, etc. *are forbidden* **~recht** n [pl] *economic privileges of the feudal lord* [pl] **~spruch** m *exorcism*; ⟨ec⟩ *excommunication* **~strahl** m *anathema*; *fulmination* (gegen *against*); den ~ schleudern gegen *to excommunicate a p, to fulminate against a p* **~ware** f *contraband* **~wart** m Sw = Flur-, Waldhüter

b·annen vt [h] **A. 1.** (vertreiben) (Geister etc) *to lay* od *exorcize*; *to conjure* od *charm away* **2.** (jdn) *to ban, banish, exile* || ⟨ec⟩ *to excommunicate* **3.** ⟨übtr⟩ (Furcht, Not, Sorge etc) *to banish*; *to drive away*; *to lift* **B.** (festhalten) **1.** (jdn) *to bind by a spell, to charm, to enchant, to spell*; festgebannt *spell-bound* || wie gebannt s *to be spell-bound* || *to captivate, to enthral(l), to fascinate*; *to subdue* (: *subdued by* . .); *to get a hold on (a p)* **2.** (das Glück) *to get hold of*; *to master* **3.** (Rede, Lied) auf die Schallplatte ~ *to record*

B·anner n ~s/~ ⟨mil⟩ *banner*; *flag, standard*; ⟨hist⟩ *gonfalon* || ein ~ entrollen *to unfurl a banner*; ⟨mst fig⟩ jds ~ folgen *to follow* (od *join*) *the banner of a p, to march under the standard of a p* | ⟨übtr⟩ *banner, sign* **~herr** m *banneret* **~träger** m *standard-bearer*

°**b·annig 1.** a [nordd] ⟨fam⟩ *beastly, confounded*; *deuced*; ich habe ~e Kopfschmerzen ⟨sl⟩ *I've got a beast of a headache* **2.** adv ⟨fam⟩ *beastly*; *confoundedly (cold)*; *wildly*

B·anschaft f (in Südslawien) *administrative district*

B·anse f ~/~n [nd] *bay, recess (for corn)* || *storeroom (for coal)* **b·ansen** vt [h] (Garben) *to pile up*

B·antam n ~s/~s ⟨zoo⟩ (Zwerghuhn) *bantam* **~gewicht** n ⟨box⟩ *bantam-weight* (nicht über 108 Pfd, engl 118 lbs)

B·anteng m ~s/~s ⟨zoo⟩ *banteng species of wild ox*

B·antu [pl] (Negerstämme in Afrika) die ~ *the Bantu* **~sprachen** f [pl] *the Bantu*

Bany·an m ~s/~e ⟨bot⟩ = Baniane

B·anzai (Japanisch) intj *banzai, hurrah*; ~ rufen *to shout banzai*; [a. als s; pl *banzais*]

B·aobab m ~s/~s ⟨bot⟩ = Affenbrotbaum

Bapt·ist m ~en/~en ⟨ec⟩ **1.** → Täufer **2.** ⟨ec⟩ *Baptist*, die ~en *the Baptists* (ggr 1633) || ~engemeinde f *the Baptist Church*; ~enkapelle, ~enkirche f *Baptist chapel* **Baptist·erium** n *baptist(e)ry*

Bar m ~s/~e ⟨Ger Lit⟩ *song of several stanzas composed according to the rules of tabulature*

Bar f ~/~s *bar*; *nightclub*; ⟨golf⟩ die ~ im Klubhaus ⟨sl⟩ *the nineteenth hole* | ~dame, °~fliege [f] *barmaid*; ~hocker [m] *bar-stool*; ~inhaber [m] *barkeeper, bartender*; ~mixer [m] *dispense barman*, ⟨Am⟩ *bartender*; ~theke [f] *canteen*; ~wagen [m] ⟨rail⟩ *buffet* od *cafeteria car*

Bar n ~s/~ ⟨meteor & phys⟩ (Einheit des Drucks) *bar*

bar I. a **1.** (nackt) nur in Zus-setzungen → ~fuß etc **2.** e–r S ~ s *to be destitute* (od *devoid*) *of a th, to be lacking in a th*; *to be without a th*; jedes Schamgefühls ~ (*or* ~ jedes Sch.) *barefaced* **3.** ⟨übtr⟩ (rein) *pure, downright, sheer,* *arrant* (*nonsense*) **4.** ⟨com⟩ **a.** ~e 50 Mark, 50 M. ~ *50 marks* (*in*) *cash, 50 m. down*; ~es Geld *cash*; *ready money*; ~e Auslage *actual outlay* ‖ ⟨übtr⟩ etw f. ~e Münze nehmen *to take a th as* (od *for*) *gospel* **b.** gegen ~ *cash down*; gegen ~ verkaufen *to sell for cash*; sie verkaufen nur gegen ~ *their terms are cash only* ‖ in ~ (*in*) *cash*; in ~ bezahlen *to pay cash* (*down*) **II.** adv ~ bezahlen, ~ auf den Tisch legen *to pay cash* (*down*); ⟨sl⟩ *to pay on the nail*; ~ verkaufen *to sell for cash* ≚**frost** → d.

B·ar- [in comp] *cash* .. **~auslagen** f [pl] *cash* (od *out-of-pocket*) *expenses* [pl] od *outlay* **~bestand** m *cash* (od *balance*) *in* od *on hand*; *bullion reserve* **~betrag** m *amount in ready money* **~bezahlung** f → Barzahlung **~deckung** f *cover in ready money* **~geld** n *cash, ready money* ‖ ~ lacht *money talks* ≚**geldlos** a *cashless* (*by cheque or transfer*) **~geschäft** n *dealing for cash* od *money*; *cash business, spot cash* **~kauf** m *cash purchase* **~leistung** f ⟨ins⟩ *cash payment* **~mittel** n [pl] *ready money*; *financial resources* [pl] **~schaft** f *cash, ready money*; m–e ~ beträgt 10 Mark *I have ten marks in cash* **~scheck** m *cash-cheque* **~verkauf** m *cash-sale* **~verlust** m *clear* (od *net*) *loss* **~wert** m *cash-value* ≚**zahlend** a *cash-paying* **~zahlung** f *cash payment* ‖ bei ~ 3% Rabatt *3% discount for cash*; gegen ~ *cash down*; nur gegen ~ *cash terms only* ‖ ⟨Am⟩ *cash and carry* ‖ e–e ~ v £ 20 verlangen *to want £ 20 cash* | ~srabatt [m] *cash discount*

Bär m ~en/~en **A. 1.** ⟨zoo⟩ **a.** (*he-*)*bear*; ~in f *she-bear* ‖ der braune ~ *the brown bear*; ⟨ent⟩ der Braune ~ *tiger-moth*; Grau≚ *grizzly bear*; der schwarze ~ → Baribal; Höhlen≚ *cave bear*; → Eis≚, Wasch≚ **b.** ⟨fig⟩ wie ein Bär schlafen *to sleep like a top* od *log*, ⟨sl⟩ *to hog it* ‖ ehe man den ~en hat, soll man sein Fell nicht verkaufen *don't count your chickens before they are hatched* ‖ e–n ~en anbinden *to contract debts* ‖ jdm e–n ~en aufbinden *to hoax a p, to impose upon a p*; ich laß mir k–n ~en aufbinden *that's a long-tailed bear* **2.** (a. Teddy ≚) (Spielzeug) *teddy bear* **3.** ⟨fig⟩ (P) *bear*; er ist ein rechter ~ *he is a regular lout* ‖ → Bären- **B.** ⟨astr⟩ der Große ~ *the Great Bear, Charles's Wain*; ⟨Am⟩ *the* (*Great*) *Dipper*; der Kleine ~ *the Little Bear* **C.** ⟨tech⟩ (a. Ramm≚) *monkey, tup*; *ram*(*mer*); *drop-hammer* **D.** [in comp] → Bär–, Bären–

B·är-≚**beißig** a *gruff, surly*; *morose* **~beißigkeit** f *moroseness, surliness*

Bar·acke f ~/~n ⟨mil⟩ *barrack*; *hut*; (Truppen) in ~n unterbringen *to barrack, to hut*; in ~n liegen *to hut* | ⟨übtr⟩ *barrack, rambling house*; *hut* | ~nbau [m] ⟨bes mil⟩ *hutting* ~nkomplex [m] ⟨arch⟩ ⟨bes Am⟩ *compound*; ~nlager [n] *hutments, hut-camp, hutted camp* ~nmaterial [n] ⟨bes mil⟩ *hutting*

Baras·inga m ~s/~s ⟨zoo⟩ (ind. Zackenhirsch) *barasingha*

Baratter·ie f ⟨mar⟩ *barratry* **Bar·atthandel** m = Tauschhandel

Barb·ados, Barb·adoes n (östlichste der Kleinen Antillen) *Barbadoes*

Barbak·ane m ~/~n ⟨fort⟩ *barbican*

Barb·ar m ~en/~en *barbarian* ‖ ~entum n *barbarism*

B·arbara- ~befehlsmeldung [f] *estimated compound meteorological message* ‖ ~kraut [n] ⟨bot⟩ *winter-cress* ‖ ~meldung [f] *meteorological report*

Barbar·ei f ~/~en *barbarism* (: *state of b.*); *heathenism* ‖ (Grausamkeit) *barbarity, cruelty, savagery* **barb·arisch 1.** a *barbarous* (*ignorance, cruelty*); *barbaric* (*taste, splendour, costume*); *barbarian* (*tribe, king*) ‖ *rude, uncivilized*; *coarse*; *bad* (*Latin*) ‖ *cruel, savage* **2.** adv *barbarously*; *cruelly, exceedingly, extremely*; ⟨sl⟩ *beastly, confoundedly, deucedly* (*cold*) **Barbar·ismus** m (Sprachwidrigkeit) *barbarism*

Barbar·ossa m ~s/~s ⟨fig hum⟩ *Rufus, Ginge, Sandy*

B·arbe f ~/~n ⟨ich⟩ *barbel*; gr ind. ~ *mahseer*; See≚ (*grey*) *mullet*

Barb·ette f ~/~n ⟨mil⟩ (Geschützbank) *barbette*

Barb·ier m ~s/~e *barber*; *hairdresser*; *coiffeur*; beim ~ *at the barber's* od *hairdresser's*

Barbier- [in comp] *barber's tonsorial* **~becken** n *shaving bowl* **~gehilfe** m *barber's assistant* **~innung** f *the Barber's Company* **~laden** m *barber's* (od *hairdresser's*) *shop*, ⟨Am⟩ *barber-shop* **~lehrling** m *barber's apprentice* **~salon** m = Barbierladen; ⟨Am⟩ *tonsorial parlor* **~schild** m *barber's sign*; ⟨engl⟩ *barber's pole* **~stube** f *barber's shop*

barb·ieren vt [h] [mst: rasieren] *to shave*; sich ~ l *to get shaved* | ⟨fig⟩ jdn über den Löffel ~ *to overreach, to cheat a p*

Barcel·ona n [–ts–] ⟨Span⟩ [–θ–] (Stadt)

b·archen a *fustian* **B·archent** m ~s/~e *fustian*; geköperter ~ *dimity*

°**bard·auz** intj ~! *bang*!, *crash*!, *plump*!, *kerbang*!

B·arde m ~n/~n *bard*; ~ndichtung f *bardic poetry*; ~ngesang m *bardic song* | ⟨übtr⟩ *epic poet*

B·arde f ~/~n *slice of bacon as a cover for roast poultry*

Bard·iet, Bard·it n ~s/~e ⟨Ger Lit⟩ *bardic song*

B·ären- [in comp] *bear, bear's* **~beißer** m = Bullenbeißer **~dill** f ⟨bot⟩ = Bärwurzel **~fell** n *bearskin* **~fett** n *bear's grease* **~führer** m *bear-leader* **~fuß** m (⟨hist⟩ Schuhmode) *bear-paw* **~haut** f *bearskin* ‖ auf der ~ liegen *to waste one's time in idleness*; *to loaf about*; *to dawdle*, **~häuter** m *lazy-bones* [pl] [sg konstr], *sluggard* **~hetze** f *bear-baiting* **~hunger** m ⟨fig⟩ *insatiable* od *enormous hunger*; ich habe e–n ~ *I'm as hungry as a hunter* **~jagd** f *bear-hunting* **~klau** f ~/ & m ~s/ ⟨bot⟩ **1.** *acanthus, bear's breech, brank-ursine* **2.** *cow-parsnip* **~lauch** m ⟨bot⟩ *ramson* **~marder** m = Binturong °≚**mäßig** a ⟨fig⟩ *enormous, incredible* **~mütze** f *bearskin cap*; → Pelzmütze **~raupe** f ⟨ent⟩ *woolly bear*, → Bärenspinner **~ruhe** f ⟨fig⟩ *perfect coolness* **~spinner** m ⟨ent⟩ *tiger-moth* **~tanz** m *bear-dance* **~tatze** f *bear's paw* **~traube** f ⟨bot⟩ *bearberry* **~wurz(el)** f → Bärwurz(el) **~zwinger** m *bear-garden, bear-pit*

Bar·ett n ~(e)s/~e ⟨univ⟩ *barret*; *cap*; ⟨engl⟩ (viereckiges) (*trencher-*)*cap, mortar-board* ‖ ⟨ec⟩ *barret, biretta*

B·arfrost m *black frost*

***barft; barfuß** [pred] a *unshod*; *barefoot*(*ed*)

B·arfüßer m ⟨ec⟩ *barefooted friar* **b·arfüßig** a [attr & pred] *barefooted*

b·arhaupt a [pred] *bareheaded*

B·aribal m ~s/~s ⟨zoo⟩ *American black bear*

Bar·illa [ba'rilja] f (Span) (Asche) *barilla*

B·ariton m ~s/~e ⟨mus⟩ **1.** (~stimme, ~sänger) *baritone* **2.** (Blechblasinstrument) (a. ~horn) *barytone*

B·arium n ~s/ ⟨chem⟩ **1.** *barium* **2.** [in comp] *barium* (*hydrate*); ~chlorid [n] *chloride of b.*; ~sulphat n *sulphate of b.*

Bark f ~/~en ⟨mar⟩ (Dreimaster) *bark, barque*

Barkar·ole f (Gondellied) *barcarole, –rolle*

Bark·asse f ~/~n ⟨mar⟩ *launch* ‖ *long-boat*

B·arke f ~/~n *Mediterranean fishing-boat*

B·ärlapp m ~s/ ⟨bot⟩ *club-moss, lycopodium* (L); ~samen m *lycopodium powder, witch-meal*

B·arlauf m ~spiel n *prisoners' base* od *bars* [pl]; *chevy, chivy*

B·arlowsche Krankheit f ⟨med⟩ *Barlow's disease*

Barmak·iden, Barmek- [pl] (pers. Geschlecht) *the Barmecides* [pl]

B·ärme f ~/ [nd] *barm, leaven, yeast* || *foam*

b·armen vi [h] *to lament*

barmh·erzig a *charitable, compassionate, merciful* || ~er Bruder m *hospitaller* || ~e Schwester f *Sister of Charity* od *Mercy* || der ~e Samariter *the good Samaritan* ⟨a. übtr⟩ **Barmh·erzigkeit** f ~/ *charity, compassion, mercifulness, mercy* (aus ~ *in m.*)

Barn m ~s/~e *crib, manger; rack for fodder*

Barn n (Flächeneinheit der Kernphysik) *barn*

bar·ock a **1.** ⟨arts⟩ *baroque* || das ≗ *the b.* (: *a study of the b.*); Periode des ≗ *b. period* | ⟨übtr⟩ *b., bizarre, grotesque, odd; bombastic* **≗dichtung** f *baroque poetry* **≗kunst** f *b. art* **≗stil** m *b. style, the baroque*

Barogr·amm n *barogram* **Barogr·aph** m *barograph*

Barom·eter n ~s/~ *barometer; weather-glass;* das ~ steigt ⟨fam⟩ *the glass is going up* || Heber-≗ *siphonbarometer* | ⟨übtr⟩ *barometer* (*of conditions*) **~schwankung** f *barometrical variation* **~stand** m *height of the barometer*

barom·etrisch a *barometric(al)*

Bar·on m ~s/~e **1.** ⟨engl⟩ **a.** ⟨hist⟩ (Pair) *baron* **b.** ⟨mod⟩ (niedrigste Adelsstufe) *baron* (Anrede: *My Lord*); [koll] die ~e *the baronage* **2.** ⟨Ger⟩ (Freiherr) *baron* **3.** ⟨übtr⟩ *baron, magnate* **Baron·esse** f ~/~n *baroness* **B·aronet** ['bærənit] m ~s/~s ⟨engl⟩ (oberer Grad des niederen erblichen Adels; Anrede *Sir* [*Sir John Smith*]) *baronet* (abbr *Bart.*); [koll] die ~s [pl] *the baronetage* || (jdn) zum ~ m *to baronet* || ~srang [m] *baronetage* || ~swürde [f] *baronetcy* **Baron·ie** f ~/~n (Grundbesitz e-s Barons) *barony* **Bar·onin** f ~/~nen *baroness* **baronis·ieren** vt/i [h] **1.** vt (jdn) *to create* (*a p*) *a baron* **2.** vi ⟨fig⟩ *to be a gentleman; to idle* od *lounge about; to be out of work; to play the fine gentleman* **Bar·onstück** n ⟨cul⟩ (Rücken & Keule) *baron of lamb*

Barosk·op n ~s/~e = Barometer

B·arras m ~/ [sd] ⟨mil sl⟩ beim ~ ⟨m. m.⟩ *square-bashing* (*in the army*)

B·arre f ~/~n **1.** (Stange) *bar; turnpike* **2.** (Sandbank an Flußmündung) (sand) *bar* **3.** (Brandung in Flußmündung) *bore, eagre*

B·arren m ~s/~ **1.** *bar*; ein ~ Eisen *a bar of iron*; (f. Edelmetalle) *ingot*; ein ~ Gold *an ingot of gold*; ~gold [n] *ingot-gold, gold in ingot(s)* **2.** ⟨gym⟩ *parallel bars* [pl]

Barri·ere [bar'jerə] f ~//~n **1.** ⟨hist⟩ *turnpike* **2.** ⟨rail, etc.⟩ *barrier*; ⟨sport⟩ *railing, railings*

B·arriereriff ['bæriərif] n Großes ~ (an austral. Küste) *Great Barrier Reef*

Barrik·ade f ~/~n ⟨mil⟩ *barricade*; durch ~n versperren *or* schützen *to barricade*

Barrister ['bæristə] m ⟨engl⟩ *barrister*; → berufen; Berufung

Barsch m ~es/~e ⟨ich⟩ *perch*; ~e [pl] *perch* (: *p. are* . .) || Kaul≗ *ruff*

barsch **1.** a (of persons & manners) *blunt, rough, rude* (gegen *to*); *coarse, harsh; abrupt;* ~es Wesen *bluntness*, etc. || *short* (*answer*); *grim* (Befehl) || *harsh, sharp* (*taste*) **2.** adv *bluntly, abruptly* **B·arschheit** f ~/~en *bluntness, harshness, roughness, rudeness, sharpness; incivility*

Bars·oi m ~s/~s ⟨zoo⟩ *Russian* (*long-haired*) *greyhound*

Bart m ~(e)s/≗e **1.** (P) **a.** (Voll≗) *beard*; ⟨sl⟩ *beaver*; →Backen≗, Spitz≗ etc **b.** (Schnauz≗, Schnurr≗, Knebel≗) *moustache*; → Fliege **c.** ⟨ich⟩ *wattle* **d.** Wendungen: sich e–n ~ wachsen l *to grow a b.*; sich den ~ stehen l *to allow one's b. to grow* || sich den ~ streichen *to stroke one's b.* | in den ~ brummen *to mumble* od *speak in one's beard, to mutter between one's teeth* || in den ~ lachen *to laugh in* od *up one's sleeve* | jdm um den ~ gehen, jdm Honig um den ~ schmieren *to butter a p up, to cajole, humour, jolly a p; to get round a p*; → Gunst || um des Kaisers ~ streiten *to dispute about trifles*, ein Streit um des K. ~ *a dispute about t.* | bei m–m ~!, beim ~ des Propheten! *by Jove* || so ein ~ (= e–e Geschichte, die so alt ist, daß sie e–n ~ h könnte)! *Queen Anne is dead!* ⟨sl⟩ *froze!* **2.** ⟨übtr⟩ **a.** (T) *beard* (*of a goat*, etc.); *whiskers* [pl] (*of cats*, etc.) || *barb, wattle* (*of fish*); *beard* (*of oysters*) | *gills, wattles* [pl] (*of fowl*) **b.** (*of plants*) *beard* (*of grain*); *barb* **c.** *web* (*of a feather*) **3.** (S) *bit, ward* (*of a key*) || *rough edge* (*of note-paper*) || ⟨met⟩ (Grat) *burr*; (Gußnaht) *seam* **~affe** m ⟨zoo⟩ *wanderoo* **~binde** f *moustache-trainer* **~faden** m ⟨ich⟩ *barb(el)* **~flechte** f **a.** ⟨bot⟩ *beard-moss* **b.** ⟨path⟩ *sycosis, barber's itch* **~geier** m ⟨orn⟩ *bearded vulture*, → Lämmergeier **~gras** m ⟨bot⟩ *beard-grass* **~grind** m = Bartflechte b. **~grundel** f ⟨ich⟩ *the common loach* **~haar** n *hair of the beard* **~hafer** m *wild oat* °**~kratzer** m ⟨hum⟩ *shaver* **~lappen** m [pl] ⟨orn⟩ *gills* [pl] **≗los** a *beardless* **~männchen** n **~meise** ⟨orn⟩ *bearded titmouse* **~moos** n ⟨bot⟩ *beard-moss* **~nelke** f ⟨bot⟩ *sweet-william* **~scherer** m *barber, hairdresser* **~tracht** f *beard* (od *moustache*) *fashion* **~wal** m ⟨zoo⟩ *whale-bone whale* **~wichse** f *cosmetic for the moustache*

B·ärtchen n ~s/~ *small beard*

B·arte f ~/~n **1.** †(Beil) *broad-axe* **2.** (Fischbein) *whalebone, baleen, horny plate of bone*

B·artel f ~/~n ⟨ich⟩ = Bartfaden

B·ärtel m ~s/ = Werg

B·arthel (aus Bartholomäus) °⟨übtr⟩ (Brecheisen) *crowbar*; er weiß, wo ~ den Most (sc Geld) holt *he knows which side his bread is buttered; he knows the ropes* od *his onions, he knows the price of old iron, he knows a th or two*

B·artholinsche Drüsen f [pl] (nach K. Bartholin, † 1738) ⟨anat⟩ (bei der Frau) *the glands of Bartholin*; → Cowpersche Drüsen

Bartholom·äusnacht f *St. Bartholomew's Night* (zum 24. Aug. 1572)

B·ärtierchen n [pl] (Spinnen) *tardigrades* [pl]

b·ärtig a *bearded*

B·ärwurz(el) f ⟨bot⟩ **1.** *baldmoney* **2.** *saxifrage* || → Mutterwurz

B·arysphäre f ~/~n *barysphere*

Bar·yt m ~s/~e ⟨min⟩ *barytes, barite; heavy spar*; → Bariumsulphat **~beton** m (Strahlenschutz) *baryte concrete* **~erde** f *baryta* **~gelb** n *barium yellow* **~weiß** n *permanent white*

baryz·entrisch a *barycentric*

Bas·alt m ~(e)s/~e ⟨geol⟩ **1.** *basalt*; glasig ausgebildeter ~ *tachylyte* **2.** [in comp] *basalt; basaltic* **≗artig** a *basaltic* **~felsen** m *basaltic rock*

bas·alten, bas·altisch a *basaltic*

Bas·ane f ~/~n (Schafleder) *basan, bazan*

Basan·it m ~s/~e ⟨minr⟩ *basanite*

Bas·ar m ~s/~e **1.** (orient. Markt) *bazaar* **2.** Wohltätigkeits≗ *bazaar, fancy-fair* **3.** (billiges Warenhaus) *bazaar, sixpenny stores* [pl]; ⟨Am⟩ *ten cent store*

Baschk·iren m [pl] (türkische Gruppe der altaischen Völker) *Bashkirs* [pl]

B·aschlik m ~s/~s (Wollkapuze) *bashlik*

B·ase f ~/~n (*female*) *cousin* || † & Sw (Muhme) *aunt* | Klatsch≗ *gossip, tell-tale*

B·ase f ~/~n ⟨chem⟩ *base* | ~bildner [m] *base-forming element*

Baseball ['beisbɔ:l] m (amer. Nationalballspiel) *baseball* || ~spiel n ⟨Am⟩ *ball-game*

B·asedowsche Krankheit f (nach K. v. Basedow, † 1854) ⟨med⟩ *exophthalmic goitre, Graves' disease*

B·asel n (schweiz. Kanton & Stadt) *Basle*

B·aseler m, **~in** f *inhabitant of Basle*

B·as(e)ler Konzil n *the Council of Basle* (1431–48)

bas·ieren vt/i [h] **1.** vt (etw) *to base, found* (auf *on, upon*) || e–e Aussage auf etw ~ *to predicate a statement on a th* **2.** vi *to be based* (*on, upon*)

Basili·aner m *Basilian monk*

Bas·ilienkraut n ⟨bot⟩ *basil*

Bas·ilika f ~/-ken ⟨ec arch⟩ *basilica* (L)

Bas·ilikum n ~s/ ⟨bot⟩ = Basilienkraut

Basil·isk m ~en/~en **1.** (Fabelwesen) *cockatrice, basilisk*; ~enblick m *basilisk glance* **2.** ⟨zoo⟩ (Leguan) *basilisk*

B·asis f ~/B·asen **1.** (Grundfläche) ⟨arch & math⟩ *base* || ⟨mil⟩ Flotten≈ *naval base*; → Operations≈ **2.** ⟨übtr⟩ (Grundlage) *basis*, auf e–e breite ~ stellen *to place on a broad b.* **3.** ⟨chem⟩ = Base **4.** [in comp] ~metall [n] ⟨tech⟩ *parent metal*; ~welle [f] ⟨at⟩ *base surge*

b·asisch a ⟨chem⟩ *basic*; ein~ *monobasic*; zwei~ *dibasic* || ~e Medizin [f] *antiacid* [s]

Basizit·ät f ~/ *basicity*

B·asken m [pl] die ~ *the Basques* [pl] **~land** n *Basque country* **~mütze** f ⟨sport⟩ *beret* || *tam-o'-shanter*

B·asketball m ⟨engl⟩ *basket-ball*

b·askisch a *Basque* (*provinces*; *languages*)

Bask·ül, Basküleverschluß m (an Fenstern etc) *fastener on the bascule principle*

Basreli·ef [bɑreli'ef] n ~s/~s ⟨arts⟩ *low relief, bas-relief, basso-relievo* It; *anaglyph*

B·aß m B·asses/B·ässe **1.** ⟨mus⟩ *bass* || *bass, lower part of the keyboard* **2.** (~stimme) *bass, basso*; Buffo≈ *basso buffo* **3.** **~geige** f *contrabass, double-bass*; *violone* **~geiger** m *double-bass player* **~posaune** f *bass-trombone* **~saite** f *bass-string* **~schlüssel** m *bass-clef* **~stimme** f *bass, basso*, sehr tiefer ~ *basso profundo* **~tölpel** m ⟨orn⟩ *gannet*

†**baß** adv *very, very much, highly* (erstaunt)

B·asse m ~n/~n ⟨zoo⟩ *male wild boar*

Bass·ett n ⟨mus⟩ *bass-viol* **~horn** n ⟨mus⟩ *basset-horn*

Bassin [ba'sɛ̃:] n ~s/~s **1.** (gr. Behälter) *reservoir* (*for water*) || (f Nilpferd etc) *basin*; *pond* || Hafen≈ *harbour-basin*; *dock* **2.** (Gefäß) *tank*

Bass·ist m ~en/~en *bass* (*singer*)

B·asso m ⟨mus⟩ *bass*

B·ast m ~es/~e **1.** ⟨bot⟩ (Zellgewebe) *inner fibrous bark*; *bast*; Raphia≈ *raffia* || *harl* (*of flax*) **2.** ⟨hunt⟩ (Reh) im ~ *in velvet*; mit zerfetztem ~ *in rags and tatters* **~hanf** m *undressed hemp* **~hut** m *chip-hat, bast-hat* **~matte** f *bast-mat* **~papier** n *Manillapaper* **~seide** f *raw silk*

b·asta intj (It) damit ~! *that is all!*, (*so*) *that's that!, so there!, there's an end of it!* || und damit ~! *and that's all about it* (od .. *all there is to it*)!

B·astard m ~(e)s/~e **1.** (uneheliches Kind) *bastard*; (jdn) zum ~ erklären *to bastardize* **2.** (Mischling) **a.** ⟨biol, zoo & bot⟩ *hybrid*; *crossbreed*; *mongrel* **b.** ~s [pl] *hybrid race descended from Hottentots and Europeans* **3.** [in comp] **a.** (unehelich) *bastard* **b.** ⟨biol, zoo & bot⟩ *hybrid, mongrel* || ⟨bot & zoo⟩ (abnorm) *bastard* (*apple*; *type*) **~art** f *cross-breed, hybrid species* || *bastard type* **≈artig** a *hybrid* || *bastard* **~hund** m *mongrel, mongrel dog* **~klee** m ⟨bot⟩ *alsike* **~pflanze** f *hybrid* (*plant*) **~rose** f *hybrid rose* **~rasse** f *hybrid race, mongrel race* **~schaft** f (unehel. Geburt) *bastardy* **~schrift** f ⟨typ⟩ *bastard fount* || **~wechsel** m = Kellerwechsel

bastard·ieren vt [h] (Tiere) *to hybridize*

†**Bast·arner** pl (germ. Volk zw Karpathen u Donaumündung)

Bast·ei f ~/~en *bastion, bulwark*; → Bastion

B·astel- **~arbeit** f [abstr] *manual work*; *elementary* (*wood*)*work, sloid, sloyd* || [konkr] *elementary woodwork* **~buch** n *do-it-yourself book* **Bastel·ei** f [abstr] *elementary* (*wood*)*work* **b·asteln** **I.** vt/i [h] **1.** vt (etw) *to rig up*; *to put* od *paste together* || (Kleid) *to mend* **2.** vi *to potter* || **~ an** etw *to mend, repair a th*; *to muddle with a th* **II.** ≈ n = Bastelarbeit

b·asten, b·astig a *bast, made of bast*

Basti·on f ~/~en ⟨fort⟩ *bastion*; *crenallation*

Bast·it m ~s/ ⟨minr⟩ *bastite*, → Schillerspat

B·astler m ~s/~ *amateur constructor*, ⟨fam⟩ *do-it-yourselfer*

Baston·ade f ~/~n *bastinado* || er bekam die ~ *he was bastinadoed*

Bas·uto [pl] (Negerstamm) *Basuto* || ~land n *Basuto-Land* (heute Lesotho)

Bat·aille [bɑ'taljə] f ~/~n *battle*

Bataill·on [bɑtal'jo:n] n ~s/~e ⟨mil⟩ *battalion* || ⟨übtr⟩ (Menge) *battalion, large number* | **~s-** ~exerzieren [n] *b. drill*; ~geschäftszimmer [n] *orderly-room*; ~kommandeur [m] *b.-commander*; *major*; ~tambur [m] *drum-major*

Bat·ate f ~/~n ⟨bot⟩ *batata, sweet potato*; ⟨S.-Am⟩ *yam*

B·ataver m [pl] (Volksstamm an Rheinmündung) ⟨hist⟩ *the Batavi* (L) || = Holländer **Bat·avia, Bat·avien** n (Stadt auf Java) *Batavia* **bat·avisch** a *Batavian* (*republic*)

B·athmetall [ba:θ-] n *white brass*

Bathol·ith m ~en/~en ⟨geol⟩ *batholith*

B·atik m (Färbverfahren) *batik*; ~stoff *batik cloth*

Bat·ist m ~es/~e *batiste, cambric, lawn* || ~taschentuch n *cambric handkerchief* **bat·isten** a *lawny cambric*

Batr·achier [pl] ⟨zoo⟩ (Froschlurche) *Batrachia* [pl] (L)

b·atschen [engl] vt [h] (benetzen) (Jutefaserbündel) *to batch*

Batter·ie f ~/~en **1.** ⟨mil⟩ *battery*; Feld≈ *field-b.* || ⟨mar⟩ *battery*; schwimmende ~ *floating b.* **2.** ⟨el⟩ *battery*; Akkumulatoren≈ *accumulator b.*; galvanische ~ *galvanic b.* || ⟨wir⟩ Gerät mit ~anschluß *battery-operated set* **3.** ⟨tech⟩ *battery*; Kessel≈ *b. of boilers* **4.** ⟨fig⟩ *bottles* [pl]: abgekämpfte *or* verschossene ~ (leere Flaschen) *dead soldiers* od *marines* **5.** [in comp] *battery* **~chef** m, **~führer** m *battery-commander* **~gerät** n *battery* **~kasten** m ⟨mot⟩ *battery-box* °**~krokodil** n, °**~nuttchen** n ⟨sex⟩ *garrison hack* **~offizier** m *gun position officer* **~(klein)tonbandgerät** n ⟨rec⟩ *miniphone* **~trupp** m *b. head-quarters detail* **~zündung** f ⟨mot⟩ *battery coil ignition*

Bat·um (Hafenstadt in Georgien, am Schwarzen Meer) *Batum*

B·atzen m ~s/~ (frühere Silbermünze in Schweiz etc) *batz* || ⟨übtr⟩ ein schöner ~ Geld *a nice bit of money*, ⟨sl⟩ *a pot of m.*; er hat k–n ~ *he has not a penny* od *farthing* (*to bless himself with*)

B·atzen m ~s/~ (Klumpen) *clot, clotted* od *caked mass* || *blot*

Bau m ~s/~ten, ~e **A.** ⟨abstr⟩ (Bauen) **1.** *building, construction, erection* || in ~ *under construction*, im ~ befindlich s *to be in process of construction, to be on the stocks*; das Haus ist im ~ begriffen *the house is being built, the h. is building* || ⟨fig⟩ vom ~ s *to be of the trade, to be in the know*; jd, der vom ~ ist *an expert* **2.** *establishment, planning*, Städte≈ *town p.* || ⟨rail⟩ *construction* (*of a line*); Straßen≈ *road-building* od *making* **3.** (~ des Bodens etc) *cultivation, culture, growth*; Feld≈ *tillage* || [bes in comp] *culture*, → Acker–, Garten–, Wein≈ **4.** ⟨tech⟩ *building, construction*; Maschinen≈ *construction of machines*; Wagen≈ *carriage-building, car-*

-construction **5.** ⟨übtr⟩ *erection* (*of a system*) **B.** (das Gebaute) **1.** *building, edifice, structure* || ⟨theat-sl⟩ *shop*; e–r vom ~ *a professional*; der ~ ⟨sl⟩ *the profesh* || Schwund⁓ *jerry-built house* || öffentliche ~ten [pl] *public works* [pl]; ⟨engl⟩ Behörde f. öffentl., bes historische ~ten *Office of Works* || ⟨film⟩ ~ten [pl] *set* | Pfahl⁓ m *lake-dwelling* **2.** ⟨min⟩ (Anlage) *working* [oft pl *workings*] **3.** (Tier⁓) *burrow, den, earth kennel, hole lodging* || (of fox) in den ~ schliefen *to earth*; (Fuchs) aus dem ~ sprengen *to bolt* vt **4.** ⟨übtr⟩ den ganzen Tag im ~ sitzen *to stay in one's den all day* || (Hütte) *kennel, mean hovel* || ⟨theat-sl⟩ *shop* || ⟨mil-sl⟩ (Gefängnis, Arrest) *jug, clink*; im ~ *limbered*, 6 Tage ~ *sixpence over the wall*; er bekam 3 Tage ~ ⟨mil sl⟩ *he had to go to the glass-house for 3 days* → Loch, Kittchen **C.** (inneres Gefüge) **1.** (Körper⁓) *build, frame*; er war von schlankem ~ *he was of slender build* (od *slender of build*) || *organism* **2.** *fabric, frame* (: *the f. of society*); *structure* (*of a language*); *architecture* **3.** ⟨übtr⟩ *framework*; *plan* (*of an essay*, etc) **4.** ⟨tech⟩ *mechanism*

B·au- [in comp] *building*; *constructional*; *architectural* (*task*) **~abnahme** f *examination of a new building by the Board of Surveyors* **~abschnitt** m *building campaign* **~akademie** f *school of architecture* **~amt** n ⟨m. m.⟩ *Office of Works* **~anschlag** m *builder's estimate* **~arbeiten** f pl *construction ahead* ⟨a mot⟩ **~arbeiter** m *builder's labourer* **~art** f *architecture, structure*; *fabric*; *style*; *model*; *design* ⟨bes mach⟩ || unsolide ~ *jerry-building* **~aufseher** m *surveyor of the works, inspector of buildings* || *builder's foreman* **~aufzug** m *hoist* **~behörde** f = ~amt [n] **~beratungsstelle** f *advisory office for prospective builders* **~block** m *block* **~element** n ⟨tech⟩ *component, c. part* **~erlaubnis** f *building permit* (od *licence*) **~fach** n *architecture*; *profession of* (*an*) *architect, building trade* **~fachausstellung** f *exposition of works of architecture* **⁓fällig** a *tumble-down*; *out of repair*; *crazy, dilapidated, decayed, ruinous*; *ramshackle, rickety*; ~ s *to be in disrepair* **~fälligkeit** f *ruinous state, disrepair*; *craziness, state of decay* **~firma** f *construction company* **~flucht (linie)** f *alignment, alinement* (*of buildings in streets*) **~forderungen** f [pl] *charge for building-expenses* **~form** f *type of construction* **~führer** m *foreman* (od *overseer*) *of a new building* **~führung** f *building supervision* **~gelände** n *building land*; *building sites* [pl] **~genehmigung** f (*building-*)*licence* **~genossenschaft** f *building society* **~gerüst** n *scaffolding* **~gesetzgebung** f *building legislation* **~gewerbe** n *building trade*; ~ausstellung f *Building Trades Exhibition* **~gewerkschule** f *builder's technical school* **~glied** n *structural member*; *limb* **~grube** f *excavation*; *building pit* **~handwerker** m *artisan in the building trade* **~herr** m *builder* (*p for whom a house is built*) **~hof** m *timberyard* **~höhe** f *overall height* **~holz** n (*structural*) *timber*; ⟨Am⟩ *lumber*; (zugeschnittenes) *scantling* | ~einschlag [m] ⟨for⟩ *timber operations*; ~recht [n] *right to timber* **~hütte** f *association of builders, artisans*, etc.; *stone-cutter's yard* **~ingenieur** m *structural engineer, civil engineer* **~inspektor** m *surveyor*; *inspector of works* **~jahr** n *date when built, year in which constructed* **~kasten** m (f Kinder) *box of bricks*; Stabil⁓ *meccano* | ~konstruktion [f] ⟨mach⟩ *unit construction*, ~möbel [n pl] *modular furniture*; ~prinzip [n] ⟨tech⟩ *unit construction* (od *building-block*) *system*; *unit construction principle* **~keramik** f *architecturally applied ceramics* [pl] **~klotz** m (f. Baukasten) *brick* || da staunt man Bauklötze *that takes one's breath away* **~kolonne** f (P) *construction unit*; *gang* **~kosten** [pl] *building-costs* (od *expenses*) [pl] | ~anschlag [m] *contractor's estimate*; ~zuschuß [m] *key money* **~kunst** f *architecture*; Lehre v der ~ *architectonics* [pl] **~künstler** m *architect* **~land** n *arable land* || *building land, construction area* | ~beschaffungsgesetz [n] *Building Site Requisitioning Act* **~last** f *obligation for the upkeep of ecclesiastical buildings* **~lebung** f ⟨hist jur⟩ *heriot* **~leiter** m *building supervisor* **~leute** [pl] *workmen* [pl] *employed on a building* **~lust** f *building activity* (od *enthusiasm*) **⁓lustig** a *fond of building* **~markt** m *building-market* **~materialien** n [pl] *building-materials* [pl] **~meister** m *architect, master-builder*; ⟨fig⟩ *builder* (*of Modern Italy*) **~muster** n ⟨tech⟩ *model, type* **~normen** f pl *standards of building* **~opfer** n (*custom of*) *walling in of humans*, etc. *as protection against evil spirits* **~ordnung** f *building-regulations* [pl] **~plan** m ⟨tech⟩ *construction diagram*; ⟨arch⟩ *building-plan*; *architect's plan*; -pläne [pl] *details* [pl] **~planungsbehörde** f *planning authorities* pl **~platz** m *building plot* (od *site*); *estate* **~polizei** f = Baubehörde; **⁓lich** verboten *forbidden by the Surveyors* **~projekt** n *building scheme* **~rat** m (P) *surveyor*; *member of the board of works* **~recht** n *building bye-laws* [pl] **⁓reif** a ⟨tech⟩ *developed* **~riß** m = Bauplan **~sand** m *mortar sand* **~schaltplan** m ⟨el⟩ *wiring diagram* **~schlosser** m *locksmith* **~schule** f *school* (od *academy*) *of architecture* **~schutt** m *rubble* **~sohle** f ⟨min⟩ *level* **~sparkasse** f ⟨Ger⟩ *Loan and Building Association* **~sparvertrag** m *building* (*society*) *loan contract* **~spekulant** m *real estate investor* **~stahl** m *engineering st.* **~stätte** f *building-ground* **~stein** m *building-st.* || = Bauklotz || ⟨comp⟩ ~e [pl] *turret sections* || ⟨fig⟩ *component, component part* | ~verfahren [n] *building block technique* **~stelle** f = Baustätte; ⟨mot⟩ *road works* **~stil** m *style of architecture* **~stoff** m *building material* | ~händler [m] *builder's merchant* **~strecke** f ⟨el⟩ *field* **~tätigkeit** f *building activity* **~techniker** m *technical architect* **~teil** m *part*; *subassembly*; ~e herstellen *to prefabricate* (*a house*) | ~gruppe f *subassembly* **~tempo** n *rate of building* **~tischler** m *builder's joiner* (od *carpenter*) **~trupp** m (P) *construction unit* od *gang* **~unternehmer** m *builder, contractor*; (privater *private*) *builder* **~vertrag** m *building contract* **~vorhaben** n *building project*, **~weise** f *construction*; *arrangement* (od *disposition*) *of houses*; ⟨tech⟩ *design* **~werk** n *edifice, building* || *monument, monumental structure* **~wesen** n *architecture*; *building*; *building trades* [pl] **~wich** m *distance of a house from the neighbouring one* **~wirtschaft** f *building industry* **~wut** f *passion* od *rage for building* **~zaun** m *hoarding* **~zeit** f *time of building*; *time taken to build a th* **~zeitung** f *builder's journal*

Bauch m ~(e)s/⁓e **1.** ⟨anat⟩ *abdomen, belly* || (Leib) *bowels, entrails, intestines*; *guts*; *stomach* || vom ~ nach dem Rücken zu befindlich *ventro-dorsal* || Dick⁓ *pot-belly, paunch* | e–n ~ bek *to develop a paunch* || voller ~ studiert nicht gern *fat belly, lean brain* || sich [dat] den ~ halten vor Lachen, sich ein Loch in den ~ lachen *to shake one's sides with laughing, to split one's sides*; sich [dat] den ~ vollschlagen *to grease one's gills* | ⟨fig⟩ dem ~ dienen, sich den ~ pflegen *to make a slave* od *god of one's belly, to indulge one's belly* || vor jdm auf dem ~ liegen *to ko(w)tow*, ⟨Am fam⟩ *to cater to a p* **2.** ⟨übtr⟩ (Ausbuchtung) *belly*; *bilge* (*of a cask, ship*); die Flasche hat *or* macht hier e–n ~ *the bottle bulges out here* || *bunt* (*of a net*, etc.)

Bauch- [in comp] *abdominal, ventral*; *ventricular*; *coeliac* **~binde** f *belly-band, abdominal bandage* | (an Zigarren) *cigar-band* **~fell** n ⟨anat⟩ *peritoneum* [L]; ~entzündung f *peritonitis* [L] **~fleck** m ⟨zoo⟩ *light-coloured patch on the belly* || ⟨sl⟩ *belly-flopper* **~flosse** f ⟨ich⟩ *ventral fin* **⁓förmig** a *belly-shaped*; *bulging* **~freiheit** f (of tanks) *belly clearance* **~füßer** m ⟨zoo⟩ *gast(e)ropod* **~gegend** f *abdominal regions* [pl] **~grimmen** n *stomach* od *belly-ache, gripes* [pl], *colic*; ⟨fam⟩ *mulligrubs, collywobbles* [pl] **~gurt** m *belt*; (für Pferde) *belly-band* **~hieb** m ⟨fenc⟩ *cut in low tierce* **~höhle** f *abdominal cavity* | ~nschwangerschaft [f] *abdominal pregnancy*; *pregnancy in the fallopian tube* **~klatscher** m ⟨swim sl⟩ *belly-buster*; e–n ~ m *to gutter* **~kneipen** n = Bauchgrimmen °**~knöpfchen** n (Nabel) ⟨fam⟩ *belly button* **~kühler** m ⟨aero mot⟩ *underslung* ⟨sl⟩ *b. radiator* **~kullern** n ⟨fam⟩ *womble* **~laden** m *vendor's box* **~landung** f ⟨aero⟩ *wheels-up landing*, ⟨fam⟩ *belly landing*, ⟨sl⟩ *b. flop* **~mark** n ⟨anat⟩ *lumbar portion of the spinal c(h)ord* **~muskel** m *abdominal muscle* **~pilz** m ⟨bot⟩ *gasteromycetous fungus*, die ~e [pl] *gasteromycetes* [pl]; → Bofist **~presse** f ⟨anat⟩ *abdominal muscular pressure* **~redekunst** f *ventriloquism, ventriloquial art* **≗reden** vi [h] *to ventriloquize* **~reden** n *ventriloquism*; durch ~ äußern *to ventriloquize* **~redner** m *ventriloquist* **≗rednerisch** a *ventriloquous* **~riemen** m *belly-band, girth* **~schild** n ⟨zoo⟩ (der Schildkröte etc) *plastron* **~schmerz** m = Bauchgrimmen **~schnitt** m ⟨surg⟩ *laparotomy* **~speicheldrüse** f ⟨anat⟩ *pancreas* [Gr] **~speichel** m *pancreatic juice* **~tanz** m *hip and ventral dance* **~wand** f ⟨anat⟩ *abdominal wall*; ~bruch [m] *interstitial hernia* **~wassersucht** f ⟨med⟩ *dropsy of the abdomen, ascites* **~weh** n = Bauchgrimmen

°**B·äuchi** n ~s/~ ⟨Kinderspr⟩ *tumtum, tummy*, → Bäuchlein **b·auchig** a *bulging, bulgy, convex*; ⟨poet⟩ *bellied* ‖ ~ m *to belly*; w *to bulge, to belly* ‖ **-bauchig, -bäuchig** a [in comp] *bellied*; dick~ *big* (od *pot*)*-bellied* **B·äuchlein** n ~s/~ *little belly* → Bäuchi **b·äuchlings** adv *lying flat on one's belly* **B·auchung** f *bulge, bulging*; *swelling*

B·aude f ~/~n ⟨Ger⟩ (im Riesengebirge) *farm* ‖ *mountain-hut*

b·auen vt/i [h] **I.** vt **1. a.** (Haus) *to build*; *erect, raise*; unsolide ~ *to jerry-build* | ⟨übtr⟩ Luftschlösser ~ *to build castles in the air* ‖ Häuser ~ auf jdn *to trust a p implicitly* **b.** (Brücke) *to construct, build* ‖ (Straße) *to lay down*; *to make, build* ‖ (Maschine) *to construct* **c.** ⟨orn⟩ (Nest) *to make, build* **d.** stark gebaut *strongly built*; wohlgebaut *well-built* (P) **2. a.** Acker etc) → bebauen **b.** (Getreide, Gemüse) *to grow*; ⟨Am⟩ *to raise* ‖ (Pflanzen) *to cultivate, grow* **3.** ⟨übtr⟩ °(machen) *to pass* (*an examination*); s–n Doktor ~ *to take one's degree* ‖ (Anzug) *to build*; sich e–n Anzug ~ l *to have a suit built* od *made* ‖ wie wir gebaut sind! ⟨fam⟩ *that's us*! **II.** vi ⟨übtr⟩ **1.** (tätig s) *to be active*; *to be on the go* ‖ ~ **an** etw *to contribute to a th, to play one's part at* od *in a th* **2.** ~ **auf a.** ⟨min⟩ ~ auf Silber (etc) *to dig for silver* **b.** ~ **auf jdn** *to trust a p*; *to rely, to depend, to count on a p*; darauf kannst du ~ ⟨fam⟩ *you may count on it*; auf jds Treue ~ *to place reliance on a p's loyalty*

B·auer[1] m ~s & ~n/~n **1.** (Landmann) *peasant, farmer*; *countryman, rustic*; *husbandman*; ⟨Am sl⟩ *hayseed* ‖ ⟨Ger⟩ *small owner* od *proprietor*; kl ~ ⟨bes. Scot⟩ *crofter* ‖ begüterter russ. ~ *kulak* ‖ was der ~ nicht kennt, das frißt er nicht *you can't teach an old dog new tricks* **2.** ⟨fig⟩ *boor, churl, clown*; *lout*; *yokel*; ⟨Am sl⟩ *hick* **3.** (chess) *pawn* ‖ ⟨cards⟩ *knave*

B·auer[2] n & m ~s/~ (f Vögel) cage

-bauer [in comp] (→ Erbauer) *-builder*; *-wright*; Wagen~ *carriage-builder*; Schiff- *ship-wright*

B·äuerin f ~/~nen *female peasant*; *peasant-woman, countrywoman, peasant's wife* **b·äu(e)risch** a (grob, ungebildet) *boorish, churlish, clownish, rustic*; ~ Werk = Bossenwerk ‖ → bäuerlich **b·äuerlich a** *rural, rustic*; *country* (*sports*); ~er Grundbesitzer *peasant proprietor*

B·auermeister m ⟨hist⟩ *president of the peasants' court*

B·auern- [in comp] (→ Bauer) **~befreiung** f ⟨hist⟩ *liberation of peasants from feudal servitude* **~bengel** m *boor, lout, yokel* **~brot** n *coarse bread* **~bund** m ⟨Ger⟩ *the Peasants' League* **~bursche** m *young peasant*; *country lad* **~dirne** f *country lass* **~erhebung** f ⟨engl⟩ *the Peasants' Revolt* (*1381*) **~fänger** m (*card-*)*sharper, confidence* (⟨Am⟩ *con*) *-man*; *swindler*; *rook*; ⟨fam⟩ *shark, sharp* **~fängerei** f *card-sharping*; *confidence trick* od ⟨Am⟩ *game, take-in, swindle* **~flegel** m *churl, boor* **~frau** f = Bauersfrau **~führer** m → Reichs≗ **~gericht** n ⟨hist⟩ *the peasants' court* **~gut** n (*peasant's*) *farm*; *small holding* **~haus** n *farm-house* **~hochzeit** f *country-wedding* **~hochschule** f *peasants' academy* **~hof** m (*peasant's*) *farm*; *farm-stead* **~hütte** f (*peasant's*) *cottage* **~junge** m *peasant-boy* **~kalender** m *peasants' almanac* **~kerl** m *boor*; *lout* **~kittel** n *smock-frock* **~knecht** m *farm-servant* (od *hand*) **~komödie** f = Bauernspiel **~kostüm** n *peasant's costume* **~krieg** m ⟨Ger⟩ *the Peasant's War* (*1524/5*) **~legen** n ⟨hist⟩ *expropriation* od *dispossession of the peasantry* **~leier** f = Drehleier **~lümmel** m *bumpkin, clod-hopper*; *lout, jake*, ⟨sl⟩ *tyke*; ⟨Am⟩ *hick* **~mädchen** n *country-girl, peasant-girl* **~magd** f *farmer's maid, farmer's servant* **~regel** f *peasant's proverb* od *saying* **~rose** f ⟨bot⟩ *peony* **~schaft** f **1.** *peasantry, farmers* [pl]; ⟨Ger⟩ Reichs≗ → Reichsnährstand **2.** *farm* **~schänke** f *village ale-house* (od *inn*) **~schläue, ~schlauheit** f *peasant's cunning*; *horse-sense* **~schuhe** m pl *clodhopper shoes* **~spiel** n ⟨theat⟩ *peasant-play* **~stand** m *peasantry, peasants* [pl] **~stolz** m *peasant's pride* od *conceit* **≗stolz** a *conceited as a peasant* **~tag** m → Reichs≗ **~tanz** m *country-dance* **~tölpel** m *clown, haymaker, lout, yokel*; ⟨sl⟩ *tyke*; ⟨Am⟩ *hick* **~tracht** f *country-dress* **~tum** n = Bauernstand **~verein** m *Peasant's Union* **~verstand** m ⟨cont⟩ *stunted intellect* **~volk** n *country-people, peasantry* ‖ ⟨fig⟩ *churls* [pl] **~wirtschaft** f *rural* od *peasant economy*

B·auersame f ~/~n Sw = Bauernschaft

B·auersfrau f *peasant* od *country woman* ‖ *peasant's wife* **B·auersleute** pl *peasants* [pl]; *peasantry* **B·auersmann** m *countryman, peasant*

Bauh·inie [-iə] ~/~n f ⟨bot⟩ *bauhinia*

b·aulich a *architectural*; *structural*; die ~en Anlagen [pl] *the buildings* [pl]; in ~er Hinsicht *architecturally*; *constructional* (Schwierigkeiten) | ~er Zustand *repair*; in gutem ~en Zustand *in good repair*; in schlechtem ~en Zustand *in bad repair, out of repair* | **≗keit** f *building, edifice*

Baum m ~(e)s/≗e **1.** ⟨bot⟩ **a.** *tree*; → Laub-, Nadel-, Tannen≗ etc ‖ auf Bäumen lebend *arboreal* (*monkey*) ‖ (Tier auf *or* in) den ~ treiben *to tree* **b.** → Stamm≗ ‖ der ~ der Erkenntnis, des Lebens *the tree of knowledge, of life*; ⟨ec⟩ Jesse≗ *the Tree of Jesse* **c.** (Wagen≗) *shaft*; (Deichsel) *pole* ‖ ⟨mar⟩ *boom* ‖ (Hebe≗) *beam* ‖ ⟨hors⟩ (Flankier≗) *bar* **d.** Wendungen: ein Mann stark wie ein ~ *a man of strong frame* ‖ wie der ~ so die Frucht *as the tree is, so is the fruit*; als könnt' ich ≗e **ausreißen** *fresh as a daisy*; er kann ≗e ausreißen *he's as strong as a horse*; er wird k–e ≗e ausreißen *he won't set the Thames on fire* ‖ das ist, um auf die Bäume z **klettern** *that's the limit, that's incredible*; *that gets my dander up, that gets my goat*; *it's enough to drive one up the wall*, . . *for crying out aloud* ‖ man kann den Wald nicht vor (lauter) Bäumen **sehen** *one cannot see the wood for the tress* ‖ es ist gesorgt, daß die ≗e nicht in den Himmel **wachsen** *there is a limit* od *end to everything*; als ob die ≗e in d. H. wüchsen *as if there were no tomorrow* **2.** ⟨übtr⟩ **a.** (Rundholz) *pole, bar*;

shaft || Schlag⩪ *toll-bar, turnpike* || Lang⩪ (am Wagen) *perch* **b.** ⟨mar⟩ *boom, spar*; Besans⩪ *spanker-boom*; Klüver⩪ *jib-boom* || Lade⩪ *derrick* **c.** ⟨tech⟩ (Hebe⩪) *beam*; Weber⩪ *beam*; → Kett⩪ || ⟨mech⟩ (Dreh⩪) *arbor* **d.** ⟨mar⟩ (Hafen⩪) *boom*

B·aum- [in comp] *tree (bark)*; *arboreal (vegetation)*; *arboraceous, arboreous*; *dendri–, dendro–* ⩪**ähnlich** a *dendroid* **~allee** f *tree-avenue* ⩪**artig** a *arboraceous, arboreous*; (~ verzweigt) *arborescent*; ~e Bildung f ⟨anat⟩ *arborization* **~bart** m *beardmoss* **~bast** m → Bast **~beobachtung** f ⟨mil⟩ *observation from a tree* | ~sstand [m] *observation post in a tree* ⩪**bepflanzt** a *tree-lined* (Straße) **~bestand** m *stand, wood, growth*; mit herrlichem ~ *rich with fine old timber* **~blüte** f (Zeit) *blossoming-season, time when all the fruit-trees are in bloom* **~bürste** f *tree-scraper* **~falke** m ⟨orn⟩ *hobby* **~farn** m ⟨bot⟩ *tree-fern* **~flechte** f *lichen* ⩪**förmig** a *dendriform*; → -artig **~frevel** m *injury done to trees* **~gang** m *alley, avenue (of trees)* **~garten** m *orchard* **~gärtner** m *nurseryman* **~geist** m *tree-spirit* **~grenze** f ⟨geog⟩ *tree,- timber-line* **~gruppe** f *cluster* (od *clump*) *of trees* **~haar** n ⟨bot⟩ = Tillandsie **~harz** n *resin, soft gum* **~haus** n ⟨ethn⟩ *tree-house* ⩪**kantig** a *squared (timber)*; → bewaldrechten **~kitt** m *grafting (clay)* **~krone** f *top of a tree, tree-crown* **~kuchen** m *pyramidal cake* **~kult** m *tree-worship, tree-cult* **~kunde** f *dendrology* ⩪**lang** *as tall as a tree*; *lanky* (P) **~läufer** m ⟨orn⟩ *tree-creeper*, → *creeper* **~laus** f ⟨ent⟩ *tree-louse* **~liest** m ⟨orn⟩ *halcyon, kingfisher*; → Riesenfischer ⩪**los** a *treeless* **~marder** m ⟨zoo⟩ *pine-marten* **~nymphe** f *treenymph, (hama)dryad* **~öl** n *olive-oil, sweet oil* **~pfahl** m *prop*; *stay* **~pflanztag** m ⟨Am⟩ *Arbor Day* **~pflanzung** f *plantation of trees* **~ratte** f ⟨zoo⟩ *tree-rat* **~räumer** m ⟨tech⟩ *tree-dozer* ⩪**reich** a *wooded* **~reihe** f *set of trees* **~rinde** f *tree-bark* **~säge** f *pruning-saw* **~sarg** m *tree-trunk coffin, tree-coffin* **~schere** f *tree-pruner*; *pruningshears* pl (e–e ~ *a pair of p.*) **~schlag** m ⟨arts⟩ *foliage* **~schnitt** m *pruning of trees* **~schoner,** **~schützer** m *tree-protector* **~schule** f ⟨for⟩ *tree-nursery* **~spritze** f ⟨hort⟩ *tree spreader* **~stachelschwein** n ⟨zoo⟩ *tree porcupine* **~stamm** m *stem, trunk*; schlanker ~ *shaft* ⩪**stark** a ⟨fig⟩ *robust, strapping* **~steppe** f *savanna* **~stumpf** m *stub, stump* **~verhau** m *abatis*, ⟨Am⟩ *slashing* **~verschnitt** m *topiary work* **~wachs** n *grafting-wax* **~wachtel** f ⟨orn⟩ amerik. ~ *bobwhite*, ⟨Am⟩ *quail* **~wanze** f *tree-bug* **~woll-,** **~wolle** → d. **~zucht** f *arboriculture* **~züchter** m *nurseryman, arboriculturist*

B·äumchen n ~s/~ *small tree* **b·aumeln** vi [h] *to dangle, to hang down* (an *from*), *to swing* (an e–m Haken *from a hook*); *to sway (from the trees)*; mit den Füßen ~ *to swing* (od *waggle*) *one's legs* || (etw) ~ l *to dangle, to swing* | am Galgen ~ (gehenkt s) *to swing*

b·aumen vi ⟨hunt⟩ [s] (auf e–n Baum klettern) *to tree* || → aufbaumen

b·äumen **I.** vi/refl [h] **1.** vrefl **sich** ~ (of horses) *to rear, prance* | ⟨fig⟩ *to boggle, to jib* || sich ~ gegen *to revolt against*, → aufbäumen, -lehnen **2.** vi ⟨weav⟩ *to roll, warp on the beam* **II.** ⩪ n Sich-⩪ *prance*

B·aumwoll- [in comp] *cotton* **~abfall** m *c.-waste* ⩪**artig** a *cottony* **~baum** m ⟨bot⟩ *cotton-tree*; *kapok-tree*; *ceila* [L] **~fabrikant** m *c.-manufacturer*; reicher ~ *cotton-lord* **~garn** n *c. (yarn)* **~gewebe** n *c. fabric*; → Kaliko, Kattun **~handel** m *c. trade*; Magnaten [pl] des ~s *cottonocracy* **~industrie** f *cotton-industry* **~kapselkäfer** m ⟨ent⟩ *c.-fly* **~kuchen** m *c.-cake* **~musselin** m *leno muslin* **~saat** f *c.-seed*; ~mehl [n] *c.-seed meal* **~samen** m *c.-seed*; ~öl [n] *c.-seed oil* **~spinnerei** f *c.-mill* **~staude** f ⟨bot⟩ *c.-plant*; *Gossypium* [L] **~stoff** m geköperter ~ *jean*; gestreifter ~ *gingham*; loser ~ *sponge-cloth* **~teppich** m ind. ~ mit Fransen ⟨A Ind⟩ *dhurrie* **~waren** f pl *cottons* pl, *Manchester goods* pl **~zeug** n *cotton-cloth* **~zwirn** m *cotton-thread*

B·aumwolle f ~/ *cotton* **b·aumwollen** a *cotton (fabric)*

Bausch m ~(es)/⩪e & ~e **1.** (Wulst) *puff*, Puder⩪ *powder-puff*; → Puffärmel || *bolster, pad*; *plumper* || *wad*; Watte⩪ *wad of cotton-wool*; Mull⩪ *tampon* || → Pausche, Pauschale **2.** (dick zus-gelegtes Tuch etc); → Bausche || *bundle* **3.** [urspr surv] ⟨fig⟩ in ~ und Bogen *in the lump* (od *gross*), *en bloc* Fr; *wholesale, as a whole*; *taken all together*; (Dinge) in ~ u Bogen behandeln *to lump, to lump together*; ein Haus in ~ u B. kaufen *to buy a house, lock, stock, and barrel*

B·ausche f ~/~n ⟨med⟩ *bandage, compress*

B·äuschel m ~s/~ ⟨min⟩ *big hammer*

b·auschen vrefl [h] sich ~ (schwellen) *to swell out, to bag, to puff out*; (of skirt) *to flare* || (Falten schlagen) *to pouch* || → aufbauschen

b·auschig a *baggy, puffy*; *swelled*

B·aute f [neuer sg aus Bauten] ~/~n = Baulichkeit **B·auten** [pl] v Bau ⟨film⟩ *set-up*

Baux·it m ~s/~e ⟨minr⟩ *bauxite*

°**bauz** [intj] ~! *flop*! *bang*! *plump*! *smash*!

B·ayer m ~n/~n; **~in** f ~/~nen *Bavarian*

b·ayerisch a *Bavarian*; ~e Alpen [pl] *B. Alps*

B·ayern n ⟨Ger⟩ *Bavaria* **Bayr·euth** n (Stadt in Bayern) *Bayreuth, Baireuth* **B·ayrische Wald,** der → Böhmerwald

B·ayrum ['bɛrum] m ~s/ (Kopfwasser etc) *bay-rum*

Baz·ar m → Basar

Bazillen- **~krieg** m → Bakterien- **~träger** m (immune P) ⟨med⟩ *carrier*

Baz·illus m ~/-llen *bacillus* [pl *bacilli*]; durch Bazillen verursacht *bacillary (disease)*

Be, be → B, b

be- [unbetontes, untrennbares pref, urspr prep, → bei-] *be-* **I.** (in erstarrten Verbindungen) **1.** [urspr prep] (vor Subst.): behende **2.** (vor Adv.): bevor **3.** (vor Adj.): bereit, bequem **4.** (vor vi): beharren, beruhen **II.** [lebendes pref] **A.** (vor vt) **1.** [aus Simplex u prep] **a.** [aus urspr vi]: befahren (= fahren um), begehen, betreten etc **b.** [aus vt]: belegen (= legen auf); beschenken **2.** [aus vt] (Ausdehnung, Verstärkung etc der Handlung): beackern, bearbeiten, bekleiden, belehren **3.** [aus Subst.] (versehen mit): befruchten, bemuttern; beanspruchen **4.** [aus Adj.] (machen): befeuchten; befleißigen, beruhigen **B.** [vor von Verben abgeleiteten Subst., Adj. u. Adv.]: Belehrung, Beruhigung; bekömmlich, belehrbar, bedeutend

be·absichtigen vt [h] (etw) *to intend, to mean*; nichts Böses ~ *to have no evil intentions* || wie -sichtigt *as intended*; ob durch Zufall oder beabsichtigt *whether by accident or by design* || ~ mit *to mean by*; *to imply in (a plan)*; was ~ Sie eigentlich damit? ⟨fam⟩ *what's the big idea*? | ~ z tun *to design* (od *intend*) *doing* od *to do, to mean* (od *propose*) *to do, to be out to do*; *to contemplate doing*; ⟨Am⟩ *to plan to do* | **be·absichtigt** a *calculated*; es ist nicht ~ *it is not intended, proposed*

be·achten vt [h] **1.** (Vorschriften etc) *to pay attention to, to attend to, to give heed* (od *pay regard*) *to (a th)*; *to heed, to observe, to regard (a th)*; *to be regardful of (a th)*; ~ Sie wohl *mind you (I like him)*; es ist z ~ *it is worthy of notice* (od *worth noting*); *it is noteworthy* od *remarkable (that)* || nicht ~ *to ignore, slight, disregard (a th)*; *to pay no regard to*; *to let (a th) go by*; *to take no heed* (od *notice, note*) *of (a th)*; *to be oblivious to (a th)* | *to consider, to take into consideration*;

gehörig ~ *to appreciate* **2.** jdn ~ *to notice a p, to take notice of a p*; er beachtete sie kaum *he scarcely noticed them* || jdn nicht ~ *to ignore a p, to take no notice of a p*

be·achtenswert, be·achtenswürdig a *noteworthy, worthy of notice* od *note*; *remarkable* **be·achtlich** a **1.** = beachtenswert **2.** *considerable* (*income*); → ansehnlich

Be·achtung f ~/~en *attention*; *consideration, notice* (*of a th*); *regard* (e–r S *to* od *for a th*), *compliance* (*with*) || zur ~! *notice*! || der Plan ist nicht unserer ~ wert *the plan is not worth our notice* || ~ finden *to be noticed, to be taken notice of* || e–r S ~ schenken *to pay attention* (od *regard*) *to a th, to regard a th*; e–r S größte ~ sch. *to give one's fullest consideration to a th*; e–r S keine ~ schenken *to disregard a th, to pay no attention* (od *regard*) *to a th* | nach ~ streben *to crave* (*for*) *attention* **~swahn** m ⟨psych⟩ *idea of reference, referential idea*

be·ackern vt [h] *to till, to plough* | ⟨übtr⟩ (Gebiet) *to examine*; *to investigate*; *to work one's way through*; → bearbeiten

Be·amte: der ~ (ein ~r) m ~n/~n *official, officer*, ⟨Am a.⟩ *office-holder* || [koll] die ~n [pl] *bureaucracy, officialdom* || Staats∸r *Government official*, (*career*) *Civil Servant*; (höherer) *officer* (od *functionary*) *of State* || Polizei∸r *police officer*; Post∸r *postal official* (od *clerk*), *post-office official*; Zoll∸r *customs official* | ⟨com⟩ Bank∸r *bank-clerk*, → Angestellte

Be·amten- ~abbau m *axing of officials*; *retrenchment* **~apparat** m *staff* **~bund** m *Association of Officials and Civil Servants* **~gehalt** n *official salary* **~körper** m *staff* **~laufbahn** f *Civil Service* (untere, mittlere, höhere .. *lower, intermediate, senior grade*) **~schaft** f, **~tum** n *officialdom*; *officials* [pl], *bureaucracy* **~sprache** f *officialese* **~welt** f *officials* [pl], *officialdom* **~wohnung** f *official residence*

Be·amtin f ~/~nen *female official*; *female civil servant*

be·ängstigen vt [h] *to alarm, disquiet*; *to make anxious* od *restless, uneasy*

be·ängstigend 1. a *alarming, disquieting* (*news*), *fearful, uneasy* (*dream*) || *anxious* (*task*); *appalling* (*strength*) **2.** adv *alarmingly*; *appallingly* (*pale*) **Beängstigung** f ~/~en *anguish, anxiety*; *uneasiness, nightmare*

Be·anlagung f → Begabung

be·anspruchen vt [h] **1.** (of persons) (etw) *to demand, to require* || er hat nichts mehr zu ~ *he has no further demands* || als Eigentum ~ *to claim* (f sich *for o.s.*); *to enter a claim for, to lay claim to* (*a th*); f sich ~ *to claim* (*to be, to have done*); etw nicht ~ *to forgo a th* || Schadenersatz ~ *to lodge* (od *place*) *a claim* **2.** (of actions etc) *to call for*; *to demand, require*; Lob ~ *to call for praise* **3.** jdn, etw ~ = in Anspruch nehmen; → Anspruch B. 2. **4.** ⟨tech⟩ *to stress, strain*; stark —cht *heavily strained* **Be·anspruchung** f *demand* (m–r Zeit *on my time*); starke ~ *drain* (od *strain*) (m–r Börse *on my purse*); → Anspruch || ⟨tech⟩ *stress, fatigue, strain, load*; mittlere ~ *mean load*; zulässige ~ *safe stress*; größte ~ *toughest working strains* [pl]

be·anstanden vt [h] (etw) *to object to*; *to demur to*; *to complain of*; das —dete Produkt ⟨com⟩ *the article complained of*; *to take exception to* (*a th*) || (jds Recht) *to challenge* || (Wahl) *to contest*; *to oppose* || (Waren) *to reject, to refuse* | (jdn) *to object to* **Be·anstandung** f ~/~en *objection* e–r S *to a th*; ~en m *to raise objections* || *protestation* (e–r S *against a th*) | (Beschwerde) *complaint* | (Einspruch) *protest* | (Einwendung) *remonstration* | ~en geltend m *to bring complaints to notice*

be·antragen vt [h] (etw) *to propose, request* (*a th*); *to apply for* (*a th*) || ein Gesuch ~ um .. *to file a petition for* (*review*); den Konkurs ~ *to file one's petition in bankruptcy* || ⟨parl etc⟩ (Ablehnung etc) *to move* (*a th*); *to move for* (*a th*) || (vor Gericht) *to sue out, to solicit* **Be·antragung** f ~/~en *the proposing* od *proposal* (v Bewerbern *of candidates*); → Antrag

be·antworten vt [h] (Brief, Frage) *to answer*; jds Frage ~ *to answer* (od *reply*) *to a p's question*; alle Fragen ~ ⟨univ sl⟩ *to floor the paper*; schwer zu ~ *hard to answer*; beantwortet w *to meet with a reply* (od *response*) || ⟨übtr⟩ (Vorgehen jds) *to answer* (od *react, reply, respond*) *to*

Be·antwortung f ~/~en *answer, reply* (e–r S *to a th*); in ~ Ihres Briefes *in reply* (od *answer, response*) *to your letter* **~sschreiben** n *answer, reply*

bearbeitbar a *workable* **∸keit** f ⟨tech⟩ *workability, machinability*

be·arbeiten vt [h] **A. etw ~ 1. (zurichten) a.** (Acker, Garten) *to cultivate, till*; *work*; z ~d [a] *workable* (*soil*) **b.** (Holz etc) *to work* (*up*) (zu *into*); (Metall) *to hammer* (zu *into*); (Leder) *to dress*; (Stein) *to face, to hew, to cut*; roh ~ *to rough*; im groben ~ *to rough-hew* || (formen) *to model, to fashion* (nach *after, on*; zu *to, into*) ⟨tech⟩ *to process* || mit der Maschine ~ *to machine* **c.** ⟨chem⟩ *to treat* (*with*) || ⟨med⟩ etw (jdn) öfter u reichlich mit Salbe ~ *to give a th* (*a p*) *liberal applications of ointment*; → 2. b. **d.** (übermäßig ~) *to pound* (*the piano*) **2.** ⟨übtr⟩ **(geistig ~) a.** (Thema etc) *to deal with*; *to treat*; *to work* (*up*); → ausarbeiten || (kompilieren) *to compile* || ⟨Lit & theat⟩ *to adapt* (nach *from*); *to arrange* (f *for*); (Stück) f die Bühne ~ *to adapt*; nach dem Englischen bearbeitet *adapted from the English* || ⟨mus⟩ *to arrange* **b.** *to handle, to manipulate*; ⟨jur⟩ e–n Fall ~ *to prepare a case, to be in charge of a case* || die S wird (behördlich) —tet w *action will be taken in this matter* **c.** e–e S tüchtig ~ *to pound away at a matter* **3. neu** ~ *to revise*, gänzlich neu ~ *to rewrite*; neubearbeitete Ausgabe *revised edition* **B. 1. jdn ~ a.** (zurichten) *to belabour, to thrash*; jdn mit den Fäusten ~ *to hammer a p*, ⟨box fenc⟩ *to punish a p* **b.** *to handle, manage* || (beeinflussen) *to influence a p, to work a p up, to work* (*up*)*on a p, to hammer at a p* (*to do*); *to urge a p*; *to prevail on a p*; *to try to get round a p* (od *to win a p over*) || (Kunden) *to high-pressure* || (Abgeordnete) ⟨Am pol⟩ *to lobby* || (nachteilig) *to practise* (*up*)*on a p*; *to manipulate* **2. (Gegend)** geschäftlich ~ *to work* || (Wahldistrikt) *to canvass*

Be·arbeiter m *reviser* (of books) || *compiler* (*of an anthology*) || *adapter* (*of plays*); *arranger* | (Fach∸) *official appointed to deal with special matters*; *departmental expert* → Arbeiter

Be·arbeitung f ~/~en **1. a.** *cultivation, tillage* (*of the soil*) **b.** ⟨tech⟩ *machining, fabrication, tooling, fashioning*; (v Rohstoffen) *processing* || *working* (*of metals*); *machining*; ~ aus dem Groben *roughing* || *fashioning* || ⟨chem⟩ *treatment* (*with*) **2.** ⟨übtr⟩ **a.** *treatment* (*of a subject*); *working-up* || *preparation* (*of a case*) || *management, manipulation* || ich übersende es Ihnen zur ~ *I pass it on for you to deal with* || jdm .. zur ~ weitergeben *to pass .. to a p for attention* **b.** ⟨Lit & theat⟩ *adaptation* (*of a play*); *compilation*; ⟨mus⟩ *arrangement* || neue ~ *revision* **3.** *managing, manipulation* (*of a p*) **~skosten** pl *tooling* od *process costs* **~smetall** n ⟨tech⟩ *parent metal* **~sverfahren** n *tooling process* **~svorgang** m *machining process* **~swerkstatt** f *mechanical workshop* **~szugabe** f *machining allowance*

be·argwohnen, -wöhnen (jdn) vt [h] *to suspect* (wegen *of*; getan z h *of doing*)

Beau m [bo:] ~s/~s Fr („schöner Mann"; Stutzer) *beau*

be·aufsichtigen vt [h] *to inspect, overlook, oversee, superintend, supervise; control* ‖ (Kinder) *to look after,* (Kleinkind) *to babysit;* —tigtes Kl.kind *sittee* ‖ jdn ~ *to set a watch on a p* ‖ (Pferd) ⟨Am⟩ *to wrangle* ‖ ⟨tech⟩ *to watch, control* **Be·aufsichtigung** f ~/~en *inspection, superintendence, supervision; surveillance,* unter ständiger ~ *under s.* ‖ → Aufsicht

be·auftragen vt [h] (jdn) *to charge, commission, entrust* (mit *with* [*a task*]) ‖ (jdn) *to charge, direct, instruct, order* (z tun *to do*); ich bin beauftragt *I am directed* (*to do*) | (bevollmächtigen) *to authorize, commission, empower* (*to do*); jdn als Vertreter ~ *to delegate; to depute* (*to do*); beauftragt *delegated* ‖ ⟨jur⟩ (Barrister) *to brief;* beauftragter Richter *commissioner*

Be·auftragte; der ~ (ein ~r) m ~n/~n *commissioner* (*for*); (⟨engl⟩ amtlich) *royal c. functionary; mandatory; delegate, deputy, proxy; trustee* ‖ *appointee* ‖ ⟨com⟩ (persönlicher Vertreter) *agent representative* ‖ ⟨jur⟩ *private attorney;* (Richter) *judge in charge of a case, official referee* ‖ ⟨pol⟩ *representative;* ⟨dipl⟩ *plenipotentiary;* Regierungs≙ *commissary;* Sonder≙ *special representative*

be·äuge(l)n vt [h] ⟨fam⟩ *to eye, ogle*

be·augenscheinigen vt [h] *to inspect, view*

Be·augenscheinigung f ~/~en *inspection*

Beauté f [bo:'te:] („Schönheit", schöne Frau) *beauty*

beb·ändern vt [h] *to ribbon*

beb·artet a *bearded*

beb·auen vt [h] **1.** (Acker, Feld) *to cultivate, till; work;* nicht bebaut *uncultured;* → unbebaut **2.** *to cover with buildings;* e–n Platz ~ *to build* (*up*)*on a site;* das Land wird allmählich bebaut *the countryside is getting built over;* bebautes Gebiet *built-up area*

Beb·auer m ~s/~ *cultivator*

Beb·auung f *cultivation* (*of a field*); in ~ *in crop,* unter ~ *under crop* ‖ die ~ des Platzes *the covering of the site with buildings*

b·eben I. vi [h] **1.** *to quake, rock, shake, tremble; tingle;* → erbeben ‖ ~d [adv] *in a tremble* ‖ die Erde bebte heftig *the earth shook violently;* s–e Hand bebte *his hand was shaking,* s–e Stimme bebte *his voice trembled;* ~de Stimme *quiver* (*:with a q.*) ‖ (of knees) → schlottern ‖ am ganzen Körper ~ *to be trembling all over, to be all of a tremble, to be all in a shiver* | vor Kälte, Furcht etc ~ *to shake, shiver, tremble, with cold, with fear;* vor Erregung ~ *to quiver with emotion,* vor Wut ~ *to tremble with rage* | das Haus bebte unter dem Donner der Kanonen *the house was trembling to the sound of the guns* **2.** ~ um jdn *to tremble for a p* ‖ ~ vor jdm *to be frightened of a p* **II.** ≙ n (Erd–) *quake shake* ‖ *quiver* (*of grass*) ‖ (P) ein ~ lief durch *or* über s–e Züge *his face was quivering;* → Erbeben **b·ebend** a *trembling; vibrant* (vor *with*)

beb·ildern vt [h] *to illustrate; to adorn with pictures* od *illustrations* ‖ ⟨übtr⟩ *to illustrate by an example*

bebl·ümen vt ⟨poet⟩ *to flower*

beb·ohlen vt [h] *to plank, to line with planks*

bebr·illt a *spectacled, bespectacled*

bebr·üten vt [h] *to brood on, to hatch* ‖ ⟨übtr⟩ (*of mist,* etc) *to brood over* **B–tung** f *incubation*

B·ebung f ~/ ⟨mus⟩ *vibration*

B·echer m ~s/~ **1.** (Trinkgefäß) **a.** *cup;* gr ~ *beaker;* (ohne Henkel) *chalice, goblet;* (ohne Henkel u. Fuß) *tumbler, mug;* Bier~ *beer-mug;* Trink≙ *drinking-cup* ‖ ⟨ec⟩ (Kelch) *chalice, cup* ‖ Eis≙ *ice-bowl* | Eier≙ *egg-cup* ‖ Würfel≙ *dice-box* **b.** ⟨übtr⟩ der ~ des Leids (etc) *the cup of sorrow, misery* **2.** ⟨bot⟩ = ~hülle **3.** ⟨astr⟩ (Sternbild) *crater* **~blume** *f* ⟨bot⟩ *lesser burnet* **~farn** m ⟨bot⟩ = Baumfarn **~flechte** f *cup-moss, Lapland moss* **≙förmig** a *cup-shaped* **~glas** n ⟨chem⟩ *beaker* **~glocke** f ⟨bot⟩ *gland bell-flower* **~hülle** f ⟨bot⟩ *cupule* **~klang** m *the chinking, ringing of glasses* **~ling** m ⟨bot⟩ (Pilz) *cup-mushroom* **~voll** m *cupful* (*:a c. of..*) **~werk** n ⟨tech⟩ *chain bucket dredge; bucket elevator*

b·echern vi [h] (zechen) *to booze, tipple, tope* ‖ gerne ~ *to be fond of the cup;* er hat gebechert *he is muggy*

bec·ircen vt *to vamp*

B·ecken n ~s/~ **1.** (Schüssel) *basin;* Wasser≙ *water-basin* ‖ Wasch≙ *wash* (od *wash-hand*) *basin;* ⟨ec⟩ *piscina* [L] **2.** ⟨mus⟩ [mst pl] *cymbals* [pl] **3.** (künstl. Wasserbassin) *basin;* (Schwimm≙) *swimming pool;* Hafen≙ *harbour-basin* ‖ *pond, pool* ‖ (im zool. Garten) (*arctic, tropical*) *pool* **4.** ⟨geol⟩ *cavity, hollow; basin: Basin of Paris,* etc ‖ ⟨mar⟩ *basin: Japan B., Coral Sea B.* **5.** ⟨anat⟩ *pelvis* [L]; Nieren≙ *pelvis of the kidney* **6.** [in comp] ⟨anat⟩ *pelvic* (*brim, cavity*) **~bein** n, **~knochen** m ⟨anat⟩ *pelvic bone* **~haube** f ⟨hist⟩ *skull-cap, bascinet* **~schläger** m ⟨mus⟩ *cymbal-player*

b·eckmessern vi [h] (wie Beckmesser in R. Wagners „Meistersinger") *to cavil*

bed·achen vt [h] *to roof* | **-cht** a *roofed*

Bed·acht m [nur in folgenden festen Wendungen]: mit ~ *advisedly; considerately, deliberately* ‖ ohne ~ *thoughtlessly, headlong, rashly* ‖ ~ nehmen auf etw *to take a th into consideration; to be careful of a th;* darauf ~ nehmen z tun *to take care, to be careful to do*

bed·acht [pp v bedenken] [pred a] ~ auf *attentive to; intent, keen on;* auf Sicherheit ~ *security-minded* ‖ ~ s auf *to be out for* ‖ ~ s auf s–e Gesundheit *to be careful* (od *to take care*) *of one's health* ‖ ~ s auf s–e Interessen *to study* od *consult one's own interests; to bear . . in mind* | eifrig ~ *anxious* (z tun *to do*)

bed·ächtig 1. a *cautious; gingerly; wary; circumspect; deliberate* (im Reden *in speech*); *discreet* ‖ *slow and cautious* **2.** adv *cautiously; deliberately; gingerly;* ~ z Werke gehen *to proceed with care, to go about a th cautiously*

Bed·ächtigkeit f ~/ *caution, circumspection; deliberateness*

bed·ächtlich a adv *deliberately, cautiously*

bed·achtsam a = bedächtig **≙keit** f = Bedächtigkeit

Bed·achung f *roofing,* → bedachen, bedacht

Bed·ampfung f ⟨tech⟩ *vapo*(*u*)*r plating*

bed·anken vt [h] **1.** [nur pass] Sie sollen bestens bedankt sein! seien Sie b. b.! *my* (od *our*) *best thanks to you, accept my* (*our*) *best th.!* **2. sich ~ bei** jdm *to thank a p, to express one's thanks to a p* ‖ **sich ~ für** etw *to express one's thanks for a th* ‖ ⟨iron⟩ dafür bedanke ich mich bestens! *no, thanks!, not I!, that's a tall order!*

Bedarf m [nur sg] ~(e)s/ **1. a.** *want, need* (an *of*) ‖ ~ h an etw *to want* (od *need*) *a th, to be* (od *stand*) *in need, to be in want of a th;* gr ~ h an *to be in great want of a th;* k–n ~ h an etw *to have no need of a th, to be* (od *stand*) *in no need of a th;* ich habe k–n ~ *I don't want any* | **bei** ~ *if required* ‖ **nach** ~ *as needed* (od *required;* je nach ~ *as they* (etc) *occur* ‖ **über** ~ eingedeckt s *to have more than is required* **b.** *requirements* [pl], mein ~ ist gering *my r. are few* | Geld≙ *financial requirements;* den ~ **decken** *to meet the requirements* (*of a state*); ⟨iron⟩ mein ~ ist gedeckt ⟨sl⟩ *my cake is dough* **c.** ⟨com⟩ (Nachfrage) *demand* (an Gütern *for goods* | (Leistungs≙) *required output* | wir h z. Z. k–n ~ an Tabak *we are fully supplied with tobacco* **2.** (Verbrauch) *amount of products consumed, consumption;* f eigenen ~ *for home consumption* od *use* **3.** [konkr] *the necessary supplies* [pl], *supply, stock, material*; Kriegs∼ *war material*

bed·arf 1. & 3. sg prs v bedürfen, → d.

Bed·arfs- ∼anmeldung *f indent* **∼artikel** m *article of consumption*, [bes pl] *necessaries, necessities, consumption-goods* [pl] ‖ *necessary supplies, requisites, fittings* [pl]; ⟨Am⟩ (f. Handwerker) *findings* [pl] ‖ ∼geschäft n [konkr] *store, general shop* **∼deckung** f *supplies* **∼dekkungsschein** m ⟨Ger⟩ *promissory note* (od *bond, scrip*) **∼deckungswirtschaft** f *economic system based on satisfying the national needs rather than working for profit* **∼fall** m; im ∼ *in case of need, if need be* (od *arise*) **∼forschung** f marketing **∼halt(estelle** f) m ⟨rail⟩ *optional* od *request* od *emergency stop* **∼quote** f *required supply rate* **∼weckung** f *marketing*; ∼s– & –befriedigungs-Methoden [f pl] *marketing techniques* **∼zug** m *train run if required*; *relief train*; → Sonderzug

bed·auerlich 1. a *deplorable, regrettable*; *woeful* (*results*); es ist ∼ *it is sad* (*that*) **2.** adv *deplorably, regrettably*; *woefully* (*few men*) **bed·auerlicherweise** adv *regrettably*; *sad to say*

bed·auern vt [h] **1.** **(etw)** *to regret* (*a th*; getan z h *having done*); *to be sorry* (od *regretful*) *for* (*a th*); ich bedauere, Sie verletzt z h *I am sorry for having offended you*; es ist z ∼ *it is to be regretted, it is a matter for regret* (*that*) ‖ ∼ daß.. *to express regret that..*; ich bedauere, daß .. *it is a regret to me that.. I am afraid that* (*I cannot*) ‖ sehr ∼ *to deplore*; (mißbilligend) *to deplore* (*what has happened*); ich bedauere sehr, daß.. ⟨fam⟩ *I hate that..* | (verblaßt) ich bedauere sagen z müssen *I regret* (od *I am sorry*) *to say*; wir ∼ die Waren nicht senden zu können *we regret we cannot send the goods* ‖ er bedauert das dafür verausgabte Geld *he grudges the money spent for it* ‖ bedauere sehr! *very sorry* **2.** **(jdn)** *to pity* (*a p*), *to be sorry for* (*a p*); *to commiserate, compassionate* (*a p*); er ist z ∼ *he is to be pitied* **Bed·auern** n *regret* (über *for*); ohne Gefühle des ∼s *without regrets* ‖ z m–m ∼ *to my sorrow*, z m–m gr ∼ *to my great regret* (od *grief*) ‖ sein ∼ ausdrücken (äußern) *to regret* (*that*); *to express regret* (od *one's sorrow*) (über *for*; daß *that*) ‖ mit ∼ *regretfully*; mit (*or* unter) ∼ ablehnen *to refuse with much regret* (od *many regrets*); mit ∼ hören *to hear with regret* (von, über *of*; daß *that*), *to regret to hear* (*that*); mit ∼ denken an etw *to regret a th*

bed·auernswert, bed·auernswürdig a *deplorable pitiable, pitiful* (*fate*); [pred] (*it is*) *to be pitied*

B·ede f ⟨Ger hist⟩ *oldest direct tax*

bed·ecken vt [h] **1. a.** (Körper etc) *to cover* (mit *with*); mit e–m Mantel ∼ *to cloak*; bitte bleiben Sie bedeckt *pray remain covered* **b.** (of snow, etc) (Boden) *to cover* ‖ mit Wolken ∼ *to overcloud* (*the sky*) | Bücherregale bedeckten die Wand *bookshelves lined the walls*; → belegen **c.** (bestreuen) *to besprinkle, dot, pepper* (*with*) ‖ bedeckt mit *cluttered up with* ‖ ein mit Karten bedeckter Tisch *a table littered with maps*; bedeckt s mit.. (of the face) *to be covered with* (*freckles*); *to be smothered with*; die Wiese war ganz mit Veilchen bedeckt *the meadow was a mass of violets* **d.** ⟨astr⟩ (Gestirn) *to occult* **e.** ⟨übtr⟩ (jdn) *to cover, smother* (*with kisses*) ‖ bedeckt s mit *to be covered with* (*shame*); *to be overwhelmed* od *suffused with*; *to be cluttered up with* ‖ → schmücken **f. sich ∼** *to cover one's head*; bitte ∼ Sie sich *pray, be covered* | sich mit Ruhm, Schande ∼ *to cover o.s. with glory, ignominy* **2.** *(schützen) *to shelter*; → decken **3.** ⟨hors⟩ (Stute) *to cover* **bed·eckt** a *covered* (*carriage*; *boat*) ‖ *overcast* (*sky*) ‖ ∼es Gelände ⟨mil⟩ *ground covered with wood, buildings*, etc.; (bewachsen) *close country* **∼samig** a ⟨bot⟩ *angiospermal, –mous*; die ∼e (Ggs Nacktsamige) = Angiosperme

Bed·eckung f ∼/∼en **1.** (Körper∼) *covering*; *clothing*; Kopf∼ → Hut, Mütze etc ‖ *surfacing*; → Decke, Verdeck **2.** ⟨astr⟩ *occultation* (*of the moon*, etc) **3.** *protection* **4.** ⟨mil⟩ *escort, convoy*; ∼skommando [n] ⟨mil⟩ *escort party*; ∼smannschaft [f] *escort*; ∼ssymbol [n] ⟨metor⟩ *cloud symbol*

Bedeg·ar m ∼s/ ⟨bot⟩ (Rosenapfelgalle) *bedeguar*

bed·enken vt [h] (→ denken) **1.** **(S)** **(etw** erwägen) *to consider, ponder* (*a th*); *to take* (*a th*) *into consideration, to reflect* od *ponder* (*up*)*on* (*a th*); *to reckon with*; *to give attention to* (*a th*) ‖ wenn man sein Alter bedenkt *considering his age* ‖ jdm z ∼ geben *to make a p consider*, etc (*a th*) ‖ [ell] wenn man bedenkt *considering* (: *pretty well, c.*) **2.** (beachten) *to mind* (*a th*), *to bear* od *keep* (*a th*) *in mind, to think of* (*a th*); *to heed, remember* (*a th*) ‖ ∼ Sie wohl *mind you*; bedenke, daß.. *mind* od *remember that..*; wenn man bedenkt, daß.. *to think that..* **3.** **(P) jdn ∼** *to provide for a p*; jdn im Testament ∼ *to remember* (od *include*) *a p in one's will* ‖ jdn mit etw ∼ *to furnish* (od *provide, supply*) *a p with a th*; *to bestow a th* (*up*)*on a p*; *to bequeath a th to a p*; *to make a p a present of a th*; er wurde reichlich bedacht *he was left an ample legacy* **4. sich ∼ a.** *to consider, deliberate, reflect*; *to think a matter over*; *to take councel with o.s.* ‖ sich e–s anderen ∼ → besinnen **b.** *(zögern) *to hesitate* (*to do*)

Bed·enken n ∼s/ **1.** (Überlegen) *deliberation, consideration, reflection* (*–xion*); nach reiflichem ∼ *on mature deliberation, on reflection* **2.** (Zögern) *hesitation* ‖ (Zweifel) *doupt, scruple*; *objection* | **ohne ∼** *without hesitation* od *demur, unhesitatingly*; *unscrupulously*; wir können ihn ohne ∼ empfehlen *we have no hesitation to recommend* (od *in r.ing*) *him* ‖ **∼ äußern** *or* h *to demur* (gegen *to*) ‖ es bestand kein ∼ z tun *there was no hesitation about doing* ‖ noch einige ∼ [pl] hegen *to have some doubts left* ‖ ∼ tragen *to hesitate, to be in two minds* ‖ kein ∼ tragen z tun *not to scruple* (od *to make no scruple*) *to do*; ⟨fam⟩ *to make no bones about* (od *of*) *doing* ‖ die ∼ jds zerstreuen *to dispel a p's doubts* **bed·enkenlos** [pred a & adv] = ohne Bedenken

bed·enklich a *doubtful, dubious* (*character*); *suspicious* (*action*); ∼es Licht werfen auf *to reflect* (*up*)*on* (*a th, a p*) | *delicate, ticklish*; *critical* (*turn*; *state*); *hazardous, dangerous*; *serious* (*illness*); jds Zustand *or* e–e S ∼ finden, (⟨a.⟩ ∼ [adv] ernst) finden *to take a grave view of a p's condition* od *of a th* (*a situation*) ‖ *precarious* (*situation*); *risky* (*undertaking*); *ominous* (*sign*) ‖ → nachdenklich **Bed·enklichkeit** f ∼/∼en *doubtfulness, dubiousness* | *delicacy, gravity, seriousness*, die ∼ der Lage *the serious* (od *critical, delicate*) *character of the situation*

Bed·enkzeit f *time to consider, time for reflection*; → Aufschub

°**bed·eppert** a *perplexed*; *depressed*; er schob ganz ∼ ab *he went off with his tail between his legs*; → bestürzt, betreten [a], ratlos

bed·euten vt [h] **1.** **(S) a.** (etw) *to mean, signify*; *to be significant of*; *to stand for*; *to constitute*; was bedeutet schon ein Name? *what's in a name*? (Shak) ‖ *to imply* (*a th*; *that*); was bedeutet Ihnen der Name 'Brew'? *what does the name Brew convey to you*?; sie —tet ihm sehr viel *she is of very great importance to him* ‖ es —tet uns nichts *it is nothing to us* ‖ was bedeutet Flansch auf Englisch? *what is 'Flansch' in English*? ‖ B. A. bedeutet Bachelor of Arts *B. A. stands for Bachelor of Arts* ‖ Glück, Unheil ∼ *to spell bliss, disaster* (f. *for, to*) **b.** (vorhersagen) *to (fore)bode, portend, presage*; dies bedeutet nichts Gutes f. ihn *this bodes him no good, this b. no good for him* **c. ~, z ~ h** *to signify, to be of consequence; to count, tell, weigh; to matter* (f. jdn *to a p*) ‖ **er** bedeutet **nichts** *he does not signify*; **es hat nichts** z ~ *it does not signify, it is of no consequence, never mind, don't mention it; there is nothing in it*; das will **was** ~! *that makes all the difference*; (..,) u das will schon etw ~ *which is saying something* ‖ was soll das ~? *what is the meaning of that*? ‖ aber Nahrung bedeutet doch nicht **alles?** *but is food everything*? ‖ ich fragte ihn, was dies alles bedeute *I asked him what this was all about* | **sie** bedeutete **ihm** alles *she meant* od *was everything to him*; ..sehr viel *she was of very great importance to him* ‖ ihm —tet äußere Form alles *he sets all his store on form*; es —tet uns nichts *it is nothing to us* ‖ **2. (P) jdm ~, z tun** od **daß** *to intimate* (od *suggest*) *to a p, to make a sign to a p to do; to give a p to understand to do* od *that; to enjoin* (od *order*) *a p to do* | ***jdn ~** (belehren) *to instruct a p* (in *in*) ‖ sie lassen sich nicht ~ *they won't listen to reason*

bed·eutend **1.** a [pred] *important* (f. *for*) *significant; relevant* (f. *to*); *of consequence, noteworthy* ‖ [attr] *considerable, weighty*; ⟨Am⟩ ein ~er Erfolg *some success* ‖ *distinguished, eminent; remarkable* ‖ geistig ~ *great* (*writer*); ein recht ~er Künstler *no mean artist* | viel~ *big with significance* **2.** adv *considerably; greatly*

bed·eutsam a *significant, significative* (*look*); *pregnant* (*words*) ‖ = bedeutend **≗keit** f ~/ *significance* ‖ *importance*

Bed·eutung f ~/~en **A.** (Sinn) *meaning* (*of a word*); *significance, –cy; signification, sense; implication* (: *a word in its implications*); Wörter derselben ~ *words with the same meaning*; in der volkstümlichen ~ des Ausdrucks *in the popular acceptation of the word*; in des Wortes eigenster ~ *in the proper* od *strict sense of the word* ‖ *import* (*of his words*); *value* **B.** (Wichtigkeit) **1.** *consequence, impact, import, importance* (f. *to*); *force* **2.** Wendungen: **a.** ~e Männer *men of weight*; ein Mensch v ~ *a man of consequence*; ein M. v gr ~ ⟨sl⟩ *a big pot* ‖ Miltons dichterische ~ *Milton's importance as a poet* ‖ nichts v ~ *nothing to speak of*, ⟨fam⟩ *nothing to write home about* ‖ e–r S ~ beilegen, beimessen *to give weight to a th* **b. an ~** verlieren ⟨fig⟩ *to lose in weight* ‖ **v ~ s, ~ h** *to signify, matter; to be relevant* (od *of consequence*) (f. *to*), *to be not irrelevant* (f. *to*); *to be a consideration; to play a part* (in *in*); *to be in the picture* ‖ das ist v ~ *that makes a difference*; v gr ~ s *to be a decisive factor*; e–e S v ganz geringer ~ ⟨fam⟩ *nothing to make a song about*; das ist v gr ~ für den Erfolg *that makes all the difference to the success* ‖ es ist **kaum** v irgendwelcher ~ *it hardly counts at all* ‖ **nicht v ~ s** *to be irrelevant, to be of no consequence, to be outside the picture* ‖ **nichts v ~** (Nennenswertes) ⟨fam⟩ *nothing to make a song about*; ⟨sl⟩ *no great shakes* ‖ **ohne** ~ *of no consequence*; ⟨fam⟩ *off the map*; das ist ohne ~ *that does not make any difference* (f. *to*); ohne jede ~ s ⟨sl⟩ *to cut no ice*; er ist ohne jede ~.. *he has no case in the eyes of the world* ‖ f jdn ohne ~ s *to mean nothing to a p* **c.** e–r S ~ **beilegen** *or* beimessen *to make a big point of a th, to put a special significance on a th* ‖ e–e gr ~ einnehmen *to occupy an important position* (*in*); (S) *to bulk large* ‖ e–r S ~ geben *or* verleihen *to give point to a th* ‖ an ~ gewinnen *to gather momentum, to gain in point*; erhöhte ~ g. *to take on increased significance*; gr ~ g. *to take high rank* (in *in*) ‖ das Land verdankt s–e überragende ~ der Tatsache *the country owes its eminent position to the fact* (*that*) **C.** *(Anweisung) *direction, instruction*

Bed·eutungs- [in comp] *significant* (*element*); *significative* (*root*) **~gehalt** m *pregnancy* **≗los** a *meaningless, unmeaning, insignificant; of no consequence* **~schwere** f *pregnancy* (*of events*) **≗voll** **1.** a *significant; meaningful; pregnant* (*words*); *purposeful; suggestive*; [pred] *big with significance* ‖ *portentous; momentous* (*day*) **2.** adv *with meaning, meaningly* **~wandel** m ⟨phil⟩ *semantic change*

bed·ienbar a: leicht ~ *easy to handle; of light, quick touch* ⟨a. comp⟩, → bedienend

bedi·enen vt/i [h] **I.** vt **1.** (jdn) **a.** *to attend* od *wait, to be in attendance* (*up*)*on* (*a p*), *to attend* (*a p*), ‖ (jdn) bei Tisch ~ *to serve a p at table*; (pflegen) *to tend upon a p* **b.** ⟨com⟩ *to attend to* (*a p*); w Sie schon bedient? *are you being attended to* (⟨Am⟩ . . *waited on*)? ‖ reell bedient w to *get good value for one's money*, ausgezeichnet bedient w *to get excellent value* (*at a restaurant*) ‖ °da bin ich bedient *I had enough of it, I'm sick of it* **2.** (Pferd) *to groom* **3.** ⟨tech⟩ *to handle*; ⟨mach⟩ *work, tend*; (Geschütz) *serve* ‖ *to answer* (*the telephone*) **4.** ⟨cards⟩ Farbe ~ *to follow suit* **5. sich ~ a.** (bei Tisch) *to help o.s.*; ~ Sie sich! *help yourself*! wollen Sie sich noch einmal ~? *would you like a second helping*? **b.** sich e–s Dinges ~ *to make use of a th, to use a th*; sich e–s Angebots (etc) ~ *to avail o.s. of an offer* **II.** vi **1.** *to wait* od *serve at table* **2.** ⟨cards⟩ *to follow suit*; nicht ~ *to revoke, to refuse* | leicht zu **~d** *easy-to-use* [attr]; → bedienbar **Bedienende(r** m) f *operator* ⟨a. comp⟩

Bed·ienstete: der ~ (ein ~r) m ~n/~n *attendant, servant, footman* ‖ *= Beamte **Bed·iente:** der ~ (ein ~r) m ~n/~n (*man-*)*servant, attendant* ‖ (Lakai) *flunkey, lackey, lacquey; footman*

Bed·ienten- **≗haft** a *servile, cringing, fawning* **~kleidung** f, **~rock** m *livery* **~seele** f *flunkey; cringing soul* **~sitz** m (hinten am Wagen) *dicky, rumble* **~stube** f, **~zimmer** n *servants' room*

Bed·ienung *f* ~/~en **1.** *attendance* (jds *upon a p*) ‖ ⟨mot & mach⟩ *servicing*; einfachste ~ ⟨tech⟩ *minimum attendance*; schnelle u einfache ~ *speed and operational simplicity* ‖ (bei Tisch, im Hotel etc) *service*; ~ inbegriffen, einschließlich ~ *service included, inclusive service* Preise einschließlich (Licht u) ~ *inclusive terms* ‖ → Verfügung ‖ ~, bitte! *some service, please*! | ⟨com⟩ *attendance*; reelle ~ ⟨com⟩ (*the giving of*) *good value* **2.** ⟨tech⟩ *working* (*of a machine*) **3.** [konkr] **a.** *servants; domestics; attendants* [pl] ‖ *waiters* [pl] **b.** *crew; team* **~sanweisung** *operating* od *service instructions* [pl] **~sbühne** f ⟨aero⟩ *service platform* **~seinrichtungen** f pl ⟨tech⟩ controls **~(sgeld** n) *service* (*charge*) ‖ ~zuschlag [m] *service charge* **~sgeschwindigkeit** f *operating speed* **~sknopf** m *control knob* **~smannschaft** f ⟨mil⟩ *service personnel* od *crew*; *gunners* pl **~sturm** *m* (Rakete) *gantry tower* **~svorschrift** f = ~sanweisung

†**Bed·ing** m = Bedingung ‖ mit dem ~ daß = unter der Bedingung daß

bed·ingen vt [h] **1.** [bedang/bedungen] → ausbedingen **2.** [bedingte/bedingt] **a.** (die Bedingung *or* Voraussetzung s f. etw), (etw) ~ *to condition* (*a th*); die beiden Welten ~ e–a *the two worlds condition each other* ‖ (voraussetzen) *to presuppose, postulate* ‖ → bedingt **b.** *to cause, effect; involve, imply* **c.** (einschränken) *to qualify, restrict* **d.** ⟨gram⟩ der ~de Ausdruck *the conditional*

bed·ingt **1.** a **a.** [pred] ~ s durch *to be conditioned by, to be conditional* (od *dependent, contingent* (*up*)*on* ‖ ⟨jur⟩ *contingent* (*remainder*) **b.** [attr] *conditional* (*acceptance*); ⟨jur⟩ ~er

Straferlaß *remission of punishment conditional upon a time of probation* ‖ nur ∼e Richtigkeit *relative truth* ‖ *qualifield* (*reply*, *title*); *limited* **2.** adv *conditionally* (*correct*) ≗**gut** *n goods* [pl] *supplied conditionally* ≗**heit** f *conditionality*; *relativity* ≗**sein** n *conditional nature*

Bed·ingung f ∼/∼en **1.** (Voraussetzung) **a.** *condition* (f etw *of a th*); *provision, terms*; *proviso*; *prerequisite* ‖ geheime ∼ ⟨Am⟩ *string* ‖ unerläßliche ∼ *sine qua non* [L] ‖ ⟨com⟩ Ihren ∼en entsprechend (*finished*) *to your requirements* ‖ ⟨contr⟩ die hierfür geltenden ∼en *the terms and conditions governing such* | etw z ∼ m *to set the condition* (daß *that*); k–r ∼ unterworfen *unconditioned* ‖ (Schieß-, Übungs≗) *requirement* ‖ **mit** der ∼, daß.. *on condition that* ‖ **unter** der ∼ der Bezahlung v *conditionally upon the payment of..* ‖ unter der ∼, daß *on condition that*, ..daß er abreist *on condition of his leaving*, unter der stillschweigenden ∼ daß.. *on the understanding that..*; unter k–r ∼ *on no condition* od *account* ‖ unter sonst gleichen ∼en *other things being equal* ‖ **zur** ∼ **m** *to condition* (*that*); es zur ∼ m *to make it a condition* od *proviso* (*that*) ‖ etw als wesentliche ∼ ausmachen *to stipulate a th* ‖ ∼en stellen *to make conditions* **b.** ⟨gram⟩ Umstandsatz der ∼ *conditional clause* **2.** ⟨jur⟩ *condition*; aufschiebende ∼ *condition precedent*, auflösende ∼ *condition subsequent* **3.** [konkr] (Ausbedungenes) *stipulation*, *provision* ‖ ⟨com⟩ ∼en [pl] *terms* [pl]: Lieferungs≗en *t. of delivery*; unter jeder ∼ *on any terms*; unter günstigen (gleichen) ∼en (*to buy*) *on easy* (*equal*) *terms*; jdn zur Annahme der ∼en zwingen *to bring a p to terms* **4.** ∼en [pl] **(Verhältnisse)** *conditions* [pl]; unter günstigen ∼en (*to work*) *under favourable conditions*

Bed·ingungs- ∼**form** f ⟨gram⟩ die ∼ *the conditional* ∼**klausel** f *proviso* ≗**los 1.** a *unconditional* (Anerkennung, Unterwerfung); *unqualified* (*statement*); *unquestioning* (*obedience*, *loyalty*); *indiscriminate* (*admission*) **2.** adv *unconditionally* ∼**satz** m ⟨gram⟩ *conditional clause* ∼**schießen** n *record firing* od *practice* ≗**weise** adv *upon condition, conditionally*

bedr·ängen vt [h] (P) jdn ∼ *to close* od *press in upon a p*; *to mob, press a p*; ⟨Am⟩ *to crowd a p* ‖ *to harass, vex a p*; *to be urgent with a p* (um etw *for a th*) ‖ *to overwhelm, pelt, worry a p* (mit *with*) ‖ hart bedrängt v *hard pressed by*; hart bedrängt w *to be hard put to it* (*to do*) | (of *duties*) *to throng upon a p*; (of ideas, etc) *to crowd in upon a p*

Bedr·ängnis f ∼/-nisse *need* (in ∼ *in n.*); *plight*; *distress*; *affliction, oppression* | in gr ∼ *with one's back to the wall*; *at bay* ‖ Zeiten der ∼ *times of stress* ‖ jdn aus der ∼ befreien *to pull a p out of the fire* ‖ in ∼ geraten *to fall on evil times, to come to grief* **bedr·ängt** a [pp v bedrängen] sich in ∼er Lage, in ∼en Umständen befinden *to be hard put to it*, (*to be*) *in straitened circumstances* **Bedr·ängung** f ∼/∼en *pressure*; → Bedrängnis

bedr·äuen vt [h] ⟨poet⟩ = **bedr·ohen** vt [h] (jdn) *to threaten, menace* (mit *with*) ‖ (Frieden) *to threaten* ‖ sehr —ht s *to be in a very exposed position* **bedr·ohlich 1.** a *threatening, menacing forbidding* (*cliffs*) ‖ ∼er Zustand *gravity*; ∼es Anzeichen *threat* (*of rain*) **2.** adv *threateningly*

×**bedripst** a ⟨fam⟩ **1.** = kleinlaut, verlegen **2.** = betrübt

Bedr·ohung f ∼/∼en *threat, menace* (e–r S *to a th*) ‖ e–e ∼ des Friedens *a threat* od *menace to peace* ‖ ⟨jur⟩ *threatening a p with the commission of a crime*

Bedruckbarkeit f ⟨pap⟩ *printability*

bedr·ucken vt [h] *to print over* (od *on*); das Papier ist bedruckt *the p. is printed over* ‖ (Tuch) *to print*

bedr·ücken vt [h] (jdn) *to* (*op*)*press*; *to grind*; *to harras* | (Gemüt) *to oppress*; *afflict, depress* ‖ was bedrückt dich? *what's on your mind?* es -ckt mich schwer *it weighs heavily upon me*

bedr·ückt a *depressed* (*mood*); *in low spirits*

Bedr·ücker m ∼s/∼ *oppressor* **Bedr·ücktheit** f *oppression, depression* **Bedr·ückung** f ∼/∼en *oppression*; *tyranny, stress*; *urgency* ‖ (innere) *compunction*; → Bedrücktheit

Bedschap·ur n → Bidschapur

°**bed·udelt** a = beschwipst → d.

Bedu·ine m ∼n/∼n, **bedu·inisch** a *Bedouin*

bed·ünken 1. vt [imps] [h] (mst: dünken) es bedünkt mich *it seems to me*, † *methinks* **2.** ≗ n: m–s ∼s, nach m–m ∼ *in my opinion*

bed·ürfen vi (→ dürfen) [h] e–r S (jds) *to need, want a th* (*a p*); *to be* od *stand in need of, to be in want of a th* (*a p*); e–r S dringend (besonders) ∼ *to be in great need* (*extra need*) *of a th*; er bedarf der Ruhe *he wants rest* | es bedarf großer Anstrengung *it takes a lot* (*to do*) ‖ es bedarf k–r Antwort *no reply is needed* od *required*; der Brief bedarf keiner besonderen Beantwortung . . *calls for no special reply* ‖ es bedarf k–r Vorzerkleinerung *no preliminary crushing is necessary* ‖ es bedurfte aller unserer Kraft *it needed* od *required all our energy* (*to do*) ‖ die S bedurfte drastischer Maßnahmen *the matter called for drastic measures* ‖ es bedarf nicht wiederholt z w *it does not require repeating*

Bed·ürfnis n -nisses/-nisse **1.** *need* (nach Ruhe *of rest*; *to do*); dringendes ∼ *necessity* (nach *for*); (inneres) *urge* (*to do*); ein ∼ h nach etw *to be* od *stand in need of a th*; *to need, want a th*; es ist mir ein ∼ z tun *I feel the urge, I am urged* od *bound to do*; es liegt kein ∼ dafür *or* dazu vor *there is no need of it*; e–m sich seit langem fühlbar machenden ∼ abhelfen *to supply a long-felt want* ‖ s–e ∼se verrichten *to relieve nature* od *the bowels* ‖ –nisse [pl] *needs, requirements, wants* [pl] (:*he has few requirements*) **2.** (das Gewünschte) *a desideratum* [L], *a want*; [mst pl] *wants*; *necessaries, necessities* [pl]; Lebensbedürfnisse *the necessaries of life* ∼**anstalt** f (*public*) *lavatory, urinal*; *cloakroom*; (*public*) *convenience*; ⟨Am⟩ *comfort station, rest-room* ∼**befriedigung** f *satisfaction of one's wants* (od *needs*)

bed·ürfnislos a *having few wants* ‖ *frugal*, → anspruchslos **Bed·ürfnislosigkeit** f ∼/ *frugality*

bed·ürftig a **1.** [pred] e–r S ∼ s *to be in need* od *want of a th*; *to need, want a th*; trost∼ *in need of comfort* **2.** [attr] *indigent, needy, necessitous* ≗**keit** f ∼/ *neediness, want, destitution, indigence* | ∼snachweis [m] ⟨m. m.⟩ *means test*

°**bed·useln** [vref] sich ∼ *to get fuddled*

B·eederwand f = Beiderwand

B·eefsteak ['bi:fsteik] n ∼s/∼s **1.** (*beef-*)*steak* **2.** deutsches ∼ *Hamburg*(*er*) *steak*, (*ham*)*burger* (*steak*); *rissole*; Tat·ar≗ *steak à la tatare*

be·ehren vt [h] **1.** (jdn) *to honour, favour* (mit *with*); jdn, ein Fest mit s–r Gegenwart ∼ *to honour a p, a festival with one's presence* ‖ ⟨com⟩ *to favour* (*with orders*) **2.** ∼ Sie uns bald wieder *give us the favour of another visit* **3. sich** ∼ **a.** Herr u Frau N. ∼ sich anzuzeigen *Mr. N. and Mrs. N. have the honour of announcing* od *to annouce ..*; ich beehre mich, Sie zum Diner am 19. April einzuladen *I request the favour of your company at a dinner on April 19th* **b.** ⟨bes com⟩ ich beehre mich, Ihnen mitzuteilen .. *I beg to inform you ..* (beizufügen *to enclose*)

be·eiden, be·eidigen vt [h] **1.** (etw) *to affirm* (*a th*) *by oath, to confirm* (*a th*) *by swearing* **2.** jdn ∼ = vereidigen **be·eidet, be·eidigt** a *sworn* (*member*); ⟨jur⟩ beeidigte Aussage *sworn evidence*, schriftlich b. A. *affidavit*; ∼er Bücherrevisor *chartered accountant* **Be·eidigung** f ~/~en *affirmation* (od *confirmation*) *by oath* || → Vereidigung (jds)

be·eifern [vref] [h] sich ~ *to exert o.s., to endeavour, to strive* (*to do*)

be·eilen vt [h] **1.** (etw) beeile deine Schritte *hurry up, make haste*; → beschleunigen **2. sich** ~ *to make haste, to hurry* od *hasten* (*along*); *to hurry* (⟨fam⟩ *buck*) *up* (mit etw *with a th*); ⟨fam⟩ *to stir one's stumps*; ⟨sl⟩ *to get a move on, to step on it*; ⟨Am⟩ *to step lively*; ⟨sl⟩ *to step on the gas* || beeile dich *be quick, hurry up*; → sich eilen **Be·eilung**: *hurry*; ~! *hurry up*!

be·eindrucken vt [h] (jdn) *to impress* (*a p*), *to impress o.s. on* (*a p*); die Idee —ckt ihn in zunehmendem Maße *the idea grows upon him* || –ckt v *struck with* || (nicht) beeindruckt s *to be* (*un*)*impressed* (durch *by*) || ⟨theat⟩ das Publikum ~ *to get across* || → imponieren

be·einflussen vt [h] jdn ~ *to bring one's influence to bear* (*up*)*on a p* || (jdn, etw) *to influence* (zu jds Gunsten *in a p's favour*); *to affect* (*a p*; *an organ*; *the health*); *to exercise an influence on* (*a p*) || *to throw one's weight about* .. (*in the diplomacy*) || ⟨Am⟩ *to swing*; ⟨pol⟩ (Abgeordnete) *to lobby* || beeinflußt w durch *to yield to* (:*to y. to brandy*); beeinflußt w bei *or* durch (of organs) *to be implicated in* | (of ideas) günstig ~ *to preposses* (*a p*); *to react on* (*a p*) || (mst: nachteilig ~) *to bias, prejudice* (*a p*); *to tell on* (*a p*); (jds Urteil etc) *to warp* || (Vorgang) störend ~ *to interfere with* (*a th*) || → Einfluß ausüben **Be·einflussung** f ~/ die ~ jds *the influence* od *effect on a p*; gegenseitige ~ *mutual influence upon one another*; ungebührliche ~ *undue influence*; s–e ~ durch Goethe *the influence exerted upon him by Goethe*; → Einfluß || (~ der Presse) *inspiration*; durch ~ von seiten jds *at the i. of a p*; gegenseitige ~ *interplay* (*between*; *of forces*) | gegenseitige ~ zus-treffender Wellen *interference*

be·einträchtigen vt [h] jds Rechte ~ *to encroach* od *infringe* (*up*)*on a p's rights* || (die Gesundheit) *to affect injuriously*; *to injure, impair*; (jds Ruf) *to injure* || (jds Aussichten, Interesse) *to prejudice*; *to vitiate*; *to abrogate*; *to be prejudicial* od *detrimental to* (*a th*); *to derogate from* (*a th*); (jds Verdienst) *to detract from* (*a p's merit*); e–e S sehr (etwas) ~ *to detract much* (*somewhat*) *from a th*; jds Leistungen ~ *to cramp a p's style* **Be·einträchtigung** f ~/~en *impairment* (*of rights*) || *injury, damage* (des Rufes jds *to a p's reputation*); *detriment*; *prejudice, wrong* (e–r S *to a th*); *detraction* od *derogation* (e–r S *from a th*)

be·eist a *covered with ice*

Be·elzebub m *Beelzebub* || ⟨fig⟩ den Teufel durch ~ austreiben *to cast out devils through B.*, *to make bad worse*; → Traufe

be·enden, be·endigen vt [h] **1.** (Arbeit, Untersuchung) *to complete, end, finish*; (Dienst) *to terminate*; *to bring* (*a th*) *to an end* od *a close*; (Sitzung) *to close, to wind up*; (Rede) *to wind, finish, close up*; *to conclude* (mit *with*; indem er sagte *by saying*) || (Buch) *to end off* **2.** (e–r S ein Ende m) *to make an end of* (*a th*), *to put an end* (od *stop*) *to* (*a th*); der Vertrag beendet ihre Streitigkeiten *the treaty puts an end to their quarrel* **B.gung** f ~/~en *completion*; *concluding*; *close, conclusion, termination* (*of a journey, a quarrel*); s–e ~ finden (of a discussion) *to be concluded* (od *terminated*), *to reach its close*

be·engen vt [h] (jdn) *to cramp* (*up*); *to make* (*a p*) *clammy*; beengt sitzen *to sit cramped* | *to hamper, to impede*; durch s–e Kleidung beengt s *to be hampered by one's clothes* || (Herz) *to constrict* || sich beengt fühlen *to feel hampered* od *oppressed*; *to feel ill at ease* || → einengen, beschränken | **~d** a *confining* (Raum); *oppressed* (Gefühl)

be·engt a *narrow, small*; auf ~em Raume *in a confined space* || im Raume ~ s *to be cramped for space* || sich [acc] auf der Brust ~ fühlen *to feel tight in the chest, to feel a tightness across the ch.* || ~e Verhältnisse [pl] *straitened circumstances* [pl] | [adv] ~ leben *to be in cramped conditions*; ~ stehen *to be crowded into a small place* **Be·engtheit, Be·engung** f *constriction*; ein Gefühl der ~ h *to have the feeling of oppression*

be·erben vt [h] jdn ~ *to be heir to a p, to be a p's heir, to inherit a p's property*

b·eerblau a *bilberry blue*

be·erdigen vt [h] (jdn) *to inter, bury*; *entomb*

Be·erdigung f ~/~en *interment, burial*; *funeral*; → Begräbnis, Bestattung **~sanstalt** f *undertaker's business, undertaking b.*; (*firm of*) *funeral furnishers* [pl] **~sfeier** f = Begräbnisfeier **~sgeschäft, ~sinstitut** n = Beerdigungsanstalt || Besitzer, Direktor, Leiter e–s ~s ⟨a.⟩ *mortician* **~skosten** [pl] *funeral expenses* [pl]

B·eere f ~/~n *berry*; ×Blau≃, Heidel≃, ×Schwarz≃ *bilberry, blaeberry, blueberry, huckleberry* || ~n sammeln *to berry*; ~n bilden *to berry* | **~n- ≃förmig** n *bacciform* **≃fressend** a *baccivorous* **~obst** n *berries* [pl] **≃tragend** a *berried* (*shrub*) **~wein** m *wine from berries*

B·eermost m *must from small fruit*

Beet n ~(e)s/~e *bed*; Blumen≃ *flower bed*, Garten≃ *garden b.*, Gemüse≃ *vegetable b.* Spargel≃ *asparagus b.*; Erbsen≃ *bed of peas* || Rand≃ *border*; Mist≃ *hotbed*

Beet, Beete f → Bete

b·eetlen vt [h] [engl] ⟨tech⟩ (Stoff, Leinen) *to beetle*; → Glanz

bef·ähigen vt [h] (jdn) *to enable* (*to do*); *to make* (*a p*) *fit, to qualify* (z *for*; *to do*); er ist für die Arbeit nicht befähigt *he is not capable of doing the work, he is not fit for the w.* (od *up to the work*) **bef·ähigt** a *able, capable, gifted* (P)

Bef·ähigung f ~/~en *qualification* (für, zu *for*) || (natürl. Begabung) *aptitude* (z *for*), *capacity* (*of, for*); *talent* (*for*) **~snachweis** m [abstr] *evidence of competency* || [konkr] (Urkunde) *certificate of qualification* od ⟨off⟩ *competence* **~sprüfung** f ⟨aero⟩ *qualification test*

bef·ahl 1. & 3. sg pret v befehlen

bef·ahrbar a *passable, practicable* (*road*); nicht ~ *impassable, impracticable* || *navigable* (*river, coast*); nicht ~ *unnavigable* **≃keit** f ~/ *trafficability*

bef·ahren I. vt [→ fahren] [h] **1.** (Straße) *to drive on, to travel on* od *over, to pass over* (*a road*); ein Land im Auto ~ *to travel a country by car* || (Fluß, Meer) *to navigate*; (oft ~) *to frequent*; → II. **2.** ⟨min⟩ e–e Grube ~ *to descend* (od *go down*) *into a mine*; die Grube wird ~ *the mine is being exploited*; (e–n Schacht) *to descend* **3.** ein Feld mit Dung ~ *to cover a field with manure, to unload manure on to a field* **II.** [a] ein viel~er Weg *a much frequented road, a well-beaten track* || ⟨hunt⟩ der Bau ist ~ *the earth is occupied* || ⟨mar⟩ ~es Volk *old salts* od *tars* [pl]

Bef·all m *attack on plants and fruits by parasites, moulds*, etc.; *noxious growth on plants, trees* || ⟨at⟩ (schädlicher) ~ (*radioactive*) *contamination*

bef·allen vt [→ fallen] [h] **1.** ⟨hort, for⟩ (v. Schädlingen) *to infest* **2.** (jdn) *to befall* (*a p*), *to come* od *fall* (*up*)*on* (*a p*); *to happen to* (*a p*) || *to attack*; *to seize* (*a p*), *to catch* od *seize hold of* (*a p*) || *to catch* od *take* (*a p*) *unawares, to surprise* (*a p*) || ~ w v *to be seized* od *taken with*, v e–r Krankheit ~ w *to be taken ill*; v Schrecken ~ w *to be overtaken* od *stricken with terror* || Furcht befiel sie *fear came over them*; v gr Furcht ~ [pp] *smitten with panic, fear*

†**bef·angen** vt [→ fangen] [h] **1.** (jdn) *to enclose, encompass* **2.** ⟨übtr⟩ (jdn) *to seize; overcome, overpower* **3.** (jdn) *embarrass; to put* (*a p*) *out of countenance*

bef·angen a [pp v ~] **1.** [pred] (→ ~ vt) **a.** ~ s in *to be enslaved in*; in Sünde ~ s *to be enslaved by sin* ‖ in Vorurteilen ~ s *to be swayed by prejudice, to be bias(s)ed* (od *prepossessed, prejudiced*) (zu Gunsten jds *in favour of a p*; gegen jdn *against a p*) ‖ in e–m Irrtum ~ s *to labour under a delusion; to be mistaken* ‖ ⟨jur⟩ (parteiisch) *bias(s)ed*, ⟨Am⟩ *biased* **b.** (*to be*) *lost*; (*to be*) *lapped* (in *in*) ‖ vom Schlaf ~ s *to be overcome with sleep* **c.** *easily embarrassed, self-conscious; nervous* (betreffs *of*; gegenüber jdm *of a p*); ~ s gegenüber jdm *to be ill at ease with a p* ‖ jdn ~ m *to disconcert a p, to put a p out of countenance* ‖ ~ tun *to look embarrassed* **2.** [attr] **a.** *embarrassed, disconcerted; shy* **b.** *bias(s)ed, prejudiced, partial* (*judge*) | ≂**heit** f ~/ **1.** *self-consciousness; embarrassment*; sie nahm ihm die ~ *she put him at ease* ‖ **2.** *prejudice, prepossession; partiality* ‖ ⟨jur⟩ (Parteilichkeit) *bias*; e–n Richter wegen (Besorgnis der) ~ ablehnen *to challenge a judge on account of* (*presumed*) *partiality*

bef·assen vt [h] **1. a.** † = einschließen **b.** *to touch, handle* **2.** ⟨übtr⟩ **sich ~ mit a.** (P) *to concern* (od *occupy*) *o.s. with; to deal with; to engage in; to go in for; to attend* od *turn to* (*a th*); *to handle, undertake* (*a th*), sich mit Politik ~ *to take up politics, to dabble in p.*; *to take up* (*the study of*); sich unberufen ~ mit *to meddle with* ‖ *to take care of* (*a p, a th*) ‖ sich nicht ~ mit *to keep aloof from* **b.** (S) *to be concerned with* (*:the lecture was c. with the causes of ..*)

bef·ehden vt [h] **1.** (jdn) *to go to war with, to make war against* od *upon* (*a p*); *to fight* (*a p*) ‖ ⟨übtr⟩ *to attack* (*a p*) | (etw) *to combat; to attack* **2. sich** ~ *to fight* (*against*) *one another, to be at feud with one another* ‖ ⟨übtr⟩ *to spar; to dispute* **Bef·ehdung** f ~/~en ⟨übtr⟩ *attack, criticism* (*:to be subjected to attacks*)

Bef·ehl m ~s/~e **1.** (Gebot) **a.** *command, order; bidding*; ⟨poet⟩ *mandate* ‖ ausdrücklicher ~ *injunction* ‖ ⟨mil⟩ Tages≂ *order of the day* ‖ (Auftrag) *charge*; → Auftrag, Vorschrift ‖ ⟨comp⟩ festgelegter ~ *predetermined program of instructions* (*set up on the control panel*) **b. auf** jds ~ *at* od *by a p's command; by order of a p* ‖ bis auf weiteren ~ *till further orders* ‖ auf *or* durch mündlichen ~ *by order of mouth* ‖ ~ ist ~ ⟨hum⟩ *order is order*; z ~, Herr Major (etc)! *yes, Sir!, very good, Sir!* → Dienst, Verfügung | e–n ~ **ausführen** *to carry out an order* ‖ ~ ausgeführt! ⟨hum⟩ *delivered the goods!* ‖ den ~ erhalten h *to be ordered, to be under orders* (*to do*) ‖ ~e erteilen *to give orders* ‖ jdm ~e erteilen *to order a p about* ‖ jdm den ~ erteilen (*or* geben) z tun *to order a p to do* ‖ ~ geben z tun *to give orders* (od *the, an order*) *to do; to give the word to do*; ~ geben, daß etw geschieht *to give orders for a th to be done* (od *that a th should be done*), *to order a th to be done* ‖ dem ~ jds gehorchen *to do a p's bidding, to be obedient to a p's bidding* ‖ den ~ h z tun *to be under orders, to have a p's command to do* ‖ e–n ~ verweigern *to refuse to obey an order* **2.** ⟨jur⟩ (Urkunde) Vollziehungs≂ *warrant*; Haft≂ *warrant of arrest*; Pfändungs≂ *warrant of distress* **3.** ⟨mil⟩ (Befehlsgewalt) *command* (über *of*) ‖ unter dem ~ v *under the command* od *orders of ..* ‖ den ~ h *or* führen über *to be in command of, to command* (*a regiment*) ‖ unter jds ~ stehen *to be under the command of a p* ‖ den ~ übernehmen über *to take command of ..* ‖ → ~s–

bef·ehlen vt [befahl/befohlen] [h] **1.** ⟨bib⟩ (empfehlen) s–e Seele Gott ~ *to commend one's soul to God*; Gottes Schutz befohlen s *to be commended* (od *entrusted*) *to God* ‖ Gott befohlen! *adieu! God be with you! good-bye!* **2.** (gebieten) ~, daß jd tut; jdm ~ z tun *to command* (od *direct, enjoin, order, tell*) *a p to do; to dictate for a p to do*; ~ daß jd geschickt wird *to command* (od *direct, order*) *a p to be sent* (od *that a p should be sent*) ‖ etw ~ *to order a th*; ~, daß etw geschieht *to order* (od *direct*) *a th to be done* (od *that a th should be done*); *to give orders for a th to be done*; ⟨Am⟩ *to order* (od *direct*) *a th done*; er befahl, es z tun *he ordered it to be done* ‖ wer hat es befohlen? *who has ordered it?* er hat uns nichts z ~ *he has no right to dictate to us* (od *to order us about*); er ließ sich nichts ~ *he refused to be dictated to*; er ließ sich v niemand ~ *he r. to take orders from anybody* ‖ ⟨com⟩ was ~ Sie? *what is your pleasure?*, *what can I do for you?* ~ Sie sonst noch was? *do you wish for anything more?* | [abs] wer hat hier z ~? *who is entitled to give orders here?* ‖ wie Sie ~ *as you wish* od *please*; wie befohlen *as directed*; tu wie dir befohlen *do as you are told* ‖ → anordnen; heißen; lassen

bef·ehlend a *mandatory* (*function*); *imperative* (*tone*) ‖ = **bef·ehlerisch** a (P) *imperious, dictatorial; authoritative, peremptory; overbearing*

bef·ehligen vt [h] ⟨mil⟩ (Heer) *to command; to be in command of*; befehligt v *under the command of* ‖ *to head, lead*

Bef·ehls- ~ausgabe, ~erteilung f *issue* od *issuance of orders*; ⟨mil⟩ *briefing* **~bunker** m ⟨aero⟩ *flight line bunker* **~ebene** f ⟨mil m. m.⟩ *echelon of command* **~empfänger** m *courier* **~empfangsraum** m ⟨mar, aero⟩ *ready room* **~folgezähler** → —zählregister **~form** f ⟨gram⟩ *imperative* (*mood*) ‖ ⟨comp⟩ *instruction form* ≂**gemäß** adv *in accordance with orders* **~haber** m *commander, commanding-officer, chief* ‖ ⟨mar⟩ *admiral*; ~ der Aufklärungsschiffe *senior officer of the scouting forces* ≂**haberisch** a *imperious, dictatorial* **~repertoire** n ⟨comp⟩ *repertoire of instructions* **~schema** n ⟨comp⟩ *flow-chart, flow-diagram* **~schlüssel** m *code* **~sprache** f ⟨comp⟩ *computer language* **~stab** m ⟨rail Ger⟩ *signal disk* (⟨engl⟩ *green signal flag*) **~stelle** f ⟨aero⟩ ~ der Staffel *the flight commander's headquarters* [pl] **~ton** m *imperative tone* **~turm** m ⟨aero⟩ *control tower* **~übermittlungsapparat** m ⟨mar⟩ *transmitter gear* **~verweigerung** f ⟨mil⟩ *refusal to obey orders; disobedience* ≂**weise** adv *by way of command* **~wege** m pl ⟨mil⟩ *chains of command* **~wort** n ⟨comp⟩ *verb* ≂**widrig** a *contrary to orders* **~zählregister** n ⟨comp⟩ *address counter*

bef·einden vt [h] = anfeinden

Bef·ensterung f ~/~en ⟨arch⟩ *lights* pl; (Maßwerk) *fenestration*

bef·estigen vt [h] **1.** (Planke) *to fix, to secure; to make fast* ‖ (Seil, Draht) *to attach, to fasten, to tack, to tie* (an *to*); ein (Bergsteiger-) Seil ~ ⟨mount⟩ *to belay a rope*; (Feder) *to fix; to stick* (in *in*) ‖ (Gurt) ⟨Am⟩ *to cinch tight* ‖ (etw) mit Nägeln ~ *to pin* (an *to*); ⟨mar⟩ mit e–m Tau ~ *to lash* (an *to*); (Bugspriet) durch Tau ~ *to gammon* ‖ (Teile) durch Bindestück ~ *to tie* ‖ z ~d *tie-on* (*label*) ‖ (Straße) *to surface* (*s. d road*); (Start- u Landebahn) *to pave*; befestigt *hard-surface* [attr] (⟨aero⟩ *runway*) **2.** ⟨mil⟩ (Stadt) *to fortify*; (Grenze) *to strengthen; to secure* **3.** ⟨übtr⟩ (Wörter) *to fix* (*in the memory*) ‖ die Bande der Freundschaft ~ *to tighten the ties of friendship* ‖ (Einfluß etc) *to consolidate*; (Ruhm) *to establish; secure* ‖ (jdn) *to strengthen* (in *in*) **4. sich** ~ *to strengthen, to grow in strength* ‖ (of prices) *to harden, to stiffen* ‖ sich ~ l *to tie*; (mit Nadeln) *to pin*

Bef·estigung f ~/~en *attachment, fastening, fixing* (an *to*) ‖ ⟨mil⟩ *fortification*; ~en m *to* *fortify* **|** ⟨übtr⟩ *securing, strengthening; consolidation* **|** **~s- ~anlagen** f pl ⟨mil⟩ *defences* pl (*of a town*) **~arbeiten** f pl ⟨mil⟩ *works* [pl] *of fortification* **~bolzen** m ⟨tech⟩ (*fixture*) *stud* **~bügel** m ⟨tech⟩ *fastening bow* **~holz** n ⟨mar⟩ (f Tau) *belayingpin* **~kunst** f ⟨mil⟩ (*art of*) *fortification* **~linie** f *line of defence* **~mittel** n ⟨tech⟩ *fastener* **~schelle** f ⟨tech⟩ *mounting clip* **~werk** n ⟨mil⟩ *fortifications, defensive works*

bef·euchten vt [h] (Wäsche) *to damp, moisten, wet, humidify* **Bef·euchtung** f ~/~en *damping, moistening, wetting*

bef·euern vt (Flugplatz) *to mark with lights* **|** ≃ n **Bef·euerung** f ⟨mar⟩ *lighting, lights* [pl]; ⟨aero⟩ Flugstrecken≃ *airway-lighting*

B·effchen n ~s/~ [mst pl] ⟨ec & jur⟩, ⟨engl a. univ⟩ *bands* [pl] ‖ (*clergyman's*) *kerchief*

bef·iedern vt [h] *to cover* od *furnish with feathers*; (Pfeil) *to feather*; befiedert *feathered*

bef·inden I. vt/i [→ finden] [h] **1.** vt **a.** *to find, to deem*; etw wahr ~ *to find a th true*; der Vorschlag wurde gut befunden *the proposal was deemed good* ‖ es für richtig ~ z tun *to deem it right, to think fit* od *proper to do* ‖ ⟨jur⟩ jdn schuldig ~ *to find a p guilty* **b. sich** ~ *to be, feel* ‖ er befindet sich wohl *he is well, feels fine*; wie ~ Sie sich? *how are you*? wir ~ uns hier sehr wohl *we are quite comfortable here* ‖ es befindet sich zw .. *you will find it between* .. ‖ der Eingang befindet sich dort drüben *the entrance is over there* ‖ er befindet sich im 20. Lebensjahre *he is in his twentieth year* ‖ sie ~ sich auf Reisen *they are on their travels, they are away*; sie ~ sich viel auf R. *they travel a good deal* ‖ sich im Irrtum ~ *to be mistaken*; sich in Verlegenheit ~ *to be at a loss, to be embarrassed* ‖ er befand sich umgeben v .. *he found himself surrounded by* .. **2.** vi (entscheiden) ~ über etw *to decide a th* **II.** ≃ n ~s/ **1.** *opinion, view,* (*way of*) *thinking*, nach m–m ~ *in my opinion*; → Meinung ‖ je nach ~ *as you may think fit* **2.** *state of health*; sich nach jds ~ erkundigen *to inquire after a p's health*

bef·indlich [a] ~ s *to be, to be found* od *present*; *to be contained* (in *in*) ‖ die auf dem Dampfer ~en Passagiere *the passengers on the steamer*; die am Orte ~en Truppen *the troops stationed at the place*; irgendwo ~ s *to be somewhere or other* ‖ darin ~ war ein Juwel *contained therein was a jewel*

bef·ingern vt [h] (etw) *to finger*; *to handle with one's fingers*; *to pinch* (*a roll*) ‖ °⟨sex⟩ *to muck about*, → befummeln ‖ ⟨übtr⟩ *to manage*

befl·aggen vt [h] (Häuser etc) *to* (*be*)*flag*

befl·ecken vt [h] **1.** (beschmutzen) **a.** ⟨eig⟩ (Papier mit Tinte) *to blot* ‖ (Tuch etc) *to stain, spot* ‖ sich die Finger ~ *to spot* (od *stain*) *one's fingers* (*with*) ‖ mit Blut befleckt *blood-stained* **b.** (entweihen) (Heiligtum) *to defile, pollute* **c.** ⟨fig⟩ (Ehre, Namen, Ruf) *to asperse, besmirch, smirch, soil, stain, sully, tarnish* **2.** (mit Absätzen versehen) (Schuhe) *to heel* **Befl·eckung** f ~/~en ⟨übtr⟩ *defilement, pollution* (*of a sacred place*) ‖ ⟨fig⟩ *staining, sullying* (*of a p's reputation*)

befl·eißen [vrefl] [befliß/beflissen] [h] sich e–r S ~ [im prs mst befleißigen] *to aim at a th, to be intent on a th, to be solicitous of* (od *about*) *a th*; *to give one's mind to a th*; sich der Kürze ~ *to study brevity* ‖ sich ~ z tun *to apply o.s. to do, to endeavour to do, to be intent on doing, to be solicitous to do*; *to study* (od *to take pains*) *to do* ‖ → beflissen

befl·eißigen [vrefl] [h] [im prs & pret] = befleißen; er befleißigt sich großer Höflichkeit *he studies to be polite*

befl·iegen vt [h] ≃flog/~flogen ⟨aero⟩ (e–e Strecke) *to fly*

befl·issen a [pred] **1.** *solicitous, studious* (e–r S *of a th*; *to do*); ~ s = sich befleiß(ig)en **2.** der Medizin ~ s *to study medicine*; → dienst~

Befl·issene: der ~ (ein ~r) m *student*, ein der Medizin ~r, ein ~r der M. *a student of medicine* ‖ [oft in comp] → Dienst≃r, Handels≃r **Befl·issenheit** f ~/~en *studiousness, zeal* (*to do*); *assiduity, diligence* **befl·issentlich** adv *assiduously, studiously*; (absichtlich) *deliberately*

befl·ügeln vt [h] ⟨fig⟩ *to wing* (: *fear winged his steps*); *to lend* od *give wings to*; s–e Begeisterung beflügelte s–e Worte *his enthusiasm gave wings to his words* **befl·ügelt** a ⟨fig⟩ *winged, swift*

befl·uten vt [h] ⟨mar⟩ (Schiffsteil) *to flood*

Befl·utung f *flooding*

bef·ohlen [pp] v befehlen

bef·olgen vt [h] (Befehl, Vorschrift) *to follow, obey*; nicht ~ *to disobey* ‖ (Regel) *to comply with, to observe*; (Brauch) *to be observant of* ‖ (Grundsatz) *to abide by, to adhere to*; (Normen) ⟨tech⟩ *to observe* (*standards*); (Rat) *to act upon*; *to follow out* **bef·olgenswert** a *worth following* **|** ≃ n, **Bef·olgung** f ~/~en; die ~ e–r S [gen] *the compliance with a th*; *observance of a th*; *adherence to a th*

Beförderer m ~s/~ ⟨rail, mar, aero, etc⟩ *carrier* **bef·ördern** vt [h] **A. 1.** (fördern) (Vorgang) *to accelerate, hasten* ‖ *further* ‖ (Verdauung) *to aid, promote*; die Verdauung ~d *digestive* **2.** (jdn) *to prefer* (z *to*) ‖ ⟨bes mil⟩ *to advance, promote*; jdn zum Oberst ~ *to advance a p to be colonel, to promote a p colonel, to advance* od *promote a p to the rank of colonel*; befördert w *to gain* od *obtain promotion*; er wurde zum Oberst befördert *he was promoted* (*to be*) *c.* od *to the rank of c.* **B.** (spedieren) **1.** (Waren etc) *to forward* (mit der Bahn *by rail*); *to consign, convey, carry, dispatch, send*; (Gepäck) *to expedite*; *transport*; ⟨Am⟩ *to haul* ‖ mit der Post ~ *to post* ‖ (Holz) ⟨Am⟩ *to tote* **2.** jdn ~ *to pack a p off* (*to bed*); jdn schnell ~ *to bundle, to whisk a p* (in den Fahrstuhl *into the lift*), *to rush a p* (nach *to*) ‖ jdn aus dem Amt ~ *to fling a p out of office* ‖ jdn ins Jenseits ~ *to dispatch, kill a p* ‖ jdn z Tode ~ *to send a p to his death*; jdn z elektrischen Stuhl ~ *to send a p to the chair*

Bef·örderung f ~/~en **1.** (Förderung) *acceleration* ‖ *furtherance, promotion* (*of digestion*) **2.** *preferment* (*of a p*); *advancement, promotion* (z *to*) **3.** *forwarding*; *conveyance, dispatch, transport, haulage* (*of goods*) **~sart** f *mode of conveyance* **~skosten** [pl] *cost of transport*; ⟨rail⟩ *carriage charges* **~sleistung** f *number of passengers, etc carried* **~smittel** n (*means of*) *conveyance*; *transportation facility*; [pl] *means of transportation* **~ssteuer** f *transport-tax* **~sunternehmen** n = Beförderer

bef·orsten vt [h] *to forest*

befr·achten vt [h] (Wagen) *to load*; ⟨Am⟩ *to freight*; (Schiff) *to freight*; → chartern **Befr·achter** m ~s/~ *freighter, charterer* ‖ (Absender) *consignor* **Befr·achtung** f ~/~en *affreightment*; *the hiring of a vessel* ‖ ~svertrag = Seefrachtvertrag

befr·ackt a (*waiter*) *in a dress-coat, in tails*

befr·agen vt [h] **1.** (jdn) *to interrogate*; *to turn to* (*a p*); (den Arzt) *to consult* (über *about*); ⟨bes Am com⟩ *to contact a p* **|** ⟨übtr⟩ (die Sterne) *to consult, question*; (Wetter etc) *consult* ‖ → fragen **2. sich** ~ *to consult, to take counsel* (mit jdm über etw *with a p about a th*) **Befr·agung** f ~/~en *interrogation*; *consultation* (*of a p*) ‖ *questioning* ‖ ⟨demog, etc⟩ *personal interview*; direkte ~ *field enquiry* od *survey*

befr·ansen vt [h] *to fringe*

befr·eien vt [h] **1.** (jdn, e–n Gefangenen) *to set* (*a p*) *free* (od *at liberty*); *to release, discharge* ‖ (jdn, ein Land) *to free* (v *from* [*oppression*]); (jdn) *to liberate, release* (aus *from* [*prison*]); *to rid* (v *of*) ‖ *to deliver, rescue* (aus, v *from*) ‖ *to* *disentangle, to extricate* (aus *from* [*difficulties*]) | ⟨übtr⟩ (jdn) *to absolve* (*from an obligation*); *to dispense* (*from a task*); jdn vom Besuch ~ *to excuse a p from attendance*; ich wurde v der Aufgabe befreit *I was excused* (*from*) *the task* ‖ *to exempt* (*from taxes, duties*, etc.); befreit s v *to be exempt from* ‖ *to release* (*from cares, a promise*) ‖ *to acquit, free* (*from a charge, from suspicion*); ⟨school⟩ v Turnen befreit s *to be excused gymnastics* ‖ *to relieve* (v Furcht *from fear*; v e–r Last *of a load*) ‖ (Geist, Inneres) *to clear* (v *of* [*doubts*]) ‖ → aufatmen | (Handel etc) *to free, liberate* (v *from*) **2. sich** ~ *to shake off one's fetters, to break loose* ‖ *to extricate o.s., to disentangle* (aus *from*); sich durch e–n Ruck ~ *to shake o.s. free* | ⟨übtr⟩ *to free o.s.* (aus, v *from* [*dangers*]); *to rid o.s.* (v *of*) ‖ sich v jdm ~ *to get rid of a p*; *to shake a p off* ‖ sich v den Kleidern ~ *to divest o.s. of one's clothes, to strip*

befr·eiend a *liberating* (*action*; *angel*) ‖ ⟨übtr⟩ *relieving* (*word*); *solvent* (*power of laughter*; *influence*) **Befr·eier** m ~s/~ *liberator*; *deliverer* (aus, v *from*) **befr·eit** a *freed* (*slave*)

Befr·eiung f ~/~en *liberation, deliverance* (v *from*); *rescue, release* (aus *from*); s–e ~ finden *to be delivered* ‖ ⟨jur⟩ gewaltsame ~ *rescue* (*of a prisoner*) ‖ *disentanglement, extrication* (aus *from*) | ⟨übtr⟩ *exemption, immunity* (v Steuern etc *from taxes*) ‖ *relief* (v *from* [*pain*]) **~skriege** m [pl] ⟨Ger⟩ *the War of Liberation* (*1813—15*)

befr·emden 1. vt [h] jdn ~ *to appear strange to a p*; es befremdet mich *it strikes me as strange* (*that*) ‖ *to surprise, to astonish*; *to embarrass* (*a p*); sein Benehmen befremdet mich *his conduct surprises me* **2.** ≗ n *surprise* (über *at*); *astonishment*; z m–m ~ *to my surprise* ‖ *displeasure*; *dismay*; tiefes ~ *deep resentment* (über *at*) **befr·emdend, befr·emdlich** a *strange, odd*; *queer*; *surprising*; *embarrassing* (jdm *to a p*); jdm ~ vorkommen *to astonish, surprise*; *embarrass a p*

befr·eunden [vref] [h] **1.** sich ~ *to become friends, to make friends with one another* ‖ sich ~ mit jdm *to make friends with a p*; †*to cotton on* (od *up*) *to a p* **2.** sich ~ mit etw *to become reconciled* (od *to reconcile o.s.*) *to a th*; *to cotton on to a th, to fall in with a th* (:*with an idea*); *to take kindly to a th* (:*to a duty*) ‖ *to approve of a th*; *to adopt a th*; → sich abfinden

befr·eundet a **1.** [pred] ~ s mit jdm *to be on friendly* od *intimate terms with a p*; mit e–a ~ s *to be friends*, ich war mit ihm ~ *we were friends*; sehr (*or* eng) ~ s *to be hand and glove with* (*a p*); sie waren eng ~ *they were very close friends*, ⟨fam⟩ *they were very thick* **2.** [attr] *friendly* (*relations with*); e–e ~e Nation *a friendly nation*; bei e–r ~en Familie *with friends*

Befr·eundung f ~/~en *making of friends*

befr·ieden vt [h] *to pacify, appease*

befr·iedigen vt [h] **1.** (jdn) *to content, satisfy*; *please* (*a p*); *to give satisfaction to a p*; schwer z ~ *hard to satisfy* (od *to please*) ‖ (Gläubiger) *to satisfy* **2.** die Bedürfnisse jds ~ *to provide for the needs of a p*; *to serve the wants of a p*; jds Eitelkeit ~ *to feed a p's vanity*; jds Wünsche ~ *to meet* (od *comply with*) *a p's wishes* ‖ Verlangen, Begierde, Trieb etc) *to appease, to glut, to gratify*; *to indulge*; *to satiate*; *to satisfy*; den Durst nach Rache ~ *to slake one's thirst for revenge*; → stillen ‖ (Geschmack) *to suit* (:*to suit all tastes*) **befr·iedigend 1.** a *satisfying*; *satisfactory* **2.** adv *contentedly*; (*to nod*) *approvingly* ‖ e–e Prüfung nur (mit) ≗ bestehen *to satisfy the examiners* **befr·iedigt** a [mst pred] *satisfied*; *well-content*; ~ s über (von) *to be gratified at, with* (*the success*), *to be pleased with* (*the result*); ⟨Am⟩ *to be proud about* (*a th*) **Befr·iedigung** f ~/~en **1.** *satisfying, satisfaction* (*of a p*); *payment* (*of creditors*); ~ aus e–r Hypothek ⟨jur⟩ *foreclosure of a mortgage* **2.** *appeasement*; *gratification, fulfilment, satisfaction* (*of a desire*); *compliance with* (*a desire* [nach *for*]) **3.** (Befriedigtsein) (P) *satisfaction* (über etw *at, with a th*); *gratification* (*at*); mit gr ~ *with great satisfaction*; ~ erhalten v, finden an *to take s. from*; ~ finden (suchen) *to find* (*to seek*) *s.* (z tun *in doing*); ~ verschaffen *to give satisfaction to a p* **Befr·iedung** f *pacification, appeasement* | ~sgebärde [f] ⟨eth⟩ *appeasing gesture*

befr·isten vt [h] *to limit in time* **Befr·istung** f ~/~en *limitation*

befr·uchten vt [h] ⟨biol⟩ (Ei) *to fecundate, fertilize, impregnate*; ⟨bot⟩ (Blüte) *to fructify* ‖ (Boden) *to fertilize, to make productive* ‖ ⟨übtr⟩ (Künstler) *to fecundate*; (Geist) *to fertilize, fructify* **befr·uchtend** a *fertilizing* (*effect*); *fecundating, fructifying*; ~e Kraft *fecundity*; ~ wirken *to exert a fertilizing influence* (auf *on*)

Befr·uchtung f ~/~en ⟨biol⟩ *fecundation, fertilization, impregnation*; ⟨bot⟩ *fructification* **~sprozeß** m *fertilizing process*

bef·ugen vt [h] (jdn) *to authorize, empower*, (z tun *to do*); [mst pass] **bef·ugt** a [pred] ~ s *to be authorized* od *entitled, licensed* (z *to*; z tun *to do*); *to be competent* (*to do*); ich bin nicht ~ z erzählen *I am not at liberty to tell*; sich ~ halten *to think o.s. entitled* (*to do*) **Bef·ugnis** f ~/-nisse *authority, power, right* (*to do*); *warrant* (z *for*); aus eigener ~ *on one's own authority*; jdm die ~ erteilen *to authorize, to empower a p*; k–e ~ h *to have no right* (*to do*); s–e -nisse überschreiten *to exceed one's authority* ‖ ⟨jur ec⟩ *faculty* (zu, für *for*)

bef·ühlen vt [h] *to feel, touch, handle*; *finger* ‖ (jdn) *to run* od *pass one's hand over a p*; ⟨fam⟩ *to paw* (*a p*)

°**bef·ummeln** vt [h] (erledigen) (e–e S) *to manage, handle* (*a th*); *to deal* od *cope with* (*a th*); gründlich ~ *to handle efficiently* | (befühlen) (jdn) ⟨fam⟩ *to paw* (*a p*) ‖ ⟨sex vulg⟩ *to finger, fumble*; *to muck about with*; *to make a pass at*

Bef·und m ~(e)s/~e *result of an examination*; ⟨med⟩ *data* pl, *statement*; auf Grund des ärztlichen ~es *on the strength of the medical find, findings* od *statement* ‖ Gesundheitszeugnis ohne ~ (o. B.) *clean bill of health* ‖ → Befinden

bef·ürchten vt [h] **a.** (etw) *to apprehend, fear* (*a th*) ‖ *to be suspicious of* (*a th*) ‖ er befürchtet z fallen *he fears* (od *is afraid of*) *falling*; ~, daß .. *to apprehend, fear that* ..; es wurde befürchtet, daß .. *it was feared that* .. **b.** Wendungen: ~ Sie nichts! *never fear*! ‖ ich befürchte, mich verspätet z h *I am afraid I am late*; ich b., Sie könnten sich erkälten *I fear you might catch a cold* ‖ ~, daß .. *we fear he might come* | ohne z ~ etw umzuwerfen *without the fear of knocking something over* ‖ du brauchst nicht z ~, daß .. *you need not fear but* (od *but that*) .. ‖ hat man .. z ~? *is there any danger of* (*a summons*)? ‖ das ist nicht z ~ *there is no fear of it*; es ist nicht z ~, daß er tut *there is no fear of his doing* ‖ da Unfälle z ~ waren .. *for fear of accidents* (*they gave orders that* ..) ‖ nichts z ~ h v jdm *to have nothing to fear from a p* **Bef·ürchtung** f ~/~en *apprehension, fear* (daß *that, lest*); [oft pl] *apprehensions, fears* [pl] ‖ (böse Ahnung) *misgiving*; jdn mit ~en erfüllen *to fill a p with misgivings* | → Furcht

bef·ürworten vt [h] (Bitte etc) *to speak* od *plead for, to speak in favour of* (*a th*); warm ~ *to put in a plea for* (*a th*) ‖ (Reform) *to advocate*; *recommend*; (Antrag) *to support, second, back*

Bef·ürworter m *advocate*; *supporter, upholder, mainstay, abetter, backer, promotor, champion, exponent, partisan, sympathizer* ‖ starker ~ *vigorous advocate, etc* ‖ ⟨Am a.⟩ *proponent*

Bef·ürwortung f ~/~en *recommendation; support* (*of a th*); *plea* (e–r S *for a th*)

beg·abt a **1.** [pred] ~ s mit *to be endowed* od *gifted with*; ~ s für *to have a talent for* **2.** [attr] *gifted, talented; able, clever* (*man*); ein ~er Mensch *a man of excellent parts*; die ~esten Schüler *the most gifted* od *talented boys*; hoch~ *highly-talented* ‖ die ≗en des Landes *the talent of the country* e–e mechanisch ~e P *a mechanical mind* **Beg·abtenaufstieg** m *support and promotion of young talent* **Beg·abtenauslese** f *selection of the talented* od *of young talent*

Beg·abung f ~/~en (natürliche) *aptitude, gift, giftedness, talent* (f. *for*); (geistige) *abilities, mental endowments* [pl]; e–e geniale ~ *a genius* (f. *for*); e–e P mit mechanischer ~ *a mechanical mind*; ein Mann v hoher ~ *a man of great talents* (od *of many gifts*) ‖ → Fähigkeit

beg·affen vt [h] (etw, jdn) *to gape* od *stare at* (*a th, a p*) **Beg·affer** m ~s/~ *gaper*

beg·angen pp v begehen

Beg·ängnis n -nisses/-nisse *solemn act*; (*act of*) *celebration*; → Leichen≗

beg·asen vt [h] ⟨agr, for, tech⟩ *to gas; fumigate* **Beg·asung** f ~/~en *gassing*

Beg·asse f = Bagasse

beg·atten vt [h] ⟨orn⟩ (Weibchen) *to copulate with; to tread*; → decken ‖ mst refl **sich** ~ *to couple, copulate*; ⟨orn⟩ *to mate, pair* **Beg·attung** f ~/~en *copulation* ‖ ⟨orn⟩ *pairing* **~strieb** m *copulative* od *copulatory instinct* **~szeit** f = Paarungszeit

°**beg·aunern** vt [h] (jdn) *to cheat, to overreach*

beg·ebbar a ⟨com⟩ *negotiable* (*bill*); *realizable* (*securities*)

beg·eben vt [→ geben] **1.** ⟨com⟩ (Wechsel) *to negotiate; to dispose of, to sell* | (Schatzwechsel) *to issue* **2. a. sich e–r S** ~ *to give a th up, to desist from a th; to renounce a th*; sich e–s Anspruchs ~ *to waive a claim*; sich e–s Rechts ~ *to divest o.s. of a right, to waive* (od *renounce*) *a right*; sich e–s Vorteils ~ *to forgo* (od *waive*) *an advantage* **b. sich ~ nach** *to go, proceed, repair, resort to; to betake o.s. to; to make for*; ⟨fam⟩ *to adjourn to* ‖ sie ~ sich in .. *they take possession of* (*his drawing-room*) | **sich an** Bord e–s Schiffes ~ *to* (*go on*) *board a ship*; sich an Land ~ *to go ashore*; ..an die Arbeit ~ *to go* od *set to work* ‖ sich **auf** die Reise ~ *to set out on one's journey*, ..auf die Wanderschaft ~ *..on one's travels*; ..auf die Flucht ~ *to take* (*to*) *flight* ‖ sich **in** die Stadt ~ *to go* (*in*)*to town*, ⟨Am⟩ *to go downtown*; ..in ein Krankenhaus ~ *to enter a hospital* (: *he had to e. a hospital*); ..in Gefahr ~ *to expose* od *subject o.s. to danger*; ..in jds Schutz ~ *to place o.s. under a p's protection* ‖ sich **zu** s–m Regiment ~ *to join one's regiment*; sich zur Ruhe ~ *to go to rest* (od *bed*) **c.** [imps] mst ⟨bib⟩ *to happen, occur*; und es begab sich, daß.. *and it came to pass that..* **Beg·ebenheit** f ~/~en, **Beg·ebnis** n -nisses/-nisse *happening, event*; → Ereignis

Beg·ebung f ⟨com⟩ *negotiation* (*of a bill*); *sale* (*of securities*) ‖ *issue* (*of Treasury bills*)

beg·egnen vi [s] **A.** jdm ~ **1.** (P) **a.** *to meet a p*; (a. feindlich) *to encounter a p* ‖ (zufällig) *to come* od *run across a p, to meet* (*with*) *a p, to run into a p* **b.** e–a mit Höflichkeit ~ *to treat each other with politeness*; jdm mit Liebe *or* liebevoll ~ *to treat a p with kindness, to deal kindly with a p*; ..grob ~ *to handle, receive, treat a p roughly* **2.** (S) **a.** (zufällig) *to come* (*in*) *a p's way* (: *he imagined the triumphs which would come* [*in*] *his way*); die Züge ~ sich *or* e–a *the trains pass eachother*; das Wort begegnete mir in der Bibel *I came across* (od *met with*) *the w. in the B.* **b.** (zustoßen) *to happen* od *occur to a p, to befall a p*; was mag ihm begegnet s? *what may have happened to him?* **c.** ihre Ansichten ~ sich in nichts mehr *their views coincide no longer in any point* **B.** e–r S ~ **1.** (zufällig) *to come across, to meet with, to happen* od *light on a th*; vielen Schwierigkeiten ~ *to encounter many difficulties*; Probleme, denen wir ~ *problems we are facing* **2.** (entgegenkommen) e–m Wunsche etc ~ *to meet* (od *comply with*) *a wish* ‖ (entgegentreten) *to anticipate, prevent a th*; e–r Drohung ~ *to counter a menace*, e–r Gefahr ~ *to obviate a danger* ‖ [dat] (entgegentreten) *to contend with* (*a p, a th*) **C.** [abs] das Wort begegnet in der Bibel, bei Shakespeare *the work occurs* (od *is found*) *in the B., in Sh.*; oft ~ *to be of frequent occurrence; to be frequent*; oft ~d *often recurring* (*error*) **D. sich ~, e–a ~** *to meet*; ihre Blicke ~ sich *their eyes meet*; (of letters) *to cross, meet*

†**Beg·egnis** n -nisses/-nisse = Begegnung ‖ *occurrence* **Beg·egnung** f ~/~en *meeting*; ~ Annas u Joachims (an der Goldenen Pforte) ⟨arts, bib⟩ *Meeting of St. Joachim and St. Anne* ‖ (plötzliche, unerwartete, feindliche) *encounter*; ⟨sport⟩ *match* (*between 2 teams*); *meet*; → Treffen | †(Behandlung) *treatment, reception*

beg·ehen I. vt [→ gehen] [h] **1.** (Weg, Strecke etc) *to go over; to walk along; to travel*; ein viel begangener Weg *a well-beaten track* ⟨a. fig⟩, *a much frequented road* ‖ (besichtigend) *to inspect, survey* **2.** (feiern) (Fest) *to keep, observe*; (Sieg, Tag) festlich ~ *to celebrate, solemnize* **3.** (Sünde, Verbrechen) *to commit, perpetrate*; e–n Fehler ~ *to make a mistake* od *an error*; ein oft begangener Fehler *a mistake often made* **II.** ≗ n ~s/ das ~ des Weges *the going over* (od *walking along*) *the road* ‖ → Begehung

Beg·ehr m & n ~s/ *desire; request*; auf ~ *by request*; was ist Ihr ~? *what is your business? what is it you want? what can I do for you?* nach jds ~ fragen *to inquire a p's business* ‖ ⟨com⟩ *demand, request* (nach *for*) ‖ → Begehren

beg·ehren I. vt/i [h] **1.** vt (etw) *to desire, request* (*a th*); *to wish* (od *crave*) *for* (*a th*); ~ z tun *to wish to do* ‖ etw v jdm ~ *to apply to, to ask a p for a th* | (fordern) *to require* (v *of a p*); ⟨com⟩ *to demand* **2.** vi ~ **nach** (⟨bib⟩ † jds ~) *to crave* od *long for; to aspire* od *hanker after, to be covetous of, to covet* (*a th*) ‖ → begehrt **II.** ≗ n ~s/ *desire, request*; auf ~ *by request*; auf ~ jds *at a p's request* ‖ *demand, request* (nach *for*) ‖ → Begehr **beg·ehrenswert** a *desirable* ‖ ~er Gegenstand *plum*; die ~en Stellen (Posten) *the plums* [pl] ‖ *eligible* (*bachelor*)

beg·ehrlich a *desirous, covetous* (nach *of*); *grasping, greedy* ‖ †(begehrenswert) *desirable* | ≗keit [f] ~/~en *covetousness, greediness*

beg·ehrt a **1.** [pred] er war sehr ~ *he was in great request* (bei *with*), *he was much sought after* | ⟨com⟩ (sehr) ~ s *to be in* (*great, hot*) *demand*; wenig (*or* nicht) ~ s *to be uncalled for, to be easy* **2.** [attr] der ~este Mann *the most sought–* od *run-after man*

Beg·ehung f ~/~en **1.** *keeping, observance* (*of a feast*); *celebration* (*of an anniversary*) **2.** *commission, committal, perpetration* (*of a crime*) → Begehen

beg·eifern vt [h] *to* (*be*)*slaver, beslobber* ‖ ⟨fig⟩ (Ehre jds) *to asperse, besmirch; calumniate, slander* **Beg·eiferung** f ~/~en ⟨fig⟩ = Schmähung

beg·eistern vt [h] (jdn) *to thrill, enchant, excite; to inspire* (z *zo*) ‖ *to fill* (*a p*) *with enthusiasm* (f. *for*) | **sich** ~ *to become* (od *feel*) *enthusiastic* (f. *for*; über *at, about*); *to enthuse* (*about*) ‖ *to work o.s.* (z *into*) ‖ sich [acc] an etw ~ *to kindle at a th* **beg·eisternd 1.** a *inspiring; stirring* (*speech*) **2.** adv sich ~ äußern *to enthuse, to be thrilled* (über *about*)

beg·eistert 1. a *inspired, exalted* ‖ *enthusiastic* (*crowds; reception*); *rousing* (*welcome*); ~e Zurufe *loud cheers* [pl]; ~ über *enthusiastic at, about* || *ardent, enthusiastic, fervent, zealous* (*adherent*); ~er Angler *a keen angler, zealot of the rod* **2.** adv *with enthusiasm*; ~ aufgenommen w *to be received enthusiastically* (od *with loud cheers*) **B.rung** f ~/~en *inspiration* || *enthusiasm*; *zeal* (f. *for*); *thrill* || mit ~, voller ~ *with enthusiasm*; *enthusiastically* || ein Sturm der ~, helle ~ *an outburst of enthusiasm, a roar of cheers* || in ~ geraten *to get* od *go into raptures* (über *over*)

Beg·ier f ~/ *desire, longing* (nach *for*); *eagerness*; e–e heiße ~ *a passion* (*for*); voll ~ *desirous, eager, zealous* (*to do*); voll ~ zuhören *to listen eagerly* || → **Beg·ierde** f ~/~n *desire* (nach *for*; *to do*); *appetency* (*of, for*); *appetite, craving, longing, yearning* (*for*); vor ~ brennen *to burn with longing* || ⟨sex⟩ *appetence*, (*sexual*) *appetite, concupiscence, desire, lust* | *eagerness* || voll ~ → Begier

beg·ierig I. [pred] **1.** a *eager* (auf, nach *for*; z tun *to do*); *covetous, desirous* (nach *of*; *to do*); *anxious, impatient* (nach *for*; *to do*); *urgent* (*to do*) **2.** (neugierig) *anxious, curious* (*to know*; *how* ..) **II.** adv *anxiously* (*to wait a. for* ..) || *eagerly, zealously*

beg·ießen vt [→ gießen] [h] **1.** (Pflanzen etc) *to water, sprinkle*; *wet*; reichlich ~ *to shower* (*with*) || (befeuchten) *to moisten* || (Braten) mit Fett ~ *to baste* | jdn mit Wasser ~ *to pour water over a p* || wie ein begossener Pudel dastehen *to stand perplexed* od *ashamed* || → Nase **2.** (feiern) (Ereignis) *to celebrate*; das Geschäft ~ *to wet the deal*; ⟨fam⟩ *to wet* (⟨aero⟩ *one's props*)

Beg·inn m ~(e)s/ *beginning, commencement, inception, outset, start*; e–n ~ m *to take the initiative, first step*; *to break the ice*; .. mit *to set .. afoot, to usher in*; bei ~, z ~ *at the beginning*, etc. (*of the 19th c.*); seit .. *since the turn of the c.*; noch e–e Minute bis zum ~ *still a minute to go* || *origins* [pl] || → Anfang

beg·innen vt/i [begann / pret subj begönne, begänne / pp begonnen] [h] **I.** vt **1.** (Tätigkeit) *to begin, commence, start* || *to* (*make a*) *start on* (*a th*) || *to launch, initiate* || *to plunge into* [prep], *to start up* [adv] || *to get .. under way* | s–e Arbeit ~ *to set about one's work*; e–e Kontroverse ~ *to enter* od *launch into a controversy* (*with*); ein Unternehmen ~ *to embark upon an enterprise*; plötzlich ~ *to break into* (*a defence of* ..) || das 6. Lebensjahr ~ *to enter one's sixth year*; den Tanz ~ *to lead off* (*with a partner*) || ein neues Programm ~ *to start on a new programme* **2.** (tun) *to do, undertake*; was soll ich nun ~? *what shall I do now*? **II.** vi **1.** [abs] *to set out, to pitch in*; ⟨fam⟩ *to kick off*, ⟨bes Am fam⟩ *to get the show on the road* | (P) ~ z tun *to begin* (od *commence, start*) *to do* od *begin* (etc) *doing*; *to fall to doing* || ~ mit *to begin with*; ⟨Am⟩ *to start in with* || damit ~ z tun *to begin by doing*; er hat damit begonnen *he has taken to* (*issue more severe laws*); z reden (etc) ~ *to begin* | *to make a beginning* od *a start*; ich will ~ *I'll make the beginning* || er begann einst als Diplomat ⟨Am⟩ *he started out as a diplomat* || frisch begonnen, halb gewonnen *well begun is half done* **2.** (S) die Feier beginnt um 11 *the ceremony begins at 11 o'clock* || das Feuer begann im Schuppen *the fire originated in the shed* || → anfangen **Beg·innen** n ~s ⟨übtr⟩ (→ ≗ I. 2.) *undertaking, enterprise*

begl·aubigen vt [h] **1.** (Schriftstück) *to attest, authenticate, legalize, verify*; gerichtlich ~ *to exemplify* (*a deed*); amtlich, gerichtlich, notariell -gt *certified* ([*true*] *copy*) || ⟨Am⟩ (Scheck) *to certify* **2.** (e–n Gesandten) *to accredit* (bei *to*)

begl·aubigt a *attested* (*copy*) || → beglaubigen

Begl·aubigung f ~/~en **1.** *attestation, authentication, legalization, verification* (*of a document*); notarielle ~ *acknowledgment*; zur ~ dessen *in witness whereof* **2.** *accrediting* (*of an ambassador*); = ~sschreiben **~sschreiben** n *letter*(*s*) *of credence*; *credentials* [pl] **~svermerk** m *note testifying to the truth of a th*

begl·eichen vt [→ gleichen] [h] **1.** (Rechnung) *to balance*; *to pay* (*in full*); *to settle, to square up* (*a debt*) **2.** (Streit) *to settle*; (Differenzen) *to compose* **Begl·eichung** f ~/ *payment, settlement* (*of an account*); zur ~ unseres Kontos *in settlement of our account* | *settlement* (*of a quarrel*)

Begl·eit- ~adresse f ⟨com Ger⟩ *bill of parcels*; → Frachtbrief || = Begleitschein **~brief** m *accompanying letter*; *covering letter* **~erscheinung** f *side effect*; *accompaniment* (e–r S, z e–r S *of a th*); *by-product*; *concomitant*; *attendant circumstance*; ~en [pl] *concomitant circumstances*; *accessories* [pl] **~flugzeug** n ⟨aero⟩ *escort-plane* **~jäger** m ⟨aero⟩ *escort fighter* **~karte** f *docket* **~musik** f *accompanying music* **~papier** n, **~schein** m (Zoll–) *transire, permit*; *pass-bill*; ⟨com⟩ *way-bill* || → Frachtbrief **~schiff** n ⟨mar⟩ *convoy-ship, escort* (*vessel*); → Geleitzug || *tender* || ~ f. U-Boote *submarine depot ship* **~schiffversorgung** f *underway logistic support* **~schreiben** n *letter of advice* od *transmittal*; *cover letter*; = Begleitbrief **~schutz** m *air escort*; (f Schiffe) ~ fliegen ⟨aero⟩ *to shadow* **~text** m *accompanying text* **~umstände** m [pl] *concomitant* od *attendant circumstances* [pl] **~zettel** m (f Verwundete etc) ⟨mil⟩ *tag* || ⟨phot⟩ *identification tag* (*developing and printing* [D & P])

begl·eiten vt [h] **1.** (jdn) *to accompany*, ⟨Am⟩ *to walk* (*a p*) *to* ..; jdn nach Hause, an die Tür ~ *to see a p home, to the door*; *to walk with a p to the d.*; jdn ein Stück ~ *to set a p on his way*; jdn an die Bahn ~ *to see a p off* || (jdn) höflich ~ *to escort* (nach *to*), *to marshal*; → geleiten || (jdn dienstlich ~) *to attend* (*a p*), *to attend* od *wait upon* (*a p*) || ⟨mil⟩ (zum Schutz ~) *to escort*; ⟨mar⟩ *to convoy* **2.** ⟨mus⟩ (jdn, Gesang) *to accompany*; sie begleitete sie mit Musik in die Halle (aus der H.) *she played them into* (*out of*) *the hall* **3.** ⟨übtr⟩ (Worte) *to accompany* (mit *with*) || (Ereignis) *to attend*; begleitet s v *to be attended* od *accompanied with*; (of disaster) *to be dogged with*; in Zwischenräumen begleitet s v (of speech) *to be punctuated by* (*sobs*) || ~der Umstand *accompaniment*; *attendant* (od *concomitant, collateral*) *circumstance*; *concomitant* || ~de Umstände *circumstances that go with* (*a th*)

Begl·eiter m ~s/~ *companion, attendant* (jds *on a p*); er ist immer ein guter ~ *he is always good company*; treuer ~ *henchman* (*of a hero*) || ⟨mil⟩ *escort* || ⟨mus⟩ *accompanist* **Begl·eiterin** f ~/~nen (*female*) *companion*; ⟨mus⟩ (*female*) *accompanist*

Begl·eitung f ~/~en **1.** *company* || jdm s–e ~ anbieten *to offer one's company to a p* || in der ~ jds s, gefunden w *to be, to be found in the company of a p* (od *in a p's c.*) || in s–r ~ befanden sich mehrere Offiziere *he was attended by several officers* **2.** ⟨mus⟩ *accompaniment* (z *to*); marschieren nach (*or* unter) der ~ v .. *to march to the a. of* .. **3.** [konkr] (Gefolge) *attendants*; *following, train, retinue*; er erschien mit gr ~ *he arrived with a large retinue* || ⟨mil⟩ *escort*; ⟨mar⟩ *convoy*

begl·otzen vt (jdn, etw) *to stare goggle-eyed at* ..

begl·ücken vt [h] (jdn) *to make* (*a p*) *happy, to bless* (mit *with*) || (erfreuen) (jds Herz) *to rejoice, to cheer* || (beehren) *to favour* (mit *with*)

begl·ückend a *cheering, pleasant, joyful*; ⟨poet⟩ *gladsome* **begl·ückt** a *happy, fortunate*; ~ s mit *to be blessed with* (*children*); *to rejoice in* || ~ s über *to be rejoiced, to rejoice at, over*; ~ s z sehen (etc) *to be glad* (od *delighted*), *to rejoice to see* ‖ ⟨Am a.⟩ *proud* **Begl·ücker** m *benefactor*

begl·ückwünschen vt [h] jdn z etw ~ *to congratulate* (od *compliment, felicitate*) *a p* (*up*)*on a th*; Sie sind z ~ *you are to be congratulated*; **sich** ~ *to congratulate o.s.* (z *on*) **Begl·ückwünschung** f *congratulation, felicitation* (z *on*)

begn·adet a **1.** [pred] ~ s mit *to be blessed* (od *blest*) *with*; *to be endowed with* **2.** [attr] *highly gifted* (*artist*) ‖ gott~ *uncommonly gifted*, gott~er Künstler *genius*

begn·adigen vt [h] (jdn) *to pardon, reprieve* (*a p*); *to grant a reprieve to* (*a p*); ⟨pol⟩ *to amnesty* (*a p*) ‖ er wurde z lebenslänglichem Zuchthaus begnadigt *the death-sentence was commuted to* (*one of*) *penal servitude for life* **Begn·adigung** f ~/~en *pardon, reprieve*; *clemency* ‖ ⟨pol⟩ *amnesty* ‖ ~sgesuch [n] *petition for clemency*

begn·ügen vrefl [h] sich ~ mit (†sich ~ l an; → genügen) *to be satisfied* od *contented*; *to content o.s.* (mit etw *with a th*); sich damit ~ z tun *to content o.s. with doing* ‖ sich mit s–m Lose ~ *to acquiesce in one's fate* ‖ †**begn·ügsam** a = genügsam

Beg·onie f ~/~n ⟨bot⟩ *begonia, elephant's ear*

beg·önnern vt [h] (jdn) *to patronize* ‖ *to treat* (*a p*) *condescendingly*

beg·ossen pp v begießen

begr·aben vt [→ graben] [h] **1.** (jdn) *to bury, inter*; *entomb*; *to lay to rest*; lebendig ~ *to bury alive* ‖ da liegt der Hund ~! *there's the rub!*, *that's the point!* ‖ °laß dich ~! *hang you! hang it!*; du kannst dich ~ l *you are not up to much*, damit kannst du dich ~ l *forget it!* **2.** ⟨übtr⟩ ~ w unter *to be buried under* (*an avalanche*) ‖ die Streitaxt ~ *to bury the hatchet* | etw ~, ~ sein l *to bury a th, to lay .. to rest, to draw the curtain over a th*; → Vergangenheit ‖ ~e Hoffnung *buried hope* **3.** [pp] ~ unter ⟨fig⟩ *snowed under* **Begr·äbnis** n –nisses/–nisse **1.** *burial, interment, entombment*; (a. ~feier) *funeral*, bei dem ~ *at the f.* ‖ feierliches ~ *state f.* ‖ → Beerdigung, Bestattung, Beisetzung **2.** (Grab) *tomb, sepulchre* **3.** [in comp] *burial, funeral* **~feier** f *funeral, obsequies* [pl]; → Trauerfeier **~kasse** f *burial club* **~kommando** n ⟨mil⟩ *funeral detachment* **~platz** m *burial-ground*; *cemetery* **~stätte** f → Grabstätte

begr·adigen vt [h] (Fluß) *to straighten, regulate* **Begr·adigung** f *straightening* (*of a river*)

°**begr·apschen** vt [h] (Buch) *to thumb*; (P) *to paw*; ⟨sex⟩ *to fumble, finger* **begr·apscht** a *thumby*

begr·asen vt [h] *to cover with grass, to turf* ‖ (of cattle) (Wiese) *to graze* **begr·ast** a *grassy, grass-grown*

begr·eifen vt [→ greifen] [h] **1.** (betasten) *to touch, feel*; *handle*; *finger* **2. in sich** ~ (= umfassen) (Lösung etc) *to comprehend, comprise, include*; *contain*; → einbegreifen **3.** (verstehen) (etw) *to comprehend, conceive, understand, realize* (*a th*; *that*); *to see, to catch on* (*a th*) | *grasp, to make out*; *to get in the way of* (*a th*); den Sinn e–s Wortes ~ *to get the sense of a word*; ⟨sl⟩ *to get* (*a th*) *into one's nut*; *to tumble to* (*a th*) ‖ das begreift sich leicht *that is easily understood* ‖ es ist kaum z ~ *it is hardly conceivable* od *imaginable*; *it is incredible* ‖ etw nicht ~ *to miss the point of a th* | [abs] leicht *or* schnell ~ *to be quick of comprehension*; schwer *to be dull of understanding, to be slow of wits*, ⟨fam⟩ *to be slow in the uptake*

begr·eiflich a *comprehensible* (f. *to a p*), *conceivable, intelligible, understandable* ‖ jdm etw ~ m *to make a th clear to a p*; *to make* od *get a th understood by a p*; *to make a p understand a th*; ⟨iron⟩ *to bring* (*a th*) *home to a p*; ich werde es ihm schon ~ m *I'll bring him to reason* **~erweise** adv *as you will understand*; *as might be expected*; *of course, naturally* (*excited*) | ≈**keit** f ~/ *comprehensibleness, conceivableness*

begr·enzen vt [h] **1.** [mst pass] ⟨geogr⟩ *to bound*; Deutschland wird im Süden durch die Alpen begrenzt *Germany is bounded on* od *in the South by the Alps* ‖ (einfassen) *to border* (*the field is bordered by a forest*) ‖ ⟨opt⟩ das Feld ~ *to outline the field* **2.** ⟨übtr⟩ *to confine, limit* (auf *to*); (Sphäre) *to circumscribe* ‖ genau ~ *to fix*; *define* ‖ die Höhe der zu leihenden Gelder wird v den Banken –zt *the banks clamp ceilings on the amount of money they are willing to lend*

begr·enzt a *bounded* (*surface*) ‖ ⟨übtr⟩ *bounded* (*view*); *limited, restricted, partial* ‖ ⟨fig⟩ *narrow* (*mind*) ‖ ⟨tact⟩ *limited* (*objective*); Angriff mit ~em Ziel *l. o. attack*

Begr·enztheit f ⟨fig⟩ *boundedness, narrowness*

Begr·enzung f ~/~en *bordering*; *bounds* [pl] ‖ ⟨übtr⟩ *limitation*; technische ~ *physical l.* **~sleuchte** f *side lamp* **~sventil** n *restrictor, r. valve*

Begr·iff m ~(e)s/~e **1.** (Vorstellung) *conception, idea, notion*; unklarer ~ *crude idea, hazy notion*; falscher ~ *misconception* ‖ ⟨philos⟩ Allgemein≈ *concept*; die Allgemein≈e [pl] *the universals* [pl] ‖ Vernunft≈ *idea* ‖ (Wort≈) *definition* | **in** chemischen ~en *in terms of chemistry*; wir denken ausschließlich in ~en u Wörtern *all our thinking is done in terms of concepts and words* ‖ **nach** modernen ~en *by modern standards* | .. ist **zu** e–m festen ~ geworden ⟨m. m.⟩ *has made its way* | ⟨iron⟩ jdm e–n ~ v etw beibringen *to bring a th home to a p* ‖ e–n hohen ~ h v *to think highly of ..* ‖ er hatte e–n schönen ~ v ihr *he had a nice idea of her* ‖ k–n ~ h v *to have no idea of* ‖ ist Ihnen der Name ein ~? *is the name familiar to you? does the name mean anything to you?* ‖ sich e–n ~ m v etw *to conceive a th*; *to get* (od *form*) *an idea of a th*; *to imagine, envisage, visualize a th*; du kannst dir k–n rechten ~ davon m *you can't quite picture it*; → vorstellen **2.** (Verstehen) [nur in Wendungen:] langsam v ~ *slow in the uptake*; schwer v ~(en) *dull*; *dull of understanding* od *apprehension*; *slow*; *dense*; *blunt-witted*, → begreifen 3. ‖ über alle ~e *extremely, exceedingly, to a* (*high*) *degree* ‖ das geht über (*or* das übersteigt) alle ~e ⟨sl⟩ *that beats all*; *that is beyond all description*; das geht über m–e ~e ⟨sl⟩ *that beats* (od *licks*; ⟨Am sl⟩ *hits*) *me, that is beyond me, that passes* (od *is past*) *my comprehension* ‖ s–e Unverfrorenheit geht über alle ~e *his impudence is sublime* **3.** im ~ s *or* stehen z tun *to be about* (od *be going*) *to do*; *to be on the point* (od *in the act*) *of doing*

begr·iffen a [pp a begreifen] **a.** (P) ~ s in (e–r Tätigkeit) mst: *to be* + [prs p]: im Anmarsch, Lesen, Schreiben etc ~ s *to be advancing* od *approaching, .. reading, .. writing*; → beschäftigt ‖ in ständiger Aufregung ~ *in a state of constant anxiety* ‖ (a. of ships) auf der Ausreise (Rückreise) ~ *outward* (*homeward*) *bound* **b.** (S) in der Auflösung ~ *in process of disintegration*; im Bau ~ *in process of construction* ‖ das Haus ist im Bau ~ *the house is being built* od *is building*

begr·ifflich 1. a (Ggs konkret) *abstract, conceptional, conceptive, conceptual*; *ideal*; *notional* (*thruth*); rein ~ *abstract* ‖ ~e Erklärung f *definition* (*of a word*); ~es Denken *abstract reasoning*; ~es Hauptwort *abstract noun* **2.** adv *conceptually*; (Wort) ~ erklären, bestimmen *to define*

Begr·iffs- [in comp] *notional*; *ideal* **~bestimmung** f *definition* **~form** f ⟨philos⟩ *category* **~inhalt** m ⟨log⟩ *connotation*; persönlicher ~ *individual c.* (z. B. bei Idiosynkrasie); ~ f e–e Berufsgruppe, Rasse etc *group c.* (z. B. Baudelaire „Albatross"; allgemeiner ~ *general c.* (z. B. Rose, Schlange) **~lehre** f *ideology* **≚stutzig** a *dense, dull, obtuse* **~umfang** m ⟨log⟩ *connotation* **~verb** n *notional verb* **~vermögen** n *comprehension, intellect*

begr·ünden vt [h] **1.** (gründen, → d.) **a.** (Familie, Dynastie) *to found* ‖ (Geschäft etc) *to establish, to set up* **b.** ⟨übtr⟩ (Macht, Ruhm) *to establish* ‖ (Theorie) *to establish, to initiate* ‖ (etw) ~ auf *to base* (od *found*) *on*; *to ground on, in*; auf Tatsachen begründet *founded on fact* **2.** (Ausführungen, Behauptung etc) *to prove, to give reasons for* (*a th*); *to substantiate, to make good* ‖ (Verhalten) *to account for*; *to justify* ‖ (im Drama) (of actions, qualities) begründet w *to be motived* (od *motivated*)

Begr·ünder m ~s/~ *founder* **begr·ündet** a [pp v begründen] *substantiated*; *well-founded* (*hopes, suspicion*); *justifiable*; *justified*; *reasonable* (*doubt*) ‖ ungenügend ~ *ill-founded* (*pretensions*)

Begr·ündung f ~/~en **1.** (Gründung, → d.) *founding*; *foundation* ‖ *establisment* **2.** *argument, proof, reason, reasons* [pl] (e–r S *for a th*) ‖ *substantiation* ‖ ~ e–s Gesetzentwurfes *explanatory preamble to a Bill* | (im Drama) *motivation*

begr·üßen vt [h] **1.** (P) *to greet, salute, receive* (mit *with*); *to welcome*; ich freue mich, Herrn N. ~ z können *I am pleased to welcome Mr. N.* ‖ jdn als König ~ *to hail a p as king* ‖ jdn mit Beifall etc ~, begeistert ~ *to cheer a p, receive a p with cheers* ‖ sich [acc] herzlich ~ *to greet each other warmly* **2.** (S) (schönes Wetter; die Anregung etc jds) *to welcome*; (die Rückkehr jds) *to greet*, (den Mut jds) *to salute* ‖ (etw) warm ~ *to approve* (*a th*) *warmly*; dankbar ~ *to hail* (*a th*) *with gratitude* ‖ zu ~ s (⟨a.⟩ **~swert** s) *to be helpful, welcome, appreciated*

Begr·üßung f ~/~en *greeting* (jds *to a p*; seitens jds *from a p*); *salutation* (ein Wort der ~ *a word of s.*); *welcome* (Worte der ~ *words of w.*)

°**beg·ucken** vt [h] etw (jdn) ~ *to look at, to peep at*; (genau ~) *to peer at a th* (*a p*)

B·egum f [engl] (ind. Titel: Fürstin) *begum*

beg·ünstigen vt [h] **1.** *to befriend, countenance, encourage, patronize*; *support, to back* (*a p*) ‖ –gter Dritte ⟨ins⟩ *third party beneficiary* ‖ wenig(er) –gt *underprivileged* | (parteiisch bevorzugen) *to favour*; *to treat with partiality* ‖ begünstigt v der Dunkelheit *under cover of darknes* **2.** (S) *to favour*, (Plan) *to countenance*; *to encourage*; *to support* (*a th*) | (Verbrechen) *to* (*aid and*) *abet* ‖ *to connive in* (*a th*) **Begünstigte(r** m) f (Pfründner) *beneficiary*; (Beschenkte[r]) *donee* **Beg·ünstigung** f ~/~en *countenance, encouragement*; *support* (*of a th* od *a p*) ‖ *abetment* (*of a crime*); ⟨jur⟩ *aiding and abetting* | *patronage, protection* (*of a p*) ‖ (ungerechte) *favour* (*of a p*) **~starif** m ⟨rail⟩ *preferential tariff*

Beg·ußmasse f → Angußmasse

beg·utachten vt [h] (etw) *to pass* od *give an opinion on* (*a th*) ‖ etw ~ l *to submit a th to experts*; Begutachter [m] *expert*

Beg·utachtung f ~/~en *expertise*; *expert opinion*; → Gutachten

beg·ütert a *rich, opulent, wealthy* (*house*); *well-to-do* (*p*); die ~en Kreise *the well-to-do*, die ~en Klassen *the propertied classes* ‖ [pred] *well-off*

beg·ütigen vt [h] (jdn) *to appease, conciliate, pacify, soothe*; → besänftigen ‖ **~d 1.** a *soothing* **2.** adv (*to reply*) *soothingly*

beh·aaren vrefl [h] sein Kopf behaart sich wieder *his hair is growing again, his head is growing hair again* **beh·aart** a *hairy*; [pred] *haired* ‖ [in comp] *haired*, rot~ *red-haired* rauh~ ⟨bes zoo⟩ *hirsute* | ⟨bot & zoo⟩ *pilose, pilous*; ⟨bot⟩ *comose*; dicht ~ *to mentose* **Beh·aartheit** f ⟨bot & zoo⟩ *pilosity*

beh·aben 1. vrefl [ohne pret/pp: behabt] ~ *to behave* **2.** ≚ n *behaviour, port*

beh·äbig a *easy-going, comfort-loving* ‖ (etw beleibt) *corpulent, portly*; ~er Körperumfang *spread* ‖ †*well-to-do* ‖ → behaglich **≚keit** f ~/ *corpulence, portliness*

beh·acken vt [h] *to hoe* ‖ °(betrügen) *to cheat*

†**beh·aften** vt [h] (jdn) *to affect* (*with*); → behaftet ‖ ⟨jur⟩ = haftbar m **beh·aftet** a [pred] ~ s mit *to be affected, afflicted with* (*a disease*) ‖ *to be covered with* (*scales*) | *to be charged, loaded with*; mit Schulden ~ s *to be in debt*

beh·agen vi [h] jdm ~ *to please* od *suit a p*; *to be pleasing to a p* ‖ das behagt ihm ⟨sl⟩ *that's nuts to* od *for him*; das b. mir nicht *that doesn't suit me, I don't like it*; wie b. dir das? *how does that sound to you*? ‖ hier lasse ich es mir schon ~ *it suits me here to a T, I am quite comfortable here*

Beh·agen n ~s/ [mst nach prep] *ease, comfort*; *delight, gusto, pleasure, relish, zest*; inneres ~ *unction* ‖ mit ~ *with gusto* (od *relish, zest*), mit innerem ~ *with unction*; (etw) mit ~ genießen *to relish* (*a th*) ‖ z m–m ~ *to my delight* ‖ ~ finden an etw *to take delight* (od *pleasure*) *in, to delight in a th*; *to relish a th*; kein ~ finden an etw *to find no relish in a th*

beh·aglich 1. a (bequem) *comfortable* (*life*), ⟨fam⟩ *comfy*; *easy* ‖ *jog-trot* (*ways of old days*) ‖ sich ~ fühlen *to be* (od *feel*) *at one's ease*; sich nicht ~ fühlen *to be uneasy* (bei *with a p*); es sich ~ m *to make o.s. comfortable* (od *at home*); *to take one's ease* ‖ (traulich) *cosy, snug* | in ~en Verhältnissen *in easy circumstances* **2.** adv *comfortably*; *cosily, snugly* ‖ ~ plaudern *to talk unconstrainedly* ‖ ~ gehen *to jog-trot*; ~ arbeitend *jog-trot* (*fellow*) | das ≚-Gefühlhafte ⟨mus⟩ *pleasureful lyricism* | **≚keit** f ~/~en *comfort-*(*ableness*), *ease, easiness* ‖ *cosiness, snugness*

Beha·ismus m (moham. Lehre) *bahaism*

beh·altbar a (z behalten) leicht, schwer im Gedächtnis ~ *easy, difficult to retain* od *remember*

beh·alten vt [behielt/behalten] [h] **1.** (im Besitz ~) **a.** *to keep, retain* ‖ du kannst das Buch e–e Woche ~ *you may keep the book for a week*; darf ich es ~? *may I have it for my own*?, ⟨fam⟩ *is it for keeps*? ‖ (Gegenstand) f. sich ~ *to keep to o.s.*; ein Geheimnis f. sich ~ *to keep a secret*; etw f. sich ~ (= schweigen) *to keep a th quiet* od *dark*; *to keep one's own counsel*; behalt's f Dich! ⟨fam⟩ *keep it* (Geheimnis) *under your hat*! ‖ ⟨iron⟩ das konnten Sie auch f. sich ~ *thank you for nothing* ‖ jdn bei sich ~ *to keep a p with one*; behalte ihn bei dir *keep him with you*; Gäste bei sich ~ *to keep guests at one's house*; ich werde den Schirm bei mir ~ *I'll take the umbrella with me* **b.** ⟨übtr⟩ etw fest in der Hand ~ *to keep hold of a th*; Rechte fest in der H. ~ *to hold on to* (od *cling to*) *one's rights*; die Außenpolitik fest in der H. ~ *to keep control of foreign policy within one's own hands* ‖ ⟨com⟩ e–e Stellung ~ *to hold* od *keep down a job* **c.** die Oberhand ~, den Sieg ~ *to win the day* od *field*; *to be victorious* ‖ recht ~ *to gain one's point* **d.** wenn wir dieses Wetter ~ *if the weather keeps* **e.** ich habe kein Geld übrig ~ *I have no money left* **2.** (in e–r Lage, e–m Zustand lassen) **a.** *to keep*; den Hut auf dem Kopfe ~ *to keep one's hat on*; ~ Sie Platz *keep your seat, please* **b.** jdn (im Dienste) ~ *to retain* (*a p*); *to keep* (*a p*) *on* **c.** (beibehalten) (Brauch, Sitte) *to retain, preserve*; *maintain*; s–n Wert ~ (S) *to retain its value* **d.** die Geduld ~ *to retain* od *keep one's patience*; die Ruhe ~ *to keep one's temper* od *head* **3.** (geistige Tätigkeit) **a.** (jdn) im Auge ~ *to keep an eye on, not to lose sight of*; (etw) *to bear* (od *have, keep*) (*a th*) *in mind*; *to keep* (*a th*) *in view* ‖ in Obhut ~ *to take care of* (*a th*) **b.** im Kopfe, im Gedächtnis ~

to remember, to retain; jdn in gutem Andenken ~ *to preserve the memory of a p*; das kann ich nicht alles ~ *I can't remember all that*; leicht, schwer z ~ → behaltbar **beh·alten** a [pp v ~] ⟨mar⟩ *safe* (*ship*) **zum Beh·alten** ⟨fam⟩ *for keeps*

Beh·älter m ~s/~ *receptacle*; ⟨rail⟩ (für Waren) *container* ‖ (Vorrats≈) *depository* ‖ ⟨tech⟩ *drum*; ⟨a. chem⟩ *receiver* | (gr ~ f. Flüssirkeiten) *reservoir*; *tank* | (Kasten etc) *bin, box*; Sammel≈ *collecting box* ‖ *cage* **~beförderung** f ⟨rail⟩ *transport of goods in containers* **~depot** n (Treibstoff≈) *tank farm* **Beh·ältnis** n –nisses/–nisse *receptacle*; *depository*; → Behälter

beh·andeln vt [h] **1.** (P) *to deal with* (*a p*); *to treat, use* (gut, schlecht *well, ill*) (*he has been shamefully used*); *to handle, manage* (*a p*); jdn roh ~ *to rough-house a p*; schlecht behandelt *hard used*; er fühlt sich schlecht –lt *he thinks he is ill done by* ‖ → glimpflich, unsanft | ⟨med⟩ (jdn *to attend*; *to treat* (wegen *for*, mit *with*); behandelt w v *to receive treatment from* (*a specialist*) ‖ (T) ⟨fam⟩ *to vet* **2.** (Krankheit) *to treat* ‖ (Wunden) *to dress* ‖ ⟨chem⟩ (etw) *to treat* (mit *with*); ⟨com⟩ chemisch ~ *to process* **3.** (handhaben) (Geschütz etc) *to handle*; geschickt ~ *to manipulate* **4.** ⟨com⟩ (Ware) *to bargain for, to haggle about* (od *over*) (*a th*) **5.** (in Wort, Schrift etc ~) **a.** (P) (etw) *to deal with, to treat* (als *as*); (Frage) *to discuss* ‖ (Thema, Buch etc) *to discuss, debate, treat, handle, examine, study*; *to talk over, to go into*; *to deal with*; *to handle* ‖ eingehend ~ *to labour* (*an argument*) **b.** (of literary works, etc.) *to deal with, to be concerned with* (*the lecture was c. with* ..); *to treat of* ‖ nachlässig ~ *to treat like a stepchild*

beh·ändigen vt [h] (etw) *to hand, deliver*

Beh·andlung f **1.** *handling, treatment* (*of a p*); *management*; grausame, schlechte ~ *ill-treatment* ⟨Am sl⟩ *raw deal* ‖ ⟨med⟩ ärztliche ~ *medical treatment*; in ärztlicher ~ s *to be under the doctor's care*; der ~ zugänglich *treatable* (*disease*); in ~ *under treatment* **2.** *dressing* (*of wounds*) ‖ ⟨chem⟩ *treatment* (*with*) **3.** (Handhabung) *use* (*of tolls*); (~sweise) *handling, usage*; gute ~ *good usage* (*of an instrument*); kunstgerechte ~ *manipulation* **4.** *handling, treatment* (*of a subject, theme*); *discussion* (*of a question*) **~art, ~smethode** f ⟨med⟩ *pathy* (*I tried all pathies*) **~skosten** pl ⟨med⟩ *medical expenses* **~sweise** f *usage* (→ 3.); *mode of treatment*

beh·andschuht a *gloved* ‖ (*hands cased in white kid*) ‖ *with gloves on*

Beh·ang m ~(e)s/≈e **1.** *appendage* ‖ (Wand≈) *hangings* [pl]; schmaler ~ über Gardinenstangen *pelmet*; ausgezackter ~ über Fenstern *lambrequin* (Fr); ⟨ec⟩ *veil* ‖ (an Gegenständen) *flounce*; *decorations, ornaments* [pl] **2.** *lop-ears* [pl] (*of a hound*) ⟨a. hunt⟩ **3.** (Kötenhaar) *fetlock* (*of a horse*)

beh·ängen vt [behängte & behing/behängt] [h] **1.** (Wand etc) *to hang, drape* (*with*); *to cover* (*with*); behängt s mit *to be festooned with* | **sich** ~ *to deck o.s.* (*out*) (*with*) **2.** ⟨hunt⟩ e–n Hund ~ *to train a dog on the lead*

°**beh·arken** vt [h] ⟨artill⟩ *to rake*

beh·arren vi [h] **1.** (ausharren) ⟨bib⟩ *to continue steadfastly*; *to persevere*; *to remain firm* **2. ~ bei** *to abide by, to keep at* od *to, to persevere* od *persist in, to insist on*; *to stand by* od *to, to adhere* (od *cling, stick*) *to* (*a th*); bei s–r Meinung ~ *to stand* (od *to stick*) *to one's opinion*; ~ z tun *to persevere* (od *persist*) *in doing* ‖ (bestehen) ~ **auf** *to insist* od *stand on, to persist in* (*a th*) **Beh·arren** n *persistence* (bei *in*) *insistence* (bei *on*) ‖ ⟨jur⟩ hartnäckiges ~ *peremptoriness* ‖ ~ im Irrtum *perversity*

beh·arrlich 1. a *persistent, insistent, persevering, perseverant*; *constant, steady*; *steadfast*; *unwavering*; *unyielding*; ~e Aufmerksamkeiten *assiduities* [pl]; ~es Fortfahren *persistence* **2.** adv *persistently, perseveringly*; ~ fortfahren *to persist, to persevere* (mit *with*; z tun *in doing*) **≈keit** f ~/ *persistence, perseverance*; *steadfastness*; *insistence*; *constancy*; ~ führt zum Ziel ⟨sl⟩ *it's dogged* (*as*) *does it*

Beh·arrungs- ~vermögen n ⟨phys⟩ *vis inertiae* L **~zustand** m ⟨phys⟩ *steady-state, inertia*

beh·aucht a ⟨gram⟩ ~er Laut *aspirate*

beh·auen vt [behaute/behauen] [h] (Steine, Holz etc) *to hew, to cut*; *to dress, to trim*; vierkantig ~ *to square* ‖ (Bäume) *to lop*

beh·äufeln vt [h] (Pflanzen) *to hill*

beh·aupten vt [h] **1.** (festhalten) **a.** (Stellung, Stadt) *to maintain, keep*; das Feld ~ *to hold* od *keep the field* **b. sich** ~ *to maintain* od *stand one's ground* ⟨a fig⟩; ⟨fig⟩ *to hold* (*one's own* od) *out*; *to keep one's end up, to assert o.s.*; sich tapfer ~ *to face the facts* ‖ sich ~ gegen *to assert o.s., to bear* od *stand up against, to hold out against* ‖ ⟨com⟩ (of prices) sich ~ *to be firm* od *steady*; behauptet *firm, steady* **2.** (Ansicht etc) *to maintain*; *to state*; *to affirm*; *to say* (*so he says*) ‖ *to profess* (gefunden z haben *to have found*) ‖ (Unerwiesenes) *to allege* | ~, daß .. *to contend* (od *assert, maintain*) *that* ..; ⟨Am⟩ *to allow* od *claim that* ..; steif u fest ~, daß .. *to contend positively* (od *to swear*) *that* ..; fälschlich ~, daß .. *to pretend that* .. ‖ ⟨jur⟩ [in Parenthese] erlaube ich mir z ~ *I submit* ‖ ich habe nicht behauptet, daß .. *my case was not that* ..; ~, daß etw ist *to maintain* od *claim a th to be*; v letzterem wird behauptet, daß er es sei *it is said of the latter that he is*; *the latter is said to be* ‖ v sich ~ ⟨Am⟩ *to claim* (daß *that*; daß etw ist *a th to be*; z s *to be*; .. *to have done*) **Beh·auptung** f ~/~en **1.** *maintaining, maintenance, keeping* (*of a position*) **2.** *assertion, affirmation, contention* (*that*); *statement* (*of a p*); e–e ~ aufstellen *to make a statement*; die ~ aufstellen, daß .. *to lay it down that*; bei e–r ~ bleiben *to hold to a st.* ‖ ⟨Am⟩ *claim*; *say-so* (*of a p*) ‖ leere, nicht erwiesene ~ *allegation*, ~en aufstellen *to make allegations* ‖ e–e ~ enthaltende Verneinung ⟨jur⟩ *negative* [s] *pregnant*

beh·ausen vt [h] (jdn) *to house, lodge*; *accommodate, entertain* (*a p*); *to put* (*a p*) *up* **Beh·ausung** f ~/~en *housing, accommodation* ‖ *lodging, dwelling, habitation*

Behavior·ismus [biheiviə'rismus] m [engl] ⟨bes Am philos⟩ *behavio*(*u*)*rism*

beh·eben vt [→ heben] [h] **1.** (Schwierigkeit, Störung etc) *to clear away, to adjust, meet, obviate* (*a th*); *to resolve*; *to do away with*; (Mängel) *to make good*; (Mißstand, Übel) *to redress*; *rectify*; (Schaden) *to repair* **2.** ⟨com⟩ (Geld) ~ = abheben

Beh·ebung f *adjustment*; *obviation, removal* ‖ *redress* (*of an abuse*)

beh·eimatet a (ansässig) *domiciled, resident* (in *in*) ‖ (heimisch) Herr N., ~ in *Mr. N., a native of* (*Canada*)

beh·eizen vt [h] *to heat* **Beh·eizung** f *the heating*

Beh·elf m ~(e)s/~e *expedient, shift*; *device, dodge* ‖ *makeshift, pisaller* [Fr], *substitute* (*a poor s.*) ‖ †⟨jur⟩ (Ausrede) *excuse, subterfuge*

beh·elfen vrefl [→ helfen] [h] sich ~ *to make shift* od *do* (*with*); ⟨Am⟩ *to make out* ‖ sich nur kümmerlich ~ *to make but a poor shift* ‖ sich ~ ohne etw *to do* od *manage without a th* **Beh·elfs-** ⟨mst⟩ *emergency* [attr] (*antenna*); *makeshift* (*article*) **~bau** m *temporary construction* **~brücke** f *em.* ⟨mil fam⟩ *hasty bridge* **~dunkelkammer** f ⟨phot⟩ *improvised darkroom* **~flugplatz** m *emergency airfield* **~glied** n = Kunstglied **~heim** n *improvised* od *temporary abode* od *dwelling*; *emergency house* **~instandsetzung** f *em. repair* **≗mäßig** a *makeshift* (*dinner*) || [adv] ~ einrichten *to improvise* | ~keit [f] tentativeness **~material** n *auxiliary material* **~mittel** n *expedient*

beh·elligen vt [h] (jdn) *to bother, trouble* (*with*); *annoy, molest*; *importune* (*with*) **Beh·elligung** f ~/~en *bother*(*ation*), *trouble*; *molestation*

beh·ende 1. a *handy* (*with the pen*), *adroit, dexterous*; *agile, nimble*; *quick, spry*; (geistig ~) *smart* **2.** adv *quickly, nimbly* **Beh·endigkeit** f ~/~en *handiness, dexterity*; *quickness, agility, nimbleness*; *smartness*

B·ehennuß f ⟨bot⟩ *ben-nut* **B·ehenöl** n *oil of ben*

beh·erbergen vt [h] (jdn) *to lodge, accommodate, shelter, house* (*a p*; *to be host to* (*a p*); *to put* (*a p*) *up, to give shelter to* (*a p*) || *to harbour* **Beh·erbergung** f ~/~en *housing, lodging* || → Obdach

beh·errschen vt [h] **A.** (P) **1.** (Land, Stadt) *to rule* (*a th*); *to rule* od *reign over* (*a th*); *to hold sway over* || ⟨mil & pol⟩ (Stellung) *to command, dominate*; die Lage ~ *to rule the roost* **2.** ⟨übtr⟩ (Gegenstand, Sprache) *to master* (*a th*), *to be master of* (*a th*); *to be well up in* (*a th*); *to have a grasp of* (*a th*); vollkommen ~ *to have complete command of* (*a th*); den Text e–r Rolle völlig ~ *to be wordperfect* **3. a.** (Gefühle, Leidenschaften) *to command, control, discipline, govern, master*; ~ lernen *to conquer, subdue*; → beherrscht **b. sich** ~, sich z ~ wissen *to command* od *control o.s.*; *to control one's feelings* od *temper*; *to keep one's temper*; *to be master of o.s.*; *to keep* od *hold o.s. in check, to keep o.s. in hand*; sich nicht ~ können *to have no selfcontrol* **B.** (S) **1.** (überragen) (of towers etc.) *to command, dominate*; *to tower above*, die Türme ~ das Stadtbild *the towers dominate the city*; ~d *towering* (*heights*) **2.** ⟨übtr⟩ jdn ~ (of ideas, principles) *to dominate, govern*; *determine*; *sway, influence*; (of passions) *to ride a p*; (of feelings) *to possess a p* || die Universitäten beherrscht ein moderner Geist *the universities are informed with a modern spirit* || ein v der Maschine beherrschtes Zeitalter *a machine-ridden age* **beh·errschend** a *dominating* || *overriding* (*problem, object*)

Beh·errscher m ~s/~ *ruler*; *master, lord*; *sovereign* **Beh·errscherin** f ~/~nen *mistress*; *sovereign* **beh·errscht** a ⟨fig⟩ *restrained, self-possessed*; *level-headed* **Beh·errschtheit** f *self-possession, level-headedness* **Beh·errschung** f ~/~en **1.** *control, mastery* (e–s Gebietes *of* od *over an area*); *sway* (e–s Landes *over a country*); → Herrschaft **2.** ⟨übtr⟩ **a.** *grasp, mastery* (e–r S *of a th*); s–e ~ des Englischen *his m. of English* || *grip* (e–r S *upon a th*) **b.** (Selbst≗) *self-control*

beh·erzigen vt [h] (etw) *to take to heart, to bear in mind*; *to heed, mind*; *follow, observe, consider* **beh·erzigenswert** a *worth heeding* (od *minding*), *worth following*; *worthy of observance*

Beh·erzigung f ~/~en *the taking to heart, bearing in mind*; *consideration*; *observance*; zur ~ *by way of observance* **beh·erzt** a *game, plucky, spirited, stout-hearted*; → tapfer, mutig || *level-headed* | **≗heit** f ~/ *pluckiness, spiritedness*; *intrepidity*

beh·exen vt [h] *to bewitch, to lay a spell on*; (bei Negern) *to voodoo* || ⟨fig⟩ *to charm, enchant* || wie behext *like mad*; wie behext s *to be all in a whirl* **Beh·exung** f *bewitchment*

beh·ilflich a [mst pred] (P) *helpful*; *useful, serviceable*; jdm ~ s *to lend a p a helping hand*; *to help a p* (bei etw *with* od *in a th*; z tun *in doing, to do*, ⟨fam⟩ *do*), *to assist a p* (bei etw *with a th*, z tun *in doing*)

beh·indern vt [h] (jdn) *to* (*en*)*cumber, hamper, handicap, hinder, impede*; behindert s *or* w durch *to be clogged* od *encumbered with, to be hampered* od *handicapped by* od *with* || ⟨ftb⟩ *to tackle* || → hindern | (etw) *to hinder, impede, obstruct*; (Bewegung) *to embarrass*; *to interfere with* (*a th*); ⟨tact⟩ *to interdict* **Beh·inderung** f ~/~en *hindrance, impediment* (e–r S *to a th*), *obstruction, embarrassment, encumbrance* || im ~sfalle *in case of prevention*

beh·obeln vt [h] *to plane*

beh·olzen vt [h] *to afforest* || **sich** ~ (of a tree) *to run to wood, to form branches*

beh·orchen vt [h] *to overhear* | ⟨med⟩ *to auscultate*

Beh·örde f ~/~n *authority*, [oft pl] *the authorities, magistracy*; *board, office, department*; Staats≗, staatliche ~ *government board* od *department* od *agency*; städtische ~ *local board* od *government* || ⟨jur⟩ *jurisdiction* || örtliche ~n (Kommunal≗n) *local authorities* || vorgesetzte ~ *superior authority* | ~neigentum [n] *government property* **beh·ördlich 1.** a *authoritative, official* **2.** adv *by authority*; *officially*

Beh·uf m ~(e)s/~e [nur in festen Verbindungen:] zu diesem ~ *for this purpose*; zu m–m ~ *on my behalf*; zum ~ jds *for the benefit of a p*

beh·ufs prep [gen] *in order to, for the purpose of, with a view to*; ~ Übernahme der Leitung *with a view to taking over the control*

beh·uft a *hoofed*

†**beh·ülflich** = behilflich

°**Beh·ums** m ~es/ = Betrug | **≗en** vt/i [h] = betrügen

beh·üten vt [h] (jdn) *to guard, to keep, to preserve* (vor *from*), *to protect* (vor *from, against*) *to watch over* (*a p*) | behüt dich Gott! *may God keep and preserve you*! *God be with you*! *good--bye*! || das Behüt-dich-Gott *god-speed* [s] || davor möge uns Gott ~ *may God prevent it* || Gott behüte! *God forbid*! || behüte! *by no means*!, *no idea*!, *far from it*!

Beh·üter m ~s/~ *guardian, protector*

beh·utsam 1. a *careful, cautious, circumspect, guarded* (*advice, prognosis*); *gingerly*; *wary* (beim Lesen *in reading*) **2.** adv *cautiously, gingerly* **Beh·utsamkeit** f ~/ *care, carefulness, cautiousness, circumspection*

B·ei m [*bei*] (türk. Titel) *bey*

bei adv **1.** *by*; (hier) dicht ~ *close by, hard by* || jd, der ~ allem da~ ist *a jack of all trades, a busy-body* || da ist nichts ~ *there is no objection to it*; → dabei **2.** [mst in comp] **a.** → bei– **b.** da~, hier~ (etc)

bei prep [dat] (beim = bei dem) **I. (räumlich) A. (Nähe)** (vor S) *by, near*, nahe ~, dicht ~ *beside, close beside* (*the table*); (*near, close hard*) *by* (*the church*); *next to* (*the church*); *near Berlin*; *by the fire* | die Schlacht ~ Leipzig *the battle of Leipzig* **B.** (vor P & T) **1. a.** (neben) *by, beside*; er saß ~ ihr *he sat by her* **b.** (zus– mit) *with*; *at*; er wohnt ~ s–n Eltern *he lives with his parents*; ~ Müllers *at the Millers'*; bei s–m Onkel *with his uncle* od *at his uncle's*; *I shall stay with you for a week, I shall spend a week with you*; beim Buchhändler *at the bookseller's*, ~ allen Buchhändlern (z h) *of all booksellers*; er war ~ ihm gewesen ⟨fam⟩ *he had been to see him*; *have you got the book with you*? *no, I left it with your sister*; *with* (od *from*) *whom do you take lessons*? || *his influence with the king* **c.** *about*; *on*; *I have no money about me* || *the document was found on him* || ⟨mil⟩ beim Stabe *on the staff*; ~ der Times beschäftigt *on the Times*; ich hinterließ m–e Karte ~ ihr *I left my card on her* **d.** ~ Hofe *at court* || Sekretär beim Herzog v N. *secretary to the duke of N.*; so: *A.D.C. to the Minister, to North Africa* || eine Audienz beim Könige *an audience of the king* || ~ jdm im Dienste stehen *to be in the employ of a p* || *to have* *access to the director* || ~ uns (z Lande) *in this country, with us, at our place* || verlegt ~ N. *published by N.* || → beklagen, bestellen **2.** ⟨übtr⟩ **a. with;** ~ Gott ist kein Ding unmöglich *with God all things are possible* || ~ den Römern *with the Romans*; (not so) *among the R.* || ~ den Seehunden ist es anders *it is otherwise with the seals* || es steht ~ dir *it rests with you* || es ist die Regel ~ ihm *it is a rule with him* || er dient ~ der Marine ⟨engl⟩ *he does his service with the Royal Navy* **b. in:** *he serves in the guards*; wie es ~ Goethe heißt *as we read in Goethe*; ich lese ~ Milton *I read in M.*; *a passage in M.* | **(in jds Natur)** ~ alten Leuten *in old people*; ~ Geigenspielern *in violinists* || beim Rotwild *in red deer* (*the antlers constitute* ..) | ~ **sich** [dat] überlegen *to consider on one's mind* **C.** (vor S) **1.** Körperteilen) **a. by;** jdn ~ der Hand nehmen *to take a p by the hand*; ~ den Haaren (*to seize*) *by the hair*; beim Kragen *by the collar* **b.** ⟨übtr⟩ ~ der Hand s *to be at hand* || jdn ~ s–m Namen nennen *to call a p by his name* **2.** ⟨übtr⟩ **with** || ~ kl Gewichten *with tiny weights* || es ist nicht so beim Drama *it is not so with the drama* || ~ diesen Verben steht das Gerundium *these verbs take the gerund* **II.** (in **Beteuerungen)** ~ Gott dem Allmächtigen! *by Almighty God*! beim Zeus! *by Jove*! beim Himmel! *by Heaven*! || ~ m–r Seele! (*up*)*on my soul*! ~ m–r Ehre (*up*)*on my honour* || ~ m–r Seligkeit! *as I hope to be saved*! ~ d–r Liebe zu mir! *as you love me*! **III.** ⟨übtr auf **Vorgänge** u **Zustände**⟩ **A. 1. at;** ~ der Arbeit *at work*; *at play*; beim Essen *while eating, at dinner*; *at breakfast*; ~ Tische *at table* | ~ Tagesanbruch *at dawn* | **over** *a glass of wine*; *he never talks over his breakfast*; *she always sings over her work* || sie sah ihnen ~m Trinken zu *she looked at them drinking* | (einschränkend) ~ der Einfuhr *in regard to importation* | ~ rotem Licht hier halten! *stop here for red light* **2. by; in; during a.** ~ Tage *by day, in the day-*(*time*); ~ Nacht *by night, in the night*; *Berlin by night*; ~ hellem Tage *in broad daylight*; ~ Tag u Nacht *day and night*; ~ Mondschein *by the light of the moon*; ~ Lampenlicht *by lamplight*; ⟨phot⟩ *to develop only in red light*! ~ gedämpftem Licht *in subdued light*; → Licht **b.** ~ schönem Wetter *in fine weather*; ~ günstigem Wetter *weather permitting*; ~ Regen *in the rain*; ~ jeder Witterung *in rain* od *shine, in all weathers* || ~ dieser Hitze *in this heat*; ~ dem Gewitter *in the thunderstorm* **c.** ~ e–m Luftangriff (*killed*) *in an air-raid*, (*in a car-accident*) | **d.** *during the night*; *during her lifetime* **3. (zeitlich) on; at** (gleich) ~ s–r Ankunft (Abreise) *on his arrival* (*leaving*) || beim ersten Anblick *at first sight, at the first glance* || ~ dieser Nachricht *on receiving this news* || ~ Ebbe (Flut) *at low* (*high*) *tide* || ⟨com⟩ ~ Sicht der Wechsel *on presentation of the bills, on sight of the drafts*; ein ~ Sicht zahlbarer W. *a draft payable at sight* || ~ reiflicher Überlegung *on further consideration*; ~ flüchtiger (näherer) Ü. *on first* (*second*) *thoughts* || ~ Gelegenheit *on occasion, occasionally*; ~ dieser G. *on this occasion*; ~ der ersten G. *on the first opportunity*; ~ jeder G. *on all occasions*; bei passender G. *on a suitable occ.* **B. with; in;** ~ verschlossener Tür *with the door locked*; ~ offenem Fenster *with the window*(*s*) *open* || ~ diesen Worten *with these words* || ~ guter Gesundheit *in good health*; ~ Jahren *advanced* (od *well on*) *in years*; ~ Lebzeiten *in life* || ~ Sinnen *in one's senses*; nicht ~ Sinnen, ~ Troste s *to be out of one's senses* || ~ Kasse *in cash* (od *funds*); nicht ~ K. *out of cash* || ~ Stimme *in voice*; ~ Laune *in humour*, nicht ~ L. *out of humour* || ~ diesen Umständen *on* od *under these circumstances* || ~ s–m Reichtum *with his riches*; ~ s–r Bescheidenheit *with his modesty* **C. (einräumend = trotz)** ~ allen ihren Reizen *with all her charms*; ~ aller unserer Vorsicht *with all our caution* (*it got lost*) || er konnte uns beim besten Willen nicht helfen *try as he would, he could not help us* || ~ alledem *for all that*; → dem **D.** ~ **Strafe** der Verhaftung *under penalty of imprisonment*; ~ e–r Strafe v 10 Pfd *under penalty of £ 10*; ~ Todesstrafe *on penalty of death, on* od *under pain of d.* || → beileibe **IV. (vor Zahlen)** *about*; ~ 500 Mann *about five hundred men* **V. (vor Adj.)** ~ weitem *by far, far* od *out and away*; ~ weitem besser *far better*

bei- pref **1.** [betont] **a.** [trennbar vor Verben]: b·ei|geben **b.** [untrennbar vor Substantiven]: B·eifall **2.** [unbetont u untrennbar vor Adverben]: beinahe

b·ei|behalten vt [h] (Kurs) *to keep*; (Zustand) *to keep on* (od *up*), *to retain, to maintain*; *to continue to use*; (Plan) *to adhere* (od *keep, stick*) *to, to abide by* **B·eibehaltung** f ~/ *keeping*; *retention* (*of submarines*); *maintenance*; *adherence* (e–s Planes *to a plan*) || (im Amt) *retention*

B·eiblatt n ~(e)s/~̈er *supplement* (e–r Zeitung *to a newspaper*)

B·eiboot n ~s/~e ⟨mar⟩ *cock-boat, dinghy, dingey*; *pinnace*; *tender*; (e–s Segelschiffs) *long-boat*; kl ~ → Dingi

b·ei|bringen vt [h] **A.** (herbeibringen) (Zeugen) *to produce*; (Beweise etc) *to adduce, to bring forward*; (Gründe) *to allege*; (Argument) *to urge*; (Zeugnis) *to present* **B. 1.** (zufügen) **a.** (e–n Schlag) *to plant* **b.** jdm etw ~, jdm e–e Wunde ~ *to inflict a wound* (*up*)*on a p, to cause a p a wound*, jdm e–e Niederlage ~ *to inflict a defeat* (*up*)*on a p*; v eigener Hand beigebracht s (of wounds) *to be self-inflicted*; → versetzen || jdm e–e Arznei ~ *to administer a medicine to a p*; jdm Gift ~ *to administer poison to a p, to poison a p* **2.** (lehren) jdm etw ~ *to teach a p a th* (od *a th a p*); *to inculcate a th on* (od *in a p*; jdm ~ z tun *to teach a p to do*; jdm Gehorsam ~ *to teach a p to obey*, jdm Räson ~ *to bring a p to reason*; ich werde es ihm schon ~ *I'll teach him manners* || jdm e–n Begriff v etw ~ *to impress upon a p the idea of a th* || jdm –zu– suchen, daß .. *to try to make clear* (od *to bring home*) *to a p that* .. **3.** (mitteilen) jdm etw ~ *to impart a th to a p*; jdm etw schonend ~ *to break a th to a p*

B·eibringung f ~/~en *production* (*of witnesses*); *the bringing forward* (*of proofs*); *the sending-in* (*of a certificate*)

Beicht f ~/~en [sd] = Beichte || [in comp] ⟨ec⟩ *confessional, confessionary* **~formel** f *formula used at confession* **~geheimnis** n = Beichtsiegel **~geld** n *confession-money*; *confessor's fees* [pl] **~kind** n *penitent*; *commnnicant* **~siegel** n *seal of confession*, unter dem ~ *under the s. of c.* **~stuhl** m *confessional* **~vater** m *father confessor*

B·eichte f ~/~n ⟨ec⟩ *confession* || ~ ablegen *to confess*; zur ~ gehen *to go to confession*; *to confess*; die ~ hören *to hear confession*; jdm die ~ abnehmen *to confess a p* **b·eichten** vt/i [h] **1.** vt (Sünde) *to confess* **2.** vi *to confess, to go to confession* **B·eichtiger** m ~s/~ *confessor* **B·eichtling** m = Beichtkind

b·eidarmig a *both-handed*

b·eide I. [betont] **1.** [a] *both*; die ~n Herren kamen zur selben Zeit an *both* (*the*) *gentlemen arrived at the same time*; s–e ~n Brüder fielen *both his brothers fell* **2.** [pron] *both*; ~ sind zurück *both* (*of them*) *are back, each of them is back, they are both back, they are back both*; wir ~ *both of us*; alle ~ *both of them, both one and the other* **II.** [unbetont] **1.** [a] *two*; die ~n Herren sind angekommen *the two gentlemen have arrived*; s–e ~n Schwestern *his two sisters* **2.**

[pron] ~, die ~n *the two*; wir ~ *the two of us* welcher v ~n? *which of the two*? || → beides **III.** e–e(r) v ~n, k–r v ~n **1.** [a] e–r v ~n *either*; wenn e–r v ~ n Parteien sich weigert *if either side refuses* (*to meet the other*); setz die Lampe an irgend e–s der ~n Enden *put the lamp at either end* || in ~n Fällen *in either case*; auf ~n Seiten *on either side*; ~ Ansichten sind richtig *either view is right* | k–r der ~n Wege ist richtig *neither way* (od *neither of the ways*) *is right* **2.** [pron] e–e(r) v ~n *either*; eins v ~n (sc Büchern) genügt *either* (*of them*) *will do* || k–e(r) v ~n *neither, not .. either*; ich habe k–n v ~n gesehen, ich habe ~ nicht gesehen *I have not seen either* | k–r v uns ~n weiß *neither of us knows* (*what* ..)

b·eiderlei a *of both kinds* od *sorts, of either sort*; Ausländer ~ Geschlechts *aliens of either sex*; auf ~ Art *both ways*; *either way*

b·eiderseitig a *bilateral* (*contract*); *on each* od *either side*; f ~es Gespräch ⟨telph⟩ *for recording two-way conversations* || (gegenseitig) *mutual, reciprocal* || ⟨bes mot⟩ ~es Verschulden *both to blame collision* || [adv] ~ tragbar *turnabout, double-face, reversible* (Mantel) **b·eiderseits** adv *on both sides* || (wechselseitig) *mutually, reciprocally* || → vor || ~ angelehnt ⟨mil⟩ ⟨m. m.⟩ *interior units*

B·eiderwand f ~/ & n ~s/ *linsey-woolsey*

b·eides [pron] *either*; ~ ist richtig *either is correct*; ~ trifft zu *both things are true*

B·eid- **~händer** m ~s/~ *heavy sword* || ⟨biol⟩ *ambidexter* **≗händig** a *ambidextrous* **~händigkeit** f *ambidexterity* **~leber** m ~s/~ ⟨zoo⟩ *amphibian* **≗lebig** a *amphibious* **≗recht** a *reversible* (*cloth*) **≗seits** adv Sw = beiderseits

b·ei|drehen vi [h] ⟨mar⟩ *to bring to, to heave to*

beiein·ander adv *together* || dicht ~ *close together*; ⟨fam⟩ *cheek by jowl*

B·eifahrer m ⟨mot⟩ *assistant driver, co-dr.*; *driver's mate*; ⟨racing⟩ *team-mate* || ⟨mot cycl⟩ *passenger in side-car*; *p. on pillion*

B·eifall m ~(e)s/ **1.** (Zustimmung) *assent, approval, approbation*; ~ finden *to meet with approval, to be approved of* (bei jdm *by a p*); der Plan hat s–n ~ *he approves* (*of*) *the plan* **2.** (lauter ~) *acclamation*; *applause, cheers, plaudits* [pl] || unter starkem ~ *with loud applause* od *cheers*; e–m Publikum ~ abringen *to draw applause from an audience*; ~ finden bei, v *to be greeted with app. by*; ~ klatschen *to applaud*; jdm ~ klatschen *to applaud* od *clap a p*; jdn mit ~ begrüßen *to cheer a p*; stürmischen ~ finden *or* hervorrufen ⟨theat⟩ *to bring down the house*

†**b·ei|fallen** vi [s] **1.** = helfen **2.** = einfallen

b·eifällig **1.** a *approving, assentient, assenting, favourable*; **2.** adv *approvingly*; ~ aufnehmen *to receive* (*a th*) *with approval*

B·eifalls- **~bezeigung** f *applause*; *acclamations* [pl] **~klatschen** n *applause, clapping*; *plaudits* [pl] **~klatscher** m *clapper* **~ruf** m [mst pl ~e] *cheers* [pl] **~sturm** m *burst* od *peals* [pl] *of applause* **≗würdig** a *approvable*

B·eifilm m ~s/~e *short feature*

b·ei|folgen vi [s] ⟨com⟩ *to follow*, [mst prs p ~d] **b·eifolgend** a ⟨com⟩ *annexed, enclosed, subjoined* || ~ erhalten Sie *enclosed please find*; ~ sende ich .. *I enclose herewith* ..

b·ei|fügen vt [h] *to add* (e–r S *to a th*) || (im Briefe) *to subjoin, enclose* **B·eifügung** f ~/~en *addition* (z *to*); *enclosure* || unter ~ e–s Schecks *enclosing a cheque* (*I* ..) | ⟨gram⟩ *attribute, attributive*; ~ssatz *attributive* (od *adjective*) *clause*; *relative c.* (der Wald, wo ..; die Zeit, wo ..)

B·eifuß m ~es/ ⟨bot⟩ *mugwort, artemisia, absinth*(*e*)

B·eigabe f *addition* (z *to*); *enclosure*; *extra*; *contribution*

beige [bæ:ʒ] a [Fr] *beige*

b·ei|geben vt/i [h] **1.** vt (etw) *to add, join* (e–r S *to a th*) || (jdn) *to give*; jdn als Ratgeber ~ *to attach a p as adviser* **2.** vi (nachgeben) *to give in, to yield*; klein ~ *to submit*; *to lower one's pretensions*; *to come down a peg* od *two, to draw in one's horns, to sing small*; ⟨fam⟩ *to back* od *pipe down, to knuckle under* od ⟨Am⟩ *to, to get down from one's high horse*

B·eigeordnete [der ~, ein ~r] m ~n/~n *adjunct, assistant* (jds *to a p*) || ⟨jur⟩ *assessor*; ⟨Ger⟩ *deputy-mayor*

B·eigericht n ~s/~e *entremets*; *hors d'œuvre*(*s* ⟨engl⟩ pl) [Fr], *side-dish, extra dish*

B·eigeschmack m ~(e)s/ *after-taste, smack, tang* || ⟨übtr⟩ *dash* (*with a d. of* ..), *savour, smack* (*a ~ of*); *touch, tinge, tincture*; e–n ~ h v *to smack of, to be tinged with*; e–r S e–n ~ geben *to tinge a th*

b·ei|gesellen vt [h] (jdn) *to attach* (jdm *to a p*); *to associate* (jdm *with a p*) || sich jdm ~ *to associate with a p, to join a p*

Beignet [bæn'je:] m [Fr] ~s/~s ⟨cul⟩ *beignet, fritter*

B·eiguß m –sses/–güsse = Soße

beih·er adv (nebenher) *beside* (*to walk, run b.*) || = nebenbei

B·eihilfe f ~/~n **1.** *aid, assistance, succour* || *collaboration*, unter ~ v *with the c. of* .. | ⟨jur⟩ (bei e–m Verbrechen) *abetment*; jdm ~ leisten *to abet a p*; bei e–m Verbrechen ~ leisten *to aid and abet a crime* **2.** [konkr] (geldliche ~) *allowance*; *grants* pl (zu .. *towards the purchase of furniture*); *subsidy*; (staatliche) *subvention*

b·ei|holen vt [h] ⟨mar⟩ *to take in* (*the sail*)

B·eiklang m ~(e)s/≗e *accompanying sound*

b·ei|kommen vi [s] jdm ~ *to get at* od *near a p*; *to come up to* od *with a p, to reach a p*; *to get* od *lay hold of a p*; es ist ihm nicht –zu– *there is no getting at him, there is no arguing* od *reasoning with him* || ⟨übtr⟩ e–r S ~ *to get at a th, to get hold of a th*; e–r S –zu– suchen *to cope* (od *grapple*) *with a th, to tackle a th*; *to try to get the better of a th*; *to break the back of a th* | sich [dat] etw ~ l = .. einfallen l

Beil n ~(e)s/~e *hatchet*; → Axt || kl ~, Fleischer≗ *chopper*, (schweres) *cleaver* || → Fall≗, Kriegs≗

B·eiladung f ~/~en ⟨artill⟩ *igniting charge*

B·eilage f ~/~n *the enclosed, enclosure* (*in a letter*) || *insert, supplement* (e–r Zeitung *to a newspaper*) || ⟨cul⟩ *vegetables* pl, *etc*; Hammelkeule u ~ *leg of mutton and trimmings* || → Zugabe

†**B·eilager** n ~s/~ *nuptials* [pl] *of distinguished people*; → Beischlaf

B·eilast f ~/ ⟨mar⟩ *any luggage* od *goods exempt from freight* || *worthless goods*

b·eiläufig **1.** a *casual, incidental, passing* (*remark*); *occasional*; *secondary* **2.** adv *casually, incidentally*; *in passing*; (wie) ~ erwähnen *to mention by the way* (od *by the bye*), *to m. in passing* od *in an offhand way*; ~ e–e Bemerkung m *to throw out a remark* || (in Parenthese) ~ bemerkt *by the bye, by the way*; *by way of parenthesis* | × = etwa ≗keit f ~/ *casualness*

†**B·eilbrief** m ⟨mar⟩ *ship's register*; Sw = Schuldschein; → Zertifikat

b·eilegbar [a] jdm ~ *predicable to a p*

b·ei|legen vt/i [h] **I.** vt **1.** (dazulegen) (etw) *to enclose* || *to add, to adjoin, to join* (e–r S *to a th*); etw (e–r Zeitung) ~ (hineinlegen) *to insert* **2.** (beiseitelegen) **a.** ⟨mar⟩ die Segel ~ *to reef the sails*; ein Schiff ~ *to heave* (od *bring*) *a ship to, to make a ship lie to* **b.** ⟨übtr⟩ (Streit) *to accommodate, to arrange, to compose, to compound, to make* (od *patch*) *up, to settle, to sink*; e–n Streit gütlich ~ *to compromise*; (Differenzen) *to resolve, shelve*; *to smooth over* [adv];

e–e Unterredung mit dem Zweck e–n Streit –zu– *a fence-mending discussion* **3.** ⟨übtr⟩ **a.** (zuschreiben) jdm etw ~ *to ascribe, to attribute, to impute a th to a p, to put a th down to a p* || jdm e–n Namen ~ *to give a p a name, to surname, to nickname, to dub a p*; sie legten ihm den Namen Lackland bei *they surnamed* (od *nicknamed, dubbed*) *him Lackland* || jdm e–n Titel ~ *to confer* (od *bestow*) *a title on a p*; sich e–n Titel etc ~ *to assume, to usurp a title* **b.** (beimessen) e–r S Bedeutung (Wert etc) ~ *to attach importance* (*value*) *to a th*; dem Ereignisse ist k–e bes. Bedeutung beizulegen *no special importance attaches to the event* **II.** vi **1.** ⟨mar⟩ (of a ship) *to lie to, to heave to* (*the ship hove to*) **2.** † = sich beeilen

B·eilegung f ~/~en **1.** (Schlichtung) *adjustment* (*of controversies*), *composition, accommodation, settlement* (*of a quarrel*) **2.** *attribution*; *conferment* (*of a title*) **~sverfahren** n ⟨bes pol⟩ *amiable composition*

beil·eibe adv: ~ nicht! *not for the world! not for the life of me!*; ⟨Am fam⟩ *not by a long shot* || *by no means!, on no account!, certainly not!, no fear!*

B·eileid n ~(e)s/ *condolence* || jdm sein ~ ausdrücken *to express one's condolence with a p*; *to express sympathy with a p* (z e–m Verlust *in a loss*); jdm sein ~ bezeigen, –zeugen *to present one's condolences to a p, to condole with a p* (z etw *on a th*); *she expressed her sincere concern* **~sbesuch** m *visit of condolence* **~sbezeigung, ~sbezeugung** f ~/~en *condolence*; *sympathy* **~sschreiben** n *letter of condolence* (od *sympathy*); *sympathetic message*

b·eilfertig a ⟨mar⟩ *ready for the rigging*

b·eilförmig a *hatchet-shaped*

b·ei|liegen vi [s] **1.** †jdm ~ *to lie* od *sleep with a p* **2.** (beigefügt sein) *to be enclosed* **3.** ⟨mar⟩ (of a ship) (beigelegt h, → beilegen II. 1.) *to have heaved* od *lain to* **b·eiliegend** a **1.** [pred] ~ finden Sie .. *enclosed you will find ..* **2.** [attr] *enclosed* (*letter*)

B·eilkespiel n (Schieben v talergroßen Scheiben auf 6–7 m langem Brett) (nach 9 Kegeln) ⟨m. m.⟩ *shovelboard, shuffle-board*; *spillikins*

B·eilstein m ⟨minr⟩ = Nephrit

beim = bei dem, → bei

b·ei|mengen vt [h] etw e–r S ~ *to admix, to mix a th with a th, to add to a th*

b·ei|messen vt [h] jdm etw ~ *to ascribe, attribute a th to a p, to put* od *set down a th to a p*, jdm die Schuld ~ *to lay* (od *put, throw*) *the blame on a p, to set the blame down on a p* || e–r S Glauben ~ *to give credence to a th* | e–r S Bedeutung ~ = beilegen, → I. 3. b.

b·ei|mischen vt [h] etw e–r S ~ *to mix* (od *admix*) *a th with a th* **B·eimischung** f ~/~en *admixture*; entwertende ~ *alloy*, fälschende ~ *loading* || e–e ~ v *a dash of* (*brandy*); ⟨übtr⟩ *a smack* (od *infusion, sprinkling, tinge, touch*) *of*; Freude mit e–r ~ v Leid *joy dashed with pain*

Bein n ~(e)s/~e **I.** (Knochen) **1.** *bone* [bes in comp, → Elfen≈, Fisch≈, Nasen≈ etc] **2.** Wendungen: → Mark, Stein **II.** ⟨anat⟩ **1.** *leg*, am ~ *on the l.*; ohne ~e *legless* || dünnes ~ ⟨oft derog⟩ *shank*; lange dünne ~e [pl] *spindle-shanks* [pl] || künstliches ~ *artificial leg, joint-leg* **2.** ⟨übtr⟩ *leg* (*of a table*, etc.); Hosen≈ *leg of trousers* **3.** Wendungen: **a.** kein ~! *no idea! not a bit!* || ˣdas ist auch kein ~ ab! *that won't hurt you!* **b.** sich die ~e ablaufen *to do one's utmost* (*to do*) || sich kein ~ ausreißen ⟨fig⟩ *not to twist one's neck, to take it easy, to let things slide* || (suchend:) „es hat ~e bek" *it has walked off* || sich das ~ brechen *to break* od *fracture one's leg* || die ~e gebrauchen *to leg it* || noch junge ~e h *to be still young* || alles, was ~e hat *anybody able to run* || die ~e kreuzen *to cross one's legs, to cross one leg over the other* || ~e m *to leg it*; *to shake a leg, to stir one's stumps*; jdm ~e m *to put a p to the run, to make a p find his legs* (*that'll put legs on him*) || die ~e breit m ⟨sex⟩ *to lift one's leg* || die ~e in die Hand (*or* unter die Arme) nehmen *to put one's best leg* od *foot foremost*; ⟨fam⟩ *to leg it, to stir one's stumps, to shake a leg*; *to take to one's heels* || sich die ~e in den Leib stehen ⟨sl⟩ *to cool one's heels* || ein ~ stellen *to trip* (*to t. in football*); jdm ein ~ st. *to trip a p* (*up*), *to chip a p*; ⟨fig⟩ *to lay a mine for a p, to spring a mine on a p*; *to put a spoke in a p's wheel*; *to kipper a p* || die ~e übereinanderschlagen = die ~e kreuzen || sich die ~e vertreten *to stretch one's legs, to take a walk* || die ~e hoch werfen können (beim Tanz) *to have a high* od *good kick* **c.** [nach prep] (Forderung etc) **ans** ~ binden *to give* (*a th*) *up as a bad debt* (od *as lost*), *to get over the loss of* (*a th*) | **auf** den ~en *on one's feet* od *legs*; *afoot, astir, stirring, out and about*; sich auf den ~en halten *to keep on one's legs*; früh auf den ~en s *to be up and doing, to be up early*; gut auf den ~en s *to be a good walker*; immer auf den ~en s *to be always on the go* (od *move, trot*); wieder auf den ~en s *to be up and about* (od *doing*) *again* | auf die ~e bringen = auf die ~e stellen; jdn .. br. *to boost a p* || jdm (wieder) auf die ~e helfen *to help a p to his feet*, ⟨fig⟩ *to give a p a leg up, to give a p a lift, to pull a p round*; *to set a p on his legs* || auf die ~e k *to get on one's legs*; wieder auf die ~e k *to pull round, to recover* || sich auf die ~e m *to be off, to set out* || auf einem ~ kann man nicht stehen! *what! one cocktail? who can fly on one wing?* || (Einrichtung) auf die ~e stellten *to put* (*a th*) *on its legs*; *to launch, to start* (*a th*); ein Heer auf die ~e st. *to put an army in the field, to raise an army*; etw glücklich auf die ~e st. *to put a th across* | **mit** den ~en auf der Erde bleiben *to keep in touch with real life* (od *realities*); .. stehen *to be near to earth, to be earthy* | jdm e–n Knüppel **zwischen** die ~e werfen ⟨fig⟩ *to put a spoke in a p's wheel*; → jdm ein ~ stellen **III.** [in comp] **1.** (aus 1.) → Knochen– **2.** (aus II.) ⟨anat⟩ *crural* (*artery, vein*, etc.)

B·ein- ~asche f *bone-ash* **~berge** f ⟨hist⟩ = Beinschiene 1. **~brech** m ⟨bot⟩ *bog* od *English asphodel*; → Ährenlilie **~bruch** m *breaking* od *fracture of the leg*; er hat sich e–n ~ zugezogen *he has broken* od *fractured his leg* **~fäule** f = Knochenfraß **~freiheit** f ⟨mot⟩ *leg-room* **~geschwür** n ⟨med⟩ *varicose ulcer* **~glas** n *opaline* **~halter** m *leg-support* **~harnisch** m = Beinzeug **~haus** n *charnel-house, ossuary* **~haut** f = Knochenhaut **~heil** n ⟨bot⟩ = Beinbrech **~kleid** n ~s/~er (gewählt f Hose) *breeches, trousers* [pl]; ⟨bes Am⟩ *pantaloons*, [mst] *pants*, ⟨sl⟩ *bags* [pl]; ein ~ *a pair of trousers* (etc) || Damen≈ *drawers, knickers* [pl], ein ~ *a pair of drawers*; langes Damen≈ *pantalettes* [pl] **~kleidung** f *chausses* pl **~prothese** f *artificial leg* **~schiene** f **1.** ⟨hist⟩ (Teil der Rüstung) *greaves* [pl], → Beinzeug; ⟨hock⟩ *pad, leg-guard* **2.** ⟨med⟩ *leg-splint*; ~n [pl] *irons* [pl] || → **~schützer** m ⟨sport crick⟩ (*leg-*)*guard*, (*leg-*)*pad* **~schwarz** n *bone-black* **~stellen** n *leg-tripping*; (beim Ringen) *trip* **~strecken** n ⟨gym⟩ *leg-stretching* **~tasche** f ⟨hist⟩ (Hüftgehänge der Rüstung) *tasset* **~well** n ⟨bot⟩ *comfrey* **~wunde** f *wound in the leg* **~zeug** n ⟨hist⟩ (Teil der Rüstung) 1. (~ f Oberschenkel) *cuisses* [pl] 2. (~ f Unterschenkel) *greaves* [pl]

bein·ahe adv **1.** [bei Verben u vor Maß–, Zahl–, Zeitangaben] *nearly* (*she was nearly 20*); *close* (*up*)*on* (*40 years*), *near* (*up*)*on ten o'clock* ||

ich glaube ~ *I have half an idea*; ~ getötet w *to come within an ace of being killed* **2.** [vor Adj. u Subst.] *almost* (⟨Am⟩ *most*), *well-nigh*; *all but*; ⟨Am⟩ *near*; ~ die meisten klebrigen Flüssigkeiten *all but the most viscous liquids*; → fast

B·einame m ~n/~n *by-name, surname*; (Spitzname) *nickname, sobriquet* ‖ jdm e–n ~n geben *to surname a p*; *nickname a p*; Johann mit dem ~n Lackland *John surnamed Lackland*; man gab ihnen den ~n Methodisten *they nicknamed them Methodists*

B·einchen n ~s/~ *little leg*

b·einern a *made of bone, bony* **-b·einig** a [in comp] *legged*; zwei~ *two-legged*; lang~ *long-legged*; etc.

be·inhalten [be'in–] vt *to contain*; *to imply* ‖ was –tet das Gesetz? *what are the provisions of the law?*

b·ei|ordnen vt [h] **1.** (beigeben) (jdn) *to give*; *join* (e–m Ausschuß *to a committee*); *to appoint as a member* (*to a th*) **2.** (nebeneinanderstellen) (verschiedene Klassen *to coordinate* ⟨a. gram⟩ ‖ beigeordnet *coordinate*; → Beigeordnete ‖ beiordnend *coordinative* (*function*) **B·eiordnung** f ~/~en *coordination* (*of classes*)

b·ei|packen vt [h] (etw) *to pack* (*a th*) *up with a th*

B·eipferd n ~s/~e **1.** (Handpferd) *led-horse* **2.** (2 Pferden vorgespanntes Reservepferd) *outrunner, extra* (od *spare*) *horse*

b·ei|pflichten vi [h] jdm ~ *to agree* od *concur with a p* (in etw *in a th*) ‖ e–r S ~ *to assent* (od *agree*) *to a th*; jds Meinung ~ *to concur with a p on his opinion* ‖ *to approve* (*of*) *a th, to subscribe to .., acquiesce in a th, to endorse a th*; → beistimmen **b·eipflichtend** a *assentient* **B·eipflichtung** f ~/~en *agreement, concurrence*; *assent*; *approbation*

B·eiprogramm n ⟨film⟩ *anything in a show except the chief film* (z. B. *the news reel*); *trailers* pl; *supporting program*

B·eirat m ~s/~̈e (Körperschaft) *advisory council* ‖ [konkr] (P) *adviser*

B·eiried n ~(e)s/~e [östrr] ⟨cul⟩ = Rippen–, Rumpfstück

be·irren vt [h] *jdn ~ *to make a p vacillate* od *waver, to disconcert a p* ‖ mst: **sich ~ l** *to be*(*come*) *wavering, to falter in resolution* ‖ sich nicht ~ l *to hold firm to one's views, to stick to one's purpose* (etc); *to be persistent*; er ließ sich nicht ~ *he did not allow himself to be dissuaded* (z tun *from doing*); .. *to be deterred* od *influenced* (durch *by*) ‖ laß dich durch ihn (durch s–e Worte) nicht ~ *don't let him put you off, don't be put off by his words*

beis·ammen adv *together*; dicht ~ *close together*, er hatte nicht 3000 Mann ~ *he had not 3000 men in all* od *3000 men altogether* ‖ s–e Gedanken ~ h *to attend, to be attentive, to be all ears*; s–e G. nicht ~ h *to be absent-minded* ‖ s–e 5 Sinne nicht ~ h *to be out of one's senses, to have a screw loose* ‖ °nicht ganz ~ s *not to feel up to the mark* **~̈sein** n; geselliges, gemütliches, zwangloses ~ *forgathering, social gathering* od *meeting, sociability, sociable* [s]; *get-together* [s] **~wohnen** vi [h] *to cohabit*; **das ~̈** *cohabitation*

B·eisasse m ~n/~n *denizen, person without full citizenship*

B·eisatz m ~es/~̈e *addition* (z *to*) ‖ (Beimischung) *admixture* ‖ entwertender ~ *alloy*, ohne ~ *without alloy* ‖ ⟨gram⟩ *apposition*

b·ei|schießen vt [h] (Summe) *to contribute* (*to*)

B·eischiff n ~(e)s/~e *tender*; → Beiboot

B·eischlaf m ~(e)s/ *coition, coitus* [L], *sexual intercourse* ‖ unterbrochener ~ *withdrawal, coitus interruptus* ‖ den ~ vollziehen bei jdm (= beischlafen) *to go to bed with a p*; *to have sexual intercourse with a p*

b·eischlafen vi [h] jdm ~ ‖ → Beischlaf

B·eischläfer m ~s/~ *one who has sexual intercourse with a woman* ‖ (in gutem Sinne) *bedfellow*, ⟨poet⟩ *bedmate* **B·eischläferin** f *concubine*

B·eischlag m ~s/ **1.** ⟨arch⟩ *raised platform in front of a bilding, flight of steps ascending to the front door, perron* **2.** *counterfeit coin*

b·ei|schließen vt [h] *to enclose*; → beifügen

B·eischluß m –usses/–üsse *enclosure* (*of a letter*) ‖ (beigefügtes) *a letter enclosed*

B·eischlüssel m ~s/~ = Nachschlüssel

†**B·eischmack** m ~(e)s/ = Beigeschmack

B·eisegel n ~s/~ *studding-sail*

B·eisein n ~s/~: im ~ jds *in a p's presence* (od *hearing*), *in* (*the*) *presence of a p*

beis·eite adv *aside, apart*, [mst in Verbindung mit Verben] *aside* ‖ ~ sprechen ⟨theat⟩ *to speak aside* ‖ Scherz ~ *joking apart* ‖ ⟨theat⟩ die ~ gesprochenen Worte *the aside* **~|bringen** vt [h] **1.** (fortschaffen) (etw, jdn) *to take away, to remove*; *to carry* (*a p*) *to safety* **2.** (etw) *to appropriate*; *to abstract, to purloin*, → stehlen **3.** (umbringen) (jdn) *to do away with* (*a p*) **~|gehen** vi [s] *to step aside* **~|lassen** vt [h] ⟨übtr⟩ (etw) *to disregard* (*a th*), *to take no notice of* (*a th*), *not to take into account* ‖ *(jdn) *to pass* (*a p*) *by, to set* (*a p*) *aside* **~|legen** vt [h] (weglegen) *to put aside* (od *away*); *to set aside* ‖ (aufsparen) *to lay aside* (od *by, up*); *to put by*; *to store up*; (etw Geld) ~ ⟨fam⟩ *to salt away ..* **~|nehmen** vt [h] (jdn) *to draw* (*a p*) *aside* **~|schaffen** vt [h] = beiseite bringen **~̈schaffung** f *removal* ‖ *abstraction, stealing* ‖ *killing* (*of a p*) **~|schieben** vt [h] *tu put* od *shunt aside* ‖ (jdn) *to elbow a p out of one's way* ‖ ⟨übtr⟩ (Schwierigkeiten) *to brush aside*; *to override* ‖ (jdn) *to put on the shelf, to shelve*; ⟨Am⟩ *to side-track* **~|setzen** vt [h] (etw) *to set aside, to overrule* ‖ (jdn) *to set aside* **~̈setzung** f *setting aside* **~|stellen** vt [h] *to place* (od *put*) *aside* **~|treten** vi [s] *to stand* od *step aside*; *to stand clear*; *to clear off* | jdn ~ lassen [h] *to send a p aside* **~|tun** vt [h] *to put aside* od *away* ‖ *to put by, to set aside*

b·ei|setzen vt [h] **1.** (jdn) *to entomb*; *to bury*; *to lay* (*a p*) *to rest* **2.** (Segel) *to unfurl*; die Segel ~ ⟨mar⟩ *to make sail*; alle Segel ~ *to crowd sail* **B·eisetzung** f ~/~en *entombment, interment*; *burial*; feierliche ~ (*state*) *funeral*; → Begräbnis **~skommando** n → Begräbnis–

b·ei|sitzen vi [h] e–r Jury, Kommission ~ *to sit on a jury, a committee*; e–m Gericht ~ *to be a member of a court*

B·eisitzer m ~s/~ *associate judge*; *assessor*; *member of a court* ‖ (Geschworener) *juryman, juror* ‖ *alderman*

B·eispiel n ~s/~e **1.** †⟨hist Ger Lit⟩ *fable* **2.** † = Gleichnis ‖ ⟨reth⟩ *paradigm*(*a*) **3.** (Muster, Vorbild) **a.** *example* **b.** Wendungen: ohne ~ *without example, without precedent* od *parallel*; *unprecedented*; *unexampled* ‖ ein gutes, schlechtes ~ f jdn *a good, bad example to a p* ‖ ein warnendes ~ *an example* (für *to*) | jds ~ folgen *to follow a p's example* (od *lead*); *to take a leaf out of a p's book* ‖ (jdm) ein gutes ~ geben *to give* (od *set*) (*a p*) *a good example* ‖ jdn als ~ hinstellen *to hold* (*a p*) *up as an example* (*to a p*) ‖ sich ein ~ nehmen an jdm *to take example by a p* ‖ (jdm) mit gutem ~ vorangehen *to give* (od *set*) (*a p*) *a good example* ‖ ein ~ statuieren an jdm *to make an example of a p* **4.** (Beleg) **a.** *example, instance* (für *of*); abschreckendes ~ *deterrent*; (erläuterndes ~) *illustration*; typisches (*or*- charakteristisches) ~ *case in point*; in ihm h wir ein ~ f diese Leidenschaft *in him we have an example of this passion* || bei allen diesen ~en *in all these examples* **b.** Wendungen: zum ~ (abbr z. B.) *for example, for instance, e. g.* (= *exempli gratia*); *such as* || ich zum ~ *I for one*; ⟨Am⟩ *take me, for example*; wie z. B. Australien *as, say, Australia*; z. B. Mozart, *shall we say M.*, Leute wie z. B. *people such as ..* || zum ~? *such as?* || jdn (etw) als ~ anführen für *to adduce a p as an example of*; *to instance a p, to quote* (*a th*); zum ~ dienen *to serve as an example* || um ein ~ z geben *by way of example* (od *illustration*); um nur ein ~ z nennen *for one example* || ein ~ f e–e Regel geben *to exemplify a rule*; etw durch ~e belegen *to exemplify a th*; böse ~e verderben gute Sitten *bad examples corrupt good manners* ≗**haft** a *exemplary*; *remarkable* (Erfolg) || → exemplarisch

b·eispiellos a *unparalleled, unprecedented, unexampled, matchless, unheard-of*; [pred] *beyond* (od *without*) *example* **B·eispiellosigkeit** f ~ *matchlessness*

b·eispielshalber, b·eispielsweise adv *by way of example* (od *illustration*)

b·ei|springen vi [s] jdm ~ *to hasten to a p's aid, to run to a p's help, to hold out* (od *to lend*) *a helping hand to a p*; *to assist* od *succour a p*

Beiß- ~beere f ⟨bot⟩ *capsicum* **~korb** m *muzzle* **~zahn** m = Schneidezahn **~zange** f *nippers, pincers* [pl], e–e ~ *a pair of nippers* od *pincers*

b·eißen vi/t [biß/gebissen] [h] **I.** vi **1.** **(P)** *to bite* (auf *on*, durch *through*, in *into*) | (kauen) *to chew* (auf *on*), *to gnaw* (an *at*); am Bleistift ~ *to bite one's pencil* | ⟨fig⟩ nichts z (brechen u z) ~ h *to be without a bite and a sup*; *to have neither bite nor sup* || in den sauern Apfel ~ *to swallow a bitter pill* || ins Gras ~ *to bite the dust* (od *ground*); *to lick the dust* **2.** **(T)** beißt der Hund? *does the dog bite?*; ~ nach jdm *to snap at a p* || (of a horse) auf die Stange ~ *to champ the bit* || (of insects) *to bite, sting* **3.** ⟨übtr⟩ (jucken) *to itch* || (of spices) *to bite, sting*; *to cause a smarting pain*; der Pfeffer beißt auf der Zunge *the pepper stings my tongue* || (of the wind) *to nip* **4.** ⟨fig⟩ (of words) *to bite, sting, prick*; ~ an *to gnaw* od *prick at* **II.** vt **A. 1.** (Rinde) *to bite*; ich kann es nicht ~ *I cannot chew it*; klein ~ *to chew thoroughly* || ⟨fig⟩ die Zähne auf e–a (*or* zus–) ~ *to set one's teeth* **2.** **(T)** (jdn) ins Bein ~ *to bite a p's leg, to bite a p in the leg* || (stechen) (jdn) *to bite, sting* || → Hund **3.** ⟨fig⟩ *to prick, sting* **B.** [imps] **es beißt mich** *it itches me, my skin itches*; es beißt mich überall *I itch all over* **C. sich** ~ *to bite one another* || ⟨fig⟩ sich auf die Lippen ~ *to bite one's lip* | ⟨fig⟩ sich ~, sich herum~ *to fight, quarrel, squabble* (mit *with*) || die Farben ~ sich *the colours clash*; *this blue swears at yellow*

b·eißend a *biting, hot, pungent, sharp* (*spice*) || *cutting, nipping* (*wind*) | ⟨fig⟩ *biting* (*irony*), *pungent, trenchant* (*wit*); *mordant, sarcastic*; *cutting* (*remark*) | [adv] *tartly* (sagen)

B·eißer m ~s/~ *biter, dog given to biting* || ⟨hum⟩ (a. ~chen) *tooth*; s–e ~chen [pl] *his peggies* [pl] **b·eißig** a = bissig

B·eistand m ~(e)s/≗e **1.** *aid, assistance, help, support*; ~spakt [m], ~sverpflichtung [f] *pact of mutual assistance* || ⟨med⟩ *attendance* || ohne ~ *unaided* (v, durch *by*) || ~ leisten *to lend* (od *render*) *assistance*; jdm ~ leisten *to give* od *render assistance* (od *support*) *to a p*; *to assist a p*; *to lend a p a helping hand*; ⟨fam⟩ *to give a p a lift* **2.** [konkr] (P) *assistant, supporter* || *best man* (*of a bridegroom*) || ⟨jur⟩ *legal adviser*; *advocate, counsel*

b·ei|stehen vi [h] jdm ~ *to stand by a p, to aid, assist, help, succour, support a p*; *to give assistance* od *support to a p*; jdm tröstend ~ *to comfort a p* || Gott steh(e) mir bei! *God help me!*

B·eistehende [der ~, ein ~r] m ~n/~n *bystander*; *onlooker*

B·eisteher m ~s/~ *assistant, helper*

B·eisteuer f ~/~n *contribution* (z *to*); *pecuniary assistance, subsidy* **b·ei|steuern** vt/i [h] **1.** vt (etw) *to contribute* (z *to*) || ⟨übtr⟩ *to furnish, to supply* **2.** vi *to club together*; *to help* || z etw *to contribute to a th*; *to help to bring a th about*

b·ei|stimmen vi [h] jdm ~ *to agree* od *concur with a p* || e–r S (Ansicht etc) ~ *to accede* (od *agree, assent*) *to a th*; *to fall in with* (*a th*); → zustimmen; beipflichten

B·eistrich m ~s/~e ⟨gram⟩ = Komma

B·eitel m ~s/~ [nd] *chisel*; → Hohl≗, Loch≗

B·eitrag m ~(e)s/≗e **1.** (Geld≗) **a.** *contribution, share of money*; *sum contributed*; e–n ~ entrichten *to pay a contribution*; [abs] ~ erheben *to ask for contributions* **b.** (Mitglieds≗) *subscription* || ⟨bes Am⟩ *dues* pl **c.** ⟨ins⟩ *premium* **2.** *contribution, share* (z *to*); (Pflicht≗) *contingent, force contributed*; (verhältnismäßiger) *quota* (an *of*) || *work* od *service exacted from a p* **3.** *anything given voluntarily*; *contribution* (z e–m Buch *to a book*); *writing*; *article* (z e–r Zeitschrift *to a periodical*, etc.); ≗e f e–e Zeitung liefern *to contribute to a newspaper*

b·ei|tragen vt/i [h] **I.** vt (etw) *to contribute* (z *to*) || ⟨übtr⟩ *to furnish, to supply* **II.** vi ~ z **1.** (P) *to contribute to* (od *towards*); *to be contributor(s) to* od *instrumental in*; dazu ~ z tun *to be instrumental in doing*; viel dazu ~ etw z verbessern *to do much to improve a th* **2.** (S) *to contribute to* (*his presence contributed to my comfort*), *to conduce to, to be conducive to, to go* od *add to, to result in*, ⟨Am⟩ *to make for*; → dienen || das hatte dazu -ge- .. z m *that had some share in making him the morose, hard man he was* || z jds Ehre ~ *to redound to a p's credit* || z der Entwicklung ~ *to promote the development* || die Maßnahmen würden sehr dazu ~, den Ertrag z vermehren *the measures would go a long way to increase* od *towards increasing the output*; .. nur sehr wenig dazu ~ .. *would go only a small way to increase ..* || zur Stärkung des Ruhmes jds ~ *to add to* od *increase a p's reputation*

B·eitrags- ~einzug m (im Betriebe des Arbeitgebers) *deduction* (*from wages*); (Gewerkschaftsbeitrag) *check-off* **~ermäßigung** f ⟨ins⟩ *premium rebate*; *discount* ≗**frei** a *non-contributory* (Organisation) **~leistung** f *contribution*; [koll] ~en [pl] *contribution* **~pflicht** f *liability to contribute* ≗**pflichtig** a *liable to contribution*; *bound to contribute*; *contributory* **~pflichtige** [der ~, ein ~r] m ~n/~n *contributory* **~übertrag** m *unallocated premiums* (*reserve*) **~zahlung** f *contribution*; [koll] ~en [pl] *contribution* (*exempt from c.*)

b·ei|treiben vt [h] (Geld, Steuer etc) *to collect*; *to exact*; (Schulden) ⟨jur⟩ *to enforce the payment of ..*; (Schadenersatz) *to recover* || ⟨mil⟩ (Truppenbedarf etc) *to requisition* **B·eitreibung** f ~/~en *collection* (*of taxes*, etc.); *exaction* (*of fees*); ⟨com⟩ *recovery* || ⟨mil⟩ *requisition* (*of horses*, etc.)

b·ei|treten vi [s] **1.** e–m Antrag ~ *to accede to* (*a motion*); e–r Auffassung ~ *to agree* (od *assent*) *to a view, to concur in a view*; ich trete Ihrer Meinung bei *I concur* **2.** e–r Partei ~ *to accede to a party, to join a party* **3.** (als Partei im Gerichtsverfahren) *to intervene*

B·eitritt m ~(e)s/ *accession* (in e–e Partei *to a party*); sein ~ in den Klub *his joining the club* || ⟨ins⟩ *entry* **~serklärung** f *enrolment* **~sgebühr** f *entry-fee* **~sgesuch** n *application for membership*

B·eitun n ~s/ *support*; *countenance*; *protection*; *participation*; mst: ohne ~ jds *without a p's support* (etc.)

B·eitzger m ⟨ich⟩ = Schlammbeißer

B·eiwache, B·eiwacht f *bivouac*

B·eiwagen m ~s/~ ⟨mot⟩ *side-car* ‖ (Anhänger) *trailer* **~maschine** f *side-car motorcycle, motorcycle combination*

B·eiwerk n ~(e)s/ *the accessories* [pl] ‖ = Staffage → d.

B·eiwert m *coefficient*

b·ei|wohnen vi [h] e–r Feier (etc) ~ *to assist* (od *to be present*) *at a ceremony, to attend a c.* ‖ ⟨sex⟩ *to cohabit* | ≗ n *cohabitation*; → Beischlaf

***B·eiwohnung** f ~/~en *presence, attendance* ‖ ⟨sex⟩ *cohabitation*, → Beischlaf

B·eiwort n ~(e)s/≗er ⟨gram⟩ → Eigenschaftswort *adjective* ‖ ⟨rhet⟩ übertragenes ~ *tansferred epithet* (z. B. *dusty death*); (schmückendes) *epithet, descriptive name* (od *title*) **b·eiwörtlich** a *adjective, adjectival*

Beiz- **~falke** m ⟨hunt⟩ (weibl.) *fame falcon*; †*falcongentle* **~farbstoff** m *mordant dye* **~jagd** f *falconry, hawking* **~jäger** m *falconer* **~kraft** f *corrosive power*; *causticity* **~mittel** n *caustic, mordant*; *corrosive*

***b·eizählen** vt [h] = zurechnen

B·eizäumung f ⟨hors⟩ (of *a* horse) *correct carriage of the head*

B·eize f ~/~n **I.** (Handlung des Beizens) **1.** ⟨hunt⟩ *falconry, hawking*; *fowling* **2.** ⟨tech⟩ *immersion in salt* (od *acid*) ‖ *etching* ‖ *pickling* ‖ *staining* (*of wood*) ‖ ⟨med⟩ *cauterization* **II.** [konkr] **1.** (durch ~ jagbare Vögel) *wild fowl, wild duck, black game*; *herons* [pl] etc **2.** (Mittel zum Beizen) **a.** ⟨hunt⟩ (Vogel) *female falcon* **b.** ⟨tech⟩ *solution of salt, acid solution*; ⟨met⟩ *pickle*; (Salpeter≗) *aqua fortis* ‖ ⟨cul bes österr⟩ *marinade* ‖ (beim Gerben) *bate*; *ooze* ‖ (beim Färben) *mordant*; (Holz≗) *stain*; *stainer* ‖ ⟨med⟩ *caustic* ‖ Tabak≗ *sauce* ‖ ⟨cul⟩ *pickle, marinade, souse*

B·eizeichen n ~s/~ ⟨her⟩ *distinguishing mark, distinctive insignia* [L] [pl]; *mark of cadency*

beiz·eiten adv *in* (*good*) *time, in season, betimes*; *soon*; *early*

b·eizen **I.** vt [h] **1.** ⟨hun⟩ (Reiher etc) mit Falken ~ *to hawk* **2.** ⟨tech⟩ **a.** (Holz) *to stain* **b.** (Metall) *to pickle* (*castings*); *to etch* ‖ (Stoff) *to mordant* (mit Alaun *with alum*); (Häute) *to bate*; *to master*; *to pickle*; (Leder) *to pickle* **c.** ⟨med⟩ (Wunde) *to cauterize* **d.** ⟨cul⟩ *to pickle, marinade, souse* **e.** (Saatgut) *to disinfect* **II.** ≗ n → Beize I.

b·eizend a **1.** *caustic, corrosive*; *mordant* **2.** ⟨übtr⟩ (beißend) *mordant*; *pungent* **B·eizung** f ~/~en = Beizen ‖ ⟨phot⟩ *mordanting*

bej·ahen vt [h] (bestätigen) *to affirm* ‖ *to aver* (daß *that*) ‖ er bejahte die Frage *his answer to the question was in the affirmative*; er bejahte es *his answer was* (od *he answered*) *in the affirmative* ‖ *to assent* (od *accede, consent*) *to* (*a th*) | ⟨fig⟩ *to accept*; *to advocate and appreciate* ‖ das Leben ~ *to say yes to life, to take life cheerfully* **bej·ahend** **1.** a *affirmative* (*sentence*) **2.** adv (*to answer*) *in the affirmative*

bej·ahrt a *aged*; *aging*; *elderly* ‖ [pred] *advanced* od *along in years*; hoch~ *stricken in years*; (ehrwürdig) *venerable, patriarchal*; ⟨poet⟩ *in years* | ≗heit [f] ~/ *advanced age*

Bej·ahung f ~/~en *answer in the affirmative* ‖ *affirmation* ‖ Lebens≗ *acceptance of life*

bej·ammern vt [h] (Verlust, Tod jds, etc) *to bemoan, to bewail, to deplore, to lament* ‖ (jdn) *to pity* **bej·ammernswert, bej·ammernswürdig** a *lamentable*; *deplorable*; *pitiable*

Bej·arie f ⟨bot⟩ = Andenrose

bek·almen vt [h] [engl] ⟨mar⟩ (Schiff) *to becalm* (*a ship*), *to deprive* (*a ship*) *of wind*

bek·ämpfen vt [h] **1.** ⟨eig⟩ (jdn) *to fight* (*a p*); *to combat* od *fight against* (*a p*) ‖ (etw) aufs äußerste, stärkste ~ *to fight a th to the last ditch* **2.** ⟨übtr⟩ (Feuer, Krankheit etc) *to combat, to fight* (*off*); (Schädlinge, Ungeziefer, Epidemie) *to control* ‖ (in Worten ~) *to attack, to assail*; (Meinung) *to oppose*; ⟨Am⟩ *to battle* ‖ (Leidenschaften) *to fight* od *war against*; *to strive*; *to overcome* (od *to subdue*) **3. sich** ~ *to fight against each other*; *to have a fight* | ⟨übtr⟩ *to attack one another* **B.fung** f ~/~en, die ~ e–r S *the fighting* od *struggle against a th* ‖ *control* (*of epidemics*) ‖ *attack of a th*, ⟨Am⟩ *drive against a th* ‖ ~ der gegnerischen Artillerie *counter-battery fire* ‖ zur ~ v See– u Erdzielen *air-to-surface* [attr] ‖ (v Ungeziefer etc) (*pest*) *control*; *destruction* od *extermination* (*of mosquito larvae*)

bek·annt a [pp v bekennen] **I.** [pred] **A. 1.** *known*; *well-known, noted* (als *as*; durch, wegen *for*); z bekannt *too well-known* ‖ ⟨com⟩ Zigarren in ~ vorzüglicher Qualität *cigars of acknowledged excellence* **2.** ~ **mit** *acquainted with* (*a p, a th*); *familiar* (od *conversant with a th*); *versed in* (*a th*) **B.** Wendungen: **1.** etw ~ geben → bekanntgeben **2.** **~geben, ~machen: a.** etw ~ m → bekanntmachen; s–e Ansichten ~ geben *to air one's views* **b.** jdn ~ m *to introduce a p*; ⟨Am⟩ *to get a p acquainted*; jdn ~ m mit *to acquaint a p with* (*a th*), *to make a p acquainted with* (*a th* od *a p*); .. mit jdm *to introduce a p to a p* ‖ sie machte sie ~ *she made them known* ‖ Mitglieder mit einander ~ m ⟨Am⟩ *to acquaint members* **c. sich ~ m** *to make o.s. known* ‖ (sich berühmt m) *to make o.s. a name* od *a name for o.s.* | sich ~ m mit jdm *to make o.s. acquainted with a p, to introduce o.s. to a p* ‖ .. mit etw *to acquaint o.s. with, to make o.s. familiar with a th* **3. ~ sein a. (P)** er ist ~ in Berlin (= man kennt ihn) *he is well-known in B.*; er ist ~ dafür, daß er gründlich arbeitet *he is known* od *noted for being a good workman*; .. daß er geizig ist *he is notorious for his avarice* ‖ ~ s wegen .. *to have a reputation for* .. | er ist ~ in Berlin (= er kennt B.) *he knows B. well*; ich bin selbst nicht ~ hier *I am a stranger here myself* | wir sind ~ (sc mit einander) *we are acquainted* | ~ s mit jdm, etw *to be acquainted with a p, a th* | jdm ~ s: die Leute sind uns nicht ~ *we do not know the people* | ~ s unter dem Namen N. *to go by the name of N.* **b. (P) jdm** ~ s *to know a p* | **(S)** jdm ~ s *to be familiar* od *known to a p*; das ist mir ~ *I know that* ‖ in dem ganzen Ort ~ s (of news) *to be all over the place* | es ist ~, daß .. *it is known that*; es ist weit ~ *it is far from unknown* (daß jd tut *for a p to do*) ‖ es ist allgemein ~ *it is generally known, it is* (*a matter of*) *common* (od *public*) *knowledge* (jdm *to a p*; daß *that*); *it is notorious* (*that*) **4.** als ~ voraussetzen *or* annehmen *to take* (*a th*) *for granted* **5. ~ werden a. (P)** *to become known* od *famous*; sie wurden nicht so ~ wie .. *they did not become so well-known as ..* | ~ w mit jdm *to become* od *get acquainted with a p, to make the acquaintance of a p*; wenn ich nur mit ihm (*or* den Leuten) ~ w könnte *if I could only get a leg in* **b.** (a. ~werden) **(S)** *to get around*; *to take air*; *to leak out*; *to transpire*; ⟨Am⟩ *to develop* ‖ es wurde ~, daß .. *it transpired, it was learnt, it came to notice that* ..; wenn es ~ wird, so .. *if it comes to be known* .. **II.** [attr] **1.** *known*, Shakespeares ~e Werke (die, die wir als solche kennen) *Shakespeare's known works* ‖ ein im ganzen Lande ~er Arzt *a doctor known all over the country*; ein mir ~er Herr *a gentleman known to me* (od *acquainted with me*) **2.** [mst] *well--known*, ein ~er Dichter *a well-known poet*; s–e ~esten Werke *his best-known works* ‖ allg (öffentlich) ~e **S** *matter of public record* **Bek·annte:** [der ~, ein ~r] m ~n/~n *acquaintance; friend*; er ist ein ~r v mir *he is a friend of mine*; wir sind ~ *we are acquainted*; ein alter ~r *a crony* **Bek·anntenkreis** m (circle of) *acquaintances; friends* [pl] **bekannterm·aßen,** adv *as is well-known, as you know* || ⟨dero⟩ *notoriously* **bek·annt|geben** vt [pp –ge–] [h] (etw) *to make known; to notify* (jdm *to a p*) || (öffentlich) *to make public; to announce, proclaim; disclose, divulge; to give out; to state*; s–e Ansichten ~ → bekannt geben; es wird hiermit –ge–, daß *notice is hereby given that* .. **Bek·anntheit** f ~/~ **1.** *knowledge* (mit e–r S *of a th*); *familiarity* (*with a p*) **2.** ⟨dero⟩ (Bekanntsein) *notoriety* (*of a p*) **bek·anntlich** adv = bekanntermaßen **bek·annt|machen** vt [h] [pp bekanntgemacht] [h] (veröffentlichen, eröffnen) (etw) *to make known* od *public; to promulgate, publish* || (durch Plakat) *to bill; to post up* || (in der Zeitung) *to advertise* || etw allg ~ *to give wide publicity to a th* || (jdn) → bekannt I.B.2.b.

Bek·anntmachung f ~/~en **1.** *publication; promulgation; notification*; (feierliche) *proclamation*; (in der Zeitung) *announcement, advertisement* **2.** [konkr] (Anschlag) *public notice* || (Plakat) *placard, poster* || (offizielle) *bulletin*

Bek·anntschaft f **1.** [abstr] ~/ mit jdm *acquaintance with a p* || bei *or* nach näherer ~ *on closer acquaintance*; bei längerer ~ *with longer acquaintance* || e–e ~ anbändeln mit jdm *to scrape acquaintance with a p* || sich jds ~ aufdrängen *to impose o.s. upon a p*; ⟨sl⟩ *to gate-crash a p's acquaintance* || ~ m mit jdm *to form an acquaintance with a p; to make a p's acquaintance* od *acquaintance of a p; to become acquainted with a p* | ~ mit etw *acquaintance, familiarity with a th, knowledge of a th* **2.** [konkr] ~/~en = Bekannte

Bek·anntsein n → Bekanntheit, –schaft

bek·anntwerden 1. vi → bekannt I. 5. b. **2.** ≈ n *leaking-out, transpiration; divulgement, promulgation*

Bekass·ine f ~/~n ⟨orn & cul⟩ *snipe*; Gr ~ *double snipe*; Kl ~ *jack-snipe* || → Bd. I, *snipe*

bek·ehrbar a *convertible* **bek·ehren** vt [h] **1.** (jdn) ⟨ec⟩ *to convert* (z *to*); *to proselytize*, ⟨bes Am⟩ *to proselyte* (z *to*) | ⟨übtr⟩ *to convert* (*to*); *to bring* (*a p*) *round* (*to an opinion*); jdn zu dem Glauben ~, daß *to help a p believe that* .. || bekehrt w ⟨Am⟩ *to see the light* **2. sich** ~ *to become converted*; ⟨Am sl⟩ *to get religion* | ⟨übtr⟩ sich ~ z *to become a convert to* (*an idea*); sich z jds Ansicht ~ *to come round to a p's opinion* || → sich bessern

Bek·ehrer m ~s/~ *converter*; (zudringlicher ~) *proselytizer* **Bek·ehrte:** [der ~, ein ~r] ~n/~n; die ~ f ~n/~n *convert; proselyte* **Bek·ehrung** f ~/~en ⟨a. übtr⟩ *conversion* (z *to*); → Besserung **~seifer** m, **~ssucht** f *proselytism*

bek·ennen vt [h] [→ kennen] **A. 1.** ⟨ec⟩ (Zeugnis ablegen f.) s–n Glauben ~ ⟨bib⟩ *to testify one's faith*; Gott ~ *to declare one's faith in God, to profess God*; → B. 1. **2.** (eingestehen) (Sünde) *to confess*; (Verbrechen) *to confess, to admit, to own*; ~, getan z h *to admit* (od *own*) *doing*; (etw) offen ~ *to avow; to own up to* (*a th*) | ⟨übtr⟩ ich ~, ich war überrascht *I confess* (od *admit, own*) *I was surprised*; ~, daß etw wahr ist *to admit a th to be true* || sie bekannten sich [dat] ihre L. *they confessed their love* **3. a.** ⟨cards⟩ Farbe ~ *to follow suit*; e–e F. nicht ~ *to revoke* || ⟨fig⟩ F. ~ *to show one's colours* **b.** ⟨com⟩ (Empfang e–r S) *to acknowledge* **B. sich ~ 1. a.** ⟨ec⟩ sich z e–r Religion ~ *to profess a religion*; sich zur christlichen R. ~ *to profess Christianity, to profess o.s. a Christian* **b.** sich z e–r guten S ~ *to embrace* (od *espouse*) *a good cause*; sich z jdm ~ *to profess* od *avow o.s. loyal to a p, to declare one's faith in a p* || ich bekenne mich als s–n Freund *I confess myself* (*to be*) *his friend* **2.** ⟨jur⟩ sich schuldig ~ *to plead guilty* (des Diebstahls *to theft*; gestohlen z h *to stealing*) || sich z e–m Fehler ~ *to confess* od *own to a fault*, sich dazu ~ getan z h *to confess* (od *own*) *to doing* || sich z e–r Schuld ~ *to acknowledge a debt*; sich zu e–r Idee ~ *to subscribe to an idea* || sich nicht ~ z etw *to go back on a th* || sich als der Verfasser ~ *to avow o.s. the author*

Bek·enner m ~s/~ ⟨ec⟩ *confessor; professor*

Bek·enntnis n –nisses/–nisse **1.** ⟨ec⟩ *confession, profession*; → Glaubens≈ || ~ auf dem Sterbebett *dying confession* | (Konfession) *denomination; religion* **2.** ⟨übtr⟩ *avowal, confession*; nach d–m eigenen ~ *by* (od *on*) *your own confession* || ein ~ ablegen *to make a confession; to confess* (getan z h *to doing*) **~christ** m *professing Christian* **~freiheit** f *freedom of faith* **~kirche** f ⟨Ger⟩ *Confessional Church; professing church* **~schrift** f *formal creed* od *confession, confession of faith; symbolic book* **~schule** f *denominational* (⟨Am⟩ *parochial*) *school* **~treuer** m *confessionist*

bekl·agen vt [h] **1.** (etw) *to lament, deplore; bemoan, bewail* || den Tag ~ *to rue the day* || Menschenleben sind nicht z ~ *there are no casualties* | (jdn) *to pity* **2. sich** ~ *to complain*; sich ~ über *to complain of* od *about* (bei jdm *to a p*); *to make complaints about*; sich heftig ~ über ⟨sl⟩ *to make heavy weather about*

bekl·agenswert a *deplorable; lamentable; pitiable; sad, woeful* (*results*) || es ist ~ it is sad (*that*); es ist sehr ~ *it is a great pity*

Bekl·agte: [der ~, ein ~r] m ~n/~n; **die** ~ ~n/~n ⟨jur⟩ *defendant*; → Angeklagte || (im Berufungsverfahren, Ehescheidungsprozeß) *respondent*

bekl·atschen vt [h] **1.** (applaudieren) (jdn, etw) *to clap; to applaud* **2.** (jdn) *to slander*

bekl·eben vt [h] (Wand etc) *to paste* (mit *with*); *to paste* (*a th*) *over* (*with*); mit Papier ~ *to line with paper*; Koffer mit e–m Zettel ~ *to label a trunk*

°**bekl·eckern** vt [h] (Tischtuch) *to dirty, soil; blotch, daub, smudge, stain*; mit Tinte ~ *to ink, blot* || **sich** ~ *to daub o.s.* (*with*); ⟨iron⟩ er hat sich nicht gerade mit Ruhm bekleckert *he has come off badly enough* || °bekleckert a *perplexed*

bekl·ecksen vt [h] *to blot, ink; daub, stain* || **sich** ~ *to daub o.s.* (mit Tinte *with ink*)

†**bekl·eiben** vi = haften

bekl·eiden vt [h] **1.** (jdn) **a.** *to clothe, dress* **1.** (jdn) **a.** nicht einmal mit e–m Hemd bekleidet *without even a shirt on*; → kleiden **b.** ⟨übtr⟩ jdn mit den Insignien, e–r Würde, Ländern etc ~ *to invest a p with the insignia, a dignity, lands*, etc. **c. sich** ~ *to clothe o.s., to dress* **2.** ⟨übtr⟩ etw ~ **a.** (behängen) *malerisch*) *to drape; cover; deck* (*with*) **b.** (Oberfläche) *to coat*; (Gebäude) *to face* (*with cement*); → verkleiden (Fußboden) mit Planken ~ *to plank* || (Metall) *to plate* (*with gold*) || (Schiffsboden) *to sheathe* (*with copper*) || (Räder) *to shoe* (*with cross-bars*) || ⟨mar⟩ (Tau) *to serve* (*with*); (Anker) *to shoe* || innen ~ *to line* (*with*); mit Futterholz ~ *to fur* **3.** ⟨übtr⟩ (→ 1.b.) (Amt, Stelle) *to hold, fill; occupy*

Bekl·eidung f ~/~en **1. a.** *clothing, dressing; clothes* [pl] **b.** ⟨übtr⟩ *investiture* (*with the insignia, a dignity*, etc.) **2.** *coating, covering* (*with*); *facing* (*of a building with cement*); Wand≈ *hangings* [pl]; Planken≈ *planking; furring* (*of a ship*); Panzer≈ *plating*; → Verkleidung || (innere ~) *lining* **3.** *tenure* (*of an office*), *holding* **~sgewerbe** n *clothing industry* **~s– u Ausrüstungsnachweis** m ⟨mil⟩ *individual clothing and equipment* **~svorschrift** f ⟨mil⟩ *dress regulations* pl

bekl·emmen vt [h] jdn ~ *to press* (od *weigh*) *upon a p*; (Gemüt) *to oppress, depress*; (Herz) *to wring* || es beklemmt mir den Atem *it takes my breath away* || beklemmt s durch *to be suffocated with* **bekl·emmend** a *anxious* (*experience*); *agonizing* (*wait*) || *oppressive* (*weather*), *sultry* (*heat*) **Bekl·emmung** f ~/~en (*sense of*) *constriction*; *sense of weight* (*on the chest*) || *apprehension*; *anguish, anxiety*; *agony*; *nightmare* || ~szustand [m] *nightmare*

bekl·ommen a *anxious, uneasy* (*feeling*) || *depressed, heavy* (*heart*), *oppressed*; [pred] *sick at heart* | **≗heit** f *anxiety, uneasiness*; *heaviness* (*of heart*); *oppression*; Gefühl der ~ *sinking at the* (od *one's*) *heart*

bekl·opfen vt [h] (etw) *to tap* (mit *with*); *to beat* (*a th*) *repeatedly* || ⟨med⟩ *to percuss*

Bekl·opfung f → Perkussion

bekn·abbern vt [h] (etw) *to nibble* (*at*) (*a th*)

°**bekn·eipen** vrefl sich ~ *to get tipsy* °**bekn·eipt** a *tipsy*, → beschwipst

°**bekn·iffen** a *out of humour* od *tune* || *self--conscious*

bek·ohlen vt [h] (Schiff) *to coal* || (Ofen) *to charge*; *to feed* || ⟨min⟩ (Grube) = belegen | ⟨fam⟩ = anschwindeln **Bek·ohlung** f *coaling* || ~sanlage [f] *coaling plant*

bek·ommen vi/t [→ k] **I.** vi [s] jdm ~ (of food, etc.) *to agree with a p, to suit a p*; nicht (*or* schlecht) ~ *to disagree* (od *not to agree*) *with a p*; die Nahrung ist ihm nicht ~ *the food has upset him* | (jdm gut ~) *to do a p good*; ist der Spaziergang Ihnen gut ~? *has the walk done you good*?; ich hoffe, die Reise ist dir gut ~ *I trust you are none the worse for your journey*; die R. ist mir sehr gut ~ *I feel all the better for the journey* || wohl bekomm's! *may it do you good*! (nach dem Niesen) *God bless you*! || jdm schlecht ~ *to go hard with a p*; es wird ihm schlecht ~ *it will go ill with him, he will fare badly with it, he will be none the better for it* **II.** vt [h] **1. etw** ~ ⟨mst⟩ *to get a th* **a.** (Brief, Nachricht, Schlag etc) *to get, to receive* (v *from*); ⟨fam⟩ *to have*, kann ich ein Zimmer ~? *can I have a room*?; → Platz || *to come by* (*a th*); (Gehalt, Lohn) *to get*; (Belohnung, Preis) *to obtain*; (Kritik) *to come in for* || *to be awarded* (*the Legion of Merit*) || ⟨wir⟩ (Ort) *to get* || ⟨fig⟩ e–n Korb ~ *to get the mitten* || s–n Willen ~ *to have one's own way* | wieviel ~ Sie? *how much is owing to you*?, *what do I owe you*? || ⟨com⟩ ~ Sie schon? *are you attended to*? || ⟨exch⟩ f 1 Mark –t man 2 Schilling *a mark exchanges for 2 sh* || Bedeutung ~ *to assume importance* **b.** Strafe ~ *to get* od *receive punishment*; *to be punished* (→ erhalten); Prügel ~ *to get a thrashing*, du wirst tüchtig P. ~ *you'll get it* (*hot*), *you'll have it* || ein Jahr (Gefängnis) ~ *to get 12 months* **c.** (Krankheit) *to get*; die Masern ~ *to get* (od *to come out with*) *measles*, ⟨fam⟩ *to measle*; e–e Erkältung, den Schnupfen ~ *to catch* (*a*) *cold* **d.** Zähne ~ *to cut one's teeth* || e–n Bauch ~ *to develop a paunch* || Blasen ~ *to blister* || wieder Farbe ~ *to regain colour* || nasse Füße ~ *to get one's feet wet* || ein Geweih ~ (of stags) *to grow antlers* | Blätter ~ (of trees) *to come into leaf*; *to leaf* || Löcher ~ (of cloth) *to go into holes* || e–e Rinde ~ (of bread) *to crust* **e.** wir w Regen, besseres Wetter ~ *we'll have rain, better weather*; .. anderes Wetter ~ *there'll be a change in the w.* || ⟨fig⟩ Wind ~ v *to get wind of* .. **f.** ein Kind ~ *to have a baby* || Junge ~ *to be with young*; *to have young ones* **g.** Hunger, Durst ~ *to get hungry, thirsty* || Furcht ~ *to get into a panic* → Angst || Mut ~ *to take courage* || e–n Schreck ~ *to get a fright* || Lust ~ *to feel inclined* (z *to*), *to be in the mood* (*to do*) **2.** [mit prädik. Adj., pp u adv] *to get* || etw etw **fertig** ~ *to bring a th about, to manage a th*; er hat es f. ~ abzureisen *he has ventured to leave* || jdn v e–r Strafe frei ~ *to beg a p off* || etw **satt** ~ *to get tired of, to tire of a th* | die Uhr habe ich **geliehen** ~ *the watch was lent to me, I got the w. on loan*; .. **geschenkt** ~ *I got the w. as a present* | etw **fest** in die Gewalt (*or* Hände) ~ *to get a firm hold of a th* || z Gesicht ~ *to get a sight of* **3.** [mit inf] *to get*; **zu essen, hören** ~ *to get to eat, to hear*; z fassen ~ *to get hold of*, → fassen; z sehen ~ *to catch sight of, to get a sight of* (*a th*) **4. sich** ~: sie h sich endlich ~ *they have got married at last* **5.** (**P**) jdn **zu** etw ~ *to get a p to do a th*

bek·ömmlich a *digestible, digestive*; *consistent* (*food*); *suitable* || *salubrious* (*climate*); *healthy, wholesome*; *beneficial* (jdm *to a p*) | **≗keit** f *digestibility, digestiveness* || *salubrity*

bek·östigen vt [h] (jdn) *to furnish* (*a p*) *with food, to find* (*a p*) *in food*; *to board*; *to feed* || **sich** selbst ~ *to find o.s.*

Bek·östigung f ~/~en *board, boarding, food*; *keep, maintenance*; Art der ~ *diet* || volle ~ *all found*; Wohnung u ~ *board and lodging*

bekr·äftigen vt [h] (etw) *to confirm, corroborate, endorse*; *aver*; *to sanction, to give sanction to* (*a th*) || (Aussagen) *to substantiate*; mit s–m Eide ~ *to confirm upon* (*one's oath*); *to depose* (*that*) || → bestärken **bekr·äftigend** a *corroborative, corroboratory* **Bekr·äftigung** f ~/~en *confirmation, corroboration, endorsement*; *averment*; *substantiation* || *sanction*

bekr·änzen vt [h] (jdn, jds Haupt) *to adorn* (*a p*) *with a wreath, to wreathe*; ⟨poet⟩ *to deck with flowers* || (Häuser) *to deck out*; mit Girlanden ~ *to crown with garlands, to festoon, to garland* **Bekr·änzung** f *decking-out, festooning*

bekr·euz(ig)en vt [h] jdn ~ *to make the sign of the cross on* od *over a p* || **sich** ~ *to make the sign of the cross, to cross o.s., to ex one's chest* (*he ex-ed* ..)

bekr·iegen vt [h] (jdn) *to make* od *wage war on* od *against* (*a p*) || *to fight* (*a p*); *combat* od *fight against* (*a p*) | **sich** ~ *to be at war with one another*; *to go to war* || → bekämpfen

bekr·itteln 1. vt [h] (etw, jdn) *to crab, criticize*; *to carp at, to find fault with* (*a p, a th*) **2.** ≗ n *criticizing* (*of a th*); *fault-finding* (e–r S *with a th*)

bekr·itzeln vt [h] (Papier) *to scrawl* od *scribble on* (*paper*)

†**bekr·önen** vt [h] *to crown* || → bekränzen

bekr·usten [h] *to crust* || **sich** ~ *to crust, to become crusty* **Bekr·ustung** f *incrustation*

bek·ümmern vt [h] **1.** (jdn) *to afflict, distress, grieve* || *alarm, trouble* || es bekümmert mich *it grieves me* (*to see*) || bekümmert s *to be distressed*; .. über *to be afflicted, alarmed* (od *anxious, troubled*) *about, concerned at* (od *about*; *for*); *to care about*; *to grieve at* (od *over*) **2.** (verblaßt) (→ kümmern) das bekümmert uns wenig *we don't care*; *that's all the same to us* **3.** sich ~ um = sich kümmern um **Bek·ümmernis** f ~/–nisse *affliction, grief, pain*; *trouble* || z m–r gr ~ *to my great grief*

bek·ümmert a *afflicted*; *depressed* || → bekümmern

bek·unden vt [h] **1.** ⟨jur⟩ (etw) eidlich ~ *to declare upon oath, to depose* **2.** (kundtun) *to demonstrate, manifest, reveal, show*; (s–e Unwissenheit) *to betray*; (Gefühl, Freude etc) *to evince, to be evincive of*; (s–e Entrüstung) öffentlich ~ *to record, register* **Bek·undung** f ~/~en (eidliche) *deposition* || *manifestation*

Bel n ~s/~ ⟨el⟩ (= 10 Dezi≗) *bel*

bel·ächeln vt [h] etw ~ *to smile at a th*; verächtlich ~ *to poohpooh a th* **bel·achen** vt [h] etw ~ *to laugh at* od *over a th* || (spottend) *to deride a th, to laugh a th to scorn*

Bel·ade- ~grenze f *cargo capacity; tonnage* **~plan** m *loading* od *storage chart*

bel·aden vt [h] [→laden] (Schiff) *to load (up)* (mit *with*); *to lade, to freight* || (Magen) *to load* || (jdn) *to burden (with a parcel)* | ⟨übtr⟩ (jdn) *to burden (with taxes,* etc); *to load (with reproaches)* || (Geist, Gedächtnis) *to charge (with)*

bel·aden a [pp v ~] [pred] *laden (with)*; z sehr ~ *overweighted (with)*; *supercharged* | [attr] *loaded (stomach)*; reich ~ *laden (tables)*; voll ~ *groaning (tray)* **Bel·adung** f ~/~en *loading; lading;* → Belastung

Bel·ag m ~s/∸e **1.** ⟨cul⟩ *slices* [pl] *of meat; breadspread* **2. a.** (auf Metall) *tarnish;* → Beschlag || mit e–m ~ überziehen *to tarnish* || Kesselstein∸ *furring* **b.** ⟨tech⟩ *(thin) coat(ing); film; facing* (⟨mot⟩ *clutch f.*); *lining* || (Straßendecke) *carpet;* (Spiegel∸) *foil* **c.** (Bretter∸) *covering, flooring;* (Raum) mit Bretter∸ versehen *to floor;* mit Platten∸ versehen *to slab* || ⟨arch⟩ *incrustation* **3.** ⟨med⟩ ~ auf der Zunge *fur* || (Zunge) mit ~ überziehen *to fur* (a. sich .. ~)

Bel·agerer m ~s/~ *besieger* **bel·agern** vt [h] ⟨mil⟩ (Stadt) *to besiege, to beleaguer, to invest; to lay siege to (a town)*; belagert w *to undergo a siege* || ⟨übtr⟩ (ein Haus, Zimmer; jdn) *to throng;* ⟨Am⟩ *to crowd* **Bel·agerung** f ~/~en *siege;* die ~ aufheben *to raise the s.*

Bel·agerungs- [in comp] mst *siege* **~arbeiten** f [pl] *siege-operations* [pl] **~armee** f *besieging army* **~artillerie** f *siege-artillery* **~geschütz** n *siege-gun* **~kunst** f *siege-craft* **~münze** f *siege-piece* **~park** m *siege-train, battering-train* **~werke** n [pl] *siege-works* [pl] **~zustand** m *state of siege;* im ~ *in a state of s.* || (⟨Ger⟩ = Ausnahmezustand) *martial law;* (Ort) in ~ versetzen *to place (a town) under martial law;* den ~ verhängen *to declare the state of siege;* .. über e-n Ort *to proclaim a place;* die Stadt befindet sich im ~ *the town is proclaimed;* im ~ befindlich *proclaimed (place)*

°**bel·ämmert** a = belemmert, kläglich, dürftig

Bel·ang m ~(e)s/~e **1.** *importance, consequence, moment, relevance* (f. *to*); *case* || v ~ *of importance, important* (f *to*); v ~ s (P & S) *to count;* v gr ~ *of great moment; very important* (f. *to*) || nicht v ~, v k-m ~ *of no account* (od *importance,* etc.); nichts v ~ *nothing important;* ⟨fam⟩ *nothing to write home about;* ohne ~ *without importance; irrelevant;* das ist ohne ~ *that does not count;* gänzlich ohne ~ s *to be quite a detail;* (P) ⟨sl⟩ *to cut no ice;* die Örtlichkeit ist hier ohne ~ *locality does not matter here;* es ist ohne ~ z h *there is no case for having* **2.** die ~e [pl] *the concerns, activities, interests* [pl]; die höchsten ~e *the supreme concerns;* kulturelle ~e *cultural concerns* ∸**bar** a ⟨jur⟩ *actionable*

bel·angen vt [h] **1.** anbelangen **2.** ⟨jur⟩ jdn vor Gericht *or* gerichtlich ~ *to sue a p in the courts, to go to law with a p, to have* od *take the law of a p, to have a p up; to process, to prosecute a p*

bel·anglos a *inconsiderable, irrelevant, insignificant* (f. *to*); *petty (circumstance)*; ⟨jur⟩ *impertinent* || [pred] *of no account* (od *importance, consequence, moment*); ~ s *not to amount to much;* gänzlich ~ s *to be quite a detail* ∸**igkeit** f ~/~en *impertinence, insignificance, -cy, irrelevance* (f. *to*)

bel·angreich a *considerable, important, momentous, relevant* (f. *to*); *weighty* (matter)

Bel·angung f ~/~en ⟨jur⟩ *prosecution; action, suit* **bel·angvoll** a *important;* → wichtig

bel·assen vt [h] [→ lassen] (etw) *to leave; to maintain (in a state)* || es dabei ~ *to leave it at that;* alles beim alten ~ *to leave things as they are* || jdn in s-r Stellung ~ *to maintain, retain a p*

Bel·assung f ~/~en (im Amt) *retention,* → Beibehaltung

bel·asten vt [h] **1.** (Wagen, Schiff) *to load* (mit *with*); *to lade; to freight* || (Wagen) *to load* || (durch Gewicht, Blei ~) *to load; to weight* || ungleichmäßig ~ *to lump-load* → überladen **2.** jdn ~ **a.** *to burden; to encumber; to weight a p (with a heavy trunk)*; belastet s mit *to be clogged with;* sich ~ mit *to cumber o.s. with (baggage)* | ⟨übtr⟩ *to burden a p (with taxes); to put a burden* od *strain (up)on a p;* [oft pass] mit der Verantwortung ~ *to saddle a p with the responsibility* (f. *for*); schwer ~tet *heavily burdened (with)*; schwer ~tet s mit etwas *to carry a heavy load* od *burden of a th* || **sich** mit Schulden ~ *to incur debts;* mit Schulden belastet *saddled with debts;* mit Sünde belastet *weighted with sin* | (sein Gewissen) *to load* || (Geist, Gedächtnis) *to charge (with)*; **sich** ~ mit *to charge one's mind* (od *memory) with* || sein Hirn ist mit wertlosen Dingen belastet *his brain is clogged with useless facts* || nicht belastet s mit *to have no concerns with* **b.** (bedrücken) *to press* (od *weigh*) *(up)on a p, to oppress a p* **c.** (beschuldigen) *to incriminate, discriminate; accuse a p (of); to make a charge against a p; to charge a p (with)* | ⟨pol⟩ irgendwie belastet s *to be suspect;* minder ~tet *less incriminated* **d.** (moralisch) belastet s *to be tainted (with)*; ⟨med⟩ geistig ~ s *to be mentally affected;* erblich belastet s *to be affected with a hereditary taint, to be hereditarily afflicted; to be tainted with a hereditary disease* (od *tendency*) || (Beziehungen etc) *to impair, harm, damage, worsen, impede* **3.** ⟨com⟩ jdn *or* jds Konto ~ mit e–r Summe *to place a sum to a p's account, to debit a p* (od *a p's account*) *with a sum; to place a sum to a p's debit; to charge an acc. with;* jds Konto mit Waren ~ *to charge goods to a p's account;* belastet s *to stand debited* || (Haus) *to encumber (with debts); to charge (with)*; ein Haus mit e-r Hypothek ~ *to encumber a house with a mortgage, to mortgage a house;* belastet *mortgaged (house)* || (Etat) *to overtax, overstretch, (over)burden, strain* **4.** ⟨psych⟩ *to depress* **bel·astend** a *discriminating, incriminatory (statement)*

Bel·astete m [der ~, ein ~r] *politically incriminated (p)*

bel·ästigen vt [h] (jdn) *to annoy, bother, inconvenience, molest; trouble* (: *I am sorry to trouble you*) || *to trouble a p* (mit *on a matter*) || (quälen) *to badger, pester, trouble, worry* (mit *with*); das —gt mich *that plagues me;* dauernd ~ *to harass, harry; importune;* (of creditors) *to dun (a p)* || (Herren) (of women) *to solicit; accost* **Bel·ästigung** f ~/~en *annoyance, bother, molestation; trouble* (f. *to a p*) || (dauernde) *importunity*

Bel·astung f ~/~en **1.** *loading, lading (with)* || (Last) *burden, charge* (e-r S *on a th*); *load* || ⟨tech⟩ *load, stress* ⟨a. el⟩; angepaßte *matched,* dauernde *continnous, permanent,* gleichmäßige *uniform,* maximale *maximum,* mittlere *mean,* ruhende *dead, steady,* zulässige *safe load* || (Kessel ∸) *evaporation;* (Hochofen ∸) *consumption;* Steuer∸ *incidence of taxation* || ⟨el⟩ *demand* **2.** (Behinderung) *encumbrance* (: *without e.*); *adverse impact; burden; handicap; stress* (im täglichen Leben *of daily life*); → Anspannung schwere ~ [+ gen] *heavy burdens on the troops* **3.** ⟨jur⟩ *incrimination (of a p)* | (moralische ~) *taint* || erbliche ~ *hereditary taint* **4.** ⟨com⟩ (Konto∸) *debit, d. entry;* ~ e-s Besitztums *encumbrance* (od *burden*) *on a property* **~sanzeige** f ⟨com⟩ *debit advice* **~sart** f ⟨tech⟩ *nature of load* **~sausgleich** m *load balance* od *compensation* **~sdauer** f *load duration* **~sermächtigung** f *debit authorization* **~sfähigkeit** f *load capacity* || *yield-capacity* || *carrying capacity* (e–r Brücke etc) **~sfaktor** m *load-factor;* ⟨fig⟩ *element of encumbrance* **~sgebirge** n ⟨el⟩ *load curves* pl **~sgrenze** f *load(ing) limit;* ⟨tech⟩ *load capacity; maximum load* **~sprobe** f *load-test* || ⟨übtr⟩ *test*

⟨tech⟩ *breaking load test* **~sspitze** f *load peak* **~sspule** f ⟨el⟩ *loading* od *Pupin coil* **~stal** n *off--peak* **~szeuge** m ⟨jur⟩ *witness for the crown* od *prosecution* **~szustand** m ⟨tech⟩ *loading condition*

bel·auben vt [h] *to cover with leaves* ‖ **sich** ~ *to come* od *burst into leaf*; *to put forth leaves*; *to frondesce*; sich ~d *frondescent* **bel·aubt** a *leafy*; ⟨for⟩ *foliaged*, → benadelt; dicht ~ *frondose* ‖ (*tree*) *clad with leaves*, [pred] *in leaf*

Bel·aubung f ~/ *leafiness* ‖ (Laub) *foliage*, *leafage*

bel·auern vt [h] jdn ~ *to lie in wait for a p*; *to watch for a p*

Bel·auf m ~s/ **1.** (Betrag) *amount*; bis zum ~ v *to the amount of* **2.** *district*, *sphere of inspection* (*of a forester*)

bel·aufen vrefl [h] [→ laufen] sich ~ auf *to amount to*; *to come* od *run to*; es beläuft sich auf 3 Schilling das Stück *it works out at 3/ each* ‖ die Mannschaft belief sich auf 25 Mitglieder *the crew numbered 25*; sich im ganzen ~ auf *to total* (*up*) *to*; *to aggregate*, *to total*, sie beliefen sich im ganzen auf 25 *they totalled* (od *aggregated*) *25* ‖ sich ~ auf mehr als *to exceed*

bel·auschen vt [h] (jdn) *to overhear*; *to listen to* (*a p*) *deliberately*; jdn heimlich ~ *to spy* (*up*)*on a p* ‖ ⟨telph⟩ (Gespräche) *to milk*, *tap*

B·elche f ~/~n ⟨orn⟩ = Bleßhuhn

Belchen m ~s/~ (Berg) *ballon* Fr, *balloon* ‖ Elsässer ~ *B. d'Alsace*

bel·eben vt [h] **A.** (jdn) **1.** ⟨eig⟩ wieder ~ *to resuscitate*, *to revivify* (*a p*); *to restore* (*a p*) *to life* **2.** ⟨übtr⟩ (anfeuern) *to animate*, *encourage*, *galvanize*, *invigorate*, *vitalize*; *rouse*, *stimulate* (: *it roused his dormant energies*) ‖ *cheer* (*up*); *elevate* ‖ *to inform* (mit *with*) ‖ neu ~ *to revive*; *to galvanize into new life* **B.** (etw) **1.** (Handel, Unterhaltung) *to enliven*, *animate*; *liven* (*up*) ‖ (Gefühl) *to rouse*; *stimulate* ‖ (Brauch) wieder ~ *to revive*; *resuscitate* **2.** (lebensvoll m) *to vivify*; (e-n Charakter) *to give life to*, *to put life into* (*a th*) ‖ (durch Abwechslung ~) (Schauplatz) *to diversify*, *variegate* (*a th*), *to lend life to* (*a scene*); durch Abwechslung belebt s v *or* durch *to be variegated with* | die Parks sind sehr belebt *the parks are in full swing*; *the parks are gay* (v *with*) **bel·ebend** a *animating*, *enlivening*, *brisk* (*atmosphere*), *stimulating* (*climate*); ~er Trunk ⟨sl⟩ *reviver* ‖ *informing* (*spirit*); ~e Kraft, ~es Element *sting* **Bel·eber** m ~s/~ *stimulator*; *reviver* **bel·ebt** a *animated*; *vivacious*, *sprightly* ‖ *lively* (*woods*); *busy*, *crowded* (*streets*); ~ v *gay* (od *lively*) *with* **Bel·ebtheit** f ~/ *animation*; *liveliness* ‖ *bustle*; *busyness*; *gay appearance*

Bel·ebung f ~/~en **1.** ⟨eig⟩ Wieder≈ *resuscitation*, *revivification* (*of a drowned p*) **2.** *animation*; *invigoration*, *stimulation* (*of trade*) ‖ Neu≈ *revival* (*of shipping*, *of the drama*); *rebirth*; *resuscitation* (*of a custom*) | *vivification* ‖ *diversification*, *variegation* (*of scenery*) **~smittel** n *restorative* **~sversuch** m *attempt at resuscitation*

bel·ecken vt [h] (jds Hand etc) (of dogs) *to lick* (*a p's hand*) ‖ ⟨übtr⟩ v der Kultur beleckt *refined*, *cultivated*; wenig v der K. b. s *to have only a smattering* od *sprinkling of culture*

bel·edern vt [h] (etw) *to leather*

Bel·eg m ~s/~e **1.** *evidence*, *proof* (f. *of*, *for*); ~e [pl] *supporting documents*; ein ~ *a piece of evidence* ‖ (Quelle) (of books) *authority* (f. *for*) | (~schein) *voucher*; *receipt* | ⟨print⟩ *voucher copy* **2.** (Beispiel) *example*, *instance* (f. *of*); *illustration*; *reference*; → Beispiel 4. ‖ →Belag **bel·egbar** a *capable of being proved by an example*; *verifiable* **Beleg- ~dauer** f (e-s Zimmers) ⟨hot⟩ *occupancy* **~exemplar** n *voucher* od *author's copy* **~normen** f pl ⟨mil⟩ *billeting standards* **~nummer** f ⟨comp, etc⟩ *reference number* **~photographie** f *record photography* **~schein** m *voucher*, *receipt* **~stärke** f ⟨mil⟩ *quartering strength* **~stelle** f *reference*; *quotation* ‖ *authority*, *source* **~stück** n = –exemplar ‖ *tear sheet*, ⟨Am⟩ *ticket* ‖ *record*; *copy*; *voucher*

bel·egen vt [h] **A. 1.** (bedecken) (Boden etc) *to cover*, *to overlay* (*with*); ⟨tech⟩ *to cover* (*with liners*) ‖ etw ~ mit etw *to spread a th over a th* ‖ (etw) mit Brettern ~ *to board*; mit Dielen ~ *to board*; *to floor*; (Glas) mit Folie ~ *to silver*; mit Matten ~ *to mat*; mit Planken ~ *to plank*; mit Platten ~ *to slab*; (Straße) mit Pflaster ~ *to pave*; (Faß) mit Reifen ~ *to hoop*; (Zimmer) mit Teppichen ~ *to carpet* ‖ die Hufe ~ *to shoe a horse*; (Räder) *to shoe* ‖ (Bremse) *to* (*re-*)*line* | (Brot) *to cover with a slice of meat*, *cheese*, etc. ‖ (Zunge) [mst pass] *to fur*; die Zunge ist belegt *the tongue is furred*; **sich** ~ *to become furred* od *coated* ‖ → belegt | e-e Stadt mit Bomben ~ *to bomb a town* **2.** (Stute etc) *to cover*, *to serve* **3. a.** (e-n Platz) *to book* (: *book me 2 seats*), *to reserve*, *secure* ‖ ⟨univ⟩ Vorlesungen ~ *to enter one's name* (od *to sign up*) *for a course of lectures* | (Zimmer) *to bespeak*, *engage*; *occupy* ‖ ⟨telph⟩ e-e Leitung ~ *to seize a line* **b.** e-e Stadt mit Garnison ~ *to garrison a town*; ..mit Soldaten ~ *to quarter soldiers* (*up*)*on a town* ‖ ⟨min⟩ (Grube) *to work* **c.** etw mit Beschlag ~ *to lay an embargo on a th*, *to embargo a th*; *to arrest*, *to seize a th* ‖ ⟨übtr⟩ jdn mit Beschlag ~ *to engage a p* (*for*); (Kräfte) *to tax* **d.** ⟨mar⟩ ein Boot ~ *to belay*; *to hitch a rope round the belaying-pin* **4.** ein Land mit e-r Steuer ~ *to impose* (od *lay*) *a tax on a country*; Waren mit e-r St. ~ *to tax goods* ‖ jdn mit e-r Geldstrafe ~ *to fine a p*, (: *he was fined £ 2*), *to lay a fine on a p*; → verhängen ‖ jdn mit e-m Fluch ~ *to lay a curse on a p*, *to curse a p*; (Buch) mit dem Bann ~ *to ban*; → Bann **B.** (beweisen) (Tatsachen) durch Zeugnisse ~ *to prove*, *verify*; *authenticate*; *to demonstrate* od *support by documentary evidence*; → belegt ‖ (Behauptung) durch Quellenangabe ~ *to give one's authority* od *source for a statement* ‖ (etw) durch Beispiele ~ *to illustrate by quotations* ‖ → zitieren

Bel·egen n **1.** *covering*, *overlaying* (*with*) ‖ ~ mit Bomben *bombing* (*of a town*) **2.** *booking*, ⟨Am⟩ *reservation* (*of seats*) ‖ ⟨univ⟩ ~ v Vorlesungen *signing up for a course of lectures*; → Beschlagnahme ‖ → Belegung **†bel·egen** a *situated*

Bel·egschaft f ~/~en *shift* (*of workmen*); ⟨bes Am⟩ *crew* ‖ *employees* [pl]; *personnel*, *staff*; *worker staff*; *all hands*; *members of a firm* ‖ ⟨mar⟩ *crew* ‖ ⟨mil⟩ *hands*, → Mannschaft

bel·egt a **1.** *furred* (*tongue*); *husky*, *thick* (*voice*) ‖ ~es Brot *sandwich* **2.** *booked*, *reserved*, *occupied* (*seat*) ‖ *engaged* (*room*) **3.** urkundlich ~ *documented* **≈sein** n ~s/ *occupancy*

Bel·egung f **1.** ~ mit Steuern *imposition of taxes* ‖ (Abgabe) *imposition* ‖ (Platz≈) *booking*, *reservation* | ~ mit e-r Geldstrafe *the fining* (*of a p*) ‖ ~ mit e-m Bann *the banning* (*of a book*) **2.** *verification* (*of facts*, etc.) ‖ ~ durch Beispiele *illustration by examples* **3.** ⟨mil⟩ *quartering*, *billeting*; *occupancy* **4.** (Spiegel≈) *tin-plate*; *covering* **5.** (mit Strafe) *infliction* **6.** ⟨telph⟩ *engagement*, *holding* ⟨a. telv⟩ **~sdauer** f *holding time*

bel·ehnen vt [h] **1.** (jdn) *to enfeoff*; *to invest* (*a p*) *with a fief* **2.** Wertpapiere ~ *to raise money on securities* **Bel·ehnte** :[der ~, ein ~r] ~n/~n *feoffee* **Bel·ehnung** f ~/~en (*en*)*feoffment*; *investiture* (*with*)

bel·ehren vt [h] **1.** *(unterweisen) (jdn) *to instruct* (*in*) **2.** [mst übtr] (jdn) *to inform*, *advise* (über *about*, *on*); *to warn* (*of*) ‖ ⟨jur & aero⟩ *to brief* ‖ jdn eines Besseren ~ *to teach a p better*, *to set a p right*, *to disabuse* (od *undeceive*) *a p* | **sich** ~ l *to listen to reason*, *to take advice*, *to be* *open to conviction*; laß dich ~ *be advised* **bel·ehrend** a *instructive* (*lecture*) **Bel·ehrung** f ~/~en *instruction* (in *in*); *teaching* ‖ *information*: e-e Fundgrube der ~ *a mine of i.*; ~en [pl] *advice, instructions* (über *on*) ‖ ⟨jur & aero⟩ *briefing* ‖ ~ schöpfen aus *to glean information from* ‖ ⟨bes pol⟩ *indoctrination* ‖ **~smittel** n *tool of learning* **~sschießen** n ⟨mil⟩ *instruction firing*

bel·eibt a *burly, corpulent, obese, plump, pursy*; *fat, stout* | **≚heit** f ~/ *corpulence, embonpoint* [Fr], *obesity, plumpness*

bel·eidigen vt [h] **1.** (jdn) *to give offence to* (*a p*), *to displease* (*a p*); *to injure, wrong* (*a p*); *to rub* (*a p*) *the wrong way* ‖ (gröblich ~) *to insult, affront*; *dishonour, defame*; jdn öffentlich ~ *to put an affront upon a p* ‖ (tätlich ~) *to assault* | beleidigt aussehen *to look displeased* (über *at*) ‖ beleidigt s *to be offended, to take offence*; *to bridle* (über *at*); er ist leicht beleidigt *he is rather touchy* od *testy, he is apt to take offence* ‖ sich beleidigt fühlen *to be offended, to feel hurt, to take offence* (über *at*) **2.** (Auge, Ohr, Geschmack, Gefühl) *to offend, hurt, displease*; (jds Ohr, Nerven) *to grate* od *jar* (*up*)*on* (*a p's ear, nerves*); das Rechtsgefühl (etc) ~ *to offend against the sense of justice*; (gröblich ~) *to outrage*; jds Zartgefühl ~, aufs höchste ~ *to shock a p's feelings* **bel·eidigend** a *abusive* (*language*); *offensive* (*remarks*); *insulting* ‖ (of noise) *grating, jarring* (f. *to a p*) | (abstoßend) *disgusting* (*sight*); *repellent* **B.ger** m *offender*; *insulter* **bel·eidigt** a *offended*, etc (*p*) ‖ den ≚ spielen *to sulk* **Bel·eidigung** f ~/~en **1.** *abuse*, ~en [pl] *abuse, insulting language* ‖ ~ jds *offence to a p*; (grobe) *affront, insult to a p*; e-e ~ einstecken *to swallow an affront* ‖ e–e ~ jds (*or* f. jdn) s (of portraits) *to be a libel on a p* ‖ schwere tätliche ~ *assault and battery* ‖ → überschütten **2.** ~ e-s Gefühles (etc) *offence against a feeling* **Bel·eidigtsein** n *displeasure, resentment* (über *at*)

bel·eihen vt [h] [→ leihen] **1.** = belehnen **2.** (Papiere, Gut) *to raise money on* (*securities, an estate*) ‖ (of lender) *to lend money on* **Bel·eihung** f ~/~en *the raising of money against security* ‖ *the lending of money against s.*

bel·emmern vt [h] **1.** (Schiff) *to encumber* **2.**° (jdn) *to cheat* °**bel·emmert** [pp] a *abominable*; *miserable, poor, wretched* (*existence*); das ist ja ~ *that's very bad* ‖ *hopeless* ‖ er ist immer der ≚e *he is always the loser*

Belemn·it m ~en/~en *belemnite*

bel·esen a **1.** [pred] ~ s in *to be read in*; er war nicht sehr ~ *he was not well-read* **2.** [attr] *well--read* (*man*); der ~ste Gelehrte *the best-read scholar* **Bel·esenheit** f ~/ *reading*; ein Mann v gr ~ *a man of vast* (od *wide*) *reading* ‖ *erudition*

B·elespr·it m ~s/~s (Schöngeist) *bel esprit*

B·eletage f = Belletage

bel·euchten vt [h] **1.** (Raum) *to light* (*up*); festlich ~ *to illumin*(*at*)*e*; ⟨theat, film⟩ *to pick up* **2.** ⟨fig⟩ (Zus-hänge) *to throw* od *shed light upon* (*a th*); *to elucidate, illustrate* (*a th*), *to be illustrative of* (*a th*) **Bel·euchter** m ~s/~ ⟨theat⟩ *lighter, electrician* | ~verband m ⟨aero⟩ *marker force* **Bel·euchtung** f ~/~en **1.** *lighting* (*of a room*); elektrische ~ *electric l.*; indirekte ~ *conceiled l.*; ⟨theat⟩ (*the*) *lights*; festliche ~ *illumination*; ~ v verschied. Seiten *cross-light* **2.** ⟨paint⟩ *distribution of light and shade* **3.** ⟨phot⟩ *lighting*; ~ im Gegenlicht *l. from behind*; v unten *l. from below*; *horror*; reflexlose *antiflare l.*; seitliche *half-back* od *side l.*; halbzerstreuende *semidiffuse l.*; ~ des Aufnahmegegenstandes *subject l.* ⟨fig⟩ (Erklärung) *elucidation, illustration* **~sanlage** f *fittings* [pl] **~anordnung** f ⟨phot⟩ *lighting set-up* od *–arrangement* **~apparat** m ⟨phot⟩ *lighting unit*; *illuminator* **~seffekt** m *illuminating effect* **~sinspektor** m ⟨theat⟩ *chief electrician* **~skörper** m *lighting fixture*; *lamp*; pl *fittings* **~slinse** f *condensing lens* **~smittel** n *illuminant*; *means of illumination* **~splan** m ⟨theat⟩ *lighting* (⟨Am⟩ *light*) *plot* **~sschalter** *lighting switch* **~sschirm** m *reflector* **~sstärke** f *illumination intensity*; *lighting force* **~swirkung** f = –effekt **~szug** m ⟨theat⟩ *sky batten*

bel·eum(un)det a *pleasant-spoken* (*people*); gut (schlecht) ~ s *to be well* (*ill*) *reputed, to be in good* (*bad*) *repute*; schlecht ~ s *to be under a cloud*

°**b·elfern** vt [h] (P) *to brawl, quarrel, squabble*; *scold*; *swear*

Belfort n [Fr] (Festung an der Burgund. Pforte)

B·elfried m ~s/~e *belfry*

B·elga m ~s/~s (seit 1926) *Belgian monetary unit* (5 Fr = 500 Centimes) **B·elgien** n *Belgium* **B·elgier** m ~s/~s; **~in** f ~/~nen *Belgian* **b·elgisch** a *Belgian*

B·elgrad n (Hptst. von Jugoslawien) *Belgrade*

B·elial m ~s/ (Teufel) *Belial*

bel·ichten vt [h] ⟨phot⟩ (Platte etc) *to expose*; gut belichtet *dense* ‖ ⟨übtr⟩ (Raum) *to admit light into* **Bel·ichter** m ⟨phot⟩ *automatic exposing apparatus* **B.tung** f ~/~en ⟨phot⟩ *exposure* **~sberechner** m ⟨phot⟩ *exposure calculator* od *computer* **~sdauer** f *exposure* **~smesser** m *photometer*, (*visual*) *exposure meter* **~smessung** f *measurement of exposure time* **~srolle** f (Tonfilm) *sound-recording drum* **~sspielraum** m *exposure latitude, latitude of* od *in exposure* **~sstärke** f *strength of lighting* **~sstufe** f *stage of exposure* **~stabelle** f *exposure table, exposing chart* **~szeit** f *exposure* (*time*); die ~ bestimmen *or* vermitteln *to establish the exposure time* ‖ ⟨phot mst⟩ *shutter speed*

bel·ieben vt/i [h] **1.** vt **a.** (etw) *to like*; *to want, to wish, to wish for* ‖ was ~ Sie? *what is your pleasure*? ⟨com⟩ *what is it you want*? *what can I do for you*? ‖ ⟨com⟩ ~ Sie noch etwas? (*is there*) *anything more* od *else you want* (od *we can show you*)? ‖ ganz wie Sie ~ *just as you like* od *please, please yourself* **b.** [vor inf] *to choose, please*; Sie ~ z erwähnen *you choose* od *please to mention* (*that..*) ‖ ~ Sie einzutreten *please, walk in, will you kindly walk in* ‖ ⟨iron⟩ Sie ~ z scherzen *you are joking, Sir*; *are you in earnest, Sir*? ‖ → geruhen **2.** vi **jdm** ~ *to please a p*; *to be convenient to a p* ‖ tu, was dir beliebt *please* od *suit yourself, do as you like* (od *choose, please*); ganz wie es Ihnen beliebt *just as you like* od *please*; wenn es dir beliebt *if you please, if it is convenient to you*; *if you will be kind enough*; *if you think proper*; solange es uns beliebt *during our pleasure* ‖ [ell] wie beliebt? *Sir*? *Madam*? *I beg your pardon, madam* (etc)? **Bel·ieben** n ~s/ *convenience*; *choice, pleasure, will*; nur in folg. Wendungen: **nach** ~ *at choice* (od *discretion, will*), *at one's convenience* (od *discretion, pleasure*); ganz nach ~ *just as you like* od *please*; ganz nach (d-m) ~ *please* od *suit yourself*; je nach jds ~ *according to a p's preference*; ganz nach ~ tun können *to be welcome to do*; nach ~ imstande s etwas z tun *to be free to do a th*; tu das ganz nach d–m ~ *suit your own convenience*; nach ~ wählen *to take one's choice* ‖ es steht ganz in Ihrem ~ *it is within your discretion* (*to do*) ‖ etw in jds ~ stellen *to leave a th to a p's discretion*; ich stelle es in Ihr ~ *I leave it to you* (*to do*)

bel·iebig **1.** [a] e-e ~e Anzahl *any sum you please*; ~e Zahl *random number*; Nägel (in *or* v) ~er Größe *nails of any size desired, of any size you choose* od *like* ‖ irgendein ~er *any* (*policeman*) ‖ jede ~e P *any p whatever*; z jeder ~en Zeit *at any time that suits your convenience* | jeder ~ *anyone, anybody*; jedes ~e *anything*; e–e ~e Zahl *any* (*small*) *number you like* **2.** [adv]

(nach Belieben) *at choice* od *will* || ganze Seiten ~ auslassen *to omit whole pages at choice* || ~ viele *as many as one chooses* || ~ viele Seiten *as many pages as you like* || ~ lange *as long as you like* od *please* || ⟨comp⟩ *random* [attr]

bel·iebt a **1.** [attr] **a.** e-e sehr ~e P *a much liked p*; ein ~er Dichter *a popular poet*; der ~este Musiker in Deutschland *the most popular* (od *liked*) *musician in Germany* **b.** ein ~es Lied *a popular song*; das am wenigsten ~e s-r Werke *the least liked of his works* || ein ~er Fehler *a common* (od *much recurring*) *error* **2.** [pred] **a.** (P) (sehr) ~ s *to be* (*very*) *popular* (: *the poet is very popular*); *to be a favourite* (bei *with*) || bei jdm sehr ~ s *to be high in a p's favour, to be the favourite of a p*; sie war bei jedermann im Dorfe ~ *she was the favourite of the village* || plötzlich ~ w *to leap into popularity* || sich ~ m *to make o.s. popular*; sich bei jdm ~ m *to ingratiate o.s. with a p, to curry favour with a p*; **b.** (S) es ist sehr ~ *it is very popular*; Mathematik u Naturwissenschaften sind am ~esten *mathematics and.. are the favourites* || (of fashion) sehr ~ s *to be in full vogue*; *to be the craze*; → begehrt; ~ w *to come into vogue* **ᵡheit** f ~/ *popularity* (unter, bei *among*); *vogue*; die ~ Shakespeares *Shakespeare's popularity, the vogue for Shakespeare*; sich gr ~ erfreuen *to enjoy great popularity*; (of songs, etc.) *to be in full vogue*

bel·iefern vt [h] (jdn) *to furnish, to provide, to supply* (mit *with*) || die Armee ~ *to purvey for the army*; die Soldaten wurden mit Schuhen beliefert *the soldiers were issued with shoes*

Bel·ieferung f ~/~en *supply* (*with*)

Bellad·onna f ~/–nnen ⟨bot⟩ *belladonna* **~lilie** f ⟨bot⟩ *amaryllis*

Belle-Alli·ance [belal'jɑ̃s] n: die Schlacht bei ~ *the battle of Waterloo*

b·ellen vi [h] *to bark, to give tongue* || kz u laut ~ *to yap*; dumpf ~ *to bay*; *to wuff* | ⟨übtr⟩ (stark husten) *to bark*

Bellet·age [bele'tɑ:ʒə] f (Fr) *first floor*

Belletr·ist m ~en/~en *belletrist, man of letters*; *literary man* **Belletr·istik** f ~/~en *belles-lettres* (Fr) [pl]; *fiction*; *purely literary writings* [pl] **belletr·istisch** a *belletristic*; *literary* (*magazine*)

bel·ob(ig)en vt [h] (jdn) *to praise, to commend*

Bel·ob(ig)ung f ~/~en *praise, commendation*; namentliche ~ ⟨mil⟩ *citation* || ~sschreiben [n] *commendatory* od *laudatory letter, letter of praise*

bel·ohnbar a *rewardable*

bel·ohnen vt [h] (jdn) *to reward, recompense* (f. *for*; durch, mit *by, with*); *to pay, remunerate* (*for*); er wurde mit e-r Medaille belohnt *he was awarded a medal* || (entschädigen) *to recompense* || (nützen) *to pay* | (Dienst) *to reward* (*with*)

Bel·ohnung f ~/~en *reward* (f. etw *for a th*), *recompense*; zur ~ f. *as a r. for* || *payment, remuneration* (*for*) || Geldsumme als ~ *reward* (f. jdn *to a p*); *premium, prize* || → Lohn

Belon·it m ⟨minr⟩ [mst pl] ~e *belonites* [pl]

Belt m ~s/~e *belt*; ⟨geog⟩ der Große, Kleine ~ *the Great, Little Belt* | †*Baltic* (*Sea*)

bel·udern vrefl [h] ⟨hunt⟩ sich ~ (of game) *to stuff o.s.*

bel·üften vt [h] *to aerate, vent*; *to admit air to ..* **B.tung** f ~/~en *aeration, airing, venting*; ⟨bes tech⟩ *air inlet, air admission*; *ventilation, cooling* | ~sanlage [f] *air conditioner*; ~sart [f] *ventil.* od *cooling method*; ~sleitung [f] *vent-line*

Bel·uga ⟨ich⟩ **1.** m *beluga* **2.** f = Hausen

bel·ügen vt [h] [→ lügen] jdn ~ *to lie to a p*; *to deceive a p by lies*

†B·elur- (*or* Bolor-, richtiger Belut-) **Dagh** m (früherer Name verschiedener Gebirgszüge in Mittelasien) *Beloor-* (od *Belor-*)*Tagh*

bel·ustigen vt [h] *to amuse, divert*; *to delight* || –gt s *to be amused* od ⟨fam⟩ *tickled* || (unterhalten) *to recreate*; ⟨oft iron⟩ *to entertain* | **sich ~** *to make merry*; *to disport, to disport o.s., to enjoy o.s., to entertain o.s.* || sich ~ an *to be amused with* (*a th*); sich ~ über *to make fun of* (*a p*); *to make merry over* (*a th*) **bel·ustigend** a *amusing*; *entertaining*; *funny*

Bel·ustigung f ~/~en *amusement, diversion*; *gay entertainment*; *fun*; *merry-making*

Bel·utsche m (Eingeborener v Belutschistan) *Baluch, Baluchi*; die ~n [pl] *the Baluchis* [pl]

Belved·ere n ~s/~s *belvedere*

b·elzen vt [h] ⟨hort⟩ (pfropfen) *to graft* (auf *on*, in *in*)

B·ema n ~s/ ⟨ec arch⟩ (in orient. Kirchen) *sanctuary, chancel*

bem·ächtigen vrefl [h] **1. sich e-r S** ~ *to take possession of, to possess o.s. of a th, to seize a th*; *to seize* (*up*)*on a th*; *to get control of a th*; (widerrechtlich) *to usurp a th* (: *the throne*) **2. sich jds** ~ *to take hold of a p, to seize* (*up*)*on a p* || (of a demon, feelings, etc) *to possess a p*; *to come to a p*; *to get hold of a p*; *to grip a p*; *to steal over* od *upon a p*; Erbitterung ~gte sich s-r *exasperation got the better of him*

bem·äkeln vt [h] = bemängeln **bemakelt** a *tainted*

bem·alen vt [h] (Bild) *to colo*(*u*)*r*; *to illuminate* || (Glas) *to paint* || *to decorate* (*with*) || °**sich ~** = sich schminken

bem·ängeln vt [h] etw ~ *to find fault with*; *to carp* od *cavil at a th*; *to quarrel with a th, to pick holes in a th*; *to blame, censure, criticize*; *disapprove a th* || etw ~ an (*or* bei) jdm *to find fault with a p*; *to blame a p for a th*

Bem·ängelung f *faultfinding* (e-r S *with a th*); *criticism* (e–r S *of a th*), *complaint* (e–r S *at a th*)

bem·annen vt [h] ⟨mar⟩ (Schiff etc) *to man*; *to personnel*; *to supply with men* || –nnt [pp] *manned*, ⟨tech⟩ *attended* | °**sich ~** (of women) *to marry* **B.nnung** f ~/~en ⟨mar⟩ *crew*; *ship's company*

bem·änteln vt [h] **1.** (verbergen) (Gefühle) *to disguise*; (Unwissenheit) *to cloak* (unter *beneath, under*) **2.** (beschönigen) *to palliate, extenuate*; *minimize* **bem·äntelnd** a *palliative*

Bem·äntelung f ~/~en **1.** (Deckmantel) *cloak* (e-r S *for a th*) **2.** *palliation, extenuation* (*of a th*)

Bem·aßung f ~/~en *dimensioning*

bem·asten vt [h] (Schiff) *to mast*

°**bem·ausen** vt [h] jdn ~ *to pilfer* (⟨sl⟩ *to bone*) *a th from a p*; *to rob a p*

bem·eiern vt [h] **1.** (Farm) *to lease* **2.** ˣ ~ jdn *to take* (*a p*) *in*; *to cheat* (*a p*)

bem·eistern vt [h] (Leidenschaft) *to conquer, govern, master, subdue* | **sich ~** *to contain* (od *restrain*) *o.s.* || sich e-r S ~ *to seize* (*a th*), *to get* (*a th*) *into one's power*; → bemächtigen

†**bem·eldet** a *said, aforesaid*

bem·engen [h] sich ~ mit *to meddle with*

bem·erkbar a *observable, perceptible*; *sensible* || sich ~ m (P) *to make* od *render o.s. conspicuous*, ⟨fam⟩ *to show the flag*

bem·erken vt [h] **1.** (wahrnehmen) *to perceive* (*a th, a p*); *to notice, note, observe*; *to remark* (*a th*; *that*); ~ daß jd tut *to perceive* (od *notice, see*) *a p do* (od *doing*); etw (nicht) ~ *to be* (*un*)-*aware of a th* || er wollte uns nicht ~ *he didn't deign to notice us, he ignored* od *cut us* || nicht bemerkt w *to elude observation* | (einsehen) *to see* (: *he saw his mistake*); *to remark* (*a th*; *that*) **2.** (**äußern**) *to observe, to remark* (: '*A nice day*' *he remarked*); ~ daß *to observe, to remark that*; zu jdm ~ *to remark to a p* (: *he remarked to his wife* "*Nice lot!*") || es ist z ~ *it is noteworthy* (*that*) || bes ~ *to note*; wie oben bes bemerkt *as noted above* || er bemerkte es übel, daß wir ablehnten *he resented our refusal*; *he was displeased* od *offended at our r.* **bem·erkenswert** a *notable, remarkable*; [pred] *worth noting, noteworthy, worthy of note* od *emphasis*; *deserving of notice, conspicuous* (*men of noted intellect*) || nichts ≈es *nothing to write home about* | ~erweise [adv] *notably*; *remarkably* **bem·erklich** a = bemerkbar || *considerable* (*differences*), *remarkable* || jdm etw ~ m *to call a p's attention to a th* || sich ~ m *to make o.s. conspicuous*; *to attract attention*

Bem·erkung f ~/~en **1.** (Wahrnehmung) *observation, remark* **2.** (Äußerung) *remark, observation* (über *on*; v jdm *by a p*); einige ~en *to make some remarks* (z jdm *or* jdm gegenüber *to a p*; über *or* z etw *on a th*); ~en m über *to remark, to observe on* (*the weather*) | erklärende *or* kritische ~ *comment* (über *on*); ..~en m *to comment* (über *on*) || tadelnde ~ *stricture* (über *on*) || einige interessante ~en *some interesting points* **3.** schriftl. ~ *note, memorandum* (L); [mst pl] ~en *notes, memoranda*

bem·essen vt [h] [→ messen] (Strafe) *to proportion* (nach dem Vergehen *to the offence*) || (Eigenschaft) *to measure* (nach *by*) || so ~, daß *to rate so as to* **Bem·essung** f ~/~en *proportionment* (nach *to*), *size*; ⟨tech⟩ *rating, proportioning, dimensioning*

bem·itleiden vt [h] (jdn) *to pity, commiserate, compassionate* (*a p*); *to feel pity for* (*a p*); er ist z ~ *he is deserving of pity, he is to be pitied* **bem·itleidenswert** a *pitiable*; *worthy of compassion*; *deplorable*

bem·ittelt a *well off, well-to-do* (*classes*); ein ~er Mann *a man of* (*independent*) *means* || [pred] *in easy circumstances*, ⟨Am⟩ *on easy street*; er ist nicht ~ *he has got no means* (*of his own*), *he is not a man of means*

×**B·emme** f ~/~n [ost- md] *slice of bread*; Butter≈ *slice of bread and butter*

°**bem·ogeln** vt [h] (jdn) *to cheat, trick* (*a p*); *to take* (*a p*) *in*; *to palter with* (*a p*) | –lt w ⟨fam a⟩ *to be sold*

bem·oost a *moss-grown, mossy* || ⟨bes univ⟩ ~es Haupt n *old student, old fellow* od *stager*

bem·ühen vt [h] **1.** jdn ~ *to trouble a p* (mit *with*; um, wegen *for*; z tun *to do*); darf ich Sie ~? *may I trouble you?* || *to give a p trouble, to put a p to trouble*; es tut mir leid, Sie z ~ *I'm sorry to trouble you* || (**bitten**) jdn ~ *to apply to a p* (um *for*; z tun *to do*) **2. sich ~** *to take pains*; *to endeavour, try* (*hard*) **a.** bitte, ~ Sie sich nicht *pray, don't trouble* od *bother* || sich vergeblich ~ *to lose one's labour* || sich nicht sonderlich ~ *not to take great trouble* || ~ Sie sich bitte herauf, herein *will you please come up, step in* **b.** sich ~ z tun, bemüht s z tun *to be at pains of doing* (od *to do*); *to endeavour* (od *labour, strive, study, try*) *to do*; *to lay o.s. out* (od *make efforts*) *to do*; sich sehr ~ *to be at* (od *to go to*) *great pains*; sich aufs äußerste ~ *to strive* od *try one's hardest* (*to do*) || eifrigst bemüht s *to do one's best endeavours* (*to do*); bemüht bleiben *to keep on striving* (*to do*) **c.** sich sehr ~ **für** *or* um jdn *to exert o.s.* (od *to intervene*) *on a p's behalf*; *to be busy helping a p* **d.** sich ~ **um** (etw) *to strive* od *apply for* (*a th*); *to labour for* (*peace*) || sich eifrig, intensiv ~ um *to make a strong bid for* || er bemüht sich um.. *he attemps to find* (*an explanation*) || sich um jds Gunst ~ *to seek* od *court a p's favour* || sich um e-e Stellung ~ *to try* od *apply for a place* | sich ~ um jdn → 2. d. = sich um jds Gunst ~ **e.** sich **wegen** jds ~ *to try to help a p* **Bem·ühen** n ~s/ = Bemühung || ein vergebliches ~ *a wild-goose chase*

Bemühung f ~/~en *effort* (um *for, toward*; um e-e Lösung *for a solution*); *move* (*for*); *exertion*; eifrige ~ *endeavour* (z tun *to do, at doing*) || gehörige ~(en) *due diligence* || ~en [pl] *trouble*; *pains* [pl]; → Mühe; *services* (*rendered*); Ihre freundlichen ~en *your kind offices* [pl]; → ärztlich

bem·üßigen vt [h] [nur in:] sich bemüßigt fühlen, finden, sehen z tun *to find o.s. induced, driven, prevailed upon, compelled, obliged to do*

bemustern vt [h] ⟨com⟩ *to sample* || bitte ~ Sie uns für.. *Kindly send us samples of* (*the line* od *article*); *please sample us the article* **Be·m·usterung** f ~/~en *sampling*

bem·uttern vt [h] (jdn) *to take care of, to mother, to dry-nurse* (*a p*) || (eine junge Dame) *to chaperon, to matronize* **Bem·utterung** f *mothering*; *motherly care* || *chaperonage*

ben·achbart a *neighbouring* (*village*); *contiguous*; (*the room*, etc) *next door*; → angrenzend, anliegend

ben·achrichtigen vt [h] jdn ~ *to inform* od *notify a p* (v *of*; daß *that*); *to apprise a p* (*of*); *to acquaint a p* (v etw *with a th*); (frühzeitig) *to warn* (*of*; *that*); ⟨com⟩ *to advise a p* (*of*) || *to give a p notice, to let a p know, to send a p word* (daß *that*) || jdn sehr spät ~ *to give a p short notice* (betreffs *about*); jdn längere Zeit vorher ~ *to give a p longer notice* || benachrichtigt w *to receive notice* **Ben·achrichtiger** m ~s/~ *informant*; → Angeber

Ben·achrichtigung f ~/~en *information*; *notification*; *notice*; *warning*; ⟨com⟩ *advice* || bei kurz vorher erfolgter ~ *at short notice* || → Nachricht **~sschreiben** n ⟨com⟩ *letter of advice*

ben·achteiligen vt [h] (jdn) *to put* (*a p*) *at a disadvantage, to handicap* (*a p*); *discriminate against* (*a p*); *to injure, to wrong* (*a p*); benachteiligt s *to be handicapped*; der Benachteiligte *the loser, the victim*; körperlich B. *physically handicapped* → beeinträchtigen **Ben·achteiligung** f ~/~en: die ~ jds (e-r S) *the handicap to a p*; *the discrimination against a th* || *injury*; *prejudice* (der Rechte jds *to a p's rights*)

ben·adelt a ⟨for⟩ *foliaged*; → belaubt

ben·ageln vt [h] (Schuhe) *to nail*; die Schuhe ~ l *to have one's boots nailed*

ben·agen vt [h] (etw) *to gnaw* (*at*) (*a th*)

ben·amsen vt [h] [du benams(es)t] (jdn) *to name*; *surname, nickname, dub* (*a p*), → beilegen

ben·annt a → benennen

ben·arbt a *scarred*

Ben·ares n (Heilige Stadt in Vorderindien)

×**ben·aut** a verlegen, beklommen, schüchtern

B·endel n &m ~s/~ Sw = Bändel

B·endsel, B·ändsel [pl] ⟨mar⟩ (Reff≈) *reef-points* [pl]

ben·ebeln vt [h] ⟨fig⟩ (den Geist) *to fog, cloud*; *bemuse*; (berauschen) *to fuddle, intoxicate* || **sich ~** *to fuddle o.s.* **benebelt** a (berauscht) ⟨fam⟩ *fogged, bemused, fuddled* (v *with*); *intoxicated, tipsy*; ⟨sl⟩ *dopy, squiffy*

†**bened·eien** vt [h] (jdn) *to bless* †**Bened·eiung** f ~/~en *benediction*

Benediktion·ale n ⟨R. C.⟩ *benedictional* **Bened·ictus** [L] ⟨bib & ec⟩ *Benedictus* **Bened·iktenkraut** n ⟨bot⟩ *holy thistle*

Bened·ikt·iner m ~s/~ **1.** ⟨ec⟩ *Benedictine*; die ~ [pl] *the Benedictines* [pl] **2.** (Likör) *Benedictine* **~mönch** m *Benedictine* (*monk*) **~orden** m *Benedictine Order*

Benedikt·ion f ~/~en ⟨ec⟩ *benediction*

Benef·iz n ~es/~e **1.** ⟨theat⟩ *benefit*; ~vorstellung f *benefit-night, benefit-performance* **2.** ⟨ec⟩ = Pfründe **Benefizi·ar** m ~s/~e, **Benefizi·at** m ~en/~en ⟨ec⟩ *beneficiary* **Benef·izium** n ~s/-zien *benefice*; ⟨ec⟩ *living*

ben·ehmen vt [h] [→ nehmen] **1.** etw ~ *to take a th away*; die Schmerzen ~ (of a remedy) *to take away* (od *remove, soothe*) *the pains* || (Aussicht) *to obstruct* | jdm den Atem, die Luft ~ *to take a p's breath away*, ..den Appetit ~

to take away a p's appetite || jdm die Aussicht ~ *to intercept a p's view*; es benahm mich *I was stunned*; der Schrecken benahm ihm die Sprache *the terror tied his tongue*; ..ihm die Besinnung *the t. made his head swim* || jdm den Irrtum ~ *to undeceive a p*; jdm den Mut ~ *to discourage a p*; jdm die Lust ~ *to spoil a p's pleasure* (an *in*) || → benommen **2. sich ~** *to behave* (gegen *to*) || *to act..* || *to conduct* od *demean o.s.* || sich anständig ~ *to behave o.s.*; (z e-m Kind) benimm dich! *behave yourself!* || sich aufs beste ~ *to be on one's best behavio(u)r*; sich leichtfertig *or* unverantwortlich ~ ⟨sl⟩ *to play the giddy goat*; sich schlecht, rebellisch, ungewöhnlich ~ ⟨fam⟩ *to act up*, sich auffällig (ausgelassen, närrisch) ~ ⟨fam⟩ *to carry on*; sich (sau)-schlecht ~ ⟨sl⟩ *to behave like a ham* || benimm dich! *behave yourself!*, *play the game!* **Ben·ehmen** n ~s/ **1.** *behaviour* (gegen *to*); *conduct, demeanour* || *way(s)* || feines ~ *gentlemanlike, ladylike conduct*; *good manners* [pl], *respectability*; Regeln f feines ~ *etiquette* || sehr auf sein ~ achten *to be on one's best behavio(u)r* **2. sich ins ~ setzen** mit jdm *to take counsel with, to get into touch* od *contact with*; *to communicate* (od *consult, confer*) *with a p* (über *about*) || **im ~ mit** *on consultation with*

ben·eiden vt [h] (jdn) *to envy* || jdn um etw ~ *to envy* od *grudge a p a th* (: *she had not grudged her her beauty*); *to be envious of a p because of a th* **ben·eidenswert** a *enviable*; nicht ~ *unenviable*

B·enelux n ~/ Abk f Belgien, Niederlande (Netherlands), Luxemburg

ben·ennen vt [h] [→ nennen] (jdn) *to name, call* (nach *after*; ⟨Am⟩ *for*); *to denominate* || (etw) *to name, call* (nach *after*); *to designate*; *term*; benannte Zahl *concrete number* **ben·ennend** *denominative*

Ben·ennung f ~/~en *naming*; *appellation*; *denomination* | [konkr] (Name) *name* || ⟨arith⟩ *denomination*; (Quantitäten) unter e-e ~ bringen *to reduce to the same denomination*

ben·etzen vt [h] (→ naß) (etw) *to moisten, sprinkle* (*with*), *to wet*; (mit Tau) *to bedew* || (of liquids) *to suffuse* || ⟨tech⟩ (Faserbündel) *to batch* **Ben·etzung** f ~/~en *wetting* | ~swärme [f] *heat of wetting*

Beng·ale m ~n/~n *Bengali, Bengalese*; die ~n [pl] *the Bengalese* **Beng·alhanf** m *sunn*

Beng·ali n (bengalische Sprache): das ~ *Bengali* **beng·alisch** a *Bengali, Bengalese, Bengal* || ~es Feuer n *Bengal light* || ~er Meerbusen *Bay of Bengal* || ~e Sprache f = Bengali

Bengal·ist m → Prachtfink

B·engel m ~s/~ **1.** *rude* (od *rough, clumsy*) *fellow*; *boor, booby, clown*; *churl* || gr ~ → Schlaks; kl ~ *urchin*; ⟨hum⟩ *rascal, scamp*; → Bürschchen || dummer ~ *silly fool*; *oaf* **2.** ⟨typ⟩ *bar*; **~scheide** f *bar-handle* **Bengel·ei** f *boorishness* **b·engelhaft** a *boorish, clownish*

ben·iesen vt [h] (etw) ~ *to confirm* (*a fact*) *by sneezing*

°**Ben-imm** m ~s/ er hat k–n ~ *he has no manners*; → Benehmen

B·enne f ~/~n Sw *wheelbarrow* → Schieb-, Schubkarren

B·ennuß f ~/-nüsse *ben-nut* **~baum** m ⟨bot⟩ *ben-nut tree*

ben·ommen a [pp v benehmen] *dazed*; *dizzy, giddy* (v *with*), *vertiginous*; ~ s v *to be suffocated with* || ⟨sl⟩ *dopey* || ⁓**heit** f ~/ *dizziness, giddiness*

ben·ötigen vt [h] (etw) *to be in want of, to be* (od *stand*) *in need of* (*a th*); *to want, need* (*a th*) || nicht ~ *to be in no need of*; sehr (*or* dringend) ~ *to want* (*a th*) *badly, to be in great want of* (*a th*)

B·enthos n ~/ (Lebewesen am Meeresgrund) *benthos* [Gr]

ben·ummern vt [h] (Plätze) *to number*

ben·utzbar a *available, useful* | ⁓**keit** ~/ *usefulness*

ben·utzen, benützen vt [h] **1.** (verwenden) (etw, jdn) *to use, to make use of* (z *for*); fleißig ~ *to make good use of* (*a th*) || Sublimat wird f manche S benutzt *sublimate has many uses* || e-e Bibliothek (etc) ~ dürfen *to have the run of* (od *to have access to*) *a library* s-e Glieder ~ können *to have the use of one's limbs* **2.** (sich z Nutze m, verwerten) (etw) *to profit by*; *to utilize*; *to turn* (*a th*) *to account* || *to lay* (*a book*) *under contribution*; *to draw* (*up*)*on* (*a source*) || *to avail o.s. of* (od *to embrace, improve, seize, take*) (*the opportunity to do*) || → ausnutzen

Ben·utzer m ~s/~ *user*

Ben·utzung f ~/~en *use* (f *for*); freie ~ e-r S genießen *to have the run of a th* (: *of a library*) | (Verwertung) *utilization* **~sdauer** f *usage time*; *period of service*; *operating time* **~sgebühr** f: ~ f etw *fee for the use of a th*; (f e-n Text) *royalties* pl **~srecht** n ⟨jur⟩ *user*

B·enzaldeh·yd m ~s/ ⟨chem⟩ *benzaldehyde*

Benz·in n ~s/~e **1.** ⟨chem⟩ *benzine*; e-e Art ~ *benzoline* || ⟨mot⟩ *petrol*; ⟨Am⟩ *gas*(*oline, ..olene*); ⟨sl⟩ *juice* || geruchfreies ~ *sweet p.* (*g.*) || verbleites ~ *leaded p.* (*g.*) **2.** [in comp] *benzine* (*plant*) || ⟨mot⟩ *petrol*, ⟨Am⟩ *gas* **~abscheider** m *petrol* (⟨Am⟩ *gas*) *trap* **~behälter** m ⟨mot⟩ *petrol-*(⟨Am⟩ *gas-*)*tank* **~ersparnis** f *petrol saving* °**~hunne** m ⟨bes Am⟩ *teenicide(r)* **~motor** m *petrol(eum)* (⟨Am⟩ *gas*[*oline*]) *motor* od *engine* **~süßung** f *sweetening of p.* (*g.*) **~uhr** f *fuel-gauge*

B·enzoë f ~ ~ (~harz) *benzoin* **~säure** f ⟨chem⟩ *benzoic acid*

Benz·ol n ~s/~e ⟨chem⟩ *benzene*

be·obachten vt/i **I.** vt **1.** (betrachten) (P, T, Natur) *to observe* || (sorgsam) *to watch*; *study*; ~, wie jd ißt, jdn beim Essen ~ *to watch a p eat(ing)* || jdn heimlich ~ *to spy upon a p*, ..~ l *to set a watch on a p*; (of detectives) *to shadow*, jdn ständig ~ *to keep tab(s) on a p* | ⟨mil⟩ *to observe*; (Schuß) nicht –tet! *lost!* | (im Geiste) *to sense, view* (*with concern*) **2.** (wahrnehmen) (Eigenschaft etc) *to observe, notice* (an jdm *in a p*) **3.** (im Auge behalten) die öffentliche Meinung ~d ⟨bes Am⟩ *with the ear to the ground* || (Kinder) *to look after* || (Gesetz, Regel) *to keep, observe, to be observant of*; *to respect*; (Fest) *to observe*; (Anordnungen) *to follow, obey*, || Stillschweigen ~ *to keep* od *observe silence* **II.** vi (betrachten) *to observe* (*keenly*) **Be·obachter** m *observer*, ein aufmerksamer ~ *a close o.*; neugieriger ~ ⟨fam⟩ *Peeping Tom* || ⟨aero⟩ (*aeroplane-*)*observer* **Be·obachtung** f ~/~en **1.** *observation* (*of nature*); aus eigener ~ *from personal o.* || ~en [pl] *observations* [pl] (über *of, on*); ~en m *to observe* || *examination* || ⟨a–n⟩ e–e ~ nehmen *to take a sight* || (Verrückte) unter ~ stellen *to restrain*; unter ~ *under restraint* || .. der ~ [dat] entziehen ⟨mil⟩ *to shield ..from enemy observation* **2.** *observance* (*of a law, of Sunday*, etc.)

Be·obachtungs- ~flugzeug n *reconnaissance* od *scout-plane* **~fehler** m *personal error* **~fenster** n ⟨tech⟩ *sight port*; *viewing glass* **~gabe** f *observation* **~kompaß** m *navigator's compass* **~leiter** f ⟨artill⟩ *pulpit* **~lücke** f *gap in the observation* **~offizier** m *observation post officer* **~posten** m ⟨mil⟩ *observation-post*, ⟨sl abbr⟩ *O. Pip* **~reihe** f ⟨demog, stat⟩ *set* **~schiff** n *scout* **~stelle** f (abbr B-Stelle) *observation stand* **~vermögen** n *observation*

be·ordern vt [h] (jdn) *to direct, order, command* (*to do*); *to summon* (z etw *to a th*) || *to order* (*a p*) (*away*) (nach *to*) || *to have* (*a p*) *up* (*for a purpose*)

bep·acken vt [h] (jdn) *to load* (mit *with*) → belasten

bepfl·anzen vt [h] *to plant* (mit *with*); (Boden) *to set* (*with*) ‖ (Baugelände) *to landscape*

Bepfl·anzung f ~/~en (das Pflanzen) *planting* | [konkr] (das Gepflanzte) *plantation*

bepfl·astern vt [h] (Straße) *to pave* ‖ ⟨artill sl⟩ *to rake* ‖ ⟨aero sl⟩ *to plaster*

bep·inseln vt [h] *to paint*; *daub*

°**bep·issen** vt [h] *to piss* ‖ **sich** ~ *to wet o.s.*

bepl·anken vt [h] (Schiff) *to plank*; (innen) *to line* (*a ship*) *with planks* **Bepl·ankung** f *planking*; *planks* [pl]; Innen≗ = Garnierung ‖ ⟨aero⟩ *skin, covering*

bep·olstern vt [h] = polstern

bep·udern vt [h] *to powder* (mit *with*)

bep·utzen vt [h] (Mauer) *to render*

°**bequ·asseln** vt [h] (jdn) *to bamboozle* .. (*into doing*)

bequ·em I. a A. [attr] 1. (angenehm) *easy* (*path*; *coat*) ‖ *comfortable* (*chair*); *sprawling* ‖ *handy* (*tool*) ‖ (geräumig) *commodious* (*rooms*) 2. (leicht) *easy* od *soft* (*job*); e-e sehr ~e Lösung *a very easy* od *simple solution* ‖ ⟨sl⟩ *cushy* (*job*) 3. (passend) *convenient* (*time*); e-e ~e Gelegenheit *an opportunity*; unter ~en Bedingungen *on easy terms* ‖ ~e Einrichtung *convenience* 4. (P) *comfort-loving*; *easy-going, lazy* ‖ er ist ein ~er Gegner *he is easy meat* ‖ ein ~er Nachbar *a neighbour easy to get on with* B. [pred] 1. (S) *easy*; *comfortable* ‖ *convenient* (*to do*) ‖ (Schuhe) ~(er) m *to ease* ‖ ~ zur Hand *ready at hand, handy* (*:the station is h.*) 2. (P) (of persons) a. *at ease*; es sich [dat] ~ m *to make o.s. comfortable*; *to be at one's ease, to take it easy, to take one's ease*; *to ensconce*; m Sie es sich ~ *make yourself at home*; sitzen Sie dort wirklich auch ~? *are you sure you are comfortable there*? ‖ es ~ h *to live in comfortable circumstances* b. (passend) (S) *convenient*; jdm ~ s *to suit a p, to be convenient to a p*; tue das ganz, wie es dir ~ ist *suit your own convenience* c. (träge) *easy-going*; *lazy* (*:too lazy for..*) II. adv 1. (leicht) *easily*; ~ in 2 Stunden *easily in 2 hours*; ~ siegen *to win hands down* ‖ ⟨obs⟩ ~ (die Flöte spielen).. *with ease*; *well* ‖ ~ erreichbar *convenient* (*controls, switch*, ⟨comp⟩ *keys*) 2. (angenehm) der Rock sitzt ~ *the coat is quite comfortable*; in dem Stuhl sitzt es sich ~ *the chair is quite comfortable* ‖ mit ihm lebt es sich ~ *he is easy to get on* (od *to deal*) *with* ‖ ~ gelegen *comfortable* (*lodgings*); ⟨Am⟩ *convenient* ‖ ein ~es Leben führen *to live an easy* od *a soft life* ‖ es sich in dem Sitz ~ m *to settle in the seat*

bequ·emen vrefl [h] sich ~ 1. sich auf dem Fußboden ~ *to make o.s. comfortable* (od *to take a seat*) *on the floor* ‖ sich möglichst schnell nach Hause ~ *to make the best of one's way home* 2. sich ~ z etw *to comply* (od *put up*) *with a th, to submit to a th*; wir mußten uns schon dazu ~ *we had to submit to it* ‖ sich ~ z tun *to come round to do* **bequ·emlich** a 1. *comfortable* (*life*) ‖ *easy* (*work*); *convenient* 2. *indolent, lazy* (*p*) ≗**keit** f ~/~en 1. *convenience*; aus ~ *for c.*; jede ~ *every c.* ‖ *comfort, ease*; s-e ~ lieben *to be fond of comfort* ‖ ⟨obs⟩ schickliche ~ des Gesprächs (ungezwungene Unterhaltung) *ease of conversation* 2. (Trägheit) *indolence* 3. [konkr] (bequeme Einrichtung) *convenience*

ber·ändern vt [h] *to border, edge*

ber·appen I. vt [h] 1. (Mauer) *to rough-cast* ‖ (Baum) *to rough-hew* 2. °(Geld) *to fork* od *shell out* od *over*, → bezahlen; die Zeche ~ *to pay for one's whistle* II. vi tüchtig ~ *to come down with the money*, ⟨sl⟩ *to pay the piper, to pay for one's whistle*

ber·asen vt [h] *to* (*cover with*) *turf*

ber·aten vt/i [h] [→ raten] I. vt 1. jdn ~ a. *to advise a p, to take.. under advisement* (über *on, about*); *to give* od *offer counsel to a p* ‖ jdn gut ~ *to give good counsel to a p*; gut, übel ~ s *to be well-, ill-advised*; sie waren gut ~, als sie.. *they had their wits about them when they..*; → beraten [a] b. †jdn ~ mit = jdn ausstatten mit c. sich ~ *to be in consultation* od *conference*; *to take counsel*; *to consult, confer* (mit jdm *with a p*; über etw *about* od *on a th*); *to deliberate* (über *on*) ‖ sich mit-e-a ~ ⟨fam⟩ *to put* (*lay, knock*) *heads together* 2. (etw) *to deliberate on* (*a th*); ⟨parl⟩ etw eingehend ~ *to go into Committee on a th* ‖ (besprechen) *to discuss, debate* (*a question*) ‖ → beratschlagen II. vi **über** etw ~ *to deliberate on a th*; *to discuss a th* ‖ **mit** jdm ~ = sich ~, → I. 1. c. **ber·aten** a ‖ ≗e(r) *advisee* → ~ vt 1. a. **ber·atend** a *advisory, consultative* (*body, committee*); in ~er Eigenschaft *in an advisory capacity* ‖ ~e Versammlung f *council*; *deliberative assembly* ‖ nur ~e Stimme in dem Ausschuß h *to be a non-voting committee member*

Ber·ater m ~s/~ *adviser* (jds *of* od *to a p*; e-r Körperschaft *to a body*); *counsellor*, ⟨Am⟩ *counselor* ‖ fachärztlicher ~ *consulting physician, consultant*; fachlicher ~ *consultee*; technischer ~ *consulting engineer* **~gruppe** f *advisory group*

ber·atschlagen vt/i [h] 1. vt etw ~ *to deliberate on a th* ‖ *to debate, discuss* (*a question*) ‖ über die S wird noch beratschlagt *the matter is under consideration* | sich untereinander ~ *to be in consultation* od *conference* ‖ sich mit jdm ~ = sich beraten, → beraten I. 1. c. 2. vi ~ **mit; über** = beraten II; I. 1. c.

Ber·atschlagung f ~/~en *deliberation* (über *on*); *conference, consultation* (mit *with a p*)

Ber·atung f ~/~en 1. (Rat) *advice, counsel* (jds *to a p*) ‖ ärztliche ~ *consultation* ‖ (z. B. Auswanderer≗ *emigration*) *services* ‖ 2. (Beratschlagung) *deliberation* (über *on*), die ~en *the deliberations* (*of a Committee*); bei den ~en *at the d.* ‖ *conference, consultation* (*with a p*) ‖ ~ h *to sit* (*: they were sitting from.. to..*); *to be in conference* (od *consultation* (*with*) ‖ e-e ~ halten *to hold a consultation* od *conference*; in ~en eintreten *to enter into deliberations* ‖ das Gericht zog sich z ~ zurück ⟨jur⟩ *.. for deliberation* ‖ ⟨engl parl⟩ Stadium der ~ e-s Gesetzentwurfs *Committee*: in die ~en (od Einzel≗en) eintreten *to go into Committee* (über *on a th*) **~sausschuß** m *advisory committee*; *braintrust* **~sdienst** m, **~sstelle** f *services* pl; ⟨med⟩ *health centre*; ~ f Erziehungsfragen *Child Guidance Centre*

ber·auben vt [h] 1. jdn ~ a. *to rob, plunder, despoil a p* ‖ jdn e-r S ~ *to deprive* (od *divest, rob, strip*) *a p of a th*; jdn s-s Besitzes ~ *to fleece a p of all he possesses, to dispossess a p*; jdn e-s Gutes ~ *to expropriate a p from his estate*; jdn des Thrones ~ *to dethrone a p* ‖ s-s Geldes beraubt w *to be fleeced* (bis auf den letzten Pfennig *to one's last shilling*) ‖ der Tod beraubte ihn s-s einzigen Sohnes *death bereaved him of his only son*; durch den Tod beraubt [a] *bereaved* (*father*) b. ⟨übtr⟩ jdn s-r Ehren ~ *to strip a p of his honours*; s-s Ruhmes beraubt s *to be shorn of one's glory* ‖ jdn der Hoffnung (etc) ~ *to bereave, deprive a p of hope*; des Trostes beraubt [a] *comfortless* ‖ °dies beraubt mich des Vergnügens, Sie zu sehen *this deprives me of the pleasure of seeing you.* c. sich e-s Rechtes ~ *to divest o.s. of a right* 2. etw e-r S ~ *to sweep a th clear of a th*; ein Haus des Lichtes ~ *to deprive a house of light*; des Mobiliars ~ (of fire) *to strip a house of furniture* ‖ e-e S des Glanzes, der Anziehung ~ ⟨fam⟩ *to take the gilt off the gingerbread*

Ber·aubung f ~/~en *deprivation, plunder, plunderage, spoliation; bereavement* ‖ ⟨übtr⟩ *robbery* (*of a th*)
ber·äuchern vt [h] *to fumigate* (*with*), → beweihräuchern
ber·auschen vt [h] (jdn) **1.** *to inebriate, intoxicate*; ⟨sl⟩ *to fuddle*; *to make* (*a p*) *drunk* | ⟨fig⟩ *to inebriate, intoxicate*; berauscht v *inebriated, intoxicated with* od *by* **2. sich** ~ *to get drunk* (od ⟨fam⟩ *tipsy*), ⟨sl⟩ *to fuddle* | ⟨fig⟩ sich ~ **an** *to be intoxicated with*
ber·auschend a *intoxicating, intoxicant, heady* (*wine*); ~es Getränk n *intoxicant* **ber·auscht** a *inebriate(d), intoxicate(d); drunk*, ⟨fam⟩ *tipsy* ‖ ⟨übtr⟩ *besotted; infatuated* (v *with*)
Ber·auschung f *intoxication*
B·erber m ~s/~ **1.** *Berber, Moor* **2.** [in comp] *Berber* | ~affe [m] ⟨zoo⟩ = Magot; ~sprache [f] *Berber* **Berber·ei** f *Barbary States* **b·erberisch** a *Berber, of Barbary*
Berber·itze, B·erbesbeere f ~/~n ⟨bot⟩ *barberry* ‖ Fiederberberitze *Thin-leaved Mahonia*
Berchtesg·aden n (Luftkurort in Oberbayern)
ber·echenbar a *calculable, computable*
ber·echnen vt [h] **1.** (Einnahmen etc) *to count, to calculate; to reckon* (*up*); *to cast up*; (Betrag) *to work out*; aus e-r Reihe v Tatsachen ~, daß .. *to calculate from a number of facts that ..* ‖ ⟨Am⟩ *to figure* (*that*) ‖ falsch ~ *to miscalculate, miscount* | (abschätzen) *to compute, to estimate* (auf *at*) ‖ den Wert e-r S ~ *to evaluate a th* ‖ ⟨typ⟩ (Manuskript) *to cast off* **2.** ⟨com⟩ (Preis) *to charge, quote*; ⟨Am⟩ *to tax*; er berechnete (mir) 2 Mark dafür, er b. es mir mit 2 M. *he charged* (*me*) *2 marks for it*; was ~ Sie f ein Meter? *what do you charge* (*me*) *for a meter, what are your charges for a m.?*; ⟨Am⟩ *what's your figure?* ‖ Heizung u Licht w bes –net *fire and light are extras* **3.** ⟨übtr⟩ **berechnet s auf** (of *actions*) *to aim at; to strive after*; sein Spiel war zu sehr auf Effekt berechnet *he played too much to the gallery* ‖ berechnet s f *to be meant, intended for*; *to be calculated for* (*boys only*) **4. sich** ~ **l** *to be calculable* od *computable*; sich nicht ~ l *to be incalculable*
ber·echnend a *calculative*; z ~er Betrag *calculable, computable* | ⟨übtr⟩ (klug) *calculating, diplomatic, politic*; ⟨Am sl⟩ *hard-boiled* ‖ *mercenary*; ~e Liebe *cupboard love*
Ber·echner m ~s/~ *computer, calculator*
Ber·echnung f ~/~en *computation, calculation*; (Schätzung) *computation, estimate*; ungefähre ~ *rough estimate*; nach ungefährer ~ *calculating roughly*; nach niedrigster ~ *at the lowest computation* ‖ e-e ~ anstellen *to make a calculation* ‖ ~ des Wertes e-r S *evaluation of a th* ‖ etw in s-e ~ einbeziehen *to allow for a th in one's calculations* | ⟨übtr⟩ (kluge ~) *expediency* (:*to be based on e.*); *policy* | ⟨a–n⟩ ~ v Bahnkorrekturen *computation of flight path corrections* **~svorrichtung** f (Rechengerät) *computer*
ber·echtigen vt/i [h] **1.** vt (jdn) *to entitle*, (z *to*; z tun *to do*); *to authorize, to empower, to license* (*to do*); → ermächtigen; befähigen | berechtigt s (of claims) *to be valid, to hold good*; die Frage ist nicht b. *the question does not arise* ‖ berechtigt s (P) *to be entitled* (z *to*; z tun *to do*), *to be justified* (z tun in *doing*); *to be licensed* (*to do*) **2.** vi ~ z etw (of actions, etc.) *to entitle to a th, to justify* (od *warrant*) *a th* ‖ dies berechtigt zu der Annahme, daß .. *this justifies* (od *entitles to*) *the assumption that ..* ‖ die Expedition berechtigt z der Hoffnung, daß sie erfolgreich s wird *the expedition bids fair to be successful* ‖ er berechtigt z den größten Hoffnungen *he is a man of great promise*
ber·echtigt a **1.** [pred] → berechtigen; vollk ~ s etw z tun *to have a perfect right to do a th* wohl—tigt s *to have a perfect right* (*to do*); ⟨Am⟩ *to be well taken* **2.** [attr] *entitled* (*holder*); *justified* | *legitimate* (*claim; interests; fears*); → begründet ≈e(r m) f ⟨contr⟩ *covenantee, permittee* **~erweise** adv *legitimately*
Ber·echtigung f ~/~en *justification* (z *for*; z tun *for doing*); *warrant* (z *for*); nicht ohne ~ *not without warrant* ‖ (Recht) *right, title* (z *to*); (behördliche) *licence* ‖ ⟨Ger⟩ (~ auf Grund der Vorbildung) *qualification* (*for*); e-e ~ erwerben *to qualify o.s., to be qualified, to qualify* (f, zu *for*); .. u erhält dadurch s-e ~ *thus qualifying itself thereby*, erst dadurch s-e ~ erhalten *to be only then qualified* **~sschein** m *scrip; qualifying certificate; licence* **~swesen** n *system of qualification*
ber·eden vt [h] **1.** (etw) *to talk* (*a th*) *over; to discuss* (*with a p*); → besprechen; verabreden **2.** (jdn) *to speak ill of; to backbite, slander* **3.** (überreden) (jdn) *to persuade, induce* (z *to*; z tun *to do*); er war nicht z ~ *he was not to be persuaded*; → beschwatzen **4. sich** ~ *to confer, consult, to take counsel* (mit *with*; über *about*); sich ~ über etw *to deliberate on a th*
ber·edsam a *eloquent* **Ber·edsamkeit** f ~/ *eloquence; oratory* **ber·edt** a *eloquent* (*barrister*); *fluent* | ⟨übtr⟩ *eloquent, significant* (*silence*)
ber·egen vt [h] = erwähnen
ber·egnen vt [h] (etw) *to wet* (*a th*) *with rain*; *to shower rain upon* (*a field*)
Ber·eich m & n ~(e)s/~e **1.** (Reichweite) *compass, reach*, innerhalb m-s ~s *within my r.*; außerhalb m-s ~s *above* od *beyond, out of, my r.* ‖ *sweep*; → Ausdehnung ‖ ⟨mil⟩ *range, reach* (:*out of the r. of the guns*) ‖ *range, compass* (*of a voice*); (Seh≈) *range of vision, ken* **2.** ⟨übtr⟩ **a.** *sphere* (*of a science*) ‖ *compass* (*of a life-time*) ‖ *range* (*of understanding*) ‖ im ~ der Möglichkeit *within the range of possibility* **b.** (Spielraum jds) *range, reach, scope, sphere* (*of a p*) ‖ (Amts≈, Arbeits≈) *province, range, scope, sphere* (:*within my province*, etc.); in den ~ jds kommen (of tasks) *to come within the range of a p* ‖ Wissens≈ *ken* (:*without my k.*); (Einfluß≈) *sweep* **3.** (Gebiet) *area; precincts* [pl] (:*within the p. of the town*) ‖ *field, domain, sphere*: etw in den ~ der Fabel verweisen *to relegate a th to the domain of legend* ‖ dies ist mein ~ *this is my sphere, my little world*; in m-m kl ~ *in my own small way* ‖ im sozialen ~ *in social matters*; → Bereichs–
ber·eichern vt [h] **1.** (jdn) *to make a p rich; to enrich*; [oft pp] bereichert durch *enriched by* | **sich** ~ *to enrich o.s.*; *to feather one's nest* **2.** etw ~: (Kenntnisse) *to enrich, enlarge; to add to* ‖ (Leben) *to enrich, heighten* **Ber·eicherung** f ~/~en **1.** *enrichment* (*of a p*) **2.** *enlargement; addition* (e-r S *to a th*); e-e ~ s-r Kenntnisse *an addition to his knowledge* | er ist wirklich e–e ~ des Klubs *he is quite an acquisition to ..*
Ber·eichs- ~(um)schalter m ⟨el⟩ *range* od *band switch* od *selector*
ber·eifen vt (→ Reif) *to cover with hoar-frost; to rime* ‖ **sich** ~ *to get rimed* **bereift** a *rimy*
ber·eifen vt [h] ⟨tech⟩ (Faß) *to hoop* ‖ (Autorad) *to tyre, to fit with tyres*; ⟨Am⟩ *to tire*; → Reifen **B.fung** f ~/~en ⟨mot & cycl⟩ *tyring, tyre-fitting* ‖ [konkr] (*set of*) *tyres*, ⟨Am⟩ *tires* [pl]
ber·einigen vt [h] (Text) *to emend* ‖ (Angelegenheit, Streitfall) *to settle*; (Schwierigkeit) *to remove*; (Mißverständnis) *to clear up*
ber·eisen vt [h] ein Land ~ *to travel* od *tour a country* (im Norden u Süden *north and south*); e-e Gegend geschäftlich ~ *to work a district* ‖ → besuchen **ber·eist** a *travelled*
ber·eit a [nur pred] **1.** (P) **a.** *ready*; bist du ~? *are you ready?* ‖ ~ z *ready, prepared for,*

(*pre*)*disposed to*; z näherer Auskunft ~ (*I shall be*) *pleased to give further information* || ~ s z, z tun *to be ready* (od *game, prepared*) *for* (*a th*), *to do*; z allem ~ s *to go to any lengths* (um z erhalten *to get*) || ~stehen *to be* (od *stand*) *ready*; ⟨mar⟩ *to stand by*; ständig f jdn ~ stehen (*or* sein) *to be at everybody's beck and call* | **sich ~ erklären** *to consent* (*to do*) || sich ~ finden, sich z etw ~ finden 1 *to agree* (*to do*); *to see one's way* (*to do*) (:*I cannot see my way to do*); *to resign o.s.* (z tun *to doing*) || sich ~ halten *to hold o.s. in readiness, to stand by* || sich ~ m *to get* (od *make*) *ready* (*to do*) **b. etw ~ h** *to be ready with a th*; s-e Antwort ~ h *to have one's answer pat* || ~ halten *to keep a th ready* (od *in readiness*) (*for*); Fahrkarten ~ halten! (*have your*) *tickets ready, please*! || ~|legen *to lay out*; *to place* (*a th*) *in readiness* || → ~stellen **2.** (S) *ready*; das Essen ist ~ *dinner is ready*; alles ist ~ *everything is r.* || ~ z *ready for* (*use*) || ~|liegen *to be ready*, ~ stehen *to be ready* (:*the car is r. at the door*) || etw ~ m *to make a th ready* (f *for*) || die Waren sind zur Lieferung ~ .. *are awaiting delivery* **ber·eiten** vt [h] **1.** (Mahl) *to prepare* (aus *from*); *to make* (*a th*) *ready* || (Getränk) *to brew*; (Tee) *to make*; (e–e gute Mahlzeit) *to turn out..* **2.** (bearbeiten) (den Boden) *to work* || (Leder) *to dress, curry* **3.** ⟨übtr⟩ jdm den Untergang ~ *to bring a p to ruin* od *grief* || jdm Freuden ~ *to give a p pleasure*; jdm Kummer (etc) ~ *to cause a p grief, to grieve a p*; jdm Schande ~ *to bring disgrace on a p*; jdm gr Unannehmlichkeiten ~ *to put a p to much trouble* (od *to great inconvenience*) || jdm Vergnügen ~ *to afford amusement to a p*; **es bereitet mir** die größte Genugtuung *it affords me the greatest satisfaction* (*to do*); es b. mir viel Vergnügen *it gives me much pleasure* (*to see..*); ~ Sie mir das V., mich z besuchen *do me the pleasure of calling on me* || ihm wurde eine herzliche Aufnahme b. *he had a hearty reception*; dem Buch wurde e-e günstige Aufnahme b. *the book met with a favourable reception*

ber·eiten vt [h] (→ reiten) **1.** ein Land ~ *to ride a country, to ride over a country*; *to visit a country on horseback* **2.** (abrichten) (ein Pferd) *to break in*; *to train* **Ber·eiter** m ~s/~ (Pferde≗) *rough-rider, horse-breaker, trainer*

Ber·eiter m ~s/~ *preparer*; (Leder≗) *dresser, currier*; (Tuch≗) *dresser*; → (zu)bereiten

ber·eitfertig 1. a *willing, eager* (*to do*); *unhesitating* **2.** adv *willingly*

ber·eit|legen vt [h] → bereit 1. b. **ber·eit|liegen** vi → bereit 2. **ber·eits** adv = schon

Ber·eitschaft f ~/~en **1.** (Bereitsein) *readiness, preparedness* (z *for*) || in ~ *ready*; ⟨mil⟩ *at the ready*; (Polizei) *on the alert*; in ~ s *or* stehen *to be* od *stand ready* (z *for*); *to stand by* ⟨a. wir⟩; in ~ s ist alles *readiness is all* (Shak.); alles in ~ stellen *to get* od *put everything in readiness, to get everything ready* (*for*); sich in ~ halten *to hold o.s. in readiness*; ⟨mar⟩ *to stand by* || (latente Kraft) *potentiality, potential* || schnelle ~ *resource* (*in an emergency*) **2.** (Bereitwilligkeit) *readiness, willingness* (*to do*) **3.** [konkr] *squad of mounted police*; ⟨tech, a. aero⟩ *refuelling* (etc.) *and maintenance* (*duty*) *squad* **~seinsatz** m ⟨aero⟩ *air alert mission* **~sflugzeug** n *air alert* **~sgraben** m ⟨mil⟩ *support-trench* **~smunition** f ⟨artill⟩ *ready service ammunition* **~spolizei** f *alert police* **~sstellung** f ⟨tact⟩ *prepared position* **~stasche** f *ever*(-)*ready case* ⟨a. phot⟩

Ber·eitsein n *preparedness, readiness* (: *r. is all*, Shak.)

ber·eit|stehen vi, etc → bereit 1. a. **ber·eitstehend** a *available, disposable*

ber·eit|stellen vt [h] **1.** jdm e–n Stuhl ~ *to arrange a chair for a p* **2.** ⟨übtr⟩ (etw) *to make* (*a th*) *available*; *to furnish, provide, supply* (*a th*) || (Geld) *to earmark* (f *for*); *to commit* (*funds*); (Zeit) *to lay aside* (*for*) | jdm etw ~ *to place a th at a p's disposal*; *to throw a th open for a p* **Ber·eitstellung** f ~/~en *the making available* (*of a th*); *provision, supply* (*of a th*) || ⟨mil tact⟩ [abstr] *concentration*; *forming up*; *final assembly*; Angriff nach ~ *deliberate attack*, ~en [pl] *troops in reserve, troops ready for action* **~sflugplatz** m *marshalling airfield* **~sfond** m ⟨com⟩ *appropriation* **~sraum** m ⟨mil⟩ *assembly* od *concentration area*, ⟨aero⟩ *marshalling* od *staging area*

Ber·eitung f ~/~en *preparation* || (Herstellung) *marking, manufacture*; Leder≗ *dressing*

ber·eitwillig 1. a *ready, willing* (*to do*) || (eifrig) *eager, solicitous, desirous*; *ready and willing* **2.** adv *readily*; *willingly*; etw ~ tun *or* erzählen *to oblige with a th* **≗keit** f ~/ *readiness, willingness* (z etw *of a th*; *to do*); s-e ~ erklären *to notify one's w.* (*to do*) || gr ~ *alacrity*

ber·ennen vt [h] [→ rennen] (bestürmen) (Festung) *to storm*; (belagern) *to invest, blockade* **Ber·ennung** f ~/~en (e-r Festung, Stadt) *storm*; *blockade* → Angriff, Belagerung

ber·euen vt [h] (etw) *to repent, regret* (*a th*); *to repent of* (*a th*); *to be sorry for* (*a th*) || ~ getan z h *to repent* (od *regret*) *doing* || er wird es noch ~ ⟨liter⟩ *he will live to rue it*; du wirst den Tag ~, an dem du sie sahest *you will rue the day you saw her* **Ber·euung** f ~/ *repentance*

B·erg m ~(e)s/~e **1.** *mountain*; den ~ 'runter *downhill* || ⟨poet⟩ *mount*; [vor Eigennamen] *Mount* [abbr Mt], der ~ N. *Mount N.* || kl ~ *hill* || feuerspeiender ~ *volcano* **2.** ⟨übtr⟩ **a.** *comb, crest* (*of a wave*); → Wellenkamm **b.** ⟨fig⟩ *a mountain of books, debts, difficulties*; ~e v *heaps of, lots of* (*money*) **c.** ⟨min⟩ (= taubes Gestein) *waste rock, gob, gobbing*; ~e [pl] *deads* pl → Versatz **3. a.** da steht der Ochs **am** ~e ⟨fig⟩ *that beats me*; dastehn wie der O. am ~e *to be at the end of one's tether, to be all at sea* | **auf** e-n ~ steigen *to ascend* od *climb a mountain, to mount a hill* | **hinterm** ~e halten *to avoid coming to the point, to beat about the bush*; mit etw hinterm ~e h. *to hold a th back*; *to withhold a th* || hinterm ~e wohnen auch Leute *he is not the only pebble on the beach* | in die ~e gehen *to go into the mountains* | **über** den ~ s ⟨fig⟩ *to be over the hump*; über ~ u Tal *up hill and down dale* || ⟨fig⟩ über den ~ hinwegkommen *to turn the corner*; ich bin über den ~ hinweg *I've broken the neck* od *back of it*; wir sind noch nicht über den ~ hinweg *we are not yet out of the wood* || über alle ~e s *to be off and away, to be out of reach* | **vor** e-m ~e stehen *to be faced with unsurmountable difficulties*; *to be in a fix*; → Klemme | **zu** ~e fahren *to move to the high pasture-grounds*; *to travel upstream* || die Haare stehen mir z ~e *my hair stands on end, my hair slowly rises* **b. ~e besteigen** *to climb mountains, to mountaineer* || ~e versetzen *to remove mountains* || goldne ~e versprechen *to promise wonders* **5.** [in comp] *mountain* (*top*) || ⟨min⟩ *mining*

B·erg, ≗·ab adv *downhill*; bergauf u ~ *up hill and down dale* || ⟨fig⟩ es geht ~ mit ihm *he is going down*(*hill*); (gesundheitlich) *he is sinking fast*; (alternd) mit uns geht's ~ *the shadows lengthen* ⟨fig⟩ **~abhang** m *hill-side, slope* **≗·abwärts** adv *downhill* **~ahorn** m ⟨bot⟩ *sycamore* (*maple*) **~akademie** f ⟨min⟩ *School of Mines*; *mining-academy* **~akademiker** m ⟨min⟩ *mining engineer* **~alraun** m ⟨bot⟩ *wild mandrake* **~amt** n ⟨min⟩ *Mining Office, Board of Mines* **≗·an** adv *uphill* | **≗**fahrt [f] ⟨mot⟩ *uphill driving*; *climb* **~arbeit** f ⟨min⟩ *mining* **~arbeiter**

m ⟨min⟩ *miner*; (Kohlen) *collier* | ∼streik [m] *miners strike*; ∼verband [m] *Miners' Federation*; *miner's union* ≗**artig** a *mountainlike* ≗**·auf** adv *uphill*; → bergab, Berg·anfahrt ∼**bahn** f *mountain-railway* ∼**bau** m ⟨min⟩ *the working of mines*; *mining* (*industry*) ∼**beamte:** [der ∼, ein ∼r] m ⟨min⟩ *mining official* ∼**behörden** f [pl] ⟨min⟩ *mining authorities* [pl] ∼**besteigung** f *climb* ∼**bewohner** m *mountaineer*; *highlander* ∼**blau** n ⟨minr⟩ → Las·urstein ∼**butter** f ⟨minr⟩ *mountain butter*, *alunogen* ≗**ehoch** adv *mountains high*; → berghoch ∼**eisen** n ⟨min⟩ *jumper* ∼**erz** n ⟨min⟩ *crude ore* ∼**fach** n *mining profession*, *mining line* ∼**fahrt** f **1.** = Almfahrt **2.** *upstream voyage*, *up-passage* **3.** ⟨mot⟩ *hill--climb* **4.** *m. trip* ∼**feste,** ∼**festung** f *mountain--fort*(*ress*) ∼**fex** m *mountaineering fan* od *enthusiast* ∼**fink** m ⟨orn⟩ *brambling* ∼**flachs** m **1.** ⟨minr⟩ *amianthus* **2.** ⟨bot⟩ *mountain flax* ∼**forelle** f ⟨ich⟩ *mountain-trout* ∼**freiheit** f *mining privilege* ∼**fried** m *castle keep* ∼**führer** m (*mountain* od *alpine*) *guide* ∼**gegend** f *mountain--district* od *regions*; *highland* ∼**geist** m *gnome*, *mountain-goblin* ∼**gelb** n ⟨minr⟩ *yellow ochre* ∼**grat** m *ridge* ∼**grün** n ⟨minr⟩ *malachite*; *chry--socolla* ∼**gruß** m *miners' salute* ∼**halde** f *mountain slope*; (Schutt) *pit heap* ∼**hänfling** m ⟨orn⟩ *twite* ∼**harz** n *bitumen* ∼**hauptmann** m *overseer* (od *superintendent*) *of mines* ∼**h·eideland** n *moorland* ≗**h·och** a [attr] *mountain-high* (*waves*); → bergehoch ∼**hoheit** f *the right of supervision of mines* ∼**holz** n ⟨minr⟩ *rock-cork*, *wood* ∼**huhn** n ⟨orn⟩ *mountain-partridge* ‖ *mountain fowl* ∼**hütte** f *mountain hut* ∼**ingenieur** m *mining engineer* ∼**inspektor** m *mining inspector* ∼**kamm** m *crest* ∼**kessel** m *basin*; *gorge* ∼**kette** f *range*, *chain* od *ridge of mountains*, *mountain-range* ∼**kiefer** f → Kiefer ∼**knappe** m *miner* ∼**knappschaft** f *body of miners* ∼**kork** m ⟨minr⟩ *rock--cork* ∼**krankheit** f *mountain sickness* ∼**kraxler** m *cragsman* → Bergsteiger ∼**kristall** m ⟨minr⟩ *rock-crystal*; Art ∼ *Rhinestone*; → Pras ∼**kuppe** f *summit* (*round top of a mountain*) ∼**land** n *hill*(*y*) od *mountainous country*; [attr] *highland* ‖ v Mato Grosso (Brasilien) *Mato Grosso* ∼**leder** n **1.** *miner's apron* **2.** ⟨minr⟩ *rock-*, *mountain-cork*; → Asbest ∼**lehne** f *mountain--side* ∼**leute** [pl] *miners* [pl] ∼**mann** m [pl Bergleute] *miner*, *pitman*; (in Kohlenwerken) *collier*; *mining-engineer* ∼**männchen** n *gnome* ≗**männisch** a *mining* ∼**mannsstand** m *miners' craft* ∼**mehl** n ⟨minr⟩ *mountain flour* od *meal* ∼**meister** m *surveyor of mines* ∼**milch** f ⟨minr⟩ *mountain-milk* ∼**nymphe** f *mountain-nymph*; *Oread* ∼**parte** f *miner's pickaxe* ∼**partie** f *mountain trip* ∼**polizei** f ⟨Ger⟩ *supervising authorities of mines* ∼**predigt** f ⟨bib⟩ *Sermon on the Mount* ∼**rat** m **1.** (Körperschaft) *board of mines* **2.** (P) *mining director* ∼**rechte** n [pl] *mining-laws* [pl] ∼**regal** n *mining royalty* ∼**reihen** m *highlanders' song* od *dance* ∼**reien,** ∼**reihen** f [pl] *miners' songs* [pl] ∼**röschen** n ⟨bot⟩ = Seidelbast ∼**revier** n *mining district*; ⟨Ger min⟩ *administrative district of the* Bergpolizei ∼**rücken** m (*mountain-*)*ridge* ∼**rutsch** m *landslip*; ⟨Am⟩ *landslide*; *mountain slide* od *creep* ∼**salz** n ⟨minr⟩ *rock-salt* ∼**sattel** m *saddle* (*between two peaks*) ∼**schaden** m ⟨min⟩ *damage caused to a building*, etc. *by mining* ∼**schicht** f ⟨min⟩ *layer*, *stratum* ‖ *miners' overtime* ∼**schlucht** f *gorge*, *ravine*, ⟨Scot⟩ *corrie* ∼**schotten** m [pl] *Scotch Highlanders* [pl] ∼**schuhe** m [pl] *mountaineering shoes* [pl] ∼**schule** f *technical mining school* ∼**schüler** m *student at a technical mining-school* ∼**seife** f ⟨minr⟩ *mountain soap*, *kind of bole* ∼**spatz** m ⟨orn⟩ = Braunelle ∼**spitze** f *mountain--top*; *peak* ∼**sport** m = Bergsteigen ∼**stadt** f *mountain-town* ∼**steigen** n *mountaineering*, *alpinism*; *mountain-climbing* ∼**steiger** m *mountaineer*, *alpinist*; *climber*; geübter ∼ *cragsman* | ∼ausrüstung [f] *mountaineering outfit* ∼**steiger·ei** f *mountaineering* ∼**stock** m *alpenstock* [Ger] ‖ (Massiv) *massive rock* ∼**straße** f *mountain-road* ‖ [Ger] *the* "Bergstrasse" (*between Heidelberg and Darmstadt*) ∼**striche** m [pl] ⟨geog⟩ *hachures* [pl] (*on maps*) ∼**strom** m *torrent* ∼**sturz** m *landslip mountain-creep* od *-slide* ∼**stütze** f *spray* (f Wagen) ∼**teer** m *mineral tar* ∼**- und Talbahn** f ⟨rail⟩ *switchback* ‖ (Rummelplatz≗) *roller-coaster* ∼**versatz** m *mine filling* ∼**verwalter** m *technical director of a mine* ∼**volk** n *highlanders*, *mountaineers* [pl] ∼**wachs** n → Erdwachs ∼**wand** f *mountain wall* ∼**wanderung** f *mountain-tour* ∼**ward·ein** m *assayer* (*of mines*) ∼**werk** n *mine*, *pit* ‖ ∼saktien [pl] ⟨com⟩ *mining-stock*; *mining-shares* [pl] ‖ ∼skunde [f] (*science of*) *mining*, *metallurgy* ∼**wesen** n = Bergbau ∼**wiese** f *mountain* od *alpine meadow* ∼**wind** m *mountain breeze* ∼**zinn** n *mine* od *pure tin*

Bergam·asker Alpen pl ⟨It⟩ *Bergamask Alps*

Bergam·otte f ∼/∼n **1.** (Birne) *bergamot* **2.** (Südfrucht) *bergamot* **Bergam·ottöl** n *essence* od *oil of bergamot*

B·erge- (→ bergen vt & Berg) [in comp] ∼**brechanlage** f *rock crushing plant* ∼**geld** n, ∼**gut** n, ∼**lohn** m *salvage* ∼**schleuder** f ⟨min⟩ *stowing slinger*

b·ergen I. vt [h] [barg/geborgen] **1. a.** (Ernte, Heu etc.) *to shelter*, *to save*; *to house* | **sich** ∼ *to shelter o.s.*, → bewahren, schützen **b.** (Segel) *to furl*, *to take in*, *to shorten* **c.** ⟨übtr⟩ *to harbour*, *shelter* (:*this wood harbours much game*) ‖ (enthalten) *to hold*; in sich ∼ (S) *to contain*; *to involve* (*danger*) **2.** ⟨mar⟩ (gestrandetes Schiff, Gut) *to salvage*, *to make salvage of*, *to salve* **3.** (verheimlichen) [oft neg] (Gefühle etc.) *to conceal*, *hide*; → verbergen ‖ °sich nicht ∼ können *to be beside o.s.* (vor Freude *for joy*) ‖ → geborgen **II.** ≗ n = Bergung **B·erger** m ⟨mar⟩ *salvor* **b·ergig** a *mountainous*; *hilly*

B·ergisches Land n -en -des ⟨Ger⟩ *the Berg country* (*between the rivers Ruhr and Sieg*)

B·ergung f ∼/∼en *sheltering*, *saving* ‖ ⟨mar⟩ *wrecking*, *salvage*; (der Gerätekapsel) *recovery*

B·ergungs- ∼**arbeiten** f [pl] *salving-operations* [pl] ∼**arbeiter** m *salvor*, ⟨Am⟩ *wrecker* ∼**dampfer** m, ∼**fahrzeug** n *salvor*, ⟨Am⟩ *wrecker* ∼**kommando** n *collecting unit* ∼**kosten** [pl] *salvage--charges* [pl] ∼**mannschaft** f *wrecking crew*; (der Feuerwehr) ⟨ins⟩ *salvage-corps* ∼**schiff** n *rescue ship*, *salvor*, ⟨Am⟩ *wrecker* ∼**schlepper** m *rescue tug*

B·erib·eri f ∼/ ⟨path⟩ (Reis-Esser-Vitamin-B-Mangelkrankheit) *beriberi* (*a nervous disease*)

Ber·icht m ∼s/∼e **1.** *account*; *report* ⟨a. jur⟩ (e–s Beauftragten) *record* → 3, *list* (über *of*, *on*) ‖ ausführl. ∼ ⟨Am⟩ *write-up* | amtlicher ∼ ⟨pol⟩ *communiqué* (Fr); *return* (über *of*); Wahl≗ *statement* (an *to*; über *of*), *return*; protokollarischer ∼ *official report*, *minutes* [pl] ‖ ⟨wir⟩ *bulletin* ‖ Jahres≗ *report*; ⟨engl⟩ ∼e [pl] über Entscheidungen der Obergerichte *Law Reports* [pl] | **nach** den neuesten ∼en *from the latest accounts* ‖ e–n ∼ **abfassen** *to draw up* (od *make out*) *a report* ‖ e–n ∼ einliefern *to send in a report* ‖ ∼ erstatten *to report* (jdm *to a p*; über *on*; wegen *for*); *to give*, *return* od *render an account* (üb *of*); über den Fortgang ∼ erstatten *to report progress*; ∼ erstatten über ⟨Am⟩ *to cover* (*a meeting*) ‖ e–n ∼ liefern *to make a statement* ‖ ⟨com⟩ *return* (*on stocks*) **2.** (mündlicher ∼) *narrative*; *relation*; *statement* **3.** (historischer ∼) *record*, *tale*, *historical account*; *narrative*, *story* **4.** (Mitteilung) ⟨com⟩ [mst ∼e pl] *advices; information* || laut ~ *as per advice* od *statement*; mangels ~s (of bill) *unpaid for want of advice* **~erstatter** m ~s/~ **1.** *informant* **2.** (e–r Zeitung) *reporter*; (auswärtiger) *correspondent; interviewer* || ⟨wir⟩ *commentator* **3.** ⟨jur etc.⟩ *member of a court* od *committee appointed to deal with, and to report on a case* || *rapporteur* (Fr) (*at a conference*) **~erstattung** f ~/~en **1.** *reporting* **2.** (Bericht) *report, statement* (über *of*) || ⟨dipl⟩ *report*; zur ~ *for report*; (Botschafter) zur ~ zurückrufen *to recall to report* [vb] **3.** ⟨mil⟩ (~ über im Felde stehende Truppen) *state* (: *piles of states and returns*) **~zeit** f etc. → Berichtszeit etc

ber·ichten vt/i [h] **I.** vt **1.** jdm etw *to report a th to a p* || (mitteilen) *to inform* (od *apprise*, ⟨com⟩ *advise*) *a p of a th* || *to tell a p a th*; ~, daß .., wie.. *to report, to tell that.., how..*; es wird uns berichtet, daß.. *we are told that..* **2.** etw ~ *to report a th, to report on a th*; → II. 1. || (sagen) *to say* || von ihm wird berichtet, er sei.. *he is reported to be..*; nach allem, was berichtet wurde *when all was said*; es wird in der Bibel berichtet *it is said* (od *it says*) *in the Bible* || (etw) historisch ~ *to record* **3.** jdn ~ (= unterrichten), [nur pass]: falsch **berichtet** s *to be misinformed*; wenn ich recht berichtet bin.. *if I am well informed* **II.** vi **1.** ~ **über** etw *to report to break the news on a th* (jdm *to a p*); *to give an account of* || *to tell about* **2.** (in der Presse) ~ über etw *to report* (⟨Am⟩ *to cover*) *a th* (: *to report a fire*); über den Fortgang ~ *to report progress*; eingehend ~ über (etwas, jdn) *to write up* [vt] **3.** historisch ~ über etw *to record a th*

ber·ichtigen vt [h] **1. a.** (Fehler, Irrtum) *to correct, rectify*; *to set right* || (Grenzlinien) *to rectify* || ⟨übtr⟩ *to correct, neutralize* **b.** (jdn) *to correct* (*a p*); *to set* (*a p*) *right* **2.** (begleichen) (Rechnung) *to balance, settle*; (Schuld) *to clear off, to pay* **B.gung** f ~/~en **1.** *correction, rectification* (*of an error*) || *correction* (*of a p*) **2.** *settlement* (*of an account*) || *payment* (*of a debt*) **~sanzeige** f *notice of error* **~sbuchung** f, **~sposten** m ⟨com⟩ *adjusting entry* **~staste** f *reset key*

Ber·ichts— **~jahr** n *year reported for, year under review* od *report*; *financial year* **~periode** f *report-period* **~woche** f *weak under review* od *report* **~zeit** f *period* (*of time*) *under review*

ber·iechen vt [h] [→ riechen] (etw) *to smell* od *sniff at* (*a th*); *to smell* (*a th*) | **sich** *or* e–a ~ *to smell* od *sniff at one another* || (P) *to try to get into touch with one another*

ber·ieseln vt [h] (Land etc) *to irrigate, spray, water*; mit Jauche ~ *to sewage* **Ber·ieselung** f ~/~en *irrigation, watering* **~sgerät** n *sprinkler* **~kühler** m *spray cooler, water cooling plant*

Ber·ing m ~s/ *circumference*

ber·ingen vt [h] (Vögel) *to* (*provide with a*) *ring* || beringt *ringed* **Ber·ingung** f *the ringing* (*of birds*)

B·eringmeer n (nordöstl. Teil des Stillen Ozeans) *Bering Sea* **B·eringstraße** f (zw. Alaska u Sibirien) *Bering Strait*

Ber·itt m ~s/~e **1.** ⟨mil⟩ (Abteilung e–r Schwadron) *troop* **2.** *district of a mounted official* || ⟨for⟩ *district*

ber·itten a *mounted* (*infantry, police*); *horsed* (*regiments*); ~e Miliz *yeomanry* || (Regiment) ~ m *to mount, to horse* || ~ s *to be mounted* (od *on horseback*) || ein ≗er *a man on horseback*

Berk·an m ~s/~e (gewebter Wollstoff) *barracan, barragan*

B·erle f ⟨bot⟩ *upright water-parsnip*

berl·icke – **berl·ocke** adv *head over heels, helter-skelter*

Berl·in: du bist verrückt mein Kind, du mußt nach ~ ⟨fig⟩ *go to Bath* | Stadtteile: Berlin-Charlottenburg, -Dahlem, -Gr. Lichterfelde, -Grunewald, -Pankow, -Schöneberg, -Tempelhof, -Zehlendorf usw. **Berl·ine** f ~/~n (viersitziger Reisewagen) *Berlin* **Berl·iner** m ~s/~ **1.** *inhabitant* od *native of Berlin* **2.** °*large knapsack* **3.** [attr] *Berlin* (*opera*); ~ Kongreß *Berlin Congress* (1878) **Berl·inerbl·au** n ~s/ *Prussian* od *Berlin blue* **berl·inern** vi *to talk in a Berlin dialect* **berl·inerisch,** ⟨mst⟩ **berl·inisch** a (*of*) *Berlin, Berlinian*

B·erlitzschule f ~/~n (nach Deutschamerikaner M. D. Berlitz, †1921) *Berlitz School*

Berl·ocke f ~/~n *trinket*

B·erme f ~/~n *benching*; ⟨fort⟩ *berm*

Berm·udagras n ⟨bot⟩ = Hundszahn **Berm·udainseln, Berm·udas, Berm·uden** f pl (Inselgruppe im Atlant. Ozean) *the Bermudas* pl **berm·udisch** a *Bermudian*

Bern n (schweiz. Stadt u Kanton) *Bern*(*e*)

B·erner m, **~in** f *Bernese* **~ ·Alpen,** die pl *the Bernese Alps* pl; ~ Klause [f] (Engpaß) *Berner Klause* || ~ Konvention [f] ⟨post, rail, Lit⟩ *Berne Convention* (*1886*) || ~ Oberland [n] *Bernese Oberland*

B·ernhard, der Große (Kleine) St. ~ (Alpenberge) *the Great* (*Little*) *Saint-Bernard*

Bernhard·iner m ~s/~ **1.** die ~ [pl] (Orden) *the Bernardines* [pl]; → Zisterzienser **2.** ⟨zoo⟩ (Hund) *St. Bernard* **~krebs** m = Einsiedlerkrebs

Bern·ikelgans f ⟨orn⟩ = Ringelgans

Bern·ina m (Gebirge der Rätischen Alpen)

B·ernstein m ~(e)s/~e **1.** *amber* || (schwarzer) *jet* **2.** [in comp] *amber* **~fang** m *amber-fishing* **~farbe** f *amber* **≗farben** a *amber* **~fischerei** f *amber fishing* **~kette** f *string of amber-beads*; *amber necklet* **~küste** f *the Amber Coast* **~säure** f ⟨chem⟩ *succinic acid* **~schmuck** *m amber-ornaments* pl **~schnecke** f ⟨zoo⟩ *succinea* (L) **~schnur** f → –kette **~spitze** f *amber cigar*(*ette*)*-holder* **b·ernsteinen** a *amber*

ber·ohren vt [h] (Wand) *to* (*cover, with*) *reed*

B·erserk m ~s/~er; **Bers·erker** m ~s/~ *berserker* **Bers·erkerwut** f *Berserker rage*

B·erstdruckprüfer m ⟨tech⟩ *bursting tester*

b·ersten **I.** vi [s] [barst/geborsten] **1.** (of surfaces) *to burst, rupture*; (of ice, glass, bubbles) *to break, crack*; (of a ship) *to split* || (of timber) *to spring* || es sieht aus, als wenn es ~ wollte *it looks as if it had reached bursting-point* **2.** ⟨fig⟩ (P) ~ vor.. *to burst with* (*envy, delight*); *to explode with* (*fury*); ~ vor Lachen *to burst with laughing, to burst* od *split one's sides*; ich berste vor Begierde z tun *I'm simply bursting to do* || *to brim with* (*energy*) **II.** ≗ n *burst* || dem ~ nahe *ready to burst*; (etw) zum ~ bringen *to burst* (*a th*) || zum ~ voll s v *to be bursting with* (*a th*)

B·ertram m ~s/~e ⟨bot⟩ (= Mutterkraut) *feverfew* || Deutscher ~ ⟨bot⟩ (= Sumpfgarbe) *sneezewort, wild pellitory* **~kamille** f ⟨bot⟩ *pellitory* **~wurzel** f ⟨pharm⟩ *pellitory*

ber·üchtigt a **1.** [attr] *notorious* (*smuggler*); *ill-famed, ill-reputed* **2.** [pred] *notorious* (wegen *for*); *infamous* (in der Geschichte *in history*; *for*) **≗sein** n *notoriety* (wegen *for*)

ber·ücken vt [h] **1.** †(täuschen) (jdn) *to beguile, deceive, to impose upon* || **2.** (bezaubern) (jdn) *to bewitch, captivate, charm*, → bezaubern **ber·ückend** a *bewitching* (*smile*), *captivating, charming*; *fascinating* (*beauty*)

ber·ücksichtigen vt [h] **1.** (etw) *to have regard* od *respect to* (*a th*); *to bear* (*a th*) *in mind*; *to consider* (*a th*); *to take* (*a th*) *into consideration* od *account*; *to allow for, to make allowance for* (*a th*); die Tatsache ~, daß.. *to make allowance for the fact that..*; etw in vollem Umfang ~ *to give one's fullest consideration to a th* || nicht ~ *to disregard*; jds Gefühle nicht ~ *to have no regard to a p's feelings* **2.** (jdn) *to consider*

|| jdn f. e–e Wahl nicht ~ *to count a p out*

Ber·ücksichtigung f ~/~en *consideration* (e–r S *of a th*) || ~ finden *to be considered; to be taken into consideration* || in ~ e–r S *in consideration of a th, considering a th*; in ~, daß.. *considering that..*; → Anbetracht || ohne ~ e–r S *without regard* od *reference to a th* || unter ~ e–r S *with* od *in reference to a th*; unter ~ dieser Umstände *in the light of these circumstances*; unter gebührender ~ aller Gründe *allowing for all the reasons*

Ber·ückung f ~/~en *captivation, fascination*

Ber·uf m ~(e)s/~e **1.** (göttlicher ~) = Berufung 1. **2.** innerer ~ (*inward*) *calling*; *vocation* (z *for*); *mission*; e–n ~ in sich fühlen *to feel a calling* (*for*) || (Amt, Aufgabe) *function, province* **3.** (weltlicher ~) **a.** (*habitual*) *occupation*; *business*; *calling, vocation*; ⟨fam⟩ *job*; Sterblichkeit nach ~en *occupational mortality* **b.** *career*; *walk of life* || *line* **c.** (geistiger ~) *profession*; (akademische ~e [pl] *the professional class*); der ~ e–s Juristen *the p. of a lawyer*; Jurist v ~ s *to be a lawyer by p.*; Diplomat v ~ ⟨Am⟩ *career man* || der freie ~ *the liberal profession* || [koll] die Angehörigen e–s ~s *the profession* || e–m ~e eigentümlich *professional* **d.** (Handwerks≈) *trade*; der ~ e–s Schlachters *the t. of a butcher*; Sch. v ~ s *to be a butcher by t.* **4.** e–n ~ **ausüben** *to practise* od *follow a profession*; e–n ~ ausübend *professional* || e–n ~ ergreifen *to enter upon a career* || e–n neuen ~ erlernen *to learn a new job* || e–m ~e nachgehen *to follow* od *pursue a profession, trade* || k–n festen ~ h *to be without a regular occupation*; *to have learned no profession* || s–n ~ verfehlt h *to have missed one's vocation* | sich **auf** e–n ~ vorbereiten *to prepare* (*o.s.*) *for a profession* || **im ~** stehen *to have a profession, to be a professional man*; im ~ stehend *professional* || je **nach** dem ~ *professionally* || jeder nach s–m ~ *everyone to his trade*

ber·ufen vt [h] [berief/~] **1.** (aufrufen, ernennen) ⟨ec⟩ (jdn) *to call* (an e–e Kirche *to a church*) || jdn z e–r Aufgabe ~ *to assign a task to a p*; *to designate a p to* od *for a task*; ~ w z tun *to be called* (*upon*) *to do*; jdn in ein Amt, e–n Stab ~ *to appoint a p to an office, to a staff*; jdn auf e–n Posten ~ *to appoint* od *nominate a p to a post*; jdn zum Barrister ~ *to call a p to the bar*; jdn zum Botschafter ~ *to appoint a p* (*to be*) *ambassador* || jdn als Professor an e–e Universität ~ *to appoint a p to a professorship*; an e–e U. als P. ~ w *to get a call to a professorial chair* **2.** (zus-rufen) (Versammlung etc.) *to call* (*together*), *to convene*; *to assemble*; (amtlich) *to convoke* **3.** (behexen; schädigen) ich will es nicht ~ *I won't cast an evil spell* (od *bring ill--luck*) *on it, I won't prejudice my chances* od *case by boasting* (etc.); → beschreien **4. sich ~ auf a.** sich auf etw als Zeugnis ~ *to appeal to a th* (: *I appeal to history*) || sich zur Entschuldigung auf e–e Anordnung ~ *to plead an order*; ..auf s–e Unwissenheit ~ *to plead one's ignorance* || darauf kannst du dich nicht ~ *you cannot take it as a precedent* | sich auf jdn als Zeugen ~ *to call a p to witness* od *in testimony* (*that*); *to appeal to a p* (*to say..*) **b.** (verblaßt) sich auf etw, jdn ~ *to refer to a th, a p*; *to adduce a th, to quote a p* (als *as*) || für Ihre Behauptung können Sie sich auf k–e Autorität ~ *there is no authority for your assumption*; auf ihn können Sie sich nicht als Autorität ~ *you cannot quote* od *take him as an authority*; auf welche Quelle können Sie sich ~? *what is your source? what source can you adduce* (*for..*)?

ber·ufen a **1.** [pred] ~ s *to be authorized* (*to do*); *to be competent, qualified* (z *for*; *to do*) || sich ~ fühlen *to feel a call* (*to write a play*); *to feel authorized, competent* (*to do*); sich nicht ~ fühlen *to feel no call* (*to do*) **2.** [attr] *qualified* (*judge*); *competent* (*critic*); *able*

ber·uflich 1. a *professional, vocational*; *occupational* || *professional* (*class*) || in ~er Angelegenheit *or* Hinsicht, zu ~en Zwecken *professionally* **2.** adv *by profession, by trade* || *professionally* (*trained*); → Berufs– 2. || ~ verhindert s *to be professionally prevented* (*from doing*) || ~ tätig s *to practise a profession*; *to have a job*, ⟨Am fam⟩ *to hang out one's shingle*

Ber·ufs— [in comp] **1.** mst *vocational* (*clothing*) || *professional* (*ability, cricketer, golfer*) || *occupational* (*group, class, disease, accident, training*, etc.) || *career* (*civil servant*; *diplomatist*) || *regular* (*officer*) **2.** (= beruflich ausgebildet *or* tätig als) *professional* (*actress, gardener, politician*, etc.) **~amt** n *professional advisory board* **~arbeit** f *professional work* **~ausbildung** f *vocational education* (od *training*); enge ~ *professionalism* **~beamte:** [der ~, ein ~r] m *professional official*; ⟨engl⟩ *civil servant* **~beamtentum** n *professionalism*; → *merit system* **~berater** m *vocational adviser* **~beratung** f *vocational guidance* **~charakter** m *professional character* od *status* **~diplomat** m → 1. **~einkommen** n *professional income* **~einwirkungen** f pl *occupational exposures* **~erziehung** f *professional education, vocational training* **~fach** n *profession, line of business* **≈fremd** a (*occupation*) *foreign to* (*a p*) || ~e Elemente ⟨agr⟩ *non-farmers*; etc. *non– etc.* **~fürsorge** f *occupational welfare* **~führung** f *vocational guidance* **~geheimnis** n *secrecy* || Bruch *or* Verletzung des ~ses *breach of* (*professional*) *secrecy* **~genosse** m *colleague* **~genossenschaft** f *Employers'* od *Employees' Liability Insurance Association*; (Handwerk) *trade association*; (Einzelhandel) *cooperative association*; (freie Berufe) *Institute of..* **~gliederung** f *occupational classification* **~haftpflichtversicherung** f *professional indemnity insurance* **~heer** n *regular army* **~kleidung** f *vocational clothes*; *overalls* **~krankheit** f *industrial disease* **~kunde** f *science concerned with professions and trades* **~leben** n *professional life*; im ~ *professionally* (: *p. known as..*); im ~ stehend *professional* **~lenkung** f *vocational guidance* **~leute** [pl] *professional people* **≈los** a *professionless*; *without a profession* **≈mäßig** a *professional*; nicht ~ *unprofessional* **~mensch** m *professional man, professional*; enger ~ *professionalist* **~mobilität** f ⟨stat, demog⟩ *occupational mobility* **~musiker** m *professional musician* **~nachwuchslenkung** f *juvenile vocational guidance* **~offizier** m *regular officer* **~orientierung** f *occupational guidance* **~pflicht** f *professional duty* **~schule** f ⟨Ger⟩ *continuation school extending over 3 years* **~spezialist** m = Fachspezialist **~spieler, ~sportler** m *pro*(*fessional*) **~spielertum** n *professionalism* **~sprache** f *jargon, cant*; *terms* [pl] *peculiar to a special profession* od *trade* **~stand** m *profession*(*al status*) **≈ständisch** a *professional* **~statistik** f *occupational statistics* [pl] **~sterblichkeit** f (spezifische) *occupational mortality* **≈tätig** a *professional, practising a profession*; *career* [attr] (*woman*) || ~e Hausfrau *homemaker and careerist* | die B·gen *the occupied population* **~umschulung** f *occupational retraining* **~unfähigkeit** f *disablement* **~verbrecher** m *professional criminal* **~verkehr** m ⟨rail, etc⟩ *traffic of season--ticket holders* **~vormundschaft** f *guardianship over illegitimate children exercised by an authorized person* **~wahl** f *choise of profession* od *trade* **~wechsel** m *change of profession* od *trade* **~wettkampf** m *vocational competition* **≈widrig** a *unprofessional* (*behavio*[*u*]*r*) **~zugehörige** m/f pl ⟨demog-agr, etc.⟩ *population dependent on* (*agriculture*, etc.); (*agricultural* od *farm*) *population* **~zweck** m *professional aim*; zu ~en *professionally*

Ber·ufung f ~/~en **1.** ⟨rel⟩ (göttliche, innere ~) *call* (z *to*); *calling, vocation* (z *for*) ‖ ~ der Apostel *Call of the Apostles* **2.** *appointment* (in e–n Stab *to a staff*), *nomination* (auf e–n Posten *to a post*) ‖ ⟨univ⟩ *call* (auf e–n Stuhl *to a chair*), ~ zum Barrister *call to the bar* **3.** ⟨jur⟩ *appeal* (bei *to*; gegen *from*); ~ in Strafsachen *criminal appeal* ‖ ~ einlegen *to* (*give notice of*) *appeal* (gegen *against*); *to file a notice of appeal*; *to lodge* od *file an appeal* (gegen *against*); .. in e–r S *to appeal a case* ‖ e–r ~ stattgeben *to allow an appeal* **4.** ⟨übtr⟩ ~ **auf** (etw, jdn) *appeal to*; *reference to* (*a th, a p*); unter ~ auf *referring to*; → berufen vt 4. b. **5.** *the calling together*; *convocation* (*of Parliament*)

Ber·ufungs— [in comp] **~ausschuß** m *board of review* | ⟨jur⟩ **~beklagter** m *appellee* **~frist** f *time allowed for appeal* **~gericht** n *court of appeal* **~instanz** f *court of appeal*; *appellate tribunal* **~kammer** f *court of appeal* **~klage** f *appeal*; *writ of error* **~kläger** *appellant*; *plaintiff in error* **~recht** n **1.** *right of appeal* **2.** (Ernennungsrecht) *patronage*; → Besetzung ‖ → Rechtsmittelfrist **~verfahren** n *proceedings* [pl] *of a court of appeal*

ber·uhen vi [h] **1. ~ in a.** → ruhen in **b.** (of feelings) *to depend on* (: *ah, on what little things does happiness d.!*) **2. ~ auf** (of facts, etc.) *to be based* od *founded* (*up*)*on, to rest on*; s–e Behauptungen ~ auf Tatsachen *his assertions are based on facts*; ein Stück ~d auf.. *a play based* (*up*)*on..* ‖ *to depend on* (*happiness depends on..*) → 1. b. ‖ *to be due to*; dies beruht auf e–m Irrtum *this is a mistake* ‖ auf Gegenseitigkeit ~ *to be reciprocal* (: *their love was r.*) ‖ auf Tatsachen ~d *founded upon fact* sg **3.** etw (od die Dinge) **auf sich ~ l** *to let a matter rest, to let the thing drop, to give a th a rest, to leave things as they are*; wir können die S nicht auf sich ~ l *the matter cannot rest here*; wir wollen das auf sich ~ l *we will not labour the point* ‖ es dabei ~ l *to let it rest there*; *to leave it at that*

ber·uhigen vt **1.** jdn ~: (e–n Erregten, Erzürnten etc.) *to appease, mollify, pacify, soothe, tranquillize*; (Baby) *to lull*; *to sing* (*a child*) *to rest* ‖ (Unzufriedene) *to quiet* ‖ (v Furcht etc. befreien) *to ease, reassure*; *relieve*; *comfort*; *to cheer up* **2.** ⟨bib⟩ (of God) (Meer, Sturm) *to calm* (*down*), *to quiet* **3.** ⟨übtr⟩ (Schmerz) *to allay, alleviate, assuage, mitigate, reduce, soothe, still* ‖ (Erregung, Leidenschaft etc.) *to assuage, to calm* (*down*); *to mollify, quiet, soften, soothe, still* ‖ (Nerven) *to settle* (*one's, a p's nerves*) ‖ sein Gewissen ~ *to salve one's conscience* **4. sich ~ a.** (P) *to compose o.s.*; *to compose* od *settle one's mind*; *to set one's mind at ease*; ~ Sie sich! *compose yourself*! er beruhigte sich bei dem Gedanken.. *he found relief in the throught..* ‖ sich mit der H. ~ *so salve o.s. with the hope* ‖ er hat sich jetzt ganz –gt *his mind is now entirely at ease* **b.** (of anger, the sea) *to calm* od *quiet down*; *to lull*

ber·uhigend a *calming, quieting, soothing* (*words*); *reassuring* (*effect*); *tranquillizing* (*factor*); ~es Gefühl *feeling of relief, relief* ‖ ⟨med⟩ *sedative* (*drug*); ~es Mittel n *sedative*

Ber·uhigung f ~/~en **1.** (Beschwichtigung) *appeasement, mollification, quieting, relaxation, soothing, tempering, tranquillization* (*of an angry p*); *pacification* (*of a country*) | (innere) *reassurance* (: *to find r. in..*); *consolation* ; *ease, relief* (f. jdn *to a p*); zur ~ der Gemüter.. *in order to relieve* od *ease their minds* (*he said..*); es ist mir e–e ~ *it is a relief to me* (*to know*); .. zu ihrer ~ (*he said it*) *to set her mind at rest* **2.** ⟨bib⟩ *calming, quieting* (*of the sea*) **3.** *alleviation, mitigation* (*of pain*) ‖ *calming, quieting* (*of anger, etc.*) **~smittel** n, **~stablette** f *tranquillizer, sedative*

ber·ühmt a *celebrated, famous, noted* (wegen *for*); *illustrious, renowned*; ⟨theat⟩ ~er Sänger (etc.) *star* ‖ °ich fand den Wein nicht sehr ~ *I did not find the wine so wonderful* ‖ weit~ *far-famed* ‖ sich ~ m *to render o.s. famous, to make a name for o.s.* ‖ ~ w *to acquire reputation*; *to rise to eminence*; ⟨fam⟩ *to boom*

Ber·ühmtheit f **1.** ~/ *fame, renown*; *eminence*; ~ erlangen *to rise to e.* **2.** ~/~en (P) *man of renown*; *celebrity*; die ~en [pl] *the celebrities* [pl] ‖ ⟨fam⟩ *lion*; ⟨theat & film⟩ *star*

ber·ührbar a *touchable*; *tangible*

ber·ühren 1. vt/i [h] **A.** vt **1.** (P) (etw, jdn mit der Hand ~) *to touch*; *handle* (*a th*) ‖ *to sweep* (*the strings*) ‖ etw nicht ~ *to leave a th alone*; er hat sein Essen nicht berührt *he has not touched his meal* ‖ (Oberfläche) flüchtig ~ *to skim*; (etw, jdn) *to touch*; ~ Sie mich ja nicht! *don't dare to lay a finger on me*! **2.** (S) (etw) *to touch, to meet* (: *where the neck-muscles meet the head*); *to reach, to border on, to be contiguous to* (*a th*); leicht ~ *to graze* (: *the bullet grazed his left hand*) | sein Kopf berührt fast die Decke *his head nearly touches the ceiling* ‖ (of ships) (den Hafen) *to call* (od *touch*) *at* ‖ ⟨übtr⟩ ⟨math⟩ *to be tangent of* **3.** (erwähnen) (etw) *to touch upon, to mention*; *to allude to, to refer briefly to* (*a th*) ‖ etw nicht ~ *to slide over a th*; e–e Frage nicht ~ *to leave a question alone* ‖ (Gegenstand) leicht ~ *to touch* **4.** ⟨übtr⟩ jdn, etw ~ **a.** (betreffen) (jdn, jds Interessen) *to concern, to touch* **b.** (innerlich ~) *to affect*; berührt w *to be affected*; es –rte ihn zu sehr, als daß man darüber hätte sprechen können *it went too deep with him to be spoken of*, .., als daß er hätte darüber spr. k. *he was too deeply affected for words*; jds Gefühle ~ *to come home to a p's feelings* er wurde durch diese Sticheleien nicht berührt *he was not affected with these taunts*; s–e Bosheit berührt mich nicht *his malice leaves me cold* | **jdn (un)angenehm** ~ *to* (*dis*)*please a p*, (*to jar upon a p*) ‖ (un)angenehm –rt w *or* s *to be* (*un*)*pleasantly struck*; jdn angenehm ~ *to give a p a pleasant sensation*; es berührt uns angenehm *we are agreeably surprised* (*that*), *it is pleasing to us* (*that*) ‖ schmerzlich –rt s *to be pained*; jds Auge (etc.) unangenehm ~ → beleidigen 2.; (un)angenehm berührt (*un*)*pleasantly affected* ‖ peinlich berührt *distressed* **5. sich ~** (S) *to touch* (: *the wires t.*); *to meet*; (of events, etc.) *to concur* ‖ sich ~ mit (etw) *to be connected with* (*a th*), *to touch* (*a th*) ‖ ⟨math⟩ sich ~d mit *tangent to* ‖ ⟨math & biol⟩ sich eng ~ mit *to osculate with* | (P) sich in s–r Meinung ~ mit *to concur with* (*a p*), *to be in agreement with* (*a p*) **B.** vi **es berührt** seltsam, unangenehm *it is strange* (*that*) **II.** ≗ n durch leichtes ~ *by gently touching*; = **Ber·ührung** f ~/~en **1.** (S) *contiguity* (mit *with*) ‖ ⟨a. math⟩ *contact*; ⟨el⟩ ~ zweier Stromleiter *contact* (: *to bring into c. with*); die Drähte w in ~ gebracht.. *are made to touch* ‖ in ~ k *to touch, meet* | ⟨übtr⟩ *connexion* (*between Church and State*) **2.** (P) ⟨eig⟩ *touch*; mit e–r unterwürfigen ~ s–r Mütze *with a submissive touch to his cap* ‖ bei der leisesten ~ *on the slightest touch* ‖ in ~ s mit *to be in touch with, to be within touch of* (*a th*) ‖ ⟨med⟩ Ansteckung durch ~ *contagion*; P., die sich durch ~ angesteckt h kann *contact* | ⟨übtr⟩ *connexion, contact, touch* (mit jdm, etw *with a p, a th*); enge ~ *close contact*; → Kontakt | (Erwähnung) *mention* (*of a th*); *reference* (e–r S *to a th*) | in ~ bleiben *to keep in touch* (*with a p*) ‖ in ~ bringen *to bring into contact* (*with*); in ~ k *to get into touch, to come into contact*, ⟨fam⟩ *to rub shoulders* (*with a p*) ‖ in ~ s → oben ‖ in ~ stehen *to be in connexion* od *touch* (*with a p*)

Ber·ührungs- ~bereich m *touch* **~ebene** f ⟨math⟩ *tangent plane* **~elektrizität** f *contact electricity* **~linie** f ⟨math⟩ *tangent* **~punkt** m ⟨übtr⟩ *point of contact* (: *to have many points of c. with..*) **~schutz** m ⟨el⟩ (*shock*) *protection* (*from accidental contacts*) ‖ mit ~ versehen [a] *screen-protected, screened* | ~̲sicher [a] *all--insulated* (*switch*) **~spannung** f ⟨el⟩ *contact voltage* **~winkel** m *angle of contact*

ber·ußen vt [h] (etw) *to soot*; *to cover with soot*

Ber·yll m ~s/~e ⟨minr⟩ *beryl* **Ber·yllium** n ~s/ *beryllium, glucinum* (L)

bes·äen vt [h] (Land) *to sow, seed*; *to crop* (*with*); ⟨Am⟩ *to stock* ‖ ⟨fig⟩ *to stud, strew* (*with*); [mst pp] **besät** mit *dotted, spangled, sprinkled, sown, strewn, studded with*; (bunt ~) *dappled* od *speckled with*; wirr ~ *littered* (*with*); mit Sternen besät *star-spangled*; *alive with* (*worms*, etc.); *crowded with people*

†**bes·age** adv ~ daß *to the effect that, saying that* ‖ ~ [gen] *by virtue of*

bes·agen vt [h] (melden) (of rumours) *to say*; *purport* ‖ (bedeuten) *to import, imply* (*a th*; *that*); *mean, signify* ‖ ein Befehl ~d *an order saying* (*that..*) | dies besagt nur *this is only saying* (*that*); es besagt mehr als das *it implies more than that* ‖ das besagt viel *that is saying a good deal*; das besagt sehr viel *that makes all the difference* ‖ das besagt nichts, das will nichts ~ *that is of no consequence, that does not count* ‖ das will wenig ~ *it little matters* ‖ → bedeuten

bes·agt a ⟨off⟩ (*afore*)*said*; *specified* (*time*) ‖ v den ~en Krankheiten *of the diseases under discussion* ‖ ⟨jur⟩ unter ~er Nummer stehend *so numbered* ‖ um auf ~en Hammel zurückzukommen *to return to our muttons* (*let us suppose..*)

bes·aiten vt [h] (Geige) *to string* **besaitet** a *stringed* (*violin*) | zart ~ ⟨fig⟩ *finely* (od *delicately*)*-strung* (*mind*); *sensitive, easily affected*

B·esam m ~s/~e (Kugelfries) ⟨arch⟩ *pellet, bizant*

bes·amen vt [h] ⟨bot⟩ *to strew with seed*

Bes·amung f ~/~en ⟨physiol⟩ (*artificial*) *insemination* ‖ ⟨bot⟩ *sowing*; natürliche ~ *natural seeding* ‖ ⟨vet⟩ *artificial insemination*

Bes·an m ~s/~e ⟨mar⟩ (Gaffelsegel) *miz*(*z*)*en* (*-sail*); *spanker* **~baum** m ⟨mar⟩ *spanker-boom* **~gaffel** f ⟨mar⟩ *spanker-gaff* **~mast** m ⟨mar⟩ *miz*(*z*)*en-mast* **~segel** n = Besan

bes·änftigen vt [h] **1.** (jdn, erregte Gemüter) *to appease, assuage, mollify, pacify, soothe, tranquillize* ‖ (Unzufriedene) *to quiet* **2.** ⟨bib⟩ (of God) (Sturm) *to calm* (*down*), *to quiet* **3.** ⟨übtr⟩ (Schmerz) *to alleviate, mitigate* ‖ (Erregung, Leidenschaft) *to assuage, to calm* (*down*), *to mitigate, mollify, quiet, soften* ‖ → beruhigen, beschwichtigen **be·sänftigend** a *calming, soothing* **Bes·änftigung** f ~/~en **1.** *appeasement, mollification, soothing* (*of an angry p*) **2.** ⟨bib⟩ *calming, quieting* (*of the sea*) **3.** *mitigation* (*of pain*) ‖ *calming, quieting* (*of anger*) ‖ → Linderung **~spolitik** f *appeasement*

bes·ät a → besäen

bes·aß 1. & 3. sg pret v besitzen

Bes·atz m ~es/~̲e *border, braid*(*ing*); *edging, trimming*; Litzen~̲ *piping* ‖ ⟨mil⟩ Uniform~̲ *facings* [pl]; Streifen~̲ *stripes* [pl] ‖ Falten~̲ *falbala*; loser ~ *flounce* | (Schuh~̲) *vamp* **~artikel** m [pl] *trimmings* [pl] **~schnur** f *gimp, gymp*

Bes·atzung f ~/~en **1.** ⟨mil⟩ *garrison*; (e–n Ort) mit e–r ~ versehen *to garrison* | ⟨mar⟩ *crew, the ship's company*; *all hands*; mit der gesamten ~ (gesunken).. *with all hands* ‖ volle zulässige ~ *complement* (*of a ship*); ~setat *scheme of complement* ‖ (Ggs totes Material) *personnel* | ⟨aero⟩ *flight crew, air-crew* ‖ → Belegschaft **2.** *troops* [pl] *of a fortification* **3.** *occupation--troops, occupying forces* [pl] **4.** ⟨tech⟩ (~ am Bart des Türschlosses) *wards* [pl] **~samt** n *occupation office* **~sbehörde** f *occupying authority* **~sbereich** m *occupied zone* **~sdienst** m *occupational duties* pl **~sgeld** n *scrip money*; ⟨engl⟩ *British Armed Forces Vouchers* (*BAFVs*) **~sgericht** n *occupation court* **~sheer** n *army of occupation* **~skosten(erhebung** f) pl (*imposition of*) *occupation costs* **~smacht** f *occupying power* **~smitglied** n ⟨mar, aero⟩ *crewman* **~sstatut** n *occupation statute* **~sstreitkräfte** f pl *forces of occupation, occupying forces* **~struppen** f pl = Besatzung 3. **~szone** f *zone of occupation*; angloamerikanische ~ (1945) *bizone*, ⟨fam⟩ *bizonia*

°**bes·aufen** vrefl [h] [→ saufen] sich ~ ⟨sl⟩ *to fuddle*; *to get drunk*

bes·äumen vt [h] (Balken, Bretter) *to edge* ‖ (Blech) *to edge-plane*

besch·ädigen vt [h] (Gepäck etc.) *to damage*; (Ernte) *to injure* (: *injured by a storm*); (Blumen) *to hurt* (: *hurt by drought*); (Flugzeug etc.) *to cripple, disable* → verderben, -nichten → kriegsbeschädigt **Besch·ädigung** f ~/~en *damage, injury* (e–r S *to a th*) ‖ ⟨arts⟩ *defacement* ‖ mechanische ~ *mechanical damage* → Seeschaden

besch·affen vt [h] [pp beschafft] **1.** etw ~ *to find, procure, provide, supply, furnish a th* (f. *for a th*); Sie müssen alles Material selbst ~ *you must find everything* ‖ (nicht) z ~ (*un*)*procurable*; schwer z ~ *difficult to procure* **2.** jdm etw ~ *to find* (od *get, procure, provide*) *a p a th* (od *a th for ap*) ‖ **sich** [dat] **etw** ~ *to procure, secure a th*; *to get o.s. a th*; jeder kann es sich leicht ~ *it can readily be procured by anybody*

besch·affen a [mst pred] **1.** ~ s *to be constituted*; die Einrichtungen sind wie die unseren ~ *the institutions are constituted like our own* ‖ wie ist der Weg ~ *how is the road*? wie ist es mit s–r Gesundheit ~? *how is his health*; *what about his h.*? ‖ er ist nun mal so ~ *he is like that*; die S ist folgendermaßen ~ *the matter stands thus*; damit ist es so ~ *it is like this*; so ist die Welt ~ *that's the way of the world*; wie schlecht auch immer es ~ s mag *however bad it may be* **2.** [in comp] *conditioned*; gut ~ *well-conditioned*, schlecht ~ *ill-conditioned* ‖ gut ~ *in condition, in good repair*; schlecht ~ *out of condition* (od *repair*) | ~̲**heit** f ~/~en **1.** (Zustand) *condition* (*of a house, of goods*) ‖ *state* (: *in an unfinished state*); nach ~ der Umstände *according to circumstances* ‖ Körper~̲ *constitution* ‖ Geistes~̲ *state of mind* **2.** (natürliche ~) *the nature* (*of coal*, etc.) ‖ (charakteristische ~) *character* (*of a region*; *of poverty*); *quality* (*of art*); *turn* ‖ *structure, texture* (*of the skin*) **3.** (P) *nature*; *quality* ‖ *disposition*, charakterliche ~ *character* **4.** [a + ~ oft durch ein Subst.]: glatte ~ *slickness*; rauhe ~ *roughness*; knotenartige ~ *nodosity* ‖ Materialien ähnlicher ~ *similar materials*

Besch·affung f ~/~en *procurement, procuring*; *acquisition, attainment* ‖ ⟨Am⟩ staatl. Bedarfs~̲ *procurement* ‖ → Anschaffung **~samt** n, ~stelle f *procurement office* **~sgesetz** n *proc. act* **~sministerium** n *Ministry of Supplies*

besch·äftigen vt [h] **1.** jdn ~ **a.** (P) *to busy a p*; *to keep a p busy* ‖ (anstellen) *to employ* (f. *for*); [bes pass] *to engage*; → beschäftigt **b.** (S) (jdn) angestrengt ~ *to exercise* (*a p*); das Rätsel beschäftigt den Historiker sowohl wie den Biologen *the riddle exercises the historian as well as the biologist*; jdn ständig im Geiste ~ *to be constantly in a p's mind* **2.** (Aufmerksamkeit, Kräfte) *to absorb, to engross* **3. a.** sich geistig ~ *to exercise one's mind* **b.** sich ~ mit (P) *to concern o.s.* (od *occupy one's mind*) *with*; *to employ* od *busy o.s. with* od *in*; *to deal with*; *to engage in*; *to go into* (*a th*); *to take* (*a th*) *up*; *to work at* od *on* (*a th*); sich damit ∼ z tun *to occupy o.s. with* od *by doing* | (S) *to deal with, to be concerned with* (: *the lecture is concerned with*..); Stücke, mit denen sich dieser Abschnitt besonders beschäftigt, sind.. *plays which are the particular concern of this chapter are*.. **beschäftigt** a **1.** [pred] *busy* (mit *with*); *engaged* (*in*); eifrig ∼ mit *agog over* (*a th*) ‖ *in employ*; ∼ bei jdm *in the employ of a p*; im Tuchhandel ∼ s *to be in the drapery way* od *line* | mit sich selbst ∼ *self-centered, introspective* (*mind*) | ∼ s *to be busy* ‖ ∼ s mit *to be occupied* (od *taken up*) *with, to be engaged in* od *on* (*a th*); *to be at work over* (*a th*); *to be employed on* (*a th*); damit ∼ s z tun *to be occupied with* od *on doing*; *to be concerned* (od *employed, engaged*) *in doing*; eifrig ∼ s z tun *to be busy doing*; vor allem *or* in erster Linie –gt s mit .. *to be preoccupied with* .. **2.** [attr] *busy* (*man*) ‖ *diligent*

Besch·äftigtsein n *preoccupation* (*with*)

Besch·äftigung f ∼/∼en *employment*; *occupation* (mit *in*); *pursuit* (mit *of*) ‖ *business*; *work* ‖ gedankliche ∼ *preoccupation* ‖ ohne ∼ s, k–e ∼ h *to be out of employ* od *work*; *to be at a loose end* **∼sbedingungen** f pl *terms of service*; *conditions of employment* **∼slage** f *labo(u)r market* **≗slos** a *unemployed*; [pred] *out of employ* (od *work*; *without occupation* **≗slosigkeit** f = Arbeitslosigkeit **∼snachweis** m *employment record*; *certificate of service* **∼stherapie** f *occupational therapie*

besch·älen vt [h] (Stuten) *to cover, to horse* ⟨a. fig⟩ **Besch·äler** m ∼s/∼ *stallion, stud-horse, sire* **Besch·älseuche** f ⟨vet⟩ *dourine* (Fr) **Besch·älung** f ∼/∼en *covering* (*of a mare*) **Besch·älzeit** f *covering-season*

besch·allen vt [h] ⟨phys⟩ (S) *to expose.. to ultrasonic waves* **Besch·allung** f ∼/∼en *exposure to ultr. w.s* **∼sanlage** f *public address system*

besch·alten vt [h] *to wire* **Besch·altung** f ∼/∼en *wiring*

besch·ämen vt [h] (jdn) *to make* (*a p*) *ashamed, to fill* (*a p*) *with shame, to put* (*a p*) *to shame, to put* (*a p*) *to the blush*; *to shame* (*a p*), tief ∼ *to humiliate*; sein Fleiß beschämt alle s–e Kollegen *his industry shames all his colleagues* ‖ *to abash, discomfit*; ⟨bib⟩ *to confound*; *confuse* | (übertreffen) *to eclipse, outrival, outshine* (*a p*); *to throw* (*a p*) *into the shade* **besch·ämend** a *humiliating* (*feeling*) **besch·ämt** a *ashamed* (über *of*); *abashed* ‖ ⟨poet⟩ *shamed* **Besch·ämung** f ∼/∼en *abashment*; *humiliation, confusion* ‖ (Zustand) *shame* ‖ zu m–r ∼ gestehe ich *I confess to my shame* ‖ jdn durch ∼ dahin bringen z tun *to shame a p into doing*

besch·atten vt [h] *to shade*, (*over*)*shadow* ‖ ⟨übtr⟩ *to outshine* ‖ (P) *to shadow*, ⟨fam⟩ *tail* (*a suspect*); er wird –ttet *he is being shadowed*, ⟨Am sl⟩ *there is a tail on him*

Besch·au f **1.** *examination of meat in abattoirs* ‖ *examination of prescribed degree of fineness for gold*, etc. ‖ *customs examination* **2.** ⟨philos⟩ *contemplation*; innere ∼ *introspection*

besch·auen 1. vt [h] etw (*or* jdn) ∼, sich [dat] etw ∼ *to look* od *gaze at, to have a look at a th* (*a p*); *to view a th* (*a p*) ‖ (prüfend) *to look a p over*; *to look into* od *over a th*; *to examine, inspect a th* ‖ (im Geiste) *to contemplate a th* | **sich** innerlich ∼ *to introspect* **2.** ≗ n *gaze*; *view* ‖ *examination, inspection* ‖ → Beschau 2. **Besch·auer** m ∼s/∼ *observer* ‖ *examiner, inspector*; Fleisch≗ *meat inspector, inspector of meat* ‖ ⟨jur⟩ Leichen≗ *coroner*

besch·aulich a *thoughtful, meditative, speculative* ‖ ⟨rel & philos⟩ *contemplative*; *introspective* | *peaceful*; *quiet* (*village*); *tranquil, unruffled* ‖ *comfortable* (*life*) | ≗**keit** [f] ⟨rel⟩ *contemplativeness, contemplation*; *thoughtfulness*; *introspection* ‖ *peacefulness*; *quiet, quietness*; *quitude*; *tranquillity* ‖ *comfort* **B.uung** f → Beschau(en)

Besch·auzeichen n *inspector's mark*

Besch·eid m ∼(e)s/∼e **1.** ⟨jur⟩ *decision*; *decree, rescript* | ⟨übtr⟩ *answer*; ⟨off⟩ *reply*; (Steuer≗ etc.) *assessment note*; abschlägiger ∼ *refusal* ‖ ∼ sagen → 3. **2.** (Anweisung) [nur in]: bis auf weiteren ∼ *till further orders* od *instructions* **3.** (Nachricht, Auskunft) ∼ **erhalten** *to be informed* (*that*) | jdm ∼ **geben** *to let a p known, to tell a p*; geben Sie mir bitte zur rechten Zeit ∼ *kindly tell me in time* ‖ jdm v etw ∼ geben *to inform a p of a th* | ∼ **hinterlassen** *to leave word* (bei *with*) | jdm ∼ **sagen** *to answer a p, to give a p the word*; → ∼ geben; jdm ∼ sagen l *to send a p word* (*that*..) ‖ ⟨übtr⟩ jdm (gehörig) ∼ sagen *to give a p a piece of one's mind*; *to tick a p off* **4.** jdm ∼ **tun** (= zutrinken) *to pledge a p* **5.** (Kenntnis) ∼ **wissen** *to* (*be in the*) *know*; *to know one's way* ‖ .. über etw *to be familiar with a th, to know of a th* ‖ ⟨fam⟩ *to know one's stuff*; *to kn. what's what, the score, the ropes, the ins and outs*; *to know a th* od *trick or two* ‖ → bekannt, vertraut s mit ‖ °sie weiß ∼ ⟨sex⟩ *she's had it, she's been there*; Leute, die ∼ wissen *people that know*; wissen Sie ∼, wie man das macht? *do you know how to do it*? ‖ ich weiß ∼ hier im Hause *I know my way about the house*; ich weiß k–n ∼ hier *I am a stranger here*; in e–r S genau ∼ wissen *to know the ins and outs of a matter*; über jdn ganz genau ∼ wissen *to know all about a p*

besch·eiden vt [h] [→ scheiden] **1.** [nur pass] jdm beschieden s *to be assigned* (od *allotted, destined*) *to a p*; ihm war ein hartes Los b. *his lot had been a hard one*; ihm war es nicht b. *it was not granted* (od *given*) *to him* (*to do*) **2.** jdn ∼ = jdm Bescheid geben, → Bescheid 3. ‖ jdn abschlägig ∼ *to refuse a p, to give a p a refusal*; abschlägig beschieden w *to meet with a refusal* **3.** (beordern) jdn ∼ *to order* od *direct a p* (nach *to*; z tun *to do*); jdn z sich ∼ *to send for a p*; z s–m Regiment beschieden w *to be ordered to join one's regiment*; ich habe ihn herbeschieden *I have ordered him here* ‖ jdn gerichtlich ∼ *to summon a p* **4. sich** ∼ *to desist*; *to refrain*; *to resign o.s.* (mit *to*); sich z ∼ wissen *to know one's place* ‖ → abfinden 2. b.; sich begnügen

besch·eiden 1. a (P) *modest* (*man*), *unassuming, unpretentious, lowly* (*scholar*); *reserved*; *humble*; *demure* (*girl*); *sober* ‖ *unassuming* (*manners*) | (S) *unpretentious* (*buildings*); *modest* (*sum*); *moderate* (*claim*; *income, means, prices*); *small* (*profit*); *frugal* (*meal*); äußerst ∼ *skin-and-bone* (Etat *budget*); sich ein ∼es Ziel setzen *to aim low* (*in order to achieve something*) **2.** adv *modestly, unassumingly, unpretentiously*; *in a small way* ‖ ∼ auftreten ⟨fam⟩ *to draw in one's horns* | ≗**heit** f ∼/ *modesty, unassumingness, unpretentiousness* l *self-effacement*; *reserve*; *demureness, soberness* | *moderateness* (*of claims, prices*)

[1]**besch·einen** vt [h] [→ scheinen] etw (jdn) ∼ (of the sun) *to shine upon a th* (*a p*); → bestrahlen

[2]**besch·ein(ig)en** vt [h] (etw) *to attest, certify*; *certificate* ‖ ⟨jur⟩ ich bescheinige hiermit *I do hereby certify* (*that*..); hiermit wird bescheinigt *this is to certify* (*that*..) ‖ (bezeugen) ich bescheinige Herrn N. gern, daß.. *I have much pleasure in testifying to Mr. N. that*.. | ⟨com⟩ den Empfang e–r Summe ∼ *to give a receipt for a sum* **B.igung** f ∼/∼en *attestation, certification* ‖ [konkr] (amtlich beglaubigte) *certificate* ‖ ⟨com⟩ (Empfangs≗) *receipt*

°**besch·eißen** vt [h] [→ scheißen] ⟨übtr⟩ (jdn) *to do (a p) in the eye* || → beschissen || l Sie sich nicht ~ ⟨Am fam⟩ *don't take any wooden nickels*

besch·enken vt [h] jdn mit etw ~ *to make a p a present of a th, to make a donation of a th to a p, to present a p with a th, to bostow a th (up)on a p* || er wurde reichlich beschenkt *he was overwhelmed* od *showered with gifts, he got many presents* | **B.kte(r** m) f *recipient of a gift*; ⟨jur⟩ *donee* **B.kung** f ~/~en die ~ jds mit e–r S *the bestowal of a th on a p, the donation of a th to a p*

***besch·eren** vt [h] [→ scheren] (T) *to shear* || *to shave*

besch·eren vt [h] **1.** (zuteilen, bestimmen) jdm etw ~ *to assign* (od *allot, destine) a th to a p* || *to give a p a th* (od *a th to a p*), *to bestow a th (up)on a p*; (of God) *to send a p a th* || ihm wurde ein gutes Weib beschert *heaven sent him a good wife* **2.** (beschenken) die Kinder (*den Kindern) ~ zu Weihnachten *to present the children with gifts at Christmas*; ⟨engl⟩ Dienstboten (etc.) ~ *to give Ch. boxes to servants*; beschert w *to receive Ch.s b.s* **B.rung** f **1.** Weihnachts≗ *distribution of Christmas-presents*; *distribution of Christmas-boxes (to servants)* || Geburtstags≗ *distribution of birthday presents* **2.** ⟨fig⟩ eine schöne ~! *a pretty* (od *nice) kettle of fish*! *a pretty business* (od *pass*)! *a nice* od *pretty how--dye-do*! *a nice mess*! *a blessed nuisance*! || da h wir die ~! *here's a pretty go*! *there we* od *you are*! || [konkr] (Kram) die ganze ~ *the whole show, the whole bag of tricks*

besch·ichtet a ⟨phot⟩ *coated* (doppelseitig *on both sides*)

besch·icken vt [h] **1.** (in Ordnung bringen) *to put* od *set in order*; sein Haus ~ *to set one's affairs in order*; *to make one's will* || (besorgen) *to do, to arrange* **2.** eine Ausstellung ~ *to exhibit*; *to send exhibits (to an exhibition)*; e–e Messe ~ *to send goods to a fair*; e–n Kongreß (etc.) ~ *to send deputies* od *representatives to a congress* **3.** ⟨tech⟩ (Hochofen) *to charge, feed, fill* || (Metall) *to alloy* **4.** ***sich ~** = sich anschicken **Besch·icker** m ~s/~ (Messe≗) *exhibitor* || ⟨tech⟩ *feeder* **Besch·ickung** f ~/~en **1.** die ~ e–r S *putting* od *setting a th in order* **2.** die ~ e–r Messe *the sending of goods to a fair*; → beschicken 2. **3.** ⟨tech⟩ [konkr] *charge (of a furnace)*; die ~ aufgeben *to charge* (od *feed, fill*) *the furnace* || *alloy (of metal)*; ⟨met a.⟩ *burden*; ⟨at⟩ *feed* || ⟨aero, mar⟩ **Besch·ickungs-** [in comp] *charging* || ~anlage [f] *ch. plant* || ~kran [m] *ch. crane* ~material [n] (Hochofen≗) *charge, burden*

besch·ieden pp v bescheiden, → d.

besch·ießen vt/i [→ schießen] [h] **I.** vt **1.** ⟨mil⟩ den Feind ~ *to fire at* od *on the enemy* || (Stadt) *to bomb, bombard, cannonade, to shell*; e–e Stadt ~ können *to have got one's range on a town* (mit *with*) || (of guns) *to play on* || (Schiff) der Länge nach ~ *to enfilade, rake* || jdn aus weiter Entfernung u aus dem Hinterhalt ~ *to snipe a p* **2.** ⟨hunt⟩ ein Revier ~ *to shoot (over) a district* || (Flinte) → einschießen **3.** (Wand) *to coat, cover* **4.** ⟨tech⟩ *to bombard*, → Beschuß **II.** vi ⟨dial⟩ es beschießt (= genügt) *that will do*

Besch·ießung f ~/~en *bombardment, bombing, cannonade*; *shelling*; → Beschuß

besch·iffbar a *navigable* **besch·iffen** vt [h] (Meer) *to navigate*; *to sail on* **Besch·iffung** f ~/~en *navigation*

besch·ilft a *reeded, reedy*; *sedgy*

besch·impfen vt [h] jdn ~ *to abuse, insult, revile, affront a p*; *to call a p names, to fling dirt at a p, to swear at a p* || **sich ~** *to revile each other* || → beleidigen **besch·impfend** a *abusive, insulting, defamatory* **Besch·impfung** f ~/~en *abuse, vituperation*; ~en [pl] *abuse* || ~ jds *affront to a p, insult*; → Beleidigung

besch·indeln vt [h] *to shingle*

besch·irmen vt [h] (jdn, etw) *to protect, shelter, screen* (vor *from*); *to defend* **Besch·irmer** m ~s/~ *protector*; *defender* **Besch·irmung** f ~/~en *protection*; *defence*

°**Beschiß** m ⟨übtr⟩ *mess*, ⟨sl⟩ *sell, plant*

°**besch·issen** [pp v bescheißen] a ⟨übtr⟩ = belemmert

Beschl·ächt f ~/~en *perpendicular planking for the protection of river-banks*

beschl·afen vt [h] [→ schlafen] **1.** ⟨bib⟩ jdn ~ = jdm beischlafen **2.** e–e S ~ *to sleep upon a matter, to take counsel of one's pillow*

Beschl·ag m ~(e)s/≗e **A.** (Beschlagen) **1.** *shoeing (of horses)* || ~schmied = Hufschmied **2.** *copulation (of big game)* **B.** [konkr] **1.** (Metall≗ z Schutz u Verzierung) *fitting, mounting*; Eisen≗ *iron fitting* od *mounting*; ~ aus Holz, Planken≗ *sheeting* || ≗e [pl] *metal work* od *fittings*; *hardware*, polierte ≗e *brightwork*; Eisenbeschläge *iron work* | Tür≗ *door-fitting* od *mounting* || *sheathing (of a ship)* → Kupferhaut || (~ am Gewehr etc.) *mounting* || (~ an Stöcken u Schlitten) *metal rim, ferrule*; *shoe* || Huf≗ *shoes* [pl] || (~ an e–m Buch) *clasp* **2.** (Überzug) (am Glase) *damp, dimness* || (auf Metall) *tarnish* || (Schimmel) *mould* || ⟨chem⟩ *efflorescence* **C.** ⟨fig⟩ (Arrest) → Beschlagnahme; [nur in folg. festen Wendungen]: etw in ~ nehmen, mit ~ belegen; ~ legen auf etw ⟨jur⟩ *to arrest, attach, impound, seize*; *to confiscate, sequestrate, sequester a th*; *to distrain (up)on a th*; *to levy a distress on a th* || ⟨mil⟩ *to commandeer* od *requisition a th*; *to put a th in requisition*; (Schiff) *to embargo, to lay an embargo on* | ⟨übtr⟩ (Handel, Unterhaltung) *to monopolize*; (Aufmerksamkeit etc.) *to engross*; (jdn) *to engage, occupy* || ⟨sport⟩ ~ legen auf e–n Platz *to secure a place* || → Beschlag- ~hammer etc.

beschl·agen vt/i [h] [→ schlagen] **I.** vt **1.** (Kiste etc.) *to mount*; *to fit with metal plates* (od *ferrules*, etc.); mit Eisen ~ *to bind with iron*; mit Metall ~ *to cover* od *overlay with metal* || (Faß) mit Reifen ~ *to hoop* || (Schiff) *to sheathe* || mit Tuch ~ *to drape*; mit Wachstuch ~ *to cover with oilcloth* | (Hufeisen) *to nail, to fasten with nails*; (Pferd) *to shoe* || (Schlitten, Stock) *to shoe* || (innen ~) *to line (with)* | mit Nägeln ~ (z Verzierung) *to stud* **2.** (behauen) → beschlagen [a]; (Holz) *to square* **3.** ⟨mar⟩ (Segel) *to furl, to hand* **4.** [nur pass] **a.** *the windows are dimmed*; *the silver is tarnished*; *the pudding is covered with mould* **b.** die Ricke ist ~, geht hoch~ *the doe is impregnate* **5. sich ~** (of windows) *to be getting dimmed* || = **II.** vi (of glass, etc.) *to get covered with damp*; *to steam up* || (of metal) *to oxide, to tarnish* || (of food) *to get mouldy* **Beschl·agen** n **1.** *mounting*; (mit Nägeln) *studding* **2.** → Beschlag A. **3.** *tarnish (of metal)* **beschl·agen** a **1.** mit Silber ~ *silver-mounted (stick)* || *shod (horse)*; mit Eisen ~er Stock *a stick shod with iron* || e–e mit eisernen Nägeln ~e Tür *an iron-studded door* **2.** *clouded (lenses)*; *dimmed (windows)*; *misted (glass)* **3.** *impregnate (doe)* **4.** (P) gut ~ s in *to be (well) versed* od *skilled in, to be well up in*, er ist im Englischen gut ~ *he is a good English scholar* || auf allen Gebieten gut ~ s *to possess all-round information*; ein auf allen G. ~er Mann *an all-round man*

Beschl·agenheit f *experience* (in e–r S *of* od *in a th*); *knowledge, grasp (of a th)*

beschl·agfrei a: (Fenster) ~ machend *anti--fogging*; → beschlagen II. vi

Beschl·ag- ~hammer m *shoeing hammer* **~nahme** f ~/~en ⟨jur⟩ *arrest, attachment, distraint, distress* (e–r S *on a th*); *sequestration*; *seizure (of arms)*; *seizure* od *impounding (of*

goods) ‖ ⟨mil⟩ *impoundment, impressment, requisition*; Schiffs≈ *embargo* ‖ *confiscation (of books)* ‖ ~befehl [m] *writ of assistance* ‖ ~verfügung [f] *confiscation* od *requisition* od *vesting order* ≈**nahmen** vt (etw) *to attach, impound*; (Papiere) *to seize*; *to sequestrate, sequester (a th)*; *to distrain (up)on (a th)* ‖ (Buch) *to confiscate* ‖ ⟨mil⟩ (Wagen etc.) *to commandeer, impress, to requisition*; (Schiff) *to embargo (a th), to lay an embargo on (a th)* ~**schmied** m ~s/~e ⟨mil⟩ *farrier*, ⟨a.⟩ *horseshoer* ~**teil** n (f Möbel etc.) *decorative fitting* ~**zange** f *farrier's tongs* pl

beschl·eichen vt [h] [→ schleichen] jdn ~ **1.** (P) *to steal* od *creep up to a p, to take a p by surprise* ‖ (Wild) *to stalk* **2.** *(of sleep, old age,* etc.) *to come creeping upon a p* ‖ of feelings) *to creep over* od *(up)on a p, to steal over a p*; die A. beschleicht ihn *a feeling of fear creeps over him*

beschl·eunigen vt [h] (Geschwindigkeit) *to accelerate, to speed (up)*; Geschw. ~ *to pick up speed* ‖ (Gangart) *to quicken*; die Schritte ~ *to quicken one's steps*; (Tempo) *to force, to urge* ‖ (Arbeit, Bewegung) *to hurry, to h. along*; Erstellung ~ *to speed up the production* (⟨comp⟩ *of punched cards*); (Krise) *to precipitate* ‖ (Wachstum) *to hasten* ‖ (Beschluß, Entscheidung) *to expedite* | sich ~ *to accelerate*; *to quicken* **beschl·eunigend** a *accelerative*; *accelerating*; *quickening (factor)*; **beschl·eunigt** a *speedy (return)*; *expeditious*; *accelerated (particle)* **B–gung** f ~/~en *acceleration, increase of speed* ‖ ⟨phys⟩ *acceleration*; ⟨mot⟩ rasche ~ *quick get-away* s; negative ~ *deceleration* | ~sanode [f] *second* od *gun anode* | ~selektrode [f] *accelerating electrode* | ~skraft [f] *accelerative force* | ~smesser [m] *accelerometer* | ~smoment [n] *moment of acceleration* | ~spedal [n] ⟨mot⟩ *accelerator* | ~svermögen [n] ⟨mot⟩ *acceleration capacity*; *throttle response*; ⟨fam⟩ *zip*

beschl·ießen vt/i [h] [→ schließen] **I.** vt **1.** (umfassen) *to comprise, comprehend*; beschlossen s in *to be contained in* **2.** (beenden) (Rede, Buch) *to close, conclude, finish, terminate* ‖ den Tag so ~ *to make a day of it* ‖ s–e Tage ~ *to finish* od *end one's days* | (Diskussion) als letzter ~ *to wind up (a debate)*; e–n Zug ~ *to bring up the rear* **3.** (sich entschließen z) **a.** etw ~ *to decide* (od *determine, resolve*) *on a th*; ~ z tun *to decide* (od *determine, resolve*); ⟨Am⟩ *to conclude to do* (od *on doing*); es wurde beschlossen *it was resolved* od *agreed upon (that..)* **b.** ⟨parl, etc.⟩ *to vote a th, to carry a th by vote*; e–n Protest ~ *to pass a resolution of protest* **II.** vi ~ über etw *to decide a th* (: *they decided his fate*) **Beschl·ießer** m ~s/~, **Beschl·ießerin** f ~/~nen *care-taker*, ⟨hot⟩ *housekeeper*, (Wäsche≈) *linen-keeper*

beschl·ossen [a] e–e ~e S *an agreed matter, a settled m.*; ~ermaßen adv *as agreed upon*

Beschl·uß m -usses/-üsse **1.** (Ende) *close, conclusion, end, termination*; zum ~ *in conclusion, finally* **2.** (Willens≈) *decision, determination, resolution*, ⟨Am⟩ *resolve* ‖ mst (Beschlossenes) *resolution*; ⟨parl⟩ *vote* ‖ ⟨jur⟩ *decree, order, decision, judg(e)ment*; ⟨ec⟩ *canon*; ⟨univ⟩ *grace*, durch Senats≈ *by grace of the senate* ‖ (Entscheid) *determination*; (e–r Versammlung) *resolution*, ⟨Am⟩ *result* ‖ e–n ~ fassen *to pass a resolution*; ⟨jur⟩ *to take a decision, to decide*; (in e–r Versammlung) *to pass a resolution*; e–n Antrag zum ~ erheben *to carry a motion* ≈**fähig** a ⟨parl⟩ e–e ~e Anzahl v Mitgliedern *a quorum*; das Haus war ~ *there was a quorum in the House* ~**fähigkeit** f ⟨parl⟩ *quorum* ~**fassung** f *resolution*, ⟨Am⟩ *resolve* | ~sformel [f] ⟨jur⟩ *tenor*

°**beschm·eißen** vt [h] [→ schmeißen] *to pelt (with)*

beschm·ieren vt [h] **1.** (schlecht bemalen) (Wand) *to (be)daub, to besmear*; die Mauer mit Buchstaben ~ *to smear letters on the wall* **2.** → bestreichen ‖ mit Teer ~ *to tar* ‖ mit Fett ~ *to grease* **3.** = beschmutzen

°**beschm·ort** a = betrunken

°**Beschm·uh** n ~s/ ⟨sl⟩ *sell* ‖ nix ~! *no shine!*

beschm·utzen **1.** vt [h] **a.** (jdn) *to dirty*; *to spoil*; *to bedabble*; mit Ruß ~ *to soot* ‖ (bespritzen) *to bespatter*; *to splash*; beschmutzt *dirty* ‖ sich [dat] die Finger ~ *to spot one's fingers*, ..mit Tinte ~ *to splash ink on to one's fingers*; sich die Hände ~ *to soil one's hands* | **sich** ~ *to get dirty* od *soiled* **b.** (Fußsteige) *to foul*; (Wasser) *to defile, pollute* **c.** ⟨fig⟩ *to besmirch, defile, foul, pollute, soil*; jdn ~ *to sling mud at a p*; das eigene Nest ~ *to foul one's own nest* **2.** ≈ n *spoiling* ‖ (Wasser≈) *pollution* ‖ *mud-slinging (of a p)*; ~ der Ehre jds *a slight on a p's honour*
Beschm·utzung f = Beschmutzen

°**beschn·archen** vt [h] = (etw) beschlafen

Beschn·eide- ~**hobel** m (f. Buchbinder) *cutting* (od *plough*) *-knife* ~**maschine** f ⟨pap⟩ *cuttingmachine*; ⟨phot, etc.⟩ *trimming machine, print trimmer* ~**messer** n *edge tool*

beschn·eiden vt [h] [→ schneiden] **1. a.** (Papier) *to true*; (Seiten e–s Buchs) *to clip*; *edge*; beschnitten *cut (edges)*; ⟨phot⟩ *to trim* ‖ (Blech) *to edge off, trim* ‖ (Holz) vierkantig ~ *to square* **b.** (Bäume etc.) *to lop, prune*; → kappen (Hecke) *to clip, trim*; (Spitzen e–s Baums) *to clip, crop, tip*; (Rasenrand) *to clip, edge, trim* **c.** (Haar) *to cut, clip*; (kurz) *to crop*; die Nägel ~ *to pare one's nails* **d.** e–m Tier die Ohren, den Schwanz ~ *to crop the ears, the tail of an animal* ‖ ⟨fig⟩ jdm die Flügel ~ *to clip a p's wings* **e.** (Münze) *to clip* **2.** (jdn) *to circumcise*; beschnitten *circumcised (Jew)* **3.** ⟨übtr & fig⟩ **a.** (kürzen) (Aufsatz; Rede) *to curtail, cut*; *truncate*; *shorten* **b.** (Ausgaben) *to axe, retrench*; (Gehalt, Lohn) *to curtail*; *to cut down, to whittle away* od *down (a p's salary..)*; (Preise) *to cut* **c.** *to lessen, reduce*; (jds Wünsche) *to curb*; (Rechte) *to restrict*; *to impinge upon*; *to cut into*; jdm s–e Vorrechte ~ *to curtail a p of his liberties*, jdm s–e Hoffnung ~ *to reduce the hopes of a p*

Beschn·eidung f ~/~en **1.** *clipping, lopping*; *pruning*; *trimming* **2.** (jüdische) *circumcision* **3.** ⟨fig⟩ *truncation*; *emasculation (of a book*, etc.) ‖ *reduction*; *retrenchment (of expenses)*; *curtailment*

beschn·eien vt [h] *to cover with snow* ‖ beschneit a *snowy*; *snow-capped*

Beschn·itt m ~s/~e (→ beschneiden) ⟨pap⟩ *truing*; ⟨phot⟩ *trim*

beschn·üffeln, beschn·uppern vt [h] etw ~ *to smell* od *sniff at a th* ‖ ⟨fig⟩ *to poke* (od *put, thrust*) *one's nose into (other people's business)* | **sich** (*or* e–a) ~ *to smell* od *sniff at one another*; *to touch noses*; → beriechen

besch·olten a = anrüchig

besch·önigen vt [h] (etw) (entstellen) *to colour* od *sugar(-coat)* ‖ s–e eigene Handlungsweise ~ *to put a good face on one's actions* ‖ (bemänteln) (Fehler) *to gloss over*; (Vergehen) *to excuse, extenuate, mince, palliate*; *to thin down*; nichts ~ *not to mince matters* (od *one's words*) **besch·önigend** **1.** a *euphemistic(al)*; *extenuatory, palliative*; ~er Ausdruck *euphemism* **2.** adv *euphemistically* **Besch·önigung** f ~/~en *extenuation, palliation*; *excuse*

besch·ottern vt [h] (Straße) *to ballast, to metal*; *to macadam* **Besch·otterung** f *metalling, ballasting*

beschr·anken vt [h] ⟨rail⟩ *to guard* ‖ –nkt [a] *guarded (level crossing)*

beschr·änken vt [h] (etw) *to confine, limit, restrict* (auf *to*); *to narrow, to set limits to (a th)*; (jds Macht etc.) *to circumscribe, curtail, limit,* *restrict*; → begrenzen, Grenzen setzen; [mst pass] *to bound*, beschränkt s durch *to be bounded by* ‖ ⟨sport⟩ jdn auf ein Tor ~ *to hold a p to a goal* | **sich ~ auf** *to confine* od *limit, restrict o.s. to*; sich darauf ~ müssen z tun *to be restricted to doing* **beschr·änkend** a *restrictive*

beschr·änkt a **1.** *limited* (*space*), *narrow* (*scope*) **2.** ⟨übtr⟩ *narrow* (*means*); ~e Verhältnisse *straitened* (od *narrow*) *circumstances* ‖ *limited* (*power*) ‖ ⟨gram⟩ *narrow* (*sense*) ‖ ⟨com⟩ *conditional* (*acceptance*) ‖ ~e Haftung *limited liability*; Gesellschaft mit ~er H. *limited liability company* (abbr *Ltd*) **3.** ⟨fig⟩ *narrow* (*mind, views*); *dense, obtuse, narrow-minded*; *dull* **≃heit** f ~/~en **1.** *limitedness, narrowness* **2.** ⟨fig⟩ *narrowness, narrow-mindedness*; *denseness, density, obtuseness*; *dullness*

Beschr·änkung f ~/~en *circumscription, limit, limitation* (*of a th*), *restriction* (e–r S *of* od *on a th*); (Handels≃) *restraint of trade, tr. barriers* pl, ⟨Am⟩ *tr. curb*; ~ der Presse *restraint upon the press*; (der Industrie) *rationing* ‖ e–r S ~en auferlegen *to impose* od *place restrictions upon a th* ‖ in der ~ zeigt sich der Meister *brevity is the soul of wit* (Shak) ‖ die ~ (e–r S) aufheben *to lift the ban* (*on a th*); .. (der Geschwindigkeit) *to derestrict* (*a road* f e–e Straße) ‖ ohne ~ ⟨fam⟩ *with no strings attached*

beschr·eibbar a *describable*

beschr·eiben vt [h] [→ schreiben] **1.** (Papier etc.) *to inscribe*; *to write upon* (*paper*) ‖ beschriften) *superscribe* **2.** ⟨math⟩ (e–n Kreis etc.) *to describe*; e–n gr (weiten) K. ~ *to run* (*sweep*) *a large* (*wide*) *circle* (*of beacon*); (Figur) *to inscribe* (in *in*) ‖ ⟨übtr⟩ e–n vollen Kreis ~ (of wheels) *to come full circle*; e–n Kreis ~ (P) *to form into a ring* **3.** (schildern) *to describe, depict*; *to give a description of* (*a th*); *to picture*; *to set out*; nicht zu ~ *beyond all description* ‖ jdn ~ als.. *to draw a p as..*; etw ~ als *to represent a th as* (od *to be..*) ‖ (Wappen) *to blazon* ‖ ⟨com⟩ stückweise ~ *to specify* **beschr·eibend** **1.** a *descriptive* (*power*); nicht z ~ *indescribable* **2.** adv (*to represent*) *descriptively*

Beschr·eiber m *describer* **Beschr·eibung** f **1.** *the describing* (*of a circle*) **2.** (in Worten) *description, depiction, portrayal*; *representation* ‖ e–e ~ e–r P geben *to pencil an outline of a p* ‖ allgemeine ~ ⟨tech⟩ *general data* pl ‖ über alle ~ *past all description*; jeder ~ spotten *to beggar* (od *baffle, defy*) *description* ‖ ⟨com⟩ genaue, stückweise ~ *specification*; → Haar **3.** [in comp] *-graphy*; Natur≃ *physiography*; Orts≃ *topography*

beschr·eien vt [h] etw ~ → berufen vt 3. ‖ beschrei es nur nicht! *don't halloo till you are out of the wood! don't crow over it too soon!*

Beschr·eikraut n ⟨bot⟩ = Berufkraut

beschr·eiten vt [h] [→ schreiten] (Pferd) *to tread*; *to tread* (*up*)*on*; z ~ *walkable* ‖ (Schwelle) → überschreiten | ⟨übtr⟩ (Schauplatz) *to enter upon* ‖ den Rechtsweg ~ *to go to law*; den Instanzenweg ~ *to follow the official channels*; → Beschwerdeweg

beschr·iften vt [h] (etw) *to superscribe*; (Schild, Bild) *to letter* **Beschr·iftung** f *superscription, inscription*; *lettering*

beschr·oten vt [h] ⟨tech⟩ *to fettle*

besch·uhen vt [h] (jdn) *to furnish* (*a p*) *with shoes*; *to shoe* (*a p*) ‖ (Pfahl etc.) *to shoe, to protect with iron*

besch·uldigen vt [h] jdn e–s Verbrechens (etc.) ~ *to accuse a p of a crime, to charge a p with a crime*; *to lay a crime to a p's charge*; er wurde des Versuchs –gt.. *he was charged with attempting* (*to distort the truth*) ‖ *to arraign a p*; jdn des Mordes ~ *to arraign a p upon a charge of murder* ‖ ich beschuldige ihn k–r bösen Motive *I impute no evil motives to him* ‖ (of circumstances) *to inculpate, to incriminate a p* ‖ jdn ~ getan z h *to accuse a p of doing, to charge a p with doing* ‖ beschuldigt w *to be under an imputation* **besch·uldigend** a *inculpatory, incriminatory* **Besch·uldiger** m ~s/~ *accuser* **Besch·uldigte:** [der ~, ein ~r] m ~n/~n *the suspect* ‖ oft = Angeklagter **Besch·uldigung** f ~/~en *accusation, charge*; *imputation* (*of dishonesty*); *inculpation*; e–e ~ enthaltend *imputative*; falsche ~ *malicious prosecution*

besch·ulen vt [h] = einschulen

°**besch·ummeln,** °**beschuppen** vt [h] *to cheat, to do* od *have* od *sell* (*a p*), *to take* (*a p*) *in*; ⟨bes Am stud sl⟩ *to clip*

besch·uppen vt [h] *to cover with scales* ‖ *to scale* (*fish*)

Besch·uß m *official testing of small-arms*; *proof* ‖ *bombardment*, → Beschießen ‖ unter ~ halten *to keep under fire* ⟨hunt⟩ = Abschuß | ~meldung [f] *shelling report*; ≃sicher [a] *shell--proof* ‖ ⟨mot⟩ *self-sealing* (*tank*)

besch·ütten vt [h] jdn ~ mit etw *to throw* od *cast a th on a p, to cover a p with a th*; jdn mit Wasser ~ *to pour water over* od *on a p* ‖ das Tischtuch mit Milch ~ *to spill milk on the table-cloth*; e–e Seite mit Tinte ~ *to splash a page with ink* ‖ → überschütten

besch·ützen vt [h] (jdn, etw) *to protect* (gegen, vor *from, against*); *to screen, shelter, shield, guard, defend* (*from*) ‖ ⟨übtr⟩ (jdn) *to patronize* **Besch·ützer** m ~s/~ *protector, defender* ‖ *patron* **Besch·ützerin** f ~/~nen *protectress* ‖ *patroness* ‖ ⟨myth⟩ *dragon* **Besch·ützung** f ~/~en *protection* (gegen, vor *from, against*); → Schutz

beschw·atzen vt [h] **1.** (überreden) jed z etw ~ *to talk a p into a th, to come round* (*a p*), *to lead* (*a p*) *up the garden path*; *to coax* (z tun *to do, into doing*), *to wheedle* (z *into a th*; *into doing*); *to persuade* (*to* od *into a th*; *to do, into doing*); → bereden **2.** *etw ~ *to talk a th over*

beschw·eift a *tailed*

Beschw·er f & n = **Beschw·erde** f ~/~n **1.** (Last, Mühe) *burden, encumbrance*; *difficulty*; *hardship, inconvenience, trouble* ‖ ⟨med⟩ *complaint, trouble*; körperliche ~ *discomfort*; Herz≃ *heart trouble*; Leib≃n [pl] *abdominal discomfort*; → Gebrechen ‖ jdm ~ m *or* verursachen *to discomfort a p*; *to put a p to inconvenience, to give a p trouble*; (of food) *to disagree with a p* **2.** (Klage) *complaint* (über *about*); *grievance* (: *a statement of grievances*); ~n *gravamina* [L] [pl] ‖ e–e ~ einbringen, einlegen *to file a complaint* ‖ ~ führen über *to make complaints about, to complain of* (bei *to a p*); ~ führen bei *to appeal to*; ~ führen, daß ⟨Am⟩ *to charge that* ‖ ~n liefen ein (*or* es wurde ~ geführt), daß.. *it was complained that.., there were complaints that..* **3.** ⟨jur⟩ *declaration of dissent*; *protest* (gegen *against*), *remonstrance* (*against*) ‖ ~ einlegen *or* erheben *to make a remonstrance* (gegen *against*); *to enter* (od *lodge, make*) *a protest* (*against*; bei *with*); *to protest* (*against*) ‖ ihm steht das Recht der ~ zu gegen.. *he is entitled to protest against* **~ausschuß** m (Arbeiter≃) *grievance committee* **~buch** n *complaint-book* **≃führung** adv: sich ~ wenden an jdn *to complain* od *appeal to a p* **~führer** m *complainant, complainer* **~schrift** f ⟨engl hist⟩ öffentl. ~ *remonstrance* **~verfahren** n *grievances procedure* **~weg** m ⟨jur⟩: den ~weg beschreiten *or* einschlagen *to enter* od *lodge a protest* (*against a decree*)

beschw·eren vt [h] **1.** (durch ein Gewichtstück beschweren) (Briefe, lose Papiere) *to load*; *to weight* ‖ (Magen) *to load*; (of food) *to lie heavy on* **2.** ⟨übtr⟩ (Gedächtnis, Gewissen) *to burden, charge*; (Geist) *to clog*, beschwert s mit *or* von *to be clogged with*; jdm das Herz ~ (of thoughts, etc.) *to weigh heavily on a p, to depress, oppress, trouble a p* ‖ jdn ~ → belasten; beschwerlich; (etw) erschweren **3. sich ~** *to complain* (über *about, of*; bei jdm *to a p*) *to make complaints* (über *about*); sich ~ bei jdm *to appeal* od *complain to a p*, ⟨Am fam⟩ *to take it up with a p* **Beschw·erer** m → Brief≗

beschw·erlich a *arduous* (*task*); *difficult, hard, heavy* (*work*); *uphill* (*way, work*), *troublesome* (*job*); *fatiguing* (*journey*); *thorny* (*path*); *awkward, inconvenient* (*method*); → lästig, unbequem ‖ jdm ~ s, ~ fallen *to be a burden to a p*; *to incommode, trouble, inconvenience a p, to put a p to inconvenience*; das Gehen fiel ihm ~ *he walked with difficulty* ‖ → lästig, unbequem; belästigen | **≗keit** f ~/~en *arduousness, difficulty* (*of a task*); *inconvenience*; ~en [pl] *fatigues, exertions* [pl]

Beschw·ernis f ~/-nisse *burden, encumbrance, difficulty*; *hardship*; *inconvenience, trouble*

Beschw·erung f ~/~en *loading, weighting* (*of letters*) ‖ *encumbrance* (*of the mind*) | ~sketten [f pl] ⟨theat⟩ *chain weight*

beschw·ichtigen vt [h] (jdn) *to appease, mollify, pacify, soothe, tranquillize*; (Baby) *to hush, lull* ‖ (Unzufriedene) *to quiet* ‖ (of God) (Sturm) *to calm, quiet* | (Gewissen) *to silence* ‖ *to set a p's mind at rest* ‖ (Erregung, Leidenschaft) *to assuage, to calm* (*down*), *to lull, mollify, quiet, soften, still* **B.-gung** f *appeasement, mollification, pacification* ‖ *quieting* ‖ *silencing*; ~sbissen [m]; ~smittel [n] *sop* (für *to*) | ~spolitik [f] *appeasement*

beschw·indeln vt [h] (jdn) *to cheat, to do* (*a p*), *to do a p in the eye*; *to palter with* (*a p*); wir dürfen uns nicht ~ l *we must not be paltered with* → betrügen, beschummeln, bescheißen ‖ jdn ~ um etw *to cheat a p of* (od *out of*) *a th, swindle* (⟨sl⟩ *to bamboozle*) *a p out of a th*

beschw·ingen vt [h] ⟨fig⟩ = beflügeln

beschw·ingt a *winged*

°**beschw·ipst** a ⟨fam⟩ *boozy, fuddled, squiffy, swizzled, soused, fuzzy, tiddled, tiddley, tipsy*; ⟨Am fam⟩ *plastered* ‖ *half-seas-over, bright in the eye*; ⟨sl⟩ *moony, three sheets in the wind*; *under the weather*; → angesäuselt

beschw·ören vt [h] [→ schwören] **1.** (Geister) *to raise, conjure, evoke, to call up* ‖ (austreiben) *to conjure away, to exorcize* → bannen **2.** (bitten) jdn ~ *to conjure a p* (*to do*); *to entreat, implore* **3.** etw (Aussage etc.) ~ *to swear* (*to*) *a th*; die Identität jds ~ *to swear to a p*, kannst du es ~? *can you swear it*?; ~, daß.. *to take an oath that..* ‖ jdn etw ~ l *to swear a p on a th* | (Frieden) *to confirm by oath* ‖ vor mir beschworen *sworn to* [adv] *before me* **Beschw·örer** m ~s/~ ⟨hist⟩ *conjurer, magician, wizard*; *exorcist*

Beschw·örung f ~/~en **1.** (Geister≗) *conjuring, magical invocation* (*of spirits*); *conjuration* ‖ (Bannung) *exorcism* **2.** *adjuration, solemn appeal* (od *entreaty*) **3.** *swearing*; *confirmation* (*of a th*) *by oath* **~sformel** f *adjuration*

°**beschw·uppen** vt [h] = beschummeln

bes·eelen vt [h] ⟨mst übtr⟩ *to animate, enliven, ensoul, inspire, inspirit, inform* (mit *with*) ‖ beseelt v *informed* od *inspired with* (*new life*) **Bes·eelung** f ~/~en *animation, inspiration*

bes·ehen vt [h] [→ sehen] **1.** etw ~, sich etw ~ *to* (*have a*) *look at a th*; (prüfend) *to examine, inspect, view a th*; *to look into* od *over a th* ‖ (betrachtend) *to contemplate* | ⟨übtr⟩ etw bei Lichte ~ *to look closely into a th*; bei Lichte ~ [pp] *on closer inspection*; *strictly speaking* ‖ als ich mir den Schaden besah, wenn man den Sch. besieht *on closer inspection, on further consideration* ‖ °jdn nicht ~ können *to have a down on a p, to hate the very sight of a p* **2.** °Prügel ~ *to get a thrashing, to come in for a thrashing* **3. sich ~** *to look at o.s., to inspect one's appearance, to survey o.s.* (*in a mirror*) ‖ °sie können sich *or* e–a nicht ~ *they hate the very sight of each other*, → 2

bes·eitigen vt (h) **1.** (S) (Trümmer etc.) *to remove* ‖ (Geräusche) *to stop* ⟨a. mot⟩ ‖ (Einrichtungen) *to abolish, to do away with, to dispose of, to get rid of, to remove, to set aside*; ⟨Am⟩ *to knock out* ‖ (Fehler) *to eliminate* (aus *from*); (Schuld) *to clear off* (*by*); (Schwierigkeiten, Hindernisse) *to overcome*; (Streitigkeiten) *to settle, sink*; (Übel) *to redress*; (Abszeß) *to extirpate*; (Unklarheiten) durch Erklären ~ *to explain away* ‖ Dinge vollkommen ~ *to make a clean sweep of things* **2.** (P) *to get rid of a p*; (Beamte) *to shelve a p* ‖ (töten) *to make* (od *do*) *away with a p*; *to do for a p*; *to remove a p*; → abtun **B.gung** f ~/~en **1.** *removal* (*of debris*, etc.) ‖ *abolition* (*of abstacles*, etc. ‖ *disposal, removal* (*of institutions*, etc.); *doing away with*; *elimination* (*of errors*); ~ des Kloakenwassers *sewage disposal* ‖ *accommodation*; *settlement* (*of quarrels*); *redress* (*of evils*) **2.** *shelving* (*of an official*); *removal* (*of a p*); *making away with* (*a p*) **3.** ⟨übtr⟩ ~ v Schäden *counteracting damage*

bes·eligen vt [h] ⟨poet⟩ jdn ~ *to make a p happy, to bless a p* (*with*), *to beatify a p*

B·esemer m ~s/~ (Schnellwaage) *steelyard*

B·esemschon n (holländisch) *discount allowed for loss in leavings cleaving to barrels* (etc.)

B·esen m ~s/~ **1. a.** *broom*; grober ~ *besom*; kl, leichter ~ *whisk* ‖ Feder≗ *feather-broom, feather-duster*; Haar≗ *hair-broom* ‖ kugelförmiger ~ *Turk's head*; Hof≗ *yard-broom* ‖ (Raum) mit dem ~ auskehren *to sweep* (*out*), *to give* (*a room*) *a sweep*; *to broom* **b.** ⟨fig⟩ (etw) mit eisernem ~ auskehren *to make a clean sweep* (*of a th*) ‖ neue ~ kehren gut *a new broom sweeps clean* ‖ °ich freß'n ~ *I'll be shot* od *damned* (wenn *if*), *I'll eat my hat* od *head*, .. mitsamt der Putzfrau *I'll eat my head and my hat to boot* **2.** ⟨übtr⟩ *large brush*; *mop* ‖ ⟨cul⟩ *whisk* **3.** ⟨fig⟩ (P) ⟨dero⟩ *housemaid*, ⟨fam⟩ *skivvy* ‖ (Weibsbild) *besom, catamaran, termagant* **~binder** m *broom-maker* ~-führende Göttin ⟨fig⟩ (Putzfrau) ⟨iron⟩ *nymph*, ⟨hum⟩ *Mrs. Mop* **~ginster** m ⟨bot⟩ *broom* **~—,** (Kleider- etc.) **Kammer** f (-Schrank m) ⟨bes Am⟩ *closet* **~korn** n (Durra, Sorghum) ⟨Am⟩ *broomcorn* **≗rein** a *well-cleaned* **~stiel** m *broomstick*; er sieht aus als hätte er e–n ~ verschluckt *he's as stiff as a poker*

bes·essen a [pp v besitzen] *possessed*, vom Teufel ~ *demoniac*(*al*); ~ s v *to be possessed by* (*a spirit, the devil, an idea*); *to be in the grip of* (*an idea*) ‖ (rasend) *frantic, frenzied* ‖ ⟨übtr⟩ *infatuated*; *besotted*; *inveterate* (*player of cards*) ‖ (verblaßt) *mad* (*are you m.*?); er ist total ~ *he is as mad as a hatter*; er war v e–r fixen Idee ~ *it was an obsession with him* **Bes·essene** [der ~, ein ~r] m ~n/~n *man possessed, demoniac* ‖ *maniac*, wie ein ~r *like a maniac*

Bes·essenheit f *obsession*, → fixe Idee; *possession* (v e–m Dämon *by a demon*) ‖ (Raserei) *frenzy*

bes·etzen vt [h] **1. a.** ⟨mil⟩ (Land, Stadt) *to occupy, take*; *to take possession of*; besetzt halten *to keep occupied, to hold*; ~de Macht *occupant* ‖ (Stadt) mit Garnison ~ *to garrison* **b.** (Straße etc.) *to line* (*with soldiers*, etc.) die Straßen waren dicht besetzt *the streets were densely lined* ‖ (Gegend) mit Menschen ~ *to people* **2.** (e–n best. Platz ~) **a.** (Sitzplatz) *to take, engage*; der Platz ist besetzt *the seat is engaged* od *taken*; das Theater war gut besetzt *the house was well attented*; ⟨rail⟩ der

Wagen ist voll besetzt *the car is full up* || ⟨telph⟩ besetzt *engaged, busy* **b.** (Geschütz, Schiff) *to man* **c.** (Posten, Vakanz) *to fill*; voll –tzt s (of unit) *to be up to establishment* **d.** ⟨theat⟩ (Rolle, Stück) *to cast*, das Stück ist glänzend besetzt *the play is perfectly cast* **e.** all m–e Zeit ist besetzt *all my time is occupied* (od *taken, filled up*) **3.** ⟨tech & com⟩ **a.** *to furnish* (*with*); (Hut, Stoff etc.) *to trim* (*with*); (Saum) *to border* (*with*); (Kleid) mit Spitzen ~ *to lace*; mit Pelz ~ *to fur* || mit Juwelen ~ *to set with jewels*; *to gem* || mit Pflanzen ~ *to plant* od *set with plants* **b.** (Straßenpflaster) *to ram*; (Bohrloch) *to tamp, ram* **c.** (Ofen) → beschicken **d.** (Leitung) *to engage* **e.** (Teich) mit Fischen ~ *to stock* **bes·etzt** a **1.** [pred] → besetzen 1. 2. || ich bin ~ ⟨vulg sex⟩ *I'm hooked* (*up*) **2.** [attr] ~es Gebiet *occupied territory* || *engaged* (*seat*); ⟨theat⟩ gut ~ *well--attended* (*house*); voll ~ *full* (*houses*); (*bus*, etc.) *solid with people* || ⟨*theat*⟩ (of lights) *full up* || sehr ~ *crowded* (*day*) **≈zeichen** n ⟨telph⟩ *busy signal* || ⟨tech⟩ *blocking signal*

Bes·etzung f ~/~en **1.** ⟨mil⟩ *occupation* (*of a country*) || *lining* (*with soldiers*) **2.** ⟨theat⟩ *attendance*; Rollen≈ *cast*; mit voller ~ *with the full cast*; Vorstellung mit erster ~ *star performance* || *filling* (*of a post*); ~ e–r Stelle *appointment to a post* || ⟨sport⟩ *field*; e–e gute ~ *a big field*; 5 Rennen in gr ~ *big field for 5 races* **3.** *furnishing, trimming*; *setting* (*with*) || → Besatz; Besatzung **~srecht** n *patronage*; ⟨ec⟩ Pfründen≈ *advowson* **~swechsel** m ⟨theat film⟩ *switch*: e–n ~ v A. als.. vornehmen *to make a switch and cast A. as..*

bes·eufzen vt [h] (etw) *to bemoan, deplore*

bes·ichtigen vt [h] **1.** (Ort, Ausstellung etc.) *to visit* || z ~ *on view*; weiter z ~ bleiben *to remain on view* **2.** (prüfen) (Grundstück etc.) *to examine*; *to make an examination of* (*a th*); *to inspect*; *view*; *survey*; *to go over* (*a machine*) || (amtlich) *to perambulate*; ⟨bes mil⟩ *to inspect* || den Leichnam ~ *to view the body* **bes·ichtigenswert** a *worth visiting*; *visitable*

Bes·ichtigung f ~/~en **1.** *visit*, e–e ~ des Museums *a visit to the museum*; ~ durch geladene Gäste *private view*; ~ v Sehenswürdigkeiten *sightseeing* **2.** (Prüfung) *examination, inspection* (*of a place*); *survey*; → Leichenschau || (amtliche) *perambulation, visitation*; ⟨bes mil⟩ *inspection* **~sbericht** m (amtlicher) *perambulation* **~sdistrikt** m *inspectional district* **~sgebühren** f [pl] *inspector's fees* [pl] **~sreise** f *tour of inspection, inspection tour*; (jährliche) *perambulation*

bes·iedeln vt [h] (Land) *to colonize, plant, settle* **Bes·iedelung** f ~/~en *colonization, settlement*; (Politik der) innere(n) ~ *redistribution of population*

bes·iegbar a *conquerable*

bes·iegeln vt [h] ⟨fig⟩ (bekräftigen) (etw) *to seal, to set one's seal to* (*a th*) || (Versöhnung) *to seal* (mit e–m Kuß *with a kiss*) || den Untergang e–r Rasse ~ (of actions) *to seal the doom of a race*; sein Schicksal ist besiegelt *his fate is sealed*

Bes·iegelung f ~/~en ⟨fig⟩ *sealing*

bes·iegen vt [h] (Feind, Volk) *to conquer, vanquish*; (jdn) *to worst*; *defeat*; *overcome* || ⟨sport⟩ (jdn) *to beat, throw*; ⟨fam⟩ *to lick*; ⟨Am a.⟩ *to whip* || jdn nach Strich u Faden ~ *to knock spots off* (od *out of*) *a p* || sich f. besiegt erklären *to throw up the sponge* || besiegt w ⟨Am pol⟩ *to be snowed under* || (im Debattieren ~) *to worst, outdo a p* || besiegt w *to be defeated* od *worsted*; *to get the worst of it, to have the worst* || (Trieb etc.) → beherrschen, überwinden **Bes·ieger** m ~s/~ *conqueror, victor, vanquisher*

Bes·iegung f ~/~en *defeat* (*of the enemy*) || ⟨sport⟩ *beating* || (im Debattieren) *worsting* (*of*)

Bes·ik, Bes·ique [be'zi:k] (Fr) *bezique*; Kartenspiel ähnlich dem ~ *pinocle*

bes·ingen vt [h] [→ singen] (jdn, etw) *to sing* (*a p, a th*); *to sing of* (*a p, a th*); *to celebrate* (*in song*)

bes·innen I. vt/refl [h] [→ sinnen] **A.** vt (überlegen) [nur noch in]: erst besinn's dann beginn's *better is one forethought than two after* **B.** vrefl **sich ~ 1.** (zum Bewußtsein k.) *to recollect o.s., to recollect one's thoughts* || sich auf sich selbst ~ *to remember o.s.* **2.** (überlegen) *to bethink o.s., to reflect, to consider* (*how to do*) || sich e–s andern ~, sich anders ~ *to change one's mind*; sich e–s Besseren ~ *to think better of it* || sich hin u her ~ *to rack one's mind* || ohne sich lange z ~ *unhesitatingly, without hesitation, without thinking twice* **3.** (sich erinnern) **a.** *to remember, recollect*; jetzt besinne ich mich *I remember now*; wenn ich mich recht besinne *if I remember rightly* **b. sich auf etw** (jdn) ~ *to recall, remember, recollect a th* (*a p*), *to call a th to mind*; *to think of a th*; ich kann mich nicht darauf ~ *I cannot remember it* **II.** ≈ n *reflection, consideration*, ohne langes ~ *unhesitatingly, without hesitation* **bes·innlich 1.** a *thoughtful*; *reflective*; *contemplative, meditative* **2.** adv (*to answer*) *thoughtfully* **Bes·innlichkeit** f *thoughtfulness*; *contemplativeness*

Bes·innung f ~/ **1.** (Bewußtsein) *consciousness* || bei ~ *conscious*; nicht bei ~ *unconscious*; bei ~ bleiben *to retain one's consciousness*; wieder z ~ k. *to come to life, to recover consciousness, to recover o.s., to come to* [adv]; die ~ verlieren *to lose consciousness, to faint* (*away*); → **2.** (Überlegung) *reflection, consideration*; (Nachdenken, Besonnenheit) *reason*; die ~ verlieren *to lose one's head* || ganz bei ~ *in one's right mind*; nicht ganz bei ~ *out of one's mind, not right in the head*; (nicht) bei ~ s *to be in* (*out of*) *one's senses* || ohne ~ → Besinnen || zur ~ k. *to recover one's senses, to* (*re*)*collect o.s.*; wann wird er endlich zur ~ k.? *when will he listen to reason*? || jdn zur ~ bringen *to bring a p to his senses* od *to reason* **≈slos 1.** a **a.** *unconscious, insensible, senseless* (infolge *from*) **b.** (unüberlegt) *insensate, senseless*; *thoughtless, inconsiderate*; *rash* **2.** adv *thoughtlessly, inconsiderately* **~slosigkeit** f *unconsciousness, insensibility, senselessness* || *thoughtlessness*

Bes·itz m ~es/ **A.** [abstr] (Besitzen) **1.** *possession* || (Land≈) *tenure* || (Landnahme) *occupancy* || ⟨jur⟩ fingierter ~ *constructive possession*, unmittelbarer ~ *actual p.*; ungestörter ~ *quiet enjoyment* **2.** Wendungen: **a.** ~ ergreifen or nehmen v etw *to take poss. of a th*; ..v jdm *to grip, possess a p, to take hold of a p* **b.** im ~ e–r S *in poss. of a th*; ein Pferd im ~ v Herrn N. *a horse owned by Mr. N.*; das Hotel (sc in der Schweiz) ist im ~ e–s Deutschen *the hotel is German-owned*; Fabriken im ~ Groß-Britanniens *British-owned factories* (*in China*); Passagiere im ~ britischer Pässe *passengers holding British passports* **c.** (etw) im ~ h. *to have* (*a th*) *in one's poss., to possess* (*a th*); *to be seized* od *in poss. of* (*a th*) | im ~ e–r S s (P) *to be in poss. of a th* (: *he is in p. of the keys*); *to be seized of a th* (→ im ~ h); nicht im ~ s–r 5 Sinne s *not to be in poss. of all one's senses, to be not right in the head* || im ~ jds s (S) *to be in the poss. of a p* (: *the copy is in the p. of Mr. N.*); *to be owned by a p*; in s–m ~ s *to be in his poss.*; in staatlichem ~ s *to be state-owned* || etw in ~ nehmen (P) *to lay one's hands on a th* **d.** in den ~ e–r S k. (P) *to come into poss. of a th* (: *he came into p. of the plans*), *to become possessed of a th, to get hold of a th* || (S) *to come into the poss. of a p*; Ihr Brief kam in m–n ~ *your letter* *came to hand*; die Pläne kamen in den ~ des Herrn N. *the plans came into the poss. of Mr. N.*; *Mr. N. became possessed of the plans* | (etw) in ~ nehmen *to take poss. of a th* | (jdn) in den ~ e–r S setzen *to put a p in poss. of a th* | in den ~ e–r S treten *to enter into poss. of a th* | in den ~ jds übergehen *to become the poss. of a p*; das Geschäft ist in s–n ~ übergegangen *the business has been taken over by him*; das Haus ging in s–n ~ über *he became possessed of the house*; in den sicheren ~ jds übergehen *to be secured by a p* **B.** [konkr] (Besitztum) *possession, property, estate*; Grund~ *real estate*; Haus≈ *house property* || *possessions* [pl]; *wealth* || Miet≈, Pacht≈ *tenancy* || ein lästiger, kostspieliger ~ *a white elephant* || sein ganzer ~ war.. *all his wealth was.., all he possessed was..* || jdn aus s–m ~ (ver)treiben *to dispossess a p*

Bes·itz- **~anspruch** m = Besitztitel **≈anzeigend** a ⟨gram⟩ *possessive*; ~es Fürwort [n] *the possessive, the p. pronoun* **~art** f ⟨jur⟩ *tenure* **~aufgabe** f (dingliche) ⟨jur⟩ *dereliction* **≈betonend** a *possessive*; *proprietary* **~dauer** f *tenure* **~entziehung** f *deprivation of possession* | ~sklage [f] *action of ejection* **~ergreifer** m *occupant* || ⟨Am⟩ *squatter* (*of land*) **~ergreifung** f *occupancy, occupation*; *seizure*; ⟨jur⟩ *seizin, seisin*; widerrechtliche ~ *usurpation* (*of a th*) **≈gierig** a *possessive* **~instinkt** m *possessive instinct, sense of property* **~interesse** n *possessory interest* **≈los** a *propertyless, unpropertied, without property* || die ~losen [pl] *the have-nots* [pl] **~nahme** f *occupancy, occupation, seizure* (*of a town*) || *appropriation* **~recht** n *right of possession*; *ownership*; *possessory title* (auf *to*) || ⟨jur⟩ *estate* **~schutz** m *protection of property* **~stand** m *ownership* || (Aktiva) *assets* [pl] | ~sklausel [f] *incumbency clause* **~steuer** f *property-tax* **~störung** f *disturbance of possession* **~titel** m *title*; *tenure*; *legal estate* **~übertragung** f *transfer of property* **~urkunde** f *title-deed* **~wechsel** m *change of ownership* | ~steuer [f] → Grunderwerbssteuer **~wut** f *possessioness*

bes·itzen vt [h] [→ sitzen] **1.** †(sitzen auf) **a.** e–n Stuhl ~ *to sit upon a chair* || den Witwenstuhl ~ *to be a widow* **b.** (of evil spirits) (jdn) *to possess* (*a p*); → besessen **2.** (zu eigen h.) **a.** (Gegenstände jeder Art, Land etc.) *to possess*; *to be possessed of* (*a th*); *to be in possession of* (*a th*), *to own* (: *he owns five suits*), *to hold*; *to have* (: *he had had a fine watch*); nur ein Haus ~ *to have only one house to one's name* **b.** ⟨übtr⟩ (Eigenschaften etc.) *to possess*; *to have* || e–e gute Gesundheit ~ *to enjoy* (od *rejoice in*) *a good health*; viele Kinder ~ *to be blessed with many children*; ein gutes Gedächtnis ~ *to have a good memory*; ich besitze k–e Gelehrsamkeit *I do not pretend to learning*; gr Gaben ~ *to be a man of great abilities* **c.** (a. S) sich rühmen können etw z ~ *to boast* (*of*) *a th*; unsere Stadt besitzt ein schönes Museum *our town boasts* (*of*) *a beautiful museum* || das Zimmer besitzt e–e herrliche Aussicht *the room commands a fine view* **bes·itzend a 1.** die besitzenden Klassen [pl] *the propertied classes*; ⟨fam⟩ *the haves* [pl] **2.** [in Verbindungen v Objekt + ~] *-ed*: Geld ~ *moneyed*; Talent ~ *talented*

Bes·itzer m *possessor* || *owner, proprietor*; ⟨jur⟩ *tenant* || *occupant* (→ Eigentümer); *holder* (*of shares, of a title*); → Grund≈, Laden≈, Pfründen≈ || den ~ wechseln (of houses, etc.) *to change hands* **Bes·itzerin** f *proprietress* **besitzerlos** a *abandoned* (*ear, dog*) **Bes·itztum** n ~s/-tümer *possession, property*; *estate* **Bes·itzung** f ~/~en *possession, property*; *estate* || ⟨pol⟩ ~en [pl] *possessions* [pl] (: *the British ~s in Africa*)

Besk·iden pl (höchster Teil der Westkarpathen) *Beskids* pl (: *East & West B.*)

B·esmer = Besemer

°**bes·offen** a **1.** [pred] ⟨sl⟩ *foxed, swigged, swinny*, ⟨Am a.⟩ *cock-eyed* || total ~ *drunk as a lord* od *a newt, tight as an owl*; sinnlos ~ *dead drunk* **2.** [attr] *drunken* (*man*) °**Bes·offenheit** f ~/ *drunkenness*, ⟨vulg⟩ *crapulence*

Bes·ohlanstalt f, ⟨fam⟩ **Bes·ohlei** f ~/~en *cobbler's workshop* **bes·ohlen** vt [h] *to sole*; (dick ~) *to clump*

bes·olden vt [h] (jdn) *to salary* (*a p*), *to pay a salary to* (*a p*) **bes·oldet** a *salaried* (*classes*); *stipendiary* (*magistrate*); ⟨mil⟩ fest ~ *substantive* (*captain*), ~er Friedensrichter, Geistlicher, Lehrer *stipendiary* || die ~e Klasse *the salariat*

Bes·oldung f ~/~en *pay, salary*; (f. Geistliche, Lehrer etc.) *stipend* | ~sgruppe [f] *pay grade* | ~sliste [f] *pay record* | ~sdienstalter [n] *pay seniority*

bes·ommern vt [h] ⟨agr⟩ *to cultivate in summer* (*only*)

bes·ondere I. a [nur attr] **1.** (abgesondert) *separate* (*lodging, place, way*) || *special* (*day*) **2.** (unterscheidend) *distinct*; ~ Kasusformen *distinctive case-forms* || *individual* (*wishes*); er hat s–e ~ Methode *he has a method of his own* || *particular*; v ~r Bedeutung *of particular importance*; v ~m Interesse *of particular interest*; *peculiar* (*attention*); ⟨scient⟩ *specific* (*forms, qualities*) || *special*, s–e ~ Pflicht *his special duty*; (etw) auf ein ~s Gebiet beschränken, nach e–r ~n Richtung entwickeln *to specialize*; in der ~n Absicht (*to write*) *specially* (*to see you*); f. den ~n Zweck *for the special purpose* **3.** (außergewöhnlich) *singular* (*beauty*); *particular*; *especial* (*aversion*; *dexterity*); *extraordinary*; ganz ~ *eminent* || e–e ~ Schönheit an sich h. (S) *to have a beauty all its own* || kein ~r (= besonders guter) Wein *not much of a wine* **4.** (eigenartig) *particular* (*case*), *peculiar*; ~ Bewandtnis *peculiarity, particularity*; ~r Umstand *the particular* || (seltsam) *peculiar* (*sort of man*); *strange*; *singular* **II.** ≈ n [das ~, ein ~s] **1.** etw ~s *something separate* od *apart* **2.** das ~ ⟨log⟩ *the particular* || im ~n *in especial* (od *particular*); *particularly, specially* || etw ganz ~s *something quite extraordinary, something out of the ordinary*; nichts ~s *nothing particular, nothing much*; ⟨fam⟩ *nothing to write home about* || ein ~s tun *to go out of one's way* (um jdm z gefallen *to please a p*) **B.rheit** f ~/~en *distinctiveness*; *individuality*; ~en [pl] (e–r S) *features*; charakterliche ~ *idiosyncrasy* || *particularity, peculiarity*; *speciality* || *strangeness, peculiarity*; *singularity* (*of a p*) **bes·onders** adv **1.** (getrennt) *separately, severally, apart* || *distinctly, individually, personally* (: *to negotiate p. with a p*) **2.** *specially, expressly*; *particularly, in particular*; ich schrieb ~, um dich z sehen *I wrote specially to see you* || (etw) ~ angeben *to particularize*; (etw) ~ bezeichnen *to specialize*; sich ~ ausbilden *to specialize* (f. *for*; in *in*) **3.** (in hohem Maße) [intensiv] *especially, in particular*; *most of all, above all, chiefly*; *greatly*; ⟨Am⟩ *preferably* || ich liebe Äpfel ~ *I like apples especially*; jdm ~ ähneln *to resemble a p greatly*; ganz ~ *eminently, singularly* | (vor Adj u Adv) *highly, most, very*, ~ interessant *very* (od *most*) *interesting* **4.** [pred] nicht ~ *so-so, not very good*; *second rate*; das Essen ist nicht ~ ⟨fam⟩ *the food is not terribly good* || es geht ihm heute nicht ~ (gut) *he's not too well today*

bes·onnen vt [h] (etw) *to sun*; *to expose* (*a th*) *to* (od *to bathe, place* [*a th*] *in*) *the sun* || ⟨übtr⟩ die Gegenwart ~ *to brighten and warm the present* || besonnt *sunned, sunny* (*room*); ⟨phot⟩ *sunlit* (*landscape*) || ⟨übtr⟩ (P) *cheerful, sunny*

bes·onnen [pp v besinnen] **1.** a *collected*; *sober, sober-minded, thoughtful* || *discreet, circumspect*, *prudent, sensible* **2.** adv *collectedly* **Bes·onnenheit** f ~/ *collectedness, composure; sobriety; presence of mind; thoughtfulness* || *discretion, circumspection* || ruhige ~ *sanity*

bes·orgen vt [h] **A. 1.** (beschaffen) (etw) *to provide, supply,* ⟨euphem⟩ *to pinch (a th)*; Lebensmittel ~ f. *to cater for* || *to arrange (a table)* || jdm etw ~ *to procure* (od *provide, get) a p a th* (od *a th for a p*); jdm e–e Stellung ~ *to find a p a job*; besorge dir ein Exemplar *get a copy for yourself* | ⟨fig iron⟩ ich werde es ihm schon ~! *I'll give it to him!* **2.** (mst versorgen) jdn ~ *to provide for a p* || (die Kinder etc.) *to care for; to take care of, to look after, to watch over (a p)* || (die Pferde) *to groom* **3.** (erledigen) (etw) *to attend to; to see to (a th); to arrange for (a th)*; (Haushalt) *to manage* || (ausführen) (Versicherung) *to effect*; (Auftrag) *to carry out, to discharge, to perform* || *to do*; das Kochen ~ *to do the cooking,* die Blumen ~ *to do the flowers* || Briefe ~ *to post letters,* (durch Boten) *to forward* (od *send*) *l.* || (Gottesdienst) *to conduct*; (Geschäfte) *to transact* || etw gründlich ~ ⟨sl⟩ *to go the whole hog* || was du heute kannst ~, das verschiebe nicht auf morgen *a stitch in time saves nine* **B.** †(befürchten) → besorgt **Bes·orger** m *manager* || *executor* || ⟨jur⟩ unentgeltlicher ~ (fremder Geschäfte) *volunteer,* → Vertreter

***bes·orglich** a *solicitous, provident* ***Bes·orglichkeit** f *solicitude, providence* **Bes·orgnis** f ~/-nisse *alarm, concern, disquiet; anxiety* (um *for*), *worry; fear* (um *for*); *concern* (um *for*; über *about*); *apprehension* (über *at*); *misgiving*; –nisse [pl] *fears, misgivings* [pl]; ernste ~ *grave concern* || ernsteste ~ erregen *to cause the gravest concern*; einige ~ erregen *to cause some disquiet*; jdn mit ~ erfüllen *to fill a p with misgivings, to alarm a p* || in ~ geraten *to get alarmed, to take alarm (at)* || ~ hegen *to fear* (um *for*) || → Befangenheit

bes·orgniserregend a *alarming, causing anxiety*

bes·orgt a **1.** [pred] *solicitous*; zärtlich ~ *tender and s.*; ~ s f. (*or* um) jdn (etw) *to be careful* (od *solicitous) for a p; to care for, to look after a p* || ~ s um *to be anxious* (od *concerned, solicitous) about, (a p's health)* || ~ s um jdn *to be in fear* (od *to fear) for (a p)* || sehr ~ s *to be in great anxiety* | ich werde darum ~ s *I shall look into it* || ~ s z tun *to be anxious* (od *solicitous) to do*; sehr ~ s nicht z tun *to be fussy about not doing* || jdn ~ m *to alarm, to trouble a p* **2.** [attr] *alarmed (parents); anxious (look)* **Bes·orgtheit** f *care; solicitude (about)* **Bes·orgung** f ~/~en **1.** (Beschaffung) *procurement*; ~ v Wasser *supply with water* **2.** (Behandlung) *care, management (of the patients)* **3.** (Erledigung) *performance, execution (of a commission); management* || *posting (of letters)* || ~en m *to go on errands* | (Einkauf) *purchase,* ~en m *to do one's shoppings, to go shopping, to shop*

besp·annen vt [h] **1.** (Geige etc.) mit Saiten ~ *to string* **2.** (Wand) mit Stoff ~ *to cover with cloth* od *fabric, to drape* **3.** e–n Wagen mit Pferden ~ *to put horses to a carriage* **besp·annt** a *animal-drawn (vehicle); horse-drawn (artilley)*

Besp·annung f ~/~en **1.** = Gespann **2.** ⟨aero⟩ **a.** (Bespannen) *covering (of a wing)* **b.** [konkr] (~sstoff) *fabric,* ⟨aero⟩ *skin* **~sstoff** m ⟨aero⟩ *fabric*

besp·eien vt [h] [→ speien] jdn (etw) ~ *to spit at* (od *upon) a p (a th)*

besp·iegeln vt [h] *(etw) = beleuchten || **sich ~** *to look* (od *gaze) at o.s.,* ⟨fam⟩ *to admire o.s. in the glass* **Besp·iegelung** f → Beleuchtung; Selbst≈

besp·ielen vt [h] ⟨poet⟩ *to play on* od *in* || die Schallplatte ist bespielt worden *the record has been used*

besp·innen vt [h] (Draht) *to cover*

besp·itzeln vt [h] jdn ~ *to spy (up)on a p; to be a spy (up)on a p*

besp·ötteln vt [h] (jdn) *to deride, mock; rally, ridicule; to jeer* od *mock at (a p)*

bespr·echen vt [h] [→ sprechen] **A. 1.** (Krankheit etc.) *to bind* od *influence (an illness) by a magic spell, to put a charm* od *spell upon (an illness)* || (entzaubern) *to conjure, charm, spell away* **2.** ein Mikrophon ~ *to speak before a microphone*; (Schallplatte) *to record; to speak before a recording gramophone* **B.** ⟨übtr⟩ **1.** (etw) *to talk (a th) over* (mit *with*), *to have a chat about (a th); to discuss (a th*; mit jdm *with a p*); gründlich, ausführlich ~ *to discuss (a th) at great length*; sie besprachen es unter e–a *they discussed it among them*; wir w es mit ihm ~ ⟨fam⟩ *we'll take it up with him* **2.** (ausmachen) *to arrange, to settle (a th), to agree upon (a th)* **3.** (Buch etc.) *to review; to notice* || günstig besprochen w v jdm (of plays) *to have a good send-off from a p* || (Dinge) in der Presse ~ *to comment on* **4. sich** unter e–a ~ *to go into conference* || sich ~ mit *to confer, to consult, to take counsel, to commune with (a p)* || sich ~ über *to deliberate on (a th)* || (verabreden) sich ~ *to agree (that)*

Bespr·echer m *reviewer (of a book,* etc.) **Bespr·echung** f ~/~en **1.** *charm, incantation, spell (of a p)* || *charming (of an illness)*; an ~ v Warzen glauben *to believe in charming warts* **2.** *discussion (of a question)* **3.** *conference, consultation* (mit jdm; über etw *with a p; on a th*); *deliberation*; nach ~ mit *on consultation with* || ⟨dipl⟩ *pourparler* (Fr) **4.** *review, notice (of a book)*

bespr·engen vt [h] (etw) mit Wasser ~ *to besprinkle* (od *sprinkle) with water*; (Garten) *to water*; jdn mit Weihwasser ~ *to sprinkle a p with holy water* || leicht ~ *to bedew, moisten, damp*; → besprenkeln **Bespr·engung** f ~/~en ⟨ec⟩ *sprinkling*

bespr·enkeln vt [h] *to sprinkle* (mit *with*), nur mit einigen Tropfen besprenkelt *sprinkled only with a few drops* || → sprenkeln

bespr·ingen vt [h] [→ springen] (Wall) *to leap upon* || (T) (Weibchen) *to cover* || **Bespr·ingung** = Begattung

bespr·itzen vt [h] (etw, jdn) *to bespatter, to splash* (mit Wasser *with water*); Häuser mit Wasser ~ (*of firemen*) *to play on houses* || mit Dreck ~ *to splash* od *soil with mud*

besp·ucken vt [h] (jdn etw) *to spit at* od *upon*

besp·ulen vt [h] *to load with coils; to pupinize*

Besp·ulungsplan m *pupinization scheme*

besp·ülen vt [h] (of the sea) (Küste, Land) *to wash, bathe* || (die Augen etc.) *to bathe, wet*; ⟨poet⟩ *to lave*

bessar·abisch a *Bessarabian*

B·essemer- (nach Henry Bessemer, † 1898) [in comp] ⟨tech⟩ **~birne** f *(Bessemer) converter* **~prozeß** m *B. process* **~roheisen** n *(acid) B. pig* **~stahl** m *(acid) B. steel*

b·esser [compr v gut] **I.** a **A.** [reiner compr] *better* **1.** [attr] jds ~e Gefühle *a p's better feelings*; jds ~e Hälfte *a p's better half (his wife)* || ~e Tage gesehen h. *to have seen better days* || in ~en Umständen leben als.. *to be better off than* **2.** [pred] **a. es ist** ~ abzureisen *it is better to leave* || es ist ~, daß er bleibt *it is better for him to stay* || es ist ~ als gestern *there is an improvement on yesterday* || man kann mit ihnen ~ reden *they are easier to talk to* (als *than*) || er ist heute ~ (sc als bisher) *he is better today* || ~ s als (S) *to be better than, to be preferable* od *superior to (a th), to excel (a th)* || ~ ist ~ *in order to be on the safe side* || das wäre noch ~! *that would be the limit!* | ~ w *to improve; to (get) better*; (of the weather) *to clear up* || → sich bessern **b. ich bleibe** ~, wie ich bin *I am better as I am* || du siehst nach d–m Ausflug viel besser aus *you look much the better* *for your trip* || sich ~ fühlen (sc als bisher) *to feel better* || er hat es ~ als ich *he is better off than I* || ⟨iron⟩ es sollte noch ~ k. *worse was to follow* || das macht die S nicht ~ *that is no improvement, that does not mend matters* || jdn ~ stellen *to raise a p's wages* od *salary* || ich täte ~ z gehen *I had better go*, ⟨Am fam⟩ *I better go*; ich hätte ~ getan, z gehen *I had better have gone* **c. ~ als nichts** *better than nothing* || ~ spät als nie *better late than never*; °~ als 'n Tritt vor'n Bauch! ~ als in die hohle Hand geschissen etc. *better than a kick in the pants* | **desto ~** *all the better, so much the better*; je eher desto ~ *the sooner the better*; je mehr desto ~ *the more the better* (⟨fam⟩ *merrier*) || um so ~ *all the better, so much the better* **B.** [dem Sinne nach kein compr] **1.** (ganz gut, leidlich gut) einige ~e Hotels *some quite decent hotels* **2.** ~e Herren, Kaufleute *better-class gentlemen, merchants* || *respectable, good*; *experienced*; ein ~es Mädchen gesucht *wanted a housemaid of respectable family* **3.** es ist sein ~es Recht *it is his good right* (*to have*..) **4.** er ist ein ~er Handlanger *he is a mere drudge* **II.** adv *better*; immer ~ *better and better* || ~ daran *better off*; er ist jetzt keineswegs ~ daran *he is none the better for it*; ich bin so ~ daran *I am better as I am* | sich ~ in achtnehmen *to be more careful* (od *cautious*) || sich ~ benehmen *to behave better* || dies gefällt (*or* behagt) mir ~ *I like this better, I prefer this* || es geht ihm heute ~ (als bisher) *he is better today*; es geht ihm immer ~ *he is steadily improving* || er macht es ~ als du *he does it better than you* || oder ~ gesagt *or strictly speaking, or rather* || heute steht es ~ (sc als bisher) mit ihm *he is better today* || es sich ~ überlegen *to think better of it* || es ~ wissen *to know better* (*he ought to know better*) **III.** [in comp] ~ aussehend [a] *better-fed* || ~ unterrichtet [a] *better-informed* || **ˣ~wisser** m *knowbetter*; *faultfinder* **B·essere** [das ~, ein ~s] n *the better* || etw ~s *something better* || das ~ ist des Guten Feind ⟨biol⟩ *the best is the enemy of the good*; ⟨prov⟩ [umgekehrt] *let well* (*enough*) *alone*! ~s leisten *to do better* || ich habe ~s z tun *I have better* (od *other*) *things to do* || jdn e–s ~n belehren *to disabuse a p* || sich e–s ~n besinnen *to think better of it* || nichts ~s *no better thing, nothing better*; man kann nichts ~s v ihm erwarten *he is no better than he should be* || eine Wendung zum ~n *a change for the better* **b·essern** vt/i [h] **I.** vt **1.** ⟨mst übtr⟩ (Verhältnisse etc.) *to better, to improve*; *to ameliorate*; *to meliorate*; s e Lage ist um nichts gebessert *he is none the better for it* || (jdn) ~ *to better* || → auf–, aus–, verbessern **2. sich ~ a.** (of conditions, health, etc.) *to better, improve, mend*; *to get* od *grow better, to change for the better*; (of securities, etc.) *to advance, improve*; *rise* **b.** (P) (moralisch) *to amend, reform*; *to turn over a new leaf, to mend one's ways* || er hat sich sehr gebessert *he is greatly improved* || → sich erholen **II.** vi ~ an e–m Buch etc. *to make corrections in a book, to correct a book* **b·essernd** a *ameliorative* (*influence*)

B·esserung f ~/~en **1.** *⟨eig⟩ *melioration* (*of roads*) || → Aus–, Verbesserung **2.** (sittliche ~) *amendmend, betterment, reform* (*of a p*) **3.** (of conditions, etc.) *improvement, improve, amelioration, change for the better*; ~ der Gesundheit jds *improvement in a p's health*; auf dem Wege der ~ *in a fair way of recovery, on the improve* od *mend*; a. d. W. d. ~ s *to be improving* od *mending*; es ist e–e ~ gegenüber gestern vorhanden *there is an improvement on yesterday*; gute ~! *I hope you will soon recover*! | ⟨com⟩ *advance* (v ½% *of ½ percent*; des Zinssatzes *in the rate*); *rise* (des Gehalts *of* od *in the salary*); *recovery* (*of the market*) **~sanstalt** f *corrective institution*; *reformatory*; *house of correction*; (f. Prostituierte) *penitentiary* || ⟨Am⟩ *workhouse reform-school*, **ˣ~sfähig** a *improvable, mendable*; **~smittel** n *corrective*

B·esserwissen n ~s/, °**Besserwisser·ei** f ~/ (*his*) "*I know better*" *attitude*

B·est- (→ beste) [in comp] **~arbeit** f *best* od *record work* **ˣ~besucht** a *best-frequented* **~fall** m *optimum* (L) **ˣ~gefügt** a *best-knit* **ˣ~gehaßt** a *best-hated* **~geher** m (Buch) *best seller* **~haupt** n ⟨hist jur⟩ → Baulebung **~leistung** f *best performance*; → Höchstleistung **~mann** m ⟨mar⟩ *proxy of a master of a small coasting vessel* **ˣ~möglich 1.** a; *best*; der ~e Weg *the best way possible, the best possible way*; ~e Verhältnisse [pl] *optimum* (L); das ˣ~e tun *to do one's level best* **2.** adv *best* **~seller** m (Buch) *best seller* **~wert** m ⟨mach⟩ auf ~e arbeitend *giving the best results*

best·allen vt [h] (jdn) *to install* (*a p*) *in an office, to invest* (*a p*) *with an office*; *to appoint* (*a p*) *to an office* **best·allt** a *installed*; wohl ~ *duly installed* **B.llung** f **1.** *appointment, investiture, installation* (*of a p*) **2.** ⟨med⟩ = Approbation l. **3.** ⟨jur⟩ (Urkunde) *warrant* **4.** = ~surkunde **5.** † = Gehalt **~sbrief** m, **~sdekret** n, **~surkunde** f *patent, letters-patent*; *commission* || → Diplom

Best·and m ~(e)s/ˣ~e **A. 1. a.** (Bestehen, Fortdauer) *existence, continuance, duration, endurance*; *standing* || (Haltbarkeit) *consistence, -cy, stability, durability* **b.** v kurzem ~ *of brief* od *short duration* || e–r S ~ geben *to make a th last, to make a th durable* od *secure, to give a th a solid basis* (od *footing*) || ~ h, v ~ s *to endure, to be durable* (od *lasting*); k–n ~ h, nicht v ~ s *to be of no duration*, (of the weather) *to be unsettled*; bei jdm ~ h *to last with a p* **2.** ˣ⟨jur⟩ = Miete; Pacht **3.** ⟨forest⟩ *standing growth* **B.** (Vorrat) **1.** ⟨forest⟩ *stand, growth, wood, body, crop*; Baumˣ~ *growing crop, amount, number of trees*; Eichenˣ~ *number of oaks* **2. a.** *stock, store, supply* (an.. *of food, fuel, energy*, etc.); *amount, number, stock* (*of books, words*); *inventory* (*of furniture*); Viehˣ~ *live stock* || ⟨hunt & agr⟩ *population* (*the deer, pig p.*) Notˣ~ *reserve*, → Reserve | ⟨com⟩ Warenˣ~ *stock on hand, supply of goods, stores* [pl]; den ~ aufnehmen *to take stock of* (*goods*) || Restˣ~ *rest*; Restbestände [pl] *remainders* [pl] **b.** Kassenˣ~ (*cash or liquid*) *assets* [pl] (*of a bank*) || eiserner ~ *the gold reserve* (*of the Bank of England*); *the iron* od *last reserve*; ⟨übtr⟩ *the basic* od *constituent parts* [pl] (*of a library*, etc.), *the foundations* [pl] (*of a science*) || *cash in hand* | (Kontoˣ~) *balance in hand*; Effektenˣ~ *holdings in bonds and shares* (*of a p*) **3.** (Personenˣ~) ⟨mil & nav⟩ *establishment*; *strength* (*of a force*); → Etat **4.** Tatˣ~ *facts* [pl]

Best·and- **ˣ~bildend** a ⟨for⟩ *gregarious, social* (*tree*) **~geber** m ⟨jur⟩ = Vermieter; Verpächter **~geld** n ⟨com⟩ *cash in hand* || *cash-balance* **~nehmer** m ⟨jur⟩ = Mieter; Pächter **~teil** m → d. (*essential*) *part* **~vertrag** m ⟨jur⟩ = Miete; Pacht

best·anden a [pp v bestehen] ~e Prüfung *successful examination* || ⟨for⟩ *stocked* (Gebiet); mit Bäumen (dicht) ~ (*closely*) *grown over with trees*

best·ändig I. a **1.** [attr & pred] (P & conditions) *constant, faithful, steady* (*lover*); *firm, steadfast, steady* (*mind*); → besonnen || *fixed, invariable* (*habit*); *unvarying, unvacillating* (*conditions*); *settled* ([*good*] *weather*); *steady* (*climate*) | (zeitlich) *continuous, perpetual* || *steady* (*demand*) || *chronic* (*doubts*) **2.** [pred] *constant* (in *in one's love*) || (of barometer) *set fair* || ⟨com⟩ ~ s (of the market, etc.) *to be steady*; ~ gegen (Luft, Wasser, Hitze) *unaffected by*.. **II.** adv *continuously, perpetually* **ˣ~keit** f *constancy, steadfastness*; *steadiness* (*of a p*) || *steadiness* (*of climate, weather*) | (zeitliche) *continuance, per-*

petuance, perpetuity || ⟨tech⟩ *insusceptibility* || *permanence, stability* (*of dyes*)

Best·ands- ~aufnahme f ⟨com⟩ *stock-taking* **~buch** n, **~liste** f ⟨com⟩ *inventory, stock-book, ledger* **~karte** f ⟨com, comp⟩ *balance card* **~konto** n *holding account* **~masse** f *cubic capacity of timber in a special area* **~nachweisung** f *list of stores on charge* **~schluß** m ⟨for⟩ *crown-cover, canopy* **~verzeichnis** n *inventory, stock-book*; ein ~ aufnehmen über *to make an inventory of*

Best·andteil m (*essential*) *part, ingredient*; (*the ingredients of a cake*); ein wichtiger ~ e–s Charakters *an important ingredient in a character*; die ~e, aus denen sich ein Held zus–setzt *the ingredients that go to the making of a hero* || Grund≃ *element* || ⟨jur & chem⟩ *component* (od *constituent*) *part* (od *element*), *component, constituent*; wesentlicher ~ *essential part*, ein w. ~ s v, e–n wesentlichen ~ bilden v etw *to be part and parcel of a th*; e–n ~ der Berechnung bilden *to enter into the calculation* | ⟨aesth⟩ kennzeichnender, inhaltlicher ~ *motif*

best·ärken vt [h] **1.** etw ~ (Aussage etc.) *to confirm, corroborate, endorse, fortify* (mit *with*) || e–e Annahme ~ *to lend force to a supposition*; s–e Philosophie bestärkt s–e eigene Erfahrung *his philosophy reinforces his own experience* **2.** jdn ~ *to confirm a p* (in s–m Entschluß *in his decision*, etc.); *to encourage, fortify, strengthen, support a p* (*in*); jdn im Glauben ~ *to help a p believe* (daß *that*); jdn in s–n Leidenschaften ~ *to pander to a p's passions* **B.kung** f *confirmation, corroboration* (*of a statement*; durch *by, with*) || *encouragement, strengthening, support* (*of a p*)

best·ätigen vt [h] **1.** etw ~: (Aussage etc.) *to confirm*; (Zeugnis, Theorie) *to corroborate, validate, endorse*; *verify*; (im Brief) hiermit möchte ich ~ *this is to confirm*; (Bescheinigung) hiermit wird –gt *this is to certify* || (Annahme) *to substantiate*; *to make good* || (Empfang) *to acknowledge* (*the receipt*); wir ~ Eingang *we are in receipt* (*of your letter*); dankend ~ wir den heutigen Eingang Ihres Schreibens *we acknowledge* (*with thanks*) *your letter received today*; wir ~ dankend den Abschluß mit Ihnen *this confirms sale arranged with you* || etw amtlich ~ *to certify a th*; jdm ~, daß.. *to certify to a p that..*; hiermit wird –gt *this is to certify* (daß *that*) → bescheinigen, bezeugen | (of events) (Verdacht, Tatsache) *to bear out* (*an examination does not bear out the charges*); *to confirm, support, verify*; es jdm ~, daß.. *to bear out to a p that..*; wir ~ dankend (Ihr Schreiben..) *we have received and wish to thank you* **2.** (gutheißen) (Beschluß, Wahl etc.) *to approve, authorize*; *confirm*; (Urteil) *to sanction* (*a th*), *to give sanction to* (*a th*); *to make* (*a th*) *valid*; (Vertrag) *to ratify* **3.** jdn ~ *to confirm a p*; *to ratify the appointment of a p* **4.** ⟨hunt⟩ (Rehbock) *to ascertain*; die Hunde ~ den Hirsch *the hounds track the stag* **5. sich ~** *to be confirmed* od *verified*; *to come true*; *to prove* (*to be*) *true*

best·ätigend 1. a *confirmatory, confirmative* || *approving* **2.** adv (*to nod*) *affirmatively*; *approvingly* **Best·ätiger** m *corroborator* **best·ätigt** a *certified* (*check*); → bestätigen

Best·ätigung f ~/~en *confirmation, corroboration* (*of a statement*); *endorsement*; *verification*; *substantiation* (*of an assertion*); z ~ v *in corroboration of..* || amtlich beglaubigte ~ *certification* (*of a teacher*); → Bescheinigung || *probate* (*of a will*) || *ratification, sanction* **~surteil** n ⟨jur⟩ *confirmatory* od *corroborative judgement*

best·atten vt [h] (feierlich f. beerdigen) (jdn) *to bury, inter*; bestattet liegen *to be buried* (*in..*) || feuer~ *to cremate* (*a p*) || → begraben **Best·atter** m (Leichen≃) *undertaker*

***Best·ätter** m = Spediteur

Best·attung f ~/~en (Leichen≃) *undertaking* || (Beerdigung) *burial, interment*; *funeral* || Feuer≃ *cremation* **~sfeier** f *funeral*; *obsequies* **~sinstitut** n = Beerdigungsinstitut **~szeremonien** pl *funeral ceremonies, obsequies* [pl]

best·auben vi [s] *to get dusty*

best·äuben vt [h] (etw) *to dust*; *to cover with dust* || (mit Mehl etc.) *to sprinkle, dredge* || ⟨bot⟩ mit Pollen ~ *to pollen, to pollinate* || → zerstäuben **Best·äubung** f ⟨bot⟩ *pollination*

best·auden vrefl [h] sich ~ ⟨bot⟩ (of plants) *to grow into a bush*; *to grow bushy*

best·aunen vt [h] etw (jdn) *to gaze at a th* (*a p*), *to look at a th with astonishment* || ⟨übtr⟩ (jdn) *to admire*

b·este [sup v gut] [attr] a **1.** der, die, das ~.. *the best* [in verschiedensten Bedeutungen: edelste (*man*), vollkommenste (*mother*), gütigste (*heart*); fähigste (*general, scholar*), tüchtigste (*teacher*); vollendetste (*novel*); schönste (*view*); geeignetste (*man for..*); bequemste, passendste (*way*); feinste (*quality, cigar*) etc.] **2.** ⟨bes com⟩ *first-class, first-rate, superior* (*quality*); *prime* (*beef*; *bill*) **3.** [besondere Verbindungen:] die ~n Absichten *the best intentions* || im ~n Alter *in the prime of life, in one's prime* || ~n Dank f. *many thanks for, thanks very much for* || im ~n Einvernehmen *on the best terms* (*with*) || ~ Empfehlungen an *my best compliments to..* || im ~n Fall *at* (*the*) *best* || das kommt in den ~n Familien vor *accidents will happen in the best-regulated families* || mit ~n Grüßen *with kind regards* || ⟨jur⟩ das ~ Haupt = Besthaupt → Baulebung || in den ~n Jahren *in the prime of life* || jds ~ Kleidung *one's* (*Sunday*) *best* || nach ~n Kräften *to the best of one's power, to the top of one's bent* || der ~ Mann *the best of men*, ⟨*cards*⟩ *the winner* || im ~n Mannesalter *in the prime of manhood* || er ist der ~ Mensch v der Welt *he is the best fellow alive* (od *in the world*) || in ~r Qualität (*beef*, etc.) *in prime condition* || im ~n Schlaf *in one's best sleep* || sich v der ~n Seite zeigen *to show o.s. at one's best, to come down handsomely*; er zeigte sich dir v der ~n Seite *he was at his best with you* || im ~n Sinne *in the best sense* || die ~n Stellen (e–s Buches) *the plums* (*in a book*) || der ~ Teil v *the pick of* (*his men*) || auf dem ~n Wege s *to be in a fair way* (*to succeed*) || beim ~n Willen nicht *not for the world*; ich verstehe mit dem ~n W. nicht *I don't understand at all* (*what..*) || nach ~m Wissen u Gewissen *to the best of one's knowledge and belief* || im ~n Zuge s *to be in the middle* od *midst of one's work* (etc.)

B·este 1. der ~ m, **die** ~ f: er ist der ~ in der Klasse *he is the top of the class* || der erste ~ *the first comer* || die ~ der Ehefrauen *the best of wives* || mein ~r *my dear Sir* (od *fellow*); (herablassend) *my good man*; m–e ~ *dear Madam, dear Mrs. N.* || die neun ~n *The Nine Worthies* **2. ~s, das** ~ n **a.** *the best thing*; das ~ v *the pick* (od *cream, flower*) *of* (*the crew, of society*, etc.); das ~ v allen *the pick of the bunch* || das ~ vom ~ *the choicest of the choice*, ⟨fam⟩ *the finest ever*, → *ever* || das ~ in s–r Art *the best in its way*; das ~.. s *to be unique* od *unmatched* || das ~ ist gerade gut genug *the best is none too good*; das ~ wäre es, du schwiegest *you had better* (od *you had much best*) *not talk* || das ~ wird s *the best* (*thing*) *will be* (*to leave*) || das wäre das ~ *nothing would be better* || wir wollen das ~ hoffen *we'll hope for the best* || sein ~s geben *to do one's best* || sein ~s tun *to do one's best* od *utmost* (um ihm z helfen *to help him*) || ich will nur dein ~s *I am thinking only of your wellbeing* || fürs allgemeine ~ *for the public weal* || ich halte es f. das ~ *I think it best* (*to do*) || sein ~s tun *to do one's* (⟨fam⟩ *level*) *best* || das ~ daraus m *to make the best of things* **b. am** ≃**n** *best* || am ≃n abschneiden *to get* od *have the best of it*; *to come out on top* || dies gefällt mit am ≗n *I like this best* ‖ am ≗n s, sich am ≗n zeigen *to be at one's best* (*he was at his best in the third act*) ‖ ich täte am ≗n nicht z gehen *I had best not go*, ich hätte am ≗n getan z gehen *I had best have gone* | **aufs** ≗ *best*; → bestens ‖ etw aufs ≗ ausnutzen *to make the best of a th* | **zu jds ∼m** *to a p's advantage* (*it turned out to his a.*); *for the benefit of a p, in the interest of a p, on* od *in behalf of a p*; z d–m ∼n *for your good* ‖ etw zu s–m (eigenen) ∼ wenden *to turn a th to one's profit* ‖ zum ∼n der Armen *for the benefit of the poor* ‖ etw *or* e–n zum ≗n geben *to stand, treat*; jdm etw zum ≗n geben *to stand a p a th* (od *a th to a p*); *to favour a p with a th*; gib ein Lied zum ≗n *give us a song*; er gab ein Lied zum ≗n *he obliged* (*the company*) *with a song* ‖ jdn zum ≗n h. *or* halten *to make fun* od *game of a p, to pull a p's leg*; hältst du mich z ≗n? *are you kidding*? **3.** die ∼n [pl] *the best*; die ∼n v *the pick* (od *cream, flower*) *of* (*his men*) ‖ unter den ∼n s *to be of the best*

best·echbar a = bestechlich

best·echen vt/i [h] **I.** vt [→ stechen] **1.** *to prick, stab*; (Saum) *to stitch* ‖ ⟨min⟩ (Zimmerung des Schachts) *to sound by pricking* od *stabbing* **2.** ⟨fig⟩ **a.** (jdn durch Geld) *to corrupt, bribe* (z *to*; z tun *to do*) *to suborn* (*to do*); ⟨fam⟩ *to grease*, ⟨sl⟩ *to nobble*, ⟨Am⟩ *to buy* (*a p*) *off*; ⟨fam⟩ *to grease a p's palm* **b.** *to allure, attract*; *captivate*; *win* ‖ *mislead, dazzle* **c.** (Urteil) *to bribe* **d. sich ∼ 1** *to take a bribe, to be corruptible* | *to be captivated* ‖ *to be misled* **II.** vi *to prove an attraction, to draw*; das Bild besticht durch s–e Farben *the picture draws* (od *exercises an attraction*) *by its colours*

best·echend a ⟨fig⟩ *alluring, appealing*, (*most*) *attractive*; *captivating, engaging, exquisite*; *lovely, delightful*; *remarkable, striking*; *winning* (*ways*) ‖ (äußerlich ∼) *specious* (appearance) **Best·echer** m *briber* **–chlich** a *bribable, corruptible*; *venal* (judge) ‖ [pred] *open to bribery* ≗**keit** f ∼/ *corruptibility*; *venality* **Best·echung** f ∼/ ∼en (aktive) *bribery*; (passive) *corruption*; *subornation* ‖ ⟨Am sl⟩ *graft*; mit ∼en arbeiten *to graft* ‖ (jdn) durch ∼ verleiten *to bribe* (z *to*; *to do*); sich durch ∼en weiterhelfen *to bribe one's way* ‖ ∼sgeld [n] *bribe* ‖ ∼sversuch [m] *attempt at bribery*

Best·eck n ∼(e)s/∼e **1.** *(Futteral) *box*; *case*, ∼kasten *case of instruments* **2.** (Satz v Gegenständen) *set of tools*; ⟨med⟩ *set of surgical instruments*; *case* ‖ Eß≗ *knife, fork, and spoon*; ∼e [pl] ⟨com⟩ *table cutlery*; ⟨hot⟩ (Gedeck) *cover*; Fisch≗ *fish-cover*; Vorlege≗ *serving spoon and fork* **3.** ⟨mar⟩ *reckoning*; gegißtes ∼ *dead-reckoning*; das ∼ m *to take one's reckoning* **4.** °(P) = Kauz **∼kasten** m *case*; *box* ‖ *drawer* (*in a side-board*) **∼korb** m ⟨Ger⟩ *cutlery basket*; ⟨m. m.⟩ *knife-tray*; *plate-basket*

best·ecken vt [h] (etw) *to stick* (mit *with pins*, etc.) ‖ ⟨agr⟩ (Beet) *to plant* (*with*) ‖ (Kletterpflanzen) *to stake*

Best·eder m ∼s/∼ *a p who has given an order for the building of a ship*

best·ehen vi/t [h] [→ stehen] **I.** [vi] *to exist, subsist, stand, hold, prevail, occur*; *to be present, extant, prevalent, current* **A. 1.** (standhalten) siegreich in e–m Kampf ∼ *to come off victorious in a combat* ‖ mit Ehren ∼ *to come off with honour* ‖ vor Gott, Gottes Richterstuhl ∼ *to justify o.s. before God* ‖ er hat bestanden (sc in der Prüfung) *he has passed* (od *got through*), *he has been successful in his examination*; er hat nicht b. *he has failed in his examination* (→ durchfallen); er hat nur eben ∼ *he has satisfied his examiners, he has obtained a pass*; er bestand im Deutschen *he passed in German* **2.** (andauern; ∼ bleiben) (*to continue*) *to exist, to be in existence, to be extant, to subsist, remain* ‖ *to continue, endure, last*; *persist*; noch ∼ *to remain, subsist, survive* ‖ ∼ bleiben *to hold* od *stand good* ‖ *to continue to exist* ‖ (*of spots*, etc.) *to become fixed* (auf *in*) ‖ z Recht ∼ *to be valid, to hold* (*good*) | (existieren) *to exist*; das Geschäft besteht schon 50 Jahre *the business has existed for 50 years*; schon sehr lange ∼ *to be of old standing* ‖ ⟨sl⟩ *to carry on*; bei solchen Preisen können wir nicht ∼ *with such prices we cannot keep things going* ‖ (vorhanden sein) *to be, to exist*; es besteht ein Unterschied zwischen.. *there is a difference between*; es ∼ Zweifel *there are doubts* (*as to*); worüber kein Zweifel besteht, ist.. *what is not in any doubt is..* ‖ nicht neben–e–a ∼ können (of colours, qualities, etc.) *to be incompatible* od *inconsistent with one another*; *to clash* **3.** ∼ auf etw *to insist* od *stand on, to persist in a th, to urge a th*; fest ∼ auf *to be adamant on a th* ‖ ich bestehe darauf *I insist on it*; ich bestehe darauf, daß dein Bruder abreist *I insist on your brother('s) leaving*; ..daß er abreist.. *on him* od *his leaving*; jdm gegenüber darauf ∼, daß.. *to insist to a p that* ‖ auf s–m Lohn ∼ *to stand out for one's wages* ‖ auf s–r Meinung ∼ *to stick to one's opinion* od *to one's guns* ‖ auf s–m Recht ∼ *to be tenacious of one's right* | auf s–m Kopf ∼ *to be obstinate* **B. ∼ in** *to consist in*; *to lie in*; das Leben besteht in Arbeit *life consists in work*; darin ∼.. z s *to consist in being..* ‖ die gr Leistung des 18. Jhs bestand in der Entwicklung des.. *the great achievement of the 18th c. was in the development of..* ‖ → **2. ∼ aus** (in) etw *to consist of, to be composed* (od *made up*) *of a th*; → ausmachen, zus–setzen **II.** vt **1.** *jdn ∼ *to conquer, defeat a p* **2.** etw ∼ *to go* od *pass through a th*; *to undergo, endure, stand a th*; (Gefahren, Schwierigkeiten) *to get over, to over-come* ‖ Abenteuer ∼ *to go through..* ‖ den Kampf (siegreich) ∼ *to come off victorious, to come out winner* ‖ e–e Krise ∼ *to weather a crisis* ‖ die Probe ∼ *to stand the test* ‖ e–e Prüfung ∼ *to pass an examination*; den B.A. ∼ ⟨Cambr. univ⟩ *to go out* (*in science*); e–e Prüfung nicht ∼ *to fail in an examination*, ⟨sl⟩ *to be plucked* od *ploughed* ‖ e–n Sturm ∼ (of ships) *to weather a storm*

Best·ehen n **1.** (*existence* (*of a disease*); *subsistence* ‖ die Schule feierte gestern ihr hundertjähriges (500-jähriges) ∼ *the school celebrated its centenary* (*quincentenary*) *yesterday* ‖ *presence* (*of a danger*) ‖ (Fort≗) *continuance* (*of a quarrel*); *persistence* (*of an impression* **2.** das ∼ jds (od seitens jds) *the insistence by a p* (auf *on*) ‖ *adherence, attachment* (auf *to*) **3.** *getting over, overcoming* (*of difficulties*) ‖ ∼ e–r Prüfung *passing of an examination*; *pass* ‖ → Bestand, bestanden **best·ehend** a *existing* (*forms*); *ruling*; unter den ∼en Verhältnissen *under the circumstances, under present c.*; ∼e Versicherung [f] *insurance in force*; mit ≗em zufrieden s ⟨Am sl⟩ *to stand pat* ‖ *prevailing* (*fashion*); *ruling* ‖ lange ∼ *long-standing* (*difference*); noch ∼ *extant*; *surviving* ‖ [pred] *in existence, in being*

best·ehlen vt [h] [→ stehlen] jdn ∼ *to steal from a p, to rob a p*

best·eigbar a *ascendable*

best·eigen vt [h] [→ steigen] (Berg) *to ascend, mount*; *conquer*; noch nie bestiegen *virgin* (*peak*) (Leiter) *to ascend, mount* ‖ (Pferd) *to mount, bestride, cross* ‖ (Fahrrad) *to mount* ‖ ein Schiff ∼ *to board a ship, to go on board a ship*; *to embark*; (Zug etc.) *to board* ‖ den Thron ∼ *to ascend* od *mount the throne, to accede to the throne* ‖ °⟨sex⟩ *to scale, mount* **B.gung** f *ascension, ascent* (*of a mountain*) ‖ *mounting* (*of a horse*) ‖ ∼ des Thrones *accession to the throne*

Best·ell- (→ bestellen) **∼amt** n (der Post) *delivery office* **∼bezirk** m *postal district* **∼buch** n ⟨com⟩ *order-book* **∼gebühr** f, **∼geld** n *postage*; *charge for delivery*, (f Fracht) *carriage, portage*, *porterage* **~karte** f *order-card* **~nummer** f *order--number* **~schein** m ⟨com⟩ *order form* **~zeit** f **1.** ⟨agr⟩ *seed time* **2.** (für Briefe) *time of delivery* **~zettel** m = Bestellschein; *order form* od *blank*

best·ellbar a ⟨agr⟩ *cultivable* | *capable of delivery*; ein ~er Brief *a letter that can be delivered* **best·ellen** vt [h] **A.** (füllen) (Tisch etc.) *to cover, fill* (mit *with*) **B. 1.** (Acker, Feld) *to cultivate, till* ‖ ⟨übtr⟩ *to attend to* (*a th*); das Haus ~ *to order one's household*; ⟨übtr⟩ *to set one's house in order*; → beschicken ‖ ⟨fig⟩ es ist gut um ihn bestellt *he is quite all right*; es ist schlecht, schlimm um ihn b. *he is in an evil plight*; ..es ist kläglich um die Landwirtschaft b. *agriculture is in a miserable condition*; wie ist es um diese Welt b.? *what is the matter with this world*? **C. 1.** (P) ⟨mil⟩ (beordern) *to order, direct* (nach *to*) ‖ (berufen) *to appoint, constitute* (*a p*); jdn zum Präsidenten ~ *to appoint a p* (*to be*) *president* | (k l) ⟨jur⟩ *to call, cite, summon* (*a p*) (z jdm *before a p*) ‖ *to ask* (*a p*) *to come* (*ask the doctor to come*); jdn z sich ~ *to send for a p* ‖ jdn nach e–m bestimmten Ort ~ *to tryst a p*; ich werde ihn ins Hotel ~ *I'll ask him to come to the hotel* (od *to meet us at the h.*); ich werde ihn auf 10 Uhr ~ *I'll ask him for 10 o'clock*; was glauben Sie, weshalb ich Sie hierher bestellt habe? *what do you think I asked you to come here for*? **2.** (S) **a.** (Waren) *to order, indent* (*a th*); *to give an order for* (*a th*); etw bei jdm ~ *to order a th from a p*; bestellt s *to be on order* ‖ (Speisen) *to order* (zum Mittagessen *for dinner*); jdm etw ~ *to order a th for a p*; Getränke ~ *to call for drinks*; er bestellte e–e Flasche Wein beim Kellner *he ordered a bottle of wine from the waiter* ‖ (of waiter) *Have you given your order, sir? to ring for* (*a th*) **b.** (Tisch) *to reserve, order*; (Platz, Zimmer) *to book* (*book me 2 seats*); *to bespeak, engage*; ich bestellte mir 2 Plätze *I booked 2 seats*; jedes Zimmer ist bestellt *every room is bespoken* ‖ bestellter Platz ⟨sail⟩ *reserved seat* ‖ (Buch) *to send for* **c.** (Briefe) *to deliver* **d.** (Botschaft, Mitteilung) *to deliver* (*a message*); kann ich etw ~? h Sie etw z ~? *have you any message* (an ihn *for him*)? jdm etw ~ *to give a p a message* | Grüße v jdm ~ *to present a p's compliments* (*he presented his mother's c.*); bestelle ihm schöne Grüße v mir *give him my kind regards* **B.ller** ⟨agr⟩ *cultivator, tiller* ‖ ⟨com⟩ *orderer*; *buyer* ‖ *deliverer* (*of letters*) **Best·ellung** f ~/~en **1.** *cultivation* (*of the soil*) **2.** ~ jds *the appointment of a p* (zum Botschafter *to the post of ambassador*) **3.** ⟨com⟩ *order* ⟨a. cul⟩; ⟨cul⟩ ~(en) entgegennehmen *to take the order*(*s*) ‖ *indent* (e–r S *for a th*); *application*; ~sformular [n] *application form*; e–e ~ ausführen *to discharge an order*; unausgeführte ~ *unfilled order*; ~en m *to place orders* (auf *for*) ‖ auf ~ *on* (od *to*) *order*; auf ~ angefertigt *bespoke* (*boots, suit*) | *booking* (*of seats, rooms*) | *delivery* (*of letters*; *of a message*); mit der 10 Uhr~ *by the 10 o'clock d.*

b·estenfalls adv *at* (*the*) *best*

b·estens adv *best, in the best way*, ⟨fam⟩ *for all there's in it*; ⟨sl⟩ *o. k.*! ‖ ⟨st exch⟩ *at the best price* od *figure* ‖ ~ **ausführen** *to carry* (*a th*) *out to the best of one's ability*; ⟨com⟩ *to give* (*a th*) *one's most careful attention* ‖ etw ~ auslegen *to put the best construction on a th* ‖ etw ~ ausnützen *to make the best of a th* ‖ ich danke ~ *many thanks, thanks very much* ‖ empfehlen Sie mich ~ Ihren Eltern *remember me most kindly to your parents*; sich ~ empfehlen *to send one's compliments* od *regards* (jdm *to a p*); ich empfehle mich Ihnen ~ *my best compliments to you, with kind regards*

best·ernt a *starred*; *studded* od *set with stars* od *asterisks*; → gestirnt ‖ *starred* (*general*)

best·euerbar a *taxable*; *subject to taxation*

best·euern vt [h] (P) *to impose a tax upon, to tax* (*a p*) ‖ (S) *to put a tax upon, to tax* (*a th*) ‖ z hoch ~ *to overtax* ‖ → veranlagen

Best·euerung f ~/~en *taxation*; *taxability* ‖ jds ~ *tax on a p*; Rentner≗ *tax on the rentier*

besti·alisch a *bestial, beastly*; *brutish* **Bestiali·t·ät** f ~/~en, *bestiality* [–*ties* pl], *beastliness*

best·icken vt [h] (Tuch) *to embroider*

B·estie f ~/~n *wild beast* (*of prey*) ‖ ⟨fig⟩ *brute*

best·immbar a *ascertainable, determinable, definable*

best·immen vt/i [h] **I.** vt **1.** (anordnen) **a.** [oft pass] (durch höhere Gewalt) *to ordain, will*; *destine* (f *for*, z *to*), *to doom* (z *to*; *to do*); (vorher~) *to predestinate, predestine* (*to*; *to do*); Gott hat es so bestimmt *God has willed it so* ‖ (of laws) ~, daß..*to lay down that..* **b.** (ausersehen) jdn ~ *to design, destine, intend a p* (f die Marinelaufbahn *for the navy*; zum Juristen *to be a lawyer*; z tun *to do*); ⟨Am⟩ *to head a p* (f *for*) ‖ (Leute) *to detail* (*for duties*) ‖ (etw) *to intend*, ich hatte das Buch f dich bestimmt *I had intended the book for you* **c.** (ernennen) (jdn) *to appoint* (zum Schiedsrichter *to be umpire*) **2.** (entscheiden) **a.** (etw) *to determine, decide*; *to be decisive of*; der König hat es anders bestimmt *the king has decided otherwise* ‖ bestimmt w durch *to be determined by* (*the result was d. by*); (of things) *to go by* ‖ das habe ich zu ~ *that's my business to decide* ‖ (Frage) *to settle* ‖ (entscheidend ~) (die Politik) *to control* **3.** (festsetzen) (Preise) *to fix* ‖ (Ort, Zeit etc.) *to appoint, assign, fix* (f *for*); ⟨Am⟩ *to appropriate* (*to, for*) **4.** (~d beeinflussen) (jdn) (entscheidend) *determine* (*decide*) (z tun *to do*), *to induce* (z *to*; *to do*), *to influence*; *to prevail on* (*to do*); **sich ~ l von, durch** *to be determined* (od *influenced*) *by* **5.** (genau bezeichnen) (Lage, Merkmale, Pflichten etc.) *to determine*, (Begriff) *to define*; *to ascertain*; *to find out* ‖ (Zahlenwert etc.) *to evaluate* ‖ (Krankheit) *to diagnose* ‖ ⟨gram⟩ näher ~ *to qualify* **II.** *vi *to call the tune* ‖ ~ über (etw) *to control* (*a th*); → verfügen **best·immend 1.** a *determining, determinant* (*factor*); ⟨a. gram⟩ *determinative* ‖ objektiv ~ *constitutive* (*ideas*) | [pred] *decisive* (f *for a p*); dies ist ~ f mich gewesen, als.. *this has determined me when..* ‖ *determinant* (in *in*) | das ≗e n *the determinant, determinative* **2.** adv (*to influence*) *decisively*

best·immt I. a **1.** [pred] es ist nun mal so ~ *it is destined* (od *willed*) *so by God* | (P) ~ s z tun *to be destined to do*; zum Geistlichen ~ s *to be destined* (od *designed*) *for the Church* ‖ (S) ~ s f jdn *to be intended for* (vorgemerkt) *to be marked down for*; f e–a ~ (P) *meant for each other* | ⟨mar⟩ (of ships) ~ nach *bound for* (Hamburg) | ~ s im Auftreten *to be firm, resolute, peremptory* **2.** [attr] **a.** (durch Schicksal ~) *destined* (*end*) | *appointed, definite* (*place, time*), *fixed* (*sum*); *special* (*day*) ‖ *definite* (*answer*); *positive* (*promises*) ‖ *exact, determined* (*outlines*); *specified* (*channels*); *special* (*purposes*); ~e Gruppen *groups of a specified denomination*; ⟨tech⟩ *specific* (*design*); ⟨gram⟩ *definite* (*article*) **b.** ⟨math scient⟩ *determinate* (*number*; *order*) **c.** (entschieden) *decided, determined* (*attitude*) **II.** adv *decidedly, definitively*; ganz ~ *most decidedly* od *positively*; *without fail* ‖ (*to express*) *distinctly* ‖ er ist ~ der erste deutsche Maler *he is decisively* od *certainly the first of German painters*; nicht ~ wissen *not to know for certain*; ich habe ihn ~ nicht gesehen *I'm sure* od *positive that I've not seen him* **Bestimmtheit** f *definiteness*; *certainty* ‖ *accuracy, exactness, precision* (*of a statement*); *distinctness* | *decision, determination, resoluteness, peremptoriness*; *emphasis* | **mit ~**

definitely, certainly; confidently || *categorically, peremptorily, positively*; mit aller ~ *with all emphasis*

Best·immung f ~/~en **A.** (Bestimmen) **1.** *designation* (jds z *of a p to..*); *vocation* (*for*) | (Ort der ~) *destination* **2.** (Festsetzung) *decision* (über *as to*); *determination* (*of persons*) || *settlement* (*of a question*) || *fixation, fixing* (*of a date*) || *regulation* || ⟨Am⟩ ~ f best. Zwecke *appropriation* **3.** (genaue) *determination* (*of quantities*, etc.); *definition* || (Begriffs≃) *definition* || (zahlenmäßige) *evaluation* || ⟨med⟩ *diagnosis* (*of a disease*) **B.** (Bestimmtes) **1.** *destiny, predestination*; *decree*; Schicksals≃ *decree of fate* **2.** (behördliche) *decree* | ~en [pl] *provisions*; *procedures*; zwingende ~en *mandatory provisions* || ~en, Ausführungs≃en [pl] *regulations* (*of a law*); nach den alten ~en *on the old r.* || ~en e–s Kontrakts *stipulations of a contract*, → Maßgabe; ~en e–s Testaments *provisions of a will* **3.** ⟨gram⟩ nähere ~ *attributive adjunct, attribute* **~sflughafen** m *terminal*; *t. aerodrome* **~sgleichung** f ⟨math⟩ *defining equation* **~shafen** m *port of destination* **~sland** n *country of destination* **~smensur** f ⟨univ fenc⟩ *match appointed for equal partners* **~sort** m *destination*; *post-terminal* **~spunkt** m ⟨bes aero⟩ *point of destination*

bestirnt a = gestirnt

best·ocken vt [h] (e–e Farm mit Vieh) *to stock* || ⟨for⟩ *to stock* **Best·ockung** f ⟨bot⟩ (*the growing of side-shoots from low-lying buds*) *stumpage*; ⟨agr⟩ [konkr] *standing crop* || ⟨agr & for⟩ [konkr & abstr] *stocking*

best·oßen vt [h] [→ stoßen] ⟨tech⟩ (Kanten; Platten) *to trim*; *dress* **Best·oßhobel** m ⟨typ⟩ *dresser*; *plane*

bestr·afen vt [h] (jdn) *to punish*; (züchtigen) *to chastise*; mit Worten ~ → schelten || ⟨univ⟩ (Studenten) *to proctorize*, ⟨fam⟩ *to prog* | ⟨übtr⟩ (jdn; Fehler etc.) *to penalize*; jdn ~ mit *to visit a p with* || schwer bestraft w ⟨sl⟩ *to get it in the neck* || **Bestr·afung** f ~/~en *punishment*; die ~ jds durch.. zur Folge h *to subject a p involved to punishment by..* || z ~ gemeldet w ⟨mil fam⟩ *to be weighed off* || (Züchtigung) *chastisement* || ⟨übtr⟩ *penalization* (*of errors*, etc.) || → Strafe

bestr·ahlen vt [h] (etw) *to irradiate* (*milk*, etc.); *to shine upon* (*a th*); *to illumine* || ⟨med⟩ (jdn) mit Höhensonne ~ *to subject* (*a p*) *to sun-ray treatment*; (Stelle des Körpers) *to treat* (*a p*) *with radioactive rays, to subject to ray-treatment*; (mit Radium) *to radio* (*a p*) **Bestr·ahlung** f ~/~en *irradiation* || ⟨med⟩ (künstliche) *radiation*; *ray-treatment, ray-therapy*; Radium≃ *radio-therapy* | ~serholung [f] *radiation annealing*

bestr·eben 1. [vrefl] [h] sich ~ z tun *to make great efforts, to endeavour, to exert o.s., to strive to do*; sich ~ z gewinnen *to aim at gaining*, ⟨Am⟩ *to aim to gain* **2.** bestrebt s z tun = sich ~; eifrig bestrebt s *to do one's best endeavours*; *to be anxious* (*to do*) || *to tend* (nach.. hin *towards*) **Bestr·eben** n *effort*; *endeavour* (*to do*; *at doing*). in dem ~ z tun *in the endeavour to do* || *exertion* | *tendency* (*to do*); ein ~ zeigen *to tend* (nach *towards*; z *to*; *to do*) || → Streben; Neigung

Bestr·ebung f ~/~en [mst pl] ~en *efforts, endeavours* || *tendencies*, Selbständigkeits≃en *autarchic t.* || *attempts*; *undertakings* [pl]

bestr·eichen vt [h] [→ streichen] **1.** Oberfläche ~ mit *to spread a surface with*; Brot mit Butter ~ *to spread bread with butter, to spread butter on bread, to butter bread* || (etw) mit Fett ~ *to grease*; mit Öl ~ *to oil*; (Leinwand) mit Pflaster ~ *to plaster* || mit Farbe ~ *to paint*; Wand mit Tünche ~ *to daub a wall with whitewash, to whitewash a wall*; mit Teer ~ *to tar* **2.** (streichend berühren) **a.** (Saite) *to scrape* (*with a bow*) || *to graze*, →streifen **b.** (Glied) *to stroke, to pass one's hand repeatedly over* (*a limb*), *to massage cautiously* || das Haar leicht ~ *to make some dabs at one's hair* **c.** *to glide* od *sail along* (*a th*); (Horizont) *to rake* (*with a telescope*); die Küste ~ *to coast* || (of waves) *to lick* **d.** ⟨mil⟩ (Schiff) mit Feuer ~ *to rake*, (Gebiet) mit Feuer ~ *to sweep*; (Brücke, Straße) der ganzen Länge nach *or* schräg ~ *to enfilade*; v der Seite ~ *to flank*; bestrichener Raum *area* od *zone exposed to enfilade* **e.** sein Blick bestrich die Gegend *he swept the area with his eye*

Bestr·eichung f ~/~en **1.** *spreading* (mit *with*;) *buttering* (*of bread*) **2.** *stroking* (*of a limb*); (in mesmerism) *pass* || ⟨mil⟩ *raking*; *sweeping* (*of an area*) **~sfeuer** n *grazing fire*; ⟨hist⟩ *enfilade* **~swinkel** m *arc of training*

bestr·eikt a (→ streiken) *strike-bound*, ⟨a.⟩ *struck* (Gebiet, Fabrik)

bestr·eitbar a *contestable, disputable*; *challengeable*; *arguable*

bestr·eiten vt [h] [→ streiten] **1.** (anfechten) (Aussage, Frage) *to contest, dispute* (*a th*), *to argue against* (*a th*); *to call* (*a th*) *in question*; *to controvert a th*; (Behauptung, Tatsache) *to challenge, traverse*; jds Schlußfolgerungen ~ *to join issue with a p's conclusions*; jdm ein Recht ~ *to contest* od *dispute a p's right*; es ist nicht z ~ *it is not to be disputed, it is incontestable* od *indisputable* || (widersprechen) *to gainsay, traverse* || (leugnen) *to deny*, das kann niemand ~ *nobody can deny it*; .., dessen Richtigkeit der Käufer nicht ~ kann ⟨contr⟩ .. *and shall be accepted as accurate by the purchaser* **2. a.** (Bedürfnisse) *to meet, supply* || (bezahlen) *to cover, defray, meet* (*the expenses* aus *out of*); *to carry share* (*of*); *to bear* (*the expenses* f etw *of a th*); ich kann es nicht ~ *I cannot afford it* || den Haushalt aus eigener Tasche ~ *to bear* (od *pay for, to meet*) *all the expenses of a household out of one's own pocket* **b.** (auf sich nehmen, erledigen) || er bestritt die Unterhaltung allein *he did all the talking, all the t. was on his side* || die Arbeit, Mühe, e–e S ~ *to bear the brunt* (od *chief strain*) *of a th*; er hatte den Hauptteil des Kampfes (etc) allein z ~ *he had to bear the brunt of the fight, the brunt of the fight fell on him* **Bestr·eitung** f **1.** *the contesting, diputing* (*of a question*) **2.** *the supply* (*of wants*) | *the defraying* (*of expenses*); ~ der Kosten *defrayal*; zur ~ m–r Unkosten *to cover* od *defray my expenses*

bestr·euen vt [h] (Weg etc) *to cover, strew* (*with roses*); (Weg) mit Sand ~ *to sand*; .. mit Kies ~ *to gravel*; (Boden) dicht ~ *to bestrew* (*with papers*) || ⟨cul⟩ (Speise) *to pepper* (*with pepper*), *to sprinkle, dredge* (*with flour, etc*); → streuen **B.uung** f *covering, strewing, sprinkling*

bestr·icken vt [h] **1.** (T) *to catch* od *entangle in a net* od *in meshes, to mesh* **2.** ⟨fig⟩ (P) *to ensnare, entrap, enthral(l), mesh, captivate, fascinate*; → berücken **3.** (Ball etc) *to cover* od *enclose with netting*

bestr·ickend a *captivating, fascinating*; *charming, winning* (*ways*) **Bestr·ickung** f ~/~en *captivation, fascination*; *enthralment*

bestr·itten a (→ bestreiten 1.) *controversial*; oft ~ *oft-argued* **Bestr·ittenwerden** n *contestation*

bestr·umpft a (→ Strumpf) *stockinged* (*leg*)

best·ücken vt [h] (Schiff etc) *to arm* (*with guns*); bestückt s mit *to be mounted with* (*10 guns*)

Best·ückung f *gunnage* (*of a warship*); *armament* || *tipping* (*of cutting tools*)

best·uhlen vt [h] (Raum) *to bench* **Bestuhl·ungsplan** m ⟨theat⟩ *seating plan*

best·ürmen vt [h] **1.** (Stadt) *to storm*; *assail, assault* **2.** (Gebäude, Amt) *to besiege, to press* (od *crowd*) *in upon, to throng*, das Marineamt wurde v Neugierigen bestürmt *the Admiralty* *was besieged by inquirers*; die Bank wurde b. *there was a run* od *rush on the bank* **3.** (P) (of thoughts, etc) *to crowd* (od *press*) *in upon a p* ‖ *to assail, beset, besiege* (*a p with requests*), *to bombard, pelt, ply, overwhelm* (*with questions*); → belästigen **Best·ürmung** f *the storming* (*of a town*); *assault* (*on the town*) ‖ ~ der Bank *run* od *rush on the bank*

best·ürzen vt [h] (jdn) *to amaze, bewilder, dismay, dumbfound, perplex, stagger, stupefy* (*a p*); [mst pass] **best·ürzt I.** a **1.** [pred] *aghast* (über *at*); ~ s *to be amazed, confounded, confused, dismayed, nonplussed, perplexed, upset*; *to be struck all of a heap*; sich ~ ansehen *to look at each other in dismay*; ~ dastehen *to stand aghast*; jdn ~ m = jdn bestürzen **2.** [attr] *bewildered, bedazed, confused* (*husband*) ‖ ein ~es Gesicht m *to look confusion*, etc. **II.** adv *confusedly*; jdn ~ ansehen *to look at a p with perplexity, etc*

Best·ürzung f ~/~en *bewilderment, consternation* (*with c.*), *dismay*; *confusion, perplexity, stupefaction*; *panic*; *amazement*; *abashment, bedazement*; *embarrassment* ‖ in ~ *in dismay*; mit ~ *with consternation*; zu s–r ~ *to his consternation* (od *embarrassment*)

Bes·uch m ~(e)s/~e **I.** [abstr] **A.** ⟨hunt⟩ auf ~ gehen *to quest* (*out*) *for game* **B. 1.** *visit*; kz ~ *call* **a.** der ~ jds *the visit of a p* (*we expect the v. of my father* ‖ ein ~ bei jdm *a call upon a p* (od *at a p's house*), *a visit to a p* (*my v. to his father*); ein ~ beim Zahnarzt *a visit to the dentist* ‖ ein ~ v Herrn N. (*or* seitens des Herrn N.) *a visit from Mr. N.* (*they had a v. from Mr. N.*) **b.** ein kz ~ *a call, a brief* (od *flying*) *visit*; ⟨fam⟩ *look-in* ‖ langer ~ *long stay* (bei *with a p*); ⟨fam⟩ *visitation* ‖ der übliche ~ *the routine visit* ‖ amtlicher ~ *visitation*; beruflicher ~ *visit*; ~ der Kranken *visitation of the sick* ‖ Kranken≈ *visit* | ein ~ v 2 Tagen *a two--day visit* **c. auf** ~ *on a visit*; ich bin nur auf ~ hier → II.; auf ~ bei *on a visit to* (*a p*), .. in *on a visit to* (*a place*); auf ~ k *to come on a visit* (zu jdm *to a p*, nach Berlin *to B.*); auf ~ gehen *to go out visiting, to visit* | bei dem ~ *at the visit*; bei m–m zweiten ~ *at* od *on my second visit* | z ~ bei *on a visit to* (*a p*); z ~ in *on a visit to* (*a place*) ‖ z ~ k = auf ~ k; z ~ k z jdm = jdn besuchen ‖ z ~ s *to be on a visit* (bei *to a p*); *to stay* (*with a p*); auf kz Zeit in Berlin z ~ s *to be on a short visit to Berlin* **d.** jdm e–n ~ **abstatten** *to pay a p a visit* (od *a visit to a p*); *to call* (*up*)*on a p*, ⟨fam⟩ *to look a p up*; e–r Stadt e–n kz ~ abstatten *to be on a short visit to a place* ‖ e–r Filiale wiederholte überraschende ~e abstatten *to make periodical descents* (*up*)*on a branch*; du solltest d–e ~e bei ihr aufgeben *you should cease visiting at her house* ‖ e–n ~ **erwidern** *to repay a visit* ‖ ~e m *to make calls, to go out visiting* ‖ e–n ~ m *to pay a visit*; e–n kz ~ m *to drop in* (jdm *on a p*); e–n ~ m bei jdm *to make a call up*(*on*) *a p*, *to call* (*up*)*on a p* ‖ jdm e–n ~ m = jdm e–n ~ abstatten ‖ ich werde mit Ihnen e–n ~ bei ihm m, ich werde Sie zu e–m ~ bei ihm mitnehmen *I'll take you to see him* ‖ wir **freuen** uns auf Ihren ~ *we are looking forward to the pleasure of meeting you* ⟨a. com⟩, .. und .. ⟨com⟩ *looking .. you ..* ‖ **2.** ~ e–s Vortrags, e–r Versammlung (etc) *attendance at a lecture, at a meeting*; Theater≈ *theatre-going* ‖ häufiger ~ *frequentation* (*of a theatre*) **3.** (Besichtigung) ein ~ des Museums, des Zoologischen Gartens *a visit to the museum; to the Zoo* **II.** [konkr] (P) **1.** *visitor*; [mst pl] *visitors, callers* [pl], ich bin nur ~ hier *I am only a visitor here*; viel ~ *many visitors*; Damen≈ *lady visitor* ‖ ~ erwarten *to expect visitors* ‖ ~ h *to have visitors*; es kommt ~ *a visitor is* od *visitors are coming*; es ist ~ da *there are visitors* **2.** (~ [= Besucher] e–r Ausstellung etc) *attendance* **~saustausch** m *exchange of visits* **~sfuß** m: auf ~ stehen mit *to be on visiting terms with* (*a p*) **~skarte** f *visiting-card*, ⟨Am⟩ *calling card* **~stag** m *visiting-day*; Empfangstag (*my*) *day in* [adv] **~szeit** f *visiting-hours, visitors' hours* pl **~szimmer** n *drawing-room*

bes·uchen vt [h] (→ Besuch) **1.** jdn ~ (gesellschaftlich) *to visit a p, to call* (*up*)*on a p, to pay a p a visit* ‖ ⟨fam⟩ *to look a p up*; besuch mich mal *look me up*; *to go* od *come to* (od *and*) *see a p*, ich besuchte ihn *I went and saw him*; Herr N. hat mich besucht *Mr. N. has been to see me*; jdn auf e–n Sprung ~ *to drop in on a p*; *to step round to a p* ‖ den Arzt ~ *to see the doctor* ‖ (jdn beruflich ~) *to visit* (*a p*) **2. a.** (Ort, Museum etc) *to visit*; ⟨Am⟩ *to take in* ‖ ⟨fam⟩ *to do* (*the museums*) **b.** (Kirche; Vortrag, Konzert; Versammlung) *to attend* ‖ e–e Schule ~ *to go to* (od *to attend*) *a school, to be educated at a school*, er hatte e–e *Public School* besucht *he had been to a P. S.*, Schüler, die s–e Schule besuchten *boys who came to his school* ‖ das Theater ~ *to go to the theatre* **c.** (Ort, Bibliothek etc) öfter ~, gewohnheitsgemäß ~ *to frequent* (*a place*), *to resort to* (*a place*); (Meere) *to haunt* ‖ (Geschäft, Restaurant als Kunde ~) *to patronize* ‖ jds Privatbibliothek ~ dürfen *to have the run of a p's library* **bes·uchenswert** a *visitable*; *worth visiting*

Bes·ucher m **1.** *caller* ‖ *visitor* (jds *to a p*) ‖ (Gast) *guest* ‖ (Kunde) *customer*; (regelmäßiger) *frequenter* **2.** ~ e–s Landes, des Museums (etc) *visitor to a country, to the museum*; *viewer* **3.** ~ v Wettkämpfen *attender of matches*; ständiger ~ *habitué* (*of the turf*) ‖ die ~ [pl], ~zahl *the attendance, audience*, ⟨sport fam⟩ *gate*; die ~ der Versammlung *those present at the meeting* **4.** [in comp] *-goer*; Film≈ *film-goer*, ⟨Am⟩ *moviegoer*; Theater≈ *theatre-goer* | ~liste [f] *visiting* (⟨Am⟩ *calling*) *list*; ~zahl [f] (→ 3.), → Besuch, ~szeiten

bes·ucht a ~, gut ~ *well-attended* (*lecture, meeting*, etc.) ‖ *much-frequented, well-patronized* (*restaurant*); ⟨theat⟩ ein gut~es Haus *a full house*

bes·udeln vt [h] **1.** ⟨eig⟩ *to befoul, dirty, foul*; *contaminate* (mit *with*) **2.** ⟨übtr⟩ (Heiliges) *to defile, pollute* ‖ ⟨fig⟩ *to befoul*; (jdn, jds Ehre etc); *foul* (*a p's reputation*); ⟨Lit⟩ (Gegenstand) *to soil* **Bes·udelung** f *contamination* ‖ *defilement, pollution* ‖ *fouling*

bes·ungen a [pp v besingen] nicht ~ *unsung*

B·et- [in comp] *prayer, praying* .. **~bruder** m *bigot, devotee*; → Frömmler **~fahrt** f = Wallfahrt **~glocke** f *prayer-bell*; → Angelusläuten **~haus** n *house of prayer* **~kissen, ~polster** n *hassock* **~pult** n *prayer* (od *praying*)*-desk* **~saal** m *chapel, oratory* **~schwester** f *devotee* **~sonntag** m (vor Himmelfahrt) *Rogation Sunday* **~stuhl** m *praying stool* **~stunde** f *prayer-hour, prayer--time, prayers* [pl]; *prayer-meeting* **~tag** m *day of prayer* ‖ *fast-day* **~woche** f = Bittwoche

B·eta n [invar] (griech. Buchstabe) *beta* **~strahlen** m [pl] *beta-rays* [pl] | ~einlaß [m] ⟨at⟩ *β-port* **~teilchen** n *beta particle*

bet·agt a = bejahrt ‖ ⟨com⟩ = befristet

bet·akeln vt [h] (Schiff) *to rig* ‖ ein Tauende ~ *to wrap the slack of a rope with twine* **Bet·akelung** f ~/~en = Takelung

Bet·ankung f ~/~en ⟨bes aero⟩ *fuelling*

bet·asten vt [h] (etw) *to touch, handle, finger, feel*; ungeschickt ~ *to fumble* ‖ ⟨med⟩ (Leib) *to palpate* ‖ jdn mit der Hand ~ *to run one's hand over a p*; ⟨fam⟩ *to paw* (*over*) *a p* | ⟨übtr⟩ (Problem) *to handle* **Bet·astung** f *touch* ‖ ⟨med⟩ *palpation*

bet·ätigen vt [h] **1. a.** (Gefühl) *to manifest, show* (durch *by*); *to display* ‖ (Gesinnung, Lehre,

Philosophie) *to carry out in action, to practise, to put into practise* (*by*); *to realize*; s–e Ideale ∼ *to have the courage of one's ideals*; ∼ was man predigt *to practise what one preaches* **b. sich** ∼ *to work* (in *in*; f *for*); *to busy o.s.* (im Hause *about the house*); sich noch immer ∼ *to be still active* ‖ sich ∼ als *to act as* (*private teacher*); sich als Rechtsanwalt ∼ *to practise at the bar* ‖ sich eifrig ∼ bei etw *to play one's part in a th, to take an active part in a th* **2.** (Muskel) *to activate* ‖ ⟨tech⟩ *to actuate, operate, handle*; *to control, command* (Bremse etc) *to work, to set going* ‖ mechanisch –gt *mechanically controlled*

Bet·ätigung f ∼/ *display, manifestation* (*of a feeling*) ‖ *putting into practice* (*of a doctrine*) ‖ *activity, occupation, practice*; ⟨sl⟩ *lay* ‖ emsige ∼ *application, diligence*; → Tätigkeit ‖ → Beteiligung **|** ⟨tech⟩ *control, operation, actuation, manipulation*; willkürliche ∼ *manual control*; ∼ durch e–n Hebel *operating by a lever*; **∼sfeld** n *range of activities* **∼sfolge** f ⟨tech⟩ *sequence of operation* **∼sknopf** m *operating* od *adjusting knob* **∼sorgan** n *actuating appliance* **∼sschalter** m *act.g switch*

bet·äuben vt [h] **1.** (Ohren) durch Getöse ∼ *to deafen, din, stun* **2.** (jdn) *to make* (*a p*) *insensible, to stun* (*a p*) ‖ *to drug* (*with veronal*) ‖ ⟨med⟩ *to anaesthetize*; durch Narkose ∼ *to narcotize*; (starr m) (Glieder) *to be numb* **3.** ⟨übtr⟩ **a.** (jdn) *to daze, stun, stupefy, bewilder*; wie betäubt *as though stunned*; *dazed-like* **b.** (Schmerz) *to deaden, dull, stop* **c.** (Gefühle) *to blunt, deaden, narcotize*; *to calm, soothe* ‖ durch Alkohol ∼ *to intoxicate*; ‖ (Gewissen) *to silence, stifle, drown* **4. sich** ∼ *to relax, to seek distraction* od *relaxation* (in *in*) ‖ *to be intoxicated* (durch *by*) **bet·äubend** a *deafening* (*sounds*; *noise*; *applause*) ‖ *stunning* (*blow*) ‖ ⟨med⟩ *narcotic* (*effect*); *anaesthetic*; *stupefying* (*drug*) ‖ schmerz≈ *analgesic, pain-killing*; schmerz≈es Mittel *analgesic* **|** *narcotic* (*smell*); *soporific* **B.bung** f ∼/∼en **1.** *deafening* (*of the ears*) **2.** *stunning* (*of a p*); *state of insensibility* ‖ ⟨med⟩ *narcotization*; *anaesthesia* [L]; Operation mit ∼ *anaesthetic operation* ‖ Schmerz≈ *analgesia* **3.** ⟨übtr⟩ **a.** *stupor* (*of limbs*) ‖ *stupefaction*; *stun, stunning*; *torpidity* **b.** *deadening*; *soothing* ‖ *intoxication* **4.** ⟨fig⟩ (Ablenkung) *distraction, relaxation* (in *in*) **∼smittel** n *narcotic*; *anaesthetic*

bet·auen vt [h] *to bedew* **bet·aut** a *dewy*

B·et(e) f ∼/ ⟨cards⟩ *stake*, bes *stake lost*; ∼ m, ∼ w *to lose the game*

B·ete f ∼/∼n ⟨bot⟩ *beet*; *beetroot*

Beteig·euze [Arab] (Stern im Orion) *Betelgeuse*

bet·eiligen vt [h] **1.** ⟨com⟩ jdn ∼ *to make a p a partner, to partner a p*; jdn ∼ an etw *to interest a p in, to invest a p with a share in* (od *a title to*), *to give a p a share* (od *an interest*) *in a th* **2.** beteiligt s an *or* bei **a.** *to have an interest in* (*an industry*), *to be interested in* (*a business*); *to be in a th* **b.** *to have* od *take a share in* (*a business*; *a plot*); *to be a party to* (*a plot*), *to be concerned in* (*a murder*) **3. sich** ∼ **a.** *to play one's part* (*men and women played their part*) **b.** sich ∼ **an** *to engage in, to join in, to take part in, to participate in* (*a discussion*; *festivities*; *a game*) *to have a hand in* (*the elucidation of* ..) ‖ sich an e–m Gespräch ∼ *to enter into a conversation* **|** *to participate in* (*a crime*) **Bet·eiligte** [der ∼, ein ∼r] m *the* (*p*) *concerned*; → Teilnehmer ‖ die ∼n [pl] *those concerned, the interested parties, the parties concerned* [pl]

Bet·eiligung f ∼/∼en **1.** ∼ an **a.** *interest in, share in, participation in* (*a business*, etc.) **b.** *participation in* (*a crime*) **2.** ∼ am Gewinn, Gewinn≈ *profit-sharing, participation*; *share*; *interest* ‖ (Teilhaberschaft) *partnership* **3.** (Teilnehmerzahl) *attendance*; das Begräbnis fand unter zahlreicher ∼ statt *there was a large* od *big attendance at the funeral* ‖ (Zuhörerschaft) *attendance* **4.** (Ertrag bei Versammlungen etc) *turn-out* ‖ (Unterstützung) *support* **5.** [pl] ∼en ⟨ins bal⟩ *investments*; (Aktienbesitz) *holding share investments* **∼sgesellschaft** f ⟨com⟩ *holding-company* **∼squote** f *contingent* **∼ssystem** n *participation system*

B·etel m ∼s/∼ (Kaumittel) *betel* **∼nuß** f *betel-nut* **∼palme** f ⟨bot⟩ *betel-tree, betel-nut-tree*

b·eten vi/t [h] **1.** vi *to pray, to say one's prayers*; (bei Tisch) *to say grace* ‖ ∼ um *to pray for* (*a th*); z Gott ∼ *to pray to God, to Heaven* ‖ ∼ lernen *to learn to pray* **2.** vt ein Gebet ∼ *to pray a prayer*; sein G. ∼ *to say one's prayers*; das Vaterunser ∼ *to say the Lord's Prayer*; den Rosenkranz ∼ *to tell one's beads* ‖ jdn gesund ∼ *to heal a p by prayer*

°**bet·eppert** a = bedeppert

B·eter m ∼s/∼ *prayer*

bet·euern vt [h] (s–e Sympathie, Unschuld; daß) *to asseverate, protest* (*a th*; *that*) *to swear that*; ∼ z tun *to swear to do*; wiederholt ∼ *to reassure* ‖ *to affirm solemnly, to assert* od *aver positively* (*a th*; *that*) **Bet·euerung** f ∼/∼en, *asseveration, protestation* (*of a th*; *that*); *profession* ‖ wiederholte ∼ *reassurance*; beharrliche ∼ *insistence* ‖ *solemn affirmation*

Beth·anien n ⟨bib⟩ *Bethany*

bethlehem·itisch a *Bethlehemite*; ≈er Kindermord *Massacre* od *Slaughter of the Innocents* ⟨a. arts⟩ ‖ ≈er Orden [m] ⟨R.C.⟩ *the Bethlemites* pl

B·eting m ∼s/∼e, [a. f] *bitt*, [mst pl] *bitts* ‖ (Taue) um die ∼e winden *to bitt*

Bet·ise f ∼/∼n Fr = Dummheit

bet·iteln vt [h] **1.** (Buch etc) *to entitle* (*he entitled his book 'N. N.'*) ‖ *to designate* (als *as*) ‖ betitelt s *to be* (*en*)*titled* **2.** (jdn) *to entitle* (*they entitled him nabob*); scherzhaft ∼ *to dub* (*they dubbed him a princeling*) ‖ *to style, call*; Provost betitelt w *to be styled Provost*; → anreden **3. sich** ∼ (of books) *to be entitled* ‖ (P) *to style o.s.*; → nennen **bet·itelt** a *titled* (*psalm*); nicht ∼ *untitled* ‖ *titled* (*p*) **Bet·itelung** f ∼/∼en, *entitling* (*of a book*) ‖ *styling* (*of a p*) **|** (Titel) *title*; *name*

bet·ölpeln vt [h] (jdn) *to fool*; *to cheat, dupe*

Bet·on [be'tɔ̃:] m ∼s/∼s ⟨arch⟩ **1.** *concrete*; armierter ∼ *armoured* od *reinforced c.*; Kalk≈ *lime c.*, Traß≈ *trass c.*, Zement≈ *cement c.* ‖ Guß≈ *cast c.*; Spritz≈ *rendering c.*; Eisen≈ *armoured* (*reinforced*) *c.* ‖ Stahl≈ *steel c.* ‖ Schaum≈ *foam c.* ‖ Spann≈ *prestressed c.* ‖ Stampf≈ *stamped c.* ‖ mit ∼ belegen *to* (*pave with*) *c.* (*a floor*) **2.** [in comp] *concrete* (*bridge, floor*) **∼arbeiter** m *concreter, –tor* **∼eisen** n *reinforcement iron* **∼mischmaschine** f *concrete-mixer* **∼spritzmaschine** f *cement gun*

bet·onen vt [h] **1.** (Silbe, Wort) *to accent, accentuate, emphasize, stress*; e–e Silbe z stark ∼ *to lay too much emphasis on a syllable* **2.** ⟨übtr⟩ (Äußerung, Gedanken, Tatsachen) nachdrücklich ∼ *to accentuate, emphasize, to lay* (od *place*) *emphasis on, to lay stress on, to point up, to insist on, to be insistent on, to stress, to lay stress on* (*a th*), *to underline* ⟨bes Am⟩ *to play up* ‖ ⟨tail etc⟩ *to boast* ‖ ⟨fam⟩ *to rub* (*a th*) *in*; mit Nachdruck ∼, daß .. *to be emphatic* (od *to insist, to make the point, to point out, to stress, to urge*) *that* ..; wert, betont z w *worthy of emphasis* ‖ nicht betonen *to belittle, minimize*; *to play down*

Bet·onie f ∼/∼n ⟨bot⟩ *betony*

beton·ieren **1.** vt [h], *to* (*reinforce with*) *concrete* **2.** ≈ n *concreting* **Beton·ierung** f *concreting*

bet·onnen vt [h] (Fahrwasser) *to mark with buoys*; *to buoy* (*out*) **Bet·onnung** f ⟨mar⟩ *buoyage*

bet·ont 1. a *stressed* (*syllable*); nicht ~ *stressless* | *emphatic* (*declaration*); *insistent* (*simplicity*, *cordiality*) 2. adv *emphatically*, *insistently* (*polite*) **Bet·onung** f ~/~en 1. *accentuation* (*of a word*) ‖ (Ton) *accent*, *stress*; *emphasis*; die ~ liegt auf .. *the stress is on* ..; schwebende ~ *level stress*; *hovering accent* 2. ⟨übtr⟩ *accentuation*; *emphasizing* (*of a th*) ‖ *emphasis*, *insistence* (e–r S *on a th*)

bet·ören vt [h] (jdn) *to befool*, *bemuse*, *besot*, *infatuate*; (täuschen) *to deceive*, *delude*, *dupe* ‖ **sich ~ l** *to be infatuated*; *to let o.s. be deluded* (z tun *into doing*) **bet·ört** a *infatuated*; *besotted*

Bet·örung f ~/~en *besottedness*, *infatuation*; *delusion*; *deception*

Betr·acht m; [nur in:] 1. etw (jdn) **außer ~ l** *to leave a th* (*a p*) *out of account*, *to make no account of*; *not to consider a th* (*a p*) ‖ außer ~ stehen (*or* bleiben) *to be out of the question*; das bleibt außer ~ *there is no question of it*; *that will not be considered* 2. **in ~** k **a.** *to come into question*, ⟨fam⟩ *into the picture*, das kann in ~ k *that can be taken into consideration*, *that can be considered*; *in* ~ k.d *in question* **b.** (P) *to be in the running* (f *for*) **c. nicht** in ~ k. *to be out of the question*; ⟨sport sl⟩ *to be nowhere* ‖ es kommt nicht in ~ *there's no question of it*; Geld kommt nicht in ~ *money is no consideration* | (P) *to be out of the running* (f *for*) ‖ das kommt nicht in ~! ⟨fam⟩ *that's out*! 3. **etw in ~ ziehen** *to take a th into consideration* od *account*; *to consider a th*; *to give a th one's consideration*; *to allow for*, *to make allowance for a th*; [oft neg] (Vorschlag) in ~ ziehen *to entertain*; etw nicht in ~ z. *to take no count of* ‖ jdn in ~ ziehen *to consider a p* ‖ in ~ ziehen z tun ..; daß .. *to consider* (od *contemplate*) *doing* ..; *that*; in ~ gezogen w *to be in contemplation* ‖ wenn man alles in ~ zieht *all things considered* ‖ → Anbetracht, Betrachtung; Hinsicht **betr·achten** vt [h] 1. ⟨eig⟩ **a.** (Bild, Landschaft, jdn) *to* (*have a*) *look at*, *to view*; etw flüchtig ~ *to take a glance at a th* ‖ länger ~ *to regard*; jdn lange ~ *to have a long look at a p*; prüfend ~ *to look* (*a p*) *over*; *to look into* (od *over*) (*a th*); *to inspect* (*a th*); sorgsam ~ *to watch*; jdn v oben bis unten ~ *to eye a p from top to toe* (od *up and down*), ⟨Am⟩ *to give a p the once-over*; jdn **mit** Neugier ~ *to regard a p with curiosity* **b.** (sinnend ~) *to contemplate* (*a th*, *a p*); *to meditate up*(*on*) (*a th*) 2. (**im Geiste** ~) **a.** etw ~ *to sense*; (Zukunft) *to view* (*with concern*); *to regard* (*with distrust*; *with horror*) ‖ etw **mit** Skepsis, Pessimismus ~ *to take a dim view of a th* ‖ ⟨philos⟩ (etw) abgesondert (*or* f sich) ~ *to abstract* ‖ jdn ~ *to view a p* (*in his career*) **b.** (**halten f**) (etw, jdn) *to consider*, *regard*; *to look upon*; ich betrachte ihn **als** e–n reichen Mann *I consider him* (*to be*) *a rich man*, *I regard* (od *look upon*) *him as a rich man*; er wird als ein reicher M. betrachtet *he is considered a rich man*, *he is regarded* (od *looked upon*) *as a r. man* ‖ jdn als Vorbild ~ *to look at a p as example* ‖ als unnötig ~ *to regard a th as unnecessary*; es als ratsam ~ *to see it advisable*; er betrachtet es als ein Unglück *he considers it a misfortune*, *he regards it as a misfortune*; etw auf s–n künstlerischen Wert hin ~ *to consider a th on its artistic merits* **c. Wendungen:** in diesem Lichte betrachtet *regarded* (od *viewed*) *in this light*; etw in rosigem L. ~ *to take a bright view of a th*; genau (*or* bei Licht) betrachtet *strictly speaking*; wenn man es recht (*or* bei Licht) betrachtete *come* (od *if you came*) *to think of it*, *if it came to that*; *when all was said and done* ‖ f sich betrachtet *considered by itself* (*the problem is insoluble*) ‖ v allen Seiten ~ *to regard* (*a th*) *from every angle* ‖ v e–r anderen Seite ~ *to regard* (*a th*) *from a different angle*, *in a different light*; betrachte es einmal v m–m Standpunkt aus *regard it for a moment from my angle* (od *point of view*) ‖ im Zus–hang ~ *to consider fully* 3. **sich ~ a.** *to look at o.s.* (*in the mirror*) **b.** *to consider* (od *regard*) *o.s.*; sich v innen ~ *to listen to o.s.* er betrachtet sich als e–n gr Dichter *he considers himself* (*to be*) *a great poet*, *he regards* (od *looks upon*) *h.s. as a great poet* **betr·achtend** a *contemplative* (*attitude*); *meditative* **Betrachter** m ~s/~ *contemplator* ‖ ⟨arts⟩ *spectator*

betr·ächtlich 1. a *considerable* (*distance*; *sum*); *handsome*, *respectable* (*income*, *sum*); *heavy* (*weight*, ⟨übtr⟩ *investments*); *appreciable* (*pause*); ⟨fam⟩ *tidy* (*income*); e–e ~e Anzahl ⟨fam⟩ *a smart few*, *a smartish few*; e–e ~e Anzahl Menschen *a great many people*, ⟨fam⟩ *a smart number of people*; ein ~es Stück Geld *a pretty penny*, ⟨fam⟩ *a sight of money* ‖ **um ein ≈es** *by far*; *much* 2. adv *considerably*; *pretty*; *to a high degree*; *much*; ~ besser ⟨fam⟩ *a long sight better*; e–e ~ lange Zeit *a good long time*

betr·achtsam a = beschaulich

Betr·achtung f ~/~en 1. **a.** (Anschauen) *looking on*; *view* (*of a play*) ‖ prüfende ~ *inspection* ‖ bei näherer ~ *on nearer view*; bei oberflächlicher ~ *at a superficial glance* **b.** (sinnende ~) *contemplation*; *study*; fromme ~ *meditation*; in ~ versunken sein *to be lost in contemplation* ‖ nach längerer ~ *in the long view* 2. (geistige ~) **a.** (Überlegung) *consideration*; *reflection*, *-lexion* (über *on*, *upon*) ‖ bei näherer ~ *on reflection*, *on further consideration*, *on second thoughts*; ~en anstellen *to reflect* (*on*, *upon*) **b.** *review* (*of the German genius*); *discussion*; *study* (*of a subject*); zus–fassende ~ *comprehensive survey*; psychologische ~ *psychological investigation*; Art der ~ *approach* **~sweise** f *approach*; *outlook*

Betr·ag m ~(e)s/≈e *amount* (*of an account*, *invoice*); *sum*; Gesamt≈ *sum total*, *total*; Subskriptions≈ *subscriptions* [pl] ‖ ⟨bal⟩ *balance* ‖ ⟨comp etc⟩ *amount of the item* ‖ **im** ~e v *to the amount of*, *amounting to*; ein Scheck **über** den ~ v 10 Pfd *a cheque*, *value £ 10*, *a cheque for £ 10*; e–n ~ **auszahlen** *to pay out a sum*; ~ dankend erhalten *received with thanks*; → ergeben

betr·agen [h] [→ tragen] 1. vrefl **sich** ~ *to behave* (gegen *towards*, *to*); *to conduct* (od *comport*, *deport*) *o.s.*; sich anständig ~ (z Kindern gespr.) *to behave o.s.* (*to learn to b. o.s.*); *to act* 2. vi *to amount* (od *come*, *run*) *to*; *to work out at*; → belaufen; (e–e Summe) *to add up to* ‖ wieviel beträgt die Rechnung? *what does the bill run to*? *how much is the bill*? Ihr Guthaben beträgt 2000 Mark *the balance standing to your credit amounts to 2000 marks* ‖ im ganzen ~ *to total* (*up*) *to*; *to aggregate*, *total*; die erbeuteten Pferde betrugen i. g. 500 *the horses captured totalled* (od *aggregated*) *500*

Betr·agen n *behaviour* (gegen *to*), *conduct*; *bearing*, *demeanour*; sehr auf sein ~ achten (z Kindern) *to be on one's best behaviour* ‖ tadelloses ~ (e–s Schülers) *faultless deportment*

betr·auen vt [h] jdn ~ mit etw *to entrust* (od *charge*) *a p*; *with a th*; *to confide a th to a p* (od *to a p's care*); mit der Aufgabe betraut w *to be charged with the mission*, *to be commissioned* (od *ordered*) (*to do*); damit beauftragt w *or* s *to be commissioned* (*to do*); → anvertrauen

betr·auern 1. vt [h] jdn ~ *to mourn for a p*, *to mourn* (od *bewail*) *a p* ‖ den Tod, Verlust jds ~ *to lament a p's death*, *to mourn a p's loss*; ⟨Ger⟩ (in Anzeigen) wir ~ den Tod unseres Kameraden *we record with regret the death of our comrade* ‖ das Los jds ~ *to mourn* (od *lament, deplore) a p's lot, to mourn over a p's lot* **2.** ≗ n *the mourning; lamentation*

betr·äufeln vt [h] etw ~ *to cover* od *wet a th with drops; to besprinkle,* ⟨poet⟩ *to bedrop a th*

Betr·auung f die ~ jds mit e–r S *the entrusting of a th to a p*

Betr·eff m ~s/ [nur in:] (in Briefen): [abbr Betr.] *subject, subject matter;* (unter dem Briefkopf) *concerning:* in ≗ e–r S [gen] *with regard* od *respect to, in regard of* od *to, in respect of, in* od *with reference to a th; as to* od *for a th; as concerns, as regards, as regarding* (od *touching) a th; concerning a th;* ⟨jur⟩ *re* [L] *a th;* in ≗ s–r Ehrlichkeit *as to* (od *what concerns) his honesty* (*there is* ..); Ihre Anfrage in ~ der Bände *your inquiry re the volumes* ‖ † in dem ~ *in this respect* ‖ → betreffs

betr·effen vt [h] [→ treffen] **A.** *(jdn) *to catch;* auf frischer Tat betroffen w *to be caught in the (very) act, to be taken red-handed* **B.** [im Aktiv, nur 3. sg & pl] **1. a.** jdn ~ (of accidents, misfortune) *to assail, befall a p, to come* od *fall upon a p, to visit a p; to take a p by surprise* ‖ (of laws, etc.) *to affect a p;* nahe ~ *to touch a p* (*the question touches you nearly*); [oft pass] jeder wird davon b e t r o f f e n *everyone is affected by it;* schwer b. w v *to be stricken with (a disease);* → 2. **b.** etw ~ *to affect, touch a th* (*his position was not touched by the decree*); b. w *or* s *to be affected* od *concerned;* b. w durch (of organs) *to be implicated in* ‖ (Land) *to assail, to visit;* v e–m Erdbeben b. w *to be smitten by an earth-quake;* v e–r Epidemie b. w *to be visited by an epidemic* **2.** (angehen) jdn, e–e S ~ (S) *to concern a p, a th;* → 1. a. b. ‖ *to refer* od *relate to a p* (*these regulations refer only to children*) ‖ ⟨jur⟩ an alle, die es betrifft *to whom it may concern* ‖ es betrifft mich nicht *I am not concerned;* ⟨fam⟩ *it's not my pigeon, etc* ‖ was .. betrifft *in terms of (money, etc)* ‖ was mich betrifft, so werde ich .. *as far as I am concerned, for my part I shall ..; I, for one shall ..* | es betrifft m–e Ehre *my honour is concerned* ‖ was das betrifft *for that matter, as to that* ‖ was den Charakter betrifft *(up)on the count of character* ‖ was den ersten Punkt betrifft .., was den zweiten .. *(up)on the first count (we cannot judge), (up)on the second (it is clear that ..)* **3.** (behandeln) *to be concerned with, to deal with, to have reference to (this chapter is concerned with his position in ..);* → betroffen

betr·effend I. prs p (abbr betr., → betreffs. *concerning, regarding;* ein Bericht ~ die politische Lage *a report concerning the political situation* ‖ alle(s) ~ *universal* **II.** a **1.** [aktiver Sinn] ein die S ~er Brief *a letter concerning the matter, a letter concerned with the m.* ‖ ⟨jur⟩ z der (den Vorfall) ~en Zeit *at the material time* ‖ (zustehend) die ~e Behörde *the proper authority;* alle gingen auf ihre ~en Plätze *they all went to their respective places* **2.** [passiver Sinn] die ~e P, der ~e *the p concerned* (od *referred to), the p in question;* die ≗en *those referred to;* die ~en Bücher *the books in question* (od *referred to*) ‖ → betroffen **betr·effs** prep ~ e–r S [gen] = in Betreff e–r S

betr·eiben vt [h] [→ treiben] **1.** (ständig ausüben) (ein Geschäft etc) *to carry on, to practise, to run;* (Unternehmen, Eisenbahn) *to manage, work;* ⟨Am⟩ *to operate* | (Handwerk, Beruf) *to follow, practise, pursue;* Ackerbau ~ *to follow the plough;* sein Gewerbe ~ *to ply one's trade* | (Kunst) *to cultivate;* (Studien etc) *to prosecute, to pursue* | *to prosecute (a war)* ‖ *to pursue (a policy)* | etw nur nebenbei als Hobby ~ *to play at a th* **2.** (beschleunigen) *to urge; to push (forward);* (Arbeit) *to hurry (along);* → beschleunigen **Betr·eiben** n **1.** *the carrying on (of a business); practice* ‖ *management* ‖ *pursuit (of a profession; trade, of studies,* etc.); *prosecution; cultivation (of an art)* **2.** *urging* ‖ (Antrieb) auf ~ jds *at the instigation of a p*

betr·essen vt [h] ⟨tail⟩ (Rock etc) *to braid, frog*

betr·eten vt [h] [→ treten] **1.** (Treppe etc) *to step* od *tread on; to tread;* (Kanzel) *to ascend, mount;* er wird Sonntag die Kanzel z letzten Mal ~ *he will preach Sunday for the last time* | (Gegend, Schauplatz; Pfad) *to enter upon;* ein Land ~ *to set foot in a country;* jds Land etc unbefugt ~ *to trespass on a p's land* ‖ ⟨sport⟩ den Spielplatz, das Kampffeld ~ *to take the field* | (Haus etc) *to enter;* wieder ~ *to re-enter; to come* od *stride into (a room)* ‖ (Schwelle) *to cross;* betritt m–e Schwelle nicht wieder *don't darken my door again* ‖ → antreten **2.** ⟨orn⟩ (Weibchen) *to tread* **3.** † = ertappen

betr·eten 1. [a] **a.** viel ~ *beaten (track)* **b.** [mst pred] *startled, surprised; disconcerted, perplexed, nonplussed; embarrassed; helpless; awkward* **2.** adv *perplexedly; helplessly; awkwardly*

Betr·eten n *treading* ‖ *mounting (of the chancel)* | *entering upon (a scene)* ‖ unbefugtes ~ v Land *trespass;* das ~ des .. war ihm verboten worden *he had been forbidden the mess-room;* das ~ des Rasens ist verboten *do not walk on the grass;* unbefugtes ~ des Grundstücks ist bei Strafe verboten! *trespassers will be prosecuted!* das ~ dieses Weges ist nicht gestattet *this way is not open to the public* | *the entering (of a house,* etc.)

Betr·etung f = Betreten **~sfall** m: im ~e *in case of being taken in the act, when taken red-handed* **~srecht** n ⟨jur⟩ (Nutzungs–, Wegerecht) *easement*

betr·euen vt [h] jdn ~ *to look after, to have the care of, to care for a p (widows were cared for); to (dry-)nurse a p;* (Kranke) *to tend* ‖ ⟨Am⟩ *to handle* | die Erziehung der Kinder ~ *to attend to the education of the children* ‖ (Haus, Wirtschaft) *to do; to look after;* ich habe viel z ~ *I have a great deal to attend to* ‖ Herr N. betreute den musikalischen Teil *the musical part lay in the hands of Mr. N.* ‖ v niemandem betreut *uncared-for* **Betr·euer** m ~s/~ *mentor* ‖ ⟨soc⟩ *welfare officer* **Betr·euung** f *the looking after, (dry-)nursing (of a p); care* (e–r S, P [gen] *of* od *for a th, a p)* ‖ *welfare* ‖ ständige ~ *continuing service* ‖ ärztliche ~ *medical service* **~soffizier** m ⟨mil⟩ *recreation officer*

Betr·ieb m ~s/~e **A.** [abstr] (Ausübung) **1. a.** *the carrying on, management (of a business)* ‖ *the running, working (of an undertaking, a factory, plant; mine; farm);* ⟨Am⟩ *operation* ‖ → Betreiben **b.** *the running, working (of a machine, a railway)* **c.** ⟨rail⟩ *service* ‖ (Eisenbahn≗, Omnibus≗ etc) *traffic;* reger ~ *busy t.,* gr ~ *great t.* **d.** wissenschaftlicher ~ *the scientific work and teaching (at a university)* **e.** Wendungen: den ~ aufnehmen ⟨rail, etc.⟩ *to open* od *start a service* (nach *to*) ‖ den ~ e–r Fabrik einstellen *or* schließen *to shut a factory down;* den ~ einstellen (of factories) *to shut down* ‖ der ~ der Fabrik steht still (*or* stockt) *the factory has shut down* (od *has come to a stop*) ‖ dem ~ übergeben *to open (a line) for traffic* | **außer** ~ *out of commission* od *gear;* (of furnace) *out of blast;* ⟨tech⟩ außer ~ (befindlich) *inoperative, out of action, operation, commission* ‖ (Fabrik) außer ~ setzen *to close* (od *shut) down* ‖ (Maschinen) *to stop; to phase out* | **in** ~ *in gear; at* od *in work; operated; functioning; in operation; running; in working order;* (of furnace) *in blast;* ⟨übtr⟩ in vollem (*or* schwunghaftem) ~ *in full blast;* in ~ s *to be running;* ⟨rail⟩ *to be open for traffic;* das Hotel ist wieder in ~ *the hotel runs again* ‖ (Maschine, Unternehmen) in ~ bringen *or* halten, setzen ⟨Am⟩ *to operate* ‖ in ~ nehmen *to exploit (a* *mine*) ‖ ⟨tech⟩ in ∼ setzen *to put in operation*; *to get in working order*; *to gear*, *to start*; *to set going*; *to phase in* [*adv*] ‖ **2.** °⟨übtr⟩ **a.** (lebhaftes Treiben) *bustle*, *hustle*; *stir* ‖ ⟨fam⟩ *spree*, ⟨sl⟩ *binge*; ∼ m *to go on the binge* od *spree*, *to spree*, ⟨Am⟩ *to make whoopee*; was ist das für ein ∼! *what a hurly-burly*! **b.** ⟨sl⟩ *show* **B.** [konkr] **1.** (Arbeitsstätte) **a.** *industrial undertaking*; lebenswichtige ∼e *vital undertakings*, *industries* [pl] etc ‖ *the works*, *plant*, *factory*, *manufactory*, *workshops*, *mill*; ⟨min⟩ *workings* [pl] **b.** *concern* (*the floor had been let to other concerns*); ein gut gehender ∼ *a going concern* ‖ *business*; (*business* od *industrial*) *establishment*; *firm*; *enterprise*; *company*; *trade* **c.** ⟨agr⟩ *farm* **d.** öffentl. ∼ *public undertaking*; Kommunal≈ *communal undertaking* **e.** gemischter ∼ *mixed business*; *mixed farm* ‖ Groß≈ *largescale undertaking* od *business*; (*large*) *estate*; Klein≈ *small factory*, *workshop* **2.** (P) der ∼ (Ggs Leitung) *the staff*

Betr·iebs- [in comp] *working*; *operative*; *running*; ⟨Am⟩ *operating* ‖ ⟨rail⟩ *traffic* ‖ *business*; *trade*; *trading* ‖ *works* (*kitchen*) **~abgabe** f *tax on industrial undertaking* **~amt** n ⟨rail, etc.⟩ *traffic department* **~anlage** f *plant* ‖ ⟨bal⟩ ∼en [pl] *physical assets* pl **~anleitung, ~anweisung** f *service* od *operating instructions* **~appell** m ⟨Ger⟩ *regular meeting of managers and the staff of an undertaking* **~art** f *working method* **~arzt** m *industrial doctor* **~ausfall** m *operating trouble* od *shutdown* **≈bereit** a → –fähig **~bereitschaft** f *readiness for service* **~budget** n *operational budget* **~buße** f *fine imposed on employees for an offence* **~dampf** m *process steam* **~direktor** m *works superintendent*; *manager*, *managing director* **~ebene** f: auf ∼ *within enterprises* **~einnahme** f [pl] ⟨rail⟩ *traffic receipts* [pl] **~einrichtung** f *plant* ‖ ⟨bal⟩ ∼ u Ausstattung *property*, *plant and equipment* **~einschränkung** f *restriction of output* **~einstellung** f *shut-down* (*of a factory*) **~erweiterung** f (e–r Fabrik) *deployment*, (Modernisierung) *redeployment* **~fachleute** pl *work engineers* **≈fähig** a *workable*; *in* (*good*) *working* od *operating*, *running condition* od *order*; *ready to operate*; *fit for use*; nicht ∼ *unworkable* **≈fertig** a *ready for service* od *operation* **~fest** n *bean-feast* **~fonds** m (*working-*)*-fund* **~forschung** f *operational* od *operations research* **~führer** m *works* od *general manager*; *manager of a department*; *managing director*; *works manager*; ⟨fam⟩ *boss* **~führung** f *works management*; ⟨comp⟩ *industrial m.*; mehrfache ∼ *multiple m.* **~fürsorge** f ⟨Ger⟩ *factory welfare-work* **~gebäude** n *factory*; *works* [pl] **~geheimnis** n *business-secret* **~gemeinschaft** f ⟨Ger⟩ *fellowship and cooperation between employer and employees* **~gewerkschaftsleitung** f ⟨bes SBZ⟩ *trade union's council* **~gewinn** m *trading profit* **~ingenieur** m *working* (od *works*, *production*) *engineer* **~inspektor** m ⟨rail⟩ *traffic inspector* **~jahr** n *business* (od *working*)*-year*; *financial year* **~kapital** n *business* (od *trading*, *floating*, *working*; ⟨rail⟩ *rolling*)*-capital*; *stock-in-trade* **~klima** f *human relations* pl **~kollekt·ivvertrag** m ⟨SBZ⟩ *collective agreement of a nationally owned firm* **~kontrolle** f *quality control* **~kosten** [pl] *working* (od *running*, ⟨Am⟩ *operating*) *costs* od *expenses* **~krankenkasse** f *medical*, *surgical* od *health plan*; *plant health insurance fund* **~krankenschwester** f *industrial nurse* **~krankheit** f *occupational* od *industrial disease*; *disease caused by conditions of work* **~lehre** f = Betriebswissenschaft **~leistung** f *manufacturing efficiency*; *operating performance* **~leiter** m *managing director* ‖ *operator* ‖ ⟨tech⟩ *chief engineer* **~leitung** f *management* **~material** n *plant*; *working* (⟨rail⟩ *rolling*)*-stock* **~mitglieder-Verbesserungsvorschläge** m pl *staff suggestions* **~obmann** m *work-master*; *shop-steward* **~ordnung** f *works regulations* [pl] **~personal** n *the staff* **~prüfung** f = –kontrolle **~psychologie** f *industrial ps.* **~rat** m *factory* od *worker's council* od *committee* ⟨Ger⟩ *Works Council* °**~rübe** f ⟨fam⟩ (P) *great gun* **~schutz** m *Workmen's Compensation* **≈sicher** a *safe operating* (Zustand); [pred] *dependable in service* ‖ ⟨fam⟩ *foolproof* **~sicherheit** f *safety in operation* od *service*; *working* od *industrial safety* **~spannung** f ⟨el & wir⟩ *operating voltage* **~spesen** [pl] = Betriebskosten **~statistik** f *statistics of industrial--enterprises*; *operating statistics* **~stätte** f *workshop*, *plant* **~steuer** f *licence-duty* (*on hotels*) **~stillegung** f = Betriebseinstellung **~stockung** f *dead-lock of operation*; *interruption* (od *stoppage*) *of work*, *of traffic*; ⟨rail⟩ *break-down* **~stoff** m ⟨mot⟩ *fuel* **~stoffanhänger** m *fuel servicing trailer* **~stofflager** n *petrol*(*eum*) *dump* **~störung** f = Betriebsstockung **~stromkreis** m ⟨el⟩ *mains* pl; ⟨tech⟩ *service line* **~stunde** f *running hour* **≈technisch** a *practical*, *technical* **~überwachung** f *production* od *management control*; *works supervision* **≈unfähig** a *unserviceable* **~unfall** m *accident in a factory*; *shop* od *industrial acc.*; *acc. on the job*; *acc. occurring in the course of employment* ‖ *railway-accident* **~unkosten** f = Betriebskosten **~unterlagen** f pl *works records*; ⟨fam⟩ *job cards* **~verfassungsgesetz** n *Works Council Act*; ⟨Am⟩ *shop organization law* **~verhältnisse** n pl *plant* od *service conditions*; Untersuchung der ∼ ⟨comp⟩ *outline feasability study* **~vermögen** n *working-assets* [pl] **~versammlung** f *meeting of managers and the staff* **~versicherung** f *group insurance* **~vertretung** f *workers' representatives* pl **~verwaltung** f *factory administration*; ⟨rail⟩ *administration of traffic* **~vorschrift** f ⟨tech⟩ *service instructions* pl; (Buch) *instruction manual* **~wagen** m ⟨rail⟩ *work-train* **~weise** f ⟨tech⟩ *control* (z. B. *automatic* od *manual c.*) **~wirt** m *business economist* **≈wirtschaftlich** a *managerial* (Kenntnisse); → Operationsforschung **~wirtschaft** f *business economics planned* (od *organized*) *economy*; *economic organization*, *industrial management* **~wirtschaftslehre** f *science of industrial management*, *business administration*, *business* od *plant economy* **~wissenschaft** f *science of industrial organization* **~zählung** f *census of establishments* **~zeit** f *working* (od *business*)*-hours* [pl]; *working-period*; *hours of operation* **~zelle** f ⟨Ger hist⟩ *administrative subdivision of German Labour Service* **≈zulässig** a *safe operating* (Temperatur) **~zustand** m *working condition* **~zweig** m ⟨m. m.⟩ *operational division*

betr·iebsam a *active*; *busy*; *industrious*, *diligent*, *strenuous* ‖ *energetic*, *go-ahead*, *pushing*; ⟨dero⟩ *fussy*; ∼er Mensch m *bustler*, *hustler*; ⟨dero⟩ *busybody*; ∼ s ⟨Am⟩ *to hustle* | **≈keit** f *activity*; *industry*, *diligence* ‖ *bustle*, *go-aheadness*, *hustle*, *push*; ⟨dero⟩ *fussiness*

betr·inken vrefl [h] [→ trinken] sich ∼ *to get drunk*; ⟨sl⟩ *to fuddle*; ⟨Am⟩ *to go on a jag* ‖ sich sinnlos ∼ *to drink o.s. into a stupor*; → besoffen

betr·offen [pp v betreffen] **I.** a **1.** (v Krankheit, Unfall ∼) **a.** *affected*, *afflicted*, das (sc v der Krankheit) ∼e Kind *the afflicted child*; nicht ∼ *unaffected* ‖ die ∼e Seite *the affected side*; die v dem Erdbeben ∼en Städte *the towns afflicted*, *smitten*, *visited by the earthquake*; vom Unglück ∼ *stricken* (*area*); schwer ∼ *hard-hit* ‖ nicht ∼ *untouched*; ⟨pol⟩ *cleared* **b.** *der* ≈e *the p affected* od *concerned*; die ∼en *those affected* od *concerned* ‖ → betreffend **2.** (bestürzt) *confounded*, *embarrassed*, *perplexed*, *struck*; *amazed*, *surprised* **II.** adv *perplexedly* | **≈heit** f *embarrassment*; *perplexity*; *amazement*, *surprise*

betr·og, betr·ogen pret, pp v betrügen

betr·öpfeln vt [h] = beträufeln

betrüben vt [h] **1.** (jdn, Seele) *to afflict, distress, grieve*; es betrübt mich *it grieves me* (*to see, to think*); *I am sorry* (*to say*) || *to depress, to cast down* || (quälen) *to fret, pain* || → betrübt [a] **2. sich** ~ *to be afflicted, to grieve* (über *at, over*); *to feel distressed* od *sorry* (*about*); *to sorrow* (*at, over*) **betr·übend** a *distressing* (*news*); *sad* (f. *for*) **betr·üblich** a = betrübend || *woeful* (*results*) || *sore* (*subject*)

Betr·übnis f ~/–nisse *affliction, distress, grief*; *sorrow* (über *at*); *depression* **betr·übt** [pp v betrüben] **I.** a **1.** [pred] *afflicted* (über *at*); ~ s *to be afflicted, sad* (*at*); *to grieve* (*at, over*); *to feel sore* (*about*); *to take on* (*about*); *to be sorry* (*to hear*) || tief ~ s *to be much distressed* (*to hear*); ⟨fam⟩ *to be cut up* **2.** [attr] *afflicted, distressed, grieved* (*mother*), *sad, sorrowful*; *sore* (*heart*) || *cheerless, dismal, gloomy, sad* (*thoughts*, etc.) **II.** adv *distressedly, sadly* | **≃heit** f *distressedness, sadness*

Betr·ug m ~(e)s/ *cheat, deceit, fraud, imposture*; *dishonesty*; *falseness*; *duplicity*; *dupery, swindle*; *trick*; *fraudulent deception*; *underhand dealing*; *underhandedness*; (*sharp*) *practice*; *trickery, knavery* || frommer ~ *pious fraud* || ⟨jur⟩ *fraud*; ⟨engl⟩ Gesetz z Verhütung v Betrügen *Statute of Frauds* (1677) || (strafrechtlich) *cheating* || (beim Spiel) ⟨sl⟩ *double-cross*; ⟨cards Am sl⟩ *bunco* | ⟨übtr⟩ (Täuschung) *deception*; *deceit(fulness), fraud, imposition, juggle*; ⟨sl⟩ *fake* || *false coin* || *foul play* || e–n ~ begehen an jdm *to cheat a p*; ⟨übtr⟩ *to deceive a p*

betr·ügen vt/i [h] [betrog/betrogen] (→ °beschuppen, beschummeln) **1.** vt **a.** jdn ~ *to cheat, deceive, defraud*; ⟨Am fam⟩ *to honey-fug(g)le*, ⟨sl⟩ *to bunco, nobble a p*; ⟨Am sl⟩ *to stick, to short-change a p* || (s–e Komplizen) *to double-cross*; ⟨sex⟩ *to deceive* || betrogen w [nur pass] *to be bitten* | jdn ~ um etw *to cheat a p* (*out*) *of a th, to defraud a p of a th*; *to bamboozle, humbug, juggle, swindle*; ⟨Am⟩ *beat*, ⟨sl⟩ *bunco, diddle a p out of a th*; er betrog mich um 2 Sch. ⟨fam⟩ *he did me out of two bob*; betrogen w ⟨sl⟩ *to be stung* (um *for*) || um jdn z ~ *in fraud of, to the fraud of a p* | (täuschen) *to deceive* (⟨sex⟩: *his wife deceived him*); *to impose upon, to palter with a p*; leicht z ~(d) *deceivable*; v s–r Frau betrogen w ⟨mar⟩ *to double Cape Horn* **c. sich** ~ *to cheat o.s.*; *to deceive o.s.*; *to delude o.s.* **2.** vi *to cheat, to practise deceit* od *fraud*; *to swindle*; in der Absicht z ~ *with intent to defraud*

Betr·üger m ~s/~, Betrügerin f ~/~nen *cheat, fraud*; *impostor, swindler*; *pretender* || *quack, mountebank* || *faker* || ⟨cards⟩ *sharper* || ⟨sl⟩ *fourflusher, shark*; ⟨Am⟩ *beat, slicker*; ⟨Am sl⟩ *bunco-steerer* **Betrüger·ei** f ~/~en *cheating, deceit, fraudulence, practice, trickery*; → Betrug **b.isch 1.** a *fraudulent, deceitful*; ⟨Am sl⟩ *phon(e)y* || in ~er Absicht *fraudulently*; *with intent to defraud*; auf ~e Weise *fraudulently, on the cross* **2.** adv *fraudulently*

betr·unken [pp v betrinken] a **1.** [pred] ~ s *to be drunk, inebriated, intoxicated, groggy*; ⟨euph⟩ *tipsy* || ⟨sl⟩ *tight*; *blotto, canned, primed, sozzled*; *to be in liquor, the worse for liquor, in one's cups*; *to be up the pole* || sinnlos (*or* °sternhagel, total) ~ *beastly* od *dead, blind drunk, blind to the world*; *as drunk as a lord*; *three sheets in the wind*; *stewed to the gills* || jdn ~ m *to make a p drunk, to inebriate, intoxiate a p* **2.** [attr] *drunken* (*fellow*); *intoxicated*; ⟨sl⟩ *tight* || ~er Zustand (*state of*) *drunkenness* od *intoxication*

Betr·unkene: [der ~, ein ~r] m ~n/~n *drunken man*; *drunkard* || ein ~r *a drunk* **Betr·unkenheit** f (*state of*) *drunkenness, intoxication*

Betschu·anen pl *Bechuanas* pl

Bett n ~(e)s/~en **A.** (T) *bed, lair*; (f. Hasen) *form* **B.** (P) **1. a.** *bed*; **an** jds ~ *at* od *by a p's bedside*; Sachen ans ~ stellen *to put things by the bed* || **auf** dem ~ *on the bed* || **in** dem ~ (*the bottle is*) *in the bed* || ~ u Zubehör (Wäsche etc) *bedding*; Kopfende des ~s *bed-head*; Seite des ~s *bedside* || vierpfostiges ~ mit Vorhängen *fourposter with curtains* | (als Schlaf– u Ruhestatt e–r bes P) [nach prep ohne def art]: **im ~, aus** dem ~ (*he is*) *in bed, out of bed*, etc. → 2. b. **b.** Ruhe≃ *couch*; Schiffs≃ *berth*; Schlafwagen≃ *sleeping berth* || Deck≃, Feder≃ ⟨a–engl⟩ *feather-bed*; Stroh≃ *straw-bed, bed of straw* **c.** Fremden≃ *spare bed*; Kinder≃ *cot*; Kranken≃ *sick-bed, bed of sickness*; Sterbe≃ *death-bed* (an s–m St. *at his d.*) **d.** Braut≃ *bridal bed* || Ehe≃ *marriage-bed*; ⟨engl⟩ (zweischläfriges) *double-bed*; Tisch u ~ *bed and board* **e.** (Liege [f] der Rauschgiftsüchtigen) ⟨sl⟩ *pad* **2. a.** ein ~ **aufschlagen** *to put up a bed* || das ~ hüten *to keep one's bed, to lie up* || ein ~ lüften *to air a bed* || das ~ m *to make the bed* || ein ~ überziehen *to sheet a bed* **b. ans** ~ gefesselt s *to be confined to one's bed, to be laid low, to be laid up in bed* | **aus** dem ~ springen *to jump out of bed* || aus dem ~ steigen *to get out of bed*; mit dem linken (*or* verkehrten) Fuße aus dem ~ steigen *to get out of bed on the wrong side* || jdn aus dem ~ herausholen *to rout out a p* | **im** ~ *in bed* || im ~ bleiben *to stay in bed* || (lange) im ~ liegen *to lie* (*late*) *in bed* || im ~ liegen mit e–r Influenza *to be in bed with influenza* | **ins** ~ gehen *to go to bed, to get into bed, to go between the sheets*; ⟨fam⟩ *to turn in*; ⟨aero⟩ *to spin in*; ⟨Am sl⟩ *to hit the hay* || sich ins ~ legen (wegen Krankheit) *to take to one's bed* | jdn z ~ bringen *to put a p to bed*; ⟨fig⟩ *to give a p a piece of one's mind*; z ~ gehen = ins ~ gehen **C.** ⟨übtr⟩ **1.** (Fluß≃) *bed, channel, river-bed, river-channel*; der Fluß ist aus dem ~ getreten *the river has overflowed its banks* **2.** ⟨min⟩ *bed, layer* **D.** ⟨tech⟩ *bed*; ~ e–r Drehbank *lathe-bed* || Gieß≃ (beim Eisengießen) *pig-bed* **E.** [in comp] *bed*

B·ett- **~behang** m *valance* **~bezug** m ⟨Ger⟩ *linen cases* od *coverings for feather-bed and pillows* || ⟨engl⟩ *sheets* [pl] **~couch** f *convertible couch, bet-settee* **~decke** f (zum Zudecken) *blanket, bed-cover* || ⟨Am⟩ *bedspread*; gefütterte ~ *comforter, comfortable*; Stickerei auf e–r ~ *candlewick* || mit e–r ~ zudecken *to blanket* || (als Schutzdecke f. ~) *bed-cover, counterpane, coverlet*; (leichte) *bedspread*; (Stepp≃) *quilt* **~feder** f *bed-feather* **~gestell** n *bed-framework* °**~haserl** n ⟨sl⟩ *playmate*; (*snappy*) *undercut* **~himmel** m *canopy* **~kante** f *bed-edge* **~kissen** n *pillow* **~lade** f = Bettgestell **≃lägerig** a *bedridden*; *sick in bed*; ⟨Am⟩ *bedfast* || ~ w *to take to one's bed, to be laid, to be laid up in bed, to be confined to one's bed* **~lägerigkeit** f *bedridden state, confinement to bed* **~laken** n *sheet* **~linnen** n *sheeting* **~machen** n *bed-making* **~nässen** n ⟨med⟩ *enuresis* **~nässer** m (P) *wet-bed* **~pfosten** m *bed-post* **~pfühl** m *bolster* **~ruhe** f ⟨mst med⟩ (*complete*) *bedrest* **~schüssel** f = Stechbecken **~schwere** f ⟨fig⟩ (*state of*) *sleepiness* od *somnolence caused by drink*; die nötige ~ *one's fill* ⟨Am⟩ *one's load* (*got his load*) **~stelle** f *bedstead*; leichte ~ ⟨AInd⟩ *charpoy* **~überzug** m = Inlett **~tuch** n *sheet*; Leinwand z Bettüchern *sheeting* **~unterlage** f *waterproof sheet* **~vorhang** m *bed-curtain*; *valance*; Bettvorhänge [pl] *bed-hangings* [pl] **~vorlage** f, **~vorleger** m *bed-carpet, bed-rug* **~wärmer** m *electric warming-pan* **~wäsche** f *bed-linen, bed-clothes* **~zeug** n (Stoff) *bedding, bed-clothes* [pl] ×**~zieche** f = Inlett

B·ettchen n *small bed*; *cot* ‖ „∼gehn!" → Baba ‖ wer bringt mich ins ∼? *who tucks me in*?

B·ettel m ∼s/ **1.** (geringfügiges Ding) *trifle*; *rubbish, trash*; *trumpery* ‖ ein ∼ v 5 Penny *a beggarly 5 pence* ‖ °der ganze ∼ *the whole lot*; ⟨sl⟩ *the whole caboodle* od *show* | ⟨cont⟩ → Kram ‖ der alte ∼ *the same mess* (od *jog-trot, mismanagement*) *as before* **2.** [koll] *beggars* [pl]

B·ettel- [in comp] *beggarly*; *mendicant* **≗·arm** a *wholly destitute* **∼·armut** f *beggarliness, beggary, abject poverty* **∼brief** m *begging-letter* **∼brot** n *bread of mendicity* od *charity* **∼bruder** m *professional beggar* **∼bube** m *beggar-boy* **∼frau** f *beggar-woman* **∼geld** n *alms* [pl]; *dole* **≗haft** a *beggarly, poor*; *miserable, wretched*; ∼ aussehend *beggarly-looking* **∼junge** m *beggar-boy* **∼kram** m *trash, trumpery*; ⟨sl⟩ *caboodle* **∼leute** [pl] ⟨übtr cont⟩ *gang of beggars* [pl] **∼mann** m ∼(e)s/–lleute **1.** *beggar, mendicant*; *pauper* **2.** ⟨*at* cards⟩ *beggar-my-neighbour* **∼mönch** m *mendicant*, (*mendicant*) *friar* ‖ ind. ∼ *sunnyassee, sun*(*n*)*yasi* ‖ ∼kloster [n] *friary* ∼orden [m] die ∼ [pl] *the mendicant orders* [pl] **∼pack** n *beggarly crew* **∼sack** m *beggar's bag* od *wallet* **∼stab** m ⟨fig⟩ (jdn) an den ∼ bringen *to pauperize, beggar* (*a p*), *to reduce* (*a p*) *to beggary* od *mendicity*; (Land) *to impoverish, to reduce to poverty*; an den ∼ k. *to be reduced to beggary* **∼stolz** m → Bettlerstolz **∼vogt** m *beadle*; *inferior constable* **∼volk** n *gang of beggars, beggarly crew* **∼weib** n *beggar-woman*; *pauper* **∼wesen** n *mendicity*

Bettel·ei f ∼/∼en **1.** *begging, beggary, mendicity, mendicancy*; Verein gegen Haus≗ *Charity Organization Society* (1869) ‖ ⟨fig⟩ *importunity, solicitation* **2.** es ist e–e rechte ∼ *it's mere trash*

b·etteln I. vi/t [h] **1.** vi *to ask alms, to beg*; *to cadge*; ⟨Am⟩ *to pan-handle*; ∼ gehen *to go begging, to beg one's bread*; *to cadge* ‖ die Kunst geht ∼ *art is in a miserable condition* ‖ ∼ um etw *to beg* (*for*) *a th*; ⟨a. übtr⟩ um s Leben ∼ *to beg one's life* **2.** *vt (etw) *to beg* (*a th*) ‖ **sich** v Ort z Ort ∼ *to beg one's way from place to place* **II.** ≗ n *begging, cadging*; *calling* ‖ sich aufs ∼ legen *to take to begging* ‖ etw durch ∼ erhalten *to cadge a th* ‖ ⟨übtr⟩ ich bin nicht groß im ∼ *I am but a poor beggar*

b·etten vt/i [h] **I.** vt **1.** (jdn) *to bed, to pillow* (*a p*); *to lay* (*a p*) *in bed, to put* (*a p*) *to bed*; hoch ∼ *to pillow* (*a p*) *up* ‖ zur letzten Ruhe ∼ *to lay to rest* **2.** ⟨übtr⟩ (Steine etc) *to bed* (*in mortar*) ‖ ⟨poet⟩ gebettet in (of houses, etc.) *bosomed, embowered* (*in trees*); *sunk in* (*woods*) ‖ ⟨fig⟩ er ist nicht auf Rosen gebettet *his life is no bed of roses* (od *is not all roses*) **3. sich** ∼ *to make one's bed* ‖ wie man sich bettet, so schläft man *as a man makes his bed, so he must lie on it*; *you must lie on the bed which you made for yourself*; *you made your bed, now lie in it, do well and have well* **II.** *vi *to make the bed*(*s*)

B·ettler m ∼s/∼ *beggar, mendicant*; ⟨Am⟩ *panhandler* ‖ ⟨fam⟩ *bum* ‖ ∼ um Nachtasyl *sundowner* ‖ jdn z ∼ m *to beggar a p*; sich z ∼ m *to beggar o.s.* ‖ ⟨übtr⟩ *pauper* **∼stolz** m *beggarly* od *beggar's pride* **∼tum** n *beggardom*

B·ettlerin f ∼/∼nen *beggar*(*-woman*)

B·ettung f ∼/∼en **1.** *bedding* (*of a patient*) **2.** ⟨tech⟩ *bed, bedding, framework*; *foundation, support* ‖ ⟨rail⟩ (Schotter≗) *ballast* ‖ ⟨mil⟩ *platform* (*of a gun*)

bet·ulich a *amenable, forthcoming, obliging* ‖ *busy, officious*; → freundlich; geschäftig

×**bet·un** vrefl [h] °betu dich nicht! *don't be fussy, pettish, petulant*; *don't fuss*!

bet·üpfeln vt [h] (etw) *to dot*; *to mark with dots*; *to spot* **bet·upfen 1.** vt [h] (etw) *to dab*; *to touch lightly*; die Augen ∼ *to dab one's eyes* (*with a handkerchief*); das Haar leicht ∼ *to make some dabs at one's hair* ‖ (Wand) *to touch* (*with brown varnish*) **2.** ≗ n *dab* °**bet·uppen** vt [h] → °beschuppen

B·etze f ⟨hunt⟩ = Wölfin

B·euche f *lye*; †*buck* **b·euchen** vt [h] (Garne) *to boil in lye* (in a kier) *to steep in lye*; †*to buck*

b·eugbar a ⟨gram⟩ *flexional, inflexional* (*language*; *verb*); *declinable* (*noun*)

***B·euge** f **1.** (mst = Beugung) ‖ Knie≗ ⟨gym⟩ *knee-bending*; Knie≗n [pl] *knee-bending exercises* [pl]; tiefe Knie≗ *deepknee bending* **2.** (Werkzeug) *bender* **3.** ⟨for⟩ *stack, pile* (of *timber*) **∼muskel** m ⟨anat⟩ = Beuger **∼übung** f *bending exercise*

b·eugen I. vt [h] (→ biegen) **1. a.** den Kopf ∼ *to bend, incline, stoop one's head*; gebeugte Haltung *stoop*; gebeugte Schultern *stooping shoulders* ‖ die Knie ∼ (zur Andacht) *to bend the knees, to genuflect*; ⟨gym⟩ *to bend the knees*; gebeugte Knie [pl] *bended knees* [pl] **b.** ⟨a. übtr⟩ (jdn) *to bend*; *to bow* (*down*); *to afflict*; *to depress*; v Alter gebeugt s *to be bent* od *bowed by age*; v Kummer g. s *to be bowed* od *afflicted with grief* **c.** (of the wind) (Bäume) *to bend* **d.** ⟨phys⟩ (Licht etc) *to diffract* **e.** (das Recht) *to give a bias to, to tamper with, to twist, to warp* (*the law*) **f. sich** ∼ *to bend* (über *over*; vor *to, before*); *to incline o.s., to stoop* (*to hear, to do*) ‖ sich mit dem Hals nach vorn ∼ *to crane forward*; sich mit dem H. ∼ über .. *to crane over* .. ‖ sich in Ehrfurcht ∼ vor *to bow the knee to, to bow down to* (*a p*) | (of trees) *to bend, bow* **2.** ⟨fig⟩ (unterwerfen) **a.** (jdn, ein Volk) *to bend* (unter *to*) ‖ den Nacken ∼ unter .. *to bow one's neck under* .. ‖ (demütigen) *to humble, humiliate, mortify* **b.** sich ∼ *to submit, yield*; sich ∼ vor jdm (etw), sich jdm (e–r S) ∼ *to bow before* (*an authority*); .. *to* (*a decision, to fate*); *to defer to* (*a judgement*); *to yield to* (*force*); *to bend, submit, truckle to* (*a p*) **3.** ⟨gram⟩ (Wort) *to inflect*; (Hauptwort) *to decline*; (Zeitwort) *to conjugate* **II.** ≗ n *the bending* (*of the body head*, etc.) ‖ ⟨gym⟩ Knie≗ = Kniebeuge, → d. ‖ → Beugung **B·euger** m ∼s/∼ ⟨anat⟩ *flexor*; → Strecker **B·eugung** f *bending*; *flexion, flection, flexure* ‖ ⟨phys⟩ *diffraction* (*of light-waves*, etc.) ‖ ⟨gram⟩ *inflexion* (*of words*); *declension* (*of nouns*); *conjugation* (*of verbs*) ‖ ∼sdifferenz [f] *dispersivity* | ∼sfarben [f pl] *prismatic colo*(*u*)*rs*; ∼sgitter [n] *diffraction grating*, ∼sspektrum [n] *diffraction spectrum*

B·eule f ∼/∼n **1.** (am Körper) *bruise*; *bump, lump, swelling* ‖ (Geschwür) *boil, tumour* ‖ Frost≗ *chilblain* ‖ ⟨med⟩ Leisten≗ *bubo* ‖ ⟨vet⟩ (harte ∼) *warble* **2.** ⟨übtr⟩ *dent, dint* (*in a can*); (im Hut) *dinge*; mit ∼n versehen [a] *dented, dinted* (*armour*) ‖ → Buckel, Bosse

B·eulenpest f ⟨med⟩ *bubonic plague*

b·eulig a *full of bumps*

be·unruhigen vt [h] **1.** (jdn) *to disquiet*; *alarm, to fill* (*a p*) *with misgiving*; *to flurry* (*with*); *to perturb*; sie war beunruhigt *she was perturbed, she felt flustered* (*when she heard*) ‖ *to disconcert, discompose*; *trouble, worry* (⟨Am fam⟩ *faze*) (*a p*) | *she was rendered restless and uncomfortable by his presence* ‖ die öffentl. Meinung ∼ *to disquiet public opinion*; das politische Leben ∼ *to flutter the political dovecotes* ‖ (Land) *to disturb* | (Feind) *to harass* ‖ über etw sehr –gt s *to be much excited* (*etc*) *about a th* **2. sich** ∼ *to be troubled in mind*; .. über *to trouble, to be troubled, to trouble one's head* (od *to worry*) *about*; sich ∼ wegen *to put o.s. about for*; ∼ Sie sich nicht! *never mind*! **be·unruhigend** a *alarming, staggering, unsettling* (*news*); *disquieting* (*features*); *panicky* (*speech*) ‖ *disturbing* (f. *to*); es ist ∼, daß *it is disquieting that* .. **Be·unruhigung** f ∼/∼en *disquieting, disturbance* (*of a p, a* *country, of the weather)* || (Unruhe) *alarm* (über *at*); *anxiety* (f. *to*) (*he laboured under some vague anxiety and alarm*); *inquietude*; *trouble* || ⟨pol⟩ ~ hervorrufen *to cause comment* || kein Grund zur ~! *no cause for alarm!*

be·urkunden vt [h] *to document*; *authenticate*, *prove* (*a th*) *by documentary evidence* || *to prove*, *to verify* ⟨a. com⟩ | ⟨jur⟩ *to depose* **Be·urkundung** f ~/~en *documentary authentication* od *proof* || *verification* | ⟨jur⟩ (*deposition made before a public notary*) (notarielle) *acknowledg(e)ment* || ~en [pl] ⟨scient⟩ *documentation*

be·urlauben vt [h] **1.** jdn ~ *to give* od *grant leave* (*of absence*) *to a p*; er wurde 3 Monate beurlaubt *he was given leave of a. for 3 months* || ⟨mil⟩ *to grant a furlough to a p* | **sich** ~ *to take* (*one's*) *leave* **2.** (vom Amte) ~ *to suspend* (*an official*) **be·urlaubt** a (*absent*) *on leave* || ⟨mil⟩ *furloughed* (*man*); [pred] *on furlough* **Be·urlaubte:** [der ~, ein ~r] m *man on leave* || ~nstand [m] ⟨mil⟩ *reserve status*; *the Reserve* **Be·urlaubung** f ~/~en **1.** *leave* (*–giving*) || ⟨mil⟩ *furlough* **2.** *suspension* (*of an official*)

be·urteilen vt [h] **1.** jdn ~ *to judge a p* (nach *by* [*others*]); falsch ~ *to misjudge a p*; jdn richtig ~ *to size a p up* || etw ~ *to judge* (*of*) *a th*; *to pass* od *pronounce judg*(*e*)*ment* (*up*)*on a th*; (Wert, Verlust) *to estimate*; (Pferde etc bei Wettbewerb) *to judge* || (auffassen) *to view* | etw ernst ~ *to take a grave view of a th* || e–e Lage richtig ~ *to size up a situation* | [abs] selbst ~ *to judge for o.s.* (*how great a debt* ..) **2.** (Buch etc) *to criticize*, *review*; *discuss* || (un)günstig ~ *to* (*dis*)*approve of* (*a play*); (un)günstig beurteilt w *to meet with* (*dis*)*approval*

Be·urteiler m ~s/~ *judge* (*of a th*) || *critic*, *reviewer* (*of a book*) **Be·urteilung** f ~/~en **1.** *judgment* (*of* od *on a p, a th*); *opinion* (*of* od *on a th*) || Art der ~ *approach* (gegenüber e–r S *to a th*) **2.** *review* (*of a book*); kritische ~ *criticism* (*of a th*); günstige ~ finden bei jdm *to meet with a favourable reception with a p*; *to appeal to a p*

B·eusch(e)l n ~s/~ [österr] ⟨cul⟩ → Innereien bes Lunge; → Bäuschel

^×^**B·eute** f = Backtrog

B·eute f ~/ **I. 1.** (Kriegs≗) *booty*, *loot*, *plunder*, *spoil*; *the spoils of war* || ⟨bib⟩ *prey* **2.** (auf See) *prize*; als ~ kapern *to make prize of*, *to prize* **3.** (Raub) *loot*, *plunder*; Diebes≗ *loot*, *spoil*; ⟨sl⟩ *swag* **4.** ⟨übtr⟩ (Gewinn) *booty* (f. *for*); *haul* (an *of*); *plunder*, *prize*; *quarry*; *profits* [pl]; gemeinsame ~ ⟨Am⟩ *melons* [pl] **5. reiche ~ m** *to get a rich booty*; *to make a big haul* (an *of*) || der Feind machte reiche ~ an Gefangenen u Geschützen *the enemy took many prisoners and captured numerous guns* || **als** ~ mit sich nehmen *to carry off as spoil* || e–e ~ des Feindes w, dem Feinde **zur** ~ **fallen** *to fall into the hands of the enemy*, *to be captured* od *seized by the enemy* || **auf ~ ausgehen** *to rove in search of plunder*, *to make raids for plunder*, *to go marauding* od *plundering* **B. 1.** ⟨hunt⟩ **1.** (Jagd≗) *bag*; e–e gute ~ m *to make a good bag* **2.** (of beasts, hounds) (verfolgtes Tier) *prey*, *quarry*; ⟨poet⟩ *game* || ~ m auf *to prey upon* (*cats prey upon mice*); auf ~ ausgehen *to be after one's prey* || der L. schlug s–e ~ *the lion made its kill* **3.** ⟨übtr⟩ (Opfer) *prey*; *victim* (jds, e–r S *to a p*, *to a th*); e–e ~ s–s Hasses *a prey to his hatred* || ~ m auf (of robbers, etc.) *to prey upon* (*a p*) || jdm, e–r S zur ~ fallen *to fall a prey* od *victim to a p*, *to a th*; dem Orkan fielen 1000 Opfer z ~ *the hurricane took toll of a thousand lives* **~geschütz** n *captured gun* **~gier** f *thirst for plundering* **≗gierig**, **≗lustig** a *eager for* (od *given to*) *plundering* **~park** m ⟨mil⟩ *salvage dump for captured materiel* **~recht** n *right of seizure* (im Kriege) **~sammelstelle** f *collecting point for c. m.* **~zug** m *raid* (in *into*); *plundering* od *marauding expedition*

B·eutel m ~s/~ **1.** *bag*; (Brief≗) *bag*, *sack* || kl ~, Tabaks≗ *pouch* || ⟨AInd⟩ lederner ~ (f. Wasser) *mussuck* || (~sieb f. Mehl) *bolter* **2.** ⟨anat⟩ *pocket*, *pouch*; *purse*; e–n ~ bilden *to pouch* || ⟨biol⟩ *sac*; → Sack, Schleim≗ || ⟨zoo⟩ *pouch* **3.** Geld≗ *money-bag*, *purse* | ⟨übtr & fig⟩ ein gr Geld≗ *a heavy* od *long purse*; mit leerem ~ *with an empty purse* || das geht an den ~ *that is very expensive* || den Daumen auf den ~ halten *to tighten the purse-strings*; den ~ ziehen *or* aufmachen *to loosen the purse-strings* || in den ~ greifen müssen *to have to pay*, ⟨sl⟩ *to have to fork out*; ein Loch in jds ~ reißen (of bills) *to empty a p's purse* || den ~ spicken *to fill one's purse* **4.** ⟨billiards⟩ *pocket*; (Ball) in den ~ treiben *to pocket* **5.** ^×^ = Beitel **6.** °[in comp] (P) → Dumm≗, Lügen≗, Wind≗ **7.** [in comp] *bag*, *purse* || ⟨zoo⟩ *pouched* **~bär** m ⟨zoo⟩ *koolah*, *koala* **~dachs** m ⟨zoo⟩ = Bandikut **≗förmig** a *baggy*, *purse-shaped* || ⟨scient⟩ *sacciform* **~kammer** f (Müllerei) *bolting-house* **~kanzleipapier** n *bag paper for confectionery* **~maschine** f *bolting-mill* **~maus** f ⟨zoo⟩ *pouched mouse* **~netz** n *pursenet* **~ratte** f ⟨zoo⟩ *pouched rat*; *opossum* **~schneider** m ⟨fam⟩ *cutpurse*, *pickpocket* **~schnur** f *purse-string* **~sieb** n *bolter* **~star** m *cacique*; *icteric oriole*; *hangnest*, *hangbird*; Gattung der ~e *Icteridae* **~tier** n *marsupial*; → Bandikut **~tuch** n *bolting-cloth*; ⟨phot⟩ *cheese-cloth* (*to dry prints on*) **~voll** m *purseful*, ein ~ Geld *a p. of money* **~wolf** m ⟨zoo⟩ *thylacine*

b·eutelig a *baggy*, *bulging*; *bagged*

b·euteln vt/i [h] **I.** vt **1.** (Mehl) *to bolt*, *sift* **2.** *to shake thoroughly* **3.** °jdn ~ *to fleece*, *plunder a p* **4. sich ~** (of clothes) *to bag*, *bulge*; *pucker* (*up*) **II.** vi = sich ~ **b·eutelnd** a (*of clothes*) *bagging*

B·eutler m **1.** purse-maker **2.** ~ [pl] = Beuteltiere [pl]

B·euthen n ⟨hist⟩ (Stadt in Oberschlesien)

bev·ölkern vt (Land) *to people*, *populate*; *to make* (*a country*) *populous* **bev·ölkert** a *populated*; stark ~ *heavily pop.*; dicht ~ *populous*; dünn ~ *sparsely populated*

Bev·ölkerung f ~/~en **1.** [abstr] *population*; starke ~ *populousness* **2.** [konkr] *population*; *inhabitants* [pl] || Zahl der ~ *population* || ~ im schulpflichtigen Alter *schoolage pop.* || Wachstum [n] der ~ *pop. growth* **~sbewegung** f ⟨demog⟩ (*general*) *pop. change* od *movement*; (räumlich) *migratory m.* || Methode der natürlichen ~ *vital statistics technique* (*of* ..) **~sdichte** f *density of population*; *populousness* ⟨demog⟩ *density index* **~sdruck** m *pop. pressure* **~sentwicklung** f *pop. dynamics* **~sgeschichte** f *historical demography* **~skartei** f ⟨demog⟩ (*continuous*) *pop. registrater* **~slehre** f *theory of population*; *principle of p.* **~srückgang** m ⟨demog⟩ *decrease in population* **~sstand** m *population* **~sstatistik** f *demographic statistics* **~sstat·istiker** m *demographer* **~strennung** f ⟨demog⟩ *segregation* **~svermehrung** f = –swachstum || Anhänger der ~ *pro-natalist*; Gegner der ~ *anti-natalist* **~swachstum** m *increase of population* **~swissenschaft** f *demography* **~swissenschaftler** m *demographer* **~szuwachs** m (gesamt) *total growth*; (natürlich) *natural increase*

bev·ollmächtigen vt [h] (jdn) *to authorize*; *to empower* (*to do*); *to give* (*a p*) *full powers* || (Gesandten) *to accredit* || ⟨jur⟩ jdn ~ *to give a p* (od *to invest a p with*) *power of attorney* **bev·ollmächtigt** a *authorized* || *plenipotentiary* (*ambassador*) **Bev·ollmächtigte:** [der ~, ein ~r] m ~n/~n *deputy*, *representative*; *proxy*; ⟨com⟩ *authorized agent*; *assignee*, *trustee* || ⟨pol⟩ *plenipotentiary* || ⟨jur⟩ *attorney* **Bev·ollmächtigung** f ~/~en, *authorization*; → Vollmacht

bev·or conj *before*; er brauchte etw Zeit ~ er sprach *he took a little time to speak*; ~ du zurückkamst *prior to your coming back* ‖ [nach negat. Hauptsatz] *till*; nicht aussteigen, ~ der Zug hält! *do not get out till the train stops!* |

bev·ormunden vt [h] ⟨übtr⟩ (jdn, ein Volk geistig ~) *to tutor* (*a p*); *to hold* (*a p*) *in tutelage*; *to regiment*, bevormundet w *to be regimented* ‖ → Vormund **bev·ormundend** a *tutelary* **Bev·ormundung** f ~/ ⟨übtr⟩ (geistige ~) *tutelage*; *regimentation* (*of a people*)

bev·orraten vt/refl [h] *to set up supplies, stores, equipment, etc* (*in advance*) **Bev·orratung** f ~/~en (*the*) *setting up* (*in advance*) *of s., st., equ., etc* ‖ *stockpiling*, ⟨bes Am⟩ *hedging* **~sziel** n ⟨log⟩ *target* (*of ..*)

bev·orrechten vt [h] (jdn) *to privilege*

bev·orrechtet, -tigt a *privileged* (*classes*) ‖ *preferential* (*claim*; Forderung *debt*) ‖ –tigte Straße *major road*; nicht .. *by-road, by-street* **Bev·orrechtete** [der ~, ein ~r] m ~n/~n *privileged person* **Bev·orrechtung** f ~/~en die ~ jds *the act of privileging a p, the privileged position of a p*

bev·orschussen vt [h] (etw) *to advance money on* (*a th*); jdm e–e Summe ~ *to advance a p a sum* (auf *on*) **Bev·orschussung** f *advance* ‖ (*the*) *making available of advance monies* od *funds*

bev·or|stehen I. vi [h] **1.** (of events) *to be at hand, to be imminent* od *near, to impend*; die Zeit stand bevor *the time was at hand*; Ostern steht bevor *Easter is near* ‖ (of danger) *to threaten, impend* **2.** jdm ~ (S) *to be in store for a p* **II.** ≗ n das nahe ≗ *the imminence* (*of his marriage*), *impendence* **bev·orstehend** a (nahe ~) *imminent, impending*; *impendent* (*ceremony*); *forthcoming* (*jubilee*); *approaching* (*end*) ‖ die ~en Ereignisse *the events ahead* ‖ (drohend) *threatening, menacing* ‖ das Schlimmste steht noch ~ *the worst is yet to come* ‖ [pred] *at hand*; .. *in prospect*; .. *to come* ‖ (folgend) *ensuing* (*months*), *next*

bev·orzugen vt [h] jdn, etw ~ vor dem anderen, der anderen S *to favour a p, a th before* od *above the other*; → vorziehen ‖ ⟨jur⟩ *to privilege* ‖ bevorzugt abgefertigt w vor anderen *to take precedence of* od *over others* ‖ das Produkt wird v Publikum immer mehr –gt .. *is finding increasing favo(u)r with the public*

bev·orzugt a *favo(u)red* (vor anderen ~ *above others*; *preferred* (*method*) ‖ der v ihm bes ~e Maler *his favo(u)rite painter* ‖ in ~er Lage s *to be possessed of advantages* ‖ ~e Stellung *primacy*; *pride of place* ‖ *privileged* ‖ ~e Abfertigung *precedence*

Bev·orzugung f ~/ *preference* (vor *to, over, above*); die ~ jds *the preference given to a p, the favour shown to a p*

bew·achen vt [h] (jdn) *to watch* (*over*) (*a p*); *to guard* (*a p*) ‖ (v Detektiv) *to nose* (*a p*)

***bew·achsen** vi/t [→ wachsen] **1.** vi *to become overgrown* od *covered* (*with*); mst ~ s *to be overgrown* od *covered* (*with*) **2.** vt (Fläche) *to overgrow, to cover* **bew·achsen** a *overgrown* (*with*); *grown-up* (*with trees*); üppig ~ *rank* (*with weeds*); dicht ~ *close* (*country*) **Bew·achsung** f ~/~en *vegetation*

Bew·achung f ~/~en *custody*, jdn unter ~ halten *to keep a p in custody* ‖ (Schutz) *guard*, unter ~ jds *under the guard of a p*

bew·affnen vt [h] (jdn) *to arm* (bis an die Zähne *to the teeth*); *to armour*; *to equip* (*a p*) *with arms* ‖ ⟨übtr⟩ bewaffnet s mit *to be armed with* (*an umbrella*, etc.) ‖ **sich** ~ *to arm o.s., to arm* **bew·affnet** a *armed* | ⟨übtr⟩ mit ~em Auge *with an armed eye* ‖ mit ~er Hand *by force and arms* ‖ ~e Neutralität *armed neutrality*

Bewaffnete [der ~, ein ~r] *p equipped with arms* (od *clad in armour*), *armoured warrior*

Bew·affnung f ~/~en *arming* (*of a p*); *weaponry* (*of a country*); *equipment* (*of the infantry*) ‖ (Geschütze) *armament* (*of a ship*); das Schiff hat e–e ~ v 10 Geschützen *the ship is mounted with 10 guns* ‖ ⟨übtr, bot & zoo⟩ *armature*; *arming*

Bew·ahranstalt f Kleinkinder≗ ‖ *home* od *nursery for infants and orphans*

bew·ahren vt [h] **1.** (erhalten, aufbewahren) *to keep, preserve* ‖ ⟨mst übtr⟩ (etw) im Innern ~ *to keep* (*a th*) *in one's mind*; jds Andenken ~ *to preserve the memory of a p, to remember a p*; jdm ein treues A. ~ *to keep a p in kind remembrance*; Treue ~ *to keep faith*, jdm, e–r S die T. ~ *to stick* od *keep to a p, to a th, to abide* od *stand by a th* ‖ sich e–n guten Ruf ~ *to keep* od *preserve one's good name* | ein Geheimnis ~ *to keep a secret*; Stillschweigen ~ *to keep* od *preserve silence* **2.** (behüten) *to keep*; *to take care of* **3.** (schützen) jdn (etw) ~ vor *to guard, preserve, save from*; *to keep from* (od *out of*); jdn davor ~ z tun *to save a p from doing*; **sich** ~ vor *to protect o.s., to guard* (*o.s.*) *from* od *against* ‖ → behüten **4.** [abs] Gott bewahre!, (i) bewahre! *no! certainly not!, by no means!, no idea!, far from it!*, (*if ..!*), *defend us!, no fear!*

bew·ähren vt [h] **1.** (alten Ruf, Ruhm) *to prove, verify*; *show*; *to make good* **2. sich** ~ (P & S) *to meet a test* **a.** (P) *to stand the test* od *trial, to prove one's worth*; *to achieve success*; *to satisfy expectations*; *to make good* (*I hope he will make good*); ⟨Am sl⟩ *to be the goods* ‖ sich gut ~ *to give a good account of o.s.*; er bewährt sich durchaus *he is quite a success* (od *an acquisition*); er b. sich nicht *he is a failure* ‖ sich –rt h ⟨tech⟩ *to work well* (an *on*) ‖ es –rte sich ihm glänzend *it served him in good stead* **b.** *to stand the test, to prove its value*; *to hold*; (of qualities) *to make good*; (of principles) *to hold good* od *true* ‖ diese Musik hat sich gut bewährt *this music has worn well* ‖ sich ~ *to prove a success, to be* od *prove useful*; (of medicine) *to be good* (gegen Gicht *for gout*); sich nicht ~ *to prove a failure*; *to be of no use* ‖ → erweisen

Bew·ahrer m ~s/~ *keeper, preserver*

bew·ahrheiten vt [h] (etw) *to make* (*a th*) *good, to prove* (*a th*) *true, to verify* (*a th*) | **sich** ~ (S) *to come* od *prove true*; *to justify itself*

bew·ährt a *proved, approved* (*friend*); *reliable, trusty* ‖ *tried and true*; *proven* ‖ *successful* (*writer, medicine*); e–e ~e Kraft *a success* (als *as*; in *in*) ‖ *tested, tried* (*abilities*) ≗**heit** f *proved excellence* ‖ *successfulness* (als *as*)

Bew·ahrung f ~/ *keeping, preserving*; → Aufbewahrung, Verwahrung ‖ *preservation* (vor *from*)

Bew·ährung f ~/~en *confirmation*; *proof, verification* (*of a th*) ‖ *the putting to the proof*; *test, trial*; in der Praxis allein zeigt sich die ~ *the proof of the pudding is in the eating* **~sfrist** f ⟨jur⟩ *probation*; jdm ~ gewähren *to place a p on probation*; e–e ~ erhalten *to be placed on probation*; auf *or* mit ~ *on probation*; e–e ~ v 2 Jahren erh. *to be bound over for 2 years* | ⟨jur⟩ *remand period*

bew·aldet a *wooded* (*banks*), *woody* (*hills*); *timbered* (*land*) **bew·aldrechten** vt [h] (Rundholz) *to hew* (*timber*) *roughly in longitudinal section* **Bew·aldung** f ~/~en *woodiness*; *woodland, wooded region*; *woods, trees* [pl]

bew·ältigen vt [h] **1.** (störrisches Pferd etc) *to manage, master* **2.** etw ~ **a.** *to execute* ⟨a. mus⟩; (Hindernis) *to overcome*; (Berg) *to conquer* ‖ (Feuer) *to* (*get under*) *control*; *to subdue*; das F. wurde bewältigt *the fire was brought under c.* **b.** (Schwierigkeit, schwierige Rolle; Verkehr etc) *to cope with, to manage* ‖ (Arbeit) *to accomplish, to do*; (Gegenstand) *to master* || ich kann es nicht allein ~ *I can't manage it alone*; leicht z ~d *easy* (*task*) | ⟨übtr⟩ können Sie noch ein Glas ~? *can you manage another glass*? **3.** *jdn ~ *to overcome, overpower, worst*, → überwältigen **Bew·ältigung** f ~/ *conquest, the mastering, overcoming* (*of difficulties*) || *accomplishment* (*of work*)

bew·andern vt [h] (Länder) *to journey through, to travel*; *to see* (*he has seen many countries*)

bew·andert a [mst pred] ~ in *versed, skilled, experienced in*; *conversant, learned, well-read in*; ~ s in *to be versed* (etc) *in, to be up in*; in allem ~ s *to be clever all round*; in e–r S sehr ~ s *to know the ins and outs of a matter*

bew·andt [pp v bewenden] a [nur in:] bei (*or* unter) so ~en Umständen *under these circumstances* **Bew·andtnis** f ~/–nisse [nur in einigen festen Wendungen:] die besondere ~ e–r S *the particularity of a matter* || nach ~ der Umstände *according to circumstances* || die S hat eine ganz andere ~ *the matter* od *case is quite different, is not what one thinks*, ⟨fam⟩ *is quite another* od *different story* || das hat e–e besondere *or* eigene ~, das hat s–e ~, damit hat es e–e bes. *or* eigene ~ *there is something peculiar about it*; *thereby hangs a tale* || es hat damit *or* damit hat es folgende ~ *the circumstances connected with it are* (od *the matter is*) *as follows, the case is this*

bewässern vt [h] (Land etc) *to irrigate, to water* **B.rung** f ~/~en *irrigation, watering* | ~sanlage [f] *irrigation-works* [pl]

bew·egbar a 1. ⟨eig⟩ = beweglich 2. ⟨fig⟩ er war nicht ~ *he was not to be persuaded*; leicht ~ *easy to persuade*

bew·egen vt [h] [bewegte/bewegt; doch → C.] **I.** ⟨bib⟩ (erwägen) (Worte) *to ponder* (*in one's heart*) **II.** (in Bewegung setzen) **A.** ⟨eig⟩ **1.** *to set in motion*; *to move, stir* (*a th*); *to give* (*a th*) *a stir* || die Hand ~ *to pass one's hand* (über *across*; um *round*); die Hände lebhaft ~ *to throw out one's hands* (*with a gesture of* ..) ich kann ihn nicht v s–m Platze ~ *I cannot budge him from his place* || (regelmäßig) (Pferd etc) *to exercise* || etw hin u her ~ *to agitate, wave a th*; unruhig hin u her ~ *to flutter a th*; heftig hin u her ~ *to shake a th*; der Wind bewegt die Blätter *the wind moves, stirs, shakes the leaves* | ⟨tech⟩ (Rad) *to work*; *actuate* || *drive*; *impel* **2. sich** ~ **a.** (P) *to move, stir* || *to go, move* (entlang *along*; v *from*; nach *to, towards*); *to pass* (zwischen *between*); *to shift*; sich mühsam ~ *to work* (*one's way*) (nach *to*); sich weiter ~ *to move on* || sich im Kreise (*or* wirr) ~ ⟨sl⟩ *to mill* (um *about*); sich nicht v der Stelle ~ *not to budge* od *stir* || sich im Freien ~ *to take exercise* | ⟨übtr⟩ sich in guter Gesellschaft ~ *to move in good society*; sich ~ unter .. ⟨Am⟩ *to circulate among* .. || er bewegte sich in allgemeinen Redensarten *he uttered merly platitudes* (od *vague generalities*) **b.** (S) *to revolve* (um *round*); (of door) *to ride* (auf *on* [*hinges*]); *to shift* || (of the eye) *to go* (nach *to*), *to wander*; (of heat, etc.) *to travel* || (of currents, of questions, etc.) *to trend* (*in the same direction*; nach *towards*) || (of prices) *to fluctuate, to vary* (*between*) || sich hin u her ~ *to wave*; (unruhig) *to flutter*; → Kreis || sich krampfhaft ~ (of the face) *to work* (vor *with pain*) || sich ~ l *to be movable* **B.** ⟨fig⟩ (jdn, jds Herz, Innere) *to affect, move* (zum Mitleid *to pity*), *to stir*; [oft pass] bewegt w *or* s *to be affected*, etc. (durch *by*) (*they were deeply affected by the news*) || Probleme, die uns ~ *pr. we are facing* **C.** ⟨fig⟩ [bewog/bewogen] **1.** jdn ~ z tun *to bring, determine, get, induce, move, persuade, spur, urge a p to do*; *to prevail* (*up*)*on a p to do, to make a p do*; jdn ~ z etw *to persuade a p* (*in*)*to a th*; → (an)treiben || leicht z ~ *easy to persuade*; *persuadable, persuasible* || sich bewogen fühlen *to feel moved* od *urged*; *to find o.s. called upon* (*to do*); || sich ~ l *to be moved*; *to relent, yield* **2.** (*of feelings, motives*) (jdn) *to actuate, urge* (*a p*); bewogen v *actuated by* **Bew·egen** n *moving, stirring*; → Bewegung

bew·egend a: ~e Kraft *motive power*; *mover* || sich ~ *moving*; sich selbst ~ *self-acting, spontaneous* (*movement*) || ⟨fig⟩ *moving, touching*; → rührend **Bew·eggrund** m *motive* (z etw *for a th*; z tun *for doing*); *incentive, inducement, stimulus* (z etw *to a th*; z tun *to do, to doing*) | aus e–m ~ *from a motive* || der ~ s v etw, den ~ geben z etw *to motive, to motivate a th*; (er mochte wissen) welchen ~ sie h könnten (..) *what could motivate them* (*to do*) **Bew·egkraft** f *motive power*

bew·eglich I. a **1.** ⟨eig⟩ *movable*; ~e Lettern pl ⟨print⟩ (allg) *moving type* sg; (einzeln) *movable types* | ⟨tech⟩ frei ~ *flexible* || (biegsam) *elastic, lissom* || schnell u leicht ~ *mobile* | ~es Fest *movable feast*; ~es Eigentum, ~e Habe (Ggs Grundeigentum) *movable* od *personal estate* od *property*; *movables* pl (Ggs *real estate* od *property, immovables* [pl]) || ~e Skala *gliding scale* || *portable* (⟨rad⟩ *receiver*) **2.** ⟨übtr⟩ (P) *agile, brisk, lissom, nimble, resilient*; *mobile*; *spry*; *versatile, resourceful* (*mind*); || ~es Denken [n] ⟨mst⟩ *mental mobility* || ein Mensch v ~em Geist *a nimble mind, quick wit* || ~e Zunge *lissom* od *voluble tongue* || → lebhaft || ~e Kampfführung [f] *elastic tactics*; *mobility in combat* || ~e Kräftegruppe [f] ⟨tact⟩ *manœuvring force*; ~es Ziel [n] (z Ausbildung) *movable target*; → Augenblicksziel **3.** = rührend **II.** adv (*to pray*) *touchingly* || ⟨mil, tact⟩ *in a mobile manner*; ~ gehalten (*supplies*) *held on a mobile basis*

Bew·eglichkeit f ~/ **1.** *movability*; *movableness*; *manœuvrability*; *mobility, flexibility* **2.** *agility, briskness, resilience, –cy*; *versatility* (*of the mind*); geistige ~ *mental nimbleness* od *quickness* || *volubility* (*of the tongue*) **3.** ⟨mil⟩ *flexibility*; *mobility in combat*

bew·egt [pp v bewegen] a **1.** *agitated*; *rough* (*sea*); *heaving* (*waves*) | *trembling* (*voice*) | ⟨übtr⟩ *excited*; *lively* (*conversation*) || *eventful* (*life*; *years*); ~e Jugend(zeit) *wild youth*; *disturbed, troubled* (*reign*); *troublesome, exciting, stirring* (*times*); ⟨sl⟩ *hectic* (*history*) **2.** *moved, touched*; tief ~ *deeply moved*; mit ~en Worten *with warm-hearted words*; ~en Herzens, bis ins Innerste ~ *touched to the heart* **≗heit** f *agitation* || *excitement* || (innere) *emotion*

Bew·egung f ~/~en **I. A.** ⟨eig⟩ **1.** (P) **a.** → Bewegen **b.** (Körper≗) *motion, movement* (der Hand, mit der H. *of the hand*); *gesture* (mit der Hand *with one's hand*); schwingende ~ *sweep* (mit dem Arm, Schwert *of the arm, sword*); mit e–r schwungvollen Hand≗ *with a sweep of the hand* || e–e ~ der Ungeduld *a movement of impatience* || schnelle ~ *whisk* (mit dem Schwanz *of the tail*) || ⟨gym & dancing⟩ drehende ~ *evolution*; ⟨gym⟩ Ruck≗ *jerk* || °immer dieselbe ~ ⟨sex⟩ *fore-and-aft* **c.** regelmäßige körperliche ~ *exercise*; schöngegliederte ~ (im Tanz) *eurhythmics* [pl] || sich ~ m *to take exercise* || (T) in ~ halten *to exercise* **d.** Art der ~ *action* (*fine, clumsy action*) **e.** (~ des ganzen Körpers) Fort≗ *locomotion* || die ~en jds *the movements, comings and goings* [pl] *of a p*; scheu in s–n ~en *shy in his comings and goings* **2.** ⟨übtr⟩ **a.** *movement* (*of trains, waves, etc.*); *action* (*of an instrument*) || gleichmäßige stetige ~ *sweep* (*of the tide*) **b.** ⟨mil⟩ *movement*; taktische ~ *evolution* **c.** ⟨com⟩ *movement* (*in the market*) || *tendency* (nach *towards*) **d.** ⟨mus⟩ *movement*; Gegen≚ *counter-movement*; ⟨pros⟩ rhythmische ~ *movement* ‖ *movement* (*in a play*) **3.** ⟨phys⟩ *motion* ‖ rotierende ~ *rotatory motion* ‖ ⟨astr⟩ scheinbar rückläufige ~ *retrogradation* ‖ Rückwärts≚ *retrogression* ‖ schwingende ~ *oscillation, vibration* **4.** ⟨mech⟩ *action*; *working* (*of machines*); ~en *revolutions* [pl] (*of a wheel*) **B.** (Ggs Ruhe) **1.** (aufrüttelnde ~) *stir*; nicht die leiseste ~ *not a stir* ‖ heftige ~ *agitation*; *commotion* (*of the waves*) ‖ (gährende ~) *agitation, fermentation* (*in a country*) **C.** Gemüts≚ *emotion*; vor ~ zittern *to tremble with e.* **D. in** ~ *on the move* (*he is always on the m.*); *stirring, astir*; ⟨mech⟩ *in motion* **| in ~ bringen** *to stir up*; *to put* (od *set*) *in motion*; *to work* (*a machine*) **|** in ~ halten *to keep* (*a th*) *going*; → 1. c. **|** in ~ s *to be moving* (od *stirring, astir*); (of machines) *to be at work*; in unruhiger ~ s (of a child) *to be on the fidget*; immer in ~ s (*of the tongue*) *to wag* **|** (S) in ~ setzen *to set in motion, to set going*; *to actuate, to work* (*a machine*); in schwingende ~ setzen *to set* (*a th*) *in vibration*; die Luft in ~ setzen *to set the air vibrating* ‖ alle Hebel (*or* alles, Himmel u Erde) in ~ setzen *to move heaven and earth* ‖ jdn in ~ setzen *to actuate a p* **| sich** [acc] in ~ setzen *to move, to make a move*; *to head, strike* od *set out* (nach *for*) *to start* ‖ sich [dat] ~ m *to stretch one's legs* **II.** ⟨rel & pol⟩ *movement*; ⟨C. E.⟩ die Oxforder ~ *the Oxford Movement* ‖ ⟨Ger hist⟩ die ~ *the National Socialist M.* ‖ ⟨Lit⟩ (Strömung) *tendency* **III.** [in comp] → Bewegungs–

Bew·egungs- ~empfindung f ⟨psych⟩ *kin(a)esthesis* **~energie** f *kinetic energy* **≚fähig** a *capable of locomotion*; *mobile* **~fähigkeit** f *capacity for locomotion*; *mobility* **~freiheit** f *liberty to move* ‖ *free* od *full scope*; *rope*, sehr viel ~ *plenty of r.* ‖ Einschränkung der ~ jds *restriction on a p's liberty*; mit voller ~ *without any restrictions*; → Spielraum ‖ ~ v Körper u Gliedern *leg-and-elbow room* ⟨a. mot⟩ **~größe** f ⟨phys⟩ *impulse*; *quantity of motion, momentum of body* **~karte** f ⟨comp⟩ *current transaction card* ‖ Nicht-~ ⟨comp⟩ *card relating to unmoved accounts* **~kontrolle** f ⟨aero⟩ *flight control* **~kraft** f *locomotive power*; *motivity* **~krieg** m *open* (od *moving*) *warfare* **~lehre** f *kinetics* **≚los** a *motionless, unmoving*; *quiescent*; *impassive* (*face*) **~losigkeit** f *immobility* **~malerei** f ⟨arts⟩ (vitale) *action painting* **~moment** n = –größe **~organe** n pl ⟨zoo⟩ *locomotory system* **~schaubild** n *kinematogram* **~spiele** n [pl] *outdoor games, field sports* [pl] **~störung** f ⟨med⟩ *locomotor ataxy* **~studie** f *motion-study* **≚unfähig** a *immobilized* ⟨a. mot⟩ **~unschärfe** f ⟨phot⟩ *blurring by motion* **~vortäuschung** f *animation*

bew·ehren vt [h] **1.** = bewaffnen **2.** ⟨tech⟩ (etw) *to reinforce*; bewehrter Beton *reinforced concrete*

bew·eiben [vrefl] [h] sich ~ *to have a wife, to marry*

bew·eihräuchern vt [h] **1.** (Raum) *to incense, to cense*; *to fumigate with incense* **2.** ⟨fig⟩ (jdn) *to praise* (*a p*) *excessively and slavishly*; *to flatter* (*a p*) **Bew·eihräucherung** f **1.** *the incensing* (*of a room*) **2.** ⟨fig⟩ *pleasing* od *flattering homage* (jds *to a p*)

bew·einen vt [h] (etw, jdn) *to bewail, bemoan, weep*; *to weep for* **bew·einenswert** a *deplorable, lamentable* **Beweinung** f ⟨arts⟩ ~ des Leichnams Christi *Wailing over the Body of Christ*

Bew·eis m, –ses/–se **1. a.** *evidence* (f *of*); *proof* (f *of, for*); *substantiation*; deutlicher ~ *demonstration*; schlagender ~ *striking evidence* ‖ (Zeugnis) *witness* (e–r S, f e–e S *of* od *to a th*) ‖ (~grund) *argument*, ein auf schwachen Füßen stehender ~ *a lame* (od *weak-kneed*) *argument* ‖ ⟨jur⟩ *evidence*; *proof*; augenscheinlicher ~ *prima facie ev.*; ~ durch Augenschein(nahme) *real ev.*; Indizien≚ *circumstantial evidence*; mittelbarer ~ *hearsay ev.*; ~ durch Vorlegen des Originals (der beglaubigten Abschrift) der Urkunde *primary* (*secondary*) *documentary ev.* **b.** [koll] (~material) Beweise [pl] *evidence, case*; *proofs* [pl]; äußere Beweise *external evidence*; k–e Beweise *no case*; aufgrund authentischer Beweise *on authentic evidence* ‖ alle Beweise, die wir h, zeigen .. *all the evidence we have shows* ..; immer neue Beweise s–r guten Absichten *proof on proof of his good intentions* ‖ ein (einzelner) ~ *a piece of evidence* **2.** ⟨math, etc⟩ *demonstration* **3.** (Zeichen) *evidence, proof, token* (*of a feeling*) **4.** ⟨jur⟩ den ~ **antreten** *to produce ev.*; den ~ erbringen *to adduce ev.*; ~ erheben *to take* od *hear ev.* ‖ **als ~ dient** Byron *witness Byron*; als ~ (nenne ich ..) *as witness* (..); als ~, zum ~ s–r Treue *in token of his loyalty* ‖ mangels ~es *for want of ev.*; wegen mangelnder Beweise *in the absence* (od *in default*) *of evidence* ‖ zum ~ e–r S *in proof* od *substantiation of a th* **|** den ~ **antreten** (*or* bei–, erbringen, führen) f etw *to prove a th*; → erbringen ‖ als ~ gelten ⟨jur⟩ (of statements) *to be in evidence* ‖ den ~ liefern f etw *to prove a th*; (k–n) ~ dafür liefern, daß .. *to offer* (*no*) *proof that* .. ‖ jdm Beweise s–r Treue liefern *to give a p tokens of one's loyalty* ‖ etw unter ~ stellen *to give evidence of a th*; *to prove, to demonstrate a th* ‖ als ~ zugelassen w ⟨jur⟩ (of statements) *to be admitted in evidence*

Bew·eis- ~aufnahme f ⟨jur⟩ *taking evidence, ev.-taking*; (mündlich) *the hearing of witnesses* ‖ Aussage bei der ~ *proof* **≚bar** a *demonstrable* **≚erheblich** a *evidentiary* (*fact*) **~führung** f *demonstration, proof*; (*line of*) *argument*; *reasoning* **~grund** m *argument*; *evidence*; zwingende –gründe anführen *to clinch an argument*; es liegen nicht genügend –gründe vor *there is not enough ev.* **~kraft** f *conclusiveness, conclusive*, od *probative force*; (k–e) ~ besitzen (of statements) *to be conclusive* (*inconclusive*); gr ~ h *to carry great evidential weight* **≚kräftig 1.** a *conclusive*; *convincing, demonstrative*; nicht ~ *inconclusive* **2.** adv *conclusively* **~last** f ⟨jur⟩ *burden* od *onus of proof* **~mittel** n *evidence, proof*; direktes ~ *primary* od *best ev.* **≚pflichtig** s ⟨jur⟩ *to have the burden of proof* **~photographie** f *legal photography* **~recht** n ⟨jur⟩ *law of evidence* **~sicherung** f ⟨jur⟩ *presentation of ev.* **~stück** n, **~urkunde** f *proof*; *piece of ev.* ‖ *exhibit* s; *legal document* **~vorlage** f *submission of proof* ‖ *legal document*

beweisen vt (h) [→ weisen) **1.** (etw) *to evidence*; *to prove* (jdm *to a p*; daß etw ist *a th to be*); jdm ~, daß .. *to prove to a p that*; bewiesen ⟨Am⟩ *proven* ‖ etw schlagend ~ *to be striking evidence of a th* **|** (Tatsache) *to demonstrate*; *to show* (aus *from*); (Behauptung) *to substantiate* ‖ ⟨math⟩ (etw) *to show* (*a th*; daß etw ist *a th to be*); beweise, daß ..! *show that* ..! ‖ (Lehre, Theorie) *to establish, show* ‖ (Anspruch) *to establish*; *to make good* ‖ ~d s *to be conclusive* **|** [abs] Urkunden ~ *documents give evidence* **2.** (zeigen) (etw) *to exemplify* (durch *by*), *to manifest, prove*; gr Geschick ~ *to show great skill*; ~ daß .. *to evince, to make out that* ..; ~, daß jd etw nicht getan hat *to make out a case against a p having done a th*; °mir kann keener nischt ~ ⟨Am fam⟩ *they've got nothing on me*; jdm deutlich ~, daß .. *to make it clear to a p that* ..; z ~ suchen, daß .. *to argue that* .. ‖ jdm Ehre ~ *to show honour to a p, to honour a p* **|** ⟨tech⟩ *to demonstrate successfully* **3.** sich fähig ~ *to prove o.s. able*; sich als treuen Freund ~ *to prove o.s. a true friend* ‖ → erweisen

bew·enden vi [→ wenden] [nur in:] es dabei ~ l *to leave it at that, to let it go at that, to let it rest there*; wir wollen es dabei ~ l *we'll leave it at that*; ich will es diesmal bei dieser kl Geldstrafe ~ l *I'll leave it* (od *let it go*) *at this small fine for the present, this small fine may suffice for the the present* **Bew·enden** n ~s/ **1.** [nur in:] und dabei hatte es sein ~ *and there the matter ended*; laß es dabei (*or* es mag dabei) sein ~ h *let it go at that*; dabei muß es sein ~ h *there the matter must rest*; *there must be an end of it*; *that must suffice* **2.** † = Bewandtnis

bew·erben [vrefl] [h] [→ werben] sich ~ um *to make an application for, to apply for* (*a post*, etc); *to put in for* (*a job*) ‖ ⟨com⟩ *to tender for* (*a contract*) ‖ ⟨parl⟩ *to canvass for* (*a seat*); → werben ‖ sich um e–e Frau ~ *to woo* od *court a woman, to make love to a w.* ‖ sich mit~ um *to compete* od *enter for, to go in for* (*a th*)

Bew·erber m ~s/~ *applicant, candidate* (um *for a post*); *enrollee* ‖ Stimmen≗ *canvasser* ‖ ⟨com⟩ (bei Preisausschreiben) *entrant, tenderer, competitor* (*he won a prize out of 2000 entrants*) ‖ ⟨sport⟩ *entrant, entry* (:*few entries*) | (Freier) *suitor, wooer*

Bew·erbung f ~/~en *application* (um *for*; an *to a p*); ~en einreichen *to send in applications* ‖ *candidature* (*for*) ‖ *bid* (*for*) ‖ ⟨sport⟩ *entry* ‖ → Werbung, Wettbewerb | *the courting, courtship, wooing* (um e–e Frau *of a woman*)

bew·erfen vt [h] [→ werfen] **1.** (Weg) *to cover* (*with gravel*) ‖ ⟨arch⟩ (Mauer etc) *to plaster*; *render* (*with concrete*); im Rohen ~ *to rough-cast* (*a house*) | (Stadt) mit Bomben ~ *to bomb* (*a town*) **2.** jdn ~ *to pelt, to pepper* (*with mud, tomatoes*); jdn mit Steinen ~ *to throw stones at a p*; sich mit St. ~ *to throw stones at each other* ‖ ⟨fig⟩ jdn mit Schmutz ~ *to sling mud at a p*

bew·erkstelligen vt [h] (etw) *to bring* (*a th*) *about, to contrive* (*a th*); (mit Geschick) *to engineer, to manage* (*to do*) ‖ *to carry out, to effect*(*uate*), → ausführen ‖ den Rückzug ~ *to make good one's retreat*; glücklich ~ *to put* (*a th*) *over*, ⟨fam⟩ *to bring* (*a th*) *off* ‖ ich werde es schon ~, daß er abwesend ist *I'll arrange for him to be away* **Bew·erkstelligung** f ~/~en *contrivance*; *effecting, execution*; → Ausführung

bew·erten vt [h] (schätzen) (Schaden, Verlust etc) *to assess, estimate, value* (auf *at*) | ⟨übtr⟩ etw ~ *to value* (nach *by*); *to take into account* ‖ sein Leben ~ *to value one's life*; hoch ~ *to set a high value on* (*a th*); (jds Einfluß) sehr hoch ~ *to rate very high*; niedrig ~ *to price* (*a th*) *low*; z hoch ~ *to overrate*; zu niedrig ~ *to underrate* **Bew·ertung** f ~/~en *assessment*; *estimation, valuation* ‖ ⟨bal⟩ *valuation*, ⟨Am⟩ *appraisal* ‖ ⟨demog, stat⟩ *conjecture*

Bew·etterung f ⟨min⟩ (= Wetterführung *ventilation*

bew·ickeln vt [h] etw ~ mit *to wind a th with* (*the stick was wound with* ..); *to wrap a th round with*; etw mit Papier ~ *to wrap a th in paper, to wrap paper round a th*

bew·illigen vt [h] (etw) *to grant* (*a th*; anstandslos *readily*), *to agree to*; *to comply with* (*a th*); (Gelder) *to appropriate*; (Rabatt) *to allow*; bewilligte Menge, Ration *allowance*; bewilligte S *grant* ‖ ⟨parl (of H. C.)⟩ (Geld) *to vote* (jdm *to a p*; f *for*) ‖ jdm etw ~ *to allow a p a th*; *to grant a p a th* (od *a th to a p*); *to concede a th to a p* ‖ → einwilligen, genehmigen **Bew·illigung** f ~/~en **1.** *the granting, grant* (*of money*, etc., z jds Verwendung *to a p*) ‖ ⟨parl⟩ (Geld≗) *vote*; *appropriation* (f bes Zwecke) **2.** (Bewilligtes) *grant*; *allowance*

bew·illkommnen vt [h] (jdn) *to welcome*; *greet, receive* ‖ ⟨übtr⟩ (etw) *to greet, welcome*

Bew·illkommnung f ~/~en *welcome, welcoming, reception* (*of a p*; *of a th*)

bew·irken vt [h] **1.** (etw) *to bring about, to cause* [nie mit *that-clause*], *to effect, to occasion*; (hervorrufen) *to give rise to, to produce*; *to result in, to conduce* od *lead to*; bewirkt w durch *to be caused* (od *occasioned, effected*) *by* | dieser Schritt bewirkte eine beträchtliche Entspannung *this move produced a considerable détente* ‖ ⟨contr⟩ .. –kt nicht die .. *shall be without prejudice to the* .. ‖ etw ~ in jdm → hervorrufen **2.** ~, **daß** ..: die Medizin bewirkte, daß er sich viel besser fühlte *the medicine made him feel much better*; dies bewirkte, daß das Wasser abfloß *this caused the water to flow off* ‖ ~, daß etw geschieht *to cause a th to be done*; ich bewirkte, daß er zurückgerufen wurde *I caused him to be called back* ‖ hierdurch wurde bewirkt, daß schnelle Erleichterung eintrat *by this a speedy relief was brought about* **bew·irkend** a ⟨gram⟩ *causative* (*verb*)

bew·irten vt [h] **1.** (jdn) *to entertain* (*a p*); *to treat a p* (mit Früchten *to fruit*); jdn festlich ~ *to regale a p* (mit *with*); jdn glänzend, fürstlich etc ~ ⟨sl⟩ *to do a p proud* ‖ ⟨hot⟩ *to cater for* **2.** × = bewirtschaften

bew·irtschaften vt [h] (Acker, Boden) *to cultivative, till* ‖ (Gut) *to manage, run, work*; (verwalten) *to administer, conduct* ‖ (Geschäft, Laden etc) *to manage, run*; *to carry on* ‖ *to control* (Waren); –tet *price-controlled*; *quota* [attr] (Ware) **Bew·irtschaftung** f ~/~en *cultivation* (*of the soil*) ‖ *management, managing, running, working* (*of a farm*, etc.); *administration* ‖ Devisen≗ *regulation* (od *control*) *of business in foreign exchange* | (Waren≗) *State Control*, ⟨com⟩ *rationing* ‖ die ~ e–r S aufheben, etw aus der ~ herausnehmen *to take off allocation, to unfreeze*; der ~ unterliegen *to be controlled*; *to be put on allocation*, .. nicht mehr .. *to be taken off all.*

Bew·irtung f ~/~en *entertainment*; *reception* ‖ ⟨bib, arts⟩ ~ der 3 Engel *Entertaining of* ..

Bew·itterung f ~/~en ⟨geol⟩ *weathering*

bew·itzeln vt [h] (etw) *to ridicule*; *to turn* (*a th*) *into ridicule*; *to mock* od *sneer at* (*a th*)

bew·ogen [pp v bewegen] → d. II. C.

bew·ohnbar a *habitable, inhabitable*, nicht ~ *uninhabitable* | ≗**keit** f ~/ (*in*)*habitableness*, (*in*)*habitable condition* od *state*

bew·ohnen 1. vt [h] (Land, Haus) *to inhabit*; *to live* od *reside in* (*a country, a house*, etc.); *to occupy* (*a house*) | (T) *to people* **2.** ≗ n *habitation* (*fit for h.*), *inhabitation*

Bew·ohner m ~s/~ *inhabitant* (*of a district, region*; *house*); → Einwohner, Land~ ‖ *inmate* (*of a house*); *occupant* (*of a room*) ‖ ständiger ~ *resident* (*of a country, town*, etc.) | ⟨übtr⟩ *denizen*, die ~ des Waldes (T) *the denizens of the forest* **~schaft** f ~/ *inhabitants* [pl] **Bew·ohntsein** n ~s/ *occupancy*

bew·ölken vt [h] *to cloud, overcast* (*the sky was o.*) ‖ ⟨fig⟩ *to overcast, overshadow* **sich ~** *to become cloudy* od *overcast, to cloud over* **bew·ölkt** a *overcast* (*sky*) ‖ ⟨fig⟩ *dark, gloomy*

Bew·ölkung f ~/~en *clouding, cloudiness*; dichte ~ ⟨meteor, aero⟩ *thick cloud* | ~shöhe [f] *ceiling*

Bew·underer m ~s/~ *admirer*; *adorer* ⟨a. sex⟩ **bew·undern** vt [h] *to admire* **bew·undernswert, -würdig** a *admirable, wonderful* **Bew·underung** f ~/ *admiration* (für jdn, vor jdm *of a p*); jdm ~ abnötigen *to extort admiration from a p*; ~ auslösen *to call forth adm.*; jds ~ finden *to command a p's admiration*

Bew·urf m ~(e)s/≗e ⟨arch⟩ (Wand≗) *coating of plaster*; *parget, pargeting*; *plaster, plastering*; Beton≗ *rendering*

bew·urzeln vt [h] ⟨hort⟩ *to root*; (Setzling) *to layer*; der bewurzelte Ableger *the rooted layer* ‖ **sich** ~ (of plant) *to develop roots*

bew·ußt I. a **1.** [pred] sich [+ gen] ~ s (w) *to be(come) conscious of, to be(come) aware* od *sensible of a th*; ich bin mir k–r Schuld ~ *I am not conscious* (od *I am unconscious*) *of any guilt*; ich bin mir nicht ~, dich verletzt z h *I am not conscious of hurting you*; ich bin mir ~, daß .. *I am c. that* ‖ es ist mir nicht mehr ~ *I do not remember* (*what* ..) ‖ dessen wird sich die Regierung ~ s *that will be in the mind of the government* .. ‖ sich e–r S wohl ~ s *to be alive to a th*; es ist mir wohl ~, daß *I know very well that* .. ‖ sich e–r S ~ w *to awake to a th*; er wurde sich der Störung kaum ~ *the annoyance scarcely rose to perception in his mind* **2.** [attr] **a.** (überzeugt) *conscious* (*artist*) **b.** *intentional* (*lie*) **c.** die ~e P *or* S *the p* od *matter in question* (od *referred to*) **II.** adv **1.** ~ oder un~ *consciously or unconsciously* **2.** *deliberately, intentionally* **Bewußtheit** f *consciousness, awareness*, ⟨philos⟩ *self-consciousness*; → Bewußtsein

bew·ußtlos a ⟨med⟩ *unconscious*; *insensible* (infolge *from*) ‖ (ohnmächtig) *senseless* ‖ er fiel ~ nieder *he fell down senseless*; jdn durch e–n Schlag ~ m *to knock a p senseless*, ⟨box⟩ *to put a p to sleep*; ~ w *to lapse into insensibility*; *to swoon, to faint away* **Bew·ußtlosigkeit** f *unconsciousness*; *insensibility* ‖ (Ohnmacht) *swoon* ‖ ⟨fig⟩ bis zur ~ *with a vengeance, excessively, tremendously*; (*to torment a p*) *to death* ⟨fig⟩; ⟨fam hum⟩ *until the cows come home*

Bew·ußtsein n **1.** → Bewußtheit *consciousness*; ~ h *to be possessed of consciousness*; kein ~ habend *unconscious* (*nature*) **2.** ⟨med⟩ *consciousness* ‖ bei ~ *in a state of consciousness*; (nicht) bei ~ s *to be* (*un*)*conscious* ‖ im Besitze des ~s *conscious* ‖ ins ~ gehoben, dem ~ gegenwärtig *conscious* (*power*) ‖ ohne ~ s *to be unconscious*; (ohnmächtig) *senseless* | das ~ verlieren *to lose consciousness*; *to swoon* ‖ wieder z ~ k, das ~ wiedergewinnen *to come round, to come to* [adv]; *to recover* od *regain consciousness* **3.** (Sich-Bewußtsein) *consciousness, conviction*; Pflicht≈ *sense of duty*; Schuld≈ *conviction of guilt* ‖ **im** vollen ~ s–r Lage *with full realization of his situation*; im ~, daß .. *fully convinced that* .. ‖ das beruhigende ~, daß *the quiet knowladge that* ..; *a feeling of relief that* ‖ **mit** vollem ~ *deliberately* ‖ jdm etw **zum** ~ bringen *to convince*, (bes Irrtum) *to convict a p of a th*; *to bring a th home to a p*; jdm s–e Pflichten z ~ bringen *to recall a p to a sense of his duties* ‖ jdm zum ~ k *to go* (od *come*) *home to a p*; es kam ihm zum ~ *it dawned upon him, it became clear to him* (*that* ..); *he realized, he became aware* (*that*) **~sinhalt** m ⟨psych⟩ *object*; Mischung *or* Vertiefung der ~e (dadurch, daß mehrere Sinne [Auge, Ohr] angesprochen w) ⟨Lit⟩ *compounding of consciousness* (z. B. in *Keats' Ode to Autumn*) **~skunst** f *expressionism* **~slücke** f *blackout of consc.* **~sstrom** m ⟨Lit⟩ *stream of consc.* (z. B. *in Joyce's Ulysses, in Sterne's Tristram Shandy*) **~sverlust** m (vorübergehend) *blackout*

Bey = Bei

bez·ahlbar a *payable*

bez·ahlen vt [h] **A.** (S) **1.** (~, was man schuldet) (Schulden, Geldstrafe) *to pay, discharge*; (Rechnung), *to pay, settle*; die Rechnung (Kosten) f etw ~ *to foot the bill*; die Kosten ~ *to defray the expenses* ‖ (Wechsel) *to honour*; bezahlt w *to be duly honoured* ‖ (Lohn) *to pay*; (Geld) *to pay*, ⟨sl⟩ *to fork out* ‖ alles ~, auf Heller u Pfennig ~ *to pay in full*; auf Abschlag ~ *to pay in part*; bar, sofort ~ *to pay* (*cash*) *down*; ganz *or* voll ~ *to pay up*; im voraus ~ *to pay in advance*; nicht ~ können *to be insolvent*; nicht schlecht –lt s *to be pretty well paid* ‖ Aufnahme–, Eintrittsgeld ~ *to pay* (*for*) *one's footing* **2.** (Gekauftes [Waren etc], einmalige Leistungen u Dienste) *to pay for* (*the furniture, goods, funeral*); ich werde das Auto ~ *I'll pay for the taxi* ‖ [abs] gemeinsames Vergnügen, bei dem jeder f sich bezahlt *a Dutch treat* **3.** ⟨übtr⟩ etw teuer ~ *to pay dear for a th*; etw mit dem Leben ~ *to pay for a th with one's life* ‖ die Zeche ~ *to pay the piper*; *to pay for it* ‖ nicht z ~ *beyond* od *above price*, nicht z ~d *priceless, invaluable* (*services*) ‖ nicht bezahlt w (of actions) *to be unpaid* **4.** (etw) bezahlt m *to remunerate* (*the labours*) ‖ **sich bezahlt m** (of undertakings) *to pay, to pay one's way* (*:farming pays*); gute Sachen z kaufen macht sich immer bezahlt *it always pays to buy good things* **B. 1.** (P) *to pay a p* (f *for*); *to fee* (*a doctor*); *to remunerate*; ⟨Am⟩ *to compensate* ‖ voll ~ *to pay off*; gut bezahlt w ⟨fam⟩ *to be in the money* **2.** sie w sich schon bezahlt m *they'll know how to recoup themselves* **C.** jdm etw ~ *to pay a p a th* (od *a th to a p*); mir wurde das Geld bezahlt *I was paid the money*; → heimzahlen ‖ er hat es sich gut ~ l *he has got a nice bit of money for it* ‖ er läuft, als wenn er's bezahlt kriegte *he runs as if he got paid for it* **Bez·ahler** m ~s/~ *payer*

bez·ahlt a *paid, remunerated, salaried* (*official*); ~e Rente [f] ⟨ins⟩ *annuity paid*; dürftig ~ *poorly-salaried* ‖ *paid-for* (*labour*); ⟨Am⟩ *gainful* (*occupation*) ‖ ⟨com⟩ (abbr bez.) ~ Brief *deals were recorded, but stock was still an offer*; ~ Geld *bargains were made and stock continued to be in demand* **Bez·ahlung** f ~/~en **1.** *payment, discharge* (*of debts*); *settlement* (*of a bill*) ‖ gegen ~ *against payment*; gegen ~ v *on payment of* **2.** [konkr] (bezahltes Geld) *pay, payment*; *salary*; *wages*; ⟨Am⟩ *compensation* ‖ *fee, remuneration* ‖ angemessene, gerechte ~ (P) *a fair day's wage for a fair day's work*

bez·ähmbar a ⟨fig⟩ *restrainable*; *controllable*

bez·ähmen vt [h] ⟨fig⟩ (Leidenschaft etc) *to control, curb*; *to keep in check, to restrain, subdue* ‖ (Zunge) *to tame* | **sich** ~ *to control, govern, restrain o.s.*

bez·aubern vt [h] **1.** (jdn, ein Volk etc) *to bewitch, to lay a spell on* (*a p*) **2.** ⟨fig⟩ (jdn) *to bewitch, captivate, charm, enchant, enslave, enthral(l), entrance, fascinate*; *to cast a glamour over*; *to glamour, mesmerize* (*a p*); bezaubert s v *to be enchanted* (od *enraptured, entranced*) *with* **bez·aubernd** a *bewitching, compelling* (*smile*), *enchanting, entrancing* (*picture*), *enthralling*; ⟨sl⟩ *killing* (*dressed in a k. silk dress*); ~e Schönheit *glamour* **B.rung** f ~/~en **1.** *enchantment, witchery, witchcraft* **2.** *⟨fig⟩ *enchantment, fascination* (*of the audience*)

°**bez·echen** [vrefl] [h] sich ~ *to get drunk*; ⟨sl⟩ *to fuddle* °**bez·echt** a [pred & attr] → betrunken ‖ [pred a.] *in soak*; ~ s *to be well away*

bez·eichnen vt [h] **A.** (P) **1.** ⟨eig⟩ (Weg etc) *to mark*; (Baum) *to blaze* ‖ ein Wort mit e–m Akzent ~ *to accent a word*; Wort mit e–m Stern ~ *to denote a word by an asterisk* ‖ Waren ~ → auszeichnen ‖ → kennzeichnen ‖ ⟨arts⟩ –net (signiert) *signed, inscribed* **2.** ⟨übtr⟩ **a.** etw ~ *to put a name to a th*; *to designate, to name a th* **b.** jdn ~ als *to designate* (od *label, qualify*) *a p as*; sie ~ ihn als ihren größten Dichter *they designate him* (*as*) *their greatest poet*; die Vorsteher einiger Colleges w als Provost bezeichnet *the heads of some colleges are styled Provost*; er bezeichnete sich als Baron *he styled himself a baron*; → betiteln **3.** etw ~ *to point out, to show*; jdm etw (Weg, Haus) ~ *to point a th out to a p* ‖ ⟨übtr⟩ jdm (e–m Forscher) den Weg ~ *to blaze the way for a p* (*in* ..) **B.** (S, events; actions) (ein

Zeichen s f, an–, bedeuten) **1.** (etw) *to denote, indicate; signify; to stand for;* ein steigendes Barometer bezeichnet gutes Wetter *a rising barometer denotes the approach of fine weather* **2.** (charakterisieren) (Gesinnung etc) *to characterize, to be characteristic of; to describe, to be descriptive of; to express, show* **bez·eichnend** a *characteristic, significant* (f *of*); ∼ s f ein Buch *to set the tone of a book* ‖ ∼er Zug, ∼es Merkmal *characteristic* ‖ *expressive, significant* (*glance*) **B.nung** f ∼/∼en **1.** *the marking* (*of roads*); *blazing* (*of trees*) ‖ *pointing out* **2.** *denotation, designation;* z ∼ v *in denotation of* **3.** *denotation, designation* (f *of*); *expression, name; appellation* (*this is a ridiculous app.*) ‖ ⟨mil⟩ *identification* (e–s Zieles) **4.** [konkr] (Zeichen) *mark;* ⟨math, mus & phon⟩ *notation;* → Signatur, Zeichen **∼ssignal** n ⟨mar⟩ das ∼ setzen *to make one's number*

bez·eigen vt [h] (Gefühl etc) *to exhibit, express, manifest, show; record* (*one's satisfaction*); *to testify* (*one's eagerness*) ‖ jdm s–e Dankbarkeit ∼ *to express one's gratitude to a p;* jdm sein Beileid ∼ *to condole with a p* (z etw *on a th*); → Beileid ‖ jdm Verehrung ∼ *to display reverence toward a p* **Bez·eigung** f ∼/∼en *expression, manifestation* ‖ *intimation;* s–e Dankes≈ *the intimation of his gratitude;* mit heißen Dankes≈en *with fervent protestations of thanks* ‖ Beileids≈ *condolence;* Ehren≈en [pl] *honours* (*military h.*)

bez·eugen vt [h] **1.** etw eidlich ∼ *to testify a th, to testify* (od *attest*) *to, to bear witness to a th;* ∼, daß .. *to testify that ..* ‖ (bescheinigen) amtlich ∼ *to attest, certify* (*a th*); ich bezeuge Herrn N. gern, daß .. *I have much pleasure in certifying* od *testifying to Mr. N. that ..;* hiermit wird bezeugt *this is to certify* (*that*) **2.** ⟨übtr⟩ (S) etw ∼ *to attest a th* (*his authorship is attested*); *to be evidence of, to testify a th* (*the picture testifies his skill*), *to testify to a th* (*it testifies to the energy of the leader*), *to witness* (*to*) *a th* (*his looks witnessed* (*to*) *his disappointment*) **3.** = bezeigen **B.gung** f ∼/∼en **1.** *attestation; testification* ‖ (Bescheinigung) amtliche ∼ *certification;* ∼ durch Unterschrift *attestation, witness* ‖ (Zeugnis) *testimony;* → Zeugnis **2.** = Bezeigung

bez·ichtigen vt [h] = beschuldigen

Bez·ichtigung f ∼/∼en = Beschuldigung

bez·iehbar a *habitable* (*house*); sofort ∼ *ready for immediate occupation* ‖ ⟨com⟩ (of goods) *obtainable; procurable;* bei allen Buchhändlern ∼ *to be had of all booksellers*

bez·iehen I. vt [h] [→ ziehen] **1. a.** (Haus) *to* (*re*)*move into, to occupy, to take up residence in* (*a house*); e–e neue Wohnung ∼ *to move into new rooms;* sofort z ∼ *ready for immediate occupation* **b.** ⟨mil⟩ Quartiere ∼ *to go into quarters, to take up one's quarters;* ein Lager ∼ *to encamp,* die Truppen ein L. ∼ l *to encamp troops;* die Wache, den Posten ∼ *to mount guard;* e–e Stellung ∼ *to move into a position, to occupy a pos.* **c.** ⟨com⟩ (Messe etc) *to resort to; to frequent, visit* **d.** die Universität ∼ *to go up to the university* **2.** (bedecken) **a.** (etw) *to cover; spread* (*with*); ein Bett ∼ *to put clean linen on a bed; to sheet a bed;* (Schirm) neu ∼ *to recover* ‖ ⟨mus⟩ mit Saiten ∼ *to string* (*an instrument*) ‖ (of clouds) (Himmel) *to cover, overcast* **b. sich** ∼ (of the sky) *to cloud* (*over*) **3.** ⟨com⟩ **a.** (bek) (Waren etc) *to get, obtain, procure, receive* (aus, v *from*); *to buy* (v *of, from*); Aktien ∼ *to take up stock;* aus erster Hand ∼ *to buy at first hand;* v auswärts ∼ *to import* ‖ (Zeitung) *to take* (*in*) ‖ (Geld, Gehalt, Pension) *to draw;* ‖ °⟨übtr⟩ Schläge, Prügel, Senge ∼ *to get a thrashing;* ⟨sport⟩ *to be beaten* **b.** jdn ∼ *to draw a bill* (*up*)*on a p, to draw* (*up*)*on a p;* → Bezogene **4.** ⟨fig⟩ **a.** (Worte etc) ∼ **auf** *to apply, refer to* (*a p*), *to use with reference to* (*a p*); *to bring* (*a th*) *to bear upon* (*a th*); z ∼(d) *referable* (auf *to*) **b. sich ∼ auf** *to refer* od *relate, allude to, to have reference* od *respect to; to bear on, to have bearing on;* sich ∼d auf *relative to, relevant to* ‖ ⟨com⟩ **sich auf jdn** ∼ *to use a p's name for reference* (*you may use my name .., you can give my name as reference,* ⟨Am⟩ *you are free to refer anyone to me* **II.** n **1.** ∼ des Hauses *the moving into the house, occupation of the h.* ‖ ⟨mil⟩ ∼ der Wache *mounting the guard* **2.** *covering; sheeting* (*of a bed*) ‖ *stringing* (*of an instrument*) **3.** *procurement; purchase, supply* (*of goods*) ‖ *drawing* (*of money*) ‖ → Bezug; Beziehung

bez·iehentlich adv = beziehungsweise

Bez·ieher m ∼s/∼ ⟨com⟩ *drawer* (*of a bill*) ‖ *subscriber* (e–r Zeitung *to a paper*)

Bez·iehung f ∼/∼en ⟨fig⟩ **I.** (gedankliche ∼) **1.** *connection, connexion* (*between*) ‖ *reference, regard, respect, relation* (z *to*); *bearing* (z *on*) ‖ *relationship* (*between*); das Stück ist das Produkt vieler ∼en *the play is the product of many relationships* ‖ gegenseitige ∼ *interrelation* (zwischen *between, of*); die ∼ z e–a *the interrelation;* → einander; Wechsel≈ **2. a. in ∼ z** *in relation to* **b. in allen s-n ∼en** (S) *in all its bearings* od *relations* ‖ in anderer ∼ *otherwise; in other respects* (*he is otherwise a nice fellow*) ‖ in dieser ∼ *in this connection* (od *respect, regard*) ‖ in e–r ∼ *in a way* ‖ in gewisser ∼ *in certain ways* ‖ in jeder ∼ *in every regard, in all respects; every bit* (od *way*) ‖ in k–r ∼ *in no respect* (od *way*) ‖ in mancher ∼ *in some respects* (od *ways*) ‖ in welcher ∼? *in what way?* **c.** [in + Adj + ∼: oft durch das Adv]: **in politischer** ∼ *politically, in* kultureller ∼ *culturally,* in musikalischer ∼ *musically;* in wirtschaftlicher ∼ *economically;* etc. **d.** etw in ∼ **setzen** z etw *to relate a th to a th* (*he relates the play to the background*); *to bring a th to bear upon a th;* etw in die richtige ∼ setzen z *to put a th in its relation to* ‖ in ∼**stehen** z *to be related to, to have relation to;* in logischer ∼ stehen z *to connect with;* in k–r ∼ stehen z *to be out of relation to;* in (k–r) ∼ stehend (*un*)*related* (*to*) **e.** k–e ∼ z e–a h (of parts) *to have no reference to each other* **II.** (persönliche, gesellschaftliche ∼) **1.** *association, connection, relation* (mit, z jdm *with a p*); [mst pl ∼en] *associations,* etc.; ⟨Am⟩ *affiliations, contacts* [pl], ⟨sl⟩ *pull;* geschäftliche ∼en *commercial relations* **2.** besondere ∼en h zu *or* unterhalten mit *to have special ties with;* einflußreiche ∼en h *to be well-connected* ‖ neue ∼en anknüpfen *to establish new connexions* ‖ mit jdm vertrauliche (intime) ∼en aufnehmen *to enter upon terms of intimacy with a p* ‖ ∼en pflegen, **in** ∼ stehen mit *to have* od *maintain relations* od *contact with;* ⟨Am⟩ *to affiliate with* (*a p*); in k–r ∼ zu jdm stehen *to be unconnected with a p, to have no connection with a p;* in ∼en treten z jdm ⟨Am⟩ *to contact a p;* in freund(schaft)lichen ∼en stehen z *to be on friendly terms with* (*a p*) ‖ → abbrechen, anknüpfen; treten ‖ in ∼ zu ⟨a.⟩ *relative to* ‖ ∼en zw Mitarbeitern *human relations*

Bez·iehungs- ≈los a *irrelative* (z *to*); *unrelated* (*items*) **∼wahn** m ⟨psych⟩ → Beachtungsw. **≈weise** adv (abbr bzw) *respectively; and, or; that is to say;* bekannt als N., bzw X. *known as N. and X. respectively;* die Summe v 4 bzw 3 Mark *the respective sums of 4 marks and 3 marks* **∼wort** n ⟨gram⟩ *antecedent*

bez·iffern vt [h] **1.** (etw) *to mark with figures;* (Häuser etc) *to number;* die Seiten e–s Buches ∼ *to page a book* **2. sich ∼ auf** *to amount to; to number; to work out at* **3.** ⟨mus⟩ bezifferter Baß *figured bass* **Bez·ifferung** f *numbering; paging* (*of a book*) ‖ [konkr] *figures, numbers* [pl]

bez·innt a *battlemented,* → Zinne

Bez·irk m ~s/~e **1.** *district* ‖ der ~ N. *the d. of N.*; *division*; ⟨Am⟩ *canton, shire* ‖ in ~e einteilen *to district* ‖ Stadt≃ *urban district*; *ward* ‖ Verwaltungs≃ *administrative district*; ⟨engl⟩ e–r der 3 Verwaltungsbezirke v Yorkshire *riding*; ind. fiskalischer ~ *tahsil* ‖ ⟨engl⟩ Wahl≃ e–r Stadt *borough* ‖ ⟨engl⟩ Landes≃, Reichs≃ (e–r der 12 ~e im Falle e–s Krieges) *national region*; Leiter dieses ~s *regional commissioner* ‖ ⟨engl jur⟩ ~ f. die Assisengerichte *circuit* **2.** ⟨übtr⟩ **a.** *grounds* [pl]; Jagd≃ *hunting-ground* ‖ eingezäunter ~ *enclosure* **b.** (Bereich) *compass, domain, province*; → Bereich

Bez·irks- [in comp] *district* (*physician*; *school*) **~amt** n *District Board* **~ausgabe** f (Presse) *local edition* **~ausschuß** m *District Council* **~feldwebel** m *district-sergeant* **~gefängnis** n ⟨engl⟩ *county--gaol* **~gericht** n ⟨österr, Sw⟩ = Amtsgericht *district-court,* ⟨m. m.⟩ *country-court* **~gruppe** f ⟨Ger⟩ *district group* **~hauptmannschaft** f *Board of Administration* (*in Austria*) **~kommando** n ⟨Ger⟩ (Wehr≃) *district command*; *Enlistment* od *Selective Service Authorities* [pl] **~notari·at** n *district notary* **~polizei** f *d. constabulary* **~schulamt** n *d. school inspection* **≃weise** a *by district*(*s*)

°**bez·irzen** vt [h] (Männer) *to vamp*

Bezo·ar m ~s/~e ⟨zoo⟩ *bezoar*; *hair-balls* [pl] | ~ziege [f] ⟨zoo⟩ *bezoar-goat*

bez·ogen [pp v beziehen] ~ auf etw *relative to a th* | ≃e [der ~, ein ~r] ⟨com⟩ *drawee, acceptor* **Bez·ogenheit** f *relationship, bearing*

Bez·ug m ~(e)s/~̈e *case* **1.** ⟨com⟩ *procurement, procuring purchase, supply* (*of goods*); ~̈e [pl] *supplies* [pl] ‖ *subscription* (e–r Zeitung *to a paper*) ‖ *the drawing* (*of wages*); → Beziehen ‖ Zahlung bei ~ *payment on delivery* ‖ bei ~ v 50 Exemplaren *on orders for 50 copies* **2.** (gedanklicher ~) [nur in:] **in** ≃ *or* **mit** ~ **auf** *in* od *with reference to*; *in regard of* od *to, with regard to*; *in respect* od *terms of, with respect to*; *concerning, regarding, respecting*; *as to* od *for* ‖ in ~ auf die Fauna *faunally*; in ~ auf die Musik *musically,* → Beziehung I. 2. c. ‖ in ~ auf Frauen *when women are concerned* ‖ **unter** ~ **auf** unser Gespräch *referring* (od *with reference*) *to our talk* | **~ h auf** *to refer to, to relate to*; *to bear on*; *to have a bearing on* ‖ ~ nehmen auf *to refer to*; bitte ~ z nehmen auf .. *kindly quote* .. **3.** [konkr] **a.** *case, cover*(*ing*); Kissen≃ *slip*; → Bett≃ ‖ Daunen≃ → Inlett **b.** ~ v Saiten *set of strings* **c. Bezüge** [pl] *emoluments, fees, takings* [pl]; *salary* ‖ *drawings*

bez·üglich a **1.** a ⟨gram⟩ *relative* (*pronoun*); ~ auf *relative to*; die darauf ~en Einzelheiten *the details relative to that matter* **2.** prep [gen] ~ e–r S (= in bezug auf e–e S) *regarding, respecting a matter, relating to a matter*; *about a m.* → Bezug 2., Betreff, betreffs

Bez·ug- **~nahme** f ~/~n *reference* (auf *to*) ‖ unter ~ auf *referring* (od *with reference*) *to*; *pursuant..* | **~s-** ⟨com⟩ **~anweisung** f *delivery-order* **~bedingungen** f [pl] *terms of delivery* [pl] **~berechtigte(r** m) f ⟨st exch⟩ *allottee* **~dauer** f *duration* **~ebene** f ⟨aero⟩ *datum level* **~genossenschaft** f *cooperative buying society* **~größe** f (Richtwert) *reference value* **~kosten** [pl] *delivery-charges* [pl] **~linie** f *datum* od *reference line* **~profil** n *basic profile* **~punkt** m *check point,* ⟨surv⟩ *reference p.*; ⟨aero-phot⟩ *ref. mark* **~ort** m, **~quelle** f *source of supply*; *market* (f. *for*), *source* (f. *of*); die beste ~ *the best place* (*to get..*) **~recht** n *claim*; ⟨st exch⟩ *right*; *option*; *right of option* (f *on*) (~ auf Aktien ausüben *to take up an option*); *priority of right, preference--right* **~schein** m *voucher*; *supply ticket*; *order for delivery* ‖ (f Mangelware) *ration ticket* od *card*; (*individual*) *buying permit*; Schuh≃ *footwear p.* ‖ ≃frei [a] *off the ration* [pred] | ≃pflichtig [a] *rationed* **~spesen** pl *charges of delivery, petty ch.* pl **~temperatur** f *reference* od *ambient t.*

bez·uschussen vt [h] *to subsidize*

bezw·ecken[1] vt [h] (etw) *to have* (*a th*) *in view, to intend, purpose* (*a th*); (S) *to tend toward, to aim at*; ⟨Am⟩ *to look to* ‖ ~ mit *to intend by*; sie bezweckte damit s–n Untergang *she intended his ruin by it*

bezw·ecken[2] vt [h] (→ Zwecke) (etw) *to fasten* (*a th*) *with tacks*; e–n Teppich ~ *to tack a carpet down* ‖ *to set with tacks* (od *pegs*); (Schuhe) *to peg*

bezw·eifeln vt [h] (etw) *to doubt*; *to* (*call in*) *question*; *to be sceptical about* od *of* (*a th*) ‖ ich bezweifle, daß es der Wunsch ist, daß .. *I doubt it to be the wish that*; ich b., daß er kommt *I doubt his coming* ‖ das bezweifle ich! *I wonder*! ‖ nicht ~ *to make no question of*; ich b. nicht, daß .. *I have no doubt that* ..; (nicht) z ~ (*un*)*questionable*; es ist nicht z ~, daß .. *it cannot be questioned* (*but*) *that* .. ‖ z ~ s *to be open to doubt*

bezw·ingbar a *conquerable*; *superable* ‖ *restrainable* (*character*)

bezw·ingen vt [h] **1.** (Volk, Land) *to conquer, overcome, subdue*; *to reduce to submission*; → besiegen ‖ (jdn) *to master, overcome, overpower* | (Feuer) *to get under, to subdue* ‖ (e–n Berg) *to conquer* ‖ (Schwierigkeiten etc) *to master* **2.** (Leidenschaften etc) *to conquer, control, curb, restrain, subdue* | **sich** ~ *to control* od *r. o.s.* **B.ger** m ~s/~ *conqueror, subduer* **bezw·inglich** a = bezwingbar **Bezw·ingung** f ~/~en *conquest*; *conquering, subduing* ‖ *mastering*

Bhag·alpur n (Provinz u Stadt in Vorderindien)

Bh·aratpur n (Provinz in Vorderindien)

Bh·utan n (Himalajastaat) *Bhutan*

bi- (L) pref (zweifach, doppel) Bikarbon·at

Bi·afra n Landschaft Nigeriens

B·iarritz n (franz. Badeort)

°**b·ibbern** vi [h] = zittern

B·ibel f ~/~n **1.** die ~ *the Bible, Scripture, the* (*Holy*) *Scriptures* [pl] ‖ ein Schwur auf die ~ *a Bible oath*; in der ~ steht geschrieben *it says in the Bible* **2.** ⟨übtr⟩ *bible*; *authority*; das Buch war ihm zur ~ geworden *the book had become his Bible* | [in comp] *bible* **~ausdruck** m *scriptural expression* **~ausgabe** f *edition of the Bible* **~ausleger** m *interpreter of the Bible* **~auslegung** f *exegesis*; am Buchstaben klebende ~ *biblicism* **≃fest** a *well-read* (od *versed*) *in Scripture* **~forscher** m *Bible student*, Ernste ~ [pl] = Zeugen Jehovas **~gesellschaft** f *Bible-society* **~glaube** m: buchstabentreuer ~ ⟨Am⟩ *fundamentalism* **≃gläubig** a *bibliolatrous* **~kenntnis, ~kunde** f *biblical knowledge* **~lesen** n *Bible-reading* **~leser** m *Bible-reader* (od *student*) **~papier** n *bible paper* **~sprache** f *scriptural language* **~spruch** m *scriptural sentence, verse* (*taken*) *from the Bible*; *text, lesson* **~stelle** f *scriptural passage*; ⟨ec⟩ *text, lesson* **~stunde** f *biblical instruction*; *Bible class*; *Sunday school* **~übersetzung** f *translation of the Bible, Bible-version* **~verehrer** m *bibliolater* **~werk** n *polyglot Bible*

Bibel·ots [bi'blo:s] pl (Fr) = Nippsachen

B·iber m ~s/~ **1.** ⟨zoo⟩ *beaver* **2.** ~fell [n], ~pelz [m] *beaver*; (imitierter) *beaverette* **3.** (Baumwollstoff) *beaverteen* **4.** ⟨fig⟩ (Bart) ⟨fam⟩ *beaver*

B·iber- [in comp] *beaver-*; **~bau** m *beaver's burrow* **~baum** m ⟨bot⟩ = Magnolie **~fell** n *beaver* (*-skin*) **~geil** n (Drüsenabsonderung) *castor* **~haar** n *hair of the b.* **~hut** m *beaver*; *castor* **~klee** m ⟨bot⟩ = Bitterklee **~kraut** n ⟨bot⟩ = Tausendgüldenkraut **~pelz** m *beaver-*(*-fur*) **~ratte** f ⟨zoo⟩ *coypu*; Fell *or* Pelz der ~ *nutria* **~schwanz** m **1.** *flat* od *plain* (*roofing-*) *tile* **2.** ⟨mech⟩ *pad-saw*

Bibern·elle f ~/~n ⟨bot⟩ *burnet*

°**B·ibi** m hat ‖ ⟨fam⟩ *bowler(-hat), pot hat*

B·iblio- [in comp] (Buch-, Bücher-) *biblio* .. **~gr·aph** m ~en/~en *bibliographer* **~graph·ie** f ~/~n *bibliography* **≗gr·aphisch** a *bibliographical* **~m·ane** m ~n/~n *bibliomaniac* **~man·ie** f ~/ *bibliomania* **~mant·ie** f ~/ *bibliomancy* **~ph·ile** m *bibliophile* **~th·ek** f ~/~en *library* ‖ ~sgebäude [n] *library* ‖ ~sdirektor [m] *principal librarian*; ⟨engl⟩ *keeper of a library, librarian*; Amt e–s solchen *librarianship*; ~szeichen [n] *library-stamp* ‖ ~swesen [n] *bibliothecarial matters* [pl], *libraries* [pl] **~thek·ar** m ~s/~e *librarian*; ⟨engl⟩ *sublibrarian* **≗thek·arisch** a *bibliothecarial*

b·iblisch a *biblical, scriptural*; ~e Geschichte [f] *sacred history* **Bibliz·ismus** m ⟨theol⟩ *biblicism*

Bichrom·at n ⟨chem⟩ *bichromate*

B·ickbeere f ~s/~n [nordd] ⟨bot⟩ *bilberry*; *whortleberry*; → Heidelbeere

bid·erb [a] (bieder & derb) *Dobbin-like*

Bid·et [bi'de:] n Fr ~s/~s (Badegefäß) *bidet*

Bidschap·ur n (vorderindischer Bezirk) *Bijapur*

b·ieder a *honest, ingenuous, upright* ‖ ⟨iron⟩ *gullible, simple* **≗keit** f ~/ *honesty, ingenuousness, uprightness* ‖ ⟨iron⟩ *gullibility* **≗mann** m *honest man, honourable man* ‖ *⟨iron⟩ *philistine* **~männisch** a *honest, singlehearted* ‖ *⟨iron⟩ *philistine* **~meier** m **1.** *philistine* **2.** [in comp] *plain, homely*; *old-fashioned*; ~stil [m] ⟨Ger⟩ *style of plain, simple forms (of furniture,* etc); (1815–48) ⟨Lit⟩ *bourgeois period* (Stifter, G. Keller, Raabe, Freytag, Mörike)

b·iegbar a *flexible*

B·iege f ~/~n = Krümmung **~fähigkeit** f *bending property* ~**festigkeit** f *b. strength* **~maschine** f *bending* od *curving machine* **~stempel** m *punch* **~zange** f *bending pliers* [pl]

b·iegen vi/t [bog/gebogen] **I.** vi [s] **1.** *(of vehicles)* (fahrend ~) *to turn* (in *into*; um *round*); *to swing* (in *into*; aus *out of* [*High Street*]); um die Ecke ~ *to turn the corner*; → ab-, ein– biegen ‖ (P) *to go* (in *into*); *to walk* (um *round*) **2.** ⟨fig⟩ es mag ~ oder brechen *by hook or by crook*; besser ~ als brechen *it is better to yield in time* **II.** vt (S) → beugen **1.** (krümmen) (Draht, Rohr) *to bend* (in, z *into* [*a loop*]); *to give a twist to (a th)*; (Holz) (of the heat) *to warp*; (Metall etc) *to buckle* ‖ (Zweige etc) (of the wind) *to bend, to sway* ‖ *to curve* ‖ (Muskel, Glied) *to flex* ‖ etw nach außen, innen, oben, unten ~ *to turn a th out, in, up, down* **2.** ⟨übtr⟩ etw zurecht ~ *to manage*; *to warp* (z *into*) **3. sich ~ a.** (S) *to bend*; *curve*; (of branches) *to sway* (unter der Last v, vor *with*) ‖ (of wood) *to warp* ‖ (of metal, rails) *to buckle* ‖ sich nach außen ~ *to turn out, to curve outwards*; sich nach innen ~ *to turn in, to curve inwards* **b.** (P) sich schmiegen u ~ *to twist and turn, to creep and cringe*; sich vor Lachen ~ *to split one's sides* ‖ → gebogen **B·iegen** n *bending, curving (of a th)*; *warping* ‖ (Sich-Biegen) *swaying (of boughs)* | auf ~ oder Brechen *neck or nothing* [abs]; es geht auf ~ u B. *we must be prepared for the worst* ‖ → Biegung

b·iegsam a *flexible (wire)*; *ductile, malleable* ‖ *limp (cover)*; *pliable, pliant, supple (cane)*; *limber, lithe(some)* ‖ ⟨übtr & fig⟩ *flexible (voice), lissom*; *pliable, pliant (mind)*; *malleable, supple, tractable (character)* ‖ ~ m *to make* od *render supple*, etc; *to supple* **≗keit** f ~/ *ductility*; *flexibility (of wire)*; *pliability, pliancy, suppleness* ‖ ⟨übtr⟩ *flexibility (of the voice)*; *suppleness, tractability (of character)*

B·iegung f ~/~en **1.** *bend, bending (of a th)*; *inflection*; *flexion (of a limb)*; *flexure* ‖ konvexe ~ *camber* **2.** (Gebogenes) *bend, winding (of a river)*; *curve (of a bay)*; *flexion (of the stem)*; *turn (of the road)* ‖ → Beugung; Biegen **~sfestigkeit** f *bending strength* **~sspannung** f *bending stress* (od *strain*)

B·ielbrief m = Bailbrief

Bien m ~s/ (~envolk) *bee colony*

°**B·ienchen** n ~s/~ ⟨fig⟩ (Wanze, Laus) *b., b flat* **B·iene** f ~/~n ⟨ent⟩ *bee*; (Honig≗, Imme) *honey-bee* ‖ Arbeits≗ *worker*; → Drohne ‖ Wald≗ *wild bee* ‖ fleißig s wie e–e ~ *to be busy as a bee* ‖ ⟨teens⟩ dufte ~ (Mädchen) *slick chick*

B·ienen- [in comp] *bee* **~ameise** f *mutilla, velvet ant* **~brot** n *bee-bread*; *pollen* **~falke** m ⟨orn⟩ *bee-hawk* **~fleiß** m *unremitting assiduity* od *industry*; er entwickelt e–n ~ *he's as busy as a bee* **~fresser** m ⟨orn⟩ *bee-eater* **~harz** n *bee-glue* **~haus** n *bee-house, apiary* ‖ ⟨übtr⟩ *hive* **~kasten** m *wooden beehive* **~königin** f *queen bee* | ~-Futtersaft [m] *royal jelly* **~korb** m *hive, bee-hive* **~laus** f ⟨ent⟩ *bee-louse* **~meister** m *bee-master, bee-man* **~motte** f ⟨ent⟩ *bee-moth* **~saug** m ⟨bot⟩ *dead-nettle* **~schwarm** m *swarm of bees*; (e–s Stockes) *hive*, **~stich** m *bee-sting* **~stock** m *hive, beehive*; (Bienen) in den ~ tun *to hive* **~vater** m *bee-master*; *bee-keeper* **~volk** n *swarm of bees* | → Wabe **~wachs** n *bees-wax* **~weisel** m *queen-bee* **~wolf** m **1.** = Bienenfresser **2.** = Bienenmotte **~zelle** f *bee-cell* **~zucht** f *apiculture, bee-culture, bee-keeping* **~züchter** m *apiarist*; *bee-keeper* (od *master*)

bi·enn a ⟨bot⟩ *biennial* **Bi·ennium** n (L) *period of two years*

B·ier n ~(e)s/~e *beer*; ⟨Ger⟩ Lager≗, leichtes ~ *lager (beer)*; Münchener ~ *Munich beer*; °drei ~ *three lager* (etc) | ⟨engl⟩ gewöhnliches ~ v Faß *bitter (beer)* ‖ (bessere ~e:) gut gehopftes ~ (vgl Pils) *light (pale) ale* (weniger stark gehopft), ⟨Am⟩ *dry beer*; helles ~ *(pale) ale*; dunkles (starkes) *stout*, (exportiert) *porter* | ~ mit Schuß (Schnaps) *pot of hot* ‖ ~ vom Faß *draught-beer, beer on draught, b. from the tap* ‖ ~ auf Flaschen ziehen *to bottle beer*, Flaschen≗ *bottled beer* ‖ ~ ausschenken *to dispense beer, to sell beer retail* ‖ zum ~ gehen ⟨fam⟩ *to go to the pub*; beim ~ sitzen *to sit over one's beer, to have a glass of beer* ‖ etw wie sauer ~ ausbieten *to offer a th for a trifle*, wie sauer ~ ausgeboten w *to be had for the asking, to go begging*

B·ier- ~abend m ⟨Ger⟩ *beer-party* **~bank** f *ale-bench*, ⟨mst übtr⟩ *public house*, ⟨fam⟩ *pub*; auf der ~ sitzen *to beer*; *to sit over one's stout, to have a glass of beer*; ~politiker [m] *pot-house* od *armchair politician*; ~stratege [m] *armchair strategist* °**~baß** m *deep hoarse voice, beery voice*, ⟨engl⟩ *whiskey tenor* °**~bauch** m *paunch* **~brauen** n *beer-brewing* **~brauer** m *brewer* **~brauerei** f *brewery* °**~bruder** m *pot-companion* **~deckel** m *beer-mat* °**~dorf** n *small village in the vicinity of a university town* **~druckapparat** m *beer-engine* °**~eifer** m *bustle, hustle*; *great fuss* od *zeal* **~essig** m *vinegar made of beer*; *alegar* **~faß** n *beer-barrel* (od *cask*) **~filz** m *b.-mat* ‖ ~pappe [f] *beermat board* **~flasche** f *beer-bottle* **~garten** m ⟨bes Ger⟩ *beer-garden* **~glas** n *b.-glass*, (fuß- u henkelloses) *tumbler* **~hahn** m *b.-pump*; *tap* **~haus** n ⟨Ger⟩ *b.-hall, restaurant*; ⟨engl⟩ *public--house*, (einfaches) *ale-house*; ⟨fam⟩ *public, pub, pot-house* **~heber** m (Schwengel) *b. pull* **~hefe** f *barm* °**~idee** f *foolish* od *funny idea*; ⟨sl⟩ *sth out of a bottle* **~kaltschale** f *cold b.-soup* **~kanne** f *b.-can* ‖ (Trinkgefäß) *tankard* **~keller** m ⟨Ger⟩ *beer-cellars* od *vaults* [pl] **~kellner** m *pot-boy, potman* **~kneipe** f *pot-house*, → Bierhaus **~komment** [–kɔ'mã:] m ⟨Ger univ⟩ *student's rules for drinking* **~krug** m *beer-jug* od *mug*; ⟨Am⟩ *stein* **~kutscher** m *drayman* **~laune** f; in bester ~ *glorious* **~lokal** n = Bierhaus **~orgel** f ⟨Ger univ sl⟩ *piano* **~pumpe** f *figger* °**~rede** f ⟨Ger univ⟩ (mst *humorous*) *student's speech* *made at a b.-party* °**~reise** f *blowout, booze-up, bust-up*; ⟨Ger⟩ *pub-crawl* (e–e ~ m *to do a p.-c.*); *tour* od *beat of the public-houses*; ⟨sl⟩ *binge*; e–e ~ m *to go on the burst* ‖ auf der ~ *on the spree* od *hops* **~schank** m *right of retailing beer*; → Ausschank **~schenke** f = Bierhaus, -lokal **~seidel** n *beer-glass* (od *mug*); *tankard* **~selig** a *glorious* **~steuer** f *excise* od *duty on beer* **~stube** f ⟨fam⟩ *taproom*; = Bierhaus **~suppe** f *beer-soup* **~tisch** m ⟨übtr⟩ am ~ *in the public-house*; → Bierbank **~tonne** f *beer-vat* ‖ ⟨fig⟩ *big-bellied fellow* **~treber** pl *brewer's grains* **~trinker** m *beer-drinker*; ⟨hum⟩ *froth-blower* **~verleger** m *brewer's agent* **~wagen** m *dray* (*-cart*); ~fahrer *drayman* **~wärmer** m *beer-chiller* **~wergel** m = Bierheber **~wirt** m = Schenkwirt **~wirtschaft** f *beer-shop, public-house* ‖ ⟨Am⟩ (*beer-*) *-saloon* **~zapfer** m *tapster* **~zeitung** f ⟨Ger⟩ *humorous gazette to be read at a beer-party*

B·iese f ~/~n (am Kleid) *small seam* od *fold* ‖ (an Uniform) *coloured braid* od *edging*; *piping* ‖ (Schnur) *cord, lace, border* ‖ (an Bluse) *quilted fold*

B·iesfliege f ⟨ent⟩ = Bremse, Dasselfliege

°**B·iest** n ~es/~er (Vieh) *beast* ‖ ⟨übtr⟩ (P) *beast, brute*; dieses ~! *this beast of a fellow*

°**b·iestern** vi *to bluster*; biestere nicht so *don't be so boisterous*; mst herum~

B·iestmilch f (Kolostrum) *beestings* [pl]

b·ieten vt/i [h] [bot/geboten] **I.** vt **A.** (P) **1.** jdm e–n guten Morgen ~ *to bid a p good morning*; jdm den guten Tag ~ *to give a p the time of the day* **2.** (jdm, e–r S) die Spitze ~ *to make head against* (*a p*), *to oppose* (*a p*); *to make a stand against* (*a th*); jdm die Stirn ~ *to face, resist a p*; jdm Trotz ~ *to defy a p, to bid defiance to a p* ‖ Schach ~ *to give check*, jdm Sch. ~ *to check a p, to give check to a p* **3.** (anbieten) **a.** ⟨com⟩ (Preis etc) *to bid, offer* (f. *for*); → feil~ ‖ (at auctions) (Summe) *to bid* (f. *for*); 5 Schilling ist geboten! *five shillings I'm bid!* **b.** jdm etw ~ *to offer a p a th* (od *a th to a p*) ‖ jdm den Arm ~ *to give* od *offer one's arm to a p* ‖ jdm die Hand ~ *to offer* (od *hold out*) *one's hand to a p*; ⟨fig⟩ *to help, assist a p*; jdm die Hand zum Frieden ~ *to be willing to make one's peace with a p*; dem Glück die Hand ~ *to take one's chance, to try one's luck* ‖ jdm den Genuß e–r S ~ *to treat a p to a th* (*we were treated to a fine concert*) | das hätte man mir nicht ~ dürfen *I should not have stood* od *taken it from anybody* ‖ das lasse ich mir nicht ~ *I won't stand* (od *put up with*) *that*; das l wir uns nicht so ohne weiteres ~ *we won't take it lying down*; er läßt sich alles ~ *he submits to everything*; → einstecken, gefallen l **B.** (S) (darbieten) **1.** (Anblick, Eigenheit, Sicherheit etc) *to offer, present* (*the text presents considerable difficulties*); *to afford* (*the trees afford plenty of shade*); *to show*; das Buch bietet interessante Lektüre f .. *the book makes interesting reading for* .. ‖ Anreiz (Möglichkeiten) ~ *to hold out an inducement* (*possibilities*) (*to do*); jdm e–e Handhabe ~ *to give a p a chance* (z tun *of doing*) **2.** sich ~ *to present* (od *show*) *itself, to offer*; es bot sich e–e Gelegenheit *an opportunity presented itself* (od *offered*); es bot sich ihm e–e Aussicht *a chance came his way* **II.** vi (at auctions) *to make an offer* od *a bid*; ~ auf *to make an offer for* **B·ieten** n (at auctions) *bidding* **b·ietend** a: die sich zuerst ~e Gelegenheit *the first opportunity offering*; → höchst~, meist~

B·ieter m (at auctions) *bidder*

bifil·ar a *bifilar*; ~e Aufhängung *b. suspension*; ~e Wicklung *b. winding*

Bifok·algläser n [pl] ⟨opt⟩ *bifocal glasses* [pl] **bif·orm** a *biform*(*ed*) **Bifurkati·on** f *bifurcation*

Bigam·ie f *bigamy* **big·amisch** a *bigamous*

Bigam·ist m ~en/~en *bigamist*

bigen·erisch a ⟨biol⟩ *bigeneric*; → Gattungsbastard

big·ott a *bigoted* ‖ ⟨bes rel⟩ *hypocritical*

Bigotter·ie f ~/~n *bigotry* ‖ *hypocrisy*

Bih·ar n (vorderindischer Bezirk)

Bijouter·ie [biʒu:tə'ri:] f ~/~n [–i:ən], ~waren [pl] *jewel*(*le*)*ry, trinkets* [pl]

Bikarbon·at n ⟨chem⟩ *bicarbonate* **Bik·ephalus** m ~/–len *bicephalous, malformation*

Bik·ini m ~s/~s *bikini*; ~ ohne (Oberteil) *topless b., topless, mini-kini*

bikonk·av a *biconcave* **bikonvex** a *biconvex* **bilabi·al** a *bilabial, bilabiate*

Bil·anz f ~/~en **1.** ⟨com⟩ *balance*; (die aufgestellte ~) *b.-sheet*; Eröffnungs≗ *opening b.-sheet*; reine (rohe, Roh–) ~ *net* (*rough* od *trial*) *b.*; Unter≗ *adverse b.* **2.** ⟨übtr⟩ *result, outcome* **3.** die ~ aufstellen *to strike a b.* die ~ °frisieren, verschleiern *to cook* od *doctor the b.* ‖ die ~ ziehen *to strike a b.*; ⟨übtr⟩ *to take stock* **~aufstellung** f = –ziehung **~bogen** m *b.-sheet* **~buch** n *private ledger* **~buchhaltung** f *b. department* **~konto** n *balance-account, capital b.* **~prüfer** m *auditor* **~verschleierung** f *the cooking* (od *doctoring*) *of balances* (od *accounts*) **~wert** m *value in b.-sheet* **~ziehung** f *striking of a b.*

bilanz·ieren vt/i [h] **1.** vt (Konto) *to balance* **2.** vi (of accounts) *to balance*

bilater·al a *bilateral*

Bilch m ~s/~e ⟨zoo⟩ = Schlafmaus

Bild n ~es/~er **A.** (Gestalt) [nur in]: Manns≗, Weibs≗ **B. 1.** (Bildnis) **a.** ⟨allg⟩ *effigy*; *image* (*of a saint*); *representation* (*of a dog*) **b.** ⟨arts: sculp⟩ *effigy, image*; *cast*; Götzen≗ *graven image*; ~er [pl] *imagery, images* [pl]; → Stand≗ ‖ ⟨paint⟩ *picture*; (Gemälde *painting, piece*; (Heiligen≗) *icon*; → Altar≗, Wand≗; Familien≗, Genre≗, Schlachten≗ ‖ *drawing* ‖ (Porträt) *portrait*; *picture* (v ihm *of him*; [v ihm gemalt] *by him*) ‖ → Stich, Holzschnitt; Schatten≗ **c.** (in Büchern) *illustration, reproduction*; *figure*; ~ im Kreis *inset* ‖ (erläuterndes) *chart, diagram* ‖ → Abdruck **d.** (auf Münzen) *effigy* ‖ ⟨cards⟩ *figure*; (Karte) ~ *court-card* **e.** ⟨phot⟩ *picture*; (Diapositiv) *slide*; (ohne Zeichnung *featureless*; flau *poor*; kopfstehend *inverted*; packend *trenchant*; seitenrichtig *right-way-round*; stehende ~er [pl] *stills* (Ggs *movies*); umgekehrt *inverted*; undeutlich *vague*; unscharf *blurred, fuzzy*; verkleinert *reduced*); → Licht≗ **f.** mit ~ern schmücken *to decorate, to picture*; (Buch) *to illustrate* **2.** (Spiegel≗) *image, reflection* **3.** lebendes ~ *tableau* (*vivant*); *living picture* ‖ Bühnen≗ *scene, setting* ‖ → Film **4.** ⟨typ⟩ *face* (*of a type*) **C.** ⟨übtr⟩ **1.** (Beschreibung) **a.** *description, picture* (*of the 19th c.* etc); *representation, tableau* (*of the past*); Lebens≗ *life, life-picture* (od *story*); anschauliches ~ *portrait, graphic representation* ‖ ein ~ entwerfen v etw *to give a description of, to draw a picture* od *portrait of a th*; *to picture, to portrait a th*; ein allg ~ entwerfen *to describe a general pattern*; → schief | **im ~e s** *to be in the know, to know what's what*; ich bin im ~e *I know*, ⟨sl⟩ *I am in whatever know there is*; im ~e s über *to be abreast* (od *aware, cognizant*) *of a th*; *to know about a th*; ich bin über dich im ~e ⟨fam⟩ *I've got you* ‖ jdn ins ~ setzen ⟨sl⟩ *to put a p up to* (*the*) *ropes*, ⟨Am⟩ *to put a p wise*; ⟨mil fam⟩ *to put a p in the picture* **b.** ⟨rhet⟩ *figure* (*of speech*); *metaphor*; *simile*; *figurative expression*; in e–em ~e darstellen *to figure*; in ~ern sprechen *to speak figuratively*; → Allegorie; Gleichnis; Vergleich; (~ der Metapher) *image* (Ggs *tenor*); schiefes ~ *mixed metaphor*; dichterisches ~ *poetic i.*; ~er [pl] *imagery* **2.** (~ im

Geiste) *picture*; Welt≃ *world-picture*; lebendiges ~ ⟨Am⟩ *close-up* (*of a th*) ‖ *vision* | *idea, notion* ‖ ein klares ~ gewinnen v etw *to see a th clearly* ‖ sich ein ~ m v etw *to picture* od *figure a th to o.s., to form an idea* od *picture of a th, to visualize a th*; *to fancy, imagine a th*; um sich ein genaues ~ v e–m Orte z m *in order to get the hang of a place* **D.** ⟨fig⟩ **a.** (Sinn≃) *emblem, figure, picture, symbol* ‖ die Taube ist ein ~ des Friedens *the dove is a symbol of peace*; ein ~ der Unschuld *an embodiment of innocence*; **b.** ein ~ v e–m Mädel *a peach* (*of a girl*), *a perfect peach*; ein ~ v e–m Weib *a perfect beauty* ‖ ⟨sl⟩ *a stunner*; es ist ein ~ v e–m Mädchen *the girl is* (*as pretty as*) *a picture*; *she's a regular peach of a girl* **c.** ein ~ des Elendes *a picture of misery* ‖ ein ~ f. Götter *a sight for the gods*; ein prächtiges ~ *a sight to see* ‖ → Ab≃; Eben≃, Zerr≃

B·ild- [in comp] (→ Bilder–) **~abtaster** m ⟨telv⟩ *scanner, scanning device* **~aufklärung** f *photographic reconnaissance* **~aufnahme** f *filming, shooting* **~berichter** m *screen reporter* **~berichterstatter** m *news photographer* **~berichterstattung** f *coverage* **~betrachter** m (S) ⟨phot⟩ *viewer*; *light box* **~brief** m *telautogram, telautograph* **~bühne** f ⟨phot⟩ *image frame* **~darstellung** f *schematic representation* **~diagramm** n *pictograph* **~effekt** m *pictorial effect* **~entzerrung** f *rectification* **~fehler** m ⟨bes phot⟩ *aberration*; *image fault* **~feld** n ⟨phot⟩ *image field* **~feldzerleger** m ⟨telv⟩ = –abtaster **~fenster** n ⟨aero-phot⟩ *gate* **~fläche** f **1.** *perspective plane*; *surface* ‖ auf der ~ erscheinen ⟨fig⟩ *to appear on the scene, to make one's appearance*; (plötzlich) *to turn* (⟨fam⟩ *roll*) *up*; ⟨fam⟩ *to pop into ken* ‖ v der ~ verschwinden *to disappear* (*from the limelight*); (etw) v der ~ v. l *to wipe out, extinguish* **2.** *screen* **~format** n ⟨telv⟩ *aspect ratio* **~frequenz** f *video frequency* **~funk** m ⟨wir⟩ *radio photography, wire-photo*; *picture transmission, facsimile broadcast*(*ing*) **-funkanlage** f *facsimile apparatus* **~geschichte** f (lustige) ⟨bes Am⟩ *comics* pl **~gestalter** m ⟨theat & film⟩ *scenic designer* **~gießer** m *statue-caster*; *bronze-founder* **~gießerei** f (Werkstatt) *statue-foundry* **~grundträger** m ⟨paint⟩ *support* (z. B. *wood, canvas*) **~guß** m *bronze-foundry* **~hauer** m ⟨arts⟩ *sculptor* | ~arbeit [f] *statuary, sculpture* ‖ ~werkstatt [f] *sculptor's studio* **~hauerei, ~hauerkunst** f *sculpture*; *statuary* **≃hübsch** [pred –'–] *extremely pretty*; → bildschön (*you look as pretty as a picture*) **~karte** f ⟨cards⟩ *court-card* **~kop·ien** f ⟨film⟩ *visuals* pl **~kraft** f *formative* (od *plastic*) *power* **~landkarte** f *illustrated map* **~material** n *pictures* [pl] **~plan** m ⟨aero-phot⟩ *serial mosaic* **~reportage** f *illustrative photography* **~röhre** f ⟨telv⟩ *picture tube* **~säule** f *statue* ‖ wie e–e ~ dastehen ⟨fig⟩ *to be motionless as a statue* **~schärfe** f ⟨phot⟩ *definition*; mit *or* v gr ~ ⟨telv⟩ *high-definition* [attr] **~schirm** m ⟨telv, film⟩ *screen*; ⟨phot⟩ (*projection*) *screen*; (Radar) *display* **~schnitzer** m (*wood-*)*-carver, sculptor* **~schnitzerei** f *sculpture*; *wood-carving, ivory-carving* ‖ (*carved work*) *carving* **≃schön** a [pred –'–] *very* (od *most*) *beautiful, very handsome* od *lovely*; *dazzling*; das Kind ist ~ .. *is a picture*; e–e Frau *a beauty* **~schreiber** m *facsimile set* **~seite** *face, obverse* (*of a coin*); ⟨fam⟩ *head* **~skizze** f (→ Skizze) ⟨aero-phot⟩ *uncontrolled mosaic* **~stein** m *agalmatolite* **~stelle** f Armee≃ *army photo center*, Heeres≃ *army photographic interpretation section* **~stock** m ⟨R. C.⟩ *way-side shrine* (*of a saint* od *with a crucifix*) **~streifen** m ⟨film⟩ *film-strip* **~telegramm** n *wire-photo, facsimile* **~telegraphie** f *photo-telegraphy, telephotography* **~teppich** m *tapestry* (*-carpet*), *gobelin*; (Wand) mit ~ schmücken *to tapestry* **~ton** m ⟨phot⟩ *key* (dunkel *low*) **~übertragung** f ⟨wir⟩ *picture transmission*; → Bildtelegraphie **~unterschrift** f *legend, caption* **~wechsler** m *slide carrier* od *changer* **~weite** f ⟨phot⟩ *depth of focus* **~werfer** m *projection apparatus*, ⟨mst⟩ *projector* **~werk** n *imagery*; *sculpture* **~wirker** m *tapestry-weaver* **~wirkerei** f *tapestry-weaving* **≃wirksam** ⟨film⟩ *photogenic* **~wölbung** f ⟨opt⟩ *curvature of field* **~wurf** m *projection* **~zeilennorm** f ⟨telv⟩ *line definition standard* **~zeitung** f *illustrated paper, magazine*

B·ildchen n *small picture*

b·ilden vt [h] **I. A.** (P) **etw ~ 1.** ([künstlerisch] gestalten) **a.** *(Figur) *to form, shape*; *fashion* (aus *from, out of*); [mst formen] **b.** (Wörter, Sätze) *to form*; (Beispiele) *to make up* .. ‖ e–n Kreis ~ *to form* (*o.s. into*) *a circle* **c.** (einrichten) (Heer, Regierung, Partei) *to form, organize*; (Ausschuß) *to constitute*; sie bildeten e–e Gruppe *they constituted themselves a group* **d.** sich [dat] e–e Meinung (etc) ~ *to form an opinion* **2.** (S) (hervorrufen) (Pfützen etc) (of rain) *to form* ‖ Blasen ~ (of water) *to form bubbles, to bubble*; Klumpen ~ *to clot*; Knoten ~ (of gout) *to knot*; Knospen ~ (of plant) *to come into bud, to burgeon*; Kristalle ~ *to crystallize* ‖ es wurden Blasen gebildet *bubbles were formed* **3.** ⟨math & gram⟩ (of lines) (Winkel; Figur) *to form* (*3 lines form a triangle*) ‖ (of words) den Plural durch Umlaut ~ *to form the plural by mutation*; starke Verben ~ das Präteritum durch Ablaut *strong verbs make the preterite by ablaut* **4.** (ausmachen) *to constitute, form*; *to be* ‖ ihre Bescheidenheit bildet ihren Hauptreiz *her modesty constitutes* od *is her main charm* ‖ die Grenze ~ v *to form* od *be the boundary of, to border* (*a country*) ‖ ein Hindernis ~ *to be an obstacle* ‖ die Spitze ~ v *to head* (*a procession*); die Nachhut ~ *to bring up the rear* **B.** [mst jdn ~] **1.** (jdn; Geist, Charakter, Stil jds) *to form, mould* (nach dem Muster v *on*) **2.** (erziehen) *to cultivate, educate*; → auf–, erziehen; sie ist vielseitig gebildet *she has many accomplishments* ‖ (Volk) *to civilize* ‖ *to discipline, train* ‖ → gebildet **3.** [abs] Reisen bildet *travelling cultivates the mind* **II. sich ~ A.** (S) **1.** (of clouds; bubbles, etc.) *to form*; Eis begann sich über Europa z ~ *ice began to form all over Europe* ‖ es bildeten sich Blasen *bubbles were formed* **2.** (entstehen) (of *feelings*, etc.) *to arise, to spring up*; *to come into being* **B.** (P) *to cultivate* od *improve one's mind, to educate o.s.*

b·ildend a **1.** [pred] ~ s (of occupations) *to be educating*; *to cultivate the mind* **2.** [attr] **a.** ~e Kraft f *formative* (od *plastic, creative*) *power* ‖ ~e Kunst f *pictorial art*, die ~en Künste [pl] *the fine* (od *plastic, visual*) *arts* [pl] **b.** *educating* (*influence*); *civilizing* (*factor*)

B·ilder- [in comp] (→ Bild-) mst *picture* .. **~anbeter** m *worshipper of images*; *iconolater* **~anbetung** f *iconolatry, worship of images* **~beschreibung** f *iconography* **~bibel** f *illustrated Bible* **~bogen** m *picture-sheet* **~buch** n *picture-book* **~dienst** m ⟨rel⟩ *image-worship*; *iconolatry* **~fibel** f *illustrated primer* **~folge** f *serial pictures*; komische ~n *comic strips*; *funnies* pl **~form** f ⟨typ⟩ *form of the engravings* **~galerie** f *picture-gallery* **~handel** m *imagery* **~händler** m *picture-dealer* **~handschrift** f ⟨hist⟩ *illuminated manuscript* **~kabinett** n *collection of pictures* **~kenner** m *connoisseur in pictures, authority on pictures* **~laden** m *picture-dealer's shop* **~liebhaber** m *picture-lover, amateur collector of pictures* **~rahmen** m *picture-frame* **~rätsel** n *rebus* **≃reich** a *rich in pictures* od *illustrations* | ⟨fig⟩ *figurative, figured, picturesque* (*language*) ‖ *florid, flowery, ornate* (*style*) **~reichtum** m *rich* *imagery, wealth of metaphor, figurativeness (of poetry,* etc). **~saal** m = Bildergalerie **~sammlung** f *collection of pictures* **~schrift** f *pictography, picture-writing, hieroglyphics* [pl]; ~zeichen *hieroglyph* **~sprache** f *imagery; figurative* od *metaphorical language* **~sturm** m, **~stürmerei** f ⟨ec hist⟩ *iconoclasm, destruction of images* **≗stürmend, ≗stürmerisch** a *iconoclastic* **~stürmer** m *iconoclast* **~tafel** f *plate* **~text** m *caption, legend* **~wand** f ⟨ec arch⟩ *iconostasis*

b·ildhaft a *plastic* **b·ildlich 1.** a *painting like; figurative, metaphoric(al), tropical* ‖ ~er Ausdruck *figure, figure of speech, figurative expression* (z. B. *man's inward laboratory*); *image, trope*; ~e Darstellung *figurative representation, figuration, figurativeness, imagery*; ~e Sprache *imagery* ‖ → sinn~ **2.** adv *figuratively, metaphorically, tropically* ‖ ~ darstellen *to image*

B·ildner m ~s/~ *sculptor, statuary*; ⟨mst fig⟩ (→ bilden I.B.) *moulder (of character, a people,* etc.) **b·ildnerisch 1.** a *pictorial (art)* | *plastic (talent); formative, creative (power); pictorial (imagination)* **2.** adv *pictorially* ‖ *plastically*

B·ildnis n -nisses/-nisse **1.** †(Gleichnis) *image* **2.** (v P) *portrait, likeness*; (bes auf Münzen) *effigy*; → Bild ‖ jds ~ verbrennen *to burn a p in effigy* **~aufnahme** f ⟨phot⟩ *portraiture* **~beschreibung** f = Bilderbeschreibung **~kunde** f *iconology*

b·ildsam a *impressionable, plastic (mind); pliable, pliant; ductile*; in Wärme ~ *thermoplastic* **≗keit** f ~/ *plasticity, pliability, pliancy*

B·ildung f ~/~en **I.** (Formen) **A. 1.** *forming, shaping, formation (of a sentence, circle; salt* etc.); Staub≗ → III. **2.** *constitution (of a committee,* etc.); *formation (of a new cabinet)* **3.** *creation (of a feeling, unrest)* **B.** *forming, moulding (of a p, a character)* ‖ *cultivation (of the mind)* ‖ ~ der Persönlichkeit *personality development* ‖ → Ausbildung **II.** (Geformtes) **1.** *formation*; ~en *formations* [pl] ‖ *form, shape; fashion*; → Gefüge ‖ *institution* ‖ → Formation **2.** (durch Formung Erworbenes) *education*, höhere ~ *higher e.*; humanistische ~ *classical education; scholarship*; akademische ~, Hochschul≗ *university education* ‖ charakterliche, gesellschaftliche ~ *good breeding, refinement, culture,* (breite) *liberal education,* ein Mann v ~ *a man of refinement* (od *culture*); ohne ~ *ill-mannered, rude, boorish* ‖ (Wissens≗) *knowledge, literacy*; ohne ~ *illiterate*; allgemeine ~ *general knowledge*; Prüfung in allgemeiner ~ *general k. examination* ‖ → Fertigkeit, Kenntnis **III.** [in comp] -bildung **1.** Riß≗, Staub≗, Wolken≗ *the formation of cracks, dust, clouds*; Kristall≗ *crystallization* **2.** Miß≗ *malformation* ‖ Wissens≗ *knowledge*

B·ildungs- ~anstalt f *educational establishment* od *institution; school*; höhere ~ *institution of higher learning* → Internat, Pensionat **~art** f *formation* **~element** n ⟨fig⟩ *component* **≗fähig** a *civilizable (race)* ‖ *cultivable (faculties); capable of being cultivated* **~feind** m *obscurant(ist); opponent of progress* **≗feindlich** a *obscurant(ist)* **~gang** m *course of education* (od *instruction*) **~gewebe** n ⟨bot⟩ *meristem* **~grad** m *stage of instruction; educational status; standard of knowledge* od *learning*; ⟨Am⟩ I Q (*Intelligence Quotient*); hoher ~ *high level of education* **~hunger** m *thirst of* od *for knowledge* **~ideal** n *ideal* (od *standard*) *of education* **~kraft** f *formative power* **~mittel** n *civilizer* **~roman** m *educational novel* **~stätte** f *educational institution* **~stufe** f hohe ~ *advanced stage of social development; civilization*; auf hoher (niederer) ~ stehend *(un)civilized* **~trieb** m geistiger ~ *desire for the improvement of the mind; .. for learning; creative power* **~vorgang** m ⟨tech⟩ *process of formation* **~wärme** f *heat of formation; enthalpy* **~weise** f *manner of formation* **~wesen** n *education; educational system; things educational* [pl] **~zentrum** n *educative centre*

B·ileams Eselin f *Balaam's ass*

B·ilge f ~/~n *bilge (of a ship)* **~wasser** n *bilgewater*

Bilh·arzia (L) (Gattung der Saugwürmer) (nach Theodor Bilharz, † 1862) *Bilharzia* ‖ Bilharzi·ose [f] *bilharziasis, -ziosis*

Bil·imbibaum m ⟨bot⟩ *cucumber tree*

biline·ar a ⟨math⟩ *bilinear*

bilingu·al, bil·inguisch a (zweisprachig) *bilingual*

Bill f ⟨engl⟩ ~/~s *bill*

B·illard ['biljard] n ~/~e, ~s **1.** (Spiel) *billiards* [pl] [sg konstr: *b. is* ..]; (deutsches) *pool*; ~ spielen *to play at b.*; → Karambolage≗ **2.** (~tisch) *b.-table* **3.** [in comp] *billiard (ball; cloth)* ⟨engl⟩ **~beutel** m, **~loch** n *pocket* **~queue** n, **~stock** m *cue, queue* **~serie** f *break* **~spieler** m *b.-player,* **billiardist* **~zimmer** n *b.-room*

B·ille f ~/~n (Hacke) *bill, bill-hook*

Billet-doux [bijɛ'du:] n *billet-doux* (Fr), ⟨fam⟩ *billy-doo*

Bill·ett [bil'jet] n ~s/~e → Fahrkarte; Eintrittskarte

Billi·arde f ~/~n (1 mit 15 Nullen) *a thousand billions*; ⟨Fr & Am⟩ *quadrillion*

b·illig I. a **1.** (recht) [mst pred] *equitable, just, right; fair* ‖ → recht ‖ *reasonable*; ‖ ein ~es Verlangen *a reasonable demand* **2.** (wohlfeil) **a.** *cheap (clothes; shops; tailor); inexpensive*; (mäßig) *moderate, reasonable* ‖ ~es Hotel ⟨Am fam⟩ *flop-house*; ~es Restaurant ⟨Am sl⟩ *hash joint*; ~er Urlaub *vacation on the cheap*; z ~em Preis *at a low price*; z ~en Fahrpreisen *at cheap fares*; Ausverkauf z bes ~en Preisen *bargain-sale*; ein ~er Einkauf *a bargain* ‖ auf ~ste Art *on the cheap* ‖ ~ u schlecht *cheap and nasty*; nicht ~ *expensive, not cheap*; → spott~ **b.** ⟨übtr⟩ e–e ~e Ausrede *a poor excuse* ‖ wie ~! ⟨Am sl⟩ *a dime a dozen!* **II.** adv [mst] *cheaply*; ⟨fam⟩ *cheap (to buy, get, make,* etc. *ch.)* ‖ °~ davonk *to get off cheap* | [compr] ~er *more cheaply*; ⟨fam⟩ *cheaper* **~denkend** a *fair-minded, just*

b·illigen vt [h] (etw) *to approve of (a th); to countenance, sanction (a th)*; (Vorschlag) *to agree* (od *consent*) *to*; (Gesetz) *to pass (a bill)*; gebilligt w *to be approved of, to meet with approval* ‖ ich kann es nicht ~, daß du früher abreist *I cannot approve of you(r) leaving earlier, I cannot suffer you to leave e.*

billigerm·aßen, billigerw·eise adv *justly; with justice; fairly; reasonably*

B·illigkeit f ~/ **1.** ⟨jur⟩ *equity* ‖ *equitableness, fairness, justice, justness; reasonableness* ‖ nach Recht u ~ *according to justice* **2.** ⟨com⟩ *cheapness (of goods); low price* **~sgericht** ⟨engl⟩ n *the Court of Equity* **~sgrund** m aus -gründen *from reasons of fairness* **~srecht** n ⟨engl⟩ (ungeschrieben) *Equity* ‖ ~e [pl] *equitable interests* [pl] **≗rechtlich** a *equitable*

B·illigung f ~/ ~ e–r S *approbation, approval, sanction of a th; agreement* od *consent to a th* ‖ stillschweigende ~ *tacit acceptance*

Billi·on f ~/~en *billion*; ⟨Am & Fr⟩ *trillion*

Bill·on [bi'jɔ̃:] (Fr) m & n ~s/~s (Legierung v Kupfer u Silber) *billon*

B·ilsenkraut n ⟨bot⟩ *henbane*

b·imb·am [intj] *ding-dong!* ‖ ['—] ⟨fig⟩ heiliger ≗! *goodness gracious! dear me! o lord!*

b·imb·amb·um [intj] *ding-dong!*

Bimet·all n ⟨phys⟩ *bimetal* **Bimetall·ismus** m ⟨com⟩ *bimetallism* **bimetall·istisch** a *bimetalistic*

°**Bimmel** m ~s/~ ⟨vulg sex⟩ *pencil*

°**Bimmel** f ~/~n *bell* ‖ °~bahn = Kleinbahn; ⟨Kinderspr⟩ *choo-choo-train*

°**b·immeln** vi [h] *to tinkle*

Bims m **1.** = ~stein **2.** ° = Kommiß(brot); (Geld) *dough* ‖ = °**B·imse** f [pl] *thrashing*; ~ bekommen *to get a th.* ‖ ⟨mil⟩ *sharp drill*

b·imsen I. vt [h] **1.** (Sohlen) *to pumice* **2.** ° ⟨übtr⟩ (jdn) *to punish, thrash* ‖ ⟨mil⟩ *to drill,* → schurigeln **II.** vi ⟨sl⟩ *to swot*

B·imsstein m *pumice (-stone)*; mit dem ~ abreiben *to pumice*

b·in [1. Pers. sg, pres v sein] ich ~ *I am*

bin·är a *binary*; ⟨chem⟩ ~e Verbindung *b. compound* | ~ [adv] verschlüsselt ⟨com⟩ *binary coded* | ≈kode [m] ⟨commun⟩ *b. code*; ≈zahl [f] *b. number*, ≈ziffer [f] *b. digit*; → *bit*

B·indbaum m *hay-pole*

B·inde f ~/~n **1.** ⟨surg⟩ *bandage*; ~n [pl] *bandages*; mit e–r ~ verbinden *to bandage* ‖ ~ f den Arm *sling, triangular bandage*; den Arm in der ~ tragen *to have one's arm in a sling* ‖ → Manipel **2. a.** (Hals≈) ⟨Ger univ⟩ (bei Mensuren) *neck-bandage* ‖ *necktie, tie; cravat*; in Frack u weißer ~ *in evening-dress* ‖ ⟨mil⟩ *tie* | °e–n hinter die ~ gießen *to wet one's whistle*; ein Glas .. *to sink* (od *neck, sling*) *a glass* (*of whisky*), *a pot* (*of beer*) **b.** ~ um den Arm *armlet* **c.** Damen≈ *sanitary towel* ‖ ~ngürtel [m] *sanitary belt* **d.** die ~ fiel mir v den Augen ⟨fig⟩ *the scales fell from my eyes* ‖ → Leib≈ **3.** ⟨anat⟩ *fascia* [L]

B·inde- ~(r)balken m ⟨arch⟩ *girder, binder* **~draht** m *binding wire* **~dreieck** n (Dachstuhl) *truss* **~garn** n ⟨agr⟩ *binder twine* **~gewebe** n ⟨anat⟩ *connective tissue*; -gewebsfasern bilden *to fibrose* **~glied** n *connecting link* (*between* ..) **~grün** n *herbaceous plants* [pl] *for binding and filling bunches of flowers* **~haut** f ⟨anat⟩ (des Auges) *conjunctiva*; ~entzündung [f] ⟨med⟩ *conjunctivitis* [L]; → Flügelfell **~kraft** f *binding* (od *cohesive*) *force, cohesiveness* **~kunst** f *artistic binding of flowers* **~mittel** n *binding agent*; ⟨mas, etc⟩ *construction medium*; ⟨paint⟩ *vehicle, medium* ‖ ⟨cul⟩ *thickening*; ⟨fig⟩ *cement, link* **~strich** m ⟨gram⟩ *hyphen*; (Wort) mit e–m ~ versehen *to hyphen* (*a word*) **~stück** n *connecting piece*; *tie* **~wort** n ⟨gram⟩ *conjunction*

b·inden vt/i [h] **I.** vt **A.** (S) **1. a.** (Getreide) *to bind* ‖ (Blumen) *to twist* (z e–m Kranz *into a wreath*); (Girlande, Kranz) *to twine, weave* ‖ (Besen) *to make* ‖ (Buch) *to bind* ‖ (Faß) *to hoop* **b.** Band z e–r Schleife ~ *to tie a ribbon in(to) a bow*; *to knot*; den Schlips ~ *to tie one's tie* **c.** ⟨univ⟩ die Klingen ~ *to lock swords* **d.** (Suppe) *to bind, thicken* **e.** (Worte, Töne) *to bind*; *to run into one another*; ⟨mus⟩ durch ein Zeichen ~ *to tie* **f.** ⟨übtr⟩ (Geldmittel) *to obligate* **2. a.** (S, T) ~ **an** *to bind* (od *fasten, tie*) *to*; (Hund) fest an den Boden ~ *to tie* (*a dog*) *down* ‖ → Bein II. 3. c. ‖ (Zweige) in die Höhe ~ *to tie up* **b.** Strick ~ um e–e Kiste *to cord a box* ‖ Tuch ~ um den Hals *to tie a neckerchief round the neck* **B.** (P) **1.** *to put a p into irons, to fetter a p*; → fesseln ‖ **2.** ~ **an a.** (Gefangenen) *to bind, chain to* **b.** ⟨übtr⟩ *to bind, chain, enslave, tie to*; gebunden s an *to be chained to* (*the desk, a p*); an die Scholle g. s *to be rooted to the soil*; an die Zeit g. s *to be tied to time* ‖ sie w ihn an s–e Verlobung gebunden halten ⟨fam⟩ *they will keep him to his bargain* **3. a.** jdm die Hände ~ *to bind the hands of a p*; ⟨übtr⟩ *to tie the hands of a p* ‖ ⟨übtr⟩ sich die H. ~ *to tie one's hands*; mir sind die H. gebunden *my hands are tied*; an Händen u Füßen gebunden s *to be tied hand and foot* ‖ jdm die Zunge ~ *to tie a p's tongue* **b.** ⟨übtr⟩ jdm etw auf die Nase ~ *to let a p into a th*; *to tell a p a th*; wozu brauche ich ihm das auf die Nase z ~? *why need I tell him?* ‖ jdm etw auf die Seele ~ *to enjoin* od *urge a th on a p*; jdm auf die Seele ~ *to enjoin a p* (*to do*) **4.** (verpflichten) **a.** (durch Eid etc) *to bind, to commit a p* (*to do*); *to oblige a p* (an *to*); gebunden s *to be bound* (an *to*; *to do*); *to be guided* (an *by*), *to relie* (*on*); durch Versprechen g. s *to be pledged* (an *to*); (of oath, promise) *to be binding on* (*a, p*) **b. sich** ~ *to bind* (od *commit engage, oblige*) *o.s.* (*to do*); *to hold firm* (an *to*); ich fühle mich gebunden *I feel bound* (*to do*); sich nicht ~ *to temporize* **II.** vi *to bind*; *to be adhesive* (*the mortar does not bind*) ‖ ⟨übtr⟩ (of a promise) *to be binding* **B·inden** n *binding* ‖ *weaving, twisting* ‖ *typing* ‖ (v Suppe) *liaison, thickening* ‖ [in comp] → Binde 2. c. **b·indend** a **1.** *adhesive* **2.** ⟨übtr⟩ *cohesive*; *binding* (*promise*); ~ s f jdn *to be binding* (od *mandatory*) (*up*)*on a p* ‖ ~e Kraft *cohesive force, bindingness, validity* (*of a contract*); ~e Regel *hard and fast rule*; ~es Versprechen *undertaking* (*to do*)

B·inder m ~s/~ **1.** (Schlips) *tie* | ⟨arch⟩ (Ggs Läufer) *binder, binding stone, inbond brick, header, parpen* **2.** (Faß≈) *cooper* | ~balken m → Binde-; ~barte [f] *cooper's hatchet*

B·indfaden m ~s/≈ *string*, ein Stück ~ *a piece of st.*; starker ~ *twine*; *packthread*; mit ~ zubinden *to tie up with string* (od *twine*) ‖ ⟨fig⟩ °es regnet ≈ *it is pouring, it is raining cats and dogs* **B·indling** m ⟨bot⟩ = Zaunwinde

×**B·indsel** n ~s/~ = Schnur

B·indung f ~/~en **A.** [abstr] **1.** *adhesion*; *cohesion*; *agglutination* ‖ (v Gas in Wasser) *absorption*; ⟨chem⟩ *chemical bond* ‖ ⟨arch & tech⟩ *bond* (f *for*) | ⟨gram, phon⟩ Wort≈ *linking*; *liaison* [Fr] **2.** ⟨fig⟩ **a.** *adhesion* (an *to*); *bond, obligation* (jdm gegenüber *to a p*); frei v allen ~en *free from any obligation* ‖ (politische ~) *commitment* (an *to*); ohne jede ~ *without any c.* ‖ die feste ~ des Einzelnen an die sozialen Formen *the firm hold* (od *grip*) *of the social forms on the individual* **b.** (Zus–halt) (*bond of*) *cohesion*, der ~ entbehren *to lack c.* ‖ feste ~en [pl] *tight bonds* [pl]; die ~en der Gesellschaft *the social ties, the binding ties of society* [pl] ‖ (innere, religiöse etc ~) *sanction* **II.** [konkr] **1.** ⟨mus⟩ (~szeichen) *ligature, slur, tie* **2.** (Schnüre) ⟨skiing⟩ (Zehen≈) *binding*; ⟨mount⟩ Steigeisen≈ *cramponstraps* [pl] **~szeichen** n ⟨mus⟩ = Bindung II. 1. ‖ mit ~ versehen *to slur, tie*

B·inge f ⟨min⟩ *funnel-shaped hole*; *funnel*

B·ingelkraut n ⟨bot⟩ *dog's mercury*

B·ingen n ⟨Ger⟩ (Stadt am Rhein)

b·innen [prep] [mit dat & gen] (of time) *within*; ~ e–r Woche *within a week*; ~ e–s Jahres nach s–m Tode *within a year of his death* ‖ ~ zwei Jahren *within two years*; ~ acht Tagen *within a week* ‖ ~ kurzem *before long, shortly, in a short time*

B·innen [in comp] *inland*; *inner*; *upcountry* **≈bords** adv *inboard* **~deich** m *inner dam* **~eis** n = Inlandeis **~fischerei** f *river and lake fishery* **~gewässer** n *inland waters* ‖ ~ [pl] *fresh waters* [pl]; Lehre v den ~n *limnology*; → Luftfahrzeug **~hafen** m *inner harbo(u)r*; *inland h.* **~handel** m *inland* (od *home*) *trade* **~land** n *inland, interior*, ⟨Col⟩ *up country* **~länder** m *inlander* **≈ländisch** a *inland* ‖ *internal, interior, domestic, home*; ⟨Col⟩ *upcountry* **~markt** m *home* od *domestic market* **~meer** n *inland sea* **~reim** m ⟨pros⟩ *internal* (od *middle*) *rhyme* **~schiffahrt** f *inland navigation* **~sohle** f *intermediate sole* **~stadt** f *inland town* **~tief** n *channel, drain behind a dike* **~verkehr** m *inland traffic* **~wanderung** f *internal migration* **~wasserstraße** f *inland waterway* **~zoll** m *inland duty*; *toll*

Bin·ode f *binode* **Bin·okel** n ~s/~ ⟨opt⟩ *binoculars* [pl] **binokul·ar** a *binocular*

Bin·om n ~s/~e ⟨math⟩ *binomial* **bin·omisch** a *binomial*; ~er Lehrsatz *b. theorem*

B·inse f ~/~n ⟨bot⟩ *rush*; [koll] ~n *rush* || → Riedgras, Schilf, Simse || Betreuen u Schmükken der Kirche mit ~n z Kirchfest *rush-bearing* || mit ~n bedecken, auslegen *to rush* || °in die ~n gehen *to get lost*; *to come to nought*; *to fail*; (P) *to be ruined*, ⟨sl⟩ *to go to pot* **b·insen** a *rushy* **B·insen-** [in comp] *rush* **~decke** f *rushmat* **⁓förmig** a *rushlike* **~gebüsch** n, **~gras** n *rush-grass* **~korb** m *rush-basket* **~licht** n *rushlight* **~matte** f = Binsendecke **⁓reich** a *rushy* **~wahrheit** f *truism*, *counter word*, ⟨hum⟩ *bromide*; → Gemeinplatz

b·insig a *rushy*

B·inturong m ~s/~s ⟨zoo⟩ (Schleichkatze) *binturong*

B·io f ~/ ⟨school sl⟩ = Biolog·ie || [in comp] (Lebens–) *bio–* **~bl·ast** m ~en/en ⟨biol⟩ *bioblast* **~chem·ie** f *biochemistry* **~ch·emiker** m *biochemist* **~ch·emisch** a *biochemical* **~g·en** n ⟨biol⟩ *biogen* **~gen·ese** f ⟨biol⟩ *biogenesis* **~gen·etisch** a ⟨biol⟩ *biogenetic* (*law*); ~es Grundgesetz [n] *biogenesis*, *biogeny* **~gen·ie** f ⟨biol⟩ *biogeny* **~geograph·ie** f *biogeography* **~gr·aph** m *biographer* **~graph·ie** f ~/~n *biography*; (*a p's*) *veritable memoirs* **~gr·aphisch** *biographic*(*al*) **~klimatolog·ie** f *bioclimatology* **~l·og** m *biologist* **~log·ie** f *biology* **~l·ogisch** a *biologic*(*al*); in ~er Hinsicht *biologically* **~metr·ie** f *biometry* **~nik** f *bionics* **~m·etriker** m *biometrician* **⁓m·etrisch** a *biometric*(*al*) **~nom·ie** f *bionomics* [pl] **⁓n·omisch** a *bionomic*(*al*) **~phys·ik** f *biophysics* [pl] **~sk·op** n ~s/~e *bioscope* **~sph·äre** f *biosphere* **~t·it** m ⟨minr⟩ *biotite* **⁓z·entrisch** a *biocentric* || **Bi·ose** f ⟨chem⟩ *biose*

Bip·ede m ~n/~n *biped* **bip·edisch** a *bipedal*

bipol·ar a *bipolar*

Bir·ett n ⟨R. C.⟩ *biretta*

B·irke f ~/~n ⟨bot⟩ *birch*, *birch tree*; Weiß⁓ *white birch*; Zwerg⁓ *dwarf b.* **b·irken** a *birch*

B·irken- [in comp] *birch* **~holz** *birch*, *birch wood* **~reis** n, **~rute** f *birch-rod* **~teer** m *birch-tar*; ~öl [n] *birch tar oil* **~wald** m *birch wood* **~wasser** n *birch-water* **~zeisig** m ⟨orn⟩ *redpoll*

B·irk- [in comp] **~häher** m ⟨orn⟩ = Blaurake **~hahn** m ⟨orn⟩ *heath-cock*, *blackcock*; → Auerhahn; Schneehuhn **~henne** f *wood-hen*; (schwarze) *grey-hen* **~huhn** n *black grouse* (od *game*); *heath–* od *mountain cock*; *hazel hen* || [koll] ~hühner [pl] *black game* (*have* ..) **~wild** n *black game*

B·irma, B·urma n (in Hinterindien) *Burma* **Birm·ane** m, **Birm·anin** f *Burman*, *Burmese*; die ~n *the Burmese* **birm·anisch** a *Burman*, *Burmese* | das ⁓e *the Burmese*

Birn- [in comp] (→ Birnen–) **~baum** m *pear-tree* **~helm** m (Maurenkappe) ⟨hist⟩ *morion* **~kraut** n ⟨bot⟩ *wintergreen* **~most** m *perry* **~sauger** m ⟨ent⟩ *pear-sucker* (od *louse*)

B·irne f ~/~n **1.** *pear*; süße frühreifende ~ *jargonelle* **2.** ⟨el⟩ *bulb* || ⟨tech⟩ *Bessemer*⁓ *Bessemer converter* **3.** °(Kopf) ⟨sl⟩ *sconce*, (*k*)*nob*, *noddle*, *pannikin*, *costard*, *chump* || (du hast wohl 'ne) weiche ~! *you're dotty* od *daffy*!, *you must be nuts*!

B·irnen- [in comp] (→ Birn–) *pear* **~äther** m, **~essenz** f *pear-essence* **⁓förmig** a *pear-shaped* **~most** m *perry*

Birsch f = Pirsch **b·irschen** = pirschen

bis I. adv **A.** [vor prep] **1. ~ an a.** (örtlich) *to*, *up to*; *as far as* [*to*] (*the sea*), ~ an die Kniee *up to the knees*; ~ an den Himmel *up to the sky* **b.** (zeitlich) ~ an den Tod *till* (od *up to*) *death* || weit hinunter ~ *as low as* (*the 10th c.*) **2. ~ auf a.** (örtlich) ~ auf den Gipfel *up to the summit* || sie kamen ~ auf wenige Meter an e–a heran *they came within a few metres of each other* || naß ~ auf die Haut *wet to the skin* **b.** (zeitlich) ~ auf den heutigen Tag *till* (od *up to*) *this day* **c.** ⟨übtr⟩ ~ aufs Blut *to the quick*, *to the utmost*; ~ auf die Knochen *to the very bones*; ~ aufs Messer (*war*) *to the knife* || ~ auf den letzten Heller *to the last farthing*; ~ auf den letzten Mann *to a man*, *to the last man* || ~ auf weiteres *pending further information*; *till further notice*; *for the present* | ~ auf (= außer) *but*, *except for*, *except*; *with the exception of* (*Mr. N.*); alle ~ auf einen *all but one*; (gut) ~ auf einige Fehler (..) *except for some mistakes* **3. ~ gegen** Mitternacht *till about midnight* **4. ~ in a.** (örtlich) ~ in das Innere des Landes *as far as* (od *into*) *the interior of the country* **b.** (zeitlich) ~ in die Nacht hinein *far into the night*; ~ in die frühen Morgenstunden *into the small hours* || treu ~ in den Tod *true till death* **c.** ⟨übtr⟩ ~ ins einzelnste (*to examine*) *down to the smallest* od *slightest detail* **5. ~ nach a.** (örtlich) ~ nach Berlin *as far as Berlin*; ~ nach Schottland *up to Scotland* **b.** (zeitlich) ~ nach Ostern *till after Easter* **6. ~ nahe an a.** (örtlich) ~ nahe an die Grenze *up to near the frontier* **b.** (zeitlich) ~ nahe an Mitternacht *till near midnight* **7. ~ über a.** (örtlich) ~ über die Grenze *beyond the frontier*; das Wasser reicht mir ~ über den Kopf *the water is beyond my depth* **b.** (zeitlich) ~ über Ostern *beyond Easter* || ich wartete ~ über 8 Tage *I waited more than a week* **c.** ⟨übtr⟩ ~ über die Ohren *up to the ears* (*in debt*) **8. ~ um a.** (örtlich) ich begleitete ihn ~ um die Ecke *I saw him round the corner* **b.** (zeitlich) ~ um 6 Uhr *till 6 o'clock* **9. ~ unter** 10 Grad (*to fall*) *below 10 degrees* **10. ~ vor a.** (örtlich) ~ vor die Tür *up to the door* **b.** (zeitlich) ~ vor einigen Jahren *until a few years ago* **11. ~ zu a.** (örtlich) ~ zur Bahn *as far as the station*; ~ zur Tür etc *up to the door*, *peak*, *etc* || ~ zum Buchstaben N *down to the letter N.* **b.** (zeitlich) ~ z diesem Tage *till* (od *up to*) *this day* || ~ z m–r Rückkehr *pending my return*; noch 3 Wochen ~ zum Jahrestage *still 3 weeks to the anniversary*; noch 3 Minuten ~ zur Abfahrt *still 3 minutes to go* || ~ z Ende *to the end* || ~ zum Tode *till death* || ⟨com⟩ ~ zur Verfallzeit *till due* || v e–r Woche ~ zur anderen *from week to week* **c.** ⟨übtr⟩ ~ z 20 Pfd. hinaufgehen *to go as high as £ 20* || ~ z Betrage v *to the amount of*, *amounting to* || mutig ~ z Tollkühnheit *courageous to the point of recklessness* || ~ z Tränen gerührt w *to be moved to tears* **B.** [als prep; beschränkt] **1. a.** [vor Ortsnamen] ~ Berlin *as far as Berlin* **b.** [vor Ortsadverbien] ~ dort(hin) *up to that point*; ~ hierher *to this point* od *place*; *so* od *thus far* | ⟨übtr⟩ ~ d·ahin *up to that point*; ~ hierher u nicht weiter *as far as this but no further* || v .. ~ hinunter z *from .. down to* (*the domestics*) **2. a.** [vor Monats–, Tagesnamen u. ä.] *till*, *until*; ~ April, Montag, Weihnachten, 6 Uhr *till*, *until April*, *Monday*, *Christmas*, *6 o'clock* || ~ 1966 einschließlich *up to and including 1966* **b.** [vor Zeit-adv] ~ daher, ~ jetzt || ~ dahin *so far*, *till then*; *by that time* || ~ dato *hitherto* || ~ heute *up to this day* | ~ jetzt *till now*, *yet* (*the largest yet found*) || *as yet*, *so far* || ⟨a.⟩ *under present conditions* od *circumstances* | ~ heute (*un*)*til this day* | ~ morgen *till to-morrow* || ~ nachher *till then* | ~ spät nachmittags *until late in the afternoon*; ~ spätestens Montag *by next Monday*; ~ 3 Uhr *by 3 o'clock* || ~ tief ins 17. Jahrhundert hinein *as low as the 17th c.* || ~ wann soll ich zurück s? *by what time am I to be back*?; ~ wann bleibst du dort? *how long will you stay there*? **3. a.** v Berlin ~ München *from Berlin to Munich* | v Weihnachten ~ Ostern *from Crhistmas to Easter*; v 10 ~ 22 Uhr (abbr: 10—22) *from 10 a. m. to 10 p. m.* **b.** drei ~ vier Tage (*about*) *three or four days* **4.** [vor best. Maßangaben u Zahlen] ~ drei Meter hoch *as high as 3 meters* ||

~ 20 Mark bieten *to bid as high as 20 marks* || ~ drei zählen *to count three*; er kann nicht ~ 3 zählen ⟨fig fam⟩ *he can't say bo to a goose* || (übersetze) ~ (Zeile 9) .. *as far as* .. **II.** [conj] ~, ~ daß **1.** *till, until* (*till I return*); [nach neg oft] *until* (*not until he returned did we start*) **2.** *before*; drei Monate vergingen, ~ wir v ihm hörten *three months elapsed before we heard of him*; es wird lange dauern ~ .. *it will be long before* || es dauerte lange, ~ Neuigkeiten ihren Weg fanden nach .. *it took a long time for news to find its way to* ..

B·isam m ~s/~e **1.** = Moschus **2.** (Fell der ~ratte) *musquash* **3.** [in comp] *musk* **~duft, ~geruch** m *muskiness* **~ente** f *Muscovy duck* **~fell** n → Bisam 2. **~flockenblume** f ⟨bot⟩ *sweet sultan* **~kraut** n ⟨bot⟩ *moschatel* **~ratte** f *musk-rat, musquash*; *beaver-rat*; Fell der ~ *musquash, musk-rat* **~rüßler** m, **~spitzmaus** f ⟨zoo⟩ *desman*

B·ischof m ~(e)s/~̈e *bishop*; ⟨engl⟩ Anrede: *My Lord*; Anschrift: *The Right Rev. the Lord Bishop of* ..; [koll] die gesamten Bischöfe *the episcopate, –acy* || Amtsbezirk e–s ~s *see* **b·ischöflich** a *episcopal*; ~e Verfassung; *episcopacy*; ⟨engl⟩ Kirche nach ~er Verfassung *the Episcopal* od *Anglican church*

B·ischofs- ~amt n *bishopric, episcopate* **~mantel** m *pallium* **~mütze** f *mitre*; mit der ~ bekleiden *to mitre* (mst pp) **~stab** m *crosier* **~stadt** f *episcopal seat* **~stuhl** m *bishopstool, bishop's throne* **~würde** f *episcopate*; *mitre*, jdm die ~ verleihen *to confer a mitre upon a p*

bish·er adv *hitherto, till* (od *up to*) *now*; *so far, as yet*

bish·erig a *hitherto existing*; *all-time* (Rek·ord)

bisexu·ell a ⟨bot & biol⟩ *bisexual* **Bisexualit·ät** f *bisexuality*

Bisk·aya f; Golf v ~ = folg

Bisk·ayischer M·eerbusen m *Bay of Biscay*

B·iskuit [bis'kwi:t] [Fr] n ~s/~e **1.** (Keks) *biscuit*; ⟨Am⟩ *cracker*; → Gebäck **2.** (a. ~porzellan) *biscuit* | ~kuchen [m] *sponge*-cake

bisl·ang adv = bisher

†**B·ismarck-Archip·el** m *Bismarck Archipelago*

†**B·ismut** n = Wismut

B·ison m ~s/~s ⟨zoo⟩ **1.** (Wisent) *bison* **2.** nordamer. ~ → Büffel

B·iß m B·isses/B·isse **1.** (Beißen) *bite, biting* **2.** (~wunde) *bite*; *sting* **3.** ⟨fig⟩ → Gewissens~̈

b·iß 1. u 3. P sg pret v beißen

B·ißchen n ~s/~ (Häppchen) *tot*

b·ißchen: ein ~ **a.** *a* (*little*) *bit, a little*; ⟨fam⟩ *a mite*; ⟨Am⟩ *a snack* (*of* ..); kein ~ ⟨übtr⟩ *not a morsel*; warte ein (klein) ~ *wait a bit* od *minute*; ein ~ z Mittag essen *to have a bit* od *spot of lunch* od *dinner*; mit e–m ~ vorliebnehmen *to be content with a little* || auch nicht ein ~, kein ~ *not a bit* (od *jot*); *no*(*t a*) *whit* **b.** ein ~ Geld, Schlaf, Musik *a spot of cash, sleep, music*; kein ~ Geld *not a bit of money*; kein ~ Schlaf *not a wink of sleep* || sein ~ Geld *his little bit of money* || [vor Abstr.] *an atom* od *element of* (*truth*) **c.** [vor Adj. & Adv] *somewhat, rather, slightly*; ein ~ nervös *somewhat* (od *a little, a whit,* ⟨fam⟩ *a mite*) *uneasy*; ein ~ besser *rather better*; nicht ein ~ besser *not a bit better* || das ist ein ~ stark! ⟨sl⟩ *that is the limit! that's a bit thick!* || ~ fix! *make it snappy!* || sie machte ihn ein kl ~ unruhig *she made him the least bit uneasy* || ×**b·issel** = bißchen

B·issen m ~s/~ **1.** *bit, morsel*; kl ~ *nibble*; eingetauchter ~ *sop* || (nicht) ein ~ Brot *not a bit of bread* **2.** (Imbiß) e–n ~ essen *to have a bit* (od *mouthful, spot*) *of lunch* **3.** ⟨übtr⟩ ein fetter ~ *a good bargain*; *a nice bit of money*; *a great piece of luck*; ein harter ~ *a piece of hard luck* (f jdn *for a p*) || leckerer ~ (hübsches Mädel) ⟨vulg⟩ *bit* || sich den ~ vom Munde absparen f jdn *to pinch* od *stint o.s. in food for a p*; mir blieb der ~ im Halse stecken *the words stuck in my throat* || Beschwichtigungs~̈ *sop* (*as a sop to a p*) **~̈weise** adv *by bits, bit by bit*

b·issig a **1.** *ferocious, savage, snappish* (*dog*); *vicious* (*horse*); ist der Hund ~? *does the dog bite?* **2.** ⟨übtr⟩ *bitter* (*cold*) || ⟨fig⟩ *cutting* (*remark*); *biting* (*irony*; *tone, tongue*); ~er Ton *or* Charakter *bitingness* (*of an article*) **~̈keit** f ~/~en *ferociousness, snappishness* (*of a dog*); *viciousness* (*of a horse*) | ⟨fig⟩ *biting sarcasm, bitterness*; *bitingness* (*of a remark*) || ~en [pl] *biting remarks*

B·ißwunde f *wound caused by a bite*; ⟨poet⟩ *bite*

b·ist [2. P sg pres v sein] du ~ *you are*; ⟨† & bib⟩ *thou art*, → sein

bistab·il a *bistable*

b·isten vi [h] (of hazel-hens) *to call*

B·ister m & n ~s/~ (braune Farbe) *bistre*

Bisto·uri m & n ⟨med⟩ (Klappmesser) *bistoury*

B·istum n ~s/~̈er *bishopric, diocese, see*; das ~ N. *the see of N.* || → Erz~̈

bisw·eilen adv *occasionally, sometimes, now and then*

Bit n ~s/~s *bit* (Abk. f *binary digit*), → Bin·ärziffer; durch 4 ~ dargestellt ⟨comp⟩ *represented by 4 binary digits* || Sechs-~-Zeichen [n pl] ⟨comp⟩ *six bit characters* pl

†**Bith·ynien** n (antike Landschaft im nordwestl. Kleinasien) *Bithynia*

B·itt- ~brief m *begging letter*; *petitionary* (od *supplicatory*) *letter* (an *to*) **~gang** m ⟨R. C.⟩ *Blessing of the Earth*; *penitential procession* || –gänge [pl] *gang days*; (an den 3 Tagen vor Himmelfahrt) *rogations* [pl] **~gebet** n *supplication*; *petitionary prayer* **~gesuch** n → Gesuch **~schreiben** n = Bittschrift **~schrift** f *petition* (an *to*; um *for*); ⟨parl⟩ *memorial* || e–e ~ einreichen *to send in a petition*; ⟨parl⟩ *to present a memorial*; e–e ~ richten an jdn, jdm e–e ~ einreichen *to petition a p* (um *for*; *to do*) **~steller** m ⟨jur⟩ *petitioner, suppliant* **~woche** f ⟨R. C.⟩ (→ Bittgang) *rogation-week*

B·itte f ~/~n **1. a.** *request*; *solicitation, suit*; dringende ~ *entreaty* || demütige ~ *prayer*, *supplication* (an Landesherrn etc) *petition* || → Verlangen **b. auf** jds ~ *at* od *on a p's request*; ⟨com⟩ auf Ihre ~ (*we send*) *as requested* | e–e ~ **einlegen** bei jdm *to intercede with a p* (f jdn, etw *for a p, a th*) || jds ~ gewähren *to grant a p's suit* (od *petition*) || ich habe e–e ~ an Sie *may I ask a favour of you?* || e–e ~ richten, stellen, tun an jdn *to make a request to a p*; *to request a p* || jdn mit ~n bestürmen *to besiege a p with requests*; .. belästigen *to importune a p* **2.** ⟨ec & bib⟩ (Gebet) *petition, prayer*; die 7 ~n *the seven petitions* (*of the Lord's prayer*) || (~ der Mönche) *miserere* [L]

b·itte → bitten II. 5., II. 6.

b·itten vt/i [h] [bat/gebeten] *to plead, coax* **I.** vt **A.** ⟨eig⟩ *to entreat* (*a p to do, that*); *beseech* (*a p, a p that* od *to do*); *to implore* od *urge* (*a p to do*); schmeichelnd *to wheedle* (*into doing, into good temper*) **1. jdn etw** ~ [nur in Wendungen wie:] das eine bitte ich dich, verlaß uns nicht *I ask you one thing, don't leave us in the lurch* **2. jdn um etw** ~ *to ask* (od *solicit*, [in Fragen] *trouble*) *a p for a th*; *to beg* od *solicit a th of a p*; dringend ~ *to beseech a p*, flehentlich ~ *to implore* od *pray a p for a th*; → erbitten | jdn um die Erlaubnis ~ *to ask a p's permission, to ask a p for permission* (*to do*) || jdn um e–n Gefallen ~ *to ask a favour of a p* od *a p a favour* || jdn um Vergebung ~ *to beg forgiveness of a p* || jdn um e–e Zugabe ~ *to encore a p* || dürfte ich Sie um den Zucker ~? *may I ask you for the sugar?* ||

⟨iron⟩ ich möchte Sie ~ um .. *I will thank you for* | ich bitte Sie um alles in der Welt (*or* um Gottes willen), was ..? *for goodness' sake tell me what* ..? **3. jdn ~ z tun** *to ask* (od *beg, request, solicit*) *a p to do*; *to beg of* (od *plead with*) *a p to do*; dringend ~ *to beseech*, jdn ernstlich ~ *to entreat*; flehentlich ~ *to implore* od *pray a p to do*; (schmeichelnd) jdn fußfällig (*or* auf den Knien) ~ *to go on one's knees to a p* ‖ die Herren w gebeten *gentlemen are requested* (*not to smoke*); es wird g. *it is requested* [*not*] (*to do*) ‖ dürfte ich Sie ~? *may I ask you* .. (*to do*)? ‖ ⟨iron⟩ ich möchte Sie ~ *I will thank* od *trouble you* (*to mind your own business*); ich werde dich noch lange ~, dies z tun *I'll trouble you to do this* **4. jdn** ~ *to ask a p*; 'ich bitte Euch', sagte er, 'sprecht'! '*I beg* od *pray of you*', *he said*, '*speak out*'. ‖ [mst nur in Paranthese u Ausruf:] ist dies — ich bitte Sie — ein Leben? *is this a life*? *I ask you* | ich bitte Sie! *you don't say so*! *is that so*? aber ich b. Sie! *goodness gracious* | sich lange ~ l *to want a lot of asking* **5. darum ~, daß** etw geschieht *to beg* od *request that something should be done* ‖ darum ~, tun z dürfen *to beg to do, to request to be allowed to do* ‖ ich bitte, sich z entschuldigen *I beg you will apologize* **B.** (einladen) jdn ~ *to ask a p* (z Tee *to tea*); wir l Herrn N. ~ (einzutreten)! *please show Mr. N. in*; jdn z sich ~ *to ask a p round* (od *home*); wie nett, uns hierher z ~! *how nice to ask us here* ‖ Sie w zum .. gebeten *kindly come to* (⟨Am⟩ *contact*) (*the information desk*) **II.** vi **1.** ~ **um etw** *to ask* od *request a th, to make a request for a th*; (dringend) *to solicit for*, (demütig) *to supplicate for*, (flehentlich) *to pray for a th, to beg* od *implore a th*; demütig ~d *supplicatory, suppliant* | darf ich um gefällige Antwort ~? *may I be favoured with an answer*? ‖ um gefälligst baldige Antwort wird gebeten *an early reply will oblige*; *the favour of an early r. is requested* ‖ um Erlaubnis ~ *to ask* (od *beg*) *leave, to request permission*; um die E. ~ *to request permission* (*to do*; *that*) ‖ um Gnade ~ *to beg for mercy* ‖ um Hilfe ~ *to implore help* ‖ um jds Leben ~ *to beg a p's life* ‖ darf ich um Ihren Nanem ~? *Give me the favour of your name*; *may I ask your name*? ‖ ich bitte um Ruhe! *silence, please*! *now then*! ‖ um Verzeihung ~ *to beg* (od *ask for*) *pardon* ‖ um Wiederholung e–s Liedes ~ *to encore a song* **2. wenn ich ~ darf** [in Antworten] *yes, thank you*; *if you please*; *I don't mind if I do* ‖ da muß ich doch sehr ~! *now then*!, *here, you*! *mind what you are saying*! **3. wir l** ~ *please, show them in*, die Herrschaften l ~ *will you step this way, please* **4. ~ f jdn bei jdm** *to intercede* (od *plead*) *for a p with a p* **5. bitte** [f ich bitte] **a.** *please, pray*; ⟨poet⟩ *prithee* ‖ sag mir den Grund, bitte *tell me the reason, pray* ‖ bitte, vergib ihm *pray, forgive him* ‖ bitte, sage mir *do tell me* ‖ setzen Sie sich, bitte *sit down please, please sit down* ‖ bringen Sie die Kiste herein, bitte *bring the box in, will you*? ‖ geben Sie mir bitte z rechten Zeit Bescheid *kindly tell me in time* ‖ wie stellen Sie das fest, bitte? *how do you make that out, come now*? ‖ wollen Sie nicht bitte Platz nehmen *take a seat, will you not*? ‖ Ich kann das machen. Bitte *I can do that. Let me* ‖ komm, aber schnell, bitte *come quickly now* **6.** [in Antworten] ‚darf ich helfen?' ‚Bitte (sehr)' '*May I help you*?' '*Thank you*'; '*Please* (od *Pray*) *do*' ‖ ‚Wünschen Sie noch ein Glas?' ‚Bitte sehr' '*will you have another glass*?' '*Yes thank you*' ‖ **b.** ‚h Sie eine Zigarette?' ‚Bitte sehr.' '*Have you got a cigarette*?' '*Here you are*' ‖ Wie bitte? (*I beg your*) *pardon*? ‖ ‚Ich danke f das schöne Buch.' ‚O bitte' '*Many thanks for the nice book*.' '*Oh, please, don't mention it*'; '*you are welcome*'; ‚Erlauben Sie?' — ‚Aber bitte!' ⟨fam⟩ '*Mind*?' — '*Go right ahead*.' **c.** (im Anruf) ~ schön! Achtung ~! *Thank you*! **d.** (im Spiel) ~! *play*!

B·itten n *asking, praying* ‖ auf ~ jds *at the instance* od *request of a p*

b·itter I. a **A.** [attr] **1.** ⟨eig⟩ *bitter* (*medicine*; *taste*); sehr ~ *acrid, sharp*; → sauer ‖ ein ~es Getränk, e–e ~e Substanz *a bitter*; ~e Tropfen [pl] *bitters* [pl] ‖ ~e Mandel *bitter almond* ‖ etw ~ m *to bitter* **2.** ⟨übtr & fig⟩ *bitter, severe, sharp*; *biting, mordant, poignant, pungent* ‖ ~e **Armut** *abject poverty*; ~es **Elend** *abject misery*; bis z ~en Ende *to the bitter end*; ~e Enttäuschung *keen disappointment*; ~e Erfahrung *painful* od *unpleasant experience*; es ist mein ~er Ernst *I am in real earnest*; ~e **Feindschaft** *virulent animosity*; ~es **Gefühl** *bitterness, bitter feeling*; ~e **Ironie** *biting irony*; ~e **Kälte** *bitter* (od *keen, severe*) *cold*; ~er Kampf *sharp conflict*; ~e Klage *bitter complaint*; ~er Kummer *bitter* od *poignant grief*; ~es **Lächeln** *sardonic smile*; ~es Los *sad lot*; ~e **Not** *bitter hardship*; ~er **Schmerz** *bitter pain*; ~er Spott *biting sarcasm*; ~er Streit *acrimonious* od *rancorous quarrel*; ~er **Tadel** *severe criticism*; ~e Tränen weinen *to weep bitterly*; die ~e **Wahrheit** *the very* od *naked truth*; ~e Worte [pl] *bitter* (od *sharp, stinging*) *words* [pl] **B.** [pred] das ist ~ *that's bad*; es ist ~ *it is sad* (daß *that*; f *for a p*) ‖ jdn ~ m *to embitter a p* ‖ ~ w (P) *to become embittered*, → verbittern **II.** adv **1.** *bitterly* ‖ **~böse** *extremely angry* **~·ernst** *intensely serious* ‖ **~ kalt** *bitter*(*ly*) od *bitingly cold* ‖ es ist **~ nötig** *it is badly wanted* ‖ **~schwer** *awfully difficult* | **~ weinen** *to weep bitterly* **2.** er ist uns **~ feind** *he is our sworn enemy* ‖ e–e Reform tut **~ not** *a r. is badly wanted* ‖ er tut ihm **~ Unrecht** *he wrongs him unjustly* **III. der** ≗, ≗e (≗schnaps) *the bitter*; e–n ≗en trinken *to have a b.*

B·itter- ~apfel m ⟨bot⟩ *bitter-apple* (od *gourd*), → Koloquinta **~bier** n ⟨engl⟩ *bitter* **~erde** f ⟨chem⟩ *bitter-earth, magnesia* **~holzbaum** m ⟨bot⟩ *quassia* **~kalk** m ⟨minr⟩ *dolomite* **~klee** m ⟨bot⟩ *buckbean, marsh trefoil* **~kresse** f ⟨bot⟩ *cardamine*; *bitter cress* **~mandelöl** n = Benzaldehyd **~mittel** n [pl] *bitter herbs* od *plants* [pl] **~salz** n *Epsom salts* [pl], *sulphate of magnesia*; *saline* **~schwamm** m ⟨bot⟩ = Röhrenpilz **~spat** m ⟨minr⟩ *bitter-spar* **~stoff** m *bitter principle* **~süß** n ⟨bot⟩ *bitter-sweet, woody nightshade* **≗süß** a *bitter-sweet* **~wasser** n *bitter mineral water*; *saline water* **~wurz** m ⟨bot⟩ *bitter-wort*

B·itterkeit f ~/~en **1.** *bitterness, bitter*; *sharpness* **2.** ⟨fig⟩ *bile*; *bitterness, sharpness, severity*; *bitingness, poignancy*; *edge* (*of a crisis*); (Schmerz) *gall* ‖ ~en [pl] *bitter words* [pl] ‖ in ~ *acrimoniously*; *severely* **b·itterlich 1.** a *somewhat bitter* (*taste*) **2.** adv ⟨fig⟩ (*to weep*) *bitterly*

B·itterling m ~s/~e **1.** ⟨ich⟩ *bitterling* **2.** ⟨bot⟩ *yellow wort* **3.** ⟨bot⟩ = Röhrling

Bit·umen n ~s/ ⟨minr⟩ *bitumen* **bitumin·ös** a *bituminous*

b·itzeln 1. [obd] vi [h] = kribbeln 2.; = prickeln **2.** [md] = schnippeln

Biv·alve f ⟨zoo⟩ *bivalve*

B·iwak n ~s/~s ⟨mil⟩ *bivouac*

biwak·ieren vi [h] *to bivouac*

biz·arr a *bizarre, eccentric, queer* (*p*) ‖ *bizarre, fantastic, grotesque* (*taste, style*) ‖ *strange, odd*

Biz·arre f ⟨hort⟩ (Blume mit breitem Farbenstreifen) *bizarre* **Bizarrer·ie** f ~/~n *bizarrerie, bizarre character*; *strangeness, oddity*

B·izeps m, –pses/–pse ⟨anat⟩ *biceps*

blach a *flat, bevel, plain* (*ground*) **Bl·ache** f *flat country* ‖ ⟨poet⟩ *battle-field* **Bl·achfeld** n *flat country*; *plain, field*

Bl·ackfisch m ⟨ich⟩ *cuttle-fish*

blaff [intj] ∼! *bang*! *pop*! **Blaff** m *bark* (*of a dog*); ⟨artill⟩ *pluft* **bl·affen** vi [h] *to bark, to yelp* (⟨a.⟩ ≗) ‖ ⟨artill⟩ *to plonk*

Bl·ag n ∼s/∼en; **Bl·age** f ∼/∼n *tiresome urchin* od *child*

Blague [blɑ:g] [Fr] f *blague* [Fr], *humbug*; → Aufschneiderei **Blag·eur** [blɑ'gœr] m = Aufschneider

Bl·ähe f ⟨com⟩ *inflation* ‖ [in comp] *inflatory*

bl·ähen vt/i [h] **1.** vt (Backen, Segel) *to puff out, to swell*; *to inflate* | **sich** ∼ (of sail) *to belly, puff, swell* ‖ ⟨fig⟩ *to be inflated* (od *puffed up*); *to peacock o.s.* **2.** vi (of food) ⟨med⟩ *to cause flatulence*; *to prove flatulent*

bl·ähend a *flatulent* **Bl·ähhals** m ⟨med⟩ *swelling of the thyroid gland*, → Kropf **Bl·ähsucht** f *flatulence, –ncy*

Bl·ähung f ∼/∼en **1.** (Blähen) *puffing, swelling* (*of sails, cheeks*); *inflation* **2.** (geblähter Zustand) ⟨med⟩ *flatulence, –ncy*; *flatus, wind* ‖ ∼en h *to be troubled with wind*; ∼en verursachen *to produce flatulence, to prove flatulent*; ∼en vertreibend *carminative*; ∼en vertreibendes Mittel *carminative*

Blak m ∼s/ [niedd] *fume, smoke* **bl·aken** vi [h] *to fume, smoulder, smoke*; → schwelen, rußen

bl·äken vi [h] (of children) *to bawl*

bl·akig a *smouldering*; *smoky*

blam·abel a *shameful*; *compromising*

Blam·age [bla'mɑ:ʒə] f ∼/∼n *scandal, shame, disgrace* ‖ *come-down*; *humiliation* ‖ *fiasco, complete failure*; ⟨sl⟩ *sell*

blam·ieren vt [h] jdn ∼ *to cast aspersions on a p*; *to bring shame* (*up*)*on a p, to bring a p to shame* ‖ *to compromise* od *discredit a p* | **sich** ∼ *to compromise* od *commit o.s.*; *to make a fool* od *an ass of o.s.*; sich unsterblich ∼ *to stultify o.s. hopelessly*; du hast dich schön blamiert! *you have put your foot in it nicely*!

blanch·ieren vt [h] ⟨cul⟩ *to blanch*

bl·ank a **1.** (glänzend) *bright, glossy, shining* (*pewter*); ∼ v *glossy with* ‖ mit ∼en Talern bezahlen *to pay* (*in*) *cash* | *shiny* (*boots*); *sleek* (*hair*); *smooth, polished*; → blitz∼, schmuck ‖ der ∼e Hans *the sea, North Sea* **2.** (bloß) *naked*; *open*; *uncovered*; *bare* (*floor*) ‖ mit ∼en Fäusten *with naked fists* ‖ *bare, naked* (*wire*) ‖ *naked* (*sword*); *barebacked* (*horse*), auf ∼em Pferd (*to ride*) *barebacked*, mit ∼er Waffe *with a naked blade*; ∼ ziehen *to draw one's sword* | ⟨fam⟩ (ohne Geld) [pred] *without a penny*, ⟨sl⟩ *stoney--broke* **3.** (sauber) *clean* (*dish*) ‖ (unbeschrieben) *blank, clean* (*paper*) **4.** [pred] (P) ∼ s *to be broke* od *skint* **5.** ⟨fig⟩ *absolute, mere, plain*; *sheer* (*nonsense*) ‖ *flat* (*lie*) **6.** ⟨cards⟩ das Karoas saß ∼ *the ace of diamonds was blank* **7.** ∼ glühen ⟨tech⟩ *to anneal* ‖ ∼ m, ∼ putzen *to brighten, burnish, furbish, polish*; ⟨fam⟩ (Stiefel) *to shine* ‖ (Kessel etc) ∼ scheuern *to scour* ‖ ⟨typ⟩ ∼ schlagen *to leave blank* **∼beizen** vt [h] *to scour* **≗film** m *trailers* pl **≗glühen** n *bright annealing* **≗lack** m *varnish*

***Bl·änke** f *brightness* ‖ *bright* (od *shining*) *surface* **bl·änkern** vi [h] = glitzern

Blank·ett n ∼s/∼e ⟨com⟩ *blank* (*form* od *cheque*)

blank·ieren vi ⟨com⟩ = in blanko verkaufen

bl·anko adv ⟨com⟩ *blank*; in ∼ *in blank, short*; in ∼ verkaufen *to sell short* **≗akzept** n *blank--acceptance* **≗auftrag** m *blanket order* **≗giro, ≗indossament** n *blank-endorsement* **≗kred·it** m *blank credit* **≗verkauf** m *short, short sale* **≗vollmacht** f ⟨jur⟩ *unlimited power of attorney*; ⟨Am⟩ *blanket authority*

Bl·ankscheit n ∼s/∼e *busk*

Bl·ankvers m *blank verse*; in ∼en *in b. v.*

Bl·äschen n ∼s/∼ **1.** ⟨anat & bot⟩ *vesicle*; *small bladder*; *bleb*; aus ∼ zus–gesetzt *vesicular, vesiculate* | (Haut≗, Brand≗ etc) *vesicle, small blister*; *bleb* ‖ Eiter≗ *pimple, pustule*; → Pustel **2.** Luft≗, Wasser≗ *small bubble*; *bleb* ‖ ⟨glass⟩ *bubble* **≗artig, ≗förmig** a *vesicular* **∼flechte** f ⟨med⟩ *herpes* (L)

blas·é Fr (blasiert) a *sophisticated, blasé*

Bl·ase f ∼/∼n **A. 1. a.** ⟨anat⟩ (Harn≗) *bladder*, ⟨bes med, vet⟩ *vesica* (L); die ∼ entleeren *to pass urine*; → Gallen≗ ‖ → Zyste **b.** (Haut≗, Brand≗, ∼ am Fuß) *blister*; ⟨vet⟩ *gall*; mit ∼n bedeckte Füße *blistered feet*; sich mit ∼n bedecken *to vesicate*; ∼n bek. *to become covered with blisters*; ⟨med⟩ ∼n ziehen *to raise blisters*; *to vesicate* **c.** ⟨übtr⟩ (Gummi≗ in Bällen etc) *bladder* **2. a.** (Luft≗, Wasser≗) *bubble*; ∼n werfen *to send up bubbles*; *to bubble, effervesce*; voll ∼n *bubbly* **b.** (in Metall) *blister, bubble, flaw*; (im Glas) *bubble, bleb*; ⟨pap⟩ *bell*, ∼n [pl] ⟨pap⟩ *froth* **B. 1.** (Destillier≗) *alembic, matrass* **2.** (Ofen≗) *boiler* **C.** ⟨ich⟩ (∼ des Hausens) *isinglass* **D.** °⟨cont⟩ *crew, set*; die ganze ∼ *the whole lot*, ⟨sl⟩ *the whole caboodle*

Bl·ase- → blasen **∼balg** m (Hand≗) *bellows* [pl]; ein ∼ *a pair of bellows*; ∼ der Orgel → Balg 4. **∼balken** m ⟨mar⟩ (am Boot) *washboards*

bl·asen vi/t [h] [blies/geblasen] **I.** vi **1.** (of the wind, etc.) *to blow* (v Norden *from the north*); *to breeze* ‖ (of bellows) *to blow* ‖ (v Wal) *to blow* | ⟨übtr⟩ in die Hände ∼ *to blow one's fingers* ‖ ⟨fig⟩ jdm in die Ohren ∼ *to whisper in a p's ears* **2.** ⟨mus⟩ **a.** (P) *to play*, ⟨poet⟩ *to blow, sound* (auf *on*); auf der Flöte ∼ *to* (*play on a*) *flute*; auf der Trompete ∼ *to* (*blow* [*a blast*] *on the*) *trumpet*; auf dem Horn ∼ *to bugle* ‖ (tuten) *to toot*; wiederholt ∼ *to tootle* ‖ blas mal drauf *have a blow at it* ‖ (of trumpets) zum Angriff, Rückzug ∼ *to sound the charge* (od *attack*), *the retreat* **b.** mit jdm in dasselbe Horn ∼ *to take sides, to make common cause with a p*, er bläst mit s–m Bruder in dasselbe Horn *he holds the same opinions as his b.*; die ganze Presse blies in dasselbe H. *the whole press voiced the same opinion* **II.** vt **1. a.** (Luft etc) *to blow* (in *into*; durch *through*) ‖ (of the wind) jdm Staub (etc) ins Gesicht ∼ *to blow, carry, drive, send dust into a p's face* **b.** (Suppe) kalt ∼ *to chill* (*soup*) *by blowing upon* **2.** ⟨tech⟩ (Glas) *to blow* ‖ (Eisen) *to smelt* **3. a.** e–e Flöte ∼ *to* (*play a*) *flute*; ein Horn ∼ *to* (*sound a*) *bugle*; e–e Trompete ∼ *to* (*blow* od *sound a*) *trumpet* ‖ e–e Fanfare ∼ *to sound a fanfare* ‖ (Lied etc) *to play* (auf *on*) **b.** Trübsal ∼ *to be in the blues* od *sulks* **c.** °jdm den Marsch ∼, jdm e–n Schweinehund ∼ *to haul a p over the coals* ‖ °ich werde dir etw ∼ *I'll see you further first* **4.** (beim Damespiel) (Stein) *to huff* (*a piece* od *man*)

Bl·asen n *blowing* (*of the wind*), *blow* ‖ *blast* (*of a band, trumpet*)

Bl·asen- **∼ausschlag** m ⟨path⟩ (of skin) *pemphigus* (L) **∼bahn** f ⟨mar⟩ *furrow* od *track* (*of a torpedo*) **∼bildung** f *vesication*; *formation of bubbles*; *bubbling* **∼entzündung** f ⟨med⟩ *cystitis* **∼fuß** m ⟨ent⟩ *insect of the family thrips* **∼füßer** m [pl] ⟨ent⟩ *thrips*; Ordnung der ∼ *thysanoptera* (L) [pl]; Erkrankung durch ∼ ⟨bot & agr⟩ *fly* **∼grieß** m ⟨med⟩ *gravel* **∼grind** m ⟨path⟩ *impetigo* **∼käfer** m ⟨ent⟩ *blister beetle*; Familie der ∼ *Meloidae* (L) [pl] **∼katarrh** m *cystitis* **∼kirsche** f ⟨bot⟩ *alkelengi, winter-cherry* **∼kraut** n ⟨bot⟩ *bladder-wort* **∼leiden** n *bladder complaint* od *trouble* **∼mole** f ⟨med⟩ *cystic mole* **∼pflaster** n *blister* **∼robbe** f ⟨zoo⟩ *large species of seal* **∼schnitt** m ⟨surg⟩ *lithotomy* **∼spiegel** m ⟨med⟩ *cystoscope* **∼sprung** m ⟨med⟩ *rupture of the foetal membranes* **∼stahl** m ⟨tech⟩ *blister-steel* **∼stein** m ⟨med⟩ *calculus* (L) **∼strauch** m ⟨bot⟩ *bladder senna* **∼tang** m ⟨bot⟩ *bladder-wrack*

~wurm m ⟨zoo⟩ *bladder-worm*; ~krankheit [f] *echinococcosis* (L) **~ziehen** n *vesication* **~̈-ziehend** a ⟨med⟩ *epispastic, vesicant*; ~es Mittel *epispastic, vesicatory, vesicant*

°**Bl·aser** m (Sportmütze) *cap*

Bl·äser m ~s/~ **1.** ⟨tech⟩ *blower* ‖ Horn~̈ *bugler* ‖ [koll] ⟨mus⟩ die ~ [pl] *the wind* (a. P) **2.** ⟨min⟩ (Ausbruch v Grubengas) *blower*

blas·iert a *blasé*; *smug* **~̈heit** f *smugness*

bl·asig a *blistered* (*steel*, etc.)

Bl·asinstrument n *wind-instrument* ‖ [koll] die ~e [pl] *the wind*; die Holz~̈e *the wood* ‖ *wind*; die Spieler [pl] der ~e *the wind*

Blas·on [blaˈsɔ̃:] m (Fr) ~s/~s (Wappenschild) *blazon* **blason·ieren** vt [–o:n] [h] (Wappen) *to blazon*

Bl·asorchester n *brass-band*

Blasphem·ie f ~/~n *blasphemy*; *profanity*

Bl·asrohr **1.** ⟨tech⟩ *blow-pipe*; *exhaust* (od *eduction*)*-pipe* (*of steam engine*) **2.** (~ zum Schießen v Pfeilen) *blow-pipe*; (z Schießen v Erbsen) *pea-shooter*

bl·aß a **1.** *colourless*; *pale, pallid* (*cheeks, complexion*); ~ vor *pale with* (*fear*); (kränklich) *wan*; toten~ *dead-pale* ‖ ~ w *to pale, to turn pale*; → verblassen ‖ → bleich | *dim* od *pale* (*light*); *wan* (*glimmer*); *faint* od *pale* (*colour*) ‖ ⟨übtr⟩ blasser Neid *pure* od *mere envy* **2.** (gering) *dim* (*recollection*), *faint*, *slight*; nicht e–n blassen Schimmer, k–e blasse Ahnung *not the slightest idea* **3.** [in comp] *pale* **~bl·au** *pale blue* **~̈gesicht** n *pale-face* **~gr·ün** a *pale green*; ~e Farbe *eau-de-Nil* °**~̈kopf** m = Glatze **~r·ot** *pink*

Bl·ässe f ~/ **1.** *paleness, pallidness, pallor*; *wanness* ‖ v des Gedankens ~ angekränkelt *sicklied o'er with the pale cast of thought* (*Shak*) **2.** → Blesse **Bl·äßhuhn** n ⟨orn⟩ = Bleßhuhn

bl·äßlich a *palish*; *sallow*; ~e Farbe *sallowness*

Blast·em n ~s/~e ⟨biol⟩ *blastema* (L) **Blasto·d·erm** n ~s/ ⟨biol⟩ *blastoderm* **Blast·om** n ~s/~e = Geschwulst **Bl·astula** f ⟨biol⟩ *blastula* (L)

Blatt n ~(e)s/~̈er **1.** ⟨bot⟩ *leaf*; [koll] Blätter *foliage, leafage*; → Laub ‖ wieder ~̈er ansetzen *to become young again with leaves*; ~̈er entwickeln *to leaf, to come into leaf*; ~̈er treiben *to foliate* ‖ (Gras~̈, Korn~̈) *blade* | Blüten~̈ *petal*; → Keim~̈; Kelch~̈ *sepal*; Samen~̈ *seed--leaf*; Staub~̈ *stamen* (L) **2. a.** ~ Papier (als Maß) *sheet of paper* ‖ *sheet of note-paper* ‖ ⟨mus⟩ (Noten) *music* ‖ ⟨arts⟩ *print*; *drawing*; *engraving* | unbeschriebenes ~ *blank sheet*; ⟨übtr⟩ (P) *blank sheet, dark horse* (: *he is a d. h.*) **b.** fliegendes ~, Flug~̈ *fly-leaf, leaflet* ‖ (Zeitung) (*news-*)*paper, sheet*; in Ihrem ~ *in your columns*; es hat im ~ gestanden *it has been in the papers*; ⟨typ, print⟩ ins ~ geben *to pass for publication* **c.** (~ im Buch) *leaf*; nur auf der Vorderseite numeriertes ~ *folio*, Folio~̈ *folio*; Vorsatz~̈ *fly-leaf* ‖ auf dem nächsten ~ (Verweis) *over a leaf*; ein ~ weiter umschlagen *to turn over a leaf*; Album mit auswechselbaren ~̈ern *loose-leaf album*; (Buch) nach ~̈ern zählen *to foliate, to folio* ‖ ⟨fig⟩ unbeschriebenes ~ (P) *empty canvas* **d.** ⟨cards⟩ ein gutes, schlechtes ~ *a good, wretched* od *terrible hand* **e.** (Vorder~̈) ⟨shoe⟩ *vamp* **3.** ⟨übtr⟩ **a.** (an Werkzeugen) *blade*; Messer~̈, Schwert~̈ *blade*; Säge~̈ *saw-blade*; (e–r Kreissäge etc) *web, disc* **b.** ⟨mech⟩ *plate, thin layer* od *sheet*; *lamina*; Metall~̈ *sheet of metal*; Ziffer~̈ *hour-plate* **c.** ⟨mus⟩ (Zunge) *reed* ‖ (~ am Webstuhl) *reed* **d.** (Deck~̈ am Schuh) *vamp* **e.** ⟨carp⟩ *halved joint* **4.** ⟨anat⟩ Schulter~̈ *shoulder-blade, scapula* (L) ‖ Schulter~̈ (T) *shoulder*; ⟨cul⟩ *blade-bone, shoulder* (: *a sh. of beef*) **5. Wendungen:** ⟨fig⟩ (sich [dat]) kein ~ vor den Mund nehmen *to speak one's mind*; *to go* (*always*) *straight to the point*; *not to mince matters* od *one's words*; *to make no bones about it* ‖ vom ~ singen, spielen *to sing, play at sight*; *to play from music*; das Vom-~-Singen *sight-singing*; jd, der vom ~ spielt *a sight-player, –reader*; Spielen vom ~ *sight-playing* ‖ ⟨fig⟩ das steht auf e–m anderen ~e *that is* (*quite*) *another* (od *a different*) *thing, that is another pair of shoes, that's a horse of another colo*(*u*)*r* ‖ ⟨fig⟩ das ~ hat sich gewendet *the tables are turned, the tide has turned* **6.** [in comp] → Blatt-, Blätter-

Bl·att- [in comp] ⟨mst bot⟩ *leaf* .., *foliage* ..; *foliaceous, foliar*; *phyllo-* **~achsel** f ⟨bot⟩ *axil* **~ader** f *leaf-vein, nerve, string* **~ansatz** m *stipule* **~̈artig** **1.** a *foliate* **2.** adv ~ geschichtet *bladed* **~auge** n ⟨bot⟩ *leaf-bud* **~̈bildend** a *frondescent* **~bildung** f ⟨bot⟩ (Zeit der) *frondescence* **~blei** n *sheet-lead* **~bräune** f ⟨bot⟩ *leaf-rust* **~entwicklung** f ⟨bot⟩ *foliation* **~fall** m ⟨bot⟩ (*leaf-*)*fall* **~feder** f ⟨tech⟩ *C-spring, leaf-* od *plate-spring* **~fleckenkrankheit** f ⟨bot⟩ *leaf spot* **~floh** m ⟨ent⟩ *leaf-flea* **~füßer** m ⟨zoo⟩ *branchiopod, phyllopod*; ~krebse m [pl] *Daphnia* **~gewinde** n *garland* (L) **~gold** n (*beaten*) *gold leaf, gold foil, leafgold* **~grün** n *leaf-green* ‖ ⟨chem⟩ *chlorophyll* **~halter** m ⟨tech⟩ (an Schreibmaschine) *feed roller rod* **~häutchen** n ⟨bot⟩ (an Gräsern) *ligula* (L), *ligule* **~käfer** m ⟨ent⟩ *leaf-beetle* **~kaktus** m ⟨bot⟩ *Phyllocactus* (L); *Epiphyllum* (L) **~kelch** m ⟨bot⟩ *calyx* **~knospe** f *leaf-bud* **~laus** f ⟨zoo⟩ *leaf-louse*; *greenfly*; *aphis* (L), *aphid* **~̈los** a *leafless* **~metall** n *leaf-metal, sheet-metal* **~narbe** f *pit* **~pflanze** f *foliage plant* **~ranke** f ⟨bot⟩ *leaf--tendril* **~̈reich** a *leafy, foliate* **~rippe** f = Blattader **~roller** m ⟨ent⟩ *leaf-roller* **~rosette** f ⟨bot⟩ *leaf-rosette* **~scheide** f ⟨bot⟩ *leaf-sheath* **~schmetterling** m ⟨ent⟩ *leaf-butterfly* **~schneider** m ⟨ent⟩ (Biene) *leaf-cutter* **~schuß** m ⟨hunt⟩ *shot in* (od *through*) *the shoulder* **~silber** n *silver-leaf* **~spreite** f ⟨bot⟩ *leaf-blade* **~stellung** f ⟨bot⟩ *foliation*; *leaf-arrangement* **~stiel** m *leaf--stalk*; *stipe* **~stück** n ⟨cul⟩ *blade* **~(t)ang** m ⟨bot⟩ *tangle, seaweed* **~̈tragend** a *phyllophorus* **~vergoldung** f *leaf-gilding*; ⟨typ⟩ *gold-blocking* **~verzierung** f (an gotischem Maßwerk) *foil*; (etw) mit ~ schmücken *to foliate* **~wenden** n *page turning* **~wender** m *book-tassel* **~werk** n ⟨bot⟩ *foliage* ‖ ⟨arts⟩ *leafage* **~wespe** f ⟨ent⟩ *saw-fly* **~zählung** f *foliation* (*of a book*) **~zapfen** m ⟨carp⟩ *scarf-tenon* **~zeit** f ⟨hunt⟩ *rutting-time* **~zinn** n *tin-foil*; → Stanniol

Bl·ättchen n **1.** *leaflet* ‖ ~ Papier *slip of paper* **2.** ⟨anat⟩ *lamella*; ⟨bot⟩ *lamella* (L), *pinna* (L) **3.** Metall~̈, Blech~̈, Glanz~̈ *foil*; Aluminium~̈ *aluminium foil*; sich in ~ spalten *to foliate* **4.** das ~ hat sich gewendet → Blatt **5.** **~̈förmig** a *lamelliform* **~pulver** n ⟨artill⟩ *flake powder*

bl·atten vt/i [h] **1.** vt e–e Pflanze ~ *to strip a plant of its leaves* **2.** vi ⟨hunt⟩ *to whistle on a leaf* (*by way of decoy*)

Bl·atter f ~/~n ⟨med⟩ *pustule, pock*; ~n [pl] *pocks* **~narbe** f *pock-hole, -mark* **~̈narbig** a *pock-marked*

Bl·ätter- [in comp] ⟨bot⟩ *leaf* .., *foliage* ..; *foliaceous* **~̈los** a *leafless* **~magen** m ⟨zoo⟩ *omasum, psalterium* (L); ×*manyplies* **~meldung** f *press-news* (od *item*) **~pilz** m ⟨bot⟩ *agaric, mushroom* **~schmuck** m *foliage* ‖ ⟨arch⟩ *foliation* **~schwamm** m ⟨bot⟩ *agaric* **~tabak** m *leaf--tobacco* **~teig** m *puff-paste* (od *pastry*); gefüllter ~ *turn-over* | ~gebäck [n]; *puff pastry* | ~pastete [f] Fr *vol-au-vent* (*case*) **~wuchs** m *foliation*

bl·ätt(e)rig a **1.** ⟨bot⟩ *leafy, foliaceous, foliate* ‖ ⟨übtr⟩ *laminar*(*y*), *laminate*; *lamellar* **2.** [in comp] *-leaved*; vier~ *four-leaved*

bl·ättern vi [h] in e–m Buche ~ *to turn the pages of a book*; *to leaf through a b.*

blau I. a **A.** [attr] *blue* ⟨a. cul⟩; *blue, violet* (*eyes*); ~e Farbe *blue*(*ness*); der ~e Himmel *the blue* | ⟨her⟩ *azure* | dunkel~ *blue-black*; himmel~ *azure*; tief~ *deep-blue* [**Wendungen**]: ~es Auge n (durch Schlag) *black eye*; ⟨fig⟩ mit e–m ~en A. davonkommen *to come* (od *get*) *off cheaply* (od *pretty lightly*) ‖ das ≃e Band des Ozeans *the Blue Riband of the Atlantik* ‖ ⟨Ger Lit⟩ ≃e Blume *blue flower* ‖ ⟨fig⟩ ~es Blut *blue blood*, ~es Blut in den Adern h. *to be blue--blooded* ‖ ⟨übtr⟩ ~e Bohne f (Gewehrkugel) *bullet*; ⟨Am sl⟩ *blue pill* ‖ den ~en Brief bek. ⟨sl⟩ *to get the sack*; ⟨mil⟩ *to be given a bowlerhat* (*to have notice to quit*); jdm ~en Dunst vormachen *to bamboozle, dupe, humbug a p* ‖ ~er Fleck m **1.** (durch Schlag) *bruise*; ~e Flecken h. *to be black and blue* **2.** *Mongol patch* ‖ ~e Glockenblume f ⟨bot Scot⟩ *bluebell* ‖ ≃er Heinrich m ⟨Ger⟩ *dish of rice, pearl barley and plums* ‖ ~e Hyazinthe f ⟨bot engl⟩ *bluebell* ‖ die ~en Jungens [pl] *the blue-jackets, boys in blue* [pl] ‖ → Karpfen ‖ ~es Meer n *blue water* od *sea* ‖ °~er Montag *Saint* od *blue Monday*, ~en M. m *to keep S. M.* ‖ ~er Peter ⟨mar⟩ *Blue Peter* ‖ sein ~es Wunder erleben *to get the shock of one's life*; *to stand amazed* **B.** [pred] (Metall) ~ anlaufen l *to blue* ‖ (etw) ~ färben *to blue* ‖ °~ m *to take a day off*; ⟨sl⟩ *to whip the cat, to keep Saint Monday* ‖ jdn grün (*or* braun) u ~ schlagen *to beat a p black and blue* ‖ °~ s ⟨fam⟩ *to be ripe, pickled, in soak*; ⟨Am⟩ *lickered up* → kornblumen–, veilchen– ‖ ~ w (beim Ersticken) *to become black*; mir wurde grün u ~ vor den Augen *I turned giddy* od *dizzy*; → schwindlig | na so ~! *you don't catch me*! **II.** ≃ n (→ Blaue) ~s/~ *blue*; *blue colour*; sanftes ~ *nattier blue* ‖ der Herr in ~ *the man in blue* | Berliner ~ *Prussian blue* ‖ ⟨engl univ⟩ Dunkel≃ *Oxford blue*; Hell≃ *Cambridge blue* ‖ Marine≃ *Navy blue* | Wasch≃ *blue*, ⟨Am⟩ *blueing* ‖ → (Fahrt ins) ~e, *etc*

Bl·au- [in comp] *blue* .. ≃**äugig** a *blue-eyed* ~**bart** m Ritter ~ *Bluebeard* ~**beere** f *bilberry*; ⟨Sc⟩ *whortleberry* ⟨Am⟩ *blueberry* ≃**blütig** a ⟨fig⟩ *blue-blooded, aristocratic* ~**buch** n ⟨engl pol⟩ *Blue-Book*; → Gelb–, Weißbuch ≃**bunt** a *dapple-gray* (*cow*) ~**druck** m (gedruckter Kattun) *cotton-print*; ⟨arch, etc⟩ *blueprint* (*copy*) ~**ente** f ⟨Am⟩ *blue-bill* ~**erz** n ⟨minr⟩ *vivianite* ~**falke** m ⟨orn⟩ *bluehawk* ~**farbenglas** n *smalt* ~**farbenwerk** n (Glas) *smalt-house* ~**färber** m *dyer in blue* ~**felchen** m ⟨ich⟩ *blue char* (od *poll*) ~**feuer** n ⟨mar⟩ *blue flare-up light* ~**fisch** m ⟨ich⟩ *skipjack* ≃**fleckig** a *blue-spotted* ~**fuchs** m *blue fox* ~**fuß** m ⟨orn⟩ = Edelfalke ≃**grau** a *blue-grey* ≃**grün** a *bluish-green* ~**holz** n (Mexiko) *logwood, campeachy-wood* ~**jacke** f ⟨fig⟩ (P) ⟨mar⟩ *blue-jacket* ~**kehlchen** n ⟨orn⟩ *blue-breast, blue-throat*(*ed warbler*) ~**kohl** m = Rotkohl ~**kolbenblitz** m ⟨phot⟩ *blue-coated flashbulb* ~**kreuz** n ⟨mil⟩ (Gaskampfstoff) *cough–causing poison gas*; *Clark I* (*Diphenylchloroarsine*) ~**kuppe** f *pin* od *tack with blue head* °~**machen** n *absenteeism* ~**meise** f ⟨orn⟩ *blue-tit, nun* ~**pause** f ⟨phot⟩ *blue print, cyanotype* ~**ra(c)ke** f ⟨orn⟩ *blue roller* ~**säure** f *prussic* od *hydrocyanic acid* ~**schwarz** a *blue-black* ~**sieb** n ⟨ent⟩ *wood-leopard* ~**spat** m ⟨minr⟩ *lazulite* ~**specht** m ⟨orn⟩ *nuthatch* ~**stern** m ⟨bot⟩ *squill scilla* ~**stift** m *blue pencil* ~**strumpf** m ⟨fig⟩ *blue stocking* ~**sucht** f ⟨med⟩ *cyanosis* ~**wal** m ⟨zoo⟩ *blue whale*

Bl·aue n (→ Blau) [nur in]: das ~ vom Himmel herunterschwatzen (–lügen) *to talk* (*to lie*) *nineteen to the dozen, to talk one's head off* ‖ ins ~ hineinreden *to talk wild, to talk at random*; ins ~ schießen *to shoot wild* ‖ Schuß ins ~ *random shot*; Fahrt ins ~ *Mystery Tour*

Bl·aue m [der ~, ein ~r] (Polizist) ⟨fam⟩ *cop*(*per*)

Bl·äue f ~/ *blue colour*; *blue*(*ness*) ‖ die ~ des Himmels *the sky-blue, azure* ‖ ⟨arts⟩ (~ ferner Berger etc) *neutral tint of distant hills* | = Waschblau → Blau ‖ (Blaufäule des Holzes) *blue fungus stain*

bl·auen vi/t **1.** vi [s] *to become* od *be blue* **2.** vt [h] (etw) *to* (*dye*) *blue* ‖ (Wäsche, Stahl) *to blue* | ⟨poet⟩ *to azure*

bl·äuen 1. vt [h] = blauen 2. **2.** ≃ n *the blueing* (*of laundry, metal*) **3.** → bleuen

bl·äulich a *bluish, pale blue*; *livid* **Bl·äuling** m ⟨ent⟩ (Tagfalter) *hairstreak, Lycaenid butterfly*; Familie der ~e *Lycaenidae* (L) [pl], *Blues* pl

Bl·azer m [bleizə] ~s/~ (Klubjacke) [engl] *blazer*

Blech n ~(e)s/~e **1.** ⟨met⟩ **a.** *thin plate* od *sheet of metal*; starkes ~ *double plate*; geriffeltes, geschlagenes, gewalztes ~ *riffled, hammered, rolled plate*; gewelltes ~ *corrugated iron* ‖ Eisen≃ *sheet-iron*; verzinktes Eisen≃ *galvanized sheet--iron*; Kupfer≃ *sheet-copper*; Messing≃ *sheet--brass* ‖ Fein≃ *thin plate*; Grob≃ *thick plate* **b.** (mst verzinntes Eisen≃, Zinn≃, Weiß≃) *tin--plate, tin* **2.** (Back≃) *griddle* **3.** †(= Geld) ⟨sl⟩ *tin* **4.** °⟨fig⟩ *fudge, nonsense*; ⟨sl⟩ *bosh, rot, trash*; ~! *rubbish*, etc., ⟨Am sl⟩ *blah*!, *baloney*! rede kein ~ *don't talk rot*

Bl·ech- [in comp] *tin* .. ~**bearbeitung** f *sheet metal forming*; ~smaschine [f] *sheet metal working machine* ~**beplankung** f ⟨aero, tech⟩ *sheet-metal skin* ~**bläser** m ⟨mus⟩ *performer on a wind instrument*, die ~ [pl] *the brass wind* (a. P) ~**büchse** f ~**dose** f *tin*(*-box*), *can*; (f. Tee, Kaffee) *canister* ‖ ⟨fig fam⟩ (Auto) *tin Lizzie* ‖ e–e ~ Sardinen *a tin of sardines*; in ~n verpacken *to tin, can*; in ~n verpackt *tinned, canned* ~nöffner [m] *tin-opener* ~**druck** m ⟨typ⟩ *tin-printing*; ~maschine *tin-plate printing machine* ~**eimer** m *tin plate bucket* ~**einsatz** m *tin*(*-lined*) *case* ~**gefäß** n *tin vessel* ~**instrument** n ⟨mus⟩ *brass wind-instrument*; [koll] die ~e [pl] *the brass wind* ~**kanne** f *tin-can* ~**kasten** m *tin--box* ~**kern** m ⟨tech⟩ *plate core* ~**kuchen** m *griddle-cake* ~**lehre** *metal-gauge* ~**löffel** m *tin spoon* ~**material** n *iron sheet* ~**musik** f *music of brass instruments* ~**schaden** m ⟨mot⟩ *slight material damage* ~**schere** f *plate-shears* [pl], *p.-cutter* ~**schmied** m *tinworker, tinsmith* ~**walzwerk** n *plate-mill, p.-rollers* pl, *sheet rolling mill* ~**waren** f pl [koll] *tin-ware*

°**bl·echen** vt/i [h] **1.** vt (Geld) ⟨fam⟩ *to pay* (*up*); ⟨Am fam⟩ *to come across*; ⟨sl⟩ *to cough up, to fork* od *shell out* (od *over*), *to stump up*; er hat dafür 1000 Dollar geblecht *that has set him back a th. d.s* **2.** vi tüchtig ~ f. etw *to bleed for a th*; ⟨sl⟩ *to pay for one's whistle*; (gerne) *to put one's hand down*

bl·echern a **1.** *tin* (*can*); [pred] *made of tin* **2.** *tinny, brassy, harsh* (*sound, voice*) **bl·echern** vi [h] *to sound tinny* od *brassy*; (of tin-bells) *to sound*

bl·ecken vt [h] (of dogs) die Zähne ~ *to show the teeth*

Blei m ~s ~e ⟨ich⟩ = Brassen

Blei n ~s **1.** ⟨chem⟩ *lead* ‖ ~ in Mulden *pig-lead*; Tafel≃ *sheetlead* ‖ aus ~ *made of lead, leaden* ‖ mit ~ überziehen, füllen *to lead*; (Würfel) mit ~ belasten, beschweren *to load*; mit ~ beschwert *loaded* (*cane*) **2.** (Senk≃, Lot) *lead, plummet* **3.** (~ zum Schreiben etc) (*black*) *lead*; Reiß≃ *graphite* ‖ (~stift) *pencil*; in ~ geschrieben *pencilled, in pencil*; e–e Zeile mit ~ schreiben *to pencil a line* **4.** (~kugel, Schrot) *shot, slug* **5.** ⟨fig⟩ schwer wie ~ *as heavy as lead*; m–e Beine sind schwer wie ~ *my legs are as heavy* *as lead*; es liegt mir wie ~ in den Gliedern *my limbs feel like lead*

Bl·ei- [in comp] *lead* .. **~akkumulator** m *lead storage battery* **~arbeiter** m *plumber* **~baum** m *lead tree* **~belag** m: (Behälter) mit ~ *lead-lined* (*container*) **~benzin** n *tetraethyl lead fuel*, ⟨Am⟩ *l.-doped gasoline* **~bergwerk** n *lead mine* **~blech** n *sheet-lead* **~dach** n *leaden roof*; *leads* [pl] **~draht** m *lead wire* **~erz** n *lead ore* **~essig** m ⟨pharm⟩ *solution of basic lead acetate and lead oxide* **≈farben** a *leaden*, *lead-coloured*; *livid*; ⟨zoo⟩ *plumbeous* **~feder** f = Bleistift **~folie** f *lead foil* **~fuß** m ⟨typ⟩ *metal mount* **~gießen** n ⟨Ger⟩ *the pouring of molten lead into water* **~gelb** n *massicot* **~gewicht** n (am Lot) *plumb*, *plummet* **~gießerei** f *lead-foundry* **~glanz** m *galena*, *lead glance* (od *sulphide*) **~glas** n *lead-glass* **~glasur** f *lead-glazing* **~glätte** f *litharge* **~guß** m ⟨arts⟩ *the art of founding objects out of lead* **≈haltig** a *plumbiferous*; *lead-bearing* (Glas) **~hütte** f *lead works* [pl] **~kammer** f *leaden chamber* **~klotz** m, **~klumpen** m ⟨fig⟩ *clog*, *encumbrance* **~kolik** f *lead colic* **~kristall** m *lead crystal* **~korrektur** f ⟨typ⟩ *correcting of composition* **~kugel** *lead-ball* (od *bullet*, *shot*), *shot*, *slug*; [koll] ~n [pl] *shot* (: *a handful of sh.*), *lead* **~legierung** f *alloy of lead* **~linien** f [pl] ⟨typ⟩ *lead rules* [pl] **~lot** n *plumb-line* **~lötung** f *lead-soldering* **~mantel** m (am Kabel) *lead sheath* (od *covering*) **~mennige** f *red lead* **~muffe** f ⟨el⟩ *lead sleeve* **~oxid** n *lead oxide*; → Bleiglätte, Massicot **~pflaster** m ⟨pharm⟩ *diachylon*; *lead plaster* **~platten** f [pl] *leads* [pl] **~rohr** n *lead pipe* **~rot** n *red lead*, *minium* (L) **~rute** f (Glasmalerei) *lead* **~salbe** f ⟨pharm⟩ *lead-ointment* **~salz** n *plumbate* **~schwamm** m *spongy lead* **≈schwer** a ⟨fig⟩ *as heavy as lead* **~soldaten** m [pl] *tin-soldiers* [pl] **~stift** m *lead pencil*; *pencil*; flüssiger ~ *liquid l. p.*; Dreh–, Druck–, Füll≈ *eversharp*; → Blei 3.; Mine ‖ ~halter [m] *pencil-case*; ~hülle [f] *pencil-point protector*; ~spitzer [m] *pencil-sharpener*; ~spitzmaschine [f] *pencil-sharpening machine*; ~verlängerer [m] *pencil extension*; ~zahlen [f pl] *pencilled figures* [pl] ‖ ~zeichnung [f] *pencil-drawing*; (*black*) *lead drawing* **~streifen** m (an Fenstern) *lead-line* **~sulfat** n *sulphate of lead* **~superoxid** n *lead peroxide* **~tetraäthyl** n *tetra-ethyl lead* **~vergiftung** f *lead* (od *saturnine*) *poisoning*, *plumbism*; an ~ leidend *saturnine* **~verglasung** f: (Fenster mit) ~ *leaded windows* **~verschluß** m *leading*; unter ~ *sealed with lend* **~wasser** n *lead water* (od *lotion*), *solution of acetate of lead*, *Goulard* (*water*) **~weiß** n *white lead*; *ceruse*; *cremnitz* **~wurz** f ⟨bot⟩ *plumbago* **~zucker** m *sugar of lead*

Bl·eibe f (Obdach) *shelter* ‖ *abode*; *lodging*; *rooms* [pl]; *accommodation* ‖ *keep* ‖ k–e ~ h *to be houseless*, *to have no roof over one's head*

bl·eiben vi [s] [blieb/geblieben] **A. 1.** (ausharren) *to remain*; (⟨fam⟩ *to be here to*) *stay*; *stop* (im Bett *in bed*; bei jdm *with a p*); in London ~ *to stay up*; zum Tee ~ *to stay* od *stop to tea*, ⟨fam⟩ *to stay tea* ‖ zu Hause ~ *to stay* od *stop in*; *to stay behind*; draußen ~ *to stay out*; ich kann hier nicht (weiter) ~ *I cannot stay* (*on*) *here*; länger ~, als man willkommen ist *to outstay one's welcome*; an Ort u Stelle ~ *to stay put* | auf dem Wege ~ *to hold on one's way*; ~ Sie immer links *keep always to the left* ‖ derselbe ~ *to remain o.s.* | **es** wird schön(es Wetter) ~ *it'll keep fine*, → B. 1. **2.** ⟨übtr⟩ **a. auf** e–m Posten ~ *to continue* od *remain at a post* ‖ **in** der Kirche ~ *to remain in the Church* ‖ **der Meinung** ~ *to remain of opinion* ‖ f. sich ~ *to keep to o.s.* ‖ **auf** dem Spielplan ~ (of plays) *to continue to be played* **b. am** Leben ~ *to remain alive*; *to survive* ‖ → Ruder | → Spiel | **bei etw** ~ *to abide by*, *to keep to*; *to adhere* od *stick to*; bleib dabei! ⟨Am fam⟩ *keep at it*!; (beharrlich) *to persist in*, *to insist on a th*; bei der S, °bei der Stange ~ *to stick to the point*; nicht bei der S ~ *to wander from the point* ‖ es bleibt beim alten (*or*, wie es war) *things remain as they were*; im Grunde blieb doch alles beim alten *there was no real change after all*; es bleibt dabei *it's agreed* od *done*, *it's a bargain*; dabei kann es nicht ~ *the matter cannot rest there*; u dabei bleibt es! *and there it stands*! ‖ u wo bleib' ich? *what is there in it for me*? | **im Gange** ~ *to keep going*; im Gedächtnis ~ *to be remembered* ‖ in Gunst ~ bei jdm ⟨fam⟩ *to keep in with a p*; in der Schwebe ~ *to be kept in suspense* | **ohne Erfolg** ~ *to be of no avail* ‖ ohne Folgen ~ *to be without* (od *to have no*) *consequences* | **unter:** das muß unter uns ~ *let us keep this between ourselves* ‖ unter jds Aufsicht ~ *to be kept under a p's care* | bleib mir **vom Leibe!** *stand off*! *leave me alone*! ‖ bleib davon! *keep clear of it*! ‖ wissen, **wo** man bleibt *to know which side one's bread is buttered* ‖ wo bleibt er nur? wo ist er geblieben? *what has become of him*? ‖ wo bleibt hier die Objektivität? *where is here the required objectiveness*? **4.** (übrig~) **a.** ⟨math⟩ drei v sechs bleibt drei *three from six leaves three* **b.** e–e Hoffnung bleibt noch *one hope remains*; sechs s–r Stücke sind uns geblieben *six of his plays remain to us* **5.** ⟨typ⟩ bleibt! (= bleibt stehen) *stet* (L) **6.** (im Kampfe fallen) *to fall in battle*, *to perish*, auf dem Feld der Ehre ~ *to remain on the field of honour*; auf dem Platze ~ *to be killed* od *slain*; *to be lost at sea* **7. etw ~lassen** = unterlassen ‖ das werde ich schön ~l *I'll see you further first* ‖ ich würde das ~l *I should let that business alone*; das wirst du schön ~l *I defy you to do it* ‖ nimm's oder laß es ~! *take it or leave it*! **B.** [mit pred Ergänzung] **1. [mit Adj.]** *to continue*, *remain*, *keep* ‖ bitte, ~ Sie **bedeckt** *please, be covered, Sir*; ernst ~ *to preserve one's gravity*; fest ~ *to hold out*; *to stand fast*, *to stand it out*; gelassen ~ *to keep one's temper*; geöffnet ~ *to be kept open*; geschlossen ~ *to stay closed*; gesund ~ *to continue in good health*; bleib schön gesund! *take care of yourself*!; sich gleich ~ *to be always the same*; *to remain o.s.*; glücklich ~ *to continue happy*; ledig ~ *to remain single*; ruhig ~ *to keep quiet*; wir blieben r. *we kept our heads*; schön ~ → A. 1.; ~ Sie so (*sc.* sitzen *etc*)! ⟨arts fam⟩ *hold it*! **treu** ~ *to remain faithful*; jdm, e–r S t. ~ *to stick to a p, a th*; *to stand by* (od *to*) *a p, a th*; s–n Prinzipien t. ~ *to stick* (od *stand*) *to one's guns*; unbestraft ~ *to go unpunished*; unerledigt ~ *to stand over* **2. [mit Subst.] Christ** ~ *to stay Christian*; ich beibe dein Freund *I continue your friend*; wir ~ Freunde, wir ~ die alten *we keep friends*; sein Schicksal bleibt ein Rätsel *his fate remains* (od *rests*) *a mystery* | derselbe ~ *to remain o.s.* **3.** bleibe, was du bist *stay what you are*; es bleibt abzuwarten *it remains to be seen* **C. [mit Infinitiv]** in e–m Zustand erhalten ~ *to be preserved in a condition* | hängen~ *to catch*, *to be caught* (in *in*); → Fuß ‖ °⟨school⟩ *not to get one's remove* | kleben~ *to stick* (an *to*) | liegen~ (P) *to remain* od *stay in bed* ‖ (of work) *to stand over*; *to be discontinued* | sitzen~ *to remain sitting* (od *seated*) ‖ ⟨school⟩ *not to get one's remove* ‖ (nicht tanzen) *to sit out* ‖ sitzengeblieben s (of women) *to be on the shelf* | stecken~ *to stick* (*in the mud*) ‖ (in der Rede) *to break down* | stehen~ 1. (anhalten) *to stop* (*short*); alles blieb stehen *everybody stopped*; nicht stehen~! *move on*!; m–e Uhr ist stehengeblieben *my watch has stopped*; wo sind wir gestern stehengeblieben? *where did we leave off yesterday*? 2. *to remain standing* ‖ e–e Kirche, von der nur ein Teil der Kanzel stehengeblieben ist *a church with only a portion of the chancel left standing*

Bl·eiben n *stay* **bl·eibend** a (dauernd) *permanent, lasting*; ~er Eindruck m *lasting* (od *ineffaceable*) *impression* ‖ → frei~

bleich a **1.** *pale, pallid* (*cheeks, complexion*); *wan* ‖ ~ vor *pale with*; kreide~ *as white as a sheet*; toten~ *ashen* (*face*), *ashy-pale* ‖ ~ w *to turn pale, to pale* | [pred] (P) *off colour* **2.** *faint, faded, pale* (*colour*); ~ w (of colour, etc) *to fade* | *dim, pale* (*moonlight*)

Bl·eich- [in comp] *bleaching* **~erde** f *bleaching clay* **~flotte** f ⟨chem⟩ *bleaching bath* od *liquor* **~gesicht** n *pale-face* **~kalk** m = Chlorkalk **~mittel** n *bleaching agent* **~platz** m *bleaching-place* **~pulver** n *bleaching powder, bleach* **~sucht** f ⟨med⟩ *anaemia, chloremia, chlorosis*; *anaemic characteristics* ‖ ⟨bot⟩ *chlorosis* **≈süchtig** a *chlorotic*; *anemic*; *chloremic*; *having anemic symptoms*

Bl·eichart, Bleicher(t) m *light-red wine*

Bl·eiche f **1.** [abstr] *paleness, pallor* **2.** (Bleichen) *bleaching* **3.** (Ort des Bleichens) *bleaching-croft* (od *ground*)

bl·eichen I. vt/i **1.** vt [h] (Wäsche) *to bleach* ‖ ⟨tech⟩ (Flachs etc) *to whiten* ‖ (of age Haar) *to blanch, whiten* **2.** vi [s] *to bleach* ‖ *to whiten, to grow white*; (of hair) *to blanch* | (of colours) *to fade* **II.** ≈ n *bleaching*; *bleach* (*in the sun*) ‖ Gefäß zum ~ *bleacher* **Bl·eicher** m *bleacher*

Bl·eide f ⟨hist⟩ *medieval catapult*

Bl·eie f ⟨ich⟩ = Brassen

bl·eien vt [h] gebleit *leaded* (*fuel*)

bl·eiern a **1.** *lead* (*bullet*), *leaden* **2.** ⟨fig⟩ *leaden* (*sleep*); ~e Schwere *leadenness* | [pred] *leaden* (: *her hand was l.*); *as heavy as lead*; ~ liegen auf *to lie heavy on*

Bl·end-~arkade f ⟨arch⟩ *blind-story*; *dead* od *blank arcature* **~belästigung** f ⟨mot⟩ *glare nuisance* **~bogen** m ⟨arch⟩ *dead arcade, blind arch* **≈frei** a ⟨phot⟩ *dazzle free*; *non-glare* (Taste) **~glas** n *darkening-glass* **~laterne** f *bull's eye, dark lantern*; ⟨mot⟩ *dazzle-lamps* od *lights* [pl] **~leder** n *blinker*, [mst pl ~] *blinkers* pl **~rahmen** m *window frame* ‖ ⟨paint⟩ *wooden frame covered with canvas* **~schutz** m ⟨mot⟩ *visor, anti-dazzle, glare eliminator* | ~brille [f] *antidazzle goggles* | ~glas [n] ⟨mot⟩ *tinted glass* | ~scheibe [f] *visor*; *anti-glare screen* **~stein** m ⟨arch⟩ *facing brick* **~triforium** n ⟨ec arch⟩ *blind stor(e)y* **~werk** n **1.** ⟨fort⟩ *blindage* **2.** *frippery, jugglery, hocus-pocus*; *deception, delusion, mockery* ‖ jdm ein ~ vormachen *to delude a p* **~wirkung** f ⟨at⟩ *flash-blindness*

Bl·ende f ~/~n **A. 1.** ⟨fort⟩ *blindage*; *mantlet*; *screen* ‖ Stahl≈ *steel loop-hole plate* **2. a.** (Schutzschirm) *screen, blind*; *folding screen* **b.** (an e–r Mütze) *peak* **c.** = Blendleder **d.** ⟨tech⟩ *guard, screen* **e.** ⟨mar⟩ (vor den Kajütenfenstern) *dead-light* **f.** (Panzer≈) *shielded port* **g.** ⟨theat⟩ *shutter, blinders* pl ⟨Am⟩ *light curtain* **3.** ⟨arch⟩ *blind door* od *window*; *blind niche* **4. a.** (am Rock) *lapel* **b.** (am Kleid) *coloured* (*or glossy*) *braiding* (od *stripe*) **c.** ⟨opt & phot⟩ *aperture*; *stop*; Iris≈ *iris-diaphragm* ‖ ⟨film⟩ Sektoren≈ *sector-diaphragm* **B.** ⟨minr⟩ *blende*

bl·enden I. vt/i [h] **A.** vt **1.** ⟨eig⟩ (jdn) *to blind* **2.** ⟨übtr⟩ (jdn, die Augen) *to blind, dazzle* [oft pass] **3.** (abschwächen) (Glanz, helles Licht) *to deaden, tarnish* ‖ (Pelz) *to dye dark* ‖ → abblenden; tarnen **4.** ⟨fig⟩ (jdn, jds Sinne) *to dazzle, deceive, hoodwink, humbug*; **sich ~ l** *to be deceived* ‖ → verblenden **B.** vi **1.** (of light) *to glare*; *to dazzle the eyes*; *to be dazzling*; e–e Laterne –dete mir plötzlich ins Gesicht *I had a l. flashed in my f.* **2.** (P) *to dazzle*, ⟨Am sl⟩ *to four-flush* **II.** ≈ n **1.** *blinding* (*of a p*) **2.** ⟨übtr⟩ *dazzling, dazzle* **bl·endend I.** a **1.** *dazzling, glaring* (*light*); ~es Licht, ~er Glanz *glare* ‖ *phantasmagoric* (*brilliancy*); → leuchten; nicht ~ *glare-free, non-glare* [attr] **2.** °⟨fig⟩ *brilliant* (*ideal*); *dazzling, flashy, gorgeous, meteoric*; *specious, splendid*; ⟨Am sl⟩ *corking* (*salary*), *ripping*; das ist ~ *that's corking* (od *a corker*); °~ aussehen *to look marvellous* ‖ ein ~er Kerl, e–e ~e S ⟨sl⟩ *a corker, a ripper* (→ Pracht-); durch Schein ~e Redekunst *flash oratory* **II.** adv **1.** *dazzlingly* (*white*) **2.** °⟨fig⟩ *dazzlingly, ripping* (*rapid*); *gorgeously, splendidly*

Bl·enden- ⟨phot⟩ **~nummer** f *numerical aperture* **~öffnung** f *lense aperture*; *diaphragm* **~skala** f *l. a.* od *d. scale* **~stellung** f *stop*

Bl·ender m **1.** ⟨übtr⟩ (Pferd) *flat-catcher* **2.** ⟨fig⟩ **a.** (P) *a dazzler*, ⟨Am sl⟩ *four-flusher*; (Halbwisser) *sciolist* **b.** *dazzling expression*; *flash of wit* **Bl·endling** m **1.** = Mischling **2.** = Blender 2.

Bl·endung f ~/~en **1.** ⟨eig⟩ *blinding* (*of a p*) **2.** ⟨übtr⟩ *dazzling* (*of the eyes*); ⟨mot⟩ *glare* **3.** ⟨fig⟩ *deception, hoodwinking* (*of a p*); *delusion, illusion*

Blenheim, Blindheim (Donau-Dorf in Bayern) ‖ Schlacht bei ~ (*or* Höchstädt) *battle of B.* (1704)

Bl·enker m = Blinker 2.

Blennorrh·öe f ⟨med⟩ *blennorrhœa*

Bleß m = Blesse 2.

Bl·eßbock m ⟨zoo⟩ (Antilope) ⟨SAfr⟩ *blesbok*

Bl·esse f ~/~n **1.** (weißer Stirnfleck) (T) *blaze, white spot* **2.** *horse* od *cow with a blaze on its face*

Bl·eßhuhn n ⟨orn⟩ *bald coot*

bleu [blø:] a Fr ⟨mod, tail⟩ *blue*

Bl·euel m ~s/~ *beetle, beater*; *mallet* ‖ ~stange = Pleuelstange **bl·euen** vt [h] (jdn) *to beat*, ⟨fam⟩ *to hide* ‖ → durch~, ein~, ver~

Bl·ick m ~(e)s/~e **I.** (Aufblitzen) *blaze, flash, gleam* (*of the sun*); → Silber≈ **II.** (~ des Auges) **1.** *look* (auf, nach *at*; in *into*; über *over*); *eye* (auf *on*); *peep, sight, view* (auf *of*); ⟨sl⟩ *dekko* | auffordernder ~ *come-hither look* ‖ ausdrucksvoller ~ *speaking look* ‖ e–n besorgten ~ auf jdn werfen *to glance* (*with solicitude* od) *anxiously at a p* ‖ böser ~ *evil eye*; drohender ~ *eye of menace*; durchdringender ~ *glare*; mit erfahrenem ~ *with a knowing eye*; finsterer ~ *scowl*; e–n flehentlichen ~ auf jdn werfen *to give a p a look of appeal*; flüchtiger ~ *glance* (auf *at*; über *over*), *glimpse* (auf *of*); *dip* (in *into*); ⟨Am⟩ *peek* ‖ flüchtiger, prüfender ~ ⟨Am⟩ *once-over* ‖ offener ~ *open countenance*; *straight eyes*; prüfender ~ *scrutinizing look*; e–n scharfen ~ h f *to be sharp-eyed for*, .. bek *to develop an eye for* ..; mit gesenktem ~ *with hooded lids* ‖ starrer ~ (*steady*) *gaze* ‖ mit e–m unverschämten ~ im Auge *with an insolent look* od *glint in the eye*; verstohlener ~ *peep*; *furtive* (od *stealthy*) *glance* | ein ~ des schärfsten Mißtrauens *a glance of keen distrust* ‖ ein ~ in die Zukunft *a vision of* (*glimpse into*) *the future*; *a forward look* (od *glance*); mit e–m ~ in die Z. *with an eye to the future* ‖ s–m ~ entzogen *vanished from his gaze* **2. a. auf** den ersten ~, beim ersten ~ *at a glance, at first sight* od *view, at the first blush, glimpse* od *glance*; *on the face of it*; auf den ersten ~ sehen *to see with half an eye* ‖ mit e–m ~ *at a glance, with half an eye* **b.** sein erster ~ **war nach** der Tür *his first glance was for the door* **c.** jds ~ [dat] ausweichen *to avoid a p's eyes* ‖ jdn mit dem ~ **durchbohren** *to look daggers at a p, to look a p through* ‖ e–n ~ gleiten l über *to run a glance over* ‖ jds ~ lenken auf *to direct a p's eyes to* ‖ den ~ richten *to glance one's eye* (auf *at*) ‖ den ~ senken *to look down* ‖ jds ~ treffen *to catch a p's eye* ‖ e–n ~

tun *to have a look* (auf *at*; in *into*); ⟨sl⟩ *to take a dekko*; e–n flüchtigen ~ tun *to get* (od *catch*) *a glimpse* (in etw *of a th*) ‖ jdn mit prüfendem ~ mustern *to give a p the once-over* ‖ mit einem ~ übersehen *to see with half an eye* ‖ unter s–m scharfen ~ *under his keen eye* ‖ e–n ~ richten, werfen auf *to take a look at* (*a th*), *to cast a glance at, to cast an eye on* (*a th*) ‖ jds forschendem ~ standhalten *to meet the search of a p's eye steadily* ‖ jdn mit s–n ~en verfolgen, k–n ~ v jdm wenden *to keep a close eye on a p* ‖ e–r S e–n ~ zuwerfen *to give a look at a th*; jdm e–n (ängstlichen) ~ zuwerfen *to cast* od *shoot a* (*troubled*) *glance at a p, to shoot* od *throw a p a* (*troubled*) *glance*; jdm e–n einladenden ~ zuwerfen ⟨fam⟩ *to give a p the glad eye, to make eyes at a p, to ogle a p* ‖ jdm e–n verstohlenen ~ von der Seite zuwerfen *to steal a sideways glance at a p* **II.** (Aussicht) *view, prospect* (auf *of*); mit e–m ~ auf das Meer (*a room*) *with a view of the sea* **III.** ⟨fig⟩ (Urteilskraft) *eye, insight, imagination, intuition*; *vision*; e–n ~ h. f. *to have an eye for*; mit intuitivem ~ *with intuition, intuitively*; ein Mann mit klarem ~ *a clear head*; *a man of penetration*

Bl·ick- ~fang m ⟨com⟩ *eye-catch(er)* **~feld** n ⟨opt⟩ *vision-field, visual field, field of vision*; → Gesichtsfeld | ⟨übtr⟩ *purview, range, scope* (: *within the purview of his studies*) **~feuer** n → Leuchtfeuer **~linie** f ⟨opt⟩ *visual line, line of vision* **~punkt** m ⟨opt⟩ *visual point, point of vision* od *sight* | ⟨übtr⟩ (Brennpunkt) *focus*; in den ~ rücken *to bring into f.*; im ~ des öffentlichen Lebens stehen *to be in the public eye*, ⟨fam⟩ *to be in the news* **~winkel** m ⟨opt⟩ *visual angle*

Bl·icke f ~/~n ⟨ich⟩ *bleak, blay, ablet*

bl·icken vi [h] **1. a.** *to look* (auf, nach *at*; in *into*; über *over*); zur Seite ~ *to look sideways* | **erstaunt** ~ *to look one's astonishment* ‖ finster ~ *to scowl* (auf *at, on*) ‖ flüchtig ~ *to glance, to glimpse* (auf *at*) ‖ er blickte mitleidig *his eyes looked compassion* ‖ jdm scharf in die Augen ~ *to look a p squarely in the eyes* **b.** (betrachten) **auf jdn ~** *to look* (*up*)*on a p* (als *as*) **2.** ⟨übtr⟩ (S) *to appear, to make one's appearance, to emerge*; (of the sun) *to break* od *burst* (*through*); *to peep, to loom* (*through*) ‖ Verachtung blickte aus s–n Augen *his eyes looked contempt* **3.** ~ l *to show* ‖ das läßt tief ~! ⟨fig⟩ *that is very significant!, that does unfold a tale!, that speaks volumes* | **sich ~ l** *to make one's* (od *put in an*) *appearance*; laß dich nicht wieder ~ *I hope I have seen the last of you*; du läßt dich ja gar nicht mehr ~ *you make yourself scarce, you're quite a stranger*

bl·ieb 1. & 3. sg pret v bleiben

blies 1. & 3. sg pret v blasen

blind I. a **A.** (P) **1.** *blind* (*p*); auf e–m Auge ~ *blind of an eye* ‖ stock~ *stone-blind* ‖ jdn ~ m *to blind a p* ‖ ~er Fleck (der Netzhaut) *blind spot* **2.** ⟨übtr⟩ *blind, fond* (*parents*); *blinded*; ~ f *or* gegen *blind to* (*a p's weaknesses*), *to see nothing of* ‖ jdn ~ m *to blind a p* (gegen *to*) ‖ ~ s f etw *to be oblivious to a th*; wenn du nicht ganz ~ wärest, so würdest du .. *if you had half an eye, you would* .. **3.** ~er Passagier *deadhead*; ⟨mar⟩ *stowaway* **B. 1.** (of feelings, etc.) *blind* ‖ ~er Eifer schadet nur *more haste less speed* ‖ ~er Gehorsam *blind* (od *implicit, unquestioning*) *obedience* ‖ ~er Glaube *blind* od *implicit faith* ‖ ~er Haß *unreasoning hatred* ‖ ~e Liebe *blind love* ‖ in ~er Wut *in a blind fury* **2.** (dunkel) ~e Gewalten [pl] *blind agents* od *forces* ‖ ein ~er Zufall *a mere chance* **C.** (S) **1.** (trübe) *dull, tarnished* (mirror); *dead* **2.** (nur z Schein gemacht) ~e Tür *blind* (od *blank*) door; ~es Fenster *blind window*; ~e Mauer *dead-wall*; → Blendbogen ‖ ⟨typ⟩ ~er Bogen *blank sheet*; ~es Material *blank material* ‖ ~er Alarm *or* Lärm *false alarm* ‖ ~e Versteigerung *sham auction* ‖ → Blindgänger, Platzpatrone **3.** (versteckt) *concealed, hidden* ‖ ~e Klippe *sunken rock* **4.** ~er Fleck (im Auge) *blind spot* **II.** adv **1.** ~ entwickeln ⟨phot⟩ *to develop without visual control* ‖ ⟨fig⟩ (kopflos) *blindly*; *rashly*; ~ gehorchen *to obey implicitly* ‖ → blindlings **2.** ⟨aero⟩ ~ fliegen *to fly on instruments*; ~ fliegen zwischen 2 Wolldecken (schlafen) ⟨hum⟩ *to press blankets*; ⟨mil & aero⟩ ~ laden *to load with a blank-cartridge* ‖ ~ schießen *to fire* (*with*) *blank-cartridges*; *to fire in the air* **3.** ~ schreiben (auf der Schreibmaschine) *to write blindfold* (od *without looking at the keys*) ‖ ⟨chess⟩ ~ spielen *to play blindfold*

Bl·ind- [in comp] *blind* .. **~anflug** m ⟨aero⟩ *instrument* od *blind approach* | ~verfahren [n] *b. a. procedure* od *system* **~boden** m ⟨arch⟩ *false floor* **~bombenwurf** m *blind bombing* **~darm** m ⟨anat⟩ *caecum* (L), *blindgut*; ⟨med⟩ *appendix* | ~entzündung [f] *appendicitis* | ~operation [f] (–entfernung) *appendectomy* ‖ z ~ gehörig *caecal* **~druck** m ⟨typ⟩ *blind blocking* od *tooling*; *relief-printing* **~fliegen 1.** n ⟨aero⟩ *instrument* od *blind flying* **2.** ≗ vi [s] *to fly on instruments*; *to ride the beam* **~flug** m *instrument flight*, ~ zwischen 2 Wolldecken (Schlaf) ⟨aero hum⟩ *blanket drill* **~gänger** m *blind* od *unexploded shell* od *bomb*; ⟨sl⟩ *dud* **≗geboren** a *blind-born* **~holz** n *plywood core* (*between veneers*) **~landung** f ⟨aero⟩ *instrument landing* **~material** n ⟨print, typ⟩ *spacing material* **~maus** f ⟨zoo⟩ *blind mole-rat* **~ort** m ⟨min⟩ *dummy drift* **~prägung** f = Blinddruck *relief printing* **~sack** m ⟨med⟩ *blind pouch* **~schleiche** f ⟨zoo⟩ *slow-worm, blind-worm*; *coecilian* **~spannung** f ⟨el⟩ *reactive voltage* | ~skomponente [f] *reactive, idle* od *wattless component of voltage* **~spiel** n ⟨chess⟩ *blindfold match* **~strom** m ⟨el⟩ (Ggs Wirkstrom) *reactive* od *idle current* | ~komponente [f] *idle, reactive* od *wattless component of the current*

Bl·inde m [der ~, ein ~r] ~n/~n **1.** *the blind man*; die ~ *the blind woman* ‖ die ~n [pl] *the blind* [pl] | das sieht selbst ein ~r, das kann ein ~r mit dem Stocke fühlen *that's as clear as* (*noon*) *day* ‖ er versteht sich darauf wie der ~ auf die Farben *he knows as much about it as the man in the moon* ‖ wie der ~ v der Farbe reden *to talk without understanding* ‖ unter den ~n ist der Einäugige König *among the blind a one-eyed man is king* **2.** ⟨cards⟩ *dummy*

Bl·indekuh f *blind man*, ⟨Scot⟩ *blind-harry*; ~spiel *blind-man's buff*; ~ spielen *to play at blindman's buff*

Bl·inden- [in comp] *blind* **~anstalt** f *blind-asylum, asylum for the blind* **~druck** m *Braille* **~erziehung** f *blind education* **~hund** m *blind man's dog*; ⟨Am a.⟩ *seeing-eye dog* **~schrift** f *Braille*

Bl·indheit f ~/~en *blindness*; → Tag≗ Nacht≗ ‖ ⟨übtr⟩ *blindness* (gegen *to*) ‖ jdn mit ~ schlagen *to strike a p blind, to smite* od *strike a p with blindness*

bl·indlings a ⟨fig⟩ **1.** (kopflos) *blindly, blindfold* (: *to sail blindfold*); *at random* (: *to fire at r.*); *headlong, recklessly, pell-mell*; *slap, slap-bang, slap-dash*; *with a rush*; ~ handeln *to go it blind* **2.** (ohne Zögern) ~ gehorchen *to obey implicitly*

Bl·indlingsspiel n = Blindspiel

Blink m ~s/~e **1.** *blink*; *momentary flash* od *gleam of light*; Eis≗ *iceblink* **2.** ⟨mar⟩ = Blinkfeuer | ~bake [f] ⟨aero⟩ *flash(ing) beacon* | ~feuer [n] *flashing-light, intermittent flash-light, blinker* | ~gerät [n] *flash* od *signal lamp* | ~lampe [f], ~licht [n] ⟨mot⟩ *winker*, ~ f Fahrtrichtungsänderung (*left-, right-)turn signal* | ∼signal [n] *flash signal*

bl·inken I. vi [h] **1.** (glänzen) (*of the sun*, etc.) *to blink, to cast a momentary flash of light; to gleam* od *shine intermittently* ‖ (glitzern) *to glitter* ‖ (*of stars*) *to twinkle* (v *with*); *to wink* ‖ (of armour) *to flash, gleam* ‖ (of eyes) *to wink* | ⟨übtr⟩ *to flash, gleam* **2.** (blicken) *to blink, twinkle, wink; peep*; mit den Augen ∼ nach *to wink at* **II.** ∼̂ n **1.** *blink, blinking* (*of light*) ‖ *flash, gleam* (*of armour*) **2.** *blink, wink* (*of the eye*) **bl·inkend** a *blinking* (*light*), *flashing, gleaming, glittering,* (*sword*)

Bl·inker m **1.** (P) *blinker* ‖ ⟨mil⟩ (P) (*lamp*) *signal(l)er* ‖ ⟨mot⟩ (S) *flasher, blinker* **2.** (an der Angelschnur) *spoon-bait*

bl·inkern vi [h] **1.** (glänzen) = blinken 1. **2.** (blicken) = blinken 2. **3.** (mit Blinker angeln) *to spoon*

bl·inzeln, †bl·inzen 1. vi [h] (mit den Augen ∼) *to blink*, ⟨scient⟩ *to nictitate, twinkle, wink* (nach *at*) ‖ ohne z ∼ *unblinkingly* ‖ → an-, zu-blinzeln **2.** ∼̂ n *blink, wink*

Blitz m ∼es/∼e **1.** *lightning*; Flächen∼̂ *sheet l.*; Kugel∼̂ *ball l.*; Linien∼̂ *chain l.*; Zickzack∼̂ *forked l.* ‖ ∼strahl *flash of l.* ‖ ∼e zuckten *lightnings flashed* ‖ vom ∼ erschlagen *struck by lightning* ‖ der ∼ schlug in ein Haus *lightning struck a house* | ⟨phot⟩ ∼(licht [n]) *flash*(-light), indirekter ∼ *bounce fl.-l.* **2.** ⟨übtr⟩ (of sun, light, etc.) *flash*; ⟨mar⟩ *flash-light* **3.** ⟨fig⟩ **a.** (Aufflammen) Geistes∼̂ *flash* od *coruscation of wit* ‖ ⟨poet⟩ die ∼e *the spurts* [pl] (*of conversation*) ‖ ⟨theat⟩ ∼e [pl] (Glanzstellen) *plums* [pl], *the pick* **b.** ∼e u Donnerschläge [pl] *buffets* (*of fate*) **4.** (Schnelligkeit) *lightning speed* **5.** [intj] Potz ∼! †*zounds*! **6. wie der ∼** *like lightning, like a streak* (*of lightning*), *lightning-like*; (*it was gone*) *in a flash* ‖ wie ein geölter ∼ (*quick as* od) *like greased lightning; like old boots, like a shot, like a house on fire* ‖ er lief wie der ∼, wie ein geölter ∼ *he ran like greased lightning*; es kam über ihn wie ein ∼ *it came upon him like a thunderbolt*; wie ein ∼ aus heiterem Himmel *like a bolt from the blue, like a thunderclap in a clear sky*; wie ein ∼ aus h. H. hineinplatzen in *to drop like a bolt from the blue into* (*the troops*) ‖ sich wie der ∼ verbreiten *to spread like wildfire* | der ∼ schlage drein! *damn it! the deuce take it! the devil!* ‖ wie vom ∼ getroffen ⟨fig⟩ *thunderstruck* | **trotz ∼** u Donner ⟨fig⟩ *whatever happens, roll, bowl, or pitch*

Bl·itz [in comp] *lightning* .. **∼ableiter** m *lightning-conductor*, ⟨Am⟩ *l.-rod* | ⟨fig⟩ (Sündenbock) *scapegoat* (f *for*) ∼anlage [f] *lightning protective apparatus* **∼anschluß** m ⟨phot⟩ *nipple* **∼̂artig 1.** a *lightning* (*blow, swiftness*); *lightning-like* **2.** adv ∼ zucken ⟨übtr⟩ *to flash*; ∼ zuckend *fulgurant* (*eye*) | (schnell) *in a flash* **∼aufnahme** f ⟨phot⟩ *flash exposure* **∼ausbildung** f ⟨bes mil⟩ *crash training* **∼auslöser** m ⟨phot⟩ *flash firing switch* **∼besuch** m *flying visit* ⟨fig⟩ ‖ e–n ∼ m bei ⟨fam⟩ *to nip over to* °**∼̂bl·ank** a **1.** *shining, bright* (*knife*); ∼ putzen *to polish* (*a th*) *to a dazzling glitter* **2.** ⟨fig⟩ *dapper, smart, spruce* (*girl*); [pred] *spick and span* ‖ ein ∼es Mädel, ∼er Fratz *a peach*, ⟨sl⟩ *a smashing line* ‖ (*she keeps the house*) *like a pin* ‖ er sah ∼ aus *he looked as if he had just come out of the band box* **∼entladung** f *lightning discharge* **∼feuer** n ⟨mar⟩ *quick flashing-light* **∼flugzeug** n *high-speed airplane* **∼gespräch** n ⟨telph⟩ *lightning* od *flash* (*long distance*) *call* **∼intervall** m ⟨el⟩ *time interval between two strokes* °**∼j·unge** m **∼k·erl** m *sharp* od *smart lad, the devil of a fellow, capital fellow* **∼kopie** f ⟨phot⟩ *flash copy* **∼krieg** m *blitz*(*krieg*); durch e–n ∼ besiegen *to blitz*; ∼ mit Atomwaffen *blitz atomic war* **∼lampe** f ⟨phot⟩ *flash gun* od *lamp* **∼licht** n ⟨phot⟩ *flash-light*; ∼aufnahme *flash-light photograph, flash exposure*; ∼birne [f] *photoflash, flash bulb*; ∼bombe [f] ⟨phot⟩ *flash bomb* ∼lampe [f] *flash-lamp*; ⟨theat⟩ *flash box*; ∼pulver [n] *flashlight powder*; ∼röhre [f] ⟨phot⟩ *flash tube* **∼linie** f *zigzag* °**∼mädel** n *sharp* od *smart girl, the devil of a girl* **∼nachricht** f *flash message* **∼röhre** f (im Sand) *fulgurite*; (Elektronenblitz) ⟨phot⟩ *electronic flash* **∼̂sauber** a = blitzblank **∼schlag** m *lightning-stroke; thunderclap*; (Entladung) *lightning-discharge* **∼̂schnell 1.** a *lightning* (*blow*); *lightning-fast* (*decision*); *quick as a wink* **2.** adv *with lightning speed; like lightning; like a shot; in a flash, in the twinkling of an eye*; → schnell wie **∼schutz(sicherung** f) m ⟨el⟩ *lightning protection fuse, l. arrester* **∼spruch** m *flash message* **∼strahl** m *flash of lightning* **∼telegramm** n *lightning telegram* **∼̂vergnügt** a = kreuzfidel **∼wäscherei** f *launderette* **∼̂wenig** a *damned little* ‖ ich mache mir ∼ daraus *I do not care a damn* **∼zug** m ⟨Am⟩ *lightning train* (od *express*)

bl·itzen vi/t [h] **I.** vi **A.** (*of lightning*) *to lighten; to flash*; [mst imps] es blitzt *it is lightning* **B.** ⟨übtr⟩ **1. a.** (of the sun, light, etc.) *to flash, to shine* (*into; through*); *to blink, coruscate, sparkle, twinkle; wink* ‖ (of arms) *to glance, gleam, glitter; flash* **b.** (of eyes) *to flash, lighten; to light up*; s–e Augen blitzten v Feuer *his eyes flashed with fire* **c.** (of talk, etc.) *to flash* (v *with*) ‖ (of feelings) Mut blitzte in s–m Auge *courage gleamed in his eye* **2.** (flitzen) *to flit, to flash* (*through*) **3.** °[imps] es blitzt bei ihr *her petticoat shows*; Fräulein, es blitzt ⟨Am fam⟩ *it snows down south* **II.** vt ⟨poet⟩ Feuer ∼ *to flash fire* (: *his eyes flashed fire*) **Bl·itzen** n *flash, flashing*

bl·itzend a *flashing; gleaming, glittering*

Bl·itzesschnelle f *lightning speed*; mit ∼ *with l. s.; in a flash*; → blitzschnell

Bl·ock m ∼s/∼̂e **A. 1.** (Baumstumpf) *block, stump* ‖ (Holz∼̂) (⟨for a.⟩ Bloch ⟨obd⟩) *log*; ⟨for⟩ *butt* | (Richt∼̂) *block; stocks* [pl]; → Stock ‖ Hack∼̂ *block* **2.** ⟨mech⟩ (hölzernes Gehäuse f. Rollen am Flaschenzug) *block* ‖ ⟨tech⟩ walzfertiger ∼ *slab, bloom* ‖ ⟨mar⟩ (∼ mit 3 Löchern) *dead eye*; → Jungfer **3.** (Metall∼̂) *bar, ingot, lump, pig*; → Barren **4.** *bar, cake* (*of soap*, etc.) **B.** Fels∼̂ *block; mass of rock; boulder*; erratischer ∼ *erratic block* od *boulder* **C.** (Masse *or* Vereinigung mehrerer Teile) **1.** (Häuser∼̂) *block*; in Blöcken gebaut *built in blocks* **2.** ⟨rail⟩ (e–r v mehreren Streckenabschnitten zwischen 2 Stationen) *block*; → ∼system **3.** ⟨Ger pol⟩ *bloc; coalition of several parties* **4.** ⟨nazi Ger⟩ *smallest subdivision of the Party* **5.** (gemeinsamer Einsatz) *pool; collective stakes* [pl] **6.** (Papier∼̂, Schreib∼̂) *block*; → Abreißkalender ‖ Fahrkarten∼̂ *book of tickets* **7.** ⟨comp⟩ (Ggs Datensatz) *physical record*

Bl·ock- [in comp] *block* .. **∼abschnitt** m ⟨rail⟩ *block section* **∼anordnung** f *unitized construction* **∼bildung** f *formation of blocks* **∼buch** n ⟨hist⟩ *block-book* **∼diagramm** n ⟨geog⟩ *relief-diagram*; ⟨tech⟩ *block diagram* **∼druck** m *block-printing* (*of calico*) **∼eis** n *block-ice* **∼fett** n *briquetted grease* **∼flöte** f ⟨mus⟩ *recorder* **∼̂frei** a ⟨pol⟩ *neutral; non-aligned* (*state*) **∼freiheit** f *non-alignment* **∼haus** n **1.** *log-house, log-cabin, blockhouse* **2.** ⟨fort⟩ *blockhouse* **∼heftung** f ⟨typ⟩ *block-stitching* **∼hütte** f *log-cabin, –house* **∼lehm** m ⟨geol⟩ *boulder-clay* **∼leiter** m ⟨nazi Ger⟩ *leader of a 'Block'*, → C. 4. **∼mehrheit** f ⟨Ger⟩ *coalition majority* **∼motor** m *block-motor* **∼partei** f ⟨Ger⟩ die ∼en [pl] *the coalition* **∼schrift** f ⟨typ⟩ *block* (od *capital*) *letters* [pl], in ∼ *in b. l.* **∼seife** f *bar-soap* **∼signal** n ⟨rail⟩ *block-signal* **∼station** f ⟨rail⟩ *block-station*, *signal-box* **~stelle** f ⟨rail⟩ *block station* **~strecke** f ⟨rail⟩ *block* **~system** n ⟨rail⟩ (z Regelung der Zugfolge) *block system* **~verband** m ⟨arch⟩ *block-bond* **~wagen** m *lorry*; (niedriger) *truck* **~wart** m ⟨nazi Ger⟩ = Blockleiter **~werk** n ⟨rail⟩ *block* **~zinn** n *block-tin*

Block·ade f ~/~n **1.** ⟨mil⟩ *blockade, blocking-up*; enge (weite) ~ *close* (*distant*) *blockade*; papierne ~ *paper b.* ‖ e–e ~ aufheben *to raise a blockade* ‖ die ~ brechen *or* umgehen *to run the b.* ‖ ein Land der ~ unterwerfen *to blockade a country* | geistige ~ ⟨psych⟩ *intellectual block-out* **2.** ⟨typ⟩ *turned letters* [pl] **~brecher** m ⟨mil⟩ *blockade-runner* **~bruch** m *blackade run*(*ning*) **~erklärung** f ⟨mil⟩ *declaration of blockade* **~linie** f *blockading line*

bl·ocken vt/i [h] **I.** vt **1.** ⟨rail⟩ (Strecke) *to block by block signal* **2.** (formen) (Hut) *to block* **3.** ⟨mil⟩ = blockieren **II.** vi (of birds of prey) *to be perched* (auf *on*) **bl·öcken** vt [h] = blocken I. 2. **bl·ockieren** vt [h] **1.** ⟨mil⟩ *to blockade, to block* (*up*); ⟨rail⟩ (Strecke) *to block by block signal* ‖ ⟨tech⟩ *to interlock* ‖ ⟨wir⟩ (Leitung) *to jam* ‖ ⟨übtr⟩ *to block, obstruct* ‖ blockiert ⟨com⟩ *frozen* (*capital*) **2.** ⟨typ⟩ (Wort etc) *to mark by turned letters, thus*: ■ **Block·ierung** f ~/~en ⟨mil⟩ *blocking-up, blockade*; ⟨rail⟩ *blocking* ‖ ⟨übtr⟩ *obstruction* | ~srelais [n] ⟨el⟩ *interlocking relay*

Bl·ocksberg m ⟨Ger⟩ → Brocken

blöd a [nur pred] = blöde

bl·öde a **1.** †(schwach) *weak* (*stomach, eyes*) **2.** ⟨med⟩ (schwachsinnig) *imbecile, weak-minded* **3.** (schüchtern) *bashful, shy, timid* **4.** (dumm) *dull, imbecile, stupid, dull-witted* **5.** °[verblaßt] *fatuous* (*smile*), *foolish*; *idiotic* (*killing*); *senseless*; *silly*; ⟨sl⟩ *goofy* (*p*); *bloody*; *footling* (*play*); °~er Hund, ~es Schwein *idiotic goof, a bloody idiot*; gibt es etw ~eres? *is there anything more idiotic*? †**Blöde** f = Blödheit **bl·ödeln** vi *to talk nonsense*; *to fool* (mit *with*) **Blödesein** n ~s/ (völliges) *amentia* **Bl·ödheit** f *dullness, stupidity* ‖ → Blödigkeit ×**Blödl** m ~s/~ *duffer* °**Bl·ödian** m = Dummkopf **Bl·ödigkeit** f (Schüchternheit) *bashfulness, shyness, timidity* ‖ → **Blödheit** †**bl·ödsichtig** a *purblind, weak-sighted* **Bl·ödsinn** m **1.** ⟨med⟩ *idiocy, imbecility*; *weakness of mind*; Alters≈ *dementia senilis* [L] **2.** [verblaßt] °(Quatsch, Unsinn) *drivel, moonshine, nonsense, piffle, trash,* ⟨sl⟩ *bosh, hokum, rot*; ~ reden *to talk nonsense* od *rot*; das ist alles ~ *that is all bosh, that is all my eye*; gr ~ *big fiddlestick*; blühender ~, höherer ~ ⟨sl⟩ *tommyrot*; ~! ⟨sl⟩ *bosh*! *fiddlesticks* [pl], *fudge*! *rot*! (Unfug) *flim-flam, gaff, tricks* [pl]; ~ m *to play tricks* **bl·ödsinnig 1.** a **a.** ⟨med⟩ *weak-minded, idiotic*; (alters~) *silly* **b.** [verblaßt] °(dumm) *idiotic, silly, stupid*; *foolish*, ich bin nicht so ~ *I am not such a fool as that* **2.** adv *capitally, extremely,* ⟨sl⟩ *rippingly*; → riesig, kolossal **3.** ≈e m [der ~, ein ~r] ~n/~n *idiot*

Bl·ödsinnigkeit f *silliness, stupidity*

bl·öken 1. vi [h] (of sheep) *to bleat,* ⟨fam⟩ *to baa*; (of cattle) *to bellow, low* ‖ ⟨übtr⟩ (P) *to shout, roar* **2.** ≈ n *bleating*; *bellowing, lowing* ‖ ⟨übtr⟩ *shouting*

blond a **1.** (P) *blond*(*e*), *light auburn* (*hair*); *fair* (*complexion*); ein Mädchen mit ~em Haar, Aussehen *a fair-haired, blonde-complexioned girl* ‖ hell~ *light-blond*(*e*); dunkel~ *dark-blond*(*e*), *auburn* (*woman*); gold~ *golden-blond*(*e*) **2.** (hell) (S) *light* (*–coloured*); → Weiße ‖ ⟨poet⟩ ~e Jahre *years of youth* **Bl·ondchen** n ~s/~ ⟨fam⟩ *goldy-locks, goldilocks* **Bl·onde 1.** [der ~, ein ~r] m, die ~ *the blonde* **2.** (Seidenspitze) *blonde* (*lace*) **bl·ondgelockt** a *blonde-locked* **bl·ondhaarig** a *fair-haired* **Bl·ondheit** f *lightness of hair or complexion, blondness* **Blond·ine** f ~/~n *blonde*; *fair-haired woman*

bloß I. a **1.** (nackt) *bare, naked* (*feet, hands,* etc.); *stark*; *uncovered*; arm u ~ *very poor* ‖ mit ~en Beinen *barelegged*; mit ~en Füßen *barefoot, barefooted*; mit ~em Halse *bare-necked*; mit ~en Händen *with naked hands*; mit ~em Kopfe *bareheaded, uncovered* ‖ auf ~er Erde *on the bare ground* ‖ mit ~en Fäusten *with naked fists*; mit ~em Schwert *with a naked sword* ‖ (unbewaffnet) mit ~em Auge *with the naked* od *unaided eye* **2.** ⟨übtr⟩ (nichts als) *mere, simple*; [nur nach: *the*] *very* ‖ der ~e Gedanke *the very idea* ‖ in ~em Hemde *with only a shirt on* ‖ mit ~en 20 Mark *with a bare 20 marks* ‖ er war kein ~er Politiker *he was no mere politician* ‖ auf den ~en Verdacht hin *on the mere suspicion* ‖ v ~em Verstande beherrscht *ruled by intellect alone* od *only* ‖ sein ~es Wort *his bare* (od *naked, simple*) *word*; ~e Worte *mere* od *empty words* ‖ → nackt, rein **II.** adv (nur) **1.** *barely, merely, purely, simply*; *only*; *just* ‖ er kam ~, weil .. *he simply came, because* .. ‖ das Buch kostet ~ e–e Mark *the book costs only one mark* ‖ m Sie ~ k–n Lärm *don't you make a noise* ‖ komm ~ mal hierher *just come here* **2.** was hat er ~? *what may be the matter with him*? ‖ wo mag er ~ s? *where may he be, I wonder*? *I wonder where he is* ‖ wie kamst du ~ auf solchen Gedanken? *where on earth did you get such an idea*?; wie macht er denn das ~? *how in the world does he do it*?

°**Bl·oße** m ~n/~n; der ~ *the behind*

Bl·öße f ~/~n **1.** *nakedness, bareness* **2.** ⟨fenc⟩ *weak point* od *spot* ‖ ⟨mil⟩ ~en [pl] *weak points* od *spots* [pl] (*of a fortress*) ‖ ⟨übtr⟩ *weak side, weakness* (*of a p*) ‖ sich e–e ~ geben *to expose o.s., to commit* od *compromise o.s.*; er gab sich e–e ~ nach der andern *he left himself wide open* **3.** (Wald≈) *glade*; ⟨for⟩ *opening, gap*; *fail-place*; (Kahlschlag) *clearing*

bl·oß|legen vt [h] ⟨bes geol⟩ (Gestein etc) *to denude, expose* ‖ (alte Gebäude etc) *to uncover* ‖ ⟨tech⟩ *to visualize* | ⟨mil⟩ (e–n Flügel) *to uncover* | ⟨übtr⟩ (Verborgenes, Vergangenheit; Gefühle) *to lay bare*; *to unearth, unravel*; *disclose, reveal* **B.gung** f *uncovering* (*of the ruins of a palace*) ‖ ⟨geol⟩ *denudation*

bl·oß|stellen vt [h] ⟨fig⟩ (jdn) *to compromise* (*a p*); *to give* (*a p*) *away* ‖ **sich** ~ *to compromise* od *commit o.s.*; → blamieren

Bl·oßstellung f ⟨fig⟩ *compromise*

Bl·ücher: wie ~ *with a vengeance*

bl·ubbern vi *to give forth a bubbling sound*

°**Bl·ubo** m ⟨hum⟩ [abbr] f. ⟨nazi⟩ Blut und Boden

Bluff [blʌf, besser: bluf] [engl] m ~s/~s *bluff*; ⟨Am a.⟩ *strike* ‖ ~! *eye-wash*!; jds ~ auf die Probe stellen *to call a p's bluff* ‖ jdn durch e–n ~ bringen z *to bluff* od *bounce a p into* (*a confession*); **bl·uffen** [blʌfən] **I.** vt/i [h] **1.** vt (jdn) *to bluff* (durch *by*); *to bounce* **2.** vi *to bluff*; ⟨Am sl⟩ *to four-flush* **II.** ≈ n *bluff* **Bl·uffer** ['blʌfə] m *bluffer*; ⟨Am sl⟩ *four-flusher*

bl·ühen vi [h] **1. a.** ⟨eig⟩ *to bloom, blossom, blow, flower*; *to be in bloom* od *blossom* **b.** ⟨fig⟩ (of poets) *to flourish*; (of genius) *to flower* ‖ (of life, etc.) *to bloom, flower* **2.** (gedeihen) ⟨fig⟩ (of trade, art, etc.) *to flourish, prosper, thrive* **3.** (of evils) *to prosper, thrive* **4.** sein Weizen blüht jetzt *conditions are favourable for him now* ‖ wer weiß, was ihm noch blüht *who knows what is in store for him*; das kann ihm auch noch ~ *that may happen to him too*

bl·ühend a **1. a.** ⟨eig⟩ *blooming, blossoming, blossomy, flowering* ‖ *flourishing, verdant* (*landscape*); *flowery* (*meadow*) **b.** ⟨fig⟩ er starb im ~en Alter *he died in the prime of life* od *in* *his prime* ‖ ∼es Aussehen *rosy complexion* ‖ ∼er Stil *florid* od *flowery style* **c.** °∼er Unsinn ⟨sl⟩ *tommy-rot* **2.** (gedeihend) ⟨fig⟩ *flourishing* (*town*; *practice*); *prospering*, *prosperous* (*business*); *thriving*, ⟨fam⟩ *humming*, *booming* (*trade*)

Bl·ümchen n ∼s/∼ *floweret*, *floret*; → Mauer-≗ ‖ °die ∼ gießen ⟨fig, f sex⟩ *to pick* od *do a sweet pea*, ⟨euph⟩ *to pluck a rose*, *to gather violets* °**∼kaffee** m (*weak*) *husbands' coffee*

Bl·ume f ∼/∼n **A. 1.** (Blüte) *flower* (*of a plant*); (bes Frucht≗) *blossom* | (Pflanze mit Blüte) *flower*, *flowering herb* od *plant*; ∼en streuen *to strew flowers*; Schnitt≗n [pl] *cut flowers* [pl] | laß ∼ sprechen *say it with flowers* ‖ ∼n verbeten *no flowers by request* ‖ °die ∼n begießen *to water the flowers*, ⟨fig f sex⟩ *to do a sweet pea* ‖ „Blaue ∼" ⟨Ger⟩ "*blue flower*" (*symbol of romantic longing esp. for romantic poetry since 1799 Novalis' Heinrich von Ofterdingen*) **2.** künstliche ∼ *artificial flower*; Papier≗ *paper flower* ‖ ⟨arts⟩ mit ∼n schmükken *to flower* ‖ in Stein ausgeführtes Gehänge v ∼n *festoons* [pl]; (Kreuz–, Giebel–, End≗) ⟨arch⟩ *flower* ‖ ⟨paint⟩ Streu≗ [pl] *scattered flowers* [pl] (*on porcelain*) ‖ Eis≗n [pl] *frostwork* **3.** ⟨übtr⟩ **a.** (Duft) *aroma*, *bouquet*, *flavour* (*of wine*) **b.** *froth* (*of beer*); *head*, *top* (*on a glass*), die ∼ (ab)trinken *to take the top off*, trink die ∼ ab *take the t. off it*; jdm die ∼ bringen *to pleadge a p the first draught of one's glass* **4.** ⟨fig⟩ **a.** Rede≗n [pl] *flowers of speech* [pl] **b.** etw durch die ∼ sagen *to say a th indirectly* (od *allusively*, *by way of innuendo*); durch die ∼ (*speaking*) *in metaphors*; → ∼nsprache ‖ jdm ∼n auf den Weg streuen *to make life pleasant to a p* **B.** ⟨übtr⟩ **1.** (weißer Stirnfleck bei Tieren) *blaze* **2.** ⟨hunt⟩ (Schwanz) *scutt*, *tail* (*of a hare*); (*white*) *tag* (*of a fox's brush*) **3.** *softest and thickest fleece* (*of a sheep*) **4.** ⟨cul⟩ *cut of beef over the aitch-bone* **5.** *maidenhead*

Bl·umen- [in comp] *flower* .. **≗ähnlich, ≗artig** a *fl.-like* **∼ampel** f *hanging fl.-pot* **∼asch** m *fl.-pot* **∼ausstellung** f *fl.-show* **∼bau** m *floriculture* **∼beet** n ⟨hort⟩ *parterre*; *fl.-bed* **∼binderei** f = Bindekunst **∼binse** f ⟨bot⟩ *fl.-ing rush* **∼blatt** n = Blütenblatt **∼duft** m *fragrance of fl.s* **∼erde** f *fine mould*, *garden-mould* **∼fest** n *feast of fl.s* **∼fliege** f ⟨ent⟩ *fl.-fly* **∼flor** m *show of fl.s*; *bloom* **∼freund** m *lover of fl.s*, *fl.-fancier* **∼garten** m *fl.-garden* **∼gärtner** m *florist*, *floriculturist* **∼gehänge** n = Blumengewinde **∼gelb** n (wasser[un]löslich) *xanth*[*e*]*in* **≗geschmückt** a *fl.-decked* (*carriage*) **∼gestell** n *fl. stand* **∼gewinde** n *festoon*, *garland*; (etw) mit ∼n schmükken *to festoon*, *to garland* **∼göttin** f ⟨ant⟩ *Flora* **∼händler** m *florist* **∼kante** f (in e–m Garten) ⟨hort⟩ *border bed* **∼kasten** m *fl.-box* **∼kelch** m *calyx*, *fl.-cup* **∼kenner** m *botanist* **∼kohl** m *cauliflower* **∼korb** m *fl.-basket* **∼korso** m *fl.-corso* **∼kranz** m *wreath of fl.s* **∼krepp** m *florist's crepe paper* **∼kresse** f ⟨bot⟩ = Kapuzinerkresse **∼krippe** f *fl.-stand* **∼krone** f ⟨bot⟩ *corolla* **∼laden** m *fl.-shop* **∼lese** f ⟨fig⟩ *collection of select poems*; *anthology*, *florilegium* ‖ *analects*, *analecta* pl; *literary gleanings* [pl] **∼liebhaber** m *florist*, *fl.-fancier*, *lover of fl.s* **∼mädchen** n *fl.-girl* **∼muster** n *floral design* (od *pattern*); *floriation*; mit ∼n schmücken *to flower*; Stoff mit ∼n *flowered stuff* **∼ornament** n ⟨arts⟩ *fleuret*; ⟨arch⟩ *fleuron* **∼pracht** f *floridity* **≗reich** a *rich in fl.s*, *fl.y*, ∼er Schmuck *fl.iness*, *floridity* ‖ ⟨fig⟩ *fl.y*, *florid* (*language*); ∼er Stil *floridity* **∼reichtum** m *fl.iness*, *floridity* **∼rohr** n ⟨bot⟩ *canna* **∼schale** f *fl.-bowl* **∼schmuck** m *floral decoration*; *fl.-work* **∼spende** f *floral tribute*; v ∼n bitte abzusehen *no fl.s by request* **∼spiele** n [pl] ⟨Fr hist⟩ *floral games* [pl] **∼sprache** f *language of fl.s*, *floral symbolism* **∼ständer** m *fl.-stand*; *jardinière* [Fr] **∼stengel, ∼stiel** m *flowerstalk*, *peduncle* **∼stilleben** n *flower-painting* **∼stock** m *pot-fl.* **∼strauß** m *bunch of fl.s*, *bouquet*, *nosegay*, *posy* **∼stück** n ⟨paint⟩ *flower-piece* **∼tag** m ⟨m. m.⟩ *flag-day* **∼tee** m ⟨com⟩ *true imperial tea* **∼tiere** n [pl] ⟨zoo⟩ = Korallentiere **∼topf** m *fl.-pot* (od *jar*) ‖ (Preis) *pot*; da ist kein ∼ z gewinnen ⟨fig fam⟩ *he* (etc) *won't win any medals there* **∼vase** f *fl.-vase* **∼wasser** n *fl.-water* **∼wespen** f [pl] = Bienen **∼zucht** f *floriculture* **∼züchter** m *florist*, *floriculturist* **∼zwiebel** f *bulb*

bl·ümen vt [h] ⟨übtr⟩ (Stoff) *to flower*; geblümt *flowered* (*cretonne*, etc.) ; ⟨ceram, etc⟩ *to floriate*

Bl·umenau n (⟨Ger⟩ Siedlung in Südbrasilien)

°**blümer·ant** a: mir ist *or* wird ganz ∼ *I feel quite dizzy* od *queer*, ⟨fam⟩ *all-overish*

bl·umig a *full of flowers*, *flowery* ‖ (geblümt) *flowered* (*chintz*); *floral* (*pattern*, *design*) | ⟨fig⟩ *florid*, *flowery* (*language*)

Bl·use f ∼/∼n *blouse*; Hemd≗ *shirt-blouse*; ⟨Am⟩ *shirt-waist* | ⟨mar⟩ (Matrosen≗) *blouse* ‖ ⟨mil⟩ Feld≗ *blouse*, *field service jacket*

ˣ**Blust** m ∼es/ [obd] = Blüte

Blut n ∼s/ **1. a.** ⟨anat⟩ *blood*; ⟨sl⟩ *claret* ‖ geronnenes ∼ *clotted blood*; ins Gewebe ausgetretenes ∼ → ∼erguß ‖ das ∼ Christi *the blood of Christ* **b.** → Fleisch ‖ ⟨fig⟩ bis aufs ∼ *to the quick*, *to the marrow of one's bones*; *to the utmost*; *to death* ‖ mit ∼ befleckt *stained with blood* | es ist viel ∼ geflossen *much b. has flown* (od *was shed*) ‖ sein ∼ hingeben *or* l *to give* od *shed one's b.* (f *for*) ‖ ∼ husten *to spit b.* ‖ ∼ lecken (*of beasts*, etc.) *to taste b.* ‖ ∼ stillen *to sta*(*u*)*nch b.* ‖ mit *or* von ∼ überströmt s *or* w *to be bled over* ‖ ∼ vergießen *to shed b.*; sein ∼ vergießen *to shed one's b.* (*for*) **2.** ⟨übtr⟩ **a.** (Gemütsverfassung) böses ∼ m *to engender choler*, *to breed bad* od *ill b.*, *to make trouble* (unter *among*); jds ∼ z Kochen *or* in Wallung bringen *to make a p's b. boil*; sein ∼ gerät in Wallung *his b. is up*, sein ∼ kommt leicht in W. *he has a hot temper* ‖ ∼ gerinnen m (of terror) *to freeze a p's b.*, *to make a p's b. run cold* ‖ das ∼ schoß ihm ins Gesicht *the b. rushed to his face* | heißes ∼ *hot b.* ‖ kaltes ∼ *cold b.* (: *the situation called for c. b.*); kaltes ∼ bewahren *to keep one's temper* (od *a cool head*); in kaltem ∼ *in cold b.* ‖ ruhig ∼! *keep cool!* ⟨sl⟩ *keep your hair on!* ‖ leichtes ∼ *light character* ‖ ∼ schwitzen *to sweat b.*, *to be in extreme anxiety* **b.** (Leben, Kraft) feuriges ∼ *fiery b.* od *disposition* ‖ Lebens≗ *blood*, *sap*; (e–r S) frisches ∼ zuführen *to bring fresh b. to a th* ‖ ∼ u Eisen *b. and iron* **c.** [konkr] (P) ein junges ∼ *a young b.* [koll] junges ∼ *the young bloods* [pl] **3.** (Erbmasse, Rasse) **a.** *blood*, *race* ‖ *birth*, *descent*, *lineage*; *family* ‖ v reinem ∼ *full-blooded* (German); Kinder desselben ∼es *children of the same b.* ‖ Bande des ∼es *the ties of b.* ‖ ⟨nazi Ger⟩ ∼ u Boden *b. and soil* ‖ adliges ∼ *high* od *blue b.*; blaues ∼ *blue b.*, blaues ∼ in den Adern h *to be of noble birth* od *descent* ‖ im ∼e liegen (of qualities) *to run in the b.*; Schauspielern liegt *or* steckt ihr im ∼e *the theatre is in her b.* ‖ das ∼ sprach in ihm *the b. spoke in him* ‖ ∼ verleugnet sich nie *b. never dies*; → Art ‖ **b.** (T) *good breed* od *pedigree*; → Voll≗, Halb≗ ‖ da steckt ∼ drin ⟨hors⟩ *it's a bit of b.* **4.** ⟨übtr⟩ (of plants) *juice*, *sap*; Reben≗, Trauben≗ *the juice of the grape* **5.** (∼farbe) [mst in comp] → ∼apfelsine, ∼buche etc ‖ → Milch ‖ ⟨com⟩ Koralle ersten ∼es *blood of the first quality* **6.** [in comp] **a.** (→ Blut–, Bluts–) *blood* ..; ⟨scient⟩ *haemal*, *haematic*, *haemato–*, *haemo–* **b.** [mit doppeltem Ton als Intensiv] (= sehr, überaus) *very*, *extremely*; → ≗·arm 2., ≗j·ung,

~w·enig **Bl·ut-** mst *blood* **~ader** f *vein* **~alge** f ⟨bot⟩ → Blutregen **~·alkoholspiegel** m ⟨bes mot⟩ *blood alcohol level* **~andrang** m ⟨med⟩ *congestion*; ~ nach dem Kopfe *rush of b. to the brain, cerebral congestion* **~apfelsine** f *b.-orange* **~arm** *anaemic* **~·arm** a (→ Blut 6. b.) *extremely poor, poor as a church-mouse* **~armut** f *deficiency of b.*, ⟨med⟩ *anaemia* [L]; progressive ~ *Addison's disease* **~auffrischung** f ⟨biol⟩ *fresh b.* **~austritt** m ⟨med⟩ punktförmiger ~ in der Haut *ecchymosis* [L] **~bad** n *carnage, massacre, slaughter*; ein ~ anrichten *to massacre, slaughter* **~bahn** f *bloodstream* **~bank** f *blood bank* **~bann** m ⟨hist⟩ *power of life and death* **~befleckt** a *b.y, b.-stained, sanguinary* (*hands*) **~bildung** f *formation of b., sanguification* **~blase** f *b. blister* **~blume** f ⟨bot⟩ *b.-flower* **~brechen** n ⟨med⟩ *haematemesis* **~buche** f ⟨bot⟩ *copper-beech* **~druck** m ⟨med⟩ *b.-pressure*; Messung des ~s *measurement of the b.-p.* | ~messer [m] (S) *sphygmomanometer* **~drüse** f ⟨anat⟩ *endocrine gland* **~durst** m ⟨fig⟩ *b.thirstiness* **~dürstig** a ⟨fig⟩ *b.thirsty, sanguinary* **~egel** m ⟨zoo⟩ *leech*; ~ setzen *to apply leeches* (an *to*) **~entnahme** f *extraction of b.* (*from the veins of a p*) **~erguß** m *extravasation, haematoma* [L]; *effusion of b.* (*in the brain*); *haemorrhage* (*of the lungs*) **~fahne** f *red flag* ‖ ⟨nazi Ger⟩ (9. XI. 1923) *b.-stained swastika flag* **~faserstoff** m *fibrin* **~fink** m ⟨orn⟩ **1.** ein Prachtfink, → d. **2.** *bullfinch* **~fleck** m **1.** *stain* od *spot of b., b.-stain* **2.** ⟨ent⟩ = Blutströpfchen 2. **~fluß** m *haemorrhage* ‖ Heilung der –flüssigen Frau ⟨bib arts⟩ *the Woman with the Issue of Blood* **~fr·emd** a (→ Blut 6. b.) *utterly strange* **~gebunden** a *b.-bound*; *b.-cemented* **~gefäß** n *b. vessel* **~geld** n *b.-money* **~gerinnsel** n *clot of b.* **~gerinnung** f *b.-coagulation*; → Thrombose **~gerüst** n *scaffold* **~geschwür** n ⟨med⟩ *furuncle* **~gier** f ⟨fig⟩ *b.-thirstiness, sanguinary disposition* **~gierig** a ⟨fig⟩ *b.thirsty, b.y-minded, sanguinary* **~gruppe** f ⟨biol⟩ *b.-group, b. type*; ~n [pl] *the b.-grouping* (*of parents and children*) **~harnen** n ⟨med⟩ *haematuria* [L] **~heil** n ⟨bot⟩ → Johanniskraut **~hochzeit** f: Pariser ~ *St. Bartholomew's Night* **~holz** n = Blauholz **~hund** m ⟨zoo⟩ *b.hound* ‖ ⟨fig⟩ *b.y tyrant, blood-drinker* **~husten** m ⟨med⟩ *haemoptysis, spitting of b.* **~igel** ⟨zoo⟩ = Blutegel **~j·ung** a (→ Blut 6. b.) *very young* **~konserve** f *blood* (*stored*) *in a b. bank*; Bereitung e–r ~ *adtevac* (*adsorption + temperature + vacuum*) **~körperchen** n ⟨anat⟩ *corpuscle, corpuscule*; rote ~ [pl] *red corpuscles, erythrocytes* [pl]; weiße ~ [pl] *white corpuscles, leucocytes* [pl] **~kreislauf** m *blood-stream, circulation of the b.* **~kuchen** m *clotting of b.* **~kügelchen** n *globule of b.* **~lache** f *pool of b.* **~lauf** m *b.-flow, b.-stream*; → Blutkreislauf **~laugensalz** n ⟨chem⟩ gelbes ~ *potassium ferro--cyanide, yellow potassium*; *prussiate*; rotes ~ *red prussiate of potash, potassium ferri-cyanide, red p. prussiate* **~laus** f ⟨ent⟩ *wooly aphis* → Blattlaus **~leer** a *b.less, exsanguine* ‖ ⟨fig⟩ *b.less* (*system*); *cold-b.ed* (*sciences*) **~leere** f *b.lessness* **~linie** f *line of descent, pedigree* **~los** a *b.less* (*victory*) ‖ → blutleer **~mal** n = Muttermal **~mangel** m *deficiency of b. b.lessness* **~nelke** f ⟨bot⟩ *maiden-pink* **~orden** m ⟨nazi⟩ *B.-Order* **~pfropf** m ⟨med⟩ *clot of b., thrombus* [L] **~plasma** n ⟨biol⟩ *b.-plasma* **~plättchen** n [pl] *b.-plaques* (od *platelets*), *thrombocytes* [pl] **~probe** f *b.-test* ⟨a. mot⟩; e–e ~ m *to examine the b.*; die ~ nehmen *to take the b. a. l.* → -alkohol- **~rache** f *b.-feud*; *vendetta* [It] **~rausch** m *b.-lust* **~regen** m (durch e–e Alge verursachtes Rot) *b.-rain* **~reich** a *plethoric* **~reinigend** a ⟨med⟩ *depurative, purgative* **~reinigung** f *purification* od *depuration of the b.*; ~smittel *depurative, purgative* **~rinne** f (e–s Degens) *groove* **~r·ot** a *b.-red, ruby-red, haematic*; *dark crimson*; *sanguine* (*lips*); ~ w *to colour up* (*to the eyes*), *to blush* **~rünstig** a *b.y, sanguinary* **~s·auer** a (→ Blut 6. b.) ⟨fig⟩ *very hard* (od *laborious, toilsome*) **~sauger** m ⟨fig⟩ *b.-sucker, vampire, vulture*; *extortioner* **~sauger·ei** f ⟨fig⟩ *b.-sucking* **~schande** f *incest* **~schänder** m *incestuous p* **~schänderisch** a *incestuous* **~schuld** f *b.-guilt*(*iness*), ⟨poet⟩ *murder* **~schwamm** m ⟨bot⟩ = Bofist **~senkung** f *hypostasis, blood sedimentation* | ~untersuchung [f] *sed*(*imentation*) *rate test* **~serum** n *b.-serum* **~spender(in** f) m *blood donor* **~spukken** n *spitting of b., haemoptysis* **~spur** f *b.-stain, b.-mark* **~stauung** f ⟨med⟩ *passive* (od *venous*) *hyperaemia* [L] **~stein** m ⟨minr⟩ → Roteisenstein **~stillend** a *b.-stanching*, ⟨med⟩ *styptic*; ~es Mittel [n] *haemostat*(*ic*), *styptic* **~stillung** f ⟨med⟩ *haemostasis* [L] **~stockung** f *stagnation of b.*; *discontinuance of menstruation* **~strahl** m *jet of b.* **~strom** m *torrent of b.* **~sturz** m ⟨med⟩ *haemoptoë, haematemesis* [L], *violent haemoptysis* ‖ e–n ~ h *to break a b.-vessel* **~tat** f *b.y deed*; *murder* **~taufe** f ⟨ec hist⟩ *b.-baptism* **~triefend** a *b.y, reeking with b.*; *sanguinary* **~tropfen** m *drop of b.* **~überströmt** a *b.y* (*face*); ~ s *to be all b.* **~übertragung** f ⟨med⟩ *transfusion of b., b.-transfusion* **~unterlaufen** a *b.-shot* (*eye*) ‖ ~sein [n] *suffusion, effusion of b.* **~vergießen** n *b.shed, effusion of b., slaughter* **~vergiftung** f *b.-poisoning*, ⟨med⟩ *pyaemia, sepsis*; *toxaemia* [L] **~verlust** m *loss* od *effusion of b.* **~vorrat** m *blood bank* **~wallung** f = Blutandrang **~w·arm** a *as warm as b.* **~wärme** f *b.-heat* **~wasser** n *lymph*; *serum*; *ichor* **~welle** f *wave of b., blush* **~w·enig** a (→ Blut 6. b.) *extremely little, very little*; *next to nothing* **~wolle** f *fell* od *carrion wool* **~wurst** f *black-pudding* **~wurz** f ⟨bot⟩ *blood-wort* ‖ *b.-root, tormentil* **~zehnt** m ⟨hist⟩ *tithe of live stock* **~zelle** f *b.-cell* **~zeuge** m ⟨ec hist⟩ *martyr*; ⟨a. übtr⟩ **~zirkulation** f = Blutkreislauf **~zucker** m *b.-sugar*

Bl·üte f ~/~n **I. A.** ⟨eig⟩ **1.** [abstr] (Blühen) *blooming, flowering,* (*ef*)*florescence* **2.** [konkr] *flower,* (zarte) *bloom*; (bes Fruchtbaum~) *blossom*; Frucht~ *female flower*; Zwitter~, eingeschlechtige ~ *monoclinous flower*; dikline, zweigeschlechtige ~ *diclinous flower*; Entstehung v ~n am Stamm *or* Zweig *cauliflory* ‖ [koll] ~n [pl] *flowerage, inflorescence*; (Fruchtbaum-~n) *blossom* **B.** ⟨fig⟩ **1.** [abstr] **a.** (P) die ~ *the prime* (*of a p*); *the bloom* (*of manhood*); in der ~ des Lebens, der Jahre *in the prime of life, in his prime, in the flower of his age*; *in the pride of his years* ‖ die ~ der Jugend *the bloom of youth*; die höchste ~ *the flower* (*of his genius*) **b.** (S) ⟨arts⟩ *bloom,* ⟨lit, mus⟩ *efflorescence*; ⟨drama⟩ *climax, maturity*; *flowering* (*of civilization*); → ~zeit ‖ *prosperous condition, prosperity* (*of an undertaking*) **2.** [konkr] **a.** *blossom* (: *the first blossoms of literature*); *product,* ~n der modernen Zivilisation *products of modern civilization* ‖ Rede~n, Stil~n [pl] *trimmings, flowers of speech* [pl] **b.** die ~ *the cream, the elite, the flower* (*of the army, chivalry, society*) **C. in** ~ *in bloom*; *in blossom*; (of maize) *in tassel*; in voller ~ *in full bloom* ‖ (Pflanze) **zur ~ bringen** *to flower*; ⟨fig⟩ (etw) *to bring* (*a th*) *to a peak* ‖ s–e ~ **erreichen** *to reach one's full flowering* (od *one's meridian, zenith*) ‖ **in ~ stehen** *to be in* (*full*) *bloom*; ⟨fig⟩ *to flower, flourish*; *to be in one's heyday* (: *the Guilds were in their heyday*) ‖ ~n **treiben** *to put forth blossoms*; *to bloom, blossom*; seltsame ~n t. *to produce strange phenomena* **II.** ⟨übtr⟩ **1.** (~ auf der Haut) *acne, pimple, pustule*; ~n [pl] *eruption*; voller ~n *full of pimples* **2.** °(in Gaunersprache) *forged* (od *counterfeit, queer*) *money* **3.** ⟨chem⟩ → Schwefel≃ **∼zeit** f ⟨fig⟩ *flowering time; floruit* [L] (*of an author*)

bl·uten I. vi [h] **1.** *to bleed* (aus vielen Wunden *from many wounds*; wie ein Schwein *like a pig*) ‖ mir blutet das Herz *my heart bleeds* (um ihn *for him*) ‖ ∼ f etw *to bleed* (od *die; shed one's blood*) *for a th* ‖ jdn ∼ l *to bleed a p* | (of trees, etc.) *to bleed* **2.** °(zahlen) *to bleed,* ⟨sl⟩ *to fork out*; ⟨cul⟩ nun muß er ∼ *he shall have to pay for his whistle*; → blechen ‖ tüchtig ∼ müssen *to pay through the nose*; er wird dafür ∼ müssen *he will have to pay for it* ‖ jdn (gehörig) ∼ l *to bleed* od *fleece a p* (*to take a p for all he is worth*) **II.** ≃ n *bleeding*

Blüten- [in comp] *flower* .. **∼ähre** f *spike* **∼bestäubung** f *pollination* **∼bildung** f *efflorescence* **∼blatt** n *petal,* → apetal **∼hüllblätter** n [pl] **∼hülle** f *perianth* **∼kelchblatt** n *sepal* **∼knospe** f *bud* **∼kolben** m *spadix* [L] **∼köpfchen** n *fl.-head* **∼lese** f = Blumenlese **≃los** a *fl.less*; ∼lose Pflanze *cryptogam* **∼öl** n *oil distilled from fl.s* **∼pflanze** f *phanerogam* **≃reich** a *floriferous, fl.y* ‖ → blumenreich **∼reichtum** f *fl.age, fl.iness* **∼scheide** f *spathe* **∼schmuck** m *fl.ing* **∼stand** m *inflorescence*; razemöser ∼ *raceme,* zymöser ∼ *cyme*; männl. ∼ des Mais *tassel* **∼staub** m *pollen* **∼stecher** m ⟨ent⟩ *weevil* **∼stiel** m *fl.-stalk* **≃tragend** a *floriferous, fl.ing* (*plant*) **∼träger** m (Pflanze) *bloomer, flowerer* **∼zweig** m *blooming* (od *flowering*) *twig*

Bl·uter m ⟨med⟩ *bleeder* **∼krankheit** f ⟨med⟩ *bleeding, haemophilia*

-blüter [in comp] **-blütler** [in comp] → Korb∼, Schmetterlings∼

Bl·ütezeit f **1.** *flowering–* od *blooming-time, (ef)florescence* **2.** ⟨fig⟩ *efflorescence; time of flourishing* od *prosperity, peak-time; the golden age* (*of German music*); *high-water mark* | (P) *flower, heyday, meridian, prime; palmy days; floruit* (*of an author*); in s–r ∼ *in his heyday* (od *palmy days, prime*); die ∼ hinter sich h *to be past one's meridian*

bl·utig a **1.** *bloody, blood-covered, –stained; sanguinary* (*hands,* etc.); sich die Hände ∼ m *to stain one's hands with blood* ‖ ∼e Wunde *bleeding wound* ‖ jdn ∼ schlagen *to beat a p black and blue*; jdm die Nase ∼ schl. *to tap a p's nose* ‖ ⟨fig⟩ sich ∼e Köpfe holen *to be bloodily beaten* **2.** *bloody* (*deed*); *murderous, sanguinary* (*battle, day*); *dire* (Rache) (an *upon*) **3.** ⟨fig⟩ ∼e Tränen weinen *to shed tears of blood* ‖ es ist mein ∼er Ernst *I am in dead earnest*; ein ∼er Laie *an utter dilettante, a beginner, complete layman,* ⟨fam⟩ *greenhorn,* ⟨sl⟩ *a numb hand*

-blütig [in comp] *–blooded*: halb∼ *half-blooded,* → heiß∼, voll∼ etc **-blütig** ⟨bot⟩ [in comp] *–flowered*; weiß∼ *white-flowered*

Bl·uts- ∼brüderschaft f *blood-brotherhood* **∼gemeinschaft** f *blood-community* **∼tröpfchen** n **1.** ⟨bot⟩ = Blutnelke **2.** ⟨ent⟩ *burnet-moth, –fly* **∼tropfen** m → Bluttropfen **≃verwandt** a *consanguine, consanguineous*; → verwandt ‖ ≃e(r m) [f] *blood-kin*; ≃e [pl] *kinsfolk; relations by blood* ‖ Heirat zw ≃en *consanguineous marriage* **∼verwandtschaft** f *consanguinity*; Grad v ∼ *degree of c.* od *relationship*

Bl·utung f *bleeding, haemorrhage*; ∼en [pl] *haemorrhages* [pl]

Blyde f = Bleide

Bö f ∼/∼en ⟨mar⟩ *flaw, gust, scud, squall; air bump*; Sturm≃ bei heiterem Himmel *white squall*; ∼ mit Wolkenbogen *black squall*; ∼ mit Hagel u Schnee *thick squall* | ∼geschwindigkeit [f] ⟨meteor⟩ *gust velocity*

B·oa f ∼/∼s ⟨zoo⟩ **1.** *boa-constrictor* **2.** (mst Feder≃) *boa*

B·ob m ∼s/∼s **1.** = Bobsleigh ‖ im ∼ fahren *to bob* ‖ kl ∼ (f 2 P) *boblet* **2.** [in comp] *bob* .., *bobsleigh* .. **∼bahn** f *bobsleigh-course* **∼fahren** n *bobbing* **∼fahrer** m *bob(sleigh) rider* **∼rennen** n *bob race*

B·obak m ∼s/∼s ⟨zoo⟩ *bobac*

B·obaum m ⟨bot⟩ *peepul, pipal*

B·obbel f ∼/∼n *bubble* **b·obbeln** vi [h] *to bubble*

b·obben vi [h] *to bob*

Bob·ine f ∼/∼n (Spule) ⟨spin etc⟩ *bobbin*

Bobin·et m ∼s/∼s (engl Tüll) *bobbinet*

B·ob(o)link m ⟨orn⟩ *bobolink, rice-bird*

Bobsleigh [ˈbɔbslei] m ∼s/∼s (→ Bob) **1.** *bobsleigh, bob* ‖ im ∼ fahren *to* (*ride on a*) *bob* **2.** [in comp] *bob(sleigh)*; → Bob 2.

B·ochum n ⟨Ger⟩ (Stadt)

B·ock m ∼(e)s/≃e **A. 1.** ⟨zoo⟩ **a.** (Ziegen≃) *he-goat,* ⟨fam⟩ *billy-goat* ‖ → Gems≃, Schaf≃; Stein≃ **b.** ⟨hunt⟩ (Reh≃) *(roe)buck*; angehender (jagdbarer) ∼ *fair roe*; ∼ v ersten Kopf *roe* od *buck of the first head* **c.** *buck, male* (*of a hare, rabbit*) **d.** ⟨fig⟩ (bockiges Tier) *butter* ‖ → Sünden≃ **2.** ⟨fig⟩ (P) ein alter ∼ *an old goat* od *rake* ‖ ein steifer ∼ *a clumsy fellow* **3.** (Fehler) *blunder, mistake, slip*; grober ∼ ⟨sl⟩ *howler* **4.** e–n ∼ h, ein ∼ s *to be obstinate* od *stubborn* (*as a mule*) ‖ e–n ∼ schießen ⟨fig⟩ *to commit a blunder, to make a slip*; ⟨fam⟩ *to pull a boner* **5.** ihn stößt der ∼ *he mopes* od *sulks; he sobs convulsively* ‖ den ∼ zum Gärtner m *to set a thief to catch a thief, to put the cat among the pigeons* **B.** ⟨übtr⟩ (Gerät) **1.** *frame, horse, jack, stand, stock, support, trestle*; ⟨tech⟩ *dog* ‖ Säge≃ *saw-buck, buck, jack* ‖ Kamin≃ *andiron* **2.** (Ramme) *beetle, ram*; → Prell≃, Sturm≃ **3.** (Sitz≃) *stool*; (hochbeiniger) *high stool* ‖ Kutscher≃ *coach-box, seat* **4.** ⟨gym⟩ *buck(-horse)* ‖ (über den) ∼ springen *to vault over the b.-h.* ‖ ∼ springen (Spiel) *to play leap-frog*; jdm ∼ stehen *to give a back to a p* **5.** (Sünden≃) (⟨bib⟩ T) & ⟨übtr⟩ (P) *scapegoat* **C.** (starkes Bier) = ∼bier **D.** [in comp] → Bock–, Bocks–

B·ock- ≃beinig a ⟨fig⟩ *obstinate, pigheaded, recalcitrant, stubborn* (*as a mule*) **∼beinigkeit** f *pigheadedness, stubbornness* **∼bier** n *bock(-beer)* ‖ °das geht mir über ein ∼fest (mit Würstchen) *this beats cock-fighting* ‖ °es war mir ein ∼fest mit Würstchen *it was a treat* od *picnic, it was as good as a play* **∼brücke** f ⟨tech⟩ *trestle-bridge* **∼gestell** n *trestle* **∼kran** m *frame crane* **∼leder** n *buckskin* **≃ledern** a *buckskin* **∼leiter** f *double ladder* **∼mist** m °⟨fig⟩ *bilge, rubbish* (= *nonsense*) **∼mühle** f *post windmill* **∼sattel** m *stock-saddle* **∼springen** n *leap-frogging* ‖ ⟨gym⟩ *vaulting over the buckhorse* **∼sprung** m **1.** *leap-frog*; e–n ∼ m über jdn *to l.-f. over a p* ‖ ⟨gym⟩ *vault over the buckhorse*; e–n ∼ m *to vault over the b.-h.* **2.** ⟨fig⟩ (Kapriole) *caper, gambol*; –sprünge m *to cut capers, to caper* **∼wurst** f ⟨Ger⟩ *bock sausage* (→ Bockbier)

B·öckchen n ∼s/∼ ⟨zoo⟩ *kid, small species of South African antelope, oribi*

b·ocken vi [h] **1.** (of female animals) *to be in heat, to rut* **2.** ⟨übtr⟩ **a.** (of horses) *to buck, to jib* **b.** ⟨fig⟩ (P) *to be recalcitrant* od *be refractory; to kick* ‖ °**sich** ∼ *to feel dull* **c.** (of engines, motors) *to conk; to misfire*; (of a car) *to buck, bounce* **b·ockig** a **1.** *goatish* (*smell*); *hircin(e)* **2.** *jibbing*; ∼es Pferd *jibber* ‖ ⟨fig⟩ *obstinate, pigheaded, obstinate, recalcitrant, stubborn*

B·ocks- ∼bart m ⟨bot⟩ *goat's beard; salsify* **∼beutel** m ⟨Ger⟩ *'Bocksbeutel'* (*a Franconian wine in a rounded bottle*) **∼dorn** m ⟨bot⟩ *box thorn* **∼fuß** m *goat's foot* **∼horn** n **1.** *buck's horn* **2.** ⟨bot⟩ = Johannisbrot **3.** jdn ins ∼ jagen *to intimidate* od *bully a p; to frighten a p out* *of his senses* **~hornklee** m ⟨bot⟩ *fenugreek* **~melde** f ⟨bot⟩ *goose-foot* [pl *goose-foots*]

B·odden m *shallow bay on the Baltic, partly separated from the sea*

×**B·odem** ['bɔdəm] m = Boden

B·oden m ~s/⩪ **I. A.** ⟨eig⟩ **1.** (Meeres⩪) *bottom, ground*; den ~ berühren *to touch ground*; → schlagen vi ‖ Erd⩪ *ground* (auf dem ~ *on the g.*); fester ~ *firm ground*; ein Fuß über (*or* v) dem ~ *a foot from the ground* ‖ ⟨racing⟩ *going* (: *the g. was good*) **2.** (Acker⩪) *ground, soil*; den ~ bearbeiten *to work on the ground* ‖ Heimat⩪, Mutter⩪ *homeland, native soil*; auf deutschem ~ *in* od *on German soil*; → Blut, Grund **3.** Lehm⩪ *clay soil*; Moor⩪ *marshy* od *swampy ground*; Sand⩪ *sandy ground*; Wiesen⩪ *meadow ground* **|** (~beschaffenheit) ⟨sport⟩ *the going*; ⟨golf⟩ rauher, unebener ~ (zw *tee* u *green*) *the rough* ‖ ⟨crick⟩ ~, auf dem der Ball gut (schlecht) springt *lively* (*dead*) *pitch* **4.** ⟨übtr⟩ *soil, field*; die Musik hat e–n fruchtbaren ~ in Deutschland gefunden *music has found a fertile soil in G.* **5. a.** ein Künstler, der neuen ~ betritt ⟨fig⟩ *an innovating artist* ‖ → **brennen** I. 3. a. ‖ ⟨fig⟩ jdm den ~ **ebnen** *to smooth the way for a p* ‖ (Stadt) dem ~ **gleich m** ⟨fig⟩ *to make* (*a town*) *even with the ground, to level to* od *with the ground, to raze to the ground* ‖ den ~ unter den Füßen **verlieren** *to lose the ground under one's feet*; ⟨fig⟩ *to go beyond one's depth*; *to go off the deep end* **b. am** ~ liegen ⟨a. fig⟩ *to lie prone*; ⟨bot⟩ am ~ liegend *decumbent* **|** sich **auf** den ~ setzen *to seat o.s. on the ground* ‖ auf den ~ springen *to spring to the ground* ‖ sich auf den ~ werfen *to fling o.s. prostrate* **|** → Pilz **| vom** ~ loskommen ⟨aero⟩ *to unstick* **| zu** ~ *to the ground*, [in Verbindung mit Verben mst] *down*: (jdn) z ~ drücken, ⟨fig⟩ *to crush* (*a p*) *down* ‖ z ~ fallen, sinken (P) *to fall* od *slump down* ‖ z ~ schlagen (jdn) *to knock* (od *strike, crush*) *down*; die Augen z ~ schlagen *to cast down one's eyes* ‖ z ~ schleudern → z ~ werfen ‖ z ~ strecken (jdn) *to floor*; → z ~ schlagen ‖ z ~ treten ⟨fig⟩ *to crush* od *trample down*; *to suppress* ‖ (jdn) z ~ trinken *to drink* (*a p*) *down* ‖ z ~ werfen *to throw* od *fling down*; ⟨sl⟩ *to lay a p out*; ⟨fig⟩ (Widerstand) *to crush* od *put down*; (Feind) *to crush, overwhelm* ‖ er warf ihn krachend z ~ *he brought him crashing to the ground*; *the explosion lifted him clean off his feet* **B.** ⟨übtr⟩ **1.** (**Raum, Gebiet**) *ground, room* ‖ **an ~ gewinnen** *to gain ground, to gather way*; an ~ verlieren *to lose ground* ‖ jdm ~ abgewinnen *to gain ground* (*up*)*on a p* **2.** (**Halt**) **fester** ~ *footing*; festen ~ fassen, gewinnen *to obtain a footing* (*in*); *to take root* ‖ sicheren ~ (unter den Füßen) fühlen *to feel one's feet* od *legs* ‖ jdm den ~ zu heiß m *to make a place too hot for a p* ‖ (Grundlage) *basis, base* ‖ jdm den ~ unter den Füßen nehmen *or* abgraben *to cut the ground from under a p's feet* ⟨a. fig⟩, ⟨fig⟩ *to pull the rug from a p* ‖ e–r S den ~ entziehen *to knock the bottom out of a th* **| auf dem ~ der** Verfassung stehen *to be founded* od *based on the constitution, to be in accordance with the c.*; sich auf den ~ der Tatsachen stellen *to take one's stand on reality, to start from facts, to base one's arguments on facts* **C.** (**untere Fläche**) (e–s Dinges) **1.** *floor* (*of a room*) **2.** (of objects) **a.** *bottom* (*of a ship, glass*, etc.); **am** (*or* **auf dem**) ~ des Glases *at the bottom of the glass* ‖ *head* (*of a cask*) ‖ ein Koffer mit doppeltem ~ *a trunk with a double bottom* ‖ (etw) mit e–m ~ versehen *to bottom* (*a th*) ‖ → Faß **b.** Hosen⩪ *breech, seat* ‖ → Resonanz⩪ *sound-board* **D. 1.** † = Stockwerk **2.** (Dachgeschoß) *top-storey*; *attics* [pl], *loft* ⟨a. Hänge⩪⟩; *garret*; Heu⩪ *hay-loft* ‖ ⟨theat⟩ Schnür⩪ *gridiron*; Rollen⩪ *barrel loft* **2.** Fecht⩪ *fencing room* ‖ Tanz⩪ *dancing-floor, -room* **3.** *store, storehouse* ‖ Schrot⩪ *grist-barn*

B·oden- ~analyse f *analysis of the soil* **~art** f *nature of the soil* **~ausbildung** f ⟨aero⟩ *synthetic training* **|** ~sausrüstung [f] *synthetic equipment* **~auszug** m ⟨phot⟩ *extension* **~bearbeitung** f *cultivation of the soil* **~(be)deckung** f ⟨geog, agr, mil⟩ *vegetation* **⩪bedingt** a *edaphic* **~belag** m *floor-covering*; *bottom-covering*; (Fliesen) *pavement* **~beschaffenheit** f *the natural features* [pl] *of the earth's surface*; ~ e–s Landes *geographical features of a country* ‖ *soil-condition* (*of a district*) ‖ ⟨racing⟩ *going* **~brett** n *floor-board*; *bottom-board* **~-Bord-** ⟨aero⟩ *ground-to-air* [attr] (*calling, communication*) **|** ~-Verkehr– [m] ⟨aero wir⟩ *ground-air communication* **~bürste** f ⟨el⟩ *electric polisher* **~chemie** f *chemical composition of the soil* **~eis** n *bottom-ice* **~dienste** m pl ⟨aero⟩ *base services* **~erhebung** f *elevation of the ground, rise in the gr.* **~ertrag** m *agricultural produce*; *return on the land* **~fenster** n *dormer(-window)* **~fläche** f *floor-space* **~fräse** f ⟨agr⟩ *rotary hoe, ground-mill* **~freiheit** f ⟨mot⟩ *ground* (⟨Am⟩ *road*) (⟨fam⟩ *belly*) *clearance* **~gare** f ⟨agr⟩ (*bacteriological*) *ripeness of soil*; *proper state of tillage* **⩪gebunden** a *soil-bound*; *attached* od *rooted to the soil* **~geschwindigkeit** f ⟨aero⟩ *ground speed* **~gestalt** f ⟨geog⟩ *features* pl (*of a country*) **~haftung** f ⟨mot⟩ *ground adhesion, traction of the road* **~höhe** f ⟨aero⟩ *zero altitude* **~kammer** f *attic* **~kredit** m *credit on land, loan on security of land*; ~bank *land mortgage bank* **~kultur** f *cultivation of the soil* **~luke** f *garret-window* **~mannschaft** f ⟨aero⟩ *ground crew* **~mosaik** n *tesselated pavement* **~navigation** f ⟨aero⟩ *terrestrial navigation* **~nebel** m *ground fog* **~nutzung** f *agricultural politics* **~parzelle** f → Bauplatz **~personal** n ⟨aero⟩ *ground crew* od *personnel*, ⟨hum⟩ *penguins, kiwis* pl **~probe** f *soil sample*; ⟨a–n⟩ *document example* **~raum** m *attic* **~reform** f *land reform* **~reformer** m *land-reformer* **~rente** f *pure rent for land* **~satz** m *sediment, dregs, grounds, lees* [pl]; ⟨chem⟩ *precipitate*; (Malz⩪) *draff* **~schätze** m [pl] *the natural resources* od *treasures* (*of the earth*); *mineral wealth* ‖ ~ u ihre Nutzung *resources and development* **~schätzung** f *land classification, soil evaluation of the soil* **~schwelle** f ⟨geog⟩ 1. *hummock*, (*low ridge*) 2. *submarine ridge* **~see** m *Lake Constance* **~senkung** f [abstr] *submergence of ground* ‖ → Senkung *declivity* **~sicht** f ⟨aero⟩ *ground visibility*; mit ~ fliegen *to fly by contact*; Flug mit ~ *contact flight* **~spekulation** f *land speculation* **⩪ständig** a *homesteady, redolent of the soil, attached to the soil* ‖ *static* (Luftverteidigung) **~ständigkeit** f *homesteadiness* **~station** f ⟨aero, a–n, etc⟩ *ground station, down-range station, earth station* **~stein** m *the nether millstone* **~stewardeß** f ⟨aero⟩ *ground hostess* **~struktur** f *texture of soil, soil condition* **~stück** n *breech* (*of a gun*) **~treppe** f *garret* od *attic stairs* pl **~turnen** n *exercises on the floor* **~verbesserung** f ⟨agr⟩ *soil improvement* od *amelioration* **|** ~smittel [n] *soil conditioner* **~verhältnisse** n [pl] *ground* od *soil conditions* **~verschiebung** f *landslide* **⩪verwurzelt** a *rooted in the soil* **~welle** f ⟨geog⟩ *swell*, (*low ridge*), Fr. *rideau* **~wert** m *land value* **~wind** m *ground-wind* **~zeit** f ⟨aero⟩ *ground time* **~zins** m *ground-rent* **~zünder** m *base* od *tail fuse*

b·odenlos 1. a *bottomless*; *fathomless* ‖ °⟨fig⟩ *outrageous, amazing, enormous, excessive, unbounded* **2.** adv °~ *exceedingly, excessively, outrageously* (*stupid*); ~ unverschämt *nervy, insolent, impudent*

B·odensee, der *the Lake* (*of*) *Constance*

b·odmen vt [h] **1.** ⟨mar⟩ *to secure a loan on a ship, to raise money on a bottomry-bond*;

(Schiff gegen Anleihe verpfänden) *to bottomry* (*a ship*) **2.** (Faß) *to head* **Bodmer·ei** f ~/~en ⟨mar⟩ **1.** *bottomry* **2.** [in comp] *bottomry*; ~brief [m] *bottomry-bond*

Boehm·eria (L) ⟨bot⟩ = Ramie

B·ofist m ~s/~e ⟨bot⟩ *puff-ball, fuzz-ball*

b·og 1. u 3. sg pret. v biegen

B·ogen m ~s/~ & ≃ **I.** (Biegung, gebogene Linie) [pl ≃] **1. a.** *bend, bow, curved* (*out*)*line*; ⟨skating⟩ *curve, sweep*; e–n ~ beschreiben *or* m (P & S) *to describe a bend* (od *bow, curve*); in e–m ~ fließen *to flow in a curve* (um *round*); → Umweg, Runde ‖ ⟨skating⟩ ~ fahren *to cut pigeon-wings, to practise figure-skating* ‖ im ~ hinausfahren *to swing out* (aus e–m Tor *at a gate*) ‖ e–n großen ~ machen: *the path swings wide* ‖ in hohem ~ springen *to vault* (über *over*); im ~ nach links fliegen *to take a swing to the left* ‖ ⟨mot⟩ weiter, enger ~ *wide, narrow turn* | ⟨tech⟩ (scharfes Knierohr) *elbow, sharp bend* | ⟨**fig**⟩ e–n gr ~ um jdn m *to shun a p, to keep clear of a p* ‖ er hat den ~ 'raus (S) *he's got the hang of it* ‖ gr ~ [pl] spucken (= angeben) *to draw the long bow, to long-bow* [vi]; ⟨sl⟩ *to shoot one's mouth off*; *to sling* od *throw the hatchet* ‖ → Bausch **b.** ⟨math⟩ (Kreis≃) *arc* (*of a circle*) (schlagen *to describe*) ‖ (Licht≃) *arc*; → Regen≃ **c.** ⟨mus⟩ Halte≃ *bind, tie* ‖ ⟨typ⟩ *curve* **d.** Krocket≃ *hoop* **2.** ⟨arch⟩ *arch* ‖ gotischer ~, Spitz≃ *ogive*; gleichseitiger Spitz≃ *equilateral arch*; Schwib≃ *flying-buttress* romanischer ~, Rund≃ *Roman* od *semicircular arch* ‖ Brücken-≃ *arch*; Kiel–, Wellen≃ → Eselsrücken; Korb≃, gedrückter ~ *baskethandle* od *elliptic, flat arch*; Gurt≃ *transverse arch*; Hakenstein≃ *arch with joggled joints*; überhöhter ~ *horseshoe* od *stilted arch*; Entlastungs–, Übergangs≃ *discharging arch* ‖ Blend≃ *dead arcade* ‖ ⟨theat⟩ *cut cloth*, ⟨Am⟩ *cut-out drop* ‖ → Triumph≃ **II. 1.** [pl ≃] **(Schußwaffe)** *bow*; Lang≃ *long-bow*; → Armbrust ‖ e–n ~ spannen *to bend* od *draw a bow*; den ~ überspannen *to overdraw the bow* ‖ Flitz≃ *boy's bow* **2.** ⟨**mus**⟩ (Geigen≃) *bow*; den ~ führen *to bow*; die den ~ führende Hand *the bow-hand* **III.** [pl ~] **~ Papier** *sheet of paper*; ~ Schreibpapier, Brief≃ *sheet of note-paper* ‖ ⟨bookb⟩ *sheet* **IV.** [in comp] *bow ..* ‖ ⟨arch⟩ *arch ..* **~anleger** m ⟨typ⟩ *feeding apparatus* **~ansatz** m ⟨arch⟩ *summer* **~bohrer** m ⟨tech⟩ *bow-drill* **~brücke** f *arched bridge*; (alte) *hump-back bridge* **~einfassung** f ~ im Schlingstich (am Kleid) *scallops* [pl] **~feld** n *tympanum* **~fenster** m *arched window* **≃förmig** a ⟨arch⟩ *arched, arch-shaped*; ~er Ausschnitt (am Kleid) → Langette ‖ etw ~ m *to arch* (*a th*) **~führung** f ⟨mus⟩ *bowing* **~gang** m **1.** ⟨anat⟩ (im inneren Ohr) *semicircular canals* [pl] **2.** ⟨arch⟩ *arched arcade* **~geradleger** m ⟨typ⟩ *jogger-up* **~gerüst** n *centre* (entfernen *to strike*) **~gewölbe** n *arched vault* **~größe** f ⟨typ⟩ *folio* **~kalander** m ⟨pap⟩ *plate glazer* **~korrektur** f ⟨typ⟩ *proof in sheets* **~lampe** f ⟨el⟩ *arc-lamp* **~licht** n ⟨el⟩ *arc-light* **~lilie** f ⟨bot⟩ *Cyrtantus* (L) **~linie** f *curvature, curve* **~minute** f ⟨math⟩ *minute of arc, arc minute* **~rücken** m *extrados* **~säge** f *bow-saw* **~schießen** n *archery*; Zeitalter des ~s *bow and arrow period* **~schneider** m ⟨typ⟩ *sheet-cutter* **~schuß** m ⟨mil⟩ *high-angle fire* **~schütze** m *archer, bowman, toxophilite* **~sehne** f *bow-string* **~sekunde** f *second of arc, arc sec.* **~signatur** f ⟨typ⟩ *sheet signature* **~strich** m ⟨mus⟩ *stroke of the bow*; *bowing*, ~e [pl] *bowings* **~sprung** m ⟨hors⟩ *curvet* **≃weise** adv *in* od *by sheets* **~widerlager** n *arch abutment* (⟨bes⟩ e–r Brücke) **~zähler** m ⟨typ⟩ *sheet counter* ‖ *counting machine* **~zapfen** m *pendant, –dent* **~ziffer** f ⟨typ⟩ *sheet signature* **~zirkel** m *bow-compasses*, ⟨fam⟩ *bows* [pl]; ein ~ *a pair of b.* **~zuführung** f ⟨typ⟩ automatische ~ *automatic sheet feeder*; pneumatische ~ *pneumatic feeding arrangement*

B·ogheadkohle ['bɔghed–] (engl) f *boghead coal, torbanite*

b·ogig a *bent, curved*

Bogom·ilen m [pl] ⟨ec hist⟩ *Bogomils* [pl]

Boheme [bo'æ:m] (Fr) f *Bohemia* (L); ~tum [n] *Bohemianism* **Bohemien** [boe:'mjɛ̃:] m *Bohemian*; → Böhme

B·ohle f ~/~n *thick board* od *plank*; (Weg) mit ~n versehen *to plank* **~nbelag** m *planking, plank bottom* **b·ohlen** vt [h] *to board, plank*

B·öhme m, **B·öhmin** f *Bohemian* **B·öhmen** n *Bohemia* **B·öhmerwald** m *Bohemian Forest*

b·öhmisch a **1.** *Bohemian*; ~e Brüder *Bohemian-Moravian Brethren* [pl] **2.** ⟨fig⟩ (fremd) *strange*; das sind mir ~e Dörfer, das kommt mir ~ vor *that is Greek to me*

B·öhnchen n ~s/~ *small bean* ‖ °jedes ~ hat sein Tönchen *beans do talk with one* ‖ ⟨übtr⟩ sag mal ~! *purse your lips!*

B·ohne f ~/~n **1.** ⟨bot⟩ **a.** *bean*; Garten≃ *garden-bean*; Stangen≃ *runner bean* ‖ grüne ~n [pl] *French* (⟨Am⟩ *string*) *beans*, (kl) (Wachs≃) *kidney beans* [pl]; türkische ~n *scarlet runners* ‖ weiße ~n (*dried*) *haricot beans*, ⟨cul⟩ *white beans* ‖ dicke ~n, Puff≃n, Sau≃n *broad beans*; Pferde≃n *horse-beans* ‖ Feuer≃ *scarlet runner*, → Lupine **b.** Kaffee≃ *coffee bean*; Kakao≃ *cocoa bean* **c.** °⟨fig⟩ nicht die ~ *not one jot* od *tittle, not a bean*; ⟨Am sl⟩ *not a hoot*(*er*); er ist nicht die ~ wert *he is not worth a straw*; (in Antworten) nicht die ~! *nothing doing!* ‖ ich mache mir nicht die ~ draus *I do not care a bean* od *damn* (od *a straw*, ⟨Am sl⟩ *a cuss*); niemand kümmert sich die ~ um .. *nobody cares a hoot for ..*; sie macht sich nicht die ~ aus Blumen *she does not care a hang for flowers*; er versteht nicht die ~ davon *he does not understand a bit of it* **2.** °blaue ~ *bullet*; ⟨Am sl⟩ *blue pill* **3.** ⟨vet⟩ = Kunde f ⟨vet⟩

×**b·ohnen** vt [h] = bohnern

B·ohnen- [in comp] *bean* (*flower*; *field*) **~fest** n ⟨hist⟩ *Twelfth-Night festivities* [pl] **~kaffee** m *coffee* **~kraut** n ⟨bot⟩ *savory* **~kuchen** m ⟨hist⟩ *Twelfth cake*; → Bohnenfest **~lied** n ⟨fig⟩ das geht über's ~ *that's the limit, that beats all, that takes the cake* **~salat** m ⟨cul⟩ *salad of French beans* **~stange** f *bean-pole* (⟨a. fig⟩ P), *bean-stick* ‖ ⟨fig⟩ (P) *hop-pole* ‖ lang wie e–e ~ *as tall as a h.-p.* od *May-pole* **~strauch** m ⟨bot⟩ ind. ~ *cajan* **~stroh** n *bean-straw* ‖ ⟨fig⟩ grob (dumm) wie ~ *uncouth*; *extremely coarse* od *rude* (bzw *silly*) **~suppe** f *beansoup*

B·ohner m (P) *polisher* **~besen** m ⟨el⟩ (*floor-*) *-polisher* **~bürste** f *polishing-brush* **~lappen** m *rubber* **~maschine** f ⟨el⟩ *floor polisher* **~masse, ~wichse** f *polish, polishing-paste for floors* **~wachs** n *floor-wax* (od *varnish*); *rubbing-wax*

b·ohnern vt [h] (Fußboden) *to polish, wax*; *to* (*polish with*) *bees-wax*

B·ohnerz n ⟨minr⟩ *granular* od *pisiform limonite, pea-ore*

Böhnli n [mst pl] ⟨cul Sw⟩ = Bohnen

B·ohr- ~anlage f ⟨tech⟩ *boring plant* **~arbeit** f *boring*; ~en [pl] *drilling work* **~assel** f ⟨zoo⟩ *gribble* **~brunnen** m *Artesian well* **~eisen** n *bit* **~futter** n *drilling chuck* **~gerät** n *boring tool* **~gerüst** n *bore-frame* **~gezähe** n *drilling tools* **~hammer** m *boring* (od *drilling*)*-hammer* **~käfer** m ⟨ent⟩ *death-watch* **~klinge** f *drill* **~knarre** f ⟨tech⟩ *ratchet-brace* (od *drill*) **~loch** n *bore-hole*; *boring* **~löffel** m ⟨min⟩ *metal cylinder for enclosing the bore-meal*; *bailer* **~maschine** f *drilling* (od *boring*)*-machine*; (Gesteins≃) *rock drill* ‖ ⟨dent⟩ *dental engine* **~mehl** n *bore-meal*; ⟨min⟩ *quarry dust* **~muschel** f ⟨zoo⟩ *stone-borer*;

→ Bohrwurm **~ratsche** f ⟨tech⟩ = Bohrknarre **~schmand** m *ooze of borings* **~schwamm** m ⟨zoo⟩ *boring-sponge* **~späne** m [pl] *borings* [pl], *boring--dust* **~spitze** f → Bohrerspitze **~turm** m ⟨tech⟩ *high boring-scaffold*; (oil) *derrick* **~werk** n *drilling-plant* **~winde** f ⟨carp⟩ *brace and bit* **~wurm** m ⟨zoo⟩ *ship-worm, teredo*

b·ohren I. vt/i [h] **A.** vt **1.** (Loch) *to bore, drill*; mit e–m Handbohrer ~ *to gimlet* ‖ ein Loch in (etw) ~ *to poke a hole in(to)*; (Brunnen) *to bore, drill, sink* ‖ (Tunnel) *to drive* | (Bretter) *to bore*; (Metall, Stein) *to drill* ‖ ⟨fig⟩ das Brett ~, wo es am dünnsten ist *to shun hard work*; hartes Holz ~ *to fight severe opposition* **2.** ⟨übtr⟩ (Stock etc) *to bore, dig, pierce* (in *into*) ‖ jdm ein Schwert in den Leib ~ *to pierce a p with a sword* ‖ (Schiff) in den Grund ~ *to sink a ship* **3. sich** ~ *to bore* od *make one's way* (in *into*; durch *through*) ‖ (of eyes) *to bore* (in *into*) | ⟨übtr⟩ sich ~ in etw *to dig into a th*; *to penetrate, pierce a th*; Kummer bohrte sich in sein Herz *sorrow pierced his heart* (od *pierced him to the heart*) **B.** vi **1.** ~ **auf** *or* **nach** etw *to bore* od *dig for a th* **2.** ⟨übtr⟩ *to bore, dig* (in *in*) ‖ (drängen) *to prod* ‖ jdm im Schädel (herum)~ (of feelings) *to rack, torment a p* ‖ sie bohrte so lange, bis er nachgab *she harassed* (od *tormented, worried*) *him till he yielded* **II.** ≗ n *boring, drilling*; Tief≗ *deep boring* od *drilling* **b·ohrend** a *boring* ‖ ⟨übtr⟩ *piercing*; *lancinating* (*pains*); *penetrating* (*glance*); *probing, searching* (*question*)

B·ohrer m ~s/~ **1.** (P) *borer* **2.** (an insect) *borer* ‖ Lege≗ *ovipositor* (*of an insect*) **3.** ⟨tech⟩ (Werkzeug) *borer*, ⟨carp⟩ Hand≗, Nagel≗ *gimlet*; gr ~ *auger*; mit e–m Hand≗ bohren *to gimlet* ‖ Drill≗, Stein≗ *drill*; Gesteins≗ *rock drill*; Metall≗ *metal drill*; → Krauskopf ‖ ⟨dent⟩ *dental drill* ‖ Gewinde≗ *screw-tap*; Knarren≗ *ratchet-borer*; Spiral≗ *spiral drill* ‖ Preßluft≗ *pneumatic borer*; → Bohrmaschine, -winde **~einsatz** m *auger-bit* **~spitze** (auger-)bit

B·ohrung f ~/~en **1.** = Bohren **2.** (Bohrloch) *bore(-hole), boring* ‖ ⟨mot⟩ *bore*

B·oi m ~(e)s/~s (Flanellstoff) *baize*

b·öig a *gusty, puffy, squally* (*wind*, etc.) ‖ ⟨meteor⟩ *turbulent* ‖ ⟨aero⟩ *bumpy* (*air*); ~e Beschaffenheit, ≗keit [f] *gustiness*; *puffiness*; *turbulence*; *bumpiness*

Boj·ar m ~en/~en ⟨hist⟩ (russ.) *boyar*

B·oje f ~/~n ⟨mar⟩ *buoy*; Rettungs≗ *life--buoy*; runde, an beiden Enden spitz zulaufende ~ *nun-buoy* ‖ an die ~ gehen (of ships) *to make fast to a buoy*; durch ~n kennzeichnen *to buoy* ‖ [koll] ~n [pl], ~system *buoyage*

†**Bojer** pl (keltisch. Volk) *Boji* [L] pl

Bol m ~s/ ⟨minr⟩ = Bolus

×**B·olchen** n ~s/~ = Bonchen, Bonbon

Bol·ero m ~s/~s **1.** (span. Tanz) *bolero* **2.** (kz Jacke) *bolero*

Bol·etus m (L) ⟨bot⟩ *boletus*, → Röhrling

Bol·ide m ⟨meteor⟩ = Feuerkugel

Bolivi·aner m ~s/~, **bolivi·anisch** a *Bolivian*

×**b·ölken** vi [niedd] = schreien, brüllen

B·olle f ~/~n **1.** ⟨bot⟩ (Zwiebel) *bulb* ‖ (Samenkapsel) *boll* **2.** °⟨übtr⟩ = Taschenuhr; Nase

B·öller m ~s/~ **1.** ⟨hist mil⟩ *mortar(-piece)* **2.** ⟨übtr⟩ *mortar*; jdn mit ~schüssen empfangen *to salute a p with a discharge of cannon*

b·ollern vi [h] **1.** (poltern) *to rumble*; *to boom* ‖ *to bluster* **2.** ~ gegen *to knock against* ..

b·öllern vi [h] ⟨übtr⟩ *to shoot with a mortar*; *to fire, shoot*

Bolletr·ieholz n *horse-flesh mahogany*

b·ollig a *bulbous*

B·ollmehl n ~s/~e *shorts* pl

B·ollwerk n ~s/~e **1.** ⟨fort⟩ *bulwark, bastion*; *rampart*; mit ~en versehen *bastioned* | ⟨mar⟩ *bulwark*; *mole* **2.** ⟨fig⟩ *bulwark, bastion*; *stronghold* (gegen *against*)

Bol·ogna n ⟨It⟩ (Stadt) *Bologna* **Bologn·eser(in** f) m *Bolognese, Bolognian*; *Bologna dog* **Bologn·eser** f ~/~ (⟨a.⟩ ~wurst f) ⟨m. m.⟩ *boloney*

Bolom·eter n (z Messen der Strahlungsenergie) *bolometer*

B·olor-Dagh m → Belur-Dagh

Bolschew·ik m = –w·ist –**wis·ierung** f ~/~en *bolshevization* –**w·ismus** m ~/ *bolshevism* –**w·ist** m ~en/~en *Bolshevist, Bolshevik*; ⟨cont⟩ *Bolshy*, –*shie* **b–w·istisch** a *Bolshevist(ic), Bolshevik* ‖ ~ m *to bolshevize*

B·olus m ⟨minr⟩ *bole, bolus*

B·olzen m ~s/~ **1.** (kz Pfeil) *bolt*; *short arrow* od *dart* **2.** ⟨übtr⟩ **a.** (gr Nagel) *bolt, peg, pin*; ⟨mach⟩ *gib*; *pintle*; ⟨rail⟩ (Schienen≗) *spike*; Schrauben≗ *screw bolt* ‖ (Schlag≗) *striker* ‖ mit e–m ~ befestigen *to bolt* **b.** (Plätteisen≗) *heater* **c.** *upright beam* **3.** °(P) Dienst≗ ⟨dero⟩ *skivvy* **4.** [in comp] *bolt* .. **~büchse** f *air-gun* **~kopf** m *bolt-head* **~schloß** n *padlock*

°**b·olzen** vt [h] = prügeln

Bomb·age f ~/~n *blown tin*

†**Bomb·arde** f ~/~n **1.** ⟨hist⟩ (gr Geschütz) *bombard* **2.** = Bomhart **Bombardem·ent** [bɔmbardəˈmɑ̃:] n (Fr) ~s/~s *bombardment* (e–r Stadt, auf e–e St. *of a town*); *the bombarding* od *bombing, shelling* ‖ ⟨übtr⟩ *bombarding* †**Bombardier** m ~s/~e *bombardier* **bombard·ieren** vt [h] (Stadt etc) *to bombard*; *to batter, bomb, shell*; ⟨sl⟩ *to crump* | ⟨fig⟩ (jdn) *to bombard* (mit *with*); *to assail, pound* (*with*); → bestürmen **Bombard·ierkäfer** m ⟨ent⟩ *bombardier beetle* **Bombard·ierung** f → Bombardement

Bombard·on [bɔ̃:barˈdɔ̃:] n ~s/~s ⟨mus⟩ (Blechinstrument) *bombardon* ‖ → Euphonium; Tuba

B·ombay n (Vorderindien: Provinz u Hptst.)

Bombas·in m ~s/~e (Kleiderstoff) *bombasine*, –*bazine*

Bomb·ast m ~es/ *bombast, highfalutin, highfaluting, orotundity*; *verbiage, verbosity* **bomb·astisch 1.** a *bombastic, highfalutin(g), inflated, orotund* (*style*) **2.** adv *bombastically*

B·ombe f ~/~n **1.** (Sprengkörper) **a.** ⟨aero & mil⟩ *bomb, bomb-shell, shell*; ⟨sl⟩ *crump, pine-apple*; Brand≗ *incendiary bomb* ‖ (Hand≗) *small bomb, grenade*, → Granate ‖ ⟨mar⟩ → Wasser≗ | ~n (ab)werfen *to drop* od *throw bombs*; ~n (ab)werfen auf e–e Stadt *to bomb a town* ‖ mit ~n beschießen = bombardieren ‖ die ~ platzt *the bomb explodes* ‖ → ~ntreffer **b.** ⟨fig⟩ *bomb(shell)*; wie e–e ~ einschlagen *to strike like a b.* ‖ potz ~n u Granaten! *dash it all!* **2.** ⟨übtr⟩ ⟨geol⟩ (Lavastück) *volcanic bomb* **3.** ⟨cul⟩ Eis≗ (*ice-cream*) *bomb* **4.** °⟨fig⟩ **a.** (P) *tub*; *barrel-bellied man* **b.** ⟨ftb⟩ *heavy shot* **c.** (Hut) ⟨sl⟩ *pot*

B·omben- A. ⟨aero⟩ **~(ab)werfen** n, **~(ab)-wurf** m *bomb-throwing, bombing* **~·abwurf** m *bomb release* **~angriff** m *bombing-raid* **~·aufhängevorrichtung** f *bomb carrier* od *gear* **~·auslösevorrichtung** f *bomb release control* **~(·einsatz)flug** m *bombing mission* **~einschlag** m *bomb impact* **~f·allkurve** f *bomb flight path* **~falltafel** f *bomb trajectory table* ≗**fest** a *bomb-proof, shell--proof*; → B **~flugzeug** n *bomber* ‖ ~schütze [m] ⟨aero⟩ *bomb aimer*; *gunner* **~gr·oßangriff** m ⟨sl⟩ *clobbering* **~kalorimeter** n ⟨phys⟩ *bomb calorimeter* **~kasten** m *bomb container* **~klappe** f *bomb-bay door* **~n·otwurf** m *emergency release* **~p·unktwurf** m *pin-point bombing* **~-R·äum- u Spr·engkommando** n *bomb disposal unit* **~reihe** f *train of bombs* **~r·eihenwurf** m *trail bombing* **~schacht** m *bomb bay* **~schaden** m *air-raid damage* **~schüttkasten** m *bomb chute* **~schütze**

m ⟨aero⟩ *bombardier*, ≗**sicher** a = bombenfest; → B **~sturzflug** m *bombing dive* **~teppich** m *bomb carpet*, *bombing pattern* ‖ das Belegen mit einem ~ *area bombing* ‖ e–n ~ legen auf *to plaster* (*a station*) **~t·iefwurf** m *low altitude bombing* **~treffer** m *bomb impact*; e–n ~ erhalten *to be bombed*; jdn durch ~ aus dem Haus vertreiben *to outbomb a p* **~werfer** m *bomb-thrower* **~wurf** m ~ aus gr Höhe *high-level bombing* | ~bahn [f] *bomb flight path* | ~vorhaltewinkel [m] *bombing angle* **~zielanflug** m *bombing run* **~zielgerät** n, **~zielvorrichtung** f ⟨aero⟩ *bomb sight* **B.** °⟨fig⟩ [als Intensiv] = Mords–, Riesen– *huge, immense, terrific, tremendous*; ⟨fam⟩ *rattling, ripping*; ⟨sl⟩ *stunning, topping* **~attraktion** f *big draw* **~element** [intj] ~! *dash* od *hang it all*! *damn it*! **~erfolg** m *rattling success*; ⟨Am sl⟩ *wow* ‖ e–n ~ h. *to score a hit* ≗**fest** a *quite certain*, das steht ~ *that is quite c.*; → A. **~kerl** m *ripper, stunner*; **~sache** f *ripper, stunner* ≗**sicher 1.** a *quite certain, deadsure*; ⟨fam⟩ *cocksure* (*of a p's applause*); das ist ~ *that is as sure as eggs are eggs, that is as sure as a gun*; → A. **2.** adv *certainly, for certain*

B·omber m ⟨aero⟩ *raider, bomber, bomb-dropper*; ⟨fam⟩ *cuckoo*

bomb·ieren vt [h] ⟨tech⟩ (wölben) *to curve, chamfer, flute*; bombiertes Blech = Wellblech

°**b·ombig** a *huge, terrific*; ⟨fam⟩ *rattling* (*success*), *ripping, stunning, topping*

B·ombus (L) ⟨ent⟩ (Hummelgattung) *Bombus* (L), *humble-bees* [pl]

Bomhart, Bommert m ~s/~s ⟨mus⟩ (altes Holzblasinstrument) *bombard(o)*

Bon [bɔŋ] m (Fr) ⟨com⟩ **1.** (Gutschein) *draft, order* ‖ *credit note* (f. *for*) **2.** (Kassenzettel) *coupon*; *voucher*; *ticket*; *check*

bona fide (L) *bona fide* (L), *in good faith*; *genuinely* **bona fides** (L) *bona fides* (L), *good faith*

Bonapart·ist m *bonapartist*

Bonb·on [bɔŋ'bɔŋ] m & n (Fr) ~s/~s *bonbon, sweet, sweetmeat*; ⟨bes Am⟩ (*hard*) *candy*; gr ~ *humbug*; e–e Tüte ~s *a bag of sweets*; Brust≗ *lozenge*; runder Frucht≗ *drop* ‖ [koll] ~s [pl] *lollipops, sweet meats* [pl], *confectionery, comfit*; (*boiled*) *sweets*, ⟨sl⟩ *bullets* **~dose** f = Bonbonniere **~laden** m *sweet-shop*, ⟨sl⟩ *tuck-shop* **~schachtel** f = Bonbonniere

Bonbonni·ere [bɔ̃bɔ'nje:rə] f (Fr) *sweetmeat-box, comfit-box*

×**B·onchen** n ~s/~ = Bonbon

B·onde m ⟨Ger⟩ *freeholder*; ~ngut [n] *freehold*

B·onebed ['bounbed] n (engl) ~s/ ⟨geol⟩ *bone-bed*

°**b·ongfortion·ös** a ⟨sl⟩ *go–, galuptious*

B·ongo f ⟨zoo⟩ (afrik. Waldantilope) *bongo*

Bonhom·ie f *bonhomie, good nature*

Bonhomme [bɔ'nɔm] m (Fr) *bonhomous p*

Bonifikati·on [ts] f ~/~en *indemnity*; *bonus* (L) **bonifiz·ieren** vt [h] (jdn) *to bonify*; *to indemnify* (f. *for*)

Bonif·atiusstraße f (Meerenge zw. Korsika u Sardinien) *Straits of Bonifacio*

Bonit·ät f ⟨com⟩ *solvency*; *credit, reliability, stability* (*of a p, of a firm*) **bonit·ieren** vt [h] (Land) *to classify* (*land*) *according to the quality of the soil* **Bonit·ierung** f *classification of landed property*

Bon·ite m ~n/~n ⟨ich⟩ *bonito, striped tunny*

Bonm·ot [bɔ̃'mo:] n ~s/~s (Fr) *bon mot* (Fr), *witty saying*; *witticism*

Bonn n ⟨Ger⟩ Bundesrepublik-Hptst.

B·onne f ~/~n *French bonne*; *nursery governess, children's nurse*

B·onus m (L) ~/~(se) ⟨com⟩ *bonus*; *premium*

Bonvivant [bɔ̃vi'vɑ̃] m (Fr) *bon-vivant*

B·onze m ~n/~n **1.** (buddhist. Priester) *bonze* **2.** ⟨übtr⟩ **a.** ⟨cont⟩ = Pfaffe **b.** *bigwig*; ⟨sl⟩ *big bug, would-be big bug* ‖ ⟨a. pol⟩ *boss*; Ober≗ *head boss*; Partei≗ *party boss* **~ntum** n *bigwigs* pl ‖ [abstr] *bigwiggedness*; *bossdom* ⟨Am⟩ *spoils system, boss rule*

Boos f niederländ. = Viehstall

B·oot n [×a. f] ~(e)s/~e *boat*; ~e [pl] *boats* [pl], *craft*; das ~ des Kommandanten *the captain's gig*; → Bei≗, Einbaum; Fischer≗; Rund≗; Segel≗ | ein ~ voll Matrosen *a boatful of sailors*, .. voll Fische *a boat-load of fish* ‖ ein ~ aussetzen *to get a boat out*; .. einsetzen *to hoist a b. in*; → fieren, heißen ‖ in e–m ~ fahren *to boat*; ⟨fig⟩ im selben ~ sitzen *to be in the same boat* ‖ etw im ~ befördern *to boat a th* ‖ ein ~ an ein Schiff anlegen *to lay a boat alongside of a ship*

Boot [bu:t] m [engl] ~s/~s (Hufschoner) *boot*

B·ootfahren n *boating* **B·ootfahrt** f *boating-trip*

Bö·otien n ⟨Gr⟩ *Bœotia, Beotia*, ⟨poet a.⟩ *Aonia* **B·öot(i)er** m, **~in** f, **bö·otisch** a *Bœotian, Bœotic*, ⟨a.⟩ *Beotian, Beotic*

B·oots- [in comp] *boat* .. **~anlageplatz** m *marina* **~anker** m *grapnel, anchor* **~bau** m *boat-building* **~dienst** m *boat drill* **~führer** m *boatman*; ⟨racing⟩ *cox*; als ~ fungieren *to cox* **~gast** m *oarsman* **~haken** m *boat-hook* **~haus** n *boat-house* **~klampen** f [pl] ⟨mar⟩ *chocks* [pl] **~kran** m *davit* **~leine** f *tow-rope* **~leute** [pl], **~mannschaft** f *boat's crew, sailors* [pl] **~mann** m *boatswain*; ~smaat [m] *boatswain's mate* **~manöver** n *boatdrill* **~motor** m *marine motor* **~pfropfen** m *boat-plug* **~rennen** n = Bootwettfahrt **~steuermann** m *coxswain* **~tau** n ⟨mar⟩ *painter* **~unglück** n *boating accident* **~verleiher, ~vermieter** m *boatman* **~wettfahrt** f *boat-race* **~winde** f *boat-hoist*

B·ootschwanz m ⟨orn⟩ *boat-tail*

°**b·opmäßig** a ⟨sl⟩ *spiffing*

B·or n ~s/ ⟨chem⟩ **1.** *boron* **2.** [in comp] *boric* **~salbe** f *boracic ointment* ≗**sauer** a *boric*; ~es Salz *borate* **~säure** f *boric* (od **boracic*) *acid*; Salz der ~ *borate*

B·ora f (It) (Nordostwind) *bora*

Boraginaz·een f [pl] *Boraginaceae* [pl] (L)

Bor·assuspalme f ⟨bot⟩ *borassus* (L)

Bor·at n ⟨chem⟩ *borate*

Borax m ~es/ ⟨chem⟩ *borax*; roher ~ *tincal, tinkal*

Boraz·it m ~s/~e ⟨minr⟩ *boracite*

Bord, Bort n ~s/~e & B·örde, B·örter **1.** (Brett) *board*; *plank* **2.** (Brettgestell) *shelf*; Wand≗ *wall-shelf* ‖ Blumen≗ *flower-shelf* ‖ (Bücher≗) (*book-*)*shelf*; ein ~ voll Bücher *a shelfful of books*

Bord m ~s/~e **1.** ⟨mar⟩ *board*; → Back≗, Luv≗, Steuer≗; Frei≗ | **an** ~ (des Schiffes) *on board, aboard, on shipboard, on board ship*; an ~ e–s Schiffes *on board a ship*; an ~ der ‚Bremen' *on board the 'Bremen'*; an ~ desselben *on board her, on board of it* ‖ frei an ~ (abbr fob) *free on board* (abbr *f.o.b.*) ‖ alle (Reisenden) an ~! *all aboard*! ‖ (etw) an ~ bringen *to ship*; *to take on board* ‖ an ~ gehen *to go aboard* (od *on board*); *to embark*, ⟨aero⟩ *in-, enplane*; an ~ e–s Schiffes gehen *to go aboard a ship, to board a ship* ‖ (Schiff) an ~ (e–s anderen) legen *to lay* (*a ship*) *on board* ‖ an ~ nehmen *to take in, to ship* | **über** ~ *overboard*; Mann über ~! *man overboard*; *to go by the board* ‖ (Waren) über ~ werfen *to throw overboard, to jettison*; ⟨fig⟩ (Ideen, Einrichtungen) *to scrap, to discard*; *to throw to the winds* od *dogs*; über ~ geworfen w *to go by the board* | **von** ~ *from board the ship*; v ~ gehen *to disembark*, ⟨aero⟩ *to deplane* **2.** (Rand) *border, edge*; *brim, rim* **~anlasser** m

⟨aero⟩ *cockpit starter* **~-Boden-** *air-to-ground* (*attack, communication*) **~-~-verkehr** m ⟨wir aero⟩ *inter-aircraft communication* **~buch** n ⟨aero⟩ *journey log book, flight log* **~dienst** m *duty on board* **~funker** m ⟨aero⟩ *aircraft wireless operator* **~geschütz** n ⟨aero⟩ *cannon* **~küche** f ⟨mar, aero⟩ *galley* **~maschinengewehr** n ⟨aero⟩ *aircraft machine-gun* **~mechaniker, ~monteur** m *air mechanic, flight-engineer* **~radar(gerät** n) m *air* od *nose radar* | ~ z Erfassung v Überwasserfahrzeugen *air-to-surface vessel radar* **~stein** → d. **~stewardeß** f *air-hostess*; ⟨Am⟩ *stewardess* **~telefon** n *interphone* **~verpflegung** f *catering*; *flight ration* **~verständigungsanlage** f *intercom(munication system)* **~vorräte** m pl *aircraft stores* **~waffen** f pl *aircraft weapons* od *armament* | ~angriff [m] *strafing attack*; *air-to-ground* (*range*) **~wand** f ⟨mar⟩ *ship's side* **~wart** m = –monteur **~-zu-~-** *air-to-air* [attr]

B·orde f = Borte

B·örde f *flat, fertile tract of land*

Bordeaux- [bɔr'do:] **~brühe** f ⟨hort⟩ Bordeaux mixture **⩯rot** a *claret-red* **~(wein)** m *B. wine, claret* **Bordelaiser(in)** m, **-lese** m, **-lesin** f [–'lɛ:–] *Bordelese, inhabitant of B.*

Bord·ell n ~s/~e *brothel, disorderly house, bawdy-house, whorehouse*, ⟨sl⟩ *knocking shop*

B·ördel- ~eisen n *edging tool* **~maschine** f *flanging machine* **~rand** m (Konservendosen⩯) *flange* **b·ördeln** vt [h] (Rand) *to crease*; *border*; *flange*; (Blech) *to cup*; ⟨tech⟩ (abbiegen) *to fold*; (Dosen ⟨a.⟩) *to bead*; ⟨num⟩ (rändern) *to edge(-raise)* **B·ördelung** f ⟨num⟩ (Perlrand) *border of dots*

b·orden vt [h] *to border* (*a th*) *with boards* od *planks* ‖ (Schiff) *to board*

bord·ieren vt (Rand) *to border, edge, trim*; *lace*

B·ording m ~s/~e ⟨Ger, mar⟩ *one-masted lighter* (*on the Vistula*)

B·ordkante, -schwelle f, **-stein** m (am Bürgersteige) *kerb* ‖ –stein *edge stone* ‖ –steintaster [m] ⟨mot⟩ *kerb feeler*

Bord·un m ~s/~e ⟨mus⟩ **1.** *drone, bass-pipe* (*of a bagpipe*) **2.** (Orgelregister) *bourdon, burdoun*

Bord·üre f ~/~n *edging, trimming, braiding* ‖ ⟨bookb⟩ (Zierleiste) *border* ‖ (Ornament⩯) *frame*

B·ore f [engl] ~/~n (Flutwelle) *bore*

B·oreas m (L) (Nordwind) *Boreas*

B·oretsch m ~s/ ⟨bot⟩ → Borretsch

Borg m ~s/ *borrowing* ‖ *credit, trust* ‖ auf ~ *on credit* (od *trust*); *on loan*; ⟨sl⟩ *on tick* ‖ (etw) auf ~ geben *to lend* (jdm *to a p*) ‖ (etw) auf ~ nehmen *to take on credit, to borrow* (v jdm *of* od *from a p*)

b·orgen I. vt [h] **1.** (entleihen) (etw) *to borrow* (v jdm *of* od *from a p*) ‖ ⟨arith⟩ *to borrow* (: *I borrow 10*) **2.** (leihweise geben) jdm etw ~ *to lend a p a th* (od *a th to a p*) **II.** ⩯ n *borrowing* ‖ ~ macht Sorgen *who goes a-borrowing goes a-sorrowing* **B·orger** m ~s/~ *borrower*

B·orgis f ~/ (ein Schriftgrad) *Long Primer*

B·orgtau n ~s/~e ⟨mar⟩ *preventer*

B·orke f ~/~n [niedd] **1.** *bark, rind* (*of a tree*) **2.** *crust, scab* (*of a wound*)

B·orken- ~flechte f ⟨med⟩ *herpes tonsurans* (L) **~käfer** m ⟨ent⟩ *bark-beetle*, ⟨Am⟩ *bark-borer*

B·orn m ~s/~e ⟨poet⟩ *spring* | (Brunnen) *well*; *salt-well*

B·orneo n (Sunda-Insel)

Borne·ol n ⟨chem⟩ *borneol*

born·iert a *borné, narrow, narrow-minded*; *dense, obtuse*; *stupid* **⩯heit** f ~/~en *narrow-mindedness*; *denseness, density, obtuseness*; *stupidity*

B·orre m (Fr) ⟨bot⟩ = Porree

B·orretsch m ⟨a.⟩ Boretsch, *borage*

Borrom·äische Inseln f pl (Inseln im *Lago Maggiore*) *Borromean Islands* pl

×**B·örs** m ⟨ich⟩ = Barsch

Borschtsch (russ. Suppe) *borsch, bortsch*

B·orsdorfer m ⟨Ger⟩ *Borsdorf pippin*; Backen wie ein ~ Apfel *rosy cheeks like an apple*

B·örse f ~/~n **1.** (Geldbeutel) *purse*; ⟨Am⟩ *pocket-book* | ⟨übtr⟩ (Geldmittel) *means* **2.** ⟨com⟩ **a.** *Exchange, Change*, ⟨a-engl⟩ *Bourse*; ⟨fam⟩ *the House*; Effekten⩯ *Stock Exchange*, (Geldmarkt) (*money-*)*market*; Produkten⩯ *Produce Exchange* ‖ an, auf der ~ *on 'Change, on* (*the*) *Exchange, on the Stock Exchange, in the market* ‖ die ~ besuchen, zur ~ gehen *to go on 'Change* **b.** (Gebäude) *Exchange*, auf der ~ *at the E.* ‖ *Stock Exchange* ‖ ⟨Am⟩ (Getreide⩯) *pit*

B·örsen- ~beginn m: zu ~ *in early dealings* **~bericht** m *exchange-report* (od *advice*), *stock exchange* (od *market*)*-report*; (in der Presse) *city article* **~besuch** m *attendance on the Exchange* **~blatt** n *exchange list, stock-report* ‖ *financial newspaper* **⩯fähig, ⩯gängig** a *quoted on the Exchange*; *marketable, negotiable* **~gericht** n *Stock Exchange Committee* **~geschäft** n *Stock Exchange transaction* **~handel** m *Stock Exchange business* **~kurs** m *price-current on 'Change, market-rate* **~makler** m *stock-broker* **~ordnung** f *Exchange regulations* [pl] **~papiere** n [pl] *stocks, shares, securities* [pl] *quoted on the Stock Exchange* **~platz** m *Exchange* ‖ *place on 'Change* **~preis** m *market price* **~recht** n *Stock Exchange law* **~schluß** m *closing-time of the Exchange* **~schwindel** m *Stock Exchange swindling*, ⟨Am⟩ *bucket-shop business* **~spekulant** m *stock-jobber, stag* **~spiel** n *Exchange gambling* **~steuer** f *Stock Exchange tax, stock-transfer tax* **~sturz** m *break* **~umsatzsteuer** f *tax on Stock Exchange transactions* **~verein** m der deutschen Buchhändler *association of German book dealers* **~vorstand** m *Exchange Committee* **~wert** m *Stock Exchange value, market value* **~zeitung** f *financial paper* (od *news* [pl]) **~zettel** m *market-report, stock-list*

×**Borst** m ~es/~e = Riß; → bersten

B·orste f ~/~n *bristle, stiff hair*; ~n [pl] ⟨zoo⟩ *pelage*; ⟨bot & zoo⟩ *seta*; mit ~n versehen *bristled*

B·orsten- ⩯artig a *setaceous* **~besen** m *bristle-broom* **⩯förmig** a *setiform* **~gras** n ⟨bot⟩ *mat-grass* **~igel** m → Tanrek **~pinsel** m *bristle-brush* **⩯tragend** a *setigerous* **~vieh** n = Schwein **~wisch** m (f. Kamin) *hearth-brush*

b·orstig a *bristly*; ⟨bot & zoo⟩ *hirsute, hispid, setaceous* | ⟨fig⟩ *crabbed, gruff, irritable, sour, surly* **⩯keit** f ~/ *bristliness* ‖ ⟨fig⟩ *crabbedness, gruffness, sourness*

Bort n = Bord n **Bört** n = Bord n

B·orte f ~/~n *border* (*of a carpet, wall-paper*); *selvage* (*of cloth*); *edging, trimming*; *braid(ing), galloon*; seidene ~ *silk binding*; gestickte ~ *purls* [pl]; → Tresse ‖ mit e–r ~ besetzen *to braid*; mit e–r ~ einfassen *to purl* **~nmacher, ~nwirker** m *braid* (od *lace*)*-maker* **~nwirkerei** f *lace-braiding* od *-trimming*

†**Bor·usse** m *Prussian*

bös = böse **b·ösartig** a *malignant, malicious, virulent* (*press campaign*; *tone*); *bad, evil-minded, wicked* ‖ *wild, vicious, mean* (*horse*) | ⟨med⟩ *malign(ant)* (*tumour*), *virulent* (*disease*); *infectious* **B·ösartigkeit** f *badness*; *malignancy, malignity* ‖ ⟨med⟩ *malignancy, malignity, virulence, -cy*

b·öschen vt [h] = abböschen

B·oschhorn n ⟨mot el⟩ (Marke) *horn*

B·öschung f ~/~en *slope*; *talus* (L) ‖ ⟨mil⟩ *scarp*; ⟨geog, fort⟩ *escarpment*; innere Graben⩯ (e–s Unterstandes) *escarp* ‖ waagerechter Absatz e–r hohen ~ *berm* **~(sabsatz** m) (→ Berme) *benching*, ⟨fort⟩ *berm* **~spflasterung** f *pitching* **~swinkel** m *gradient of a slope*

b·öse I. a [compr ärger, schlimmer] **A.** [attr] **1.** (S) **a.** *bad* (*habit, reputation*), *evil, ill* (*repute*: *news*; *wind*); *wicked* (*thoughts*) ‖ ~ Absicht *malice* ‖ ~er Blick *evil eye*; mit ~m B. behaftet *evil-eyed* ‖ ~s Gewissen *bad* od *guilty conscience* ‖ e–e ~ S, ~ Geschichte *a bad business* od *affair*; das ist e–e ~ S *that's a great nuisance* ‖ ~ Wetter [pl] → Wetter ‖ ~r Wille *malice* ‖ ~ Zeiten *hard times* ‖ ~r Zufall *unfortunate coincidence* ‖ ~ Zunge *evil* od *sharp tongue* ‖ → Miene **b.** (krank) *bad, sore* (*finger, leg*) ‖ (groß, heftig) *bad* (*blunder*); ~ Erkältung *bad cold* **2.** (P) **a.** (schlecht) *bad, wicked*; ein ~r Bursche *a bad egg* od *hat*; ein ~s Pack *a bad lot* ‖ (gottlos) *ungodly, impious* **b.** (boshaft) *evil, malicious, vicious*; *mischievous* ‖ ~ Geister *evil spirits* ‖ ~ Sieben, ~s Weib *shrew* **3.** (T) *vicious* (*dog, horse*) **B.** [pred] (ärgerlich) ~ s *to be angry* od *cross, to be ill-tempered* (od *in a bad temper*), ⟨sl⟩ *shirty*; ~ w *to get angry* ‖ jdm ~ s *to bear a p a grudge*; *to have a g. against a p* ‖ auf jdn (*or* mit jdm) ~ s *to be angry* od *vexed with a p*, ⟨Am⟩ *to be mad at a p* ‖ jdn ~ m *to make a p angry, to rile a p* ‖ sich ~ stellen, ~ tun *to feign anger* **II.** adv *badly* ‖ ~ dran s *to be badly off* ‖ es nicht ~ meinen *to mean no harm*

B·öse 1. [~s, das ~] n *the evil, the ill* ‖ ~s tun *to do evil* od *ill*; ~s meiden *to shun evil* ‖ jdm ~s zufügen *to inflict evil* od *an injury upon a p* ‖ ~s mit Gutem vergelten *to return good for evil* ‖ jetzt heißt es: ~s mit ~m bekämpfen *desperate cases require desperate means* **2.** der ~ (Teufel) *the evil one, the foul fiend* | die ~n [pl] (Gottlosen) *the ungodly*

b·osen vrefl [h] sich ~ = sich ärgern

B·ösewicht m ~s/~e(r) *miscreant, ruffian, scoundrel, villain, wretch* ‖ ⟨hum⟩ *rogue, scamp*

b·oshaft a *cussed, evil(-minded), malicious, mischievous, spiteful, wicked* **≗igkeit** f = **B·osheit** f ~/~en *malice, maliciousness, malignancy, malignity, spite, wickedness*; aus ~ *out of spite*

Bosk·ett n ~s/~e ⟨hort⟩ *plantation* (*in a garden*), *shrubbery, bosket, bosquet, bosk*

b·öslich a & adv = böswillig

Bosni·ak m ~en/~en (Bosnier) *Bosniac*

°**B·osnickel** m ⟨sl⟩ *a bad egg*

B·osnien n *Bosnia*

B·osnier m ~s/~ *Bosnian* **b·osnisch** a *Bosnian*

B·osporus m *Bosp(h)orus*; der (Thrazische) ~ (*Thracian*) *Bosp(h)orus* (= *Strait(s) of Constantinople*); †der Kimmerische ~ *Cimmerian B.* (*between the Black Sea and the Sea of Azov*)

†**Bosquet** n = Bosket

Boß m [engl] ~/Bosse (Arbeitgeber etc) *boss*

Boss·age [bɔ'sa:ʒə] f (Fr) = Bossenwerk

B·osse f ~/~n **1.** ⟨sculp⟩ *rough-hewn form of a plastic work* **2.** (Buckel) *boss* **bossel·ieren** vt [h] = bossieren **b·osseln** vt [h] **1.** = bossieren **2.** = basteln **B·ossen(mauer)werk** n ⟨arch⟩ *rustic work, bossage-work*; *quarry-faced masonry*; –quader [m] *rusticated ashlar* **boss(el)·ieren** vt [h] **1.** (Stein, Holz) *to rough-hew, to hew* (od *shape out*) *roughly* | (ausklopfen) *to deboss* (Ggs hohlprägen *emboss*) **2.** *to model in wax* **Boss·ier-~hammer** m *embossing hammer* **~wachs** n *modelling-wax* **Boss·ierer** m *modeller*

B·oston n (Stadt) *Boston* (*Mass. U.S.A.*) **B·oston** [bɔstn] m ~s/~ (Tanz) *Boston*

b·öswillig 1. a *malevolent* ‖ ~e Absicht *wilful malice*; ⟨jur⟩ in ~er Absicht, ~ u mit Vorbedacht *with malice prepense* (od *aforethought*) ‖ ~e Verlassung *wilful desertion* **2.** adv *maliciously*; jdn ~ verlassen *to abandon a p wilfully* **≗keit** f *malevolence*

Bosw·ellia f (L) ⟨bot⟩ *Boswellia*

bot 1. & 3. sg pret v bieten **B·ot** n ~(e)s/~e = Gebot | Sw = Mitgliederversammlung

Bot·anik f ~/ *botany* **~er** m ~s/~ *botanist*

bot·anisch a [mst] *botanical*; (in festen Verbindungen:) *botanic*; der ≗e Garten *the Botanic Gardens* [pl] **Botanis·ierbüchse, -trommel** f *botanizing-tin, collecting-box* **botanis·ieren** vi [h] *to botanize*

B·ote m ~n/~n **1.** *messenger*; geheimer ~ *emissary* ‖ ⟨bib⟩ *apostle* ‖ → Friedens≗, Liebes≗, Unglücks≗ | (Laufbursche) *errand-boy*; *runner* ‖ e–n Brief durch ~n schicken *to send a letter by hand*; → Eil≗ ‖ Brief≗, Post≗ *postman*, ⟨Am⟩ *mail man* ‖ → Dienst≗ **2.** (Vor≗) *harbinger, herald* (*of spring*)

B·oten- ~frau f *female messenger* **~gang** m *errand, commission*; –gänge besorgen *to run errands* **~läufer** m *runner, errand-boy* **~lohn** m *messenger's fee, porterage*

B·otin f ~/~nen *female messenger*

b·otmäßig a *subject*; jdm etw ~ m *to subject a th to a p* **≗keit** f ~/ *dominion, jurisdiction, rule, sway*

Botok·ude m ~n/~n (Brasil-Indianer) *Botocudo*

botr·ytisch a ⟨bot⟩ *botryose, racemose*

B·otschaft f ~/~en **1.** *message* (an jdn *to a p*); *communication*; → Schreiben ‖ *news*; Freuden≗, frohe ~ *good news, glad tidings* (pl); Willkommens≗ *message of welcome* ‖ jdm ~en auftragen *to give a p messages* (an, f *to*); jdm e–e ~ zukommen l *to send a p a message*; etw als ~ mitteilen *to message a th* | ⟨pol⟩ amtliche ~ *message* (an die Nation *to the nation*) **2.** (Auftrag) *errand, message, mission*; e–e ~ ausrichten *to deliver a message, to go on an errand* **3.** (Gesandtschaft) *embassy*; die ~ bei *or* an e–m Hofe *the Embassy to a court* ‖ (~sgebäude) *Embassy*; → Gesandtschaft **B·otschafter** m ~s/~ ⟨pol & dipl⟩ *ambassador* (an e–m Hofe *to a court*) | **~in** f ~/~nen *ambassadress*, ⟨Am⟩ *lady ambassador*

B·otschafts- [in comp] *ambassadorial* **~attaché** m *attaché* **~rat** m *Counsellor of Embassy*

B·öttcher m ~s/~ *cooper*; *barrel-maker* **~handwerk** n *cooper's trade, cooperage, coopery* **~lohn** m *cooperage*

Böttcher·ei f ~/~en **1.** (Handwerk) *cooper's trade, cooperage, coopery* **2.** (Werkstatt) *cooper's workshop, cooperage, coopery*

b·otten vt [h] (Flachs) *to break*

B·otter m ~s/~ *one-masted Dutch fishing--smack*

B·otthammer m *bott-hammer*

B·ottich m ~s/~e *tub, tun, vat*; Holz≗ *wooden tub*; Maisch≗ *mash-tun*; Rühr≗ ⟨tech⟩ *dolly* ‖ in e–n ~ tun *to tub, to vat* | ~schwimmer [m] ⟨brew⟩ *attemperator*

B·ottnische M·eerbusen, der *the Bothnian Gulf, the Gulf of Bothnia*

Botul·ismus m (Wurstvergiftung) *botulism*

Boudoir [bu'dwɑ:r] n (Fr) ~s/~s *boudoir*

Bougainv·illea [bugɛ̃'vilea] f ⟨bot⟩ *bougainvillaea*

Boug·ie [bu'ʒi:] f (Fr) ~/~s ⟨med⟩ (Kautschukstab) *bougie*

Bouill·on [bul'jɔŋ] f (Fr) ~/~s *bouillon, strong broth, beef-tea* **~würfel** m *soup-tablet* (od *square*)

Bo·ulevard ['bulvɑr] m (Fr) ~s/~s *Boulevard* **~presse** f = Asphaltpresse

Boul·ogne [bu'lɔɲ] n ⟨Fr⟩ (Stadt) **Boul·ogner Hölzchen** od **Wäldchen** n (Paris) *Bois de B.*

Bouquet n = Bukett

Bourb·onen m [pl] (Fr) *the Bourbons* [pl]

Bourb·ontee [bur'bɔ̃–] m *Bourbon* (od *Faham*)-*tea*

Bourd·on [bur'dɔ̃] m (Fr) = Bordun

Bourgeois [bur'ʒwɑ] m (Fr) ~/~ *bourgeois* (Fr)

Bout·ique [bu'ti:k] f (Fr) = Budike

Bov·iden [pl] *Bovidae* (L) [pl] *bovine animals*

Bov·ist m ⟨bot⟩ = Bofist

B·owdenzug ['baudən–] m *Bowden wire*

B·owiemesser ['boui–] n ⟨bes Am⟩ *bowie-knife*

×**Bowke** m = Lümmel *hooligan*

B·owle ['bo:lə] f ~/~n **1.** (Gefäß) *bowl*; ~ f Punsch *punch-bowl* **2.** (Getränk) *cup*; *spiced wine*; ~ auf Eis *iced cup*; Rotwein≈ *claret cup*; Punsch≈ *bowl of punch* ‖ e–e ~ brauen *to brew a bowl*

Box f [engl] ~/~en (Stand f Pferd im Stall) *box, bay, stall* | ⟨photo⟩ *box camera* | ⟨mot⟩ (*for 1 car*) *lock-up*

B·ox- (→ boxen) [in comp] *boxing* **~ball** m *punch-ball* (od *bag*), *punching-ball* **~gewicht** n *boxing-weight*, ‖ ~e [pl] → Bd. I. S. 91 **~haltung** f: ~ einnehmen *to adopt a boxer's demeanour*, ⟨fam⟩ *to square up* **~handschuh** m *boxing-glove* ‖ ~e ⟨sl⟩ *mittens* [pl] **~kampf** m *bout, boxing-match*, ⟨engl⟩ maßgebende Vorschriften f den ~ *Queensberry Rules* [pl] ‖ *spar(ring match)* **~kunst** f *art of boxing*; *pugilism* **~motor** m *opposed-cylinder* (⟨sl⟩ *pancake*) *engine* **~ring** m *prizering* **~sport** m *boxing*; *pugilism* **~stellung** f: → –haltung; in ~ gehen *to take up a boxing stance* **~wettkampf** m *boxing match* od *bout*; (ohne Handschuhe) *prize-fight*

B·oxbeutel m = Bocksbeutel

°**B·öxe** f = Buxe

b·oxen I. vi/refl **1.** vi *to box*; *to spar* ‖ *to fight* (um *for*) **2.** refl **sich** ~ *to box*; *to box each other* ‖ ⟨übtr⟩ *to spar*; → knuffen, puffen **II.** ≈ n *boxing* ‖ ~ ohne Gegner *shadow-boxing*; → Boxkampf

B·oxer m ~s/~ **1.** *boxer*; (Berufs≈) *pugilist*, (Preis≈) *prize-fighter*; ~stellung einnehmen *to spar* (gegen *at*) ‖ ⟨übtr⟩ *fighter* **2.** (Hund) *small bulldog* **Boxer·ei** f ⟨übtr⟩ *boxing, fighting*

B·oxkalf ['bɔkskɑ:f] n (engl) ~s/~s (Leder) *boxcalf*

Boy [bɔi] m (engl) ~s/~s *boy, page*

Boyk·ott m (engl; nach Iren Boycott) ~s/~e *boycott(ing)*; ~ fremder, bes britischer Waren in Indien *Swadeshi* ‖ jdn in ~ erklären, den ~ verhängen über jdn *to boycott a p* **boykott·ieren** vt [h] *to boycott*; ⟨Am fam⟩ *to freeze* (*a p*) *out* **Boykott·ierung** f *boycotting*

Boy-Scouts pl (engl) (engl. Jugendorganisation) *Boy-Scouts* [pl]

Br, br(r) intj **1.** (uh) ~! *ugh*! *whew*! **2.** (halt) ~! (*gee*) *whoa*!, *wo*!, *woa*!

Brabanç·onne [–bɑ̃'sɔn] f ~/ F belgische Nationalhymne **Brab·ant** n (holl.-belg. Provinz) *Brabant*

br·abbeln vi [h] *to mumble, mutter*; *speak indistinctly* od *carelessly*; vor sich hin ~ *to mutter to o.s.*

brach 1. u 3. sg pret v brechen

brach a [mst pred] ⟨agr⟩ *fallow, waste*; ~ liegen *to lie fallow* (od *waste*); (Land) ~ liegen l *to fallow* | ⟨übtr⟩ *fallow, uncultivated*; *waste*; ~ liegen (of business) *to lie idle*; *to run to waste* ‖ *dull, monotonous*; ~ liegen (of the market) *to be dull* **Br·ach- ~acker** m *fallow*; *fallow ground* **~distel** f ⟨bot⟩ **1.** *sea-eryngo* **2.** *creeping thistle* **~feld** n *fallow field*; *fallow* **~huhn** n ⟨orn⟩ = Brachschwalbe **~land** n *fallow* **~monat** m *the month of June* **~pilz** m = Champignon **~schnepfe** f ⟨orn⟩ = Brachvogel **~schwalbe** f ⟨orn⟩ *plover* **~vogel** m *curlew*; (kl Art ~) Regen≈ *whimbrel*; Eskimo≈ ⟨Am⟩ *doughbird*; → *curlew* **~zeit** f *fallowing-season*

Br·ache f ~/~n **1.** ⟨agr⟩ (Acker) *fallow* ‖ (Brachliegen) *fallow, fallowness* **2.** ⟨übtr⟩ *idleness*; *dullness*; *waste*

br·achen vt/i [h] **1.** vt (umbrechen) (Land) *to fallow* ‖ (brach liegen l) *to fallow* **2.** vi *to lie waste* **Br·achet** m = Brachmonat **Br·achling** m ⟨bot⟩ = Champignon

brachi·al a (Arm–) *brachial* ≈**gewalt** f ⟨übtr⟩ *brachial* od *bodily strength*; *brawn* [Ggs *brains*] ‖ etw mit ~ durchsetzen *etc to steam-roller*

Brachiop·ode m ⟨zoo⟩ *brachiopod*

Br·achse(n m) f [~/~n f, ~/~ m] ⟨ich⟩ *bream*; See≈ *sar* **~kraut** n ⟨bot⟩ *quill-wort*

Brachy- [in comp] (Kurz–) *brachy–* **~·uren** [pl] (Krabben) *Brachyura* (L) **~zephal·ie** f ⟨anthr⟩ *brachycephaly*

Brack n ~s/~e **1.** (Schund) *refuse, trash* **2.** *amber, fur* (etc.) *of inferior quality* **brack** a *worthless, inferior* | *brackish* (*water*); → brackig

Br·acke 1. m ~n/~n (Spürhund) *hound*; (langhaariger) *spaniel*; (Hasenhund) *harrier*, (kl) *beagle* → Jagdhund **2.** f ~/~n *brach*

Br·acke f ~/~n (am Wagen) *swing-tree*

br·acken vt [h] ⟨com⟩ (Vieh, Waren) *to cull, to sort*; *to cast out*

Br·acker m ~s/~ ⟨com⟩ *official sorter*

Br·ackgut n *article of inferior quality*

br·ackig, br·ackisch a *brackish*; *partly fresh, partly salt* **Br·ackvieh** n *cull*; *sorted-out cattle*

Br·ackwasser n *brackish water*

Brahm·ane m ~n/~n *Brahmin, Brahman*; Anrede e–s ~n *Swami* ‖ **Brahm·anin** f ~/~nen *Brahminee* **brahm·anisch** a *brahminic(al)* **Brahman·ismus** m *Brahmanism* **Brahm·ine** m, etc. → Brahmane

Braille-Alphabet [brɑ:j] n (f Blinde; nach L. Braille) *Braille-System*

Braisi·ère [brɛ:'ziɛ:r] f [Fr] ⟨cul⟩ *braising-pan*

Brakte·at m ~en/~en (Hohlmünze) *bractea*

Brakt·ee f ~/~n ⟨bot⟩ (Deckblatt der Seitenblüte) *bract*; Wirtel v ~n *involucel* **Brakte·ole** f ~/~n ⟨bot⟩ (Vorblatt der Seitenblüte) *bracteole*

Br·am [brɑ:m] m ~s/~e ⟨mar⟩ = Bramstange **~rahe** f *topgallant-yard* **~segel** n *topgallant-sail* **~stange** f *topgallant mast*; Groß≈ *main-topgallant mast*; ~nstag [m] *breast-backstay*

×**Bram** [brɑ:m] m ⟨bot⟩ = **1.** Brombeere **2.** Ginster

Bram·arbas m ~/–basse *braggart, swaggerer*, (Maulheld) *miles gloriosus* (⟨ant⟩ & It *in commedia dell'arte*); (feiger) *scaramouch* ≈**·ieren** vi [h] *to brag*

Br·äme f ~/~n **1.** (Rand) *border, brim, edge* ‖ *enclosure*; *encompassing wood* **2.** = Besatz

Br·amme f ~/~n ⟨tech⟩ (walzfertiger Block) *slab*

Br·anche ['brɑ̃ʃə] f ~/~n ⟨com⟩ *business, line, trade*; in der Tuch≈ s *to be in the drapery line* od *drapery way* ‖ → Zweig | ~nadreßbuch [n] *trade* od *classified directory*

Br·anchie f ~/~n [mst pl] ~n *branchiae* (L), *gills*

Branchiop·ode m ⟨zoo⟩ *branchiopod*

Brand m ~s/≈e **I.** [abstr] **1.** ⟨eig⟩ (Brennen) **a.** *burning* ‖ (Feuer) *fire, conflagration*; → Verbrennung **b.** e–n ~ **entfachen** *to start a fire* ‖ der ~ griff um sich *the fire spread* ‖ **in** ~ *ablaze, on fire*; in ~ geraten *to catch* (od *take*) *fire*; in ~ setzen, stecken *to set* (*a th*) *ablaze* (od *on fire*), *to set fire to* (*a th*); *to fire, to kindle* (*a th*); in ~ stehen *to be on fire* ‖ ⟨fig⟩ → Mord **2.** ⟨übtr⟩ *burning* (*of bricks, lime*, etc.); *baking* (*of pottery*); *refining* (*of gold, silver*) **3.** (Hitzewirkung) **a.** *burning, baking*; *burning heat* (*of the sun*); Sonnen≈ *sunburn* **b.** (Rauschdurst) *hot coppers* [pl]; e–n üblen ~ h *to have an awful morning-after thirst, to be parched*; wenn man den ~ hat *when the c. are hot*; den ~ löschen *to cool one's c.* **c.** (Leidenschaft) *ardour, fire* **4.** (~geruch) *smell of burning*; nach ~ riechen *to smell* *of burning* ‖ (~geschmack) *burnt taste*; nach ~ schmecken *to taste burnt* **II.** [konkr] **1.** (brennendes Stück Holz) *brand*; *piece of burning wood*; → Feuer≃; Zünder **2.** = Feuerung **3.** (durch ~ hergestellte Waren) *batch* (*of loaves*); ein ~ Ziegelsteine *a b. of bricks* ‖ Wein≃ *brandy, cognac* **4.** (eingebranntes Zeichen) **a.** *brand* (*on cattle, horses*); *burn*; *mark made by burning*; → ~mal **b.** ⟨com⟩ *brand, trade-mark* (*on goods*) ‖ → Marke, Sorte **5. a.** ⟨med⟩ (Gewebstod) *gangrene, mortification, necrosis*; feuchter, kalter, trockener ~ *moist, cold, dry gangrene* **b.** ⟨bot⟩ *brand, blight, fire-blast, rust*; (Getreide-≃) *ergot*; *mildew, smut*, (des Weizens) *bunt*; durch ~ vernichten *to blight, to mildew* **6.** ⟨poet⟩ (Schwert) ⟨poet⟩ *brand*

Br·and- [in comp] *incendiary*; *fire* .. **~abschirmung** f *cutoff* **~bekämpfung** f *fire fighting* **~binde** f *bandage for burns* **~blase** f *blister* **~bombe** f ⟨aero⟩ *incendiary* (*bomb*) **~brief** m **1.** ⟨jur⟩ *letter* (etc) *threatening with arson* **2.** *begging l.* ‖ *threatening l.* ‖ *urgent l.* ‖ (Mahnbrief) *dunning l.* **~direktor** m *chief officer of the fire-brigade*; ⟨Am⟩ *fireward*(*en*) **~eisen** n *branding-iron* **~ente** f ⟨orn⟩ *sheldrake* **~fackel** f *torch-brand*; ⟨fig⟩ *torch* (*of war*) **~fieber** n *inflammatory fever* **~flasche** f ⟨mil⟩ *incendiary bottle*; *Molotov cocktail* **~fleck** m *burn mark*; ~e [pl] *scorching, burn, scald* **~fuchs** m **1.** *brant-fox* **2.** (Pferd) *sorrel* **3.** ⟨univ; m.m.⟩ *fresher* **~gans** f = Brandente **~gasse** f *small space between blocks of houses* **~geruch** m *smell of burning* **~geschoß** n = Brandkugel **~giebel** m *gable-end*; *gable-wall* **~glocke** f *fire-bell* **~grab** n *praehistoric grave containing relics of burnt persons* **~granate** f *incendiary shell* **~kasse** f *fire insurance office* **~kugel** f *fire-ball, incendiary* (*bullet, shell, etc*) **~kanister** m *incendiary canister* **~kasse** f *fire-*(*insurance*) *office* **~lattich** m ⟨bot⟩ → Alpenlattich **~leder** n *leather for insoles* **~leiter** f *fire-ladder* od *–escape* **~mal** n *brand* ‖ ⟨ec & fig⟩ *stigma* **~malerei** f *poker-work, pyrography* **≃marken** vt [h] (jdn) ⟨hist⟩ *to brand* ‖ ⟨fig⟩ *to brand, stigmatize*; ge–rkt s *to be branded* ‖ *denounce* **~markung** f ⟨fig⟩ *branding*; *stigmatization* ‖ *denouncement* ‖ *excoriation* **~mauer** f *fire-*(*proof*) *wall, partition-wall, party-wall, cutoff* **~meister** m *divisional officer of the fire-brigade* **~munition** f *incendiary ammunition* **~narbe** f *scar resulting from burns* **~opfer** n *burnt offering* (od *sacrifice*), *holocaust* **~pfeil** m ⟨aero⟩ *incendiary arrow* **~pflaster** n *plaster for burns* **~pilz** m ⟨bot⟩ *smut-fungus* **~rede** f *inflammatory* (od *incendiary*) *address* **~salbe** f *ointment for burns* **~satz** m *incendiary charge* od *compositon* **~schaden** m *damage caused by fire* **≃schatzen** vt/i [h] **1.** vt *to lay* (*a town*) *under contribution* ‖ ⟨übtr⟩ (jdn) *to fleece* **2.** vi (plündern) *to ravage, plunder* **~schätzer** m ⟨ins⟩ *fire-loss assessor* **~schatzung** f *war-contribution* ‖ *plundering, ravage* **~schiefer** m ⟨geol⟩ *bituminous schist* **~schott** n *firewall*; *fireproof bulkhead* **~silber** n *refined silver* **~sohle** f *inner sole, welt* **~spur** f *trace of burning* **~stätte, ~stelle** f *scene* (od *place*) *of conflagration* **~stifter** m *arsonist, fire--raiser, incendiary*; ⟨Am fam⟩ *fire-bug* **≃stifterisch** a *incendiary* **~stiftung** f *arson, incendiarism*; *fire-raising* | ~sgetriebene(r [m]) [f] *pyromaniac* | ~strieb [m] *pyromania* **~verletzung** f (Hitze≃) *burn*; (Verbrühungs≃) *scalding injury* **~versicherung** f → Feuerversicherung **~wache** f ⟨mil⟩ *fire piquet* **~wart** m *fire-watcher* od *–fighter* **~wirtschaft** f ⟨agr⟩ *burnbeating* **~wunde** f *burn, scald, scorching*; leichte ~ *singe*; → –verletzung **~zeichen** n = Brandmal **~zettel** m = Brandbrief **~ziegel** m *fire-brick*

br·anden 1. vi [h] ⟨mar⟩ *to break into foam, to surge* (gegen *against*) **2.** ≃ n *surging, welter*

Br·andenburg n ⟨Ger⟩ *Brandenburg*; die Mark ~ *the March of B.* **Brandenburger** m, **~in** f *B.er* **br·andenburgisch** a (*of*) *B.*

Br·ander m ~s/~ ⟨mar & mil hist⟩ *fire-ship*

br·andig a **1.** (angebrannt) ~ riechen *to smell of burning*, ~ schmecken *to taste burnt* **2. a.** ⟨med⟩ *gangrenous*; ~ w *to become gangrenous, to gangrene*; (Fleisch) ~ m *to gangrene* **b.** ⟨bot⟩ *mildewed, blasted, blighted* ‖ ~ w *to mildew, to smut*; (Getreide) ~ m *to smut*

Br·andung f ~/~en *breakers, breaking waves* [pl], *surf, surge*; *wash* (*of the waves*) **~swelle** f *breaker*

Br·anntkalk m *burnt lime*

Br·anntwein m ~s/~e **1.** *brandy*; *spirits* [pl]; ⟨Am sl⟩ *hooch*; ⟨Scot⟩ Korn≃ → Whisky; Wacholder≃ *gin* ‖ → Kognak ‖ ~ brennen *to distil spirits* **2.** [in comp] *spirit* .. **~brenner** m *distiller* **~brennerei** f *distillery* **~flasche** f *spirit-bottle* **~handel** m *spirit-trade* **~händler** m *spirit-dealer* **~monopol** n *spirit* (od *brandy*)*-monopoly, monopoly of spirits* **~nase** f *bottle-nose* **~schenke** f *dram* (od *gin*)*-shop*; *pot-house* ‖ feine ~ *gin--palace* ‖ nicht konzessionierte ~ *shebeen* **~steuer** f *spirit-duty* (od *tax*), *duty on spirits*

Br·ante f = Pranke (v Bär, Fuchs) *pad*

Bras·il f *Brazilian cigar* **Brasil·ian** m ⟨minr⟩ *Brazilian topaz* **Brasili·aner** m ~s/~ *Brazilian* **brasili·anisch** a *Brazilian* **Bras·ilien** n *Brazil* **Bras·ilienholz, Brasili·ettoholz** n *Brazil-wood* **Bras·ilnuß** f = Paranuß

Br·asse f ~/~n ⟨mar⟩ *brace*; ~ des gr Segels *main-brace* **br·assen** vt [h] ⟨mar⟩ *to brace*; *to trim*

Br·asse(n m) f ~/~n (~s/~) ⟨ich⟩ = Brachsen *bream*

Br·at- ~aal m ⟨cul⟩ *spitchcock* **~apfel** m *baked apple* **~fisch** m *fried fish* **~fleisch** n *broil* **~hering** m *grilled herring* **~hähnchen** n *roast chicken*; *chicken for roasting* **~hendlstation** f *chicken inn*; → Backhendl **~huhn** n *roast fowl* **~kartoffeln** f [pl] *roast* od *fried* (⟨Am a.⟩ *pan-browned*) *potatoes* [pl] **~ofen** m *roasting-oven* **~pfanne** f *roasting-tin, frying-pan*; ⟨mst el⟩ *frier* **~rost** m *gridiron, grill* **~spieß** m *spit*; ~fest ⟨Am⟩ *barbecue* | ~dreher [m] (P *or* Hund) *turnspit* **~spill** n ~s/~e ⟨mar⟩ *windlass*; mit e–m ~ heben *to windlass* **~wurst** f *sausage for frying*; *fried sausage*

br·äteln vt [h] *to roast* (od *grill, bake*) *slightly*

br·aten I. vt/i [briet (bratete)/gebraten] [h] **A.** vt **1.** (Fleisch etc) am Feuer ~ *to roast* (am Spieß *on the spit*) ‖ (auf dem Rost ~) *to broil* ‖ *grill* ‖ (in der Pfanne) *to fry* ‖ (Äpfel) *to bake* ‖ z wenig gebraten *underdone*; gerade recht g. *well-done, done to a turn*; z sehr g. *overdone* | **sich ~ l** *to roast* **2.** ⟨übtr⟩ **sich** in der Sonne ~ l *to bask in the sun, to take a sun-bath* ‖ da brat mir einer 'nen Storch! *well, I never*! *that beats all*! **B.** vi **1.** *to roast*; *broil, grill*; *fry* **2.** (P) *to bake, to roast* (*in the sun*); *to be scorched* **II.** ≃ n *roasting* ‖ *grilling*

Br·aten m ~s/~ **1.** *joint*; *roast* (*meat*); ⟨Am⟩ *roast* ‖ Hammel≃ *roast mutton*, Kalbs≃ *roast veal*; Rinder≃ *roast beef*, etc. **2.** ⟨fig⟩ ein fetter ~ *a nice bit of money*; ⟨sl⟩ *a great catch* ‖ da hast du den ~! *there now*! *there you are*! *a nice state of affairs*! den ~ riechen *to smell a rat*; er roch den ~ *he got wind of it* **~brühe** f *gravy* **~fett** n *dripping* **~rock** m ⟨hum⟩ = Gehrock **~wender** m *roasting-jack*

Br·ätling m ~s/~e **1.** ⟨ich⟩ *sprat* **2.** ⟨bot⟩ (Pilz) *agaric* **3.** ⟨cul⟩ (*roast*) *meat-ball, ball of soy*

Br·atsche [ɑ:] f ~/~n ⟨mus⟩ *viola* **~nspieler** m = Bratschist

Br·atsche [ɑ:] f ~/~n *paw* (*of a bear*)

br·atschen [ɑ:] vi [h] *to play the viola* **br·atschig** [ɑ:] a *unusually broad*

Bratsch·ist m ~en/~en *viola-player*

Br·atze f ~/~n *paw*

Br·au- **~̈berechtigt** a *having the privilege of brewing; licensed to brew* **~bottich** m *brewing-tub* (od *vat*), *ale-vat* **~gerechtigkeit** f *privilege of brewing* **~haus** n *brewery* **~innung** f *corporation of brewers* **~kessel** m *brewing-copper* **~meister** m *master brewer* **~ordnung** f *regulations* [pl] *for brewing* **~wesen** n *brewing industry*

Bräu n **1.** (Brauen) *brew(ing)* **2.** (Gebrautes) **a.** *brew(age)*; ⟨Ger⟩ '*Hofbräu*', '*Löwenbräu*' ‖ (auf einmal Gebrautes) *brewing* **b.** ⟨übtr⟩ *brewage, brewing* **3.** (Brauhaus) *brewery, brew-house*

Brauch m ~s/~̈e (Übung, Sitte) *usage, use; habit, practice; custom* ‖ ~̈e [pl] *customs, ways* [pl] ‖ allgemeiner ~ *common usage*; anerkannter ~ *convention*; gewohnheitsmäßiger ~ *routine* (→ Geleise); herkömmlicher ~ *customary observance; tradition*; fester ~ *custom, usage* ‖ es ist ~ *it is the custom* (*to do*); nach altem ~ *according to ancient use*; wie es der ~ mit sich bringt *according to custom* | Seemanns~̈ *sailor's custom* ‖ religiöser ~ *ordinance*; ritueller ~ *use*; → Ritus ‖ ⟨com⟩ Handels~̈ *usance* ‖ → Gebrauch, Verwendung; Sitte; Praxis **~̈bar** a (S) *serviceable, usable, useful; suitable for use* ‖ (P) *able, competent, efficient* **~barkeit** f ~/ *serviceableness, usefulness, usability*

br·auchen vt/aux [h] **I.** vt **1.** = gebrauchen, verwenden **2.** (nötig h) (etw) *to need, want; to be in need* (od *want*) *of, have need of, to require* (*a th*); jds Dienste ~ *to have need of a p's services* ‖ dringend Ruhe ~ *to want rest badly* ‖ wozu braucht ein Beamter Bildung? *what does an official want with* (⟨Am⟩ *of*) *education?* ‖ etw nicht mehr ~ *to have finished* (od *done*) *with a th* ‖ er hat so viel Geld wie er braucht *he has all the m. he needs* ‖ ich brauche nur eine Zigarette u bin glücklich *give me a cigarette and I am happy* ‖ ⟨mot⟩ der W. braucht 4 l für 20 Meilen *the car does 20 miles on the gallon* | (Zeit) *to require, take* ‖ ich brauche nicht einmal e–e Minute *I won't take a minute*; du wirst 2 Stunden ~ *it will take you 2 hours* (*to do*); er brauchte ¾ Std *he gave himself 3 quarters of an hour* (*to do*) ‖ die Hörner ~ Monate zum Wachsen *the horns take months to grow* | (jdn) *to want*; ich brauche dich nicht weiter *I have no further use for you* ‖ → bedürfen **II.** [v aux] [vor inf] [mit (⟨vulg⟩ ohne) ‚zu', neg & interr] **1. a.** [nur prs & pret] *need*; wer ‚~' nicht mit ‚zu' gebraucht, braucht ‚~' überhaupt nicht **zu** ge~! ⟨m. m.⟩ *mind your P's and Q's!*; das hätte er nicht (zu) tun ~ *there was no need for him to do it*; er braucht nicht (zu) eilen *he need not hurry; he does not need to hurry*; er brauchte nicht (zu) eilen *he need not hurry, he did not need to hurry*; er hätte nicht (zu) eilen ~ *he need not have hurried*; sie hätten nicht einbegriffen (zu) w ~ *they need not have been included*; wozu brauchte er (zu) eilen? *why need he hurry? why did he need to hurry?* **b.** du brauchst nicht traurig (zu) s *you have no business to be sorry* **c.** *to require, want*; ich brauche die Bitte nicht immer (zu) wiederholen *there is no need for me to keep on asking* ‖ du brauchst dich nicht zu fürchten *there's no call for fear* **2.** [imps] **es** braucht kaum hinzugefügt (zu) w *it scarcely needs* (od *requires, wants*) *repeating*

brauchgemäß adv *according to custom*

†**br·äuchlich** a = gebräuchlich **Br·auchtum** n *customs* [pl], *usage and customs* [pl]; *tradition* **br·auchtümlich** a *customary, traditional*

Br·aue f ~/~n = Augenbraue

br·auen I. vt/i [h] **A.** vt **1.** (Bier etc) *to brew* ‖ (Punsch, Bowle) *to mix, brew*; (Tee, Kaffee) *to make, brew*, ⟨fam⟩ *to brew up* **2.** ⟨übtr⟩ *to make, prepare*; (e–n Aufsatz) *to compile* ‖ (Unheil) *to brew, contrive; to concoct* | **sich** ~ → zus-~ **B.** vi **1.** *to brew* **2.** ⟨übtr⟩ (of mountains, etc.) *to be covered with mist; to be steaming*; (of mist) *to rise in vapour* **II.** ~̈ n *brewing*

Br·auer m ~s/~ *brewer* | **~·ei** f ~/~en *brewery*; ~anlage *brewery plant* **Br·äuhaus** n *brewery, brewhouse*; → Brauhaus

braun 1. a **a.** *brown*; die ~e Farbe *the brown* (*-ness*) ‖ ~es Pferd *bay*; ~er Schmetterling *brown*; [koll] ~e Wildhühner [pl] *the bown* [pl], ~e Butter *fried butter*; ⟨fig⟩ → Butter | gelb~ *tan, tawny*; gelb~e Farbe *tan*; gelblich~, schmutzig~ *lurid* ‖ grau~, dunkel~ *dark-brown; bistre dun*; dunkel~e Farbe *bistre, dun*; dunkel~es Pferd *dun* ‖ rot~ *russet, sorrel*; rot~es Pferd *sorrel* ‖ schwarz~ *nut-brown* (*maid*) ‖ hell~ ⟨paint, etc⟩ *dead leaf shade* ‖ (etw) ~ m, ~ färben *or* beizen *to brown*; ~ w *to brown* | (jdn) ~ u blau schlagen *to beat* (*a p*) *black and blue* **b.** (sonnverbrannt) *brown, sunburnt, tanned*; ~ w *to become sunburnt*; sehr *or* leicht ~ w *to take on a deep sunburn* **c.** ⟨Ger⟩ ⟨nazi⟩ ~̈es Hemd → Braunhemd **2.** ~̈ n; das ~ *the brown*; das Gelb~̈ *the tan*; das Grau~̈ *the dun*, etc.

Br·aun- [in comp] *brown* .. **~̈äugig** a *brown–* (od *dark*)*-eyed* **~bier** n *brown beer*; ⟨engl⟩ *brown stout* ‖ aussehen wie °~ u Spucke *to look corpsey* ⟨sl⟩ **~eisenerz, -stein** m ⟨minr⟩ *brown haematite; limonite* **~erz** n ⟨geol⟩ *brown ore; vivianite* **~fäule** f ⟨bot⟩ (Holz-, Gemüse~̈) *brown-rot*; (des Weizens) *brown-rust* **~fisch** m ⟨zoo⟩ *porpoise* **~̈fleckig, ~̈gefleckt** a *brown-speckled* **~̈gelb** a *yellowish brown* **~̈haarig** a *brown-haired* **~heil** n ⟨bot⟩ → Braunelle **~hemd** n ⟨nazi⟩ (P) *Brown-Shirt* **~holz** n Fernambuk– **~kehlchen** n ⟨orn⟩ *whinchat* **~kohl** m *kale, kail; colewort* **~kohle** f *brown* (⟨Am⟩ *soft*) *coal, lignite* | ~nöl [n] *pyrocarbonic oil*; die ~nformation [f] ⟨geol⟩ *the tertiary*; ~nrevier [n] *lignite fields* [pl]; ~nzeit [f] ⟨geol⟩ *tertiary era*; ältere ~nzeit *oligocene age* **~̈rot** a *brownish red* **~̈schwarz** a *dark-brown* **~spat** m ⟨minr⟩ *brown spar* **~stein** m ⟨minr⟩ *brown-stone, manganese ore* od *dioxide; pyrolusite* **~wurz** f ⟨bot⟩ *brown-wort*; ~gewächse [pl] *Scrophularia* [L]

Br·aune m [der ~, ein ~r] ~n/~n (Pferd) *chestnut* od *bay* (*horse*); der Rot~̈ *the sorrel*

Br·äune f ~/ **1.** *brown colour, brownness* **2.** ⟨med⟩ (eitrige Mandelentzündung) *quinsy, angina* [L] ‖ häutige ~, Hals~̈ *croup*; → Diphtherie ‖ Herz~̈ → angina pectoris | ⟨vet⟩ *angina* (*in horses*); *pip* (*in birds*)

Braun·elle f ~/~n **1.** ⟨orn⟩ (Hecken~̈) *hedge-sparrow, dunnock* **2.** ⟨bot⟩ *self-heal* ‖ = Günsel

bräunen vt/i [h] **1.** vt (etw) *to brown, to bronze, to make* (od *roast*) *brown*, (Fleisch ⟨a.⟩) *to sear* ‖ (of the sun) (Gesicht, jdn) *to sunburn; to tan* **2.** vi *to brown, to become brown* ‖ *to become sunburnt* od *tanned*

Braun·it n ~s/ ⟨minr⟩ *braunite*

br·äunlich a *brownish* ‖ ~ gefärbt *brownish-coloured*

Br·aunsche Röhre *cathode-ray tube*

Br·aunschweig n ⟨Ger⟩ (Stadt u †Land) *Brunswick* **Br·aunschweiger** m, **~in** f *Brunswicker* **Braunschweiger-** [in comp] ⟨chem⟩ *Brunswick* (*black; -green*) **br·aunschweigisch** a (*of*) *Brunswick*

Braus m → Saus u ~

Br·ausche f ~/~n *bruise*; (Beule) *bump*

***br·auschen** vi [s] → anschwellen

Br·ause f ~/~n **1.** (Ansatzteil der Gießkanne etc) *rose*, (*perforated nozzle*) **2.** (Gießkanne) *watering-can* | (Dusche) *shower(-bath), douche, spray*; sich unter die ~ stellen *to douche* **3.** ⟨fam⟩ *pop*, ⟨bes Am⟩ *soda(-)pop* = ~limonade **~bad** n *shower-bath, douche* **~kopf** m ⟨fig⟩ *hot-*

headed fellow, hothead, hotspur **≃köpfig** a *hot-headed, impetuous* **~limonade** f *effervescent lemonade; sherbet* **~pulver** n *soda-powder, effervescent powder* || ⟨med⟩ *Seidlitz powder* **~wind** m ⟨fig⟩ = Brausekopf

br·ausen I. vt [h] **1.** (rauschen) (of water, the sea, wind) *to bluster, rage, storm; surge* || *to sweep* (über *across*); *to rush*; dahin~ *to rush along*; über das Land ~ (of storm) *to sweep the country* | (of sound; of the sea, wind) *to roar, bellow; to roll, to thunder*; (of organ) *to peal; resound*; (dröhnen) *to boom, chunk; buzz, hum* **2.** (aufwallen) *to effervesce, fizz, sparkle; to ferment* **3.** ⟨übtr⟩ (lärmen) *to bluster* || (of blood) *to boil* || (of emotions, etc.) *to surge* (durch *through*), *to thrill* || die Kunde brauste durchs Land *the news thrilled through the country* **II.** ≃ n **1.** *raging, surging* || *roar; roll* **2.** *effervescence, fizz* **3.** *surge; thrill*

br·ausen (→ Brause 2.) vt [h] (begießen) (Pflanze etc) *to shover, water*

br·ausend a *roaring; boisterous* (*wind*) || *rousing* (*applause, welcome*), ~er Beifall *thunders of applause*

Br·aut f ~/≃e **1.** (Verlobte) *fiancée* [Fr]; die ~ m–s Bruders *the fiancée of my brother*; m–e ~ *my fiancée* || „~" des Soldaten ⟨fig⟩ (Gewehr) *soldier's friend* | [nur nach pron poss] *betrothed*; ⟨fam⟩ *intended*; m–e ~ *my betrothed* od *intended* || ~ s *to be engaged*; sie ist die ~ m–s Bruders *she is engaged to my brother* **2.** (~ am Hochzeitstage) *bride*; ~ u Bräutigam *bride and bridegroom* (⟨Am⟩ *groom*) **3.** Gottes≃ *the Virgin* (*Mary*); *a nun* **4.** = Geliebte ⟨euphem⟩ *bride* **5.** ⟨übtr bot⟩ ~ in Haaren *love-in-a-mist* || → Winds≃ **6.** [in comp] *bridal* **~bett** n *bridal bed* **~führer** m ⟨Ger⟩ *young unmarried man who accompanies a bridesmaid* || ⟨R. C. & engl⟩ *the best man, bridesman, groomsman* **~führerin** f ⟨Ger⟩ (= Brautjungfer) *bridesmaid* || ⟨R. C. & engl⟩ *the chief bridesmaid,* ⟨Scot⟩ *best maid* **~gemach** n *bridal chamber* **~geschenk** n *wedding-present* **~jungfer** f *bridesmaid*; erste ~ *principal b.*; ⟨Am⟩ *maid of honour* **~kammer** f *bridal chamber* **~kauf** m *the buying of the bride* **~kind** n *love-child legitimated by the parents' marriage* **~kleid** n *bridal gown, wedding-dress* **~kranz** m *bridal garland* od *wreath* **~lauf** m ⟨hist⟩ *nuptials* [pl] **~leute** [pl] = Brautpaar **~nacht** *nuptial night, wedding-night* **~paar** n das ~ **1.** (die Verlobten) *the betrothed; the engaged couple* **2.** (am Hochzeitstage) *bride and bridegroom* (⟨Am⟩ *groom*) **~ring** m *wedding-ring* **~schatz** m *dower, dowry* **~schau** f *looking for a wife*; auf (die) ~ gehen *to look out for a wife, to go courting* **~schleier** m *bride's veil* **~schmuck** m *the personal ornaments* [pl] *of the bride* **~staat** m *bridal attire* **~stand** m *state of being affianced; time of engagement* **~vater** m *the bride's father* **~werber** m *suitor, wooer* **~werbung** f *wooing* **~zug** m *bridal procession*

Br·äutigam m ~s/~e **1.** (Verlobter) *fiancé* [Fr]; (er ist) der ~ m–r Schwester .. *the fiancé of my sister*; er ist mein ~ *he is my fiancé* || [nur nach *pron poss*] *betrothed,* ⟨fam⟩ *intended*; mein ~ *my betrothed* od *intended* || ~ s *to be engaged*; er ist der ~ m–r Schwester *he is engaged to my sister* **2.** (am Hochzeitstage) *bridegroom,* ⟨Am⟩ *groom*; ⟨engl⟩ Beistand *or* rechte Hand des ~s (bei der Hochzeit) *best man, groomsman* **3.** ⟨ec⟩ Seelen≃ *Jesus Christ* **4.** = Geliebter

br·äutlich a *bridal, nuptial*

br·av I. a **1.** (anständig, wacker) *honest, upright; worthy*; ein ~er Kerl *a jolly good fellow* **2.** (artig) *good*; mustergültig ~ *as good as gold*; ein ~es Kind *a good* (od *wellbehaved*) *child*; (Abschied) sei ~ u daß mir k–e Klagen k ⟨hum, m. m.⟩ *be good and if you can't be careful* **II.** [adv] sich ~ benehmen *to behave well* || ~ gemacht! *well done! very good!* **≃heit** f ~/ **1.** (Anständigkeit) *honesty, uprightness* **2.** *good behaviour*

brav·issimo, br·avo [intj It] *bravissimo! bravo! capital! well done!* ⟨Am⟩ *good for you!* ⟨Am sl⟩ *attaboy!* **≃ruf** m *bravo*

Br·avo m ~s/~s (Räuber) *bravo, hired assassin*

Brav·our [bra'vu:r] f [Fr] ~/ *bravura* [It], *dash* || *great skill, brilliancy of execution* **~arie** f ⟨mus⟩ *bravura-aria* **~stück** n ⟨mus & übtr⟩ *bravura* [It]; *brilliant passage* || *feat*

Break [bre:k] (engl) **1.** m ~s/~s *break, large wagonette* **2.** n ~s/~s ⟨racing⟩ *break*

Br·ech- [in comp] *breaking*; ⟨tech⟩ *crushing* **~bank** f *kneading board* || = Breche **~bohne** f ~n [pl] *broken beans* **~durchfall** m ⟨med⟩ *the European* (od *Summer*) *cholera; cholerine* **~eisen** *crowbar; jemmy*; ⟨Am⟩ *jimmy, jenny*; mit e–m ~ öffnen *to jemmy* **~kraft** f (Stärke) e–r Linse ⟨opt, phot⟩ *lens power* || ≃los [a] ⟨opt⟩ *zero-power* ([*correcting*] *lens*) **~maschine** f ⟨tech⟩ *breaking-engine; breaker; crusher; crushing-machine* || (f Flachs) *brake* **~mittel** n **1.** (Arznei) *emetic, vomit, vomitive* **2.** ⟨fig⟩ (P *or* S) *vomit; disgusting p* od *th*; (P) *perfect horror, sickener* **~nuß** f ⟨bot⟩ (Samen) *nux vomica* || ~baum [m] *nux vomica* **~pulver** n *emetic powder* **~punkt** m ⟨phys⟩ *point of incidence* **~reiz** m *retching*; ~ h *to be* od *feel sick; to heave*; jdm ~ geben, verursachen *to nauseate a p* **~ruhr** f = Brechdurchfall **~schnecke** f ⟨tech⟩ *crusher-worm* **~stange** f = Brecheisen; *pinch bar* **~walzwerk** n *crushing mill* **~weinstein** m *tartar emetic* **~wurzel** f ⟨bot⟩ *ipecacuanha* **~zange** f *pincers* [pl]; e–e ~ *a pair of pincers*

br·echbar a *breakable; brittle; fragile*

Br·eche(l) f ~/~n (Flachs≃) *brake*

br·echen vt/i [brach/gebrochen] **I.** vt [h] **A.** ⟨eig⟩ **1. a.** (Stock etc) *to break* || (Steine) *to quarry*; (Erz) *to break, to dig* || (Brot) *to break*; nichts z ~ u z beißen h → beißen I. 1. **b.** (in Stücke ~) *to break up*; kz u kl ~ *to smash* (*in*)*to atoms* **c.** (Zweig) *to break* (v *from*); ⟨poet⟩ (Blumen) *to pluck, gather* **d.** (Acker) *to break; to dig up* **e.** (Flachs etc) *to brake*; (Wolle) *to card*; (Malz) *to crush*; (Leder) *to scrape smooth* **f.** (Falten) (Bogen) *to fold*; auf e–r Seite e–n Rand ~ *to provide a page with a margin* **2.** (Glied) *to break*; sich den Arm, 3 Rippen ~ *to break* od *fracture one's arm, three ribs*; das Genick ~ *to break one's neck*; er hat beide Beine (ihm sind b. B.) gebrochen *he has both legs broken*; (Knochen) v neuem ~ *to rebreak* || ⟨fig⟩ es brach ihm den Hals *it broke his back, it ruined him* || e–r Flasche den Hals ~ *to crack* (od *empty*) *a bottle* **3.** ⟨opt⟩ (Licht etc) *to refract* || (Lichtstrahl) *to diffract*; → Sonnenstrahl || ⟨gram⟩ [mst pass] (Vokal) *to break* (z *to*) || ⟨typ⟩ (Wort) *to divide* **4.** gebrochen deutsch sprechen *to speak broken German*; → gebrochen **5.** (Blut etc) *to vomit* **B.** ⟨übtr & fig⟩ **1.** → Bahn 2. d. || das Eis ~ *to break the ice* || e–e Lanze ~ f jdn *to intercede* (od *plead*) *for a p*; e–e L. ~ mit jdm *to break a lance with a p* || den Stab ~ über jdn *to give a dog a bad name and hang him; to condemn a p* || etw übers Knie ~ *to hurry over a th, to hasten a th unduly, to do a th hastily* od *cursorily* || (etw) vom Zaun ~ *to seek occasion for* (*a th*); *to begin* (*a th*) *abruptly* (od *without reason*); *to hasten on, to precipitate*; e–n Streit v Z. ~ *to pick a quarrel* (*with a p*) **2.** (Macht, Willen; Eigensinn jds) *to break; to break down*; den Widerstand e–r S ~ *to break the back of a th*; der W. des Feuers wurde gebrochen *the back of the fire was broken* || (Bann) *to break* || Not bricht Eisen *necessity knows no law* || (unter~, aufheben) (Stillschweigen) *to break*; *to stop for the time* ‖ Reichsrecht bricht Landesrecht *national law precedes regional law* **3.** (verletzen) (Eid; Frieden; Vertrag, Wort) *to break*; *violate* ‖ die Ehe ~ *to commit adultery* **4.** jdm das Herz ~ *to break a p's heart*; mit gebrochenem Herzen *broken--hearted* ‖ seelisch gebrochen s *to be broken* (durch *by*) **C. sich ~ 1.** (of waves) *to break*; sich ~ an *to dash* (od *surge*) *against* ‖ ⟨übtr⟩ sich ~ an .. *to be resisted* (od *foiled*) *by* .. **2.** ⟨opt⟩ (of rays) *to be refracted* **3.** (sich erbrechen) *to vomit, retch, sputter* **II.** vi **1.** [s] (zerbrechen) *to break*; *burst, crack, go, spring*; *snap*; der Stock brach unter dem Gewicht *the stick snapped under the weight*; die Achse war gebrochen *the axle was broken*; mir ist der Mast g. *I have sprung my mast* ‖ (sich spalten) *to part, rip* **2.** [s] ⟨übtr⟩ (of wine) *to become turbid* ‖ (of the weather) *to change* ‖ die Stimme des Knaben beginnt z ~ *the boy's voice begins to break* ‖ die Freundschaft brach bald *their friendship soon broke down* ‖ das Herz will mir ~ *my heart will break* **3.** [h] (of boars) *to root* | **aus** dem Gefängnis ~ *to break prison*; aus dem Lager ~ (of game) *to break cover*; aus den Wolken ~ (Sonne) *to break through the clouds* ‖ Tränen brachen ihr aus den Augen *tears gushed from her eyes* ‖ → aus–, einbrechen | ~ **mit** *to break with* (*a p*); mit der Vergangenheit ~ *to break with the past* ‖ mit e–r Gewohnheit ~ *to abandon* od *discontinue a habit* **4.** [h] (= sich ~) *to vomit, retch, sputter*

Br·echen n **1.** *breaking* ‖ ⟨ec⟩ *fraction* (*of the bread*) | ⟨fig⟩ → Biegen ‖ zum ~ voll *cram*– od *chok*(*e*)-*full*; *full to bursting point* (od *to overflowing*) **2.** *breach* (*of contract*, etc.), *violation* **3.** (Erbrechen) *vomit, retch* ‖ → Brechung, Bruch **br·echend 1.** a *breaking* **2.** adv ~ voll *cramp-full*; *full to bursting point* (od *to capacity*) **Br·echer** m **1.** (P) *breaker* (*of the law*) **2.** (Sturzwelle) *breaker, comber* **3.** = Brechmaschine

Br·echung f ~/~en **1.** ⟨opt⟩ *refraction* **2.** ⟨gram⟩ *breaking* (*of a vowel*) **~sebene** f ⟨opt⟩ *plane of refraction* **~sfehler** m *refraction error* **~sindex** m *refraction index* **~sstreifen** m ⟨opt⟩ *refraction fringes* pl **~swinkel** m *angle of refraction*

Bredouille [brə'duj], °**Bred·ulje** f *mess, scrape*

Br·egen m ~s/~ (Gehirn) *brain* ‖ °= Kopf, Schädel, „Birne"

Br·egma n ~s/ ⟨anat⟩ *bregma*

Br·ei m ~s/~e **1.** (Nahrung bes f Kinder) *pap*; Mehl~́ *meal pap*; Reis~́ *rice pap* ‖ Hafer~́ *porridge*; Kartoffel~́ *mashed potatoes* [pl], ⟨cul, sl⟩ *mash*, → Püree ‖ Maismehl~́ ⟨Am⟩ *mush* ‖ süßer ~ ⟨fig⟩ *mealymouthed things* pl | (wie die Katze) um den heißen ~ (herum)gehen, (herumreden) *to beat about the bush*; *to stop to look at the fence*; (*to hedge, dodge, side-step*); *to follow a roundabout course, to avoid coming to the point* ‖ er schmierte ihr ~ ums Maul *he soft-soaped her* ‖ (jdn) z ~ schlagen ⟨fam⟩ *to knock into a cocked hat* **2.** ⟨übtr⟩ (klebrige Masse) *mash, mush, pap, pulp*; Papier~́ *pulp* ‖ z ~ m *to mash, pulp, squash, stodge* ‖ z ~ w, ein ~ w *to pulp*; (of berries) *to go to squash* ‖ ~́**artig** a *pappy, pulpy, masly* **~umschlag** m (heißer ~) *cataplasm, poultice*; e–n ~ auflegen auf etw *to poultice a th*

Br·eiha(h)n m Broyhan

br·eiig a *mushy, pappy, pulpous, pulpy, squashy* ‖ ~ m *to pulp, squash*; ~ w *to pulp*

Br·eisgau m & n ⟨Ger⟩ (Landschaft in Baden)

breit I. a **1.** [Ggs schmal] *broad*; *wide* (*bed*; *door*; *river*; *road*, etc.); ~er Rand *wide margin*; *broad-based* (*heel*); ~es Schwert *broadsword* ‖ *square* (*chin, shoulders*); ~ in der Schulter *broad in the shoulder*, .. w *to fill out*; er ist sehr ~ *he has a broad chest*; ~e Stirn *wide forehead* ‖ ⟨fig⟩ er hat e–n ~en Buckel *he can stand a good deal* ‖ (etw) ~ m *to broaden*; ~er w *to broaden* | (ausgedehnt) *broad, extensive, spacious*;*diffuse* (*masses of light*) ‖ ⟨typ⟩ *extended, expanded* (*type*) **2. a.** ⟨oft com⟩ (bei Messungen [Ggs lang]) ⟨mst⟩ *wide*; ein Meter ~ liegen (of cloth) *to be one metre wide* (od *in width*); wie ~ ist es? *how wide is it*?; ein Meter ~ *one metre wide*; ein 3 Zoll ~er Streifen *a three-inch wide strip*; 3 Meter lang u 2 M. ~ *three metres by two* ‖ *broad*; 3 Hände, Finger ~ *three hands, fingers in width* od *breadth*; k–n Finger ~ weiter *not any farther*; → Finger~, Hand~ **b.** ⟨mil⟩ *wide* (Front) **c.** (*the lake is 2 miles*) *across* **3.** ⟨übtr⟩ **a.** die ~e Masse *the vast numbers* [pl]; die ~e Öffentlichkeit *the public at large*, ein ~eres Publikum *a wider public* ‖ ein ~es Feld *a wide field* (*for experiments*); ~es Wissen *wide knowledge* **b.** (weitschweifig) *diffuse, wordy* (*style*); *lengthy* (*statement*) **c.** (plump) *broad* (*accent, pronunciation*) **4.** Wendungen: es ist **so** ~ wie es lang ist *it is as broad as it is long* | da steht er, **groß** u ~ *there he is as large as life*; → ~beinig | **ein langes u ~es,** des langen u ~en erzählen *to spin a long yarn, to talk at large* | weit u ~ *far and wide* ‖ → ~machen, ~schlagen, ~treten **II.** adv *broadly, widely* ‖ *squarely* ‖ ~ angelegt *broadly laid down* (od *planned*) ‖ hier ist es gr u ~ z lesen *here it is clearly to be seen* ‖ lang u ~ erzählen *to talk at great length* ‖ ~lachen *to laugh freely*

breit- [in comp] *broad* .., *wide* .. **~ästig** a *broad-boughed* ~́**bandscheinwerfer** m *wide-band headlamp* ~́**beil** n *broad-ax*(*e*) **~beinig 1.** a *straddle-legged* **2.** adv *squarely*; ~ gehen, stehen *to straddle*; ~ stehen auf etw *to straddle a th*; sich ~ vor jdn hinstellen *to square up to a p* ‖ ~́gehen [n] *straddle* **~|drücken** vt [h] *to flat*(*ten*) **~füßig** a *broad-footed* **~gedrückt** a *flattened, flat* (*nose*) **~gesichtig** a *broad-faced* **~gestirnt** a *having a wide forehead* **~getreten** a *beaten* (*path*) ‖ ⟨fig⟩ *worn out*; *hackneyed* ~́**hacke** f *mattock, twibill, twybill* ~́**hammer** m *sledge-hammer*; *flatting h.* **~köpfig** a *broad-headed* (*nail*) ‖ ⟨engl⟩ ~er Pfeil (als Eigentumszeichen) *broad arrow* **~krempig** a *broad* (od *wide*)-*brimmed* **~|machen** vt [h] sich ~ ⟨fig⟩ *to parade, to show off, to strut*; *to behave ostentatiously*; *to make o.s. at home*; → sich aufblähen; prahlen ‖ (of evils) *to spread*; → einreißen ~́**nase** f ⟨zoo⟩ [koll] ~n [pl] *New World monkeys* [pl] **~|quetschen** vt [h] *to squash*; *to crush into a flat pulp* ‖ ⟨fig⟩ *to dilate* (od *expatiate, palaver*) *on* (*a th*) ~́**rand** m ⟨ent⟩ *dytiscus* **~randig** a *broad-brimmed* **~|schlagen** vt [h] *to flat*(*ten*) ‖ ⟨fig⟩ jdn ~ *to talk a p over* od *round, to cajole* od *persuade a p* (z tun *into doing*); *to prevail upon a p* (*to do*) ‖ **sich ~ l** *to let o.s. be persuaded*; *to yield*; *to strain a point* **~schnablig** a *broad-billed* **~schulterig** a *broad*– od *square-shouldered, square-built* ~́**schwanz** m **1.** (= Persianer) *broadtail* **2.** ⟨orn⟩ (a. ~lori) *lory* ~́**seite** f *broadside* (*of a ship*) ‖ Geschütze nach e–r ~ *broadside* (a. deren Salven-Feuer) ‖ jdn mit der ~ (des Geweihs) fassen (of stags) *to catch a p broadside on* ~́**spur** f ⟨rail⟩ *wide gauge* [⟨a.⟩ attr] = **~spurig** a ⟨rail⟩ *broad gauge* (*line*) ‖ ⟨fig⟩ *conceited*; *arrogant, bumptious, snobby*; ~es Wesen *bumptiousness, arrogance*; → aufgeblasen 2. **~streifig** a ⟨hort⟩ *bizarre* **~|treten** vt [h] (Gerücht) *to promulgate, to make public* ‖ *to dilate* od *expatiate on* (*a th*) ~́**wand** f ⟨film⟩ *cinerama*; *wide-screem* | ~film [m] *cinemascope* ®; *w.-sc. film*; *vista-vision* [attr] „~́**-wie–hoch**": Herr, Frau ~ *Mr, Mrs Fife-by-five* **~würfig 1.** a ⟨hort⟩ *broadcast* **2.** adv ~ säen *to sow broadcast*

Br·eite f ~/~n **A.** [abstr] **1.** *breadth, width*; Haares≃ *hair's breadth*; → Hand≃ ‖ größte ~ (e–s Schiffes) *beam* ‖ *extensiveness, spaciousness*; ⟨hum⟩ *latitude* **2.** ⟨com⟩ (bei Messungen) *width, breadth* ‖ in die Länge u ~ *in the lengthwise and breadthwise direction*; der L. u ~ nach *lengthwise and breadthwise* **3. a.** ⟨geogr⟩ *latitude*; 53 Grad, 15 Minuten (53°15′) nördlicher ~ *53°.15′ north latitude* **|** ⟨übtr⟩ in diesen, unseren ~n *in these, our latitudes* (od *climes, parts, regions*) **b.** ⟨astr⟩ *latitude* **4.** ⟨übtr⟩ *breadth* (*of a p's outlook*; ⟨arts⟩ *of treatment*); *wideness*; an ~ gewinnen *to gain in breadth* (od *extension*) ‖ in die ~ gehen *to expand in width*; *to get stout, to grow broader*; ⟨übtr⟩ *to become diffuse* (od *prolix, lengthy*); in die ~ gehend *diffuse*; *lengthy* **B.** [konkr] (Stoffmaß) *breadth, width*; die ~n e–s Rockes *the breadths of a skirt* ‖ ⟨agr⟩ (Acker≃) *breadth*; e–e ~ säen *to sow a breadth*

Breiten- ~feuer n ⟨mil⟩ *traversing fire* (Ggs Tiefen–) **~gliederung** f ⟨tact⟩ *distribution in width* **~grad** m ⟨geog⟩ *degree of latitude* **~kreis** m ⟨geog⟩ *parallel*; *parellel* od *circle of l.* **~wirkung** f ⟨artill⟩ *spreading effect* ‖ kulturelle ~ *influence in the cultural field*

Br·eitling m ~s/~e ⟨ich⟩ *whitebait, sprat*

Br·ekzie f ~/~n (Felsmasse) *breccia* [It]

†**Br·eme** f ~/~n ⟨ent⟩ = Bremse

Br·emen n ⟨Ger⟩ (Hansestadt) **Br·emer**(in f) m *inhabitant* od *native of Bremen* **~bl·au** n *Bremen blue*

Br·emmer m ~s/~ ⟨min⟩ *small shaft*

Br·ems- [in comp] *brake* .. **~anlage** f *brake assembly* **~backe** f *brake-shoe* (od *–block*) **~band** n *brake* (od *braking*)*-band* **~baum** m *brake-shaft* **~belag** m ⟨mot⟩ *brake lining* **~belege** m pl *brake-linings, disc brake pads* **~berg** m ⟨min⟩ (steile Seilbahn) *jig*; *jig-brow* **~dynamometer** m *absorption dynamometer* **~einrichtung** f *braking arrangement*; *brake gear* **~elektrode** f *decelerating electrode* **~fallschirm** m ⟨aero⟩ *brake* od *drogue parachute* **~feder** f *brake spring* **~flüssigkeit** f *brake fluid*; ⟨artill⟩ *recoil oil* **~fußhebel** m *brake pedal* **~gefühl** n ⟨mot⟩ *feel of the brake* **~gummi** m [*n] ⟨cycl⟩ *brake pad* **~handhebel** m *handbrake* **~haspel** f *brake winch* **~hebel** m *brake handle* (od *lever*), *hand lever* **~keil** m *sprag* **~klappe** f ⟨aero⟩ *flap* **~klaue** f *holder of a brake-shoe* **~klotz** m *skid*; *brake block*; ⟨aero⟩ *chock* ‖ (e–m Rad) e–n ~ anlegen *to skid* (*a wheel*) **~kurbel** f *brake handle* (od *crank*) **~länge** f ⟨mot⟩ *braking distance* **~leistung** f ⟨mot⟩ *braking capacity*; *brake HP* **~licht** n ⟨mot⟩ *stop light* **~luft-** ~behälter [m] *compressed-air brake cylinder* ‖ ~druck [m] ⟨mot⟩ *brake air pressure* **~pedal** n *brake pedal* **~prozeß** m ⟨phys⟩ *slowing down process* **~prüfer** m ⟨bes mot⟩ *decelerometer* **~rad** n *brakewheel* **~rakete** f ⟨astronaut⟩ *retro-rocket* **~scheibe** f *brake pulley* **~schuh** m *brakeshoe* (od *block*) **~segment** n *quadrant of a brake* **~spur** f ⟨mot⟩ *skid mark* od *track*[*s* pl] **~stange** f *brake rod* **~stock** m *brake shaft* **~stoß** m ⟨mot, rail, etc⟩ *shock of braking* **~strahlung** f ⟨Kerntechnik⟩ *bremsstrahlung* **~strecke** f (ausreichende *enough*) *room in which to stop* **~trommel** f *brake drum* **~vorrichtung** f *braking equipment* od *device*, *brake gear* **~wagen** m ⟨rail⟩ *brake car* (od *van*); (im Güterzug) ⟨Am⟩ *caboose* **~weg** m *stopping* od (*panic-*) *braking distance* **~welle** f *brake shaft* **~zylinder** m *cataract* od *brake cylinder* ‖ ⟨artill⟩ *recoil buffer*

Br·emse f ~/~n **1.** (Nasenklammer f Pferde) *barnacle, twitch* ‖ e–m Pferd die ~ geben *to apply a barnacle to a horse* **2.** ⟨cycl, mot, rail⟩ *brake*; angreifende, fassende ~ ⟨m. m.⟩ *grabbing of brakes*; die ~n greifen gleichmäßig an *the brakes take hold evenly*; Backen≃ *shoe-brake*; Band≃ *band-brake*; Druckluft≃ *air-brake*; Wirbelstrom≃ *magneto-electric brake*; → Notbremse ‖ ohne ~ *brakeless* ‖ die ~ (an)ziehen, anlegen *to apply* (od *put on*) *the brake* (: *the brake is applied*); die ~ betätigen *to actuate the brake*; die ~ lösen *to release the brake*; die ~ ziehen *to put on the brakes* ⟨a. a–n⟩ **3.** °= Ohrfeige

Br·emse f ~/~n ⟨ent⟩ (Vieh≃) *gad-fly*; (Pferde≃) *breeze*(*-fly*), *horse-fly* ‖ ~n(larven)-schwindel ⟨vet⟩ *the bot*(*t*)*s* [pl]

br·emsen I. vt/i [h] **1.** vt (Wagen) *to brake* (*a car*); *to apply the brake to* (*a car*); scharf ~ *to jam the brakes* **|** ⟨fig⟩ (Übermut) *to check* **2.** vi *to apply* (od *put on*) *the brake* **|** ⟨fig⟩ *to pull up*; bei ihm muß man immer ~ *he always wants being kept in check* **|** °(Arbeit einschränken) *to ca'canny, to show up*, ⟨sl⟩ *to mike* **II.** ≃ n *brakeage* ‖ (Verlangsamen der Arbeits– *or* Produktionsleistung) *ca'canny*

Br·emser m ~s/~ ⟨rail⟩ *brakesman*, ⟨Am fam⟩ *brakey*; ~ s ⟨Am⟩ *to brake* (*on a train*) ‖ ~häuschen [n] ⟨Am rail⟩ *caboose*

Br·emsung f ~/~en ⟨at⟩ *retardation moderation* **|** ~smittel [n] *moderator*

Br·enn- [in comp] *burning* .. ‖ ⟨phys⟩ *focal* **~apparat** m *tools* [pl] *for wood-etching* ‖ (f Branntwein) *distilling-apparatus, still* ‖ ⟨surg⟩ *galvanocaustic apparatus* **~dauer** f ⟨mil⟩ *burning rate* od *time* ‖ ⟨el⟩ (*burning*) *life of a lamp* **~ebene** f ⟨phys⟩ *focal plane* ‖ **~eisen** n *branding-iron, brand* ‖ ⟨surg⟩ *thermo-cautery* ‖ = Brennschere **~fläche** f ⟨phys⟩ *focal plane* **~glas** n ⟨phys⟩ *burning-glass* **~haar** n ⟨bot⟩ *sting* (*of a nettle*) **~haus** n *distillery* **~hexe** f *very small stove* **~holz** n *firewood* **~kammer** f ⟨tech⟩ *combustion chamber* **~kasten** m, **~kapsel** f ⟨ceram⟩ *saggar*, **~länge** f (e–s Zünders) *setting of a fuse* **~linie** f ⟨phys⟩ *caustic curve, caustic*; (bei Spiegeln) *catacaustic curve*, (bei Linsen) *diacaustic curve* **~material** n *fuel* **~meister** m *head distiller* **~(n)essel** f ⟨bot⟩ *stinging-nettle, urtica* [L]; wie ~n stechen *to urticate*; ⟨med⟩ (jdn) mit ~n bearbeiten *to urticate*; ~behandlung, ~kur [f] *urtication* **~ofen** m (f Ziegel) *kiln*, ⟨met⟩ *refining-furnace* **~öl** n *lamp-oil* **~palme** f ⟨bot⟩ *jaggery* (od *toddy-*)*palm*; Saft der ~ *toddy* **~punkt** m **1.** ⟨phys⟩ *focal point, focus* ‖ auf ~ gestellte Lampe ⟨microscope⟩ *focused illuminator* ‖ bildseitiger ~ ⟨opt⟩ *principal focal point* ‖ mit 2 ~en *bifocal* ‖ im ~ *in focus*; nicht im ~ *out of focus* ‖ im ~ eingestellt ⟨theat⟩ *sharp focussed*, ⟨Am⟩ *sh. forcus* [attr] ‖ in den ~ rücken *to bring into focus*; (Strahlen) in e–m ~ sammeln *to focus* **2.** ⟨fig⟩ *focus* (*of a revolt*; *disease*); *focal point* (*of a play*); *centre, hive* (*of industry*) ‖ (Aufmerksamkeit) in e–m ~ konzentrierten *to focus*; (etw) in den ~ rücken *to bring* (*a th*) *into focus* ‖ im ~ des Interesses stehen *to be* (*in*) *the centre of interest* **~schere** f *curling-tongs* (od *irons*) [pl] (e–e ~ *a pair of curling-t.*) **~schluß** m (v Raketen) (völliger) *burnout* (auf Kommando, nach Erreichen e–r bestimmten Höhe *or* Geschwindigkeit, ⟨a.⟩ ~gabe [f]) *cut-out* **~spiegel** m ⟨phys⟩ *concave mirror, burning-mirror* **~spiritus** m *methylated spirit* **~staub** m ⟨tech⟩ *fuel powder* **~stelle** f ⟨el⟩ *light*(*ing*)*-point* **~stift** m *cautery* **~stoff** m *fuel*; *combustible* ‖ ~ einspritzen ⟨m. m.⟩ *to prime an engine* ‖ (etw) mit (frischem) ~ versehen *to* (*re*)*fuel* ‖ Schiff mit ~ *fueller* **|** ~ f Düsenflugzeug *jet fuel* ‖ ~aggregat [n] *fuel assembly* **|** ~behälter [m] *fuel-tank*; ~ersparnis [f] *fuel saving* (od *economy*); ~messer [m], ~uhr [f] *fuel gauge*; ~motor [m] *fuel engine*; ~standhöhe [f] *fuel level*; ~verbrauch [m] *fuel consumption*; ~zufuhr [f] *fuel feed*; → Kraftstoff **~stunde** f *burning-hour* **~weite** f ⟨phys⟩

focal length (od *distance*) || hintere ~ ⟨opt⟩ *rear focal length*; Objektiv mit verstellbarer ~ *variable focus lens* **~wert** m = Heizwert **~winde** f ⟨bot⟩ *Chili-nettle* **~wirtschaft** f = Brandwirtschaft **~wurz** f ⟨bot⟩ = Seidelbast **~ziegel** m *kiln-burnt brick* **~zünder** m *combustion fuse*; (*variable*) *time-fuse* | ~-Mine [f] *anti-personnel mine* **~zündung** f *ignition fuse*

br·ennbar a *combustible* | **≃keit** f ~/ *combustibleness, combustibility*

br·ennen vi/t [h] [brannte/gebrannt] **I.** vi **1.** ⟨eig⟩ **a.** (of fire) *to burn*; hell, lichterloh ~ *to blaze* || es brennt! *fire*! es brennt im Dorfe *there is a fire in the village*; wo brennt es? *where is the fire*?, ⟨fig⟩ *what's the matter*?; → I. 3. c. **b.** (of candles, gas, etc.) *to burn, shine*; das Gas brennt noch *the gas is still alight*; ~ bleiben *to remain alight* || die Zigarre will nicht ~ *the cigar will not burn* **c.** (of a building, etc.) *to burn, to be on fire*; lichterloh ~ *to be ablaze* **d.** (brennbar s) *to be combustible* **2.** ⟨übtr⟩ **a.** die Sonne brennt *the sun is burning* (od *shines hot*) **b.** (of nettles) *to sting* **c.** (of spices, etc.) *to bite, to be hot, to sting*; Senf brennt auf der Zunge *mustard burns* od *stings the tongue* **d.** (of wounds, eyes, etc.) *to burn*; *to smart* **e.** der Himmel brannte in der Glut der Abendsonne *the sky was ablaze with the evening glow* || ganz Europa brannte *the whole of Europe was ablaze* (od *in a flame*) **3.** ⟨fig⟩ **a.** mir brennt der Kopf *my head is burning* || ihm brannte der Boden hier unter den Füßen, ihm brannten die Sohlen *the place was getting too hot* od *warm for him* || das Geld brennt ihm in der Tasche *or* in den Händen *the money burns a hole in his pocket* || jdm auf den Nägeln (*or* Nähten, Fingern) ~ *to press upon a p*; die S brannte ihm auf den N. *the matter was pressing* || das Geheimnis brannte ihm auf der Seele *the secret burned in his heart* (od *weighed heavily upon him*) || in jdm ~ (of remorse) *to sear a p* **b.** wo brennt **es** denn? *why* (*in*) *such a hurry*? → I. 1. a. || die Sache brennt sehr *the matter is urgent*; die Sache brennt nicht! *there is no hurry*! *that matter will keep*!; → I. 1. a. **c.** (**P**) **auf** etw ~ *to crave, to long, to yearn for a th*; er brannte (darauf) zurückzusein *he was anxious* (od *dying*) *to be back*; ich brenne darauf, dich zu verprügeln *I itch to get my hands on you* | **vor** Liebe ~ *to be aflame with love*; ~ vor Ehrgeiz, Erwartung etc *to burn with ambition, impatience*, etc; er brannte vor Begierde *he was tingling with eagerness*; .. vor Verlangen *he itched with the desire* (*to do*) **II.** vt **1.** (Holz, Kohle) *to burn*; (Holz) schwarz ~ (of fire) *to char*; z Asche ~ *to reduce to ashes* || (Kerze etc) *to burn*; Gas ~ *to burn gas* || (Schiff) rein ~ *to bream* || ein Loch ~ in *to burn a hole in* (*a table-cloth*) **2. a.** (Ton, Ziegel, Porzellan etc) *to bake, burn, fire*; (Kalk) *to burn* **b.** (Metall) *to roast*; (Erze) *to calcine*; (Stahl) *to anneal* || (Silber) *to refine* | ⟨fig⟩ jdn weiß ~ (= v Verdacht reinigen) *to exculpate, exonerate a p*; sich weiß ~ *to exonerate o.s.* **c.** (Kaffee) *to roast* || gebrannte Mandel *burnt almond* **d.** (Branntwein) *to distil* **e.** (das Haar) *to curl*; sich das Haar ~ *to curl one's hair* **3. a.** (Vieh) *to brand, mark* **b.** ⟨übtr⟩ jdm eins aufs Fell ~ *to fire* od *take a shot at a p*; ⟨fig⟩ *to give a p a thrashing* **4.** ⟨surg⟩ (Wunde) *to cauterize, sear* || ⟨vet⟩ (Pferd) *to fire* **5.** jdn ~ *to injure* (od *to cause pain to*) *a p by fire*; **sich** ~ = sich verbrennen || gebranntes Kind scheut das Feuer *a burnt child dreads fire* || ⟨übtr poet⟩ *to sting*; *hurt*

Br·ennen n **1.** (→ ≃ I.) *burning* || *stinging* (*of a nettle*, etc.) || *smarting* (*of the eyes* **2.** (→ ≃ II.) *burning* (*of coal, gas*) || *baking, burning* (*of bricks*, etc.) *roasting* (*of coffee, metal*) || *distillation* (*of brandy*) || *curling* (*of the hair*) || *branding* (*of cattle*) || ⟨surg⟩ *cautery, searing*

br·ennend I. a **1.** *burning* (*candle*) || *on fire, ablaze, alight*; die Zahl der ~en Kerzen *the number of candles alight* || *lighted* (*cigar*) | *burning hot, scorching* (*day*) || *burning* (*desert*) **2.** *burning, smarting* (*eyes*) || *acute, biting*; *pungent* (*pain*) || *burning* (*thirst*); *violent* || *glaring* (*red*) || ⟨surg⟩ *caustic* **3.** *ardent, burning* (*ambition, love, passion, sorrow, zeal*) || ⟨bot⟩ ~e Liebe *Cross of Jerusalem, scarlet lychnis* **4.** ~e Frage *burning question*; die Frage wird ~ *the question becomes acute* (od *arises*) **II.** [adv] ~ heiß *scorching* od *scalding hot*; *broiling* (*sun*) || ~ gern wissen mögen *to be anxious* od *dying to know* || ~ nötig h *to want very badly, to be in dire need of*

Br·enner m ~s/~ [mst in comp] **1.** (P) (Branntwein≃) *distiller* || Ziegel≃ *brick-burner* (od *maker*) || → Mord≃ **2.** (S) (Lampenteil) *burner*; Gas≃ *gas-burner*; Spiritus≃ *spirit lamp*; → Bunsen≃; Schweiß≃ || (Kaffee≃) *roaster* **b.** ⟨bot⟩ (Pflanzenkrankheit) *brand, rust* **c.** ⟨ent⟩ = Blütenstecher

Br·enner m (Bergpaß in Tirol) *Brenner*

Brenner·ei f ~/~en (Branntwein≃) *distillery, still* || Ziegel≃ *brick-kiln*

Brenz m ~es/~e: [mst pl] ~e (brennbare Mineralien) *inflammables* [pl] **~säure** f *pyro-acid*

br·enzlich, –lig I. a **1.** ~ riechen *to smell of burning*; ~ schmecken *to taste burnt*; ~er Geruch (Geschmack) *burnt smell* (*taste*) **2.** ⟨fig⟩ (a. –lig) *critical, snickersneed* (*condition*); e–e ~e Lage *a touch-and-go*; e–e ~e S *a delicate* od *ticklish matter*; die S ist sehr ~, es steht sehr ~ *it is touch-and-go* (mit, um jdn *with a p*) **II.** adv *awfully, extremely*; ⟨sl⟩ *deuced* (*cold*)

Br·esche f ~/~n ⟨mil⟩ *breach, gap* || e–e ~ legen (*or* schlagen, schießen) *to* (*make a*) *breach*; *to break through a line of defence*; e–e ~ legen in etw, etw in ~ legen *to breach a th, to make a breach in a th*; ⟨fig⟩ *to break the back of a th* || in die ~ springen *to stand in the breach*; ⟨fig⟩ *to step* (od *throw o.s.*) *into the breach*

Br·escia n ⟨It⟩ (Stadt u Provinz) *Brescia*

Br·eslau n ⟨†Ger⟩ (Hauptstadt Schlesiens)

†br·esthaft a = kränklich

Brest-Litowsk n (⟨†poln.⟩ Stadt) (jetzt Russ: Brest) *B.-Litovsk* (Friede v. ~ 1918)

Bret·agne [brəˈtaɲ] f ⟨Fr⟩ *Bretagne, Brittany*, ⟨a.⟩ (*Little* od *Lower*) *Britain*; in der ~ *in Brittany* **Bret·agner, bretagnisch** → **Bret·one** m, **Bret·onin** f *Breton, native of Little Britain* **bret·onisch** a *Breton, of Little Britain*

Brett n ~s/~er **1.** (Stück Holz) **a.** *board*; dünnes längliches ~ *batten*; halbzölliges ~ *half-inch board*; äußeres, rindiges ~ *slab*; ein Stoß ~er *a stack of boards* || Fuß≃ *footboard*; Plätt≃ *ironing-board*; Sprung≃ *spring-board*; Wasch≃ *washing-board* || dickes ~ *plank* (*of a ship*, etc.); → Bohle, Planke; ~ mit Nut u Feder *match-board* || die ~er [pl] am Boden e–s offenen Bootes, vorn u hinten *sheet*; Lauf≃ *gang-way, plank-way* || (etw) mit ~ern bedecken *or* beschlagen *to board*; mit ~ern vernageln *to board up*; → täfeln **b.** ⟨fig⟩ kein ~ vor dem Kopf h *to know a th or two*; ein ~ vor dem Kopf h *to be blindfold*(*ed*); *to be stupid* (od *dull of comprehension*) || er kann durch ein ~ sehen *he can see through a brick-wall* || in die ~er gehen (sc. in den Sarg gehen) *to die* || hier ist die Welt mit ~ern vernagelt *here we are in an impasse*; *here is the end of civilization*; *things are terribly dull here*; jdm das ~ unter den Füßen wegziehen *to cut the grass from under a p's feet* **2.** Bücher≃ *shelf*; Wand≃ *wall-shelf*; Eck≃ *corner-shelf* || (Tablett) Kaffee≃, Servier≃ *tray*; Präsentier≃ (aus Metall) *salver* **3. a.** (Spiel≃) *board, table*; ~ f Damespiel *draught-board*; Puffspiel≃ *back-*

gammon-board; Schach≗ *chess-board* ‖ auf demselben ∼ stehen (S) *to be much the same*; *to be equally concerned* ‖ → Stein **b.** herzförmiges ∼ mit Rollen u Schreibvorrichtung bei spiritist. Sitzungen *planchette* **4.** Zahl≗ *counter* ‖ (etw) auf e–m ∼ bezahlen *to pay down in cash* ‖ ⟨univ⟩ Schwarzes ∼ *notice* (⟨Am⟩ *sign*) *board* **5.** Griff≗ *finger-board* (*of a violin*) **6.** (erhöhter Sitz an e–r Tafel) am ∼ s *to be at the top of a table*; ⟨fig⟩ *to be at the top of the tree* **|** ⟨theat⟩ ∼er [pl] *boards* [pl], *stage*; die ∼er betreten *to tread the boards*; über die ∼er gehen (of plays) *to be* (*en*)*acted*; ∼er, die die Welt bedeuten vgl: *all the world's a stage* (Shak) → aufführen 3. **7.** ∼er [pl] (Skier) *skis* [pl] **8.** [in comp] → Brett–, Bretter–

Br·ett- ∼mühle f *saw-mill* **∼nagel** m *board-nail* **∼säge** f *rip*(*ping*)*-saw*; mit der ∼ sägen *to ripsaw* **∼schneider** m *sawyer* **∼spiel** n **1.** *game played on a board*; → Dame–, Puff–, Schachspiel ‖ japanisches ∼ *yobang* **2.** ⟨ent⟩ (Augenfalter) *satyr* **3.** ⟨bot⟩ *fritillary* **∼stein** m (im Damespiel) *draught*(*s*)*man*

Br·ettchen n ∼s/∼ *small board* ‖ ⟨weav⟩ Lese-≗ *hole-board*

Br·etter- [in comp] *made of boards* od *planks boarded, planked* **∼bekleidung** f *board-lining* (*of a window*) **∼bude** f *booth* **∼dach** n = Schindeldach **∼siedlung** f (am Stadtrand) ⟨Am⟩ *city shantytown* **∼stapel** m *board pile* **∼steg** m *duckboards* [pl] **∼verkleidung** f *plank revetment*; *boarding, board-lining* **∼verschlag** m, **∼wand** f *partition of boards* od *planks* **∼zaun** m *hoarding*; ⟨Am⟩ *board-fence*

Brettl n ∼s/∼ *cabaret*

Br·etzel m = Brezel

Br·eve n ∼s/∼s (päpstliche Urkunde) (*papal*) *brief*; *breve*

Br·evet n ∼s/∼s ⟨hist⟩ (Gnadenbrief) *brevet* ‖ (Patent) *brevet, patent*

Brev·ier n ∼s/∼e **1.** ⟨R. C.⟩ *breviary* **2.** ⟨typ⟩ *brevier*

Br·ezel f ∼/∼n *cracknel*, ⟨Am⟩ *pretzel* **∼backen** n: °wie's ∼ ⟨fig⟩ *like a shot, like anything*; °das geht wie's ∼ ⟨fig⟩ *you are very quick indeed* **∼frau** f *cracknel-seller*

br·ich imp sg. **brichst** 2. sg **bricht** 3. sg v brechen

Br·icke f ∼/∼n ⟨ich⟩ = Neunauge

Bride f (Fr) ∼/∼n (am Spitzengrund) *bride*

Bridge n ⟨cards⟩ *bridge*; ∼ spielen *to play b.*

Brief m ∼s/∼e **1. a.** *letter* (an *to*; v *from*); ⟨rhet⟩ *epistle*; kz ∼ *note, chit* (an *to*) ‖ ∼e [pl] *letters* [pl], *correspondence* ‖ eingeschriebener ∼ *registered l.*; postlagernder ∼ *letter "general delivery"*; ∼ mit Aufschrift ‚Amtlich' (u portofrei) *letter marked* '*On Her* od *His Majesty's Service*'; unbestellbarer ∼ *dead* od *returned l.*; Büro f unbestellbare ∼e *Dead* od *Returned Letter Office*; ∼e [pl] fürs Inland *inland letters*, ∼e fürs Ausland *foreign letters* [pl]; → Leerung, Zustellung ‖ ⟨com⟩ Ihr werter ∼ vom 5. d. Mts. *your favour of the 5th inst.*; in Beantwortung Ihres ≗es *in reply to your letter* ‖ Karten≗ *letter-card*; Begleit≗ *covering letter* ‖ e–n ∼ frankieren, frei m *to stamp a letter*; e–n ∼ zur P. geben *to post* ⟨Am⟩ *mail a l.*; ∼e wechseln *to correspond* (mit *with*) **b.** ⟨ec⟩ *Epistle* (an die Römer *to the Romans*) **c.** ⟨pol⟩ offener ∼ *open letter* (an *to*) **2. a.** ⟨jur⟩ (Urkunde) *written document*; *charter*; *letters-patent* ‖ blauer ∼ → blau I. A. 2. ‖ *edict* ‖ → Frei≗ **b.** ⟨com⟩ Wechsel≗ *bill* (*of exchange*), *draft* ‖ ⟨st exch⟩ (abbr *B.*) *offer*; ∼ u Geld *bills* [pl] *and money, asked and bid* **c. unter ∼ u Siegel** *under my hand and seal* ‖ jdm ∼ u Siegel geben *to assure* (od *wager*) *a p* (*that*); ich gebe Ihnen ∼ u Siegel *I'll warrant* (*you*), *I'll be bound* **3.** ein ∼ Stecknadeln *a paper of pins*

Br·ief- ∼abfertigung f *dispatch of the mails* **∼adel** m *nobility obtained by letters-patent* **∼annahme** f (Schalter) *receiving-window* **∼anrede** f –schluß → *letter* I. 2. **∼aufschrift** f *address of a letter* **∼beschwerer** m *letter-weight* (od *weigher*); *paper-weight* **∼bestellung** f *delivery* **∼beutel** m *letter-bag*, ⟨Am⟩ *mail pouch* **∼bild** n *telautogram* **|** ∼sender [m] *telescriptor, telautograph* **|** ∼telegramm [n] *telautogram* **|** ∼telegraphie [f] *telautography* **∼bogen** m *sheet of note-paper* **∼bote** m = Briefträger **∼buch** n *letter register*, *–book* od *copy-book* **∼einwurf** m (in e–r Mauer) (*slot of a*) *letter box*; ⟨Am⟩ *letter-drop*; → Briefkasten **∼fach** n (e–s Pults etc) *pigeonhole* ‖ (bei der Post) *post-office box* **∼form** f: ∼romane [m pl] → Briefroman *epistolary fiction* (z. B. *Richardson, Pamela* [1740], *Clarissa* [1747–48]) **∼freund** m *pen-friend* **∼geheimnis** n *secrecy of private correspondence* **∼halter** m *letterclip*; (Behälter) *letter-rack* (od *case*) **∼karte** f *card sent in an envelope* **∼kassette(n)** f [pl] *boxed stationery* **∼kasten** m **1.** ⟨Ger⟩ *letter-box*, ⟨Am⟩ (in Straße u Haus) *mail-box* **|** ⟨engl⟩ (freistehender ∼ in Säulenform) *pillar-box*; (in der Mauer) *letter-box*; *posting-box* ‖ „toter ∼" *hiding place* (*for letters etc*) ‖ Leerung des ∼s *collection*; den ∼ leeren *to collect letters* (*from the pillar-box*); ∼öffnung [f], ∼schlitz [m] *slot of a letter-box* **2.** ⟨Ger⟩ (e–r Zeitung) *question-and-answer column* **∼klammer** f (= Bürokl.) *paper-clip*, *letter-clip* **∼kopf** m (gedruckter) *letter-head*(*ing*) **|** ∼papier [n] *letter-head* **∼kopierbuch** n *letter–book* **∼korb** m, **∼körbchen** n *letter tray, office basket*; ∼ f Ein–, Ausgänge *in–, out-tray* ⟨Am⟩ *-box* **∼kurs** m ⟨com⟩ *selling* od *asked* (⟨Am⟩ *posted*) *rate* (od *price*) **∼mappe** f *letter-case*; *file*; → Aktenmappe **∼marke** f (*postage-*) *stamp* ‖ ∼n-album [n] (*postage-*) *stamp album* ‖ ∼nkunde [f], ∼nsammeln [n] *philately*; in der ∼nkunde *philatically* ‖ ∼nsammler [m] *stamp-collector, philatelist* ‖ ∼nsammlung [f] *stamp-collection* **∼öffner** m *letter-opener* od *–knife* **∼ordner** m *file*, *letter-file* (od *book*); die im ∼ befindlichen Briefe *the file*, unter den Briefen *or* Akten im ∼ *on the file* **∼papier** n *note-paper*; (Quartformat) *l.-p.*; ⟨bes Am⟩ *stationery*, ⟨com⟩ *printed letter-heads*; **∼porto** n *postage* **∼post** f *post*; (bes ausländische) *mail* ‖ ⟨Am post a.⟩ *first-class* (*matter*) **∼roman** m ⟨Lit⟩ *epistolary novel* → Briefform **∼schaften** [pl] *correspondence, letters*; *documents, papers* [pl] **∼schluß** m *conclusion of a letter* ‖ *formula concluding a letter*; *complimentary ending*; → ergeben **∼schreiber** m *letter-writer*; *correspondent* ‖ (Buch) *guide to letter-writing, letter-writer* ‖ (Absender) *sender of the letter* **∼schulden** f [pl] **1.** *debts not inscribed in the register* **2.** ⟨fam⟩ *arrears of correcpondence* **∼steller** m *epistoler*; *letter-writer* **∼stempel** m = Poststempel **∼stil** m *epistolary style* **∼tabak** m *tobacco in packets* **∼tasche** f *wallet, pocket-book, note–* od *letter-case*, ⟨Am a.⟩ *bill-fold*; dicke ∼ (f Geld) *well-lined wallet* **∼taube** f *carrier-pigeon, homing-pigeon* **∼telegramm** n ⟨Ger⟩ *letter t.* (*delivered by mail*) **∼träger** m *postman*; ⟨Am⟩ *mailman* **∼umschlag** m *cover, envelope* **∼verkehr** m *correspondence* (*he has a large c.*) **∼waage** f *letter-balance* **∼wahl** f *absentee ballot, postal vote* **∼wechsel** m *correspondence*; mit jdm in ∼ stehen *to be in correspondence with a p*; e–n ∼ unterhalten mit *to carry on* (od *keep up*) *a correspondence with* (*a p*)

Br·iefchen n ∼s/∼ *note*; *chit*; *billet* (an *to*)

br·ieflich 1. a *epistolary* (*communication*) **2.** adv *by letter*

Bries m –ses/–se **1.** ⟨anat⟩ = Thymus **2.** (⟨a.⟩ Kalbs≗, ∼chen [n]) ⟨cul⟩ = Kalbsmilch (*neck*)*sweetbread*

briet 1. u 3. sg pret v braten

Brig·ade f ~/~n ⟨mil⟩ *brigade* (⟨Ger⟩ *consisting of 2(–4) regiments*; ⟨engl⟩ .. *of 3 regiments 3 batteries*); Artillerie≈ *artillery brigade* **~general, ~kommandeur** m ⟨engl mil⟩ *Brigadier* (bis 1918: *Brigadier-General*; bis 1928: *Colonel-Commandant, Colonel-on-the-Staff*); *Brigade-General*

Brigadi·er [brigaˈdjeː] m ~s/~s **1.** †⟨Ger⟩ *brigadier* | ⟨engl⟩ *brigadier*; → Brigadekommandeur **2.** [Fr] *corporal*

Brig·ant m ~en/~en (Räuber) *brigand*

Brigant·ine f ~/~n **1.** ⟨mar⟩ (zweimastiges Segelschiff) *brigantine* **2.** ⟨hist⟩ *shirt of mail*

Brigg f ~/~s ⟨mar⟩ (Zweimastsegler) *brig*

Brik·ett n ~s/~e *briquette*; ~s [pl] *patent fuel*

Brikett·ieranlage f *briquetting plant* **brikett·ieren** vt [h] *to briquette, to form into briquettes*

Brik·ole f [Fr] ~/~n ⟨bill⟩ *bricole*

Brill m ⟨engl⟩ ~s/~s ⟨ich⟩ (Plattfisch) *brill*

brill·ant [brilˈjant] [Fr] **1.** a (glänzend) ⟨fig⟩ *brilliant* (*prospects*; *idea*); *splendid* **2.** adv *brilliantly* **Brill·ant** [brilˈjant] m [Fr] ~en/~en **1.** *brilliant*; *diamond of the finest cut*; → Straß **2.** [f] ⟨typ⟩ (kleinste Schriftgröße) *brilliant* **~feuerwerk** n *brilliant fireworks* [pl] **~nadel** f *brilliant necktie-pin* **~ring** m *brilliant-ring, ring set with a brilliant* **~schmuck** m *set of brilliants* od *diamonds* **~schrift** f ⟨typ⟩ *brilliant*; ⟨Am⟩ *ruby*

Brillant·ine [briljantˈtiːnə] f [Fr] *brillantine*

Br·ille f ~/~n **1.** *spectacles, glasses,* ⟨fam⟩ *specs,* ⟨sl⟩ *goggles, blinkers* [pl] ‖ e–e ~ *a pair of spectacles*, etc.; goldene ~ *gold-rimmed glasses*; Horn≈ *horn-rims, horn-rimmed glasses* ‖ rosarote ~ ⟨fig⟩ *rose-tinted spectacles* ‖ (Schutz≈ f Autofahrer) *goggles* (*a pair of g.*) | die ~ absetzen *to take off one's glasses* ‖ die ~ aufsetzen *to put on one's g.*; ⟨fig⟩ jdm e–e ~ aufsetzen *to dupe, to hoax a p* ‖ ⟨fig⟩ (etw) durch e–e rosige ~ ansehen *to look at a th through rose-coloured spectacles, to take a rose-coloured view of a th* ‖ ⟨fig⟩ durch e–s anderen ~ sehen *to see with another p's eyes* ‖ e–e ~ tragen *to wear spectacles* **2.** (Sitz des Aborts) *lavatory seat*

br·illetragend a *bespectacled*

Br·illen- [in comp] *spectacle-* .. ‖ ⟨zoo⟩ *spectacled* **~bär** m ⟨zoo⟩ *spectacled bear* **~einfassung** f *spectacle-frame* **~futteral** n *spectacle-case* **~glas** n *spectacle-glass* **~kaspar** m ⟨fam⟩ *gig-lamps* [sg konstr] **~macher** m *spectacle-maker, optician* **~rand** m *spectacle-rim* **~schlange** f ⟨zoo⟩ *hooded snake, spectacled serpent*, (südasiatische) *spectacled cobra* (*de capello*); *naja* **~schleifer** m *spectacle grinder* ≈**tragend** a *spectacled* (*p*) **~träger** m *spectacled person, wearer of glasses*

brill·ieren [brilˈjiːrən] vi [h] (glänzen) ⟨fig⟩ (of wit) *to sparkle* ‖ (P) *to cut a dash*

Br·imbeere f (Kreuzung zw Him- u Brombeere) *loganberry*

Brimb·orium n ~s/–orien *brimborium*; *frills* pl; *embroidery*; ein gr ~ m um *to make a fuss about*

Br·indisi n ⟨It⟩ (Hafenstadt an der Adria)

Brin·ell- (nach dem Schweden *I. A. Brinell*; † *1925*) **~härte** f *Brinell hardness* **~probe** f *Brinell test*

br·ingen vt [h] [brachte/gebracht] **I.** Grundbedeutungen **A. 1.** (**her~**, zum Sprecher hin~) (etw) *to bring*; jdm etw ~ *to bring a p a th* od *a th to* (od ˣ*for*) *a p*; bring mir das Buch *bring me the book*; bring ihn her *bring him here* **2.** ⟨übtr⟩ **a.** Bescheid, Nachricht ~ *to bring word* ‖ was ~ Sie? ⟨fam⟩ *what's up*?; was ~ Sie Neues? *what is the news*? ‖ *to bring* (*peace to a country*) ‖ (jdm) Hilfe ~ *to bring* (*a p*) *help* ‖ Opfer ~ *to make sacrifices* ‖ (Schaden) *to cause* od *bring injury* (jdm *to a p*) ‖ jdm ein Ständchen ~ *to serenade a p. to play a serenade to a p* ‖ etw vor jdn ~ *to lay a th before a p*; → II. 10. **b.** (S) *to bring, offer* ‖ (veröffentlichen) *to publish* ‖ (of newspapers, etc,) (etw, nichts) *to mention, to say* (über *about*); *to contain* ‖ was bringt Sie hierher? *what brings you here*? ‖ im Gespräch bringt eins das andere *in talk one th leads to another* ‖ Tränen in die Augen ~ *to bring tears into the eyes* **B.** (**hin~**, vom Sprecher *or* Ort **fort~**) **1.** (etw) *to take* (in das Zimmer *into the room*); ⟨fam⟩ *to get* ‖ *take* (*this letter to the post-office*) ‖ ich brachte ihm Blumen *I took him some flowers* **2.** (tragen) *to carry, convey* **3.** (führen, geleiten) (jdn) *to conduct, lead, take*; er brachte ihn schnell hin *he hurried him there* ‖ jdn **auf** den Weg ~ *to go along with a p*; bring mich auf den W. *come along with me*; jdn auf den richtigen W. ~ *to put a p in the right way* | **in** die Garage ~ *to garage* | etw **mit sich** ~ *to cause, to occasion, to produce*, etc → *verursachen* (*time has worked* od *wrought many changes*) | jdn **nach** Hause, **zur** Tür ~ *to see a p home, to the door* ‖ jdn zu Bett ~ *to put a p to bed* ‖ jdn zur Bahn ~ *to see a p off* **C.** (**hervor~, verursachen**; **ein~**) *to bring, cause, produce* ‖ *to bear* (*fruit*) Gewinn ~ *to yield profit* (jdm *to a p*); Nutzen ~ *to be of use* (jdm *to a p*); → Zinsen ‖ jdm Glück (Unglück) ~ *to bring a p good* (*bad*) *luck* ‖ Ärger, Verdruß ~ *to cause* (od *give rise to*) *trouble*; → bereiten ‖ Unheil ~ über jdn *to bring trouble upon a p*; Ruin über sich ~ *to draw one's own ruin on o.s.*; → Verderben **II.** ⟨übtr⟩ in bes. Verbindungen **A.** [mit präpositionalem Ausdruck] **1. an** den Bettelstab ~ → Bettelstab; desgl → Glocke; Mann | ans Land ~ *to land* ‖ ans Licht, an den Tag ~ *to bring to light, to bring forth*; (Wahrheit) *to elicit* ‖ (Pferd) ans Ziel ~ *to land* **2.** (jdn) (in der Unterhaltung) **auf** etw (jdn) ~ *to bring a p to a th* (*a p*); die Rede auf etw ~ *to turn the conversation to a th*; jds Gedanken auf etw ~ *to lead a p's thoughts to, to make a p think of,* ⟨Am⟩ *to put a p up to* (*a th*) | → Bein II. 3. c. ‖ auf die Bühne ~ *to bring on* (od *to*) *the stage* ‖ jdn auf e–n Gedanken ~ *to suggest an idea to a p*; jdn auf den G. ~, daß *to convey the idea to a p that*; jdn auf andere G. ~ *to divert a p's thoughts* ‖ → Markt; Nenner ‖ etw auf die Seite ~ *to shuffle a th away*; jdn auf e–e S. ~ *to bring a p round*; *to get a p alongside one* ‖ → Tapet; Trab | **3.** jdn **aus** der Fassung, Ruhe ~ *to discompose*; *to disquiet a p* ‖ jdn aus dem Gleichgewicht ~ *to throw a p off his balance*; → Konzept; Text **4.** er brachte es (**bis**) **auf** 80 Jahre *he lived to be eighty years*; .. bis auf 60 Punkte *he achieved 60 points* | **etw ~ (bis) auf:** er brachte sein Einkommen (bis) auf monatlich 1000 Mark *he managed to make as much as .. a month* ‖ (Maschine) ~ bis auf *to bring* od *get* (⟨Am⟩ *whack up*) *to* ‖ **.. bis zum** Oberst *he rose to the rank of colonel* ‖ → 11. b. **5. ~ in a.** jdn in e–e schiefe Lage ~ *to land a p in an awkward position*; → Harnisch; Verdacht; Verlegenheit **b.** [~ in + Verbalabstraktum oft = entsprechendes trans. Verb]: etw in Ordnung ~ = etw ordnen; → Anwendung; Aufnahme; Berührung; Einklang; Erfahrung; Erinnerung; Gang; Mode; Ordnung; Rechnung; Schwierigkeit; System; Umlauf; Wallung **c. ins** Gleichgewicht ~ *to equilibrate* ‖ → Grab ‖ ins Reine ~ *to settle*; (Bücher) *to post up* **6. ~ über**: ich konnte es nicht über das Herz ~ *I could not find it in my heart* od *I could not bring myself* (*to do*); .. nicht über die Lippen, Zunge ~ *I could not bring myself to utter it* ‖ → I. C. **7. jdn um etw ~** *to deprive* (od *rob*) *a p of* (*his money*, etc.); *to defraud a p of* (*his savings*); *to let a p down by* (*£ 50*); *to do a p out of* (*his job*); *to lose a p a th* (od *a th to a p*); die Dummheit brachte ihn um s–e Stellung *the folly lost him his place*; gebracht w um *to be disappointed* od *balked of* (*one's desires, hopes*) ‖ → Leben **8. ~ unter** → Gewalt; Hammer; Hut ‖ **unter die Leute ~** (Geld) *to spend freely* (od *lavishly*); (Gerücht) *to circulate, to spread* **9. vom** Fleck, von der Stelle ~ *to* (*re*)*move*; [mst neg] *to budge* **10.** (jdn) **vor** Gericht (*or* den Richter) ~ *to bring a p into court* (od *to trial*), *to put a p on one's trial* ‖ etw vor jdn ~ *to lay a th before a p*; → I. A. 2. a. **11. ~ zu a.** jdn z etw ~ *to drive* (od *impel, incite*) *a p to a th*; jdn dazu (*or* dahin) ~ z tun *to bring* (od *get, induce, prompt, tempt*) *a p to do, to prevail on a p to do, to lead a p into doing*; → Pferd ‖ sich dazu (dahin) ~ .. *to bring o.s.* (*to do*) **b. es zu etw ~** im Leben *to make one's way* (od *to succeed*) *in life*; es z nichts ~ *to fail* (*in life*); er wird es nie zu etw ~ *he will never amount to anything*; es z nichts gebracht h *to be a complete failure* ‖ er brachte es zu .. *he managed to achieve* (*a high position*) → 4. | er kann **sich nicht dazu** *or* **soweit** ~, es z tun *he cannot bring himself to the point of doing it*; → C. **c.** → Ende ‖ z Fall ~ (jdn) *to* (*over*)*throw, ruin* (*a p*); (etw) *to bring* (*a th*) *to nought, to frustrate* ‖ z Papier ~ *to commit* (*a th*) *to paper* ‖ zustande ~, zuwege ~ *to bring* (*a th*) *to pass, to bring* (*a th*) *about*; *to manage, to contrive* (*to do*) **d. zum**: zum Halten ~ *to bring* (*a th*) *up, to bring* (*a th*) *to a halt* (od *standstill, stop*) ‖ zum Kochen ~ *to make* (*a th*) *boil, to cause* (*a th*) *to boil, to bring* (*a th*) *to the boil* ‖ (jdn) zum Lachen (etc) ~ *to make a p laugh, to set a p laughing* ‖ jdn zum Reden ~ *to make a p talk* ‖ jdn zum Schweigen ~ *to silence a p* | → Abschluß; Bewußtsein; Gehorsam; Opfer **e. zur**: etw zur Anzeige ~ *to bring a th to the notice of the authorities* ‖ → Aufführung; Besinnung; Entscheidung ‖ jdm etw zur Kenntnis ~ *to bring a th to a p's notice* ‖ zur Macht ~: *the class which floated the Nazis into Power* ‖ → Sprache ‖ jdn zur Vernunft ~ *to bring a p to reason, to his senses* ‖ jdn zur Verzweiflung ~ *to drive a p to despair* ‖ etw zur Vollendung ~ *to bring* od *carry a th to completion* ‖ zur Welt ~ *to bring into the world*; *to bring forth* **B. 1.** (etw) **an sich** [acc] ~ *to appropriate, to acquire* (*a th*), *to take possession of* (*a th*) **2. mit sich** ~ (S) (*or* (Belohnung) *to bring* (*a th*) *along with it* (od *them*), *to carry* (*a th*) *with it* (*them*), *to hold*; (Mühe) *to entail, involve* (*a th*); Gefahren, die diese Laufbahn mit sich bringt *dangers incidental to this career*; das Leben bringt es so mit sich *such is life* **3.** etw (Strecke) **hinter sich** ~ *to cover* ‖ *to get through* (*one's work*) ‖ das Schwerste (e–r Aufgabe etc) hinter sich ~ *to breack the back of* (*a th*) **4.** etw **über sich** ~ z tun = über das Herz ~ → II. A. b. **5.** (viel, wenig etc) **vor sich** ~ *to achieve, accomplish, perform*; *do* **6.** jdn **zu sich** ~ *to bring a p to* [adv], *to bring a p to himself* **C.** [mit Adj. u Adv.] (etw) fertig ~ → fertigbringen ‖ **es dahin, zustande, zuwege** ~ .. *to manage* (*contrive, accomplish*) *to do it* ‖ **es weit** ~ *to get on in the world*; er wird es weit ~ *he will go far*; es weit gebracht h in *to be* (*a*) *proficient in* (*a th*) ‖ es so weit ~, es dahin ~, daß .. *to bring things to such a pass that* **III.** °etw ~ = fertigbringen

Br·inger m ~s/~ (v bringen I. A.) *bringer* (*of hope*); *bearer* (*of a letter*); *carrier*; ~ e–r Botschaft *messenger*

Br·ingschuld f ⟨jur⟩ *debt bound to be brought and paid to the creditor* (Ggs Holschuld)

Br·ingung f ~/ (Holznahtransport) *logging, lumbering*

×**Br·ink** m = Anger

br·io [It] (Schneid) *brio* [It]

Bri·oche [bri'ɔʃ] f [Fr] ~/~s (Eiergebäck) *brioche* [Fr]

bris·ant a (zermalmend) *brisant* (*explosive*)

Bris·anz f (Sprengwirkung) *brisance*; ~bombe *brisant bomb*; ~geschoß [n] *brisant explosive*

Br·ise f ~/~n *breeze*; e–e leichte ~ *a cat's paw, a faint drift* (*of cold air*)

Br·isling m ⟨ich⟩ (Art Sardine) *brisling*

Brisol·ett n ~s/~e **Brisol·ette** f [Fr] ~/~n ⟨Ger⟩ *meat-ball*

Br·ißlauch m ⟨bot⟩ = Schnittlauch

Bristol n ⟨engl⟩ Hafenstadt **~kanal** m ⟨engl⟩ *Bristol Channel*; **~papier** (nach engl. Stadt) n *Bristol-board*

Brit·anniametall n ⟨chem⟩ *Britannia-metal*

Brit·annien (Groß≈) *Great*(*er*) *Britain* **br·itisch** a *British*; → d.

Br·ite m ~n/~n **1.** (keltischer Bewohner Britanniens) *Briton* **2.** (Angehöriger Großbritanniens *or* des Brit. Weltreichs) *Briton*; *Englishman*; ⟨Am⟩ *Britisher*; die ~n [pl] *the British* od *English, the Britons*

br·itisch a **1.** (keltisch) *British* **2.** (großbritannisch) *British*; *English* ‖ die ≈en Inseln [pl] *the British Isles*; das ≈e Museum *the British Museum*; das ≈e Weltreich *the British Empire*

Broadway ['brɔ:dwei] m (Hauptgeschäftsstraße v Neuyork etc) *Broadway*, am *or* auf dem ~ *on Broadway*

Brocat·ellmarmor m *variegated marble*, → Brokatello

Br·öckchen n ~s/~ *bit, small piece* ‖ (Brot≈ [pl] zur Suppe) *croûtons* [Fr], *sippets* pl

br·öckelig a *crumbling, crumbly*; ⟨cul⟩ *friable*; *crisp* **Br·öckelkohl** m ⟨cul⟩ *broccoli* **br·öckeln** vi [h] *to crumble* ‖ → ab–, zerbröckeln

Br·ocken m ~s/~ **1.** *small particle* od *piece*; *bit*; ein ~ Brot *a scrap of bread, a crumb* ‖ → abweisen; zuwerfen; in ~n zerfallen *to crumble* **2.** ⟨übtr⟩ *lump* (*of coal*); ~ Erde *clod* ‖ ⟨mil⟩ °dicke ~ [pl] *heavy bombs* od *shells* **3.** ⟨fig⟩ [mst pl] ~ *fragments* (*of a speech*), *scraps* [pl] (*of news*); ein paar englische ~ *or* ~ Englisch *a few scraps of English* ‖ allerlei ~ [pl] *odds and ends* [pl]; das war ein harter ~ *that was a hard* (od *tough*) *nut*

br·ocken vt [h] **1.** Brot ~ *to put small morsels of bread* (in *in*) **2.** (pflücken) *to pluck*

Br·ocken m ⟨Ger⟩ (höchster Harzgipfel); *Mount Brocken* **~anemone** f ⟨bot⟩ *pulsatilla* **~moos** a ⟨bot⟩ *Iceland moss* **~myrte** f ⟨bot⟩ *crowberry*

br·ockenweise adv *bit by bit, crumb by crumb, piecemeal*

†**Br·odel** m = Brodem **br·odeln** vi [h] (of water) *to bubble, hum*; *simmer*; *to boil with a bubbling sound* ‖ (of the stomach) *to rumble* ‖ ⟨sociol⟩ *to simmer, seethe, fume*; *to reflect volcanic undertones*; *to breathe fire and fury*; *to presage a violent eruption* od *explosion*; *to seethe with volcanic emotion*

Br·odem m ~s/ *steam, vapour, exhalation*

Broder·ie f = Stickerei

Brögger·it m ⟨minr⟩ (nach W. C. Brögger) *bröggerite*

Br·oihahn m = Broyhan

Brok·at m ~s/~e (Seidenstoff) **1.** *brocade*; mit ~muster schmücken *to brocade* **2.** [in comp] *brocade* (*gown*); *brocaded* (*silk*) **Brokat·ell** m ~s/~e (gemusterter Baumwollstoff) *brocatelle*

Brokat·ello m *brocatello*; *brocade marble*

Br·okkoli = Bröckelkohl

Brom n ~s/ ⟨chem⟩ *bromine* ‖ ⟨phot⟩ mit ~ behandeln *to bromize*

Br·om- [in comp] *bromic, bromine* **~druck** m ⟨phot⟩ *bromide print* **~k·alium** n *bromide of potassium*, ⟨fam⟩ *bromide* **~metall** n *bromide* **~öldruck** m ⟨phot⟩ *bromoil print* **~ölumdruck** m ⟨phot⟩ *bromoil transfer* **~säure** f *bromic acid* ‖ ≈saures Salz *bromate* **~silbergelatine** f ⟨phot⟩

bromide emulsion **~silberpapier** n ⟨phot⟩ *bromide paper* **~spat** m = Bromit **~vergiftung** f *bromism*

Bromargyr·it m ⟨minr⟩ = Bromit

Brom·at n ⟨chem⟩ *bromate* **Brom·atik** f *bromatology*

Br·ombeere f ~/~n ⟨bot⟩ *blackberry*; *brambleberry*; ⟨Scot⟩ *bramble* **Br·ombeerstrauch** m *bramble*, *blackberry-bush*

Br·omberg ⟨†Ger⟩ (Stadt in Westpreußen)

Brom·elie f ~/ ⟨bot⟩ *bromelia* [L]

brom·ieren vt [h] *to brominate*, *bromize* **Brom·it** m ~s/ ⟨minr⟩ *bromyrite*

Br·ommeis m ⟨orn⟩ = Gimpel

Br·onchen m [pl] ⟨anat⟩ *bronchi* [L]; *bronchial tubes* [pl] **bronchi·al** a *bronchial* **Bronchi·al-** ⟨med⟩ [in comp] **~erweiterung** f *bronchiectasis* **~katarrh** m *bronchial catarrh*, *bronchitis* **Br·onchien** f [pl] = Bronchen **Bronch·itis** f ⟨med⟩ *bronchitis* **Broncho-** [in comp] ⟨med⟩ *broncho-* **~pneumon·ie** f *bronchopneumonia* **~skopie** f *bronchoscopy* **Br·onchus** m [L] ~/–chen ⟨anat⟩ *bronchus* [L] → Bronchen

Bronn m ~s/~e, **Br·onnen** m ~s/~ ⟨poet⟩ = Brunnen, Quelle

Brontos·aurus m ~/–rier (fossile Riesenechse) *brontosaurus*

Br·onze [ˈbrɔŋsə] f ~/ **1.** (Mischmetall) *bronze*; Glocken≃ *bell-metal*; Stahl≃ *steel bronze* **2.** (Gegenstand aus ~) [pl ~n] *bronze* **3.** [in comp] *bronze* .. **~-Diab·etes** m ⟨med⟩ *a serious kind of diabetes* **~farbe** f *bronze*; *bronze paint* od *ink* ≃**farben** a *bronze*, *bronze-coloured* **~gießer** m *bronze-founder* **~krankheit** f *Addison's disease*, *Bronzed Skin* **~kunst** f *the craft of bronze-working*, *art of executing implements*, *statues* (etc.) *in bronze* **~lager** n ⟨tech⟩ *bronze bearing*; ein neues ~ anbringen *to remetal a bearing* **~pest** f ⟨arts⟩ *plague* **~waren** f [pl] *bronze-ware*

br·onzen a *bronze* **bronz·ieren** [brɔŋˈsiːrən] **1.** vt [h] (Metall etc) *to* (*coat with*) *bronze* **2.** ≃ n *bronzing* **Bronz·ierer** m *bronzer*

Br·osame (m) f ~(n)/~n *crumb* [mst pl] ~n *crumbs* ‖ ⟨übtr⟩ letzte ~n *remnants* [pl]

Br·osche f ~/~n *brooch*

Br·öschen [sç] n ~s/~ [südd] → Bries(chen)

brosch·ieren vt [h] (Buch) *to sew*, *to stitch*; (mit Draht) *to stab* ‖ ⟨weav⟩ → broschiert 2. **brosch·iert** a **1.** *sewed*, *stitched*, *in paper cover* ‖ steif broschiert *in boards* **2.** ⟨weav⟩ *broche* (*silk*), *embroidered*

Brosch·üre f ~/~n *book in paper cover* (od *in boards*) ‖ *booklet*, *pamphlet*; → Prospekt | ~ndruck [m] *brochure printing*; ~nschreiber [m] *pamphleteer*

Br·ösel m, [österr] n ~s/~ [südd] = Brosamen, geriebene Semmel

Brot n ~s/ **1. a.** *bread*; e–e Scheibe ~ *a slice of bread* ‖ (un)gesäuertes (*un*)*leavened*, altbackenes *stale*, frischgebackenes *new*, hausbackenes ~ *home-made bread*; lockeres (gut aufgegangenes) ~ *light bread*; das Weiche im ~ *the crumb*, *bread-crumb* (Ggs Kruste) | Gersten≃ *barley-bread*; Grau≃, Land≃ *brown bread*; Reib≃ *white breadcrumbs*; Roggen≃ *rye-bread*; ⟨a-engl⟩ Schwarz≃ *blackbread* ‖ Kasten≃ *sandwich loaf* ‖ ungesäuertes ~ *azyme*; Fest der ung. ~e *azymes* ‖ Weizen≃, Fein≃ *wheat-bread*; ⟨engl⟩ Weizenschrot≃, Graham≃ *brown bread* | belegtes ~ (offen) *canapé*, (zugeklappt) *sandwich*; Käse≃ *cheese s.*, Schinken≃ *ham s.* | ~ brechen *to break bread* ‖ → Wasser **b.** [pl ~e] ein (Laib) ~ *a loaf of bread* ‖ das ~ ist gestiegen *the loaf has risen* **2.** ⟨ec⟩ Abendmahls≃ *consecrated* od *sacramental bread*; ~ u Wein *bread and wine* **3.** ⟨übtr⟩ (Nahrung, Unterhalt) *bread*, *livelihood* ‖ (das tägliche ~, liebe ~ *the daily bread*; sein tägl. (karges) ~ verdienen *to earn one's* (*scanty*) *living*; jdn um ~ u Lohn, um sein ~ bringen *to take the bread out of a p's mouth* ‖ → Kunst ‖ sein ~ h *to enjoy a modest competence*; sein gutes ~ h *to be well-off* ‖ in ~ u Lohn bei jdm stehen *to be in the employ of a p* ‖ (sich) sein ~ verdienen *to earn one's bread* od *livelihood* ‖ sein ~ mit Nichtstun verdienen *to eat the bread of idleness*

Br·ot- [in comp] *bread* .. **~arbeit** f ⟨arts⟩ *pot-boiler* **~aufstrich** m *spread* **~backen** n *bread-baking* **~bäckerei** f *bakery* **~baum** m ⟨bot⟩ *bread-fruit tree*; Frucht des ~s *bread-fruit* **~beutel** m *bread-bag*; (*shepherd's*) *scrip*; ⟨mil⟩ *haversack*, *field bag*; ⟨hum⟩ *nose-bag* **~brei** m *pap*, *panada* **~erwerb** m *bread-winning*; *living* ‖ ~s- [in comp] *bread-winning* (*work*) **~getreide** n *bread-stuffs* [pl] **~herr** m *master*, *principal*, *patron*; *employer*; ⟨sl⟩ *boss* **~kammer** f *bread-room* **~karte** f (bei Rationierung) *bread-card* **~kasten** m *bread-bin*; ⟨fig⟩ °~ (auf Rädern) (Kleinauto) (*tin-*)*Lizzie* **~korb** m *bread-basket* ‖ ⟨fig⟩ jdm den ~ höher hängen *to make a p tighten his belt*, *to cut* od *keep a p short*, *to put a p on short allowance* od *on rations* **~krume** f *bread-crumb* **~kruste** f = Brotrinde **~laib** m *loaf*, ~e [pl] *loaves* ≃**los** a **1.** (P) *breadless*, *unemployed* ‖ jdn ~ m *to throw a p out of employment*; ~ w *to loose one's livelihood*; → arbeitslos **2.** [nur in]: ~lose Kunst *unprofitable* od *unremunerative occupation* **~mangel** m *scarcity of bread* **~maschine** f *bread–cutter* od *-slicer* **~meister** m ⟨hist⟩ *pantler* **~messer** n *bread-*, *table-knife* **~neid** m *professional envy*, *commercial* (od *trade*) *jealousy*; der reine ~ *pure jealousy* **~nußbaum** m ⟨bot⟩ *bread-nut tree* **~reste** m pl *broken bread* **~rinde** f *bread-crust* **~röster** m (*electric*) *toaster*; ⟨engl⟩ *toasting fork* **~säge** f *serrated knife* **~scheibe** f *slice of bread* **~schieber** m *peel* **~schneidemaschine** f *bread-cutter* **~schnitte** f *slice of bread*; (geröstete) *toast* **~schrank** m *bread-cupboard* **~schrift** f ⟨typ⟩ *body* (od *book*)*-type* **~studium** n *professional study*, *study for bread-winning purposes* **~suppe** f ⟨Ger⟩ *bread-soup* **~teig** m *dough*; in ~ ⟨cul⟩ *en croûte* **~verdiener** m *bread-winner* **~würfel** m kl gerösteter ~ (in Suppen) *croûton* [Fr] **~wurzel** f ⟨bot⟩ *yam*

Br·ötchen n ~s/~ *roll*, ⟨Scot⟩ *cookie*; [oft pl] ~ *rolls* [pl] ‖ belegtes ~ *sandwich* ‖ kl ~ backen ⟨fig⟩ *to eat humble pie* °**~geber** m ⟨sl⟩ *boss*

Br·owning [ˈbrauniŋ] f ⟨engl⟩ ~/~ Selbstladepistole, nach *Mr. John Browning*

Br·oyhan m ~s/ *pale sweetish-sourish beer*

Brr, brr! [intj] = Br

Bruch [brux] m ~s/≃e [ˈbryçə] **A.** (Brechen, Gebrochenes) **1.** *break*(*ing*); *breach*; *rupture*; *rift* ‖ ⟨bes com⟩ *breakage* (frei v ~ *free from breakage*); *fracture* ‖ Rad≃ *breakage of a wheel* (→ Damm≃; Schiff≃; Wolken≃) ‖ ⟨aero⟩ *smash-up* [s]; ~ m *to smash* [vi], *to pile up* [vi] **2.** ⟨surg⟩ *fracture* od *breaking* (*of the arm*); Knochen≃ *fracture of the bone*; → Bein≃; Krampfader≃ ‖ einfacher, komplizierter ~ *simple*, *compound f.* ‖ e–n ~ einrichten *to set a fracture* **3. a.** ⟨min⟩ (Zus–bruch) *break*(*ing*)*-down*; z ~e gehen *to break down* **b.** ⟨aero⟩ *crash*; e–n ~ m *to crash an aeroplane* **4.** ⟨fig⟩ *breach*, *break* (*with a tradition*); *rupture* (*of relations*; *between friends*, etc.; *with a p*); diplomatischer ~ *diplomatic rupture*; es kam zum ~ zwischen ihnen *their relations came to a rupture*; (e–e S) zum ~ treiben *to push* (*a th*) *to a break* od *rupture* ‖ *infringement*, *violation*, *infraction* (*of a treaty*); Friedens~ *breach of the peace*; → Ehe≃, Eid≃, Treu≃ **B. 1.** (Trennungsfläche) *breach*, *break* (*in a wall*); *breakage*; *breaking* (*in a pipe*); *crack*, *gap*; *snap* | ⟨minr⟩ *fracture*, *surface of fracture* ‖ ⟨geol⟩ *break*, *fault*

|| ⟨met⟩ *flaw* || (Knick in Papier etc) *fold, crease* **2.** ⟨path⟩ (Eingeweide≈) *hernia, rupture*; falscher ~ *prolapse*; → Leisten≈, *inkarzeriert* || e–n ~ bek, sich e–n ~ heben *or* zuziehen *to be ruptured* **C.** ⟨arith⟩ *fraction*; (un)echter ~ *(im)proper fraction*; gemeiner ~ *vulgar fraction*; Dezimal≈ *decimal fraction* || ⟨fig⟩ in die Brüche gehen *to fail, to come to nothing* (od *nought*; *grief*); *to be wrecked*; ⟨fam⟩ *to go to pot* **D.** [konkr] (Abge–, Zerbrochenes) **1.** ⟨com⟩ (~ware) *breakage*; *chips* [pl] | ⟨fig⟩ es ist viel ~ unter ihnen *there are many failures* (⟨sl⟩ *duds*) *among them* **2.** Wind≈ *windfall* **3.** Stein≈ *quarry* **4.** ⟨hunt⟩ (Laubzweig) *brush*

Bruch [bru:x] m & n ~s/≈er [ˈbryçər] *marshy meadow*; *fen*; *bog, moor, marsh*

Br·uch [brux] [in comp] ⟨tech⟩ oft *broken* (*coal*, etc.), *refuse* .. **~anlage** f ⟨med⟩ *disposition to hernia* **~band** n ⟨med⟩ *truss* **~beanspruchung** f *breaking strain* **~beere** f ⟨bot⟩ = Heidelbeere **~belastung** f *breaking load* **~bergungs- u Feuerwache** f ⟨aero⟩ *crash and fire station* **~bude** f *jerry-built house*; *wretched hovel* **~dehnung** f *breaking elongation, fracture strain* **~eisen** n *scrap-iron* **≈fest** a *proof against fracture* **~festigkeit** f *breaking strength*; (gegen äußeren [inneren] Druck) *crushing* [*bursting*] *strength* **~festigkeitsprüfer** m *breaking tester* **~fläche** f *fracture, surface of fracture* **≈frei** a *free from breakage* **~front** f ⟨geol⟩ *fault scrap* **~glas** n *cullet, broken glass* **~kraft** f *breaking-strain* **~kraut** n ⟨bot⟩ *rupturewort* **~kupfer** n ⟨tech⟩ *shruff copper* **≈landen** vi [s] ⟨aero⟩ *to crash-land* **~landung** f ⟨aero⟩ *crash* (*-landing*), ⟨fam⟩ *prang*; ⟨sl⟩ *touch-bottom*; ~ m *to crash the aeroplane* **~last** f *ultimate strength* od *load* **~lastvielfaches** n *breaking factor* **~linie** f ⟨geol⟩ *line of faulting, fault line* **~rechnung** f ⟨arith⟩ *fractions* [pl], *fractional arithmetic* **~reis** m *broken rice* **~schaden** m *breakage* **~schiene** f ⟨surg⟩ *splint* **~schlange** f ⟨zoo⟩ = Blindschleiche f **~schrift** f ⟨typ⟩ = Fraktur **≈sicher** a *unbreakable*; (Glas) *shatter proof* **~sicherheit** f *safety against fracture* **~sicherung** f *security against breakage* **~silber** n *scrap silver* **~spannung** f *tensile strength*; *breaking strain* od *stress* **~stein** m *quarry stone, ashlar*; (Abfall) *rubble-stone* | ~mauer [f] *rubble-wall* **~stelle** f (*point of*) *fracture* **~strich** m ⟨math⟩ (*horizontal*) *line*; unter, über dem ~ *below, above the line* **~stück** n *fragment* || ⟨übtr⟩ [mst pl] ~e *fragments, scraps* (*of a conversation*), *snatches* [pl] (*of a song*); ein Manuskript in ~en *a fragmentary manuscript* | ≈artig [a] *fragmentary*; ⟨geol⟩ *fragmental*; ≈artige Beschaffenheit [f] *fragmentariness*; ≈weise [adv] *fragmentarily, in fragments*; (*to tell a story*) *in bits and pieces* **~teil** m ⟨math⟩ *fraction* (*only a small f.*); ~ e–r Pferdestärke *fractional horsepower*; in e–m (innerhalb e–s) ~(s) v .. *within a sliver of* .. **~weide** f ⟨bot⟩ *crack-willow* **~zahl** f ⟨math⟩ *fraction*(*al number*)

br·üchig a **1.** *full of breaks*; *brittle, fragile* || (of metal, etc.) *flawy, short*; (etw) ~ m *to flaw*; ~ w *to flaw* | ⟨übtr⟩ *brittle, fragile* || ⟨fig⟩ *fragmentary, gappy, incomplete* **2.** (geborsten) *broken*; *cracked*; *damaged* **3.** [in comp] → treu~

Br·ücke f ~/~n **1. a.** *bridge* (über den Rhein *over the Rhine*) || → Ausleger≈, Balken≈, Bogen≈, Dreh≈, Hänge≈, Ketten≈, Zug≈; Eisenbahn≈, Schiffs≈ || schwimmende ~ *floating bridge*; fliegende ~ *flying bridge* || Seufzer≈ (in Venedig) *Bridge of Sighs* || ⟨theat⟩ (Arbeits≈) *fly-bridge*; (Beleuchtungs≈) *lighting* (⟨Am⟩ *light*) *bridge* || ⟨mar⟩ (Kommando≈) *bridge* **b.** ⟨fig⟩ *bridge, link* (zwischen *between*); *bridge* (für, z *for*); *road* (z *to*) **c.** (Damenhut) *half-hat* **d.** (schmaler Teppich) *runner* **e.** e–e ~ **schlagen** über *to build* (od *construct, make, throw*) *a bridge over, to bridge* (*a river*); ⟨a. fig⟩ || e–e ~ führt über .. *a bridge leads over* .. | ⟨fig⟩ alle ~n hinter sich **abbrechen** *to burn one's boats* || jdm e–e goldene ~ bauen *to build a golden bridge for a p* || e–e ~ bilden v .. z *to form a bridge from* .. *to* || wenn das Wort e–e ~ wäre .. *if I could rely on your word* .. **2.** ⟨mar⟩ (Kommando≈) *bridge* (*of a steamer*) **3. a.** ⟨dent⟩ *bridge* **b.** ⟨el⟩ Wheatstonesche ~ (Gerät) *Wheatstone bridge*, → Widerstand **c.** (kl Teppich) *rug* → 1. d. **d.** ⟨gym⟩ *back bend*

Br·ücken- [in comp] *bridge–* .. **~bau** m *bridge-building* **~bauer** m *bridge-builder* **~bock** m *br. trestle* **~bogen** m *bridge-arch, arch* od *span of a bridge* **~boot** n *pontoon* **~echse** f ⟨zoo⟩ *tuatara* **~geländer** n *parapet*; *railing of a bridge* **~geld** n *bridge-toll, pontage*; ~einnehmer [m] *toll-gatherer* **~joch** n *space between two pillars of a bridge* **~kleid** n (der Kommandobrücke) *canvas screen* **~kolonne** f *br. train* **~kopf** m ⟨mil⟩ *bridge-head, barbican* **~lehne** f = Brückengeländer **≈los** a *bridgeless* **~pfeiler** m *bridgepier* **~rampe** f *bridge approach* **~schanze** f = Brückenkopf **~waage** f *weighing machine* || (für Wagenlast) *platform balance* od *scales* pl; *weigh-bridge* **~zoll** m = Brückengeld

Br·ückner m *keeper* od *warden of a bridge*; *bridgemaster*

Brüde f ~/~n, **Brüden** m ~s/~ [water] *vapo*(*u*)*r* (*and gypsum dust*) | ~nkondensator [m] *vapo*(*u*)*r condensor*

Br·uder m ~s/≈ **1.** *brother*; ≈ [pl] *brothers* [pl] || ~ väterlicherseits *brother on the father's side*; leiblicher ~, Voll≈ *brother-german*; Stief≈ *step-brother*; Halb≈ *half-brother* || die ≈ Grimm *the brothers Grimm*; → Gebrüder || gleiche ≈ gleiche Kappen *share and share alike, birds of a feather flock together* || der Ring ist 50 Mark unter ≈n wert *the ring is a bargain at 50 marks*; .. *is worth every penny of 50 m.* **2.** ⟨übtr⟩ (Freund; Mitbürger; Landsmann; Volksgenosse) *brother*; s–e ≈ *his brothers*; s–e schottischen ≈ *his brother Scots* [pl] **3.** (Mitglied e–r Gesellschaft) *brother*, [pl] *brethren*; christlicher Bruder *Christian brother*; m–e Brüder *my dear brethren* | geistlicher ~, Ordens≈ *brother*; *monk, friar* || barmherziger ~ *hospitaller*, die barmherzigen Brüder *the knights Hospitallers* [pl], die mährischen B. *the Moravians* [pl] **4.** Amts≈ ⟨ec⟩ *brother clergyman*; m–e Amtsbrüder *my brother clergymen* || Waffen≈ *brother-in-arms* **5.** (als Titel) ein ~ Studio *a student*; ~ Liederlich *debauchee* || ~ Jonathan (Spitzname f das amer. Volk) *Brother Jonathan* || ~ Straubinger *itinerant journeyman* **6.** (Bursch, Kerl) **a.** *fellow*; *bird, dog*; ⟨sl⟩ *bloke*; ⟨Am sl⟩ *guy*; ein lustiger ~ *a jolly dog*; ein böser ~ *a bad lot* od *egg*, das sind böse ≈ *that's a bad lot* || °ein warmer ~ *a homosexual*, ⟨fam⟩ *backgammoner, pansy*(*-boy*), *Oscar* **b.** [in comp] Fecht≈ *beggar* || Kneip≈, Sauf≈ *boon companion* || Radau≈ *rowdy*

Br·uder- **~herz** n *brother's heart* || (als Anrede) *dear brother* **~krieg** m *fraticidal strife* **~kuß** m *fraternal kiss* **~liebe** f *brother's love, brotherly love* **~mord** m *fraticide* **~mörder** m *fraticide* **≈mörderisch** a *fraticidal, internecine, civil* (*war*) **~volk** n *nationals* [pl] *of the same blood* od *race, cousins* [pl] (*across the sea*) **~zwist** m *fraternal quarrel*

Br·üderchen n ~s/~ *little brother*

Br·üdergemeine f (*fraternity of*) *the Moravians* [pl], *United Brethren* [pl] **Br·üderlein** n ~s/~ = Brüderchen

br·üderlich **1.** a *brotherly, fraternal* **2.** adv *brotherly, in a brotherly manner* || ~ teilen *to go halves* || ~ u treu zus–stehen *to stand by each* other steadfastly | ~̈**keit** f ~/ brotherliness, fraternity **Br·uderschaft** f fraternal tie, brotherly companionship **Br·üderschaft** f ~/~en **1.** brotherhood, fraternity confraternity, fellowship | ⟨rel⟩ chapter **2.** ⟨Ger⟩ mit jdm ~ m or trinken to chum up (od fraternize) with a p; l Sie uns ~ trinken let us address each other as ‚du'

Br·uders- **~kind** n brother's child; sein ~ the child of his brother, a child of his brother's **~sohn** nephew; ein ~ ihres Mannes a nephew of her husband's **~tochter** f niece

Br·ügge n (Stadt in Belgien) Bruges

Br·üh- (→ Brühe) **~faß** n scalding-tub **~futter** n scalded fodder ~̈**heiß** a boiling (od scalding)--hot, scalding **~kartoffeln** f [pl] potatoes [pl] boiled in broth **~näpfchen** n sauce-boat ~̈**warm** **1.** a **a.** = brühheiß **b.** ⟨fig⟩ quite new od fresh; hot, just received (news) **2.** adv ⟨fig⟩ (to report a th) immediately, straight away **~würfel** m ⟨cul⟩ meat extract cube **~würstchen** n hot sausage

Br·üh(e) f ~/~en **1.** (Fleisch~̈) broth; Kraft~̈ beef-tea | (Bratensoße) gravy; sauce **2.** °~ slop, wash **3.** ⟨fig⟩ da kostet die ~ mehr als die Brocken it is not worth the rattle, it will eat its od his head off; mehr ~ als Brocken more sauce than pig ‖ e–e lange ~ a tirade, a long palaver, e–e l. ~ um etw m to palaver about a th ‖ in der ~ sitzen to be in a nice fix

br·ühen vt [h] (etw) to scald, to treat with (od soak in) boiling water ‖ (Wäsche) to wash in hot lye **br·ühend** **1.** a scalding (water) **2.** adv ~ heiß scalding hot; scalding

†**Br·ukterer** pl (altdeutsch. Volksstamm) Bructeri [L] pl

Br·üllaffe m ⟨zoo⟩ howler; howling monkey

br·üllen **I.** vi/t [h] **A.** vi **1.** (of oxen) to bellow (of cows) to low ‖ (of lions, etc.) to roar; (of bullfrog) to trump; → rören **2.** ⟨übtr poet⟩ (of the sea, etc.) to bellow; (of cannon) to roar **3.** (P) to bawl, bellow; ⟨Am⟩ to yip; über das ganze Haus ~ to bawl about the house ‖ (heulen) to howl, roar (with pain); to cry ‖ (lachen, ~ vor Lachen) to guffaw, yell; to roar with laughter; to laugh uproariously **B.** vt (ein Kommando etc) to roar **II.** ~̈ n **1.** bellow(ing); low(ing) ‖ roar(ing) **2.** (of persons) bawl(ing), roar(ing) ‖ howl(ing) ‖ (T) durch ~ verjagen to boo ‖ es ist zum ~! it's too funny (for words)! ⟨Am fam⟩ it keeps me in stitches

br·üllend **1.** a roaring; ~es Gelächter roar of laughter | °~ heißer Tag scorcher **2.** [adv] ~ lachen to guffaw, yell

Br·üllfrosch m ⟨zoo⟩ bullfrog

Br·umm- ×**~bär**, °**~bart** m ⟨fig⟩ grumbler, growler, snarler; der alte ~ the old martinet **~baß** m ⟨mus⟩ **1.** (Orgelstimme) bourdon **2.** (Blasinstrument) bombardon ‖ = Baßgeige **3.** ⟨übtr⟩ deep voice; bass **~eisen** n ⟨mus⟩ Jew's-harp **~fliege** f ⟨ent⟩ = Brummer 1. **~hahn** m ⟨orn⟩ = Birkhahn **~käfer** m ⟨ent⟩ dung-beetle **~kreisel** m humming-top °**~ochse** m blockhead **~pfeife** f ⟨mus⟩ drone, bass-pipe (of a bagpipe) °**~schädel** m ⟨fig⟩ (vom Trinken) headache; e–n ~ h ⟨fam⟩ to have a head

°**Br·umme** f ~/~n ⟨teens sex⟩ (⟨a.⟩ Wucht~̈) A-bomb

br·ummen **I.** vi/t [h] **A.** vi **1.** (of flies, etc.) to buzz, hum, drone ‖ (of machines) to buzz; boom; purr; (of aeroplanes) to zoom ‖ mir brummt der Schädel my head whirls; I have a head **2.** (P) to mutter; murmur **3.** **ärgerlich ~ a.** (T) to growl ‖ (P) to growl, grumble (über at, about, over), to grunt, snarl; er grüßte ~d he grunted a greeting; (etw) ~d äußern to grumble, grunt; → Bart 1. **4.** °~ **a.** to serve time (to be in prison); ⟨vulg⟩ to lag **b.** ⟨school⟩ to be kept in, to be detained **B.** vt (etw) to mutter; hum; e–e Melodie vor sich hin~ to hum a tune to o.s., etw vor sich hin~ to growl something to o.s. **II.** ~̈ n **1.** buzz ‖ boom **2.** (vor Ärger) grumble, growl, grunt (über at, about) **3.** ⟨mot⟩ humming

Br·ummer m ~s/~ **1.** ⟨ent⟩ (Fliege) blow-fly, bluebottle **2.** °⟨übtr⟩ heavy gun; shell **3.** (P) = Brummbär

br·ummig a ⟨fig⟩ grumbling, growling, growly; cross, gruff

Br·ummse f, **Br·ummser** m = Brummer 1.

Brun·elle f ~/~n ⟨bot⟩ **1.** = Braunelle **2.** = Günsel **Brün·elle** f = Prünelle

brün·ett a brunette od brown-haired, brown--complexioned (woman) | ~̈**e** f ~/~n brunette

Brunft f ~/~~̈e ⟨hunt⟩ (of deer only; → Brunst) rut ‖ in der ~ s to be rutting, to be in a state of rut **~hirsch** m rutting-stag **~schrei** m bell (of a stag) **~zeit** f rutting-time

br·unften vi [h] ⟨hunt⟩ (of stags) to rut

br·unftig a rutting (deer)

brün·ieren vt [h] (Metall) to brown; burnish

Brünn n (Hauptstadt Mährens)

Br·ünne f ~/~n ⟨hist & poet⟩ (coat of) mail

Br·unnen m ~s/~ **1.** (Quelle) spring **2.** gegrabener ~, ~anlage well; → artesisch, Spring~̈, Zieh~̈, Pumpe **3.** (~wasser) spring-water; Heil~̈, Mineral~̈ mineral spring, (mineral) waters [pl]; ~ trinken, brauchen to drink od take the waters ‖ → Weih~̈ **4.** ⟨fig⟩ well (the w. of life); Jung~̈ the well of juvenescence

Br·unnen- [in comp] well .. **~anlage** f well **~arzt** m physician at a spa **~bau** m well-sinking **~bauer** m well-sinker (od borer) **~bohrer** m (P & S) well-borer **~eimer** m well-bucket **~einfassung** f; obere ~ well-head (of a draw-well); well-curb **~faden** m ⟨biol⟩ filamentous iron-bacterium **~gehäuse** n pump-barrel **~gräber** m well-digger **~halle** f well-room **~haus** n (of a spa) well-room; pump-room; (Kloster–, Waschraum) lavatory **~kresse** f ⟨bot⟩ nasturtium [L], water– (od fen, well)-cress **~kur** f course of treatment at a spa, cure at a spa; e–e ~ m to take a course, to drink the waters **~meister** m inspector of the wells ‖ fountain maker **~mündung** f well-head **~pest** f = Brunnenfaden **~röhre** f well-tube; pipe of a pump; conduit-pipe **~salz** n spring-salt **~schwengel** m well-beam **~stange** f pole of a draw-well **~vergifter** m ⟨fig⟩ poison-pen **~vergiftung** f well--poisoning ‖ ⟨fig⟩ politische ~ poisonous political propaganda **~wasser** n pump-water, spring--water

Br·unnquell m ⟨bib & fig⟩ = Quell

Br·unst f ~/~̈e **1.** ⟨† & poet⟩ = Feuers~̈ | ⟨übtr⟩ = Inbrunst **2.** (T) (→ Brunft) oestrum L; heat, rut, in der ~ s to be in a state of rut ‖ ⟨übtr⟩ appetence, sexual excitement; lust **~zeit** f rutting-season (od time) **br·unsten** vi [h] to be in heat; to rut, to be rutting; (of swine) to brim

br·ünstig a **1.** † = inbrünstig **2.** (geschlechtlich) rutting (elephant); ~ s to be rutting; ~ w to come into rut ‖ ⟨übtr⟩ lascivious, lewd, lustful

brüsk **1.** a brusque; blunt, rough **2.** adv brusquely; bluntly **brüsk·ieren** vt [h] (jdn) to treat (a p) brusquely; to defy; ⟨bes Am fam⟩ to stand a p on his ears **Brüsk·ierung** f defiance, rebuff (durch by)

Br·ussa n (Stadt in der asiat. Türkei, das ehem. Prusa) Brusa, Broussa

Br·üssel n (Hauptstadt v Belgien) Brussels **1.** m, **~er(in)** [inhabitant (od native)] of Brussels **2.** a Brussels ‖ ~ Kohl [m] ⟨bot⟩ = Rosenkohl ‖ ~ Spitze(n [pl]) f Brussels lace

Brust f ~/~̈e **A.** (P) **1.** ~ [pl] Brüste breast ‖ die weibliche ~, die Brüste the breasts [pl]; ⟨med⟩ mammae (L); bust ‖ ein Kind an der ~ a child at od on the breast; e–r weibl. ~ ähnlich mastoid → 4. ‖ ⟨fig⟩ die Brüste der Weisheit the breasts of wisdom **2. a.** (~korb) chest, thorax L **b.** (Lunge) e–e schwache ~ a weak chest;

schwach auf der ~ s *to have a weak chest, to be chesty*; ⟨fig⟩ *to be rather hard up* **c.** (Herz, Inneres) *breast, bosom*; *heart, soul* | ⟨cul⟩ *brisket* **3.** (Teil der Kleidung) *breast* (*of a coat*), *bosom*; *front* (*of a shirt*); Schnür≈ *bodice* **4.** ~ **an** ~ *abreast, side by side, neck and neck*; ~ an ~ kämpfen *to fight neck and neck* (*with*) | jdn an die ~ **drücken** *to press a p to one's breast* || ein Kind der ~ **entwöhnen** *to wean a child* || e–m Kind die ~ **geben** *to give a child the breast, to nurse* od *suckle a child* || es auf der ~ h 1. *to have a cold on the chest* 2. *to have a weak chest* || zur ~ **nehmen** 1. (Kind) *to suckle*, etc. 2. °⟨fig⟩ (Getränk) *to swill, sink*; e–n z ~ n. *to wet one's whistle* || sich an die ~ **schlagen** *to feel pangs of contrition* || aus voller ~ singen *to sing with a full voice* || an jds ~ sinken *to sink on a p's breast* || sich in die ~ **werfen** *to square one's shoulders*; *to bridle* (*up*), *to preen o.s.*; *to strike an attitude* **B.** (T) ⟨a. cul⟩ *brisket* || *chest* (*of a horse*) || → ~stück **C.** ⟨übtr⟩ (S) **1.** ⟨mus⟩ *face, front* (*of an organ*) **2.** *curved projection*

Br·ust- [in comp] *breast–*; *chest–*; *pectoral* ..; *thoracic* **~arznei** f *pectoral*; *pectoral medicine* **~band** n *breast-band*; *stay-lace* **~baum** m ⟨weav⟩ *breast-beam* **~beere** f ⟨bot⟩ *jujube*; schwarze ~ *sebesten*; *–tan* **~bein** n ⟨anat⟩ *breast-bone, sternum* (L) || *merrythought, wish*(*ing*)*-bone* (of *fowl*) **~beklemmung** f *asthma* **~beschwerden** f [pl] *chest-trouble* **~bild** n *halflength portrait*; ⟨phot⟩ *head-and-shoulder portrait*; ⟨sculp⟩ *bust* **~blatt** n *breast-plate* (*of an armour*) || *breast-collar* (*of a harness*) **~bonbon** n *pectoral lozenge, cough-drop* (od *lozenge*); *jujube* **~drüse** f ⟨anat⟩ *mamma*; *mammary gland*; ~nentzündung [f] *mastitis* || innere ~ *thymus* (L) **~einsatz** m (am Damenkleid) *plastron*; (im Herrenhemd) *front* **~entzündung** f ⟨med⟩ = Lungen–, Brustfellentzündung **~fallschirm** m ⟨aero⟩ *chest-pack parachute* **~fell** n ⟨anat⟩ *pleura* || [in comp] *pleural* (*sac*) || ~entzündung [f] *pleurisy* || Luft-ansammlung in der ~höhle *pneumothorax* **~fernsprecher** m *head-and-chest set* **~flossen** f [pl] ⟨ich⟩ *pectorals, pectoral fins* [pl] **~gang** m ⟨anat⟩ *thoracic duct* **~grube** f ⟨vet⟩ *counter* (*of a horse*) **~gurt** m *breast plate* (*of a harness*) || (Schwimm≈) *breast-belt* **~harnisch** m *breast-plate*; *cors*(*e*)*let* || ⟨mil⟩ *cuirass* ≈**hoch** a *breast-high* **~höhle** f *chest-cavity, thoracic cavity* **~kasten** m *chest* **~kind** n *breast-fed infant, child at the br.* **~korb** m ⟨anat⟩ *thorax* (L); *chest* **~krampf** m **1.** *asthma* **2.** = Herzkrampf **~krebs** m ⟨med⟩ *cancer of mamma* **~kreuz** n ⟨ec⟩ *pectoral*; *pectoral cross* **~leder** n *leather-apron* **~leier** f ⟨carp⟩ *brace and bit* **~mark** n ⟨anat⟩ *the dorsal portion of the spinal cord* **~messer** m ⟨med⟩ *thoracometer, stethometer* **~mikrophon** n ⟨wir⟩ *chest-type m., breast transmitter* **~mittel** n *pectoral remedy* **~muskel** m ⟨anat⟩ *pectoral muscle* **~nadel** f *breast-pin*, ⟨Am⟩ *stick-pin* **~packung** f ⟨med⟩ *cold-water compress for the chest* **~panzer** m *breast-armour cuirass* **~pulver** n ⟨Ger⟩ *a mild aperient* **~schild** n *breast-plate*; *plastron* **~schmerzen** m [pl] *pains* [pl] *in the chest* **~schwimmen** n *breast-stroke* (od *swimming*) **~seuche** f ⟨vet⟩ (in horses) *pleurisy* **~stich** m ⟨surg⟩ *thoracotomy* **~stiche** m [pl] *sharp stings* [pl] *in the chest* **~stimme** f *chestvoice* **~stück** n ⟨zoo⟩ *thorax* (*of an insect*) || ⟨cul⟩ *brisket*, (v Hammel) *breast* **~tasche** f *breast-pocket* **~tee** m *pectoral tea* **~ton** m *natural note of virile quality*; ⟨fig⟩ mit dem ~ der Überzeugung sprechen *to speak with a ring of deep conviction in one's tone* **~tuch** n *tucker* **~umfang** m *the capacity of the chest* **~warze** f ⟨anat⟩ *nipple, teat*; ⟨scient⟩ *mamilla* (L) **~wassersucht** f ⟨med⟩ *hydrothorax*; *dropsy of the chest* **~wehr** f ⟨fort⟩ *breastwork* **~werk** n ⟨mus⟩ *breastwork* (*of an organ*) **~wurz** f ⟨bot⟩ *angelica*

Br·üstchen n = Mieder

br·üsten vrefl [h] sich ~ *to bridle* (*up*), *to give o.s. airs, to strut*; ⟨fam⟩ *to put on dog* (od *side*); ⟨sl⟩ *to side* || sich ~ mit etw *to boast of, to preen o.s. over, to pride* (od *plume*) *o.s. on a th, to vaunt a th*; sich mit s–r Bildung ~ *to vaunt one's education*; .. mit s–n Kräften *to air one's powers* || sich (damit) ~ .. z h *to boast of having*

-brüstig a [in comp] *–breasted, –bosomed, –chested* || eng~ *narrow-breasted*

Br·üstung f ~/~en ⟨fort⟩ *breastwork, parapet* || ⟨übtr⟩ *balustrade*; *shoulder* || ⟨mar⟩ Deck≈ *railing*

Br·ut f ~/~en **1.** †(Brüten) *brooding, hatch*(*ing*); in der ~ s (of hens) *to be sitting* **2.** [konkr] (Ausgebrütetes) **a.** *brood, hatch*; (Enten etc) *team* || e–e ~ junger Hühner *a clutch* || flügge ~ *flight*; *flock of fledgelings*; e–e ~ Rebhühner *a covey of partridges*; → Aufflug || (of fish) *fry, spawn* **b.** ⟨übtr bot⟩ *offset, offshoot* **c.** ⟨fig⟩ (P) ⟨cont⟩ *brood, spawn*; *set*; ⟨sl⟩ *caboodle, lot* || (Kinder) *brats* [pl], ⟨hum⟩ *fry* **~anstalt** f (Fisch≈) *hatchery* **~apparat** m (f Eier) *hatcher, incubator, brooder*; *foster-mother, chicken-raising apparatus*; Benutzung v ~en *fosterage* || (Fisch≈) *hatching-apparatus* **~blatt** n ⟨bot⟩ *bryophyllum* (L) **~ei** n *hatching-egg* **~henne** f ⟨orn⟩ *brood-hen, sitting-hen* **~hitze** f ⟨fig⟩ *burning* (od *excessive*) *heat* **~instinkt** m *incubatory instinct* **~kasten** m *nesting home* **~knospe** f *offset* **~maschine** f = Brutapparat **~ofen** m *hatching-oven, incubator* **~pflege** f *parental care in breeding time* **~reaktor** m *breeder reactor* **~schrank** m = Brutapparat **~stätte** f *breeding* (od *hatching*) *–place*; (Hühner≈) *hennery* || ⟨fig⟩ *breeding-ground, hotbed, hothouse* **~tasche** f ⟨anat⟩ *brood-space*; *marsupium* (L) **~trog** m (Fisch≈) *breeding-box* **~zeit** f *brooding-time* **~zwiebel** f ⟨bot⟩ *offset-bulb, bulbil*

brut·al **1.** a *brutal*; *inhuman, cruel*; ~es Wesen *brutality*; ~er Mensch *brute* **2.** adv *brutally*; ~ behandeln *to brutalize*

Brutalit·ät f ~/~en *brutality*

br·üten **I.** vi/t [h] **A.** vi **1.** (of birds) *to breed, brood, incubate, sit*; auf den Eiern ~ *to sit on eggs, to hatch* od *incubate eggs* **2.** ⟨fig⟩ **a.** (P) (grübeln) *to brood, pore*; ~d sitzen *to sit brooding* || ~ über etw *to brood over* od *pore on, to hatch* od *incubate a th, to chew on a th* || über Büchern ~ *to pore over books* **b.** (of clouds, etc) *to brood, hover* (über *over*) || ⟨poet⟩ (lasten) ~ auf *to weigh on* **c.** ⟨poet⟩ (of the sun) *to shine hot* **B.** vt **1.** *(Kücken) = ausbrüten **2.** ⟨fig⟩ (ersinnen) *to brew*; *to hatch* (*out*); *to contrive, plan* **II.** ≈ n **1.** *brooding, breeding, hatch*(*ing*); *incubation* **2.** ⟨fig⟩ *brooding, poring* (über *over*)

Br·üter m (Henne etc) *brooder, hatcher* (*a good h.*) **br·ütig** a *broody* (*hen*); ~ w *to become broody*

Brutsch f ~/~en *mone*

br·utto adv (Ggs netto) *gross*

Br·utto- [in comp] *gross* .. **~betrag** m *gross amount* **~einnahme** f, **~ertrag** m *gross receipts* [pl]; *gross profit* **~gewicht** n *gross weight* **~gewinn** m *gross profit* **~preis** m *gross* (od *long*) *price* **~raumgehalt** m (of a ship) *gross registered tonnage* (abbr *G.R.T.*) **~registertonne** f *gross register ton, gr. registered tonnage* **~-Sozi·alprodukt** n *gross national product*

br·utzeln vi [h] *to sizzle, frizz*

Bruy·ereholz [bry'jæ:r–] n *brier* (od *briar*) *–root*; *brier* || Tabakspfeife aus ~ *briar, brier*

Bruzell·ose f ~/ ⟨vet⟩ *brucellosis*

Bruz·in n ⟨chem⟩ *brucine* **Bruz·it** m ⟨minr⟩ *brucite*

Bryolog·ie f ⟨bot⟩ (Mooskunde) *bryology*

Bryoph·yten [pl] ⟨bot⟩ (Moose) *bryophyta*
Bryoz·oen [pl] (Moostierchen) *bryozoa* [pl]
bst! *hist! hush!*
B-Stelle f ⟨mil⟩ = Beobachtungsstelle
Bub m ∼en/∼en = Bube 1. a. **B·übchen** n ∼s/∼ *little boy*; ⟨Am⟩ *bub(by)*
B·ube m ∼n/∼n **1. a.** *boy*; *lad, youth*; Schul∼̈ *school boy* **b.** ⟨cards⟩ *knave*, ⟨Am⟩ *jack*; (in euchre) *bower* **2.** (Schurke) *scoundrel, rascally fellow*; ein feiger ∼ *a mean coward* ‖ → Laus∼̈, Lotter∼̈, Rotz∼̈; Spitz∼̈
B·uben- **∼̈haft** a **1.** *boyish* **2.** *knavish, rascally* **∼kragen** m *Peter Pan collar* **∼streich** m, **∼stück** n ∼(e)s/∼e (Schurkerei) *knavery, roguery, knavish* od *rascally trick*
Buber·ei f ∼/∼en *foul play*; = Bubenstreich
B·ubikopf m (of a girl) *bobbed hair* **B·übin** f (Schurkin) *rascally woman* **b·übisch** a (schändlich) *foul, rascally* (*trick*); ∼es Verhalten *foul play*
B·ubo m ∼s/Bub·onen ⟨med⟩ *bubo* (L)
Buch n ∼(e)s/∼̈er **1. a.** *book* ‖ ein Stapel Bücher *a pile of books*; e–e Flut v Büchern *a stream of books*; nie ein ∼ ansehen *never to look into a book*; → aufschlagen, blättern; illustrieren ‖ das ∼ ist vergriffen *the book is out of print* ‖ das ∼ der Bücher *the Bible* ‖ → Lehr∼̈, Lese∼̈, Rechen∼̈ etc **b.** ⟨übtr⟩ das ∼ des Lebens, der Natur, des Schicksals *the book of life, nature, fate* ‖ ein ∼ mit 7 Siegeln *a book with 7 seals* **c.** Wendungen: er **redet wie** ein ∼ *he speaks like a book* (od *with a great flow of words*) ‖ das war ein Sommer, wie er **im** ∼e **steht** *that was a glorious* (od *first-class, perfect*) *summer* ‖ über Büchern hocken, sitzen *to be at one's books, to pore over books* **d.** ⟨fig⟩ offenes ∼ (P) *open book* **2. a.** ⟨com⟩ *book*; [oft pl] ∼̈er *books*; Haupt∼̈ *ledger*; die ∼̈er führen *to keep accounts, to keep the books* (⟨übtr⟩ *the records*); (etw) z ∼ bringen, in die ∼̈er eintragen *to book* (*a th*); *to enter* (*a th*) *in the books*; z ∼ stehen mit .. (of estates) *to be entered* (od *valued*) *at* (*£ 1000*); z ∼ stehender Wert *book value* ‖ (jdn) aus den ∼̈ern streichen *to cross* (*a p*) *off one's books* ‖ wir können diesen Posten in unsern B. nicht feststellen *this item does not figure in our books* ‖ ∼ führen über .. *to keep a record of* (*sums*, etc.) **b.** (Wett∼̈) *book* **c.** = Heft **3.** (Teil e–s ∼es) *book*; *chapter*; die ∼̈er des Alten, Neuen Testaments *the Books of the Old, New Testament*; die ∼̈er der Könige *the Book of Kings*; das erste ∼ Moses *Genesis* (*in G.*) **4.** (Mengenmaß f Papier; 24 bzw. 25 Bogen) [pl ∼] *quire*; 3 ∼ Schreibpapier *3 quires of note-paper* **5.** ⟨cards⟩ *full suit, complete set* (*of cards*) ‖ ⟨whist⟩ *six tricks* [pl] **6.** ⟨vet⟩ = Blättermagen **7.** [in comp] → Buch–, ∼̈er– *book–* .. **∼abschluß** m ⟨com⟩ *closing* od *balancing of books* **∼ausstattung** f *get-up of a book* **∼auszug** m *extract*; ⟨com⟩ *abstract of account* **∼auto** n ⟨Am⟩ *bookmobile* **∼beschneidemaschine** f *booktrimmer* **∼besprechung** f *book review*(*ing*) **∼bestand** m *bookstock* **∼beweis** m *book-test* **∼binder** m (*book*)*binder*; das Buch ist beim ∼ *the book is binding* (od *at the binder's*) | ∼geselle [m] *journeyman bookbinder*; ∼gold [n] *gold-leaf*; ∼handwerk [n] *bookbinding, trade of a bookbinder*; ∼leinwand [f] *calico* **∼binder·ei** f *bookbinding* ‖ *bookbinder's* (*work*)*shop*; ⟨Am⟩ (*book*)-*bindery* ‖ *binding department* **∼branche** [–brɑ̃ʃə] f *book-field* **∼decke** f *board, side* (*of the cover*) **∼deckel** m *book-case, book-cover* **∼drama** n ⟨Lit⟩ *book-drama, closet-play, literary drama* **∼druck** m *letter-press printing*; → Druck | ∼ätzung [f] *photo-engraving* ‖ ∼betrieb [m] *printing plant* ‖ ∼farbe [f] *printing-ink* ‖ ∼presse [f] *printing-press* **∼drucker** m *printer*; *typographer* ‖ ∼kunst [f] *art of printing, typography* ‖ ∼lehrling [m] *printer's devil*; ∼prinzipal [m] *master printer* ‖ ∼schnellpresse [f] *high-speed printing machine* **∼druckerei** f *printing-office*; ⟨Am⟩ *printing plant* **∼eignerzeichen** n *ex-libris* (L) (*an ex-libris*) **∼einband** m *binding* **∼forderung** f ⟨com⟩ *book claims* pl, ⟨Am⟩ *accounts receivable* **∼führer** m *book-keeper* **∼führung** f *book-keeping*; *accounting* ‖ einfache (doppelte) ∼ *book-keeping by single* (*double*) *entry, single* (*double*) *entry* ‖ f dopp. ∼ *double-entry* [attr] (*book-keeper*) ‖ ∼sarbeiten erledigen *to do book-keeping* **∼gelehrsamkeit** f *book-learning* (od *lore*), *bookishness* **∼gemeinschaft** f *book club, subscription library*; ⟨Am⟩ *literary guild* **∼gesellschaft** f (*scientific*) *book guild* **∼gestalter** m *book designer* **∼gewerbe** n *book-manufacture* (od *trade*) **∼halten** n *book-keeping* **∼halter** m **1.** *book-keeper* **2.** *accountant, clerk*; (Haupt∼̈) *comptroller* **3.** ⟨übtr⟩ *recorder* **∼halter·ei** f *countinghouse book-keeping department* **∼halterin** f *girl clerk* **∼haltung** f **1.** = Buchhalterei **2.** *book-keeping*; *accounts*; ⟨comp⟩ *routine accounting* ‖ Kosten [pl] der ∼ *operating costs in the accounting department* ‖ ∼unterlage [f] ⟨comp⟩ *accounting detail* **∼handel** m *book* (od *bookselling*) *-trade*; im ∼ erhältlich bei *to be sold by* .. **∼händler** m *bookseller*; beim ∼ *at the bookseller's* ‖ Verlags∼̈ *publisher* ‖ ⟨engl⟩ ∼börse [f] (in London) die ∼ *Stationers' Hall* (*at St.-H.*); ∼gilde [f] ⟨hist⟩ *the Stationers' Company* **∼handlung** f *bookshop, bookseller's shop*, ⟨Am⟩ *book-store* ‖ Verlags∼̈ *publishing house* **∼hülle** f *book jacket* od *wrapper* **∼kredit** m *book-credit* **∼laden** m = Buchhandlung **∼macher** m ⟨racing⟩ *book-maker*; ⟨Am⟩ *handbook man*; ⟨sl⟩ *bookie*; der Gehilfe des ∼s *tick-tack* **∼maler** m ⟨hist⟩ *miniaturist* **∼malerei** f *miniature-painting*; *illuminations* [pl] **∼̈mäßig** a *as shown by the books*; *book* [attr] (*b. loss, b. profit*); ∼er Nachweis [m] *account* ‖ ∼ [adv] nachweisen *to account for* **∼messe** f *book fair* **∼nummer** f *book-number* **∼porto** n *book-postage* **∼post** f *book-post* **∼prüfer** m = Bücherrevisor **∼rücken** m *the back of a book* **∼schlager** m *best seller* **∼schmuck** m *book ornamentation* **∼schnitt** m *edge* (gesprenkelt *sprinkled*) **∼schrift** f ⟨typ⟩ *book face* **∼schuld** f *bookdebt* **∼schuldner** m *book-debtor* **∼stabe** m etc → d. **∼stütze** f *book rest* **∼titel** m *title of a book* **∼umschlag** m: flexibler ∼ *limp binding* **∼wert** m *book-value* **∼wesen** n *bibliology* **∼wissen** n *book-learning* (od *-lore*); *bookishness* **∼zeichen** n *bookmark*(*er*) **∼zwang** m *duty obligatory on a p to keep books*
Buch- (→ Buche; vgl Buchen–) [in comp] *beech–* .. **∼ecker** f ⟨bot⟩ *beech-nut* **∼esche** f ⟨bot⟩ = Bergahorn) **∼fink** m ⟨orn⟩ *chaffinch* **∼marder** m ⟨zoo⟩ *beech marten* **∼mast** f *beechmast, buckmast* **∼weizen** m ⟨bot⟩ *buckwheat* | ∼grütze [f] *b. porridge*
B·uche f ∼/∼n **1.** *beech*(*-tree*); Rot∼̈ *red* (od *purple*) *beech*, ⟨Am⟩ *beech*; Blut∼̈ *copper-beech*; Hopfen∼̈ *Hop Hornbeam*; → Hain∼̈ **2.** [in comp] → Buch–; Buchen–
Buchel f *beech-nut*; ∼n [pl] (als Futter) *mast* | ∼öl [n] *beech-nut oil*
B·üchelchen n ∼s/∼ *booklet, small book*
b·uchen a *beech, beechen*
b·uchen vt [h] **1.** ⟨com⟩ (Aufträge, Summen) *to book, to enter* (*in a book*); *to make an entry of* (*a th*); korrekt ∼ *to enter up*; (etw) auf jds Konto ∼ *to book* (*a th*) *to a p's credit*; → eintragen **2.** ⟨übtr⟩ *to record, register* ‖ (Namen etc) *to list* | *to represent, to write down*; etw als e–n Erfolg, Mißerfolg ∼ *to write a th down a success, a failure*; als ausgezeichnet ∼ *to vote* (*a th*) *excellent*; e–n Erfolg f sich [acc] ∼ *to score a success* **II.** ∼̈ n *booking*, etc ‖ ⟨comp⟩ ∼̈ auf 2 Formularen *posting two forms*

B·uchen- (→ Buche; vgl Buch–) [in comp] *beech–* .. **~hain** m *beech-grove* **~öl** n *beech-oil* **~schwamm** m ⟨bot⟩ *beech-agaric* **~spinner** m ⟨ent⟩ *notodontid moth, puss-moth* **~wald** m *beech-wood*

Bücher- (→ Buch; vgl. Buch–) oft *biblio–* **~abschluß** m ⟨com⟩ *balancing of the books* **~auktion** f: ~ des Buchhändlerverbandes *trade-sale* **~austausch** m *exchange of books* **~bord** n, **~brett** n *bookshelf, book-stand* **~freund** m *book-lover, bibliographil(e)* **~gestell** n *book-stand, book-rack; open bookcase*; drehbares ~ *revolving book-rack* **~halle** f *public library* **~halter** m = Bücherstütze **~kenner** m *bibliographer* **~kenntnis,** **~kunde** f *bibliography* **~laus** f, –milbe [f] ⟨ent⟩ *book-louse* **~marder** m ⟨fig⟩ *book-stealer* **~markt** m *book-market* **~narr** m *bibliomaniac* **~regal** n = Büchergestell **~reihen** f [pl] *rows* (od *tiers*) *of books* [pl] **~reisender** m *book travel(l)er,* ⟨Am⟩ *b.-agent* **~revision** f *audit* **~revisor** m *accountant, auditor*; Diplom-~ *certificated* (⟨Am⟩ *certified*) *public accountant*; vereidigter ~ *chartered* (⟨Am⟩ *public*) *accountant* **~saal** m *library* **~sammlung** f *collection of books, library* **~schatz** m: die –schätze der Staatsbibliothek *the treasures* [pl] *of the National Library* **~schau** f (in e–r Zeitschrift) *New Books; Reviews* [pl] **~schrank** m *bookcase* **~skorpion** m ⟨ent⟩ *book-scorpion* **~stand** m (auf Bahnhöfen etc) *bookstall*; an allen –ständen *on all bookstalls* **~ständer** m = Büchergestell **~stütze** f *book prop* (od *support*); ~n [pl] *book-ends* [pl] **~sucht** f *bibliomania* **~verleiher** m *owner of a circulating library* **~verzeichnis** n *catalogue* od *list of books* **~wart** m *librarian* **~wurm** m ⟨zoo & fig⟩ *bookworm,* ⟨sl fig⟩ *swot* **~zettel** m *form for ordering a book* (*in a library*)

Bücher·ei f ~/~en *library*; → Volks≃

B·üchlein n ~s/~ *booklet*

Buchs m Buchses/ ⟨bot⟩ **1.** = ~baum **2.** *milkwort* ‖ *bearberry*

B·uchsbaum m ⟨bot⟩ **1.** (⟨a.⟩ Immergrüner ~) *Common Box-Tree*; *box(-tree)* **2.** [in comp] *box*; *boxwood* **~hecke** f *hedge of boxwood* **~holz** n *box(-wood)* **~wald** m *boxwood forest*

B·uchse f ~/~n **1.** ⟨mach⟩ = Büchse 2. **2.** °~ = Buxe, Büxe

B·üchse f ~/~n **1. a.** ~ aus Ton, Porzellan (→ Salbe etc., → Dose) *jar, pot* | Blech≃ *can, tin*; (f Tee etc) *canister*; e–e ~ kondensierte Milch *a tin of condensed milk*; e–e gr ~ Tee *a chest of tea* ‖ in ~n einmachen *to can, tin*; in ~n eingemacht *canned, tinned*; aus ~n leben *to live out of tins* **b.** Geld≃ *money-box*; (→ Sammel≃; Spar≃) ‖ Puder≃ *powder-box* **2.** (a. Buchse) ⟨mach⟩ (Hohlzylinder) *socket*; (f Kabel) *drum* ‖ (Metallfutter) *bush, metal lining, liner; shim* ‖ ⟨mot⟩ Stopf≃ *stuffing-box* **3.** (Jagdgewehr f Kugel; → Flinte) *rifle, gun*; ⟨hist⟩ *musket* ‖ → Haken≃; Knall≃

B·üchsen- **~fisch** m *tinned fish* **~fleisch** n *tinned* (od *canned, potted*) *meat*; (Rindfleisch) *corned beef* ‖ ⟨mil⟩ *iron rations* [pl] **~futteral** n *gun-case* **~gemüse** n *tinned vegetables* [pl] **~konserven** f [pl] *potted preserves* [pl] **~kugel** f *rifle-bullet* **~lauf** m *rifle* (od *gun*) *barrel* **~macher** m *gunmaker, gunsmith* **~öffner** m *tin-opener* **~rohr** n *gun-barrel* **~schaft** m *gun-stock* **~schuß** m *rifle-shot* **~spanner** m *loader* **~spargel** m *tinned asparagus* **~waren** f [pl] *canned goods* [pl]

B·üchsflinte f *double-barrelled gun with a smooth and a rifled bore*

B·uchstabe m ~n/~n **1.** *letter; character* ‖ ⟨typ⟩ *type* ‖ gr ~ *capital*; gr Anfangs≃ (e–s Eigennamens) *initial*; in gr lateinischen ~n *in block capitals*; kl ~ *small letter*; (etw) mit kl ~n schreiben ⟨typ⟩ *to lower-case* **2.** ⟨übtr & fig⟩ der ~ des Gesetzes *the letter of the law* ‖ etw dem Sinn (*or* Inhalt) u ~n nach ehren *to honour a th in letter and spirit* ‖ (etw) bis auf den letzten ~n erfüllen *to carry* (*a th*) *out to the letter, to fulfil* (*a th*) *up to the hilt* ‖ °die 4 ~n (= Popo) *b.t.m.* (f. *bottom*); °setz dich auf d–e 4 ~n ⟨vulg⟩ *park your stern*

B·uchstaben- **~folge** f *alphabet; alphabetical order* **~glaube** m *biblilatry; bigotry; dogmatism* **~gleichung** f *algebraic equation* **~mensch** m *pedant,* → Bürokrat **~rätsel** n *anagram; logogriph* **~rechnung** f *algebra* **~setzmaschine** f *type-setting machine* **~versatzspiel** n *anagrams* [sg konstr] **~versetzung** f *transposition of letters*

Buchstab·ier- **~alphabet** n ⟨commun⟩ *phonetic alphabet,* → Bd. I. S. 1105 **~buch** n *spelling-book, primer*; ⟨hist⟩ *horn-book* **≃en** **1.** vt/i [h] *to spell* ‖ falsch ~ *to misspell* **2.** ≃ n *spelling* **~(wett)spiel** n ⟨Am⟩ *spelling-bee*

b·uchstäblich **1.** a *literal* | ⟨übtr⟩ *technical* (*assault*) ‖ *arrant* (*nonsense*), *sheer, thorough* **2.** adv *literally, word for word* | ich fiel ~ auf ihn *I fell literally on him*

Bucht f ~/~en **A. 1.** (Biegung) *bend(ing), curve* ‖ ⟨bot⟩ *sinus* **2.** (See≃) *bay*; kl ~ *bight, cove, creek, inlet, voe* ‖ die Helgoländer ~ *Heligoland Bight*; die Danziger ~ *the Gulf of Danzig* od *of Gdansk*; die Kieler, Lübecker ~ *the bight of Kiel, Lübeck*; → Meerbusen ‖ e–e ~ m in e–e Küste *to indent a coast* **3.** (Schleife im Tau) *bight* **B. 1.** (Pferch) *pen, fold* **2.** °~ = Bett **≃en** vt [h], [pass] gebuchtet w (of a coast) *to become indented* ‖ sich ~ *to be indented*

b·uchtenreich, b·uchtig a *indented* (*coast-line*)

B·uchtung f → Aus≃, Ein≃

B·uchung f ~/~en ⟨com⟩ *booking, entry*; Gegen≃ *cross-entry*; e–e ~ m *to make an entry* ‖ ⟨comp⟩ *record posting operation* ‖ ⟨übtr⟩ *registration*; die ~en m *to keep the records* **~sablauf** m ⟨comp⟩ *accounting operations* pl **~sautomat** m ⟨comp⟩ *office automation equipment; accounting machine* (mit Kartenlocher *with card punch control unit*) **~sbeleg** m ⟨bes Am⟩ *voucher* **~smaschine** f *acc. machine*

B·uckel m ~s/~ **1.** *convex projection* ‖ (erhabene Verzierung) *boss*; mit ~n verziert *bossy* ‖ (Schild≃) *boss, umbo* ‖ (Metallbeschlag) *knob, stud* **2.** ⟨anat⟩ **a.** *hump, hunch* (*of a p; of a camel*); Rücken mit e–m ~ *humpback; hunchback*; e–n ~ h *to be humpbacked* (od *hunch–*) | ⟨übtr⟩ *hump, hummock* (*of a hill,* etc.) ‖ ⟨bot⟩ = Knorren **b.** (krummer Rücken) *stoop* ‖ e–n ~ m (of a cat) *to arch one's back*; (P) *to make a bow* od *kowtow; to bow; to kowtow* (vor *to a p*) **c.** °(Rücken) *back*; → Rücken ‖ ⟨fig⟩ e–n krummen ~ m *to cringe, kowtow* (vor *to a p*); → kriechen ‖ °rutsch mir den ~ herunter (*or* lang) *I'll see you further* (⟨sl⟩ *in hell*) *first; no, thanks; not I* ‖ *go chase yourself* ‖ rutsch mir mit d–n Vorschlägen den ~ herunter ⟨sl⟩ *go to blazes with your proposals* ‖ ein ~ voll Keile! *a sound thrashing*! ‖ sich e–n ~ lachen *to split one's sides* **~ochse** m ⟨zoo⟩ *zebu* **~urne** f ⟨praeh⟩ *embossed urn* **~wal** m ⟨zoo⟩ *humpback whale* **~zirpe** f ⟨ent⟩ *cicade*

b·uckeln vt/i [h] **1.** vt **a.** (jdn) *to carry* (*a p*) *on one's back* ‖ sich ~ *to plod, to plough*; → katz~ **b.** (Metall) *to emboss; to fashion in relief* **2.** vi *to hump one's back* (*up*) **B·uckelung** f ⟨arts⟩ *embossing; embossment*

b·ucklig a *humpbacked, hunchbacked; humped* ‖ (Rücken) ~ m *to hump; to arch* | ⟨übtr⟩ *humpy* ‖ sich ~ lachen ⟨fig⟩ *to split one's sides* **B·ucklige** m [der ~, ein ~r] ~n/~n *humpback, hunchback*

b·ücken vt & sich ~ [h] *to bend,* vt [h] **1.** (Kopf, Nacken) ~ = beugen I.1.a. | [pass] v Alter gebückt *bent* od *bowed by age*; gebückter Mann *stooping man* ‖ gebückt gehen *to walk with* *a stoop*; sich g. halten *to stoop*; gebückte Haltung *on one's back* ‖ sich ~ *to plod, to plough*; → *stoop* **2.** sich ~ **a.** *to lean down*; *bend* (über *over*); *incline o.s., stoop* (um z tun *to do*); sich nach e–r Blume ~ *to stoop to pick a flower* ‖ sich ~ (beim Bockspringen) *to give* od *make a back* | (sich verneigen) *to bow* (vor *to*); sich tief ~ *to bow down* **b.** ⟨fig⟩ sich ~ vor jdm *to bend, to submit to a p* ‖ (kriechen) *to cringe* (vor *to a p*)

B·ück(l)ing m ~s/~e *red herring, bloater*

B·ückling m ~s/~e *bow, obeisance*

B·uckram [ˈbʌkrəm] m (engl) ~s/ *buckram*

B·uckskin m (engl) ~s/~s **1.** (Schafleder) *buckskin* **2.** (Tuch) *buckskin* **3.** [in comp] *buckskin* (*breeches*)

°**B·uddel** f ~/~n (Fr = *bouteille*) *bottle*

°**b·uddeln** vi/t [h] **1.** vi *to dig, delve* ‖ ⟨übtr⟩ *to* (*s*)*puddle* (in *in*) **2.** vt (Kartoffeln) *to dig*

Buddh·ismus m ~/ *Buddhism* **Buddh·ist** m ~en/~en *Buddhist* **≗isch** a *Buddhist*(*ic*)

buddis·ieren vt (nach C. C. L. Budde) [h] (Milch) *to sterilize by peroxide of hydrogen*

B·ude f ~/~n **1.** *small house*; *hut*; *outhouse*; ⟨Am⟩ *shack* **2.** (Bretter≗, Markt≗) *booth, stall, stand*; (Schau≗) *show* ‖ (Laden) *shop*; die ~ zumachen *to shut up shop*; *to close down* **3.** °⟨cont⟩ e–e ärmliche ~ *a squalid dwelling*; *a hovel*; *a ramshackle house*; e–e elende ~ ⟨sl⟩ *a beastly hole* **4.** °⟨bes univ⟩ *lodgings, rooms* [pl]; ⟨fam⟩ *den, diggings, digs* [pl]; ⟨Am sl⟩ *shebang*; komm auf m–e ~ *come to my digs* ‖ ⟨übtr⟩ *office* ‖ *school* **5.** Wendungen: jdm auf die ~ rücken *to pay a p a surprise-visit*; *to come unawares upon a p*; ⟨fig⟩ *to take a p to task* ‖ °er brachte Leben in die ~ *he imbued the whole show* od *place with new life*; jetzt kam Leben in die ~ *now things became lively and interesting*

B·uden- **~besitzer** m *stall-holder* **~geld** n *stallage* °**~zauber** m ⟨univ⟩ *rag*; *spree in one's* od *a p's digs*; ~ m *to rag*

B·udeng m ⟨zoo⟩ ein Stummelaffe, → d.

Budg·et [byˈdʒeː] n ~s/~s *budget* ‖ ein ~ aufstellen *to budget* (f *for*); etw im ~ vorsehen *to budget a th*; → Etat; Haushaltsplan **~jahr** n *financial year* **~kommission** f *the Committee of Ways and Means* **~rechnung** f *budgeting* **~überwachung** f *budgetary control*

°**Bud·ike** f ~/~n *small shop* ‖ ⟨cont⟩ = Bude 3. ‖ ⟨fam⟩ *pub*, → Kneipe

B·üdner m ~s/~ **1.** *stall-holder* **2.** *cottager, cotter*

Bu·enos ·Aires n (Hauptstadt Argentiniens) *Buenos Aires*

Büf·ett [byˈfeː] n (Fr) ~s/~s **1.** (Anrichte, Tellerschrank) *buffet* ‖ → Imbißhalle **3.** kaltes ~ *luncheon* (*etc*) *served buffet style*; *table with refreshments*, (*cold*) *buffet* **~dame** f *barmaid* **~kellner** m *barman*

Büfett·ier [byfeˈtjeː] m (Fr) *manager of a bar*, ⟨bes hot⟩ *barman*; ⟨Am⟩ *bartender, barkeeper*

B·uffalo **1.** n (Stadt) (N.Y., USA) **2.** m (engl) ~s/~s ⟨zoo⟩ (amerik. ~) *buffalo, bison*

B·üffel m ~s/~ **1.** *buffalo* [pl oft *buffalo*]; Haus≗ *tamed buffalo* ‖ indischer ~ *water-buffalo* (od *cow*) **2.** = Buffalo **3.** °(P) *lout*; → Ochse **~beere** f ⟨bot⟩ *buffalo-berry* **~haut** f *buffalo-skin* (od *hide*) **~jagd** f *buffalo-hunting* **~leder** n *buff-leather* **~ochs** m *buffalo*

°**Büffel·ei** f *drudgery, grind, toil*; ⟨sl⟩ *cram, sap*; *cramming, swotting, cribbing*

°**b·üffeln** **I.** vi/t [h] **1.** vi *to drudge, grind, stew, plod, toil* (an *at*); ⟨sl⟩ *to swot, mug*; ⟨Am⟩ *to bone up* (an *on*) ‖ tüchtig ~ müssen *to keep one's nose to the grindstone* **2.** vt Geschichte (etc) ~ *to cram history*; *to grind history into one's head* ‖ → ochsen **II.** ≗ n = Büffelei °**B·üffler** m ~s/~ *plodder*, ⟨Am⟩ *dig*; ⟨sl⟩ *sap, smug, swot, mug*

B·uffo m (It) ~s/~s (Sänger komischer Rollen) *buffo*

Bufon·it m ~s/~en ⟨geol⟩ (Krötenstein) *bufonite*

Bug m ~s/~e **A.** **1.** ⟨zoo⟩ (Gelenk e–s Gliedes) *joint* ‖ (des Hinterbeins) *hock, hough* ‖ ~ der Schulter *shoulder*; (v Rind) ⟨cul⟩ *brisket* **2.** ⟨übtr⟩ (Ggs Heck *bow* (*of a ship*); an ihrem ~ *at her bow*; über Backbord≗, Steuerbord≗ liegen *to be on the port bow, starboard bow* ‖ (Schiffsschnabel) *prow* ‖ ⟨aero⟩ *bow* (*of an aeroplane*); *nose*; mit dem ~ nach unten *nose-down* **3.** (Vorderseite) *front* (*of a roof*, etc.) **B.** (Bogen, Biegung) *bend, bow*; *curvature, curve*; *flexure* **~anker** m *bow-anchor, bower* **~figur** f ⟨mar⟩ = Gallionsfigur **~flagge** f ⟨mar⟩ = Gösch **~geschütz** n *bow-chaser* **~kanzel** f ⟨aero⟩ *nose compartment*; (fMG.) *nose turret* **≗lahm** a ⟨vet⟩ *splayshouldered* (*horse*) **≗lastig** a ⟨aero⟩ *nose-heavy* **~licht** n (weiß) ⟨aero⟩ *headlight* **~mann** m (beim Rudern) *bowman*, ⟨fam⟩ *bow, bow-oar* **~rad** n ⟨aero⟩ *nose wheel* ‖ ~fahrwerk [n] *nose* od *tricycle landing gear* **~ruder** n *bow-rudder* **~schütze** m ⟨aero⟩ *nose* od *front gunner* **~schutzgerät** n *paravane* **~spriet** n *bowsprit*; → befestigen **~stück** n ⟨cul⟩ *brisket* **~welle** f *bow-wash* (od *wave*)

B·ügel m ~s/~ **1.** (gebogenes Holz, Metall etc) *semicircular piece of wood* (etc); *bow*; *hoop, ring*; (Griff) *handle*; Kleider≗ *coat-hanger* ‖ (am Gewehr) *trigger-guard* **2.** (Steig≗) *stirrup*; → Steig≗ ‖ ⟨tech⟩ (U-förmiger ~) *stirrup*; eiserner ~ *U-shaped piece of iron*; *shackle* ‖ *frame* (*of a fretsaw*) ‖ ⟨el⟩ Stromabnehmer *pantograph collector* **3.** ⟨tech⟩ (Joch) *yoke*; (Verstärkung) *strut* **~brett** n *ironing-board* **~eisen** n (*flat* od *smoothing, laundry*) *iron* ‖ (~ des Schneiders) *goose* [pl *gooses*] **~falte** f (in Hosen) (*iron*) *crease, press*; ~n [pl] *creasing*; die Hose mit e–r ~ versehen *to crease one's trousers* **≗fest** a ~ s *to be firm in one's stirrups* **≗frei** a *wash-and-wear, no*(*n*)*-iron* (*shirt*) **~meßschraube** f *micrometer caliper* od *gauge* **~riemen** m *stirrup-leather* (od *strap*) **~säge** f *bow-saw* **~stahl** m (Bolzen) *heater*

B·ügelhorn n [aus engl *bugle*] ⟨mus⟩ **1.** ⟨hist mil⟩ (Signalhorn) *bugle* **2.** (~ mit Ventilen) *cornet*; *saxhorn*; *tuba*

b·ügeln **1.** vt (Wäsche) *to iron, smooth*; (Kleider) *to press* **2.** ≗ n *ironing, pressing*

^×^**b·ugen** vi [h] = sich beugen

B·üglerin f *ironer*; *ironing woman*

B·ugra f abbr f. Internationale Ausstellung f. **Bu**chgewerbe u **Gra**phik

Bugs·ier- (→ bugsieren) **~boot** n *tow-boat, tug*(*-boat*) **~dampfer** m *steam tug* **~lohn** m *towage* **~tau** n, **~trosse** f *tow*(*ing*)*-rope*

bugs·ieren **1.** vt (Schiff) *to tow*; *to take* (*a ship*) *in tow*; *to tug* | ⟨übtr⟩ (etw) *to put*; *to smuggle* (in *into*) ‖ (jdn) *to lead, to take*; → hinein~, hinaus~ **2.** ≗ n *tow, towage, towing*

^×^**B·ühel** m ~s/~, **Bühl** m [obd] ~s/~e *hill*

B·uhle m ~n/~n ⟨dero & poet⟩ *paramour* ‖ †*lover, sweetheart* **B·uhle** f ~/~n (a. Buhldirne) ⟨dero & poet⟩ *prostitute, paramour, mistress* ‖ †*lover, sweetheart*

b·uhlen vi [h] **1.** **a.** ~ mit jdm *to have illicit intercourse with a p* **b.** ⟨poet⟩ der Wind buhlte mit den Blättern *the wind courted* od *wooed the leaves* **2.** ⟨übtr⟩ **a.** ~ um etw *to court a th* ‖ ~ um jds Gunst (etc), ~ um jdn *to curry favour with a p, to court a p*; um e–n Staat ~ *to court a state*; *to woo the friendship of a state* ‖ um Applaus ~ *to court applause* **b.** (wetteifern) mit jdm ~ um etw *to compete* (od *strive, vie*) *with a p for a th* **c.** ~ nach etw *to long for, to strive after* **b·uhlend** a *courting, wooing* (*wind*) †**B·uhler** m ~s/~ *lover*; *paramour* ‖ *courter, wooer* (um etw *of a th*)

Buhler·ei f ∼/∼en 1. *illicit intercourse* (*with a p*) ‖ (Gefallsucht) *coquetry* 2. ⟨übtr⟩ die ∼ um etw *the courting of a th*; *the striving for a th* **B·uhlerin** *courtesan*; *strumpet*, *wanton*; *prostitute* **b·uhlerisch** a *lewd*, *wanton* **B·uhlin** f = Buhle f **B·uhlschaft** f ∼/∼en *illicit intercourse*

B·uhne f ∼/∼n *groyne*; *breakwater*; *dam*; (Ufer) durch e–e ∼ schützen *to groyne* ‖ (Zaun v Reisern f Fischer) *crawl*

B·ühne f ∼/∼n 1. (Brettergerüst) *scaffold*(*ing*), *stage*; *estrade*; *raised platform*; Redner≃ *platform* ‖ ⟨min & tech⟩ (am Hochofen) *gallery*, *platform* ‖ ⟨macro-phot⟩ (*camera-*)*rostrum* 2. ⟨theat⟩ **a.** *stage*; *the boards* [pl] ‖ ⟨ant⟩ *scene* (*of a Greek theatre*) ‖ → Dreh≃, Freilicht≃ ‖ auf der ∼ *on the stage* ‖ sich auf der ∼ halten (of plays) *to hold the stage* ‖ (Stück) auf die ∼ bringen *to bring on* od *to the stage*; *to stage* (*a play*) ‖ auf die ∼ k (of actors) *to come on to the stage*; auf die ∼ treten *to step on to the stage* ‖ (Stück) f die ∼ bearbeiten *to adapt for the stage*; über die ∼ gehen (of plays) *to be* (*en*)*acted* od *performed* ‖ zur ∼ gehen *to go on the stage*, *to take to the stage* | im Hintergrund der ∼ (befindlich) *up-stage* ‖ ∼ frei! *clear please* **b.** [koll] die deutsche ∼ *the German stage* **c.** provisorische ∼ *fit-up* **d.** ⟨fig⟩ v der politischen ∼ abtreten *to retire from the political stage* ‖ ∼ des Lebens, Welt≃ *the scene*, v der W. abtreten *to quit the scene*, *to die*

B·ühnen- [in comp] *stage–*; *scenic*; *theatrical*; *acting* **∼angst** f *stage-fright* **∼anweisung** f *stage direction* **∼arbeiter** m *stage hand* **∼architekt** m *st. designer* **∼auftreten** n *stage-appearance* (*of an actor*) **∼ausgabe** f *acting-edition* **∼ausstattung** f *scene*(*ry*), *set*(*ting*) **∼bearbeitung** f *adaptation for the stage* **∼bild** n *scene*, *scenery*, *set*(*ting*) ‖ ∼ner(in f) m *st.* od *scenic designer* ‖ ∼projektion [f] *projected scenery* **∼darstellung** f *stage--production* (od *setting*) **∼dekoration** f = Bühnenausstattung **∼deutsch** n *standard German as spoken on the stage* **∼dichter** m *playwright*, *dramatist* **∼erfahrung** f *stage-craft* **∼erfolg** m *stage-success* **≃fähig** a *stage-worthy* (*play*) **∼fex** m *stage-struck youth* **≃gerecht** a *theatrical*, *fit for the stage*, *suitable for stage production*; *acting* (*play*), *actable* (*script*) **∼haus** n *frame--work of the stage* ‖ *play-house* **∼held** m *hero* **∼heldin** f *heroine* **∼hintergrund** m *upstage*; im ∼ *up-stage* **∼kenntnis** f *stage-craft* **∼kritiker** m *stage-critic* **≃kundig** a: ∼er Mann *p. with theatrical experience* **∼kunst** f *art of acting* **∼laufbahn** f *stage career* (*of an actor*) **∼leiter** m *stage-manager* **∼leitung** f *stage-management* **∼maler** m *scene-painter*, *scenic artist* **∼malerei** f *scene-painting* **∼manuskript** n *play-house manuscript* **≃mäßig** a *theatrical* **∼meister** m (*master*) *carpenter* **∼musik** f *incidental music* **∼ordnung** f (*scenery*) *stage directions* **∼portier** m *stage door-keeper* od *doorman* **∼requisiten** [pl] *stage-properties* [pl], *fit-up* **∼schriftsteller** m *playwright* **∼sprache** f: deutsche ∼ = Bühnendeutsch **∼star** m *top-flight performer* **∼stück** n *stage-play*; *stage* (Ggs *television*) *drama* **∼tanz** m *ballet* **∼technik** f *stagecraft* **≃technisch** a *scenic*, *theatrical*; in ∼er Hinsicht *scenically* **∼teppich** m *drugget*; *stage* (⟨Am⟩ *ground*) *cloth* **∼tradition** f *stage--tradition* **∼version** f *acting* (od *stage*) *-version* **∼vorhang** m *act drop* **∼vorstellung** f *stage play* **∼wagen** m *truck*, ⟨Am⟩ *wagon* **∼werk** n ⟨Lit⟩ *stage-work*; *dramatic work* **∼wesen** n *acting*; *theatrical matters*; *theatres* **≃wirksam** a = –gerecht; *acting* (*play*) **∼wirkung** f *stage-effect* **∼zubehör** f = Bühnenrequisiten

B·uhurt m ∼s/∼e [Ger-Fr] ⟨hist⟩ *tournament*

Buk·anier m (Seeräuber) *buccaneer* **bukan·ieren** vt [h] (Fleisch) *to buccan*; *boucan* (Fr)

B·ukarest n (Hptst. Rumäniens) *Bucharest*

Buk·ett n ∼s/∼e 1. ⟨bot⟩ *bouquet*, *nosegay*, *posy* 2. (of wine) *bouquet*, *aroma*, *flavour* **∼zweig** m *short twig of a fruit-tree*

Buk·oliker m *bucolic poet* **buk·olisch** a *bucolic*

Bukow·ina f, die ∼ *Bukovine* **Bukow·iner** m ∼s/∼ *inhabitant of Bukovine*

B·ulb m [engl] (Wulst) *bulb* **≃förmig** a *bulb-like*

Bulb·ärparalyse f ⟨med⟩ *bulbar paralysis*

Bulb·ille f ⟨bot⟩ (Brutzwiebel) *bulbil*

Bülb·ül m ∼s/∼s ⟨orn⟩ *bulbul*

B·uleine f ∼/∼n ⟨mar⟩ *bowline*

Bul·ette f ∼/∼n (Fr) *small meat-ball*; *rissole*; ⟨Am⟩ *hamburger* ‖ °wie Hektor (*dog*) an die ∼n *like a shot*, *like the devil*

Bulg·are m ∼n/∼n, **bulg·arisch** a *Bulgarian*

Bul·ine f (Haltetau) → Buleine

B·ulkladung f ⟨mar⟩ *load*(*ing*) (*grain*, *etc*) *in bulk*

B·ull- ∼auge n ⟨mar⟩ *bull's eye*, *light-port*, *port-hole* (od *light*); *scuttle* **∼dogge** f ⟨zoo⟩ *bulldog*; **∼dozer** m *bulldozer*; kl ∼ *muledozer* **∼terrier** m ⟨zoo⟩ *bull-terrier*

B·ulle m ∼n/∼n ⟨zoo⟩ *bull* ‖ junger ∼ ⟨Am⟩ *steer* ‖ Seehund– etc-≃ *bull seal etc*, → Kuh | ⟨übtr⟩ (P) 1. *he-male*, *he-man*, *cave-man*; ein ∼ v e–m Kerl *a bull of a man* 2. = Tolpatsch ‖ → Gemeinde≃

B·ulle f ∼/∼n ⟨ec⟩ (päpstl. ∼) *bull* ‖ ⟨Ger⟩ die Goldene ∼ *the Golden Bull*

b·ullen vi [h] (of cows) *to be in heat*, *to take the bull*

B·ullen- ∼beißer m *mastiff bulldog*; *bandog* ‖ ⟨fig⟩ *grumpy person* °**∼h·itze** f e–e ∼ *a hell of a heat*; es ist 'ne ∼ *it's hot as blazes* **∼kalb** n *bull-calf*

°**B·ullerjahn** m *noisy blatant fellow*; ⟨fam⟩ *paddy* **b·ullern** vi [h] 1. = poltern 2. ∼ gegen *to knock against* 3. (of water) *to popple*, *bubble*

Bullet·in [byl'tɛ̃] n (Fr) ∼s/∼s *bulletin*

B·ullion ['buljən] n (engl) ∼s/ (ungemünztes Gold etc) *bullion*

B·ullrichsalz n *bicarbonate of soda*

bum intj ∼! *bang*!

B·ully n [invar] ⟨hock⟩ *bully*

°**B·umann** m (Kindersprache) *bog*(*e*)*y*(*man*)

Bumbum m *rub-a-dub*

B·umerang m ∼s/∼e *boomerang*

°**b·umfiedeln** vt [h] (jdn) = jdm um den Bart gehen, → Bart 1. c.

B·ummel m ∼s/ 1. *promenade*; *stroll*, *lounge*, *saunter*; auf den ∼ gehen *to go for a stroll*; e–n ∼ m *to take a stroll* | (Straßen≃) ⟨hum⟩ *monkey-parade* 2. (Straße) *the grand strut*, ⟨hum⟩ *monkey's parade* 3. (Bierreise) *spree*; ⟨sl⟩ *binge*, ⟨Am⟩ *bum*; auf den ∼ gehen *to go on the loose* (od *racket*, *spree*) ⟨sl⟩ *bend*, *ooze*, *fly*, *rantan*, *bust*, *razzle-dazzle*; ⟨Am sl⟩ *to go on the bat*

B·ummel- °**∼fritze** m *dawdler*, *slow-coach*; *idler*, *lazy-bones* **∼leben** n *idle* (od *disorderly*) *life*; ein ∼ führen *to lead an idle life*; → Bummeln **∼streik** m *go-slow strike*, *working to rule*; e–n ∼ m *to work to rule*; → „Adler", „Igel" °**∼zug** m ⟨rail⟩ *slow train*; *stopping train*

°**Bummel·ant** m = Bummelfritze

Bummel·ei f ∼/∼en *dawdling*, *idleness*, *loafing*, *lazy life*; diese ∼ von ihm ist entsetzlich *it is scandalous the way he is dawdling* ‖ (Nachlässigkeit) *carelessness*, *slipshodness*, *slovenliness*; *forgetfulness* **b·ummelig** a → bummlig

b·ummeln I. vi [h] 1. = baumeln 2. (schlendern) *to stroll*, *to saunter* (*into*; *through*); durch ein Land ∼ *to travel slowly through a country* ‖ *to beat the streets*; ∼ gehen *to go for a stroll*; → umher≃ ‖ *to dawdle*; *to be sluggish*; bummele nicht so *look sharp, please* 3. *to loaf*; *to be idle*, *to waste one's time* ‖ *to knock about* ‖ ⟨Am⟩ *to* *bum*; ⟨sl⟩ *to bat round* **4.** sich amüsieren; (ohne Damen) ~ gehen *to stag it* **II.** ~̈ n *stroll* || *dawdle, dawdling* || *flanerie* (Fr); *idling*; *laziness*; sein Leben mit ~ verbringen *to eat the bread of idleness* ..

B·ummersalat m [östrr] = Kopfsalat

B·ummler m ~s/~ **1.** *stroller, saunterer*; ⟨mil⟩ Schlachten~̈ *civilian at the front*; → Welten~̈ || *dawdle*; *slow-coach* **2.** *idler, loafer*; *tramp*; *flaneur* (Fr) || ⟨Am fam⟩ *bum(mer)*; ⟨sl⟩ *dead-beat*

b·ummlig 1. a *dawdling*; *idle, slow*; ein ~er Mensch *a dawdle* | *careless, slipshod*; *forgetful* **2.** adv *carelessly, slovenly*

bums intj ~! *bang*! *pop*! || *plump, smack, smash*; ~ rennen gegen, in *to run smash against, into* **Bums** m **1.** (Schlag; Fall) *bang, plump, smack, smash, thump, whump* **2.** (Furz) e–n ~ m *or* l *to make a noise* **3.** °⟨dero⟩ (Lokal) *gaff*; *drinking-den* | ⟨Am sl⟩ *dive, joint, honky-tonk* **b·umsen** vi [h] *to bang*; *to bump, to plump (against)*; *to smash, to thump* (auf *on*) || ⟨euphem⟩ *to make a noise* **B·umslandung** f ⟨aero⟩ *bumpy* (od *squash*) *landing*; ⟨sl⟩ *pancake*

B·umslokal n = Bums 3.

B·una m & n ~/ ⟨Ger chem⟩ (Butadien-Natrium) *synthetic rubber*; *buna* || ~reifen [m] ⟨mot⟩ ~ *tyre*

B·und m & n (→ I. A.; I. B.; II.) **I.** [konkr] **A.** (Bindendes) m ~es/~̈e **1.** *circular band, ring*; *hoop* || Schlüssel~̈ *key-ring*, → B. **2.** (Einfassung an Hosen, Rücken) *band, waistband, neckband* || *cording (of a book)* **3.** ⟨tech⟩ (Ring an e–r Welle, etc) *collar* || ⟨aero⟩ (am Gehäuse) *stop-flange* **4.** ⟨arch⟩ = Bindebalken **5.** ⟨mus⟩ (Querleiste an Saiteninstrumenten) [mst pl]: ~̈e *frets* [pl] **B.** n (Gebundenes, Bündel) **1.** ~es/~e: ~ Schlüssel, Schlüssel~̈ *bunch of keys*; ein Schlüssel an dem ~ *a key on the bunch* **2.** ~es/~ (Maßeinheit f zus–gebundene Dinge) ⟨mst com⟩ ein ~ Holz *a bundle of sticks*, drei ~ Holz *three bundles* [pl] *of sticks*; .. *a hank (of flax)*; *a knot (of yarn)*; *a bottle* od *truss (of hay, straw)*; *a bolt (of canvas)*; *a rope (of onions)*; drei ~ Stroh *three bottles* [pl] *of straw* **II.** (Verbindung) m ~es/~̈e **1.** ⟨bib & ec⟩ *covenant, dispensation*; der Alte, Neue ~ *The Old, New Testament* **2.** *bond of union, knot, tie*; der ~ der Ehe, ~ fürs Leben, Ehe~̈ *the marriage knot* **3.** ⟨pol⟩ *alliance, federation, league*; Staaten~̈ *confederation, union*; ⟨Ger hist⟩ der Deutsche ~ *the 'Bund', the German(ic) Confederation* (1815–1866) || Völker~̈ *the League of Nations* | *association, league*; *union* || ⟨Ger⟩ ~ der Landwirte *the Agrarian League*; ⟨nazi⟩ der ~ Deutscher Mädel (abbr B.D.M.) *the German Maidens' Organization*; ~ der Kinderreichen ⟨nazi⟩ *the National Union of Big Families* **4.** ~es/~̈er ⟨univ⟩ *club, fraternity* **5.** (geheimer ~) *confederacy, conspiracy*; *collusion* **6.** Wendungen: den ~ der Ehe **eingehen,** sich die Hand z ~e reichen *to tie the knot*; *to marry* || e–n ~ schließen *or* eingehen mit .. *to enter into an alliance, to cement* (od *form, make*) *an alliance with* ..; *to ally* od *league o.s. with* .. || **im** ~e mit *in company* od *league with* || in geheimem ~e mit *in collusion with* || in engem ~e stehen mit *to be hand in glove with* .. || in geheimem ~e stehen mit *to be in with (a p)*

rohren) *bunching*; (v Triebwerken) *clustering*

B·und- ~axt f ⟨carp⟩ *mortise-axe* **~garn** n *bundle-yarn* **~mutter** f *collar-nut* **~schraube** f *collar-bolt* **~schuh** m **1.** *peasant's strapped clog*; ⟨Scot⟩ *brogue* **2.** ⟨fig hist⟩ *the Peasant's rising* (1493–1517); *Bundschuh Insurrections* [pl] **~sparren** m ⟨arch⟩ *chief rafter* **~steg** m ⟨typ⟩ *side-stick* **~̈weise** adv *by* od *in bundles* **~weite** f ⟨tail⟩ *waist measurements*

B·ündchen n ~s/~ *small band*; *neckband*, → Bund I. A. 2.

B·ündel n (→ Bund I. B.) ~s/~ *bundle, bunch*; ein ~ Banknoten *a bundle* od *sheaf of (bank-) -notes*, ⟨Am⟩ *a wad (of bills)*; *a bundle (of asparagus)*; *a sheaf (of arrows)*; *a bottle (of hay*, etc.); *a bolt (of canvas)* || kl ~ *wisp (of hay*, etc.) || (etw) in ein ~ packen *to bundle* || Bomben~̈ ⟨aero⟩ *cluster*; → Faser~̈; Strahlen~̈ | *packet, parcel* || Reise~̈ *bag*; das ~ in der Hand *bag in hand*; sein ~ schnüren *to pack up one's things* od *traps* [pl]; *to be off* || sie ist ein ~ Nerven *she is a bag* od *mass of nerves* **b·ündeln** vt [h] (etw) *to bundle*; (Strahlen) *to focus* ⟨a. at⟩ **B·ündel- ~elektrode** f *focussing electrode* **~pfeiler** m ⟨arch⟩ (in Gotik) *pier composed of cylindrical columns* **~spule** f *focussing coil* **~ung** f ~/~en *bundling, focussing*; (v Elektronen in Vakuumrohren) *bunching*; (v Triebwerken) *clustering*

b·ündelweise adv *by* od *in bundles* od ⟨aero⟩ *clusters (of bombs)*

B·ünden n → Graubünden, Bündner

B·under m ~s/~ ⟨zoo⟩ (Affe) *rhesus*

B·undes- [in comp] *federal*; *confederate, federative* || (Ggs Länder-) *Federal, National*; *State-* **~abgabe** f ⟨Am⟩ *Federal Tax* **~akte** f *act of the German(ic) Confederation* **~amt** n *Federal Office* || ⟨Ger⟩ ~ f das Heimatwesen *the Supreme Administrative Court for Welfare-Associations* **~angelegenheit** f *Federal Concern* **~anwaltschaft** f *National Bar* **~anzeiger** m *Federal Herald* **~bahn** f *Federal Railway* | **auf ~ebene** [f] ⟨Ger⟩ *on the level of the Federation* **~fürst** m ⟨Ger hist⟩ *sovereign of one of the principalities of the German Confederation* **~geheimpolizei** f ⟨Ger⟩ *Federal Bureau of Investigation* **~genosse** m *confederate, ally* **~genossenschaft** f *alliance* **~gericht** n Schweizer ~ ⟨jur⟩ *the Supreme Court of Switzerland*; ⟨Ger⟩ *Federal Court* **~gesetzblatt** n *Federal Gazette* **~grenzschutz** m *frontier police of the GFR* **~kanzler** m ⟨Ger⟩ *Chancellor*, ⟨hist⟩ *the Prime Minister of the North German Confederation* (1866–71) **~krimin·alamt** n ⟨Ger⟩ *Federal Bureau of Criminal Investigation* **~lade** f ⟨bib⟩ *the Ark of the Covenant* **~länder** n pl ⟨Ger⟩ *Federal Lands* **~minister** m f Atomfragen *F. Minister for Atomic Affairs* **~mitglied** n *member of a confederation* || ⟨sport⟩ *member of a club* **~präsident** m ⟨Ger⟩ *the (Federal) President* **~rat** m ⟨Ger hist⟩ *Federal Council* (1871–1918); ⟨Ger mod⟩ *the (Federal) Upper House*; *(legislative chamber in Bonn)* **~regierung** f *Federal Government* **~republik** f *Federal Republic (of Germany)* **~reservebank** f U.S.A. *the Federal Reserve Bank* **~staat** m **1.** *federation of states organized on a federal basis* **2.** *federal state, member of a federation* **~̈staatlich** a *federal* **~tag** m ⟨Ger⟩ *the (Federal) Lower House, F. Diet* ⟨hist⟩ *the Assembly of the German Diet* (1815–66) **~verfassung** f *federal constitution* **~versammlung** f ⟨Ger⟩ *Federal Assembly* **~versorgungsgesetz** n *Federal Assistance Law* **~wehr** f *Federal German Armed Forces* pl

b·ündig I. a **1.** ⟨arch⟩ [pred] ~ mit (= in gleicher Ebene mit) *flush with*; ~ m *to make flush (with)* **2.** ⟨übtr⟩ *concise, curt*; kz u ~ *succinct*; *brief*; *terse* || (überzeugend) *convincing (proof)*, *conclusive* **3.** †(rechtsgültig) *binding, valid* **II.** [adv] kz u ~ *succinctly, tersely*

B·ündigkeit f ~/ *conciseness*; *succinctness, terseness* || *conclusiveness*

b·ündisch a *federal (youth)*

B·ündner m ~s/~ *member of a confederation* || (⟨Sw a.⟩ = Grau~̈) *inhabitant of the canton* Graubünden

B·ündnis n –nisses/–nisse *alliance, league* (mit *with*); ein ~ bilden *to ally o.s., to league (with)* ||

confederacy, confederation **~fall** m *event of alliance* **≈frei** a = blockfrei

B·ungalow [ˈbʌŋgəlou] m (engl) ~s/~s (leichtes Landhaus) *bungalow*

B·ungar(um) m (Giftschlange) *bungar(um)*

B·unge f ~/~n **1.** *drum* ‖ (Reuse) *drum-net* **2.** ⟨bot⟩ = Bach≈

B·unker m ~s/~ ⟨ich⟩ *menhaden*

B·unker m ~s/~ **1.** (Kohlen≈) *bunker* ‖ ⟨mill⟩ *storing silo* **2.** ⟨golf⟩ (Sandloch) *bunker* **3.** ⟨mil & fort⟩ *armed and sheltered concrete dug-out*; *bunker*; ⟨fam⟩ *pill-box*; ⟨sl⟩ *elephant dug-out* **|** ⟨mil fam⟩ (Arrestlokal) *cooler, fizzer*; im ~ *limbered* **~auslauf** m ⟨tech⟩ *escape gate* **~kohlen** f pl *bunker coal, bunkers* pl **~ofen** m *brazier* **b·unkern** vi [h] *to bunker* ‖ ⟨mar⟩ (Kohle) *to coal*

B·unsenbrenner m (nach R. W. Bunsen † 1899) ⟨chem⟩ *Bunsen burner*

b·unt I. a **1.** (vielfarbig) **a.** *many-coloured, parti* (od *party*)*-coloured, vari-coloured*; *motley* (*coat*), *pied, variegated* (*plants*); ~es Glas *stained glass* **|** (lebhaft) *bright, gay* (*colours*); *bright* (od *gay*)*-coloured, gaudy* (*decorations*); sehr ~ ⟨Am a.⟩ *chrome* (*postcard*) ‖ *multicolo*(*u*)*red* (*search lights, etc*); e–e ~e Wiese *a meadow gay with flowers* **|** ⟨zoo⟩ (*gefleckt*) *dappled*; *pied, spotted, piebald* (*bird*) ‖ (kariert) *chequered, checkered*; ~e Fensterscheibe *checkerpaned window*; ~es Muster *chequer, checker*; (etw) ~ m *to chequer* ‖ ~ farbig **b.** bekannt wie ein ~er Hund *known all over the place* ‖ den ~en Rock anziehen *to go soldiering* ‖ es wird mir ~ vor den Augen *my head begins to whirl* od *swim* **2.** (gefärbt) *coloured, rouged* (*cheeks*) **3.** ⟨übtr⟩ (abwechslungsreich, gemischt) *motley* (*population*), *mottled*; *variegated, varied* (*life, scene*); *chequered* (*history*); *promiscuous*; ~es Gemisch *motley, mottle* **|** ~er Abend *variegated evening entertainment* ‖ ~e (Abend– etc) Gesellschaft [f] *mixed party* ‖ ~e Reihe *ladies and gentlemen in alternate order*; ~e R. m *to pair a party off, to arrange a party in couples* **4.** ⟨fig⟩ (verwirrend; toll) das ist aber doch z ~, die S wird mir z ~ *that's the limit, that's a tall order, that is going too far* ‖ hier sieht's ~ aus *this is a nice confusion* → II. 2. **II.** adv **1.** gaily; ~ gefärbt *fancy-coloured*; ~ geschmückt *pied* (*with*); *gaily-decorated* (*streets*); ~ gemischt mit *variedly mingled with*; *variegated* od *gay with*; ~ gestalten (Laufbahn) *to chequer*; (Unterhaltung etc) *to variegate*; *diversify* **2.** ~ durch e–a *higgledy-piggledy*; *topsyturvy* ‖ es ging dort ~ zu *everything was at sixes and sevens there* ‖ treib es nicht z ~ *mind your health*; *don't go too far*

B·unt- ~bock m **1.** ⟨zoo⟩ *bontebok*, → Kuhantilope **2.** ⟨ent⟩ ein Bockkäfer, → d. **~druck** m **1.** (*the art of*) *colour-printing, chromotypography*; lithographischer ~ *chromolithography* **2.** [konkr] (Abdruck) *colour-print*; *chromolithograph*; ⟨fam⟩ *chromo* **≈farbig** a *coloured*; *variegated*; ⟨übtr⟩ *varied* (*scene*) **~feuer** n *pyrotechnic light* **≈fleckig** a *speckled, spotted* **≈kariert** a ~er Stoff *tartan* **~kupfererz** n ⟨minr⟩ *bornite* **~metalle** n pl (Nichteisenmetalle) *non-ferrous m.s* **~papier** n *coloured* od *fancy, stained paper* **~sandstein** m ⟨geol⟩ *variegated sandstone* **≈scheckig** a ⟨zoo⟩ *dappled, piebald*; *pied*; *spotted* ‖ ⟨übtr⟩ *motley* (*crowd*); *chequered* (*history*); *promiscuous* **≈schillernd** a *opalescent, chatoyant* **~specht** m ⟨orn⟩ *great spotted woodpecker* **~stickerei** f *coloured embroidery, crewelwork* **~stift** m *coloured pencil* **~waschmittel** n ⟨chem⟩ *detergent for colo*(*u*)*red wash* **~weberei** f *coloured weaving*

B·untheit f *motley*; *piebaldness* ‖ *variegation, variety*

B·unya-B·unya f ⟨bot⟩ *bunyal*(*-bunya*)

Bur, ~e ~en/~en *Boer* ‖ der ~enkrieg *the Boer Wars* [pl] (SAfr 1899–1902); → Bur(e)

B·ürde f ~/~n *burden, load* ‖ ⟨mst fig⟩ *burden* (f jdn *to a p*); *charge* (f jdn *on a p*), *load, weight*; unter der ~ der Jahre *under the weight of years* ‖ jdm e–e ~ auflegen *to lay* od *impose a burden on a p, to burden a p*

B·ur(e) m, **B·urin** f *Boer* **B·urenfreund** m, **-freundlich** a *pro-Boer*, **-krieg** m *Boer War*

B·üre f = Bettüberzug

Büreau [byˈroː] n (Fr) → Büro

Bür·ette f ~/~n ⟨chem⟩ (Glasröhre) *burette* Fr

Burg f ~/~en ⟨hist⟩ *castle, fort*; *'burg'*; (Stadt≈) *citadel* **|** ⟨übtr⟩ *house* ‖ ⟨zoo⟩ *burrow* (*of a beaver*)

B·urg- [in comp] *castle-* .. **~bann** m ⟨hist⟩ *castle-guard* ‖ *jurisdiction of a castle* **~bau** m *castle-building* **~flecken** m *borough*, ⟨Scot⟩ *burgh* **~frau** f *lady of the castle* **~fräulein** n *young l. of the c.* **~friede** m *precincts* pl *of a castle held inviolable* ‖ ⟨übtr⟩ *cessation of hostilities, peace*; ~n halten *to keep the peace*; ~n schließen *to make truce* **~graben** m *fosse, castle-moat* **~graf** m ⟨hist⟩ *burggrave, governor of a castle* **~grafschaft** f *burggraviate* (*the ~ of N.*) **~herr** m *lord of a castle* **~hof** m *bailey*; *courtyard of a castle*; äußerer ~ *outer ward* **~keller** m = Burgverlies **~mauer** f *bailey*; *castle-wall* **~ruine** f *castle-ruin* **~turm** m *keep*; (äußerer) *barbican* **~verlies** n *keep*; *dungeon, donjon* **~vogt** m *castellan, warden of a castle* **~wache** f *castle-guard* **~warte** f *keep, watch-tower*

B·urgenland n ⟨geog⟩ (Teil der ungarischen Tiefebene; ⟨a.⟩ österr. Bundesland)

B·ürge m ~n/~n *bondsman*; ⟨jur⟩ **1.** (Strafrecht) ~ f jdn, f jds Erscheinen *bail, surety for a p*; *for a p's appearance* (*in court*) ‖ ~ s *to be bail, to go bail* (*for*), *to stand surety* (*for*) ‖ sich ~n verschaffen *to find bail*; e–n ~n stellen (of a prisoner) *to give* od *offer bail*; e–n ~n zulassen *to admit a p to bail* **2.** ⟨Zivilrecht & übtr⟩ ~ f etw *security, surety for a th* (*for the payment of a debt*, etc.); (*the*) *guarantor*; *guarantee* (f e–e Schuld *of a debt*); ~ s f etw *to be the guarantor* (od *-tee*) *of a th, to guarantee* od *warrant a th, to answer for a th*; jdm ~ s, daß *to guarantee to a p that* ‖ e–n ~n stellen *to give security* (*for a th*) ‖ er muß zwei Mitglieder als ~n h *he must be vouched for by two members*

b·ürgen vi [h] ⟨jur⟩ (→ Bürge) **1.** ~ f jdn *to be bail, to go bail* (od *to stand surety*) *for a p* (od *a p's appearance*) **2.** ~ f etw *to give security for a th* (*for a debt*); *to answer* (od *vouch*) *for a th*; *to guarantee* (od *warrant*) *a th*; jdm ~ f etw *to answer to a p for a th*; wer bürgt mir für s–e Ehrlichkeit (*or* daß er ehrlich ist)? *who answers for his honesty*? *who warrents him honest*? (jdm) dafür ~, daß .. *to guarantee to a p*) *that* .. **|** ⟨übtr⟩ (S) *to guarantee a th* (*the training guarantees rapid progress*)

B·ürger m ~s/~ **1.** (e–r Stadt) *citizen, townsman* ‖ ⟨a-engl⟩ *burgher* ‖ (~ e–s *borough*) *burgess*; Voll≈ e–r Stadt *freeman of a city*; ~ e–r St. w *to get the freedom of a city*; Mit≈ *fellow citizen* ‖ Welt≈ *citizen of the world*; → Pfahl≈, Spieß≈ **2.** (Staats≈) *citizen, commoner* **3.** (Ggs Soldat) *civilian* **4.** akademischer ~ *gownsman* (Ggs *townsman*) **5.** ⟨dero⟩ *bourgeois*; → Philister

B·ürger- [in comp] *civic*; *civil*; *citizen* **~ausschuß** m ⟨Ger hist⟩ *committee of citizens* **~brief** m *certificate of burgess-ship*; ⟨Am⟩ *c. of citizenship*; (of aliens) *letter of naturalization* **~eid** m *freeman's oath* **~garde** f ⟨Fr hist⟩ *national guard, town-militia*; → Bürgerwehr **~haus** n *community centre* **~krieg** m der ~ *civil war* (*civil war was* *over*); *intestine war* ‖ der englische ~ *the* (*English*) *Civil War* (*1642 to 46*; *48–49*); der amerik. ~ *the War of Secession* (*1861–65*) **~krone** f ⟨ant⟩ *civic crown* **~kunde** f (Staats≗) *civics* [pl] **~mädchen** n *girl of the middle classes* **~meister** m ⟨a–engl⟩ *burgomaster*; ⟨Ger a.⟩ *Bürgermeister*; Ober≗ *Oberbürgermeister*; ⟨Fr⟩ *maire* ‖ Amt e–s ~s *burgomastership* | ⟨engl⟩ *mayor*; (of London, York & Dublin) *Lord Mayor*; Amt, Würde, Amtszeit e–s ~s *mayoralty* **~pflicht** f *civic duty*; *duty of a citizen* **~recht** n *citizenship*, *burgess-ship*; *civic rights* [pl], *freedom of a city* ‖ ⟨a-engl⟩ *burghership* ‖ das ~ erwerben *to get the freedom of a city*; jdm das ~ verleihen *to make a p free of a city* ‖ → naturalisieren ‖ ~surkunde [f] *certificate of naturalization* **~schule** f ⟨Ger (bis 1918)⟩ *middle-class school*, *higher-grade elementary school*, *central school* ‖ höhere ~ *lower-grade secondary school* **~sinn** m *civil* od *public spirit* **~stand** m = Bürgertum **~steig** m *pavement*; *causeway*; ⟨bes Am⟩ *banquette*, *sidewalk* **~steuer** f *rate* **~stolz** m *civic pride* **~tugend** f *civic virtue* **~vorsteher** m *town-councillor* **~wehr** f ⟨mil⟩ *militia*; ⟨mod⟩ *Local Defence Volunteers* [pl] (abbr *L. D. V.*)

b·ürgerlich I. a **1.** (dem Bürgerstand angehörig) **a.** *civil* (*liberty*, *life*, *society*, etc.); *civic* (*activity*, *virtue*; *guest*) **b.** (⟨a.⟩ ~e Mitte) *middle class* ‖ (Ggs sozialistisch) *non-socialist*; *bourgeois* (*government*) **c.** ~es Drama ⟨Lit⟩ *domestic drama*; ~e Tragödie *domestic tragedy* ‖ ~es Gesetzbuch ⟨jur⟩ *civil code*; ⟨Ger⟩ (abbr BGB) *the German Civil Code* ‖ ~es Jahr *civil year* ‖ ~es Recht *civil law* **2.** (Ggs militärisch, geistlich) *civilian*, *nonmilitary*; *civil* **3.** (dem Bürger eigentümlich) *characteristic of the citizen* od *middle class* ‖ *plain*, *simple*, *unpretentious* ‖ ~e Küche *plain cooking* ‖ ⟨dero⟩ *bourgeois* **II.** [adv] wir essen ~ *we prefer plain cooking*; sie kann ~ kochen *she understands plain cooking* **B·ürgerliche** [der ~, ein ~r] ~n/~n *commoner*

B·ürgers- [in comp] *middle class* .. **~frau** *woman belonging to the middle class* **~leute** [pl] *middle class people*, *townspeople* **~mann** m *townsman*, *citizen* **~tochter** f *daughter of a citizen*

B·ürgerschaft f ~/~en *citizens* [pl]; *townspeople* ‖ ⟨univ⟩ *town*; ~ u Studentenschaft *town and gown*

B·ürgertum n *rank* od *status of a citizen*; *citizenship* ‖ [konkr] *citizens*, *middle-classes* [pl] ‖ ⟨dero⟩ *bourgeoisie*; *habits and modes* [pl] *of thought of the middle classes*

B·ürgschaft f ⟨jur⟩ **1.** (Kaution im Strafrecht) (f jdn *for a p*); ~ leisten f jdn *to go bail*, *to stand surety for a p* (od *for a p's appearance*); → bürgen 1. ‖ die ~ wurde abgelehnt *bail was refused*; jdn gegen ~ freilassen *to release a p on bail* od *bond*; jdn durch ~ aus der Haft befreien *to bail a p out*; gegen ~ aus der Haft entlassen ⟨jur⟩ *to allow bail*; ~ übernehmen *to act as surety* ‖ ~ zulassend *bailable* (*crime*); gegen ~ freizulassen(d) *bailable* (*prisoner*); Freilassung gegen ~ *bailment* **2.** ⟨Zivilrecht & übtr⟩ (*contract of*) *guarantee* (od *-ty*); (f etw *of a th* [*of peace*]); *security* (f etw *for a th*) ‖ ⟨bank⟩ (*deed of*) *suretyship* ‖ ~ leisten *to give security* (*for a th*); ~ leisten f etw *to guarantee* (od *warrant*) *a th*; → bürgen 2. ‖ jd, dem ~ gegeben wird *guarantee* ‖ → Bodmerei

B·ürgschafts- ⟨jur⟩ **≗fähig** a *bailable* (*crime*) **~gesellschaft** f *surety company* **~leistung** f *suretyship*; *sponsorship*; *the giving of security* **~schein** m *bail-bond*; *bond*, *security-bond*, *deed of suretyship* **~vertrag** m *contract of guarantee* (od *-ty*); *contract of surety*

Burg·und n ⟨Fr⟩ *Burgundy*

Burg·under m ~s/~ *Burgundian* **Burg·under** m ~s/~, ~wein *Burgundy*, *Burgundywine*; deutscher ~ *German Burgundy* ‖ ~farbe [f], ~rot [n] *Burgundy* **burg·undisch** a *Burgundian*

Bur·iti f ⟨bot⟩ *South American fanpalm*

Burj·äten [pl] (Mongol. Volk in Ostsibirien) *Buriats*, *Buryats* [pl] **burj·ätisch** a *Buriat*(*ic*)

B·urka m (russ. Mantel) *burka*

B·urko f (Schleier) *burka*, *burko*

burl·esk a ⟨Lit⟩ *burlesque*; *mock-heroic*; ~e Darstellung *burlesque* ‖ (etw) ~ darstellen *or* behandeln *to burlesque* **Burl·eske** f ~/~n **1.** ⟨Lit & theat⟩ *burlesque*; heroische ~ *mock-heroic* **2.** ⟨mus⟩ *burlesca*

B·urma n → Birma

B·urnus m ~/–sse (orient. Mantel) *burnous*(*e*)

Bür·o n ~s/~s **1.** † = Schreibtisch **2.** *office*; ⟨Am⟩ *bureau* ⟨a. hot⟩ ‖ (amtliches ~) ⟨pol & scient⟩ *bureau*; → Amt ‖ Auskunfts≗ *information b.*; Reise≗ *travel b.*; Stellenvermittlungs≗ *employment b.* **~angestellter** m *clerk* **~arbeit** f *desk-work* **~beamte** m *clerk*; *official*; ⟨Am⟩ *officer* **~bedarf** m *office supplies* (od *requirements*, *appliances*) pl **~chef** m *head-clerk*, *head* od *chief of an office* ‖ ~ der *Quarter Sessions* ⟨engl⟩ *Clerk of the Peace* **~diener** m *office-boy* **~direktor** m *chief clerk*; des *H. L.* ⟨engl⟩ *Clerk of the Parliaments* **~hilfe** f (P) *office hand* **~klammer** f *letter* od *paper clip* **~maschine** f *business*, *desk* od *office machine* **~mensch** m *office-drudge* **~personal** n *staff*; *employees* [pl] **~schluß** m *closing-time* **~sprache** f *officialese* **~stunde** f *office-hour* **~tätigkeit** f *desk-work* **~vorsteher** m = Bürochef

Bürokr·at m ~en/~en ⟨dero⟩ *bureaucrat*, *red-tapist*; *jack-in-office*; ⟨fam fig⟩ *barnacle* **Bürokrat·ie** f ~/~n **1.** [abstr] *bureaucracy*, *officialism* ‖ (bes ihr Unwesen) *bureaucratism* **2.** [konkr] *officials* [pl], *officialdom* ‖ → Bürokratismus **bürokr·atisch 1.** a *bureaucratic* (*system*) ‖ ⟨dero⟩ *red-tape* **2.** adv *bureaucratically* **Bürokrat·ismus** m [abstr] **1.** = Bürokratie 1. **2.** ⟨mst dero⟩ *officialdom*, *red-tapism*; *bumbledom*, *beadledom* ‖ wie weit der ~ gehen kann *the extent to which officialdom can go*

b·urren vi [h] (of partridges) *to drum*

B·ursch, ~e m ~en/~en **1.** ⟨univ⟩ (Ggs Fuchs) *senior*; *senior undergraduate*; → Leib≗ **2.** ⟨übtr⟩ *chap*, *fellow*; *comrade*; ⟨fam⟩ *galoot*; *josser* ‖ ⟨Am, fam⟩ *gink*; ⟨AInd⟩ [oft in comp] *wallah*; ⟨sl⟩ *blighter*, *bloke*, *dog*; *johnny*; ⟨Am⟩ *guy*, *pup* ‖ tapferer ~ *hearty*; junger ~ *boy*, *lad*, *youth* ‖ heller ~ *live wire* ‖ Bauern≗ *country lad*, ⟨poet⟩ *swain* ‖ → Lauf≗; Schlaf≗ **3. a.** *journeyman*, → Handwerks≗ **b.** ⟨mil⟩ *batman* (bei e–m Offizier *to an officer*), *officer's servant* **4.** ⟨dero⟩ *bird*, *customer*; ein seltsamer ~ *a queer bird*, ⟨sl⟩ *a rum cove*; ein alter ~ *an old buffer* (od *bird*) ‖ ⟨cont⟩ *fellow* (*the f. is drunk*); der blöde ~ ⟨sl⟩ *the blighter*; ein übler ~ ⟨sl⟩ *a bad lot* od *egg*

B·ürschchen n, ~s/~ *little boy* od *lad*; *laddie* ‖ ⟨hum⟩ *rogue*, *rascal*; ⟨dero⟩ *stripling*; *old boy*; freches ~ *whipper-snapper*

b·urschenhaft a (studentenhaft) *student-like*

B·urschenschaft f ⟨Ger univ⟩ *students' association* od *fraternity based on national principles* **B·urschenschafter** m *member of a Burschenschaft*

burschik·os 1. a *student-like*; *jolly*, *free and easy*, *gay* (*life*); *devil-may-care* ‖ ~e Redensarten *homely expressions of a style which is called slang* (*Thack.*) ‖ ⟨dero⟩ *unmannerly*; *ostentatious*, *showy* (*manners*) **2.** adv *freely* ‖ ⟨dero⟩ *coarsely*; → auffällig

B·urse f ⟨univ⟩ *hostel*; ⟨Am⟩ *dormitory*

B·ürste f ~/~n **1.** *brush*; Haar≗ *hair-brush*; Roßhaar≗ *horsehair-brush*; Draht≗ *wire-brush* ‖ Kleider≗ *clothes-brush*; Hut≗ *hat-brush*; Stiefel≗ *blacking-brush*; Zahn≗ *tooth-brush*;

→ Bohner≗; Scheuer≗ ‖ (~ f Vergolder) *mop* **2.** *bristly hair* **3.** (Schnurrbart) *tooth-brush* **4.** ⟨tech & el⟩ *brush* **|** ⟨comp⟩ (verstellbar) *designation reading brush* (*set optionally*); Abfühl≗ *reading br.*; Vergleicher≗ *comparing br.*; *br. for punch comparison*

b·ürsten I. vt [h] **1.** (Hut etc) *to brush*; sich die Zähne ~ *to brush one's teeth* ‖ glatt~ *to brush up*; rein~ *to brush clean* ‖ sich ~ *to brush o.s.* **2.** °~ *to drink*; ⟨sl⟩ *to mop* **3.** °⟨sex⟩ *to bounce* **II.** ≗ n *brushing, brush*; Glatt≗ *brush-up*

B·ürsten- ~abzug m ⟨typ⟩ *brush-proof* **≗artig** a ⟨el⟩ ~e Entladung *brush, brush-discharge* **~binder** m **1.** *brush-maker* ‖ °laufen wie ein ~ *to put one's best foot* od *leg foremost*; saufen wie ein ~ *to drink like a fish* **2.** ⟨ent⟩ (a. ~raupe) *tussock caterpillar*; → Bürstenspinner **~halter** m *brush-holder* **~rad** n ⟨tech⟩ *brush-wheel* **~scheibe** f ⟨tech⟩ *circular revolving brush* **~walze** f *brush-roller* **~waren** f [pl] *brushware*

B·ürzel m ~s/~ **1.** ⟨orn⟩ *rump*; ⟨scient⟩ *uropygium* [L] **2.** ⟨hunt⟩ *tail* (*of a badger*, etc.) **~drüse** f ⟨orn⟩ *uropygial gland*

Bus m (= Omnibus) *bus* ‖ im ~ fahren ⟨fam⟩ *to bus it* **|** ~fahrer [m] (*bus*) *driver*, ⟨Am⟩ *operator*; ~haltestelle [f] *bus stop*

B·usch m ~(e)s/≗e **A. 1.** (Strauch) **a.** *bush, shrub*; Dorn≗ *thorn, thorn-bush* **b.** Büsche, ~dickicht *shrubbery*; *brushwood, coppice, cospe, underwood*; ⟨Am⟩ *brush* **2.** (Wald) *wood* ‖ (Urwald) *bush* (*to live in the b.*) **3.** ⟨fig⟩ **auf** den ~ klopfen (sc um etw herauszubekommen) *to draw a* od *one's bow at a venture*; bei jdm auf den ~ .. *to sound a p*; vgl. Brei l. ‖ wie Zieten **aus** dem ~ (*to appear*) quite *unexpatedly* ‖ sich (seitwärts) in die Büsche schlagen *to slope off, to slip away*; ⟨euphem⟩ *to look upon a hedge, to go round the corner* **B.** (Büschel) **1.** *bunch of twigs* od *of foliage*; *cluster*; ˣ = Blumenstrauß ‖ ⟨hunt⟩ → Bruch D. 4. **2.** ⟨übtr⟩ (Feder≗) *plume* (*of a helmet*) **~dickicht** n = Busch A. 1. b.; ⟨geog⟩ *scrub* **~egge** f *bush-harrow* **~hemd** n (geblümt) *floral shirt* **~holz** n *underwood, brush-wood, copse-wood* **~hornblattwespe** f ⟨ent⟩ *pine saw-fly* **~katze** f ⟨zoo⟩ *bush-cat, serval* **~klepper** m *bushranger, highwayman* (*in the bush*) **~kohle** f = Holzkohle **~krieg** m *bush-fighting* **~land** n ⟨geog⟩ *scrub*, ⟨bes Am⟩ *brushland* **~männer** m [pl] (afr. Stamm) *Bushmen* [pl]; ~mann [m] *bushman* **~meister** m ⟨zoo⟩ (brasil. Giftschlange) *bush-master* **~messer** n *bush knife, cutlass*; ⟨Burma⟩ *dah*; ⟨Malaya⟩ *panga parang*; ⟨L Am⟩ *machete* **~neger** m *maroon* **~obst** n *bush fruit* **~pause** f: e–e ~ m *or* einlegen ⟨euph⟩ *to pluck a rose, to gather violets, to pick* od *do a sweet pea* **~pflanzung** f *shrubbery* **~wald** m *brushwood*; ⟨geog⟩ *scrub* **~werk** n *brushwood*; *shrubs, bushes* [pl] **~windröschen** n ⟨bot⟩ *wind-flower*; *wood-anemone*

B·üschel m & n ~s/~ **1.** *bunch, cluster*; ~ Haare *bunch* (od *tuft, wisp*) *of hair*; ~ Stroh, Gras *wisp of straw, grass*; *rip* (*of hay*) ‖ kl ~ ⟨bot⟩ *fascicle, fascicule* **|** ~ bilden (S) *to tuft* ‖ (etw) in ~n binden *to bunch*; in ~n gruppiert *clustered*; in ~n hängen um *to wisp about*; in ~n wachsen *to cluster* (um *round*); in ~n wachsend *bunchy, clustery, tufty* ‖ (etw) mit ~n versehen *to tuft*; mit ~n versehen [a] *tufted* **2.** Feder≗ *tuft of feathers*; (als Schmuck) *plume, aigrette* **3.** Strahlen≗ ⟨el⟩ *brush*; ⟨geom⟩ *pencil*

b·üschelförmig, b·üschelig a *clustered*; *tufted, tufty*; ⟨bot⟩ *fascicular* (*-late*) **B·üschellicht** n *brush-light*

b·uschig a *bushy, shrubby* ‖ *shaggy* (*hair*)

B·üse f ~/~n ⟨mar⟩ *small boat, fishing-boat* (f Heringe)

B·usen m ~s/~ **1.** [mst sg] *bosom, breast*; (weiblicher ~) *breast*(*s*) ‖ an jds ~ sinken *to sink on a p's breast* ‖ °auf den ~ kommt's an ⟨Am sl⟩ *it's what's up front that counts*; vgl: vorn u hinten alles dran **2.** ⟨übtr⟩ (Inneres, Seele) *bosom, breast*; *heart, soul* ‖ (Gefühl) im ~ hegen *to cherish in one's bosom* od *mind*; die Schlange der Eifersucht am ~ nähren *to nurse the worm of jealousy in one's breast*; (etw) im ~ verschließen *to lock in one's bosom* **3.** ⟨tail⟩ *bosom, breast*; *shirt-frill*; (etw) in den ~ stecken *to put into the bosom* **4.** (Meer≗) *gulf, bay* **~freund** m *bosom-friend*; *chum* **~nadel** f *breast* (od *scarf*)*-pin*

°**Bus·ento** m (⟨hum⟩ = Busen) wogender ~ ⟨vulg⟩ *panters* pl ‖ ⟨eig⟩ Fluß in Italien

Bush·ido n (Ehrenkodex in Japan) *bushido*

-b·usig a [in comp] *bosomed*; voll~ *big-b.*

Buß- (→ Buße) [in comp] ⟨ec⟩ *penitential, penitentiary* **~buch** n ⟨ec⟩ *penitential* **≗fertig** a *penitent, repentant*; *contrite* **~fertigkeit** f *penitence, repentance*; *contrition* **~gang** m → Bittgang **~lied** n *penitential chant* **~prediger** m *preacher of penitence*; *Lenten pr.* **~predigt** f *penitential homily* (od *sermon*) **~psalmen** m [pl] *penitential psalms* **~tag** m *day of repentance*; *fast-day*; Buß- u Bettag *day of prayer and repentance* **~übung** f *penitential exercise* **~zahlung** f *fine* **~zelle** f *penitentiary cell* **~zucht** f *penitential discipline*

B·ussard m ~s/~e ⟨orn⟩ *buzzard*, → d. Bd. I

B·uße f ~/~n **1.** ⟨jur⟩ (Sühne) *atonement, payment, reckoning* (f etw *for a th*), *expiation* (f ein Verbrechen *of a crime*); jdm e–e ~ auferlegen f etw *to make a p atone for a th*; sich e–e ~ auferlegen *to set o.s. a penance* (f *for*) ‖ Geld≗ *fine, mulct*; *forfeit*; jdm e–e ~ auferlegen, jdn z e–r ~ verurteilen *to fine* od *mulct a p*; er wurde z e–r ~ v £ 10 verurteilt *he was fined £10* ‖ ~ auf sich nehmen *to assume a penance* ‖ → Entschädigung, Ersatz, Genugtuung **2.** ⟨ec⟩ *penance, penitence, repentance*; ~ tun *to do penance*; jdm ~ auferlegen *to subject a p to penance, to penance a p*; sich ~ auferlegen *to penance o.s.* ‖ → Reue **|** ⟨R. C.⟩ (*Sakrament*) *penance*

ˣ**Buss(e)l** n = Busserl

b·üßen vt/i [h] **I.** vt **1.** ˣ = wiederherstellen **2.** (Missetat etc) *to expiate* (*a th*); *to atone, to make amends for* (*a th*); *to make* (*an*) *atonement for* (*a th*) ‖ er büßte es mit £ 10 *he was fined £10 for it* ‖ (Dummheit etc) *to pay* (od *suffer*) *for* (*a th*); er büßte es mit dem Leben *he atoned* od *paid for it with his life*; du wirst es ~ müssen *you'll be in for it*; ⟨sl⟩ *you'll get it in the neck*; das sollst du mir ~ *you shall smart* od *suffer for it*; *I'll pay you back in your own coin* **3.** *⟨ec⟩ (Sünde) *to undergo penance for* (*a th*) **4.** ˣ = durch Besprechung heilen, → besprechen A. 1. **II.** vi **1.** ~ f etw *to atone for a th*; *to pay* (od *suffer*) *for a th*; schwer ~ müssen f etw *to be punished severely for a th* ‖ jdn ~ l f etw *to make a p atone* (od *pay*) *for a th*; ich will ihn f die S nicht ~ l *I won't have the matter visited on him* **3.** ⟨ec⟩ *to do* od *undergo penance* (*for a th*)

B·üßer m ~s/~ *penitent* ‖ → Lücken≗ **~bank** f *penitent-form*; ⟨Am⟩ *anxious seat* od *bench* **~gewand** n *penitential robe* **~hemd** n (härenes) *hair-shirt, hair-cloth* **~schnee** m ⟨geog⟩ *variety of sérac*; [Span] *penitentes* [pl]

B·üßerin f ~/~nen *penitent*

ˣ**B·usserl** n *kiss, smack*; ⟨poet & dial⟩ *buss* ‖ jdm ein ~ geben *to kiss a p*; ⟨poet & dial⟩ *to buss a p* **|** ⟨cul⟩ (*cream-*)*meringue* Fr

Buss·ole f ~/~n ⟨mar⟩ *mariner's compass*

B·üßung f *expiation* (e–r S *of a th*)

B·üste f ~/~n **1.** (Bildnis) *bust* **2.** (weibl. Brust) *bust, bosom* **B·üstenhalter** m *brassière* [Fr], ⟨fam⟩ *bra*; *bust-bodice* (od *holder, improver*); trägerloser ~ *strapless bra*; (Oberteil e–s Bikinis) *halter* | ∼körbchen [n] *cup*; ⩪los [a] *no-bra* [attr]

Butad·ien n ∼s/ ⟨chem⟩ *butadiene*; → Buna

But·an n ⟨chem⟩ *butane* **Butan·on** n ∼s/ ⟨chem⟩ *butanone*

×**b·uten** adv *outside* (Ggs binnen *inside*) ×⩪**land** n *outland*

°**But·ike** f ∼/∼n (Fr boutique) → Budike

Butt m ∼s/∼e **1.** ⟨ich⟩ *butt, flounder, plaice*; → Heil⩪, Stein⩪ **2.** ×∼ *thickset* (od *short and thick*) *person*; *small thick animal* ‖ ×**butt** a *blunt, stumpy*

B·utte f ∼/∼n **1.** ⟨ich⟩ = Butt 1.; ⟨ich cul⟩ *brill* **2.** ×∼ *thickset woman* **3.** ⟨bot⟩ Hage⩪ *haw, hip, hep*

B·ütte, B·utte f ∼/∼n *tub, vat*; *trough*; ⟨engl⟩ *gr* ∼ (als Wein–, Biermaß [ca 572,5 l]) *butt* ‖ (Korb) *basket*; *coop* ‖ ⟨fig⟩ die Hand v der Butte (*or* Butter)! *hands off*!

°**B·uttel** f, ×**B·uddel** f ∼/∼n *bottle*

B·üttel m ∼s/∼ *apparitor, bailiff,* ⟨fam⟩ *catchpoll*; (Kirchspiel⩪) *beadle* ‖ (Henker) *Jack Ketch* ‖ ⟨derog⟩ (Polizist) *cop*

b·ütten vt [h] (etw) *to vat, to tub*

Bütten- **∼druckpapier** n *handmade printings* [pl] **∼papier** n *handmade paper with rough edge* ‖ handgeschöpftes ∼ *handmade deckle-edged paper* **∼rand** m *deckle* (*edge*), *jagged edge* ⟨a. phot⟩ **∼rede** f (*carnival*) *comic speech*

B·utter f ∼/ **1.** *butter* ‖ (un)gesalzene ∼ (*un-*)*salted b.*; Land⩪ *farmhouse b.*; geklarte ∼ *clarified b.*; Koch⩪ *cooking b.*; zerlassene ∼ (als Soße) *melted b.*; ohne ∼ frühstücken *to breakfast butterless* ‖ Rahm z ∼ schlagen, kernen *to churn cream* ‖ Brot mit ∼ bestreichen, ∼ aufs Brot schmieren *to butter bread* | die Hand v der ∼! → Butte ‖ ihm war die ∼ vom Brote gefallen *he looked perfectly blank*; *he was disagreeably disappointed* ‖ sie läßt sich nicht die ∼ vom Brote nehmen *she does not allow herself to be put upon, she keeps a stiff upper lip,* ⟨Am fam⟩ *you can't put anything over on her* ‖ das Geld zerrann wie ∼ an der Sonne *the money melted away like butter in the sun* ‖ °in ∼ ⟨fig⟩ *in apple-pie order*; ⟨Am sl⟩ *hanky-panky*; es ist alles in ∼ *everything is okay* (od *O.K.*) **2.** ⟨chem⟩ *butter*; → Kunst⩪, Schi⩪, Mahwa⩪

B·utter- [in comp] *butter–* ‖ ⟨chem⟩ *butyric, butyraceous* ⩪**artig** a *buttery*; ⟨chem⟩ *butyraceous* **∼bällchen** n *butter-pat, pat of butter* **∼baum** m **1.** *shea* **2.** (indischer) *mahwa, máhwa-tree* **∼birne** f *butter-pear, beurré* [Fr] **∼blume** f ⟨bot⟩ *buttercup* ‖ *marsh-marigold* ‖ ⟨fig⟩ (Hut) *boater* **∼brot** n *bread and butter*; ein ∼ *a slice of bread and butter*; ein belegtes ∼ *a sandwich* ‖ ⟨fig⟩ du brauchst es mir nicht immer aufs ∼ z schmieren *you need not rub it in anymore* ‖ etw f ein ∼ erwerben, kaufen *to buy* od *get a th for a song* | ∼dose [f] *sandwich box*; ∼papier [n] *grease-proof paper, sandwich paper* **∼creme** f *butter cream* **∼dose** f *b.-dish* **∼ersatz** m *b. substitute* **∼fertiger** m *b. churn* **∼faß** n *b.-cask* (od *tub*) ‖ (zum Buttern) *churn* **∼fett** n *butter-fat* **∼fisch** m ⟨ich⟩ *butterfish, spotted gunnel* **∼form** f *butter-print*; *butter-mould* **∼former** m *b.-curler* **∼frau** f *butter-woman* **∼glocke** f = Butterdose ⩪**haltig** a *butyraceous* **∼händler** m *butter-man* **∼karte** f (bei Rationierungen) *butter-ticket* **∼keks** m *milk-biscuit* **∼krebs** m ⟨zoo⟩ *crayfish after the moult* **∼kühler** m *butter-cooler* **∼land** n ⟨mar⟩ *illusionary coast* (od *island*) *produced by clouds* **∼mann** m *butter-man* **∼messer** n *butter--knife* **∼milch** f *butter-milk* **∼nuß** f *butter-nut* **∼pergament** n *butter parchment paper* **∼pilz** m = Röhrling **∼portion** f *individual pat of butter* **∼röllchen** n *butter-pat, pat* od *curl of b.* **∼säure** f ⟨chem⟩ *butyric acid*; Salz der ∼ *butyrate* **∼schmalz** n *clarified* (od *run*) *butter* ‖ *mixed fat and b.* **∼schnitte** f *slice of bread and butter* **∼semmel** f *buttered roll*; → Semmel **∼soße** f *melted* od *drawn butter* **∼weck** m, **∼wecke** f *buttered roll*

b·utt(e)rig a *buttery* ‖ ⟨chem⟩ *butyric, butyraceous* **b·uttern** vi [h] *to churn*; *to make butter*

B·üttner (vgl Bütte) m ∼s/∼ → Böttcher

Butyr·at n ⟨chem⟩ *butyrate* **Butyrom·eter** n *butyrometer*

Butz m **1.** = Butt **2.** *bugbear* **3.** = Butzen

B·utze f **1.** m = Butt, Butz **2.** f **a.** = Butte **b.** *partition of boards* ‖ *partitioned-off room*

B·utzemann m *bog(e)y* (*man*)

B·utzen m ∼s/∼ **1.** *clotted mass*; *thickened mucus*; *mucous clot*; ⟨dial⟩ *gob*; vgl Batzen **2.** (Kerngehäuse) *core* ‖ (Knospe) *butt* **3.** (Schnuppe) *snuff* **4.** ⟨min⟩ *pocket of ore*

B·utzenscheibe f *bull's eye pane*

B·utzkopf m ⟨ich⟩ *grampus*; *orc, ork*

B·ux m → Buchs **∼baum** m ⟨bot⟩ *box-tree*

°**B·uxe, B·üx** f *buckskin breeches, buckskins* [pl] ‖ = Hose ⟨fam⟩ *pants* pl, ⟨sl⟩ *bags* pl

Büxe f → Büchse

°**buxen** vt [h] (stehlen) ⟨sl⟩ *to filch, pinch*

Buxteh·ude n ⟨Ger⟩ (Stadt); ⟨fig⟩ *Gotham*

B·yssus m **1.** ⟨hist⟩ (Leinengewebe) *byssus* **2.** ⟨zoo⟩ (Muschelseide) *byssus*

Byzant·iner m ∼s/∼ ⟨ant⟩ *Byzantine* **byzant·inisch** a ⟨arts, arch⟩ *Byzantine* (*round arch, cross, dome,* etc) ‖ ⟨fig⟩ (kriechend) *obsequious* **Byzantin·ismus** m ∼/ *Byzantinism* ‖ ⟨fig⟩ *sycophancy* †**Byz·anz** n *Byzantium, Constantinople*

C

Unter C (bzw. Ch) nicht anzutreffende Wörter suche man unter K, Z (bzw. Sch)

C, c [tseː] n ∼/∼ **1.** (Buchstabe) C, c; → Abc ‖ [∼ lebt in deutschen Wörtern nur in den Verbindungen ch, ck & sch]. Die Aussprache in fremden Wörtern ist 1. vor a, o, u & allen Konsonanten [k] 2. vor e & i [ts]; in jüngeren frz u engl Wörtern [s], in italienischen [tʃ] schreibe Bacchus mit 2 c *B. is spelt with 2 c* **2.** ⟨mus⟩ C *do* [It] ‖ C-dur *C major*, c-Moll *c minor* ‖ ∼ Schlüssel *C clef* **3.** C-Falter m *comma butterfly*

Caboch·on [–ˈʃɔ̃ː] m Fr (Rundschliff) *cabachon*

Cab·oclo m (Mischling v Weißen u Indianern) *caboclo*

Cachenez [kɑʃneː] n [Fr] ∼/∼ *scarf for the neck*

Cacho·u [kɑˈʃuː] n [Fr] ∼s/∼s *cachou* [Fr]

C·addie [ˈkædi] m ⟨engl⟩ ∼s/∼s ⟨golf⟩ *caddie*

C·adiz n ⟨Span⟩ (Stadt) *Cadiz*

Café [kɑˈfeː] n [Fr] ∼s/∼s *café*, ⟨Am⟩ *coffee--shop*

Cagot [kɑˈgoː] m [Fr] *cagot*

Cairn [kɛən] n [engl] (Hügelgrab) *cairn*

Caiss·on [kɛːˈsɔ̃] m [Fr] ∼s/∼s (Senkkasten z Tiefbau unter Wasser) *caisson* [Fr] | ∼arbeiter [m] ⟨fam⟩ *ground* od *sand hog*

Cake walk [ˈkeik wɔːk] m [engl] (Negertanz) *cake-walk*

Cal·ais [kɑˈlɛ] n ⟨Fr⟩ (Stadt)

Calembour(g) [kalɑ̃ˈbuːr] m [Fr] *calembour* [Fr], *pun*

Callgirl n [ˈkɔːlgəːl] ∼s/∼s (Prostituierte mit Telephonanschluß) *call-girl*

Cambr·ai [kɑ̃'brɛ] n ⟨Fr⟩ (Stadt)
C·ambric ['keimbrik] m [engl] (Leinengewebe) *cambric*
Cambridge ['keimbridʒ] ⟨Engl⟩ Universitätsstadt **C·ambridgestudent** m ⟨engl⟩ *Cantabrigian*, ⟨fam⟩ *Cantab*
Camembert ['kamɑ̃bɛ:r] m [Fr] ∼s/∼s *camembert* [Fr]
C·amholz n (Rotholz) *camwood*
Cam·orra f [It] (Geheimbund) *camorra* [It]
Camoufl·age [kamu'flɑ:ʒə] f [Fr] *camouflage*
Camp·agna (Römische) f *Campagna*
Campan·ile m [It] ∼/∼ ⟨arch⟩ (alleinstehender Glockenturm) *campanile* [It]
Camp·echeholz n *campeachy wood*
c·ampen ['kæmpən] vi [h] *to camp* **C·amping-∼anhänger** m (P) *camping fan* | (S) *trailer*, ⟨Am⟩ *caravan* **∼platz** m *camping site*, ⟨mot⟩ *caravan site*
Can·aille [ka'nɑj; ka'naljə] f [Fr] **1.** die ∼ *the canaille* [Fr], *mob, rabble* **2.** (P) *scoundrel*
Can·angaöl n *ihlang-ihlang*
Canapé n ∼s/∼s Fr ⟨cul⟩ *canapé*
C·andia n → Kreta
C·andlenußbaum ['kændl–] m *candle-nut tree*
Canevas [kan'vɑ] m [Fr] *canvas*
C·añon ['kænjən] m [engl] ∼s/∼s *canyon*
Cant [kænt] m ⟨engl⟩ ∼s/ *cant*
cant·abile a [It] *cantabile* [It] **C·antus** m [L] ⟨bes ec⟩ *cantus* [L]; *chant, song*; e–n ∼ steigen l *to strike up a song*
Cape [keip] n [engl] ∼s/∼s *cape*
C·apri ⟨It⟩ (Insel)
Capt·atio benevol·entiae f [L] *captation*
Car alp·in [kar al'pɛ̃] m ∼s/∼s [Sw] ⟨m. m.⟩ *char-à-banc(s)*
C·aravan ['karavan] m ∼s/∼s ⟨mot⟩ (Wohnwagen-Anhänger) *trailer*, ⟨Am⟩ *caravan*
Carbox·yl-Ende n der Peptidkette ⟨biochem⟩ *C-terminal*
C·aritas f [L] *charity* ‖ ⟨R. C.⟩ ∼verband [m] (*Catholic*) *Charity Organization Society* (abbr *C. O. S.*) **caritat·iv** a *charitable*; *charity* ..
Carn·et n [–'nɛ] ∼s/∼s Fr ⟨aero⟩ (als Ausweis); ⟨aero–mot⟩ (f. internat. Tanken); ⟨mot–cust⟩ (f freien Grenzübertritt) *carnet*
Carot·in n ∼s/ *carotene*
Carpent·aria-Golf m (Australien) *Gulf of C.*
Carr·ara n ⟨It⟩ (Stadt) *Carrara*
carte [kart] f [Fr] *card* ‖ à la ∼ (Ggs table d'hôte) *à la carte* ‖ ∼ *blanche* [Fr] *full power of action, carte blanche*
Casabl·anca n (Hafenstadt in Marokko)
Cäs·aren- **∼wahnsinn** m *Caesarean madness*
C·atboat ['kætbout] n [engl] ∼s/∼s (kl Segelboot) *catboat*
Causerie [ko:z'ri] f [Fr] ⟨Lit⟩ *causerie*
Causeuse [ko:'zøzə] f [Fr] *small sofa, causeuse*
Cay·enne [kɑ'jɛn] n (Hptst. v Fr.-Guayana) **∼pfeffer** [ka'jen–] m *cayenne* (*pepper*)
Cédille [se'dij] f [Fr] ∼/ *cedilla* [Span]
Cel·ebes n [ts–] (Sundainsel) *Celebes*
Cel·esta [tʃe'lesta] f [It] ∼/∼s & –ten ⟨mus⟩ (Tasteninstrument) *celesta*
Cell·ist [tʃɛ'list] m [It] ∼en/∼en ⟨mus⟩ *cellist*
C·ello ['tʃelo] n [It] ∼s/∼s (*violon*)*cello*
Celloph·an [ts–] n ∼s/ *cellophane*
C·elsius (A. ∼, † 1744) ∼skala *centigrade* (od *Celsius*) *scale*; ∼ thermometer *centigrade thermometer*; 30 Grad ∼ *30 degrees centigrade* (abbr 30° C)
Cembal·ist [tʃemba'list] m *player of a harpsichord* **C·embalo** ['tʃembalo] n [It] ∼s/∼s ⟨mus⟩ *harpsichord, cembalo*; ∼ spielen *to play on the harpsichord*
Cen·is, Mont [mɔ̃ se'ni] m → Mont Cenis
C·ensus m ∼/∼ (Vokszählung) *census*
Cent [sent] **1.** m (niederl. = $^{1}/_{100}$ Gulden) *cent* ‖ ⟨Am⟩ (= $^{1}/_{100}$ Dollar) *cent*; 5-∼-Stück *picayune*, ⟨sl⟩ *jitney*; silb. 10-∼-Stück *dime*, *short bit*; 25-∼-Stück *quarter*; Summe v $12^{1}/_{2}$ ∼ ⟨Am⟩ *bit* **2.** n = Zent **Cent·esimo** [tʃen'tezimo] m [It = $^{1}/_{100}$ Lira] *centesimo* **Cent·ime** [sɑ̃'ti:m] m [Fr = $^{1}/_{100}$ Franc] *centime* **C·éntimo** ['θentimo] m [Span. = $^{1}/_{100}$ Peseta] *centimo*
Cercle ['serkl] m [Fr] *reception*; ∼ halten *to hold a r*
ces, Ces n ∼/∼ ⟨mus⟩ *C flat*
Cest·oden [pl] ⟨zoo⟩ (Bandwürmer) *cestoids*
Cetac·een [pl] ⟨zoo⟩ (Wale) *cetaceans* [pl]
Cet·an n ∼s/ *cetane* | ∼zahl [f] ⟨mot⟩ *c. rating*
C·etische Alpen [ts–] pl *eastern part of the Central Alps*
Cev·ennen [s–] pl *Cévennes* pl
C·eylon ['tsailɔn] n : Bewohner v ∼, aus ∼ *Sin(g)halese, Cingalese* | ∼tee [m] *Ceylon tea*
CGS-System n (abbr f Centimeter-Gramm-Sekunden-System) *C.G.S. system*
ch, Ch [tse'hɑ:] n ∼/∼ Aussprache: **1.** in deutschen Wörtern **a.** nach hellen Vokalen [ç]; z B ich; lechzen; aber: Orchester [ɔr'kestə] **b.** nach dunklen [x], z B auch; doch **2.** in Lehn- u Fremdwörtern **a.** in griech-lat. vor hellen Vokalen [ç], z B Chemie, Chinin ‖ vor dunklen Vokalen & l, r [k]; z B Chaos, Charakter; Cholera; Chlor; Christ **b.** in englischen [tʃ]; z B Cherry Brandy **c.** in französischen [ʃ]; z B Chiffon **d.** in intalienischen [k]; z B Chianti
Chac·onne [ʃa'kɔn] f [Fr] ∼/∼s & ∼n ⟨hist mus⟩ (Tanz) *chaconne*
Chagr·inleder [ʃɑ'grɛ̃–] n *shagreen*
Ch·aiberpaß [k–] m → Khaibarpaß
Chaise ['ʃɛ:zə] f [Fr] ∼/∼n *chaise* ∼longue ['ʃɛz'lɔ̃g] f ∼/∼n *long chair*; *couch, lounge*
Chal·aza [k] f ⟨zoo & bot⟩ *chalaza*
†Chald·äa [ç–] n (später = Babylonien) *Chaldea*
Chald·äer [k] m ∼s/∼ ⟨ant⟩ *Chaldean* **chald·äisch** a *Chaldean, Chaldee*
Ch·alko- [k-] (Kupfer-) *chalco-*
Chalzed·on [k] m ∼s/∼e ⟨minr⟩ *chalcedony*: heller ∼ *mocha*; → Karneol, Onyx, Sarder
Cham·äleon [k] n ∼s/∼s ⟨zoo & fig⟩ *chameleon*
Chamois [ʃa'mwa] n (weiches [urspr] Gemsenleder) → chamois | [a] ∼ ⟨phot⟩ (leicht getönt) *cream*
Champ·agne [ʃɑ̃m'paɲə] f *Champagne*, **∼r** m (Wein) *champagne* **Champ·agner** [ʃam'panjə] m ∼s/∼ (Schaumwein) *champagne* (herb, trocken *dry*) **∼bowle** f *ch.-cup* **∼flasche** f *champagne-bottle* **∼pfropfen** m *tampion*
Ch·ampignon ['ʃampinjɔ̃] m ∼s/∼s ⟨bot⟩ (*cultivated* od *button*) *mushroom*
Champlevé [ʃɑ̃lə've] n [Fr] (Grubenschmelz) *champlevé enamel* (Ggs Cloisonné)
Chams·in [k] m ∼s/∼s (heißer ägypt. Südwind) *k(h)amsin*
Chance ['ʃɑ̃sə] f [Fr], ∼/∼n *chance, opportunity*; ⟨Am⟩ *break*; e–e ∼ ausnutzen *to take advantage of an opportunity*; e–e ∼ vorübergehen l *to miss an opportunity*: gib ihm e–e ∼ *give him a chance*; er hat s–e ∼ *he has his time*; er hat nicht die geringste ∼ z gewinnen ⟨fam⟩ *he hasn't a show of winning*; neben jdm e–e ∼ h ⟨bes Am⟩ *to have a look-in with a p* | ∼n [pl] *chances of success, prospects* (auf *of*); *odds* [pl]; ∼n h *to have prospects*, k–e ∼n h *to have no prospects*; ⟨sl⟩ *to have not an earthly*; die ∼n waren gegen (für) ihn *the odds were against him* (*in his favour*); die ∼n stehen 10 : 1 *the odds are 10 to 1*; die ∼n sind gleich *it's a toss-up*; → Schanze **≈nvoll** a ⟨exch⟩ *promising, hopeful*
change·ant [ʃɑ̃'ʒɑ̃] **1.** a [Fr] (schillernd) *iridescent, shot* (*silk*) **2.** ≈ m *shot-silk* **Change·antstoff** m *shot fabric* od *material*

chang·ieren [ʃɑ̃ˈʒiːrən] vi [h] **1.** (schillern) *to be iridescent* ‖ (of silk) *to be shot* **2.** ⟨hors⟩ (of rider) *to change hand*; (horse) *to change step* **Chans·on** [ʃɑ̃ˈsɔ̃] f, n [Fr] ⟨Fr Lit⟩ *chanson, song* **Chanson·ette** [ʃɑ̃sɔˈnetə] f [Fr] ~/~n *female singer in a cabaret* (od *variety theatre*)

Ch·antefable [ˈʃɑ̃təˈfabl] f Fr (*prose tale with laisses of verse*) *chantefable* (*e. g. Aucassin et Nicolette*)

Chaos [ˈkaːɔs] n ~/ *chaos*; *utter confusion* ‖ ⟨übtr⟩ *muddle*; *tumult*; *welter* (*of passions*, etc.) **cha·otisch** [k–] **1.** a *chaotic*; *confused*; *muddled*; ⟨Am sl⟩ *snafu* **2.** adv *chaotically*

Chapeau cl·aque [ʃapoˈklak] m [Fr] *opera* (od *crush*)*-hat*

Chaper·on [ʃaˈprɔ̃] m [Fr] ~s/~s **1.** ⟨hist⟩ (Kopfbedeckung) *chaperon* **2.** ⟨fig⟩ (Anstands–P) *chaperon*; jdm als ~ dienen *to chaperon a p*

chaptalis·ieren [ʃ–] vt (nach A. Chaptal, † 1832) [h] (entsäuern) (Wein) *to chaptalize*

Char·akter [k–] m ~s/Charakt·ere **A.** (S) **1.** (Schriftzeichen) [oft pl –t·ere] *character, letter* **2.** (Merkmal) *characteristic* od *distinctive mark* (od *stamp*; *quality*); *characteristic*; *trait*; *characteristic features* [pl]; *character, nature* (*of a region, a mineral, a history, an art, a novel,* (etc.); dem Krieg den ~ e–s Kreuzzugs verleihen *to give to the war the character of a crusade* ‖ [Adj. + ~ oft durch abgeleitetes Abstraktum auf *–ness*] würziger ~ *spiciness*, finsterer ~ *gloominess*, tragischer ~ *tragicalness* **B.** (P) **1.** (natürliche Anlage) *character, disposition, fibre, spirit, nature, aptitude*, (⟨Am sl⟩ *make-up*) (*of a p, a race*, etc.); ererbter ~ *strain*; Züge heroischen ~s *features* [pl] *cast in a heroic mould*; ein Mann v rauhem ~ *a man of coarse fibre* ‖ s–n wahren ~ zeigen *to unmask* **2.** (sittliche Veranlagung) *character*; *stamina*; ein Mann v ~ *a man of character*; ohne ~ *characterless* **3.** (amtl. Eigenschaft) *capacity, character, position, official rank*; sein königlicher ~ *his royal ch.* ‖ ⟨mil⟩ Offiziers≃ *brevet*; ein Hauptmann mit dem ~ e–s Majors *a brevet major*; den ~ e–s Majors erhalten *to be breveted a major* **4.** [konkr] (P) [oft pl –tere] *character, personality*; er ist ein ~ *he is quite a character*; ein schlechter ~ *a bad ch.* **5.** ⟨Lit⟩ *character* (*in a play*, etc.) ‖ ⟨theat⟩ *character, part, role*; dem ~ gemäß *in ch.*; im Widerspruch mit dem ~ *out of ch.*; e–r Figur ~ verleihen *to characterize a part* **6.** [in comp] **~ähnlichkeit** f *similarity in ch.* **~anlage** f *character, disposition*; *natural bent, strain* **~bild** n *portrait(ure), portrayal* (*of a p*) **≃bildend** a *ch.-building* **~bildung** f *ch.-building* (od *forming, moulding, training*) **~darsteller** m ⟨theat⟩ *ch.-actor*, ⟨bes Am film⟩ *feature player* ‖ ~in [f] *character-actress* **~darstellung** f *depiction* (od *description, portraiture*) *of characters* od *of a p's character*, ⟨theat⟩ *ch.-work* **~eigenschaft** f *characteristics* pl **~erziehung** f *ch.-training* (od *forming*) **~fehler** m *defect of ch., shortcomings* pl **≃fest** a *of firm ch.*; *resolute, staunch* **~festigkeit** f *decision* (od *firmness, strength*) *of ch.*; *backbone, grit, resolution*; *stamina*; *staunchness* **~film** m (erster Besetzung) *feature film* **~komödie** f ⟨Lit⟩ *ch.-comedy*; ⟨engl⟩ *Comedy of Humours, C. of Manners* **~kopf** m *face strongly expressive of character* **~kunde** f *characterology* **~rolle** f ⟨theat⟩ *character part* **~schilderung** f *depiction* (od *delineation, description, portraiture*) *of a p's character, characterization* (*of a p*) **~schulung** f *character-training* **≃schwach** a *weak, weak-kneed* **~schwäche** f *weakness* (*of ch.*) **~skizze** f *ch.-sketch* **~stärke** f *character*, ⟨sl⟩ *guts* [pl] **~stück** n ⟨theat⟩ *ch.-play*; *drama with skilful ch.-drawing* **~studie** f *ch.-study* **~tragödie** f *tragedy of recoil* **≃voll** a (*man*) *of principles* (*when women are concerned*); *principled*; *fair* **~zeichnung** f *characterization, delineation of characters*; *character-drawing* (od *sketching*) **~zug** f [qual] *characteristic*; *strain*; (Einzel≃) *trait*, (ausgeprägter) (*characteristic*) *feature*

charakteris·ieren vt [h] **1.** (P) jdn ~ *to characterize a p, to delineate* (od *depict, draw, limn*) *the character of a p, to give a character-sketch of a p* | –sierter Major *brevet major* **2.** (S) jdn, etw ~ *to be characteristic* od *significant of a p* od *a th*; die Bücher charakterisieren einen philosophischen Geist *a philosophic mind sets the tone of the books* **Charakteris·ierung** f *characterization* (*of an art*, etc.); *delineation* od *description of the characteristics* (*of a th*) ‖ *characterization* (*of persons in a play*)

Charakter·istik f **1.** *characterization* (*of a p*); kz ~ *character-sketch*; e–e ~ geben *to give a characterization* ‖ *characterization* (*of a language*); *description of the characteristics* (*of a th*) **2.** ⟨math⟩ *characteristic* (*of a cubic*) **Charakter·istikum** n ~s/–ken *characteristic*; (*characteristic*) *feature*; Haupt≃ *chief characteristic* ‖ –ken [pl] (Kennlinien) *characteristic curves*

charakter·istisch **1.** a *characteristic* (f *of*); *distinctive*; ~e Eigentümlichkeit *distinctiveness*; ~e Eigenschaft, ~er Zug, ~es Merkmal *characteristic*; *strain*; in ~er Weise *characteristically* **2.** adv *characteristically* (*German*) **char·akterlich** [a] ~e Anlage *strain*; ~e Ausbildung *character-training* **char·akterlos** a *characterless*; *fickle*; *unprincipled, weak for character*; ein ~er Geselle ⟨fam⟩ *a stinking bad lot*; ⟨übtr⟩ *expressionless*; (Gesicht) *without character* **≃igkeit** f *want of character* (od *principles*)

Ch·arge [ˈʃarʒə] f ~/~n **1.** ⟨mil⟩ *rank*; ~n [pl] *officers and non-commissioned officers* [pl] ‖ Hof≃n [pl] *court officials* [pl] **2.** ⟨tech⟩ (Beschickung) *charge* **~nnummer** f *batch number* **~npferd** n *charger* **~nrolle** f ⟨theat⟩ *subordinate part* **Charg·ierte** [ʃarˈʒiːrtə] [der ~, ein ~r] m ~n/~n ⟨Ger univ⟩ die ~n [pl] *the leaders* od *delegates* [pl] *of a students' club*

Char·isma [k] n ~s/~ta *charism, charisma* (L)

Charité f ~/ *hospital* (bes in Paris u Berlin)

Char·iten [k] f [pl] (Grazien) *the Charites* [pl]

Chariv·ari [ʃ–] n (Fr) ~s/~s *charivari* (Fr)

Ch·arkow [ç–] n ⟨Russ⟩ (Stadt) *Kharkow*

Ch·arleston [ˈtʃaːlstən] m (engl) ~s/~s (Tanz) *charleston*

charm·ant a *charming* **Charme** [ʃarm] m *charm* **Charm·euse** [–ˈmøz] n ⟨tex⟩ *locknit*; verkehrtes ~ *reverse locknit*

Ch·arta [ˈkarta] f ~/~n *c(h)arta*; ⟨pol⟩ *charter*

Chartepart·ie [ʃart–] f (Fr) ⟨com⟩ *charter-party*

ch·artern [tʃ] vt [h] (engl) (Schiff) *to charter* ⟨a. übtr⟩ (Wagen, Auto)

Chart·ismus [tʃ] m ⟨engl⟩ *chartism* (1837–48)

Char·ybdis [k]: zwischen Skylla u ~ *between Scylla and Charybdis, between the devil and the deep sea*

Ch·assis [ʃaˈsiː] n (Fr) ⟨mot⟩ *chassis, under-car* ‖ ⟨wir⟩ *radio chassis*

Chateaubri·and n [ʃatoːbriˈɑ̃] ~s/~ ⟨cul⟩ *chateaubriand*

Chaude·au [ʃoːˈdoː] m (Fr) ~s/~s *sweet wine-cream*

Chauff·eur [ʃoˈføːr] m (Fr) ~s/~e *chauffeur*

chauff·ieren vt/i [h] ⟨mot⟩ *to chauffer*

†**Ch·auken** [ç–, x–] pl (altdeutsch. Volksstamm) *Chaucians* pl

Chaulmoograöl [tʃɔːlˈmuːgrə–] n (engl) *chaulmoogra oil*

Chauss·ee [ʃoˈseː] f (Fr) ~/~n **1.** (Landstraße) (*high*) *road, highway*; *turnpike* (*-road*) ‖

(in Städten) *road, avenue* **2.** [in comp] *road-* **~bau** m *road-making* °**~floh** m ⟨fig⟩ (Motorrad) ⟨sl⟩ *road-hog*; (zweitakter) *pip-squeak* **~geld** n ⟨hist⟩ *turnpike-toll*; ~einnehmer [m] ⟨hist⟩ *turnpike-man* **~wanze** f = –floh

Chauvin·ismus [ʃo–] m ~/ *chauvinism*, ⟨engl⟩ *jingoism* **Chauvin·ist** [ʃo–] m ~en/~en *chauvinist, jingo(ist)* **chauvin·istisch** [ʃo–] a *chauvinistic, jingo(istic)*

Chay·ote [tʃa'jo:tə] f ⟨bot⟩ *chocho, chayote*; die Frucht der ~ *chayote*

Ch·aywurzel [tʃei–] f *chay, choy*

Chef [ʃɛf] m ~s/~s **1.** ⟨mil, mar & pol⟩ ~ des Stabes *Chief of (the) Staff*, ~ e–s höheren Stabes *adjutant-general*, ~ des Generalstabes .. *Chief of the General Staff*, ⟨engl⟩ *Chief of the Imperial General Staff*; → Admiralstab ‖ Kompanie~ *captain*; ~ e–s Regiments (als Ehrenbezeichnung) *honorary colonel of a regiment* ‖ ⟨Ger⟩ ~ des Protokolls *Director of the Protocol*; ⟨engl⟩ *Master of (the) Ceremonies* **2.** ⟨com⟩ *chief, governor, head, principal*; *employer*; ⟨sl⟩ *boss* **3.** ⟨hot⟩ ~ d'étage *floor--waiter* ‖ ~ de service *head waiter* **4.** ⟨teens sl⟩ (Vater) *governor* **~arzt** m *medical superintendent*; *senior medical officer*; *head physician* **~ingenieur** m *chief engineer* **~kameramann** m ⟨film⟩ *operator*; *director of photography* **~konstrukteur** m *chief designer* **~pilot** m *chief test pilot* **~redakteur** m *editor* **~sache** f *secret*

Ch·efin ['ʃefin], ⟨hum⟩ **Chefeuse** [ʃe'føzə] f *female chief*; *mistress* ‖ *chief's wife*

Chelléen [ʃele:'ɛ̃] n (Fr) ~s/ *the Chellean culture*

Chem·ie [ç–, ˣk–] f ~/ *chemistry*; angewandte ~ *applied ch.*; organische ~ *organic ch.*; anorganische ~ *inorganic ch.*; Experimental~ *experimental ch.*, Elektro~ *electro-chemistry*; Bio~ *biochemistry*; Agrikultur~ *agricultural ch.* | ~fasern [f pl] *man-made fibres*, ⟨Am⟩ *fibers* (Fasern & Fäden) ~werker [m] *chemical worker* ‖ ~werte [m pl] ⟨st exch⟩ *chemical stocks, chemicals* pl **Chemigr·aph** m ⟨typ⟩ *chemigrapher* **Chemigraph·ie** f ⟨typ⟩ [abstr] *chemigraphy* ‖ [konkr] (Bild) *chemigraph* **Chemik·alien** [pl] *chemicals* [pl] ‖ ⟨med⟩ *fine chemicals, medicinal compounds*; *drugs* [pl] ‖ mit ~ behandeln *to chemicalize* **Ch·emiker** m ~s/~ *(analytical) chemist* ‖ → Apotheker, Drogist

ch·emisch 1. a **a.** *chemical* (*structure, plant, works*; *warfare agents* Kampfstoffe); in ~er Beziehung *chemically* ‖ ~e Formel *chemical formula*; ~e Grundstoffe [pl] *chemical elements* [pl]; ~es Labor *chemistry laboratory*; ~e Produkte *or* Stoffe [pl] *chemicals* [pl] ‖ ~e Verbindung *chemical combination* od *compound* **b.** [in comp] *chemico–*, ~-dynamisch *chemico-dynamic*; ~-technisch *chemico-technical* **2.** adv *chemically* (*pure*) ‖ ~ behandeln, herstellen, reproduzieren [vt] *to process*; ~ reinigen *to dry--clean(se)* ~e Reinigung *dry-cleaning*

Chemis·ett [ʃəmi'zɛt] n ~s/~s **1.** (Vorhemd) *dick(e)y* **2.** (Einsatz f Damenkleid) *chemisette*

Ch·emnitz [k–] n ⟨Ger⟩ (Stadt)

Chemo- ~sph·äre f (32–50 km über NN) *chemosphere* **~t·echniker** m *chemical engineer* **~therap·ie** f *chemotherapeutics, –therapy*

-chen [dim suff] **1.** *–ie, y*: Hünd~ *doggy, doggie* **2.** *–kin*: Lämm~ *lambkin* **3.** *–let*: Häkchen *hooklet*; Flügelchen *winglet*

Chen·ille [ʃe'nij, ʃə'niljə] f (Fr) ~/~n *chenille*; ~teppich *chenille-carpet*

Cherry Brandy ['tʃeri 'brændi] m (engl) ~s/~s *cherry brandy*

Cherson(n)·es [ç–] m *Chersonese* (= Halbinsel); †Kimbrischer ~ (= Jütland) *Cimbric Ch.*; †Taurischer ~ (= Krim) *Tauric Ch.*; †Thr·akischer ~ (= Halbinsel v Gallipoli) *Thracian Ch.*

Ch·erub m ~s/~im & ~·ine(n) *cherub* [pl *cherubs, cherubim*]

†**Cher·usker** m [pl] (⟨Ger⟩ Volk) *Cherusci* (L) **ch–kisch** a *Cheruscan*

Ch·esterkäse ['tʃestə–] m (engl) *Cheshire cheese*

chevaler·esk [ʃəval'resk] a *chivaleresque, –rous*

Ch·eviot ['tʃeviət] m (engl) ~s/~s (Stoff) *cheviot*

Chevreau [ʃə'vro:] n (Fr) ~s/ *goat-skin leather*

Chianti(wein) [ki'anti–] m (It) *Chianti*

Chicor·ée [ʃikɔ're:] f Fr (*vegetable of*) *chicory*

Ch·iemsee [k–] m ⟨Ger⟩ (Voralpensee)

Chiff·on [ʃi'fɔ̃] m (Fr) ~s/~s (Stoff) *chiffon* (Fr)

Ch·iffre ['ʃifər] f (Fr) ~/~n *cipher* (*cy–*); *code*; Code~ *cipher-code* (od *key*); in ~n schreiben *to cipher, code* | ⟨ad⟩ *box-number*; unter ~XY *under cipher XY* **~brief** m *cipher--letter, code-message* **~schlüssel** m *cipher code* **~schrift** f *cryptography*; *cipher, code* **~telegramm** n *cipher* (od *code*)*-telegram*

Chiffr·ier- [ʃ–] **~maschine** f *ciphering machine* **~offizier** m *cipher officer* **~stelle** f *cipher office, code centre*

chiffr·ieren [ʃi–] vt [h] (Brief etc) *to cipher* (*cy–*), *to code* **Chiffr·ierung** f ~/~en *coding*

Chik·ago [ç–] n *Chicago* (Stadt) (*U.S.A.*)

Chil·ene [ç, tʃ] m ~n/~n *Chilian* (*–lean*) **chil·enisch** a *Chilian* (*–lean*) **Ch·ilesalpeter** ['tʃili–] m (engl) *Chili* (od *Chile*) *saltpetre*

Chili·ade [ç] f ~/~n *chiliad* **Chili·asmus** [k] m ~/ *chiliasm, millenarianism*

Chim·äre [ç] f ~/~n **1.** ⟨myth⟩ *chimera, –maera* **2.** ⟨ich⟩ *chimaera, chimaeroid*

Chimbor·asso m *Chimborazo*

Ch·ina- [ʃ–] **~muster** n (blau) ⟨ceram⟩ *willow-pattern* **~rinde** *China* (od *cinchona, Peruvian*) *–bark*; ⟨pharm⟩ *cinchona, quinquina* ‖ ~nbaum [m] ⟨bot⟩ *cinchona* **~säure** f *cinchonic* (od *quinic*) *acid* **~silber** n *China silver* **~wein** m *quinine wine*

Chinch·illa [tʃin'tʃilja] (Span) ~/~s **1.** f ⟨zoo⟩ *chinchilla* **2.** n & m *chinchilla* (*fur*)

Chin·é [ʃi'ne:] n (Fr) ~s/~s *chiné silk* od *fabric* **chin·iert** a *chiné*

Chin·ese m ~n/~n *Chinese, Chinaman*; ⟨sl⟩ *Chinee, Chink, Chinkie* ‖ (jdn) zu e–m ~n m *to sinify* ‖ die ~n [pl] *the Chinese* | ~nart [f] (etc) *sini(ci)sm*; ~nhasser [m] *sinophobe*; ~nhut [m] *coolie hat* **chin·esisch** a **1.** *Chinese* (*art*, etc.) ‖ *sinic, sinian* | in ~em Sinn abwandeln, beeinflussen, verändern *to sinify, sinicize* ‖ ~er Talg *Chinese tallow* ‖ ~es Grün *Chinese green* **2.** [in comp] *Chino–, Sino–*; ~-japanisch *Chino* (od *Sino*) *–Japanese* **Chin·esisch**: das ~e *Chinese*; auf ~ *in Ch.*

Ch·inga ['tʃiŋgɑ] f ⟨zoo⟩ *chincha, chinche*

Chin·in n ⟨chem⟩ *quinine* **~rausch** m *cinchonism, quinism*

Chinoiser·ie [ʃinwɑzə'ri:] f (Fr) ⟨arts⟩ *chinoiserie* (Fr)

Chinol·in n ⟨chem⟩ *chinoline*

Chin·one [pl] ⟨chem⟩ *chinones* [pl]

Chintz [tʃints] m (engl) (Baumwollstoff) *chintz*

Ch·ippendalestil [tʃipendeil–] m (engl, nach Th. Chippendale, † 1779) *the Chippendale style*

Chips [ʃ–] pl ⟨cul⟩ (Kartoffel~ etc) *chips* pl

Chir-, Ch·iro- ⟨scient⟩ (Hand–) *chir–, chiro*

Chiro- ~m·ant m *chiromancer, palmist* **~mant·ie** f *chiromancy, palmistry* **~pr·aktik** f *chiropractic* **~praktiker** m *chiropractor* **~pt·eren** [pl] ⟨zoo⟩ *cheiroptera, chiro–* (pl) **Chir·urg** m ~en/~en **1.** ⟨med⟩ *surgeon*; ⟨sl hum⟩ *sawbones* ‖ erster ~ *surgeon-in-chief*; ~ mit eigenen neuen Methoden *creative surgeon* **2.** ⟨ich⟩ *surgeon-fish*

Chirurg·ie f ~/ *surgery*; kosmetische ~ *plastic s.* **chir·urgisch 1.** a *surgical*; die ~e Abteilung (*or* Klinik) e–s Krankenhauses *the surgical side of a hospital*; ~e Behandlung *surgery, surgical treatment*; in ~er Beziehung *surgically* **2.** adv *surgically*

Chit·in n ~s/ *chitin*

Chit·on m ~s/~e ⟨ant⟩ *chiton*

Ch·ittagongholz n *Chittagong wood*

Chlamydosp·ore f ~/~n ⟨bot⟩ *chlamydospore*

Chl·amys [k] f ~/~ ⟨ant⟩ *chlamys*

Chloanth·it [k] m ~s/~e ⟨minr⟩ *chloanthite*

Chl·or [k] n ~s/ ⟨chem⟩ *chlorine* ‖ (etw) mit ~ behandeln *to chlorinate* **~äth·an** n ⟨chem⟩ *clorethane* **~äth·yl** n *ethyl chloride* **~bleiche** f *chlorine bleaching* **~di·oxid** n *chlorine dioxide* **≗haltig** a *chlorous*; *chloric* **~kalk** m *chloride of lime*; *calcium chloride* **~lauge** f ⟨pap⟩ *bleach liquor* **~ph·osphor** n *phosphorus chloride* **~pikr·in** n *chloropicrin* **≗sauer** a *chloric*; –saures Salz *chlorate*; –saures Kalium *chlorate of potassium* **~säure** f *chloric acid* **~stickstoff** m *chloride of nitrogen* **~verbindung** f *compound of chlorine* **~wasser** n *chlorine water* **~w·asserstoff** m *hydrochloric acid*

Chlor·al n ⟨chem⟩ *chloral* ‖ **~hydrat** n *chloral-hydrate*

Chlor·at n ⟨chem⟩ *chlorate* **chl·oren** vt [h] (Wasser) *to chlorinize*; gechlortes Wasser *chlorurated water* **Chlor·id** n ⟨chem⟩ *chloride*

Chlor·ierung f ~/ *chlorination* **chl·orig** a *chlorous* (*acid*) **Chlor·it** n ⟨chem⟩ *chlorite* **Chloro·f·orm** n ⟨chem⟩ *chloroform* ‖ ~narkose *ch.-narcosis* **chloroform·ieren** vt [h] (jdn) *to chloroform* **Chloroph·yll** n ⟨bot⟩ *chlorophyll* **Chlor·ose** f ⟨med⟩ (Bleichsucht) *chlorosis* **Chlor·ür** n ⟨chem⟩ *chloride*; **chloruret*

Cholag·og n ⟨med⟩ *cholagogue* **Choläm·ie** f ⟨med⟩ *cholaemia* **Cholelith·iasis** f ⟨med⟩ *cholelithiasis*

Ch·olera [k] f ~/ **1.** (*Asiatic, epidemic, malignant*) *cholera* **2.** = Brechdurchfall **~bazillus** m *comma-bacillus* **~tropfen** [pl] *remedy for 'Brechdurchfall'* **Chol·eriker** [k] m ~s/~ *choleric* od *irascible person*

Choler·ine [k] f ~/ (leichte Choleraart) *cholerine* **chol·erisch** [k] a *choleric*

Cholester·in n ~s/ ⟨chem⟩ *cholesterin* **Cholezystektom·ie** f ⟨med⟩ *cholecystectomy* **Cholezyst·itis** f ⟨med⟩ *cholecystitis* (L)

Chol·in [k] n ~s/ *choline*

Ch·olo [ˈtʃolo] m (Indianer) *Cholo*

Chom·ageversicherung [ʃɔˈmɑːʒ–] f (Fr) ⟨com⟩ *loss of profits insurance*; *consequential loss insurance*

Chondr·in n (Leim) *chondrin*

Chondrolog·ie f (Knorpellehre) *chondrology* **Chondr·om** n *chondroma* **Chondr·ose** f *chondrosis*

Ch·or [k] m ~s/≗e **1.** ⟨ant⟩ (in drama) *chorus* ‖ (Sänger≗) *chorus*; ⟨ec⟩ *choir*; Knaben≗ *boys' choir*; gemischter ~ *choir of men & women* ‖ (~gesang) *chorus* ‖ *burden, refrain* ‖ (etw) im ~ singen *to chorus*; *to choir* ‖ ⟨mus⟩ *chorus* (*of instruments*) **2.** ⟨übtr⟩ (Geschrei etc) *chorus*; Sprech≗ *speaking chorus* ‖ im ~ *in chorus*; im ~ äußern *to chorus*; im ~ sprechen *to speak in chorus* | der ~ der Vögel *the feathered tribes* [pl] ‖ °n *group, crowd, multitude*; ⟨sl⟩ *lot, caboodle* **3.** [in comp] *choral* **~amt** n *Cathedral Service* **~drama** n *choral drama* **~frau** f ⟨R.C.⟩ *choir nun* od *sister* **~führer** m *chorister* **~gesang** m *chorus, choral song* **~gestühl** n ⟨ec⟩ *stalls* pl **~haupt** n *apse* **~hemd** n *surplice, alb*; (f Bischof) *rochet* **~herr** m = Domherr **~knabe** m *chorister, choir* (od *chorister*) *-boy* **~konzert** n *choral concert* **~leiter** m *choirmaster* **~rock** m *cope*; (f Bischof) *rochet* **~sänger** m *chorus singer*; (bezahlter) *singing-man* ‖ ⟨theat⟩ *member of chorus*, ⟨Am⟩ *chorus boy, .. girl* **~schranke** f ⟨a. arch⟩ *closure--slab* **~umgang** m ⟨ec arch⟩ *ambulatory*; *processional path* **~verein** m *choral society* **~werk** n *choral work*

Ch·or m & n ⟨ec arch⟩ **1.** ⟨engl & R. C.⟩ (Ort, wo der ~ sitzt) *chancel, choir* **2.** ⟨Ger⟩ *gallery* **~altar** m *high altar, great altar* **~empore** f *rood-loft* **~gang** m (in der Kirche) *aisle* **~nische** f *apse* **~pult** n *lectern, reading-desk* **~stuhl** m (*choir*) *stall*

Chor·al [k] m ~s/≗e *choral(e), sacred hymn, sacred choral, song*; *chant*

Ch·orda [k] f (L) ⟨anat⟩ (Saite) *chorda* | ~tiere = **Chord·aten** pl [k], **Chord·onier** pl [k] ⟨zoo⟩ *chordata*; → Art

Chor·ea [k] f (Veitstanz) *chorea* (L)

Choreograph·ie [k] f *choreography* **Chor·eutik** [k] f *choreutics* [pl]

Chorim·oyia f ⟨bot⟩ *sweet-sop*

Choripet·ale [k] f ⟨bot⟩ *choripetalous* od *polypetalous plant*

Chor·ist [k] m *chorister*; *member of a choir*

Chor·istin f *chorister, female member of a choir*; *singing girl* ‖ ⟨theat⟩ *chorus-girl*

Chorograph·ie [k] f ⟨geog⟩ *chorography* **chorogr·aphisch** a *chorographic* **Chorolog·ie** [k] f ⟨geol⟩ *chorology*

Chrestomath·ie [k] f ~/~n [–iːən] *chrestomathy, anthology*

Chr·ie f *theme*

Chr·isam n & m, **Chr·isma** n [ç–] (Salböl) *chrism*

Chr·ist [k] m ~en/~en *Christian*; e–m ~en geziemend *christianlike* ‖ Heiliger ~ *Holy Christ, Child Christ* ‖ zum ~en m *to christianize* (*a p*) **~abend** m *Christmas eve* **~baum** m *Christmas tree* ‖ sie war behängt wie ein ~ *she was wearing everything but the kitchen sink* **~bescherung** f *distribution of Christmas-presents* [pl] **~blume** f ⟨bot⟩ (*black*) *hellebore, Christmas rose* **~dorn** m ⟨bot⟩ *Christ's thorn* **~fest** n *Christmas* ‖ *the Nativity* **~geburtspiel** n *nativity* **~gehen** n *singing Christmas carols and asking alms* **~geschenk** n *Christmas-present*; ⟨engl⟩ (~ f Dienstboten etc) *Christmas-box* **~kind(lein)** n *Infant* od *Child Jesus, the Christ-child* **~markt** m *Christmas fair* **~messe, ~mette** f *Christmas matins* [pl] **~monat, ~mond** m *Christmas--month, December* **~nacht** f *Christmas-night* **~rose** f ⟨bot⟩ = Christblume **~woche** f *Christmas week* **~wurz(el)** f ⟨bot⟩ → Nieswurz

Chr·isten- **≗feindlich** a *antichristian* **~gemeinde** f *community of Christians* **~lehre** f *instruction in Christian religion* **~pflicht** f *Christian's duty* **~seele** f *Christian*; k–e ~ *not a soul* od *p* **~verfolgung** f *persecution of early Christians*

Chr·istenheit f *Christendom* **Chr·istentum** n *Christianity* ‖ das ~ annehmen *to adopt* od *espouse Christianity* ‖ sich zum ~ bekennen *to profess Christianity* ‖ e–m Lande das ~ predigen, bringen *to evangelize a country*; (jdn) zum ~ bekehren *to christianize*; Bekehrung zum ~ *christianization*

christianis·ieren vt [h] *to christianize* **Christianis·ierung** f *christianization*

chr·istlich a *Christian* (*church, era*; *art*) ‖ *christianlike* (*conduct*) ‖ ~e Lehre *Christian doctrine*; ~er Glaube *Christian faith, Christianity*; ~e Tat *Christian act, charitable act* ‖ die ~e Welt *Christendom* ‖ ~er Verein Junger Männer *Young Men's Christian Association* (abbr *Y.M.C.A.*) ‖ ~e Wissenschaft f ⟨rel⟩ *Christian Science* (ggr. 1866) ‖ ⟨ec⟩ ~-soziale Bewegung f *Christian Socialism*

Christolatr·ie f *christolatry* **Christolog·ie** f *christology*

Chr·istophskraut n ⟨bot⟩ *herb Christopher; baneberry*

Chr·istus m ~ & Christi/ *Christ* ‖ 1833 nach ~ (*or* Christi Geburt) *in the year 1833 of our Lord, 1833 Anno Domini* (abbr *A. D.*); 1833 vor ~ (*or* Christi Geburt) *1833 before Christ* (abbr *B. C.*); → Zeitwende ‖ Christi Wunder [pl] *Christ's miracles* [pl]; Christi Geburt *the Nativity*; Verspottung Christi *Mocking of C.*; ~ am Ölberg *C.'s Agony in the Garden*; Christi Schaustellung *C. before the People*; Christi Geißelung ⟨arts⟩ *Flogging of C.*; Beweinung Christi ⟨arts⟩ *Mourning (over the Body) of C., Lamentation for C.*; Christi Himmelfahrt *the Ascension*; Christi Auferstehung *the Resurrection*; ~ erscheint Maria Magdalena ⟨paint⟩ *Noli-Me-Tangere*; Christi Höllenfahrt *Harrowing of Hell*; thronender ~ *C. in Majesty* | um Christi willen! *for Christ's sake!*

Chr·istus- [in comp] **~akazie** f ⟨bot⟩ *honey-locust* **~auge** f ⟨bot⟩ *Christ's eye* ‖ *lychnis; scarlet campion* ‖ *hawkweed* ‖ = Stiefmütterchen **~bild** n *representation of Jesus Christ*; (Kreuzigung) *picture* od *figure of Christ on the Cross; crucifix; crucifixion* **~dorn** m ⟨bot⟩ = Christusakazie **~monogramm** n **1.** *the monogram of the Greek name of Christus* (*I H Σ*) **2.** *sign of the fish* **3.** I H S [statt I H Σ] (= *Iesus Hominum Salvator*) **~orden** m ⟨R. C.⟩ *the Order of Christ*

Chrom [k] n ~s/ ⟨chem⟩ *chromium* [L] ‖ (Farbe) *chrome* (→ Chrom–)

Chr·om- [in comp] ⟨chem⟩ *chromium; chrome* **~alaun** m *chrome alum* **~bad** n *chrome bath* **~·eisenstein** m ⟨minr⟩ *chrome iron ore* od *stone; chromite* **~farbe** f *chrome dye* **~fluorid** n *chromic fluoride* **~gelat·ine** f *chrome gelatine; bichromated gelatine* **~gelb** n *chrome yellow* **~gerbeextrakt** m *chrome tanning extract* **~gerbung** f *chrome tanning* **~grün** n *chrome green* **~kali** n *potassium bichromate* **~karbid** n *chromium carbide* **~leder** n *chrome leather* **~leim** m = Chromgelatine **~metall** n *chromium metal* **~oxid,** –yd n *chromic oxide* **≚sauer** a; –saures Salz *chromate*; –saures Kali *potassium chromate* **~säure** f *chromic acid*; mit ~ behandeln *to chromicize* ‖ ~anhydrid *chromic anhydride* **~sulfat** n *chromium sulphate* **~stahl** m *chrome steel* **~tr·ioxid,** –yd n *chromium trioxide*

Chrom·at [k] n *chromate* **Chrom·atik** [k] f **1.** ⟨mus⟩ *chromatic* **2.** ⟨phys⟩ (Farbenlehre) *chromatics* [pl] **Chromat·in** [k] n *chromatin*

chrom·atisch [k] a **1.** ⟨mus⟩ *chromatic (scale)* **2.** ⟨phot⟩ ~e Abweichung f *chromatic aberration; chromatism*

Chrom·ato- [in comp] *chromato–* **~meter** n *chromatometer* **~phor** n ~s/~en *chromatophore* **~sphäre** f *chromatosphere* **~skop** n *chromatoscope*

Chr·omi- [in comp] *chromic* **~salz** n *chromic salt* **~sulphat** n *chromic sulphate*

chrom·ieren vt [h] (Wolle etc) *to chrome*

Chr·omo- [in comp] *chromo–* **~g·en** n *chromogen* **~l·ith** m *chromolith* **~lithogr·aph** m *chromolithographer* **~lithograph·ie** f [abstr] *chromolithography* ‖ (Abdruck) *chromolithograph*; ⟨fam⟩ *chromo* **~m·er** n *chromomere* **~s·om** n ~s/~e *chromosome* | ~entheorie [f] der Vererbung *gene-chr. theory* **~sph·äre** f *chromosphere*; → Gasschicht **~trop·ie** f *chromotropy*

Chr·onik [k] f ~/~en *chronicle* ‖ in e–r ~ auszeichnen *to chronicle* | ~drama [n] ⟨engl theat⟩ *chronicle play*; → d. **Chr·onika** f ⟨bib⟩ Bücher [pl] der ~ *the Chronicles* [pl]

chr·onisch [k] **1.** a ⟨med⟩ *chronic*; ~er Zustand *chronicality* **2.** adv *chronically*

Chron·ist m ~en/~en *chronicler*

Chrono- [k] [in comp] (Zeit–) *chrono–* **~gr·amm** n *chronogram* **~gr·aph** m (Apparat z Messung kl Zeitteile etc) *chronograph* **~log·ie** f *chronology* **≚l·ogisch** **1.** a *chronologic(al)*; in ~er Beziehung *chronologically* **2.** adv *chronologically* **≚logis·ieren** vt [h] *to chronologize; to arrange in chronological order* **~m·eter** n *chronometer, timepiece* **~metr·ie** f *chronometry* **~m·etrisch** a *chronometric(al)*

Chrysal·ide [k] f (Puppe e–r Raupe) *chrysalis* [pl *–lises*]

Chrys·anthemum [k] n ~s/Chrysanth·emen ⟨bot⟩ *chrysanthemum* **~orden** m (japan.) *the Order of the Chrysanthemum* (ggr. 1877)

Chryso- [k] [in comp] (Gold–) *chryso–* **~ber·yll** m ~s/~e ⟨minr⟩ *chrysoberyl* **~l·ith** m ~s/~e ⟨minr⟩ *chrysolite* **~phen·in** n (ein Farbstoff) *chrysophenine* **~pr·as** m ~/–prase ⟨minr⟩ *chrysoprase*

chth·onisch a *chthonian, chthonic*

Ch·ylus m [L] ⟨physiol⟩ *chyle*; → d. Bd. I

Ch·ymus m [L] ⟨physiol⟩ *chyme*

C·icero ['tsitsəroː] f ⟨typ⟩ *pica* [L]

Cicer·one [tʃitʃe'roːne] m [It] ~/~ni *cicerone*

Cinchon·in n ⟨chem⟩ *cinchonine*

Cinquec·ento [tʃiŋkwə'tʃento] n [It] ~s/ ⟨arts⟩ (16. Jh.) *cinquecento*

c·irca adv [L] *circa* [L], *about*

C·irce f ~/~n ⟨fig⟩ *tantalizer; man-trap; enslaver*

Cis n ~/~ ⟨mus⟩ *C sharp* **C·isis** n ⟨mus⟩ *C double sharp*

C·ity ['siti] f ⟨engl⟩ die ~ (Altstadt) *the City*

Civ·ette f ⟨zoo⟩ (Zibetkatze) *civet*

Clam [klæm] f ⟨engl⟩ (eßbare Muschel) *clam*; ⟨Am⟩ *quahaug, –hog*

Clan [k] m (Sippe) *clan*

Claqu·eur klɑ'kør] m [Fr] ⟨theat⟩, ~e [pl] [koll] *claque*

Cl·earing ['kliəriŋ] n ⟨engl⟩ ~s/~s *clearing*

Clem·atis f ~/~ ⟨bot⟩ (Blaue) ~ *(Blue) Traveler's Joy*

Clement·ine f ~/~n ⟨bot⟩ *clementine*

Cl·eve [k–] n ⟨Ger⟩ (Stadt) *Cleves*

Cl·eveland ['kliːvlənd] n *Cleveland* (*O., U.S.A.*)

cl·ever ['klɛvə] a (klug, ⟨mst⟩ → gerissen) *clever; artful*

Cl·ique ['klikə] f ~/~n *clique, coterie, gang, set; caste; clan* **cl·iquenhaft** a *cliquish, cliqu(e)y* **Cl·iquenwesen** n, **Cl·iquenwirtschaft** f *cliquism, cliquedom, cliquery*

Cl·ivie f ['kliːviə] ⟨bot⟩ *clivia*

Cl·oche f [klɔʃ] ~/~n [–ʃən] ⟨cul⟩ *cover*

Cloisonné [klwɑzɔ'ne] n [Fr] (Zellenschmelz) *cloisonné enamel* (Ggs Champlevé)

Clou [kluː] m [Fr] ~s/~s *clou* [Fr], *chief attraction*

Clown [klaun] m [engl] ~s/~s *clown*; den ~ spielen *to clown it* | ~artig [adv] (Rolle) ~ darstellen *to clown (a part)*; ~tracht [f] *motley*

Clowner·ie f *clownery*

Clun·y [kly'ni] n ⟨Fr⟩ (Stadt) *Cluny*

Coach [koutʃ] m [engl] ⟨sport⟩ *coach*

C·obbler m [engl] (Getränk) *cobbler*

C·oblenz n → Koblenz

C·oburg n ⟨Ger⟩ (Stadt u †Land) *Coburg*

C·oca-C·ola f ~/~ *coca-cola*, ⟨Am, fam⟩ *coke*

Cochen·ille f [kɔʃə'niljə] *cochineal*

C·ockney n ⟨engl⟩ *cockney*

C·ocktail ['kɔkteil] m [engl] *cocktail* | ~anzug [m] (f Damen) *c. trouser snit* ‖ ~kleid [n] *c. dress*

Code m [Fr] *code*; → Chiffre | ~-Ent–, ~-Verschlüßler [m] *cipher clerk* od *officer*; ~-Schlüsseltext [m] *cipher text*; ~tafel [f] ⟨accmach⟩ *tape encoder* **Cod·ierung** f ~/~en *encoding*

Coeur [køə] n [Fr] ⟨cards⟩ *heart* ‖ (~farbe) *hearts* [pl]; ~ ist Trumpf *hearts are trumps*; ~neun f *nine of hearts*

C·olanuß f (→ Nuß) ⟨bot⟩ *cola nut*
C·ollege [ˈkɔlidʒ] n ⟨engl⟩ *college*
Coll·ier [kɔlˈjeː] n [Fr] ~s/~s *necklace*
Coloc·asie f ⟨bot⟩ *colocasia* [L]
Col·ombo n (Hauptstadt Ceylons)
C·omer See m ⟨It⟩ *Lake Como*
Compiègne [kɔ̃piɛɲ] n ⟨Fr⟩ (Stadt)
Compr·ette f ⟨med⟩ *a sort of tablet*
Complet [kɔ̃ˈple] n ~s/~s Fr *ensemble*
Comp·uter m ~s/~ (z Rechnen & Datenverarbeitung) → *computer*, Rechner
Conc·ours hipp·ique m [kɔ̃ˈkuːr iˈpik] Fr (Reit- u Fahrturnier) *equestrian contest*
Conférenci·er [kɔ̃feːrɑ̃ˈsjeː] m [Fr] ~s/~s *announcer*; *conferencier* [Fr]; ⟨rad, telv⟩ *compère* [Fr], ⟨Am⟩ *Master of Ceremonies*; ⟨fam⟩ *emcee* (= M. C.) (dazu: *to emcee a show*) ‖ → Komm-Franz-und-geh
Conn·ecticut [–ət] n (Staat der U.S.A.)
Cont·inuo m [It] ⟨mus⟩ *(basso) continuo*
C·ookinseln f pl (im Stillen Ozean) *Cook* od *Hervey Islands*
C·ookstraße f (Neu-Seeland) *Cook Strait*
Copyright n ~s/~s © (Urheber-, Verlagsrecht) → *copyright*
Coqu·ito [koˈkiːto] m ⟨bot⟩ *coquito*
Cord m [engl] (Stoff) *cord*
C·órdoba, C·ordova n ⟨Span⟩ (Stadt) *Cordova*
Cor·olle f [L] ⟨bot⟩ *corolla* [L]
Corom·andelküste f (Madras, Indien) *Coromandel Coast*
Corpor·ale n [L] ⟨R. C.⟩ *corporal*
Corps [koːr] n [Fr] ⟨Ger univ⟩ *oldest kind of German students' societies*; → Korps
C·ortisches Org·an n ⟨anat⟩ (im Ohr) *Cortian organ*
Cort·use f ⟨bot⟩ *cortusa* [L]
Cottbus ⟨Ger⟩ (Stadt) Niederlausitz
Couch [ˈkautʃ] f [engl] ~/~es (Liegesofa) *couch*; ⟨Am⟩ *davenport*
Coué|·ismus m (nach Coué, † 1926) *couéism*
Couleur [kuˈløə] f [Fr] f ~/~en ⟨Ger univ⟩ *distinctive colours* [pl] *of a students' society* **~student** m *st. belonging to a soc. wearing colours*
Couloir [kulˈwɑːr] m [Fr] (Schlucht) *couloir*
Coulomb [kuˈlɔ̃] n [Fr] (nach Ch. A. de ~, † 1806) ⟨el⟩ *coulomb*
Countd·own [–au–au–] m ~s/~s (Abzählen) *countdown*; der ~ ging stark auf null *the c. neared zero*
Coup [kuː] m [Fr] ~s/~s *coup*; *move*, *stroke*; e–n ~ m *to make a coup, to strike a blow*
Coupé [kuˈpeː] n [Fr] ~s/~s **1.** (Kutsche) *coupé* ‖ ⟨mot⟩ (geschlossener Zweisitzer) *coupé* **2.** ⟨rail⟩ = Abteil
Couplet [kuˈpleː] n [Fr] ~s/~s *music-hall song*; *light comic song with a rhyming couplet*; *verses* [pl] *of topical or piquant character* **~dichter** m *music-hall poet, song writer* **~sänger** m, **~sängerin** f *comic singer*
Coup·on [kuˈpɔ̃] m [Fr] ~s/~s → Kupon
Cour [kuːr] f ~ **1.** (bei Hofe) *court*; *levee*; e–e ~ abhalten *to hold a cour* od *levee* **2.** nur in: jdm (bes e–r Dame) die ~ m *or* schneiden *to court a p, to make* od *pay court to a p*; *to pay one's addresses to a p* ‖ sich gern die ~ m l *to be fond of flirtation* **~macher**, **~schneider** m *beau, lady's* od *ladies' man, lady-killer*
Cour·age [kuˈrɑːʒə] [h] [Fr] *courage*; ⟨sl⟩ *guts* [pl]; ⟨Am sl⟩ *spunk*; Zivil≈ *the courage of one's convictions*; → Schneid **courag·iert** [kurɑˈʒiːrt] a *courageous*
Cour·ante [kuˈrɑ̃t] f [Fr] ~/ ⟨mus⟩ *courante*
Court·age [kurˈtɑːʒə] f ~/~n [Fr] ⟨com⟩ *brokerage*; *courtage* [Fr]
Courtois·ie [kurtwɑˈzi] f [Fr] ~/~n [–iːən] *courtesy*
Cous·in [kuˈzɛ̃] m [Fr] ~s/~s *cousin* **Cous·ine** [kuˈziːnə] f *(female) cousin*
C·owboy [ˈkaubɔi] m [engl] *cowboy* | ~fest [n] ⟨Am⟩ *rodeo* ‖ ~hose [f] *(blue) jeans* pl
C·owpersche [kau–] **Drüsen** f [pl] [engl] (nach W. Cowper, † 1709) ⟨anat⟩ (beim Mann) *Cowperian* od *Cowper's glands* [pl]; → Bartholinsche Drüsen
Cox Orange f ⟨bot⟩ *Cox's Orange Pippin*
Cr·abwood [ˈkræbwud] n [engl] *crab-wood*
Creme [krɛːm] f [Fr] → Krem ‖ ⟨cul⟩ englische ~ *custard*; gekochte ~ *pastry cream*; | ≈farbig [a] *c.-coloured*; ~es Papier *c.-white paper*; ~schnitte [f] *cream-slice, iced slice* ‖ ⟨cosm⟩ → Krem
Crem·ona n ⟨It⟩ (Stadt)
cresc·endo [kreˈʃendo] [It] ⟨mus⟩ *crescendo*
Crew [kruː] f [engl] ⟨mar⟩ *crew* ‖ ⟨Ger nav⟩ *cadets* [pl] *of the same year of entry*
Cr·ibbage [ˈkribidʒ] n [engl] ⟨cards⟩ *cribbage*
Cro·issant n [ˈkroaʃɑ̃] ~s/~s ⟨cul⟩ (Hörnchen) *crescent (roll)*
Crookessche [kruːks–] **Röhre** f [engl] (nach W. Crookes, † 1919) ⟨phys⟩ *Crookes tube*
Crout·ons n pl [kruˈtɔ̃s] = Bröckchen
Cryptom·erie [–iə] f ⟨bot⟩ *cryptomeria* [L]
cum grano salis [kum ˈgrɑːnoː ˈzɑːlis] L *take it with a grain of salt*
C·umuluswolke (Haufenwolke) f *cumulus*
Cuph·ee f ⟨bot⟩ *cuphea* [L]
C·upula f ⟨bot⟩ *cupule* (*–la* [L])
Curaç·ao [kyrasao] n (Insel bei Venezuela) | m (Likör) *curaçao*
Cur·ie [kyˈriː] n *curie* (*unit of radium emanation*)
Curi·osa [L] [pl] *curiosities* [pl]
C·urry [ˈkʌri] m & n ⟨cul⟩ *curry (powder)* (Ingwer, Koriander, Kümmel, Curcuma, Pfeffer etc) ‖ mit ~ *curried*
°**Cut** m ~s/~s ⟨fam⟩ = Cutaway [kʌtəˈwei] m [engl] ~s/~s *cutaway, morning dress*
C·utter [ˈkʌtə] m ~s/~ ⟨film⟩ (Schnitt[meister(in)]) *cutter*
C·ypern [tsy–] n (Insel im Mittelmeer) *Cyprus*

D

D, d [deː] n ~/~ **1.** *D*, *d* **2.** ⟨mus⟩ *D* ‖ *re* [It] ‖ D-Banken [f pl] ⟨Ger⟩ (4 gr Banken mit D beginnend) *'D'-banks* pl ‖ D-dur *D-major* ‖ d-Moll *d-minor* **3.** D-Zug m ~(e)s/–züge ⟨rail⟩ *through-train, corridor-train, express train*; ⟨Am⟩ *vestibule-train*
da adv **I.** **(örtlich)** **A.** ⟨eig⟩ **1.** **(dort)** *there* : [oft bei intr. Verben]: ~liegen *to lie there*; ausgestreckt ~liegen *to sprawl*; → stehen Georg war ~ *George was there*; ~ ist er *there he is* od *goes*; ~ kommt er *there he comes*; ~ ist es *there it is* | **(hier)** ~ bin ich *here I am*; er war ~ *he was here*; der Frühling ist ~ *spring is in* ‖ die Seuche hatte in dem Dorfe gewütet u nur ~ *the plague had raged in the village, and only here*; ~ ist Ihr Frühstück *here is your breakfast*; ~, nimm es *here, take it* | ~ u dort *here and there* | **~ ungefähr** *thereabouts*, od ungefähr ~ *or thereabouts* ‖ er sagte, er hätte ihn ~ u ~ gesehen *he said he had seen him at such and such a place* **2. du ~, Sie ~** *you there* ‖ das Buch ~ *that book there*, ⟨vulg⟩ *that there book*, dies Buch ~ *this*

book here, ⟨vulg⟩ *this here book* ‖ der ~ *that one*, dieser ~ *this one* ‖ ⟨mil⟩ wer ~? *who goes there*? ‖ wo ~? *where*? wo denn ~? *where then*? **3. v ~** *from there*; *thence* **4. ~ draußen** *out there*; ~ drinnen *in there*; ~ drüben *over there*; ~ herum *thereabouts*; ~ hinauf *up there*; ~ hinaus *out there*; ~ hinein *in there*; ~ hinunter *down there*; ~ oben *up there*; ~ unten *down there* ‖ ~ z Lande *in those parts* od *regions* **5.** ~, wo ich wohne .. *where I live* .. **B.** ⟨übtr⟩ **1. (anwesend)** *there, here, present*; *at hand*; er war nicht ~ *he was not present*; ist er schon ~? *has he arrived already*; .., ob er ~ ist (*I'll see*) *if he is come*; ich bin schon wieder ~ *I'm here again, back again*; bleib doch noch ~ *stay a little longer* | **(vorhanden)** das deutsche Blut war ~ (*sc* in ihm) *the German blood was there*; ist die Post schon ~? *is the mail in already*? ist Post ~ f mich? *are there any letters for me*? ‖ wenn noch etw ~ ist, so .. *if there is something left* .. ‖ hier ist alles ~ *here is full measure* ‖ der Frühling ist ~ *spring is in* **2. ~ ist ein Mann** an der Tür *there is a man at the door* ‖ ~ liegt die Schwierigkeit, ~ ist der Haken *there is the difficulty, there's the rub* ‖ ~ war noch etw mehr, das .. *there was something more that* .. **3. (in dem Falle)** *there, here*; *then*; *in that* od *this case* od *matter*: was läßt sich ~ m? *what can be done there* (od *in such a case*)? ~ stimme ich nicht mit Ihnen überein *there* od *here I do not agree with you* **4. wozu** ist das ~? *what's the use of this*? *what purpose does it serve*? er ist dazu ~, das z tun *it is incumbent upon him* (od *it is his duty*) *to do that* **5.** (verallgemeinernd) **wer ~, der** *he who*; einerlei wer ~ kommt *whoever may come* ..; einerlei was ~ geschieht *whatever may happen*; ⟨bib⟩ wer ~ suchet, der findet *he that seeketh findeth* ‖ es gibt Leute, die ~ glauben .. *there are people who do believe* .. **6. hier u ~** *here and there*; *in some places*; → II. **7. ~ sind wir** schon *here we are* ‖ ~ habe ich dich! *I have you there*! ‖ ~ ist es, ~ hast du's (*sc* was du suchtest) *here you* (od *we*) *are* ‖ ~ h wir's! *there we are*! ~ hast du's! *there* (od *so*) *now*! *there you are*! ‖ u schon ist's ~ *and there you are* ‖ ~ sieht man mal! *now there*! aber ~ sah man's wieder *but there it was* ‖ ~ hört doch alles auf! *that's the limit*! *that beats all* (⟨Am⟩ *the band*)! ‖ sieh ~, sieh ~! *look at that now*! *well I never*! *just fancy*! ‖ → II. 3. **8. Platz ~**! *get out of the way there*! nichts ~! *nothing of the kind*! *not a bit*! **C.** [in comp] → ~bei, ~mit etc ‖ °~ behüte mich Gott vor = davor behüte mich G., → behüten **II. (zeitlich) 1.** *then*; *at that time*; *at that moment*; ah, ~ waren wir noch jung *ah, we were young then* ‖ °wenn ich ~ noch lebe! *if I am still alive then* ‖ (in der Erzählung) *now*; ~ gab es gr Freude *there was great joy now* | **~ erst** *not till then* ‖ **v ~ an** *from that time onwards, thenceforward, thenceforth* **2. hier u ~** *here and there*; *sometimes, now and then, now and again* **III. (relativisch) 1.** *when, that*; in dem Augenblick, ~ der Vorhang hochging *at the moment when the curtain rose*; der Tag, ~ Heinrich starb *the day that poor Henry died* ‖ das erstemal, ~ sie ihn gesehen hatte *the first time* (*that*) *she had seen him* ‖ *while*; ~ er noch reich war, ~ hatte er viele Freunde *so long as he was rich he had many friends* **2. nun ~**, jetzt ~ *now, now that*; nun ~ du es erwähnst, will ich .. *now you mention it I will* ..

da conj **[kausal] 1.** *as*; ~ es dunkel wurde, kehrten wir um *as it was getting dark we turned round* ‖ ~ er jung war, schlief er fest *being young he slept heavily*; das Gesetz ist e–e viel wichtigere Verfügung, ~ es nicht nur die Beamten betrifft, sondern auch alle die .. *the law is a much more important enactment affecting as it does not only officials but all those* .. ‖ ~ sie ein ehrliches Kind war, wollte sie .. *for the honest child that she was she wanted* .. ‖ ~ ja *since*; *inasmuch as* ‖ ~ nun ⟨Kanzleistil⟩ *whereas* **2.** (→ da adv III.) ~ doch *when* (: *how could you tell him when you knew it would hurt him*?)

Da ⟨wir⟩ (= Strich) *dash*

Dabb m ~s/~s ⟨zoo⟩ *dabb, agamoid ground-lizard*; *uromastix* (L)

dab·ei [conj]: ~ (ist es dreimal so groß) *and yet*

dabei (Betonung → u) adv **A.** [dab·ei] **1.** nahe ~, dicht ~ *near by, close by, hard by* ‖ [in Verbindung mit Verben]: ~sitzen *to sit by* ‖ ~stehen *to stand by*, (untätig) *to look on*; → Beistehende **2. ~ sein a.** (P) *to be at it* (*sc at work, play*, etc.) ‖ ~ s z tun *to be about to do, to be on the point of doing* | (mitmachen) *to be on, to be in the movement* od *swim*; ganz ~ s *to be ready* od *game* (*to do*); ⟨sl⟩ *to be all there* ‖ (teilnehmen) *to be of the party, to share a th, to take part*; ich bin ~! *count me in*!; bin ich ~? *am I to be in on this*? **b.** (S) es ist doch nichts ~ *there is no harm in it*; was ist denn ~? *what of that*? *what harm is there in it*? was wäre denn ~, wenn ..? *what if* ..? **B.** [d·abei, dab·ei] **1.** [mst ′– –, am Satzanfang] *thereby, therewith*; *by that, with that*; ~ sah er mich an *with that he looked at me*; ~ (atmete er auf) *as he did so* (*he* ..) u ~ verirrte ich mich *and thereby I lost my bearings* **2.** (außerdem) *besides, moreover*; *in addition, into the bargain*; *as well*; *to boot*; die Ware ist schlecht u ~ teuer *the article is bad and expensive as well* **C.** [unbetont; den Ton hat das Verbum] **1.** ein Haus u ein G·ärtchen ~ *a house with a garden attached to it* **2.** er st·and (s·aß) ~ (*sc* während er sprach etc) *he was standing* (*sitting*) *all the time* ‖ Licht genug, um ~ z lesen *light enough to see by* ‖ ich habe mir nichts ~ gedacht *I meant no harm by it*; was denken Sie sich eigentlich ~? *what's the big idea*?; es kommt *or* springt nichts ~ heraus *it's of no use, it's no good, there is not much in it* **3. ~ bleiben a.** (P) *to abide by it, to persist in it, to insist on it, to keep to it*; bleibe ~ (*sc* bei d–m Plan) *keep to it* ‖ ich bleibe ~, daß *I maintain that* **b. es bleibt ~**! *it's a bargain*! *agreed*! ‖ u ~ bleibt es *and there it stands* **4 es ~ lassen** *to leave it at that* **5.** (daran) [unbetont] er ist w·ieder ~ *he's at it again*

d·a|bleiben vi [s] *to stay, to remain*; bleib doch noch da *stay a little longer* ‖ ~ müssen ⟨school⟩ *to be detained* (od *kept in*)

da c·apo adv (It) *da capo, encore* ‖ → Dakapo ‖ ~ rufen *to encore*

D·ach n ~(e)s/~̈er **1.** (Haus~) *roof*; ~̈er [pl] *roofs* [pl], [koll] *roofage*; abhängendes ~ zw 2 Giebeln *saddleback* ‖ Schiefer~ *slated roof*; Stroh~ *thatch*(*ed roof*); Vor~ ⟨arch⟩ *canopy*, Kabinen~ ⟨aero⟩ *canopy*; gebrochenes, französisches ~ *broken roof*; *attic*; → Pult~; Sattel~; Walm~; Zelt~ ‖ ohne ~ *roofless* ‖ ein ~ aufsetzen *to put a roof on* ‖ ein ~ decken *to cover a roof* (mit *with*); ein ~ mit Schiefer decken *to slate a roof*, mit Schindeln .. *to shingle a roof*, mit Stroh .. *to thatch a roof* **2.** ⟨übtr⟩ **a.** (of a vehicle) *roof*; *head* ‖ (of trees, etc.) *roof* (: *the trees formed a roof*); *vault* | ⟨anat⟩ Schädel~ *cranial vault* | ⟨min⟩ *roof*; *stratum lying over a bed of coal* **b.** (Haus) *roof, house*, unter m–m ~ *under my roof*; mit jdm unter e–m ~e wohnen *to live with a p under the same roof*; ein niedriges ~ *a modest dwelling* **3.** ⟨fig⟩ (Schutz) *shelter, protection* **4.** Wendungen: eins (*or* einen) aufs ~ bek ⟨fam⟩ *to get a clip over the head*; *to get a crack on the nut* ‖ *to get a scolding, to be slated* od *rebuked*; jdm eins aufs ~ geben *to hit a p over the head* ⟨a. fig⟩; *to slate, rebuke a p*;

jdm aufs ~ steigen *to haul a p over the coals*; *to talk to a p like a Dutch uncle*; *to comb a p's hair for him*; → abkanzeln, zurechtsetzen ‖ .. da ist bei ihm gleich Feuer im ~e .. *he flies into a passion*, ⟨sl⟩ .. *he loses his wool* ‖ (ein Haus) unter ~ bringen *to roof*; jdn, etw unter ~ u Fach bringen *to shelter, to house a p, a th*; *to bring a th to completion* ‖ unter ~ u Fach k *we are under cover* (od *safely housed*) *at last*; das Projekt ist nun unter ~ u F. *the project is finished* (od *complete*) *now*

D·ach- [in comp] *roof-* **~antenne** f ⟨wir⟩ *overhouse aerial* **~arbeit** f *roofing* ‖ (Achtung!) ~en! *works overhead* **~̊artig** a *roof-shaped, roof-like* **~aufsatz** m *skylight* **~balken** m *roof--tree*; schräger ~ *rafter*; → Hahnenbalken **~begriff** m → Ober- **~boden** m *loft* **~decker** m *roofer*; *tiler, slater, shingler*; (Stroh~̊) *thatcher*; → -leiter **~deckung** f *roofage*; *roofing*; *tiling, slating* **~fenster** n *dormer(-window)*; *skylight* **~filz** m *roofing felt* **~first** m *roof-ridge* ‖ ~balken m *ridge-pole* **~fläche** f *roofage* **~(garten)häuschen** n ⟨mod⟩ (im Hochhaus) *maison(n)ette* **~gesellschaft** f *holding company* **~gleichenfeier** f ⟨öster⟩ = Richtfest **~kammer** f *garret, attic, cock--loft* **~kantprisma** n ⟨opt⟩ *ridge* od *pentagon prism, roofprism* **~lauch** m ⟨bot⟩ = Dachwurz **~(decker)leiter** f *cat ladder* **~luke** f *scuttle*; *exit opening* **~organisation** f ⟨com, etc⟩ *over-all organization* **~pappe** f *tar-board*; → Dachfilz **~pfanne** f *pantile* **~reiter** m *wood-* od *ridge-turret*, ⟨hist⟩ *louver* **~rinne** f *gutter*; °du kannst ja aus der ~ frühstücken! ⟨fam⟩ *reach me down a star* °**~rutscher** m (Tiefflieger) ⟨fam⟩ *sky-hog, hedge-hop(per)* **~schaden** m ⟨fig fam⟩ *mental deficiency*; er hat e–n ~ *he's not quite right in the top stor(e)y* **~schiefer** m *roofing-slate* (od *-tile*) **~schindel** f *shingle* **~sparren** m *rafter* **~stein** m *slate, tile* **~stroh** n *thatch*; mit ~ decken *to thatch* **~stube** f *attic, garret* | ~nbewohner m *garreteer* **~stübchen** n *garret* **~stuhl** m *frame* (od *wood*)*-work* od *timbering, truss* **~traufe** f *eaves* [pl] **~türmchen** n *louver* **~werk** n *roofage, roofing* **~wohnung** f *garret*; ⟨bes Am⟩ (auf Hochhaus) *penthouse* **~wurz** f ⟨bot⟩ *houseleek, Sempervivum* (L) **~ziegel** m *tile*; → über–e–a legen

D·achl n ⟨österr⟩ = Dach **D·ächlein** n ~s/ *small roof, rooflet*

Dachs m D·achses/D·achse; → 1. c. **1.** ⟨zoo⟩ **a.** *badger*; ⟨dial & †⟩ *brock*; wie ein ~ schlafen *to sleep like a top* **b.** Australischer ~ *wombat*; Beutel~̊ *bandicoot* **c.** = ~hund **2.** ⟨fig⟩ (P) ein frecher ~ *a saucy customer*

D·achs- [in comp] *badger-* **~bau** m *badger's burrow* **~beil** n = Dechsel *adze* **~̊beinig** a *badger-legged* **~eisen** n *badger-gin* (od *trap*) **~fänger** m *terrier*; = Dachshund **~fell** n *badger's skin* **~fett** n *badger-fat* **~haar** n *b. bristle* | ~pinsel [m] *b. brush* **~hetze** f *badger--baiting* (od *drawing*) **~hund** m *badger-dog, badgerer*; *basset*; *dachshund* [Ger]

d·achte 1. & 3. sg pret v denken

°**D·achtel** f = Ohrfeige

D·ächsel m **1.** ⟨zoo⟩ = Dackel **2.** = Dechsel

D·ächsin f ~/~nen ⟨hunt⟩ *sow*, → *boar*, Dachs

°**D·ackel** m ⟨zoo Ger⟩ → Dachshund

Dada·ismus m ⟨arts⟩ *dadaism* (seit etwa 1917)

dadurch (Betonung → u) adv **A.** [dad·urch] **1. (örtlich)** [in Verbindung mit Verben] *through that, through it*; er eilte ~ *he ran through it* (sc *the gate*, etc.) **2.** ⟨übtr⟩ *by it*; *through it*; *with it*; *thereby*; er profitierte nichts ~ *he did not profit by* od *from it*; er war ~ erfreut *he was pleased with it*; er verlor ~ s–e Stellung *it lost him his position* ‖ → davon **B.** [d·adurch, am Satzanfang] **1.** *by this means*; *in this way, thus*; ~ gelang es ihm *in this way he succeeded* **2. ~ daß** conj *in that* (: *the success is all the more singular in that the book has captured the masses and pleased the critics*) ‖ ~ daß man Eisen erwärmt, dehnt man es aus *by warming iron you expand it*; ~ daß man Eisen erwärmt, dehnt es sich aus *by your warming iron, it expands*

dafür (Betonung → u) adv **A.** (daf·ür, dafür **1.** *for it* (od *that*), *for them*; ich bin ganz ~ [–′–] *I am all in favo(u)r of it*; er kann nichts ~ *he is not to blame for it*; ich zahlte 3 Mark ~ *I paid 3 marks for it* (sc *the book*), *for them* (sc *the books*) ‖ ich werde ~ sorgen, daß er dort ist *I'll see to it that he is there, I'll arrange for him to be there* ‖ er ist (mir) gut ~, er steht (mir) ~ *he answers* (od *is answerable*) *for it* (*to me*) ‖ häßlich, ~ aber reich *plain but rich* **2.** (an Stelle v) gib mir dies ~ *give me this instead of it, give me this in return* ‖ **3.** er ist bekannt ~ *he is known for it* ‖ ich kann nichts ~ *it is not my doing* (od *fault*), *I can't help it* **4. ~ sein** *to be on*; ich bin ~ *I am for* (od *in favour of*) *it, I vote for it* ‖ [ell] entschieden –′–! ⟨bes mil fam⟩ *flat out for it*! ‖ ⟨parl⟩ die Mehrheit ist ~ *the ayes have it*; die, welche ~ sind *those in favour* ‖ ~ s z tun *to be for doing, to advocate doing* ‖ ich halte ~, daß .. *I am of opinion that* .. **B.** [d·afür; am Satzanfang] **1.** (Ggs hierfür) ~ zahlte ich 3 Mark *for that one I paid 3 marks* ‖ ~ kenne ich kein Mittel *for this I know no remedy* ‖ ~ bedanke ich mich *no, thanks* **2.** er kann das, ~ ist er König *he can do that, for* (od *because*) *he is king* **3. ~ daß** *because* (: *he was punished because he had been late*)

Daf·ürhalten n [nur in]: nach m–m ~; m–s ~s *in my opinion, according to my judgment*

dagegen (Betonung → u) adv **A.** [dag·egen] **1.** er stieß ~ *he knocked against it* (sc *the staircase*); das Schiff stieß ~ *the ship struck against it* (sc *the rock*) **2.** ⟨übtr⟩ er eiferte ~ *he exclaimed against it* (sc *the church*); man schützte ihn ~ *they protected him from* (od *against*) *it* ‖ s–e Abneigung, Abscheu ~ *his aversion* od *reluctance to it* (sc *alcohol*), *his dislike of it* **3.** nichts ~ (einzuwenden) **haben** *to have no objection*; ich habe nichts ~ *I don't mind* (*it*), .. *if I do*; wenn Sie nichts ~ h *if you don't mind*; ⟨iron⟩ *if you please* ‖ h Sie etw ~, wenn geraucht wird? *do you mind smoking*? .., wenn ich rauche? *do you mind my smoking*? **4. ~ sein** *to be against it*, ⟨Am⟩ *to be down on it* ‖ *to the contrary*; Berichte, die ~ waren *reports* [pl] *to the contrary* **5.** (im Vergleich damit) *compared to it, in comparison to it*; die Musik ist nichts ~ *this music is nothing to it* (sc *German music*) ‖ wenn ich diese Uhr ~ halte .. *if I compare* (od *contrast*) *this watch with it* .. **6. (indessen)** *however*; *on the other hand*; .. was ~ nicht der Fall war .. *which, however, was not the case*; ~ muß man bedenken, daß .. *on the other hand we must remember that* .. **7.** das ist nichts ~ *that's nothing by comparison* **B.** [d·agegen; am Satzanfang] ~ habe ich nichts einzuwenden *to that I have no objection* ‖ ~ kenne ich kein Mittel *for that* (sc *rheumatism*) *I know no remedy* ‖ ~ kann man die Entwicklung halten, die .. *with that we may compare* (od *confront*) *the development which* ..; ~ kann man die Tatsache halten, daß .. *against that we may put the fact that* ..

d·agewesen [pp v. d·asein]; ist jemand ~? *has anybody called*?; noch nicht ~ *without precedent, unprecedented, unheard-of*; noch nicht ~ s *to be unprecedented* ‖ der größte Saal, der größte, der je ~ (ist) *the largest hall, the largest ever* ‖ alles ~̊e in den Schatten stellen *to eclipse all records*

Dagg m & n ~s/~en *rope's-end* ‖ durch die ~en laufen *to taste the rope's-end*; jdn durch die ~en laufen l *to rope's-end a p*

D·ag(h)estan n *Daghestan*

Daguerreotyp [da'gɛro–] n (Fr; nach L. J. M. Daguerre; † 1851) ⟨phot⟩ (Bild) *daguerreotype* **~·ie** f *daguerreotypy*

Dag·ussa f = Korakan

Dahab·ieh [–'i:e] f (Nilschiff) *dahabiah, –bieh*

dah·eim adv *at home*; ~ bleiben *to stay at home* ‖ *home*; er wird bald ~ s *he will be home soon* ‖ *in one's own country*

daher (Betonung → u) adv **A.** [dah·er] **1.** *from there*; wir k gerade ~, da k wir gerade her *we've just come from there* **2.** [mit intr. Verben der Bewegung] → daher– **B.** [d·aher] **1.** ~ weht der Wind *that's where the wind sits* **2.** 'Aus Österreich?' '~ stamme ich' *that's where I come* od *am from* **3.** ⟨übtr⟩ *from this, from that*; *hence, thence* ‖ ~ kommt es, daß .. *hence it comes that* ..; ~ k die Irrtümer *hence arise* (od *to this are due*) *the mistakes* ‖ *hence, thence, therefore, on that account*; *for that reason*; *consequently, accordingly*; *in that case* od *event*; *under the circumstances, the condition being this*; *by the same token*; *likewise* ‖ ~ dürfen wir annehmen, daß .. *hence we may assume that* .. ‖ sehr alt u ~ schwach *very old and thence feeble*

dah·er|- (→ daher A. 2.) **~brausen** vi [s] *to roar up* (*in a car*) **~eilen** vi [s] *to hurry along* **~gelaufener** m *anybody who comes* od *came along* **~gewesen** : alles ~e übertreffend *precedent-breaking* **~kommen** vi [s] *to come along* (: *Mr. N. came along*) **~reden** vi red nicht so dumm daher ⟨fam⟩ *don't talk rubbish*; geschwollen ~ *to mouth it* **~rennen** vi *to run along*; ~gerannt k *to come running along* **~sausen** vi [s] *to dash about* **~stapfen** vi [s] *to plug along* ‖ → einher–

d·aherum adv *thereabouts*; oder ~ *or thereabouts* †**dah·ier** adv ⟨off⟩ *here*

dahin [Betonung → u] adv **I.** [dah·in] **A. 1.** (dorthin) *there, thither*; er kam ~ *he came there*; er gehört ~ *he belongs to the place* **2.** (zeitlich) ~ s *to be gone, to be over* (od *past*); ~ waren die Freuden *gone were the pleasures* ‖ ~ *away, lost* **3.** ⟨übtr⟩ das gehört nicht ~ *that does not belong there*; *that has nothing to do with it*; *that has no bearing on it* ‖ er hat sein Teil ~ *he has got his share*; alles ~ geben *to give* (od *sacrifice*) *everything* (*in order to* ..) ‖ es steht noch ~ *it is still uncertain* (od *undecided, questionable*) ‖ ich lasse es ~gestellt *I leave it undecided*; es bleibt ~gestellt *it remains to be seen* **B.** [in Verbindung mit mst intr. Verben der Bewegung] → dahin– **II.** [d·ahin] **1.** ~, wo .. *to that place where* .. **2.** (zeitlich) bis ~ *till then*; *by then* (*they had lost everything*) **3.** ⟨übtr⟩ **a.** [bei intr u refl. Verben]: ~ ist es gek *it has come so far*; ~ war es gek, daß .. *it had come to this that* ..; laßt es nicht ~ k *don't let it come to that* ‖ m–e Ansicht geht ~, daß .. *my opinion is that* .. ‖ er äußerte sich ~, daß .. *he spoke to the effect that* ..; er äußerte sich ~ *he spoke to that effect* | wir einigten uns ~, daß .. *we agreed that* .. ‖ er strebte ~, er arbeitete ~, ihnen z helfen *he aimed at helping them* | °es steht mir bis ~ *I am sick of it* **b.** [bei trans. Verben]: jdn ~ bringen *to bring* (od *get, induce, lead, persuade*) *a p, to prevail upon a p* (*to do*) ‖ es ~ bringen, daß jd tut *to cause a p to do, to make a p do*; es ~ bringen, daß etw geschieht *to cause a th to be done*; er brachte es ~, daß der Plan scheiterte *he caused the plan to fail, he succeeded in thwarting the plan* ‖ ~ rechne ich .. *among those* (od *in that class*) *I reckon* ..

dah·in|- (→ dahin I. B.) [in comp oft: Verb + *along*] **~eilen** vi *to hurry along* **~fahren** vi *to drive along*; *to slip along*; schnell ~ *to spin along* ‖ mit Wucht ~ (of ship) *to forge*; *to forge one's way* **~fliegen** vi *to fly along* ‖ (of time) *to pass away*; schnell ~d *transient, transitory* (*life*) **~fließen** vi ⟨übtr⟩ *to flow* od *glide easily* od *smoothly*; (of verse) *to go with a swing* **~gehen** vi *to go along* ‖ (sterben) *to pass out* od *away, to depart this life* ‖ (of time) *to drag* (od *go*) *by*; *to pass away* **dah·ingestellt** [pp] bleiben *to remain to be seen*; *to be doubtful*; es ~ s l *to leave it undecided* (od *an open question* **~gleiten** vi (of a ship) *to sail*; auf der Straße ~ (of a car) *to glide along the road* °**~hauen** vt ⟨übtr⟩ (etw) *to dash off* **~jagen** vi *to spank along* **~leben** vi *to rub along*; stumpf ~ *to vegetate*; gedankenlos ~ *to go on existing with no thought for the future*; nur so ~, ohne Sinn u Zweck ~, ohne Zweck u Ziel ~ *to be at loose ends* **~raffen** vt (jdn) *to cut* (*a p*) *off*; → hin(weg)-raffen **~rasen** vi (of a car) *to spank along* **~sausen** vi (P) ⟨fam⟩ *to hurtle, whisk along* **~scheiden 1.** vi *to depart this life* **2.** ≈ n *the passing* (*of a p*) **~schlachten** vt *to slaughter* **~schlendern** vi *to slouch* od *tag along* **~schreiten** vi *to stamp* od *stride along*; über die Welt ~ (of death, etc.) *to stalk the world* **~schwanken** vi *to swing along* **~schwinden** vi *to dwindle* (od *melt, thin*) *away* ‖ (of time) *to pass away*; *to pass by* ‖ (of feeling) nicht so leicht ~ *to die hard* **~siechen** vi (vor Gram) *to pine* od *waste away* **~stapfen** vi [s] *to plug along* **~strömen** vi *to pour along* **~traben** vi *to trot along* **~träumen** vt die Tage ~ *to dream away one's time* **~trotten** vi *to trudge along* **~vegetieren** vi *to vegetate* **~welken** vi *to fade* (od *wither*) *away*; *to go into a decline* °**~wetzen** vi *to breeze along* **~ziehen** vi *to go* od *tag along*; *to travel*; (of vessels) *to ride*; (of the moon) *to ride* (: *the moon rode in a starless sky*)

d·ahinab adv *down there* **d·ahinauf** adv *up there* **d·ahinaus** adv **1.** *out there* **2.** ⟨übtr⟩ bis ~ *utterly*; verschuldet bis ~ *up to the eyes in debt* **d·ahinein** adv *into that place*; *in there* **dahing·egen** adv = dagegen A. 6.

dah·inten adv *behind* (*there*); *at the back*; weit ~ *far behind*; ~ l *to leave behind*

dah·inter adv **1.** *behind that* od *it*; *at the back of it*; ⟨Am⟩ *back of it* ‖ ~ gehen, stehen *to go, to stand behind it* **2.** ⟨fig⟩ **a.** *behind the scenes* ~|stecken, ~|stehen *to be at the bottom of it*; es steckt etw dahinter *there is more in it than meets the eye, there's sth at the back of it* od *behind* (*it*), ⟨Am⟩ *there's sth back of it* ‖ es steckt nichts ~ *there is nothing in it* **b.** ich werde bald ~|kommen *I shall soon unravel it, I shall soon find it out* (od *clear it up*) ‖ ich werde mich tüchtig ~|setzen *I shall take every pains with it, I shall do my best* ‖ was steckt ~? *what is it all about*? **c.** sehr ~her s *to be very keen on* .., *to be dead set on* ..; *to be out* (*to do*); er ist sehr ~her, es z erhalten *he does his utmost to get it*

ˣ**d·ahlen** vi [h] = tändeln

D·ahlie f ~/~n ⟨bot⟩ *dahlia*; Kaktus≈ *cactus dahlia*

D·ahome [–e:] n (W.-Afrika) *Dahomey*

Dak·apo n *encore* (Fr); drei ~s *three encores* [pl] → da capo

†**D·akien, D·azien** n *Dacia*

Dak·ota pl → Sioux

dakt·ylisch a *dactylic* **Daktylogr·aph** m ~en/~en ⟨Sw⟩ *typist* **Daktylolog·ie** f *dactylology* **D·aktylus** m ~/Dakt·ylen ⟨pros⟩ *dactyl* (– ∪ ∪)

D·alarna, D·alerne n (schwed. Landschaft) *Dalarne* **Dalek·arlien** n (schwed. Landschaft) *Dalecarlia*

D·albe f ~/~n ⟨mar⟩ (Pfahl) *dolphin*; *bollard*

Dalb·ergie [–iə] f ~/~n ⟨bot⟩ *Amerimnon, Dalbergia* (L); *sissoo*

d·a|liegen vi [h] → da adv I. A. 1.

°**D·alles** m ~/ *impecuniosity* || den ~ h, im ~ s *to be hard up, to be short* od ⟨Am⟩ *flat, to be flat broke*

°**d·alli** adv ~! ein wenig ~! *hurry up! be quick about it! look sharp!; make it snappy!*

Dalm·atien n (Küstenlandschaft am Ostufer des Adriatischen Meeres) *Dalmatia* **dalm·atisch, dalmat·inisch** a *Dalmatian*

Dalm·atika f (L) ~/-ken ⟨R. C.⟩ *dalmatic*

Dalmat·iner m ~s/~ **1.** *Dalmatian* **2.** ⟨zoo⟩ *Dalmatian, Dalmatian dog* **dalmat·inisch** a *Dalmatian*

D·alsland n (schwed. Landschaft) *Dalsland*

Dalton·ismus m *daltonism*

D·altonsches Gesetz (nach J. Dalton, † 1844) n ⟨phys⟩ *Dalton's law*

Dam m ~s/~e ⟨zoo⟩ = Damhirsch **~geiß** f, **~schmaltier** n (im 2. Jahr) *pricket's sister*

d·amalig a *then* || der ~e Botschafter *the then Ambassador* || die ~en Sitten *the customs of that time* || ihr ~es Alter *her then age*

d·amals adv *then; at that time; in those days* || bis ~ *till then*; seit ~ bis jetzt *from then until now* || schon ~ *even then* || seit ~ *from that time*

Dam·askus n (Hauptstadt Syriens) *Damascus*

Dam·ast m ~s/~e **1.** *damask* **2.** [in comp] *damask (linen, paper)*; ~stoff [m] *damask* **dam·asten** a *damask* **Damasz·ene** f ~/~n ⟨bot⟩ *damson, damascene* **Damasz·ener** a, ~ Klinge [f] ~ Säbel [m] *damask* (od *damascus*) *blade* || ~ Pflaume [f] *damson* || ~ Rose [f] ⟨bot⟩ *damask rose* || ~ Stahl [m] *damask* **damasz·ieren** vt [h] (Stoff) *to damask*; (Stahl) *to damascene* **damasz·iert** a *damascene (work), damascened (hilt); damsk(ed)*; ~e Arbeit [abstr] *damaskeening* **Damasz·ierung** f *damascening*

D·ämchen n ~s/~ ⟨fam⟩ *damsel*

D·ame f ~/~n **1. a.** *lady*; m-e ~ *madam*; m-e ~n (u Herren) *ladies (and gentlemen)* || (beim Tanz) *partner* || ohne ~ gehen ⟨Am⟩ *to go stag* || vornehme ~ *gentlewoman*; ⟨poet⟩ *dame* || Anstands≈ *chaperon*; Hof≈ *lady-in--waiting*; junge ~ ⟨fam⟩ *damsel*; junge ~, die zuerst in die Gesellschaft eingeführt wird *débutante*, ⟨Am fam⟩ *deb* || ~ des leichten Milieus *lady of ease virtue* || die gr ~ spielend *ladyfied*, .. spielen *to pretend to be a lady* **b.** ⟨fam⟩ m-e alte ~ *my mater* (= *mother*), *the old lady* **c.** die Weiße ~ *the White Lady* **2.** ⟨übtr⟩ ⟨bot⟩ ~ in Trauer *iris* **3.** (im Spiel) **a.** (Siegerstein im ~spiel) *king* || eine ~ m *to crown a man*; in die ~ k (of a man) *to be crowned* | (~spiel) *draughts*; ⟨Scot⟩ *dams*; ⟨Am⟩ *checkers* [pl] || ~ spielen *to play at draughts*; laß uns eine Partie ~ spielen *let us have a game of draughts* **b.** ⟨chess⟩ *queen*; die ~ ziehen, sich e-e ~ m *to go to queen, to queen a pawn* **c.** ⟨cards⟩ *queen* **4.** [in comp] → Dame–; Damen–

D·ame- (→ Dame 3.) **~brett** n *draught* (⟨Am⟩ *checker*) *-board* **~spiel** n *draughts* [pl]; ⟨Am⟩ *checkers*; → Dame 3. a. **~stein** m *man*; ⟨Scot⟩ *dam*

°**D·ämel,** °**D·äm(e)lack** m ~s/~s *fool, noodle, blockhead* **Dämel·ei** f *foolishness; foolish act*

D·amen- (→ Dame 1.) [in comp] *lady's, woman's*; (oft [vor pl mst]) *ladies'* **~abteil** n ⟨rail⟩ *ladies' compartment* **~bekleidungsgeschäft** n *women's outfitters* pl **~besuch** m *lady-visitor* **~binde** f *sanitary towel* **~brett** n = Damebrett **~doppel(spiel)** ⟨ten⟩ *the women's doubles* [pl] **~einzelspiel** n ⟨ten⟩ *the women's singles* [pl] **~flor** m (*array of*) *ladies* [pl] **~frisör** m *hair stylist* **~gemach** n *bower, lady's chamber* **~gesellschaft** f *ladies' party*, → ~klatsch; das kann in ~ nicht gesagt w *it cannot be said in mixed company* **~hand** f *lady's hand* **~held** m *lady's* (od *ladies'*) *man, squire of dames; lady--killer* **~handschuh** m *lady's glove*; ~e [pl] *ladies' gloves* [pl] **~hemd** n *chemise; camisole; vest* **~hose** f (lange, weite) *slacks* pl **~hut** m *lady's hat*; (ohne Krempe mit Bändern) *bonnet*; (eng anliegender) *cloche* °**~klatsch** m *henn-* od *cat--party* **~kleid** n *frock*; (f Gesellschaft) *gown, lady's dress* **~kleidung** f *lady's dress*; phantastische ~ *Dolly Varden* **~konfektion** f *ladies' outfitting; millinery*; ~sgeschäft *the milliner's, millinery* **~kostüm** n *lady's tailor-made costume* **~oberbekleidung** f *women's outer wear* **~putzwaren** f [pl] *millinery* **~reitkleid** n *lady's riding-habit* **~sattel** m *lady's saddle, side-saddle* **~schlüpfer** m (enger) ein ~ *a pair of tighties* **~schneider** m *ladies' tailor*; ~in [f] *dressmaker* **~schneiderei** f *ladies' tailoring* **~stein** m = Damestein **~stift** n *charitable institution for gentlewomen* **~tampons** m pl ⟨Am⟩ *absorbencies* pl **~toilette** f *powder-room* **~unterwäsche** f *lingerie* (Fr) **~wahl** f *the ladies' turn* od *choice* **~welt** f *the realm of ladies; ladyhood*

d·amenhaft a *ladylike; resembling a lady*

D·am- hirsch m ⟨zoo⟩ *fallow-deer*; (im 5. Jahr) *bare buck* **~wild** n *fallow deer*; → Dam

ˣ**d·amisch** a → albern, dumm; betäubt; ungeheuerlich

damit [Betonung → u] adv **A.** [dam·it] **1.** *with it, with them*; er nahm das Buch (die Bücher) u ging ~ fort *he took the book(s) and went away with it (with them)*; was soll ich ~? *what am I to do with it?* || es ist nichts ~ *it's no good* || *therewith*; jeder, der ~ verbunden war *every man connected therewith* || sich ~ begnügen z tun *to content o.s. with doing* **2.** *by it, by them*; ja, er fuhr ~ *yes, he went by it* (sc *the train*); was meinen Sie ~? *what do you mean by it?* **3.** *to it*; ich bin ~ einverstanden *I agree* (od *consent*) *to it*; ich bin ~ einverstanden, daß er abreist *I consent to his leaving* **4.** her ~! heraus ~! *out with it!* || es würde ~ aus s *there would be an end to it* **B.** [d·amit] **1.** *with that* od *it*; ~ eilt es nicht *there is no hurry with it*; ~ hat es noch Zeit *that can wait* **2.** *therewith*; ~ erhob er sich *therewith he rose* || u ~ *and therewith; and consequently, and thus*; u ~ basta or abgemacht! *and there's an end of it!*

dam·it conj **I. 1.** *that, in order that, to the end that* (.. *may; might; should*); er hielt inne, ~ er sähe *he stopped that he might see*; ich habe sie hergebracht, ~ du sie ansiehst *I have brought them in order that you may look at them*; .., ~ nichts vergessen wird .. *in order that nothing may* (bzw *might*) *be forgotten; turn him round so I can see his back* **2.** er war vorsichtig, ~ er sie nicht störte *he was careful not to disturb her*; er lag ruhig da, ~ er sie nicht störte *he would lie there quietly so as not to disturb her*; der Nagel wurde angestrichen, ~ er nicht zu sehen war *the nail was varnished so as not to show* || er muß sein Gepäck vorzeigen, ~ der Beamte es prüft *he must show his luggage for the official to examine* **3. ~ nicht** *lest* (.. *should* ..); ich verberge es, ~ er es nicht findet *I'll hide it lest he should find it*, ⟨poet⟩ *lest he find it* **II.** ⟨mst poet⟩ [pron rel] = womit; mit dem etc

°**d·ämlich** a *foolish, silly, stupid, sheepish* °**D·ämlichkeit** f *silliness, stupidity, sheepishness*

Damm m ~(e)s/≈e **1.** (Erderhöhung) **a.** (gegen Wasser) *dam*; (etw) durch e-n ~ schützen *to dam* || (Deich) *dike, dyke* || (Fluß≈) *dam, embankment; barrage*; ⟨Am⟩ *levee*; (Stau≈) *retaining dam* || (Hafen≈) *breakwater; jetty, mole, pier; quay* **b.** (verbindender ~) *causeway*; (Marschland) durch e-n ~ überbrücken *to causeway* || *bank; raised ground*; → Wall || ⟨rail⟩ Bahn≈ *embankment* **c.** ⟨fig⟩ *bar; barrier, breakwater* (gegen *against*); *impediment, obstacle*; e-r S e-n ~ setzen *to place a check on a th* **2.** (gepflasterter Fahr≈) **a.** *roadway* || (Straße) *avenue, boulevard, highroad* **b.** 1. (jdn *or* etw) (wieder) **auf den ~** bringen *to give (a p) a leg up; to set (a p) on his legs* (od *feet*) *(again), to brush (a th) up* 2. (jdn) auf den ~ bringen *to make (a p) find his legs; to put (a p) to the run* ‖ = zurechtsetzen ⟨fig⟩ | **auf dem ~ s** 1. *to be alive* od *astir; to be wide awake,* ⟨fam⟩ *to be on one's pins* od *toes* 2. *to be up to date* 3. wieder ganz auf dem ~ s *to be quite all right again* 4. nicht (ganz) auf dem ~ s *not to feel up to the mark,* ⟨fam⟩ .. *up to snuff; to be out of sorts;* ⟨sl⟩ *to feel blue* (od *green, yellow, queer) about the gills* ‖ wieder auf dem ~ s ⟨fam⟩ *to be on one's feet* **3.** ⟨anat⟩ *perineum* (L) **~arbeit** f; **~bau** m *the building of a dam* (etc) **~bruch** m *bursting of a dike,* ⟨Am⟩ *crevasse* **~erde** f *mould* **~grube** f *casting-pit* **~riß** m ⟨surg⟩ *rupture of the perineum, perineal rupture* **~rutsch** m *landslip,* ⟨Am⟩ *landslide* **~stein** m *a medium-sized amber* **~straße** f *quay* **~weg** m *causeway*

D·ammarharz n *dammar*

ˣ**d·ammelig** a *foolish,* → Dämel, dämlich

d·ämmen vt [h] **1.** *to dam (up); to dike, to dyke* **2.** ⟨fig⟩ *to dam (up); to stop (up); to block, obstruct; confine, check; restrain*

***D·ämmer** m *half-light, twilight;* = Dämmerung **~grau** n: im ersten, frühen ~ liegen *to be shrowded in the grey of early dawn* **~licht** n, **~schein** m *dusk, twilight* (beim ~ *by t.*) **~schlaf** m *twilight-sleep* **~schoppen** m *early-evening drink,* ⟨bes Am⟩ *sundown(er)* **~stunde** f *twilight;* in der ~ *by twilight, at dusk* (bzw) *dawn* **~zustand** m *semi-trance, semi-conscious state*

d·ämmerhaft a *dusky, twilight* [attr] ‖ ⟨fig⟩ *dim, obscure* **d·ämmerig** a *twilight, dusky;* es wird ~ *it is getting dusky* (od *dark*) ‖ ⟨fig⟩ *dim, obscure; shadowy*

d·ämmern I. vi & imps [h] **1.** vi *to dawn;* der Tag dämmerte *the day dawned* ‖ (of a candle) *to burn dimly* | ⟨fig⟩ *to dawn;* (of feelings) *to begin to appear* od *arise* ‖ vor sich hin ~ *to doze; walk leisurely* **2.** [imps] **es dämmert** *it is getting dusky* od *dark;* (bei Tagesanbruch) *it is dawning* | ⟨fig⟩ es –rt mir schwach *I remember dimly, I have a vague idea;* jetzt –rte es bei mir (*or* in m–m Kopfe) *it dawned upon me; it became clear to me; I began to see (what* .. od *that* ..) **II.** ~̈ n ⟨fig⟩ noch im ~ s *to be dawning* **d·ämmernd** a *dawning; dusky, twilight* ‖ ⟨fig⟩ *dawning (hope); nascent* **D·ämmerung** f ~/~en (Abend~̈) *twilight, gleaming, dusk;* in der ~ *by twilight, at dusk* (od *nightfall*) ‖ (Morgen~̈) *dawn, the grey of dawn* (od *of the morning*); ⟨poet⟩ *dawning;* astronomische ~ *nautical twilight* **~sschein** m *twilight glow*

D·amno m, **D·amnum** n (L) ~s/ ⟨com⟩ *damage; deduction, loss; rebate*

D·amoklesschwert n *sword of Damocles*

D·ämon m ~s/Däm·onen ⟨myth & übtr⟩ *demon, daemon* ‖ ~enverehrung f *demonolatry*

däm·onisch a **1.** (teuflisch) *demoniac (spirit), demoniacal (expression, look); demonic (character); ghoulish* **2.** (v übernatürlicher Kraft) *daemonic (man);* das Dämonische *the daemonic element (in man)* **Dämonolog·ie** f *demonology*

D·ampf m ~(e)s/~̈e **1.** (Wasser~̈) **a.** *steam;* vom ~ beherrscht *steam-ridden (era)* ‖ gesättigter ~ *saturated steam;* überhitzter ~ *superheated st., steam-gas* **b.** ⟨fig⟩ *steam, energy; go* **c.** Wendungen: ~ ablassen *to let* od *blow off steam* ‖ ~ aufsetzen *to get up* (od *put on*) *steam;* ⟨cycl⟩ *to accelerate* ‖ ~ erzeugen *to generate steam* ‖ ~ geben ⟨mot⟩ *to step on the gas, to open the throttle;* ~ spannen *to increase the tension of steam* ‖ mit vollem ~ *at full steam; with full steam on* ‖ (etw) mit ~ behandeln *to steam;* (Umschlag) mit ~ öffnen *to steam* .. *open* ‖ unter ~ liegen (of ships) *to lie with steam up;* unter ~ s (of ships) *to be under steam;* (Lok) ⟨rail⟩ unter ~ .. *with steam up;* (of machines) *to be under* (od *in*) *steam* | ⟨fig⟩ mit ~ arbeiten *to get up steam;* → Voll~̈ ‖ das ging wie mit ~ *that went swimmingly* od *smoothly* ‖ ~ dahinter machen (*or* setzen) *to step on the gas, to get up steam, to make things hum* ‖ Hans ~ in allen Gassen *Jack of all trades, the lad of the village* **2.** (Wasserdunst) *vapour; damp;* (etw) in ~ verwandeln *to vaporize* ‖ (Nebel) *mist, fog* **3.** (Rauch) (Pulver~̈) *smoke;* Tabaks~̈ *reek of tobacco; smoke* **4.** (Ausdunstung) **a.** *exhalation (from the body)* ‖ ~̈e [pl] *fumes* [pl]; voll v (giftigen etc) ~̈en *fume filled;* ⟨min⟩ *damps* [pl] **b.** ⟨fig⟩ °~, Heiden~̈ ⟨sl⟩ *(blue) funk;* ~ h *to be in a blue funk;* ~ bek *to get into funk, to get the wind up* **5.** ⟨vet⟩ (Kurzatmigkeit) *broken wind;* den ~ h *to be broken-winded* **~ableitung** f : Rohr f schnelle ~ *quick vent pipe* **~absperrventil** n *steam-stop valve* **~anlage** f *steam-power plant* **~antrieb** m *steam drive* **~̈artig** a *vaporous, vapo(u)ry* **~auslaßrohr** n *exhaust-steam pipe* **~bad** n *vapo(u)r-bath* **~bagger** m *steam-dredger* **~barkasse** f *steam-launch* **~blasenbildung** f *vapo(u)r lock (in fuel pipe)* **~betrieb** m *steam-driving* (od *drive*); *steam-driven plant* **~bildung** f *formation of vapo(u)r* od *steam* **~boot** n *steamboat; steamer* **~bremse** f *steam-brake* **~bügeleinrichtung** f *steam press* **~̈dicht** a *steam-tight* **~dom** m *steam-dome* **~druck** m *steam-pressure,* ⟨tech⟩ *head of steam;* ~messer [m] *steam gauge, elaterometer;* kolbenlose ~pumpe [f] *pulsometer* **~dusche** f = Dampfstrahl **~einlaß** m *steam inlet* **~entnahme** f *extraction* **~entöler** m *oil extractor* **~entwässerer** m *steam-drier* **~entwicklung** f, **~erzeugung** f *generation of steam; steam-raising* **~fähre** f *steam-ferry* **~̈fixieren** vt [h] *to st. set* **~̈förmig** a *vaporous* **~gebläse** n *steam blast* od *blower* **~hammer** m *steam-hammer* **~heißmangel** f *cylindrical st. press* **~heizung** f *steam-heating* **~jacht** f *steam-yacht* **~kanal** m *steam-passage* **~kasten** m *steam-box* (od *chest*) **~kessel** m *steam-boiler; generator;* ~anlage [f] *boiler-plant;* ~rohr [n] *boiler-tube* **~̈klar** a ; ~ s *to be under steam* **~kochtopf** m *steamer; autoclave, digester* **~kohle** f *steam-coal* **~kolben** m *steam-piston* **~kompresse** f ⟨med⟩ *hot wet-compress* **~kraft** f *steam-power;* ~anlage [f] *steam-power plant* **~leitung** f *steam-piping;* ~srohr [n] *steam-pipe* **~lokomotive** f *steam locomotive* **~mantel** m *steam jacket* **~maschine** f *steam-engine; steam-raiser;* oszillierende ~ *oscillating st.-e.,* rotierende ~ *rotary st.-e.;* ~ mit Umsteuerung *reversing st.-e.;* → Verbund~̈ ‖ ~nalage [f] *steam-power plant;* ~nbauer [m] *steam-engine builder* **~messer** m *steam meter* **~nudeln** f [pl] ⟨Ger cul⟩ *stewed dumplings* [pl] **~pfeife** f *steam whistle* **~pflug** m *steam-plough* **~pumpe** *steam-punp* **~raum** m (über dem Kessel) *steam-room* (od *space*); (unter dem Kessel) *steam-pocket* **~rohr** n *steam-pipe* **~roß** n *locomotive* **~schiff** n *steamboat, steamship, steamer, steam-vessel;* → Dampfer **~schiffahrt** f *steam-navigation;* ~sgesellschaft [f] *steam-navigation company;* ~slinie [f] *steam-navigation line* **~schlange** f *steam-coil* **~spannung** f *steam-pressure* **~speicher** m *steam accumulator* **~spritze** f *steam fire-engine* **~strahl** m *steam-jet;* ~gebläse [n] *steam-jet blower;* ~luftpumpe [f] *steam-jet air pump* **~turbine** f *steam-turbine* **~·überdruck** m *effective steam pressure above atmospheric* **~überhitzer** m *steam-superheater* **~verbrauch** m *steam-consumption* **~verbraucher** m (of engines) ⟨fam⟩ *steam-eater* **~v·orwärmer** m *feed heater* **~wagen** m *steam-car* **~walze** f *steam-roller* ⟨a. fig⟩; mit der ~ vernichten *to steam-roller* **~waschanstalt** f *steam-laundry* **~winde** f *steam-winch* **~zuleitung** f *steam supply*

d·ampfen vi/t [h] **I.** vi **1.** (ausdunsten) **a.** (of hot liquids, food; of animals; of meadows, etc.) *to steam, to emit hot vapour, to smoke with heat*; ⟨poet⟩ *to fume*; ⟨dial⟩ *to reek* (v *with*); die Wiesen ∼ *the meadows are steaming* **b.** (rauchen) *to smoke, fume*; der Schornstein dampfte *the chimney smoked* **c.** (of mist) *to steam*; *to rise in the form of vapour*; ∼d aufsteigen *to rise in vapour* ‖ *to fume* **2. a.** (of engines) *to steam, to generate steam* **b.** (of a ship, train) *to steam* **c.** (P) *to* (*go* od *to travel by*) *steam*; → ab∼ **3.** ⟨fig poet⟩ *to steam*; *to work vigorously* ‖ das Land dampft v Kraft *the country radiates energy* **II.** *vt (rauchen) *to smoke* (*one's pipe*)

d·ämpfen vt [h] **A.** (auslöschen) **1.** ⟨eig⟩ (Feuer) *to damp* (*down*), *quench, smother*; *extinguish* **2.** ⟨übtr⟩ (Aufstand) *to suppress*; *to put down*; *to quell* **3.** (mäßigen, mildern) **a.** (Schall) *to deaden*; [mst pass] *to muffle*; (Geräusch) *to blimp*; (Stimme) *to soften*; mit ge–fter Stimme (*to speak*) *in a low voice* ‖ *to cushion* (*blow, impact, fall*) ‖ (Licht, Farbton) *to soften* (*down*), *to subdue*; ⟨el⟩ *to attenuate*; → gedämpft **c.** (Leidenschaft) *to soften*; *conquer, smother, subdue*; *check* ‖ (Stimmung, Gefühle) *to damp*(*en*), *depress*; *to mute* (*down*); *to cast a damper on, to be a damper to* (*a p's spirits*) **B. 1.** ⟨cul⟩ [bes Sw = schmoren] *to stew*; gedämpft w *to be stewed, to stew* **2.** ⟨tech⟩ (Holz, Gewebe) *to steam*

D·ampfer m ∼s/∼ ⟨mar⟩ *steamer, steamboat, steamship* (abbr *S.S.* [vor dem Schiffsnamen: *S.S. Niobe*]); ⟨fam⟩ *boat* ‖ Fluß∼̊ *river-boat, waterbus*; Fracht∼̊ *cargo steamer*; Schrauben∼̊ *screw steamer*; Schlepp∼̊ *steam-tug*; Tramp∼̊ *tramp*; Übersee∼̊, Passagier∼̊ *liner* ‖ mit dem ∼ *by steamer*; mit dem ersten ∼ *by the first boat*; mit dem ∼ fahren *to go* (od *travel*) *by steamer* (od *by liner, by steam*); *to steam* (hinüber nach *over to*)

D·ampfer- ∼gesellschaft f *steamship-company, shipping company* **∼hafen** m *steamer pier* **∼linie** f *steamship-line*

D·ämpfer m ∼s/∼ **1.** ⟨mus⟩ (am Klavier) *damper*, (am Harmonium) *sourdine* ‖ (vom Streichinstrument) *mute* (: *with a mute on his cello*), *sordine* | ⟨at⟩ *moderator* | ⟨fig⟩ [dat] (Freude, Wünschen etc) e–n ∼ aufsetzen *to cast a damp on a th, to damp a th*; jdm e–n ∼ aufsetzen *to put a check* od *damper on a p*(*'s self--assertion*); ⟨fam⟩ *to take a p down a peg* **2.** ⟨tech⟩ *damper*; ⟨wir⟩ (am Lautsprecher) *baffle--board*; ⟨mot⟩ (Schall∼̊) *silencer*, ⟨Am⟩ *muffler*; ⟨aero⟩ *stabilizer* ‖ (Stoß∼̊) *shock-absorber*; (an e–r Bogenlampe) *dash-pot* **3.** ⟨cul⟩ *steamer*

d·ampfig a *steamy, vaporous*

d·ämpfig a ⟨vet⟩ *broken-winded* (*horse*), ∼es Pferd ⟨fam⟩ *piper* **∼̊keit** f ⟨vet⟩ *broken wind* (*in a horse*)

D·ampfl n ∼s/∼ [österr] ⟨cul⟩ = Hefestück

D·ämpfung f ∼/∼en **1.** *damping, quenching* (*of a fire*) ‖ *suppression* (*of a rebellion*) **2.** *deadening, muffling* (*of a sound*); *softening, subduing* (*of light*) ‖ ⟨phys⟩ *damping* (*of oscillations*); *cushioning*, → dämpfen; *attenuation* ⟨a. el, telv⟩ **3.** *damping* (*of spirits*); *checking* (*of passion*) **4.** ⟨cul⟩ *stewing* (*of meat*) ‖ ⟨tech⟩ *steaming* (*of fabrics*) **∼sentz·errung** f *attenuation compensation* **∼sfeder** f *supplementary spring* **∼sfläche** f, **∼sflosse** f ⟨aero⟩ *tail-plane* (⟨Am⟩ *horizontal*) *stabilizor* **∼smaß** n ⟨logar⟩ → Dezibel, *decibel* **∼smesser** m *decremeter* **∼sverz·errung** f *attenuation distortion*

D·amspiel, D·amstein = Damespiel, –stein

danach [Betonung → u] **I.** adv **1.** [mst danach] *after that, after it* (: *he could not sleep after that*) ‖ (zeitlich) *upon that, thereupon*; bald ∼ *soon* (od *shortly*) *after* **2.** [dan·ach, danach] **a.** *for it*; er fragte, verlangte ∼ *he asked for it*; ich frage nichts ∼ *I don't care a pin*; wer fragt ∼? *who cares?* ‖ er sehnte sich ∼ *he was longing for it*; er sehnte sich ∼ zu heiraten *he was longing to marry* ‖ er strebte ∼, der erste z s *he aimed at being the first* ‖ der Sinn steht mir nicht ∼ *I have no mind to do it* **b.** *accordingly, according to that*; handle ∼ *act in accordance with it* ‖ das Papier ist billig, ist aber auch ∼ *the paper is cheap and thus of inferior quality* ‖ er ist nicht der Mann ∼ *he is not the man for it, he is not equal to it* ‖ er sieht ganz ∼ aus *he looks* (*very much like*) *it* **3.** [d·anach] ∼ habe ich nicht gefragt *for that I did not ask* ‖ ∼ sieht er auch aus *he looks like it indeed* **II.** ⟨mst poet⟩ [pron rel] = wonach; nach dem etc

†**D·anaer** [ˈdɑːnaər] m pl ⟨Gr⟩ *Danaï* [L] pl **∼geschenk** n *Greek* (od *treacherous*) *gift*

Dana·idenarbeit f *Danaidean* od *futile task*

D·andy [ˈdændi] m ∼s/∼s *dandy*; ⟨sl⟩ *toff*

D·äne m ∼n/∼n *the Dane*; [pl] *the Danes* [pl]

D·änemark n *Denmark*

dan·eben adv **1.** *beside* (od *near*) *it*; *next to it* od *that*; dicht ∼, gleich ∼ *close by, hard by* | *beside the mark*; ∼ gehen (of a missile, etc.) *to fail to hit, to pass by without touching*; der Versuch ging dan·eben *the attempt miscarried*; °∼|hauen [vi] [h] *to miss the mark*; ∼|treten *to miss one's footing* ‖ ⟨fig⟩ °sich ∼ benehmen *to misbehave*; ∼ raten *to miss one's guess* ‖ ∼ schießen (im Reden etc) *to miss one's mark* (od *guess, aim*), *to draw the wrong conclusion* | **sich** ∼|setzen *to miss* (*the seat, etc*) **2.** (außerdem) *besides, moreover*

D·anebrog m ∼s/ *Dan*(*n*)*ebrog*

d·ängeln vt → dengeln

†**dan·ieder** adv *on the ground, down*; *low* ‖ → nieder **∼|liegen I.** vi [h] **1.** (krank s) *to be lying ill, to lie up, to be laid low, to be taken ill*; an Influenza ∼ *to be laid up* (od *to be down*) *with i.* **2.** ⟨fig⟩ *to be brought down*; *to be lacking in vigour* (od *activity*) ‖ ⟨com⟩ *to languish*; (of trade) *to be depressed* **II.** ∼̊ n *depression*

D·aniell-Element [ˈdænjel–] n [engl] (nach J. Fr. Daniell, † 1845) ⟨phys⟩ *Daniell cell*

d·änisch 1. a *Danish* ‖ ∼es Recht in England z Zeit der ∼en Eroberung *Danelaw* (*–lagh*) **2.** das ∼̊e *Danish* (auf ∼̊ *in D.*)

Dank m ∼(e)s **1.** *thanks* [pl]; *gratitude* ‖ → ∼barkeit; Lohn **2. a. aufrichtigen ∼** (*my*) *sincerest thanks*; herzlichen ∼ (*my*) *cordial th.*; tiefgefühlten ∼ (*my*) *heartfelt th.* ‖ besten ∼ *best th.*, vielen ∼, schönen ∼ *many thanks*; vielen herzlichen ∼ *best th.*, vielen ∼, schönen ∼ *many thanks*; vielen herzlichen ∼ *thanks very much, thank you very much indeed*; tausend ∼ *a thousand thanks*; ⟨vulg⟩ *thanks ever so* ‖ **habe** ∼ f *accept my thanks for*; h Sie vielen ∼ *thank you very much* ‖ unser ∼ ist dir gewiß *you can be confident of our gratitude*; das ist der ∼ dafür *this is how you are thanked* (od *repaid*) *for it* ‖ unser ∼ gebührt ihm zuerst *our thanks are due to him first* ‖ Gott sei ∼! *thanks be to God!, thank God!*; dem Himmel sei ∼! *Heaven be thanked!* **b.** s–n ∼ **abstatten,** ausdrücken, aussprechen *to express one's thanks* (*for*); jdm s–n ∼ abstatten *to render thanks to a p, to thank a p* ‖ jdm s–n ∼ ausdrücken *to speak one's thanks to a p, to tender a p one's th.* ‖ jds ∼ entgegennehmen *to accept a p's th.* ‖ wenig ∼ habe ich dafür geerntet *small thanks I got for it* ‖ jdm ∼ **sagen** *to return thanks to a p*; *to thank a p* ‖ jdm ∼ schulden *to be indebted to a p* (*for*) ‖ jdm ∼ **wissen** *to be grateful* od *obliged to a p* (f *for*); du wirst es mir ∼ wissen *you will thank me for it, you will feel indebted* od *be grateful to me for it*; jdm schlechten ∼ wissen *to give a p no thanks* **c. mit** (vielem) ∼ *with* (*many*) *thanks*; **mit ∼**

annehmen *to accept* (*a th*) *with th.*; .. zurückgeben *to return* (*a th*) *with th.* | jdm etw **zu ~e m** *to please a p* (: *you'll never p. him*) || du würdest mich **zu** (gr) **~ verpflichten**, wenn du schicktest .. *you would* (*highly*) *oblige me by sending* ..; jdm zu ~ verpflichtet s *to be* (*very much*) *obliged* od *indebted to a p* (*for*); wir sind Ihnen sehr zu ~ verpflichtet, daß Sie .. *we appreciate having you* (*take up this matter for us*); sich [dat] jdn zu ~ verpflichten *to deserve well of a p* || zum (*or* als) ~ erhielt ich vom ihm .. *in token of his gratitude I received* .. **3.** [in comp] → Dank–; Dankes–

dank prep [mit dat & * (vor Abstr.) gen] *thanks to, owing to*; *through*; ~ deiner Hilfe *thanks to* (od *through*) *your help*

D·ank- (→ a. ~es–) **~adresse** f *vote of thanks* **~́beflissen** a *studiously grateful* **~́erfüllt** a *full of gratitude* **~fest** n *Thanksgiving*; ⟨Am⟩ *Thanksgiving Day* (im Nov.) **~gebet** n *thanksgiving* **~gottesdienst** m *th. g. service* **~lied** n *thanksgiving hymn* **~opfer** n *offering* **~sager** m *thanksgiver* **~sagung** f *thanksgiving*; *note* od *rendering of thanks* **~schreiben** n *letter of thanks* od *of acknowledg*(*e*)*ment*; ⟨Am fam⟩ *bread-and-butter note*

d·ankbar I. a **1.** (P) *thankful, grateful* (jdm *to a p*; f etw *for a th*); ~ s, daß .. *to be thankful that* ..; ich wäre Ihnen ~ f *I will thank you for* (*a cup of tea*); sich ~ erweisen, zeigen *to show gratitude*; sich ~ zeigen *to be thankful* (*for*) || ⟨com⟩ f Begleichung sind wir ~ *a settlement will oblige* || ein ~es Herz *a thankful heart* **2.** (S) *acceptable*; *agreeable*; *satisfactory* (*task*) | (lohnend) *lucrative, paying, profitable*; e–e ~e Aufgabe *a rewarding task* **II.** adv *gratefully, thankfully*; *with gratitude*: (etw) ~ begrüßen *to hail* (*a th*) *with g.* **~́keit** f ~/ *thankfulness, gratitude*; aus ~ f *in gratitude for*

d·anken vi/t [h] **I.** vi **1.** jdm ~ *to thank a p* (f *for*); ⟨parl⟩ *to tender one's thanks* || ich danke dir, daß du .. geschickt hast *I thank you for sending* ..; ich danke Ihnen tausendmal *I thank you ever so much*; → 1000 Dank; ich lasse ihm bestens ~ *give him my best thanks*; *my best thanks to him*; ~d erhalten (auf Quittung) *received* (*with thanks* od), *thank you*; ich darf Ihnen nochmals bestens ~ *let me express once again my very great thanks* || s–m guten Stern ~ *to thank one's lucky stars* || Gott sei gedankt *God be thanked* **2.** [abs] **a.** *to express one's thanks* || nichts z ~ *you are welcome, don't mention it*; er läßt bestens ~ *he thanks very much* **b.** im **voraus** ~d *thanking you in anticipation* || ~d *with thanks*; ~d **ablehnen** (*or* ablehnend ~), annehmen *to decline, accept with th.*; ⟨com⟩ ~d erhalten [pp] *received with th.* **c.** (f e–n Gruß) ~ *to return a bow* || ich danke f deine Hilfe (ablehnend) *no, thanks, I can do without your help*; °ich danke f Obst! *no, thanks*! *thank you for nothing*! **d.** ich danke! danke! *thanks*! danke sehr *or* schön! *many thanks*! || nein, danke *no, thanks* | ⟨iron⟩ ich danke! *indeed*! na, ich danke! ⟨sl⟩ *my hat*!; du bist ein schönes Exemplar, ich danke *you* **are** *a fine specimen* **II.** vt **1.** (lohnen) deine Mühe dankt dir niemand *nobody will thank* (od *repay*) *you for your pains* **2.** (verdanken) jdm etw z ~ h *to be indebted to a p for a th* || das hast du dir selbst z ~ *you have only yourself to thank for it*

d·ankenswert a *meritorious, praiseworthy, deserving acknowledgement* || *kind* (*permission*) in ~er Weise *kindly* (adv)

D·ankes- (→ a. Dank–) **~brief** m *letter of thanks* **~erklärung** f *vote of thanks*; e–e ~ beantragen *to propose a v. of th.* **~schuld** f *debt of gratitude* || *indebtedness* **~worte** n [pl] *vote of thanks*; ~ sprechen *to return thanks*

dann I. adv **1.** (zeitlich) *then*; *after that* || was soll ~ folgen *or* k? *what do you want to follow*? || wenn .., ~ ist es Zeit *when .. then is the time* (*to do*) .., u ~ ging ich .., *when I went* || erst ~ *not till then* || was ~ noch? *what next*? || ~ u wann (*every*) *now and then*; *once and again, then* od *here and there, between whiles, by fits and starts*; ⟨Am⟩ *every so often*; er trank ~ u wann e–e Flasche Wein *he drank an occasional b. of w.* **2.** (bedingend) *then, in that case*; ~ u nur ~ *then and then only* || wenn .., ~ *if .. then* || selbst ~, wenn *even if* ..; selbst ~ nicht, wenn *not even if* .. **II.** [conj] (außerdem) *then, besides, moreover*; ~ sind da die Spielleute *then there are the minstrels*

d·annen adv [nur in:] v ~ *thence*, [aber fast nur in Verbindung mit Verben:] v ~ gehen, ziehen (etc) *to go away* od *off*

dant·esk a *Dantesque*

D·anzig n ⟨hist Ger⟩ (Stadt) *Danzig* **~er Bucht** f *Gulf of Danzig*

D·aphne f ⟨myth & bot⟩ *Daphne*

dar adv [nur in comp mit Präpositionaladverbien (→ ~an, ~auf etc) u Verben (→ ~bieten, ~bringen etc)] || → da, dahin

daran [Betonung → u] adv (→ dran) **I.** (dar-·an, daran) **1.** ⟨eig⟩ *at it* (sc *the corner*; *the school*); *at them* || *to it*; befestige es ~ *fasten it to it* (sc *the door*), *to them* (sc *the doors*) || *on it* (sc *the coast*), *on them* (sc *the coasts*) || nahe ~ *near it, close by it* (sc *the house*); *near them* **2.** ⟨übtr⟩ **a.** *at it*; er ist jetzt ~ *he is at it* (sc *the work*) *now* | [bei vielen Verben] *of it*, denke ~ *think of it*; es fehlte ihnen ~ *they were short of it* (sc *water*); ich zweifle nicht ~ *I have no doubt of it*; ich z. ~, daß *I doubt that* ..; ich z. ~, daß es sein Wunsch ist *I doubt it to be his wish*; ich z. ~, daß er kommt *I doubt his coming* | *in it*; ich nehme nicht ~ teil *I do not participate in it* || ist etw ~? *is there anything to it*? es ist nichts Wahres ~ *there is no truth in it*; es ist nichts ~ *there is nothing in it* od *to it*; ~ s, Wirklichkeit z w *to be on the way to realization*; es fehlen noch 3 Minuten ~ *it wants 3 minutes to it* (sc *ten o'clock*) **b. es liegt mir ~** z wissen *it is of great consequence to me to know, I am anxious to k.*, was liegt mir schon ~? *what of that*? *what do I care*? || nahe ~ s z tun *to be about to do, to be on the point of doing, to be near doing* || **übel ~ s** *to be badly off* || er **tat gut ~** *he did well* (*to leave*); *it was clever of him* (*to l.*) || er will nicht groß ~ *he is undecided, he is loath* od *reluctant to do it* **c. ~|gehen,** sich ~|m *to set to work, to set out* (*to do*), *to set o.s. to do a th*; sie alle machten sich ~ *they all set to* || sich ~|halten *to hurry up*; *to try one's best* (*to get*) || alles ~|setzen *to do one's utmost* od *best* (*to obtain* ..); *to make every effort* **II.** [d·aran] ⟨mst übtr⟩ ([oft relativ] = woran) **1.** ~ leidend *suffering from same*; ~ liegt es *that's what it is* || ~ liegt (mir) sehr viel *I attach great importance to it* || das liegt ~, daß .. *that is owing to the fact that* .. || ~ ist nichts Wahres *in it there is no truth* || ~ zweifelte er nicht *of that he had no doubt*

darauf [Betonung → u] adv (→ drauf) **I.** [dar·auf] **1.** ⟨eig⟩ **a.** (*up*)*on it* (sc *the river, the journey*), (*up*)*on them* (sc *the rivers*); ich ließ den Pelz ~ *I left the fur on* (sc *the cape*) || *in it* (: *the street*), *in them* (: *the streets*); ⟨Am⟩ *on it, on them* **b.** (Richtung) *towards it* (: *the house*); *towards them*; gerade ~los|gehen, ~zu|-gehen *to go straight at* (od *towards*) *it* **2.** (zeitlich) ein Jahr ~ *a year after* (*that*); den Tag ~, am ~folgenden Tage *the day after*; *the next* od *following day*; bald ~ *soon after*; gleich ~ *directly after that* **3.** ⟨übtr⟩ [bei Verben u Subst] **a.** *to it*; ohne e–e Antwort ~ *without an* *answer to it* **b.** es ~ ankommen l *to take one's chance; to wait and see* || er arbeitet ~hin, es z erhalten *he aims at getting it* || ~aus|gehen, ~aus|sein *to be out* (*to do*) || er bestand *or* drang ~ *he insisted on it, he persisted in it*; er besteht ~, daß ich abreise *he insists on my leaving*; er ging (*or* ließ sich) ~ ein *he agreed* od *consented to it* || er hält sehr ~ *he sets great store by it; he lays great stress on it* || wir k noch ~ *we come to that still*; ich kann nicht ~ k *I cannot think of it; I cannot rememver it*; wie kam er nur ~? *what put the idea into his head*? || ich gestatte mir, Ihre Aufmerksamkeit ~ z lenken *I beg to draw your attention to it*; .. ~ z lenken, daß .. .. *to call your attention to the fact that* .. || ich kann ~ schwören *I can swear it*; er schwört ~ *he swears by it* (sc *iodine*) || es steht der Kopf ~ *it is a hanging matter* || verlaß dich ~ *depend on it* **c.** er ist stolz ~ *he is proud of it* (sc *his hat*); er ist st. ~, Soldat z s *he is proud of being a soldier* **d.** ~|gehen (S) *to go, to be consumed*; viel Geld ging ~ *much money went towards it*; das ganze G. ging ~ f Zigarren *all the money went* (od *was spent*) *in cigars* || ~los|arbeiten *to work away* **II.** [mst d·arauf, oft *relativ* = worauf] **1.** (zeitlich) *upon that; after that; next, then; thereupon* || u ~ *whereupon; after which*; ~ folgend [a] *ensuing* (Periode) || ~ sagte er *he went on to say* **2.** ⟨übtr⟩ **a.** ~ falle ich nicht herein! *not I! catch me doing that*! || ~ war ich gefaßt *for that I was prepared* || ~ kommt alles an *on that everything depends* || ~ kannst du dich verlassen *on that you may depend* || alle s–e Sorge war ~ gerichtet .. z erhalten *all his care was bent on getting* .. || die Verzögerung ist ~ zurückzuführen, daß .. *the delay is owing to the fact that* ..; gerade ~ zu *straight towards it* **b.** mit Rücksicht ~, daß .. *making allowance for the fact that* .. **c.** ~hin *on that; on the strength of it*; (er hatte nur ein geringes Gehalt) u ~ heiratete er *and on that he got married*

daraus [Betonung → u] adv **I.** [daraus, dar·aus] **1.** ⟨eig⟩ (*out*) *of it*; ~ gemacht *made of it* (sc *of stone*) **2.** ⟨übtr⟩ *of it*; er machte das Beste ~ *he made the most of it* || *from that* od *this*; † *therefrom* || ~ ableitbar *deducible from that* || °ich mache mir nichts ~ (⟨fam⟩ draus) *I don't care* od *mind*; was du dir schon ~ machst *for all* od *aught you care* || was ist ~ geworden? *what has become of it* (sc *the hydrogen*)? || nichts Gutes wird ~ w *no good will come of it* **II.** [oft: d·araus, oft *relativ* = woraus] ⟨übtr⟩ *from that; hence*; ~ folgt, daß .. *hence* od *thence it follows that*; ~ schließen wir .. *hence we infer* .. || ~ wird nichts w *that will come to nothing, that won't do, it cannot be done*

d·arben vi [h] *to want* (: *he must not be allowed to want*); *to live in want; to go short; to be pinched, to pinch o.s.*; jdn ~ l *to allow a p to want* || sehr ~ *to starve*

D·arbietung f ~/~en **1.** *presentation; exhibition* || ⟨arts⟩ *display* (szenische ~en *scenic displays*); ⟨theat⟩ *performance*; allerlei ~en [pl] *all kinds of entertainments* [pl] **2.** ⟨ec⟩ *porrection*

d·ar|bieten vt [h] **1.** (P & S) (etw) *to offer; present* (jdm *to a p*; e–r S *to a th*); *to hold out; to promise* || (Speisen) *to dispense* || (Anblick) *to offer, exhibit, display* || (Resultate) *to represent, to set forth* od *out* || ⟨theat & mus⟩ *to give, perform*; Werke v Bach ~ *to play works of Bach* **2. sich ~** (S) *to present o.s.* (: *no other difficulty presented itself*); *to emerge* (: *new facts emerged*); *to arise*; wenn sich e–e Gelegenheit darbietet *if an occasion offers*; es bot sich uns ein wundervoller Anblick dar *a magnificent view met our eyes*

d·ar|bringen vt [h] (etw) *to offer*, (Opfer) *to present* (jdm *to a p*); jdm e–e Ovation ~ *to give a p an ovation* **D·arbringung** f ~/~en *offering, presentation*

Dardan·ellen [pl] die ~ *the Dardanelles* [pl]

Dardsch·iling n *Darjeeling*

dar·ein (⟨fam⟩ drein) adv **1.** *⟨eig⟩ *into that* od *it* **2.** ⟨mst übtr⟩ || finde (*or* füge, schicke) dich ~ *put up with it*; gib dich geduldig ~ *submit patiently to it* || er mischt sich immer ~ *he is always interfering* od *meddling* || es ist Zeit sich ~ z mischen *it is time to intervene* (od *interpose, interfere*) || rede nicht immer ~ *don't always interfere*; er redet immer ~ *he is a meddlesome fellow* || er willigte ~ *he agreed* od *consented to it*

Daressal·am n (Hauptstadt Tansanias)

darf 1. & 3. pres sg v dürfen

Darf·ur, Darf·or n (Prov. im Sudan) *Darf(o)ur*

D·arién, Golf von [m] *Gulf* (*Isthmus*) *of Darien*

darin [Betonung → u) adv **I.** [dar·in] **1.** ⟨eig⟩ *in it* (sc *the town*), *in them* (: *the towns*); ein schöner Garten, um ~ z spielen *a fine garden to play in* || † *therein* || u ~ *wherein* || es ist nichts ~ (⟨fam⟩ drin) *there is nothing in it*; was ist denn da drin? *what is in there*? || *on it* (sc *the committee, staff*), *on them* **2.** ⟨übtr⟩ *in that matter* od *affair*; all sein Glück lag ~ *all his happiness was there* **II.** [mst d·arin, oft *relativ* = worin] ~ war er wie sein Vater *in that he was like his father* || dies Mißverständnis findet s–e Erklärung ~, daß .. *this misunderstanding finds its explanation in that* (*we did not realise* ..); dies unterscheidet sich v den anderen ~, daß .. *this differs from the others in that* (*it does not need* ..) || ~ ist alles einbegriffen *these terms are inclusive* || ~ irren Sie sich *there you are mistaken* || ~ stimme ich Ihnen bei *I agree with you there*

dar·innen adv in there

d·ar|legen vt [h] ⟨cust⟩ (Inhalt) *to display* | ⟨übtr⟩ (s–e Absichten etc) offen ~ *to lay open, to reveal* (jdm *to a p*); (Absichten) *to show*; (Plan) *to expose; disclose; to make known* || (auseinandersetzen, erläutern) *to explain*; die S muß noch klarer –ge–gt w *the matter requires clearer statement*; (Resultate) *to set forth* od *out; to state*; (Anspruch) *to put forward*; s–e Ansichten im einzelnen ~ *to elaborate one's views* || gut dargelegt *well put* || geordnet ~ *to formulate*

D·arlegung f ~/~en *explanation, exposé* [Fr]; *exposition* (über *of*); *statement*; = Ausführung

D·arleh(e)n n ~s/~ *loan* (an jdn *to a p*); *advance*; kurzfristige ~ [pl] *short loans*, ⟨exch⟩ *fixtures*; unbefristetes ~ *undated loan*; ~ gegen Sicherheit *loan against security*; ungesichertes ~ *loan on trust, unsecured loan*; ein ~ auf e–e Hypothek *a mortgage loan*; jdm ein ~ gewähren *to grant a p a loan* || (jdm) Geld als ~ geben *to lend out* (⟨Am⟩ *to loan*) *money to*

D·arlehns- ~bank f = Darlehnskasse 2. **~geber** m *loaner* **~jobber** m *loan-contractor* od *-shark* **~kasse** f **1.** ⟨engl⟩ *loan-society* **2.** ⟨Ger⟩ (bis 1924) *loan-bank*; ~nschein [m] *loan bank-note* **~schuld** f *loan-debt* **~stelle** f (f öffentl Arbeiten) (*Public Works*) *Loan Board*

d·ar|leihen vt [h] (Geld) *to lend* (*out*); ⟨Am⟩ *to loan* (jdm *to a p*) **D·arleiher** m ~s/~ *lender*

D·arleihung f *the lending, letting out*; ⟨Am⟩ *loaning* (an *to*)

D·arm m ~(e)s/⸚e **1.** ⟨anat⟩ (~kanal) ⟨med⟩ *bowel, intestine*(*s* [pl]); *gut*; ⟨zoo⟩ *gut*; Dick⸚ *large intestine; colon*; Dünn⸚ *small intestine* || Mast⸚ *rectum* [L]; (Medizin) durch den ~ eingegeben *administered rectally*; (Temperatur) im ~ gemessen *taken rectally* || (Rohr) in den ~ einführen *to pass* (*a tube*) *into the rectum*; den ~ entleeren *to move one's bowel(s)*; jds ~ öffnen (z Abführen) *to open a p's bowels* | ⸚e [pl] (Leib) *bowels, entrails, intestines* [pl]; (a. T) *guts* [pl] **2.** (Tier≃ z tech. Zwecken) *gut*; ≃e [pl] *guts* [pl] ‖ Seiden≃ *gut*

Darm- [in comp] **a.** ⟨med⟩ *intestinal*; *rectal*; *enteric* **b.** ⟨tech⟩ *gut* **~abschnürung** f *strangulation* **~anhang** m *intestinal appendage* **~aufblähung** f *inflation of intestine* **~bad** n *enema* [L] **~bakterien** [pl] *intestinal bacteria* [pl] **~bein** n ⟨anat⟩ *iliac bone*; *ilium* [L]; [in comp] *iliac* **~bereiter** m ⟨tech⟩ *gut-dresser* **~bewegung** f = Darmperistaltik **~blutung** f *instetinal h(a)emorrhage* **~bruch** m ⟨med⟩ *enterocele* **~einklemmung** f ⟨med⟩ *incarceration, strangulation of intestine in a hernia* **~entzündung** f ⟨med⟩ *enteritis* **~fieber** n *gastric fever* **~fistel** f ⟨med⟩ *intestinal fistula* **~gase** n [pl] *intestinal gases* [pl] **~geschwür** n ⟨med⟩ *intestinal ulcer* **~grimmen** n *colic* **~inhalt** m *faeces* [pl] [L] **~kanal** m ⟨anat⟩ *intestinal canal* **~katarrh** m ⟨med⟩ *enteritis* [L] **~krankheit** f *intestinal* od *bowel complaint* **~krebs** m ⟨med⟩ *cancer of the intestine*; *intestinal carcinoma* [L] **~lähmung** f ⟨med⟩ *intestinal paralysis* **~netz** n ⟨anat⟩ → Netz **~papier** n *paper skin* **~peristaltik** f ⟨anat⟩ *peristalsis* [L] **~rohr** n ⟨med⟩ *intestinal tube* **~saft** m *intestinal juice* **~saite** f ⟨tech⟩ *catgut, gut-string*; kz ~, die die Angelhaken mit der Angelschnur verbindet *snell* **~schnitt** m ⟨surg⟩ *enterotomy* **~stein** m ⟨vet⟩ *enterolite, –lith* **~trägheit** f → Verdauungsträgheit **~tuberkulose** f ⟨med⟩ *intestinal tuberculosis* **~verschlingung** f ⟨med⟩ *volvulus* [L] **~verschluß** m *intestinal obstruction*; *ileus* [L] **~wand** f *intestinal wall* **~waren** f [pl] ⟨tech⟩ *goods* [pl] *from guts* **~zotte** f *villus* [L]

D·armstadt n ⟨Ger⟩ (Stadt)

***darn·ach** adv = danach ***darn·eben** adv = daneben ***darn·ieder** adv → danieder ***dar·ob** adv = darüber

D·arr- [in comp mst] *kiln* **~anlage** f *kiln-plant* **~arbeit** f ⟨brew⟩ *drying work* **~malz** n *kiln-dried malt* **~ofen** m *drying-oven, kiln* **~sucht** f ⟨vet⟩ *consumption in animals*, ⟨orn⟩ *roup, pip* **≃süchtig** a ⟨vet⟩ *consumptive*

D·arre f ~/~n **1.** [abstr] (Dörren) *kiln-drying* **2.** (Darrvorrichtung) *drying-oven, (air-)-kiln*; Hopfen≃ *hop-kiln*; *oast* **3.** ⟨vet⟩ = Darrsucht

d·ar|reichen vt [h] jdm etw ~ *to reach* od *hand a p a th*; *to proffer a th* (od *to hold a th out*) *to a p*; (Speisen) *to dispense* ‖ ⟨ec⟩ *porrect*

D·arreichung f ~/~en *handing, presenting*; *offering* ‖ ⟨ec⟩ *porrection*

d·arren vt [h] (Hopfen etc) *to kiln-dry, to dry in a kiln*

d·arstellbar a *representable*; *fit for representation*

d·ar|stellen vt [h] **1. a.** (bildlich ~) (Landschaft etc) *to represent*; *depict, delineate, exhibit, limn, portray*; *to set off* (auf e–m Hintergrunde *against a background*); (Figur) graphisch ~ *to figure* ‖ *to map out* ‖ weißt du, wen (*or* was) diese Photographien ~? *can you identify these photographs*? | symbolisch ~ (S) *to represent, to be representative of, to symbolize* **b.** ⟨theat⟩ (Rolle, Figur) *to act*, (*im*)*personate, represent*; *interpret* ‖ (jdn) *to do* (in *in* [*a play*]); *to play* (*a part*); im Film ~ *to feature* **2.** (in Worten ~) (etw) *to put forward*; (jdn, etw) *to represent* (als *as*); *to hold* (*a p*) *up* (*as*) ‖ jdm etw ~ *to* (*re*)*present* od *picture a th to a p* ‖ (Vorgänge etc) *to delineate, depict, describe, exhibit, picture*; *to set forth* od *out* ‖ (Gegenstand, Thema) *to handle, to treat* ‖ (Problem) *to pose* ‖ (etw) anschaulich, lebendig ~ *to depict, illustrate, portray vividly*; ausführlich ~ *to elaborate*; *to treat* (*a th*) *in detail*; *to write up*; etw falsch ~ *to belie a th*; treffend, überzeugend ~ *to hit* (*a th*) *off*; im Umriß ~ *to outline*; in gr Zügen ~ *to skeletonize* ‖ (etw) falsch ~ *to misrepresent*; (Bericht) falsch ~ ⟨sl⟩ *to salt*; etw entstellt ~ *to colour a th* | (etw finanziell) ~ können *to afford, manage* **3.** ⟨chem⟩ (e–n Stoff) *to prepare*; *to produce*; *to obtain* (aus *from*) **4.** [refl] **sich ~** *to represent o.s.* (als *as*) ‖ sich jdm ~ (S) *to present o.s. to a p*

d·arstellend a; ~e Kunst *pictorial art* ‖ *descriptive*; ~e Geometrie *descriptive geometry*

D·arsteller m ~s/~ ⟨theat⟩ *actor, impersonator* (of a part), *representer*; stummer ~ → Figurant, Statist **~besetzung** f *cast*

D·arstellerin f ~/~nen *actress*; stumme ~ → Statistin

D·arstellung f ~/~en **1.** ⟨ec⟩ (~ vor Gott) *presentation*; die ~ Christi im Tempel *the Presentation of Christ in the Temple* (2. Febr.); ~ Mariä *the P. of the Virgin Mary* (21. Nov.) **2. a.** ⟨arts⟩ (~ im Bild) *figuration, representation*; *rendering* (*of effects of light*); *depiction*; bildliche ~ *pictorial representation, graphic reproduction*; *picture*; graphische ~ (v Kräften, Werten) *diagram, graph*, .. in Kreissektoren *pie-chart* ‖ symbolische ~ *symbolization* **b.** ⟨theat⟩ *acting, embodiment*, (*im*)*personation, interpretation* (*of a part*); Charakter≃ *character impersonation* ‖ ⟨film⟩ *featuring* **3.** (~ in Worten) *presentation* (*of facts*), nach s–r eigenen ~ *according to his own words* (od *account, version, story*); *representation* (*of one's views*); v etw e–e genau den Tatsachen entsprechende ~ geben *to give an exact account of a th* ‖ ⟨Lit⟩ *depiction, description, exposition*; Charakter≃ *delineation of characters* ‖ *account*; *narrative*; *statement* ‖ (Fassung) *version* ‖ anschauliche ~ *graphic description*; *portrayal*; genaue ~ *detailed description*; ~ im Umriß *outline*; bildliche ~ *figurative representation*; falsche ~ *false representation, misrepresentation*; (wissentlich) *distortion of truth* **4.** ⟨chem⟩ *preparation*; *production*; *obtaining* (aus *from*) **5.** ⟨comp⟩ *notation*

D·arstellungs- ~art f *manner* od *style of representation* ‖ ⟨chem⟩ *process of production* **≃fähig** a *representable* **~gabe, ~kraft** f *descriptive power*; ein Schriftsteller v gr ~ *a descriptive writer* **~kunst** f *art of representation* od *description*

d·ar|tun vt [h] (etw) *to evince, prove*; *show*; handgreiflich ~ *to demonstrate*

dar·über [Betonung → u] **adv** (→ drüber) **I.** [dar·über; ⟨fam⟩ drüber] **1. a.** ⟨eig⟩ *above*; *above it* (sc *the bridge*), *above them* (: *the bridges*); (*a rug*) *over it* (sc *the bed*), *over them*; ~|liegen *to lie over it* ‖ quer ~ *across it* **b.** er machte sich ~ (her) *he fell upon it*; *he set about it* **2.** (über .. hinaus) **a.** ~ hinaus *beyond* ‖ *beyond it* (:*the village*); *beyond them* **b.** 20 Jahre u ~ *twenty years and upwards*; 20 Mark u ~ *20 marks and over* ‖ er ist ~ hinaus *he is past* (od *beyond*) *it* (: *its youth*) **c.** ⟨übtr⟩ ~ hinaus *over and above this*; *in addition*; *apart from this* ‖ ⟨fig⟩ er ist ~ erhaben *he is above it* **3.** (zeitlich) *in the meantime, by that time*; wir w ~ sterben *we shall die before that* **4.** ⟨fig⟩ (bei Adj., Subst. u Verben) **a.** ärgerlich ~ *angry at it* od *about it* od *that*; erfreut ~ *pleased with it*; er war glücklich ~, daß er e–n Sohn hatte *he was happy at having a son*; er war überrascht ~, daß .. *he was surprised* (*to find*) *that* .. **b.** sprich nicht ~ *don't talk about it*; er beklagte sich ~ *he complained of it, on it* od *that, on that matter* od *point* ‖ sich ~ entscheiden, wie .. *to decide how* .. **5.** ~gelagert, –liegend a *overlying, superjacent* **II.** [d·arüber] **1.** ~ hinaus wollte er nicht gehen *beyond that he would not go* ‖ ~ geht nichts *there is nothing like it* **2.** (zeitlich) ~ würde viel Zeit vergehen *that would take much time* **3.** ⟨fig⟩ ~ sprechen wir später *about that we shall talk* *later on* || ~ besteht kein Zweifel *of that there is no doubt*

darum [Betonung → u] adv **I.** [dar·um, ⟨fam⟩ drum] **1.** (*a*)*round it* od *that*; (*a*)*round them*; *about it* od *that, about them* || ~|legen *to put* (*a*)*round it* | ⟨übtr⟩ wir sind noch mal ~ herum gek *we have had a lucky escape*; er ist ~ (*sc* um sein Geld) gek *he has lost all of it* **2.** ⟨übtr⟩ **a.** *for it*; ich bat ihn ~ *I asked him for it* (od *that*) **b.** (betreffs) *about it* (od *that*); er weiß ~ *he knows about it, he is in the know* || er kümmert sich nicht ~ *he does not care*; wer kümmert sich ~? *who cares*? || es ist mir sehr ~ z tun, daß er nichts erfährt *what I attach great importance to is that he does not learn anything*; es ist mir sehr ~ z tun z erfahren .. *I am most anxious to learn* ..; es ist ihm nur ~ z tun z erfahren .. *his only object is to learn* .. || es sei ~! *let it be then*! *I'll risk it*! *for all I care*! **II.** [d·arum] **1.** ~ handelt es sich eben! *that's the very point in question* **2.** (deswegen) *on that account, for that reason*: *therefore*; *that's why* (*he left so early*) || ~ daß .. *because*

darunter [Betonung → u] adv (→ drunter) **I.** [dar·unter; ⟨fam⟩ drunter] **1.** ⟨eig⟩ *below*; direkt ~ *underneath, beneath* || *below* (od *beneath, under, underneath*) *it* (sc *the surface*); *below* (etc) *them*; ~|liegen *to lie below*; ~liegend *subjacent* (*stratum*) **2.** (bei Preisangaben etc) *less*; (im Werte v) 20 Mark u ~ .. *20 marks and under* (od *less*); eher ~ als darüber *rather less than more*; wir können sie nicht ~ liefern *we cannot supply them for less* **3.** (dazwischen) *among them, among* (od *in, of*) *the number* || *between them*; es ist kein Unterschied ~ *there is no difference between them* **4.** ⟨übtr⟩ was verstehst du ~? *what do you understand by it*? || ich kann mir nichts ~ vorstellen *I cannot conceive what it means* **II.** *[d·arunter] *among those* (*he will not be*) || *between those* | ~ kann ich mir nichts vorstellen *of that I cannot form any idea, I can't make heads or tails of it*

D·arwin-Gebirge n ⟨Aust⟩ *Darwin Mountains* **Darwin·ismus** m ~/ *Darwinism* **Darwin·ist** m ~en/~en *Darwinist* **darwin·istisch** a *Darwinian, Darwinistic*

das [pron dem abs] **A.** [nom] **1. a.** *that*; dies od ~? *this or that*? || ~ mag s *that may be* || ~ sollte man w *that was a thing to be* || ~ heißt *that is to say* || Liebe? ~ war es nie gewesen! *Love*? *That it had never been*! || ist es ~? *is that it*? || wer ist ~? *who is that*?; ⟨telph⟩ Sind Sie ~, Herr Doktor? (*is*) *that you, doctor*? || ~ waren die Kinder (= h die K. getan) *that was the children*; vgl. 2. **b.** *the thing*; *a thing like that* (*could not be*) **c.** (im Ausruf) ~ ist mal ein braver Junge! *there's a good boy*! [betont] ·~ Armband! *the* [ðiː] *bracelet*! *a glorified br.*! **d.** *so*; 'Sind Sie Herr N.?' '~ bin ich' '*Are you Mr. N.*?' '*So I am*', 'du siehst müde aus'. '~ bin ich auch' '*You look tired.*' '*So I am*' || .. u ~ mit Recht .. *and justly so* **e.** u ~ *which*; .., u ~ ist der Grund f .., *which is the reason for* .. **f.** ~, was .. *that which*; *the thing that*; *what*; nach dem, was Sie sagen *from what you say* **2.** [hinweisend auf folg. Subst.] ~ ist der Mann, den .. *that is the man that* ..; das sind die Männer, die .. *those are the men who* .. || ~ waren Zeiten! *those were the times*! **B.** [acc] gut, ~ gebe ich zu *all right, I give you that* || ~ wird er niemals tun *that is what he will never do* || nennst du ~ e–n Dichter? *do you call that a poet*? || er sagte ~ *he said as much* || ja, ich wußte ~ *yes, I knew* **3.** daß du arbeitest, ~ sehe ich *that you are working I see* || → der

d·a|**sein** vi [s] **1.** (anwesend s) *to be there, to be present* **2.** (existieren) *to exist* || → dagewesen

D·asein n ~s/ **1.** *being, existence* || das politische ~ *the political condition* (*of a country*) || ins ~ treten *to come into being* | *life, existence*; ein elendes ~ *a wretched* od *miserable existence* || der Kampf ums ~ → ~skampf **2.** †*presence*; → dortsein, hiersein **~sberechtigung** f *raison d'être* [Fr], *right to exist* **~skampf** m *struggle for existence* od *life* **~sstufe** f *plane of existence*

das·elbst adv *there*; *in that* (*very*) *place*

d·a|**sitzen** vi [h] *to sit* (*and ponder, etc*) || ⟨fig⟩ *to be at a loss*

d·asjenige → derjenige

°**d·asmal** adv *this time, this once*; *for once*

daß [conj] **I.** [in Substantivsätzen] **A.** [in Subjekt– u Objektsätzen; in letzteren oft ausgelassen] **1.** [durch engl Konj.] **a.** *that*; ich glaube, ~ er Recht hat, ich glaube, er hat R. *I believe* (*that*) *he is right* || es ist unmöglich, ~ er z Zeit zurückkommt *it is impossible that he should return in time* || kein Wunder, ~ .. *no wonder that* .. || es ist 2 Jahre her, ~ er starb *it is 2 years that he died* **b.** [nach neg, *doubt, deny*, etc.] *but that*; es war k–e Frage, daß er ehrlich war *there was no question but that he was honest* **c.** [nach *to fear*, etc.] *that*; *lest* (.. *should*); er befürchtete, ~ er unterlag *he feared lest he should succumb* **d. ~ nicht** *lest* (.. *should*); .. ~ wir nicht vergessen .. *lest we should not forget* **2. a.** ich wünsche, ~ du besser lernst *I wish you to learn better*; dies bewirkte, ~ er glaubte .. *this made him believe* (*that* ..) || es ist üblich, ~ er so spricht *it is usual for him to talk like that*; .., ~ Hüte getragen w .. *for hats to be worn* **b.** entschuldige, ~ wir z spät k *excuse our being late* || ist es nicht seltsam, ~ wir so zus-treffen? *isn't it strange our coming together like this*? **3.** [ohne regierenden Satz] **1.** oh, ~ es doch wahr wäre! *oh, that it were true*! (*I*) *would it were true*! || ~ dich der Teufel hole! *the devil take you*!; ~ du es ihm ja sagst! *be sure and tell him*! **2. nicht ~** *not that* (*he was miserable*); nicht ~ er es nicht glaubte *not but that he believed it* || nicht ~ ich wüßte *not that I know of* **B. 1. f den Fall ~** *in case*; im Falle ~ er krank ist *in case he should be ill, in case of his being ill* (*we shall* ..) || unter der Bedingung ~ *on condition that*; vorausgesetzt ~ *provided* (*that*) || es sei denn ~ *unless* **2.** dadurch ~, dafür ~, damit ~, davon ~, darin ~, darüber ~, darum ~; → dadurch, dafür, damit, daran, darin, darüber, darum **II. 1.** = damit [conj], → d. **2. so ~** *so that*; schreib es so, ~ du sie nicht verletzst *put it so as not to hurt them*; der Mond erhellte den Raum hinreichend, so daß sie .. erkennen konnte *the moonlight lit up the room sufficiently for her to distinguish* ..; bist du so ein Narr (= solcher N.), ~ du das glaubst? *are you a fool for believing that*? *are you such a fool as to believe that*? **3.** [nach prep] **anstatt ~** → anstatt 2. || **auf ~** → auf adv III. || **außer** ~ → außer II. || **bis ~** → bis II. || **ohne ~**: ich beobachtete sie, ohne ~ sie mich sahen *I watched them without their* (⟨fam⟩ *them*) *seeing me* **4.** z schwierig **als ~** → als II. A. 3. b.

D·assel f ~/~n ⟨ent⟩ *bot-fly*; *gad-fly*; ⟨Scot⟩ *cleg*; Larve der ~ *bot*(*t*) **~beulen** f [pl] ⟨vet⟩ *bots, botts* [pl] **~fliege** f = ~ **~plage** f = ~beulen

dass·elbe → derselbe A. 2. b.

d·a|**stehen** vi [h] **1.** *to stand there*; er stand da in Gedanken *he stood there thinking*; er stand da u tat nichts *he stood doing nothing* **2.** ⟨übtr⟩ gut (schlecht) ~ *to be well* (*badly*) *off*; glänzend ~ ⟨fam⟩ *to be on velvet* || (S) *to be in a good* (*bad*) *condition* || wie stehe ich nun da! *I have made a fool of myself, indeed*! wie angewurzelt ~ *to be rooted to the floor* || unerreicht ~ *to stand alone*; *to be unequalled* od *unmatched*; einzig ~de Leistung *unprecedented achievement* || als Rebell ~ *to stand confessed as a rebel*

Dasym·eter n ~s/~ ⟨phys⟩ *dasymeter*

Dat·ei f ~/~en *file* ⟨a. comp⟩ (⟨a.⟩ Datenbank)

D·aten n [pl] → Datum ‖ die wichtigsten ~ der Geschichte *the most important dates in history* ‖ ⟨comp⟩ eingegebene ~ *incoming raw data*; zu verarbeitende ~ *input data for processing* ‖ ⟨tech⟩ *specifications* **~endstelle** f ⟨comp⟩ *terminal* **~eingabe** f ⟨comp⟩ *data input* **~feld** n ⟨comp⟩ *array* **~fernübertragung** f ⟨comp⟩ *teleprocessing* **~satz** m ⟨comp⟩ (*logical*) *record* **~verarbeiter** m (S) (*electronic*) *data processing machine*; *data processor* **~verarbeitung** f *data processing*, (elektronische) *electronic d. pr.*; ~ mit Lochkarten *punched card d. pr.* | ~sanlage [f] *automatic d. pr. devices*; *computer*; ~ssystem [n] *data processing system* **~wort** n ⟨comp⟩ (*data*) *item* od *word*

dat·ieren vt/i [h] **1.** vt (Brief) *to date*; falsch ~ *to misdate* ‖ datiert s *to be dated, to date* (v *from*) **2.** vi *to date* (v *from*); *to be dated* ‖ ⟨übtr⟩ *to date* (aus *from*); dies datiert aus e–r Zeit vor dem Kriege *this dates from before the war*

Dat·ierung f ~/ *dating* (*of a letter*) ‖ *date line* (e–s Briefes, e–r Zeitung)

D·ativ m ~s/~e ⟨gram⟩ *dative*; *dative case*; → Wemfall ‖ ~objekt *indirect object* (*in dat.*)

d·ato adv ⟨com⟩ 3 Monate ~ *at three months' date* ‖ bis ~ *till now, hitherto* ‖ nach ~ *after date* **~wechsel** m ⟨com⟩ *time-bill, -draft, bill after date*

°**Däts** m **1.** (Schädel; ⟨sl⟩ *noddle, chump*, ⟨Am⟩ *knob* **2.** = Hut

D·attel f ~/~n *date* **~baum** → Dattelpalme **~fieber** n *dengue* **~kern** m *date-kernel* **~muschel** f ⟨zoo⟩ *date-shell*; Gattung der ~n *lithodomus* [L] → Bohrmuschel **~öl** n *date-oil* **~palme** f *date*(*-palm* od *tree*) **~pflaume** f ⟨bot⟩ *date plum*; ⟨Am⟩ *persimmon*

°**D·atterich** m = Tatterich

D·atum n ~s/-ten *date*; vom heutigen ~ *of this date*; ~ des Poststempels *date as per postmark, date as shown on postal cancellation hereof*; unter dem ~ des 16. Februar *under date of February 16*; ohne ~ s *to be undated*; welches ~ h wir heute? *what day of the month is it? what is today's date?* ‖ ⟨übtr⟩ jungen ~s s *to be of recent date* | Daten [pl] 1. *dates* [pl] 2. (Angaben) *data* [L] [pl]; → D·aten pl **~presse** f ⟨rail, etc⟩ *ticket dating machine* **~sgrenze** f ⟨geog⟩ *date-line* **~stempel** m *dater* **~suhr** f *calender watch*

Dat·ure f ⟨bot⟩ *datura* [L]; *thorn-apple*

Dau f [Arab] ~/~en = Dhow (bes Nilboot) *dhow*

D·aube f ~/~n *stave*; (Faß) aus ~n zusstellen *to stave* (*a cask*) ‖ ~nholz n *stave-wood*

D·auer f ~/ **1.** (Andauern) **a.** *duration* (*of a p's life*; *of a flight*; *of a war*, etc.); *continuance* (*of a process, a state*); *length* (*of a stay, visit*; *of a note*); *permanence, -cy* **b.** auf die ~ *in the long run*; → 2. ‖ f die ~ *lastingly* ‖ v ~ s *to be permanent* (od *lasting*); nicht v ~ s *to have no permanency* ‖ v kz ~ *of brief* od *short duration*; v kz ~ s *to be short-lived*; Freuden v kz ~ *ephemeral* (od *short-lived*) *pleasures*; ⟨fig⟩ ein Aufflammen v kz ~ *a flash in the pan* ‖ v langer ~ *of long duration* od *standing* ‖ e–e P, S, Stellung v ~ *a permanency* ‖ e–e ununterbrochene ~ *a run* (*of an exhibition*); Amts≈ *run of office* **2.** (Zeitabschnitt) *period, term*; auf die ~ v *for a period* (od *term*) *of* (*22 years*); auf unbestimmte ~ *for an indefinite time*; *indefinitely* **3.** (Dauerhaftigkeit) Leucht≈ *period of lighting* → Bestand; Beständigkeit

D·auer- [in comp] *permanent, lasting* (*peace*; *value*); *around-the-clock* [attr] (~besetzung ⟨telph⟩, *operation* ⟨techn⟩); *long-life* [attr] (*mould, pattern*) ‖ ⟨sport⟩ *endurance .., long-distance ..* **~äpfel** m [pl] *keeping-apples* [pl], *good keepers* [pl] **~auftrag** m *standing order* **~bad** n ⟨med⟩ *water-bed* **~belastung** f ⟨tech⟩ *permanent load* **~betrieb** m *continuous working* od *running* **~brandkochherd** m *heat storage cooker* **~brandofen** m, **~brenner** *slow combustion stove, continuous burning stove, anthracite stove* **~erhitzer** m (Molkerei) *holder method pasteurizer* **~erhitzung** f *holder pasteurization* **~fahrer** m ⟨cycl⟩ *stayer* **~feuer** n ⟨mil⟩ *continuous* od *sustained fire* ‖ ⟨mar, aero⟩ *fixed light* **~flamme** f *by-pass* **~fleisch** n *preserved* (*smoked, pickled*) *meat* **~flug** m ⟨aero⟩ *endurance, duration* (od *long-distance*) *flight* **~frostboden** m *permafrost* **~funktionstasten** n *continuous typing at one single key depression* **~geschwindigkeit** f *maintainable speed* **~güter** n pl *durable goods* **~karte** f ⟨rail⟩ *season* (⟨Am⟩ *commutation*)*-ticket*; Inhaber e–r ~ ⟨Am⟩ *commuter* **~lauf** m *endurance-run, long-distance run* od *race, Marathon* (*race*); (Straßen≈) *grind* **~laut** m ⟨phon⟩ *continuant* **~leistung** f *normal output, n. power, n. rating* °**~lufterschütterung** f ⟨fam⟩ *talkathon* °**~lutscher** m *laster* (*toffee*) **~magnet** m *permanent magnet* **~mieter** m *permanent tenant* **~milch** f *sterilized milk* **~prüfung** f *fatigue test* **~rede** f; e–e ~, ~n halten *to talk a horse's hind leg off* **~regen** m *permanent* od *steady rain* **~ritt** m *endurance-ride* **~schlafmittel** n *long-acting soporific* **~schlagversuch** m *fatigue impact test* **~schwingbeanspruchung** f *fatigue load* **~schwingungsfestigkeit** f *fatigue limit* **~speicherung** f ⟨comp⟩ *preservation of records, maintenance on tape* **~stellung** f *permanent position* ⟨a. mil⟩ **~strich** m ⟨telg⟩ *continuous dash* **~ton** m *continued buzz, steady hum* **~tonsektor** m ⟨aeronav⟩ *on-course sector* od *zone* **~versuch** m *endurance-test* **~ware** f *food* (od *other product*) *that keeps well*; dies ist ~ *this will keep well* **~wellen** f [pl] *permanent waves* [pl]; ⟨fam⟩ *perm*; ~ bek. *to be permed* **~wirkung** f *lasting effect* **~wurst** f *hard sausage* **~zeilenschaltung** f ⟨typewr⟩ *continuous line spacer* **~zustand** m *steady state*; *permanency*

d·auerhaft 1. a *durable* (*cloth, material*); *lasting* ‖ *stable*; *solid* (*structure*), *strong, stout*; sehr ~ *perdurable* ‖ *fast* (*colour*) ‖ *durable, lasting* (*peace*, etc.) | [pred] ~ s (of cloth, etc.) *to wear well*; *to last* **2.** adv *durably*; *solidly*; ~ gemacht *made to last* ≈**igkeit** f ~/ *durability, durableness, sturdiness, lastingness*; *lasting quality*; *wear* (: *of great w.*); *fastness* (*of dyes*)

d·auern vi [h] (währen) *to last, continue*; *endure*; *to take* (: *the hearing took 2 hours*) ‖ ewig ~ *to last for ever* ‖ die Freude sollte nicht lange ~ *the pleasure was not to continue long* | es wird (nicht) lange ~ (z tun) *it will* (*not*) *take long* (od *a long time*) (*to do*); *I shall not be long*; diese Dinge ~ ihre Zeit *these things take time*; es dauert mir z lange *it takes me too long* ‖ je weiter wir fort sind, je länger dauert es, daß das Echo uns erreicht *the farther we are away the longer it takes the echo to reach us* | es wird nicht lange ~, dann (*or* so) blühen die Bäume *it won't be long before the trees blossom*; es dauerte nicht lange, so bot sich e–e Gelegenheit *it was not long before an opportunity presented itself*

d·auern vt [h] **1.** das dafür verausgabte Geld dauert mich, es dauert mich, das Geld .. *I grudge the money spent for it* ‖ laß dich das Geld nicht ~ *don't grumble at* (od *over*) *the money, don't regret the m.* ‖ laß dich die Anstrengungen nicht ~ *don't repent the efforts* ‖ es dauert mich, .. getan z h *I regret* od *repent having done .., I am sorry to have done*; es dauert mich, daß .. *I am sorry that ..* **2.** der arme Kerl dauert mich *I am sorry for* (od *I pity*) *the poor fellow*; du dauerst mich wirklich *I do pity you*

d·auernd **1.** a *continuous* (*laughter*), *lasting* (*comfort*); *permanent* (*position*; *residence*); ~es Gefrorensein [n] *permafrost*; *abiding* (*menace*) ‖ das ganze Jahr ~ *perennial* (*supply*); ewig ~ *perennial* (*youth*) **2.** adv *continuously*; *permanently*; er rauchte ~ *he kept smoking*; sie proklamieren ~ *they never cease to p.*

D·aumen m ~s/~ **1.** *thumb* ‖ (etw) mit dem ~ befühlen *to thumb*; mit dem ~ beschmutzen *to thumb* (*a book*) | ⟨fig⟩ (die) ~ drehen *to twiddle one's thumbs* od *fingers* ‖ jdn unter dem ~ halten, jdm den ~ auf's Auge setzen *or* drücken *to have* od *keep a p under one's thumb* (od *rule*, *sway*) ‖ er hält den ~ auf dem Geld *he's a tightwad* ‖ jdm den ~ halten *or* drücken *to wish a p good luck* od *success*; *to think of a p*; ⟨Am fam⟩ *to root for a p*; drück mir den ~! *keep your fingers crossed*! ‖ **über** den ~ (gepeilt) *by guess and by God*; ⟨aero sl⟩ (*to fly*) *by the seat of one's pants* **2.** (of a glove) *thumb* **3.** ⟨übtr mech⟩ *cam* **4.** [in comp] **~abdruck** m *thumb-print* **≗betätigt** a *thumb-actuated* **~kappe** f = Däumling 1. **~lutschen** n *thumb sucking* **~lutscher** m *th.-sucker* **~nagel** m *thumb-nail* **~-Peilverfahren** n *guess-work* **~register** n ⟨bookb⟩ *thumb index*; mit ~ *thumb-indexed* **~ring** m (beim orient. Bogenschießen) *thumb-ring* **~scheibe** f ⟨mech⟩ *jumping cam* **~schmutzfleck** m *thumb-mark* **~schraube** f ⟨hist⟩ *thumb-screw*, jdm die ~en anlegen *to thumb-screw*, *to torture a p* **~spur** f *thumb-mark*; mit ~en beschmutzt *thumby*

D·äumling m ~s/~e **1.** (Kappe) *thumb-stall* **2.** ⟨myth & übtr⟩ *Tom Thumb*

D·aumschraube f = Daumenschraube

D·aune f ~/~n *down*; Eider~n [pl] *eider-down*

D·aunen- [in comp] *down-* ..; *downy* **~bett** n *down-bed* **~decke** f *down-quilt*, *eider-down* **~feder** f *down*; *downy feather* **≗weich** a *downy*

da·unten adv *down there* ‖ (südlich) das Leben ~ *life down there* (⟨Am⟩ *down south*)

Dauphiné [dofi'ne:] f ⟨Fr⟩ *Dauphiny*

Daus n D·auses/D·äuser **1.** (Zwei im Würfel- u Kartenspiel) *deuce* **2.** *the highest throw*; ⟨cards⟩ *ace*; Däuser spielen *to play aces* **3.** ⟨übtr⟩ (P) ⟨sl⟩ *ripper*, *topper*, ein ~ im Spiel *a crack*; ein Kerl wie ein ~ ⟨fam⟩ *a regular brick*

°**Daus** m D·auses/ (Teufel) nur in Verwünschungen: ei der ~! potz ~! *deuce* (od *devil*) *knows* (*what*, *who* ..)?; was der ~! *what the d.*!

D·avid | ~sschild, ~sstern [m] *Star of D.*

D·avis-Pokal ['deivis-] m (engl; nach D. F. Davis) *Davis Cup*

D·avit ['dævit] m (engl) ~s/~s *davit*

davon [Betonung → u] adv **I.** [dav·on, davon] **A.** ⟨eig⟩ **1.** *off it*; *off them* ‖ iß nur ~ *please, eat off it* (sc *the plate*) **2.** *from it*; *from them*; nimm 5 ~ ab *subtract 5*; ziehen Sie 3% ~ ab *deduct 3 per cent* ‖ er ist nicht weit ~ *he is not far off*; er ist nur 2 Jahre ~ entfernt *he is only 2 years short of it* (sc *sixty*) ‖ er trennte sich ~ *he parted with it* (sc *the house*) ‖ bleib ~ *keep off*, *leave it alone* ‖ frei ~ *free from it* (sc *pain*); *free of it* (sc *debt*) | er lief auf u ~ *he ran away* ‖ → davon- **B.** ⟨übtr⟩ **1.** (von = aus, durch) *of it*; das kommt ~ *that comes of it* (sc *disobedience*); das kommt ~, wenn man lügt *that comes of lying* | *from it*; er hatte wenig Nutzen ~ *he derived little profit from it*, *he was none the better for it*; was hab ich ~? *what have I got* (od *do I get*) *out of it*?; was hätte ich ~? *what would it profit me*? *what would be the profit of doing that*? ‖ er starb ~ *he died from it* (sc *the fatigue*) | *with it*; *with them*; er war ~ angetan *he was pleased with it* ‖ *again*: .., bis das Tal ~ widerhallte .. *till the valley echoed again* **2.** *on it*; *on them*; das hängt in der Tat ~ ab *that depends partly on it* (sc *the result*) *indeed* **3.** [von = betreffs; oft bei Verben] *of it*, *of that*; *of them*; sprich nicht ~ *don't talk of it*; man sprach ~, sein Los leichter z m *they were talking of making his lot easier*; ich erlaube mir, Sie ~ in Kenntnis z setzen, daß .. *I beg to inform you that* ..; er hält wenig ~ *he thinks little of it* ‖ (in Antworten) Operation – nichts ~ *operation – nothing* **4.** (von als Formwort) *of it*; *of them*; Teile ~ *parts of it* (sc *the village*); nichts mehr ~ *no more of that* ‖ das Resultat ~ *the upshot of it* **II.** [d·avon] ~ h wir gar nichts *it does not profit us at all* ‖ ~ hatte ich k–e Ahnung *of that I had no idea* ‖ ~ hängt alles ab *on that everything depends*

dav·on- (→ davon I. A. 2.) [in comp] **~|eilen** vi [s] *to hurry away* od *off*; *to be off* **~|fahren** vi [s] (of a car) *to roll away* **~|gehen** vi [s] *to move off*; v jdm ~ *to walk away from a p* **~|kommen** vi [s] *to come off*; *to get away* (od *off*) ‖ glücklich ~ *to have a lucky escape*; mit dem Leben ~ *to escape* ‖ mit knapper Not ~, mit e–m blauen Auge ~ *to have a narrow escape* (od ⟨sl⟩ *squeak*) ‖ ohne Schaden ~ *to escape scotfree* ‖ ohne Strafe ~ *to be let off*; *to go unpunished*; jdn ohne St. ~ l *to let a p off* **~|laufen** **1.** vi [s] *to run away*, *to be off*; → davon I. A. 2. ‖ heimlich ~ *to abscond*; *to steal away* (od *off*); ⟨mil & mar⟩ *to desert*; vor Schreck ~ *to be* od *get scared away* **2.** ≗ n °es ist z ~ *it is intolerable*, *it is simply awful* **~|machen** vrefl [h] sich ~ *to take to one's heels*, *to make off*; ⟨fam⟩ *to clear out*, *to cut and run*, *to skip*, *toddle*; .. mit etw *to walk off with a th*; sich gerade noch ~ (können) *to get just away in time* ‖ °(sterben) *to shuffle off this mortal coil* ‖ sich heimlich ~ *to abscond*; *to steal away* (od *off*) **~|schleichen** vrefl [s] sich ~ *to slip away*, *to sneak off*, *to steal away* od *off* **~|stehlen** vrfl [h] sich ~ *to slink off* od *away*; ..v jdm *to lurk out of a p's reach* **~|tragen** vt [h] **1.** ⟨eig⟩ *to carry away* **2.** ⟨übtr⟩ (e–e Krankheit) *to catch*, *contract*, *get*; e–e Erkältung ~ *to catch a cold* ‖ (Verlust etc) *to incur* ‖ (Ehren) *to carry off*; (Preis) *to bear* od *pull off* ..; e–n Sieg ~ *to score a victory* ‖ den Sieg ~ *to carry* od *win the day*; ⟨übtr⟩ *to sweep the board*, ⟨sl⟩ *to bring home the bacon* ‖ °**~wetzen** vi [s] ⟨fam⟩ *to skid*

davor [Betonung → u] adv **I.** [dav·or, davor] **1.** ⟨eig⟩ *before it* (sc *the door*); *before them* (sc *the doors*); (*he stood*) *in front of it*, *in front of them*; er trat ~ *he stood* (od *moved*) *in front of it* **2.** ⟨übtr⟩ **a.** *of it*; die Furcht ~ *the fear of it*; ich fürchte mich nicht ~ *I am not afraid of it*; hüte dich ~ *beware of it* **b.** *from it*; bewahre ihn ~ *save him from it*; schütze ihn ~ *protect him from* (od *against*) *it*; jdn ~ bewahren z tun *to save a p from doing* **c.** *for it*; man konnte nicht ~ arbeiten *you could not work for it* (sc *the noise*) **II.** [d·avor] ~ brauchst du k–e Angst z h *of that you need not be afraid* ‖ Gott bewahre uns ~! *God forbid*!

Dav·os n (Alpental u Kurort)

D·awes- [dɔ:z–] (nach Ch. G. Dawes) **~anleihe** f *Dawes-loan* **~plan** m *Dawes-plan*

daw·ider adv = dagegen A. 3. u B.

dazu [Betonung → u] adv **I.** [daz·u, dazu] **A.** **1.** [bei intr Verben → dazu–] **2.** geben (*or* legen, tun) Sie noch 3 Äpfel ~ *give* od *add another three apples* (od *three more apples*), *please* **B.** ⟨übtr⟩ **1.** (obendrein) *at that*; ein Lügner u ein dummer ~ *a liar and a stupid liar at that* ‖ er war 2 Meter gr u breit ~ *he was 2 metres in height and broad with it* ‖ *in addition*, *besides*, *moreover*; noch ~ *to boot*, *into the bargain*, *on top of that*, *on the back of it*; .. u sehr viel mehr ~ .. *and a great deal more thrown in* **2.** *to it*; *to them*; eine Vorrede ~ *a preface to it* (sc *the book*) ‖ er schlug den Takt ~ *he beat time* *to it* ‖ er sang u spielte (Klavier) ~ *he sang and she accompanied him* (*on the piano*) ‖ er hatte das Zeug ~ *he had it in him* ‖ Gott gebe s–n Segen ~! *may God grant it His blessing* **| es gehört** wirklich ~ *it does belong to it* (sc *the class*) ‖ es gehört nicht ~ *it is not germane to it* (sc *the question*) ‖ mit ~ gehören (P) *to be one of the party*; ⟨übtr⟩ *to be in it*; *to be in the swim*; nicht mehr ~ gehören *to be out of the swim* **3.** laßt es nicht ~ **kommen** *don't let it come to that* ‖ ich kann nicht ~ k (z tun) *I cannot find time* (*to do*) ‖ wie k Sie ~ z behaupten ..? *how do you come to assert* ..? ‖ wie k Sie ~? *what's the idea of it*? *what is the meaning of that*? ‖ ⟨iron⟩ wie käme ich ~? *not I*? **| halte** dich ~ *keep to your work*; *get along*; *hurry up* ‖ ich konnte leider nichts ~ tun *unfortunately I couldn't do anything in the matter* **4.** was **sagst** du ~? *what do you say to it* (sc *a visit to* ..) **5. ~ ausersehen**, bestimmt s z tun *to be destined to do*; ~ beitragen z tun *to contribute to do*; ~ bereit s .. *to be ready to do*; ~ fähig s .. *to be able to do, to be capable of doing*; ~ übergehen z tun *to set out to do, to start doing* **6.** *for it*; es ist **z dick ~** *it* (sc *the board*) *is too thick for it* ‖ er ist nicht der Mann ~ *he is not the man for it* **II.** [d·azu] ⟨übtr⟩ ~ ist er hier *that is what he is here for*; ~ ist er zu sehr Gentleman, es z tun *he's too much the g. to do it* ‖ ~ wird es nicht k *to that it won't come* ‖ ~ kommt noch, daß .. *add to this that* .. ‖ ~ gehört Zeit *that requires time* ‖ ~ gehört nicht viel *that I could do with ease* (⟨sl⟩ *on my head*)

daz·u- (→ dazu I. A.) **~|eilen** vi [s]: er eilte dazu *he hastened to the spot* **~|gehören** vi [h] (S) was –rt *what goes with it* ‖ (P) (z dem Klub) *to belong* (zu *to*), ⟨Am fam⟩ *to be in the swim*; *they all belonged* **~|gesellen** [vrefl] [h] sich ~ *to join the company, etc* **~|kommen 1.** vi [s] (P) *to come along*; *to appear on the scene*; er kam zufällig dazu *he happened to come along* **|** (of a disease) *to supervene*; als Bronchitis dazukam, war er .. *bronchitis supervening he was* .. ‖ wo viel ist, kommt mehr dazu *money breeds money* ‖ dazu kommt .. *not to mention* .., *not including* .. ‖ nicht ~, jdn z sehen *to have no chance to see a p* **2.** ≈ n *unexpected appearance* (*of a p*) ‖ *supervention* (*of a th*)

daz·ugehörig a *belonging* od *pertinent to it*

Daz·ukunft f = Dazukommen

d·azumal adv *then, at that time*

dazw·ischen adv *between them* (sc *the houses*), *among them* **~|drängen** vrefl sich ~ *to squeeze in between* **~|fahren** vi [s] *to jump in, to intervene* (*in a quarrel*) **~|kommen I.** vi [s] **1.** ⟨eig & übtr⟩ *to interfere* ‖ wie konntest du ~? *how could you come* (od *interpose, stand*) *between them* (sc *the combatants*)? **2.** (of events) *to intervene*; .., sollte nichts ~ .., *should nothing intervene* ‖ etw Neues kam ~ *sth new turned up* **II.** ≈ n = ≈**kunft** f = Dazwischentreten **~|legen** vt [h] (etw) *to interpose* **~|liegen 1.** vi: der Teil liegt dazwischen *that part intervenes between them*; ~d [a] *intermediate, intervenient, -vening*; ~de Seiten [pl] *intervening pages* [pl] **2.** ≈ n *intervention* **~|reden** vi [h] *to cut in*; *to interrupt* (jdm a p) **~|setzen** vt (etw) *to interpose* **~|treten 1.** vi [s] = -kommen **3.** ≈ n *interference, interposition, intervention* (*of a p*; *of a power*) **~|werfen** vt ⟨übtr⟩ (Bemerkung) *to interject, interpose*; *to throw in*; -geworfen [a] *interjectional* (*question*)

„**Deb**"- (= Debütantinnen) -**Star** m *star of starlets*

†**Deb·akel** n (Fr) *débâcle* (Fr), *collapse, breakdown*

Deb·atte f ~/~n **1.** ⟨parl⟩ die ~ *the debate* ‖ ⟨engl⟩ gedruckter Bericht der ~n *the debates* [pl]; Führer der ~ ⟨Am⟩ *floor-leader* ‖ die ~ eröffnen (schließen) *to open* (*to closure*) *the debate* ‖ (Antrag auf) Schluß der ~ *closure, gag*; den Antrag auf Schl. der ~ stellen *to apply the closure* (*to* [*motion, speakers*]); in die ~ eingreifen *to engage in the debate*; ⟨Am⟩ *to be on the floor* ‖ Festsetzung e–s best. Tages f den Abschluß der ~ *guillotine* (Fr) ‖ Mitglieder hinterer Bänke, die nicht viel in die ~ eingreifen *the backbenchers* [pl] **2.** *discussion*; in e–e ~ eintreten *to enter into* od *upon a discussion*; zur ~ stehen (S) *to be under* (⟨Am⟩ *up for*) *discussion*; etw zur ~ stellen *to make a th a matter* (od *subject*) *for discussion*; wir w es z ~ st. *we shall discuss it*

debatt·ieren vt/i [h] **1.** vt (Frage) *to debate, discuss*; *argue* **2.** vi *to debate* (über *on*); erregt ~ ⟨Am sl⟩ *to chew the rag* **Debatt·ierklub** m *debating-club* (od *society*)

D·ebet n ~s/~s ⟨com⟩ *debit*; = ~seite, → d. ‖ im ~ stehen *to be on the debit*(*-side*) od *debtor-side* **~note** f *debit-note* **~posten** m *debit-entry* **~saldo** m *debit-balance* **~seite** f *debit*(*-side*), *debtor*(*-side*) (abbr *Dr.*) ‖ ⟨Am⟩ die ~ mit etw belasten *to put a th in the red* (sc *red ink*); (S) auf die ~ k (*or* gesetzt w) *to go into the red, to be put in the red*; aus der ~ k *to come out of the red*

Debilit·ät f ⟨med⟩ *debility*

Deb·it [de'bi] m (Fr) ⟨com⟩ **1.** *sale*; *market* **2.** [in comp] † = Konkurs– **debit·ieren** vt [h] **1.** (belasten) jdn, jds Konto ~ mit etw *to debit a p, a p's account with a th* (: *a sum*); *to place a th to a p's account*; → belasten 3. **2.** (verkaufen) *to sell*; *to dispose of* **D·ebitor** m ~s/Debit·oren *debtor* ‖ ⟨bal⟩ ~en *debitors*

†**debouch·ieren** vi [h] ⟨mil⟩ *to debouch*

D·ebreczin [–tʃin], **D·ebretzin** (ungar. Stadt)

Deb·üt [de'by] n (Fr) ~s/~s *début* (Fr), *first appearance in public* (*of an actor*, etc.); sein ~ m *to* (*make one's*) *debut* **Debüt·ant** m ~en/~en *debutant* (Fr)

Debüt·antin f *débutante*, ⟨fam⟩ *deb*, ⟨Am a.⟩ *bud* **debüt·ieren** vi [h] *to* (*make one's*) *début*

Dechan·ei f ~/~en ⟨ec⟩ *deanery* **Dech·ant** m ~en/~en ⟨ec⟩ *dean*

Dech·arge [de'ʃɑrʒ] f ⟨com⟩ *discharge* (v *from*); → Entlastung

D·echer n ⟨obs⟩ (10 Stück [Felle]) *dicker*

dechiffr·ieren [deʃi'fri:rən] vt [h] (Geheimschrift) *to decipher*; (Codetelegramm) *to decode*

×**D·echsel** f ~/~n *adze*; (etw) mit der ~ bearbeiten *to adze*

Decidu·aten [pl] ⟨zoo⟩ *deciduata* (L) [pl]

D·eck n ~(e)s/~e **1.** ⟨mar⟩ *deck*; (am Heck) *poop*; → Achter≈ ‖ Haupt≈ *main deck*, Ober≈ *upper deck*; Zwischen≈ *middle deck*; Unter≈ *lower deck*; → Orlog≈ ‖ an ~, auf ~ *on deck*; unter ~ *below d.*; klar ~ (überall)! *clear decks*!; an ~ gehen *to go on d.* **2.** ⟨übtr⟩ *roof, top* (*of a vehicle*) **3.** [in comp] *deck* **~abstand** m ⟨aero⟩ *distance between wings* **~aufbauten** m pl ⟨mar⟩ *superstructure*; (e–s ⟨aero⟩-Trägers) *island* **~balken** m *deck-beam* **~haus** n *deck-house* **~ladung** f *deck-load* **~landebahn** f ⟨aero⟩ *deck runway* **~landeflugzeug** n *deck-landing plane* **~offizier** m ⟨Ger nav⟩ *warrant-officer* **~passagier** m *deck-passenger* **~sitz** m *roof-seat*

D·eck- (→ decken) [in comp] **~adresse** f *cover address* **~anruf** m ⟨telph⟩ *code-call* **~anschrift** f *closed address* **~anstrich** m *finishing* od *final coat* **~bett** n ⟨Ger⟩ *feather-bed* **~blatt** n *paster* ⟨a. mil⟩; ⟨bot⟩ *covering-leaf*; (~ e–r Seitenblüte) *bract* ‖ (of a cigar) *wrapper* ‖ (e–s Gesetzes etc) *amendment* **~creme** f ⟨cosm⟩ *make-up, rouge* **~emulsion** f ⟨cosm⟩ *cover fluid* **~fänger** m ⟨crick⟩ *cover-point* **~farbe** f ⟨arts⟩ *body-colour*; *opaque colour* ‖ ~nmalerei [f] *gouache* **~federn** f [pl] ⟨orn⟩ *tectrices* [pl]; *feathery covering* (*of* *a leg)* **~firnis** m *covering varnish* **~gang** m *covered way* **~glas** n ⟨opt⟩ *protecting* od *cover glass* **~haut** f ⟨anat⟩ *integument* **~hengst** m *stallion* **~kraft** f ⟨paint⟩ (einer Farbe) *hiding power* **~lage** f (e–r Straße) *wearing course* **~mantel** m ⟨fig⟩ *cloak* (e–r S *for a th*); unter dem **~** der Freundschaft *under the cover* (od *in the guise*) *of friendship* || *disguise*; *mask*; *veil*; unter dem ∼ der Bescheidenheit *under the cloak* (od *disguise, mask*) *of modesty*; *under colour* (od *cover*) *of modesty* **~name** m *cover name*; ⟨mil⟩ *nickname* || *pseudonym*; ⟨Lit⟩ *pen-name*; unter e–m ∼n *pseudonymously*; die Verwendung e–s ∼ns *pseudonymity* **~netz** n (f Fuchsfang) *loaded net* **~platte** f *cover-plate* **~serviette** f *napkin, serviette* (*to cover the table-cloth*) **~stuhl** m (bei Dacharbeit) *roof-trestle* **~weiß** n *zinc white* **~wort** n *code word*

D·eckchen n (Tellerunterlage) *doily*

D·ecke f ∼/∼n **A.** (Zimmer≃) *ceiling*; an der ∼ *on the c.*; ein Raum mit tiefer ∼ *a low--ceil(ing)ed room* || ⟨min⟩ *roof* || ⟨fig⟩ vor Freude bis an die ∼ springen *to jump* od *leap for* (od *with*) *joy*, ⟨sl⟩ *to jump to the moon* **B. 1.** (∼ auf etw) *outer cover(ing)*; *coat(ing)*; Rasen≃ *covering of turf*; Schnee≃ *covering* (od *field*) *of snow*; (Eis≃) *sheet*; Staub≃ *coat of dust* || *surface*; *layer* || ⟨mot⟩ Reifen≃ *cover* || (auf Flüssigkeiten) *head*; *top* || (Geigen≃) *covering board* **2.** (aus Tuch etc) *cover, cloth*; wollene ∼, Bett≃ *blanket*; → Pferde≃, Reise≃, Sattel≃, Stepp≃, Wagen≃ || → Haube | ⟨fig⟩ sich nach der ∼ strecken *to cut one's coat according to the cloth, to make both ends meet, to make the best of it, to accommodate o.s. to circumstances* || unter e–r ∼ stecken *to conspire together*; ⟨sl⟩ *to be in cahoots*; mit jdm unter e–r ∼ stecken *to combine in a plot* (od *to plot together, to be hand in glove*) *with a p*; .. bei, in e–r S *to connive at a th*; sie stecken unter einer ∼ *they stick together* **3.** (Hülle) (Schutz≃) *cover, jacket, wrapper* (*of a book*) || *envelope* || ⟨zoo⟩ *coat, skin*; *tegument*; *vestiture*; ⟨hunt⟩ *hairy skin* (*of deer, etc.*) **4.** ⟨geol⟩ *nappe* Fr **C.** [in comp] → Decken–

D·eckel m ∼s/∼ **1.** *cover, lid* (*of a kettle*), *top* (*of a bottle*), *cap* || *movable flap*; *lid* (*of a box*); *shutter*; Schiebe≃ *sliding-shutter* || aufklappbarer ∼ *hinged lid*; ∼ zum Ab–, Aufschrauben *screw-top* (od *cap*) || mit ∼ versehen [a] *lidded* **2.** (Buch≃) *cover*; *binding* || ⟨typ⟩ *tympan* **3.** ⟨ich & bot⟩ *operculum* (L) **4.** °(= Hut) ⟨sl⟩ *lid* || eins auf den ∼ bek *to be hauled over the coals*; jdm eins auf den ∼ geben *to haul a p over the coals* **~glas** n *glass with a lid* **~kanne** f *pitcher with a lid* **~krug** m *tankard* **~rahmen** m ⟨typ⟩ *tympan--frame* **~stuhl** m ⟨typ⟩ *gallows* [pl] **~verschluß** m *lid locking*

d·ecken vt/i [h] **I.** vt **A.** ⟨eig⟩ **1.** (P) (Dach) *to cover* (mit *with*); (Dach) mit Ziegeln ∼ *to tile*; mit Schiefer ∼ *to slate*; mit Stroh ∼ *to thatch*; ein Haus ∼ *to roof* (od *cover in*) *a house* (*with glass*) || (Hand) wölbend ∼ *to cup* (über *over*) | den **Tisch** ∼ *to lay the cloth*; *to lay the table*; ∼! *cover*!; es ist gedeckt *the table is laid*; f 8 Personen ∼ *to lay covers for 8 persons* **2.** (S) **a.** Schnee deckt die Flur *snow covers the fields* **b.** ihn deckt nun der Rasen *he is below* (*the*) *ground now* **3.** (T) (Stute etc) *to cover* **4.** ⟨artill⟩ (Ziel) *to straddle* **B.** ⟨übtr⟩ (schützen) **1.** (T) (Junge) *to cover, to protect* (*with*) **2.** ⟨mil⟩ (schützend geleiten) *to convoy, escort* || (Flanke etc) *to cover* (*the retreat*; gegen *from*) || ⟨übtr⟩ jdm den Rücken ∼ *to back a p* **3. jdn ~ a.** *to cover* od *secure a p* (gegen Schläge *from blows*); *to protect, shield a p*; er ist nicht gedeckt *he has no security* **b.** (Verbrecher) *to screen, shield* **c.** jds Handlung(sweise) ∼ *to take the responsibility for a p's action* **4.** ⟨bib & poet⟩ (verbergen) (Schande) *to conceal*; *hide* **5.** ⟨chess & fenc⟩ *to guard* **6.** ⟨com⟩ (Ausfall) *to replace*; ein Defizit ∼ *to cover a deficit, to make good a deficiency*; jds Kosten ∼ *to cover* (od *defray, reimburse*) *a p's expenses*; e–n Schaden ∼ *to cover* (od *make good*) *a loss*; → Bedarf 1. b. || ein Akzept ∼ *to provide for acceptance*; e–n Wechsel ∼ *to meet a bill*; der Scheck ist (nicht) gedeckt .. *is* (*not*) *covered* **C. sich ~ 1. a.** ⟨math⟩ (of lines, etc.) *to coincide* (: *the superposed triangles c.*); *to be identical* od *equal* || (of areas, events) sich ∼ mit *to coincide with*; sich teilweise ∼ *to overlap* || sich ∼de Begriffe *coextensive concepts* **b.** ⟨übtr⟩ **sich ~ mit** *to coincide* (od *correspond, fall in line, square, tally*) *with*; *to conform to*; *to be identical, to be in accord with*; diese Behauptung deckt sich nicht mit den Tatsachen *this statement does not tally with the facts*; unsere Ansichten ∼ sich völlig *our views are in full accord* **2.** *to cover* od *defend o.s.*; ⟨chess & fenc⟩ *to guard* (gegen *against*) **3.** ⟨com⟩ *to provide cover*; *to reimburse o.s.* || *to insure o.s.* **II.** vi **1.** die Farbe deckt gut *this colour covers the ground well* **2.** decke f ihn da drüben *lay for him over there* **3.** der Boxer deckte gut *the boxer guarded well*

D·ecken n **1.** *the covering* (*of a roof*); *roofing* (*of a house*) **2.** *the laying* (*of the table*) **3.** *the covering* (*of a mare*) || → Deckung

D·ecken- (→ Decke) **~balken** m *ceiling-beam* **~beleuchtung** f *ceiling-lighting* (od *lamp*); ⟨mot⟩ *interior lighting*; → Deckenlicht **~feld** n → Paneel **~gebirge** n *overthrust mountains* **~gemälde** n *painted ceiling* **~gewölbe** n *arched roff* **~lager** n ⟨mach⟩ *hanger* **~licht** n *top light, ceilinglight*; *lighting from above*; ⟨mot⟩ *dome light* **~malerei** f *decoration of ceilings* **~projektor** m (f Wolkenhöhe) *ceiling projector* **~transmission** f *overhead transmission* **~wulst** m ⟨mot⟩ *head over the cover*

D·ecker m = Decher

-decker m [in comp] **1.** ⟨mar⟩ Zw·ei∼ (etc) *two-decker* **2.** → D·ach∼, Sch·iefer∼, Str·oh∼

D·eckung f ∼/∼en **A.** [abstr] (Decken) **1.** ⟨eig⟩ → Decken ⟨phot⟩ die 2 Teile e–s Schnittbildes zur ∼ bringen *to bring 2 parts of a split image into register*; (2 Bilder) z ∼ br. *to bring into coincidence, to make coincide, to superimpose* **2.** ⟨übtr mil⟩ *covering* (*of the flank, of a retreat*); → Bedeckung || Rücken≃ *backing* (*of a p*) **2.** *covering*; *protecting* (*of a p*) || *screening, shielding* (*of a culprit*) **3.** ⟨chess & fenc⟩ *guard* **4.** ⟨com⟩ *covering* (*of a deficit, a loss*); *reimbursement* (*of expenses*) **B.** [konkr] (etw, das deckt) **1.** ⟨mil⟩ *cover, shelter* (gegen *from*) || Truppen in ∼ *protected troops*; ∼! *take cover*!; in ∼ gehen *to run for cover, to take cover* || ohne ∼ *uncovered*; unter ∼ *under cover*; (Flügel) außer ∼ bringen, ohne ∼ l *to uncover*; über die ∼ springen *to go over the top*; ∼ suchen *to take cover*; eiligst ∼ suchen *to make a dash for cover* || (Sicht≃) ⟨mil⟩ *concealment* | ⟨übtr⟩ *covering* **2.** ⟨hunt⟩ (f T) *cover(t)* **3.** ⟨com⟩ (Geld≃) *cover* (f *for* [*a draft*]), *security* (*for*); *funds* [pl]; *margin* || → Papiergeld | genügende ∼ *ample cover*; ohne ∼, keine ∼ *no effects* (abbr *N/E*), *no funds*; *without cover* (od *funds*); ohne ∼ verkaufen *to sell short* || ∼ finden, f ∼ sorgen *to provide cover, to cover* || ∼ in den Händen h *to be covered* || ∼ schaffen f *to provide for* || jdm ∼ zugehen l *to provide a p with funds* || mangels ∼ zurückgehen (Scheck) *to go* (⟨fam⟩ *bounce*) *back* **4.** ⟨ins⟩ (Schadens≃) *coverage*

D·eckungs- ~betrag m *cover(-money)*; *margin* **≃fähig** a *valid as legal cover* **~feuer** n *cover(ing) fire* **~graben** m *shelter trench* **~kauf** m ⟨com⟩ *covering-purchase* **~klausel** f *covering-clause* **~loch** n ⟨mil sl⟩ *foxhole* **~mannschaft** f *covering troops* pl **~papier** n (mündelsicheres) ⟨st exch,

m. m.⟩ *floater* **~rückstellung** f ⟨ins⟩ *reserves* **~winkelmesser** m *angle-of-sight instrument*

decresc·endo [–kreʃ–] adv (It) ⟨mus⟩ *decrescendo*

Dedikati·on [–ts–] f ~/~en *dedication* (an, f jdn *to a p*) ‖ ~sexemplar [n] *presentation copy*

dediz·ieren vt [h] jdm etw ~ *to dedicate a th to a p*

Dedukti·on f ~/~en ⟨philos⟩ (Ggs Induktion) *deduction* **dedukt·iv** a *deductive*; ~e Methode, ~es Verfahren *d. method* **deduz·ieren** vt [h] (etw) *to deduce* (aus *from*)

×**Deern** f *girl, wench* (: *a buxom w.*)

Deeskalati·on [ts] f ~/ *deescalation*

de facto adv (L) *de facto* (L); *in fact*

Defait·ismus m ~/ [defɛ–] *defeatism* **–t·ist** m *defeatist, wet blanket* **d–t·istisch** a *defeatist*

Defäkati·on f ⟨med⟩ *defecation*

D·efa f ~/ ⟨SBZ⟩ Deutsche Film-AG

def·ekt a *defective* (*machine, condition*); *out of order*; *wanting examining*; *faulty*; *incomplete* (*work*) ‖ ⟨typ⟩ *battered, spoiled* (*letter*); ~er Buchstabe *batter* ‖ *damaged* (*goods*)

Def·ekt m ~(e)s/~e **1.** *defect* (an e–r Maschine *in a machine*); Maschinen≗ *engine trouble* → Panne ‖ ⟨typ⟩ ~e [pl] *sorts* [pl] | (P) *defect, deficiency* (: *mental d.*); *fault, imperfection* | → Fehlbetrag **2.** ⟨typ⟩ **~bogen** m [pl] *overplus sheets* [pl] **~buch** n *sorts register* **~buchstabe** m *batter* **~kasten** m *fount-case*

defens·iv a *defensive* ‖ sich ~ verhalten *to act* (od *stand*) *on the defensive* **Defens·ive** f ~/~n *defensive* ‖ sich in der ~ befinden *to be on the defensive*; sich in der ~ halten *to act* od *stand on the d.* **Defens·ivkrieg** m *defensive war*

Defil·ee n (Engpaß) *defile* **defil·ieren** vi [h] ⟨mil⟩ *to defile, to file* (*off*); *to march past* **Defil·iercour** f *défilé* (Fr) *of the courtiers*; *levee*

defin·ierbar a *definable* **defin·ieren** vt [h] *to define* **Definiti·on** f ~/~en *definition*; e–e ~ geben *to provide a definition*; ⟨opt⟩ *definition* **definit·iv 1.** (endgültig) *definitive* (offer, *verdict*), *final* **2.** adv *definitely*; *definitively*

D·efizit n ~s/~e *deficit, deficiency*; *shortage*; ⟨Am⟩ *wantage*: ein ~ v $ 100 h *to be $ 100 short* ‖ → decken I. A. *b.*

Deflagrati·on f ⟨phys⟩ *deflagration*

Deflati·on f **1.** (of air, wind) *deflation* **2.** ⟨com⟩ (Ggs Inflation) *deflation, disinflation*; ~sbewegung *deflationary movement*; Wiederherstellung der Kaufkraft nach e–r ~ *reflation*

deflor·ieren vt [h] (entjungfern) *to deflower*

Deformati·on f ⟨phys & anthr⟩ *deformation* ‖ (der Erdkruste) *diastrophism* **deform·ierbar** a *deformable* **≗keit** f *deformability*

deform·ieren vt [h] *to deform, distort, strain*

Deformit·ät f ~/~en *deformity*

Defraud·ant m ~en/~en *defrauder* **–dati·on** f ~/~en = Betrug **d–d·ieren** vt/i *to defraud, cheat*

×**d·eftig 1.** a *heavy* (*blow*); *sound* (*price*); *square, good* (*meal*); *good long* (*walk*); → tüchtig, derb ‖ *strong, vigorous* (*p*) **2.** adv; jdn ~ anfassen *to rough-house a p*

D·egen m ~s/~ (P) ⟨poet⟩ *thane*, ⟨hist⟩ *thegn*; *retainer* ‖ ⟨übtr⟩ *soldier, warrior*; *champion*

D·egen m ~s/~ ⟨mil⟩ *sword*; den ~ senken *to lower the s.* ‖ ⟨fenc⟩ *épée*; *small-sword* ‖ ⟨fig⟩ e–n ~ verschluckt h *to be* (*too*) *straight-necked* **~band** n *sword-knot* **~fechten** n *épée-fencing* **~fechter** m *épé*(*e*)*ist* **~gefäß** n *sword-hilt* **~gehenk** n *sword-belt* **~griff** m *sword-hilt* **~klinge** f *sword-blade* **~koppel** f *sword-belt* **~quaste** f *sword-knot* **~stich** m *s.-stab* **~stoß** m *s.-thrust*; *épée-thrust*

Degenerati·on f *degeneration* **degener·ieren** vi [s] *to degenerate*; degeneriert [a] *degenerate*

Degradati·on f *degradation* **degrad·ieren** vt [h] ⟨mil & nav⟩ (jdn) *to degrade* (z *to, into*); *to demerit*; *to reduce* (*a p*) *to a lower rank*, ⟨fam⟩ *to demote*; (Offizier) *to break* **Degrad·ierung** f ~/~en = Degradation

Degressi·on d *degression* (*of taxes*) **degress·iv** a *degressive* (*taxation*)

D·egu m ⟨zoo⟩ (e–e Trugratte) *degu*

degumm·ieren vt [h] ⟨tech⟩ (Fäden) *to degum*

d·ehnbar a **1.** (aus~) *extensible* (*skin*), *dilatable* ‖ (of metal) *ductile, flexible*; *malleable*; *pliable*; *yielding*; ⟨tail⟩ *stretch* [attr] **2.** ⟨übtr⟩ *ductile* (*law*); *elastic* (*conscience*); *flexible* (*wording*); *vague* (*statement*); *loose* od *ambiguous* (*notion*), *equivocal* **≗keit** f ~/ **1.** *extensibility, dilatability* ‖ ⟨met⟩ *ductility*; *flexibility*; *pliability* **2.** ⟨übtr⟩ *flexibility* (*of a law*); *vagueness*; *ambiguity* **3.** ~sprobe [f] ⟨tech⟩ *elasticity test*

d·ehnen vt [h] **A. 1.** ⟨eig⟩ **a.** (etw) *to hammer out*; *to pull out*; *to pull lengthwise*; ⟨tech⟩ *to extend* ‖ (Glieder beim Foltern) *to stretch* ‖ (v innen weiten) *to dilate, distend, expand, stretch*; *lengthen*; *widen* ‖ (die Brust) *to expand*; *to swell out* **b.** ⟨phon⟩ (Vokal) *to lengthen* (*out*); gedehnt w *to lengthen*; gedehnte Silbe *lengthened syllable* ‖ Worte ~ (*or* gedehnt aussprechen) *to drawl* (*out*) *words*; *to speak words with lazy slowness*; gedehnte Aussprache *drawling pronunciation*; gedehntes Sprechen *drawl*; in gedehntem Tone *drawlingly* **2.** ⟨übtr⟩ *to extend*; (Gesetz etc) *to make ductile* (od *elastic, flexible*); *to put a suitable construction on* (*a th*) **B. sich ~ 1.** ⟨eig⟩ **a.** ⟨phys⟩ (of air, etc.) *to expand*; (*of wood*) *to distend, dilate*; *stretch*; (of material) *to creep*; (of areas) *to extend* (*o.s.*); *to stretch* ‖ (of the chest) *to expand*; *to swell out* **b.** (P) *to stretch o.s.*; sich recken u ~ *to give a stretch* (: *he gave a st.*) **2.** (of time) *to lengthen* **3. sich ~ l** = dehnbar s

D·ehnung f ~/~en **1. a.** *dila*(*ta*)*tion, distension*; *stretching* ‖ *expansion*; Wärme≗ *expansion due to heat* ‖ *expansion, swelling out* (*of the chest*) ‖ ⟨tech⟩ elastische ~ *longitudinal stress* **b.** *lengthening* (*of a vowel*); Vokal≗ *vowel lengthening* **2.** ⟨übtr⟩ *extension* ‖ *suitable interpretation* (*of a law*) **~sapparat** m *dilator* **≗sfähig** a *extensible, expansible* **~sfähigkeit** f *extensibility, flexibility, expansibility* ‖ *elasticity* **~skoeffizient** m *modulus of extension* **~smesser** m (f Flüssigkeiten, durch Wärme) *dilatometer* **~sversuch** m ⟨tech⟩ *tensile test* **~swärme** f *heat of elastic extension* **~szahl** f *coefficient of expansion, etc* **~szeichen** n ⟨gram⟩ *lengthening mark*

dehydr·ieren 1. vt [h] ⟨chem⟩ *to dehydrate* **2.** ≗ n *dehydration*

D·eibel m ⟨ich⟩ = Karausche ‖ ×~ = Teufel; °wie der ~ ⟨fam⟩ *like sin*; wie der ~ festhalten *to hold on like grim death* (an *to*)

Deich m ~(e)s/~e **1.** (am Meeresufer) *dike, dyke*; *causeway, dam*; (Land) durch e–n ~ schützen *to dike, dam, causeway* ‖ (Fluß≗) *dam, embankment*; ⟨Am⟩ *levee* ‖ mit e–m ~ versehen *to dam, embank* ‖ → Damm **2.** ⟨fig⟩ *bulwark* (*against*); *barrier* **3.** [in comp] **~amt** n *dike-office* **~aufseher** m *overseer of the dikes* **~bau** m *diking, dyking* **~bruch** m *breach in a dike* **~damm** m *jetty* **~genossenschaft** = Deichverband **~graf, ~-hauptmann** m *dike-reeve* **~land** n *diked land* **~meister** m *dike-master* **~recht** n *dike-laws* [pl] **~schleuse** f *dike* (od *drainage*) *lock* **~-verband** m *dike-building association* **~vorstand** m *dike-managing committee* **~wesen** n *diking*

d·eichen vi [h] *to build a dike*

D·eichsel f → Dechsel (Querbeil)

D·eichsel f ~/~n (f Zweispänner) *shaft, thill*; *pole* ‖ Gabel≗ (f Einspänner) *shafts, thills* [pl] ‖ °~ nach Norden ⟨sex vulg⟩ *hard-on* **~arm** m *shaft-bar, futchel*(*l*) **~blech** n *pole-plate* **~haken**

m *pole-hook* **~nagel** m *pole* (od *thill*)-*pin* **~pferd** n *thill* (od *shaft*)-*horse, wheeler*

°**d·eichseln** vt [h] (etw) *to arrange*, ⟨fam⟩ *wangle*, ⟨Am⟩ *to fix* (*a th*) *up* ‖ *to bring about*; *to put through*; (durch Geschick) *to engineer, manage*; *to pull off*; (durch List) ⟨sl⟩ *to wangle* ‖ er deichselt die ganze S *he bosses* (⟨Am a.⟩ *fixes*) *the show*, ⟨sl⟩ *he swings it*

de·iktisch a *deictic* (*action*)

dein I. [pron poss] **A.** [mst attr] **1. a.** *your* (*brother*; *hat*, etc.) ‖ ~ Exemplar ist herrlich *yours is a fine specimen*; ist er e–r ~er Freunde? *is he a friend of yours*? immer wieder ~ falscher Tritt! *that false step of yours*! | ⟨dial, bib & poet⟩ *thy*, (vor Vokal) *thine* **b.** [pred] *yours* (: *this book is y.*) ‖ ⟨dial, bib & poet⟩ *thine* **B.** [abs] **1.** das ~e → mein **2. a.** der (die, das) ≗e *yours*; dies Buch ist das ~e *this book is yours*; tu du das ≗e *do your duty* (od *best*) ‖ (im Brief) immer der ≗ *Yours ever* | ⟨dial, bib & poet⟩ *thine* **b.** die ≗en [pl] *yours* (: *kind regards to you and yours*), *your people* **II.** [gen pron pers] ~, ~er *of you* ‖ ich werde ~(er) gedenken *I shall remember you*

d·einerseits adv *for* (od *on*) *your part* **d·eines-gl·eichen** adv *your like*(*s*); ⟨fam⟩ *the like*(*s*) *of you* ‖ verkehre mit ~ *mix with your likes*

d·einethalben, d·einetwegen adv *on your account, for your sake, on* od *in your behalf*; *for all* od *aught you care* **d·einetwillen** adv; um ~ = deinetwegen

D·einige: der, die, das ~/die ~n → dein I. B.

D·eining f ~/~en ⟨mar⟩ *swell* (*of the sea*)

d·einsen 1. vi [h] ⟨mar⟩ *to back* od *fall astern* **2.** ≗ n ⟨mar⟩ *stern-way* (*of a ship*)

×**d·eisig** a = diesig

De·ismus m ~/ ⟨ec⟩ *deism* **De·ist** m ~en/~en *deist* **de·istisch** a *deistical*

D·eister m ⟨Ger⟩ (Gebirge)

×**Deiwel,** ×**D·eixel** m (f Teufel) ei der ~! pfui ~! → °Daus

déjà-vu n [invar] Fr ⟨psych⟩ ~-Erlebnis [n] (Erinnerungsfälschung) *déjà vu*

Deka- (Gr = zehn) [in comp] *deca–* **~·eder** n ⟨math⟩ *decahedron* **~g·on** n ⟨math⟩ *decagon* **~gr·amm** n *decagram*(*me*) **~l·iter** n *decalitre* **~l·og** m ⟨bib⟩ *decalogue* **~m·eter** n *decametre* **~p·ode** m ⟨zoo⟩ *decapod*

Dek·ade f ~/~n *decade*, ⟨fam⟩ *ten-day batch*

dekad·ent a *decadent* (age, art), *degenerate* (*family, person*) **Dekad·enz** f ⟨arts⟩ *decadence*; ~erscheinung *symptom of d.* ‖ *degeneracy* (*of a people, class*)

dek·adisch a (→ Dekade) *decadal* ‖ ~e Logarithmen pl *decimal logarithms*

Dek·alo m ⟨com⟩ *loss in weight, shrinkage*

Dek·an m ~(e)s/~e ⟨ec⟩ *dean* ‖ ⟨univ⟩ *dean*; *chairman of a faculty* **Dekan·at** n ~(e)s/~e ⟨ec & univ⟩ **1.** (Amt u Würde e–s Dekans) *deanery, deanship* **2.** (Bezirk u Amtshaus) *deanery*

dekant·ieren vt [h] (abgießen) ⟨chem⟩ *to decant*

D·ekar n ~s/~e, [Sw], **Dek·are** f ~/~ = 10 Ar → d.

dekarbur·ieren vt [h] = ⟨tech⟩ entkohlen

Dekat·iermaschine f ⟨tech⟩ *decatizing machine*

dekat·ieren vt [h] ⟨tech⟩ (Wollstoff) *to decatize*; *steam, sponge* **Dekat·ierung** f ~/ *decatizing*

D·ekkan, D·ekhan m (Vorderindien) *Deccan*

Deklamati·on f ~/~en *declamation*; *recitation*

Deklam·ator m ~s/Deklamat·oren *declaimer, reciter* **deklamat·orisch 1.** a *declamatory* (*passage*) **2.** adv *in a declamatory manner* **deklam·ieren** vt/i [h] **1.** vi *to recite*; ⟨bes Am⟩ *to declaim* **2.** vt (Gedicht) *to declaim, recite*; ⟨fam⟩ *to spout*

Deklar·ant m ~en/~en ⟨jur⟩ *declarant*

Deklarati·on f ~/~en ⟨com⟩ *declaration* ‖ amtliche ~ *return*; Einkommensteuer≗ *income-tax return* ‖ Zoll≗ *declaration, entry*; (f zollfreie Waren) *entry for duty-free goods* | ~sschein [m] *bill of entry* **deklar·ieren** vt [h] (Waren) *to declare* (: *have you anything to d.*?); *to enter*; z wenig ~ *to enter short*

Deklinati·on f ~/~en ⟨astr & phys⟩ *declination*; → Mißweisung ‖ ⟨gram⟩ → Beugung **deklin·ierbar** a ⟨gram⟩ *declinable* **deklin·ieren** vt [h] ⟨gram⟩ → beugen I. 3.

Dekod·ier- ~einrichtung f *decoder, decoding installation* | dekod·ieren vt [h] *to decode*

Dek·okt n ~s/~e ⟨chem⟩ → Abkochung

Dekollet·é n ~s/~s (Fr) *neckline*; tiefes ~ *lownecked dress*; sie hat ein zu tiefes ~ *she wears her dress too low*, ⟨Am⟩ *she has a too low neckline*

Dekolletee n ~s/~s *decolletage*

dekollet·iert [pp v dekolletieren] *decolleté* ‖ *low-cut, low-necked* (*dress*) ‖ *decolletée* (*lady*)

Dek·or n ~s/~e *decoration, pattern, style* **~ofen** m ⟨ceram⟩ *decoration kiln* **~stoff** m ⟨tex⟩ *furnishing fabric*

Dekorat·eur [–tør] m ~s/~e (Zimmer≗) *upholsterer*; *curtain hanger* | *house-painter*; Maler u ~ *painter and decorator*; Theater≗ *scene--painter* **Dekorati·on** f ~/~en **1.** *decoration*; Schaufenster≗ *window-dressing* ‖ ⟨theat⟩ *scenery, setting*; geschlossene ~ *box set* **2.** (Orden) *decoration, cross*

Dekorati·ons- ~bezeichnungen f pl ⟨film⟩ *names of the settings* **~damast** m *furnishing damask* **~lager** n ⟨theat⟩ *scenery store*, ⟨Am⟩ *sc. storage* **~maler** m (*painter and*) *decorator* ‖ ⟨theat⟩ *scene-painter* **~malerei** f *pouch–* od *house-painting* ‖ ⟨theat⟩ *scene--painting* **~plan** m ⟨theat⟩ *scenic plot*, ⟨Am⟩ *production blueprints* pl **~probe** f *scene rehearsal*, ⟨Am⟩ *technical r.* **~stück** n **1.** ⟨theat⟩ *revue* **2.** ⟨übtr⟩ (P) *figure-head* **~wand** f (versteift) ⟨theat⟩ *French flat*

dekorat·iv a *decorative* (*art*)

dekor·ieren vt [h] **1.** (etw) **a.** (schmücken) *to adorn* (mit *with* [*flowers*] etc); (Stadt) *to decorate* (f *for*); *to ornament* **b.** (malen) (Haus, Zimmer) *to decorate* **c.** (ausstatten) *to upholster* ‖ (behängen) *to drape* **2.** jdn ~ *to decorate a p* (*with an order*) **dekor·iert** a ⟨arch⟩ ~er Stil (sc der engl. Gotik des 14. Jhs) *decorated style*

Dekor·ierung f *decoration, ornamentation*

Dek·ort m ~s/~e ⟨com⟩ *deduction, discount*; *abatement*; jdm e–n ~ bewilligen (*or* zugestehen) *to allow* od *grant a p a deduction* **dekort·ieren** vt [h] ⟨com⟩ *to deduct*

Dek·orum n ~s/ *decorum* (L), *proper behaviour*; das ~ wahren *to keep up decorum*

Dekrem·ent n ~s/~e ⟨math⟩ *decrement*

dekrepit·ieren vi [s] ⟨chem⟩ *to decrepitate* ‖ ~ l *do decrepitate*

Dekrepitati·on f ⟨chem⟩ *decrepitation*

Dekr·et n ~(e)s/~e *decree*; ein ~ erlassen *to issue a d.* **Dekret·ale** n ~(s)/~n, –lien ⟨ec jur⟩ (päpstliche) *decretal* **dekret·ieren** vt [h] (etw) *to decree*; ~, daß .. *to decree that* ..

Dek·ubitus m ⟨med⟩ *decubitus, bed-sore*

Dek·urio m ⟨Rom ant⟩ *decurion*

dekuss·iert a ⟨bot⟩ (of leaves) *decussate*

Delag·oa-Bai (S.-O.-Afrika) *D.-Bay*

Delati·on f ⟨jur⟩ *delation* **delat·orisch** a ⟨jur⟩ *criminative, criminatory*

D·elaware 1. m (Fluß in Nordamerika) **2.** n (Staat der U.S.A.)

Dele·atur n (L) ~s/~ ⟨typ⟩ (abbr ₰) *dele*

Deleg·at m ~en/~en ⟨R. C.⟩ *delegate* **Delegati·on** f ~/~en **1.** [abstr] (Abtretung) ⟨jur⟩ *delegation* (an jdn *to a p*) **2.** [konkr] (Ausschluß) *delegation* **deleg·ieren** vt [h] **1.** ⟨jur⟩ (etw) *to delegate* (jdm *to a p*) **2.** (jdn) *to delegate* **Deleg·ierte** [der ~, ein ~r] ~n/~n *delegate*; Stellvertreter e–s ~n *substitute delegate*

delekt·ieren vt [h] (jdn) *to delight, to regale* || sich ~ *to regale o.s.* (an *with*); *to regale* (an *on*)

Delft (Stadt in Holland) **D·elfter Fay·ence** [fa'jɑ̃s] f (nach Stadt Delft, Holland) *delft(-ware)*; → Steingut

D·elhi n (Stadt v Vorderindien) *Delhi*

delik·at I. a **1.** (schmackhaft) *delicate, dainty, delicious, exquisite, savoury (food)* **2.** (zart) *delicate, fine*; *tender*; ~e Beschaffenheit *delicacy* **3.** (heikel) *delicate, nice (question), ticklish* **II.** adv *deliciously, exquisitely (cooked)*

Delikat·esse f ~/~n **1.** (Zartheit) *delicacy, daintiness* **2.** [konkr] (Leckerbissen) *delicacy (for the table), dainty*; ⟨com⟩ ~n [pl] *dainties, groceries*; *delicatessen* [Ger pl] **~nhändler** m *grocer*; *dealer in delicatessen* || beim ~ *at the grocer's* **~nhandlung** f *grocery-store, grocer's shop*; ⟨Am⟩ *delicatessen-shop* (od *store*)

Del·ikt n ~(e)s/~e ⟨jur⟩ (Strafrecht) *delict, misdemeanour*; *crime* || (Zivilrecht) *tort(ious act)* | ~sklage [f] *action in tort*

Delinqu·ent m ~en/~en *delinquent, offender*; ⟨mil⟩ *defaulter*

delir·ant a ⟨med⟩ *delirious* **delir·ieren** vi [h] ⟨med⟩ *to be delirious* **Del·irium** n ~s/–rien *delirium, wandering*, [mst pl] *wanderings*; ⟨hum⟩ *bottle-ache* || im ~ (befindlich) *delirious* || **~ tremens** *delirium tremens* (abbr. *D. T.*), ⟨hum⟩ *bottle-ache*, ⟨sl⟩ *jim-jams* pl

D·elisches Problem n ⟨math ant⟩ *Delian problem*

Delkr·edere n (It) ~/ ⟨com⟩ *del credere*; *guarantee, –ty*; ein ~ bieten *to offer a guaranty*; ~ stehen *to stand del credere* **~konto** n *del credere account*

D·elle f ~/~n *delve, depression (in a hat)*

†D·elphi n ⟨Gr⟩ *Delphi*

Delph·in m **1.** ⟨zoo⟩ *dolphin*; → Schwertwal, Butzkopf **2.** ⟨astr⟩ *Delphinus* (L)

d·elphisch a *Delphian, Delphic (oracle)*

D·elta n (Gr) ~s/~s **1.** (gr. Buchstabe) *delta* **2.** ⟨hist & geol⟩ (Fluß≈) *delta* **3.** [in comp] *delta (formation)* || *deltaic (population)* **~arm** m *distributary* ≈**förmig** a *deltoid (muscle)* **~metall** n *delta metal* **~muskel** m ⟨anat⟩ *deltoid* **Delto·id** n ⟨math⟩ *deltoid*

d·em ⌊dat sg⌋ **1.** ⌊pron dem⌋ **A.** ⌊abs⌋ **1.** n (→ das) *to that*; ~ habe ich nichts hinzuzufügen *to that I have nothing to add* || wenn ~ so ist *if that be the case, if that is so* || es sei ~, wie es wolle *be that as it may* | es ist (nicht) an ~ *it is (not) so* (od *the case*) || bei all(e)~ *for all that*; *nevertheless, notwithstanding* || nach all(e)~ *after all* || → zu~ **2.** m (→ der I.) **B.** [def art] ~ Mann(e) *to the man* || er folgte ~ Mann(e) *he followed the man*, ..~ Vater .. *his father*; → der II. **II.** [pron rel] *to whom; to which* || *whom (he followed)*; *which*; *that* || → der III.

Demag·og(e) m ~en/~en *demagogue* **Dema·g·ogentum** n *demagogy, –gogism* **Demagog·ie** f ~/~n *demagogy* **demag·ogisch** a *demagogic*

D·emant m ~s/Dem·anten ⟨poet⟩ = Diamant

Demarche [de'marʃ] f (Fr) ⟨dipl⟩ *démarche* Fr

Demarkati·on f *demarcation* **~slinie** f *line of demarcation*

demask·ieren vt [h] (jdn) *to unmask* || **sich ~** *to unmask* **Demask·ierung** f *the unmasking (of)*

d·ementgegen adv *over against this* || → demgegenüber

Dem·enti n ~s/~s ⟨dipl⟩ *dementi*; *official contradiction* (od *denial*) *(of a statement)* **dement·ieren** vt [h] *to contradict* od *deny officially*

Dem·entia f (L) ⟨med⟩ *dementia*

d·ementsprechend adv *accordingly*; *conformably, pursuantly* **d·emgegenüber** adv *against this* || *as against that*; ~ gibt es Leute *as against that there are people (who ..)* **d·emgemäß** adv = dementsprechend

D·emijohn ['demidʒən] m (engl) ~s/~s (gr Korbflasche) *demijohn*

Demim·onde [dəmi'mɔ̃d] f (Fr) ~/ *demimonde* (Fr)

Demissi·on f ~/~en *demission*; *resignation* || s–e ~ einreichen *to hand* (od *send*) *in one's resignation* **demission·ieren** vi [h] *to resign* (: *the Prime Minister has resigned*); *to resign office*

d·emnach adv (demgemäß) *accordingly* || (folglich) *consequently, therefore*; (also) *then*

d·emnächst adv *soon, shortly*; → bald **d·emnächstig** a *impending, approaching*

demobilis·ieren vi [h] *to disarm*; *to reduce the forces to peace footing*; ⟨fam⟩ *to demob* **Demobilis·ierung, Demob·ilmachung** f *demobilization*

Demodulati·on f ~/~en (Radar-Zielauffassung) *detection* **demodul·ieren** vt [h] ⟨wir⟩ *to demode*

Demograph·ie f ~/ (analytische) *population analysis*; (qualitative) *study of population quality* **demogr·aphisch** a *demographic*

Demokr·at m ~en/~en *democrat* **Demokrat·ie** f ~/~n *democracy* **demokr·atisch 1.** a *democratic* || ⟨Am pol⟩ die ≈e Partei *the Democratic Party, the Democracy*; organisierte ~e Partei in New York City ⟨oft dero⟩ *Tammany, T. Society*; Mitglied der ~en Partei *Democrat* **2.** adv ~ gesinnt *democratically minded* **demokratis·ieren** vt [h] *to democratize* **Demokrat·ismus** m *democratism* °**Demokrat·ur** f ~/~en *dictatorial democracy*

demol·ieren vt [h] *to destroy*; (Festung) *to raze*

Demol·ierung f ~/~en *destruction*

demonetis·ieren vt [h] (außer Kurs setzen) (Münze) *to demonetize* **Demonetis·ierung** f *demonetization*

Demonstr·ant m ~en/~en *demonstrator* **Demonstrati·on** f ~/~en **1.** *demonstration* (vor e–m Publikum *to a public*) || → Darlegung || ~ der Macht *show of force* **2.** ⟨pol⟩ (Kundgebung) (public) *demonstration*; e–e ~ veranstalten *to make a demonstration* **3.** (Scheinmanöver) *demonstration* **demonstrat·iv** a ⟨a. gram⟩ *demonstrative (behaviour)* || ⟨übtr⟩ *pointed*; *disapproving (silence)*; *illustrative, clear, distinct*; *ostentatious*; *open (display of emotion)* **demonstr·ieren** vt/i [h] **1.** vt (etw) *to demonstrate, to be demonstrative of (a th)*; *to show*; ad oculus ~ → Auge I. C. 3. h. **2.** vi ⟨pol⟩ *to demonstrate, to take part in a demonstration*

Demont·age [demɔn'tɑ:ʒə] f ~/ *dismounting, dismantling* **demont·ierbar** a ⟨tech⟩ *separable* (Zündkerze) **demont·ieren** vt [h] *to dismount, dismantle* || ⟨tech⟩ = abmontieren; *to disassemble, to knock down*

Demoralisati·on [–tsio:n] f ~/~en *demoralization* **demoralis·ieren** vt [h] *to demoralize* || ~d *demoralizing (f to)*

Demoskop·ie f ~/ *public opinion research*

dem·otisch a & n (Volksschrift) *demotic*

d·emungeachtet adv *nevertheless, notwithstanding*

D·emut f ~/ *humbleness, humility, lowliness, meekness* || *submissiveness*; *modesty*

d·emütig 1. a *humble*; *lowly (scholar)*; *meek, modest* || *submissive*; ⟨iron⟩ *meek* **2.** adv *lowly*; *submissively*

d·emütigen vt [h] **1.** (jdn) *to humble, humiliate*; *mortify*; *to put down* || (→ ducken) *to take a p down a peg* (od *two*) | (unterwerfen) *to subdue*; gedemütigt liegen vor *to lay prostrate before* **2. sich ~** *to humble* od *prostrate o.s.* (vor *before*); *to abase* od *degrade o.s. (before)*; *to grovel (before, to)* | *to submit*; *to eat humble-pie*

D·emütigkeit f ~/ = Demut **D·emütigung** f ~/~en *humiliation, mortification*; *prostration*; ~en einstecken *to put one's pride in one's pocket*

d·emutsvoll a & adv = demütig

d·emzufolge adv *accordingly* || *consequently*; → demnach

den I. m acc **1.** [v betonten pron det] **a.** (P) *that one, him*; ~ kenne ich nicht *that one I do not know, him I do not k.* || ~, der .. *him who* .. **b.** (S) *that*; ich habe ~ (*sc* Hut) lieber *I like that better* **c.** ~ Mann kenne ich nicht *that man I do not know*; ~(jenigen) Menschen, der .. *that man who* .. **2.** [v def art] *the* **3.** [v pron rel] *whom*; *which*; *that* **II.** dat m, f & n **1.** [v betonten pron det] *those*; ~ Leuten folge ich nicht *those people I do not follow*; → denen **2.** [v def art] *the*

Den·ar m ~s/~e *denarius* (L) (abbr *d*); ~e [pl] *denarii* (L)

denaturalis·ieren vt [h] *to denaturalize*

denatur·ieren vt [h] ⟨chem⟩ (etw) *to denature*; denaturierter Spiritus *methylated spirit*; *industrial* (*alcohol*)

Dendr·it m ~en/~en ⟨minr⟩ *dendrite*; ⟨übtr a. in Neurologie⟩ **Dendrolog·ie** f = Baumkunde **dendrol·ogisch** a *dendrologic*

d·enen [dat pl] m, f & n **1.** [v betonten pron det abs] (P & S) *to those* (*ones*); ~ erklärte ich es *to those I explained it* || ~ folge ich nicht *those I do not follow* || ~, die .. *to those* (*ones*) *who*; *those* (*ones*) *who* **2.** [v pron rel] *to whom*; *to which* || *whom*; *which*; *that* (*he followed*)

D·engelmaschine f (*scythe-*)*whetting machine*

d·engeln vt [h] (schärfen) (Sense etc) *to sharpen, whet*

D·enguefieber [ˈdeŋge–] n *dengue*

denitr·ieren vt [h] ⟨chem⟩ *to denitrate* **Denitrifikati·on** f ⟨agr⟩ *denitrification* **denitrifiz·ieren** vt [h] ⟨chem⟩ *to denitrify*

D·enk- (→ denken) **~arbeit** f *thinking, thought* **~art** f *mode* od *manner, way of thinking*; *disposition*; *mentality*; *ideology*; = Denkungsart **≈fähig** a *endowed with the faculty of thinking, intelligent* **~fähigkeit** f *thinking faculty* || *intelligence* **≈faul** a *disinclined to think* || *indolent, inert, slow, sluggish*; *dull*; *slow-witted*; *stolid*; *torpid* **~faulheit** f *intellectual indolence* (od *torpidity*) **~fehler** m *false reasoning*; *fallacy* **~form** f *thinking-form*; *mode of thinking* (od *reasoning*) **~freiheit** f *freedom of thought* **~hemmung** f *blocking of thought* **~kraft** f *intellectual power* **~lehre** f → Logik **~mal** n *monument* (f jdn *to a p*; z jds Erinnerung *to a p's memory*), *memorial* || ⟨übtr⟩ *monument* (*of learning*) | ~amt [n] *Department for Ancient Monuments*; ~spflege [f] *care and preservation of monuments* (od *works of art*); ~sschutz [m] *preservation of ancient monuments, etc*; unter ~ stehen (*of monuments, etc*) *to be protected by an Act of Parliament* **~maschine** f, **~zeug** n ⟨comp⟩ *electronic brain* **~münze** f *commemorative medal* **~prozeß** m *thinking-process, process of thought* **~psychologie** f *thought-psychology* **~säule** f *memorial column* **~schabl·one** f *mould of thought* **~schrift** f ⟨dipl⟩ (Eingabe) *memorial, pro-memoria*, ⟨pol⟩ *aide-mémoire* Fr || ⟨pol⟩ *memorandum*; *exposé* (Fr) | (wissensch. Abhandlung) *memoir* **~sport** m *mnemonic sport, mnemonics* [pl] **~sportaufgabe** f *quiz*; *intelligence test* **~spruch** m *aphorism, apophthegm, maxim, motto, sentence* **~stein** m *memorial stone* **~system** n *thought-system* **~tafel** f *memorial tablet* **~tätigkeit** f *thinking* (od *intellectual*) *activity* **~übung** f *mental exercise* **~vermögen** n *capacity of thinking*; *intelligence, intellectual power* **~weise** f *mode* od *way of thinking* od *thought*; *habit of thought*; *turn of mind*; *mentality*; → Denkart **≈würdig** a *memorable, noteworthy, remarkable* **~würdigkeit** f *memorability, memorableness* || ~en [pl] *memoirs* [pl]; *reminiscences* **~zettel** m ⟨übtr⟩ *reminder*; *object-lesson* (f *to a p*) || (Strafe) *punishment*; *flapper* || jdm e–n ~ geben *or* verpassen *to give a p an object-lesson* (od *a thrashing* etc.); *to give a p something to think about* **~zeug** n → –maschine

d·enkbar 1. a *conceivable, imaginable, thinkable*; *possible*; || kein ~er Grund *no earthly reason* || kein Zweifel über irgend e–e nur ~e Frage *no doubt on any conceivable question* || es ist durchaus ~, daß .. *it's on the cards that* .. **2.** adv; die ~ äußerste Grenze *the utmost conceivable* (od *imaginable*) *limit* od *the utmost l. conceivable* || auf die ~ einfachste Weise *in the most simple way conceivable* || die ~ kürzeste Zeit *the shortest possible time* od *the sh. time possible* || ~ schlechtestes Klima *the worst climate imaginable* || ~ vereinfachen *to make as simple as possible*

d·enken vt/i [dachte/gedacht] [h] **I.** vt **A. 1.** ⟨eig⟩ (etw) *to think* || was ~ Sie darüber? *what do you make of it*? || ich möchte wissen, was du jetzt denkst *a penny for your thoughts*; das mögen sie im geheimen ~ *that may be at the back of their minds* | ⟨philos⟩ *to cogitate*; (e–n Gedanken) logisch zu Ende ~ *to reason* (od *think*) *out* || → aus~, über~ | **Böses ~** *to think evil* **2.** (meinen, glauben) *to believe, think*; *suppose*, ⟨Am⟩ *guess* || wer hätte das gedacht? *who would have thought it possible*? || ich habe es nicht v ihm gedacht *I never thought it of him* || er denkt wunder was v .. *he thinks the world of* (*his invention*) || er denkt immer gleich das Schlimmste bei allem *he always sees things at their worst* | (der Ansicht s) *to be of the opinion* | **~, daß ..** *to think, feel, believe that* ..; ich denke, er wird k *I think he will come* || °ich denke, mich laust der Affe, ich denke, ich falle aus den Wolken ⟨fam⟩ *well, I never*! *my food* od *hat*! || ich d. .. *what I say is* .. || ich dächte *I* (*should*) *think*; ich dächte, du brauchtest dich nicht z fürchten *I think you need not be afraid* **3. ~ z tun a.** (glauben) er denkt, berechtigt z s *he thinks he is authorized* (*to do*) **b.** (im Sinn h) *to contemplate doing, to think of doing*; er denkt morgen abzureisen *he thinks of leaving to-morrow* || (beabsichtigen) *to intend* od *mean to do*; was ~ Sie z tun? *what do you intend to do*? **c.** (erwarten) ich dachte nicht, dich hier z finden *I did not think to find you here* **B. sich** [dat] etw ~ **1.** *to think a th*; ich dachte es mir doch (*or*: das habe ich mir gleich gedacht) *I thought as much* || das hättest du dir ~ können *you might have known* od *imagined that* || denk an e–e Zahl *think of a number* || du kannst dir ~, was s–e Worte bedeuten *you may infer what his words* .. || besseres als wir uns ~ können *better things that we can dream* || ich habe mir nichts (Böses) dabei gedacht *I didn't mean anything by it, I meant* (od *thought*) *no harm*; niemand würde sich etw dabei ~ *nobody would think anything of it* **2.** (sich vorstellen) *to conceive, fancy, imagine, think a th*; [neg] *to conceive of a th*; → vergegenwärtigen, vorstellen || wir ~ es uns als ein Ganzes *we think of it as a whole*; ich kann mir e–e Lösung nicht ~ *I cannot conceive of a solution* || ich denke ihn mir sehr groß *I fancy* od *imagine him* (*to be*) *very tall, I fancy that he is v. t.* || sich ~, daß jd tut *to conceive* od *imagine a p doing*; ich d. ihn mir, wie er .. predigt *I fancy him preaching*; ich dachte mir, daß er käme *I imagined that he might come* || ich kann mir ~, was du meinst *I have an idea what you mean* || ~ Sie sich nur! *just imagine*! || denkt euch nur, er ist da! *just fancy, he is here*! || ⟨iron⟩ er lud mich trotzdem ein, denk dir (nur) *he invited me after all, if you please* || du kannst dir nicht ~, wie .. *you cannot think how* .. || man denke sich! *to think of it*! || so gastfreundlich wie man sich nur ~ kann *as hospitable as you please* **3.** (glauben) *to believe, deem, think*; er denkt es sich leicht *he thinks it easy*; → glauben, halten (für) **C. sich ~ in ..** *to think o.s. into* (*a position*, etc.) **II.** vi **A. 1.** ⟨eig⟩ **a.** *to think, to be* *thinking* ‖ der Mensch denkt, Gott lenkt *man proposes, God disposes* ‖ ich denke schon! *I think so* ‖ ich d·enke d·och! *I am sure*! ‖ ⟨iron⟩ denkste! (= .. du) *catch me*! ‖ bei sich ~ *to think to o.s.*; laut ~ *to think aloud* ‖ solange ich ~ kann *since I can remember, within my remembrance* od *recollection* ‖ wie Sie ~ *as you think fit, as you like* ‖ wo ~ Sie hin? *what (ever) ·are you (what c·an you be) th·inking of*? *you don't mean it*! ⟨fam⟩ *just fancy*!, *what's the idea*? ‖ jdm z ~ geben *to set a p thinking, to give pause to a p, to puzzle a p*; .. stark z ~ g. *to strike a p as significant*; das gibt z ~ *that's puzzling, there is food for thought* ‖ → nach~ **b.** edel ~ *to be noble-minded*; rechtschaffen ~ *to be of an upright mind* ‖ gering, niedrig ~ v jdm *to think little* od *meanly of a p*; → halten ‖ deutsch ~ *to think German* ‖ kleinlich ~ *to be of a petty turn of mind* ‖ vernunftmäßig, logisch ~ *to reason* **2.** (glauben) *to believe, think*; (Werdet Ihr abreisen?) Ich denke (..) *I think so*, ⟨Am a.⟩ *I expect so* **3.** (sich vorstellen) ~ Sie (sich) nur! *only* od *just fancy* od *imagine*! *think of it*! ‖ das läßt sich ~ *that's easy to imagine* od *understand* **B. 1. ~ an a.** *to think of (a th)*; *to give (a th) a thought* | **gern** ~ an *to have happy recollections of .., to remember .. with pleasure*; an etw nicht **länger** ~ wollen *to refuse to entertain the thought of a th*; **nicht mehr** an Rückkehr ~ *to abandon all thought of returning* | **wenig** an etw ~ können *to have little thought to give to a th* | es ist **schwer,** an e–e Lösung z ~ *it is hard to conceive of a solution* | **daran** ~ z tun *to think of doing*; ich dachte halb u halb daran z tun *I had some thoughts of doing* ..; er sagte, man dächte nicht daran abzureisen *he said there was no idea of leaving*; daran ist nicht z ~ *that's out of the question* ‖ °es (*sc* Urteil) denkt nicht daran, umfassend z s *it does not begin to be comprehensive* ‖ er soll daran ~ *I'll make him remember it* ‖ ⟨iron⟩ ich denke nicht (im Traum) daran! *not I!, no thanks!, catch me (at it)*! ‖ denk mal an! *fancy*! *indeed*! **b. an jdn ~** *to think of a p, to give a p a thought* ‖ *to remember a p*; ~ Sie an mich *remember me*; er soll an mich ~ *I'll make him remember me*; wir w an Sie ~, wenn sich e–e Gelegenheit f Sie bieten sollte *we shall keep you in mind should anything come along for you*; wenn man an den *or* die Menschen denkt! *in human terms*! **2. ~ über** *to think about* od *over*; wie ~ Sie über die Lage? *what are your views on the situation*? ‖ wie denkst du über ..? *what do you say to (Mozart; a visit to ..; to going to ..)*? ‖ wie denkst du jetzt über d–n Freund? *what price your friend now*?; ⟨Am sl⟩ *how's about* od *for* ‖ → nach~

D·enken n *thinking, thought* (: *modern th.*); verwirrtes ~ *muddled thinking*; wissenschaftliches ~ *scientific th.g* ‖ ⟨philos⟩ *cogitation*; logisches ~ *reasoning*; nur durch ~ gewonnen *rational* ‖ jdn z ~ anregen, veranlassen *to make a p think* | besorgtes ~ *thought* (an *of*) ‖ → Nach~

d·enkend 1. a *thinking*; ~es Wesen *thinking* (od *reasoning, rational*) *being* ‖ edel~ *noble-minded* | (nachdenklich) *thoughtful (people)* **2.** ~: der, die ~e: jeder vernünftig ~e *all thinking men*

D·enker m ~s/~ *thinker*; *philosopher*

D·enkungsart f *mentality* | (Gesinnung) *feelings* [pl]; *mind*; edle, vornehme ~ *noble* (od *high*)*-mindedness*, v edler, vornehmer ~ *noble* (od *high*)*-minded*; die Milch der frommen ~ *the milk of human kindness*

d·enn I. adv **1.** [betont] wo ~? *where else*? *at what other place*? es sei ~, daß .. *unless*; *provided (that)*, daß es regnet *p.d (that) it doesn't rain* ‖ ⟨bib⟩ ich laß dich nicht, du segnest mich ~ *I will not let thee go, except thou bless me* **2.** [unbetont] (= also, nun) wohl·an ~ *well then*; nun gut ~ *all right then* ‖ nimm es ~ *take it then* ‖ so war es ~ auch *and so it was* (od *came about*) ‖ er kam ~ auch *he came after all, he did come* | wo ~? *where then*? ‖ weiß ich's ~? *how should I know*? ‖ was hat er ~? *what may be the matter with him*? ‖ wo war er ~? *where then was he*? ‖ wer ist ~ da? *who is it now*? ‖ wo mag er ~ s? *where may he be, I wonder*? ‖ wie ist es dir ~ gelungen? *how then did you manage it*? Was gibt's ~ schon wieder? was ist ~ los? *what is it now*? **II.** [conj] **1.** [beiordnend; nach compr] *than*; → als II. 2. ‖ mehr ~ je *more than ever* ‖ bekannter als Philosoph ~ als ein Dichter *better known as philosopher than as poet* **2.** [unterordnend, begründend] *for* (: *yes please, for I like it*) **3.** (als Antwort) ~ nicht! [ell] *don't then*!

d·ennoch [conj] *yet, nevertheless, still, notwithstanding*; *however*; der Stil ist nicht elegant, ~ ist er korrekt *the style is not elegant, yet* (od *but, still, however*); wenn der Stil auch nicht elegant ist, so ist er ~ korrekt *though not elegant the style is yet* od *nevertheless correct* ‖ [stets am Satzende] *though* (: *I wish you had told me though*)

Denominat·iv n ~s/~e ⟨gram⟩ *denominative*

Densim·eter n ~s/~ *densimeter, pycnometer*

Densit·ät f ~/ *density*

dent·al 1. a *dental* **2.** ~ m ⟨gram⟩ *dental*

dental·iert a *dentel(l)ated*

Dent·in n *dentine* **Dent·ist** m *dental practician* (Ggs Zahnarzt)

Denudati·on f ~/~en ⟩geol⟩ *denudation* | ~sniveau [n] *base level*; ~sterrasse [f] *rock terrasse*

Denunzi·ant m ~en/~en *(common) informer, denouncer*; ⟨Am sl⟩ *rat* **Denunziati·on** f ~/~en *denunciation* **denunz·ieren** vt/i **1.** vt [h] jdn ~ *to inform against a p, to denounce a p* **2.** vi *to be a common informer*; ⟨sl⟩ *to squeal*

D·enver n (Hauptstadt v Colorado, U.S.A.)

De·odorans n ~/–ranten ⟨cosm⟩ *deodorant*

Departem·ent [depart'mã] n [Fr] ~s/~s ⟨pol, mil & com⟩ *department*

Depend·ance [depã'dãs] f [Fr] Hotel~ *appurtenance to a hotel, dependency (of a hotel)*

Dep·esche f ~/~n **1.** ⟨dipl⟩ (durch Boten) *dispatch, despatch* ‖ chiffrierte ~ *code message* **2.** = Telegramm ‖ Kabel~ *cablegram* → drahtlos, Funk– **~nboot** n *dispatch-boat* **~nschlüssel** m *code* **depesch·ieren** vt/i [h] = telegraphieren; kabeln

Dephlegm·ator m ~s/–mat·oren (am Destillierapparat) *dephlegmator*

Deplacem·ent [deplas'mã] n [Fr] ⟨mar⟩ *displacement (of 10000 tons)*

Depolarisati·on f ~/ ⟨phys & el⟩ *depolarization*

Dep·onens n [L] ~/Depon·enzien ⟨gram⟩ *deponent, deponent verb* **Depon·ent** m ~en/~en **1.** ⟨com⟩ *depositor* **2.** ⟨jur⟩ (Ggs Depositar) *bailor* ‖ (aussagender Zeuge) *deponent*

depon·ieren vt [h] **1.** ⟨com⟩ (Geld) *to deposit*; *to place (a th) on deposit*; *to lodge (in a bank)* ‖ (Waren) *to bail* †**2.** ⟨jur⟩ = aussagen **Depon·ierung** f ⟨com⟩ *deposition*

Dep·ort m ~s/~s ⟨st exch⟩ *backwardation*; ~geschäft [n] *backwardation-business* ‖ ~kurs [m] *backwardation-rate* ‖ *discount*

Deportati·on f ~/~en *deportation* **deport·ieren** vt [h] (jdn) *to deport*; (Verbrecher) *to transport*

Deposit·ar, -t·är m ~s/~e ⟨jur⟩ (Ggs Deponent) *bailee, depositary*

Depos·iten n [pl] [v Dep·ositum] ⟨com⟩ **1.** *deposits*; *trust-funds* [pl] ‖ *valuables* [pl] *deposited in a bank*, etc. **2.** [in comp] *deposit–* **~bank** f *deposit-bank, bank of deposit* **~gelder** n

[pl] *deposit-money, deposits* [pl] **~kasse** f *deposit-department* || (Filiale) *branch-office* (*of a bank*) **~konto** n *deposit-account* **~schein** m *deposit-receipt* || (*for goods*) *deposit-warrant* **~verkehr** m *deposit-traffic*

Dep·ositum n ⟨jur & com⟩ *deposit* || [mst pl] Depos·iten → d.

Dep·ot [de'po:] **1.** (Lagerplatz) **a.** ⟨mil & mar⟩ *depot* **b.** ⟨com⟩ (Waren≈) *depository, depot*; *storehouse, warehouse*; ⟨Am⟩ *deposit* **2.** (Deponiertes) ⟨com⟩ *deposit*; *commodities, valuables* [pl] *deposited in a bank*, etc. || als ~ *on deposit*; in ~ geben *to place* (*money*) *on deposit* || ins ~ geben *to put in store* od *safe-keeping* **~brief** m ⟨com⟩ *letter of deposit* **~geschäft** n = Depositengeschäft **~schein** m = Depositenschein **~wechsel** m *bill of exchange deposited as security*

×**D·epp** m = Dummkopf, Tölpel; ≈eter ~, ≈eter!

Depressi·on f ~/~en **1.** [abstr] (Senkung) *depression* (*of a curve*) || ⟨astr⟩ → Höhenkreis || ⟨meteor⟩ *depression* || ⟨com⟩ *depression* (*of trade*) | ⟨fig⟩ (Niedergeschlagenheit) *depression*; ⟨fam⟩ *the blues, doldrums*; ⟨sl⟩ *jim-jams* [pl] **2.** [konkr] (Vertiefung) *depression*; *hollow* || *low part* **~szone** f ⟨meteor⟩ *suction zone*

deprez·ieren vi = abbitten

deprim·ieren vt [h] ⟨fig⟩ (jdn) *to depress*; *discourage* | ~d *depressing, discouraging, demoralizing* (f *to*) | –iert [pp pred] *unhappy, dejected, depressed, downhearted, downcast*; *discouraged, disheartened, dispirited*; *feeling low*; *in low spirits*, ⟨fam⟩ *down in the month, in the doldrums* od *dumps*; ⟨poet⟩ *woebegone*

Deput·at n ~(e)s/~e, *emolument* || *allowance in kind*; ~holz *a. of wood*; ~kohle *a. of coal* (etc), *concessionary coal* || ⟨jur⟩ *estovers* pl

Deputati·on f ~/~en [konkr] *deputation*; *delegation*; *committee*

deput·ieren vt [h] (jdn) *to depute*, ⟨Am a.⟩ *to deputise* **Deput·ierte** m, f [der ~, ein ~r] ~n/~n *deputy* || ⟨Fr parl⟩ ~nkammer [f] *Chamber of Deputies*

der m (die f, das n) **I.** [betont] [pron det] (→ das; dem; den; die; dessen; deren; derer; denen) **A.** [abs] **1.** (P) ~ [m] (die f, das n) [sc Kind] *that* (od *the*) *one*; *he, she, it* (sc *the child*); [pl] *those* (od *the*) *ones*; *they* || ~ ist es *he* od *that is the man* od *one* || ⟨Ger⟩ Die (sc Herren) v Lützow *Barons* [pl] *Lützow* || ~ und bezahlen! *he pay? Not he*! || ~ u ~, ~ u jener *So-and-so, somebody* od *other*; ~ u ~ wird sagen *So-and-so will say* || ~ (die, das), welcher (welche, –s); derjenige etc, welcher *the one who, he who*; die, welche *she who*; [pl] die(jenigen), welche *those* (od *the ones*) *who*, †*they who*; ~ würde ein Tor s, welcher .. *he would be a fool who* .. **2.** (S) *that*; *the one*; [pl] *those*; ~ (sc Hut) ist ein wenig z hoch *that* (*one*) *is a little too high*; ist es ~? *is that it*? das (sc Buch) da drüben *that* (od *the one*) *over there*; ~ (sc Brief) v m–m Vater *that from my father*; oh, was das f ein Leben war! *oh, the life that it was* || ein Wimmern gleich dem e–s Kindes *a whimper like a child's* **B.** a; *that*, [pl] *those* || ~ **Feigling**! *that coward*!, *coward that he is*! ~ u ~ Mann *such and a man* || ~ Garten da *that garden there*, ⟨vulg⟩ *that there garden* || Rotwein ist d·as Getränk fürs Alter *claret is the drink for old age*; das ist einfach d·er Hut! *that's th·e hat*! | ~ (*or* derjenige) Mann, welcher .. *that man who* ..; die Männer, welche .. *those men who*; das (*or* dasjenige) Stück, welches *that play which* || (alle) die (*or* diejenigen) Stücke, die existieren .. *such plays as exist* || das, was .. *that which*; *what* **II.** [unbetont] [def art] **1.** *the*; ~ Verfasser des Stückes *the author of the play* || das Deutschland v heute *the Germany of today* || die hübsche Frau Sh. *pretty Mrs. Shandon* || die protestantische Religion *the Protestant Religion*; die zivilisierte Welt *the civilized world* || die Müllers [pl] *the Millers* [pl] | das Schöne *the beautiful* || das Beste *the best thing* | die doppelte Höhe *double the height* **2.** die Schweiz *Switzerland* || die Gerechtigkeit wird siegen *justice will carry the day* || das nördliche England *Northern England* || die deutsche Literatur *German Literature* || die Gotische Kunst *Gothic art* || der Senator N. *Senator N.* || die Breitestraße *Broad Street* || in der Schule, Kirche *at school, church* **3.** 2 Schilling das Pfund *2 shillings the* od *a pound* **4.** er gab widerwillig die Hand *he gave a reluctant hand*; er stampfte ärgerlich mit dem Fuße *he stamped an angry foot* **5.** er steckte die Hand in die Tasche *he put his hand into his pocket* || er öffnete mir die Augen *he opened my eyes* **6.** → am, beim, im, vom, zum, zur; ans, aufs, durchs, fürs, ins, ums; hinterm, überm, unterm; hinters, übers, unters; hintern, untern **III.** [pron rel] **A. 1. a.** *who*; der Mann, ~ .. *the man who* ..; der M., dessen Frau .. *the man whose wife* ..; den M., dem er es versprach .. *to whom he promised it* || .. *with whom her chief occupation was to quarrel* || die Dichter, v denen alle (*or* die alle) .. *the poets all of whom* .. || ein Mann v komischem Aussehen, der .. *a man of comical appearance and who* .. || wie e–r, der sagen wollte *as who should say* || er ist ein Mann, der, wie ich weiß, zuverlässig ist *he is a man who I know is trustworthy* (od *whom I know to be t.*) || ich, der diese Zeilen schreibt, hatte .. *I who write these lines had* ..; wir, die wir die Listen ausstellen, müssen .. *we who make out these lists must* .. **b.** das Haus, das .. *the house which* ..; das H., dessen Dach .. *the house whose roof* (od *the roof of which*) ..; das Kloster, dessen Hauptwohltäter er war *the convent of which he was the chief benefactor* || .., v denen alle (*or* .. die alle) .. *all of which* .. || Vorträge, f die allein der Vortragende verantwortlich ist *lectures* .., *the responsibility for which rests solely on the lecturer* || in den 50 Jahren, die er Führer ist .. *in the fifty years for which he has been leader* || .., e–e Größe, die am beliebtesten ist .. *which size is the most popular* (od *which is the most popular size*) **2.** *that* [in einschränkenden Sätzen; wie nach prep; als Akk. oft ausgelassen] k–r, ~ .. *no one that* ..; jedes Buch, das .. *any book that* ..; jede zweite P, die man trifft, ist .. *every other p one meets is* .. || am selben Tage, an dem ich ankam *on the very day* (*that*) *I arrived* || das ist die Welt, in der wir leben *this is the world we live in* | alles (vieles, wenig), das .. *all* (*much, little*) *that*; was auch immer .., das .. *whatever* .. *that* .. **B.** [besondere Fälle] **1.** ich war e–r der ersten Leute, die mit ihm sprachen *I was one of the first people to speak to him* || keine Bücher, die gelesen w mußten *no books to be read* || ein passender Ausdruck, mit dem man es beschreiben kann *a suitable term by which to describe it* || ein Freund, von dem er leicht Geld bek könnte *an easy friend to get money from* || der Punkt, den wir im Auge behalten müssen, ist .. *the point for us to remember is* .. **2.** ein Mann, der nach Macht verlangt *a man wanting power*; der Stuhl, der neben ihm stand .. *the chair standing near him* .. **3.** die Dinge h ein Stadium erreicht, in dem .. *matters have reached a stage when* .. || (er empfahl), alle Reste aufzulesen, die sie finden könnten (..) *to pick up what trifles they might find* || die Geschicklichkeit, über die er verfügt, ist .. *such skill as he commands is* .. (→ I. B.) **4.** diese knochigen Hände, die er hatte *those bony hands of his*

5. .., die er errichtet hatte *barriers of his erecting*

der I. gen & dat f sg [v die] **1.** [v pron det] → der (die, das) I. **2.** [v def art] → ebd II. **II.** dat f sg [v die] [v pron rel] → ebd III. **III.** gen pl m f & n [v die] **1.** [v pron det] → ebd I. B. **2.** [v def art] → ebd II.

derang·ieren [derɑ̃ˈʒirən] vt [h] *to derange*

d·erart adv *so, in such a manner; to such a degree*; ⟨fam⟩ *that* (: *that angry*); ~ groß war sein Schrecken *such was his fright* **d·erartig 1.** a *such, of such a kind*; ein ~es System *such a system, a system such as this*; ~e Schwächen *weaknesses such as these*; ein ~es Geschick, über das er verfügt *such a skill as he commands*; ein ~es Zeichen *one such sign*; das einzige ~e Ereignis *the only such incident*; der Tumult war ~, daß .. *the tumult was such that* .. ‖ ^~es *that kind of thing*; etw ^~es *that sort of thing* **2.** adv; ~ ärgerlich ⟨fam⟩ *that angry* ‖ ~ groß war sein Schrecken *such was his fright*

derb I. a **1.** ⟨eig⟩ (fest) *compact* (*texture*), *dense, firm* (*flesh*); *solid* ‖ *robust* (*man*), *strong* (*fists*) ‖ (grob) *coarse* (*cloth*); *rough*; *gross* **2.** ⟨übtr⟩ (stark) *hardy, robust, stout* (*boots*), *strong, sturdy* (*body*); *broad* (*humour*); *unrefined* (*taste*) ‖ (tüchtig) *hearty*; *keen* (*wind*); *smart* (*punishment*); *severe* (*blow*) ‖ e–e ~e Lektion f *a sound talking-to, a home lesson* ‖ e–e ~e Tracht Prügel *a sound thrashing, a good hiding* | (grob) *coarse, blunt, gross, rough, uncouth, unpolished* ‖ ~e Manieren *rustic manners*; ~ komisch *rustic and grotesque* ‖ ein ~er Scherz *a broad joke, a gross jest* ‖ e–e ~e Lüge *a great lie*, ⟨fam⟩ *a plumper* od *whopper*, ⟨sl⟩ *a corker* **II.** adv ⟨übtr⟩ *heartily*; *severely* ‖ *bluntly, roughly*; jdn ~ anfassen *to treat a p rough, to handle a p roughly*; ⟨sl⟩ *to man-handle a p* ‖ sich ~ ausdrücken *to express o.s. bluntly* (od *in plain terms*)

D·erbheit f ~/~en **1.** *compactness, firmness, solidity* **2.** (Kräftigkeit) *robustness, sturdiness* ‖ *heartiness*; *severity* (gegen *on a p*) | (Grobheit) *bluntness, roughness*; ~en [pl] *smart things* [pl]; *indecency*; ~en sagen *to say coarse* od *rough things*; → Zote

Derby [ˈdɑ:bi] n (engl); (nach *the Earl of Derby*): das ~, ~rennen *the Derby* (im Juni bei Epsom); (in Hamburg) [ˈdə:bi]

der·einst adv [nur v der Zukunft] in (*the*) *future, some day*; *yet* (: *he may succeed yet*)

der·einstig a *future*

Derelikti·on f ~/~en ⟨jur⟩ (= Besitzaufgabe) *abandonment of possession of chattel by owner with intent to relinquish property*

d·eren 1. [pron det] **a.** [gen f sg] ~ (sc der Frau) Gatte *her husband* ‖ ~ (sc der Hütte) Dach *its roof* **b.** [gen pl] ~ (sc der Frauen) Männer *their husbands* **2.** [pron rel] *whose*; *of whom* ‖ die Männer ~ er gedachte *the men whom he remembered* ‖ *which he remembered*

d·ere(n)thalben, –wegen; –willen (⟨a.⟩ um ~) adv **1.** [deren = pron det] *on her, their, its account*; *for her, their sake* **2.** [deren = pron rel] *on whose account*; *for whose sake* ‖ *because of which*

d·erer [pron det, gen pl, abs] die Fragen ~, die .. *the questions of those who* ..

d·ergestalt adv *in such a manner*; *so* ‖ ~ daß *so that*; *insomuch that, to that* (od *such a*) *degree that*; *with that restriction that*

dergleichen 1. [abs] **a.** [am Satzanfang ˈ– ..] *such a thing*; *the like*; ~ habe ich nie gehört *the like I never heard, I have never heard anything like that* **b.** [sonst: .ˈ–.] u ~ *and the like, and so forth* ‖ oder ~ *or the like, or suchlike* ‖ all ~ ⟨fam⟩ *all that sort of thing* ‖ nichts ~ *no such thing, nothing of the sort* (od *kind*) ‖ ~ wie *such as* ‖ ~ tun, als ob man tun (*or* s) wolle *to feign* od *pretend to do* (*to be*); ⟨dial⟩ er tat nicht ~ *he pretended not to see him* (*her, it*) | [relativisch] zwei Männer, ~ kaum je wieder gefunden w *two men whose like will scarcely ever be found again* ‖ Worte, ~ ich nie zuvor gehört hatte *words the like of which I had never heard before* **2.** a [unflektierbar attr] [mst d·ergleichen] *suchlike*; *similar*; Fleisch u ~ Dinge *meat and suchlike things* (od *and such kind of things*) ‖ ~ Leute [pl] *suchlike*

Deriv·at n *derivate*, ⟨chem⟩ *derivative*, ⟨pharm⟩ *body* (: *pyrazolone b.*) **Derivati·on** f *derivation* **derivat·iv** a *derivative* **Derivat·iv** n ⟨gram⟩ *derivative* **Deriv·ierte** f ⟨math⟩ die ~ *the derivate*

d·erjenige [d·iejenige, d·asjenige/d·iejenigen] [pron det] **1.** [a] → der I. B. **2.** [abs] ~, welcher *he* (od *the one*) *who*; diejenige, welche *she who* ‖ dasjenige, welches *that which* | diejenigen, welche *those* († *they*) *who* ‖ (S) *diesenigen*, welche *those which*

d·erlei a [invar attr] (dergleichen) *of that sort* od *kind, suchlike*; ~ Dinge *suchlike things*

D·erma n ~s/~ta ⟨anat⟩ *derm*(*a*) **derm·al** a *dermal*

dermal·einst adv = dereinst

†**d·ermalen** adv *now*; *at present* †**d·ermalig** a *present*

d·ermaßen adv *to such a degree, in such a manner, to such an extent, so much, so*; ⟨fam⟩ *that* (: *that angry*); ~ gr war sein Schrecken *such was his fright* ‖ ~, daß *insomuch that*

Dermat·itis f ⟨med⟩ *dermatitis* **Dermatol·og(e)** m *dermatologist* **–log·ie** f ⟨med⟩ *dermatology* **–myk·ose** f ⟨med⟩ *dermatomycosis* [L] **–pl·astik** = Dermoplastik **Dermat·ose** f ⟨med⟩ *dermatosis* **Dermopl·astik** f *dermatoplasty*

†**d·ero** [pron] **1.** = deren **2.** ^~ [in Anrede] *Your*, ^~ Gnaden *Your Honour* ‖ *His, Her* ‖ ~halben, ~wegen = derenthalben, ~wegen

Derogati·on f ⟨jur⟩ *derogation*

ders·elbe m [dies·elbe f, dass·elbe n] [pron] **A.** [betont] **1.** [a] *the same* (*p, th*; wie *as*); ein u ~ .. *one and the same* ..; eben~, ganz ~ Hut *the very same* (⟨liter⟩ *the selfsame*) *hat*; genau ~ *exactly the same* .. ‖ z demselben Preise, wie (*or* z dem) .. *at the same price as* ..; z ~n Zeit, in der .. *at the same time that* .. ‖ v ~n Art wie diejenigen .. *of the same nature with those* .., v ~n Art wie *of a piece with* ‖ in ~n Weise wie *the same as* (: *they look at things the s. as we do*) **2.** [abs] **a.** ~ s *to be the same*; (: *he was always the same to me*) ‖ er ist nicht mehr ~ *he is no longer the same man* ‖ an denselben (sc wie die vorhergehenden) *to the same* **b. dasselbe** *the same, the same thing* (wie *as*); genau dasselbe *just the same* ‖ dasselbe s (*or* bedeuten) *to be the same*; es ist ziemlich dasselbe *it is much the same*; es kommt auf d. hinaus *it comes to the same thing* ‖ dasselbe ist hier der Fall *the same here*; dasselbe tun *or* sagen *to ditto* **B.** [unbetont; verblaßt = er, sie, es] [abs] **1.** *he, she, it*; denselben *him, it*, etc. → er ‖ der Vater desselben *his father* ‖ der V. derselben (sc der Frau) *her father*; (sc der Kinder etc) *their father* ‖ ein Freund desselben *a friend of his*; .. derselben *a friend of hers*; .. *of theirs* **2.** ⟨com & jur⟩ (*the*) *same*; (mit Bezug auf Ihren Brief vom 15.) u Ihre Antwort auf denselben (..) *and your answer to same*; wir h an denselben (sc e–n Herrn N.) geschrieben *we have written to same* **3.** †höchst~ = der selbe ‖ was befehlen Höchstdieselben? *what is your Highness*'s etc. *pleasure*?

†**ders·elbige** m [dies·elbige f, dass·elbige n] = derselbe

†**derw·eil 1.** [adv] *the while*; *in the meantime, meanwhile* **2.** [conj] *while* ‖ **derw·eile(n)** adv = derweil

D·erwisch m ~es/~e *dervish*

d·erzeit adv **1.** (jetzt, öfterr = zur Zeit) *at present, just now; for the time being* **2.** (damals) *at that time, then*; [attr] → **d·erzeitig** a **1.** *present, the present mayor, the treasurer for the time being* **2.** der ∼e Bürgermeister *the then mayor*

des [gen sg] 'm & n [v der, das] **1.** [v pron det] → der, (die, das) I. B. **2.** [v def art] → ebd. II.

Des n ∼/∼ ⟨mus⟩ *D flat* ‖ ∼-Dur *D flat major*; ≗-Moll *d flat minor*, → A-Dur etc

desavou·ieren [de:zavu'i:rən] vt; jdn ∼ *to go back on a p*; = abrücken v

Desensibilis·ator m ∼s/–t·oren ⟨phot⟩ *desensitizer* **desensibilis·ieren** vt ⟨phot⟩ (unempfinglich m) *to desensitize* **desensitiv·ieren** vt ⟨med⟩ *desensitize*

Desert·eur [–'tør] m ∼s/∼e ⟨mil⟩ *deserter*

Deserti·on f ∼/∼en *desertion*

desert·ieren vi [s] *to desert*; → Fahnenflucht

d·esfalls adv *in that case*

desgl·eichen [abbr desgl.] adv **1.** sie h nie vorher ∼ gesehen *they have never seen the like (of that) before* ‖ [relativisch] *the like of which (they had not seen)* **2.** (ebenso) *also; as well (: it had been a disaster for him as well); likewise*; ⟨dial⟩ *by the same token* ‖ (der Direktor des .. wird vermißt), ∼ der des Warenhauses (..) *and so the manager of the stores*; (Ich ging heim.) Mein Bruder ∼ (..). *So did my brother* ‖ (Hals- u Beinbruch!) ∼! (..) *The same to you!*; → auch, ebenso | ⟨com⟩ *item; ditto; same*; (20 Pfd gezahlt an Herrn N.), ∼ an Herrn X. (..) *ditto to Mr. X.*

d·eshalb adv *on that account, for that reason* od *matter; therefore; for it (: he did not look the worse for it)*; ∼ ging er so früh *that's why he left so early* ‖ [relativisch] *wherefore*

Desider·at n ∼s/∼e *desideratum* [L]; ∼e [pl] *desiderata* **Desider·atum** n [L] ∼s/–ten = Desiderat ‖ –tenliste *list of desiderata*

Designati·on f ∼/∼en *designation* (z *to*) **design·ieren** vt (jdn) *to designate* (z *to, for*) **design·iert** a *designate*, der ∼e Bischof *the bishop designate* od *elect*

Desinfekti·on f ∼/∼en *disinfection*

Desinfektions- [in comp] *disinfectant (liquor); disinfecting (officer)* **∼apparat** m *disinfector* **∼mittel** n *disinfectant, deodorizer*

Desinfektor m (P) *disinfector (–ter)*

desinfiz·ieren vt [h] *to disinfect* ‖ *to fumigate*, → entlausen ‖ (Abort) → desodorisieren ‖ ∼d *disinfectant; disinfecting*

Desintegrati·on f *disintegration*

Desinter·esse n ∼s/ *indifference* (an *to[wards]*)

desinteress·iert a *indifferent* (an *in*); *unbiased by personal interest* | *impartial (with regard to)*

Desinteressem·ent [desẽterɛs'mɑ̃] s [Fr] *disinterestedness*

Desjat·ine f ∼/∼n (russ. Flächenmaß; = 1,093 ha) *dessiatine, desya–*

deskript·iv a *descriptive*

D·esman m ⟨zoo⟩ = Bisamspitzmaus

Desmidiaz·een f [pl] → Bandalge

Desm·in n ⟨minr⟩ *stilbite, desmine*

Desmo·id n = Fasergeschwulst

Desodorisati·on f *deodorization*

desodoris·ieren vt [h] (Raum) *to deodorize* | ∼des Mittel [n] *deodorant* **Desodoris·ierung** f ⟨cosm⟩ *deodorization* | ∼smittel [n] ⟨chem⟩ *deodorizing compound*

Desorganisati·on f *disorganization* **desorganis·ieren** vt [h] *to disorganize*

Desorient·ierung f ∼/∼en (P) *disorientation* ⟨a. psych⟩

Desoxydati·on f ⟨chem⟩ *deoxydation*

Desoxyribonukleinsäure f (DNS) *deoxyribonucleic acid (DNA)*

despekt·ierlich a *disrespectful, contemptuous*

Desper·ado m ∼s/∼s *desperado* [Span]

desper·at a *desperate*

Desp·ot m ∼en/∼en *despot; tyrant* **Despot·ie** f ∼/∼n *despotism* **desp·otisch** **1.** a *despotic*; in ∼er Weise *despotically* **2.** adv *despotically* **Despot·ismus** m *despotism*

D·essau n ⟨Ger⟩ (Stadt) *Dessau*; der alte ∼er *Leopold I., Prince of Anhalt-D.* (1676–1747)

d·essen **I.** [pron det] **1.** er war sich ∼ wohl bewußt *he was well aware of it*; ∼ bin ich sicher *of that I am certain* **2.** (= derselbe B. 1.) (ein Beamter folgte dem Oberbürgermeister) mit ∼ Insignien (..) *with his insignia* **II.** [pron rel] *whose* ‖ *whose, of which*; → der (die, das) III.

d·essenthalben, d·essentwegen adv **1.** [dessen = pron det] *on his account, for his sake* ‖ *on its account, for its sake* **2.** [dessen = pron rel] *for whose sake* ‖ *for the sake of which, because of which* **d·essentwillen** adv um ∼ = dessenthalben ‖ der Grund, um ∼ wir .. *the r. why we ..*

dessen·ungeachtet adv *notwithstanding (that), that notwithstanding; nevertheless, however, all the same*

Dess·ert [de'sɛ:r] n ∼s/∼s **1.** *dessert, sweet (course)*; → Nachtisch **2.** [in comp] *dessert*; ∼löffel *d.-spoon*; ∼wein *d.-wine*

Dess·in [de'sɛ̃] n ∼s/∼s **1.** *design* (f *for*), *pattern*; ⟨fam⟩ *trick* ⟨a. sex⟩ **2.** [in comp] *figuring (machine)* **∼zeichnen** n *figuring, patterning*

Dessinat·eur [–'tør] m –s/–e *designer, pattern--designer* (od *drawer*)

dessin·iert a [pp v dessinieren] *patterned*

Dessous [də'su:] n ∼/∼ [–s] Fr *sheer lingerie*

Destill·at n *distillate* **Destillat·eur** [–'tør] m ∼s/∼e *distiller*

Destillati·on f ∼/∼en **1.** [abstr] *(act of) distilling, distillation*; fraktionierte ∼ *fractional distillation*, trockene ∼ *dry* od *destructive d.*; nasse ∼ *vaporization* **2.** [konkr] (Ort) → Branntweinbrennerei ‖ → Branntweinschenke

Destillati·ons- [in comp] *distilling* **∼apparat** m *distilling apparatus, distiller; alembic, still* **∼raum** m *still-room*

°**Dest·ille** f = Branntweinschenke, Kneipe

Destill·ier- **∼apparat** m *still* **∼blase** f, **∼gefäß** n *(boiler of a) still* **∼kolben** m *distilling flask; matrass, retort, alembic*

destill·ieren vt [h] *to distil*

Destinat·ar m ∼s/∼e ⟨mar com⟩ → Empfänger

d·esto adv *the*; ∼ besser *all the better, so much the better*; ∼ schlimmer *so much the worse* ‖ je .. ∼ *the .. the*; je mehr er erhält, ∼ mehr verlangt er *the more he gets the more he wants* (od *does he want*)

destrukt·iv a *destructive*

desult·orisch a (unbeständig, ohne Ausdauer) *desultory; unmethodical*

d·eswegen adv *because of it; for that; on that account; for that reason, therefore*; eben ∼ *for that very reason* ‖ → deshalb **d·eswillen** adv; um ∼ = um dessentwillen

Deszend·ent m ∼en/–en *descendant* **Deszend·enz** f *descent* ‖ ∼lehre, ∼theorie [f] *theory of descent; Darwinism; evolution*

Detachem·ent [detaʃ'mɑ̃], Sw [–m·ent] n, ∼s/∼s Sw ∼s/∼e ⟨mil & mar⟩ *detachment*

Detach·eur [deta'ʃør] m ∼s/∼e (Mahlmaschine) *detacher* **detach·ieren** [deta'ʃi:rən] vt [h] (Truppen) *to detach; detail* **Detachiermittel** n *stain removing agent*

Det·ail [de'taj] n ∼s/∼s **1.** (Einzelheit) *detail, particular point* ‖ ⟨phot⟩ ohne ∼s *featureless*; ∼s auflösen *to separate* od *resolve details* ‖ ins ∼ gehen, auf ∼s eingehen *to go into detail(s), to go into particulars; to individualize* ‖ bis ins kleinste ∼ (*or* bis in die kleinsten ∼s) schildern *to describe (a th) down to the smallest detail, to* *give a detailed description of* (*a th*); *to particularize* (*a th*) **2.** ⟨com⟩ *retail*; im ~ *retail, by* (⟨Am⟩ *at*) *retail*; im ~ verkaufen *to sell* (*by*) *retail, to retail*; im ~ verkauft w *to retail* (z *at*)

Det·ail- ~arbeit f ⟨arts⟩ *detail* **~bericht** m *detailed* (od *minute, circumstantial*) *account* (od *report, statement*) **~geschäft** n [abstr] *retail dealing* (od *trade*) || [konkr] (Laden) *retail shop* **~handel** m *retail trade* **~händler** m *retail dealer, retailer* **~handlung** f *retail-shop* **~konstrukteur** m *draftsman* **~preis** m *retail price* **≗reich** a ⟨phot, etc⟩ *with fine definition* **~schilderung** f *detail, detailed description*; *particularization* (: *his power of p.*) **~verkauf** m *retail* **~zeichnung** f ⟨bes tech⟩ *detail drawing*

detaill·ieren [deta'ji:rən] vt [h] (etw) *to detail, particularize* **Detaill·ierung** f ~/~en *particularization*; *detailed description* **Detaill·ist** [deta'jist] m ~en/~en *retailer, retail dealer*

Detekt·iv m ~s/~e *detective, plain-clothes man*, ⟨fam⟩ *sleuth*; ⟨sl⟩ *split*; ⟨Am sl⟩ *dick*; *fly cop*; den ~ spielen *to sleuth* **~kamera** f *detective camera* **~roman** m *detective story*

Det·ektor m ~s/Detekt·oren ⟨wir⟩ *detector* (früher): *coherer* Kristall≗ *crystal detector* (od *rectifier*); Empfangsapparat mit Kristall≗ *crystal-set* (od *receiver*) **~nadel** f ⟨fam⟩ *cat's whisker* **~röhre** f *detector valve*, ⟨Am⟩ *d. tube*

Deterg·entien [–ts–] pl *detergents*

Determin·ante f ~/~n ⟨a. math⟩ *determinant* **Determinati·on** f ⟨log & math⟩ *determination* **determinat·iv** a *determinative* (*pronoun*) **Determin·ismus** m *determinism*

Detonati·on f ~/~en *detonation, explosion* || (etw) zur ~ bringen *to detonate*, .. vorzeitig *to pre-detonate* | ~sdruck [m] *blast pressure* **deton·ieren** vi [h] *to detonate*, vorzeitig *to pre-detonate* || ⟨mus⟩ *to sing out of tune, to descend*

Detr·itus m [L] ⟨geol & med⟩ *detritus* [L]

D·etroit n (Stadt) (*Mich. U.S.A.*)

°**Dets, Detz** m → Däts

d·etto adv [bay, österr] = dito

°**D·eubel** m = °Deibel = Teufel || auf ~ u komm heraus ⟨sl⟩ *split arse* [attr]

deucht 3. sg prs [fast †, f dünkt; → dünken] mir *or* mich ~, es ~ mir *or* mich, er hat e–n falschen Namen benutzt *it seems to me* (od *I think, I fancy*; † *me thinks*) (*that*) *he has used an alias*; *he has used it seems to me* (od *I fancy*) *an alias*; *he seems to have used an alias* **d·euchte** 3. sg. pret [fast †, f dünkte; → dünken) mir *or* mich ~, es ~ mir *or* mich, er hätte es erwähnt *it seemed to me* (od *I thought*; † *me thought*) (*that*) *he had mentioned it*

Deul m ~s/~e = Luppe

deus ex machina L ⟨theat & fig⟩ *God from the machine*; *deus ex machina*

D·eut m ~s/~e ⟨übtr⟩ *doit*; *farthing*; *mite*; *rap*; (Bißchen) *bit, atom* || k–n ~ wert *not worth a doit*; k–n ~ besser (als) *not a bit better* (*than*), *no whit superior* (*to*); es macht k–n ~ aus *it doesn't matter* (*a*) *sixpence*; ich gebe k–n ~ dafür *I don't give a rap for it*; → scheren

d·eutbar a *explainable, explicable, interpretable* || es ist anders ~ *it admits of another explanation, it can be explained in a different way* **Deutel·ei** f ~/~en *quibble, sophistry*; *sophistication, sophistical argumentation* **d·euteln** vt/i [h] **1.** *vt (etw) *to sophisticate, to subtilize* **2.** vi *to sophisticate, to use sophistical arguments*; *to subtilize* || **~ an** *to quibble at* (*a th*)

d·euten vt/i [h] **I.** vt **1.** (Text, Gesetz) *to explain, expound, interpret*; (Zeichen, Traum etc) *to read* || falsch ~ *to misinterpret* || jdm etw ~ *to point out* (od *explain*) *a th to a p* **2.** ⟨übtr⟩ e–e Bemerkung übel ~ *to construe a remark unfairly, to put an unfair construction on a remark* || etw als Faulheit ~ *to put a th down to indolence*; jdm etw als Stolz ~ *to put* (od *set*) *a th down to a p's pride*; → auslegen I. B. 2. **II.** vi **1. ~ auf** etw, jdn *to point to* (od *at*) *a th, a p*; mit dem Finger ~ auf *to point one's finger at* (*a p*); ernst .. *to p. a stern f. at a p*; der Schweif des Kometen deutet nach Osten *the tail of the comet points to* (od *towards*) *the east* **2.** ⟨übtr⟩ **~ auf** etw *to argue* (od *betoken, indicate, signify*) *a th, to be suggestive of a th*; es deutete auf gr Zuversicht ihrerseits hin *it argued great confidence on her part*; **darauf hin ~, daß** *to indicate that*; alles deutet darauf hin, daß .. *there is every indication that* .. || **~ auf** (Gutes, Böses, Sturm etc) *to* (*fore*)*bode, portend*; dies deutet auf ein glückliches Ende hin *this bodes a happy ending*; alles deutete auf e–e Erneuerung des Konfliktes hin *everything portended a renewal of the conflict*

D·euter m ~s/~ *expounder, interpreter*; [oft in comp] → Stern≗, Traum≗ **-deutig** [in comp] → ein~, zwei~

Deut·erium n ~s/ ⟨chem⟩ (Wasserstoff vom Atomgewicht 2,01410) *deuterium, heavy hydrogen*

Deutero- (zweit) [in comp] *deutero–* **~n·omium** n ⟨bib⟩ *Deuteronomy*

d·eutlich I. a **1.** (sichtbar) *clear* (*outline*), *distinct*; *conspicuous, obvious, plain* (*view*); *spectacular* || *distinct, legible, readable* (*writing*); *plain* (*print*) | *clear* (*remembrance*); *distinct* (*improvement*) **2.** (hörbar) *articulate* (*voice*); *clear, distinct*; *plain* (*articulation*); sein Vortrag war klar u ~ *his delivery was clear and distinct* **3.** (verständlich) *clear* (*statement*), *intelligible, perspicuous* || *evident, obvious, plain*; *definite* (*answer*) || etw ~ m *to make a th clear* (od *plain*); vollends ~ m *to make .. so patently clear, to prove so conclusively*; jdm etw ~ m *to explain* (od *point out*) *a th to a p*; *to bring* (od *drive*) *a th home to a p* | ~e Ausdrucksweise *perspicuity* || ~e Erklärung *lucid explanation* || ~e Sprache *plain speaking* || ~er Wink *broad hint* **4.** (derb) *blunt*; *plain-spoken* || *insistent* || *pointed* || sehr ~ w *to speak in very plain terms*; e–e ~e Sprache mit jdm führen *to speak to a p quite sharply, not to mince matters* (od *one's words*) **II.** adv (→ I.) **1.** *clearly, distinctly*; *conspicuously*; ~ hervortretend (*or* sichtbar) *obvious, in evidence* || *legibly*; *plainly* **2.** *clearly, distinctly* **3.** *clearly*; *intelligibly, perspicuously* || *evidently, obviously* || *bluntly* || jdm ~ sagen *to tell a p plainly* (od *in plain words*) *what* ..) **≗keit** f ~/ **1.** *clearness, distinctness*; *conspicuousness* || *distinctness, legibility* (*of writing*); *plainness* (*of print*) || || ⟨opt & phot⟩ *definition* (*of a telescope*; *photograph*) **2.** *clearness, distinctness* (*of the voice*) **3.** *clearness, plainness* (*of a statement*); ~ im Ausdruck *perspicuity* | *bluntness, plain-spokenness*; *insistence*; *pointedness* || mit aller ~ *bluntly, insistently* es an ~ nicht fehlen l *to make one's sentiments abundantly clear*; s–e Antwort läßt an ~ nichts z wünschen übrig *his answer could not have been plainer* | ~sweite [f] ⟨phot⟩ (Sichtweite) *sight distance, visual range*

deutsch I. a **1.** *German* || ~ m *to Germanize* (*a country*); ~e Sitten annehmen *to Germanize* [vi] **2.** ⟨geog⟩ die ≗e **Bucht** *Heligoland Bight* || der ~e Kaiser *the Kaiser*; die ~e Nation *the German nation* || das ≗e Reich *the Reich*; *the German Empire* || der ~e Gruß ⟨nazi⟩ *the German salute*; den Arm z ~en G. erheben *to raise one's arm in the G. salute* || ≗es Nachrichtenbüro (abbr DNB. ⟨hum⟩ darf nichts bringen) *the German News Service* || ≗e Bundesbahn *the German Federal Railways* [pl] || ~es Wesen *the German national character* **c.** ⟨hist⟩ der ≗e Bund (1815–66) *The German*(*ic*) *Confederation*; → nord~ || die Brüder vom ≗en Hause *the Teutonic knights* [pl]; der ≗e Orden *the Teutonic Order* od *O. of T. Knights* || das

Heilige Römische Reich ≃er Nation *the Holy Roman Empire* ‖ ≃er Reichstag [m] *German Imperial Diet* **d.** die ~e Schrift *the German text; black letter* ‖ die ~e Geschichte *German History* ‖ die ~e Kunst, Literatur, Musik *German art, literature, music* ‖ der ~e Tanz *the German dance, the waltz* | ⟨ec⟩ ≃e Christen [pl] *German Christians* [pl]; die ≃e Glaubensbewegung *the German Faith Movement* **II.** adv *in a German manner* (od *way*) ‖ ~ denken, fühlen *to think, feel German* | ⟨übtr⟩ ~ reden *to speak plainly*; mit jdm (echt) ~ reden *to speak to a p in the vernacular* (od *in plain German*); *not to mince one's words*

Deutsch n *German, the German language*; → Hoch≃, Nieder≃ ‖ ~ sprechen *to speak German* ‖ ein gutes ~ *good German*; ein möglichst klares ~ *the clearest possible German* ‖ auf ~ *in German*; auf gut ~ *in plain German* ‖ aus dem ~en, in das ~e übersetzen .. *from G. into G.*

D·eutsch- [in comp] **I. ~amerikaner** m *German-American*; ⟨Am⟩ *hyphenated American* (dies auch: = *Italo-* od *Dutch-American, etc*) **≃amerikanisch** a *German-American* (*literature*) **~balte** m *the Baltic German* **≃feindlich** a *Germanophobe* (*attitude, etc*) **~herr** m; ~en [pl] *the Teutonic knights* [pl] **~kunde** f **1.** *part of Germanic philology* **2.** ⟨school⟩ *systematic instruction in what is German and in what Germans have achieved in the world* **≃kundlich** a; ~er Unterricht *instruction dealing with* Deutschkunde **~lehrer** m *teacher of German* **~meister** m ⟨hist⟩ *Grand Master of the Teutonic Order* (*for the German territories*) **≃nation·al** a ⟨pol⟩ ~e Volkspartei f *German National People's Party* **~ordensland** n *Lands* [pl] (*formerly*) *in the possession of the Teutonic Order* **~russe** m *German-Russian* **~schweizer** m *German-Swiss* **≃sprachig** a *German-speaking* ‖ ~es Schrifttum *publications of German-speaking countries* **≃stämmig** a *ethnic*(*al*) *German*; ~es Volk *people of German origin* **II. ≃-·englisch** a *Anglo-German* (*fellowship*) **~-franz·ösisch** a *Franco-German* od *Prussian* (*war*; 1870/71) **~-Ost·afrika** n *German East Afrika*, ⟨engl⟩ *Tanganyika Territory* **~-Südwest·afrika** n *German South-West A.* ⟨engl⟩ *Southwest A.*

Deutsche m [der ~, ein ~r] ~en/~en *the German*; ⟨fam⟩ *Teuton*; ⟨mil sl⟩ *Jerry, Fritz*; v ~n gemacht *German-made* ‖ → Auslands≃r

D·eutsche Bucht f → Helgoländer Bucht

D·eutschen- ~feind m *Germanophobe* **~freund** m *Germanophil* **≃freundlich** a *Germanophil* **~haß** m *Germanophobia*

d·eutscherseits adv; darüber ist man sich ~ einig *on this there is no division of opinion in Germany*; .. *there is opinion united in G.*

D·eutschheit f *the German popular character*

D·eutschland 1. *Germany*; in ~ hergestellt *made in G.* ‖ das nördliche (etc) ~ *Northern G.*; das mittelalterliche ~ *Medieval G.* **2.** (Schiff) die ~ *the Deutschland* **~lied** n *the German national anthem* '~, ~ über Alles' v Hoffmann v Fallersleben (1841) **~sender** m ⟨wir⟩ *Deutschlandsender Radio*

D·eutschtum n **1.** [abstr] *the German character*; *Germanity*; *Teutonism* **2.** [konkr] *Germans* [pl]; das gesamte ~ *Germans everywhere*; das ~ im Auslande *Germans living abroad* **Deutschtümel·ei** f ~/ *Germanomania, Teutomania*; *affectation of things German* **d·eutschtümeln** vi *to be possessed with Germanomania* **D·eutschtümler** m ~s/~ *Germanomaniac, Teutomaniac*

D·eutung f ~/~en *explanation, interpretation* (*of a text*); falsche ~ *misinterpretation* ‖ *construction, interpretation* (*of facts, words, actions*); irrige ~ *misconstruction*; e–r S e–e günstige ~ geben *to put a favourable construction on a th*; e–r anderen ~ unterliegen, e–e andere ~ zulassen *to be open to* (od *to admit of*) *another construction*

D·eutzie [–iə] f ⟨bot⟩ *Deutzia*

Deux-Pièces [ˈdøː piˈɛːs] pl ⟨tail⟩ Fr *two-piece*

Devalvati·on f ⟨com⟩ *devaluation*

Deviati·on f ⟨mar⟩ *deviation*; die ~ bestimmen *to ascertain the d.*

Dev·ise [deˈviːzə] f ~/~n **1.** *motto*; ⟨her & poet⟩ *device*; → Wahlspruch **2.** ⟨com⟩ *foreign* [v England aus gesehen] *bill of exchange* ‖ *foreign exchange* od *currency*

Dev·isen- ~abgabe f *sale of foreign* [v England aus gesehen] *bills* **~beschaffungsstelle** f *office for procuring foreign exchange* **~bestände** m pl *f. e. assets* **~bestimmungen** f [pl] *foreign exchange regulations*; *currency* (*control*) *regulations* pl (umg·ehen *to circumvent*) **~bewirtschaftung** f *exchange control* **~geschäft** n *business in foreign exchange* **~gesetz** n *f. e.* od *c. law* **~handel** m *transactions* [pl] *in foreign exchange* **~knappheit** f *shortage of f. c.* **~kurs** m (*rate of*) *foreign exchange* **~markt** m *foreign exchange market* **~-politik** f *foreign exchange policy* **~schieber** m *currency-profiteer* **~schiebung** f *currency-manipulation*; *illegal transfer of f. c.* **~schmuggel** m *currency-smuggling* **~sperre** f *embargo on foreign exchange* **~stelle** f *foreign exchange department* (od *office*) **~überw·achungsstelle** f *exchange control anthorities* pl **~vergehen** n *currency--offence* **~werte** m pl *f. e. assets*, ⟨Am⟩ *f. security* **~zentrale** f *Clearing-House for foreign bills* **~zwangswirtschaft** f *exchange control*

Devoluti·on [–ts–] f ⟨ec jur⟩ *devolution*

Dev·on n (nach Grafschaft ~shire), **~formation** f ⟨geol⟩ *Devonian*; *D. formation* **dev·onisch** a ⟨geol⟩ *Devonian* (*formation*)

dev·ot [deˈvoːt] a *devout, pious* ‖ (unterwürfig) *respectful, obsequious, submissive* **≃ion·alien** f pl *religious* od *devotional articles* (*medals, etc*)

D·exel f = Dechsel

Dextr·in n ~s/ *dextrin*

Dextrop·ur n ⟨Ger⟩ (Kräftigungsmittel) *pure grape-sugar* **Dextr·ose** f *dextrose*; *starch sugar*

Dez·ember m ~s/~ *December* (im ~ *in D.*) ‖ ~tage [pl] *December days* [pl]

Dez·emvir m ~n & ~s/~n *decemvir* **Dezemvir·at** n ~(e)s/ *decemvirate*

Dez·ennium n ~s/–nien *decennium* L pl *–nia, decade, decennary*

dez·ent 1. a (anständig) *decent* (*story*) ‖ (unaufdringlich) *unobtrusive* (*manners*); *modest* (*behaviour*); *retiring*; *restrained*; *dignified* ‖ *moderate* (*demands*), *reasonable* **2.** adv *decently*; *unobtrusively*

Dezentralisati·on f *decentralization* **dezentralis·ieren** vt [h] *to decentralize* **dezentr·ieren** ⟨phot⟩ **1.** vt [h] *to put out of centre* **2.** ≃ n *decentering*; → 1.

Dezern·at n *department appointed to deal with special matters* ‖ *sphere* (od *functions* [pl]) *of a* **Dezern·ent** m (*one appointed to report on* (od *deal with*) *special matters*) ‖ (*departmental expert*) *chief of the .. desk*: NN ist ~ f: *N.N. sits at the* (*Middle East*) *desk* ‖ *spokesman* (*for*)

D·ezi- (Zehntel–) [in comp] *deci–* **~·ar** n ~s/~e, Sw **~·are** f ~/~n $^1/_{10}$ Ar [abbr da] **~gr·amm** n *decigram*(*me*) **~liter** n *decilitre* **~meter** n *decimetre*

Dezib·el ~s/~ ⟨phys⟩ *decibel* → d. Bd. I

Dezim·al a *decimal* **~bezeichnung** f *decimal notation* **~bruch** m *decimal*; *decimal fraction*; → Dezimalzahl ‖ periodischer ~ *repeater* **~rechnung** f *decimal arithmetic* **~stelle** f *decimal place*; *digit*; *decimal digit* **~system** n *decimal system* ‖ (der Maße, Gewichte) *decimal s. of weights and measures*; *metric system* ‖ (der

Münzen) *decimal coinage* || nach dem ~ *decimally*; (etw) auf das ~ zurückführen *to decimalice* **~waage** f *decimal balance* **~währung** f *decimal currency* **~zahl** f *decimal*; periodische ~ *circulating d.*; unendliche ~ *repeating* (od *recurring*) *d.*

Dez·ime f ~/~n ⟨mus⟩ *tenth*

D·ezimeter- *decimetric*; → Dezi- **~welle** f *d. wave* **dezim·ieren** vt [h] (Heer; Volk) *to decimate*

Dezim·ierung f *decimation*

Dh·akbaum m ⟨bot⟩ *Dhak tree*

Dhau, Dhaw, Dhow [*dau*] f (arab. Segelboot) *dhow*

di- pref (Gr) (zwei; doppelt) *di-*

D·ia n ~s/~s (= **Diapositiv**) ⟨phot⟩ (*transparent*) *slide* **~betrachter** m (S) *dia* od *transparent viewer* **~·einfaßstreifen** m *slide binding* (*strip*) **~fassung** f = -rahmen **~film** m *transparence film* **~projektor** m (S) *transparence projecting apparatus* **~rahmen** m *slide frame* od *mount* **~transport** m (*forward and backward*) *slide change* **~vorführung** f *performance* od *show of slides*

dia- pref (Gr) (durch; auseinander) *dia-*

Diab·as m ~es/~e ⟨minr⟩ *diabase*

Diab·etes m ~/ ⟨med⟩ *diabetes* (*mellitus*) L

Diab·etiker m *diabetic* **diab·etisch** a *diabetic*

diab·olisch a *diabolical*; *devilish*, *fiendish* (*cruelty*) **Di·abolo, ~spiel** n *diabolo*

Di·achylonpflaster n ⟨med⟩ *diachylon* (*–lum* L)

Diad·em n ~s/~e *diadem*; *coronet*

Diad·ochen m [pl] *Diadochi* (L) [pl], *successors of Alexander the Great* || ~zeit [f] *Diadochian period*

Diagen·ese f ⟨geol⟩ *diagenesis*

Diagn·ose f ~/~n ⟨bes med⟩ *diagnosis* ⟨a. übtr⟩; e–e ~ stellen *to make a d.* **Diagn·ostik** f ⟨med⟩ *diagnostics* [pl] **Diagn·ostiker** m *diagnostician* **diagn·ostisch** 1. a *diagnostic*; in ~er Hinsicht *diagnostically* 2. adv *diagnostically*

diagnostiz·ieren vt/i [h] 1. vt *to diagnose* 2. vi *to make a diagnosis* .. || .. ist *or* wird selten –rt *the diagnosis of .. is often missed*

diagon·al 1. a *diagonal*; *cater-cornered*; in ~er Richtung *diagonally* 2. ≗ n ~s/ *diagonal cloth*; *diagonal* || ≗schnitt [m] *angle-cutting* **Diagon·ale** f ~/~n ⟨math⟩ *diagonal*

Diagr·amm n ~s/~e *diagram*, *graph*; *schematic drawing*; ⟨bes wir⟩ *schematic*; in Form e–s ~s *diagrammatically*

diak·austisch a ⟨phys⟩ ~e Linie *diacaustic curve*, *diacaustic*

Diak·on m ~s/~e ⟨R.C. & C.E.⟩ *deacon* || ⟨in evang. Kirche⟩ *deacon*, *layman* **Diakon·at** n ~s/~e (Amt e–s Diakons *diaconate*, *deaconhood*, *deaconry*, *deaconship* **Diakon·ie** f *devotion to works of charity* **Diakon·isse** f ~/~n (der evang. Kirche) *Lutheran nurse* (*affiliated with one of the* ~nhäuser) || ~nanstalt [f], ~nhaus [n] *Lutheran nurses' institute* (od *institution*)

Diakon·issin f ~/~nen = Diakonisse

Di·akonus m (L) = Diakon

diakr·itisch a *diacritic*(*al*); ⟨gram⟩ ~es Zeichen *diacritic*; *diacritic sign*

Dial·ekt m ~(e)s/~e 1. *dialect*; ~ sprechen *to speak d.*; → Mundart 2. [in comp] *dialectal* (*poetry*)

Dial·ektik f ⟨philos⟩ *dialectic*, die Methode der ~ *the method of d.* | **–tiker** m ~s/~ ⟨philos⟩ *dialectician*, *logician* | **d–tisch** a 1. *dialectal*; *dialectic*(*al*); in ~er Beziehung *dialectally*, *dialectically* 2. ⟨philos⟩ *dialectic*(*al*)

Diall·ag m ⟨minr⟩ *diallage*

Dial·og m ~s/~e *dialogue*, *duologue* || ⟨Lit⟩ *dialogue* (: *written in d.*); Begabung f den ~ *gift of d.* | ~autor [m] ⟨film⟩ *dialogue writer* **dial·ogisch** a *dialogic* **dialogis·ieren** vt [h] *to write* (*a th*) *in dialogue*

Dialypet·ale f ⟨bot⟩ = Choripetale

Dial·yse f ⟨chem⟩ *dialysis* (L); (etw) durch ~ trennen *to dialyse* **dial·ytisch** a *dialytic*

diagmagn·etisch a *diamagnetic* **Diamagnet·ismus** m *diamagnetism*

Diam·ant m ~en/~en 1. *diamond* (fassen *to set*); geschliffener, ungeschliffener ~ *cut*, *rough d.*; (etw) mit ~en schmücken *to diamond* || imitierter ~ *rhinestone* || schwarzer ~ *black diamond* (= Steinkohle) || ~en pl ⟨sl vulg⟩ *rocks* 2. (Gerät z Schneiden) (*cutting*) *diamond*; ⟨engr⟩ (z Gravieren) *diamond-point* 3. ⟨typ⟩ f (Schriftgröße) *diamond* 4. ≗**artig** a *adamantine*; *diamond-like* **~fink** m ⟨orn⟩ ein Prachtfink, → d. **~glanz** m *adamantine lustre*; Material mit ~ *diamanté* (Fr) **~grube** f *diamond-mine*; Aktien [pl] e–r ~ *diamonds* [pl] ≗**haltig** a *diamondiferous*, *diamantiferous* **~kitt** m *galbanum* (L) **~ring** m *diamond-ring* **~schleifer** m *diamond-cutter*, *-polisher* **~schmuck** m *set of diamonds* **~schneider** m *diamond-cutter* **~schwarz** n *diamond black* **~spat** m *adamantine spar* **~staub** m *diamond-powder* (od *dust*) **~vogel** m ⟨orn⟩ *diamond-bird*

diam·anten a *diamond*; *adamantine* || ~e Hochzeit f *diamond jubilee* od *wedding* **Diam·antenfasser** m *diamond-setter*

Diam·at m ~s/ *dialectical materialism*

Di·ameter m ~s/~ *diameter* **diametr·al** I. a 1. *diametral*, *diametrical* (*direction*) 2. (genau entgegengesetzt) *diametrical* (*difference*) II. adv ~ entgegengesetzt *diametrically opposed*, *poles apart* **diam·etrisch** a *diametral*, *diametrical*

Diam·ine [pl] ⟨chem⟩ *diamines* [pl]

Di·ana-Affe m ⟨zoo⟩ *diana monkey*

Dianth·ee f ['e:ə] Gattung der ~n *dianthus*

diaph·an a (durchscheinend) *diaphanous*

Diaphor·ese f ⟨med⟩ *diaphoresis* **diaphor·etisch** a ⟨med⟩ *diaphoretic*; ~es Mittel n *diaphoretic*

Diaphr·agma n ~s/–men ⟨anat & opt⟩ *diaphragm*

Diaph·yse f ~/~n ⟨anat⟩ *diaphysis*

Diapositi·v n ~s/~e ⟨phot⟩ *lantern slide* || ⟨film⟩ *diapositive* | ~abzugsfilm [m] *transparent stripping film*; → Dia

Diär·ese f ⟨gram & pros⟩ *diaeresis* (L)

Di·arium n ~s/–rien *diary*; *memorandum-book*

Diarrh·öe f ⟨med⟩ 1. *diarrhoea* 2. [in comp] *diarrhoeal*

Diarthr·ose f ⟨anat⟩ *diarthrosis* (L)

Diask·op n ~s/~e *projector*

Diaspor·a f ~/ ⟨ec⟩ *diaspora* (L)

Diast·ase f ~/~n 1. ⟨chem⟩ *diastase* 2. ⟨path⟩ *diastasis* (L) **diast·atisch** a ⟨chem⟩ *diastatic*

Di·astole f ~/–st·olen ⟨med⟩ *diastole*

Di·ät f ~/ ⟨med⟩ *diet*; *regimen*; e–e strenge ~ halten *to diet*; *to observe a strict regimen* || nach ~ leben *to diet* (*o.s.*) || jdn auf ~ setzen *to put a p on a diet*, *to diet a p* || sich e–e ~ auferlegen *to diet o.s.* **di·ät** adv ~ leben *to diet* (*o.s.*); streng ~ leben *to observe a strict regimen*; → Diät

Di·ät [in comp] **~brot** n *diet-bread* **~fehler** m *dietary indiscretion* **~kost** f *dietary* **~krankheit** f *dietetic disease* **~küche** f *dietary table* od *kitchen* **~kur** f *regimen*, *dietary* || e–e ~ m *to slim* **~vorschrift** f *dietary prescription*; *diet*

Diät·ar m *one who gets a daily allowance*

Di·äten f [pl] *daily allowances* (*for attendance*; *for expenses*, etc.)

Diät·etik f ~/~en *dietetics* [pl] [sg konstr] **Diät·etiker** m *dietician* **diät·etisch** 1. a *dietetic*; *dietary*; *dietetic* 2. adv *dietetically*

diatherm·an a *diathermanous*, *diathermic*

Diatherm·ie [–i:] f ~/ ⟨med⟩ *diathermy* || mit ~ behandeln *to diathermize*

Diath·ese f ⟨med⟩ *diathesis* (L)

Diäthyl- [in comp] ⟨chem⟩ *diethyl-*

Diatom·ee [eːə] f ⟨bot⟩ *diatom*; *diatomaceous plant*; Gattung der ~n *Diatomaceae* ‖ ~n-schlamm [m] ⟨geol⟩ *diatomaceous deposits* [pl]
Diatom·it n ~s/ ⟨geol⟩ *diatomite*
Diat·onik f ⟨mus⟩ *diatonic system*; *diatonism*
diat·onisch a ⟨mus⟩ *diatonic* (*scale*)
Di·azo- [in comp] ⟨chem⟩ *diazo-* .. **~verbindung** f *diazo compound*
diazot·ieren vt [h] (etw) *to diazotize*
d·ibbeln **1.** vt/i [h] [engl] ⟨agr⟩ *to dibble* **2.** ≃ n *dibbling* **D·ibbel(sä)maschine** f *dibbling machine*
°**d·ibbern** vi *to talk low*; *to whisper*
dich **1.** pron pers acc [v du] *you* ‖ ⟨bib, poet & †⟩ *thee* **2.** [pron reflex] *you*; sieh unter ~ *look below you* | mach ~ fort † *get you* (od *thee*) *gone*; setz ~ *sit down*, † *sit you* (od *thee*) *down*
Dich·asium n ~s/–sien ⟨bot⟩ *dichasium*
Dichl·or- [in comp] ⟨chem⟩ *dichlor-*, *dichloro-*
Dicho- (entzwei) [in comp] *dicho-* **~gam·ie** f ⟨bot⟩ *dichogamy* **~tom·ie** f *dichotomy*
Dichro·ismus m ⟨minr⟩ *dichroism* **dichro·itisch** a ⟨minr⟩ *dichroic* **Dichromas·ie** f *dichromatism*
Dichrom·at n ⟨chem⟩ *dichromate* **Dichrosk·op** n ~s/~e *dichroscope*
dicht **I.** a **A.** **1.** = gediegen, → d. **2.** (aus vielen Teilen, fest zus–hängend) *compact*, *firm*, *solid*; *close* (*tissue*); *dense* (*fog*) ‖ *thick* (*cloth*) ‖ ~er w *to thicken*; die Finsternis wurde ~er *darkness gathered* | *dense*, *thick* (*foliage*; *crowd*; *forest*); ~e Bevölkerung *dense population*; ~es Gedränge *dense mass* od *crowd* ‖ *bushy* (*eyebrows*); ~es Haar *bushy* od *thick hair* ‖ ~e Hecke *thick*(*set*) *hedge* ‖ in ~en Reihen ⟨gard⟩ *in close rows* ‖ ~es Unterholz *matted undergrowth* ‖ ~e Straßen *crowded streets*; *heavy* (*traffic*) ‖ der ~este Teil *the thick* (*of a fight*) ‖ ~ stehen *to stand thick* **B.** (abgedichtet) *tight* (*cask*); *watertight* (*ship*); ~ gegen *impervious to light*, etc.) → luft~, schall~, wasser~; ~ m *to make* (*a th*) (*water*)*tight*; ⟨fig⟩ *to close down* ‖ ~ halten *to be tight*; *to hold water*; → ~halten II. 3. ⟨com⟩ ~ s *to be reliable* **II.** adv **1.** *closely*, *densely* ‖ ~ schließen *to shut tightly*; ~ schließend *closely fitting* (*door*, *window*) ‖ mit Vorhängen ~ verschlossen *close-curtained* ‖ ~ zus–drängen *to compact*, *compress* ‖ ~ die Straßen füllen (of people) *to crowd* od *throng the streets* **2.** (nahe) **a.** sich ~ **am** Ufer halten *to hug the shore*; ~ am Winde *close-hauled*; ~ am W. fahren *to sail close to the wind* ‖ ~ am Ziel *near the goal* ‖ ~ an *hard on* (*nonsense*) ‖ ~ an (*or* bei) e–a *close together*; *cheek by jowl* ‖ jdm **~ auf** den Fersen s *to be at* (od *on*) *a p's heels*, *to tread* (od *to press close*) *upon a p's heels*; e–r S ~ auf den F. folgen (S) *to tread upon the heels of a th* ‖ **~ bei** *close by* (od *to*); ~ dabei *close* (od *hard*) by ‖ **~ hinter** jdm *at* (od *on*) *a p's heels*; ~ hinter jdm folgen *to follow hard after* (od *behind*) *a p*; e–e ~ hinter e–a folgende Reihe v Schlägen *a thick shower of blows*; die Schläge kamen ~ hinter–e–a *the blows came* od *fell fast and thick* **b.** **~ vor** s–m Tode *just before his death* **3.** [in comp] **~anliegen** *to fit tight*(*ly*); *to sit close*; ~anliegend *tight* (*jacket*); *tight* (od *close*) *-fitting* (an *to*) ‖ ~ansitzend a *close* (*cap*); *tight* **~bedeckt** a *thickly covered* ‖ ~behaart [a] *thick with hair*; *hairy*; *with thick growth of hair* ‖ ~belaubt [a] *thick with leaves* ‖ ~besät, ~besetzt [a] *thick* (mit, von *with*); die Bäume waren ~ mit Blättern besät *leaves were thick on thre trees* ‖ ~beschrieben *closely written* (*page*) ‖ ~besiedeltes Gebiet *congested district* [aber: .. ist dicht besiedelt] ‖ ~bevölkert [a] *densely populated* [aber: .. ist dicht bev.] **~gedrängt** a *compact*; *tightly packed*; *thick*; ~ voll Menschen *thronged with persons*; ~stehen *to stand crowded together* ‖ ~gepflanzt [a] *thickset* (*hedge*) ‖ ~geschlossen [a] *closely shut up*; *tight* ‖ ~gewebt [a] *closely woven* ‖ → ~halten ≃**masse** f ⟨tech⟩ *jointing compound* **~schließend** a *tight* **~verwachsen** a *tightly woven*
D·ichte f ⟨phys⟩ *concentration*, *density* ‖ ⟨demog⟩ landwirtschaftliche *or* physiologische ~ *density of the agricultural population per unit of cultivable area* ‖ größtmögliche ~ *population carrying capacity* ‖ → Dichtheit | ~maßzahl [f] ⟨demog⟩ *comparative density index* ‖ ~messer [m] → Aräometer, Densimeter ‖ ~unterschied [m] *differency in density*
d·ichten **1.** (→ dicht a) vt [h] (Faß etc) *to make* (*water*)*tight*; (Schiff) *to caulk* ‖ (luftdicht m) *to lute* (*with*); *to stop* ‖ (Fugen) *to flush* ‖ *to seal* (*a container* od *gap*) **2.** ≃ n *caulking* ‖ *luting* ‖ *flushing*
d·ichten **I.** vt/i [h] **A.** vt **1.** † = sinnen **2.** = ersinnen, erdichten **3.** (Verse, Lied etc) *to compose*, *write* **B.** vi *to compose* od *write poetry*, *to make verses*; *to write in verse* **II.** ≃ n **1.** (Sinnen) all sein ~ u Trachten *all his thoughts and endeavours* **2.** *composing*; *composition* od *writing of poetry* od *verses*
D·ichter m ~s/~ *poet* ‖ (engl) Hof≃, gekrönter ~ *Poet Laureate* **Dichetr·ei** f ~/~en *rhyming* **D·ichterin** f ~/~nen *poetess*
d·ichterisch **1.** a *poetic* (*genius*; *imagination*; *diction*, *justice*; *vein*); ~e Freiheit *poetic licence* ‖ *poetical* (*expression*; *subject*; *works*) ‖ ~e (rhythmisierte) Prosa [f] *polyphonic prose* ‖ in ~er Hinsicht *poetically* **2.** adv (*to treat*) *poetically*; ~ behandeln, verherrlichen *to poet*(*ic*)*ize*
D·ichterling m ~s/~e *poetaster*, *rhymester*; *scibbler of verse*; *versifier*; *would-be poet*
D·ichthalten n *tightness* (*of a cask*)
°**d·icht|halten** vi [h] ⟨fig⟩ *to keep silence*; ⟨fam⟩ *to hold one's tongue*; *to keep one's own counsel*, *to keep mum* ‖ er kann nicht ~ ⟨fam⟩ *he's leaky*, *he's likely to blab*
D·ichtheit, D·ichtigkeit f ~/ **1.** *closeness* (*of a tissue*), *compactness* ‖ *consistence*, *–cy*; *denseness*, *density*; *thickness* (*of hair*; *of a forest*, etc.) **2.** *tightness*, *leakproofness* (*of a cask*)
D·ichtkunst f ~/; die ~ (*the art of*) *poetry*; die griechische ~ *Greek poetry* ‖ †*poesy*
D·ichtung (→ dicht) f ~/~en **1.** [abstr] *caulking* (*of a cask*) ‖ *luting* ‖ *jointing* **2.** [konkr] (Material) ⟨tech⟩ (an Maschinen) *packing*, *package*; *seal*; (aus Hanf, Gummi, Metall, Werg) *gasket*; → Stopfbuchse ‖ ~sdraht [m] ⟨el⟩ *seal wire* ‖ ~sleiste f = –streifen ‖ ~s-manschetten [f pl] *gaskets* pl ‖ ~smasse [f], ~smaterial [n], ~mittel [n] *sealing* od *leakproofing material*; *sealant*; *lute*, *luting* ‖ *packing* ‖ ~sring [m] *packing–* od *sealing-ring*; *washer* ‖ ~sscheibe [f] *washer* ‖ ~sstreifen [m] *draught excluder* (f. Fenster etc), *weatherstrip*
D·ichtung f ~/~en **1.** → Dichten **2.** (Erdichtetes) *fiction* ‖ ~ u Wahrheit *Fiction and Reality* **3.** **a.** = Dichtkunst **b.** [konkr] *poem*; *poetical work* ‖ [oft pl] ~en *poems* [pl], *poetry* (: *Goethe's p.*) ‖ Prosa≃ *fiction* ‖ ~sart f *kind* od *form of poetry* ~svermögen n *poetic faculty* od *power*
D·ichtwerk n *poem*; [mst pl] ~e *poetical works*; *poems* [pl]; *poetry*
dick a **A.** (dicht) **1.** *dense* (*fog*); *thick* ‖ (trübe) *turbid* (Flüssigkeit) ‖ °es ist ~e Luft *there is something afoot* (od *in the air*) → dicht I. A. 2. | *thick* (*soup*; *blood*); *curdy*; ~e Milch = ≃milch ‖ ~ w (of jelly) *to set*; *syrupy* (*fruit juice*) **2.** ⟨übtr & fig⟩ *intimate* (*friendship*); sie sind ~e Freunde *they are thick*; *they are as thick as thieves* ‖ durch ~ u dünn *through thick and thin* **B.** (massig) **1.** **a.** *big*; *thick* (*legs*, *fingers*, *lips*); *large* (*stomach*), *big*, *fat* (⟨fam⟩ *belly*) ‖ *chubby*, *round*, *plump* (*cheeks*, *face*); ⟨med⟩ ~e

Backe *swollen cheek* || *stout* (*oak*); *thick, heavy, warm* (*coat*); *heavy* (*raindrops*); *large* (*tears*) **b.** (P) *big, burly, corpulent, fat, plump, stout*; *heavy-set* (*man*); *obese*; ~e P *fatty* || ~ und rund(lich) *roly-poly* (*child*); e–e ~e u rundliche P *a roly-poly* || ⟨mot⟩ sich auf der Straße ~ m *to hedge the road* || ⟨mil⟩ °die ~e Bertha *Big Bertha* || sich ~ (u fett) essen *to eat one's fill, to eat to excess*; *to overeat o.s.* || °~ (= schwanger) s *to be big with child* || ~ auflaufen, anschwellen *to bulge, to swell* || ~ m *to stouten* || ~(er) w *to swell*; (P) *to stouten* **c.** *big, bulky* (*book*), *voluminous* || das ~e Ende *the butt-end* (*of a gun* etc.); **d.** ⟨übtr & fig⟩ das ~e Ende *the crux, the knotty point* (*of a th*); das ~e E. kommt nach *this is where the catch comes in*; das ~e E. kam nach *worse followed* || °ein ~es Fell h *to be thick-skinned*; *to be insensitive* || °~e Gelder h *to have money to burn, to have heaps of money* || e–n ~en Kopf h *to be pigheaded* (od *thick-headed, stubborn, obstinate*) || °~e Töne reden *to talk big* (od *tall*) || etw ~ h *to have one's fill of, to be fed up with, to be sick of a th* **2.** (als Maß, bei Flächen) *thick*; ~e Scheibe Brot *thick slice of bread* || ein 4 Zoll ~er Stock *a stick four inches thick, a stick four inches in thickness* (od *breadth*); *a four-inch stick* || ~e Fläche *thickness* || Butter ~ aufstreichen *to spread butter thick*; ~ mit Butter bestrichenes Brot *br. thickly spread with b.* || ⟨fig⟩ ~ auftragen *to lay it on thick* || °ich hab's ~! *I'm fed up with it*! || er hat es (faust)dick hinter den Ohren *he is a slyboots*; *he is not frank*; *he looks as if butter wouldn't melt in his mouth* || °**sich ~ tun** *to swank*; → angeben; → ~tun **C.** [subst.] **das** ≈e (e–r Flüssigkeit) = Bodensatz

d·ick- **~bäckig** a *chubby*(*-faced*) **≈bauch** m *pot-belly, paunch* || (P) *pot-belly* **~bäuchig** a *paunchy, pot-bellied*; *ventripotent*; ~ w *to belly* **≈bein** n = Oberschenkel **≈blatt** n ⟨bot⟩ *sedum* L; *house leek*; *Crassula* **≈darm** m *colon*; *large intestine*; → Faserschicht || ~katarrh [m] *colitis* **~fellig** a ⟨fig⟩ *thick-skinned*; *pachydermatous*; *stolid*; ~e P *pachyderm* **≈felligkeit** f ⟨fig⟩ *stolidity* **~flüssig** a *glutinous, ropy*; *viscid, viscous*; *syrupy* **≈flüssigkeit** f *ropiness, viscidity, viscosity* **≈fuß** m **1.** ⟨orn⟩ *a kind of plover* **2.** ⟨bot⟩ *boletus* **~gepolstert** a *heavily upholstered* **≈häuter** m ⟨zoo⟩ *pachyderm* ⟨a. fig⟩ **~häutig** a *thick--skinned*; → dickfellig **≈horn** n ⟨zoo⟩ (wildes Schaf) *bighorn* **≈kopf** m **1.** ⟨ich⟩ = Döbel **2.** ⟨ent⟩ *skipper* **3.** ⟨fig⟩ (P a.) °–kopp *pigheaded fellow*; *blockhead*; *hard nut* **~köpfig** a ⟨fig⟩ *pigheaded, thick-headed, obstinate* **≈köpfigkeit** f ⟨fig⟩ *pigheadedness*; *stolidity*; (*pertinacious*) *obstinacy* **~leibig** a *corpulent*; → dickbäuchig || (of books, etc.) *bulky, voluminous*; *plethoric* **≈leibigkeit** f *corpulence, –cy* || (von Büchern) *bulkiness* **~lippig** a *thick-lipped* **≈maul** n ⟨ich⟩ *capelin* **≈milch** f *curds* [pl]*, and whey*; *junket* **~nasig** a *having a thick, fat nose*; ⟨fig⟩ *arrogant, snobby*; *bumptious*; → aufgeblasen **≈rübe** f = Runkelrübe **≈saft** m (v Zucker) *meladura* **~schalig** a *thick-shelled* (od *skinned*); ⟨bot⟩ *husky* **≈tuer** m *boaster, braggart* **≈tuer·ei** f *boast*(*ing*) (mit *of*); *brag*(*ging*); *tall talk* °**~|tun** vi & vrefl [h] ~, sich ~ *to talk big* od *tall, to brag*; *to* (*make*) *boast* (mit *of*); → aufschneiden || *to peacock o.s.*; *to put on airs* (⟨sl⟩ *side*; ⟨Am sl⟩ *lugs*); ~d *peacockish, peacocky* **~wandig** a *thick-walled* **≈wanst** m → Dickbauch

°**D·ickchen** n [oft voc] *fatty* || (Kind) *roly-poly*

D·icke f (→ dick) **1.** *density* (*of fog*) || *thickness* (*of soup*) **2. a.** *thickness* (*of legs*); *plumpness* **b.** *corpulence, –cy, fatness, obesity, stoutness* (*of a p*) **c.** *bigness, bulk*(*iness*) **3.** (als Maß) *thickness* (*of a board*); Seil≈ *diameter of rope*; ⟨tech⟩ *gauge*, ⟨pap⟩ *cal*(*l*)*iper* (*in callipers ranging from .. to*) → Dickte || ~nmeßgerät *thickness gauge*; ⟨pap⟩ *micrometer*; → Taster

°**d·icke** adv & a **1.** etw ~ h → dick B. d. || (sich) ~tun → dicktun || (Spiel) → gewinnen *to win hands down* | (in Antwort) reicht das? – °~! *rather*! *ra·ther*! **2.** °~ *groggy, fuddled*

D·ickerchen n ~s/~ ⟨fam⟩ *fatty*

D·ickicht n ~(e)s/~e **1.** (Busch≈) *thicket*; *brake, brushwood, copse, coppice, shrubbery*; ⟨Am⟩ *brush* **2.** (Wald≈) *natural wood*; *bush* || Sumpf≈ *jungle* **3.** ⟨fig⟩ *thicket*; *labyrinth*

d·icklich a *bulky, thickish* (*volumes, liquid*) || *fattish* (*legs*) || (P) *burly*; *chubby* (*baby*); *plump* (*child*); *stoutish* (*man*); *well-rounded*; rund u ~ *roly-poly*

Dicks·onie [–iə] f ⟨bot⟩ *Dicksonia* [L]

D·ickte f = Dicke 3. **D·icktenhobelmaschine** f *thicknessing-machine*; *thicknesser*

D·ickung f ~/~en ⟨hunt⟩ *covert*

Did·aktik f ~/ *didactics* [pl] [sg konstr]

did·aktisch **1.** a *didactic*; in ~er Beziehung *didactically* **2.** adv *didactically*

didd ⟨telg⟩ (= Punkt [kz Ton]) *dot*; ~ u da *dot and dash*

dideld·um [intj] *tweedledum, tweedledee*

didyn·amisch a ⟨bot⟩ *didynamic, didynamous*

die [nom & acc, f & pl] **1.** [betont] [v pron der] → der (die, das) I. A. B. **2.** [unbetont] [v def art] → ebd II. | ~ F. ⟨theat, etc⟩ *the Fotheringay* **3.** [unbetont] [v pron rel] → ebd III.

D·ieb m ~(e)s/~e **1. a.** *thief*; *sneak-thief*; ⟨Am sl⟩ *snooper* || Pferde≈ ⟨Am sl⟩ *rustler* || (~ kl Mengen) *pilferer* | ein abgefeimter ~ *an old bird* || haltet den ~! *stop thief*! || Gelegenheit macht ~e *opportunity makes the thief*; die kl ~e hängt man, die gr läßt man laufen *great rogues get off unscathed and the small fry get hanged* || → Einbrecher; Hochstapler; Laden≈; Räuber; Taschen≈, Wild≈ **b.** ⟨übtr⟩ wie ein ~ *thiefwise*; wie ein ~ in der Nacht *like a foe in the dark* || ~ geistigen Gutes *plagiarist, plagiary* || → Tage≈ **2.** (Lichtschnuppe) ⟨fam⟩ *thief*

Dieber·ei f ~/~en *thievery, thieving*; *theft* || *pilferage*

D·ieb(e)s- [in comp] *thief–, thieves'–* **~ameise** f ⟨ent⟩ *thief-ant* **~bande** f *gang of thieves* **~falle** f *thief-detector* **~finger** m: ~[pl] h *to be light-fingered* **~geselle** m *thief's accomplice* **~gesicht** n *hang-dog look* **~gesindel** n (*pack of*) *thieves* **~gut** n *stolen goods* [pl]; ⟨fam⟩ *stuff* **~herberge** f *thieves' den* **~höhle** f *nest of thieves* **~käfer** m ⟨ent⟩ Gattung der ~ *Ptinidae* [L] **~laterne** f *dark lantern* **~nest** n *nest of thieves* **~schlüssel** m *thief-key, skeleton key* **≈sicher** a *thief-proof* **~sprache** f *thieves' Latin* **~trick** m ⟨bes Am⟩ *shenanigan*

D·iebin f ~/~nen (*female*) *thief*

d·iebisch **1.** a **a.** *thievish*; *priggish*; *light-fingered* || auf ~e Art *in the manner of thieves*; ~e Freude, ~es Vergnügen *malicious joy* od *pleasure*; ~es Wesen *thievishness* || *pilfering* (*magpie*) **b.** ⟨fig⟩ *capital, immense* (*delight*); *splendid* (*fun*); → kolossal, riesig **2.** adv *jolly* (*cold*); er freute sich ~ *he was immensely pleased* (*with himself*), *he gloated* (*over a th*); *he was as pleased as Punch*

D·iebsinseln f pl → Marianen

D·iebstahl m ~(e)s/–stähle **1.** ⟨jur⟩ *larceny*; einfacher ~ *simple*, ⟨jur⟩ *petty l.*; schwerer ~ *aggravated*, ⟨jur⟩ *grand l.*; → Einbruch≈ || *the prisoner indicted of larceny committed the theft on May 6*; → | *theft*; *sneak-thieving*; (geringfügiger) *pilfery* || dreister ~ *bold* od *daring robbery* **2.** geistiger ~ *plagiarism* **~versicherung** f *insurance against burglary and theft*

d·iejenige [pron det] → derjenige

D·iele f ~/~n **1.** *board, plank*; (aus Kiefern–, Tannenholz) *deal* **2.** (Fußboden) *floor* **3.** (Flur,

Vorhalle) *hall, vestibule*; (in Hotels) *lounge* **4.** *small (wine) restaurant with dancing* **~ndarbietung** f (in Nachtclub) *floor-show* **~nfußboden** m *deal floor* **~nkopf** m *mutule*

di|elektrisch a *di|electric* (⟨a.⟩ D–ikum [n])

d·ielen vt [h] (Fußboden) *to board; plank* ‖ (Raum) *floor*

d·ienen vi [h] **I.** [abs] **A.** (P) **1.** *to be a servant; to serve* (in *in*); als Magd ~ *to serve as a maid*; ~ bei jdm *to be in a p's service* (od *employ*) ‖ um Geld ~ *to work for money* **2.** ⟨mil⟩ *to be a soldier* od *a sailor; to serve one's time; to serve* (in *in a regiment, in the navy*); von der Pike auf ~ *to rise from the ranks*; er dient bei den Husaren *he serves with the hussars* **B.** (S) **1. ~ als** *to serve as* od *for*; das Haus dient als Museum *the house serves as* od *for museum*; der Katalog dient als Einführung *the catalogue is by way of introduction* (f *to*); ein Gekritzel diente als Unterschrift *a scrawl did duty for a signature* **2.** ⟨com⟩ **damit** kann ich leider nicht ~ *I am sorry we don't keep that in stock* ‖ damit ist mir nicht gedient *that is of no use to me* **3. ~ zu etw** *to serve for a th*; zum Vorwand ~ *to serve as a pretext*; zur Zierde ~ *to serve for decoration* ‖ wozu dient dies? *what purpose does this serve? what is the use of this? what is that for?* ‖ dazu ~ z tun *to serve* (od *go*) *to do*; dies dient dazu, das Ganze z stützen *this serves* od *goes to support the whole* **II.** jdm, e–r S ~ **A.** (P) **jdm ~ 1.** *to serve a p*; s–m Vaterlande ~ *to serve one's country*; ⟨bib⟩ niemand kann zween Herren ~ *nobody can serve two masters* **2.** (helfen) *to assist, to help a p*; jdm ~ mit etw *to be of use to a p with a th; to oblige* (od *interest*) *a p with a th*; ⟨com⟩ womit kann ich Ihnen ~? *what can I do for you?* wir können Ihnen nicht ~ in .. *we cannot oblige you in ..*; Ihnen z ~! *Yes, Sir; at your service, Sir* **B.** (S) **1.** den Bedürfnissen jds ~ *to minister to* (od *provide for*) *the needs of a p*; der Bildung des Charakters ~ *to go to the formation of character*; den Sinnen ~ *to cater for the senses* ‖ jds Interessen, Zwecken ~ *to serve a p's purpose, interests*; es dient der gegenseitigen Verständigung *it makes for mutual understanding*; welchem Zwecke dient dies? *what is the use of this?* **2. jdm ~ als** *to serve a p as* od *for* (: *this served him for a bed*) **3. jdm in** etw ~ *to be of use to a p in a th* | **jdm zum besten ~** *to conduce to a p's benefit*; jdm z Vorteil, z Ehre ~ *to redound to a p's advantage, credit*; e–m Lande z Vorteil ~ *to redound to the advantage of a country* ‖ laß dir sies z Warnung ~ *let this be a warning to you*

D·iener m ~s/~ **A.** (P) **1.** *(man-)servant, footman* ‖ *attendant; subordinate* ‖ (neben dem Kutscher) *tiger* ‖ hochherrschaftlicher~ *gentleman's gentleman* ‖ ⟨univ⟩ (College≗) ⟨Oxf⟩ *scout*; ⟨Cambr⟩ *gyp*; ⟨Trin. Coll. Dublin⟩ *skip* ‖ (im Brief) (Ihr) gehorsamer ~ *Your obedient servant*; ich bleibe Ihr g. ~ *I beg (leave) to remain Your o.s.* ‖ Ihr ~! *your servant, Sir!* **2.** *official*; ~ des Staates *servant of the state* ‖ ~ Gottes *divine*; *(humble) servant of God*; ~ des göttlichen Willens *minister of the Divine Will* ‖ ein ~ der Kunst, der Gemeinschaft *a servant of art, of the public*; ~ des Volkes *public servant*; → ~in **B. 1.** (Verbeugung) *(deep) bow* (vor *to a p*); *curts(e)y, reverence*; e–n ~ m vor jdm *to drop* od *make a curts(e)y to a p; to bow* od *curts(e)y to a p* (bis auf den Boden *to the ground*) **2.** stummer ~ (Tisch) *dumb-waiter* **D·ienerin** f ~/~nen **1.** *(maid-)servant; female attendant* ‖ ~, die im Hause etc schläft *sleep-in servant* **2.** ⟨übtr⟩ *handmaid(en)* (*of politics, virtue*)

d·ienern vi [h] ~ u buckeln *to bow and scrape*

D·ienerschaft f ~/ *servants, domestics* ‖ *attendants* [pl]; → Gefolge

d·ienlich a *helpful, serviceable; subservient; useful* (f *to ap*); jdm ~ s *to be helpful to a p*; e–r S ~ s *to subserve a th* ‖ in der S (nicht) ~ s *to be of (no) help in this matter*; .. nicht .. *not to be of any use in the matter* ‖ es f ~ halten *to think fit (to do)* | **≗keit** f ~/ *helpfulness, serviceableness, subservience (–cy), usefulness, expediency*

Dienst m ~es/~e **I.** (**~ als Pflicht, Beruf**) **A.** (Zustand) **1.** (häuslicher ~) *service, employ* ‖ im ~ s *to be in service*; bei jdm im ~ stehen *to be in a p's service* (od *employ*); in ~ treten *to go into* (od *out to*) *service*; bei jdm in ~ treten, in jds ~ treten *to take service with a p, to engage o.s. to a p, to enter a p's service* ‖ **~ tun als** *to function as* ‖ e–n ~ antreten *to take up* (od *enter upon*) *one's duties; to take up a position*; jdn in ~ nehmen *to take a p into service*; den ~ verlassen *to leave service* ‖ nicht mehr im ~ s *to have retired* ‖ → Beruf; Stellung **2. a.** *attendance* (bei jdm *upon a p*); vom ~ befreit *released from attendance*; im ~ s bei jdm *to be attendant (up)on a p* ‖ (~ bei Hof) *waiting*; im ~, vom ~ *in waiting*; ~ h *to be in waiting*; Kammerherr vom ~ *lord-in-waiting* **b.** ⟨com⟩ *attendance* (an jdm *upon a p*) **3.** (öffentlicher ~) *public utility* **a.** Staats≗ *the Civil Service*; im Staats≗ stehen *to be in the C. S.* ‖ in preußischen ~en *in the Prussian Service* **b.** ⟨mar, mil & aero⟩ Heeres≗, Militär≗ *military service*; Marine≗ *naval service* **c.** (~ zur Erhaltung öffentl. Einrichtungen) Eisenbahn≗ *railway service*; Nachrichten≗ *news service*; Presse≗ *press service*; Telephon≗ *telephone service*; → drahtlos **d. aus** dem ~ entlassen w *to be dismissed the service* ‖ jdn s–s ~es entheben *to suspend a p* ‖ (P) außer ~ stellen *to inactivate* ⟨bes mil⟩ ‖ (Schiff) **außer** ~ stellen *to put (a ship) out of commission; to dehumidify, to scrap (a ship)* ‖ (Schiff [wieder]) **in** ~ stellen *to put (a ship) in commission, to [re]commission (a ship)* ‖ (of ship) in ~ stellen [vi] *to commission*; die 'Scharnhorst' stellte in ~ *the 'Scharnhorst' commissioned*; im ~ e–r guten S stehen *to serve* (od *to be devoted to*) *a good cause*; sich in den ~ e–r S stellen *to devote o.s. to a th* **B.** (**einzelne ~leistung**) **1.** ⟨hist⟩ Feudal≗ *feudal service*; Ritter≗ *knight('s) service* | ~ **an** der Gemeinschaft *community service* | niedrige ~e verrichten *to fetch and carry* (f *for*) **2.** ⟨a. mil⟩ *service, duty* ‖ der ~ bei der Fahne *the service with the colours* ‖ im aktiven ~ *on active service* od *list* ‖ im ~ s, ~ h *to be on duty*; nicht im ~ s, k–n ~ h *to be off duty*; Offizier vom ~ *officer of the day, orderly officer* ‖ Major außer ~ *half-pay major; major on half-pay*; Offizier außer ~ *retired* (od *unattached*) *officer* jdn außer ~ stellen *to retire a p, to place a p on half-pay* (od *on the retired list*) ‖ ~e nehmen *to take service; to enlist; to enter the army* ‖ ⟨mar⟩ ~ tun als *to ship as ..* ‖ **zum** ~ antreten ⟨mil⟩ *to report for duty* **3.** ⟨übtr⟩ *function, office, service*; die Augen versagen ihren ~ *the eyes refuse their office* **II.** (**freiwilliger ~**) **1.** *service, turn; office*; ⟨ec & rel⟩ *ministry* (an *to a p*) ‖ guter, nützlicher ~ *a yeoman('s) service*; gute ~e *kind offices*; jdm e–n gr ~ erweisen, leisten, tun *to do* od *render a p a great service, to do a p a good turn*; jdm e–n schlechten ~ erweisen *to do a p a (grave) disservice, to disserve a p* ‖ ~e, die er der Wissenschaft geleistet hat *his services to the cause of learning* **2. jdm zu ~en stehen** (P) *to be at a p's service* (od *command, disposal*); er steht immer z ~en *he is always at command* | (S) was steht Ihnen z ~en? *what is your pleasure? what can I do for you?* schöne Worte standen ihr z ~en *fine words were her pleasure*; jedes Buch steht Ihnen gern z ~en *you are welcome to any book*;

any book is at your disposal | stets gerne zu Ihren ~en *assuring you of our best attention* (od *of our desire to be of every assistance) at all times*; *we assure you of our best services at all time* **III.** ⟨übtr arch⟩ (Halbsäule) *respond*; *attached* od *imbedded shaft*

D·ienst- **~alter** n *seniority*; nach dem ~ *by s.*; (⟨bes Am & mil⟩ & jüngeres ~) *longevity* N | ~sgrenze [f] *age limit* | ~sliste [f] *seniority roll* **⁓älter, ⁓ältest** a *senior* (*lieutenant*); der ~e *the senior* **~anruf** m *official call* **~anschluß** m *official telephone* **~antritt** m *entrance into* (od *upon*) *an office, assumption of office* **~anweisung** f *service directives* od *instructions* pl **~anzug** m ⟨mil etc⟩ *service dress*; gr ~ *dress uniform* **~aufsicht** f ⟨mil⟩ *command supervision* **~auszeichnung** f ⟨Ger mil⟩ *decoration in recognition of services in the army* **⁓beflissen** a *assiduous in office*; *conscientious*;. *full of zeal*; (übertrieben ~) (*over*)*eager*, (*over*)*fervent*, (*over*)*zealons in one's duty*; *officious* | [adv] ~ um jdn herumtanzen *to dance attendance upon a p* **~beflissenheit** f *assiduity* od *zealousness in office* **~bereich** m *competence, competency*; *sphere of duty* **⁓bereit** a *obliging*; → dienstfertig **~beschädigung** f *accident incurred while on duty* **~bezüge** m [pl] = Diensteinkommen **~bote** m *servant, demostic*; *domestic servant* || ⟨Am⟩ *help*; *hired woman* od *girl* | ~ntreppe [f] *back-stairs* **~dolch** m ⟨mar etc⟩ *cutlass* **~eid** m *oath of office*; den ~ ablegen *to be sworn in* **~eifer** m (*professional*) *zeal*; *obligingness*; (übertriebener) *officiousness* **⁓eifrig** a *full of zeal*; *zealous, eager* **~eingang** m (P) *service entrance* **~einkommen** n *official income*; *salary* **~einteilung** f ⟨mil⟩ *roster* **~eintritt** m *entry into service*; frühester ~ 1. Mai *available May 1st at the earliest* **~enthebung, ~entlassung** f *dismissal* (*from service* od *office*); vorläufige –enth. *suspension* **⁓fähig** a ⟨mil⟩ *fit for military service*; *effective*; ~er Soldat *effective* **~fähigkeit** f *fitness for m. s.* **~fanatiker** m *servicey fellow* **⁓fanatisch** a *servicey* **⁓fertig** a *obliging, serviceable*; übertrieben ~ *officious* **~fertigkeit** f *obligingness*; (übertriebene) *officiousness* **⁓frei** a *exempt* od *released from attendance* od *service*; ⟨mil⟩ ~ s *to be off duty* || ~ nehmen *to take time off* || ~e Zeit ⟨mil⟩ *silent hours* **~gebrauch** m: nur f den ~ *for official use only*; *restricted, "private document"* **~geheimnis** n *secrecy* **~gespräch** n ⟨telph⟩ *service* od *official call* **~gewicht** n ⟨rail, mot⟩ *weight in working order* (*of vehicle*) **~gipfelhöhe** f ⟨aero⟩ *service* od *operational ceiling* **~grad** m ⟨mil⟩ *rank* (→ Charge); ~ e–s Generals *rank of general*; Mannschafts⁓ *rank of private* | ~abzeichen [n pl] *insignia* pl *of grade* od *rank* **⁓habend** a ⟨mil⟩ *duty* [attr]; *on duty* || (bei Hof) *in waiting* **~herr** m ⟨hist⟩ (*feudal*) *lord* || (Arbeitgeber) *employer, master, principal*; ⟨sl⟩ *boss* **~jahr** n ⟨com (mil)⟩ *year of* (*active*) *service*; besoldungsmäßig anrechnungsfähige ~e *pay-service creditable* **~kleidung** f (f Diener) *livery* || ⟨mil etc⟩ *uniform* → Dienstanzug **~lehen** n ⟨engl⟩ *soc(c)age* **⁓leistend** a *rendering service, s.-r.* **~leistung** f *service*; *office* || kl~en *odd jobs* [pl] | **~s-** *service* ~betriebe [m pl] *s. industries*; ~gewerbe [n] *s. trade*; ~verkehr m *supply of s.s* **~leitung** f ⟨telph⟩ [konkr] *order wire* **~leute** [pl] ⟨hist⟩ *feudatories, retainers, vassals* [pl] || (Dienerschaft) *servants* [pl] → Dienstmann **~liste** f ⟨mil⟩ *roster* **~lohn** m (*servants'*) *hire, wage*[*s* pl] **~mädchen** n, **~magd** f *maid-servant, servant-girl* (od *maid*), *help*; ⟨cont & fam⟩ *skivvy*; ⟨Am⟩ *hired girl* **~mann** m ⟨rail etc⟩ *commissionaire* (Fr), (*railway-, street-*) *porter*; *messenger*; ⟨hist⟩ *ticket-porter* **~miete** f = Dienstvertrag **~mütze** f ⟨mil⟩ *service cap* **~ordnung** f *labour* (od *staff, official*) *regulations* [pl] **~personal** n *domestics* [pl] || *menial staff*; *personnel, staff* **~pferd** n *troop horse* **~pflicht** f ⟨mil⟩ allgemeine ~ *universal compulsory military service*; *conscription*; ⟨Am⟩ *draft* || ⟨engl⟩ *liability to national service*; *compulsory military training* (*1939*); ~gesetzesvorlage *Military Training Bill* (*1939*) | ~en [pl] ⟨allg⟩ *job duties* **⁓pflichtig** a ⟨mil⟩ *liable* od *subject to conscription*; ⟨engl⟩ *liable to national service* || im ~en Alter s ⟨mil⟩ *to be of military age* **~pflichtige** [der ~, ein ~r] ⟨mil⟩ *conscript* || ⟨engl⟩ *trainee* **~plan** m ⟨mil⟩ *roster* **~platz** m ⟨theat⟩ *house seat* **~prämie** f *service bonus* **~rang** m *rating* **~reise** f *official tour* **~rock** m ⟨mil⟩ *field service jacket* **~sache** f *official business* (od *matter*) || ⟨engl⟩ (auf Briefen) *On Her, His Majesty's Service* (abbr *O.H.M.S.*); ⟨Ger, Am⟩ *Official Business* **~siegel** n *official stamp* || *official seal* °**~spritze** f ⟨vulg⟩ *slummy, skivvy, slavey*; → ~mädchen **~spruch** m ⟨telph etc⟩ *service message* **~stelle** f *office* (in jeder ~ *at every o.*); *branch*; *agency* **~stellung** f *appointment* **~stempel** m *official stamp* **~strafrecht** n *disciplinary law* **⁓strafrechtlich** a *disciplinary* **~stunden** f [pl] *office-hours* [pl], *hours* [pl] *of attendance*; *duty hours*; *business hours* **⁓tauglich** a ⟨mil⟩ = dienstfähig **⁓tuend** a ⟨mil⟩ *on duty*; *orderly* (*officer*) || ~er Kammerherr *lord-in-waiting* || → amtieren **~übergabe** f *handing over of duty* ⟨a. mil⟩ **⁓unfähig** a ⟨mil⟩ *unfit for military service*, .. *for duty*; → kriegsbeschädigt; Invalide **~unfähigkeit** f ⟨mil⟩ *unfitness for military service* **⁓untauglich** = dienstunfähig **~vergehen** n *official misdemeanour*; *disciplinary offence* **~verhältnis** n (*domestic*) *service* **~vernachlässigung** f *neglect of duty* **~verpflichtete(r** m) f *commandeered p* || ⁓ Arbeitskräfte [f pl] *requisitioned labour* **~verpflichtung** f *conscription*; (ins Amt) *installation* **~verrichtung** f *function* **~vertrag** m *contract of service* **~vorschrift** f ~en [pl] *rules* [pl] *of the service, official service publication* **~weg** m *official way* (od *channels* [pl]) || auf dem ~ (abbr a.d.D.) *through official*(*s* od *o. channels*); *officially* **~widrig** a *contrary to rules and regulations* **⁓willig** a = dienstbereit **~wohnung** f *official residence* **~zeit** f *length of service*; *seniority*; s–e ~ abdienen *to serve one's time* **~zeugnis** n ⟨mil⟩ → Führungszeugnis **~zulage** f *allowance for special duty*

D·ienstag m ~(e)s/~e *Tuesday*; [→ Montag]

d·ienstbar a **1.** jdm ~ s *to be subservient to a p*; *to be dependent on a p* || (S) e–r S ~ s *to be in service to a th*; e–r S ~ w *to go into service to a th* | (jdn) ~ m *to sway* (e–r S *to a th*) | **sich** [dat] **jdn ~ m** *to make a p subservient to o.s.*; natürliche Prozesse menschlichen Bedürfnissen ~ m *to bend natural processes to man's needs* **2.** [attr] ~er Geist *ministering angel*; ⟨übtr⟩ *domestic*; *servant, maid* | **⁓keit** f ~/ *bondage, subjection, servitude* || ⟨jur⟩ (Servitut) *easement*; ⟨Scot⟩ *servitude*

d·ienstlich 1. a *official* (*duties*) **2.** adv *officially*; ~ verhindert s *to be detained by official duties*

dies [pron dem, n, abs] *this* **A.** [nom] **1.** [ohne pl] ~ oder das? *this or that*?; v diesem od jenem *of this or that* || ~ mag s *this may be* || ~ war vor Jahren *this was years ago* || ~ alles *all this*; aus all diesem (*or* allem diesen, diesem allen) *from all this* **2.** [hinweisend auf folg. Subst] *this* [pl *these*]; ~ ist mein Sohn *this is my son*; ~ sind m–e Söhne *these are my sons* || ~ ist ein prachtvoller Raum *a beautiful room this* || (daß ihr Vater .., daß ihre Mutter ..,) ~ war nicht ihre S (..) *this was not their business* | ~ ist die Lage *here is the situation* | **B.** [acc] ~ liebe ich *this is what I like*; gut, ~ gebe ich zu *all right, I give you this* | ~ od gar nichts nehmen *to take Hobson's choice* || (sie drehte sich um) u wie sie ~ tat, sprach er

|| *and as she did so he spoke* **d·iesbezüglich** a *referring* (od *relating, pertinent*) *to this*; *corresponding, relevant*; in ~em Sinne *in the relevant sense*; Ihre ~e Entscheidung *your decision in this connection* od *matter*

D·iesel- ~antrieb m *Diesel propulsion*; mit ~ *D.-powered* **~betrieb** m *compression ignition*; Umstellung auf ~ *dieselization*; auf ~ umstellen *to dieselize* **~elektrisch** a *D.-electric*, ⟨Am⟩ *oil--electric* (Antrieb *drive*) **~kraftstoff** m *D. fuel--oil* **~motor** m (nach R. Diesel, † 1913) *Diesel* (od *compression-ignition*) *engine* **~(öl)** n *Diesel oil* **~-Pkw** m *Diesel engined passenger car* **~triebwagen** m *D. rail-car* **~zugmaschine** f *D. tractor*

d·ieser (d·iese, d·ieses *or* dies) [pron dem] **I.** [abs] **1.** (P) *this one, the latter*; diese [pl] *these ones* [pl], *the latter*; ~ u jener *this one and that one*; ⟨fam⟩ = der Teufel **2.** (S) *this, the latter*; diese [pl] *these*; *the latter*; ~ hier *this one*; diese [pl] hier *these ones* [pl]; ich habe diesen (sc Hut) diese [pl] (sc Hüte) viel lieber *I like this, these much better*; ist es dies (sc Buch)? *is this it?* | [ell] am vierten (*or* den vierten) dieses (sc Monats) *the fourth instant* || ⟨com⟩ bei Empfang dieses *on receipt of the present*; Schreiber dieses *the present writer*; *the undersigned* || Überbringer dieses (sc Briefes) *the bearer* **II.** [a] **1.** *this* (*man*); *that* (*man*); diese Leute *these people* || dieses (dies) e–e Mal *this once* || dieses nämliche Buch *this same book*; an diesem selben Tage *this very day* || ~ Morris! *that Morris*! || diese Ihre Heirat *this marriage of yours*; diese s–e Bemerkungen (*or* diese B. v ihm) *these remarks of his* **2.** (gegenwärtig) dieses Jahr *this year*; diese drei Wochen *these* (od *this*) *three weeks* || dieser [gen] Tage *one of these days*

†**d·ieserhalb** adv *for this, on account of this*

d·iesig a *hazy* (*weather*), *misty* || ~ w *to haze*; (Wetter) ~ m *to haze*

d·iesjährig a *of this year*; *this year's*; das ~e Festspiel *this y.'s festival, the festival of this year*

d·iesmal adv *this once* (od *time*, **bout*); f ~ *for this once* (od *time*); genug f ~ *enough for now*

d·iesmalig a *happening this once*

d·iesseit prep = diesseits 2.

d·iesseitig a **1.** das ~e Ufer des Flusses *this side of the river*; auf dem ~en U. des Flusses *on this side* (*of*) *the river* || die ~en Gebäude *the buildings on this side* **2.** ⟨übtr⟩ *secular*; *terrestrial, worldly*; die ~e Welt *this world* | ≃**keit** f ⟨übtr⟩ *secularity*; *worldliness*

d·iesseits 1. [adv] *on this side* **2.** [prep] ~ des Kanals (*on*) *this side* (*of*) *the Channel* **3.** ≃ n *this* (od *the present*) *world* **~ gerichtet** a *this-wordly*; *worldly* (*people*), *worldly-minded*

D·ietrich m ~(e)s/~e *picklock, false* (od *skeleton*) *key*; ⟨sl⟩ *dub, jenny, bitty*; ein Schloß mit dem ~ öffnen *to pick a lock* **d·ietrichen** vi *to use a p.*, etc.

D·ietwart m ~(e)s/~e *guardian* (od *protector*) *of national customs, sports, and life in general*

diew·eil 1. †adv = inzwischen **2.** conj **a.** *as* (od *so*) *long as*; = während **b.** (weil) *because* || (Kanzleistil) ⟨off⟩ all ~ *whereas*

Diffamati·on f *defamation* **diffam·ieren** vt [h] (jdn) *to defame* **Diffam·ierung** f = Diffamation

differenti·al 1. a *differential* **2.** ≃ n ~s/~e *differential* || ⟨com⟩ *increment*

Differenti·al- [in comp] ⟨bes math⟩ *differential* **~bremse** f *d.l brake* **~flaschenzug** m *d.l pulley* **~getriebe** n *d.l gear*; *d.l* **~gleichung** f ⟨math⟩ *d.l equation* **~koeffizient** m ⟨math⟩ *d.l coefficient*; *derivative* **~quotient** m ⟨math⟩ *d.l quotient* **~rechnung** f ⟨math⟩ *d.l calculus*; *the calculus*; *method of fluctuations* **~schraube** f *d.l* od *Hunter's screw* **~sperre** f *lock of d.l* **~tarif** m *d.l tariff*; ⟨com⟩ *load-rate tariff* **~zoll** m *d.l duty*

Differ·enz f ~/~en **1.** *difference* (: *a d. of £ 10*); *the spread* (*between two prices*) || (Rest) *balance*; *residual* || sich in die ~ teilen *to split the difference* **2.** (Uneinigkeit) *difference*; *disagreement, dissension, dispute* || ~en h *to have differences*; e–e ~ beilegen *to adjust* od *settle a difference* **~betrag** m = Differenz **~geschäft** n ⟨st exch⟩ *spot and forward exchange deal with a margin* || *option* **~handel** m ⟨com⟩ *speculation in differences*; = Differenzgeschäft **~methode** f ⟨demog⟩ *calculus of finite differences* **~ton** m ⟨mus⟩ *difference* (od *differential*)*-tone* **~zoll** m = Differentialzoll

differenz·ieren vt [h] ⟨a. math⟩ (etw) *to differentiate* || –iert *distinctive* ⟨a. mus⟩ || **sich ~** *to be differentiated, to differentiate* **Differenz·ierung** f *differentiation*

differ·ieren vi [h] *to differ* (v jdm *from a p*)

diffiz·il a *difficult*; *delicate*; = heikel

diffund·iren vi [h & s] *to diffuse, transpire, permeate* (durch *through*); in–n–a ~ *to inter-diffuse*

diff·us a *diffuse* **Diffusi·on** f ⟨chem⟩ *diffusion* || ~ schneller Neutronen ⟨at⟩ *fast diffusion* ≃**sfest** a ⟨phys⟩ *fast to d., nondiffusing* **~skreis** m ⟨opt⟩ *circle of confusion* **~svermögen** n ⟨opt⟩ *diffusivity, diffusibility*

ˣ**d·ifteln** vi [h] = tüfteln

Dig·amma n ~s/~(s) (Gr) *digamma*

Dig·esten [pl] ⟨jur⟩ die ~ *the Digest, the Pandects* [pl]

diger·ieren vt [h] ⟨chem⟩ (auflösen) *to digest*

Digesti·on f ⟨chem⟩ *digestion*

Digit·al- ~rechner m *digital computer*

Digital·in n ~s/ ⟨med⟩ *digitalin* **Digit·alis** f ~/ ⟨bot & med⟩ *digitalis* (L)

Dignit·ar m ⟨R. C.⟩ *dignitary*

dig·yn a ⟨bot⟩ *digynous*

Dihybr·ide [der ~, ein ~r] m, die ~ f ⟨biol⟩ *dihybrid*

Dij·on [di'ʒɔ̃] n ⟨Fr⟩ (Stadt) *Dijon*

D·ikabrot n *dika-bread* **D·ikafett** n *dika-fat*

dikl·in, dikl·inisch a ⟨bot⟩ *diclinous* **Dikot·yle, Dikotyled·one** f ⟨bot⟩ *dicotyledon*

Diktaph·on® n ~s/~e *dictaphone* (*magnetic disc dictation machine*), *magnetic dictation disc* (od *tape*) *equipment*

Dikt·at n ~s/~e **1.** (Befehl) *dictate*; *dictation* (gemäß jds ~ *at a p's d.*) || das ~ v Versailles *the dictated* od *dictatorial treaty of V.* **2.** (Nachgeschriebenes) *dictation*; ~ (*or* nach ~) schreiben *to write from dictation* || ~ bitte! *take down, please*! **~aufnahme** f ⟨steno⟩ *taking dictation, take* **~zeichen** n pl *reference initials* **Dikt·ator** m ~s/–tat·oren *dictator* **diktat·orisch 1.** a *dictatorial*; **2.** adv *dictatorially* **Diktat·ur** f *dictatorship*; die ~ des Proletariats *the d. of the proletariat*

Dikt·ier- ~apparat m, **~maschine** f *dictating machine*; *dictaphone*; ⟨Am⟩ *voicewriter, voice recorder*; *dictograph*

dikt·ieren vt/i [h] **I.** vt **1.** (auferlegen) (etw) *to dictate* (jdm *to a p*) **2.** (Brief) *to dictate* (jdm *to a p*) **II.** vi **1.** jdm ~ *to d. to a p* **2.** *to d. letters*

Dikti·on f ~/~en *diction* (: *poetic d.*); *style*

Diktogr·aph m ~en/~en (f weite Entfernungen) *dictograph*

D·iktum n [L] ~s/Dikta *dictum* [L] [pl *dicta*]

Dilatom·eter n *dilatometer* **d–t·orisch** a *dilatory*

Dil·emma n ~s/~s *dilemma*, ⟨fam⟩ *fix* || *crux*

Dilett·ant m ~en/~en *layman, amateur* || ⟨sport sl⟩ *rabbit* ≃**enhaft,** ≃**isch** a *amateurish*; *dilettante* **~entum** n ~s/ = **Dilettant·ismus** m *dilettantism, amateurism, amateurishness*

D·ill m ~(e)s/~e, [österr] ⟨a.⟩ **D·ille** f ~/~n ⟨bot⟩ *dill*

Dill·enie [–iə] ⟨bot⟩ *dilleniad*; Gattung ~ *Dillenia* || ~ngewächse [pl] *Dilleniaceae* [L pl]

diluvi·al a ⟨geol⟩ *diluvial*; ≗-Zeit *diluvial epoch* **Dil·uvium** n [L] ∼s/ ⟨geol, obs⟩ *diluvium* [L], *pleistocene*, → -zän

Dimensi·on f ∼/∼en ⟨a. math & phys⟩ *dimension* ‖ ⟨übtr⟩ [mst pl] ∼en *dimensions, proportions* [pl]; v gr ∼en *of great d.*, gr ∼en annehmen *to increase in extension* **dimension·al** a *dimensional*; drei∼ *three-dimensional*

D·imeter m ∼s/∼ ⟨pros⟩ *dimeter*

Dimeth·yl- [in chem comp] *dimethyl-* **∼anil·in** n *dimethylaniline*

Diminu·endo adv ⟨mus⟩ *diminuendo* **Diminut·iv** n ∼s/∼e ⟨gram⟩ *diminutive*

Dimissi·on f *dismissal* ‖ → Entlassung

dimitt·ieren vt/i [h] **1.** vt (jdn) *to dismiss* ‖ *to exclude* **2.** vi *to resign*

dim·orph a *dimorphic, dimorphous* **Dimorph·ismus** m *dimorphism*

DIN- (abbr = Deutsche Industrie-Normung) **∼format** n ⟨Ger⟩ *normalized size of writing paper*, etc. (DIN A 4: 210 × 297 mm)

Din·ar m ∼s/∼e (Währungseinheit in Irak [= 1000 Fils], Jugoslawien [= 100 Para], etc) *dinar*

din·arisch a die ∼e Rasse *the Dinaric Race*

Din·arische Alpen pl *Dinaric Alps* pl

Din·er [di'ne:] n [Fr] ∼s/∼s *dinner (-party)* ‖ jdm ein ∼ verabreichen *to dine a p*

Ding n ∼(e)s/∼e **I.** ⟨hist & †⟩ (Volksversammlung; Gericht) *'thing', judicial assembly*; *legislative council* ‖ ⟨jur⟩ *court of law* ‖ → Storthing; Thing; Thingstätte **II. A. [abstr] 1.** ⟨† jur⟩ *cause* **2.** (Lage) [nur in:] guter ∼e s *to be quite all right, to be in good spirits*; gesund u guter ∼e s *to be alive and kicking*; sei guter ∼e *cheer up* **3.** (Angelegenheit, Sache) **a.** *thing, matter*; das is'n ∼! *that's quite* (od *isn't that*) *something* (?), *that's smashing*; *splendid!*, ⟨sl⟩ *ripping!*; → B. 2. **b.** nach Lage der ∼e *in the circumstances*; das ist ein **ander** ∼ *that's a different thing* ‖ das ist ein ∼ der Unmöglichkeit *that's quite impossible* ‖ alle(r) **guten** ∼e sind drei *all good things come in* od *go by threes* ‖ gut ∼ will Weile h *it takes time to do a th well* ‖ ⟨iron⟩ das sind mir **schöne** ∼e!, was sind das f ∼e! was macht ihr bloß f ∼e? *fine doings these! that's a nice thing* (od *a pretty mess*)! ‖ **jedes** ∼ hat s-e Zeit *there is a time for everthing* ‖ er hat viele ∼e im Kopf *he has many things to think about* | nach Lage der ∼e *in the circumstances*; wie die ∼e **liegen** *as things* od *matters stand*; *in the circumstances*; *in the present state of affairs*; wie die ∼e lagen *as it was* ‖ so (einfach) liegen die ∼e doch nicht *this is not the way to look at the matter* (*things are not so simple as that*) | wir wollen die ∼e beim rechten Namen **nennen** *let's call a spade a spade* (⟨vulg⟩ *some call it a bloody shovel*) ‖ laß den ∼en ihren Lauf *let things slide* | das geht nicht (*or* da geht etw nicht) **mit rechten ∼en** zu *there is sth fishy about it*; *there is some jugglery about it*; *all is not as it should be there*; das ist nicht mit r. ∼en zugegangen *that is due to foul play* ‖ **vor allen ∼en** *above all, first of all, first and foremost*; [nur auf Subjekt *or* Objekt bezüglich] *of all things* (: *unemployment, of all ths, should be the subject of* ..) **4.** ⟨theol⟩ die Lehre v den letzten ∼en *eschatology* **5.** °(= Verbrechen) ein ∼ drehen *to do mischief, to play a trick*; ⟨sl⟩ *to do the trick*; *to do a job, to pull the job* **B. [konkr] 1.** (Gegenstand) das ∼ (⟨cont⟩ ∼s), [pl] die ∼e (⟨cont⟩ ∼er) *thing, object* | ⟨fam⟩ *thing, gadget, contraption*; das ∼(s) da *this th here*, ⟨fam⟩ *that there thing*; ∼e aller Art *things of every description* **2.** ⟨übtr⟩ (P) [pl oft ∼er] *thing, creature*; ein liebes kl ∼ (= Wesen) *a dear little th*; das is'n ∼! *she's a smasher* od *peach*; ein dummes, junges ∼ *a silly, young thing* (od *girl*); ein niedliches kl ∼ *a pretty little thing*; das arme ∼! *poor little thing*! sie ist ein nettes ∼ *she is a decent sort*; niedliche kl ∼er *pretty little things*; die kl ∼er (sc Kinder) *the little tots* [pl]; die süßen ∼er (sc Frauen) *pastry* **3.** ⟨vulg euph sex⟩ *thing(ummy), funny bit, machine* **III.** ⟨philos⟩ das ∼ **an sich** *the thing itself*

d·ingbar a *hir(e)able*

D·ingelchen n ∼s/∼ *little thing*

d·ingen vt/i [dingte & dang / gedingt & gedungen] [h] **1.** vt (Arbeiter, Dienstboten etc) *to hire*; *engage*; *to take on* ‖ (e-n Mörder etc) *to hire*; *bribe* ‖ → chartern **2.** vi = feilschen

D·inger n [pl] → Ding II. B.

D·ingerich m ⟨cont⟩ *fellow*; *customer* ‖ = Dingsda

d·ingfest a [pred] jdn ∼ m *to seize, arrest a p*, *to put a p in prison* **D·inggedicht** n ⟨Lit⟩ *poem picturing a thing*

D·ingi ['diŋgi] n [engl] ∼s/∼s ⟨mar⟩ (kl Beiboot) *dinghy*

d·inglich a ⟨jur⟩ *real*; ∼e Klage *real action*; ∼e Lasten [pl] *real liabilities* [pl]; ∼es Recht *real right* | [adv] ∼ gesicherter Anspruch ⟨jur⟩ *lien*; Zusicherung des Nichtbestehens e-s ∼en [a] Anspruchs *lien covenant*

Dings n ∼/Dinger **1.** *thing*; → Ding II. B. ‖ das obere ∼ *the top thingumajig* **2.** = ∼da, → d. 2. °**∼da 1.** (S) n [nach prep] in ∼ *in Thingamy* (od *Thingumajig*); *in What-do-you-call-it*; *in What's-its-name* **2.** m; Herr ∼ *Mr. Thingamy* (od *Thingummy, Thingumbob*), *Mr. What's-his--name*, ⟨Am⟩ *Mr. Whatdyecallem* °**∼kirchen** = Dingsda

D·ingwelt f *the world of (concrete) things*; *the material world* **D·ingwort** n ⟨gram⟩ = Hauptwort

din·ieren vi [h] *to dine* (mit *with*) ‖ an dem Tisch können 10 Personen ∼ *the table dines ten persons*

Din·itro- [in chem comp] *dinitro-* **∼benz·ol** n *dinitrobenzene*

D·inka [pl] (ägypt. Negervolk) *dinkas* [pl]

D·inkel m ∼s/∼ ⟨bot⟩ *spelt*

Dinoflagell·aten [pl] ⟨zoo⟩ *dinoflagellates* [pl]

Dinos·aurier [-iər] m ∼s/∼ ⟨zoo⟩ *dinosaur*; *iguanodon* **Dinoth·erium** n ∼s/-rien ⟨zoo⟩ *dinothere, dinotherium* **Dinozer·at** m ∼en/∼en ⟨zoo⟩ *dinoceras*

Di·ode f ∼/∼n *diode*

dion·ysisch a *Dionysiac, Dionysian*

Di·opter n ∼s/∼ *diopter*; *vane* ‖ *theodolite* ‖ ⟨phot⟩ *sighting notch*

Dioptr·ie f ⟨opt⟩ *dioptric* **Di·optrik** f ⟨phys⟩ *dioptrics* [pl] **di·optrisch** a *dioptric*

Dior·ama n *diorama*

Dior·it m ∼s/∼e ⟨geol⟩ *diorite, greenstone*

Diosk·uren [pl] ⟨ant⟩ *Dioscuri* [L] [pl] ‖ ⟨astr⟩ *Castor and Pollux*

Diox·id, -yd n ∼s/ ⟨chem⟩ *dioxide*

Diözes·an m ∼en/∼en *diocesan* **Diöz·ese** f ∼/∼n *diocese* (die ∼ N. *the d. of N.*)

Diöz·ie f ⟨bot⟩ *dioecism* **di·özisch** a ⟨bot⟩ *dioecious*

Diphenyl- [in chem comp] *diphonyl* **∼am·in** n *diphenylamine*

Diphther·ie, Diphther·itis f ⟨med⟩ *diphtheria* [L] ‖ des Kehlkopfes → Krupp **diphth·erisch** a *diphtheric, diphtheritic*

Diphth·ong m ∼s/∼e ⟨gram⟩ *diphthong*

diphthong·ieren vt [h] *to diphthongize*

Diphthong·ierung f *diphthongization* **dipth·ongisch** a *diphthongal*

Dipleg·ie f ⟨med⟩ *diplegia* [L]

Diplo- (doppelt, zweifach) [Gr] [in comp] *diplo-* **∼k·okkus** m *diplococcus* [L]

Dipl·om n ∼s/∼e *diploma, charter* ‖ ⟨bes univ⟩ *diploma, certificate* ‖ die Ausstellung e-s

∼s an jdn *the certification of a p* ‖ mit e–m ∼ versehen = ∼- [in comp]

Dipl·om- [in comp] *diplomaed*; *certificated*, ⟨Am⟩ *certified* (*interpreter*, *midwife*); *fully qualified* **∼ingenieur** m *certificated* od *commissioned* (⟨Am⟩ *graduate*[*d*]) *engineer*; *engineer holding a diploma* **∼kaufmann** m *Bachelor of Commerce* **∼prüfung** f *examination conferring the right to hold a diploma*

Diplom·at m ∼en/∼en *diplomat*(*ist*); ∼ v Beruf *diplomatist of career*, ⟨Am⟩ *career man* | ∼enpudding [m] *trifle* **Diplomat·ie** f ∼/ *diplomacy* **Diplom·atik** f ∼/ *diplomatics* [pl] **Diplom·atiker** m ∼s/∼ ⟨übtr⟩ *diplomatist*; *crafty person*, *cunning fox*

diplom·atisch I. a **1.** *diplomatic* ‖ ∼er Dienst *Diplomatic Service*, ∼er Handelsdienst *Commercial Diplomatic S.*; das ∼e Korps *the Diplomatic Corps* (od *Body*); ∼er Schritt *démarche* [Fr]; ∼e Beziehungen aufnehmen *to enter into diplomatic relations* (mit *with*), die ∼en B. abbrechen *to break off d. r.* **2.** ⟨übtr⟩ *diplomatic*; *crafty*, *cunning*; *wily* **II.** adv *diplomatically*

Dipn·oer m ⟨ich⟩ *dipnoan*; Ordnung der ∼ *dipnoi* [Gr]

Dipod·ie f ∼/ ⟨pros⟩ *dipody*

D·ipol m ∼s/∼e *dipole*

×**D·ippel** m ∼s/∼ [südd] = Döbel, Zapfen

°**D·ippelschisser** m ⟨sl⟩ *nit-picker*

d·ippen I. vt/i [h] **1.** vt (untertauchen) *to dip* **2.** vi (= Fahne senken) *to dip the flag* **II.** ∼̂ n ⟨mar⟩ *dipping the flag*; *salute by striking colours*

Dipsakaz·een [pl] ⟨bot⟩ *Dipsacaceae* [L]

Dipsoman·ie f ⟨med⟩ (Trunksucht) *dipsomania*

D·iptam m ∼s/ ⟨bot⟩ **1.** *fraxinella*, *dittany*; *burning-bush* **2.** Kretischer ∼ *dittany* (*of Crete*)

Dipt·eren [pl] ⟨zoo⟩ *Diptera* [L]

D·iptychon n ∼s/–chen ⟨ant⟩ *diptych* **D·iptyk** n ∼s/∼s ⟨mot cust⟩ *diptych* (ausgeben *to issue*)

dir 1. [pron pers] [dat v du] *you* (: *he handed you the letter*); mit ∼ *with you*; wenn es nach ∼ ginge *for all* (od *aught*) *you care* | *to you*; *for you* (: *I bought a book for you*) ‖ ist er ein Freund von ∼? *is he a friend of yours*? ‖ °das ist die schöne Feder von ∼ *that is your fine pen* | ⟨bib, poet & †⟩ *thee*, *to thee* **2.** [pron, refl] [nach prep] *you* | ⟨bib etc⟩ *thee*

dir·ekt 1. a **a.** *direct* (*road*, *route*, *way*) **b.** *direct*, *immediate*, *first-hand* (*information*) **c.** *direct*, *exact* (*opposite*) **d.** ⟨pol⟩ ∼e Aktion *direct action* ‖ ∼e Fahrkarte *through-ticket* ‖ ∼e Lüge *direct lie* ‖ ∼e Rede *direct speech* ‖ ∼e Steuer [f] *direct tax* ‖ ∼er Wagen ⟨rail⟩ *through-carriage* **e.** (unverblümt) s–e Ausdrucksweise ist sehr ∼ *he is very blunt* od *outspoken in his manner of expression* **2.** adv **a.** *direct*; ∼ unmöglich *simply impossible* ‖ ∼ nach Berlin fahren *to go d. to Berlin*; ∼ nach Hause k *to come home right away*; an jdn ∼ schreiben *to write a p direct*; nur ∼ vom Verlag *only from the publishers direct* ‖ *directly*; jdn ∼ ansehen *to look directly at a p* ‖ ∼ hinter *in the wake of* (*a p*; *a ship*) **b.** *directly*, *immediately*, *at first hand*; *without intermediary* **c.** ∼ in die Mitte *plumb in the middle* ‖ ∼ gegen die Bestimmungen handeln *to go flat against orders* ‖ ich sagte das auch ∼ z ihm *I said as much to him* ‖ er sah ihm ∼ in die Augen *he looked him squarely in the eyes* ‖ er sprang ∼ aus dem Fenster *he jumped bang out of the window* ‖ ∼ gegenüber v *straight across from*; jdm ∼ gegenüberstehen *to face a p squarely* ‖ ∼ auf der Haut tragen *to wear next to the skin*

Dir·ekt- ∼aufnahme, ∼sendung, ∼übertragung, ∼wiedergabe f ⟨telv⟩ *on-the-spot pick-up*, *outside* od *live transmission* od *broadcast* **∼verbindung** f ⟨mil, telph, wir⟩ *point-to-point communication*

Direkti·on f ∼/∼en **1.** [abstr] (Leitung) *administration*, *direction*; *management* (*of a th*); unter der ∼ v *under the direction of* **2.** [konkr] *direction*, *body* od *board of directors* od *managers* ‖ *directors' office* ‖ → Direktorium **∼sassistent** m ⟨hot⟩ *assistant-manger* **Direkt·ive** f ∼/∼n *directive rule*; ∼n [pl] *directions*, *instructions*

Dir·ektor m ∼s/Direkt·oren ⟨com⟩ *director*; (of a bank) *governor*; Betriebs∼̂, geschäftsführender ∼ *managing director*, *manager* (: *commercial m.*; *technical m.*); ⟨Am⟩ *president*; General∼̂ *Director-General*; ∼enkonferenz [f] *boardmeeting* ‖ ⟨school⟩ *headmaster*; *principal* ‖ Ministerial∼̂ *chairman of a department* ‖ Theater∼̂ *business manager* ⟨Am⟩ *producer* ‖ ⟨hot⟩ *manager* ‖ Gefängnis∼̂ *governor*; ⟨Am⟩ *warden*

Direktor·at n ∼s/∼e *directory*; *directorship* **direktori·al** a *directorial* **Dir·ektorin** f ⟨school⟩ *headmistress*; *principal*

Direkt·orium n ∼s/–rien [–iən] *directory*, *body of gevernors* od *managers* ‖ ⟨Fr hist⟩ (1795/99) *Directory*, *Directoire* [Fr]

Direktr·ice [–ˈtriːsə] f ∼/∼n *directress*, *directrix* [pl –trices]; *manageress*; ⟨tail⟩ (*female*) *head cutter* (*in clothing factory*)

°**D·irex** m ⟨school⟩ = Direktor

Dirig·ent m ∼en/∼en ⟨mus⟩ *conductor*, *leader*; ⟨theat⟩ *musical director* ‖ ∼enpult [n] *conductor's desk*; ∼enstab [m] *baton* [Fr] ‖ = Leiter ‖ → Besteder

dirig·ieren vt [h] (etw) *to direct*, *manage*; *to be in control of* (*a th*) ‖ ⟨mus⟩ (Orchester etc) *to conduct* | (senden) *to direct*, *forward* (an, nach *to*) **Dirig·ismus** m ∼/ ⟨pol⟩ *dirigism*, *statism*

Dirim·entien [–tsiən] [pl] ⟨jur⟩ *diriment impediments* [pl]

Dirl·itze f ∼/∼n ⟨bot⟩ = Korn·elkirsche

×**Dirndl** n ∼s/∼ *lass*, *lassie*; *girl*; *dirndl* ‖ ⟨bot⟩ [österr] = Korn·elkirsche

D·irne f ∼/∼n **1.** [mst Dirn] *girl*, *lass*; *maid*, *wench*; e–e dralle Dirn *a buxom w.* **2.** (Hure) *woman of pleasure*, *prostitute*, *cocotte* [Fr]; *baggage*, *hussy*, *strumpet*, *trollop*, *trull*; ⟨sl⟩ *bird*; ⟨vulg⟩ *bitch* ‖ Straßen∼̂ *street-walker*, *deadly nightshade*

Dis n ∼/ ⟨mus⟩ *D sharp* ‖ → Des

Dis- [pref] *dis–*

Dis·agio [disˈɑːʒio] n [It] ∼s/ ⟨com⟩ *loss on exchange*; *rate under par*; *discount*; ∼kurs *discount quotation*

Discount- [disˈkaunt] ∼laden [m] *discount store* od *house*

Disfunkti·on f ∼/∼en *malfunction*

Disharmon·ie f ∼/∼n ⟨mus⟩ *disharmony*, *discord*, *discordance*; *dissonance* | ⟨übtr⟩ *discord*, *discordance* **disharmon·ieren** vi [h] *to disharmonize* **disharm·onisch** a *discordant*, *dissonant*, *inharmonious*

D·isis n ⟨mus⟩ *D double sharp*

Disjunkti·on f ⟨log⟩ *disjunction* (z. B. a oder b)

disjunkt·iv a ⟨log & gram⟩ *disjunctive*

Disk·ant m ∼s/∼e ⟨mus⟩ **1.** *treble*, *soprano* **2.** (of a piano) *the treble pitch* **∼sänger** m *treble singer* **∼schlüssel** m *tr. clef* **∼stimme** f *tr. voice*

Disk·ont m ∼s/∼e ⟨com⟩ *discount*, *rebate*; ∼ gewähren *to allow discount* ‖ Reichsbank∼̂ *bank-rate*, den ∼ erhöhen (herabsetzen) *to raise* (*to lower*) *the bank-rate*

Disk·ont- ∼bank m *discount-bank* **∼fuß** m = Diskontsatz **∼geschäft** n ⟨bank⟩ *discounting* (*business*) ‖ (Laden) ⟨bes Am⟩ *discount store*, *cut-price store* **∼kredit** m *discount-credit* **∼makler** m *discount-broker* **∼nehmer** m *discounter* **∼note** f *note of interest* **∼rechnung** f *discount-*

-account; → Diskontnote **~satz** m *bank-rate, rate of discount* **~wechsel** m *bill to be discounted*

diskont·ierbar a *discountable, bankable* **diskon·t·ieren** vt [hl] ⟨com⟩ (Wechsel) *to discount*
Disk·onto n = Diskont

Diskoth·ek f ~/~en *discotheque*

diskredit·ieren vt [h] (jdn) *to discredit*; (etw) *to bring discredit on* (*a th*)

diskrep·ant a *discrepant* **Diskrep·anz** f *discrepancy*

diskr·et I. a **1.** (P) *discreet; judicious; tactful* **2.** *separate* ‖ ⟨math⟩ *discrete* (*quantity*); *discontinuous* **II.** adv *discreetly* **Diskreti·on** f ~/ *discretion, discreetness* ‖ vollste ~ wahren *to preserve strict confidence* **diskretion·är** a *discretionary* (*powers*)

diskrimin·ieren vt [h] (jdn) *to discriminate against* (*a p*) **diskrimin·ierend** a *discriminatory* **Diskrimin·ierung** f *discrimination*

Disk·urs m ~es/~e, *discourse, conversation, talk* **diskurs·iv** a ⟨philos⟩ (Ggs intuitiv) *discursive*

D·iskus m ~/~ *discus; disk, disc* **~werfen** n *throwing the discus* **-werfer** m *thrower of the discus* ‖ ⟨arts⟩ *disk-thrower* **~wurf** m *discus-throw*

Diskussi·on f ~/~en *discussion; debate; argument* ‖ offene ~ *open forum* ‖ z ~ stehend *under discussion*; (etw) z ~ stellen *to invite .. to discuss, to put .. up for discussion*; die Frage wird z ~ gestellt w .. *will come up for discussion*; als Grundlage f weitere ~ *for the sake of argument* ‖ Gegenstand der ~ *matter for discussion* | ~steilnehmer [m] *panellist* **diskut·abel** a *discussible*

diskut·ieren vt/i [h] **1.** vt (etw) *to argue, to discuss, debate* **2.** vi *to argue; debate*; um weiter ~ z können *for the sake of argument* ‖ offen ~ *to air; to bring out into the open*; (e–e Frage) zu Ende ~ *to argue out*; darüber läßt sich ~ *that is worth considering*

Dislokati·on f ~/~en ⟨geol & med⟩ *dislocation*

Disp·ache [dis'paʃə] f [Fr] ⟨mar⟩ *adjustment* (od *statement*) *of average* ‖ die ~ aufnehmen *to make* od *draw up the average statement* ‖ → Schadensberechnung **Dispach·eur** [–'ʃør] m ⟨mar ins⟩ *adjuster* **dispach·ieren** vi [h] *to adjust the average*

dispar·at a *disparate* **Disparit·ät** f *disparity*

Disp·ens m –nses/–nse (⟨ec⟩ f ~/~e) *dispensation*; ~ erteilen *to grant dispensations* (jdm *to a p*); ~ erteilen in .. *to dispense in* ..

Dispensati·on f ~/~en = Dispens **dispens·ieren** vt [h] (jdn) *to dispense* od *excuse* (v *from*)

Dispersi·on f ~/~en *dispersion*

Dispon·enden [pl] *books* [pl] *not sold by the bookseller and placed at the disposal of the publisher*

Dispon·ent m ~en/~en ⟨com⟩ *manager, managing clerk*

dispon·ibel a *available, disposable*

dispon·ieren vi [h] *to make arrangements* ‖ ~ über (etw, jdn) = verfügen; er kann über s–e Zeit frei ~ *his time is his own* **dispon·iert** a gut (schlecht) ~ *well (ill)-disposed,* (*to be*) *in good* (*bad*) *form* ‖ ⟨med⟩ ~ z *susceptive to, liable to* (*a disease*)

Dispositi·on f ~/~en **1.** *disposition, arrangement; order*; s–e ~en treffen *to make one's dispositions* **2.** = Verfügung **3.** (Anlage, Neigung) *disposition* (z *to*) **4.** ⟨a. mil⟩ zur ~ *on half-pay*; jdn z ~ stellen *to reduce* od *put a p on half-pay*; z ~ gestellt *unattached* (od *retired*) (*officer*) **≗sfähig** a ⟨com⟩ *entitled to contract* **~sfonds** m *fund at the disposal of a ministry, etc*

disposit·iv a (maßgebend) *dispositive* (*clause*)

disproportion·iert a *lopsided*

Disp·ut m ~(e)s/~e *dispute* **Disputati·on** f ~/~en *disputation, debate* **disput·ieren** vi [h] *to dispute* (über *on*); *to debate; to argue* (*about*)

Disqualifikati·on f ~/~en *disqualification* **disqualifiz·ieren** vt [h] (jdn) *to disqualify* **D–z·ierung** f (Startverbot) ⟨sport bes mot⟩ *suspension*

Dissertati·on f ~/~en ⟨univ⟩ *dissertation, thesis; treatise*

Dissid·ent m ~en/~en *dissident*; ⟨engl ec⟩ *dissenter, nonconformist*

Dissimilati·on f ~/~en *dissimilation*

Disson·anz f ~/~en ⟨mus⟩ *dissonance* ‖ ⟨übtr⟩ *discordant note*

Dissoziati·on [tsiats] f ⟨a. psych⟩ *dissociation* | ~sgrad [m] *degree of d.* ‖ ⟨el⟩ *coefficient* od *degree of electrolytic d.*

dist·al a *distal*

Dist·anz f ~/~en ⟨mst übtr⟩ *distance*; → Entfernung ‖ ~ bewahren *to condescend* (gegenüber jdm *to a p*); *to keep aloof* (*from a p*); ~ halten *to keep one's distance*

Dist·anz- [in comp] *distance–*; ⟨sport⟩ → Dauer– ‖ **~geschäft** n *d. trade* **~lauf** m ⟨sport⟩ *long-distance run* od *race* **~ritt** m = Dauerritt **~wechsel** m ⟨com⟩ *bill of exchange payable in another town than that in which it was made out*

distanz·ieren vt [h] sich ~ v jdm *to distance a p*; → abrücken **Distanz·iertheit** ~/ *remoteness, detachment*

D·istel f ~/~n ⟨bot⟩ *thistle*; voll v ~n *thistly*; Feld≗ *field-thistle* **~blume** f *thistle-flower* **~falter** m ⟨ent⟩ *painted-lady, nymphalid* **~fink** m ⟨orn⟩ *thistle-finch, goldfinch* **~frucht** f Haarschopf der ~ *thistle down* **~orden** m ⟨Scot⟩ *the Order of the Thistle*

Disth·en m ~s/ ⟨minr⟩ *disthene*

D·istichon n ~s/–chen *distich*

Dist·ickstoffoxid n *nitrous oxide*

distingu·iert [–'giːrt] a *distinguished*

distribut·iv a ⟨math⟩ *distributive*

Distr·ikt m ~(e)s/~e *district; quarter*; ⟨Am⟩ *section*; → Bezirk ‖ Regierungs≗ ⟨Ind⟩ *taluk*

Diszipl·in f ~/~en **1.** (Zucht) *discipline*; auf ~ halten *to enforce d.* **2.** ⟨univ⟩ (Wissenszweig) *branch* od *department of a science* **3.** ⟨ec⟩ *the discipline; mortification*

Disziplin·ar- [in comp] *disciplinary* **~gewalt** f *disciplinary power* **~strafe** f *summary punishment* **~verfahren** n *disciplinary action* (od *proceedings* [pl]) **~vergehen** n *breach of discipline* **~vorgesetzter** m *commanding officer*

disziplin·arisch a *disciplinary* (*punishment*) | adv ~ vorgehen *to take disciplinary action*

disziplin·ieren vt [h] *to discipline* **Diszipli·n·ierung** f ⟨dero⟩ *regimentation* **diszipl·inlos** a *wanting in discipline* **≗igkeit** f *indiscipline, lack of d.*

D·ithmarschen n (Landschaft in Holstein) *Dithmarschen, Ditmarsh*

Dithyr·ambe f ~/~n *dithyramb* **dithyr·ambisch** a *dithyrambic*

d·ito adv *ditto* (abbr do, dto) ‖ ⟨fam⟩ *ditto brother smut!* ‖ 'Du bist ein Lügner.' '~'. ⟨sl⟩ '*You are a liar.*' '*You are another!*' ‖ danke ~ (doppelt *or* mit Zinsen)! *same to you* (*with bells* od *knobs on*)

Diverg·enz f ~/~en *divergence* **diverg·ieren** vi [h] *to diverge* ‖ (Strahlen) ~ l *to diverge*

div·ers a *divers, sundry*

Div·ersa [L], **div·erse** pl ⟨com⟩ *sundries* pl

divide et impera! L *divide and rule!*

Divid·end m ~en/~en ⟨math⟩ *dividend*

Divid·ende f ~/~n ⟨com⟩ **a.** *dividend*; einschließlich ~ *cum d.*; ausschließlich ~ *ex d.* ‖ die Zahlung e–r ~ ankündigen *to declare a dividend* **b.** ⟨ins⟩ *bonus*

Divid·enden- **~ausschüttung** f *payment of dividend* **~berechtigung** f *dividend rights* pl **~bogen** m *coupon-sheet* °**~jauche** f *small-beer,* *bilge-water, legs and arms* (sc *no body*); ⟨sl⟩ *squirt, bilge* **~papier** n *security entitling to dividend* **~schein** m *dividend-warrant* od *coupon* | ~bogen [m] *coupon sheet* **~verteilung** f *distribution of dividend*

Divid·ivi [pl] ⟨bot⟩ *divi-divi*

divid·ieren vt [h] (Zahl) *to divide* (durch *by*), 8 durch 2 ~ *to divide eight by two*

Divinati·on f ~/ *divination* **divinat·orisch** a *prophetic; predictive; visionary*

Divisi·on f ~/~en **1.** ⟨math⟩ *division;* ~saufgabe *sum in division;* ~szeichen *division mark* **2.** ⟨mil⟩ *division;* ~skommandeur *divisional commander*

Div·isor m ~s/ Divis·oren *divisor*

D·iwan m ~s/~e (orient. Empfangssaal; Liedersammlung) *divan* ‖ (Polsterliege) *divan,* ⟨Am⟩ *davenport*

Dnjepr ⟨a.⟩ **Dnieper** m ⟨Russ⟩ (Fluß) *Dnieper*

Dnjestr ⟨a.⟩ **Dniester** m ⟨Russ⟩ (Fluß) *Dniester*

Do n [It] ⟨mus⟩ (= C) *do*

D·öbel m ~s/~ **1.** ⟨tech⟩ (a. Dobel, Dübel) *dowel; peg* (od *pin, plug*) *of wood; tampion* ⟨mar⟩ *tre(e)nail* ‖ (etw) mit e–m ~ befestigen (etc) *to dowel* | ~bohrer [m] *pin drift* **2.** ⟨ich⟩ *chub; alderman*

D·obermann m ⟨zoo Ger⟩ *Dobermann pinscher*

×**D·obostorte** f *eight-layer cake*

Dobr·udscha f die ~ (Rumänien) *the Dobruja*

doch I. adv **A.** [betont] **1.** (dennoch) *yet, nevertheless, notwithstanding,* seltsam u ~ (*or* aber ~) wahr *strange and yet* (od *but yet*) *true;* wenn auch der Stil nicht elegant ist, so ist er ~ korrekt *though not elegant the style is yet correct* ‖ ich werde ~ gehen *I shall go nevertheless* ‖ das Buch ist also ~ nicht hier *the book isn't here after all* ‖ [immer am Ende stehend] *though* (: *human nature is the same now, though*) **2.** [in Entgegnungen] 'Bald wird man nicht mehr wissen, was man malen soll.' 'Oh ~.' '*They soon won't know what to paint.*' '*Oh yes they will.*' ‖ 'Siehst du das nicht ein?' '~.' '*Don't you see that?*' '*Oh yes, I do.*' ‖ ~, ~! *Yes, yes!* **B.** [unbetont] **1. ja ~** *yes to be sure; yes, yes;* hast du's gehört? Ja ~ *do you listen? Yes I do* ‖ **nicht ~**! *no indeed! certainly not! don't!* **2.** [verblaßt] **a.** *surely; indeed, really* ‖ das ist ~ z arg *that's really too bad* ‖ das ist ~ e–e Schande! *if that isn't a shame!* ‖ das müßte ich ~ wissen *surely I should know* ‖ er kann es ~ nicht s *it surely cannot be he* ‖ Sie h ~ gehört ..? *surely you will have heard ..* ‖ Sie wissen ~ .. *you know I suppose* od *hope* ‖ du begleitest uns ~? *surely you'll accompany us* **b.** komm ~ *do come; come, do* ‖ treten Sie ~ bitte näher *do come in, please* ‖ sag mir ~ *just tell me* **c.** (**aber**) ~: er, der ~ ein so unruhiger Mensch war, ertrug es geduldig *he, for so restless a man, was patient of it* ‖ ⟨Am⟩ *sure* (: *last year you sure let him buzz round you plenty*); → aber **d. wenn** ich ~ wüßte ..! *if I only knew ..!* ‖ möchte es ~ wahr s *I would* od *wish it were true* **II.** [conj] **a.** [unbetont] *yet, but, still, however, nevertheless;* der Stil ist nicht elegant, ~ ist er (*or* ~ er ist) korrekt *the style is not elegant yet* (od *but, still,* etc.) *it is correct;* → I. A. 1. **b.** [betont] und d·och .. *yet ..*

D·ocht m ~(e)s/~e (Kerzen≗, Lampen≗) *wick* **~kohle** f ⟨Am⟩ *cored carbon* **~öler** m *w. oiler* **~schmierung** f *w. lubrication* **~schraube** f (e–r Lampe) *w.-rack*

D·ock n ~s/~s ⟨mar⟩ *dock;* → Hafenbecken ‖ in e–m Flusse ~s anlegen *to dockize a river* ‖ aus dem ~ gehen *to leave the dock* ‖ (Schiff) ins ~ bringen *to dock* ‖ ins ~ gehen (of ship) *to* (*go* od *come into*) *dock; to lie up* ‖ Unterbringung im ~ *dockage* | Ausbesserungs≗ *repair-dock* ‖ Schwimm≗ *floating-dock* ‖ Trocken≗n *dry* (od *graving*)*-dock* **~arbeiter** m *docker, docksman;* ⟨bes Am⟩ *longshoreman* **~gebühren** f [pl] *dock--dues* [pl], *dockage* **~hafen** m (Bassin n) *wet dock* **~schein** m *dock-warrant* **~schwelle** f *dock-sill* **~verschlußponton** m *dock-pontoon*

D·ocke f ~/~n **1. a.** ⟨× & †⟩ = Puppe **b.** (Spielzeug) *turned doll of wood.* **c.** *baluster;* ~ngeländer [n] *balustrade; open parapet; baluster railing* **2.** (Maß Garn in Strähnen) *skein, hank;* (Garn) z ~en formen *to skein* **3.** ⟨bot⟩ = Herbstzeitlose

d·ocken vt/i [h] **1.** vt (Schiff) *to dock* **2.** vi (of ships) *to dock*

Dodeka·eder n ~s/~ ⟨math⟩ *dodecahedron*

Dodekan·es m ⟨Gr⟩ (Inselgruppe) *Dodecanese*

D·odo m ~s/~s ⟨orn⟩ (ausgestorb. Taubenvogel) *dodo*

Dogcart ['dɔgkɑ:t] m [engl] ~s/~s *dog-cart*

D·oge ['do:ʒə] m ~n/~n *doge* ‖ Amt *or* Würde e–s ~n *dogate* **~npalast** m *ducal palace*

D·ogge f ~/~n ⟨zoo⟩ ⟨engl⟩ (schwere, plumpe ~) *mastiff;* → Bull≗ ‖ ⟨Ger⟩ (*Great*) *Dane*

D·ogger m ~s/ ⟨geol⟩ *middle strata in the Jurassic system; the oolites* [pl]

D·ogger m ~s/~ ⟨mar⟩ (zweimast. Fischerfahrzeug) *dogger* **~bank** f *the Dogger Bank;* Schlacht an der ~ (24. 1. 1915) *naval battle of the D. B.*

D·ögling m ~s/~e *black species of sperm--whale*

D·ogma n ~s/~men *dogma* ‖ (Lehre) zum ~ erheben *to dogmatize* **Dogm·atik** f ~/ *dogmatics* [pl] [sg konstr] **Dogm·atiker** m ~s/~ *dogmatist*

dogm·atisch 1. a *dogmatic;* in ~er Hinsicht *dogmatically* ‖ *doctrinal* **2.** adv *dogmatically;* ~ erklären *to state d.*

Dogmat·ismus m *dogmatism;* juristischer ~ *legalism* **D·ogmengeschichte** f *history of dogmatic theology*

D·ogskinleder n [engl] *dog-skin*

D·ohle f ~/~n ⟨orn⟩ (*jack*)*daw* | → Dole

°**Döhnchen** n *joke, fun; funny story*

D·ohne f ~/~n (Schlinge) *springe; gin, noose, snare;* e–e ~ aufstellen *to set a springe;* (Tier) in e–r ~ fangen *to noose, to springe* **~nstieg, ~nstrich** m *line* od *series of springes*

d·oktern vi [h] *to doctor;* an jdm (herum)~ *to doctor a p* (*up*)

D·oktor m ~s/–t·oren (abbr Dr.) **1.** ⟨univ⟩ (Titel, akad. Grad) **a.** *doctor* (abbr. *D.;* vor Namen *Dr.*); (f Frauen) *woman* (od *lady*)*--doctor; doctress* ‖ Anrede: ⟨Ger⟩ Herr (~) N., ⟨engl mst⟩ *Mr. N.,* ⟨Am immer⟩ *doctor;* → 1. c. ‖ ~ der Medicin (Dr. med.) *Doctor of Medicine* (*M. D.*); ~ der Naturwissenschaften (Dr. rer. nat.) *D. of Science* (*D. Sc.*); ~ der Rechte (Dr. jur.) *D. of Laws* (*LL. D.*); ~ der Theologie (Dr. theol.) *D. of Divinity* (*D. D.*); ~ der Philosophie (Dr. phil.) *D. of Philosophy* (*D. Ph.* od *Ph. D.*); ~ der Literaturwissenschaften *D. of Literature* (*D. Lit.*) ‖ → Backalaureus, Magister **b.** jdn als ~ anreden *to doctor a p* ‖ jdn z ~ m *to confer the degree of doctor on a p* ‖ den ~ m (*or* °bauen), ~ w *to take one's* (od *obtain the*) *degree of doctor;* er hat s–n ~ in Marburg gemacht *he got his doctor's degree at M.* **c.** Herr ~ N. *Dr. N.* ‖ Sehr geehrter Herr ~! S. g. H. Dr. N.!; Lieber Herr ~! *Dear Doctor,* → 1. a.: *Dear Mr. N.* **2.** °(= Arzt) (*the*) *doctor;* unser ~ *our medical man;* den ~ holen, zum ~ schicken *to send for the doctor* ‖ die Frau ~ (Gattin e–s ~s) ⟨mst⟩ Frau N. *the doctor's wife* **~arbeit** f *thesis* (*for the doctor's degree*) **~diplom** n *doctor's diploma* **~examen** n *examination for a doctor's degree* **~grad** m *degree of doctor, doctor's degree, doctorate* **~hut** m *doctor's cap* ‖ = Doktorwürde; ⟨engl⟩ *the hood;* den ~ erwerben *to* receive the hood ~**rechnung** f doctor's bill ~**titel** m doctor's degree; → Doktorwürde ~**vater** m ⟨Ger⟩ supervisor ~**würde** f doctorate, doctorship; status od dignity of a doctor; → Doktorgrad ‖ jdm die ~ verleihen to confer the degree of doctor on a p ‖ die ~ erhalten, erwerben = den Doktor m; → Doktor

Doktor·and m ~en/~en doctorand; candidate for a doctor's degree **Doktor·at** n ~(e)s/ = Doktorwürde **doktor·ieren** vi [h] to take one's degree, to obtein the degree of doctor

Doktr·in f ~/~en doctrine; (racial) creeds [pl] ‖ ⟨Am⟩ Monroe≃ Monroe doctrine **Doktrin·är** m doctrinaire **doktrin·är** a doctrinaire

Dokum·ent n ~(e)s/~e document; ⟨jur⟩ instrument, deed ‖ ~e [pl] ⟨allg⟩ papers ‖ ~en-film [m] ⟨phot⟩ document copying film ‖ ⟨com⟩ ~en-Akkreditiv [n] d.ary letter of credit | ⟨übtr⟩ evidence, proof –**t·ar** m ~s/~e (P) documentalist | ~bericht, ~film [m] record od educational film **d–t·arisch** a documentary –**tati·on** f ~/~en documentation ~**entratte** f d.ary draft **d–t·ieren** vt [h] to document; to authenticate documentarily ‖ ⟨übtr⟩ to demonstrate, to reveal, to show

D·olch m ~(e)s/~e ⟨a. fenc⟩ dagger, poniard; → Stilett ‖ malaiischer ~ kris | (als Waffenschmuck) ⟨mil, mar & pol⟩ dirk | (jdn) mit e–m ~ (er)stechen to dirk, poniard, stab (a p) ‖ den ~ zücken to draw one's dagger ‖ ⟨übtr⟩ s–e Blicke waren gleich ~en his eyes looked od spoke daggers ≃**artig** a dagger-like ~**messer** n → Jagdmesser ~**stich,** ~**stoß** m dagger-stab (od thrust); thrust with a dagger ~**stoßlegende** f stab--in-the-back mongering; legend of the "Stab in the Back"

D·öldchen n ~s/~ ⟨bot⟩ umbellet, umbellule

D·olde f ~/~n ⟨bot⟩ umbel ‖ ⟨übtr⟩ cluster (: in clusters)

D·olden- [in bot comp] umbellar, umbellate(d), umbelliferous ≃**artig** a umbellar, umbellate(d) ~**blume** f umbellate flower, umbellifer ~**blüter** [pl] Umbelliferae [L pl] ≃**blütig** a umbellar, umbellate ≃**förmig** a umbelliform; umbellar, umbellate(d) ~**gewächs** n umbelliferous plant, → Doldenblüter ~**rebe** f ⟨bot⟩ Virginia creeper ~**rispe** f ⟨bot⟩ inflorescence paniculate ~**tragend** a umbelliferous ~**traube** f ⟨bot⟩ corymb

d·oldig a ⟨bot⟩ umbellate(d), umbelliform

D·ole f (Abzugsgraben) drain, culvert

Doler·it m ~s/~e ⟨minr⟩ dolerite

d·olicho- [in comp] (Lang-) dolicho– ⟨anthr⟩ ~**zeph·al** a dolichocephalic ≃**zeph·ale** m dolichocephal

Dol·ine f ~/~n ⟨geol⟩ round depression

°**doll** a = toll

D·ollar m dollar (abbr $) ~s/~; 50 ~ $ 50 ‖ ⟨Am sl⟩ bone, buck, plunck; 1000 ~ grand, 4000 ~ four grand ‖ ein Tausendstel ~ mill ~**noten** f pl ⟨Am fam⟩ (folding) greenbacks pl ~**zeichen** n dollarmark ([$] seit 1779)

D·ollart m ⟨Ger⟩ (Bucht vor Emsmündung)

D·ollbord n ⟨mar⟩ gunwale, gunnel, saxboard

D·olle f ⟨mar⟩ thole(-pin); swivel, gudgeon, rowlock | ~nboot [n] in-rigged boat

D·ölling m ⟨ich⟩ young zander; pike-perch

D·olman m ~s/~e (türk. Leibrock) dolman

D·olmen m ~s/~ ⟨praeh⟩ (Steingrab) dolmen

D·olmetsch m ~(en)/~e ⟨übtr⟩ interpreter, mouthpiece, spokesman; advocate ‖ sich zum ~ e–r S m to interpret od advocate a th ‖ → ~er

d·olmetschen vi/t [h] **1.** vi to interpret; to act as an interpreter **2.** vt (Gedanken) to interpret ‖ → verdolmetschen **D·olmetscher** m ~s/~ interpreter ‖ (im Orient) dragoman ‖ Amt or Stellung e–s ~s interpretership ‖ ~prüfung [f] examination for an interpretership ‖ ~zeugnis [n] interpreter's certificate | ⟨übtr⟩ → Dolmetsch

D·olmetscherin f ~/~nen interpretress; female interpreter

Dolom·it m ~(e)s/~e ⟨minr⟩ dolomite ‖ ⟨geog⟩ die ~en [pl] the Dolomites [pl]

dol·os a ⟨jur⟩ dolose **D·olus** m ⟨jur⟩ dolus [L]

D·om m ~(e)s/~e **1.** cathedral, minster; der Kölner ~ Cologne Cathedral **2.** † ⟨arch⟩ = Kuppel vault **3.** [in comp] (→ a. Kathedral–) ~**chor** m cathedral choir ~**dekan** m dean of a cathedral ~**frau** f canoness ~**freiheit** f the Close ~**herr** m canon, prebendary ‖ ~npfründe, ~nwürde [f] canonry ‖ ~nornat [n] canonicals [pl] (: in full c.) ≃**herrlich** a canonical (buildings) ~**kapital** n chapter ~**kirche** f cathedral church ~**pfaff** m ⟨orn⟩ redbird, bullfinch; vom ~ getraut married over the broomstick; sich v ~ trauen l to jump od hop the b. ~**prediger** m cathedral preacher ~**probst** m provost of a cathedral ~**schol·aster** m school-divine ~**schule** f endowed school attached to a cathedral ~**stift** n chapter

Dom·äne f ~/~n **1.** crown (od state) demesne (od domain); ⟨engl⟩ royal demesne, crown-land **2.** ⟨übtr⟩ domain, province, sphere; realm

Dom·änen- ~**amt** n crown-land office ~**gut** n domanial estate; ⟨engl⟩ Crown-estate ~**pächter** m crown-land lessee

Domest·ik m ~en/~en domestic **Domestikati·on** f domestication (of animals)

domin·ant a ⟨biol⟩ dominant; ~er Erbgang [m] dominant | ≃akkord [m] dominant-chord; ≃septakkord [m] dominant seventh **Domin·ante** f ~/~n ⟨mus⟩ dominant

domin·ieren vi [h] (P) to domineer, to lord it, to rule (über over) | ⟨mst übtr⟩ to be pre-eminent (unter among); to hold a commanding position (in in) ‖ (S) to (pre)dominate, prevail, to be prevalent (in in) ‖ ~ in e–m Gebiet to dominate a sphere **domin·ierend** a dominating (influence); commanding (position); prevailing (trait) ‖ pre--eminent ‖ ~e Eigenschaft [f] ⟨biol⟩ dominant

D·ominik·aner m ~s/~ ⟨ec⟩ Dominican; die ~ [pl] the Black (od Preaching) Friars [pl] ~**kloster** n Dominican monastery ~**orden** m the Order of St. Dominic; the Dominicans [pl]

Dominik·anerin f ~/~nen Dominican nun

dominik·anisch a Dominican (Republik [auf Haiti])

D·omino 1. m ~(s)/~s (Maskentracht) domino ‖ P im ~ domino; als ~ verkleidet dominoed ‖ **2.** n ~s/~s (~spiel) dominoes [pl]; e–e Partie ~ a game of d.; ~ spielen to play at d. ~**maske** f domino ~**spiel** n dominoes pl ~**stein** m domino

Domiz·il n ~s/~e domicile ‖ ⟨com⟩ domicile (of a bill of exchange) **domizil·ieren** vt [h] ⟨com⟩ (Wechsel) to make (a bill) payable, to domicile (a bill) (bei at, nach to) **Domiz·ilwechsel** m ⟨com⟩ domiciled bill

Dompt·eur [dɔ̃'tør] m [Fr] ~s/~e tamer

Don m ⟨Russ⟩ (Fluß) Don

Don (span. Titel) Don **Doña** ['dɔnjɑ] [Span] Doña, Donna ‖ °unsere ~ our maid

D·onar ⟨myth⟩ Thor

Don·ator m ~s/–·oren donor

D·onau f (europ. Fluß) Danube [in comp] Danubian (trade) ~**länder** n pl countries on the Danube ~**monarchie** f Danube-monarchy ~**raum** m Danubian area ~**staaten** m [pl] Danube states ~**tiefland** n Danubian lowlands [pl] od plain

°**D·önchen** n → Döhnchen

D·onegal (nach ir. Grafschaft) m ~s/~s (Ulsterstoff) Donegal tweed

D·onie [–iə] f ~/~n ⟨bot⟩ glory-pea, Donia

D·onja [Span] f ~/~s ⟨hum⟩ = Dienstmädchen; Geliebte

Don Juan m ['dɔn xu'an] ~/~s Don Juan, libertine; ⟨Am⟩ Valentino

D·onner m ~s/~ **1.** *thunder; clap crash;* der ~ rollt *the thunder roars* od *rumbles* ‖ Blitz u ~ *thunderbolt* ‖ wie vom ~ gerührt *thunder-struck* ‖ der ~ s–r Stimme *the roar of his voice;* °~ u Doria! = Donnerwetter!, ⟨sl⟩ *thunder and turf* **2.** ⟨übtr⟩ *thunder(ing)* (*of guns*) **≗ähnlich, ≗artig 1.** a *thundering, thunderous;* ~es Geräusch [n] *thunder;* ~es G. m *to thunder, roar* **2.** adv *like a thunder* **~axt** f = Donnerkeil **~bart** m ⟨bot⟩ *houseleek* ‖ = Fetthenne **~blech** n ⟨theat⟩ *thunder-sheet* **~büchse** f ⟨hist⟩ *blunderbuss;* → Bombarde **~gepolter, ~getöse** n *the grumbling of thunder; thunder(ing)* **~gott** m *Thunderer, Thor* **~keil** m ⟨myth⟩ *thunderbolt* ‖ ⟨geol⟩ *belemnite, thunderbolt* °**~lüttchen** intj ~! = Donnerwetter! **~maschine** f ⟨theat⟩ *thunder machine* **~schlag** m *clap* od *crash of thunder, thunder-clap* ‖ ⟨fig⟩ *thunderbolt:* wie ein ~ ⟨fig⟩ *like a th., like a bolt from the blue* **~ u Doria!** *thunder and lightning!* **~stimme** f *thundering voice* **~wetter** n *thunderstorm;* ⟨fig⟩ *explosion, row* ‖ ~! zum ~ (noch einmal)! *Great Scot!* da soll doch gleich das (ein) ~ dreinfahren! *confound it!, hang it all!, by all that's holy!* ⟨sl⟩ *dash it! damn it! hot dog!* ‖ zum ~! *in thunder!* (: *why in th. did you interfere?*) | (anerkennend) *I say!* | er ist wie ein ~ dreingefahren *he rushed upon it like a thunderbolt,* ⟨Am⟩ .. *like a duck on a june-bug; made a terrific row about it; he fulminated* od *protested vehemently against it* ‖ .. (dann) mach dich nur auf ein schönes ~ gefaßt .. *just look out for squalls* ‖ das wird ein schönes ~ setzen *we shall be in for it properly* (*when* ..); das ~ ging über ihn nieder ⟨fig⟩ *the thunderbolt descended upon his head*

d·onnern A. vi **1.** v imp [h] ⟨eig⟩ es donnert *it thunders, it is thundering* **2.** vi [h] ⟨übtr⟩ (of sound) *to roll;* (of gun) *to poop* ‖ (P) *to thunder; to roar, to rage; to fulminate* (gegen *against*) **B.** ≗ n *thunder(ing)* ‖ *roll(ing); poop* ‖ *roar(ing)*

d·onnernd 1. a *thundering* (*applause*); ~e Reden [pl] *thunders* [pl] **2.** adv ~ fallen, rollen, stürzen (S) *to thunder* (v *from;* auf *upon*); ~ schlagen an *to thunder at* (*the door*); (etw) ~ äußern *to thunder*

D·onnerstag m ~(e)s/~e *Thursday;* → Montag ‖ Grün≗ *Maundy-Thursday* ‖ °~ & Freitag ⟨sl⟩ *thunder and turf! Great Scott! Christmas!*

Donquichotter·ie [–kiʃ–] f *quixotism, quixotry*

D·ontgeschäft [dɔ̃–] n (Fr) ⟨com⟩ *option-business; option-rate* ‖ → Börsenwesen

°**doof** a *boring; monotonous* ‖ (dumm) ⟨sl⟩ *blithering, goofy, mushy* | adv der guckt aber ~ aus der Wäsche! *what a duffer!* **≗kopf, ≗mann** m *blitherer, stupe, stupid, coot, mutt(on-head),* ⟨Am⟩ *numbskull;* ⟨mil & school sl⟩ *gubbins*

D·oornkaat® m ⟨Ger⟩ *corn brandy, whisky*

d·open vt [engl] (Perde, etc) *to dope*

D·oppel 1. n ~s/~ *double, duplicate* **2.** m ~s/~ = Zweier

D·oppel- (→ doppelt I.A.) [in comp mst] *double* ‖ *duplex; twin; dual; diplo–* ‖ → Zwei– **~achter** m ⟨rowing⟩ *sculling-eight* **~adler** m ⟨her⟩ *double eagle* **≗adrig** a *two-pole* [attr] → zwei– **~agent** m *double agent,* ⟨Am sl⟩ *double crosser* **~arbeit** f *duplication* **≗armig** a ⟨tech⟩ *double-armed* (*lever*) **≗atomig** a *diatomic* **~ausschalter** m ⟨el⟩ *double cutout* | **~-B** n ⟨mus⟩ *double B flat* **~backenbremse** f *double block brake* **~belichtung** f ⟨phot⟩ *super-imposition, double exposure* **~bereifung** f ⟨mot⟩ *twin-tyres,* ⟨Am⟩ *double tires* pl **~besteuerung** f *double taxation* **~bett** n (2 Betten) *twin beds;* französisches ~ *double bed* ‖ Schlafzimmer mit ~ = Doppelzimmer **~bewußtsein** n ⟨psych⟩ *double consciousness; dissociation* **~bild** ⟨phot⟩ *divorced image;* ⟨telv⟩ *ghost* | ~kamera [f] *double-frame camera* **~boden** m *double bottom, false floor* **~brechung** f ⟨phys⟩ *double refraction;* ⟨opt⟩ *birefringence* **~brenner** m *duplex gas-burner* **~bruch** m ⟨math⟩ *compound fraction,* ⟨med⟩ *compound fracture* **~büchse** f = Doppelflinte **≗chromos·omig** a *bivalent* **~decker** m ⟨aero⟩ *biplane;* ⟨a. mot⟩ *double-decker* **~drucker** m ⟨comp⟩ *dual printer* **~druckknopf** m ⟨comp⟩ *dual print head* **~ehe** f *bigamy* **~endball** m ⟨box⟩ *punching-ball* **~faden** m ⟨wear⟩ *flat* **≗fädig** a ⟨tech⟩ *bifilar* (*suspension*) **~fahrbahn** f ⟨mot⟩ *dual carriage-way* **~fehler** m ⟨ten⟩ *double fault* **~fenster** n *double window* **~fernrohr** n *binocular telescope* **~flak** f ⟨Ger⟩ *double anti-aircraft gun* **~flasche** f *double bottle; magnum* (*2 quarts*) **~flinte** f *double-barrel(led) gun; double barrel* **~fokusglas** n ⟨opt⟩ *bifocal glass* **~gänger** m *double, fetch, wraith; counterpart, complement, correspondent; double-ganger; doppel-ganger* [Ger]; **≗gängig** a *double-threaded* (*screw*) **~getriebe** n *double gear* **~gewebe** n *double cloth* **~gleis** n *double rail* od *track* **≗gleisig** a *double-railed* **~griff** m ⟨mus⟩ ~e [pl] *double-stopping;* in ~en spielen *to double-stop* **~hammerbrecher** m *twin hammer breaker* **~haus** n (*two*) *semi-detached house(s),* ⟨Am⟩ *duplex row-house* ‖ halbes ~ *semi-detached h.,* ⟨fam⟩ *semi* **~hebel** m *double lever* **~-Ich** n ⟨psych⟩ *dual* (*dissociated, split*) *personality* **~insel** f *twin island* (: *New Zealand, Novaya Zemlya*) **~kasten** m ⟨typ⟩ *a pair of cases* **~kinn** n *double chin* **≗kohlensauer** a → doppeltkohlensauer **~kolbenmotor** m *double-piston motor* **~kondensator** m *twin condenser* **~konsonant** m *double consonant* **~kopf** m ⟨Ger⟩ *a card-game for four players* **~kreuz** n ⟨mus⟩ *double sharp* **~lauf** m *double barrel;* Gewehr mit ~ → Doppelflinte **≗läufig** a *double-barrelled* (*gun*) **~läuten** n *double change* **~läutewerk** n *double-stroke bell* **~leiter** m ⟨el⟩ *twin-conductor* **~leitung** f ⟨el⟩ *double-circuit line* **~leitungskabel** n ⟨el⟩ *twisted pair cable* **~leitwerk** n ⟨aero⟩ *twin tail* **~linie** f ⟨typ⟩ *double rule* **~lochkontrolle** f ⟨comp⟩ *double punch detection device* **~luftschraube** f *tandem propellers* pl **~magazinsetzmaschine** f ⟨typ⟩ *double-magazine composing machine* **~magnet** m *dual magnets* pl **~maschine** f (Schuh≗) *sole stitcher* **≗mäulig** a ⟨tech⟩ *double-ended* (*spanner*) **~monarchie** f *Dual Monarchy* **~muffe** f *double socket* **~nummer** f *double number* **~objektiv** n ⟨opt⟩ *doublet* **~packung** f *magnum* (*of a washing agent*) **~partie** f ⟨ten⟩ *doubles match* **≗polig** a *two-pole* (Draht) **~prismenglas** n *prism binoculars* pl **~programm** n ⟨film⟩ *fill-up* **~punkt** m ⟨gram⟩ *colon* ‖ ⟨match⟩ *double point* **~quittung** f ⟨com⟩ *receipt in duplicate* **~reifen** m pl ⟨mot⟩ *twin tires* ⟨od Am⟩ *tyres* **~reihe** f ⟨mil⟩ *double file, file* od *column of two(')s* **~salz** n *double salt* **~schalter** m ⟨el⟩ *duplex switch* **~scherkopf** m ⟨tech⟩ *bi-ax shaving head* **~schicht** f *double layer* **~schlag** m ⟨mus⟩ *turn* **~schlußmaschine** f ⟨tech⟩ *compound dynamo* **~schraube** f *twin-screw;* ~ndampfer [m] *twin-screw;* ~nschiff [n] *twin-screw ship* **≗seitig** a *bilateral;* ~e Lungenentzündung [f] *double pneumonia;* ~er Verdichter [m] ⟨aero-mot⟩ *dual entry impeller* | [adv] *on both sides* **~selbstlaut** m ⟨gram⟩ *diphthong* **~sinn** m *double meaning; ambiguity* **≗sinnig** a *ambiguous, double-barrelled, equivocal* **~sinnigkeit** f *ambiguousness, ambiguity* **~sitz** m *tandem seat* | ~er [m] ⟨aero⟩ *two-seater* **≗sitzig** a ⟨tech⟩ *double-beat* (*valve*) **~skuller** m = Doppelzweier **~sohle** f *double sole;* dicke ~ *clump(-sole);* (Schuh) mit ~n beschlagen *to clump* **~spat** m *Iceland* (od *double*) *spar* **~spiel** n ⟨ten⟩ *doubles* [pl] ‖ ⟨fig⟩ *double-dealing;* ⟨sl⟩ *double-cross* **~spieler** m ⟨film etc⟩ *double* **~sprechen** n *duplex telegraphy*

~spur f ⟨rec⟩ *twin* od *dual track*, ⟨film⟩ *double track* **~stecker** m ⟨el⟩ (*two-way*) *adapter* **~stern** m ⟨astr⟩ *double star*; ~e [pl] *binary stars, binaries* [pl] | ~motor [m] ⟨aero⟩ *two-row* od *-bank radial* (*engine* od *motor*) **~steuerung** f ⟨aero⟩ *dual control* **~stickerei** f *top and bottom embroidery* **~tarif** m *maximum-minimum tariff, two-rate* (od *time-of-day*) *tariff* **~-T-Eisen** n *H girder, H iron* **~tür** f *double* od *storm door* **~verdiener** m *two-job man*; (v Eheleuten) *independent wage-earners* **~vers** m ⟨pros⟩ *distich* **~versicherung** f *double insurance* **~vierer** m ⟨rowing⟩ *sculling-four* **~währung** f *double standard* (Gold u Silber), *bimetallism* **~wandig** a *double-walled* **~wesen** n *twofold nature* **~zählung** f ⟨demog⟩ *multiple counting* ‖ *overregistration* **~zeile** f *double line* **~zentner** m (im Dezimalsystem) *quintal* **~zimmer** n *double room with one bed, d. r. w. two beds*; *double* (*bed*)*room, double* **~zünder** m *double-acting fuse*; *time/super-quick* (*fuse*) **~zündmagnet** m *dual magnets* pl **~züngig** a *deceitful, double-dealing*; ~es Gerede [n] *double(-)talk* | adv ~ reden *to speak with two voices* **~züngigkeit** f *double-dealing, double-talk, duplicity, deceitfulness* **~züngler** m *deceitful person* **~zweier** m ⟨rowing⟩ *sculling-pair*

D·oppelheit f *doubleness, duplicity*

***d·oppeln 1.** vt [h] *to double*; *to duplicate* ‖ → verdoppeln; mehren **2.** ~ n *reproducing*; automatisches ~ ⟨comp⟩ *automatic transfer* (*of repetitive data*)

d·oppelt I. a **A.** (oft = Doppel-) **a.** *double, twofold, duplicate*; ⟨tech⟩ *duplex* **b.** ~es **Ale** *double ale* ‖ ~e Arbeit leisten *to do double work* ‖ in ~er Ausfertigung *in duplicate*; *bipartite* (Urkunde); in ~er A. herstellen *to duplicate* ‖ ~e **Blüte** *double blossom* ‖ ein ~er Boden *a double bottom*; *false floor* ‖ ~e Buchführung (*book-keeping by*) *double-entry* ‖ ~es Gesicht ⟨fig⟩ *dual nature* ‖ jdm mit ~er **Kraft** *zusetzen to double-team on a p*; ~e Kraftstoffpumpe f *dual fuel pump* ‖ ⟨fig⟩ ~e **Moral** *double set of morals, double(-barrelled) morality* ‖ *dual* (*nationality*) ‖ ⟨tech⟩ in ~er **Richtung** wirkend *double-acting* ‖ Wirkung in ~er Richtung *double-action* ‖ e e ~ e **Schneide** *a double edge* ‖ ~er **Sinn** *double meaning* ‖ ~es Spiel *double-dealing* (*with*); *double-cross*; ein ~es S. spielen mit jdm *to double-cross, to deal double with a p* ‖ ~e Übersetzung ⟨mot⟩ *two-speed gear* ‖ ~es Vorhandensein *duplicity, doubleness* ‖ ein ~er Vorteil *a double advantage* **c.** Tuch ~ **legen** *to place cloth double* (über *over*) ‖ etw ~ h *to have duplicates of a th* ‖ nehmen Sie noch eins, ~ hält besser *have another one, one* (*glass, etc.*) *won't do* **B.** (~ soviel) [mst mit def art] die ~e Anzahl, Summe *double the number, double* od *twice the sum* ‖ ein Würfel v ~em Rauminhalt *a cube of twice its cubic content* ‖ v ~er Dicke *double-ply* **II.** adv **1.** *double, twice, twofold* ‖ ~ **oder nichts**! *win the mare or lose the halter*!; ~ oder Nichts spielen *to play double or quits* ‖ ~ **geben** *to give double* ‖ ~ **gewebt** *double-ply, two-ply* (*linen*) ‖ ~ gezahnt *double-cogged* ‖ ~ sehen *to see double* ‖ (Tür) ~ verschließen *to double-lock* ‖ ~ zus-legen *to double* | ⟨fig⟩ ~ u dreifach entschädigt w *to be fully* (od *to the full*) *repaid* **2.** [vor Adj.] *doubly*; ~ **glücklich** *doubly happy* ‖ es ist ~ so groß als es war *it is double what it was* ‖ ~ so hell *double as bright* ‖ ~ so viel *twice as much* **III.** ~e [n] ~n/ : es zählt das ~ u dreifache *it counts far more* **IV.** [in comp] **~kohlensauer** a ⟨chem⟩ ~es Natron *bicarbonate of soda*, ⟨Am⟩ *saleratus*; ~es Salz *bicarbonate* **~sehen** n ⟨med⟩ *diplopia* (L); *double vision* **~wirkend** a ⟨tech⟩ *double-acting* (*engine*)

D·oppelte n das ~ *the double* (: *take the d. of* ..); das ~ davon *double that amount*; *twice as much, twice the sum*; → doppelt III.

D·oppelung f *doubling*; *extra layer of planking*

D·öpper m ~s/~ ⟨tech⟩ *header*; *snap die*

D·oppler m ~s/~ ⟨comp⟩ *comparing reproducing punch*; (Karten~) *reproducer* ‖ ~ mit automatischer Prüfung = Doppler; ~ mit Nummerndruck *end printing reproducing punch*; ~ mit Zeichenlochung *mark sensing reproducer*

D·opplereffekt m (nach Ch. Doppler, † 1853), a. Dopplersches Prinzip *Doppler effect*

Dor·ade f ⟨zoo⟩ *dorado, dolphin*

Dor·ado n ~s/~s; das ~ = Eldorado

Dor·ant m ⟨bot⟩ → Löwenmaul, Enzian, Sumpfgarbe

D·orer [pl] → Dorier

D·orf n ~(e)s/~er *village*, das ~ Uldale *the village of Uldale*; *Uldale village* ‖ ⟨Aust⟩ *township*; ⟨SAfr⟩ dorp ‖ ⟨fig⟩ → böhmisch

D·orf- ~au(e) f *common* **~bewohner** m *villager* **~gemeinde** f **1.** (Distrikt) *country-parish, rural parish* **2.** (die Einwohner) *villagers* [pl] **~gemeinschaft** f *village-community* **~geschichte** f *village story* **~jugend** f, **~kinder** [n pl] *village children* [pl] **~krug** m *village-inn* **~leben** n *country* (od *village*)*-life* **~pfarrer** m *country parson* **~rand** m *outskirts* pl *of a village* **~richter** m ⟨hist⟩ *village magistrate* **~schenke** f *village inn* **~schule** f *village school*; ⟨Am a.⟩ *district-school* **~schulmeister** m *village schoolmaster* **~schulze** m *village magistrate* **~verfassung** f *village constitution* **~wirtschaft** f [abstr] *village economy* ‖ → -schenke

D·örfchen n ~s/~ *small* od *little village, hamlet*

D·örfler m ~s/~ *villager* **d·örflich** a *village* (*life*); → ländlich, bäuerlich

D·orfschaft f ~/~en **1.** (Dorf) *village*; → Kirchspiel **2.** *villagers* [pl]

D·orier m ~s/~ ⟨ant⟩ *Dorian* **d·orisch** a *Dorian* (*movement*); ⟨mus⟩ die ~e Tonart *the Dorian mode* ‖ ⟨Lit⟩ *Doric* (*dialect*); ~er Dialekt *the Doric* ‖ ⟨arts⟩ *Doric* (*column*; *order*)

D·orn m [~(e)s/ [pl → u] **A.** [pl ~en] **1. a.** ⟨bot⟩ *prickle, thorn* (*of a rose*, etc.); *spine* ‖ kl ~ *spinule* ‖ ohne ~en *thornless*; voller ~en *thorny* ‖ k-e Rose ohne ~en *no rose without a thorn* ‖ → Stachel **b.** ⟨fig⟩ jdm ein ~ im Auge s *to be a thorn in a p's side*; s-e Beredsamkeit war dem Ministerium immer ein ~ im A. *his eloquence was always a thorn in the side of the ministry* ‖ ~en [pl] *hardships, sufferings* [pl] **2.** ⟨bot⟩ (~busch) *thorn*; *bramble, brier, briar*; → Hage~, Rot~, Weiß~ **B.** [pl ~e, Dörner] (Spindel) *mandrel* (*-ril*); *triblet, tribolet*; *arbor* ‖ (Stift) *spike, tang*; *bolt, pin* (*of a hinge*); *tongue* (*in a buckle*) **C.** [in comp] → Dorn-, Dornen-

D·orn- ~apfel m ⟨bot⟩ = Dature **~auszieher** m ⟨arts⟩ *Boy Extracting a Thorn* **~busch** m *thorn*(*-bush*), *bramble*(*-bush*); *brier* **~dreher** m ⟨orn⟩ *red-back*(*ed*) *shrike* **~echse** f ⟨zoo⟩ = Schleuderschwanz **~fisch** m ⟨ich⟩ = Stichling **~fortsatz** m ⟨anat⟩ *spinous process* **~grundel** m ⟨ich⟩ = Schmerle **~kaat** m → Doorn– **~röschen** n ⟨myth⟩ *Sleeping Beauty*; aus dem ~schlaf erwachen *to wake up to reality* **~schuhe** m [pl] *shoes with spiked soles* [pl] **~strauch** m ⟨bot⟩ = Dornbusch **~teufel** m ⟨zoo⟩ (Eidechse) *thorn-devil* **~zikade** f ⟨ent⟩ = Buckelzirpe

d·ornen vt [h] (durchbohren) ⟨tech⟩ *to pierce*

D·ornen- ~hecke f *quickhedge*; *thorn-hedge*; → Hecke **~krone** f ⟨ec⟩ *crown of thorns, thorn-crown* **~krönung** f *crowning with thorns* **~pfad** m *thorny path* **~stock** m *thorn-stick* **~voll** a *thorny* | ⟨fig⟩ *thorny* (*path*); *distressing, painful*; → dornig

d·ornig, *d·ornicht a *briery, thorny*; ⟨bot & zoo⟩ *spinose, spinous, spiny* | ⟨fig⟩ *difficult, thorny* (*problem*); *unpleasant*; *delicate*

d·orren vi [s] *to dry* (*up*), *wither*; *fade*

d·örren vt [h] (Gemüse, Obst etc) *to dry* ⟨a. brew⟩; (im Darrofen) *to kiln-dry* ‖ Sw (Brot) *to toast* ‖ ~ u salzen *to drysalt* | ⟨übtr⟩ (härten) *to bake* ‖ → (aus)trocknen, rösten **D·örrgemüse** n *dried vegetables* pl **D·örrobst** n *dried fruit*

dors·al a *dorsal*

D·orsch m ~es/~e ⟨ich⟩ *cod(fish), torsk*

Dorst·enie [iə] f ⟨bot⟩ *dorstenia* [L]

d·ort adv **1.** ⟨eig⟩ ~ ist er *there he is* od *goes*; ~ kommt er *there he comes*; → da ‖ ich werde gleich ~ s *I'll be right along* ‖ ~ würde der Tee stattfinden *that was where tea would be* ‖ v ~ (aus) *from there, from that place*; † *thence* ‖ hier u ~ *here and there*; *in some places* ‖ jenes Dorf ~ *yonder village* ‖ ~ drüben *yonder*; *over there*; ⟨dial⟩ *yon*; ~ drüben gelegen *yonder* (*house*) ‖ ~ hinten, ~ oben etc = da hinten, da oben etc → da I. A. 4. ‖ ~, wo .. *where* (:*turn to the left where* ..) **2.** (im Jenseits) *in the other world, beyond the grave* **3.** [in comp] **~her** adv (v ~) *from there, from that place*; † *thence* **~herab** adv *down there* **~herauf** adv *up there* **~heraus** adv *out there* **~herunter** adv *down there* **~hin** adv *there*; *that way*; ⟨liter⟩ *thither* ‖ bis ~ *as far as that* **~hinab** adv *down there* **~hinauf** adv *up there* **~hinaus** adv *out there*; °bis ~ [räumlich] *to the end of the world*, [zeitlich] *till Doomsday* **~hinüber** adv *over there* **~hinunter** adv *down there* **≗sein** n während m–s ~s *during my stay* (*while I was present*) *there*

d·orten adv ⟨poet⟩ = dort

d·ortig a; die ~en Verhältnisse *the conditions there* od *of that place, country*, etc. ‖ das ~e Buch ⟨vulg⟩ *that there book*

D·ortmund n ⟨Ger⟩ (Industrie- u Universitätsstadt)

D·öschen [-sc] n ~s/~ *little* od *small box*, → Dose ‖ °⟨vulg sex⟩ *snatch-box, jam(-pot)*

D·ose f ~/~n **1.** *box*; *pot*; Puder≗ *powder-box*; Tabaks≗ *snuff-box* ‖ (Blech≗) *tin, can*; in ~n einmachen *to tin, to can* ‖ in ~n verpacken *to pack* ‖ ⟨hum⟩ Musik in ~n ⟨rec⟩ *canned music* ‖ → Steck≗ ‖ °⟨sex⟩ → vor. ~nkonserven [f pl] *canned food* ~öffner [m] *tin-opener* **2.** [bes pl ~n] = Dosis

°**d·ösen** vi [h] *to doze*; *maunder*; ⟨fam⟩ *to think about breakfast* ‖ (dahinleben) *to vegetate*

°**d·ösig** a *dizzy*; *dull*; → dumm ‖ *dozy*; *sleepy*

dos·ieren vt [h] *to administer* (*a th*) *in doses*; *to dose, to proportion* | -rt *in measured quantites*; sorgfältig -rt *carefully measured*, richtig -rt *in correct doses*

Dos·ier- **~pumpe** f *metering pump, proportioning pump*

Dos·ierung f *dosage*

D·osis f ~/Dosen **1.** *dose*; *draught*; ⟨med fam⟩ *shot*; in Dosen verabreichen *to administer in doses*; jdm e–e ~ verabreichen *to dose a p* ‖ z starke (schwache) ~ *overdose* (*underdose*); jdm e–e z st. ~ geben *to overdose* (*underdose*) *a p* ‖ **2.** ⟨übtr⟩ *dose*; e–e starke ~ *strong meat, a tall order*; e–e reichliche ~ v *a hand-out of* (*applause*); e–e gründliche, gute, kräftige ~ Selbstbewußtseins *a full share of self-confidence* ‖ → Schuß **~leistung** f ⟨at⟩ *dose rate*

Doss·ierung f = Böschung

D·ost m ~es/~e ⟨bot⟩ *origanum* [L], *common* od *wild marjoram*

Dot·alsystem n ⟨jur⟩ *dotal system*

Dotati·on f ~/~en ⟨jur⟩ *dotation, endowment*

dot·ieren vt [h] ⟨jur⟩ *to endow* ‖ e–e gut –rte Stelle *a well-paid* (od *-endowed*) *post*, e–e gut–rte Stiftung *a richly endowed foundation*

D·otter m & n ~s/~ **1.** *yolk* (*of an egg*) ‖ ⟨biol⟩ Bildungs≗ *ooplasm*; Nahrungs≗ *deutoplasm* **2.** ⟨bot⟩ (a. Flachs≗, Lein≗) *cameline*; *Gold of pleasure* **~blume** f ⟨bot⟩ *marsh marigold*; *Caltha* [L] **≗gelb** a *yolky* **~haut** f *yolk-membrane* **~loch** n *blastospore* **~öl** n *cameline oil* **~sack** m ⟨ich⟩ *yolk-bag* (od *sac*)

d·ott(e)rig a *yolky* ‖ zwei~ *double-yolked* (*egg*)

Dou·ane [du'ɑːnə] f [Fr] *customs* [pl]; *custom-house*

D·ouble n [-uː-] ~s/~s ⟨film⟩ *stand-in*, ⟨theat⟩ *understudy* **doubl·ieren** vt [h] *to line* (*a canvas*)

Dougl·asie [du'glɑːziə], **D·ouglastanne** ['dʌgləs-] f ⟨bot⟩ *Douglas spruce*

D·over n (südengl. Hafenstadt) *Dover* **Straße von ~** f *Strait of Dover*

Downs [daunz] [pl] ⟨engl⟩ (Kreidekalkhügel) *downs* [pl]

D·owsongas ['dausen-] n [engl] *Dowson gas*

Doxolog·ie f ~/~n ⟨ec⟩ *doxology*

Doyen [dwa'jɛ̃] m [Fr] ⟨pol⟩ *doyen*

Doz·ent m ~en/~en ⟨univ⟩ *university-teacher inferior in rank to the professor*; ⟨Am⟩ *instructor* | *lecturer, reader*; *professor*; ⟨fam⟩ *don*; die ~en ⟨a.⟩ *the college divines*; ~ f Geschichte *professor of History*

Doz·entenschaft f ⟨univ⟩ *teaching-staff* **Doz·entenzimmer** n *Senior Common Room* (abbr *S. C. R.*), *Staff Room*; die Mitglieder des ~s *the S. C. R.* **Dozent·ur** f *qualification for a professorship, right to profess*

doz·ieren vi/t [h] **1.** vi *to profess* (in *in*); *to lecture* (über *on*) **2.** vt (etw) *tp profess*

Drac·äne f ~/~n ⟨bot⟩ *dracaena*

Dr·ache m ~n/~n **1. a.** ⟨myth⟩ *dragon* **b.** ⟨bib⟩ *the dragon, the old serpent*; → Satan **c.** ⟨zoo⟩ (Eidechse) *flying lizard* **d.** ‖ ⟨übtr⟩ (zänk. Weib) *catamaran, dragon, termagant, battle-axe* **2.** ⟨astr⟩ *Draco* [L]; *the Dragon* **3.** (Spielzeug) *kite*; e–n ~ steigen l *to fly a k.*

Dr·achen- [in comp] *dragon–*; ⟨bes bot & astr⟩ *dragon's* **≗artig** a *dragon-like*; *dragonish* **~ballon** m ⟨aero⟩ *kite-balloon* **~baum** m ⟨bot⟩ *dracaena* [L]; *dragon-tree* **~blut** n **1.** *dragon-blood* **2.** ⟨übtr⟩ (Harz) *dragon's blood* ‖ *red Rhine wine of Drachenfels* **~fabel** f ⟨Lit⟩ *dragon-legend* **~kampf** m *dragon-fight* **~kopf** m ⟨bot & astr⟩ *dragon's head* **~maul** n ⟨bot⟩ *Pyrennean Dead-Nettle* **~saat** f ⟨fig⟩ *dragon-seed*; *dragon's teeth* [pl] **~schwanz** m ⟨astr⟩ *dragon's tail* **~töter** m *dragon-killer* **~wurz(el)** f ⟨bot⟩ *dragon* (*Arum*)

Dr·achme f ~/~n **1.** (Münze) **a.** ⟨ant⟩ *drachm* **b.** (griech. Währungseinheit, = 100 Lepta) *drachma* **2.** (Apothekergewicht) *drachm, dram*

Drag·ée [drɑ'ʒeː] n [Fr] ~s/~s *dragée*; *sugar-coated pellet* od *pill*

Dr·agge f ~/~n, **Dr·aggen** m ~s/~ ⟨mar⟩ (ein Anker) *grapnel*; *grappling-iron*

Dr·agoman m ~s/~e *dragoman* [pl *d.s* & *-men*]

Dragon·ade f ~/~n [Fr] ⟨ec hist⟩ *dragonnade*

Drag·oner m ~s/~ **1.** ⟨mil⟩ ⟨Ger⟩ *light cavalry soldier* (*up to WW I*), ⟨mst⟩ *dragoon* **2.** °⟨übtr⟩ (Weibsbild) *virago*; *jade*; → Besen **~regiment** n *regiment of Dragoons*

Dr·aht m ~(e)s/≗e **1.** (gedrehter Faden) Pech≗, Schuster≗ *cobbler's wax* **2.** (Metall≗) **a.** *wire*; Eisen≗, Kupfer≗ etc *iron wire, copper wire*; gewundener Gold≗, Silber≗ *purl* ‖ Aufreih≗ (f Papiere) *file*; Blumen≗ *flower-wire*; Heft≗ *stitching wire*; ⟨el⟩ Leitungs≗ *wire*; Stachel≗ *barbed wire* **b.** Telegraphen≗ *telegraph wire*; Telephon≗ *telephone wire* **c.** (Telegraphie) *wire*; per ~ *by wire* **3.** °(Geld) *cash, money*; ⟨fam⟩ *tin, brass*; ⟨sl⟩ *boodle, dough*; → °Moos, °Pinke, °Kies, °Zaster **4. a. ~ ziehen** *to draw wire*; ~ walzen *to roll w.*; (Metall) z ~ ausziehen *to wiredraw*; *to draw* (*metal*) *out into wire* **b.** (Haken) mit ~ umwickeln *to gange*; mit ~ umsponnen, umflochten *wire-wound* **c.** (Papiere) **an** ~ aufreihen *to file papers* ‖ Garten **durch** ~

abgrenzen *to wire a garden in* || etw **auf** ~ ziehen *to wire a th* || °auf ~ s *to know the ropes*, ⟨Am sl⟩ *to be on the ball* || etw **mit** ~ zus–binden *or* befestigen *to wire a th*; Buch mit ~ heften *to staple a book* || ⟨wir⟩ **über** den ~ leiten *to pipe*

Dr·aht- [in comp] → a. Telegramm, telegraphisch **~abschneider** m *wire cutter* **~anschrift** f *cable* od *telegraphic address* **~antwort** f *telegraphic reply, reply by wire* **~anweisung** f *telegraphic money order* **~arbeit** f: Zier≈ *filigree* **~aufnahmegerät** m *wire recorder* **~auslöser** m ⟨phot⟩ *cable release* **~bericht** m *telegraphic report*; *telegram, wire* **~bruchmelder** m *electric break alarm* **~bürste** f *wire-brush* **~feder** f *wire-spring* **~flechtmaschine** f *wire-plaiting machine* **~funk** m *wire broadcasting services* pl, *wired wireless, line radio*; ⟨wir⟩ *carrier transmission*, ⟨Am⟩ *wire program distribution* **~geflecht** n; feines ~ *wire-netting*; Zier≈ *filigree* **~geschütz** n *wire-gun, wire-wound gun* **~gewebe** n *wire-gauze, wire fabric* **~gitter** n *wire-grate*; ⟨opt⟩ (f Gitterspektren) *grating* **~glas** n *wire(-reinforced) glass, armoured glass* **~haar** n *wire hair* **~haarterrier** m ⟨zoo⟩ *wire-haired fox-terrier, wire(hair)* **~haspel** f *pay-out reel* **~heftmaschine** f *wire-stitching machine*; (Buch≈) *stapling-machine* **~hindernis** n ⟨mil⟩ *wire-entanglement* **~igel** m ⟨mil⟩ *gooseberry (obstacle)* **~käfig** m *wire-cage* **~klemme** f *wire terminal* °**~kommode** f ⟨mus⟩ (Klavier) *tinkling-box*, ⟨Am⟩ *juke box* | die ~ bearbeiten *to pound the box* **~korrespondent** m (Presse) *string correspondent* **~lehre** f (Werkzeug) *wire-gauge* **~leitung** f ⟨el⟩ *telegraph* (od *telephone*)*-wires* [pl]; Haus mit ~ versehen *to wire a house* **~magnetophon** n *wire recorder* **~meldung, ~nachricht** f *telegraphic message*; *telegram, wire* **~nachrichtenbüro** n, –**dienst** m *news wire bureau*, ⟨Am⟩ *wire service* **~nagel** m *wire-nail* **~netz** n *wire-gauze, wire-netting*; → Netz **~öse** f *staple* **~puppe** f *marionette, puppet* **~rohrgeschütz** a = Drahtgeschütz **~rolle** f *coil of wire* **~rundfunk** m *wire broadcasting, line radio* **~saite** f *wire (-string)* **~schere** f *cropper, wire-cutter* **~schneider** m (P) *wire-cutter* **~seele** f *wire core* **~seil** n *wire-rope, tight-rope* || ~akrobat [m] *wire-walker* (od *dancer*) || ~bahn [f] *cableway*; elektr. ~ *telpher line* || ~brücke [f] *wire-bridge*; **~säge** f *stone-sawing strand* **~sieb** n *wire-sieve*; *griddle* **~speichenrad** n ⟨mot⟩ *wire (spoke) wheel* **~sperre** f ⟨mil⟩ *wire apron* **~stärke** f *diameter* (od *size*) *of a wire* **~stift** m *wire-nail* (od *tack*) **~verarbeitungsmaschine** f *wire-working machine* **~verbindung** f ⟨telph⟩ *wire communication* od *connection* **~verhau** m ⟨mil⟩ *protective wire, wire-entanglement, barbed wire*; durch ~ schützen *to wire* **~walze** f (aufziehbare Stachel~) ⟨mil⟩ *concertina (roll)* **~walzwerk** n *wire mill* **~waren** f [pl] *wire-goods* [pl] **~weg** m: auf dem ~e *by wire* **~wurm** m (Schnellkäferlarve) *wire-worm* **~zange** f *wire-pliers* [pl] **~zaun** m *wire-fence* **~ziehbank** f *w.-drawing bench* **~zieher** m **1.** ⟨met⟩ *wiredrawer* **2.** ⟨fig, pol⟩ (unsichtbarer) *wire-puller* || ⟨Am⟩ *pipe-layer* od *-fitter*; *politician* || der ~ s *to pull the wires*; er ist der eigentliche ~ *he is the boss of the roost* **~zieherei** f ~/~en ⟨tech⟩ *wire drawing mill*

dr·ahten vi/t [h] **1.** vi *to telegraph*; ⟨fam⟩ *to wire* (jdm *to a p*) **2.** vt (etw) *to telegraph*, ⟨fam⟩ *to wire*; jdm etw ~ *to telegraph* (⟨fam⟩ *to wire*) *a p a th* (od *a th to a p*); jdm ~ *to wire to a p* (*to do*; *that*)

dr·ahtig a *wiry* (*fellow*) **dr·ähtig** a [in comp] drei~ *three-threaded*; grob~ *coarse-wired* (od *threaded*) **dr·ahtlich 1.** a *telegraphic* **2.** adv *by wire* **dr·ahtlos 1.** a *radio*; *wireless* (*telegraphy, telephony*); ~e Bildübertragung *w.l. image transmission*; ⟨Ger⟩ ~er Dienst *w.l. service*; Nachrichten des ~en Dienstes *News Service*; ~er Empfang *w.l. reception* ~e Fernsteuerung *w.l. remote control*; ~es Fernsehen *television*; ~e Nachricht *radio, wireless*; ~e Ortsbestimmung *radio direction finding*; ~e Peilung *radio bearing*; Station f ~e Telegraphie *wireless station*; ~er Verkehr *wireless* **2.** adv *by wireless*; ~ senden, telegraphieren *to radio, to wireless* (jdm etw *a p a th* od *a th to a p*) || ~ gesteuertes Flugzeug *radio controlled plane* || ~ übermitteltes Telegramm *wireless telegram, radiogram*

Drain [dre:n] m (engl) = Drän **Drain·age** [ɑ:ʒə] f = Dränage **drain·ieren** vt = dränieren

Drais·ine f (nach K. von Drais, † 1851) ~/~n **1.** ⟨hist⟩ (Laufmaschine) *draisine, dandy-horse* **2.** ⟨rail⟩ *rail-bicycle*; *light troll(e)y*

drak·onisch 1. a *Draconian, draconic* (*measures*) **2.** adv *draconically*

Drakont·iasis f [Gr] ⟨vet & med⟩ *disease caused by the guinea worm*

Drall m **1.** ⟨phys⟩ *twist* **2.** ⟨spin⟩ (Anzahl der Drehungen auf best. Fadenlänge) *twist* || ⟨mil⟩ (des Geschosses u im Gewehrlauf) *rifling*; *twist*; Progressiv≈ *progressive twist* || ⟨ball⟩ *spiral movement* **2.** ⟨fig⟩ *tenseness*; *discipline* **3.** °= Ulk, Spaß **~verhältnis** n ⟨tech⟩ *lay ratio* **~wirkung** f *twist effect*

dr·all a *buxom, crumby, crummy, strapping* (*girl, woman*); *plump, well-covered* (*cheeks*)

Dr·allheit f *buxomness*; *plumpness*

Dr·ama n ~s/–men *drama* ⟨a. fig⟩ *drama*; –mengattung *kind of drama* || das ~ ⟨a. =⟩

Dram·atik f ~/ *dramatic art, the drama*

Dram·atiker m ~s/~ *dramatist, playwright*; *writer of dramas* (od *plays*); *dramaturge* **dram·atisch 1.** a *dramatic* (*art*); in ~er Hinsicht *dramatically* || ⟨fig⟩ *dramatic*; *thrilling* **2.** adv *dramatically* || ~ darstellen *to dramatize*

dramatis·ieren vt [h] (Roman etc) *to dramatize*

Dramatis·ierung f *dramatization*

Dramat·urg m ~en/~en *dramatic critic* || ⟨Ger⟩ *adviser* (*who arranges repertoire and cooperates with the producer*) **Dramaturg·ie** f ~/~n *dramaturgy* **dramat·urgisch** a *dramaturgic*

dran I. adv **1.** = daran || °da ist alles ~ = das ist Sache! || °an der *or* ihr ist alles ~ *she's lush*, → reizend **2.** [bes Wendungen] **a.** ich **denke nicht** ~! *not I!, catch me doing that!* || komm ja nicht ~ *don't touch it* || du bist allein ~ schuld *it is all your doing* **b.** ~ (sc am Spiel) s *to be in*; wer ist ~? *whose turn is it?*; ⟨fam⟩ *who's up?*, ⟨Am⟩ *who goes?* ich bin ~ *it is my turn*; ich komme jetzt ~ *it is my turn now*; ⟨bes mil⟩ er ist ~ (zur Bestrafung) *he's in for it* || es kam nicht ~ (zur Erörterung) *it was not reached* | man weiß nie, wie man mit ihm ~ ist *you never know where you are with him* || wie bist du ~? *how are you up for cash?* || gut (übel) ~ s *to be well* (*badly*) *off*; schlimm ~ s *to be up a tree* **c.** ~ **glauben** müssen *to be in for it*; *to have to suffer* (od *die*) *for it* || = ~ k (→ u) || feste ~ müssen *to have to work hard* (od *vigorously*) | °~ k (= sterben) *to kick the bucket* **d. jdn ~ nehmen** *to attend to a p, to serve a p* || jdn tüchtig ~ nehmen *to make a p work hard* **e.** drauf u ~ *touch and go* (: *it was t. and g. that* ..); drauf u ~ s z tun (P) *to be on the point of doing, to be about to do, to be near doing*; (bes S) *to be within an ace of doing*; der Wagen war drauf u ~ umzukippen *the car was within an ace of turning over* **II.** [rel pron] = woran **III.** ≈ n → drum

Dr·än m ~s/~s **1.** ⟨agr⟩ (Abflußgraben, –rohr) *drain* **2.** ⟨med⟩ *drainage-tube* **~rohr** n *drain-pipe* **~strang** m *drain* **~system** n *drainage, system of drains*

Drän·age [dre'nɑʒə] f **1.** [abstr] (Dränieren) *drainage* || ⟨med⟩ *drainage* **2.** [konkr] (Anlage) *drains* [pl], *drainage* **3.** [in comp] *drainage*

Drang m ~(e)s/ **1.** (S) *press(ure), rush, urgency*; im ~ des Augenblicks *on the spur* (od *impulse*) *of the moment*; der ~ der Geschäfte *the pressure of business, the urgency of affairs* **2.** (P) (Trieb) *desire, eagerness, search, thirst* (nach *for*); *drift, drive* (nach *towards*); der ~ nach Osten *the desire for expansion eastwards*; ~ nach dem Süden *longing, yearning for the South* ‖ ⟨Am⟩ (innerer ~) *urge* (z *to*; *to do*); der elementare ~ *the elemental urge* ‖ ⟨Lit⟩ Sturm u ~ *Storm and Stress* **~zustand** m ⟨psych⟩ *drive*

Drängel·ei f = Gedränge

dr·ängeln vt/i [h] **1.** vt (jdn) *to press, push*; *rush* ‖ **sich** ~ *to crowd* (durch *through*); *to crush* (in *into*; um *round*); *to push one's way* (nach, zu *to*) ‖ → drängen **2.** vi **nicht** ~! *don't push* (od *thrust*) *yourself* (*–selves*) *forward*

dr·ängen I. vt/i [h] **A.** vt **1.** (treiben) **a.** (jdn) *to force, press, push, thrust*; *urge, prod, nudge* (in *into*; v *off*); *to elbow* (aus *out of*); *to edge, urge* (z *to*; *to do*); jdn in e–e Lage ~ *to dragoon a p into a position*; *to hurry* (z *into*; z tun *into doing*); ich will nicht gedrängt w *I won't be rushed*; z dem Schluß gedrängt w *to be forced to the conclusion* **b. sich** ~ *to elbow* (od *push, squeeze, thrust*) *o.s.* (**in** *into*; **durch** *through*); *to elbow* (od *force, push, shoulder, shove, urge*) *one's way* (*into*; *through*); *to crowd, crush, hustle, push, squeeze* (*into*; *through*) ‖ er drängte sich dicht **an** die Schutzwehr *he pressed up against the rampart* ‖ sich ~ **um** jdn *to close* (od *press*) *in upon a p* ‖ man drängte sich um Karten *there was a rush for tickets* **2.** (Schuldner) *to dun*; *press* (*for payment*) **3.** (etw) *to cram, crowd* (in *into*) ‖ (S) *to hurry, urge*; ein Fest drängte das andere *one festival followed close upon the other* ‖ → gedrängt **4. es drängt mich** *I feel called upon* (od *moved*) (*to do*); *the spirit moves me* (*to do*); *I feel compelled to thank you*; *I feel I must thank you* **B.** vi **1.** = drängeln 2. **2.** nach vorwärts ~, an die Spitze ~ *to forge ahead* **2.** ~ **auf** *to insist* (*up*)*on*; *to press for* (*payment*); darauf ~, daß .. *to insist, to be insistent* (od *urgent*) *that* ..; die Not –gte ihn **dazu** *necessity drove him to it*; sich ge–gt fühlen zu *to feel prompted to*, .. *an impulse to* ‖ **sich** zu etw ~ *to be very keen on a th, to do a th* **3. die** S **drängt**, es drängt *the matter presses* (od *is urgent*) *the m. admits of no delay* ‖ die Zeit drängt *time presses, time is growing short* **II.** ≃ n **1.** *the pressing, pushing*; *urging* (z *to*) **2.** ständiges ~ *insistence, urgency* (*of a p*)

Dr·änger m ~s/~ (ungeduldiger Gläubiger) *dun*

Dr·angsal f ~/~e & n ~(e)s/~e *affliction, distress, grief, tribulation*; *trial*; ~e [pl] *hardships* [pl] ‖ °**drangsal·ieren** vt [h] (jdn) *to annoy, harass, importune, vex*; *bully, persecute, torment*; *to make* (*a p's*) *life a misery*

Drän·ier- [in comp] **~pflug** m *draining-plough*

drän·ieren 1. vt (Boden) *to drain* ‖ (of the soil) dräniert w, sich ~ l *to drain* **2.** ≃ n = **Drän·ierung** f ~/~en ⟨a. med⟩ *drainage*

Dr·ansein (→ dran) n ⟨crick⟩ *innings* [pl] [sg konstr]

Draper·ie [–iː] f, ~/~n [–iːən] *drapery*

drap·ieren vt [h] (Stoffe) *to drape* **Drap·ierung** f *draping*

Dräs·ine f → Draisine

dr·astisch 1. a *drastic* (*remedies*); *kill or cure* (*remedy*) | ⟨übtr⟩ *drastic, thorough-going* (*reforms*) ‖ *realistic, effective* **2.** adv *drastically*; (*to describe*) *in a most graphic manner*

Drau, Dr·ave f (Nebenfluß der Donau) *Drave*

†**dr·äuen** vi = drohen

drauf adv = darauf, worauf ‖ was ist denn da ~? *what is on there?* ‖ ~ u dran → dran I. 2. e.

Dr·auf- ~gabe f ⟨com⟩ *earnest*(*-money*) (auf *of*); *premium* **~gänger** m *live wire*; *dare-devil*; *hearty*; *pusher*; *pushing* (od *go-ahead*) *fellow*; ⟨hunt⟩ *thruster*; ⟨Am⟩ *go-getter*; waghalsiger ~ *neck or nothing goer*; junger ~ *young blood* ‖ ⟨dero⟩ *plunger*; *rake* ‖ → Fanatiker, Chauvinist **≃gängerisch** a *aggressive*; *pugnacious, combative* ‖ *dare-devil, go-ahead, pushing* **~gängertum** n *dashing carriage*; *pugnacity* ‖ *go-ahead*(*ed*)*ness* ≃|**geben** vt [h] (etw) beim Kauf ~ *to throw* (*a th*) *into the bargain* ≃|**gehen** vi [s] (P) *to perish*; *to die* ‖ (Geld) *to go* (f *on*); *to be spent* (bis auf den letzten Pfennig *to the last farthing*); viel ~ l *to spend a great deal* (*on*); bei dem Geschäft geht viel Geld ~ *this b. swallows up much m., much m. is swallowed up in this b.* **~geld** n = Draufgabe ≃|**legen** vt [h] (Geld) *to pay in addition* | ich mußte noch ~ *I had to sell it at a loss* **≃los** adv *along, away* ‖ ~|arbeiten vi *to work* (⟨fam⟩ *to peg*) *away* (an *at*) ‖ ~|gehen vi *to make straight for it* ‖ °~|pfeffern vi/t ⟨fam⟩ *to fire* od *blaze away*; *to let fly* ‖ ~|reden vi *to ramble* ‖ ~|reiten vi ⟨a.⟩ *to ride for a fall* ‖ ~|schießen vi *to blaze* (od *fire*) *away* (auf *at*) ‖ ~|wirtschaften vi *to manage recklessly*; *to be wasteful of one's means* **~sicht** f *top* od *plan view*

draus adv ⟨fam⟩ = daraus

dr·äuschen vi [h] = platschen; pladdern

dr·außen adv **1.** *out, outside, without*; *out of doors*; *away* ‖ † *without doors* ‖ ~ s *to be out*; ~ bleiben *to keep out* ‖ ~ halten *to keep .. out* (P & S) ‖ da ~, dort ~ *out there*; da weit ~ *away out there*; ~ auf der Terrasse sitzen *to sit out on the terrace*; ~ auf See *out at sea* ‖ weit ~ ⟨Am⟩ *way off*; *she lives away out in the country* **2.** (in der Fremde) *abroad*; *out*; ~ in Afrika *out in A.*; hier (sc Afrika) ~ *out here* **3.** (nicht im Kittchen) *outside* **4.** (Ggs im Büro) *in the field*

Dr·ave, Drau f (Nebenfluß der Donau) *Drave*

Draw·idasprachen f [pl] *Dravidian languages*

Dr·eadnought [ˈdrednɔːt] m (engl) ~s/~s ⟨mar⟩ *dreadnought*

Dr·echsel- (→ drechseln) [in comp] *turning* **~bank** f (*turning-*)*lathe*

Drechsel·ei f ⟨fig⟩ *affectedness*; *affectation*

dr·echseln vt/i [h] **1.** vt (etw) *to shape* (*a th*) *on a lathe, to turn* (*a th*) (aus *out of*) | ⟨übtr⟩ (Phrasen) *to turn* ‖ *to shape*; *devise* ‖ °e–e S ~ → deichseln, gedrechselt **2.** vi *to work with a lathe, to turn* **Dr·echsler** m ~s/~ *turner*

Dr·echsler- ~arbeit f *turner's work, turnery* **~geselle** m *journeyman turner* **~handwerk** n *turner's trade* **~kunst** f *turnery* **~meister** m *master-turner* **~waren** f [pl] *turned goods* [pl], *turnery ware* **~werkstatt** f *turner's shop* **~werkzeug** n *turning-tool*

Drechsler·ei f ~/~en **1.** *turnery* **2.** *turner's shop*

Dreck m ~(e)s/ **1.** (Kot) *dirt, excrements* [pl], *ordure*; *dung*, Mäuse≃ *mouse-dung*; → Teufels≃ **2.** °(Schmutz) ⟨oft fig⟩ *dirt, mire, muck, mud, slush*; *dust* ‖ häßlicher ~ *filth* ‖ macht euren ~ allein(e) *do your own dirty work* | ⟨fig⟩ ~ **am** Stecken h *to have a skeleton in one's closet*; ⟨mst °fig⟩ (etw) **aus** dem ~ ziehen *to drag* (*a th*) *out of the mud*; aus dem größten *or* gröbsten ~ bin ich jetzt heraus *I have broken the back of it now* ‖ **durch** den ~ ziehen *to drag* (*a p, a th*) *through the mire* ‖ tief **im** ~ sitzen *or* waten *to be deep in the mire*, ⟨fig fam⟩ *to be hard up* ‖ die Karre in den ~ gefahren h *to stick in the mud* ‖ (jdn) in den ~ ziehen *to drag* (*a p*) *in the mud*, ⟨fam⟩ *to smear*; **mit** ~ (be)werfen *to fling* (od *throw*) *dirt* (od *mud*) *at a p* ‖ jdn **wie** ~ unter den Füßen behandeln *to treat a p as the mud beneath one's feet*; frech wie ~ (as) *bold as brass* **3.** ⟨fig⟩ (Wertloses) ~, °Scheiß≃ *muck, rubbish*; *garbage*; reiner ~ *sheer muck* ‖ der ganze ~ *the whole damn thing* ‖ sich **um** jeden ~

kümmern, s–e Nase in jeden ~ stecken *to concern o.s. with every trifle*; *to poke one's nose into things where one is not wanted* ‖ er kümmert sich (k)einen ~ darum ⟨fam⟩ *he doesn't care a damn* ‖ ich mache mir e–n ~ daraus *I don't care a damn* (od *farthing, pin, straw*) ‖ du verstehst e–n ~ davon *you understand damned little of it* ‖ (in Antworten) 'en ~ kann er! *deuce a bit he can*! **4.** °⟨aero sl⟩ *thick cloud*; ⟨fam⟩ *dirty, foul, nasty* (*weather*)

Dr·eck- [in comp] **~bürste** f *scrubbing-brush* | °**~fink,** °**~hammel** m *mudlark, muckworm*; *sloven* **~käfer** m ⟨ent⟩ *muckworm, dung-beetle* **~karren** m *dung-cart* | °**~kerl** m *nasty dirt* | °**~loch** n ⟨sl⟩ *beastly hole*; → Pfuhl **~schleuder** f *evil tongue* | °**~spatz, ~vogel** m = Dreckfink **~winkel** m = Dreckloch

dr·eckig I. a **1.** *dirty* (hands), *muddy* (*boots*); *grimy* ‖ widerlich ~ *foul* (v *with*); *filthy*; *mucky* ‖ ~er Zustand *state of dirt*; *dirtiness, muddiness* ‖ (etw) ~ m *to dirty*; sich die Hände ~ m *to soil one's hands* | *dirty, foul, nasty* (*weather*) **2.** ⟨übtr & fig⟩ (gemein) *dirty, mean* (*fellow*); *filthy* (*talk*); *nasty* (*mind*) **II.** adv **es geht mir** heute sehr ~ ⟨sl⟩ *I feel blue today* ‖ es geht ihm ~ *he is badly off* ‖ ~·lachen *to grin*; *smirk, sneer*

Dr·edsche f (Grundnetz) *dredge*

Dreesch m ~es/~e [a. n & f] ⟨agr⟩ = Brachfeld

Dr·eganker m, **Dr·egge** f ⟨mar⟩ = Dragge

Dreh m ~s/~e (→ ~e) **1.** = Drehung **2.** °⟨fig⟩ (Wendung, Kniff) *trick, artifice, twist, thing*; ⟨bes Am⟩ *gimmick* ‖ e–r S e–n neuen ~ geben *to give a new twist to a th*; der richtige ~ *the right twist*; den ~ e–r S heraushaben *to have the knack of a th*

Dr·eh- [in comp] *pivot* ..; *rotary, revolving*; *turning*; *swivel* **~achse** f *rotary axis*; *pivot* → Drehungs– **~arbeiten** f pl ⟨film⟩ *shooting* **~automat** m *automatic lathe* **~bank** f *lathe, turning machine*; *turn-bench*; selbsttätige ~ *automatic*; Revolver≈ *turret-lathe* **~basse** f ⟨hist, mar⟩ *swivel-gun* **~bewegung** f *rotary motion*; *rotation*; → –moment **~bleistift** m *propelling* (od *revolving*) *pencil* **~blende** f ⟨phot⟩ *revolving diaphragm* **~blinkfeuer** n *rotating beacon* **~brücke** f *turn* (od *swing, swivel*)*-bridge*; *pivot-bridge* **~buch** n ⟨film⟩ *word-book, scenario*, ⟨Am a.⟩ *script*; endgültiges ~ *final* (*shooting*) *script* **~buchschreiber** m *scripter, scenarist* **~bühne** f ⟨theat⟩ *revolving stage* **~durchmesser** m *swing* **~feld** n; magnetisches ~ *magnetic alternating current field* **~feuer** n ⟨mar⟩ *revolving light* **~flügelflugzeug** n ⟨aero⟩ *rotary plane* **~flügler** m ⟨off⟩ = Hubschrauber **~frucht** f ⟨bot⟩ *Cape primrose*; *Streptocarpus* [L] **~funkfeuer** n ⟨aero, mar⟩ *rotating radio beacon* **~funkpeilung** f *omnirange bearing* **~gestell** n ⟨rail⟩ *bogie* **~griff** m ⟨mot⟩ *twist grip* **~hals** n ⟨orn⟩ = Wendehals **~herz** n ⟨tech⟩ *lathe dog* **~käfer** m ⟨ent⟩ *whirligig* **~kolben** m *rotary piston* **~kondensator** m ⟨el⟩ *adjustable* od *variable disc condenser* **~kraft** f ⟨mech⟩ *torque* **~kran** m ⟨a. mar⟩ *slewing crane* **~krankheit** f ⟨vet⟩ (in sheep) *staggers* [pl] **~kranz** m ⟨artill⟩ (der Lafette) *racer*; *base ring* ‖ ~lafette [f] *ring-type mounting* **~kreis** m *turn*(*ing*)*-circle* **~kreuz** n (auf Fußwegen) *turnstile* **~leier** f ⟨mus⟩ *hurdy-gurdy* **~leiter** f (Feuerwehr) *turnable ladder* **~maschine** f *turning m.*; *lathe* **~meißel** m ⟨tech⟩ *lathe tool, turning tool* **~moment** n ⟨mech⟩ *torque*; *turning moment* **~ofen** m ⟨tech⟩ *turning furnace, rotary kiln* **~orgel** f ⟨mus⟩ *barrel-organ* **~pause** f ⟨film⟩ *stretch*; während der ~e *between takes* **~plan** m ⟨film⟩ *shooting schedule* **~platz** m ⟨film⟩ *location* **~punkt** m *centre of motion* od *rotation*; *fulcrum* ‖ ⟨fig⟩ → Angelpunkt **~rad** n *revolving-wheel* **~rahmenantenne** f *rotating loop antenna* **~ring** m *swivel* **~rolle** f (f Wäsche) *mangle* **~schalter** m ⟨el⟩ *turn-switch* **~scheibe** f ⟨rail⟩ *turn-table*; *traverser* ‖ → Töpferscheibe ‖ (Geschütz–) ~ *racer* **~schieber** m *rotary slide valve* **~sitz** m *swivel seat* **~späne** m [pl] *turnings* [pl] **~spannung** f ⟨mech⟩ *torsional strain* **~spiegel** m *cheval-glass* **~spieß** m ⟨cul⟩ *rotisserie* Fr **~spulinstrument** n ⟨el⟩ *adjustable coil instrument* **~stahl** m *turning* (od *lathe*)*-tool* **~stift** m (in der Uhr) *turning-arbor* **~strom** m ⟨el⟩ *three-phase* (od *polyphase, triphase*) *current* ‖ ~motor [m] *three-phase motor, three-phaser* **~stuhl** m *swivel-chair* **~stütze** f (f Geschütze) *swivel* **~sucht** f ⟨vet⟩ = Drehkrankheit **~tag** m ⟨film⟩ *shooting day* **~tür** f *revolving door* **~turm** m ⟨mil⟩ *revolving turret* **~ventil** n ⟨tech⟩ *rotary valve* **~waage** f ⟨el⟩ *torsion balance*; → Drall **~wähler** m ⟨telph⟩ *rotary selector* **~würfel** m *teetotum* **~wurm** m ⟨zoo⟩ *hydatid*; → Drehkrankheit **~zahl** f *number of revolutions* (od *rotations*); *speed of rotation* ‖ ~begrenzer [m] ⟨tech⟩ *governor* ‖ ~bereich [m] *speed range* ‖ ~einstellung [f] ⟨aero⟩ *power setting* ‖ ~messer [m] *rev*(*olution-*)*counter* ‖ ≈regelbar [a] *speed control* (Motor) ‖ ~regler [m] *speed control* od *regulator*; ⟨bes aero⟩ *constant-speed control unit* ‖ ~schwankung [f] (Pendeln) ⟨tech mach⟩ *hunting* **~zapfen** m *swivel*; *trunnion*; *fulcrum pin*

dr·ehbar a *revolving, rotating, rotatory*; *swivel*; ~es Büchergestell *revolving case* | adv ~ gelagert ⟨tech⟩ *pivoted* ‖ → Dreh–

°**Dr·ehe** f (= Gegend): in dieser ~ wird es s *it will be hereabout*(*s*)

dr·ehen vt/i [h] **I.** vt **A. 1.** (um e–e Achse ~) **a.** (Maschine) *to revolve*, (Globus) *to rotate*; (Rad) *to turn*; ⟨fam⟩ *to rev* ‖ (etw) schnell ~ *to spin* (*a th*), *to give* (*a th*) *a spin*, ⟨fam⟩ *to rev up* ‖ auf e–m Zapfen ~ *to swivel*; *his chair was skewed to one side* **b.** (Kurbel) *to turn*; (Orgel, Lied) *to grind* **c.** → Film **2.** (~d formen) **a.** = drechseln **b.** (Faden, Seide etc) *to twist* (z *into*); (Haar) *to curl* ‖ (in pottery) *to throw* ‖ (Kränze) *to twine* ‖ (Bart) *to twirl* ‖ (Tabak, Zigarette) *to roll* ‖ (Pillen) *to make*; *form* **3.** (in e–e Richtung ~) **a.** (Schiff) *to veer* ‖ (Scheinwerfer) *to turn* (auf *on*); abwärts ~ *to tilt* **b.** den Kopf ~ *to screw one's head*; jdm den Rücken ~ *to turn one's back on a p* **4.** ⟨übtr & fig⟩ **a.** (Tanz) *to dance* ‖ → Daumen **b.** → Mantel ‖ jdm e–e Nase ~ *to make a long nose at a p, to lead a p by the nose* ‖ jdm e–n Strick ~ aus etw *to turn a th to a p's disadvantage* **c.** (verdrehen) (etw) *to twist*; *to distort* **d.** °e–e S ~ *to manage a th*, wir w es schon irgendwie ~ ⟨sl⟩ *we shall wangle it somehow* ‖ °e–n ~ *to paint the town red* ‖ ein Ding ~ → Ding II. A. 5. **B. sich** ~ **1.** (S) **a.** *to revolve, rotate, turn* (um e–e Achse *on an axis*; um e–n Punkt *round a point*); ⟨fam⟩ *to rev* ‖ sich schnell ~ *to spin, gyrate* (um *round*); ⟨fam⟩ *to rev up* ‖ das Rad hat sich einmal gedreht *the wheel has come full circle* ‖ sich wirbelnd ~ (of a top) *to sleep* ‖ sich auf e–m Zapfen ~ *to swivel* ‖ sich ~ l *to turn*; *screw* **b.** (Schiff) *to veer* ‖ (Wind) *to shift round, to veer*; → schralen **c.** (Augen etc) *to reel, revolve* ‖ der ganze Raum drehte sich ihr im Kopfe *the whole room reeled about her* ‖ mir dreht sich der Kopf *my head is spinning* ‖ mir dreht sich alles im Kopfe *my head reels* (od *swims, turns*), *my brain whirls* (vor *with*) **2.** (P) **a.** *to turn* (nach *to*); sich im Kreise ~ *to spin round*; sich in s–n Gedanken im K. ~ *to argue in a circle* ‖ sich im Tanze ~ *to whirl* (in e–m Raum *round a room*); sich kreiselartig ~ *to pirouette* (auf e–m Bein *on one leg*) | **sich um sich selbst** ~ *to slew, slue* **b.** ⟨übtr⟩ (lavieren) sich ~ *to veer*; sich ~ u wenden *to hedge, shuffle, tergiversate* **c.** ⟨übtr⟩ die ganze

Familie dreht sich um ihn *all the family gyrate around him* **3.** ⟨übtr⟩ (S) **sich ~ um** *to pivot on* od *round*; *to hinge on*; *to turn on* (: *the split turned on principles*) ‖ der Streit dreht sich um etw .. *revolves around a th* ‖ die Unterhaltung drehte sich um .. *the conversation was of* ..; das ist der Punkt, um den sich alles dreht *that is the pivot on which everything turns*, es dreht sich darum, ob .. *the point is whether* ‖ *to depend* (od *hang*) *on* ‖ der Gedanke, um den sich alles dreht *the core idea* ‖ es dreht sich um dich *it's you who matter* **II.** vi **1.** (Wind) *to veer round* (nach Osten *to the east*) ‖ (Schiff) *to turn* (nach *to*); ⟨aero⟩ nach rechts ~ *to veer*; → wenden **2.** ~ **an etw** *to turn a th*; *to twist a th*; an e–m Knopf ~ *to twiddle a knob* ‖ ⟨phot⟩ v e–r Aufnahme z anderen weiter ~ *to wind from one exposure to the next* **III. Dr·ehen** n *revolving*; *turning* ‖ *twist* ‖ etc → I. & II. ‖ ⟨film⟩ *shooting* ‖ Hang z ~ ⟨tech⟩ *verticity*

dr·ehend a sich ~ *revolving*, *rotating* (*shaft*) *rota(to)ry* (*motion*), *rotative*; *gyratory* (*movement*); ~e Bewegung *rotation*, *turn*; *twist*; *whirl*

Dr·eher m ~s/ [pl] ~ **1.** (P) ⟨tech⟩ *turner* ‖ °Pillen≈ = Apotheker **2.** (S) = Kurbel **Dreher·ei** f ~/~en 1. *turnery* 2. *turner's shop* **Dr·ehling** m ⟨bot⟩ *agaric*

Dr·ehung f ~/~en **1.** (um e–e Achse) *turn* (*of a wheel*); *gyration*, *rotation*, *revolution*; ⟨fam⟩ *rev* ‖ ganze ~ ⟨hors⟩ *pirouette* ‖ schnelle ~ *spin*, *whirl* ‖ (etw) in ~ versetzen *to rotate*, *revolve*, *gyrate* ‖ e–e ~ m = sich drehen **2.** (schraubenförmige ~) *torsion* **3.** *twist* (⟨a.⟩ *of the body*); (Windung) *turn*; *twine* **4.** (~ in e–r Richtung) *turn* (nach rechts *to the right*); → Kamera ‖ e–m Ball e–e ~ geben *to screw a ball* **5.** ⟨übtr⟩ = Wendung | **~s- ~achse** f *axis of rotation* **~elastizität** f *torsion* **~festigkeit** f *torsional strength* **~vermögen** n *rotatory power* **~winkel** m *angle of rotation*; *angle of torsion*

dr·ei I. a [attr & abs] **1.** *three* ‖ ~ gleich ausgeführte Exemplare *triplicates* [pl] ‖ ⟨phot⟩ ein Pack v ~ Filmen *a tri-pack* ‖ ~ Fuß lang *three-foot* (*board*) ‖ Gestell mit ~ Füßen *tripod* ‖ ~ Jahre alt *three-year-old* (*child*); alle ~ Jahre e–e Beförderung *a triennial promotion* ‖ → König; Leib ‖ Periode v ~ Monaten *trimester* ‖ Flugzeug mit ~ Motoren *trimotor* ‖ ~ Pence *threepence*; ~ Pence wert *threepenny* ‖ ~ P betr, aus ~ P bestehend *triangular* (*talk*); *three-cornered* (*fight*) ‖ Satz v ~ P *or* Dingen *triplet* ‖ aus ~ Stücken bestehend *threefold* ‖ (etw) in ~ Teile gabeln *to trifurcate*; .. teilen *to trisect* | wir waren unser ~ *we were three* (*in number*) ‖ noch ehe man (bis) ~ zählen konnte *in a twinkling* od *trice*; *in the twikling of an eye*; er sah aus, als ob er nicht bis ~ zählen könnte *he looked as if butter would not melt in his mouth* ‖ → Ding | diese ~ *these three*; sie alle ~ *all three of them* ‖ *ich nehme alles ~es *I'll take all three* (*things*) **2.** ~ Uhr *three o'clock* ‖ halb ~ *half past two* **II.** ≈ f ~/~en (*the number*) *three*; e–e ~ *a three*; zwei ~en [pl] *two threes* ‖ z ~en *in threes*; ⟨golf⟩ Spiel z ~en (einer gegen zwei) *threesome* ‖ zw ~en abgeschlossen *tripartite* (*treaty*) ‖ mit ~en fahren *to drive three-in-hand* ‖ z ~en antreten *to form threes* → acht, fünf **III.** [in comp] *three–*, *tri–* **~achsfahrzeug** n mit Vierradantrieb ⟨mot⟩ *six-by-four* **~achser** m ⟨mot⟩ *six-wheeler* **~achteltakt** m ⟨mus⟩ *three-eight time* ≈**adrig** a ⟨el⟩ *three-core* (*cable*) **~akter** m *three-act play* °**~angel** f = Triangel ≈**armig** a *three-armed* ≈**atomig** a *triatomic* ≈**basisch** a *tribasic* ‖ **~bein** n *tripod*; *gin* ‖ ~fahrwerk [n] ⟨aero⟩ *tricycle landing gear* ‖ ~lafette [f] *tripod mount* ‖ ~wettlaufen [n] *three-legged race* ≈**beinig** a *three-legged* **~blatt** n **1.** ⟨bot⟩ *trefoil*; *clover* **2.** ⟨arch⟩ *trefoil* **3.** ⟨cards⟩ = Tippen ‖ ~schraube [f] ⟨aero⟩ *three-bladed airscrew* ≈**blätt(e)rig** a *trifoliate* **~bund** m *Triple Alliance*; *triplice* [It] (1882) **3-D** (= dimensional) ⟨film etc⟩ *3-D* **~decker** m ⟨mar⟩ *three-decker* ‖ ⟨aero⟩ *triplane* ‖ °in **~deibelsnamen,** ja! (*stay* od *go*, etc.) *and be hanged* ≈**dimension·al** a *three-dimensional* ‖ ~er Klang *spherical* od *stereophonic sound* ‖ D–·alfilm [m] *cinemascope*, *cinerama* ≈**drähtig** a *three-cord* [attr] **~eck** n *triangle*; *trigon*; (Land) in ~en vermessen *to triangulate* ‖ Zeichen≈ (Lineal) *set square* ‖ ~flügel [m] ⟨aero⟩ *delta wing* ‖ ~(s)rechner [m] (*triangle*) *computor*, ⟨aero⟩ *time*, *distance*, *speed* (*TDS*) *computer*, *course and speed calculator* (*CSC*) ‖ ⟨surv⟩ ~smessung [f] *triangulation* ‖ ~slehre [f] *trigonometry*; ~hös|chen [n] *Y-front pants* ‖ ⟨el⟩ ~schaltung [f] *delta connexion* ≈**eckig** a *three-cornered* (*hat*); *triangular*; *trigonal*; ~e Form *triangularity*; ~es Bogenornament *triquetra* [L] ‖ ~es Segel *lateen sail* ‖ ~es Stück (im Kleid) *gore*, *gusset* ‖ ~e Verabredung (1 Mann–2 Frauen *or* umgekehrt) *sandwich date* ≈**einh·alb,** ~ und einhalb a *three and a half*; ~ Pence *threepence halfpenny* ≈**·einig** a *triune* **~·einigkeit** f *Trinity* ‖ ~s-fenster [n] ⟨arch⟩ *triple lancet* ‖ ~s- *Triune* (Nummer) ‖ ~slehre [f] *trinitarianism* **~elektr·odenröhre** f ⟨el⟩ *triode*; *three-electrode* ≈**fach** adv ~zus–legen *to fold .. into three* ‖ das D–e nehmen *to take three times* (*as much* od) *the amount* **~fächer** m *spread salvo of 3 torpedos* **~fachrevolver** m ⟨microscope⟩ *triple nosepiece*, ⟨opt⟩ *triple-lens turret* **~f·altigkeit** f *Trinity* ‖ ~sfest [n] = Trinitatisfest **~f·arben-** [in comp] *three-colour*; *trichromatic* ‖ ~druck [m] 1. *colo(u)rtype process*; *three-colour process* od *printing* 2. (Bild) *three-colour print* ‖ ~photographie [f] *three-colour photography* ‖ ~system [n] ⟨film⟩ *tricolo(u)r system* ≈**farbig** a *tricolo(u)red*, *trichromatic* **~f·elderwirtschaft** f *three-field system* **~flach** n *trihedron*; ≈- *trihedral* ≈**flügelig** a *three-blade(d)* (Schraube) ≈**förmig** a *triform* **~fuß** m *tripod*; (f Kochgefäß) *trivet* ≈**füßig** a *tripedal* ≈**gablig** a *trifurcate* **~ganggetriebe** n *three-speed gear* od *transmission* ≈**gängig** a *three-thread* (*screw*) **~gespann** n *three-in-hand*; *three-horse carriage*; russisches ~ *troika* **~gestell** n *tripod* **~gestirn** n ⟨übtr⟩ *triumvirate* ≈**gestrichen** a ⟨mus⟩ *three-marked* **~gitterröhre** f ⟨wir⟩ *pentode* ≈**gliederig** a *trinitarian* (*group*) ‖ ⟨math⟩ *trinomial* (*equation*); ~e Zahlengröße *trinomial* ‖ ⟨bot & zoo⟩ *trinomial* ≈**geteilt** a *tripartite* ≈**gleisig** a ⟨mot⟩ *three-lane* (Fahrbahn) ≈**gliedrig** a *triangular* (⟨mil⟩ Division) **~glied(e)rung** f *triangular organization* **~gr·oschenoper** f ⟨mus⟩ *Beggars' Opera* **~herrschaft** f *trierarchy* ≈**holmig** a ⟨aero⟩ *with 3 spars* ≈**h·undert** a *three hundred* ‖ ~jährig a *tercentenary*; ~jähriger Gedenktag *tercentenary* ≈**hundertste** a *three-hundredth* ≈**jährig** a *three-year(s)-old*; *three-years'*; *triennial* ≈**jährlich** a *triennial* **~k·aiserschlacht** f ⟨Ger⟩ *the Battle of Austerlitz* (1805) **~k·aiserverhältnis** n *the League of the Three Emperors* (1872) **~kampf** m ⟨sport⟩ *triathlon* °**~k·äsehoch** m *manikin*, *hop-o'-my-thumb*, *Jack Sprat* **~kant** m *trihedron* ≈**kantig** a *triangular* (*wire*) **~klang** m ⟨mus⟩ *triad* **~kl·assenwahlrecht** n ⟨Ger hist⟩ *three-class franchise* **~konchenchor** m *trefoiled apse* **~k·önigsfest** n ⟨ec⟩ *Epiphany*, *Twelfth-Night* ≈**köpfig** a ⟨anat⟩ ~er Muskel (am Oberarm) *triceps* **~k·örperproblem** n *problem of three bodies* **~kreiser** m ⟨wir⟩ *three-circuit receiver* ≈**lappig** a ⟨bot⟩ *trilobate* **~laut** m ⟨gram⟩ *triphthong* **~leiterkoaxi·alkabel** n ⟨el⟩ *triple concentric cable* **~m·ächte-** [in comp] *tri-power* (*discussions*) ≈**mal** adv *three times*, *thrice*; ~ so groß *threefold*; ~ wöchentlich (erscheinend etc) *tri-weekly* ≗**malig** a *done* od *repeated three times*; nach ~em Versuch *after three attempts* **~m·ännerskat** m ⟨Ger⟩ *three-man skat* ≗**maschiges** (Fischer-)Garn n *net of 3 meshes* **~mastbark** f *three-masted bark* **~-master** m **1.** ⟨mar⟩ *three-master, bark, barque* **2.** (Hut) *cocked hat, three-cornered hat*; → Dreispitz **~m·eilenzone** f *three-mile zone* ≗**monatig** a *three-months'*; *lasting three months* ≗**monatlich** a *three-monthly*; *quarterly* ≗**motorig** a ⟨aero⟩ *trimotor* [attr] ≗**namig** a *trinomial* **~paß** m ⟨arch⟩ *trefoil* **~p·encestück** n *threepenny bit* (od *piece*) **~pfünder** m ⟨mil⟩ *three-pounder* **~ph·asenstrom** m ⟨el⟩ *three-phase* (od *triphase*) *current* **~phasig** a ⟨el⟩ *triphase, three-phase* ≗**polig** a ⟨el⟩ *triple-pole* (Umschalter *reverser*) ≗**prozentig** a ⟨com⟩ *three-percent*; ~e Staatspapiere [pl] *three-percents* [pl] **~punktlandung** f ⟨aero⟩ *three-point landing* | –system [n] ⟨mill⟩ *three-point system* **~rad** n ⟨cycl⟩ *tricar, tricycle*, ⟨fam⟩ *trike*; zweisitziges ~ *sociable* ‖ ~fahrgestell [n] *three-wheeled undercarriage*; ~kraftwagen [m] *tricar* ≗**räd(e)rig** a *three-wheeled*; ~er Kraftwagen *tricar, three-wheeler* ≗**reihig** a *three-row*; *treble riveted* (*joint*) **~reim** m ⟨pros⟩ *triplet* **~r·öhrenapparat** m ⟨wir⟩ *three-valve set* **~ruderer** m ⟨ant⟩ (Schiff) *trireme* **~s·aiteninstrument** n ⟨mus⟩ *trichord* **~satz** m ⟨math⟩ *rule of three* **~scharpflug** m *three-furrow plough* (⟨Am⟩ *plow*) **~schenkel** m ⟨arch⟩ *triquetra* (L) ‖ ~zirkel [m] *triangular compasses* [pl] ≗**schenkelig** a *three-legged* ≗**schichtig** a *three-ply* (*wood*) ≗**schiffig** a *three-bayed* **~schlag** m ⟨hors⟩ *amble* **~schlitz** m ⟨ant arch⟩ *triglyph* ≗**schneidig** a *three-edged* **~schr·aubendampfer** m *triple-screw steamer* **~seilverankerung** f ⟨aero⟩ *three-wire mooring* ≗**seitig** a *three-sided, trilateral*; *triangular* (*pyramid*); ⟨bot⟩ *trigonal* ≗**silbig** a *trisyllable*; ~es Wort *trisyllable* **~sitzer** m ⟨mot⟩ *three-seater* ≗**sitzig** a *provided with three seats* ≗**spaltig** a ⟨typ⟩ *three--columned*; ⟨bot⟩ *trifid* **~spänner** m = Dreigespann **~spitz** m = Dreimaster 2. ≗**sprachig** a *trilingual* **~sprung** m ⟨sport⟩ *hop, step, and jump* **~stab** m ⟨crick⟩ *wicket*; die weiße Linie vor dem ~ *popping-crease* ≗**stellig** a (Zahl) *of 3 digits, to 3 decimal places*; ~e Zahl *three figures* [pl] ≗**stimmig** a *for three voices* ≗**stöckig** a *3-, 4-storied* (*house*) ≗**stoffig** a *ternary* **~stufen-**, ≗**stufig** a *with 3 steps*; *three stage* (Rakete) ≗**stündig** a *three-hour*; *three-hours'* ≗**stündlich** a *every three hours* ≗**tägig** a *three-day*; *three-days'*, *lasting three days*; → Tertianfieber **~t·ausend** a *three thousand* (*men*) ≗**t·ausendste** a *three-thousandth* ≗**teilig** a *triform, tripartite*; *three-sectional* [attr]; ~es Objektiv ⟨opt⟩ *triplet*; ⟨bot & zoo⟩ *trifid*; ⟨mus⟩ *triple* ‖ ~es Kostüm *three-piece costume* **~teiligkeit** f *trichotomy* **~teilung** f *tripartition, trisection* **~undzwanzig** a *twentythree*, **three and twenty*; ⟨Ger⟩ ~ Uhr *eleven o'clock p. m.* **~verband** (zw Frankreich, England, Rußland) m ⟨pol⟩ *Triple Entente* **~v·iertel** **1.** n ~ des Lebens *three quarters* (od *parts*) *of life* **2.** a *three-quarter* (*length, chime*) **3.** [in comp] ⟨Rug ftb⟩ ~reihe [f] *three quarters* [pl] ‖ in ~stunden *in three quaters of an hour* ‖ ~takt [m] ⟨mus⟩ *three-four time* | ~wendung [f] *three-quarter view* **~w·egeventil** n *three-way valve* **~weg** m *point where a road forks*; *bifurcation* | ~kontakt [m] ⟨el⟩ *three-terminal contact* ≗**wertig** a ⟨chem⟩ *trivalent*; ~es Element *triad* ≗**wöchentlich**, ≗**wöchig** a *tri-weekly* **~zack** m **1.** *trident*; *tridental spear* **2.** ⟨bot⟩ *arrow-grass* ≗**zackig** a *three-pronged*; *tridental*; *trifurcate*; ~er Speer *trident* **~zahl** f *triad* **~zahn** m ⟨bot⟩ *spinifex* (L) **~z·ehenmöwe** f ⟨orn⟩ *kittiwake* **~zehn** → d. **~zeiler** m ⟨pros⟩ (*interlinked*) *tercet*, It *terza rima* ≗**zeilig** a *trilinear* **~zinkig** a *three-pronged* ≗**zipflig** a ⟨bot⟩ *trifid* ≗**zöllig** a *three-inch* ≗**zon·al**, **~z·onen-** *trizonal* ‖ –zonen-Farbbandeinstellung *f* ⟨typwr⟩ *three colo(u)r device* ≗**zonig** a *trizonal*

Dr·eier m ~s/~ ⟨hist⟩ *German coin of 3 pfennig* ‖ nicht (für)'n ~ *not* (*for*) *a ha'p'orth*; °ich gebe nicht e–n ~ dafür *I don't give a rap for it* **~gemisch** n ⟨mot⟩ *ternary fuel* **~gespräche** n pl *tripartite talks* **~komitee** n *tripartite committee* **~pakt** m *Pact Tripartite*

dr·eierl·ei a ~ Bedingungen *three kinds of conditions*; ~ Farben *three different colours*; ~ Arten Bücher *books of three* (*different*) *kinds*

dr·eifach **1.** a *threefold, trine, triple*; ≗expansionsmaschine *triple expansion engine*; in ~er Ausführung *in triplicate* ‖ *three-ply* (*thread, linen*) ‖ ⟨mot, cycl⟩ ~e Übersetzung *three--speed gear* **2.** adv *threefold*; ~ ausgefertigt *tripartite, triplicate*

Dr·eiheit f *threeness*; *triad*; *trichotomy*; *triplicity*

°**dr·ein** adv = darein ‖ → oben~ **~blicken** = –schauen **~|fahren** vi [s] da soll der Teufel ~! *the devil take it!* **~|reden** vi *to interfere*; *to meddle* (in *in*) ≗**|reden** n *interfering*; *interference* (in *in*); *meddling*; *meddlesomeness* **~|schauen** vi; blöde ~ *to stare stupidly*, ⟨Am⟩ *to gawk* ‖ ruhig ~ *to have* od *wear a calm expression* **~|schlagen** vi *to lay about one*; sie schlugen ~ *they laid about them*

Dreisch m = Dreesch

dr·eißig **1.** a *thirty*; vgl achtzig **2.** ≗ f *thirty* ‖ in den ~en *in the thirties* ‖ er ist Mitte ≗ *or* Mitte der ≗er *he is half-way between thirty and forty*

Dr·eißiger **1.** **a.** ~ m ~s/~; ein ~ *a man of thirty* (od *in the thirties*) **b.** die ~ (*or* ~jahre) [pl] *the thirties* [pl] (: *to be in the th.*); ein Mann in den ~n (~jahren) *a man in the thirties*; vgl achtzig **2.** ≗ a die ~ Jahre des 19. Jhs. *the thirties* [pl] *of the 19th century*

dr·eißigjährig a *thirty years old*; *of thirty years*; ein ≗er → Dreißiger 1. ‖ der ≗e Krieg *the Thirty Years' War*

dr·eißigste a *thirtieth* **Dr·eißigstel** n ~s/~ *the thirtieth*

dr·eist a *bold, free*; *audacious*; er war so ~ z tun *he presumed* (od *made bold*) *to do* ‖ *confident*; *courageous, daring* ‖ *blatant* (*lie*) | (frech) *bold, forward*; ⟨fam⟩ *cheeky, saucy*; ⟨Am sl⟩ *fresh* **~frech** a ⟨m. m.⟩ *impudently saucy* ≗**igkeit** f ~/~en *impudence, boldness*; *audacity* ‖ *confidence, assurance*; *courage, daring* | *boldness, forwardness*; ⟨fam⟩ *cheek, sauciness* (: *it's frightful cheek on my part*) ‖ es würde e–e unerhörte ~ s *it would be infernal cheek* (*to do*); ~en *liberties* [pl], sich ~en gegenüber jdm herausnehmen *to take liberties with a p* ‖ so e–e ~! *you've* (od *he's*) *got your* (*his*) *nerve with you* (*him*) od .. *got the cheek of the devil*

dr·eizehn a *thirteen*; *a baker's dozen* ‖ ⟨Ger⟩ ~ Uhr *one o'clock p. m.* ‖ nun schlägt's ~ *that takes the cake!*; *so it's come to this!* **dr·eizehnte** a *thirteenth* **Dr·eizehntel** n *thirteenth* **dr·eizehntens** adv *thirteenthly*; *in the thirteenth place*

Drell m ~(e)s/~e *drill, tick, ticking* **dr·ellen** a *drill* (*jacket*)

Dr·empel m ⟨arch⟩ *short projecting part of a wall* ‖ ⟨mar⟩ *sill*

Dr·esch- (→ dreschen) [in comp] *threshing* **~flegel** m *flail* **~maschine** f *threshing-machine, thresher* **~mühle** f *threshing-mill* **~tenne** f *threshing-floor*

°**Dr·esche** f ~ *beating, thrashing*; *belting*; ⟨sl⟩ *larrup*; ⟨Am sl⟩ *whaling*; ~ bek *to get a beating* od *thrashing*; → verdreschen

dr·eschen I. vt/i [drosch/gedroschen] [h] **A.** vt **1.** (Korn etc) *to thresh,* **thrash* || gedroschenes Getreide *threshing* || ⟨fig⟩ leeres Stroh ~, Phrasen ~ *to utter platitudes* (od *empty words*), ⟨sl⟩ *to let off hot air* || Skat ~ *to indulge in playing skat* **2.** ⟨übtr⟩ jdn ~ *to thrash a p*; jdn windelweich ~ *to thrash the life out of a p* **B.** vi ⟨eig⟩ *to thresh* **II.** ≗ n *threshing*

Dr·escher m ~s/~ *thresher*; °essen wie ein ~ *to play a good knife and fork*

Dr·esden n ⟨Ger⟩ (Stadt) *Dresden*

Dreß m [invar] (⟨bes⟩ *sport*) *suit*; in vollem ~ ⟨fam⟩ *in full get-up*

Dress·eur [dreˈsør] m (Fr) *trainer* **Dress·ier-** ~beutel, ~sack [m] ⟨cul⟩ *piping–, forcing-bag* | ~nadel [f] ⟨cul⟩ *trussing-needle* **dress·ieren** vt [h] **1.** (T) *to train*; (Hund) *to teach*; (Pferd) *to break in*; ein Hund auf den Mann dressiert *a dog trained to attack a p when commanded* || (Löwen) *to tame*; **2.** (Tuche) *to dress, steam* **3.** (Geflügel) ⟨cul⟩ *to truss* **4.** (Blech) *to temper roll* **Dress·ur** f ~/~en *training; breaking-in* || *taming* || ⟨circus⟩ (~nummer) *trained-animal act*

dr·ibbeln vt [h] ⟨ftb⟩ *to dribble*

Driesch m ~es/~e [a. n & f] ⟨agr⟩ = Brachfeld **Dr·ieschling** m ⟨bot⟩ = Champignon

dr·ieseln vt [h] = drehen 2. b.

Drift f ~/~en (engl) ⟨mar⟩ (Strömung) *drift*

Dr·iften n ~s/ *drifting* ⟨a. a–n⟩

Drilch m = Drillich **Drill** m = Drell

Dr·ill m ~s/ ⟨bes mil⟩ *drill; military training* od *discipline* || ⟨übtr⟩ *drill*; strammer ~ *rigorous discipline; strict methodical instruction* **~bogen** m *drill-bow* **~bohrer** m *drill* **~meister** m ⟨mil⟩ *drill-sergeant, –master* **~platz** m ⟨mil⟩ *drill--ground*

dr·illen vt [h] †**1.** (drehen) *to twist; turn* **2.** ⟨mil⟩ (Rekruten) *to drill* || ⟨übtr⟩ (jdn) *to discipline, drill, instruct, train* (in *in* [*a subject*]) || *to subject* (*a p*) *to a rigorous discipline; to regiment* (*a p*)

dr·illen vt [h] ⟨agr⟩ (in Reihen säen) (Saat) *to drill*; → Drillmaschine

Dr·illich m ~(e)s/~e ⟨bes mar⟩ (coarse linen) = Drell || ~rock ⟨mil⟩ *fatigue jacket* || Drilchanzug [m], –zeug [n] ⟨mil⟩ *denims* pl, *fatigues* pl, *fatigue dress*

Dr·illing m ~(e)s/~e **1.** *triplet*; ~e [pl] *triplets* [pl] **2.** (Gewehr) *three-barrelled gun* **~sblume** f ⟨bot⟩ *bougainvillaea* (L) **~s(dampf)-maschine** f *three* (od *triple*)*-cylinder engine* **~sturm** m ⟨mar⟩ *triple turret*

Drillmaschine f ⟨agr⟩ *drill(-machine, –plough)*

Dr·illung f ~/~en *torsion*

°**drin** adv = darin; worin || ⟨übtr⟩ mitten ~ s *to be in the movement* || ~ sitzen (in der Patsche *or* Tinte) *to be in it*

dr·ingen vi [drang/gedrungen] **A.** [s] **1.** ⟨eig⟩ **a.** (P) **~ aus** (etw) *to break out of* (*a th*) | **~ bis** (nach) .. *to get* od *go as far as*; → vordringen | **~ durch** (etw) *to break through, to force one's way through; to get* od *pass through* (*a th*) || *to penetrate* (*a forest*) || → durchdringen | **~ in** (etw) *to break into* (*a house*); *to enter by force, to force one's way into* (*a th*) || *to invade* (*a country*) || *to penetrate* (od *search, see*) *into* (*a secret*) || *to penetrate* (*a mystery*); *to go to the bottom of* (*a th*); → eindringen **b.** (S) **~ aus** (etw) *to spring from*; (of sounds) *to break* od *come from* (*a th*) | ~ bis z *to reach* (*to*) (*the bottom*) | **~ durch** (etw) (of a bullet, knife; of light, etc.) *to enter, pierce, penetrate* (*the skin*); *to plough one's way through* (*the flesh*); *to strike through* || (of liquids) *to permeate* (*the soil*); *to pass through* (*the surface*); *damp seeps through; a cry rang into the night*; (of wind) *to search* || laut ~ (of noises) *to rip through* (*the door*) || (of ideas) *to permeate* (*a community*) | **~ in** etw *to enter, penetrate, pierce* (*the flesh*); (of the sea) *to gain upon* (*the land*) || in die Öffentlichkeit ~ (of news) *to gain publicity, to get abroad* | **zum** Herzen ~ *to stir the soul; to move* (od *go straight to*) *a p's heart* **2.** ⟨übtr⟩ **in jdn ~ z tun** *to press* od *urge a p to do; to make a p do* || mit Bitten ~ in jdn *to plead with a p, to prevail upon a p* (*to do*) || mit Fragen ~ in jdn *to ply a p with questions* **B.** [h] **1.** die Stunde dringt *time presses* **2. auf etw** ~ *to insist* (od *to be insistent*) *on a th; to persist in a th; to demand a th* || darauf ~, daß .. *to insist that; to be urgent that*; bei jdm auf etw ~ *to press a p for a th* **C.** sich **gedrungen** fühlen *to feel called upon* od *compelled* (*to do*)

dr·ingend 1. a *pressing* (*problem*); ⟨med⟩ *emergency* (*case*); *imperative* (*necessity*); *urgent* (*need, action,* ⟨telph⟩ *call*); *priority* (*message, call*); ~e Not *urgency, exigency; crying need* || *exigent* (*demand*); ~es Bedürfnis *or* Erfordernis *exigence, –cy*; ~er Fall *emergency*; ~e Gründe *compelling* od *cogent reasons*; ~e Vorstellungen [pl] *urgencies* [pl] || *instant, imminent* (*danger*) || ⟨telph⟩ ~es Gespräch *emergency call* || ~er Verdacht *strong suspision* **2.** adv *urgently, pressingly* || ~ benötigt, nötig *badly needed* || ~ notwendig *imperative* || jdn ~ auffordern *to urge* od *press a p* (*to do*); jdn ~ ersuchen *to request a p earnestly* || jdm ~ empfehlen, nahelegen, raten *to press* od *urge* (*a th*) *upon a p; to advise a p strongly* (*to do*) || ~ bitten um *to press for*

dr·inglich 1. a *pressing, urgent* (*duties, problems*); *instant* (*response*); ~ s *to be pressing* od *urgent* **2.** adv *urgently, pressingly* | **≗keit** f ~/ *urgency, pressure* (*of business*); *instancy; emergency*; → dringend || ⟨bes mil⟩ *priority*

Dr·inglichkeits- [in comp] *urgency* **~antrag** m *urgent application* || ⟨parl⟩ *motion of urgency*; es wurde ~ gestellt *urgency was moved* **~bescheinigung** f *certificate of priority* **~beschluß** m *urgency resolution* **~folge** f *order of priority* **~grad** m *degree of pr.* **~liste** f *pr. list* **~maßnahme** f ⟨parl⟩ *urgency* **~meldung** f *urgent message* **~stufe** f *degree of importance* **~zeichen** n *urgency signal*

dr·innen adv *in; inside, within* || da ~ *there in, in there*; hier ~ *here in, in here* || ~ im Hause *within the house*

Dr·ischel m ~s/~ = Dreschflegel

drischt 3. prs sg v dreschen

dritt 1. a *third*; der ~e April *the third of April*; jedes ~e Wort *every third word*; | Verwandter ~en Grades ⟨Scot⟩ *third of kin* || aus ~er Hand *at third-hand*; [attr] *third-hand* (*information*) || das „~e Haus" ⟨Am pol⟩ *the lobby* || ~e Klasse ⟨a. rail⟩ *third class, third*; ~er Klasse [attr] *third-class* (*carriage*); zwei Billets ~er Kl. *two thirds* || ~er Mann *thirdman, third p; arbiter* || e–e ~e Möglichkeit (*or* ein ~es Mittleres) *zw* zweien *a tertium quid* (L) || ~e P ⟨gram⟩ *third person*; ⟨jur⟩ *third party*; ⟨allg⟩ *another p, disinterested p* || ⟨math⟩ ~e Potenz *cube, the third power*; e–e Zahl in die ~e Potenz erheben *to raise a number to the third power, to cube a number* || ~en Ranges [attr] *third-rate* (*ship*) || ⟨Ger pol⟩ das ≗e Reich *the Third Reich* || ⟨pol⟩ der ~e Stand *the third estate*; ⟨engl⟩ *the Commons* [pl] || sein ~es Wort *his favourite saying* (*was* ..) **2.** [abs] zu ~ *in threes* (: *to march in th.*); wir waren z ~ *there were three of us*

dr·ittbeste a *third best* **Dr·itte 1.** [der ~, ein ~r] m, die ~e [f] *the third p; the third*; im Beisein ~r *in the presence of other people; before witnesses*; e–m ~n gegenüber erwähnen *to mention to anyone else, to another p* || ⟨jur⟩ ein ~r *a third party*; ohne ~en *between ourselves* || Vertrag zugunsten ~er ⟨jur⟩ *third-party beneficiary contract*; → Drittschuldner || ⟨engl jur⟩ (bei Ehescheidung) der mit eingeklagte ~

the co-respondent || ⟨sport⟩ ~n abschlagen *to play third* **2.** das ~ [ein ~s] *the third thing* od *point* || ein ~s gibt es nicht *there is no other way, we have no alternative* || z ersten, z zweiten, z ~n! *going, going, gone!* **dr·itt(e)halb** a *three and a half*

Dr·ittel n ~s/~ *third; the third part* || ⟨math⟩ ⅔ *two thirds; two over three* || ⅔ Mehrheit *two--thirds majority* **dr·itteln** vt [h] (etw) *to third; to divide into 3 parts* **Dr·ittenabschlagen** n (Spiel) *twos-and-threes* [pl]; *tierce* **dr·ittens** adv *thirdly; in the third place* **dr·ittl·etzte** a [a. abs] der ~ *the last but two* || ⟨gram⟩ *antepenultimate*; ~e Silbe *antepenultimate* **drittrangig** a *third-string* [attr] **Dr·ittschrift** f *triplicate original* **Dr·itt-schuldner** m ⟨jur⟩ *garnishee*; (Forderung e–s Schuldners) bei e–m ~ beschlagnahmen *to garnishee*

†**drob** adv = darob, → darüber

dr·oben adv (*high*) *up there; above there; there at the top* || die Sterne ~ *the stars overhead* || ~ im Himmel *on high*; v ~ *from on high*

ˣ**drög** a = trocken → Droge

Dr·oge f ~/~n *drug* || (etw) mit ~n versetzen, mischen *to drug*; (~) spritzen *to fix*

Dr·ogen- [in comp] *drug* .. **~erprobung** f an lebenden Tieren *bioassay* **~geschäft** n = Drogenhandlung **~händler** m *druggist* **~handlung** f *druggist's shop*; ⟨Am⟩ *drug-store, pharmacy*; **~waren** f [pl] *drugs* [pl]

Droger·ie f ~/~n = Drogenhandlung **Drog·ist** m ~en/~en *druggist; chemist and druggist; pharmaceutist, pharmacist* || beim ~ *at the druggist's*

Dr·ohbrief m *threatening letter*

dr·ohen vi [h] **A.** (P) **1.** *to threaten, menace*; **2. jdm** ~ *to threaten* od *menace a p; to fulminate against a p; to bluster at a p*; ⟨Am sl⟩ *to bullgrag a p* **3.** (jdm) **mit** etw ~ **a.** mit dem Finger etc ~ *to threaten* od *menace* (*a p*) *with one's finger; to wag* od *shake one's f.*; → Faust **b.** ⟨übtr⟩ mit Strafe (etc) ~ *to threaten a penalty* (jdm *upon a p*); man drohte ihm mit dem Tode *they threatened him* (od *he was threatened*) *with death* || er drohte mit dem Austritt *he threatened secession* || **damit ~ z tun** *to threaten* (od *menace*) *to do*; er drohte zurückzutreten *he threatened to resign, he threatened his resignation*; damit ~, daß .. *to threaten that* .. **4.** ⟨übtr⟩ er drohte zus–zubrechen *he threatens to collapse; his collapse is impending*; die Verhandlungen ~ fehlzuschlagen .. *are in danger of going wrong* **B.** ⟨übtr⟩ (S) **1. Gefahr** droht, es droht G. *danger threatens, danger is imminent* (od *impending*) || ihm droht G. *danger threatens* (od *hangs over*) *him; he is threatened by danger* **2.** das **Wetter** droht mit Regen *the weather threatens rain; the weather is threatening; there is a threat of rain* **3.** sein **Herz** droht z versagen *his heart threatens to fail*

dr·ohend 1. a *threatening, menacing* (*attitude*) || *imminent, impending* (*disaster*) || ~e Gefahr *threat, menace, imminence* (f jdn *to a p*) || jdm *or* e–r S ~ bevorstehen *to threaten* od *menace a p* od *a th*; die Hand ~ erheben *to raise a threatening hand* || das Barometer kündigt ~en Sturm an *the barometer threatens a storm* **2.** adv *threateningly* (*near*)

Drohn m ~s/~e, **Dr·ohne** f ~/~n ⟨ent⟩ *drone* || ⟨übtr⟩ *drone, idler, loafer*

dr·öhnen 1. vi [h] **a.** ⟨mach⟩ *to hum, throb, thud; chunk* || (of steps, etc.) *to thud* || (of thunder, etc.) *to boom, roar, rumble* || (of places) *to re-echo, resound, ring, roar* (v *with*) | (of noises) in den Ohren ~ *to boom* od *ring in a p's ears*; mir dröhnt der Kopf *my head is ringing* **b.** ˣ(P) *to drawl, to drone* **2.** ~̈ n *the hum; throb; thud* (*of engines*) || *boom, roar, rumble* (*of thunder*)

dr·öhnend 1. a *humming, thudding* || *booming, roaring* || *ringing* (*voices*) **2.** adv *thuddingly*

Dr·öhnung f ~/~en *portion of drug* (od ⟨Am⟩ *dope*)

Dr·ohung f ~/~en *threat* (mit etw *of a th*; gegen jdn *to a p*); schwere ~ *fulmination* (*against a p*), *menace* || leere ~ *bluff, bluster*; jdn durch leere ~en einschüchtern *to bluff a p* || jdn unter ~en treiben z tun *to bully a p into doing*

dr·ollig a *droll; amusing, comical, facetious, funny, ludicrous, waggish*; ~e P *droll*; ~es Wesen *drollery, drollness* | (seltsam) *funny, odd, queer, quaint*; es ist z ~ *it is too funny* (*for words*); e–e ~e S *a funny thing* | ~̈**keit** f ~/ *drollery, facetiousness*

Dromed·ar n ~s/~e **1.** ⟨zoo⟩ *dromedary* **2.** ⟨fig⟩ (P) *blockhead, ass*

Dromm·ete f ~/~n ⟨poet⟩ = Trompete

Dr·onte f ⟨orn⟩ = Dodo

Dr·ontheim n (norw. Stadt) *Trondhjem*

Drops pl **1.** *drops* **2.** ⟨fig aero⟩ *bird-seed*

drosch 1. & 3. sg pret v dreschen

Dr·oschke f ~/~n (vierrädrige Kutsche, Mietwagen) *dros(h)ky; cab, fly, four-wheeler*, ⟨fam⟩ *growler*; ⟨Am⟩ *coach*, ⟨mst⟩ *hack* || ⟨engl⟩ (zweirädrig) *hansom; h. cab* || in e–r ~ fahren *to cab* (*it*) || Auto~̈ *taxi(-cab)*; in e–r Auto~̈ fahren *to taxi*

Dr·oschken- ~auto n *taxi(-cab)* **~gaul** m *cab--horse* **~halteplatz** m *cab-stand*; ⟨mot⟩ *taxi--rank*, ⟨Am⟩ *cab-stand* **~kutscher** m *cabman, cab-driver* **~tarif** m, **~taxe** f *table of cab-fares*

Drosom·eter n ~s/~ *drosometer*

Dr·ossel f ~/~n ⟨orn⟩ *thrush*; Mistel~̈ *missel-thrush*; Schwarz~̈ = Amsel; Sing~̈ *song-thrush*, ⟨liter⟩ *throstle* || Frucht~̈ → Bülbül

Dr·ossel f **1.** ⟨hunt⟩ (Kehle des Rotwilds) *throat*; ⟨fam⟩ *throttle* **2.** [in comp] *throttle* .. **~ader** f ⟨anat⟩ *jugular vein* **~kette** f ⟨el⟩ *choke--filter* **~klappe** f ⟨mot & tech⟩ *throttle; throttle* (od *butterfly*)*-valve* **~schieber** m ⟨tech⟩ *sliding thr.* **~spule** f ⟨wir⟩ *choke; choke* (od *choking, inductance*)*-coil* **~ventil** n = Drosselklappe

dr·osseln vt [h] **1.** (jdn) *to choke, to throttle* **2.** ⟨tech⟩ (Motor, Geschwindigkeit etc) *to choke* (*up*); *to throttle*; (Lautstärke) *to tune down* **3.** ⟨fig⟩ Ausgaben, (Verkehr etc) *to choke* (*up*), *to throttle*; → einschnüren

Drost m ~es/~e ⟨hist⟩ *prefect* od *head of a* **Drost·ei** f ~/~en ⟨hist⟩ *administrative district in Hanover*

dr·üben adv ~, da *or* dort ~ *over there; on the other side; yonder*; ~ v Uldale *from Uldale yonder* || v ~ *from America, East Germany*

°**dr·über** = darüber → drunter

Dr·uck m ~(e)s/~e **I.** [pl ~̈e] (→ drücken) **1.** (vorübergehender ~) *press(ure); strain*; leichter ~ (*light*) *touch*, ein ~ der Hand, Hände~̈ *a squeeze of the hand*; ein ~ auf den Knopf *a pressure of the button* || ~ im Kopf *pressing* (od *straining*) *sensation in the head* **2.** (längerer ~) **a.** *pressure* (*of a weight*, etc.) **b.** ⟨phys⟩ *pressure*; atmosphärischer ~ *atmospheric* (od *barometric*) *pressure*; physischen ~ ausüben auf *to impose physical strain upon*; hydraulischer ~ *hydraulic pressure, water-pressure*; Einheit des ~s *bar, atmosphere*; ⟨met, tech⟩ (Wucht) *force* → Blut~̈, Luft~̈; Hoch~̈, Tief~̈ **c.** (horizontaler ~) *compression* || ⟨arch⟩ *push*; Seiten~̈ *thrust* || → Erd~̈ **3.** ⟨übtr⟩ **a.** *pressure* (*of taxes*, etc.); *weight, burden* || *hardship*; ⟨poet⟩ *oppression* || seelischer ~ *nightmare*, → Alp; übermäßiger ~ *overpressure* || ~ ausüben auf (of feelings) *to press* (od *weigh*) *on* || starkem ~ ausgesetzt ⟨fig⟩ *under heavy fire*; (P) unter ~ halten *or* setzen (zwingen) *to turn* *the heat on* (*a p*); *to pressure* (zu *into*); ohne Gnade e–m ~ ausgesetzt *squeezed unmercifully* **b.** ⟨com⟩ ~ auf dem Markt *depression*; e–n ~ auf die Preise ausüben *to force prices down* **c.** (Zwang, moralischer ~) *compulsion, force, strain* (auf *on*); *screw*; ⟨jur⟩ *duress*(*e*) ‖ unter ~ *under pressure* (od *compulsion* ⟨jur⟩ *duress*[*e*]); unter ~ handeln *to act under pressure*; e–n ~ ausüben auf *to exert a pressure on* (*a p*); *to bring pressure to bear upon* (*a p, a th*); *to force a p's hand*; e–n ~ ausüben nach .. hin *to bring pressure to bear towards* (*a p, a th*); jdn unter ~ setzen *to pressurize* (*to put pressure on*) *a p, to put the screw on a p* ‖ dem ~e weichen *to yield to pressure* (od *force*) **d.** (Drang) *press*(*ure*) (*of business*); ~ der Verhältnisse *pressure of circumstances* **II.** (→ drucken) [pl ~e] **1.** [abstr] **a.** ⟨typ⟩ *impression, printing* (*of a book*); *press, press work* ‖ im ~ *in the press*; im ~ s *to be printing* ‖ in ~ geben *to* (*put into*) *print, to send to the press*; in ~ gehen *to go to the press*; z ~ fertig m *to get ready for the press* ‖ ~ u Verlag v .. *printed and published by* .. **b.** (Tuch≈) *printing*, (Oberfläche) durch ~ kennzeichnen *to print* **2.** [konkr] (Gedrucktes) **a.** ⟨typ⟩ *print, type*; verwischter ~ *mackle*; gr ~ *large print* od *type*; kl ~ *small print*; → Fest≈ ‖ *impression, edition*; erster ~ *first edition* od *impression* ‖ (Ggs: Abbildungen im Buch) *letter-press* ‖ (of a coin) ~ auf Wachs *squeeze* ‖ schwacher ~ *faint impression* ‖ → Abzug; Buch≈; Stein≈ **b.** *print*, → Tuchdruck

Dr·uck- [in comp] **1.** ⟨phys & tech⟩ *pressure* (*pre.*) .. **2.** ⟨typ⟩ *printing* (*pri.*) .. **~abfall** m *drop in pre.* **≈abhängig** a *pre.-controlled* **~achse** f ⟨typ⟩ *pri. shaft* **~änderung** f *change of pre.* **~anstieg** m *increase of pre.* **~anzeiger** m ⟨tech⟩ (S) *manometer*; *pre. ga*(*u*)*ge* **~anzug** m ⟨aero, astronaut⟩ *high-pre. suit* **~apparat** m ⟨typ⟩ *pri. apparatus*; (Tank) *tank apparatus* **~-aufbereitung** f ⟨comp⟩ *editing* (*process*) **~-ausbreitung** f *propagation of pre.* **≈ausgleichend** a *pre.- equalizing* **~beanspruchung, ~belastung** f *compressive strain* od *stress*; *pre. load*(*ing*) **~behälter** m *pre. tank* **≈belüften** vt [h] ⟨aero⟩ *to pressurize*; –ftete Kabine *pressurized cabin* **~belüftung** f *pressurization* **~berichtiger** m (*proof-*)*reader corrector* (*of the press*) **~berichtigung** f *correction of the press* **~binde** f ⟨med⟩ *pressure-bandage* **~bleistift** m *ejector* od *push pencil*; → –füller **~bogen** m *printed sheet* **~buchstabe** m *letter, type* **~einheit** f ⟨comp⟩ *pri. unit* **~einspritzung** f ⟨tech⟩ *injection under pre.* **~elastizität** f *elasticity of compression* **~entlastung** f *depression* **~erlaubnis** f *imprimatur* [L] **~fahne** f *galley-proof* **~farbe** f *pri.-ink* **~feder** f *compression spring* **~fehler** m *printer's error, erratum* [L] *misprint* ‖ ~teufel [m] *demon of misprints*; ~verzeichnis [n] *errata, corrigenda* [L pl] [a. sg konstr] **≈fertig** a *ready for the press* **≈fest** a *pre.-proof* (*casing*); ⟨tex⟩ *crush resistant* **~festigkeit** f *compressive strength* (od *pre. resistance*) **~filter** m *pre. filter* **~filz** m *blanket* **~fläche** f ⟨typ⟩ *impression surface* **~form** f ⟨typ⟩ *form, pri.-block* **~formular** n *printed form* **~füller** m (mit Vorlaufmine) *push* (od *automatic, repeater*) *pencil*; → –bleistift **~gas** n *pre. gas*; ~generator [m] *pressure gas generator* **~gefühl** n *feel* od *sensation of pressure* **~gewerbe** n *the printing trade*; *the press* **~höhe** f *pre.-height*, (*pre.* od *effective*) *head* | ~nmesser [m] ⟨aero⟩ *pre. altitude-meter* **~hub** m *pre. stroke* **~kabine** f ⟨aero⟩ *pressurized cabin* **~kammer** f *compression chamber* ⟨a. aero⟩ **~kattun** m *print*; *chintz* **~kessel** m *pressure-boiler* **~klappe** f *pressure-valve* **~knopf** m ⟨tail⟩ *press*(*ure*) *button*; ⟨Am⟩ *snap* ‖ ⟨el⟩ *push-button*; ⟨wir⟩ ~abstimmung [f] *p.-b. tuning*; ~anlasser [m] *p.-b. starter*; ~krieg [m] *p.-b. war*; ~steuerung [f] (*p.-*)*b. control* **≈kochen** vt *to pre.-cook* **~kocher** m *pre. cooker* **~kolben** m ⟨tech⟩ *ram* **~kombination** f ⟨aero⟩ *pressure suit* **~kopf** m ⟨comp⟩ *pri.-head* (= *group of pri. sectors*) **~kosten** [pl] *pri.-expenses* [pl]; *print-price* **~kraft** f (*power of*) *pressure*; *compressive force* od *energy* **~kunst** f *printer's art* od *trade*; *pri.* **~lager** n *thrust-bearing* **~legung** f *impression*; *pri.* **~leitung** f ⟨tech⟩ *pre.-pipes* [pl] **~luft** f *compressed air*; ~anlage [f] *pressurization system* ‖ ~antrieb [m] *pneumatic drive* ‖ ~anzeiger [m] ⟨mot⟩ *air-pre. ga*(*u*)*ge* ~bremse [f] *compressed air brake*; *pneumatic brake* ‖ ~bremssystem [n] *c. a. b. system*; ≈gesteuert a *pneumatic-controlled* ‖ ~hammer [m] *pneumatic h.* ‖ ~krankheit [f] *caisson disease*, ⟨fam⟩ *bends* pl; ~maschine [f] *air-compressing engine*; *compressor* ‖ ~spannung [f] *air chucking* ‖ ~zerstäuber [m] *compressed-air atomizer* **~lüfter** m *pre.-fan* **~maschine** f *pre. engine* ‖ ⟨typ⟩ *pri. machine* **~messer** m (Dampf~) *manometer*; *pre.-gauge*; ⟨mot⟩ *tyre* (⟨Am⟩ *tire*) *g.* **~mittel** n ⟨übtr⟩ *compulsion* (*by c.*); ~ [pl] gebrauchen *to bring pre. to bear, to use* od *exercise pre.* **~mittelpunkt** m ⟨tech⟩ *centre of pre.* (*c. p.*) **~ort** m *place of pri.*; → Impressum **~papier** n *pri.-paper* **~platte** f ⟨typ⟩ *pri.-block* (od *plate*) **~pöstchen** n *soft* od *bobby's job* **~presse** f ⟨typ⟩ *pri.-press* **~probe** f *pre.-test* ‖ ⟨typ⟩ *proof, specimen* **~pumpe** f *pre.-pump* **~punkt** m *centre of pre.* ‖ *aerodynamic centre*; (Gewehr) *pull-off*, ~ nehmen (beim Schießen) *to take up the slack* (*of the trigger*), *to hold on*; °(sich drücken) *to shirk* (*one's duty*) [a. abs] **~raster** m *printer's screen* **~regler** m ⟨tech⟩ *pre. governor*; (Druckminderer [m]) *pre. reducing valve* **≈reif** a druckfertig **~rückgang** m *depression* **~sache** f *printed matter*; ⟨Am⟩ *printings*; als ~ *by book-post* **~schaden** m ⟨at⟩ *blast damage* **~schlauch** m *forcing hose* **~schmierpresse** f *grease gun* **~schmierung** f *forced lubrication* **~schraube** f *setscrew*; ⟨aero⟩ Flugzeug mit ~ *pusher* **~schrift** f ⟨typ⟩ *print, type*; in ~ schreiben *to write in block-letters*, ⟨Am⟩ *to print* ‖ (Buch) *printed book*; ⟨Am⟩ *print* ‖ *prospectus, pamphlet* **~schwankung** f *fluctuation of pre.* **~seite** f *printed page* **~spannung** f *compressive stress* **~spüler** m (Klosett≈) (*flushing*) *press* (*in W. C.*) **~stellbügel** m ⟨typ⟩ *impression adjuster bar* **~stelle** f (an Körper, Obst etc) *bruise* **~stempel** m *pre.-stamp* **~stock** m *cut*; *electro block*; ⟨mill⟩ *pre. yoke*; ⟨typ⟩ *process-block*; *cliché* [Fr] | ~abzug [m] *block pull*, ⟨Am⟩ *engraver's proof* **~tasten-** ~abstimmung [f] ⟨wir⟩ *push-button tuning* ‖ ~bedienung [f] *p.-b. operation* ‖ Radio mit ~einstellung [f] *p.-b. radio* ‖ ~stellwerk [n] ⟨rail⟩ (Apparat) *p.-b. circuitry*, (Raum) *p.-b. control signal-box* **~telegraph** m *pri.-telegraph* **~tinte** f *lithographic ink* **~topf** m ⟨cul⟩ *pre. cooker* **~type** f *pri. type* **~ventil** n *pre.-valve, surge v.* **~verfahren** n *pri.-process*; *pri.-method* **~vermerk** m *imprint*; *printer's address* **~verminderungsventil** n *pre.-reducing valve* **~versorgung** f ⟨aero⟩ (*cabin*) *pressurization* **~walze** f ⟨typ⟩ *pri.-roller* (od *cylinder*) ‖ *presser*; *pressing-roller* **~waren** f [pl] *printed goods* [pl] **~wasser** n *water under pre.* **~wasserreaktor** m *pressurized water reactor* **~welle** f (bei Explosion) *blast*; ⟨at⟩ *shock wave* **~werk** n ⟨num⟩ [abstr] *coining* **~zeilen** f pl ⟨typ⟩ *lines of print* **~zeug** n ⟨weav⟩ *printed stuff* ‖ ⟨typ⟩ *print, printer, pri.-cloth* **~zylinder** m *pre.-cylinder* ‖ ⟨typ⟩ *impression-cylinder*

dr·uckbar a *printable*

°**Dr·ückeberger** m ~s/~ *stand-backer, malingerer*; *dodger*; *shirk*(*er*); *skulker*; ~ v der Arbeit *shirker of work, slacker* ‖ ⟨mil⟩ *scrimshanker*,

⟨Am⟩ *draft-dodger*; (v Truppendienst) ⟨sl⟩ *goldbricker* ‖ ⟨sl⟩ *passenger*; ⟨Am sl⟩ *quitter, crawfish* ‖ → Angsthase

dr·ucken vt [h] *to print*; gedruckt w *to be printing* ‖ (etw) ~ l *to print (a th)*; *to get (a th) printed, to bring (a th) out*; 20 Expl (= Emplare) ~! *run off 20 copies*! ‖ wie gedruckt lügen *to lie like a book* od *by the b.*

dr·ücken vt/i [h] **I.** vt **A.** **(P)** **1.** etw ~ **a.** (seitlich zus–drücken) *to give a th a press*; jds Hand ~, jdm die H. ~ *to press* (od *clutch, squeeze*) *a p's hand, to give a p's hand a squeeze* od *grip* **b.** (Form, Zeichen v oben ~) *to (in)print*, (auf *on*); (Stempel) *to impress* (*on*); das Siegel auf ein Dokument ~ *to seal a document* ‖ (Marke) *to press* (auf *on* [*a letter*]) ‖ ⟨tech⟩ *to force* ‖ (Kuß) *to imprint, press* (auf *on*) **c.** etw ~ gegen .. *to press a th against* .. ‖ den Hut ins Gesicht ~ *to pull one's hat over one's eyes* ‖ jdm etw heimlich in die Hand ~ *to slip a th into a p's hands* ‖ gedrückt w *to gravitate* (in *into*) **d.** ⟨fig⟩ die Schulbank ~ *to go to school, to be kept at school* **e.** (Registrierkasse) *to register*; *to ring up* **f.** ⟨st exch⟩ (Papiere) *to pound* ‖ (Preise) *to beat* od *bring down, to depress, lower* ‖ (Rekord) *to beat* **2.** jdn an die Brust, ans Herz ~ *to clasp* od *press a p to one's breast*; *to embrace* od *hug a p*; er drückte sie an sich *he clasped* (od ⟨sl⟩ *crushed*) *her to him* ‖ ⟨fig⟩ jdn an die Wand ~ *to drive* od *thrust a p to the wall, to corner* od *ruin a p*; an die W. gedrückt w *to go to the wall* | jdn z Boden ~ *to press a p to the ground*; ⟨fig⟩ *to crush* (od *keep, strike*) *a p down* **3.** ⟨hors⟩ *to gall (a horse)* **B.** **(S)** **1.** (jdn, etw) *to press* (gegen *against*, nach .. hin *towards*); (of gloves, shoes, etc.) *to pinch, press* (: *my shoe presses the toes*); ⟨fig⟩ niemand weiß, wo ihn der Schuh drückt *nobody knows where the shoe pinches him* ‖ etw breit *or* platt ~ *to flatten a th*; platt gedrückt w *to be squeezed flat* **2.** ⟨fig⟩ jdn ~ *to depress*; *to oppress a p* (mit *with*), *to weigh a p down*; *the thought weighs (up)on my mind* (mich); es drückt sein Gewissen *it weighs (up)on his c.*; die Pflichten drücken ihn *duties throng* (od *weigh*) *upon him*; die Schulden ~ ihn sehr *the debts press* (od *weigh*) *heavily upon him*; → II. 2. b. ‖ gedrückt s *to be depressed*; *to feel oppressed* (v *with* [*grief*]) **3.** ⟨com & sport⟩ (Tätigkeit; Markt, Preise) *to bring* (od *beat, force, weigh*) *down, to depress*; *to lower*; den Rekord ~ *to beat the record* (um *by*) **C.** **sich** ~ **1.** *to get injured by pressure* **2.** = sich drängen (I. A. 1. b.) **3.** *to crouch* (in *into*); *to stoop*; sich aus dem Hause ~ *to skulk from one's house* **4.** °⟨fig⟩ **a.** (ausreißen) *to decamp, scuttle*, ⟨fam⟩ *skedaddle*; *to sneak off* od *away*; ⟨Am sl⟩ *to beat it*; sich französisch (*or* heimlich) ~ *to take French leave* ‖ *to hedge, dodge*, → Drückeberger, (v Truppendienst) *to crimshank, funk, shirk*, ⟨Am sl⟩ *to goldbrick* ‖ (v der Schule) *to play hookey* **b.** ⟨mil sl⟩ *to scrimshank*; *to get out of the rain, to take evasive action*; ⟨mar sl⟩ *to swing the lead* **c.** **sich** ~ **um** (*or* v) etw *to shirk a th* (: *to shirk work*); *to work one's ticket*; sich um s–e Pflichten ~ *to skulk*; sich v der Arbeit ~ *to sugar*; sich v e–m Versprechen ~ *to skulk from a pledge*; ⟨pol⟩ sich vom Wählen ~ ⟨Am⟩ *to take to the woods* | sich **vor** (etw) ~ *to duck, dodge (a task)*, *to back out of (a th)* **II.** vi **1.** (of shoes, etc.) *to nip, pinch, to be tight* ‖ (fig) wissen, wo der Schuh drückt *to know where the shoe pinches* **2.** **a.** ~ **auf** etw *to press (upon) a th*; auf den Knopf ~ *to press the button* **b.** ⟨fig⟩ ~ auf jdn *to press a p*; *to weigh* od *press upon a p*; lastend ~ auf *to weigh heavily upon (a p)* ‖ → I. B. 2. **3.** (niederdrücken) die Sonne, Hitze drückt *the heat is oppressive* ‖ Not drückt *distress is depressing, distress causes depression* **4.** ⟨cards⟩ falsch ~ *to discard the wrong cards*

dr·ückend a *heavy, oppressive (rule; heat)*; (schwül) ⟨meteor⟩ *muggy (hot moist) (weather)* ‖ *depressing*; *dismal*; *gloomy (wood)* ‖ *onerous (terms)*

Dr·ucker m ~s/~ (Buch≃) *printer*; (bes an der Handpresse) *pressman* ‖ (Tuch≃) *presser*; ⟨print⟩ (*letterpress*) *printer*; *pressman* ‖ ⟨comp⟩ ~: 36 000 Zeilen je Stde maximal *printed output*: *operates at a speed of up to 600 lines a minute* **~arbeit** f *press-work* **~ballen** m ⟨typ⟩ *plug* **~lohn** m *printer's wages* [pl] **~presse** f *printing--press*; Schnell≃ *printing-machine* **~schwärze** f *printer's ink, printing-ink* ‖ ⟨fig⟩ *printing-ink, printed matter* **~zeichen** n *printer's mark*

Dr·ücker m ~s/~ **1.** (Türklinke) *handle* ‖ (Türschloß mit Riegel) *latch*; (Tür) durch ~ verschließen *to latch* ‖ (Schlüssel dazu) *latch* (od *pass*)*-key* **2.** (am Gewehr) *trigger*

Drucker·ei f ~/~en (Buch≃) *printing office* od *works* od *plant press* (: *the Clarendon Press*); ⟨Am⟩ *printing shop* ‖ ~besitzer *printer* ‖ (Tuch≃) *printworks* [pl] [sg konstr]

°**dr·ucksen** vi [h] *to boggle*; *dawdle, hesitate, linger, tarry, waver* ‖ *flounder*; *to hum and ha(w)*; *to beat about the bush*; *not to know one's mind*

Dr·ude f ~/~n *evil female demon* (od *incubus, spirit*); *witch*; †*nightmare*

Dr·uden- [in comp] **~baum** m *tree under which witches meet* **~fuß** m *pentacle, pentagram* **~kraut** n ⟨bot⟩ = Bärlapp **~mehl** n *lycopodium--powder*

°**druff**! (= d(a)rauf) [adv] *at him*!, ⟨Am⟩ *attaboy*!: immer feste ~!

Dru·ide m ~n/~n *Druid* ‖ ~nstein, ~ntempel [m] *Druid stone*

°**dr·um** **1.** adv = darum; alles, was ~ und dran hängt *everything connected with it*, ⟨sl⟩ *the whole bag of tricks* ‖ sei's ~! *well then*! (*come if you like*; *say no more*) **2.** ≃ n; das ≃ u Dran *the paraphernalia* [L pl], *accessories, belongings* [pl] ‖ mit allem ≃ u Dran *lock, stock, and barrel*, ⟨ec⟩ *bell, book, and candle*

dr·unten (= da unten) adv *there below, down there*

dr·unter = darunter ‖ ~ und drüber *helter--skelter, topsyturvy, upside-down*; alles ging ~ u drüber *things were all topsyturvy, everathing was at sixes and sevens*

Drusch m ~es/~e *threshing*

Dr·use f ~/~n [pl] **1.** ⟨geol & minr⟩ *druse* ~ntextur *drusy structure* **2.** ⟨hors, vet⟩ *glanders, strangles* [pl] [sg konstr]; → Rotz **3.** → Drusen

Dr·use m ~n/~n ⟨ec⟩ *Druse*, die ~n [pl] (moham. Sekte in Syrien) *the Druses* [pl]

Dr·üse f ~/~n **1.** ⟨physiol⟩ *gland* ‖ ~n mit äußerer Sekretion *glands* [pl] *of external secretion*; → Bauchspeichel≃, Lymph≃, Speichel≃, Tränen≃; geschwollene ~n h *to have (got) the mumps* ‖ ~n mit innerer Sekretion *glands* [pl] *of internal secretion*; *ductless* od *endocrine glands* [pl]; *endocrines* [pl]; → Hormon; Hypophyse; Inkret **2.** ⟨bot⟩ *gland* (of a plant)

Dr·usen f [pl] *wine-lees* [pl]

Dr·üsen- [in comp] *gland* ..; *glandular* ..; *adenoid* .. **≃artig** a *gland-like*; *glandular* **~fieber** n *gland-fever* **~geschwulst** f ⟨med⟩ *adenoma* [L] **~grübchen** n *follicle* **~haar** n ⟨bot⟩ *glandular hair* **~schwellung** f *swelling of the glands* **~verhärtung** f *scirrhous glands* [pl]

Dr·usenkopf m ⟨zoo⟩ *large inguanid lizard*; *conobophus* [L]

dr·usig a ⟨geol⟩ (→ Druse 1.) *drusy*

dr·üsig a *glandular, glandulous*

Dry·ade f ~/~n *dryad*

Dsch·aina m [Ind] *Jain* ‖ ~lehre [f] *Jainism*

Dsch·aipur n ((indische Provinz) *Jaipur*

Dschat m (Angehöriger e–r ind. Stammeskaste) *Jat*

Dschib·uti n (Stadt an Somaliküste) *Djibouti*

Dschih·ad m [moham.] *jihad, jehad*; → Krieg

Dschinn m ∼s/∼s (moham. böser Geist) *jinnee*

Dsch·ungel m, n, f *jungle* ‖ Bewohner [m] der ∼n *jungli* ‖ ∼fieber [n] *jungle-fever*

Dsch·unke f ∼/∼n ⟨mar⟩ (Segelschiff) *junk*

d·u 1. [pron, pers] *you*; bist ∼ es? *is it you*? ∼ da *you there*; → mir ‖ ⟨bib & poet⟩ *thou* **2.** ∸ n *you* ‖ jdm das ∼ anbieten *to ask a p's permission to address him by the pronoun* Du ‖ mit jdm auf Du und Du stehen (*or* sich stellen) *to be on intimate terms, hand in glove, to hobnob, to be on first-name basis with a p*

Du·al m ∼s/∼e, **∼is** m ⟨gram⟩ *dual, dual number* **|** ∼zeichen [n] (Zweierschritt an Büromaschinen) *binary digit*, → Bit **Dual·ismus** m ∼/ ⟨philos, rel & pol⟩ *dualism* **dual·istisch 1.** a *dualistic* **2.** adv *dualistically*

Dualit·ät f ⟨math⟩ *duality*

Du·alsystem n *dual* od *dyadic system*

D·ubben n (Übersprechen e–s Films) *dubbing*

D·übel m = Döbel 1.

dubi·os a ⟨com, bal⟩ *doubtful* (Forderung *debt*) **Dubi·ose(n)** [pl] *bad* od *doubtful debts*

D·uble ['dʌbl] m ⟨engl⟩ = Doppelspieler

Dubl·ee n ∼s/∼s *plated metal* **∼gold** n *rolled gold*, e–e Taschenuhr aus ∼ *a rolled gold watch* **∼waren** f [pl] *plated goods* [pl]

Dubl·ette f ∼/∼n *duplicate, duplicate copy* ⟨a. arts⟩, *double* ‖ ⟨gram⟩ (of words) *doublet* (: '*to catch*' *is a doublet of* '*to chase*') ‖ ⟨hunt⟩ *right-and left, right-and-left shot* **dubl·ieren** vt [h] **1.** (Seide) *to double* ‖ ⟨typ⟩ (unscharf drucken) *to double*; *mackle* **2.** (Metall) *to plate*

D·ublin n (Hauptstadt Irlands)

Dubl·one f ∼/∼n ⟨Span, hist⟩ (Goldmünze) *doubloon*

D·uce [du:tʃə] m [It] *duce* (Mussolini)

Duchob·orzen m pl [Russ] (Sekte) *Doukhobors*

Ducht f ∼/∼en ⟨mar⟩ **1.** (of a rope) *strand* **2.** (Ruderbank) *thwart*

D·ückdalbe f ∼/∼n ⟨mar⟩ *dolphin*

d·ucken vt/i [h] **I.** vt **1.** den Kopf ∼ *to duck* (od *lower, stoop*) *one's head* **2.** jdn ∼ **a.** (untertauchen) *to dip* od *duck a p* **b.** (den Gegner) *to down*; *beat, worst a p* ‖ ⟨fig⟩ *to bring* od *put a p down*; *to humble a p*; *to take a p down a peg* (*or two*), *to snub a p* ‖ geduckt s *to sing small* **3. sich** ∼ **a.** *to cower, crouch, stoop*; ⟨Am⟩ *to scrooch*; sich vor etw ∼ *to dodge a th* (: *a blow*) ‖ (untertauchen) *to dip, dive, duck* **b.** ⟨fig⟩ *to duck* (vor *to*); (vor Angst) *to cringe, to knuckle under* (vor *to a p*) **II.** vi ∼ = sich ∼ a. ‖ geduckt gehen *to stoop* **D·ucken** n *duck* (*of the head*); *ducking*

D·ucker m ⟨zoo⟩ (Schopfantilope) *duiker*

D·ücker m ∼s/∼ *sluice pipe*

D·uckmäuser m ∼s/∼ **1.** *cringer, shuffler, sneak, mouse* ⟨fig⟩; *hypocrite* ‖ ⟨school⟩ *informer* **2.** = Kopfhänger, Spießer **d·uckmäuserig** a; *cringing, sneaking*; *underhand*; *hypocritic*(*al*) ‖ = spießig, philisterhaft **d·uckmäusern** vi [h] *to cringe, sneak* **d·ucknackig** a *stooping*

D·udeldumd·ei [intj] = Dideldumdei

°**Dudel·ei** f ∼/∼en ⟨mus⟩ *strum*(*ming*); *skirl* (*of the gabpipes*) ‖ (Gesang) *monotonous song*; *chant* °**D·udelkasten** m *barrel-organ* **d·udeln** vi/t [h] **1.** vi *to tweedle*; *drum, thrum, strum, twang* (auf .. *on an instrument*) ‖ (of instruments) *to pipe*; (of a bagpipe) *to skirl*; (blasen) *to tootle* ‖ (singen) *to chant* **2.** vt Melodie, (ein Stück) *to strum, thrum* (auf *on*); ⟨Scot⟩ *to doodle* ‖ (singen) *to chant*

D·udelsack m *bagpipe*; *pipes* [pl], auf dem ∼ spielen *to play on a bagpipe, to skirl*; jdm etw auf dem ∼ vorspielen *to give a p a skirl on the pipes* **∼pfeifer** m *bagpiper*

Du·ell n ∼s/∼e **1.** *duel* (zw *between*; mit *with*); ein ∼ auf Pistolen (Säbel), Pistolen∸ *a duel with pistols* (*swords*) ‖ ein ∼ ausfechten *to fight a duel* (*with*) ‖ → herausfordern **2.** ⟨übtr⟩ *contest, duel, fight* ‖ ∼regeln [f] pl] *code* (od *laws*) *of honour* **Duell·ant** m ∼en/∼en *duellist, dueller*

duell·ieren [vrefl] [h] sich ∼ *to duel*; *to fight a duel* (*with*)

Du·ero m (Fluß der Pyrenäenhalbinsel) *Duero, Douro*

Du·ett n ∼(e)s/∼e *duet*

D·üffel m ∼s/∼ (Wollstoff) *duffel, duffle*; ⟨mar⟩ *pilot-cloth*

D·uft m ∼(e)s/∸e **1.** ⟨poet⟩ (feiner Dunst) *emanation*; *exhalation*; *effluvium* [L] ‖ *haze* ‖ *hoar-frost*; *rime*; ∼bruch [m] *r.-break* **2.** (Wohlgeruch) *fragrance, perfume, redolence*; *pleasant smell*; *aroma*; *fragrant odour*; *sweet scent*; lieblicher ∼ *sweet scent* (*of roses*); reiner ∼ *virgin scent* (*of flowers*); zarter ∼ *faint odour*; *waft*; der ∼ e–r guten Zigarre *the whiff of a good cigar*; (of wine) → Blume A. 3. a. **|** unangenehmer ∼ *unpleasant* (od *bad, offensive, nasty*) *smell* od *scent* (*of tobacco*); → Geruch **3.** ⟨übtr & fig⟩ *fragrance, perfume*; *savour*; rosiger ∼ *bloom* (*of youth*); e–e S ihres ∼es berauben *to take the bloom off a th* ‖ e–r S ∼ verleihen *ro scent a th*

°**d·ufte** a (gerissen) *crafty, cunning, sly, wily* (*customer*); ein ∼r Bursche *a deep one* ‖ (famos) ⟨fam⟩ *corking, rattling, ripping*; *booming*; ⟨sl⟩ *swank*; ein ∼er Kerl ⟨fam⟩ *a brick, a corker*; *a duck of a fellow*; das ist e–e ∼ S *that's a corker*

d·uften vi/t [h] **1.** vi *to exhale fragrance*; *to smell sweet*(*ly*); (ganz) frisch ∼ *ro smell new*; (stark) ∼ nach *to be redolent of*; ∼ v *to be scented with* (: *the air was sc. with fresh grass*), *to be fragrant* od *sweet with*; die Rosen ∼ süß *the roses smell sweet*; der Abend duftete süß v. .. *the evening was sweet with* .. ‖ unangenehm ∼ *to smell strong* (od *offensively*); ∼ nach *to smell of* **2.** vt ⟨poet⟩ (= atmen) (Jugend) *to breathe*; *to be redolent of*

d·uftend a *fragrant, odorous, odorant, odoriferous* (*substance*); *redolent* (nach *of*; v *with*); lieblich ∼ *sweet* (v *with*)

d·uftig a **1.** *fragrant, odorous*; *sweet* ‖ ⟨übtr⟩ *delightful, fragrant* (*memories*) ‖ *savoury*; *aromatic* **2.** (of fabrics) *gauzy, filmy, vaporous, delicate*

Duft- ∼n·ote f *fragrance* od *perfume of a special flavour* **∼organ** n ⟨ent⟩ *scent-gland* (od *organ*) **∼stoff** m *perfume*; ∼e [pl] *aromatics*

D·ugong m ⟨zoo⟩ *dugong*

ˣ**duhn** a [pred] *drunk*; → bezecht ‖ halb ∼ *half-seas over*

D·uisburg n ⟨Ger⟩ (Stadt) *Duisburg*

Duk·aten m ∼(s)/∼ *ducat* **∼falter** m ⟨ent⟩ *copperwing butterfly*; → Bläuling **∼gold** n *ducat* (od *fine*) *gold*

Duk-Duk → Geheimbund

D·üker m ∼s/∼ **1.** ⟨arch⟩ (gebogene Rohrleitung) *siphon* **2.** ⟨orn⟩ *ducker*

dukt·il a *ductile* **D·uktus** m [L] **1.** (Feder–, Schriftzug) *duct*; *stroke* **2.** ⟨anat & bot⟩ (Gang) *duct*; *conduit*

d·uldbar a *endurable, sufferable, tolerable* **|** ∸**keit** ∼/ *endurability*; *tolerableness*

d·ulden vt/i **I.** vt **A.** etw ∼ **1.** (ertragen, –leiden) (Unrecht, Verfolgung) *to bear, endure, suffer, sustain*; er kann viel ∼ *he can stand a lot* **2.** (hingehen l, zulassen) **a.** (Kränkung etc) *to countenance, endure, tolerate*; *to acquiesce in, to put up with* (*a th*); *to stomach*; geduldet w *to pass muster* ‖ (erlauben) *to permit* ‖ (Unrechtes) stillschweigend ∼ *to connive at, to wink at* (*a th*) **b.** [neg] ich will solches Benehmen **nicht** ~ *I will not permit* (od *suffer, tolerate*) *such conduct* || ich dulde es nicht *I will not have it, I draw the line at it* || er kann k–n Widerspruch ~ *he cannot bear* (od *brook, suffer*) *contradiction*; diese S duldet k–n Aufschub *this matter brooks no delay* **B.** ~, daß jd tut *to suffer* (od *allow, permit*) *a p to do*; ~, daß etw geschieht *to suffer a th to be done*; *to countenance a th being done* **C.** jdn ~ *to bear with a p*; *to countenance, tolerate a p*; [mst neg] Intriganten dulde ich **nicht** *I have no use for intriguers*; → leiden || geduldet w *to gain tolerance*; *to pass muster, to be accepted*; sie sind hier nur geduldet *they are here only by* (od *on*) *sufferance* **II.** vi (P & T) *to suffer*; lerne ~ ohne z klagen *learn to suffer without complaining*

D·ulder m ~s/~, **~in** f ~/~nen *sufferer*; er ist ein stiller ~ *he suffers in silence* **~miene** f *patient look*; *martyred expression*; e–e ~ (z Schau) tragen *to wear a m. exp.* **~sinn** m *resignation* **d·uldsam 1.** a *indulgent* (gegen *to*); *patient* (*towards, with*); *tolerant* (*of*); ~ s gegen *to tolerate* (*a p*; *a th*); → dulden I. A. 2. a. **2.** adv *patiently* | **≗keit** f ~/ *tolerance, toleration* (gegen *of*)

D·uldung f (Einwilligung) *acceptance*; *permission, sufferance*; *tacit consent* (*of a p*); stillschweigende ~ *tacit permission*; *connivance*; unter stillschweigender ~ *on sufferance* || (Nachsicht) *tolerance*; *toleration*; unter ~ v *in tolerance of*

Dul·ie f ~/ ⟨R. C.⟩ *dulia*

Dulong-Petitsche Regel f ⟨phys⟩ *Dulong and Petit's Law*

×**Dult** f ~/~en [bay] = Jahrmarkt, Messe

Dulz·in n ⟨chem⟩ *dulcin* **Dulz·it** m ~s/ ⟨chem⟩ *dulcite*; ~manna [f] *Madagascar manna*

Dulzin·ea f [L] *sweetheart*; [Span] *Dulcinea*

Dumd·um-Geschoß n (engl) *dumdum*; *dumdum bullet*

dumm a **I.** (mst P) **A.** (beschränkt) (P, actions, thoughts, etc.) ⟨mst dero⟩ **1.** *dense, dull, obtuse, opaque*; *slow of understanding*; *addle-pated* (od *headed*), *stupid*; ⟨sl⟩ *goofy*; ⟨Am⟩ *dumb, fool* || auf e e ~e Frage gehört e–e ~e Antwort a *stupid qu. deserves a stupid answer* **2.** (unerfahren, unklug) *imprudent*; *foolish, silly*; *gullible* || [abs als subst] → Dumme **3. a.** ~er **August** *clown, buffoon* || die ≗sten Bauern h die dicksten Kartoffeln! *fools for luck*! °~e **Gans** *goose*; ⟨fam⟩ *silly owl* || ein ~es **Gesicht** m *to look foolish* od *silly* || ~er **Junge** *young shaver*; *greenhorn, jackanapes, mug, stripling*; (to adults) *fool*; *yellow dog* || °~er **Kerl** *dolt, blockhead*; *flat*; *silly*; *stupid*; °sau~er Kerl *damfool* od *blithering idiot* || ~e **Streiche** [pl] *capers*; *silly pranks* od *tricks*; *practical jokes* [pl] || ~e **Witze** [pl] *silly jokes, clownish jests* [pl] **b.** [pred] da müßte ich schön ~ s (da mußt du dir e–n ≗eren suchen)! *not I*! *I am not such a fool as that*! *catch me doing that*! || °~ **wie** e–e Gans, ~ wie Bohnenstroh *as stupid as an owl* || es war ~ v dir *it was foolish* od *silly of you*; *you were silly* (*to do*) || jdn ~ m, jdn f ~ verkaufen *to stultify a p, to make a fool of a p* **c. sich ~ anstellen,** ~ tun *to behave* od *answer foolishly*; sich bei e–r S ~ anstellen *to be an idiot at a th* || er ist nicht so ~ wie er **aussieht** *he is not such a fool as he looks* || ich bin nicht so ~ wie ich aussehe, seh ich so ~ aus? *I'm not so green as I'm cabbage-looking* || seh ich so ~ aus? *do you see any green in my eye*? *I didn't fall off a Christmas tree* || **frag** nicht so ~ *don't ask such foolish* od *silly questions, don't be so stupid*! **B.** (schwindlig) *dizzy, giddy* (v *with*); mir wird ganz ~ im Kopfe *my head swims, I have a swimming in my head* **C.** (of horses, etc.) *staggery*; *affected with staggers* **II.** (S) *ridiculous*; *silly* (*book*); *footling* (*play*); ⟨Am⟩ *fool* (*story*) || ~es Zeug! *nonsense*! ⟨sl⟩ *bosh*! *fiddlesticks*! *rubbish*! ⟨Am⟩ *fool nonsense*! || lauter ~es Z. *a lot of piffle* | (ärgerlich, peinlich) *awkward, disagreable* || das ist ja ~ *that's a great nuisance*; das ist z ~ *that's too bad*; wie ~! *what a nuisance*! *bother*! *botheration*! || jetzt wurde mir die S z ~ *now I lost* (*my*) *patience* || das hätte ~ ablaufen können *that might have had bad consequences*

dumm adv → vor. I. A. 3. c., II.

D·umm- [in comp] °**~bart, ~beutel** m *silly*; *simple*(*ton*); *simple Simon*; ⟨Am sl⟩ *dumbbell* **≗dreist** a *forward, impudent, minxish, saucy*; *pig-headed, stupid* **~erjungenstreich** m *lark*; *prank*; *teenery* **~kopf** m *addle-head* (*–brain, –pate*); *blockhead, mud-head, booby, dolt, duffer, dullard*; *thick-head*; *nitwit*; ⟨fam⟩ *noddy*; ⟨sl⟩ *chump, juggins* || ⟨Am⟩ *dumbhead*, ⟨sl⟩ *boob, dope, dumbbell, dummy, ninny* || eingebildeter ~ ⟨fam⟩ *squirt* → Dummbart **~köpfig** a *doltish, pig-headed*; *stupid* **≗stolz** a *self-conceited, snobbish, snobby*

D·umme [der ~, ein ~r]: der ~ s *to be the loser, to pay the piper*, ⟨Am⟩ *to hold the bag* || die ~n w nicht alle *there are fools around*, ⟨Am⟩ *there's a sucker born every minute* || das ist das ~ *that's what's the matter with the world*

°**Dummerchen** n *silly*; *silly boy* od *girl* **d·ummerhaft(ig)** a *foolish, silly* °**D·ummerjan** m = Dummbart **dummerw·eise** adv ich habe das Stück ~ z kurz geschnitten *I have gone and cut the piece too short*; er war ~ gestorben *he had gone and died*

D·ummheit f ~/~en **1. a.** *dullness*; *obtuseness*; *stupidity*; *asininity* **b.** *imprudence*; *folly*; es ist e–e ~ *it is folly* od *foolish* (*to do*); es ist bloße ~ *it is mere folly* **2.** *foolish action*; *blunder* (: *a tactical b.*), *gaff*(*e*) [Fr]; e–e ~ begehen *to do a foolish th, to commit folly* (od *a gaffe, an indiscretion*) || ~en [pl] *foolish pranks* od *tricks* [pl]; ~en m *to cut capers, to play the fool, to indulge in buffoonery*

D·ümmling m = Dummkopf

D·umpalme f ⟨bot⟩ *doum*(*-palm*)

D·umper [–ʌ–] m ~s/~ (Schütter-Lkw) *dumper*

d·umpf I. a **1.** = dumpfig **2.** (of sound, etc.) *dull, hollow, dead*; *deep* (*groan*); *muffled* (*thunder*; *voice*); *indistinct* || (undeutlich) *dim, faint* || ~er Klang *thump*(*ing*); ~er Ton *thud* **3.** ⟨übtr⟩ **a.** *dull* (*pain*); *stuffy* (*feeling*); ~ im Kopfe *heavy* (v *with sleep*); *darkling* (*sensations*) **b.** *depressed, dull, gloomy* (*mood*); (jdn) in e–e ~e Stimmung versetzen *to cast a damper on* (*a p*) **II.** adv *dimly, faintly*; *indistinctly* || ~ aufschlagen *to* (*fall with a*) *thud*; ~ äußern *to cluck* [vi]; ~ tönen → dröhnen | **≗heit** f ~/ *dul*(*l*)*ness, hollowness* (*of sound*) || *dimness, faintness* || (e–s Raumes) *musty, fusty atmosphere* | ⟨übtr⟩ *dul*(*l*)*ness, gloominess*; *monotony*

d·umpfig a (feucht) *damp, dank, moist*; etw ~ *dampish* || (modrig) *mouldy, musty*; ~ riechen *to smell mouldy* od *stale* || (muffig, beengend) *close, frowzy, fusty, poky* (*room*); *stale, stifling, stuffy* (*air*); (schwül) *sultry* → muffig | **≗keit** f ~/ *dampness* || *mustiness* || *closeness*; *fustiness*

D·umping ['dʌmpiŋ] n [engl] ~s/~s ⟨com⟩ *dumping* || ~praktiken [f pl] *dumping*

D·üna f ⟨Russ⟩ (Fluß) *Dvina*

D·üne f ~/~n *dune, sand-hill*; → Downs || Wander~ *drifting* od *driving dune*

D·ünen- ~distel f ⟨bot⟩ *eryngo* **~hafer** m ⟨bot⟩ = Strandhafer **~kette** f *range of dunes*

D·ung m ~(e)s/ *dung, manure*; *muck* | [in comp] *dung* .., *manure* ..; *manurial* (*quality*)

~erde f *terramara, –mare* **~fliege** f ⟨ent⟩ *dung-fly* **~haufen** m *dunghill*; *muck* (od *manure*)*-heap* **~käfer** m ⟨ent⟩ *dung-beetle* (od *chafer*) **~karren** m *dung-cart*; kl ~ *manure barrow*

Dung·ane m: ~n [pl] (moham. Mongolenvolk) *Dungas* [pl]

Dünge- [in comp] *fertilizing* **~mittel** n *fertilizer*, ~fabrik [f] *fertilizer factory* **~salz** n *fertilizer salt*

d·üngen vt/i [h] **1.** vt (Boden) *to dung, manure, muck* ‖ mit Mergel ~ *to marl* **2.** vi *to dung*

D·ünger m ~s/ *dung, manure*; *fertilizer*(*s* [pl]): ⟨agr⟩ wirtschaftseigener ~ *farmgard manure*; Kunst≃ *chemical* od *artificial manure* od *fertilizer*; Kali~ *potash manure*; Stickstoff≃ *nitrogenous manure*; → Guano **~grube** f *dung--pit* (od *cistern*) **~haufen** m = Dunghaufen **~stätte** f *dung-yard* **~streumaschine** f *manure distributor*

D·üngstoff m (künstl. ~) *fertilizer* **D·üngung** f ~/~en *dunging, manuring*; künstliche ~ *artificial manuring*

d·unkel I. a **A.** (Ggs hell) *dark* (*clouds, hair*); *black*; *obscure*; –kle Beleuchtung *dim lighting* ‖ dunkle Farben [pl] *darks, dark colours* [pl] ‖ v –kler Hautfarbe *dark-skinned* ‖ (trübe) dark, *sombre* (*sky*) ‖ (düster) *dusky, swarthy* (*complexion*); *murky* (*light, night*) ‖ ~ m *to darken*; *to turn out the light, to draw the curtains* ‖ ~ w *to get dark*; *to darken, darkle, dim*; *dusk* (:*it began to d.*); ~ werdend *darkling* (*wood*) ‖ es wurde ihm ~ vor den Augen *his head began to swim* od *to go around* **B.** ⟨übtr & fig⟩ (Ggs klar) **1.** (undeutlich) *dim, faint* (*idea, recollection*); *darkling, misty*; *obscure* (*feelings*); *opaque*; *vague* (Erinnerung *recollection*) ‖ (S) ~ vor jdm liegen *to be wrapped in obscurity* ‖ *recondite* (*style, author*); die Zukunft liegt ~ vor uns *we cannot see in the future* ‖ ⟨derog⟩ –kles Kapitel der Geschichte .. *black chapter in the h. ..*; ~kle Pläne pl *deep designs* **2.** (unergründlich) *dark* (*subject*); der dunkle Erdteil *the Dark Continent*; *mysterious* (*hints*), *obscure* (*motives*; *origin*; *passage*); *opaque*; *secret* (*ways*); *mystic*; *puzzling* ‖ ⟨fig⟩ (finster) *dark* (*vice*); *evil, sinister* (*instincts*); *darksome, sombre* (*character*); *weird* **3.** (trübe) *dark* (*hour*), *dismal, gloomy, sad, sombre* (*outlook*) **4.** ⟨phon⟩ *obscure* (*sound*) **II.** adv (*to feel*) *dimly, faintly*; *vaguely*; ~ brennen *to burn dimly*; *mysteriously, obscurely*; ich erinnere mich ~ *I remember dimly, I seem to remember* ‖ (*he spoke*) *darkly* **III.** ≃ n **1.** *the dark* ‖ im ~(n) *in the dark*; *darkling* (:*to sit d.*) ‖ im ~ bleiben *to remain obscure*; sich im ~n halten ⟨fig⟩ *to keep in the background*; *to shun light*; jdn im ~n l *to keep a p in the dark*; im ~ der Zukunft liegen *to lie hidden in the f.*; im ~n tappen *to be* (od *to grope*) *in the dark* (über *on*); ein Sprung ins Dunkle *a leap in the dark*, im ~n liegend *darkling* **2.** (Schleier) *mist, veil*; das geheimnisvolle ~, das ihn umgab *the air* od *veil of mystery that clung about him* ‖ ein ~ über etw breiten *to throw a v. of m. over a th*

d·unkel- [in comp mst] *dark-* .. ≃**adaptation** f ⟨opt⟩ *dark adaptation* **~äugig** a *dark-eyed* **~blau** a *deep* (od *dark*)*-blue* **~blond** a *off-blond* ≃**entladung** f ⟨el⟩ *silent discharge* **~farbig** a *dark, swarthy* ≃**feldbeleuchtung** f (im Mikroskop) *dark-wells* [pl] **~feldmikroskopie** f *dark field m.*, → Hellfeld- **~häutig** a *swarthy* ≃**kammer** f ⟨phys⟩ *camera obscura* [L]; ⟨phot⟩ *dark-room* ≃**mann** m (Lichtfeind) *obscurant*(*ist*), ⟨fam⟩ *back-stage conspirator* ≃**männerbriefe** m [pl] ⟨Ger Lit⟩ *Epistolae virorum obscurorum* [L] **~nachtjagd** f ⟨aero⟩ *dark night fighting* **~pause** f (im Kino) *obscuring* od *cut-off period* **~rot** a *dark-red*; er wurde ~ im Gesicht *his face became a deep pink*; *she flushed darkly* **~schalter** m ⟨el⟩ *dimmer* (*of light*) ≃**werden** n *dark, dusk*; *nightfall*; vor dem ~ *before dusk*; bei ~ *at dusk* ‖ *darkling* ([a & adv] *in the dark*)

D·ünkel m ~s/ *conceit*; *priggery, priggishness, priggism*; *arrogance, presumption* ‖ Klassen≃ *snobbery* ‖ e–n ~ h *to be conceited, to be a prig* od *snob, to be arrogant* od ⟨bes Am fam⟩ *stuck-up* | ≃**haft** a *conceited*; *priggish*; *arrogant, presumptuous*; *snobbish*; ⟨bes Am fam⟩ *stuck-up*

D·unkelheit f ~/ (→ dunkel) **A.** *darkness* (:*in the d.*); *murk*; tiefe ~ *black darkness* ‖ *swarthiness* (*of complexion*) ‖ (beginnende ~) *dusk*; bei anbrechender ~ *at nightfall, at dusk* **B.** ⟨übtr & fig⟩ **1.** *dimness, faintness* **2.** *darkness, mystery*; *obscurity*; in ~ gehüllt *wrapped in obscurity*; *opacity* (*of meaning*) ‖ *reconditeness* (*of style, author*) **3.** *darkness*; *gloom* **~sangst** f ⟨psych⟩ *scotophobia*

d·unkeln vi [h] *to grow dark, to darken, darkle* ‖ → verdunkeln

d·ünken vi [h] **1.** [v imps] *to seem, appear* ‖ dünkt dir das gut? *does that seem a good idea to you?* mir *or* mich dünkt, es dünkt mir *or* mich → deucht, deuchte **2.** [vref] **sich ~ a.** sie ~ sich besser z s *they fancy* (od *imagine, think*) *themselves* (*to be*) *better, they fancy they are b.* **b.** sie ~ sich etw Großes *they fancy themselves*; *they have a high opinion of themselves*; → einbilden

D·ünkirchen n ⟨Fr⟩ (Stadt) *Dunkirk*

dünn, † **~e I.** a **1.** (Ggs dicht) *thin, rare*; ~e Luft *rarefied atmosphere* ⟨a. fig⟩; *tenuous* (*air*); sein Haar ist ziemlich ~ *his hair is rather thin*; ~(er) w *to thin*; (etw) ~(er) m *to thin* ‖ → dick A. 2. ‖ (of liquids) *thin* (*soup*), *weak* (*tea*), *poor* (*wine*), *small* (*beer*); [pred] (*this beer is*) *all arms and legs* (sc *without body*) **2.** (Ggs dick) **a.** *thin* (*fingers*); (zart) *fine* (*thread, wire*), *delicate, slender* ‖ (schlank) *fine-drawn*; *slender, slight* (*figure*), *slim*; *tenuous*; lang u ~ *lank*; ~ wie ein Faden *spindly, lanky* ‖ (mager) *lean, meagre* ‖ ~ aussehen *to look thin* ‖ ~(er) m *to thin*; sich ~ m *to squeeze o.s. together*, → dünn(e)machen; → sich drücken ‖ ~ w (of ladies) *to slim*, Lebensweise mit dem Ziel ~ z bleiben *or* z w *slimming* **b.** *thin* (*paper*; *slice*) **3.** ⟨fig⟩ (schwach, gering) *poor* (*horse*); *weak* (*tone*), *lean* (*voice*) **II.** adv **1.** *thinly* (*covered*; *peopled*) **2.** *thinly* (*clad*); *delicately*; *finely*

d·ünn- ~backig a *thin-faced* **~beinig** a *spindle--legged* (od *shanked*); ~er Mensch m *spindle--shanks* pl [sg konstr] ≃**bier** n *small* od *near beer*; ⟨sl⟩ *swipes* ≃**blech** n *light-gauge steel* pl ≃**darm** m ⟨anat⟩ *small intestine* ≃**druckausgabe** f *thin--paper edition* ≃**druckpapier** n *India paper, thin printing paper* **~fädig** a *thin-spun* **~flüssig** a *liquid*; *of thin, flowing consistency*; *thin-bodied* (Öl); *sloppy, watery* **~gehämmert** a *rolled*; *beaten into plates* **~gesät** a *thin-sown*; *thinly scattered* ≃**lauge** f *deconcentrated liquor* **~(e)machen** [vrfl] sich ~ = °abhauen (weglaufen) ‖ aber: sich dünn m, → dünn °≃**pfiff,** ≃**schiß** m ⟨sl⟩ *squitters* (= *diarrhoea* [L]) **~schalig** a *thin-skinned* (*fruit*) ≃**schliff** m ⟨geol⟩ *thin section* ≃**schnäbler** m ⟨orn⟩ *tenuiroster* [L], *tenuirostral bird*

D·ünne f **1.** (Ggs Dichte) *thinness*; *tenuity* (*of air*) **2.** (Ggs Dicke) **a.** *delicacy*; *slenderness*; *slimness* ‖ ⟨fig⟩ *thinness*; *poverty* **b.** *thinness* (*of a seam, layer*) ‖ † **d·ünne** a → dünn **D·ünnheit** f ~/ → Dünne

D·unst m ~es/≃e **1.** † = Staub(wind); °⟨artill⟩ *heavy stuff*; °Mords≃ bek *to be fired at, to be under heavy fire* **2.** (leichter Dampf) **a.** *vapour, damp*; Wasser≃ *water-vapour* ‖ (Küchen≃) *steam* (*from boiling*); *smoke* (*from frying*) ‖ in ~ verwandeln *or* auflösen *to vaporize*; → Dampf ‖ (Nebel) *haze, mist*; *fog* **b.** (schlechter Geruch, Rauch) *fume*; *reek* (*of* *tobacco*), *smell*; *smoke* **3.** (Ausdünstung) **a.** ⟨physiol hist⟩ ∸e [pl] *exhalations* (*from the body*), *vapours* pl ‖ schädliche ∸e *mephitic vapours* od *fumes* (*from the earth*, etc.) pl; *miasma* [L] (:*full of miasma*); ⟨min⟩ *damps* pl **b.** ⟨fig poet⟩ *fume* (*of fear*); *intoxicated state* **4.** ⟨fig⟩ (Nichtigkeit) *vapour*; *vaporous* (od *vapoury, unsubstantial*) *matter* od *th* **5.** Wendungen: er hat k–n (**blassen**) ~ v der S *he has not the vaguest notion* od *the faintest idea of the matter* ‖ **blauer** ~ ⟨fig bes Am fam⟩ *baked wind, hot air* ‖ sich in blauen ~ auflösen *to vanish* od *melt into thin air*; jdm e–n blauen ~ vormachen *to throw dust in a p's eyes*; *to dupe, hoodwink, humbug, mystify a p*; ⟨sl⟩ *to bamboozle a p*; blauer ~! *all foam–no beer*! *hot air*! ∸**artig** a *vaporous*; *vapory* ~**haube** f ⟨tech⟩ *vapour hood* °~**kiepe** f = Helm ~**kreis** m ⟨fig⟩ *atmosphere*; *environment*; *milieu* [Fr] ~**masse** f: schwere ~n [pl] *masses of heavy vapour* ~**obst** n *stewed fruit* ~**rohr** n *ventilating pipe* ~**schleier** m *haze*; *vapory veil* ~**(sperr)filter** m ⟨phot⟩ *haze* (*cutting*) *filter*

***d·unsten** vi [h] **1.** (dampfen) *to emit vapour*; (rauchen) *to fume, reek* (v *with*); → schwitzen ‖ (of mist) *to steam*; *to rise in the form of vapour* **2.** (riechen) *to fume*; *reek*; *smell* (nach *of*)

d·ünsten vt/i [h] **1.** vt (Obst etc) *to stew*; ⟨cul⟩ braun ~ (schmoren) *to* (*dry-*) *braise* ‖ gedünstet *stewed* (*fruit*) **2.** *vi *to stew* ‖ = dunsten

d·unstig a *vaporous* (*atmosphere*; *hills*); *vapory* (*veil*) ‖ *damp*; *misty* (*weather*); *foggy* ‖ *steamy* (Waschküche) ‖ (rauchig) *reeky, smoky* ‖ *miasmal* (*place*); *miasmatic* (*jungle*) ‖ → dumpfig, muffig

D·ünung f ⟨mar⟩ *swell*(*ing*); tiefe ~ *ground-swell*

D·uo n ~s/~s ⟨mus⟩ *duo*; → Duett

Duod·ez n ~es/~ ⟨typ⟩ (Format) *duodecimo, twelvemo* (abbr *12mo*) ‖ Buch in ~ *duodecimo*

Duod·ez ~ausgabe f *duodecimo edition* ~**band** m *duodecimo volume* ~**fürst** m *duodecimo* od *petty prince*; *princeling*

duodezim·al a *duodecimal* ∸**bezeichnung** f *duodecimal notation* (od *scale*) ∸**rechnung** f *duodecimal calculation*; *duodecimals* pl, *cross-multiplication* ∸**system** n *duodecimal system*

Duod·ezime f ⟨mus⟩ *duodecimo*

düp·ieren **1.** vt [h] (jdn) *to dupe*; *befool, cheat, delude*; ⟨sl⟩ *bamboozle, dope, kid* **2.** ∸ n *dupery*

Düp·ierte [der ~, ein ~r] m *the dupe*

D·uplex- [in comp] *duplex* ‖ ~telegraphie [f] *d. telegraphy* ‖ ~verkehr [m] ⟨wir⟩ *d. communication*

†**Dupl·ik** f ~/~en ⟨hist jur⟩ (Gegenerklärung des Beklagten auf die Replik des Klägers) *duply*, [mst pl] ~en *duplies*; *rejoinder*

Duplik·at n ~(e)s/~e *duplicate*; *exact copy*; *counterpart* ‖ ⟨comp⟩ *tally* (z *of*); ⟨arts⟩ *replica* ‖ im ~ herstellen *to duplicate* ‖ Wechsel∸ *second copy of a bill* ~**i·onskontrolle** f *duplication controls* pl **Duplizit·ät** f *duplicity* **Dupnegativ** n ⟨phot⟩ *dupe* (= *duplicate*) *negative*

Düppel m ~s/~ ⟨anti-radar⟩ *window* ‖ ~straße [f] *window cloud*; ~streifen [m pl] *rope, chaff*

Dur n ~/ ⟨mus⟩ *major*; C-~ *C major* ‖ ~tonart f *major key* ‖ ~tonleiter [f] *major scale*

dur·abel a *durable*

Duralum·in n ⟨met⟩ *duralumin*

D·urban n (Hafenstadt in Natal, Süd-Afrika)

d·urch I. prep [mit acc] **A.** (Ort) **1.** *through*, ⟨Am a.⟩ *thru* (*the air*); jdm ~ die Brust dringen *to pass through a p's chest*; jdm durchs Herz (*or* ~ Mark u Bein) gehen *to pierce a p's heart* (od *a p to the heart*); *to cut* od *touch a p to the quick*; ein Gedanke schoß mir ~ den Kopf *a thought crossed my mind*; *an idea occurred to me*; .. plötzlich .. *flashed across my mind* ‖ ⟨fig⟩ jdm ~ die Finger sehen *to indulge a p*; *to be lenient* od *indulgent to a p* ‖ (quer ~) *across* (*the river, city, room, meadow*); *through* (*the country*); ~ e–e Wüste gehen *to cross a desert*; ~ die ganze Stadt g. *to walk right across the town* ‖ e–n Querstrich ziehen ~ etw *to cross a th* **2.** (Weg) **a.** *by way of, through* (*the window*); ~ die Nase sprechen *to speak through the nose* ‖ sie gingen ~ ein Kloster nach .. *they went by way of a monastery to ..* ‖ ~ die Tür eintreten *to enter by* od *at the door*; wir w ~ M. k *we shall come/travel through M.* | *of* (: *our tour of Spain, of the city*) | *over* (: *we showed him over the house*; *we travelled over the whole* [od *all over the*] *continent*) | ~ ganz .. *all over* ..; *throughout*.. (: *we travelled thr. Spain*) **b.** er kletterte ~ das (*or* zum) Fenster hinein *he climbed in at the window* ‖ er flog ~ e–e Seitentür hinaus *he flew out at a side door* **3.** ⟨com⟩ ~ die Post schicken *to send through the post, to send by* (od *per*) *post*; ~ Überbringer *per bearer* ‖ *it was transmitted by wireless* ‖ *through* od *by the medium* od *intervention of Mr. N.* **B.** ⟨übtr⟩ (Zeit) ~ s–e ganze Regierung hindurch *through all his reign* ‖ ~ e–e Reihe v Gefahren, Krisen, Nöten *through a series of dangers, crises, anxieties* ‖ → hindurch **C.** (Mittel, Ursache) **1.** *through, by means of*; *in consequence of*; *by dint of*; ~ wiederholtes Klopfen *by dint of constant hammering* (*on the door*); ~ s–e gr Anstrengungen *through* (od *by dint of*) *his great efforts*; ~ Ihre Hilfe *through your help*; ~ anhaltenden Regen *in consequence of continual rains* **2.** ~ Arbeit *by working* ‖ ~ Zufall *by chance* ‖ *impressed by* .. ‖ *influenced by* .. ‖ *to die by poison* **3.** *with* (: *distorted with age*) ‖ (*to cure with fasting*) ‖ *from* (*to suffer from the war*), er starb ~ Ermüdung *he died from fatigue* **4.** ~ jdn *through a p* ‖ etw ~ jdn erleiden *to sustain a th at the hands of a p* ‖ *England became a sea power through Cromwell* ‖ *through my fault*; *through you, through gambling* od *waste* **II.** adv **A.** (Zeit) das ganze Jahr ~ *throughout the year*; die ganze Nacht ~ *all the night*; *the whole n. through* ‖ er schlief den ganzen Tag ~ *he slept the clock round*; .. den ganzen Sommer (hin)~ (*the flowers blossom*) *all through the summer* ‖ es ist 5 (Uhr) ~ *it is past five* **B. 1.** wir **dürfen** nicht ~ *we are not allowed to pass* ‖ ich **habe** das Buch ~ *I have read the book through, I have done with the book*; wann wirst du die Aufgabe ~ h? *when shall you get through your task*? ‖ sie konnten nicht ~ *they could not get throught* (od .. *not pass*); wir **müssen** ~ *we must get* od *break through* **2.** ~ **sein a.** (P) *to be through* [adv]; er ist ~ *he is through* [prep] *his examination, he has passed* (*in his e.*) ‖ ~ s mit etw *to be through with a th* (: *he is through with his lessons*); ist er mit dem Examen ~? *is he through his exam*? ‖ ⟨fig⟩ er ist bei mir (unten) ~ *I have done* od *broken with him* **b.** (S) der Käse ist ~ .. *is ripe* ‖ (of clothes, etc.) *to be the worse for wear*; die Stiefel sind ~ *the boots are worn out* ‖ der Zug muß ~ s *the train must be through* **3.** [als pref bei Verben etc] → durch–, bes I. B. 2. **C.** ~ u ~ *through and through*; er war ~ u ~ naß (*or* naß ~ u ~), er war ganz u gar ~ *he was wet through* (*and through*), *he was wet to the skin* ‖ sie handelten als Deutsche ~ u ~ *they acted as Germans through and through* ‖ ein Deutscher ~ u ~ *a German through and through*; *a thoroughbred German* ‖ ~ u ~ ein Ehrenmann *a g. to his fingertips* ‖ ~ u ~ ehrlich *thoroughly honest* ‖ er war ein General ~ u ~ *he was a general every inch of him*; ein Sozialist ~ u ~ *a thorough-going socialist, a socialist to the backbone* ‖ ein Schurke ~ u ~ *a thorough-paced* (od *an out-and-out*) *scoundrel, a s. out-and-out* ‖

→ hindurch, mittendurch | jdn ~ u ~ kennen *to be able to sum up a p, to know a p thr. and thr.*

durch- pref **I.** [in Verbalkompositen] [Allgemeines] **1.** [die Verbindung ~ + Verb entspricht stets = engl Verb + *through*]: ~br·echen vt *to break through*; ~·eilen vt *to run through*; ~|brechen vi *to break through*; ~|lesen vt *to read .. through* ‖ [statt des Kompositums kann oft auch ein Verbum anderer Bildung (mst aus Frz. Lat.) verwandt werden]: ~b·ohren vt *to pierce*; ~br·echen vt *to break*; ~dr·ingen vt *to penetrate*; **2.** ~qu·eren *to cross* [die Partikel *through* kann sein]: **a.** [prep]: ich ~br·eche das Hindernis *I break through the barrier*; ich ~·eile die Straßen *I run through the streets* **b.** [adv]: ich arbeite das Buch ~*I work through the book*; die Sonne bricht ~ *the sun breaks through*; das Hindernis wurde ~br·ochen *the barrier was broken through* **A.** [mit untrennbarem, unbetontem pref] **1.** [alte Transitiva]: ~br·echen [~br·ach/~br·ochen] ~s·uchen [pp ~s·ucht] **2.** [jüngere Transitiva aus urspr Intr.]: ~·eilen [ich ~·eile (die Straßen); [pp ~·eilt]; ~l·aufen [pp ~l·aufen] **B.** [mit trennbarem betontem pref] **1.** [alte Intransitiva]: ~brechen [ich breche ~/~gebrochen]; ~fallen [ich falle ~/~gefallen] (oft begegnet dasselbe Verbum dieser Art, also intransitiv, neben einem transitiven, → A. 2.): ~fahren vi: [ich fahre ~/pp (er ist) ~gefahren] neben ~fahren vt [ich ~f·ahre (das Meer)/pp ~f·ahren] **2.** [jüngere Transitiva, deren pref urspr. adv war (= hin~, mitten~; ganz ~, ~ u ~; ~e–a)]: ~arbeiten [ich arbeite ~/pp ~gearbeitet]; *to work through*; ~lesen *to read .. through*; [*through* kann adv wie prep s]: ich arbeite das Buch ~ *I work* od *go through* [prep] *the book*; *I work the book through* [adv], (Vorsicht bei Übersetzung!), → ~ackern, ~beraten, ~lassen; [oft begegnet dasselbe trans. Verbum dieser Art neben den unter A. 1.]: ~suchen [ich suche ~/pp ~gesucht] neben ~s·uchen [ich ~s·uche/pp ~s·ucht] **3.** [Reflexiva derselben Art wie 2.] **a.** [mst Grundverb + *one's way*]: sich ~arbeiten [ich arbeite mich ~/pp ~gearbeitet] *to work one's way* (durch *through*); sich ~betteln *to beg one's way* **b.** [reflexiv]: *to work o.s.* (*through*) | [intransitiv]: *to work* (*through*) **II.** [in Nominalkompositen, stets untrennbar] **A.** [alle, mit betontem pref] **1.** [engl Nomen + *through*]: ~bruch ⟨mil⟩ *break-through* [′– –] **2.** [engl] *through* + Nomen]: ~gang *through passage* [′–͵–]: ~reisender [m] *through passenger* [′–͵–] **3.** [durch andere Bildungen] ~fall [m] (in Prüfung) *failure*; ⟨med⟩ *diarrhoea* **B.** [v Verben abgeleitete] **1.** (vgl A. 1.) [mit unbetontem pref]: ≈br·echung; ≈s·uchung; ~d·acht; ~f·orscht [auch hier im Engl oft e–e andere Bildung]: ≈dr·ingung *penetration*; ≈f·orschung *exploration* **2.** (vgl I. B. 2.) [mit betontem pref]: ≈bildung (*through*) *training*

durch·ackern vt [h] [pp –ackert] (Feld) *to plough* **d·urch|ackern** vt [h] [pp –ge–t] ⟨fig⟩ ein Buch ~ *to plough through a book*; *to work a book through*; das Gebiet ~ *to go over the ground*; ich habe es hin u her –geackert *I have gone* od *been over and over the ground*

durch·ädern vt [h] (etw) *to rein* **-·ädert** *veined* (v *with*)

d·urch|arbeiten vt/i [h] **I.** vt [pp –ge–t] **1. a.** ein Buch ~ *to work* od *go through a book, to work a book through,* .. gründlich .. *to make a thorough study of a b.*; ein Gebiet tüchtig ~ *to go over and over the ground* ‖ *to work up* (f *for*) **b.** (Körper etc) *to exercise, train*; beim Gehen wird der ganze Körper –ge–t *walking exercises the whole body* **2. sich** ~ durch .. *to work o.s.* (od *one's way*) *through* .., *to work through* ..; (sich drängen) *to elbow* od *make one's way through*; sich mühsam ~ *to beat* od *toil* (*through*) **II.** vi wir arbeiten durch *we are working without a break*; bis z Abend ~ *to work without break till evening* **D·urcharbeitung** f *training* (*of the body*)

durch·atmen vt [h] [pp –atmet] **1.** vt ⟨fig⟩ (etw) *to pervade*; jds Werke ~ *to breathe through a p's works*; –atmet s v *to be informed with*

d·urch|atmen vi [h] [pp –ge–t] *to breathe briskly* od *thoroughly*

durch·aus [a. **d·urchaus** vor Adj] adv **A.** [vor Adj. u Adv.] ~ wahr *quite* (od *absolutely, entirely, really*) *true* ‖ (in jeder Hinsicht) *in every way*; *quite* (*possible*) ‖ (vollständig) *down to the ground* ‖ ~ unerfreulich *downright* (od *thoroughly*) *unpleasant*; ~ ungesetzlich *positively unlawful* ‖ ~ demokratisch *democratic throughout*; *nothing if not democratic* ‖ ein ~ ehrlicher Mann *an honest man throughout* (od *out and out*) ‖ e–e ~ andere S *quite another th* | ich bin ~ bereit .. *I am game* (*to do*); es ist ~ denkbar *it is on the cards* (*that*); es ist ~ möglich *it is just possible* (*that*) ‖ ~ sicher *safe enough*, ⟨Am⟩ *good and safe*; Ist sie wieder wohl? Ja, ~ wohl '*Is she well again?*' '*Oh yes, well enough*' **B.** [bei Verben] **1.** *quite*; *absolutely, entirely*; *positively* ‖ ich verstehe ~ *I quite understand*; ich schätze ihn ~ *I quite like him* | ich erwartete ~ *I half expected* (*to find*); das erwartete ich ~ *that's very much what I expected* ‖ 2 Schilling würden ~ genügen *2 shillings would do nicely* ‖ er will es ~ sehen *he will see it*; *he insists on* (od *persists in*) *seeing it* ‖ .. u hoffen, daß Sie damit ~ zufrieden s w .. *and hope you will find they are in every way satisfactory* **2.** [neg] ~ .. **nicht** *not .. at all* ‖ ⟨Am⟩ *not .. any* ‖ ~ nicht gehorchen wollen *to refuse to obey* ‖ ihn rührte das ~ nicht *he did not mind this at all*; ⟨Am⟩ *he did not mind this any* ‖ ~ nicht unzufrieden *far from displeased* ‖ er verstand ~ k–n Spaß *he understood no sort of humour* **C.** [alleinstehend, in Antworten] **1.** ~! *quite! quite so! just so! all right! at all events! by all means! absolutely! positively! exactly! precisely! definitely!* **2.** ~ **nicht**! *not at all! by no means! not in the least!* ‖ ~ niemand *no one at all* ‖ ,Du mußt müde s' ,Oh nein, ~ nicht', .. '*Oh no, thank you*'.

d·urch|backen vt [h] (Brot) *to bake* od *do properly* od *thoroughly* ‖ –ge– *well-baked*

durchb·eben vt [h] ⟨fig⟩ (jdn) *to thrill*; *inform, pervade, stir* (*a p*) ‖ durchb·ebt v *informed with*; *thrilled with*; *quivering with* (*fright*)

d·urch|beißen vt [h] **1.** die Leine ~ (of dogs) *to bite the line through* (od *asunder, in two*) **2. sich** ~ ⟨fig⟩ *to bite one's way through*; *to fight one's way*; *to fight it out*; *to get across* (od *ahead, along*); *to get over the difficulties*

d·urch|bekommen vt [h] [pp ~] etw ~ *to get a th through*; *to get through with a th* ‖ ⟨parl⟩ e–e Vorlage ~ *to make a bill pass*

d·urch|beraten vt [h] [pp –beraten] e–e S gründlich ~ *to go over and over the ground*; *to discuss a th in detail*

d·urch|beten vi [h] [pp –gebetet] *to pray without a stop* ‖ die Nacht ~ *to spend the night in prayer*

d·urch|betteln vrefl [h] [pp –ge–t] sich ~ *to get one's livelihood by begging*; *to beg one's way* (durch *through*)

d·urch|beuteln vt [h] [pp –ge–t] (Mehl etc) *to shake* (*flour*) *thoroughly*; *to sift*

D·urchbiegung f (e–r Linie) ⟨opt⟩ *incurvation* ‖ ~skraft [f] ⟨mech⟩ *deflecting force*

d·urch|bilden vt [h] [pp –ge–t] (den Körper) *to exercise*; ⟨a. mil⟩ jdn ~ *to set a p up*; *to train a p* | (den Geist) *to train* (*thoroughly*) ‖ jdn ~ *to perfect a p's education* ‖ –ge–t (körperlich) *set-up* || *accomplished, finished*; *consummate*; *drilled* (in *in*); technisch –ge–t *technically trained*; ein allseitig –ge–ter Mann *an all-round man* **D·urchbildung** f ∼/∼en ⟨mil⟩ *drill*; *thorough training* od *education* (*of a p*)

d·urch|blasen vt [h] [pp –geblasen] (Luft) ∼ durch .. *to blow* (*air*) *through* (*a pipe*) || (ein Rohr etc) *to blow* (*a pipe*) || sich ∼ l (vom Winde) *to get a blow*

d·urch|blättern vt [h] [pp –ge–t] ein Buch ∼ *to turn over the leaves of a book*; ein B. (nur) ∼ *to glance over* ⟨Am⟩ *leaf a book*; *to have only a glance at a book*; .. schnell ∼ *to run through a book*; (Prospekt) *to glance through*; (Papiere) ⟨bes Am⟩ *to leaf through* **durchbl·ättern** vt [h] [pp –bl·ättert] = d·urchblättern

d·urchblenden vt [h] [pp –ge–t] ⟨film⟩ *to dissolve* (*from to*)

°**d·urch|bleuen** vt [h] [pp –ge–t] = d·urchhauen

D·urchblick m ∼(e)s/∼e *peep* (in *or* auf den Garten *of the garden*); *view, vista* (auf *of*); flüchtiger ∼ *glimpse* (auf *of*) || k–n ∼ h zu *to have no glimpse of* das Gute in ihm blickt in s–n Handlungen durch *his good nature is apparent in his actions* **∼fenster** n *viewing window*

d·urch|blicken vi [h] [pp –geblickt] **1.** *to look through* [adv]; durch e–e Öffnung *to look through* [prep] *an aperture*; blick mal durch *have a look through* (*it*) **2.** ⟨übtr⟩ (sichtbar w) (S) *to appear*; *to peep out* | etw ∼ l *to hint a th*; → andeuten || ∼ l, daß .. *to imply* od *insinuate that* .. || jdm gegenüber ∼ l, daß *to convey the thought to a p that* ..

durchbl·icken vt [h] [pp –kt] jdn ∼ *to look a p through*; → durchsch·auen

durchbl·utet [pp, a] *blood-stained* (*bandage*) || frisch ∼ *fresh* (Teint *complexion*); die Haut ist gut ∼ .. *is well nourished*, .. sieht gut ∼ aus *the appearance of the skin signifies good circulation*; der Teint erhält e–e gut ∼e Tönung *the c. gets the rosy hue of g. c.* **Durchbl·utung** f *blood supply* (verbessern *to promote*) **∼sstörung** f *circulatory disturbance*

durchb·ohren vt [h] [pp –bohrt] **1.** (etw) *to pierce* (mit *with* [*a spear*]) || jdn, jds Korper ∼ *to pierce* (od *run*) *a p through* [adv], *to transfix a p*; *to run a p through* [prep] *the body*; er –bohrte ihn mit dem Schwerte *he passed* od *thrust his sword through him*; sich [dat] die Ohrläppchen ∼ l *to have one's ears pierced*; sein Herz war –bohrt v .. *he had been run through the heart by* ..; → Horn || ⟨bot⟩ ein vom Stengel –bohrtes Blatt *a perfoliate leaf* || → durchlöchern | ⟨übtr⟩ jdn mit den Blicken ∼ *to impale a p with one's eyes*; *to look a p through and through*; *to look daggers at a p* **2. sich** ∼ *to stab o.s.*

d·urch|bohren vt [h] [pp –gebohrt] ein Brett ∼ *to bore* (*through*) *a board*; *to make a hole through a board* || **sich** ∼ (T) *to bore* (*one's way*) (durch *through*) | **∼d** a *piercing* (*frost*; *wind*); *keen, penetrating, piercing* (*glance, voice*); *acute, agonizing, excruciating, lancinating* (*pain*)

Durchb·ohrung f ∼/∼en *the piercing* (*of a p*)

d·urch|braten vt [h] [pp –ge–] (Fleisch) *to roast thoroughly* od *well* || –ge– *well done, done to a turn*; nicht –ge– *underdone*; ⟨Am⟩ *rare* (*meat*)

d·urch|brausen vt [h] [pp –ge–t] (of a train) durch den Bahnhof ∼ *to go* (od *run*) *roaring through the station*

durchbr·aust a; vom Sturm ∼ *storm-tossed*; *wind-swept*; *wind-whipped* (*streets*)

durchbr·echen vt [h] [pp –br·ochen] **1.** ein Hindernis ∼ *to break through an obstacle* | (Oberfläche) *to breach* || to perforate ⟨a. arts⟩ || ⟨mil⟩ (Mauer) *to breach* ⟨a. übtr⟩; die Linie ∼ *to break* (*through*) *the line* (*of defence*); *to pierce the lines*; → Blockade **2.** ⟨übtr⟩ die Regeln des beruflichen Anstands ∼ *to violate the rules of professional conduct* || (Gesetz etc) *to break, to infringe* || (Stille) *to break*; → brechen

d·urch|brechen vt/i [pp –gebrochen] **1.** vt [h] etw ∼ *to break a th through, to break a th asunder* (od *in two*) || e–e Verbindung ∼ *to cut a passage through* (*to a place*); e–e V.–sstraße ∼ *to open a thoroughfare* → durchbrochen **2.** vi [s] **a.** *to break*; *to break to pieces* || der Appendix ist (in die Bauchhöhle) –gebr. *the app. has perforated* (*into the abdominal cavity*) **b.** (hervorkommen) (of buds, etc.) *to break*; *to break* od *come forth*; (*of teeth*) *to erupt*; (*of buds*) *to burst*; bei dem Kinde brechen schon die Zähne durch *the child is cutting its teeth* || (of the sun) *to break through* || (of features) *to peep out*; *to appear, show*; s–e wahre Natur bricht durch *his true character asserts itself*; die Wahrheit bricht durch .. *comes out*, .. *comes to light* **c.** ⟨mil⟩ *to break through* [adv]; *to force one's way, to break* (durch .. *through* ..)

d·urch|brennen vt/i [pp –gebrannt] **1.** vt [h] (Faden) *to burn* (*a thread*) *through*; *to affect* (*a th*) *by burning*; die Tasche ∼ *to burn a hole in the pocket* || ⟨el⟩ *to fuse*; *to burn out*; e–e Sicherung ∼ *to blow a fuse*; die Sicherung ist –gebrannt *the fuse is gone* **2.** vi [h] **a.** ⟨el⟩ *to fuse, blow*, (of fuse) *to blow out* **b.** ⟨fig⟩ °(P) *to slip away* od *off* || *to abscond*; ⟨Am sl⟩ *to vamo*(*o*)*se*; → ausreißen || ∼ mit etw *to bolt* (od *walk off*) *with a th*; *to bilk a th*; → d·urchgehen || mit der Kasse ∼ *to make off with the cash* || heimlich mit der Miete ∼ *to shoot the moon* || e–m Gläubiger ∼ *to bilk* od *cheat a creditor* **D·urchbrennen** n ⟨fig⟩ *bolting*; *elopement* (*of a woman*) **D·urchbrenner** m *absconder*

d·urch|bringen vt [h] [→ –gebracht] **A. 1.** jdn ∼ *to see* od *take a p through*; (durch Nöte) *to bring a p through*; (e–n Kranken) *to bring a p round* od *through*; *to pull a p through* || etw ∼ *to get a th through*; ⟨parl⟩ (Antrag) *to carry*; e–e Vorlage ∼ *to get a bill adopted*; (Gesetz) *to pass*; (Gesetz) in Eile ∼ *to rush*; etw im Senat ∼ *to hustle* (*a th*) *through the senate* **2.** ⟨übtr⟩ (Geld) *to get through*, (: *you got through half your fortune*), *to go through* (*a fortune*); *to dissipate, squander*; *consume*; sein Geld ∼ ⟨sl⟩ *to blow one's money*; viel G. ∼ *to run* od *go through a lot of m.* || die Zeit ∼ *to idle away one's time*; *to kill time* **B. sich ehrlich** ∼ *to make both ends meet*; *to make an honest living* || sich anständig, bequem ∼ *to get along quite comfortably* || sich kümmerlich ∼ = sich d·urchschlagen

durchbr·ochen a; ∼e Arbeit *open work*; ∼e Strümpfe [pl] *openwork stockings* pl; → durchbrechen, –löchern; Filigran || *perforated* (*rim*) ⟨a. arts⟩; ⟨arts⟩ *openwork* [attr] || geschnitzt ∼e Arbeit *fretwork*; (Decke etc) mit geschnitzt ∼er Arbeit verzieren *to fret*

D·urchbruch m ∼(e)s/∼e **A.** [abstr] **1.** *break*; *breaking-through* || (of buds) *burst* || *breakthrough* (*of scientists to new discovery*); ⟨aero⟩ *of sound barrier* | ⟨mil⟩ *break-through*; ∼sschlacht *break-through battle* || → Bresche; Bruch **2. a.** (of the sun) *break* (*in the clouds*) || plötzlicher ∼ der Sonne *sun-burst*; → Tagesanbruch || (of floods) ⟨Am⟩ *wash-out* **b.** ⟨übtr⟩ *breaking forth*; *burst* (*of activity*); *outburst* || zum ∼ k *to come to a head*; (of features, etc.) *to come into view, to peep out* **B.** [konkr] (Kanal) *cut*(*-off*); → Durchlaß, Öffnung **∼soperation** f ⟨tact⟩ *breaching op.* **∼stal** n *transverse valley*; *water gap*

d·urch|bummeln vi [h] die ganze Nacht ∼ *to make a night of it*

durchd·acht a; wohl∼ *reasoned* (*statement*), *well-thought-out, well-weighed*; fein ∼ *studied*; *carefully excogitated* (*plan*) || nicht ∼ *crude* (*judgement*)

durch|d·enken vt [h] [pp –dacht] (etw) logisch ~ *to reason* (*a th*) *out*; die Rede war glänzend –dacht *the speech was admirably reasoned* | (überlegen) *to think* (*a th*) *over*; *to revolve* (*a th*) *in one's mind*; *to meditate* (od *muse*) *on* (*a th*); (gründlich ~) *to think* (*a th*) *out*

d·urch|drängen vrefl [h] [pp –ge–t] sich ~ *to elbow* (od *push*, *squeeze*) *o.s.* (durch *through*); *to elbow* (od *force*, *push*) *one's way* (*through*); *to hustle*, *push* (*through*); er drängte sich durch *he forced his way through the crowd*; → sich drängen

d·urch|drehen vt [h] [pp –ge–t] **1.** (Fleisch etc) *to pass* (*meat*) *through a mincing-machine*; *to mince* (*meat*) ‖ (Wäsche) *to pass* (*a th*) *through a wringer* **2.** → verrückt w; °vollkommen –gedreht s *to be down and out*; *to be at the end of one's tether*; ⟨Am⟩ *to be all-in* ‖ m–e Nerven waren wie –gedreht *my nerves were rattled*

°**d·urch|dreschen** vt [h] jdn ~ *to thrash a p*, *to give a p a thrashing* od *beating*

durchdr·ingen vt [h] [pp –drungen] **1.** (jdn, jds Körper etc) (of a bullet, knife) *to penetrate*, *pierce* ‖ (of cold, etc.) *to pierce*, *search*; → dringen **2.** (Boden) (of liquids) *to permeate*; *to pass* (od *permeate*) *through* (*the soil*) **3.** (Dunkelheit) (of eyes, etc.) *to penetrate* ‖ (Tiefen) *to plumb* **4.** ⟨übtr⟩ **a.** (Geheimnis) *to penetrate*; *to see* (od *penetrate*) *into* (od *through*) *a th* **b.** (of influence) *to permeate*, *pervade* (*a country*) **5.** ⟨übtr⟩ ~ mit **a.** **(etw)** ~ **mit** *to interfuse* od *interpenetrate with* (*another th*); (Land) *to leaven with*, *to imbue* (*a country*) *with* (*a spirit*); →–setzen ‖ e–a ~, sich gegenseitig ~ *to interfuse*, *interpenetrate*; *interlock*; ⟨phys⟩ (of 2 substances) *to* (*inter*)*mingle* **b.** **jdn** ~ **mit** etw *to fill* (od *to imbue*, *impress*, *inspire*, *inform*, *saturate*) *a p with* (*a feeling*); *to instil*(*l*) *a th into a p*; jdn mit neuem Leben ~ *to breathe fresh life into a p*; sich v Kraft –drungen fühlen *to feel o.s. infused with str.*, –drungen v *imbued with* (*hatred*, *love*); *inst·inct with* (*life*); –drungen s v *to be informed* (od *imbued*, *impressed*) *with* (*a new spirit*); v Wert dessen, .., –drungen s *to cherish a belief in the value of that* (*for which one is fighting*)

d·urch|dringen vi [s] [pp –gedrungen] **1.** *to get through*; Licht –gt durchs Fenster .. *enters the w.* ‖ ⟨mil⟩ ~ bis *to advance* (od *get*) *as for as* (*Lyon*); ~ bis z *to win through to* (*the port*) **2.** (of news) ~ z jdm *to get through to a p* ‖ *to penetrate*; s–e Stimme konnte nicht ~, er konnte mit s–r St. nicht ~ *his voice could not come through*; *his v. was drowned* **3.** ⟨übtr⟩ **a.** (of ideas) *to penetrate* **b.** (P) ⟨fig⟩ *to make a way for o.s.* mit s–r Meinung (etc) ~ *to carry one's point*; *to prevail* (gegen *against a p*) ‖ *to succeed*; ⟨Am⟩ *to come through*

durchdr·ingend, d·urchdringend a **1.** *biting*, *piercing* (*cold*); *searching*, *sharp* (*wind*); *pungent* (*taste*) ‖ *deep*; *plangent* (*sound*); *shrill*, *thrilling* (*voice*); (ohrenbetäubend) *ear-piercing* (*noise*) **2.** *cutting*, *penetrating*, *piercing* (*glance*) ‖ *acute*, *incisive*, *keen*, *penetrative* (*mind*); *sharp* **3.** *pervasive* (*influence*); sich gegenseitig ~ *interpenetrative* (*power*) ‖ *trenchant* (*reform*) ‖ ~es Erlebnis *thrill* ‖ → durchb·ohrend

Durchdr·ingung f *penetration* (durch *by*); *permeation*; *pervasion*; friedliche ~ *peaceful penetration* ‖ ~ mit *interfusion with*; gegenseitige ~ *interpenetration*

durch|dr·öhnen vi [h] *to boom*, *rumble*, *resound*, *ring*

d·urch|drücken vt [h] [pp –ge–t] **1.** die Knie ~ *to straighten one's legs*, *to keep one's l. straight*; *to draw in one's knees*; –ge–ckte Hosenbeine *baggy trouser legs* **2.** etw ~ *to press* (od *push*, *squeeze*) *a th* (durch *through*); (Kartoffeln) ⟨cul⟩ *to rice* **3.** ⟨übtr⟩ (Anspruch) *to push* ‖ s–n Willen ~ *to force acceptance of one's will*; *to carry one's point* ‖ (Gesetz) *to force acceptance of* (*a law*) ‖ Vorlage im H.C. ~ *to hustle* od *rush a bill through the H.C.*; → d·urchbringen, d·urchsetzen **4.** sich ~ (of ink) *to come through* (*on the other side*) **D·urchdrückverfahren** n ⟨engr⟩ *soft ground*

durchdr·ungen a → durchdr·ingen

durchd·uften vt [h] [pp –d·uftet] (e–n Raum) (of flowers, etc.) *to perfume*, *scent* (*a room*); *to fill* (*a room*) *with odour* od *perfume*

durch·eilen vt [h] [pp –lt] (die Straßen) *to hasten* (od *hurry*, *rush*) *through* (*the streets*) ein Land ~ *to travel* od *traverse a country in haste* ‖ ⟨übtr⟩ (Buch) *to run through* (*a book*)

d·urcheilen vi [s] [pp –geeilt] er ist schnell –geeilt *he has passed* (*through*) *in great haste*

durchein·ander **1.** adv *in confusion* od *disorder*; *confusedly*, *promiscuously*; *higgledy-piggledy*, *topsyturvy*; *upside-down*; ⟨Am⟩ *afoul*; es ist alles ~ *it is all topsyturvy*, ⟨Am⟩ *it's all gone haywire*; bunt ~ *higgledy-piggledy* | (P) ich bin ganz ~ *I'm off the hinges* **2.** ≗ n *confusion*, *disorder*; *muddle*, *mess*(*-up*); *jumble*; *medley*; *pell-mell*, *mix-up*, *topsyturvy*(*dom*); ⟨bes Am⟩ *hugger-mugger*; ein wirres *or* wüstes ~ *an up--and-down disorder*; das tolle ~ *the bedlam* (*of the distant noise*) ‖ ein ~ aufräumen *to clear up*, *to straighten up a mess*, *a chaos*; ein möglichst gr ~ m ⟨fig⟩ *to make as much hay as possible* **3.** [betontes, trennbares pref]: **~|bringen** vt [h] *to confuse*; *to turn topsyturvy* ‖ (Pläne) *to upset* ‖ alles ~ ⟨Am fam⟩ *to ball things up* **~|laufen** vi = ~rennen **~|liegen** vi [h] *to be in confusion*, *to be in a tumble*; wirr ~ *to be in utter confusion* **~|mengen** vt [h] *to mix up* (od *thoroughly*); → ~werfen **~|mischen** vt [h] *to mix* ‖ (Dinge) wild ~ *to scramble* **~|rennen** vi [s] wirr ~ *to run in utter confusion* (nach *to*); alles rannte durche–a *there was an utter confusion among them* **~|rufen** vi [h] *to shout simultaneously* **~|werfen** vt [h] *to throw* (*a th*) *into confusion*, *to turn* (*a th*) *topsyturvy*; *to jumble*; in e–m Raum alles ~ *to turn a room upside down* ‖ ⟨übtr⟩ (verwechseln) (Begriffe) *to confuse*; *to mix up*; *to muddle* **~|wirbeln** vt/i [h] *to whirl round and round* vt/i ‖ vt (Papiere) *to throw in disorder*

d·urch|fädeln vt [h] [pp –ge–t] (Faden) *to pass* (*a thread*) *through a needle's eye*

durchf·ahren vt [h] [pp ~] **1.** (of ships, etc.) das Meer ~ *to sail* od *cross the sea*; *to sail* (od *glide*) *over* od *across the sea* ‖ (P) die Straßen ~ *to drive* (od *pass*; *ride*) *through the streets* (*in a bus*, etc.); ein Schauder durchfuhr ihn *a shiver ran through his body* (od *down his spine*); ein plötzlicher Schreck durchfuhr ihn *he was seized with sudden fear*; ein Gedanke durchfuhr ihn *an idea rushed into his mind* (od *crossed his mind*), *an idea flashed upon him*; → durchzucken

d·urch|fahren vi/t [pp –gefahren] **1.** vi [s] (of a train) *to go through without a stop*; (of a ship) *to sail through* (od *past*) *without landing* ‖ unter e–r Brücke ~ *to shoot a bridge* ‖ er ist –gefahren *he has passed* (*through the village*, etc.) *without stopping* **2.** vt [h] (Straße) *to wear* (*a road*) *out by driving*

D·urchfahrt f ~/~en **1.** [abstr] *passage* (durch *through*); ~ verboten! *no thoroughfare!* ‖ *transit* (*of goods*) ‖ journey (*through* od *across a town*) **2.** [konkr] (Straße) *passage*, *passageway*; *thoroughfare* ‖ (Tor) *gate*(*way*) ‖ → Kanal, Straße, Tunnel etc **~(s)höhe** f (e–r Brücke) *headroom*, (*overhead clearance*) (*under a br.*), → lichte Höhe **~(s)kontrolle** f *passing c.* **~srecht** n *right of passage* (od *way*) **~szoll** m *transit-duty*

D·urchfall m ~(e)s/≗e **1.** (Durchfallen in der Prüfung) *failure*; ⟨sl⟩ *plough*, *pluck*; ⟨Am⟩ *fizzle* **2.** ⟨med⟩ *diarrhoea*; plötzlich ~ bek ⟨fam⟩ *to* *be taken short*; ~ h *to be troubled with diarrhoea* **~asche** f *riddlings* pl

d·urch|fallen vi [pp –gefallen] **1.** ⟨eig⟩ *to fall through* (adv); ~ durch etw *to fall through* (*the skylight*) || (of light) *to come through*; ~der Strahl *transmitted ray* **2.** ⟨fig⟩ **a.** in e–r Prüfung ~ *to fail* (*in*) *an examination*; ⟨fam⟩ *to pip*; ⟨sl⟩ *to get ploughed, to take a plough, to be ploughed* od *plucked*; ⟨Am sl⟩ *to fizzle, plunk* || jdn ~ l *to fail* (od ⟨sl⟩ *to plough, pluck*) *a p*; ⟨Am⟩ *to flunk a p* || –ge– *plucked of all fine feathers* **b.** ⟨parl⟩ (bei e–r Wahl) *to be unsuccessful*; ⟨Am⟩ *to lose out* || der Antrag fiel durch .. *was rejected*; **c.** (of plans) *to fall through* || ⟨theat⟩ (of a play, etc) *to be* (od *turn out*) *a failure*; *to fail to find favo(u)r*; *to be damned*; ein Stück ~ l *to damn* od *reject a play*

d·urch|fechten vt [h] [pp –gefochten] **1.** er muß es ~ *he is in for it*; *he must fight* (od ⟨sl⟩ *whack*) *it out, he must fight to a finish* || er wird es ~ *he will carry his point* **2. sich** ~ *to fight one's way* (durch *through*) || (betteln) *to beg one's way*

d·urch|feiern vi/t [Nacht] ~ *to make a night of it* || –rt *white* (Nacht)

d·urch|feilen vt [h] [pp –ge–t] *to file* **1.** (etw) *to file* (*a th*) *in two* **2.** (Stil) *to file, polish*

durchf·euchten vt [h] [pp –feuchtet] (etw) *to wet* (*a th*) *thoroughly* **Durchf·euchtung** f *soaking, imbition*

d·urch|feuern vt/i [h] **1.** vt (Ofen) *to fire* (*a furnace*) *thoroughly* **2.** vi Nacht ~ *to fire the furnace all the night* || ⟨mil⟩ *to fire incessantly*

d·urch|finden vrefl [h] [pp –gefunden] sich ~ *to find one's way* (durch *through*); ich kann mich wirklich nicht mehr ~ *I am at the end of my tether*

durchfl·ammt a (v Leidenschaft) *inflamed* od *aflame* (*with passion*)

durchfl·echten vt [h] [pp –fl·ochten] (etw) *to interlace, intertwine, interweave*; *entwine* (mit *with*)

durchfl·iegen vt [h] [pp –fl·ogen] **1.** e–n Ort ~ (of birds) *to fly over a place* || (of the earth) (Raum) *to fly through* (*space*) **2.** (of the eye) *to sweep over* (*the country*) || ⟨aero⟩ e–e Strecke ~ *to fly a distance*; *to cover a d. by air* **3.** ⟨fig⟩ ein Buch ~ *to skim a book*, *to gallop* (od *run, tear*) *through a book*; er durchflog im Geiste die Vergangenheit *his mind rushed over the past, he skimmed* od *ran over the past in his mind* || ~ *to race through* (*a country*)

d·urch|fliegen vi [s] [pp –geflogen] **1.** *to fly through* || ⟨aero⟩ *to fly past without a stop* **2.** ⟨fig⟩ = d·urchfallen 2. a.

durchfl·ießen vt [h] [pp –fl·ossen] (of rivers) (Land) *to flow* (od *run, rush*) *through* (*a country*) || ⟨übtr⟩ *to traverse* || → überschwemmen, durchfluten

durchfl·ochten a (→ –flechten) die Rede ist ~ mit .. *intertwined with*

D·urchflug m ~(e)s/⁓̈e ⟨aero⟩ *flying through*; *transit by air*

D·urchfluß m –flusses/–flüsse *the flowing through*; *circulation* (: *in a state of constant c.*) | ~indikator [m] ⟨tech⟩ *flowmeter*; ~menge [f] *rate of flow*; ~messer [m] *fluidmeter, delivery meter*; ~volumen [n] *discharge*

durchfl·uten vt [h] [pp –fl·utet] **1.** (Land) *to flow* (od *run, stream, surge*) *through* (*a country*) || (of liquids) *to pour through* (*a body*) **2.** ⟨übtr⟩ (P) *to sweep* (*the country*) || (of colour, etc.) (Gesicht) *to suffuse* (*the face*); –flutet s v *to be suffused with* || (of feelings, etc.) jdn ~ *to flow* (od *go, pass, run, spread*) *through a p*; *to penetrate, to pervade a p*; Wärme –flutete ihn *warmth flooded him*; ein Schauer –flutete ihn *a shiver ran through him*

durchf·orschen vt [h] [pp –f·orscht] (Land) *to explore* | ⟨übtr⟩ (jds Gesicht, Herz) *to search* || (Gebiet) *to investigate, to explore*; (genau ~) *to scrutinize*; *to examine thoroughly*; (etw) *to make an exhaustive study* (*of*), *an exh. research* (*into*) **Durchf·orschung** f ~/~en *exploration* (*of a country*) || *examination, investigation*; *scrutiny*

durchf·orsten vt [h] [–f·orstet] (Wald) *to clear* (*a wood*) *methodically of trees, to thin* (*out* [*adv*]) **Durchf·orstung** f *planned deforestation*

D·urchfracht f ⟨com⟩ *through-freight*

d·urch|fragen vt [h] [pp –gefragt] **1.** ⟨school⟩ er fragte die Aufgaben durch *he heard them their lessons* || (Zeugen etc) *to question in succession* **2. sich** ~ *to find one's way by asking*

durchfr·essen vt [h] [pp ~] (of acids) (Metall) *to eat away*; *to erode, corrode* || (Tuch) *to eat into* **d·urch|fressen** vt [h] [pp –gefressen] **1.** (of mice, etc.) (Zeug) *to eat into* (*the cloth*) **2.** ° **sich** ~ *to eat one's way* (durch *through*) || sich kümmerlich ~ *to live from hand to mouth*

durchfr·ieren vt [h] [pp –fr·oren] ganz –froren s *to be chilled through*; *to be frozen to death*; *to feel icily cold*; *to be chilled to the bones*

d·urch|frieren vi [s] [pp –gefroren] = durchfr·ieren

d·urch|fühlen vt [h] [pp –ge–t] (etw) *to have a dim sensation of* (*a th*); *to realize* (*a th*) *dimly*

D·urchfuhr f ~/~en **1.** ⟨com⟩ *transit* (*of goods*) **2.** [in comp] *transit–* .. || ~erlaubnis [f] ⟨com⟩ *transit permit* || ~handel [m] *transit-trade* || ~verbot [n] *transit-embargo, prohibition of transit* || ~zoll [m] *transit-duty*; (in China) *likin*

d·urchführbar a *practicable, feasible, workable*; *realizable* (*plan*) | ⁓̈keit f *practicability, feasibility, workability*

d·urch|führen vt [h] [pp –ge–t] **1.** (hin~) (jdn) *to lead* (*a p*) *through* (: *he led the horse through*); *to convey, transport* (durch .. *through* ..; nach *to*) || (Draht) *to pass .. through* **2.** ⟨übtr⟩ (ausführen) Pläne ~ *to carry* (⟨Am⟩ *to put*) *one's plans through* od *out* || (Angriff) *to press home*; (Kampf etc) *to carry on* || (Untersuchung) *to conduct*; *prosecute*; (Geschäft) *to pursue* || (Haltung, Rolle) *to support* || (Bau etc) *to accomplish*; *complete* || (etw) mit Erfolg ~ *to bring .. across* || (Angriff) mit Nachdruck ~ *to press* || etw glücklich ~ ⟨Am sl⟩ *to put a th across* od *over* || etw zwangsweise ~ *to enforce a th* || etw durch Kniffe ~ *to wangle a th* | → ausführen 2.

D·urchführung f **1.** *conveyance, transport*(*ation*) (durch *through*); *actual conduct* **2.** ⟨übtr⟩ *carrying-through* (od *out*) (*of an undertaking*) || *arrangement* (*of courses, of cultural activities*); ~ der Volkszählung *census operations* pl || ⟨math⟩ *working* || *prosecution* (*of a plan*); *pursuit* (*of a business*) || *completion* (*of a building*) || gewaltsame ~ *enforcement* || ⟨mus⟩ (in der Fuge) *modulation* || → Ausführung **~sbestimmung** f ⟨Ger⟩ *rule of application* || ⟨mst pl⟩ *regulations* (*of a law*) **~svorschriften** f pl ⟨cust, etc⟩ *implementing* od *–tary regulations*

durchf·urchen vt [h] [pp –f·urcht] (of a plough) (Acker) *to furrow, plough* || (of a ship) (Wasser) *to plough, ridge* || ⟨übtr⟩ *to gouge* (mit *with*) **durchf·urcht** a (of a face) *furrowed*; (tief) *deeply lined* (v Gram *with sorrows*); *furrowy, rugged, wrinkled, wrinkly* (*face*)

d·urch|füttern vt [h] Vieh im Winter ~ *to feed cattle through the winter*; *to winter cattle*; ⟨übtr⟩ (jdn) *to feed, support* (*a p*) | **sich ~ l** v jdm *to live on a p*

D·urchgabe f [abstr] → durchgeben || [konkr] *delivery hatch*

D·urchgang m ~(e)s/⁓̈e **1.** [abstr] (Durchgehen) *passage* (durch *through*; nach *to*);

traverse ‖ ~ verboten! *no thoroughfare*! ‖ ⟨com⟩ *transit* (*of goods*) ‖ ⟨astr⟩ *transit*; → Kulmination 2. [konkr] (Weg) *passage*; *through-passage*; *thoroughfare*; *cut*; ~ gesperrt, kein ~! *closed to traffic*! *no thoroughfare* od *trespassing*, *private road*! kein ~ f .. *no* (*passengers*) *allowed* ‖ (zw Sitzreihen) *gangway* ⟨a. aero⟩; ⟨Am⟩ *aisle*

D·urchgänger m ~s/~ (Pferd) *runaway*; *runaway horse*; *bolter* ‖ (P) *absconder* | ⟨fig⟩ (P) *pleasure-seeking person*; *fast man*

d·urchgängig 1. a *general*, *universal*; *usual* 2. adv = durchgehends

D·urchgangs- [in comp] ⟨com⟩ *transit–* **~bahnhof** m *through-station*, ⟨Am⟩ *way station* **~flugverkehr** m *through airline operation* **~gleis** n ⟨rail⟩ *through line* **~güter** n pl *tr.-goods* pl **~handel** m *tr.-trade* **~hotel** n *commercial* (⟨Am⟩ *tr.*) *hotel* **~instrument** n ⟨astr⟩ *tr.-instrument*; *tr.-circle* **~lager** n *tr. camp* **~lazarett** n ⟨mil⟩ *casualty clearing station* **~öffnung** f *passage-opening* **~punkt** m *point of transition* **~stadium** n *tr. stage* od *period* (*in life*) **~station** f → –bahnhof **~straße** f *thoroughfare* **~-Summenprozente** pl ⟨tech⟩ *cumulative percentage of undersize* **~tal** n ⟨geog⟩ *corridor* **~verbindung** f ⟨telph⟩ *through connection* **~verkehr** m *through* (od *tr.*)*-traffic* **~visum** n *tr.-visa* **~wagen** m ⟨rail⟩ *through* (od *corridor*)*-carriage*; ⟨Am⟩ *vestibule car* **~zoll** m *tr. duty* **~zug** m *through* od *nonstop train*; (D-Zug) *corridor-train*, ⟨Am⟩ *vestibule train*

d·urch|geben vt [h] [pp –ge–] (Speisen) *to pass*, *reach* (durch *through* [*the window*]) ‖ ⟨übtr⟩ (Befehl, Nachrichten etc) *to pass on* (jdm *to a p*); *to announce*, *send* (*to a p*); ⟨wir⟩ *to broadcast*; *to give out by wireless*; e–e Nachricht ~ ⟨wir⟩ *to make an announcement* ‖ (Alarm) *to relay* (an *to*)

d·urchgebildet a → durchbilden

d·urchgebraten a ⟨cul⟩ *well done*; nicht ~ *underdone*

d·urchgebrochen a (Magengeschwür etc) *perforated*; → d·urchbrechen

°**d·urchgedreht** a *crazy*, *mad*; *queer*; *at the end of one's tether*; ⟨Am⟩ *all-in*; ~ s ⟨fam⟩ *not to know whether one's going or coming*

d·urchgefallen a *unsuccessful* (*candidate*)

d·urchgefärbt a (völlig ~) *dyed throughout*

d·urch|gehen vi/t [pp –gegangen] I. vi [s] A. (P) 1. *to go through* [adv]; *to pass* (durch .. *through the gate*); darf ich ~? *may I pass*?, *may I go through*? gehen Sie nur weiter durch! *pass along, there*! das Wasser ist so niedrig, daß man ~ kann *the water is so low that you can pass through it* ‖ jdn ~ l *to let a p pass* ‖ sich nicht ~ l *to discipline o.s.* ‖ ~ durch *to pass*; *cross*; *traverse* (*a country*) 2. ⟨fig⟩ er geht gerade durch *he is a thoroughly straight fellow*; *he is a fair* (od *an unbiassed*) *man* B. 1. ⟨hors⟩ *to run away* (mit *with*); *to bolt*, *stampede* 2. ⟨übtr⟩ (of a car) *tu run away*; (of engines) *to race* ‖ (P) ~ mit *to bolt with* (*the money*; *a p's wife*); *to go off with* (*a woman*); mit e–m Mädel ~ *to elope with a girl*; → ausreißen, durchbrennen ‖ das Temperament ging mit ihm durch *his temper ran away with* (od *got on top of*) *him*; er ließ die Phantasie mit sich ~ *he let imagination run away with him* ‖ l Sie Ihren Unmut nicht mit sich ~ *let not your spirits carry you away* C. (S) 1. *to get out of hand*; *to pass* (durch *through*); der Regen ging bei mir bis auf die Haut durch *the rain soaked me to the skin* ‖ ~ durch *to pass*; *penetrate*, *permeate*, *pierce*; durch viele Hände ~ *to pass through many hands* → durchdringen 2. ⟨astr⟩ ~ durch *to transit* (*the disc of the sun*) 3. (of a train) *to go through* 4. ⟨übtr⟩ a. (of a motion) *to go through*; *to be carried* ‖ (of a bill) *to pass*, *to be passed* od *carried*; die Vorlage ist im Hause –gegangen *the bill has passed the house*; etw ~ l *to pass a th*; geht einstimmig durch (abbr g.e.d.) *carried unanimously* (abbr: *nem. con.* = nemine contradicente) b. (geduldet w) *to pass*, *to be allowed* od *tolerated*; das mag ~ *that may pass* ‖ ihm geht alles durch *he is alway successful* ‖ ~ l → dulden; derartige Entschuldigungen l wir nicht ~ *such excuses will not pass muster with us* II. vt [h] 1. (Schuhe) → d·urchlaufen 2. ⟨fig⟩ (Bücher, Vorschläge) *to go* (od *pass*) *through* (*books*, *proposals*); s–e Aufgaben ~ *to go over one's lessons* ‖ flüchtig ~ *to run over*, *to skim over* (od *through*) (*a book*) → d·urchlesen, –sehen **D·urchgehen** n 1. *running-away*; *bolting* ‖ *passing*, ⟨Am⟩ *passage* (*of a bill*) ‖ → Durchgang 2. *going through*; *perusal*

d·urchgehend a 1. ~er Bolzen *through-bolt*; ~e Stange *through-rod* 2. ~e Waren [pl] *transit goods* pl 3. ⟨rail⟩ ~e Fahrkarte *through ticket*; ~er Wagen *through* od *direct car* (od *carriage*); ~er Zug *through* (od *direct*, *non-stop*) *train*; *non-stop* **d·urchgehend(s)** adv *generally*, *universally*, *usually*, *as a rule*; *all the way* (*through*); *in every particular*; *throughout* (: *it has been fine th.*); ~d geöffnet *open throughout*; s–e Aufsätze sind ~(s) schlecht *his papers are all bad*; ~ im Betrieb sein *to run fulltime*

durch·geistigt a: ~es Gesicht *face reflecting a high mentality*, *a face suggestive of a high spiritual refinement* ‖ ~e Gesichtszüge *spiritual features*, ~er –sausdruck *spiritual expression*

d·urch|gerben vt [h] [pp –gegerbt] (Leder) *to tan thoroughly* ‖ ⟨fig⟩ (jdn) *to curry*; → durchprügeln

d·urchgesiebt a *sifted* ‖ ≗es n *siftings* [pl]

d·urch|gießen 1. vt [h] [pp –gegossen] (Flüssigkeit) *to pass* od *pour* (durch *through*); *to filter*; *strain* 2. ≗ n *filtration*, *percolation*

durchgl·ühen vt [h] [pp –gl·üht] ⟨fig⟩ (jdn) *to inflame*, *inspire*; –glüht s v *to be informed* (od *imbued*, *inspired*) *with*; *to glow with* (*enthusiasm*); → durchdr·ingen **d·urch|glühen** vt [h] [pp –ge–t] (Eisen) *to heat* (*thoroughly*); *to make red-hot*

d·urch|graben vt [h] [pp –ge–] (Loch) *to dig* (durch *through* [*the trench*])

d·urch|greifen I. vi [h] [pp ich habe –gegriffen] 1. ⟨eig⟩ mit der Hand ~ *to pass one's hand* (durch *through*); greif mal durch *pass your hand through it* 2. ⟨übtr⟩ rücksichtslos ~ *to resort to drastic measures*; *to go all lengths*, ⟨sl⟩ *to go the whole hog*; er greift r. durch *he is a thorough-going uncompromising fellow*; in e–r S r. ~ ⟨fam⟩ *to crack down on a th* II. ≗ n *uncompromising proceeding*; *sweeping change*, *drastic measures* [pl]

d·urchgreifend 1. a ⟨fig⟩ *drastic* (*measures*, *remedies*), *strong* ‖ *radical*, *sweeping*, *thorough* (*change*); *trenchant*, *uncompromising*, *thorough-going* (*reform*) 2. adv *drastically*, *radically*, *thoroughly*; *completely*

D·urchgriff m *penetration coefficient* ‖ ⟨el⟩ *durchgriff*; *penetration factor*; *reciprocal amplification factor*

durchgr·übeln vt *to* [h] [pp –ge–t] *ponder* od *brood over* (*a th*)

d·urch|gucken vi [h] [–ge–t] *to look through* [adv]; *to look* (od *peep*, *peer*) (durch *through*); laß mich mal ~ *let me have a look* od *peep through* (*it*)

°**d·urch|haben** vt [h] [pp –gehabt] → durch II. B. I.

d·urch|hacken vt [h] [pp –gehackt] (etw) *to hew* (*a th*) *asunder* (od *to pieces*)

durchh·allen vt [h] [pp –h·allt] (of sound) *to penetrate* (*a room*)

d·urch|halten I. vt/i [h] [pp –ge–] 1. vt (ertragen) *to endure*; *to see* (*a th*) *through* ‖ ⟨mar⟩ den Kurs ~ *to keep the course* ‖ jdn den Winter

~ (of supply) *to last a p through the winter* || ich kann's nicht ~ ⟨Am fam⟩ *I can't take it* **2.** vi **a.** *to hold out*; *to hold one's ground* (od *one's own*); *to carry on*; *to rub along* od *on*; || ~! *stick it* (*out*), *lads*! || (of patients) *to last out, to pull through* || mutig ~ *to keep one's end up, to keep one's shoulder to the wheel*; *to keep it up* || ⟨sport⟩ *to stay*; bis z Ende ~ *to stay one's course* **b.** (of supply) *to last out* **II.** ≈, **Durchhaltevermögen** n *endurance, holding-out* || *stay*; → Ausdauer

D·urchhang m *sag*

d·urch|hauen vt [h] [pp –ge–] **1.** (etw) *to cut* (*a th*); *to chop* (od *cut, hew*) (*a th*) *in two*; → d·urchschlagen || den Gordischen Knoten ~ *to cut the Gordian knot* **2.** jdn ~ [pret: haute .. durch] *to cudgel, curry, flog* (*a p*) → verhauen || ⟨sl⟩ *to give* (*a p*) *socks* **3. sich** ~ [pret: haute sich durch] *to force* od *cut one's way* (durch *through*)

d·urch|hecheln vt [h] **1.** (Flachs) *to hackle* (*thoroughly*) **2.** ⟨fig⟩ jdn ~ *to speak ill* od *maliciously of* (od *to talk about*) *a p behind his back*; *to sneer at a p*; *to backbite a p* || (Verhältnisse) *to pooh-pooh*; *to criticize* (*a th*) *adversely*; *to pick holes in* (*a th*)

d·urchheizen vt/i [h] [pp –ge–t] **1.** vt; e–n Raum gut ~ *to heat a room thoroughly* **2.** vi; die Nacht ~ *to keep the fire burning all the night*

d·urch|helfen vi [h] [pp –geholfen] **1.** jdm ~ *to help a p to get through, to see a p through* (bei etw *with a th*); *to help a p over his trouble* **2. sich** ~ **mit** etw *to eke out a th*; *make shift with a th*; sich kümmerlich ~ *to eke out a scanty living*; → durchbeißen, –schlagen

D·urchhieb m *long narrow opening in a wood*; → Schneise || ⟨min⟩ *stenting, stenton*

°**durchh·in** adv; ganz ~ k [s] ⟨fig⟩ *to be confused* od *perplexed*

durchh·itzen vt [h] [pp –h·itzt] (etw) *to heat* (*a th*) *thoroughly*

durchh·öhlen vt [h] [pp –h·öhlt] (etw) *to hollow* (*a th*) *out*; *to undermine* || ⟨übtr⟩ *to sap, weaken*

d·urch|holen vt/i [h] [pp –ge–t] **1.** vt (etw) *to haul* (*a th*) *in* **2.** vi; gut ~ *to pull well*

d·urch|huschen vi [s] [pp –ge–t] *to move* od *pass quietly, to flit* (durch *through*)

durch·irren vt [h] [pp –irrt] die Wälder ~ *to roam* od *rove the woods*; *to ramble* (od *roam, rove, wander*; ⟨poet⟩ *stray*) *through the woods*

durchj·agen vt [h] [pp –jagt] die Straßen ~ *to dash* (od *gallop, hurry, rush*) *through the streets* || die Wälder (nach Beute) ~ *to scour the woods*

d·urch|jagen vi/t [pp –ge–t] **1.** vi [s] *to pass in haste* || *to rush* (durch *through*) **2.** vt [h] (T, P) *to chase, drive* (durch *through*)

d·urch|kämmen vt [h] [pp –ge–t] (Haar) *to comb* (*thoroughly*); *to comb out* ⟨a. fig mil⟩

d·urch|kämpfen vt/i [h] [pp –ge–t] **A.** vt **1.** er hat manche Schlacht –ge–t *he has fought many a battle* || er muß es ~ *he must fight it out* | ⟨übtr⟩ etw ~ *to maintain a th by fighting*; e–n Prozeß ~ *to fight a case*; → bestehen II. 2. **2. sich** ~ *to fight* (od *cut, force*) *one's way* (durch *through*; in *in* [*the world*]; *into*) **B.** vi *to fight to a finish*

d·urch|kauen vt [h] [pp –ge–t] (Speise) *to chew thoroughly* || ⟨fig⟩ (etw) *to repeat* (*a th*) *over and over again*; → wiederholen

d·urch|klingen vi [s] [pp –geklungen] s–e Stimme klang deutlich durch *his voice could be distinctly heard* || ⟨fig⟩ durch s–e Worte klang durch, daß .. *I understood him to say that* ..

durchkn·eten vt [h] [pp –knetet] = **d·urchkneten** vt [h] [pp –ge–t] (Teig) *to knead* od *work* (*thoroughly* od *well*)

d·urch|kochen vt [h] [pp –ge–t] (etw) *to boil thoroughly* || durchgekocht *well done*

d·urch|kommen I. vi [s] [pp –ge–] **1.** ⟨eig⟩ *to get through* || *to pass through* (v *from*); ~ durch .. *to pass through* **2.** ⟨übtr⟩ **a.** *to get through* (⟨Am⟩ *by*); (of a patient) wieder ~ *to come* od *pull through* || (im Examen) *to get through, to pass*; eben noch durch e–e Prüfung ~ *to shave through* [prep] *an examination*; mit knapper Not ~ *to shave through* [adv] **b.** (of news, etc.) *to come through* (daß *that*) **c.** ~ **mit** etw *to get along* (od *by, away, through*) *with a th*; *to do* (od *to manage*) *with a th*; mit e–m geringen Einkommen ~ *to eke out a scanty income* || *to be successful in a th* || er wird mit dieser Entschuldigung nicht ~ *this excuse won't help him*; bei ihr wird er mit dieser E. nicht ~ *this excuse won't pass muster with her* **II.** ≈ n *getting through*; hier ist kein ~ *you cannot get through* (od *along*) *here* || ⟨übtr⟩ *passage* (*of a bill*) || ⟨fig⟩ es ist kein ~ *I can't manage it alone*

d·urch|können vi → durch II. B. 1.

D·urchkonnossement [–kɔnɔsmã, –ment] ⟨com⟩ *through-bill of lading*

d·urch|kosten vt [h] [pp –ge–t] Speisen ~ *to taste one dish after the other* || ⟨übtr⟩ (Freuden) *to go* od *pass through* (*a th*); *to experience*; (Leiden) *to undergo*

durchkr·euzen vt [h] [pp –kreuzt] **1.** (Gebiet, Land) *to cross*; *traverse* (*a district*); *to pass through* (*a th*) **2.** ⟨com⟩ (Scheck) *to cross* **3.** ⟨fig⟩ (jds Pläne) *to baffle, balk, foil, frustrate, spoil, thwart*; *to run counter to* (*a th*); jds Pläne gründlich ~ *to queer the pitch for a p* || *to cut across* (*a p's policy*) **Durchkr·euzung** f *traverse* (*of a country*) || *crossing* (*of a cheque*) || *frustration*; *prevention* (*of a plan*)

d·urch|kriechen vi [s] [pp –gekrochen] *to creep through*; *to creep* (durch *through*)

d·urch|kriegen vt [h] (etw) = *durchbekommen, –bringen*

d·urch|langen vz [h] (etw) *to hand* od *pass* (*a th*) (durch *through*)

D·urchlaß m –lasses/–lässe **1.** [abstr] (Durchlassen) *passing*; *passage*; *pass* || um ~ bitten *to ask for the permission to pass*; ~ erhalten *to be allowed to pass*; jdm ~ gewähren *to let a p pass* **2.** (Weg z Durchlassen) *pass*; *passage*(*-way*); *lane* (durch *through*); *cut* || (unterirdischer) *channel, conduit, culvert* || (Öffnung) *opening* (in *in*); *inlet*; *outlet*; (verschließbarer) *shutter* **~band** n ⟨opt⟩ *pass band* **~karte** f (Flughafen≈) *gate pass* **~schein** m *pass-check* **~zoll** m *pass-duty*

d·urch|lassen I. vt [h] [pp –gelassen] **A.** (P) **1.** jdn (*or* etw) ~ *to let a p* (od *a th*) *pass*; *to let* (*a p*) *through* (: *let me th.*); *to allow a p* (*a th*) *to pass* || **2.** ⟨übtr⟩ jdn ~ (sc in der Prüfung) *to pass a p* || ⟨parl⟩ (Beschluß) *to pass*; = durchgehen I, → durchgehen || (Fehler) → dulden I.A.2.a. **B.** (S) **1.** ⟨phys⟩ (etw) *to suffer* (*a th*) *to pass, to transmit* (*a th*); Licht, Wärme ~ *to be pervious* (od *permeable*) *to light, heat* (: *glass is pervious to light*); kein Licht etc ~ *to be impervious to light* || Wasser ~ *to leak* (: *the kettle is leaking*); *to be pervious to water*; (of boots) *to ooze*; kein W. ~ *to be impervious to* (od *proof against*) *water*; → luft-, schall-, wasserdicht || ⟨Am⟩ (of a pipe) (Gas) *to leak* **II.** ≈ n *passing* (*of a bill*); *pass*

d·urchlässig a *porous*; *leaky* (*boots*) || (f Wärmestrahlen) *diathermic, diathermanous* (*power*) || [pred] *permeable, pervious* (f *to*) | **≈keit** f *permeability, perviousness* (f *to*); *diathermancy* | ~sbereich [m] ⟨opt⟩ *pass band*; ⟨phot⟩ (Filter) *filter range* || ~sdichte [f] ⟨phot⟩ *transmission density of a negative*

D·urchlaucht f ⟨engl⟩ (Titel) (f Herzog, Erzbischof) Seine ~ *His Grace* || ⟨a-engl⟩ *His Serene Highness* **durchl·auchtig** a *serene*; *illustrious* || ~st *most serene* od *illustrious*

D·urchlauf m ~(e)s/⁓e [abstr] *running through*; *run* (durch *through*) || °⟨med⟩ = Durchfall || ⟨comp⟩ *run*; während des ~s (of cards) *on the move* | ~erhitzer [m] *continuous-flow waterheater* || bei e–r ~geschwindigkeit [f] v *at a speed of .. passages* || ~kopierer [m] ⟨phot⟩ *continuous paper processor* || ~kopiermaschine [f] *continuous printer*

durchl·aufen vt [h] [pp –laufen] **1.** die Straßen ~ *to run through the streets*; → durcheilen, –jagen || eine Strecke ~ *to cover* (od *run, travel*; ⟨sport⟩ *(to lap)*) *a distance* **2.** ⟨übtr⟩ etw ~ *to go* (od *pass, run*) *through a th*; e–e Schule ~ *to pass through a school* || das Gerücht durchlief die Stadt mit Windeseile *the rumour spread like wildfire over the town* **d·urch|laufen** vi/t [pp –ge–] **1.** vi [s] durch ein Gebäude ~ *to run* (od *rush*) *through a building* || er lief durch *he passed through in haste* || (of liquids) *to filter, ooze, percolate* (durch *through*) **2.** vt (Strümpfe etc) *to wear out* || sich die Füße ~ *to walk one's feet sore*

d·urchlaufend **1.** a *continuous* (*brake*) || ⟨rail⟩ → durchgehend *direct* (*car, train*) || ⟨phot⟩ *continuous* (*slide projector*) **2.** adv *continuously*

durchl·eben vt [h] **1.** (überl·eben) wird er die Nacht noch ~? *will he live through* (od *out* [adv]) *the night*? **2.** ⟨übtr⟩ (erleben) e–e Krise ~ *to live* (od *go, pass*) *through* [prep] *a crisis*; *to experience*; gute u böse Zeiten –bt h *to have seen good days and bad* || fröhlich –bte Tage *days happily spent*; *happy days* || angstvoll –bte Stunden *anxious hours*; → d·urchmachen **d·urch|leben** vt [h] [pp –ge–t] = durchl·eben 2.

d·urch|lesen **1.** vt [h] [pp –gelesen] ein Buch ~ *to read a book through* od *over* (adv); *to peruse* (od *finish*) *a b.*; hast du das Buch –gelesen? *have you finished the book*? || (= lesen) laß mich die Briefe nochmal ~ *let me go through* [prep] (od *read*) *the letters again*; etw schnell ~ *to run over a th, to skim* (*over*) *a th* **2.** ⁓ n *reading*; *perusal*

durchl·euchten vt [h] [pp –leuchtet] **1.** (Eier) *to candle* || ⟨med⟩ (jdn, Organ etc) *to transilluminate*; *to radio, to radiograph*; *to subject* (*an organ*) *to a transillumination*; ⟨mst⟩ *to screen* (auf *for*) || sich ~ l *to submit o.s., to a tr.* || → bestrahlen **2.** ⟨übtr⟩ (erhellen) (etw) *to illumine*; (aufklären) *to clear* (*a th*) *up, to examine into* (*a th*) **D–l·euchtung** f ~/~en ⟨phot⟩ *light transmission* || ⟨med⟩ *transillumination*; (am Röntgenschirm) *radioscopy*; *fluoroscopy, röntgenoscopy*; ⟨mst⟩ *screen examination, screening* → Bestrahlung || ⟨übtr⟩ *clearing-up* | ~skopie [f] ⟨phot⟩ *direct-* (od *transmitted-*)*light copy* || ~sschirm [m] *fluorescent* od *fluoroscopic screen*

Durchl·ichtung f ⟨for⟩ *improvement cutting*

d·urch|liegen **1.** vrefl [h] [pp –gelegen] sich ~ *to develop bed-sores* (od *a bed-sore*; ⟨med⟩ *decubitus* L) **2.** ⁓ n *decubitus* (L)

durchl·ochen **1.** vt [h] *to hole*; *prick*; → lochen, perforieren **2.** ⁓ n *pricking*

durchl·öchern **1.** vt *to perforate*; *to hole*; ~d *perforative* || wabenartig ~ *to honeycomb* || (Leder etc) kunstvoll ~ *to pink*; *pounce*; → perforieren || (jdn; Schiff) wie ein Sieb ~ *to riddle* (mit *with* [*shot*]); → durchbohren **2.** ⁓ n *perforation* **durchl·öchert** a *full of holes*; *in holes*; nicht ~ ⟨bot⟩ *imperforate* || v Kugeln ~ *riddled* (*like a sieve*) || (Strumpf) an den Fersen ~ *out at heels* || ~e Arbeit *open work*

durchl·üften vt [h] [pp –lüftet] (Raum) *to air, ventilate* **d·urch|lüften** vt [h] [pp –ge–t] = durchl·üften **Durchl·üftung** f *ventilation*

d·urch|lügen vrefl [h] [pp –gelogen] sich ~ *to get out of a scrape* (od *to get off, to make one's way*) *by lying*; *to resort to lies if possible*

d·urch|machen vt [h] [pp –ge–t] (e–e Zeit etc) *to go* od *pass through* (*a time*); e–e Schule ~ *to pass through a school*; s–e Lehrzeit ~ *to serve one's apprenticeship*; etw nicht ganz ~ *not quite finish* od *complete a th* || (Mühsal etc) *to experience*; vieles ~ *to go through a lot of trouble* || sie hat viel im Leben –gemacht *she has gone through a great deal in her life* || (Operation etc) *to undergo*; *endure*; *suffer*

D·urchmarsch m ~(e)s/–märsche **1.** *march*(*ing*) *through, way through*; den ~ erzwingen *to force one's way* (durch *through*) **2.** °⟨med⟩ *squitters* [pl]; → Durchfall **d·urch|marschieren** vi [s] *to march through* (adv) || *to march* (durch *through*); ~ durch *to traverse*

durchm·essen vt [h] [pp ~] *to pass* (od *travel*) *over, to traverse* (*an area*) || *to cover* (od *run, travel, traverse*) (*a distance*); (z Fuß) *to walk a d.*; (e–n Raum) *to walk up and down* (*a room*), *to stride through* (*a r.*), *to pace* (*a r.*) *up and d.* **d·urch|messen** vt [h] [pp –ge–] e–n Raum (genau) ~ *to take the* (*exact*) *measure of a room* || (noch einmal messen) *to measure a th over again*; → nachprüfen **D·urchmesser** m ~s/~ *diameter*; äußerer (innerer) ~ *outside* (*inside*) *d.*; im ~ *in diameter* (: *one inch across in d.*); ⟨tech⟩ (Stärke) *gauge* || das Gewehr hat e–n inneren ~ v 0,3 Zoll *the rifle is .33 calibre*; → Kaliber || Kreis⁓ *d. of circle*; Rohr⁓ *d. of pipe* || ⟨num⟩ *module*

d·urch|mischen vt [h] [pp –ge–t] *to mix* (*a th*) *thoroughly*

d·urch|müssen vi → durch II.B.1.

durchm·ustern [pp –mustert] **d·urch|mustern** vt [h] [pp –ge–t] (s–e Sachen) *to look carefully through* (*one's things*); *to scan*; *examine* (od *review*) (*a th*) *in detail*; (Papiere) *to scrutinize* **Durchm·usterung** f *inspection, examination*; *scanning*

durchn·agen [pp –nagt] **d·urch|nagen** [pp –ge–t] vt [h] (etw) *to gnaw* (*a th*); *to gnaw* (*a th*) *in two* || *to gnaw into* (*a th*)

durchn·ähen vt [h] (etw) *to fasten* (*a th*) *together by lines of stitching*; → steppen

durchn·ässelt a *somewhat damp*; → –lt, –ln

durchn·ässen vt [h] [pp –näßt] etw ~ *to soak* od *wet a th* (: *the rain will soak your clothes*); || –näßt w (P) *to get wet through*; (S) ⟨scient⟩ *to be wetted through* || –näßt s v *to be soaked* od *wetted with* || jdn (ganz) ~ *to wet* (od *soak, souse*) *a p to the skin*; –näßt w *to get a souse*

durchn·äßt a **1.** [pred] *soppy, wet*; (*a ground*) *sodden with wet* | (P) ganz ~ *wet through*; *wet* (od *soaked, sopped, soused*) *to the skin*; *sopping-wet* **2.** [attr] *soppy, wet* (*clothes*); *soggy* (*packet*)

d·urch|nehmen vt [h] [pp –genommen] **1.** etw (: e–n Stoff) ~ *to go over* od *through a th* (mit jdm *with a p*), *to deal with a th, to treat a th* || ⟨school⟩ was wollen wir heute ~? *what do we take up today*?; wir h heute viel –genommen *we covered much ground t.* **2.** ˣjdn ~ = durchhecheln, vornehmen

durch·örtern vt [h] ⟨min⟩ e–n Berg etc ~ *to drive two levels through a mountain in opposite directions*; *to cut across a mountain from two opposite points*

d·urch|parieren vi [h] [pp –rt] ⟨hors⟩ *to draw rein*

d·urch|passieren vi [s] [pp –rt] *to pass through* [adv]; *to pass* (durch *through* [prep])

°**d·urch|pauken** vt [h] es ~ ⟨sl⟩ *to whack it out*; → d·urchfechten

d·urch|pausen vt [h] [pp –ge–t] (Zeichnung) *to trace* (*a drawing*); *to take the tracing of* (*a d.*) || (Muster auf Tuch) *to pounce* || *to write, draw through carbon paper*

d·urch|peitschen vt **1.** (jdn) *to whip soundly* **2.** ⟨parl⟩ *to rush* (od *hustle*, ⟨Am⟩ *railroad*) *a bill through the House* || (Stoff in der Klasse) *to* *hurry over (a subject); to hustle (a s.) through*

durchp·ilgern vt [h] [pp –pilgert] das Land ~ *to travel* (od *wander) over* (od *through) the country, to travel* (od *traverse, walk) the c.* **d·urch|pilgern** vi [s] [pp –ge–t] *to pass through* [adv]; *to pass* (durch *through* [prep])

°**d·urch|plumpsen** vi [s] ⟨school⟩ → durchrasseln

d·urch|pressen vt [h] [pp –ge–t] (etw) *to press* od *squeeze (a th) through* [adv]; *to press* (durch *through*); (Flüssigkeit) *to strain* (durch *through*)

D·urchpreßgeräusch n ⟨med⟩ *stenotic* (od *systolic) murmur*

d·urch|prügeln vt [h] [pp –ge–t] *to beat, belabour, cudgel, curry, drub, thrash (a p)*; ⟨fam⟩ *to lick (a p)* ‖ *to give (a p) a beating, dressing, thrashing; to give (a p) the stick*; ⟨Am sl⟩ *to dust off*

durchqu·eren vt [h] [pp –quert] **1.** ein Land (etc.) ~ *to cross* (od *travel, traverse) a country; to pass* (od *travel) over the c.; to wander through a c.* **2.** ⟨übtr⟩ (jds Pläne) = durchkreuzen 3.

Durchqu·erung f *crossing, traversing, traverse*

d·urch|quetschen vt [h] [pp –ge–t] (etw) *to press* od *squeeze* (durch *through*) ‖ **sich ~** *to squeeze* (durch *through*)

durchr·asen vt [h] [pp –rast] ein Land (etc) ~ *to dash* (od *race, rush) through a country*; e–e Strecke ~ *to run* od *travel a distance at full speed* ‖ → rasen **d·urch|rasen** vi [s] [pp –ge–t] durch das Land ~ *to rush through the country*; er raste durch *he rushed through at full speed*

°**d·urch|rasseln** vi [s] [pp –ge–t] (im Examen) ⟨sl⟩ *to pip, skew; to take a plough; to be ploughed* (od *dipped, plucked*); → durchfallen

durchr·äuchern vt [h] [pp –räuchert] **1.** (Zimmer) *to fill (a room) with smoke*; –räuchert *smoky (room)* **2.** (Schinken) *to smoke* ‖ (reinigen *to fumigate* (mit *with*) **d·urch|räuchern** vt [h] (Schinken) *to smoke* od *fumigate thoroughly*

d·urch|rechnen vt [h] (etw) *to count* od *reckon (a th); to count (a th) over* [adv]; (Summe) *to go over (a sum), to examine (a th)*; ⟨Am⟩ *to check (a th) up* **D·urchrechnung** f ⟨math⟩ *working (of a sum)*

d·urch|regnen vi [imp] [h] [pp –ge–t] es regnete durch *the rain came* od *got through* **durchr·egnen** vt [h], –regnet s *to be soaked with rain*

d·urch|reiben vt [h] [pp –gerieben] **1.** (wund reiben) (den Nacken etc) *to chafe, gall, rub*; er hat sich die Ferse –gerieben *he has rubbed his heel*; –gerieben [a] *sore* ‖ **sich ~** (of limbs) *to get chafed* **2.** (Stoff am Rande) *to fray, frazzle* ‖ sich ~ *to fray*; die Leine ist (*or* hat sich) –gerieben *the cord is frayed*

d·urch|reichen vt [h] = durchlangen

D·urchreise f ~/~n *passing through; transit*; auf der ~ *on one's way through* [adv]; auf der ~ durch *on one's way through* [prep] **|** ~vermerk [n], ~visum [n] *visa of transit, tr.-v.* **durchr·eisen** vt [h] [pp –reist] ein Land ~ *to travel a country, to pass* (od *travel) over a c.; to journey* (od *wander) through a c.* **d·urch|reisen** vi [s] [–gereist] ~ durch = durchr·eisen ‖ er ist –gereist *he has passed through without stopping*

D·urchreisende [der ~, ein ~r] *transit passenger*, ⟨Am⟩ *transient*; ⟨rail⟩ *through passenger; passenger*; (Emigrant) *transmigrant*

durchr·eißen vt [h] [pp –rissen] (Strick) *to part (: the strain will part the cord); to sever* ‖ oft ⟨übtr⟩ (Bande) *to part, sever; disunite, separate* **d·urch|reißen** vt/i [pp –gerissen] **1.** vt [h] (etw) *to tear (a th) asunder* (od *in two*); in der Mitte ~ *to tear (a th) across* **2.** vi [s] *to break, sever, tear (: the rope will tear)*

durchr·eiten vt [h] [pp –ritten] das Land ~ *to ride (over) the country; to pass over the c. on horseback* ‖ e–n Fluß ~ *to cross* od *traverse a river on horseback* **d·urch|reiten** vi/t [pp –geritten] **1.** vi [s] *to ride through; to pass through on horseback without stopping* **2.** vt [h] **a.** (Hose) *to wear out by riding* **b.** (Pferd) *to gall by riding* ‖ (ein Glied) *to chafe; to make sore*; er hatte sich –geritten *his seat was sore with riding*

durchr·ennen vt [h] [pp –rannt] **1.** e–n Ort ~ *to race* (od *run, rush) through a place* ‖ *to run (a distance)* **2.** jdn ~ *to run a p through* [adv], *to pierce a p* (mit *with*); → durchb·ohren

d·urch|rennen vi [s] [pp –gerannt] er rannte durch *he passed through at full speed*

durchr·ieseln vt [h] [pp –rieselt] **1.** den Boden ~ *to trickle through* (od *to permeate) the soil*; der Bach –lt (rieselt durch) die Wiese *the br. ripples across the m.* **2.** ⟨fig⟩ (of feelings, etc.) jdn ~ *to flow* (od *pass) through a p; to pervade, to thrill a p*; ein wohliges Gefühl v Wärme –lte ihn *a pleasurable feeling of w. pervaded him*; es durchrieselte mich kalt *a shivering thrill ran through me* **d·urch|rieseln** vi [s] [pp –ge–t] (of liquids) *to trickle (through*; unter *under); to penetrate*

d·urch|ringen vrefl [h] [pp –gerungen] ⟨fig⟩ (P) **sich ~** *to make one's way; to win one's way* **sich ~ z** *to come round to (a standpoint); to win through to (civilization); to arrive at (a conclusion)* ‖ (S) *to win through (more and more)*

durchr·innen vt [h] [→ rinnen; pp –ronnen] = durchr·ieseln **d·urch|rinnen** vi [s] [pp –geronnen] = durchrieseln l.

D·urchritt m ~(e)s/~e *riding-through*; ~ durch *ride through (the wood)*

d·urch|rollen vt [h] [pp –ge–t] (Wäsche) *to mangle (thoroughly)*

durchr·udern vt [pp –rudert] e–n See ~ *to row across a lake* ‖ e–e Strecke ~ *to row a distance*

d·urch|rudern vi [s] [pp –ge–t] *to row (through)*

d·urch|rufen vt/i = telephonieren

d·urch|rühren vt [h] [–ge–t] (etw) *to stir* od *mix up (thoroughly)*; ⟨cul⟩ *to toss*

d·urch|rutschen vi [s] [pp –ge–t] *to slide* od *slip through* [adv]; *to slide, slip* (durch *through*)

durch|r·ütteln vt [h] (etw) *to shake (thoroughly)* ‖ (jdn im Wagen) *to jolt (a p)*

durchs = durch das

d·urch|sacken vi [s] [pp –ge–t] ⟨aero⟩ *to pancake*

D·urchsage f ~/~n *communication, announcement*

d·urch|sagen vt [h] [pp –gesagt] ⟨telph⟩ (etw) *to telephone*, ⟨fam⟩ *to phone (a th); to communicate (a th) over the telephone* (jdm *to a p*) ‖ ⟨wir⟩ *to broadcast; to give out* (od *make known, to spread) by wireless*; es wurde –gesagt, daß *it was given out by wireless that ..*; e–e Meldung ~ ⟨wir⟩ *to transmit a message, to make an announcement* ‖ *information was passed on to them over the telephone*

durchs·ägen vt [h] [pp –sägt] (Baum) *to saw*

d·urch|sägen vt [h] [pp –ge–t] ein Brett ~ *to saw a board through*; .. quer ~ *to saw a b. across*

durchs·alzen vt [h] [pp –salzen] (etw) *to salt*

d·urch|salzen vt [h] [pp –ge–] *to salt thoroughly*

D·urchsatz m *weight rate of flow*; (Leistung) *throughput*; ≈e pl ⟨a.⟩ *output* **|** ~leistung [f] *throughput (feeding) capacity*

durchs·äuern vt [h] (etw) *to leaven*

durchs·äuseln vt [h] [pp –säuselt] (of the wind) die Blätter ~ *to blow gently through the leaves*

durchs·ausen vt [h] [pp –saust] (of the wind, etc) (Wälder) *to roar* od *rush through (the woods)*

durchsch·allen vt [h] [pp –schallt] (of the voice) (e–n Raum) *to echo* (od *resound, ring) through (a room); to penetrate (a r.)* **d·urch|schallen** vi [s] [–ge–t] = d·urchtönen

D·urchschau- ⟨mod⟩ *see-through (dress, blouse)*

durchsch·auen vt [h] [pp –schaut] jdn ~ *to see through* [prep] *a p*; *to take a p's measure*; ⟨sl⟩ *to rumble a p* ‖ etw ~ *to see through* od *into a th*; *to get to the bottom of a th*; *to be up to a th* ‖ er hat mich –schaut *he's rumbled me* ‖ jds Pose ~ *to divine a p's attitude*

d·urch|schauen vi [h] [pp –ge–t] *to look* (durch *through*); laß mich mal ~ *let me have a look through it*

durchsch·auern vt [h] [pp –schauert] jdn ~ *to thrill a p*, *to affect* (od *pass through*) *a p with a thrill*

durchsch·einen vt [h] [pp –schienen] (etw) *to illumine*, *irradiate* **d·urch|scheinen** vi [h] [pp –geschienen] (of light) *to come* od *get through* ‖ (of cloth) *to be translucent* od *diaphanous* ‖ (*of writing*) *to show* ‖ ⟨übtr⟩ *to appear with clearness*, *to be* od *become clearly visible* od *evident* (durch *through*) ‖ er ließ Enttäuschung ~ *dis. was revealed* od *apparent* (*in his words*) **d·urchscheinend** a (of cloth) *diaphanous*; *translucent*; → durchsichtig

d·urch|scheuern vt [h] [pp –ge–t] = d·urchreiben

D·urchschießblatt n ⟨typ⟩ *interleaf*

durchsch·ießen vt [h] [pp –schossen] **1.** jdn ~ *to shoot a p* (*through*) ihm wurde der Helm –schossen *he had his helmet shot through* **2.** ⟨übtr⟩ (of birds) die Luft ~ *to shoot through the air* ‖ (of blood) die Adern ~ *to shoot through the arteries* **3.** (Buch) *to interleave* ‖ ⟨typ⟩ (Zeilen) *to lead* ‖ ⟨fig⟩ –schossen mit *shot* (*through*) *with*

d·urch|schießen vi [h] [pp –geschossen] durch e–e Wand ~ *to shoot through a wall*; ⟨a. übtr⟩

durchsch·iffen vt [h] [pp –schifft] das Meer ~ *to navigate* (od *sail*; *cross*, *traverse*) *the ocean*; *to sail* od *glide across* od *over the ocean*

d·urch|schiffen vi [s] [pp –ge–t] ~ durch *to sail through* (*the straits*)

durchsch·immern vt [h] [pp –schimmert] ⟨poet⟩ etw ~ *to pass glimmeringly through* (*a th*), *to imbue od suffuse* (*a th*) *with a glimmer*; ⟨mst⟩ *to gleam through*

d·urch|schimmern vi [h] [pp –ge–t] (of light) *to come* od *get faintly through* ‖ *to glimmer* (*through*)

durchschl·afen vt [h] [pp –schlafen] Nächte ~ *to pass* od *spend nights in sleep*; sein Leben ~ *to sleep one's life away* **d·urch|schlafen** vi [h] [pp –geschlafen] die ganze Nacht ~ *to sleep the whole night through* (od *throughout the night*) **D-fmittel** n *intermediate-acting soporific*

D·urchschlag m ~(e)s/⁓e **A.** [abstr] **1.** *cutting*; *piercing* (*of a tunnel*) ‖ Öffnung, Weg) *cut*; *cutting*; *opening* (durch *through*); → Durchbruch, –laß **2.** ⟨el⟩ *break-down*; *puncture* (*of an insulation*) ‖ ⟨mot⟩ (Reifen⁓) *puncture* **3.** ⟨mil⟩ *complete penetration* **B.** [konkr] **1.** (Schreibmaschinen⁓) (*typewritten*) *copy*, (*carbon*) *copy*, ⟨fam⟩ *carbon* ‖ *duplicate* ‖ das Schreiben v ⁓en *multi-copy work* **2.** (Sieb) ⟨cul⟩ *cullender* od *colander*; *strainer*; *sieve*, *screen*; ⟨pharm⟩ *filter*; (etw) durch den ~ pressen = durchschlagen I.A.3. **3.** (z Lochen) *punch*; *piercer* **~eisen** n *punch*, *piercer* **~hammer** m *driving-hammer* **~papier** n *copying paper*, *carbon-paper* **⁓sicher** a ⟨el⟩ *puncture proof* **~sicherung** f *puncture cut-out*

durchschl·agen vt [h] [pp –schlagen] (etw) *to penetrate*, *pierce* (: *the bullet penetrated* od *pierced the wall*) ‖ ⟨übtr⟩ *to break*; = zerschlagen, –reißen **d·urch|schlagen** vt [h] [pp –geschlagen] **I.** vt **A. 1.** (P) **a.** e–e Wand ~ *to breach* (od *to make a breach in*) *a wall*; *to break through a wall* ‖ ein Loch ~ *to cut* (od *make a hole*) (durch *through*) ‖ e–n Nagel ~ *to drive a nail through* [adv]; ~ durch *to drive through* .. **b.** etw ~ *to cut a th in two*, *to slash a th through*; → d·urchhauen **2.** ⟨el⟩ (Isolation) *to puncture* **3.** ⟨cul⟩ (Erbsen etc) *to pass* od *rub* (*peas*) *through a colander*, *to colander*; *strain* **4.** (Brief) *to make a carbon copy of* (*a letter*); *to copy* (*a l.*) **B. sich ~ 1.** ⟨mil⟩ *to break through*; sich ~ durch .. *to force* (od *cut*, *fight*) *one's way through* .. **2.** ⟨fig⟩ sich (durchs Leben) ~ *to contrive to live*; sich auf eigene Faust ~ *to live by one's own wits* sich eben so ~ *to keep the pot boiling*; *to make but a poor shift*, *to crack a crust*; *to pull through*, *to rub along*; ⟨Am⟩ *to beat one's way*; sich als Werkstudent ~ ⟨Am⟩ *to work one's way* ‖ sich ehrlich ~ *to turn an honest penny* (mit *by*); sich kümmerlich *or* mühselig ~ *to scrape through*, *to scrape a living*; *to rough it*; *to live from hand to mouth*; *to eke out a scanty livelihood* **II.** vi **1.** (P) (bei Wetten etc) schlagen Sie durch! *make it a bargain*! **2. a.** (of rain, etc.) *to get through*; *to penetrate*; (of cold) *to be penetrating*; → durchdr·ingend **b.** (of medicine) *to act* (od *operate*) *on the bowels* **3.** ⟨fig⟩ **a.** (of features) *to appear*; *to peep out*; *to show*; im Enkel schlägt der Großvater durch *characteristic features of the grandfather peep out in the grandchild* **b.** (Erfolg h) *to be successful*; *to get across*

D·urchschlagen n ~s/ (früheren Anstrichs) *soaking through*

d·urchschlagend a **1.** *effective*, *impressive*; *telling* (*effect*); *thorough* ‖ *brilliant*; *striking*; *sweeping* (*success*, *victory*) **2.** *convincing* (*proof*), *conclusive*; *decisive* (*argument*); ~e Kraft *convincingness*

D·urchschlags- [in comp] **~festigkeit** f ⟨el⟩ *insulation-resistance* **~kraft** f **1.** *penetrating*, *-tive power* ‖ *effect* ‖ *penetration* (*of a gun*); *striking force* (*of a bullet*) **2.** *potency* (*of a drug*, *a drink*) **3.** ⟨fig⟩ *drive*; *urge* ‖ *convincingness*, *conclusiveness* (*of an argument*); *conviction*

d·urch|schlängeln vrefl [h] [pp –ge–t] sich ~ (of a river, etc.) *to meander* od *to wind* (durch .. *through a valley*) ‖ (P) *to thread one's way* (*through*)

durchschl·eichen vt [h] [pp –schlichen] e–n Raum ~ *to steal* (od *slink*, *sneak*) *through a room*

d·urch|schleichen vi [s] & vrefl [h] [pp –geschlichen] ~, sich ~ *to steal* od *sneak* (*through*)

d·urch|schleppen vt [h] [pp –ge–t] etw ~ *to drag a th* (durch *through*) ‖ ⟨fig⟩ (jdn) *to pull* (*a p*) *through* [adv] | **sich ~** *to pull through*; → sich durchschlagen

d·urch|schleusen vt [h] [pp –ge–t] ein Schiff ~ *to pass a ship through a lock*

D·urchschlupf m *slipping-through*; *way out*, *way in*; ~ durch *slip through* ‖ *sloping passage*

d·urch|schlüpfen vi [s] [pp –ge–t] *to slip through*; *to slip* (durch *through*) ‖ jdn ~ l *to let a p pass*; → übersehen

d·urch|schmecken vt/i [h] [pp –ge–t] **1.** vt (etw) *to taste* (: *I t. the lemon distinctly*) **2.** vi die Zitrone schmeckt durch *the taste of the lemon gets* od *comes through*

d·urchschmelzen vt [h] (Email) *to melt* ‖ ⟨el⟩ *to blow*, *fuse*

durchschm·ettern vt [h] (of sound) *to echo* (od *resound*, *ring*) *through* (*a room*)

d·urch|schmuggeln vt [h] (etw) *to smuggle* (*a th*) *through* od *over*

durchschn·eiden vt [h] [pp –schnitten] **1.** (Tau) *to cut* ‖ jdm die Kehle ~ *to cut a p's throat*; → d·urchschneiden **2.** ⟨übtr⟩ die Luft ~ (mit der Hand) *to saw the air* ‖ (of ships) das Meer ~ *to plough* (od *cleave*, *cross*, *cut*, *traverse*) *the ocean* ‖ (of a railway, etc.) (Weg) *to intersect* ‖ ⟨math⟩ (of lines) *to cut*, *intersect* ‖ quer ~ *to cross-cut* **3.** ⟨fig⟩ (Bande) *to part*; *sever* **4. sich ~, e-a ~** (of lines) *to cut* (od *cross*) *each other*; *to intersect* **d·urch|schneiden** vt [h] [pp –geschnitten] (etw) *to cut* (*a th*) *asunder* od *in two*, *to cleave* od *divide* (*a th*); in der Mitte ~ *to cut* (*a th*) *across*; → durchschn·eiden **Durchschn·ei-dung** f *cutting, division*; *intersection* ‖ ⟨surg⟩ *section* (*of a muscle*); Sehnen≈ *tenotomy*

D·urchschnitt m ~(e)s/~e **1.** ⟨eig⟩ = Durchschneidung **2.** (of a building, etc.) *section*; senkrechter ~ *profile*; *vertical section*; → Schnitt **3.** ⟨übtr⟩ **a.** *average*; *mean*; annähernder ~ *rough average* ‖ im ~ *on an a.*; → ≈lich ‖ (S) im ~ betragen, liegen, e–n bestimmten ~ erreichen *to average* ‖ über (dem) ~ *better than a.* ‖ den ~ nehmen, feststellen *to strike an average*; den ~ berechnen, nehmen v etw *to average a th* **b.** *average, standard, level* ‖ Methode des gleitenden ~s *moving averages* ‖ der gr ~ der Menschen *the majority of people, people in general*; ein guter ~ ⟨sl⟩ *not half bad*; über (unter) dem ~ *above* (*below*) *the average* od *standard* ‖ die Schriftsteller im ~ *the general run of writers* ‖ den ~ nicht erreichen *not to be up to the average* od *level* | ⟨dero⟩ der ~ *the ruck*

d·urchschnittlich 1. a *average, mean, medium, normal* (price) ‖ *common, normal, ordinary* (*height*); ~e Art v Leuten *common run of people* **2.** adv *on an average*; = im Durchschnitt → d. 3.a. ‖ die Preise fielen ~ um 3 Pfg pro Tag *the prices fell at an average of 3 Pfg. a day* ‖ er studierte ~ 3 Stdn täglich *he studied 3 hours daily on average* ‖ es ~ auf .. bringen *to average ..*

D·urchschnitts- [in comp] *average* (*age*) **~aufwand** m *average expense* **~ausbringung** f *av. output* **~belastung** f *av. load* **~bestimmung** f *av. analysis* **~betrag** m *av. amount* **~erzeugnis** n *common run-of-the-mill* **~frequenz** f *mean fr.y* **~geschwindigkeit** f *av. speed*; e–e ~ v 100 km die Stde erreichen *to average 62 m.p.h.* **~jahres-temperatur** f *mean annual temperature* **~klasse** f *common, general ordinary run* **~mensch** m *av. p, every-day man*; ~en [pl] *common people* ‖ ⟨derog⟩ *very ordinary* od *insignificant p* ‖ der ~ *the man in the street*; er ist nur ein ~ *he is nothing out of the common run* od *out of the ordinary* **~preis** m *average, normal, medium price* **~qualität** f ⟨a.⟩ *run* (des Mehles *of the mill*) **~satz** m ⟨ins⟩ *av. rate* **~summe** f *av.* (od *mean*) *sum* **~verhältnis** n *average*; *mean proportion* **~wert** m *standard value* **~zahl** f *av.* (od *mean*) *number* **~zeichnung** f *profile*; *cross-section drawing*

durchsch·ossen a ⟨typ⟩ *leaded* ‖ *interleaved* (*book*) ‖ ⟨weav⟩ *interwoven* **~schn·üffeln** vt [h] *to ferret, nose, rummage through*

D·urchschreib(e)- ~buch [n] *duplicating b.* | ~feder [f] *manifold pen*; ~formular [n] *carbon-ized form*; ~papier [n] *duplicating* od *manifold paper*, ⟨fam⟩ *flimsy*; ~stift [m] *stylus*

durchschr·eiten vt [h] [pp –schritten] ein Gebiet ~ *to cross* (od *travel, traverse*) *an area*; *to pass* od *travel over an a.* ‖ (z Fuß) *to walk* (*a country*); e–n Raum mit langen Schritten ~ *to stalk* od *stride a room*; die Straßen prunkend or stolz ~ *to parade the streets* ‖ ein Tor ~ *to pass through a gate* | (S) (Stufen) *to pass through* (*stages*) **d·urch|schreiten** vi [h] [pp –geschritten] *to pass through* [adv]; (z Fuß) *to walk through* ‖ ~ durch .. *to pass through* [prep]

D·urchschuß m –schusses/–schüsse **1.** (Ggs Steckschuß) *shot-through*; e–n ~ erhalten *to be shot through* **2. a.** ⟨typ⟩ (kl Bleistück) *lead*; *slug*; †*space-line*; *white line*; *white page*(*s*); Holz≈ *reglet* **b.** *interleaves* pl **~blatt** n = Durchschießblatt **~kasten** m ⟨typ⟩ *lead and slug case*

d·urch|schütteln vt [h] [pp –ge–lt] (etw) *to shake* od *stir* (*a th*) *thoroughly*

d·urch|schütteln vt [h] [pp –ge–t] (etw) *to pour* (*a th*) *through*; ~ durch .. *to pour through ..*

durchschw·ärmen vt [h] [pp –schwärmt] (of bees, etc.) die Luft ~ *to swarm through the air* ‖ ⟨übtr⟩ (P) die Wälder ~ *to rove the woods*; = **d·urch|schwärmen** vi [h] [pp –ge–t] sie h die ganze Nacht –(ge)–mt *they have made a night of it*

durchschw·eben vt [h] [pp –schwebt] (of birds) die Luft ~ *to sail the air*

durchschw·eifen vt [h] [pp –schweift] die Wälder ~ *to rove* od *range the woods*; *to wander through the w.* ‖ s–e Augen ~ den Himmel *h. e. range* od *sweep over the sky*

durchschw·immen vt [h] [pp –schwommen] den Fluß ~ *to swim the river, to swim across the r.*; *to swim* (*a distance*) **d·urch|schwimmen** vi [s] [pp –geschwommen] *to swim through* [adv]; ~ durch *to swim across* od *through* (*a river*)

d·urch|schwindeln vrefl [h] *to get by* (als *as*)

d·urch|schwingen vt [h] ⟨sport⟩ e–n Schlag ~ *to follow through* [adv]

d·urch|schwitzen vt [h] [pp –geschwitzt] mst [pass] ich bin ganz –geschwitzt *I am wet through with sweat, I am all in a sweat*; das Hemd ist –geschwitzt *the shirt is soaked with sweat*; das Pferd ist –ge–tzt *the horse is covered with sweat*

durchs·egeln vt [h] [pp –segelt] (of p, ships, etc.) das Meer ~ *to sail* (od *cross, navigate*) *the ocean*; *to sail* od *glide over* od *across the o.*; *to sail* (*a distance*); → segeln **d·urch|segeln** vi [s] [pp –ge–t] *to sail through* [adv]; ~ durch .. *to sail over* od *across* (*the ocean*)

d·urch|sehen I. vi/t [h] [pp –gesehen] **1.** vi ~ durch .. *to look through ..*; sieh mal durch *have a look through it* ‖ (of objects) *to emerge, peep*; *to become visible* (durch *through*) ‖ ⟨fig⟩ °ich sehe in dieser S nicht durch *I am not quite clear in this matter* **2.** vt **a.** man kann das Haus ~ *you can see the house distinctly* **b.** ⟨übtr⟩ etw ~ *to look* (od *go*) *over a th*; (prüfend) *to examine*; *to review*; wieder ~ *to revise* (*revised edition*); → nachprüfen ‖ (s–e Aufgaben) *to go over* [prep]; *to con*; die Hefte ~ *to mark* od *correct the books* ‖ gründlich ~ *to overhaul*; flüchtig ~ *to glance* (*one's eye*) *over* (*a th*); schnell ~ *to skim*; *to run an eye over* (*a th*) **II.** ≈ n → Durchsicht

d·urch|seihen vt [h] (Flüssigkeit) *to filter, percolate, strain* (*a th*); *to pass* (*a th*) *through a filter* **D·urchseihung** f *filtration, percolation*

d·urch|sein vi → durch II. B. 2.

durchs·etzen vt [h] [pp –setzt] [oft pass –setzt s] **1.** ⟨eig⟩ (Boden, Luft) *to impregnate, interfuse* (mit *with*); *to saturate* (*with*); –setzt mit *saturate with*; → dopen ‖ –setzt s mit (of fabrics) *to be shot with*; (of light, etc.) *to be suffused with* | (schmücken) (Erzählung) *to intersperse* (*with*); *to diversify, interlard, interlace* (*with*) **2.** ⟨übtr⟩ (of spirit, feeling) (Land, Volk) *to impregnate, to leaven, to penetrate* (*with*); alle Teile e–s Landes ~, ein L. in allen s–n Teilen ~ *to interpenetrate a country*; e–e neue Moral –setzte die Gesellschaft *a new moral spread through society*; Ernst mit Heiterkeit ~ *to leaven gravity with wit* ‖ –setzt s *to be interfused*; –setzt s mit *or* von *to be infused* od *saturated with, to be shot with* (*irony*); = durchdrungen s, → durchdr·ingen

d·urch|setzen vt [h] [pp –ge–t] **A. 1.** (Haus) *to partition*; *to intersect* **2.** ⟨min⟩ Erz ~ *to sift* od *sieve ore* **3.** ⟨fig⟩ **a.** (etw) *to carry* (*a th*) *through*; *to effect* (*a th*); (*he'll get the tax program through*); (Antrag) *to carry*; s–e Ansicht ~, s–n Willen ~ *to carry one's point*; (jds Vernichtung) *to compass* ‖ *to enforce*; *to make good* ‖ (Anspruch) *to push* ‖ s–e Pläne mit Gewalt ~ *to forge ahead with one's plans*, (*he pushed, forced his plan through*); → d·urchführen **b.** er hat bei ihm nichts –gesetzt *he did not succeed with him* **c.** ~, daß jd tut *to prevail upon a p to do, to make a p do*; ~, daß etw geschieht *to cause a th to be done*; wir setzten durch, daß er zurückgerufen wurde *we caused him to be called back*

B. (P) jdn ~ *to establish a p* | **sich** ~ **1.** *to make* (od *fight, push, win*) *one's way* (: *they have made their w.*); *to make good*; *to gather way*; *to make ready headway*; *to assert* (od *reassert*) *o.s.*, *to prevail* (gegen *against a p*); *to succeed* (: *he* ~*ed in life*) ‖ ⟨Am⟩ *to get there*; *to win out* ‖ (politisch) *to make a political breakthrough* ‖ sich bleibend, siegreich ~ *to establish o.s. permanently, triumphantly* ‖ sich trotz Unfähigkeit ~ *to muddle through* **2.** (v S) **sich** ~ *to gain ground, to gain in use*; *to prove its worth*; *to penetrate*; *to make its way, to prevail* (: *his authority prevailed*); *to win through*; *to come true* (: *the seeds do not c. t.*) ‖ Blut setzt sich durch *blood will out* **D·urchsetzen** n *carrying-through*; → Durchführung **D–·etzung** f **1.** *impregnation, saturation* (mit *with*); *suffusion* ‖ *interspersion* (*with*) **2.** ⟨übtr⟩ *impregnation, penetration* (*with*); → Durchdr·ingung

durchs·euchen vt [h] [pp –seucht] (Land) *to infect* (mit *with*) ‖ ⟨übtr⟩ = verseuchen

D·urchsicht f ~/~en **1.** *⟨eig⟩ ~ durch *look through*; *vista*; → Durchblick ‖ ⟨phot⟩ in der ~ gesehen *seen by transmitted light* **2.** mst ⟨übtr⟩ (sorgsame) *perusal*; *examination, inspection*; nochmalige ~ *revision*; *supervising* (*of proofs*) ‖ bei flüchtiger ~ *on a cursory perusal*; (Überprüfung) *proving*; z (gefälligen) ~ *for* (*your kind*) *perusal* **d·urchsichtig** a **1.** *transparent, diaphanous*; → d·urchscheinend **2.** ⟨übtr⟩ (klar) *pellucid* (*style*); *clear, lucid* ‖ ⟨fig⟩ *manifest, transparent* (*manœuvre*); *translucent* (*treachery*) ‖ nicht ganz ~e Sachlage *not quite clear position* | ≈**keit** f *transparency* ‖ ⟨übtr⟩ *lucidity, pellucidity* (*of style*) ‖ ⟨fig⟩ *transparency*; → Durchschau-

D·urchsicht(s)- ~bild n *translucent picture* ‖ ⟨phot⟩ *lantern slide* ‖ ⟨tech⟩ *ghosted* od *exploded view* **~fenster** n ⟨typewr, etc⟩ *little window* **~schirm** m ⟨telv⟩ *transparent screen* **~sucher** m ⟨phot⟩ *direct-vision* (*view*)*finder* (*D. V. finder*)

durchs·ickern vt [h] [pp –sickert] den Boden ~ *to trickle* (od *ooze*) *through the soil* **d·urch|-sickern I.** vi [s] [pp –ge–t] **1.** ⟨eig⟩ *to trickle* (od *ooze*) *through* [adv]; *to seep, transude*; ~ durch .. *to trickle* (od *infiltrate, filter, ooze, percolate, sift*) *through* .. ‖ (etw) ~ l *to percolate* ‖ Durchgesickertes *seepage* **2.** ⟨fig⟩ (of news) *to leak out* ‖ (of secrets) *to ooze out, to transpire*; es sickerte durch, daß .. *it transpired that* ‖ ~ l *to ooze* **II.** ≈ n *leakage, seepage* ‖ ⟨fig⟩ *leakage* (*of news*)

d·urch|sieben vt [h] (Korn) *to riddle*; (Kohlen) *to screen*; *sift* ‖ ⟨übtr⟩ *to sift*

d·urch|singen vt [h] [pp –gesungen] (Lied) *to sing* (*a song*) *through* (od *to the end*)

d·urch|sitzen vi/t [h] [pp –gesessen] **1.** vi *to sit* od *stay up*; die ganze Nacht ~ *to sit up all night* **2.** vt (Stuhl, Hose) *to wear out by much use*

d·urch|spielen vt/i [h] [pp –gespielt] **1.** vt ⟨mus⟩ ein Stück ~ *to play a piece through*; immer wieder ~ *to practise* ‖ e–e Rolle mit Erfolg ~ *to support a rôle* **2.** vi; wir h die ganze Nacht –gespielt *we have been playing the whole night through*

d·urch|sprechen vt [h] [pp –gesprochen] etw ~ = besprechen

d·urch|sprengen vi [s] [pp –gesprengt] *to pass through at full speed*

d·urch|springen vi [s] [pp –gesprungen] *to leap* od *jump through*

d·urch|staffeln vt [h] (Steuer) *to graduate thoroughly*

durchst·änkern vt [h] [pp –stänkert] **1.** *to fill* (*a room*) *with smoke* **2.** = –stöbern

d·urch|starten vt [h] Flugzeug ~ *to go around*

durchst·echen vt [h] [pp –stochen] **1.** (jdn) *to pierce* (*a p*) *through*; *to pierce* (mit *with* [*a dagger*]); *to pink* (*a p*); er –stach ihn mit dem Messer *he ran* od *thrust his knife into him*; die Nadel –stach s–n Finger *the needle ran through his finger*; → durchbohren **2.** (Papier etc) *to prick*; (Haut) *to prick, puncture*; → durchlöchern **3.** (Damm etc) *to cut* **d·urch|stechen** vt/i [h] [pp –gestochen] **1.** vt e–e Nadel ~ durch .. *to pass a needle through* (*a th*) ‖ (ein Muster) *to perforate by a roulette* ‖ (das Feuer) tüchtig ~ *to stir, poke* ‖ (Getreide) *to turn* **2.** vi **a.** *to pierce through* [adv] **b.** *⟨fig⟩ *to crop up*; *to emerge* **c.** † mit jdm ~ *to be* (od *act*) *in collusion, to collude with a p*

Durchstecher·ei f ~/~en *collusion, underhand scheming, plotting*; *intrigue, plot* ‖ ~ treiben *to play into each other's hands* **Durchst·echung** f *cutting* (*of a dike*)

d·urch|stecken vt [h] (Band) ~ durch .. *to pass* (*a ribbon*) *through* (*a th*) ‖ er steckte den Kopf durch *he poked his head through*

d·urch|stehen vt/i **1.** vt = aushalten **2.** vi *to hold out* → Durchhalten 2. **D·urchstehvermögen** n ⟨mil⟩ *holding power*

d·urch|stehlen vrefl [h] [pp –gestohlen] **1. sich** ~ durch .. *to steal* (od *slink*) *through* (*a th*) **2.** *to make a living out of stealing*

d·urch|steigen vi [s] [pp –gestiegen] *to climb through* [adv] ‖ ⟨fig⟩ °da steige ich nicht durch *that's beyond me*

D·urchstich m ~(e)s/~e **1.** [abstr] *piercing* ‖ *cutting* (*of a tunnel*) ‖ *cutting* (*through river loop*) **2.** [konkr] ⟨a. rail⟩ *cutting, tunnel*; ⟨Am⟩ *cut*

durchst·öbern vt [h] [pp –stöbert] (Zimmer, Taschen) *to ransack* (nach *for*), *to rummage*; (Gebiet) *to scour* ‖ ⟨hunt⟩ (Dickicht) *to draw*; (Wald) *to beat*; (Buch) *to rake* (*for*)

durchst·oßen vt [h] [pp –stoßen] **1.** jdn ~ *to thrust* (od *pierce, run*) *a p through*; → durchb·ohren ‖ etw ~ *to pierce a th*; *to push through a th* **2.** ⟨mil⟩ die Linie ~ *to break* (*through*) *the line of defence* **d·urch|stoßen** vt/i [pp –ge–] **1.** vt [h] (Stoff) durch Gebrauch ~ *to fray, frazzle*; **sich** ~ *to fray, ravel*; der Ärmel ist (*or* hat sich) –ge– *the sleeve is frayed* ‖ –ge–e Socken, Schuhe h *to have holes in the toes* **2.** vi [s] ⟨mil⟩ *to break through*; *to penetrate* **3.** ≈ n ⟨aero⟩ *descent--through-cloud*

durchstr·ahlen vt [h] [pp –strahlt] (of sun) (Zimmer) *to illumine, irradiate*; *brighten* ‖ ⟨übtr⟩ Güte –strahlte sein Antlitz *g. shone in his face*

durchstr·eichen vt [h] [pp –strichen] die Wälder ~ *to rove* (od *range, scour, traverse*) *the woods*; *to wander through the w.*; → durchstreifen

d·urch|streichen vt/i [pp –gestrichen] **1.** vt [h] (Geschriebenes) *to cross* (od *strike*) *out*; *to cancel*; *to run one's pen through* (*a word*); Nichtzutreffendes bitte ~ *please cross out the words not required* **2.** *vi [s] (of birds, etc.) *to pass*; *to pass through*

durchstr·eifen vt [h] *to roam* od *sweep* (*the seas*); *to rove, range, scour, traverse* (*the woods*); *to tramp, walk* (*the streets*); *to range over* (*the past*); sein Auge –streifte das Zimmer his eye *roamed the room*

D·urchstrich m *passage* (*of birds*); *route* ‖ → Streichung

durchstr·ömen vt [h] [pp –strömt] ein Land ~ (of river) *to flow* (od *run*) *through a country*; (of soldiers) *to sweep a c.*; → überfluten ‖ (of blood, etc.) jds Körper ~ *to pour through a p's body* ‖ (of colour, etc.) *to suffuse* (: *blushes suffused her face*); –strömt sein v *to be suffused with* **d·urch|strömen** vi (of people) *to rush through*; ~ durch *to rush* (od *sweep*) *through* ..

d·urch|studieren vt [h] [pp –studiert] vt ein Buch ~ *to study a book minutely*

durchst·ürmen vt [h] [pp –stürmt] ein Gebiet ~ *to rush* (od *sweep*) *through an area; to sweep an a.* ‖ ⟨poet⟩ sein Leben ~ *to lead a wild life* ‖ (of feelings) (jdn) *to thrill* **d·urch|stürmen** vi [s] = d·urchrasen

d·urch|stürzen vi [s] *to tumble* od *fall through*

durchs·uchen vt [h] [pp –sucht] **1.** *to search* (*a room*) *to go over* (*a r.*); (gründlich) *to ransack* (*a r.*), *to search* (*the pockets*), *to go through* (*the p.*); (Schublade) *to rifle* ‖ *to search*; (⟨Am sl⟩ bes nach Waffen) *to frisk* (*a p*) **2.** (of police, etc) (Stadt) *to hunt, ransack* (nach *for*); (Gegend) *to comb* ‖ (plündernd) *to rifle* ‖ (Land) *to scour* (*for*) | ⟨hunt⟩ (Wald, Dickicht) *to beat, draw* **Durchs·ucher** m ~s/~ *searcher* **Durchs·uchung** f ~/~en *search* (*of the luggage*); → Haussuchung ‖ ~sbefehl [m] *search warrant* ‖ ~srecht [n] ⟨mar⟩ *right of search*

d·urch|tanzen vt/i [h] [pp –getanzt] **A.** vt **1.** (Schuhe) *to wear out by dancing, to go through* (*two*) *pairs of shoes* **2.** e–n Walzer ~ *to dance a waltz through* (od *to the end*) **B.** vi *to dance through*; die ganze Nacht ~ *to dance the whole night through*

D·urchtarif m *through tariff*

d·urch|tasten vrefl [h] ⟨übtr⟩ sich ~ *to feel one's way along*

d·urch|telephonieren vt [h] → durchsagen ‖ es wurde –telephoniert, daß .. *the call came through that ..*

durcht·oben vt [h] [pp –tobt] Volksmassen –tobten die Straßen *tumultuous* od *uproarious crowds walked* od *thronged the streets*

durcht·önen vt [h] [pp –tönt] = durchschallen

d·urch|tönen vi (of sounds) *to come* od *get through*; *to be heard*

durcht·osen vt (of waters) *to rush through* (*a place*) *in a roar*

d·urch|trainieren vt [h] jdn ~ *to set a p up*

d·urchtrainiert a; gut ~ *well set-up* od *trained*

durchtr·änken vt [h] [pp –tränkt] **1.** (of liquids) (etw) *to impregnate, infiltrate, saturate*, –tränkt s v *to be infused* od *saturate(d) with*; *to be steeped in*; v Blut –tränktes Taschentuch *handkerchief sodden with* (od *steeped in*) *blood* **2.** ⟨fig⟩ *mst* [pass] *to imbue, to impregnate, to saturate* (*with*); → durchs·etzen **Durchtr·änkung** f *impregnation, saturation* (mit *with*) ⟨a. fig⟩; → Durchdringung

durchtr·äumen vt [h] [pp –träumt] *to spend in dreams*

d·urch|treiben vt [h] [pp –getrieben] (Vieh; Nagel) *to drive* (*cattle*, etc.) *through*; ~ durch .. *to drive through ..*

D·urchtrieb m ~(e)s/~e (f Vieh) *cattle-road* (od *way*); *driftway* ‖ *right of way for cattle*

durchtr·ieben a *artful, crafty, cunning, dodgy, sharp, shifty, sly, smart, tricky, trickish, tricksy*; ~er Schurke *arrant rogue, thorough-paced* (od *out-and-out*) *scoundrel, an out-and-out* ‖ → gerieben, gerissen | ≃heit f ~/ *cunning*, etc

D·urchtrift f = Durchtrieb

durchw·achen vt [h] [pp –wacht] (Nächte) *to pass waking*

d·urch|wachsen vi [s] [pp –ge–] *to grow through* [adv]; ~ durch .. *to grow through* (*a hedge*) **durchw·achsen** a *streaky* (*bacon, beef*), *streaked*; *marbled* ‖ ⟨fig⟩ (so–s·o) *like the curate's egg* **D·urchwachskraut** n ⟨bot⟩ = Bitterling 2. **Durchw·achsung** f ⟨bot⟩ *diaphysis*

durchw·acht a *white* (*night*)

d·urchwagen vrefl [h] [pp –ge–t] sich ~ *to venture through* (adv); sich ~ durch .. *to venture through* (*a line*)

d·urch|walken vt [h] [pp –ge–t] **1.** (Tuch) *to full well* **2.** ⟨übtr⟩ (jdn) *to trash*; → durchprügeln

†**durchw·allen** vt [h] *to wander through* (*a meadow*) ‖ (of odour, etc) *to pervade*

°**d·urch|wamsen** vt [h] = durchprügeln

durchw·andeln vt [h] [pp –wandelt] ⟨bib⟩ (Land) *to walk* od *pass through* (*a country*)

durchw·andern vt [h] [pp –wandert] ein Gebiet ~ *to range over an area, to wander through an a.*; *to traverse an a.*; mühsam ~ *to trudge*

d·urch|wandern vi [s] [pp –ge–t] *to wander through* [adv]; ~ durch *to w. through* (*a country*)

durchw·ärmen vt [h] [pp –wärmt] (etw, jdn) *to warm* (*a th, a p*) *through* [adv] **d·urch|wärmen** vt [h] [pp –ge–t] = durchw·ärmen

d·urch|waschen vt [h] [pp –ge–] (etw) *to wash thoroughly*

durchw·ässern vt [h] = bewässern ‖ → durchweichen

durchw·atbar a *fordable* **durchw·aten** vt [h] [pp –watet] e–n Fluß ~ *to wade* (od *ford*) *a river*; *to wade through a r.* **d·urch|waten** vi [s] [–ge–t] *to wade through* [adv]

durchw·eben vt [h] [pp –webt] ⟨fig⟩ (etw) *to interweave*; = verweben ‖ den Hintergrund e–r Zeit mit e–r Erzählung ~ *to weave a narrative through the background of a period* ‖ –woben mit *shot through with* **d·urch|weben** vt [h] der Stoff ist –gewebt *the pattern comes through on either side of the cloth*

D·urchweg m ~(e)s/~e *passage, passageway*; ~ durch *way through* ‖ → Durchgang

d·urchweg, durchw·eg, ×~s adv *altogether*; *consistently*; *without distinction* od *exception*; *throughout*; sie *or* es sind fast ·~ Arbeiter *nearly all of them are w.*; = durch die Bank, → A. 6. ‖ (allezeit) *every time, always*

durchw·ehen vt [h] [pp –weht] (of wind) (etw) *to blow through* (*a th*) ‖ mst ⟨fig⟩ *to flow* (od *pass*) *through* (*a th*); *to pervade* (*a th*); → –dringen **d·urch|wehen** vt [h] [pp –ge–t] sich (v Winde) ~ l *to get* (od *to go for*) *a blow*

durchw·eichen vt [h] [pp –weicht] (etw) *to soak*; *to sop* (*up*); v Regen –weichter Boden *ground sodden with rain, soggy g., sop*; v Wasser –weicht *sodden* (*paper*); → durchnässen **d·urch|weichen** vt [h] [pp –ge–t] *to soak thoroughly* ‖ ⟨tech⟩ *to impregnate* (mit *with*)

durchw·einen vt [h] [pp –weint] (Nächte) *to pass weeping* (od *in tears*)

d·urch|werfen vt [h] [pp –geworfen] (etw) *to cast* od *throw* (*a th*) *through*; → durchsieben

d·urch|wetzen vt/i [pp –ge–t] **1.** vt *to wear down* (*trousers, etc*) **2.** vi °~ → °abhauen

°**d·urch|wichsen** vt [h] = durchprügeln

durchw·inden vt [h] [pp –wunden] *to entwine* (mit *with*) **d·urch|winden** vrefl [h] [pp –gewunden] sich ~ durch (of river, etc.) *to wind* (od *twist*) *through ..* ‖ ⟨übtr⟩ (P) *to pick* (od *thread, wind*) *one's way through* (*a thicket*); *to wriggle through* (*a hole*); *to pull through* (*an illness*); *to struggle through* (*hardships*)

durchw·intern vt [h] [pp –wintert] (Pflanzen) *to winter* ‖ → überw·intern **Durchw·interung** f *the wintering* (*of plants*)

Durchw·irbelung f *turbulence* ⟨a. aero⟩ → Wirbel–

durchw·irken vt [h] [pp –wirkt] (etw) *to interweave, work* (mit *with*); –wirkt mit *shot* (*through*) *with* **d·urch|wirken** vt [h] (Teig) = durchkneten

°**d·urch|wischen** vi [s] = d·urchschlüpfen

durchw·ogen vt [h] [pp –wogt] = durchfl·uten

durchw·ühlen vt [h] [pp –wühlt] **1.** (of rabbits) (Boden) *to burrow* **2.** ⟨übtr⟩ e–e Schublade ~ *to rummage through a drawer, to root about in a d.*; → durchst·öbern ‖ ⟨fig⟩ (jds Innere) *to agitate, excite, stir*; *thrill* ‖ v Leidenschaft –lt *torn by passion* **d·urch|wühlen** vt [h] [pp –gewühlt] = durchw·ühlen ‖ °**sich** ~ = sich mühsam durcharbeiten

D·urchwurf m ~(e)s/≃e (Sieb) *screen, riddle*

d·urch|würgen vrefl [h] [pp –ge–t] sich ~ = sich (mühsam) durcharbeiten

durchw·ürzen vt [h] [pp –würzt] (Speise) *to season* (mit *with*) ‖ (Raum) mit Geruch ~ *to scent* ‖ ⟨übtr⟩ (Unterhaltung) *to season* (*with*)

durchz·ählen vt [h] [pp –zählt]; **d·urch|zählen** vt [h] [pp –gezählt] *to count over*

durchz·echen vt [h] (Nacht) *to pass .. in a carousal* **d·urch|zechen** vi [h] *to carouse throughout the night*

d·urch|zeichnen vt [h] (Zeichnung) *to trace*; → pausen ‖ durchz·eichnet a ⟨phot⟩ *with fine definition* D·urchzeichnung [f] ⟨phot⟩ *tone separation*

durchz·iehen vt [h] [pp –zogen] **1.** (P) **a.** = durchqu·eren, –schw·eifen, –w·andern ‖ (Gegend) als Wahlredner ~ ⟨Am⟩ *to stamp* **b.** (etw) mit Fäden ~ *to thread* ‖ v grauen Haaren –z·ogen (*a beard*) *shot with grey* **2.** (S) **a.** (of valleys, rivers) (Land) *to traverse*; oft [pass] –zogen s v *to be traversed by* ‖ mit Furchen ~ *to furrow*; (Boden) mit Gräben ~ *to trench*; mit Kanälen ~ *to canalize, to furnish with canals*; (Boden) mit Dränrohren ~ *to drain* ‖ v Rauch –zogen *filled* od *dense with smoke*; *smoky* **b. sich ~ mit** *to be saturated* od *impregnated with* **c.** ⟨übtr⟩ *to permeate, pervade*; *thread* (: *one spirit threads the whole*) ‖ (Gedanke) *to pass through* (*a p's brains*)

d·urch|ziehen vi/t [pp –gezogen] **A.** vi [s] **1.** (P) *to pass* (od *travel, walk*) *through* [adv]; ⟨mil⟩ *to march through*; jdn ~ l *to let a p pass* ‖ ~ **durch** *to pass* od *travel through* (*a country*); *to cross, traverse* (*a country*); Flugzeug durch die Wolkendecke ~ *to break cloud* **2.** (of air, damp) *to penetrate* **B.** vt [h] **1.** (etw, jdn) *to draw* od *pull* (*a th, a p*) *through* [adv] ‖ e–n Faden ~ durch *to pass a thread through* (*a needle's eye*) **2.** (Scheitel) *to draw* ‖ ⟨sport⟩ e–n Schlag ~ *to follow through* **3.** jdn ~ = durchhecheln 2. **|** °⟨sex⟩ *to have, make*; *to go through* (*a woman*) **4. sich ~ durch** etw *to pervade, to thread a th*, → durchz·iehen 2. c. **D·urchzieher** m ⟨Ger fenc⟩ *deep cut slitting the cheek*; *gash*

durchz·ittern vt [h] [pp –zittert] = durchb·eben

D·urchzoll m ⟨com⟩ *transit-duty*

durchz·ucken vt [h] [pp –zuckt] **1.** ⟨eig⟩ Blitze –zuckten die Finsternis *lightnings flashed their light through the darkness* **2.** ⟨fig⟩ e–e Erregung –zuckte die Menge *a stir beat through the multitude* ‖ (of feelings) *to thrill a p*; ein Schmerz –zuckte ihn *a pang* (*of* ..) *shot through him*; ein Gedanke –zuckte mich *an idea rushed* (od *flashed*) *into my mind, it flashed upon me*

D·urchzug m ~(e)s/⁓e **1.** (P) *passage through, march through* ‖ ~ durch *journey* od *march through* (*a country*); ~ durchs Rote Meer ⟨arts⟩ *Crossing of the Red Sea* ‖ (T) *passage* **2.** (of air) *circulation*; *through-blow*; *draught*; macht ~ *let fresh air in*; e–n ~ m *to make, create a* (*through*) *draught* **3.** [konkr] ⟨arch⟩ *girder, summer* ‖ ~srecht [n] ⟨mil⟩ *right-of-way* (durch *through*) **D·urchzügler** m ⟨orn⟩ *bird of passage*; *transient, transmigrant*; → Zugvogel **D·urchzugs- ~kraft** f *pulling* od *tractive power* **~moment** n ⟨mach⟩ *lugging capacity* **~schaltung** f *progressive system of gear shifting*

d·urch|zwängen vt [h] [pp –ge–t] **d·urch|zwingen** vt [h] [pp –gezwungen] (etw) *to force* od *squeeze through* ‖ **sich** ~ *to force* (od ⟨fam⟩) *beef*) *one's way* (durch *through*)

d·ürfen v aux [h] [prs darf/pret durfte/pp gedurft; nach inf ~] **A.** [vor inf] **1.** (= brauchen, das mst dafür verwandt wird) [nur prs & pret]: er darf (durfte) nur befehlen *he need* (*need*) *only command, he needs* (*needed*) *only to c.*; er hätte nur schreiben ~ *he need only have written* **2.** (Erlaubnis h) **a.** *to be allowed* od *permitted*; hast (wirst) du ausgehen ~? *were you* (*shall you be*) *permitted to go out*? nein, ich habe (es) nicht gedurft *no, I was not* **b.** [nur prs]: ich darf (etc) .. *I may* ..; darf ich mich darauf verlassen? *may I rely on it*? Ja, du darfst es *Yes, you may*; nein, du d. es nicht .. *no, you may* od *must not* **c.** [nur neg & nur prs & *pret]: ich darf (etc) nicht .. *I must not* .. du darfst hier nicht eintreten *you must not enter here* ‖ du darfst das nicht (tun) *you are not to do that*, → B. 2. **d.** noch etw Fleisch, **wenn ich bitten darf** *some more meat, if you please*; ja, wenn ich bitten darf *yes,* (*if you*) *please* **| nicht** tun ~ *not to be authorized to do* ‖ **hier darf nicht** geraucht w *smoking is not allowed here*; *no smoking, please*; → verboten ‖ das darf niemand außer dir wissen *nobody must know this but you* **3.** [verblaßt] **a. ich darf wohl** behaupten, *I dare say*; man d. wohl erwarten *it is to be expected* (*that*); man d. sich nicht wundern *you must not be surprised* (*if* ..) **b. das durfte** nicht k! *of all appalling things!, it wanted only that!* **c. jetzt dürfte es** z spät s *now it may be* (od *will probably be*) *too late*; es dürfte ein leichtes s *it should* (od *would*) *be an easy matter* (*to do*) ‖ dies dürfte N. s *this is N. I suppose* ‖ sie dürften wohl k *they are likely to come* ‖ daher dürfte heute ein gewisser Entwicklungstrend dahin gehen *threrefore, it seens that there is a trend nowadays* ‖ es dürfte genug s *it would seem to be enough* **d.** das **hättest** du nicht tun ~ *you ought not to have done that*; das hätte nicht geschehen ~ *that should not have occured* **B.** [mit scheinbarem Objekt] **1.** [mit 'es'] (als Ersatz f vorhergeh. Verb) → A. 2. **2.** [ell f tr. Verb + ~] er darf (sc tun) *he is allowed* (od *he has permission*) *to do it*; das darfst du nicht *you must not do it*; *it isn't done*; → A. 2. c. ‖ °darf ich noch e–e Birne? *may I have another pear*? **C.** [ell f intr Verb + ~; mit adv]: wir durften nicht hinaus (sc gehen) *we were not allowed to go out*; es darf niemand hier herein *no one is admitted here* ‖ darf ich mit? *may I go with you*? ‖ er darf mir nicht ins Haus *I will never have him in my h.*

d·ürftig I. a **A.** (S) **1.** (notleidend) *indigent*; *needy*; *straitened* (*circumstances*) **2.** ⟨übtr⟩ (unzulänglich) **a.** *poor* (*clothes*), *scanty* (*crop*); *meagre, slim* (*income*); *inadequate, paltry, petty* (*village*); *humble* (*cottage*) ‖ ~e Beschaffenheit *poorness* **b.** *poor* (*consolation*); *thin* (*light of a bulb*); ⟨liter⟩ *sorry excuse*); *slim, thin* **B.** (P) *inferior, poor* (*player*); *insignificant* ‖ ⟨Am fam⟩ *ornery, one-horse* **II.** adv *poorly*; *inadequately, insufficiently* **| ⁓keit** f ~/ **1.** *indigence*; *neediness*; *poverty* (*of people*) **2.** *scantiness* (*of crops*); *inadequacy, insufficiency* ‖ *poorness*; *inferiority* (*of a player*) ‖ ~ der Ausschmückung *bareness*

D·urian m ⟨bot⟩ *durian* ‖ Frucht des ~s *durian*

Dur·ine f ⟨vet⟩ = Beschälseuche

dürr a **1.** (unfruchtbar) *arid, barren*; *thirsty* (*soil*); *poor*; *sterile*; *dry* (*summer*) ‖ ~ w; ~ m *to dry up* **2.** (verwelkt) *dried up, dead, withered* (*plant*; *branch*); ⟨poet⟩ *sere, sear* (*leaf* [*Shak., Macbeth* V, 3]) ‖ → welk **3.** (P, Glieder) *gaunt, lean, meagre, scraggy, skinny, thin*; ⟨Am⟩ *scrawny*; → dünn ‖ *wizen(ed)* ‖ klapper~ *bony, weedy*; spindel~ *spindly*; → dünnbeinig **4.** ⟨übtr⟩ **a.** (dürftig) *meagre, thin* **b.** (schlicht, kz) mit ~en Worten *in plain* (od *few*) *words*; *in short*; *bluntly, curtly*

D·ürr- ~erz n ⟨minr⟩ *ore poor in silver* **~futter** n (Ggs Grünfutter) *fodder*; *dried food* **~wurz** f ⟨bot⟩ *fleabane*

D·urra f ⟨bot⟩ *sorghum*, ⟨Am a.⟩ *broomcorn*

D·ürre f ~/~n **1.** *aridity, barrenness, dryness* (*of a soil*) ‖ (trockenes Wetter) *drought* **2.** *with-*

ered condition (*of trees*) **3.** *gauntness, leanness* (*of a p*) **4.** ⟨übtr⟩ *dearth, drought* (: *dramatic d.*)

D·urst m ∼es/ **1.** *thirst* (auf .. *for a drink*) ‖ heißer ∼ *burning th.* ‖ ∼ h *to be thirsty* (*for*); gr ∼ h ⟨sl⟩ *to have a thirst*, ⟨vulg⟩ *to be dry* ‖ den ∼ löschen *to slake* od *quench one's thirst* ‖ ∼ m *to cause thirst*; *to make thirsty*; die Arbeit macht ∼ *this is thirsty* (⟨vulg⟩ *dry*) *work* ‖ er hat e–n über den ∼ getrunken *he has had a drop too much*; *he's overshot*; → betrinken ‖ vor ∼ verschmachten *to be parched with thirst* **2.** ⟨fig⟩ *thirst* (nach .. *for knowledge*; z tun *to do*); *eagerness* (*for adventure*); *thirsting, longing* (*for*) ‖ ∼ h nach *to thirst for* ‖ brennender ∼ *craving* (*for justice*)

d·ursten vi [h] *to suffer thirst*; *to go thirsty*; wir h tagelang gedurstet *we have been without any drink for days*

d·ürsten vt/i [h] **1.** vt [imp] ⟨eig⟩ es dürstet mich, mich d. *I am thirsty* **2.** vi ⟨fig⟩ ∼ nach *to thirst for* od *after*; *to long for*; *to be itching* (*for a th* od *to do*)

d·urstig a **1.** *thirsty* (auf *for*); ⟨vulg⟩ *dry* ‖ e–e ∼e Kehle *a parched throat*; e–e ∼e Seele ⟨fam⟩ *a bone-dry man, a Wet Quaker* ‖ ∼ m = Durst m **2.** ⟨fig⟩ *desirous* (nach *of*); *eager* (*for*)

d·urstlöschend, d·urststillend a *thirst-quenching*; ∼es Mittel n ⟨fam⟩ *thirst-quencher*

Dusch- **∼ecke, ∼kabine** f *shower cabinet*

D·usche f ∼/∼n *douche*; *shower*; *shower-bath* ‖ ⟨fig⟩ kalte ∼ *wet blanket* (f jdn *on a p*); *cold douche*; e–e tüchtige ∼ bek *to get a good ducking*; e–e kalte ∼ bek *to be damped* (: *his joy was d.*)

d·uschen vt [h] ⟨a. sich ∼⟩ *to take a shower*

D·üse f ∼/∼n ⟨tech⟩ *nozzle*; *spray*; *blast* (*pipe*); (an Springbrunnen) *adjutage*; ⟨mot⟩ *jet*

D·usel [u:] m ∼s/ **1.** (Schwindel) *dizziness, giddiness*, im ∼ s *to be* od *feel dizzy* od *giddy* **2.** *drowsiness, sleepiness*; *doze*; im ∼ s *to doze* **3. a.** (Trunkenheit) *inebriation, intoxication*; ⟨sl⟩ *fuddle*; im ∼ s *to be intoxicated, in one's cups, inebriated*; *tipsy* **b.** ⟨übtr⟩ (Rausch) *inebriation, intoxication*; → Rausch, Wahn ‖ oft [in comp] *extravagant enthusiasm*; *fad, mania* (f *for*); *gush, nonsense*; Freiheits≃ *flush for liberty*; → Duselei, Fimmel **c.** °⟨fig⟩ (Glück) *luck, score*; so ein ∼! *what a score! what luck!* ein gr ∼, ein Mords≃ *a great score, a grand piece of luck* ‖ ∼ h *to be in luck, to be lucky*; ⟨sl⟩ *to click*; da hast du ∼ gehabt *you were lucky*; den ∼ h *to have the luck* (*to be* ..); wenn man ∼ hat *with luck*; ∼ h mit *or* bei *to make a strike with* **4.** = Dussel **Dusel·ei** f ∼/∼en ⟨übtr⟩ (→ Dusel 3. b.) *daydream, reverie* ‖ mst [in comp] Humanitäts≃ *humanitarian nonsense, humanity-mongering*; → Gefühls≃ **d·uselig** [u:] a **1.** (betäubt) *muzzy*; *giddy, dizzy*; mir ist ganz ∼ im Kopfe *my head swims, I feel quite giddy* **2.** = betrunken → gefühls∼ **3.** = dusselig

d·useln [u:] **I.** vi [h] **1.** *to doze, to be half asleep*; angenehm ∼ *to be daydreaming*; → dösen **2.** vor sich [acc] hin∼ *to maunder along* ‖ = tuscheln **II.** ≃ n *dozing, doze*

D·üsen- **∼antrieb** m ⟨aero⟩ *jet propulsion* **∼bomber** m *jet bomber* **∼flugzeug** n *jet plane, jet aircraft*, ⟨fam⟩ (*jumbo-*) *jettie*, ⟨Am⟩ *blow-torch* **∼hubschrauber** m *jet helicopter* **∼jäger** m ⟨aero⟩ *jet fighter* ‖ (2motorig) *twin-jet fighter* **∼kopf** m *hose top* ‖ *nozzle tip* **∼motor** m *jet engine, thermojet* **∼ring** m ⟨mach⟩ *port ring* **∼strahl** m *jet stream* **∼triebwerk** n *jet-engine* **∼verkehrsflugzeug** n *turboliner* **∼zerstäubung** f ⟨chem, tech⟩ *pressure atomization*

°**D·ussel** m *goof, nincompoop, simpleton*; *idiot* ‖ ∼kopf [m], ∼tier [n] = ∼ °**d·usselig, d·ußlig** a *dozy*; *goofy*; *silly, stupid*; › dumm

D·üsseldorf n ⟨Ger⟩ (Stadt)

†**Dust** m = Staub ×[niedd] = Dunst, Staub

×**d·uster** [u:] a = **d·üster I.** a **1.** ⟨eig⟩ (dämmernd) *dusky*; *dim, shadowy*; *dim, faint* (Schein *light*); ⟨poet⟩ *dusk*; es fängt an ∼ z w *it is getting dusky, it begins to dusk* ‖ (finster) *dark* **2.** ⟨übtr⟩ (gefühlsbetont) **a.** *dark, murky* (*night*); *cloudy, sombre* (*sky*); *gaunt* (*wood*); *gloomy* (*church, staircase*); ∼ aussehen (of the sky) *to gloom* **b.** *dark, sad, sombre* (*colour*) **c.** (of sound) = dumpf **d.** *mournful, sullen* (*face, scene*); *lurid* (*light*), ein ∼es Licht werfen auf *to cast a lurid light on* **e.** ⟨fig⟩ *black, dark* (*days*); *black* (*mood*); *gloomy, melancholy, sad, somber* (*thoughts*); *drab* (*existence*); *dismal, gloomy, sullen* (*silence*), *sombre* (*outlook*) ‖ in ∼em Brüten versunken *sunk in gloomy meditation* ‖ *dismal, black, depressed, dull, gloomy, melancholy* (*mood*) ‖ ∼e Vorahnung *dark, dire forebodings* ‖ die Lage sieht ∼ aus *things look black*; → dunkel; *finster*; *unheimlich* **II.** adv *dismally, gloomily, sullenly*; ∼ blicken *to gloom* **III.** ≃e n; im ∼n = im Dunkeln; → Dunkel n

D·üsterheit f **1.** → Dunkelheit **2.** ⟨übtr⟩ *darkness*; *gloom* (*of a church*) ‖ *sullenness* (*of a face*) ‖ *luridness* (*of light*) ‖ ⟨fig⟩ *gloom* (*of poverty*), *gloominess*; *melancholy, sadness* **d·üstern** vi [h] = düster (*or* dunkel) w, → düster I. 1., dunkel **D·üsternis** f = Düsterheit

D·üte f, **D·ütvogel** m ⟨orn⟩ *golden plover*

×**D·üte** f, ×**Dutt** f = Tüte

°**Dutt** m, **∼e** f *tuft of hair* ‖ *heap* ‖ = Knirps ‖ ⟨fig⟩ in die ∼en gehen *to get lost*; *to fail*; *to come to grief*

D·utzend n ∼s/∼e **1.** [alleinstehend, pl ∼e] *dozen*; ein volles ∼ *a round d.*; ein ∼ kleiner Nägel *a d. of small nails*; → 2. ‖ Bäcker≃ (13) *baker's* (od *devil's, printer's*) *dozen, the* (od *a long*) *dozen* ‖ ⟨com⟩ gr ∼, 12 ∼ *a gross* ‖ etwa ein ∼ Pn *some dozen people* ‖ ∼e [pl] *dozens* [pl]; ∼e v Leuten *dozens of people*; einige, mehrere, viele ∼e v *some, several, many dozens of* .. ‖ ≃emal *dozens of times* ‖ z ∼en *in dozens* **2.** (= zwölf) [unflektiert]: ein ∼ kleine Nägel *a dozen small nails*; zwei (etc) ∼ Flaschen *two dozen bottles*; mehrere, viele ∼ Leute *several, many dozen people*; einige ∼ L. *some dozens of p.* **D·utzend-** **∼artikel** m = Dutzendware **∼bild** n *mediocre picture* **≃mal**: ein ∼ *a dozen times*; einige ∼ *some dozens of times* **∼mensch** m *ordinary, commonplace p*; *mediocrity, p of mediocre talents*; → Durchschnittsmensch **∼preis** m *price per dozen* **∼ware** f *article sold by the dozen*; *mass-produced articles*; *mediocre, cheap, poor things* **≃weise** adv *by the dozen*

D·uz- **∼bruder** m *intimate friend*; ⟨fam⟩ *chum* **∼fuß** m: auf dem ∼e stehen *to be very intimate* (mit *with*), *to be on intimate terms* (*with*); *to fraternize, to hobnob* (*with*); sie stehen zus– auf dem ∼e *they are on first-name friendliness*; *they are great chums*, ⟨fam⟩ *they are very thick* **∼schwester** f *intimate friend*

d·uzen vt [h] jdn ∼ *to address a p as* 'du'; *to thou* (*and thee*) *a p* ‖ **sich** mit jdm ∼ *to be very intimate with a p*; wir ∼ uns *we are very intimate, we are great chums, we are on first-name friendliness*

dw·ars adv ⟨mar⟩ = quer; ∼ v *abeam* (od *abreast*) *of*; ∼ vor *athwart* (*the bows*) **≃linie** f *line abreast* **≃saling** f *cross-trees* [pl] **∼schiffs** adv *athwart-ships* **≃see** f *beam* (od *athwart, broadside*) *sea* **≃wind** m *beam-wind*

Dweil m ∼s/∼e ⟨mar⟩ *mop, swab* **dw·eilen** vt [h] *to mop, swab*

Dw·ina f ⟨Russ⟩ (Fluß) (*Northern*) *Dvina*

Dy·adik f ⟨math⟩ → Dualsystem

D·yas f, **∼formation** f ⟨geol⟩ *the dyas*; *the Permian formation*

Dyn n (alte Maßeinheit der Kraft) *dyne* **Dyna·m·eter** n *dynameter*

Dyn·amik f ~ **1.** ⟨phys⟩ (Ggs Statik) *dynamics* [pl] [sg konstr] **2.** ⟨übtr⟩ *dynamic, dynamics* [pl], *energy; motive force; forces* [pl] (*of evolution*, etc.) **dyn·amisch** a (Ggs statisch) *dynamic(al)* ‖ ⟨übtr⟩ *dynamic, effective, energetic, potent*; ~e P ⟨fam⟩ *forceful personality*; ~es Gleichgewicht ⟨biochem⟩ *steady state-level*; ~e Kraft *dynamism* **Dynam·ismus** m ⟨philos⟩ *dynamism* **Dynam·it** n ~s/~e ⟨chem⟩ *dynamite*; → Gelatine≈ ‖ (etw) durch ~ in die Luft sprengen *to dynamite* ‖ ~verbrecher [m] *dynamiter*

Dyn·amo m ~/~s (= ~maschine) *dynamo* (*-electric machine*); → Antriebs≈ ‖ Erreger≈ *exciter* **~bürste** f *collecting brush* **≈el·ektrisch** a *dynamo-electric* **~maschine** f = *Dynamo* **~m·eter** n *dynamometer*

Dyn·ast m ~en/~en *dynast; hereditary ruler of a dynasty* **Dynast·ie** f ~/~n *dynasty; ruling house* **dyn·astisch** a *dynastic(al)*

D·yne f = Dyn

Dys- [Gr pref] (miß–, schlecht) ⟨med⟩ *dys-* **~enteri·e** f *dysentery* **≈g·enisch** a ⟨biol, demog⟩ *dysgenic* (*union*) **~peps·ie** f *dyspepsia* **~p·eptiker** m *dyspeptic* **~ton·ie** f ~/~n ⟨physiol⟩ *dystonia* **~troph·ie** f *dystrophy*

D-Zug m → D 3, → Zug

E

E, e n ~/~ **1.** (Buchstabe) *E, e* **2.** ⟨mus⟩ *E; mi* ‖ **E-dur** *E major*; **e-Moll** *e minor* **E-Lok** f *electric locomotive* **E-Offizier** (Ersatz-Offizier) ⟨fam⟩ *dug-out* **E-Werk** = Elektrizitätswerk

Eau de Cologne [o:dəkɔ'lɔɲ] [s] [Fr] *Eau de Cologne* [Fr]

Ebbe f ~/~n **1.** *ebb, ebb-tide, low-tide* (od *water*); → Flut; Nippflut ‖ ~ und Flut *the tides* [pl], *ebb and flow* (od *flood*) ‖ bei ~ *at ebb, at low-tide* ‖ es ist ~ *the tide is down*; es tritt ~ ein *the tide is going out* **2.** ⟨fig⟩ *ebb, decline*, → Tiefstand ‖ in meiner Börse ist ~, bei mir ist ~ *my purse is at a low ebb, I am low in my pocket, I am in low-water* (od *at low tide, on the rocks*)

·ebben vi [h] **1.** (of the tide, etc.) *to ebb, to retreat*; [mst imps] es ebbt *the tide is going out* ‖ ~ u fluten *to ebb and flow*; die Gezeiten ~ u f. *the tides ebb and flow* **2.** ⟨übtr & fig⟩ (of blood, feeling, etc) *to ebb* (*away*); *to decline*; → ab-, verebben

·eben I. a *even, flat, level* (*ground, surface*); *plane; smooth* (*slope*); ~e Fläche, ~er Boden *the flat, level*; auf ~em B. *on the flat*; ~es Gelände *level ground*; ~es Land *open country* ‖ ~ m = ebnen ‖ ⟨math⟩ *plane* (*geometry; triangle*) ‖ zu ~er Erde *on the groundfloor* ‖ → uneben **II.** adv **A.** (gleichmäßig) *evenly, regularly* **B.** ⟨übtr⟩ **1.** (gerade) **a.** *just* ‖ ~ an der Stelle *just on that spot* ‖ ~ groß genug um .. *just big enough to admit* .. ‖ ~ nur einige Zeilen *just a few lines* | ~ damals *just then* ‖ ~ an dem Tage *on that very day* ‖ ~ erst *very recently*; er kam ~ erst *he arrived but that very moment*, etc ‖ es ist ~ 1 Uhr *it is just one o'clock* | das ist es ~ *that is just it, that's the state of affairs, the nature of things, the way it goes* ‖ das wollte ich ~ sagen *that's just what I was going to say* ‖ damit k wir ~ aus *that will just do for us* ‖ das geschieht dir ~ recht *that serves you right* ‖ ich habe den Zug nur so ~ noch erwischt *I caught the train, but I cut it very fine* **b.** (zustimmend) ~! *exactly!, certainly!, that's right!* **c.** ~ **nicht!** (eindringlich als Antwort) *well no!* das nun ~ nicht *not exactly* (od *precisely*) *that; not quite so* ‖ nicht ~ viel *not particularly much*; er ist nicht ~ klug *he is not what I should call clever* **d.** (zeitlich) *just* (*he is* [*just*] *coming*: so oft in progressiver Form) ‖ er ist ~ gek. *he has just arrived*; ~ erst (*only*) *just now, but now* ‖ ~, als er ankam .. *just at the moment when he arrived* ‖ er wollte ~ gehen *he was about* (od *going*) *to leave* ‖ (nur) ~ recht *just in time, at the very nick of time* ‖ der ~ Genannte *the same* ‖ → genau; gerade **3.** [Füllwort, gefühlsbetont] sag mir doch ~ *just tell me* ‖ komm doch ~ mit mir hinein *do just get in with me* ‖ man muß es ~ hinnehmen *it can't be helped; there is nothing for it but to submit* ‖ er ist ~ nicht z gebrauchen *he is no good as I told you* ‖ er ist ~ ein Schurke *he is a scoundrel, he is* **4.** [in comp] **~da** adv *at that very place* **~daher** adv *from the same place* **~d·aher** = ebendarum **~dahin** adv *to the same place* **~d·arum** adv *for that very reason*; ~ kam er *that is it why he came* **~das·elbst** adv *at* (od *in*) *the very same place* **~der(selbe)** a *the very same* (*man*), *the identical* **~d·eshalb, ~desw·egen** adv = ebendarum **~dieser** a: ~ Tag *this very day* **~dort** adv = ebenda **~falls** → d. **~jener** a *that very same* (*man*) **~so** etc → d.

·Ebenbild n *image, likeness, picture*; das ~ Gottes *God's image*; → Abbild ‖ das (ganze) ~ jds *to be the* (*very*) *image* (od *model*, ⟨fam⟩ *moral, spit, fetch*) *of a p*, ⟨sl⟩ *to be the* (*post-*) *-moral of a p* (*he is the very moral of his father*)

·ebenbürtig a **1.** [pred] jdm ~ s *to be of equal birth with a p* ‖ ⟨übtr⟩ *to be of equal rank, to be on a par with a p, to be the equal of a p*; er ist ihm nicht ~ *he is not his equal*; nicht ~ s *not to be equal in rank* (od *of e. r.*); → gewachsen, nachstehen **2.** [attr] ~e Kinder *children of equal birth* **b.** *worthy* (*adversary, successor*) | **≈keit** f *equality of birth*

·Ebene f ~/~n **1.** (Flachland) *plain*; (tiefliegende ~ zw Bergen *creek* **2.** (Fläche) **a.** ⟨math⟩ *plane* ‖ schiefe ~ *inclined plane* ‖ ⟨golf⟩ schiefe z Holzschlagen geeignete ~ *loft* **b.** *flat surface; flat; level* ‖ in der ~ darstellen *to represent* (*a th*) *in the flat* ‖ in gleicher ~ ruhen *to rest flush* (auf *on*); in der gleichen ~ liegen *to be on a level, to be flush* (wie, mit *with*) **c.** ⟨übtr⟩ *level, plane; pitch, standard*; hohe ~ *high level* (od *plane*); auf allseitiger, breitester ~ *extensionally*; Besprechung auf höchster ~ (Gipfelkonferenz) *conference at the highest level, top-level conference* ‖ auf e–e ~ heben *to lift to a plane* ‖ auf derselben ~ liegen *to be on the same level, to be on a par* (wie *with*); das liegt auf der ~ der Biologie *that belongs to the province of biology, that is a matter of b.*; das liegt auf e–r anderen ~ *that lies on another plane* od *in a different field* ‖ (S) auf dieselbe ~ stellen *to place* od *put on the same level* (od *on a level*); jdn auf s–r ~ treffen *to meet a p on his ground*; → Stufe ‖ auf die schiefe ~ geraten *to slide downhill* (od *into evil ways*), *to go astray; to come to grief, to fail*; jdn auf die schiefe ~ bringen *to bring a p to grief* (od *ruin*); *to be a p's ruin*

ebenen vt → ebnen **·ebenerdig** a *ground-floor* (*room*) **·ebenfalls** adv *also, likewise; as well; too*; → auch 1.a.; desgleichen 2. **·Ebenheit** f *planeness; levelness; smoothness* **·Ebenhoch** m ⟨hist⟩ = Belagerungssturm

·Ebenholz n *ebony*; Stab aus ~ *ebony wand*; schwarz wie ~ *ebony* (*hair*) ‖ ⟨fig⟩ (Negerin) *a*

bit of ebony **~baum** m *ebony-tree* **eben·ieren** vt [h] (Holz) *to ebonize* †**Eben·ist** m *ebonist*

·**Ebenmaß** n *symmetry*; *due proportion*; *poising*; *evenness*, *regularity*, *harmony* (*of a p's features*) ‖ ins ~ bringen *to harmonize* ·**ebenmäßig 1.** a *symmetric*(*al*); *duly* (od *well*) *proportioned*; *harmonious* **2.** adv *symmetrically*; *harmoniously*

·**ebenso** adv **1.** *in the same way*; *equally*; *the same*; ~ wie *in the same way as* (od *that*); *just as*; *the same as* (*I do not judge things the same as you do*); ich werde abreisen ~ wie er *I shall leave equally with him*; mit ~ eleganten wie unmißverständlichen Gesten *with gestures as elegant as they are clear*; ~ alt s wie *to be of the same age as* **2.** (ebenfalls) *likewise*, *as well*; *also*; *too*; → auch 1. a., desgleichen 2. ‖ alle Theater sind geschlossen, ~ alle Wirtshäuser *all theatres are closed as are* (od *and so are*) *all public houses*; (der Krämer verkauft jeden Tag ..) ~ der Fleischer (..) *so does the butcher* **3.** [vor a & adv] **a.** [vor a] ~ arm (gut) *just as poor* (*good*); ~ gefürchtet *equally dreaded*; ~ arm wie .. (*just*) *as poor as* .. e–e ~ wichtige P wie du *no less a p than you* **b.** [vor adv] ich möchte ~gern bleiben wie abreisen *I would as soon* (†*lief*) *stay as leave* ‖ ~gut *just as well*; *as well* (*we may as well start at once*); → sowohl ‖ ~lange (*just*) *as long* ‖ ~oft *as many times* (wie *as*); ~oft wie *no less than* ‖ ~sehr *just as much*; bei Goethe ~sehr wie bei Schiller, *with G. no less than with Sch.* ‖ ~viel *just as much*; ~viel wie *no less than* ‖ ~viel bedeuten wie (P) *to be on a par* (od *an equality*) *with*, *to be the equal of* (*a p*); (S) *to be equivalent* od *tantamount to* (*a th*) ‖ ~wenig (*just*) *as little*; ~wenig wie *not any more than*, *no more than*

·**ebensohlig** a ⟨min⟩ *horizontal*

·**Eber** m ~s/~ ⟨zoo⟩ (wild) *boar*; → Hirsch-≃, Wildschwein ‖ ~fleisch [n] *boar*; *boar's meat* **~esche** f ⟨bot⟩ *mountain ash*, *rowan*(*-tree*); → Sperberbaum **~fleisch** n *boar*(*'s meat*) **~raute** f, **~reis** n ⟨bot⟩ *southernwood*, *lad's love*, *abrotanum* [L]; → Artemisie f **~wurz** f ⟨bot⟩ *earline*

ebnen 1. vt [h] (etw) *to even*, (Rasen) *to level* ‖ (glätten) *to plane*, *smooth*, *surface*; *to make even* (od *level*, *plain*, *smooth*) ‖ (Wege) *to grade*; ⟨Am⟩ *to graduate* | ⟨fig⟩ die Wege f etw ~ *to clear the ground for a th*; e–r S, jdm den Weg ~ *to smooth* od *pave the way for* od *to a th*, *a p* **2.** ≃ n *levelling*; *planing*; *smoothing* ·**Ebnung** f = Ebnen; ⟨phon⟩ *smoothing*

Ebon·it n *ebonite* ‖ [in comp] *ebonite*; ~rohr [n] *ebonite tube*

·**Ebro** m ⟨Span⟩ (Fluß) *Ebro*

Ebulliosk·op *n ebullioscope*

Ecce Homo ⟨arts⟩ L *Christ before the people*

Echappement [eʃap'mɑ̃] n ⟨tech⟩ *escapement*

echauff·ieren [eʃɔ'fi:rən] vt (jdn) = aufregen, erhitzen

Echev·erie [-iə] f ⟨bot⟩ → Nabelkraut

Echin·it m → Seeigel

·**Echino-** [in comp] (stachlig) *echino-* **~d·ermen** [pl]; → Stachelhäuter **~k·aktus** m [L] ⟨bot⟩ *echinocactus* [L] **~k·okkus** m ⟨med⟩ *echinococcus*

Ech·inus m **1.** = Seeigel **2.** ⟨ant, arch⟩ *echinus* [L]

·**Echo** n ~s/~s **1. a.** *echo*; ~s hervorrufen (of sound) *to echo*; *to produce echoes*; (wie) im ~ wiederholen *or* wiedergeben *to echo* ‖ ohne ~ *echoless* **b.** (Radar≃) *return* **c.** ⟨fig⟩ ein ~ finden *to be echoed*, .. lebhaftes .. *to meet with a lively response*; .. finden bei jdm *to find* (od *evoke*) *a l. r. in a p* **2.** (P) er ist nur das ~ s–r Frau *he is a mere echo of his wife* **≃ähnlich**, **≃artig** a *echoic* **≃frei** a *anechoic* (*room*)

*·**echoen** vi [h] *to echo*; es echot *there is an echo* **Echolal·ie** f ⟨path⟩ (sinnloses Nachsprechen) *echolalia* ·**Echo-** **~lot** n *echo-sounder*; ⟨aero⟩ *terrain clearance indicator*; ⟨mil⟩ *sonar* | ~aufzeichnung, ~kurve [f] *echogram* **~sperre** f ⟨telph⟩ *echo-suppressor* **~zeichen** n (Radar) *pip*

·**Echse** f ~/~n ⟨zoo⟩ **1.** *reptile*; *saurian*; Riesen≃ *iguanodon* **2.** = Eidechse

·**echt I.** a **A.** (S) **1.** *real* (*silk*, *pearls*) ‖ *pure* (*gold*), *unalloyed* (*metal*) ‖ *natural* (*hair*) ‖ ⟨bot oft⟩ *common* (Jasmin, Lorbeer) **2.** (waschecht) *fast*, *lasting* (*colour*); waschechtes Blau *true-blue*; → Induline **3.** *authentic*, *genuine* (*signature*); *true* (*copy*); ein ~er Dürer *a genuine Durer* ‖ (etw) als ~ erweisen *to substantiate* (*a th*) **4.** ⟨übtr⟩ *pure* (*blood*) ‖ *natural*, *unaffected* (*language*); *pure* (*English*) ‖ *natural* (*talent*); *genuine* (*feeling*); *unalloyed* (*joy*); *unadulterated* (*praise*); *significant* (*difference*) **5.** ⟨math⟩ *proper* (*fraction*) **B.** (P) *legitimate*, *natural*, *true* (*child*); → rasse~ ‖ e–e ~e Frau *a womanly woman* ‖ *true-born* (Engländer) ‖ ein ~er Deutscher *a dyed-in-the-wool G*; er ist ein ~er Londoner *he was born and bred in London* ‖ *natural* (*poet*); *true*; *thorough-going* (*socialist*), *thorough-paced* (*gentleman*); = durch u durch → durch II. C. | ein ~er Kerl *a faithful fellow* od *chap* ‖ die ~e P, die er z s vorgibt *the real Simon Pure* | ~e Freude *true*, *unmixed joy* **II.** adv *truly* (*English*); *genuinely* ‖ ~ gefärbt *fast-dyed* ‖ das ist ~ Hans *that is typically* (od *just like*) *John*, *that is J. all over* ·**Echtheit** f **1.** *purity* ‖ *reality*, *real nature* (*of a th*); *trueness*; Stempel der ~ *hall-mark*; (Metall) mit dem St. der ~ versehen *to hall-mark* ‖ *authenticity*, *genuineness* (*of a document*) **2.** ⟨übtr⟩ *purity* (*of thought*, etc) ‖ *naturalness*, *unaffectedness* (*of feeling*) ‖ *legitimacy* (*of a child*) ‖ ⟨Lit⟩ (Offenheit) *sincerity*

×·**Eck** n [sonst fast nur in math. Fachwörtern u Eigennamen] = Ecke, → Drei≃, Recht≃, → über≃ ‖ Deutsches ~ (in Koblenz) *at the confluence of Rhine and Moselle*

·**Eck-** [in comp] *corner-*; *angle-* **~ball** m ⟨Ass ftb⟩ (freier) ~ *corner*(*-kick*) **~blech** n *gusset* **~brett** n *bracket*; *corner-shelf* **~fahne** f (e–s Fußballfeldes) *corner-flag* **~fenster** n *corner-window* | ≃l [n]: aus dem ~ ⟨fig⟩ *out of the tail of her eye* | mit jdm **≃fensterln** *to give a p the glad eye* **~flügler** m ⟨ent⟩ *vanessa* **~haus** n *corner-house* **~hölzer** n [pl] = Kanthölzer **~kegel** m (des Spiels) *corner-pin* **~klammer** f (f Papier) *corner-* od *hook-clip* **~loch** n ⟨billiards⟩ *corner-pocket* **~mann** m ⟨crick⟩ *slip*, erster (etc) ~ *first slip*; Feld des ~s *slip* ‖ weit zurückstehender ~ *third man* **~pfeiler** m *corner-pillar* ‖ ⟨fig⟩ *bedrock* (*of a policy*) **~pfosten** m *corner-post* (od *stake*) **~platz** m = Ecksitz **~säule** f *angle-column* **~schlag** m ⟨hock⟩ freier ~ *corner*(*-hit*) **~schrank** m *corner--cupboard* **~sitz** m ⟨a. rail⟩ *corner-seat* **~stange** = Eckfahne **~stein** m *corner-stone*; *quoin*; mit e–m ~ versehen *to quoin* ‖ ⟨cards⟩ = Karo ‖ ⟨fig⟩ *corner-stone*, *bedrock* **~stoß** m = Eckball **~trichter** m ⟨arch⟩ (Trompe) *squinch* **~turm** m *angle-turret* **~ventil** n *angle valve* **~verband** m ⟨arch⟩ *edge bond* **~winkel** m *angle bracket* **~zahn** m *canine tooth* **~ziegel** m *corner* (od *hip*)*--tile* **~zimmer** n *corner-room*

·**Eckart** m ⟨Ger, Lit⟩ ein getreuer ~ *a Faithful Eckart*

·**Eckchen** n ⟨fig⟩ = Ecke A. 1. c.

·**Ecke** f ~/~n **A.** (äußerer Winkel) **1.** (Spitze) *corner* (*of a table*), mit runden ~en *round--cornered* ‖ *angle* ‖ (*of* a wall, etc) *quoin*, *coign* ‖ (Käse≃) *wedge* ‖ (Kante) *corner*, *edge* ‖ (am Stehkragen) *wing* ‖ angeschliffene ~ (e–s Brillanten) *facet* **2.** (Straßen≃) **a.** *corner* ‖ an der ~ *at the corner*; Grundstück an der ~ ⟨Am⟩ *corner-lot* ‖ auf der ~ *on the corner* ‖ um die ~ *round the corner*; um die ~ biegen *or* gehen *to* *turn the corner* ‖ e–e ~ abschneiden *to cut off a corner* | (Biegung) *turning*, an der ~ *at the t.* **b.** ⟨übtr⟩ an allen ~n u Enden *everywhere, on all sides, on every side* ‖ **an** allen ~n brennen *to burn from end to end*; ⟨fig⟩ es brannte **an** allen ~n *there was a tremendous stir* ‖ an allen ~n *here, there, and everywhere*; es fehlt ihnen an allen ~n u E. *they are short of everything* ‖ **in** allen ~n u Winkeln *in every hole and corner* ‖ **um** die ~ gehen *to turn (round) the corner*; ⟨fig⟩ *to go west*; *to go* (od *drop*) *off the hooks* (= *to die*) ‖ jdn um die ~ bringen *to make* (od *do*) *away with a p, to put a p out of the way*; ⟨sl⟩ *to do a p in*; *to bump a p off*; sie wollten ihn um die ~ br. ⟨Am, fam⟩ *they took him for a ride* ‖ etw (Geld etc) um die ~ br. *to make away with, to squander* ‖ um die ~ verwandt *remotely related* (mit *to*) ‖ ich traue ihm nicht um die ~ *I do not trust him round the corner, I wouldn't trust him an inch* | **von** allen ~en u Enden *from everywhere under the sun* **c.** ⟨fig⟩ (Entfernung) *distance*, e–e ziemliche ~ *quite a distance*; ich will dich e–e kl ~ (*or* ein Eckchen) begleiten *I will go with you a short distance* **B.** (innerer Winkel e–s Zimmers etc) *corner, nook*; *recess*; in der ~ sitzen *to sit in the corner* ‖ (Kind) in die ~ stellen *to stand* od *put* (..) *in the corner* ‖ in allen ~n u Winkeln *in every nook and corner*; *in all quarters, everywhere*; Hans in allen ~n = Hans Dampf in allen Gassen, → Dampf 1. c. ‖ ⟨ftb⟩ = Eckball **C.** ⟨fig⟩ (Gegend) *corner, quarter*; die vier ~n der Erde *the four corners of the earth*; der Wind wehte aus allen ~n *the wind blew from all quarters* (od *sides*) ‖ e–e gefährliche ~ *a warm corner* ‖ in allen ~en suchen .. *high and low*

·Ecken- °**~gucker** m *corner-man* (od *boy*); *loafer*; neugieriger ~ *rubberneck* **~kragen** m *wing-collar* °**~steher** m *street-porter*, ⟨fam⟩ *corner boy* = Eckengucker

·Ecker f ~/~n **1.** ⟨bot⟩ *acorn* ‖ → Buch≃ **2.** ⟨Ger, cards⟩ ~n [pl] *clubs* [pl] **~ich** m ⟨for⟩ *mast proper*

×**·Eckergiek** n (Versteckspiel) *peek-a-boo*; → Ecke, gucken

·eckig a **1.** *angular*; (mst [in comp]:) *cornered* ‖ scharf≃ *sharp-cornered*, → drei~ ‖ ~e Klammer *square bracket* ‖ *square* (*chin, jaw, shoulders*) **2.** ⟨fig⟩ (P) *angular*; *awkward* ‖ *cantankerous, unaccommodating*

·Eckigkeit f ~/ *angularity* ‖ ⟨fig⟩ *angularity, awkwardness*

·Edamer Käse m *Edam, E. cheese*

ed·aphisch n ⟨bot⟩ *edaphic* **·Edaphon** n ~s/ *edaphon*

·Edda f ⟨Lit⟩ **1.** *Edda* **2.** [in comp] *Edd(a)ic* (*poems*)

°**·Ede** m ~n/~n *Ted(dy)* ‖ = Genosse

·edel I. a **1. a.** †*ligitimate*; *true* **b.** (adlig, vornehm) *noble* (*birth*); v edler Abstammung *of noble birth* od *extraction*; ein Mann v edler A. *a high* (od *well*)-*born man*; → Edle **c.** *noble, high-bred* (*horse*) **2.** ⟨übtr⟩ (S) **a.** *noble* (*countenance*; *name*) ⟨a. iron⟩ ‖ *aristocratic, famous, distinguished* ‖ e–e edle S, Tradition *a noble cause, tradition*; im edelsten Sinne des Wortes *in the noblest acceptation of the word*; ⟨engl⟩ die edle Kunst *the noble art* (sc of *boxing*) ‖ *elevated, noble* (*style*) **b.** (kostbar) *noble* (*metal*; *opal*); *excellent*; *generous, rich* (*soil, wine*); ⟨min⟩ *rich* (*vein*) ‖ ⟨mus⟩ *rich* ‖ ⟨com⟩ *superior* (*quality*); *rare*; *special* ‖ ⟨school fam⟩ *noble* ‖ edle Teile [pl] *noble* (od *vital*) *organs* od *parts, vitals* [pl] **3.** (of the mind, etc.) *noble* (*mind*; *action, sentiment*); *noble* (od *high*)-*minded* (*p*), *generous* (*spirit*); *lofty* (*character*); *magnanimous*; edle Gesinnung *nobility of mind, magnanimity, high-mindedness* **II.** adv *nobly* (*to act n.*); *in a noble manner*; *magnanimously* ‖ *magnificently* ‖ ~ entschlossen *magnanimously resolute* | oft [in comp] ~geformt *nobly formed*

·Edel- [in comp] **1.** [in Subst] *noble* **2.** [in Adj] **a.** *nobly* (*born*; *shaped*) **b.** *noble* (~-*minded* ⟨noble mind⟩ + -*ed*) **~bürger** m *patrician* ≃**bürtig** a = edelgeboren **~dame** f = Edelfrau ≃**denkend** a *high* (od *noble*)-*minded* **~erden** f [pl] *noble* (od *rare*) *earths* [pl] **~erzeugnis** n *superior product* **~erz** n *rich ore* **~falke** m ⟨orn⟩ *peregrine falcon*; *perfalcon* **~fäule** f *decay of ripe grapes caused by the* '~pilz' *Botrytis cinerea* **~fink** m ⟨orn⟩ = Buchfink **~frau** f *noble lady, noblewoman, gentlewoman, lady of noble rank* ‖ (Gemahlin e–s *baronet*, etc.) *Dame* **~fräulein** n *unmarried lady of noble birth* **~gase** n [pl] ⟨chem⟩ *noble* (od *rare*; *inert*) *gases* [pl] ≃**geboren** a *nobly-born* ≃**gesinnt** a *noble-minded* **~gleitsitz** m *medium force fit, wringing fit* **~haftsitz** m ⟨tech⟩ *medium force fit* ≃**herzig** a *noble-hearted* **~hirsch** m *stag* **~hof** m *mansion* (od *country seat*) *of a nobleman* **~holz** n *precious wood* **~kastanie** f ⟨bot⟩ (*edible* od *sweet*) *chestnut* **~knabe** m *page* **~leute** [pl] *noblemen, nobles* [pl] **~mann** m *noble, nobleman*; Hochland≃ ⟨Scot⟩ *duniwassal*; spanischer ~ *hidalgo* **~metall** n *noble* (od *precious*) *metal*; ~ in Barren *bullion* ‖ ~industrie [f] *precious metal industry* **~mut** m *noble-mindedness, magnanimity, generosity* ≃**mütig** a *generous, nobleminded, big-hearted, magnanimous*; *handsome* (*it was ~ of him to do*) **~obst** n *dessert fruit* **~passung** f ⟨tech⟩ *force fit* **~pilz** m = Champignon **~rassig** a ⟨hors etc⟩ *high*– od *true-bred* **~reis** n ⟨hort⟩ *slip fit for grafting* **~rost** m *patina* **~sinn** m = Edelmut ≃**sinnig** a = edelmütig **~stahl** m *special* od *high-grade steel* **~stein** m *precious stone*; *jewel*; (geschliffener) *gem*; mit ~en schmücken *to gem, to jewel* ‖ ~händler [m] *jeweller*; ~schneider [m] *lapidary* **~tanne** f ⟨bot⟩ *silver-fir* **~weiß** n ⟨bot⟩ *edelweiss, lion's foot* **~wild** n *red deer* **~zellstoff** m ⟨pap⟩ *textile pulp*

·Edeling m ~s/~e = Edle 1.

·Eden n ~s/ *Eden, Paradise*

Edent·aten [pl] ⟨zoo⟩ *Edentata* [L pl]

-eder [suff] ⟨math⟩ -*hedron* ‖ Hexa~ *hexahedron*

ed·ieren vt [h] *to edit, publish*

Ed·ikt n ~(e)s/~e *edict*

·Edinburg n (Hauptstadt Schottlands) *Edinburgh*; ⟨poet⟩ *Edina*

Editi·on f ~/~en **1.** *edition*; ~stechnik [f] *the technique of editing* **2.** ⟨jur⟩ *exhibition, producing* (*of a deed*)

·Edle 1. [der ~, ein ~r] m ~n/~n *man of noble birth, noble(man)* ‖ ⟨Ger⟩ ~r (als Titel) '*Edler*', ⟨engl⟩ *baronet* ‖ ⟨übtr⟩ die ~n [pl] *the noble-minded* **2.** *noble* | **die** ~ ~n/~n *lady of noble birth*

Ed·ukt n (Ggs Produkt) *educt* **Edukt·ion** f ⟨com⟩ *eduction*

·Efeu m ~s/~s ⟨bot⟩ **1.** *ivy* ‖ ≃bekränzt, mit ~ bewachsen *ivied*; *ivy-clad*; v ~ umwunden *wreathed with ivy* ‖ Sommer≃, Schnell≃ *mikania* **2.** [in comp] *ivy*; *hederaceous* **~blatt** n *ivy-leaf* **~ranke** f *ivy branch*

°**Effeff** n [nur in]: etw aus dem ~ verstehen *or* kennen *to have the knack of a th, to have a th at one's fingers' ends, to know the ins and outs of a th, to know a th inside out*

Eff·ekt m ~(e)s/~e **1.** Licht≃ *light effects* [pl]; Bühnen≃ *stage effect* ‖ ⟨film⟩ ~lampe [f] *effects lamp* | mit gr ~ *with great effect*; auf ~ berechnet *calculated for e.*; um ~ z erzielen *for e.* ‖ nach ~ haschen *to aim at* (od *to strive after*) *effect*; *to play to the gallery* ‖ gr ~ m *to cause a sensation, to produce a striking effect*; *to be effective* **2.** ⟨phys⟩ (Leistung) *effect, power* ‖

⟨el⟩ *effect* (*the Faraday e.*) ‖ (starker Einfluß) *impact* **∼apparat** m ⟨theat⟩ *effects projector* **∼beleuchtung** f ⟨bes theat⟩ *glamour lighting*; ⟨phot⟩ *effect* od *dramatic lighting* **∼haschen** n *striving after effect* **≃haschend** a *claptrap*, ⟨theat⟩ *stag(e)y* ‖ ∼e Aufmachung, ∼es Wesen *staginess* **∼hascherei** f *ostentatious display*; ⟨Am fam⟩ *grandstand play* ‖ *theatricality*; (in der Sprache) *claptrap* **≃voll** a *effective*; *impressive, striking*

Eff·ekten [pl] **1.** (*personal*) *effects, movables, goods and chattels* [pl]; *stock* **2.** ⟨st exch⟩ *securities, stocks* (*and bonds*), *shares* [pl]; *paper(-money)* | [in comp] stock **∼abteilung** f *Securities Department* (*of a bank*) **∼bestand** m *stocks* [pl] *on hand*; ⟨Am⟩ *stockholding* **∼börse** f *Stock-Exchange* **∼geschäft** n, **∼handel** m *Stock-Exchange transactions* (od *operations*) [pl] ‖ *stock-jobbing* (od *jobbery*) **∼händler** m *stock-jobber* (od *broker* **∼kurs** m *rate* (od *price, quotation*) *of stocks*, (etc.); *stock-rate* **∼liquidationsbüro** n *Stock Exchange Clearing House*; (in London) *Settlement Department* **∼makler** m *stock-broker* **∼markt** m *stock-market* **∼stempel** m *finance-stamp*

effekt·iv I. a **1.** (wirksam) *effective* (*blockade*); *efficient* **2.** (tatsächlich) *actual*; *effective, real*; *virtual* (Höhe ⟨com⟩); ∼e Leistung ⟨tech⟩ *effective power* ‖ ⟨com⟩ *actual*; ∼e Waren *actual* (od *spot*) *goods* [pl] **II.** adv *actually, really*; *indeed*

Effekt·iv- [in comp] ⟨com⟩ mst *cash* **∼bestand** m ⟨bank⟩ *actual balance* **∼geschäft** n ⟨com allg⟩ *trade in actual goods* ‖ ein ∼ *a cash-sale* (od *transaction*) **∼preis** m *cash-price* **∼stand** m ⟨mil⟩ *effective strength* od *part* (*of an army*); *number of effectives* **∼weizen** m *cash-wheat* **∼wert** m (Ggs Nennwert) *effective* (od *actual*) *value*

effektu·ieren vt [h] ⟨com⟩ (Aufträge etc) *to carry out, to execute*, ⟨Am⟩ *to fill*; (Kauf) *to effect*

Effet [e'fe:] m [Fr] ∼s/∼s **1.** ⟨billiards⟩ *side*; e–m Ball ∼ geben *to put on* [adv] *side* **2.** ⟨sport (ten etc)⟩ *screw, twist*; e–m Ball ∼ geben *to put a screw on a ball, to give a twist to a ball* | | ∼ball [m], ∼kugel [f] ⟨ten, golf, etc⟩ *slice*

in effigie [L] (verbrennen *to burn*) *in effigy*

effil·ieren vt [h] ⟨cosm⟩ *to thin* (*hair*) **Effil·ierschere** f *thinning shears*; e–e ∼ *a pair of th. sh.*

Effloresz·enz f ⟨bot & minr⟩ *efflorescence*

effloresz·ieren vi [h] *to effloresce*

Effusi·on f ∼/∼en *effusion* **Effus·ivgestein** n ⟨geol⟩ = Ergußgestein

eg·al 1. a **a.** *equal*; *uniform* **b.** °[pred] (= einerlei) das ist ganz ∼ *that makes no difference* ‖ es ist mir ∼ *it's all the same* (od *all one*) *to me, it's immaterial to me, it does not matter with me, I don't care* ‖ ganz ∼ wie, v wem, wohin (etc) *no matter how, by whom, where*; .. ganz ∼, wohin er geht *wherever he goes*; → einerlei **2.** adv **a.** ∼ schneiden *to cut in equal parts*; *to cut uniformly* (mit *with*) **b.** °·egal *always*; ∼ wiederholen *to repeat over and over again*; er rauchte ∼ weiter *he kept on smoking*

Egalis·ier- [in comp] *equalizing*; ∼maschine [f] *e. -machine* **egalis·ieren** vt [h] *to equalize*; *to make equal*; ⟨tex⟩ *to level*

·Egartenwirtschaft f ⟨agr⟩ (in the Alps, etc.) = Feldgraswirtschaft

·Egel ⟨zoo⟩ = Blut≃ **∼kraut** n ⟨bot⟩ *spearwort* **∼schnecke** f ⟨zoo⟩ = Ackerschnecke

·Eger 1. f (Fluß) *Eger* **2.** n (böhm. Stadt) *Eger* **·Egerland** n *Egerland* **·Egerländer** m ∼s/∼ *inhabitant of northwestern Bohemia*

·Egge f ∼/∼n *harrow*; schwere ∼ *drag* ‖ ∼nzinken [m] *harrow-tooth* **·eggen** vt/i [h] **1.** vt (Land) *to harrow*; *drag* **2.** vi *to harrow*; sich ∼ l (of land) *to harrow*

Ego·ismus m *egoism, selfishness*

Ego·ist m ∼en/∼en *egoist*; *selfish p*; *egotist*; *self-seeker*: abscheuliche ∼en *selfish pigs* **ego·istisch 1.** a *egoistic(al), selfish*; *egotistic(al)* **ego·zentrisch** a *egocentric, self-centred*; ∼es Verhalten *or* Wesen *egocentricity, self-centredness*

egren·ieren vt [h] (Baumwolle) *to gin* **Egren·iermaschine** f (Baumwoll≃) (*cotton-*) *gin*; *ginning-machine* **Egren·ierung** f *ginning*

eh [conj] **1.** = ehe **2.** ⟨dial⟩ = sowieso (∼ schon) **3.** seit ∼ u je *for ages*

†**eh** [intj] (oft in Frage) ∼? *eh? well?*

·Ehe f ∼/∼n **1.** *marriage* (mit *to*); *matrimony*; rechtmäßige ∼ *legal* od *lawful marriage* ‖ ⟨jur⟩ *wedlock*, in (außer) der ∼ geboren *born in* (*out of*) *wedlock*; während des Bestandes der ∼ *during coverture* ‖ → ∼bett ‖ ⟨ant⟩ Gott der ∼ *Hymen* ‖ morganatische ∼, ∼ z linken Hand *morganatic* (od *left-handed*) *marriage* ‖ ∼ zw Angehörigen verschied. Stämme *intermarriage* ‖ aus erster ∼ *by a first m.* ‖ ein Knabe aus ihrer ersten ∼ *a boy of her first m.*; viele Kinder aus dieser ∼ *many children by this m.* ‖ wilde ∼ *concubinage*; *common law marriage*; ⟨fam⟩ → Doppel≃; in wilder ∼ leben *to live tally, to have hopped the broom(stick)*; .. mit jdm *to cohabit with a p* ‖ → Kameradschafts≃ **2.** Wendungen: e–e ∼ anfechten ⟨jur⟩ *to contest the validity of a m.* → anhalten ‖ die ∼ brechen *to commit adultery* ‖ ∼n eingehen (of members of different tribes, etc.) *to intermarry with* (*the blacks*) ‖ e–e zweite ∼ eing. *to remarry* ‖ e–e glückliche ∼ führen *to live* (od *lead*) *a happy married life* ‖ eine ∼ scheiden *to dissolve a marriage*; die ∼ jds sch. *to divorce a p* ‖ e–e ∼ schließen (mit allem Zeremoniell) *to solemnize a m.*; e–e ∼ schließen mit *to contract a m. with, to get married to* (*a p*); ∼n w im Himmel geschlossen (Sprichw.) *marriages are made in heaven* ‖ die Ehe wurde getrennt *the m. was dissolved* ‖ in dem (stillen) Hafen der ∼ landen *to settle down to married life* ‖ in den Stand der ∼ treten *to marry, to get married*

·ehe [conj] *before*; ⟨poet⟩ *ere* ‖ ∼ daß sie sich ergäben, stürben sie *they would die before surrendering*; → ∼dem, ∼tunlichst

·Ehe- [in comp] *marriage–* ..; *conjugal*; *matrimonial* (*adventures*) **∼akt** m; den geschlechtl. ∼ vollziehen *to consummate the marriage*; Vollziehung des ∼es *consummation of the m.* **∼anbahnungsinstitut** n *matrimonial agency* **∼aufhebung** f *annulment of marriage* **∼auflösungsziffer** f ⟨demog⟩ *m. dissolution rate* **∼band** n ∼e [pl] *bonds of* m., *m.-ties, conjugal ties* [pl]; *m.-knot*; gültiges ∼ *valid m.* **∼berater** m *m. consultant* **∼beratung** f *marital counselling* | ∼sstelle [f] *m. c. council* od *bureau* **∼betrug** m *deceitful concealment of any disqualification for*, od *impediment to, a m.* **∼bett** n *m.-bed*; ⟨a. übtr⟩ (= Ehe) **≃brechen** vi [h] [nur inf; daher: ich breche (etc) die Ehe] *to commit adultery* **∼brecher** m *adulterer*; ∼in [f] *adulteress*; die –in ⟨bib arts⟩ *The Woman Taken in Adultery*; rückfällige –in ⟨hist⟩ *free lance* **≃brecherisch** a *adulterous* **∼bruch** m *adultery*; *misconduct*; ⟨jur⟩ *criminal conversation*; → Ehescheidungsprozeß ‖ ∼ begehen *to commit adultery*; *to misconduct o.s.* (mit *with*) **∼bund** m, **∼bündnis** n *marriage, matrimony*; *marriage-tie, matrimonial union* **∼darlehen** n *m. loan* **∼dauer** f bis z ersten Kind ⟨demog⟩ *interval between m. and the first birth* **∼delikt** n *misconduct*; → Ehebetrug, –bruch, Doppelehe **∼erschleichung** f ⟨jur⟩ *m. under false pretences* **≃fähig** a (nicht) ∼ (*non-*) *m. –able* (*population*) **∼feind** m *misogamist* **∼frau** f *wife, spouse*; (in Titeln) *consort*, → Gemahl ‖ ⟨jur⟩ *feme covert*; Stand der ∼ *coverture*

~freuden f [pl] *connubial joys* [pl] **~gatte** m (Mann *or* Frau) *spouse*; die ~n [pl] *the spouses* [pl]; → Ehemann; auf ~n lautender Grundstückstitel *tenancy by the entirety* **~gattin** f = Ehefrau **~gefährte** m *partner* **~gelübde** n *marriage-vow* **~gemahl** m *husband*; *spouse*; ~in [f] *wife, spouse* **~gesetz** n ⟨engl⟩ ~e [pl] *Marriage Acts* [pl] **~gesundheitsgesetz** n ⟨nazi⟩ (1935) *law for the preservation and safeguard of a healthy and racy stock* **~glück** n *marital happiness, connubial bliss* od *felicity* **~güterrecht** n → ehelich **~hälfte** f *marital partner*; m–e ~ *my better half*; ⟨hum⟩ *my rib* **~hindernis** n *impediment to m.*; aufschiebendes ~ ⟨jur⟩ *suspensive i. t. m.* **~joch** n *matrimonial yoke* ‖ das ~ auf sich nehmen *to do the double act* **~konsens** m *parental consent* (od *that of a guardian*) *to the marriage* **~kontrakt** = Ehevertrag **~krüppel** m ⟨hum⟩ = Ehemann **~leben** n *conjugal* (od *married, wedded*) *life* **~leute** [pl] *married people*; *spouses* [pl]; die jungen ~ *the young couple* **~lösung** f *dissolution of m.* **~mann** m *husband*; rechtl. Gewalt des ~s *marital power* **~mündigkeit** f *marriageable age*; (e–r Frau) ⟨jur⟩ *nubility*; *age of consent* (⟨engl⟩ *minimum age*: *16*) **~nichtigkeit** f ⟨jur⟩ *nullity of marriage* | ~sklage [f] *action for annulment of m.* **~paar** n *married couple* **~pakten** m [pl] = Ehevertrag **~pflicht** f *conjugal duty* **~prozeß** m ⟨jur⟩ *procedure in matrimonial matters* **~recht** n *marriage law* **~ring** m *wedding* (od *marriage*)*-ring* **~sache** f ~n [pl] *matrimonial matters* od ⟨jur⟩ *causes* [pl]; Gerichtshof f ~n *divorce-court* **~schänder** m *adulterer* **~scheidung** f *divorce* | ~sklage [f], ~sprozeß [m] *divorce-suit, action* od *suit for divorce*; → Urteil; Beklagte(r) im ~sprozeß *respondent*, Mitschuldiger im ~sprozeß (gegen e–e Frau) *co-respondent* | ~sziffer [f] nach -schließungen ⟨demog⟩ *number of divorces per new m.* **~scheu** f *misogamy* **~schließung** f *marriage* (zivile *civil m.*) ‖ *wedding*; *solemnization of marriage*; *ceremony of m.*; ⟨engl⟩ Erlaubnis z ~ *m. licence* | ~salter [n] ⟨demog⟩ *age at m.* | ~sdarlehen [n] *wedding-loan* | ~surkunde [f] *m. certificate* **~segen** m *nuptial benediction* od *blessing* ‖ *issue, children* [pl] **∸stand** m *married state, matrimony*; ⟨jur⟩ *wedlock*; in den ~ (ein)treten *to enter into matrimony* | ⟨Ger⟩ ~sbeihilfe [f], ~sdarlehen [n] *state dowry, wedding-loan* **~statistik** f *statistics* [pl] *of m.* **~stifter** m *match-maker* **~stiftung** f *match--making* **~streit(igkeiten)** f [pl] m *matrimonial squabbles, conjugal dispute*; kl ~ [pl] *little domestic* od *connubial tiffs and quarrels* **∸tauglich** a *fit to marry* **~tauglichkeitszeugnis** n ⟨Ger⟩ *certificate of qualification as required by the* 'Ehegesundheitsgesetz' **~vermittlung** f = Heiratsvermittlung **~versprechen** n *promise of m.* ‖ Verletzung des ~s *breach of promise* **~vertrag** m *m. settlement*; vorehelicher ~ *ante-nuptial settlement*; *m. articles* [pl] ‖ °**~weib** n = Ehefrau **∸widrig** a: ~e Beziehungen *illicit relations*; *misconduct* (*his wife was guilty of m. with N.*) **~zerrüttung** f *breaking up of a m.*

·**ehedem** adv *formerly*; → ehemals ·**ehegestern** adv = vorgestern

·**ehelich I.** a **1.** *conjugal* (*duty*; *right*); *matrimonial* (*difficulties*); *married, wedded* (*happiness, life*); in ~er Hinsicht *matrimonially* ‖ Wiederherstellung der ~en Rechte *restitution of conjugal rights* ‖ ~er Aufwand *or* Haushalt ⟨jur⟩ *joint household* ‖ ~er Gesamtgrundbesitz *tenancy by the entirety* ‖ ~es Güterrecht ⟨Ger⟩ *law relating to the rights of property of the spouses*; ⟨engl⟩ Gesetz über das ~e Vermögen der Frau *Married Women's Property Act* (1882) **2.** *legitimate, true* (*child*); ~e Geburt *legitimacy*; ~ geboren *legitimate*; Häufigkeitsziffer [f] der ~ Geborenen *legitimate birth rate* ‖ (Kind) f ~ erklären *to legitimate, legitim(at)ize* **II.** adv *matrimonially* ‖ ~ geboren *born in wedlock*, ~ verbinden *to join in w.*; ⟨sl⟩ *to slice* ·**Ehelichkeit** f ⟨jur⟩ *legitimacy* (*of a child*) | ~sanfechtung [f] *contestation legitimation* ‖ ~serklärung [f] *legitimation* (*of a child*) ·**ehelos** a = ledig ‖ ⟨ec⟩ *celibate, celibatarian*, jd, der ~ lebt *celibate* ·**Ehelosigkeit** f *single life* ‖ ⟨ec⟩ *celibacy* ‖ Verlängerung der ~ *postponement of marriage*

·**ehemalig** a *of ancient times* ‖ *late* (*bishop*); ~e Freunde *former friends* [pl] ein ~er Schüler der Schule *an old boy*, ⟨Am⟩ *a graduate* (*of Harvard*) ‖ *ex-* (*ex-combatant*); ~e Militär- *ex-army* (*huts*); die ~e Königin *the ex-queen* ‖ *former* (*ambassador, etc*) ‖ → früher ·**ehemals** adv *formerly*; *in former times*; *in the past*; *of old, of yore*

·**eher** adv **1.** *sooner, earlier, at an earlier time*; ich konnte nicht ~ k *I could not come earlier*; ich kann nicht ~ k als 7 Uhr *I cannot come sooner than 7 o'clock* (od .. *come before 7 o.*); umso ~, desto ~ *the sooner*; je ~, je lieber *or* je ~, desto besser *the sooner the better* ‖ ~ stürzt der Himmel ein *sooner the heavens will fall* **2.** [Steigerungspartikel: mehr; vielmehr] **a.** *rather*; ~ gelb als grün *rather yellow than green, yellow rather than g.* **b.** so wird es ~ gehen *this way will work more easily*; es geht ihm ~ besser *he is, if anything, better*; sie sah ~ (sogar) jünger aus, als vorher *she looked, if anything, younger than she had looked before* ‖ das läßt sich schon ~ hören *that sounds more reasonable* **3.** (lieber) *rather, sooner*; *first*; (er sagte) er würde ~ sterben *he said he should prefer to die*, .. *he should die first*; sie würden ~ sterben als sich ergeben *they would rather* (od *sooner*) *die than surrender, they would die before surrendering* ‖ alles andere ~ als das *anything but that*; ~ aus Vernunft als aus Liebe *from reason rather than from love*; ~ ein Hindernis als ein Vorteil sein *to be more of a handicap than an advantage* (f jdn *to a p*); ein Erfolg oder ~ ein Triumph *a success or rather a triumph*; (es ist nicht die Folge v ..,) ~ ist es die Ursache davon (..) *rather it is the cause of it* ‖ umso ~, als (*or* da) .. *all the more so because* (od *as*) ..; umso ~, als ich .. *all the more so that I* ..

·**ehern** a **1.** *brazen* (*image*); *of brass* ‖ das ~e Zeitalter *the Brazen Age* **2.** ⟨übtr⟩ *hard, strong, unbreakable* (*chains*); ⟨poet⟩ *pitiless* **3.** ⟨fig⟩ *brazen, shameless* ‖ mit ~er Stirn *brazen--facedly, brazenly*; *impudently*

·**ehest** adv; am ~en = ~ens ‖ er wird dir am ~en helfen *he is most likely to help you*

·**ehestens** adv *earliest, soonest*; *at the earliest* (od *soonest*) ‖ *the easiest*

·**ehetunlichst** adv *as soon as possible*

·**Ehr-** (→ Ehre) [in comp] **~abschneider** m *calumniator, defamer*; → Verleumder **~abschneiderei** f *defamation*; → Verleumdung **~auffassung** f (*sense of*) *hono(u)r* (*the boy's h. is a very high one*) **~begierde** f *desire for distinction* (od *h.*); *ambition* **∸begierig** a *ambitious* **~begriff** m *idea* od *conception of hono(u)r* **∸erbietig** a *reverent, reverential, respectful* **~erbietigkeit** f *respectfulness* **~erbietung** f *duty*; jdm s–e ~ darbringen *to present one's duty to a p* ‖ *deference* (vor *to*); *respect* (vor *for*), *reverence* (*for*); *veneration*; aus ~ vor *out of respect for*; mit der gehörigen ~ *with due reverence*; bei aller ~ vor .. *with all due deference to* .. **~furcht** f *awe* (vor Gott *of God*); *piety*; *respect, reverence* (vor .. *for the law*), tiefe ~ *profound reverence*; → Demut ‖ aus ~ vor *in awe of*; ~ gebietend a *awe--inspiring, awesome* ‖ ~ haben vor Gott *to fear God* ‖ (etw) mit ~ betrachten *to venerate*; jdm ~ einflößen, jdn mit ~ erfüllen *to inspire a p with* *awe, to awe a p*; v ~ erfüllt s vor *to stand in awe of*..; v ~ erfüllt vor dem Gesetz *law-abiding* (*p*); v ~ ergriffen *awestruck* ‖ ≃slos, ohne ~ *aweless*; *disrespectful, irreverent* ‖ ≃svoll a = ehrfürchtig **≃fürchtig** a *awe-filled, awestruck*; *respectful*; *reverential* **~gefühl** n *sense of h.* ‖ (Selbstachtung) *self-respect*; *pride*; k–n Funken ~ *no self-respect whatever*; jds ~ kränken *to hurt a p's pride* **~geiz** m *ambition*; übertriebener ~ *inordinate a.*; sich über alles hinwegsetzender ~ *vaulting ambition* (Shak) ‖ v ~ eingegeben *ambitious* (*plan*) ‖ (Strebsamkeit) *push* (*a man of p.*) ‖ berechtigter ~ *pride*; s–n ~ dareinsetzen z tun *to take a pride in doing* **≃geizig 1.** a *ambitious*; *high-flying*; *pushful, pushing* (*p*) ‖ ~e Bestrebungen *ambitions* pl; ~er Draufgänger *high-flier* (*–flyer*); ~es Streben *ambition* (nach *for*); in ~er Weise *ambitiously*; ~e Ziele h *to fly high* (od *at high game*); s–e ~en Ziele erreichen *to gain one's ambitions* | (aufstrebend) *aspiring* (*classes*); → aggress·iv **2.** adv *ambitiously*; ~ trachten nach *to aspire to* (od *after*) **≃liebend** a *honour-loving* **~sucht** f (*inordinate*) *ambition*; *ambitiousness* **≃süchtig** a *ambitious, filled with inordinate ambition*; *greedy of distinction* (od *honour*); ein ~er Mensch *an honour-seeker* **≃vergessen** a *without selfrespect*; *reprobate, unprincipled* **~verletzung** f *insult* **~verlust** m ⟨jur⟩ → Ehrenrecht **≃widrig** a *dishono*(*u*)*rable, disgraceful, disreputable* **~würden** f ⟨ec⟩ (Titel) Euer (Ew.) ~ *Reverend Sir* (⟨R. C.⟩ *dear father*); ⟨Ir⟩ *Your Reverence*; an Seine ~ Henry N. *to the Reverend Henry N.* **≃würdig** a *venerable, respectable, reverend, worshipful* **~würdigkeit** f *venerableness, respectableness*

·**ehrbar** a *hono*(*u*)*rable, reputable, respectable* (*man*; *character*; *life*) ‖ *chaste* (*maid*) ‖ (anständig) *decent, modest*; ⟨fam⟩ ein ganz ~er Kerl *a quite honest fellow* | **≃keit** f ~/ *hono*(*u*)*rableness*; *reputability, respectability* ‖ *decency, modesty*

·**Ehre** f ~/~n **A.** (äußere ~, Achtung durch andere) [a. pl] ~n **1.** (Ruhm) ⟨rel⟩ *glory*; z ~n Gottes *to the glory of God*; ~ sei Gott in der Höhe *Glory to God in the highest* **2.** (guter Ruf *or* Name; Ansehen) *credit, honour*, ⟨Am⟩ *honor*; *character, reputation*; *high respect* (od *esteem*) ‖ ⟨sl⟩ *kudos* ‖ ein Fleck auf jds ~ *a blot on a p's h.* **3.** (~nbezeugung) *distinction*; [oft pl] ~n *honours* [pl] ‖ militärische ~n *military h.s*; kriegerische ~n *h.s of war* ‖ nach ~n trachtender Mensch *h.-seeker* **B.** (innere ~, Selbstachtung, Ehrgefühl) **a.** *honour, self-respect*; *moral dignity* (od *rectitude*); *pride* ‖ ein Mann v ~ *a man of h.*; ein Gebot der ~ *a dictate of h.* ‖ die nationale ~ *national h.* **b.** (of women) *hono*(*u*)*r, chastity* **c.** *standard of conduct*; Standes≃ *professional honour*; Ritter≃ *knightly h.* **C.** (verblaßt) **a.** (Anstand) → D. 2. a. (in ~n) **b.** ⟨fam & com⟩ *compliment, pleasure*; *leave* → **D. 1. a. aller ~n wert** *quite honourable*; *very handsome* (*of you*) ‖ es ist mir e–e ~ *I deem it an honour*; es ist mir e–e ~, ich habe die ~ tun z können *I am privileged to do*; es ist mir immer e–e ~, wenn .. *it is always a feather in my cap when* .. **b.** jdm die ~ **abschneiden** *to speak ill of a p, to backbite, slander, vilify, libel, defame a p*; *to ruin a p's good name*; → ~ rauben ‖ → angreifen I. B. 2. ‖ jdm die ~ antun = .. erwiesen, → u ‖ jds ~ beflecken *to cast aspersions on a p*; *to defame a p* ‖ s–e ~ dreinsetzen z tun *to take a pride in doing* ‖ auf dem Felde der ~ fallen *to die on the field of h.* ‖ jdm gr ~ einbringen = zur ~ gereichen, → u ‖ ~n einheimsen *to gain h.s* (⟨sl⟩ *kudos*) ‖ mit ihnen (*or* mit dem Buche) wirst du ~ einlegen *they* (*the book*) *will do you credit*; damit wirst du (dir) k–e ~ einlegen *that will not reflect much credit on you* | jdm ~ **erweisen** *to give* (od *pay, show*) *h. to a p*; *to confer h. on a p*; *to do a p proud* ‖ jdm die ~ erweisen *to do a p the h.* (*to come*); *to do a p the compliment* od *pleasure* (*of coming*) ‖ würden Sie uns die ~ erweisen, ein Lied z singen? *would you favour us with a song?* ‖ jdm die kriegerischen ~n erweisen *to grant a p the h.s of war* ‖ jdm die letzte ~ erweisen *to render the last h.s to a p* | Herr u Frau N. geben sich die ~, Herrn X. .. einzuladen *Mr. and Mrs. N. request the pleasure of the company of Mr. X.* (*to dinner*) ‖ ⟨com⟩ ich gebe mir die ~ Ihnen mitzuteilen *I beg leave to inform you* ‖ der Wahrheit die ~ geben *to tell* (od *speak*) *the truth* | die ~ **gebührt** dir *the credit is yours* ‖ ~, dem *or* wem ~ gebührt *h. where* (od *to whom*) *h. is due*; *give credit where cr. is due*; ihm gebührt alle ~ *all h. to him* | jdm z ~ gereichen *to reflect great credit on a p* | (k–e) ~ im Leib **haben** *to have* (*no*) *self-respect*; → Leib ‖ ich habe die ~ *I have the h.* (z tun *to do, of doing*) ‖ ich habe nicht die ~, Sie z kennen *you have the advantage of me* ‖ mit wem hab ich die ~? *whom have I the pleasure of speaking to?* ‖ ich hatte schon die ~ *I had the pleasure already* ‖ ˣhab die ~! *good day!*; *good--by!*; † *Your servant!* | (viel) auf s–e ~ halten *to set* (*great*) *store by one's h.* ‖ jds Andenken in ~n halten *to hono*(*u*)*r a p's memory* | jdm ~ **machen** *to be a credit* (od *creditable*) *to a p, to do a p credit*; jdm alle ~ m *to reflect great credit on a p*; jdm k–e ~ m *to be discreditable to a p* ‖ sich e–e ~ daraus m *to deem it an h.* (*to do*) ‖ s–m Ruf ~ m *to live up to one's reputation* | jdm die ~ rauben *to take away a p's character* ‖ es s–r ~ schuldig s → ~npflicht ‖ s–e ~ darein setzen *to make it a point of h.* ‖ s–e ~ steht auf dem Spiel *his h. is at stake* (od *is affected*) ‖ s–e ~ verpfänden *to pledge one's h.* ‖ was verschafft mir die ~? *what gives me the pleasure* (*of your visit*)? ‖ s–e ~ wegwerfen *to fling one's h. away* **2. a. auf ~! bei** m–r ~! (*up*)*on my h.! h. bright!* ⟨Am⟩ *honest! honest Injun!* | **in** ~n *in h.*; (*to hold an office*) *worthily* (od *honourably*) ‖ dein Wort in ~n *with all due deference to your word* ‖ ein Kuß in ~n *an honest kiss* ‖ sein Alter in allen ~n *all due respect to his age* ‖ in allen ~n sagen *to say quite candidly* (od *without unfair motives*) | **mit** ~n *with h.*; *honourably, creditably* | **zu** ~n jds, e–r S *in honour of a p, of a th*; z ~n der Gefallenen *in h. of the fallen* **b. auf ~ halten** *to act with due regard to one's h.* | jdn **bei** der ~ **packen** *to put a p on his h.* ‖ in ~n halten *to hold in h.*; *to honour* ‖ e–e Prüfung **mit** ~n **bestehen** *to do* (od *to acquit o.s.*) *well in an examination, to come off with flying colo*(*u*)*rs* ‖ mit ~n aus e–m Kampfe hervorgehen *to come off honourably in a combat* | **nach** ~(n) streben *to aspire to h.* | darf ich **um** die ~ **bitten**? *may I have the honour* od *pleasure* (*of your visit*, etc.)? ‖ (jdn) **um** s–e ~ **bringen** *to dishonour*; (ein Mädchen) *to seduce, to violate* | jdm etw **zur ~ anrechnen** *to lay a th to the credit of a p*; ich rechne es mir z ~ an *I take credit for it* ‖ jdm z ~ gereichen *to do a p credit, to redound to a p's credit*; Ihr Besuch gereicht mir zu gr ~ *I take your visit as a great h.*; dies g. ihnen nicht gerade zur ~ *this reflects none too creditably on them*

·**ehren** vt [h] **1.** (achten) (jdn) *to honour*, ⟨Am⟩ *honor*; *to respect*; *revere, venerate* ‖ Ihr Vertrauen ehrt mich *I feel honoured by your confidence* ‖ sich geehrt fühlen *to feel honoured* (od *complimented*); → geehrt | (etw) *to respect, to regard with deference* ‖ (Gottes Namen) *to reverence* **2.** (auszeichnen) *to honour* (mit *with*); *to confer honour on* (*a p*)

·**Ehren-** [in comp] *honorary, unpaid* ‖ *honourable*; *of honour*, → ~kodex, ~mann etc ‖ *memorial* ‖ *complimentary* **~abzeichen** n *deco-*

ration; *medal* **~akzept** n = Ehrenannahme **~amt** n *honorary post* ‖ *honourable office*; *dignity* **≈amtlich** a *honorary, unpaid*; ~e Stellung → Ehrenamt ‖ adv ~ tätig s *to serve in an honorary capacity* **~annahme** f ⟨com⟩ *acceptance for honour* **~banquet** n *complimentary* (od *testimonial*) *dinner* **~begleiter** m *tour director* **~bezeichnung** f *honorific* **~bezeigung, ~bezeugung** f *honour, respect, tribute* (f *to a p*), [oft pl] ~en *honours*, etc. [pl]; → Ehre A. 3. ‖ jdm s–e ~en erweisen *to pay one's respects to a p* ‖ ⟨mil⟩ *salute*; jdm s–e ~ m *to salute a p*; ~en erweisen *to give a salute, to salute* **~bogen** m = Ehrenpforte **~bürger** m *honorary freeman* (*of a city*) ‖ ~recht [n] *honorary freedom* (*of a city*); jdm das ~ e–r Stadt verleihen *to bestow the h. f. of a city on a p* **~dame** f *maid of honour* **~degen** m *sword of honour* **~denkmal** n = Ehrenmal **~dienst** m (am Hofe) *honorary service* **~doktor** m *honorary doctor* (*of a university*) **~eintritt** m ⟨com⟩ *intervention on protest* **~erklärung** f *vindication of a p's character* ‖ (*full*) *apology*; e–e ~ abgeben *to make an a., to apologize* **~friedhof** m *memorial cemetery* **~gabe** f *complimentary gift*; *testimonial*; jdm e–e ~ m *to testimonialize a p* **~gast** m *guest of honour* **~gefolge** n *suite* (*of a king*); *retinue* **~geleit** n *escort of hono*(*u*)*r*; = Ehrengefolge **~gericht** n; ~shof [m] *Court of Honour* **~geschenk** n = Ehrengabe **~grad** m *honorary degree* **~halle** f *hall of honour*; *Pantheon* **~hain** m *memorial grove* ‖ °**~hand**! ⟨fam⟩ *honest Injun* (od *Indian*)!, *honour bright* **~handel** m *affair of honour* **~hof** m ⟨arch⟩ *principle courtyard* **~karte** f *complimentary ticket* **~kleid** n *festive* (od *honorary*) *dress* **~kodex** m *code of honour*; ~ des japan. Rittertums *bushido* **~kränkung** f *defamation*; ~ jds *insult to a p's honour*; *slander of a p* **~kranz** m *crown of honour* ‖ ⟨Rom ant mil⟩ *civic crown* **~kreuz** n ⟨Ger⟩ *medal* **~krone** f ⟨ec⟩ *crown of glory* **~legion** f [Fr] *Legion of Honour* **~lohn** m *honorary reward* **~mal** n *honorary monument*; *memorial*; ~ f die Gefallenen *war m.*; ⟨engl⟩ (*in Whitehall*) *the Cenotaph* **~mann** m *man of honour, honourable* (od *respectable, worthy*) *man*; als ~ handeln *to play the game* **~mitglied** n *honorary member* **~pflicht** f *honorary obligation*; [Ir] *geis* [pl *geasa*]; es ist s–e ~ *he is bound in h.*; durch ~ gebunden s *to be on one's honour* (*to do*); durch ~ g. *bound in honour* **~pforte** f *triumphal arch* **~platz** m *pride of place* **~posten** m *honorary post* **~preis** m **1.** *prize* **2.** ⟨bot⟩ *speedwell, veronica*; → Bachbunge **~rat** m *Court of Honour* **~recht** n *law of honour* ‖ bürgerliche ~e [pl] ⟨jur⟩ *civil rights* [pl] ‖ Aberkennung *or* Verlust der bürg. ~e *deprivation* (od *extinction, loss*) *of civil rights*; *civil death* ‖ ⟨engl hist⟩ *attainder*; jdn dem Verlust der bürg. ~e aussetzen *to attaint a p* **~retter** m ~ jds *vindicator of a p's honour* (od *character*) **~rettung** f ~ jds *vindication of a p's honour*; *whitewash*(*ing*) *of a p*; ⟨fam⟩ *face-lifting* **~rolle** f = Ehrentafel **≈rührig** a *defamatory, calumnious, slanderous* (*insult*) ‖ *disgraceful, shameful* (*conduct*) **~rührigkeit** f *defamation, calumny* ‖ *disgracefulness, shamefulness* **~säbel** m = ~degen ‖ ~! ⟨mil fam⟩ *honest Injun*; → ~hand **~sache** f *affair of honour* ‖ es als ~ betrachten *to make it a point of h.* ‖ es ist mir e–e ~ *it is my* od *a p. of h.* **~säule** f *honorary monument* (od *statue*; *memorial*) **~schänder** m *defamer, calumniator, libeller* **≈schänderisch** a *defamatory, calumnious* **~schuld** f *honorary debt, debt of honour* **~schuß** m *salute* **~sitz** m = Ehrenplatz **~schutz** m *patronage* **~sold** m *honorary payment* **~standpunkt** m *point of hono*(*u*)*r* ⟨a. Lit⟩, *cf.* Fr *noblesse oblige* **~stelle** f = Ehrenamt, -posten **~strafe** f ⟨Ger⟩ *punishment involving the loss of certain civil rights* ‖ ⟨mil⟩ *degrading punishment* **~tafel** f *memorial tablet* ‖ ⟨fig⟩ *honour-roll*; die ~ der Gefallenen *the roll of honour* **~tag** m = Respekttag **~tanz** m *complimentary dace*; ~ f jdn *dance inserted to honour a p* **~tempel** m = Ehrenhalle **~titel** m *honorary* (od *honorific*) *title*; der ~ e–s Stammvaters der Familie *the h. t. of an ancestor of the family* **~tod** m *honourable death* **~trunk** m *complimentary cup*; → Toast **~verleihung** f die ~en am Geburtstage des Landesherrn *the Birthday Honours* [pl] **~verpflichtung** f *honorary engagement* **≈voll 1.** a *honourable* (*task, mention*) **2.** adv *honourably* **~wache** f *guard of honour* **≈wert 1.** a *honourable, respectable*; *creditable*; *worshipful* (*company*) ‖ ~e Stellung *dignity* | ⟨engl⟩ ≈ (als Titel) *Honourable* (*Captain the Honourable N. N.*); Sehr ≈ (f Adlige unter dem Marquis) *Right Honourable* (*The Right H. the Earl of N.*); Höchst≈ (f Marquis) *Most Honourable* **2.** adv *honourably*; *creditably*; ~ handeln *to act straight* **~wort** n *word of honour*; auf mein ~ *on my w. of h.* ‖ jdm das ~ abnehmen *to put a p on his h.* (*not to do*); sein ~ geben *to pledge one's word* ‖ ⟨mil⟩ *parole, parole of honour*; sein ~ brechen *to break one's parole* ‖ auf ~ verpflichtet *on parole*; ein Gefangener, der sich auf ~ verpflichtet (nicht z fliehen) *a man on parole*; jdn auf ~ verpflichten *to parole a p* **~zahlung** f ⟨com⟩ *payment for honour*, → Ehrenannahme **~zeichen** n *badge of honour, mark of distinction*; *decoration*; *medal*; jdm ein ~ verleihen *to decorate a p*; mit ~ ausgezeichnet, im Besitz v ~ [pl] *medalled* (*p*)

·**ehrenhaft 1.** a *honourable, respectable, worthy* ‖ *honest, upright*; auf ~e Art u Weise *honestly* **2.** adv *honourably* ‖ *honestly*; sich ~ verhalten *to keep honest* | **≈igkeit** f ~/ *honourableness* ‖ *honesty, uprightness*

·**ehrenhalber** adv *for honour's sake* ‖ ⟨univ⟩ (abbr e.h.) *honoris causa* (abbr. *h.c.*) [L]; Doktorgrad ~ *honorary degree*; den juristischen Doktorgrad ~ erhalten *to receive the degree of LL.D, honoris causa* | nur ~ *for purely honorary reasons*

·**ehrlich I.** a **1.** (ehrenvoll) *creditable*; *honourable* (*peace*); *respectable* (*burial*); *decent*; *worthy*; der ~e Name *the good* (od *fair*) *name* (*of a firm*) **2.** (redlich) **a.** (P) *honest, straight, upright*; ~er (anständiger) Mensch ⟨fam⟩ *square shooter*; *plainspoken*; ~es (echtes) Mitgefühl *sincere sympathy*; °e–e ~e Haut *an honest fellow*; er ist e–e ~e Haut ⟨fam⟩ *he's a true penny*, ⟨Am⟩ *he's on the level* ‖ *conscientious, faithful, reliable* ‖ [pred] *above board*; ⟨sl⟩ *on the square* ‖ dabei (bei e–r S) ~ s *to play a th straight* ‖ ~ währt am längsten *honesty is the best policy* ‖ wenn ich ganz ~ s soll *to tell* (*you*) *the truth* **2.** (S) *honest* (*face*; *attempt*); *open, plain* (*speech*); *square* (*dealing*); *straight* (*answer*) ‖ es ist nicht ~ *it is not fair* od *cricket* (*to do*) **3.** °**≈es**: das hat ein ~es gekostet *that has required a good deal*; er lügt ein **≈es** zus *he lies like anything* **II.** adv *honestly*; *on the square*; ~ handeln *to act straight* (od *fair*); ~ h. gegen *to be honest in one's dealings with* (*a p*) ‖ es ~ meinen *to have honest intentions*; *to be reliable*; es mit jdm ~ m. *to act in a p's best interests*; ~ gemeint(e Ratschläge *advice*) *given in good faith* od *with the best intentions* ‖ ~ s–e Meinung sagen *to be fair and square, to be straightforward* (od *outspoken*); ~ gesagt, ~ gesprochen *honestly* (*speaking*), *to be honest* ‖ alles ging offen u ~ zu *all was open and above board* ‖ ~ spielen *to play fair* (od *cricket*), *to play the game, to play an honest* od *straight game* ‖ ~ überrascht *genuinely astonished* od *surprised* ‖ ein ~ verdienter Unterhalt *an honest living*; sich ~ durchschlagen → durchschlagen I. B. 2.

Ehrlichkeit f ~/ *honesty, straightness, uprightness; fairness*

·ehrlos a *dishonourable, disgraceful, infamous*; ein ~er Mensch *a bad character* **·Ehrlosigkeit** f *dishonourableness, disgracefulness, infamy*

·ehrsam a = ehrbar **≈keit** f ~/ = Ehrbarkeit

·Ehrung f ~/~en *compliment, honour, testimonial, tribute* (f jdn *to a p*); jdm e–e ~ erweisen *to pay a tribute to a p*

·Ei n ~(e)s/~er **A. 1.** *egg* ‖ Insekten≈ *insect egg* ‖ frisches, frischgelegtes; faules, schlechtes ~ *fresh, new-laid; addle(d), bad* (od *rotten*) *egg*; wie faule ~er riechen *to stink like rotten eggs*; jdn mit faulen ~ern werfen *to pelt a p with r. e.*; → Trink≈, Wind≈ ‖ rohes; (hart–, weich)-gekochtes ~ *raw*; (*hard–, soft-*)*boiled egg*; eingelegtes ~ *water-glass egg*; → Sol≈ ‖ ⟨cul⟩ gefülltes ~ *stuffed egg*; verlorene ~er *poached eggs* [pl]; → Rühr≈, Spiegel≈ ‖ ohne ~ *eggless* ‖ ~er legen *to lay eggs*; ⟨ent⟩ *to oviposit eggs*; → ~erlegend; mit ungelegten ~ern ist nicht gut Schmarrn kochen *you cannot make an omelette without breaking eggs*, → 3. b. ‖ → ausbrüten **2.** ⟨biol⟩ *egg, ovum* [L] [pl *ova*]; *ovale*; befruchtetes ~ *oosperm*; → Dotter **3.** ⟨fig⟩ **a.** das ~ des Kolumbus! *Sherlock Holmes!, elementary, my dear Watson!*; er fand das ~ d. K. *he just touched the button* ‖ (zerbrechlich) wie ein rohes ~ *egg-shell* [attr]; man muß ihn wie ein rohes ([österr] weiches) ~ behandeln *he has to be handled with kid gloves* ‖ sie gleichen sich wie ein ~ dem anderen *they are as like as two eggs* ‖ will das ~ klüger s als die Henne? *will you teach your grandmother to suck eggs?* **b.** wie auf ~ern gehen *to tread lightly*; *to walk gingerly* (od *warily*) ‖ er ist kaum aus dem ~ gekrochen *he is still unfledged*; ⟨Am⟩ *he is still in the shell* ‖ (er ist) wie aus dem ~ gepellt (*he's*) *as neat as a bandbox* od *as a new pin*; ⟨bes mil⟩ *quiff*; er sieht aus wie aus dem ~ gepellt *he looks spick and span, he looks as if he had just stepped out of a bandbox* ‖ kümmere dich nicht um ungelegte ~er *you never trouble trouble before it troubles you*; *don't worry*; ungelegte ~er zählen *to count one's chickens before they are hatched* **B.** ⟨übtr⟩ **1.** ⟨arch⟩ *ovolo*; *ovum* [L] **2.** °⟨aero⟩ *bomb, shell*; ⟨sl⟩ *egg*; leichte ~er *eggs*; schwere ~er *groceries*, ⟨Am⟩ *cookies*; ~er werfen *to lay eggs* (*in* ..) **3.** °~er [pl] (= Hoden) *balls, rollies, stones, nutmegs,* (*monkey*) *nuts, nick-nacks* [pl]; °jdm die ~er schleifen *to take the balls out of a p*; → ei **4.** °(= Mark) 20 ~er *twenty bob* **C.** [in comp] → Ei–, Eier–

ei [intj] ~! *ah! indeed! why!* ‖ ~, du bist krank, mein Sohn *why, you are ill, my boy* ‖ ~ ~! *now now!*; ⟨iron⟩ *fancy*; *just look*; *ah .. indeed*; '~ ~, sieh mal an', sagte er, 'seidene Strümpfe!' '*Ah*', *he said*, '*silk socks, indeed!*' ~ ~ sagte die Hegamme und siehe es war ein Knäblein! *twig and berries!* | ~ freilich *why, yes! to be sure!* ‖ ~ ja! *oh, yes!* ~ ja doch! *why, yes!, to be sure! of course!* ‖ ~ nicht doch! *don't* ‖ ~ nun! *why!* ‖ ~ was! *nonsense!* ‖ ~ warum nicht gar! *o indeed!* | °~ verflucht! *the devil! confound it!*

·Ei- [in comp] *egg–*; ⟨biol⟩ *ovi–, ovo–; ovoid; oo–* **~ausstoß** m ⟨biol⟩ *ovulation* **~bildung** f ⟨biol⟩ *ovogenesis* **~dotter** m *yolk, yelk* **~form** f *egg-form*; Figur in ~ *ovoid* **≈förmig** a *egg-shaped, oviform, oval, ovoid*; verkehrt ~ *obovate* **~gelb** n = Eidotter **~haut** f ⟨anat⟩ *amnion, caul* **~klar** n [österr] = Eiweiß **~leiter** m ⟨anat⟩ *Fallopian tube; oviduct* **~schwangerschaft** [f] *tubal pregnancy* **~pulver** n *powdered* od *dried, dehydrated egg* **≈rund** a *oval, ovate*; *elliptical* (*wire*) **~salat** m *mayonnaise egg* **~schnecke** f ⟨zoo⟩ *Egg-shell*; *ovulum* [L] **~schnee** m → Eier– **~teilung** f ⟨biol⟩ *cleavage*; → Furchung **~weiß** n → d.

·eiapop·eia [intj] ~! *lullaby! hushaby!* ‖ Kind durch ~ einschläfern *to lullaby a child*

·Eibe f ~/~n, **~nbaum** m ⟨bot⟩ *yew(-tree)* **·eiben** a *yew* **·Eibenholz** n *yew*

·Eibisch m ~es/ ⟨bot⟩ **1.** *althæa* [L]; *marsh-mallow* **2.** (Chinese) *hibiscus* [L]; *rose-mallow*; Syrischer ~ *Rose of Sharon* **3.** = Abelmosch

Eich- (→ Eiche) [in comp] *oak–* **~apfel** m *oak-apple* (od *gall*); *gall*; *gall-nut* **~baum** m *oak-tree, oak* **~hase** m ⟨bot⟩ (Pilz) *Polyporus* [L] **~hörnchen, ~kätzchen,** †**~horn** n ⟨zoo⟩ **1.** *squirrel, sciurine* **2.** [in comp] *squirrel(-hunt)*; *sciurine* | ~nest [n] *drey* **~ochs** m ⟨ent⟩ = Hirschkäfer **~pilz** m = Eichhase **~wald** m *oak-wood* (od *forest*)

Eich- (→ eichen vt) [in comp] *gauging* **~amt** n *gauger's office; Weights and Measures Office*; ⟨engl⟩ (Reichs≈) *the Standards Department* (*of the Board of Trade*) **~glas** n *gauge-glass* **~instrument** n *calibration tester* **~maß** n *gauge, standard* **~meister** m *gauger, sealer* **~sender** m ⟨wir⟩ *calibration transmitter* **~stab** m *gauging-rod* (od *rule*) **~stempel** m *gauger's stamp*

·Eiche f ~/~n **1.** ⟨bot⟩ *oak*; *oak-tree*; Gattung ~ *quercus* [L] ‖ Stiel≈, Sommer≈ *stalk-fruited oak*; Stein≈, Winter≈ *sessile-fruited oak*; Zerr-~ *Turkey Oak* ‖ kl *or* junge ~ *oaklet* **2.** (Farbe) *oak colour*; Dunkel≈ *Jacobean colour*; in Dunkel≈ *in Jacobean coloured oak*; Möbel [pl] in Dunkel≈ *Jacobean furniture*; ~ (mit Räucherbeize) geräuchert (Möbel) *fumed oak*

·Eiche f *gauging; adjustment; standardization* ‖ *gauge, standard* ‖ *calibration*

·Eichel f ~/~n **1.** ⟨bot⟩ *acorn* **2.** ⟨anat⟩ *glans* [L] (*of the penis*), ⟨vulg⟩ *bell-end, cleat* **3.** ⟨cards⟩ *club* ‖ ~ (alle ~karten [pl], ~farbe [f]) *clubs* [pl], ~ ist Trumpf *clubs are trumps*

·Eichel- ~bohrer m ⟨ent⟩ *balaninus* [L]; *oak weevil* **~entzündung** f ⟨path⟩ *balanitis* [L] ‖ **≈förmig** a *acorn-shaped, glandiform* **~häher** m ⟨orn⟩ *jay* **~kaffee** m *acorn-coffee* **~mast** f *oak-mast* **~maus** f ⟨zoo⟩ = Haselmaus **~schwamm** m ⟨bot⟩ = Stinkmorchel **≈tragend** a *glandiferous* **~tripper** m ⟨path⟩ *balanitis*

·Eichen n ~s/~ ⟨bot & biol⟩ *ovule* → Ei

·eichen I. vt [h] **1.** (Faß etc) *to gauge*; (Gewichte, Maße) *to adjust; to seal*; (Waren) *to stamp* ‖ (Metalle) *to assay* ‖ (prüfen) *to verify* ‖ → kalibrieren **2.** ⟨fig⟩ darauf bin ich nicht geeicht *that's not in my line* **II.** ≈ n *gauging*

·eichen a *oak* (*floor*); → Eichen– ‖ ⟨poet⟩ *oaken*

·Eichen- [in comp] *oak–* **~blatt** n *oak-leaf* **≈blättrig** a *oak-leaved* (*goosefoot*) **~bock** m ⟨ent⟩ *oak-beetle*, → Bockkäfer **~holz** n *oak; oak-wood* **~kranz** m *oak wreath* **~laub** n *oak-leaves* ‖ ⟨Ger⟩ das ~ (zum Ritterkreuz des E. K.) *the Oak-Leaves* (*to* ..) | °⟨hum⟩ ~ (f: Eigenlob) stinkt (*to a p who likes to blow his own trumpet*) *self-praise is no recommandation* **~rinde** f *oak-bark* **~spinner** m ⟨ent⟩ *oak-egger-moth*; → Glucken **~stuhl** m *oak chair* **~tisch** m *oak table* **~wald** m *oak-wood* (od *forest*)

·Eicher m ~s/~ *gauger*

Eichh·ornie [–iə] f ~/~n ⟨bot⟩ *Eichhornia* [L]

·Eichung f ~/~en *gauging*; ⟨opt⟩ *calibration*; → Eiche, eichen [vt]

·Eid m ~(e)s/~e **1.** *oath*; ⟨sl⟩ *davy* ‖ Vor≈ *promissory oath*; Nach≈ *assertory oath* ‖ falscher ~ *false oath*; e–n falschen ~ schwören *to perjure* (od *forswear*) *o.s.* ‖ Amts≈ *oath of office*; Lehns≈, Treu≈ *o. of allegiance*; *o. of loyalty* **2. a. an** ~es Statt *in lieu of an oath*; → eidesstattlich ‖ **auf** ~ (*up*)*on* (*one's*) *oath* ‖ **unter** ~ *under an oath*; → eidlich **b.** den ~ **ablegen** ⟨jur⟩ *to take the oath*; *to swear* (auf etw *to a th* [*a statement*]) ‖ e–n ~ ablegen *to take an* (od *one's*) *oath* (auf den Landesherrn *to the sovereign*; daß *that* ..) ‖ ⟨fam⟩ kannst du e–n ~ darauf ablegen? *can you swear to it*? ich lege e–n ~ darauf ab, daß .. *I take an oath that* .., *I swear that* ..; → beschwören, schwören | jdm den ~ abnehmen *to administer* od *tender an* (od *the*) *oath to a p*; *to put a p upon* (*his*) *oath*; → vereidigen ‖ jdm den ~ auferlegen = .. zuschieben, → u ‖ den ~ brechen *to break the oath* ‖ e–n ~ **leisten** *to take an oath*; *to swear*; *to swear an oath* (*that*); → ~ ablegen ‖ jd, der e–n ~ leistet *an oath-taker* ‖ jdn e–n leisten l *to swear a p* (auf etw *on a th*); *to swear a p in* ‖ jdm e–n ~ leisten *to take an oath to a p* ‖ den ~ verweigern *to refuse to take the oath* ‖ jdm den ~ zuschieben *to give a p the oath* **c.** etw **auf s-n ~ nehmen** *to swear to a th* | etw **durch** ~ bekräftigen, bestätigen *to swear a th* ‖ durch ~ gebunden sein *to be bound by oath* | jdn **in** ~ u Pflicht nehmen *to swear a p, to swear a p in* | **unter** ~ (*or* eidlich) aussagen → eidlich 2.; Sie sagen unter ~ aus! *you are under your oath* ‖ unter ~ verpflichtet s *to be under an oath* (*to do*); → eidlich

·Eid- **~brecher** m *perjurer*, ⟨Am a.⟩ *oath breaker* **~bruch** m (*wilful*) *breach of oath*; *perjury* **≈brüchig** a *forsworn, perjured* ‖ [pred] *guilty of perjury*; ~ w *to perjure* (od *forswear*) *o.s.*; *to break one's oath* **~brüchige** [der ~, ein ~r] m *perjurer* **~genosse** m *confederate* ‖ ⟨Swiss⟩ **~genossenschaft** f *confederation, league*; die Schweizerische ~ *Switzerland*; '*Schweizerische Eidgenossenschaft*' **≈genössisch** a *confederate, federal* ‖ *Swiss* **~schwur** m *oath* **~verweigerer** m ⟨engl hist⟩ *non-juror* (L) **≈verweigernd** a *non--juring*

†**·Eidam** m ~(e)s/~e = Schwiegersohn

·Eidechse f ~/~n *lizard*; Kletter≈ *gecko*; Schlangen≈ *seps*; ausgestorbene ~ → Dinosaurier ‖ → Agame, Leguan, Waran **~nwurz** f ⟨bot⟩ *Monarch of the East*

·Eider f **1.** (dänischer Fluß) *Eyder* **2.** ⟨orn⟩ = Eiderente **~dänen** m [pl] *designation of the Danish Nationalists before 1864* **~daunen** f pl [koll] *eider-down*; ~decke [f] *eider-down* (*quilt*) **~ente, ~gans** f ⟨orn⟩ *eider*(*-duck*)

·Eides- **~ablegung** f *taking an oath* **~abnahme** f *administration* (od *tendering*) *of an oath* **~fähigkeit** f; ~ besitzen *to be legally qualified to take an oath* **~formel** f *form of an oath* **~helfer** m ⟨hist⟩ *compurgator* **~leistung** f *the taking of an oath*; *oath-taking* (auf jdn *to a p*) **≈stattlich** a; ~e Erklärung *statutory declaration*; schriftliche ~e E. *affidavit* (L); e–e ~e E. abgeben über *to make an a. of* ..; ~e Versicherung *solemn affirmation* **~verweigerung** f *refusal to take an oath*

Eid·etik f ⟨psych⟩ *eidetics* [pl] **eid·etisch 1.** a *eidetic* (*ability, image*) **2.** adv (*to see*) *eidetically*

·eidlich 1. a; ~e Aussage *deposition* ‖ schriftliche ~e Erklärung *affidavit*; e–e ~e E. abgeben *to make an a.* **2.** adv ~ aussagen, bezeugen *to give evidence under oath*; *to swear an oath* (*that*; *to do*); (etw) *to assert* (*a th*) *on one's oath, to swear* (*to*) (*a th*) ‖ ~ gebunden s *to be on one's oath* ‖ ~ verpflichten *to bind* (*a p*) *by oath*; *to swear a p* (z *to*); *to swear a p in*; ~ verpflichtet *under an oath* (*to do*); *sworn* (*broker*); → vereidigen

·Eier- [in comp] *egg–*; ⟨biol⟩ *ovi–* **~auflauf** m ⟨cul⟩ *omelette soufflée* Fr **~becher** m *egg-cup* **~creme** f *custard*; ~ mit Karamellsoße *custard cream* **≈fressend** a *egg-eating, ovivorous* (*bird*) **~grog** m *egg-nog* **~händler** m *eggler, egg-dealer* **~kiste** f *egg-box* **~knappheit** f *dearth of eggs* **~kohle** f *egg-coal* **~kuchen** m **1.** *omelet*(*te*), *pancake*; ⟨Am⟩ (aus Buchweizen) *cake* ‖ ~teig [m] batter **2.** ⟨typ⟩ (*printer's*) *pie* **~kunde** f *oology* **~kürbis** m *vegetable marrow* **~landung** f ⟨aero fam⟩ *three-pointer, pretty perch, daisy-cutter* **~laufen** n *egg-and-spoon race* **~legen** n *egg-laying* **≈legend** a *oviparous* **~liqueur** m *egg-liqueur* **~löffel** m *egg-spoon* **~mann** m = Eierhändler **~öl** n *egg-oil* **~pflanze** f ⟨bot⟩ *egg-plant*; (Frucht a.) *aubergine* Fr; Frucht der ~ *brinjal, egg-plant*, ⟨cul⟩ *aubergine* **~pflaume** f *egg-plum* **~pulver** n *egg-powder* **~punsch** m *egg-flip, egg-nog* **~sack** m ⟨zoo⟩ *ovisac, egg-pouch* (od *sac*) **~schale** f *egg-shell* **~schlägel** m *egg-whisk* **~schnee** m ⟨cul⟩ *whites of eggs beaten* (*until stiff*), *whipped eggs* [pl] **~schneider** m *egg-slicer* **~schwamm** m ⟨bot⟩ = Pfifferling **~speis** f [österr] *scrambled eggs* pl; → Rühreier **~speise** f *dish made of eggs*; *egg-dish* **~spiegel** m *ovoscope* **~stab** m ⟨arch⟩ *egg and dart, egg and anchor*; *egg-and-tongue moulding* od *design* **~ständer** m *egg-stand* **~stich** m ⟨cul⟩ *royal* Fr **~stock** m ⟨anat⟩ **1.** *ovary* ‖ operative Entfernung des ~s *ovariectomy*; e–r Frau den ~ entfernen *to spay a woman* **2.** [in comp] *ovarian*; ~entzündung [f] *oophoritis* (L) **~tanz** m *egg-dance* ⟨a. fig⟩ **~teiler** m *egg-slicer* **~uhr** f *egg-timer, egg-glass*

·Eifel f (Teil des Rhein. Schiefergebirges) *Eifel*

·Eifer m ~s/ *eagerness, keenness, zeal* ‖ (Fleiß) *assiduity, studiousness*; *push* ‖ (Hingabe) *devotion* (f *to*); *enthusiasm* (f *for*); → Wett≈ ‖ brennender ~ *ardour* (f *for*), *fervour*; gr ~ *avidity*, mit gr ~ *with avidity*; mit ~ u Hingebung *with zest and abandon* | ⟨dero⟩ übertriebener ~ *officiousness*; *fussiness* ‖ blinder ~ *haste, rashness*; ⟨rel⟩ *bigotry, zealotry*; bl. ~ schadet nur *more haste less speed*

·Eiferer m ~s/~ ⟨rel⟩ *bigot, zealot*; *tub--thumper* ‖ *fanatic* ‖ (Pedant) *stickler*

·eifern vi [h] *to be zealous* ‖ ~ gegen jdn *to inveigh* od *declaim* (od *exclaim*) *against a p* ‖ ~ nach etw *to strain after* od *for*; *to strive for, to be a stickler for a th* ‖ → er~, wett~ **·eifernd** a *zealous* (nach *for*) ‖ *tub-thumping* (*orator*)

·Eifersucht f ~ (zw Liebenden) *jealousy* (auf *of, towards*) | *envy, grudge*; → Neid ‖ ~sanwandlung [f] *fit of jealousy* **Eifersüchtel·ei** f ~/~en [mst pl] ~en (*mean*) *envies, jealousies, rivalries* [pl] (between) **·eifersüchtig 1.** a *jealous* (auf *of*) ‖ *envious, emulous* (auf *of*) **2.** adv *jealously*; *with jealousy* ‖ ~ wachen über *to keep tabs on* ..

·Eiffelturm m *Eiffel Tower*

·eifrig 1. a *zealous, zestful* (*adherent*); *eager, keen* (*observer*); *avid* (*smoker*); *great* (*dancer*); ~ z tun *eager to do, keen to do* (od *on doing*); dienst~ *full of zeal*; übertrieben dienst~ *officious, fussy, assiduous, studious*; *pushing*; *devoted*; *enthusiastic, warm*; → rührig, betriebsam ‖ ~er Angler *zealot of the rod*; ~er Verfechter *stickler* (e–r S *for a th*) ‖ ~es Bemühen *endeavour*; *studiousness*; ~es Verlangen *anxiety* (nach *for*) **2.** adv *eagerly, zealously* ‖ ~ bedacht *zealous* (auf *for*; *to do*); *studious* (auf *of*; *to do*); ~ bestrebt *anxious* (nach *for*; *to do*); ~ bemüht sein *to do one's best endeavours*; .. s um *to hustle for* ‖ sich [acc] ~ an etw m *to knuckle down to a th*

·eigen a **A.** [attr] **1.** (den Besitz bezeichnend) *own* [⟨engl⟩ nur nach pron poss (→ B. 1. a.) *or* flexivischem Genetiv, daher]: ein ~es Haus *a house of one's own* | *non-public* **a.** (P) mein ~es Haus *my own house*; sie h ein ~es Haus *they have a house of their own*; wir h k–e ~en Kinder *we have no children of our own* ‖ mit ~en Augen *with one's own eyes* ‖ → Faust ‖ ⟨fig⟩ auf ~en Füßen stehen *to stand on one's own legs*; auf ~e Füße gestellt w *to come into one's own* ‖ ⟨fig⟩ er wird es am ~en Leibe erfahren *he will have to suffer for it* ‖ in (höchst)~er P *in one's own p*; *bodily* ‖ die Rücksicht auf das ~e Selbst *the respect to self* ‖ jdm etw **zu** ~ geben *to give a th* *to a p for his own*; sich etw Neues zu ~ m *to adopt sth new* | er ist sein ~er Arzt *he is his own doctor* || sein ~er Herr s *to be one's own man* od *master* | sein ~er Gedanke *his own idea, an i. of his own*; ein Mensch mit ~en Gedanken *an independent mind* | **aus** ~em Antrieb *of one's own accord*; (*to do a th*) *on one's own* || auf ~e Gefahr *at one's own risk* || auf ~em Kiel (of a ship) *on her own bottom* || auf ~e Kosten *at a p's own cost* od *expense* || aus ~er Kraft *on one's own* || aus ~er Macht *on one's own authority* | k–e ~en **Mittel** h *to have no resources of one's own* || f ~e Rechnung *on one's own account* | ⟨com⟩ ~es Akzept *one's own acceptance* || ~er Wechsel → Eigenwechsel | ⟨mil⟩ mit ~en Mitteln *with organic resources*; ~e Truppen *friendly troops* **b.** (S) der Stern strahlt kein ~es Licht aus *the star gives out no light of its own* || das Buch hat e–n ganz ~en Wert *the book has a value all its own* (od *a value of its own*) **2.** (~tümlich, charakteristisch) **a.** *individual* (*style*); e–e ~e Art *a particular way*; er hat so s–e ~e Art *he has a way all his own* **b.** die ihm ~e Natur *his own peculiar temperament*; mit dem ihm so ~en höhnischen Lächeln *with that sneering smile peculiarly his* (od *..smile of his*; *..smile characteristic of him*); diese ihm ~en knochigen Hände *those bony hands of his* || ein der Stadt ~er Reiz *a charm peculiar* (od *proper, special*) *to the city*; → B. 1. b. || art~ *specific* **3.** (besonder; persönlich) *special* (*room*); *separate*; *private* (*property*) || zum ~en Gebrauch *for private use*; m–e ~e Meinung *my personal opinion* || ~e Gesetzgebung *domestic law* **4.** (seltsam) *curious, odd, peculiar, queer, strange*; ein ~es Wesen *a strange being*; → komisch || es ist e–e ~e S um den Fortschritt *it's a strange th about progress* **5.** (wählerisch) *delicate, fastidious* (*taste*); *squeamish*; übertrieben ~ *pernickety*; → genau, peinlich **6.** (bedenklich) *delicate, nice*; *ticklish*; e–e ~e S *a nice question* **7.** (in gewisser Art u Weise) → ~artig; *a sort of ..., .. in a way* **8.** → leib~ **B.** [pred] **1.** *own* [nur nach pron poss, daher]: z ~ *of one's own* **a.** mein ~ *my own, mine* || etw nicht als s ~ anerkennen *to disown a th*; ein Kind als (sein) ~ annehmen *to adopt a child* || darf ich es mein ~ nennen? *may I have it for my own*? || es wird s ~ w *it will be his own, it will be his* **b.** jdm z ~ *of one's own*; ein Haus z ~ h *to have a house of one's own* || sich e–r S ganz z ~ geben *to devote o.s. entirely to a th* || sich (etw) z ~ m *to make* (*a th*) *one's own*; *to accept* (*an idea*); sich [dat] jds Meinung z ~ m *to embrace a p's opinion*; → aneignen, (in sich) aufnehmen **2.** (als Besitz ~) jdm ~ s *to be peculiar* (od *proper*) *to a p*; (of rights) *to be vested in a p*; (of qualities) *to be inherent in a p* || ein Lächeln, das ihm so recht ~ war *a smile so peculiarly his* || Wildheit ist den Tigern ~ *ferocity is proper to tigers* | e–r Stadt ~ s *to be peculiar* (od *special*) *to a city* || e–r S ~ s *to inhere in a th* **3.** (seltsam) *queer, strange*; *funny*; es ist ~, daß .. *it is strange* od *funny that* .. (*should* ..); mir wurde so ~ z Mute *I felt so strange* (od *funny*) **4.** (wählerisch) *fastidious, particular, squeamish*; ⟨fam⟩ *pernickety*; sehr ~ s in (*or* betreffs) *to be very squeamish about, as to*; übertrieben ~ *fussy, finical, finicking, finicky* (in *about*) **C.** [abs] **1.** er besitzt nichts ≗s *he has nothing of his own* || aus ~em drauflegen *to pay out of one's own pocket* **2.** ⟨poet⟩ = Eigentum

·**Eigen-** **~art** f ~/~en *characteristic, quality*; charakterliche ~ *character, temperament* (*of a p*); ~en [pl] *ways* || *characteristic* (od *peculiar, special*) *features* [pl] (*of a people*); deutsche ~ *the peculiarity of the German character* || künstlerische ~ *originality* | *character* (*of a country*) || (*particular*) *way*; die ~en des Krieges *the ways of war* | (Angewohnheit) *trick* (*the eye has the t. of fluttering*); *way* **≗artig 1.** a *curious, funny, peculiar, quaint, queer, strange*; *unaccountable*; e–e ~e Schönheit *a beauty of one's own*; (*a passion*) *of its own* || ⟨sl⟩ *rum*(*my*); mir wurde ganz ~ z Mute *I felt quite strange*; es ist ~, daß .. *it is strange that* (.. *should* ..); äußerst ~ *curiously enough* **2.** adv *curiously, strangely* **~artigkeit** f *curiousness, strangeness* **~bedarf** m *one's own requirements* [pl] **≗belüftet** a *self-cooled*, ⟨Am⟩ *self-ventilated* **~bericht** m; ~ unserer Zeitung *report from our own correspondent* **~betrieb** m *one's own management* **~bewegung** f ⟨mech⟩ *proper* od *individual motion*; (*to have*) *a movement of one's own* | ~szeit [f] (z. B. Radar) *characteristic time* **~brötel·ei** f *quaint* (od *odd, eccentric*) *ways* [pl] **~brötler** m *queer* (od *eccentric*) *p*; *odd fish*; *oddity, original*; *square-toes* [pl] [sg konstr] || *outsider* || *nonconformist* **≗brötlerisch** a *odd, queer*; *square-toed* **~dasein** n *self-existence* **~dünkel** m *egotism, self-conceit*; krankhafter ~ *egomania* (L) **~empfindlichkeit** f ⟨phot⟩ *characteristic sensitivity* **~energie** f *proper e.* **~erregung** f ⟨tech⟩ *self-excitation* **~finanzierung** f ⟨com⟩ *financing out of one's own capital* **~frequenz** f ⟨wir⟩ *natural fr.* **~geschwindigkeit** f ⟨aero⟩ *true airspeed*, angezeigte ~ *indicated airspeed* (*IAS*) **≗gesetzlich** a *having its own laws* **~gesetzlichkeit** f ⟨biol⟩ *autonomy, autonomism, organic independence* **~gewicht** n *dead weight*; *specific weight*; (Leer–) ⟨com⟩ *tare* (*of vehicle*); *empty weight* **~gut** n *allodium* (L); *estate in fee simple*; (nach dem 1. Weltkriege) *freehold* **~handel** m *trade on one's own account* **≗händig 1.** a; ~e Schrift (*or* Unterschrift) *autograph, one's own handwriting* (od *signature*) || *holographic* (*will*) || ~e Übergabe *personal delivery* **2.** adv **a.** *personally*; (auf Briefen etc) *private* **b.** *with one's own hand*; ~ geschrieben *autograph* (*letter*), *autographic*(*al*); ~ unterschrieben (u besiegelt) *under one's hand* (*and seal*); *signed in his* (*our, their*) *own hand* [sg!] || ~ trainiert *hand-trained* **~heim** n; ein ~ *a house of one's own, a separate h.*; ⟨off⟩ *owner-occupied dwelling* | ~besitzer [m] *owner-occupier* **~kapazität** f *natural cap.* **~kapital** n ⟨bal⟩ (*our*) *capital resources* || bei e–m Drittel ~ *one third equity* (*in the property*) *being purchased* **~leben** n *life of one's own*; ⟨bot⟩ *organic life* || (seelisches) *inner life* (*of a p*) **~liebe** f *self-love*; ⟨psych⟩ krankhafte ~ *narcissism* **~lob** n *self-praise*; ~! *he's tooting his own horn*; ~ stinkt *self-praise is no commendation* **≗mächtig 1.** a *arbitrary*, ~e Entschlüsse fassen *to make a. decisions*; *autocratic, dictatorial*; *high-handed, despotic* **2.** adv *arbitrarily*; (*to act*) *autocratically, despotically* || *without having* (*official*) *authority* || ~ verfahren *to take an action on one's own responsibility* || sich ~ Recht verschaffen *to take the law into one's own hands* **~name** m ⟨gram⟩ *proper name* (od *noun*) **~nutz** m *self-interest, selfishness, egoism* **≗nützig 1.** a *selfish, self-benefiting, self-seeking*; *egoistic*(*al*) **2.** adv *egoistically* **~nützigkeit** f *self-interestedness, egotism, selfishness* **~peilung** f *self-bearing*, ⟨aero⟩ *air-to-ground direction finding*; *homing* **~periode** f ⟨el⟩ *natural* od *free period of circuit* **~produktion** f *home production* **~resonanz** f ⟨el⟩ *natural* od *period resonance* **~schwingung** f ⟨phys⟩ *self-oscillation*; *characteristic vibration*; *natural oscillation* | ≗sfrei [a] ⟨el⟩ *strongly damped* **~sinn** m *obstinacy, stubbornness, wilfulness*; *perversity* || das ist nur ~ v ihm *that's only this stubbornness of his* || sie ist ein kl ~ *she will always have her own way* **≗sinnig 1.** a *headstrong, hardheaded*, ⟨fam⟩ *bullheaded, pigheaded*; *obdurate, obstinate, obstreperous*; *stubborn* (*as a mule*); *wayward, wilful*; *unreason-*

able; *unyielding*; *intransigent*, *inflexible*, *uncompromising*; *set in one's ways* || → eigenwillig, launisch **2.** adv *obstinately*, *stubbornly* **~staatlichkeit** f (*autonomous*) *statehood* **~ständig** a ⟨arts⟩ *original* **~start** m ⟨aero⟩ *non-assisted take-off* **~strom** m *own electricity* **≗ventiliert** a = –belüftet **~veredelungsverkehr** m ⟨cust⟩ *customable goods which have been cleared for processing to be made for a firm's own account* **~verständigung(sanlage** f) f ⟨telph⟩ *interphone*; ⟨aero⟩ *audio(-)control*, *intercom(munication)* **~wechsel** m ⟨com⟩ *promissory note* **~wert** m *intrinsic value*; ⟨at⟩ *eigenvalue* **~wille** m *self--will*, *wilfulness* **≗willig 1.** a *opinionated*, *opinionative*; *individual*; *dogmatic*; *unorthodox*; *self-willed*, *wilful*; → eigensinnig **2.** adv *wilfully* **~willigkeit** f *opinionatedness*, *wilfulness*; *stark individuality* **~zustand** m ⟨at⟩ *eigenstate*

·Eigenheit f ~/~en **1.** (Eigentümlichkeit) *characteristic* (od *peculiar*) *quality*; *peculiarity* (*of a p*) || *property* (*of a th*; *of glass*, etc.); sprachliche ~ *idiom*; *idiomatic expression* (od *turn*) | ⟨dero⟩ [mst pl ~en] kl ~en im Benehmen *little peculiarities* [pl] (im Benehmen *of manner*); *idiosyncrasies* [pl] **2.** (Seltsamkeit) *oddity*, *peculiarity*, *queerness*, *singularity*, *strangeness* **3.** *fastidiousness*, *particularity* (in etw *as to a th*)

·eigens adv *particularly*; *express(ly)*, (*e*)*specially*; er reiste ~ nach B. *he made a special trip to B.*; *on purpose* (nach B. k) || ~, damit .. *on purpose that ..* || ~ f den *or* zu dem Zweck *for that particular purpose*; *for the nonce*; ein ~ geprägtes Wort *a nonce-word*

·Eigenschaft f ~/~en **1.** (P) *quality* (*the –ties of a hero*); *attribute* (*an a. of God*); *characteristic* || (S) *property* (*the –ties of iron*), *quality* || besondere ~ *peculiarity* (*a p. of German music is ..*); *point* **2.** (verblaßt) *capacity*, *character*, *position*; in dieser ~ *in this capacity*; in s–r ~ als Bürger, Individuum *in his civil*, *individual capacity*; in s–r ~ als Vorsitzender *in his capacity as chairman*, *qua chairman*; der Staat in s–r ~ als soziale Form *the state qua establishment* **~swort** n ⟨gram⟩ *adjective* || durch ein ~ ausgedrückt *adjectival*; in Form e–s ~s *adjectivally*

·eigentlich I. a **1.** (Ggs übertragen) *literal meaning*; *primary*; im ~en Sinne (des Wortes) *in the literal* (od *strict*) *sense* (*of the word*) || (*his*) *real* (*name is J.*) || → wahr **2.** (wirklich) *proper* (hinter dem Subst.); die ~e Kunst *art proper*; es gehört nicht zur ~en Literatur *it does not belong to literature proper* || *actual*, *real*; der ~e Herrscher *the virtual ruler* (: *the Prime Miniter is the v. r. of the country*) || s–e ~en Worte *his exact words* || der ~e Wert *the intrinsic value* || das ≗e *the actual matter* od *business at hand* **II.** adv **1.** *properly*; *properly* (od *strictly*) *speaking* **2.** (v Rechts wegen) *by rights* (*it ought to be mine by r.*) **3.** (wirklich) *actually*, *really*, *technically*; *virtually*; *in fact* **4.** (verblaßt) was hat sich ~ ereignet? *what has happened exactly*? || was soll das ~ (bedeuten)? *what do you mean*? *what do you mean you are doing*? *what is the use of that*? || was willst du ~ ? *now*, *now* (od *come now*), *what is it you want*?

·Eigentum n ~(e)s/≗er **1.** ⟨allg⟩ *property* || bewegliches ~ *personal pr.* (od *estate*); geistiges ~ *literary pr. personalty*; *chattels*, *movables*; *effects* [pl] || unbewegliches ~ *real pr.* (od *estate*), *realty*; *immovables*; souveräne Gewalt über Privat≗ ⟨Am⟩ *right of Eminent Domain* || ihr ~ *her belongings* [pl]; dies ist mein ~ *this is my pr.*, *this is mine*, *this belongs to me* || z unbeschränktem ~ besitzen ⟨jur⟩ *to have and to hold .. absolutely and forever* **2.** (Besitzung) *possession*; *estate*; → Eigengut **·Eigentümer** m ~s/~ *owner*, *proprietor*, *holder* (*of a bill*) || v ~ bewohnt *in owner-occupation* **~in** f ~/~nen *proprietress* || → Eigentums–

eigent·ümlich I. a **1.** = eigen A. 2. b. **2.** (seltsam) *odd*, *peculiar*, *quaint*, *queer*, *strange*; *funny*; *eccentric*; es ist ~, daß *it is strange that* (.. *should* ..); → eigen B. 3., eigenartig **II.** adv (seltsam) (*to behave*) *peculiarly*; *queerly*; *strangely* || es berührt mich ~ *it strikes me as strange* (*that* ..); *I am surprised to see* (od *find*) (*that* ..) **~erweise** adv *curiously enough*

Eigent·ümlichkeit f ~/~en **1.** *peculiarity*; *characteristic quality*, *peculiar feature* || sprachliche ~ *idiom* || typische ~ *character* || abnorme ~ *twist*, *abnormality* **2.** (Seltsamkeit) *oddity*, *peculiarity* (an jdm *about a p*); *queerness*; *strangeness*; ~en im Benehmen *peculiarities of manner*

·Eigentums- *proprietary*, *proprietorial* (*right*) **~anspruch** m *claim of ownership* **~begriff** m *conception of property* **~klage** f *replevin*; ~ erheben *to replevin* [vi] **~lehre** f *theory of property* **~merkmal** n *earmark* **~recht** n ⟨jur⟩ *right of ownership*, *proprietary right*, *ownership*, *proprietorship* **~steuer** f *property-tax* **~übergang** m *devolution of pr.* **~übertragung** f *property* od *title transfer* **~urkunde** f *title deed*; *tranfer of ownership*; ⟨jur⟩ (Rechtsänderung) *change of title* **~vorbehalt** m *reservation of property* od *title*; *hold on pr. reservation* **~wohnung** f *owner--occupied apartment* od *flat*; *flat of one's own*; *freehold flat* || ~en [pl] *co-operative apartments* | ~sinhaber [m] *owner-occupier* || ~sgesellschaft [f] *condominium* [pl *–nia*]

·eignen vt/i [h] **I.** vt **1.** ⟨poet⟩ (etw) *to have*, *to possess* **2.** mst [pass] geeignet s = sich ~ || es f geeignet halten *to think proper* (od *fit*) (*to do*) || → geeignet **3. sich** ~ *to be* od *prove suitable* (od *adequate*, *fit*); *to work well* | **sich ~ für a.** sich ~ f etw (P & S) *to be suitable* (od *suited*) *for* (*a post*; *the country*) || sich ~, **um** z zeigen *to be adequate* od *suitable to show*; die beiden Szenen ~ sich bes. (um) die Entwicklung z zeigen *the two scenes aptly illustrate the development* **b.** (S) **sich** ~ f jdn *to suit* (od *fit*) *a p*; *to be adequate to a p* || sich ~ z *or* f *to lend o.s. to* (*a th*); sein Kopf eignet sich zur Karikatur *his head lends itself to caricature*; der Gegenstand eignet **sich** nicht z dem Zweck *the subject does not lend itself to that purpose* **II.** vi; jdm ~ *to be peculiar* od *proper to a p*; → eigen B. 2.

·Eigner m ~s/~ *owner*, *proprietor*

·Eignung f ~/~en *appropriateness*; *fitness*, *suitability* (f *or* z *for*) || (Tauglichkeit) (P) *aptitude*, *qualification* (f *or* z *for*) **~sprüfung** f *qualification* od *fitness*, *aptitude test* || ~ auf Höhentauglichkeit ⟨aero⟩ *pressure test* || (Berufs≗) *trade test*; (jdn) e–r ~ unterziehen *to trade-test*

·Eil- (→ eilen) [in comp] *express* **~auftrag** m *rush-order* **~beförderung** f = Eilbestellung **~bestellung** f *express* (⟨Am⟩ *special*) *delivery* **~boot** n *express boat* **~bote** m *express messenger*; *express*; *courier* [Fr] || durch ~n zu bestellen! *by dispatch*! **~brief** m *letter sent by express* (⟨Am⟩ *special*) *delivery*; *express letter* || *express*!, ⟨Am⟩ *special delivery* ! **≗fertig 1.** a *hasty*, *speedy*, *rash*, *reckless* **2.** adv *hastily*; *in haste* || *recklessly* **~fertigkeit** f *hastiness*, *speediness* || *rashness*, *recklessness* **~fracht** f ⟨rail⟩ *dispatch* (od *express*)*-freight* **~gut** n ⟨rail⟩ *dispatch* (od *express*) *goods* [pl]; ⟨Am⟩ *fast freight* || ~! *by express*! || als ~ *by fast train* | ~tarif [m] *passenger train tariff* **~marsch** m ⟨mil⟩ *forced* od *quick march* **~post** f *express* (⟨Am⟩ *special*) *delivery* **~schritt** m ⟨mil⟩ *quick step* od *time*; im ~ marschieren *to double* **~sendung** f *express* (⟨Am⟩ *special*) *delivery letter* (od *parcel*) | im **~tempo** *in a hurry* **~zug** m ⟨rail⟩ *semi-fast* *train* ~**zustellung** f *express* (⟨Am⟩ *special*) *delivery*

·**Eiland** n ~(e)s/~e ⟨poet⟩ *island* | ⟨übtr⟩ *place, region, spot*; ein friedliches ~ *a peaceful quiet spot* ‖ *oasis*

·**Eile** f ~/ **1.** *dispatch, haste, speed* ‖ gr ~ *hurry, great haste* ‖ dringende ~ *urgency* **2. a. in** ~ (*to act*) *in haste*; ⟨Am fam⟩ *on the jump*; nur e–e Zeile in ~ *just a hasty line* ‖ in aller ~ (*built up*) *in a hurry* ‖ in gr ~ (*to write*) *in great haste*; du warst in gr ~, als .. *you were hurried when you* ..; in größter ~ *hurriedly*; *in a hurry*; *double-quick time* ‖ in der ~ hatte ich es vergessen *I had forgotten about it in the hurry*; .. in *or* **mit** größter ~ *he came* (*at*) *full speed* | **mit** größter ~ ⟨com⟩ *with the utmost dispatch*; *at full speed* **b. etwas** ~! *get a move on*! ‖ nur keine ~! *don't hurry*! *there is no hurry*! *heaps of time*! **c.** ~ **haben** (P) *to be in a hurry*; er hatte gr ~ damit *he was in a hurry to get it done*; *he made a run for it* ‖ (S) *to be urgent*; die S hat gr ~ *the matter is very urgent*; es hat k–e ~ *there is no hurry*; die Briefe h k–e ~ ⟨fam⟩ *the letters can wait* ‖ jdn z ~ antreiben *to speed a p on his way*, *to hurry a p*

·**eilen** vi & vrefl **I.** vi[s & h] **1.** (P) **a.** *to haste*(*n*), *to make haste*; geschäftig ~ *to bustle*; schnell ~ *to flit* ‖ warum eilst du so? *why are you in such a hurry*? ‖ (im Gespräch) schnell weiter ~ *to sweep on* ‖ Eile mit Weile *more haste less speed*, *haste makes waste* **b.** er eilte **an** das Krankenbett s–s Kindes *he hastened to the sick-bed of his child* ‖ ~ **aus, nach** *to hasten* (od *to run, scurry*) *out of, to*; z Bahnhof ~ *to get along to the station*; er eilte auf .. zu *he ran up to Laura*; schnell ~ nach *to hurry* (*over*) *to*; .. **durch** *to hustle through*; **zur** Stelle ~ *to hasten to the spot* ‖ z jds Verteidigung ~ *to fly to a p's defence*; → Waffen ‖ jdm z Hilfe ~ *to run to a p's aid* **c.** ich eile, Sie wissen z l *I hasten to let you know* **d.** ~ **mit** e–r Arbeit *to hurry a work* ‖ er eilte sehr damit *he was in a hurry to get it done*; er eilte nicht sehr damit *he took it rather easy*; *he took his time over it* **2.** (S) **a.** die **Zeit** eilt *time flies* **b. die S eilt** *the matter is urgent*; die S eilt nicht *there is no hurry* ‖ **es eilt sehr** *it is a matter of great urgency, there is no time to lose* ‖ es eilt ihm sehr damit *it is a matter of great urgency to him* ‖ (auf Briefen) Eilt *immediate* **II. sich** ~[h] *to make haste*; *to hasten along* ‖ eil dich ein wenig *hurry a bit, hurry up, be quick, look sharp*; eil dich nicht *don't hurry, there is no hurry* ‖ → sich beeilen ·**eilend** a *hastening, hurrying*; *hurried* (*steps*) ·**eilends** adv *hastily, in* (*great*) *haste*; *in a hurry*; → eilig II.

·**eilig** **I.** a **1. a.** (schnell) *hurried* (*meal*); *rushing* (*footsteps*); *quick* (*journey*); *speedy* (*reply, return*) ‖ ⟨Am⟩ *hurry* (*meal, visit*) ‖ etwas ~! *get a move on*! *look sharp*! ⟨fam⟩ *make it snappy*! ⟨sl⟩ *step on it*! nur nicht so ~ *don't hurry* **b.** (übereilt) *hasty* (*judgement*); ich war z ~ *I was too hasty* **2.** (dringend) *pressing* (*duties*), *urgent*; ~e S ⟨bes mil⟩ *priority* ‖ die S ist ~ *the matter is urgent* **II.** adv (*to act*) *in haste*; (*to leave*) *hurriedly*; *hot-foot* ‖ **es sehr** ~ **h** *to be in a hurry* (*to do*) ‖ er hatte es sehr ~ damit *he made a run for it*; *he was insistent upon it* ‖ jdn ~ **befördern,** bringen *to hurry a p* (aus *out of*; in *into*); ~ fahren über (of a ship) *to speed across* (*the waves*); ~ s–n Weg gehen *to speed one's way*; sie h es damit nicht ~ *they are not very quick at it*; Truppen ~ senden *to hurry troops* ‖ ~st *at full speed*; *with the utmost dispatch*; → spornstreichs **III.** [abs] **etw** ≗**es** *some pressing* (od *urgent*) *matter* ‖ er hatte nichts ≗eres z tun, als es z verbreiten *he did his best endeavours to disseminate it most quickly*; *he was very quick to disseminate it*

·**Eimer** m ~s/~ *pail*; (Schöpf≗) *bucket*; ein ~ Wasser *a pail of water* ‖ Aschen≗, Müll≗ *ash-bucket, dust-bin, refuse-pail*; Milch- *milk pail*; Spül≗ *slop-pail*; ~ f Marmelade *pot* | ⟨min⟩ (eiserner ~) *skip* ‖ ⟨tech⟩ (Schöpf≗) *bucket, scoop* ‖ °im ~ ⟨fig fam⟩ *all at hell* ‖ °in'n ~ gehn ⟨sl⟩ *to go to pot*; etwas in'n ~ gehn l (vergeuden) ⟨fam⟩ *to put .. down the drain* ~**(ketten)-bagger** m ⟨tech⟩ *bucket-dredge*(*r*) ~**leiter** f *articulated ladder* ~**voll** m *bucketful, pailful*: ein ~ Wasser *a p. of water*; ~ [pl] Wasser *pailfuls of w.* ≗**weise** adv *in bucketfuls, in pailfuls* ~**werk** n ⟨tech⟩ *bucket-elevator*

·**ein**[1] (Zahlwort [betont]) **I.** ⟨eig⟩ **1.** [abs] ~s *one*; hundert u ~s *a hundred and one* ‖ ~s v 10 bleibt 9 *one from ten leaves nine* ‖ Numero ~s *number one*; Kapitel ~s *chapter one* ‖ 100 z ~s *a hundred to one* | es ist ~s (*or* ~ Uhr) *it is one* (*o'clock*); um ~s *at one*; halb ~ *half past twelve*; ~s, 2, 3, los! ⟨sport⟩ *on your marks, get set, go*! **2.** [attr] **a.** ~ Tausend *one thousand* ‖ ~und-zwanzig *twenty-one*, **one and twenty*; ⟨Ger⟩ ~undzwanzig Uhr *9 o'clock p. m.* ‖ ~(und)-einhalb *one and a half* **II.** ⟨übtr⟩ (P & S) **A.** [abs] **1. a.** ~**er** m, ~**e** f, ~**s** n *one* ‖ ~er v ihnen *one of them* ‖ nur ~e(r) auf einmal *only one at a time* ‖ °du b·ist mir ~er! *you ·are a one*! ‖ °er lief wie nur ~er *he ran like anything* (od *like mad*) ‖ e–e Familie so alt wie nur ~e *a family as ancient as any* (*in* ..) ‖ ~er f alle, alle f ~en *work of each for weal of all*; *each for all, all for each* ‖ ~er z viel *one too many* ‖ °sieh mal ~er an *look at that now* ‖ alle bis auf ~en *all but one* ‖ ~s (sc ein Buch) behalte ich *I'll keep one* **b.** ~ **u derselbe** (*one and*) *the same* **c.** ~er v **beiden** *either*; e–n v beiden angreifen heißt beide angreifen *to attack either is to attack both*; ~e v beiden Seiten *either side* ‖ der ~e .. der andere *the one .. the other*; ~er nach dem anderen (*to be dismissed*) *one by one* ‖ ~s hinter dem anderen k (S) *to come one on top of the other* ‖ ~er nach dem anderen *one by one* **2.** ~**s (e–e S)** n **a.** *one thing* ‖ ~s gefällt mir nicht an ihm *there's one th I don't like about him* ‖ (wenn ..), so ist ~s klar (*if* ..) *there is one plain thing* ‖ ~s kann man nur *you can't have it both ways* ‖ ~s ins andere gerechnet *taking one th with another* ‖ das ~e *or* das andere *the one th* od *the other* ‖ noch ~s (in Unterhaltung) *there is another th* (od *point*); *wait a minute* | ~ **u dasselbe** *one and the same* (*thing*) ‖ sie ist ihm sein ~ u alles *she is everything* (od *all il all*) *to him*; *she is one and all with him, she is his all in all* **b.** [pred] ~s s *to be one* | (gleich) es ist (mir) alles ~s *it is all one* (od *the same*) *to me* ‖ Kaution u Bürgschaft sind ~s *'Kaution' u 'Bürgschaft' are the same* ‖ sie sind alle ~s *they are all the same, .. all identical* ‖ es kommt (*or* läuft) auf ~s heraus *it comes to the same thing* **c.** [pred] ⟨fig⟩ ~s s mit jdm *to be at one with, to be of the same opinion with, to agree with a p*; (S) *to be of a piece with, to be in keeping with a th* ‖ (sich) ~s w *to agree*; ⟨Am⟩ *to get together*; ~s w mit jdm *to settle with a p*; ~s w über etw *to agree on a th* ‖ er wußte (*or* fühlte) sich ~s mit uns *he knew he was* (od *he knew himself to be*) *in perfect harmony with us, he felt himself in p. h.* .. **d.** kalt u warm **in** ~**em** *at once cold and hot* ‖ **in** ~**em fort** *continuously*; *incessantly* ‖ das geht so **in** ~**em hin** *I expected as much* ‖ **mit** ~**s** *all of a sudden* **B.** [attr] **1.** ~e Mark wert *worth one mark* ‖ ~e Stunde arbeiten *to work for one hour* **2. a.** *one, a* ‖ auf die ~e oder andere **Art** *some way or the other*; in ~er oder der anderen Art *one way or the other* ‖ das ~e **Gute** war .. *one good thing was* .. ‖ ~ **Herz** u ~e Seele s *to be bound up with each other in one affection*; ⟨iron⟩ *to be thick friends* ‖ in ~em **Lauf** *in a single run* ‖ ~ f allemal → einmal, → V. ‖ noch ~en **Schritt** (und ..) *one step more* ‖ nicht ~e lebende **Seele** war in Sicht *not another living soul was in sight* ‖ Rom wurde nicht an ~em **Tage** erbaut *Rome was not built in one day* ‖ ~ Tag um den anderen *every other* (od *second*) *day*; → Tag ‖ ~en um den anderen Montag *alternate Mondays* (*he had* ..) ‖ nicht ~ Ton *not a sound* ‖ °in ~er **Tour** *continuously, incessantly* ‖ in ~em **Wort** *in a word* ‖ in ~em **Zug** *at a draught* **b. (gleich)** *one, the same* ‖ alle v ~er Größe *all of a size, all the same size* ‖ ich bin mit Ihnen ~er Meinung *I am entirely of your opinion, I judge things the same as you do* ‖ an ~em Tische mit .. *at the same table with* (*a p*) ‖ ⟨theol⟩ ~es Wesens s *to be one in substance*; *to be co-essential* od *consubstantial* **III.** [reines Substantiv] → Einer; Eins **IV.** [in comp mit Adj u Subst] → ein–1 **V.** [adv, betont] **~ für allemal** *once for all*; *for good and all*; → allemal, einmal

ein2 [unbetont] **I.** [pron] **1.** *one* ‖ ~er v ·uns *one of our people* ‖ ~er m–r Fr·eunde *a friend of mine* ‖ ~er vom ·Adel *one of the nobility, a noble* ‖ er ist wie ~er, der .. *he is as one who* ..; wie ~er, der t·ot war *like one dead* ‖ eine Bibliothek so gut wie ~e in der St·adt *a library as good as a town one* ‖ manch ~er *many a one* **2. a.** [nom] = man, jemand ‖ °wenn ~er dir sagt *if a fellow tells you* ‖ unser~ *the likes of me* **b.** [acc & dat] *you*; e–e Kraft, die ~en niederwirft *a force that knocks you down*; das kann ~em alle Tage passieren *that can occur to you any day*; es ist ~nem, als ob .. *you feel as if* .. **II. [indef art] A. 1.** *a* [vor Kons.] ‖ *an* [vor Vokalen]; **~ Buch** *a book*, ~ Ei *an egg* (aber: *a unit, a history*; *an M. P.* [ˈemˈpiː], etc.) ‖ ~e Tracht Prügel *a thrashing* ‖ ~ gewisser Herr N. *a* (od *one*) *Mr. N.* | **~ Ratschlag** *a piece of advice*; ~e Torheit *a piece of folly* | wie **~ Toter** *like one dead*; so ~ Unbeständiger *one so fickle* ‖ ~ oder zwei Bücher *one or two books* (*were lost*); *a book or two* (*was lost*) | manch ~ Tag *many a day* ‖ **noch** ~ Glas *another glass*; noch ~ Mal *a second time* ‖ **solch** ~ Pferd! *such a horse*; solch ~ Rat *such advice* ‖ (in Frage) **was f** ~ Wein ist dies? *what wine is this*?; (im Ausruf) was f ~ Leben! *what a life*! was f ~ Unsinn! *what nonsense*! ‖ → jeder; irgend ~ | der Rang ~es Generals *the rank of general*; der Titel ~es Herzogs *the title of duke* ‖ wenn je ~ Mann .. hatte, so hatte er es *if ever man had* .., *he had.* **2. ~ Goethe,** ~ Schiller *a Goethe, a Schiller*; *the Goethes, the Schillers* [pl]; er hält sich f e–n G. *he fancies himself a sort of G.* ‖ ein vollständiger G. *a complete set of G.'s works* **3.** das w·ar e–e Hitze *the heat was terrific*; sie hatten e–n K·affee! *they had coffee of a kind*! **B. [abs] [ell** = ~ Schlag, Stück etc] *one*; ~en ins Auge bek *to get one in the eye* ‖ jdm ~en *or* ~s langen (*or* auswischen) *to land a p one* ‖ ~ fahren l *to pass a wind, to do a fart* ‖ ~en trinken *to take a drop* ‖ °~en (*sc* Platz) rauf (runter)! *go up* (*down*) *one*! ⟨a. fig⟩ ‖ (*I lose a neighbour and you gain*) *one* ‖ such mir ~en guten/~e gute/~ gutes aus *pick me out a good one*

ein3 adv **1.** °es will mir nicht ~ *I cannot see your point* ‖ nicht ~ noch aus wissen; nicht wissen, wo ~ u aus *to be at the end of one's tether, to be at one's wits' end, to be nowhere* ‖ ~ u ausgehen *to come in and out*; *to be in and out*; *to come and go* (*people were always coming and going*); → püttjern ‖ bei jdm ~ u ausgehen *to associate with a p, to be a p's friend*; in e–m Hause ~ u ausgehen *to frequent a house* | ⟨aero⟩ ~! *On*! *Switch on*! **2.** [in comp mir Verben] → ein–2

ein-1 [betontes pref in Adj u Subst] *one–, single–* ‖ ⟨scient⟩ *uni–, monp–*

ein-2 [betontes pref] **1.** [in Verben] **a.** *in* [adv]; ~nehmen *to take in* **b.** [in frz. u lat. Verben] *in*, ~zahlen *to pay in* ‖ *in–*: ~schreiben *to inscribe*; *im–*: ~kerkern *to imprison* ‖ *inter–*: ~greifen *to interfere* ‖ *intro–*: ~führen *to introduce* **2.** [in Subst. Adj u Adv] **a.** *in–*: ≈kommen *income* **b.** [in frz. u lat. Wörtern] *in–*: ≈drängen *intrusion*; *im–*: ≈sperrung *imprisonment* ‖ *inter–*: ≈mischung *interference* ‖ *intro–*: ≈führung *introduction*

-ein [suff] *in*; tagaus, tag~ *day in day out* ‖ → querfeld

·einachsig a ⟨scient⟩ *monaxial*; *uniaxal, uniaxial* | **≈keit** f ~/ *uniaxiality*

·Einachsschlepper m *two-wheeled tractor*

·einad(e)rig a *single-core* (*cable*)

·Einakter m ~s/~ *one-act play* (seit 1887, Paris)

ein·ander adv **1.** *one another, each other* ‖ zwei Charaktere ~ gegenüberstellen *to introduce two opposite characters, to contrast two characters* | ~ beeinflussen *to interact*; → gegenseitig ‖ sie sahen ~ ins Gesicht *they looked each into the other's face* **2.** [in comp nach prep] → an~; bei~; durch~; hinter~; neben~; über~; etc

·ein|arbeiten vt [h] **1.** etw ~ *to work* od *introduce a th* (in *into*); *to insert a th* (in *in*) **2. a.** jdn ~ in etw *to train a p for, to introduce a p to, to make a p familiar* (od *acquianted*) *with, to familiarize a p with a th* **b. sich** ~ *to get one's hand in*; sich ~ in etw *to familiarize o.s. with a th*; *to make o.s. familiar* (od *acquainted*) *with a th* ‖ sich miteinander ~ *to work in with each other* ‖ → hineinarbeiten **·Einarbeitungszeit** f *breaking-in period* ⟨a. mot⟩

·einarmig a *one-armed*

·ein|äschern vt [h] **1.** (Stadt etc) *to burn* (od *reduce*, *to ashes*, *to lay in ashes*; *to burn down* **2.** (jdn) *to cremate, incinerate* **·Einäscherung** f ~/~en *incineration, cremation* | ~sofen [m] *cremation furnace*; *cremator*

·ein|atmen vt [h] *to breathe in, to inhale*; tief ~ *to draw breath*

·Einatmung f *inhalation*; ~ v Staub (etc) → Silikose **·einatomig** a ⟨chem⟩ *monatomic*

·ein|ätzen vt [h] *to etch in* **·einäugig** a *one-eyed*; *monocular* ‖ ⟨phot⟩ *single-lens* (*reflex camera*)

E·in-Ausgabe-Steuerung f *i*(*nput*)-*o*(*utput*) *control*

·Einbahn- ~straße f ~/~n *one-way street* od *road* **~verkehr** m *one-way traffic*

·ein|ballen, ein|ball·ieren vt [h] ⟨com⟩ *to pack up*; *to pack in bales*

·einballig a (Schuh) *made to fit either foot*

·ein|balsamieren vt [h] (jdn) *to embalm, to mummify* ‖ °⟨fig⟩ = einseifen ‖ laß dich ~! → abmalen **·Einbalsamierung** f ~/~en *embalming, embalmment, mummification*

·Einband m ~(e)s/≈e ⟨bookb⟩ *binding*; [abstr] *finishing* | ~decke [f] (*book-*)*cover, binding* **·einbändig** a *in one volume, one-volume* (*novel*)

·einbasig, ·einbasisch a ⟨chem⟩ *monobasic*

·Einbau m *additional alteration* (in *in*); *insertion*; *installation* (*of a motor*); ~ im Fahrzeug *vehicular inst.* ‖ *mounting* (*of a compass*) | ~küche [f] *kitchen* od *sink unit, built-in k.*; ~möbel [n pl] *built-in furniture, built-ins* pl **·ein|bauen** vt [h] **1.** (etw) ~ *to build* (in *into* [*a house*]) ‖ ⟨tech⟩ *to fit* (*into*); *to install* (*in*); (Motor) *to mount* **2.** (einschließen) *to build in* (*our garden is entirely built in*) ‖ (Fluß) *to embank*

·Einbaum m (Boot) *canoe, dugout, pitpan*

·ein|bedingen vt [h] *to stipulate*; *to include in the bargain*

·Einbeere f ⟨bot⟩ *herb paris*

·ein|begreifen vt [h] [→ greifen] *to comprise, to include; to be inclusive of* (*a th*) || (begrifflich) mit ~ *to connote* || –griffen s in *to be included in*; in diese Preise ist alles –griffen *these terms are inclusive*; er ist mit –griffen *he is among the number* **·einbegriffen** *including*; dein Vater ~ *including your father, inclusive of your f.*; Frühstück ~ *with breakfast thrown in*; → einschließen

·ein|behalten vt [h] [→ halten] (etw) *to keep back, to detain* **·einbeinig** a *one-legged* **·ein|beißen 1.** vi *to bite* (in *into*); → anbeißen **2.** [vrefl] **sich** ~ in *to bite into,* ⟨fig⟩ *to work one's way into* (*a th*)

·ein|bekommen vt [h] [→ kommen] (Beiträge) *to get in*; (Geld) *to take in* || °= (jdn) einholen **·ein|berufen** vt [h] [→ rufen] **1.** (Versammlung etc) *to call, to convene*; (amtlich) *to convoke* || (Reichstag) *to summon* **2.** ⟨mil⟩ (jdn) z Heeresdienst ~ *to call* (*a p*) *up* (*for service*); *to summon* (*a p*) *to the colours*; *to induct*; → aufrufen | *≈***er** m *inductee*; ⟨Am⟩ *enlisted man* **·Einberufer** m ~s/~ *convener* **·Einberufung** f ~/~en **1.** *calling together*; *summoning*; *convocation* (*of Parliament*); (e–r Versammlung) *convening* **2.** ⟨mil⟩ (~ z Heeresdienst) *calling up* (*of the reserves, of a p*); *induction* || ⟨com etc⟩ ohne daß es e–r (bes) ~ bedarf (*the assembly shall meet*) *as of right* | ~sbefehl [m] ⟨mil⟩ *induction order* || ~sort [m] *induction station*

·ein|betonieren vt ⟨tech⟩ *to embed* od *set, encase in concrete*

·Einbett- ~abteil n ⟨rail⟩ *roomette* **~zimmer** n *single room*

·ein|betten vt [h] ⟨übtr⟩ (Draht etc) *to embed, imbed* (in *in*); [mst pass]: eingebettet s in (of *houses*, etc.) *to be sunk in* (*a wood*); ⟨poet⟩ *to be bosomed in*; der Ort ist im Tal –ge–et *the place nestles in the valley*

·ein|beulen vt [h] (etw) *to dent, to dint*; (Hut) *to batter* **·Einbeulung** f ~/~en *dent, dint* || ⟨tact⟩ *bulge*

·ein|beuteln vt [h] *to put* (*a th*) *in a bag*

·ein|beziehen vt [h] (etw) *to bring* od *integrate* (in *into*); *to include, to incorporate* (in *in*) **·Einbeziehung** f *inclusion* (in *in*); *incorporation* (in *into, in*)

·ein|biegen I. vi/t [h] **1.** vi: in e–n Weg ~ *to turn* od *swing into a road*; *to join a path* (*that* ..) || auf *or* in die Hauptstraße ~ ⟨bes mot⟩ *to turn on to the main road* || in die gerade Bahn ~ *to round into the straight* || in ein Tor ~ *to turn in at a gate, to swing into a gateway* || (nach) rechts, links ~ ⟨bes mot⟩ *to turn right, left* || nach rechts (⟨engl⟩ links) ~ *to filter*; *to move out* od *turn to one's left*; *to pull in* od *turn to one's right* (⟨engl⟩ *vice versa*) **2.** vt (etw) *to bend* od *turn in* (od *inward*[*s*]) **II.** *≈* n turn(ing)

·Einbiegung f *inward bend* || e–e ~ m *to curve inward*

·ein|bilden [vrefl] [h] sich [dat] ~ **1.** (mst = sich fälschlich vorstellen) *to fancy, imagine* (daß *that*; daß etw *or* jd ist *a th* od *a p to be*; daß jd tut *a p to do, a p doing*); *to flatter* od *persuade o.s., to be under the delusion* (*that* ..); ich bilde mir ein, ihn gesehen z h *I imagine myself to have seen him*; sich nur etw ~ *to imagine a th* **2.** (sich groß dünken) sich etwas (*or* °was Rechtes, °wer weiß was) ~, sich viel ~ *to be conceited, to be full of conceit, to have a high opinion* (od *to think a lot*) *of o.s.*; ⟨fam⟩ *to fancy o.s.*; bilde dir nur nichts ein *don't put on side*; ich bilde mir nicht ein, gelehrt z sein *I do not pretend* (od *profess*) *to be a scholar* || **sich etw ~ auf etw** *to boast of a th*; *to presume on a th*; *to vaunt a th*; *to pique* (od *plume, peacock, pride, value*) *o.s. on a th*; *to preen o.s. over a th*; *to fancy o.s. at* (*bridge*) || du brauchst dir nichts darauf –zu– *that's nothing to be proud of* | **was** bildest du dir eigentlich ein? *what do you think you are* || → sich brüsten || → eingebildet

·Einbildung f ~/~en **1.** *fancy, imagination*; *delusion*; es ist alles nur ~ v Ihnen *it's all your imagination*; das war k–e bloße ~ *that was not entirely imagination*; nur in der ~ vorhanden *imaginary* **2.** (Dünkel) *conceit* **~skraft** f *power of imagination, imaginative faculty*; mit höchster Anstrengung der ~ *by a vivid stretch of the imagination* || ⟨engl Lit⟩ schöpferische ~ *imagination*; spielerisch-belebende ~ *fancy*

·ein|binden vt [h] [→ binden] (Buch) *to bind*

·einbindig a ⟨chem⟩ *univalent*

·ein|blasen vt [h] **1.** ⟨tech & med⟩ (etw) *to blow in*; *to blow, inject* (in *into*); Jodoform in die Nase ~ *to insufflate the nose with iodoform* || ⟨bib⟩ (Odem) *to breathe* (jdm *into a p*) **2.** ⟨fig⟩ jdm etw ~ *to whisper a th to a p*; → eingeben

·Einbläser m ~s/~ *prompter, whisperer* || *instigator* **·Einblasung** f ⟨md⟩ *injection, insufflation*

·Einblatt n ⟨bot⟩ (Name versch. Pflanzen) *one-blade* **~druck** m ⟨print⟩ *one-side print*; *broadside, broadsheet*

·ein|bläuen vt [h] (Wäsche) *to blue*

·ein|blenden vt [h] ⟨film etc⟩ (Bild, Ton) *to fade in*; (langsam) *to sneak in* (z. B. *music*); in–e–a ~ *to cross-fade* **·Einblendung** f ⟨film etc⟩ *cross fade*, ⟨Am⟩ (Trick *≈*) *tie-in*

·ein|bleuen vt [h] jdm etw ~ **a.** (durch Prügel) *to beat* (od *cane, flog, whip*) *a th into a p* **b.** (einprägen) *to grind* (od *hammer, pump, rub*) *a th into a p, to knock* (od *drum*) *a th into a p's head*; → einprägen, einbläuen

·Einblick m ~(e)s/~e *insight* (in etw *into a th*); ⟨Am⟩ *close-up* (in etw *of a th*) || e–n ~ gewinnen *to gain* od *get an insight* (*into*); *to get an idea* (*of*); jdm e–n ~ in etw geben *to give a p the hang of a th*; e–n ~ in etw h *to be well up in a th, to have the knack of a th* | kurzer ~ *glimpse* (in etw *of a th*); e–n kz ~ gewähren in *to afford a glimpse of* (*a th*); geben Sie uns e–n kz ~ in s–e Kunst *give us* (od *favour us with*) *a glimpse of his art*

·einblumig a ⟨bot⟩ *uniflorous*

·ein|bohren [vrefl] [h] sich ~ (of beetles) *to bore, to bore one's way* (in *into*) || ⟨fig⟩ sich ~ in etw *to work o.s., to work one's way into a th*; *to penetrate into a th*

·ein|brechen vt /i **I.** vt [h] (einschlagen) *to break*; *to break down* (od *open*); *to smash, to smash in* **II.** vi [s] **A.** (of persons) **1. a.** (einfallen) in ein Land ~ *to invade a country, to make an inroad* od *irruption into a c.*; *to burst upon a c.* **b.** in ein Haus ~ *to burgle*; *to burglarize a h., to break into a h., to commit burglary*; ⟨fam⟩ *to crack a crib*; in das Haus wurde –gebrochen *the house was broken into*; bei uns wurde –gebrochen *our house was broken into* || in e–e Wohnung ~ ⟨sl⟩ *to gate-crash a flat* **c.** ⟨übtr⟩ (überraschen) bei jdm ~ *to break upon a p*; → eindringen **2.** auf dem Eise ~ *to fall through the ice* **B.** (S) **1.** *to collapse*; *to fall down* (od *in*); *to give way*; *to come to grief*; ⟨Am⟩ *to go out* **2.** (*of daylight*, etc) *to break*; *to dawn* || die Nacht bricht ein *night is falling*; bei ~der Nacht *at nightfall* || → Einbruch

·Einbrecher m ~s/~ *burglar, housebreaker, picklock*; ⟨Am sl⟩ (Wander*≈*) *yegg, yeggman*

·einbrennbar a *ceramic* (Abziehbild) **·Einbrenne** f [österr] (Mehlschwitze) ⟨cul⟩ *roux* [ru:] (pl [ru:z])

·ein|brennen I. vt [h] (hineinbrennen) *to burn in* || (auf *or* festbrennen) *to stove, bake* || (jdn ins Fleisch ~) *to brand* (*a p*) || ⟨fig⟩ **sich** ~ in *to burn*

into (*this spectacle burnt into his soul*) **II.** ~̈ n ⟨ceram⟩ *annealing*

·ein|bringen I. vt [h] **A.** ⟨eig⟩ (P) **1.** *to bring in*; (Ernte etc) *to bring* (od *gather, get*) *in, to harvest, to store* (*up*); → eingebracht ‖ (Schiff) *to conduct* ‖ viele Gefangene ~ *to bring in many prisoners* **2.** e–e Gesetzesvorlage ~ *to bring in* (od *to introduce, pass*) *a bill*; e–n Antrag ~ *to bring, forward a motion*; *to put a m. before the House* **B.** ⟨übtr⟩ (S) **1.** (etw) *to bring in, to yield, return*; jdm etw ~ *to bring* (od *gain*) *a p a th* (*this work brings him hundreds a year*); *to earn* (od *win*) *a p a th* od *a th for a p*; es bringt mir nicht e–n Pfennig ein *it does not pay me a farthing*; was bringt dir das ein? ⟨Am fam⟩ *what does that buy you*?; es bringt mehr ein *it is more profitable* ‖ Gewinn ~ *to bring in* (od *produce, yield*) *a profit, to pay well*; jdm G. ~ *to pay a p* ‖ (Summe) *to realize* ‖ hohe Preise ~ *to fetch high prices* ‖ (Zinsen) *to command* ‖ es wird nicht viel ~ *it won't bring* (od *fetch*) *much*; das Geschäft bringt nichts ein *the business does not pay*; das G. wird dir nichts ~ *the b. won't pay you*; die Stellung bringt 1000 Pfd ein *the post is worth £ 1000.* **2.** Glück (etc) ~ *to produce happiness*; jdm Macht ~ *to bring a p power* ‖ die Folgen, die der Schritt ihm einbrachte *the consequences the step brought on him* **3.** etwas wieder ~ *to make up for a th* (jdm *to a p*); *to repair*; jdm e–n Betrag wieder ~ *to recoup a p an amount* (*of his outlay*); jdm e–n Verlust wieder ~ *to make good a loss to a p*; *to compensate* (od *recoup*) *a p for a loss*; → einholen **4.** ⟨typ⟩ (Zeile) *to get in* **II.** ~̈ n *bringing-in*; *harvesting* (*of the corn*) **einbrinlich** a = einträglich **·Einbringung** f = Einbringen ‖ = das Eingebrachte

·einbrocken vt [h] **1.** ⟨eig⟩ → brocken ‖ e–e Suppe ~ *to cover* (od *thicken*) *a soup with morsels of bread* **2. a.** viel –zu– h *to have money to burn, to live in plenty* **b.** jdm etw Schlimmes (⟨fam⟩ Schönes) ~ *to get a p into trouble, to bring trouble upon a p* (*to land a p in a nice fix* [⟨Am⟩ mess]) ‖ er hat **sich** etw Schönes –ge–kt *he's got himself in a nice mess*, du hast es dir selbst –ge–kt *you've only yourself to thank for it* ‖ sich etw ~ *to let o.s. in for a th, to get into trouble*; da hat er sich e–e schöne Suppe –ge–kt *now he is in for it properly* ‖ da hat er uns e–e schöne S. –ge–kt! *there now, he has made a pretty muddle* (od *a fine mess of it*)! → anrichten 2. ‖ was man sich –ge–kt hat, muß man ausessen *as you have brewed, so you must drink*; *as you have made your bed, so you must lie on it*

·Einbruch m ~(e)s/~̈e **1. a.** ⟨mil⟩ *breaking-in*; *incursion, inroad, irruption* (in ein Land *into a country*); *invasion* (in ein Land *of a country*); *sudden attack, inroad* (in die Front *on the front*); e–n ~ m in *to burst upon* (*a country*) **b.** (unerlaubtes Betreten) *trespass* ‖ → Eindringen **c.** *house-breaking*; *burglary*; Schaufenster~̈ *smash-and-grab raid* (od *robbery*); sicher gegen ~ *burglar proof*; sicher gegen Feuer u ~ *fire and thief-resisting* (*safe*) ‖ e–n ~ begehen *to commit burglary* **2.** (of the sea) *invasion* (in das Land *of the land*) ‖ ~ der Nacht *nightfall* **~sdiebstahl** m *housebreaking, break-in, burglary* | ~versicherung [f] *insurance against burglary and theft* **~sbecken** n ⟨geol⟩ *structural basin* **~sfront** f ⟨mil⟩ *front of penetration* **~sgebiet** n ⟨geol⟩ *structural depression* **~stelle** f ⟨mil⟩ *breach*

°**·ein|buchten** vt [h] (jdn) = einsperren

·Einbuchtung f ~/~en (Küsten~̈) *bight*; *indentation*

·ein|bürgern vt [h] **1.** (Ausländer) *to naturalize*; [mst pass] *to denizen*; *to make* (*a p*) *a denizen* ‖ ⟨übtr⟩ (fremdes Wort etc) *to naturalize*; *to adopt* **2. sich** ~ *to naturalize*; *to be naturalized* od *denized*; *to become a denizen*; sich fest ~ (S) *to come to stay* **·Einbürgerung** f ~/~en *naturalization* (*of an alien*) ‖ *naturalization, adoption* (*of a foreign word*, etc.)

·Einbuße f ~/~n *forfeiture*; *loss* (an *of*); → Schaden ‖ ~ erleiden *to lose*; *to suffer loss*; gr ~ erl. *to lose heavily*; ~ erl. an etw *to lose in a th*; *to lose* (od *forfeit*) *a th*; *to be deprived of a th* ‖ ~ erl. durch *to lose by*; *to be a loser by* (*a bargain*); ⟨fam⟩ *to be damaged by* (*an earthquake*); dadurch erleidet sein Verdienst k–e ~ *that does not detract from his merit* ‖ **unter** ~ s–r Ehre *at the expense* od *cost of his hono(u)r* od *reputation*

·ein|büßen vt/i [h] **1.** vt (Vermögen etc) *to forfeit, lose*; sein Leben ~ *to forfeit one's life* ‖ durch die Dummheit büßte er s–e Stellung ein *the folly lost him his place* ‖ er hat 1000 Mark –gebüßt *he is 1000 marks out* ‖ ⟨sport sl⟩ (Punkte) *to concede* **2.** vi *to lose*; er wird dabei nur ~ *he will only lose by it, he will be a loser by it* ‖ ~ **an** etw *to lose in a th*; *to lose a th*, → Einbuße

·Eincentstück n ⟨Am fam⟩ *penny*

·ein|dämmen vt [h] **1.** (Fluß etc) *to dam up*; *to embank* ‖ (hemmen) (Flut) *to stem* ‖ (Land) *to dike, to dyke* ‖ (Feuer) *to control* **2.** ⟨fig⟩ (Redefluß) *to stem*; (Gefühle) *to dam up*; *to restrain* ‖ (Unsitte etc) *to check, stop* **·Eindämmung** f ~/~en *damming up*; *embankment* ‖ *stemming* (*of a current*) ‖ ⟨fig⟩ *stemming*; *check*

·ein|dampfen vt [h] ⟨chem⟩ = abdampfen vt

·Eindampfgerät n *evaporator*

·ein|decken vt [h] **1.** (Dach) *to cover*; → decken **2.** (Pflanzen f den Winter) *to cover with earth, to earth up* **3.** ⟨übtr com⟩ (voll) eingedeckt s *to be* (*fully*) *supplied* (od *provided, stocked*) (mit *with*); über Bedarf –gedeckt s *to have more than is required* **4.** ⟨com⟩ **sich** ~ *to provide o.s.* (mit *with*); sich ~ mit etw *to buy* (od *lay*) *a th in*; *to stock, to store a th*; sich mit Kartoffeln ~ *to lay in potatoes* ‖ ⟨ad⟩ decken Sie sich genügend ein! *don't get caught short*; *get plenty of ..* (*for the weekend*)!

·Eindecker m ~s/~ ⟨aero⟩ *monoplane, single-decker* **·Eindeckung** f *covering* ‖ ⟨übtr⟩ *buying-in*; ~stag *buying-in day*

·eindeichen vt [h] (Land) *to dike, dyke, empolder*

·eindeutig 1. a *having but one meaning*; *unambiguous* (*answer*), *unequivocal*; *clear, plain*; *unmistakable*; *manifest perceptible, apparent, patent*; *evident*; *unreserved*; *categorical*; *absolute*; *unrestricted*; *definite*, (*well-*)*defined*; *straightforward* (*behaviour*) ‖ es ist ~! *there are no ifs, ands* od *buts* **2.** adv *unambiguously, unequivocally*; ~ klar *u. clear*; s–e Ansicht ~ äußern ⟨a.⟩ *to express o.s. one way or the other*; ~ ausgedrückt *expressed in clear* od *plain terms* **~̈keit** f *unambiguousness, unambiguity*; *unequivocalness*; *straightforwardness*

·ein|deutschen vt [h] (Wort) *to germanize* ‖ (Land etc) *to make* (*a country*) *German in character*; *to assimilate to German thought* **·Eindeutschung** f *germanization, germanizing*; ~sprozeß [m] *germanizing process*

·ein|dicken vt [h] ⟨cul⟩ (Saft etc) *to boil down, to thicken*; ⟨cul, chem a.⟩ *to inspissate*; → kondensieren, verdicken

·Eindicker m *concentrator* **·Eindicktrommel** f ⟨tech⟩ *condensing drum* **·Eindickung** f *thickening*

·eindimensional a *one-dimensional*

·ein|dosen vt [h] ⟨cul ind⟩ *to pack*

·Eindrahtleitung f ⟨el⟩ *single-wire circuit*

·ein|drängen [vrefl] [h] sich ~ *to push one's way, to thrust o.s.* (in ein Amt *into an office*) ‖ (S) *to intrude itself* (zw *between*; in *into*) | sich störend ~ *to insinuate o.s., to intrude* (in *into* [*a company*]); ⟨sl⟩ *to barge in* [adv]

·ein|drehen vi [h] ⟨aero⟩ (v Jägern z Angriff) *to close in*

·**Eindring-** **~tiefe** f *penetration depth*

·**ein|drillen** vt [h] ⟨mil⟩ *to drill*; *to knock* (*a p*) *into shape*; → drillen ‖ (jdn f ein Examen) *to coach* ‖ jdm etw ~ = einpauken

·**ein|dringen** **I.** vi [s] **A.** *to break in* ‖ *to get in* **B.** ~ in **1.** (P) **a.** (störend) ~ in *to impinge on* (*a th*); *to insinuate o.s.*, *to intrude into* (*a company*); bei jdm ~ *to break in upon a p* (od *a p's peace*); *to forage on a p* | (gewaltsam ~ in) *to break into* (*a house*); *to enter* (*a house*) *by force*; *to force one's way into* (*a th*); ⟨sl⟩ *to gate-crash* (*a flat*) ‖ *to invade* (*a country*) | tief in die Archive ~ *to dig deeply into the archives* **b.** (durchdenken) *to penetrate* (od *dive*, *examine*, *probe*, *search*, *see*) *into* (*a matter*, *a secret*); *to go to the bottom of* (*a th*); *to penetrate* (*a mystery*) **2.** (S) (of the sea) *to gain upon* (*the land*) ‖ *to enter* od *penetrate*, *pierce* (*the flesh*) ‖ (of liquids) *to infiltrate* (od *ooze*, *sink*) *into* ‖ (of impressions) tief ~ *to enter deep into* (*a p*); ⟨Am⟩ *to seep into* **C.** ~ **auf jdn** **1.** (P) *to close in upon a p*; *to fall upon a p* ‖ ~ auf jdn, daß er tut *to be urgent with a p to do* ‖ mit Fragen auf jdn ~ *to press* od *ply a p with q.*, mit Bitten .. *to plead with a p* **2.** (od duties) *to throng* (od *press*) *upon a p*; (of feelings, thoughts) *to crowd* (od *press*) *in upon a p* **II.** ≗ n **1.** (P) (störendes) *intrusion* (in *into*); *irruption* (in *on* [*a p's peace*]); *influx* (*of aliens*) | (gewaltsames) ~ in ein Haus *breaking into a house*, *entering a h. by force*; ~ in ein Land *invasion of a country* | (gedankliches) ~ in *penetration of* (*a th*); *examination of* od *into* (*a th*) **2.** (S) *infiltration* (in *into*); *influx*; das ~ neuer Wörter in e–e Sprache *the impact of new words upon a language* ·**eindringlich** **1.** a ⟨fig⟩ **a.** *insistent* (*demand*), *pressing*, *urgent* (*request*); *imperative* (*command*) **b.** *compelling*, *engaging*; *insistent*, mit ~en Worten *with great insistence* (od *insistency*) ‖ *effective*, *forceful*, *incisive*, *pithy* (*style*); *trenchant* ‖ auf das ~ste *most emphatically* (od *insistently*) ‖ ~er Appell *moral suasion* **2.** adv *insistently*, *urgently*; *emphatically*; *with great insistence*; (*to express*) *forcefully*; jdm ~ nahelegen *to bring* (*a th*) *home to a p*; jdm etw ~ vorstellen *to impress a p with a th*, *to urge a th upon a p* ·**Eindringlichkeit** f *insistency*, *urgency*; *emphasis*; *force*; mit aller ~ *with great insistence*; *with all the emphasis at one's command* ‖ *convincingness* (*of a style*); *forcefulness*, *pith*, *pithiness*; *trenchancy* (*of contrast*) ‖ *insistence* (*of a melody*); ⟨Lit⟩ *urgency* (*of a character*); → eindringsam

·**Eindringling** m, *intruder*; ein ~ in diese Einsamkeit *an i. upon this solitude*; *interloper*; ⟨Am⟩ *gate-crasher* ·**eindringsam** a *drastic* (Mittel); ~er Appell *moral suasion*

·**Eindringungs-** **~bereich** m ⟨aero-mil⟩ *air raid zone*, *zone of penetration* **~tiefe** f *depth of penetration*, → Aktionsradius **~vermögen** n *penetrating power*

·**Eindruck** m ~(e)s/≗e **I.** ⟨eig⟩ (*of objects*) *impress*, *impression*, *imprint*, *mark*, *stamp* (auf *on*); *impression* (*of shoes on the ground*, *of the head on a pillow*) **II. A.** (~ auf die Seele etc) *impression* (auf *on*); bleibender (*or* nachhaltiger), tiefer, unauslöschlicher ~ *lasting*, *deep*, *indelible i.*; kläglicher ~ *poor i.*; übler ~ *bad* (od *unfavourable*) *i.* **B. 1.** e–n **guten** ~ **erhalten** v *to be favourably impressed by ..* ‖ er erweckte (*or* machte) den ~, als ob er .. *he gave the impression that he ..* ‖ sich [acc] des ~s nicht erwehren *not to escape the i.* ‖ den ~ h, daß (*or* als ob) .. *to have an i. that ..*, ⟨fam⟩ *to feel that ..* ‖ e–n ~ hervorrufen *to create* (od *produce*) *an i.* ‖ e–n ~ bei jdm hinterlassen *to leave an imp. on a p*, *to leave a p with an i.*; (of books, etc.) *to make one's mark with a p* | ~ m = Aufsehen m; ⟨theat⟩ *to get across* ‖ nur um ~ z m *only for show* ‖ (ezw tun,) um ~ z m .. *for effect* ‖ e–n weit älteren ~ m als dem Alter entspricht *to appear far older than one's years* ‖ e–n ~ m (of rooms) *to strike a note* ‖ ~ m auf jdn *to impress a p*; *to take a hold on a p* ‖ e–n ~ auf jdn m *to make* (od *produce*) *an imp. on a p* ‖ (S) e–n guten ~ m ⟨fam⟩ *to be going down well* ‖ den ~ e–s Träumers m *to make* (od *give*) *the i. of being a dreamer* ‖ k–n ~ m (of a speech, etc.) *to fall flat*; k. ~ machend *unimpressive* ‖ | **auf jdn** ~ **m** *to impress a p*, *to register with a p*; was f e–n ~ sie auf ihn gemacht hat! *how she has struck him!* ‖ k–n ~ auf jdn m *to be lost upon a p*; *not to cut much ice with a p* ‖ Drohungen m auf mich k–n ~ *I am not impressed by threats* ‖ °~ schinden → schinden | der ~, der in mir zurückblieb .. *the impression that was left with me* **2. für** ≗e empfänglich *impressionable* | ohne jeden ~ **auf** jdn bleiben *to go off a p* (od *to leave a p*) *like water off a duck's back*; *to be lost on a p* | **unter** dem ~ der Neuigkeit *under the novelty* ‖ unter dem ersten ~ *on the spur of the moment* ‖ unter dem ~ der kürzlichen Ereignisse *in the light of recent events* ‖ sie stehen noch unter dem ~ s–s Todes *the impression of his death is still fresh in their minds*

·**ein|drucken** vt [h] ⟨typ⟩ (etw) *to imprint*, *impress*, *overprint*; (Bilder etc) *to insert* ‖ (bei Kattundruck) (Farbe) *to re-enter*, *to ground in*

·**ein|drücken** vt [h] **1.** (einbeulen) (etw) *to dent*, *dint*; *indent*; *to mark* (*a th*) *with a depression* ‖ (Hut) *to batter*, *crush* **2.** (plattdrücken) (Nase) *to flatten* ‖ *to compress*, *crush*; *squeeze* **3.** (durchbrechen) (Fenster) *to blow in*; (F.scheibe) *to push* od *press*, *in*, (*panes broken* od *shattered*, *the door was blown in by the explosion*) ‖ (Mauer etc) *to breach* ‖ ⟨mil⟩ die Front ~ *to break through the front*; ([befestigte] Linien) ~ ⟨mil⟩ *to dent* ‖ ihm wurde der Brustkorb –gedrückt *he had his ribs broken* (od *fractured*); → 2.

·**eindrücklich** a = eindrucksvoll

·**Eindrucks-** ≗**fähig** a *impressionable* **~fähigkeit** f *receptiveness* (f *for*) **~kunst** f ⟨arts⟩ *impressionism* ≗**los** a *unimpressive*, *unimposing* ‖ *flat* (*speech*); *lame* (*story*); *monotonous*; *tame* (*ending*; *retort*) ≗**voll** a *impressive* (*scene*); *commanding* (*speech*); *effective* (*picture*), *imposing*, *striking*; *emphatic*, *forcible*, *telling* (*effect*) | (das) ≗e *impressiveness*

·**Eindünst-** **~apparat** m *evaporator* ·**ein|dünsten** vt [h] *to stew* od *evaporate down*

°·**einduseln** vi [s] *to doze off*

·**ein|ebnen** vt [h] (Hügel) *to level*; *to even*; *to make flat* ·**Einebnung** f *levelling*

Ein- (→ (Zahl) eins) **~ehe** f *monogamy* **~eiig** a → Zwilling; → –gänger, –glas, –gottglaube, –hand-, –häusig, –horn, –hufer etc ≗**gleisig**, ≗**spurig** a *single-track* [attr] **~kreiselkompaß** m *s.-gyro c.* ≗**polig** a *s.-pole* ≗**stufig** a *s.-stage* **~schichtfilm** m ⟨phot⟩ *s.-coated film*, etc, etc

·**einen** vt [h] (ein Volk) *to unify*, *to unite*; innerlich geeint sein *to be unified within* → geeint ‖ **sich** ~ *to unite*; *become one* (od *a whole*)

·**ein|engen** vt [h] **1.** *to constrain* ‖ (den Hals) *to constrict* (durch *by* [*a collar*]) ‖ *the dress cramps me* od *restricts my movements*; die Bewegungsfreiheit ~ *to hamper movements* ‖ (jdn) *to confine*, *to crib*; *to shackle* → behindern ‖ ⟨fig⟩ (Handel, Macht; Geist) *to constrict*, *to contract*, *to cramp*; **2.** (begrenzen, reduzieren) (Bereich) *to confine* (auf *to*); *to narrow in* (durch *by*); → einschließen, umgeben ‖ (s–e Wünsche) *to limit*; (Begriff, Zahl) *to narrow*; *to narrow down* (auf *to*); *to restrict* (*the sense*, *meaning*; *sphere of activity*); ⟨mil⟩ den Angriff ~ *to canalize the attack* **3.** ⟨chem⟩ (konzentrieren) *to concentrate*
·**Einengung** f **1.** *constriction*, *contraction*; *cramping* **2.** *confinement*; *limitation*; *narrowing* (*of an*

idea), *narrowing(-down)*; *reduction* || *restriction* (*of law*) *by new clauses*

·**Einer** m ~s/~ **1.** ⟨math⟩ *unit* || → einzeln | ~stelle [f] *unit's place* **2.** ⟨sport⟩ (Renn≈) *skiff* || ≈ → ein

einerlei [Betonung → u] **I.** a **A.** [attr] [·einerlei] **1.** (gleichartig) *one and the same* (*colour*), *the same*; ~ Tuch *cloth of the same kind* **2.** (eintönig) *dull*, *hundrum*, *monotonous* (*diet*) **B.** [pred] [einerl·ei] **1.** *all one*, *all the same*; (gleichgültig) *indifferent*; es ist ganz ~ *it is six of one and half a dozen of the other*, *it makes no difference* (od *odds*), *that comes to the same th* || es ist mir ~ *it is immaterial* od *indifferent to me*, *it is all one* (od *all the same*) *to me*; *I don't care* || es ist schließlich ~ *it makes no odds* **2.** [abs] **a.** ~, her damit! *all the same*, *let's have it*! **b.** [a. ·einerlei] ~, ob .. *no matter if* .. || ~, wie, wieviele *no matter how*, *how many* | ~, wann .. *whenever* || ~, was .. *whatever* || ~, welches .. *whichever*; ~ welchen Ursprungs *of whatever origin* || ~, wer .. *whoever* || ~, wohin .. *wherever* (*he goes*) **II.** ≈ [Einerl·ei] n *sameness*, *monotony*; *humdrum*; das gewöhnliche ~ *the routine things*; ~ der Fabrikarbeit *factory r.*; ein greuliches ~ *a horror of routine*; das ewige ~ des menschl. Daseins *the deadly sameness in life*

·**ein|ernten** vt [h] (Getreide etc) *to gather*, *to gather in*, *to reap*, *to harvest*; → ernten

·**einerseits**, ·**einesteils** adv; ~ .. andererseits *on* (*the*) *one hand* .. *on the other* (*hand*); *for one thing* .. *for another thing*

·**ein|exerzieren** vt [h] ⟨mil⟩ (Soldaten) *to drill*, *to train*; *to knock into shape*; → drillen || ⟨übtr⟩ (P, T) *to exercise* (in *in*; z tun *in doing*); (Pferd) *to school*

·**einfach** **I.** a **A.** [attr] **1.** (Ggs doppelt; zus–gesetzt) **a.** *single* (*flower*; *vowel*; *birth*, *delivery*); *simplex* | bes ⟨tech & com⟩ ~er Adler ⟨her⟩ *single eagle* || ~es Bier → 2. || ~e Buchführung *book-keeping by single entry* || ⟨rail⟩ ~e Fahrkarte, ~e Fahrt [f] *single ticket*; *single* (*3 singles to Berlin*) || e–e Feile mit ~em Hieb *single-cut file* || ~er Kolben *single-acting piston* || ~e Lage *single ply* || ~e Nietung *single--riveted joint* || ~e Option *single option* || ~es Ventil *single valve* **b.** *simple*; *pure* | bes ⟨scient; bot; med; math & log; mus; jur⟩ *simple*; ⟨chem⟩ *simple* (*substance*), *uncombined* (*state*), *elementary* (*body*) || ⟨phys⟩ *primary* (*colo[u]r*) || ~er Bankrott *simple bankruptcy* || ~er Bruch ⟨med⟩ *simple fracture* || ~es Fest ⟨ec⟩ *simple feast* || ~e Gleichung ⟨math⟩ *simple equation* || ~e Größe ⟨math⟩ *simple quantity*, *monomial* || ~e Havarie *simple average* || ~er Körper *simple solid* || ~e Zeiten ⟨gram⟩ *simple tenses* **2.** ⟨übtr⟩ (schlicht) **a.** *simple* (*mode of life*); *austere* (P); *frugal* (*meal*); *homely*; *homespun* ⟨fig⟩; *plain* (*clothes*); *austere*, *Spartan* (*diet*) || ~es Bier *small* (od *weak*) *beer* || ~e Postkarte *plain postcard* || ~e Worte *plain words* || etw ≈es *something simple* **b.** *common*, *ordinary*, *plain*, *simple*, *primitive* (*man*, *people*) **3.** ⟨übtr⟩ (leicht verständlich) *simple* (*explanation*, *task*); *easy* || *primitive* (*methods*) || ~ u klar *terse* (*style*) || → II. 4. **B.** [pred] (leicht) *simple*, *easy*; *plain sailing*; es ist bestimmt nicht ~ *it is certainly not a simple matter*; das ist sehr ~ *there is nothing in it*; so weit war alles ~ *so far all was plain sailing* || es ist gar nicht so ~ *it's quite a business*, *it takes a bit of doing* **C.** [in comp] ⟨tech & chem⟩ *single*; *simplex* || ≈-Betrieb [m] *simplex-operation* || ≈-Expansionsmaschine [f] *single-expansion machine* **II.** adv **1.** ⟨tech⟩ ~-wirkend *single-acting* **2.** (schlicht) *simply*, *plainly*; ~ gekleidet *plain-clothed*; ~ leben *to live simply* **3.** (unkompliziert) *simply*; *clearly*; die S liegt ganz ~ *the matter is quite simple* || (ohne Schwierigkeit) *simply*, *easily* (*to be answered quite simply*) **4.** [verblaßt] **a.** das ist ~ Schmutz *that is garbage pure and simple*; .. Unsinn *that is pure nonsense*; .. ~ Wahnsinn *that is simple madness*; das ist mehr als ~ Flirt *that is more than just a flirtation* || die S ist ~ die, daß *the point is this that* .. **b.** er fürchtet sich ~ vor nichts *there really isn't anything he is afraid of* || du gehst ~ hin u fragst *you just* (od *simply*) *go and ask* || du verschwindest ~ so u *you just disappear and* .. || ~ großartig, °~ Puppe *simply magnificent*, *just splendid* || ich verstehe dich ~ nicht *I don't understand you at all* ≈**leitung** f ⟨telph⟩ *single-wire line* ≈**telegraphie** f *simplex telegraphy* ≈**wendellampe** f *single-coil lamp* || → ⟨a.⟩ I. C.

·**Einfachheit** f ~/ **1.** *simplicity* (*of a problem*); der ~ [gen] halber *for the sake of simplicity* **2.** (Schlichtheit) *simplicity* (in *in* [*dress*]), *plainness*; strenge (*or* spartanische) ~ *austere* (od *Spartan*) *simplicity*; *austerity* || weise ~ *frugality and prudence*

·**ein|fädeln** vt [h] **1.** (Nadel) *to thread* || (Zwirn) *to pass through the eye of a needle* | **sich** (in Marschkolonne) ~ *to get into line*, *to join* (*a column*) **2.** ⟨fig⟩ *to arrange*; (Plan) *to contrive*, *to devise*; *to manage*; (Intrigue etc) *to engineer*, *to scheme* e–e S schlau ~ *to go* od *set about a matter subtly* ·**Einfädelung** f *threading* || ⟨übtr⟩ *arrangement*; *contrivance*; *approach* ~**spunkt** m ⟨mil⟩ (e–r Kolonne) *initial point* ·**Einfädler** m *threading wire*

·**ein|fahren** vi/t **I.** vi [s] **1.** in e–e Stadt ~ *to drive* od *pull into a town* || ⟨min⟩ *to descend*, *to go down*; in e–e Grube ~ *to descend a mine* || ⟨hunt⟩ (in den Bau, *of fox*) *to go to ground* **2.** (of trains) *to pull in*; in e–n Bahnhof ~ *to pull* (od *draw*) *into a station*, *to enter a station*; → erreichen || ⟨mot⟩ in auf .. *to join* (*the motorway* || **II.** vt [h] **1.** (Korn) *to bring* (od *carry*, *get*) *in* **2. a.** ein Pferd ~ *to break a horse to harness*; *to break a h. in* || (Wagen) *to run* .. *in*, *to road-test*; .. wird –ge–! *Running-in*! || ⟨aero⟩ (Fahrwerk, Landeklappen) *to raise* **b. sich** ~ *to practise driving*; *to get one's hand in*

·**Einfahrt** f ~/~en **1.** [abstr] *entrance* ⟨a. mot⟩ (~! *way in*!, *IN* || *turn-in* || *merging traffic*, ⟨Can⟩ *merge*) || *entry* ([a. mot⟩ *to*, *into one-way street*) || ~ freihalten! *keep entrance clear*! || ⟨min⟩ *descent* (*into*) | (of trains) *pulling in*; der Zug hat ~ *the signal is up* (⟨engl⟩ *down*) *for the train*, *the train is signalled*; der Z. hat keine ~ *the signal is down* (⟨engl⟩ *up*) *for the train* **2.** [konkr] (Weg; Öffnung) *drive*; *approach*; ⟨Am⟩ *driveway* || (*carriage-*) *entrance*; *entry* || *gateway*; *entrance* (*of a tunnel*) || *entrance*, *mouth* (*of a port*) || (Fuchs≈) *drain* ~**geschwindigkeit** f *running-in speed* ~**signal** n (Apparat) *home-signal* ~(**stelle** f) ⟨mot⟩ (z Autobahn) (*intermediate*) *access point*, ⟨Am, Can⟩ *Merge* ~**zeichen** n *up-signal*

·**Einfahrzeit** f ⟨mot⟩ *breaking-in period*

·**Einfall** m ~(e)s/≈e **1.** (Einsturz) *falling*; *in* (od *down*); *collapse* || ⟨geol⟩ → Einfallen **2. a.** ⟨mil⟩ (feindl.) ~ in ein Land *invasion of a country*; *incursion* (od *foray*, *inroad*, *irruption*, *raid*) *into a c.*; die Wikingereinfälle [pl] *the Viking raids* [pl] || e–n ~ in ein L. m *to invade* od *raid a country* **b.** ⟨phys⟩ (of lines, rays) *incidence*; → Einfalls- **c.** (of a lock) *clicking*; (of a latch) *catching* **d.** ⟨hunt⟩ *fall* (*of snipe*) **e.** ⟨fig⟩ → Einbruch 1. b.; Eindringen 1. **3.** ⟨fig⟩ (gedanklicher ~) *sudden fancy* (od *inspiration*; *idea*, *thought*) || ein späterer ~ *an afterthought* || geistreicher, kluger ~ *brain-wave*; lustiger, spaßiger ~ *fun*, *joke*, *jest*; witzige –fälle [pl] *quips*; *sallies* (*of wit*), *starts of fancy*; auf den richtigen ~ k, den r. ~ h *to hit the right idea*; wunderliche (*or* seltsame) -fälle *freaks*, (*queer*) *kinks, whims* [pl]; *vagaries* (*of fashion, fortune*); ⟨hum⟩ er hat „-fälle" wie ein altes Haus *he has whims of a sort*; *the idea*! → Grille, Laune ‖ sonderbarer ~! *the idea*! | ⟨Lit⟩ (of style) gesuchter witziger ~ *concetto, conceit* | es war nur ein ~ v ihm *it was merely a sudden inspiration on his part* (od *of his*) ‖ ich habe e-n ~, es kommt mir ein ~ *a fresh idea occurs to me* ‖ es kam mir der ~, daß *I had a fancy that* ..; *it occured to me that* ..; *it struck me that* .. **~energie** f ⟨opt⟩ *incident energy*; → Einfalls-

·ein|fallen vi/t **I.** vi [s] **A.** ⟨eig⟩ (of buildings) *to collapse*; *to fall down* (od *in*); *to founder*; → einbrechen I. B. 1. ‖ über jdm ~ *to come down on a p* ‖ ich glaubte, der Himmel fiele ein *I thought the sky* (od *heavens*) *would fall* **2.** ⟨geol⟩ (of ground, stratum) *to dip, sink* **3.** ⟨übtr⟩ (of the face, etc.) *to fall in, to shrink*; *sink*; sein Gesicht war -ge- *his face had fallen in*; **B. 1. a.** ⟨mil⟩ *to make inroads* ‖ in ein Land ~ *to invade* (od *foray, raid*) *a country, to impinge on a c.*; → Einfall **b.** störend bei jdm ~ *to break* (od *pounce*) *in upon a p* (od *upon a p's peace*); → einbrechen II. A. 1. c.; eindringen B. 1. **2.** (of birds) ~ in *to alight on* (*the water*); *to swoop down upon* (*a tree*) **3.** (of the wind) plötzlich ~ *to come on* (od *to set in*) *unexpectdly* **3.** (of light) *to break, fall, penetrate, shine* (durch *through* [*the window*]) **4.** (of a lock) *to click*; (of a latch) *to catch* **5.** ⟨übtr⟩ **a.** (in Worten) *to break* (od *cut, nip*) *in* (*he broke in 'Leave him'*); ~ mit *to break* (od *strike*) *in with* (*a jest*) ‖ [abs] *to answer*; *retort*; *to put in a remark* **b.** ⟨mus⟩ (of instruments, etc.) *to chime* (od *come, join*) *in* **c.** (of ducks, etc) *to flight*; (of snipe) *to fall* **C.** ⟨fig⟩ (gedanklich ~) **1.** [nur 3. sg & pl] jdm ~ (of *thoughts*, etc.) *to come into a p's head*; *to occur to a p* (od *to a p's mind*); zwei Beispiele fallen mir ein *two examples occur to my mind*; der Gedanke an .. fiel ihm ein *the thought of* .. *crossed* (od *flashed across*) *his mind*; der Name fällt mir nicht ein *I forget the name*; sein N. wollte mir nicht ~ *I could not think of his n.*; da fällt mir gerade ein .. *it has just struck me* ..; dabei fällt mir e-e Geschichte ein *that puts me in mind of a story*; [abs] da(bei) fällt mir ein: .. *that reminds me* (*of* .., *that*) ..; halt, da fällt mir gerade ein, daß .. *wait a minute, it just occurs to me that* .. ‖ jdm wieder ~ *to come back to a p* **2.** [imps] (ich werde nicht gehen) **das fällt mir nicht ein**! das sollte mir im Traume ~! (..) *not I*! (..) *catch me doing that*!; es fällt mir nicht ein z tun *I have not the slightest intention to do, I do not think* (od *dream*) *of doing* ‖ was fällt Ihnen (nur) ein? *what the hell is the idea*? *what's the big idea*? *what do you think you are doing*? *what(ever) are you thinking of*? **3. sich ~ l** *to dare*; *to take into one's head* (*to do*); laß dir das ja nicht ~ *don't dare to do that*!, *you just try it*! ‖ sich etw Neues ~ l *to think up sth new*; du könntest dir etw Besseres ~ l *you might think of sth better* **II.** vt; sich [dat] den Schädel ~ *to break one's skull by a fall* **·Einfallen** n **1.** *collapse*; *falling-in* (*of the face*) **4.** → Einfall **·einfallend** a ⟨phys⟩ *incident* (*beam*) ‖ ⟨min⟩ *inclined* (Strecke)

·Einfalls- ⟨phys⟩ **~ebene** f *plane of incidence* **≈los** a *lacking in ideas* **~pforte** f *gateway* (*in to*) **~punkt** m *point of incidence* **≈reich** a: ~er Mann *idea man* **~reichtum** m *ingenuity*; *fertility of ideas* **~winkel** m *angle of incidence*

·Einfalt f ~/ **1.** *simplicity* (*of a child*); *ingenuousness*; *innocence*; *artlessness, naturalness* **2.** (P) *simple p*; die ~ vom Lande *a simple country girl* **3.** = Einfältigkeit °**~spinsel** m *gaby, greenhorn, josser, nincompoop, ninny, noodle, simpleton*; ⟨Am⟩ *gump*

·ein|falten vt [h] *to fold* od *turn down, to turn in*

·einfältig a **1.** *simple*; *ingenuous, innocent*; *artless, natural* ‖ ein ~es Gemüt *a simple soul* **2.** ⟨dero⟩ = *cerdulous, simple*; ⟨fam⟩ *gullible*; → dumm **≈keit** f ~/ mst ⟨dero⟩ (sonst = Einfalt) *gullibility*; → Dummheit

·ein|falzen vt [h] ⟨carp⟩ *to rabbet* ‖ (Papier) *to fold*

·Einfamilienhaus n *single-family house*

·Einfang m ⟨at⟩ (*fission*)*capture* | ~experiment [n] mit Gammastrahlen *capture gamma experiment*

·ein|fangen I. vt [h] **1.** (Vogel) *to catch, seize*; (Dieb) *to capture, to catch* od *lay hold of* ‖ (Gefangene) wieder ~ *to recapture* | ⟨übtr⟩ (jdn) *to rope in*; *take in*; jdn f s-e Zwecke ~ *to exploit a p* ‖ (Strahlen etc) *to catch*; (Elektronen) *to trap, capture* ‖ (Seelisches) in Worte ~ *to put into* (od *express in*) *words* **II.** ≈ n ⟨at phys⟩ *capture*

·ein|färben vt [h] ⟨weav, etc⟩ *to dye* ‖ ⟨print⟩ *to ink the form* ‖ ⟨theat⟩ (Lampe) *to dip*

·Einfarbendruck m *single-colo(u)r* (od *monochrome*) *print*

·einfarbig, [österr] ≈ a *unicoloured, uniform in colour* ‖ (*of cloth, flowers*) *self-coloured*; *plain* (*wall-paper*) ‖ ⟨paint⟩ *monochromatic*; ~es Gemälde *monochrome* | **≈keit** f *uniformity of colo(u)r*

Einfaß- ~band n ⟨tail⟩ *edge binding*; → u.

·ein|fassen vt [h] **1.** (Edelstein) *to enchase, mount, set* (in Gold *in gold*); (etw) ~ mit *to set with* (*diamonds*) ‖ (etw) in e-n Rahmen ~ *to frame*; (Bild) *to frame*; -gefaßt in *framed in* .. **2.** (Mantel etc) *to trim* (mit *with* [fur]); (Waffe, Teppich) mit Borte ~ *to bind*; (Kleid) mit gestickter Borte ~ *to purl*; mit Spitzen ~ *to lace* **3.** (Rasen, Weg) *to border, edge* (mit *with* [*flowers*]); (Straße) *to line* (*with trees*); e-e v Bäumen -gefaßte Straße *a tree-lined road* ‖ (Garten) *to enclose* (mit *with*); (etw) mit e-m Zaun ~ *to fence*; *a wall encloses the garden*; (Quelle) *to curb*; → einschließen **Einfaß- ~mauer** f (Stütz-) *retaining wall* **~streifen** m ⟨phot⟩ *binding strip*

·Einfassung f ~/~en **A.** [abstr] (Einfassen) **1.** *mounting, setting* (*of jewels*) ‖ *framing* (*of a picture*) **2.** *trimming* (*of a dress*) **3.** *enclosure* (*of a garden*) **B.** [konkr] **1.** *mount* (*of a picture*); ⟨phot⟩ (v Dias) *mounting*; → Rahmen **2.** *border, edge*; → Rand, Saum ‖ genähte Leder ≈ *welt* (*of a shoe*); Sohlen mit e-r ~ versehen *to welt*; → Borte **3.** *enclosure*; *fence*

·ein|fetten 1. vt [h] *to grease, lubricate*; *to smear* (mit *with*); → einschmieren ‖ mit Öl ~ *to oil*; mit Talg ~ *to tallow*; → einölen ‖ **sich** ~ *to smear o.s.* (mit *with*) **2.** ≈ n *greasing*; *lubrication*

·ein|feuern vi [h] (tüchtig einheizen) *to fire up*

·ein|finden vrefl [h] sich ~ *to appear, come*; *to make one's appearance* ‖ *to be, to be present* (z etw *at a th*) ‖ *to assemble, muster* ‖ sich zufällig ~ *to turn up* | ⟨übtr⟩ sich ~ in (etw) *to acclimatize to, to get accustomed to* (*a th*); → sich (ab)finden

·ein|flechten vt [h] **1.** (Haare) *to braid* (od *plait*) *together* ‖ (Muster etc) ~ in *to inweave* (od *enweave, work*) *into a th* **2.** ⟨übtr⟩ (Bemerkung, Lob) *to interpose*; *to insert, to introduce*; *to put* (od *throw*) *in* ‖ ein Ereignis (etc) ~ in etw *to weave an incident into a th* (*a narrative*) **·Einflechtung** f ~/~en *inweaving* (in *into*) ‖ ⟨übtr⟩ *interposition*; *interposed remark* od *word*; *insertion, introduction*

·ein/flicken vt [h] (etw) *to put* (*a th*) *in as a patch*; ~ in etw *to patch* (*a th*) *into a th* ‖ ⟨übtr⟩ = einflechten

·**ein|fliegen I.** vi/t ⟨aero⟩ **1.** vi [s] ~ in ein (fremdes) Land *to fly into a country, to enter a c. by aircraft* **2.** vt [h] (Flugzeug) *to test (out) an aeroplane* || **sich** ~ *to practise flying* **II.** ≃ n ⟨aero⟩ *trial flight, test-flight* (od *fly*) ·**Einflieger** m ⟨aero⟩ *test-pilot*

·**ein|fließen** vi [s] **1.** *to flow in*; ~ in *to flow into (a country)* || (of money) *to come in* **2.** ⟨übtr⟩ (Worte etc) ~ l *to interpose; insert, introduce; to put* (od *throw*) *in*; e–e Bemerkung ~ l *to make* (od *drop*) *a remark* (über *on*; z *to*) *in passing*

·**einflößbar** a *capable of being instilled*

·**ein|flößen** vt [h] **1.** (Medizin) in Tropfen ~ *to instil; to administer, to give* (jdm *to a p*); e–m Kranken die Nahrung ~ *to feed a patient* **2.** ⟨fig⟩ **a.** Achtung ~ *to command respect*; Vertrauen ~ *to command* (od *give*) *confidence*, → 2. b. **b.** jdm etw ~ *to instil(l)* (od *infuse, transfuse*) *a th (new ideas, life) into a p* (od *into a p's mind*); jdm Schrecken ~ *to strike terror into a p* || → eingeben || *to fill* (od *imbue, inform, infuse, inspire*) *a p with a th (comfort, confidence, courage; fear; hope*, etc.) || → einprägen, –schärfen ·**Einflößung** f ~/~en **1.** *instillation; administration (of medicine)* **2.** ⟨fig⟩ *infusion, instillation*; → Eingebung

·**ein|fluchten** vt [h] ⟨surv⟩ (etw) *to align* od *arrange according to the prescribed line of frontage*

·**Einfluchtung** f ⟨surv⟩ *alignment*

·**Einflug** m ~(e)s/≃e ⟨aero⟩ **1.** *air-raid; flight* (in *into*); *entrance (into ..) by aircraft*; ~erlaubnis [f] *entry-permit*; ~punkt [m] *point of entry*; ~schneise [f] *approach funnel* od *track*; *lane of approach*; ~zone [f], ~abschnitt [m] *air-corridor* **2.** *test-flight*

·**Einfluß** m –flusses/–flüsse **A.** ⟨eig⟩ **a.** (Einfließen) *inflow, inflowing (of a liquid), influx*; ~ in *the flowing (of ..) into* **b.** (Ort des –sses) *influx, confluence; mouth* **c.** ⟨chem⟩ *action* **B.** ⟨fig⟩ **1.** *influence* (auf *on, upon*); der ~ Goethes auf ihn *the i. of Goethe upon him* || (Macht) *influence* (bei *with*; über *over*); *authority* od *interest* (bei *with*); *ascendancy, purchase* (über *over*); *foothold, grip (on), hold* (auf, über *on, over [a people]*); *sway (over)*; polit. ~ ⟨Am⟩ *pull* **2. a. erhebender** ~ *moral influence*; ⟨Am⟩ *uplift*; (ihre Ermahnungen, Drohungen) blieben nicht ohne ~ auf ihn *he was not (left) unimpressed by ..* || schädlicher (*or* unheilvoller, verderblicher) ~ *blight* (auf *on*), *blast* || schlechter ~ *infection* **b.** s–n ~ **aufbieten,** geltend m, z Geltung bringen in e–r S; ~ nehmen auf e–e S *to bring one's influence to bear upon a th; to make one's influence on a th felt* || (gr) ~ **ausüben** *to exercise an (a great) influence (on); to influence (a p); to bear* od *work upon*; e–n schädlichen ~ ausüben auf .. *to cast a blight upon ..* | s–n ~ **geltend m f** *to pull a few strings for; to throw one's weight about in (the diplomacy)* || *to use one's influence (in favo(u)r of .., to the disadvantage of ..)* || s–n ~ zugunsten jds in die Waagschale legen *or* geltend m *to throw one's weight on the side of a p* || gr ~ gewinnen *to gain a great ascendancy (over a p)* || ~ gewinnen (*or* sich ~ z verschaffen wissen) bei jdm *to gain upon a p*; (of habits) *to grow on a p* | ~ **haben** *to have influence* (auf *over*); *influence* (od *authority, interest, weight*) (bei jdm *with a p*) || ~ h in e–r S *to have a voice in a th* || *(his name) carries great weight* (bei, auf *with*) || k–n ~ h auf etw *to be beyond a p's control*; → rückwirkend || welchen ~ hat diese Veränderung auf das Licht? *what difference does this change make to the light?* | k–n ~ hinterlassen *to remain uninfluential* || s–n ~ verlieren *to lose one's grip (on a p)* **c. an** ~ gewinnen (verlieren) *to gain (to lose) in influence* | ein Mann **ohne** jeden ~ *an uninfluential man* | **unter** jds ~ geraten, k *to come under the influence of a p; to fall under a p's sway* || unter e–m ~ stehen *to be under an influence* || unter jds ~ stehen *to be under the i. of a p* || unter dem ~ e–s Gefühls stehen *to be in the grip of a feeling* | **von** ~ auf, in *influential on, in* || ein Mann v gr ~ *a man of great consequence* (od *credit, weight*); *an influential man* || v k–m ~ s (a. S) *to cut no ice, not to cut any* (od *much*) *ice* ~**gebiet** n, ~**sphäre** f ⟨pol⟩ *sphere of influence* ≃**reich** a *influential (p)*; ⟨pol⟩ *string-pulling* [adj]; (Mann, Zeitung) → angesehen; *(a p) of great consequence*; ⟨Am pol fam⟩ *big-time* (od *shot*); e–n ~en Gönner h *to have a friend at court*; ~e Beziehungen *connexions* [pl]; ~e Beziehungen *or* Verwandte h *to be well connected* ~**röhre** f *inflow* (od *inlet*) *-pipe*

·**ein|flüstern** vt [h] jdm etw ~ *to convey* (od *suggest*) *a th to a p by way of innuendo* ·**Einflüsterung** f ~/~en *prompting, suggestion*; böse ~ *incitement, instigation* || ⟨pol⟩ [oft pl] *indirect suggestion; innuendo, (malicious) insinuation*

·**ein|fluten** vi ⟨fig⟩ ~ auf jdn *to pour in upon a p*

·**ein|fordern** vt [h] (Münzen; Schulden) *to call in* od *up*; e–e Summe Geldes ~ *to demand payment of a sum*; → eintreiben || ⟨com⟩ Kapital ~ *to make a call for funds; to call up capital*; noch nicht –ge–rt *uncalled* | e–n Bericht ~ *to call for a report*; → einholen, –ziehen || etw ~ v (*or* bei) jdm *to indent upon a p for a th* ·**Einforderung** f ~/~en *calling in (of debts)*; → Eintreibung || ~ v Kapital *call for funds*

·**einförmig** a *uniform; homogeneous* || (eintönig) *monotonous*; ~e Ebene *dead level* || *dull (life); tedious*; → eintönig || *featureless* | ≃**keit** f ~ *uniformity; homogeneity*; ⟨übtr⟩ *monotony, sameness; dullness; featurelessness*

·**ein|fressen** vt & refl [h] **1.** Kummer (etc) ~ → fressen **2. sich ~ in** (of moths, etc.) *to cut into (a cloth)*; (of acids) *to bite* od *gnaw into (a th)*; *to bite* (od *corrode*) *a th* || ⟨übtr⟩ (of habit) *to bite into (a p)*; (of sorrow) *to eat* (od *gnaw*) *into (a p)*; sich in die Seele ~ *to gnaw at one's heart*; (of ideas) *to eat one's way into, to take root in (a country); to pervade (a people)*; → eindringen in || –ge– *pitted (metal); deep-rooted (hatred)* ||

·**ein|friedigen,** ·**ein|frieden** vt [h] (Garten etc) *to enclose, fence, hedge; to fence in*; → einhegen || –ge–detes Gelände *(in Asia) compound*

·**Einfriedigung,** ·**Einfriedung** f ~/~en **1.** [abstr] *enclosing, enclosure; fencing, walling* **2.** [konkr] **a.** (das Eingefriedigte) *enclosure; enclosed land* (etc); (Feld) *close*; → Domfreiheit **b.** (Mauer etc) *enclosure; fence* (etc.); ~ aus Stein ⟨Am⟩ *stone fence* ~**smauer** f *enclosing wall*

·**ein|frieren** vi [s] *to freeze (the water in the basin was frozen)*; ~ in *to freeze in (the Baltic)* || *to freeze in (the ship was frozen in)* || ⟨fig⟩ (P) *to freeze up* | vt [h] *to freeze* (⟨cul⟩ *vegetables*, ⟨com⟩ *capital*)

°·**ein|fuchsen** vt [h] jdm etw ~, jdn auf etw ~ *to coach* (od *train*) *a p in a th; to drum* (od *hammer*) *a th into a p*; → abrichten

·**ein|fügen I.** vt [h] **1.** ⟨eig, tech⟩ (Stein etc) *to interpose, insert* (zw *between*); (etw) ~ zw *to place between*; (Wort) zw den Zeilen ~ *to interline*; (etw) ~ in *to dovetail (a th) into; to enter (a th) in* || e–n Tag ~ *to fit in a day* (f *for*); ~ in *to fit in* od *into* || *to integrate* (in *into*) **2.** ⟨übtr⟩ (Bemerkung etc) *to interpose; insert* (in *into*); → einschieben; ~ in *to put in*; [abs] → einfallen **3. a. sich ~ in** (S) *to fit into*; sich gut ~ in *to fit in well with (a plan); to group well in (a landscape)* || sich fest ~ *to fit down* (auf *on*) **b.** (P) sich ~ *to toe the line; to conform* (od *adapt o.s.*) *to custom* (etc); sich ~ in *to fit in with, to become one with (a party)*; sich in (e–e Gruppe) ~ *to become an integral part of ..* → (ab)finden **II.** ≃ n ⟨eig & übtr⟩ *interposing, interposition; insertion, inter-*

polation ‖ → ·**Einfügung** f ~/~en **1.** [abstr] → Einfügen ‖ *adaptation, conforming* (in *to*) **2.** [konkr] (Eingefügtes) *interposition, interposed remark*; *insertion, inserted word*; *interpolation*; ~ zw den Zeilen *interlineation* **~ssatz** m ⟨gram⟩ *parenthetical clause*

·**ein|fühlen** vrefl [h] sich ~ in etw *to feel one's way* (od *to project one's personality*) *into a th* (*a subject*) ‖ sich ~ in *to humour* (*a p, a p's wishes*); *to achieve a sympathetic understanding of, to get into the spirit of a writer's work* ·**Einfühlung(svermögen** n) f ~/ *emotional penetration* (in etw *of a th*); ⟨psych, arts⟩ *empathy* ‖ *ability to feel* (f *with a p*); *appreciative perception* od *understanding*; *a sense* (f *of*); *flexibility*

·**Einfuhr** f ~/~en ⟨com⟩ **1.** [abstr] *importation, import* (*of goods*) **2.** [konkr] (Eingeführtes) *import*; [mst pl] *imports, inwards, import goods*; ~ u Ausfuhr *imports and exports* [pl]

·**Einfuhr-** [in comp] *import–* .. **~abgabe** f *i. duty*; *i.* od *customs duties* (*and taxes*) **~artikel** m *import*; *article imported* **~beschränkung** f *i. restrictions* pl **~bewilligung** f *i. certificate*; e–e ~ erteilen *to issue an i. authorization* **~deklaration** f ⟨cust⟩ *declaration inwards* **~erlaubnis** f *permission to import* **~hafen** m *port of entry* **~handel** m *i.-trade* **~händler** m *importer* **~kontingent** n *i. quota* **~land** n *importing country* **~-liste** f *list of imports* **~monopol** n *i.-monopoly* **~prämie** f *import-bounty* **~schein** m *import-permit* **~überschuß** m *i.s in excess of exports*; *surplus of imports* **~verbot** n *embargo on* (od *prohibition of*) *imports* **~waren** f [pl] *imports*; *import(ed) goods* [pl] **~zoll** m *import* (od *customs*) *-duty*; *customs* [pl] | ~schuld [f] *i. duty debt*; *debt of i. duties*; (un)bedingte (*unconditional*) .., *hypothetical* ..; Erlaß v ~ *dispensation from i. duties*

·**einführbar** a ⟨com⟩ *importable*

·**ein|führen** vt [h] **1.** jdn ~ *to introduce a p*; *to usher a p in* ‖ jdn ~ in *to bring* (od *initiate, introduce, lead, usher*) *a p into* (*a room, a company*) ‖ jdn ~ bei jdm *to introduce a p to a p*; jdn in die Gesellschaft ~ *to launch a p*; jdn bei Hofe ~ *to introduce* (od *present formally*) *a p at Court* ‖ jdn redend ~ *to introduce a p as speaking* ‖ e–e junge Dame in die Gesellschaft ~ *to bring a young lady out, to introduce a y. l. to society*; sie wurde in die G. eingeführt *she had her coming-out party* | jdn (feierlich) in ein Amt ~ *to install a p in an office*; *to inaugurate a p*; (e–n Geistlichen) in s–e Pfründe ~ *to induct to a benefice, to institute into a b.* | jdn in (e–n Gegenstand etc) ~ *to initiate* (od *instruct*) *a p in* (*a subject*); (durch Übung) *to rehearse in* (*an author*) **2. a.** (Neuheit, Währung) *to introduce*; *adopt* ‖ e–e Mode (wieder) ~ *to launch* (*revive*) *a fashion*; (Artikel) *to bring into fashion*; der Artikel ist bei dem Publikum gut –geführt *the article takes on well*; → Anklang ‖ (Gesetz, Sitte etc) *to establish, institute*; *to set up* ‖ (neue Ära; System) *to initiate, inaugurate, herald, introduce, start*; *to usher in*; (System) *to adopt* ‖ (etw) zwangsmäßig ~ *to enforce* **b.** (Waren) *to import*; ~ bei *to bring to the notice of* (*a p*) **3.** (Sonde) *to introduce, to insert* (in *into* [*a wound*]); (etw) *to enter* (*into a th*) ‖ ⟨tech⟩ *to run in*; ⟨mill⟩ *to feed* (*to the m.*); *to lead a cable* od *wire into a house*

·**Einführung** f ~/~en **1.** (P) *introduction* (bei jdm *to a p*; in *into*) | *initiation* (*into an office*); (feierliche) *installation*; *induction* (*of an official*) | *initiation* (in *into*); *instruction* (*in*) **2.** (S) **a.** *introduction*; *institution*; *establishment* ‖ *initiation, inauguration* (*of a new era*) ‖ zwangsmäßige ~ *enforcement* **b.** ⟨com⟩ *importation* (*of goods*) **3.** ⟨med⟩ *introduction, insertion* (in *into*)

·**Einführungs-** [in comp] ⟨tech⟩ *leading-in* **~draht** m *leading-in wire* **~gesetz** n *introductory* (od *preliminary*) *law* (z *to*) **~kabel** n *leading-in cable* **~kurs** m (kurzer *brief*) *orientation* od *appreciation course* **~schreiben** n *letter of introduction*

·**Einfüll-** [in comp] ⟨tech⟩ *filling–*; *feed–* **~hahn** m *feed-cock* **~öffnung** f ⟨tech⟩ *filling hole* (*aperture, mouth*) **~rohr** n *filling pipe* **~stutzen** m *feed-cock*; ⟨mot⟩ *tank filler* (*cap*)

·**ein|füllen** vt [h] (Flüssigkeit) ~ in *to put* od *to pour into* (*a bottle*); → füllen II.

·**einfüßig** a *one-footed*; ⟨min⟩ *one-foot* (*vein*)

·**Eingabe** f ~/~n *application* (an *to*; um *for*) (Bericht) *statement* (an *to*); e–e ~ m um etw *to make an application for, to apply for a th* (an jdn *to a p*) ‖ ⟨dipl & parl⟩ (Bittschrift an Behörde) *memorial*; *petition* (an *to*; um *for*); e–e ~ richten an jdn *to address a memorial to a p*; *to memorialize* (od *petition*) *a p* (um *for*) | ~frist [f] *time limit for application* ‖ ⟨comp⟩ *input*; ~ u Ausgabe *selection*; ~/Ausgabepuffer [m] *input/output "buffer store"*; neue ~datenmengen [f pl] (*minimal*) *amounts of new input data*; ~einheit [f] *input unit*

·**ein|gabeln** vt [h] ⟨mil⟩ (Ziel) *to bracket*

·**Eingang** m ~(e)s/⁓̈e **I.** [abstr] (Eingehen) **1.** (P) *entrance* (in *into*; z *to*), *entry, ingress*; → Eintritt, Zutritt ‖ verbotener ~ *no admittance, no entrance* **2.** (S) **a.** *entry* (*of gold*; *money*); *receipt* (*of goods, letters*); nach ~ v *on receipt of*; → bestätigen ‖ *arrival* (*of a ship, train*) **b.** ⟨com⟩ *arrival(s* pl) **3.** ~ **erlangen** z *to obtain entry to* (*the Embassy*) ‖ ~ finden (S) *to come into vogue, to become popular*; ⟨com⟩ *to find a market*; ~ finden bei jdm *to find admittance* (od *entry*) *into a p's mind*; *to meet with the approval of a p*; *to be adopted by a p*; *to appeal to a p*; ~ finden in *to be introduced into* (*a country*); → Aufnahme, Anklang ‖ jdm freien ~ gewähren z etw *to give a p the run of a th* ‖ jdm ~ verschaffen in .. *to introduce a p into* (*a society*); jdm ~ versch. z *to give a p access to* (*a p, a th*), *to obtain access for a p* ‖ e–r S ~ versch. *to bring a th into fashion* ‖ Mißbräuchen ~ versch. *to open the door to misuse* ‖ **sich** ~ versch. z *to force one's way to, to obtain entry to* (*a p, a th*) ‖ ⟨com⟩ ~ vorbehalten (abbr E. v.) *under usual reserve* **II.** ⟨übtr⟩ (Zeit) (Anfang) *beginning* (am ~ des 19. Jhs *at the b. of the 19th c.*); *opening* (*of a letter*); *exordium* (*of a speech*); → Anfang, Einleitung **III.** [konkr] **1.** (Ort des ~s) *entrance* (z *to the house*), ⟨bes Am⟩ *entry*; der ~ des Hauses *the entrance of the house*; ~ nach *entrance upon* (*the street*); das Tor bildet den ~ z .. *the gate gives entrance to* (*the link*) ‖ ⟨min⟩ *adit* ‖ *approach, access* (z *to*); *channel, opening* (*into a bay*); *passage* ‖ *doorway*; *gate*; ~ f Boten (etc) *back-door* ‖ *mouth* (*of a river*) ‖ ⟨rail, aero⟩ (z Bahnsteig etc) *gate* ‖ ⟨film⟩ (am Mischpult) *channel* **2.** (Eingegangenes) *money* (od *mail*) *received*; [mst pl] ⁓̈e *goods received*; (Einnahmen) *incomings, receipts, takings* [pl] ‖ ⟨comp⟩ *input*

·**Eingänger** m ⟨hunt⟩ *solitary wild boar*

·**eingangs** adv *at the beginning* (od *outset*); ~ erwähnt *above-mentioned*

·**Eingangs-** [in comp] ⟨com⟩ oft = Einfuhr– **~bestätigung** f ⟨com⟩ *acknowledgment of receipt* **~buch, ~journal** n ⟨com⟩ *book of entries* **~daten** pl ⟨comp⟩ *initial data* **~energie** f ⟨tech⟩ *input* **~halle** f *entrance-hall* **~information** f ⟨comp⟩ *input* **~stelle** f ⟨cust⟩ *point of entry* **~stück** n ⟨theat⟩ *curtain-raiser* ‖ **~tor** n ⟨sport⟩ *gate*; die durch das ~ eingelassene Menge Personen *the gate*[*s* pl]; → Eintrittsgeld **~werte** m pl ⟨comp⟩ *incoming data*

·**eingebaut** a *built-in* (*shelves, furniture*); in die Wand ~er Schrank *built-in wardrobe* ‖ *fixed*

(⟨a. mil⟩ *machine gun*) ‖ ⟨tech⟩ *embodied*; ⟨mot⟩ *integral* (Anlasser)

·ein|geben vt [h] **1.** (Arznei etc) *to administer*; *to give* (jdm *to a p*); tropfenweise ~ *to instil(l)*, jdm Gift ~ *to poison a p* **2. a.** ⟨übtr⟩ (Denkschrift) *to present*; *to put in*; (Gesuch) *to hand* (od *send*) *in*; → einreichen **b.** jdn ~ z e–r Beförderung, f e–n Orden *to propose* (od *name*, *recommend*) *a p for a preferment*, *for a decoration*; e–n Geistlichen f e–e Pfründe ~ *to present a clergyman a benefice* **3. a.** (durch höhere Macht ~) jdm etw (Gedanken, Gefühle) ~ *to infuse a th into a p*; *to inspire* (od *arouse*, *awaken*) *a th in a p*, *to inspire a p with a th*; v Gott –ge– *inspired* (*word*); das hat ihm der Teufel –ge– *the d. put this idea into his head* **b.** ⟨übtr⟩ (etw) *to dictate*, *inspire*, *prompt*, *suggest* (jdm *to a p*) **c.** ⟨comp⟩ *to put in*, *to list* ‖ –ge– w (of cards) *to be fed* (in *into the machine*) ‖ (Programmbefehle) *to code* ‖ wieder ~ *to feed back*

·einge- ~bildet a **1.** [pass] *imagined* (*illness*) **2.** [act] *conceited* (*p*); ~ auf *c. of*; *vain of* ‖ *supercilious*; ⟨fam⟩ *swell-headed*; → anmaßend ‖ ~ s *to be a snob*; *to suffer from swelled head*; *to be stuck up*, .. *smug*; ⟨fam⟩ *to have side*; ⟨Am⟩ *to be snooty*; ~ w *to get too big for one's boots* | ≃heit [f] *conceit*, *superciliousness*, *priggishness*, *etc* **~blindet** a ⟨arch⟩ *worked in low relief* **~bogen** a *bent* **~boren** a **1.** ⟨ec⟩ der ~e Sohn *the only begotten son* **2.** *aboriginal*, *native* **3.** [mst pred] *inborn* (jdm *to a p*); *inherent*, *innate* (jdm *in a p*) ≃**borene** [der ~, ein ~r] m ~n/~n *indigene*, *native*; die Häuser der ~n *the native houses* ‖ ~er v Australien *blackfellow* **~bracht** [pp v einbringen] das ~e Gut, das ≃e *a woman's marriage-portion*; *the dowry*

·Eingebung f ~/~en (göttliche) *infusion* (v Gott *on God's part*); *inspiration* (v oben *from above*) ‖ künstlerische ~ *inspiration* (v *from*) ‖ die ~en der Vernunft *the dictates* [pl] *of reason* | *prompting*, *suggestion*; ~ z Bösen *instigation* ‖ (plötzlicher Einfall) *quick hunch*; *brain-wave* (*I had a b.*) ‖ ~en [pl] ⟨a.⟩ *lights* ‖ e–r plötzlichen ~ folgend *on the spur of the moment*

·einge- ~bürgert a *naturalized*; ~er Ausländer *denizen* ‖ ⟨übtr⟩ *naturalized*; ~es Wort (etc) *denizen* **~denk** a [nur pred] e–r S ~ *remindful of a th* (*one's duty*); *remembering a th*; *heedful of a th*; e–r S ~ sein *to mind* (od *remember*) *a th*; *to bear a th in mind* **~fahren** a *run-in* (*car*) **~fallen** a *dilapidated* (*house*) ‖ *pinched* (*features*) *hollow*, *sunken* (*cheeks*, *eyes*); *shrunken* (*face*); er, sein Gesicht war ganz ~ *he*, *his face was all fallen-in* ‖ ~ aussehen *to look haggard*, *gaunt*, *peaked* **~fleischt** a ⟨fig⟩ *confirmed* (*bachelor*); *engrained*, *inveterate* (*sportsman*); ein ~er Sozialist *a thorough-going socialist*, *a s. to the backbone*; → durch II. C. ‖ *deep-rooted*, *deep-seated*, *engrained*, *inveterate* (*habits*, *enmity*) ‖ *dyed-in-the-wool*, *die-hard*, **~froren** [pp v einfrieren] a *icebound* ‖ ⟨fig com⟩ *frozen* (*capital*, *credit*) **~führt** [pp v einführen] a **1.** ⟨com⟩ *imported* (*goods*) ‖ neu ~er Artikel *novelty* ‖ gut ~ *well-connected* (*agent*) **2.** *established*, *received* (*custom*, etc.) **~glast** a ⟨phot⟩ *glass-bound* (Dia) **~hakt**, °**~häkelt**, °**~henkelt** a (Arm in A.) ⟨sl⟩ *crooky* ‖ ~ gehen *to crooky* **~hängt** a *crooked* (Schirm)

·ein|gehen vi/t **I.** vi [s] **A.** ⟨eig⟩ **1.** ⟨bib & poet⟩ *to enter*; *to go in* ‖ in die ewige Ruhe ~ *to go to* (*one's*) *rest* **2. a.** ein u ausgehen → ein [adv] **b.** ⟨com⟩ (S) *to enter*, *to come in*, *to come to hand*; (of money) *to be cashed* (od *paid*); (of goods) *to be imported* ‖ (of trains) *to arrive*, *to come* (od *pull*) *in* **B.** ⟨übtr⟩ **1.** jdm ~ *to become clear to a p*, *to be plausible to a p*; das will mir nicht ~ *that won't go down with me*; das wird ihm schwer ~ *it will be difficult to make him understand that*; *he will not easily be reconciled to that*; es geht ihm glatt ein *he grasps it easily*; das Latein geht ihm glatt (schwer) ein *he learns Latin with ease* (*with difficulty*); jdm lieblich ~ (of news, etc.) *to go down well with a p* ‖ jdm nicht ~ *not to cut much ice with a p*; *to elude a p* (*the sense eludes me*) **2. ~ auf a.** (untersuchen) *to enter* (od *go*, *inquire*, *look*) *into a matter*; *to take kindly to*; auf jds Gedanken ~ *to enter into a p's ideas*; die Debatte ging kaum auf die S ein *the discussion scratched scarcely the surface of the matter*; auf Einzelheiten ~ *to descend to particulars*; ich werde des näheren nicht darauf ~ *I shall not go into detail(s)* od *particulars* **b.** *to accede to* (od *comply with*) (*a request*), *to agree* (od *consent*) *to* (*an offer*; *to conditions*); *to comply with* (*instructions*); *to fall in with* (*a th*); *to welcome*; *to yield to* (*a demand*); er ging darauf ein *he agreed* ‖ auf e–n Vorschlag ~ *to accept a proposal*; ich kann auf den V. nicht ~ *I cannot entertain the p.* **c.** *to react* (od *respond*) *to* (*an argument*, *orator*); *to humour* (*a p*) **C.** ⟨fig⟩ **1. a.** (of cloth, etc.) *to shrink*; *to run up* **b.** (of a tumour) *to melt away*; *to dwindle* **2.** (aufhören) *to cease to exist*; (of a family) *to die* (*off*); *to become extinct*, *to be extinguished*; (of plants) *to perish*, *die*; *decay*, *wither*; der Baum ist –gegangen *the tree is gone* ‖ (of institutions, etc.) *to come to an end*; *to drop* (: *our correspondence dropped*); (of a newspaper) *to perish* ‖ (Brauch etc) ~ l *to discontinue*; *to drop*; ein Geschäft ~ l *to give up business*, *to go out of b.* ‖ die Zeitung ist –gegangen .. *has ceased to appear* **II.** vt [h] etw (Beziehungen, Verpflichtungen, Vertrag) ~ *to enter into a th* (*relations*, *obligations*, *treaty*); e–e Ehe ~ *to contract a marriage* (*with*); ein Geschäft ~ *to contract for a piece of work*; e–n Handel ~ *to make* od *strike a bargain*; ein Risiko *to chance a risk*, ~ *to embark upon a venture*; e–e Schuld ~ *to contract a debt*; e–e Wette ~ *to make a bet* (od *wager*), e–e W. ~, daß .. *to wager* (od *bet*) *that* **·Eingehen n 1.** → Eingang I. **2.** ⟨übtr⟩ ~ auf etw *accession* (od *agreement*, *consent*) *to a th*; *compliance with a th* ‖ *reaction to a th* ‖ ~ in etw *entering into a th* **3.** *shrinkage* (*of cloth*) **4.** *extinction* (*of a family*); *death*; *decay* (*of a plant*); *cessation*; *decline* (*of institutions*) ‖ *discontinuance* (*of a correspondence*) **5.** das ~ e–r S *the entering into a th* ‖ *contraction* (*of a marriage*, etc) ‖ ~ e–r Wette *making a bet*

·eingehend I. a **1.** ⟨eig⟩ *incoming* (*mail*, *message*) ‖ → einlaufend **2.** ⟨fig⟩ *detailed* (*discussion*); *circumstantial* (*report*); *careful*, *exhaustive*, *thorough*, *close* (*investigation*), *searching* (*examination*); → gründlich **II.** adv *in detail*; ~ an-, wiedergeben *to particularize*

·einge- ~klemmt a ⟨surg⟩ *strangulated* (*hernia*) ‖ ⟨übtr⟩ *sandwiched* (*between*) **~lassen** a *sunk* (*screw*; *pool*); *sunken*; *flush* (*headlight*, *switch*) **~laufen** a ⟨mot⟩ *seasoned* (*car*) → einlaufen **~legt** a; ~e Arbeit *inlay*; *inlay work*; *inlaid work*; ~e A. v farbigem Holz *marquetry*, *-terie*; ~e A. in Holz *intarsio*, *-sia* [It] ‖ ~es Ei *water-glass egg* ‖ ~es Stück *inlet*; *interpolation* **~macht 1.** a *preserved* (*fruits*, *vegetables*); *tinned*, ⟨Am⟩ *canned* (*fish*, *fruits*); *potted* (*meat*) ‖ in Zucker ~ *candied* (*fruits*); in Essig ~ *pickled* (*cucumbers*, etc.) ‖ ≃es *preserves* [pl]; *tinned* (⟨Am⟩ *canned*) *goods* [pl]; (in Essig) *pickles* [pl]; (Frucht in Syrup) *compote* ‖ ⟨österr⟩ ~es Kalbfleisch, Huhn = Kalbs-, Hühner-Frikassee

·ein|gemeinden vt [h] (Land etc) *to communalize*; *to incorporate* ‖ (Vorort) *to annex* **·Eingemeindung** f ~/~en *communalization*; *extension of borough boundaries*; *inclusion of .. into*

the borough of; *annexation* (in, nach *to*), *conurbation*

·einge- ~nommen [pp v einnehmen] a **1.** [attr] e–n ~en Kopf h *to feel giddy* (od *dizzy*) **2.** [pred] ⟨fig⟩ ~ s f jdn *to be biassed* (od *prepossessed*) *in favour of a p*; .. f etw *to be biassed in favour of a th*; *to be enthusiastic about* (od *at*) *a th*; *to be partial to a th* ‖ ~ s gegen jdn, etw *to be biassed* (od *to have a bias*) *against*; *to be prejudiced* (od *to have a prejudice*) *against a p, a th* ‖ ~ s v jdm *to have a high opinion of a p*; *to fancy a p*; *to be infatuated with a p*; *to be wrapped in a p* (*in one's children*) ‖ **v sich ~** *opinionative, opinionated*; (eingebildet) **v sich ~ s** *to be full of o.s.* (od *of conceit*), *to be conceited, to be taken up with o.s., to be full of one's own importance* ‖ (zu) sehr v sich ~ s *to get above o.s.* | ≗heit [f] ~/ *bias, prepossession* (f jdn *in favour of a p*); *bias, prejudice* (gegen jdn, etw *against a p, a th*) ‖ ~ v sich selbst *selfconceit* **≗richte** n *interior mechanism of a lock* **~rostet** a **1.** *rusty* (*sword*) **2.** ⟨fig⟩ **a.** *rusty* (*knowledge*); mein Englisch ist etw ~ *my English is a little r.* ‖ *out of practice* (*in*) ‖ *antiquated* (*he is a bit a.*) **b.** *hoarse, thick* (*voice*) **≗sandt** n (Zeitungs≗) *Letter to the Editor* **~schaltet** a *intercalary* (*day*) ‖ alle Lichter sind ~ .. *are on* **~schlafensein** n *numbness* (*of limbs*); ⟨fam⟩ *pins and needles*

·eingeschlechtig a ⟨bot⟩ *unisexual*; *one-sex*

·einge- ~schlossen [pp v einschließen] a *enclosed* (*letter*) ‖ v Land ~ *landlocked* (*bay*); v Eis ~ *ice-bound* (*island*) | ≗heit [f] ~/ ⟨fig⟩ *confinement, isolation, seclusion* °**~schnappt** a ⟨fig⟩ [pred] *cross*, ⟨sl⟩ *shirty*; haushoch ~ *c. as two sticks*; leicht *or* oft ~ *stuffy, miffy*; er ist ~ *he has the hump on*; warum ist er ~? *what's eating him?* → einschnappen **~schnitten** a: ~e Tasche ⟨tail⟩ *inset pocket* **~schränkt** **1.** a *restricted* (*diet*) ‖ *straitened* (*circumstances*) ‖ *narrow* (*sense*) | *modified* (*right*); *qualified* (*reply*) **2.** adv; ~ leben *to live in straitened circumstances*; *to live economically* **~schrieben** [pp v einschreiben] a **1.** ⟨math⟩ *inscribed* (*circle*) **2.** *registered* (*letter*); nur ~e Aktien (ohne Besitzerschein) *inscribed stock* | ~es Mitglied *enrolled member* (*of a party*) ‖ ~er Student *matriculant* **~schworen** a [pred] auf s–e Arbeit ~ *wedded to his job* **~sehen** a ⟨tact⟩ *exposed* **~sessen** a *resident* (*stranger*); *domiciled*; *long-established* (*family*); [pred] *settled for a long time*; → alt~, ansässig **~setzt** a *inserted* (*piece*) | ~er Ärmel [m] ⟨tail⟩ *set-in sleeve* **~spielt** a ⟨fig⟩ *well established* (*system*) **~sprengt** a ⟨minr⟩ *disseminated* **~standenerm·aßen** adv *avowedly* **≗ständnis** n –nisses/–nisse *confession* (*of a crime*); nach Ihrem eigenen ~, auf Grund Ihres –nisses *by* (od *on*) *your own confession* ‖ ⟨übtr⟩ *admission, avowal, confession* **·ein|gestehen** vt [h] [→ gestehen] ein Verbrechen (etc) ~ *to confess* (*to*) *a crime*; ~ getan z h *to confess to having done*; ~, daß .. *to confess* (od *give in*) *that* ‖ ⟨übtr⟩ (etw) *to admit, acknowledge avow*; ⟨fam⟩ *to confess* (*a th*); *to own to* (*a th*); sein Unrecht ~ *to stand corrected* **~stellt** a *indexed*; ~e Werte *what is i.* ⟨a. comp⟩ **~strichen** a → eins ⟨mus⟩ (im Violinschlüssel) die ~e Oktave *the second octave* **~tastet** a ⟨comp etc⟩ *indexed* (*on the keyboard*) **~tragen** a (amtlich) *registered* (*company*); ~er Verein *registered association* (od *club*) **≗tropftes** n ⟨österr cul⟩ = Einlauf ⟨cul⟩ **≗weide** n ~s/~ ⟨anat⟩ *bowels, entrails, guts, intestines*; *viscera* [L pl] ‖ ~ v Wild *gralloch*, das ~ e–s Tiers ausnehmen *to gralloch an animal* ‖ Lehre v den ~n *splanchnology* ‖ Sektion der ~ *splanchnotomy* | [in comp] *intestinal, visceral* (*cavity*); *splanchnic* (*nerves*); *entero-, splanchno-* ~arterie [f] ⟨anat⟩ *coeliac artery* ~bruch [m] ⟨med⟩ *hernia* [L] ~senkung [f] ⟨path⟩ *enteroptosis* [L] ~würmer [m pl] ⟨zoo⟩ *intestinal worms* pl, *entozoa* [Gr pl] **~weiht** a *initiated* (*members*); *adept, initiate*; ~ s ⟨fam⟩ *to be in the know* ‖ in etw ~ *privy to a th*, od *on the inside of a th* ‖ ein ≗er *an initiated p*; *an adept* od *initiate*, ⟨fam⟩ *insider*; die ≗en *the initiated*; *adepts, initiates*; ⟨fam⟩ *the insiders* [pl]

·ein|gewöhnen vt (jdn) *to acclimatize*; ⟨Am⟩ *to acclimate*; –ge–hnt s *to feel quite at home* **sich ~** *to acclimatize*; *to shake down*; ⟨Am⟩ *to acclimate* ‖ sich ~ in *to settle in* (*a job*) ‖ → einleben; –passen; gewöhnen

·einge- ≗wöhnung f *acclimatization*; ⟨Am⟩ *acclimation* **~wurzelt** a ⟨fig⟩ *deep-rooted, engrained, inveterate* (*habit, prejudice*); *deep-seated* (*faith*) **~zogen** [pp v einziehen] a ⟨fig⟩ **1.** *confiscated* (*property*) **2.** † = zurückgezogen **3.** ≗e [m] [der ~, ein ~r] *conscript*

·ein|gießen vt [h] *to pour in*; ~ in *to infuse* (od *pour*) *into*; den Tee ~ *to pour the tea* ‖ eine Tasse Tee ~ *to pour out a cup of tea*; sie goß sich e–e T. Tee ein *she poured out herself a cup of tea* (od *a cup of tea for herself*)

·Einglas n –ses/–gläser *monocle*

·eingleisig a ⟨rail⟩ *single*(*-line*) (*railway, tunnel*)

·ein|gliedern vt [h] (System) ~ in *to dovetail* od *integrate into*; *to incorporate in* ‖ jdn ~ in *to enrol* od *enter a p in*; jdn e–r Organisation [dat] ~ *to enrol a p in an organization*; sich e–r O. ~ *to join an o.* ‖ ⟨tact⟩ *to assign* ([dat *or* in] *to*)

·Eingliederung f = Einordnung

·eingliedrig a ⟨math⟩ *monomial*

·Eingottglaube m *monotheism*

·ein|graben vt [h] **1. a.** (Tote) *to bury* **b.** (Dung) *to dig in* ‖ (etw) ~ in *to dig into*; die Sporen ~ in *to dig* (od *sink*) *one's spurs into* (*a horse*) ‖ e–n Pfahl ~ *to drive a stake in*; ~ in *to sink* (*a th*) *into* (*the ground*) **c. sich** (in die Erde) ~ *to dig o.s. in*; ⟨mil⟩ *to entrench o.s.* ‖ sich ~ in *to burrow* (od *dig*) *one's way into*; ⟨fig⟩ *to burrow* (od *dig, penetrate*) *into* (*a subject*) **2.** ⟨tech⟩ (Namen) *to carve, to cut* (in *into*); *to engrave* (auf *on*) ‖ ⟨fig⟩ (etw) dem Gedächtnis ~ *to engrave upon a p's memory, to stamp upon a p's mind*; **sich** dem G. ~ *to be engraved upon the m.* ‖ tief –ge– s in *to be deeply bitten into* **3.** ≗ n: das (Sich-)~ *digging in*

·ein|gravieren vt [h] (Namen) *to engrave* (*on*)

·Eingreif- ~division f *strike* [attr] *d., reserve d.* **~flotte** f *striking fl.* **~truppe** f *mobile striking force*

·ein|greifen **I.** vi [h] **1.** (P) **a.** (of police) *to step in* (um z tun *to do*); mit der flachen Klinge ~ *to use the flat of one's sabre* **b.** in die Unterhaltung ~ *to engage in the discussion*; → Debatte **c.** (sich ins Mittel legen) ⟨mst pol⟩ *to interfere, intervene* (in *in*; um z tun *to do*) ‖ ⟨Am sl⟩ *to horn in* | unrechtmäßig ~ *to interfere, meddle*; ~ in etw, den Gang (e–r S) *to meddle in* od *with* (*a th*); *to interfere with* (*a course*); in jds Rechte ~ *to encroach on a p's rights*; *to invade a p's rights*; in jds Macht ~ *to impinge upon a p's authority* **2.** (S) ⟨tech⟩ (of a wheel) *to bite* (*the wheels would not b.*); ~ in *to engage* od *mesh with* (*the perforation*, etc); *to gear into*; → ineinandergreifen **II.** ≗ n **1.** (P) *interference* (in *in, with*); *interposition, intervention* (*of police*); → Eingriff **2.** (S) ⟨tech⟩ (v Zahnrädern) *engagement*; ~ in *the gearing* (*of the wheels*) *into* **3.** ⟨aero⟩ ~ in den Erdkampf *air-to-ground fighting* **·eingreifend** a ⟨fig⟩ → durchgreifend

·Eingrenzung f *localization*

Eingriff- (→ (Zahl) eins) ~abstimmung [f] *one-knob-tuning*

·Eingriff m ~(e)s/~e **1. a.** *interference* (in, *in, with*); → Eingreifen 1., 2. ‖ unrechtmäßiger ~ in etw *encroachment* (od *impingement, usurpation*)

on a th; *inroad into* (*a p's freedom*) od *upon*; (in das Recht) *infringement*; *invasion of a th* **b.** *act performed*; *measure*; operativer ~ *operative treatment*; *operation*; e–n ~ m *to operate*; *to perform an operation* (bei jdm *on a p*); ⟨jur⟩ verbotener ~ → Abtreibung 3. **2.** ⟨tech⟩ *gearing*, *meshing*; *gear*; im ~ *in gear*, außer ~ *out of g.*; im ~ stehen *to be in gear*; *to gear* (*with*) **~sbereich** m *zone of contact* **~getriebe** n (Synchron-) *meshed gear* **~swinkel** m (Zahnrad≃) *pressure angle*; *angle of action*

·**ein|gruppieren** vt [h] *to classify*, *grade* ‖ (Blut) *to blood-type*

·**Eingruppierung** f *grading*; → Einstufung

·**Einguß** m, –gusses/–güsse **1.** *instillation*, *infusion*, *pouring* (in *into*) **2.** ⟨tech⟩ (*founding*) *sprue*; *feeder* ‖ ⟨aero⟩ Kühler≃ *radiator filler*

·**ein|hacken** vi [h] (*of a bird*) ~ auf *to strike with the bill at*, *to pick at* (*a p*, *a th*) ‖ ⟨fig⟩ °auf jdn ~ *to pick holes in a p*, *to carp at a p*

·**ein|hageln** vi [h] (*blows*) *fall as thick as hail*

·**ein|haken** vt/i [h] **1.** vt (Fenster) *to hook in* ‖ jdn ~ *to take a p's arm*; sie hakte sich bei ihm ein *she linked her arm through his*; ich hakte ihn ein, ich h. mich bei ihm ein *I hooked my arm in his* **2.** vi *to break* (od *cut*) *in*; °ich weiß nicht, wo ich ~ soll .. *where to begin*; → eingehakt

·**ein|hallen** vt [h] ⟨aero⟩ *to bring in*; *to berth*

·**Einhalt** m ~(e)s/ [nur in der Wendung:] e–r S ~ tun *or* gebieten *to put a stop to*, *to impose* (od *place*) *a check on a th*; *to check* (od *stop*; *prohibit*) *a th* ·**ein|halten** vt/i [h] **I.** vt **1.** (hemmen) (e–e Bewegung) *to stop*, *check* ‖ (verbieten) *to prohibit* **2.** (Stoff) *to gather*, *pucker* **3.** ⟨fig⟩ (innehalten) e–e Verabredung (nicht) ~ *to keep* (*break*) *an app.*; (Bestimmung, Regel, Vertrag) *to observe*, *hono(u)r* (*terms*); *to be observant of*; *to adhere* (od *keep*, *stick*) *to* (*a plan*, *terms*); (Kurs, Weg) *to follow*, *keep*; *to hold on* (*one's course*) ‖ e–e best. Zeit, Frist ~ *to observe the appointed time*, *to be punctual*; die Zahlungen ~ *to be punctual in paying*, *to pay* (*to keep one's payments*) *punctually* ‖ (Termin) nicht ~ *to trangess* **II.** vi = innehalten II.; (im Sprechen) *he checked himself*

·**Einhaltung** f *observance* (*of a rule*, *of terms*) (streng *strict*); ~ e–s Planes *adherence to a plan*

·**ein|hämmern** vt [h] ⟨fig⟩ etw fest ~ *to knock a th home*; den Gedanken ~, daß .. *to rub in the idea that* ‖ jdm etw ~ *to drub* od *hammer*, *knock a th into a p*; *to drive* od *pound a th into a p's head*; ⟨sl⟩ *to cram a th down a p's throat*

·**Einhand-** [in comp] *one-handed*; *single-hand* **~fahrt** f *single-handed cruise* **~feuerzeug** n *one--handed lighter* **~segelboot** n *single-hand* **~segler** m *single-handed cruiser*

·**ein|handeln** vt [h] (Länder) *to acquire by bargaining* (od *haggling*); ~ gegen *to barter* (*a th*) *for* (*a th*)

·**einhändig** a *one-handed*, *single-hand*(*ed*) adv (*to play the piano*, *to ride the bicycle*) *with one hand*; → Einhand– ·**ein|händigen** vt [h] jdm etw ~ *to hand a p a th* (od *a th to a p*); *to deliver a th to a p* ·**Einhändigung** f ~/~en *delivery*; *handing over* (an jdn *to a p*)

·**Einhandsgut** n ⟨jur⟩ *exclusive* od *separate property of husband* od *wife*

·**Einhänge- ~blende** f ⟨phot⟩ *interchangeable diaphragm* **~draht** m *slinging wire*

·**ein|hängen** vt/i [h] die Türkette ~ *to put the chain on the door*; e–e Tür (etc) ~ *to hang a door*; *to place a d. on its hinges* ‖ ⟨telph⟩ (Hörer) *to replace* ‖ **sich** bei jdm ~ → einhaken, eingehängt | vi ⟨telph⟩ *to hang up* (mitten im Gespräch *on a p*)

·**ein|hauchen** vt [h] jdm neues Leben (etc) ~ *to breathe* (od *infuse*, *instil*[*l*] *new life into a p*; *to inspire a p with new l.*

·**ein|hauen** vi/t [h] **I.** vi **1.** ~ auf jdn *to strike* (*out*) *at a p*, *to strike a p violent blows*, *to slip into a p* ‖ wir hauten mit dem Schwerte ein *we laid about us with our swords*; mit dem Säbel auf jdn ~ *to sabre a p* ‖ tüchtig ~ *to lay on* **2.** ⟨fig⟩ °tüchtig ~ *to play a good knife and fork*; *to plough* od *pitch* (in, bei *into*); *to take one's teeth* (*to*); *to lay in* (*a good meal*); er haute t. ein *he helped himself generously*; hauen Sie nur t. ein *cut and come again* ‖ ⟨Am fam⟩ *to pitch in* ‖ ~ in *to walk into* **II.** vt (etw) *to break*, *crack*; *to cut open*; → einschlagen ‖ (Loch) ~ in *to make* (*a hole*) *in*

·**einhäusig** a **1.** ⟨bot⟩ *monoecious*, *androgynous*, → eins | **2.** (P) *stay-at-home*

·**ein|heben** vt [h] e–e Tür ~ *to hang a door*; *to heave* od *place a d. on its hinges* ‖ ⟨typ⟩ die Form ~ *to lay the form*(*e*) *on*, *to put the f. into the press* ‖ → Boot; einhieven

·**ein|heften** vt [h] (Buch) *to stitch*; *sew* ‖ (Briefe) *to file*

·**ein|hegen** vt [h] (Land) *to fence*, *hedge* (*in*); *enclose* ·**Einhegung** f *fencing*, *enclosure* (*of land*)

·**einheimisch** a **1.** (P) **a.** (beheimatet) *domiciled*, *resident* (*alien*); ~ in *resident in* ‖ (gebürtig) *born in a place* od *country*; er ist in Kanada ~ *he is a native of Canada* ‖ *home-born*; *home-bred* (*farmstock*); *home-grown* (*fruit*, *etc*); *local* (*population*); *intestine* (*rebel*) ‖ v früh auf ~ *aboriginal* ‖ → ansässig, gebürtig; heimisch; seßhaft, ureingesessen | **der** ≃**e** *the native*, *resident*, *inhabitant* ‖ **die** ≃**en** [pl] *the residents*; *the natives* [pl] **b.** (außereuropäisch) *native* (*troops*) ‖ **die** ≃**en** = Eingeborenen **2.** (T, of plants) *endemic*, *indigenous* (*flora and fauna*); *native*; ~es Tier, ~e Pflanze *native* ‖ ~ s in *to be indigenous to*; beide Arten sind in Deutschland ~ *both the species are natives of Germany* od *are indigenous to G.*; → heimisch **3.** (S) **a.** *native* (*customs*; *dress*) ‖ ⟨com⟩ *indigenous* (*growth*, *origin*); ⟨bes Am⟩ *domestic*, *home-born*, *native* (*product*, *word*) ‖ *home-bred* (*mutton*); *home-made* (*bread*); *internal*, *inland* (*fuel*); ~er Handel, Markt *home-trade*, *home-market* **b.** ~ geworden *endemic* (*disease*) **c.** (of language) *native*, *vernacular*; die ~e Sprache *the vernacular*; in der ~en Sp. geschrieben *vernacular* (*poetry*); in der ~en Sp. schreibend *vernacular* (*poet*)

°·**ein|heimsen** vt [h] **1.** (Ernte etc) *to garner*; *to gather* od *get in*; *to harvest*; *reap*; *to store up* **2.** (Geld, Gewinn) *to pocket* (*he pocketed a nice sum*); *to pouch*; *to rake* od *get in*; Geld ~ ⟨Am sl⟩ *to clean up* ‖ den Gewinn ~ *to scoop the pool*; die Vorteile der Arbeit ~ *to reap the benefits of work*; die Ehre ~ *to grab the credit*

·**Einheirat** f: die ~ jds in e–e Familie (etc) *the marrying of a p into a family* ·**ein|heiraten** vi [h] ~ in e–e Familie *to marry into a family*

·**Einheit** f ~/~en **A.** (in eins zus–gefaßte Größe *or* Zahl) **1.** ⟨math⟩ *unit*; *one*; *unity* **2.** (~ e–s Maßsystems) *unit*; *standard*; *fixed basis*; *official gauge* ‖ Energie≃ *unit of energy*; Gewichts≃ *u. of weight*; Längen≃ *u. of length*; Maß≃ *u. of measurement*; Wärme≃ *u. of heat*, *thermal u.*; *calorie* | ⟨stat⟩ ~en [pl] der Grundgesamtheit *elements* **3.** ⟨übtr⟩ (P & S) **a.** *unit undivided whole*; *one* od *single entity*, *unity*; e–e ~ wie s–e Familie *an entity as his own family*; f ihn ist Natur e–e ~ *for him nature is one* ‖ Teile zu e–r ~ verschmelzen *to weld parts into a homogenous* od *integrated whole* **b.** ⟨mil⟩ *unit* (~ f ~ *unit-wise*); ⟨Am a.⟩ *organization* ‖ Gefechts≃ *fighting* od *armed unit* **c.** ⟨sport⟩ *unit*, *fixed number* (*of runs*, *strokes*, etc.) ‖ ⟨golf⟩ ~ (*or* Platz≃) v Schlägen (f guten Spieler) *bogey*; (f Vorgabe-Null-Spieler) *par*; einer (sc

Schlag) unter der ~ *birdie*; zwei unter der ~ *eagle* **B.** [abstr] (Einssein) *unity*, (*the u. of subject and object*); *oneness* (*a sense of oneness*); die ~ der Nation *national unity*; die drei ~en des Dramas *the dramatic unities* [pl] (*action, time, place*) ‖ *unity, union* (*in perfect union*); *harmony* ‖ (Volk) z e–r ~ zus-schließen *to unify*; Zus–schließung z e–r ~ *unification* **·einheitlich 1.** a *uniform* (*dress, weight*, etc.); *homogeneous* (*structure*); *coherent* (*in mind*); *consistent*; *unitary* (*distance, sound*) ‖ ⟨com⟩ *flat*; → Einheits– ‖ ~ m *to standardize*, ⟨mech⟩ *homogenize* ‖ ⟨mil⟩ *organic* (Gerät *equipment*); ⟨bes Am⟩ *unified* (Kommando, Führung) ‖ ⟨scient⟩ *integrated*; ~es Maßsystems ⟨bes Am⟩ *standard system of measurements* **2.** adv *uniformly* ‖ *unitedly*; *harmoniously*; ~ ansetzen *to employ under coordinate control* **≃keit** f *uniformity* (in *in*); *homogeneity*; *cohesion*; *conformity to one form* od *standard*; *consistency*; *unity*

·Einheits- [in comp] *unit–*; *standard*; *uniform*; ⟨com⟩ *flat*; ⟨pol⟩ *unitary*; *united* **~auftrieb** m ⟨aero⟩ *specific lift*; *lift coefficient* (*in kg per m*^{3}) **~bestrebungen** f [pl] *unitary tendencies* [pl] **~bewegung** f ⟨pol⟩ *unitary movement* **~bohrung** f *basic hole* **~boot** n *one-design* (abbr *O.D.*) *boat*; *one-designer* **≃eigen** a ⟨mil bes Am⟩ *organic, organizational* **~form** f *standard form* **~front** f *united front* **~führer** m ⟨mil⟩ *commanding officer* **~gebühr** f *uniform* od *standard rate* **~gewicht** n *standard* (od *uniform*) *weight* **~klasse** f ⟨mar⟩ *one-design class*; Jacht der ~ *one-designer* **~kurs** m ⟨st exch⟩ *uniform quotation* **~ladung** f ⟨el, phys⟩ *unit charge* **~mark** f ⟨Ger⟩ *standard mark* **~maß** n *unit-measure*; ~ der Zeit *unit of time* **~partei** f *unity party* **~pol** m *unit magnetic pole* **~porto** n *uniform postage* **~preis** m ⟨com⟩ *one* (od *single*)*-price*; ~geschäft [n] *one-price shop, single-price store* **~satz** m ⟨com⟩ *flat-rate* **~schule** f ⟨Ger⟩ *uniform type of primary* (od *junior*) *school, standard school* **~staat** m *unitary state* **~steuer** f *single tax* **~tarif** m *uniform* (od *standard*) *tariff* | ~münzzahler [m] ⟨tech⟩ *single-rate prepayment meter* **~versicherung** f *all risks insurance* **~ware** f *standardized article* **~welle** f ⟨tech⟩ *basic shaft* **~wert** m ⟨Ger⟩ *standard value* (e–s Grundstücks) **~zeit** f *standard time* **~zoll** m *uniform duty*

·ein|heizen vi [h] **1.** *to heat a room*; *to make up a fire*; tüchtig ~ *to fire up* **2.** jdm tüchtig ~ ⟨fig⟩ *to build fires under a p*; *to give a p a piece of one's mind*; *to haul a p up*; *to urge a p on* ⟨fam⟩ *to make it hot for a p, to give it a p hot* ‖ ⟨sex⟩ *to rub* od *touch up* (*a p*) **3.** tüchtig ~ (essen) *to stoke* (*up*); er hatte tüchtig –geheizt *he had drunk a lot*

·ein|helfen vi [h] ⟨fig⟩ jdm ~ (beim Rezitieren etc) *to prompt a p* **E–fer** ⟨theat⟩ *prompter*

·einhellig 1. a *unanimous, uniform*; *consistent* (*sense*) ‖ [pred] *alike*; *of one mind, of a piece* ‖ nicht ~es Urteil *split decision* → eindeutig, –mütig, –stimmig **2.** adv *unanimously*; *with one accord* (od *consent, voice*) | **≃keit** f ~/ *unanimity, uniformity*; mit ~ *with one accord* (od *consent, voice*)

·einhenk(e)lig a *one-handled*; *having but one handle*

°**·ein|henkeln** [vt & refl] [h] ich henkelte ihn ein, ich h. mich bei ihm ein *I hooked my arm in his* ‖ henkle dich ein *take my arm* ‖ eingehenkelt gehen *to walk arm in arm* ‖ → eingehakt

einh·er- [trennbares, betontes pref bei Verben] *along, forth* **~|gehen** vi [s] *to walk* (od *go, move*) *along*; auf der Straße ~ *to march* od *walk the street*; → einherschreiten ‖ °**~|latschen** vi [s] *to mouch* od *mooch along* **~|schreiten** vi [s] *to stride* (od *stamp*) *along*; *to prance*; → einhergehen ‖ stolz ~ *to stalk* (od *strut, sweep*) *along*; auf den Straßen ~ *to sweep along the streets*; *to stalk the streets*; triumphierend ~ *to galumph* **~|stolzieren** vi [s] → einherschreiten **~|ziehen** vi [h] *to move along*; → einhergehen

·ein|hetzen vt [h] ⟨hunt⟩ (Hunde) *to break in*; *to train*

·ein|hieven vt [h] ⟨mar⟩ (Kette) *to heave in*

·ein|holen vt/i [h] **I.** vt **A.** ⟨eig⟩ **1. a.** (einkaufen) *to buy, purchase*; → II. **b.** (Ernte) *to harvest*; → einbringen **c.** ⟨übtr⟩ → Akzept ‖ jds Ansichten ~ *to ask for a p's views* ‖ e–n Bericht ~ *to call for a report* ‖ jds Einwilligung ~ *to obtain a p's consent* ‖ Erkundigungen (*or* Auskünfte) ~ *to make inquiries* (bei jdm über .. *of a p on* [od *about*] ..) ‖ jds Erlaubnis ~ *to ask, get, procure, obtain a p's permission* od *consent* ‖ Instruktionen ~ v jdm *to apply to a p for instructions* ‖ ein Gutachten ~ *to get* od *have an opinion*; das G. e–s anderen ~ *to get another opinion* ‖ Rat ~ v jdm, jds R. ~ *to seek advice from a p* ‖ Stimmen ~ *to collect votes* ‖ ein Zeugnis ~ *to call in a testimony* **2.** (Leine, Tau) *to haul in* ‖ (Fahne) *to haul down, to strike* ‖ (Segel) *to take in* **3. jdn** feierlich ~ *to* (*go to*) *meet a p, to go to receive a p with all due ceremony*; *to go and conduct a p in procession to a place* **B.** ⟨übtr⟩ **1. a. jdn ~** *to catch a p up* (*in walking*), *to catch up on* od *to a p*; *to draw level with a p*; *to overtake a p*; *to come up with a p*; *to pull up to* (od *with*) *a p*; ⟨Am fam⟩ *to catch up to a p* **b.** ⟨sport⟩ jdn ~ *to lap a p* ‖ ⟨engl⟩ ein Boot ~ (u berühren) *to bump a boat* → Einholrennen **c.** (Klassenkameraden) im Lernen ~ *to catch up in learning* **2.** (Verlust) wieder ~ *to recoup, recover, repair, retrieve*; verlorene Zeit wieder ~ *to make up for lost time*; es kann nicht wieder –geholt w *it cannot be made good* **II.** vi *to shop, to go shopping* (in *at*); ~ gehen *to go shopping*

·Einholen n ⟨eig⟩ **1. a.** *buying*; *shopping*; Tasche z ~ *shopping-bag* **b.** *asking for* (*a p's views*); *applying for* (*instructions*); *obtaining* (*of a p's consent, permission*); *collection* (*of votes*); das ~ e–s Gutachtens *the getting of an opinion* **2.** *hauling in* (*of a rope*) **3.** feierliches ~ *ceremonious reception* (*of a p*) **B. 1.** *catching up, overtaking* (*of a p*) **2.** *recoupment, recovery* (*of a loss*); *retrieval*

·Einholrennen n ⟨engl⟩ *bumping-race* ‖ → einholen B. 1. b. **·Einholung** f → Einholen

·Einhorn n ⟨arts & Lit⟩ *unicorn* ‖ See≃ n, ~fisch [m] ⟨ich⟩ *unicorn-fish*; *narwhal*

·Einhufer m ~s/~ *soliped, solidungulate*; *solid-hoofed* (od *solidungulate*) *animal* **·einhufig** a *solid-hoofed, solidungulate*

·ein|hüllen vt [h] **1.** (jdn, etw) *to envelop, to wrap, to wrap up* (in *in*); den Kopf ~ *to muffle one's head*; → einmummeln ‖ dicht ~ *to smother* (in *in*); (S) *to engulf* (*darkness engulfed us*); etw ringsum ~ *to wrap a th about* | –gehüllt s in *to be wrapped* (od *enveloped, –lopped*) *in*; in Nebel eingehüllt *enveloped in mist*; ein Haus in Efeu –gehüllt *a house swathed in ivy*; in Rauch –gehüllt (*a town*) *smothered in smoke* ‖ in Dunkel –gehüllt *wrapped in darkness*; ⟨fig⟩ *enveloped in mystery* **2. sich ~** *to wrap up*; *to envelop o.s.* (in *in* [*a blanket*]) ‖ sich in s–e Würde ~ *to be wrapped in one's dignity, to stand on one's d.*

einh·undert = hundert *a* od *one hundred*

·ein|hüten vi [h] bei jdm *to take care of a p's house, apartment, children*; *to baby-sit*

·einig I. a **1.** [attr & pred] (geeint) *united*; ein ~es Volk *a united people* **2.** [nur pred] (e–s Sinnes) ~ s *to be at one*; *to agree, to be in agreement*; (mit *with*) *to be at unity* (*with*) ‖ in der Überzeugung ~ s, daß .. *to share the conviction that* | **(sich) ~ s** *to be of one mind*; *to be unanimous* (über *on*; z tun *in doing*); *to be agreed* (über *on*); ⟨Am⟩ *to be a unit* (über *on*) ‖ ~ z s scheinen *to seem agreed* (*that* ..); man ist sich ~, daß .. *it is agreed that* ‖ sich noch nicht ~ s *to be still in two minds*; sie sind sich darüber noch nicht ~ *they have not yet made up their minds on that*; darüber sind (sich) die Gelehrten noch nicht ~ *on that opinions are still divided* | **sich ~ w** *to agree* (über *on*; daß *that*); ⟨Am⟩ *to get together* (*the jury was unable to g. t.*); ~ w mit jdm *to settle with a p* ‖ → ein[1] II. A. 2. c. **II.** adv mit jdm ~|gehen → u.

·einige [pron] **1.** [attr] **a.** ~ Zeit *for some time*; nach ~r Zeit *shortly after* ‖ v ~r Größe (*an object*) *of reasonable size*; ein Mann v ~r Belesenheit *a man of some reading* **b.** ~ [pl] *some*; *certain*; *a few*; *several*, *sundry*; ~ hundert *some hundred*; ~ Meilen *a couple of miles*; ~ 20 Meilen *some twenty miles*; ~ Auserwählte *a select few*; ~ junge Leute *a sprinkling of young people*; ~ Zeilen weiter *some lines further on* ‖ ~ sechzig Jahre *sixty odd years*; ~ zweihundert Seiten *two hundred odd pages*; 200 u ~ Mann *two hundred and odd men*; ein Mann v ~n Sechzig *a man of sixty odd* **2.** [abs] **a.** ~s *something*; er wird dir ~s erzählen können *he will be able to tell you something*; das hat ~s f sich *there is something in that* ‖ ~s verstehen v *to know a thing* od *two about* .. **b.** ~ [pl] *some* (*some went home and some stayed*; *I'll give you some* [*or other*]); *a few*: ~ s–r Freunde *a few of his friends*; ~ wenige *some few* (*people*)

·ein|igeln vrefl [h] sich ~ *to hedgehog*; *to make all-round defence* **·Einigelung** f ⟨fig⟩ *seclusion*

·einigemal adv *several times*; *now and then*

·einigen vt [h] **1.** (Volk) *to unite*, *unify* **2. sich** ~ *to agree* (über *on*; daß *that*); ⟨Am⟩ *to get together* ‖ sich auf die Hälfte der Differenz ~ *to split the difference*; man einigte sich dahin, daß .. *it was agreed that*; man hat sich darüber ge–gt *agreement was reached*; sich nicht ~ können; ⟨Am⟩ (of the jury) *to be hung* ‖ sich ~ mit *to come to terms*, *to settle with* (*a p*); *to strike* (*one's*) *hands with* **·Einiger** m *unifier* **einigerm·aßen** adv ein ~ ausführlicher Bericht *a quite* od *fairly detailed report* ‖ *to some* (od *a certain*) *extent*; *after* (od *in*) *a fashion*; *somewhat*; *pretty* od *reasonably* (*p.* od *r. well*, *good*); → ziemlich ‖ wenn sie ~ hübsch sind ⟨Am⟩ *if they've any looks*; ich habe ~ e–e Idee, worum es geht *I've got some idea what it is all about*

·einiges pron (*I have*) *some* od *a few things* (*to tell him*)

·einig|gehen vt [s] ⟨com⟩ *to be in agreement* (mit *with*); ~ mit jdm in etw *to agree with a p in a th*

·Einigkeit f ~/ (Eintracht) *unity* (*between*), *union*; *concord*, *harmony*, *unanimity*; in völliger ~ *in perfect unity*; ~ macht stark *unity is strength*, *unity makes a* (*powerful*) *nation* | (~ der Meinungen) *agreement* (über *on*); *accordance in opinion*; es herrscht völlige ~ *there is complete agreement* (über *on*)

·Einigung f ~/~en **1.** ⟨pol⟩ *unification*; *union* **2.** ⟨jur & com⟩ *agreement* (über *on*), *arrangement*, *settlement*, *understanding*; zu e–r ~ k, e–e ~ erzielen *to come to an agreement*, etc.; *to arrive at* (od *bring about*) *an agreement*, *to reach a settlement*; e–e ~ zw 2 Parteien zustandebringen *to bring 2 parties to an agreement*; es konnte k–e ~ erzielt w *the matter was deadlocked*

·ein|impfen vt [h] **1.** (Serum etc) *to inoculate* (jdm *on* od *into a p*) **2.** ⟨fig⟩ jdm etw ~ *to implant a th in a p* (od *in a p's mind*); *to inject* od *instill a th into a p*; *to inoculate* od *inspire a p with a th*; uns allen –geimpft s (of feelings) *to be instilled into all our minds* **·Einimpfung** f ~/~en **1.** *inoculation* (e–s Serums *with a serum*) **2.** ⟨fig⟩ *implantation*, *inoculation*

·ein|jagen vt [h] jdm Angst, Furcht, Schrecken ~ *to throw a p into a fright*, *to strike fear* od *terror into a p*; *to frighten* (od *scare*, *terrify*) *a p*; *to give a p a fright*; ⟨fam⟩ *to put the wind up to a p*

·einjährig a **1.** *one-year-old*; ~es Tier (bes Fohlen) *yearling animal*, *yearling* **2.** *annual*; *lasting for one year*; *of one year*; *one-year* ‖ ~e Pflanze *annual plant*, *annual* ‖ ~e Dienstzeit ⟨Ger⟩ (*before 1919*) *one year's military service*

·Einjährige 1. das ~ n ⟨Ger⟩ (*before 1919*) *examination qualifying the candidate for serving one year only* ‖ ~nschein *one-year service certificate* **2.** der ~ [ein ~r], der Einjährig-Freiwillige m ⟨Ger⟩ (*before 1919*) *conscript who by passing the qualifying examination was liable to one year's service only*

·ein|kacheln vt [h] *to line* (*bathroom*) *with tiles* | °vi [h] ⟨fam⟩ *to light a roaring fire*

·ein|kalken vt [h] *to limewash* (*trees*)

·ein|kalkulieren vt [h] *to take* .. *into account*; *to figure in* (*extras*)

·Einkammersystem n ⟨parl⟩ *single chamber system*

·ein|kampfern vt [h] *to put moth balls* od *moth powder in* (*clothes*)

·einkanalig a ⟨tech⟩ *monaural*

·ein|kapseln vt [h] **1.** (etw) *to encyst* (in *in*) **2.** ⟨fig⟩ *to embed*, *encyst* (*in*) ‖ °**sich** ~ *to cloister o.s.*, *to shut o.s. up* **·Einkapselung** f *encystation*, *encystment*

·ein|kassieren vt [h] (Außenstände) ⟨com⟩ *to recover outstanding debt* (Beiträge, Geld, Schulden) *to collect*; (*en*)*cash* ‖ (Wechsel etc) *to cash* ‖ (als Tageseinnahme) *to take* .. *as daily total*

·Einkassierung f ~/~en *collection* (*of contributions*, etc.); *encashment* ‖ *cashing*; → Inkasso

·Einkauf m ~(e)s/≃e *purchase*; Weihnachts~ *Christmas p.*; billiger ~ bargain ‖ ≃e m *to make purchases*; *to do one's shoppings*, *to shop*, *to go shopping*

·ein|kaufen I. vt/i [h] **1.** vt (etw) *to buy*, *purchase*; *to make a purchase of* (*a th*); (Vorräte) *to lay* (od *buy*, *take*) *in* | **sich** in eine Anstalt ~ *to buy a place in an institution*; *to buy one's admission to a home*; sich in e–e Lebensversicherung ~ *to insure one's life* **2.** vi *to shop* (in *at*); *to be shopping* **II.** ≃ n *buying*; *shopping*

·Einkäufer m ~s/~ *purchaser*, *buyer*, *shopper* ‖ ⟨com⟩ *buying* od *purchasing agent*

·Einkaufs- [in comp] ⟨com⟩ *buying*, *purchasing* **~abteilung** f *purchasing department* **~berater** m *buying adviser* **~buch** n *purchase-book*; *purchase-ledger* **~genossenschaft** f *co-operative buying society* **~leiter** m *purchasing manager* **~liste** f (Hausfrau) *shopping list* **~netz** n *marketing* (*string*) *net* **~order** f ⟨com⟩ *buying-order*; *indent* **~preis** m *cost-price*; *first* (od *prime*) *cost* ‖ unter ~ *below cost*; zum ~ *at prime cost* **~tasche** f *shopping-bag* **~verband** m *buying association* **~zentrum** n *shopping area* od *centre*

·Einkehr f ~/ **1.** (Einkehren) **a.** *putting up* (in e–m Wirtshaus *at an inn*) **b.** ⟨fig⟩ (innere) (*self-*)*communion*, *introspection*; (*spiritual*) *contemplation*, *meditation* ‖ ~ bei sich halten *to hold communion with o.s.* ‖ Friede hielt bei ihm ~ *p. came into his heart* **2.** [konkr] = Herberge, Wirtshaus **·ein|kehren** vi [s] **1.** *to put in* (um z essen *for dinner*); *to put up* (in e–m Gasthaus *at an inn*); *to drop* (od *look*) *in* (bei jdm *upon a p*); ⟨Am⟩ *to stop by* (od *in*) ‖ wir w unterwegs ~ *we shall stop for a drink on the way* **2.** ⟨fig⟩ bei sich ~ *to hold communion with o.s.*, *to feel remorse*

·ein|keilen vt [h] (etw) *to wedge in*; fest ~ *to wedge* (zw *between*; in *into*) ‖ ⟨typ⟩ die Form ~

to quoin the forme ‖ –ge–lt ⟨med⟩ *impacted* (*fracture, tooth*)

·**einkeimblättrig** a ⟨bot⟩ *monocotyledonous* (*plant*); ≗e f *monocotyledon*

·**ein|kellern** vt [h] (etw) *to cellar, to lay in*

·**ein|kerben** vt [h] (etw) *to indent, to nick*; (Bogen, Pfeil) *to nock*; (Tisch) *to notch*; (Brot etc) *to score* ‖ ⟨her⟩ (Rand) *to engrail* **Einkerbung** f *indent; nick, notch*

·**ein|kerkern** vt [h] (jdn) *to imprison, to incarcerate; to put* (*a p*) *in prison* ·**Einkerkerung** f ~/~en *imprisonment, incarceration*

·**einkernig** a ⟨at⟩ *mononuclear*

·**ein|kesseln** vt [h] ⟨hunt⟩ (Fuchs) *to encircle, to hem* (od *shut*) *in*

·**Einkindschaft** f ⟨jur hist⟩ *legal equality among children of different marriages*

·**ein|kitten** vt [h] (etw) *to fix* (*a th*) *with cement* od *putty; to putty* (*a th*) *in*

·**einklagbar** a *suable, actionable; enforceable in proceedings*

·**ein|klagen** vt [h] *to sue for, to enforce* (*a debt*); e–n Anspruch ~ *to prosecute a claim*

·**ein|klammern** vt [h] ⟨tech⟩ *to cramp* ‖ (Wörter, Sätze) *to bracket, to put* od *enclose in brackets; to parenthesize* ‖ Eingeklammertes *the word(s) in brackets*

·**Einklang** m ~(e)s/ **1.** ⟨mus⟩ *unison* **2.** ⟨fig⟩ *accord, unison*; [nur in festen Verbindungen]: **a. in ~ mit** *consonant, in accord* (od *accordance, conformity, unison*) *with; of a piece with* ‖ in vollem ~ mit *in key with* ‖ nicht in ~ mit *incongruous with, in opposition with; out of tune with* **b.** (Dinge) **in ~ bringen** *to coordinate*, (Meinungen) *to harmonize* ‖ (etw) in ~ bringen mit *to bring* (*a th*) *into accordance* (od *consonance, line*) *with; to harmonize* od *reconcile* (*a th*) *with*; .. u dadurch zu höchster Wirkung bringen *to make .. mutually effective*; .. wie er die Forderung mit der Tatsache in ~ bringt, daß .. *how he squares the demand with the fact* (*that* ..); den Geist in ~ bringen mit *to put the spirit in tune with* | **in ~ stehen mit** *or* **zu** (S) *to be of a piece with; to chime* (od *fit*) *in with; to square with; to be compatible* od *consonant with; to be in keeping* (od *harmony, tune*) *with* ‖ (P) *to be of one mind* (od *of the same mind*) *with, of the same opinion as* (*a p*) ‖ nicht im ~ stehen mit *to be out of keeping* (od *harmony, tune*) *with; to be incompatible with*; (nicht) im ~ stehend (*in-*) *compatible* (*with*)

·**einklappbar** a *stow-away* (*armrest*)

·**ein|klarieren** vt [h] (Schiff) *to clear in; to enter*

·**einklassig** a: ~e Schule *all-age class*

·**Einklebe- ~album** n ⟨phot⟩ *paste-on album* **~buch** n *scrap-book* ·**ein|kleben** vt [h] (Bilder) *to paste, stick, glue* (in *in, into*); nur an einer Kante ~ *to tip in*

·**ein|kleiden** vt [h] **1.** (jdn) *to clothe* (in *in*); *to array, invest* (*in*) ‖ ⟨mil⟩ *to accoutre, equip* **2.** ⟨übtr⟩ (etw) *to cover, envelop, invest* ‖ ⟨fig⟩ (Gedanken) ~ *to clothe, couch* (in *in*); in Verse ~ *to put into rhyme*; → kleiden

·**Einkleidung** f ~/~en **1.** *clothing* (in *in*); (feierliche ~) *investitute*; ⟨R. C.⟩ *taking the veil* ‖ ⟨mil⟩ *accoutrement, equipment* **2.** ⟨übtr⟩ *cover(ing), envelopment* ‖ ⟨fig⟩ *clothing* (*of thoughts*); *wording*; → Fassung **~sbeihilfe** f *clothing allowance*

·**ein|klemmen** vt [h] **1.** (etw) fest ~ *to jam* (zw *between*; in *into*); (*the dog*) *put* (*his tail*) *between* (*his legs*) ‖ –geklemmt w, sich ~ *to jam* ‖ ⟨med⟩ (Darmteil) *to strangulate*; eingeklemmter Bruch *incarcerated hernia* ‖ *to nip* od *pinch one's finger, catch one's coat in the door* ‖ *gallstones became impacted* **2.** ⟨übtr⟩ (jdn) *to sandwich* (*in*) (zw *between*) ‖ sich in die Tür ~ *to wedge o.s. in at the doorway* ·**Einklemmung** f *jamming* ‖ ⟨med⟩ *strangulation*

·**ein|klinken** vt/i [h] **1.** vt (Tür) *to latch*, die Tür ist –geklinkt *the door is on the latch* **2.** vi (of doors) *to latch* (*the door won't l.*) ‖ ⟨tech, aero⟩ *to engage*

·**ein|knicken** vt/i **1.** vt [h] (Blatt im Buche) *to fold; to double; to dog-ear* ‖ (Tuch) *to crease; to wrinkle*; –geknickt w *to crumple* ‖ mit Gewalt ~ *to crack, to flaw* **2.** vi [s] *to bend; to sag*; ⟨arch⟩ *to fall*; s–e Knie knickten ein *his knees began to buckle, his knees gave way*

·**Einknopfbedienung** f ⟨wir⟩ *single-dial control*

·**ein|kochen** vt/i [h] **1.** vt (Saft) *to boil down* ‖ *to make jam, to preserve* ‖ ⟨cul⟩ *to reduce* **2.** vi (of liquids) *to boil away; to be reduced* (od *to thicken*) *by boiling*

·**ein|kommen** vi [s] **1.** (P) *to apply, petition* (um etw *for a th*); bei jdm (Behörde etc) um etw ~ *to apply to a p for a th, to petition a p for a th* ‖ um s–n Abschied ~ *to hand* (od *send*) *in one's resignation*; → einreichen **2.** (of money) *to come in, to be paid in* ‖ –ge–e Gelder [pl] *moneys paid in, incomings, receipts, takings* [pl]

·**Einkommen** n ~s/Einkünfte **1.** *income* (*of a p*); ein hohes ~ *a big i.*; ~ durch Arbeit *earned i.*; ~ aus Vermögen *unearned i.* ‖ festes ~ *settled, fixed, regular, steady i.* ‖ Einkünfte *emoluments* (*of a judge*) ‖ ~ durch Miete, Pacht *rental*; Jahres≗ *annuity*; er hat ein jährliches ~ v 10000 Mark *he is worth 10 thousand marks a year* ‖ → Auskommen **2.** *revenue* (*of a state, a public body; a ruler*, etc.); fundiertes ~ *revenues* [pl] ‖ → Ertrag **~klasse** f *income bracket* **~steuer** f *income-tax* ‖ ~erklärung [f] *income-tax return* (⟨Am⟩ *statement*); ~formular [n] *schedule* ‖ ~hinterzieher [m] *i.–t. dodger* ‖ ~hinterziehung [f] *i.–t. evasion* ‖ ≗pflichtig [a] *liable to i.–t.* ‖ ~überprüfung [f] *means test*

·**ein|kopieren** vt [h] *to overprint*

·**Einkorn** n ~(e)s/ ⟨bot⟩ *one-grained spelt* (od *wheat*); → Dinkel

·**ein|krallen** vt/refl (sich) ~ *to dig one's nails in*

·**ein|kramen** vt [h] (Waren) *to pack* (od *put*) *up*

·**ein|kratzen** vrefl [h] sich bei jdm ~ *to get under a p's skin*

·**Einkreisgerät** n ⟨wir⟩ *single-circuit receiver*

·**ein|kreisen** vt [h] ⟨a. pol⟩ *to encircle* ‖ ⟨mil⟩ (Feind etc) *to close in upon; to envelop* ·**Einkreisung** f ⟨pol⟩ *encirclement*; ~smanöver [n] ⟨tact⟩ *e. manoeuvre*; ~spolitik [f] *encircling policy*; ~sschlacht [f] *battle of encirclement*; ~sversuch [m] *attempted e.*

·**Einkristall** m *single crystal*

·**Einkünfte** pl → Einkommen

·**ein|kuppeln** vi [h] ⟨mot⟩ *to let in* [adv] *the clutch; to couple, clutch; to engage; to throw in gear*

·**ein|kuscheln** vt [h] *to tuck in* ‖ **sich** ~ *to snuggle up in bed, in one's blanket*

·**einkurbelig** a ⟨tech⟩ ~e Welle *single-throw crank-shaft*

·**ein|kurven 1.** vi [s] ⟨aero⟩ *to pitch out; to turn in* **2.** ≗ n *turn-in*

·**Einlad** m ~s/ ⟨Sw⟩ = Ein–, Verladung

·**ein|laden I.** vt [h] **1.** (Waren) *to lade, load, ship*; → einnehmen **2.** jdn ~ *to invite a p* (zum Tee etc *to tea*; in sein Haus *to one's house*); *to ask a p* (*to sit down, for tea*); *to entertain a p* (zum Essen etc *at* od *to dinner*); ich darf Sie wohl *or* bitte ~ *it is my treat*; z Essen –ge– w *to be entertained at* (od *to*) *dinner; he welcomed us to a share of his wine*; jdn z sich aufs Land ~ *to invite a p down*; jdn ~ l *to send to invite a p* | **sich** selbst ~ (schmarotzen) *to cadge o.s.* **3.** vi *to give invitations* **II.** ≗ n *lading, shipment* (*of goods*) ‖ → Einladung ·**einladend** a *inviting; attractive; promising* (*weather*) ·**Einlader** m

∼s/∼ *loader* ·**Einladung** f ∼/∼en **1.** → Einladen **2.** *invitation*, ⟨Am a.⟩ *bid* (an jdn *to a p*; z Tee *to tea*); e–r ∼ Folge leisten *to accept an i.*; e–r ∼ folgend ging ich .. *in response to an invitation I went* ..; auf jds ∼ *at* (od *on*) *the i. of a p*; → Aufforderung **∼skarte** f *invitation-card* **∼sschreiben** n *letter of invitation*

·**Einlage** f ∼/∼n **I.** [abstr] → Einlegen **II.** [konkr] (Eingelegtes) **A. 1.** (im Brief) *enclosure, the enclosed*; in der ∼ übersende ich Ihnen ein Exemplar v *I enclose a copy of* .. **2.** ⟨cul⟩ Suppe mit ∼ *soup with meat-balls* od *vegetable*, etc. **3.** (∼ im Zahn etc) *filling* ‖ (in Zigarre) *filler* ‖ (im Schuh) *instep raiser* (*to wear supports* od *padding*) ‖ (Reifen≗) (*inside*) *tyre protector* **4.** weiche ∼ *wadding* (im Hut) ‖ *padding* ‖ (steife ∼) *stiffening* ‖ → –stück **5.** (im Schrank etc) *case, compartment* **B.** (Geld≗) **1.** (beim Spiel) *stake* **2.** ⟨com⟩ *deposit*; feste ∼n *fixed deposits* [pl]; Spar≗ *deposit in a savings bank* **3.** (Kapital≗ e–s Gesellschafters) *money* (od *capital*) *paid in* (od *invested*), *investment* **C. 1.** ⟨mus & theat⟩ musikal. ∼ *inserted piece, intermezzo*; Gesangs≗ *inserted song*; Tanz≗ *inserted dance* ‖ (*lyrical*) *passage* (*in a play*) **2.** (in Büchern) *insertion, intercalation, interpolation*; *insert*; *inset* **3.** ⟨cul⟩ (Zwischengang) *entremets* [mst pl] (Fr), *side-dish* **4.** → eingelegt(e Arbeit) **∼bestand** m *amount of deposits in a bank* **∼blatt** n *loose leaf* **∼bogen** m ⟨post⟩ (f Ersttagsstempelung) *stuffer* **∼buch** n *depositor's book* **∼kapital** n *capital invested* **∼tisch** m ⟨tech⟩ *feed-table*

·**ein|lagern** vt [h] ⟨com⟩ (Waren) *to warehouse*; (Möbel) *to store*; (Getreide) *to silo, store*; (Vorrat) *to stockpile* ·**Einlagerung** f *warehousing* (*of goods*); *storage, storing* (*of grain*) ‖ *stockpiling* ‖ ∼ v Kalzium ⟨biol⟩ *deposit of c.* | **∼s-** ∼maßnahme [f] *arrangement for st.* ‖ ∼verbindung [f] *interstitial* od *intercalation compound*

·**Einlaß** m –lasses/ **1.** [abstr] (P) *letting in, admission, admittance, entrance* (z *to*); ∼ 12 Uhr *doors are opened at 12 o'clock*; ∼ nur gegen Karte *admission only by ticket*; jdm ∼ gewähren *to grant a p admittance* (*to*); jdm ∼ verschaffen *to get a p admitted, to gain a p('s) admittance* (in, zu *to*); sich mit Gewalt ∼ verschaffen in (*or* z) *to force an entrance into* **2.** [konkr] *inlet, opening*; *wicket*; *wicket-gate*; ⟨rail, aero⟩ *gate* **∼karte** f *ticket* (od *card*) *of admission* ‖ Eintritt nur mit bes. ∼ *by special order* ‖ ∼ f Ersatzvorstellung *rain check* ‖ ⟨aero⟩ *gate pass* **∼öffnung** f *inlet* ⟨a. mot⟩ **∼schinder** m ⟨sport⟩ *gate--crasher* **∼ventil** n *admission* (od *inlet*) *-valve*; ⟨aero mot⟩ *suction valve*

·**ein|lassen I.** vt [h] **A. 1.** jdn ins Haus ∼ *to admit a p, to let a p in*; ∼ in *to admit* od *let a p into* (*a room*) **2.** (Luft etc) *to admit*; *to let in*; ∼ in *to admit to* ‖ Wasser in das Bad ∼ *to turn water on into the bath* **3.** ⟨carp & arch⟩ (Platte, Tafel) *to let in* ‖ ∼ in *to let into* (*the wall*); *to fix* (od *fasten*) *in*, *to fit into* (*the wall*); (Brett) an e–m Ende in die Wand ∼ *to tail in*; mit e–m Zapfen ∼ in *to mortise into* ‖ (Stein) *to sink*; ∼ in *to sink into* ‖ (Bolzen, Nietkopf) *to counter--sink* ‖ ⟨östrr⟩ *to wax* (*the floor*) ‖ → eingelassen **B.** (Kleid) *to take in* **C.** [refl] **sich ∼ 1.** (ins Haus) *to let o.s. in* **2.** ⟨fig⟩ **a. sich ∼ auf** *to embark on* (*a th, an action*); *to let o.s. in for* (*a th*); *to let o.s. involved in* (*discussion*), *mixed up in* (*a quarrel, politics*); *to accede to* od *comply with* (*a request*); *to agree* od *consent to* (*an offer, conditions*); *to comply with* (*instructions*); *to yield to* (*a demand*); er ließ sich darauf ein *he agreed* ‖ man läßt sich zu leicht darauf ein *it is entered into too lightly* ‖ *not to go into* (*explanations, details*); *not to be satisfied with* (*mere promises*); ich will mich mit diesen Leuten nicht ∼ *I won't have anything to do with these people*; laß dich nicht darauf ein! *don't go in on it* ‖ sich auf e–n Vorschlag ∼ *to accept a proposal*; ich kann mich auf den V. nicht ∼ *I cannot entertain the p.* ‖ sich auf Einzelheiten ∼ *to descend to particulars* **b. sich ∼ in** (etw) *to engage in*; sich in ein Gespräch ∼ *to enter into conversation* (*with a p*) ‖ sich in Spekulationen ∼ *to venture on speculations* **c. sich ∼ mit** (jdm) *to enter into intimate relations with a p*; *to associate* od *mix with* (*a p*); *to make free with* (*a girl*); sich mit e–r Frau ∼ *to have intercourse* od *intimacy with a woman* ‖ laß dich nicht z weit mit ihm ein ⟨allg & sex⟩ *don't be too intimate with him* **II.** ≗ n (S) **1.** *letting-in* (*of air*); *admission* (in *to*) ‖ → Einlaß 1. **2.** *letting-in* (*of a slab*); *sinking* (*of a stone*); *countersinking* **3.** Sich-∼ = Eingehen → d. 2. 5. ‖ → Umgang, Verkehr ·**einläßlich** a ⟨Sw & österr⟩ *thorough* (*discussion, inquiry, etc*) ·**Einlassung** f ⟨jur⟩ (Klage≗) *appearance*; (∼ des Beklagten) *formal entry of a suit*; *litiscontestation* | ∼sfrist [f] *time to serve* od *interpose an answer*

·**Einlauf** m ∼(e)s/ ≗e **1.** = Einlaufen **2.** ⟨com⟩ ≗ [pl] *mail received*; *incoming mail, goods* **3.** ⟨med⟩ *enema* (L) **4.** ⟨found⟩ *runner* **≗echt** a **∼sicher** a ⟨tex⟩ *non-shrink* [attr], *shrink-resistant, pre-shrunk* **∼suppe** f ⟨cul⟩ *consommé aux œufs filés* Fr **∼zeit** f ⟨mot⟩ *breaking-in period*

·**ein|laufen** vi/t **I.** vi [s] **A. 1.** (of a train) *to come* od *pull in*; in den Bahnhof ∼ *to pull* (od *draw*) *into the station*; der Zug läuft um 11 Uhr in Berlin ein *the train gets to B. at 11.* ‖ (of ships) in den Hafen ∼ *to enter harbour*; *to put into port*; in den Heimathafen ∼d *inbound* (*ship*) ‖ Badewasser ∼ l *to run the bath* **2.** ⟨übtr bes com⟩ (of letters, etc.) *to enter*; *to come in*; *to come to hand*; (of orders, etc.) *to drop in*; in Mengen ∼ *to pour in*; zahlreiche Beschwerden liefen ein *it rained complaints* **B.** (of cloth) *to shrink*; *to run up* **II.** vt [h] **1.** jdm das Haus ∼ *to pester a p with trouble-some visits*; *to importune a p* **2.** (Maschine) ∼ *or* ∼ l *to run in* ‖ (Schuhe) *to break in* **3.** [refl] **sich** ∼ (of a machine) *to run itself in* **III.** ≗ n **1.** (of trains) *pulling in* ‖ (of ships) *entrance, entry* (in *into*) ‖ ∼ u Auslaufen *entry and departure* (*of a ship*) **2.** (of cloth) *shrinkage* **3.** ⟨übtr⟩ *entry*; *coming in* ·**einlaufend** a *shrinkable* (*cloth*); nicht ∼ *unshrinkable* ·**Einläufer** m **1.** = Eingänger **2.** *one-barrelled gun*

·**einläufig** a *one-barrelled* (*gun*)

·**ein|laugen** vt [h] *to steep in an alkaline lye*

·**ein|läuten** vt [h] (das Neue Jahr) *to ring in*

·**ein|leben** vrefl [h] **sich** ∼ = sich eingewöhnen; *to settle down in a new place* ‖ er wird sich bald in die Schule ∼ *he will soon shake down at his school* ‖ sich ∼ in die Umgebung (etc) *to accustom o.s.* (od *to get accustomed*) *to the surroundings* ‖ *to make o.s. familiar with*; .. in e–e fremde Sprache *to familiarize o.s. with a foreign language* ‖ wie h Sie sich –ge–bt? *how are you shaping*?

·**Einlege- ∼arbeit** f = eingelegte Arbeit **∼keil** m *inserting quoin, laid-in key* **∼platte** f (am Tisch) *leaf* **∼sohle** f *inner sole*; *insole*; *boot-sock* (od *sole*); → Filzsohle **∼stück** n ⟨mach⟩ (aus Holz *or* Metall) *shim*; (Fuge) mit e–m ∼ ausfüllen *to shim* **∼tisch** m ⟨print⟩ *feed-board*

·**ein|legen I.** vt [h] **A. 1.** (Kartoffeln, Kohlen) *to lay in*; *to store*, *warehouse*; im Keller ∼ *to cellar* **2.** (Fleisch etc) *to pot*, *preserve*; *salt*; (Heringe) *to pickle* ‖ (Eier) *to pot*; → eingelegt **B.** etw ∼ in *to enclose* od *put a th in* (*a letter*) **C. 1.** (Blatt, Platte) *to insert*, *introduce* (in *into*); *to inset*; *intercalate*; *interpolate* ‖ ⟨tail⟩ (Watte) *to pad* (*the shoulders*) ‖ (Lied, Tanz) *to insert, interpolate* ‖ e–e Arbeitsstunde ∼ *to put in an hour's work*; e–n Zug ∼ *to run an extra-train* (*between* ..); mehr Züge ~ *to put on more trains* **2.** ⟨print⟩ (Schrift) *to lay*; (Papier) *to feed* **3.** (Holz) *to inlay*; mit Elfenbein –gelegt *inlaid with ivory*; → eingelegt **4.** eine Lanze ~ *to couch a lance* || ⟨fig⟩ f jdn e–e L. ~, f jdn ein gutes Wort ~ *to intercede* (od *plead*; *speak*; *stand up*) *for a p*; *to put in a* (*good*) *word for a p* **5.** ⟨rec⟩ (Band) *to feed in* **D.** ⟨übtr⟩ **1.** Berufung ~ *to appeal*; *to lodge an appeal* (gegen *against*) || eine Beschwerde ~ *to lodge a complaint* (*against a p*) || Protest, Verwahrung ~ *to enter* (od *lodge*, *make*) *a protest* (bei jdm gegen *with a p against*) || ein Veto ~ gegen etw *to put a* od *one's veto on a th* **2.** mit ihm, mit dem Buche wirst du Ehre ~ *he, the book will do you credit* **II.** ≈ n **1.** *laying in*; *storing* **2.** *preserving*; *salting*; *potting* **3.** *enclosing* (*of money*) **4.** *insertion*; *interpolation* || *putting in* || (des Films) *loading* (*of the camera*) **5.** *inlaying*; Holz z ~ *wood for i.* **b.** ~ e–r Berufung *the lodging of an appeal*; ~ e–s Protestes *the entering of a protest*

·**Einleger** m ~s/~ **1.** ⟨hort⟩ *layer*; *shoot* **2.** ⟨print⟩ *feeder*; *layer-on* **3.** (P) *inlayer*

·**ein|leiten** vt [h] **1.** (Buch) *to preface* || ⟨übtr⟩ (Bemerkungen, Rede etc) *to preface* (mit *by*, *with*; damit daß man sagt *by saying*); *to prelude* (*by*, *with*) || *to begin*, *open*, *start* (mit *with*); etw durch e–n Prolog ~ *to prologue* || (neue Methode, Zeit) *to inaugurate*, *to introduce*; *to usher in*; *to pave the way for* || ⟨gram⟩ (Satz) *to introduce* **2.** (etw) *to open*, *start*; *to set on foot*; e–e Untersuchung ~ *to institute an inquiry* || e–n Prozeß ~ *to bring an action*, *to take proceedings* (gegen .. *against a p*) || ein Verfahren ~ *to institute* (*criminal*, *bankruptcy*, *etc*) *proceedings*; *to prosecute*; *to start legal proceedings*; .. gegen jdn *to prosecute a p* (wegen *for*) ·**einleitend** a *introductory*, *prefatory*, *preliminary* (*remarks*); *opening*; *lead-off* (*part*) || ~er Teil *exordium*, *introduction*, *opening*, *preamble* (*of a speech*, *story*) || ~e Schritte [pl] *preliminary steps* [pl] || ~e Worte [pl] *a word of introduction* ·**Einleiter-** (→ eins) **~antenne** f *single-wire a.* **~kabel** n *single*(*-core*) *cable* ·**Einleitung** f ~/~en **1. a.** *introduction*, *preface* (z .. *to a book*; ein Buch mit e–r ~ versehen *to preface a book* || ⟨mus⟩ *prelude*; → Ouvertüre | ⟨übtr⟩ *preamble*, *preface*, *prelude*, *prologue* (z .. *to a speech*; *to a war*) || lange ~en m, mit e–r ~ beginnen *to preamble* (*begin without preambling*); als ~ dienen z etw *to preface*, *prelude* **b.** (Wegweiser) *introduction* (in etw) *to a th*) **2.** *beginning*, *opening*, *starting* (*of proceedings*); *instituting* (*of an inquiry*) ·**Einleitungs-** → einleitend

·**ein|lenken** vi [h & s] **1.** *to turn in* (in den Torweg *at the doorway*) || ~ in e–e Straße *to turn into a road*, *to join a r.* || wieder in e–e Straße ~ *to rejoin a road*, *to join a r. again* **2.** ⟨fig⟩ (nachgeben) *to cave* od *give in*; *to relent*, *yield*; *to come down a peg* od *two*; *to come around* (*to a p's view*) ~ solange es Zeit ist *to go while the going is good* || → umschwenken

·**ein|lernen** vt [h] **1.** sich [dat] etw ~ *to learn a th thoroughly* (od *by heart*) || jdm etw ~ *to teach a p a th* **2.** jdn ~ *to initiate* od *instruct a p*

·**Einlesemaschine** f ⟨weav⟩ *reading machine*

·**ein|lesen** vt [h] **1.** = einsammeln **2.** [refl] **sich ~ in** etw *to familiarize o.s. with a th by reading*; *to get into* (*a foreign language*) *by reading* || *to get into the spirit of a book* || *to get used* (*to the style of an anthor* | *to read a th up*

·**ein|leuchten** vi [h] ⟨fig⟩ (S) *to be clear*, (od *evident*, *obvious*, *plausible*); es leuchtet ein, daß .. *it is obvious that* || das leuchtet mir wohl ein *that's quite plausible*, *I agree*; *there's something in that*; || das will mir nicht ~ *I cannot see that*; der Sinn will mir nicht ~ *the sense eludes me* ·**einleuchtend** a *evident*, *clear*, *obvious*, *comprehensible*, *plausible*; nicht ~ *implausible* || ~er [compr] *with greater show of reason*

·**ein|liefern** vt [h] (etw) *to deliver*; *to hand in* (jdm *to a p*) || (Bericht, Zeugnis) *to submit* (jdm *to a p*) | (P) *to commit* .. *to prison*

·**Einlieferung** f ~/~en *delivery* (*of goods*); *handing in*; ~sschein [m] *receipt*; → Lieferung || ~ jds (ins Krankenhaus) *the admission of a p* | ~sbefehl [m] *warrant of commitment* (in Untersuchungshaft *upon remand*, nach Schuldigsprechung *upon conviction*); ~szeit [f] *time of admission*

·**einliegend** [v †einliegen] **1.** [prs p] ⟨com⟩ ~ übersende ich Ihnen ein Exemplar v *I enclose a copy of* .. **2.** [a] ~er Kreis *inscribed circle*

·**ein|lochen** vt [h] (Golfball) *to putt* || °(jdn) *to lock up*, *to run in*; ⟨sl⟩ *to jug*, *quod*

·**ein|logieren** [–ʒi:rən] vt [h] = einmieten

·**einlösbar** a ⟨com⟩ *redeemable* (*bond*)

·**ein|lösen** vt [h] **1. a.** (Pfand) *to redeem* **b.** (Schuldschein etc) *to redeem*; *discharge*, *pay* || (Wechsel) *to honour* (pünktlich *duly*), *to meet*, *protect*, *retire*; *to take up*; zum Fälligkeitstermin –gelöst w *to find due protection* || (Verpflichtung, Versprechen) *to keep*, *redeem*; (*to keep one's word*); nicht ~ *to dishono*(*u*)*r* (*one's promise*) **2.** (in Geld umsetzen) (Coupon) *to cash*; e–n Scheck ~ *to cash* od *pass a cheque*; → Scheck

·**Einlösung** f **1.** *redemption* (*of a pledge*; *a bond*) || *discharge*, *payment*; *protection* (*of a bill of exchange*) || *redemption* (*of a promise*); *the keeping* (*of one's word*) **2.** *the cashing* od *passing* (*of a cheque*); *encashment*

·**ein|lullen** vt [h] **1.** *to lull* (*a child*) *to sleep* **2.** ⟨fig⟩ (jdn) ⟨oft iron⟩ *to allay*; *appease*; *calm*, *soothe* || jdn ~ in *to cajole* od *to lull a p into* (*a sense of security*)

·**Einmach** f ~/~e [österr] *flour slightly roasted in fat*

·**Einmach(e)-** [in comp] *preserving* **~apparat** m *preserving* (od *sterilizing*)*-apparatus* (od *boiler*); *preserver*, *sterilizer* **~büchse** f *tin*, ⟨bes Am⟩ *can* **~glas** n *preserving-glass* (od *bottle*, *jar*) **~hilfe** f *easy-jel* **~verfahren** n *method of preserving* od *canning* **~zucker** m *jamming sugar*

·**ein|machen 1.** vt [h] (Früchte etc) *to preserve*; (in Büchsen ~) *to tin*, ⟨bes Am⟩ *to can*; ⟨Am fam⟩ *to put up*; (in Dosen ~) *to pack*; (Fleisch) in e–m Topf ~ *to pot* || in Zucker ~ *to candy* || in Essig ~ *to pickle*; *to marinade*, *marinate* **2.** ≈ n *preserving*; (in Büchsen) *canning*, *tinning*

·**ein|maischen** vt [h] ⟨brew⟩ *to mash* od *dough in* ·**Einmaischtemperatur** f ⟨brew⟩ *initial t.*; *striking heat*

einmal [Betonung → u] adv **I.** [ˈeinmal] **1.** *once*; *on one occasion*; nur ~ *one time only*, *only once*; ~ eins ist eins *once one is one*; ~ Null ist Null *once nought is nought* || ~ u nicht wieder *once and never again* || ein f allemal *for good and all*; *once* (*and*) *for all*; *first*, *last*, *and all the time*; *quite finally*; ein über das andere Mal *once* (od *time*) *and again*; *repeatedly* || ~ .., dann .. *for one th* .. *for another*; ~ in Paris, ~ in London *one time in P.*, *another t. in L.*; ~ lachte, ~ weinte sie *she laughed and cried in turns*; ~ ja ~ nein sagen *to say yes one moment*, *and no the next* | ~ täglich *once every day* || ~, als .. *once upon a time when*; → II. **1.** || ~ .., ~ .. *now* .. *now* || ~ darfst du mehr nehmen *once in a way you may take more* **2. auf** ~ (plötzlich) *all of a sudden*, *all at once* | (zugleich) *at once*, *at a time* (*only two at a time*) | **mit** ~ *all of a sudden* **3.** noch ~ *once again*; *this once* (*I will permit it this once*), *for once*; wenn ich dich noch ~ fasse, dann .. *if I catch you again* (*you* ..) || **noch** ~ [ˈ– – od –ˈ–] *once more*; || noch ~ so gr *twice as large*; noch ~ so breit, lang wie *double the breadth*, *length of* **II.** [unbetont] **1.** (zeitlich)

a. *once; once upon a time; in times past; formerly;* er war schon *or* früher ~ dort *he has been there before;* es war ~ ein König *once (upon a time) there was a king, there once lived a k.;* → I. 1. **b.** *once; some day* (od *time*); *one of these days;* du wirst es ~ bereuen *you will repent it some day or other;* die Zeit war ~, als .. *time was when ..;* das war ~ *the time is gone* **c.** ab u z ~ *once in a way* ‖ endlich ~ *at the long last* ‖ laß mich erst ~ ausruhen *let me rest first* ‖ schon längst ~ *long ago; long since* **d.** als ~, sobald ~, wenn ~ *once, once that* [conj]; sobald er erst ~ dort war (..) *once there (he did not care)* **2.** [verblaßt] wieder ~ *again (he is naughty a.)* ‖ laß ihn, er ist ~ so *let him alone, he is like that* ‖ es ist nun ~ so in der Welt *such is the world; it is the way of the w.* | ich ~ nicht *not me for one* | denk dir ~ *just fancy;* komm ~ her *just come here;* hör ~ *just listen, look here* | nicht ~ *not even, never even;* ich kenne ihn nicht ~ *I don't so much as know him;* sie machte nicht ~ ihr Bett *she never so much as made her own bed* ‖ → mal ≗**behälter** m *disposable container* ≗**kanüle** f *d. tubule* od *canula* ≗**skalpell** n *d. scalpel* ≗**spritze** f *d. syringe;* etc

Einmal·eins n ~/ *multiplication-table(s)* ‖ er kann das ~ bis 10 *he can multiply up to the 10-times table*

·einmalig a *done* (od *happening*) *but once* ‖ *single (sum)* ‖ *non-recurring (payment)* ‖ sie ist ~ (e–e Perle) *she's a oner* ‖ ~e Abfindung *lump-sum payment* ‖ ~e Gelegenheit *unique chance* od *opportunity;* "*once only*" *purchase* | ≗**keit** f *uniqueness;* ⟨fig⟩ *matchlessness*

·Einmalprämie f ⟨ins⟩ *single premium*

·Ein-M·ann- [in comp] *one-man (company)* ‖ ~gesellschaft [f] ⟨jur⟩ *corporation sole* ‖ ~loch [n] ⟨mil⟩ *(one-man) foxhole* ‖ ~torpedo [n] *human t.*

·ein|marinieren vt [h] *to pickle; marinade, marinate*

·Einmarsch m ~(e)s/≗e *march(ing) in;* ~ in *march(ing) into; entry into (a country)*

·ein|marschieren vi [s] *to march in;* ~ in ein Land *to march into a country, to enter a c.*

·Einmaster m ~s/~ ⟨mar⟩ *single-masted vessel* **·einmastig** a *single-masted (ship)*

·ein|mauern vt [h] **1.** (Bild etc) *to build in(to) a wall, to immure in a wall* ‖ ⟨fig⟩ (etw) fest ~ *to embed, imbed* (in *in*) **2.** (Stadt) *to wall in* ‖ → z umauern

·ein|meißeln vt [h] (etw) ~ in *to cut* (od *carve, engrave*) *with a chisel into (a slab)*

·ein|mengen vt [h] → einmischen **·Einmengung** f → Einmischung

·ein|messen; ≗ n → eichen, Eichung

·ein|mieten[1] vt [h] **1.** jdn ~ *to find a p lodgings, to find l. for a p* (bei *with a p;* in *in*) **2. sich** ~ *to take lodgings (with a p; in)*

·ein|mieten[2] vt [h] (Gemüse) *to pit;* (Kartoffeln) *to clamp, pit; to store in a clamp;* (Gemüse) *to pit;* (Getreide) *to silo, store* **·Einmietung** f *pitting; clamping; storing*

·ein|mischen vt [h] **1.** etw ~ in *to mix a th in* od *with; to add a th to* ‖ ⟨comp⟩ *to file* **2. sich** ~ (P) *to interfere, intervene; to put one's oar in* ‖ sich ~ in *to butt in; to break in (a conversation); to interfere* (od *intermeddle, intervene, meddle*) *in (matters); to mingle in (a dispute);* ⟨fam⟩ *to poke one's nose into (other people's business)* **·Einmischung** f ~/~en *interference* (in *in*); *tampering (with)* ‖ ⟨pol⟩ *intervention (in)*

einm·onatlich a; ~e Kündigung *a month's notice* **·einmotorig** a *one-engined (plane)*

·ein|motten vt [h] (Kleidung) *to mothball*

°**·ein|mummeln** vt [h] **1.** (jdn) *to envelop; muffle; to wrap (up);* er war –ge–lt bis z *he was muffled to (the eyes)* **2. sich** ~ *to wrap up; to envelop o.s.* (in *in*); sich im Bett warm ~ *to cuddle (up)*

·ein|münden vi [h] ~ in (of a river, etc) *to flow into, to enter (the sea), to debouch into, to discharge* (od *empty*) *itself into;* (of a brook) *to join (a river)* ‖ ⟨übtr⟩ in die Landstraße ~ (of a lane) *to run into, to join the high-road;* wieder ~ in *to rejoin* ‖ ⟨anat⟩ (of arteries) *to anastomose with* | ~d a *approach-(road)* **·Einmündung** f (Straßen≗) *intersection, junction;* ~ zur Autobahn *entrance to a motorway*

·Einmut f ⟨poet⟩ = Einmütigkeit

·einmütig 1. a *unanimous, harmonious;* [pred] *solid* (f *for, in a p's favour;* gegen *against*) **2.** adv *with one accord* (od *consent, voice*); ~ stimmen für, gegen *to vote* (od *go*) *solid for, against; to be solid for, against;* ~ hinter jdm stehen *to be solidly behind a p* ‖ ~ zus-stehen *to be united in solidarity* ≗**keit** f ~/ *concord, harmony, unanimity;* es herrschte volle ~ in *there was perfect u. in (this matter)* ‖ *fellowship; solidarity*

·ein|nachten vi [h] ⟨Sw⟩ es nachtet ein *night is setting in;* → Nacht w

·ein|nähen vt [h] **1.** (etw) ~ in *to sew (up) in (a bag)* **2.** (Kleid) *to take in; to make a tuck in* ‖ → umnähen

·Einnahme f ~/~n **A.** [abstr] (Einnahmen) **1.** ⟨mil⟩ die ~ e–r Stadt *the taking possession of a town, the taking* (od *capture, occupation*) *of a t.* (durch *by*) **2.** *the taking (of seats)* **3.** *the taking in, taking on board, loading (of goods, provisions); the receiving (of money); collection (of taxes)* ‖ *the taking (of a meal);* nach ~ des Frühstücks *after breakfast* **B.** [konkr] (Eingenommenes) *cash* (od *money*) *received;* → Einkommen ‖ [mst pl] ~n *earnings, proceeds, receipts, takings* [pl]; ~en u Ausgaben *receipts and expenses* ‖ ~en im Bundes–, Reichshaushalt *revenue;* ~en durch inländische Steuern *inland* (⟨Am⟩ *internal*) *revenue*

·Einnahme- [in ⟨com⟩ comp] **~buch** n *receipt-book;* ⟨theat, m. m.⟩ *box office returns* **~quelle** f *source of revenue (of a state); s. of income (of a p)* **~überschuß** m ⟨com⟩ *credit balance*

·ein|nebeln vt [h] ⟨mil⟩ (Truppen) *to smoke--screen* **·Einnebelung** f *smoke-screening*

·einnehmbar a *capable of being taken*

·ein|nehmen vt/i [h] **I.** vt **A. 1.** ⟨mil⟩ *to take possession of, to take;* (Land) *to conquer, occupy; to take in* **2. a.** den (angewiesenen) Platz ~ *to take one's seat;* jds Stelle ~ *to replace a p; to act as a substitute for a p* | ⟨mil⟩ (Stellung) *to occupy;* ⟨tact⟩ *to seize* **b.** (S) (Raum) *to occupy; to take up* ‖ die Stelle e–r S ~ *to replace a th* **c.** ⟨übtr⟩ e–e hervorragende Stelle ~ *to hold* od *occupy a cardinal place; to adopt a menacing posture* **3.** ⟨übtr⟩ **a. jdn** ~ (of emotions, etc.) *to occupy; captivate, engage, fascinate a p* ‖ *to bias* od *predispose a p* (f *to*); *to prejudice* od *prepossess a p* (f *in favour of*) ‖ *to prejudice a p* (gegen *against*); *to set a p (against)* ‖ (Publikum, Stadt) f sich ~ *to capture; to take by storm;* jdn f sich ~ *to gain a p's favo(u)r;* ⟨fam⟩ *to suck up to a p* ‖ (jds Interesse) ganz ~ *to consume* **b.** den Kopf ~ *to make one's head dizzy, to make one feel giddy* ‖ → eingenommen; er schien v der S nicht sehr eing. z s ⟨fam⟩ *he didn't seem to fall for it* **B. 1.** (of a ship) (Ladung) *to take in; to take on board* ‖ Kohlen ~ f ein Schiff *to coal a vessel* ‖ (Segel) *to take in* **2.** (Geld etc) *to receive; take* ‖ (Steuern) *to collect, gather* **3.** (Arznei) *to take;* e–e Mahlzeit ~ *to take a meal, to partake of a m.;* e–e M. mit jdm (gemeinsam) ~ *to share a m. with a p;* das Frühstück, Mittagessen, Abendessen ~ *to breakfast, dine, sup (with); to have (one's) breakfast, dinner, supper* (in .. *at* [*the hotel*]); → verzehren **II.** vi; er nimmt durch sein Wesen f sich ein, sein Wesen nimmt f ihn ein *his engaging ways captivate you, one is prepossessed by his engaging* *manners* **·Einnehmen** n (v Medizin) *ingestion*; → Einnahme A. **·einnehmend** a ⟨fig⟩ *engaging, prepossessing, taking, winning, winsome*; ⟨fam⟩ *fetching* ‖ *attractive, captivating, charming, appealing* (*personality*) ‖ sein ∼es Wesen *his taking* od *winning ways* od *manner, his engagingness* | [adv] ∼ angeboten ⟨sex⟩ *fetchingly offered* **·Einnehmer** m ∼s/∼ *collector* od *receiver* (*of taxes*) ‖ Lotterie≈ *collector*

·ein|nicken vi [s] *to nod*; *to fall* (od *drop*) *asleep*

·ein|nisten [vrefl] [h] sich ∼ **1.** (of birds) *to build* od *make one's nest* (in *in*); *to nest, nestle, nidificate, nidify* (in *in*; auf *on*) **2.** ⟨übtr⟩ (P) *to establish o.s., to settle* (in *in*); *to gain* od *get a footing* (*in*); → einschleichen ‖ ⟨fig⟩ (of habits) *to take root*; *to become established*; → festsetzen

·ein|norden vt [h] *to orient* (*plan, map*)

·Einöde f ∼/∼n *desert, solitude, wilderness*

·ein|ölen vt [h] *to oil* ⟨a. fig⟩; → einfetten

·ein|ordnen vt [h] **1.** (etw) *to arrange* (od *dispose, range*) *a th in proper order*; (Briefe) *to file* ‖ in Klassen ∼ *to classify*; → ordnen ‖ (etw) ∼ in *to dovetail into*; *to fit into* ‖ **sich** ∼ *to fit in, to drop into place, to take one's place in a queue*; ⟨mil⟩ *to come* od *fall into line*; ‖ ⟨mot⟩ *to get into the correct traffic line*; (nach links, rechts) *to filter l., r., to move into the l., r. lane* ‖ sich in–e–a ∼ *to dovetail into one another* ‖ (System) ∼ in *to incorporate in*(*to*) **2.** jdn ∼ in etw, jdn e–r S [dat] ∼ *to enrol* od *enter a p in a th* ‖ **sich** e–r S ∼ *to join a th* **·Einordnung** f *arrangement in proper order*; *classification* ‖ *integration* (in *into*) ‖ *incorporation* (*in*) ‖ *enrolment*

·ein|packen vt [h] **I.** vt **1.** (Sachen) *to pack up* (in *in*) ‖ (Waren) *to put up* (in *in*); in Ballen ∼ *to bale* **2.** (jdn) *to envelop, wrap*; *to wrap up* (in *in*) ‖ sich im Bett warm ∼ *to cuddle* (*up*); *to tuck up o.s. in bed* ‖ (Patienten in feuchte Tücher) *to pack* **II.** vi **1.** *to pack* (*up*) **2.** °⟨fig⟩ **a.** packen Sie ein! *bundle off* od *out!, be off!*, ⟨Am⟩ *pack up!* ‖ pack ein mit d–n Witzen *none of your jokes* ‖ mit den Ausreden kannst du ∼ *you can keep your excuses* **b.** (er hat derartiges geleistet), da können wir ∼ (..) *he is more than a match for us* ‖ (wenn ..), dann können wir nur ∼ (..) *we shall be at the end of our tether* (od *at our wits' ends*) **·Einpackpapier** n *packing-paper*

·Einpackung f ⟨med⟩ (feuchte *wet*) *pack*

·ein|passen I. vt [h] **1.** (etw) *to adjust*; *to fit in*; (Rohr) ∼ in *to fit in* od *into* (*the wall*) **2. sich** ∼ in (P) *to fit o.s. in to* (*he fitted himself in to life*) ‖ (S) *to fit in to, to fit into* **II.** ≈ n *fitting* (in *into*) **·Einpassung** f (→ Eingliederung, Einordnung); *integration* (in *into*)

°**ein|pauken** vt [h] **1.** etw ∼, sich etw ∼ *to cram a th* (f *for*) ‖ jdm etw ∼ *to drum* od *hammer a th into a p's head* (od *into a p*); → einbleuen **2.** ⟨univ⟩ (jdn) *to cram, coach* (f *for*); *to train* ‖ mit jdm e–e Lektion ∼ *to hammer away at a lesson with a p* ‖ sich ∼ l *to be coached* **3. sich** ∼ *to practise fencing*

·Einpauker m ∼s/∼ ⟨univ⟩ *crammer, coach*; ⟨school⟩ *cram, grinder* ‖ als ∼ tätig s *to coach*

·Einpeitscher m ⟨engl parl⟩ (∼ e–r Partei) *whip*; ∼ der regierenden Partei *government whip*; ∼ der O. *opposition whip*; Haupt≈ der Regierung *Patronage Secretary to the Treasury*

·ein|pfählen vt [h] *to fence in*; *to enclose with pales*

·einpfarren vt [h] (Dorf) *to parochialize*; *to make parochial*

Einpf·ennigstück n ⟨Ger⟩ *one-penny piece*

·ein|pferchen vt [h] **1.** (T) *to pen*; (*im*)*pound* **2.** ⟨übtr⟩ (jdn) *to pen up* od *in*; *to coop* (od *shut*) *up*; *to sandwich* (*in*) (zw *between*); –gepfercht s mit *to be cooped up with*

·ein|pflanzen vt [h] **1.** (Baum) *to plant* (in *into*); (Kartoffeln) *to set*; (Sämling) *to prick in* **2.** ⟨fig⟩ jdm etw ∼ *to plant a th in a p*; jdm etw tief ∼ *to engrain a th in a p*; etw dem Geiste tief ∼ *to engraft a th in the mind*; = einimpfen

·Einpflanzung f ∼/∼en **1.** *planting* **2.** ⟨fig⟩ *implantation*; *inoculation*

·ein|pflöcken vt [h] *to peg* (in *in*); *to fasten with a peg* (*in*) ‖ (Gebiet) *to peg out*; *to enclose with pegs*

·ein|pfropfen vt [h] **1.** ⟨hort⟩ (Zweig) *to engraft, ingraft* (auf *upon*; in *into*) **2.** (etw) *to cram, pack, squeeze* (in *into*) **3.** jdm Nahrung ∼ *to overfeed a p, to fill a p to satiety* ‖ ⟨fig⟩ jdm Wissen ∼ *to stuff* od *cram a p with knowledge*

·einpfündig a *one-pound* [attr]

·Einphasen- [in comp] *single-phase*; *monophase* **∼generator** m *single-phase alternator* **∼motor** m *monophase motor* **∼strom** m *single-phase alternating current*

·einphasig a *single-phase* (*current*); *monophase*

·ein|pökeln vt [h] (Fleisch) *to salt*; *cure, corn, pickle* ‖ eingepökeltes Fleisch *salt meat, corned beef*; ⟨mar sl⟩ *salt horse* od *junk*

·einpolig a *unipolar*

·ein|prägen vt [h] **1.** ⟨eig⟩ (Bildnis) *to imprint* (auf *on*) ‖ (Linien) *to indent* (*on*) **2.** ⟨fig⟩ **a.** etw dem Geiste ∼ *to engraft* od *engrain a th in the mind, to imprint a th on* od *in a p's mind, to impress* od *stamp a th on a p's mind*; etw dem Gedächtnis ∼ *to fix a th* (jds Bild *a p*) *in one's mind*; *to engrave* od *stamp a th on the memory* ‖ (Lehre) mit Nachdruck ∼ *to enforce* (jdm *upon a p*); → einbleuen **b.** sich [dat] etw ∼ *to note a th* ‖ *to retain* (*an exercise*) ‖ ⟨theat⟩ *to memorize* (*one's part*) **3.** [refl] sich ∼ (of words, etc) *to sink in*; sich jdm ∼ *to sink into a p's mind, to be fixed in a p's mind*; sich dem Gedächtnis ∼ *to imprint o.s. on the memory*; es hat sich mir eingeprägt *it is imprinted on my mind* **·einprägsam** a *impressible*; *impressive*

·ein|prasseln vi [s] (*of blows, rain etc*) *to come pouring down* (auf *on a p*)

·ein|pressen vt [h] Falten ∼ in Stoff *to gather cloth in pleats*; eingepreßte Falten [pl] *plissé* ‖ etw ∼ zw, in *to wedge a th between, to squeeze .. in between* | **sich** ∼ in *to force* od *squeeze o.s. into* (*stays*)

·ein|proben vt [h] ⟨theat⟩ *to practise, rehearse*

·ein|pudern vt [h] (Kind etc) *to powder thoroughly*; *to sprinkle with powder* ‖ sich ∼ mit *to dust o.s. with*

·ein|pumpen vt [h] **1.** (Wasser) *to pump* (in *into*) **2.** ⟨fig⟩ °jdm etw ∼ *to pump a th into a p*

·ein|puppen vt [h] **1.** (jdn) *to wrap up* (in *in*) **2. sich** ∼ (of moths, etc.) *to change* (od *develop, turn*) *into a chrysalis*

·ein|quartieren vt [h] *to accomodate*; ⟨bes mil⟩ (Truppen) *to quarter, billet* (bei jdm *on a p*; in .. *at, in a place*); –quartiert s *to be quartered* (*on*); *to be in billets* ‖ **sich** ∼ *to quarter* od *billet o.s.* (bei *on a p*); *to take up quarters* (bei *with a p*; in *at, in a place*) **·Einquartierung** f ∼/∼en **1.** *quartering, billeting* **2.** [konkr] (die Soldaten) *soldiers* [pl] *quartered* od *billeted* (*on a p*) ‖ ⟨fig fam⟩ (Läuse) *colonists, lodgers* [pl]; *live stock*

·ein|quellen vt [h] (Hülsenfrüchte) *to soak, steep*

·ein|quetschen vt [h] (etw) *to squeeze, press* (in *into*) ‖ jdm die Rippen ∼ → eindrücken

·Einradanhänger m *monowheel trailer*

·ein|rahmen vt [h] (Bild) *to frame, mount* ‖ ⟨fig⟩ –gerahmt in .. (*a village*) *framed* od *sunk in* (*a wood*); *set in*; in musikalische Darbietungen –ge–mt *put in a musical setting* ‖ *provided* od *adorned with* **·Einrahmer** m ∼s/∼ *framer*

·ein|rammen vt [h] (Pfahl) *to ram* (od *drive*) *in*; fest ∼ in *to ram down into* (*the ground*)

·ein|rangieren [-raŋʒiːrən] vt [h] = einordnen, einreihen

·ein|rasten vt/i [h] *to lock, engage; snap, catch, stop* ‖ ⟨phot⟩ *to click in* **·Einrastknopf** m *locking knob*

·ein|räuchern vt [h] **1.** (Fleisch) *to smoke* **2.** *to fill with smoke*; –geräuchert *smoky* (*room*) ‖ → ausräuchern **·Einräucherung** f ~/~en *smoking* (*of meat*)

·ein|räumen I. vt [h] **A. 1.** (ein Zimmer) ~ *to place* od *set the furniture in a room in right order* **2.** (Möbel) *to place* od *put* (in *into a room*); *to stow* (*into*); → unterbringen ‖ → aufräumen **B.** ⟨fig⟩ **1.** (Gebiet) *to cede; to make over; to resign* (jdm *to a p*); → abtreten | (Recht, Vortritt etc) *to concede, grant, yield* (jdm *to a p*) ‖ ⟨com⟩ (Abzug, Nachlaß, Rabatt) *to allow a p* (*a discount*) ‖ (Kredit) *to open*; jdm e–n Kredit ~ in Höhe v *to give a p credit for* (*1000 marks*) ‖ (jdm, e–r S) genügend Zeit ~ *to allow sufficient time to* ‖ jdm ein Zimmer bei sich ~ *to acommodate* od *house a p* **2.** (zugeben) (etw) *to admit, own* (jdm gegenüber *to a p*); → zugeben **II.** ≚ n *the placing* od *moving* (*of furniture*) (in *into*); ⟨theat⟩ *get-in*, ⟨Am⟩ *take-in* **·einräumend** a ⟨gram⟩ *concessive* (*clause*)

·Einräumung f ~/~en **1.** → Einräumen **2.** ⟨fig⟩ *concession, grant* (*of rights*) (an *to*) ‖ *admission* **~ssatz** m ⟨gram⟩ *concessive clause*

·ein|rechnen vt [h] (etw) *to count in; to include*; die Sondereinnahmen –ge–net *counting in the extra fees*; .. nicht –ge–net *not allowed for* .. ‖ ⟨fig⟩ alles –ge–net *all things considered*; → einbegriffen, einschließen **·Einrechnung** f *inclusion*

·Einrede f ~/~n **1.** ⟨jur⟩ *defence*; ⟨engl hist⟩ (vor 1875) *plea*; aufschiebende ~ *dilatory plea* od *defence*; dauernde ~ *peremptory d.* **2.** = Einspruch, Einwand

·einreden vt/i [h] **A.** vt **1.** jdm Mut ~ *to inspire a p with courage; to encourage a p* **2.** jdm etw ~ *to talk a p into believing; to argue* (od *persuade, talk*) *a p into a th; to make a p believe a th*; jdm ~, daß .. *to persuade a p that* .. ‖ sich etw ~ *to get a th into one's head*; **sich** [dat] ~, daß .. *to make o.s. believe* (od *to persuade o.s.*) *that* ..; das lasse ich mir nicht ~ *I won't be argued into that* **B.** vi **1.** **~ auf jdn** *to talk insistently to a p; to work a p up* **2.** † = hineinreden

·ein|regnen vi & refl [s] **1.** vi *to be detained by the rain* **2.** es hat sich –ge–net *the weather has set in rainy, a continuous rain has set in* ‖ ⟨fig⟩ auf jdn ~ *to pour in on a p*

·ein|regulieren vt [h] *to adjust, regulate; to tune* (*an engine*) ‖ ⟨theat el⟩ *to dead, to make level*, ⟨Am⟩ *to trim* ‖ (Zündung) *to adjust the timing of the spark*

·ein|reiben I. vt [h] **1.** (Salbe) *to rub in*; ~ in *to rub into* (*the skin*) **2.** (Gesicht) *to smear* (mit *with*); jdm den Kopf ~ *to rub a p's head* (with ..); reib es tüchtig ein *give it a thorough rub* | (jdn) *to rub in*; ⟨med⟩ *to embrocate* ‖ **sich ~ mit** (Salbe) *to rub* (*ointment*) *into one's skin, to rub one's skin with* (*oi.*) **II.** ≚ n *rubbing in* ‖ Mittel z ~ *liniment* **·Einreibung** f ~/~en *rubbing in; rub* ‖ ⟨med⟩ *embrocation*

·ein|reichen vt [h] (Petition) *to present; submit* ‖ (Gesuch) *to send* (od *hand*) *in*; ⟨Am⟩ *to file* ‖ ein Gesuch ~ um etw *to apply for a th*; s–n Abschied ~ *to tender* (od *send in, give*) *one's resignation* | ⟨jur⟩ (Urkunde) *to put in* ‖ (Klage) *to lodge, prefer* (bei *to*; gegen *against*) | ⟨com⟩ (Rechnung) *to hand in*; → Angebot

·Einreichung f ~/~en *presentation* (*of a petition*) ‖ *sending in; tendering; handing in* ‖ *lodging* (*of a charge*)

·ein|reihen vt [h] **1.** (Papiere etc) *to file* **2.** ⟨übtr⟩ (Gesetz) *to subsume* (in *in*; unter *under*) ‖ (jdn) *to enrol* (unter *among*); *to range* (in *in*); *to enter a p's name* (*in*); (jdn) in e–e Klasse ~ *to class* (mit *with*); in e–e Kategorie ~ *to assign to a definite c.y*; unter die Besten ~ *to place among the first*; → rechnen | **sich** ~ *to fall into line*; ⟨mot, etc⟩ *to filter in* ‖ ⟨fig⟩ *to enrol o.s.* (in *in the struggle for* ..) ‖ sich ~ in etw *to join a th; to range o.s. on the side of a th*; sich unter die Besten ~ *to rank among the best*; → einfügen **3.** (Kleid) *to shir(r); to gather in small pleats*

·Einreiher m ~s/~ ⟨tail, com⟩ *single-breaster*

·einreihig a *single-breasted* (*coat*) ‖ ⟨tech⟩ ~e Nietung *single-riveted joint* **·Einreihung** f *filing* (*of papers*) | ⟨übtr⟩ *subsumption* (in *in*; unter *under*) ‖ *enrolment* (*of a p*)

·Einreise f *entry* (in *into*) ‖ ~bewilligung, ~erlaubnis [f] (entry) *permit* ‖ ~visum [n] (*entry*) *visa* **·einreisend** a nach F. ~e Ausländer *foreigners entering France*

·ein|reißen vt/i **A.** vt [h] **1.** e–n Rock (etc) ~ *to make* (od *tear*) *a hole* (od *rent, slit*) *in a coat* | sich [dat] den Nagel ~ *to split one's nail* **2.** (Häuser etc) *to pull* (od *knock, take*) *down; to demolish* **B.** vi [s] **1.** *to tear; rend, rupture; to be torn* (od *rent, split*) **2.** ⟨fig⟩ (of a nuisance) *to gain ground, to spread* ‖ –gerissene Schlamperei *widespread slovenliness*

·ein|reiten vi/t **1.** vi [s] *to ride in*; ~ in *to ride into* **2.** vt [h] (Pferd) *to break in*

·ein|renken vt [h] **1.** ⟨surg⟩ (Knochen) *to set; reduce* ‖ **sich wieder** ~ (of a bone) *to set* **2.** ⟨fig⟩ e–e S (wieder) ~ *to settle a matter; to straighten .. out, to bring* (od *put, set*) *a m. to rights*; es wird sich schon wieder ~ *it'll dry straight* **·Einrenkung** f ⟨surg⟩ *setting; reduction*

·ein|rennen vt [h] (etw) *to force open*; ⟨fig⟩ offene Türen ~ *to force an open door* ‖ etw mit dem Kopf ~ *to run one's head against a th* | ⟨fig⟩ **sich** [dat] den Kopf ~ *to crack one's skull*, ⟨fig⟩ *to come to grief, to land in disaster*

·ein|richten vt [h] ***A. 1.** ⟨surg⟩ = einrenken **2.** ⟨math⟩ (Bruch) *to reduce* **B. 1. a.** (Haus) *to furnish; equip; to fit* (od *get*) *up*; das Hotel ist nett –ge–tet *the hotel is well furnished* ‖ (herrichten) *to dress* ‖ ⟨tech⟩ *to install* (Leitung) **b.** er ist pompös –ge–tet *his house is luxuriously furnished* ‖ ⟨tech⟩ modern –ge–tet *equipped with modern machinery* **c.** ⟨theat⟩ *to fit* (⟨Am⟩ *set*) *up, to lower* (⟨Am⟩ *drop*) *in* **2.** (errichten) (Geschäft) *to set up; to start*; jdm ein G. ~ *to set a p up* (od *to settle a p*) *in business* ‖ (Institut) *to establish, found*; (Kloster) *to plant*; (System) *to constitute; institute; introduce*; er richtete Schulen in dem Lande ein *he brought schools to the country* ‖ → einführen 2. **3.** ⟨übtr⟩ (ordnen) (Bewegung) *to organize* ‖ ⟨a. mus⟩ (etw) *to arrange* (f *for the violin*) ‖ sein Verhalten ~ nach .. *to regulate one's conduct according to* .. ‖ s–e Politik ~ nach .. *to align one's policy with* (*another country*) | es ~ *to arrange*; es ~, daß .. *to arrange* od *contrive that*; wir w es so ~, daß wir dich treffen *we'll arrange* od *contrive to see you*; wir w es ~, daß er dort ist *we'll arrange for him to be there*; wir w es ~, dort z s *we'll arrange* (od *contrive*) *to be there* **C. sich** [acc] ~ **1.** *to obtain the necessary furniture* ‖ jdm helfen sich einzurichten *to settle a p in* **2. sich neu** ~ *to establish o.s. in a new style* ‖ sich häuslich ~ *to make o.s. comfortable* (od *at home*) **3.** (wirtschaften) *to economize, manage; to make both ends meet*; sich sparsam ~ *to cut and contrive* **4. sich ~ auf** *to make arrangements for; to lay o.s. out for; to prepare for* **5. sich** [dat] ~: ich kann's mir nicht ~, wie ich möchte *I can't make it as I would like it*

·Einrichtung f ~/~en **A.** (Einrichten) **1.** *furnishing* (*of a house*); *equipment*; ~ des Arbeitsraums ⟨tech⟩ *site preparation* ‖ *lay-out* (*of a workshop*) **2.** *establishment* (*of a route*); *foundation, institution*; *introduction*; → Einführung ‖ ~en [pl] betreiben *to operate facilities* **3.** *arrangement* (*of a library*); *regulation*; *organization, installation* (*of a plant*) **4.** ~ f Orchester *scoring* **B.** (Eingerichtetes) *adjustment*; *arrangement* ‖ *plan*; *scheme* ‖ e–e feste *or* stehende ~ *an establishment* od *institution*; *established custom*; e–e feste ~ w *to attain a permanent standing*; ⟨Am⟩ *to come to stay*; → Institut ‖ e–e bequeme *or* nützliche, notwendige ~ *a convenience*; öffentliche ~en [pl] *public utilities* pl; soziale ~en *social services* | ⟨tech⟩ *contrivance, device*, ⟨mach⟩ *feature*; e–e ~ z Steuern *a steering contrivance*; → Vorrichtung **C.** [konkr] **1.** *appurtenances* [pl], *furniture* (*of a room*); Möbel≗ *set of furniture* ‖ *furnishings* pl (*of a hotel*); (z Hause gehörige ~) *fixtures* pl ‖ ⟨tech⟩ *installation*; *fittings, fitments, fixings* pl, ⟨Am⟩ *accommodations, facilities* pl (*production f., recreational f.*); Betriebs≗ *plant* **2.** (of a machine) *mechanism*; *working parts* pl **3.** ⟨fig⟩ e–e alte ~ (P *or* S) *a fixture*; alte ~en [pl] *rookeries* pl **~sgegenstand** m, **~sstück** n *fixture*; *fitment*; ein ~ *a piece of furniture*

·**ein|riegeln** vt [h] ⟨übtr⟩ (jdn) = einschließen

·**Einritt** m ~(e)s/~e *entrance* od *entry* (*of a p*) *on horseback*

·**ein|ritzen** vt [h] = einschneiden ‖ ⟨med⟩ (Haut) *to scarify* ·**Einritzung** f *scarification*

Einr·öhrenapparat m ⟨wir⟩ *single-valve set*

·**ein|rollen** vt [h] (etw) *to roll up*; ~ in *to roll in* (*paper*)

·**ein|rosten** vi [h] *to rust, to grow rusty* ‖ ⟨fig⟩ *to rust*; → eingerostet

·**ein|rücken I.** vi/t **1.** vi [s] **a.** ⟨mil⟩ = einmarschieren ‖ (z Truppe) *to join the services* **b.** in jds Stelle ~ *to replace* od *succeed a p*; *to fill a p's post* **c.** (Anzeige) ~ l *to insert* (in *in*); *to put in* **2.** vt [h] **a.** (Maschine) *to throw into gear, to engage* **d.** ⟨typ⟩ (Zeile) *to indent* **II.** ≗ n, ·**Einrückung 1.** = Einmarsch **2.** *insertion*

·**ein|rühren** vt [h] **1.** etw ~ in *to mix a th in* (od *with*) **2.** ⟨fig⟩ jdm etw ~ = einbrocken 2. b

·**ein|rüsten** vi/t [h] *to erect a scaffold* | vt *to scaffold* (*a building*)

Eins f ~/·Einsen **1.** *the number one* ‖ e–e arabische (römische) ~ *an Arabic* (*a Roman*) one; e–e Reihe Einsen *a row of ones*; s–e E. sind undeutlich *his ones are not clear* **2.** (beim Würfelspiel) *ace* **3.** ⟨engl⟩ die Prüfung mit ~ bestehen *to get* (od *obtain, take*) *a First Class* ‖ → ein

·**Einsaat** f = Saat

·**ein|sacken** vt/i **1.** vt [h] ⟨fig⟩ (etw) *to bag, sack*; *pocket*; → einheimsen 2.; einstecken **2.** vi (of the ground) *to sag, sink, subside*; in den Knien ~ *to sag at the knees* ‖ (P) *to collapse*

·**ein|sagen** vt [h] (jdm zuflüstern) *to whisper* (*a word to a p*), *to prompt* (*a p*)

·**einsaitig** a ⟨mus⟩ *one-stringed* (*instrument*)

·**ein|salben** vt [h] (jdn) *to anoint, embalm*

·**ein|salzen 1.** vt [h] → einpökeln **2.** ≗ n *salting* ‖ ·**Einsalzer** m *salter*

·**einsam** a *lonely, lonesome, solitary* (*p*; *life*) ⟨Am a.⟩ *lone*; sich ~ fühlen *to feel lonely* od *lonesome*; ~ leben *to live in solitude*; → zurückgezogen ‖ (T) *solitary* ‖ (of places) *lonely, lonesome, secluded*; *out-of-the-way* (*spot*) ‖ *isolated*

·**einsamenlappig** a ⟨bot⟩ einkeimblättrig

·**Einsamkeit** f ~/ *loneliness, lonesomeness* (*of a p*); *solitariness, solitude, secrecy*; ⟨poet⟩ ~en [pl] *lonely places*; → Zurückgezogenheit

·**ein|sammeln** vt [h] (Früchte) *to gather, to gather in* ‖ (Beiträge, Fahrgeld) *to collect*

·**Einsammler** m ~s/~ *gatherer* ‖ *collector*

·**Einsammlung** f *gathering* ‖ *collection* (*of contributions*)

·**ein|sargen** vt [h] *to coffin* ‖ ⟨fig⟩ *to bury*

·**Einsatt(e)lung** f ⟨geol⟩ *saddle*

·**Einsatz** m ~es/≗e **I.** [abstr] **A.** → einsetzen I. B. **1.** *application, employment* (*of machines*; f *for*); *use* (*of one's powers*; *of police*); ‖ ⟨comp⟩ ~ in der Wirtschaft, Wissenschaft *industrial, scientific applications*; → Aufbietung, Aufgebot, Aufwand ‖ ⟨com⟩ *deposit* (*on bottles, etc*) → II.B. ‖ (*vigorous*) *activity*; *active help* **2.** ⟨mil⟩ *action, engagement*; *attack*; ⟨Am⟩ *induction* (in *into*); ⟨aero⟩ *mission*, (Fla≗) gegen Erd– u. Seeziele *surface mission*; mit konzentriertem ~ *with a concentrated effort*; (zum) ~ fliegen *to fly a sortie*, ⟨hum⟩ *to go to the movies* ‖ *commitment, employment, deployment* (*of troops*); (Truppen) z ~ bringen *to engage*; ⟨Am⟩ *to induct*; z ~ k *to be engaged* | ⟨a–n⟩ *mission*; auf ~, im ~ (6′ 15″) *into m.* **3.** *risk*; *venture*; *help assistance, risk venture*; *sacrifice*; *sacrificing* (*of means*); ~ des Lebens *risking one's life*; unter ~ des Lebens *at the risk of one's life* ‖ → Einsetzen; Einsetzung ‖ bis z ~ des L.s *up to the pledging of life itself*; selbstloser ~ *selfless efforts* **B.** (→ einsetzen II. 2.) ⟨mus⟩ *entry*; sicherer ~ *attack*; *entrance* (*of the strings*) ‖ (beim Rudern) *catch* **II.** [konkr] (Eingesetztes) **A. 1.** *inserted part* (od *piece*); *inset*; *insertion* ‖ (im Koffer) *tray*; → ~platte ‖ (Satz v ineinanderpassenden Gegenständen) *nest*; → Satz **2.** (Brust≗ im Kleid) *inset*; *plastron*; *insetbreast* (*of linen*); ~ im Oberhemd *shirt-front*; ⟨Am⟩ *bosom* ‖ dreieckiger *or* keilförmiger ~ *godet* [Fr], *gusset* **3.** Eck≗ (auf Bild) *inset* **4.** ⟨tech⟩ *charge* (*of a furnace*); *case* **B.** (Geld≗) **1.** *stake* (*they played for high stakes*); das Spiel ist nicht den ~ wert *the game is not worth the candle* ‖ ⟨racing⟩ *stakes* [pl] **2.** *pledge, pawn* **3.** ⟨com⟩ *capital paid up*; *share*

·**Einsatz-** ⟨oft⟩ *operational* (*car, team, aircraft, etc*) **~anweisungen** f pl ⟨aero etc⟩ *briefing* **≗bereit** a ⟨mil⟩ *ready for action* od *battle, ready to be used in battle*; ⟨aero⟩ *ready for sortie*; *on alert* ‖ ~ s (of a soldier) *to be open to commitment, to be willing to play one's part* ‖ (Gerät) *serviceable, ready for service, prepared* **~bereitschaft** f *sense of commitment*; *spirit of involvement* ‖ *combat readiness, r. to be used in battle*; *preparedness for battle*; *alertness* **~besprechung** f ⟨mil⟩ *briefing* **≗fähig** a *capable of being used* (f *for*); *roadworthy* (*vehicles*) **~fähigkeit** f ⟨mil⟩ *combat availability* **~flott(ill)e** f *task force* **~flug** m *sortie* | ~höhe [f] *operational height*; ~zeug [n] *op. aircraft* **≗härten** vt ⟨tech⟩ *to case-harden* **~härten** n ⟨tech⟩ *case-hardening* **≗mäßig** a ⟨mil⟩ *operational* (Übung) | Prüfung der **~möglichkeit(en)** f (pl) *feasibility studies* pl **~platte** f (am Tisch) *leaf* **~platz** m ⟨aero⟩ *combat airfield* **~preis** m (bei Auktionen) *upset* (od *reserve*)*-price*, (Spiel) *bet* **~streifen** m, **~stück** n *inserted piece*; *insertion*; farbiges ~ (am Kleid) *panel*; (Kleid) mit ~ versehen *to panel* ‖ ⟨tech⟩ *adapter* **~teich** m *fishpond* **≗unfähig** a ⟨mil⟩ *inoperative* **~zeichen** n ⟨mus⟩ *entry sign*; *the conductor's sign* **~zirkel** m *compasses* [pl]

°·**ein|sauen** vt [h] (etw) *to befoul, bemire, dirty*

·**ein|säuern** vt [h] **1.** (Brot) *to leaven* ‖ (Fleisch) *to pickle in vinegar* **2.** (Futterstoffe) *to ensil(ag)e*; → Süßpreßfutter ·**Einsäuerung** f *ensilage* (*of fodder*), *ensilation*

·**ein|saugen I.** vt [h] **1.** (P) **a.** (Milch; Luft) *to suck in* **b.** ⟨übtr⟩ (Duft) *to inhale*; in sich ~ *to absorb, imbibe* **2.** (of the ground, etc.) (Regen) *to soak* (od *suck*) *up*; *to absorb*; *imbibe* **II.** ≗ n **1.** *sucking in* **2.** *absorption* ·**Einsaugungsmittel** n *absorbent*

·ein|säumen vt [h] (Kleid) *to hem* || mit Borte (etc) ~ *to purl* || ⟨übtr⟩ (S) (Weg etc) *to line; to hem in; to border* (od *edge, trim*) (mit *with*); –ge–mt v (*a path*) *bordered* od *edged with; enclosed in*; → säumen

·ein|schachteln vt [h] **1.** ⟨tech⟩ *to interlock* **2.** ⟨fig⟩ ~ in *to dovetail into; to incorporate in*; → eingliedern, –schalten

·ein|schäkeln vt [h] (Kabel) *to shackle in*

·einschalig a ⟨zoo⟩ *univalve*; ~es Tier *univalve*

·Einschalt- ~bild n ⟨print⟩ *inset* **~blatt** n *insertion leaf* **~brett** n ⟨sl⟩ *starting panel* **~-dauer** f *duration of connection* (od *operation, of voltage application* **~hebel** m *starting lever* **~knopf** m *closing push-button* **~(relais)stellung** f *on-position* **~strom** m *making current* **~verzug** m ⟨el⟩ *make time* **~vorrichtung** f ⟨el⟩ *switch gear* **~zeichen** n ⟨print⟩ *insertion mark*

·ein|schalten vt [h] **1.** (Wort) *to insert, to interpolate* (in *into*); *to intercalate; to put* (od *slip*) *in* || (Tag) *to intercalate*; → einlegen **2.** ⟨el & wir⟩ (Licht etc) *to switch* (od *turn*) *on*; ⟨theat⟩ *to plug in* || ⟨tech⟩ *to engage*; ⟨mot⟩ die Kuppelung ~ *to slip in the clutch*; den ersten Gang ~ *to go into low* (od *bottom*) *gear, to have the lowest gear in*; den dritten G. ~ *to go on top-gear* **3.** ⟨übtr⟩ (jdn) ~ in *to bring into, to incorporate in* || (Fabrik, Industrie in ein Programm, e–n Erzeugungsgang) ~ *to gear* (*to*) || ⟨fig⟩ **sich ~ in** *to get* (od *slip, strike*) *into* (*the conversation*); *to join* (*a movement*); → einreihen || (sich ins Mittel legen) *to interfere, interpose, intervene*; → Mittel

·Einschaltung f ~/~en **1.** *insertion; interpolation* (in *in the text*); *intercalation* **2.** *switching on* (*of the light*) **~szeichen** n ⟨typ⟩ (V) *caret*

·ein|schärfen vt [h] ⟨fig⟩ jdm etw ~ *to enjoin* (od *impress, inculcate, urge*) *a th upon a p*; jdm ~ z tun *to enjoin* od *urge a p to do*; jdm dringend ~ *to give a p strict injunctions* (*not to do*) || → einprägen **·Einschärfung** f ~/~en *inculcation, injunction*

·ein|scharren vt [h] **1.** (Tote) *to bury* **2. sich ~** (T) *to burrow* (in *into*)

·ein|schätzen vt [h] **1.** (jdn zur Steuer) *to assess; to rate*, hoch –ge–tzt s *to be highly rated* **2.** ⟨übtr⟩ **(etw)** *to value* (nach *by*); etw hoch ~ *to value a th highly, to set a high value on a th*; (jds Einfluß) sehr hoch ~ *to rate very high*; etw niedrig ~ *to set little store by a th, to price* (*a th*) *low*; z niedrig ~ *to underrate*; z hoch ~ *to overrate* || **jdn** ~ *to take a p's measure, to take the full m. of a p*; jdn hoch ~ *to have a high* (niedrig *poor*) *opinion of a p, to rate a p high*; jdn richtig ~ *to take a true m. of a p; to form a true estimate of a p*; ⟨fam⟩ *to jump* (od *size*) *a p up* || → schätzen **·Einschätzung** f ~/ ~en **1.** *assessment* (*of a p's*) *income* **2.** *estimation, valuation*

·Einscheiben- ~antrieb m *single-pulley drive* **~bremse** f ⟨mot⟩ *single-disk brake* **~drucklager** n *s.-d. thrust bearing* **~kupplung** f *s.-d. clutch*

·ein|schenken vt/i [h] **1.** vt (ein Glas Wein etc) *to pour out*; schenk ihm noch ein Glas ein *pour him* (*out*) *another glass*; er schenkte sich e–n Whisky, e–n Trunk ein *he poured himself a whisky, a drink* (aus *from the bottle*); er schenkte sich tüchtig ein *he helped himself liberally* | ⟨fig⟩ jdm reinen Wein ~ *to tell a p the naked* (od *plain*) *truth, to come out in the open* **2.** vi jdm ~ *to fill a p's glass* || sich [dat] ~ *to fill one's glass*

·ein|scheren vt [h] ⟨mar⟩ (Tau) *to reeve*

·einschichtig a *having but one layer* || → vereinzelt, einsam, eigenbrötlerisch || (ledig) *single, unmarried* | adv ~ leben *to live alone*

·ein|schicken vt [h] (etw) *to send in* (jdm *or* an jdn *to a p*) || (Geld) *to remit* (*to a p*)

·einschiebbar a *extensible* (*tripod*); ~e Bodentreppe *folding ladder staircase*

Einschiebe- ~brett n *extra* od *extension leaf* (*of a table*) **~schablone** f *dovetail templet*

·ein|schieben I. vt [h] **1.** (etw) ~ in *to shove* (od *push*) *into; to put in* (⟨a⟩ Stück Arbeit als Teil e–s Ganzen) || (einschalten) *to insert, intercalate, interpolate* (in *in*); (zw 2 Dinge) *to sandwich; to thrust in* (zw *between*) || (Stück Papier) *to slip in* (unter *among*); *to feed* (*paper*) *into the typewriter* || –geschoben *interpolated clause* | **jdn ~ als**: *they ran me in for bridesmaid* **2. sich ~ in** *to thrust o.s. into; to slip into* **II.** ≈ n = Einschiebung

·Einschiebsel n ~s/~ *insertion, interpolation inserted piece* **·Einschiebung** f ~/~en *insertion, intercalation, interpolation* (*of a word*)

·Einschienenbahn f *monorail* (*railway*)

·Einschieß- ⟨artill⟩ **~(bezugs)punkt** m *registration point* **~punkt** m *ranging point* **~ziel** n *registration* od *adjustment* (⟨oft⟩ *check*) *target*

·ein|schießen I. vt/i **A.** vt [h] **1. 1. a.** (Brot) ~ in *to shove into, to put in* (*the oven*) || ⟨typ⟩ (Form) *to impose* || ⟨weav⟩ *to shoot* **b.** ⟨fig⟩ (Geld) *to invest; to pay in*; Geld ~ in *to put money into* (*a business*), *to invest m. in* (*an undertaking*) **2.** ein Gewehr ~ *to try* (od *test*) *a gun by shooting at a mark*; ⟨artill⟩ *to adjust*; ⟨a.⟩ sich ~ *to register the firing elements* || **sich ~** *to practise shooting; to find the range; to register*; sich ~ auf ein Ziel *to practise shooting at a mark*; sich –geschossen h auf etw *to have found the range of a th* **B.** vi [s] ⟨med⟩ (of the milk) *to shoot in*; ~ in *to shoot into* (*the breast*) **II.** ≈ n ⟨mil⟩ *independent fire to find the range*; (Eingabeln) *bracketing; range adjustment*

·ein|schiffen vt/i **1.** vt [h] (Truppen, Waren) *to embark; to ship* || **sich ~** *to go on board ship, to embark* (auf *in a steamer*) **2.** vi [s] = einlaufen I. A. 1. **·einschiffig** (→ eins) (*church*) *consisting of one nave only* **·Einschiffung** f ~/~en *embarkation, shipping* (*of troops*); *Emb.* (*for Cythera*) || *shipment, shipping* (*of goods*) **~shafen** m *port of emb.* **~soffizier** m *emb.-officer* **~sraum** m *emb. area*

·ein|schirren vt [h] *to harness*

·ein|schlachten vt [h] (T) *to kill for household use*; ein Schwein ~ *to kill one's own pig*

·ein|schlafen I. vi [s] **1.** (P) *to fall* (od *drop*) *asleep, to go to sleep*; ⟨fam⟩ *to go* (od *drop*) *off*; endlich ~ *to get to sleep*; u im Augenblick war er –ge– *and instantly he was asleep* || *to die*; sanft ~ *to pass peacefully away*; ~ u nicht wieder erwachen *to die in one's sleep* **2.** (of limbs) *to get* (od *go*) *to sleep*; mein rechtes Bein war (*or* das r. Bein war mir) –ge– *my right leg had gone to sleep* **3.** ⟨fig⟩ (of a custom) *to die out* || (of correspondence, etc.) *to drop; to be discontinued*; → nachlassen | (Brauch) ~ l *to discontinue; drop* || (Gefühl) ~ l *to desiccate* || die S schlief damit ein *there the matter rested* **II.** ≈ n *falling* (od *going*) *to sleep* || ⟨med⟩ ~ der Glieder *paraesthesia, paraesthesis*

·ein|schläfern vt [h] **1.** *to make* (*a p*) *fall asleep*; (*of reading*) *to send .. to sleep*; (Kind) *to lull to sleep*; (durch ein Wiegenlied ~) *to lullaby* || ⟨med⟩ (jdn) *to chloroform, narcotize* **2.** ⟨fig⟩ (etw) *to lull*; (Gewissen) *to silence* || (jdn) ~ in *to lull* (*a p*) *into* (*a sense of security*) **·einschläfernd** a ⟨med⟩ *narcotic, somniferous, soporific* (*drug*); *somnolent* (*effect*)

·Einschläferung f ~/~en *lulling to sleep* || ⟨med⟩ *narcotization, soporification* **~smittel** n *narcotic; opiate*; → Schlafmittel **·Einschlafmittel** n *short-acting soporific*

·einschläfrig a *single* (*bed*)

·Einschlag m ~(e)s/≈e **A.** (Einschlagen) **1.** *impact* (*of a shot; shell*) || *striking* (*of lightning*); der ~ in ein Haus *the striking of a house* **2.** = Handschlag **3.** ⟨fig⟩ *dash* (*a strong d. of Roman-*

esque); *infusion, infused element, admixture* (in *in*); *suggestion* (*with a s. of the bizarre*); *touch*; mit starkem ∼ westlichen Dialekts (*a voice*) *with a West-country tang*; mit stark o. ∼ *showing marked oriental characteristics*; Bücher mit religiösem ∼ *books with a religious twist*; → Beimischung **B.** [konkr] **1.** *cover, wrapper* ‖ *enclosure* **2.** ⟨weav⟩ (Querfäden) *weft, woof*; → Kette **3.** (∼ am Kleid) *fold, tuck*; *pleat*; e–n ∼ m *to turn up the hem* **C.** (∼stelle → d.) *place* (od *point*) *of impact* ‖ *hit* (auf *on*)

·Einschlag- ∼lupe f ⟨opt⟩ *folding magnifier* **∼messer** n *clasp-knife*; gr ∼ *jack-knife* **∼papier** n *packing* (od *wrapping*)*-paper*; *wrappage* **∼seide** f ⟨com⟩ *tram*; *tram* (od *shot*) *silk* **∼stelle** f ⟨artill, etc.⟩ *place of impact, point of burst* **∼(s)winkel** m *angle of impact*; ⟨mot⟩ (Räder∼) *angle of lock*

·ein|schlagen vt/i **I.** vt [h] **A. 1.** ⟨eig⟩ **a.** (Nagel) *to drive* (od *knock*) *in*; ∼ in .. *to drive into*; fest ∼ *to drive* (*a nail*) *home* ‖ (Pfahl) ∼ in *to sink into, to plant in* (*the ground*) **b.** ein Loch ∼ in *to make* (od *strike*) *a hole in*; .. in ein Faß *to stave a cask in*; → schlagen **c.** (Tür etc) *to batter* (od *break, smash*) *in*; (Fenster) *to smash, break* **d.** jdm den Schädel ∼ *to break a p's head* (mit *with*); *to smash a p's head in*; *to dash a p's brains out*; (Zähne) *to kick .. in* **e.** Eier ∼ *to crack eggs* ‖ (Holz) ⟨for⟩ *to cut, fell* **2.** ⟨fig⟩ e–n Weg ∼ **a.** *to enter upon a road*; *to strike* (*into*) *a path* (über *across*); *to take a* (od *one's*) *course* od *route* (nach *to*); den Weg nach rechts, in die Felder ∼ *to strike to the right, into the fields* ‖ e–e Richtung ∼ *to set o.s. on a course* ⟨a. fig⟩; die R. ∼ nach .. *to take the direction of* (*the palace*) ‖ *to follow* od *choose* (*the path of virtue*) ein schnelles Tempo ∼ *to strike out, to speed* (*up*), *to quicken one's pace* **b.** ⟨übtr⟩ *to adopt* (od *pursue*) *a course*; e–n eigenen W. ∼ *to strike out a line of one's own*; → Beschwerdegang ‖ e–n Beruf, e–e Laufbahn ∼ *to embrace a profession, a career* **B. 1.** (einhüllen) *to envelop*; *to enwrap, to wrap up* (in *in*); *to lap* (*in*); (Brief) *to put in an envelope* **2.** ⟨hort⟩ (Baum) *to earth* **3.** (Korn etc) *to sack* ‖ *to store* (*up*) ‖ (Pflanze in Erde) *to heel in* [adv]; *to bed .. in earth* **C.** ⟨tech⟩ (Falte, Saum) *to tuck*; (Kleid) *to take in* **II.** vi [h & s] **1.** [h & s] (of lightning, etc.) *to strike*; in ein Haus ∼ *to strike a house* ‖ (of shell) ∼ in *to hit* (*a place*); → Bombe 1. b. **2.** [h] (in die Hand ∼) es ist abgemacht, schlag ein *it's a bargain, reach out and take my hand* **3.** [h] ∼ **auf** jdn *to strike out at a p*; *to hail blows down on a p* **4.** ⟨fig⟩ **a.** (S) *to turn out well*; *to sell well, to go down* (*well*), ⟨theat⟩ *to take*; *to be successful* od *effective*; nicht ∼ *to fail* ‖ ∼d *never--failing* (*joke*) **b.** (P) *to be successful*; *to be a success*; nicht ∼ *to be a failure* ‖ → Fach **·Einschlagen** n **1.** *driving in* (*of a nail*) ‖ *battering in*; *smashing in* (*of a door*) **2.** *adoption* od *pursuance* (*of a course*); *embracing* (*of a profession*) **3.** *enveloping*; *wrapping up* **4.** → Einschlag A.

·einschlägig a *apposite, pertinent* (*remarks*) (f *to*) *relevant*; ∼es Beispiel *case in point*; die ∼e Literatur (e–s Gegenstandes) *the bibliography*; *the lit. on the subject*; die ∼en Paragraphen *the sections bearing on the matter*

·ein|schleichen vi & refl **1.** vi [s] ∼ in *to creep* (od *steal, slip*) *into* (*a room*) **2. sich** ∼ [h] *to creep* (od *slip, steal*) *in*; (Dieb) *to go upon the sneak*; sich ∼ in *to creep* (od *steal*) *into*; sich heimlich ∼ in *to insinuate o.s. into*; *to twine one's way into* (*a p's confidence*); *to worm one's way into* (*a p's favo[u]r*) | (of errors) *to creep in*; sich ∼ in *to creep into* (*the text*) ‖ (of thoughts) *to insinuate o.s. into*; (of feelings) sich unbemerkt ∼ bei jdm *to steal over a p* ‖ ∼der Reiz *creeping stimulus*

·ein|schleifen vt [h] *to cut, grind in*; *to reseat* (*a valve*) ‖ –geschliffen *ground* (*glass stopper*)

·ein|schleppen vt [h] **1.** (Schiff) *to tow, to tow in*(*to port*); *to take* (*a ship*) *in tow*; ∼ in *to tow into* (*the harbour*); → schleppen **2.** (Waren) *to smuggle in* ‖ (Krankheiten) *to bring in, to import* **·Einschleppung** f ∼/ *bringing in, importation, introduction* (*of a disease*)

·ein|schleusen vt [h] *to pass* (*a ship*) *into a lock*; *to lock in* ‖ ⟨fig⟩ –ge–st *infiltrating* (*agent*)

·Einschleusung f ⟨tech, el⟩ *charging* **∼spreis** m (z Schutz der eigenen Wirtschaft) *inhibitive* od *curbing price*

·ein|schliefen vi [s] (*of fox, etc*) *to kennel*; *to go to earth*

·einschließen vt [h] **A.** ⟨eig⟩ **1.** (jdn) **a.** *to lock* (od *shut*) *in*; *to hem in*; ∼ in *to lock* od *shut in* (od *into*); *to imprison* **b. sich** ∼ *to lock* (od *shut*) *o.s. in*; sich ∼ *to lock o.s. up* od *closet o.s. in* (*a room*) **2.** (Hund) *to immure* (in *in a room*) ‖ (Papiere) *to lock up* (in *in*); *to enclsoe* (in *in a drawer*) ‖ (etw) in ein Gehäuse ∼ *to encase* **3.** ⟨mil⟩ (Stadt) *to beset, blockade, invest* ‖ (Feind) *to close in upon*; *to round up*; *to surround*; → einnehmen **B.** ⟨übtr⟩ **1.** (Garten) *to surround* (in *in*; mit *with*) (Wort) in Klammern ∼ *to bracket* ‖ (S) *to enclose* (*a wall encloses the park*); *to close* (od *hem*) *in*; *to edge* (*hills e. the plain*); jdn ∼ *to close about a p* (*mists closed about him*) ‖ –geschlossen s *to be surrounded* (*with*); *to be enclosed* (v *by*); → eingeschlossen **2. a.** jdn ∼ in *to include a p in* (*one's prayers*) **b.** (etw) *to include* (in *in*) ‖ (S) *to take in, to comprise*; alle Fälle ∼ *to cover all cases* ‖ *to be inclusive of a th*; Frühstück –geschlossen *breakfast thrown in*; → einbegreifen, –begriffen

·einschließend a; alles ∼ *all-in* (*cost*); ⟨Am⟩ *blanket*; alle ∼ ⟨Am⟩ *blanket* (*law*) **·einschließlich** **1.** [adv] vom 1. bis z 31. April ∼ *from April 1st to 31st inclusive*(*ly*); Preise ∼ Licht u Bedienung *inclusive terms* **2.** [prep] ∼ der Gäste *including the guests, inclusive of the g.* **·Einschließung** f ∼/∼en **1.** *locking* (od *shutting*) *in* (*of a p*); → Haft ‖ *locking up, enclosure* (*of a th*) **2.** ⟨mil⟩ *blockade, investment* (*of a town*) ‖ *closing in upon* (*the enemy*), *surrounding* (*of an army*) **3.** *enclosure* (*of a park*) **4.** → Einschluß

·ein|schlucken vt [h] *to swallow down*

·ein|schlummern vi [s] *to doze off*; = einschlafen; = entschlafen (sterben) *to take one's last sleep*

·ein|schlürfen vt [h] *to sip*; (gierig) *to gulp down, to lap up* | ⟨übtr⟩ (Duft) durch die Nase ∼ *to sniff* ‖ *to drink in*

·Einschluß m –schlusses/–schlüsse **1.** [abstr] (→ einschließen B. 2.) *inclusion* (*of a p, a th*; in *in*); mit ∼ jds, e–r S *with the inclusion of, inclusive of a p, a th*; *including a p, a th*; unter ∼ der Fragen, die .. *with the inclusion of the questions which ..* ‖ → Einschließung **2.** [konkr] (Eingeschlossenes) **a.** *word*(*s*) *in brackets* **b.** = Einlage **c.** ⟨minr, geol, glass⟩ *inclusion*

·ein|schmeicheln vrefl [h] sich bei jdm ∼ *to ingratiate o.s. with a p, to creep* (od *insinuate o.s. into a p's favour, to curry favour with a p*; ⟨Am⟩ *to play up to a p*, ⟨fam⟩ *to polish apples* (*for a p*); → einschleichen **·einschmeichelnd** a *caressing* (*look*), *endearing* (*words*); *ingratiating* (*ways*), *silky* (*voice*), *suave* (*manners*); ⟨fam⟩ *smarmy* **·Einschmeich(e)lung** f *ingratiating ways* [pl]; *insinuation*

°**·ein|schmeißen** vt [h] = einwerfen

·ein|schmelzen vi/t **1.** vi [s] *to melt* **2.** vt [h] (Münzen etc) *to melt down*; ⟨Am⟩ *to melt up* ‖ –geschmolzen ⟨el⟩ *seal-in* (*contact*) ‖ in Glas ∼ *to seal in, to fuse in*(*to*) od *with glass*

·ein|schmieren **I.** vt [h] **1.** (etw) *to smear* (mit *with*); ⟨tech⟩ *to lubricate* ‖ (Haar) ⟨fam⟩ *to smalm, to smarm* ‖ mit Talg ∼ *to tallow*; → einfetten, –ölen **2.** °= einschmutzen, be–, verschmieren **II.** ≃ n ⟨tech⟩ *lubrication*

·ein|schmuggeln vt [h] **1.** (Waren) *to smuggle in*; (etw, jdn) ∼ in *to smuggle into* (*a country*) || → Konterbande **2. sich** ∼ *to infiltrate*; **in** *to get illegal admittance to* (*a place*) || ⟨übtr⟩ *to insinuate* (od *worm*) *o.s. into, to worm one's way into* (*society*)

·ein|schmutzen vt [h] (Buch) *to soil, dirty*

·ein|schnallen vt [h] etw ∼ *to fasten* (od *secure*) *a th with a strap, to strap a th*

·ein|schnappen vi [s] **1.** (of a lock) *to catch, click* **2.** °⟨fig⟩ (P) *to get angry, to feel vexed* (über *at*); *to cut up rough*; *to lose one's hair* (od *wool*) || ⟨fam⟩ *to take on*, eingeschnappt *shirty*

·ein|schneiden I. vt/i [h] **A.** vt **1.** (Brot) *to cut up* (in *into the soup*); (Sauerkraut, Bohnen) *to shred* **2.** (Muster, Namen) *to cut in*; *to carve, engrave, incise* (auf *on*) || (Fläche) *to incise*; *score* || (tief) –geschnitten (*deeply*) *incised* (*cross*; *rock*); –geschnittenes Bild *engraving* || → einkerben, –prägen **B.** vi **1.** ∼ in etw *to cut a th, to cut into a th*; *to make a cut* od *incision in*(*to*) *a th* **2.** (of a whip, etc) *to cut*; ∼ in *to cut* od *dig into* (*the flesh*) || (of tools) *to bite* (in *in, into*) **3.** ⟨fig⟩ **a.** (of words, etc.) ∼ in *to imprint o.s. in, to sink into* (*a p's mind*); *to penetrate* (*the mind*); tief in jds Seele ∼ *to cut a p to the heart* **b.** (of reforms) tief ∼ *to be trenchant* (od *effective*) **II.** ≃ n *cut* (in *in, into*); *carving, engraving, incision* (auf *on*) **·einschneidend** a ⟨fig⟩ = durchgreifend; *incisive, stringent* (*measures*)

·einschneidig a (→ eins) *single-edged*

·ein|schneien vi/t **1.** vi [s] (S, P) *to be enveloped in snow*; *to be snowed up* (⟨Am⟩ *in*) | ⟨fam⟩ (P) *to drop in* (in *into*) **2.** vt [h] (jdn) *to snow up* (⟨Am⟩ *in*); mst [pass] –geschneit *snow-bound*, .. s *to be snowed up* (⟨Am⟩ *in*)

·Einschnitt m ∼(e)s/∼e **1.** = Einschneiden **2. a.** (Schnitt) *cut, incision* (in *in*); *indentation*; *recess*; → Kerbe || ⟨med⟩ ∼ in die Haut *scarification*; e–n ∼ m in *to scarify* (*the skin*) **b.** *cleft, cut, rent* (*in a hill*); *opening* || ⟨rail⟩ *cutting* **c.** ⟨pros⟩ (Vers≃) *caesura* [L] **d.** ⟨fig⟩ *cleavage, incision, scission* (in *in*; zw *between*) || *turning-point*; *critical point, decisive moment* (*in a p's life*)

·einschnittig a ⟨tech⟩ ∼e Nietung *single-shear riveted joint*

·ein|schnitzen vt [h] (etw) *to carve* (in *into*)

·ein|schnüren vt [h] **1.** (Paket) *to tie* (*up*) **2.** (of collars) (den Hals) *to strangle* | ⟨fig⟩ (jds Tätigkeit) *to hamper* (durch *by restrictions*); *to strangle, to throttle*; *to trammel* **3. sich** ∼ (of cytoplasma, etc) *to lace o.s.*; *to constrict* || –ge–rt (P) *straight-laced* **·Einschnürung** f *strangling* || ⟨med⟩ *strangulation* || ⟨fig⟩ *hampering*; *check* (e–r S *to a th*) || ⟨tech⟩ *constriction*

·ein|schränken vt [h] **1. a.** (jds Tätigkeit, Freiheit) *to restrict*; *to keep in check*; *to hamper*; → einschnüren, beschneiden || (s–e Wünsche) *to restrain* | (Produktion, Umfang e–r S) *to reduce*; (Bestände) *to run down*; (Ausgaben) *to cut down, to reduce, to retrench* || ⟨com⟩ (Markt, Währung) *to peg*; → beschränken **b. sich** ∼ *to reduce one's standard* od *style of living*; *to economize* (in bezug auf *on*); *to retrench* || *to tighten one's belt* || *to stint o.s.* (in *in*; mit *of*); sich aufs Nötigste ∼ *to restrict* od *confine o.s. to what is most essential* **2.** (Bedingungen, Urteil) *to modify, qualify* || → eingeschränkt

·einschränkend 1. a *limitative*; *restrictive* (*measures*); ∼e Klausel *limitation* || *modificatory, qualificatory* **2.** adv *reservedly*

·Einschränkung f ∼/∼en **1.** *inroad, restriction* (der Freiheit jds *on a p's liberty*); *check* (e–r S *to a th*) || *limitation* || *reduction* (*of expenses*) || ∼ des freien Wettbewerbs *restraint of trade* || ∼ des Alkoholverkaufs ⟨Am⟩ *lid*; (der Währung) ∼en auferlegen *to peg*; (Währung) v ∼en befreien *to unpeg* | wirtschaftl. ∼ *economizing, retrenchment*; (nach *or* bei Notstand) äußerste ∼ der Lebenshaltung *austerity* || sich ∼en auferlegen *to economize, retrench* **2.** *modification*; *qualification*; *reserve* || mit ∼en *with* (*certain*) *qualifications*; ohne jede ∼ *without any qualification*; *without reserve* od *stint*; *unreservedly* || mit ∼ in bezug auf *allowing for* (*age*) **∼serleichterung** f *easing of restrictions* **∼smaßnahme** f *restrictive* od *economy measure*; ∼n [pl] ⟨fam⟩ *squeeze*

·Einschraub- ∼automat m ⟨el⟩ *screw-in type circuit breaker* **∼filter** m ⟨phot⟩ *s.-i. f.* **∼gewinde** n (*s.-in*) *thread* **∼maschine** f *screw driver* **∼objektiv** n ⟨phot⟩ *s.-on lens* **∼stutzen** m *threaded socket* od *bushing* **∼zapfen** m *screwed male*

·ein|schrauben vt [h] (etw) *to screw in* || eine Schraube ∼ in *to drive a screw into* (*the door*)

·ein|schrecken vt [h] = einschüchtern

·Einschreibe- ∼brief m *registered letter* **∼gebühr** f *registration* (od *booking*; ⟨Am⟩ *registry*) *-fee* **∼sendung** f *registered letter* (od *packet*, etc)

·ein|schreiben I. vt [h] **1.** ⟨com⟩ (etw) *to enter* (in *in, into*; f jdn *to a p*) || (amtlich ∼) (Brief) *to register*; → Gepäck || Brief ∼ l *to register a letter*; ∼! *to be registered*; –ge–rieben (*by*) *registered* (*post* od *mail*) **2. a.** jds Namen ∼ *to enter* (od *inscribe*) *a p's name* (in *in*); (als Mitglied in e–e Körperschaft) *to enrol* (in *in a club*); ⟨mil⟩ in die Musterrolle ∼ *to enlist, enrol*; → eingeschrieben; matrikulieren **b. sich** ∼ *to enter* (od *inscribe*) *one's name* (in *in*); (im Hotel) ⟨Am⟩ *to register*; sich als Mitglied ∼ *to enrol one's name* (in *in*); sich in die Musterrolle ∼ *to enlist*; ⟨univ⟩ sich ∼ *to matriculate* **3.** e–e Feder ∼ *to make a pen suitable for one's hand* **II.** ≃ n *entering, entry* (*of a th*; in *in*) || (amtliches) *registration* (*of a letter*); → Einschreibung **·Einschreibung** f ∼/∼en *entry* (*of a p's name*); *enrolment*; ⟨mil⟩ ∼ in die Musterrolle *enlistment* || ⟨univ⟩ *matriculation* || → Einschreiben

·ein|schreiten I. vi vi [s] ⟨übtr⟩ **1.** (of police) *to step in* (um z tun *to do*); mit Waffengewalt ∼ *to employ force* (*to do*) || energisch ∼ gegen *to take drastic measures against* ..; sofort .. *to take immediate corrective action*; hier sollte –geschritten w *something ought to be done about this* || ⟨pol⟩ *to interfere, intervene* (in *in*) || → eingreifen **2.** ⟨jur⟩ gerichtlich ∼ *to prosecute*; ∼ gegen jdn *to take action* od *to proceed against a p*; → verfolgen **II.** ≃ n *stepping in* || ⟨pol⟩ *interference, intervention* (in *in*) || ⟨jur⟩ *proceedings* [pl] (gegen *against*); *the taking of legal proceedings*

·ein|schrumpfen 1. vi [s] *to shrink* (z *into*); *to shrivel* (*up*); *to contract* || –ge–ft *wizened* (*p*) **2.** ≃ n *shrinkage*; *contraction*

·Einschub m ∼(e)s/≃e **1.** = Einschiebung **2.** [konkr] *inserted piece* (od *part*); *insertion, intercalation*; *interpolation* (*in a text*)

·ein|schüchtern vt [h] (jdn) *to daunt, intimidate, cow, outface, overawe*, ⟨bes Am⟩ *bulldoze*; *to put* (*a p*) *out of countenance* || –ge–rt s *to be abashed* od *confounded*; nicht –ge–rt durch *undaunted by* | durch Bluff ∼ *to bluff*; | (durch Drohung etc ∼) *to browbeat*; (durch Gewalttätigkeit), *to bully, to hector*; ⟨Am sl⟩ *to bullyrag* || [abs] *to use scare tactics*

·Einschüchterung f ∼/∼en *intimidation* || (durch Drohung etc) *browbeating*; *bullying*; ⟨pol⟩ *bluffing*; sich durch ∼en treiben l z *to be browbeaten into* (*an admission*) **∼smanöver** n ⟨pol⟩ *bluff* **∼sversuch** m *attempt at intimidation* || *bluff*; ⟨Am a.⟩ *strike*

·ein|schulen vt [h] (jdn) *to school*; *to put* od *send* (*a p*) *to school* || (Pferde) *to school, train* ||

⟨fig⟩ → drillen **·Einschulung** f *putting* (od *sending*) *to school* ‖ *training* ‖ *schooling* (*of a horse*)

×**·einschürig** a (of sheep) *only once shorn* ‖ (of a meadow) *mown only once a year*

·Einschuß m –schusses/–schüsse **1.** *entrance* od *entry* (*of a bullet*); *point of impact* **2.** ⟨weav⟩ = Einschlag **3.** ⟨com⟩ *capital* (od *money*) *invested, investment* (in *in*); *share* **4.** ⟨vet⟩ (am Fuß des Pferdes) *phlegmon* **~(wunde** f) *wound of entry*

·ein|schütten vt [h] *to pour in*; ~ in *to pour* (od *shoot*) *into* (*a th*) ‖ Koks ~ ⟨tech⟩ *to feed, charge* (*blast furnace*) *with coke*; → eingießen **·Einschütttrichter** m *hopper*

·ein|schwärzen vt [h] *to blacken, ink* ‖ † = einschmuggeln

°**·ein|schwatzen** vt [h] jdm etw ~ = einreden

·ein|schwenken vi/t **1.** vi [s] ⟨mil⟩ *to swing into line* ‖ ~ in *to swing* (od *move, turn*) *into* ‖ hinter jdm ~ *to fall in behind a p* **2.** vt (Pferd) *to make* (*a horse*) *move* (in *into*)

·ein|segnen vt [h] (Kind) *to confirm* ‖ ⟨engl⟩ (Bischof, König) *to consecrate* | ⟨ec⟩ (etw) *to consecrate, bless* ‖ (e–e Kirche etc) *to consecrate*

·Einsegnung f ~/~en *confirmation, churching* (*of a child*); *consecration* (*of a bishop, king*; *of a church*); ⟨liter⟩ *sacring*; → Segen

·einsehbar a *open to* (*available for*) *examination* od *inspection*

·ein|sehen vi/t [h] **A.** vi **1.** ⟨eig⟩ laß mich mal ~ *let me look into it, let me have a look into* (od *at*) *it* ‖ ~ in *to look into, to have a look into* (*a room*) | ⟨übtr school⟩ bei jdm ~ (sc im Buche) *to look on* (od *over*) *with a p* **2.** (vorsprechen) *to look* (od *drop*) *in* **B.** vt **1.** ⟨eig⟩ etw (Akten etc) ~ *to look into* (od *over*) *a th, to consult* (*books, etc*); *to look through* (*papers*); *to have a look at* (od *into*) *a th*; *to examine* od *inspect a th* **2.** (erkennen) *to apprehend, grasp, understand*; *realize*, ⟨Am a.⟩ *recognize*; (die Bedeutung e–r S) *to appreciate*; (Lage, Möglichkeit) *to realize*; *to see* ‖ sein Unrecht ~ *to stand corrected*; er sah s–n Irrtum ein *he owned* (od *saw*) *that he was wrong* ‖ ~, daß .. *to appreciate* (od *decide, realize, see*) *that* ..; er sah nicht ein, warum er abreisen sollte *he saw no reason for departing* (*I see no r.* (*at all* od *on earth*) *why I should do that*); es war schwer –zu– *it was hard to see* (*why* ..) **3.** ⟨mil⟩ (Truppe) schützen –ge– z w *to shield .. from enemy observation*, –ge– s *or* w ⟨mil⟩ *to be under observation*

·Einsehen n **1.** (= Einsicht) ~ h *to be reasonable* od *sensible, to hear reason, to listen to reason*; kein ~ h *to refuse to listen to r.*; → Einsicht, Verständnis **2.** ein ~ h *to strain a point*; *to be propitious*; der Wettergott hatte ein ~ *the clerk of the weather was p.*; ich will noch mal ein ~ h *I'll let it pass* (od *put up with it*) *this once, I'll bear with you once more*

·Einseifbecken n *bowl of lather*; *lather-bowl*

·ein|seifen vt [h] **1.** ⟨eig⟩ (Wäsche) *to soap*; *to treat with soap*; jds Kopf ~ *to soap a p's head*; (Kind) *to lather, to soap* ‖ (Bart) *to lather* ‖ sich ~ *to soap* **2.** °⟨fig⟩ jdn tüchtig °~ *to soap a p down*; *to cajole* (od *coax, hoax, dupe, humbug, stuff*) *a p*; *to get round a p*

·Einseilgreifer m *monocable grab bucket*

·einseitig I. a **1.** ⟨bot, zoo & path⟩ (nur [od bes] auf e–r Seite entwickelt) *unilateral*; *one-sided*; *unilateral* (*sciatica*, ⟨mot⟩ *parking*); ⟨wir⟩ *unidirectional* (*communication*); (*pressure*) *applied from* od *on one side* **2.** (nur e–e Seite betreffend, bindend) *unilateral* (*acceptance, contract*); ⟨com jur⟩ *independent* (*agreement*) **3.** ⟨übtr⟩ ein ~er Mensch *a one-sided p*; *a p having a small range of interests* ‖ *one-sided* (*report*); *biassed, partial*; *prejudiced* ‖ (geistig) ~ s ⟨fam⟩ *to have a one-track mind* ‖ *ill-balanced* (*course of study*) **II.** adv *all one way* ⟨a. fig⟩ ‖ ~ befestigen *to fix at one end*; Papier nur ~ beschreiben *to write on paper on one side only* ‖ ~ glatt *machine glazed* (*paper*) ‖ *unilaterally* (*binding*) ‖ *onesidedly* (*logical standpoint*) ‖ ~ beeinflußt *prejudiced*; (etw) ~ darstellen *to represent* od *treat* (*a th*) *from a one-sided point of view* ‖ zu ~ auf etw eingestellt *too one-sided in one's attitude to a th* ‖ ~ gehandhabt ⟨Am⟩ *jug-handled*

·Einseitigkeit f ~/~en *one-sidedness*; *unilaterality* ‖ ⟨übtr⟩ *one-sidedness*; *one-sided* (od *partial*) *character*

·ein|senden vt [h] = einschicken ‖ → Eingesandt; inserieren **·Einsender** m ~s/~ *sender, transmitter* ‖ e–s (Briefes f Zeitung) *correspondent*

·Einsendung f ~/~en *sending in* (an *to*); → Übersendung ‖ *remittance* (*of money*)

·ein|senken vt [h] (etw) ~ in *to plant in, to sink into* (*the ground*) ‖ ⟨hort⟩ ~ *to set in, to plant*; ~ in *to plant* (od *stick*) *in*(*to*) (*the ground*), → absenken **·Einsenkung** f ~/~en *planting* ‖ ~ in *sinking into*; *planting in*(*to*) ‖ *depression*

·Einser m ~s/~ = Einer

·ein|setzen vt/i [h] **I.** vt **A. 1.** ⟨eig⟩ (etw) *to fix, place, plant, set* (in *in*); –gesetzt in *fixed* (od *placed, set*) *in* ‖ (Stein) ~ in *to sink into* (*the ground*) ‖ e–n Boden ~ in ein Kleidungsstück *to seat a garment* ‖ (Fische) in e–m Teich ~ *to stock a pond*; *to put* (*plants in the ground*) ‖ ⟨tech⟩ *to position* ‖ (Motor) *to install*; (Mast, Ruder etc) ⟨mar⟩ *to ship*; → Boot ‖ (einfügen) *to insert, to inset*; *to put in*; → inserieren ‖ ein anderes Wort ~ *to substitute another word* (f *for*) **2.** jdn ~ *to set a p up, to put a p in*; *to install a p* (in ein Amt *in an office*); *to appoint* od *nominate a p* (in ein Amt *to an office*); jdn wieder in sein Amt ~ ⟨fam⟩ *to put a p back on the saddle* ‖ amtlich ~ *to ordain, bench*; (feierlich) *to inaugurate a p*; (Bischof) *to enthrone* ‖ jdn als *or* zum Direktor ~ *to install a p headmaster*; jdn als, zum Erben ~ *to appoint a p* (*to be*) *one's heir*; *to make a p one's heir*; .. als Vorsitzer *to constitute a p chairman* ‖ e–n Ausschuß ~ *to appoint* (od *constitute*; *set up*) *a committee* **3.** ⟨übtr⟩ (einrichten) (etw) *to establish, found, institute, plant*; *start* **B. 1. a.** (Geld) *to stake*; *to make available* (*public funds*) **b.** sein Leben (etc) ~ *to risk* (od *stake, venture*) *one's life*; *to lay down one's life* (f *for*) **2.** bes ⟨mil⟩ (Truppen) *to get ready*; *bring into action*; *to engage, commit*; (Polizei) *to call in* (gegen *against*) ‖ –gesetzt w *to be committed, engaged* ‖ *to employ, use, utilize* (f *for*) ‖ s–n Einfluß ~ f etw *to use one's influence for*; *to bring one's influence to bear upon a th* ‖ (Kräfte) *to gather, to put forth*; s–e ganze Kraft ~, alles ~ *to muster all one's powers, to strain every nerve, to summon all one's energy*; *to be all out* (f *for a th*); → aufbieten **3. sich** ~ **a.** ⟨mil⟩ *to play one's part in battle*; *to venture one's life in b.* ‖ *to toe the mark* **b. sich** ~ **f** *to go for* (*a th*); *to push, encourage* (*a th*); *to identify o.s. with* (*a th*), *to stake o.s. on, to throw o.s. into* (*a th*); *to take up the cudgels for* (*a th*); *to stand up for* (*a p*) | sich mit allen Kräften ~ f *to go all out for, to be a go-getter for* (*peace*); .. voll u ganz .. *to throw one's full weight behind a th*; sich mit Begeisterung ~ f etw *to enthuse about a th* ‖ .. f jdn *to stand up for a p*; .. warm .. *to espouse warmly the cause of a p*; ⟨Am pol⟩ *to shout for a p*; ⟨Am sl⟩ *to root for* (*a team*); sich blindlings ~ *to go it blind*; sich ganz ~ *to play one's full part* **II.** vi **1.** (of a fever, the tide, weather) *to set in*; der Sommer hat bei uns plötzlich mit e–r

Hitzewelle –gesetzt *summer has burst upon us with a heat-wave* ‖ *to begin, open* (od *start off*) (mit *with*) ‖ (of a gale) *to blow up* **2.** ⟨mus⟩ *to come in simultaneously*; sicher ~ *to attack* **3.** (of cavalry, etc.) *to come into play* **4.** (of a story) wieder ~ *to be resumed* **·Einsetzen** n (→ einsetzen II.) *setting-in* (*of the fever*, etc.) ‖ (e–r Glasmalerei) *laying* ‖ ⟨comp⟩ (~ des Steuersatzes) *positioning* ‖ Wieder≗ *resumption* ‖ → Einsatz; Einsetzung

·Einsetzung f ~/~en (→ einsetzen I. A.) **1.** *fixing, placing, planting* (in *in*) ‖ *installation* (*of a motor*) ‖ *insertion*; *putting in* **2.** *setting up*; *installation*; *appointment* (*of a p*; in ein Amt *to an office*); Beschluß z ~ e–s Konkursverwalters *receiving-order* ‖ *constitution, setting up* (*of a committee*) **3.** *establishment, foundation, institution, plantation* (*of a th*) ‖ → Einsatz; Einsetzen **~sworte** n [pl] ⟨ec⟩ *sacramental words* [pl]

·Einsicht f ~/~en **1.** ⟨eig⟩ *examination* (in etw *of* od *into a th*), *inspection* (*of a th*); *perusal*; zur ~ *for p.* ‖ ~ nehmen in etw *to look* (od *examine, have a look*) *into a th*; *to look carefully at a th*; *to examine, peruse a th* ‖ ⟨jur⟩ ~ in die Akten *access to files* **2.** (innere ~) **a.** *discernment*; *comprehension*; *penetration* (*a man of p.*); intuitive ~ *vision*; nach bester ~ *according to one's lights*; nach b. ~ handeln *to do as one thinks best*; → Einblick, Verständnis **b.** *reason*; *reasonable view*; *sensible conduct* ‖ ~ h, z ~ k *to be reasonable* od *sensible, to listen to reason*; (jdn) z ~ bringen *to bring* (*a p*) *to reason*; *to make a p see* od *realize a th* ‖ *understanding* ‖ ~ kommt mit den Jahren *we get wiser as we grow older* | nach **~nahme** f *after heaving read it*; zur ~ *for your attention* **~slosigkeit** f *lack of discernment* od *insight*

·einsichtig, ·einsichtsvoll a *discerning, judicious*; *reasonable, sensible, understandable*; *of insight* ‖ ⟨fam⟩ *judgematic*(*al*)

·ein|sickern vi [s] ~ in *to ooze* (od *filter, soak*; ⟨Am⟩ *seep*) *into* ‖ ⟨tact⟩ *to infiltrate*

·Einsiedeglas n ⟨österr⟩ → Einmachglas

Einsiedel·ei f ~/~en *hermitage, anchorage*

·Einsiedler m ~s/~ **1.** *anchoret, anchorite*; *eremite, hermit, recluse, solitary* ‖ ⟨übtr⟩ *hermit, recluse* **2.** ⟨orn⟩ *solitaire*; → Dronte **3.** = Eingänger **·Einsiedlerin** f *anchoress*; *female recluse*

·einsiedlerisch a *solitary* (*life*) **·Einsiedler-~krebs** m ⟨zoo⟩ *hermit-crab*; *pagurian* **~leben** n *life as a hermit* od *recluse*

·einsilbig a ⟨gram⟩ *monosyllabic*; ~es Wort *monosyllable* ‖ = wortkarg

·ein|singen vt [h] **1.** (Kind) *to sing to sleep* ‖ der Chor war gut –gesungen *the singing of the choir was well practised* **2. sich** ~ *to practise singing*

·ein|sinken vi [s] (of the ground) *to sink, subside*; *to cave in*; → einstürzen ‖ (P) *to sink* (in *into*) ‖ –gesunken *sunken, hollow* (*eyes*)

·Einsitzer m ⟨mot⟩ *single-seater* ‖ ⟨aero⟩ Jagd≗ *single fighter-plane*

·einsitzig a *single-seated* (*car*)

·Einskuller m ⟨mar⟩ *skiff*

·ein|spannen vt [h] **1.** (etw) *to fix* (in *in*); auf beiden Seiten ~ *to fix at both ends*; –gespannter Träger *built-in beam* ‖ mit Zwingen ~ *to clamp*; (Zeitung) *to fix* (od *put .. into the holder*) ‖ *to mount, clamp, grip* (*a tool, workpiece*) **2. a.** ein Pferd ~ *to put a horse in*; den Wagen ~ *to harness* od *put a horse to the carriage* **b.** ⟨übtr⟩ oft [pass] jdn in e–n Beruf ~ *to harness a p to a profession*; in das Ehejoch –gespannt *yoked in marriage* ‖ ⟨fig⟩ (jdn) *to keep in check*; jdn (sehr) stark ~ *to work a p* (*terribly*) *hard*; ⟨Am sl⟩ *to rope a p in* (*for a job*)

·Einspänner m ~s/~ *one-horse carriage*; *fly* [pl *flys*]; ⟨AInd⟩ *ekka* ‖ ⟨fig⟩ ~ s *to plough a lonely furrow* **·einspännig** a *one-horse* (*carriage*) ‖ ~ fahren *to drive with one horse*

·ein|sparen vt [h] Ausgaben ~ *to reduce* od *retrench one's expenses*; *to economize, to retrench* ‖ (Stellen) *to axe*; *to do away with* **·Einsparung** f *retrenchment*; *economizing*; ~en m *to retrench, economize*

·ein|speicheln vt [h] (etw) *to insalivate*

·Einspeisung f *feed* **~s-** *feed* ⟨a. at⟩

·ein|sperren vt [h] (jdn) *to lock* od *shut in*; ~ in *to lock* od *shut in*(*to*) (*a room*) ‖ *to imprison, to commit to prison*; ~ in *to confine in* (*a cell*); → einspinnen; einengen, –pferchen, –schließen

·Einsperrung f ~/~en *confinement, imprisonment*

·ein|spielen vt [h] **1.** ⟨mus⟩ (Stück) *to practise* ‖ (Instrument) *to play up*; *to bring into suitable condition by playing* | auf e–a –ge–lt s *to play up to each other*; → Zus–spiel ‖ ⟨fig⟩ (of spies) *to play into each other's hands* **2. sich** ~ *to practise* (auf *on*; f *for*); *to practise playing*; *to get the feel of an instrument by playing it* ‖ er hat sich gut –ge–lt *he has acquired great skill in playing*; ⟨theat⟩ *to get the feel of a role*; ⟨fig⟩ *he has learned to play his part* ‖ sich gut auf–e–a –ge–lt h *to work together as a perfect team, to be well coordinated*

·ein|spinnen vt [h] **1.** (of a spider) (Fliege) *to enclose* (*a fly*) *with a web*; *to spin a web round* (*a fly*) **2.** °jdn ~ ⟨sl⟩ *to jug* od *shop a p* (*to put a p into gaol*); ⟨mil⟩ *to run a p in*, –gesponnen w *to be run* **3. sich** ~ **a.** ⟨ent⟩ *to form a cocoon*; *to cocoon* **b.** ⟨fig⟩ *to seclude o.s., to live in seclusion, to live a solitary life* ‖ sich ~ in *to wrap o.s. in, to be wrapped up in* (*one's work*)

×°**·Einsprache** f ~/~n = Einspruch; ⟨Sw⟩ = Einrede

·einsprachig a *unilingual*

·ein|sprechen vt/i [h] **1.** vt jdm Trost ~ *to comfort* od *reassure a p*; → einreden A. 1. **2.** † vi *to look* (od *drop*) *in* (bei jdm *upon a p*)

·ein|sprengen vt [h] (Wäsche) *to sprinkle* (od *besprinkle*) *with water* ‖ ⟨minr⟩ in dem Gestein ist Kupfer –ge–gt *the rock contains sprinklings of copper*; *copper is scattered here and there in the r.*

·Einsprengling m ⟨minr⟩ *phenocryst*

·ein|springen I. vi [s] **1. a.** *to jump in*; ~ in *to jump into* (*the car*) **b.** auf jdn ~ *to fall upon a p* **2.** ⟨übtr⟩ (of rocks) = vorspringen **3.** ⟨fig⟩ ~ *to step in* (um z tun *to do*) ‖ (aushelfend) *to step into the breach*; ~ f jdn *to deputize* (od *to act as a deputy*) *for a p*; *to take a p's place*; ⟨theat⟩ ~ f e–n Schauspieler *to understudy an actor*; ein Sch., der –springt *an understudy* ‖ ⟨bes ftb⟩ als Ersatzmann ~ ⟨fam⟩ *to pinch-hit* **II.** ≗ n **1.** *jumping in* **2.** ⟨fig⟩ ~ f jdn *deputizing for a p* **·einspringend** a *recessed* (*opening*) ‖ ⟨math⟩ *re-entering, re-entrant* (*angle, corner*)

·Einspritz m *jet* **~anlasser** m *engine primer* **~druck** m *injection pressure* **~düse** f *fuel inj. nozzle* **~motor** m *inj.-type engine* **~pumpe** f *priming* od *inj. pump* **~ventil** n *atomizer valve*

·ein|spritzen vt [h] (Flüssigkeit) *to inject* (in *into*); ⟨med⟩ *to give a shot* **·Einspritzung** f ~/~en *injection* (in *into*); ⟨med⟩ *shot* ‖ ⟨fam⟩ (Schnaps) *shot*; noch so 'ne ~! *one glass more of that stuff!* ‖ °⟨sex vulg⟩ *letch-water, comings* [pl]

·Einspruch m ~(e)s/≗e *exception, objection* (gegen *to*); *protest, protestation* (*against*); *veto* (*on*); *remonstrance* (jdm gegenüber *to a p*); → Einwand; Protest; Veto ‖ auf Grund des ~s v *on the remonstrance of* ‖ ohne ~ *without contestation* ‖ ~ erheben *to object*; *to* (*enter* od *lodge a*) *protest*; ⟨Am fam⟩ *to kick* ‖ ⟨jur⟩ *to demur* ‖ ich erhebe ~ *I object*; es erfolgte (*or* erhob sich) kein ~ *nobody objected*; ~ erheben gegen (etw) *to take exception* od *objection to, to make an objection to*; *to make a plea against*;

to except against (*a witness*); *to protest* od *remonstrate against*; ⟨Am⟩ *to protest* (*a th*) ‖ schriftlichen ~ erheben *to make a written protest*; es wurde kein ~ gegen den Antrag erhoben *the motion was carried unanimously* **~s-recht** n ⟨engl jur⟩ (des Königs) *veto*; → Veto

·ein|spunden vt [h] *to bung* ‖ ⟨fam⟩ (jdn) = einsperren

·einspurig a ⟨rail⟩ *one-track*; ~e Eisenbahn *single-line* (⟨Am⟩ *-track*) *railway*, ⟨Am⟩ *railroad*

einst adv **1.** (früher) *at one time*; *one day*; *once, once upon a time*; *erstwhile, previously, earlier, in the past, in times past*; *hitherto, heretofore*; → einmal II. 1. a. ‖ besser als ~ *better than of old*; wie ~ *as in the past*; ~ wie jetzt *now as ever* **2.** (künftig) *some day* od *time*; *once*; → einmal II. 1. b.

·ein|stallen vt [h] (T) *to stable*

·ein|stampfen vt [h] (etw) *to press, ram* (in *into*) ‖ (Papier, Schriften) *to* (*re*)*pulp* ‖ ~ l *to sell as waste paper*

·Einstand m ~(e)s/⁓e **1.** ×(= Antritt) *entrance into* (od *upon*) *an office*; s–n ~ feiern *to celebrate one's start in the new job*; etw z ~ zahlen → ~sgeld **2.** ⟨ten⟩ *deuce* **~sgeld** n ⟨com⟩ *entrance-fee* (od *-money*) ‖ *footing*: ~ zahlen *to pay* (*for*) *one's footing* **~spreis** m *cost-price, delivery price* **~srecht** n = Vorkaufsrecht

°**·ein|stänkern** vt [h] (Raum) *to fill with a stink*

·ein|stechen vt [h] (etw) *to prick*; *puncture* ‖ (Nadel) *to stick in*; ~ in *to stick into* (*one's finger*) ‖ ein Loch ~ in *to make a hole in*; *to pierce* od *perforate* (*a th*) ‖ ⟨med⟩ *to thrust home* ‖ auf–e–a ~ *to stab at one another*

·Einsteck- ~blende f ⟨phot⟩ *presetting diaphragm* **~kamm** m *back-comb* **~kurbel** f *removable crank* **~schlitz** m ⟨phot⟩ *anchoring slit* (*of a spool*) **~schloß** n *mortise-lock*

·ein|stecken vt [h] **A. 1.** (Schwert) *to put up, to sheathe* **2.** (in die Tasche stecken) *to pocket*; *pouch*; (Geld) *to rake* (od *get*) *in*; den Gewinn ~ *to scoop the pool*; → einheimsen 2. **3.** (Brief) *to post*; *to drop in a pillar-box* **4.** ⟨fig⟩ (Beleidigung etc) *to take .. lying down*; *to put up with*; *to sit down under* (*an insult*); *to stomach, swallow*; *accept* **B.** °jdn ~ = einlochen

·ein|stehen vi [s] ~ f jdn *to be* (od *go*) *bail for, to stand surety for a p* ‖ ~ f etw *to give security for a th* (*for a debt*); *to stand up for* (*one's conviction*); *to answer* (od *to be answerable*; *to vouch*) *for a th*; *to guarantee* od *warrant a th*; dafür ~, daß .. *to guarantee that ..*

·ein|stehlen vrefl [h] sich ~ *to steal in*; sich ~ in *to steal into* (*a room*)

·Einsteig- ~dieb m *sneak-thief* **~eisen** n (f Kabelschacht) *manhole step* **~karte** f ⟨aero⟩ *boarding pass* **~klappe** f ⟨aero⟩ *hatch cover* **~leiter** f *entrance ladder* **~loch** n *manhole* **~luke** f (*entrance*) *hatch* ⟨a. aero⟩ **~schacht** m *manhole*; *inspection shaft*

·ein|steigen vi [s] *to get in*; ⟨Am rail⟩ *to get on the train, to intrain*, ⟨aero⟩ *to embark* ‖ ~ in ⟨rail, mar, aero⟩ *to board* [vt] ‖ ⁓! ⟨rail⟩ *take your seats*!, ⟨mar⟩ *all abord*! ‖ ~ in *to get* od *slip into*; *to enter* (*a car*); *to climb* (*a house*)

·Einsteinsche Gl·eichung f *Einstein equation* ($m = \frac{E}{c^2}$ [m = *mass*; E = *energy*; c = *speed of light*])

·Einstell- [in comp] ⟨tech⟩ *adjusting*; *regulating*; *setting* ‖ ⟨opt⟩ *focussing* **~dauer** f *response time* (*of instruments*) **~halle** f *garage* **~hebel** m *adjusting* (od *regulating*) *lever* **~knopf** m *adjusting* (od *control*) *knob* **~kurbel** f *adjusting handle* **~(l)ehre** f *adjusting* od *setting gauge* **~lupe** f ⟨phot⟩ *focussing magnifier* **~marke** f *index*; *reference* (od *guide-*) *mark* ‖ (Totpunkt-⁓) ⟨mot⟩ *timing mark* **~scheibe** f ⟨phot⟩ *setting dial* **~skala** f *adjusting* (⟨phot⟩ *distance, range, focussing*) *scale* **~vorrichtung** f *adjusting device* (od *mechanism*); *control*; ⟨opt⟩ *focussing mechanism*

·einstellbar a *adjustable*

·ein|stellen I. vt [h] **A. 1.** (Wagen) ~ in *to place* od *put in* (*a shed*); *to garage* (*a car*); im Park ~ *to park* ‖ (Bücher) *to arrange, shelve*; falsch –ge–llt w *to go to the wrong place*; (Gepäck, Ware) *to deposit* **2.** ⟨tech & wir⟩ (Apparat) (richtig) ~ *to adjust, adapt* (auf *to*); *to regulate*; falsch –ge–llt *maladjusted* (Instrument); → ausrichten ‖ (Fernrohr etc) *to focus* (auf *on*); [abs] ~ auf *to focus on*; auf Unendlich ~ ⟨phot⟩ *to set at* od *to infinity*; auf (5 m) ~ *to focus for ..*; richtig –ge–llt *in focus*; nicht r. –ge–llt *out of f.*; auf etw scharf ~ ⟨opt⟩ *to sharpen the f. on a th* das Visier ~ *to set the sight* ‖ (Radio) *to tune in, to tune* (auf *to*); den Apparat ~ auf *to tune in to*; (Sender) *to dial* ‖ (Fabrik, Industrie in ein Programm, e–n Erzeugungsgang) ~ *to gear .. to* **3.** ⟨übtr⟩ (Aufmerksamkeit etc) *to concentrate, to focus* (auf *on*); (*his thoughts are centered on ..*); (das Innere) *to attune* (auf *to*); den Geist ~ auf *to put the spirit in tune with*; darauf –ge–llt s, daß *to face the fact that*; ⟨mil⟩ muß d. –ge–llt s auf *must be alert to* **4.** (Arbeiter) *to employ* ‖ ⟨mil⟩ (jdn als Rekruten ~) *to enlist, enrol, recruit*; Soldaten ~ ⟨Am⟩ *to muster in troops, to muster troops into service* ‖ (Arbeiter) *to engage*; *to put .. in* (als *as*); ⟨Am⟩ *to put .. on, to sign .. up, to take .. on* **5.** ⟨übtr⟩ –ge–llt auf (*a heart*) *attuned to ..* ‖ .. auf die Praxis *practically minded*; .. auf den Sommer *summer-minded* ‖ er ist materialistisch –ge–llt *he is materialistically minded* (od *orientated*) ‖ –ge–llt s gegen *to be unfavourably disposed towards* (*a p*) **B.** (ruhen l) (etw) *to cease, stop, stay* (*one's play*); *to leave off* (*playing*) ‖ die Arbeit ~ *to strike*; *to strike* (od *knock off*) *work*; *to down tools*; (Betrieb) *to close* od *shut down* ‖ ⟨rail⟩ (Zug) *to take off* ‖ (Dienst; Zahlung) *to suspend*; Zahlungen ~ *to cease* od *stop payments*; das Erscheinen (e–r Zeitung) *to cease publication* od *to appear* od *to be published* (Feindseligkeiten) *to suspend*; das Feuer ~ *to stop firing* ‖ ⟨jur⟩ (Verfahren) *to stay*; ⟨Am⟩ *to nolle-pros* ‖ (Gewohnheit etc) *to discontinue*; *to drop*; *to knock off*; das Rauchen ~ *to knock off smoking*; → abbrechen **C. sich** ~ **1.** (P) *to appear*; *attend*; *to come up*; *to make one's appearance, to put in an appearance*; *to present o.s.* ‖ sich wieder ~ *to come back, to return* **2.** (of cold, rain) *to set in*; (of a disease) sich plötzlich ~ *to supervene* ‖ (*of words*) *to come* ‖ *demand arises* ‖ *fever develops*; (of mistakes) *to creep in* **3.** (of events) *to occur, happen*; *to show up*; (of conditions) *to arise*; *to ensue* (infolge v *from*); *to spring up*; (of help) *to be forthcoming*; wenn sich e–e Meinungsverschiedenheit ~ sollte *if it came to a difference of opinion* ‖ (of difficulties etc.), *to insinuate* od *present o.s.* ‖ (of an idea) *to suggest itself*; *to come into play*; (of fever, symptoms, pains, etc) *to set in*; sich ~ bei jdm *to come* (od *occur*) *to a p*; sich wieder ~ bei jdm *to recur to a p* **4. sich ~ auf** *to adjust* (od *adapt*) *one's mind to*; *to respond to*; *to play up to* (*a style*); *to study* (*a p's wishes*) ‖ sich auf jede Möglichkeit ~ *to provide for every contingency*; sich auf die Vorschriften ~ *to toe the line* ‖ sich auf jdn ~ *to react to a p*; *to humour* (od *study*) *a p* **II.** ⁓ n = Einstellung A.

·einstellig a ⟨math⟩ ~e Zahl *digit*

·Einstellung f ~/~en **A.** (→ einstellen A.) **1.** *placing* (in *in*); *parking* ‖ *arrangement, shelving* (*of books*) **2.** ⟨tech⟩ *adaptation, adjustment* (auf *to*); *regulation* ‖ ⟨opt & phot⟩ *focus*; *focussing* (auf *on*); Scharf⁓ *sharp focus*(*sing*) ‖ *setting* (*of the distance*) ‖ ⟨wir⟩ *tuning in* ‖ ⟨artill⟩

setting (der Libelle the bubble) || richtige ~ ⟨mot⟩ correct alignment (of headlights) **3.** concentration (of toughts), focussing (auf on); approach (zu to [work]) **4.** ⟨mil⟩ enlistment, enrolment, recruitment; ~sjahr age of enlistment || engagement; putting in (of a p) **B. 1.** (→ einstellen B.) cessation (of an action); stoppage; → Stillegung, Streik || discontinuance (of a habit); dropping; suspension (of hostilities) || ⟨jur⟩ discontinuation || stay (of proceedings); nolle-prosequi (L) || ⟨mil⟩ ~ der Feindseligkeiten cease-fire || ⟨at⟩ suspension (of atomic weapons tests) **2.** (→ einstellen C. 4.) (innere ~) **a.** attitude; view(s pl); leanings pl; (frame of) mind || geistige ~ mental attitude || spirit || mode of thought || ~ z contact with; relations with (a p); was ist Ihre ~ dazu? ⟨Am⟩ what stand do you take? e–e falsche ~ z Leben a faulty attitude to(wards) life; feindselige ~ gegen animosity against **b.** ⟨psych⟩ feeling; (Erwartungszustand) set || ~ auf reaction (od response) to

·Einstich m: e–n ~ m to make a puncture

·ein|sticken vt [h] ein Muster ~ in ein Taschentuch to embroider (od stitch) a handkerchief with a pattern

·Einstieg m ⟨mountain⟩ start || ⟨bus etc⟩ entrance

·einstig a (vergangen) former; late (bishop); one-time (owner) || (the city) that was || former (Freunde) || (the territory of) what was once (the Roman Empire)

·ein|stimmen vi [h] **1.** ⟨mus⟩ to join in (they joined in); to chime in || ~ in den Chor, das Lied to join in the chorus, the song || ~ in e–n Willkommensgruß to concur in a welcome **2.** † = überein-, zustimmen

·einstimmig I. a **1.** ⟨mus⟩ ein ~es Lied a song for one voice **2.** ⟨fig⟩ unanimous; ~er Beschluß unanimous vote **II.** adv **1.** ⟨mus⟩ in unison **2.** ⟨fig⟩ (to resolve, vote) unanimously; (to reject) with one accord (od consent, voice; unanimity) ⟨parl⟩ ~ angenommen, geht ~ durch (abbr g.e.d.) carried unanimously (abbr nem. con. für: nemine contradicente)

·Einstimmigkeit f ~/ accord, agreement, unanimity; es herrschte or bestand unter ihnen volle ~ in, z tun they were unanimous in, in doing

°**·ein|stippen** vt [h] = eintauchen

·einstmalig a onetime (Freunde); → einstig

·einstmals adv once; once upon a time; one-time (that o.-t. fashionable square)

·einstöckig a two-storeyed (house)

·ein|stopfen vt [h] (etw) ~ in to stuff into

·ein|stöpseln vi/t [h] to plug in [adv]

·ein|stoßen vt [h] **1.** (etw) ~ in to drive into; to push od thrust into || ⟨med⟩ to thrust home || **2.** (Tür) to force open; (Fenster) to smash (⟨Am⟩ kick) in; to knock in || (Mauer) to knock down

·Einstrahlung f ~/ irradiation

·ein|streichen vt [h] (Geld) to grab; pocket; den Gewinn ~ to scoop the pool; to sweep the board; ⟨fam⟩ to rake in (a commission)

·ein|streuen vt [h] **1.** (Stroh etc) to strew in; ~ in to strew about (a place); to litter down the stable **2.** ⟨fig⟩ (Bemerkung) to intersperse (in in); to throw in **·Einstreuung** f ~/~en ⟨fig⟩ interspersion

·Einström- ~druck m flow-in pressure **~düse** f inlet nozzle **~verlust** m intake loss

·ein|strömen 1. vi [s] to flow (od run, stream) in; ~ in to flow (od run, rush) into (the lake) | ⟨übtr⟩ (S) to flow (od pour) in || to flow (od stream) in; ~ in to crowd (od stream) into (the hall) || ~d ⟨tech⟩ intake [attr] (Luft) **2.** ≈ n inflow(ing); inset (of the tide); (schnelles) rush (of water, gas) | ⟨übtr⟩ inflow, influx (of money; aliens) || ⟨ec⟩ influx (of grace)

·ein|stückeln vt [h] to patch (a th) (in into)

·ein|studieren 1. vt [h] ⟨theat⟩ (Rolle etc) to study; mit jdm to coach a p in (a part), to go through (a p.) with a p || e–e S ~ to get up (on) a subject || (Stück) to produce; (proben) to rehearse, to practise; gut –studiert well prepared by rehearsal; –studiert w to be in rehearsal || ⟨übtr⟩ (emsig lesen) to pore over (a th) || gut –studiert studied (bow, courtesy) **2.** ≈ n ~ der Rolle study

·ein|stufen vt [h] to assign to a group; to grade (a. in bezug auf Gehalt, Stellung); classify, range || ⟨for⟩ to dibble || ⟨tax⟩ to rate, graduate

·einstufig a single-stage (⟨a.⟩ rocket) **·Einstufung** f grading, classification || ⟨tax⟩ rating, graduation; → einstufen

·einstündig a one hour's (use)

·ein|stürmen vi [s] ~ auf jdn to close in upon, to come down upon, to fall (od set) upon; to rush at; to attack, assail a p || ⟨übtr⟩ → eindringen

·Einsturz m ~es/≈e collapse (of a house, roof), falling-down (od -in); downfall; tumbling-in || ~gefahr [f] danger of collapse || caving-in, sinking (of the ground); → Erdrutsch

·ein|stürzen vi/t **1.** vi (of buildings) to collapse, founder; to come down (über jdm upon a p); to fall down (od in); to tumble in || (of the ground) to cave in; to sink | ⟨übtr⟩ sie glauben, der Himmel stürze ein, wenn .. they think the heavens must fall if ..; → zus–brechen

·einstweilen [a. ∪·–∪] adv in the meanwhile od meantime, for a while; meantime, meanwhile; ⟨jur⟩ in the interim || (vorläufig) for the present; for the time being; provisionally; for the nonce (od occasion)

·einstweilig a interim, temporary, provisional (arrangement, measure) || ~e Regelung ⟨R C hist⟩ the Interim || ~e Verfügung ⟨jur⟩ restraining order, ⟨Can⟩ interim injunction

·eintägig a one-day's, one-day || ⟨med, bot & ent⟩ ephemeral (fever, flower, insect)

·Eintagsfliege f ⟨ent⟩ ephemeral fly; ephemerid, ephemera (L); may-fly

·ein|tanzen vrefl [h] sich ~ to practise dancing

·Eintänzer m ~s/~ gigolo; professional dancing-partner

·Eintauch- ~fläche f immersed part of a (filter) surface **~gitter** n wet lattice **~kolorimeter** n dipping colorimeter **~marke** f immersion mark **~refraktometer** n dipping refractometer **~vergoldung** f water gilding

·ein|tauchen vt/i [h] **1.** vt (etw) to dip in; (Brot) to sop; ~ in to dip (od sop, steep) in; to dip in; (Finger) ~ in to dip in od into (milk); to immerse (in) || → einweichen **2.** vi (mit den Fingern) ~ in to dip in(to); to dive into

·ein|tauschen vt [h] etw ~ f = umtauschen || (in Zahlung geben) to trade in | ·Eintauschwagen [m] trade-in car

·ein|teilen vt [h] (etw) to divide, parcel (in into); to arrange (in in); to dispose; → phrasieren; in Abschnitte ~ to arrange in sections, to section; (Dinge, Menschen) in Klassen ~ to arrange in classes, to classify; to seperate into groups || nach Größe, Rang ~ to grade; (Gefäß) in Grade ~ to graduate; to mark out in degrees; in Grade –geteilt graduated (scale); ein Maß –geteilt in Zoll, Meter (etc) a measure marked in inches, metres | (Zeit) passend ~ to apportion; to distribute suitably; to map out; sich [dat] die Zeit ~ to plan how to spend one's time, to use one's t. economically, budget your time! | sein Geld richtig ~ to make both ends meet | ⟨mil⟩ (z Dienst) to detail **·einteilig** a one-piece [attr]; solid (tool)

·Einteilung f ~/~en division, parcelling (in into); arrangement (in in); → Phrasierung || ~ in Abschnitte arrangement in sections, sectioning; ~ in Klassen arrangement in classes; classification; ~ nach Arten division into types; ~ nach

Größe, Rang *gradation*; Grad≈ *graduation, scale* | gleichmäßige ~ *apportion*; *proportional distribution* (*of time, work*) ‖ die Rede etc hat k–e ~ .. *has no proper plan* **~sgrund** m, **~sprinzip** n *principle of classification*

·eintönig a ⟨mus & theat⟩ *monotonic* (*recitation*); *monotonous* (*voice*) ‖ ⟨übtr⟩ *drab, dull, monotonous* (*life*); *humdrum* (*sermon, talk*); ~e Unterhaltung *humdrum*; ~e Wiederholung *monotone* **·Eintönigkeit** f ~/ ⟨mus⟩ *monotone*; *monotony* ‖ ⟨übtr⟩ *dullness, sameness, monotony, monotonousness*; *humdrum*; höchste ~ *dead level*

·ein|tonnen vt [h] (Heringe) *to barrel*

·Eintopf m (a. ~gericht) *one-dish meal, single-boiled* od *one-course dish*; *stew*; *hot-pot*; ⟨Am⟩ *boiled* (od *plate*) *dinner* **~sonntag** m ⟨Ger⟩ *Stew Sunday*

·Eintracht f ~/ *concord, harmony, union* (*in perfect u.*); alles ist in bester ~ *all is concord*; in ~ leben mit *to be at peace with* (*the world*) ‖ ⟨prov⟩ ~ vermehrt, Zwietracht zerstört *united we stand, divided we fall*

·einträchtig 1. a *harmonious* (*family*); *peaceable*; → einmütig **2.** adv *at peace*; ~ leben mit *to be at peace with*

·Eintrag m ~(e)s/≈e **1.** [abstr] (Schaden) nur in: e–r S ~ tun → Abbruch 3. **2.** [konkr] **a.** ⟨com⟩ *entry*; *item* ‖ amtlicher ~ *register, registry*; dokumentarischer ~ *record* **b.** ⟨weav⟩ = Einschlag

·ein|tragen I. vt [h] **1.** ⟨eig⟩ (hineintragen) (etw) *to carry in*; ~ in *to carry into* ‖ (Ernte) *to bring* (od *gather, get*) *in*; *to harvest*; → einbringen | ⟨pharm⟩ *to add* **2.** ⟨übtr⟩ **a.** ⟨com⟩ (Posten) *to book, enter, to make an entry of*; *to pass*; *post* (in *into*); in das Hauptbuch ~ *to post*; etw falsch ~ to *make a wrong entry of a th*; korrekt ~ *to enter up* **b.** (Namen) *to enter, inscribe* (in *in*); *to put down*; jdn als Mitglied ~ *to enrol a p as a member*; neu ~ *to re-enter* | –ge–er Kunde ⟨fam⟩ *reggie*; (etw) amtlich ~ *to register* (auf jds Namen *in a p's name*) ‖ (etw, jdn) in (amtliche) Liste ~ *to list*; → Liste ‖ ⟨jur⟩ protokollarisch ~ *to record*; → eingetragen‖ (jdn) in die Wahlliste ~ *to poll*; sich in die W. ~ l *to be polled* | **sich** ~ *to put o.s. down, to register o.s.* ‖ sich als Mitglied ~ *to enrol o.s.* (in *in*) **c.** (Bemerkungen) *to write in*; (Verbesserungen) *to put down* ‖ (Wort) *to insert*; → einschieben **d.** (etw auf e–r Figur ~) *to mark* (*in*) ‖ (etw) auf e–r Landkarte ~ *to map* ‖ *to plot* (*in a coordinate system*) **3.** ⟨fig⟩ = einbringen → d. I. B. 1. ‖ *to yield* (*profit*) ‖ das trug ihm viele Feinde ein *that made him many enemies* **II.** ≈ n *carrying in*; ~ in *carrying into* ‖ *bringing* (od *gathering*) *in* (*of the harvest*) ‖ → Eintragung

·einträglich a *gainful, lucrative* (*trade*); *remunerative* (*position*); nicht ~ *unremunerative* ‖ *profitable* (*business*); *fat* (*job*); ein ~es Geschäft *a paying game* (od *concern*); es ist nicht ~ *it does not pay* (*to do*) ‖ *productive* (*mine, soil*); *payable* (*mine*); nicht ~ *unproductive* ‖ etw ~ m *to put .. on a paying basis*

·Einträglichkeit f *lucrativeness, remunerativeness* ‖ *profitableness*; *productiveness* **·Eintragung** f ~/~en **A.** [abstr] (Eintragen) **1.** → Eintragen **2.** ⟨com⟩ *booking, entering, entry, posting* (in *in*) ‖ *recordation* ‖ *entry, inscription* (*of a name*) ‖ (amtliche) (*vital*) *registration* ⟨a. demog⟩; *registry*; *enrolment* (*of a deed*) ‖ *insertion* (*of a word*) **B.** [konkr] = Eintrag 2. a. ⟨mill⟩ *feed* **~sgebühr** f *registration fee*

·ein|tränken vt [h] (etw) = eingießen, –schenken ‖ mst °⟨fig⟩ ich werde es ihm schon ~ *I'll give it to him, he shall smart* (od *suffer*) *for it*

·ein|träufeln vt [h] (etw) *to infuse in drops*; *to pour in drop by drop*; ~ in *to instil(l) into*; *to pour into* (*the ear*) *in drops* **·Einträufelung** f *instillation, instilment*

·ein|treffen I. vi [s] **1.** (⟨eig⟩ ins Ziel treffen) (of statements, etc) *to come true*; *to be realized*; *to be verified* (od *confirmed*) ‖ (of events) *to come to pass*; *to happen* **2.** ⟨übtr⟩ (ankommen) *to arrive* (in *at*; *in*); *to appear*; plötzlich *or* unerwartet ~ *to turn up*; ⟨Am⟩ *to blow in* ‖ (of letters, etc.) *to arrive, to come to hand* **II.** ≈ n **1.** *coming true*; *realization*; mögliches ~ *contingency* **2.** *arrival*; *appearance*

·eintreibbar a *recoverable* (*debt*); *collectible*

·ein|treiben I. vt [h] **1. a.** (Vieh) *to drive in*; ~ in *to drive into* **b.** ⟨übtr⟩ (Geld, Steuer) *to exact* (v jdm *from a p*); (Schuld) *to call in, to collect*, ⟨com⟩ *to recover* (*debt*) **2.** (Keil etc) *to drive in* od *home*; ~ in *to drive into* ‖ °(Hut) *to batter, crush* **II.** ≈ n *driving in* (*of cattle*; *of a nail*) **·Eintreibung** f ~/~en ⟨übtr⟩ *exaction* (*of fees*); *collection* (*of debts*); → Eintreiben

·ein|treten vi/t **I.** vi [s] **A.** (P) **1.** ⟨eig⟩ *to enter* (durch e–e Tür *by a door*); *to come* (od *turn, walk*) *in* (durch e–e Tür *at a door*); bitte, treten Sie ein *come* (od *walk*) *in, step inside, please*; *this way, please* ‖ ~ in ein Haus (etc) *to enter*; plötzlich ~ in *to strike in* (*at a p's house*), *plunge into* (*a shop*); ungebeten ~ ⟨fam⟩ *to horn in* | ⟨mil⟩ (ins Glied) *to join the ranks* **2.** ⟨übtr⟩ **a.** in jds Dienst ~ *to enter a p's service*; in das geschäftliche Leben ~ *to enter upon a business life*; als Teilhaber jds ~ *to enter into partnership with a p*; wann treten Sie bei uns ein? *when do you start work with us?* ‖ in das Heer, e–e Partei ~ *to enter* (od *join*) *the army, a party*; in ein Kloster, e–n Beruf ~ *to enter a monastery, a profession* **b.** in das 50. Lebensjahr ~ *to enter the 50th year of one's age* ‖ *to embark* (*on a debate*); in Verhandlungen ~ *to enter into negotiations* **c.** **f jdn** ~ *to intercede for a p*; *to espouse the cause of a p*; *to side with a p*; *to stand out* (od *take up the cudgels for a p*), ⟨Am⟩ *to stick up for a p*; (sich f. jdn) einsetzen, (f. jdn) einspringen; bei jdm f jdn (e–e S) ~ *to use one's influence with a p on behalf of a p* (*of a th*) ‖ ~ f (etw) *to argue for, to espouse* (*a cause*); *to stand for* (*progress*); *to take up the cause of* (*freedom*); *to advocate* od *champion* (*a th*); mannhaft ~ f den Sozialismus *to come out strong on the side of socialism*; ⟨com⟩ → Wechsel **B.** ⟨übtr⟩ (S) **1.** (of the tide) *to come in* ‖ (of a bullet; river) ~ in *to enter* (*the skull*; *the plain*) ‖ (of a movement) in ein neues Stadium ~ *to enter upon a new stage* **2.** (of events, etc.) *to come on*; *to come to pass*; *to ensue*; *fall*; *happen*; *occur*; *materialize*; *to take place*; ⟨Am⟩ *to eventuate* ‖ (of circumstances) *to arise*; ⟨contr, etc⟩ *to intervene* ‖ Dunkelheit trat ein *darkness fell*; e–e Stille trat ein im Saal *a silence fell on the hall*; e–e Besserung ist heute –ge– *there is an improvement today* ‖ Schweigen trat ein *silence fell* (*for a moment*) ‖ der Tod trat um 2 ein *death ensued, came, occured at 2* ‖ die Unterstützung ist nicht –ge– *the support has not been forthcoming* ‖ –ge–er Verlust *actual loss* ‖ e–e günstige Wendung trat ein *there has been a change for the better* ‖ plötzlich ~ (of disease) *to supervene*; ⟨Am⟩ *to blow in* **II.** vt [h] **1.** (Tür) *to kick* (od *force*) *open* **2.** sich [dat] e–n Nagel (in den Fuß) ~ *to run a nail into one's foot* **3.** (neue Schuhe) ~ *to make shoes elastic by walking* **·eintretend** a *entering*; *incoming*; ein neu ~er Pächter *an incoming tenant* ‖ bei ~er Dunkelheit *as darkness fell* ‖ bei ~em Bedarf *if required* ‖ ~enfalls [adv] *in case this should happen*; *in such an event*

°**·ein|trichtern** vt [h] ⟨fig⟩ jdm etw ~ *to drum* (od *hammer*) *a th into a p*; → einfuchsen

·Eintritt m ~(e)s/~e **A.** (→ eintreten) **1.** *entering, coming in*; *entrance* (*of a p*), *ingress*; beim ~

at the entrance (*of the men*); bei s–m ~ *as he entered* (od *came in*) | der ~ in das Haus *the entering of the house, the entrance* (od *entry*) *into the house* **2.** ⟨übtr⟩ ~ ins Heer, Leben, in e–n Beruf *the entrance into the army, into life, into a profession* ‖ ~ in e–e Stellung *taking up, starting a job*, .. Dienststellung *entering into service* ‖ *passing* (*into old age*) **3.** der ~ f etw *the championship* (od *espousal*) *of a th* **4.** (Zulassung) *admittance* (in *or* z *to*); *admission* (z *to, into*); *entrance* od *entry* (*into*); ~ zum Stehplatz *admission to standing room*; freier ~ *free entrance*; kein ~, ~ verboten *no entrance*!, *keep out*! ‖ ~°schinden ⟨fam⟩ *to gate-crash* **B.** *coming in, incoming* (*of the tide*); *coming, approach* (*of spring*); *beginning*; *setting-in* ‖ ⟨astr⟩ *ingress* (*of a planet*) ‖ *incidence* (*of an event*); *occurrence* (*of a loss*) ‖ beim ~ der Dunkelheit *as darkness fell*; → Einbruch ‖ unerwarteter ~ *supervention* (*of a disease*) **~schinder** m *gate-crasher* **~spannung** f *admission pressure*; ⟨el⟩ *a. potential*

·Eintritts- ~geld n *admission-money*; *entrance--fee* (od *money*); ⟨sport⟩ *gate*(*-money*) **~karte** f *card of admission*; *ticket*; Zulassung nur mit ~ *admission only by ticket*; ⟨sport⟩ ~nschinder ⟨Am sl⟩ *gate-crasher* **~preis** m *charge for admission* **~recht** n *right of entrance* od *entrée*; *ingress*

·ein|trocknen vi/t **1.** vi [s] (of a stream) *to dry up*; *to shrink* ‖ ⟨übtr⟩ (of skin, etc.) *to shrink*; *shrivel* | ⟨fig⟩ (of resources) *to shrink*; *to be exhausted* ‖ (of talk) *to become barren*; *to slacken* **2.** vt [h] *to dry up* ⟨a. fig⟩; *to desiccate*

·ein|tröpfeln vt [h] = einträufeln

·ein|trüben vrefl *to become overcast* od *dull*

°**·ein|tun** vt [h] = –bringen; –gießen; –räumen

°**·ein|tunken** vt [h] (etw) = eintauchen

·ein|üben vt [h] (Gedicht, Rolle) ~ *or* sich [dat] ~ *to study*; (Stück, Tanz) *to practise* ‖ ⟨theat⟩ (Stück) → einstudieren | (jdn) *to exercise, practise* (in *in*); –geübt s *to be exercised* (*in*); *to be in practice* ‖ sich ~ *to exercise o.s.* (in *in*); *to exercise, to practise* (f *for*) **·Einübung** f ~/~en *study*; *practice*; *systematic exercise*

·Ein- u ·Austöner m *sound fading equipment*

·Einung f = Einigung

·ein|verleiben vt [h] **1.** (Land) ~ *or* sich [dat] ~ *to annex*; *to take in* ‖ ~ in *to annex to*; e–m Lande –leibt w *to be annexed* (od *joined*) *to a country* **2.** ⟨übtr⟩ etw ~ in *to incorporate a th with* od *into, in* (*a th*); *to embody* od *include a th in*(*to*) (*a th*); e–m Buch –verleibt w *to be incorporated in a book* ‖ e–r Sammlung ~ *to add* **3.** (verzehren) °sich [dat] etw ~ *to consume*; *to dispose of*; *to eat*; *to drink* **·Einverleibung** f ~/~en *annexation* (in *to*); die ~ e–s Landes in e–m Staat *the incorporation of a country with* (od *into, in*) *a state* ‖ ⟨übtr⟩ *incorporation* (in *into, in*); *inclusion* (*in*) ‖ *integration*

×**·Einvernahme** f ⟨Sw, österr⟩ ⟨jur⟩ = Vernehmung

·Einvernehmen n ~s/ **1.** (Eintracht) *agreement, concord, harmony, understanding* ‖ ein gutes ~ zw *a good understanding* (od *a goodwill*) *between* ‖ ⟨pol⟩ das gute ~ unter den Nationen *the comity of nations*; gutes nachbarliches ~ *good neighbourliness* ‖ in bestem ~ *in perfect union* | im ~ arbeiten *or* handeln mit *to concert with*; *to act in harmony with*; in geheimem ~ handeln mit *to act in collusion with* (*a p*) ‖ in gutem ~ stehen mit *to have a good understanding with*; in bestem ~ stehen mit *to be on the best* (*of*) *terms with* (*a p*) **2.** (Benehmen) sich ins ~ setzen mit *to communicate* (od *consult*), *to take counsel with*

·einverstanden a [nur pred] ~ s *to agree, to be agreed* od *in agreement* (über *on*); sind Sie ~? *do you agree*?; ~! *agreed*! *that's a bargain*!, *very good*!, *all right*!; ⟨Am sl⟩ *Roger*! sind Sie ~, daß .. (*or* z tun)? *are you willing that* .. (od *to do*)? ‖ in Betracht ziehen, ob jd ~ ist *to consult a p's convenience* | ~ s mit etw *to agree* (od *assent, consent*) *to a th*; *to be agreeable to a th*; *to acquiesce in a th* ‖ mit jdm ~ s *to fall in with a p* ‖ sich [acc] ~ erklären mit jds Ansicht *to associate o.s. with a p's words*; *to concur with a p in an opinion*; ich erkläre mich damit ~ *I agree to it*; sich damit ~ erklären z tun *to agree* (od *consent*) *to do*; → einwilligen

·einverständlich a ⟨österr⟩ (*action*) *undertaken by common consent*; *concerted* (*action*)

·Einverständnis n –nisses/–nisse **1.** (Zustimmung) *approval, assent, consent* (z *to*); *acquiescence* (z *in*); ⟨jur⟩ geheimes ~ *covin* ‖ mit jds ~ *with a p's approval*; *if a p agrees*; zum Zeichen des –nisses *in acquiescence* ‖ jds ~ einholen *to obtain a p's consent* ‖ jds ~ in Betracht ziehen *to consult a p's convenience* **2.** (Einvernehmen) *harmony, understanding* (zw *between*); *agreement*; im ~ mit *in agreement with* (*a p*) ‖ geheimes ~ *collusion*; in geheimem ~ mit *in collusion with* ‖ → Einvernehmen **~erklärung** f *declaration of* (*one's*) *approval*

·Einwaage f ~/ *initial weight*

·ein|wachsen[1] **1.** vi [s] *to grow inwards*; ~ in *to grow into* (*the flesh*) ‖ –ge– [a] *ingrown* (*nail*) **2.** ≗ n *ingrowth*

·ein|wachsen[2] vt [h] (etw) *to* (*treat with*) *wax*

·Einwand m ~(e)s/≗e *objection* (gegen *to*); *exception* (*to*) ‖ ≗e erheben *or* m *to raise objections*; *to take objection* (od *exception*) (gegen *to*); → ⟨bes jur⟩ Einspruch, Einwendung ≗emacher m ⟨fam⟩ *butter*

·Einwanderer m ~s/~ *immigrant* ‖ ⟨Am⟩ deutscher *or* skandinav. ~ *squarehead*; italien. ~ ⟨sl⟩ *wop* **·ein|wandern** vi [s] *to immigrate* (in *into*) ‖ –ge–rt [a] *immigrated* **·Einwanderung** f ~/~en *immigration* (in *into*) ‖ ~sauslese [f] *selective imm.*

·einwandfrei **1.** a *unexceptionable, faultless, unobjectionable*; *impeccable, irreproachable* (*conduct*); *perfect* (*condition*); *unimpeachable* (Deutsch, Verhalten, Charakter, Beweis); ⟨comp⟩ *positive*; nicht ~ *objectionable, contestable, impeachable*; nicht ganz ~ *somewhat shady* (*character*) ‖ (unanfechtbar) *incontestable, undeniable*; ⟨scient⟩ *valid* (Versuchsergebnis); ⟨jur⟩ *good* (*title*), *perfect* (*alibi*) **2.** adv *incontestably*; *conclusively*; (*to ascertain*) *with certainty* ‖ es steht ~ fest *it is beyond doubt* od *question*

·einwärts adv *inward, inwards*

·einwärts- pref [bei Verben] ~|**biegen** vt *to bend* (od *curve*) *inwards* ~|**gehen** vi; er geht einwärts *he goes with his toes turned in* ~|**kehren** vt (Muskel) *to introvert* ~|**setzen,** ~|**stellen** vt; die Füße ~ *to turn the toes in*

-·einwärts suff; land~ *inland*; → feld~

·ein|wässern vt [h] (Hülsenfrüchte) *to steep in water*; *to soak* ‖ (Heringe) *to free from salt by soaking in water*

·ein|weben vt [h] (Muster) *to weave in*; ~ in *to weave into* ‖ ⟨fig⟩ = einflechten, verweben

·ein|wechseln vt [h] (Geldnote) *to change* (gegen for); e–n Scheck ~ *to change a cheque* ‖ (fremdes Geld) *to exchange* (gegen *for*) **·Einwechs(e)lung** f ~/~en *changing* ‖ *exchange*

·ein|wecken vt [h] (Früchte etc) = einmachen

·Einwegflasche f ⟨com⟩ (ohne Rückgabe) *disposable bottle*; → Einmal-

·ein|weichen vt [h] (etw in Wasser) *to soak*; *to give* (*a th*) *a soak*; *to steep*; (geschmeidig m) *to macerate* ‖ ~ in *to soak* (od *steep*) *in* (*water*) ‖ → aufweichen ‖ –ge–cht *sodden* (Brot) ‖ ⟨fig⟩ °jdn ~ (of rain) = durchnässen

·ein|weihen vt [h] **1. a.** (Kirche) *to consecrate, dedicate* | (Denkmal) *to inaugurate*; *open*

formally; ⟨Am⟩ *to dedicate*; ein (neues) Haus ~ *to have* od *give a housewarming*; → eröffnen **b.** °e–n Hut (etc) ~ *to wear a hat for the first time* **2.** (jdn) *to initiate* (in *into* [*a secret*]); *to admit* (in *to*, *into*); jdn in das Geheimnis ~ *to let a p into the secret* || *to instruct*, *initiate* (in *in*) || –ge–ht s *to be in the secret*; in jds Leben –ge–ht s *to be in the s. of a p's life* || → eingeweiht

·**Einweihung** f ~/~en **1.** ⟨ec⟩ *consecration*; *dedication* || *inauguration*; *formal opening* (*of a library*); *opening ceremony* **2.** *initiation* (*of a p*; in *into*) **Einweihungs- ~feier** f, **~fest** n *inaugural ceremony* od *celebration* || ~sfest [n] ⟨bes Am⟩ *house warming* (*party*) **~ansprache, ~rede** f *inaugural address*

·**ein|weisen** vt [h] (jdn) ⟨mil⟩ *to brief*; ⟨ec⟩ *to induct* (in .. *to*, *into*); *to initiate* (in *into*); *to install* (in ein Amt *in an office*) || ⟨aero⟩ (mit Radar etc) *to vector*, ⟨fam⟩ *to talk down* ·Einweisung [f] ~/~en ⟨mil⟩ *orientation* | ~sflug [m] *familiarization flight*

·**ein|wenden** vt [h] **1.** [nur mit pronom. Objekt: etw, nichts etc] ich habe nichts –zu– *I do not object*, *I have* od *see no objection* (gegen *to*); h Sie etw dagegen –zu–, daß die Frage gestellt wird? *do you object to the question being asked*?; vieles ~ *to have many objections*; dagegen läßt sich nur einwenden, daß .. *the only th to be said against it is* ..; es ist nichts dagegen –zu– *there is no objection to it*; ich hätte gegen ein Glas Wein nichts –zu– *I wouldn't mind* (od *say no to*) *a g. of w.* **2.** (einwerfen) *to protest*; *demur* (*he demurred* '*Not quite*'); *to nip in* || *to object*, *to say in reply* (*that* ..) || → einwerfen; erwidern

·**Einwendung** f ~/~en **1.** *exception*, *objection* (gegen *to*); *demur*; ohne ~en *without d.* || ~en erheben (*or* m) gegen *to raise* od *urge an objection against* (*a book*); *to demur to*; *to argue against*; → Einwand, –spruch **2.** *interposition*, → Einwurf, Erwiderung

·**ein|werfen** vt/i [h] **A.** vt **1.** ⟨eig⟩ **a.** (etw) *to throw in*; ~ in .. *to drop into* (*the box*) **b.** (Fenster) *to smash*, *break* **2.** ⟨fig⟩ (Bemerkung) *to interpose*; *to put* (od *throw*) *in*; *to inject* .. (*into a discussion*) || zustimmend ~ *to chime in* || *to break* (od *burst*, *cut*) *in*; *to interpolate*; 'Einen Augenblick', warf er ein '*One moment*', *he broke in* **B.** vi ⟨sport⟩ *to throw in*

·**einwertig** a ⟨chem⟩ *univalent*, *monovalent*

·**Einwickel- ~papier** n *wrapping paper*

·**ein|wickeln I.** vt [h] **1. a.** (etw) *to envelop*, (*en*)*wrap* (in *in*); (Rosen) *to swathe* **b.** (jdn) *to wrap up*; (Kranke) *to swaddle*, *swathe* (in *in*); → wickeln | **sich ~** *to envelop o.s.* (in *in*); *to wrap o.s. up*; *to wrap up*; sich im Bett ~ *to tuck o.s. up in bed* **2.** °jdn ~ *to coax* (od *dupe*, *hoax*, *humbug*, *stuff*) *a p*; *to get round a p* || **sich ~** l *to be coaxed* od *duped* (v *by a p*) **II.** ≈ n *enveloping*, *envelopment*; *wrapping* (in *in*); Stoff z ~ *wrappage*; Papier z ~ *wrapping-paper* ·**Einwick(e)lung** f = Einwickeln

·**ein|wiegen** vt [h] (Kind) *to rock to sleep* || ⟨fig⟩ = einlullen

·**ein|willigen** vi [h] *to agree*, *to consent*, *to acquiesce*; *to yield consent* || ~ in (etw) *to agree* (od *assent*, *consent*, *subscribe*) *to* (*a proposal*); *to accede to* (*a demand*); *to acquiesce in* (*a p's resignation*); *to comply with* (*a request*); (darin) ~ z tun *to agree* (od *consent*) *to do*; → billigen ·**Einwilligung** f ~/~en *approval* (*with a p's a.*); *assent*; vorherige ~ ⟨jur⟩ *authorization* (v *from*), → Genehmigung; s–e ~ geben *to give one's assent* || ~ in *acquiescence in* (*a demand*) || ~ zu *agreement* (od *consent*) *to*; jds ~ erhalten z *to obtain a p's consent to*; s–e ~ geben z *to agree* (od *consent*) *to* (*a th*); (jdm) *to give* (*a p*) *one's consent to* (*a th*)

·**ein|winken** vt [h] ⟨aero⟩ (Piloten) *to direct* ·**Einwinkpersonal** n ⟨aero⟩ *marshallers* pl

·**ein|wintern** vt [h] (etw) *to accustom* (*a th*) *to wintry conditions*; *to* (*keep* .. *during the*) *winter*

·**ein|wirken** vt/i [h] **1.** vt =· einweben **2.** vi **~ auf a.** (S) ⟨chem⟩ *to react*, *affect* (*up*)*on* || (of drugs, etc.) *to act* od *operate on* (*the heart*; *a p*); *to affect* (*the health*; *a p*); *to influence* (*conditions*; *a p*) || (of light, etc.) *to impinge* (*up*)*on a th*; *upon a p* || *to have an effect on* || (etw) ~ l auf *to bring* (*a th*) *to bear upon* (*conditions*) || ein– u zurückwirken auf *to react* (*up*)*on* (*a p*) || schädlich ~ auf *to tell on a p*; → beeinflussen, Einfluß **b.** (P) ~ auf (jdn) *to work* (*up*)*on* (*a p*); *to work* (*a p* od *a th*) *up*; *to influence* (*a p*, *a th*); → bearbeiten B.1.b. || ~ auf jdn z tun (*or* daß er tut) *to prevail on a p to do*; *to cause* (od *get*, *persuade*, *urge*) *a p to do*, *to make a p do* **c.** auf e–a ~ *to react* (*up*)*on each other*; *to interact* ·**Einwirkung** f ~/~en **1.** ⟨phys⟩ *action* (*of a force*); *operation*; *working*; *influence* (*of a current*) || ⟨chem⟩ *reaction* (auf *on*) || *effect*; *impingement* (auf *on a th*) || unter der ~ v (Alkohol) *under the influence of* .. **2.** *impression*, *influence* (jds auf jdn *of a p on a p*); → Beeinflussung

·**ein|wissen** vi [h]: nicht ein– noch auswissen ⟨fam⟩ *to be nowhere*

·**ein|wohnen** vi/t [h] **1.** vi; ~ bei jdm *to lodge* (od *to live as a lodger*) *with a p* || → innewohnen **2.** refl **sich** ~ *to accustom o.s. to one's surroundings*; *to make o.s. at home* (in *in*) ·**Einwohner** m ~s/~ *inhabitant*; N. hat 2 Millionen ~ *N. has a population of 2 millions* | ~meldeamt [n] ⟨Ger⟩ *Residents' Registration Office* ·**Einwohnerschaft** f ~/ *inhabitants* [pl], *population* ·**Einwohnerzahl** f *population*; ~en [pl] *population figures* [pl]

·**Einwölbung** f ⟨arch⟩ *vaulting*

°·**ein|wühlen** vrefl: sich ~ [h] = sich eingraben

·**Einwurf** m ~(e)s/≈e **A.** [abstr] **1.** ⟨eig sport⟩ *throw-in*; den ~ haben *to throw in* || *smashing*, *breaking* (*of windows*) **2.** ⟨übtr⟩ *interposition* (*of a remark*) || *objection*; *demur*; e–n ~ m *to demur*; → Entgegnung **B.** [konkr] (Schlitz) *slit*; *narrow opening*; (an Automaten) *slot* **~automat** m *coin*(*-operated*) *machine* **~grube** f *receiving pit* **~klappe, ~öffnung** f *charging opening* **~trichter** m *feed hopper*

·**ein|wurzeln** vi & refl **1.** ⟨eig⟩ ~ [s], sich ~ [h] (of plants) *to take* (od *strike*) *root* **2.** ⟨übtr⟩ ~ *to become established*, *to take* (od *strike*) *root*; tief –ge–lt s bei jdm *to be deeply rooted in a p*; → eingewurzelt || = sich eingewöhnen

·**Einzahl** f ~/ ⟨gram⟩ *singular* (*in the s.*); *singular number*

·**ein|zahlen** vt [h] (Geld) *to pay in*, *to deposit*, *lodge*; (Aktien) voll ~ *to pay up* || (Summe) auf ein Konto, in e–e Bank ~ *to pay* (*a sum*) *into an account*, *into a bank*; ~ beim Gericht *to pay into Court*

·**ein|zählen** vt [h] (Eier) ~ in *to count into* (*a basket*) || = einrechnen ·**Einzahlung** f ~/~en **1.** [abstr] *paying-in*, *payment* (*of a sum*); ~ (e–r Summe) in *the paying* (*of a sum*) *into* (*a bank*); ~en m in *to pay into* (*a fund*) **2.** [konkr] *sum paid in*, *payment* **~saufforderung** f (f Aktien etc) ⟨bank⟩ *call* **~sbeleg** m ⟨com⟩ *credit slip* **~sschein** m *pay*(*ing*)*-in slip*, ⟨Am⟩ *deposit slip* **~ssumme** f *sum paid in*

·**ein|zäunen** vt [h] *to fence*, *hedge*; *to fence* (od *hedge*) *in* ·**Einzäunung** f = Einfriedigung

·**einzehig** a ⟨zoo⟩ *monodactyle*, *monodactylous*

·**ein|zeichnen** vt [h] **1.** ⟨math⟩ (Figur) *to inscribe* (in *in*) || (etw auf e–r Figur) *to mark in* || (etw auf e–r Karte) *to map*; *to mark* **2. sich ~ a.** = sich eintragen I.2.b.; ⟨Am⟩ *to sign up* **b.** sich ~ auf (of footsteps) *to mark* (*the earth*)

·**Einzeichnung** f ⟨math⟩ *inscription* (*of a figure*) || *mark*(*ing*) || → Zeichnung

·**einzeilig** a *single-line* (*motto*)

·**Einzel-** [in comp] *individual; single* ‖ *detailed* ‖ ⟨com⟩ *retail* **~abteil** n ⟨rail⟩ *single compartment* **~achsenantrieb** m *individual transmission* **~anfertigung** f *single-piece work* **~antrieb** m *individual drive* | soziale **~arbeit** f → –betreuung **~aufhängung** f (of wheels) *independent suspension*; ∼ h *to be independently sprung* **~aufstellung** f *itemized schedule* **~aufzählung** f *detailed enumeration* **~ausbildung** f *individual training* **~ausgabe** f *separate edition* **~ausstellung** f ⟨arts⟩ *one-man show* **~auswechslung** f (v Schienen) *replacement of single rails* **~befehl** m *separate order* **~behandlung** f ⟨Lit⟩ *particularization* **~beispiel** n *indiv. ex.*; *isolated instance* **~beratung** f ⟨parl⟩ *committee*; in ∼en über e–e Gesetzesvorlage eintreten *to go into c.* **~betrachtung** f ⟨Lit⟩ *individualization* **~betrag** m *single* (od *separate*) *amount* | soziale **~betreuung** f (*social*) *casework* **~bett** n *single bed* **~bildaufnahme** f ⟨film⟩ *successive* (od *single-*)*frame exposure*; *f.-by-f. exp.*; *stop-motion* **~darstellung** f *monograph*; *detailed presentation* **~ding** n *individual thing* **~erscheinung** f *isolated phenomenon* **~erwägungen** f pl *detailed considerations* **~fahrkarte** f ⟨rail⟩ *single*; *single ticket* **~fall** m *individual case* **~fertigung** f *single--piece* (⟨Am⟩ *indiv.*) *production* **~feuer** n *single--shot firing*; *independent fire* **~firma** f *single* (od *separate*) *firm* **~formular** n ⟨comp⟩ *single sheet*, → Endlos– **~gabe** f ⟨med⟩ *single dose* **~gänger** m ⟨hunt⟩ *solitary animal* ‖ ⟨übtr⟩ *loner*, ⟨fam⟩ *lone wolf* (P); → Eigenbrötler **~haft** f *solitary* od *close confinement* **~handel** m *retail*; *retail-trade* | ∼sgeschäft [n] [abstr] *retail outlet*, [konkr] *retail business* **~händler** m *retailer*; *retail dealer* **~haus** n *detached house*; *cottage* | ∼halt [m] *one-person household* **~hof** m ⟨agr⟩ *separate farm* **~kabine** f *single* (od *separate*) *cabin* **~kampf** m *hand-to-h. fight*; ⟨sport⟩ *indiv. match*; ⟨aero⟩ *dog-fight* ‖ –kämpfe [pl] ⟨mil, tact⟩ *individual actions* **~kämpfer** m *indiv. fighter* **~leistung** f *indiv. performance* **~mensch** m *indiv. being* **~nummer** f (Zeitung) *copy* **~preis** m *retail price* ‖ *separate price* **~radantrieb** m *indiv. wheel drive* **~radaufhängung** f *independent wheel suspension* **~richter** m ⟨jur⟩ *judge sitting alone* **~schlafabteil** n ⟨rail⟩ *roomette* **~spiel** n ⟨ten⟩ *single* **~staat** (e–s gr Reiches) m *constituent state* | ≗lich [a] *national* (*Organisation*) **~stehende** m → alleinstehend **~steuerung** f *indiv. drive* **~tabelle** f *indiv. table* **~tanz** m *solo* **~teile** n pl *single* od *indiv. parts* od *components* **~übung** f *individual exercise* **~unterricht** m *indiv. tuition* **~verkauf** m *retail*; *sale by retail* **~wesen** n *individual*; *individual being* **~wirtschaft** f *private enterprise* **~wurf** m (Bomben≗) *single release* **~zeichnung** f *detail drawing* **~zimmer** n ⟨hot⟩ *single room*

·**Einzelheit** f ∼/∼en **A.** †[abstr] *singleness*; *individuality, singularity* **B.** [konkr] **1.** (einzelner Teil, Gegenstand) *separate part*; ⟨arts⟩ *detail* ‖ *item*; *particular article* (*in a list*) **2.** (einzelner Punkt) *detail, particular, point*; *item*; *particular point* ‖ [oft pl] ∼en *details, particulars, facts* (*of the matter*) [pl]; die kleinsten (oft: unbedeutenden) ∼en *the minutiae* [L pl] ‖ alle ∼en *all particulars, the ins and outs* [pl], in allen ∼en *in detail*; (etw) in allen ∼en darstellen *to detail* ‖ bis in die kleinsten (*or* in alle) ∼en *down to the smallest* od *slightest detail*; → einzeln ‖ ⟨contr⟩ die [rel] genügend ∼en enthalten *in sufficient detail* ‖ sich in ∼en verlieren *to go into detail*(*s*) (od *particulars*); *to particularize*; er verliert sich z sehr in ∼en *he does not see the wood for the trees*; er verliert sich nicht in ∼en *with him the wood is not lost in the trees*

·**Einzeller** m ∼s/∼ ⟨zoo⟩ die ∼ [pl] *the protista* (L pl), *protozoa* (Gr pl) ·**einzellig** a *unicellular* ‖ ∼e Lebewesen [pl] = Einzeller [pl]

·**einzeln** **I.** a **A.** [attr] **1.** (als eine(r), –s f sich betrachtet) *individual, separate, several, single* (*book; act; impression; thought*); jedes ∼e Schiff *each several ship*; → Einzel- | (besonders) *particular, several* (*case*); *special* (*subject*); ∼er Teil *detail*; ∼er Punkt *or* Umstand *particular*; ∼er Posten .. *individual item* (*of supply*), jeder ∼e P. *each/and every point* **2.** (allein, f sich) *single*; *solitary*; ein ∼er Herr z Pferde *a solitary gentleman on horseback* ‖ *unrelated* (*p*) ‖ ein ∼er Mensch *one man standing alone, one man by himself* ‖ → allein; einsam; ledig | ein ∼er Band, Schuh *an odd volume, boot* **3.** (nur f e–n berechnet) *single* (*bed, room*) **4.** ∼es Geld (*small*) *change*; kein ∼es G. *no change*; ∼es Silbergeld *loose silver* **B.** [pred] → II. adv **C.** **~e** [pl] **1.** (→ A. 1.–3.) *individual, separate, several, certain, single* (*parts, acts*); in ∼en Exemplaren *in ones* ‖ die ∼en Teile (sc e–s Ganzen) *the component parts* (*of a drama*) | *particular, several*; ∼e Punkte *or* Umstände *details, particulars* [pl] | *solitary, single* ‖ ∼e Bände (e–s Werkes) *odd volumes*, ∼e Nummern (e–r Zeitschrift) *odd numbers* | *single* (*rooms*) **2.** (mehrere) *several, some* (*people*); → einige **II.** adv *individually*; *separately, severally, singly* ‖ (etw) ∼ angeben *to detail, particularize, specify* ‖ ∼ angetrieben *independent* (*machine*) ‖ ∼ benutzen *to use singly*; *to use piecemeal* ‖ ∼ behandeln *to treat separately* ‖ ∼ betrachtet (*or* genommen) *individually*; *severally* ‖ ∼ eintreten *to enter one at a time, to enter one by one* (od *in singles*) ‖ (Bücher) ∼ verkaufen *to sell separately* ‖ (Ware) ∼ verkaufen *to retail*, ∼ verkauft w *to retail* (*z at*) ‖ → einzelne 2.

·**einzelne** [abs & s] **1.** [der ∼, ein ∼er] m *single p, single man* ‖ *individual*; *person* ‖ jeder ∼ *every one*; *each one* (*of them*) ‖ die Interessen aller u jedes ∼n *all and singular interests* ‖ ∼ [pl] *several persons* (od *individuals*) [pl]; *several* (*of you*); *some* **2.** das ∼ [ein ∼s] *single thing*; *particular point*; *detail, particular* ‖ ∼s *one point, some points* | **im** ∼n (→ einzeln II.) *individually*; *separately*; *severally* ‖ im ∼n behandeln *to treat in detail*; im ∼n beschreiben *to describe in detail*; *to detail, particularize* ‖ das Ganze im ∼n wie in der Gesamtheit genommen *the whole severally and collectively* ‖ **ins** ∼ gehen *to go into* (od *come down to*) *detail*; *to individualize*; bis ins einzelnste *down to the smallest* od *slightest detail*; jdm bis ins einzelnste erzählen, wie .. *to tell a p to the smallest d. of how* ..; → Einzelheit

·**Einzieh-** **~band** n *sliver* ≗**bar** a *retractable* **~fahrgestell, ~fahrwerk** n ⟨aero⟩ *retr. landing gear* **~geschwindigkeit** f *web-feeding speed* **~getriebe** n (Kran) *luffing* od *derricking gear* **~haspel** f *feeding-in winch* **~kran** m (*level*) *luffing crane* **~schacht** m *downcast shaft* **~stellung** f *retracted position* **~vorrichtung** f *retracting gear* **~walzen** f pl *feed rollers*

·**ein|ziehen** vt/i **I.** vt [h] **A.** etw ∼ **1.** (Luft) *to draw in*; *to inhale*; (durch die Nase) *to sniff* **2. a.** e–n Faden in e–e Nadel ∼ *to thread a needle* **b.** (Balken) *to put in*; *to insert*; *set*; → einsetzen **3. a.** (Fahne) *to lower, strike* **b.** (Segel) *to take in*; *to furl* **c.** (die Hörner, den Bauch) *to draw in* ‖ (of dog) mit –gezogenem Schwanz *with his tail between his legs* **4.** ⟨typ⟩ (Zeile) = einrücken **5.** (zurückziehen) (Münzen) *to call in*; (Banknoten) *to retire* ‖ (Boje etc) *to withdraw*; (Fahrwerk) *to retract* ‖ ⟨mil⟩ (etw) wegen Untauglichkeit ∼ *to condemn* ‖ (Führerschein) ⟨mot⟩ *to take away, to impound* ‖ (Paß, Veröffentlichung) *to withdraw* ‖ (Stelle) → abbauen, einsparen **6. a.** (Beiträge, Steuern) *to collect*; (Schulden) *to call in* ‖ (Wechsel) *to cash* **b.** (Lehen, Eigentum) *to confiscate, seize*; → verwirken, → eingezogen **c.** Erkundigungen ~ *to collect* (od *gather*) *information, to make inquiries* (bei jdm über etw *of a p on* [od *about*] *a th*) **B.** jdn ~ **1.** ⟨mil⟩ *to call up*; *to conscript, induct*; → einberufen ‖ zur Übung –gezogen w *to be recalled to the colours* **2.** = einsperren **II.** vi [s] **1.** (P) **a.** ⟨mil⟩ *to march in*; ~ in *to march into, to enter* (*a town*) **b.** ⟨parl⟩ *to come in* (*with a big majority*) **c.** (in ein Haus etc ~) *to move* (od *settle*) *in*; ~ in *to move into* (*a house*) **2. a.** (of months) *to come in* ‖ der Winter ist –gezogen *winter has made its appearance* (od *has appeared on the scene*) **b.** (of liquids) *to be absorbed*; ~ in *to ooze* (od *penetrate, percolate*) *into*; *to percolate, penetrate, permeate* (*a th*) ·**Einziehen** n **1.** *drawing in*; *intake* (*of a breath*) **2.** ~ e–s Fadens in e–e Nadel *the threading of a needle* **3.** *lowering* (*of a flag*); *taking in* (*of the sail*) **4.** ⟨typ⟩ *indentation, indention* (*of a line*) **5.** (of liquids) *percolation, penetration* (in *into the soil*) ‖ → Einzug

·**Einziehung** f ~/~en **1.** → Einziehen **2.** *calling in*; *withdrawal* (*of a buoy*); ~ wegen Untauglichkeit *condemnation* (*of a fire-arm*) **3.** *collection* (*of taxes*); *cashing* (*of a bill*) **4.** *confiscation* (*of property*); *seizure* **5.** ~ v Erkundigungen *the gathering of information* **6.** ⟨mil⟩ *calling up* (*of a p*); *conscription* ‖ → Einzug

·**einzig I.** a **A.** [attr] **1.** (P) *only*, ein ~es Kind *an only child*; ⟨Am⟩: *C.'s all the daughter we have* ‖ ihr ~([st!])er Sohn *their one and only son*; die ~en Leute *the only people* ‖ *sole* (*heir*); → alleinig ‖ [neg] *single*: nicht ein ~er Mensch *not a single man* (*was to be seen*) **2.** (S) *only, single, sole* ‖ mit der ~en Ausnahme *with the single exception* (*of* ..) ‖ das ~e Buch über .. *the only book on* .. ‖ ⟨emph⟩ *the one and only* (*hope*) ‖ ein ~es Mal *only once*; nicht ein ~es Mal *not once* (*they had never once quarelled*); es ist m–e ~e Sorge .. *all I am worrying about is* ..; nicht ein ~es Wort *not a single word, never a word* | tu mit die ~e Liebe abzureisen *do leave, do it to please me* ‖ e–e ~e Stimme ging durch das Volk *the people spoke with a single voice* (od *with one v.*) | [nur nach *a, one*] *solitary*; (nicht) ein ~es Beispiel (*not*) *a solitary instance*; mit e–r ~en Ausnahme *with one solitary exception* (→ o.) **B.** [pred] *unique*; *singular*; *unexampled, unparalleled, unrivalled*; es ist ~ in s–r Art *it is unique of its kind* (od *unique*); ~ dastehen *to be unique, to stand alone, to be without parallel* **II.** adv **1.** *only*; *merely*; ~ u allein, weil .. (*simply and*) *solely because* .. ‖ das steht ~ da *this is without parallel* **2.** [vor Adj. u Adv.] *exceedingly, singularly* (*beautiful*), *extremely*; es ist das ~ Wahre *that's just the thing* **III.** [abs] **1.** der ~e *the only one*; die ~en [pl] *the only ones, the only people* [pl] ‖ unser ~er *our only son* ‖ nicht ein ~er *not a single one* od *p* **2.** das ~e *the only thing*

·**einzigartig 1.** a *unique* (*scholar*); *singular*; *remarkable* ‖ *signal* (*victory*); *rare* (*event*) ‖ *outstanding, extraordinary* (*merits*) ‖ [pred] = einzig B. **2.** adv *uniquely*; *splendidly* | **~keit** f *oneness, uniqueness, etc*

·**einzimmerig** a *one-roomed* (*cottage*)

·**einzöllig** a *one-inch* [attr]

·**ein|zuckern** vt [h] *to* (*preserve in*) *sugar*

·**Einzug** m ~(e)s/≟e **A.** [abstr] **1. a.** *march*(*ing*) *in* (*of troops*); ~ in *marching into* (*the town*); ‖ *entry* (*of the king*; in *into*) ‖ s–n ~ halten *to march in*; .. halten in .. *to enter* (*a town*) **b.** (of a season) *coming in*; *appearance, coming* (*of spring*); s–n ~ halten *to make one's appearance* **2.** *moving in*; ~ in *moving into* (*a house*) ‖ → Einziehen; Einziehung **~sgebiet** (e–s Flusses) *catchment* od *drainage basin* od *area*: (e–s Stroms) *headwaters* pl **B.** [konkr] **1.** ⟨weav⟩ *warp* **2.** ⟨typ⟩ (eingerückte Zeile) *inden*(*ta*)*tion* **~smarsch** m ⟨mus⟩ *march celebrating the entry of a p* **~sschmaus** m *house-warming* (*party*)

·**ein|zwängen** vt [h] **1.** (etw) *to jam* od *squeeze in*; ~ in .. *to cram* (od *intrude, jam, squeeze*) *into* ..; ~ zw *to sandwich* (*in*) *between* .. ‖ jdn ~ = einengen **2. sich ~ in** *to squeeze o.s. into*

·**Einzylindermaschine** f *single-cylinder machine*

Eis n ·Eises/ **1. a.** *ice* ‖ Kunst≟ *artificial ice* ‖ mit ~ bedeckt s *to be iced over* ‖ → einbrechen II. A. 2. ‖ aufs ~ gehen *to go skating* ‖ (etw) auf ~ legen, in ~ kühlen *to ice*; Champagner auf ~ *iced champagne* ‖ ⟨cul⟩ auf ~ kühlen *to refrigerate* ‖ → gefrieren ‖ etw auf ~ legen *to put* od *place a th into cold storage* ⟨a. fig⟩; (Nahrungsmittel) *to put .. on ice* ‖ ⟨fig⟩ auf ~ legen (aufschieben) *to shelve, pigeon-hole* **b.** ⟨übtr & fig⟩ ein Herz v ~ *a hard* (od *unfeeling*) *heart* ‖ das ~ war gebrochen *the ice was broken* ‖ jdn aufs ~ führen *to lead a p astray* (od *on dangerous ground*); *to impose upon a p*; *to involve a p in difficulties*; → einwickeln, nasführen ‖ aufs ~ gehen *to be led astray* **2.** ⟨cul⟩ (Speise≟) *ice*, (~creme) *ice-cream*; → Sorbett ‖ ein ~ essen *to have* (od *take*) *an ice*; drei ~, bitte *three ices, please*; ~ am Stiel *ice lolly*; (Martini) mit ~ (*M.*) *on the rocks*

·**Eis** n ~/ ⟨mus⟩ ['eis] *E sharp*; → Dis

·**Eis-** [in comp] *ice* ‖ ⟨geol⟩ *glacial* **~axt** f *ice-axe* **~bahn** f (*ice-*)*rink* **~baiser** n *ice-cream meringue*, → Baiser **~bank** f *field of ice* **~bär** m ⟨zoo⟩ *polar* od *white bear* **~barre** f *ice-barrage* **~baum** m (am Schiff) *ice-beam* **~becher** m ⟨cul⟩ *ice-bowl*, (*i.-c.*) *coupe* Fr ≟**bedeckt** a *ice-covered* **~behälter** m *i.-pail* **~bein** n → d. **~berg** m *iceberg*; *hummock* **~beutel** m ⟨med⟩ *ice-bag* **~bildung** f ⟨bes aero⟩ *formation of ice*, ⟨meteor⟩ *glaciation* **~blase** f ⟨med⟩ *ice-bag* **~blick, ~blink** m *iceblink* **~block** m *ice-block* **~blume** f ⟨bot⟩ = Eiskraut ‖ ⟨übtr⟩ ~n [pl] (auf Glas) *frostwork*; *ice-ferns* [pl]; *patterns* **~bombe** f ⟨cul⟩ (*ice-*)*-bomb, mazarine* Fr **~brecher** m (Schiff) *ice-breaker, ice-boat*; (Brückenschutz) *ice apron*; *dolphin*; (Getränk) *toddy* **~creme** f → –krem **~decke** f *layer of ice*; *ice-sheet*; *frozen surface* **~diele** f *i.-c. parlo*(*u*)*r* **~ente** f ⟨orn⟩ *hareld*; *old wife* **~essig** m ⟨chem⟩ *glacial acetic acid* **~fabrik** f *ice*(*-making*) *plant* **~feld** n *ice-field*; (Pack≟) *ice-pack* **~fläche** f *frozen surface*; *expanse* (od *sheet*) *of ice* ≟**frei** a *ice-free* (*port*) ‖ ⟨com⟩ Verschiffung erst bei ~em Wasser *f. o. w.* (= *first open water*) **~fischerei** f *ice-fishing* **~fjord** m *Ice Fjord* **~gang** m *the breaking up and drifting of the ice* ≟**gekühlt** a *ice-cooled*; ~e Flasche *iced bottle* **~glas** n ⟨tech⟩ *frosted glass* **~glätte** f *silver frost* ≟**grau** a *hoary* (vom Alter *with age*) **~grenze** f ⟨geol⟩ *glacial limit* od *boundary* **~gürtel** m (der Arktis) *ice-foot* **~haken** m *ice-hook* **~hang** m *ice slope* | die 3 **~heiligen** m pl (Maifröste) *May 11th to 13th*, → Eismänner **~hockey** n ⟨sport⟩ *ice-hockey*; | ~scheibe [f] *puck* ~stock [m] *i.-h. stick* **~hügel** m *hummock* **~jacht** f *ice-boat, ice-yacht* **~kaffee** m *iced coffee, c. ice-cream* ≟**kalt** a *icily* (od *very*) *cold* **~kälte** f *icy cold*(*ness*) **~kammer** f, **~kasten** m *ice-box* (od *closet*); *refrigerating-chamber* **~kegeln** n = Eisschießen **~keller** m *ice-house* **~kluft** f (Frostriß) *frost shake* **~klumpen** m *ice-lump* **~kompresse** f ⟨med⟩ *ice-compress* (od *poultice*) **~kraut** n ⟨bot⟩ *ice-plant*; *mesembryanthemum* [L] **~krem** m *cream ice*, ⟨Am⟩ *i.-c.*; ~ mit Schokoladen– *or* Buttersoße ⟨Am⟩ *sundae*(*s*) | ~hütchen [n] *i.-c. cone* **~kristallansatz** m ⟨aero⟩ *ice accretion* **~kübel** m (f Wein) *ice-pail* **~kunstlauf** m *figure-skating* **~kunstläufer** m *figure-skater* **~laden** m *ice-shop* **~landschaft** f *ice-scape* **~lauf** m, **~laufen** n *skating* **~läufer** m *skater* **~laufmeisterschaft** f *figure-skating championship* **~loch** n *ice-hole*; → Eisspalt **~mann** m *iceman*,

⟨fam⟩ *ice(-cream) Jack*; die ≃er *the Ice Saints, Icemen*, → –heilige **~maschine** f ⟨cul⟩ *ice-machine*; *ice-maker*; ⟨Am⟩ *i.-c. freezer* **~masse** f ausgedehnte ~ *sheet of ice, ice-sheet* **~meer** n *the frozen ocean*; Nördliches (Südliches) ~ *the Arctic* (*Antarctic*) *Ocean* **~milch** f *iced milk* **~nadel** f *ice-needle, ice-particle* **~nagel** m (auf Schuhsohlen) *ice-spur*; → Eisstollen **~packung** f ⟨med⟩ *ice-pack* **~papier** n *ice-paper* **~pflanze** f ⟨bot⟩ = Eiskraut **~picke** f, **~pickel** m *ice-axe* **~punkt** m *freezing point* **~punsch** m *iced punch* **~regen** m *sleet* **~rinde** f *layer* (od *coating*) *of ice* ⟨a. fig⟩ **~salon** m *i.-c. parlour* **~scharbe** f ⟨orn⟩ = Kormoran **~schieben** n = Eisschießen **~schießen** n ⟨engl⟩ *curling* **~schmelze** f *ice--melting* **~schnellaufen** n *speed-skating* **~schnell-läufer** m *speed-skater* **~scholle** f *cake* (od *layer*) *of ice*; treibende ~ (*ice-*)*floe*; *floating sheet of ice*; *ice-raft* **~schrank** m *refrigerator*, ⟨fam⟩ *fridge*, ⟨Am⟩ *icebox*, (f Fleisch) *ice-safe* ‖ ⟨Am a.⟩ *kelvinator* **~schuh** m = Schlittschuh **~segelboot** n, **~jacht** f *ice-boat, ice-yacht* **~segeln** n *ice-boating*; *skate-sailing* **~segler** m *ice-boatman* **~spalt** m; tiefer ~ *ice-gorge* **~spat** m ⟨minr⟩ *adularia* [L]; → Orthoklas **~spiel** n *ice-game* ‖ ⟨engl⟩ *curling* **~sporen** m [pl] *ice-spurs*; *creepers* [pl] **~sport** m *ice-sports* [pl] **~sprosse** f (2. Sprosse am Geweih) *bez-antler* **~spur** f *ice-mark* **~stock** m (beim Eisschießen) *curling stone* **~stollen** m (am Hufeisen) *calkin* **~stück** n; ~e [pl] *broken ice* **~tätigkeit** ⟨geol⟩ *ice-action* **~taucher** m ⟨orn⟩ *ember* **~technik** f (Kunstlauf) *ice-craft* **~treiben** n *drift*(*ing of*) *ice, ice-drift* **~tüte** f *ice-cone* **~vergiftung** f *ice--poisoning* **~verkäufer** m *iceman* **~vogel** m ⟨orn⟩ *halcyon*; *kingfisher* ‖ ⟨ent⟩ *white admiral* **~wasser** n *iced water* **~würfel** m ⟨cul⟩ *ice-cube*; auf ~n (*drink*) *on the rocks* **~wüste** f *frozen waste* **~zacke**, f **~zapfen** m *icicle* **~zeit** f ⟨geol⟩ *glacial period* (od *epoch, era*); *ice-age* **≃zeitlich** n *glacial* (*deposit*) **~zone** f *frigid zone*

·**Eisbein** n **1.** ⟨cul⟩ *pig's knuckles, pettitoes* pl (*pickled*) *pig-trotters* [pl] **2.** °⟨fig⟩ ~e [pl] *cold feet*

·**Eisen** n ~s/~ **A.** (Metall) **1.** *iron*; U-~ *channel iron*; Roh≃ *pig-iron*; → Ballast≃ ‖ Guß≃ *cast iron*; Schmiede≃ *wrought iron* ‖ aus ~ *made of iron*; ein Tor aus ~ *an iron gate* ‖ (etw) mit ~ beschlagen *to iron* ‖ e–n Stock mit ~ beschlagen *to put a ferrule on a stick*; mit ~ beschlagen [a] *ironed* (*trunk*), *iron-sheathed* (*door*); *iron-bound* (*gate*); mit ~ gepanzert *ironclad* ‖ ~ schmieden *to work iron* | ⟨chem⟩ *iron*; → Eisen– 2.; essigsaures ~ *iron acetate*; kohlensaures ~ *iron carbonate* | altes ~ *scrap*; *scrap iron*; ⟨fam⟩ *junk* **2.** ⟨fig⟩ **a.** Not bricht ~ *necessity knows no law*; zwei ~ im Feuer h *to have two strings to one's bow*; noch ein ~ im F. h *to have still a shot in one's locker*; viele ~ im F. h *to have quite a number of irons in the fire*, z viele ~ im F. h *to have too many irons in the f.* ‖ man muß das ~ schmieden, solange es heiß ist *strike while the iron is hot* ‖ ein heißes ~ ⟨fig⟩ *a hot brick* ‖ (Maschine, System) zum alten ~ werfen *to throw .. on the scrap heap*; *to scrap*; ⟨fam⟩ *to junk*; (jdn) *to shelve*; ⟨Am⟩ *to throw into the discard*; z alten ~ getan s *to be on the shelf*; er gehört z alten ~ *he's no longer any use* **b.** hart wie ~ *as hard as iron* (od *steel*) ‖ eine Gesundheit wie aus ~ *an iron constitution*; Muskeln (wie) aus ~ *muscles of iron* ‖ → Blut **B. 1.** (Gerät aus ~) **a.** *iron, iron tool* od *instrument*; → Brech≃; Stech≃; Stemm≃ **b.** ~, Plätt≃ *iron*; ~, Bügel≃ *flat iron* **c.** = Sense **d.** → Fang≃ **e.** ~, Fesseln aus ~ *irons, fetters, shackles* [pl]; (jdn) in ~ legen *to put in irons*; in ~ liegen *to be in irons* **f.** → Hufeisen **g.** ⟨golf⟩ → Schläger **2.** ⟨mst poet⟩ *sword, weapon* ‖ *dagger* ‖ ⟨sl⟩ *fire-arm, iron*; *pistol* **C.** ⟨med⟩ (~präparat) *iron, steel*; ~ nehmen *to take iron*

*·**eisen** vt/i [h] ⟨poet⟩ **1.** vt (jds Blut) *to ice*; *to freeze*; → vereisen **2.** vi *to ice*; *to turn to ice*; *to freeze*

·**Eisenach** n ⟨Ger⟩ (Stadt)

·**Eisen-** [in comp] **1.** *iron*; ⟨minr⟩ *ferro–* **2.** ⟨chem⟩ (dreiwertig) *ferric, ferri–* ‖ (zweiwertig) *ferrous, ferro–* **3.** ⟨med⟩ *ferruginous* **~abfall** m *iron scrap*; *scrap-iron* **~alaun** m *iron alum* **~arbeit** f ⟨tech⟩ *ironwork* **≃arm** a *poor in iron* **~zetat** n ⟨chem⟩ *ferric acetate* **~bahn** f → d. **~bakterien** f [pl] ⟨biol⟩ *iron-bacteria* [L pl] **~band** n *iron hoop* **~barren** m *pig of iron*; *billet* **~bau** m [konkr] *iron building*; *structure of iron* **~baum** m ⟨bot⟩ *ironwood tree* **~beize** f *iron mordant*; *iron acetate*; ⟨bookb⟩ *iron-liquor* **~bergwerk** n *iron-mine* **~beschlag** m ⟨tech⟩ *ironwork fittings* (od *mountings*) [pl], ≃e [pl] *ironworks* **~beton** m *ferro-concrete*; *reinforced concrete*; ~ mit Backsteinverkleidung *reinforced concrete faced with bricks* ‖ ~brücke [f] *ferro--concrete bridge* **~blau** n ⟨minr⟩ *vivianite* ‖ ~säure [f] ⟨chem⟩ *ferro-cyanic acid* **~blech** n ⟨tech⟩ *iron-plate*; *sheet iron*; → –walzwerk **~blüte** f ⟨minr⟩ *aragonite* **~draht** m *iron wire*; ~seil [n] *iron rope* | (gegen) **~einfall** m ⟨mill⟩ (*to prevent*) *tram iron from entering* **~erz** n ⟨min⟩ *iron ore* **~farbe** f *iron colour*; *iron pigment* **~feilicht** n → Eisenspäne **≃fest** a *hard* (od *firm*) *as iron* **~fleck** m *iron-mould* **~fresser** m ⟨fig⟩ *bully, hector, braggart* **~gang** m ⟨min⟩ *iron-lode* **~gans** f *iron-pig* **~gehalt** m *ferruginous ingredients* [pl] **~gewinnung** f *iron-production* (od *yield*) **~glanz** m *iron-glance* **~gießer** m *iron--founder* **~gießerei** f [abstr] *iron-founding* ‖ [konkr] *iron-foundry*; *ironworks* [pl] **~gitter** n *iron grating* **~glanz** m *specular iron ore* **~glimmer** m ⟨minr⟩ *micaceous iron-ore* **≃grau** a *iron-grey* **~graupen** f [pl] *granular bog iron ore* **~grube** f ⟨min⟩ *iron-mine* **~guß** m *iron casting*; *cast iron* ‖ ~ware [f] *cast-iron ware* **≃haltig** a *ferriferous, ferruginous*; *ferrous*; (of water) *chalybeate* **~hammer** m (Werkzeug) *forge* (od *sledge*)--*hammer* ‖ (Fabrik) *forge*; *ironworks* [pl] **~handel** m *iron-trade* **~händler** m *ironmonger*; beim ~ *at the ironmonger's* **~handlung** f *ironmongery, ironmonger's shop* **≃hart** a *hard as iron* **~holz** n *ironwood* **~hut** m ⟨bot⟩ *aconite*; *monk's-hood* ‖ Gelber ~ *wolf's bane* **~hütte** f *ironworks* [pl]; *forge* ‖ ~nbesitzer [m] *iron-master* ‖ ~nkunde [f], ~nwesen [n] *iron-metallurgy* **~hydroxid** n ⟨chem⟩ *ferric hydroxide* **~-industrie** f *iron-industry*; *iron-manufacture* **~industri·eller** m *ironmaster* **~jodid** n ⟨chem⟩ *ferrous iodide* **~karbid** n ⟨chem⟩ *iron-carbide* **~karbonyl** n ⟨chem⟩ *iron carbonyl* **~kies** m ⟨minr⟩ *iron pyrites* [pl] **~kitt** m *iron cement* **~klumpen** m → Bramme, Luppe **~kraut** n ⟨bot⟩ *vervain*; *verbena* [L] **~kur** f ⟨med⟩ *use of iron*; *course of tonics*; e–e ~ m *to take iron* **~lack** m *iron-varnish* **~laden** m *ironmongery*; *ironmonger's shop*; er ist im ~ *he is at the ironmonger's* **~ocker** m ⟨minr⟩ *iron-ochre* **~oolith** m ⟨minr⟩ *iron-oolite* **~oxalat** n ⟨chem⟩ *iron-oxalate* **~oxid** n ⟨chem⟩ *ferric oxide* **~platte** f *iron plate* **~präparat** n ⟨med⟩ *preparation of iron* **~quelle** f *chalybeate spring* **~rost** m *iron-rust* **~sau** f (Barren) *sow* od *pig of iron* **~säuerling** m *chalybeate water* **~säure** f ⟨chem⟩ *ferric acid* **~schiene** f ⟨med⟩ ~n [pl] *irons, iron-supports* [pl] **~schlacke** f *iron slag* **~schmelze** f *iron--foundry* **~schmied** m *blacksmith* **~schmiede** f *smithy, forge* **≃schüssig** a → eisenhaltig **~-schwamm** m ⟨tech⟩ *iron-sponge* **~schwelle** f ⟨tech⟩ *iron sleeper* **~sorten** f pl *irons* **~späne** m [pl] *iron--filings* [pl] **~spat** m ⟨minr⟩ *siderite*; *spathic iron-ore* **~spitze** f (Zaun≃) *spike* **~stange** f *iron* *rod* **~stein** m ⟨minr⟩ *ironstone* **~sulfat** n ⟨chem⟩ *iron-sulphate* **~sulfid** n ⟨chem⟩ *iron* od *ferrous sulphide* **~teilchen** n *particle of iron* **~tinktur** f *iron-tincture, tincture of iron* **~träger** m ⟨arch⟩ *iron girder* **~tropfen** m [pl] ⟨med⟩ *steel-drops* [pl] **~vitriol** n ⟨chem⟩ *iron-vitriol; green copperas* **~(blech)walzwerk** n *flattening mill* **~waren** f [pl] *hardware, ironmongery, ironware* | ~händler *ironmonger*; ⟨Am⟩ *hardware dealer* **~wasser** n *chalybeate water* **~werk** n (Fabrik) *ironworks* [pl] **~zaun** m *iron railing*; ⟨Am⟩ *iron fence* **~zeit** f ⟨praeh⟩ *the iron age* **~zucker** m *iron saccharate* **~zyanid** n ⟨chem⟩ *ferric cyanide* **~zyanür** n *ferrous cyanide*

·**Eisenbahn** f ~/~en *railway, rail*; ⟨Am⟩ *railroad, rail*; → Bahn 5. ‖ auf der ~ [koll] *on the railways* ‖ mit der ~, per ~ *by rail, by train*; (*to travel*) *by rail* ‖ frei ~ *free on rail* (abbr *f. o. r.*) ‖ (Güter) mit der ~ befördern *to rail* | ⟨fig⟩ es ist die höchste ~ *it is high time, there is no time to lose*

·**Eisenbahn-** [in comp] *railway*; ⟨Am⟩ *railroad*; → Bahn– **~abteil** n *r. compartment* **~aktie** f *r. share*; ~n [pl] *rails* [pl] **~arbeiter** m → Bahn– **~artillerie** f *r. artillery* **~aufmarsch** m ⟨tact⟩ *strategic concentration by rail* **~bau** m **1.** [abstr] *railroading* **2.** [konkr] *r. building* (od *construction*) | ~bataillon [n] *r. c. battalion* **~bauer** m *r. engineer*; ⟨Am⟩ *railroader* **~beamte** [der ~, ein ~er] m *r. official*; *r. man* **~betrieb** m *r. service* od *operation* | ~swerk [n] *r.-repair shop* **~bezirk** m ⟨Ger⟩ *r. district* **~brücke** f *r. bridge* **~damm** m *r. embankment* **~dienst** m *r. service* **~direktion** f ⟨Ger⟩ *r. administration* (*of a province*) ‖ ⟨engl⟩ *body of managers, board of directors* **~fähre** f *r. ferry* **~fahrkarte** f (*r.*) *ticket* **~fahrplan** m *time-table* **~fahrt** f *r.* (od *train*) *journey*; ⟨Am⟩ *train ride* **~flak** f *r.-mounted A.A.A.* **~fracht** f *r. freight* **~fundbüro** n *R. Lost Property Office* **~geschütz** n *r.-mounted gun* **~gesellschaft** f ⟨engl⟩ *r. company* **~gleis** n *r. track* **~karte** f *r. map* **~knotenpunkt** m *r. centre* **~lafette** f ⟨artill⟩ *r. mount* **~linie** f *r. line* ‖ ⟨Am⟩ *railroad, road*; kürzeste ~ ⟨Am⟩ *air-line* **~minister** m ⟨engl⟩ *Minister for R.s* **~netz** n *network of r.s, r. network* **~projekt** n *r. scheme* **~schaffner** m *r. guard* **~schiene** f (*r.*) *rail* **~schranke** f *level crossing gate* **~schwelle** f *sleeper* **~station** f *r. station* **~strecke** f *line, section*; ⟨Am⟩ *division* **~tarif** m *r. rates* [pl] **~transport** m *transport by rail* **~unfall** m *r. accident* **~unglück** n *r. disaster*; ⟨Am a.⟩ *wreck* **~verbindung** f *communication by rail*; → Anschluß **~verkehr** m *r. traffic* **~wagen** m *r. carriage* (od *coach*); ⟨Am⟩ *railroad car* ‖ → Güterwagen **~wesen** n [koll] *r.s* [pl]; ⟨Am⟩ *railroads* [pl] ‖ *r. system* **~zug** m *train*; ⟨Am a.⟩ *the cars* [pl]

·**Eisenbahner** m ~s/~ *rail(way)-man* (od *worker*) ⟨Am⟩ *railroad-man; trainman*

·**eisern** a **1.** ⟨eig⟩ **a.** *iron* (*gate*; *helmet*; *safe*) **b.** ~e Fahrt ⟨min⟩ *iron ladder* (*in a shaft*) ‖ ≈es Kreuz ⟨Ger⟩ *the Iron Cross* (seit 1813) ‖ ≈e Krone ⟨hist⟩ *the Iron Crown* (*of the kings of Lombardy*) ‖ ~e Lunge ⟨med⟩ *iron lung*(*s*) ‖ ≈es Tor ⟨geogr⟩ *the Iron Gates* [pl] ‖ ~er Vorhang ⟨theat⟩ *fire-proof curtain* ‖ ~es Zeitalter *the iron age* **2.** ⟨übtr⟩ **a.** ⟨jur⟩ *inalienable*; *inviolable*; *irreducible* **b.** ~er Bestand *iron* (od *last*) *reserve*; *permanent fund* ‖ ~es Lohngesetz [n] ⟨engl hist⟩ *the iron law of wages* **3.** ⟨fig⟩ **a.** der ≈e Herzog *the Iron Duke* (= *Wellington*) ‖ ⟨Ger⟩ der ≈e Kanzler (sc Bismarck) *the Chancellor of Blood and Iron* **b.** *iron* (*will*); *hard, strong, unyielding* ‖ ein ~er Besen ⟨fig⟩ *a new broom*; mit ~em B. regieren *to rule with a rod of iron* ‖ ~er Bestand ⟨fin⟩ *reserve* ‖ mit ~er Faust *with an iron grip* ‖ ~es Gesetz [n] ⟨fig⟩ *cast-iron rules* [pl] ‖ ~e Miene *stony look*; e–e ~e Miene aufsetzen *to set one's face like iron* ‖ die ~e Ration *the iron* od *emergency ration* ‖ ~es Sparen ⟨Ger⟩ *saving rigidly*; ~e Sparsamkeit f *rigid economy* ‖ mit ~er Stirn *brazen-facedly, brazenly*; *impudently* ‖ der ≈e Vorhang ⟨pol⟩ *the I. Curtain* **c.** *robust, strong*; ~e Gesundheit, Konstitution *iron constitution, a c. of iron* ‖ ~er Magen *cast-iron digestion* **d.** *unflinching, untiring, unwearying* (*industry*); *unflagging, unremitting* (*energy*), *unyielding*

·**eisig I.** a **1.** *icy* (*air, wind*; *water*); *glacial* (*weather*); ~e Kälte *iciness* **2.** ⟨fig⟩ *cold, frigid, icy* (*politeness, reception*); *cutting* (*callousness*); ~e Höflichkeit *icy, chilly, chilling, frigid politeness* **II.** adv *icily* (*cold*) ‖ ⟨fig⟩ (das Blut) ~kalt m *to freeze*; ~kalt w *to be frozen* (durch *by*) **≈keit** f ~/ bes ⟨fig⟩ *iciness*; *coldness*; *frigidity, frigidness*

·**eitel** a **A.** [unflektiert] (= nichts als; lauter; bloß) *pure* (*gold*); *sheer, simple*; ~ Betrug *fraud pure and simple*; *sheer* (*delight*); *pure* (*nonsense*); *sheer* (*waste of time*) ‖ jdm ~ Dunst vormachen *to throw dust in a p's eyes*; *to hoodwink* (od *humbug, mystify*; ⟨sl⟩ *bamboozle*) *a p* ‖ es ist nicht alles ~ Freude *it is not all cakes and ale* ‖ ~ Tand *vanities* pl, *vain trifles* pl **B.** [flektiert] **1.** (leer, nichtig) *vain* (*dream, pleasures, wish*); *idle* (*hope*); *empty* (*promises, words*); eitles Geschwätz *idle talk* ‖ *trivial*; *unsubstantial*; *frivolous* **2.** (eingebildet) *conceited, self-complacent, vain* (*p*); ~ auf *vain of* ‖ (putzsüchtig) *given to showy dressing*; *dressy, peacocky, showy*; ~ wie ein Pfau *proud as a peacock*

·**Eitelkeit** f ~/ **1.** *emptiness, futility, vainness, vanity* (*of human wishes*) **2.** *self-conceit, vanity* (*of a p*); ~en [pl] *vanities* [pl]; gekränkte ~ *injured vanity*

·**Eiter** m ~s/ ⟨path⟩ *matter, pus*; → eit(e)rig

·**Eiter-** [in comp] *pus–*; *purulent*; *suppurating*; → eit(e)rig **~ansammlung** f → Empyem; Hypopyon **~ausfluß** m *purulent discharge* **~beule** *abscess*; *ulcer* → Karbunkel ‖ kl ~ *boil* ‖ ⟨fig⟩ *festering boil* (an *on*); e–e ~ aufstechen *to cut open a f. b.* **~bildung** f *purulence, –cy* **~bläschen** n *pustule, blister* **~erreger** m *pus-former, pus-forming germ* **~fieber** n ⟨path⟩ *pyaemia* [L] **~flechte** f ⟨med⟩ *impetigo* [L] **~geschwulst** f **~geschwür** n *abscess* **~herd** m *pus-focus*; Abflußkanal e–s ~es *fistula* **~höhle** f *pus-cavity* **~körperchen** n *pus-corpuscle* **~vergiftung** f ⟨path⟩ *pyaemia* [L] **~zelle** f *pus-cell*

·**eit(e)rig** a *purulent*; *suppurating, suppurative*; *ulcerated*; ~er Ausfluß *gleet*; *purulent discharge*

·**eitern I.** vi [h] **1.** *to suppurate*; *fester*; *ulcerate*; (of pustules) *to maturate*; das Geschwür eitert *the ulcer discharges matter* **2.** ⟨fig⟩ *to fester, rankle*; *to come to a head*; → Eiterbeule **II.** ≈ n *festering*; z ~ bringen *to fester, to ulcerate*; *to bring to a head*; z ~ bringend *maturative* | **~d** a *festering*; *ulcerative, ulcerous*; ~e Wunde *fester* | ⟨fig⟩ *festering* (*sore*); *rankling* (*poison*); → eiterig, Eiterbeule ·**Eit(e)rung** f ~/~en *suppuration, festering*; *maturation*; ~ hervorrufend *suppurative*

·**Eiweiß** n *white of egg, albumen*; *protein* ‖ ~ z Bestreichen *glair* ‖ mit ~ bestreichen *to glair* ‖ ~ z Schnee schlagen ⟨cul⟩ *to beat the whites of egg until it is stiff* **~abbau** m ⟨physiol, chem⟩ *breaking down* (od *decomposition*) *of protein* **~spaltung** f *cleavage of pr.*; *proteolysis*

·**Eiweiß-** [in comp] *albuminoid* ‖ *glaireous, glairy* **≈haltig** a *albuminous, albuminoid* **~harnen** n ⟨path⟩ *albuminuria* [L] **~körper** m ⟨chem⟩ einfacher ~ *protein*; zus–gesetzte ~ [pl] *proteids* [pl] **≈spaltend** a *proteolytic* **~stoff** m ⟨chem⟩ → –körper **~substanz** f *albuminoid substance*

Ejakulati·on f *ejaculation* **Ejekti·on** f *ejection*

Ej·ektor m ~s/–·oren ⟨tech⟩ *ejector* → Auswerfer

Ekart·é n [Fr] ~s/~s ⟨cards⟩ *écarté* (Fr)

Ekchym·ose f (Blutaustritt) *ecchymosis* [L]

·Ekel I. m ~s/ **1.** *disgust* (*to eat with d.*); *nausea*; *satiety*; *surfeit* **2.** (Abscheu) *disgust* (über, vor *at*; gegen *for*) ‖ (Widerwille) *aversion* (gegen *to*, *from*); *distate* (*for*); *dislike* (od *horror*, *satiety*) (*of*); *loathing* (über, vor *at*) ‖ e–n ~ bek *to take a disgust* (vor *at*); *to be sickened* (beim Anblick v *by the sight of* ..) ‖ *repulsion* (vor *for a th*), *aversion* (*for meat*); ~ vor sich selbst *self--loathing* ‖ ~ empfinden *to nauseate*; *to shudder*, *sicken* (über, vor *at*); *to be disgusted* (über *at*; vor *with*); er empfand ~, ~(gefühl) stieg in ihm hoch *his gorge rose* ‖ (jdn) mit ~ erfüllen *to nauseate*, *sicken* ‖ e–n ~ h vor *to feel an aversion to* od *for* (od *a horror of*); *to abhor*, *abominate*, *loathe* (*a th*) **3.** (Gegenstand des ~s **a.** *object of disgust* ‖ *abhorrence*; *aversion*; °diese Krawatten sind mir ein ~ *these ties are my chief* (⟨hum⟩ *pet*) *aversion* ‖ er ist ihnen ein ~ *he is an eyesore to them* ‖ es ist mir zum ~ (geworden) *I am sickened* (od *sick*) *of it*; *I loathe it* ‖ s–e übertriebene Unterwürfigkeit wird einem zum ~ *his servility disgusts* od *nauseates one*; etw bis z ~ wiederholen *to repeat a th ad nauseam*; → anekeln **II.** °~ n ~s/~ (P) *disgusting* (⟨fam⟩ *pestilent*) *fellow*; das ~ *the wretch* ‖ ⟨sl⟩ *sickener*, *stinker*, *cuss*, *stiff*; ⟨Am sl⟩ *shag nasty* → Nörgler | **~gefühl** n = Ekel m

·ekelerregend a *disgusting*, *loathsome*; *nauseating*, *nauseous*; *sickening*; *nasty*; *unpleasant*; *repugnant*; → **·ekelhaft 1.** a **a.** *disgusting sickly*, *offensive* (*smell*); *loathsome*; *nauseous*; *sickening*; *hideous*; in ~er Weise *disgustingly* ‖ *detestable*; *heathenish*; *foul* (*crime*) **b.** °⟨übtr⟩ *nasty*; *beastly*; *troublesome* (*job*); *unpleasant*; *wretched* (*pain*; *weather*); ~es Gefühl *wretchedness* | ⟨fam⟩ *vile* (*hat*, *pen*); *foul* (*journey*); *pestilential* ‖ ⟨sl⟩ *putrid* (*book*, *play*); *sticky* (*business*) ‖ ⟨Am⟩ *pesky* (*idleness*) ‖ m–e Erkältung ist wirklich ~ *my cold is perfectly foul*; ein ~er Schlag *a sickener of a blow* ‖ e–e ~e Nacht ⟨sl⟩ *a beast of a night* **c.** (P) ein ~er Kerl ⟨fam⟩ *a pestilent* od *sickening fellow*, ⟨sl⟩ *a sickener*; ~e Gesellschaft *nasty fellows* ‖ ⟨sl⟩ *slimy* (*liar*) ‖ °er ist ihnen ~ *he is an eyesore to them* ‖ → widerlich, widerwärtig, zuwider **2.** adv *disgustingly loathsomely*; *sickeningly* ‖ *wretchedly* ‖ ein ~ langweiliger Mensch ⟨fam⟩ *a pestilential bore*

·Ekelhaftigkeit f *disgustingness*, *loathsomeness* ‖ *nastiness*, *wretchedness*; *fulsomeness*

·ekeln 1. vt [imps & refl] [h] es ekelt mich (*or* mir) vor Fisch, ich ekle mich vor F. *fish sickens me*, *f. makes me sick*; *I hate fish* ‖ es ekelte ihn bei dem Anblick *he was sickened by the sight* ‖ es ekelt mich, wenn ich denke, daß .. *it makes me sick to think that* ..; es ekelt mich (an) *or* davor *it disgusts me*; *it makes me sick* | ⟨übtr⟩ es ekelt mich (*or* mir) vor etw, ich ekle mich vor etw *I am disgusted with a th*; *I feel an aversion to* (od *for*); *I feel a horror of a th*; *I loathe* (od *abhor*, *abominate*, *detest*, *hate*) *a th*; (*he*, *it*) *gives me a pain in the neck* | es ekelt mich (an) z tun *it disgusts me to do*, *I loathe to do*, *I hate to do* (od *doing*), *I detest doing* ‖ → anekeln, –widern **2.** ≗ n; es ist zum ~ *it is disgusting*

Eklamps·ie f ⟨med⟩ *eclampsia* [L]

Ekl·at [e:ˈkla] m [Fr] ~s/~s **1.** *explosion* **2.** ⟨fig⟩ *éclat* (Fr); *success* ‖ *sensation*; → Aufsehen **eklat·ant** a *conspicuous* (*case*); *striking* ‖ *sensational* ‖ *blatant* (Lüge)

Ekl·ektiker m ⟨philos⟩ *eclectic* **ekl·ektisch** a *eclectic* **Eklektiz·ismus** m *eclecticism*

·eklig I. a **1.** = ekelhaft **2.** ° = gehörig, tüchtig **3.** °~ w *to get angry* (od *rough*, *rude*); sei nicht ~! *don't be sickening*! **II.** adv °~ *exceedingly*, *very*; *beastly* (*cold*); → verflucht ‖ *thoroughly*

Ekl·ipse f ~/~n ⟨astr⟩ *eclipse* **Ekl·iptik** f ~/ *ecliptic* **ekl·iptisch** a *ecliptic*

Ekl·oge f ~/~n ⟨Lit⟩ *eclogue*

Eklog·it m ~s/~e ⟨minr⟩ *eclogite*

Ekoss·aise f ~/~n [ekɔˈsæz] Fr = „Schottischer" Tanz

Ekras·it n ~s/ *ecrasite*

ekrü a [Fr] *écru* ⟨Am⟩ *ecru* ‖ ≗seide [f] *ecru silk*

Ekst·ase f ~/~n *ecstasy*, *rapture*, *trance* ‖ in ~ *in an ecstasy*, *in ecstasies* (über *over*), *in raptures* (*at*) ‖ in ~ versetzen *to throw into ecstasies*; *to trance* ‖ in ~ geraten *to ecstasize*; *to be enraptured* od *entranced*; *to go into ecstasies* od *raptures* (über *over*)

ekst·atisch 1. a *ecstatic* **2.** adv *ecstatically*

Ekto- [Gr] [in comp] (äußer) *ecto–* **~bl·ast** m ~s/~e ⟨biol⟩ *ectoblast* **~d·erm(is** f) n ~s/~e *ectoderm* **~pl·asma** n *ectoplasm*

Ekz·em n ~s/~e ⟨med⟩ *eczema*

°**·Ekzer** n ~s/~ ⟨school, sl⟩ (Ekzerzitium) ⟨fam⟩ *ekker*

Elabor·at n *elaborate investigation* (od *study*)

Elaid·insäure f *elaidic acid*

El·an [eːˈlɑ̃] m ~s/ *élan* [Fr]; *energy*, *vivacity*; *dash*; ⟨Am, sl⟩ *pep*

Eläo- [in comp] (Öl–) *elaeo–* **~pl·ast** m ~en/~en *elaioplast*

El·astik f ~/~en *elastic web* **el·astisch** a *elastic*, *giving*, *stretch* (*web*), *resilient*; *springy* ‖ *pliant*, *supple* (*limbs*); *flexible* (Kupplung) ‖ ~ m *to supple* | ⟨übtr⟩ *elastic* (*needs*; *regulations*) ‖ *buoyant*, *resilient* (*temperament*); *springy* (*in*, *one's bearing*) ‖ ~e Unterlage ⟨tech⟩ *suspension buffer* ‖ ⟨fig⟩ *adaptable* (*mind*) **Elastizit·ät** f ~/ *elasticity* ‖ ⟨fig⟩ *elasticity*, *resilience*; *buoyancy* (*of spirit*) **~sgrenze** f *elastic limit*

Elater·it m ~s/ ⟨minr⟩ *elaterite*

·Elba n ⟨It⟩ (*island of*) *Elba*

·Elb- (**·Elbe** f ⟨Ger⟩ (Fluß) *Elbe*) **~florenz** n "*Florence on the Elbe*", *i. e. Dresden* **~kähne** m [pl] ⟨fig⟩ (Schuhe) *boats* **~sandsteingebirge** n ⟨Ger⟩ *Elbsandstein Mountains* [pl]; *Saxon Switzerland*

·Elbrus m (Berg im Kaukasus) *Elbrus*

Elch m ~(e)s/~e ⟨zoo⟩ *elk*; amer. ~ *moose*

Eldor·ado n ~(s)/~s *El Dorado* [Span]; *ideal land of plenty*; *Tom Tiddler's ground*; → Dorado

Ele·aten m [pl] ⟨Gr philos⟩ *the Eleatics* [pl] **ele·atisch** a *Eleatic*

Elef·ant m ~en/~en ⟨zoo⟩ *elephant* ‖ aus e–r Mücke e–n Elefanten m *to make a mountain out of a molehill* ‖ (er benahm sich) wie ein ~ im Porzellanladen (..) *like a bull in a china-shop*

Elef·anten- [in comp] *elephant–* **~farn** m ⟨bot⟩ *Crape fern* **~führer** m *elephant-driver* **~gras** n ⟨bot⟩ *napier grass* **≗haft** a(dv) *elephantine*(*ly* adv) **~krankheit** f ⟨med⟩ *elephantiasis* ‖ °**~küken** n *jumbo*; *baby blimp* **~laus** f ⟨bot⟩ *cashew-nut* **~orden** m (dänischer) *the Order of the Elephant* **~robbe** f *sea-elephant*, *elephant-seal* **~rüssel** m *proboscis*, (*elephant's*) *trunk* **~spitzmaus** f ⟨zoo⟩ *elephant-shrew* **~treiber** m ⟨AInd⟩ *mahout* **~tritt** m ⟨tail, com⟩ *shepherd's plaid* **~zahn** m *elephant's tusk*

Elefant·iasis f ⟨med⟩ = Elefantenkrankheit

eleg·ant 1. a *elegant*, *fashionable*, *smart*; *tony*; *dressy*, *showy* (*clothes*) ‖ ⟨sl⟩ *dossy*; *nobby* (*gentleman*); *posh* (*shoes*); *swank*, *swish* ‖ ⟨Am a.⟩ *nifty* **2.** adv *elegantly*, *fashionably*; ~ gekleidet *dressy* (*p*) **Eleg·anz** f ~/ *elegance* ‖ *delicacy*; *polish*, *refinement* höchste ~ *the last word in e.*

Eleg·ie f ~/~n [–ˈiːən] ⟨Lit⟩ *elegy*; e–e ~ schreiben auf jdn *to elegize a p*; ~en sch. *to* *elegize* (über *on*) **El·egiker** m ~s/~ *elegist* **el·egisch** a ⟨ant Lit⟩ *elegiac*; → Distichon; ~e Verse in Distichen *elegiacs* ‖ ⟨übtr⟩ *elegiac, mournful, sad*

Elektor·at n ⟨Ger hist⟩ *electorate*

Elektrifikati·on f [–'tsio:n] ~/ Sw *electrification* **elektrifiz·ieren** vt [h] ⟨rail, etc⟩ *to electrify*

Elektrifiz·ierung f ~/~en *electrification*

El·ektriker m ~s/~ *electrician* **el·ektrisch I.** a **1.** (mit Elektrizität geladen, durch E. getrieben) *electric*; ⟨fam⟩ *lectric* (*shave*) ‖ ~e Anlage *e. plant*; ⟨theat⟩ *decorative fitting* (od ⟨Am⟩ *fixture*); ~e Bahn *e. tramway* ‖ ~er Draht *live wire* ‖ ~e Klingel *electric bell* ‖ der ~e Körper *the electric* ‖ ~e Kraft *e. force*, Einheiten der ~en K. *electrical units* [pl] ‖ ~e Ladung *electric charge*; ~e Lampe *e. lamp*; ~e Leitung *e. circuit*; ~es Licht *e. light*; ~es Lichtbad *e. light bath*; ~e Lok(omotive) *e. locomotive* od *engine*; ~es Messer ⟨med⟩ *electrotome*; ~er Schlag *e. shock*; ~er Strom *e. current*; ~er Stuhl *e. chair*, ⟨Am sl⟩ *hot seat* od *squat* (⟨a.⟩ Tod auf d. e. St.); ~e Schwingungen [pl] *electromagnetic waves* [pl] ‖ ~er Zähler *electric light meter* ‖ ~e Zentrale *generating* (od *power*)-*station* **2.** ⟨fig⟩ *electric*(*al*) ‖ → Elektrizität **II.** adv *electrically*; ~ beleuchtet *electrically-lighted*; ~ geheizt *electrical* (*de-icer*); ~ geladen *electricity-laden*; ~ gel. Draht [m] *live* (⟨Am fam⟩ *hot*) *wire* ‖ → Elektrolyt **III.** die ≗e f *the electric tramway* (od *tramcar*)

Elektris·ier- [in comp] *electrifying* **~maschine** f *electrostatic generator*

elektris·ieren vt [h] *to electrify*; *electrize* ‖ (jdn) *to give .. an electric treatment*; sich ~ *to get an el. shock*; ⟨fig⟩ *to electrify*; *galvanize* **Elektris·ierung** f *electrification, electrization*

Elektrizit·ät f ~/~en ⟨phys⟩ **1.** *electricity*; Reibungs≗ *frictional e.* ‖ durch ~ getrieben *electrically driven*; → Elektron ‖ (jdn) durch ~ hinrichten *to electrocute*; Hinrichtung durch ~ *electrocution* ‖ durch ~ zersetzen *to electrolyse* ‖ Beleuchtungskörper [pl] für ~ *electric light fixtures* [pl]; Bücher über ~ *electrical books*; Unfälle durch ~ verursacht *electrical accidents* **2.** = ~slehre

Elektrizit·äts- [in comp] *electrical* (*conditions*) **~automat** m *prepayment meter* **~gesellschaft** f *electric light* od *supply company* **~industrie** f *electric manufacturing industry* **~lehre** f *electricity* **~messer** m *electrometer* **~netz** n *grid* **~versorgung** f *electricity* (od *power*)-*supply* **~werk** n *electric plant*; *generating* (od *power*)-*station*; *electricity works* [pl] [sg konstr]: ein ~ *an e. works* ‖ [abstr] *electricity supply authority*, ⟨Am⟩ *electric utility company* **~zähler** m *electricity meter* **~zentrale** f *generating* (od *power*)-*station*

El·ektro- [in comp] *electro–*; *electric*(*al*) **~anal·yse** f ⟨chem⟩ *e.o-analysis* **~antrieb** m *e.c traction* **~(bedarfs)artikel** m pl *e.cal supplies* od *appliances* pl **~backofen** m *e.c baking oven* **~biologie** f *e.o-biology* **~bohrer** m *e.c drill* **~bus** m *e.c bus* **~chem·ie** f *e.o-chemistry* **~diagnose** f *e.odiagnosis* **~dyn·amik** f *e.o-dynamics* [pl] [sg konstr] **≗dyn·amisch** a *e.o-dynamic* ‖ ~er Lautsprecher *dynamic loud-speaker* **~-Enzephalogramm** n *e.o-encephalogram* **~fahrzeug** n *electric vehicle* **~geschäft** n *electrician's* **≗graphisches Verfahren** n *mark sensing* **~hängebahn** f *telpher-line* **~herd** m *e.c range* od *cooker* **~horn** n *motor* (od *electric*) *horn* **~-Hubwerk** n *e.c lifting gear* **~industrie** f *e.cal industry* (od *engineering*) **~ingenieur** m *e.cal engineer* **~installateur** m *electrician* **~kardiogr·amm** n (*e.o-*)*cardiogram* **~karren** m *e.c truck* od *barrow* **~k·auter** m ⟨med⟩ *e.otome*; *radio knife* **~kauterisation** f *e.c cautery* **~kin·etik** f *e.o-kinetics* [pl] [sg konstr] **~kühlschrank** m *e.c refrigerator* **~kult·ur** f ⟨agr⟩ *e.o-culture* **~magn·et** m *e.o-magnet* **≗magn·etisch** a *e.o-magnetic* **~mech·anik** f *e.o-mechanics* [sg konstr] | ~er [m] *electrician* **≗mechanisch** a *e.o-mechanical* (Hirn *brain*) **~messe** f *e.cal goods fair* **~metallurg·ie** f *e.o-metallurgy* **~m·eter** n *e.ometer* **~mob·il** n *e.o-mobile* **~mont·eur** m *e.cal mechanic* **~mot·or** m *e.omotor* **≗mot·orisch** a *e.omotive* (*force*); ~ [adv] angetrieben *e.cally driven*; ~er Antrieb *e.c motor drive*; ~e Kraft (EMK) *e.omotive force* (*E.M.F.*); ~e Spannung in Volts *voltage* **~narkose** f ⟨med⟩ *e.c sleep, e.onarcosis* **≗negat·iv** a *e.o-negative* **~ofen** m *e.c furnace* **~plastik** f *e.oplating* **~rasierer** m (S, P) *e.c shaver* **~schalldose** f (am Grammophon) *pick-up* **~schiff** n *e.o-ship* **~schocktherapie** f *e.o-convulsive therapy, e.o-shock th.* **~schweißung** f *e.c. welding* **~sil·age** f *e.o-silage* **~stahl** m *e.c steel* **~st·atik** f *e.ostatics* [pl] [sg konstr] **≗statisch** a *e.ostatic*(*al*) **~t·echnik** f *e.o-technics* [pl] [sg konstr]; *e.cal engineering* **~t·echniker** m *e.o-technician* **~t·echnisch** a *e.o-technical* **~therap·ie** f *e.o-therapeutics* [pl] [sg konstr]; *e.o-therapy* **≗th·ermisch** a *e.o-thermal* (od *thermic*) **~typ·ie** f *e.o*(*type*) **~werkzeug** n *e.c tool* **~werte** m [pl] *shares* [pl] *of e.cal concerns*

Elektr·ode f ~/~n *electrode*, ⟨fam⟩ *plate*; → Anode, Kathode **Elektr·oden-** **~abstand** m *e. gap* od *spacing* **~durchführung, ~fassung** f *e. collar* ⟨met⟩ **~mehl** n *crushed electrodes* **~spitze** f *e. tip* **Elektrol·yse** f *electrolysis* **elektrol·ytisch** a *electrolytic*

Elektr·on n ~s/~en (negativ el. geladenes Atomteilchen) *electron* **Elektronen-** [in comp] *electronic* (*theory*); **~aufprall** m *cathodic bombardment* **~bahn** f *e. path* od *orbit* **≗beraubt** a *stripped* (*atom*) **~beschießung** f *e. bombardment* **~beschleuniger** m *electron accelerator* **~bildfang** m *e. image pick-up* **~blitz** m *e.ic flash* **~bremsung** f *deceleration of e.s* **~bündel** n *cathode ray* **≗emittierendes Metall** *metallic e. emitter* **~gehirn** n *e.ic brain*; ⟨Am⟩ *Univac* **~herd** m *e.ic range* **~rechenmaschine** f, **~rechner** m *e.ic calculator* od *computer* (mit Magnettrommelspeicher *with magnetic drum store*; mit steuerbarer Rechenfolge *selective sequence e.ic comp.*) **~röhre** f (*e.*) *tube* **~schleuder** f *betatron* **~stauung** f *e. accumulation* **~steuerung** f *electronic control* **~strahlabtaster** m ⟨telv⟩ *iconoscope* **~strahlerzeuger** m *e. gun* **~strahlpeiler** m *cathode-ray direction finder* **~technik** f *electronics* [sg konstr] **~unterschale** f *subshell* (*of e.s*) **~vervielfacher** m *electron multiplier* **~wächter** m *e. watchman* **Elektr·onik** f *electronics* [sg konstr] **elektr·onisch** a *electronic* (*computer*) **Elektroph·on** n *electrophone* **Elektroph·or** n *electrophore, –phorus* **Elektrosk·op** n *electroscope*

Elem·ent n ~(e)s/~e **A. 1. a.** ⟨chem⟩ *element* **b.** ⟨phys⟩ galvanisches ~ *galvanic cell*; Volta-~ *Voltaic element*; Daniell-~ *Daniell cell*; Trocken≗ *dry cell* **c.** ⟨biol, etc.⟩ *element* **d.** ⟨ec⟩ die ~e [pl] *the elements* [pl] **2.** (Grundbestandteil; S *or* P) *element* (*an e. of cant*); das keltische u germanische ~ *the Celtic and Teutonic elements* [pl] ‖ anrüchige ~ e [pl] *shady individuals*; unbequeme ~e *undesirables* [pl] **3.** ⟨math⟩ *element*; *integral* **B. 1.** die vier ~ (Feuer, Wasser, Luft, Erde) *the four elements* [pl] ‖ das Toben der ~e *the war of the elements*; *elemental tumults* [pl] **2.** ⟨übtr⟩ *element*; (so recht) in s–m ~e s *to be in one's* (*proper*) *element*; nicht in s–m ~ s *to be* od *feel like a fish out of water*; er war in der Stadt mehr in s–m ~ als .. *he was in town more at home than ..* **3.** die ~e [pl] (Anfangsgründe) *the elements* (*of a science*, etc.); *the first principles*; *the rudiments* **~klemme** f *battery clip*

element·ar a **1.** ⟨chem⟩ *uncompounded; uncombined* (*carbon*) ‖ (urkräftig) *elemental* (*forces, passions*); mit ~er Gewalt *with an elemental force* **2.** (rudimentär) *elementary, rudimentary* (*knowledge*) ‖ ⟨übtr⟩ *elementary* (*maxims*); *first, primary; primitive* ‖ *fundamental, basic* (*right, rule, needs*; *basic* (*human rights*)

Elementar- [in comp] (urkräftig) *elemental* ‖ (Anfangs–) *elementary, primary* **~buch** n *primer; elementary manual* **~ereignis** n *elemental tumult; hurricane; tornado* **~geister** m [pl] *elemental spirits* [pl] **~klasse** f *elementary class, junior school* (od *form*) **~kraft** f *elemental force* **~lehrer** m *primary teacher* **~quantum** n elektrisches ~ *elementary electric charge*; → Elektron, Proton **~schadenversicherung** f *insurance against damage caused by natural force* **~schule** f *elementary* (od *preparatory, primary*) *school* **~schüler** m *primary scholar* **~stufe** f *primary education* **~teilchen** n ⟨at⟩ (Proton, Neutron, Meson etc) *elementary particle* **~teiler** m ⟨math⟩ *invariant factor* **~unterricht** m *elementary* (od *primary*) *education; the three R's* (*reading, writing,* [*a*]*rithmetic*)

El·emi n ~s/ (Baumharz) *elemi*

·Elen m & n ~s/~s ⟨zoo⟩ **1.** *elk* **2.** *eland*

·Elend n ~(e)s/ **1.** *desolateness, desolation; despondency* ‖ *affliction, calamity, distress, misery; troubles* [pl]; *hard lines* [pl]; das ~ des menschl. Lebens *the miseries of human life* | °das graue (*or* heulende) ~ bek ⟨fam⟩ *to get the horrors* ‖ °das heulende ~ bek *to get maudlin* ‖ es ist ein ~ mit ihm *he is a* (*great*) *trial; he is a nuisance, he makes a nuisance of himself* **2.** (Armut) *destitution, distress, misery, poverty, wretchedness* ‖ in ~ geraten *to become destitute; to come to grief, to go under* ‖ im ~ umkommen *to die a dog's death* ‖ das soziale ~ schreit zum Himmel *the social conditions are scandalous* (od *a scandal*) ‖ das glänzende ~ *the shabby-genteel* **·elend I.** a **1.** (P) **a.** *desolate, despondent; miserable, wretched*; sich ~ fühlen *to feel miserable*, ⟨sl⟩ *lousy, mean* (vor *with*) ‖ Sich-elend-fühlen *wretchedness* ‖ sich ~ u verlassen fühlen *to feel miserable and lonely* ‖ er sieht ~ aus *he looks very ill, pale, wan* **b.** *funny, ill, unwell; sick*; sich ~ fühlen *to feel funny*; es wurde ihr ~ *she came over funny* **c.** *mean, miserable* (*scoundrel*); ~er Schurke *despicable creature; wretched* (*sinner*) **2.** ⟨übtr⟩ (S) *miserable* (*hut*); *poor; shabby; wretched* (*place; stuff*); *pitiable, pitiful* (*fate*) ‖ *paltry, petty* ‖ *rotten* (*performance*); *shameful* (*exploitation*); *mean* (*fraud*); *terrible* (*heat*) ‖ ~e Schinderei *drudgery* ‖ in ~en Umständen leben *to live in distressed circumstances* od *in dire poverty* **II.** adv **1.** *miserably, wretchedly; pitifully*; ~ z Grunde gehen *to die a dog's death* **2.** °~ = enorm; ~ viel *a whale of* **·Elende 1.** [der ~, ein ~r] *the wretch*; ~r! *poor wretch* **2.** die ~ *the wretch* **3.** die ~n (u Verlassenen) [pl] *the wretched* (*and forlorn*) **·elenden** vt [h] (jdn) *to pester; torment; worry* **·elendig, ~lich** adv = elend II. 1. **·Elends- ~viertel** n (in London etc) *slums* [pl] ‖ Beseitigung der ~ *clearance of slum areas* **~wohnung** f *squalid dwelling; shanty, hovel*; ⟨Am, Can⟩ *shack*

Elephant·iasis f = Elefantenkrankheit

Eleus·inisch a ⟨ant⟩ *Eleusinian* (*mysteries*)

Elevat·ion f ~/~en ⟨astr. ec⟩ *elevation* ‖ ⟨mil⟩ (Erhöhungswinkel) *elevation*

Elev·ator m ~s/–t·oren ⟨tech⟩ *elevator*

El·eve m ~n/~n *student of agriculture* (od *forestry*) *during his practical training*

Elf m ~en/~en, **·Elfe** f ~/~n *elf; fairy; pixy, –xie* ‖ *elf, goblin* ‖ → Fee

·elf 1. a *eleven* ‖ [in comp] *hendeca–* **2.** ≗ f **a.** *the eleven* **b.** = Elfermannschaft **≗eck** n *hendecagon* **~eckig** a *hendecagonal* **~mal** *eleven times* **≗m·eter(stoß)** m ⟨ftb⟩ *penalty kick* **~silbig** a ⟨pros⟩ *hendecasyllabic*; ~er Vers m *hendecasyllabic*

·Elfen- [in comp] *elfin; elf–* **~kind** n *elf-child* **~königin** f *elf-queen* **~land, ~reich** n *elf-land; fairyland* **~reigen, ~tanz** m *elf* (od *fairy*) *–dance* **~schuh** m ⟨bot⟩ = Akelei

·Elfenbein n ~(e)s/ *ivory* ‖ gebranntes ~ *ivory black* ‖ künstliches ~ *artificial ivory; celluloid* ‖ geschnitzte Gegenstände aus ~ *ivories* [pl] | [in comp] *ivory–* **~drechsler** m *ivory-turner* **~küste** f ⟨geog⟩ *Ivory Coast* **~nuß** f *ivory nut; corozo palm* **~palme** f ⟨bot⟩ *ivory-palm* **~schnitzerei** f *ivory-carving, scrimshaw* **~turm** m ⟨fig⟩ *Ivory Tower, tour d'ivoire* Fr (*cf. A. de Vigny*) **~schwarz** n *ivory-black*

·elfenbeinern a *ivory*

·elfenhaft a *elf-like, fairy-like*

·Elfer m ~s/~ ⟨ftb⟩ = Elfmeterstoß

·elferlei a *elevenfold*; [pred] *of eleven kinds* od *sorts* **·Elfermannschaft** f ⟨sport⟩ *the eleven*

·elffach a *elevenfold* **·elfte** a *eleventh*; zur ~n Stunde *at the e. hour* **·elftehalb** a *ten and a half*

·Elfin f ~/~nen *female elf*

·elftel 1. a *eleventh* (*part*) **2.** ≗ n *the eleventh; eleventh part* **·elftens** adv *in the eleventh place*

elid·ieren vt ⟨gram⟩ (Vokal, etc) *to elide*

Eliminat·ion f ~/~en ⟨bes math⟩ *elimination*

elimin·ieren vt [h] ⟨bes math⟩ (Größe) *to eliminate* (aus *from*)

Elis·ion f ~/~en ⟨gram⟩ *elision*

El·ite f [Fr] ~/; die ~ *the élite* (Fr), *the cream* (od *flower*) (*of society*) ‖ moralische ~ *salt of the earth* **El·ite-** [in comp] *crack, exclusive; choice, select* **~kampfflieger** m *ace* **~regiment** n *crack* (od *exclusive*) *regiment* **~spieler** m *crack player* **~truppen** f [pl] ⟨mil⟩ *corps d'élite* (Fr)

Elix·ier n ~s/~e **1.** *elixir*; Lebens≗ *e. of life* **2.** (Heiltrank) *elixir; sovereign remedy*

Elk m ⟨zoo⟩ *elk*; ⟨Am⟩ *moose*

·Ellbogen m ~s/~ *elbow* ‖ die ~ gebrauchen *to use one's elbows; to elbow one's way* (durch *through*); er verstand s–e ~ z g. *he knew how to assert himself* ‖ am ~ durchgestoßen *out at the elbow*(*s*) ‖ (jdn) mit dem ~ stoßen *to elbow* ‖ die ~ aufstützen, sich auf die ~ stützen *to rest on one's elbow, to prop o.s.* **~fahrer** m ⟨mot⟩ *bully* **~freiheit** f *elbow-room* **~gelenk** n *elbow-joint* **~knochen** m *funny-bone* **~mensch** m *pusher* **~raum** m ⟨a–n⟩ *elbow-room*

·Elle f ~/~n **1.** ⟨anat⟩ *ulna* (L) **2.** †(altes Längenmaß f Gewebe) **a.** ⟨a-engl⟩ (Ger = 55–85 cm) *ell* **b.** ⟨engl⟩ (= *1.142* m) *ell* ‖ nach der ~ verkaufen *to sell by the ell* **3.** (jetzige der ~ entsprechende Längenmaßeinheit in England) *yard* (= *0,914* m) ‖ Meister v der ~ *knight of the needle, shears, timble*

·Ellen- [in comp] **~bogen** m = Ellbogen **≗lang** a *sesquipedalian* (*word*) ‖ *lengthy* (*report*); *tedious* **~maß** n *ell-measure* **~reiter** m ⟨hum⟩ *travelling haberdasher* **~waren** f [pl] = Schnitt–

×**·Eller** f ~/~n ⟨bot⟩ = Erle

Ell·ipse f ~/~n **1.** ⟨gram⟩ *ellipsis* [pl –ses] **2.** ⟨math⟩ *ellipse* **Ell·ipsen-** [in comp] ⟨math⟩ *elliptic*(*al*) **≗förmig** a ⟨math⟩ *elliptic*(*al*) **~zirkel** m *trammel*

Ellipso·id n ⟨math⟩ *ellipsoid* **ell·iptisch** a **1.** ⟨gram⟩ *elliptical* **2.** ⟨math⟩ *elliptic*(*al*)

·Ellok f ~/~s *electric locomotive*

·Elmsfeuer n (Sankt-Elms-Feuer) ⟨phys⟩ *corposant, St. Elmo's fire*

Elongati·on f ⟨astr⟩ *elongation*

Eloqu·enz f *eloquence*; → Bered(t)samkeit

Elox·al n (eloxiertes Aluminium) *Alinox* **~verfahren** n *anodizing* **elox·ieren** vt [h] ⟨met⟩ *to anodize* ‖ –rt [pp] *electrolytically oxidized*

·Elritze f ~/~n ⟨ich⟩ *minnow*

·**Elsaß** n –asses/ : das ~ *Alsace* ·**Elsässer** m ~s/~; ~in f ~/~nen *Alsatian* ·**elsässisch** a *Alsatian* ·**Elsaß-L·othringen** n *Alsace-Lorraine* ·**elsaß-l·othringisch** a *of* (od *pertaining to*) *A.-L.*

·**Elsbeerbaum** m, ·**Elsbeere** f ⟨bot⟩ *service-tree*

·**Else** f ~/~n ⟨bot⟩ = Erle || ⟨ich⟩ = Alse

·**Elster** f ~/~n ⟨orn⟩ *magpie* || sie ist geschwätzig wie e–e ~ *she is a talkative m.*

·**Elster** f ⟨Ger⟩ (zwei Flüsse) Weiße u Schwarze *White and Black Elster* ~**gebirge** n ⟨Ger⟩ *Elster-Mountains*

·**Elten** m ~s/~ ⟨ich⟩ = Döbel

·**elterlich** a *parental*; ~e Gewalt *p. authority*; in ~er Weise *parentally*

·**Eltern** [pl] *parents* [pl] || der Witz ist nicht v schlechten ~ *that's a good 'un* (= *one*) ~**beirat** m ⟨Ger school⟩ *parent's advisory council*; Mitglied des ~s *juvenile* (*guidance*) *officer* ~**haus** n *parental home*; dem Kind fehlt das ~ .. *wants family background* ~**liebe** f *parental love* ~̈**los** a *unparented*; *orphaned* ~**schaft** f **1.** [abstr] *parentage*, *parenthood* **2.** [konkr] *the parents* (*of the boys* etc. *of a school*, etc.),

elys·äisch, el·ysisch a *Elysian* (*fields*) || die Elys·äischen Felder [m pl] *les Champs Elysées* Fr (in Paris)

El·ysium n (L) ~s/ *Elysium* (L)

·**Elzbeere** f ⟨bot⟩ = *Elsbeerbaum*

·**Elzevirdruck** m ⟨typ⟩ *elzevir*

Em·ail [e'maj] n (Fr) ~s/~s, **Em·aille** [e'maljə] f ~/~n *enamel*; → Schmelz || (Malerei) *enamel*, → Bd. I. *enamel* || [in comp] *enamel*; *enamelled* ~**arbeit** f *enamel-work* ~**arbeiter** m *enameller* ~**badewanne** f *enamelled bath* ~**draht** m *enamelled wire* ~**farbe** f *enamel-paint*; *vitreous pigment* ~**geschirr** n *enamelled culinary utensils* [pl] ~**maler** m *enamellist*; *artist in enamel* ~**malerei** f *enamel-painting* ~**waren** f [pl] *enamelled ware*

Emaill·ier- [in comp] *enamelling* ~**ofen** m *enamelling-stove* **emaill·ieren** vt [h] *to enamel*

Emanat·ion f ~/~en **1.** [abstr] ⟨philos⟩ *emanation*; ~slehre *doctrine of e.* **2.** [konkr] ⟨chem⟩ (abbr Em) *radium emanation*; *niton*; *radon* || ~stherapie f *radio-therapy*

Emanzipati·on f ~/~en *emancipation* || ~smaßnahme f *emancipatory measure*

emanzip·ieren vt [h] *to emancipate*; sich ~ *to e. o.s.* **emanzip·iert** a ⟨jur & übtr⟩ *emancipated*

Emball·age (ãba'la:ʒə] f ~/~n *packing*; *wrapping*; *packing-material* || ~kosten f [pl] *packing-charges* **emball·ieren** vt [h] *to pack into bales*; *to bale*

Emb·argo n ~s/~s ⟨mar⟩ *embargo* (auf *on*) || ein ~ verhängen *to impose an e.*, das ~ aufheben *to lift the e.* || ein ~ legen auf ein Schiff *to lay an e. on a ship*; *to lay a ship under an embargo*; *to embargo a ship*

Embl·em n ~(e)s/~e *emblem* **emblem·atisch** a *emblematic*

Embol·ie f ⟨path⟩ *embolism* **emb·olisch** a *embolic*

Embonpoint [ãbɔ̃'pwɛ̃] n (Fr) ~s/~s *embonpoint*

·**Embryo** m ~s/–;onen **1.** *embryo*; → Eihaut **2.** [in comp] *embryo–* **Embryolog·ie** f *embryology* **embryon·al** a *embryonal*; *embryo* ·**Embryosack** m ⟨bot⟩ *embryo-sac* **Embryotom·ie** f ⟨surg⟩ *embryotomy*

Emd n ~es/ Sw = Öhmd → Grummet

·**Emden** n ⟨Ger⟩ (Stadt) *Em*(*b*)*den*

Emendati·on f ~/~en *emendation* **emend·ieren** vt [h] (Text) *to emend*

Emerg·enz f ⟨bot⟩ *emergence*

emerit·ieren vt [h] ⟨Ger univ⟩ *to discharge* (*a p*) *from active service*; → pensionieren **emerit·iert** a *emeritus* (*professor*) **Em·eritus** m ~/–ti L *emeritus professor*

Emigr·ant m ~en/~en ⟨bes pol⟩ *emigrant*; *émigré* (Fr); → Flüchtling **Emigr·anten-** [in comp] *emigrant*

·**Emil** ⟨aero hum⟩ = (Luftbeobachter) *shock-absorber*, *pop-eye*; → Franz

emin·ent **1.** a *eminent* **2.** adv *eminently*; *outstandingly*; e–e ~ wichtige Frage *a question of prime* od *extreme importance*; *an extremely important qu.*

Emin·enz f ⟨R. C.⟩ ⟨mst⟩ (Titel e–s Kardinals) Seine ~ *His Eminence* || graue ~ *éminence grise* Fr, *gray eminence* (Mönch u Vertrauter des Kardinals Richelieu, der sog. *éminence rouge*)

·**Emir** m ~s/~e (arab. Titel) *emir*; *ameer*

Emir·at n ~s/~e *emirate*

Emiss·är m ~s/~e *emissary*

Emissi·on f ~/~en **1.** ⟨com⟩ *issue* (*of shares*, etc.); *float* (*coupon fl.*) || ⟨Am⟩ *issuance* **2.** ⟨phys⟩ *emission*

Emissi·ons- [in comp] mst ⟨com⟩ ~**bank** f *bank of issue*; *issuing bank*, ⟨Am⟩ *investment b.* ~**geschäft** n *business of issuing shares* od *loans to the public* ~**haus** n *issuing house* ~**kraft** f ⟨phys⟩ *emissivity* (ε) ~**kurs**, ~**preis** m *issue-price* ~**theorie** f ⟨phys⟩ *theory of emission*, *e. theory* ~**vermögen** n = –kraft

Em·itter m ~s/~ (Teil des Transistors) *emitter*

emitt·ieren vt [h] (Aktien) *to issue*

·**Emmental** n (schweiz. Landschaft)

·**Emmer** m ~s/ ⟨bot⟩ (Dinkel) *emmer*

·**Emmerich** **1.** n (am Rhein) ⟨Ger⟩ (Stadt) **2.** m Vorname

·**Emmerling** m ⟨orn⟩ = Ammer

Emolum·ente [pl] *emoluments* [pl]

Emoti·on [-ts-] f ~/~en *emotion*

Emp·ästik f *empaestic art*

†**empf·ahen** = empfangen

Empf·ang m ~(e)s/~̈e **1.** (Erhalten) bes ⟨com⟩ *receipt* (*of a letter*; *goods*; *money*) || *the receiving* (*of congratulations*) || bei *or* nach ~ v *on receipt of* ..; bei ~ der Ware *on delivery of the goods* || den ~ e–r S bestätigen *to acknowledge receipt of a th*; den ~ e–r S bescheinigen *to give* (od *make out*) *a receipt for a th*; e–r Tratte guten ~ bereiten *to acknowledge a draft* || (Dinge) in ~ nehmen *to receive*; die Urkunden wurden v Herrn N. in ~ genommen *the deeds were received by Mr. N.* || ~ quittieren *to acknowledge receipt* **2.** (Aufnahme) *reception* (*of a p*; *of a deputation*); ⟨hot⟩ *reception* || feierlicher ~ *reception* (beim Könige *by the king*); (informeller Nachmittags-~̈) *at-home* || ~ abhalten *to hold a reception* | ihm wurde ein begeisterter ~ zuteil *or* bereitet *he had* (od *met with*) *an enthusiastic reception*; der ~, den Sie mir bereitet h, hat .. *your reception of me has* .. | *reception* (*of a proposal*; *of a play*); → Aufnahme **3.** ⟨wir⟩ *reception*; der ~ war gut *the r.* (*by wireless*) *was good*; auf ~ bleiben *to stand by*

empf·angen vt/i [h] [empfing/empfangen] **I.** vt **1.** (erhalten) **a.** (Brief, Geld) *to receive* (v *from*); *obtain*, *get*; *to be the recipient of* (*a th*) || ⟨com⟩ etw ~ h *to be in receipt of a th*; Wert ~ [pp] *value received* || → erhalten **b.** (Einladung, Geschenk) *to receive*, *get* || *take*; → annehmen || das Abendmahl ~ *to take the Sacrament* || Almosen ~ *to be on the dole* || die Taufe ~ *to be baptized*; die Weihen ~ *to take holy orders* **c.** (Eindruck) *to receive* || Strafe ~ *to get punished* **2.** (aufnehmen) **a.** (jdn) *to receive*; *see* (*do you think he would see me?*) || ⟨engl⟩ Besuch, Gäste ~ *to receive*; *to be at home*; sie ~ heute k–n Besuch *they are not receiving today* **b.** (jdn) feierlich ~ *to receive*; *welcome* || (Redner, Rede) *to receive*; *to greet*, *salute* (mit Herzlichkeit, Zischen *with cordiality, hisses*) **c.** (S) *to meet; greet, salute*; ein milder Wind empfing sie *a mild wind met* (od *saluted*) *them* **II.** vi **1.** *to receive* ⟨a. wir, telv⟩ **2.** (of a woman) *to conceive*; *to become pregnant*

Empf·änger m ~s/~ **1.** (P) *receiver, recipient* ‖ *addressee* (*of a letter*); *consignee* (*of goods*) ‖ *acceptor, payee* (*of a bill of exchange*) **2.** (Reiz~̊) *receptor* **3.** ⟨wir⟩ (Apparat) *receiving set, receiver* ‖ ⟨tech⟩ *receiver* **~empfindlichkeit** f ⟨wir⟩ *receiver sensitivity* **~gehäuse** n ⟨wir⟩ *cabinet* **~röhre** f *receiving valve*, ⟨Am⟩ *r. tube* **~staat** m (v Entwicklungshilfe) *recipient nation*

empf·änglich a **1.** [attr] (f Eindrücke ~) *impressionable* (*man*; *soul*); ein ~es Alter *an i. age* ‖ *receptive* (*mind*) **2.** [pred] (P) ~ s f etw, sich ~ zeigen f etw *to be susceptible* (od *accessible, alive, sensitive*) *to a th*; *to make a response to* (*an appeal*) ‖ f Schönheit ~ *alive to the beautiful* ‖ f Krankheit ~ *prone* od *liable to* (*catch*) *disease* ‖ jdn ~ m *to predispose a p*

Empf·änglichkeit f ~/~en *impressionableness, impressionability*; *receptivity* ‖ *sensibility, susceptibility* (f *to*) ‖ ⟨med⟩ *predisposition* (f *to*)

Empf·ängnis f ~/ *conception*; ⟨R. C.⟩ Mariä ~ *Immaculate Conception* | zeitweilige **~unfähigkeit** *sterile period* **~̊verhütend** a *contraceptive*; *birth control* [attr] (*methods*) **~verhütung** f *contraception*; ⟨demog⟩ *limitation* od *restriction of births* ‖ ~smittel [n] *contraceptive, anticonceptive* ‖ **~wahrscheinlichkeit** f *fecundability*; Periode geringer ~ ⟨biol⟩ *safe period* **~zeit** f *period of* (*possible* ⟨bes jur⟩) *conception*

Empf·angs- [in comp] **~abend** m *reception* (f *to*) **~amplitudenschwankung** f ⟨wir⟩ *fading* **~antenne** f ⟨wir⟩ *receiving aerial* **~anzeige** f = Empfangsbestätigung **~apparat** m ⟨tech⟩ *receiver, receiving apparatus* ‖ ⟨wir⟩ *receiver*; *receiving set*; ~ mit Kristalldetektor *crystal set* **~̊berechtigt** a; ~ s *to be authorized to receive* **~bereitschaft** f *readiness to receive* (od *to absorb*) **~bescheinigung** f *receipt* (*for goods*) **~bestätigung** f *acknowledgement* (*of an account, offer*); bitte um ~! *please acknowledge receipt*! **~chef** m *head-receptionist, reception clerk* **~dame** f (bei Ärzten etc) *receptionist* **~gerät** n = Empfangsapparat **~herr** m ⟨com⟩ *shop-walker*; *floorwalker* **~nachmittag** m *at-home* **~prämie** f ⟨st exch⟩ *premium for the put* **~quittung** f *receipt*; (am Scheck) *counterfoil* **~raum** m *reception room*; (Hotel~̊) *salon* **~schein** m *receipt* (*for goods*) **~staat** m (Ggs Entsendestaat) *receiving State* **~station** f ⟨wir⟩ *receiving station* **~tag** m ⟨engl⟩ *at-home*; ~ h *to be at home, to receive* **~zimmer** n *reception room*; ⟨bank, etc⟩ *parlour*; ⟨mil⟩ *ante-room*

empf·ehlbar a *recommendable*

empf·ehlen vt [h] [empfahl/empfohlen] **A. 1.** (anvertrauen) s–e Seele Gott ~ *to* (*re*)*commend one's soul to God* ‖ etw (*or* jdn) der Obhut jds ~ *to* (*re*)*commend a th* (od *a p*) *to a p's care* **2.** bitte ~ Sie mich bestens Ihren Eltern *remember me most kindly to your parents*; *give my kindest regards to your p.*; *please give my compliments to him* **3. a.** etw ~ *to encourage* (*participation is –ged*); (als geeignet) ~ *to recommend a th* (als *as*; f *for*); jdm etw ~ *to recommend a p a th* od *a th to a p*; (ein–, nachdrücklich) *to urge a th on a p* ‖ jdm ~ z tun *to r.* od *advise a p to do*; wir ~ Ihnen, sobald wie möglich f die S Sorge z tragen *we recommend your attending to the matter as soon as possible*; mir wurde empfohlen *I was recommended* (*to do*) **b.** jdn (als geeignet bestens) ~ *to recommend a p highly*; könnten Sie mir e–n Schneider ~? *would you recommend me a tailor*? ‖ wir halten uns Ihnen bestens empfohlen *we shall be happy to be at your service* **B. sich ~ 1.** *to send one's compliments* od *regards* (jdm *to a p*) ‖ (ich) empfehle mich Ihnen! *good-bye*!, ⟨fam⟩ *so long*! **2.** *to take one's leave*; sich französisch ~ *to take French leave, to walk one's chalks* **3.** (S) sich (selbst) ~ *to be advantageous* ‖ (of a method) *to commend* (od *suggest*) *itself* ‖ dieses Vorgehen empfiehlt sich sehr *this procedure has much to be said for*; *there is m. to be s. for this pr.* ‖ es empfiehlt sich z tun *it is advisable to do*; es würde sich ~ z tun *it would be well to do*; .., daß jd tut *it would be well for a p to do* **empf·ehlend** a *commendatory, recommendatory* **empf·ehlenswert** a *recommendable*; *fit, suitable* ‖ nicht ~ s *to be impertinent* (od *inexpedient*); → angebracht, ratsam

Empf·ehlung f ~/~en **1.** *recommendation* (*of a th, of a p*); *commendation* (*of a p*) ‖ auf ~ jds *upon the recommendation of a p* ‖ (of qualities) e–e gute ~ s *to be a good passport* (f *to*) ‖ ⟨com⟩ beste ~en [pl] *best references* [pl] **2.** (Gruß) *respects, compliments* [pl] (an *to*)

Empf·ehlungs- ~brief m, **~schreiben** n *letter of introduction* (od *recommendation*); *credentials* [pl] **~karte** f *card of introduction*; ⟨com⟩ *businesscard*

empf·indbar a *perceptible, sensible* **Empf·indbarkeit** f ~/ *perceptibility*

empf·inden vt/i [h] [empfand/empfunden] **I.** vt **1.** (sinnlich wahrnehmen) *to perceive through the senses*; *to feel*; *to have a sensation of* (*cold*; *hunger*); *to be sentient of* (*a th*) **2.** (fühlen) *to feel* (*I f. the cold very much*) ‖ *to experience*; das Gefühl, das diejenigen –fanden, die .. *the feeling which came to those who ..* ‖ etw lebhaft ~ *to be sensitive to a th* ‖ tief ~ *to feel deeply*; tief ~funden [a] *whole-hearted* ‖ ich werde s–n Fortgang schmerzlich ~ *I shall suffer the loss in him* ‖ Ekel, Widerwillen ~ *to be sickened* (über *at*); Groll ~ *to cherish a grudge* (*against*) ‖ Mitleid ~ mit jdm *to feel for a p*; *to have* (od *feel*) *sympathy with* (od *for*) *a p* **3.** (geistig erfassen) *to be aware* (od *sensible*) *of* (*a th*); *to perceive*; *to realize*; (Gefahr) *to sense*; (ein milder Regen fiel hernieder), aber er –fand es nicht (..), *but he did not realize it*; es wurde als unzweckmäßig –funden *it was felt to be inexpedient* **II.** vi *to feel*; ich –fand durchaus nicht so *I did not feel that way at all* ‖ tief ~ mit jdm *to feel for a p*; mit jdm *or* f jdn ~ *to share a p's feelings*

Empf·inden n *perception* (*artistic p.*) ‖ *feeling* ‖ nach m–m ~ *in my opinion*; *to my mind*

empf·indend a **1.** *sensible* (*world*); *sensitive*; *sentient* **2.** (tief ~) *feeling* (*heart*); *sympathetic* ‖ jeder ~e Mensch *every p with any feeling*

empf·indlich I. a **1.** *sensitive, tender* (*ear*); ~ f *or* gegen *sensitive to* ‖ → licht~ *sensitive* **2.** *sensitive, tender* (*skin, wound*); *weak* (*stomach*); e–e ~e Stelle *a sore* od *tender place* od *spot* (*on one's head*); s–e Haut ist ~ gegen .. *his skin is sensitive to* (*sudden movements*) **3.** (P) *delicate*; *fastidious* ‖ *sensitive*; *thin-skinned*; *irritable, miffy, testy, tetchy*; ~ in bezug auf *sensitive about* (*one's poverty*); *touchy on*; sei nicht so ~ *don't be* (*so*) *touchy* ‖ nicht mehr ~ f *lost to* (*a th*) ‖ ~ gegen *susceptible of* (od *to*) ‖ ⟨path⟩ *susceptible* (f *to*); *vulnerable* (*point*) ‖ die ~e Stelle jds *the sore place of a p*; die ~en Stellen jds *the vulnerabilities, susceptibilities of a p*; jdn an e–r ~en Stelle treffen *to touch a p on a sore place*; jdn an der ~sten Stelle treffen *to hit a p where it hurts most* **4.** ⟨übtr⟩ (S) *delicate* (*organ*); *fragile*; *tender* (*plant*) ‖ *fugitive* (*colours*) ‖ *instantaneous, superquick* (Zünder *fuse*) **5.** ⟨fig⟩ (merklich) *sensible* (*difference*; *error*; *reduction*) ‖ *considerable*; *noticeable* (Lücke *gap*); *heavy* (*loss, blow*); *serious* (*blow to a p's prestige*) ‖ *distressing, grievous* (*harm*); *biting, painful, sharp* (*pain*); *severe* (*blow*); *poignant* (*grief*) ‖ [pred] *vulnerable to hard use*, etc **II.** adv **1.** *sensitively* **2.** *perceptibly, sensibly* (*weaker*) **3.** ⟨fig⟩ *acutely*;

extremely; grievously; intensely; severely; bitterly, piercingly (cold a) || jdn ~ beleidigen *to hurt* (od *wound) a p grievously*; er war ~ verstimmt *he was grievously annoyed*; er fühlte den Schlag ~ *he poignantly felt the stroke* | **≃keit** f **1.** *sensitiveness, sensitivity* (gegen *to*) **2.** *soreness, tenderness* (*of a wound*) **3.** (P) *delicacy; fastidiousness* || *feelings* pl || *sensitivity; tetchiness, touchiness; irritability* || ~ gegen *susceptibility to* || übermäßige ~ *allergy* **4.** ⟨übtr⟩ *delicacy; sensibility* (*of an organ; of instruments*) **5.** ⟨fig⟩ *sensibility* || *grievousness, heaviness* (*of a loss*); *sharpness* (*of pain*); *severity* (*of a blow*) **~keits-~angabe** f ⟨phot⟩ *indication of speed* **~einstellung** f ⟨phot⟩ ~ von 15, 18, 21 Din *setting of 25, 50, 100 Asa* **~messer** m ⟨phot⟩ *sensitometer*

empf·indsam a **1.** (leicht u tief empfindend) *sensible, sensitive* (*child*); *sentient*; ~er Mensch *sensitive* || *tender* || (unmännlich) ⟨fam⟩ *soft* (*p*; gegen *with a p*) || → empfindlich **2.** ⟨Lit⟩ *sentimental*; → sentimental **≃keit** f ~/~en **1.** *sensibility; sensitiveness, sensitivity; sentience* || *feelings* pl **2.** *sentiment*; ⟨fam⟩ *softness* || ⟨Lit⟩ *sentiment; sentimentality; sentimentalism*; Zeitalter der ~ *Age of Sentimentalism*; die Schriftsteller dieses Zeitalters *the Sentimentalists* [pl]

Empf·indung f ~/~en **1.** (Sinnes≃) *sensation; sentience, -cy*; ⟨anat⟩ Organ der bewußten ~en im Gehirn *sensorium* [L] **2.** *feeling, sense; sentiment* (*of pity*); in jdm sanfte ~en erwecken *to touch a p with gentle feelings* **3.** *perception; sensibility* | **~s-** [in comp] *sensational; sensorial* **~eigenheit** f *idiosyncrasy* **≃fähig** a *sensitive, sensible* **~fähigkeit** f *sensitivity, sensitiveness* **~grenze** f ⟨psych⟩ *limen* [L]; *threshold* **≃los** a **1.** *insensible; dead, numb* (*limb*) **2.** (herzlos) *callous; hard-hearted, remorseless, unfeeling* **~losigkeit** f **1.** *insensibility; deadness, numbness* **2.** *callousness; unfeelingness* **~störung** f ⟨med⟩ *paraesthesia* [L] **~vermögen** n *sensibility; sensitive* od *perceptive faculty, capacity* (od *power*) *of sensation* **~wort** n ⟨gram⟩ *interjection*

empfohlen a (→ empfehlen) ~er (Richt-)Preis *recommended price*

Emph·ase f ~/ *emphasis*; → Nachdruck || ⟨mus⟩ *intensity* **emph·atisch** | a(dv) *empatic(ally* adv)

Emphys·em n ~s/~e ⟨med⟩ *emphysema* [L]

Emp·ire [ɑ̃'pi:r] n [Fr] *Empire* [Fr] **~stil** m *Empire style*

Empir·ie f ~/ *empiricism; empirical method*

Emp·iriker m ~s/~ *empiric; empiricist* **emp·irisch** **1.** a *empiric(al)* **2.** adv *empirically*

Empir·ismus m *empiricism; empirical science*

Empir·ist m ~en/~en *empiricist*

emp·or adv *up, upwards; on high; high up*

emp·or- [betontes trennbares pref bei Verben] mst ⟨übtr⟩ **~|arbeiten** [vrefl] [h] sich ~ *to work up* (z *to*); sich v unten ~ *to work one's way up from the bottom* **~|blicken** vi [h] *to look up* **~|bringen** vt [h] ⟨übtr⟩ (etw) *to advance; forward; to help forward; to further; promote* || (Gedanken im Geist) *to bring up* **~|dringen** vi [s] *to break* (od *burst*) *forth* (aus *from*); *to force* od *make one's way up* (z *to*) || (of water, etc.) *to flow forth; to spring up* (aus *out of*); (in Mengen) *to gush* (v *from*) **~|fahren** vi [s] *to go up; to ascend up* (*to heaven*) **~|führen** vt [h] (jdn) *to lead up* (z *to*) **~|heben** vt [h] *to lift* (*up*); *to raise*; (die Hostie) *to elevate* || (jdn) *to raise* (auf die Schultern *to the shoulders*; in die Höhe *to the heights*); die Augen in Ekstase zu ihr -gehoben *his eyes raised in an ecstasy to her face*; → erheben **~|kommen I.** vi [s] **1.** (of fish) *to rise* **2.** ⟨fig⟩ in der Welt ~ *to rise in the world; to get on in the world* || -ge- [a] ⟨fig⟩ *upstart* **II.** ≃ n ⟨fig⟩ *rise* (*in life*) **≃kömmling** m *parvenu* [Fr]; *upstart; upstart pusher; arriviste* Fr; die ~e ⟨a.⟩ *the jumped-up kind* **~|raffen** [vrefl] [h] sich ~ *to pull o.s. together* **~|ragen** vi [h] **1.** (of buildings, etc.) *to lift one's head; to rise; to shoot up* (bis z e-r Höhe v *to a height of* ..); *to tower*; (of hair) *to stand up; to stand on end* **2.** (P) ~ über ⟨eig & fig⟩ *to tower above* **3.** ⟨fig⟩ *to stand out* **~ragend** a *towering; lofty* **~|ranken** vi [s] *to climb* (od *creep*) *up*; ~ an e-m Hause *to climb a house* **~|recken** vt [h] **1.** (den Kopf) *to toss* || *to stretch up* (*one's arms, hands toward heaven*) || *to crane* (*one's neck*) **2.** sich ~ *to straighten up* || (of mountain) *to shoot upwards* **~|reißen** vt [h] ⟨fig⟩ jdn ~ *to pull a p round; to rouse a p to action* **~|richten** vt [h] **1.** *to raise up* **2. sich** ~ *to straighten up*; sich stolz ~ *to draw o.s. up* **~|schießen** vi [s] *to shoot up*; (of weeds) *to spring up* **~|schnellen** vi [s] (P) *to* (*give a*) *jump* || (of prices) *to jump* **~|schwingen** [vref] [h] sich ~ *to soar* (z *to*); *to mount, to rise* (*into the air*) || ⟨übtr⟩ *to rise to be* (*director*) **~|sehen** vi = emporblicken **~|senden** vt [h] *to send up* || (Dank, Gebet) *to put up* (z Gott *to God*) **~|stehen** vi → emporragen **~|steigen** vi [s] **1.** *to ascend; to climb* (z *to*), *to mount* || (of a plane) *to rise* (*in the air*) || (of birds) *to soar* | ⟨fig⟩ *to rise* (*in the world*) **2.** (of a path) *to ascend* || (of a mountain) *to rise* (z *to*) **~|streben** vi [h] *to aspire* (z *to*); *to aim* (od *soar*) *high* || → emporragen **~strebend** a *soaring* || ⟨übtr⟩ *aspiring* (*spirit*) **~|strecken** vt [h] (Hände) *to raise; to put up* **~|tauchen** vi [s] *to break water* **~|treiben** vt [h] **1.** (etw, jdn) *to cause* (*a th*) *to rise, to make* (*a th*) *rise* **2.** ⟨übtr⟩ *to force up* || *to produce* (*a th*) *by force* || (Preise) *to send up* || (Gefühle) *to work up* (z *into*) **~|ziehen** vt [h] *to draw* (od *pull*) *upwards* || ⟨übtr⟩ (jdn) *to lift* (aus *from*); *to raise; to elevate* **~|züngeln** vi [s] (of flames) *to leap high* (*in the air*); die Wände ~ *to lick the walls*

Emp·ore f ~/~n ⟨arch⟩ *gallery* || (in a cathedral) *choir*

emp·ören vt [h] **A. 1.** (erregen) (jdn, jds Gefühle) *to excite, rouse; stir* **2.** (aufbringen) *to exasperate, enrage* || (anwidern) *to disgust, nauseate, revolt, shock, sicken* || es empört mich *it disgusts me, it makes me sick* (*to hear*) || empört s *to be disgusted* (od *scandalized, shocked*) (über *at*); *to revolt* od *sicken* (*at*); *to be revolted* od *shocked* (über *by*; z hören *to hear*); ‚nein', rief er empört *'no' he cried, revolted* || → empört **B. sich ~ 1.** *to rebel, revolt, rise* (gegen *against*); → meutern **2.** ⟨übtr⟩ *to revolt* (gegen *against*; über *at*); sich ~ über etw *to be outrayed at a th, to resent a th* || = empört s, → A. 2. **3.** (of the sea) *to surge* **emp·örend 1.** a *disgusting* (*it is d.*), *revolting, shocking* **2.** *adv *disgustingly* (*ridiculous*); *shocking, shockingly* **Emp·örer** m ~s/~ *insurgent, mutineer, rebel* **emp·örerisch** a *rebellious, mutinous*

emp·ört a [pp v empören] *revolted* (*feeling*); *outraged* (P) (über *by*) || *insurgent*; die ~e Menge *the surging crowd*

Emp·örung f ~/~en *rebellion, revolt; insurrection* || (innere ~) *disgust, indignation* (über *at*); *revolt* (*against*); starke ~ *deep resentment* (*at*)

Empy·em n ~s/~e ⟨path⟩ *empyema* [L]

Empyr·eum n [L] ~s/ ⟨ant⟩ *empyrean*

Ems 1. f ⟨Ger⟩ (Fluß) **2.** n ⟨Ger⟩ (Stadt) *Ems*

·Emse f ~/~n † = Ameise *ant* **·emsig 1.** a *assiduous, diligent, industrious, sedulous* || *active, busy* (*mind*); *expeditious* (*traveller*) || ein überaus ~er Arbeiter *a demon for work* || *ant-like* (*activity*); *busy* (*bee*) ⟨a. fig⟩ **2.** adv *assiduously, sedulously; busily*; ~ arbeiten *to work hard* **≃keit** f ~/ *assiduity, diligence, industry, sedulity; busyness*

·Emu m ~s/~s ⟨orn⟩ *emu*

emulg·ieren vt [h] (etw) *to emulsify* **Emulsi·on** f ~/~en *emulsion*

en bloc [ɑ̃ˈblɔk] [Fr] *en bloc*; *in the lump*
End n ⟨engl⟩: happy ~ *happy ending*
·End- [in comp] *terminal* ‖ *final*; *ultimate* **~absicht** f *end*; *final design*, *ultimate purpose* **~anflug** m ⟨aero⟩ *final approach* **~bahnhof** m = Endstation **~band** n ⟨film etc⟩ *trailers* pl **~beleg** m ⟨comp⟩ *final document* **~betrag** m *total*; *sum total* **~buchstabe** m *final letter* **~ergebnis** n *final* (od *ultimate*) *result*; *the upshot* (*of the trouble*); *conclusion*; *resultant* **~erzeugnis** n *final* (od *ultimate*) *product* **~feinheit** f ⟨mill⟩ *product fineness* | benötigter ~sgrad *degree of fineness for the product* **~feuchtigkeit** f ⟨tech⟩ *residual moisture* **~geschwindigkeit** f *remaining* od *final velocity* **≈gültig 1.** a *definite* (*answer*), *definitive* (*offer*), *final* (*result*), *conclusive* (*proof*); *utter* (*refusal*) ‖ ~er Abschluß *finality*; der ~e Betrag *the grand total*; ~er Scheidungserlaß m ⟨jur⟩ *decree nisi* | [pred] *for good and all* ‖ der Anschein des ≈en *the appearance of finality* **2.** adv *definitely*; *finally*; *once and for all* ‖ (etw) ~ erledigen *to clinch*; damit ist die S ~ entschieden *that clinches the matter* **~gültigkeit** f *finality* **~hafen** m *navigation head* **~handlung** f ⟨eth, biol⟩ *consummatory act* **~kampf** m = Endspiel **~klemme** f ⟨el⟩ *terminal* **~konsonant** m *final consonant* **~lage** f *final position* **~maß** n *stop-measure* **~montage** f ⟨mot etc⟩ *final assembly* **~moräne** f *terminal moraine* **~produkt** n *final* od *finished product* **~punkt** m *end* (*of a line*); *termination*; *final point*; äußerster ~ *final extremity* ‖ → Endziel **~reim** m *end-rhyme* **~resultat** n *the upshot* (*of a trouble*) **~sieg** m *final* od *ultimate victory* **~silbe** f *final* od *last syllable*; *termination* **~spiel** n ⟨sport⟩ *final*; Teilnehmer am ~ *finalist* **~spurt** m ⟨sport⟩ *final efforts* [pl] **~stadium** n *terminal stage* (*of disease*) **≈ständig** a ⟨chem⟩ *terminal* (*group*) **~station** f ⟨rail⟩ *terminus*; ⟨Am⟩ *terminal* ‖ ⟨el⟩ *tramhead* **~stecker** m ⟨wir⟩ *terminal* **~stellung** f *final position* **~stück** n *terminal*; ~e [pl] *ends* [pl] **~stufe** f *final* od *output stage* **~temperatur** f *final temperature* **~termin** m *final date* **~ursache** f *final cause* **~urteil** n *final decree* (od *judgement*) **~verbraucher** m *ultimate* od *final consumer* **~wert** m *final value* **≈zeitlich** a *final* (*character of our present days*) **~ziel** n *end* ‖ *final goal* ⟨a. fig⟩ ‖ *final aim* ‖ *terminus* [L]; *destination* (*of a journey*) **~zweck** m *end*; *final aim* (od *purpose*); *ultimate object* od *aim*

·Endchen n ~s/~ *end*; (letztes ~) *fag-end* ‖ °⟨fig⟩ *short distance*; °jdn ein ~ begleiten *to accompany a p for a bit*; noch ein ~ *a little farther*

·Ende n ~s/~n **I.** [konkr] **1.** (Endpunkt) *end* (*of a line*); *extremity*, *termination*; das äußerste ~ *the final extremity* | ⟨hunt⟩ (Geweih≈) *tine* (10 ~n *10 tines*) → -ender **2.** das andere ~ *the other end* (*of the street*) → II. C. 3. a ‖ (er lebt) am anderen ~ der Stadt .. *across the city* ‖ das ~ der Welt *the ends of the earth* → II. C. 3. c.; das obere ~ *the head* (*of a table*; h *to take*); das untere ~ *the bottom* (*of the t.*); das vordere ~ *the distal end* (*of a limb*) ‖ schlaff herabhängendes ~ (e-r Leine) *slack* (*of a line*); Tau~ *rope's end* | *bit*; ein ~ Stoff *a length of material*; ein ~ Schnur *a piece of string*; ein ~ Wurst *a cut* (od *piece*) *of sausage* ‖ letztes ~ *fag-end* (*of a cigar*), *heel* (*of a loaf*); *remnant*; → II. C. 1. **3. Wendungen**: noch ein gutes ~ entfernt *a good distance off* ‖ am richtigen (falschen) ~ anfassen *to attack* od *begin at the right* (*wrong*) *end*; an diesem ~ muß man es anpacken ⟨fig⟩ *it's the right end of the stick*; am unrechten ~ sparen *to be penny-wise and pound-foolish* ‖ → Ecke ‖ mit dem ~ nach vorn, mit dem vorderen ~ *on end* ‖ (Dinge) mit den ~n aneinander|legen *to place* (od *put*) *end to end*; Bretter an den ~n an-e-a-legen *to butt*; an den ~n an-e-a-stoßen (of boards) *to butt* ‖ v e-m bis z anderen ~ *from end to end*; *end to end*; v allen ~n *from all quarters* **II.** ⟨übtr⟩ **A.** (zeitlich) *end* (*of the year*); *close* (*at the close of the 11th c.*); *termination* ‖ z ~ des Jahres *at the end of the year* am ~ der neunziger Jahre *in the late nineties* ‖ ~ Juli ⟨bes Am⟩ *the last of July*, ~ der Woche *the last of the week* ‖ → C. Wochen≈ *week-end* ‖ Lebens≈ *end*, *ending*; *death* **B.** ⟨fig⟩ **1.** (Ausgang) *end*, *ending*; *result*, *termination* ‖ *the upshot* (*of a business*) **2.** (Schluß) *end* (*of a chapter*, *book*, etc.); *ending* (*the happy e. of a play*); *termination* ‖ ⟨telph⟩ „~!" geben, rufen, ⟨wir⟩ das ~ des Programms ansagen *to sign off*; „~!" ⟨mil telph, wir⟩ "*out!*" **3.** † = Zweck **C. Wendungen: 1.** ein ~ mit Schrecken *a terrible* (od *violent*) *end* | das ~ war, daß .. *the end of it was that* .. ‖ es wird sein ~ s *it will be the end of him* ‖ °da ist das ~ v weg! *there is no end to it!*, *that's the limit!*, *won't you put an end to that!* °daß's ~ v weg ist ⟨fam⟩ *with a vengeance* ‖ dem ~ des Leids hoffnungsvoll entgegensehen *to see land* ‖ das ~ vom Liede war .. *the upshot of it was* ..; *the long and the short of it was* ..; u dann, was ist das ~ v Lied? *and then, where are you?* ‖ das **dicke** ~ kommt nach *the worst is still to come*, *this is only the thin end of the wedge*; *this is where the catch* od *rub comes in* ‖ als ihr ~ nahte *as her end drew near* ‖ ~ gut, alles gut *All's well that ends well* ‖ es kann nur ein schlechtes ~ nehmen *it can only end badly*, → II. B. 1.; das Erstaunen nahm kein ~ *there was no end of astonishment* | **letzten ~s** *ultimately*; *in the end*; *in the last analysis* (od *instance*, *resort*); *in the long run*; *when all is said* (*and done*); *after all*; letzten ~s hinauslaufen auf ⟨fam⟩ *to boil down to* .. **2.** das ~ absehen [mst neg] *to foresee the end* ‖ sein ~ erreichen *to end*, *finish*; *result* (in *in*) ‖ ein ~ finden *to come to an end*; *to end* (in *in*; bei *with*) ‖ alles hat mal ein ~ *there is an end of everything*; es muß ein ~ h mit .. *there must be an end of* .. ‖ e-r S ein ~ m *or* setzen *to make an end of a th*; *to put an end* (od *a stop*) *to a th*; *to give the quietus*; *to ring down the curtain* ‖ s-m ~ nahe s *to be near one's end* ‖ sich dem ~ nähern *or* zuneigen *to draw to a close* ‖ ein ~ nehmen *to come to an end*; *to end*, *to stop*; ein schlimmes (gewaltsames) ~ nehmen *to come to a bad* (*violent*) *end* **3.** [nach prep] **a. am ~** 1. am ~ des Zuges ⟨rail⟩ *at the back* od *rear of the train*; am ~ des Zuges kamen die Soldaten *bringing up the end of the procession came the soldiers* ‖ am ~ (s-r Kräfte) sein *to be at the end of one's tether*, *not to be able to go on* ‖ ganz am ~ *at the far end* (*of the street*) ‖ am ~ (sc des Wortes) *finally* 2. (als das ~ kam) *by the end* 3. (schließlich) *in the end*; = letzten ~es → C. 1. 4. (vielleicht) *perhaps*, *possibly* ‖ bis ans ~ der Welt *to the last* **b. mit** dem ~ nach vorne, mit dem vorderen ~ *end on* [adv] **c.** Kette **ohne** ~ *endless chain*; Schraube ohne ~ *endless screw*; Geschichte ohne ~ *never-ending*, *interminable*, *long-winded story* **d. zu ~** *at an end* ‖ v Anfang **bis z ~** → Anfang ‖ bis z bitteren ~ (Tode) *to the end of the chapter* ⟨fig⟩ ‖ bis z ~ des Stückes *to the end of the play* ‖ bis z ~ der Welt ⟨bib⟩ *unto the consummation of the w.* | (etw) bis z ~ aushalten *to stand out* | etw **z ~ bringen,** führen *to bring a th to an end* (od *a close*, *conclusion*); *to go through with a th*; *to close* (od *finish*, *terminate*) *a th* ‖ etw z ~ denken *to think a th out* | **z ~ gehen** *to come to an end*, *to draw near the end*; der Tag ging z ~ *day was declining*; April ging z ~ *April was running out* ‖ *the stock is running low*; *his leave will be up tomorrow*; (aufhören) *to cease*; ⟨fam⟩ *to go phut*; ⟨Am⟩ *to give out*; ⟨sl⟩ *to peter out*; (of a lease) *to expire* ‖ es geht z

~ *the sands are running low* ‖ es ging rasch mit ihm z ~ *he sank fast* | jdn **z ~ hören** *to hear a p out*; Stück z ~ hören *to sit a play through* (od *out*); (stehend) *to stand out* | (etw) restlos z ~ **kämpfen** *to fight .. to a definite finish* ‖ z ~ k *to come to an ˈend*; (of a speaker) *to wind up*; (of a treaty) *to be wound up* | z ~ **reden**: *I'll have my say out* | z ~ **sein** *to be at an end* (*my patience is at an end*); *to be over*; es ist z ~ *it's finished*; *the day is out*; ⟨ftb⟩ das Spiel ist z ~! *no side*! ‖ z ~ spielen *to play* (*a game*) *out* | **z ~ s mit** *to be at the end of ..* ‖ °mit s–m Latein z ~ s *to be past one's Latin, to be at one's wits' end, to be at the end of one's tether*; damit wird es z ~ s *that'll by the end of it*

Endem·ie f ⟨med⟩ *endemic* **end·emisch** a *endemic(al)*

·enden vi/t [h] **I.** vi **1.** (S) *to* (*come to an*) *end*; *to cease, to terminate* (an *at*; in *in*); (alle Züge) ~ hier .. *finish here* ‖ ~ mit *to end with*; es endete damit, daß er ging .. *it ended in his leaving* | (of words) *to end* od *terminate* (auf *in*) | (of a treaty) *to expire* ‖ *to end, result* (in *in*) **2.** (P) *to end* od *finish* (*up*); ⟨Am⟩ *to fetch up* (in *in*) ‖ er endete mit den Worten *he wound up by saying* ‖ *to die*; ⟨sl⟩ *to end up* | nicht ~ wollend *unending, ceaseless, continuous*; *undying* (*hatred*) ‖ auf dem Scheiterhaufen ~ ⟨m. m.⟩ *to perish at the stake* **II.** vt (etw) *to end* (mit *with*); *to bring to an end*; *to conclude*; *finish*; *terminate* ‖ sein Leben mit eigener Hand ~ *to do away with o.s.*

-ender [im comp] ·Acht≃ *stag with 8 antlers*

·Endesunterzeichnete [der ~, ein ~er] m ~n/~n *the undersigned*; die ~[n pl] *the undersigned*

en détail [ɑ̃ deˈtaj] [Fr] ⟨com⟩ (by) *retail*; ~ verkaufen *to sell retail*

·endigen vi/t [h] = enden

End·ivie f ~/~n ⟨bot⟩ (krause *curled*) *endive*; ⟨Am⟩ *chicory* ‖ glatte ~ *Batavia endive*

endlich I. a **1.** ⟨philos & math⟩ *finite* **2.** (am Ende eintretend) *final, last, ultimate*; → endgültig **II.** adv *at* (*the*) *last, at the long last*; *at length*; *finally*; ~ sind wir da! *here* (*we are*) *at last*!; *last of all* (*came* ..) ‖ er ist ~ fort *he's gone for good* **≃keit** f ~/ *finiteness* **·endlos 1.** a *endless, interminable, unending*; *incessant, unceasing*; *perpetual* ‖ *boundless, unbounded, infinite* **2.** adv *endlessly*; *unceasingly*; *perpetually* | **≃formular** [n] ⟨comp⟩ *continuous stationery* **~garn** n ⟨spin⟩ *filament yarn* **~windel** f *disposable nappie roll*

·Endlosigkeit f *endlessness* ‖ *boundlessness, infiniteness*

Endo- [in comp] (inner) *endo–* **~d·ermis** f ⟨bot & biol⟩ *endoderm* **~gam·ie** f *endogamy* **≃g·en** a ⟨geol & biol⟩ *endogenous* **~k·ard** n ⟨anat⟩ *endocardium* [L] **~k·arp** n ⟨bot⟩ *endocarp* **≃kr·in** a *endocrine, ductless* (*glands*) **~sk·op** n ⟨med⟩ *endoscope* **~sp·erm** n ⟨bot⟩ *endosperm* **~th·el** n ⟨anat⟩ *endothelium* [L] **≃th·erm** a ⟨chem⟩ *endothermic, endothermous*

·Endung f ~/~en ⟨gram⟩ *ending, termination*; ~ auf –ble *ending in –ble*

·Eneis m ⟨bot⟩ *anise*

Energ·etik f ⟨scient⟩ *energetics* [pl] [sg konstr]

energetisch a *energetic*

Energ·ie f ~ **1.** *energy* (mit ~ *with e.*); *force, vigour*; *drive, grit, push*; ⟨fam⟩ *kick*; ⟨Am sl⟩ *go, pep, sand* ‖ s–e ganze ~ einsetzen *to apply* (od *devote*) *one's energies* (*to do*); ⟨fam⟩ *to pick up* od *put on unusual steam* **2.** ⟨phys⟩ *energy* ‖ das Gesetz v der Erhaltung der ~ *the law of the conservation of e.* ‖ Bewegungs≃, kinetische ~ *kinetic e.*; ~ der Lage, potentielle ~ *potential, static, latent e.* ‖ aufgewandte *or* zugeführte ~ *input* ‖ Joule (Einheit elektr. ~) *joule* **~abfall** m *e. drop* **~aufspeicherung** f *storage of e.* **~auslösung** f *e. resolution* **~freigabe** f *e. release* **≃geladen** a ⟨übtr⟩ *high-voltage* (*personality*) **~haushalt** m ⟨physiol⟩ *regulation* (*of the supply*) *of e.* **~inhalt** m ⟨el⟩ *potential* od *stored e.* **~leitung** f ⟨el⟩ *power transmission line* **~quelle** f *source of e.* **≃reich** a *high-e.* [attr] **~sprung** m *e. gap* **~umsatz** m *e. conversion* **~- u Wärmewirtschaft** ⟨ind⟩ *power engineering and heat economy* **~verbrauch** m *consumption of e.* **~verlust** m *loss of e.* **~versorgungsanlage** f *power plant* **~v.einrichtung** f *e. supply equipment*, ⟨comp⟩ *power packs* pl **~wirtschaft** f *power industry* od *economy*

energ·ielos a *energyless*; *lacking energy*; *languid, listless, spiritless*; *effeminate, soft, soppy*; ~er Mensch *sop* **Energ·ielosigkeit** f *lack* (od *want*) *of energy*; *softness*

en·ergisch 1. a *energetic, forceful, strong* (*man*), *vigorous*; *enterprising, go-ahead, live, pushing* (*fellow*); *active* (od *strong*)*-mined* (*girl*) ‖ *imperative* (*gesture, step*); mit ~er Hand *with a strong hand* ‖ ⟨Am fam⟩ *two-fisted*; *peppy* ‖ *determined, resolute, firm* (*tone*) ‖ [pred] ⟨fam⟩ *full of beans* **2.** adv *energetically*; *with energy*; *strongly* ‖ ~ auftreten *to put one's foot down* (gegen *against*); (*to deny*) *emphatically*; mit jdm ~ verfahren *to deal firmly with a p*; ~ vorgehen *to take a strong line*

Enfil·ierfeuer n ⟨mil⟩ *enfilade*

·eng, *·enge I. a **A.** (schmal) **1.** *narrow* (*river, road*, etc.); ~e Straße ⟨geogr⟩ *narrow* ‖ ~(er) m *to narrow*; ~er w *to narrow* **2.** ⟨übtr⟩ ~e Verhältnisse *narrow circumstances* ‖ ⟨tech⟩ *exact* (Toleranz) **3.** ⟨fig⟩ (geistig ~, kleinlich) *narrow, small* (*mind*); *petty*; *dense, obtuse*; ~ s in *to be hidebound in* (*one's ideas*); e–n ~en Horizont h *to be narrowminded* ‖ *blinkered* (*life*); *parochial* (*opinions, politics*) ‖ (beschränkt:) in ~erem Sinne *in a narrower sense*; *strictly speaking* **B.** (dicht, gedrängt) **1.** *close* (*texture, writing*); in ~en Reihen *close-ranked* ‖ ~, z ~ *tight* (*shoe, hat*) ‖ (Gürtel) ~er m *to tighten*; (Rock) ~er m *to take in* **2.** ⟨fig⟩ (nahe) *close, firm* (*friends*); ~e Berührung *close contact* ‖ ~er Ausschuß *select committee* ‖ jds ~erem Kreise angehören *to belong to a p's intimate circle* ‖ ~ste Freunde *intimates* [pl] ‖ ~ster Kreis *immediate circle* (*in his i. c.*) ‖ ~ere Wahl ⟨parl⟩ *short list*; in die Wahl ~ere k *to be put on the sh. l.*; in die ~ere W. stellen *to put on the sh. l., to short-list* (*a p*) ‖ ~erer Wettbewerb *close competition* **II.** adv **1.** *narrowly* (*selfish*); (Worte) ~ auslegen *to read narrowly* **2.** (gedrängt) ~ sitzen *to sit close together, to sit cheek by jowl* (*with a p*) ‖ ~ schreiben *to write closely* ‖ ansitzen (of clothes) *to sit close*; ~ ansitzend *close* (*cap*); ~ anliegende Hose *tights* [pl] (e–e H. *a pair of t.*); ⟨tail⟩ ~ sitzend, ~ tailliert *hugging*; *waisted*; *tight-fitting* **2.** ⟨übtr⟩ sich dem Original ~ anschließen *to follow the original closely* ‖ ~ befreundet sein *to be on intimate terms* (*with*); er u ich sind ~ befreundet ⟨fam⟩ *he and I are very thick* ‖ ~ verbunden *closely allied* (mit *to, with*) **III.** [in comp] **~·anliegend, ~·anschließend** a *close fitting*; *tight*(*-fitting*); *waist hugging* (*jacket*) ‖ –anliegende Ohren *ears close to the skull* **~begr·enzt** a *narrow*; *limited close* **~brüstig** a *narrow-chested*; → asthmatisch **≃brüstigkeit** f *narrowness of chest*; *pursiness* **~herzig** a *narrow* (*mind*); *narrow-minded* (*p*); *hidebound*; *illiberal*; *parochial* **≃herzigkeit** f *narrowness*; *narrow-mindedness*; *pettiness*; *lack of generosity* **~maschig** a *fine-meshed* **≃paß** m *defile*; *narrow pass*; *narrow*; ⟨mot⟩ „~!" "*Road Narrows*" ‖ ⟨fig⟩ *bottleneck* (*bottlenecks in the production of ..*; .. *in supplies*) | ~güter [pl] *items in short supply* ⟨a. mil⟩ **~spaltig** a *narrow-spaced* **≃stellung** f ⟨path⟩ (*spastic*) *constriction* **~stirnig** a *cramped, dense, hidebound, narrow, narrow in mind*; *narrow* (od *small*)*minded* (*p*); *obtuse*; ⟨Am⟩

peanut (politician) **~zeilig** a ⟨typ⟩ *single-spaced*

·**Engadin,** das (Tal des Inn) *the Engadin(e)*

Engagem·ent [ãgaʒ'mã:] n [Fr] ⟨theat⟩ *engagement* ‖ ⟨com⟩ *commitment* **engag·ieren** [ã:ga'ʒi:rən] vt [Fr] [h] (jdn) *to engage; to take* od *put on*

·**Enge** f ~/~n **1. a.** *narrowness* ‖ *narrow passage* od *place;* → Meer≗; Engpaß **b.** ⟨übtr⟩ *confinement (of office life); narrowness* ‖ (Klemme) *difficulty, dilemma, straits* [pl]; *trouble* ‖ jdn in die ~ treiben *to corner a p, to drive a p into a corner; to cut the ground from under a p's feet* od *from underneath a p; to press a p hard; to nonplus* (od *stalemate) a p; to put a p on the spot* ‖ (mit der Zeit) in die ~ k *to run it fine;* in die ~ gedrückt s *to have one's back to the wall;* in die ~ getrieben ⟨fam⟩ *in a tight corner* od *spot; when his* od *her back is* od *was to the wall* **c.** ⟨fig⟩ *narrowness (of mind); narrowmindedness* **2.** (Gedrängtheit) *closeness; tightness* ‖ ⟨übtr⟩ *closeness, firmness (of an alliance)* **~laut** n ⟨phon⟩ *spirant*

·**Engel** m ~s/~ **1.** *angel* ‖ Schutz≗ *guardian angel;* sein böser ~ *his evil genius;* sein guter ~ *his good angel;* ein ~ schwebt durchs Zimmer *an angel is passing* od *is flying over (sudden hush)* ⟨fig⟩ (schweigsame Gesellschaft) *it's a Quaker-meeting* ‖ Todes≗ *angel of death;* Würg≗ *destroying angel;* gefallener ~ *fallen a.* **2.** ⟨übtr⟩ (P) *angel;* °du bist ein ~ ⟨fam⟩ *you are a dear;* mein ~ *my cherub* **3.** [in comp] → Engel–, Engels–

·**Engel-** (→ Engels–) [in comp] **~bild** n *angelic* (od *angel-)face* **~blume** f ⟨bot⟩ *cat's foot* **~brot** n *angelic food; manna* | die 9 **~chöre** m *the (nine) companies* od *hosts of angels* **~fisch** m ⟨ich⟩ *angelfish* **≗fromm** a *angelic* **≗gleich** a *angelic(al); angel-like* **~kunde** f ⟨theol⟩ *angelology* **~macherin** f *babyfarmer* **≗rein** a *angelic* **~schar** f *host of angels; angelic host* **≗schön** a *angelic; angel-bright* **~stimme** f *angelic voice* **~verehrung** f *angel-worship, angelolatry* **~wurz** f ⟨bot, cul⟩ *angelica*

·**Engels-** [in comp] **~bild** n = Engelbild **~bote** m *angel* od *angelic messenger* **~burg** f (in Rom) *Castle of St. Angelo* | ihm wachsen schon **~flügel** ⟨iron⟩ *his wings are sprouting* **~geduld** f *patience of Job* **~gestalt** f *angelic figure* **~gruß** m *Angelic Salutation; Ave Maria; Angelus, Annunciation* **~kopf** m *cherub's head* **~stimme** f *angelic voice* **~unschuld** f *angelic innocence* **~zunge** f *angelic voice* ‖ ⟨übtr⟩ ~n [pl] *the tongues of angels*

Engelchen n *little angel; cherub* ·**engelhaft** a *angelic(al); angel-like*

·**engen** vt [h] = be–, einengen

·**Engerling** m ~s/~e *larva of the cockchafer*

·**Engheit** f ⟨bes fig⟩ *narrowness; narrow-mindedness; smallness (all his s.)*

·**England** n *England* [oft fem konstr: *she*]; → Bezirk ‖ ⟨sl⟩ *Blighty* ‖ das südliche ~ *Southern E.;* das protestantische ~ *Protestant England* ‖ das ~ des 19. Jahrhunderts *the E. of the 19th c.* **~freund** m *Anglophile* **~hasser** m *Anglophobe*

·**Engländer** m **1.** *Englishman;* ⟨Scot⟩ *Englisher;* ⟨Am⟩ *Britisher* ‖ in Indien geborener ~ *Anglo-Indian* ‖ ~ v Geburt begann N. .. *British by birth N. began ..;* er ist kein ~ *he is not an Englishman, he is not English;* er sprach ohne Akzent, als wenn er ~ wäre *he spoke without an accent as though he were English* ‖ die ~ [pl] *Englishmen; the English* **2.** (Schraubenschlüssel) *monkey-wrench* ·**Engländerin** f *English woman*

·**Englisch**[1] a (→ Engel) *angelic (salutation)*

·**englisch**[2] **1.** a *English;* ⟨Am⟩ *Anglican (tradition);* ~ m *to Anglicize* ‖ die ~e Kirche *the Anglican Church;* die ~e Literatur *English Literature;* die ~e Sprache *English; the English Language;* Nachahmer ~er Spr., etc. ⟨Am⟩ *dude* ‖ ~e Nationalität *British nationality* ‖ ~e Bevölkerung in Irland *Englishry* ‖ ≗es Gras [n] = Seidendarm ‖ der ≗e Kanal *the English Channel* ‖ ~e Krankheit [f] ⟨med⟩ *rickets* [pl] [sg konstr] ‖ ~es Pflaster [n] *court-plaster* **2.** adv; ⟨cul⟩ ~gebraten *underdone,* ⟨Am⟩ *rare* **3.** ≗ n; das ≗e; auf (gut) ~ *in (plain) English;* Standard-~ *Standard E., the king's English;* ins ~e übersetzen *to English* **4.** [in comp] *English; Anglo–* **≗leder** n *moleskin* **~sprechend** a *English-speaking*

en gros [aŋ'gro:, ã:'gro:] adv [Fr] ⟨com⟩ *by* (⟨Am⟩ *at) wholesale; wholesale (to buy wh.)*

Engr·os- [in comp] *wholesale* **~firma** f *wholesale firm* **~geschäft** n, **~handel** m *wholesale business* od *trade* **~händler** m *wholesale dealer* od *merchant* **~preis** m *wholesale price*

Enharm·onik f ⟨mus⟩ *enharmonics* [pl]

enharm·onisch a ⟨mus⟩ *enharmonic (change)*

enigm·atisch 1. a *enigmatic(al)* ‖ [pred] *a can of worms* **2.** adv *enigmatically*

Enjambem·ent [ãʒãb'mã:] n (Fr) ⟨pros⟩ *enjambment* (Fr)

Enk·austik f ⟨arts⟩ *encaustic; encaustic painting*

·**Enkel**[1] m ~s/~ *grandson; grandchild;* ⟨übtr⟩ *descendant*

·**Enkel**[2] m ~s/~ ⟨anat⟩ *ankle, ancle; talus* [L]

·**Enkelin** f ~/~nen *granddaughter* ·**Enkelkind** n ~(e)s/~er *grand-child*

Enkl·ave f ~/~n *enclave*

Enkl·ise f ⟨gram⟩ *encliticism* **Enkl·itikon** n *enclitic* **enkl·itisch** a *enclitic*

en masse [ã:'mas] adv (Fr) *en masse* (Fr); *in a mass; as a whole*

ennuy·ant a [any'jant] Fr = langweilig; lästig

en·orm 1. a *enormous, huge, immense, tremendous (building); mammoth (shoulders)* | ⟨übtr⟩ *enormous (difference)* ‖ ⟨fam⟩ *mighty; howling; roaring (trade);* ein ~er Arbeiter ⟨fam⟩ *a whale for work* ‖ → riesig, ungeheuer **2.** adv *enormously; tremendously* ‖ ~ interessant ⟨Am⟩ *mighty interesting* ‖ ~ viel Zeit ⟨fam⟩ *a whale of time*

en passant [ã pa'sã:) adv (Fr) *en passant* (Fr); *in passing; by the way*

Enqu·ete [ã'kæ:tə] f [Fr] *expert inquiry; survey; investigation by experts*

enrag·iert a → leidenschaftlicher (Spieler); adv l. (spielen)

En(n)s 1. f (Nebenfluß der Donau) *Ens* **2.** n (Stadt) *Ens* ·**Ennstaler Alpen** pl *Enstal Alps*

Ens·emble [ã'sã:bl] n [Fr] ~s/~s ⟨theat & mus⟩ (⟨Am⟩ *permanent) company, ensemble;* mit vollem ~ ⟨theat⟩ *withe the full cast* **~spiel** n ⟨mus⟩ *ensemble;* ⟨theat & sport⟩ *team work*

Ensil·age [ãsi'la:ʒ] f [Fr] ⟨agr⟩ *ensilage*

Enstat·it m ~s/ ⟨minr⟩ *enstatite*

ent- [lebendes, unbetontes, untrennbares Verbal–pref] [mit Knacklaut, also ohne Bindung, vor Vokalen: ent|arten]; (mst Trennung ausdrückend) **1.** (= fort) *away; off;* ~führen *to carry off;* ~laufen *to run away* **2.** (= los) *un–;* ~runden *to unround;* ~spannen *to unbend* ‖ *de–; dis–;* ~lausen *to delouse;* ~erben *to disinherit;* ~wurzeln *to disroot* ‖ ~ölen *to free from oil*

ent- ~·adeln (→ ent–!) vt [h] (jdn) *to deprive of nobility; to degrade* **~·arten** (→ ent–!) vi [s] *to degenerate* (in zu *into*); *degrade, deteriorate* **~·artet** a *degenerate;* (moralisch) *corrupt; decadent* ‖ ~er Mensch, ~es Wesen *degenerate* **≗·artung** f ~/~en *degeneracy, degeneration; deterioration* ‖ ⟨biol⟩ *degradation* ‖ (moralische) *corruption; decadence, –cy* **≗·aschung(sanlage)** f *ash removing (plant)*

Ent·ase, ·Entasis f ⟨Gr ant arch⟩ *bulge*

ent- (→ ent-!) **~·äußern** [vrefl] [h] sich e–r S ~ *to get rid of, to dispose of a th; to sell a th;* → veräußern ‖ *to discard a th; to give a th up, to part with a th;* sich e–s Rechtes ~ *to divest o.s. of a right, to resign a right* **≃·äußerung** f ~/~en die ~ e–r S *the getting rid of, the selling of a th* ‖ *the discarding of, the giving up of a th; the parting with a th* ‖ → Veräußerung **~b·ehren I.** vt [h] **1.** (nicht h) etw ~, *[gen] ~ *to lack* od *want a th* (*the edition wants two important speeches*) ‖ das Gerücht entbehrt jeder Grundlage *the rumour is without any foundation* **2.** jdn, etw ~ *to feel the want of, to miss a p, a th* ‖ er –rt nichts *he goes short of nothing* **3.** [mst mit ‚können'] *to do* (od *go, manage*) *without* (*a th*); *to dispense with* (*a th*); *to forgo* od *renounce* (*a th*); ich kann es ~ *I can do without it; I cannot afford it;* ich kann ihn nicht ~ *I cannot spare* (od *do without*) *him* **4.** [abs] *to be temperate* (od *abstinent, frugal*); *to practise economy* **II.** ≃ n *abstinence; frugality; temperance;* → Entbehrung **~behrlich** a *dispensable, unnecessary; not wanted;* → überflüssig; übrig ‖ (nebensächlich) *non-essential* (*elements*) ‖ ist er jetzt ~? *can you spare him just now;* er ist nicht ~ *I cannot spare him* | ≃keit [f] *dispensability; superfluousness* **≃b·ehrung** f ~/~en *privation, want; need;* ~en [pl] *hardship* ‖ sich [dat] ~ auferlegen *to suffer privation; to be frugal* (od *abstinent, temperate*); *to economize, retrench; to make both ends meet* **~b·ieten** vt [h] [→ bieten] **1.** (wissen l) jdm etw ~ *to make a th known to a p; to announce a th to a p* ‖ jdm s–n Gruß *to send* (od *present*) *one's compliments to a p;* er entbot ihnen e–n guten Morgen *he bade them good morning;* jdm ein Willkommen ~ *to bid* od *make a p welcome; to extend a* (*warm*) *welcome to a p* **2.** (befehlen) jdn z sich ~ *to send for a p; to summon a p* **~b·inden** vt [h] [→ binden] **1.** (e–e Frau) *to deliver;* entbunden w v *to be delivered* (od *confined*) *of; to be brought to bed of* (*a child*); sie wurde v Zwillingen entbunden *she was brought to bed of twins* **2.** (frei m) ⟨chem⟩ (Wärme) *to set free;* (Gase) *to liberate* **3.** (befreien) ⟨fig⟩ jdn v e–r Pflicht (etc) ~ *to release* (od *dispense, exonerate*) *a p from a duty;* jdn v dem Besuch (e–r S) ~ *to relieve a p of attendance, to excuse a p from a.;* jdn v der Leitung ~ *to suspend a p;* jdn ~, etw z tun *to absolve a p from doing a th* **≃b·indung** f ~/~en **1.** ⟨med⟩ *confinement, delivery; childbirth; accouchement* [Fr]; → Gebären ‖ sie stand vor der ~ *she was near her time* **2.** ⟨fig⟩ *exemption, exoneration, release, relief* (v *from*) | ~sanstalt [f] *lying-in hospital, maternity hospital* ~ssaal [m] *delivery room* ~sstuhl [m] *obstetric chair* **~bl·ättern** vt [h] *to defoliate; strip of leaves;* (Zuckerrohr) *to trash* | **sich** ~ (of a plant) = abblättern 2. ‖ (P) °*to peel off;* ⟨mst theat⟩ *to strip* **≃bl·ätterungs-** ~akt [m], ~szene [f] *strip tease* od *scene;* ~tänzerin [f] *stripper* **~bl·öden** [vrefl] [h] * = sich erkühnen | sich nicht ~ z tun *not to be ashamed to do; not to be deterred from doing; not to scruple to do; to be impudent enough to do* **~bl·ößen** vt [h] **1.** (das Gesicht etc) *to uncover;* den Arm ~ *to bare* od *expose one's arm* (bis an den Ellbogen *to the elbow*) ‖ (jdn) *to undress; strip* (bis auf die Haut *to ste skin*) ‖ s–n Körper ~, sich ~ *to strip; to take one's clothes off; to undress* **2.** ⟨übtr⟩ *to denude, to dismantle;* ein Land der Wälder ~ *to denude* (od *deprive, strip*) *a country of woods;* die Erde war jeder Spur .. entblößt *the earth was swept clear of any vestige of them* **~bl·ößt** a *bare* (*face*); *naked, nude; unclothed;* vollkommen ~ *stark naked* ‖ ⟨übtr⟩ *bare;* ein Distrikt v Bäumen ~ *a district stripped of trees* ‖ v allen Mitteln ~ *destitute; in absolute want* **≃bl·ößung** f ~/~en *baring; denudation* (*of a country*) ‖ ~ v allen Mitteln *destitution* °**~bräunen** vt [h] ⟨anti-nazi⟩ *to clear* **≃br·äunter** m *purgee* **~br·ennen I.** vi [s] [→ brennen] **1.** *⟨eig⟩ *to catch* od *take fire; to be ignited* **2.** mst ⟨übtr⟩ **a.** (of war) *to break out* ‖ (of anger) *to break forth; to burn;* sein Zorn entbrannte gegen .. *his rage burnt against* (*the clergy*) **b.** (P) in Wut, Zorn ~ *to fly* od *get into a passion; to blaze* (od *flame*) *up; to be enraged* od *raging;* in Leidenschaft etc ~ *to be inflamed with passion, to be seized with passion, anger, hatred;* in Liebe z jdm ~ *to fall in love with, to be smitten with a p;* v Begierde nach .. ~ *to burn* (od *to be smitten*) *with the desire for* .. **II.** ≃ n *breaking-out* (*of a war*) ‖ *outburst* (*of rage*); *blaze* (*of passion*)

·Entchen n *duckling* ‖ (P) (häßliches *ugly*) *d.*

ent- **~d·eckbar** a *discoverable, detectable* **~d·ecken** vt [h] **1. a.** ⟨geog & astr⟩ (neues Land; Stern) *to discover* ‖ ⟨chem⟩ (Radium) *to discover* **b.** (aufdecken) (Verschwörung) *to discover; to expose;* (Geheimnis) *to disclose;* (Motiv) *to descry* ‖ (Fehler etc) *to detect; to find* (in *in*); *to find* (od *make*) *out;* (Spur) *to pick up;* (Verbrechen) *to spot;* (Tatsache) *to ascertain; to recognize;* e–n Fehler plötzlich ~ *to pounce upon a mistake* ‖ –ckt w *to come to light,* nicht –ckt w *to baffle* (od *escape*) *detection* **c.** jdn ~ *to spot a p;* ⟨sl⟩ *to rumble a p* **2.** jdm etw ~ *to disclose* od *reveal a th to a p* ‖ sich jdm ~ *to open one's mind to a p; to reveal one's feelings, to unbosom o.s. to a p* **≃d·ecker** m ~s/~ *discoverer* **≃d·eckung** f ~/~en **1.** *discovery;* ~sreise [f] *voyage of discovery* **2.** *exposure* (*of a plot*); *disclosure* ‖ *detection; finding* (*out*); e–e trügerische ~ *a mare's nest* ‖ *spotting* (*of a p*) ‖ auf ~en *or* ~sreisen ausgehen *to go exploring* **≃düppelung** f ⟨radar⟩ *antijamming*

·Ente f ~/~n **1.** ⟨orn⟩ *duck;* wie e–e bleierne ~ schwimmen *to swim like a brick* ‖ oft [koll] ~n [pl] *duck;* drei ~n *three duck(s);* junge ~ *duckling* ‖ ~n pl → Bd. I. *golden-eye, pochard, scoter, sheldrake, shelduck, teal* ‖ [in comp] → Enten– **2.** ⟨aero⟩ = Entenflugzeug **3.** ⟨fig⟩ *false report; hoax; fake; dope; canard* (Fr), ⟨Am sl⟩ *grapevine;* → Schwindel **4.** kalte ~ (Getränk) ⟨m. m.⟩ *cobbler, sangeree* **5.** (P) ⟨hum fig⟩ lahme ~ *lame duck* od *pup*

ent- (→ ent–!) **~·ehren** vt [h] *to dishonour; disgrace* ‖ (Mädchen) *to deflower, dishonour, ravish* **~·ehrend** a *dishonouring, disgraceful* (*for a p to do*); *degrading* (*punishment, etc*) ‖ *discreditable* (*action*) **≃·ehrer** m ~s/~ *ravisher* (*of a woman*) **≃·ehrung** f ~/~en *disgrace, dishonour; degradation* ‖ *defloration, ravishing* (*of a woman*) **~·eignen** (→ ent–!) vt [h] (jdn) *to expropriate, to disposses;* ⟨jur⟩ *to forjudge* ‖ (Land) *to expropriate* **≃·eignung** f ~/~en *expropriation, deprivation, dispossession;* ⟨jur⟩ *forjudgement* ‖ ⟨Am⟩ das Recht der Eigentums≃ (innerhalb e–s Staates) *the right of Eminent Domain* **~·eilen** (→ ent–!) vi [s] *to hasten* (od *hurry*) *away* (jdm *from a p*) **~·eisen** *to free from ice* | **Ent·eiser** m, **Ent·eisungs-** ~anlage [f] *ice eliminating system;* ~vorrichtung [f] *anti-icer,* ⟨aero⟩ *de-icer, defroster;* → Eis

ent·eisenen (→ ent–!) vt (Wasser) *to free* (*water*) *from its ferruginous ingredients* | Ent·eisenungsanlage [f] *iron extraction plant;* → Eisen

°**enten oder weder** ⟨hum⟩ → entweder oder: jetzt heißt es ~ *if you don't like it you may do the other thing* (= *lump it*)

·Enten- (→ Ente) [in comp] °„**~beine**" n pl (zu kurz) ⟨hum⟩ *duck's disease* **~braten** m *roast duck* **~ei** n *duck's egg* **~falle** f *decoy* **~fang** m *duck-decoying; duck-hunting; ground for duck-hunting* **~fleisch** n *duck* **~flott** m ⟨bot⟩ = Wasserlinse **~flugzeug** n ⟨aero⟩ *tail first* *machine* od *aeroplane* **~gang** m → ~krankheit **~grün** n ⟨bot⟩ = Wasserlinse **~herd** m = Entenfalle **~jagd** f *duck-shooting*; ⟨fam⟩ *ducking* ‖ °**~krankheit** f → –beine **~klein** n *giblets* **~kü(c)ken** n *duck-chicken* **~muschel** f *barnacle* **~pfuhl** m *duck-pool* **~schnabel** m *duck's bill* **~teich** m *duck-pond* **~vögel** m pl → Bd. I. *duck*, Ente, Eider **~züchter** m *ducker*

Entente [ɑ̃'tɑ̃:t] f (Fr) *entente* (Fr); ~ cordiale (zw England u Frankreich; 1904) *entente cordiale* (Fr); die Kleine ~ *the Little Entente*

·Enter m & n *one-year-old horse*

·Enter- (→ entern) ⟨mar⟩ [in comp] *boarding* **~beil** n *pole-axe* **~brücke** f *boarding-bridge* **~haken** m *grapnel, grapple, grappling-iron* **~mannschaft** f *boarding party* **~messer** n *cutlass*

enter·al a ⟨med⟩ *enteric*

ent·erben (→ ent–!) vt [h] (jdn) *to disinherit* (*a p*): *to cut* (*a p*) *off with a shilling* ‖ die Enterbten ⟨soc⟩ *the underprivileged classes* **Ent·erbung** f ~/~en *disinheritance* ‖ *cut-you-off-with-a-shilling* (*is out of date*)

·Enterich m ~s/~e ⟨orn⟩ *drake*; wilder ~ *mallard*

ent·erisch a ⟨med⟩ *enteric* **Enter·itis** f ⟨med⟩ *enteritis*

·entern vt [h] ⟨mar⟩ (Schiff) *to board* ‖ (mittelst Enterhakens festhalten) *to grapple*

ent- **~f·achen** vt [h] ein Feuer ~ *to kindle a fire*; e–n Brand ~ *to start* (⟨Am⟩ *to set*) *a fire* ‖ ⟨fig⟩ (Begeisterung etc) *to kindle*; *to nurse* (z *into*); *to stir up*; e–e Leidenschaft voller Glut ~ *to fann a passion into flame*; (Kampfgeist) *to rouse*; (Begierde) *to arouse, awaken*; *produce*; *to give rise to* **~f·ahren** vi [s] (→ fahren) das Wort entfuhr ihm (*or* s–n Lippen) *the word escaped him* (od *his lips*); *the word fell from his lips*; es entfuhr ihm: Gott! *he burst out*: *Lord*! ‖ (entfallen) das Schwert entfuhr s–r Hand *the sword slipped from his hand* **~f·allen** vi [s] (→ fallen) **1.** jds Händen ~ *to slip from a p's hands* ‖ ⟨tech⟩ *to be eliminated* ‖ ⟨mst übtr⟩ dem Gedächtnis ~ *to slip from* (od *out of*) *the memory*; jdm ~, jds G. ~ *to slip a p's memory* (od *mind*); sein Name ist mir ~ *his name has escaped me* **2.** auf jdn ~ (of a sum) *to fall to a p's share* **3.** (wegfallen) *to drop out*; *to cease*; daher ~fällt hierfür unsere Verantwortung *so we are no longer responsible for it, so our r. no longer exists*; **~fällt** *does not apply, is not applicable*; (auf Formularen) *nonapplicable* (*N/A*) **~f·alten** vt [h] **1. a.** ⟨eig⟩ (Fahne) *to unfurl, to break* ‖ (Blüte) *to unfold*; *to expand* ‖ ⟨mil⟩ (Truppe seitlich ~) *to deploy* **b.** ⟨übtr⟩ (Fähigkeiten) *to develop, evolve* ‖ (Tätigkeit, Eigenschaft) *to display, exhibit*; *unfold* ‖ man soll die Persönlichkeit e–s Kindes sich frei ~ l *a child should have full scope to develop its personality* ‖ alle Reize voll ~ *to release all one's charms*; s–e Fähigkeiten voll ~ *to do o.s. justice* **2. sich ~ a.** (S) *to unfurl* ‖ *to develop* (z *into*); *to effloresce*; *to unfold*; (of a story) *to unfold itself* ‖ *to display* (od *reveal*) *itself* **b.** (P) *to develop o.s.* **≗f·altung** f ~/~en **1.** *breaking, unfurling* (*of a flag*) ‖ *unfolding*; ⟨mil⟩ seitliche ~ *deploy*(*ment*) **2.** ⟨übtr⟩ *development* ‖ *display*; Leistungs≗ *show--down*; plötzliche ~ *burst* (*of activity*); prunkende ~ *flash*; ~ v Leidenschaft, Witz ⟨fam⟩ *fire-works* ‖ zur ~ k *to develop, to effloresce*; *to display o.s.* | ~smöglichkeit [f] *scope* **~f·ärben** vt [h] *to decolour, to decolo*(*u*)*rize*; *to bleach*; (Gesicht) *to make pale* | **sich** ~ = sich verfärben **≗f·ärber** m ~s/~ ⟨pap⟩ *de-inker* **≗f·ärbung** f ~/~en *loss of colour, decolo*(*u*)*ration, decolo*(*u*)*rization* **~f·asern** vt [h] (Bohnen) *to string* **≗feindung** f *dehostilization* **~f·ernen** vt [h] **1. a.** (etw) *to remove* (aus, v *from*); *to put aside*; *to take away*; etw sorgfältig ~ *to filter a th out* ‖ –fernt w ⟨Am⟩ *to be stricken out* ‖ (Flecke) *to take out* (*ammonia takes out the stain*); sich durch Wasser ~ l *to wash out* ‖ (Zahnstein) *to scale* ‖ anstößige Stellen in e–m Buch, Text ~ *to bowdlerize a book, a text* ‖ (Gedanken) *to dismiss* (aus dem Sinn *from one's mind*) **b.** (jdn) *to dismiss* (aus *from a place*); *to remove* (v e–r Schule *from a school*); (Truppen) *to withdraw* (aus *from*) ‖ ⟨sport⟩ (Spieler) *to bench* ‖ jdn v s–m Gegenstande ~ *to make a p deviate from his subject* ‖ (töten) *to do away with* (*a p*) ‖ → beseitigen **2. sich ~ a.** *to absent* (od *remove*) *o.s.*; *to draw away* (v *from*); *to retire, to withdraw*; sich heimlich ~ *to abscond* **b.** ⟨übtr⟩ sich v der Arbeit ~ *to wander from one's work* ‖ (abweichen) *to depart, to deviate, to diverge* (v *from*) ‖ sich v e–a ~ (of opinions) *to differ, vary* ‖ ⟨fig⟩ sich v rechten Wege ~ *to leave the path of rectitude*; *to stray* **~f·ernt I.** a **1.** [attr] *distant, far* (*country*); *remote* (*village*); *far-away, far-off* ‖ (Tabak) mit nicht ~en Rippen, Stielen *unstemmed* ‖ ⟨übtr⟩ *distant, remote* (*relation*); nicht die ~este Ähnlichkeit *not the remotest* (od *faintest*) *resemblance*; sie hat nicht die ~este Ä. mit ihrer Mutter *she doesn't look at all like her m.* **2.** [pred] **a.** ~ v *away from*; *distant* (od *remote*) *from*; ein wenig ~ v *a little way from*; 2 Meilen ~ *two miles away*; einige Schritte ~v ihm *within a few steps of him* **b. weit** ~ *far* (⟨Am⟩ *way*) off; ⟨fig⟩ (= keineswegs) *far from it* ‖ ziemlich weit ~ *a good distance off* | weit ~ v *far from* (*the town*); *at a distance from*; *a far cry from* (*London*) ‖ ⟨übtr⟩ *far* (od *a long way*) *from* (*solution*) ‖ weit ~ z tun *far from doing*; weit ~, vollendet z s *far from completed* (od *completion*) **c.** ⟨übtr⟩ ~ v *remote from* ‖ sich ~ halten *to stand* (od *hold, keep*) *aloof*; jdn v sich ~ halten *to keep a p at a distance* ‖ ~er liegend *ulterior* (*ends*) **II.** adv ⟨übtr⟩ ~ verwandt *remotely related*; das bezieht sich nur ~ darauf *that has but remote bearing on it*; er hat nicht im ~esten daran gedacht *he hasn't had the faintest idea of it* **III.** [abs] nicht im ~esten *not in the least, in no way, not at all*; niemand ähnelt ihm im ~esten *no one even faintly resembles him*; sie sehen e–a nicht im ~esten ähnlich *they haven't the slightest resemblance to one another, they don't resemble each other at all*; nicht im ~esten so gut *not anything like so good* ‖ die Angabe ist nicht im ~esten umfassend genug ⟨Am⟩ *the statement does not begin to be c. enough* **≗f·ernung** f ~/~en **1.** (Entfernen) *removal* (v *from*); *dismissal* (*of a p*; v *from*); *withdrawal* (*of troops*) ‖ *ejection, eviction* (*of a p*; aus *from*) | ⟨übtr⟩ *deviation, departure* (v *from*) ‖ ⟨mil⟩ unerlaubte ~ v der Truppe *absence without* (*official*) *leave* (*AWOL*) **2.** (Abstand) **a.** *distance* ⟨a. opt, phot⟩; auf kurze ~ sieht er gut, aber nicht auf gr *he can see close things well but not distant ones* ‖ e–e weite ~ *a far cry* (nach *to*) ‖ auf gr ~ hin *at a great distance*; *a good distance off* ‖ aus der ~ *from a distance* ‖ aus einiger ~ *from a d.*; *from some little d.*; jdn aus weiter ~ niederschießen *to snipe a p* **b.** ⟨mil⟩ (Schußweite) *range*, die ~ feststellen, messen, schätzen *to ascertain* od *take the r.* ‖ aus naher ~ *at close range* ‖ auf gr ~ *at long range* ‖ in e–r ~ v *at a range of ..* **c.** (Strecke) ⟨rail⟩ f größere ~en *on long runs* | ~sanzeiger [m] *range-indicator* | ~sbake [f] (vor Anschlußstelle) ⟨mot⟩ *sign indicating distance to turn-out* | ~seinstellung [f] ⟨phot⟩ *distance setting* | ~schätzen [n] *judging distance* | ~smesser [m] **1.** (P) *range-taker* **2.** (Gerät) *range-finder, telemeter*; *distance measuring equipment*; → Telemeter

ent- **~fesseln** vt [h] **1.** (jdn) *to unchain, to unfetter, to set free* **2.** (Krieg) *to unleash* ‖ (Sturm) *to unchain*; die entfesselten Elemente *the furious* (od *raging*) *elements* || (Leidenschaft) *to unchain* || *to let loose* (*forces* ⟨a. fig⟩, *passion*) || (verblaßt) *to produce*; *to give rise to*; *to raise a storm* (*of laughter*) || –lt (Prometheus) *unbound* **≗f·esselung** f *unchaining* || *unleashing*|| *furiousness* | ∼skünstler [m] *escapologist* **∼f·etten** vt [h] *to remove* od *extract* (od *skim off*) *the fat from* (*a th*) || *to reduce the corpulence of* (*a p*) **≗f·ettung** f ∼/∼en; die ∼ jds *the reduction of obesity of a p* | ∼skur [f] *treatment for obesity*; ⟨engl⟩ ∼ nach W. Banting († 1878) *banting* || Mittel f e–e ∼ *anti-fat* (*dragée*) || e–e ∼ m *to slim* || ∼svermögen [n] ⟨tech⟩ *degreasing power* **∼fl·ammbar** a *inflammable*; schwer ∼ *high flash-point* [attr] **∼fl·ammen** vt [h] ⟨mst fig⟩ (→ entzünden) jdn ∼ *to inflame a p*(*'s mind*); jdn ∼ z *to fire a p into ..* || (die Einbildungskraft) *to fire, to inflame, to kindle*; *to awaken*; *to stimulate* || jds Zorn ∼ *to rouse a p to fury, to enrage a p* || neu ∼ ⟨bes poet⟩ *to relume* || entflammt s *to be ablaze* (v *with*) **∼fl·echten** vt [h] *to disetangle* || ⟨ind⟩ (Konzerne) *to decentralize, decartelize, unscramble* (*pools*) **≗fl·echtung** f ∼/∼en *decentralization*; *dissolution*; *decartelization* (*and industrial deconcentration*) || ⟨mil-pol⟩ *disengagement* **∼fl·iegen** vi [s] (→ fliegen) *to fly away* (od *off*); jdm ∼ *to fly away from a p* **∼fl·iehen** vi [s] (→ fliehen) *to flee* (aus *from*); *to run away*; *to escape*; jdm ∼ *to run away from a p*; der Gesellschaft ∼ *to flee* (*from*) *society*; ∼ in *to slip off into* (*a house, cellar*); → fliehen || die Zeit entflieht *time flies* || das Glück ist ihm –flohen *his luck has left* od *deserted him* **∼fl·ießen** vi [s] (→ fließen) e–r Quelle ∼ (of a river) *to flow from a source* || ⟨fig⟩ *to flow* (od *spring*) *from a source*; → herrühren **∼fr·emden** vt [h] (jdn, jds Zuneigung) *to alienate, to estrange* (jdm *from a p*; e–r S *from a th*) || (etw) dem nationalen Leben ∼ *to denationalize* || **sich** jdm ∼ *to alienate a p*, ⟨Am⟩ *to antagonize a p*; sich gegenseitig ∼ *to become estranged* **≗fr·emdung** f ∼/ *alienation, estrangement* (v *from*); *coolness* (zw *between*) || ⟨jur⟩ (der Ehegatten) *alienation of affection* **≗fr·oster** m *defroster* **∼f·ühren** vt [h] **1.** (Beute) *to carry off* || jdn (Kind etc) gewaltsam ∼ *to abduct, to kidnap a p* || ein Mädchen ∼ *to elope with a girl*; die Entführte *the eloper* **2.** °(jdm) etw. ∼ → ausspannen A. 2. c. **≗f·ührer** m ∼s/∼ *abductor*; *kidnapper* (*of a p*) **≗f·ührung** f ∼/∼en *abduction* (*of a woman*); *kidnapping* (*of a p*); ∼ e–s Mädchens *elopement with a girl* || ∼sgeschichte f *kidnapping story* **≗fusion·ierung** f ⟨com⟩ *demerger* **∼g·asen** vt [h] *to degas* **≗g·asung** f *degasification, degassing*

entg·egen 1. prep [mit dat]; ∼ den Wünschen, den W. ∼ *against the wishes, adversely* od *contrary to the wishes* || *in opposition to*; *in the face of* (*the decree*) **2.** adv; dem Wind ∼ *against the wind*; *in the wind's eye*; *in the teeth of the wind*; *with the wind in one's face* || e–r S ∼ s *to be opposed to a th*; *to oppose a th* || jdm ∼ s *to oppose* (od *resist*) *a p*; → entgegen-

entg·egen- [lebendes, betontes, trennbares pref] **1.** [mit Verben der Bewegung] (Richtung auf – zu bezeichnend): ∼gehen **2.** ⟨übtr⟩ (feindlichem Widerstand [∼arbeiten] *or* freundlicher Annäherung [∼sehen] bezeichnend) ∼|**arbeiten** vi [h] jdm, e–r S *to counteract* (od *counterplot, oppose*) *a p, a th*; e–r S ∼ ⟨Am⟩ *to antagonize a th*; jdm ∼ *to thwart* (od *counterwork*) *a p, to work against a p* ∼|**blicken** vi [h] = entgegensehen ∼|**bringen** vt [h] **1.** ⟨eig⟩ jdm etw ∼ *to carry a th towards a p*; *to go to offer a th to a p* **2.** ⟨übtr⟩ jdm etw (Freundlichkeit, Nachsicht etc) ∼ *to extend a th to* (od *towards*) *a p, to grant a th to a p*; jdm Respekt ∼ *to treat a p with respect*; jdm Sympathie ∼ *to show sympathy for a p, to be sympathetic towards a p* || e–r S Interesse ∼ *to show i. in a th*; .. Verständnis ∼ *to show understanding toward a th* ∼|**eilen** vi [s] jdm ∼ *to hasten to meet a p* ∼|**fahren** vi [s] jdm ∼ *to go in one's car to meet a p* ∼|**gehen** vi [s] **1.** ⟨eig⟩ jdm ∼ *to go to meet a p* || (e–r Gefahr) mutig ∼ *to face*; *to confront* || jdm ein Stück Weges ∼ *to go part of the way to meet a p* || *to be heading for* (*happy times*; *disaster*); *to be going to* (*certain death*) **2.** ⟨übtr⟩ *to approach*; *to draw near to* (*a state*) || (S) dem Ende ∼ *to draw to a close*; *to come to an end* || der Vollendung ∼ *to be nearing completion, to be well on the way to completion* **∼gesetzt** a **1.** [pred] e–r S ∼ *opposed* (od *contrary, opposite*) *to a th*; Ansichten den Ihren ∼ *opinions opposite to yours* || genau ∼ → Gegenteil **2.** [attr] *contrary* (*wishes*); *opposite* (*direction, opinion*) || *antagonistic* (*forces*); *opposing* (*interests*; *strains*); *warring* (*influences*) ∼|**hallen** vi/t [h] jdm ∼ *to come echoing* (..) *to a p* ∼|**halten** vt [h] **1.** ⟨eig⟩ jdm die Hand ∼ *to hold out* (od *extend*) *one's hand to a p* **2.** ⟨übtr⟩ jdm etw ∼ *to confront a p with a th* || (erwidern) *to rejoin*; wenn Sie mir ∼, daß er .. *if you say by way of objection that he ..*; *if you say in reply that ..* ∼|**handeln** vi [h] e–m Befehl ∼ *to act against* (od *in opposition to*) *an order*; e–m Gesetz ∼ *to contravene* (od *infringe*) *a law* || einander unbewußt ∼ *to be* (od *play*) *at cross--purposes* ∼|**jauchzen** vi [h] jdm ∼ *to meet a p with exultation* (od *shouts of joy*) ∼|**kommen** **I.** vi [s] **1.** ⟨eig⟩ jdm ∼ *to come to meet a p* (*shall I come to meet you?*); jdm ein Stück Weges ∼ *to come a little way along the path to meet a p*; sie kam mir auf der Treppe entgegen *she met me on the stairs* || jdm auf halbem Wege ∼ *to meet a p half-way*, ⟨a. übtr⟩ **2.** ⟨übtr⟩ das Glück kam ihm entgegen *good fortune came his way* || *to benefit a p*; *to indulge* (od *oblige*) *a p* (mit *with a th*) || jds Geschmack, Temperament ∼ *to appeal to a p's taste, t.* || jdm in e–r S ∼ *to make concessions to a p in a th* || jds Wünschen ∼ *to humour a p's wishes*; *to play up to* (*a p's sense of ..*) || jedem Geschmack ∼ *to suit every taste*; *to lend o.s. to* (*a policy*) **II.** ≗ n *concession*; *obligingness, oncomingness, willingness*; ∼ zeigen *to compromise* (betreffs *on*); jdm gr ∼ z. *to be very accommodating toward a p*; kein ∼ v irgende–r Seite *no advances from any quarter* **∼kommend** a *oncoming* (*traffic, vehicle*) || ⟨übtr⟩ *accommodating, forthcoming, obliging, oncoming*; nicht ∼ *unaccommodating* || sich [acc] ∼ verhalten *to be, to show o.s. obliging* od *accommodating* || ∼erweise *accommodatingly, obligingly* ∼|**laufen** vi [s] jdm ∼ *to run to meet a p* **∼nahme** f *acceptance* (*of a th*); → An-, Aufnahme; Empfang ∼|**nehmen** vt [h] *to take* (*orders, gifts, instructions*) || jds Dank ∼ *to accept* (*a p's thanks*) || (Antrag, Bitte) *to take .. under consideration*; (Vorschlag) *to close with*; *to subscribe to* || ⟨telph⟩ (Gespräch) *to take* | (Besuch) *to receive* ∼|**reifen** vi [s] ⟨fig⟩ e–r S ∼ *to ripen* (od *develop*) *into* (od *towards*) *a th* ∼|**reisen** vi [s] jdm ∼ *to go by train to meet a p* ∼|**reiten** vi [s] jdm ∼ *to ride on horseback to meet a p* ∼|**schicken** vt [h] ihm jdn ∼ *to send a p to meet him* ∼|**schlagen** vi [h] jdm in Zuneigung ∼ (of the heart) *to go out* (*in sympathy*) *to a p* (*my heart goes out to all*) ∼|**sehen** vi [h] e–m Ereignis mit Freude ∼ *to expect an event*; e–r Entscheidung gelassen ∼ *to await a decision calmly, with composure*; *to look forward to an event*; Ihrer Antwort ∼d *awaiting your reply*; e–r (baldigen) Antwort ∼d *in anticipation* od *expectation of a* (*speedy*) *reply, .. of the pleasure of hearing from you* || e–r Gefahr mit Mut ∼ *to confront* (od *to face out*) *a danger* ∼|**sehnen** vrefl [h] sich e–r S ∼ *to be longing* od *yearning for a th*

~|sein vi → entgegen 2. **~|setzen** vt [h] etw e–r S ~ *to oppose a th to a th*; *to contrast a th with a th*; *to come up with a th against a th* ‖ sich e–r S ~ *to oppose o.s. to a th* ‖ → entgegenstellen **~|stehen** vi [h] *to be in* (*marked*) *contrast* ([dat] *with*); dem steht nichts entgegen *there is no objection* (od *I have no o.*) *to it* ‖ [dat] ~de Bestimmung *regulation in conflict with* **~|stellen** vt [h] jdm ein Heer ~ *to draw up* (od *march*) *an army against a p* ‖ jdm (e–r S) Widerstand ~ *to offer resistance to a p* (*a th*) ‖ **sich** e–r S ~ *to set o.s. against*, *to oppose o.s. to a th*; sich jdm ~ *to confront* (od *oppose*, *resist*) *a p* (od *a th*) ‖ → entgegensetzen **~|stemmen** vref [h] sich e–r S ~ *to set o.s.* (od *to battle*) *against a th* ‖ (of a ship) *to stem a th*; sich der Flut ~ *to stem the tide* **~|strecken** vt [h] jdm die Hand (etc) ~ *to stretch*, *put*, *hold out one's hand to a p* ‖ **sich** e–r S ~ *to reach out towards a th* (*he reached out towards the ball*) **~|treten** vi [s] jdm ~ *to confront* (od *face*, *head*, *meet*, *oppose*) *a p*; *to go into opposition to a p* (betreffs, über *on*) ‖ e–r S *to confront*, *counter*, *face*, *meet*, *oppose*, *resist a th*; e–r Gepflogenheit ~ *to join* (od *take*) *issue with a custom*; e–m Gerücht ~ *to contradict a rumour*; *to take steps against* (*abuse*); e–r Situation mutig ~ *to show a bold front*; e–m Übel ~ *to counter a trouble* **~|wehen** vi [h] jdm ~ (of a feeling, etc.) *to go out in sympathy to a p* ‖ aus den Bildern weht echtes Gefühl entgegen *genuine feeling is emanating* (od *flowing*) *from the pictures* ‖ ein ekliger Geruch wehte e–m entgegen *a disgusting smell met you* (*at the door*) **~|wirken** vi [h] e–r S ~ *to counter* (od *resist*, *control*, *counteract*, *oppose*) *a th*; *to act in opposition to* ..; *to take a stand against* ..; *to strive against*; *to go contrary to a th*; ⟨Am⟩ *to antagonize a th*

ent- **~g·egnen** vt/i [h] **I.** vt **1.** [Objekt ist ein Satz(inhalt)] **a.** *to reply*, *rejoin*; kz ~ *to retort*, *snap*; „Sicherlich", entgegnete er "*Certainly*", *he replied* **b.** ~, daß .. *to reply* (od *rejoin*; *say in reply*) *that* .. ‖ jdm ~, daß .. *to answer a p that* ..; *to reply to a p that* .. ‖ jdm ~ auf etw, daß .. *to answer a p to a th*, *that* **2.** [Objekt: 'etwas', 'nichts'; 'was'] er entgegnete nichts *he replied nothing*, *he made no reply*; was e. er? *what did he reply*? **3.** (jds Gruß) *to return* **II.** vi; *to reply*, kz ~ *to retort*, *snap* ‖ ~ mit *to counter* (od *respond*) *with* (*a gesture*); er entgegnete, indem er fragte, wo .. *he countered by asking where* .. **≃g·egnung** f ~/~en *answer*, *reply*, *rejoinder*; treffende ~ *retort* (auf *of*); schlagfertige ~ ⟨sl⟩ *comeback*; schroffe ~ *counterblast* (jdm gegenüber *to a p*) **~g·ehen** vi [s] (→ gehen) **1.** dem Tode ~ *to escape death*; .. knapp *to brush elbow with death* ‖ der Gefahr (etc) ~ *to escape* (od *elude*) *a danger*; der Gefahr, verlacht, geplündert z w ~ *to escape being laughed at*, *being looted* ‖ der Strafe ~ *to escape punishment*; *to get off* **2. a.** den Verfolgern ~ *to elude the pursuers* **b.** ⟨übtr⟩ (S) jdm ~, jds Aufmerksamkeit ~ *to escape a p*, *to elude a p's observation* (od *notice*) ‖ s–n Augen (ihm) entging nichts *his eyes missed nothing* ‖ kein Wort ist mir entgangen *no word has escaped me* ‖ der Fehler ist mir entgangen *the fault escaped me* ‖ es war ihm nicht entgangen, daß .. *it had not escaped him that* .. ‖ es wird Ihnen sicher nicht entgangen s, daß .. *you will not have failed to notice that* .. **c.** sich etw ~ l *to let a th slip*, *to miss a th*; *to pass up* (*a chance*); ich habe mir leider die Anzeige ~ l *I am sorry to have missed* .. **~g·eistern** vt [h] (etw) *to despiritualize* (*a th*); *to deprive* (*a th*) *of its spiritual character* **entg·eistert** a [mst pred] *beside o.s.*; *disconcerted*; ⟨fam⟩ *flabbergasted*; ⟨sl⟩ *flummoxed* **~g·elt** n (†m) ~(e)s/ (Ersatz) *compensation*; (Lohn) *recompense*, *remuneration* (f *for*); ein geringes ~ f *some slight recompense for* ‖ ohne ~ = unentgeltlich **~g·elten** vt [h] (→ gelten) etw ~ *to atone* (od *pay*, *suffer*) *for a th*; er soll es mir ~! *he shall pay for this*! ‖ er wird es ~ müssen *he will have to suffer for it* ‖ jdn (*or* jdm) etw ~ l *to make a p pay for a th*, ⟨fam⟩ *to take it out on a p* **≃g·iften** vt [h] (etw) *to decontaminate* ‖ ⟨übtr⟩ (die Atmosphäre) *to clarify* **≃g·iftung** f *detoxification*, *decontamination* ‖ ⟨übtr⟩ *clarifying* | ~strupp [m] *decontamination squad* **~gl·änzen** vt [h] (Glas) *to frost* **~gl·eisen I.** vi [s] **1.** ⟨rail⟩ (of a train, etc) *to derail*, *to run* (od *get*) *off the lines*; *to jump the rails*; *to leave* (od *run off*) *the metals*; *to be wrecked* ‖ ⟨Am⟩ *to leave* od *jump the track*; *to be ditched* **2.** ⟨fig⟩ (P) *to fail*; ⟨fam⟩ *to come a cropper* ‖ *to make a faux pas*; *to make a slip* **II.** ≃ n ⟨rail⟩ *derailment*; ⟨Am⟩ *ditching* ‖ e–n Zug z ~ bringen *to derail* od *wreck a train*, ⟨Am⟩ *to ditch a t.*; → Entgleisung **~gl·eist** a *off the lines*; ⟨Am⟩ *off the track* ‖ ≃e: [der ~, ein ~er] *a failure* **≃gl·eisung** f ~/~en **1.** ⟨eig⟩ Entgleisen **2.** ⟨fig⟩ (*moral*) *lapse* (in *into*); *slip* ‖ *faux pas* (Fr) (*of an orator*) **~gl·eiten** vi [s] jdm (*or* jds Händen) ~ *to slip from a p's hands*; *to slip from a p's grasp*, *power*, *control* ‖ sich etw ~ l *to let* (*money*) *slip through one's fingers*; → gleiten ‖ → entfallen **~gl·immen** vi [s] (→ glimmen) *to begin to glimmer*; *to catch fire*; *to kindle*; → entbrennen **~g·öttern** vt [h] (Volk) *to deprive* (*a people*) *of its religion*; *to make* (*a people*) *indifferent to religion*; *to make* (*a p*) *irreligious* od *material*; (S) *to lose a people its religion* **~gr·annen** vt [h] ⟨agr⟩ *to hummel* **≃gr·anner** m ⟨agr⟩ (Maschine) *hummel*(*l*)*er*; *hummelling-machine* **~gr·aten** vt [h] (Metall etc) *to trim*, *deburr* **~gr·äten** vt [h] (Fisch) *to bone*, *to fillet* **~gr·enzung** f ⟨psych, arts⟩ (*feeling* od *impression of*) *having no bounds* **~g·ürten** vt [h] (etw) *to ungird*; entgürtet *ungirded*, *ungirt* **~h·aaren** vt [h] (jdn; Tier) *to depilate*; (Fell; Haut) *to unhair*, *to grain* **≃h·aarung** f *depilation*; *unhairing* | ~smittel [n] *depilatory* **~h·aften** vt [h] (jdn) *to set free*; *to release*

Enthalp·ie f ~/ ⟨thermodynamics⟩ *enthalpy*; *heat content*

ent- **~h·alten** vt [h] (→ halten) **1. a.** (etw) *to contain*, *hold*; *comprise*, *comprehend*, *embrace*, *embody*, *include*; (S a.) *to lodge* ‖ (of measures) *to contain*; *to be equivalent to* ‖ nicht im Programm ~ s *to be out of the programme* ‖ ⟨übtr⟩ *to hold*; ich bin gespannt, was die Zukunft ~ mag *I wonder what the future may hold* **b.** ⟨math⟩ ~ s in *to be contained in*; 5 ist in 15 dreimal ~ *five goes into fifteen three times*, *five is contained in fifteen three times* **2. sich** e–r S ~ *to abstain* od *refrain from a th*, *to forbear a th*; sich der Nahrung ~ *to abstain* ‖ sich der Stimme ~ *to abstain from voting* ‖ *to keep back* (*one's tears*) ‖ sich ~ z tun [mst neg] *to abstain* od *refrain from doing*; ich kann mich nicht ~ z tun *I cannot forbear to do* od *doing*, *I cannot help doing*; ich konnte mich des Lachens nicht ~ *I could not help laughing* **~h·altsam** a *abstemious*, *abstinent*; *continent*; *temperate* ‖ ⟨sex⟩ *continent* ‖ [pred] ⟨Am fam⟩ *on the water-wagon* **≃halt·samkeit** f *abstemiousness*, *abstinence*; *temperance* ‖ ~sbewegung [f] *temperance movement* ‖ ⟨sex⟩ *continence*; periodische ~ *rhythm method* ‖ moralische ~ *moral restraint*

Enth·altung f ~/~en *abstention* (v *from*; z tun *from doing*); *forbearance* (z tun *of doing*) ‖ Stimm≃ *abstention* (*there were 60 abstentions*) ‖ ~ v Genüssen → Enthaltsamkeit

ent- **~h·ärten** vt [h] (Wasser) *to soften*; → tempern | (Wasser-) ≃härtungsmittel [n] (*water*) *softener*; *softening powder* **~h·aupten** vt [h] (jdn) *to behead*, *decapitate* **≃h·auptung** f ~/~en *beheading, decapitation* **~h·eben** vt [h] (→ heben) [gen] **1.** (befreien) jdn e–r Pflicht ~ *to free* (od *dispense, excuse, exempt, release*) *a p from a duty* (od *an obligation*); .. e–r Last ~ *to relieve a p of a load*; jdn der Mühe ~ *to save a p the trouble* (z tun *of doing*); jdn (v) der Verpflichtung der Teilnahme ~ *to relieve a p of attendance, to excuse a p from attendance*; ich wurde der Aufgabe enthoben *I was excused from the task, I was excused the task*; dies enthebt uns nicht der Aufgabe, .. z bestimmen *this does not dispense us from the task of determining* .. ‖ aller Sorgen u Nöte –hoben s *to be released* od *free from all cares and anxieties*; der Tod hat ihn aller S. –hoben *death put him beyond all cares* ‖ sich (e–r S) –hoben fühlen *to feel free from* **2.** jdn des Amtes, der Stellung ~ *to eject* (od *remove, oust*) *a p from* (*his*) *office, from his post*; *to relieve a p of his office, of his post*; *to dismiss* od *suspend a p*; e–n Offizier des Kommandos ~ *to remove an officer from his command*; → entkleiden **≈h·ebung** f ~/~en **1.** = Befreiung **2.** (Amts≈) *removal* (*from office* od *service*) ‖ *suspension*; *deposition, dismissal* (*of a p*); ⟨ec⟩ *deprivation* **~h·eiligen** vt [h] (etw) *to profane*; *desecrate* **≈h·eiligung** f ~/~en *profanation*; *desecration* **~h·irnen** vt [h] ⟨zoo, scient⟩ *to decerebrate* **~h·üllen** vt [h] **1.** (Gesicht) *to uncover, unveil* ‖ (Denkmal) *unveil* **|** ⟨fig⟩ (Geheimnis, Plan) *to disclose, reveal* (jdm *to a p*); *uncover, unveil* ‖ jds wahres Wesen ~ *to unmask* (⟨Am fam⟩ *debunk*) *a p* ‖ (Tatsache) ⟨Am⟩ *to develop* ‖ jdm sein Herz ~ *to uncover one's heart to a p*; jdm s–e Gefühle ~ *to divulge one's feelings to a p* ‖ den Blicken jds -hüllt w *to be revealed* (od *to lie open*) *to a p's eyes, gaze* **2. sich** ~ ⟨fig⟩ *to unveil*; *to reveal, betray o.s.*; sich als echter Dichter ~ *to r. o.s.* (*as*) *a real poet* **≈h·üllung** f ~/~en *unveiling* (*of a face*; *of a statue*) ‖ ⟨fig⟩ *disclosure, revelation* (*of a secret*); unbeabsichtigte ~ *give-away* **~h·ülsen** vt [h] (Mais, Reis) *to husk, shuck, hull*; (Mandeln) *to blanch*; (Erbsen, Bohnen) *to shell* **≈h·ülsung** f *hulling, husking*; *shelling* ‖ ~smaschine [f] *hulling* (od *shelling*)*-machine*

enthusiasm·ieren vt [h] (jdn) *to fill with enthusiasm*; –miert w *to enthuse* (über *about*)

Enthusi·asmus m ~/ *enthusiasm* (f *for*; über *about, over*) **Enthusi·ast** m ~en/~en *enthusiast* (f etw *for* od *of a th*) **enthusi·astisch 1.** a *enthusiastic* (über *about, at*) **2.** adv *enthusiastically*

Enthym·em n ⟨log⟩ *enthymeme*

Entit·ät f ⟨philos⟩ entity

ent- ~j·ochen vt [h] *to unyoke* **~j·uden** vt [h] (Land) *to desemitize* **≈j·udung** f *desemitization* **≈j·ungfern** vt [h] (Mädchen) *to deflower*; *ravish* **≈j·ungferung** f ~/~en *defloration* **~k·alken** vt [h] *to decalcify* **≈kalker** m ⟨chem⟩ *decalcifying agent* **≈k·alkung** f *decalcification* **~k·eimen** vi/t **1.** vi [s] = entsprießen **2.** vt [h] (Kartoffeln) *to free from germs* od *buds* ‖ (Getreide, Malz) *to degerminate* ‖ (Milch) *to pasteurize*; (Watte) *to sterilize* **≈k·eimung** f *sterilization*; *germ removal* **|** ~smaschine [f] ⟨brew⟩ *malt cleaning machine* **~k·ernen 1.** vt [h] (Frucht) *to core, stone*; *to remove the seeds* od *pips of* ..; *to seed* (*grapes*); entkernt *cored, stoned* **2.** ≈ n *coring, stoning* **~k·irchlichen** vt [h] ein Volk ~ *to alienate* (od *estrange*) *a people from the church*; *to make a p worldly*; die Erziehung ~ *to secularize education* **≈k·irchlichung** f *secularization* **~kl·eiden** vt [h] **1.** (jdn) *to undress, to unclothe*; *to strip* (bis auf die Haut *to the skin*) ‖ s–n Körper ~, **sich** ~ *to strip, undress*; *to take one's clothes off* **2.** ⟨übtr⟩ **a.** e–n Baum der Rinde ~ *to strip the bark from a tree* ‖ = entblößen 2. **b.** jdn s–r Ehren ~ *to strip a p of his honours* ‖ sich e–r S ~ ⟨fig⟩ *to divest o.s. of a th* ‖ → entheben ‖ (S) e–r S –kleidet s *to be deprived* (od *shorn, stripped*) *of a th* **≈kl·eidung** f *Spoliation* (Christi) ~s|akt [m], ~snummer [f] ⟨theat⟩ *strip-tease* ~stänzerin [f] *stripper* **~kl·ettern** vi [s] e–m Flugzeug ~ *to climb from* (od *out of*) *an aeroplane* **~kn·echten** vt [h] (Volk) *to free from slavery*; *to set free*; ⟨übtr⟩ *to unfetter, to unshackle* **~kn·oten** vt [h] (etw) *to undo*; *to unknot*; *to untie* ⟨a. fig⟩ **~k·ohlen** vt [h] ⟨chem & min⟩ (Metall) *to decarbonize, decarburize* **≈k·ohlung** f *decarbonization, decarburization* **~k·ommen I.** vi [s] (→ kommen) *to escape* (aus *from*); *to get away*; *to make one's escape* od *one's get-away*; *to break loose, to flee* (aus *from*), *to run away*; aus dem Gefängnis ~ *to escape* (*from*) *prison* ‖ glücklich ~ *to get off safely*; *to have a lucky escape*; sie sind nur mit Mühe ~ *they had narrow escapes* ‖ ungestraft ~ *to get off*; *to go unpunished* ‖ jdm ~ *to escape from a p*; *to give a p the slip* ‖ der Gefahr ~ *to escape danger* ‖ → davonkommen; entfliehen **II.** ≈ n ~s/ (knappes *close*) *escape* (aus, v *from*); bes ⟨Am⟩ *getaway* ‖ ein ~ mit knapper Not *a hairbreadth* od *narrow escape, a narrow* od *tight squeak* **≈koppeler** m *decoupling network* **~koppeln** vt [h] *to un–, decouple*; *to neutralize*; *to tune* od *balance out* (*balanced antenna*) **≈koppelung** f *decoupling, etc*; *disconnection* ‖ ~ v Störern *balancing-out of jamming* **| ~s-** ~glied [n] *declutching member*; ~kondensator [m] *decoupling condenser*; ~kreis [m] *anti-resonant circuit*; ~schaltung [f] *decoupling network*; ~widerstand [m] *decoupling resistance* **~k·orken** vt [h] (Flasche) *to uncork, unstop* **~k·örnen** vt [h] (Baumwolle) *to gin* **~k·örperlichen** vt [h] (Seele) *to disembody* **≈k·örperlichung** f *disembodiment* **~k·örpern** vt [h] = entkörperlichen **~kr·äften** vt [h] **1.** (jdn, jds Körper) *to debilitate, enfeeble, weaken*; *devitalize, enervate*; *exhaust*; *reduce*; durch Krankheit –kräftet s *to be reduced by sickness, to be prostrated with s.* ‖ jdn vollkommen ~ *to bleed a p white* ‖ jds Gesundheit ~ *to sap a p's health* **2.** ⟨fig⟩ (Argument) *to weaken*; (e–e Theorie) *to refute* ‖ (Anspruch) *to invalidate*; (jds Zeugnis) *to make* (od *declare*) *null and void, to nullify*; (Gesetz) *to annul* **~kr·äftet** a *effete* (*race*); *enervate* (*p*); *exhausted*; *prostrate* (*industry*) ‖ sehr ~ s v *to be prostrate with* (*sickness*) **≈kr·äftung** f ~/~en **1.** *debilitation, debility* (*of the body*); *devitalization, enervation, enfeeblement*; *exhaustion*; ⟨path⟩ *marasmus*; *inanition* (an ~ z Grunde gehen *to perish of i.*) ‖ vollkommene ~ *prostration* (*of a country*, etc.) **2.** ⟨fig⟩ *weakening*; *refutal, refutation* (*of a theory*) ‖ *invalidation* (*of a claim*); *nullification* (*of evidence*) **~kräuseln** vt [h] (Haar) *to de-kink* **~kr·iechen** vi [s] dem Neste ~ *to creep from* (od *out of*) *the nest* **~k·uppeln** vt [h] ⟨tech⟩ (etw) *to uncouple*; *to throw out of gear*; *to disengage*; ⟨mot⟩ *to declutch* **≈l·ade-** (→ entladen) [in comp] *unlading, unloading*; *discharging* ‖ Beginn des ~s *breaking bulk* **|** ~gebühr [f] ⟨rail⟩ *unloading charges* pl **|** ~vorrichtung [f] *unloading device* **~l·aden** vt [h] [→ laden] **A. 1.** ⟨eig⟩ (Schiff etc) *to unlade, unload* ‖ (Gewehr) *to unload, discharge* ‖ (Akkumulator) *to discharge*; ~ [pp & a] *discharged* ‖ *to evacuate, relieve*, → leeren **2.** ⟨übtr⟩ das Herz ~ *to disburden one's mind*; *to free one's mind from a load*; *to relieve one's bosom* **B. 1.** (S) (Inhalt) *to discharge* (*the chimney discharges smoke*); *to emit* ‖ *to evacuate* (*the lift evacuated a girl*); *to send forth* (od *out*) ‖ (Flüssigkeit etc) *to pour* (auf *on*); *to shed, to spill* **2.** ⟨fig⟩ (Gefühle) *to pour* (od *send*) *forth* (od *out*); Ströme v Flüchen ~ auf .. *to pour forth torrents of curses on* (*a p*) ‖ s–n Ekel ~ *to vent one's disgust* (in *in*) **C. sich** ~ **1.** (of a gun, etc.) *to go off*; *detonate, explode* ‖ *to break forth, to vent itself* **2.** (of a cloud) *to burst*; ein Gewitter entlud sich *a storm broke forth* od *raged* (*over* ..) ‖ (of volcano) *to erupt* **3.** sich e–r S ~ *to unload o.s. of a th, to disburden one's mind of a th*; *to throw a th off* **4.** (of a feeling) *to vent itself* ‖ s–e Wut entlud sich gegen .. *his rage burnt fiercely against*; *he fulminated* (od *raged*) *against* (*the clergy*); *he vented his fury on the clergy* **∸l·ader** m ~s/~ **1.** (P) *discharger* **2.** ⟨el⟩ (Vorrichtung) *discharger*; *discharging rod* **∸l·adung** f ~/~en **1.** *discharge*; *unloading, unlading*; *evacuation* **2.** *discharging, going off* (*of a gun*) ‖ *discharge, emission* (*of water*); *eruption* ‖ elektrische ~ *electric discharge* ‖ heftige ~ *explosion* (*of gun powder*); (etw) zur ~ bringen *to explode* ⟨a. fig⟩; *to detonate* | ⟨übtr⟩ *explosion*; *eruption, outburst* (*of passion*) | ~sröhre [f] ⟨el⟩ *discharge-tube* | ~sstrom [m] *discharge-current* | ~sventil [n] *discharge-valve* **~szeit** f ⟨el⟩ *service life*

entl·ang 1. [adv] *along, down*; an (*or* auf) dem Pfad ~ *along* (od *down*) *the path*; am Ufer ~ *along the shore*; auf dem Wege ~ *along the road* ‖ → entlang– **2.** [prep] **a.** [mit acc] *along, down*; [mst nachgestellt]: die Straßen ~, das Ufer ~, *~ die Straße, *~ das Ufer *along* (od *down*) *the street, the shore* **b.** *[mit gen & dat] ~ der Küste *along the coast, alongshore*

entl·ang- [betontes, trennbares pref] **~|baumeln** vi [h] *to bob along* ⟨a. a–n⟩ (P.) **~|bewegen** vt [h] etw auf e–r Fläche ~ *to move a th along a surface* ‖ **sich** ~ auf *to move along* (*a surface*) **~|fahren** vi [s] die Straße ~ *to drive along* (od *down*) *the road*; an der Küste ~ *to sail along the coast, to skirt the coast* **~|gehen** vi [s] die Straße ~ *to go along* (od *down*) *the road*; den ganzen Zug ~ *to walk the whole length of the train*; die Terrasse ging am ganzen Hause entlang *the terrace ran the whole length of the house* ‖ ~ an (*or* auf) *to walk* (od *pass*) *along* (*the path*); an dem See ~ *to skirt the lake* **~|kommen** vi [s] die Straße ~ *to come along the road* (a. of currents) ‖ ~ an *to skirt* (*a lake*) **~|laufen** vi [s] die Straße ~ *to run along* (od *down*) *the street*; → entlanggehen **~|reisen** vi [s] an der Küste ~ *to travel along* (od *down*) *the coast* **~|rollen** vi [s] auf dem Boden ~ *to roll along the ground*; a. vt (etw ..) **~|rutschen** vi [s] ~ an *to slither down* (*the pipe*) **~|schreiten** vi [s] an den Reihen ~ *to walk along the ranks* **~|strömen** vi [s] die Straße ~ (of a crowd) *to pour along the road* **~|werfen** vt [h] (Ball) den ganzen Weg ~ *to throw* (*a ball*) *the length of the path*

ent- ~l·arven vt [h] (jdn, etw) *to unmask*; *expose*; ⟨Am⟩ *to show* (*a p*) *up* ‖ jdn als Lügner ~ *to expose a p for a liar* **∸l·arvung** f ~/~en *unmasking*; *exposure* (*of a p, a th*) **~l·assen** vt [h] [→ lassen] **1.** jdn ~ *to allow a p to go* (od *leave*); *to dismiss, discard, discharge* (fristlos *to sack*) *a p*; jdn aus dem Krankenhaus ~ *to discharge a p from hospital* ‖ ⟨mil⟩ ~ s *to be allowed to stand down* | (Gefangenen) *to release*; *to set free*; jdn aus dem Gefängnis ~ *to release a p from prison* **2. a.** (Truppen) *to disband*; ⟨mar⟩ *to pay off*; Soldaten ~ ⟨Am⟩ *to muster out troops, to muster troops out of service* **b.** jdn (aus Dienst, Stellung) ~ *to discharge* (od *dismiss, suspend*) *a p*; *to part with a p* **c.** fristlos (*or* °Knall u Fall) ~ *to fling a p away* (od *off*); *to pack a p off, to send a p packing* (od .. *a p about his business*) ‖ ⟨fam⟩ *to give a p the sack* (⟨sl⟩ *the boot* od *the push*); *to sack a p* ‖ ⟨Am⟩ *to bounce a p*; *to lay a p off*; ⟨sl⟩ *to fire a p*; ⟨pol⟩ jdn ohne Federlesen ~ *to decapitate a p* ‖ ~ w ⟨fam⟩ *to get the sack* (⟨sl⟩ *the boot* od *the push*) ‖ → entpflichten **d.** ⟨mil & nav⟩ jdn aus dem Heer ~ *to dismiss a p from the army*; *to retire a p* (mit dem Rang e–s Oberst *with the rank of colonel*); aus dem Heer ~ w *to be dismissed the army* ‖ mit Pension ~ *to pension a p off* ‖ (unter Verlust des Rangs) *to cashier* (*an officer*) **~l·assen** [pp] ⟨com etc⟩ *off the pay roll* **∸l·assung** f ~/~en **1.** *dismissal* (aus *from* [*hospital*]) **2. a.** *disbandment* (*of troops*) **b.** (aus Stellung etc) *discharge*; *dismissal*; *release from service* ‖ fristlose ~ ⟨fam⟩ *sacking* **c.** ⟨mil & nav⟩ (v der Dienststelle aus) *dismissal* (aus .. *from the army*); (v der P aus.) *retirement*; (auf Gegenseitigkeit) *separation* N; s–e ~ einreichen *or* nehmen *to resign*; *to send in* (od *give*) *one's papers* od *resignation* ‖ (unter Verlust des Rangs) *cashierment* ‖ ~ wegen Arbeitsmangels *layoff* ‖ ~ wegen Wehrunwürdigkeit *dishonourable discharge* ‖ → Entpflichtung, Pensionierung | ~sanzug [m] ⟨mil⟩ *demob suit* | ~sgeld [n] ⟨mil⟩ *discharging* (⟨Am⟩ *severance*) *payment* | ~sgesuch [n] *resignation* | ~slager [n] *seperation centre* | ~sschein [m] *certificate of discharge* | ~sstelle [f] ⟨mil⟩ *discharge centre* | ~szeugnis [n] = –schein **~l·asten** vt [h] **1.** etw ~ *to decrease* (od *reduce, remove*) *the pressure on a th* ‖ *to release, relieve* ‖ *to remove* (*a load*) ‖ den Arm ~ *to ease* (od *disengage*) *one's arm* ‖ e–e Leitung ~ *to relieve a circuit of some of its traffic*; (Stromnetz) *to ease the load on* ..; (Verkehr) *to ease* ‖ entlastet *balanced* (*valve*; ⟨aero⟩ *aileron, surface*) | (Inneres) *to free from a burden*; *to disburden*; *to ease*; *to relieve*; (Gewissen) *to unburden* **2.** jdn *to lighten the burden of a p, to relieve the strain on a p* ‖ ⟨mst com⟩ **a.** *to free a p from excessive work* (od *from overwork*); *to relieve a p of some of his work*; *to reduce a p's work* od *responsibility* **b.** (Angeklagten etc) *to discharge*; *exonerate, release* (v .. *from a charge*); *to exculpate, clear* ‖ ~de Umstände [pl] *exonerating circumstances* ‖ –tet a ⟨tech⟩ *equilibrated*, ∸lasteter [m] ⟨pol⟩ *exonerated p*, [pred] *p cleared of political charges*; → entbinden ‖ den Schatzmeister ~ *to approve* (od *pass*) *the accounts of the treasurer* **c.** jdn ~ f e–e Summe *to credit a p for* (od *with*) *a sum, to give a p credit for a sum*

Entl·astung f ~/~en **1.** ~ e–s Bordes *reduction* (od *removal*) *of the pressure on a shelf*; *easing* ‖ *disburdening, release, relief* (*of the mind, heart*; v *from*) **2. a.** ~ jds *reduction of a p's work* od *responsibility* **b.** *discharge* (*of a bankrupt*); *exoneration* (v *from*); *relief* (*from*) ‖ z unserer ~ *to our discharge* ‖ ~ des Schatzmeisters *approval* (od *passing*) *of the accounts of the treasurer*; jdm ~ erteilen = jdn entlasten 2. c. **c.** *credit* ⟨a. bank⟩; z jds ~ *to a p's credit, to the credit of a p's account* ‖ (steuerliche *tax*) *relief* ‖ *liquidity* (*of the money-market*) | ~sangriff [m] *diverting* od *relief attack* | ~sanzeige [f] ⟨com⟩ *credit note* | ~sgründe [m pl] ⟨contr etc⟩ *reliefs* | ~sbogen [m] ⟨arch⟩ *discharging-arch* | ~sstraße [f] (f den Verkehr) *by-pass* (*road*) | ~sventil [n] *relief vent* | ~sversuch [m] ⟨mil⟩ *attempt to relieve pressure* | ~szeuge [m] ⟨jur⟩ *witness for the defence* | ~szünder [m] *release fuse*

ent- ~l·auben vt [h] = entblättern ‖ die Bäume ~ sich *the trees shed* od *lose their leaves* **~l·aubt** a (Baum) *bared, denuded, stripped of leaves*; *dismantled* (*wood*) **~l·aufen** vi [s] [→ laufen] jdm ~ *to run away* (od *escape*) *from a p* **~l·ausen** vt [h] (jdn) ⟨mil⟩ *to delouse, fumigate* **∸l·ausung,** **∸wesung** f *delousing, disinfection* **~l·edigen** vt [h] **1.** jdn s–r Fesseln ~ *to free* od *release a p from his fetters, to unfetter* od *unshackle a p*; *to set a p free* (od *at liberty*) **2.** **sich** ~ **a.** sich s–r Kleider ~ *to strip*; *undress*; *to take one's clothes off* **b.** sich jds, e–r S ~ *to get rid of a p, of a th* ‖ *to throw a th off* ‖ *to do away with a p* **c.** ⟨fig⟩ sich e–r S ~ *to come through a th*; sich e–s Auftrags ~ *to acquit o.s. of a task, to execute a t.*; sich e–r Pflicht ~ *to acquit o.s. of a duty*; *to discharge* od *perform a* *duty* **≃l·edigung** f ~/~en ⟨fig⟩ *acquittal; discharge; execution, performance* (*of a duty*, etc.) **~l·eeren** vt [h] (etw) *to deplete; empty* ‖ (Ballon) *to deflate* ‖ den Darm ~ *to evacuate*, (od *relieve*) *the bowels* ‖ (Kot, Urin) *to void* | sich ~ (v Darm, v Fluß) *to open* (*into*) | (*of fluids*) *to drain* (*into*) **≃l·eerung** f ~/~en *depletion, emptying* ‖ *deflation* (*of a balloon*) ‖ *evacuation, voidance* (*of the bowels*) ‖ ⟨tech⟩ *discharge* | ~shahn [m] *drain-cock* | ~sventil [n] ⟨aero⟩ *deflation-valve* **~l·egen** a *remote, distant; far-away, far-off, out-of-the-way*; weit ~ ⟨dero⟩ *outlandish* (*place*) **≃legenheit** f ~/ *remoteness; distance*

entl·ehnen vt [h] mst ⟨übtr⟩ etw e–m Buche, Schriftsteller (etc) ~ *to borrow a th from a book, from an author*; er hat vieles Goethe –lehnt *he drew amply on Goethe*; → ausschreiben I. 3. ‖ ~ aus *to take* (*a word from the French*) ‖ s–e Informationen e–r Quelle ~ *to draw one's information from a source* ‖ der Erfahrung entlehnt s (S) *to be derived from experience* **≃l·ehner** m ~s/~ *borrower* (v *from*) **≃l·ehnung** f ~/~en **1.** (Entlehnen) *borrowing* (aus, v *from*); *derivation* (v *from*) **2.** (Entlehntes) *borrowing*; (of customs, etc.) *loan* (aus, v *from*); (Lehnwort) *loan-word* ‖ → Diebstahl 2. **~l·eiben** vrefl [h] sich ~ *to commit suicide; to do away with o.s.* **~l·eihen** vt [h] Geld (v) e–r Bank ~ *to borrow money from a bank* ‖ (Buch) *to take out*; das Buch war –liehen *the book had been taken out* °**~l·ieben** vrefl [h] ⟨fam⟩ sich „~" *to fall out of love* **~l·oben** vrefl [h] sich ~ *to break off the engagement* **≃l·obung** f *disengagement* **~l·ocken** vt [h] jdm etw ~ *to draw* (od *bring, elicit, extract*) *a th from a p*; jdm ein Geheimnis ~ *to worm a secret out of a p* **~l·ohnen** vt [h] (Mannschaft) *to pay* (*off*) **≃l·ohnung** f, *pay*(*ing off*) **~l·üften** vt [h] etw ~ *to exhaust the air from a th*, (Wasser) *to be-aerate* | (Raum [v verbrauchter Luft befreien]) *to ventilate* **≃lüfter** m *air-vent* **≃l·üftung** f ~ e–s Rohres *exhaustion* od *evacuation of air from a pipe*; *de-aeration* (*of water*) ‖ ⟨tech⟩ *bleeding* (*of brakes*) ‖ *ventilation* (*of a room*) | ~(sanlage) [f] *ventilating arrangement* od *plant* | ~shutze [f] ⟨aero⟩ *gas shaft hood* | ~ventil [n] *bleeder valve* **~magnetis·ieren** vt [h] *to demagnetize*, (Schiff) *to degauss* **≃magnetis·ierung** f, *demagnetization* **~m·annen** vt [h] *to castrate, emasculate* ‖ ⟨übtr⟩ (verweichlichen) *to emasculate, unman*

ent- **~m·annt** a *emasculate* ‖ ⟨fig⟩ *effeminate, emasculate, enervate* | ≃e [der ~, ein ~r] m *spado* [L] **≃m·annung** f *castration, emasculation* ‖ ⟨fig⟩ *emasculation; enervation* **~m·asten** vt [h] (Schiff) *to dismast* **~materialis·ieren** vt [h] *to dematerialize* **≃materialis·ierung** f *dematerialization* **~m·enschen, ~m·enschlichen** vt [h] *to dehumanize; brutalize; unman* **~m·enscht** a *inhuman; barbarous, brutal, trute, brutish; cruel* **~militaris·ieren** vt [h] (besetztes Gebiet) *to demilitarize*; –siert *demilitarized* (*zone*) **≃militaris·ierung** f ~/ *demilitarization* **~m·ischen** vt [h] (Verbindung) *to resolve; separate*; → auflösen I. B. 2. **≃mischung** f ⟨phys⟩ *decomposition, dissociation* **~m·ummen** vt [h] *to unmask* (a. sich ~) **~m·ündigen** vt [h] (Erwachsenen) *to place* od *put a p under the care* od *control of a trustee* od *guardian* **≃m·ündigung** f ~/~en *declaration of a p's disability, incapacity*; die ~ jds *the placing of a p under the control of a trustee* ‖ ⟨jur⟩ *interdiction* **~m·utigen** vt [h] (jdn) *to discourage, dishearten, unnerve; deject, depress; cow*; → einschüchtern ‖ (Gesellschaft) *to cast a damper on, to be a damper to* (*a party*) ‖ sich (nicht) ~ l *to loose heart, to get discouraged* (*not to let o.s. be got down, to keep one's chin up*) **~m·utigt** a *dejected, depressed; crestfallen* **≃m·utigung** f ~/~en *discouragement, disheartenment* **≃n·ahme** f ~/ **1.** (Entnehmen) **a.** ~ v Geld *drawing* (od *taking out, withdrawal*) *of money* (v .. *from a bank*) **b.** *order; taking, purchasing* (*of goods*); bei ~ v 1000 Bogen erhalten Sie .. *taking 1000 sheets you will get* ..; bei ~ v großen Mengen *taking a large order you* .. **c.** ⟨tech⟩ (Dampf≃) *extraction*, (Leistungs≃) *taking of power*, (Öl≃ etc) *withdrawel* **2.** (Entnommenes) oft [pl] ~n v Geld *drawings* [pl] ‖ ~n v Proben *samplings* [pl] | ~schein [m] *withdrawel form* | ~ventil [n] *bleeder valve* **~nazifizieren** vt [h] *to denazify* **≃nazifizierung** f *denazification* | ~s-ausschuß [m] *d. panel* | ~verfahren [n] *d. proceedings* pl **~n·ebeln** vt [h] e–n Raum ~ *to clear a room of vapour* **≃n·ebelung** f ~ e–s Raums *absorption of vapour in a room* **~n·ehmen** vt [h] [→ nehmen] **1.** etw e–m Gefäß, Buch ~ *to take a th from a vessel, a book* ‖ Beispiele etc ~ aus, v *to extract* (od *collect, pick up, quote*) *examples from* ‖ ⟨übtr⟩ etw e–r Quelle ~ *to draw a th from a source*; er hat vieles den Dramatikern des 16. Jhs. –nommen *he has drawn largely upon the dramatists of the 16th c.*; → entlehnen **2.** ⟨com⟩ (etw) *to get* (v *from*); Waren beim Großkaufmann ~ *to purchase goods of a wholesaler* ‖ (Geld) *to draw, to take out, to withdraw* (v .. *from a bank*) ‖ e–e Summe ~ auf jdn (*or* jds Namen) *to draw a p for a sum*; Geld bei e–r Bank auf jds Konto ~ *to draw upon a p's banker* **3.** ⟨fig⟩ (schließen) etw ~ aus *to gather* (od *conclude, deduce, infer*) *a th from* ..; Ihrem Briefe entnehme ich, daß .. *from your letter I learn* (od *understand*) *that* .. ‖ aus den Angaben läßt sich nicht ~, wer .. *we* (od *you*) *don't learn* (od *see*) *from the statements who* .. ‖ was würden Sie daraus ~? *what inference would you draw from that?* **≃n·ehmer** m ~s/~ *purchaser* (*of goods*), *drawer* (*of a bill*) **~n·erven** vt [h] (jdn) *to emasculate, enervate, unnerve* **~n·ervt** a *emasculate, enervate* **≃n·ervung** f ~/ *emasculation, enervation, unnerving* **~n·üchtern** vt [h] = ernüchtern ‖ *to give* (*a p*) *to eat* | sich ~ *to breakfast* **~·ölen** (→ ent–!) vt [h] (etw) *to free* (*a th*) *from oil* **≃·öler** m *oil-remover* (od *separator*) **~pers·önlichen** vt [h] *to take away* (*a p's*) *personality, individuality* **≃pers·önlichung** f ⟨psych⟩ *depersonalization*

Ento- [Gr] (innen) [in comp] *ento-* **~bl·ast** n ⟨biol⟩ *entoblast* **~z·oen** [pl] ⟨zoo⟩ *entozoa* [L pl]

Entomol·og m ~en/~en *entomologist* **Entomolog·ie** f ~/ *entomology* **entomol·ogisch** a *entomological*

ent- **~pfl·ichten** vt [h] (jdn) *to pension, retire; to place* (*a p*) *on the retired list*; → Pension ‖ wegen Erreichung der Altersgrenze ~ *to superannuate* **≃pfl·ichtung** f *retirement* ‖ *superannuation* **~pl·omben** vt [h] *to unseal* ⟨a. aero⟩ **~p·uppen** vrefl [h] sich ~ **1.** (of insects) *to burst* od *split the cocoon* **2.** ⟨fig⟩ *to reveal* od *show o.s.* (als *to be*); *to unmask* ‖ (of character) *to peep out* ‖ er –puppte sich als Dichter *he revealed himself* (*as*) *a poet; he proved himself* (*to be*) *a poet*; er –puppte sich als sein Sohn *he turned out* (*to be*) *his son*; die S –puppte sich als Fehlschlag *the matter turned out* od *proved* (*to be*) *a failure* **~qu·ellen** vi [s] [→ quellen] dem Felsen ~ (of water) *to spring from the rock* ‖ ⟨übtr⟩ e–m Instrument ~ (of sounds) *to flow* (od *issue*) *from an instrument; to pour forth from* (*a p's throat*) **~r·affen** vt [h] jdm etw ~ = entreißen **~r·ahmen** vt [h] (Milch) *to skim*; (durch Zentrifuge) *to separate* **~r·aten** vi [h] [→ raten] jds ~, jds Hilfe ~ *to do without, to dispense with a p's services* **~r·ätseln** vt [h] (Geheimnis) *to unravel* (*a mystery*); *to unriddle, solve; to clear up* ‖ (Schrift, dunkles Wort) *to decipher; to make* od *puzzle out*; (Zeichen) *to interpret, read*; → erklären **~r·echten** vt [h] (jdn) *to deprive (a p) of his rights* (od *of a right*) || (Bürger) *to disfranchise* **≃r·echtung** f ~/~en *disfranchisement*

·Entreakt [ˈɑ̃trakt] m [Fr] ~s/~e ⟨theat⟩ *entr'acte* (Fr) **Entrechat** [ˈɑ̃trʃa] m [Fr] ~s/~s ⟨danc⟩ *entrechat*

Entree [ɑ̃ˈtreː] n [Fr] ~s/~s **1.** †(Zutritt) *entree* (z .. *of a house*) **2.** *entrance money* (od *fee*) **3.** ⟨cul⟩ *entrée* **4.** ⟨mus⟩ *entrée*; *opening piece*

entr·eißen vt [h] [→ reißen] **1.** jdm etw ~ *to snatch* (od *tear, wrench, wrest*) *a th from a p*; *death has torn him from his family* **2.** jdn e–r S (Gefahr, Feuer etc) ~ *to rescue* (od *save*) *a p from a th* || etw der Vergessenheit ~ *to rescue a th from oblivion* || ⟨mil⟩ (dem Feind) *to seize* .. (*from*) || **sich** den Armen jds ~ *to tear o.s. from a p's arms* (od *embrace*)

Entrem·ets [ɑ̃trˈmeː] n (Fr) ~/~ *entremets* [sg]

entre nous! [ɑ̃tr nuː] Fr → unter uns, ungezwungen, vertraulich

Entrep·ot [ɑ̃trˈpoː] n ~/~s [Fr] *entrepot* (Fr); *warehouse* || im ~ *in bond*; (etw) in ~ geben *to put in bond*; aus dem ~ nehmen *to take out of b.*

Entres·ol [ɑ̃trˈsɔl] n [Fr] ~s/~s *entresol* (Fr)

ent- ~r·ichten vt [h] (Abgaben) *to render* (*dues*); (Beitrag) *to discharge*; (Schuld) *to pay, to pay off*; (Pauschalsumme) *to compound*; → begleichen, –zahlen **≃r·ichtung** f ~/~en *discharge, payment*; *compounding*; → Begleichung **~r·inden** vt [h] (Baum) *to (un)bark, decorticate* **~r·ingen** vt [h] [→ ringen] **1.** jdm e–e Waffe ~ *to wrench* (od *wrest*; *snatch, tear*) *a weapon from a p* || jdm ein Geheimnis ~ *to elicit* (od *draw, extract, wring*) *a secret from a p, to worm a secret out of a p* **2.** (of words, etc.) sich jds Lippen ~ *to break from a p's lips*; ein tiefer Seufzer entrang sich ihrer Brust *she heaved* od *fetched a deep sigh*; *a groan escaped her lips* **~r·innen** vi [s] [→ rinnen] *to escape* (aus *from*); aus dem Gefängnis ~ *to escape* (*from*) *prison* || e–r Gefahr ~ *to escape a danger*; er ist mit knapper Not dem Ertrinken –ronnen *he had a hairbreadth* od *narrow escape from drowning*; er ist nur mit knapper N. –ronnen *he had a narrow* od *tight squeak* || jdm ~ *to escape from a p*; s–n Verfolgern ~ *to evade* (od *elude*) *one's pursuers* || → entkommen, –wischen | Tränen –rannen ihren Augen *tears gushed* od *rushed into her eyes* || die Stunden ~ *time flies* **~r·ollen** vi/t **1.** [s] jds Händen ~ *to roll from a p's hands* **2.** vt [s] **a.** (Fahne) *to unfurl*; *unfold*; *unroll* **b.** ⟨fig⟩ (of plays, etc.) (ein Bild) *to display, exhibit, expose, show, unfold* || **sich** ~ *to unfold*; *to unroll itself* (*the future will u. itself before his eyes*); *to be unrolled*

Entrop·ie f ~/ ⟨phys⟩ *entropy*

ent- ~r·osten vt [h] etw ~ *to remove the rust from, to rub the r. off a th*; *to derust, unrust* **~r·ücken** vt [h] ⟨bib⟩ *to translate* || –rückt w nach *to be carried off* (od *removed, shifted*) *to* .. || jdn dem Leben ~ *to carry a p off*; .. den Sorgen ~ *to relieve a p of his cares* || etw e–r S ~ *to remove* (od *withdraw*) *a th from a th* | –rückt *in ecstasy*; *ecstatic* || bald war sie ganz s–n Blikken –rückt *soon he lost sight of her* (od *lost her to sight*) *altogether* || der Wirklichkeit –rückt s *to lose o.s. in speculations*; *to be lost to the world, to withdraw within o.s.*; → Ekstase, entzücken **≃rückung** f ⟨bib⟩ *translation* (Hebr. 11, 5) **~r·ümpeln** vt [h] (Raum) *to clear* (*a room*) *of lumber, rubbish*, etc. **≃r·ümpelung** f ~ e–s Raumes *removal of lumber from a room*; *clearance* (*of the attic*) **~r·unden** vt [h] ⟨phon⟩ (Laut) *to unround* **≃r·undung** f ⟨phon⟩ *unrounding* **~r·üsten** vt [h] (jdn) *to anger, exasperate, enrage, infuriate, pique, provoke* (*a p*); *to make* (*a p*) *angry*; *to get* (od *put*) *a p's back up* || [mst pp] –rüstet s *to flare up*; *fume, kindle* (über *at*); sittlich ~ s *to be shocked* (od *outraged, scandalized*) (über *at*) || **sich** ~ *to chafe*; *huff*; *to lose one's temper*; ⟨sl⟩ *to get* od *put one's monkey up* **~r·üstet** a *angry* (über etw *about, at a th*; über jdn *with a p*); *indignant* (über *at*) || etw ~ zurückweisen *to resent a th with indignation* **≃r·üstung** f *anger, indignation* (über *at*) || starke ~ *deep resentment* (über *at*); ein Schrei der ~ *an outcry* **≃s·after** m *juicer* **~s·agen** vi [h] e–m Anspruch, Rechte ~ *to abandon* (od *disclaim, resign, waive*) *a claim, right*; *to forgo* (*one's claim*); dem Thron ~ *to abdicate* | e–m Beruf ~ *to abandon* (od *give up*) *a career*, e–r Gewohnheit ~ *to relinquish* (od *discontinue, give up, renounce*) *a habit*, dem Rauchen ~ *to renounce* (od *discontinue, leave off*) *smoking* || der Nahrung ~ *to abstain* (od *refrain*) *from food*; den Freuden der Welt ~ *to forsake* od *renounce the world* || dem Alkohol ~ *to abstain*; ein Versprechen geben, dem Trunk z ~ *to take the pledge* | ~ z tun *to desist* (od *refrain*) *from doing*; du tätest besser z ~ *you had better* (⟨Am⟩ *you better*) *desist* **≃s·agung** f ~/~en *abandonment, renunciation, renouncement, resignation*; *relinquishment* (auf *of*); *restraint*; Selbst≃ *self-restraint, (self-)abnegation*; *abstinence* || Thron≃ *abdication* || sich [dat] ~ auferlegen in bezug auf *to deny o.s.* (*a th*) **~s·agungsvoll 1.** a *full of resignation*; *resigned* (*life*) **2.** adv *resignedly* **≃s·alzung** f ~/ *desalin(iz)ation* (*of water, soil*) **≃s·atz** m ~es/ ⟨mil⟩ *relief* (*of a fortress*) **~s·äuern** vt [h] *to deacidify*; *deoxidize* || (Most) *to chaptalize* **≃s·äuerung** f *chaptalization* **~sch·ädigen** vt [h] **1.** jdn ~ *to indemnify* (od *compensate, recoup, repay, reimburse*) *a p* (f *for*); *to make up to a p for a th*; jdn f e–n Verlust ~ *to recoup a p a loss* | sich ~ *to indemnify* (od *recoup, reimburse*) *o.s.* (f *for*) || → ersetzen **2.** [abs] ~ *f etw* (S) *to compensate for a th*; *to make good a th*; *to remunerate a th* (*this remunerates the labour*) **≃sch·ädigung** f ~/~en **1.** [abstr] *compensation, indemnification* (*of a p*); *reimbursement*; *recompense* **2.** [konkr] (~ssumme) *compensation*; *damages* [pl] || ⟨pol⟩ *indemnity*, Kriegs≃ *war indemnity* | ~sanspruch [m] *claim for compensation*; ~ssumme [f] *compensation*; *damages* [pl] || ⟨pol⟩ *indemnity* **~schärfen** vt [h] (Bombe etc) *to unprime*; (Sprengkörper) *to disarm* **≃schärfung** f .. || ⟨übtr pol⟩ *lessening of* (*political*) *tensions* **≃schäumer** m ⟨chem⟩ *defoamer* **≃sch·eid** m ~es/~e *decision* || ⟨jur⟩ *decree*; *judgment*; *ruling*; *verdict*; Gerichts≃ *judicial ruling*; Schiedsgerichts≃ *award* || ~, dem beide Parteien zustimmen *agreed verdict*, ⟨Am⟩ *consent verdict* **~sch·eidbar** a *decidable*; *determinable* **~sch·eiden** vt/i [h] [→ scheiden] **I.** vt [fast nur mit Sachobjekt] der Richter –det *the judge rules* **1.** (Streit, Schicksal, Schlacht) *to decide* (f *for, in favour of a p*; gegen *against*); *to settle*; *to be decisive of* (*a war*) || (durch Schiedsspruch) *to arbitrate* || (Rennen) *to run off* || ~, daß .. *to decide* (od *decree*; ⟨jur⟩ *rule*) *that* .. || Waffengewalt soll die S ~ *armed force has been made the issue* **2.** (Frage etc) *to decide, determine*; *settle*; (Problem) *to resolve* || endgültig ~ *to clinch*; damit ist die S –schieden *that clinches* od *settles the matter*; alles ist –schieden *everything is settled* **3. sich** ~ **a.** (P) *to come to a decision* od *resolution*; *to make up one's mind* || sich ~ z tun *to decide* (od *determine, fix, resolve, settle*; *to make up one's mind*) *to do*; *to decide* (od *determine, resolve*) *on doing*; sich ~ nicht z tun *to decide against doing* || sich ~ f jdn *to decide for* (od *in favour of*) *a p*; *to pitch upon a p*; .. f etw *to be for* (*walking*); *to decide* (od *determine, fix,* *settle) on a th* (*I shall settle on this car*); sich beruflich ~ f *to opt for* (*medicine*); sich f e–n Austritt aus .. ~ *to opt out of* .. ‖ sich ~ über etw *to decide* (od *settle*) *on*; sich darüber ~, wer .., was .. *to decide* od *settle who* .., *what* .. **b.** (S) *to be decided* od *settled* (*against*; *in favour of*) **II.** vi *to decide* (f *for, in favour of*; gegen *against*; zw *between*); der König hat anders –schieden *the king has decided otherwise* ‖ in e–r S ~ *to decide* (od *settle*) *a th*; *to be decisive of a th* ‖ ~ über *to decide on* (*a th*) ‖ ⟨jur⟩ ~ über jdn *to pass sentence on a p*; (durch Schiedsspruch) *to arbitrate* (*between*) ‖ über die Klage ~ *to try* od *adjudicate the action* ‖ → Urteil **~sch·eidend 1.** a *decisive* (*blow, battle*); ~er Schlag ⟨sl⟩ *sockdologer* ‖ ~es Argument *clincher*, ⟨sl⟩ *sockdologer* ‖ *conclusive* (*evidence*) ‖ *crucial* (*difference, point*) ‖ im ~en Augenblick *at the critical moment* ‖ ~er Kampf *showdown* ‖ ~e Stimme *casting vote* | [pred] ~ s f *to be decisive of, to decide* (*the whole war*); (S) *to be decisive for* (*a p*) ‖ ~ s in *to be determinant in* . . ‖ ~ w f *to become decisive of* (od *for*); *to decide* (*the situation*) **2.** adv *decisively* ‖ ~ beitragen zu *to be a decisive factor in*; ~ b. z tun *to be decisive in doing* **≚sch·eidung** f ~/~en *decision* (e–r S *of a th*; über *on, over*); *determination* ‖ ⟨comp⟩ logische ~en *logical discriminations* ‖ ~ durch Krieg *arbitrament of war* ‖ der ~ ausweichen ⟨bes Am⟩ *to dodge the issue* ‖ etw z ~ bringen *to bring a th to a head* ‖ z e–r ~ k *to come to a decision* ‖ die ~ ist gefallen *the outcome* od *result is decided* od *settled* ‖ die ~ fiel z s–n Gunsten aus *the d. was in his favour*; e–e ~ wird bald fallen *a d. will soon be reached* ‖ e–e ~ herbeiführen *to bring about a d.* ‖ die ~ liegt bei dir *it is for you to decide* ‖ e–e ~ treffen *to take a d.*; die ~ treffen, daß .. *to decide that* | gerichtliche ~ *order*; *verdict*; *judicial decision*; *ruling*; e–e gerichtl. ~ treffen *to give a ruling* (über *on*); die gerichtl. ~ treffen, daß *to rule* od *decree that* ..

Entsch·eidungs- [in comp] → entscheidend **~gründe** m pl ⟨jur⟩ *opinion of court* **~kampf** m ⟨fig⟩ *showdown*; ⟨sport⟩ *final*; (nach e–m 'Unentschieden') *decider* **~runde** f = Entscheidungsspiel **~schaltung** f ⟨cyb⟩ *decision element* **~schlacht** f *decisive battle* **~schlag** m ⟨sport⟩ *knock out blow*; ⟨sl⟩ *sockdologer* **~spiel** n ⟨sport⟩ *final*; → ~kampf **~stunde** f *hour of trial*; *critical moment*

ent- ~sch·ieden I. a **1.** *decided* (*attitude, success*); *determined* (*effort*) ‖ *decisive, definite, marked* (*improvement*); *unquestionable* (*superiority*); *positive* (*proof*) ‖ *distinct* (*loss*) ‖ *categorical* (*statement*) ‖ *positive* (*turn to the better*) ‖ *dogmatic, peremptory* (*tone*) **2.** *determined, declared* (*foes*); *firm, resolute, steadfast, thorough-going, unyielding* (*adversary*) ‖ aufs ~ste *most decidedly* **II.** adv *decidedly*; ganz ~ *certainly*; *assuredly*; *emphatically*; *definitely, positively*; ~ dagegen *full against it* ‖ sich ~ (f etw) aussprechen *to pronounce strongly* ‖ ich habe ~ kein Glück ⟨fam⟩ *I'm unlucky, and no mistake* ‖ ~! *definitely*! ‖ aufs ~ste (*to deny*) *categorically* **≚schiedenheit** f ~/ *determination, firmness, resoluteness, decisiveness resolution* (*of a p*) ‖ *decisiveness, definiteness, distinctness*; *peremptoriness* (*of tone*) **~schl·acken** vt [h] etw ~ *to remove the cinders* od *slags from a th* ‖ (Ofen) *to clinker* ‖ (P) sich ~ *to purge* **≚schl·ackung** f ~/~en *slagging*; *removal of cinders* od *slags* (*from a th*) **~schl·afen** vi [s] [→ schlafen] *to fall asleep* ‖ (sterben) *to close one's eyes, to take one's last sleep, to depart this life, to pass away* ‖ der, die ≚e *the deceased* **~schl·agen** vrefl [h] sich e–r S (Sorgen etc) ~ *to rid o.s. of, to get rid of, to part with*; *to throw off a th*; sich der Sorgen ~ *to banish care*; sich aller Rachegedanken ~ *to dismiss all thoughts of revenge* **~schl·ammen** vt [h] *to clear of mud* **~schl·eichen** vi [s] *to steal away* od *off*; *to slip out* od *away*; *to escape quietly* (aus *from*) **~schl·eiern** vt [h] (Gesicht) *to uncover, unveil* ‖ ⟨fig⟩ (Geheimnis) *to disclose, reveal*; *uncover, unveil* **~schl·eimen** vt [h] *to clear of slime* **E–mung** f (der Atemwege) *expectoration* **~schl·ießen** vrefl [h] [→ schließen] sich über etw ~ *to decide* od *settle upon a th* ‖ sich ~ z etw *to decide* (od *determine, resolve*) *on a th*; *to make up one's mind to a th* ‖ sich ~ z tun *to decide* (od *determine, fix*; *make up one's mind*; *to get around*; *to resolve, settle*) *to do*; *to decide* (od *determine, resolve*) *on doing*: sich nicht ~ können z tun *to decide against doing* ‖ sich fest ~ *to set one's teeth* ‖ → entschlossen **≚schl·ießung** f ~/~en *resolution*; → Entschluß; Entscheidung **~schl·ossen I.** a **1.** [pp v entschließen & pred a] ~ s z etw *to be determined* od *resolved on a th*; *to be resolute for a th* (*he was ~ for war*) ‖ zu allem ~ *determined on extreme measures*; *ready to go to all lengths* ‖ ~ s z tun *to be determined* od *resolved to do*; *to be bent* (od *determined, resolved*) *on doing* ‖ fest ~ *stiff* (betr. *about*); fest ~ s ⟨Am⟩ *to be bound* (*to do*) ‖ → halb ‖ kurz ~ *without thinking twice*; *without a moment's hesitation* (*I turned back*) **2.** [attr] *determined* (*foe*), *resolute, resolved, steadfast*; *energetic*; *inflexible*; *purposeful* (*man, character*); ein ~er Mann *a man of determination* ‖ *firm* (*attitude*) **II.** adv *determinedly, resolutely, resolvedly*; *with finality* ‖ ~ aussehend *determined-looking* ‖ ~ verweigern z tun ⟨Am⟩ *to refuse flat-footed to do* **≚schl·ossenheit** f ~/ *decision, determination, resolution, resoluteness, resolve*; *energy, firmness*; ⟨fam⟩ *go, grit*; *push*; ⟨Am sl⟩ *pep, sand* **~schl·ummern** vi [s] *to doze off*; *to fall asleep, to fall into a slumber* ‖ → entschlafen **~schl·üpfen** vi [s] *to slip away* od *out* ‖ jdm ~ *to escape from a p, to slip a p*; *to give a p the slip*; → entrinnen ‖ jds Gedächtnis ~ *to slip a p's memory* od *mind* ‖ e–e Gelegenheit ~ l *to let an opportunity slip* ‖ das Wort ist mir törichterweise –pft *it was a foolish slip of the tongue*; das Wort ist ihm nur –pft *the word slipped out of him* ‖ sich [dat] ~ l *to let* (*money*) *slip through one's fingers* **≚schl·uß** m –l·usses/ –l·üsse *decision* ⟨a. mil⟩; *determination* (*it is our d. to do*); *resolve*; ⟨parl⟩ *resolution* ‖ e–n ~ annehmen *to pass a resolution* ‖ jds ~ bekräftigen *to confirm a p's purpose* ‖ e–n ~ fassen *to form a resolution*; *to take a desision*; den ~ fassen z etw *to resolve a th*; *to decide* (od *determine, resolve*) *on a th*; den ~ fassen z tun *to decide* (od *determine, resolve*) *to do* od *on doing* ‖ z e–m ~ k *to arrive at a decision, to come to a d.* od *determination*; z dem ~ k *to make up one's mind* (*to do*) ‖ z e–m ~ k in e–r S *to resolve a th*; *to decide* (od *determine, resolve*) *on a th*; *to make up one's mind to a th* ‖ es ist mein fester ~ *I have quite made up my mind*; *I am bent upon it, I've set my teeth* ‖ e–n ~ in die Tat umsetzen *to exercise* (od *put into action*) *a resolve* | ~kraft [f] *initiative*; *determination*; *strength of purpose*; schwach an ~ (*or* ⟨a.⟩ ohne ~) *weak of purpose* **~schlüsseln** vt [h] *to decipher, decode*; –lter Text *decipherment* **≚schlüsselung** f *deciphering, decoding*; *breaking a code* **≚schlüßler** m (P) *decoder, etc*; (v Geheimnachrichten) *cryptographer* **~sch·uhen** vt [h] jdn ~ *to slip a p's shoes off* **~sch·uldbar** a *excusable, pardonable* (*mistake*) **~sch·ulden** vt [h] (Land) *to clear* od *free from debt* ‖ ⟨Ger⟩ ein Gut ~ *to reduce the liabilities of an estate* **~sch·uldigen** vt [h] **1.** (jdn) *to excuse*; *pardon*; sie hat s–e Fehler immer –gt *she always found excuses for* ..; → entlasten, freisprechen ‖ bitte mich z ~ *I beg* *to be excused*; entschuldige mich bei ihm *make my excuses to him* | (etw) ~ *to excuse, pardon*; *to condone* (bei jdm *in a p*) ‖ ~ Sie die Störung *excuse my intrusion*; ~ Sie den Ausdruck! (*God*) *save the mark*! ‖ ~ Sie (*or* Sie ~), daß (*or* wenn) ich z spät komme *excuse* (od *pardon*) *me for being late* (od *my being late*) ‖ ~ Sie, aber ich .. *excuse me* (od *if you'll e. me*) *but I* (*must be off*) ‖ er –schuldigte es damit, daß .. *he apologized for it by saying that* .. ‖ nicht z ~ s *to be inexcusable* **2. sich** ~ *to send apologies* (⟨Am⟩ *regrets*); **bei** jdm *to excuse o.s. to a p*; *to make* od *offer an excuse to a p*; *to apologize to a p* (wegen .. *for a th*) ‖ **für**: *he was very apologetic about* ..; ‖ ich möchte mich f heute abend ~ *I should like to be exensed from coming tonight* ‖ sich ~ **mit** etw *to plead a th* (*they pleaded the direct orders of* ..), *to make* (*work*) *one's excuse* ‖ er **ließ** sich ~ *he begged to be excused from attendance* ‖ sein Verhalten läßt sich nicht ~ *there is no excuse for his conduct*; *his conduct admits of no excuse* **≈-sch·uldigung** f ~/~en *excuse*; *apology* ‖ e–e klägliche ~ *a poor excuse* ‖ als ~ kann er sagen *for excuse he may say* .. ‖ als (*or* zur) ~ f *in excuse of*, *in apology for* ‖ jdn um ~ bitten *to apologize to a p* (wegen *for*) ‖ ich bitte um ~! *excuse me*, *I am sorry* (*but* ..) ‖ als ~ dienen f, e–e ~ finden f etw [mst neg] *to excuse a th* (*I cannot e. his conduct*) ‖ dafür gibt es k–e ~ *there is no excuse for it* ‖ hast du k–e bessere ~ vorzubringen? *have you no better excuse to give*? ‖ jdm e–e ~ schreiben *to write a note of excuse for* bzw *to a p* ‖ → Ausrede, Vorwand | ~sgründe [m pl] *excuses* (f *for*) ~sschreiben [n] *letter of apology, written apology* ~svorwände [m pl] = –gründe ~szettel [m] ⟨school⟩ *note of excuse* **≈sch·uldung** f ⟨Ger⟩ *reduction of the liabilities* (*of an estate*) **~schw·eben** vi [s] *to disappear*; *to pass out of sight*; *to vanish* ‖ → entschwinden **~schw·efeln** vt [h] *to desulphurate*, *to desulphurize* **≈schw·efelung** f *desulphurization* **~schw·eißen** vt [h] (Wolle) *to scour* **~schw·inden** vi [s] [→ schwinden] *to disappear*, *to pass away*; *to pass out of sight*; *to vanish* ‖ (S) in die Ferne ~ *to recede into the distance* ‖ aus jds Augen ~ *to recede from a p's view* ‖ den Blicken ~ *to drop from sight* ⟨a. fig⟩ ‖ dem Gedächtnis ~ *to fade from m.*; der Name ist m–m G. entschwunden *the name has slipped my m.*, *the name has escaped me* **~s·eelen** vt [h] (Körper) *to deprive of soul* od *life*; *to render lifeless* ‖ *to deprive of spirit*; *to devitalize* ‖ (Leben) *to deaden*; *to* (*render*) *dull*; *to mechanize* | ~de W. *soul--destroying effect* **ents·eelt** a *inanimate*, *lifeless*, *soulless*; *dead* ‖ *dull*; *soulless*, *spiritless*, *mechanical* ‖ ~e Kunst *art without soul* **~s·enden** vt [h] [→ senden] (Boten) *to dispatch*; *to send*; *to send off* **≈s·endestaat** m (Ggs Empfangs-) *sending State* **~s·etzen** vt [h] **1.** ⟨mil⟩ (Festung) *to relieve* **2.** (absetzen) jdn s–s Amtes ~ *to eject* (od *displace, remove, oust*) *a p from* (*his*) *office*; *to relieve a p of his office*; *to dismiss* od *suspend a p*; er wurde des Kommandos –setzt *he was removed from his command*; → entthronen **3.** ⟨fig⟩ (erschrecken) **a.** jdn ~ *to appal* (od *dismay, frighten, horrify, shock, startle*) *a p*; [mst pass] –setzt s *to be frightened* od *horrified* (über *at*; *to see* ..); ganz ~setzt s *to be staggered* (über *by*); *to be scandalized* (od *shocked, startled*) (über *at*); *to shudder* (*at*); → erschrecken ‖ → entsetzt **b. sich** ~ *to get a fright*, *to take fright*; sich ~ vor *to be frightened* (od *terrified*) *of* | sich ~ über = entsetzt s → 3. a. ‖ sich vor jdm ~ *to be seized with horror by a p* **≈s·etzen** n *dismay, fright, horror* (vor *of*); gr ~ *terror* (*of* ‖) z s–m ~ sah er .. *to his horror he saw* .. ‖ ich höre mit ~, daß .. *I shudder to hear that* ..; ich sehe mit ~, daß .. *I am horrified to see that* .. ‖ jdn mit gr ~ erfüllen *to strike a p with horror* (od *terror*), *to strike terror into a p* ‖ voller ~ *horror-stricken* ‖ ~ stand in s–n Augen *his eyes were horrified*; vor ~ aufschreien *to cry out in horror* **~s·etzlich I.** a **1.** ⟨eig⟩ *dreadful*, *frightful*; *ghastly* (*murder*); *hideous, horrible, shocking* (*crime*); *terrible* (*pain*); *cruel* (*fate*); *appalling* (*weather*) ‖ in ~en Schmerzen sterben *to die in agonies* **2.** °⟨übtr⟩ [intensiv] ⟨fam⟩ *awful, horrid* (*nuisance*); *dreadful, frightful* (*time*); *egregious, thundering* (*folly*); *horrible, nightmarish* (*noise*); *shocking* (*weather*); *terrible* (*heat*); *tremendous* (*fright*); ⟨Am a.⟩ *fierce* (*the weather was f.*) ‖ ein ~er Lärm *a hell of a noise*; ein ~er Skandal *an awful* od *unholy row* ‖ ein ~er Mensch *a horrid man* ‖ es ist ganz ~ mit den Kindern! *bother the children*! ‖ ganz ~ aussehen *to look a perfect fright* ‖→ riesig **II.** adv **1.** [bei Verben] (*to suffer*) *dreadfully, frightfully, terribly* ‖ *enormously*; *immensely*; *exceedingly*; *excessively*; → riesig **2.** [bei adj & adv] *enormously*; *immensely*, *prodigiously*, *disgustingly* (*rich*); *terribly* (*dangerous*) | ⟨fam⟩ *awfully*; *fearfully* (*weary*); *ghastly* (*pale*); *horribly* (*poor*); *terribly* (*hungry*) ‖ ein ~ dürftiges Stück ⟨sl⟩ *a shocking poor play* ‖ ~ kalt ⟨sl⟩ *cruel cold* ‖ ~ krank aussehen ⟨sl⟩ *to look like the devil* ‖ ein ~ langer Weg ⟨sl⟩ *a tremendous long way* ‖ ein ~ langweiliger Mensch ⟨fam⟩ *a ghastly* od *horrible bore* ‖ → riesig **≈s·etzlichkeit** f *atrociousness*, *dreadfulness*, *frightfulness*, *terribleness* **~s·etzt** a *aghast* (*at*) | adv (*to recoil*) *in horror* **≈s·etztwerden** n (in den Himmel) ⟨bes theol⟩ *rapture* **≈s·etzung** f ~/~en **1.** ⟨mil⟩ = Entsatz **2.** *dismissal, removal* (*of a p*; v .. *from office*); *suspension* (*of a p*); → Entthronung **~seuchen** vt [h] (Gebiet) *to decontaminate* **≈seuchung** f = Desinfektion | ~smittel [n] *decontaminant* **~s·ichern** vt [h (Schußwaffe) *to unlock* **~s·iegeln** vt [h] *to unseal* **~s·ilbern** vt [h] *to desilverize* **≈s·ilberung** f *desilverization* **~s·inken** vi [s] [→ sinken] das Schwert entsank s–r Hand *the sword dropped out of his hand* ‖ ⟨übtr⟩ der Mut entsank ihm *his heart sank* (*within him*); *his courage failed him* **~s·innen** vrefl [h] [→ sinnen] sich e–r S [gen] ~ *to call* .. *to mind*; *to recall* (*recollect*, *remember*) *a th*; wenn ich mich recht entsinne *if I remember rightly* **~s·ittlichen** vt [h] *to demoralize* **~s·ittlichend** a *demoralizing* (*influence*) **≈s·ittlichung** f ~/ *demoralization* **~sp·annen** vt [h] **1. a.** (Bogen) *to release*, *to relax*, *to unbend*; (Harfe) *to unstring* ‖ (Seil) *to unfasten*, *to slacken* ‖ (Feder) *to release*, *decock* ‖ (Zunge) *to loose*, *to loosen* ‖ (Leib) *to loosen*, *relax* **b.** (Dampf, Gas) *to expand* **2.** ⟨übtr⟩ (Verhältnisse) *to ease*; (Gemüt) *to ease* ‖ (Gefühle) *to relieve* ‖ (Geist) *to relax*, *unbend*, *unbrace* ‖ (Nerven) *to unbrace*, *unstrain* | **sich** ~ *to relax*, *unbend* (⟨a.⟩ of features); *to ease o.s.*; ⟨fam⟩ *to let o.s. go slack* ‖ (S) *to loosen*, *slacken* ‖ (die Lage) –nnt sich .. *eases* **~sp·annt** a *slack* ‖ *unbent* **≈sp·annung** f ~/~en **1. a.** *release*, *relaxation*; du brauchst ~ *you want a rest* ‖ *loosening* **b.** *expansion* (*of gas, steam*) **2.** ⟨übtr⟩ *easing* ‖ *relaxation*; *unbending* (*of the mind*); *unbracing*, *unstraining* ‖ ⟨pol⟩ *détente* [Fr]; e–e ~ trat ein *a d. set in* (od *was brought about*) ‖ ⟨Lit⟩ (komische *comic*) *relief* (*e.g. the porter* (*Macbeth*), *the grave diggers*, *Ophelia's songs* (*Hamlet*) | ~spause [f] (*stretch*) *break* | ~sübungen [f pl] *loosening-up exercises* **~sp·innen** vt [h] [→ spinnen] ⟨übtr⟩ **1.** (Gedanken) *to develop* **2. sich** ~ (S) *to arise* (aus *from*; *out of*); *develop*; *ensue*; *evolve*; *to take one's rise* (aus *from*); *to originate* (aus *in*, *from*) ‖ *to come into being*; (*friendship*) *sprang up* ‖ → beginnen **~spr·echen** vi [h] [→ sprechen] **1.** [dat] ~ *to answer to a th*; *to be answerable* od *conformable* *to*; *to correspond to* (od *with*); *to tally with a th* ‖ es –spricht (s–r Würde) *it is in accordance with* .. ‖ genau ∼ *to be on all fours with a th* ‖ um speziellen Wünschen z ∼ *to meet individual circumstances* ‖ e–r S **nicht** ∼ *to come* od *fall short of a th*; der Erfolg entsprach nicht den Anstrengungen *the success was not commensurate with the efforts*; die beiden Fälle ∼ sich nicht genau *the two cases are not on all fours* ‖ (of books, etc.) (e–m Vorbild) ∼ *to come* od *be up to* (*a standard*); *to be equal to*; *to equal, match* (*a th, a p*) **2.** (jds Auffassung) ∼ *to be in line with* ..; e–r Behauptung *to stand up to a claim*; jds Geschmack ∼ *to suit a p's taste*; jds Wünschen ∼ *to comply* (*to fall in*) *with, to be equal to, to meet a p's wishes*; *to accede to a p's request* ‖ e–r Aufgabe ∼ *to acquit o.s. of a task, to fulfil a t.* ‖ jds Zweck ∼ *to serve a p's purpose* **∼spr·echend 1.** a; e–r S [dat] ∼ (angemessen) *answerable* (od *adequate, appropriate, corresponding*) *to a th*; *in compliance* od *conformity with*; *suitable to* od *for a th* ‖ dem∼ → daher ‖ im ∼en Verhältnis stehend *proportional, proportionate* (z *to*) ‖ ein dem Appetit ∼es Essen *a dinner commensurate with one's appetite* ‖ e–e dem Gewicht ∼e Geschwindigkeit *a speed proportionate to the weight* ‖ (die deutsche Arbeitsgruppe) u die ∼en kanadischen Stellen .. *and its Canadian counterparts* **2.** adv *correspondingly, suitably, proportionately, accordingly* ‖ dem∼ handeln *to act accordingly*; jds Wünschen ∼ handeln *to act according to* (od *in conformity with*) *a p's wishes*; *to comply with, to meet a p's wishes* ‖ ∼e Anwendung finden *to apply by analogy*; findet ∼ Anwendung *shall apply mutatis mutandis* **≁spr·echung** f ∼/∼en *corresponding case* od *instance*; *analogy* ‖ ⟨phil & scient⟩ *analogous* od *equivalent word* (*in a language*); (Pflanze, Tier, Wort etc) *analogue* ‖ ⟨Lit⟩ ∼en *correspondence* sg (*e.g. in symbolism, surrealism, cf. Baudelaire's "Correspondences", Rimbaud's "Voyelles"*) **∼spr·ießen** vi [s] [→ sprießen] (of plants) dem Boden ∼ *to spring* (od *germinate, grow, shoot, sprout*) *from the soil* ‖ (of men) e–r Rasse ∼ *to be descended from a race* ‖ ⟨übtr⟩ *to arise, derive, emanate* (aus, v *from*); *to originate* (aus, v *in* od *from*) **∼spr·ingen** vi [s] [→ springen] **1.** (P) *to run away*; → entfliehen; dem Gefängnis ∼ *to escape* (*from*) *prison* **2.** (S) **a.** (of a river) *to rise* (auf .. *in the hills*); *to spring* (v *from*) **b.** ⟨übtr⟩ ∼ aus *to arise* od *spring from*; *to derive from*; *to originate in* od *from*; *to result from*; *to have* od *take its rise* (aus *from*; in *in*) ‖ *to originate* (*from*) es gt aus .. *it is the outcome* (od *upshot, result*) *of* .. ‖ e–r Quelle ∼ *to flow from a source* ‖ ihre Unsicherheit entsprang der Tatsache .. *her uncertainty came from* (od *was due to*) *the fact that* .. **∼spr·ühen** vi [s] (of sparks) *to fly out* od *flash* (v *from*); (of liquids) *to gush* (v *from*) ‖ ⟨übtr⟩ [dat] ∼ *to flash* od *sparkle from a th* ‖ → sprühen **∼st·aatlichen** vt [h] (Betrieb) *to denationalize* ‖ (Kirche) *to disestablish* **≁st·aatlichung** f *denationalization* ‖ *disestablishment* **∼st·ammen** vi [s] [dat] **1.** (Familie) ∼ *to be born of, to be descended from*; *to spring* od *come, issue from* **2.** ⟨übtr⟩ e–r S ∼ *to arise* od *spring from*; *to derive* od *flow from* (*words are derived from* ..); *to be due to*; *to originate in* od *from*; *to result from a th*; alle diese Fehler ∼ der Nachlässigkeit *all these mistakes spring from* (od *are the outcome of*) *carelessness*; → entspringen **∼st·auben** vt [h] *to clear* (od *free*) *from dust*; *to dust*; *to wipe clean* **≁staubung** f; ∼ e–r S *removal* (od *extraction*) *of dust from a th* | ∼s-anlage [f] *dust removal* (od *suction, extraction*) *plant*; *de-dusting device* ‖ El·ektro-∼sfilter [m, ⟨tech mst⟩ n] ⟨mill⟩ *electrostatic precipitator* **∼st·ehen** vi [s] [→ stehen] *to bud, to grow, to pullulate* (aus *from*; *out of*) ‖ neu ∼ aus (of buds) *to bud off from* .. | ⟨mst übtr⟩ *to come in*; *to spring up*; *to come to pass*; *to come about*; *to begin*; *to rise* (auf *on*; vor .. *before a p's eye*) ‖ *to arise, accrue, develop, flow, spring* (v, aus *from*); *to have* od *take its rise* (aus *from*; in *in*); *to pullulate* (in *in*); *to originate* (aus, v *in* od *from*); *to proceed* od *result* (*from*); (of offices) *to come into being* od *to birth*; allmählich, langsam ∼ *to emerge gradually, slowly*; plötzlich ∼ *to spring into existence* ‖ (of thoughts) *to be born* (aus *of*); (of feelings) *to burgeon* (*from*) ‖ als Folge ∼ *to result* (*a flowering of civilization resulted*); (niemand weiß,) was daraus noch ∼ mag .. *what it may lead to* ‖ ∼ durch: *heat is generated, produced, developed by*; *damage, the fire was due to* od *caused by* (*carelessness*) ‖ das Gedicht –stand 1805 *the poem was written* (od *dates from*) *1805* ‖ was auch daraus ∼ mag *come what may* ‖ etw ∼ l *to give birth to* ⟨fig⟩; e–e Lage ∼ l *to evolve* (od *to conduce to, to give rise to*) *a situation*; *to bring a s. about* ‖ –standen *resulting* (*damage, consequences*) ‖ → beginnen **≁st·ehen** n; im ∼ begriffen → Entstehung **∼st·ehend** a *nascent* **≁st·ehung** f ∼/∼en *birth, creation, formation* (*of words*); *gensis* (*of a system*), *origin* ‖ ⟨biol⟩ *pullulation* ‖ in der ∼ begriffen *to be in train* (*plans are in t.*); *incipient* (*lunacy*); *nascent*; *coming into being* (*of new industries*); (*history in*) *the making*; ⟨biol⟩ *origin* (*of species*)

Entst·ehungs- [in comp] *genetic* (*history*) **∼art** f *way* od *manner of origin*; *mode of formation* **∼lehre** f ⟨biol⟩ *genetics* [pl] [sg konstr] **∼ort** m *place of origin* **∼stadium** n erstes ∼ *incipience* **∼weise** f = Entstehungsart **∼zeit** f *date* | im **∼zustand** *nascent* (*element*)

ent- ∼st·eigen vi [s] [→ steigen] dem Wagen ∼ *to alight* (od *descend*) *from the car* ‖ ⟨übtr⟩ (*of smells*, etc.) *to come* (od *emanate, flow, issue, rise*) (v, aus *from*) (*Venus risen from the sea* **∼st·einen** vt [h] (Obst) *to stone* **∼st·ellen** vt [h] **1.** (jdn) *to deform, disfigure* **2.** ⟨übtr⟩ (Kunstwerk) *to deface, disfigure* ‖ (Schönheit) *to mar* ‖ (Ende e–s Stückes) *to botch* ‖ (Landschaft, Natur) *to blur, to deface, disfeature, disfigure*; → verschandeln ‖ ⟨theat⟩ (Rolle) *to travesty* | (Tatsachen) *to distort* (bis z Unkenntlichkeit *out of all resemblance to the facts*) ‖ (Bericht) *to belie, fudge, garble, misstate, misdescribe, misrepresent*; → fälschen ‖ (Sinn e–s Wortes, Wahrheit) *to pervert*; *to wrest* (v .. z *from* .. *to*) ‖ (Gedanken) *to deform* ‖ (Urteilskraft) *to warp* ‖ (Charakter) *to flaw* ‖ (Ideal) schändlich ∼ *to defile*; *to prostitute* | ∼d beschreiben, wiedergeben *to misdiscribe, misrepresent* | –llt *corrupt* (*text*) **≁st·ellung** f ∼/∼en **1.** *deformation, disfiguration, disfigurement* (*of a p*) **2.** *defacement*; *disfigurement* (*of a statue*); (an Gebäuden durch Verfall) *dilapidation* ‖ *marring* (*of beauty*) ‖ *travesty* (*of a role*) ‖ *defacement, disfigurement* (*of nature*); → Verschandelung | *distortion* (*of facts*) ‖ *garbling* (*of an account*); *misrepresentation, misstatement* ‖ *perversion* (*of sense, truth*) ‖ *travesty* (*of a case*) ‖ schändliche ∼ *prostitution* (*of an ideal*) **∼st·ielen** vt [h] (Obst) *to pick* **∼stören** vt [h] ⟨wir⟩ *to screen, dejam*; *to suppress* (*interference*) **≁störer** m ⟨wir⟩ (S) *suppressor*; (P) *faultsman* | ∼geschirr [n] ⟨wir mot⟩ *interference eliminator* od *suppressor* **∼stört** a *interference free* **≁störung** f *interference suppression, radio-shielding*; *antijamming* | ∼s-kondensator [m] *generator condenser* **≁störzusatz** m *antij. attachment* **∼strömen** vi [s] e–m Quell ∼ *to flow* (od *pour, stream*) *from a source*; (of rain) den Wolken ∼ *to gush forth from the clouds* ‖ ⟨übtr⟩ e–r S ∼ (of smells, etc.) *to emanate* (od *flow, issue*) *from a th*; (of books) *to flow from a Press*; (of words) jds Munde ∼ *to gush* (*forth*) *from a p's mouth* **∼st·ürzen** vi [s] e–r

S ~ *to drop from, to rush from a th* ‖ ⟨übtr⟩ *to break* (od *burst forth*) **~s·ühnen** vt [h] (etw) *to expiate*; *to atone for* (*a th*) ‖ sich ~ *to purify o.s.* **~s·umpfen** vt [h] (Land) *to drain*; *to clear from swamps* **~s·ündigen** vt [h] (jdn) ⟨ec⟩ *to absolve*; *acquit*; *to free from sin* ‖ *to purify* (v *of, from*) **≗s·ündigung** f ~/~en ⟨ec⟩ *absolution*; *purification* **~t·äuschen** vt [h] jdn ~ *to disappoint a p, to frustrate* (od *thwart*) *a p's expectations*; *not to be up to a p's e.* ‖ –täuscht *disillusioned, disenchanted, disappointed*; (über etw *at, with a th*; in jdm *in a p*); ⟨fam⟩ *to be had* (über *over*); er war sehr –täuscht, als .. *he was badly had* (*when he* ..); angenehm –täuscht *agreeably disappointed* ‖ *life has disillusioned him* ‖ –täuscht w *to meet with a disappointment* **≗täuschung** f ~/~en *disappointment* (über etw *at a th*; in jdm *in a p*; f jdn *for a p*); *disillusion*(*ment*) (über *with*); *discomfiture* ‖ ⟨ped⟩ *frustration* ‖ die ~ darüber, daß er getan hat *the disappointment at his doing* ‖ es gab nichts als bittere ~en *there was nothing but heartburnings* ‖ e–e gr ~! ⟨sl⟩ *a complete frost*! ‖ ~en erleben *to be disappointed* (mit jdm *in a p*); gr ~en erleben w *to be doomed to disappointment*; wir h an ihm e–e ~ –bt *he has been a disapp. to us* **~thr·onen** vt [h] (König) *to dethrone, unthrone*; *depose* ‖ ⟨übtr⟩ (etw) *to dethrone* **≗thr·onung** f *dethronement*; *deposition* **~trümmern** vt [h] *to remove rubble from* **≗trümmerung** f *rubble clearing* **Ent-u Beladen** n ⟨rail, mar⟩ *turn-round* **~v·ölkern** vt [h] (Land) *to depopulate, unpeople* **≗v·ölkerung** f *depopulation* ‖ ⟨soc⟩ *decongestion* **~w·achsen** vi [s] [→ wachsen] e–r S ~ *to outgrow a th* ‖ den Kinderschuhen ~ s *to be no longer in leading-strings* (od *no longer a child*); kaum (*or* noch nicht) den Kinderschuhen ~ s *to be still in leading-strings*; den K. ~ *out of one's infancy* **~w·affnen** vt [h] (Land, Volk) *to disarm*; ⟨a. fig: jdn, etw⟩ **~w·affnend** a *disarming* (*smile*) **≗-w·affnung** f ~/~en *disarming* (*of a p*); *disarmament* (*of a country*) **~w·alden** vt [h] (Gebiet) *to strip* od *clear of wood* od *forest*; *to deforest, dis*(*af*)*forest* **≗w·aldung** f ~/~en *dis*(*af*)*forestation* **~w·arnen** vi [h] ⟨aero⟩ *to sound* (*the*) *All Clear* **≗w·arnung** f ~/~en, ~ssignal [n] *the All Clear*; *'raiders passed' signal*; ~ssignal geben *to give* od *sound* (*the*) *All Clear*

entw·ässern vt [h] ⟨agr⟩ (Boden etc) *to drain, dewater* (*dewatered* Gips); *dehumidify* **≗w·ässerung** f *drainage* ~sanlage [f] *drainage* ‖ *dehydration* ~sgebiet [n] *drainage-basin* ~spresse [f] *moisture expeller* ~rohr [n] *drainage-tube*

entw·eder [conj] ~ .. oder *either .. or*; ~ du oder ich bin .. *either you or I am* ..; ~ sein Bruder od s–e Eltern sind .. *either his brother or his parents are* .. ‖ [abs] ~ oder! *take it or leave it*!, *like it or lump it*!

ent-w·eichen vi [s] [→ weichen] **1.** *to abscond*; *escape* ‖ jdm ~ *to escape from a p*; *to run away from a p*; den Verfolgern ~ *to evade* od *elude one's pursuers* ‖ aus dem Gefängnis ~ *to escape* (*from*) *prison*; dem Tode ~ *to escape death* ‖ e–n Gefangenen ~ l *to permit the escape of a prisoner* → entfliehen, –rinnen **2.** ⟨übtr⟩ **a.** (of liquids) *to leak, to ooze* (*through*) **b.** (of gases) *to escape* **c.** ⟨übtr⟩ *to vanish* (v, aus *from*; in *into*) **≗w·eichung** f ~/~en *escape, flight* (*of a p*) ‖ *leakage* (*of a liquid*); *escape* (*of gas*) **~w·eihen** vt [h] (etw) *to desecrate, pollute*; *profane, violate* **≗w·eihung** f ~/~en *desecration, pollution*; *profanation, violation* **~w·enden** vt [h] [→ wenden] (etw) *to abstract, filch, pilfer, purloin, steal* (aus *from*); jdm etw ~ *to steal* (od *take*) *a th from a p* ‖ (Geld) *to peculate*; → veruntreuen **≗w·endung** f ~/~en *abstraction, purloining, theft*; *peculation* **~w·erfen** vt [h] [→ werfen] *to design*; *lay down*; *outline, project, sketch* (*out*), *trace* (*out*) ‖ etw flüchtig, grob ~ *to make a rough sketch* od *draft of a th* ‖ ⟨tech⟩ *to design*; *to blueprint* ⟨a. fig⟩ ‖ (Garten) *to lay out* ‖ (Schriftstück) *to draw up*; (Figur, Karte) *to project*; (Kurve) *to plot* (auf *on*) ‖ ⟨parl⟩ (Vorlage) *to draft*; (Vertrag etc) *to block out* ‖ *to chart* (*future strategy*) ‖ (Gedanken) *to conceive, devise, frame* ‖ schnell ~ *to knock up* ‖ in gr Zügen ~ *to block out*; *to skeletonize* **≗werfer** m ⟨typ, print⟩ *layout man* | ⟨tail, com⟩ *designer*; → Entwurf, entwerfen **~w·erten** vt [h] (Valuta) *to depreciate, devaluate* ‖ (Münzen) *to call in*; *to debase*; *demonetize*; *devalue* ‖ (Briefmarken) *to cancel, deface, obliterate* ‖ (Zeugnisaussage) *to devaluate* ‖ (etw) völlig ~ *to render .. valueless* **≗w·ertung** f ~/~en *depreciation, devaluation* (*of currency*), *debasement, demonetization* (*of coins*) ‖ *cancellation, obliteration* (*of stamps*) **≗wesung** f *disinsec*(*tiza*)*tion* **~w·ickeln** vt [h] ⟨nur übtr⟩ (→ auf–, loswickeln) **A. 1.** (Theorie, Plan) *to develop*; *evolve*; *set forth*; *unfold*; (Idee) *to work out* ‖ ⟨Am a.⟩ *to evolute* ‖ (Zustand) *to evolve*; *to give rise to*; *to bring about*; *to produce* ‖ (Eigenschaften etc) *to develop* (z *into*; aus *from, out of*) ‖ (Geschwindigkeit etc) *to develop*; (Mut; Tätigkeit) *to display, exhibit, show* ‖ näher ~ *to elaborate* (*one's proposals*); *to enlarge upon* (*a th*), *to point* (*a th*) *out*; ich werde jetzt näher ~, wie .. *I shall now point out how* .. **2.** ⟨mil⟩ (Truppen) in breiter Front ~ *to deploy, develop* **3.** ⟨chem⟩ (Gas) *to disengage, evolve, generate*; *liberate*; *produce* (aus *from*) ‖ ⟨phot⟩ (Bild) *to develop* ‖ ⟨tech⟩ *to engineer* ‖ –lt s aus *to derive from* **B. sich ~ 1.** (of buds) *to effloresce* (z *into*); *to unfold* | ⟨übtr⟩ *to flower* (z *into*) ‖ (of ideas, etc.) *to develop* (aus *from, out of*; z *into*); *to work* (z *to*) ‖ (of a system) *to develop* (od *unfold*) *itself*; *to* (*d*)*evolve*; *to be evolved*; die Stücke mögen sich folgendermaßen entwickelt h *the plays may have been evolved as follows*; *to blossom out* (z .. *into a state of perfection*) ‖ (of events) *to go, to shape*; alles entwickelte sich besser, als ich erwartete *everything went better than I expected* | (P) *to fulfil o.s.*; er entwickelt sich z unserer vollen Zufriedenheit *he is shaping very satisfactorily* ‖ sich z e–m K. ~ *to make o.s. into an artist* **2.** ⟨mil⟩ sich in breiter Front ~ *to deploy* **3.** ⟨chem⟩ (of gas, etc.) *to be disengaged* **≗w·ick(e)lung** f ~/~en **1.** *development* (*of a plant*; *an industry*; *civilization*); *evolution, working out* (*of a drama*); *unfolding*; *formation, growth* ‖ nähere ~ *elaboration* (*of a theory*); zu voller ~ k *to develop fully*; *to attein full growth*; weitere ~ *future trends in the development* ‖ ~en vorantreiben *to spur new developments* | ⟨biol⟩ *evolution* ‖ auf dem Wege der ~ *evolutionally* ‖ in der ~ *in the making* ‖ die ~ der Dinge abwarten *to await the turn of events* ‖ *display, exhibition* (*of an activity*) **2.** ⟨mil⟩ ~ in breiter Front *deploy, deployment* **3.** ⟨chem⟩ *disengagement*; *generation* (*of a gas*); *production* ‖ ⟨phot⟩ *development* ‖ die ~ e–s Films vornehmen *to develop a film* **≗w·ickler** m ⟨phot⟩ (Flüssigkeit) *developer* ‖ ⟨chem⟩ *generator*; Azetylen≗ *acetylene generator* **Entw·icklungs-** [in comp] **1.** .. *of development* **2.** ⟨biol⟩ *evolutional*; *evolutionary*; *nascent* **3.** ⟨phot⟩ *developing* **~bad** n ⟨phot⟩ *developing bath* **~dose** f ⟨phot⟩ *daylight developing tank* **~gang** m *path of development*; *course of development* (od *formation*); *evolution* **~gedanke** m *idea of evolution* **~gefäß** n ⟨chem⟩ *generating vessel* **~gerät** n ⟨phot⟩ *developing dish* **~geschichte** f ⟨biol⟩ *biogenesis, biogeny* **≗geschichtlich** a *biogenetic* **~hilfe** f *economic aid, development assistance* **~jahre** n [pl] ⟨biol⟩ *adolescence* ‖ ⟨übtr⟩ *formative years, years of growth* **~land** n *developing country* **~lehre** f

⟨scient⟩ *Doctrine* (od *Theory*) *of Evolution*; Anhänger der ~ *evolutionist* **~möglichkeit** f *possibility* **~programm** n ⟨ind, com⟩ *development policy* **~richtung** f *line of development* **~stadium** n *nascent stage* (od *state*); ⟨fig⟩ *chrysalis stage* **~stufe** f *stage of development*; *phase* **≈technisch** adv jung *or* rückständig *less* od *under-developed* (*Land*), jetzt besser: –land **~trend** m *trend* **~- u Kopieranstalt** f *development and printing* (*D* & *P*) *laboratory* **~zeit** f *period of development* od *growth*; ~ des Keims *incubation* **~zustand** m = –stadium **ent- ~w·inden** vt [h] [→ winden] jdm etw ~ *to wrench* od *wrest a th from a p* ‖ sich jds Umarmungen ~ *to extricate o.s. from a p's embraces* **~w·irren** vt [h] (Knäuel etc) *to disentangle, undo, unravel, untwist*; (die Fäden e–s Gewebes) *to unwind* ‖ (Verkehrssalat) *to unsnarl* ‖ ⟨fig⟩ (Geheimnis, Lage) *to disentangle, ravel out, unravel*; *to set in order*; (Verwicklung) *to straighten out* **≈w·irrung** f ~/~en *disentanglement, unravelling* ⟨a. fig⟩ **~w·ischen** vi [s] *to* (*make one's*) *escape*; *to steal away*; aus dem Gefängnis ~ *to escape* (*from prison*) ‖ jdm ~ *to escape from a p*; *to give a p the slip*; den Verfolgern ~ *to evade* (od *elude*) *the pursuers*; laß ihn uns nicht ~ *don't let him give us the slip* **~w·öhnen** vt [h] **1.** (Kind) *to wean* **2.** jdn e–r S (*or* v e–r S) ~ *to disaccustom a p to a th, to wean a p from a th*; *to break a p of* (*a habit*) ‖ sich e–r S ~ *to become disaccustomed to a th*; *to wean o.s. from a th*; *to discontinue a th*; sich des Rauchens ~ *to leave off smoking* **~w·öhnt** a *weaned* (*child*); vor kurzem ~es Kind *weanling* **≈w·öhnung** f *weaning* (*of a babe*) ‖ *weaning* (*of a p*; v .. *from a habit*) | ~sanstalt [f] *restrictive establishment for drug addicts*; *inebriates' home*, ⟨Am a.⟩ *asylum for alcoholics* **~w·ölken** vt [h] **1.** (S) (den Himmel) *to clear* (od *free*) *from clouds* ‖ ⟨fig⟩ (Stirn; polit. Lage) *to free from gloom*; *to clear* (*up*); *to uncloud* **2. sich ~** *to be cleared* (od *freed*) *from clouds* ‖ ⟨fig⟩ *to be freed from gloom*; *to clear* (*up*); *to brighten* **~w·ürdigen** vt [h] (jdn, s–n Namen) *to degrade, disgrace*; *abase*; *dishonour* ‖ → entweihen **≈w·ürdigung** f ~/~en *degradation*; *derogation* **≈w·urf** m ~(e)s/≈e **1.** [abstr] (Entwerfen) *designing, projektion, plan*(*ning*), *scheming, boasting* ⟨bes arts⟩ **2.** [konkr] (Entworfenes) *design* (e–s Baus, z e–m Bau *of* od *for a building*) ‖ *outline*; (erster ~) *sketch* (z etw *of a th*); *skeleton*; im ~ *in outline* ‖ *draft* (*of a document*), ⟨Am⟩ *draught*; erster ~ *rough draft* (od *copy*) ‖ *design* (*of a novel, play*); *outline, plan, project, scheme* ‖ ⟨comp⟩ ~ der Karte *card design* ‖ ⟨print⟩ *layout* ‖ Gesetz≈ *bill*; e–n G. annehmen (ablehnen) *to pass* (*to throw out*) *a bill*; → einbringen I. A. 2. ‖ ⟨pol⟩ Vorschlags≈ *plan* | e–n ~ m. ausarbeiten *to draw up a plan* od *sketch*; *to sketch out* (od *work out*) *a scheme* ‖ e–n ~ m z *or* v etw *to make a sketch of a th*; *to lay down a plan for a th*; *to design* (od *outline, plan, scheme, sketch*) *a th* | ~zeichenpapier [n] *rough drawing paper* ‖ ~skizze [f] ⟨tech, print⟩ *layout* **~w·urzeln** vt [h] **1.** (Bäume) *to unroot, uproot*; *disroot*; → ausrotten **2.** ⟨übtr⟩ **a.** jdn ~ *to uproot a p from his homeland*; innerlich –wurzelt w *to be swept from one's mental moorings* **b.** (Gewohnheiten) *to uproot*; (Überzeugungen etc) *to depolarize, unsettle, upset* **~w·urzelt** a *uprooted* (*tree*) ‖ ⟨übtr⟩ *rootless*; *uprooted*; *not rooted in the soil* **≈w·urzelung** f ~/~en *unrooting, uprooting* ‖ ⟨übtr a.⟩ *upsetting* **~z·aubern** vt [h] (jdn, etw) *to disenchant, to take the spell of* ‖ –rt w *to loose one's spell* od *magic* **≈z·auberung** f *disenchantment* **~z·erren** vt [h] ⟨phot⟩ *to correct for distortion* **≈z·errer** m ⟨rec⟩ *equalizer* **≈z·errung** f ⟨phot⟩ *restitution*; ⟨tech⟩ *equalization* **~z·iehen** vt [h] [→ ziehen] **A. 1.** jdm etw ~ *to withdraw a th from a p*; *to stint a p of a th* (*don't stint them of their rice*); *to take a th from a p* ‖ *to deprive* od *strip a p of a th*; *to exclude a p from a th*; jdm den Boden ~ *to cut the ground from under a p's feet, from underneath a p*; *to take heat from a p's body*; jdm das Kommando ~ *to remove* (od *suspend*) *a p from the command* ‖ | [dat] -zogen w *to be kept from* (*work*); das Haus wurde m–n Blicken –zogen *the house was hidden from my sight* ‖ ihm wurde der Tabak –zogen *he was forbidden tobacco, he was f. to smoke* | (jdm) das Taschengeld ~ *to cut off* (*a child's*) *p.-m.*; *to deprive a p of food*; *to take away* od *to stop a p's pension*; etw jds Zugriff ~ *to put a th out of a p's reach* od *grasp, to prevent a p from getting it* **2. sich ~ a.** (P) sich jds Umarmungen ~ *to extricate o.s. from a p's embraces* | sich den Verfolgern, der Verfolgung ~ *to elude* od *evade the pursuers, to elude* od *evade pursuit*; sich dem Gericht durch die Flucht ~ *to flee from justice* ‖ sich e–r Gefahr ~ *to escape a danger* ‖ *to avoid* od *shun* (*a society*); sich der G. jds ~ *to avoid* od *shun a p* ‖ *to avoid discovery* od *detection* = *to go undetected, unnoticed* ‖ sich dem Militärdienst ~ ⟨fam⟩ *to dodge military service* | sich e–m Kontrakt ~ *to get off a contract* ‖ sich der Zahlung ~ *to elude payment* ‖ sich e–r Pflicht ~ *to evade* od *shirk a duty* ‖ sich e–r Verantwortung ~ *to sneak out of a responsibility* ‖ sich s–n Verpflichtungen ~ *to go back upon one's obligations* | niemand kann sich ihren Reizen ~ *nobody can resist her charms* | [abs] *to remain aloof* **b.** (S) gewisse Vergehen ~ sich der Aufdeckung *certain offences are beyond detection* ‖ sich der Beobachtung ~ *to elude observation* ‖ das entzieht sich jeder Berechnung *that is past counting* ‖ das entzieht sich m–r Beurteilung *that is beyond my judgement* ‖ sich der Erkenntnis der Wissenschaft ~ *to elude the grasp of science* ‖ das entzieht sich m–r Kenntnis *that is unknown to me* ‖ das entzieht sich m–r Machtbefugnis *that is not within my powers* **B.** ⟨chem⟩ mst [pass] (etw) *to extract*; *abstract*; Sauerstoff ~ *to deoxidize* ‖ e–r S etw ~ *to extract a th from a th* **≈z·iehung** f ~/~en die ~ e–r S *the taking away* od *the deprivation of a th*; *the withdrawal* (*of subsidies*) ‖ ⟨mot⟩ Führerschein≈ auf 3 Jahre *suspension of driving licence for 3 years* ‖ ⟨ec⟩ Pfründen≈ *removal from a benefice*; *deprivation* **~z·ifferbar** a *decipherable* **≈z·ifferer** m ~s/~ *decipherer* **~z·iffern** vt [h] (Hand-, Inschrift) *to decipher*; *to make out* ‖ (Codetelegramm) *to decode*; → dechiffrieren **≈z·ifferung** f ~/~en *deciphering*; *decipherment* ‖ *decoding* **~z·ücken 1.** vt [h] (jds Auge, Herz) *to captivate, delight*; *to ravish* (*a p's eye, heart*) ‖ *to enchant, enrapture, entrance* (*a p*); *to captivate, charm, delight, fascinate, please* (*a p*); *to fill* (*a p*) *with delight*; *to go down well with* (*a p*) ‖ **~zückt** [pred a] *delighted* (über *at* od *with*); *pleased*; *overjoyed*; *rapt* (*at, with*); ~ s *to be in raptures* (über *over*); *to be delighted* od *enchanted* (über *at*; v *with*); *to be taken with a p*; *to be enraptured*, od *transported*, od *thrilled* (*with*); *to make a display* (über .. *over a p*); ganz ~ s v *to be wild about* (*a th*) **2. E.cken** n **a.** = Entzückung **b.** *delight* (über *at*); *enthusiasm* (über *over*); *thrill* (*at*); *transport*; v ~ erfüllt *delighted, overjoyed*; in ~ geraten *to enthuse* (*about*); jdn in ~ versetzen *to delight a p*; *to move a p to ecstasy*; *to fill a p with delight* **~-z·ückend 1.** a *entrancing* (*tale*); *ravishing* (*melodies*) ‖ [mst verblaßt] *bewitching*; *charming* (*girl*); *delightful* (*place*); *lovely*; *fascinating* **2.** adv *charmingly*; *delightfully* **≈z·ückung** f ~/~en *ecstasy, entrancement, rapture, ravishment, transport*; in ~ geraten *to go into raptures* (od *transports*); jdn in ~ versetzen *to enchant, to* *entrance a p* **'~z·ug** m ~(e)s/'~e = Entziehung **~z·ündbar** a; leicht ~ *combustible*; (*in*)*flammable* (*substance*); nicht ~ *non-flammable*; leicht ~e Stoffe [pl] *inflammables* [pl] ‖ ⟨fig⟩ *excitable*, *inflammable* (*temperament*) **'~z·ündbarkeit** f ~/ leichte ~ *combustibility*, (*in*)*flammability* **~z·ünden** vt [h] **1. a.** (Feuer) *to kindle*, *light*; (Stoff) *to ignite* **b.** (Auge) *to inflame*; (Wunde) *to irritate* **c.** (Leidenschaft etc) *to excite*, *inflame*, *rouse* **2. sich** ~ **a.** *to catch* od *take fire*; *to ignite*; (of sparks) *to kindle*; *to blaze up* **b.** (of the eyes) *to become inflamed* od *sore* **c.** (of passion) *to inflame*; *to blaze up*; (of feelings) *to be roused*; s–e Begeisterung –zündete sich an .. *his enthusiam kindled at* .. **~z·ündlich** a = entzündbar **'~z·ündung** f ~/~en **1.** *kindling* (*of a fire*); *ignition* (*of coal*) ⟨a. chem⟩ **2.** ⟨med⟩ *inflammation* (*of the lungs*); *irritation* (*of a wound*); ~ am Ballen *bunion*; → Phlegmone **3.** ⟨fig⟩ *excitement*, *rousing* (*of passion*) **| ~s-** ~fieber [n] *inflammatory fever* | ~gemisch [n] *ignition mixture* | ~geschwindigkeit [f] *speed of ignition* | ~punkt [m] ⟨phys⟩ *ignition* od *flash point* (*of kerosene*) | ~temperatur [f] *temperature of ignition*; *ig.n t.*

entzw·ei adv **1.** *in two*, *asunder*; *in half*; ⟨Am sl⟩ *on the bum*; → entzwei– **2.** ~ s *to be broken*, *to be in pieces* ‖ *to be torn* ‖ der Wagen ist ~ *the car is broken down*

entzw·ei- [betontes, trennbares pref] *asunder*, *in two*, *in half* **~|brechen** vt/i **1.** vt [h] *to break asunder*; *to break in half*; *to snap* **2.** vi [s] *to break* **~|fallen** vt [h] sich ein Bein ~ *to break one's leg by falling* **~|gehen** vi [s] *to break*, *burst*; *to go* od *fall to pieces*; *to go fut* ‖ *to tear* | ⟨übtr⟩ (*of friendship*) *to break up* **~|reißen** vt/i **1.** vt [h] *to tear in two*; *to snap* **2.** vi [s] *to tear* **~|schlagen** vt [h] *to smash* **~|schneiden** vt [h] *to cut in two* **~|springen** vi [s] *to snap in two*

entzw·eien vt [h] **1.** (Menschen) *to set at variance*; *to disunite*; *divide*; *separate*; *split*; alte Freundschaft, jetzt entzwei *olf friends now at variance*; → Zwietracht **2. sich** ~ *to fall out* (*they have fallen out*); *to split* (über *on*) ‖ sich mit jdm ~ *to fall out* (od *to quarrel*, ⟨sl⟩ *split*) *with a p* **Entzw·eiung** f ~/~en *disunion*, *dissension*, *variance*; *quarrel*, *strife*

En·uresis f [Gr] ⟨path⟩ *enuresis*

Env·ers [ɑ̃'væə] m = Kehrseite; *reverse* (*of a coin*) **en vogue** [ɑ̃'vo:g] adv (Fr) *in vogue*

×**·Enzeler** m = Enzianschnaps

Enzephal·itis f ~/~tiden Gr ⟨path⟩ *encephalitis*

·Enzian m ~s/~e ⟨bot⟩ *gentian*, gr ~ *gentianella* [L] **~bittermedizin** f ⟨pharm⟩ *gentian-bitter* **~gewächse** n [pl] Gattung der ~ *Gentianaceae* [L pl] **~schnaps** m *spirituous liquor distilled from the gentian-root*

Enz·yklika f [L] ~/–ken ⟨R. C.⟩ *encyclic*, *encyclical*

Enzyklopäd·ie f ~/~n *encyclop*(*a*)*edia*, *cyclop*(*a*)*edia* [L] **enzyklop·ädisch** a *encyclopaedic*(*al*), *cyclopaedic* **Enzyklopäd·ist** m *encyclopaedist*

Enz·ym n [Gr] ~s/~e ⟨chem⟩ *enzyme*

Eol·ith m [Gr] ~s & ~en/~e(n) ⟨praeh⟩ *eolith* **eol·ithisch** a *eolithic*

Eos·in n ~s/ *eosin*(*e*)

Eoz·än n [Gr] ~s/ ⟨geol⟩ (mittlere Alttertiärstufe) **1.** *eocene* **2.** [in comp] *eocene* (*rock*); ~formation f *eocene formation*; → –zän

Ep·akte f [Gr] ~/~n ⟨astr⟩ *epact*

Ep·arch m [Gr] ~en/~en ⟨ant⟩ *eparch*

Epaul·ett [epo'let] n [Fr] ~s/~s; **Epaul·ette** [epo'lɛtə] f ~/~n ⟨mil & nav⟩ *epaulet*, *epaulette* [Fr]; *shoulder-strap*

Epenth·ese f [Gr] ~/~n ⟨gram⟩ *epenthesis*

Eph·ebe m [Gr] ~n/~n ⟨ant⟩ *ephebe*; *ephebus* **Ephebiatr·ie** f *ephebiatry*

Ephedr·in n ~s/ ⟨med⟩ *ephedrin*(*e*)

ephem·er a [Gr] *ephemeral* (*insect*, *flower*) ‖ ⟨fig⟩ *ephemeral*, *fleeting*, *fugitive*, *transient*, *transitory* (*pleasures*) **Ephem·ere** f ⟨ent & bot⟩ *ephemera*, *ephemeron* [pl *–rons*, *–ra*] **Ephemer·ide** f ⟨ent⟩ *ephemerid*

·Epheserbrief m ⟨bib⟩ *Epistle to the Ephesians*

·Ephesos, ·Ephesus n ⟨Gr⟩ (Stadt in Kleinasien) *Ephesus*

Ephor·at n ~s/~e *ephoralty*, *ephorate*

Eph·ore m [Gr] ~n/~n ⟨ant⟩ *ephor* **·Ephorus** m [L] ~/–·oren ⟨ec⟩ *ephor*

Epi- [Gr lebendes Präfix z Bezeichnung der Oberfläche, des Daraufseins u –folgens etc] **~dem·ie** f ~/~n [–i:ən] *epidemic*; *epidemic disease*; ⟨a. übtr⟩ ‖ → Epizootie **'~d·emisch** a *epidemic*(*al*); ⟨vet⟩ *epizootic* **~d·ermis** f ~/–men Gr ⟨anat⟩ **1.** *epidermis* [L], *cuticle* **2.** [in comp] *epidermal*, *epidermic* **'~dermoid·al** a *epidermoid*(*al*) **~diask·op** n [Gr] ~s/~e *epi*(*dia*)*scope*; *reflecting projector* **~d·ot** m [Gr] ~s/~e ⟨minr⟩ *epidote* **~gen·ese** f [Gr] ~/ ⟨biol⟩ *epigenesis* (L) **~g·one** m ~n/~n ⟨Gr myth⟩; die ~n [pl] *the Epigoni* [L pl] ‖ ⟨Lit⟩ die ~n [pl] *the epigons*; *the unoriginal successors* [pl] (*of a generation*); *mere imitators of great models* **'~g·onenhaft** a *imitational*, *imitative*; *unoriginal* **~g·onentum** n ~(e)s/ ⟨Lit⟩ *mere imitative activity in art and literature*; *mere imitation* ‖ = Epigonen [pl] **~gr·amm** n [Gr] ~s/~e *epigram* **'~gramm·atisch 1.** a *epigrammatic*; in ~er Weise *epigrammatically* **2.** adv *epigrammatically*; ~ behandeln, ausdrücken *to epigrammatize* **~gramm·atiker** m *epigrammatist* **~gr·aph** n ~s/~e *epigraph* **~gr·aphik** f *epigraphy* **'~gr·aphisch** a *epigraphic*

·Epik f ~/ ⟨Lit⟩ die ~ *epic poetry*; → Epos

Epi- (→ o.) **~k·ard** n ~s/ ⟨anat⟩ *epicardium*

·Epiker m ~s/~ *epic poet*; → Epos

Epi- **~kur·eer** m ~s/~ ⟨fig⟩ *epicure*, *epicurean* **'~kur·eisch, '~k·urisch** a *epicurean* **~kur·ismus** m *epicurism* **~leps·ie** f ⟨path⟩ die ~ *epilepsy* (*e. may occur* ..) **~l·eptiker** m ~s/~ *epileptic* **'~l·eptisch** a *epileptic*; ~er Anfall *e. fit* **~l·og** m ~s/~e *epilogue* **~ph·ania** f [L], **~ph·aniasfest** n, das ~ (6. Januar) *the Epiphany*; → Dreikönigsfest **~phora** [.'...] f [Gr] ~/ ⟨rhet⟩ *epiphora* **~ph·yse** f [Gr] ~/ ⟨anat⟩ *epiphysis* (L) **~ph·yt** m [Gr] ~en/~en ⟨bot⟩ *epiphyte*

†**Ep·irus** n ⟨Gr ant⟩ (Landschaft) *Epirus*

·episch 1. a *epic* (*poem*, *poet*); frühe ungeschriebene ~e Dichtung *epos* ‖ in ~er Manier *epically* **2.** adv *epically*

Epi- **~sk·op** n ~s/~e *episcope*, *delineascope* **'~skop·al** a ⟨ec⟩ *episcopal* **~skop·ale** m ~n/~n ⟨ec⟩ *episcopalian* **~skop·alkirche** f *episcopal church* **~skop·alsystem** n *episcopalism* **~skop·at** n ~s/~e [abstr & konkr] *episcopate* **~s·ode** f ~/~n *episode*; *incident* (*it had become an i.*) ‖ in der Form e–r ~ *episodically* | ~nhaftigkeit [f] ⟨mus⟩ *interpolation* **'~s·odisch 1.** *episodic*(*al*) **2.** adv *episodically* **–·istel** f [.'..] ~/~n ⟨ec⟩ *epistle* ‖ ⟨fig⟩ *jdm e-e* ~ *lesen to read a p a homily* ‖ ~verleser [m] *epistoler* **~st·yl** n [Gr] ~s/~e ⟨arch⟩ *epistyle* **~t·aph** n [Gr] ~s/~e → Grabschrift, –mal **~t·asis** f ~/ (in drama) *epitasis* **~th·el** n [Gr] ~s/~e ⟨biol⟩ **1.** *epithelium* (L) **2.** [in comp] *epithelial* (*cell*) | ~körperchen [n pl] *parathyroid glands* [pl] **~theton** n [.'...] (Gr) ~s/–ta *epithet* **~z·entrum** n ~s/–ren *epicentre*, ⟨Am⟩ *epicenter* **~z·oon** n (Gr) ~s/–z·oen ⟨zoo⟩ *epizoon* (Gr) [pl *–zoa*] **~zoot·ie** *f* ⟨vet⟩ *epizootic* **~z·ykel** m [Gr] ~s/~ ⟨astr⟩ *epicycle* **'~z·yklisch** a ⟨mot⟩ *epicyclic* (*gear*) **~zyklo·ide** f ~/~n *epicycloid*; –dverzahnung f *epicycloidal gear*

epoch·al a *epochal*; *marking an epoch*; *epoch-making* **Ep·oche** f ~/~n *epoch*; *era*; *period* (*of*

national revival) ‖ *epoch*; *new era*; ~ m *to make* od *mark an epoch* (in *in*); *to create a profound sensation* ≗**machend** a *epoch-making*; *epochal*

Ep·ode f [Gr] ~/~n ⟨ant⟩ *epode*; → Epi–

***Epop·öe** f [Gr] ~/~n *epopee*; *epic poem*, *epic poetry* **·Epos** n ~/·Epen *epic poem*, *epic*; National≗ *national epic* ‖ → episch; Epopöe

·Eppich m ~s/~e ⟨bot⟩ **1.** verschiedene Doldenblüter wie *parsley* (Petersilie), *celery* (Sellerie) **2.** → Attich; Efeu

Eprouv·ette f [epru'vɛt(ə)] ~/~n [österr] *test-glass*

·Epsilon n [Gr] ~s/~s *epsilon*

Epsom ['epsəm] ⟨engl⟩ (Stadt südwestl. v London); → Pferderennen **~salz** n *Epsom salt*

Equ·estrik f ⟨hors⟩ *equestrianism*

Equ·ide m [L] ⟨zoo⟩ *equid*; [koll] ~n [pl] *Equidae* [L pl]

equilibr·ieren = äquilibrieren

Equip·age [eki'pɑːʒə] f [Fr] ~/~n **1.** *carriage*; †*equipage* [Fr] **2.** *equipment*, *outfit*; *turnout* **e–p·ieren** vt [h] ⟨mil & mar⟩ (jdn) *to equip*; *to fit out*; *to dress* ‖ **sich** ~ *to equip o.s.* **E–p·ierung** f ~/~en *equipment*; *equipage*; *outfit*

er [pron pers 3. sg masc] **1.** (P) **a.** *he*; → sie; es **b.** [betont, alleinstehend] *himself*; 10 Jahre jünger als ~ *ten years younger than himself* ‖ ~ selbst *he* (*went there*) *himself* **c.** [alleinstehend] ⟨fam⟩ *him*; das ist ~ *that's him* **d.** ~ hat ein seltsames Schicksal gehabt *his had been a curious fate* ‖ ~ hatte e–e egozentrische Natur *his was a self-centred nature* **2.** (T) **a.** ⟨allg⟩ *it*; *he* (sc *the dog*; *lion*; *fish*; *sparrow*, etc.) **b.** (of males) *it*; *he* **3.** (S) **a.** *it*; da ist ~ (sc der Hut) *there it is* ‖ °⟨sex⟩ *it* **b.** *she* (sc *the moon*) **c.** ⟨poet & liter⟩ *he* (sc *death*; *war*) **4.** °~ und sie, **ein** ≗ und e–e Sie ⟨fam⟩ *cock and hen*

er- pref [unbetont, untrennbar; bei Verben u Ableitungen; es macht imperfektive Verben, die e–n dauernden Vorgang *or* Zustand bezeichnen, zu perfektiven, welche dann den Beginn *or* das Ende e–s solchen kennzeichnen (tönen — ~tönen; frieren — ~frieren), und oft intransitive zu transitiven (blicken — ~blicken; warten — ~warten)] **1.** [intr. Verben] **a.** *a–*: ~stehen *to arise*; ~wachen, [~wecken] schrieben durch passende Verben; durch.] *to get*, *obtain* + *by* + Gerundium des einfachen Verbs: (etw) ~betteln *to get by begging* ‖ durch *to make*, *render* + stammverwandtes Adj.: ~wärmen *to make warm* [Knacklaut vor Vokal]:

er·achten vt **1.** (etw) ~ (als) *to consider*, *deem*, *esteem*, *hold*, *judge*, *think*; e–e Leistung als ein bes. Verdienst ~ *to consider* od *think a performance to be a special merit* ‖ *to regard as*; ich erachte ihn, das Buch f e–e Gefahr *I regard him*, *the book as a danger*; jdn f kompetent ~ *to judge* (od *think*) *a p to be competent*, *to regard a p as c.*; jdn der Berücksichtigung f würdig ~ *to think a p worthy of consideration*; *to think a p worthy to be considered* ‖ f genügend erachtet w *to pass muster* → betrachten, halten **2.** ⟨mst⟩ es ~ als (*or* [vor Adj.] für): ich erachte es als m–e Pflicht *I deem* (od *think*) *it my duty*; ich erachte es als e–e Ehre *I esteem it an honour* ‖ ich erachte es f recht *I consider* od *deem it right* (*to do*); *to awake* **b.** [oft umschrieben durch andere passende Verben: durch] *to begin* + einfaches Verb: ~glühen *to begin to glow* ‖ *to become*, *grow*, *turn* + stammverwandtes Adj.: ~blinden *to become blind* **c.** [wiedergegeben durch pass e–s trans. Verbs]: ~beben *to be agitated* **2.** [trans. Verben] **a.** *a–* ~warten *to await* **b.** *einfaches* Verb + *out*: ~kunden *to find* od *make out* ‖ einfaches Verb + *up*: ~heben *to lift up* **c.** [umman erachtete die S f untunlich *the matter was felt to be inexpedient*

Er·achten n ~s/ *judgement*, *opinion*, *view*; m–s ~s *to my mind* od *thinking*; *in my opinion* od *view*; ⟨fam⟩ *to my thinking* (a.: m–**m** ~ nach)

er·arbeiten vt [h] (etw; ⟨a.⟩ sich [dat] etw ~ *to work for a th by the sweat of one's brow*) *to obtain by hard working*; *to extract laboriously* (aus *from*); *to quarry* (*from*, *out of*) ‖ ⟨comp⟩ *to produce* | schwer, sauer –tet *hard-won* (*fortune*, *knowledge*)

·Erb- [in comp] *hereditary*; *patrimonial* **~adel** m *hereditary nobility* **~änderung** f ⟨biol⟩ *mutation*, → Mutation **~anfall** m *inheritance*; *legacy*; → Erbschaft **~anlage** f *constitution*(*al factor*); *hereditary* (od *innate*) *disposition* ‖ ~n [pl] *genetic heritage*; *heredity* **~anspruch** m *hereditary title* **~anteil** m = Erbteil **~baurecht** n *building rights* pl **~begräbnis** n *family vault* ≗**berechtigt** a *inheritable*; *having a right of inheritance* **~besitz** m *hereditary possession* (od *tenure*) ~**bild** n *genotype*; → Erscheinungsbild **~biologie** f *genetics*; *study of human heredity* ≗**eigen** a *possessed by inheritance*; *inherited* ≗**fähig** a *capable of inheriting* **~fähigkeit** f *capability of inheriting* **~faktor** m ⟨biol⟩ *factor* **~fall** m *death of a testator* **~fehler** m *hereditary defect* **~feind** m *sworn enemy* **~folge** f (*hereditary*) *succession* ‖ ⟨jur⟩ bestimmte unveränderliche ~ *entail*; e–e ~ aufheben *to break* (od *cut off*) *an entail*; die ~ für ein Gut bestimmen *to entail an estate* | ~krieg [m] der Spanische ~kr. *the War of the Spanish Succession* | ~streit [m] *dispute of s.* **~gang** m → Erbfolge; Vererbung ‖ dominanter ~ ⟨biol⟩ *inheritance of dominant characteristics* ≗**(an)gesessen** a *long established* (*old family*) ≗**gesund** a ⟨bes nazi⟩ *of healthy stock* **~gesundheit** f *hereditary qualities guaranteeing a healthy stock*; ~slehre [f] *eugenics* [pl] [sg konstr] **~graf** m *hereditary earl* od *count* **~grind** m ⟨med⟩ *favus* [L]; *skin-disease affecting the scalp* **~großherzog** m ⟨Ger⟩ *hereditary grand duke* **~gut** n **1.** *heritage*; *estate of inheritance*; *ancestral estate*; *patrimony*; freies ~ *allodium* ‖ ⟨Ind⟩ ~ e–s Eingeborenen *taluk*, *–look*; Inhaber e–s ~s *taluk* **2.** ⟨übtr & fig⟩ *heritage* **3.** ⟨biol⟩ = Erbmasse **~herr** m *lord of the manor* **~hof** m ⟨Ger hist⟩ *inalienable*, *entailed*, *farm not exceeding 125 hectares* ≗**krank** a *of tainted stock* **~krankheit** f *hereditary disease* **~lande** n [pl] *patrimonial dominions* [pl] (of a king, etc) **~lasser** m (*decedent*) *testator*; *legator*; (of real property) *devisor*, *deviser*; → lassen, (aber erbl·assen!) **~lasserin** f *testatrix* **~laster** n *hereditary vice* **~leh(e)n** n ⟨hist⟩ *entail*; *entailed estate* **~lehre** f *genetics* [pl] [sg konstr]; *science of the principles of heredity* **~leiden** n *hereditary trouble* (od *disease*) ≗**los** a *heirless*; *having no heir* **~masse** f **1.** ⟨jur⟩ *assets* [pl] **2.** ⟨biol⟩ *hereditary mass*; *genes* [pl] ‖ *hereditary qualities*; *genetic constitution*; *parental characteristics* pl **~merkmal** n *hereditary characteristic* **~onkel** m *wealthy old uncle from whom one has expectations* **~pacht** f ⟨hist⟩ *hereditary lease* (od *tenure*); ⟨jur⟩ *emphyteusis* [L] **~pächter** m *tenant* (od *holder*) *of a hereditary lease* **~pflege** f *improvement of the conditions for a healthy stock* **~prinz** m *hereditary prince* **~recht** n **1.** *law of inheritance* (od *succession*) **2.** *right of inheritance* (od *succession*) (*of a p*) **~schädigung** f *impairing of the genes by harmful bacteria* (od *bacilli*) **~schein** m *grant of probate*; Bestätigung e–s ausländ. ~s *re-sealing* **~schleicher** m *legacy-hunter* **~schleicher·ei** f *legacy-hunting* ‖ ~ begehen *to angle for a l.* **~stamm** m *biotype* **~stück** n *heirloom*; ein ~ v m–m Onkel *an h. inherited from my uncle*; Familien≗ *family heirloom* **~sünde** f ⟨ec⟩ *original sin* **~tante** f *wealthy old aunt from whom one has expectations* **~tauglichkeit** f ⟨nazi⟩ *hereditary qualities* [pl] *guaranteeing a healthy and valuable stock* **~teil** n, ⟨jur⟩ m *portion* od *share of inheritance*; *inheritance*; väterliches ~ *patrimony* || ⟨übtr⟩ → Erbe [n] **~teilung** f *division of an inheritance* **~tochter** f (*rich*) *heiress* **~tüchtigkeit** f ⟨bes nazi⟩ *hereditary qualities* [pl] *of a high grade*; → Erbtauglichkeit **~übel** n *never-ending trouble* **~verbrüderung** f *mutual agreement of succession* (*between dynasties*) **~vertrag** m *irrevocable settlement concerning a succession* **~vermächtnis** n *legacy* **~zins** m *quitrent*, *ground-rent*

erb·armen vt [h] **1.** *jdn ~ *to move a p* (*to pity*); ihr Jammer erbarmte ihn, *or* es erbarmte ihn ihr J. *her misery moved him* (*to pity*); *he had mercy on her misery* || ein Elend, daß es e–n Hund ~ könnte! *an unheard-of* (od *unspeakable*) *misery*! || ein Leben, daß es Gott erbarm! *a miserable life*; ein Essen, daß es G. e. *an altogether wretched food* || es würde e–n Stein ~ *it would melt a heart of stone* **2. sich** jds (*or* über jdn) ~ *to pity a p*, *to have mercy* od *compassion upon a p*, *to show mercy to a p*; *to have* od *take pity on a p* || ⟨ec⟩ Herr erbarme Dich unser! *Lord have mercy upon us*! || daß sich Gott erbarm! → 1. **Erb·armen** n ~s/ *compassion*, *mercy*; *pity* || das unendliche ~ Gottes *God in his infinite mercy* || ~! ⟨vulg⟩ *blimey*! || ohne ~ *without mercy*; *pitilessly*, *ruthlessly* || ~ fühlen *or* h mit jdm *to have compassion* od *mercy upon a p*; *to have* od *take pity on a p* || kein ~ kennen *to have no pity*; mit jdm kein ~ kennen *to be dead against a p* || es ist **zum** ~! *it is pitiful* (od *pitiable*)! *it is a thousand pities* || er führte ein Leben z ~ *his was a miserable* (of *pitiable*, *wretched*) *life* || ein Stück z ~ *a shocking poor play* || er sah z ~ aus *he was a pitiable* (*pitiful*) *sight*; *it was pitiful to see him* || er singt z ~ *he is a wretched* (*deplorable*) *singer* || → erbärmlich

erb·armenswert a → erbarmungswert

Erb·armer m *merciful person* || Gott der ~ *Father of mercy*

erb·ärmlich I. a **1.** *miserable*, *wretched* (*life*); *pathetic* (*appearance*); *pitiable* (*condition*); *pitiful* **2.** ⟨übtr⟩ (kläglich, wertlos) *pitiable*, *poor* (*show*); (*very*) *poor* (*coffee*); *wretched* (*food*, *place*); *beggarly*; *paltry*, *squalid* (*quarrelling*); *shoddy*; °⟨Am⟩ *bum* (*novel*) || *object*, *base*, *contemptible*, *mean* (*coward*, *flatterer*); *wretched* (*intrigue*) || *despicable* (*fellow*) || sich ~ fühlen *to feel wretched* **II.** adv **1.** (*to live*) *miserably*, *wretchedly* **2.** [intensiv] (*to cry*) *miserably*; *horribly*, *terribly*; *exceedingly*; *extremely* (*small income*) | **≗keit** f ~/ **1.** *misery*, *pitifulness*, *wretchedness* **2.** ⟨übtr⟩ *pitiableness*, *wretchedness* (*of food*); *paltriness*, *shoddiness* || (Gemeinheit) *abjectness*, *baseness*, *meanness* (*of a p*)

***Erb·armung** f = Erbarmen **≗slos 1.** a *pitiless*, *relentless*; *ruthless*; *grim* **2.** adv *relentlessly* **≗svoll** a *compassionate*, *pitiful*, *relenting* **≗swert**, **~swürdig** a *pitiable*, *pitiful* (*fate*)

erb·auen vt [h] **1.** (Haus) *to build* (nach jds Plan *to a p's plan*); *to construct*, *erect*, *raise*; → errichten, gründen | ⟨übtr⟩ *to build up* **2.** ⟨fig⟩ (jdn) *to edify* || *to delight*, *to please* | **sich** ~ *to be edified*, *uplifted* (an *by*) || *to be pleased* (an *with*) || erbaut s *to be uplifted*, *pleased*, *edified* (v *by*); nicht gerade erbaut *not exactly pleased* (v *with*) **erb·auend** a *edifying* (f *to a p*); *elevating* (*thoughts*) **Erb·auer** m ~s/~ **1.** *builder*; *constructor* || *founder* (*of a town*) **2.** ⟨fig⟩ *edifier* (*of youth*)

erb·aulich a ⟨fig⟩ *edifying*, *uplifting* (*sermon*); *elevating* (*thoughts*) || *delightful*, *pleasant*; nicht gerade ~ *not very pleasant*; ⟨iron⟩ das ist ja recht ~ *that's very edifying*

Erb·auung f ~/~en **1.** *building* (*of a house*), *construction*, *erection* || ⟨übtr⟩ *building up* **2.** ⟨fig⟩ (innere ~) *edification*; *spiritual elevation*; ⟨Am⟩ *uplift*; → Andacht **~sbuch** n *book of devotion* **~sliteratur** f; religiöse ~ *devotional literature* **~sschrift** f; religiöse ~ *religious tract* **~sstunde** f *hour of devotion*

·**Erbe** m ~n/~n **1.** *heir*; gesetzlicher ~ *heir-at--law*, *legal* od *lawful heir*; gesetzmäßiger ~ (e–s noch Lebenden), dessen Erbrecht nicht zerstört w kann *heir-apparent*; mutmaßlicher ~ *heir-presumptive* || ⟨jur⟩ ~, der (nach Abzug der Schulden etc) den Überschuß an beweglicher Habe erhält (*residuary*) *legatee* (→ *devisee* v Immobilien) || männlicher ~ *heir-male* ([pl] *heirs-male*) || ohne leibliche ~n *without issue* || er ist der ~ s–s Vaters *he is the heir of his father*, *he is heir to his father*; er ist ~ des Gutes *he is heir to the estate*; → Thronerbe || jdn z s–m ~n einsetzen *or* m *to make* (od *constitute*) *a p one's heir* || °die lachenden ~ warten schon ⟨m. m.⟩ *they are waiting for dead men's shoes* **2.** ⟨übtr⟩ *heir* (e–r S *of* od *to a th*); *inheritor*

·**Erbe** n ~s/ **1.** *inheritance*, *heritage*; *heirship*; väterliches ~ *patrimony* || das ~ jds antreten *to enter into the heritage of a p* **2.** ⟨übtr⟩ *heritage* (*our island h.*) || ⟨bib⟩ *inheritance*; Gottes ~ antreten *to come into God's inheritance* || ⟨biol⟩ *inerited disposition*; → Erbanlage

erb·eben 1. vi [s] (P) *to thrill* (über *at*; vor *with*); *tremble* (bei .. *at the sound*; vor *before*); *vibrate* (vor *with*); *quake*, *shake* (vor .. *with*); *shiver*; *shudder* || (of the earth, etc.) *to quake*, *shake*, *tremble*; *vibrate*; *to be agitated* **2.** ≗ n *thrill*; *tremble*

·**erben** vt [h] (Haus etc) *to inherit* (v .. *from a p*); *to fall* (od *to be*) *heir to* (*a house*); (Geld) *to come in for* || ein Vermögen ~ *to come* (od *drop*, *step*) *into a fortune*; er erbte den Titel, als .. *he came into the title when* ..; das Wenige, das er hatte, erbte s–e Frau *what little he had went to his wife* | ⟨übtr⟩ (Eigenschaft) *to inherit*; *to be heir to* (*one's father's will-power*) || °hier ist nichts z ~ *there is nothing to be gained here*; ⟨fam⟩ *nothing doing*! **≗haftung** f *liability of heirs*

***erb·eten** vt [h] (etw) *to obtain by prayer*

erb·eten [pp v erbitten] a *asked*; *asked-for* (*assistance*); *requested* (*information*)

erb·etteln vt [h] etw ~, sich [dat] etw ~ *to cadge a th* (v *from*); *to obtain* od *get a th by begging*

erb·euten vt [h] (etw) *to carry off* (od *gain*) *as booty* od *spoil*; *to capture*; → Beute I. 5.

erb·ieten vrefl [h] [→ bieten] sich ~ *to offer*, *volunteer* (*to do*)

·**Erbin** f ~/~nen *heiress* (e–r S *of* od *to a th*) || reiche ~ *an heiress* (*to marry an h.*)

erb·itten vt [h] [→ bitten] **A.** jdn ~ [nur in Wendungen wie:] er ließ sich ~ *he yielded* (od *he was accessible*) *to entreaties*; *he relented* (*at last*); er ließ sich nicht ~ *he was inexorable* (od *relentless*, *unyielding*); → erweichen **B.** etw ~ **1. a.** Essen, Geld v jdm ~ *to beg food*, *money of a p* **b.** e–e Gefälligkeit v jdm ~ *to ask a favour of a p*, *to ask a p a favour* **c.** Hilfe (etc) v jdm ~ *or* jds Hilfe ~ *to ask a p's help*, *to ask a p for help*, *to enlist* od *invite a p's help*; *to seek help from a p*; *to solicit help of* od *from a p* || jds Erlaubnis ~ *to ask a p's permission*, *to ask a p for permission* || jds Kundschaft ~ *to solicit a p for his custom* **2.** etw ~ **a.** *to beg for a th*; *to ask for a th*; Hilfe ~ *to ask for help* || Rat ~ *to ask advice* **b.** (Fragen) *to invite*; (Angebote) *to request*; oft ⟨com⟩ & [pass] Zeichnungen w erbeten *subscriptions are requested* (f *for*); wie e. *as requested*; → erbeten

erb·ittern vt [h] **1.** (jdn) *to exacerbate*, *exasperate*, *incense*, *irritate*; *to arouse a feeling of resentment in a p* || erbittert *exasperated*, *irritated*, (über *at*, *by*); *indignant* (*at*); auf jdn erbittert s *to be angry with a p*; ⟨fam⟩ *cut-throat* (*competition*) || (Stimmung) *to embitter*;

(Kampf) *to intensify* **2.** [abs] *to be embittering*; *to cause embitterment*; od *resentment*; Undank erbittert *ingratitude causes e.* **erb·ittert 1.** a *hot* (*fight*), *violent* (*struggle*); *fierce, intense, vehement* (*hatred*) **2.** adv *fiercely*, etc.

Erb·itterung f ~/~en **1.** *exacerbation*; *exasperation*; *indignation* (über *at*); *gall, irritation*; *embitterment* || *animosity, enmity, hatred* (*of a p*) **2.** *impetuosity, intensity, vehemence* (*of a fight*); mit gr ~ *with great v.*

erb·ittlich a *exorable*; *accessible to entreaties*

·**Erbium** n ~s/ ⟨chem⟩ *erbium*

erbl·assen vi [s] (P) *to grow* od *turn pale* od *pallid*; *to lose colour* || ⟨poet⟩ *to die*; *to pass away*

erbl·eichen vi [s] –blich/–blichen (→ d.)/ –bleich(e)! *to turn white* od *pallid*

·**erblich 1.** a *hereditary* (*title*); *hereditable* (*interest*); *heritable*; ~e Monarchie *hereditary monarchy* || *inheritable* (*blood*) || → vererbbar **2.** adv *hereditarily*; ~ belastet → belasten 2. d. || ~ besitzen *to posses by inheritance* | ≈**keit** f ~/ *hereditary character*; *heritability, hereditability, hereditariness* (*of a disease*; *of features*) || ~ der Kaiserwürde *hereditary imperial succession* || *heredity* (*of a fief*) || → Vererbung, Vererbbarkeit

erbl·ichen a *deceased, dead*; → erbl·eichen

erbl·icken vt [h] **1.** (etw, jdn) *to catch sight of, to catch a glmipse of* (*a th, a p*); *to behold, see*; *discern, discover, perceive* (*a th*) || (sichten) *to sight, descry, espy* || er erblickte sein Gesicht in dem Licht *he caught his face in the light* || das Licht der Welt ~ *to see the light, to come into the world*; er erblickte das Licht der W. im Jahre 1800 *he first saw the light* (od *he was born*) *in 1800* **2.** *to see*; ich erblicke die Hauptaufgabe in .. *I see the chief task in, in my opinion the ch. t. lies in ..*; → entdecken, erkennen; in ihm e. ich e–e Gefahr f *I hold* (od *judge, think*) *him to be a danger to ..*; *I regard him as ..*

erbl·inden vi [s] *to become* od *go blind*; –det *blind*

erbl·ühen vi [s] mst ⟨fig⟩ = aufblühen

erb·orgt a ⟨mst fig⟩ *borrowed* → borgen

erb·osen vt [h] **1.** (jdn) *to enrage, exacerbate, to exasperate, incense, irritate* || erbost s *to be angry* (über .. *at, about a th*; *with a p*); *to be exasperated, irritated* (über *at, by a th*); *to be indignant* (*at*) **2. sich** ~ *to get angry* (*with a p*); *to become enraged* od *exasperated* (über *at*)

erb·ost 1. a *angry, indignant*; *exasperated, irritated* (*man*) **2.** adv *angrily*; *indignantly*

erb·ötig a [nur pred] ~ s *to be ready* (od *willing, prepared*) (zur Annahme e–r S *to accept a th*; sich z ergeben *to surrender*)

erbr·ausen vi (of sound: the sea, wind) *to begin to roar* (od *roll, thunder*) || (of an organ) *to begin to peal* (od *ring*); *to resound*; ~ l *to peal*

erbr·echen I. vt [h] [→ brechen] **1.** (Tür) *to break open* od *down* | *to force* (*open*); (Schloß) *to prize*; *to prize up* od *open*; mit Eisen ~ ⟨Am⟩ *to jimmy* | (Siegel) *to break*, (Brief) *unseal* **2.** (**sich**) ~ *to retch, vomit, regurgitate*; *to be* (od *feel*) *sick* **II.** ≈ n *nausea, sickness*; *vomit*(*ing*); *regurgitation*; *retch* || ~ verursachend *vomitive, vomitory* || ⟨fig⟩ *disgust, nausea*; ~ erregen *to cause disgust*

· **erbr·ingen** vt [h] [→ bringen] den Beweis ~ f etw *to prove a th*; *to demonstrate, establish* (*truth, etc*); den B. ~, daß .. *to offer proof that .., to prove that* || ⟨jur⟩ Sie müssen den B. dafür ~ *you will have to bring* (od *produce*) *evidence to that effect*; → Beweis

·**Erbs-** [in comp] (→ Erbsen–) *pea*; *pease* ~**brei** m *pease-pudding* ~**kohle** f *pea-coal* ~**mehl** n *pease-meal* ~**mus** n = Erbsbrei ~**wurst** f ⟨Ger⟩ *pea-sausage*

·**Erbschaft** f ~/~en **1.** [abstr] *inheritance*; *heirship* (e–r S *to a th*) **2.** [konkr] (Geerbtes) *inheritance*; *heritage, legacy*; Schulden waren s–e einzige ~ *debts were his only heritage* ⟨a. fig⟩; → Erbe [n] **3.** e–e ~ **antreten** *to enter upon an inh.*; e–e ~ ausschlagen *to refuse, renounce an inh.* || e–e ~ m *to come* (od *drop, step*) *into a fortune* || jdm durch ~ zufallen *or* anheimfallen *to devolve to* (od *on*) *a p* (*the crown devolved on his son*)

·**Erbschafts-** ~**anspruch** m *claim to an inheritance* ~**gericht** n *Probate-Court* ~**masse** f *estate* (od *property*) *to be divided among the heirs* ~**steuer** f ⟨allg⟩ *death-duty, transfer tax* || (f bewegl. Habe) *legacy-duty*; (f unbewegl. Habe) *succession-duty*

·**Erbse** f ~/~n ⟨bot⟩ **1.** *pea* (*einzelne*); ~n [pl] *peas* pl; Kicher~ *chick-pea* || grüne ~n *small peas* || enthülste, gespaltene u getrocknete, halbe ~n *split peas* || ⟨fig⟩ so ähnlich wie zwei ~n *as like as two peas* || [koll] ~n *pease* [pl] (*pease are* ..) || wie auf ~n gehen ⟨fam⟩ *to walk as if one had stones in his shoes* **2.** [in comp] → Erbs–, Erbsen–

·**Erbsen-** [in comp] (→ Erbs–) ~**bein** n ⟨anat⟩ *pisiform bone* ~**brei** m = Erbsbrei ≈**förmig** a *pea-shaped, pea-like*; *pisiform* ~**gericht** n *dish of peas* ~**hülse** f *pea-pod* ~**mehl** n = Erbsmehl ~**schote** f *pea-pod* ~**sprache** f (Kinderspr.) *adding* –erbsen *to every word* ~**stroh** n *pea-straw* ~**suppe** f *pea-soup* ⟨a. fig⟩

·**Erd-** [in comp] (→ Erde–, Erden–) *earth*; *earthy* || *of the earth, earthy*; ⟨scient⟩ *geo-* || ⟨mil, aero & mar⟩ *ground* || *terrestrial*; *subterranean*; *underground* || ⟨chem⟩ *mineral*; *natural* ~**achse** f *axis of the earth* ~**alkalien** [pl] ⟨chem⟩ *alkaline earths* [pl], *earth metals* [pl] ~**alkalimetall** n *alkaline earth metal* ~**altertum** n ⟨geol⟩ *Palaeozoic Era* ~**anschluß** m ⟨wir⟩ → Erdleitung ~**apfel** m [österr u sd] = Kartoffel, cf. *Irish apricot* (= *potato*) || °die ≈ v unten anschauen *to push up daysies* ~**arbeit(en** pl) f *trench work*; *digging*; *excavation-work*; *ground-work* ~**arbeiter** m *excavator*; *groundsman*; *digger*; bes ⟨rail⟩ *navvy* ~**art** f ⟨chem⟩ *kind* od *sort of earth* od *clay* ≈**artig** a *earthy* (*smell*) ~**artischocke** f ⟨bot⟩ *Jerusalem artichoke* ~**aufklärung** f ⟨mil⟩ *ground reconnaissance* ~**bahn** f *orbit of the earth* ~**ball** m *terrestrial globe*; *the earth* ~**bank** f *earth-bank*; *bank* (od *mound*) *of earth*; ⟨fort⟩ *earthwork* ~**bau** m ⟨fort⟩ *earthwork*; –bau = Erdarbeiten ~**beben** n (*earth*)*quake*; ⟨Am a.⟩, *shake, t*(*r*)*emblor* ~**beben** [in comp] *seismic* || ~anzeiger [m] *seismograph*; *seismoscope* || ~gebiet [n] *seismic area* || ~herd [m] *seismic focus* [L]; Gebiet über dem ~herd *epicentre, –trum* [L] || ~kunde [f] *seismology* || ~messer [m] *seismometer* || ~welle [f] *seismic wave*; Bild der ~wellen *seismogram* ~**beer-** ⟨bot⟩ [in comp] *strawberry* (*leaves*); ~baum [m] *strawberry--tree, arbutus* [L]; kriechender ~baum ⟨Am⟩ *mayflower* || ~pflanze [f] *strawberry-plant* || ~pocken [pl] ⟨med⟩ *framboesia* [L]; *yaws* [pl] ~**beere** f ⟨bot⟩ *strawberry*, (Wald– *wild st.*) ~**beobachtung** f ⟨mil⟩ *ground-observation* ~**beschleunigung** f *acceleration due to gravity* ≈**beschreibend** a *geographical* ~**beschreibung** f *geography* ~**beschuß** m *terrestrial fire* ~**bewohner** m *terrestrial*; *inhabitant of the earth* ~**biene** f ⟨ent⟩ *ground-bee* ~**bildmessung** f *terrestrial photogrammetry* ~**birne** f ⟨bot⟩ *Jerusalem artichoke* || → ~apfel ~**boden** m *ground, soil*; *groundsheet* || ungepflasterter ~ ⟨Am⟩ *dirt floor* || die Gesamtheit der im ~ vorhandenen Lebewesen *edaphon*; durch den ~ bedingt *edaphic* || etw dem ~ gleichmachen *to level a th to* (od *with*) *the ground, to raze a th to the ground* ~**bohne** f ⟨bot⟩ *ground-bean*; = Erdnuß ~**bohrer** m *earth-borer* ~**buchse** f

⟨telph⟩ *grounding sleeve* **~damm** m = Erdbank **~drehung** f *rotation of the earth* **~druck** m ⟨geol⟩ (in der Erdrinde) *thrust* **~durchmesser** m *diameter of the earth* **~eichel** f ⟨bot⟩ *earth* (od *pea*)*-nut* **~eichhörnchen** n ⟨zoo Am⟩ *gopher* **~einsturz** m = Erdfall **~erkundung** f ⟨mil⟩ *ground-exploration* **~erschütterung** f *concussion of the earth*; *earth-shock* (od *tremor*) → Erdbeben **≚fahl** a *earthy*; *earth* (od *clay*)*-coloured*; → fahl **~fall** m ⟨geol⟩ *funnelled sinking* (od *caving-in*) *of the earth's surface* **~farbe** f → ~pigment *earth-colour*; *mineral colour* (od *dye*) ‖ [pl] *pigments* **≚farben, ≚farbig** a *earth* (od *clay*)*-coloured*; *earthy* **~ferkel** n ⟨zoo⟩ *aardvark*; *orycteropus* [L] **~ferne** f ⟨astr⟩ *apogee* **~fernrohr** n *terrestrial telescope* **~feuer** n *subterranean fire* **~fläche** f *surface of the earth* **~flachs** m ⟨minr⟩ *amianthus* [L] **~floh** m ⟨ent⟩ *flea-beetle*; *turnip-flea* **~forscher** m *geologist* **~forschung** f *geology* **~früchtler** m ⟨bot⟩ *hypogean* (od *hypogeous*) *plant* **~galle** f ⟨bot⟩ *earth-gall* **~gang** m ⟨min⟩ *vein*; *gallery*, *tunnel* **~gas** n *natural gas*; → Sumpfgas **≚gebunden** a ⟨fig⟩ = erdnahe **~gebundenheit** f *earthiness* **~geist** m ⟨myth⟩ *earth-goblin*; *gnome*; *spirit of the earth* **~gelb** n ⟨chem⟩ *yellow ochre* **~geruch** m *earthy smell* **~geschichte** f ⟨geol⟩ *earth's history*; *development of the geological formations*; Studium der ~ *historical geology* **~geschmack** m *earthy taste* **~geschoß** n *ground-floor*, ⟨Am⟩ *first story* od *floor*; im ~ *on the g.* **~globus** m *terrestrial globe* **~grille** f ⟨ent⟩ *mole-cricket* **~grün** n *mineral green* **~gürtel** m *zone* **~hälfte** f *hemisphere* **≚haltig** a *earthy*; *containing earth* **~harz** n ⟨minr⟩ *asphalt*, *bitumen* **~haufen** m *heap of earth* ‖ ⟨golf⟩ kl ~ (f den Ball) *tee*; den Ball auf den ~ legen *to tee the ball* **~haus** n ⟨hort⟩ = Gewächshaus **~höhle** f *cave*; *cavern* **~hügel** m (*earth-*)*mound*; *hillock* **~induktor** m ⟨el⟩ *earth-inductor* **~innere** n: das ~ *the interior of the earth* ‖ ⟨geol⟩ im ~n entstanden *endogenous* (*structure*) ‖ glutflüssiges ~ *magma* **~kabel** n *underground cable*; *buried cable* **~kampf** m ⟨aero⟩ *ground-fighting* **~kampf-** *ground-to-ground* [attr] (*missile*), → *air-to-air* **~karte** f *map of the world* **~kastanie** f ⟨bot⟩ *pignut* **~kern** m *earth's core* **~klemme** f ⟨el⟩ *ground terminal* **~kobalt** m ⟨minr⟩ roter ~ *cobalt bloom*; schwarzer ~ *earthy cobalt* **~körper** m (Ggs Himmelskörper) *terrestrial body* **~krebs** m ⟨ent⟩ *mole-cricket* **~kreis** m *globe*, *sphere*; *the earth*; ~bahn [f] *orbit*; der gesamte ~ *the whole world* **~kruste** f *earth's crust*; *lithosphere* **~kugel** f *terrestrial globe* **~kunde** f *geography*; mathematische ~ *mathematical g.*, *geodesy*; physikalische *or* physische ~ *geophysics* [sg konstr]; (→ Geophysik); → Anthropo–, Biographie **~kundler** m *geographer* **≚kundlich** a *geographical* (*subject*) **~leitung** f **1.** *underground main*; *underground pipe-line* **2.** ⟨el & wir⟩ *earth*; *ground-* od *earth-connexion* ‖ ~, ~sdraht [m] *earth-wire*, ⟨Am⟩ *ground-wire* **~licht** n ⟨astr⟩ *earth-shine* **≚magnetisch** a *geomagnetic* ‖ ~e Kraft *terrestrial magnetic force* **~magnetismus** m *earth* (od *terrestrial*) *magnetism* **~mandel** f ⟨bot⟩ *earth-almond*; ⟨Am⟩ *chufa* **~männchen** n **1.** ⟨myth⟩ = Erdgeist **2.** ⟨bot⟩ = Alraun **3.** ⟨SAfr⟩ *ground squirrel* **~mantel** m (bis 2900 km) *intermediate layer of the earth* (zw –kruste u –kern) **~maus** f *field* (od *ground*)*-mouse* **~messer** m (P) *geometer* **~messung** f *geodesy* **~metall** n *earth metal* **~mine** f *subterranean mine* **~mittelalter** n ⟨geol⟩ *Mesozoic Era* **~mond** m (künstlicher) *moonlet* **~moos** n *club-moss* **~mutter** f ⟨myth⟩ *Earth-Mother* **≚nahe** a ⟨fig⟩ [pred] *of the earth*, *earthy*; *close* (od *near*) *to earth* (od *nature*); *bound up with the soil* ‖ [attr] *earthy*; *earth-bound* **~nähe** f **1.** ⟨astr⟩ *perigee* **2.** ⟨fig⟩ *earthiness* **~neuzeit** f ⟨geol⟩ *Neozoic Era* **~nullpunkt** m (bei ⟨at⟩ –Bombenabwurf) *ground zero* **~nuß** f *earth* (od *ground*)*-nut*; *earth almond*; *pea-nut*; *pignut*; *monkeynut* | ~(brot)aufstrich [m] ⟨cul⟩ *peanut butter* **~oberfläche** f *surface* (od *crust*) *of the earth*, *earth's surface*; *ground* (*on the g.*); → Erdkruste **~öl** n *petroleum*; *mineral* (od *crude*) *oil*; *rock-oil*; *naphtha* ‖ ~lager [pl] *crude oil storage tanks* [pl] **~pech** n *mineral pitch*; *asphalt*; → Erdharz **~peilgerät** n *earth direction finder* **~pfahl** m ⟨aero⟩ *ground-peg* **~pfeiler** m → Erdpyramide **~pigm·ent** n (= Erdfarbe) *natural pigment* **~pistazie** f ⟨bot⟩ = Erdnuß **~pol** m *earth-pole* **~pyramide** f ⟨geol⟩ *earth-pillar* **~rauch** m ⟨bot⟩ *fumitory* (Klimmender .. *climbing* ..) **~räumer** m *scraper* **~reich** n (gewählter Ausdruck ⟨bes bib⟩ f Erde, → d. I. 1., II. 2., III. 2. b.) *earth*, *ground*; *soil* **~rinde** f *crust of the earth*; *earth's crust* | Entstehung der ~ *tectogenesis* **≚rüchig** a *redolent of the soil*; *earthy*; → erdnahe **~rücken** m *ridge* (od *elevation*) *of earth* | Netz [n] mit **~rückleitung** f *earth* (⟨Am⟩ *ground*) *return circuit* **~rutsch** m *landslide*, *landslip*; ⟨Am⟩ *slip of earth*; *cave* **~sack** m ⟨fort⟩ *earth-sack* **~satellit** m (⟨a.⟩ *artificial*) *earth satellite*; *moon* **~schicht** f *layer of earth*; *stratum* [L]; ~ unmittelbar unter der Erdoberfläche *subsoil* **~schlipf** m Sw = –rutsch **~schluß** m ⟨el⟩ (*leakage of current*) *earth* (⟨Am⟩ *ground*) *fault* | ~prüfer [m] *earth detector* **~scholle** f *clod* (*of earth*); ⟨poet⟩ *glebe* ‖ ~nbrecher *m* (Maschine) *clod-crusher* **~schwamm** m *mushroom*; *fungus* [L] **~schwein** n ⟨zoo⟩ = Erdferkel **~sicht** f ⟨aero⟩ *visibility of the ground* **~sieb** n ⟨hort⟩ *riddle*; *screen* **~stampfe** f *beetle* **~stern** m ⟨bot⟩ *earth-star* **~stoß** m *earth-shock* | ~welle [f] ⟨at⟩ *ground shock wave* **~strich** m *region*, *zone* **~strom** m ⟨el⟩ *earth-current*; vagabundierende ≚e *stray currents* **~stufe** f *terrace* **~sturz** m *landslip*, *landslide*; ⟨Am⟩ *cave* **~teer** m *mineral tar* **~teil** m *continent*; *division of land*; *part of the world*; → Festland, Kontinent ‖ fremde ~e [pl] *foreign parts* [pl] **~temperatur** f *earth-temperature* **~truppen** f [pl] ⟨aero⟩ *ground organization* **~umsegler** m *circum-navigator* (*of the globe*) **~umseg(e)lung** f *circum-navigation* (*of the globe*) **~- u Seezielbeschuß** m ⟨artill⟩ *terrestrial fire* **≚verlegt** a *underground* (Rohr) **~wachs** n ⟨minr⟩ *earth-wax*; *mineral wax*; *ozokerite* **~wall** m *mound*; ⟨fort⟩ *earthwall*, *earthwork*; ⟨mod⟩ *berm* (→ Schützenauftritt, Straßengefälle) **~wand** f ⟨arch⟩ *mud-wall* **~wärme** f *earth-temperature* **≚wärts** adv *earthward*(*s*) **~welle** f *rising ground* **~werk** n ⟨fort⟩ *earthwork* **~winkel** m (einsamer) *lonely spot* **~wolf** m ⟨zoo⟩ *aardwolf*; *earth-wolf* ‖ = Erdgrille **~zeitalter** n ⟨geol⟩ *geological era*; *formation* **~ziel** n ⟨mil⟩ *ground-target* | ~beschuß [m] ⟨artill⟩ *terrestrial fire*; ⟨aero⟩ *air-to-ground firing* **~zusschrumpfung** f *earth-shrinkage*

erd·acht a [pp v erdenken] *devised* (*plan*); *invented*; ⟨dero⟩ *fabricated* ‖ nur ~ *speculative*

·Erde f ~/~n **I.** (als Boden) **A.** (als Oberfläche *or* fester Boden) **1.** *earth*, *ground* ‖ seltene ~n [pl] *rare earths* ‖ ⟨pol⟩ verbrannte ~ *scorched earth* ‖ ~ zu ~ ⟨rel⟩ *ashes to ashes*, → I. A. 2. b. **2. Wendungen a.** ⟨fig⟩ die ~ **küssen** *to kiss* (od *bite*) *the dust* **b. auf der** ~ *on the ground* ‖ ⟨fig⟩ vor jdm auf der ~ rutschen *to cringe to a p*; *to fawn upon a p* ‖ mit beiden Beinen auf der ~ stehen *to have both feet on the earth* ‖ **auf die** ~, **zur** ~ *to the ground* od *earth*; .. fallen *to come* od *fall to the earth* od *ground* ‖ .. niederstürzen (of a plane) *to crash to the earth* ‖ den Fuß .. setzen *to set foot to earth* ‖ .. springen *to spring* od *drop to the ground* ‖ .. werfen *to throw* (*a th*) *to* (od *on*) *the ground*; sich .. werfen *to throw o.s. down* | ⟨fig⟩ wie Pilze **aus** der ~

schießen *to shoot up like mushrooms* || (etw) aus der ~ stampfen *to improvise* | (jdn) **in** die ~ legen *to bury, to inter* || in die ~ sinken *to sink into the grave* | **über** der ~ *above* (*the*) *ground* (*the kitchen is above g.*) || über der ~ befindlich *overground; overhead* (*erections*) | **unter** der ~ *under ground, underground* (*to work u.*); (begraben [pp]) *below-the ground* || unter der ~ befindlich *underground* (*cable*); unter der ~ lebend *hypogean, hypogeous* (*insect*); unter der ~ reifende Pflanze → Erdfrucht || jdn unter die ~ bringen *to bring a p to his grave*; er wird mich noch unter die ~ br.! *he will be the death of me*! | **von** der ~ abfliegend ⟨a–n⟩ *earth-leaving*; Reise v d. ~ aus *journey outwards from earth* | **zu** ebener ~ wohnen *to live on the ground-floor* || zur ~ → o. auf die ~ **B.** (als Wohnort) **1.** (Ggs Wasser) *earth; land, country; soil*; Heimat≗ *native soil; homeland*; auf deutscher ~ *on* od *in German soil*; rote ~ → II. A. **2.** (Ggs Himmel) *the earth, the world*; die ganze ~ *the whole world* || Himmel u ~ *heaven and earth* | *earthly life* **3. Wendungen**: Himmel u ~ in Bewegung setzen *to move heaven and erath* | **auf** der ~ *on earth; under the sun*; ⟨Am⟩ *on God's footstool* || ⟨oft bib⟩ auf ~n *on earth, here below*; im Himmel u auf ~n *in heaven and earth* || auf der ~ leben *to walk the earth* || ⟨fig⟩ auf die ~ herunter *down to earth* || **über** die ganze ~ *all the world over* **C.** (als Acker) *earth, ground, soil*; die ~ bebauen *to till the ground* od *soil* || ⟨myth⟩ Mutter ~ *Mother Earth* **D.** (Verbindung mit der ~) ⟨el & wir⟩ [pl ~n] *earth* [pl *earths*]; *ground*; → erden [vt] **II.** (als Stoff) **A.** *earth, soil*; ⟨fam⟩ *dirt*; lockere Garten≗ *mould* || (etw) mit ~ füllen *to fill with earth* (od *dirt*) || die Rote ~ ⟨Ger⟩ *Westphalia* || ⟨bib⟩ wieder z ~ w *to turn to dust and ashes, to turn to clay* **B.** ⟨chem⟩ **1.** ⟨hist⟩ (Element) *earth* **2.** [pl ~n] *earth* [pl *earths*]; alkalische ~n [pl] → Erdalkalien || blaue ~ *blue earth, earthy vivianite* || gelbe ~ *yellow ochre* **III.** (~ als Stern) ⟨astr⟩ [stets mit best. Art.] *the earth; the* (*terrestrial*) *globe* **IV.** [in comp] → Erd–, Erden–

·Erde- ~essen n *geophagy* **~esser** m *geophagist*

·erden vt [h] ⟨el⟩ (Leiter) *to earth, to ground* || geerdete Rückleitung *earth* (⟨Am⟩ *ground*) *circuit* od *return*

·Erden- [in comp] oft *earthly* **~bürger** m *denizen* od *inhabitant of the world; human being; mortal* || kl ~ ⟨fam⟩ *arrival* **~glück** n *earthly happiness* (od *joys*) **~kind** n *human being; mortal* **~kloß** m *clod; lump of earth* (od *clay*) || ⟨bib⟩ *man, mortal* **~last** f *burden of life* **~leben** n *earthly life; earthlife* **~los** n; das ~ *the human fate* (od *destiny*) **~rund** n; das ~ *the globe, the world* **~sohn** m = Erdenkind **~tal** n ⟨fig⟩ *the miseries of human life* **~wallen** n *life's pilgrimage; man's life on earth* | der letzte **~winkel** *the back of beyond* **~wurm** m ⟨fig & poet⟩ *poor worm of earth; poor creature*

erd·enkbar a = erdenklich || → denkbar

erd·enken vt [h] [→ denken] (etw) *to devise, excogitate; to think out; to contrive, invent*; ⟨dero⟩ *to fabricate*; → erdichten, –sinnen

erd·enklich a *conceivable, imaginable*; alle ~en Entschuldigungen *all the excuses imaginable; all imaginable excuses* || sich [dat] alle ~e Mühe geben *to strain every nerve; to take every pains; to do one's utmost* | alles ≗e *everything you could think of*; ich will alles ≗e tun *I will do anything in reason*

·erdhaft a ⟨fig⟩ = erdnahe

erd·ichten vt [h] (Unwirkliches, e–e Geschichte) *to feign, invent*; ⟨poet⟩ *to fable* || ⟨dero⟩ *to concoct, fabricate; feign; to trump up* || → ersinnen **erd·ichtet** a *fabled, fictitious, invented* (*name*); *imaginary* || ⟨dero⟩ *fabricated, feigned* (*excuse*); *trumped-up* **Erd·ichtung** f ~/en *fiction, invention; fable* || ⟨dero⟩ *concoction, fabrication* || reine ~ *all made up story*

·erdig a *earthy*

erd·olchen vt [h] (jdn) *to stab* (*a p*); *to run* (*a p*) *through; to poniard*

erdr·eisten vrefl [h]: sich ~ z tun **1.** *to dare* [mit reinem *inf*; wenn mit *do* umschrieben: mit *to-inf*; aber a.: *he dares to insult me*] er erdreistet sich, es z tun *he dare do it*; erdreistet er sich, es z tun? *dare he do it* od *does he dare to do it*? er erdreistet sich nicht z gehen *he dare not go* od *he does not dare to go*; er ersreistete sich nicht z gehen *he dared* od *durst not go* od *he did not dare to go*; er wird sich nicht ~ .. *he won't dare to go*; er hätte sich nicht erdreistet, es z tun, wenn .. *he dare not have done it if ..*; erdreiste dich nicht .. *don't you dare* (*to do*); wie können Sie sich ~? *how dare you*? **2.** *to presume* od *venture to do; to be* od *make bold to do; to have the audacity to do; to take the liberty to do* od *of doing*

erdr·öhnen vi [h & s] (of thunder, etc.) *to roar, rumble* || (*of a place, room*) *to resound; ring; crack* (*the walls cracked with laughter*)

erdr·osseln vt [h] (jdn) *to strangle, throttle*; ⟨sl⟩ *scrag* || ⟨hist⟩ → garrottieren || ⟨fig⟩ *to strangle*; (Handel etc) *to throttle; smother, suppress*; (Reklame etc) *to jugulate* **Erdr·osselung** f ~/ *strangulation; throttling* ⟨a. fig⟩

erdr·ücken I. vt [h] **1.** (jdn) *to crush* od *squeeze to death* || ⟨fig⟩ [mst pass] erdrückt w v *to be overwhelmed with*; v Gram erdrückt w *to be oppressed with grief*; v Geschenken (etc) erdrückt w *to be swamped* od *smothered with gifts* **2.** (Pflanze) (of rain) *to choke* || ⟨fig⟩ (Gefühl, Regung) *to choke; crush; suppress; swamp* **II.** ≗ n ⟨fig⟩ zum ~ voll *cramp-full, full to bursting point* **erdr·ückend** a ⟨fig⟩ *crushing*; ~e Mehrheit *overwhelming majority* || *potent; weighty*; ~es Beweismaterial *cumulative evidence*

Erdr·usch m ~s/ (→ dreschen) *yield of threshing*

erd·ulden 1. vt [h] (etw) *to endure, suffer*; → dulden **2.** ≗ n *endurance* **Erd·uldung** f ~/~en *endurance; suffering*

·Erdung f ~/~en ⟨el & wir⟩ *ground-connexion; earth*; → Erdleitung | ~sanschluß [m], ~sklemme [f] *earth* (⟨Am⟩ *ground*) *terminal*

er·eifern vrefl [h] sich ~ *to excite o.s., to get excited* (über *over*); *to put o.s. out* (über *about*); *to get angry* (über etw *at a th*; über jdn *with a p*); *to get exasperated* (od *worked up, enraged, irritated*; ⟨Am fam⟩ *hot*) (*at, by a th*) || *to fly into a passion; to flare* (od *blaze*) *up; to fume*; ~ Sie sich nicht! *keep your temper*! ⟨fam⟩ *keep your shirt on*! er ereiferte sich *his temper boiled up* **Er·eiferung** f ~/~en *excitement* (über *over*); *exasperation, indignation* (*at*); *heat*

er·eignen vrefl [h] sich ~ (of incidents) *to befall, come to pass, happen, occur, take place*, ⟨Am⟩ *eventuate* || es ereignete sich, daß .. *it happened that*; → sich treffen

Er·eignis n –nisses/–nisse *event, happening, incident, occurrence*; die Dynamik der –nisse *the dynamic of events* || ein (gr) ~ *a great occasion* || ein imposantes ~ *an impressive occasion* || mögliches ~ *eventuality*; ein seltenes ~ *quite an event*; ein unerwartetes ~ *an unexpected e.*; zufälliges ~ *coincidence, contingency*; | das ~ festlich **begehen** *to celebrate the occasion* || sie sieht e–m freudigen ~ entgegen *she is in the family way* **≗leer, ≗los** a *uneventful; blank* (*day*); *workaday* (*life*) **≗reich** a *eventful*

er·eilen vt [h] (jdn) *to come up with; to overtake* (*a p*) || mst ⟨übtr⟩ (of death, etc.) *to befall* (*a p*); *to happen to* (*a p*); das Geschick ereilte ihn *his fate overtook him*; ein trauriges G., ein plötzlicher Tod ereilte ihn *a sad fate, a sudden death befell him*; der Tod .. *he met his death*

erekt·il a ⟨anat⟩ *erectile (tissue)* **Erekti·on** [*ts*] f ~/~en *erection*

Erem·it m ~en/~en *hermit; eremite; anchoret* **~·age** [–ˈtɑːʒə] f ~/~n *hermitage*

·Er(e)n m ~/~ [obd] = Hausflur, –gang

Ereps·in n ~s/ (Darmsaftferment) *erepsin*

er·erben vt [h] (etw) *to inherit* **er·erbt** a *inherited (qualities)*; ⟨biol⟩ *hereditary (disease)* || *inbred, inherent, innate*

Ereth·ismus m (L) ~/ ⟨physiol⟩ *erethism*

er·ethisch a *erethismic, erethic*

erf·ahren vt/i [h] (→ fahren) **I.** vt **1.** (z hören bek) (etw) *to get* od *come to know (a th)*; *to hear*; *to learn* (über *about, of*); *to know* (v jdm *from a p*); *to get wind of (a th)*; = in Erfahrung bringen || ~, daß .. *to hear* (od *learn, to be told*) *that* ..; man erfährt, daß .. *it is learned that*; ich erfahre aus zuverlässiger Quelle, daß .. *I learn* od *understand from a reliable source that* .. **2.** (kennen lernen) (Liebe, Unbill) *to experience*; (Elend) *to know*; *to meet with (we met with a rough treatment)* || *to undergo, suffer (a th)*; *to go through (a th)* **3.** [das Passiv umschreibend, daher *engl* oft durch pass] (S) e–e Aufbesserung ~ (of salary) *to be increased* od *raised* (um *by*; auf *to*); e–e Behandlung ~ (of books) *to be dealt with*; *to be treated*; Berücksichtigung ~ *to receive consideration, to be considered*; Billigung ~ *to meet with approval*; Kritik ~ *to come in for criticism*; e–e Steigerung ~ *to be increased* od *raised*; e–e Verbesserung ~ *to undergo an improvement* **II.** vi; ~ v (etw) *to hear about*; *to learn of*; *to have heard tell of (a th)*; w h Interesse daran z ~, ob .. *we are interested in knowing if* .. **erf·ahren** [pp v ~] **1.** [attr] *experienced (teacher, speaker)*; *expert, skilled, veteran (carpenter, rider)*; *skilful (surgeon)*; ⟨Am⟩ *seasoned (airtravelers)* **2.** [pred] ~ s in *to be versed in (a subject)*; *to be expert at* od *in (a th)*; .. im Autofahren *expert at* od *in driving a car* || *to be conversant* od *familiar with (a th)*; *to be at home in* od *with (a th)* **|** **≃heit** f ~/ *experience* (in *of, in*); *familiarity* (in *with*); *skill* (in *in*); *skilfulness*

Erf·ahrung f ~/~en **A.** (Erfahren, → erfahren I.) [nur in der Wendung]: (etw) in ~ bringen *to hear, learn (a th)*; in ~ br., daß .. *to ascertain, learn, understand that* .. **B.** (durch Erfahren gewonnen) **1.** (Erlebnis) *experience*; sechsjährige ~ *six years' experience* || schlechte, üble ~ *trying experience*; *racket* || interessante ~en m *to have* (od *go through, undergo*) *interesting experiences* || wir h gute (schlechte) ~en mit ihm gemacht *he has been a success (a failure)*; .. ganz gute ~en damit g. *it has proved quite serviceable, our experiences are quite satisfactory*; e–e kürzlich gemachte ~ *a recent experience* **| auf** dem Wege prakt. ~ *by (the) rule of thumb*; *experimentally* || **aus** (eigener) ~ *from* (od *by*) *my own experience*; ich weiß aus ~ *I know by experience (how ..)*; ich weiß es aus eigener ~ ⟨sl⟩ *I' ve been there* || **durch** ~ lernen *to learn by experience*; durch ~(en) klug w *to go* (od *to have been*) *through the mill*; *to cut one's wisdom-teeth*; *to gain discretion*; ⟨Am sl⟩ *to get wise* || **nach** s–n ~en *in his experience* **2.** (Wissen, Kenntnis) *experience* (in *of, in*); *knowledge (of)*; *skill (in)*; *familiarity* (in *with*); ⟨fam⟩ *know-how* || Welt≃ *experience of the world* || ~ h in etw *to have experience of* (od *in*) *a th*; *to know a th*; Lebens≃ h *to know life*; er hat gründliche ~ auf dem Gebiet *he is very familiar with the subject*; *he knows the subject thoroughly*; praktische ~ h im Unterricht *to have experience of teaching* || ausgezeichnete ~en (mit e–r Methode) m *to achieve excellent results* || sammeln or m *to gain experience* (in *in*; im Unterricht *in teaching*) **3.** ⟨scient⟩ *experience*; menschliche ~ *human e.* || auf ~ gegründetes Denken *or* Verfahren → Empirie || e–r, der auf ~ baut *an empiric* || auf ~ gegründete Philosophie *experimental philosophy* || auf ~ gegr. Wissenschaften *empirical sciences* || auf dem Wege der ~, durch ~ *empirically, experimentally* || ⟨math & chem⟩ aus ~ abgeleitet *empiric(al)*

Erf·ahrungs- [in comp] *empiric(al)*; *experimental* **~austausch** m ⟨cyb, etc⟩ *theoretical and experimental findings* **~formel** f ⟨chem⟩ *empirical formula* **≃gemäß, ≃mäßig 1.** a *empiric(al)* **2.** adv *(to know) by experience* **≃reich** a *experienced* **~satz** m *maxim* (od *principle*) *based on experience* **~verfahren** n *empirical method* || praktisches, nicht auf Wissenschaft gegründetes ~ *the rule of thumb* **~wissen** n *knowledge gained through experience* **~wissenschaft** f *empirical science*

erf·allen vi [s] Sw ⟨mount⟩ = ab|stürzen

erf·aßbar a ⟨übtr⟩ *get-at-able*; *accessible* || ⟨mil⟩ *capable of being earmarked*

erf·assen I. vt [h] **A. 1.** ⟨eig⟩ (etw, jdn) *to catch* (od *lay, seize, take*) *hold of (a th, a p)*; *to grasp at (a th)*; (jdn) *to seize* (bei der Hand *by the hand*); → (er)greifen, fassen **2.** ⟨übtr⟩ **a.** (etw) *to lay hands on (land)*; *to collect* || *to seize (up)on (a th)*, wichtige Punkte ~ *to seize on salient points* || ⟨mil⟩ *to earmark* (f *for*); Fahrzeuge ~ *to e. vehicles* **b.** mit dem Auge alles ~ *to inventory everything* **c.** ⟨bes mil⟩ (jdn) *to inspect* (f .. *for military service*); e–n Jahrgang ~ *to draw on a class* || alle Fälle ~ (of a law) *to cover all cases* || erfaßt w durch e–n Plan *to be covered by a schedule*; die durch die Verordnung erfaßten Berufe *the scheduled occupations* **d.** etw statistisch ~ *to deal with a th statistically, to make a statistical survey of (an age group)* **3.** ⟨übtr⟩ (feelings, etc.) jdn ~ *to seize (up)on a p* || ein Schrecken erfaßte sie bei der Nachricht *they were seized with panic at the news* || ein Verlangen nach .. hatte ihn plötzlich erfaßt *a passion for (building) had sprung upon him* || das Bild erfaßt uns mit unwiderstehlichem Reiz *the picture appeals to us with an irresistible charm* **| –ßt w** *to be overcome (by fear), moved (by pity)* **B.** ⟨fig⟩ (begreifen) (etw) *to comprehend, fathom, grasp*; *to take in*; *to understand*; *to penetrate*; klar ~ *to realize* || ⟨sl⟩ *to tumble to, to get the hang of (a th)* || (Situation) *to take in*; *to appreciate (a fact)* **II.** ≃ n **1.** *catching hold of (a th)* **2.** ⟨übtr⟩ *seizing on (a th)* || ⟨mil⟩ *earmarking (of vehicles)* **3.** ⟨fig⟩ *(geistiges ~) apperception*; *comprehension grasping (of a meaning)*; *taking-in*; *uptake (quick in the u.)* || ⟨off, stat, demog⟩ *(direct) measurement* (z B. *of migration*) **4.** *interception (of signals)* ⟨a. mil⟩

Erf·assung f = Erfassen 2.

***erf·echten** vt [h] (→ fechten) ⟨übtr⟩ = erringen

erf·indbar a *contrivable*

erf·inden vt [h] (→ finden) **1.** ⟨tech⟩ (etw) *to invent* || ⟨com⟩ *to devise* **|** ⟨fig⟩ er hat das Pulver nicht erfunden *he won't set the Thames on fire* || er hat die Arbeit nicht erf. *he is no glutton for work* **2.** (erdichten) ⟨mst dero⟩ (e–e Geschichte) *to concoct, fabricate, invent*; ⟨fam⟩ *to think* od *dream* od *make up*; die ganze G. ist v A bis Z (frei) erfunden *the whole story is an entire fabrication*

Erf·inder m ~s/~ *inventor, contriver* **Erf·inderin** f ~/~nen *female inventor*; *inventress* **erf·inderisch** a *inventive, ingenious*; ⟨poet⟩ *daedal (hand)* || ~e Gabe *inventiveness* || (schöpferisch) *constructive, creative, imaginative* || [verblaßt] *inventive* (in etw *of a th*) **erf·indlich** a: aus k–m ~en Grunde *for no reason I (etc) could see* **Erf·indung** f ~/~en **1.** [abstr] *invention (of the* *telescope*) ‖ (Erdichtung) ⟨dero⟩ *concoction, fabrication* (*pure f.*), *invention* (*of the press*) **2.** [konkr] (Erfundenes) *invention* ‖ *contrivance*, (*mechanical*) *device*; ⟨fam⟩ *contraption*; e–e neue ~ *a new-fangled c.* ‖ kl technische ~ ⟨fam⟩ *gadget* **~sgabe** f *invention, inventiveness*; *creative faculty*; *power* (od *faculty*) *of invention* **~sgeist** m *inventive genius*; *ingenuity* **~skraft** f *inventiveness*; *ingenuity*; *resource* (*in an emergency*); → Erfindungsgabe **≃sreich** a *inventive, ingenious*; *resourceful*

erfl·ehen vt [h] (Schutz, Vergebung) *to implore*; *to beg* (v jdm *of a p*) ‖ (durch Flehen erlangen) *to obtain by entreaty*

Erf·olg m ~(e)s/~e **1.** (glücklicher Ausgang) *success*; *favourable issue*; *desired result*; (*a diplomatic*) *victory* ‖ ⟨fam⟩ *fetch* ‖ ⟨com, theat⟩ sensationeller ~ *hit*, ⟨Am sl⟩ *wow* **2.** *issue, outcome, result*; *effect* **3. a.** es wird ihm k–n ~ **bringen** *he will get nowhere* ‖ jdn z ~ führen *to make a p a success* ‖ ~ **haben** *to achieve* od *attain success*; *to succeed* (bei jdm *with a p*); *to get away with it* ‖ *to be successful* (in *in*); ⟨Am⟩ *to make the grade*; ⟨fam⟩ *to come through*; *to go over* (*big*); *to get there* ‖ durch etw ~ h *to score by a th* ‖ Aussicht auf ~ h *to have a fighting chance* ‖ in der Welt ~ h *to rise* (*to get on*) *in the w.*; *to carry the w. before one* ‖ k–n ~ h *to fail* ‖ gr (weniger) ~ h *to make much* (*less*) *headway* (in *in*) ‖ ~ h mit *to make a success* (⟨fam⟩ *a go*) *of* (*a th*) **|** (S) *to be effective*; (of a song, etc.) *to catch on*; (of a play) *to draw* ‖ m–e Untersuchungen h nicht viel ~ *my inquiries do not lead to much* ‖ nichts hatte ~ bei ihm *all efforts were lost* (od *nothing had any effect*) *on him* **|** ein ~ s *to turn out* (*to prove*) *a s.*; (Buch, etc) *to be* od *make a hit* **|** e–m Stück ~ **sichern** *to put a play over* **b.** ⟨sport⟩ sie hatten ihm **gegenüber** k–e Aussicht auf ~ *they had no chance against him* **| mit** ~ *with success*; *successfully*; mit ~ arbeiten ⟨Am⟩ *to make the grade* ‖ mit gutem (geringem) ~ *to some* (*little*) *purpose* ‖ mit bestem ~ *perfectly* **| ohne** ~ *without success* (od *effect, result*); *in vain* ‖ alles ohne ~ *all to no purpose* ‖ ohne jeden ~ *without any success*; *like water off a duck's back* ‖ ohne ~ bleiben (*or* sein) *to hang fire*; ohne ~ s bei jdm *to be lost upon a p*; s–e Bemühungen waren ohne ~ *he drew a blank* **|** von ~ gekrönt s *to be crowned with success* ‖ v ~ s (S) *to be a success*; *to prove successful* ‖ v ~ z ~ schreiten *to achieve a series of successes* **≃los** a *fruitless*; *ineffective, ineffectual*; *inconclusive*; *unavailing*; *unsuccessful, vain* (*efforts*); [pred] *in vain* ‖ ~ bleiben *to meet with failure* ‖ ~ s bei jdm (S) *to be lost upon a p* ‖ = ohne Erfolg (3. b.) ‖ ein –loser Bewerber *an also ran* **|** adv ~ (zurückkehren) .. *emptyhanded* ‖ ~! ⟨sl⟩ *no go*! **~losigkeit** f *ineffectiveness*; *failure*; *lack* od *want of success* **≃reich 1.** a *effective*; *successful, proficient* ‖ *booming* ‖ nicht ~ *unsuccessful* ‖ ~es Unternehmen *bonanza* ‖ ~ s als *to be a success as* (*a speaker*); .. mit ⟨fam⟩ *to make a go of* (*a th*) **2.** adv *successfully*; ~ tätig s *to be a success* (*in a firm*); *to get along well* (*in business*) ‖ e–e Prüfung ~ ablegen *to pass an ex.* **~versprechend** a *hopeful, promising* (*beginning*) ‖ *conducive to success*

erf·olgen vi [s] (nur S) **1.** (sich einstellen) (of events) *to come on* (*a severe fit came on just when ..*); *to ensue*; *fall*; *happen*; *to take place*; → eintreten I. B. 2. ‖ (of conditions) *to arise*; *ensue, follow* (aus *from*); (of help) *to be forthcoming*; unvermutet ~ *to supervene*; → einstellen I. C. 3. **2.** [engl mst durch pass]: ⟨tech⟩ *to be exercised* ‖ ist auf die Anfrage irgend etw erfolgt? *has any answer been given to the question*? ‖ Antwort ist noch nicht erfolgt *there has been no answer yet, no a. has been received yet* ‖ sein Eintritt kann sofort ~ *he may enter at once* ‖ die Erledigung Ihres Briefes wird vom Auswärt. Amt ~ *an answer to your letter will be given by the Foreign Office* ‖ Kündigung muß vor dem 1. April ~ *notice must be given before April 1st* ‖ Zahlung wird bis spätestens 1. Mai ~ *payment will be made by ..*

Erf·olgs- ~aussichten f pl: ~ h *to have a fighting chance* **~bilanz** f ⟨com⟩ *statement of surplus* **~buch** n *bestseller* **~honorar** n *contingent fee* **~rechnung** f *profit and loss accounting* od *statement* **~serie** f *lasting* od *repeated success* ⟨sport⟩ *no-defeat run*

erf·orderlich a **1.** [attr] *requisite* (*means*; *patience*); → nötig ‖ die f den Geist ~e Nahrung *the food necessary* (od *requisite*) *for the mind* ‖ *significant* (⟨a. comp⟩ Nullen) **2.** [pred] *necessary* (f *for, to*), *requisite* (*for*); *indispensable* od *needful* (*to, for*) ‖ ~ s *to be called for*; *to be required* (*for*; um z tun *to do*); es ist ~, daß es geschieht *it is necessary that it should be done* ‖ (etw) ~ m *to call for* (*drastic measures*); *to necessitate* (daß etw geschieht *a th being done*) ‖ wenn ~ *if required* **3.** das ≃e (Geld etc) *the necessary, the needful* ‖ mit der Bitte das ≃e z veranlassen ⟨oft⟩ *for necessary action please*

erf·orderlichenfalls adv *if necessary, if need be, if required*

erf·ordern vt [h] (nur S) (etw) *to demand, require, necessitate*; *need, want*; → bedürfen ‖ die Not erfordert es *the emergency requires it* ‖ die S erfordert e–n Artikel f sich *the matter requires an article to itself*; die S erfordert sorgsame Behandlung *the matter wants careful handling* ‖ drastische Maßnahmen ~ *to call for drastic measures* ‖ Energie, Geduld (etc) ~ *to demand energy, patience*; das Buch erfordert die größte Aufmerksamkeit *the book exacts the closest attention* ‖ es erforderte s–e ganze Kraft *it needed* (od *required*) *all his energy* (*to do*) ‖ es erfordert viel Zeit *it takes much time* (z tun *to do, in doing*) **|** es würde e–n Goethe erfordert h *it would have called for a Goethe* (*to do*)

Erf·ordernis n –nisses/–nisse *requirement* (f *for*) ‖ dringendes ~ *exigence, –cy, necessity* (f *for*; *to do*); das notwendige ~ *the requisite* (f *for*); *the prerequisite* (f *to*) → Bedürfnis

erf·orschen vt [h] **1.** (Land) *to explore*; (Tiefen des Meeres) *to sound* **2.** ⟨übtr⟩ (untersuchen) (etw) *to examine*; *to examine* (od *inquire*) *into* (*a th*); *to investigate*; *to explore*; *to sift* ‖ (Geheimnis) *to penetrate*; *to search into* (*a th*); (jds Gedanken) *to probe, fathom*; *to search* (*out*) ‖ jds Ansicht ~ *to sound a p* **Erf·orscher** m ~s/~ *explorer* (*of new countries*) ‖ *investigator*; → Forscher **Erf·orschung** f ~/~en *exploration* (*of a country*); *sounding* **|** (Untersuchung) *examination, investigation, inquiry* (e–r S *of* od *into a th*); *exploration* (*of a th*) ‖ *fathoming* (*of thoughts*)

erfr·agen vt [h] (etw) *to inquire*; Näheres hier (im Laden, im Büro etc) z ~ *inquire within, at the office* ‖ → erkunden, –mitteln

erfr·echen vrefl [h] sich ~ z tun *to have the audacity* (od *effrontery, impudence*) *to do*

erfr·euen vt [h] **1.** (jdn) *to cheer*; *delight* (mit *with*); *to gratify, please, rejoice* (*a p*); *to fill* (*a p*) *with delight*; *to give* (*a p*) *pleasure*; jds Herz ~ *to gladden a p's h.*; die Gesellschaft mit e–m Lied ~ *to indulge the c. with a s.* ‖ (erquicken) *to comfort, regale*, [mst pass] (*he was comforted with a cup of tea*) ‖ erfreut s *to be gratified* (od *rejoiced, glad*) (über *at, over*; z hören *to hear*); sie war am meisten v ihnen erfreut *she was the best pleased of them*; höchst erfr. s *to be charmed* (od *enchanted*) (*to see you*); er sah uns erfr. an *he looked at us delightedly* **|** (jds Ohr etc) *to delight, to rejoice*; (die Augen) *to gladden*; jds Herz ~ *to* *warm the cockles of a p's heart* **2. sich ~ a. ..an** (etw) *to take delight* od *pleasure in*; *to delight* od *glory in* (*a th*); *to be pleased with* (*a th*); *to be gladdened by* (*the sight of a th*) || *to regale o.s. with* (*a th*) **b. .. über** (etw) *to rejoice at* (*a th*); *to be delighted* od *pleased with* (*a th*) **c. sich e-r S ~** *to enjoy a th* || höchster Achtung .. *to be held in high esteem* || sich der Dienste des Herrn N. ~ *to rejoice in the services of Mr. N.* **erfr·eut** a *delighted, etc*; ⟨Am a.⟩ *proud*

erfr·eulich 1. a *enjoyable, gladsome* (*sight*), *pleasant*; *glad* (*tidings*) *welcome* (*news*); *happy* (*idea*); *refreshing* (*frankness*); nicht ~ *disagreeable* | [pred] *gratifying* (f jdn z hören *to a p to hear*) **2.** adv; ~ klar *beautifully clear*; ~ weniger Schäden *b. less damage* **~weise** adv *fortunately*; *mercifully*; es wurde ~ verschoben *it was m. postponed*

erfr·ieren I. vi/t (→ frieren) **1.** vi [s] *to freeze to death, to be frozen to death*; *to die from frost*; *to perish with cold* || (of plants) *to be blighted* (od *frosted*), *to be killed by frost* | ~ m *to freeze* || (Pflanzen) *to blight*; *to frost* **2.** vt [h] **a.** ich habe mir die Zehen erfroren *or* mir sind die Zehen erfroren *I have frozen my toes* || erfroren *frozen* (vor *with*); erfroren s *to be frozen to death* || halb erfroren *pinched with cold*; → erfroren **b.** ⟨fig⟩ wir waren ganz erfroren *we were frozen to death* **II.** ≙ n *frostbite* (*of the limbs*) **Erfr·ierung** f ~/~en *frost gangrene*; *frostbite* | ~stod [m] *death by freezing*

erfr·ischen vt [h] **1.** (jdn) *to freshen* (*up*); *to refresh* (durch *by*) || *to brace*; *revive* || (den Geist) *to recreate* **2. sich ~** *to refresh o.s.*; Sie müssen sich etw ~ *you must take some refreshment*; sich durch e–n Trank ~ ⟨fam⟩ *to refresh* || sich geistig ~ *to recreate o.s.* (durch *by*; mit *with*); *to take recreation* **erfr·ischend 1.** a *refreshing* (*drink*; *breeze*); *bracing* (*air*); *stimulating* **2.** adv ⟨übtr⟩ *refreshingly* (*clear*; *outspoken*)

Erfr·ischung f ~/~en **1.** [abstr] *refreshment* (f jdn *to a p*) || (geistige) *recreation*; *relaxation*; → Erholung **2.** [konkr] *refreshment*; (Trank) *refresher* || ~en [pl] *refreshments* [pl]; ~en einor z sich nehmen *to take refreshments*; ~en wurden herumgereicht *r. were handed round* | **~s- ~bude** f; **~zelt** n *refreshment-booth*, ⟨Am fam⟩ *soda-jerk* **~insel** f (im Atlant. Ozean) *Tristan da Cunha* **~karren, ~wagen** m ⟨rail, etc⟩ *running buffet* **~raum** m *refreshment room* (od *bar*) **~trank** m; **~trunk** m *refresher, reviver*; e–n ~ nehmen ⟨fam⟩ *to refresh*

erfr·oren [pp v erfrieren] a *frostbitten* (*ears*)

erf·üllbar a *capable of accomplishment*

Erf·üllbarkeit f ~/ *capability* od *possibility to fulfil* od *of fulfilment* **erf·üllen** vt [h] **A. 1.** ⟨eig⟩ (S) *to fill* (mit *with*); *to crowd, throng*; Gartendüfte ~ die Luft *gardenscents are crowding the air* **2.** ⟨übtr⟩ **a.** jdn ~ (of feelings, etc.) *to fill* (od *imbue, impress, inform, infuse, inspire*) *a p* (mit .. *with fear*); [oft pass] erfüllt s v *to be informed* (od *possessed*; *consumed*) *with* || jds Herz ~ *to fill a p's heart*; jds Innere ganz ~ *to be uppermost in a p's heart* (a. P) **b.** (e–e Bewegung) *to imbue* (od *leaven*) (*with*) **c.** ⟨bib⟩ (Zeit) *to fulfil*; *complete* **3.** (jds Anforderungen) *to meet*, ⟨Am⟩ *to measure up to* || (Bedingungen) *to carry out*; *to comply with*; *to fulfil* || (jds Bitte etc) *to comply with*; (jds Erwartungen, Hoffnungen) *to fulfil* | (s–e Pflicht) *to discharge, fulfil, perform*; (öffentliche Pflicht) *to serve* vi || (s–e Verpflichtungen) *to fulfil, meet* || (sein Versprechen) *to fulfil, keep*; *to make good*; *to stand up to*; sein Versprechen ~ ⟨Am fam⟩ *to deliver the goods* || sein Versprechen nicht ~ *to go back on one's promise* | (e–e Aufgabe) *to carry out*; *to fulfil, perform* || (e–n Vertrag) *to fulfil*; ⟨Scot⟩ *to implement* || *to satisfy* (*a desire*) || (e–n Zweck) *to achieve, answer, fulfil*; es wird s–n Z. ~ *it will serve its purpose* **B. sich ~** (of hopes) *to be fulfilled* od *realized*; *to materialize*; die Hoffnung erfüllt sich (nicht) *the hope is* (*not*) *borne out*; (of dreams) *to come true* || sich nicht ~ *to fail*; *to come to nothing*

Erf·üllung f ~/~en **1.** *filling* (*of a room with* ..) **2.** ⟨übtr⟩ *imbuing, inspiration* (*of a p with* ..) **3.** ~ e–r Bitte (etc) *compliance with a request* || *satisfaction* (*of a desire, condition*) || *realization* (*of hopes*) || *discharge, fulfilment* (*of a duty*); *fulfilment* (*of a hope, promise*, etc.) || *performance* (*of a task*) ⟨a. contr⟩ || bei ~ aller dieser Bedingungen *if all these c. are fulfilled* (od *complied with*) || in ~ gehen = sich erfüllen; sein Wunsch geht in ~ *he gets his wish*

Erf·üllungs- ~ort m *place of performance* (od *fulfilment, payment, settlement, delivery*) **~politik** f ⟨Ger⟩ (nach 1921) *politics* [pl] *of fulfilment* od *compliance* **~tag** m *day of payment*; *setting-day*; *settlement day* **~zeit** f *time of performance* od *fulfilment*

·Erfurter (nach ⟨Ger⟩ Stadt Erfurt) a; ~ Kongreß (1808) *Congress of Erfurt*

Erg n [Gr] ⟨phys⟩ (Arbeitseinheit) *erg*(*on*)

erg·änzen vt [h] **1.** (Fehlendes, e–e Summe) *to make* (od *fill*) *up, to supply* || (Unvollständiges) *to piece out*; *to complete* || *to restore* (*text*), *finish* (*sentence*) || *to complete, replenish* (*stores*) || (Heer) *to recruit* (aus *from*); (Verluste) *to replace* | (Aussage, Bericht) *to complement*; *to supplement*; *to be supplementary* (od *supplemental*) *to* (*a report*); (e–e Geschichte) *to piece out* (aus, v *from*); etw ~ mit, durch .. *to eke a th out with* ..; (Werk) durch ein zweites ~ *to follow up with a second* | (jdn) *to supplement* (*a p*) **2. sich ~ a.** (of an army) *to be recruited* (aus *from*) **b.** *to complement* (od *supplement*) *each other*; die beiden Bücher ~ sich durchaus *the two books are complementary one to the other* || (P) *to be complementary* (*to each other*); *to complement each other* **erg·änzend** a *supplemental, –tary*; *additional* (*remarks*) || ~ sagen *to add*

Erg·änzung f ~/~en **1.** [abstr] *making up*; *supplying* (*of a deficiency*) || *completion* (*of a statue*); *piecing out* (*of a story*) || *replenishment* (*of stores, wardrobe, etc*) || *replacement* (*of losses* ⟨a. mil⟩ [P & S]); *recruitment* (*of an army*) || *complementing, supplementation* (*of a report*); zur ~ unsrer Akten *with a view to completing our records* **2.** (Ergänztes) *complement* (e–r S, z etw *of a th*); → [in comp] *supplemental, supplementary* | **~s- ~band** m *supplement*; *supplementary volume* **~farben** f [pl] = Komplementärfarben **~heft** n = Ergänzungsband **~käufe** m pl *fill-in buying* **~mannschaft** f ⟨mil⟩ *relief, reserves* [pl] **~satz** m ⟨gram⟩ *completive clause* **~steuer** f *supplementary tax*; *supertax* **~stück** n *complement*

×**erg·attern** vt [h] (etw) *to manage to get*; *to come by*; *to get hold of* (*a th*); (e–e Tasse Tee) *to snatch*; *to cadge* || (e–n Platz) *to secure* || (Neuigkeiten) *to pick up*

erg·aunern vt [h] (etw) *to get .. by trickery* || *to swindle* (v jdm *out of a p*), *to trick* (*a p out of a th*)

erg·eben vt [h] [→ geben] **I.** (S) **1.** (Ertrag, Resultat etc) *to yield* (*it yielded a good result*) || den Gesamtbetrag v 50 Mark ~ *to amount* (od *total*) *to 50 marks*; 2 Zentner ~ *to work out at two hundredweight* || e–e Situation, Folgen ~ *to result in a situation*; *in consequences* || ⟨phil⟩ die Form hätte neuenglisch [ei] ~ *the form would have yielded modern English* [ei] **2.** (erweisen) (Tatsache; jds Unschuld) *to demonstrate, to prove*; *to show*; ~, daß *to prove that* .. || wenn die Tatsachen e–n Rechtsanspruch ~ sollten *if the facts should establish a right to claim* **II. sich ~ A.** (P) **1.** ⟨mil⟩ *to surrender*; *to cry* *craven* || sich jdm ~ *to surrender to a p*; sich jdm auf Gnade u Ungnade ~ *to surrender at discretion*; *to throw o.s. on a p's mercy, on Providence* **2. sich e-r S** (Gewohnheit etc) ~ *to give o.s. up to, to addict o.s. to a th*; *to devote o.s. to* (*a pursuit, study*); sich dem Trunk (°Suff) ~ *to take to drinking*; *to yield* (*to sin*) **3. sich in etw** ~ *to resign o.s.* (od *to be resigned*) *to a th* (*to the decrees of fate*; *to the will of God*); *to submit to a th* || *to acquiesce in*; *to put up with a th* **B.** (S) **1.** *to arise*; *emerge*; *ensue*; *occur, happen*; *to take place*; *to come off* od *about*; *to come to pass*; *to turn out*; (sich herausstellen) *to transpire*; (*of new aspects*) *to emerge*; (*of problem*) *to pose*; es ~ sich interessante Gedanken *interesting ideas emerge*; es ~ sich viele Schwierigkeiten *there arise many difficulties*; es ergab sich, daß .. *the result* (od *upshot*) *of it was that* .. **2. sich** ~ **aus** *to accrue* (od *arise, ensue, flow, follow, issue, result, spring*) *from*; *to be the consequence of* ..; daraus ergibt sich, daß .. *hence it follows that* ..

erg·eben [pp v ~] a **1.** [pred] jdm (treu) ~ s *to be attached* od *devoted to a p*; dem Sport ~ s *to be devoted to sport* || dem Trunk ~ *addicted to drink, given to drinking* || ~ s in etw *to be resigned to a th* (*to one's fate*) **2.** [attr] **a.** ~, treu ~ *devoted* (*advocate*; *servant*); aufrichtig ~ *genuinely devoted*; sein ihm ~er Enkel *his adherent grandson* **b.** Ihr (sehr) ~er (als Briefschluß) 1. ⟨com⟩ *Yours faithfully* (od *faithfully Yours* (*N. N.*) 2. (formell) *Yours truly* 3. (vertraulich) *Yours sincerely* (*N. N.*) | Ihr ganz ~er *Your humble servant* | (to newspapers) *Your obedient servant* || → ergebenst **Erg·ebenheit** f *submission* (*with all due s.*); *submissiveness* || in ~ = Ihr sehr ergebener | *attachment*; *devotion* **erg·ebenst** **1.** a; Ihr ~er = Ihr sehr ergebener 2. **2.** adv *respectfully* || ich teile Ihnen ~ mit *I beg to inform you* || (als Briefschluß) ≗ = Ihr (sehr) ergebener

Erg·ebnis n –nisses/–nisse *result, end, effect*; *upshot*; *consequence*; *issue, outcome, outgrowth*; *achievement*; → Ertrag || das ~ war, daß er abreiste *the result was that he left*; *as a result he l.*; mit dem ~, daß .. *with the consequence that* .. || z e–m ~ k *to arrive at, come to a conclusion*; wir k z folgendem ~ *the result of our discussion is as follows*; *let me sum up*; → End≗; Wirkung || bearbeitete ~se ⟨demog, stat⟩ *refined figures*; wissenschaftliche –nisse [pl] *findings* [pl] (auf dem Gebiete der Biologie *in biology*) || das entgegengesetzte ~ zeitigen, z entg–ten ~ führen *to work to opposite ends, to achieve the exact opposite* || (*an arithmetic book with*) *answers* || Aufklärungsergebnisse *reconnaissance information*; Ortungs≗e *targeting information* **erg·ebnislos** **1.** a *resultless*; *fruitless, ineffective, negative* (*criticism*) **2.** adv *without result*; ~ verlaufen *to fail*; *to come to nothing* **erg·ebnisreich** a *fruitful* (*labours*); *fructuous*

Erg·ebung f ~/ **1.** ⟨mil⟩ *surrender* **2.** ⟨fig⟩ *submission*; *resignation* (in Gott *to God*); mit ~ (*to endure*) *resignedly*

erg·ehen **I.** vi, refl, imps [→ gehen] **A.** vi [s] **1.** (of decrees, etc.) *to be issued* od *passed*; e–e Verordnung erging, es erging e–e V. *a decree was issued* || ~ **an**: (*an appeal*) *was made to* ..; (*an order*) *was sent to* ..; an uns ist k–e Einladung ergangen *we have not received an invitation, we have not been invited* || ⟨Ger⟩ es ist an ihn ein Ruf als Professor an die Universität .. ergangen *he has had* (od *received*) *a call to a professorial chair at the university* (*of Berlin*) **2.** **(etw)** ~ **l** *to give out*; *to issue*; *to make public* || ein (*or* das) Urteil ~ l *to pass* (od *pronounce*) *judgement, to pass sentence* (über *on*) || Gnade f Recht ~ l *to show mercy* **3.** **(etw) über sich** ~ **l** *to bear, to endure*; *to submit to*; *to suffer*; *to undergo*; *to acquiesce in, to put up with* (*a th*) || sie l alles über sich ~ ⟨Am fam⟩ *they let him step all over them* **B.** v imps [s] **es erging mir gut** (schlecht) *I fared well* (*ill*); .., wie es ihm ergeht .. *how things are going with him*, .. *how he is getting on*; es wird ihm schlecht ~ *it will be hard on him, it will go ill with him*; wie ist es dir ergangen? *how did you fare? how has the world used you?* wie wird es dir ~, wenn ..? *what will become of you if* ..? möge es dir gut ~! *may heaven prosper you!* || ⟨poet⟩ *fare thee well!* || es erging ihm ebenso *he met with the same fate* **C. sich** ~ [h] **1.** sich im Park ~ *to take a walk* od *stroll in the park*; *to walk about in the park* **2.** sich ~ in (ausschweifen) *to launch into* (*expense, strong language*); sich in e–r Leidenschaft ~ *to indulge* (*o.s. in*) *a passion* || sich in Dankesbezeigungen ~ *to be profuse in one's gratitude*; .. in lauten Beteuerungen (s–r Unschuld) ~ *to make loud protestations of* ..; sich in langen Reden ~ über .. *to expatiate on, to hold forth at length about* (*a th*); .. in Schmähungen .. *to break out into a stream of abuse*; sich in Greuelerzählungen ~ *to indulge* (od *luxuriate*) *in horrors* || sich in Kraftausdrücken ~ *to indulge in strong language*; sich in Lobreden ~ *to go off* (od *launch*) *into praises*; sich in überschwenglichen Reden ~ *to gush* (über *about*); *to plunge into* (*details*); *to extol* (*the virtues of a p*) **II.** ≗ n **1.** = Befinden 2. **2.** Sich-~ *indulgence*

erg·etzen etc = ergötzen etc

erg·iebig a *productive, rich, copious* (*mine*; *soil*); → fruchtbar || ~e Goldmine *bonanza*; e–e sehr ~e Farm *a bonanza farm* || ⟨übtr⟩ *rich* (*source*); → einträglich | **≗keit** f ~/ *productiveness, productivity*; *richness*; *fertility* (*of soil*)

erg·ießen vt [h] [→ gießen] **1.** (of river) (sein Wasser) *to discharge, pour* (in *into*) || ⟨übtr⟩ (S) (Rauch) *to discharge*; (Licht) *to pour* (od *send*) *out, to shed* (auf *on*); *to diffuse* | ⟨fig⟩ Ströme v Schimpfworten ~ *to pour forth* od *out torrents of abuse* (über .. *on a p*); s–n Zorn ~ *to vent* (od *let loose, pour out*) *one's wrath* (über *on*) **2. sich** ~ (of river) *to discharge* (od *empty, pour*) *itself*; *to discharge* (od *debouch, disembogue, empty, fall*) (in *into*) || (of water) *to pour, spill* (aus *from*; über *over*); *to gush forth in* (*torrents*); (of blood) *to flush* || ⟨übtr⟩ (of light) *to be shed* (*on* ..); (of sounds) *to gush* (aus *from*; in *into*) | ⟨fig⟩ (of feelings, etc.) sich ~ über jdn *to flood in upon, to surge over a p*; sein Zorn, die Schale s–s Zorns ergoß sich über sie *his wrath was let loose on them*; helle Röte ergoß sich über ihre Wangen *a blush spread* (*came, rose*) *to her cheeks*; s–e Wut ergoß sich auf ihr *his fury was vented upon her* **Erg·ießung** f *discharge* || *pouring forth* (od *out*) || ⟨fig⟩ → Erguß

ergl·änzen vi [s & h] (S) *to flash, radiate*; (of the face) *to shine* (vor *with*); (of eyes) *to flash, glow, sparkle* (vor *with*) || → erstrahlen

ergl·immen vi [s] [→ glimmen] *to begin to glimmer*; *to begin to glow faintly*

ergl·ühen **1.** vi [s] *to glow* || ⟨fig⟩ (of the face) *to blush, flush, glow* (vor *with*) || in Liebe ~ z jdm *to fall in love with*, ⟨sl⟩ *to be smitten with a p* || in Begeisterung ~ f etw *to become enthusiastic* (⟨fam⟩ *to enthuse*) *about a th* **2.** ≗ n; (Gesicht) zum ~ bringen (*or* erglühen l) *to flush*

erg·odisch a ⟨stat⟩ *ergodic* (Quelle)

Ergogr·aph m ~en/ ~en (Apparat) *ergograph*

Ergot·in n ~s/ ⟨med⟩ *ergotin*

Ergot·ismus m *ergotism*

erg·ötzen **I.** vt [h] (amüsieren) **1.** (jdn) *to amuse* (mit *with*); *to delight, to entertain* **2. sich** ~ **an** *to delight in, to take delight in* (*a th*); *to be amused by* (*a joke*) **II.** ≗ n *amusement*; zum ~ der Nachbarn *to the amusement of his neighbours* (*he* ..) **erg·ötzend** a = ergötzlich

erg·ötzlich 1. a *amusing, delightful* 2. adv *amusingly* **Erg·ötzung** f ~/~en *amusement, delight, pleasure*

ergr·auen vi [s] *to (become) grey, to grizzle*; im Dienst ~ *to grow old in service*

ergr·eifen vt [h] [→ greifen] 1. (S) *to catch* (od *get, lay, seize*) *hold of* (*a th*); *to grasp*; jds Hand ~ *to grip* od *seize a p's hand*; *to seize a p by the hand* ‖ (aufnehmen) *to pick up*; die Feder ~ *to take pen in hand*; *to take* (od *pick*) *up one's pen* ‖ gierig ~ *to snap*; hastig ~ *to grab*; *to grasp at, to make a grab at*; *to swoop up*; plötzlich u krampfhaft ~ *to clutch*; *to clutch at* 2. (P) *to lay* od *get one's hands on a p*; (Dieb) *to apprehend, arrest*; *seize* 3. ⟨übtr⟩ a. die Zügel ~ *to assume* (*take up*) *the reins* b. ~ + Abstraktum mst *to take*: (Beruf) → 3. c.; Besitz ~ v *to take possession of, to seize* (*a th*) ‖ die Flucht ~ *to take to flight* ‖ e–e Gelegenheit ~ *to embrace* (od *seize, take*) *an opportunity*; die G. ~ *to take* (*jump at an*) *occasion* (od *seize the occasion*) (*to do*); *to seize upon* (*a chance, pretext*) ‖ die Macht ~ *to seize the reins of power*; *to take over* ‖ Maßregeln (*or* Mittel, Schritte) ~ *to take action, to take measures* od *steps* (*against*) ‖ die Offensive ~ *to take the offensive* ‖ jds Partei ~ *to take sides with*; *to side with a p*; f e–e S Partei ~ *to espouse a cause* ‖ das Wort ~ *to speak*; ⟨bes Am⟩ *to take the floor*; c. e–n Beruf ~ *to embrace* (od *learn*; *take up*; *choose, adopt*) *a profession* 4. ⟨übtr⟩ (S) (of fire, etc) (etw) *to catch*; *to lay hold of* 5. ⟨fig⟩ jdn ~ a. (of feelings) *to seize upon a p*; Furcht ergriff ihn *fear gripped his heart*; ein Schrecken ergriff sie bei der Nachricht *they were seized with panic at the news*; Traurigkeit ergriff mich *sadness settled upon me*; → erfassen I. A. 3. ‖ (of a disease) (jdn, Organ) *to attack*; [oft pass] *to be attacked by* (*gout*, etc.) b. *to affect, move, thrill, touch* ‖ [oft pass] ergriffen w *to thrill* (vor *with*); *to be thrilled* od *deeply stirred* (v *by*); ergriffen s v *to be moved* od *touched by*; plötzlich ergriffen (v dem Verlangen) *visited* (*by the sudden desire* ..); *overcome with fear*; alles war bis ins Innerste (z Tränen) ergriffen v .. *all were moved* (od *touched*) *to the heart* (od *to tears*) *by* .. ‖ alles war v s–n Worten ergriffen *all were deeply impressed* (od *affected*) *by his words* ‖ es ergreift mich stets, wenn ich dies Elend sehe *I am always deeply touched by this misery* **ergr·eifend** 1. a ⟨fig⟩ *affecting* (*sight*), *moving* (*words, moment*), *pathetic, touching* (*scene*) ‖ *impressive* (*ceremony, speech*) 2. adv *pathetically*; *touchingly* ‖ (*to speak*) *impressively* 3. das ≗e *the touchingness* (e–r S, an e–r S *of a th*) ‖ *the impressiveness* (*of his speech*) **Ergr·eifung** f ~/~en 1. *seizure* (*of a th*) ‖ *apprehension* (*of a thief*); *capture* (*of a prisoner*) 2. ⟨übtr⟩ ~ der Macht, Macht≗ *seizure* (od *assumption*) *of power* (jds *by a p*) ‖ *the taking* (*of an opportunity, of measures*)

ergr·iffen a → ergreifen 5. b. **≗heit** f ~/ *emotion*, (*state of being emotionally moved*)

ergr·immen vi/t 1. vi [s] *to become angry*; *to blaze up*; ° *to lose one's hair* 2. vt [h] (jdn) *to anger*; *to get a p's goat*

ergr·ünden vt [h] (Tiefen des Meeres) *to plumb*; *to pierce* | *to go deeply* od *thoroughly into* (*a matter*); *to get to the bottom of* (*a th*); (Geheimnis) *to penetrate*; (Tiefe der Seele) *to plumb*; (jds Gedanken) *to fathom* ‖ etw z ~ versuchen *to probe deeply into, to search* od *fathom the bottom of* (*a matter*) ‖ → erforschen 2.

Ergr·ündung f ~/~en *penetration*; *fathoming*

ergr·ünen vi [s] (S) *to begin to green*; *to become green*

Erg·uß m –gusses/–güsse 1. *discharge* (*of water*); *efflux, outpour*; → Blut ≗ | ⟨fig⟩ *effusion*; *outpour*; *outhburst* od *torrent* (*of abuse*), Herzens≗ *effusion of heart*; Rede≗ *gush*; *flood of words* 2. [konkr] –güsse [pl] *effusions* (*poetical e.*); *outpourings* [pl] (*of a p's mind*) **~gestein** n ⟨geol⟩ *volcanic rock*; → Eruptivgestein

erh·aben [altes pp v erheben] a A. [bes attr] 1. ⟨eig⟩ a. *elevated* (*places on* ..) *raised* (*mark of skin*) ‖ *lofty* (*summit*) b. ⟨opt⟩ *convex* (*mirror*) c. ⟨arts⟩ ~e Arbeit *relief*; *relievo* (od *ri–*) (It); *embossment*; *embossed work*; ⟨arch⟩ *mouldings* [pl]; flach ~e A. *low relief, bas-relief, basso relievo*; *anaglyph*; halb ~e A. *half relief, semi-relievo*; ganz ~e A. *high relief, alto relievo* (It) ‖ (etw) in ~er A. anfertigen *to emboss* ‖ mit ~er A. verzieren *to emboss, to enchase*; (Metall) *to snarl* ‖ Verzierung in ~er A. *boss* 2. ⟨fig⟩ *high-pitched, lofty* (*aim*) ‖ *elevated, exalted, grand* (*style*); *lofty* (*diction*); *noble* (*lines*) ‖ *grand, impressive, majestic* (*sight*) 3. ⟨philos⟩ *sublime* (*beauty*) B. [pred] ⟨fig⟩ ~ s über etw *to be above a th* (*I am above it*); über (Neid) ~ s *to be superior to* (*envy*) ‖ über alles Lob ~ *above* (od *beyond*) *all praise*; über jeden Tadel ~ s (of a work) *to be above criticism* ‖ sich ~ dünken *to be above o.s., to have a high opinion of o.s.*; sich z ~ dünken z tun *to be above doing*; sich ~ dünken über andere *to fancy o.s. to be above others*; *to look down on other people* C. das ≗e ⟨philos⟩ *the sublime* | **≗heit** f 1. ⟨eig⟩ *elevation* 2. mst ⟨fig⟩ *elevation, grandeur* (*of style, thoughts*); *loftiness*; *nobility*; *majesty* ‖ ⟨philos⟩ *sublimity*; *sublime character*

Erh·alt m ~(e)s/ *the obtaining* (*of a licence*); *receipt* (*of a letter*); → Empfang

erh·alten vt [h] (→ halten) A. (aufrecht~) 1. etw (in e–m Zustand) ~ a. *to maintain a th* (*the house is maintained just as he left it*); sein Leben, s–n Ruf ~ *to maintain one's life, one's reputation* ‖ Nahrung erhält das Leben *food sustains life*, (sich) s–e Gesundheit, Kräfte ~ *to conserve one's health, one's strength* ‖ sich [acc] v jdm ~ l *to live on a p* ‖ [pp = a] ⟨demog⟩ (v e–r Erwerbsperson ~) *dependent* b. (Fleisch etc) frisch, kühl ~ (mst halten) *to keep* (*meat*) *fresh, cool*; in gutem Zustand ~ *to preserve* ‖ (Haus) in gutem Z. ~ *to keep* (*a house*) *in good repair*; gut (schlecht) ~ s (of a house) *to be in good* (*bad*) *repair*; gut ~ s (*of coins*) *to be in mint state* od *condition*; (of manuscript) *to be in good preservation*; bis auf den heutigen Tag ~ [pp] *extant to this day*; .. hat sich bis auf unsere Zeit ~ .. *has come down to our time*; [pp = a] (P, S) gut, schlecht ~ (*to be*) *in good, poor condition* 2. **sich ~ v** *to keep* (od *support*) *o.s. on, to subsist on* ‖ sich gesund ~ *to keep well*; *to conserve one's health* ‖ sich am Leben ~ *to keep alive* ‖ **sich ~ h (S)** = ~ s, → d. 3. B. (etw bek) 1. ⟨allg⟩ *to get*; [gewählt:] (Belohnung etc) *to obtain*; (Einladung) *to receive* ‖ ich erhielt heute e–n Brief *I got* (od *had*) *a letter today*; ich erhielt Ihren B., als .. *your letter reached me when* ..; ⟨com⟩ Ihren B. ~ [pp] *your letter* (od *yours*) *to hand* ‖ (Kritik) *to come in for* .. ‖ die Note 1 ~ in *to obtain* od *gain a first class in* (*history*) ‖ ⟨parl⟩ die Hälfte der Stimmen ~ *to poll half of the votes cast*; das Wort ~ ⟨bes Am⟩ *to get the floor* | e–n Auftrieb ~ *to be promoted* od *encouraged* (durch *by*); s–e Erziehung ~ *to receive one's education*; *to be eduated* (*at* ..); Nachricht ~ *to receive word* od *to learn* (*that* ..); N. *or* Kunde ~ v etw *to be informed* (od *to hear*) *of a th* 2. *to come by*; *to get hold of*; *to secure*; dies Buch ist schwer z ~ *this book is hard to come by*; Exemplare kann man leicht ~ *copies can easily be obtained* 3. (erben) (Geld) *to come in for* 4. ⟨chem⟩ (etw) *to obtain*; Silber erhält man aus .. *silver is obtained from* ..

Erh·alter m ~s/~ (Retter) *preserver* (*of a p's life*) ‖ (Ernährer) *maintainer, supporter* (*of a p*)

erh·ältlich a *obtainable; procurable* || → käuflich

Erh·altung f ~/ **1.** *maintenance, preservation; upkeep (of a building)* || *conservation (of energy)* || *survival (of the fittest)* **2.** *maintenance, sustenance (of a p); support (of institutions);* → Unterhalt **3.** *retention (of a custom)* || *maintenance (of peace)* | **~s- ~gesetz** n der Energie *law of the conservation of energy* **~trieb** m → Selbst≈ **~zustand** m ⟨arts, arch⟩ *state of preservation*

erh·andeln vt [h] (etw) *to acquire by bargaining* od *haggling*

erh·ängen I. vt [h] **1.** jdn ~ *to hang a p (by the neck) (he was hanged)* **2. sich** ~ *to hang o.s.* **II.** ≈ n *hanging (of a p)* **Erh·ängte(r** m) f *p who has been hanged, p who has hanged himself*

erh·ärten vt [h] **1.** ⟨eig⟩ (etw) = härten **2.** ⟨fig⟩ (Beweis, Behauptung) *to confirm, corroborate, substantiate* || etw durch Eid (*or* eidlich) ~ *to assert a th on oath; to swear to a th, to swear a th* || (s–e Meinung durch Tatsachen) ~ *to strengthen* od *reinforce (.. by ..)* **Erh·ärtung** f ~/~en ⟨fig⟩ *confirmation, corroboration, substantiation*

erh·aschen vt [h] **1.** (T etc) *to catch*; (im Netz) *to net* || (jdn) *to catch, seize*; ⟨sl⟩ *to nab* **2.** (etw) *to catch; snatch* | ⟨übtr⟩ e–n Blick v jdm ~ *to catch a glimpse of a p* || e–n Kuß ~ *to snatch a kiss* || nur einige Worte ~ *to catch only a few words*

erh·eben I. vt [h] (→ heben) **A.** (etw) **1.** die Hand ~ *to lift* (od *hold up, raise*) *one's hand*; die Hand z Schwur ~ *to lift (up) one's hand* || sein Glas ~ *to raise one's glass* || die Augen ~ *to lift (up)* od *raise one's eyes* (z jdm *up to a p*) **2.** ⟨übtr⟩ **a.** (Abgaben etc) *to levy, impose, raise*; v den Mitgliedern wird kein Beitrag erhoben *no contribution is required from the members*; → eintreiben, -ziehen || (Zinsen) *to charge; claim* || ⟨jur⟩ Schadenanspruch ~ *to make a claim for damages; to claim* **b.** Anspruch ~ auf etw *to enter* (od *put in*) *a claim for a th* || → Beschwerde, Einspruch, Einwand, Protest || e–e Klage ~ gegen *to bring* (od *enter, lodge*) *an action against; to claim against (a p)*; → Anklage || gegen jdn e–e falsche Beschuldigung ~ *to bring a false accusation against a p* **c.** die Hand ~ gegen *to lift (up) one's hand against* || s–e Stimme ~ *to lift up one's voice, to speak up; no one spoke; to raise one's voice (against)* || ein gr Geschrei ~ *to lift up a cry; to set up a clamour* od *a howl* **3.** etw ~ *to lift a th* (in .. *into a higher region*); etw aus der Alltäglichkeit ~ *to lift a th out of the commonplace* || e–n Antrag z Beschluß ~ *to adopt a proposal as a resolution; to carry a motion* || etw fast zur Sicherheit ~ *to strengthen a th near to certainty* || *to adopt (a proverb as motto* = zum M.) **4.** ⟨math⟩ (Zahl) in die dritte Potenz ~ *to raise to the third power, to cube*; ins Quadrat ~ *to square* **5.** ⟨off, stat⟩ *to collect, extract* **B.** (jdn) **1.** ⟨übtr⟩ **a.** *to elevate, exalt* (z *to*) || auf den Thron ~ *to raise to; to put, seat, instal on the thr.* || in den Adelstand ~ *to raise to the peerage* || er wurde zum Außenminister erhoben *he was exalted to the position of Foreign Secretary*; er wurde z Oberst erhoben *he was advanced* od *promoted to be colonel* od *to the rank of colonel; he was raised to the rank of c.* **b.** jdn aus der Dunkelheit ~ *to lift a p out of obscurity* **2.** ⟨fig⟩ (preisen) *to exalt, extol*; jdn in den Himmel ~ *to extol a p to the skies* **3.** ⟨fig⟩ *to elate; stimulate* || *to elevate; to raise to a higher moral level; to improve*; → erbauen; ergreifen **C. sich** ~ **1.** (P) **a.** ⟨eig⟩ *to get up, to rise*; (v .. *from one's chair*), *to rise to one's feet*; ⟨Am⟩ *to arise* || sich schwankend ~ *to stagger to one's feet* || (of an aeroplane) sich in die Luft ~ *to rise in the air*; ⟨aero⟩ *to lift* **b.** ⟨übtr⟩ sich ~ gegen *to rise against* (od *on*) | sich ~ aus *to rise out of (the ruck)* || sich ~ über *to rise above (a p)*; sich hoch ~ über *to tower above (all other poets)* | sich gern ~ über = sich erhaben dünken **c.** ⟨fig⟩ = sich erbauen **2.** (S) **a.** (of a building, etc.) *to lift its head; to lift (above the sea); to tower* (bis z *to*; über *above*) || sich hoch ~ *to rise to a considerable height* || *to stand out* || sich wuchtig darüber ~ *to tower above; to rise majestically above* **b.** (of wind) *to spring up*; (of gale) *to blow up* **c.** (of the voice) *to rise; to be raised; to be heard* || (of language) *to rise (to greatness)* **d.** ⟨fig⟩ (of questions) *to arise*; es erhebt sich die Frage *the question arises* (ob *whether*); (of difficulties) *to spring up*; → entstehen, eintreten **II.** ≈ n *the lifting* od *raising (of hands)*; durch ~ der Hände *by show of hands*

erh·ebend a ⟨fig⟩ *elevating (thoughts); edifying, exalting (sight)* || ~er Einfluß *lift*; (seelischer) ⟨Am⟩ *uplift*; ⟨Am⟩ *uplifting (thought)*; → ergreifend || wenig ~ *rather unpleasant (sight)*

erh·eblich 1. a *considerable (distance, weight); important, weighty (matters); grave (responsibility)* || e–e ~e Summe *a handsome, sizable, tidy sum of money; sizable (fortune); heavy (debts)* || *serious, extensive (damage)*; ⟨mil⟩ *heavy (losses), large (majority)* | [pred] *important, relevant* (f *to*) || *extensive* || das ist nicht ~ *that is of no consequence* od *importance* **2.** adv *considerably (more)* || ~ viel *a good* od *great deal of*; ⟨Am⟩ *considerable of* || ~ viele *a great many (mistakes)* || *to a considerable* (od *high*) *degree; to a great extent* || ⟨sport⟩ er ist ~ besser als .. *he is points better than ..* | **≈keit** f ~/ *consequence, importance, relevance, weight(iness), extensiveness; considerable size (of damage)*; ⟨jur⟩ *materiality*

Erh·ebung f ~/~en **A.** [abstr] **1.** ⟨eig⟩ = Erheben **2.** ⟨übtr⟩ **a.** *elevation* (jds z .. *of a p to the peerage*); *exaltation, promotion* (z Oberst *to the rank of colonel*) **b.** ⟨pol⟩ (Umbruch) *rise, upheaval; awakening (the national a.)* || (Aufstand) *rising; rebellion, revolt, uprising* **c.** *imposition, levy(ing) (of taxes)* **d.** *inquiry; investigation*; ~en über die Löhne *wage survey* || ~en anstellen über *to make inquiries about* (od *into*) *a th; to investigate* (od *inquire into*) *a th* || ⟨demog⟩ *inquiry* || ⟨off, stat⟩ *collection*; vollständige ~ *complete coverage* || statistische ~en anstellen über *to investigate* (od *deal with*) *a th statistically*; durch stat. ~en feststellen, daß .. *to prove statistically that ..* **e.** ⟨math⟩ ~ in e–e Potenz *involution*; ~ ins Quadrat *squaring* **f.** ⟨jur⟩ ~en [pl] *investigations* || ~ des Beweises *taking evidence*; ~ e–r Klage *bringing an action*, ..Zivilklage *commencement of an action*, .. öffentlichen Kl. *presentment of a true bill*, ⟨mst⟩ *filing of information*; ~ des Tatbestandes *fact-finding* **3.** ⟨fig⟩ **a.** (Lobes≈) *extolling, laudation (of a p)* **b.** (innere ~) *elation, exaltation*; ein Gefühl der ~ *a feeling of elation* || *elevation (of the mind)*; (seelische ~) *edifying effect*; ⟨Am⟩ *uplift*; → Erbauung **B.** [konkr] (Boden≈) *elevation (the highest e. of ..); rise* || ⟨geol⟩ *uplift (of the earth's surface)*; vulkanische Boden≈ *upheaval* || *rising, swelling (on the skin)* **~sbogen** m ⟨off, stat⟩ *basic document* **~sorgan** n ⟨jur⟩ *fact-finding organ*

erh·eiraten vt [h] (etw) *to acquire* (od *get, obtain*) *by marriage*

erh·eischen vt [h] (S) (Beobachtung, Sorgfalt) *to require (the work requires great care); to demand* || uneingeschränktes Lob ~ *to call for unstinted praise* || größte Aufmerksamkeit dringend ~ *to exact the closest attention* || (jds Achtung, Sympathie) ~ *to command*

erh·eitern vt [h] **1.** (Gemüt, jdn) *to brighten up; to cheer (up); to enliven, to exhilarate; to gladden* || (Gesicht) *to light up* **2. sich** ~ (of the face) *to brighten; to become cheerful; to light up*

erh·eiternd a *exhilarating, gladdening*; → ergötzlich **Erh·eiterung** f ~/~en *amusement, exhilaration*; *recreation*

erh·ellen vt/i [h] **I.** vt **1.** ⟨eig⟩ (Raum) *to illuminate*; *to light up*; → aufhellen **2.** ⟨übtr⟩ (Frage etc) *to elucidate*; *to clear up*; *to illuminate*; *clarify*; *to shed* (od *throw*) *light* (*up*)*on* (*a th*); *to hammer* (*a th*) *out* **3. sich** ~ = aufhellen 3. **II.** vi imp [nicht in zus–gesetzten Zeiten] aus s–r Angabe, hieraus erhellt, daß .. *from his statement, from this it becomes patent* (od *evident, obvious*) *that*; aus s–m Brief erhellt sehr deutlich *his l. makes it abundently clear*; wie aus .. erhellt *as becomes clear* od *patent from* **Erh·ellung** f *illumination* | ⟨übtr⟩ *elucidation*; *clearing up*

erh·eucheln vt [h] (etw) *to obtain by hyprocrisy* ‖ (vorgeben) (Gefühl) *to feign, sham, simulate* ‖ –lte Liebenswürdigkeit *artificial* (⟨fam⟩ *put on*) *charm*; *artificial, assumed* (*gaiety*); *artificial, false, crocodile* [attr] (*tears*)

erh·itzen vt [h] **1.** ⟨eig⟩ (Wasser etc) *to heat* (auf 40 Grad *to 40°*) ‖ ⟨chem⟩ bis zur Verbrennung ~ *to ignite* ‖ (Wein) ~ u würzen *to mull* **2.** ⟨übtr⟩ (jdn) *to make* (*a p*) *hot*; *to make* (*a p*) *perspire* (od *feel hot*) | erhitzt s durch, v *to be flushed* od *heated with* (*wine*; *exercise*) ‖ *to be excited with* **3.** (Blut) *to heat* ‖ (die Gemüter) *to inflame, to rouse* (*the minds* od *spirits*) | (ein Pferd) *to sweat* **4. sich** ~ **a.** *to become hot* od *warm* **b.** (of feelings) *to be roused* **c.** ⟨fig⟩ *to become angry* (über *at, about*); *to get heated* (od *excited*) (*about*); *to blaze up*; *to flush*; *to fly into a passion* **erh·itzt** a *heated* ‖ ⟨fig⟩ (P) *angry, excited, flushed, heated*; ⟨Am sl⟩ *het up* ‖ *heated, fierce* (*argument*) ‖ die Gemüter sind ~ *feeling runs high* **Erh·itzung** f *heating* ⟨a. übtr⟩

erh·offen vt [h] (etw) *to hope for* ‖ *to anticipate*; *to expect*; *to look forward to* (*a th*) **erhofft** a *hoped-for*

erh·öhen vt [h] **A.** (etw) **1.** ⟨eig⟩ (Damm) *to elevate, raise* ‖ (Turm) *to heighten* ‖ ⟨artill⟩ (Rohr) *to elevate* ‖ (Wasserspiegel) *to force up* ‖ **2.** ⟨mus⟩ e–n Ton ~ *to raise a tone in pitch*; *to r. the pitch of a tone*; (Note) um halben T. ~ *to sharp* | ⟨paint⟩ *to heighten, enliven* **3.** ⟨übtr⟩ (Zahl) *to increase*; dieser Fall erhöht die Zahl der Verwundeten auf 50 *this case brings the number of wounded to 50* ‖ (Preis) *to advance, to raise*; ⟨Am⟩ *to lift* ‖ (Summe) ⟨Am⟩ *to whoop up* (auf *to*) ‖ (Gehalt, Lohn) *to raise* (um *by*; auf *to*); ⟨Am⟩ *to lift* ‖ (Geschwindigkeit) *to increase* ‖ (Temperatur) *to raise* ‖ (Produktion) *to step up* ‖ (Leistung e–r Maschine) *to tune up* | (Zahl, Preis) um das Doppelte ~ *to double* (*the number, price, wages*, etc.) **4.** ⟨fig⟩ etw (Einfluß, Wirkung etc) *to add to a th* (*it adds to my pleasure to do*); *to increase* (*resistance*) ‖ *to enhance*; *to heighten*; *to raise* ‖ *to promote* (*speed and efficiency*) ‖ (Eindruck, Gefühl) *to deepen*; (Tätigkeit) *to intensify* ‖ (Appetit etc) *to sharpen* **B. 1.** jdn im Rang ~ *to exalt* (od *raise*) *a p in rank*; *to advance* (od *promote*) *a p to a higher rank* **2.** ⟨bib⟩ *to exalt*; → erheben B. 1. **C. sich** ~ **1.** ⟨übtr⟩ *to increase*; *to be increased* (od *raised*); die Zahl der Verwundeten hat sich auf 40 erhöht *the number of wounded has risen* (od *been brought, increased*) *to 40* ‖ sich stark *or* plötzlich ~ v 10 auf 50 *to jump from 10 to 50* **2.** ⟨fig⟩ *to be increased* (od *enhanced, intensified*) **erh·öht** a **1.** *elevated, raised* (*way*) **2.** *increased* (*speed*); ~e Löhne [pl] *higher wages* [pl] **3.** *added, heightened* (*respect, interest*); *enhanced*; *exaggerated*; *intensified* ‖ ⟨med⟩ *raised* (*temperature*) **E–hung** f ~/~en **A.** [abstr] **1.** *elevation, raising* (*of a way*) ‖ *heightening* (*of a house*) **2.** ⟨mus⟩ ~ e–s Tons *the raising of a tone in pitch*; → Kreuz **3.** ⟨übtr⟩ *increase* (*of a number, of speed*; *salary* [um *by*]); *advance* (*in prices*); (absichtlich) *raising*, (unabsichtlich) *rise* (*of prices*); ~ der Löhne *increase in wages* ‖ ⟨Am⟩ *raise* (des Gehalts *in salary*) **4.** ⟨fig⟩ *increase*; *enhancement*; → Ausweitung **B.** [konkr] *elevation*; *high ground, rise of the ground, height, hill, mound, eminence* ‖ runde ~ *nipple* ‖ → Erhebung B. **~swinkel** m ⟨mil⟩ (~ der Rohre) *elevation* **~szeichen** n ⟨mus⟩ → Kreuz

erh·olen vt & refl [h] **A.** vt **1.** sich Rats ~ bei jdm *to seek advice* od *counsed from a p* **2.** [pass] erholt s *to be recovered* (*he is not quite r.*); gut erholt zurückkehren *to return well rested* **B.** vrefl **1. sich** ~ **a.** *to get well*; *to convalesce, recuperate, recover*; *to recover o.s.*; ⟨fam⟩ *to pick* (od *perk*) *up* ‖ sich wieder ~ *to pull round*; *to recover* (od *recruit, regain*) *one's health* (od *strength*) ‖ sich ~ v *to recover from* (*a sickness*), *to come through, to come* od *get along*; sich gut, schnell ~ *to make a good, quick recovery* ‖ sich erholt h = erholt s → A. 2. **b.** (ausruhen) *to recreate*; *to indulge in recreation*; *to take a rest* **2.** ⟨übtr⟩ **a.** sich ~ v *to recover from* (*a disaster, the agitation*); sich v s–m Staunen ~ *to recover from one's astonishment* **b.** ⟨ind⟩ *to make a good recovery*; (of a country, an industry) *to recover* (v *from*); ⟨fam⟩ *to pick up* ‖ ⟨com⟩ (of prices, etc.) *to rally*; (of shares) *to rise* (auf *to*) **c.** * = sich schadlos halten **erh·olsam** a *recreative, refreshing*

Erh·olung f ~/~en **1.** *recovery* (v *from*) ⟨a. übtr⟩ **2.** (Ausruhen) *recreation*; *respite, rest* (v .. *from one's labours*) ‖ ~ finden *to find rest*; (Zerstreuung) *relaxation*; *resource* (*to find r. in* ..) sich der ~ hingeben, widmen *to relax* ‖ zur ~ fort s *to be on* (*one's*) *holiday*; z ~ gehen *to go on* (*one's*) *holiday, to take a holiday*; er ging z ~ in ein Bad *he went to a health-resort for a rest* od *holiday* (od *to recover his health*) **3.** ⟨com⟩ *recovery* (*of the market, prices*) **4.** ⟨golf⟩ *recovery*

Erh·olungs- [in comp] **~aufenthalt** m [abstr] *holiday*, ⟨Am⟩ *vacation* **~bedürfnis** n *need of recovery* **≗bedürftig** a *wanting a rest*; (höchst) ~ s *to want* (od *need, require*) *a rest* (*very badly*) **~fürsorge** f *recreation services* pl **~heim** n *convalescent home, rest centre* **~ort** m *health resort* **~pause** f *relief period*; *break* **~reise** f *pleasure trip* ‖ e–e ~ m *to take a rest*; *to go on* (*one's*) *holiday* **~stunde** f *hour of recreation*; *leisure-hour* **~übungen** f [pl] *recreative exercises* [pl] **~urlaub** m (*recreation*) *leave*; ⟨med⟩ *convalescent l.*, ⟨mil⟩ *sick-l. holiday*; *rest*; ~ antreten *to go on* (*one's*) *holiday*; ~ nehmen *to take a h.* **~zeit** f *time of recreation*; *holiday*

erh·ören vt [h] (Bitte, Gebet) *to hear, grant*; –re mein Gebet! *hear my prayer*!; sein Gebet wurde (nicht) erhört *his prayer was* (*not*) *granted* od *found a hearing* (*no. h.*) ‖ °ist dies wohl erhört? *would you think it credible* od *possible*?

Erh·örung f ~/~en *hearing*; *granting* (*of a prayer*); ~ finden *to find a hearing*

·Eriaseide f *eria silk*

·Erie n (Stadt am:) **·Eriesee** m *Lake Erie*

erig·ieren vt [h] ⟨physiol⟩ *to make erectile*

·Erika f ~/–ken ⟨bot⟩ *heath*; *Erica* [L]

er·innerlich a *recallable* (*my first r. scrap of verse*) ‖ jdm ~ s *to be remembered by a p*; soviel mir ~ ist *so far as I remember*; *within my remembrance* (*more than once within* ..) ‖ es ist mir nicht mehr ~ *it is beyond my recollection, I do not remember it, it has escaped* od *slipped my memory*

er·innern vt/i [h] **I.** vt **A.** (etw) **1.** etw ~ = sich e–r S ~ → C. **2.** etw bei jdm ~ *to put a p in mind of a th*; *to call* (od *draw*) *a p's attention to a th*; ich habe hierbei *or* hierzu vieles z ~ *I have a good deal to say to that*; dazu ist nichts z ~ *there are no objections to it* **B.** jdn ~ **1.** .. an etw *to remind a p of a th*; *to recall a th to a p*(*'s mind*); *to bring a th back to a p*; *to put a p in* *mind of a th* **2.** (die Erinnerung wachrufen an) du erinnerst mich an d–n Bruder *you remind me of your brother* || dies erinnert mich an den Streit, der .. *this makes me remember* (od *think of*) *the quarrel which* .. || dies erinnert mich, daß .. *this reminds me that* .. **C. sich e-r S** (*or* an e–e S), jds (*or* an jd) ∼ *to remember* od *recall a th, a p; to recall a th, a p to one's mind; to remind o.s. of a th, of a p* || *to recollect a th*; ⟨mst⟩ *I don't remember* aber: *I can't recollect* || *I don't rightly recollect when I saw her last*; *to call* (od *bring back*) *a th to mind*; ⟨Am a.⟩ *to remember of a th* || wir ∼ uns, Sie getroffen z h *we remember to have met you, we remember* od *recall having met you*, ⟨Am a.⟩ *we remember of having* .. || wir ∼ uns, daß er .. *we remember that he* ..; || *we r. him telling us how he did it; it is in my recollection that* .. || ich –re mich gern an .. *my memories of .. are pleasant*; sich dunkel ∼ *to remember vaguely*; er –rte sich dunkel *the memory came to him hazily*; ich –re mich jetzt daran *it comes back to me now* || wenn ich mich recht –re *if I remember rightly*; soviel wir uns ∼ konnten *to the best of our recollection*; mehr als einmal, soweit ich mich –re *more than once within my remembrance* **II.** vi **1. daran ∼, daß ..** *to call to mind* (od *to recall*) *that* .. (*he recalled that* ..) **2. ∼ an** etw (S) *to be a reminder of a th* (*the scene is a r. of the times when* ..); *to be reminiscent* (od *evocative, redolent, suggestive*) *of a th* || *the twist is suggestive of an eel* || nur entfernt ∼ an *to be only a distant reminder of* .. || *he took a note* (die ihn erinnern sollte) *to remind himself of the date* || *the view recalled to him his native village* || *the man reminded her of her first husband* || sich ∼ an: *I can still remember every detail*

er·innernd a; e–e an etw ∼e Melodie *a melody suggestive of a th*

Er·innerung f ∼/∼en **A.** [abstr] **1.** *recollection* (deutliche *distinct, clear*); *remembrance, reminiscence* (an *of*); || blasse ∼ *faint recollection* || e–e dunkle ∼ *an impression* (*I have an i. that* ..) || → Gedächtnis, Andenken 2. || wenn mich die ∼ nicht täuscht *if memory serves me*; **2.** (Mahnung) *reminder* (an *of*) **3. a.** die ∼ an .. **auslöschen** *to erase the memory of* ..; die ∼ **wachrufen** an *to be reminiscent of*; ∼en w., zurückrufen *to bring recollections to a p's mind, to revive memories* (an *of*); bei *or* in jdm ∼en w. *to draw recollections from a p*; (S, P) traurige ∼en w. *to be* (od *come as*) *an unhappy reminder*; → erinnern I. B. 2. **b. aus** der ∼ *off the map* || aus jds frühesten ∼en *from a p's earliest memories* || (etw) aus der ∼ verlieren *to forget* | sich (etw) **in** ∼ bringen *to call* (*a th*) *to mind, to recall, to remember* (*a th*); jdm etw in ∼ b. *to bring a th to a p's recollection, to recall a th to a p; to call* (od *draw*) *a p's attention to a th*; jdm in ∼ br., daß *to remind a p that* .. || jdn in empfehlende ∼ br. *to remember a p* (bei jdm *to a p*) || (etw) in der ∼ h *to have in remembrance*; etw ziemlich gut in ∼ h *to have a fair recollection of a th* (*a p*); etw noch gut in ∼ h *to remember a th still well*; etw in klarer ∼ behalten *to retain* od *have a clear memory* od *recollection of a th*; jdn in guter ∼ behalten *to keep a good rec. of a p* || in jds ∼ deutlich geblieben s *to remember .. clearly; to stand out quite clearly in a p's memory* || sich (etw) in die ∼ rufen *to call to remembrance* || es ist mir wohl in ∼ *it is within my recollection*; es ist mir nicht mehr in ∼ *it is beyond my recollection* || in ∼en schwelgen *to reminesce* || bei jdm in guter ∼ stehen *to be well remembered by a p* | (..) wo **nach** s–r ∼ der Tisch stand (*he stopped*) *where his memory told him the table stood* | → zehren | **zur** ∼ an *in remembrance* (od *commemoration, memory*) *of*; z freundlichen ∼ an .. "*to remind you of*" **B.** [konkr] ∼en [pl] ⟨Lit⟩ *recollections, reminiscences*; *memoirs* [pl]

Er·innerungs- [in comp] (→ Gedächtnis–, Gedenk–) *reminiscential* (*vision*) **∼bild** n *visual memory* od *remembrance*; ⟨psych⟩ *memory image* **∼hilfe** f *reminder* **∼kraft** f *memory*; (*power of*) *recollection* **∼lücke** f *gap in one's memory* **∼marke** f ⟨post⟩ *commemorative stamp* **∼posten** m ⟨Ger com⟩ *entry* (od *item*) *pro memoria* [L] **∼schreiben** n *written reminder*; *r. in writing* **∼spange** f ⟨mil⟩ *battle clasp* **∼vermögen** n *memory; power of recollection*

Er·innyen [pl] ⟨Gr ant⟩ *Erinyes*; *Furies* pl

Eritr·ea (Land am Roten Meer) *Eritrea*

erj·agen vt [h] (Wild) *to hunt for*; → jagen | mst ⟨übtr⟩ (etw) *to hunt for*; *to search* (od *seek*) *after, to strive for* (*a th*); → erreichen

erk·alten vi [s] (of a stove) *to get* od *grow cold, to cool* || im Tode ∼ *to die* | ⟨fig⟩ (of affection, zeal, etc.) *to cool*; *to cool down* || (etw) ∼ l *to cool* || jdn bis ins Innerste ∼ l *to strike chill to a p's marrow* || ∼de Leidenschaft *dying passion*

erk·älten vt [h] **1.** sich [dat] etw ∼ *to expose* (od *subject*) *a th to cold*; *to affect a th by cold*; *to give a th a chill*; ich habe mir den Magen erkältet *I have a cold in the stomach*; → Erkältung | erkältet s *to have a cold* **2. sich** ∼ *to catch* (od *take*) (*a*) *cold* (od *a chill*); sich stark erkältet h *to have a bad cold*; sich auf den Tod ∼ *to catch one's death of c.* **Erk·ältung** f ∼/∼en *cold*; e–e starke ∼ *a bad* (od *severe, heavy*) *c.* || sich e–e ∼ zuziehen (*or* °holen) = sich erkälten || e–e ∼ loswerden *to shake off a c.* || sich vor e–r ∼ schützen *to keep a cold out* || die ∼ hat sich auf den Magen gelegt *the cold has affected* od *attacked the stomach*

erk·ämpfen vt [h] etw ∼ *to contend* (od *fight, struggle*) *for a th*; → erringen; *to gain by force*

erk·annt pp v erkennen; *confirmed* (*battery*)

erk·aufen vt [h] ⟨übtr⟩ **1.** (Leben, Sieg) *to buy, to purchase* (mit *with*); teuer erkauft *dearly purchased* || ⟨fig⟩ *dear-bought, d.ly b.* (Sieg) **2.** (bestechen) jdn ∼ *to bribe*

erk·ennbar a *discernible, perceptible*; *distinguishable*; *recognizable*; (*no*) *perceivable* (*difference*) **∼keit** f ∼/ *discernibility*, etc.

erk·ennen vt/i [h] [→ kennen] **I.** vt **A.** (sinnlich erfassen) *to descry, detect, discover*; *to find out*; *to perceive*; *discern*; schwer z ∼ *difficult to descry* **B. 1.** (geistig) **a.** (etw) *to grasp*; *to know* (an *by*); den Baum an s–n Früchten ∼ *to know a tree by its fruits* || ⟨philos⟩ *to cognize* || *to appreciate*; *perceive*; *realize*; *see*; (Situation) *to take in*; (genau herausfinden) *to spot* (*errors, etc*); *to pick* (*a th*) *out*; etw wohl ∼ *to be alert* od *alive to a th*; ⟨Am⟩ *to be wise to a th* **b.** (jdn) *to make out*; (richtig ∼) *to size up*; ⟨fam⟩ *to tick*; ⟨sl⟩ *to rumble* || jdn erkannt h ⟨sl⟩ *to get* (od *have*) *a p taped* (*I've got your number*) || leicht erkannt w ⟨sl⟩ *to be* (od *get*) *easily taped*; man kann ihn leicht an .. ∼ *he is easily known by* ..; → durchschauen **2.** ⟨bib⟩ (im Beischlaf) *to know* (*a woman*) **2.** (wiedererkennen) (Gesicht etc) *to identify*; *to know again, to recognize* (an *by*); er erkannte mich sofort *his recognition of me was immediate* **3. a.** jdn ∼ als (*or* für) .. *to know a p for* ..; wir würden sie als solche ∼ *we should know them for themselves* **b.** ⟨com⟩ jdn f e–e Summe ∼ *to credit a p with* (od *for*) *a sum* **4. sich** ∼ *to know o.s.*; sich prüfend ∼ *to analyse o.s.* **5.** † = anerkennen **6. a.** ∼, daß .. *to know* (od *see*) *that* ..; ∼ an .., daß .. *to recognize* (od *to tell*) *by .. that* .. (*I can tell by your hands that you are young*) **b.** ⟨jur⟩ f recht (*or* z recht) ∼, daß .. *to decide that* ..; → II. **c.** (etw) **z ∼ geben, ∼ l** *to indicate, show* (*a th*; *that*); *to permit to recognize* (*that*); *to give evidence* (*of a th*; *that*); *his words make it plain* (*that*); ⟨sl⟩ *to let on* (*that* ..); durch Lächeln s–e Anerkennung über etw z ∼ geben *to smile acknowledgement of a th* ‖ jdn ∼ l, daß *to let a p see that* .. ‖ etw deutlich ∼ l *to throw a th into relief* ‖ den Charakter e–r S deutlich ∼ l (of a novel, etc.) *to strike the key-note of a th* ‖ **sich** z ∼ geben *to make o.s. known*; *to disclose one's identity, to discover o.s.* (*to a p*); *to declare o.s.* **II.** vi → I. B. 6. b.; ⟨jur⟩ auf etw ∼ *to pass sentence of* ..; auf Freisprechung ∼ (of the jury) *to return a verdict of not guilty*; auf Mord ∼ *to r. a v. of murder*; gegen jdn auf 3 Jahre Gefängnis ∼ *to sentence a p to three years' imprisonment* **III.** ≃ n ⟨bes theat⟩ *recognition*

erk·enntlich a *grateful, thankful* (jdm *to a p*) ‖ ∼ sein f etw, sich ∼ zeigen f etw *to reciprocate for a th*; *to acknowledge* (od *appreciate*) *a th*; sich ∼ zeigen *to show* (*a p*) *one's appreciation, to show o.s. grateful* (*to a p*); .. durch *or* mit *to reciprocate with* (*a th*) **|** ≃**keit** f ∼/∼en *gratefulness, gratitude, thankfulness* ‖ *acknowledgment* (f *of*) ‖ *appreciation*

Erk·enntnis 1. n –nisses/–nisse ⟨jur⟩ *decision*; *judg(e)ment, sentence* ‖ e–e ∼ auf Freisprechung *a verdict of not guilty* **2.** f ∼/–nisse *comprehension*; *knowledge* (*of the truth*); *perception*; *realization*; *recognition* ⟨a. bes theat⟩ ‖ ⟨scient⟩ wertvolle ∼se [pl] *valuable information*; (*basic*) *findings* pl **| zur** ∼ gelangen *to come to realize* ‖ z ∼ k *to hear* od *see reason, to listen to reason* **|** ⟨philos⟩ *cognition*; ∼ aus der Erfahrung *induction*, → Deduktion **∼drang** m *thirst of knowledge* **∼funktion** f ⟨philos⟩ *cognitive function* **∼grund** m *basis of cognition* od *knowledge* **∼lehre** f *epistemology* ≃**theoretisch** a *epistemological* **∼theorie** f *theory of cognition*; *epistemology* **∼vermögen** n *cognition*; *power of mental comprehension*; *intellectual power*; ⟨philos, psych⟩ *cognitive faculty*

Erk·ennung f ∼/∼en *mental comprehension*; *perception*; *realization* ‖ (Wieder≃) *identification*; *recognition* (*of a p*)

Erk·ennungs- ∼dienst m ⟨police⟩ *modus operandi* (L); *department of finger-prints*; ⟨engl⟩ *Habitual Criminals' Registry* (*Scotland Yard*) **∼karte** f *identification card* **∼marke** f ⟨mil⟩ *identification* (od *identity*) *disk*; ⟨Am⟩ *i.-tag*, ⟨sl⟩ *dog-tag* **∼merkmal** n *distinguishing mark*; *characteristic* **∼signal** n ⟨mar⟩ *recognition* od *distinguishing signal* **∼wort** n *catchword, password, watchword*; ⟨mil⟩ *parole, countersign*; (Stichwort) *test word* **∼zeichen** n *mark* od *sign of identification*; *distinctive mark*; *badge*; *countersign*; ⟨aero⟩ *aircraft markings* pl; ⟨med⟩ *symptom*

·Erker m ∼s/∼ ⟨arch⟩ *oriel*; *projecting bay* ‖ °⟨fig⟩ (Nase) *handle, beacon* **∼fenster** n *oriel* (od *bay*)*-window* **∼türmchen** n *brattice* **∼stube** f, **∼zimmer** n *oriel*

†**erk·iesen** vt [h] = (aus)erwählen

erkl·ärbar a *explainable, explicable* ‖ nicht ∼ *inexplicable* **|** ≃**keit** f ∼/ *explicability*

erkl·ären vt [h] **A.** (klar m) **1. a.** (Satz etc) *to explain*; (Text) *to expound, interpret*; (Wort) *to define*; (Rätsel) *to solve* ‖ jdm etw ∼ *to explain* (od *point out*) *a th to a p, to make a th clear to a p* ‖ → erläutern **b.** (a. S) *to account for*; das erklärt die S! *that accounts for it*! ich kann es mir nicht ∼ *I cannot account for it* **2. sich** ∼ (S) *to be explicable* (durch *by*); es läßt sich leicht ∼ *it explains itself easily*; → erläutern, zeigen **B.** (deutlich kundgeben) **1. a.** (etw) *to declare* (jdm *to a p*); (bestimmt ∼) *to pronounce* (*to a p*) ‖ s–e Bereitwilligkeit ∼ *to signify one's willingness* (*to do*) ‖ (e–e Farbe) als Trumpf ∼ *to declare* ‖ jdm den Krieg ∼ *to declare war on a p* ‖ jdm s–e Liebe ∼ *to declare one's love to a p* **b.** ∼, daß .. *to declare* (od *affirm, point out*) *that* ..; ⟨Am⟩ *to allow that*; → behaupten ‖ ∼, daß jd *or* etw ist *to declare* od *pronounce a p* od *a th to be* ‖ jdm ∼, daß .. *to tell a p that* .. **c.** ⟨mar⟩ ∼ z fahren → klarieren **2.** ich erklärte ihn f m–n Freund *I declare* od *pronounce him* (*to be*) *my friend*; jdn f e–n geeigneten Nachfolger ∼ *to vouch a p* (*as* od *to be*) *a fit successor* ‖ etw f eröffnet ∼ *to declare a th open* ‖ *he voted the two most agreeable men* ‖ ⟨med⟩ jdn f gesund ∼ *to pass a p sound* ‖ ⟨jur⟩ jdn f (un)schuldig ∼ *to bring a p in* (*not*) *guilty* ‖ in die Acht ∼ → Acht[2] **3. sich ∼ a.** sich bereit ∼ *to declare o.s. willing*; *to express o.s. as willing* (*to do*) ‖ sich deutlicher ∼ *to express* od *explain o.s. more clearly, to be more explicit* ‖ sich f besiegt ∼ → besiegen ‖ sich zum Erben ∼ *to declare o.s.* (*to be*) *the heir* **b.** sich ∼ f jdn, gegen jdn *to declare* od *pronounce for a p, against a p*; → entscheiden I. 3. a. **c.** *to declare o.s.*; *to speak one's mind*: *she hoped he would declare his love to her* **d.** †sich mit jdm ∼ = sich aussprechen **erkl·ärend** a *explanatory* (*remarks*); *explicative*; ∼e Erläuterung *comment*; ∼e Bemerkungen m z *to comment on* **|** ≃**e(r** m) f ⟨jur⟩ *declarant* **Erkl·ärer** m *commentator*; *expounder*; *interpreter*

erkl·ärlich a *accountable, explicable*; → erklärbar ‖ *obvious* ‖ es ist mir jetzt ∼, warum *now I know* (od *can see*) *why* ‖ (etw) ∼ m *to account for* (*a th*); das ist leicht ∼ *that may easily be accounted for* **∼erweise** adv *as a matter of course*

erkl·ärt a *avowed, declared* (*advocate*); *professed* (*enemy*) **∼ermaßen** adv *declaredly, professedly*

Erkl·ärung f ∼/∼en **1.** (Erläuterung) *explanation* (f etw *of a th*) ‖ *interpretation* (*of a text*); ⟨theol⟩ *exegesis* ‖ *comment* (z *on*) **|** z ∼ v, als ∼ f *in explanation of* ‖ e–e ∼ geben f etw *to give an explanation of*; *to account for a th* ‖ hier ist die ∼ f *here is the e. of* ‖ k–r ∼ bedürfen *to need no comment* **2.** (Aussage) *declaration*; auf dem Sterbebett *dying d.*; e–e (öffentliche) ∼ abgeben *to make a*(*n official*) *statement* ⟨a. jur⟩; die ∼ abgeben, daß .. *to declare that* .. ‖ öffentliche ∼ ⟨Am pol⟩ *outgiving* ‖ beteuernde ∼ *profession*; schriftliche eidliche (*or* eidesstattliche) ∼ *affidavit*; e–e eidliche ∼ abgeben über *to make an a. of* .. ‖ e–e ∼ vorbringen *to offer an explanation* **| ∼s- ∼art** f *mode* (od *way*) *of explanation* ≃**bedürftig** a *needing expl.* **∼kunst** f *art of commentation* od *interpretation*; → Hermeneutik **∼versuch** m *attempt at expl., attempted expl.*

erkl·ecklich a *considerable* (*sum*); *substantial, valuable* ‖ *lucrative*; *profitable* ‖ e–e ∼e Anzahl ⟨fam⟩ *a good few* ‖ → beträchtlich ‖ er hat auf dem Gebiete ≃es geleistet *he can boast many achievements in the field*

erkl·ettern vt [h] (Berg) *to climb, scale*

erkl·immen vt [h] [→ klimmen] **1.** ⟨eig⟩ = erklettern **2.** ⟨fig⟩ höchste Stufen e–r S ∼ *to climb*, od *to scale the height of a th* ‖ (S) den Höhepunkt ∼ *to reach its culminating point* (*in*)

erkl·ingen vi [s] [→ klingen] (of the bell, intrument, etc.) *to* (*re*)*sound, ring* (*out*); (of music) *to roll out* ‖ hell ∼ *to tinkle*; laut ∼ *to clang* **|** (etw) ∼ l *to ring, sound*; *tinkle*; ein Lied ∼ l *to strike up a s.*; jds Lob ∼ l *to resound a p's praises*

erkl·ügeln vt [h] = austüfteln, –denken

erk·oren [pp v erkiesen] a (*s*)*elect, chosen*

erkr·anken vi [s] *to fall ill*; *to be taken ill* (an *with*); lebensgefährlich –kt *dangerously ill*; s–e r. L. ist –kt *his right lung has been affected* **Erkr·ankung** f ∼/∼en *falling ill*; *illness* (*of a p*) ‖ *disease* (*of the glands*) ‖ *affection* **|** ∼shäufigkeit [f] *morbidity* ‖ ∼sziffer [f] *incidence rate*

erk·ühnen vrefl [h] sich ∼ z tun *to presume* od *venture to do*; *to be* od *make bold to do*; *to have the audacity to do*; → erdreisten ‖ sich ∼ z sagen *to say boldly* || was –nst du dich! *how dare you!*

erk·unden vt [h] (Land) *to explore; spy out* || ⟨mil⟩ (Gebiet) *to reconnoitre*; (Stellung) *to locale, spot* || ⟨übtr⟩ *to search out; to reconnoitre*

erk·undigen vrefl [h] sich ~ *to inquire; to make inquiries* || sich ~ **nach** etw *to inquire a th* (bei jdm *of a p*); *to inquire for a th, about* (*the price*); er erkundigte sich bei ihr nach dem Wege *he inquired of her the way* (*to* ..), *he asked her the way* (*to* ..) || sich nach jdm (*or* jds Befinden) ~ *to inquire* od *ask after a p* || er ließ sich nach m–m B. ~ *he sent to inquire after me* | sich ~ **über** *to inquire about* (*a th*) || sich bei jdm über jdn (*or* jds Eignung etc) ~ *to make inquiries of a p on* (od *about*) *a p's qualification* | **sich ~, ob ..** *to inquire whether*

Erk·undigung f ~/~en *inquiry*; ~en [pl] *inquiries* [pl], *information* || ~en einziehen *or* einholen *to gather information; to make inquiries* (bei jdm über etw *of a p on* [od *about*] *a th*)

Erk·undung f ~/~en *exploration; location;* **reconnoitre* || ⟨mil⟩ *reconnaissance, reconnoitring*, (⟨fam⟩ *recon*) || *spotting* || Fern≃ *long distance reconnaissance*, Nah≃ *short d. r.*; Luft≃ *aerial spotting* **Erk·undungs-** [in comp] *reconnaissance, reconnoitring, spotting* **~fahrt** f ⟨Am mar sl⟩ *snoop cruise* **~flieger** m *spotter* **~flugzeug** n *scout; spotting-aeroplane* **~offizier** m *spotting officer*

erk·ünstelt a *affected; artificial, constraint, forced* (*laugh, smile*) **Erk·ünstelung** f ~/ *affectation, artifice*

†**erk·üren** vt [h] [→ küren] = erkiesen

†**erl·aben** vrefl [h] sich ~ = sich erquicken

Erl·ag m [österr] ≃e pl = Depositen **~schein** m [österr] = Zahlkarte

erl·ahmen vi [s] **1.** *to become lame* **2.** ⟨fig⟩ **a.** (P) ~ in *to relax* od *slacken in* (*one's efforts*) **b.** (of action, business) *to slacken; diminish* **c.** (of interest, etc) *to flag, languish, wilt; die* **d.** ⟨mil⟩ (of attack) *to lose momentum*

erl·angbar a *obtainable; attainable* | **≃keit** f *procurability*

Gent n (belg. Stadt) *Ghent*

erl·angen vt [h] ⟨übtr⟩ [nur mit abstr Objekten: Achtung, Freiheit, Gnade etc] *to get, to obtain* || (erreichen) *to attain, to attain to; to achieve, acquire, gain; reach*; Macht ~ *to attain to power*; Vergebung der Sünden ~ *to gain remission* || etw (Glück, Ruhm etc) z ~ suchen *to reach after a th*; Beliebtheit z ~ suchen *to make a bid for popularity* || etw [konkr] ~ *to secure a th*; es war schwer z ~ *it was hard to come by* **Erl·angung** f ~/ *attainment; acquisition; getting, reaching*

Erl·aß m Erlasses/Erlasse **1.** (→ erlassen 1.) **a.** (Befreiung) *dispensation* (e–r S *from* od *with a th*); *discharge* (od *exemption, release*) (e–r S *from a th*); *remission* (e–r S *of a th* [*of a debt; of a punishment, of sins*]) || → Ablaß **b.** (Nachlaß) *remission* (*of taxes*); → Nachlaß **2.** (→ erlassen 2.) **a.** = Erlassung 2. **b.** (Erlassenes) *decree, edict, enactment, issue, ordinance; order*; königlicher (*or* behördlicher) ~ *writ*; ⟨engl⟩ königl. ~ ohne Parlamentsbefragung *Order in Council*; ⟨Am⟩ ~ des Präsidenten (ohne Kongreßgenehmigung) *Executive Order*

erl·assen vt [h] [→ lassen] **1.** (Strafe, Sünden; Steuern) *to remit*; jdm .. ~ *to exempt a p from ..* || (Eid, Verpflichtung) *to dispense with* | jdm etw ~ *to excuse a p a th* (*they excused him the fee*); *to forgive* (*debt*); *to release a p from a th*, → befreien; ihm wurde die Gebühr ~ *he was excused the fee*; mir wurde die Aufgabe ~ *I was excused the task* (od *from the task*) || jdm die Strafe ~ *to pardon a p* **2.** (Gesetz) *to enact; to put through*; (Verordnung) *to issue, to promulgate, to publish*

erl·äßlich a *remissible* (*fine*); *dispensable* (*oath*); *pardonable, venial* (*sin*) || (entbehrlich) *dispensable; omissible* | **≃keit** f ~/ *remissibility* (*of a fine*); *dispensability; pardonableness*

Erl·assung f ~/~en **1.** = Erlaß 1. **2.** *enactment* (*of a law*); *passage* (*of a bill*); *promulgation, publication* (*of an order*)

erl·auben vt [h] **A. etw ~ 1. a. (P)** *to allow, permit, suffer, tolerate*; Rauchen ist hier nicht –bt *smoking is not allowed here* | [abs] ~ Sie, bitte *allow me; look here, please* || Sie ~ doch? *I hope you don't mind*, ⟨Am fam⟩ (*do you*) *mind?* || in der Liebe ist alles –bt ⟨Am fam⟩ *anything* od *everything goes in love* || wenn Sie ~ *by your permission* (od *leave*) **b. (S)** *to permit; to allow* (od *admit, permit*) *of* (*a th*); so weit es die Gesundheit –bt *so far as health permits*; wenn es die Zeit –bt hätte *if time had permitted*; wenn es die Z., das Wetter –bt *time, weather permitting* || meine Mittel (*or* Verhältnisse) ~ das nicht *I cannot afford it* | ⟨tech⟩ *to provide for* (*being stretched, etc*) **2. wir ~, daß** du gehst *we allow you to leave* || er –bte, daß das Buch gedruckt wurde *he allowed the book to be printed; he gave permission for the book to be printed* **B. 1. jdm etw ~** *to allow* od *permit a p to do*; jdm e–e Frage, den Eintritt ~ *to allow a p to ask, to enter* || jdm den Zutritt z e–r Bibliothek ~ *to make a p free of a library*; man –be mir nur einige Beispiele *permit me* (od *let me be permitted; I beg leave*) *to add only a few examples* **2. jdm ~ z tun** *to allow* od *permit a p to do*; es wurde mir –bt *I was allowed* od *permitted* (*to do*); ihm wurde –bt auszugehen *he was allowed out* **3. a. sich etw ~** *to allow* od *permit o.s. a th; to indulge* (*o.s.*) *in a th* || sich den Luxus ~ .. z s *to allow o.s. the luxury of being ..*; darf ich mir die Frage ~, wo ..? *may I ask where ..?* sich Freiheiten jdm gegenüber ~ *to take liberties with a p*; was ~ Sie sich! *how dare you!* || das kann ich mir nicht ~ *I cannot afford that* **b. sich ~ z tun**; *to permit o.s. to do; to venture* (od *take leave*) *to do; to take the liberty of doing*; wenn ich mir ~ dürfte *if I might venture* || ⟨com⟩ wir ~ uns, Sie zu benachrichtigen *we beg* (*leave*) *to inform you*; .. beizufügen *we beg to enclose* || sich ~ z sagen *to take leave to say* || ich erlaube mir (sc auf Ihr Wohl z trinken)! *your health, Sir!*

Erl·aubnis f ~/ **1.** *permission* (*to do*); (gewählt:) *leave* (*to do*) | **mit** ~ .. (gedruckt) *by courtesy*; mit Ihrer ~, bitte *by your leave, please*; mit ~ v jdm *by* (od *with*) *perm. of, with the leave of* (*a p*); *by* od *with a p's perm.*; mit besonderer ~ *by special perm.*; mit m–r ausdrücklichen ~ *by my leave and perm.* || e–e ~ auszugehen *a leave out*; e–e ~ fortzugehen *a leave off* | **um** ~ bitten *to ask leave* || jdn um ~ bitten *to ask a p's permission, to ask a p for perm.* (*to do*) || v jdm die ~ erhalten *to obtain a p's perm., to obtain perm. from a p* (*to do*) || jdm die ~ erteilen z tun *to give a p perm. to do, to give perm. for a p to do*; die ~ erteilen, daß etw geschieht *to give perm. for a th to be done* || die ~ h *to be at liberty, to be allowed* od *permitted to do* **2.** (behördliche ~) *licence* (*–nse*) || Ehe≃ *licence*; e–e ~, z jeder Zeit ohne Aufgebot z heiraten *a special licence* || ~, e–n Hund z halten *dog licence* **~schein** m (behördlicher) *permit; licence* (*–nse*); ~ f Radio *wireless licence*

erl·aubt a *permissible* || ⟨jur⟩ *legal* (*abortion*) || nicht ~ *off-limit* (*area*), [pred] *off-limits* | **≃heit** f *permissibility* (*of an argument*)

erl·aucht a *illustrious* (*lineage*); *exalted; noble*

·Erlaucht f ⟨Ger⟩ (ehemal. Titel f Reichsgrafen) Euer ~ *Your Lordship; Your Grace*

Erl·auchtheit f *illustriousness*

erl·auschen vt [h] (etw) *to get to know .. by listening intently, .. by careful observation*; *to learn by overhearing people*

erl·äutern vt [h] *to make clear*; *to clear up, to elucidate*; (S) *to show, depict, demonstrate, explain, illustrate*; *to be illustrative of*; → erklären ‖ durch Beispiele ~ *to exemplify, to illustrate*; → veranschaulichen

erl·äuternd a *elucidative, elucidatory*; *illustrative gesture*; ~e Figur *or* Zeichnung *diagram, graph* **Erl·äuterung** f ~/~en *elucidation, illustration*; (durch Beispiele) *exemplification*; z ~ v *in exemplif.* od *illustr. of* ‖ → Erklärung

·Erle f ~/~n ⟨bot⟩ *alder*

erl·eben I. vt [h] **1. (P)** (etw) *to experience, see, witness*; *have*; *know* (*he has known deep desolation*); *to prove*; *to see* (*we have seen great changes*; *did you ever see the likes of it*?) er sagte, er hätte nie e–e solche Stunde –bt *he said he never had* (⟨Am⟩ *struck*) *such an hour*; sie hatte nie –bt, daß er so etwas tat *she had never known him do such a thing* ‖ *to witness* (*I did not w. the incident*); wir ~ e–e gr Zeit *we are witness*(*es*) *of a great time*; wir w es nicht ~ *we shan't live to see it*; (es freut mich,) es –bt z h .. *to have lived as long* ‖ er –bte es selbst, erpreßt z w *he lived to be blackmailed himself* ‖ so: *he would live to be hanged* ‖ e–e Krise ~ *to live through a crisis*; (Kunst) *to sink o.s. in a work of art*; (Liebe:) *the love she had held for him*; e–n Rückschlag ~ *to sustain a set-back*; Schlimmes ~ *to be through a bad time* ‖ ⟨fam⟩ (*you'll*) *be in for* (*a big disappointment*); allerhand –bt h *to have been around*; er hat viel –bt *a lot happened to him* ‖ wenn .., kannst du was ~! *if .., you will have cause to regret it* od *you'll be in for it*! → durchmachen **2. (S)** *to see, witness*; die letzten 20 Jahre h e–n gr Fortschritt erlebt *the last 20 years have seen a notable advance* ‖ (of a book) e–e zweite Auflage ~ *to go into* (od *to reach*) *a new edition*; viele Auflagen ~ *to go* (od *run*) *through many editions* **II.** ∼̂ n: beim ~ v 70 Jahren *surviving to the age of 70* **|** ~sfall [m] → Erlebnisfall **|** **∼̂de(r** m) f ⟨stat, demog⟩ (nicht) ledig das Alter v xy –de [pl] *single*, (*ever-married*) *survivors*

Erl·ebnis n –nisses/–nisse *experience*; *episode, event, occurrence*; –nisse [pl] *experiences, doings* [pl]; ein gr ~ *a great adventure* (f jdn *to a p*); ein aufregendes ~ *a thrill* ‖ ein ~ h *to have an experience* ‖ es wurde ihm z e–m tiefen ~ *he was deeply affected* od *impressed by it* ‖ ~religion *experimental religion* **|** im **~fall** m zahlbar ⟨ins⟩ (*sum*) *payable if insured survives* **erl·ebt** a *true* (*story*), *real* (*life*) **|** **∼̂es** n *actual* od *personal experience*

erl·edigen vt [h] **1.** etw ~ **a.** (Geschäfte, Streit etc) *to adjust, arrange, settle*; *handle, manage, negotiate*; (ausführen) *to do* (*have you done your writing*?); *to attend to*; *to deal with*; *to dispose of*; *to effect*; *to execute*; *to clear* (*e.g. a triptique*) ‖ die Briefe ~ *to get the letters done, to finish with the l.*; *to get the l. off*; Fragen ~ *to answer questions*; die Post ~ *to get* od *go through the mail*; es wird erledigt w *it will be attended to*; e–e S ~ *to get over a th*; e–e S z ~ h *to have a th on hand*; was zuerst z ~ ist *what to put one's hands to first*; z ~de Kleinigkeiten *loose ends* **b.** endgültig ~ *to clinch*; damit ist die S –gt *that clinches the matter*; damit ist alles –gt *that's all there is to it*; das wäre –gt *and that was that* ‖ etw selbst ~ *to see to a th o.s.* ‖ e–e Vorstellung ~ *to kill a notion* ‖ (etw) endgültig ~ *to set .. at rest*; *to close* **|** (etw) leicht ~ *to turn off* ‖ eiligst ~ *to rush* ‖ schnell ~ *to dispatch, to finish* (od *polish*) *off*; *to mop*; *to shuffle through* (*a th*); ⟨fam⟩ *to knock* od *toss .. off* (*problems*); ⟨Am⟩ *to dash .. off* **|** ° die Sache gründlich ~ *to go the whole hog* **|** kz ~ *to dismiss*; *to dispose of*; die neue Literatur wird auf einigen Seiten –gt *the new literature is disposed of* (od *dismissed*) *in a few pages* **2. a. jdn ~** ⟨sport⟩ *to account for a p*; *to dispose of a p*; *to finish a p off* (mit *with*); (durch e–n Schlag) *to double a p up* ‖ ⟨box⟩ *to knock out* **b.** ⟨übtr⟩ (ruinieren) ⟨vulg⟩ *to do a p's job for him*; *to dish*, ⟨sl⟩ *skunk a p, to polish off a p*; er wird bald erledigt s *he will soon come to the end of his tether*; er ist total erledigt *he is done for* (od *played out*); ⟨Am fam⟩ *he's all washed up* ‖ sie ist ein f allemal erledigt *her goose is cooked* ‖ Frauen waren f ihn –gt *he was through with women*; → erledigt A. **3. sich ~**: damit ~ sich wohl die Hoffnungen derer, die .. *this disposes of the hopes of those who ..*; damit erledigt sich die S *that clinches the matter* ‖ der zweite Punkt der Frage erledigt sich *the second point of the question does not arise* ‖ dieses hat sich erledigt *this is finished* **erl·edigt** a **A.** [pred] **1.** (abgetan) → erledigen 1. b. ‖ er ist f mich ~ ⟨fam⟩ *I've finished with him, I've had enough of him, I'm fed up with him* **2.** (unfähig gemacht) *down and out*; (*I'm*) *dead-beat*, (*I'm*) *done up* od *for* (⟨a.⟩ = erschöpft); ⟨Am fam⟩ (*I'm*) *all in*; (*I was*) *nowhere*; ⟨sl⟩ *he's cooked* (od *washed-up*); → erledigen 2.; ⟨pol, etc⟩ „Fall, Sache ~" *closed file* **B.** [attr] †e–e ~e Stelle *a vacancy* **Erl·edigung** f ~/~en **1.** *arrangement, settlement*; *management* ‖ *disposal*; *execution*; in ~ Ihres Auftrages *in pursuance of your commission*; in ~ Ihres Briefes *in reply to your letter* ‖ kz oberflächliche ~ *patch-up* ‖ ⟨com⟩ schnelle ~ (*quick*) *dispatch* ‖ etw an jdn zur ~ weitergeben *to pass a th to a p for attention* od *to deal with* **2.** *doubling up* (*of a p*); *finishing off* ‖ schnelle ~ *massacre* (*of opponents*)

erl·egen vt [h] **1.** ⟨hunt⟩ *to catch, capture*; *kill*; *bag* ‖ der Bär war v s–r Büchse –legt worden *the bear had fallen to his gun* **2.** (Geld) *to pay down* **Erl·egung** f ~/ **1.** *catch*; *capture*; *killing*; *bagging* **2.** *paying down*; *payment*

erl·eichtern vt [h] **A. 1.** ⟨eig⟩ *to lighten* ‖ ⟨med⟩ (Darm) *to unload* **2.** ⟨übtr⟩ °jdm die Taschen ~ *to ease* (od *deprive*) *a p of his purse*; °jdn um etw ~ *to ease a p of a th* **3.** ⟨fig⟩ **a.** jdn ~ *to lift a pressure from a p*; jdm das Herz ~ (*or* jds H.) ~ *to ease* od *relieve a p* (v *from*); *to ease* od *relieve a p's mind*; *to lift a burden from a p's heart*; (jds Los) *to alleviate* ‖ (Druck, Lage) *to ease* (*off*), *to relieve*; (Lasten) *to lighten*; → entspannen ‖ erleichtert aufatmen *to breathe freely* **b. sich ~** *to unload o.s.*; *to relieve one's mind, to unburden o.s.* (⟨a.⟩ sich [dat] das Herz ~) **B.** [nur mit Sachobj.] etw (Arbeit etc) ~ *to facilitate a th*; jdm die Arbeit ~ *to facilitate a p's work*; *to afford working facilities for a p*; *to help a p forward*; *to facilitate* (*payment*) **erl·eichtert** a ⟨fig⟩ ~ s *to be easier in one's mind* ‖ ~ rufen, ausrufen *to cry out with relief* **Erl·eichterung** f ~/~en **1.** *alleviation*; *facilitation*; *ease* (v *from*); *relief* (über *at*; v *from*); *respite* ‖ e–m Kranken ~ verschaffen *to give a patient ease*; *to respite a patient* **2. a.** (Erleichtern) *facilitation* **b.** *facility* [mst pl] ~en *facilities* [pl]

erl·eiden vt [h] [→ leiden] (ertragen) *to suffer, endure*; *bear* ‖ *to sustain* (*a defeat, a setback, a loss*); Verluste ~ *to lose* (durch jdn *by a p*); → durchmachen, erfahren; → Einbuße; Schiffbruch ~ *to be shipwrecked*; den Tod auf dem Schlachtfeld ~ *to be killed in the battle-field* das Schiff erlitt ernsten Maschinendefekt *the ship developed serious engine-trouble*

·erlen a ⟨bot⟩ *alder* **·Erlen-** [in comp] *alder* **~bruch** m & n *alder-swamp* **~busch** m *alder-grove* **~dickicht** n *alder-brake* **~meyerkolben** m *erlenmeyer flask* **~wald** m *alder-wood*

erl·ernbar a *learnable* **erl·ernen** v [h] (etw) *to learn*; (Geschicklichkeit etc) *to acquire*; *to take to* (*a th*) || leicht z ~(d) *easy* (*to learn*) **Er-l·ernung** f ~/ *learning*; *acquisition* (*of a skill*)

erl·esen vt [h] [→ lesen] **1.** ×(auswählen) *to select*; *choose*; *pick* **2.** *to acquire by reading*

erl·esen a [pp v ~ 1.] *elect*, *select*; *choice*, (*fruit*), *picked*; *exquisite*; *precious*

erl·euchten vt [h] **1.** ⟨eig⟩ (Raum etc) *to light*(*en*); *to illumin*(*at*)*e*; festlich ~ *to illuminate* || erleuchteter Himmel *lighted sky*; hell erleuchtet v (*a room*) *bright with* (*many lamps*) **2.** ⟨fig⟩ (jdn) *to enlighten*; *illumin*(*at*)*e*; → begeistern || erleuchtet v *alight with* (*the knowledge that* ..) ⟨hist rel⟩ –tete Schwärmer [pl] *illuminati* [L]

Erl·euchtung f ~/~en **1.** *illumination* (*of a room*) **2.** ⟨fig⟩ (religiöse) *illumination*; *inspiration* || (geistige) *enlightenment* || die ~ kam ihm *he saw* (*the*) *light*

erl·iegen **1.** vi [s] [→ liegen] *to go under*; *to succumb* || jdm *to succumb to a p*; *to fall a victim to a p* || *he fell a v.* (*they fell v.s*) *to the plague*; *he fell v. to his passion, a v. to her charms* || s–n Verletzungen ~ *to succumb to one's injuries*; der Versuchung ~ *to succumb to a temptation* || der Gewalt ~ *to yield to force* || drei Löwen erlagen s–r Flinte *three lions fell to his rifle* **2.** ≃ n ⟨tech⟩ *dead-lock* || ⟨min⟩ z ~ k (of a mine) *to be closed down*

erl·ischt [3. sg prs] v erlöschen

erl·isten vt [h] (etw) *to obtain by artifice*

·Erlkönig m ⟨Ger myth⟩ *Erl-king*; (Elfenkönig) *king of the elves*

erl·ogen a [pp v erlügen] *false*, *untrue*; die Geschichte ist °erstunken u ~ *the story is cut* od *manufactured out of whole cloth*

Erl·ös m Erl·öses/ *proceeds* [pl], *takings* [pl]; gemeinsamer ~ *melon*, *melons* [pl]

erl·oschen [pp v erlöschen] a **1.** ⟨eig⟩ *extinguished*; *extinct*, *non-active*, *burnt-out* (*volcano*); das Licht ist ~ *the light is out* **2.** ⟨übtr & fig⟩ *extinct* (*passion*; *custom*); *dead* (*past*); (*the last hope was*) *extinct* || *dull* (*colour*) || in ihm ist jedes Gefühl f .. ~ *he is dead to all sense of* .. || sein Haß ist ~ *hatred has gone out of his heart*

erl·öschen **I.** vi [s] [3. sg prs erlischt/pret erlosch/pp erloschen] **1.** ⟨eig⟩ (of fire, etc) *to be extinguished*; *to go out* **2.** ⟨übtr & fig⟩ **a.** (of eyes) *to become dim* od *lifeless*; *dying* (*eye*) **b.** (of life, passion) *to be extinguished*; *to become extinct*; (of feelings, traces) *to be effaced* (od *obliterated*); *to fade*; → verschwinden **c.** (of customs, etc) *to cease to exist*, *to go* (od *to pass*) *out of use*; (of interest) *to die out*; (of a family) *to die off* || das Geheimnis erlosch mit ihm *the secret died with him* **d.** (of a right, etc) *to expire*, *to be extinguished*, erloschen ⟨ins⟩ *expired* (*policy*); (of a grant) *to lapse* **II.** ≃ n **1.** *extinction* (*of a fire*) **2.** ⟨übtr & fig⟩ *extinction* (*of a passion, hope; race*); *effacement* (*of a feeling*); *fading* || *expiration* (*of a right*); *expiry* (*of a period, truce, etc*)

erl·ösen vt [h] **1.** ⟨ec⟩ (jdn) *to deliver*, *redeem*, *save* (v *from*); erlöse uns v dem Übel *deliver us from evil*; aus der Verdammnis ~ *to save from damnation* **2.** ⟨übtr⟩ (jdn, Gefangenen etc) ~ *to deliver*, *redeem*, *relase*, *rescue*; jdn v (*or* aus) etw ~ *to release* (od *deliver*) *a p from a th*; jdn v e–m Fluch ~ *to break a curse on a p*; → loskaufen || er ist v s–n Leiden erlöst *his sufferings are over* || das ~de Wort *the relieving word* || das erlöste Geld *the proceeds* [pl], *the money realized* (*from business*)

Erl·öser m ~s/~ *deliverer*, *redeemer* || ⟨bib⟩ der ~ *the Redeemer*, *the* od *our Saviour*

Erl·ösung f ~/~en **1.** ⟨ec⟩ *Redemption* (v *from*); *salvation* **2.** ⟨übtr⟩ *deliverance*, *release* (v *from*); die Stunde der ~ *the hour of deliverance* **~swerk** n ⟨ec⟩ *the work of redemption*

erl·ügen vt [h] [→ lügen] (etw) *to invent* od *fabricate lyingly*; → erlogen

erm·ächtigen vt [h] jdn ~ *to authorize* od *empower a p* (*to do*); er wurde zur Unterzeichnung der Urkunde –gt *he was authorized to sign the document* || –gt s *to be authorized* od *empowered*; *to have authority* (*to do*); zu etw –gt s *to be licensed to a th* | **sich** ~ = sich erdreisten **E–gung** f ~/~en *authorization* (v jdm *from a p*); *authority*, *warrant* (z *for*); auf Grund m–r ~ *in virtue of my authority* || jdm die ~ erteilen (z tun) = jdn ermächtigen; jdm die ~ erteilen, als Arzt zu praktizieren *to license a p to practise as a doctor* **~sgesetz** n ⟨engl⟩ (1920) *Enabling Act* (od *Bill*) (das der C. E. weite Befugnisse der Selbstverwaltung gab) || ⟨Ger⟩ *law empowering the Government to enact laws on their own authority*; *Emergency Powers Act*

erm·ahnen vt [h] (jdn) *to admonish*, *exhort*, *warn* || jdn ~ z tun *to admonish* (od *exhort*, *urge*) *a p to do* || jdn ~ z etw *to exhort a p to a th*; jdn zur Zahlung ~ *to urge a p to pay*; zum Gehorsam, zur Mäßigkeit ~ *to exhort a p to obedience* (od *to be obedient*), *to temperance* (od *to be temperate*); (streng:) *aunt dared us to make any noise* (k–n Lärm z m) **erm·ahnend** a *admonitory*, (*ex*)*hortative*, (*ex*)*hortatory*; *monitorial*

Erm·ahner m ~s/~ *monitor*; *admonisher* **Er-m·ahnung** f ~/~en *admonition*, *exhortation*

Erm·ahnungs- [in comp] = ermahnend **~rede** f *admonitory discourse*; *exhortation* **~schreiben** n ⟨ec⟩ *hortatory letter*

erm·angeln vi [h] **1.** [gen] (S) **a.** (P) *to be short of a th*; sie –lten der Nahrung (†es –lte ihnen an N.) *they were short of food*; *food failed them* **b.** (P & S) *to lack* od *want a th*; *to be lacking* od *wanting in a th*; er –lt des Mutes (†es –lt ihm an Mut) *he lacks* od *wants courage*, *he is lacking* od *wanting in courage*; das Stück –lt der Einheit (†es –lt dem St. an E.) *the play fails in unity*, *the play lacks unity* || e–r Eigenschaft ~ *to be void of a quality*; eine Landschaft, die aller Schönheit –lt *a landscape void of all beauty* **c.** er –lte nicht, ihr z schreiben *he did not fail to write to her* **2.** †es –lt (uns) an etw = es fehlt an **3.** †es ~ l an = es fehlen l an

Erm·angelung f ~/ ⟨jur⟩ *failure* (*of issue*) [fast nur in der Verbindung:] in ~ e–r S *in default of a th*; *failing a th*; in ~ dieser Dinge *failing these things*; in ~ e–s anderen Mittels nahm er .. *failing of any other remedy he took* ..; in ~ des Weins *failing wine* || .. (e–s Dienstsiegels) *in the absence of* .. || *in the absence of any further information* || in ~ dessen *failing this*; *in default hereof*; *failing which* od *which failing* || in ~ e–s Besseren *for want of a better*; *faute de mieux* (Fr)

erm·annen vrefl [h] sich ~ *to man o.s.*; *to pull o.s. together*; *to take heart* (*of grace*); *to take courage*; *to pluck up courage* od *heart* || *to recover* od *brace o.s.* || *to regain one's self-control* || sich z etw ~ *to man o.s. to a th*; sich ~ z tun *to will o.s.* od *to bring o.s. to do*

erm·äßigen vt [h] (Preise etc) *to abate*, *reduce* || zu ermäßigten Preisen *at reduced prices* od *rates* || ermäßigter Fahrpreis *reduced fare*; z ermäßigtem F. *at a reduced f.* **Erm·äßigung** f ~/~en *discount*, *abatement*, *reduction* (der Kosten *in the cost*); *rebate* || gr ~en [pl] ⟨fam⟩ *big cuts* (*in prices*) || e–e ~ bewilligen (*or* eintreten l) *to make a reduction* || ~ bei Mengenabnahme *discount for quantities*

erm·atten vi/t **A.** vi [s] **1.** (P) **a.** *to tire*, *flag* (vor *with*); *to become exhausted* (od *tired*, *weary*); → erlahmen **b.** ⟨übtr⟩ ~ in etw *to release* (od *slacken*) *in a th* **2.** ⟨fig⟩ **a.** (of colours) *to fade* **b.** (of action) *to slacken* **c.** (of interest, etc.) *to* *flag, languish, wilt* **B.** vt [h] (jdn) *to fatigue, tire; exhaust*; ermattet niederfallen *to sink exhausted on the ground*

Erm·attung f ~/ *lassitude, tiredness; exhaustion; faintness* **~sstrategie** f *exhaustion* (od *attrition*) *-strategy*

erm·essen vt [h] (→ messen) (abschätzen) *to calculate, compute, estimate* ‖ *comprehend, realize* ‖ *to fathom* (*the sorrow*) ‖ ⟨jur⟩ (beurteilen) *to estimate, judge*; ~ aus .., daß .. *to conclude from .. that ..* ‖ das läßt sich leicht ~ *that is easily estimated; that is easy to understand*; sich nicht ~ l *to be inestimable; to be past estimation*; das *or* es läßt sich nicht ~ *there is no way of telling, knowing*

Erm·essen n ~s/ *estimate; estimation, judg(e)ment;* (*judicial*) *discretion*; [nur in folg. Wendungen]: nach eigenem (*or* freiem) ~ *at discretion*; nach eigenem ~ handeln *to use one's own discretion* ‖ nach m–m ~ *in my opinion* (od *estimation*); *as I see it* ‖ nach billigem ~ entscheiden ⟨e.g. contr⟩ *to decide what is fair and reasonable* ‖ nach menschlichem ~ *to judge by* (od *from*) *human standards* ‖ dem ~ jds überlassen bleiben *to be left to the discretion of a p* ‖ in jds ~ liegen *or* stehen *to lie* (od *to be*) *within the d. of a p* ‖ ich stelle es in dein ~ *I leave it to your d.* **~sbefugnisse** n pl ⟨jur⟩ *discretionary powers* **~smißbrauch** m ⟨jur⟩ *abuse of discretion* **~srecht** n *discretionary power*

erm·itteln vt [h] (etw, jdn) *to ascertain, detect, discover; to find out*; Tatsachen ~ *to find facts* ‖ nicht z ~ s *to escape* (od *baffle*) *detection* ‖ ~, daß .. *to ascertain that*; v jdm (*or* durch jdn) ~, daß *to ascertain from a p that ..*

Erm·itt(e)lung f ~/~en *ascertainment, detection, discovery* ‖ *inquiry, investigation, research*; ~en [pl] *inquiries; information*; ~en anstellen *to make inquiries* (bei jdm über etw *of a p on* [od *about*] *a th*) ‖ ~ der Schadenbearbeitungskosten *allocating the claim adjustment expenses* **~sbeamter** m *investigator* **~shilfe** f ⟨Ger jur⟩ *institution to find out the facts conducive to the formation of a considered opinion on an accused* **~sverfahren** n ⟨jur⟩ (*preliminary inquiry into a criminal case previous to the accusation*) *judicial inquiry*

G·enua n ⟨It⟩ (Stadt) *Genoa* **Meerbusen v** ~ *Gulf of Genoa* **Genu·ese** m, **Genu·eserin, Genu·esin** f *Genoese* **genu·esisch** a *Genoese*

erm·öglichen vt [h] (etw) *to render* (od *make*) *possible* (od *feasible, easy*); *to enable* (*it enables the inclusion of ..*) ‖ jdm die Durchführung e–r S ~ *to enable a p to perform a th*; jdm ~ z tun *to enable a p to do* ‖ ~, daß etw geschieht *to enable a th to be done*; ~, daß etw benutzt wird *to allow* od *permit a th to be used* (*for ..*); der Verkauf ermöglichte, daß Ermäßigungen der Unkosten gemacht wurden (*or* .. ermöglichte Ermäßigungen der U.) *the sale enabled reductions to be made in the cost*

erm·orden vt [h] (jdn) *to murder*; (meuchlerisch) *assassinate* ‖ der Ermordete *the murdered man; the murderee* **Erm·ordung** f ~/~en *murder*; (jds durch jdn *of a p by a p*); *assassination*

erm·üden vi/t **1.** vi [s] (P) *to tire* (vor *with*); *be become exhausted* (od *tired, weary*) ‖ ⟨übtr⟩ ~ in etw *to relax* (od *slacken*) *in a th* **2.** vt [h] **a.** (jdn) *to fag, fatigue; knock up; tire; weary; to strain* (*the eyes*) ‖ ermüdet s *to be fagged* (*out*), *to be worn* (v *with*) ‖ sich ~ *to tire* od *fag o.s.* **b.** ⟨übtr⟩ (jdn) *to weary* (durch *or* mit *with*); *to wear out; to bore* **c.** [abs] (S) *to be fatiguing*; diese Arbeit –det sehr *this work is very fatiguing* ‖ es –det sehr z tun *it is very tiring to do* ‖ ⟨übtr⟩ das Stück –det *the play drags* **erm·üdend 1.** a *fatiguing, tiring* (*work*) ‖ *sleepy* (*morning*) **2.** adv *fatiguingly* ‖ ~ wirken *to be fatiguing*; (of a play) *to drag* **erm·üdet** a *fagged out; exhausted; fatigued; jaded* (*mind; man*) **Erm·üdung** f ~/~en *exhaustion; fatigue; lassitude; tiredness, weariness* ‖ ⟨physiol⟩ *fatigue* ‖ ⟨tech⟩ *fatigue* (*of material*) | **~s-** ~bruch m ⟨tech⟩ *fatigue failure* ~erscheinung f (P ⟨mot⟩) *drowsiness* ~festigkeit f ⟨tech⟩ *fatigue life* ≁frei a *f.-proof* ~stoffe m pl *f. products* ~versuch m ⟨tech⟩ *endurance test*

erm·untern vt [h] (jdn) **1.** (munter m) **a.** (aus dem Schlaf) *to awake, rouse* (*a p*) **b.** ⟨übtr⟩ (aufrütteln) *to rouse* (durch *by*); *to stir up* ‖ (aufheitern) *to cheer* (*up*), *to enliven, gladden* (*a p*); *to animate* **2.** ⟨fig⟩ jdn ~ z etw, z tun *to rouse* (od *encourage, incite, stimulate*) *a p to a th, to do* **Erm·unterung** f ~/~en *rousing* ‖ *cheering* | ⟨fig⟩ *encouragement, incitation, incitement, stimulation* (z *to*; z tun *to do*)

erm·utigen vt [h] (jdn) *to encourage,* (*en*)*hearten; embolden*; ⟨fam⟩ *to buck up*; (wieder) *to reassure; to put new heart into a p* ‖ (Rebellen) *to countenance, to keep in countenance*; jdn durch Zurufe ~ *to shout encouragement to a p*; jdn ~ in *to abet a p in* (*a th*); jdm ~d zusprechen *to praise a p* ‖ jdn z etw ~ *to encourage* (od *inspirit*) *a p to a th* ‖ [abs] z Anfragen ~ *to invite questions* **erm·utigend** a *encouraging; heartening* (*news*) **Erm·utigung** f ~/~en *encouragement* (z *to*) ‖ *countenance*

ern·ähren vt [h] **1.** (jdn) *to feed, keep, nourish* (v *on*); kräftig ~ *to feed up*; gut ernährt *well-fed; sleek*; schlecht –rt *poorly fed* ‖ (erhalten) *to keep, maintain; to provide for; to support*; er hat e–e Familie z ~ *he has a family to maintain* ‖ v s–n Eltern ernährt w, sich v s–n E. ~ l *to live on one's parents; to be dependent on one's p.* **2. sich ~ v** *to live on* (*meat*); *to keep* (od *maintain, support*) *o.s. on; to live* (od *subsist*) *on* (*one's salary*); sich durch Schriftstellern ~ *to live by writing*; sich selbst ~ *to be independent, to be on one's own; to shift for o.s.* ‖ sich ungenügend ~ *to underfeed* ‖ → nähren **Ern·ährer** m ~s/~ *earner, bread-winner, nourisher; maintainer, supporter* ‖ ~ des Haushalts *principal earner*

Ern·ährung f ~/~en **A.** [abstr] **1. a.** *feeding, nourishing* (*of a p*); *nourishment*; schlechte ~ *malnutrition*; → Unter≁ ‖ künstliche ~ ⟨med⟩ *artificial feeding*; vorgeschriebene ~ *diet*(*ary*); der ~ dienend *nutritive* | ⟨scient & med⟩ *nutrition* (*of the body*) ‖ *alimentation* **b.** *maintenance, sustenance; support* **B.** [konkr] (Nahrung) *food, nourishment, nutriment*; vorgeschriebene ~ *diet*(*ary*)

Ern·ährungs- [in comp] *nutritive; alimentary*; ⟨scient & med⟩ *trophic* **~abfälle** m pl ⟨physiol⟩ *waste products of nutrition* **~amt** n *Food Office* **~art** f *way of feeding* **~bedingungen** f [pl] *nutritive conditions* [pl] **~behandlung** f *dietetic treatment* **~fachmann** m *nutrition expert, nutritionist, dietitian* **~index** m *index figure for food* **~lage** f *food situation* **~lehre** f *dietetics* **~minister** m ⟨Ger⟩ (Reichs≁) *Minister of Food and Agriculture*; ⟨engl⟩ *Minister of Agriculture and Fisheries*; (im Kriege) *food-controller* **~organ** n *nutritive organ* °**~schlacht** f ⟨Ger⟩ *battle of production*, ⟨fam⟩ *dig for victory* **~stoff** m *nutrient* **~störung** f *dystrophy; defective nourishment* **~therapie** f *dietetics* [pl], *dietotherapy* **~vorgänge** m pl ⟨physiol⟩ *processes of nutrition nutritive pr.* **~weise** f *way of feeding; regime* ‖ zweckmäßige ~ *rational feeding*; Lehre v der zweckmäßigen ~ *dietetics* pl [sg konstr] **~wirtschaft** f *food production* od *industry* **~zustand** m *state of nutrition, nutritional st.*

Ern·annte [der ~, ein ~r] m ~n/~n *nominee*

ern·ennen vt [h] (→ nennen) (jdn) *to appoint, nominate; designate* ‖ jdn zum Botschafter, Präsidenten ~ *to appoint a p* (*to be*) *ambassador, president* ‖ jdn zum Richter ~ *to constitute a p a judge* ‖ jdn zum Professor des Griechischen ~

to nominate a p Professor of Greek || jdn zum Konsul ∼ ⟨Am⟩ *to name a p consul* || → einsetzen I. A. 2.; berufen, machen; übertragen **Ern·enner** m ∼s/∼ *nominator* **Ern·ennung** f ∼/∼en *nomination appointment*; *designation* || *creation* (*of peers*) || die ∼ zum Hauptmann *the appointment to the post of Captain*; die ∼ vom Obersten zum Brigadekommandeur *the a. from Colonel to be Brigadier* || s–e ∼ zum Präsidenten *his appointment to be president* || die ∼ zum Barrister *the call to the Bar* || s–e ∼ zum Professor des Griechischen *his nomination to be Professor of Greek* || durch ∼ z besetzend *appointive* (*office*) | **∼s-** **∼recht** n *nomination* || ⟨ec⟩ *patronage* **∼urkunde** f *letter* (od *deed*) *of appointment*; → Offizierspatent

ern·euen vt [h] (etw) = erneuern || → erneut

ern·euern vt [h] (etw) **1.** (auffrischen, –füllen) **a.** (Farbe, Vorrat) *to renew* ⟨tech⟩ *to change*; (Fußboden) *to put in a new floor*; (Hosenboden, Sitzfläche e–s Stuhls) *to reseat*; (Lauffläche) ⟨mot⟩ *to retread*; ⟨mot⟩ (Öl) *to change* **b.** ⟨übtr⟩ (Gesundheit) *to renew* || (Kenntnisse) *to brush up* || (Gefühl etc) *to revive* **c. sich** ∼ (of feeling; fashion) *to revive*; *recover*; *recur* **2.** (Gebäude etc) *to do up*; *recondition, renovate, repair*; *refit* || (Gemälde) *to restore* **3.** (Bewerbung, Versprechen) *to renew, repeat* **Ern·euerung** f ∼/∼en **1.** *renewal* (*of a supply*); (des Hausanstrichs) *repainting*; ⟨fig⟩ *revival* **2.** *reconditioning*; *renovation*; *repair* (*of a house*) || *restoration* **3.** *renewal, repetition* (*of a proposal*) **∼sgebühr** f *renewal fees* **∼schein** m ⟨bank⟩ *talon*

ern·eut [pp v erneuen] **1.** [a] *fresh, new* (*start*) || *repeated,* (*re*)*iterated* (*attempt*) || *twice-told* (*story*) || *recurrent* || ∼e Tätigkeit, ∼er Ausbruch *recrudescence* (*of a disease*, etc.); ∼es Auftreten *recurrence* (*of a crime*) || mit ∼er Kraft gingen wir wieder an die Arbeit *renewed in body and soul we resumed our work* || ein ∼es Zeichen *another sign* (*of his will-power*) **2.** [adv] *anew*; *repeatedly* || ∼ auftreten *to recur*; ∼ auftretend *recurrent*; ∼ ausbrechen *to recrudesce*; ∼ ausbrechend *recrudescent* || ∼ behandeln *to re-treat* || ∼ hinweisen auf etw, ∼ etw vorbringen *to repeat a th*; *to insist on a th*; jdn ∼ auf etw hinweisen, jdm etw ∼ z Bewußtsein bringen *to recall a th to a p's mind*; *to call a p's attention to a th* || → wieder, oft

ern·iedrigen vt [h] **A. 1.** jdn ∼ **a.** (im Rang) *to degrade* **b.** (demütigen) *to abase, humiliate, humble* || (s–e Ehre) *to prostitute* **c.** es würde dich ∼, wenn du tätest .. *it would degrade you to do* **2. sich** ∼ *to degrade* od *lower o.s.* (z tun *to do*); *to stoop* (tief *low*); *to demean o.s.* (durch *by*; dadurch, daß man tut *by doing*; z tun *to do*); sich so weit ∼ z tun *to condescend to do*; *to demean o.s. so far as to do* || du erniedrigst dich, wenn du das tust *you derogate if you do that* **B.** (etw) **1.** ⟨mus⟩ (Ton) *to lower*; um e–n halben Ton ∼ *to flatten*; um e–n h. Ton erniedrigt *flat* (*note*) **2.** (Preise etc) *to lower, reduce, sink*

Ern·iedrigung f ∼/∼en **1.** *degradation* (*of a p*) **2.** ⟨fig⟩ *abasement*; *come-down*; *humiliation* (*of a p*) || *derogation*; *prostitution* **3. a.** *lowering* (*of a note*); ∼ um e–n halben Ton *flattening* || *diminution, fall* (*of temperature*) **b.** *reduction* (*of prices, salary*)

Ernst m ∼es/ **A.** (Ggs Scherz) *earnest* || **es war ihm** ∼ (damit) *he was in earnest* (*about it*); *he was serious*; *he meant it* || **ist es dein** ∼? *are you in earnest*?, *are you serious*?, ⟨fam⟩ *do you say so*?; es ist mein ∼! *I mean it*!; es ist mein blutiger ∼ *I am in dead earnest, I am perfectly in earnest* | **im** ∼ *in earnest*; *serious*; im ∼ s *to be serious* (od *in earnest*) | *seriously now* (od *though*); aber nun im ∼ *and now to be serious* (*do you believe* ..?) || meinst du im ∼, was ..? *do you mean seriously what* (*you say*)? || **in allem** (*or* vollem) **∼, allen ∼es** *in good earnest*; *quite seriously*; sich allen ∼es fragen *to ask o.s. in all seriousness* | **∼ m** *to get down to* (od *to mean*) *business*; ∼ m mit etw *to mean a th*; *to be serious about a th*; ∼ m mit e–m Versprechen *to make a promise good*; er machte ∼ mit s–n Drohungen *he carried his threats out* | **es schien ∼ z w** *matters seemed to be getting serious*; es wurde ∼ aus den Vorbereitungen *the preparations assumed a serious appearance* | den ∼ **des Lebens** kennen lernen *to experience the vicissitudes of life* **B. 1.** (strenge, sittliche Auffassung) *earnestness, earnestness of purpose*; *seriousness*; *gravity* (*of a p's mind*); *moral stability*; *his attitude* od *bearing was full of seriousness and dignity* || er kann keiner S mit ∼ begegnen *he can't give a serious thought to a th* || feierlicher ∼ *solemnity, solemnness* **2.** *severity*; → Strenge **3.** *importance, seriousness* || *gravity, seriousness* (*of an injury*; *a situation*) **ernst I.** a **A.** [pred] es ist ihm sehr ∼ damit *he is much in earnest about it*; es war ihm vollkommen ∼ damit *he meant every word of it*; *he was perfectly in earnest about it* **B.** [pred & attr] **1.** *grave*; *sedate*; *serious* (*man*); *unsmiling*; ein ∼er alter Mann ⟨Scot⟩ *a dour old man*; ein ∼es Gesicht m *to keep one's face straight* (od *a str. face*) || ∼ bleiben *to keep one's countenance* || (streng) *severe*; *stern* (*parents*) **2.** (sittlich) ∼ *earnest* (*Christian*; *worker*) | *earnest* (*desire*); *genuine* (*offer*); *serious* (*scholar*); *zealous* | *serious* (*book, talk*) **3.** (wichtig) *grave, important, serious* (*rival*); *weighty* **4.** (kritisch) *severe, grave*; *serious* (*illness*; *situation, damage*); *dangerous*; *nasty* (*accident*); *stern* (*fact, necessity, reality*) **II.** adv *seriously*; → ernstlich || er sieht die politische Lage sehr ∼ an *his political outlook is very gloomy* || es ∼ meinen *to be in earnest* (mit etw *about a th*); *to be serious*; *to mean business* || etw ∼ nehmen *to take a th seriously*; nimm es nicht so ∼! *don't take it so hard*; (etw) nicht ∼ nehmen *to trifle with* (*a cold*) || jdn nicht recht ∼ nehmen *to look upon a p as sth of a joke*; er ist kein ∼ z nehmender Gegner *he is easy meat* **∼́fall** m *case of war*; im ∼e *in case of war*; *in a case of emergency* od *need*; *when it comes to the point*; *if need be* **∼-komisch** a: (*with a tipsy profundity and a*) *serio-comic* (*air*) **∼́mäßig** a *emergency* (*signal*) **∼́gemeint** a *meant seriously*; ein ∼es Anerbieten *a serious, genuine offer*; *an offer meant in earnest*; ∼e Drohungen *no empty threats* **·ernsthaft 1.** a = ernst B. || ∼e Absichten *earnest* (od *serious*) *intentions* || ⟨fig⟩ *weighty, ponderous, grave*; *serious*; *solemn*; *fateful* **2.** adv (= ernst II.) *earnestly*; *seriously*; *in all seriousness* || etw ∼ meinen *to be in earnest about a th* || er glaubte ∼ an *he was an earnest believer in* (*Christian science*); → ernstlich | **∼́igkeit** f ∼/ *earnestness*; *seriousness*

·ernstlich 1. [a] *earnest* (*desire, intentions*); *genuine*; *zealous* | = ernst I. B. 3. 4. **2.** [adv] **a.** *earnestly*; *ardently, fervently*; **∼ dringen auf ..** *to insist earnestly on ..* || ich meine es ∼ *I really mean it* || etw ∼ wollen *or* erstreben *to be in earnest for a th* || *seriously, in all seriousness*; jdn ∼ warnen *to warn a p seriously* | *seriously, severely*; **∼ erkrankt,** verwundet *seriously ill, wounded* || ∼ glauben *to really believe* (*a th*) → ernsthaft

·Ernte f ∼/∼n **1.** (Ernten jeder Art) *harvest*; Heu∼́ *hay h.*; Reis∼́ *rice h.*; Weizen∼́ *wheat h.*; Apfel∼́ *apple h.* **2. a.** (reifes Getreide) *harvest*; ∼ auf dem Halm *standing crop* || die ∼ einbringen *to harvest* **b.** (eingebrachte ∼; ∼ertrag) *crop*; die gesamte ∼ *the crops* [pl] || Farmpächter (Einwanderer) mit Beteiligung an der

~ ⟨Am⟩ *share-cropper* **c.** ⟨fig⟩ *harvest*; *vintage*; → Ertrag ‖ e–e reiche ~ ergeben *to yield a rich harvest* (an *of*) ‖ e–e reiche ~ halten *to obtain* (od *gather in*) *a rich harvest* ‖ e–e furchtbare ~ halten (Krankheit, Tod) *to take a heavy toll*

·Ernte- [in comp] *harvest* .. ‖ *harvesting* **~arbeit** f *harvest* (od *harvesting*)*-work* **~arbeiter** m *harvestman*; *harvest-worker* **~bräuche** m [pl] *harvest-customs* [pl] **~dankfest** n *harvest-festival*; *Thanksgiving* **~einsatz** m *harvest-work* **~ertrag** m *harvest-yield*; *crop* **~feld** n *harvest-field* **~fest** n *harvest home*; ⟨Scot⟩ *kirn* **~kranz** m *harvest--wreath* **~maschine** f *harvesting* (od *reaping*)*-machine*; *harvester* **~monat** m *harvest-month*; *August* **~mond** m *harvest-moon* **~schmaus** m *harvest feast* **~segen** m *abundant* (od *rich*) *harvest* **~tag** m *harvest-day* **~urlaub** m *agricultural leave* **~wagen** m *harvesting-cart* **~zeit** f *harvest*; *harvest time*

·ernten vt/i [h] **A.** vt **1.** (Getreide etc) *to harvest*, *gather* (*in*); *reap* **2.** ⟨fig⟩ *to win* (*applause*); (Belohnung, Früchte s–r Arbeit; Undank) *to reap*; k–n Dank ~ *not to get any thanks* (f *for*); (Ruhm) *to earn, gain, obtain*; den Dank jds ~ *to earn the thanks of a p*; Lorbeeren ~ *to win* (od *gain*) *laurels* **B.** vi *to harvest*; *reap*

ern·üchtern vt [h] **1.** ⟨eig⟩ jdn ~ *to sober a p*; *to make a p sober* **2.** ⟨fig⟩ *to disenchant, to disillusion, to disillusionize*; *to undeceive a p*; *to disabuse a p*; *to bring a p* (*rudely*) *down to earth* ‖ ernüchtert w *to sober down*

Ern·üchterung f ~/ **1.** *sobering* **2.** ⟨fig⟩ *disenchantment, disillusion*(*ment*) (über *with*) | **~s-**~mittel n *sobering agent*

Er·oberer m ~s/~ *conqueror*

er·obern vt [h] **1.** ⟨mil⟩ **a.** (Land) *to conquer*; erobertes Gebiet *conquest* ‖ (Festung) *to capture, take*; im Sturm ~ *to take* (*a fort*) *by storm* **2.** ⟨übtr⟩ etw ~, sich [dat] etw (Ehren, Märkte) ~ *to acquire, gain a th*; *to capture* (*new markets*) **3.** ⟨fig⟩ jdn ~ *to capture* od *win a p*; *to win* od *gain a p over*; *to make a conquest of a p*; *to captivate a p* ‖ (sich) alle Herzen ~ *to win all hearts*; (sich) alle H. im Sturm ~ *to take all h. by storm* **Er·oberung** f ~/~en **1.** [abstr] (Erobern) *the conquering* (*of India*); *conquest* ‖ *the capture* od *taking* (*of a town*) ‖ e–e ~ m *to make a conquest*; (ein Land) jdm durch ~ nehmen *to conquer a country from a p* | ⟨übtr⟩ *acquisition*; *gaining* **c.** ⟨fig⟩ *conquest* **2.** [konkr] (Erobertes) [oft pl ~en] *conquest* | ⟨übtr⟩ *acquisition*; *gain*; *investment* | ⟨fig⟩ *capture, conquest*

Er·oberungs- **~durst** m *thirst for conquest* **~krieg** m *war of conquest* **~lust, ~sucht** f = Eroberungsdurst **~süchtig** a *eager for conquests* ‖ *coquettish, flirty* (*woman*) **~zug** m *inroad, raid*

erod·ieren vt [h] *to erode*; → Erosion

er·öffnen vt [h] **A.** † = öffnen **B.** ⟨übtr⟩ **1.** (Geschäft) *to open*; *establish*; *to set up*; *to start*; e–n Laden ~ *to set up shop* **2.** (Ausstellung, Theater etc) *to open*; *to inaugurate*; *to throw* (od *declare*) *open*; feierlich ~ ⟨Am⟩ *to dedicate* **3.** (beginnen) ein Konto ~ *to open an account*; mir wurde ein Kredit bei Ihnen eröffnet *I had a credit opened with you* ‖ (Ball, Debatte, Feldzug, Feuer, Konzert, Verhandlung etc) *to open* (mit *with*); *to lead off* (*dance, debate*); ⟨engl parl⟩ (im H L) der Lord Chanceller eröffnete die Sitzung *the L. Ch. took his seat on the Woolsack*; (im H C) der Speaker eröffnete die Sitzung *the Speaker took the chair* ‖ e–e Versammlung ~ *to open the proceedings*; ⟨Am⟩ *to call a meeting to order* **4.** ⟨jur⟩ den Konkurs über jds Vermögen ~ *to adjudicate a p a bankrupt* ‖ das Testament ~ ⟨engl⟩ (vor Gericht) *to prove the will in solemn form* **5.** ⟨fig⟩ Ausblicke ~ *to open* (*up*) *prospects* ‖ ein verheißendes Feld der Untersuchung ~ *to open out a promising field of investigation* ‖ e–e neue Ära ~ *to inaugurate* (od *open*) *a new era* **C.** ⟨fig⟩ jdm etw ~ *to disclose* (od *make known*; *open, reveal*) *a th to a p*; *to break* (od *communicate, notify*) *a th to a p*; *to inform a p about a th*; *to put a p up to a th* **D. sich** ~ **1.** (of a prospect) *to present itself*; *to offer* **2.** sich jdm ~ *to open o.s.* (od *one's heart*) *to a p*; *to unbosom o.s. to a p*

Er·öffner m *inaugurator*; *initiator* **Er·öffnung** f **A. 1.** *opening*; *establishment, setting up* (*of a business*) **2.** *inauguration, opening* (*of an exhibition, a theatre*) **3.** (Beginn) *beginning, opening* (*of an account*; *of a ball, concert*; *of Parliament*, etc.); *start*; bei der ~ *at the opening* **4.** ⟨jur⟩ ~ des. Konkurses *adjudication* ‖ ~ des Testaments *the official proving of the will in solemn form* **5.** *opening up* (*of prospects*); *inauguration* (*of a new era*) **B.** *communication, disclosure* (über *about*); *notification*; jdm e–e ~ über etw m = jdm etw ~ → eröffnen C.; jdm die ~ m, daß *to notify a p that* ..

Er·öffnungs- [in comp] *opening*; *inaugural* **~abend** m *opening night*; am ~ *on the o. n.* **~ansprache** f *inaugural* (od *opening*) *address* **~bilanz** f ⟨com⟩ *first* (od *opening*) *balance-sheet* **~feier** f *inauguration* **~feierlichkeiten** f [pl] *opening ceremonies* [pl] **~inventar** n ⟨com⟩ *first* (od *opening*) *inventory* **~kurs** m ⟨com⟩ *opening--rate* (od *price*) **~periode** f (der Geburt) ⟨med⟩ *first stage of labo*(*u*)*r, period of dilatation* **~preis** m *starting pr.* **~tag** m *opening-day, first day*

erog·en a *erogenous* (*zone*); *ero*(*to*)*genic*

er·örtern vt [h] (Frage) *to argue, debate, discuss* (mit *with*); *to moot, raise*; *to comment on*; *to examine, review* ‖ (lebhaft) erörtert w *to be under* (*active*) *discussion* ‖ eingehend ~ *to discuss fully* (od *in detail*); sie hatten es viele Male eingehend erörtert *they had had it out many times* ‖ (Plan) gründlich ~ *to canvass*; *to thrash* od *thresh out* ‖ offen *or* frei ~ *to ventilate* ‖ (Unangenehmes) wieder ~ *to rip up* **Er·örterung** f ~/~en *arguing, argument* (über *on*); *debate, discussion*; ⟨off⟩ *active consideration*; allgemeine ~en [pl] *generalities* [pl] ‖ eingehende ~ *detailed* (od *full*) *discussion*; lebhafte ~ *active d.*; offene ~ *ventilation* ‖ ich lasse mich auf weitere ~en nicht ein *I do not allow* (od *I refuse*) *any further discussions* ‖ in e–e ~ eintreten *to enter into* od *upon a discussion* ‖ etw zur ~ bringen = erörtern; immer wieder z ~ bringen *to rip up* ‖ z ~ k (of subjects) *to come up for discussion*; *to be discussed* ‖ z ~ stehen *to be under discussion* ‖ ⟨parl⟩ ~sstadium e–r Vorlage vor der 3. Lesung *report stage*

·Eros m ~/–oten Gr ⟨arts⟩ *god of love, Love*; pl *Cupids*

Erosi·on f ~/~en *erosion*; → erodieren | ~smarken f pl ⟨geol⟩ *flute casts*

Er·otik f *eroticism*; *erotics* [pl] **er·otisch 1.** a *erotic*; *amatory* ‖ ~es Gedicht *erotic*; ~e Literatur *erotica* (L) [pl] **2.** adv *erotically* **Erotoman·ie** [–i:] f *erotomania* (L)

·Erpel m ~s/~ ⟨zoo⟩ = Enterich ‖ °mit dem ~ huren ⟨fig⟩ *to oscar*

erp·icht a [nur pred] ~ s auf *to have set one's heart on*; *to be bent* (od *set, intent, keen*) *on* (*enjoyment, work*); *to be agog* (od *eager, zealous*) *for* (*a th*); *to be hard up for* (*news*); *to be a maniac for* (*punctuality*); *to be greedy for* (od *of*) (*gain, money*); *to be mad for* (od *after, on*) (*a th*); *to be crazy about* (*a th*) ‖ keineswegs ~ s auf *to be none too* (od *not at all*) *anxious for* (*an investigation*) | **darauf ~ s z tun** *to be bent* (od *intent, keen*; *dead set*; *sharp-set* (*on doing*; *to be eager*, (od *crazy, zealous*) *to do*; ⟨Am sl⟩ *to be hell-bent to do*

erpr·essen vt [h] jdn ~, Geld v jdm ~ *to blackmail* od *squeeze a p*; *to levy blackmail upon a p*;

to exact od *extort money from a p*; Geld, ein Geständnis ~ v jdm *to squeeze* od *wring money, a confession from* (od *out of*) *a p*; *to wrest a confession from a p* ‖ –ßt *extorted* (*confession*) ‖ Geld ~ ⟨Am sl⟩ *to shake down money* **Erpr·esser** m –s/~ *blackmailer, extortioner*; ⟨Am sl⟩ *racketeer* **erpr·esserisch 1.** a *extortionate* **2.** adv *extortionately* **Erpr·essung** f ~/~en *blackmail, blackmailing, extortion*; *exaction*; ⟨sl⟩ *shakedown*, ⟨Am sl⟩ *racket* **~sversuch** m *attempt at extortion*; *attempted extortion*

erpr·oben vt [h] etw (jds Ehrlichkeit, Mut, Treue etc) ~ *to prove* (od *test, try*) *a th*; *to put a th to the test* (od *proof*); *to give a th a trial* ‖ jdn ~ *to put a p to the test* | **sich** in e–r S ~ *to try one's hand in a th*

erpr·obt a *tested* (*gold*) ‖ *proved, tested* (*by experience*); *tried* (*friendship*; *abilities*); *established* (*remedy*); die ~e Feder *the practised pen* ‖ *approved* (*friend*); *experienced* (*men*); *reliable*; *skilful*; *trustworthy, trusty*; alles ~e Leute *all people who have proved* od *shown themselves reliable* | ≗**heit** f *reliability* (*of p, method*); *efficacy* (*of medicine*) **Erpr·obung** f ~/~en *proof, proving*; *test*; (*product*) *testing*; *try*; *try-out* **~sstelle** f *experimental station*; *testing ground*

erqu·icken vt/i [h] **1.** vt (of food, etc.) (jdn, jds Glieder) *to refresh, reanimate*; *reinvigorate, strengthen* ‖ (of a picture) (jds Auge) *to refresh*; (of music) (jdn) *to delight, regale* ‖ s–e Augen ~ an *to feast one's eyes on* ‖ (jdn in Trübsal) *to cheer, comfort, solace* | **sich** ~ *to refresh o.s.* (mit, durch *with*); *to regale o.s.* (an *on, with*); *to delight* (an *in*) **2.** vi *to be refreshing* ‖ *to solace* (*good literature solaces*) **erqu·ickend 1.** a *refreshing* ‖ *delightful* ‖ *cheering*; *comfortable* **2.** adv *refreshingly* **erqu·icklich** a *edifying* (*sight, book, talk*) **Erqu·ickung** f *refreshment* ‖ *delight*; *regalement* ‖ *comfort*

err·affen vt [h] *to make* (*a fortune*) *hand over fist*

err·aten vt [h] (→ raten) (Rätsel) *to guess, to solve*; (jds Gedanken) *to guess*; (Absichten) *to divine*; ich errate Ihre Absicht *I see what you are driving at* ‖ du hast es richtig ~ *you've just hit it, you've hit the right nail on the head* ‖ ich kann nur ~, was du meinst *I can only guess at what you mean* ‖ jds Wünsche z ~ suchen *to study a p's wishes*

err·atisch a ⟨geol⟩ *erratic*; ~er Block *erratic block*; *erratic*

err·echnen vt [h] *to calculate*; *tally*; *compute*; (Betrag) *to work out*; es ist einfach z ~ *it is simple to compute*; errechnet w können *to become calculable*; ~, daß .. ⟨Am⟩ *to figure* (*out*) *that* .. ‖ –net (*the sum*) *arrived at* **Err·echnung** f ~/~en *calculation*; *computation*

err·egbar a *excitable, irritable* ‖ leicht ~ (P) *quick to flare up*; *hot-headed*; *nervous, nervy, touchy*; *jumpy* ‖ ⟨sex⟩ *sexy* **Err·egbarkeit** f ~/ *excitability, irritability* ‖ leichte ~ *nervousness*; *touchiness*; *sexiness*

err·egen vt [h] **1. a.** (jdn) *to agitate, excite, heat*; *to put out*; *to upset*; *to incur a p's displeasure*; *to move to* (*pity*); → aufregen ‖ erregt w *to be excited* (etc.); *to come* od *go it strong*; *to become roused in one's feelings* (über *about*); ⟨Am⟩ *to go haywire* **b.** (Gefühle) *to rouse, to stir up*; erregt w (of the blood) *to boil*; die Gefühle sind leidenschaftlich erregt *the feelings run high*; die Gemüter ~ *to stir up emotions, reactions* **c.** erregt s *to be* (od *get*) *excited* (od *upset*); *to fume*; *to be on the fret* **d. sich** ~ *to put o.s. out, to upset o.s.* (über *about*); *to chafe* (*at*); *to feel strong*(*ly*) (*about*); *to fuss* (od *get fussed*) (*about*); *to work o.s. into quite a state* (*about*) **2.** (Nerven) *to excite*; *stimulate* ‖ (elektr. Strom etc) *to excite* **3.** (hervorrufen) *to cause, provoke*; *to give rise to* (*a th*); *to provoke* (*anger*), *create* (*interest*), *arouse* (*pity, fear, mistrust*) ‖ ein Gefühl der Kälte ~ *to create a sense of cold* ‖ → Anstoß A. 2.; Aufmerksamkeit; Aufsehen ‖ Besorgnis, Furcht, Staunen, Verdruß ~ *to cause anxiety, fear, wonder, discontent* ‖ jds Bewunderung, Teilnahme ~ *to command a p's admiration, sympathy* ‖ Freude, Heiterkeit ~ *to provoke mirth, amusement*; jds Verdruß, Zorn ~ *to excite a p*; *to get a p's goat* ‖ Interesse, Verdacht ~ *to arouse* od *awaken interest, suspicion* **4.** ⟨tech⟩ *to excite* ‖ ⟨el⟩ *to energize* **err·egend** a **1.** *exciting, moving, thrilling* (*scene*); *stirring* (*incident*); *tense* (*moment*) ‖ ⟨med⟩ *excitant, stimulant*; ~es Mittel *excitant, stimulant* **2.** [Objekt + ~ oft durch passendes Adj.] **a.** Anstoß ~ *invidious*; = anstößig ‖ Besorgnis ~ *anxious* ‖ Bewunderung ~ *challenging, extraordinary*; → bewundernswert ‖ Heiterkeit ~ *amusing*; *comic* ‖ Mitleid ~ *pitiable, pitiful* ‖ Schrecken ~ *horrible, terrible* ‖ Verdacht ~ *suspectable, suspicious* **b.** → aufsehen~; staunen~ **Err·eger** m **1.** ⟨med⟩ *excitant, stimulant* ‖ unsichtbarer Krankheits≗ *virus* [L] **2.** *exciting agent* (od *force*) ‖ *cause*; *the virus* (*of sedition*) **3.** ⟨el⟩ (Maschine) *exciter* | ~strom [m] ⟨el⟩ *exciting current* **err·egt 1.** a *excited* (*magnetic field*) ‖ *agitated, excited* (*feelings*) ‖ *stirred up* ‖ *heated, high* (*words*); *impassioned, spirited* (*debate*); ~e Auseinandersetzung *flareup* ‖ *stirring* (*times*) ‖ *agog, vibrant* (vor *with*); ⟨sl⟩ *windy* (über *about*) ‖ leicht ~ *nervous, nervy, touchy*; *jumpy* | geschlechtlich ~ *sexually excited*, ⟨fam⟩ *sexy* **2.** adv *excitedly*; (*to speak*) *heatedly*; (*to dream*) *wildly* | ≗**heit** f = Erregung 2. **Err·egung** f **1.** ⟨med⟩ ~ e–s Nerven *excitation* (od *stimulation*) *of a nerve*; *nerve-excitation*; ~sfaktor [m] *stimulus* [L] **2.** *agitation, excitement, flutter*; *fluster*; innere ~ *tumult*; → Aufregung ‖ geschlechtliche ~ *sexual excitement*, ⟨fam⟩ *sexiness* ‖ innere, seelische ~ *anguish* (über *of*); *thrill, throb* ‖ in gr ~ *white-hot*, ⟨Am sl⟩ *on the jump* ‖ in höchster ~ *agog with excitement*; *at white heat*; ⟨fam⟩ *in a terrible taking* ‖ vor ~ zitternd *quivering* od *shaking with excitement* ‖ e–e gr ~ hervorrufen *to flutter the dovecotes* **3.** ⟨tech⟩ ~ e–s Signalapparates ⟨el⟩ *activation of signals* | ~senergie [f] ⟨el⟩ *excitation energy*

err·eichbar a *attainable, available*; *securable* ‖ [pred] *get-at-able*; *within reach* (od *call, range*); leicht ~ *handy* (*the station is h.*); vom Bahnhof leicht ~ *within easy reach of the station*; zu Fuß (mit dem Wagen) leicht ~ *within easy walking* (*motoring*) *distance* ‖ leicht ~ (*goal*) *easy to attain* ‖ nicht ~ *out of* (od *not within*) *reach* ‖ jdm etw ~ m ⟨fig⟩ *to bring a th within a p's means* | ≗**keit** f ~/ *attainableness, attainability*

err·eichen vt [h] **A. 1.** (herankommen an) (etw) *to reach*; *to get at* (*a th*); ich kann den Apfel (auf dem Baum) nicht ~ *I cannot reach the apple* **2.** (Ort etc) *to reach*; *to arrive at*; *to get to* (*we got to London at ten*); den Hafen ~ *to make port* | vom Bahnhof leicht z ~ *within easy reach of the station* ‖ (Zug) *to catch*; ich –chte den Zug noch in letzter Minute *I cut it fine*; den Anschluß ~ *to achieve connexion* ‖ ⟨Am⟩ *to make, strike*: das Ufer ~ *to make shore*; (*he made the door in two jumps*; [Zug] *can I still make the 3:20*) **3.** jdn ~ **a.** *to reach a p*; jdn nach langem Suchen ~ *to run a p down*; wo kann ich Sie ~? *where can I find* od *meet you*? sind Sie telephonisch z ~? *are you* (od *can I get you*) *on the phone*? *can I ring you up*? ‖ man kann ihn nie ~ *one can never get hold of him* ‖ (einholen) *to catch a p up*; *to come up with a p* **b.** (gleichkommen) *to equal* (*a p*) (an *in*); *to be the equal of* (*a p*); *to match* (*a p*); jdn nicht ~ *to be inferior to a p* **c.** (S) *to reach* (*your letter reached me in Berlin*); *to come to* (*news came to him in London*) **B.** ⟨übtr⟩ (Absicht, Ziel etc ~) **1.** *to achieve*; *to arrive at*; *to attain, to attain to*; *to come by*; *to gain*; *obtain*; *reach*; *secure*; *to work up to*; schwer z ~ *hard to come by* ‖ s–e Absicht ~ *to carry one's point* ‖ ein hohes Alter ~ *to live to a great age*; *to reach old age* ‖ → Altersgrenze ‖ das Gegenteil wurde erreicht *the reverse was the result* ‖ ein gr Geschick ~ in .. *to reach a stage of great skill in* ‖ ⟨engl univ⟩ e–e Klasse bei der Honoursprüfung ~ *to be classed* (*he was not c.*) ‖ ⟨sport⟩ *to score* (*10 points*) ‖ ein Ziel ~ *to achieve an end* ‖ das Ziel ~ *to meet* (od *fulfil*) *the requirements*; *to be successful* ‖ sein Z. ~ *to gain one's end, to reach one's aim, to win one's goal*; ⟨Am⟩ *to get there* ‖ s–n Zweck ~ *to achieve* (od *compass*) *one's purpose*; bei jdm etw ~ *to have success* (od *get somewhere*) *with a p*; bei jdm (s–n Zw. nicht *or*) nichts ~ *to fail with a p* ‖ nichts wurde –cht *nothing came out of it*; *nothing was won by it* ‖ (etw) durch Winkelzüge ~ *to scrounge* **2.** (S) der Betrag –chte nicht die Summe des vorigen Jahres *the amount did not come up to the figure of last year* ‖ sein Ende ~ *to end*; *to come to an end* (od *a close*) ‖ e–e Geschwindigkeit v ~ *to attain a speed of* ‖ e–n Preis ~ *to fetch a price*; den tiefsten Stand ~ *to touch bottom*; das Ausfuhrsoll ~ *to hit the export targets* **3. ~, daß ..**: ich –chte, daß ich zugelassen wurde *I managed to be admitted*; *I succeeded in being admitted*; ich –chte, daß er zurückgerufen wurde *I succeeded in his being called back*; hierdurch wurde –cht, daß eine Besserung eintrat *by this a recovery was brought about* **E–chung** f ~/ **1.** *reaching*; *getting at* ‖ *catching* (*of a train*) **2.** ⟨übtr⟩ *achievement*; *accomplishment, accomplishing*; *acquiring*; *attainment* (*of majority*); *reaching*; zur ~ s–s Zieles ging er .. (*in order*) *to reach his aim* (od *for reaching his aim*) *he went* ..; → Altersgrenze

err·etten vt [h] (jdn) *to save*; *deliver, rescue* (v, aus *from*); → retten **Err·etter** m ~s/~ *saviour* (*of a nation*); *deliverer, rescuer* (aus *from*); → Erlöser; Retter **Err·ettung** f ~/~en *saving, salvation,* (aus, v *from*); *rescue, deliverance* (*from*)

err·ichten vt [h] **1.** (Haus, Denkmal etc) *to build, construct, erect, raise* ‖ (Pfahl) *to erect*; (Bude, Zelt) *to pitch* ‖ Erdbefestigungen ~ *to throw up earthworks* **2.** ⟨math⟩ ein Lot (*or* e–e Senkrechte) ~ auf .. *to raise a perpendicular upon* (*a line*) **3.** ⟨übtr & fig⟩ (Geschäft, Praxis) *to build up, to open*; *to set up*; (Dynastie) *to found*; (Orden) *to institute*; (Stadt, Universität; Kirche, Kloster) *to establish, found*; *plant* ‖ ein Testament ~ *to make* (od *draw up*) *one's will* ‖ (Religion, System) *to constitute, establish*; (Theorie) *to establish* **Err·ichtung** f ~/ **1.** *building, construction, erection* (*of a house*) ‖ ⟨tech⟩ *assembly, erection, mounting*; e–s Gerüstes *scaffolding* **2.** ⟨math⟩ *raising* (*of a perpendicular*) **3.** *establishment, foundation*; *institution*; *plantation* (*of churches*); *drawing up* (*of a will*)

err·ingen vt [h] [→ ringen] ⟨fig⟩ **1.** (etw) *to achieve*; *gain, win* ‖ ⟨sport⟩ e–n Erfolg, Vorteil ~ *to score a success, an advantage* (→ erreichen) ‖ e–n Vorteil ~ *to gain an advantage* (über *over*) ‖ e–n gr Erfolg ~ *to achieve a great success* ‖ e–n Sieg ~ *to gain a victory* (über *over*); den Sieg ~ *to achieve victory*; *to gain* (od *win*) *the day*; *to be victorious* ‖ e–n Preis ~ *to gain* (od *win*) *a prize* **2.** (sich [dat] etw) *to acquire, gain, secure, win* (*a th*); (sich) die Achtung jds ~ *to win a p's estimation*; sich die allgemeine A. der Menschen ~ *to win golden opinions*; sich Ruhm (*or* e–n Namen) ~ als .. *to establish one's reputation as* ..; sich e–n Namen ~ durch *to make o.s. a name by* .. ‖ mühsam errungen *acquired by effort* od *with difficulty* ‖ → erwerben, gewinnen **Err·ingung** f ~/~en *achieving, achievement*; *gaining, winning* ‖ *acquiring, acquisition*

err·öten 1. vi [s] (P) *to blush*; *colour* (*up*); *to grow* od *turn red*; (tief) ~ *to flush* (*a deep pink*) (vor *with*); über u über ~ *to blush up to the ears* (od *to the roots of one's hair*); (of the face) *to blush, flush* (*with*); (of the cheeks) *to flush, glow* (*with*) ‖ jdn vor Scham ~ l *to put a p to the blush*; (Gesicht) ~ l *to flush, redden* **2.** ≗ n *blush, flush*; zum ~ bringen = erröten l **err·ötend** a *blushing*

Err·ungenschaft f *acquisition* (f *to*), *acquirement* ‖ *accomplishment, achievement, attainment* ([mst pl] ~en *accomplishments*, etc.); *improvement*; *invention*; k–e besondere ~ *no catch* ‖ die ~en der Wissenschaft, des Geistes *the portents, prodigies, triumphs, trophies* [pl] *of science, of the intellect* ‖ die neueste ~ *the latest achievement*; neue technische ~ *gadget*; die neuste tech. ~ *the last word* (in .. *in wireless*); mit allen ~en ausgestattet equipped with every modern technical device ‖ ⟨tech & sport⟩ ~en [pl] ⟨sl⟩ *stunts* [pl]

†**ers·ättigen** vt [h] = befriedigen, sättigen ‖ das Herz ~ an = laben an

Ers·atz m ~es/ **A.** [abstr] **1.** (Entschädigen) *compensation* od *indemnification* (f *for*); *reparation* (f *for, of*); *restitution* (*of*); *indemnity*; → Entschädigung ‖ → B. **2.** (Ersetzen) *replacing, replacement, supersession* (durch *by*); *supplementation*; *substitution*; der ~ v Phrasen durch Taten *the substitution of facts for phrases*; der ~ e–s Originals durch e–e Imitation *the substitution of an imitation for the original* **B.** [konkr] **1.** Schaden≗ *compensation*; *damages* [pl]; *amends* [pl] [oft sg konstr]; *indemnity* **2. a.** (S) *substitute*; *succedaneum* (⟨a.⟩ ~mittel) (f *for*); *surrogate* (f *for, of*) ‖ *alternative* (f *to*), als ~ f Kaffee bot sie (..) *as an alternative to coffee she offered* (..); *apology* (f *for*); *equivalent* (f *of*); *makeshift*, es stellt nur e–n ~ dar *it is only in the nature of a m.*; *make-weight* (f *for*); ein bloßer ~ f *a mere apology for* (*a dinner*) **b.** (P) *substitute*; *deputy*; *supply*; → ~mann **c.** [koll] (P) ⟨mil⟩ *replacement* **C. Wendungen**: **als** ~ [abs] *in lieu* ‖ *as* od (*by way of*) *compensation* (*for*); als ~ f *in exchange* od *return for* ‖ ~ **bieten,** geben f *to compensate for* ‖ ~ erhalten f etw *to recover a th*; Schaden≗ erhalten *to recover damages* ‖ ~ leisten *to make reparation*; ~ leisten *to make good*; ~ leisten f *to make compensation* (od *amends*) *for, to compensate for*; *to make restitution of* (*a th*) ‖ (e–n) ~ (→ o B. 2. b.) schaffen *to find* (od *procure*) *a supply* ‖ sich nach e–m ~ umsehen *to look for* (P → B. 2. b.), ⟨fig⟩ *for a second string to one's bow* **D.** [in comp] **1.** (→ Ersatz–) **a.** *relief*; *replacement*; *substitute*; *supplementary* **b.** *duplicate*; *extra*; *spare* **c.** ⟨mil⟩ *reserve* (*army, battalion*) **d.** *alternative* (Gelände *site*) **2.** –≗ *substitute*; *ersatz* ‖ Butter≗ *butter s.* ‖ ⟨bes Am⟩ *near*; Bier≗ *near beer*; Woll≗ *near wool*

Ersatz- [in comp] → Ersatz D. **~abteilung** f ⟨mil, bes artill⟩ *replacement training battalion*; ⟨engl⟩ *depot battalion* **~anspruch** m *claim for compensation* od ⟨ins⟩ *indemnity* **~arbeiter** m *relief worker* **~ausgabe** f *in lieu issue* **~bataillon** n ⟨bes *infantry*⟩ = –abteilung **~batterie** f *refill* (od *spare*) *battery* **~bereifung** f ⟨mot⟩ *spare-tyre equipment* **~beschaffung** f *the procuring of a supply* od *substitute*; *replacement purchase* ‖ ~en [pl] *replacements* **~blatt** n ⟨typ⟩ *cancel* **~blei** n *spare lead* **~dehnung** f ⟨phil⟩ *compensatory lengthening* **~dienststelle** f ⟨mil⟩ *recruiting centre* **~einheit** f *reserve unit. replacement training unit* **~fahrer** m *substitute driver* **~faser** f *substitute* *fibre* **~freiheitsstrafe** f *substituted penalty of confinement* (*in default of payment*) **~füllung** f *refill* **~geschworener** m *talesman* **~heer** n ⟨Ger⟩ *supplementary army*; *forces* [pl] *outside the regular army* **~kabel** n *spare cable* **~kasse** f ⟨Ger⟩ *health insurance society* **~käufe** m pl *fill-in buying* **~kosten** [pl] *replacement cost* **~lehrer** m *supply-teacher* **~leistung** f *compensation*; *indemnification*; *payment of damages* **~lieferung** f *compensation delivery* **~linse** f *duplicate lens* **~mann** m *substitute*; *supply*; *deputy*; *replacer*; (Geschworener) *talesman* ‖ ⟨sport⟩ *reserve*; *stand-in*; ⟨Am⟩ *scrub, scrubman*, tüchtiger ~ ⟨fam⟩ *pinch-hitter* ‖ ⟨engl mil⟩ *substitute* **~mannschaft** f *reserve team*; ⟨sport Am⟩ *scrub*; *scrub team* **~maschine** f *stand-by engine*; *supplementary e.* **~mine** f *refill* **~mittel** n *substitute*; *surrogate* **~pferd** n *spare horse* **~pflicht** f *liability to compensation* **≗pflichtig** a *liable to compensation* **~rad** n *spare wheel*; ⟨mot⟩ *stepney* (*-wheel*) **~reifen** m ⟨mot⟩ *spare tyre* **~reserve** f *the Army Reserve* ‖ *third line* ‖ ⟨engl⟩ freiwillige ~ *the Territorial Army* (seit 1908); *Territorials* [pl]; ⟨hist⟩ (vor 1782) *Volunteers* [pl] **~route, ~straße** f *alternative route, street* **~schaltung** f ⟨el⟩ *equivalent circuit* od *network*; *rerouting* **~spieler** m ⟨sport⟩ *emergency-man*; ⟨theat⟩ *understudy*; ⟨theat, sport⟩ *stand-in* **~stoff** m *substitute*; Baumwoll≗ *cotton s.* **~stück** n, **~teil** n *spare* (od *repair, replacement*) *part*; *spare*; *refill* | ~kasten [m] *spare part kit* ‖ ~lager [n] *spare part depot* **~-truppe** f ⟨Ger mil⟩ *body of troops for the training of the* 'Ersatzheer' **~wahl** f ⟨parl engl⟩ (e–s Abgeordneten) *by-election* **≗weise** adv [⟨a.⟩ abs] = als Ersatz **~wert** m *replacement value* **~wesen** n ⟨mil⟩ *recruiting and replacement* **~zündkabel** n ⟨mot⟩ *spare high-tension cable*

°**ers·aufen** vi [s] [→ saufen] (P) *to be* (od *get*) *drowned*; ~ l = ersäufen | ⟨fig⟩ (S) *to be flooded*, das Getreide wird ~ *the corn will be destroyed by inundation*; das Bergwerk ist ersoffen *the mine is drowned*

ers·äufen vt [h] (jdn) *to drown* ‖ sich ~ *to d. o.s.* ‖ ⟨fig⟩ die Sorgen ~ in .. *to drown one's cares in* (*whiskey*) ‖ ⟨min⟩ *to inundate* **Ers·äufung** f ~/~en *drowning*

ersch·affen vt [h] [→ schaffen] *to create* ‖ ⟨übtr⟩ *to produce* **Ersch·affer** m ~s/~ *creator*; der ~ *the Creator* **Ersch·affung** f ~/~en *creation*

ersch·allen vi [s] [pret erscholl & erschallte] (of the voice) *to sound, resound*; *to ring out*; Beifall erschallte aus 1000 Kehlen *applause rang out from a thousand throats* ‖ (of music) *to roll out*; *to thrill* (durch *through*) | (etw) ~ l *to ring, sound*; jds Lob ~ l *to resound a p's praises*

ersch·audern vi [s] *to shudder*; *to be shaken* (vor *with*)

ersch·auern vi [s] *to shiver, thrill* (über *at*; vor *with*); *vibrate* (vor *with*); vor Ehrfurcht ~ *to be awestruck*; → erbeben

ersch·auen vt [h] ⟨poet⟩ = erblicken

ersch·einen I. vi [s] [→ scheinen] **A. (P) 1.** *to appear, to make one's appearance, to put in an appearance*; *to come along*; ⟨fam⟩ *to happen*; *to turn up*; sie wird jeden Augenblick ~ *she'll be along at any moment* | *to emerge* (aus *from*); *to come forward*; auf der Bühne, vor Gericht ~ *to appear*; persönlich ~ *to put in a personal appearance*; als Ankläger ~ *to appear for the prosecution*; als Verteidiger ~ *to appear to defend* ‖ z erstenmal ~ *to make one's début* ‖ junge Dame, die erstmalig in der Gesellschaft erscheint *débutante* ‖ ⟨theat⟩ die Spieler mußten zehnmal ~ *the players took ten curtains* ‖ vor jdm ~ *to come before a p, before a meeting* ‖ nicht vor Gericht ~ ⟨jur⟩ *to* (*make*) *default* ‖ nicht erschienen s *to be absent* **2.** (of ghosts) *to appear* (jdm *to a p*) ‖ in körperlicher Gestalt ~ *to materialize* (*in the room*) **3.** ⟨übtr⟩ **a.** vor der Öffentlichkeit ~ *to appear in public* **b.** in e–m Roman ~ *to figure in a novel*; er erscheint in dem Stücke als Held *he figures in the play as the hero* ‖ jdn leidlich ~ l *to make a p look tolerably* (*on canvas*) **B. (S) 1.** *to appear*; *to make its appearance*; ⟨fam⟩ *to happen* (*in the hope that the ten* [die Zehn] *would h. again*) ‖ *to emerge* (aus *from*); *to come forth*; *to show*; ⟨phot⟩ (im Entwickler) schnell ~ *to flash up*; (of plants) *to spring* **2.** (of books, etc.) *to appear, to come out*; *to be published*; eben erschienen *just out, just published* ‖ ~ l *to bring out*; *to publish*; demnächst ~d *out soon* **3.** (of motifs, traits) *to figure* **4.** (den Anschein, Eindruck erwecken) glaubwürdig ~ *to sound true*; jdm unglaublich ~ *to seem* (od *appear*) *incredible to a p* ‖ es erscheint mir seltsam *it strikes me as strange* (*that* ..) ‖ es erscheint mir nicht als bes glücklich *it strikes me not as singularly felicitous* ‖ jdm in e–m neuen Lichte ~ *to strike a p in a new light* ‖ vorteilhaft (im besten Licht) ~ *to show up* ‖ (of a p) wie erschien er Dir? *how did he look to you?* **II.** ≗ n ~s/ **1.** *appearance* (*of a p*; *a th*) ‖ ~ auf der Bühne *appearance on the stage*; ~ vor Gericht *appearance*; persönliches ~ *personal a.*; *a. in person* ‖ Nicht≗ *absence*; ⟨jur⟩ *default*; *non-appearance* **2.** *appearance, publication* (*of a book*, etc.); im ~ begriffen *forthcoming* (*book*); gleich nach ~ *immediately after publication* ‖ erstes ~ e–r S *the first dawn*(*ing*) *of a th* (*of civilization*, etc.) ‖ → Auftreten; Erscheinung

Ersch·einung f ~/~en **1.** = Erscheinen ‖ *appearance* (*of a ghost*) ‖ ⟨ec⟩ die ~ des Heilands *the Epiphany of Christ*; das Fest der ~ (6. Januar) *the Epiphany*; → Dreikönigsabend; (nach der Auferstehung) *the apparition of Our Lord* | in (die) ~ treten (of actions, states) *to appear, to make its appearance*; *to become visible*; *to come to light* od *view*; deutlich *to become evident*; nicht in ~ tr. *to keep in the background* ‖ (of feelings) *to come out*; *to emerge* (in *in*); *to be forthcoming* (*their help was not f.*); *to make itself felt*; *to show*; deutlich in ~ tr. *to stand out* (aus *from*); (etw) in ~ tr. l. *to disclose, display* **2. a.** (Zeichen) *indication, sign*; (Krankheits≗) *symptom*; Dekadenz≗en *symptoms of decadence*; ~en [pl] des Verfalls *signs of decay* **b.** *fact, thing*; *phenomenon*; (Charakteristik) *feature* ‖ ~en [pl] *phenomena*; es ist e–e eigentümliche ~, daß .. *it is a curious phenomenon* (od *fact, thing*) *that* .. **c.** ⟨philos⟩ *phenomenon*; die ~en der Natur *the phenomena of nature*; die Lehre v den ~en *phenomenalism*; politische, soziale ~en *political, social phenomena* **3.** *appearance* (*a curious a. in the sky*); *spectacle*; *sight*; e–e flüchtige ~ *a spurt* ‖ *appearance*; *aspect*; *look* (*of a p*; *a th*); jds äußere ~ *a p's outward appearance* (od *show*), *a p's figure*; *the cut of a p's jib* ‖ e–e stattliche ~ *an imposing figure*; *a handsome presence*; er war e–e st. ~ *he was a man of fine presence*; sie war e–e reizende ~ *she was a lovely vision*; → Anblick, aussehen A. 2. a. **4. a.** (Phantasie, Traumbild) *vision* **b.** e–e geisterhafte ~ *an appearance*; *a presence* ‖ Geister≗ *apparition, phantasm, phantom, spectre*; *ghost* **E–nungs- ~form** f *outward form* od *shape*; → Erscheinung 2. c. ‖ ⟨biol⟩ erbmassebedingte ~ e–s Lebewesens *genotype*; umweltbedingte ~ *ph*(*a*)*enotype* **~tag** m *day of publication* **~welt** f *the external world*

ersch·ießen vt [h] [→ schießen] **1.** (jdn) (standrechtlich ~) *to fusillade*; *to shoot* (mit *with*); *to shoot* (*a p*) *dead*; *to blow a p's brains out*; erschossen gefunden w *to be found shot dead* | **sich** ~ *to shoot o.s.*; *to blow one's brains out* **2.** ⟨fig⟩ °er war erschossen *he was at his wits' end* od *at the end of his tether*; vollkommen ~ *down and out*, ⟨fam⟩ *cooked, knocked up, done for*, ⟨mil⟩ *shagged* **Ersch·ießung** f ~/~en *the shooting* (*of a p*);

the shooting dead (*of a p*); standrechtliche ∼ *execution by firing squad* | ∼skommando [n] *firing squad*

erschl·affen vi/t **A.** vi [s] **1. a.** (of muscles) *to relax* **b.** (P) *to tire* (vor *with*); *to become tired* (od *exhausted, weary*) (*with*); *to sink* ‖ ⟨übtr⟩ ∼ in etw *to relax* (od *slacken*) *in a th* **2.** ⟨fig⟩ (of action) *to slacken* ‖ (of interest, etc.) *to flag, languish, wilt*; *diminish* **2.** vt [h] (Darm, Muskeln) *to relax* ‖ (jdn) *to fatigue, tire*; *exhaust* ‖ (jds Kräfte) *to prostrate* ‖ (Interesse) *to relax* ‖ **erschlafft** *prostrate*; erschlafft s *to be prostrated* (vor *with*) ‖ → erlahmen, –matten **Erschl·affung** f ∼/∼en *relaxation* (*of the bowels*) ‖ *prostration* (*of a p*; *of the mind*); *enervation*; *attrition*; ∼ der Nerven *sag of nerves* | ∼skrieg *war of a.*

erschl·agen vt [h] [→ schlagen] **1.** ⟨eig⟩ (jdn) *to kill*; ⟨poet & gewählt⟩ *to slay* ‖ (niedermetzeln) *to massacre, slaughter* ‖ vom Blitze ∼ w *to be struck by lightning* **2.** ⟨fig⟩ **a.** wie (*or* vollkommen) °∼ s *to be completely bowled over* (durch *by*); ⟨fam⟩ *to be flabbergasted* (od *struck dumb*); → erschießen 2.; **b.** °jdn ∼ = °anpumpen

erschl·eichen vt [h] [→ schleichen] etw ∼ *to obtain* od *get a th in an underhand way* (od *by insidious means, by trickery, by guile*); *to obtain a th surreptitiously* (v *from a p*); ⟨fam⟩ [abs] *to wangle a th* ‖ jds Gunst *etc* ∼ *to creep into a p's favour*; *to insinuate o.s. into a p's f.*; *to ingratiate o.s.* (od *to curry favour*) *with a p*; *to worm o.s.* (od *one's way*) *into a p's confidence* **Erschl·eichung** f ∼/∼en *the obtaining* (*of a th*) *in an underhand way* ‖ durch ∼ erlangen *to obtain by underhand dealing* ‖ ∼ des Beischlafs *carnal knowledge under false pretences*

erschl·ichen a *surreptitious*

erschl·ießbar a ⟨übtr⟩ *developable*; *capable of being opened up* ‖ *deducible* (aus *from*); *inferable*

erschl·ießen vt [h] [→ schließen] **A. 1.** *⟨eig⟩ = öffnen ‖ **sich** ∼ = sich öffnen **2.** ⟨übtr⟩ jdm sein Herz ∼ *to open one's heart* (od *mind*) *to a p*; *to unbosom o.s. to a p*; sich jdm ∼ *to reveal o.s. to a p* **3.** ⟨übtr⟩ (etw) *to disclose, open, reveal, unfold*; *develop* (⟨a.⟩ Gelände) ‖ e–r S e–n Weg ∼ *to open a way to a th* ‖ das Geheimnis wurde ihm erschlossen *the secret was revealed to him* | **sich** ∼ (S) *to develop* (od *unfold, reveal*) *itself* (jdm *to a p*); *to open*; *develop*; e–e gr Laufbahn erschließt sich ihm *a great career is opening for him* **4.** ⟨übtr⟩ **a.** (Land) *to open up* (jdm *for a p*); *to throw open* (*to a p*); (Gelände) der Bebauung ∼ *to break fresh ground* ‖ (Gebiet, neuen Markt, Quellen) *to open up*; *to tap*; ein neues Gebiet ∼ *to break new ground* **b. sich** ∼ *to be opened up* **B.** (Bedeutung, Sinn) *to conclude, to infer* (aus *from*); (Methode) *to deduce* (*from*); (Ursprung e–r S, e–s Wortes) *to derive* (aus *from*) **Erschl·ießung** f ∼/∼en *disclosure* (*of a secret*) ‖ *opening up* (*of land, sources*, etc.) ‖ die ∼ neuen Gebietes *the breaking of new ground*

***erschm·eicheln** vt [h] *to obtain by flattery*

erschn·appen vt [h] (etw) *to catch*; gierig ∼ *to snap up*; *to snatch* ‖ °⟨übtr⟩ *to get hold of*; *to secure* ‖ °(jdn) *to catch* (bei *at*)

ersch·oll pret, **ersch·ollen** pp v erschallen

ersch·öpfen vt [h] **1.** *⟨eig⟩ = (aufbrauchen), ausschöpfen, leeren **2.** ⟨übtr⟩ **a.** (jdn) *to exhaust*; *to knock up*; (diese Art Klima) –ft einen *takes it out of a man* ‖ (schnelles Laufen) –ft mich *pumps me* ‖ jdn durch Laufen ∼ *to run a p off his legs* ‖ ganz –ft s *to feel quite exhausted*; *to be washed out*; ⟨Am sl⟩ *to be frazzled out*; → –ft | **sich** vollkommen ∼ *to spend o.s.* (bei, durch *in*); *to wear o.s. out* ‖ *to exhaust o.s.* (in *in*) **b.** (jds Kasse, Kräfte) *to drain, exhaust* ‖ (Hilfsquellen etc) *to exhaust* ‖ s–e Geldmittel –ft h *to have come to the end of one's resources*; ⟨ins⟩ sein Anspruch ist –ft *he has no more benefits to his credit*, → –ft ‖ (Thema) *to exhaust*; *to run dry*; *to treat fully* ‖ alle Möglichkeiten ∼ *to explore all possible avenues, to exhaust all possible combinations* ‖ m–e Geduld ist –ft *my patience is exhausted* ‖ m–e Weisheit ist –ft *I am at the end of my tether* | **sich** ∼ *to be exhausted* ‖ *to peter out*; das Drama –fte sich allmählich *the drama gradually played itself out* **ersch·öpfend 1.** a *exhaustive* (*study, treatment*) **2.** adv *exhaustively*; ∼ behandeln *to exhaust*; *to be exhaustive of* (*a th*) **ersch·öpflich** a *exhaustible* **ersch·öpft** a (P) *done*; *done up*; *exhausted*; *prostrate*; *run to seed*; völlig ∼ *effete*, ⟨fam⟩ *dead-beat*; ganz *or* völlig ∼ ⟨Am sl⟩ *washed-up*; *run ragged*; ∼ zum Umsinken ⟨fam⟩ *fit to sink* ‖ (S) *done with*; *finished*; *depleted*, (bes ⟨at⟩) *spent* (*fuel*); *run-down* (⟨el⟩ *battery*); ⟨min⟩ *worked out*; *played out* (*the drama is p. out*) **Ersch·öpfung** f ∼/∼en *exhaustion* (*of a p*); ⟨Am sl⟩ *frazzle*; bis zur ∼ *to a f.* ‖ ∼ durch Hunger *inanition*; vor ∼ umfallen *to drop with exhaustion* ‖ *depletion* (*of natural resources*) | *drain* (der Kasse jds *on a p's purse*); *exhaustion* (*of supplies*) | ∼skrieg *war of exhaustion* od *attrition*; ∼szustand *state of exhaustion*

erschr·ecken I. vt/i **1. vt [h] [erschreckte/erschreckt**/erschrecke!] (in Schrecken setzen) (jdn) *to alarm, appal, dismay, frighten*; *scare*; *startle*; *to give* (*a p*) *a start* ‖ (entsetzen) *to shock* ‖ *to nonplus*; *stagger* (*we were staggered by* ..); ⟨Am⟩ *to rattle* ‖ (die Nachricht) –ckte ihn (gar) sehr .. *gave him quite a turn* ‖ jdn furchtbar ∼ ⟨fam⟩ *to give a p a fit* od *jump* ‖ jdn zu Tode ∼ *to frighten* od *scare a p out of his wits* ‖ es erschreckte sie z Tode *it gave her the fright of her life, it frightened the soul out of her* ‖ **sich** ∼ *to be alarmed* (od *frightened, startled*) (über *at*); *to be frightened* (od *terrified*) (vor *of*) **2. vi [s] [erschrak/erschrocken**/erschrick!] (in Schrecken geraten) *to be frightened* (*don't be f.*); *to take alarm* (od *fright*) (über *at*); *to be affrighted*; *to get a fright*; *to start, panic* (*at the thought*) **erschrocken** [s] → d. (*to be*) *dismayed* (durch *by*); ∼ s über *to be frightened* od *shocked at* (*a th*); ∼ s vor *to be frightened* od *terrified of* (*a p*) ‖ tief ∼ *appalled* ‖ z Tode ∼ s *to have the fright* (od *to get the shock*) *of one's life, to be frightened out of one's senses*; *to have one's heart in one's mouth* ‖ ∼(er Blick) *startled, horrified* | ich habe mich ∼ = ich erschrak → 1. & 2. **II.** ∸ n *start*; *shock*; → Schrecken **erschr·eckend 1.** a *frightening, alarming, appalling, startling*; *terrible* **2.** adv *appallingly* (*long*); *bewilderingly*; *horribly* (*poor*); *monstrously* (*clear*) **erschr·ecklich** a & adv = erschreckend, schrecklich

erschr·ocken a *frightened* (*child*); *terrified*; [pred] *in terror*; → erschrecken 2. | ∸**heit** f ∼/ = Schrecken

ersch·üttern vi/t **A.** *vi [s] *to shake*; *to be shaken* **B.** vt [h] **1.** ⟨eig⟩ (of detonations, etc.) (den Boden) *to convulse* (*the ground was convulsed by an earthquake*); (Haus) *to shake* (bis in das Grundwerk *to its foundations*); –rt w *to be shaken*; *to shake* ‖ jdm das Zwerchfell ∼ *to throw a p into convulsions of laughter*; *to make a p split his sides* ‖ (Fenster) laut ∼ *to jar* ‖ ⟨phot⟩ (Apparat) *to jar, jerk, jolt* **2. a.** (ein Land) *to agitate, convulse, stagger, disturb* ‖ *to upset, unsettle* (*political situation*) **b.** (jds Stellung, Entschluß, Glauben etc) *to shake* ‖ *to break* (*confidence*) **c.** (Nerven) *to rack* **c.** (erschrecken) jdn ∼ *to stagger a p* (*we were staggered by the audacity* ..); ⟨Am⟩ *to rattle* **d.** (innerlich ∼) *to shock, thrill*; *to send a shock through* (*a p*); es –rt mich im Innersten *it gives me quite a shock*; es –rte sein Inneres plötzlich *it gave him a sudden thrill* ‖ –rt durch, über *thrilled by, at*; –rt w *to be convulsed* (v .. *with civil strife*); *to vibrate* (*with*); *to thrill* (über *at*; v *with*) **ersch·ütternd** a & adv =

ergreifend **Ersch·ütterung** f ~/~en **1.** *concussion*; Gehirnˣ~ *c. of the brain* || *concussion* (*of the air, ground*); *shaking*; *vibration* (*on a steamer*) || ⟨phot⟩ *jarring, jerking, jolting* **2.** ⟨fig⟩ **a.** innere ~ e–s Landes *civil convulsion of a country* || *upset(ting), unsettling* (der Wirtschaft) **b.** (seelische ~) *emotional upset*; *inner turmoil*; *strong emotion*; *shock*; *thrill* **ˣ~sfest, ~sfrei** a *shock-proof, vibration-proof* | ~sfreie Spezialaufhängung [f] *special suspension free of vibration, special vibration-free mounting*

erschw·eren vt [h] (jds Bewegung, Handlung) *to embarrass* (durch *by*); *hinder, impede*; *to render difficult* || jds Lage ~ *to handicap a p* (*by*) || e–e Frage (*or* die Dinge) noch ~ *to complicate a question, matters*; *to make a q.* (*matters*) *complicate* (od *intricate, involved*) | jdm die Arbeit ~ *to render the job* (*more*) *difficult for a p*; *to complicate* (od *increase*) *a p's job*; es jdm ~ z tun *to make it difficult for a p to do* || er –rt sich das Leben unnötig *he unnecessarily complicates his life* || erschwert *less favo(u)rable* (*conditions*); → verschlimmern **erschw·erend** a *complicating*, ⟨bes jur⟩ *aggravating* (*circumstances*) **Erschw·erung** f ~/~en *embarrassment*; *impediment* (e–r Tätigkeit *to an activity*); *drag, handicap* (e–r S *on a th*) || *complication, intricacy* (*of a question*); zusätzliche ~ *added difficulty* || ⟨jur⟩ *aggravation*

erschw·indeln vt [h] (etw) *to obtain by swindling*; (sich) etw v jdm ~ *to swindle a th out of a p*; ⟨Am sl⟩ *to con a th from a p*

erschw·ingen vt [h] [→ schwingen] [nur in Wendungen wie]: das kann ich nicht ~ *I cannot afford it*; .. ich kaum (*or* gerade noch) ~ *I can hardly* (*just*) *afford it*; mehr als ich ~ konnte *more than I could a.* || nicht zu ~ *unattainable*; *beyond a p's means* **erschw·ingbar, erschw·inglich** a *attainable*; (nicht) *within* (*beyond*) *a p's means*; ~ f jedermann *within reach of everyone*

ers·ehen vt [h] [→ sehen] **1.** (erkennen) (etw) *to learn* (aus *from*); *to notice, observe*; wir ~ aus Ihrem Briefe, daß .. *we learn from your letter that ..* || wie z ~ ist aus .. *as becomes patent from* (*your letter*); .. nicht z ~ s aus: *your l. does not make clear* || wie Sie aus den Zahlen ~ *as you see by these figures* || es läßt sich [acc] leicht ~ *it shows clearly* **2.** = ausersehen | ˣsich [dat] e–e gelegene Zeit ~ *to avail o.s. of an opportunity*; *to profit by an o.* || er kann mich nicht ~ *he has a down on me*

ers·ehnen vt [h] (etw) *to crave* od *long for*; *to have a desire* od *longing for* (*a th*); *to hanker* od *yearn after* od *for* (*a th*); *to desire* (*a th*) *earnestly*

ers·essen a [pp v ersitzen] ⟨jur⟩ ~es Recht [n] *prescriptive right*

ers·etzbar a *replaceable*; *replenishable* (durch *by*)

ers·etzen vt [h] **1.** (wiedergutmachen) (Schaden, Verlust) *to make good* (jdm *to a p*); *to repair* (*a th*); *to compensate* (od *make amends, make up*) *for* (*a th*); (Verluste) *to recover* (durch *by*) || (Auslagen, Unkosten) *to refund* (jdm *to a p*); *to reimburse*; *to make good* **2.** (an die Stelle setzen v) **a. (etw)** *to replace, oust, subsede* (durch *by*); etw ~ durch etw *to substitute a th for a th*; das Original durch Imitation ~ *to substitute an imitation for the original*; Worte durch Taten ~ *to substitute facts for phrases* || das Rad wurde ersetzt *the wheel was replaced by another* || ⟨übtr⟩ (*this appliance*) *does the work of* (*three*) **b. (jdn)** *to replace, to supersede* (durch *by*) || jdn, jds Stelle ~ *to fill a p's place*, → Arbeitsplatz einnehmen; er wird nicht leicht z ~ s *his place will not be easily filled*; es gibt k–n, der nicht z ~ wäre *there are as good fish in the sea as ever came out of it* || *to make up for* (*there are more Swedes and Danes than usual but that does not make up for our old friends*) **c.** (S) **(etw)** *to help out* (*soup will help out our meal*) || → Ersatz

ers·etzlich a *reparable*; → ersetzbar

Ers·etzung f ~/~en = Ersatz A.

ers·ichtlich 1. a [mst pred] *clear, evident, obvious* (*advantage, fact*); *patent* (aus *from*); aus dem Schreiben ist ~, daß .. *it appears from the letter that ..*; wie ~ ist aus .. *as becomes patent from ..* **2.** adv *obviously*; ~ ein grober Irrtum *obviously a gross error*

ers·innen vt [h] [→ sinnen] (Mittel; Plan) *to devise, plan, excogitate*; *contrive, invent*; *to strike out*; *to think* od *study .. out* || ⟨fam⟩ *to dream .. up* || ⟨dero⟩ *to concoct, fabricate*; (Ausrede) *to feign*; e–e Lüge, Geschichte ~ *to spin a yarn*; → erdenken, erdichten ***ers·innlich** a = erdenklich

ers·itzen vt [h] [→ sitzen] ⟨fig jur⟩ (ein Recht) *to acquire by prescription*; → ersessen || (ein Zeugnis) *to obtain .. by sitting an unusual stretch of time in a class* **Ers·itzung** f ~/~en ⟨jur⟩ (Eigentumserwerb durch) ~ *prescription*

ers·offen a (→ ersaufen & ˣ~) ⟨min⟩ *drowned* (*shaft*) || (*of float chamber*) *flooded*

ersp·ähen vt [h] (etw, jdn) *to espy*; *to catch sight of* || *to detect, spot*; *to descry*

ersp·aren vt [h] **1.** (sparen) etw ~, sich [dat] etw ~ *to save*; *to lay* od *put by*; ein Vermögen ~ *to make a fortune by saving* **2.** (unnötig m) **a.** (etw) *to save*; Rückverweise ~ *to save referring back*; Sie w viel Benzin ~ *you'll save much petrol*; viel Gerede wurde erspart *much talk was avoided* **b.** jdm etw (Geld, Mühe, Zeit) ~ *to save* od *spare a p a th*; es wird mir 100 Mark ~ *it will save me 100 marks*; erspare mir diesen Lärm *spare me this noise*; jdm die Mühe ~ z tun *to save* (od *spare*) *a p the trouble of doing*; sie –rte ihm e–n Sekretär *she saved him a secretary*; mir wurde diese Demütigung –rt *I was spared this humiliation*; es bleibt uns nichts –rt *we are spared nothing* **c.** sich [dat] etw ~ *to save a th*, → o. 2. a. || sich die Mühe ~ z tun *to save* (od *spare*) *o.s. the trouble of doing*; sie würden sich viele Enttäuschungen –rt h *they would have saved themselves many disappointments* || er konnte es sich nicht ~ z erwähnen *he could not help mentioning* | **-ersp·arend** a [in comp] ·arbeit~ *labour-saving*; z·eit~ *time-saving* **ersp·art** a; ~es Geld *saved money, savings* [pl] || das ˣ~e *savings* [pl]

Ersp·arnis 1. f ~/–nisse [abstr] *saving, economy* (an *of*); Zeitˣ~ *saving* (od *economy*) *of time*; der ~ halber *for economy's sake* || (S) *saver*; diese Erfindung erweist sich als e–e gr Arbeitsˣ~ *this invention is a great labour-saver* (od *saver of labour*) **2.** n –nisses/–nisse & f ~/–nisse [konkr] (Erspartes) *savings* [pl] (*all my s.*); *saved money* || –nisse [pl] (in der Wirtschaft) *economies* [pl] **Ersp·arung** f ~/~en *saving* (an *of*)

†**erspr·ießen** vi [s] = entsprießen **erspr·ießlich** a *beneficial* (f jdn *to a p*); *salutary*; *profitable, useful* **Erspr·ießlichkeit** f ~/ *beneficialness* (f *to*); *salutariness*; *usefulness*

erst adv **A.** ⟨eig⟩ ([stets betont] = zuerst) *at first*; *first*; ⟨Am⟩ *first off* || er fragte ~ nach m–m Namen *at first he asked my name, he first asked my name*; ~ kommt er, er kommt ~ *he comes first*; ~ mußt du fertig s *you must get ready first*; ich muß das ~ fertigmachen *I must get this done first* || ~ .. d·ann *first .. then*; ~ wollte er, dann wieder nicht *first he agreed then declined* || °~ (ein)mal so u d·ann so *first one way and then the other*; fang doch ~ mal an *make a start, though* || aller~ *first of all*; *first and foremost*; ich werde dies z aller~ erledigen *I shall do it first thing* **B.** ⟨übtr⟩ [verblaßt] **1.** [betont; = vorher] ~ sagtest du doch, daß .. *before you said that ..* **2.** [unbetont] .., **aber ..** ~ meinen .. *but you should just see mine* **nun** ~ wird mir klar *now at last I see* **3.** [unbetont (doch vgl. c.); = nur] mst *only*; *not until* **a.** ich bin ~ auf Seite 20

I got only as far as page 20; *I am only at page 20* || er hat ~ die H·älfte erledigt *he has finished only half of it* **b. ~ d·ann** *not till then* || ·eben ~, ~ j·etzt *only just* (*now*) || es ist ~ 9 Uhr *it is only nine o'clock*; er ist ~ 50 *he is only fifty* || ~ g·estern *only yesterday, not until yesterday*; ~ h·eute, m·orgen *not until today, tomorrow* || †~ **noch**! [abs] *well I never!*; *you don't say so!* || ~ noch ·Ostern *as recently as Easter*; ~ noch e–e Stunde vorher *as recently as an hour before*; ~ noch vor e–m Jahre *as recently as a year ago* || ~ **spät** *not until late*; ~ einige Wochen später erwachte sein Gewissen *only some weeks after did his conscience awaken*; *his conscience awakened not until some weeks later* || das Testament wurde ~ am 2. Mai gemacht *the will was made as lately as May 2.* || ~ im letzten Augenblick erkannte er .. *only at the last moment did he recognize* .. || ~ nach e–r langen Zeit entdeckte er .. *it was a long while before he discovered* .. || ~ vor drei Wochen *not later back than three weeks* **c.** [betont] **~ als, ~ nachdem, ~ wenn** *not until*; ~ als er zurückgekehrt war, brachen wir auf *not until he returned* (od *only when he returned*) *did we start*; ~ als .. *it was not till the child was two years old, that he ventured to let himself grow fond of it* **4.** [ganz verblaßt] **a.** der soll ~ noch geboren w *he is not yet born* **b. ~ r·echt** *more than ever*; *more than before*; *with a vengeance*; er schlug nun ~ recht um sich *he laid about him with a v.*; nun ~ recht nicht! *much less than before*! *much less still*! || das macht es ~ recht schlimm *that makes it all the worse*; (*now we shall have to be*) *even more* od *doubly* (*careful*); ~ recht nicht (*he would like that*) *even less* **c.** das **war** ~ ein Triumph *that was a triumph, by Jove* od *indeed* **d. wäre** ich nur ~ daheim, **wenn** ich nur ~ daheim wäre! *would I were home at last*! *if I only were h. at last*!

·Erst- [in comp] (→ erste) mst *first* .., *initial* .. **~aufführung** f ⟨theat⟩ *first-night*; *first performance*; → Ur– || gewohnheitsmäßiger Besucher v ~en *firstnighter* **~ausbildung** f *initial training* **~ausfertigung** f ⟨off⟩ *original copy* **~ausführung** f ⟨tech⟩ *prototype*; *original model* od *pattern* **~ausgabe** f *first edition*; *first-edition copy* **~ausstattung** f *initial issue* **≈beste**; der ~ → erste **~besteigung** f (Berg≈) *first climbing* od *ascent* **~druck** m *first edition* od *printing* || *incunabulum* **≈erwähnt** a *aforementioned, first-mentioned* **≈gebärend** a ⟨demog⟩ *primiparous* | **≈e** [f] *primipara* **≈geboren** a *first-born* || ≈e [der ≈e, ein ≈er] m ≈en/≈en *first-born*; ⟨bib⟩ *first-begotten* **~geburt** f **1.** *first-born child*; *first-born* **2.** ⟨jur⟩ (~srecht) *primogeniture*; ⟨bib⟩ *birthright* **~geburtsrecht** n ⟨jur⟩ *primogeniture* **≈genannt** a *aforesaid* **≈klassig 1.** a *first-class* (*article, writer*), *first-rate*; *first-quality* (*merchandise*); *principal*; *superior* (*butler*); *tip-top*; *A 1*; *thoroughbred* || ⟨com⟩ *exclusive* (*models, store*); *first-chop*; *prime* (*beef*); *gilt-edged* (*securities*); *best* (*references*); ~e Exemplare *plums* [pl] || ⟨fam⟩ *clinking, rattling*; *top-notch*; *topping* || ⟨sl⟩ *bang-up*; *posh*; *slap-up* (*dinner*); *top-hole*; e–e ~e S *a clinker*; ein ~er Arbeiter *a top-notcher* | ⟨Am⟩ *A No 1*; *bang-up* (*salaries*); *banner* (*investment*); *bully-dandy* || [pred] *perfectly good*; *the best type of* **2.** adv ⟨fam⟩ (*to play*) *first-class*; *first rate*; *clinking, rattling*; *toppingly* **≈malig 1.** a *occuring for the first time*; *unprecedented* **2.** adv = erstmals; → Verbrecher **≈mals** adv *for the first time* **~markierer** m ⟨mil aero⟩ *initial target marker* **~meldung** f *earlier* od *exclusive news*; *piece of first-hand information*; ⟨Am sl⟩ *scoop*; (Zeitung) durch e–e ~ ausstechen ⟨sl⟩ *to scoop* **~montage** f ⟨tech⟩ *green* od *new assembly* **~prüfung** ⟨tech⟩ *virgin test* **≈rangig** a = erstklassig **~stufentriebsatz** m *first-stage power plant* **~zus-bau** = –montage

erst·arken vi [s] *to strengthen*; *to grow* (*strong* od) *in strength*; *to recuperate*; ⟨bes Am⟩ *to lift up one's head* ⟨a. fig⟩ **Erst·arkung** f *strengthening*; *recuperation*

erst·arren vi/t **A.** vi [s] **1.** ⟨phys⟩ *to set, solidify coagulate* || (of limbs) *to be* od *get benumbed* (*my fingers were benumbed*); *to become numb* od *torpid*; *to stiffen, to grow stiff* || (vor Kälte) *to be chilled* || (of liquids) *to solidify* **2.** ⟨fig⟩ vor Schreck ~ *to be chilled with terror*; *to freeze with horror*; das Blut erstarrte ihm in den Adern bei dem Anblick *the sight made his blood curdle*; das Blut war ihm vor Schreck erstarrt *terror had made his blood curdle*; *his b. froze in his veins*; *his b. ran cold* || *the smile froze on her lips*; (of the face) *to become rigid*; *to freeze* od *stiffen* (z *into*) || (of conditions) *to stiffen*; *to be congealed* (z *into*) **3.** (Glieder) ~ l *to* (*be*)*numb* (vor .. *with cold*) || jdn ~ l *to freeze a p, to chill a p*; jds Blut ~ l *to curdle* od *freeze a p's blood*, → o. 2. || (Gefühle) ~ l *to deaden, numb* || (Erscheinungen) ~ l *to stiffen* (durch *by*) **B.** *vt ⟨poet⟩ (Blick) *to render lifeless* od *motionless* **erst·arrt** a (*be*)*numbed* (*limb*); *numb, torpid*; *stiff* || ⟨fig⟩ *numbed* (*faculties*) || *an iron-bound tradition* **Erst·arrung** f ~/~en *numbing*; *numbness, torpidity, –pidness, –pescence*; *stiffness* || ⟨phot, etc⟩ *chilling, setting* (*of gelatine*) || *solidification* (*of a liquid*); ⟨fig⟩ *numbness, torpor, torpidity* | ~spunkt *solidifying* od *solidification, setting point*; ~szustand ⟨phys⟩ *congealed state*; *rigidity*

erst·atten vt [h] **1.** (ersetzen) (Unkosten) *to refund* (od *repay, restore*) (jdm *to a p*); → zurückerstatten **2.** (bieten, leisten) = erstatten → Bericht 1. b. || Dank ~ → abstatten

Erst·attung f ~/~en **1.** *refund*(*ment*); *repayment* (*of expenses*) **2.** *the making* (od *drawing up*) (*of a report*); *the giving* od *rendering* (*of an account*) || → Berichterstatter, Berichterstattung

erst·aunen I. vi/t **1.** vi [s] *to be astonished* od *amazed, to marvel* (über .. *at a th*); ich bin (höchst) erstaunt über dich ⟨dero⟩ *I am surprised at you, I wonder at you*; ich bin erstaunt, dich hier z treffen *I wonder at seeing* (od *to see*) *you here*; .., daß Sie abreisen wollen *I am surprised to hear that you are leaving* **2.** *vt [h] jdn ~ = in Erstaunen setzen **II.** ≈ n *astonishment* (über *at*); *bedazement*; höchstes ~ *amazement, surprise* (*at*) || z m–m ~ *to my astonishment* (od *amazement*); z m–m ~ ist er noch nicht hier *I wonder he is not here yet* || jdn mit ~ erfüllen, jdn in ~ setzen *to fill a p with amazement*; *to astonish* (od *astound*) *a p*; in höchstes ~ setzen *to amaze* (od *surprise*) *a p*; *to put a p out*; *to take a p's breath away*, ⟨Am⟩ *to take a p's breath* || sich v s–m ~ erholen *to recover from one's astoishment* (od *bedazement*) || mit vor ~ aufgerissenen Augen (*she gazed*) *wide-eyed* || schmerzliches ~ *amazed distress* **erst·aunend** a & adv = erstaunlich

erst·aunenswert, –würdig a = erstaunlich

erst·aunlich I. a **1.** [attr] *astonishing, astounding*; *marvellous, remarkable*; *wonderful* (*courage*); höchst ~ *amazing, surprising*; *prodigeous, stupendous* (*mistake*) || ~e S ⟨fam⟩ *brow-raiser* **2.** [pred] *amazing, surprising*; *marvellous, remarkable*; es ist ~ *it is amazing*; das ≈e daran ist .. *the amazing th about it is* .. **II.** adv *amazingly, astoundingly*; *surprisingly* || .. kostet ~ wenig, z ~ kl Preis *at a cost which every user can afford*

erst·aunt 1. a *astonished, astounded*; *amazed* (über *at*); *put out* **2.** adv *amazedly*; *in astonishment* (*she asked him in a.*); *in wonder*

·erstb·este a der, die ~ *anybody* || das ~ *anything*

·erste a → ≈ (u.) **A.** der, die, das ~ **1.** *the first* (*p; th*); die ~ Straße rechts *the first turning to the right* || beim ~n Blick *at first sight* || die ~n beiden *the first two* | (zeitlich) *first*; *earliest* || im ∼n Augenblick → Augenblick 2. b. || die ∼n Früchte [pl] *the first fruits* [pl] || ⟨ec⟩ die ∼ Gebetsstunde *prime* || der ∼ Teil des Jahres ⟨Am⟩ *the first of the year* || die ∼ Blüte *the prime* (*of poetry*) || das ∼ gedruckte Buch *the first-printed book* **2.** ⟨übtr⟩ *chief*, *foremost*, *head*; *leading*, *principal*; *superior* (*quality*); *top*; ⟨Am⟩ *ranking*; → erstklassig **B.** der ∼ Januar *the first of January*, (geschrieben:) *January 1st* **C. bes. Verbindungen**: ∼r Anflug ⟨aero⟩ *initial approach* || der ∼ geschäftsführende Beamte ⟨Am⟩ *the executive*; → u. ∼e Lord, Offizier || der ∼ beste, der ∼ x-beliebige *the first comer*; ⟨Am⟩ *the next man* || jeden ∼n besten *any chance comer* || *the first* (sc *train*) || die ∼ Geige, der ∼ Geiger *the first violin* || Rindfleisch v ∼r Güte *prime beef* || aus ∼r Hand *at first-hand*; Informationen aus ∼r H. *first-hand information* || ∼ Hilfe *first-aid*; ∼ H. leisten *to render first-aid* || ∼ Klasse ⟨rail⟩ *first-class*; ∼r Kl. (*to travel*) *first-class* || Fahrkarte, Wagen ∼r Kl. *first* (*3 firsts, please*) || ⟨engl school⟩ die ∼ Kl. (= Prima) *the sixth form* || e–e ∼ Kraft *a first-rate man* (od *hand*) || in ∼r Linie *in the first place*; *first of all*; *first and foremost* || der ≗ Lord der Admiralität *the First Lord of the Admiralty* || das ∼ Mal *the first time*; z ∼n M. *for the f. t.* || beim ∼n Male *at the first go-off* || der ≗ Offizier ⟨mar⟩ *the executive officer*; (auf Handelsschiff) *mate* || im ∼n Moment *for the moment* || der ∼ Offizier der britischen Flotte ⟨Am⟩ *the ranking officer of the British navy* || → Parkett; Platz; Post; Preis || ∼r Qualität *of the finest brand* (od *quality*); Waren ∼r Q. *firsts* [pl] || ∼n Ranges *first-rate*; *first-class*; → Rang; ∼ Rede *maiden speech* || an ∼r Stelle *in the first place*; *to begin with*; *first thing*; *first of all*, *first and foremost* || er steht an ∼r St. *he is A 1*; ⟨Am⟩ *A No 1* || die wichtigsten Sachen immer an ∼r St. *first things first* || ∼r Stock *first floor*; im ∼n St. *on the f. f.* || ∼ Stufe (in der Prüfung) ⟨univ⟩ *first* || bei der ∼n Überlegung *at first glimpse* || ∼er Versuch *maiden effort* || ⟨fig⟩ auf den ∼n Wurf *at the first go-off* **D.** [subst.] er war der ∼, der ankam *he was the first to arrive*; er ging als ∼r aus dem Kampfe hervor *he came out the winner* || zeitlich das ∼ *the first in date*

·Erste A. → ≗ (o.) [∼r, der ∼; ∼, die ∼] (P) *the head* (od *top*) *boy* (*girl*) *of the form*; *the head* (od *top*) (*of a school*) || der ≗ (Kleinschreibung!), der erfindet, erfand, erfinden wird *or* sollte *the first man to invent* || als ≗r grüßen → grüßen || (S) der ∼ *the first day of the month*; am ∼n *on the first* **B.** ≗s, das ≗ **1.** *the first thing* || als ≗s *first thing*; *to begin with* (*there is, to b. with, the incident of* ..) **2. am** ≗n = am besten **3. fürs** ≗ *for the moment* (od *present*); *for the time being*; das wird genügen fürs ∼ *that will do to go on with*; fürs ≗ wohl kaum ⟨fam⟩ *not .. in a hurry* **4. vom** ≗n bis letzten *from first to last* **5. zum** ≗n .. zum zweiten *firstly .. secondly*; zum ≗n, zum zweiten, zum dritten! *going, going, gone*!

erst·echen vt [h] [→ stechen] (jdn) *to stab* (*a p*); *to run* (*a p*) *through*; hinterrücks ∼ *to stab* (*a p*) *in the back*; → erdolchen

erst·ehen vi/t [→ stehen] **1.** vi [s] **a.** ⟨ec⟩ = auferstehen **b.** *to arise*; das Land ist neu erstanden *the country has arisen anew* **c.** (entstehen) *to arise*, *to spring up*; *to come into being*; (of buildings) *to rise* (auf *on*); (of images) *to rise* (vor .. *before my mind's eye*) **d.** es w dir gr Unannehmlichkeiten daraus ∼ *you'll be put to great inconvenience by it*; → erwachsen **2.** vt [h] (durch Stehen erwerben) (etw auf Auktion) *to buy*, *to purchase* | ⟨hum⟩ → ersitzen **Erst·ehung** f ∼/∼en (auf Auktion) *purchase* (*of a th*)

erst·eigbar a *climbable*, *scalable* (*mountain*)

erst·eigen vt [h] **1.** ⟨eig⟩ (Berg, Treppe) *to ascend*, *climb*, *to mount*, *to scale* || (Mauer) *to scale*; *to climb*; ⟨hist mil⟩ (mit Sturmleitern) *to escalade*, *scale* **2.** die höchsten Stufen der Ehren ∼ *to gain the highest honours*; .. der Macht ∼ *to climb the heights of power* **Erst·eigung** f ∼/∼en *ascent* (*of a mountain*), *ascension*, *climbing* || ⟨hist mil⟩ *escalade*

erst·ellen vt [h] *to put* (od *set*) *up*; *erect*; *institute*; ⟨mach, comp⟩ *to produce* | ∼d a *originating* (Abteilung) **Erst·ellung** f *putting up*; *erection* || ∼ e–r Garantie *issue of a g.* || ⟨comp etc⟩ *setting up*, ∼ v *provision of*

·erstemal n: das ∼ = das ·erste Mal; → erste

†·ersten adv = soeben **∼mal**: beim, zum ∼ = beim, zum ersten Mal, → erste C.

·erstens adv *firstly*, *in the first place*, *for one th*; *to begin with* (*there is, to begin with, the incident of* ..) || ∼ .. zweitens *in the first place .. in the second place*; ⟨fam⟩ *first .. second*; ∼, weil .. zweitens, weil .. *for one th .. for another* || ∼ einmal *first of all*; *for one th*; ∼ einmal .. dann *for one th .. then*

erst·erben vi [s] [→ sterben] ⟨fig⟩ der Befehl erstarb auf s–n Lippen *the order died on his lips* || (of sound) *to die away* (od *down*); *to fade away* | ⟨† & hist⟩ ich ersterbe Eurer Majestät gehorsamster Diener *I remain Your Majesty's most humble and devoted servant* || in Demut ∼ *to cringe* (vor .. *to a p*), *to fawn* (*on a p*)

·erstere [pron] [∼r, der ∼; ∼, die ∼; ∼s, das ∼/; ∼e, die ∼n pl] *the former*; der ∼ .. der letztere *the former .. the latter*; die ∼n [pl] *the former* (.. *the latter*)

erst·icken I. vi/t **A.** vi [s] **1. (P)** *to choke*; *to be choked* (od *suffocated*); er ist an dem Kern erstickt *the kernel has choked him* || ich werde ∼, wenn ich hier bleibe *I shall smother* (od *suffocate*) *if I stay here* || im Schlamm –ckt *bogged down* || das Gefühl h ∼ z müssen *to feel stifled* od *suffocating* **2.** ⟨übtr⟩ *to choke* (vor .. *with anger*, etc.); *to be choked* od *suffocated* (*with*) || möge er an der Lüge ∼! *may the lie choke him*! || in der Arbeit ∼ *to be overwhelmed with work* ⟨fam⟩ *to be up to one's neck in w.* **b.** (of the voice, etc.) *to be choked* (od *smothered*); –ckte Stimme *strangled voice* || (of a riot) *to be stifled*; im Keim ∼ *to be nipped in the bud* **B.** vt [h] **1. a.** (of gas, etc.) **(jdn)** *to choke*, *stifle*, *suffocate* || (gewaltsam ∼) *to smother* (*he was smothered in the Tower*); *to stop a p's breath* **b.** (of weed) (Pflanzen) *to choke*, *stifle* **c.** der Nebel erstickt mich *the fog is smothering me* **2. (etw) a.** (Stimme) *to smother*; *to stifle*; *to drown*; mit erstickter Stimme *in a suffocated voice* **b.** (Gefühle; Lachen etc) *to smother*, *to suppress*; (Furcht) *to quell*; (Kummer) *to smother*, *to steep* (in *in*); (Seufzer) *to strangle* || (Bemühungen) *to stifle*; (jds Kräfte) *to strangle* || (Freundschaft) ⟨Am⟩ *to abort* **c.** (Aufruhr, Lärm) *to put down*, *to quell*, *to stifle*, *to suppress* || im Keime ∼ *to nip in the bud*; *to burke*; ⟨fam⟩ *to pip* **II.** ≗ n (→ ersticken A.) *choking*; *suffocation*, *asphyxia* [L] || nahe am ∼ s *to be in danger of suffocation*; *to be on the point of being choked* (od *suffocated*) || die Luft hier ist zum ∼ *the air here is suffocating*; zum ∼ heiß *stiflingly hot* || zum ∼ voll *chock-full*, *choke-full* (an, v *of*); *full to suffocation*; zum ∼ voll s v *to be choked up with* **erst·ickend 1.** a *asphyxiating* (*gas*) || ⟨übtr⟩ *choking*, *stifling*, *suffocating* (*air*, *heat*) **2.** adv *stiflingly*, *suffocatingly* **E–kung** f ∼/∼en **1.** = Ersticken **2.** (→ ersticken B.) **a.** *suffocation*, *asphyxiation* (*of a p*) **b.** *smothering*, *stifling*, *suppression* (*of a feeling*, *rebellion*) **∼sanfall** m *attack of choking* **∼stod** m *death from suffocation* od *asphyxiation*

·erstlich adv *firstly*, *in the first place*; → erstens

·**Erstling** m ~(e)s/~e **1.** *first-born*; *first-born child* **2. a.** ⟨bib⟩ (of animals) *firstling* **b.** ⟨fig⟩ [mst pl] ~e *the first fruits* [pl]; *the first products* [pl] (*of a p's work*) | **~s- ~arbeit** f *tyro's work, beginner's work* **~bekleidung** f ⟨tail com⟩ *layette* **~druck** m ~s/~e *first impression* od *edition* ‖ ⟨hist⟩ *incunabulum* **~erfolge** m [pl], **~leistungen** f [pl] *the first fruits* [pl] ‖ **~roman** m *first novel* ‖ → Jungfern–

erst·orben a [→ sterben] *sightless* (*eyes*)

erstr·ahlen vi [s] (*of eyes*) *to light up* (vor .. *with joy*); *to gleam, to be gleaming* (v *with*); *to be agleam* (*with*) ‖ Freude um sich ~ l *to radiate happiness around one*

erstr·eben vt [h] etw ~ *to aspire to* (od *after*) *a th*; *to strive after* (od *for*) *a th*; Ehren ~ *to aspire to honours*; die Führung ~ *to aspire to lead*; die Herrschaft ~ *to aspire to rule* ‖ den Sieg ~ *to strive for victory* ‖ (Glück, Ideal) *to reach after* (..) ‖ es wird –bt, daß *the aim is that* ‖ ⟨dero⟩ (e–e Stellung) *to covet*

erstr·ebenswert a *worth aspiring after*; *worth getting possession of*; *valuable* ‖ e–e ~e S *or* Partie ⟨sl⟩ *a great catch*; nicht ~ *not desirable*; k–e bes ~e S *not much of a catch*

erstr·ecken vt [h] **1.** (Forschungen etc) *to extend, spread* (über *over*) **2. sich** ~ (S) **a.** (sich ausdehnen) *to extend, stretch, run* (über *over*; nach allen Richtungen *in all directions*); *to reach* (bis hinunter z *down to*; v .. bis *from* .. *to*; über *over*); (breit) *to sprawl* (über *across*) ‖ (liegen) *to range* (an der Küste entlang *along the coast*; nach Osten *east*; v O. nach Westen *from east to west*); sich ~ zw *to intervene* (od *be situated*) *between* | (of time) *to spread* (über .. *over three years*); *to reach* (bis z, bis in *into*): *to stretch* (bis z *to*) **b.** ⟨übtr⟩ (of measures, laws) *to reach* (über *over*), *to range* (*from* .. *to*); s–e Studien ~ sich über ein weites Feld *his studies cover a wide field*; **c.** sich auf jdn *or* etw ~ *to concern a p* od *a th*; *to refer* (od *relate*) *to a p* od *a th*; *to embrace a th*; sich auf alles ~d *all-in*; ⟨Am⟩ *blanket* (*order*) ‖ → betreffen; beziehen; belaufen; umf·assen

erstr·eiten vt [h] = erkämpfen, erringen

°**erst·unken** a; es ist ~ und erlogen *it is a shameless lie*

erst·ürmen vt [h] (Festung) *to* (*take by*) *storm*

Erst·ürmung f ~/~en die ~ der Stadt *the taking of the town by storm*; *the storming of the t.*; *the sudden assault on the t.*

ers·uchen I. vt/i [h] **1.** vt; jdn (e–n Untergeordneten) ~ um etw *to call upon a p for a th*; *to request* (od *call upon*) *a p to do a th*; jdn um die Beantwortung e–r Frage ~ *to request a p to answer a question* ‖ jdn dringend ~ um etw *to beseech* od *solicit a p for a th* | jdn ~ z tun *to call upon* (od *request*) *a p to do*; (dringend) *to beseech* (od *entreat, implore, solicit*) *a p to do* ich ersuche Sie dringend .. *I'll trouble you* (*to answer my question*); m–e Eltern l Sie ~ *my parents send to request you* (..) **2.** vi; **~ um etw** *to request a th* ‖ höflich ~ um *to petition for* ..; ⟨com⟩ wir ~ höflich um baldmögliche Antwort *we request the favour of a reply at your early convenience* **II.** ≃ n *request*; dringendes ~ *entreaty, solicitation*; *petition* ‖ auf jds ~ (hin) *at a p's request*; *by request of* (*the town authorities*) ‖ das ~ an jdn stellen .. *to request a p to do*

ert·appen 1. vt [h] (Dieb etc) *to catch* (*out*) (bei etw *at* od *in a th*); *to detect, surprise*; ⟨sl⟩ *cop* (bei *at*) ‖ jdn auf frischer Tat ~ *to catch a p in the* (*very*) *act, to take a p red-handed*; beim Diebstahl ~ *to catch* .. *with the goods* ‖ wir ertappten ihn, während er es tat *we caught him doing it* ‖ er hat sich dabei ~ l *he got caught in the act*; da hab ich mich schön ~ l ⟨sl⟩ *that was a fair cop* | jdn bei e–r Unaufmerksamkeit ~ *to catch a p napping*; ich ertappte mich bei dem Gedanken *I caught myself thinking* **2.** ≃ n *catching*; *detection*; *surprise*

ert·asten vt [h] etw ~, den Weg nach .., zu .. ~ *to grope one's way towards*

ert·eilen vt [h] [nur mit bestimmten Objekten] **a.** jdm e–e Antwort ~ *to give a p an answer*; *to answer a p*; mir wurde die A. erteilt *I was answered* ‖ *to impart* (*information*); → Auftrag, Befehl; Erlaubnis ‖ jdm e–e Lektion ~ *to admonish* (od *lesson, rebuke*) *a p*; jdm ein Lob ~ *to commend* od *praise a p* (f *for*); jdm e–n Tadel, Verweis ~ *to administer a rebuke to a p*; *to censure* (od *rebuke, reprimand*) *a p* ‖ jdm Rat ~ *to tender advice to a p*; jdm e–n R. ~ *to give a p a piece of advice* ‖ jdm ein Recht ~ *to give a right to a p*; *to entitle a p* (*to do*) ‖ jdm e–e Strafe ~ *to deal out* (od *administer*) *a punishment to a p* ‖ jdm Vollmacht ~ *to authorize* od *empower a p* (*to do*) **b.** → Auskunft; Dispens ‖ Stunden *or* Unterricht ~ *to give lessons* od *instruction* (in *in*) **c.** jdm den Abschied ~ → Abschied 3. **E–lung** f ~/~en *grant*; *the giving* od *granting* (*of an answer*, etc.) ‖ *the administering* (*of a rebuke*) ‖ *the tendering* (*of advice*) ‖ die ~ e–r Antwort erfolgte nicht *no answer was given*; die ~ der Erlaubnis erfolgte erst gestern *permission was not given until yesterday* ‖ befähigt z ~ v Unterricht *qualified for giving lessons* (*in*)

ert·önen vi [s] **a.** (of an instrument, etc.) *to* (*re*)*sound*; *to ring out*; *to roll out*; *to thrill* (durch *through*); → erklingen, erschallen ‖ die Glocke ertönte *the bell came through*; e–e G. ertönte laut *a bell gave a resonant sound* ‖ die Sirenen ~ *the sirens go*; schrill ~ *to shrill* **b.** (of the voice, etc.) *to resound*; *to come* ('*be seated*' *came the king's command from the throne*) **c.** (of places) *to resound* (unter, von *with, to*); die Straßen ertönten unter dem Getrampel .. *the streets resounded to the tramp* (*of the soldiers*)

ert·öten 1. vt [h] ⟨fig⟩ **a.** ⟨ec⟩ (Fleisch, Gelüste) *to mortify*; die sinnlichen Begierden in sich ~ *to m. the flesh* **b.** (Liebe, Regung) *to deaden*; *to stifle*; *to kill* **2.** ≃ n ⟨ec⟩ *mortification*

Ertr·ag m ~(e)s/≃e **1.** *produce* [nur sg] (of the fields; of a factory); *output* (*of a mine*); *yield* (*of a farm*); ⟨com⟩ *turn-out*; ~ an *yield of* (*gold*) ‖ ~ s–r Arbeit *fruits of his labo*(*u*)*r* ‖ ~ einbringen *to produce, to yield*; guten ~ geben *to yield well*; .. gebend *high-yielding*; (etw) als ~ geben *to yield*; Rein≃ *net produce* ‖ *profit, return*; mit festem ~ *fix-yielding* (*investment*) | ≃e [pl] *produce*; *returns* [pl]; *proceeds, profits* [pl]; → Einnahme; Gewinn **2.** ⟨fig⟩ ~, ≃e [pl] *produce, output* **≃reich** a = einträglich

ertr·agen vt [h] [→ tragen] **1.** (aushalten) (Operation, Schmerz) *to bear, endure, suffer*; lerne Leiden z ~ *learn to endure suffering* ‖ (gr Hitze) *to stand* ‖ es ~ *to live through it*; ⟨sl⟩ *to stick it*; (nicht) z ~ (*un*)*bearable*, (*un*)*endurable*; (nicht) z ~der Zustand (*un*)*bearableness*; → erdulden, vertragen ‖ (of countries, plants) (e–n Zustand) *to sustain*; → erleiden ‖ [neg] ich kann ihn, es nicht ~ *I cannot bear* (od *endure*; ⟨sl⟩ *stick*) *him, it*; .. es .. *I can't face it* .. sein Benehmen nicht ~ *I cannot abide his conduct*; e–n Verlust ~ können *to afford to incur a loss*; er erträgt k–n Widerspruch *he brooks no opposition*; → ausstehen, dulden, leiden **2.** (hinnehmen) *to endure, suffer, tolerate*; *to put up with*; etw ruhig ~ ⟨sl⟩ *to stand the gaff* ‖ das wirst du wohl ~ müssen *you'll just have to make the best of it*, ⟨fam⟩ .. *to grin and bear it*

ertr·äglich 1. a [mst pred] *bearable, endurable, supportable*; → ertragen ‖ *passable, tolerable*; ~er Zustand *tolerableness*; → leidlich **2.** adv (*he plays*) *tolerably* **≃keit** f *bearableness*

***Ertr·ägnis** n –nisses/–nisse = Ertrag **ertr·agreich** a *productive* (an *of*); *rich* (an *in*); ~e Beschaffenheit *productiveness, productivity* || ⟨min & com⟩ *payable, profitable, paying* (*concern*)

ertr·aglos a *unproductive*

Ertr·ags- ~anschlag m *estimate of yield*; *e. of proceeds* **~bilanz** f *balance showing profit* (od *yield*) **≃fähig** a *productive*; ⟨agr u fig⟩ *fertile* **~fähigkeit** f *productiveness, productivity* **~schein** m ⟨com⟩ *dividend–warrant* **~wert** m *income value*; Jahres≃ *purchase*

Ertr·agsteuer f *tax on a single source of income*

Ertr·agung f ~/~en *bearing, endurance, toleration*; → Duldung

ertr·änken vt [h] (jdn) *to drown* || sich ~ *to d. o.s.* || ⟨fig⟩ die Sorgen ~ *to drown one's cares*

ertr·äumen vt [h] (etw) *to dream of* (*a th*); *to imagine, vision* (*a th*); *to see* (*a th*) (*in one's imagination* od) *as in a vision* **ertr·äumt** a *chimerical, fantastic, imaginary, Utopian, visionary*; *dreamed-up* (*luck*); nie ~ *undreamt-of* (*bliss*)

ertr·inken 1. vi [s] [→ trinken] *to be* od *get drowned*; *to drown*; im Meere ~ *to go to Davy Jones's locker* || ertr·unken *drowned* (*p*); ein Ertrunkener *a drowned man* **2.** ≃ n *drowning*; Tod durch ~ death by d. **Ertr·inkende** [der ~, ein ~r] m ~n/~n *drowning man*

ertr·otzen vt [h] (etw) *to obtain* (*a th*) *by importunity* od *pertinacity, obstinacy*

ert·üchtigen vt [h] jdn ~ *to make a p effective* od *able, fit* || *to make a p strong* od *vigorous*; *to fortify* (od *harden, steel, strengthen*) *a p*; ertüchtigt in *steeled in* (*the struggle*) || *to discipline* (od *drill, train*) *a p* **Ert·üchtigung** f ~/~en *the fortifying, hardening, steeling, strengthening* (*of a p*) || *the drilling* (*of a p*); *training* (*of mind and body*); körperliche ~ *physical training* (abbr *P. T.*)

er·übrigen vt [h] **A. 1.** (Geld etc) *to save*; *to lay* (od *put*) *by*; er hat sich [dat] e–e schöne Summe –gt *he has put by a pretty penny*; nichts –gt h *not to have a penny left* **2.** (z Verfügung h) [mit 'können']: (Raum, Zeit) *to spare*; es erfordert mehr Raum als wir ~ können *it requires more space than we can spare* (f *for*) || können Sie e–e Minute f mich ~? *can you spare me a minute?* || ich habe k–e Zeit z ~ *I have no time to spare* **3.** (übrig bleiben; nötig sein) [imps] **es -gt** nun noch z erwähnen *it now remains for me to mention* (*that* ..); es –gt die Einsendung .. *it is unnecessary for you to send in* (*a certificate*) **B.** (unnötig m) **1.** (e–e Handlung) *to make unnecessary* od *useless* **2. sich** ~ **a.** *to be not necessary, to be useless, to be of no avail* (*material aid will not be necessary*) **b.** [imps] **es -gt sich** *it is superfluous* || **es** dürfte sich ~ z tun *it is hardly necessary to do*; *it will be no use to do*; es –gt sich z sagen *needless to say*; es –gt sich z sagen, daß er nicht erschien *needless to say, he did not turn up* **er·übrigt** a = erspart

eru·ieren vt [h] = ergründen, –mitteln

Erupti·on [ts] f ~/~en ⟨geol & med⟩ *eruption*

erupt·iv a ⟨geol⟩ *eruptive* **≃gestein** n ⟨geol⟩ *igneous* (od *eruptive*) *rock*

·Erve f ~/~n ⟨bot⟩ *lentil vetch*

erw·achen 1. vi [s] **a.** ⟨eig⟩ *to wake* (*up*), **to waken* (*up*) (aus *from*); ich erwache früh, um 7 *I wake early, at seven*; es war ein kalter Tag, als er –wachte *he woke to a cold day* || *to awake*(*n*) **b.** ⟨übtr⟩ der Tag –cht *the day breaks* od *dawns* || (lebendig w) (a. of plants) *to wake*(*n*) (*up*); ~ z *to wake* od *awaken to* (*new life*); *to flash into* (*the consciousness of* ..) || (of feelings) *to wake* (*his conscience woke*); *to be wakened* (*up*) od *roused* || in ihr –chte die Reue *she began to feel remorse* || der nationale Sinn –wachte *the national spirit* (*a*)*woke* **2.** ≃ n *waking, wakening* || ⟨übtr⟩ ~ z *wak*(*en*)*ing to*; ein schlimmes ~ *an evil waking* || *the* (*a*)*wakening* (*of a nation*) | ⟨fig⟩ beim ~ des Tages *at the first blush of dawn* || *the dawn* od *dawning* (*of art, life*) | (etw) zum ~ bringen *to wake* (*up*); *to* (*a*)*waken*

erw·achsen vi [s] **1.** ~ s *to be grown-up*; **2.** ⟨fig⟩ (entstehen) **a.** (of events, actions, etc.) *to arise, develop, flow, proceed, spring* (aus *from*); daraus kann Schaden ~ *damage can accrue from that*; daraus können Unannehmlichkeiten ~ *that can bring trouble* **b. jdm** ~: es w dir gr Ausgaben daraus ~ *you'll be put to great expense by it*; die A., die dem Staat ~ aus .. *expenses accruing to the state from* .. || es sind mir gr Unannehmlichkeiten ~ *I have been put to great inconvenience* || viel Kummer wird dir daraus ~ *much grief will come to you from it*; *by it you'll bring much g. upon yourself* || gr Nutzen kann ihm daraus ~ *he may derive great benefit from it* || gr Schwierigkeiten w ihm daraus ~ *this will involve you in great difficulties* **erw·achsen** a **1.** [pred] → ~ vi 1. **2.** [attr] *grown*; *grown up* (*son*) **3.** ≃e [der ~, ein ~r] *grown-up*; *adult*; die ≃en [pl] *the grown-ups, adults* [pl] || ~enbildung [f] *adult education* || ~enerziehung [f] *adult education* | ⟨demog⟩ Alter des ~seins *maturity*

erw·ägen vt [h] [→ wägen] e–e S ~ *to consider a th*; *to give a th one's consideration*; *to think a th over*; etw nicht ~ *to give a th no consideration*; etw ernstlich ~ *to give a th one's careful consideration* || (Möglichkeiten, Vorschlag) *to canvass, contemplate*; [oft neg] *to entertain*; *ponder*; *to revolve in one's mind*; sorgsam ~ *to weigh* || (noch) erwogen w *to be* (*still*) *under consideration* od *examination* || wohl erwogen *considered* (*judgement*) | ~, wie .., was .. *to deliberate* (od *ponder, reflect*) *how* .., *what* ..; ~, ob .. *to consider whether* || ~ z tun *to consider* (od *contemplate*) *doing* | [abs] erwäge sorgsam, bevor du schreibst *consider carefully before writing* **Erw·ägung** f ~/~en *consideration*; nähere ~ *reflection, –xion*; bei *or* nach näherer ~ *on reflection, on further consideration*; ~en [pl] finanzieller Art *cost considerations*; → Überlegung || in der ~, daß .. *considering that* .. || (etw) jds ~ [dat] anheimstellen *to bring before a p's consideration* || (Vorschlag) in ~ ziehen *to take into consideration*; *to canvass*; [oft neg] *to entertain*; etw ernstlich in ~ ziehen *to give a th one's careful c.n*

erw·ählen vt [h] = (aus)wählen || das bessere Teil ~ *to choose the better part* **Erw·ählung** f ~/~en **1.** ⟨theol⟩ *election, predestination*; durch ~ *by election* **2.** = Wahl

erw·ähnen vt [h] (etw, jdn) *to mention* (jdm gegenüber *to a p*); *to make mention of*; *to refer to, to make reference to*; *to remark upon* (*a th, a p*); etw nicht (weiter) ~ *to make no* (*further*) *reference to a th*; sein Name wurde –wähnt, er wurde mit Namen –wähnt *he was named* (od *mentioned by name*) || bleibt noch z ~ *there remains to be mentioned* || erwähnt w muß noch .., *mention must be made of* ..; es sei noch –wähnt *let me still mention* (*that* ..) || wie –wähnt *as was mentioned* (od *said*) || oben erwähnt *above-mentioned* **erw·ähnenswert** a *worth mentioning*; *interesting to note*; nicht ~ *nothing to speak of*; *nothing much* | nichts ≃es *nothing to write home about* **E–hnung** f ~/~en *mention* (*of a th* od *a p*); *reference* (e–r S *to a th*); s–e ~ der Kirche *his reference to the church* || ⟨com, etc.⟩ eherenvolle ~ *honourable mention* || nicht der ~ wert *nothing to speak of* || e–r S ~ tun = etw erwähnen || ehrenvolle ~ *accolade*

erw·ärmen vt/i **1.** vt [h] **a.** ⟨eig⟩ (mst = wärmen) || (Zimmer) *to heat, to warm* **b.** ⟨übtr⟩ jds Herz ~ *to warm* (od *animate*) *a p's heart* || (jdn) *to cheer, gladden, warm*; erwärmt v *warmed with* **jdn f etw** ~ *to arouse a p's interest in a th* | **sich** ~ **f jdn, etw** *to warm* (od *take*) *to a p, a th*; *to soften* *to* (*a p*); *to sympathize with a p, a th*; *to take an interest in a th*; *to take to a th*; *to feel enthusiasm for a th*; → warm w **2.** vi [s] *to warm* (*up*); *to become* (od *get*) *warm* (*his limbs warmed by and by*) **Erw·ärmung** f ~/~en *warming*; *heating* ‖ ⟨übtr⟩ *warming, animation*; *cheering*

erw·arten vt [h] **I.** (P) **A.** **(etw) 1.** (entgegensehen) ⟨allg⟩ *to expect*; *to be in expectation of*; *to await*; (Vorteil) *to look for*; (Vergnügen, Widerspruch) *to anticipate* ‖ was können Sie anders ~? *what do you expect?* ‖ gute Resultate ~ l *to promise g. r.* ‖ etw (Strafe etc) z ~ h *to be in for a th* ‖ etw zuversichtlich ~ *confidently to look forward to a th* ‖ etw jeden Augenblick ~ *to be in momentary expectation of a th* ‖ ich habe hier nicht viel Gutes mehr z ~ *the future will not have much happiness in store for me* | [mst neg] *to bargain for*; das hatte er nicht –tet *he had not bargained for* (od *expected*) *that* ‖ etw nicht (*or* kaum) ~ können *to await a th with impatience*; er konnte es nicht (*or* kaum) ~, sie z sehen *he was impatient to see them* **2. etw ~ v jdm** *to expect a th of* (od *from*) *a p*; *to anticipate a th from a p*; ganz wie ich v ihm –tete *just what I expected of him* ‖ Schutz v jdm ~ *to look to a p for protection*; ich werde v euch allen ~, daß ihr dasselbe tut *I shall look to all of you to do the same* **3.** [abs] **wir z ~** *as one would* [have] *expect*[*ed*] **B. (jdn)** *to expect* (z Tee *to tea*); Besuch ~ *to expect visitors*; *to await* ‖ wann –test du ..? *when is* (*your wife*) *due?* ‖ ich werde um 8 Uhr bei Herrn N. –tet *I am due at Mr. N.'s at eight*; wir werden schon lange bei Müllers –tet *we are overdue at the Millers* **2.** (of a woman) ein Kind ~ *to expect a child*; *to be expecting*; ein K. wurde –tet *a child was on the way* **C. 1. ich erwartete, daß** er kommt *I expect* (*that*) *he will come*; *I e. him to come*; .. v dir, daß du pünktlich bist *I e. you to be punctual*; .., daß es geschieht *I e. it to be done*; man kann v uns nicht ~, daß wir nachgeben *we cannot be expected to give in* ‖ man –tet nicht, daß .., es wird v dir nicht –tet, daß *you are not expected* od *supposed to do this* **2.** ich –tete nicht, dich hier z sehen *I did not expect to find you here* **II.** ⟨übtr⟩ (S) (jdn) **1.** *to await* (*a p*) (*a terrible sight awaited her*) **2.** *to be in store for* (*a p*); den Chirurgen ~ gr Aufgaben *great tasks are in store for the surgeon* **Erw·arten** n [nur in den Wendungen]: über ~ *beyond expectation*; wider ~ *contrary to expectation*(*s*) od *anticipation* **erw·artet** a *expected* (*form*) **Erw·artung** f ~/~en **1.** *expectation, anticipation*; *foreknowledge* ‖ spannende ~ *expectance, –cy* (*a feeling of e.*) **2. a. in** ~ e–r S *in anticipation of a th*; *awaiting a th* ‖ in der ~, daß .. *in the expectation that ..* ‖ (als Briefschluß) in angenehmer ~ *with pleasant anticipation* ‖ in freudiger ~ e–r S entgegensehen *to look forward to a th* ‖ in höchster ~ *in a ferment* (od *flutter*) *of expectation* ‖ brennend **vor ~, voller ~** *on the tiptoe of expectation* **b.** der ~ Ausdruck geben *to express one's expectation* (*that ..*) ‖ jds ~en (nicht) entsprechen (*not*) *to come up to a p's expectations*, (⟨fam⟩ *it doesn't come up to scratch*); das Buch hat m–e ~en getäuscht (*or* hat mich in m–n ~en enttäuscht) *the book falls short of* (od *does not come to*) *my expectations* ‖ in s–n ~en enttäuscht s *to be disappointed* ‖ den ~en entsprechen, die ~en erfüllen *to fill the bill*; ⟨Am pol⟩ *to deliver the goods* ‖ den ~en (nicht) entsprechend *up to* (*under*) *the mark* ‖ den ~en entsprechend verlaufen *to run true to form* od *type*; ~en wecken *to excite expectations* **≃s-mäßig** a ⟨demog, stat⟩ *expected* (*deaths*) **≃voll 1.** a *expectant, full of expectation* **2.** adv *expectantly* **~szustand** m ⟨psych, eth⟩ *set*

erw·ecken vt [h] **1.** ⟨†eig⟩ = (auf)wecken **2.** ⟨bib⟩ jdn v den Toten ~ *to raise a p from the dead*; → wieder(auf)~ **3.** ⟨fig⟩ **a.** (ein Volk) *to wake*(*n*) (z .. *to new life*); (jdn) *to rouse, to waken* (aus .. *out of lethargy*) **b.** (Aufruhr etc) *excite, to provoke, raise* **c.** (Gefühle) *to arouse, awaken, evoke, excite, provoke, raise*; *to stir up*; *to wake*(*n*) ‖ den Anschein ~ *to create the impression* ‖ alte Erinnerungen ~ *to raise old memories* ‖ Eifersucht ~ *to wake rivalry* (unter *among*) ‖ (falsche) Hoffnungen ~ *to raise* (*false*) *hopes* ‖ *to fire* (*inspiration*) ‖ (Interesse) *to arouse, to excite* ‖ Vertrauen ~ *to inspire* (od *to give rise to*) **c.** ‖ (Zweifel) *to provoke* | Furcht in jdm ~ *to frighten a p*; *to fill* od *inspire a p with fear* ‖ in jdm den Glauben ~, daß .. *to make a p believe that* .. **d.** er erweckt den Anschein, als wäre er *he makes believe* od *pretends to be*; er wollte den A. ~, daß .. *he made it appear that* ..; → Anschein ‖ den Eindruck ~, daß .. *to give the impression that* **Erw·eckung** f ~/~en **1.** ⟨bib⟩ ~ v den Toten *the raising* (*of a p*) *from the dead* **2.** ⟨fig⟩ **a.** ⟨rel bes Am⟩ *revival* **b.** *resurrection* (*of a nation*) ‖ *arousing, awakening, evocation, excitation, raising, waking* (*of a feeling*)

erw·ehren vrefl [h] [mst neg & mit 'können'] **1.** ⟨eig⟩ sich e–s Gegners ~ *to resist* (od *withstand*) *an adversary successfully* **2.** ⟨übtr & fig⟩ er konnte sich s–r Ränke nicht (*or* kaum) ~ *he could not* (od *hardly*) *resist* (od *withstand*) *his wiles* ‖ sich e–s Gefühls ~ *to hold back* (od *restrain*; *control*) *a feeling*; sich des Eindrucks nicht ~ können, daß .. *not to be able feeling that* ‖ sich e–r S ~ *to refrain from a th*; *to resist a th*; er konnte sich des Lachens nicht ~ *he could not help laughing*; sie ko. sich der Tränen nicht ~ *she was unable to keep back her tears, she could not help crying* ‖ man ko. sich des Eindrucks nicht ~ *you could not help thinking* (od *being under the impression*) (*that ..*)

erw·eichbar a ⟨fig⟩ *malleable*; *pliable* (*mind*)

erw·eichen I. vt [h] **1.** ⟨eig⟩ *to soften*; = einweichen, weich m **2.** ⟨fig⟩ jdn, jds Sinn ~ *to mollify* (od *to move, touch*) *a p*; *to prevail* (*up*)*on a p* ‖ jds Herz ~ *to soften* (od *melt*) *a p's heart* ‖ er war nicht z ~ *he could not be prevailed upon* **II.** ≃ n ⟨met, chem⟩ (vor dem Schmelzen) *emollescence* **erw·eichend** a ⟨med⟩ *emollient* (*pountice, remedy*); ~e Mittel n [pl] *emollients* [pl] **Erw·eichung** f ~/~en *softening* ‖ ⟨fig⟩ *mollification, moving* (*of a p*); *softening* (*of a p's heart*)

Erw·eis m ~/~e [nur in wenigen best. Wendungen]: (= Beweis) den ~ erbringen f etw → erbringen ‖ Brauchbarkeits≃, ~ der Brauchbarkeit *try-out*; *test of efficiency*

erw·eisen vt [h] [→ weisen] **A. (etw, jdn) 1. a. etw ~,** erwiesene [pp] Beileidsbezeugungen *kind expressions of sympathy*; die Existenz *or* Echtheit e–r S ~ *to prove* od *show a th*; (Gesetz, Theorie) *to establish*; *to exemplify*; *to illustrate* (an *from*); (Anspruch) *to establish*; *to make good* ‖ die Richtigkeit e–r S (e–s Verdachts etc) ~, etw als wahr ~ *to verify a th* ‖ es ist erwiesen *it is proved* (⟨Am⟩ *proven*), eindeutig *it has been proved* (*beyond doubt* od) *conclusively*; wie erwiesen wird durch .. *as is proved by* .. ‖ das Gericht sieht als erwiesen an, daß .. *the Court is satisfied that* .. **b. jdn** als Lügner ~ (of actions) *to prove* (od *argue*) *a p* (*to be*) *a liar* **c.** (S) **~, daß** *to prove that*; ~, daß etw ist *to prove a th to be* **2. sich ~ a.** (P) er hat sich als treuer (*or* treuen) Diener erwiesen *he has proved* (⟨Am⟩ *proven*) *himself* (*to be*) *a faithful servant, he has turned out a f. s.*; er erwies sich als unversöhnlich *he showed himself unforgiving*; er erwies sich als Zweitbester *he turned* (⟨Am⟩ *came*) *out second--best* ‖ sich als fähig ~ *to prove o.s.* (*to be*) *able* (od *efficient*) | (sich ∼ = sein) sich dankbar (etc) ∼ *to be grateful, to show o.s. g.* (*I shall be g. to you*) **b.** (S) sich als wahr ∼ *to be verified; to prove* (*to be*) *true; to come true*; das Gerücht erwies sich als wahr, trügerisch *the rumour proved* (od *turned out*) (*to be*) *true, false* ‖ die Freundschaften w sich als glücklich ∼ *the friendships will turn up trumps* ‖ sich als nützlich ∼ *to come in useful* ‖ das wird sich bald ∼ *that will soon become clear* ‖ es erwies sich, daß er .. hatte *it turned out that he had .., he turned out to have* (*£ 500*) **B. jdm etw** ∼: jdm e–n Dienst ∼ *to do* od *render a p a service* ‖ → Ehre D. 1. b. ‖ jdm Freundlichkeiten ∼ *to extend kindnesses to a p* ‖ jdm e–n Gefallen, e–e Gefälligkeit ∼ *to do a p a favour*; .. den G. ∼ .. *the favour* (*of answering*) ‖ jdm Gnade ∼ *to show mercy to a p* ‖ jdm e–e Gunst ∼ *to grant a p a favour* ‖ jdm (nur) Gutes ∼ *to do good to a p,* (*to never show a p anything but kindness*) ‖ jdm Wohltaten ∼ *to confer benefits on a p, to heap favours on a p* **er·w·eislich 1.** a *provable; capable of being proved; demonstrable* (*influence*) **2.** adv *provably; as may be proved* ‖ *evidently* (*false*) ‖ ∼ermaßen = erwiesenermaßen **Erw·eisung** f *the rendering* (*of services*); *the granting* (*of a favour*); *the conferring* (*of benefits*); → Ehrenbezeigung

erw·eitern vt [h] **1.** ⟨eig⟩ (Straße) *to extend* (nach *to*); (Graben) *to widen* ‖ (Buch) *to expand; to dilate* (z *into*); *to enlarge* ‖ (Kleid) *to let out; to ream out* (*a hole*); (Rock) *to enlarge; to expand* (*a tube*); (etw) nach außen ∼ *to flare* (*out*) ‖ (Brust) *to expand* ‖ ⟨physiol⟩ (Herz) *to dilate*; sein Herz ist krankhaft –rt *he suffers from cardiac dilatation* **2.** ⟨übtr⟩ (Abgrund, Kreis) *to extend* ‖ (Gesichtskreis, Horizont) *to widen, to broaden one's outlook* ‖ (Handel) *to expand* ‖ (Kenntnisse) *to enlarge, extend* (*one's range of knowledge*) ‖ (Einfluß, Interessen) *to extend* (auf *to*); *to spread* (über *over*) ‖ (Macht) *to aggrandize, extend* ‖ die Grenzen des Wissens ∼ *to push back the frontiers of knowledge* ‖ die Bedeutung e–s Wortes ∼ *to extend the conception* od *meaning of a w.* **3. sich** ∼ **a.** ⟨eig⟩ *to expand* (infolge v, durch *with*); *to dilate; to diverge* ‖ ⟨path⟩ *to distend* **b.** ⟨übtr⟩ (of trade) *to expand*; (of knowledge) *to extend; widen* **er·w·eitert** a *expanded* (*version*) ‖ ⟨gram⟩ *extended* (*sense*) **Erw·eiterung** f ∼/∼en **1.** *extension; enlargement* (*of a tube*) ‖ *expansion* (*of the chest*); *dila(ta)tion* (*of the heart*); → Diastole ‖ *distension* (*of an artery*); krankhafte ∼ der Pulsader *aneurism*; → Herz≃ ‖ ⟨tech, comp⟩ *progressive installation* **2.** ⟨übtr⟩ *extension; enlargement* (*of knowledge*); *widening* (*of the spiritual horizon*) ‖ ⟨pol⟩ Macht≃ *aggrandizement* **∼sbau** m *addition to* (od *extension of*) *a building* **∼sfähigkeit** f *expansibility* **∼sgebäude** n *addition*

Erw·erb m ∼(e)s/∼e **1.** (Erwerben) *acquiring, acquisition* **2.** (Erworbenes) **a.** (Brot≃) *livelihood, living*; s–m ∼ nachgehen *to earn one's living; to work for one's l.*; → Beruf, Arbeit **b.** (Verdienst) *earnings* [pl]; = Einkommen; Lohn, Gewinn

erw·erben vt [h] [→ werben] **1.** sich [dat] sein Brot ∼ *to earn* od *gain one's livelihood* od *living; to earn one's daily bread* ‖ (sich) Geld ∼ *to make money*; (sich) ein Vermögen ∼ *to make a fortune*; (etw) durch Kauf ∼ *to purchase* ‖ (sich) Reichtum ∼ *to gain* (od *acquire*) *wealth* ‖ (Recht, Titel) *to acquire*; das Urheberrecht e–s Buches ∼ *to copyright a book* **2.** (Fähigkeiten, Kenntnisse etc) *to acquire* ‖ sich gr Verdienste ∼ um etw *or* jdn *to deserve well of a th, a p* ‖ sich die Achtung jds ∼ *to win a p's estimation*; sich Ruhm (*or* e–n Namen) ∼ als *to establish one's reputation as ..*; → erringen ‖ Ruhm ∼ *to gain kudos* ‖ → erworben **Erw·erber** m ∼s/∼ *acquirer; purchaser* (*of a house*); ⟨jur⟩ *cessionary, transferee; assign* ‖ gutgläubiger ∼ *purchaser in good faith*

Erw·erbs- ∼beschränkte, ∼geminderte [der ∼, ein ∼r] m ∼n/∼n *disabled p*; ∼nfürsorge *care of disabled persons* **∼beschränktheit** f *partial incapacity* **∼bevölkerung** f *labo(u)r force; economically active population* **∼einkommen** n, **∼einkünfte** f pl *professional earnings* ‖ auf ∼ ausgerichtet *gainful* (*occupation*) **≃fähig** a *capable of earning one's living* **∼fähigkeit** f *capability of earning one's living* ‖ Beeinträchtigung der ∼ *impaired earning capacity* **∼fleiß** m *industry* **∼genossenschaft** f *co-operative association* **∼gesellschaft** f *trading company* **∼interesse** n *acquiring interest; acquisitiveness* | Alter beim Eintritt ins **∼leben** ⟨demog⟩ *age at entry into labo(u)r force* **≃los** etc → d. **∼minderung** f *reduction of working capacity* **∼mittel** n *means* [pl]; *money; resources* [pl] **∼personen** f pl (*total number of*) *employees* ‖ ⟨demog⟩ *working population*; ∼ der Industrie *industrial pop.*; landwirtschaftliche ∼ *agricultural workers* ‖ Nicht-∼ *economically inactive pop.* **∼preis** m *purchase price* **∼quelle** f *means of living; source of income* **∼quote** f *activity rate* **∼sinn** m *business sense, commercial acumen*; ⟨dero⟩ *passion for money, acquisitiveness* **∼steuer** f *tax on the income from business* od *from industrial enterprises; profit tax*; = Ertragsteuer; → Grund≃ **∼sucht** f = Erwerbstrieb **≃süchtig** a *acquisitive* **≃tätig** a *gainfully employed; employed in industry and trade* ‖ ⟨übtr⟩ *industrious, working* ‖ ∼ s *to earn* (od *work for*) *one's living* ‖ ∼e Bevölkerung *labo(u)r force* **∼tätige(r** m) f *employed* (P) **∼tätigkeit** f ⟨übtr⟩ *industry* ‖ (durchschnittliche) ∼sdauer (*expectation of*) *working life* **∼titel** m = Erwerbsurkunde **∼- und Wirtschaftsgenossenschaft** f *co-operative industrial society* **≃unfähig** a *unable to earn one's living; disabled* **∼unfähigkeit** f *inability to earn one's living; disablement* **∼urkunde** f ⟨jur⟩ *title-deed* **∼zweig** m *branch of industry* od *trade, profession; line* (*his l. is grocery*)

erw·erbsam a *industrious* | **≃keit** f ∼/ *industriousness, industry*

erw·erbslos a, **Erw·erbslose** m, **Erw·erbslosigkeit** f → arbeitslos, Arbeitslose etc

Erw·erbung f ∼/∼en = Erwerb 1.

erw·idern vt/i [h] **I.** vt **1. a.** (Besuch, Blick, Gefallen, Gruß etc) *to return*; jds Verbeugung ∼ *to return a p's bow; to bow back to a p* ‖ *to reciprocate* (*I r. your good wishes*) **b.** ⟨mil⟩ das feindliche Feuer ∼ *to reply to the enemy's fire; to reply* ‖ (Angriff) *to reply* (mit *by*); er –widerte jeden Angriff mit e–m Schlag *he reciprocated to every attack with a blow* ‖ (Beleidigung) *to requite* (mit .. *with a blow*); *to retort* **c.** (Gefühle) *to reciprocate* (mit *with*); (jds Liebe) *to return* **2.** (in Worten ∼) **a.** (etw) *to reply* (auf *to*); er hatte nichts darauf z ∼ *he had nothing to reply to it* ‖ was h Sie darauf z ∼? *what have you to say in reply to this?* ‖ ‚Keineswegs', –widerte er '*Not at all*' *he replied* (auf s–e Frage *to his question*), .. –widerte er frech .. *he answered back*, ⟨Am a.⟩ *he came back*; .. hastig .. *he flung back*; .. schroff .. *he snapped* (*out*); .. treffend .. *he retorted* **b. ∼, daß** *to reply* (od *argue*) *that ..; to say in reply that*; auf s–e Frage –widerte sie .. *in reply to his question she said* (*that ..*); schroff ∼ .. *to snap out* **II.** vi **1.** *to* (*make a*) *reply* ‖ ∼ f (*or* an Stelle v) *to reply for* (*Mr. M.*); mit *to reply by* (*a blow*) **2.** ⟨jur⟩ *to rejoin* **3.** jdm ∼ *to reply* (od *answer*) *to a p; to answer a p* (auf *to*) **Erw·iderung** f ∼/∼en **1.** *return* (*of a visit*) ‖ *reciprocation* (*of a feeling*) **2.** (∼ in Worten) *reply, answer* (e–r S, auf e–e S *to a th*); treffende ∼ *retort*; als ∼ *in reply*; in ∼ auf *in reply to* (*a letter*) ‖

⟨jur⟩ *answer, reply*; (~ des Klägers auf Antwort des Beklagten) *replication*; (~ des Beklagten auf die *replication* des Klägers) *rejoinder*

erw·iesenermaßen adv *provedly* (*3 plays are p. his*) ‖ *evidently, obviously* ‖ *as has been proved* od *demonstrated, established*

erw·irken vt [h] (etw) *to effect*; *to obtain* (*divorce, acquittal, injunction*); *to bring about*; *to procure* (f *for a p*); → erhalten B.; erreichen B. ‖ e–e Genehmigung ~ *to take out a licence*; e–e Vorladung ~ *to take out a summons* (gegen *against a p*) ‖ (erlangen) *to secure*

erw·irtschaften vt [h] *to get* od *obtain .. by careful management* od *by good economy* ‖ *to produce* (*high financial yields*)

erw·ischen vt [h] (jdn) *to catch* (bei .. *at* od *in a th*); *to get hold of*; ⟨sl⟩ *to nab* ‖ sie w ihn bald ~ *it won't be long before they put salt on his tail* ‖ sich ~ l *to get caught* | (Zug) *to catch*; e–e Tasse Tee ~ *to snatch a cup of tea* ‖ → ertappen: ihn hat's –scht ⟨mil⟩ *he's cashed in*, ⟨sl⟩ *he's had it*; sich nicht ~ l *to obey the 11th commandment*

erw·ogen pp v erwägen

erw·orben a [pp v erwerben] *acquired*; *earned*; sauer ~ *hard-earned*; unrechtmäßig ~ *ill-got*(*ten*); wohl ~ *vested* (*rights*) ‖ ~e Fertigkeit *accomplishment, acquirement*; ~e Kenntnisse [pl] *accomplishments, acquirements* ‖ vor anderen ~ *pre-empted* ‖ das ≗e *acquisition*

erw·ünscht a **1.** [attr] *desired* (*effect*), *wished--for* (*aid*) **2.** [pred] jdm ~ s (Besuch, Gelegenheit) *to be opportune* (*to come most opportunely*) *to a p* ‖ d–e Gegenwart ist hier nicht ~ *you are not wanted here* ‖ Besucher nicht ~! *no visitors, please*! es ist ~ *it is desirable* (*that he .. should*); e–e Hilfe ist sehr ~ *a help is very welcome* ‖ das ist (*or* kommt) mir sehr ~ *that suits me admirably* (od *to a T*)

erw·ürgen vt [h] (jdn) *to scrag, strangle, throttle*; *choke*; → erdrosseln **Erw·ürgung** f ~/~en *strangling*; *strangulation*

Erysip·el n ~s/ ⟨med⟩ = Wundrose

Eryth·em n ~s/~e ⟨med⟩ *erythema*

Erythr·äa n *Eritrea*; → Eritrea

Erythr·in n ~s/ ⟨minr⟩ *erythrine*

Erythroz·yten [pl] ⟨physiol⟩ *erythrocytes* [pl]

Erz n ~es/~e ⟨minr⟩ **1.** *ore*; *native mineral* od *metal*; *ore-bearing rock*; armes ~ ⟨min⟩ *halvings* pl ‖ → aufbereiten; ~ gewinnen *to dress ore*; *to extract mineral from ore* **2.** † ⟨übtr⟩ (Kupfer) *brass* **3.** ⟨übtr⟩ (schmiedbares Metall) *metal* ‖ ⟨poet⟩ = Eisen; Schwert ‖ *precious metal*; ⟨poet⟩ *ore* **4. a.** aus ~ gegossen *brazen* (*image*); *of brass*; *iron*; → ehern **b.** ⟨fig⟩ wie in (*or* aus) ~ gegossen *as firm as a rock*; *rock--firm*; *strong as brass*; *as hard as iron*

Erz-[1] [pref] **1.** (in Titeln & ⟨bib⟩, [mit dem Ton auf ~]: ~bischof) *arch–* **2.** ⟨übtr⟩ (als Verstärkung bes vor Scheltwörtern, Subst & Adj [mit Doppelbetonung]: ·~sch·urke) *arch–*, *arrant*; *absolute*; *notorious*, *out-and-out*; *thorough*(*-going*); *unmitigated*; *double-dyed*; ⟨bes Am⟩ *dyed in the wool* **~bischof** m *archbishop* (⟨engl⟩ Anschrift: *The Most Rev. His Grace the Lord Archbishop of* ..; Anrede: *My Lord Archbishop* od *Your Grace*) **≗bischöflich** a *archiepiscopal* **~bistum** n *archbishopric*; *see*; das ~ C. *the s. of Canterbury* **~b·ube** m *arrant rascal* (od *knave*) **·~d·ummkopf** m *arch-dunce, utter fool* **~engel** m ⟨bib⟩ *archangel* **·~f·aulenzer** m *complete* od *utter lazybones* sg **~feind** m ⟨bib⟩ *archfiend* **~g·auner** m *arrant cheat* (od *swindler*) **~gr·obian** m *absolute bully* **~halunke** m *perfect rogue* **~herzog** m ⟨a. engl hist⟩ (habsburgischer Prinz) *archduke* **~herzogin** f *archduchess* **≗herzoglich** a *archducal* **~herzogtum** n *archduchy* **~kämmerer** m ⟨Ger hist⟩ *arch-chamberlain* **~kanzler** m ⟨Ger hist⟩ *arch-chancellor* **~katho·l·ik** m *ultra-Catholic* **≗kath·olisch** a *ultra--catholic* **~k·etzer** m *arch-heretic* **~kn·auser** m *arch-niggard* **~l·ügner** m *arrant liar* **~marschall** m ⟨Ger hist⟩ *arch-marshal* **~mundschenk** m ⟨Ger hist⟩ *arch-cupbearer* **~priester** m ⟨hist⟩ *archpriest* **~sch·elm** m *arch-rogue, arrant knave* **~schenk** m = Erzmundschenk **~sch·urke** m *arch-villain*; *most unmitigated cad*; *thorough-going scoundrel* **~sp·itzbube** m = Erzschelm **~stift** n *archbishopric* **~truchseß** m ⟨Ger hist⟩ *arch-dapifer* **~vater** m *patriarch*; = Patri·arch **≗väterlich** a *patriarchal*

·Erz-[2] (→ Erz) [in comp] *ore* **≗arm** a *mute, attle* **~arten** f pl (Ggs Gangarten) *ore-minerals* **~abfälle** m pl *tailings* **~aufbereitung** f *ore dressing* **~ausbeute** f *yield of ores* **~becherwerk** n *ore-elevator* **~bergbau** m *hard-work mining* **≗beschlagen** a *studded with bronze* **~bergwerk** n *metalliferous mine* **~blüte** f = Grünspan **~bunker** m *ore bin* **~fall** m *ore-shoot* **≗führend** a *ore--bearing* (*soil*) **~gang** m *ore vein* (od *lode*); → Stollen **~gebirge** n ⟨Ger geog⟩ *the Erzgebirge* **~gewinnung** f *exploitation of mineral deposits* ‖ *ore-dressing* **~gießer** m *founder* **~grube** f = Erzbergwerk **≗haltig** a *ore-bearing*; nicht ~ *barren* (*rock*) **≗höffig** a *promising a good yield of ores* **~hütte** f *smelting works* **~klauber** m *ore picker* **~körper** m *ore-body* **~lager** a *pocket* **~lagerstätte** f *ore-deposit* **~mineral** n *ore mineral* **~möller** m *ore burden* **~mühle** f *edge mill* **~nest** n *ore pocket*; *corbond* **~pochwerk** n *ore stamp*(*er*) **~probe** f [abstr] *assay* **≗reich** a *rich in ore* **~schlämmen** n *ore washing* **~schleiche** f ⟨zoo⟩ *snake lizard*; Gattung der ~n *Chalcididae* [L pl] **~seife** f *alluvial ore deposit* **~stufe** f *glebe* **~verladeanlage** f *ore handling equipment* **~vorkommen** n *mineral sources* pl **~wäscher** m *vanner* **~wespe** f ⟨ent⟩ *chalcididan, chalcid*

erz·ählbar a *fit to be told* od *recited*

erz·ählen vt/i [h] **I.** vt **1.** (etw) **a.** ⟨allg⟩ *to tell*; *to tell the tale* (od *story*) *of*; *to give* (ausführlich *a detailed*) *an account of* (*a th*) ‖ ⟨gewählt & liter⟩ *to narrate, relate, recount* **b.** ⟨bib & poet⟩ *to celebrate, sing*; *to tell of* **c.** e–e **Geschichte** ~ *to tell* (od *recount*) *a story* (e–e lange G.) *to spin a yarn*; lange Geschichten ~ ⟨fam⟩ *to yarn*; nicht z ~(d) *untellable* (*story*) ‖ ⟨übtr⟩ Geschichten ~ → flunkern ‖ Märchen ~ *to tell fairy-tales*; erzähle k–e M. *don't tell fibs*; → flunkern; Quatsch ‖ den Tatbestand ~ *to give* (*an account of*) *the facts* ‖ er kann etwas ~ *he knows* (od *has seen*) *life*; *he has seen a great deal* ‖ etw eingehend (*or* im einzelnen) ~ *to detail* od *retail a th* | (Geheimnis) weiter ~ *to repeat, to spread* **2. jdm etw ~** *to tell a p a th* (od *a th to a p*) ‖ man –lte es mir *they told me about it*; man –lte mir die Wahrheit *I was told the truth* ‖ –le mir doch nichts! Du kannst mir nichts ~! *don't tell me*! ‖ ich habe es mir ~ l *I had it told to me*; *I have been told about it* ‖ man –lt sich wunderbare Dinge über *astonishing things are told about* .. ‖ sich lange Geschichten ~ *to talk a long time*; ⟨fam⟩ *to yarn* ‖ sich v jdm die ganze Geschichte ~ l *to take a p over the story* ‖ wem ~ Sie das? *don't tell me*! **3. er -lt, daß** .. *he says* od *narrates that* ..; man –lt sich, daß .. *they say that* ..; *a tale goes about that* .. ‖ er –lte mir, daß .. *he told me that* ..; man –lte mir, daß .. *I was told that* ..; *it was told me that*; man –lte v ihr, daß sie .. sei .. *it was told of her that* ..; *she was reported* od *said to be* .. **II.** vi; ~ **über** *to tell about* ‖ ~ v *to tell of*; (of things) *to give evidence of*; *to be indicative of* ‖ jdm ~ über, v *to tell a p about, of* ‖ ~ hören v *to hear tell of*

Erz·ählen n *telling*; *narrative* ‖ (of a story) beim ~ nichts v dem Wert verlieren *to lose nothing in the telling*; → Erzählung 1.

erz·ählend a *narrative* (*form, literature*); *epic* (*poetry*); ~es Gedicht *epic*; *epic poem* ‖ in ~er Form *narratively* ‖ ~er Teil *narrative part*

erz·ählenswert a *worth* (*the*) *telling* **Erz·ähler** m ~s/~ *narrator, relator*; *reporter* ‖ ⟨Lit⟩ *story-teller*; *narrative writer* ‖ gewandter ~ *conversationalist* **E–lung** f ~/~en **1.** [abstr] *narration, relation* (*of a fact*); *account* ‖ ~en u Märchen *stories and fairytales* ‖ ein Meister der ~ *a master of narration* ‖ was die ~ betrifft *narratively* **2.** [konkr] *tale, story*; *narrative, relation* ‖ lange wirre ~ *rigmarole*

Erz·ählungs- [in comp] *narrative* (*literature*) **≈weise** adv *narratively*; *by way of narrative*

erz·eigen vt [h] jdm etw ~ = erweisen B.

·erzen a *brazen*; → ehern

erz·eugbar a *producible* **≈keit** f *producibleness*

erz·eugen vt [h] **A.** (P etc) **1.** (zeugen) (Kinder) *to beget*; *generate*; *to give birth to*; *to bring forth*; → gebären ‖ (Junge) *to bring forth*; *to produce* **2.** → bauen, ziehen; züchten ‖ → an–, verfertigen, herstellen **B.** ⟨übtr⟩ (S) **1.** (of plants, trees) (Früchte) *to bear, to bring forth, to produce*; (of the soil) (Korn etc) *to bring forth, to produce* **2.** ⟨phys & chem⟩ (Dampf, Strom) *to generate* (*friction generates electricity*); *to produce* **3.** (Durst) *to engender*; (Krankheit) *to breed* **4.** ⟨fig⟩ (Gefühl, Zustand etc) *to engender, evoke, produce* ‖ *to bring about*; *to originate*; *to give rise to* ‖ *to beget*; Gewalt erzeugt Gewalt *violence begets violence*

Erz·euger m ~s/~ **1.** *begetter* **2.** ⟨fig⟩ **a.** (P) *begetter*; *originator*; *producer* ‖ *maker, manufacturer* **b.** (Maschine) ⟨tech⟩ (Gas≈) *producer*; elektr. Kraft≈ *generator* **~kosten** [pl] *production costs* [pl] **~land** n *producer country*; *country of origin* **~preis** m *producer's price*

Erz·eugerin f ~/~nen → Mutter

Erz·eugnis n –nisses/–nisse **1. a.** (Boden≈) *produce*; –nisse [pl] *produce* ‖ die Tomaten sind fremdes ~ *the tomatoes are of foreign growth* **b.** ⟨com & tech⟩ *produce, product, production*; *manufacture, make*; *creation* ‖ unser eigenes ~ *our own make*; (auf Waren) Deutsches ~ *Made in Germany* ‖ –nisse [pl] *produce*; *products, productions* (*of a factory*); die neuesten nisse *the latest creations* **2.** geistiges ~ *product, production*; –nisse [pl] *products, productions* [pl] (*the dramatic p. of an era*)

Erz·eugung f ~/~en **1.** *begetting* (*of children*); *bringing forth* ‖ *production* (*of fruits*) ‖ *generation* (*of bacteria*) **2.** ⟨übtr & fig⟩ *generation* (*of heat, pressure*) ‖ *creation* (*of unrest*) ‖ *evocation* (*of an image*); *origination*; *production* (*of a feeling*) | **~s-** ~grammatik [f] *generative grammar*; ~schlacht [f] ⟨Ger⟩ *battle of production, pr. for victory*

erz·iehbar a *educable* ‖ schwer ~ *hard to control* (od *handle, manage*); *problem* [attr] (*child*)

erz·iehen **1.** vt [h] [→ ziehen] (jdn) = aufziehen ‖ ~ z *to bring up to*; *to train to*; jdn z Arbeit, z Gehorsam ~ *to train a p to work, to obey* | (geistig etc bilden) *to educate, tutor*; *train*; (moral. Sinn) *to cultivate*; (Geschmack, Ohr) *to educate* ‖ **sich** ~ *to educate* od *tutor o.s.* ‖ → erzogen **2.** ≈ n *tutoring*; *training*

Erz·ieher m ~s/~ *educator*; *instructor*; *pedagogue*; *teacher*; ⟨engl univ⟩ *tutor* **Erz·ieherin** f ~/~nen (in e–r Familie) *governess*

erz·ieherisch **1.** a *educational* (*progress*); *educative* (*centre*); *pedagogic*(*al*); *instructional* ‖ in ~er Hinsicht *educationally, pedagogically* **2.** adv *educationally, pedagogically* **erz·iehlich** a & adv = erzieherisch ‖ ~ wirken auf jdn *to have an educative effect on* ..; *to cultivate a p's mind*; *to educate a p*

Erz·iehung f ~/ **1.** die ~ *the breeding* od *upbringing, training* (*of a p*; f, z *for*) ‖ körperliche ~ *physical* od *bodily training* **2.** (gesellschaftl. Formen) *manners* [pl]; gute ~ *good m.*; Mangel an ~, schlechte ~ *bad m.*; *ill-breeding*; ihm fehlt jede ~ *he has no manners* **3.** (geistige, sittliche ~) **a.** *education*; *training of body and mind* (z *for*); jdm e–e ~ geben *to give a p a training* ‖ *instruction* (in *in*) **b.** *cultivation, training* (*of the mind*) **c.** (staatliche) die ~ *education*; die ~ ist ein wichtiger Faktor in .. *e. is an important factor in* .. ‖ Kunst≈ *art education* ‖ Volks≈ *popular e.* ‖ die englische ~ *English e.*; die ~ in England *education in England*; in Sachen der ~ *in the matter of e.*; was die ~ betrifft *educationally, pedagogically* ‖ → Unterricht(s–)

Erz·iehungs- [in comp] *educational*; *educative*; *pedagogic*(*al*) **~anstalt** f *educational institution* (od *establishment*); → Schule; *reformatory* **~arbeit** f ⟨mil⟩ *preparation drill* **~art** f *mode of education, educational method* **~beihilfe** f *pecuniary aid granted by the state* (etc.) *to parents of talented boys* **~beratungsstelle** f *child guidance clinic* **≈berechtigt** a (of parents) ~ s *to be vested with the rights and duties of education* | ≈e(r [m]) f *legal guardian* (*of a minor child*) **~faktor** m *educative factor* **~gedanke** m *educational thought* **~heim** n *private educational establishment* | Institut f **~hilfe** f = –beratungsstelle **~kunde** f = Erziehungslehre f **~kunst** f *pedagogics* [pl] [sg konstr] **~lehre** f *educational science*; *pedagogy* **~system** n *system of education* **~theoretiker** m *educational theorist* **~wesen** n *education*; *systems of education* **~wissenschaft** f *educational science*

erz·ielen **1.** vt [h] (etw) *to arrive at*; *to attain*; *obtain, reach*; *secure*; (Resultat) *to compass, yield*; Erfolg ~ ⟨fam⟩ *to score* (*a success* od) *points* | (Summe Geldes) *to realize*; e–n Gewinn ~ aus *to make a profit on* .. ‖ die Autos erzielten glänzende Preise *the cars fetched excellent prices* ‖ *to* (*arrive at* od) *reach* (*an agreement* | ⟨sport⟩ (Sekunden) ~ *to clock* **2.** ≈ n *attaining* (*of a th*)

erz·ittern vi [s] ⟨fig⟩ *to tremble, shake, shiver*; *thrill, vibrate* (vor *with*)

erz·ogen a [pp v erziehen] gut ~ *well-bred, well-educated* (*child*); schlecht ~ *ill-bred*

erzürnen vt [h] **1.** (jdn) *to anger, exasperate, excite, incense, irritate* (*a p*); *to make* (*a p*) *angry* ‖ ⟨fam⟩ *to get in a p's hair* ‖ erzürnt *angry, indignant*; erzürnt s *to be angry* (über .. *at, about a th*; *with a p*) **2. sich** ~ *to get* od *grow angry*, etc. | × = sich veruneinigen

erzw·ingbar a *enforceable*

erzw·ingen vt [h] [→ zwingen] **1.** *to obtain* od *get by force*; *to coerce* ‖ sich [dat] e–n Eingang ~ *to force an entry* (in *into*); sich e–n Weg ~ *to force one's way* (in *into*; durch *through*); sich den Eingang in e–e Festung ~ *to force a fortress*; sich den Weg über e–n Paß ~ *to force a pass* ‖ (Lächeln; jds Rücktritt; Übergabe) *to force* **2.** (Maßnahme) durch Gesetz ~ *to enforce by law* ‖ (Gehorsam etc) *to compel*; *to enforce* (v jdm *upon a p*); *to exact* (v .. *from a p*) ‖ Liebe läßt sich nicht ~, man kann Liebe nicht ~ *you cannot force love* ‖ v jdm etw (Geständnis, Versprechen etc) ~ *to extort* od *wrest a th from a p*; *to wring* od *force a th from a p*; jds V. ~ *to force a promise out of a p* ‖ (Achtung, Bewunderung, Liebe) kann nicht erzwungen w .. *cannot be compelled* **Erzw·ingung** f ~/ *the forcing* (*of an entry*; *of a smile*) ‖ *enforcement* (*of obedience*)

erzw·ungen a *forced* (*resignation*; *smile*) ‖ *coerced* (*silence*)

Es n ~/~ **1.** ⟨mus⟩ *E flat* ‖ Es-dur *E-flat major*; es-Moll *e-flat minor* **2.** ⟨psych⟩ *id* L (Freud)

es [pron pers] [3. sg. n] (z ‚er' m, ‚sie' f) **I.** (S & P) **A.** [nom & acc] *it*; ~ (sc das Buch) ist im Pult *it is in the desk*; du wirst ~ dort finden *you will find it there* | ⟨sex⟩ *it*; das ≈

(*Freudian*) *id* L („*basic drives of the human soul: incest, cannibalism, murder*") **B. 1.** (of a woman) *she*; [acc] *her* **2.** (of a child) *it*; *he, she* || [acc] *it*; *him, her* **3.** (T) *it*; *he* || [acc] *it*; *him*; bring ~ (sc das Pferd) in den Stall *take him to the stable* **4.** (of a *country, ship*, etc.) *it*; *she* || [acc] *it*; *her* **C.** [als acc unübersetzt]: der Reisende muß sein Gepäck zeigen, damit ~ der Beamte untersucht *the passenger must show his baggage for the official to examine* **II.** [imps] (⟨fam⟩ abbr 's) **A.** [als Subjekt bei imps Verben] **1.** ~ regnet *it rains*; *it is raining* || ~ friert *it freezes* **2.** [bei imps Verben u Ausdrücken der Empfindung u Gemütsbewegung] [⟨engl⟩ mst *pers.* Konstruktion]: ~ friert mich (= mich friert, [jetzt] ⟨fam⟩ ich friere) *I am* (od *feel*) *cold* || ~ dürstet mich *I am thirsty* || ~ reut mich, ~ tut mir leid *I am sorry for it* || ~ ist mir übel *I feel sick*; ~ geht mir besser *I feel better* **3.** [vor anderen *imps*-Ausdrücken]: ~ is kalt *it is cold* || ~ ist Mitternacht, 10 Uhr, Montag *it is midnight, ten o'clock, Monday* **4.** [ell] mag s *may be*; wird in Ordnung k. (*I'll*) *get it right* **B.** (verblaßt) [als Subjekt] **1.** [in pass. u. refl. Wendungen]: ~ wurde viel getanzt *there was much dancing* || ~ wird gesagt *they say*; *it is said* || ~ wird sich herausstellen *it will be cleared up*; *we'll see* || ~ füllte sich die Halle *the hall was filling* **2.** [vor intr. Verben] **a.** [vor sein]: ~ war einmal ein König *once there was a king* **b.** ~ lebe der König! *long live the king*! || ~ leben die Frauen! *here's to the women*! ~ lebe die Freiheit! *liberty for ever*! || ~ komme, was wolle *come what will* od *may* **c.** ~ gibt zwei Arten v .. *there are two kinds of* .. || ~ standen einige Gläser auf dem Tisch *there stood some glasses on the table* **d.** ~ klingelt *there is a ring at the door* || ~ folgen uns Leute *some people are on our heels, there are some people on our h.* **3.** [bei ‚sein' auf Vorhergehendes Bezug nehmend] **a.** (‚Wer ist da?') ‚≈ ist dein Br·uder' (..) *It is your brother* || bist du ~? *is it you*? || hier ist ~ *here you are* || war ~ das? *was that it*? **b.** ‚Wer ist der Herr (die Dame)'? ≈ ist Herr N. (Frau N.) '*Who is the gentleman* (*the lady*)?' '*He is Mr. N.* (*she is Mrs. N.*)' || sie hatte e–n Liebhaber, aber wer war ~? *she had a lover, but who was he*? || ~ waren alle (sc v denen die Rede war) Komponisten v Rang *they were all of them first-rate composers* || ~ waren ihrer drei *they were three of them* **c.** [pred] [als nom] (‚Wer ist da') ‚·Ich bin ~' (..) *It is me*; oh, du warst ~ *oh, it was you* || der ist ~ *he is the one* od *the man*; er war ~, der .. *he it was who* .. | ‚Ich war euere Mutter, ich bin ~ nicht mehr' *I was your mother*; *I am so no more* || er war betrunken u Herr N. war ~ beinahe *he was drunk and Mr. N. nearly so* || ihre Mutter war e–e Dame u sie war ~ nicht *her mother was a lady and she was not* || sie ist glücklich; ich bin ~ auch *she is happy*; *so am I* **4.** [hinweisend auf folg. Nebensatz]: ~ ist ganz richtig, was er sagt *what he says is quite correct* || (~) freut mich, daß es dir gefällt (*I'm*) *glad you like it* || ~ bleibt nichts übrig als z warten *there is nothing for it but to wait* || ~ fragt sich, ob .. *the question is whether* || es läßt sich nicht sagen, wann .. *there is no telling when* .. **5.** (gänzlich verblaßt) wie geht ~? *how are you*? || wie kam ~, daß ..? *how was it that* .. || ~ macht nichts *never mind* || ~ schien ernst z w *matters seemed to be getting serious* || ~ war ihm gut ergangen *things had gone well with him* || so ist ~ brav! *there is a good boy*! || u schon ist ~ da! *and there you are*! || so steht ~! *there it is*! *well, there you are*! || ~ heißt in der Bibel *it says in the Bible* **C.** [als Objekt] **1.** er machte ~ richtig *he did it right* || niemand glaubte ~ *nobody believed it* || bitte, sag ~ mir *please, tell me* **2.** [hinweisend auf vorhergehenden Satzinhalt] **a.** ich glaube ~ nicht (= bin nicht der Meinung) *I do not think so* || ich hoffe ~ I hope so || ‚drehen Sie die Marke um.' Ich tat ~ '*Turn the stamp over.*' *I did so* || ich sagte ~ dir ja *I told you so* **b.** (‚Du könntest ihm schreiben.') ‚Du hast recht, ich könnte ~' (..) '*You are right, I could*'; ‚ich tat ~ fast auch' *I nearly did* **c.** er ist hier, ich weiß ~ *he is here, I know* **3.** [hinweisend auf folg. Satz]: wir wissen ~ heute, daß .. *today we know that* .. || ich halte ~ f das beste .. *I think it best* (*to write at once*) || ich halte ~ f richtig *I think fit* od *proper* (*to do*) **4.** (gänzlich verblaßt) k–e Stadt kann ~ (sc an Natur) mit e–m Dorf aufnehmen *no town is in it with a village* || da hast du's! da haben wir's! *there you are*! *there now*! || Du wirst ~ sehen! *see if I don't*! || aber da sah man's wieder! *but there it was*! || nun weißt du's! *there now*!, *so now*! || er wußte ~ besser *he knew better* || wag ~! *go it*! || hol's der Teufel! *confound it*!, *damn it*! **III.** (verdunkelt) [aus urspr. gen] er war ~ müde *or* satt *he was sick of it* || ich bin ~ zufrieden *I agree*; *all right* || sie wollte ~ nicht Wort h *she refused to own it*

×**Esch** m, **~e** f *piece of arable land*

·**Eschatolog·ie** f [esça–] ⟨theol⟩ *eschatology*

·**Esche** f ~/~n ⟨bot⟩ *ash*(*-tree*) || Blumen–, Manna-, Trauer≈ *flowering, Manna, weeping ash*; → Eber≈

·**Eschel** m ~s/ ⟨chem⟩ (*finest grade of*) *smalt*

·**eschen** a *ashen* ·**Eschen-** [in comp] *ash* **~baum** m *ash-tree* **~blatt** n *ash-leaf* **~holz** n *ash-wood*; *ash* **~wurz(el)** f ⟨bot⟩ = Digtam

·**Eschlauch** m ⟨bot⟩ *shallot* **Eschsch·oltzie** [–iə] f ⟨bot⟩ (nach J. F. Eschscholtz) *eschscholtzia*

·**Esel** m ~s/~ **1. a.** ⟨zoo⟩ *donkey*; *ass*; ⟨Am fam⟩ *burro*; Fleisch e–s ~s *asinine* (od *ass's*) *flesh* || männl. ~ *jackass* || → schreien **b.** °⟨fig⟩ (P) *ass* (ich ~ *I'm an ass, a fool*); *donkey, jackass*; *blockhead*; *booby, dunce, dunderhead, fool, noodle, oaf, owl* || ⟨sl⟩ *chump, moke*; ⟨Am sl⟩ *boob* (*every b. knows that*); *dub*; *dumb-bell*; *mutt*; → Dumm–, °Schafskopf; Kamel (etc) || so'n ~ *fool that he is*; *the silly ass* || dumm wie ein ~ *as stupid as an owl* || der alte ~ *the silly ass* od *fool*, ein gr (*or* richtiger) ~ *an utter ass* || wenn's dem ~ z wohl ist, geht er aufs Eis *Pride will have a fall* || der faule ~ trägt sich auf einmal tot *that's a lazy man's load* || das kann jeder ~ *any cow could do that* || ein ~ schilt den andern Langohr *the pot calls the kettle black--(arse)* || auf den ~ k *to come down in the world* **2.** ⟨übtr⟩ (Gestell) *horse*; Maler≈ *easel* **3.** [in comp] → Esel–, Esels–

·**Esel-** [in comp] *ass–, donkey–* **~füllen** n *ass--colt* (od *foal*) **~karren** m *donkey-drawn cart* **~treiber** m *donkey-driver*

Esel·ei f ~/~en *stupid* (od *silly*) *thing*; *stupidity*; *jackassery* || e–e ~ begehen *to do sth idiotic*

·**eselhaft** a ⟨fig⟩ *foolish, silly, stupid* ·**Eselin** f ~/~nen ⟨zoo⟩ *she-ass*, ⟨fam⟩ *henny*

·**Esels-** [in comp] °**~bank** f ⟨school⟩ *form for lazy* (od *stupid*) *boys* **~brücke** f **1.** ⟨hist geom⟩ *pons asinorum* [L]; *asses' bridge* **2.** ⟨school⟩ *key, crib, cram*; ⟨Am⟩ *pony*; e–e ~ benutzen *to crib*; nach e–r ~ übersetzen *to construe from crib* **~haupt** n ⟨mar⟩ (Verbindungsteil zw Mast u Stange) *cap* **~kopf** m *ass's head* || ⟨fig⟩ = Esel 1. b. **~milch** f ⟨bot⟩ = Wolfsmilch **~ohr** n **1.** *ass's ear* **2.** ⟨übtr⟩ (im Buch) *dog-ear, dog's ear*; *crease*; durch ~en verunstaltet s (of books) *to be dog* (od *dog's*)*-eared* **~rücken** m ⟨arch⟩ (got. Bogen) *ogee-arch, Tudor arch*; ⟨rail⟩ (z Rangieren) *hump*

Eser·in n ⟨chem⟩ *eserine*

·**Es·es** n ⟨mus⟩ *E double flat*

Esk·ader f ~/~s ⟨mar⟩ = Geschwader

Eskadr·on f ~/~en ⟨mil⟩ squadron; → Schwadron

eskalad·ieren vt [h] (Mauer) to escalade

Eskalati·on [-ts-] f ~/ ⟨bes mil-pol⟩ escalation; → Ausweitung

Eskamot·age [–taːʒə] f [Fr] jugglery **eskamot·ieren** vt [h] (etw) to juggle (away)

Eskap·ade f ~/~n escapade

Esk·arpe f ~/~n ⟨fort⟩ escarp

Eskarp·in m [–'pɛ̃] ~s/~s Fr = 1. Schnallen–, Tanzschuh 2. Kniehose

·Eskimo m ~(s)/~(s) Eskimo [pl –os, –oes] Esquimau [pl –maux] **~frau** f Eskimo **~hund** m husky, malamute **~sprache** f husky

†**Esk·ompte** [es'kɔ̃t] m = Diskont

Esk·orte f escort **eskort·ieren** vt [h] to escort

esot·erisch a esoteric(al)

Espars·ette f ~/ ⟨bot⟩ sainfoin

Esp·arto m esparto; esparto-grass; alfa

·Espe f ~/~n ⟨bot⟩ aspen(-tree) **·espen** a aspen

·Espen- [in comp] aspen **~baum** m aspen-tree **~blatt** n aspen-leaf **~holz** n; aus ~ gefertigt aspen **~laub** n ⟨fig⟩ wie ~ zittern to tremble like an aspen-leaf

·Esper m ~s/ = Esparsette

Esperanto n ~(s)/ Esperanto **Esplan·ade** f ⟨a. fort⟩ esplanade **espressivo** adv It expressive, eloquent ⟨a. mus⟩ **Espresso- ~bar** f coffee-bar **~-Maschine** f instant coffeemaker **Espr·it** [–'priː] m [Fr] ~s/~s esprit; wit

·Eß- (→ essen) [in comp] **~apfel** m eating-apple **~besteck** n → Besteck; single set of knife, fork, and spoon; ~e [pl] table-cutlery **~eisen** n ⟨tech⟩ (Lufteintrittsrohr in Wand v Hochofen) tuyère [Fr] **~gefäß** n ⟨Am⟩ dinner-pail **~gelage** n banquet, feast; sumptuous repast **~geschirr** n table plate; t.-service; plates and dishes ‖ ⟨mil⟩ mess tin; ⟨mar⟩ mess-service; (Arbeiter≃) ⟨bes Am⟩ lunch-pail; ⟨fam⟩ mess-traps pl **~gewohnheiten** f pl table manners; eating od food habits **~gier** f craving for food; gluttony; voracity **≃gierig** a voracious; greedy **~kastanie** f ⟨bot⟩ Spanish od sweet chestnut; edible ch. **~korb** m picnic– od provision-basket **~löffel** m table-spoon **~lust** f appetite **~manieren** f [pl] eating-manners [pl], ⟨dero⟩ mannerisms [pl] **~nische** f dining alcove od nook; ⟨bes Am⟩ dinette | ~nmöbel [n pl] dinette set **~pause** f meal break **~saal** m dining (od banqueting)-hall **~tisch** m dining-table; mahogany ‖ refrectory-table **~unlust** f lack od loss of appetite, ⟨med⟩ anorexia **~waren** f pl comestibles, edibles; provisions; eatables, victuals pl; ⟨school sl⟩ grub ‖ ⟨Am⟩ eats [pl] **~zimmer** n dining-room ‖ ~einrichtung °⟨fig⟩ (Zähne) ⟨vulg⟩ dining-room chairs, dinner-set; ⟨sl⟩ parlies

Ess·äer m ~s/~ die ~ [pl] (jüd. Sekte) the Essenes [pl]

Essay [ɛ'seː] m ~s/~s essay; Verfasser v ~s essayist **Essay·ist** [ɛse'ist] m ~en/~en esaayist

·eßbar a edible (chestnut); → essen ‖ etw ≃es something to eat; ~e Sachen eatables [pl]; ⟨Am⟩ eats [pl] | **≃keit** f edibility

·Esse f ~/~n 1. (Schmiede) forge 2. ⟨bes omd⟩ (Schornstein) chimney; flue, funnel; hohe ~ chimneystack ‖ → Kamin, Rauchfang, Schlot, Schornstein 3. °⟨fig⟩ (Zylinderhut) ⟨fam⟩ chimneypot; ⟨hist⟩ pot-hat ‖ → Essen–

·esse-·esse! ⟨Kindersprache⟩ din-din!

·essen vt/i [h] [aß/gegessen/iß!] **I.** vt **1.** (Brot etc) to eat ‖ (etw) gern ~ to relish; etw (f sein Leben) gern ~ to be (very) fond of; to like (fruit) (very much) ‖ jdm etw z ~ geben to feed a th to a p ‖ es ist nicht z ~ it is not eatable, it is uneatable ‖ sich [dat] etw über or zuwider ~ to be sated with a th; to feel an aversion to a th ‖ → Weisheit **2.** (Teller) leer ~ to empty; to clear (one's plate) **3.** ⟨fig⟩ jdn arm ~ to eat a p out of house and home **II.** vi **1. a.** to eat; ⟨sl⟩ to grub ‖ jdm z ~ geben to feed a p ‖ gut or tüchtig ~ to eat well; tüchtig ~ to take a hearty meal; tüchtig u viel ~ to play a good knife and fork; to be a great eater; iß nur tüchtig cut and come again; ich esse nicht viel I am no great eater ‖ sich satt or voll ~ to eat one's fill; mit etw to cram o.s. with a th; wenig ~ to be a small eater; v etw nur wenig ~ to be a sparing eater of a certain food **b.** wann eßt Ihr? when do you take od have your meals? wir ~ nur zweimal am Tage we take only two meals a day ‖ er ißt f drei he eats enough for three ‖ z Mittag ~ to dine; to have dinner; ⟨engl⟩ to (have) lunch ‖ kaltes Fleisch z M. ~ to dine off od on cold meat ‖ z Abend ~ to sup; to have supper; to dine ‖ außer dem Hause ~ to dine out ‖ wer nicht arbeitet, soll auch nicht ~ no work, no dinner **2.** ~ bei to eat od dine with (a p), ich esse bei m–r Tante I dine at my aunt's ‖ ⟨mil & mar⟩ (gemeinsam) ~ to mess (mit with); wir ~ z viert zus we are four of a mess | ~ v to eat of (a pudding) ‖ v e–m Teller ~ to eat off a plate **3.** der Kuchen läßt sich ~ the cake eats well

·Essen n ~s/~ **A.** [abstr] the eating (of food) **B.** [konkr] **1.** (Nahrung) food; diet; ⟨sl⟩ grub ‖ jdm etw ~ geben to give a p something to eat (⟨sl⟩ some grub) ‖ ~ u Trinken bread and butter **2.** (Speise, Gericht) dish; Austern sind ein hervorragendes ~ oysters are excellent eating ‖ → abdecken **3.** (Mahlzeit) meal, repast; dinner; supper ‖ ⟨mil & mar⟩ mess; ⟨Am mil⟩ chow ‖ (..) beim ~ (we'll discuss it) as we eat; beim ~ sprechen to speak at meals; ⟨dero⟩ to speak with one's mouth full; wir sind vier beim ~ we are four of a mess ‖ nach dem ~ after dinner; after mess ‖ über dem ~ during dinner ‖ ein Gast zum ~, Teilnehmer am ~ diner ‖ darf ich dich z ~ einladen? ⟨fam⟩ I'll give you a snack ‖ mit dem ~ warten auf .. (it's a trying th) waiting supper for (lovers) **4.** → Festessen

·Essen n ⟨Ger⟩ (Stadt im Ruhrgebiet) → Esse

·Essen- (→ Esse) **~aufsatz** m chimney-pot **~kehrer** m chimney-sweeper; sweep **~klappe** f damper; register

Ess·ener m = Essäer

·Essenholerschlange f ⟨mil sl⟩ chow-line

·Essenszeit f meal-time (zur ~ at m.-t.) ‖ dinner-time; supper-time

Ess·enz f ~/~en essence

·Esser m ~s/~ eater ‖ (kein) starker ~ (no) great eater; schwacher ~ poor eater; unnütze ~ [pl] useless mouths

°**Esser·ei** f ~/ = Essen B.; ⟨fam⟩ guzzling

·Essig m ~s/~e **1.** vinegar; (etw) in ~ verwandeln to acetify; (etw) mit ~ behandeln to vinegar; mit ~ gewürzt vinegar-flavoured **2.** °⟨fig⟩ es war ~ mit der Reise; die R. war (z) ~ geworden the journey (had) ended in smoke (od .. (had) failed, had come to nothing); es ist alles ~! it's no go! it's all up! ⟨Am⟩ that's out!, no soap! **3.** [in comp] vinegar– ..; ⟨chem⟩ acetous **~älchen** n vinegar-eel **≃ähnlich, ≃artig** a vinegary **~baum** m ⟨bot⟩ vinegar-plant; sumach **~bildung** f acetification **~essenz** f vinegar-essence **~fabrik** f vinegar-(manu)factory **~fabrikant** m vinegar-manufacturer **~faß** n vinegar-cask **~fläschchen** n cruet **~flasche** f vinegar-bottle **~früchte** f [pl] eingemachte ~ mixed pickles [pl] **~gärung** f acetous fermentation; souring **~geist** m ⟨chem⟩ acetone **~gemüse** n pickles pl **~gurke** f pickled cucumber; kl ~ pickled gherkin **~händler** m dealer in vinegar **~lösung** f acetous lotion **~mutter** f ⟨chem⟩ mother of vinegar; vinegar-mother (od plant) **~pilz** m vinegar-plant **≃sauer** a ⟨chem⟩ acetic ‖ –saure Tonerde [f] ⟨chem⟩ aluminium acetate ‖ –saures Ammoniak (Blei, Eisen, Natrium etc)

[n] *ammonium* (*lead, iron, sodium,* etc.) *acetate*; .. Eisenoxid [n] *ferric acetate*; .. Eisenoxidul [n] *ferrous acetate* ‖ –saures Salz *acetate* **~säure** f ⟨chem⟩ *acetic acid* ‖ ~anhydrid [n] *acetic anhydride* **~siederei** f *vinegar-(manu)factory* **~-stich** m *vinegar-plant* **~- u Ölständer** m *cruet--stand*

·Este m *Est(h)onian*; *native of Est(h)onia*; die ~n [pl] *the Esths* od *Est(h)onians* [pl]

·Ester m ~s/~ ⟨chem⟩ *ester* | ~bildung [f] *esterification*

Esther·ie f ⟨zoo⟩ Gattung der ~n *Estheria*

·Estland *Est(h)onia*; *Eesti* **·Estländer** m = *Este* **·estländisch** a = *estnisch* **·estnisch** a *Est(h)onian* ‖ das ≃e *Est(h)onian* (auf ~ *in E.*)

Estr·ade f ~/~n *estrade*; *raised platform*

Estrag·on m ⟨bot u cul⟩ *tarragon*

·Estrich m ~s/~e *plastered stone floor(ing)*; *plaster* (od *puddle*) *floor(ing)* ‖ Sw *attic*

·Et(Zeichen) n (&) *ampersand*

etabl·ieren vt [h] *to establish, found*; *to set up* (*shop*) | **sich** ~ *to set up in business*; sich ~ als *to set up as* .., *to settle down as* .. **Etablissem·ent** [–blis'mã] n ~s/~s *establishment, settlement* ‖ Vergnügungs≃ *place of amusement*

Et·age [e'tɑːʒə] f ~/~n *floor, stor(e)y*; *flat*; → Stock(werk) ‖ in der ersten ~ *on the first floor*; in der ersten ~ (e–r einstöckigen Villa) wohnen *to live in the upstairs rooms* ‖ ein Fenster in der zweiten ~ *a third-story window*

Et·agen- ~bad n ⟨hot⟩ *public bathroom* **~geschäft** n *business on first* od *higher floor* **~haus** n *house divided into flats*; ⟨Am⟩ *apartment-house* **~heizung** f *floor-heating* **~ventil** n ⟨tech⟩ *multiple valve* **~wohnung** f (abgeschlossene) (*self-contained*) *flat*; *suite of rooms*; ⟨Am⟩ *apartment*, (Dach≃) *maison(n)ette*

Etag·ere [eta'ʒeːrə] f [Fr] *étagère*; *whatnot*

Etam·in m, n ~s/ (feiner grobfädiger Stoff) *estamin, –mene*; *étamine* [Fr]

Et·appe f ~/~n **1.** ⟨† & hist⟩ (Stapelplatz) *staple* **2.** (Halteplatz) *stopping-place* ‖ *half-way house* ‖ (Strecke) *stage* (*in a journey*); ≃nweise adv *by stages*; in kz ~n reisen *to travel by short stages* ‖ ⟨sport⟩ *lap*; ⟨aero⟩ ~ e–s Dauerfluges *hop* **3.** ⟨mil⟩ (*area between the scene of operations and the frontier*) *communications zone* ‖ (Sammelpunkt) *base*; Verbindungslinien in der ~ *base-line*; *lines of communication along which the supplies* (etc.) *are despatched* **4.** ⟨übtr⟩ *stage* (*in a p's life*) | **~n-** [in ⟨mil⟩ comp] **~arzt** m *base--surgeon* **~kommandant** m *base-commandant* **~lazarett** n *base-hospital* °**~schwein** n ⟨mil sl⟩ *base-wallah*; (Offizier) *brass hat, carpet knight*, ⟨sl⟩ *slacker* **~straße** f *base-line*; *road* od *railway connected with the base* **~wesen** n *system of communications*; Inspekteur des ~s *General of Communications*

Et·at [e'tɑː] m [Fr] ~s/~s **1. a.** (Staatshaushalt) *budget*; veranschlagter ~ f das folg. Jahr *the Estimates* [pl] (*the Navy E.*); ⟨parl⟩ Ausgabe-≃ *supplies* [pl]; **b.** ⟨übtr⟩ *budget* ‖ ⟨com⟩ → Bilanz **c.** e–n ~ aufstellen *to* (*draw up a*) *budget* (f *for*) ‖ den ~ überschreiten *to exceed the Estimates* ‖ das war nicht im ~ vorgesehen *that had not been budgeted for* **2.** (Kopfstärke der Truppen etc) *establishment*; Militär≃ (⟨Ger⟩ bis 1918) *the Military Establishment*; Marine≃ *the Naval E.*; Friedens≃ *peace-establishment*, Kriegs≃ *war-e.* ‖ ~ der Staatsbeamten *the Civil Service Establishment*; *the list of Civil Servants* **~beratung** f *budget debate*

etatis·ieren vt [h] (etw) *to budget for* (*a th*)

et·atmäßig 1. a *permanent* (*post, rank*); *permanently appointed* (*official*) **2.** adv *according to the Budget* ‖ *permanently* (*appointed*)

Et·ats- ~jahr n *fiscal* od *financial year* **~überschreitung** f *the exceeding of the Estimates* ‖ *excess of expenditure over the Estimates* od *over the income*

et cetera (abbr etc.) L *etcetera, et cetera* L

°**·etepet·ete 1.** a *affected, ceremonious*; *finicky*; *prissy*; *exact*; ⟨fam⟩ *niminy-piminy, namby--pamby*; sehr ~ s betreffs .. *to be very particular about* **2.** adv *ceremoniously*; tu nicht so ~ *don't be so ceremonious* od *particular*

Et·esien [–iən] pl *Etesian winds*

·Ethik f ~/ *ethics* pl [sg konstr]; *morality*; *moral science* **·Ethiker** m ~s/~ *ethicist*; *moralist*; *moral philosopher* **·ethisch 1.** a *ethical*; in ~er Beziehung *ethically*; → sittlich **2.** adv *ethically, morally*

·ethnisch 1. a *ethnic(al)*; in ~er Beziehung *ethnically* **2.** adv *ethnically*

Ethno- [Gr] [in comp] *ethno–* **~gr·aph** m *ethnographer* **~graph·ie** f *ethnography* **≃gr·a-phisch** a *ethnographic(al)*; in ~er Beziehung *ethnographically* **~l·og(e)** m –gen/–gen *ethnologist* **~log·ie** f *ethnology* **≃l·ogisch** a *ethnologic(al)*; in ~er Hinsicht *ethnologically*

Etho- ~gr·amm n ~s/~e ⟨biol⟩ *ethogram* **~log·ie** f *ethology*

·Ethos n [Gr] *ethos* [Gr]; *ethical sense* od *content*; *moral sense* od *atmosphere*

Etik·ett n ~s/~e *label, ticket*; *docket*; *tab, tag* ‖ ein ~ zum Festmachen *a tie-on label*; zum Aufkleben *a stick-on label* ‖ etw mit e–m ~ versehen, e–r S ein ~ aufkleben *to label* (od *docket, tag, ticket*) *a th*

Etik·ette f ~/~n **1.** (Hofsitte) *etiquette* [Fr]; *ceremony* (*with all due c.*); *ceremonies* [pl]; *formalities* [pl]; ein Verstoß gegen die ~ *a breach of etiquette*

etikett·ieren vt [h] (mit Etikett versehen) etw ~ *to label, docket, tab, tag, ticket a th* **Etikett·iermaschine** f *labeller*

·etliche pron pl (⟨hum a.⟩ etzliche) **1.** [a] *some*; *a few*; *several, sundry*; ~ Male → einigemal; es sind ~ Tage her, daß .. *it is several days since* ..; nach ~r Zeit *after some time*; nach ~n 30 Tagen *after a month or so*; ~ 100 = mehrere 100 (Bücher); → einige 1. b. **2.** [abs] **a.** ~ v ihnen *some of them*; ~ m–r Freunde *a few of my friends*; → einige 2. b. **b. ~s** n *something*; *a thing* od *two*; um ~ älter .. *considerably older*; → einige 2. a.

·Etmal n ~s/~e ⟨mar⟩ (die in e–m Tag v Mittag z Mittag zurückgelegte Strecke) *the day's run* (*of a ship*)

·Eton ['iːtn] n ⟨engl⟩ (Stadt in Buckinghamshire) [in comp] **~schnitt** m (of women) *Eton crop*; im ~ *Eton-cropped* **~schüler** m *Eton scholar*; *Etonian* **~tracht** f *Etons* [pl]

†**Etr·urien** n ⟨It ant⟩ (Landschaft) *Etruria* †**Etr·urier** m, **~in** f *Etrurian* **etr·urisch, etr·uskisch** a *Etrurian, Etruscan*

Etr·usker m ~s/~ *Etruscan* **etr·uskisch** a *Etruscan* ‖ das ~e *Etruscan*

Etsch, die [Ger] ⟨It⟩ (Fluß) *the Adige* **~tal** n *valley of the Adige*

etsch [eːtʃ] ~ (~ ausgelacht)! *snooks*!

Et·üde f ~/~n ⟨mus⟩ *étude* (Fr), *study*

Etu·i n ~s/~s *case*; Zigarren≃ *cigar case* | ~kleid [n] *sheath dress*; ~samt [m] *chenille*

·etwa adv **1.** (ungefähr) **a.** *about*; ⟨Am⟩ *around* ‖ ~ 50 *about fifty*; ~ 60 Jahre *about 60 years or so*; (*it will cost*) *round about* (£ 10); ~ e–e Sekunde *a second or so*; ein Kind v ~ 14 Jahren *a child of fourteen or thereabouts* ‖ ~ 5 Uhr, 6 Fuß *just on 5 o'clock, 6 feet* ‖ ~ um 10 *somewhere about 10*; oder ~ soviel *or somewhere about that* ‖ ~ im August *some time in August* ‖ es war ~ e–e Viertelstunde später *it was some quarter of an hour later* **b.** (⟨a.⟩ **in ~**) *let us say*; *say* ‖ ~ nächsten Sonntag? *shall we say next Sunday*? **c.** es wird ~ aussehen wie

Figur 12 *it will look something* od *much like figure 12*; ~ wie .. *much as* (od *as if*); (*he interrogated him much as a schoolmaster would examine his* ..); ~ als wenn er sagen wollte *as much as to say* **2.** [modal; oft reines Füllwort] **a.** (vielleicht) *perhaps, possibly*; er könnte ~ krank w (*perhaps*) *he might fall ill*; ich fürchtete, er könnte sich ~ verlieren *I was afraid that* (*perhaps*) *he might lose his way* ‖ Sie können dies nehmen, wenn Sie nicht ~ vorziehen z warten *you may take this unless* (*perhaps*) *you would prefer to wait* ‖ wenn er ~ k. sollte *if he should happen to come* **b.** [interr & neg] **nicht** ~ als ob .. *not that* .. ‖ du willst doch nicht ~ sagen, daß ich Unrecht habe? *you don't mean to say I am wrong*? ‖ Sie h ihn nicht ~ aufgesucht heute morgen? *you have not been to see him this morning, by any chance*? ‖ Sie könnten nicht ~ selbst gehen? *I suppose you couldn't go yourself* (*and* ..)? ‖ ~ noch etwas? *what next*? ‖ Sind ~ Knochen gebrochen? *are any bones broken, do you think*? ‖ bin ich ~ im Wege? *would I be in the way*? ‖ Sind Sie ~ taub? *are you at all deaf*? ‖ einige v den Birnen ~? *some of those pears, now*?

·etwaig a *possible*; *contingent*; *eventual*; ~e Ansprüche (etc) *any claims*; ~es Eintreffen *contingency, eventuality* (*of a th*) **~enfalls** adv *possibly*; *in a contingency*; *under certain conditions*

·etwas pron (⟨fam⟩ oft: was) [invar] **I.** [abs] n **A. 1.** (in Aussagesätzen) **a.** *something*; irgend ~ *something or other* ‖ in ~ *in a th*; mit ~ *with a th* ‖ noch ~ *something more*; noch ~! *I say*! ‖ so sicher wie nur ~ *as sure as fate* ‖ sonst ~ *something else* ‖ ~, was .. *something that* .. ‖ ich habe ~ über ihn gehört *I have heard something about him* | ~ Altes *something old*; ~ anderes *another th*; *something else*; das ist ~ anderes *that is another th* ‖ ~ Besseres *something better, a better th*; ~ so Dummes! *what a stupid th* od *business*!; ~ Scharfes *some pointed th*; er tat ~ sehr Rührendes *he did a very touching th*; ~ Ungewöhnliches *an uncommon th* ‖ es liegt ~ Unsicheres in .. *there is something of uncertainty in* .. ‖ ⟨emph⟩ ~ Bedeutendes *something* (*that is s.*) **b.** *some* (*will you have some*?); gib ihm ~ [acc] v *give him some of* (*your bread*); ~ davon *some of it* **2.** [in fragenden u bedingten Sätzen] **a.** *anything*; gibt es ~ [acc], was ich tun kann? *is there anything I can do*? ‖ kaum ~ *scarcely anything*; überhaupt ~ *anything at all* ‖ irgend ~ *anything* | ~ Neues *anything new*; *any news* ‖ k–e Fälschung oder ~ Ähnliches *not a forgery or anything like that* **b.** *something*; möchten Sie noch ~ [acc] mehr *do you want something more*? **c.** *any* (v .. *of a th*); ich wünschte, ich hätte ~ [acc] (sc Geld) *I wish I had any*; wünschen Sie noch ~ (sc Tinte)? *do you wish any more*? **3. Wendungen a.** das ist schon *or* doch ~! *that's not bad, is it*?; wenn du ~ [acc] bedeuten *or* vorstellen willst, so .. *if you wish to be anybody* .. ‖ alle, die ~ [acc] bedeuten *everybody who is anybody* (*will agree*) ‖ es bedeutet schon ~ [acc], daß .. *it is something that* ..; das will was [acc] bedeuten *that makes all the difference* ‖ er bildet sich ~ [acc] ein *he has a high opinion of himself*; *he is very conceited* ‖ er wird es zu ~ bringen *he will go far* ‖ ~ gelten bei *to carry weight with* (*a p*); er gilt ~ *he is a p of consequence* ‖ ~ an sich h v *to have a tinge of* (*a diplomat*) ‖ ~ auf dem Herzen haben *to have something at heart* ‖ er hat ~ gegen mich *he is down on me* ‖ das hat ~ f sich *there is something in that* ‖ ich will Ihnen ~ sagen *I will tell you what it is*; ⟨dial⟩ *I'll tell you what* ‖ das ist wenigstens ~! *that is at least something*! ‖ das ist so sicher wie nur ~ *that is as sure as eggs is* (od *are*) *eggs* ‖ ~ verstehen *to know what's what*; ~ verstehen v *to know a th or two about* .. **b. so** ~ *such a th*; *that sort of the*; *a th like that* ‖ so ~ v Dummheit! (Ich ..) *bother this stupidity*! *bless my stupidity*! (*I had not* ..) ‖ so ~ gibt es *there is such a th* ‖ so ~ gibt's nicht wieder! *there won't be anything like that* ‖ so ~ ist noch nicht dagewesen *that is unprecedented* ‖ so ~ wie ein Pascha *a pasha of sorts* ‖ er ist so ~ wie ein Dichter *he is something of a poet* (od *something like a poet*); *he is a poet of sorts, he is a poet or something* **II.** a **1.** *some* (*money, time*) **2.** [in fragenden u bedingenden Sätzen] **a.** *any*; wenn ich ~ Geld hätte .. *if I had any money* .. **b.** *some*; kann ich ~ Tinte h? *can I have some ink*? **III.** ≗ n *something*; ein gewisses ≗ *a certain something*; das gewisse ≗ *it* (= *sex appeal*), ⟨sl⟩ *oomph* ‖ ein fremdes *or* verdächtiges ≗ *a catch* (*in a p's voice*) ‖ aufgeregt durch das geringste ≗ *excited by just anything* **IV.** adv **1. a.** *somewhat* (*difficult, stout, damp*); *a little, rather*; ⟨Am sl⟩ *kind of* (*fatter*) ‖ ⟨Am⟩ *some* ‖ ~ besser (*I feel*) *rather better* ‖ das ist ~ stark! *that's too much of a good th* **b.** [vor Adj oft] *–ish*: ~ lang *longish*; ~ steif *stiffish* **2.** [bei Verben] er lügt ~ *he is something of a liar*; die Geschichte verliert ~ beim Erzählen *the story loses somewhat in the telling* ‖ °schäm dich ~! *shame on you*! → °was

†**·etwelche** [pron pl] = einige **~rmaßen** adv Sw = einigermaßen

Etymol·og(e) m ~en/~en *etymologist* **Etymolog·ie** f ~/~n *etymology* **etymol·ogisch 1.** a *etymologic*(*al*) **2.** adv *etymologically* **etymologis·ieren** vi [h] *to etymologize*

·Etzeichen n → Et †**·etzlich** a = etlich

Eub·öa n (Insel im Ägäischen Meer) *Eubœa*

euch 1. pron pers [dat & acc z ‚ihr'] **a.** [acc] *you*; f ~ *for you* ‖ ⟨Am⟩ *you*; *you all* ‖ ⟨bib & poet⟩ *ye* ‖ ⟨dial⟩ *yer* **b.** [dat] *you*; *to you, for you*; wenn es nach ~ ginge, so würde ich .. *for all you care I should* ..; ein Freund v ~ *a friend of yours* **2.** pron refl **a.** *yourselves*; schämt ~ *be ashamed of yourselves* **b.** *you*; seht unter ~ *look below you* **c.** *each other*; *one another*

euchar·istisch a *eucharistical* ‖ ≗er Kongreß *Eucharistic Congress*

Eudämon·ismus m *eud(a)emonism*

Eudiom·eter n *eudiometer*

·euer m & n, ·eu(e)re f & pl [pron poss] **1.** *your* ‖ ~ Exemplar ist herrlich *yours is a fine specimen*; ist er e–r ~er Freunde? *is he a friend of yours*? | (in Briefen) ≗ *your*; *yours*; [im Briefschluß] *Yours* (*sincerely, etc*) ‖ ich erinnere mich ≗ [nicht anders!] *I remember you* (*well*) | [pred] *yours*; es ist ~ (*or* das eure) *it is yours* ‖ ihr seid ~ vier *there are four of you* **2.** ≗ Gnaden *Your Grace*; Eure Hoheit *Your Highness* **3.** das Eure *your property*; *your things* [pl]; tut das ~ *do your duty* ‖ die Euren (*or* Euern) [pl] *yours*; *your people* **·euerseits** adv *for* (od *on*) *your part*; ihr ~ *you for your part* **·euresgleichen** adv *your like*(*s*); ⟨fam⟩ *the like*(*s*) *of you*; Leute ~ *people of your kind*; u ~ *and the likes of you* **·euerthalben** adv *for your sake*; *on your account* ‖ (= wenn es nach euch ginge) *for all you care* (*I should* ..); ~ hätte sie sterben können *she might have died for all you cared* **·euertwegen** adv = euerthalben **·euertwillen**: um ~ = euertwegen

Eug·englanz m ⟨minr⟩ *polybasite*

Eug·enik f ~/ *eugenics* pl [sg konstr] **eug·enisch** a *eugenic* (Unfruchtbarmachung)

Eugen·ol n ⟨chem⟩ *eugenol*; *eugenic acid*

Eug·ensäure f ⟨chem⟩ *eugenic acid*

Eukal·yptus m (L) ⟨bot⟩ *eucalyptus* (L) ‖ ~öl [n] *eucalyptus oil*

Eukl·as n ~es/~e ⟨minr⟩ *euclase*

eukl·idisch a; ~e Geometrie *Euclid*
Eukol·it m ⟨minr⟩ *eucolite*
eulanis·ieren vt [h] (trade mark) *to secure* (*wool, carpets*) *against damage done by moths* | **-rt** a *moth-proof*
·Eule f ~/~n **1.** ⟨orn⟩ *owl*; kl ~, junge ~ *owlet*; Schleier⁓ *barn* (od *white, church, sreech*)-*owl*; Wald⁓ *wood* (od *tawny*)-*owl* || ~n(vögel) → *owl* || häßlich wie e–e ~ *very ugly* || .. alte ~ (*she looks like a*) *stuffed owl* || ⟨teens⟩ flotte ~ *slick chick* || ⟨fig⟩ ~n nach Athen bringen *to carry coals to Newcastle* || ˣwat dem eenen sin Uhl, ist dem annern sin Nachtegal *what is one man's meat is another man's poison* **2.** ⟨ent⟩ *moth*; *noctuid*; *noctuid moth* **3.** ⟨übtr⟩ (kugelförmiger Besen) *Turk's head*
·Eulen- **⁓artig** a *owl-like*; *owlish* **~geschrei** n *the hooting of owls* °**~schiffe** f (Bier) *piss*; ⟨mar⟩ *tiger-piss*; (Whiskey) *snake-juice* **~spiegel** m (P) ⟨Ger⟩ Meister ~ *Master Tyll Eulenspiegel*; ⟨engl⟩ *Owlglass* | ~·ei [f] = ~streich [m] *waggish trick*; *tomfoolery*; → Schelmenstreich **~vögel** m pl *owls*, → *owl*
·eulenhaft a *owlish*; *owl-like*
Eumen·iden pl ⟨ant⟩ *the Eumenides* (Gr) pl
Eun·uch m ~en/~en *eunuch*; *spado*
Eu- **~phem·ismus** m ~/–men *euphemism, heterophemy* (*e.g.* "*go to Heligoland*" [= *hell*]) **⁓phem·istisch** **1.** a *euphemistic* **2.** adv *euphemistically* **~phon·ie** f ~/~n [–iːən] *euphony* **⁓ph·onisch** a *euphonic*(*al*) **~ph·onium** n (L), ~s/–nien ⟨mus⟩ (Blasinstrument) *euphonium* (L) **~phorbiaz·een** pl ⟨bot⟩ *Euphorbiaceae* (L) pl **~ph·orbie** [–iə] f ⟨bot⟩ *Euphorbia* (L) **~phor·ie** f gr *euphoria* **~phr·asia** f (L) ⟨bot⟩ *euphrasy* **~phu·ismus** m ~/ ⟨engl Lit⟩ (nach Lyly's Roman Euphues [1579/80]) *euphuism*; in der Manier des ~ *euphuistically* **⁓phu·istisch** **1.** a *euphuistic* **2.** adv *euphuistically*
·Euphrat m *Euphrates*
Eurafrik·aner m (Mischling v afrikan. Eingeborenen mit Weißen) *Eurafrican* **eurafrik·anisch** a *Eurafrican*
Eur·asien n *Eurasia* **Eur·asier** m (Mischling v Europäern u Eingeborenen v Indien) *Eurasian* **eur·asisch** a *Eurasian*
Eurat·om f [invar] *Euratom* (*European Atomic Energy Community*)
·euerseits adv (etc) = euerseits (etc)
Eurhythm·ie f ~/~n *eurhythmics* pl [sg konstr] **eurh·ythmisch** a *eurhythmic*
·Eurige **1.** der ~ (im Briefschluß) *Yours* **2.** das ⁓ *yours*; es ist das ⁓ *it is yours* || → euer 3.
·Eurokarte f ⟨hot⟩ *Eurocard* (*International S. A., 88 Brook St., London W. 1.*) **Eur·opa-** **~dienst** m ⟨wir, rad⟩ *European Services* **Eurovision(snetz** n) f (Fernsehprogramm-Austausch in Europa) *Eurovision*
Eur·opa n ~s/ *Europe* | ~rat [m] *Council of E.*
Europ·äer m ~s/~; **~in** f ~/~nen *European*
europ·äisch a *European*; ⁓es Amt f Fernmelde-Weitverbindungen *European Long Lines Agency* (ELLA); ~es Gleichgewicht ⟨pol⟩ *Balance of Power* || ⁓e Wirtschaftsgemeinschaft f (EWG) *European Economic Community* (*EEC*)
eust·achisch a ⟨anat⟩ ⁓e Röhre *eustachian tube*
Eut·ektikum n ⟨met⟩ *eutectic* **eut·ektisch** a ⟨met⟩ *eutectic* (*mixture*)
·Euter n ~s/~ ⟨zoo⟩ *udder, dug*; → Zitze **~entzündung** f ⟨vet⟩ (Kuh⁓) *garget*
Euthanas·ie f ~/ (Gnadentod) *euthanasia* (L); *mercy killing*
evaku·ieren vt [h] (Behälter) *to pump down* od *out, to exhaust* | (Gebiet) *to evacuate*
Evaku·ierte: die ~n [pl] *the evacuated*
Evaku·ierung f ~/~en *evacuation*
Evangeli·ar n ~s/~e & –rien *evangeliar*
Evang·elien- [in comp] *evangelic* (*text*) **~harmonie** f ⟨Lit⟩ *arrangement of the evangelic text in the form of a harmony* **~seite** f ⟨R. C.⟩ *gospel side* **Evang·elimann** m *exhorter*
evang·elisch a **1.** ⟨bib⟩ *evangelic* (*dogma; text*) **2.** ⟨ec⟩ **a.** ⟨Ger⟩ ~, ~-lutherisch *evangelical, Protestant*; *Lutheran* (*church*) **b.** ⟨C. E.⟩ *evangelical*; *Low Church* (*party*) || Anhänger der ~en Partei *evangelical*; Lehre der ~en P. *evangelicalism*
Evangel·ist m ~en/~en *evangelist* | **~enzeichen** n pl *Evangelistic symbols*
Evang·elium n [L] ~s/–lien **1.** [abstr] **a.** (Lehre nach den –lien) *gospel* (*to preach the g.*); *evangel*; e–m Lande das ~ verkündigen *to evangelize a country* **b.** ⟨übtr⟩ *evangel* (*of love*); ein neues ~ *a new e.* **2.** [konkr] **a.** ⟨bib⟩ *gospel*; *evangel*; das ~ Matthäi, Matthäus⁓ *the gospel according to St. Matthew* **b.** ⟨ec⟩ *text from the gospels*
Evekt·ion [ts] f ~/~en ⟨astr⟩ *evection*
Eventualität f ~/~en *eventuality, contingency*
eventu·ell **1.** a *possible* (*loss*); *contingent, eventual*; *potential* (*readers*); *that may occur* od *arise* [pred] **2.** adv *possibly*; *perhaps, should the occasion arise* || → gegebenen–, nötigenfalls
·Everest m *Mount E.* (im Himalaja)
evid·ent a *evident*; *clear, manifest, obvious*
Evid·enz f ~/ *evidence*; *clearness* (*with c.*); mit absoluter ~ *most obviously* (od *clearly*); (etw) bis zur ~ erweisen *to prove by evidence*; *to prove clearly*
Evol·ute f ~/~n ⟨math⟩ *evolute* **Evolut·ion** [ts] f ~/~en ⟨biol⟩ *evolution*; ~stheorie [f] *Doctrine* (od *Theory*) *of Evolution* **Evolv·ente** f ~/~n ⟨math⟩ *involute* **evolv·ieren** vt → entwickeln
·Ewer m ~s/~ ⟨mar⟩ *lighter* **~führer, ~mann** m *lighterman*
·ewig **I.** a **1.** *eternal* (*God*) || (zeitlos) *eternal* (*life*; *laws*; *right*; *snow*); *endless, everlasting*; *timeless* (*laws of nature*); *interminal* (*filibuster*); z ~en Andenken an *to the e.* (od *immortal*) *memory of* || die ⁓e Stadt *the Eternal City*; *Rome* || der ⁓e Jude *the Wandering Jew* || das ⁓e Licht *sanctuary lamp*; *tabernacle light* || das ⁓weibliche (Goethe, Faust II. Teil) *the divine in woman* || seit ~en Zeiten *from time immemorial* || in die ~en Jagdgründe eingehen *to go west* **||** ⟨übtr⟩ ~es Einerlei *unending monotony* **2.** (endlos) **a.** *continuous*; *eternal, everlasting* (*bliss*); *perpetual* (*damnation*); *unending*; *immutable, unchanging* **b.** ⟨jur⟩ ~e Rente *perpetual annuity*; *perpetuity* **c.** °(unerträglich) *eternal* (*chatter*); *deadly, dull* (*monotony*) **II.** adv **1.** *eternally, infinitely, endlessly, interminably*; *to the end of time* || ~, auf ~ *without end*; *for ever, forever* **2.** *continuously*; *perpetually* **3.** (als Intensivum) sie blieb ~ lange *she stayed an eternity*; in ~ langer Zeit *in a month of Sundays* | (= sehr lange) ich habe dich ~ nicht gesehen! *you are quite a stranger*! ⟨fam dial⟩ *we an't seen you this ever such a time*! || ~ warten *to wait for ages* | das tut mir ~ leid *I am terribly sorry about it* || es ist ~ schade *it is a thousand pities* zank doch nich ~! *don't keep quarreling*! **·Ewige** **1.** der ~ [des ~n] *the Eternal*; *God* **2.** das ~ [des ~n] *the eternal*; *the divine*
·Ewigkeit f ~/~en **1.** *the eternity* (*of God*) || *eternity*; *everlastingness*; *timelessness*; *time without end* || ⟨bib⟩ v ~ z ~ *world without end* || in die ~ eingehen *to pass into eternity*; *to go home*, (*to die*) **2.** *eternity*; *perpetuity* || in alle ~ *into eternity*; *in perpetuity*; *for ever and ever* **3.** °(sehr lange Zeit) e–e ~ *an endless time*; ~en pl *ages* || sie blieb e–e ~ *she stayed an eternity*; → ewig 3. || es ist e–e ~, seit .. *it is an*

age since .. ‖ e–e ~ warten *to wait for ages* ‖ in alle ~ *to the days of eternity*

·**ewiglich** adv *eternally* ‖ *everlastingly*; *perpetually*

°**ex** adv [L] *over, up*; *finished, settled*; die S ist ~ *the game is up*; → trinken ‖ ~ cathedra L ⟨R C⟩ *ex cathedra*; *from the Holy See* ‖ ⟨fig⟩ *infallible, infallibly*

Ex- [in comp] *ex–*; *quondam* [L]; *late* ‖ °**~bummel** m ⟨Ger univ⟩ *excursion on the day after a students' festival* **≗-Dividende** f *ex dividend* **~kaiser** m ⟨Ger⟩ *ex-emperor* °**~(-trinken)**! *bottomer*!

ex·akt 1. a *exact* (*experiment, expression*); die ~en Wissenschaften *the exact sciences* ‖ *accurate, exact* (*scholar*); ~ in *exact in* **2.** adv *exactly*; *accurately* **Ex·aktheit** f ~/~en *exactness*; *exactitude*; *accuracy* ‖ militärische ~ *military precision*

exalt·iert a *exalted*; *overexcited, wrought up*; *excentric* **Exalt·iertheit** f *exaltation*; *eccentricity*

Ex·amen n ~s/~&–mina *examination*; ⟨fam⟩ *exam* ‖ ⟨univ⟩ (Reihe v Prüfungen) *schools* [pl] ‖ → Prüfung | ein ~ ablegen *to take* (od *sit for*) *an exam(ination)* ‖ durchs ~ fallen → Durchfallen ‖ ins ~ gehen (°steigen) *to go up* (od *in*) *for one's examination* ‖ vor dem ~ stehen *to be in for one's schools*; *to be sitting for one's schools*; *his exams come up soon*

Examin·and m ~en/~en *examinee*; *candidate*

Examin·ator m ~s/–nat·oren *examiner* ‖ ⟨Oxf & Cambr⟩ *moderator* [L] **examin·ieren** vt [h] (jdn) *to examine* ‖ ⟨fig⟩ *to catechize, question*

Exanth·em n ~s/~e ⟨med⟩ *exanthema* [L]

Exarati·on [ts] f ~/~en *exaration*

Ex·arch m ~en/~en Gr ⟨byzant. hist⟩ *exarch* ‖ ⟨ec⟩ → Archimandrit **~·at** n ~s/~e *exarchate* (*of Ravenna*)

Exartikulati·on f ~/~en ⟨surg⟩ *disarticulation*

Ex·audi [L] (6. Sonntag nach Ostern) *Exaudi*

·**Exedra** f ~/–dren ⟨arch⟩ *exedra*

Exeg·ese f ~/~n ⟨theol⟩ *exegesis* [Gr] **Exeg·et** m ~en/~en *exegete*; *interpreter*; *commentator* | **~ik** f ~/ ⟨theol⟩ *exegetics* [pl] **≗isch 1.** a *exegetic(al)* **2.** adv *exegetically*

exekut·ieren vt [h] = vollstrecken

Exekuti·on f ~/~en ⟨jur⟩ (Zwangsvollstrekkung) *execution*; → Hinrichtung ‖ ~sverfahren [n] *execution*; *distress*; → Beschlagnahme ‖ ~sverkauf *forced sale* **Exekut·ive** f ~/ die ~ *the executive* (G gs *legislative*); *executive government*; ⟨pol a.⟩ *law enforcement* ‖ ⟨Am⟩ *administration*

Exekut·ivgewalt f = Exekutive

Ex·empel n ~s/~ **1.** (Beispiel) *example, instance* ‖ an jdm ein ~ statuieren *to make an example of a p* **2.** ⟨math⟩ (Rechen≗) *sum, problem*; ~ aufgeben *to set sums*; ~ rechnen *to do sums*; → Probe

Exempl·ar n ~s/~e ⟨allg⟩ *specimen*; (of books) *copy*; Frei≗ *specimen copy* ‖ (T) *head* (*wellgrown heads are rare*); 30 ~e *30 head* (*of cattle*) | (P) *specimen* **exempl·arisch 1.** a *exemplary* (*severity*) **2.** adv *by way of example* ‖ jdn ~ bestrafen *to punish a p severely, to make an example of a p*

Ex·emte, Exim·ierte [der ~, ein ~r] m ~n/~n *the exempt* **Exemti·on** [ts] f ~/~en *exemption*

Exequ·atur n [L] (amtl. Anerkennung e–s ausländ. Konsuls durch die Landesregierung) *exequatur* [L] (Erteilung *delivery*)

Ex·equien [pl] [F] *exequies* [pl], *obsequies* [pl]; *funeral ceremonies* [pl]

exequ·ieren vt [h] = vollstrecken

·**Exer** n ~s/~ ⟨school sl⟩ *ekker*, → ~zitium

Exerz·ier- (→ exerzieren) [in comp] ⟨mil⟩ *drill* **~halle** f, **~haus** n *drill-hall*, ⟨Am⟩ *armory* **~meister** m ⟨mil⟩ *drill-sergeant* (od *instructor*); ⟨übtr⟩ *drill-master* **~munition** f *dummy* (od *practice*) *ammunition* **~patrone** f *dummy* (od *drill, practice*) *–cartridge* **~platz** m *drill-ground* **~reglement** n *drill-book* **~vorschrift** f *drill regulation*

exerz·ieren I. vt/i [h] ⟨mil⟩ **1.** vt (Griffe etc) *to exercise* ‖ → einexerzieren **2.** vi *to drill* **II.** ≗ n *drill*; beim ~ *at drill*

Exerz·itium [ts] n ~s/–tien [–tsiən] *exercise*; *written task*

Exh·austor m ~s/–st·oren ⟨tech⟩ *exhauster*; *fan*

Exhibition·ismus [ts] m *exhibitionism*

exhum·ieren vt [h] *to exhume*

Ex·il n ~s/~e *exile, banishment* ‖ ins ~ gehen *to go into exile*; jdn ins ~ schicken *to exile* od *banish a p* | ~regierung [f] *refugee government*

Existenti·al- [ts] [in comp] **~philosophie** f ⟨Ger⟩ *existentialism*; *existential philosophy* **~satz** m *existential proposition*

Exist·enz f ~/~en **1.** [abstr] *existence* ‖ (Unterhalt) *living, subsistence* ‖ Frage der ~ → ~frage; e–e auskömmliche ~ h *to have enough to subsist upon*; gesicherte ~ *secure living*; e–e neue ~ gründen *to build* od *start a new life*; sich e–e ~ gründen *to establish o.s.* **2.** [konkr] (P) *existence*; merkwürdige ~ *curious individual*; dunkle, zweifelhafte ~en *shady, dubious i.ls*; viele verkrachte ~en [pl] *many ruined existences* [pl] **~bedingungen** f pl *terms of ex.* **~berechtigung** f *right to exist* | das ist e–e **~frage** *it is a matter of life and death* **~minimum** f ⟨physiol⟩ *subsistence level* od *minimum*; *living wage* **~mittel** n [pl] *means* [pl] *of existence* | (niedrige) **~stufe** f (*low*) *level of ex.* **~verlust** m *loss of the means of ex.*

exist·ieren vi [h] **1.** *to exist, to be*; *to subsist* ‖ (a. S) noch ~ *to be extant* (*only three manuscripts are e.*); *to be still in existence*; *to survive*; noch ~d *extant* (*letter*); es existiert nicht mehr *it does not exist any more*; → bestehen **2.** (P & T) ~ v *to live* od *subsist* (*up*)*on*

Exkav·ator m ~s/–vat·oren *excavator*

Exkl·ave f ~/~n *region of a state situated in a foreign dominion*

Exklusi·on f ~/~en *exclusion*; *expulsion*

exklus·iv a *exclusive* (*circles*), *select* (*society*); ~es Wesen *exclusiveness* ‖ *he is very exlusive*

exklus·ive adv *exclusive of*; bis ~ Seite 50 *up to exclusive of page 50*; Preise ~ Licht u Bedienung *exclusive terms* **Exklusivit·ät** f ~/ *exclusiveness*; *exclusivism*

Exkommunikati·on [ts] f ~/~en ⟨ec⟩ *excommunication* **exkommuniz·ieren** vt [h] (jdn) *to excommunicate*

Exkrem·ent n ~s/~e [mst pl] ~e *excrements* [pl]

Exkr·et n ~s/~e ⟨physiol⟩ [mst pl] ~e *excreted substances* [pl], *excreta* L [pl] → Sekret

Exkreti·on [ts] f ~/~en *excretion*

Exk·urs m –ses/–se **1.** *digression*; *excursion* (in *into*) **2.** *excursus* [L]; *appendix*

Exkursi·on f ~/~en *excursion* (auf .. *on an e.*)

Exl·ibris n ~/~ *ex-libris* [L]; *book-plate*; Sammler v ~ *ex-librist*

Exmatr·ikel f ~/~n ⟨univ⟩ *leaving-certificate*

Exmatrikulati·on [ts] f ~/~en die ~ jds *the removal of a p's name from the books* (*of a university*) **exmatrikul·ieren** vt [h] jdn ~ *to remove a p's name from the books* (*of a university*) ‖ sich ~ l *to take one's name off the books* (*of a university*); ⟨fam⟩ *to go down*

Exmissi·on f ~/~en ⟨jur⟩ *ejectment*; *eviction*

exmitt·ieren vt [h] ⟨jur⟩ (jdn) *to eject*; *evict*

·**Exodus** m ~/ [L] ⟨bib⟩ *Exodus* [L]

ex off·icio adv [L] *ex officio* [L]; *officially*

Exogam·ie f ~/ *exogamy* **exog·amisch** a *exogamic, exogamous* **exog·en** a *exogenous* **Exok·arp** n ~s/ ⟨bot⟩ *exocarp* **·exokrin** a *exocrine,* → [Ggs] endokrin

exorbit·ant a *exorbitant; excessive;* ⟨fam⟩ *steep (prices)* **Ex·ordium** n ~s/–dien ⟨Lit⟩ *proem*

Exorz·ismus m ~/–men *exorcism*

Ex·ot m ~en/~en, **Ex·ote** m ~n/~n (ausländ. Pflanze etc) *exotic* ‖ (P) *foreigner*

exot·erisch 1. a *exoteric; *exoterical* 2. adv *exoterically* **exoth·erm(isch)** a ⟨chem⟩ *exothermic*

ex·otisch a *exotic (plant, word)* ‖ der ~e Charakter, das ≗e = **Exot·ismus** m ⟨Lit⟩ *exotism (e.g. Chateaubriand's Atala)*

Expansi·on f ~/~en ⟨phys⟩ *expansion*

Expansi·ons- [in comp] ⟨phys⟩ *expansion* .. **~(Dampf)maschine** f *expansion-engine* **~kraft** f = Expansivkraft **~krieg** m *war of expansion* **~politik** f *policy of expansion; expansionism;* Anhänger [m] der ~ — **~politiker** m *expansionist* **~ventil** n *expansion-valve*

expans·iv a *expansive* **Expans·ivkraft** f *expansive force*

Expedi·ent m ~en/~en *dispatching* (od *forwarding, shipping) clerk* **exped·ieren** vt [h] ⟨com⟩ (etw) *to consign, to dispatch (des–), forward, send* ‖ (Gepäck) *to expedite* ‖ °⟨übtr⟩ (jdn) → befördern B. 2.

Expediti·on [ts] f ~/~en I. [abstr] 1. (Beförderung) *dispatch (des–); forwarding, sending (of goods); consignment* 2. (Forschungsreise) *expedition;* auf e–r ~ *on an e.* 3. (Feldzug) *expedition* II. [konkr] 1. *dispatching-office* ‖ Zeitungs≗ *newspaper office; Office* 2. (P.en) *expedition*

Expediti·ons- [in comp] ⟨mil⟩ *expeditionary*

Expektor·antien [–tsiən] n [pl] ⟨med⟩ *expectorants* [pl] **Expektorati·on** [ts] f ⟨med⟩ *expectoration*

Experim·ent n ~(e)s/~e ⟨scient⟩ *experiment* (an T.en *on animals;* in *in*) ‖ ein ~ m *to make an e.; to experiment* (an *on;* mit *with*) ‖ ⟨übtr⟩ ein gewagtes ~ *a bold experiment* **≗·al** a *experimental* ‖ ≗chemie [f] *experimental chemistry* **~·ator** m *experimenter* **≗·ell** a *experimental;* auf ~em Wege *experimentally* **≗·ieren** vi [h] *to (make an) experiment* (an *on*)

Exp·erte m ~n/~n *expert* (in *at, in;* auf dem Gebiet e–r S *on a th*) **Expert·ise** f ~/~n *expertise, assessment, survey*

Explikati·on f ~/–en *explication*

expliz·ieren vt [h] *to explain* **expl·izite** adv [L] *explicitly*

explod·ierbar a *explosible* **explod·ieren** 1. vi [s] a. *to explode;* bes ⟨chem⟩ *to detonate* ‖ *to burst* b. ⟨übtr⟩ *to break, to burst* ‖ ⟨fig⟩ (P) *to explode* (vor .. *with rage*); *to burst;* ⟨fam⟩ *to blow off the lid* 2. ≗ n *explosion* ‖ (etw) z ~ bringen *to explode; to detonate*

Exploitati·on f ~/~en [ɛksplɔata'tsio:n] (= Ausbeutung [⟨mst⟩ menschlicher Arbeitskraft]): *exploitation* = (*unjust* or *improper use of another p for one's own profit* or *advantage*)

Explosi·on f ~/~en *explosion;* bes ⟨chem⟩ *detonation;* Stoß der ~ *blast* ‖ zur ~ bringen *to explode; to detonate* | ⟨fig⟩ *explosion*

Explosi·ons- ~gefahr f *danger of explosion* **≗geschützt** a *explosion proof* **~kasten** m ⟨theat m. m.⟩ *bomb tank* **~motor** m → Verbrennungs– **~ventil** n *explosion vent*

explos·iv a *explosive* **≗geschoß** n *explosive projectile; shell* **≗laut** m ⟨phon⟩ *explosive* **≗stoff** m *explosive;* Hoch≗ *high e.*

Expon·at n ~(e)s/~e (Ausstellungsstück) *exhibit*

Expon·ent m ~en/~en ⟨math⟩ *exponent;* (e–r Potenz) *index* ‖ ⟨fig⟩ *exponent (of a th)* **Exponenti·al-** [ts] [in comp] ⟨math⟩ *exponential (curve, series)* **expon·ieren** vt (jdn, etw) *to expose; to lay open* (e–r S *to a th*) ‖ ⟨phot⟩ (Platte) *to expose* ‖ sich *to expose o.s.; to lay o.s. open* (e–r S *to a th*); [abs] ⟨fam⟩ *to stick one's neck* od *head out* **expon·iert** a *exposed*

Exp·ort m ~s/~e ⟨com⟩ *export; exportation;* → Ausfuhr **~artikel** m *article for export* **~gut** n ⟨com⟩ *export* **~handel** m *export trade* **~land** n *exporting country*

Exporteur [–'tør] m [Fr] ~s/~e *exporter*

export·ieren 1. vt [h] *to export* (nach *to*) 2. ≗ n *exporting, exportation*

Exposé n (Fr) ~s/~s *exposé;* ⟨Am⟩ *expose*

Expositi·on f ~/~en ⟨Lit & mus⟩ *exposition*

expr·eß adv *express;* ~ schicken *to send express*

Expr·eß m ⟨rail⟩ *express; express-train;* mit dem ~ reisen *to travel express* (od *by express*) **~brief** m *express* (od *special delivery*) *letter* **~gut** n *express-goods* ‖ als ~ *by express; marked express* (⟨Am⟩ *special*) *delivery* | ~dienst [m] ⟨Am rail⟩ *express freight service* **~zug** m = Expreß **~zustellung** f *special delivery*

Expression·ismus m ~/ ⟨arts⟩ *expressionism*

Expropriati·on [ts] f ~/~en ⟨jur⟩ = Enteignung **expropri·ieren** vt [h] ⟨jur⟩ = enteignen

exquis·it a *exquisite; choice; select; soigné (fashion); raffiné (delicacy, subtlety, cleverness)* Fr

Exsikk·ator m ~s/–kat·oren *desiccator*

exspirat·orisch a ⟨gram⟩ ~er Akzent *ex(s)piratory accent*

Exstirpati·on [ts] f ~/~en ⟨surg⟩ *extirpation*

Exsud·at n ~s/~e ⟨med⟩ *exudate* **exsudat·iv** a ⟨med⟩ *exudative (diathesis)*

Extempor·ale n ⟨school⟩ *test-paper, extempore exercise* (od *composition*); *exercise done in class*

ex tempore [L] *extempore (to speak e.)*

Ext·empore n ~s/~s ⟨Lit theat⟩ *extemporization; improvisation;* ⟨sl⟩ *gag* **extempor·ieren** vt/i [h] 1. (etw) *to extemporize, improvise* 2. vi *to extemporize, improvise;* ⟨sl⟩ *to gag*

extens·iv a *extensive*

Ext·ensor m ⟨anat⟩ = Streckmuskel

Exterieur [–riør] n [Fr] ~s/~s *exterior; outward appearance*

ext·ern a *external* **Ext·erne** [der ~, ein ~r] m, **Extr·aneer** m ~s/~ *day-boy* (od *scholar*); ⟨bes Eton⟩ *oppidan* **Extern·at** n ~s/~e *day-school*

exterritori·al a *exterritorial, extraterritorial* ‖ ≗rechte [n pl] *rights* [pl] *of extrality* (od *extraterritoriality*) **Exterritorialit·ät** f *ex(tra)territoriality; extrality*

·extra adv 1. *extra;* dies wird ~ berechnet w *this will be charged for extra;* Heizung u Licht sind ~ z zahlen *heating and light are extras* ‖ (als Zugabe) *extra; in addition; into the bargain* 2. *specially;* ~ dafür gemacht *made specially for that purpose;* ~ deswegen *for that very reason* 3. °es gibt heute etw ≗es *there will be something special* (od *extra-special*) *to-day*

Extra- [in comp] *extra; additional; special* **~ausgabe** f *extra;* (*extra*) *special edition* **~ausgaben** [pl] *extra expenses* [pl] **~belohnung** f = Extravergütung **~blatt** n *special edition; extra* **~dienst** m ⟨engl mil⟩ *fatigue; fatigue duty* **~dividende** f *bonus* [L] **≗fein** a *extra-fine; superfine, superior;* ~e Waren [pl] *superfines* [pl] **~gericht** n *extra; extra-dish* **~nummer** f *additional number; extra* **~ordinari·at** n ⟨univ⟩ *readership* **~ordin·arius** m ⟨univ⟩ *reader;* ⟨Am⟩ *assistant professor* **~polation** f *extrapolation* **~schlüssel** m *pass-key* **~spesen** [pl] = Extraunkosten **~strom** ⟨el⟩ *extra current* **~stunden** f [pl] *over-hours* [pl], *overtime* **~unkosten** [pl] *extras* [pl]; *sundries* [pl] **≗uter·in** a *extra-uterine* od *ectopic (pregnancy)* **~vergütung** f *bonus* [L]; *extra fee* °**~wurst** f er möchte immer e–e ~ gebraten h *he always wants something special* (od *extra-special*), ⟨Am⟩ *he likes to be* *catered to* **~zahlung** f *bonus; extra fee* **~zoll** m *additional duty* **~zug** m ⟨rail⟩ *special train*; ⟨Am fam⟩ *wild cat*

extrah·ieren **1.** vt [h] (etw) *to extract* **2.** ~̽ n *extraction* E–**akt** m ~s/~e **1.** ⟨pharm⟩ *extract, essence*; ⟨brew⟩ *balling* ‖ Malz~̽, *malt e.*; Fleisch~̽ *meat e.*; *extract* (od *essence*) *of beef* **2.** (aus Buch etc) *extract*; *excerpt* **Extrakti·on** [ts] f ~/~en *extraction* | ~sapparat [m] *extractor*; ~sflüssigkeit, ~slauge [f] ⟨chem⟩ *extraction liquor*; ~slehre [f] ⟨dent⟩ *exodontia* ~sspezialist *m exodontist* **extrakt·iv** a *extractive* (*industry*) ‖ ~̽stoff [m] *extractive substance*

Extr·aneer m = Externe

extravag·ant **1.** a *extravagant, exorbitant* (*demands*); → verschwenderisch **2.** adv *extravagantly* **Extravag·anz** f *extravagance* (*of action, opinion*) ‖ *extravagant action, notion*

Extravas·at n ⟨med⟩ *extravasation of blood*

extr·em a ⟨pol & theol⟩ *extreme* (*views*); *ultra–* ‖ e–e ~e Richtung vertreten *to hold e. views* (in *in*); ein Politiker ~er R. *an extremist*; *ultra* ‖ Konservativer ~er R.; ~̽konservativer *an extreme* (od *thorough-going*) *conservative*; *ultra--conservative*; *die-hard* **Extr·em** n ~s/~e *the extreme* ‖ ⟨math⟩ die ~e [pl] *the extremes* ‖ (die) ~e berühren sich *extremes meet* ‖ in das entgegengesetzte ~ verfallen *to fly* (od *go*) *to the opposite extreme*; sich in ~en bewegen *to move* (od *run*) *in extremes* ‖ (etw) ins ~ treiben *or steigern to carry to an extreme* ‖ v e–m ~ ins andere fallen *to go from one extreme to the other*

Extrem·ist m ~en/~en *extremist* ‖ ⟨bes Am pol⟩ *hard-liner*

Extremit·ät f ~/~en; die ~en *the extremities*

·Extro- **~invertierte** [der ~, ein ~r] ~n/~n ⟨psych⟩ *ambivert* **~vert·ierte** m ~n/~n *extrovert*; Zustand e–s ~n *extroversion*

Exzell·enz f ~/~en ⟨engl⟩ (Titel f Botschafter, Statthalter u deren Gemahlinnen) *excellency*; Seine ~ *His E.* ‖ (Titel f Adlige unter dem Marquis) *Right Honourable* (*the Right H. the Earl of N.*); (Titel f Marquis) *Most Honourable*

Exz·enter m ⟨tech⟩ (außermittige Scheibe) *eccentric* (*disc*) **~bügel** m *eccentric strap* **~scheibe** f *eccentric sheave* **~stange** f *eccentric rod* **~triebwerk** n *cam-gear*

Exz·entriker m ~s/~ *eccentric*; ⟨sl⟩ *wack*

exz·entrisch **1.** a **a.** ⟨tech⟩ *eccentric* (*circles, load*) **b.** ⟨fig⟩ *eccentric, wacky* (*p*); ~er Mensch *eccentric*; ⟨Am sl⟩ *screwball* **2.** adv *eccentrically* **Exzentrizit·ät** f ~/~en **1.** ⟨tech⟩ *eccentricity* **2.** ⟨fig⟩ *eccentricity*

exzeption·ell [ts] *a exceptional*

exzerp·ieren **1.** vt [h] *to excerpt, extract* (aus *from*) **2.** ~̽ n *excerption* **Exz·erpt** n ~s/~e *excerpt, extract*; → Abriß, Auszug

Exz·eß m –z·esses/–z·esse (moral. ~) *excess*; (*act of*) *outrage*; *violation* ‖ (Aufruhr) *riot*; –zesse [pl] *rioting*

F

F, f n ~/~ **1.** (Buchstabe) *F, f* ‖ nach Schema ~ *schematically*; nach dem Sch. ~ gemacht *cut-and-dry*; es ist ganz nach dem Sch. ~ *it is quite conventional* od *schematic*; *it is without originality* **2.** ⟨mus⟩ *F* ‖ *fa* [It] ‖ F-dur n *F major* ‖ f-Moll n *f minor* ‖ F-Loch n ⟨mus⟩ *sound-* od *f-hole* (*of the strings*) ‖ F-Schlüssel *F-key*

Fa n [It] ⟨mus⟩ (= F) *fa* [It]

F·abel f ~/~n **1.** *fable; legend, myth* ‖ *fictitious story*; *fiction* ‖ das Reich der ~ *the domain of legend* **2.** (Tier~̽) *fable*; *apologue* **3.** (of a play, etc) *plot, story* **~buch** n *fable-book* **~dichter** m *fabulous writer*; *fabulist* **~gestalt** f = Fabeltier **~land** n *world* (od *land*) *of fables*; *fairyland* **~schmied** m *fabler*; *romancer*; *fabulous historian* **~tier** n *fabulous* (od *legendary*) *beast* (od *monster*); *unicorn* **~wesen** n = Fabeltier **Fabel·ei** f ~/~en *fabulous story, fable*; *fiction* **f·abelhaft** **I.** a **1.** ⟨eig⟩ *fabulous* (*story*); *legendary, mythical* **2.** ⟨übtr⟩ *fabulous* (*wealth*) ‖ *grand, imposing*; *marvellous*; *phenomenal*; ⟨fam⟩ *ripping, topping*; in ~em Tempo *at a rattling pace* ‖ °ein ~er Kerl *a mighty fine fellow*; (e–e) ~e Frau! *an immense fine woman*!; → famos **II.** adv *fabulously* ‖ *immensely* **f·abeln** vt/i [h] (e–e Geschichte) *to fabricate*; *invent* **2.** vi *to tell stories* od *tales* (über, v *about*); *to romance* **Fabli·au** [-bli'o:] n ~s/-iaux ⟨Fr Lit⟩ *fabliau*

Fabr·ik f ~/~en **1.** (*manu*)*factory*; *mill*; *works* [pl] [sg konstr]: *a glass-works*; in e–r ~ *at a works* ‖ Baumwoll~̽ *cotton-mill*; Papier~̽ *paper--mill*; in die ~ gehen *to work in a factory* | (Gebäude) (*manufacturing*) *plant* **2.** ⟨übtr⟩ *factory* **~anlage** f *plant*; ~n [pl] *manufacturing plants* [pl] ‖ → Fabrikgebäude **~arbeit** f [abstr] *work done in a factory* ‖ [konkr] *manufacture*; *factory* (od *machine*)-*made goods*; *manufactured goods* [pl] **~arbeiter** m *factory* (od *mill*)-*hand*; *hand, operative*, (*industrial*) *workman* **~arbeiterin** f *factory* (od *mill*)-*girl* **~aufseher** m *overseer* **~besitzer** m *factory* od *mill-owner*; *manufacturer* **~direktor** m (*general*) *manager* **~distrikt** m *manufacturing district* **~erzeugnis** n *manufactured article* **~gebäude** n *factory*; *factory-building*; *premises* [pl] **~gegend** f *manufacturing district* **~gesetze** n [pl] ⟨engl⟩ *Factory Acts* [pl] (*1802–1833*) **~herr** m = Fabrikbesitzer **~konzern** m *manufacturing trust* **~mädchen** n *factory-girl* **~marke** f *trade-mark* ~̽**mäßig** **1.** a *factory* (od *machine, ready*)-*made* **2.** adv ~ herstellen *to manufacture*; ~ hergestellt *factory* (od *ready*)-*made* **~möbel** n [pl] *factory-made furniture* ~̽**neu** a *factory-new, f.-fresh*; ⟨fam⟩ *brand-new* **~niederlage** f *branch office* **~nummer** f *serial number* **~packung** f *original packing* **~preis** m *factory-price* **~schornstein** m (*smoke-*)*stack* **~stadt** f *manufacturing* od *mill town* **~ware** f *manufactured article* (od *goods* pl); *factory-made goods* pl **~wesen** n *factory system* **~zeichen** n = Fabrikmarke **Fabrik·ant** m ~en/~en *manufacturer*; *maker* ‖ alleiniger ~ *sole maker* **Fabrik·at** n ~s/~e **1.** *manufacture, manufactured article*; *make, brand*; (of textiles) *fabric* ‖ eigenes ~ *our own make* ‖ *product*; *article*; (auf Waren) deutsches ~ *made in Germany* | ~nummer [f] *maker's number*; ~steuer [f] *tax on manufactured article* **2.** ⟨übtr⟩ → Produkt **Fabrikat·ion** [ts] f ~/~en **1.** *manufacture*; *production*; *making* **2.** ⟨übtr⟩ *manufacturing* (*of poems*) **Fabrikati·ons-** *manufacturing* **~abfälle** m pl *broke*(*s* pl); ⟨pap⟩ *waste* **~abteilung** f *man.-ring department* **~anlage** f *production equipment* **~auftrag** m *job order* **~betrieb** m (*man.ring*) *plant* **~fehler** m *flaw* **~gang** m *process* **~geheimnis** n *trade secret* **~kosten** [pl] *man.ring costs* [pl] **~leiter** m *superintendent* **~nummer** f *serial* od *maker's number* **~programm** n *man.ring schedule* **~prozeß** m *man.ring process* **~steuer** f *tax on the manufacture of an article* **~vorgang** m (*man.ring*) *operation* **~zweig** m *man.ring branch*

fabriz·ieren vt [h] **1.** *to manufacture*; *produce*; *construct*; in Deutschland fabriziert *made in*

Germany || (etw) ~ *to be a manufacturer of* **2.** ⟨fig⟩ (Gedichte) *to manufacture* || (Lügen etc) *to fabricate; invent;* ⟨fam⟩ *to trump up (charges)*
fabul·ieren vi [h] = fabeln 2
Fac·ette [fa'setə] f [Fr] ~/~n *facet; facet-edge; bevelled-surface* **~nauge** n *facet-eye* **~nhalter** m [pl] ⟨typ⟩ *flanges* pl **~nsteg** m ⟨typ⟩ *catch; claw* **facett·ieren** [-se't-] vt [h] *to cover with facets* -·**iert** a *faceted (diamond)*
F·ach n ~es/~̈er **A.** ⟨eig⟩ **1.** ⟨arch⟩ **a.** (Raum zw 2 Gegenständen) *bay*; Dachwerk~̈ *bay of roofing* || → Dach u ~ **b.** (viereckige Fläche) *pane (the window was divided into several panes)* || *panel (of a wall, door)*; (Tür) mit ~̈ern versehen *to panel* **2.** ⟨carp⟩ **a.** *compartment (of a shelf); division, partition (of a cupboard)* || Schub~̈ *drawer (in a table); pigeon-hole*; (etw) in ein ~ legen, mit ~̈ versehen *to pigeon-hole*; in ~̈er trennen *to partition off* || ⟨bank⟩ *safe*; ⟨comp⟩ *pocket*; ⟨weav⟩ *shed*; → Geheim~̈ || *cell (of a honey-comb*, etc.) **b.** (Regal) *shelf* **c.** ⟨fig⟩ *recess* **B.** ⟨übtr⟩ **1.** *(branch of) business, profession; trade, branch; field; domain, line*; er studiert Bau~̈ *he studies architecture* || *branch (of learning); department, province (of philology)* || (Unterrichts~̈) *subject* || (Studien~̈) *study*; Spezial~̈ *speciality; special profession* **2. Wendungen**: in allen ~̈ern, in jedem ~ *in every walk of life*; ein Mann vom ~ *an expert, an adept* || er ist vom ~ *he is a specialist, an expert (in that), he belongs to our profession, he is a colleague of ours* || sein ~ verstehen *to know one's business; to be master of one's subject*; er versteht das ~ *he is an expert on that subject* || das ist mein besonderes ~ *that is my particular line* (od *his speciality*), ⟨Am sl⟩ *down my alley* || das gehört nicht in mein ~ *that is not* (od *does not come, lie*) *in my line* od *way* || das schlägt nicht in mein ~ *that's not in my line*; (ist nicht m–s Amtes) *that is not within my province* **F·ach-** [in comp] *professional; special; specialist(ic); technical* **~abteilung** f *special branch* **~anwalt** m ⟨jur⟩ f Grundstücksangelegenheiten *conveyancing counsel*; ~ f Steuersachen *tax counsel* **~arbeit** f *expert work* **~arbeiter** m *expert* (od *specialized, skilled*) *worker* **~arzt** m *specialist* (f nervöse Krankheiten *in nervous diseases*); ~ f innere Medizin *internist*; ~ f Geschlechtskrankheiten *venereologist* **~̈ärztlich** a *specialist* [attr]; ~e Praxis *consulting practice* **~ausbildung** f *professional, occupational* od *technical, trade education* od *training*; technische ~ *special (technical) training* || *professionalism* **~ausdruck** m *technical term* **~ausschuß** m *professional committee; c. of experts* **~berater** m *technical* (etc) *adviser; consulting engineer* **~beruf** m *skill trade* **~bildung** f = Fachausbildung **~bücherei** f *special library* **~einsatz** m *vocational employment* **~gebiet** n → Spezialgebiet **~gelehrte**: [der ~, ein ~r] m *specialist* **~̈gemäß** **1.** a *expert; skilled (work)* **2.** adv *expertly; in an expert way; skilfully* **~genosse** m *colleague* **~̈gerecht** a *proper* **~geschäft** n *special(ity) shop* (⟨Am⟩ *store*); wir sind ein ~ *we are stockists* od *specialists (in)* **~größe** f *authority*; → Fachmann **~gruppe** f *trade group* **~händler** m *dealer* **~kasten** m → ~̈erkasten **~kenntnis** f *special* (od *professional, technical*) *knowledge* **~kräfte** f pl *skilled labo(u)r* **~̈kundig** a *expert (driver); competent* **~lehrer** m *teacher in a special branch; subject teacher; technical instructor* **~literatur** f *special* od *technical literature* **~mann** m *expert* (auf dem Gebiete der Geschichte *on history*; in etw *in* od *at a th*); *specialist* (in *in*); *authority* (auf .. *on history*); *professional* || ⟨Am a.⟩ *sharp* **~̈männisch** **1.** a *expert, professional (gardener); specialistic (knowledge); technical (term); workmanlike (performance)* || ⟨com⟩ ~e Beratung *service; specialists' advice*; ~e Güte, ~es Geschick *expertise* **2.** adv *expertly*; jdn ~ beraten *to act as an expert to a p* **~ordnung** f *classification* **~personal** n *technical personnel* **~photograph** m *professional photographer* **~presse** f *technical press* **~prüfung** f *professional examination* **~richtung** f *nature of activity* **~schule** f *technical school* **~schulung** f = Fachausbildung **~̈simpeln** **1.** vi [h] *to talk shop* **2.** ~̈ n *shop-talk* **~spezialistentum** n *professionalism* **~sprache** f *professional language; technical* (etc) *language*; z. B. *scientese, journalese* **~studium** n *professional study* od *training* **~tüchtigkeit** f *craft ability* **~verband** m *Special Association* **~vertreter** m *specialist*; ⟨univ⟩ *Professor-in-Ordinary* **~werk** n ⟨arch⟩ *half-timbering; half-timber(ed) work*; ⟨tech⟩ *truss(ing)*; (Buch) *special work* | ~füllung [f] *lath and plaster* || ~haus [n] *half-timbered house*, ⟨Am⟩ *frame-building, f.-house* **~wissen** n *special* (od *expert, professional, technical*) *knowledge* **~wissenschaft** f *technical* (od *professional*) *science; special branch of science; specialty* **~wort** n *technical term* **~wörterbuch** n *technical dictionary*; ⟨hot, etc⟩ *d. of hotel*, etc *tech. terms* **~zeitschrift** f *technical journal* od *periodical; trade paper*
-fach [in adj. comp] → ein~, zwei~, drei~ etc. mannig~, mehr~, viel~ || *..times, ..-fold*
f·ächeln vt/i [h] **1.** vt (jdn) *to fan* (mit *with*) || (of air) *to fan; to play upon* || **sich** ~ *to fan o.s.* **2.** vi (of the wind) *to blow gently* (durch *through*)
f·achen[1] vt [h] ⟨poet⟩ (Feuer) *to fan* (z *to*); (Leidenschaft) z e–r Flamme .. *into a flame*
f·achen[2] vt ⟨tech⟩ (Haar, Wolle) *to prepare with the bow; to felt*
F·ächer m ~s/~ *fan* || Zimmer~̈ (an der Decke; z Ventilation) ⟨A Ind⟩ *punka(h)*; → Luftkühlapparat || e–n Torpedo~̈ abschießen *to launch a spread* **~antenne** f ⟨wir⟩ *fan aerial* **~̈artig** a *fan-like; fan-shaped*; ~er Gegenstand (Blatt, Schwanz etc) *fan* **~fenster** n (über Türen) *fan-light* **~flügler** m ⟨ent⟩ *stylops* [Gr]; *strepsipterous insect*; Gattung der ~ *Strepsiptera* [L] [pl] **~̈förmig** **1.** a = fächerartig **2.** adv; sich ~ ausbreiten, ⟨mil⟩ entfalten *to fan out* **~gebläse** n ⟨tech⟩ *fan* **~gewölbe** n ⟨arch⟩ spätgotisches ~ *fan-tracery, fan-vaulting* **~kasten** m *compartmented case* od *cabinet* **~magen** m ⟨zoo⟩ = Blättermagen **~palme** f ⟨bot⟩ *fan-palm* **~tasche** f (f Strümpfe) *stocking bag*; → Fach **~werk** n ⟨arch⟩ *lattice work; fan-like tracery*
f·ächern vt [h] *to fan* || sich ~ *to fan o.s.*
f·achlich **1.** a *professional, technical*; in ~er Hinsicht *technically* **2.** adv *professionally, etc*
F·achschaft f ~/~en *brotherhood*, die medizinische ~ *the medical b., medical association* || ⟨Ger⟩ ~ f .. *department for the organization and advancement of ..; vocational union; industrial federation* ⟨hist⟩; Reichs~̈ .. *Central Department for ..*
F·ackel f ~/~n **1.** ⟨eig⟩ *torch*; gr ~ *flambeau* [Fr] [pl *-eaus, -eaux*] || ⟨hist⟩ Pech~̈ *link* **2** ⟨fig⟩ *torch (of poetic inheritance; of learning*, etc.); die ~ der Kultur *the flame of culture*; die ~ der K. weitergeben *to hand on* [adv] *the torch* || die ~ der Vernichtung schleudern *to hurl the torch of destruction* (in *into*) **~beleuchtung** f *torchlight*; bei ~ *by t.* **~blume** f ⟨bot⟩ = Königskerze **~distel** f ⟨bot⟩ *columnar cactus* (od *cereus*) [L]; *torch-thistle* **~feuer** n ⟨mar⟩ *flare-up light* **~kraut** n ⟨bot⟩ = Königskerze **~laufen** n ⟨ant⟩ *torch-race* **~schein** m *torchlight*, bei ~ *by t.* **~serenade** f n *torchlight serenade* **~tanz** m *torch-dance* **~träger** m *torch-bearer*; ⟨hist⟩ *link-boy* (od *man*) **~zug** m *torchlight procession*; (veranstalten *to form*) || ~ u gr Zapfenstreich *retreat by torchlight*
f·ackeln vi [h] **1.*** ⟨eig⟩ = flackern **2.** °⟨fig⟩

to hesitate; nicht ~ z tun *not to hesitate to do*; *not to shrink from doing*; *not to think twice about doing* || hier wird nicht lange gefackelt *I am in no mood for trifling*; er fackelt nicht lange *he is not to be trifled with*; *he is not a man to trifle with*; er fackelte mit ihnen nicht lange *he did not think of sparing them*

Façon f = Fasson **fad** a = fade

F·ädchen n ~s/~ *threadlet* || *fibre*; *fine cord*

f·ade I. a **1.** ⟨cul⟩ *flat* (*beer*), *insipid*, *stale* (*wine*), *tasteless* (*soup*); ~ schmecken *to be without taste*; der Wein hat e–n ~n Geschmack *the wine is stale* (od *tasteless*) **2.** ⟨fig⟩ *dry* (*as dry as dust*), *dull*, *flat* (*speech*), *insipid*, *monotonous*, *vapid*; *empty*, *hollow* (*pleasures*); *washy*, *watery* (*style*); *stale* (*joke*); ~s Zeug *empty talk*, *vapid platitudes* [pl], → Gewäsch | (P) *boring*, *stodgy*; ein ~er Mensch *a bore* **II.** adv *insipidly*; *monotonously*

f·ädeln vt [h] → auf–, einfädeln **F·aden** m ~s/~̈ [doch → A.] **A.** (ein Maß) **1.** ⟨mar⟩ (Längen– u Tiefenmaß) *fathom* (= 1,83 m; ⟨engl⟩ *6 feet*); [pl] ~; 10 ~ tief *ten fathoms deep*; (etw) mit dem ~ messen *to fathom* **2.** (Garnmaß) *thread* **B.** ⟨tech⟩ **1.** ⟨eig⟩ **a.** *thread*; ⟨myth⟩ *clew* (*of Ariadne*); ausgezupfte ~̈ *ravel(l)ing*; feiner ~ *film*, *filament*; *fine cord*; Flachs~̈ *harl(e)*; Seiden~̈ *silky thread*; → Garn, Schnur, Seil, Strick; Bind~̈, Zwirns~̈ || Aufreih~̈ *file*; (Papiere) an e–m ~ aufreihen *to file* || ausgefaserter Woll~̈ *ravel* || (etw) mit Fäden durchziehen *to thread*; Durchziehen des ~s *stitch* || → Kettfäden, Schußfäden **b.** ⟨el⟩ (of electric bulbs) *filament* || Metall~̈ → Draht **c.** ⟨her⟩ *bendlet* **d.** ⟨bot⟩ → Staub~̈ || (an Bohnen) *string* **e.** langer ~ klebriger Substanz (in Wein etc) *rope* **2.** ⟨fig⟩ **a.** Lebens~̈ *thread of life*; verflochtene ~̈ [pl] *skeins* [pl]; *web* (*of fate*); → Gewebe, Netz **b.** *thread* (*of a narrative*, *conversation*) **3. Wendungen a.** ihm war der ~ abgerissen, er hatte den ~ verloren *he had lost the thread*; den ~ wiederaufnehmen *to resume* (od *pick up*, *take up*) *the thread* **b.** er hatte k–n trockenen ~ mehr am Leibe *he had not a dry stitch* (od *thread*) *on him* || k–n guten ~ an jdm l *to backbite a p*; *to cast aspersions on a p*; → Haar **c.** ein roter ~ *a continuous thread*; der Gedanke zieht sich wie ein roter ~ durch alle s–e Werke *the thought threads all his works* || den ~ fallen l ⟨fig⟩ *to break the thread* || an e–m ~ hängen *to hang by a thread*, *to hang on by the eyelids* || am seidenen ~ hängend *snickersneed* (*condition*) **d.** die verwickelten ~̈ aufdecken *to unravel the skeins* (*of a policy*) || die ~̈ sind kunstvoll verflochten *the skeins* (*in the play*) *are ingeniously twisted* || ⟨fig⟩ alle ~̈ in der Hand h *to hold all the strings in one's hand* (*his hands are on all the ropes*); die ~̈ des Unternehmens laufen alle in s–r Hand zus– *he pulls the strings of the whole enterprise*; *he pulls the wires* **e.** → Strich u ~; besiegen **~abnehmen** n (Kinderspiel) *cat's cradle* **~̈artig** a *thready*, *threadlike*; ⟨zoo & biol⟩ *filamentous* **~bakterien** [pl] *filamentous iron-bacteria* [L pl] **~führer** m (Vorrichtung beim Spinnen) *thread-guide*; (beim Stricken) *thread-carrier* **~(buch)heftmaschine** f *thread-stitching machine* **~heftung** f *thread-stitching* | **~̈lose** Bindung *paperback(-bindung)* **~kreuz** n ⟨opt⟩ *hairline cross*; *cross hairs* pl; ⟨mil, mar⟩ *graticule*, ⟨aero⟩ *web*; ⟨weav⟩ *lease* **~nudeln** f [pl] *vermicelli* pl It **~̈scheinig** a **1.** ⟨eig⟩ *threadbare* (*trousers*); *worn-out*; *shabby* || ein ~es Gewebe n ⟨weav⟩ *a sleazy fabric* **2.** ⟨fig⟩ *trivial*; *flimsy*; *poor*, *thin* (*excuse*) || *empty*, *hollow*; *sham* (*morals*); *spurious* || *insipid*; *namby-pamby* (*conversation*) **~schlag** m Sw *loosely sown seam* || ⟨übtr⟩ *preparation*, → Vorbereitung **~strahl** m ⟨electro⟩ *thread beam* **~verdickung** f ⟨spin⟩ *slub* **~verkreuzung** f ⟨weav⟩ *interlacing* **~werk** n (e–r Feder) *barbule* **~wurm** m ⟨zoo⟩ *threadworm*; Ordnung der –würmer *nematodes* L **~̈ziehend** a *stringy*, *ropy*

F·adheit f ~/~en **1.** *flatness*, *insipidity*; *staleness*, *tastelessness* **2.** ⟨fig⟩ *dullness*, *flatness*, *insipidity*, *monotony*; *vapidness* || *wateriness* (*of style*)

-fädig [in comp] d·ünn~ *thin-spun*; grob~ *coarse-spun*

F·ading ['feidiŋ] n ⟨engl⟩, ~s/~s ⟨wir⟩ *fading* | ~ausgleich [m], ~automatik [f] *automatic volume control* || ~effekt [m] *f. effect*

Fagaz·een f pl ⟨bot⟩ (Gattung) *Fagaceae* [L] pl

Fag·ott n ~s/~e ⟨mus⟩ *bassoon* **~bläser** m

Fagott·ist m ~en/~en *bassoonist*

F·ähe f ~/~n *bitch*; *bitch-fox*, *vixen*; *female otter*; *bitch-wolf* || *fur of minever*, → Feh(e)

f·ahen vt ⟨poet & †⟩ = fangen

f·ähig a **1.** [attr] *able*, *capable*, *clever*; *competent*, *qualified*; *gifted*, *talented*; ein ~er Kopf *a man of wits*; e–r der ~sten Köpfe *one of the first-rate wits* **2.** [pred] **a.** ~ z etw *capable of a th*; ~ (etw) z tun *able* od *competent to do*, *capable of doing* || nicht ~, es z tragen, warf er .. *unable to bear it he threw* ..; → unfähig || ~ m → befähigen; sich ~ m *to qualify* (f *for*) **b.** ⟨dero⟩ e–r S (*or* z etw) ~ s *to be capable of a th*; ~ (etw) z tun *capable of doing* || er ist z allen Schandtaten (*or* z allem) ~ *he is capable of doing* (od *he might do*) *anything*; *he is up to any mean trick* **3.** [in comp] → **-fähig** [in comp] ·arbeits~̈ *able to work*; *capable of working* || z·ahlungs~̈ *able to pay*; (S) verb·esserungs~̈ *capable of improvement* **F·ähigkeit** f ~/~en; ~ z etw, (etw) z tun *ability* (od *competence*, *-cy*) *for a th*, *to do*; *capability of a th*, *of doing* od *to do*; *capacity of* od *for a th*, *to do* || *power to do* (od *of doing*) *a th* || Aufnahme~̈ *capacity*; → Leistungs~̈ (etc) || → Befähigung, Eignung || *qualification* || *gift*, *talent*, *faculty* || ⟨physiol⟩ *fitness* | ~en [pl] (= geist. Anlagen) *skills*, *abilities*, *lights*; *mental powers* [pl]; nach, s–n geistigen ~en *according to his lights* || s–e ~en entwickeln *to find one's feet* od *legs*

f·ahl a; ~es Licht, ~er Schein *pale light* || *dim*, *dull* || *livid* (*sky*) | (of complexion) *sallow*; *ashy*; *bloodless*, *colourless*; *sickly* (*skin*); ~ im Gesicht, vor Zorn *livid in the face*, *with anger*; er wurde leichen~ im Gesicht *he went the colour of the ashes in the grate*; ~e Farbe *sallowness* **~̈band** n ⟨geol⟩ *fahlband* [Ger]; *orebearing stratum in archaean rock* **~̈erz** n ~es/~e ⟨minr⟩ *tetrahedrite*; *fahlerz* [Ger], *fahlore*; *grey copper-ore* **~gelb** a *fallow*, *lutescent* **~̈leder** n *russet upper leather* **~rot** a *tawny*

F·ähnchen n ~s/~ **1.** ⟨eig⟩ (Ulanen~̈) *pennon*; *streamer*; Pfahl mit ~ *flagged pole* || ⟨bot⟩ *banner* (e–r Schmetterlingsblume) || ⟨mus⟩ (Noten~̈) *hook* **2.** °⟨fig⟩ (Frauenkleid) leichtes ~ *light and cheap* od *wispy dress*

f·ahnden vi [h] ~ nach jdm *to search for a p*; *to try to find* (od *catch*) *a p* || ~ nach etw *to search a th out*; *to be in search of a th*; *to spot a th*

F·ahndung f ~/~en *search* (nach *for*) || *spotting* || *capture*, *seizure* (*of a criminal*)

F·ahne f ~/~n **A.** (Tuch) **1. a.** ⟨allg⟩ *flag*; kl ~ *streamer*; mit ~n schmücken *to flag*; mit ~n geschmückt *beflagged* **b.** ⟨pol & ec⟩ *banner*; ⟨hist⟩ *oriflamme* (Fr) || (Schützen~̈) *standard* **c.** ⟨mil⟩ (*military*) *flag*; ⟨engl⟩ (Infanterie~̈) (*regimental*) *colours* pl || ⟨mar⟩ *colours* pl, *ensign* | weiße ~, Parlamentär~̈ *white flag*, *flag of truce* **d.** e–e ~ **ausbreiten**, entfalten *to break a flag* || die ~ einziehen *to strike one's flag*; → streichen || e–e ~ heraushängen *to fly a flag* || auf (*or* aus) jedem Haus hing e–e ~ *every house was flying a flag* || e–e ~ hissen *to hoist a flag* (auf *from*); ~n raus! *flags aloft*!; die ~n senken *to lower one's* *colours*; die ~ zum Gruß senken *to dip one's ensign* (vor *to*) | **bei** der ~ dienen *to serve with the colours* || mit der ~ grüßen *to dip the flag* || mit fliegenden ~n *with flying colours* || (jdn) zu den ~n rufen *to call to the colours* **2.** ⟨fig⟩ (als Sinnbild) *banner* (*of freedom*); unter der ~ Christi *under Christ's banner* || *oriflamme* (*under a divine o.*) || die ~ der Empörung *the red flag* || die ~ hochhalten *to keep the flag flying* **3.** °= Fähnchen 2. **B.** ⟨übtr⟩ **1.** Rauch⁓ *trail* (od *wisp*) *of smoke* || °(Alkohol⁓) er hatte so 'ne ~ *he was fishy about the gills* || → Wetter⁓ **2.** ⟨typ⟩ = ~nabzug || in ~n abziehen *to pull in slips* | (Akten⁓) *tab* **3.** ⟨hunt⟩ *tail* (*of a hare*, etc.)

F·ahnen- **~abzug** m ⟨print⟩ *slip, slip* (od *galley*)-*-proof* **~eid** m *oath of enlistment* od *loyalty*; den ~ leisten *to take the o. of l.* **~flucht** f *desertion* **⁓flüchtig** a *deserting* (*regiment*); ~ w *to desert* **~flüchtig** [der ~e, ein ~er] m *deserter* **~junker** m *ensign*, ⟨cav⟩ *cornet* **~kompanie** f ⟨Ger⟩ *colour-company* **~korrektur** f ⟨typ⟩ *proof reading* **~mast** m *flag-pole* **~parade** f (the) *trooping* (*of*) *the colour*(*s*); die ~ abnehmen *to troop the colour*(*s*) **~schmied** m *farrier* **~schmuck** m *drapery of bunting* **~stange** f, **~stock** m *flagstaff*, ⟨Am⟩ *flagpole* **~stoff** m = Fahnentuch **~träger** m *colo*(*u*)*r* od *standard-bearer*; → Fähnrich || ⟨fig⟩ *standard-bearer*; *pioneer* **~tuch** n *bunting* **~unteroffizier** m *colour-sergeant* **~wache** f *colo*(*u*)*r guard* **~weihe** f *consecration* od *presentation of colours* **F·ähnlein** n ⟨übtr mil⟩ (P) *detachment*, *troop*; *squad*; ein ~ Bewaffneter *a troop of armed men* **F·ähnrich** m ~s/~e ⟨mil⟩ *ensign*; ⟨mar⟩ *midshipman* | ~smesse [f] ⟨mar⟩ *gun-room*; ~sstelle [f] *ensigncy*

F·ahr- (→ fahren) [in comp] **~ausweis** m ⟨mil⟩ *trip*(-)*ticket*; ⟨rail⟩ *ticket* **~bahn** f *carriageway*, doppelte ~ *dual c.*, zweispurige ~ *two-lane c.* || ⟨Am Can⟩ *lane* || Straße mit zwei ~en *two-lane highway* | ~rand [m] *verge* (*adjacent to a c.*) || linke Seite der ~ ⟨off⟩ *left-hand lane*; ⟨fam⟩ (in r. [l.] fahrenden Ländern) *fast* [*slow*] *lane*; die r. ~hälfte einhalten *to keep the right* || ~wechsel [m]! *single c.*! → Bahn | ⟨tech⟩ (f Riemen, Seil etc) *track*, *rails* [pl] **~befehl** m *driving order*; ⟨mil mot⟩ *work*(*ing*) *ticket* **~bereich** m ⟨mar u mot⟩ *radius of action* **⁓bereit** a *in working* od *running order* od *condition*; ⟨mar⟩ *ready to sail* **~bereitschaft** f *motor-pool* **~bühne** f ⟨rail⟩ *traverser* **~damm** m *roadway*; ⟨Am⟩ *pavement* || ⟨mot⟩ *motor-road* || ⟨rail⟩ *trackway* | ~decke [f] *road surface* **~dienst** m ⟨rail⟩ *train-service* | ~leiter [m] *despatcher*; ⟨engl⟩ *guard* **~draht** m ⟨rail⟩ *contact* od *trolley wire* | ~kreuzung [f] *overhead crossing* || ~weiche [f] *trolley frog* **~eigenschaft** f ⟨bes mar⟩ *manœuvrability*; ⟨mot⟩ *roadability* **~gast** m **1.** ⟨rail, mar & aero⟩ *passenger* | ~gondel [f] *passenger-car*; ~liste [f] *p. list* od *record*; ~raum [m] *p.-compartment* (od *cabin*); ~schiff [n] *p.-ship* **2.** ⟨mot⟩ *fare* **~geld** n *fare*; ⟨el⟩ *tram-fare*, ⟨Am⟩ *car-fare* **~gelegenheit** f; es gibt k–e ~ nach .. *there is no train* (od *bus*, *boat*; *public vehicle*) *to that place* **~gemeinschaft** f *car pool* **~geschwindigkeit** f *speed* (*at a s. of* ..) **~gestell** n ⟨mot⟩ *chassis* Fr || ⟨aero⟩ (Fest⁓ *fixed*, einziehbares *retractable*) *under-carriage*, *chassis*; serienmäßiges ~ *series-built ch.* || ⟨hum fig⟩ (Beine) *under-pinners*, *under-standings*, *locomotives* pl | ~rahmen [m] *chassis frame* **~handschuhe** [pl] ⟨mot⟩ *driving gloves* **~karte** f *ticket*; Saison⁓ *season-t.* || zwei ~n 1. Klasse *two first class*, ⟨fam⟩ *two firsts*; verbilligte ~ *curt-price t.*; e–e ~ hin u zurück *a return ticket* || (während der Fahrt) ⟨Am⟩ *hat check*; Kilometer⁓ ⟨Am⟩ *mileage ticket*; Dauer⁓ *season-ticket*, ⟨Am⟩ *commutation t.* (*good for 10* od *20 trips*) || ⟨fig mil hum⟩ (Fehlschuß) *wash-out*, ⟨sl⟩ *bos* | bitte die ~n! *tickets, please!* || e–e ~ lösen *to take a ticket*, *to book* (nach *for*) | ~nausgabe [f] = ~nschalter [m] || ~nautomat [m] *ticket machine* || ~ndrucker [m] (S) *passimeter*; *t. printing machine* || ~nknipser [m] ⟨engl⟩ (Apparat) *bell-punch* || ~nkontrolleur [m] *ticket-collector*; ⟨Am⟩ *chopper* || ~nschalter [m] *booking-office*, *t. window*; ⟨Am⟩ *ticket-o.* || ~nstempelpresse [f] *ticket dating machine* || ~nverkauf [m]; der ~ beginnt um 8 Uhr *the booking-office opens at 8 o'clock* || ~nverkäufer [m] *booking-clerk*; ⟨Am⟩ *ticket-agent* **~kolonne** f *transport column* **~korb** m *lift car*, ⟨Am⟩ *elevator cab* **~kostenentschädigung** f *travel allowance* **~kunst** f *art of driving*, *motoring*; *skill in d.* **⁓lässig** a *negligent*; *careless*; → Tötung **~lässigkeit** f *neglect negligence*; grobe ~ *gross n.* **~lehrer** m *driving teacher* od *instructor* **~leitung** f ⟨el⟩ *trol-l*(*e*)*y line* | ~sjoch [n] *arched catenary support* || ~smast [m] *catenary support* **~liste** f *itinerary* **~ordnung** f *the rule of the road* **~plan** m **1.** *timetable*; ⟨Am⟩ *schedule* || nach dem ~ soll das Schiff am 27. Mai abfahren *the ship is scheduled to start on May 27* **2.** (alphabetischer ~) *railway-guide*; ⟨engl⟩ *the ABC* **⁓planmäßig** **1.** a *schedule* [attr], *regular*; [pred] *in time*; zur ~en Zeit *on* (od *to*) *schedule*(*d*) *time*; ~e Abfahrtszeit *scheduled time of departure* **2.** adv (*according*) *to schedule*; *on schedule*; ~ abfahren *to leave according to sch. t.*; der Zug soll ~ um 10 Uhr ankommen *the train is due at 10 o'clock*; ~ .. dauern *to be scheduled to take* (*4 hours*) **~preis** m (*passenger*) *tariff* od *fare*; ~ 2. Klasse *second-class fare* | ~anzeiger [m] (Apparat) *taximeter* || ~ermäßigung [f] *reduction of fare* || ~grenze [f] *fare-stage* **~prüfung** f ⟨mot⟩ *driving test* **~rad** n *bicycle*, *cycle*; ⟨fam u mst⟩ (*push*-)*bike*; ⟨Am⟩ *wheel*; ~ mit Hilfsmotor *motor-assisted pedal cycle*; → Laufmaschine; fahren I. B. || ~anhänger [m] *cycle-trailer* || ~klingel [f] *bell* || ~pumpe [f] *inflator*, *pump* || ~sattel [m] *saddle*, ⟨Am⟩ *seat*; ~schlüssel [m] *monkey-wrench*; ~ständer [m] *cycle-stand* **~rinne** f ⟨mot etc⟩ *rut*; ⟨mar⟩ = Fahrwasser **~schein** m **1.** ⟨rail⟩ *ticket* | ~heft [n] *book of tickets*; zus–gestelltes ~heft *coupon-ticket* **2.** ⟨mot⟩ *driving-licence* **~schiene** f *rail* **~schule** f ⟨mot⟩ *driving* od *motor-school* || [abstr] *driving instruction*, „~!" *L* (= *learner*) **~schüler** m *driving pupil*; *learner* (*driver*) **~spur** f ⟨mot⟩ *lane* (richtige *appropriate*), die ~ wechseln *to change lanes* || Einordnungsspur *filter lane* || Überholspur *passing l.* **~straße** f *high-road*, *highway*; → Fahrdamm **~strecke** f = Fahrbereich; *itinerary* | ~ngrenze [f] *fare-stage* **~stuhl** m **1.** (f Kranke) *wheel-chair*; *bath-chair* **2.** ⟨tech⟩ **a.** (= Aufzug) (P) (*passenger*) *lift*; ⟨Am⟩ *elevator*; Wohnung ohne ~ ⟨Am fam⟩ *walk-up flat* || f Lasten (*goods*) *lift*; *hoist* **b.** (~kabine, ~korb) *cage*; ⟨Am⟩ *car* | ~führer [m] *lift-boy* (od *man*) || ~landung [f] ⟨aero⟩ *squash landing* **~stunde** f ⟨mot⟩ *driving-lesson* **~truppen** f [pl] ⟨mil⟩ *motorized forces* [pl] **~tüchtig** a → –bereit; nicht ~ *immobilized* **~verbot** n *driving prohibition*; ~! *prohibited* (f .. *to vehicles*) **~verkehr** m *vehicular traffic* **~vorschriften** f [pl] = Fahrordnung **~wasser** n **1.** ⟨mar⟩ (*shipping*) *channel*, *lane*, *fairway*; *navigable water* **2.** ⟨fig⟩ *channel*; das richtige ~ *the proper channels* [pl] || ⟨fig⟩ das politische ~ *the province* (od *sphere*, *domain*) *of politics* || ⟨fig⟩ ins polit. ~ abgleiten *to drift into political channels* || in s–m (*or* im richtigen) ~ s *to be right in one's groove* od *in one's* (*proper*) *element* | ~tiefe [f] ⟨mar⟩ *depth* **~weg** m *roadway*, *carriageway* || (vor herrschaftl. Hause) *drive*; ⟨Am⟩ *driveway* || gewundener ~ *sweep* **~werk** n ⟨aero⟩ *landing gear*; ⟨a.⟩ *running g.* → Fahrgestell || ~ eingefahren u gesichert *gear up and locked* || ~ aus(ge)fahren! ⟨aero⟩ *gear* down!; ~ einziehen fold up!; mit eingezogenem ~ wheels up | ~ abfederung [f] l.-g. cushioning || ~ auskreuzung [f] l.-g. bracing || ~klappe [f] undercarriage door || ~spurweite [f] u. track || ~schacht [m] wheel well **~widerstand** m ⟨mot⟩ tractive resistance **~zeit** f schedule || travelling time **~zeug** n conveyance, vehicle; → Wagen || vessel, → Boot, Schiff; Schlitten | wenn ~e ausfallen if vehicles become casualties | ~batterie [f] ⟨cl⟩ traction battery od motor || ~funkgerät [n] ⟨mil, etc⟩ vehicular radio set || ~grenze [f] ⟨tact⟩ dismount line; bei Tage (Nacht) daylight (night) traffic line || ~kolonne [f] convoy of vehicles || ~lichtgrenze [f] ⟨mil⟩ no-vehicle-light line || ~profil [n] vehicle ga(u)ge || ~schlange [f] queue || ~verkehr [m] wheeled traffic

F·ähr- (→ Fähre) [in comp] ferry .. f. service **~boot** n ferry; f.-boat **~geld** n fare, ferriage **~haus** n f.house **~lohn** m = Fährgeld **~mann** m f.man **~schiff** n f.boat; ⟨mot a.⟩ roll-on-roll-off-ship **~stelle** f f. site

f·ahrbar a passable, practicable (road) || ⟨mar⟩ navigable || mobile (shop, crane); portable (radio station, etc) **≈keit** f ~/ passableness || ⟨mar⟩ navigableness || mobility

F·ährde f ~/~n ⟨poet⟩ = Gefahr (Not u ~)

F·ähre f ~/~n ⟨mar⟩ **1.** (Boot) ferry; ferry-boat || jdn in e–r ~ befördern to ferry a p (über .. over od across a river); in e–r ~ hinüberfahren to ferry across [adv] || Überfahrt in e–r ~ ferriage **2.** (Ort) ferry || Eisenbahn≈ ferry-bridge

f·ahren vi/t [fuhr/gefahren] **I. vi** [s] **A.** ⟨allg⟩ **(P)** (wandern) **1.** to wander; to go, to travel; ⟨bib⟩ gen Himmel ~ to ascend into heaven; zur Hölle ~ to descend into hell || in die Grube ~ ⟨min⟩ to descend the shaft; ⟨übtr⟩ to sink into the grave || zu Berg ~ to go uphill || → ~d, wandern **2.** fahre(t) wohl! farewell! good-bye! God speed you! **3. (etw) ~ l** to let go; er ließ das Seil ~ he let go the rope || (Freunde, Habe) to abandon; (Recht) to waive; (Stellung, Hoffnung) to give up; (Sorgen) to banish || °⟨vulg⟩ e–n ~ l to make a noise, to break wind **B. (P) 1.** (im **eigenen** or gemieteten Wagen) to drive (in a carriage, car, etc.); to go; ⟨sl⟩ to tool || ⟨Am⟩ to ride (in a carriage) || wir wollen ~! let's cab it! || er fuhr zur Bahn he drove to the station || mit Vieren (or vierspännig) ~ to drive four-in-hand || um die Ecke ~ to turn a corner || spazieren ~ to go for a drive, to take a drive || im Schlitten ~ to go (od travel) by sledge; **2.** ⟨cycl⟩ **auf** dem Rad ~ to ride (on) a bicycle; (mit dem) Rad ~ to go by b.; to (bi)cycle; to pedal; to wheel **3.** ⟨mot⟩ **im** (or **mit** dem) Auto ~ to drive (od go, travel) by car (od in one's car), od by road; to motor (nach to) || er fuhr selbst he drove himself, he d. his own car; he took the wheel himself || er fuhr im Auto **eiligst** nach .. he rushed his car to .. **4. im Fluge** ~ to whisk (through ..) || er fährt **gut** he is a good driver; ⟨mot⟩ he has road-sense, ⟨hors⟩ he is a good whip; rücksichtsvoll, vorsichtig ~ to be traffic-minded; rücksichtslos ~ to scorch; to road-hog || gemächlich ~ to dawdle (durch through); langsam ~ to crawl || **schnell** ~ to speed; wir sind schnell ge~ we made good time **5.** ~ **auf** or **gegen** etw to hit od strike a th (he hit a lorry); ~ **in** to run into .. **6.** (im **öffentl.** Verkehrsmittel ~) ⟨allg⟩ to ride; ich fuhr nur bis .. I rode only as far as (Cambridge); rückwärts ~ to ride with the back towards the engine; vorwärts ~ to face the engine || mit dem (or im) Omnibus ~ to ride (od go, travel) by bus || **mit** der Bahn, dem Zuge ~ to go od travel by train od rail; to ride in the lift, elevator || erster Klasse ~ to go first (class) || durch das Land ~ to travel the country **7.** ⟨**mar**⟩ to sail; to steer (nach for); to steer one's way (aus out of; in into); to move (into ..) || to cruise; to go, to travel; mit dem Dampfer ~ to travel by steamer (od steam); ⟨Am⟩ to ride in a steamer || mit dem D. ~ nach to steam to || aus dem Hafen ~ to leave port || über das Meer ~ to cross (od traverse) the ocean; to navigate the seas; über e–n Fluß ~ to cross a river || über e–e Stromschnelle ~ to shoot a rapid || tastend ~ to feel one's way (up and down the river) || zur See ~ to go to sea **8.** ⟨aero⟩ to voyage; im Luftschiff ~ to travel by air (od in an aeroplane) || im Karusell ~ to ride in a merry-go-round **C. (S) a.** (of vehicles) to run (auf Schienen on rails; nach to); to travel (along rails); der Omnibus fährt zweimal am Tage the bus runs twice a day; .. zw .. the bus plies between .. || der Zug fährt nach Berlin the train goes to Berlin || schwungvoll ~ durch (of a car) to swing through (a village) **b.** ⟨mar⟩ to run (auf .. on a rock); to sail; to steam || gegen, auf e–n Felsen ~ to strike a rock; auf Grund ~ to run aground **c.** (Omnibus, Schiff etc) ~ **lassen** to run || ⟨übtr⟩ e–e Gelegenheit ~ l to let a ch. go od slip by **D.** ⟨**übtr**⟩ **1. (T & S)** to dash; rush; shoot || der Hund fuhr auf ihn los the dog flew at him od jumped, rushed upon him || die Kugel fuhr in die Wand the bullet went into the wall || (of the wind) ~ über .. to sweep (a country) **2. (P) a. aus** dem Bette ~ to start from one's bed || in die Höhe ~ to (give a) start; to be startled; er fuhr zus– he was startled || er fuhr **mit** dem Löffel **in** die Suppe he thrust the spoon into the soup || er fuhr in das Jacket, die Stiefel he slipped into his jacket, boots || das Messer fuhr ihm aus der Hand the knife slipped from his hand || **mit** der Hand ~ **durch**, über .. to pass od run one's hand through (one's hair), over (one's) face; along od over (the keys) **b.** der Teufel ist **in** ihn ge~ the devil has possessed him (od laid hold of him); was ist in dich ge~? what's come over (⟨Am⟩ got into) you? ⟨mil sl⟩ what's crawling on you? **c.** °⟨fig⟩ **aus** der Haut ~ to jump out of one's skin, to fly into a rage || °sich (or e–a) **in** die Haare ~ to fall out with one another, to fly at one another; to fall by the ears || °jdm **über** den Schnabel ~ to cut a p short; to snap a p up **d. gut, schlecht** ~ **mit, bei** .. to fare well, ill with; to get on well, ill with (a p); to be successful in (a th); er fuhr am besten dabei he came off best **3.** ⟨**fig**⟩ (of thoughts, etc.) ein Schatten fuhr über ihr Gesicht a shadow flashed over her face || der Gedanke fuhr mir durch den Kopf the thought shot across (od crossed) my mind; es fuhr mir plötzlich durch den Sinn, daß .. it flashed upon (od across) me, it f. across (od into) my mind that .. || der Schrecken fuhr ihm durch alle Glieder he was struck dumb with terror; die Nachricht fuhr ihm in die G. the news gave him a bit of a jar (od a nasty jar); the news struck him all of a heap **II. vt** [h] **A. 1.** (e–n **Wagen**) to drive; to steer; (e–n Karren) to wheel || ⟨sl⟩ to tool || Auto ~ to drive (can you d.?); laß uns ein wenig A. ~ let us go motoring a bit || (ein) Rad ~ to ride a bicycle || Schlitten ~ to go sledging; to ride in a sledge || Karussell ~ to ride in a merry-go-round **2.** (ein **Schiff**) to navigate; sail, steer || (Boot) to row, sail || ein Schiff in e–e Bucht ~ to run a ship into a creek || .. auf Grund ~ to run a ship aground **B. 1.** (Gepäck etc) to drive, carry, convey in a vehicle; to transport || ⟨Am⟩ to ride || (Heu, Mist) to cart **2.** (jdn) to drive (nach to); to wheel; ⟨sl⟩ to tool || (im Auto) to motor; jdn in den Graben ~ to run a p into the ditch || jdn spazieren ~ to drive a p out, to take a p for a drive || jdn über den Haufen ~ to run over a p; to knock a p down in driving; jdn tot ~ to kill a p by running over him || jdn über den Fluß ~ to put a p across the river **3.** (e–e **Marke**, ein Rennen) to run; welche M. ~ Sie? what make of car do you drive? || e–e Kurve ~ to turn a curve || (Strecken etc) to cover, run, traverse; to motor **C. 1. sich fest ~** to be stuck (auf on); to stick (im Schlamm in the mud);

⟨mar⟩ *to run aground*; ⟨fig⟩ *to stick* ‖ sich müde ~ *to tire o.s. by driving* **2. es fährt sich** gut auf dieser Straße *this road is easy to drive* (od *travel*) *on*; ⟨sport⟩ es fuhr sich gut auf der Bahn *the going was good* ‖ es fährt sich gut (*or* läßt sich gut ~) in dem Wagen *the car runs smoothly* od *drives well* od *pleasantly* **F·ahren** n ~s/ **A. 1.** *driving* (*in a carriage*) ‖ Auto≈ *motoring*; *motor--travelling*; das ~ erlernen *to learn driving* ‖ Sinn (*or* Instinkt) f richtiges ~ *road-sense* ‖ *riding* (*on a bicycle*) **2.** *riding* (*in a bus*) ‖ *going*; *travelling*; das ~ in der Bahn kann sie nicht vertragen *travelling by train does not agree with her* **3.** *sailing, steering*; *travelling* (*by steamer*) **B. 1.** *the driving* (*of a carriage*); wegen zu schnellen ~s angehalten w *to be stopped for exceeding the speed limit* (od *for speeding*) ‖ *the riding* (*of a bicycle*) ‖ *the navigating* od *steering* (*of a ship*) **2.** *the driving* (*of luggage, of a p*) **f·ahrend** a **1. (P)** *travelling, wandering*; *roaming, strolling, wayfaring* ‖ ~e Leute [pl], ~es Volk *vagrants* [pl], *tramps* [pl]; *vagabond classes* [pl] ‖ ⟨hist⟩ ~er Gesell, Scholar *vagrant* (od *travelling*) *scholar*; ~er Sänger *vagrant minstrel, vagabond singer*; ~er Spielmann *vagrant musician* ‖ ~er Ritter *knight-errant* **2. (S)** *moving* (*train, weight*); *travelling* (*crane, weight*) ‖ schnell, langsam ~ *fast–, slow-moving* (*cars*) ‖ ~e Habe *movables* [pl]; → Fahrnis

F·ahrenheit (nach D. G. ~, † 1736): (bei) 20 Grad ~ (*at*) *20 degrees Fahrenheit* (abbr 20 °F.) ‖ [in comp] *Fahrenheit* (*scale, thermometer*); → Anhang IV, Measures, Thermometer

f·ahren|lassen vt [h] [→ lassen] ⟨fam⟩ *to abandon* (*a plan*); ich ließ .. fahren, habe .. ~

F·ahrens- ~mann m [pl –leute] ⟨mar⟩ *sailor*

F·ahrer m ~s/~ **1.** (Berufs≈) *driver* (*of a carriage, motorcar*, etc); *chauffeur* ‖ (*motorcycle*) *rider* ‖ *motorman* (*of a bus*, etc) | (Autoliebhaber) *motorist* ‖ rücksichtsloser ~ *scorcher*; wilder ~ *road* (od *speed*)*-hog* ‖ er ist ein sicherer *or* der geborene ~ ⟨mot⟩ *he's got road-sense* ‖ ~ vom Dienst *duty driver* **2.** ~ zur See *runner*; → See≈ ‖ ⟨aero⟩ *pilot* **~flucht** f *hit-and-run driving*; *failing to stop after collision* **~haus** n ⟨mot⟩ *cab* **~zimmer** n *staff-room* **f·ahrig** a *flighty, giddy* (*child*); *unbalanced*; *volatile* ‖ *careless, reckless*; ⟨fam⟩ *harum-scarum* | **≈keit** f *flightiness, giddiness*

†f·ährlich a = gefährlich | **≈keit** f → Gefahr

F·ahrnis f ~/~se ⟨jur⟩ *movables* [pl]; *choses* [Fr pl] *in possession*

F·ahrt f ~/~en **A.** (Wanderung) *wandering*; *travel*; *journey*; *expedition* ‖ *excursion, trip*; *tour* ‖ **B.** (~ in e–m Fahrzeug) **(P) 1.** *drive* (*in a carriage, car*), *ride*; *run* (auf der ~ *on the r.*); *spin* ‖ *ride* (*on a bicycle*) ‖ *ride* (*in a bus, train*); *journey* (*in a train*); ~ ins Blaue *mystery drive* od *tour* **2.** ⟨mar⟩ *passage, voyage*; Vergnügungs≈ *cruise*; Dampfer≈ *excursion, outing*; ⟨Am⟩ *ride* ‖ → Hin≈; Rück≈, Rund≈ **3.** ⟨aero⟩ *flight, voyage*; *cruise* **C. (S) 1.** (of ships) *running, sailing* ‖ gr ~ *foreign-going* ‖ kl ~ m → D. ‖ halbe ~ ⟨mar⟩ *half speed* ‖ e–e glatte, ruhige (stürmische) ~ h *to have plain, smooth* (*rough*) *sailing* ⟨a fig⟩ ‖ (Lauf) *course* **2.** (~geschwindigkeit) *speed*; *running power* ‖ an ~ gewinnen, in ~ k → D. ~ aufnehmen; volle ~ *full speed* **D. Wendungen**: e–e ~ v 6 Meilen *a six-mile* (od *a six miles'*) *ride*; .. v 3 Tagen *a three-day* (od *a three days'*) *journey* od *tour* | **auf** ~ gehen *to go on a trip* ‖ sich auf die ~ m *to set out* (od *forth*) *on a journey*; .. nach *to set out for, to make for* .. ‖ das Signal steht auf freie ~ *the s. is up* (⟨engl⟩ *down*) *for the train* | **in** ~ *under way* ‖ in ~ gehen *to get under way* ‖ ⟨fig⟩ in ~ k *to get into one's stride* (od *into swing*) ‖ ⟨Am aero⟩ *to gain momentum* ‖ in ~ s (of ship) *to be under way*; *to be well on the way*; ⟨übtr⟩ *to be in swing*; (P) *to be on the go* od *run* ‖ in voller ~ (*at*) *full speed*; in voller ~ daherk. *to come along full swing* ‖ in langsamer ~ *at a slow pace* | ~ **aufnehmen** *to gather* od *pick speed* ‖ ⟨rail⟩ freie ~ h *to have got a free pass* (f e–e Linie *over a line*) ‖ was kostet die ~? *what is the fare?* ‖ hohe ~ laufen (of ship) *to run* od *steam at full speed* ‖ e–e ~ **m** *to go for a drive* (od *run, spin*), *to take a drive*; (zur See) *to go on a cruise*; ⟨aero⟩ *to take a flight* ‖ kl (*or* nur wenig) ~ m *to go* od *sail at reduced speed* od *dead-slow* (od *at d.-s. speed*) (infolge Havarie) nur kl ~ m *to limp* ‖ die ~ unterbrechen *to break the journey*; ⟨Am⟩ *to stop over* od *off* ‖ (an) ~ verlieren ⟨mar, aero⟩ *to loose headway*; → verlangsamen, vermehren, vermindern **~anzeiger** m ⟨mar⟩ *speed-light* | darf ich um die **~ausweise** [m pl] bitten *tickets please* **~ball** m *speed-ball* **~dauer** f *duration of voyage* (od *flight, journey*) **~laterne** f ⟨mar⟩ (bei Nacht) *position-light* **~messer** m *speed-gauge*; *speedometer*; ⟨aero⟩ *airspeed indicator* (*A.S.I.*) **~richtung** f *driving direction*; ⟨mar⟩ *course*; ⟨aero⟩ *direction of voyage*; ⟨rail⟩ in der ~ sitzen *to face the engine* ‖ die ~ freigeben *or* sperren: *the policeman reversed the direction of his white sleeves* ‖ ~sanzeiger [m] *direction-indicator*; (Lampe) *turn indicator light* **~schreiber** m ⟨aero⟩ *course recorder* **~stufe** f *rate of speed* **~unterbrechung** f *break* (*in* od *of a journey*), ⟨Am⟩ *stop--over* ‖ ⟨mar⟩ *layover* **~weg** m *prescribed route* **~wind** m *air stream*

F·ährte f ~/~n ⟨hunt⟩ *scent*; *trace, track, trail* ‖ ⟨übtr⟩ *scent, track, trail*; → Spur ‖ **auf** der ~ ⟨hunt⟩ *on the trail* od *scent* ‖ auf jds ~ *on a p's trail* ‖ auf der falschen ~ ⟨hunt & übtr⟩ *at fault, on the false* od *wrong scent*; *off the track*; .. s ⟨bes police⟩ *to bark up the wrong tree* ‖ jdn auf e–e ~ bringen ⟨übtr⟩ *to set* od *put a p on the scent* od *trail* (*of a th*) ‖ auf die rechte (falsche) ~ k ⟨übtr⟩ *to get on the right* (*wrong*) *track* ‖ jdm auf der ~ s *to be* (*hot*) *on the traces of a p* ‖ (Hund) auf die ~ setzen ⟨hunt⟩ *to lift* | jds ~ **finden** *to get on a p's track* ‖ der ~ folgen, die ~ verfolgen *to follow the scent* ‖ (*of hounds*) die ~ halten *to carry the scent, to hold the line*; auf die ~ stoßen, die ~ aufnehmen *to hit the line*; v der ~ abk, die ~ verlieren ⟨hunt⟩ *to lose* (od *to be thrown off*) *the scent* ‖ jdn v der ~ abbringen, -lenken *to put* (od *throw*) *a p off the scent* ‖ (Hund) **zur** ~ legen ⟨hunt⟩ *to lift*

Fahrten- ~buch n ⟨mot⟩ *log*(*-book*)

F·aible ['fɛ:bl] n (Fr), ~s/~s: ein ~ h f *to have a preference* od *weakness for* (*a p, a th*)

fair fɛə] a [engl] *fair*; ~ play *fair play* ⟨a. fig⟩

fäk·al a *faecal* **Fäk·al-** [in comp] *faecal*; ~stoffe [m pl] = **Fäk·alien** [pl] *faeces* L pl, *sewage*

F·akir m ~s/~e *fakir*

Faks·imile n [L] ~s/~s *facsimile*; in ~ *facsimiled*; in ~ reproduzieren etc *to facsimile* **F·akta, F·akten** [pl] → Faktum **F·aktis** m *factis* **f·aktisch 1.** a *factual*; *actual*; *practical* (*ruler*); *real* **2.** adv *actually, practically*; *in fact* **faktit·iv** a ⟨gram⟩ *factitive* (*verb*)

F·aktor m [L] ~s/–t·oren **A.** (P) **1.** ⟨com⟩ *factor*; (*mercantile*) *agent*; Geschäft *or* Amt e–s ~s *f.ship, factor* **2.** ⟨typ⟩ *overseer*; *foreman* **B.** (S) **1.** ⟨math⟩ *f.* (gemeinsamer ~ *common f.*); in ~en auflösen *to f.ize*; Auflösung in ~en *f.ization* ‖ Produkt e–r Reihe v ~en in arith. Reihe *f.ial* **2.** (mitwirkender Umstand) **a.** *f.*; *element*; *constituent*; der bestimmende ~ in .. *the determining f.* (od *the determinant*) *in* ..; ein wichtiger ~ w in *to become an important element in* .. **b.** ⟨biol⟩ (Erb≈) *f.*; *hereditary determinant* **c.** ⟨phys⟩ Sicherheits≈ *f. of safety* **Faktor·ei** f ~/~en ⟨com⟩ *factory*; *foreign trading-station of a merchant company* **Fakt·otum** n ~s/-ten *facto-*

tum (L) [pl] *factotums* ‖ ⟨fam⟩ *Jack of all work, bottle-washer* **F·aktum** n ~s/-ta & -ten *fact*; das ~ steht fest *that's a fact* ‖ Fakten [pl] *facts* [pl]; (bekannte, gegebene F.) *data* (L) [pl] **Fakt·ur** f ~/~en *invoice*; *docket*; laut ~ *as per invoice, as invoiced* **Fakt·ura** f ~/-ren = Faktur **Fakt·ura-, F·akturen-** [in comp] *invoice* **~buch** n *i.-book* **~preis** m *i.-price* **~wert** m *i.-value* **faktur·ieren** vt [h] ⟨com⟩ *to invoice* | ~̈ n *billing*

Fakult·ät f ~/~en ⟨univ⟩ *faculty*; Mitglieder [pl] der ~ *faculty* ‖ juristische ~ ⟨engl⟩ *law school*; die medizinische ~ *the Faculty* ‖ ~, die (Honours-) Prüfungen abhält *School*

fakultat·iv a *facultative*; *optional* (*stop*)

Fal·ange f ~/~n ⟨Span⟩ die ~ *the Falange*

Falang·ist m ~en/~en *Falangist*

falb a *fallow*; *dun, dun-coloured* **F·albe** [der ~, ein ~r] m ~n/~n *dun*; *dun(-coloured) horse*

F·albel f ~/~n *falbala, flounce, furbelow*; *frill* ‖ ~n [pl koll] *frillery*; Material f. ~n *flouncing* ‖ (Kleid) mit ~n besetzen *to flounce, to furbelow* ‖ mit ~n besetzt, Falbel- *flouncy*

Faldist·orium n (L) ~s/-rien ⟨ec⟩ *faldstool*

Fal·erner m ~s/ *Falernian*; *F. wine*

f·älisch a ⟨anthr⟩ *Falian, Nordic* (*race*)

F·alke m ~n/~n ⟨orn⟩ *falcon*; Wander~̈ *peregrine falcon* ‖ ⟨hunt⟩ weiblicher ~ *falcon*; (weibl.) Edel~̈ *peregrine f.*; *gerfalcon* ‖ männlicher ~ *tercel, tiercel*; junger ~, Nest~̈ *eyas* ‖ mit ~n jagen *to hawk* **~nauge** n *hawk's eye* ⟨a. fig⟩ **~nbeize** f *hawking, falconry* **~nhaube** f *hood* **~njäger** m *falconer, hawker* **~nvögel** pl → Bd I. *falcon* **Falken·ier** m ~s/~e; **F·alkner** m ~s/~ *falconer, hawker* **Falkner·ei** f ~/ *falconry*

F·alklandinseln f pl *Falkland Island* od *Isles*

F·all[1] m ~(e)s/~̈e **A.** ⟨eig⟩ (Fallen) **1. a.** *fall, drop*; *tumble* (*the crash of the t.*); ein ~ aus e–r Höhe v 10 Metern *a drop of 10 metres*; → Sturz ‖ *fall* (*of drops*; *leaves*; *a tree*); → Wasser~̈ **b.** ⟨phys⟩ *fall* (*of a body*) **c.** *hang* (*of a coat, dress*) **2.** ⟨**übtr**⟩ **a.** *fall* (*the f. of Troy*); *capitulation, surrender* (*of a fortress*) ‖ *fall, downfall* (*of an empire*), *overthrow*; *decline, decay*; *ruin* ‖ *mortality* (*of game*) **b.** ~ der Preise *fall in* (od *decline of*) *the prices*; *collapse* (*of the money-market*) **c.** (P) ⟨fig⟩ *downfall, disgrace, dishonour* **d.** ⟨pros⟩ *cadence* **3.** (moral. ~) *fall, lapse* (*of a p*); ⟨bib⟩ der Sünden~̈ *the Fall, the F. of man* ‖ → Fallen, Gefälle **B.** ⟨**gram**⟩ (Kasus) *case*; erster ~ → Wer~̈; zweiter ~ → Wes~̈; dritter ~ → Wem~̈; vierter ~ → Wen~̈ **C.** ⟨**übtr**⟩ **1.** ⟨jur⟩ *case* (*of murder*); → Präzedenz~̈ ‖ ⟨police⟩ ~ erledigt ⟨m.m.⟩ *closed file* ‖ ⟨med⟩ *case* (*of measles*) **2.** *case, event*; *occasion* (*there are occasions when* ..); ⟨contr⟩ in allen übrigen ~̈en *save as aforesaid*; im ~e der Abweisung *in the event of rejection*; im ~ e–s Unfalls *in the event of an accident*; → Bedarfs~̈, Ernst~̈, Not~̈, Übertretungs~̈, Wiederholungs~̈, Zweifels~̈ ‖ besonderer (*or* einzelner) ~ *instance* **D. Wendungen**: **1. a.** ⟨eig⟩ heftiger ~ *purl(er)*, ⟨sl⟩ *smeller* ‖ schwerer, übler ~ *heavy* od *nasty fall*; ⟨fam⟩ *mucker* ‖ ein ungefährlicher *or* leichter ~ *an easy drop* **b.** ⟨übtr⟩ hoffnungsloser ~ *hopeless case* ‖ klarer ~! *no problem*! dieser ~ ist selten *the case occurs seldom* ‖ der vorliegende ~ *the given instance* ‖ ein zutreffender ~ *a case in point* **2.** → Knall u ~; → entlassen 2. c. **3. es ist auch der ~ bei** *it is also the case with* (*Byron*); dasselbe ist hier der ~ *the same* (*is the case*) *here* ‖ .., wie oft bei diesen Gelegenheiten der ~ ist .. *as is often the case* (od *way*) *on these occasions* ‖ das ist nicht der ~ *that is not the case* | °das ist (nicht) ganz **mein** ~ *that suits me to a T*; *I like that best*; ([*that, she is*] *not exactly in my line*); das ist nicht m·ein ~ (S) *that's not my cup of tea* ‖ wenn der ~ eintritt *in that case* ‖ der ~ liegt doch so *the case is this* ‖ der ~ wird verwickelt *matters are getting complicated* **4.** e–n ~ **beraten** *or* untersuchen ⟨jur⟩ *to sit on a case* ‖ ich setze den ~, daß .., gesetzt den ~, daß .. *put the case that* ..; *suppose* od *supposing* (*he failed*) ‖ e–n ~ tun *to have* od *sustain a fall*; *to get* od *have a tumble*; *to fall* (*down*) **5. a. auf** jeden ~ *in any case* od *event*; *anyhow, anyway*; *rain or shine*; *r. or no r.*; auf jeden (möglichen) ~ bereit *ready for every contingency* → jedenfalls ‖ auf k–n ~ *in no case, on no account*; *by no means*; *not* .. *anyhow, not* .. *anyway*; → keinesfalls ‖ auf alle ~̈e *in any case, at all events, by all means* **b. für** den ~, daß .. (*or* **im** ~e, daß ..) *on the chance that* ..; f den ~ (im ~e), daß er abreist *in the event of his leaving*; f diesen ~ *in* od *for this case* ‖ ⟨hum⟩ im ~e e–s ~es *in case of need, in any c.* **c. im** ~e, daß er abreist *in case* (od *suppose, supposing*) *he should leave*; *in the event of his leaving* ‖ im ~ Schmidt *in the case of Smith* ‖ im ~e m–r Abwesenheit *in the event of my absence*; im ~ der Not *in case of necessity* → Notfall ‖ im anderen ~e *otherwise* ‖ im besten *or* höchsten ~e *at* (*the*) *best*, *if any* ‖ im ersten ~e (v zweien) *in the first instance* ‖ im günstigen ~e *if circumstances are favourable* ‖ im schlimmsten ~e *at the worst*; *if the worst comes to the worst* ‖ im vorliegenden ~e *in the given instance* | in dem ~e *in that case*; *if so*; *then* ‖ in diesem einen ~e *in this instance* ‖ in d–m ~e *in your instance* ‖ nur in diesem ~e *for the nonce* ‖ in allen nur denkbaren Fällen *in any and every case* ‖ denken Sie sich nur in den ~ hinein *imagine the way that things happened* **d. mit** dem ~ betraut s (of police) *to be on the case* **e. zu ~ bringen** (jdn) *to lay low*; *to trip up*; *to tumble*; *to give a fall*; er war schon z ~ gebracht *he had succumbed already* ‖ ⟨fig⟩ *to bring* (*a p*) *to grief*; *to lay a mine for* (*a p*); *to spring a mine on* (*a p*); *to ruin*; ⟨Am sl⟩ *to slip a banana peel in(to) a p's path* ‖ (Regierung) *to overthrow* ‖ (Mädchen) *to seduce* ‖ (Antrag, Gesetz etc) *to defeat, to kill* ‖ (Plan) *to wreck* | **zu ~ k.** *to* (*have a*) *fall*; *to be tripped* (*up*); gefährlich z ~ k *to come a cropper*, ⟨sl⟩ *mucker*; *to come* (od *take*) *a fearful purler* ‖ ⟨fig⟩ *to collapse*; (of persons, plans) *to come to grief* | **v ~ z ~** *singly*; *separately*; *as the case may be*; *according to its* (*etc*) *merits*; etw v ~ z ~ entscheiden *to decide on a th according to circumstances*; *to decide .. on a case by case basis*

Fall[2] n ~es/~en ⟨mar⟩ (Ziehtau) *halyard*

Fall·azien [-iən] pl ⟨log⟩ *fallacies*; *fallacious reasonings* [pl]

F·all- (→ fallen) [in comp] **~behälter** m ⟨mot⟩ *top* od *gravity tank* **~beil** n *guillotine* (Fr); jdn mit dem ~ hinrichten *to guillotine a p* **~benzin** n *petroleum by gravity* **~beschleunigung** f ⟨phys⟩ *acceleration of gravity* **~blatt** n ⟨decor⟩ → Überfall **~blech** n ⟨weav⟩ *chopper bar* **~bö** f *wind squall*; ⟨aero⟩ *(air-)pocket*; *down gust* **~brücke** f = Zugbrücke **~gatter** n *portcullis* (*of a castle*) **~geschwindigkeit** f ⟨phys⟩ *speed* (od *rate, velocity*) *of a* (od *the*) *fall*; *v. of impact*; → Geschwindigkeit **~gesetze** n [pl] ⟨phys⟩ *laws* [pl] *of falling bodies, law of gravitation* **~grube** f ⟨a. fig⟩ *pitfall*; *shoal* **~hammer** m ⟨tech⟩ *drop-hammer*; *h. drop* **~höhe** f *height of a fall*; e–e ~ v 3 Metern *a fall of 3 metres* **~holz** n *windfalls* pl; *dead wood branches* pl *blown from the trees* **~klappe** f (*switchboard*) *drop indicator* **~klinke** f *latch*, (e–s Schlosses ⟨a.⟩) *bolt* **~masche** f ⟨weav, etc⟩ *dropped stitch* **~maschine** f ⟨phys⟩ Atwoodsche ~ *Atwood's machine* **~mast** f ⟨for⟩ *half-mast* **~obst** n *windfall* **~reep** n ⟨mar⟩ *ladder-rope*; *rope ladder*; *gangway*; das ~ herunterlassen *to lower the g.* ‖ ~streppe [f] *gangway* (od *accommodation, companion-*)*ladder* **~rohr** n ⟨tech⟩ *down-pipe* **~scheibe** f ⟨phot⟩ *drop-shutter* **~schirm** m ⟨aero⟩

parachute, ⟨Am⟩ chute, ⟨fam⟩ umbrella, ⟨sl⟩ brolly ‖ mit ~ abgesetzt para .. (parabomb, paratrooper) ‖ mit ~ abspringen to parachute; ⟨Am fam⟩ to bail out | ~absprung [m] parachute jump, descent by p., ⟨sl⟩ brolly-hop ‖ (Soldat der) ~abwehr [f] parashot ‖ ~abwurf [m] parachute drop ‖ ~anzug [m] parasuit ‖ ~ausrüstung [f] parachute assembly ‖ ~einspringer [m] test parachutist ‖ ~gurt [m] parachute harness ‖ ~jäger, ~springer [m] parachutist, paratrooper, ⟨fam⟩ sky(-)man, umbrella man; ⟨sl⟩ brolly-hop ‖ ~jägerflugzeug [n] paratroop-dropper ‖ ~(fang)leine [f] shroud od ripping line ‖ ~leuchtkugel, ~lichtrakete [f] parachute od reconnaissance flare ‖ ~sack [m] pack ‖ ~sanitätspersonal [n] paramedics pl ~truppe [f] parachute force; airborne troop ‖ ~truppen-Division [f] Airborne Division ‖ ~truppen-Transportflugzeug [n] parachute force carrier, ⟨fam⟩ paratrooper **~schloß** n hasp-lock **~stoß** m ⟨Rugb ftb⟩ punt **~streifen** m ⟨meteor⟩ [pl] fall streaks **~strick** m snare; ⟨übtr⟩ gin, net, trap **~sucht** f ⟨med⟩ epilepsy **~treppe** f trap-stairs pl; rope ladder **~tür** f trap-door **~werk** n ⟨tech⟩ = Fallhammer **~wild** n dead game; carrion **~wind** m gravity od katabatic wind (wind blowing down a mountain-side) **~winkel** m inclination; angle of i.

F·alle f ~/~n **1. a.** ⟨eig⟩ trap; ⟨Am⟩ deadfall; (f kl Tiere, Vögel) gin, snare ‖ → Mause~, Ratten~ ‖ ~n aufstellen to set traps; in e–r ~ fangen to snare, trap **b.** ⟨fig⟩ net, pitfall, shoal, snare, (booby-)trap; ⟨Am⟩ deadfall, plant ‖ in die ~ gehen to fall od walk into the trap; to be trapped; → 2. ‖ in der eigenen ~ gefangen hoist with his own petard (Shak) ‖ jdm e–e ~ stellen to lay (od set) a p a trap (od a trap for a p); to set a booby-trap for a p; to snare od trap a p ‖ e–e ~ umgehen to avoid a pitfall **2.** °**in die ~ gehen**, sich in die ~ hauen or rollen (z Bett gehen) to turn in, ⟨Am⟩ to hit the hay **3.** = Fallklinke

f·allen vi/t [fiel/gefallen] **I. vi** [s] **A.** ⟨**eig**⟩ **1.** (aus e–r Höhe) to fall od to drop (auf on; aus .. from, out of the window; durch .. through the ceiling; in .. into the river; v .. from the horse); to have a fall; (of leaves, rain) to drop, fall | ~ auf to fall (od land, light) on (the edge of a box); (of bomb) to hit (the aerodrome) | gefährlich ~ to come a mucker, to come (od go) a purler (⟨sl⟩ a cropper) ‖ heftig u schwerfällig ~ (to have od get a) tumble ‖ plumpsend ~ to flop, plop, plunk (in into) **2.** (hin~, um~) to fall (auf .. to the pavement; to the carpet); to fall down; to sag (über across); to tumble ‖ to stumble (gegen against; über .. over a chair); to trip (up) ‖ er fiel mit dem Kopf gegen .. he hit od struck his head against; plötzlich nach vorn ~ to plump forward; er saß nach vornüber ge~ im Stuhl he was sitting slumped forward in his chair **3.** (Ggs steigen) (of thermometer, etc) to fall, sink; subside; um 5 Grad ge~ s to be down by 5 degrees ‖ (of fever) to decline ‖ (of land) to fall, to sink, to slope; to descend (the hill descended .. to a plain) ‖ der Vorhang fiel the curtain fell (nach dem 2. Akt on the second act) **4.** ⟨übtr⟩ D. **B.** ⟨**übtr**⟩ **1.** (of light, etc.) ~ auf .. to beat down (od impinge) (up)on; (of the sun) to beat upon; (of shadow) to fall (auf, an .. on the wall; durch through) **2.** (P) to fall; to be killed (in battle); auf dem Felde der Ehre ~ to fall on the field of honour; → gefallen ‖ (T) to fall; to be killed; drei Tiger fielen durch s–e Flinte three tigers fell to his rifle **3.** (of a fortress) to fall; to be taken **4.** ⟨com⟩ (of prices, etc.) to decline, drop, fall; (stürzen) to plummet (v .. auf from .. to); to be on the fall; to sag; sink; ⟨sl⟩ to tumble ‖ (of demands) to fall off **5.** (of the voice) to drop ‖ to die away **6.** ⟨pol⟩ (of p, state, etc.) to fall (durch .. through); to be overthrown od ruined; to perish **7.** (of a nation, etc.) to be defeated ‖ to be abolished **8.** (moralisch ~) to fall; → gefallen **9.** (of time) Ostern fällt auf den 8. April Easter comes on the 8th of A., fällt früh falls early; die Jahrhundertfeier fällt in dieses Jahr the centenary falls this year; (his chief works) fall in this period ‖ Christmas falls on Sunday this year **C. jdm leicht, schwer ~** to be easy, difficult for a p (to do); die Übersetzung fällt mir sehr leicht I find no difficulty whatever with the translation; I can do the t. quite easily; die Ü. fällt mir sehr schwer I find great d. with the t.; → leicht, schwer ‖ → ab~, an~, auf~, aus~, be~, durch~, ein~, hin~, über~, um~, ver~, vor~, zu~ **D. Wendungen**: **1.** → Apfel ‖ die Bemerkung fiel v s–r Seite the remark fell from him ‖ es fielen beleidigende Worte strong language was used, .. harte W. words ran high ‖ der Würfel ist ge~ the die is cast ‖ .. fielen die ersten Schüsse at ten the first shots were fired **2.** mst ⟨übtr & fig⟩ **~ an**: ⟨jur⟩ to fall (od descend, escheat) to (the estate fell to the Crown); to the crown devolved on his son; the money went to his sister | **~ auf** (→ B. 1. 2. 9.): auf den Boden, die Erde ~ to fall down (to the floor od ground); to drop; to fall to (the) earth; der Länge nach auf den B. ~ to sprawl to the floor ‖ 12 inches go to the foot ‖ ⟨fig⟩ ~ to fall on one's feet ‖ es fiel mir schwer aufs Herz it went to my heart ‖ my eye fell (od lighted) upon him; the lot, the choice fell on him; → Verdacht ‖ the chief labour devolved upon (od fell to) him ‖ auf die Knie ~ vor to go on one's knee to (a p) ‖ er war nicht auf den Kopf (or den Mund) ge~ he had his wits about him, he had a ready answer ‖ jdm auf die Nerven ~ to get on a p's nerves ‖ das gr Los fiel auf Nummer 90 the prize went to number 90 ‖ die Haare fielen ihr auf die Schultern her hair fell (od drooped, strayed) over her shoulders | **~ aus**: it dropped (od slipped) from his hand ‖ °er war aus allen Himmeln (or Wolken) ge~ he was dumbfounded (od struck dumb) (vor with) ‖ das fällt ganz aus dem Rahmen that does not match with the rest; that doesn't fit at all ‖ aus der Rolle ~ to drop a brick | **~ durch**: durchs Examen ~ → d·urchfallen | **~ in**: (P) → einfallen ‖ (of river) to fall (od flow, discharge) into (the sea) ‖ → zerfallen | jdm in den Arm ~ to seize a p by the arm; to restrain od stop a p ‖ sie fielen sich in die Arme they sank into each other's arms ‖ → Auge I. C. 3. d. ‖ ins Extrem ~ to run to the extreme ‖ das fällt nicht ins Gewicht that is of no consequence; that makes no difference ‖ Räubern in die Hände ~ to fall into the hands of robbers ‖ mit der Tür ins Haus ~ to act blunderingly ‖ this falls into the same category ‖ in hysterische Krämpfe ~ to go off into hysterics ‖ → Ohnmacht ‖ jdm in die Rede, ins Wort ~ to cut a p short, to interrupt a p ‖ jdm in den Rücken ~ to stab a p in the back ⟨a. fig⟩ ‖ → Schlaf; Schoß ‖ to fall to pieces ‖ to fall into sin (od from grace) ‖ → Ungnade; Waagschale ‖ ins Wasser ~ (of hope) to fall through; to come to nothing; to fail ‖ → Zügel | **~ um**: sie fiel ihm um den Hals she fell upon his neck | **~ unter**: unter e–e Bestimmung ~ to come within the terms of a decree ‖ unter die Diebe ~ to fall among thieves ‖ unter das Gesetz ~ to fall within the rule of law ‖ to come (od fall) under a category, class ‖ → Tisch | **~ von**: es fiel mir wie Schuppen v den Augen the scales fell from my eyes ‖ es fiel mir ein Stein vom Herzen, als ich hörte .. I was much relieved to hear .. ‖ kein Meister fällt vom Himmel no man was born a master ‖ °ich bin fast vom Stengel ge~ I was struck dumb (vor .. with amazement) | **~ zu**: jdm zur Beute or zum Opfer ~ to fall a victim to a p; (S) to fall a prey to a th ‖ to fall to (the) earth; to drop to the ground ‖ jdm z Füßen ~ to fall at a *p's feet* || → Last E. **~ lassen 1.** ⟨eig⟩ (etw) *to drop*; (heftig) *to dump* || e–e Bombe ~ l *to release a bomb* (v .. *from the aeroplane*); e–e Masche ~ l *to drop a stitch* **2.** ⟨**übtr**⟩ **a.** (Bemerkung, Worte etc) *to drop, to let fall* (*she let fall no word*); *to throw out* **b.** (Gegenstand) *to drop*; (Frage) *to dismiss*; (Absicht) *to give up*; (Plan) *to abandon* **c.** (die Stimme) *to drop* || → Maske **d. jdn ~ l** *to drop a p; to break away* (od *dissociate o.s.*) *from a p* || *she threw him over for Mr. N.* **3. sich ~ l** *to drop, sink, subside* (in .. *into a chair*) **II. vt** [h] er hat sich [dat] ein Loch in den Kopf ge~ *he has cut his head by a fall*

F·allen n **1.** *the falling* (*of leaves, snow*) || *drop, fall* (*of a p*); *tumble*; jdn im ~ auffangen *to break a p's fall*; jdn zum ~ bringen *to trip a p* (*up*); *to tumble a p*; → Fall || ~lassen [n] *release* (*of a bomb*) **2.** (Ggs Steigen) *descent, slope*; *gradient* || *fall* (*of the curtain, tide, barometer*) || ~ [gen] *fall* od *drop in the prices*; *collapse* od *decline of prices* **3.** ⟨fig⟩ *downfall* (*of an empire*) || *anticlimax* (*in a p's life, work*)

f·ällen I. vt [h] **1.** ⟨eig⟩ **a.** (Baum) *to fell*; *to cut* (od *hew*) *down* **b.** ⟨poet⟩ (jdn) *to fell*; *to knock down* || (T etc) *to fell, kill*; *shoot* **c.** → Bajonett; mit gefällter Lanze *with lance couched* **2.** ⟨chem & cul⟩ (Stoff) *to precipitate* **3.** ⟨math⟩ ein Lot ~ auf *to let fall a perpendicular upon* (*a line*) (v .. *from a point*) **4.** ⟨fig⟩ **a.** ⟨jur⟩ das Urteil ~ *to pass sentence* (über jdn *on a p*); das Todes≗ ~ *to p. s. of death* **b.** ⟨übtr⟩ ein U. ~ *to p.* (od *pronounce*) *judgement* (über etw *on a th*); *to p. sentence* (*on a th*); *to give an opinion* (über *of*) **II.** ≗ n → Fällung

. **f·allend** a *falling* (*body*) || ~e Krankheit = Fallsucht || *descending* (*diphthong*; *pipe line*)

F·allensteller m *trapper*

fall·ieren vi [h] ⟨com⟩ *to fail, to go bankrupt*; fallierte Firma *failed firm*

f·ällig a **1.** [pred] (of a ship) *due*; in Hamburg ~ am 25. August *due at Hamburg the 25th of A.* || (of money, etc.) *due* (seitens jds *from a p*); (*dividends*) *payable*; *accured* (*pay rolls*); ~, aber nicht bezahlt (*interest*) *due, but no received* am 1. ist die Miete ~ ⟨Am fam⟩ *the month's up on the first*; ~ w *to fall* (od *become*) *due*; *to mature* (zur Zahlung *for payment*) || ~, aber nicht bezahlt ⟨ins⟩ *outstanding* (*premium*) | °da wird allerhand ~ s, wenn .. *there will be something special on when* ..; ⟨sl⟩ *there will be dirty work at the cross-roads when* .. || bei ihm *or* für ihn ist was ~ (= Strafe) *he's in for it* **2.** [attr] *incoming* (*payment*); *mature* (*bill*); *payable* | ≗**keit** f ~/~en ⟨com⟩ *maturity*; bei ~ *at m.* | ~sklausel [f] ⟨jur⟩ *acceleration clause*; ~stermin [m] *maturity*; ~sdatum [n] *due date*

Fallim·ent n ~s/~e; **Fallissem·ent** [falis'mɑ̃:] n ~s/~s ⟨com⟩ *bankruptcy, failure*

†**fall·it** a [pred] *bankrupt, insolvent* **Fall·it** m ~en/~en ⟨com⟩ *bankrupt*; *insolvent* || ~engericht [n] ⟨com⟩ *Court of Bankruptcy* || ~enmasse [f] *bankrupt's estate*

Fall·ot m ~en/~en [österr] *scoundrel*, etc, → Schurke

Fall·out [fɔl'aut] m ~s/ (radioaktiver Niederschlag) *fall-out*

falls conj *in case*; *if*; *suppose* od *supposing* (*that*); ~ er abreisen sollte *in the event of his leaving, in case he should leave* || ~ N. stirbt, ist er der nächste E. *failing N. he is the next heir*

-falls (→ Fall C. 2.) [in comp] → allen~, andern~, besten~, eben~, eintretenden~ etc

F·ällung f ~/~en **1.** *cutting-down, felling* (*of a tree*) **2.** ⟨chem⟩ *precipitation* || (~sprodukt) *precipitate* | ~smittel [n] *precipitant* **3.** ⟨fig jur⟩ *the pronouncing* (*of a sentence*)

falsch I. a **1.** (**unaufrichtig**) (P) *false* (*prophet*), (gegen . . *to a p*); *false-hearted*; *deceitful, faithless*; *insincere, perfidious, treacherous*; *backbiting* || *false* (*love*); ~ wie e–e Katze *as treacherous as a cat*; e–e ~e Katze (P) *an old cat*; ° ein ~er Hund *a dirty dog* || ~es Spiel *foul play*; ~es Spiel treiben mit jdm *to play a p false* **2.** (**unwahr**) *false* (*evidence, witness*); ~e Darstellung *misrepresentation, fraudulent representation*; *bogus* (*message*); ⟨Am⟩ *phon*(*e*)*y* || unter Vorspiegelung ~er Tatsachen *under false pretences* || *deceptive*; *false* (*impression*) **3.** (**unecht**) *false* (*hair, teeth*), *artificial* || *base, counterfeit, false* (*coin*); *bogus* (*money*); *forged* (*stamp*); *sham*; *spurious* (*bank-note*); ⟨sl⟩ *dud* || ⟨fig⟩ ° ~er Fuffziger (P) *bad penny* ⟨fam⟩, ⟨Am⟩ *as phony as a wooden nickel* **4.** (**unrichtig**) **a.** *wrong* (*date, opinion, step, view, way*) || ⟨comp⟩ *incorrect* (*punching*) || *false* (*idea, note*; *verdict, weight*; ~e Scham *false shame*; ~er Stolz *false pride* || auf ~er Fährte *on the wrong tack*; *at fault* || unter ~er Flagge segeln *to sail under false colours*; ⟨a. fig⟩ || → Hase || → Kehle; Name **b.** [**pred**] *wrong* (*it would be wrong to believe* . .) || *his observation has not been at fault*; *his thought had not been far out* **c.** [**attr**] [oft durch pref] *mis-*: ~e Angabe *misstatement*; ~e Anwendung *misapplication*; ~e Auskunft *misinformation*; ~e Auslegung *misconstruction*; ~er Gebrauch *misuse*; ~e Rechnung *miscalculation, miscount* **5.** (**unangebracht** → d.) *unsound* || *improper* (*to do*) **6.** °(**wütend**) **a.** *angry* (auf .. *with a p*); ~ w ⟨sl⟩ *to lose one's wool* **b.** *vicious* (*horse*) **II.** adv **1.** (Ggs wahr) *falsely*; ~ schwören *to perjure* (od *forswear*) *o.s.* || ~ spielen ⟨cards⟩ *to sharp* **2.** (Ggs richtig) **a.** *wrongly*; [bei häufig gebrauchten Verben] *wrong*; *to answer, punch, etc wrong*; ~ raten *to guess w.*; ~ spielen *to play w.*; ~ singen *to sing w., to sing out of tune*; ~ tippen *or* setzen *to miss one's guess* || ~ gehen (of a watch) *to go w.* || ich habe es ~ dargestellt (*or* ausgerechnet) *I've got it w.*; ~ verbunden! ⟨telph⟩ (*sorry*,) *w. number*! er hat es ganz ~ verstanden *he got it all w.*, ⟨fam⟩ *he got hold of the w. end of the stick* **b.** ⟨liter⟩ [vgl I. 4. c. oft durch pref] *mis-*: ~ anwenden *to misapply*; ~ auffassen *to misconceive*; ~ auslegen *to misconstrue* || *to mispronounce*; *to misdate*; *to misuse*; ~ schreiben *to misspell*; (jdn) ~ unterrichten *to misdirect, to misinform* || *to misunderstand*; *to misquote* **c.** [vor pp] *wrongly*; ein ~ geschriebenes Wort *a wrongly spelt word* **Falsch** m *deceit, guile, wiliness*; es ist kein ~ an ihm, er ist ohne ~ *he is without guile, there is no guile in him*; ⟨bib⟩ seid ohne ~ wie . . *be ye* . . *harmless as doves* **~anzeige** f ⟨tech⟩ *error in indication* **~eid** m ⟨jur⟩ *false statement made unintentionally by a witness upon his oath*; (außergerichtlich) *false swearing*, → Meineid **~einstellung** f ⟨phot, etc⟩ *maladjustment* ≗**gelocht** a ⟨comp⟩ *faulty* (*column*) ≗**herzig** a *false-hearted* **~meldung** *f false report*; *bogus message* ⟨Am sl⟩ *grapevine* ≗**münzen** vi [h] *to forge coin* **~münzer** m *coiner, forger*; *maker of counterfeit coin* | ~werkstatt [f] *coiner's den*; ⟨Am⟩ *forger's hide-out* **~münzer·ei** f *forging, forgery*; *coining*; *the making of counterfeit coin* **~schreiber** m *bad speller* **~spiel** n ⟨cards⟩ *card-sharping* ≗|**spielen** vi [h] er spielt falsch *he is a card-sharper* (er hat –ge–lt) || aber: falsch spielen → falsch **~spieler** m ⟨cards⟩ *card-sharper*

f·älschen vt/i [h] **1.** vt (Metall, Münzen, Scheck) *to counterfeit, forge* || (Gewicht, Würfel) *to load*; *to render counterfeit* || (Nahrungsmittel) *to adulterate*; *to doctor* | (Urkunde) *to falsify, forge*; jds Unterschrift ~ *to forge a p's signature* || (Bericht, Zahlen) *to doctor, crook*; *to tamper with* || (Bilanz) *to cook* || ⟨arts⟩ (Bild, Handschriften) *to fake* (*up*) **2.** vi *to forge*; *to commit forgery* **F·älscher** m ~s/~ *counterfeiter, forger* (*of coins*) || *adulterer* (*of food, wine*) || *falsifier* (*of history*); *forger* (*of bank-notes*) || *faker* (*of manu-*

scripts) **F·alschheit** f ~/~en **1.** (P) *falseness, falsity; deceit, double-dealing, duplicity; faithlessness; guile; treachery* **2.** (S) *falseness, falsity (of a statement)* **f·älschlich 1.** adv *falsely; deceitfully; fraudulently;* ~ vorgeben *to feign, to pretend, to sham, to simulate* ‖ (irrtümlich) *erroneously, incorrectly, wrongly; by mistake* **2.** a *erroneous, incorrect; wrong (opinion)* **~erweise** adv *falsely, wrongly; by mistake* **F·älschung** f ~/~en **1.** [abstr] *falsification; debasement, counterfeiting, forgery, forging (of a coin, document)* ‖ *adulteration (of food)* ‖ *falsification (of a date); cooking (of accounts)* ‖ *faking (of a picture); fakery* | sich z e–r ~ versteigen, auf e–e ~ verfallen *to run to a forgery* **2.** [konkr] (Gefälschtes) *counterfeit, forgery; fake (the pearls are a f.), sham*

Fals·ett n ~s/~e *falsetto* (It); *head voice*

Falsifik·at n ~s/~e *counterfeit, forgery; fake*

F·alt- (→ falten) [in comp] *folding . .* **~blatt** n (Prospekt) *leaflet,* ⟨Am⟩ *folder;* (ausklappbar) ⟨bookb⟩ *pull-out,* ⟨Am⟩ *folding leaf* **~boot** n *fold(ing-)boat, collapsible boat;* ⟨aero, etc⟩ (Gummi≗) *rubber dinghy* od *dingey* **~fächer** m *(folding) fan* **~maschine** f *folding* (od *pleating*)*-machine* **~maßstab** m *folding-rule* **~prospekt** m = –blatt **~schachtel** f *folding box* **~stuhl** m *folding-chair; deck-chair* **~werk** n *folds* [pl] | ~füllung [f] *linen-scroll*

F·alte f ~/~n **A.** (natürlich *or* zufällig entstandene ~) **1.** (mst in Tuch) **a.** ⟨allg⟩ *fold (of a robe)* ‖ (of cloth, curtains) in schönen ~n fallen, schöne ~n werfen *to fall in graceful folds; to drape artistically* **b.** (fehlerhafte ~) *crease, crinkle, wrinkle;* die Strümpfe in ~n an den Beinen liegend *stockings wrinkled* [pp] *about his legs* ‖ (of cloth) ~n bek *to crease (this cloth creases easily); to crinkle; to fall into creases* ‖ ~n schlagen *or* werfen *to pouch; to pucker (up);* (of paper) *to wrinkle* **2.** (Haut≗) *pucker;* ⟨med⟩ *ruga* (L); Gesichts≗ *wrinkle* ‖ ~ n [pl] *wrinkles* [pl], *wrinkling;* (Alters≗n) ⟨euph⟩ *expression lines; facial contour;* voller ~n *puckery, wrinkly* ‖ ~n bek (of the face) *to wrinkle (up)* ‖ die Stirn in ~n ziehen *to knit* (od *gather, pucker, wrinkle*) *one's brows* **3.** ⟨übtr geol⟩ *fold* ‖ Gelände≗ *fold of the ground* **4.** ⟨fig⟩ die geheimen ~n des Herzens *the secret recesses of the heart* **B.** (absichtlich gemachte ~) *crease, fold, pleat, pleating; ply;* Quer≗ *tuck* ‖ → Bügel≗ ‖ Reih≗n [pl], *shir(r);* Preß≗n [pl] *accordion-pleats* [pl]; *plissé* (Fr) ‖ ~n in e–n Stoff m, e–n St. in ~n legen *to fold* (od *pleat*) *cloth* ‖ (Stoff) in Quer≗n legen *to tuck* ‖ (Kleid) mit ~n ausputzen *to gather*

f·älteln vt [h] (Stoff) *to gather, pleat* ‖ (Locken) *to crimp, crinkle* ‖ → folg **F·ältelung** f *pleating* ‖ *puckering (of the lips),* (Stirn≗) *wrinkling*

f·alten vt [h] **A. 1.** die Hände ~ *to clasp* (od *fold*) *one's hands, to join hands;* mit gefalteten Händen *with folded hands* **2.** (Tuch) *to fold, to pleat* → vor.; knittern ‖ (Saum) *to pucker* ‖ (Papier) *to fold* ‖ nach innen ~ *to double in* ‖ zusfalten *to d. up* **3.** die Stirn ~ *to knit* (od *gather, wrinkle*) *one's brows* **B. sich ~ 1.** (of cloth, etc.) *to pucker, wrinkle; crinkle* **2.** ⟨geol⟩ *to fold (up)* **3.** (of the face) *to pucker, crease (z . . into a smile)* **4.** sich zus–~ 1 *to double up; fold (up)* **F·alten-~balg** m → Harmonika **~besatz** m *falbala, smocking;* (Kleid) mit ~ versehen *to smock* **~-bildung** f *wrinkling,* → Falten ‖ ⟨geol⟩ *folding* **~gebirge** n *fold-mountains* pl; *folded rocks* **~-hemd** n *pleated* (⟨Am⟩ *ruffle-*) *shirt* ≗**los** a *without folds, etc; unwrinkled* **~kreme** f ⟨cosm⟩ *antiwrincle cream* **~magen** m ⟨zoo⟩ = Blättermagen **~rock** m *accordion-skirt; pleated skirt* **~rumpf** m ⟨geol⟩ *truncated fold* **~saum** m *furbelow* **~-werfen** n *puckering; wrinkling* **~werk** n = Falten [pl]; → Falte B. **~wurf** m bes ⟨arts⟩ *drapery*

F·alter m ~s/~ ⟨ent⟩ → *fritillary* ‖ Aurora≗ *orange tip;* kl, gr Heu≗ *small, large heath*

f·altig a *folded; pleated (satin)* ‖ *puckered, wrinkled (face); puckery, wrinkly* ‖ ⟨anat⟩ *rugate*

F·altung f *folding; pleating* ‖ ⟨geol⟩ *fold*

Falz m ~es/~e ⟨tech⟩ **1.** ⟨carp⟩ *rabbet, rebate; groove; notch* **2.** (Gefaltetes) **a.** (Blechverbindung) *fold,* (v Konservendose) *seam* **b.** ⟨typ⟩ (Bogen≗) *fold* **3.** (eingeheftete) *slip-fold;* ⟨bookb⟩ *guard* **~apparat** m *folding-machine; folder* **~bein** n ⟨typ⟩ *folding-stick, folder* **~hobel** m ⟨carp⟩ *rabbet-plane; fillister* **~maschine** f = Falzapparat **~messer** n *folding-blade* **~rahmen** m ⟨typ⟩ *grooved chase* **~ziegel** m *gutter-tile* **~zylinder** m ⟨typ⟩ *folding cylinder* **f·alzen I.** vt [h] **1.** (verbinden) *to rabbet, rebate* ‖ *to join by means of a fold* ‖ (mit Falz versehen) *to groove; rabbet, rebate* **2.** ⟨typ⟩ (Bogen) *to fold* **3.** (Fell, Leder) *to pare, shave* **4.** (Blechränder verbinden) *to seam* **II.** ≗ n *rabbeting* ‖ ⟨typ⟩ *folding*

F·alzer(in f ~/nen) m ~s/~ *folder*

F·ama f (L) = Gerücht n, Ruf m

famili·är 1. a *familiar (expression)* ‖ sein Benehmen war sehr ~ *his manner was very familiar* ‖ aus ~en Gründen *for compassionate* (etc) *reasons;* → Sonderurlaub **2.** adv *in a family way; familiarly; intimately* ‖ er tut sehr ~ *his manner is very familiar* **Familiarit·ät** f ~/~en *familiarity*

Fam·ilie f ~/~n **A.** (P) **1.** ⟨eig⟩ *family;* die ~ Braun *the Browns* [pl]; *the Brown f.;* ⟨fam⟩ *the Browns people* [pl]; e–e ~ Braun *a f. of Browns;* e–e Vikars≗ *a vicar's f.* ‖ m–e ~ ⟨fam⟩ *my people,* ⟨Am⟩ *my folks* ‖ ~ u Dienerschaft *the household* ‖ ein Sohn aus guter ~ *a son of good f.* **2.** (~ einschließlich Vorfahren) *family, lineage;* ein Mann aus alter, vornehmer ~ *a man of f.* ‖ ⟨Scot⟩ *clan, tribe;* → Geschlecht, Stamm **3.** ⟨fig⟩ *clan, class, f., group;* ⟨mst cont⟩ *tribe (the whole t. of actors)* **4. Wendungen:** e–e ~ gründen *to settle o.s.; to marry and settle down; to start a f.* ‖ ~ h *to have children;* e–e gr ~ h *to have a large f.;* ich habe k–e ~ *I am not a f. man; I have no children* ‖ ist ~ da? *is there any f.?* ‖ es liegt in der ~ *it runs in the f.* (od *blood*) ‖ das kommt in den besten ~n vor *accidents will occur* od *happen in the best-regulated families* **B.** (T & S) ⟨zoo & bot⟩ *family (a f. consisting of many genera); tribe;* die ~ der Hunde *the dog tribe;* → Ordnung, Gattung ‖ Sprachen≗ *family of l.s*

Fam·ilien- [in comp] *family (f.) . .* **~ähnlichkeit** f *f. likeness* **~angehörige(r** m) f → –mitglied **~angelegenheit** f *f. affair* | mit (ohne) **~anhang** [m] *(un)accompanied* **~anschluß** m; ~ suchen *to wish to be made one of the f.;* wir bieten Ihnen ~ *we offer you home from h.;* mit ~ *au pair* Fr **~-anzeigen** f pl *births, marriages, and deaths* pl ‖ ⟨fam hum⟩ *hatches, catches, matches, and dispatches* (= Geburts–, Verlobungs–, Heirats– u Todesanzeigen) **~bad** n *mixed bathing* **~bande** n pl *f. ties* pl **~begräbnis** n = Familiengruft **~betreuung** f *f. services* pl **~bild** n *f. piece* **~buch** n ⟨Ger⟩ *f. record* od *genealogic book* **~ehre** f *f. honour* **~erbstück** n *f. heirloom;* (ein Bild) *f. portrait* **~fehler** m *f. failing* **~feier** f *celebration in a small circle* **~fest** n *family festival* **~forschung** f *genealogical research* **~fürsorge** f *f. welfare-work* **~geheimnis** n ⟨engl⟩ bloßstellendes ~ *skeleton in the cupboard, f. skeleton* **~glück** n *domestic happiness* **~grabstätte** f *f. cemetery lot* **~größe** f *f. size* **~gruft** f *f. vault* **~gut** n *f. estate;* → Fideikommiß **~haupt** n *head* (od *father*) *of the f.* **~hotel** n *f. hotel* **~kreis** m *f. circle;* im ~kreise *in the f. circle* **~kunde** f *genealogy* ≗**kundlich** a *genealogical* **~leben** n *f., domestic, home life* **~-lohn** m *wages* (od *salary*) *plus f. allowance* **~mitglied** n *p belonging to the (same) f.;* ~er pl *relatives;* ⟨demog⟩ mithelfende ~er *f. helpers; unpaid f. workers* **~nachrichten** f [pl] = Familienanzeigen **~name** m *f. name, surname,* ⟨Am⟩ *last name* **~oberhaupt** n *head of the f.* **~rat** m *f. council* **~recht** n *family law* **~roman** m *saga novel* **~rücksichten** f pl *f. considerations* pl **~schmuck** m *f. heirloom* ⟨a. jur⟩ **~stammbaum** m *f. tree* **~stammbuch** n → –buch **~stammgut** n = Fideikommiß **~stand** m *a p's (legal) status in the f.* (od *in respect of f.*); *f.* od *personal status*; ⟨demog⟩ *civil, conjugal, marital status* **~statistik** f ⟨demog⟩ *prolificacy distribution* **~stiftung** f *private trust* **~stolz** m *f. pride* **~tag** m *f. meeting* (od *rally*) **~unterhalt** m, **~unterstützung** f *f. allowance* **~unternehmen** n *f.-owned, (-held) enterprise* **~vater** m *f. man, father of f.*; ⟨ant⟩ *pater familias* (L) **~verkehr** m *social intercourse* **~vorstand** m *head of the f.* **~wappen** n *f. coat of arms* **~zulage** f = –unterhalt **~zuwachs** m *f. increase; addition to the f.*; ~ erwarten ⟨fam⟩ *to be expecting (a baby)*, ~ h ⟨fam⟩ *to have a little f.*

°**fam·os** **1.** a *brilliant (idea)*; *capital (fellow)*, ⟨Am⟩ *great (guy)*; *excellent, good, splendid; tip-top* ‖ ⟨fam⟩ *great (dog); jolly (weather); roaring (health)* ‖ ⟨sl⟩ *clinking, corking, scrumptious, rattling, ripping, scorching, slap-up (dinner), stunning, topping, top-hole* ‖ ⟨Am a.⟩ *bully (headmaster)*; ~! *dandy, peachy* | ein ganz –ser Kerl (*or* Mensch) *a jolly good fellow*; ⟨fam⟩ *a brick*; ⟨sl⟩ *a corker* ‖ e–e ~e S ⟨sl⟩ *corker, scorcher, nailer* ‖ ein –ser Witz *a good 'un* **2.** adv *capitally; extremely well* ‖ du hast dich ~ bewährt *you are a brick* ‖ sie kocht ~ *she is great at cooking* ‖ er spielt ~ Klavier, Tennis *he is great on the piano; he is a whale* (⟨Am⟩ *a shark*) *at tennis*

famul·ieren vi [h] ⟨med⟩ *to walk the hospitals*

F·amulus m L ~/~se & –li *amanuensis* L

Fan [fæn] m ~s/~s („Narr", –fex) *fan(atic)*

Fan·al n ~s/~e *beacon, fire* ‖ ⟨fig⟩ *oriflamme*

Fan·atiker m ~s/~ *fanatic* (in bezug auf *on*); *extreme man*; politischer ~ *political extremist* | ⟨fam⟩ *fiend*; ⟨Am sl⟩ *bug* **fan·atisch** **1.** a *fanatic(al)*; ein ~er Verfechter der Gerechtigkeit *a fanatic for justice* ‖ *extreme*; ⟨pol⟩ *rabid (democrat); red-hot (reactionary)* **2.** adv *fanatically* **fanatis·ieren** vt [h] *to fanaticize* **Fanat·ismus** m ~/ *fanaticism, extremism*

Fanf·are f ~/~n *fanfare; flourish of trumpets*; *(tara)tantara, tarantara* ‖ ~ blasen *to sound a fanfare* **Fanfaron·ade** f ~/~n *fanfaronade; bray*

Fang m ~(e)s/⁓e **A.** [abstr] **1. a.** *catch (of an animal); capture; hunting, shooting* ‖ Fisch⁓ *catch of fish; haul; fishing*; Makrelen⁓ *catch of mackerel* **b.** erlegtem Wild den ~ geben *to kill the captured game* **2.** *catch (of a ball)* ‖ ein leichter ~ *a sitter* **B.** [konkr] (Gefangenes) **1. a.** ⟨hunt⟩ *bag, kill, take* ‖ (of fish) *catch, take, haul*; ein gr ~ *a great catch, a big haul* **b.** ⟨fig⟩ *haul; capture; acquisition* **2.** *a place where game* (etc.) *may be caught; catch*; → Enten⁓ **3.** Fänge [pl] **a.** (Zähne) *fangs* [pl] (*of a bear*) **b.** (Krallen) *claws, talons (of a vulture)* **c.** ⟨fig⟩ *clutches, fangs* [pl] **C. Wendungen**: auf ~ ausgehen *to go hunting* (od *shooting*); *to rove in search of plunder*; → Beute B. 2. ‖ ⟨fig⟩ e–n reichen ~ m *to make a fine hand* ‖ e–n ~ tun *to make a capture* **~arm** m ⟨zoo⟩ *tentacle* ‖ ⟨fig⟩ *claw, clutch; fang* **~ball** m **1.** *play-ball* ‖ ~ spielen mit jdm *to play at ball with a p* **2.** ⟨fig⟩ *shuttlecock; plaything*; ~ spielen mit jdm *to lord it over a p, to tyrannize over a p; to play blind hookey with a p* **~damm** m (bei Brückenbau) *coffer-dam* **~eisen** n *trap; hunting-spear* **~(e)mann** m ⟨fam⟩ *touch-and-run, catch-as-catch-can* **~feder** f ⟨phot⟩ *spring catch* **~frage** f *trick(y) qu.* **~gebiet** n *fishing area* **~gründe** m pl *f. grounds* **~gürtel** m ⟨hort⟩ *catch-belt* **~haken** m (Flugzeugträger ⟨mar⟩) *arrester hook* **~leine** f ⟨mar⟩ *painter*; ⟨aero⟩ (am Fallschirm) *parachute cord* **~masche** f ⟨weav⟩ *tuck-loop, t.-stitch* **~messer** n *hunting-knife* **~mutterschiff** n *factory* (od *fish-processing*) *ship* **~partei** f ⟨crick⟩ (nicht-schlagende Partei) *the fielding side* ‖ Spieler der ~ *fielder*; (direkt gegenüber dem batsman) *point*; Stellung der ~ zw *point* u *slips*: *gully* **~schnur** f ⟨mil⟩ (Achselband) *aiguillette* [Fr], ⟨Am⟩ *shoulder braid* **~schuß** m *coup de grâce* Fr, *finishing shot* **~seil** n (Flugzeugträger ⟨mar⟩) *arrester wire*; ⟨aero⟩ *lift wire* **~vorrichtung** f *catchdevice* **~ware** f ⟨weav⟩ *tuck-rib fabric* **~zahn** m *fang, tusk* **~zeit** f *catching-season; fishing-season* **f·angen** vt [h] [fing/gefangen] **1.** (T) *to catch; capture*; (Fisch) *take*; → jagen ‖ mit e–m Netz ~ *to net*; in e–r Schlinge ~ *to noose, springe*; (Fische) im Schleppnetz ~ *to trawl* ‖ (angeln) *to have sport (a fishing excursion in which he had no sport)* ‖ ⟨fig⟩ → Grillen **2.** (P) **a.** *to catch, get, capture, seize, take; net* ‖ ⟨übtr fam⟩ *to nail* ‖ mit ge~, mit gehangen *rogues of a gang on one gibbet must hang* **b.** Kunden ~ *to cater* (od *angle*) *for customers* **c.** ⟨fig⟩ *to catch; to come round (a p)*; sich leicht ~ l *to be easily caught* **3. a.** (Ball) *to catch* **b.** Feuer ~ *to catch* (od *take*) *fire*; ⟨a. fig⟩ (P) **5. sich ~ a.** *to be caught; to catch* (in *in*) **b.** ⟨aero⟩ (of aeroplane) sich wieder ~ *to straighten out* ‖ ⟨fig⟩ (P) sich wieder ~ *to cool down* **F·änger** m ~s/~ **1.** (P) *catcher* ‖ ⟨crick⟩ *fielder*; ein sicherer *or* guter ~ *a safe catch*; ~ ganz nahe dem Schläger *silly point* ‖ → Bauern⁓, Ratten⁓, Vogel⁓ **2.** (S) (Zahn) *fang, tusk* ‖ → Fliegen⁓, Hirsch⁓ **f·ängisch** a *arranged* (od *fitted*) *for catching*

Fanglomer·at n ~s/~e ⟨geol⟩ *fanglomerate*

F·ango m ~s/ *fango* **~packung** f *fango-pack*

Fant m ~s/~e *coxcomb, fop, popinjay*

Fantas·ie f ~/~n [–iːən] ⟨mus⟩ *fantasia*

Fantas·ie – (Ph) – **~papier** n *fancy paper*

°**fant·astisch**, ⟨hum⟩ **fantast·etisch** a *immense; galoptious; super (it would be simply s.!)*; ⟨school sl⟩ ~e Leistung *wizard prang* ‖ ~st [sup] *(I had the) beatest (time of my life)*; → ph –

Far·ad n (nach M. Faraday) ~(s)/~ ⟨el⟩ *farad*

Faradisati·on [*ts*] f ~/~en *faradization*

Farb- *colo(u)r* .. **~abstimmung** f ⟨phot⟩ *c. adjustment* **~anstrich** m *coat of paint* **~aufnahme** f *c. photo* od *shot* | ⟨tex⟩ (Aufnahme von Farbe) *dye take-up* **~ausgleich** m *c. balance* | ~filter [m] *c. compensating filter* **~bad** n *dye-bath* **~ballen** m ⟨typ⟩ *ink-ball* **~band** n **1.** *type-writer ribbon* | ~gabel [f] *ribbon centre guide* ‖ schaltung [f] 3-Zonen ~ *three-c. ribbon switch* ‖ ~spule [f] *ribbon-spool* ‖ ~umschaltung [f] *ribbon shifting* **2.** ⟨phys⟩ leuchtendes ~ *band of light of various c.s* **~beilage** f (Zeitung) *colo(u)r supplement* **~beize** f *mordant* **⁓beständig** a *c.-fast* | ~keit [f] *stability of dyes* **~bestimmung** f *c. specification* **~buch** n *c.-book* **~büchse** f ⟨typ⟩ *ink-box* **~dia** n *c. slide* **⁓echt** a *c.-fast; fadeless* **~entferner** m *(hair) c. remover* **~fernsehen** n *c. television* | –hsendung [f] *c. cast* **~film** m *c.-film* | ~verfahren [n] *technicolo(u)r* **~flotte** f (z Färben) ⟨tex⟩ *dye liquor; bath* **~gebung** f *c.ation* **~glas** n *c.ed glass* **~holz** n *dyewood*; → Blauholz **~kasten** m *c.-box* ‖ ⟨typ⟩ *inkduct* **~kissen** n *ink(ing)-pad* **~körper** m ⟨bot⟩ (in der Zelle) *chromosome*; → Pigment **~kraft** f = Färbe– **~kunst** f *c.ing*; Meister der ~ *c.ist* **~kuppler** m ⟨film⟩ *coupler* **~lavendel** m ⟨film⟩ *intermediate positive* **~mine** f *c.ed lead* **~mischung** f *tonal c.* **~muster** n *c. pattern* od *sample* **~photographie** f *(natural) c.-photography* **⁓richtig** a *true to c.* **~schattierung** f *hue, shading* **~scheibenzug** m ⟨theat⟩ *c. runners* pl **~schranke** f ⟨pol⟩ *c. bar* **~sehen** n *c. vision* **~spachtel** m ⟨print⟩ *palette knife* **~stern** m ⟨phot⟩ *c. star* **~stich** m ⟨phot⟩ *c. tinge, c. shade* **~stift** m *c.ed pencil*; **~stoff** m *dye(-stuff)*; gelber ~ *flavine*; tiefroter ~ *lake*; wasch- u lichtechter ~ *indanthrene* ® |

~träger [m] ⟨biol⟩ *chromatophore*; ⟨bot⟩ *chromoplast* **~temperaturmesser** m *kelvinmeter* **~ton** m *tint, tone*; *colour-tone*; *tonality*; *hue* ‖ e–n ~ treffen ⟨tail⟩ *to match a colour* ‖ **~topf** m *paint-pot* **~umkehrmaterial** n ⟨phot⟩ *c.-reversal material* **~verdünnungsmittel** n *paint thinner* **~verschiebung** f *c. shift*; *c. distortion* (⟨a.⟩ –verzerrung) **~walze** f *ink(ing)-roller* **~waren** f [pl] *c.s*, *paints* [pl]; *dyes, dye-stuffs* [pl] **~werk** n ⟨typ⟩ *inking apparatus* **~werke** n [pl] *dye-works* pl [sg konstr] **~wiedergabe** f *c. reproduction* **~zylinder** m ⟨typ⟩ *inking-cylinder* **Färb-** (→ färben) [in comp] → Färbe-

f·ärbbar a *stainable*; *capable of being dyed*

F·arbe f ~/~n → weiß **A.** ⟨phys & opt⟩ **1.** *colour*, ⟨Am⟩ *color*; (un)gemischte ~ (*pure*), *tonal c.*; → grell, matt, satt, schreiend ‖ ihr Haar hatte noch dieselbe ~, ihr H. war noch v derselben ~ *her hair was yet the same c.* ‖ *a dress the c. of violets* ‖ ich habe es in der ~ gesehen *I have seen it that c.* ‖ die Wände waren in Kupferfarbe (*or* kupferfarben) tapeziert *the walls were papered a rich copper-c.* ‖ der Himmel war v mattblauer ~ *the sky was a dull blue* ‖ → Regenbogen≗; in allen ~n schillern *to glitter in all the c.s of the rainbow* ‖ dünne, zarte ~ *tint* ‖ die gelbe ~ *the yellow c.*; *chrome*; → feldgrau, Khaki ‖ ⟨phot⟩ f alle ~n empfindlich *panchromatic, orthochromatic* **2.** (Gesichts≗) *complexion, colour, hue* ‖ blühende, rote ~ *high colour*; sehr wenig (viel) ~ h *to have very little (much) colour* ‖ sein Gesicht hatte e–e totenblasse ~ *his face was a ghastly colour* ‖ (of the face) ~ annehmen *to colour*; sein Gesicht nahm eine gräuliche ~ an *his face turned a dusty hue* ‖ die ~ wechseln *to change c.* ‖ die ~ verlieren *to lose c.* **3.** (Farbton) *colour, hue*; *tint*; *tone*; *shade* ‖ helle u dunkle ~n [pl] *lights and darks* pl ‖ (etw) in hellen (dunklen) ~n schildern *to paint in bright (dark) c.s* ‖ e–r S Inhalt u ~ verleihen *to give* (od *lend*) *life and c. to a th* **B. 1.** ~ **(als Kennzeichen)** ⟨cards⟩ *suit*; lange ~ *strong suit*; *flush*; Piek≗ *suit of spades* ‖ ~ (bedienen), bekennen *to follow suit*; ⟨fig⟩ *to show* (od *to come out in*) *one's true c.s*; nicht ~ bek. wollen *to beat about the bush to declare o.s.* **2.** (als Sinnbild) [mst pl] ~n *colours* pl (*of a college, university*; *club, crew, team*; *form*, etc.) ‖ deutsche ~n *German c.s* [pl]; den ~n treu bleiben *to stick to one's colours* ‖ die ~n wechseln *to desert one's colours*; ⟨pol⟩ *to rat*, ⟨Am⟩ *to flop* **C. (Farbstoff)** *pigment*; (aufgelöst) *dye, paint*; [mst pl] *colour* | ⟨typ⟩ *ink* | deckende ~, Deck≗ *body colour, opaque colour*; echte ~ *stable* (od *fast*) *dye* (od *colour*); unechte ~ *fugitive dye*; → durchscheinend ‖ → Grund≗; Öl≗, Wasser≗ ‖ die Tür mit blauer ~ anstreichen *to paint the door blue* | die ~ **auf|tragen** *to lay on the colour*; ⟨typ⟩ *to ink the form* | (etw) in dick –ge–en ~n malen *to impaste*; auf dem Bild sind die ~n dick –ge– *the picture is painted in impasto*; dickes A. der ~n *impasto* [It] ‖ die ~n z dick a. *to lay on the colours too thickly*; ⟨fig⟩ *to lay it on with a trowel* ‖ leicht –ge–e ~ *wash* | ~ **halten** (of cloth, etc.) *to be colour-fast*; die ~ hält *the colour will last*

F·ärbe- **~bad** n *dye-bath* **~beere** f ⟨bot⟩ *buckthorn-berry*; → Kreuzdorn **~brühe** f *dyeing liquor* **~faß** n *dye-vat* **~kraft** f *tinctorial power* **~masse** f, **~mittel** n *dyeing* (od *colouring*) *matter*; *stain, stainer* **~prozeß** m *dyeing-process*

F·arben- ⟨mst⟩ *colo(u)r* **~abstufung** f *gradation of c.*; *c.-tone* **~anordnung** f *coloration, c.ing* **~auftrag(ung** f) m (Pinseldruck) [abstr] *brush-stroke*; *touch*; [konkr] dicke(r) ~ *impasto* [It] **~bild** n ⟨phys⟩ *c.ed image*; *spectrum* [L] **≗blind** a *c.-blind* ‖ ⟨phot⟩ *non-c.-sensitive* (*emulsion*) **~blindheit** f *c.-blindness*; *achromatopsia*; → Daltonismus, Dichromasie **~brechung** f *c. refraction* **~brett** n ⟨typ⟩ *ink-board*; → Palette **~druck** m **1.** *c.-printing* **2.** [konkr] *c.-print* ‖ → Buntdruck **~drucker** m *c.-printer* **≗empfindlich** a *c.-sensitive*; *orthochromatic* **~empfindlichkeit** f *c.-sensitiveness* ‖ ⟨phot⟩ *chromatic sensitivity* | ~skurve [f] *c.-response curve* **~empfindung** f *c.-perception* **~fabrik** f *dye-works* [pl] [sg konstr] **~fabrikant** m *c.maker* ‖ ⟨print⟩ *ink-maker* **~f·estigkeitsprüfer** m *fadeometer* **~filter** m ⟨phot⟩ *c.-filter* **≗freudig**, **≗froh** a *bright, gay* (*in c.s*), *colorific* | ⟨mst übtr, fig⟩ *c.ful* **~gebung** f *colour*; *c.ation, c.ization* **~glanz** m *brightness* (*of c.*); *iridescence* **~glas** n *c.ed* (od *stained*) *glass* **~glut** f *vividness of c.* **~händler** m *dealer in dyes* od *paints*; Öl≗ *colourman* **~harmonie** f *harmony of colour* **~holz** n ⟨typ⟩ *stirring-pole* ‖ ~schnitt [m] *chrome wood-engraving* **~hören** n *colour-hearing* **~industrie** f *dyeing* od *chemical industry*; I.G.~ ® *the I.G. Farbenindustrie*; *the Dye Trust* **~karte** f ⟨paint⟩ *colour-* ⟨cosm⟩ *shade-card* **~kasten** m *colour* (od *paint*)*-box* | °**~kleckser** m *dauber, daubster* **≗korrigiert** a ⟨phot⟩ *achromatic* (*lens*) **~kübel** m *paintpot* **~lehre** f (*Goethe's*) *theory of c.*; *chromatics* [pl] [sg konstr]; *chromatology* **~lichtdruck** m [konkr] *collotype* **~linie** f *colour-line* **~lithographie** f *chromolithography* **~meer** n ⟨fig⟩ *blaze of colour* **~messer** m *colorimeter, tintometer* **~messung** f *colorimetry* **~mischung** f *mixture of colours* [a. konkr]; Kunst der ~ *chromatics* [pl] **~mühle** f *paint-mill*; *colour grinding mill* **~photographie** f [abstr] *colour-photography* **~pracht** f *wealth* od *splendo(u)r of c.(s)* ‖ ⟨fig⟩ *c.* **≗prächtig 1.** a *brightly c.ed*; *colorific*; *c.ful* (*welcome*); *c.y* ‖ *highly c.ed* (*style*) **2.** adv *c.fully* **~rand** m runder ~ *halo of c.s*; → Interferenzfarbe **~reiben** n *c.-grinding* **~reiber** m *c.-grinder* **~reibmaschine** f *c. grinding machine* **≗reich** a *c.ful*; *chromatic* (*splendour*); *vividly c.ed* (*picture of the Court*); *variegated in c.*; → farbenprächtig **~reiz** m *c. stimulus* **~schmuck** m reicher ~ *wealth of c.*; (bei Tieren) *wealth of tint* **~sehen** n ⟨physiol⟩ *chromotopsy* **~sensibilisierung** f ⟨phot⟩ *chromatic* (*dye*) *sensitization* **~sinn** m *c.-sense* ‖ ⟨physiol⟩ *chromatic sense* **~skala** f *c.-scale*; *chromatic scale*; *range of c.s*; *tonal scale*; ⟨phys⟩ *gamut of c.s* ‖ ⟨physiol⟩ *c. chart* **~spektrum** n ⟨phys⟩ *chromatic spectrum* **~spiel** n *play of c.s*; *iridescence*; *opalescence* **~sprache** f *language* of *c.s* **~steindruck** m [abstr] *chromolithography* ‖ [konkr] (Abdruck) *chromolithograph* **~stift** m = Farbstift **~strich** m mit dick aufgetragenen ~en gemalt *blottesque* **~symbolik** f *c. symbolism* **~tafel** f *cake of paint* **~topf** m *paint-pot* **≗tragend** a *wearing c.s* **~tube** f *tube of c.* **~tüchtigkeit** f ⟨med⟩ *c. perception* **~veränderung** f (T) *c.-change* **~wahrnehmung** f ⟨physiol⟩ *c. appreciation* **~wechsel** m *variation of c.*; *variegation* ‖ ⟨theat⟩ *c. change*; automatischer ~ *remotely operated c. ch.*; ⟨Am⟩ *remote-control c. ch.* **~wechsler** m ⟨pol⟩ *renegade*; *rat, ratter*; ⟨Am⟩ *flopper* **~wirkung** f *effect*; *colour-emphasis* **~zerstreuung** f ⟨opt⟩ *chromatic dispersion*; *chromatism* **~zus-stellung** f *c. scheme*

-farben a k·upfer~ *copper-coloured* ‖ ihr Kleid war orange~ *her dress was orange colour* ‖ ⟨com⟩ qualitäts~ *coloury* **f·ärben** vt/i [h] **I.** vt **A.** ⟨eig⟩ **1. a.** (Kleider, Wolle etc; Haare) *to dye*; *stain* ‖ gründlich *or* tief ~ *to grain*; in der Wolle ~ *to dye in the wool* (od *in grain*) ‖ Tuch rot ~ *to dye cloth red* (od *a red colour*); in blassem Weiß gefärbt *dyed a faded white* ‖ (Glas, Holz etc) *to stain* **b.** (Gegenstände, Wände) *to colour, paint, stain* **c. sich** [dat] das Gesicht ~ *to paint one's face* ‖ (Lippen) rot ~ *to rouge* **d.** (etw) mit Blut ~ *to stain with blood*; .. gefärbt *blood-stained* **2.** ⟨übtr⟩ (S) *to dye*;

leicht ~ *to tint, tinge* ‖ .. färbt den Himmel rosarot *the sunset dyes* (od *tinges*) *the sky a rosy pink* (od *with a rosy flush*) ‖ Schamröte färbte ihre Wangen *deep blushes dyed her cheeks*; sein Gesicht war grünlich gefärbt *his face was a greenish colour* **3.** ⟨fig⟩ **a.** (S) *to colour; tinge, tint*; die Kunst färbt das Leben *art colours life* ‖ dieser Kummer färbte sein ganzes Leben *this grief tinged his whole life* ‖ gefärbt s v *to be coloured* (od *tinted*) *by* (*all truth is tinted by* ..); gefärbt s mit *to be tinged with*; *to be infused* (od *saturated, shot, tinctured*) *with* **b.** (Rede, Worte) *to diversify, season* (mit *with*); humoristisch ~ *to season with humour* **c.** (entstellen) (Bericht) *to colour*; *slant* (*slanted report*); *distort*; → fälschen **B. sich ~ 1.** (of fruit) *to* (*take on*) *colour* ‖ sich rot ~ *to turn red* (v *with*) **2.** (sich schminken) *to paint; rouge* **3.** (rot w) *to colour* (*up*); *to take colour*; *to blush* **4.** sich ~ l *to dye*, .. läßt sich schlecht ~ *this material dyes badly* **II.** vi **1.** dieser Farbstoff färbt rot *this pigment dyes red* **2.** (Flecke m) *tea does not stain* **Färben** n *dyeing; staining*; durch ~ veränderbar *stainable* ‖ *colouring; tinting* ‖ → Färbung **F·ärber** m ~s/~ *dyer; stainer* **~distel** f *safflower; dyer's thistle* **~dorn** m = Kreuzdorn **~eiche** f *dyer's oak* **~geselle** m *dyer's assistant* **~ginster** m *dyer's broom* **~meister** m *master-dyer* **~röte** f *madder*; → Krapp **~waid** m (*dyer's*) *woad* **~wau** *dyer's weed; weld* **Färber·ei** f ~/~en *dye-house* ‖ *dye-works* [pl] [sg konstr] **~gewerbe** n *dyeing*

f·arbig [österr ⟨a.⟩ ⩪] a **1.** *colo(u)red* (*map, shirt*); *brightly-c.d* (*clothes*); *c.d* (*postcards*); *stained* (*leather*); ~e Bänder [pl] *colours* pl; ~es Herrenhemd *fancy-shirt*; sie kleidet sich wieder ~ *she is out of mourning* ‖ *chromatic* (*character, printing*) **|** ⟨anthr⟩ *colo(u)red* (*people, race*) **|** ⟨fig⟩ *c.ful, lively* (*account of an event*) **2.** [in comp] *coloured*; viel~ *fancy* (od *many*)-*coloured* **|** **⩪keit** f *colo(u)r(fulness)* **-farbig** [österr] -⩪ [suff] lavendel~ *the colour of lavender*, → -farben **F·arbige** [der ~, ein ~r] m ~n/~n *coloured man*; ⟨Am⟩ *colored gentleman*; ⟨mod a. allg⟩ *negro*, f *negress* ‖ ~ [pl] *coloured people*; Stimmrecht der ~n *coloured suffrage*

f·arblos A. a **1.** *colo(u)rless* (*water*); *hueless*; ⟨opt⟩ *achromatic* (*lens*); ~ m *to achromatize* ‖ *colourless* (*cheeks*); *bloodless; pale, pallid, sallow* ‖ *dull monotonous* (*landscape*) **2.** ⟨fig⟩ *colo(u)rless* (*p, religion*); *neutral* (*tone*); *bloodless* (*temperament*); ~e Art *colo(u)rlessness* **B.** adv (*to sing*) *colourlessly* **⩪igkeit** f *colourlessness* ⟨a. fig⟩ ‖ ⟨opt⟩ *achromatism, achromaticity* ‖ *paleness, pallidness* **F·ärbung** f ~/~en **1.** ⟨eig⟩ = Färben, → d. ‖ *colouring; pigmentation* (*of the skin*) **2.** (Farbengebung) *colo(u)ring* (*of a picture*); *colo(u)ration* ‖ (Farbton) *hue; tone* (*this gave an agreeable tone to all he said*); leichte ~ *tint, tinge* ‖ ⟨fig⟩ Politiker [pl] verschiedener ~en .. *of various hues*

F·arce ['farsə] f [Fr] ~/~n **1.** ⟨cul⟩ (Füllsel) *force-meat, stuffing*; mit ~ füllen *to stuff* **2.** ⟨fig⟩ **a.** ⟨theat⟩ *farce* **b.** *farce, mockery, sham*; reine ~ *a mere farce* **farc·ieren** vt [h] ⟨cul⟩ *to stuff*

Far·in m ~s/, **~zucker** m *brown sugar*

F·äringer m (auf den Färöer) *Faroese* [a. pl]

F·arm f ~/~en (Übersee⩪, Fuchs⩪ etc) *farm* (auf *on the f.*); kl ~ ⟨Am⟩ *ranch* ‖ *hacienda* [Span] **|** Hühner⩪ *poultry-f.* **~arbeiter** m *f.-hand* **~besitzer** m *farmer* **~haus** n *f.-house* **F·armer** m ~s/~ *farmer* **| ~hose** f *jeans*

F·arn m ~s/~e ⟨bot⟩ *fern*; (Adler⩪) *brake, bracken* ‖ [koll] ~e [pl] *fern*; Gattung der ~e *Filices* [L pl] **⩪artig** a *f.-like; ferny; filicoid* **~dickicht** n *f.-covert* **~gewächse** n [pl] Gattung der ~ *Filicales* [L pl] **~kraut** n = Farn **|** ~pflanzung, ~schonung [f] *fernery* **~säure** f *filicic acid* **~spore(n** [pl]) f *fern-seed*; → Spore

Farn·ese [It] der Palazzo ~ *the Farnese Palace* **farn·esisch** a *Farnese* (*Bull, Gardens*)

F·aro n ~s/~s ⟨cards⟩ (Glücksspiel) *faro*

F·äröer [pl] ⟨geog⟩ *the Fa(e)roe Islands* [pl] **F·äröer** m = Färinger **f·äröisch** a *Faroese* (*word*;) *Faroish; Farish* ‖ das ⩪e *Faroese*

†**F·arre** m ~n/~n *bull* **F·ärse** f ~/~n *heifer*

Fas·an m ~s/~en ⟨orn⟩ *pheasant*; männl. ~ *cock-ph.*; weibl. ~ *hen-ph.* ‖ Amherst⩪ *Amherst's ph.*; Gold⩪ *gold(en) ph.*; Jagd⩪, Kupfer⩪ *copper ph.*; Ohr⩪ *eared ph.*; Ringhals⩪ *ring-necked ph.*; Sumpf⩪ *swamp ph.*; Argus⩪ *Argus ph.* **Fas·änchen** n ~s/~ ⟨orn⟩ *pheasant-finch* **Fas·anen-** [in comp] *pheasant* .. **~braten** m *roast ph.* °**~friedhof** m *fair round belly with good capon lin'd* (Shak) **~gehege** n *ph.ry* **~jagd** f *ph.-shooting* **~küken** n *ph.-chick* **~meister**, **~wärter** m *ph.-keeper* **~zucht** f *ph.-rearing* °**fas·anenhaft** a = *famos* **Fasaner·ie** f ~/–n *pheasantry*

F·äschen [fæsçən] n *small bevel*; → Fase[3]

Fasch·ier- ~maschine f [österr] *mincing machine* **| ⩪en** vt [h] ⟨cul⟩ = hacken **| ~tes** n = Gehacktes ⩪ Laibchen *small meat ball*

Fasch·ine f ~/~n *fascine, hurdle*; [mst pl] ~n *fascines, faggots* [pl] **~nmesser** n *bill, riphook*

F·asching m ~s/~e *carnival, Shrovetide*; → Fastnacht **~skind** n *chance child* **~streiben** n *carnivaling* **~szeit** f *Shrovetide*

Fasch·ismus m ~/ [It] ⟨pol⟩ *Fascism*(o It) **Fasch·ist** m ~en/~en [It] ⟨pol⟩ *Fascist*; ~en [pl] *Fascisti* [It pl] **Fasch·isten-** *Fascist* (*leader*) **fasch·istisch** a *Fascist*, ~ m *to fascistize*

Fasch·oda n (Ort im Sudan) *Fashoda*

×**F·ase**[1] f ~/~n = Faser ‖ ~[2] ⟨arch⟩ *fillet*

F·ase[3] f ~/~n (Schrägkante) *bevel, chamfer*

†**F·asel**[1] f ~/~n = Faser, → Fase[1]

†**F·asel**[2] m ~s/~ *cub, whelp* ‖ (T) (Zucht) *breed; stock; strain; young* [pl] **~hengst** m *stallion* **~ochs** m *bull* **~schwein** n *pig for breeding*

F·asel[3] f ~/~n ⟨bot⟩ *bean*

Fasel·ei f (→ faseln[2]) ~/~en *drivel; drivel(ling) effusion; raving; twaddle* ⟨Am⟩ *flubdub*; → Quatsch, Geschwätz ‖ *flightiness* **F·aseler**, °**Faselhans** m *driveller; dodderer; drivelling fool; scatter-brain* ***f·aselhaft** a = **f·aselig** a *drivelling; doddery; idiotic, silly; scatterbrained* ‖ *flighty*

†**f·aseln**[1] vi/refl [h] ~, sich ~ *to breed, propagate*

f·aseln[2] **1.** vi [h] *to drivel, ramble* (über *about, of*); *dodder; talk rot* (od *moonshine*); *twaddle*; ⟨Am sl⟩ *to chew the rag, to chin* ‖ ⟨path⟩ *to speak incoherently; to be wandering; to rave* ‖ (of old people) *to dote* **2.** ⩪ n *drivel; twaddle*

Fase·ole f ⟨bot⟩ = Fasel[3]

F·aser f ~/~n **1.** ⟨bes anat⟩ *fibre*, ⟨Am⟩ *fiber*; synthetische ~n [pl] (Nylon, Perlon etc) *fibre; filament; threadlike body; thread*; feine ~ *film filament*; feinste ~ *fibril* ‖ Bindegewebs⩪n [pl] *fibrous tissue*; B. bilden *to fibrose*; Wurzel⩪ *root-filament; rootlet* ‖ ⟨bot⟩ mit Büscheln v langen ~n bedeckt *stupose* ‖ (in beans) *string*; Gefäß⩪ *vascular string* ‖ (etw) in ~n ausziehen *to unravel; to ravel out* ‖ sich in ~n auflösen *to fuzz* (*out*) **2.** (in wood, etc.) *grain*; in der Richtung der ~, parallel zur ~ *with the grain* **3.** ⟨fig⟩ er hing mit jeder ~ (*or* mit allen ~n) s–s Herzens an dem Werk *he gave his whole heart to the work* ‖ bis in alle ~n ein K. *an artist in his every fibre* **4.** [in comp] *fibre* ..; ⟨scient⟩ *fibro-* **⩪ähnlich**, **⩪artig** a *fibrilliform; fibroid; threadlike* **~bildung** f = Faserung **~bündel** n *bundle of raw fibre* **⩪förmig** a *fibriform* **⩪frei** a *fluffless* (*paper*) **~gerüst** n ⟨biol⟩ *stroma of fibres* **~geschwulst** f ⟨path⟩ *fibrous* (od *fibroid*) *tumour; fibroma* [L]; *fibroid* **~gewebe** n *fibrous tissue* **~holz** n ⟨pap⟩ *pulp-wood* **~korb** m ⟨anat⟩ (of the retina) *fibrebasket* **~masse** f *fibrillation* **⩪nackt** a *without a stitch of clothing* **~pflanze** f *fibre-plant* **~ring** m *fibrous circle* (od *ring)* **~schicht** f *(layer of) fibres* [pl] ‖ ⟨anat⟩ Längs≈ des Dickdarms *taenia* [L] **~schutzmittel** n ⟨tech⟩ *fibre protective agent* **~stoff** m *fibrous material* od *stuff* ‖ ⟨chem⟩ Blut≈ *fibrin* ‖ ~e [pl] *artificial fabrics* **~struktur** f = Faserung **F·äserchen** n ~s/~ *fibril; filament*

f·aserig a *fibrillate(d); fibrous, filamentous, filamentary; fuzzy; thready;* fein~ *finely fibred; fibrillar(y);* ~e Beschaffenheit *fibrousness* ‖ ~ w (of liquids) *to string*

f·asern I. vt/i [h] **1.** vt *to unravel;* (Wolle, Flachs) → krumpeln, hecheln ‖ (mit Fasern versehen) (Papier) *to mottle* **| sich ~** = fasern vi **2.** vi *to form fibres; to ravel; fray, frazzle; fuzz* **II.** ≈ n *mottling (of paper)* ‖ *fraying; ravelling*

F·aserung f *fibrillation, fibering* ‖ (in wood, etc) *grain; mottling;* ⟨a.⟩ Faser- ~bildung

F·asler m = Faselhans

Fas·ole f ~/~n Sw *bean*

F·aß n F·asses/F·ässer **A. 1.** *barrel* (Bier≈ *beer-barrel;* Herings≈ *herring-b.*) ‖ *cask; tub;* Butter≈ *butter-tub;* Regen≈ *rain-watertub;* Wasch≈ *wash-tub* ‖ → Mehl≈, Salz≈, Tinten≈; Weihrauch≈ ‖ gr ~ *hogshead, tun (the Great Tun of Heidelberg), vat* ‖ kl ~ *keg; kit* **2.** ⟨com⟩ (~inhalt; ~maß) ein ~ (zwei ~) Heringe, Schweinefleisch *a barrel (two barrels) of herrings, pork;* ein ~ Butter *a cask of butter* **|** (Stück Bier, Wein) *piece;* ein ~ Bier *(9, 18, 36 gallons* = 40,8; 80,72; 161,44 l) *a barrel of beer;* zwei ~ Bier *two barrels of b.;* kl ~ B. (40,8 l) *firkin* od *kilderkin of beer* ‖ ein ~ Whisky *a cask of whisky* ‖ gr ~ Wein *butt* (od *pipe*) *of wine (105 gallons);* → Oxhoft **3. Wendungen:** ein frisches ~ *a fresh tap* ‖ Bier (frisch) vom ~ *draught-beer, beer on draught* ‖ Wein (frisch) vom ~ *wine from the wood* ‖ auf *or* in Fässer füllen *to barrel* (in F. gefüllt *barrelled*); *to tun* ‖ in e–m ~ aufbewahren, behandeln *to vat* ‖ in ein ~ tun *to tub;* → Daube ‖ der Wein schmeckt nach (dem) ~ *the wine tastes of the cask* ‖ ⟨fig⟩ das bringt das ~ ins Rollen *that starts the matter moving;* das schlägt dem ~ den Boden aus! ⟨hum⟩ .. dem ~ die Krone ins Gesicht! *that's the limit, that puts the lid on (it); that beats everything* (od *the band*)! ‖ *that's enough to take the tiles off,* ⟨Am⟩ *that's the pay-off* ‖ °er säuft wie ein ~ *he drinks like a fish;* du ~! *you pot-belly!* **~bauch** m *bilge* **≈beinig** a ⟨hors⟩ *bow-legged* **~bier** n *draught-beer* **~binder, ~bender** m *cooper, hooper; barrel-maker;* ⟨fig⟩ wie ein ~ *(to run) like a lamp-lighter* **~boden** m *bottom* ‖ ≈ [pl] *barrel-heads* **~butter** f *barrel* (od *tub*)*-butter* **~daube** f *stave, lag;* → Daube **≈förmig** a *barrel-like, barrel-shaped* **~hahn** m *tap* **~konsum** m *barrelage* **~pumpe** f *barrel-pump* **≈reif** a *vatted (wine)* **~reifen** m *hoop* **~rumpf** m = Faßbauch **~schnecke** f ⟨zoo⟩ *tun-shell; Dolium* [L] **~wein** *wine from the wood* **≈weise** *by the barrel*

Fass·ade f ~/~n ⟨arch⟩ *exterior, facade* ⟨a. fig⟩; *front;* die ~ e–s Hauses erneuern *to reface a building* ‖ ⟨fig⟩ bei ihm ist alles ~ *he puts up a big front;* sein Wissen ist ~ *he puts* od *has all his knowledge in the window* **|** ~nkletterer [m] *cat burglar;* ⟨Am⟩ *porch-climber* ‖ ~nklettern [n] *scaling walls*

f·aßbar a ⟨fig⟩ *comprehensible* ‖ schwer ~, nicht ~ *elusive (character)* ‖ geistig nicht ~ *impalpable*

F·äßchen n ~s/~ *small cask* (od *barrel, tub*); *keg, kit;* → Salz≈ ‖ (als Maß f Bier) *firkin, kilderkin,* ein ~ Bier *a firkin of beer;* → Faß

f·assen vt/i [h] **I. vt A.** (in ein Faß *or* e–n Behälter tun) **1.** *to barrel, tun (beer); to sack (corn)* **2.** ⟨mil⟩ sein Essen (etc) ~ *to collect one's food (in the mess-traps);* s–e Löhnung ~ *to bag* (od *pocket*) *one's pay* **3.** ⟨**übtr**⟩ (in sich aufnehmen können) **a.** (of vessels, etc) *to contain,* der Raum kann 80 Pn ~ .. *can accomodate ..;* .. kann nicht alle m–e Sachen ~ .. *cannot contain all my things;* das Zelt konnte 1000 Leute ~ *the tent could seat 1000 people* **b. in sich** ~ *to comprehend, include;* → einschließen B. 2. b.; einschließend; umfassen **c.** (of the mind) *to apprehend, comprehend, grasp, understand* **d. (Sinn)** *to catch, grasp, grip, take, understand; I do not catch the meaning* = *the sense eludes me;* ich kann das nicht ~ *that beats me, it baffles me, it is beyond me* ‖ er kann (den Verlust s–r Frau) nicht ~ *he cannot (get reconciled* od) *reconcile himself to ..* ‖ → auffassen **4. (einfassen) a.** (Edelstein, Linse) *to mount, set;* (Stein) *to embed* (in *in*); Diamanten in Gold gefaßt *diamonds enchased* od *set in gold* ‖ ein Bild in e–n Rahmen ~ *to frame a picture* ‖ → einfassen **b.** ⟨**übtr**⟩ (Gedanken etc) *to clothe, couch* (in *in*); *to express* (in *in*); (Eindrücke) in Worte ~ *to put into words* ‖ sauber in e–e Formel ~ *to package neatly in a f.* ‖ etw kz ~ *to compress, to condense;* → zus–~ **c.** ⟨fig⟩ etw ins Auge ~ → Auge I. C. 3. d. **B. (ergreifen,** packen) **1. (etw)** *to catch* (od *get, lay, seize*) *hold of (a th); to grasp at (a th);* krampfhaft ~ *to clutch; to clutch at (a th)* ‖ er bekam mit der Hand ein Licht z ~ *his hand closed on a candle* **2. (jdn) a.** (Dieb etc) *to apprehend, arrest, catch, get, seize;* ⟨sl⟩ *to snaffle, nick* ‖ z ~ suchen *to hunt down* ‖ (Flüchtling) *to run down, to run to earth;* → erwischen ‖ jdn am Arm ~ *to catch a p by the arm;* jdn bei der Hand ~ *to seize a p's hand* od *a p by the hand* ‖ jdn beim (*or* am) Kragen ~ *to catch a p by the collar of his coat* **b.** ⟨**übtr**⟩ jdn bei der Ehre ~ *to appeal to a p's honour;* jdn beim Wort ~ *to take a p at his word* **c.** ⟨fig⟩ (of feelings, etc.) ihn faßte Entsetzen *fear gripped his heart* **3.** ⟨fig⟩ (P & S) (festen) Fuß ~ *to gain* (od *get, obtain*) *a footing* (in in) ‖ e–e S an der Wurzel ~ *to strike at the root of a th;* W. ~ *to root; to take root* (in *in*) ‖ *the brake does not grip the wheel* **C. (vorbereiten)** ⟨mst fig⟩ e–n Beschluß ~ *to pass a resolution;* e–n Vorsatz ~ *to conceive a purpose; to form* od *frame a plan;* den Plan ~ *to plan* od *scheme (to do)* ‖ *to conceive* (od *form*) *an idea* ‖ *to conceive an affection for (a p)* **|** Mut ~, sich [dat] ein Herz ~ *to take* (od *pluck up*) *courage* **D. sich ~ 1.** er faßte sich an den Kopf, die Stirn *his hand went to his head; he felt his forehead* **2.** ⟨**übtr**⟩ sich kz ~ *to cut a long story short; to be brief* (od *short*) ‖ fasse dich kz! *make it short (and sweet)!* **3.** ⟨fig⟩ **a.** sich ~ *to collect* (od *compose, recover*) *o.s.* ‖ sich in Geduld ~ *to possess one's soul in patience* **b.** → gefaßt ‖ ~ Sie sich! *master yourself!* **4.** sich ~ l **a.** *to get caught; to allow o.s. to be caught* **b.** ⟨übtr⟩ sich nicht in Worte ~ l *to be inexpressible in words; to elude expression in words* **c.** *to be grasped* (od *understood*); *to be understandable;* sich nicht ~ l *to elude understanding* **II. vi 1.** ~ **nach** *to grasp at;* krampfhaft ~ nach *to (make a) clutch at (a th)* ‖ er faßte mit den Händen um .. *he gripped his hands round ..;* er faßte mit der Hand an ihren Kopf *he felt* (od *touched*) *her head* **2.** ⟨**übtr**⟩ (S) *to bite; catch (the anchor will not bite)* ‖ ⟨fig⟩ → packen **3.** ⟨fig⟩ **er faßt leicht** *he is quick of apprehension* od *perception* (od *at learning*); er faßt schwer *he is slow in the uptake, .. of wit(s)* (od *in learning*) **F·assen** n **1.** *apprehension; grasping;* die Hand dient zum ~ *the hand is for apprehension* ‖ ⟨mil⟩ *collection (of wages,* etc.) **2.** *apprehension, arrest, catching, seizure (of a thief)* **3.** (geistiges ~) *apprehension, comprehension, grasp(ing); understanding* **4.** (Einfassen) *mounting, setting* ‖ *clothing, couching (of thoughts)* **5.** ⟨fig⟩ *passing (of a resolution); conception (of* *an idea)* → Fassung **f·aßlich** a *comprehensible, conceivable; intelligible; understandable* (f .. *to a p)* | **≗keit** f ~/ *comprehensibility, conceivability*

Fass·on [fa'sõ] n (Mantel-, Jackenaufschlag) *revers, lapel*

Fass·on [fa'sõ] f [Fr] ~/~s *cut, form, shape; style*; aus der ~ k (of hat etc) *to get out of shape*; der Hut war ganz außer ~ *the hat had precious little shape left in it* | ⟨übtr⟩ *fashion, mode, way* ‖ du kannst nach d–r ~ selig w! *go as you please*! **~draht** m *section wire; special wire* **~eisen** n *section iron* **~rum** m *artificial* (od *imitation) rum* **~schnitt** m *special hair cut* **~strümpfe** m pl *fully fashioned stockings* ⟨fam⟩ *three-Ds, 3-Ds* pl

fasson·ieren vt (formen) *to form, shape, profile* ‖ (Tuch) *to figure* **fasson·iert** a *special (wire)* ‖ *figured; fancy (goods)*; → Fasson-

F·assung f ~/~en **A.** [abstr] [nur sg] **1.** = Fassen **2.** ⟨fig⟩ (innere ~) *composure, peace of mind; aplomb, countenance; selfpossession* | die ~ bewahren *to keep one's countenance* (od *head)* ‖ die ~ verlieren *to blench; to go off the deep end; to lose one's aplomb*; (vor Wut) *to see red* ‖ die ~ wiedergewinnen *to recover one's aplomb* ‖ jdn aus der ~ bringen *to put a p out of countenance; to baffle* (od *discomfit, disconcert, shake) a p; to bowl a p over; to put a p out*; ⟨fam⟩ *to rattle a p*; ⟨Am sl⟩ *to get a p down* ‖ aus der ~ k *or* geraten *to be disconcerted* (od *put out)*, → die ~ verlieren ‖ außer ~ s *to be upset, embarrassed* (über *at)*; → ≗slos **B.** [konkr] **1.** (of stones, jewels) *mount(ing), setting; frame* ‖ ⟨el⟩ *(lamp) holder* od *socket*: *to mount a l. in a s.* **2.** ⟨übtr⟩ (of words, thoughts) *clothing, wording; draft* ‖ *rendering, version (of a play); edition*; veränderte ~ ⟨arts⟩ *variation* ‖ in dieser ~ ist der Text irreführend *the text is misleading as it stands*; l wir ihm e–e neue ~ geben *let's rephrase it*

F·assungs- ~gabe f *(gift of) perception* **~kraft** f *capacity; power of comprehension* (od *perception); comprehensive* (od *perceptive) faculty; grasp* ‖ v gr ~ *of great capacity, of wide grasp* ‖ jds ~ übersteigen *to be beyond a p's comprehension* **≗los** a *discomfited, disconcerted; bewildered, nonplussed; staggered* **~losigkeit** f *bewilderment; discomfit* **~vermögen** n = Fassungskraft ‖ ⟨theat⟩ *(seating) capacity* ‖ (Film≗) *footage capacity*

fast adv **I. 1.** vor Zahlen u Maß-, Zeitangaben mst *nearly; close* (od *near) upon*; ~ 20 *nearly* (od *close upon; little less than) twenty*; ~ 10 Uhr *nearly* (od *about) 10 o'clock* | [bei Verben mst] *nearly (she was nearly fainting; he was n. killed)* ‖ *all but (he all but refused it)* ‖ ich wurde ~ überfahren *I just missed being run over* ‖ jdm v etwas ~ nichts (übrig) l *to leave a p very nearly shorn of a th* ‖ → beinahe **2. a.** [vor Adj., Subst. mst] *almost; well-nigh*; ⟨Am a.⟩ *most*; sie waren ~ Bettler *they were well-nigh beggars* ‖ ~ alle (P) *almost to a man* ‖ ~ die meisten klebrigen Flüssigkeiten *all but (the) most viscous liquids* ‖ ~ betrunken *three parts drunk* ‖ ~ unfruchtbar *semi--barren* ‖ ~ ganz besetzt *about full* | ⟨Am⟩ *almost, most; near*; ~ ein Heiliger *a near-saint*; ~ e–e Knappheit *a near shortage*; ~ nackt *near-nude* **b.** ~ (genau) derselbe Geist *almost* (od *much) the same spirit*; ~ jeder *almost* (⟨Am a.⟩ *most) everyone* | [neg] ~ niemand *scarcely anyone*, ⟨Am⟩ *almost no one* ‖ ~ nichts *scarcely anything; next to nothing*; ⟨Am⟩ *almost nothing* ‖ ~ keine Straßen *scarcely any roads*; ⟨Am⟩ *almost no roads* **3.** [vor Adv.] *nearly; almost*; ~ immer *nearly always*; die Kost ist ~ i. die gleiche *the diet varies little*; wir waren ~ dort *we were nearly there*; ~ ebensooft *almost as often*; ~ sicher *almost certainly* ‖ ~ nie(mals) *scarcely ever; as good as never*; ⟨Am⟩ *almost never* **II.** × = sehr

Fast·age [fa'sta:ʒ] f [Fr] = Fustage

F·ast- ~ebene [f] ⟨geol⟩ *peneplain* ‖ ~erfolg [m] *near hit*

F·astelabend m = Fastenabend

f·asten 1. vi [h] *to fast; not to eat anything (for a whole week)* ‖ ⟨ec⟩ *to keep Lent* **2.** ≗ n *fast, fasting* ‖ *abstinence* **F·asten** [pl] (v † Faste f) (~zeit) *fast, fasting*; ⟨ec⟩ *Lent* **~abend** m *Shrove Tuesday; Pancake Day* **~brezel** f *Lenten cracknel*; vgl. *hot-cross-bun* **~brief** m *Lenten pastoral* **~predigt** f *Lenten sermon* **~sonntag** m *Sunday in Lent* **~speise** f *Lenten diet*, od *fare* **~tag** m *fast-(ing)-day* **~tuch** n *Lenten veil* **~vorstellung** f *Lenten performance* **~zeit** f *Lent, Shrovetide*

F·astnacht f **1.** *Shrove-Tuesday; Pancake Day* **2.** *Shrovetide; carnival*; → Fasching **~sdienstag** m *Shrove-Tuesday* **~scherz** m *carnival joke* **~s-spiel** n ⟨hist, Ger, Lit⟩ *Shrovetide play*

F·aszie f ~/~n ⟨arch & anat⟩ *fascia* [L]

Fasz·ikel m ~s/~ *fascicle*

Faszinati·on [*ts*] f *fascination* **faszin·ieren** vt [h] (jdn) *to fascinate; bewitch, enchant, enthrall; mesmerize* ‖ ~d *fascinating, enthralling*

fat·al a *annoying, awkward, disagreeable, dreadful; bad, nasty, nice* ‖ e–e ~e Situation *a nasty* (od *nice) situation*; es ist sehr ~ *it's a great nuisance*; wie ~! *bother*! es ist mir sehr ~, daß *it gets my goat that* .. | *(verhängnisvoll) *fatal (blunder); mischievous* **Fatal·ismus** m ~/ *fatalism* **Fatal·ist** m ~en/~en *fatalist; gambler (she was a g.)* **fatal·istisch 1.** a *fatalistic, fatalist* **2.** adv *fatalistically* **Fatalit·ät** f ~/~en *misfortune, mischance* **F·atum** n [L] ~s/–ta *fate; destiny*

°**F·atzke** m ~n/~n ⟨a.⟩ °Patent≗ *dandy, fop(ling), popinjay, prig* ‖ kl. ~ *mild bloater*

f·auchen vi [h] (of cat) *to spit*; (of tiger) *to swear* ‖ ⟨übtr⟩ (of an engine) *to puff; buzz, swear, whizz* ‖ (of the wind) *to blow* ‖ → an~

faul I. a **A. 1.** ⟨eig⟩ **a.** *bad, decayed, putrid; rotten (apple, egg); unsound (fish)* ‖ *unsound (fruit); decaying; rotted (leaves); rotten, unsound (timber)* ‖ *foul; stagnant (water); stale (air)*; → verfault **b.** *bad, foul (smell); nasty; offensive* **c.** ⟨min⟩ *slippery (lode); rotten (gallery)* ‖ *brittle, crumbling (rock); short (metal)* **d.** ~ riechen (schmecken) *to smell (to taste) rotten* (od *putrid)* | ~ **w** *to become rotten; to rot; to decay*; (Ei) *to addle* **2.** ⟨übtr⟩ (schlecht) *bad (debt, debtor, customer); rotten, unsound* ‖ ⟨com⟩ *bad; untrustworthy (shares, etc); fishy, shady (transaction); unreliable; worthless (bill); rubber* [attr] *(check)* ‖ ⟨sl⟩ *dicky* ‖ ~e Fische, ~e Ausreden *or* Redensarten *lame excuses, empty words; subterfuges* [pl]; *yarn*; → Ausrede ‖ *treacherous (peace)* ‖ fauler Kopf *addlehead* (od *pate); bad hat* (od *egg); windbag* ‖ e–e ~e S *a fishy matter*; die S steht ~ (*or* es steht ~ damit) *it looks bad, matters look bad* ‖ ~er Witz *a stale* (od *bad, poor)* ⟨sl⟩ *corny joke*; ~e Witze [pl] *nonsense, rubbish*, ⟨sl⟩ *bosh*; ~e W. m ⟨sl⟩ *to talk rot* ‖ °~er Zauber *humbug*; ⟨sl⟩ *bosh, rot* **3.** ⟨fig⟩ (verderbt) *corrupt, decayed (civilization); putrid, rotten (system); rotting, maggot-eaten (society)*; etw ist ~ im Staate Dänemark *something is rotten in the State of Denmark* (Shak., Hamlet I, 4) ‖ ~ w *to decay, deteriorate*; ~ m *to corrupt* **B.** (träge) **1.** *idle, indolent, lazy, slothful, sluggish, torpid, truant*; stinkend ~ *disgustingly idle*; °~e Bäuche [pl] *slow-bellies* pl ‖ sich auf die ~e Seite legen, auf der ~en Haut liegen *to spend one's time in idleness, to indulge in idleness, to idle* (od *lounge) away one's time* **2.** nicht ~ *quickly; suddenly; with a jack*; er, nicht ~, schlug um sich *quickly he laid about him*; ich, nicht ~, fragte ihn . . ⟨fam⟩ *I up and asked him* . . **3.** ~e See *dead calm* **II.** adv es steht ~ mit ihm, (es sieht ~ aus für ihn) *things look bad with (for) him* **F·aul- ~baum** m ⟨bot⟩ *black alder, alder buckthorn* ‖ = Traubenkirsche || ~rinde [f] *black alder-tree bark* **~bett** n ⟨fig⟩ sich aufs ~ legen *to indulge* **~-bruch** m ⟨met⟩ *brittle* (od *short*) *metal in idleness* **≗brüchig** a *brittle, short* **~brüchigkeit** f ⟨met⟩ *shortness, brittleness* **~brut** f (of bees) *foul brood* **~fieber** n ⟨fig⟩ *fit of idleness* **~gärung** f *alkalescency* **~hütte** f ⟨pap⟩ *fermenting trough* °**~pelz** m ⟨fig⟩ *idler, lounger, slug, sluggard, slow-coach*; ⟨fam⟩ *lazy-bones* [pl] [sg konstr]; → Faulenzer **~schlamm** m ⟨geol⟩ *sapropel*; gallertartiger ~ *saprocol* | ~gas [n] *sewer-gas*; Vorrichtung z Verhinderung des Aufstiegs v -gasen *trap* || ~-gestein [n] *sapropel rock* **~tier** n ⟨zoo⟩ *sloth*; dreizehiges ~ *aï* || Riesen≗ *megatherium, mylodon* || °⟨fig (P) hum⟩ = Faulpelz **F·äule** f **1.** *decay, decaying*; *rot*; → Fäulnis || → Edel≗, Trocken≗ **2.** ⟨vet⟩ (of sheep) *the rot* **f·aulen 1.** vi [s] *to decay*; *to become decomposed*; *to putrefy, rot* **2.** ≗ n *decay(ing), rotting*; → Fäule || zum ~ bringen *to rot*; *corrupt* **f·äulen** vt [h] ⟨tech⟩ (Lumpen) *to macerate* (od *to soak*) *by fermentation*; *to ferment* **f·aulend** a *putrescent*; *septic* || *decaying* **f·aulenzen 1.** vi [h] *to idle, to indulge in idleness*; *to laze*; *to be lazy*; *to lounge*; *drone*; *to take it easy* || ⟨sl & fam⟩ *to mike, mooch*; *to moon* (od *muck*) *about*; *to slack*; *slug* **2.** ≗ n *idling, lounging*; *idleness, laziness* **F·aulenzer** m ~s/~ **1.** (P) *idler, loaf(er), lounger*, ⟨sl⟩ *lounge-lizard*, ⟨fam⟩ *slacker*; ⟨Am⟩ *poke*; → Faulpelz **2.** (S) *lounge* (od *easy*)-*chair* **Faulenzer·ei** f = Faulenzen **F·aulheit** f ~/ **1.** *badness, rottenness, unsoundness*; *shadiness* (*of a th*) **2.** mst (= Trägheit) *idleness, laziness, sloth, sluggishness* **f·aulig,** † **f·aulicht** a *putrid, rotten*; *somewhat rotten* **F·äulnis** f ~/**1.** *decay, decomposition, putrefaction, putridness, putridity, rot, rottenness*; stinkende ~ *putrescence* || in ~ übergehen *to rot, putrefy* | ⟨fig⟩ *corruption, gangrene, putrefaction, rottenness* **2.** [in comp] *putrefacient*; *putrefactive* (*bacteria*); *putrescent*; *sapro–* || ⟨übtr⟩ *gangrenous* **≗erregend** a *putrefacient, putrefactive, saprogenic, saprogenous, septic* **~erreger** m *putrefactive agent*; *germ of decomposition* **≗hindernd** a ⟨med⟩ *antiseptic, aseptic* **~pflanze** *f saprophyte* **~produkt** n *decomposition product* **~prozeß** m *decomposition, putrefaction*

ˣ**Faum** m ~(e)s/≗e = Schaum *foam*

Faun m ~s/~e ⟨myth⟩ *faun*; *Satyr* || ⟨fig⟩ *lascivious fellow* **~affe** m ⟨zoo⟩ → Rollschwanz-

F·auna f L ~/–nen *fauna* [pl] *–nae*, ~s L; mit e–r reichen ~ *rich faunaed* **f·aunisch** a *lascivious*

Faust f ~/≗e **1.** *fist*, ⟨fam⟩ *bunch of fives*, ⟨Am sl⟩ *mitten* **2.** Wendungen: ⟨fig⟩ die eiserne ~ *the mailed fist, iron hand* || die ~ ballen *to clench one's fist*; ⟨fig⟩ die ~ geballt in der Tasche haltend *with an iron hand in a velvet glove* || e–e ~ m *to make a fist*; jdm e–e ~ m *to shake one's fist at a p* || wie die ~ aufs Auge passen *to clash* (od *jar*); er paßt für die Aufgabe wie die ~ aufs Auge *he is like a square peg in a round hole* | auf eigene ~ *off* (od *on*) *one's own bat, on one's own hook*; *on one's own* || jdm mit der ~ drohen *to shake one's fist at a p* || mit den ≗en losschlagen auf . . *to pound at . . with the fists* || (jdn) mit der ~ schlagen *to punch* || mit der ~ auf den Tisch schlagen *to bring one's fist down on the table, to bang one's fist upon the t.*; ⟨fig⟩ *to put one's foot down* **~ball** m ⟨Ger sport⟩ *faustball*; ⟨Ger a-engl⟩ *fist-ball* **≗d·ick 1.** [a] *big* od *thick as a fist* || er hat es ~ hinter den Ohren *he looks as if butter would not melt in his mouth*; *he is a trick(s)y fellow* **2.** [adv] ~ lügen *to lie in one's throat* **~-größe** f *fist size* **~hammer** m *locksmith's hammer* || *battle-h.*; *martel* **~handschuh** m *mitten, mitt, muffler* **~huhn** n ⟨orn⟩ *three-toed sand-grouse* **~kampf** m *pugilistic encounter* (od *match*); *bout with the gloves*; *boxing, boxing-match*; *fisticuffs* [pl] || [abstr] *pugilism* **~kämpfer** m *pugilist*; *boxer*; *prize-fighter*; ⟨Am sl⟩ *pug* **~keil** ⟨a. praeh⟩ *mallet* **~leier** f = Brustleier **~pfand** n ⟨jur⟩ *pledge, pawn* **~recht** n *fist* (od *club*)-*law*; *law of the jungle* **~regel** f *thumb-rule, r. of th.* **~-riemen** m (Portepee) *sword-knot* **~schlag** m *punch*; *cuff* (od *blow*) *with the fist*; ~ ins Gesicht *slap in the face*, ⟨Am⟩ *punch in the nose*; –schläge [pl] *fisticuffs* pl **~skizze** f *rough sketch* **~treiber** m *hoop* (od *hand*) *driver* **~verbesserung** f ⟨artill⟩ *flat correction* **F·äustchen** n ⟨fig⟩ [nur in]: sich ins ~ lachen *to laugh* od *chuckle in* (od *up*) *one's* (*roguish*) *sleeve*; *to be gloating*; *to thrust one's tongue in one's cheek*; *to gloat* (über *over, on*); *to snicker, snigger* (*at*) **F·äustel** m ~s/~ ⟨min⟩ *hammer* || = Faustkeil **f·austen** vt [h] ⟨sport⟩ (Ball) *to blow . . with the fist* **f·austisch** a *Faustian* **F·äustling** m = Fausthandschuh

Faut·euil [fo'tœ:j] m (Fr) ~s/~s *fauteuil*

Fautfracht f ⟨mar⟩ *dead freight*

Fauxpas [fo:'pɑ:] m ~/~ Fr *blunder, gaffe*; *faux pas* Fr || e–n ~ begehen *or* m *to blunder, to make a f. p.*; ⟨fam⟩ *to put one's foot in(to) it*

favoris·ieren vt [h] *to favour*, ⟨Am⟩ *favor*

Favor·it m ~en/~en *favourite*, ⟨Am⟩ *favorite* ⟨a. sport⟩; haushoher ~ (*a*) *hundred-to-one shot* | **~in** f ~/~nen *favo(u)rite* **~entum** n ~s/ *favo(u)ritism*

Fax m ~/~en *servant of students' corporation*

F·axe m ~/~n [mst pl] ~n *silly pranks* (od *tricks*) pl; *foolery, –ries* [pl]; *tricksy turns* [pl] || ~n m *to* (*play the*) *fool* || laß d–e ~n *stop your fooling* || mach k–e ~n *don't make a fuss* || jdm ~n vormachen *to befool* (od *dupe, fool*) *a p*; *to make a fool of a p*; → düpieren || sich ~n vormachen l *to be fooled* (etc.)

Fay·ence [fa'jɑ̃s] f (Fr) *faience*; *glazed earthenware and porcelain*; [attr] *faience* (*chandelier*)

F·azies [–*ies*] f ~/~ ⟨geol & scient⟩ *facies* (L)

F·azit n ~s/ *result, upshot*; *sum total*; *total* || das ~ ziehen *to sum up*

febr·il a ⟨med⟩ *febrile, feverish*

F·ebruar m, (ˣ**Feber** [österr] ~s/~) ~s/~e *February*; im ~ *in F.*

†**f·echsen** vt [h] = einernten **F·echser** m ~s/~ *cutting, slip* (*of vine-plants*, etc.)

F·echt- mst *fencing* **~bahn** f *f.-ground* **~boden** m *f.-room* (od *hall*) °**~bruder** m *loafer, tramp, vagrant*; *beggar* **~handschuh** m *f.-glove* **~-hieb** m *cut* **~jacke** f *f.-jacket, padded j.* **~klub** m *f.-club*; *Epée Club* **~kunst** f *fence*; (*art of*) *fencing*; *sword-play, swordsmanship* **~maske** f *mask* **~meister** m *f.-master* **~platz** m = Fechtbahn **~saal** m *f.-hall* (od *room*) **~schule** f ⟨hist⟩ *school of fence* || *fencing-school* **~sport** m *f.* **~stock** m *singlestick* **~stunde** f *f.-lesson* **~übung** f *practice with foils* **~-unterricht** m *f.-lessons* [pl] **~waffe** f *f.-weapon*; *rapier*; *small-sword*; *épée, foil* **f·echten I.** vi/t [h] [focht/gefochten] **A.** vi **1. a.** *to fight* (gegen *against*, mit *with*); ~de Truppe *combat* (od ⟨fam⟩ *teeth*) *arm* || ⟨übtr⟩ → kämpfen **b.** (kunstgerecht) *to fence* **c.** mit den Händen *or* Armen in der Luft ~ *to fidget with the hands, to wave one's arms, to gesticulate*; *to saw the air*; → fuchteln **2.** (betteln) *to beg from door to door*; *to beg one's way*; *to go begging*, ⟨fam⟩ *to panhandle* **B.** vt e–n Gang ~ *to fight a round*; *to take a bout of fencing* || Säbel ~ *to fence with a sabre*; *to take a bout with the sabre* (od *a bout of sabre-fencing*) **II.** ≗ n **1.** *fighting* || (kunstgerechtes ~) *fence, fencing*; *swordsmanship, sword-play* || Degen≗ *épée-fencing*; *foil-fencing* (od *–play*); Rapier≗ *rapier-f.*; Säbel≗ *sabre-f., sword-play* **2.** *begging* **F·echter** m ~s/~ *fighter* || *fencer*; *swordsman*; Degen-≗ *épée-fencer*; *épé(e)ist*; *foilist* **~abstand** m *distance between the fencers* **~sprung** m *take-off* (*with one leg*) **~stellung** f *guard*; *position in fencing*; → Auslage **~welle** f ⟨gym⟩ = Kniewelle

F·ecker m ~s/~ Sw *measure* od *milk tester*

F·eder f ~/~n **A.** (of birds) **1. a.** *feather*; *quill*, *quill-feather*; gr *or* lange ~ *plume*; ~n [pl] *feathers*; *plumes* [pl], *plumage* ‖ Deck~̽n [pl] *coverts* [pl]; Schwanz~̽ *tail-feather*; Schwung~̽ *flight* (od *wing*) *-feather*, *pinion* **b.** ⟨übtr⟩ ~n [pl] = Bett **c. Wendungen**: mit ~n bedecken *or* schmücken *to feather*, *plume*; sich mit fremden ~n schmücken *to deck o.s. with borrowed plumes*; *to plume o.s.* ‖ °jdn aus den ~n holen *to rouse a p from his bed*; noch in den ~n liegen *to be still between the sheets*, . . *still in bed* | ~n l (of birds) → federn ‖ ⟨fig⟩ *to be plucked* (od *robbed*; *to be beaten*, *to lose*; *to suffer*) **c.** (Pfeil~̽) *feather*; (Pfeil) mit ~n versehen *to feather* **2.** (Schreib~̽) **a.** *quill(-feather)*; *(quill-)pen* ‖ ⟨übtr⟩ (Stahl~̽) *pen*; → Füll~̽ | e–n Brief in die ~ diktieren *to dictate a letter* ‖ die ~ ansetzen *to put pen to paper* ‖ zur ~ greifen *to take pen in hand*, *to take up one's pen* ‖ solange die ~ in s–r Hand ist . . *so long as his pen is on the paper* . . **b.** ⟨übtr⟩ e–e gewandte ~ *a fluent pen*; e–e scharfe ~ führen *to wield a formidable pen* ‖ ein Mann der ~ *a man of pen-and-ink*, *a penman* od *writer* ‖ sich mit der ~ ernähren *to live by one's pen*, *to make a living with one's pen* ‖ ein Buch aus der ~ des Herrn N. *a book written by Mr. N.* ‖ ein Buch unter der ~ h *to be writing a book* **B.** ⟨hunt⟩ (Schwanz des Hasen, Rotwilds) *tail* **C.** ⟨tech⟩ **1.** (Sprung~̽) *spring*; flache ~ (z Rahmen) *spring arm*; Spann~̽ *tension-screw*; Spiral~̽ *spiral sp.*; gespannte ~ *tensioned sp.* ‖ geschichtete Blatt~̽ ⟨mot etc⟩ *laminated leaf sp.*; Längs~̽, (Quer~̽) *longitudinal* (*transversal*) *type sp.*; Schrauben~̽, Wickel~̽ *coil* od *helical sp.* ‖ (Wagen) mit ~n versehen *to sp.* (*a carriage*) ‖ mit e–r ~ versehen [pp] *sp.* (*balance*); → federnd ‖ leichter Wagen auf ~n *sp.-cart* ‖ v e–r ~ getrieben *sp.-driven* (*clock*) ‖ ⟨mot⟩ Fahrgestell durch ~n befestigen *to sp. the chassis* (an . . *to* . .) **2.** ⟨carp⟩ (Ggs Nut) *feather*, *tongue*; ~ u Nut *tongue and groove* **3.** Trieb~̽ **F·eder-** [in comp] *feather-* .. ‖ ⟨tech⟩ *spring-* .. **~alaun** m ⟨minr⟩ *f.-alum* | mit **~antrieb** m *actuated by sp. tension*; *sp.-driven* **~̽artig** a *f.-like*; *f.y* **~aufhängung** f ⟨tech⟩ *sp. suspension* **~ball** m *shuttlecock*; ⟨golf⟩ *f.-ball*; ~schläger [m] (badminton) *racket* ‖ ~spiel [n] *battledore and shuttlecock*; *badminton* **~band** n *buckle* **~barometer** n *aneroid* (*barometer*) **~bart** m *web* (*of a feather*) **~bein** n (P) *unstrained leg* ⟨a. sculp⟩; ⟨aero⟩ *shock strut*; *compression leg* **~besen** m *feather duster* **~bett** n *f.-bed*; ⟨hum⟩ "*Zeppelin*" **~binse** f ⟨bot⟩ *cotton-grass* **~blatt** n *sp.-plate* (od *leaf*) **~bolzen** m *sp. bolt* **~brett** n ⟨sport⟩ *sp.-board* (*with sp.s*) *for jumping* **~büchse** f *pen-case* **~busch**, **~büschel** m (*f.-*)*plume*; *tuft of f.s*; *aigrette* (Fr) ‖ ⟨orn⟩ *crest* **~fuchser** m *quill-driver*, *paper-stainer*, *ink-slinger*, (⟨Am a.⟩ *ink-spiller*); *brother of the quill*; *scribbler* **~fuchserei** f *pen-pushing*, *quill-driving*, *ink-slinging* **~̽führend** a *managing*, *authorized*; *in charge*; *writing* (*chairman*) ‖ ~ s *to be protocolist* od *secretary* ‖ *custodian* [attr] ⟨pol⟩ (*c. state*) **~führung** f *duct* **~gamasche** f = Federschutz **~gehäuse** n ⟨tech⟩ *sp.-box*; (of a watch) *barrel* **~geistchen** n ⟨ent⟩ = Federmotte **~gelenk** n ⟨tech⟩ *expansion-joint* **~gewicht** n ⟨box⟩ *f.-weight* (nicht über 114 Pfd; ⟨engl⟩ *126* lbs) **~gras** n ⟨bot⟩ *narrow small-reed* ‖ *f.-grass* **~halter** m *penholder* **~hand** f ⟨mot⟩ *dumb iron* **~̽hart** a *elastic*, *springy*; → Federstahl **~harz** n *India rubber*; *caoutchouc* **~hobel** m *tonguing plane* **~hut** m *hat with a f.*; *f.-cap* **~kasten** m = Federbüchse **~keil** m ⟨tech⟩ *f.* **~kiel** m *quill* **~kissen** n *pillow*; *cushion stuffed with f.s* **~klinke** *f sp.-latch* **~kohl** m Sw *kale* **~kraft** f *elasticity*; *springiness* **~krieg** m *paper-warfare*; *pen-and-ink war*; *book-war* ‖ *literary controversy* **~̽l·eicht** a (*as*) *light as a feather*; *feather*; *feathery* ‖ ~er Tastendruck ⟨comp, etc⟩ *f.-touch key action* | [adv] sich ~ fühlen ⟨a-n⟩ (P) *to feel springy* **~lesen** n ⟨fig⟩ ohne viel ~s *without beating about the bush*; *without much ceremony*; ⟨Am⟩ *in short order* ‖ nicht viel ~s m *not to let the grass grow under one's feet*; . . mit etw, jdm *to make short work* (od *no bones*) *of a th*; *to manhandle*, ⟨sl⟩ *to rough-house a p* **~manometer** n *scroll-sp. manometer* **~messer** n *pen-knife* **~motte** f ⟨ent⟩ *plume-moth*; → Geistchen **~nelke** f ⟨bot⟩ *sweet-william* **~puffer** m ⟨tech⟩ *sp. dash-pot* **~regler** m ⟨tech⟩ *sp. governor* **~riegel** m ⟨tech⟩ m *sp.-bolt* **~ring** m *sp.-ring* ‖ ⟨mot⟩ *sp.-washer* **~rohr** n ⟨tech⟩ *expansion-bend* **~sattel** m ⟨mot⟩ *sp. pivotseat* **~scheibe** f *locking washer* **~schließer** m ⟨tech⟩ *cotter spring* **~schloß** n *spring-lock* **~schmuck** m *f. ornament*; *plume*; (of Indians) *f.-mail* **~schutz** m ⟨mot⟩ *sp.-gaiter* | unter **~spannung** stehend *sp.-loaded* **~spiel** n *spillikins* [pl] ‖ (bei Falkenbeize) *lure* **~spitze** f *nib*; (⟨Am⟩ *pen*) *point* **~sprungbrett** n ⟨gym⟩ *high sp.-board* **~spule** f *quill* **~stahl** m *sp.-steel* **~strich** m *stroke* od *dash of the pen* ‖ ⟨fig⟩ bis zum letzten ~ erfüllen *to fulfil to the hilt* ‖ durch e–n ~, mit e–m ~ *by*, *with* (od *at*) *a stroke of the pen* ‖ mit ein paar ~en *with a few strokes* **~stutz** m *plume* **~vieh** n [koll] *f.ed animals* pl; *birds* pl, *poultry*; [koll] das ganze ~ *the f.ed world* **~vorholer** m ⟨artill⟩ *sp. recuperator* **~waage** f *sp.-balance* **~weiß** n ⟨geol⟩ *steatite*; *soapstone*; *white fibrous gypsum*; = Schneiderkreide ‖ *asbestos* **~weiße** m *fermenting new wine* **~werk** n ⟨tech⟩ *sp. drive* od *motor* **~wild** *f.ed game*, *game birds* pl; Stück ~ *game bird* **~wisch** m *f.-brush*, *f.-duster* **~wischer** m *pen-wiper* **~wolke** f *cirrus* (L) **~zange** f *pincette* (Fr); *tweezers* [pl], e–e ~ *a pair of t.* **~zeichnung** f *pen and ink drawing*; *pen-and-ink* **~zirkel** m *sp.-bows* [pl]; ein ~ *a pair of sp.-bows* **~zug** m = Federstrich ‖ ⟨tech⟩ *sp. pull* **F·ederchen** n *featherlet*; *plumule*; *small feather* **f·ed(e)rig** a *feathery*; *feathered* **f·edern** vi/t [h] **A.** vi **1. a.** (of birds) *to moult*; *to moult* (od *shed*) *feathers* ‖ ⟨übtr⟩ (of a bed) *to lose feathers* **b.** (sich leicht bewegen) *to feather* ‖ ⟨hunt⟩ (of hounds) *to feather* **2.** ⟨tech⟩ (of steel, etc) *to be elastic* (od *flexible*, *resilient*, *springy*; *supple*) | **~d** ⟨tech⟩ → d. **B.** vt ⟨hunt⟩ e–n Vogel ~ *to feather a bird* ‖ **sich ~** (of birds) *to moult* **F·edernball** m ⟨fig⟩ (Ammensprache) auf den ~ gehen → Baba gehen ‖ ⟨sex⟩ *to dance a mattress-jig* **f·edernd 1.** a *elastic*, *resilient*, *springy*; *flexible*, *supple* ‖ ~es Rad *spring-wheel*; ~e Waage *spring balance* ‖ ~e Bewegung *springing* ‖ ein Messer mit ~er Klinge *a spring-blade knife* ‖ etw ~ m *to spring a th* **2.** adv *elastically*; sich ~ bewegen *to feather*; (Angriff) ~ auffangen *to resiliently absorb* **F·ederung** f *elasticity*, *resilience*, *–cy*; *springiness*; *springing* (*of a saw*) ‖ ⟨mot⟩ *suspension* (*of a car*); weiche ~ *soft spring action(s)* | ~selement [n] *spring medium*

Fee f ~/~n **1.** *fairy*; kl ~ *pixy*, *pixie*; (Ir) e–n Todesfall verkündende ~ *banshee* **2.** ° ⟨übtr⟩ *female* (*domestic*) *servant*; Küchen~̽ *cook* **F·een-** [ˈfeːən] **~königin** f *fairy-queen* **~kreis** m (Gras–) *f.-ring* **~land** n *f.land*, *f.dom* **~reigen** m *fairy-dance* **~ring** m = Feenkreis **~tanz** m = –reigen **f·eenhaft 1.** a **a.** *fairy-like* (*creature*) **b.** mst ⟨übtr⟩ (verblaßt) *glamorous*, *magical*; *romantic* ‖ *grand*, *impressive*; *magnificent* (*illumination*); *splendid*, *sumptuous*; → bezaubernd **2.** adv *magically*; *glamorously* (*illuminated*); *magnificently* (*furnished*); *sumptuously* †**Feer·ei**, **Feer·ie** f †*faerie*, *–ry*

°**Feez** [–ts] m ~es/~e *fun*; ⟨fam⟩ *lark*, *spree*; was f ein ~! *what a lark*; e–n ~ h, sich e–n ~ m *to have a lark*; *to spree*; es würde ein Haupt~̽ s *it would be rather a spree* ‖ e–n Mords~̽ m *to paint the town red*

F·ege- ~feuer n **1.** ⟨ec⟩ *purgatory*; Leiden [pl] im ~ *purgatorial sufferings* [pl]; Messe f die im

~ Leidenden *purgatorial mass* **2.** ⟨fig⟩ *purgatory* (*of matrimony*; *of the trenches*) **~maschine** f *sweeper*; *sweeping-machine* **f·egen** vt/i [h] **I. vt A.** † & ˣ (= polieren, putzen) (Rüstung etc) blank ~ *to burnish*, *furbish* ‖ (reinigen) *to clean*(*se*); (Getreide) *to winnow* **B.** (mit dem **Besen** ~) **1.** (Schornstein) *to sweep* **2.** (Raum, Treppe etc) *to sweep*; *to give* (*a room*) *a sweep*; rein ~ *to clean*; *to scour*; → kehren **3.** (Schmutz) *to sweep away* (od *up*); *to whisk* (v . . *off a p's coat*); → weg~, den Staub v etw ~ *to dust a th* **4.** e–e Bahn ~ *to form a path* (od *to mark out an area*) *with a broom* **C.** ⟨**übtr**⟩ **1.** (of the wind, etc.) die Felder ~ *to sweep the fields*, → II. B. 2. **2.** (Laub) *to drive*, *send*, *shoot* (in *into*; v . . *off the trees*); der Wind fegte ihm den Hut vom Kopfe *the wind swept his hat off his head* ‖ (of rain) (Schmutz) *to scour* (aus . . *out of* [*the drains*]; *from*) **3.** ⟨hunt⟩ der Hirsch fegt [abs] *or* . . fegt den Bast . . *rubs his horns against trees* **II. vi A.** ⟨**eig**⟩ *to sweep*; → kehren ‖ ⟨fig⟩ vor s–r eigenen Tür ~ *to mind one's own business* ‖ der Hirsch fegt *the stag rubs the velvet off the antlers* **B.** ⟨**übtr**⟩ **1.** (P) *to dash*, *flit*, *race*, *tear*, *rush*, *whisk* (aus *from*; durch *through*); über das Land ~ *to sweep the country* ‖ er fegte mit der Hand über . . *he ran* od *swept his hand over* (*the table*); → hinunter-, vorbeifegen **2. (S) a.** (of the wind) über das Meer (etc) ~ *to sweep* (od *race*) *across the ocean*, *to sweep the ocean* ‖ ⟨Am⟩ *to cast* (durch *through*) **b.** (of waves) über das Boot ~ *to sweep the boat*; (of feelings) *to sweep* (durch *through*) **c.** (of a car) *to dash*, *race* (durch *through* . .) ‖ der Zug fegte durch den Bahnhof *the train flashed through the station* **d.** (of revolving door, etc) *to whish* **F·egen** n *sweeping*; *cleaning* **F·eger** m **1.** ⟨eig⟩ *sweeper*; → Schornstein≈ **2.** °⟨übtr & dero⟩ = Draufgänger; → °Besen 3. **F·eget**, **F·egicht**, **F·egsel** n ~s/ (Weggefegtes) *sweepings* [pl]

Feh n ~s/ (Fell v sibirischen Eichhörnchen) *grey* od *white squirrel*; *miniver*; → Fähe

F·ehde f ~/~n (Familien≈) *feud* (*a deadly f. between* . .) ‖ ⟨übtr⟩ *bickering*, *quarrel*; *warfare* ‖ in ~ leben *or* liegen mit *to be at feud* (od *warfare*) *with* (*a p*); *to war with* (*a p*) ‖ jdm ~ ansagen *to challenge a p*; *to throw down the gauntlet* (od *glove*) *to a p* **~brief** m *challenge* **~handschuh** m *gauntlet*, *glove*; *gage*; jdm den ~ hinwerfen *to throw down the g. to a p*; den ~ aufnehmen *to take up the g.* **~recht** n = Faustrecht

F·ehe f = Fähe, Feh

Fehl m ~(e)s/~e *blemish*, *fault*, *flaw*; ohne ~ *faultless*, *without a fault* **fehl** adv; ~ am Orte (*or* Platze) *amiss* [pred]; *false*, *wrong*; *erroneous*; ~ am Ort s (of a protest) *to be misplaced* (od *inappropriate*); *to be out of place* **F·ehl-** (→ fehl adv) [in comp] **~anflughöhe** f ⟨aero⟩ *missed--approach altitude* **~anzeige** f ⟨tech⟩ *error in indication* ‖ (auf Erlaß e–r Behörde) *deficiency* od *negative report*; ⟨mil⟩ *nil return*; ~! *nil*!; ~ (nicht) erforderlich! *negative report requested*, (*no nil returns*) ‖ ⟨engl jur⟩ *return of 'nihil ad rem'*; (bei Pfändung) *return of nulla bona* (L); → ~meldung **~auskunft** f *incorrect information* **~belichtung** f ⟨phot⟩ *faulty exposure* **~benennung** f *misnomer* **~bestand** m *deficiency*; *shortage* **~betrag** m *deficit*, *deficiency* (v *of*); *minus* L, *minus amount*; *shortage*; *debit balance* **~bitte** f *bootless* (od *fruitless*, *unavailing*, *useless*, *vain*) *request*; e–e ~ tun *to sue* (*for a th*) *in vain*; *to be refused*, *to meet with a refusal* **~boden** m ⟨arch⟩ = Blindboden **~bogen** m ⟨typ⟩ *imperfect sheet* **~diagnose** f ⟨med⟩ *erroneous* (od *wrong*) *diagnosis* **~druck** m = Fehlbogen ‖ ~e [pl] (Makulaturen) *misprints*, *spoils*, *spoilage* **~einschätzung** f *erroneous estimation* (*of a p*) **~einstellung** f ⟨phot, etc⟩ *maladjustment* **~entscheidung** f *wrong decision*; *misjudg*(*e*)*ment*, *wrong*(*ful*) *judg*(*e*)*ment* **~ernte** f *bad harvest* **~farbe** f **1.** *cigar in a discolo*(*u*)*red wrapper*; *off shade* (*cigar*, *diamond*) **2.** ⟨cards⟩ *renounce*, *chicane* ‖ *suit not trumps* ≈**gebären** vi [nur inf & pp; → gebären] [h] (P) *to miscarry*, *abort* ‖ (T) *to slink*; –geborenes Kalb (etc) *slink* **~geburt** f *miscarriage*; *abortion*; ⟨fam⟩ *mis*(*s*) ≈|**gehen** vi [s] **1.** *to go astray*; *to miss one's way* (of a missile) *to fail to hit*; *to pass by without touching* **2.** ⟨übtr⟩ **a.** *to err*; *to go wrong* (in der Annahme *or* wenn man annimmt *in supposing*); er war in s–n Gedanken nicht sehr –gegangen *his thoughts had not been far out* **b.** (S) *to go amiss* (*if anything should go a.*); (of a statement) *to err*; *to be incorrect* ‖ *to fail*, → fehlschlagen ≈|**greifen** vi [h] ⟨fig⟩ *to make a mistake*; *to err* **~griff** m ⟨fig⟩ *error*, *mistake*; *blunder*; *faux pas* (Fr) ‖ *failure*, *wash-out* **~guß** m ⟨met⟩ *waster* **~jahr** n; ~e [pl] *lean years* [pl] **~kauf** m *bad bargain* **~landung** f ⟨aero⟩ *balked landing* **~leistung** f *failure*; *ill success*; *non-performance* ≈|**leiten** vt [h] *to lead astray*; *to misdirect* **~leitung** f *misrouted shipment* **~meldung** f = Falschmeldung **~menge** f (in Faß etc) *ullage* ≈|**schießen** vi [h] *to miss one's aim*; *to miss the mark* ‖ ⟨fig⟩ *to make a bad shot*; °–geschossen! *far from* (od *wide of*) *the mark*!, *wrong*! **~schlag** m **1.** *wrong stroke* (od *shot*); *miss*; ⟨golf⟩ ~ auf den Boden *sclaff* **2.** ⟨fig⟩ *failure*, *miscarriage*, *wash-out*; ⟨sl⟩ *dud*, ⟨Am⟩ *bust* ‖ *disappointment*; *set-back* (f jdn *to a p*) ‖ e–n ~ erleiden *to meet with failure*, *to fail*; e–n gänzlichen ~ erleiden *to go down to complete f.* ≈|-**schlagen** vi **1.** ⟨eig⟩ [h] *to miss*; *to fail to hit* **2.** ⟨fig⟩ [s] *to fail*; *to fall flat*; *to miscarry*; ⟨sl⟩ *to peter out*; (of events) *to go wrong*; m–e Pläne schlugen fehl *my plans were thwarted* od *disappointed* ‖ –ge–e S *or* P *failure* **~schluß** m ⟨log⟩ *false* od *illogical reasoning*; *paralogism* ‖ → Trugschluß **~schuß** m *miss*; *bad shot*; ⟨phot⟩ *misfire* **~spruch** m ⟨jur⟩ *misjudg*(*e*)*ment*; *perverse verdict* **~start** m ⟨aero⟩ *unsuccessful* od *wrong take-off*; ⟨mot⟩ *false start* **~stoß** m *miss*; *wrong* (od *false*) *thrust* (od *shot*) ‖ ⟨billiards⟩ *miscue*; e–n ~ m *to miscue* ≈|**treten** vi [s & h] **1.** ⟨eig⟩ *to make* od *take a false step*; *to miss one's footing*; *to stumble*, *trip* **2.** ⟨fig⟩ = e–n Fehltritt tun **~tritt** m **1.** *false step*; *misstep*; *slip*, *trip* **2.** ⟨fig⟩ *fault*, (*moral*) *lapse*; *offence*; *slip*, *trip*; e–n ~ tun *to err*; *to cause offence*; *to trip*; (of a girl) *to go wrong* **~urteil** n ⟨jur⟩ = Fehlspruch **~weisung** f ⟨tech⟩ *error in indication* ‖ *error* (*of a compass*) **~wurf** m *miss*; *wrong* od *false throw* od *shot* **~zeiten** f pl *periods of absence* **~züchtung** f *breeding failure* **~zünden** vi [h] [nur inf & pp] ⟨mil, mot⟩ *to misfire* **~zündung** f *ignition failure*; *misfire*, *backfire* ‖ ⟨mot⟩ ~ h *to be missing* **f·ehlbar** a *fallible* | ≈**keit** f *fallibility*

f·ehlen vt/i [h] **I.** †**vt** ein Ziel (etc) ~ = verfehlen ‖ → fehlschießen **II. vi A.** **[imps] 1. a. es fehlt an** Wasser *water fails*, *is lacking* ‖ es fehlte nicht an Leuten, die . . *there were not wanting people who* . . ‖ es soll an mir (*or* v m–r Seite) nicht ~ *nothing will be wanting on my part* (*to do*) **b.** es fehlte **uns an** Wasser (→ B. 1. a.) *w. failed us* [dat]; *we were short* (od *in want*) *of w.* **c.** es fehlt ihm an Geschick *he lacks* (od *wants*) *skill*; *he fails in skill*; *he is lacking* od *wanting in skill* → ermangeln ‖ *the play fails in unity* ‖ es soll ihm an nichts ~ *he shall want for nothing* **| wo fehlt's**? *what's wrong*?, *what's the trouble*? **2. es ~ lassen an** *to fail in* (*respect*); *to be wanting in* ‖ es nicht ~ l an *to lack nothing in* . .; es an nichts ~ l *to leave nothing undone*, *to spare no pains*, *to take every pains* (*to do*, *in doing*); *to go out of one's way* (*to do*); laß es ihm an nichts ~ *let him want for nothing* **B. 1. a. das Wasser** fehlte uns (*or* es [hinweisend] fehlte uns das W.) (= A. 1. b.) ‖ das Geschick fehlt ihm (*or* es fehlt ihm das G.) (= A. 1. c.) ‖ Worte ~ mir (*or* es ~ mir W.) *words fail me* (*to tell . .*); zwei Dinge ~ ihnen (*or* es ~ ihnen zwei D.) *they are lacking in two things* ‖ es ~ mir 10 Mark *I am short of 10 marks*; *I miss* (od *lost*) *10 m.* ‖ er fehlt uns sehr *we miss him very much*; die schönen Spaziergänge w mir ~ *I shall miss the pleasant walks* (*when*) . .) ‖ der Schlag (*or* das) hat ihm noch gefehlt *it wanted only this blow*; *that was the last straw for him* **b.** es fehlt noch e–e Minute **an Zehn** *the time was within a minute of ten*; es fehlten noch 5 Minuten, bis . . *there were still 5 minutes to pass before* (*he must go*); es ~ 5 Minuten an 10 *it is five minutes to ten* **c. viel fehlte nicht** (*or* es f. nicht v.; es f. wenig), so wäre er ertrunken *he had a hairbreadth* (od *narrow*) *escape from drowning*; *within a little he got drowned*, → beinahe, fast; (um ein) Haar; es fehlte nicht viel, daß ich getötet wurde *it was a matter of touch and go whether I should be killed* ‖ es fehlte wenig, so wäre er getötet worden *by a shave* (od *by a fraction of an inch*) *he would have been killed* ‖ [neg] nicht ~ z tun → verfehlen **d. das fehlte (auch) noch**! *it wanted only that*! *I should think not*! *what next*, *I wonder*?, *that settles it*!, *that's the limit*! ‖ (Georg N. ist gek) das fehlte gerade noch! (. .) *of all appalling things*! ‖ es fehlte nur noch, daß . . *all that was wanting was* . . **2. was fehlt dir**? *what is the matter* (*with you*); *what's the trouble*? *what's wrong*? ‖ fehlt Ihnen etwas? *is anything the matter* (*with you*)?; fehlt Ihnen etw? ⟨path⟩ *are you feeling well*? ich muß sehen, ob Ihnen wirklich etw fehlt *I must see if anything is really the matter*; Ihnen fehlt immer etw *you are always ailing*; es fehlt Ihnen nichts Ernstes *there is nothing serious the matter*; mir fehlt nichts *I am quite all right* ‖ **wo fehlt's denn**? *what is the trouble*?, *what's wrong*? ‖ °bei dir fehlts wohl *you seem to have a screw loose* **3. (nicht anwesend s)** *to be absent* (in der Schule, bei e–r Feier *from school*, *from a festival*) **4. (S) (nicht vorhanden s)** *to be missing* od *wanting*; e–r S ~ *to be lacking to* (od *from*) *a th*; *to be missing from a th*; *to be wanting to a th* ‖ 2 Blätter ~ dem Bande *two leaves are missing from the volume*; *the volume wants two leaves* ‖ dies fehlt dem Programm *this is out of the pr.*; → ohne **5.** ⟨eig⟩ (nicht treffen) *to miss*; *to miss one's mark*; *to fail to hit* ‖ ⟨fig⟩ weit gefehlt! *far from* od *wide of the mark*! *wrong*! **6. (moralisch ~)** *to err*; *to go wrong*; *to sin*; ~ gegen *to offend against* **F·ehlen** n **1.** = Mangel; beim ~ v *in the absence of* **2.** *non-attendance*; ~ in der Schule *absence from school* ‖ ⟨jur⟩ ~ vor Gericht *non-appearance* | das ~ e–r Stelle in *the absence of a passage from a book* **3.** = Fehlschuß, –wurf **4.** (moralisches) = Verfehlung

f·ehlend a **1.** *lacking*; *missing* (*leaves*, *link*) ‖ ⟨com⟩ ~e Stücke [pl] *deficiencies* [pl] **2.** *absent* ‖ der ≈e *the absentee*, die Liste der ≈en feststellen *to call absence* **3.** *erring*, *sinning* **F·ehler** m ~s/~ **1. (Irrtum)** *error*, *mistake*; *fault*; ⟨sl⟩ *bloomer*; ⟨Am⟩ *break*, *slip-up* (ein böser, schlimmer ~ *a bad break*) ‖ ⟨math & jur⟩ *error* ‖ ⟨gram⟩ ~ *fault of grammar* ‖ ein ~ im Urteil *an error of judgement* ‖ grober ~ ⟨a. pol⟩ *blunder*; dummer ~ → Dummheit; Schnitzer ‖ ein ~ im Text e–s Buches *a clerical error* | e–n~ m *or* ⟨pol⟩ begehen *to make a mistake*; *to make* od *commit an error*; e–n groben ~ m *to blunder*; ⟨sl⟩ *to make a bloomer*; e–n törichten ~ m ⟨Am⟩ *to make some fool break* | ⟨sport⟩ *mistake*, *fault*; ⟨ten⟩ *fault*; Angabe≈ *mishit*, e–n ~ m *to mishit* ‖ → einschleichen **2. a. (körperlich)** *blemish*, *defect*; krankhafter ~ *vice*; Konstitutions≈ *vice of constitution*; → Herz≈ **b. (charakterl.**, sittlicher ~) *defect*, *error*, *failing*, *fault*, *imperfection*; → Fehl ‖ (~ im Verhalten) *faux pas* (Fr), *gaffe* (Fr); → Schuld ‖ ohne ~ *faultless*, *without a fault* ‖ e–n ~ begehen *to commit a fault*; *to commit* od *make a faux pas* ‖ wir h alle unsere ~ *or* e–n kl ~ hat nun mal ein jeder *we all have our little failings*, *there is always* (*a*) *sth* ‖ das ist der ~ an ihm *that's his trouble* **c. (S)** *defect* (an . . *in a machine*; in *in*); *fault*, *flaw* (*in glass*, *metal*); *feather* (*in a jewel*); ⟨com⟩ mit allen ~n *with all faults* **d.** (~ an **geistigem** Gut) *blemish*, *defect*, *fault*, *flaw* (*in reasoning*); *imperfection* ‖ ⟨Am⟩ *out* (an *about*) ‖ die ~ [pl] an der sozialen Ordnung *the vices of the social system* ‖ der Haupt≈ an dem Stück (*or* des Stückes) ist . . *the chief drawback in* (od *objection to*) *the play is* . . **~anzeige** f ⟨tech⟩ *indication of error* ⟨a. comp⟩ **~begrenzung** f *fault localization* **~berichtigung** f *correction* **~bestimmung** f ⟨tech⟩ *localization of faults* **~dreieck** n *triangle of error* ⟨a. artill, surv⟩ **≈frei 1.** a *correct*; *faultless*; *flawless* (*diamond*); (Glas) *free from flaws* ‖ *flawless* (*work*); *perfect*; *free from defect* **2.** adv *faultlessly*, *flawlessly*; ~ wiederholen *to repeat accurately* **~freiheit** f = –losigkeit **~grenze** f *margin of error* ‖ (f Gewicht etc neuer Münzen) *remedy*; ⟨bes chem u tech⟩ *tolerance* **≈haft 1.** a *defective*, *faulty*, *imperfect*; ~es Exemplar *waster*, *wastrel*; ~e Waren [pl] *wasters* [pl] ‖ *incorrect* (*reasoning*); *wrong*; *unsound* **2.** adv *faultily*, *imperfectly*, *incorrectly* **~haftigkeit** f *defectiveness*, *faultiness*; *imperfection* **~integral** n *error function* **~kontrolle** f *error indication* ⟨a. comp⟩ **~lokalisierung** f ⟨tech⟩ *flaw location* **≈los** a *flawless* (*playing*); = fehlerfrei a & adv **~losigkeit** f *faultlessness*; *soundness* ⟨a. tech⟩, *flawlessness*; *perfection* **~ortung** f ⟨tech⟩ *faultfinding* **~prozentsatz** m *error percentage* **~prüfung** f *error checking* **~punkt** m ⟨sport⟩ *bad point* **~quelle** f *source of error*(*s*); ~n [pl] ⟨a.⟩ *incidence of errors* **~schwankung** f *variation in error* **~suche** f (u Beseitigung) *trouble shooting* **~strom** m ⟨el⟩ *fault-current* **~taste** f *erasing key* **~verzeichnis** n (*list of*) *errata*

Fehme[1] f = Feme × **Fehme**[2] f = Feim

f·eien vt [h] **1.** †⟨eig⟩ (jdn, etw) *to charm* (gegen *against*) **2.** ⟨übtr⟩ *to fortify*, *to protect*

F·eier f ~/~n **1.** [abstr] *celebration* (*of a birthday*, *festival*, etc.); *commemoration*, *observance*; *solemnization*; im kl Kreise *cel. in a small circle*; zur ~ des Tages *to celebrate the occasion* **2.** [konkr] *ceremony* (e e erhebende ~ *an impressive*, *solemn*, *moving c.*) ‖ Gedächtnis≈ *commemoration*; Abschieds≈ *farewell ceremony* ‖ religiöse ~ *ritual* | (Fest≈) *festival*; e–e ~ begehen *to hold a festival*; → Fest **~abend** m ⟨hist⟩ *curfew*, ⟨Am fam⟩ *knock-off*; ⟨com⟩ *closing time* (*it is c. t.*); ~ m *to cease work for the day*; *to knock off work*; *to knock off*; (*time of*) *relaxation after* (*working*) *hours*; m wir ~! *let's call it a day*! ‖ ⟨übtr⟩ ~ des Lebens *evening of life* **~klang** m *solemn peal* (od *ringing*); **~kleid** n = Festkleid **~stätte** f *place of the ceremony*; *festive* (od *solemn*) *place* **~stimmung** f *solemnity* **~stunde** f *ceremony*; *festive hour* (od *season*) ‖ *hour of rest* **~tag** m *holiday*; *festive day*; *festival*; *red-letter day*; die ~e e–r Nation *the red-letter days of a nation* ‖ ~skleidung [f] *h. dress* **f·eierlich 1.** a **a.** *solemn*; *impressive*; *awe-inspiring*; ~e Stimmung *solemnity* ‖ *ceremonial*, *ceremonious* (*reception*; *unveiling*); *formal*; ~er Akt *ceremony* **b.** *solemn* (*assurance*, *oath*, *vow*) **2.** adv *solemnly* (*recognized*); *ceremoniously* (*opened*); (Fest) ~ begehen *to solemnize* ‖ (jdn) ~ stimmen *to solemnize* | **≈keit** f ~/~en **1.** *solemnity*; *impressiveness* ‖ *ceremonial observance*; *ceremoniousness* **2.** [konkr] *ceremony* (bei der ~ *at the c.*); ~en [pl] *ceremonies* [pl]; ⟨Am⟩ *exercises* [pl]: Eröffnungs≈en *opening e.* ‖ ⟨rel & off⟩ (Fest) *function* **f·eiern** vt/i [h] **I.** vt **1.** (Fest; Tag) *to celebrate*; *to solemnize* ‖ (Sieg) *to celebrate* ‖ Feste (*or* Orgien) ~ *to celebrate orgies* ‖ wir müssen den Tag ~ *we must celebrate the occasion* **2.** (e–n Künstler, Helden, ein Land) *to celebrate*; *extol*; *honour*;

acclaim; *praise*; 〈Am fam〉 *to lionize*; → gefeiert **II.** vi **1.** *to indulge in festivities* (od *gaieties, merry--making*) **2.** *to rest from one's labours* ‖ *to stop work for a day* od *time*; *to strike* ‖ *to be out of work* ‖ 〈übtr〉 *to be idle*; *to take it easy*

F·eifel m ~s/~ 〈vet〉 *vives* [pl]; → Ohrdrüse

feig I. a **A.** [attr] **1.** 〈min〉 (= faul) *brittle, crumbling* (*rock*); *rotten* (*gallery*) **2.** 〈übtr〉 **a.** *cowardly*; *effeminate*; *unmanly*; 〈poet〉 *recreant*, 〈sl〉 *yellow* ‖ 〈Am sl〉 *sissy* **b.** (furchtsam) *craven, faint*; *faint-* (od *pigeon-*, *weak-*)*-hearted*; *milk--livered*; *pusillanimous*; *spiritless*; *timid*; 〈sl〉 *funky* ‖ ein ~er Mensch *a faint-heart*; ~e Memme *craven*; *dastard*; *poltroon* **c.** (gemein) (a. of actions, etc) *cowardly* (*lie*); *coward* (*action*); *craven* (*fear*); *dastardly* (*act, outrage*); *mean*; *niddering* **B.** [pred] [mst ~e] *cowardly* (*he was too c.*); 〈sl〉 *yellow* ‖ du bist ~e *you are a coward*; ihr seid ~e *you are cowards* ‖ es war ~e v dir *it was* (*a*) *cowardice on your part* (*to do*) ‖ sich ~ zeigen *to show the white feather*; *to show a yellow streak*; *to have cold feet*; *to fight shy* (z tun *of doing*); *to quail* ‖ (of actions) *cowardly*; *dastardly* **II.** adv [mst ~e] *cowardly*; *cravenly*

F·ei- ~bohne [f] 〈bot〉 *fig-bean* = Lupine; ~warze [f] 〈med〉 *condyloma* L; ~wurz [f] 〈bot〉 *fig-wort*; *lesser celandine*

F·eige 1. 〈bot〉 (Eß≗) *fig* ‖ Oputien≗ *prickly pear* ‖ ein Kasten (Korb) ~n *a box* (*drum*) *of figs* **2.** 〈übtr bes hunt〉 (in deer, etc) *genitals* [pl], *genital region* ‖ e–e ~ m *to give the fig*

f·eige pred a & adv → feig I. B. u. II.

F·eigen- ~baum m 〈bot〉 *fig* (*-tree*) ‖ Bengalischer ~ → Baniane ‖ Heiliger ~ *pipal, peepul* ‖ Maulbeer≗ *sycamore* **~blatt** n **1.** *fig-leaf* **2.** 〈übtr bes hunt〉 = Feige 2. **3.** 〈fig〉 [bes pl] *fig--leaf* **~distel** f 〈bot〉 *Indian* od *Bar-Berry fig* **~drossel** f 〈orn, cul〉 *fig-pecker* **~fresser** m 〈orn〉 *beccafico*; *fig-eater* (*-pecker*) **~hain** m *fig-wood* **~kaktus** m 〈bot〉 = Feigendistel **~wespe** f 〈ent〉 *fig-wasp* **~wurz** f = Feig–

F·eigheit f ~/~en *cowardice, cowardliness*; *poltroonery*; 〈sl〉 *yellow*; *yellow streak* ‖ schmähliche ~ *recreancy* ‖ es war (e–e) ~ v ihm *it was* (*a*) *cowardice* (od *an act of c.*) *on his part*

f·eigherzig a & adv = feige | ≗**keit** f *faint--heartedness*; *funkiness*; *pusillanimity*; *timidity*

F·eigling m ~s/~e *coward, craven, dastard*; *milksop*; *niddering*; *poltroon*; *shy cock*; 〈fam〉 *sissy*; 〈sl〉 *funk, quitter* ‖ schmählicher ~ *recreant*

f·eil a **1.** 〈eig〉 ([ver]käuflich) [nur pred u mst in Verbindung mit best. Verben → ~bieten, ~halten) *for* (od *on*) *sale*; †*venal* **2.** 〈fig〉 [pred & attr] *venal* (*judge, orator*); *mercenary*; *bribable*; *corrupt* ‖ ~e Dirne *prostitute, harlot*

F·eil- (→ feilen) **~kloben** m *hand-vice* (〈Am〉 *vise*) **~maschine** f *filing-machine*; *moulding* (od *shaping*)*-machine* **~späne** m [pl] *filings* [pl]; grobe ~ *raspings* [pl] **~staub** m *file-dust*; *filings* [pl] **~strich** m *file-stroke*

f·eil|bieten (→ feil) vt [h] **1.** (Waren) *to expose* (od *lay out, put up*) *for sale*; *to hawk, peddle* **2. a.** (s–n Körper) *to prostitute*; [mst refl] **sich ~** *to prostitute o.s.* **b.** 〈übtr〉 (Ehre) *to defile, dishonour, prostitute* **F·eilbietung** f **1.** *putting up for sale* ‖ [österr] *auction sale* **2.** *prostitution*

F·eile f ~/~n **1.** *file*; einhiebige ~ *single-cut file*; Polier≗, Schlicht≗ *smooth file*; Flach≗ *flat file*; Rund≗ *round file* ‖ grobe ~ *rasp*; gr ~ *rasper* ‖ 〈med〉 Knochen≗ *raspatory* **2.** 〈fig〉 [abstr] (Feilen) *file*; *polish*; das Werk bedarf der ~ *the work wants the file*; die letzte ~ *the last touches*; die letzte ~ legen an etw *to put* od *give the finishing touches to a th*; *to finish, to perfect a th* **f·eilen I.** vt/i [h] **A.** vt **1.** 〈eig〉 (etw) *to file*; glatt ~ *to file smooth* ‖ (raspeln) *to rasp* **2.** 〈fig〉 (Verse etc) *to file, polish* **B.** vi **1.** *to file*; **~ an etw** *to file a th* **2.** 〈fig〉 ~ an etw *to file* (od *polish*) *a th*; *to finish* (*off* od *up*); *to perfect a th* **II.** ≗ n **1.** *filing*; grobes ~ *rasping* **2.** 〈fig〉 = Feile 2. **F·eilen-** (→ Feile) **~bürste** f *file-card* **~hauer** m *file-cutter* **~hieb** m *file-cut* **~muschel** f 〈zoo〉 *file-shell*; *Pholas* (L)

f·eil|halten vt [h] (Waren) *to expose* (od *offer*; *put up*) *for sale* ‖ 〈fig〉 Maulaffen ~ *to stand gaping* **F·eilheit** f ~/ *venality* (*of a judge*)

F·eilicht n ~s/ *filings* pl, → Feilstaub

f·eilschen 1. vi [h] *to bargain, palter* (um *about*); *to chaffer, haggle, higgle* (um *over*) **2.** ≗ n *chaffering, haggling*; *chaffer, haggle* **F·eilscher** m ~s/~ *bargainer, haggler*

ˣ**Feim** m ~s/~e = Schaum

ˣ**Feim** m, **Feime** f, **F·eimen** m (Schober) *mow, rick, stack* (*of corn, hay*); → Schober

ˣ**f·eimen** vi [h] = schäumen

fein I. a A. 1. (of gold, etc) *fine, refined*; *pure* **2.** (aus kleinsten Teilen) *fine* (*flour, powder, sand, sugar*); *fine* od *drizzling* (*rain*) **3.** (dünn, **zart**) *delicate* (*lines*; *edge*); *fine* (*pen*), *thin* (*thread, wire*) ‖ *delicate, fine* (*hands, skin*); *slender* ‖ *subtle* (*odour*); ~es Blau *delicate blue* | *fine-drawn* (*network*) ‖ 〈tech〉 ~es Gewinde *fine* (*pitch*) *thread* ‖ ~er Kamm *fine-tooth comb* **4.** (aus ~em Gewebe, **Stoff**) *fine* (*linen, porcelain*) ‖ *dainty* (*dish*); ~e Küche *delicate cookery*; ~es Gebäck *fancy cakes* pl, *pastry* ‖ 〈com〉 (of *wine*, etc) *choice, excellent, exquisite*; *fine, first-class*; *superior*; ~ste Sorte *choicest quality* ‖ das ≗ste vom ≗nen *the choice, pick, plums* pl; *the cream, flower* **B.** 〈**übtr** & **fig**〉 **1.** (**genau**) *accurate* (*tuning-in*); *precise* (*adjustment*) **2.** (~ **entwickelt**) **a.** *delicate* (*features*) **b.** *nice, quick* (*eye*) (f *for*) ‖ ~es Gehör, Ohr *nice* (od *quick, sensitive*) *ear* (f *for*); *delicate sense of hearing* ‖ *delicate* (*palate*), *nice* (*taste*); *delicate* (*touch*); *a good* (*nose*) (*for* . .) ‖ *nice* (od *refined, subtle*) *sense* (*of honour*) ‖ *delicate, tender* (*conscience*) **3.** (**zart**) *delicate* (*instrument*); *fine* (*design*); *minute*; *nice* (*distinctions, shades of meaning*); *subtle* (*associations*) **4.** (**~ausgeführt**) *elegant*; *neat* (*building*; *piece of work*; *stroke*); **5.** (gediegen; **vornehm**) *elegant, fine, good, refined* (*manners*; *taste*); *good* (*manners, form*) ‖ *noble, well-bred* (*man*); *good* (*player*) ‖ ~er Kopf *brilliant* (od *fine*) *mind*; ~er Gelehrter *fine* (od *distinguished*) *scholar* ‖ ~es Englisch *Standard English, the King's E.* **6.** (**äußerlich** ~) *elegant, fashionable* (*clothes*); *fine* (*lady*); *smart*; es ist nicht ~ *it is not smart* (*to wear* . .) ‖ *fashionable* (*world*) = *rank and fashion*; *the smart set* ‖ sich ~ m *to dress elegantly*; *to titivate* [vi]; *to smarten o.s. up* **7.** (**nett**, schön) *fine, goody*; *excellent, first-class, splendid*; 〈sl〉 *posh* (*shoes*) ‖ 〈iron〉 → schön ‖ ~! *excellent!*, *good!*, → famos **II. adv 1.** *delicately, finely* (*drawn, spun*); ~ gemahlen *finely ground*; ~geschnitten *fine-cut* (*tobacco*) ‖ ~ gefügt *finely wrought* (*texture*) ‖ (Teile) ~ zus–nähen *to fine--draw*; (Draht) ~ ausziehen *to fine-draw* ‖ **2.** (**genau**) *accurately* (*tuned-in*); *precisely* **3.** *to have a delicate sense of hearing*; *to have a quick* (od *nice*) *ear* **4.** 〈**fig**〉 ~aufgebaut (ersonnen, gesponnen) *fine-drawn* (*argument*); *fine-spun* (*story*) ‖ *neatly* (*carried out*) ‖ *subtly* (*blended*) **5.** *elegantly, fashionably*; *smartly* (*dressed*) **6. a.** es riecht, schmeckt ~ *it smells, tastes deliciously* **7.** das hat er ~ gemacht *he has made a neat* (od *smart*) *job of it*; *he has done well* ‖ das wird mir ~ passen *that will suit me fine* ‖ er kann ~ reiten *he is a splendid* od *good rider* od *horseman* ‖ ich konnte alles ~ sehen *I could see all fine* (*from my room*) **c.** °er ist ~ heraus *he is well-off*; *a lucky dog* (od *fellow*) *he is* **6.** °[vor Adj = schön] ~ säuberlich *nice and clean* **III.** das ≗e → Feine **IV.** [in comp] → Fein- ‖ [beachte]: ~körnig (etc) [a] *finegrained*; [compr] ~körniger *finer-grained* **F·ein-** (→ a. fein a & adv) **~abstimmung** f 〈wir〉 *sharp tuning* **~bäcker** m *pastry-cook*; *fancy-baker* **~bäckerei** f *fancy-bakery* **~bau** m ⟨phys⟩ *structure of atoms* **~blech** n (bis 3 mm) *thin sheet*; *sheet-metal* **~brenner** m *refiner* **~draht** m *fine wire* **~drähtig** a *fine-strand wire* (*rope*) **~druckpapier** n *fine printings* [pl] **~einstellung** f *precise* od *precision adjustment*; ⟨phot⟩ *fine focusing* **~empfindend** a (*finely*) *sensitive* **~faserig** a *fibrillar*(*y*); *fine-fibred*; *fine grained* (*wood*); → fein III. **~fühlend**, **~fühlig** a *delicate* (*p*); *sensitive* ‖ *tactful* **~fühligkeit** f *delicacy of feeling*; *sensitiveness* **~gängig** a *fine pitch* (*screw*) **~gebäck** n → Biskuit, Keks **~gefüge** n ⟨phys, glass⟩ *microstructure* **~gefühl** n *delicacy of feeling*; *sensitiveness*; *tact* **~gehalt** m *fineness* (*of metals*); Gold~ *carat* ‖ *standard* (*of coins*) | ~sregulierung [f] *fineness control* ‖ [konkr] *control device for the variation of the fineness*; ~sstempel [m] *hall-mark*, *plate-mark*; mit dem ~sstempel versehen *to hall-mark* **~gemahlen** a *pulverized* **~gewinde** n ⟨tech⟩ *fine-pitch thread* **~gold** n *fine* (od *pure*) *gold* (= *24 carats*) **~gut** n ⟨tech⟩ *finished product* **~höhenmesser** m *statoscope* **~hörig** a *quick* (od *open*) *-eared*; → fein III. **~kohle** f *fine* (od *small*) *coal* **~korn** n ⟨min⟩ *fine-grain* ‖ (an Waffen) *fine sight* | ~entwickler [m] ⟨phot⟩ *f. g. developer* ‖ ~film [m] *f. g. stock* **~korneisen** n *close-grained iron* **~körnig** a *close–* od *fine-grained*; *fine granular* (*product*) → fein III. **~kosthandlung** f *delicatessen* [Ger] *-shop* (⟨Am⟩ . . *store*) **~kostwaren** f [pl] *delicatessen* [Ger] pl **~kupfer** n *refined copper* **~maschig** a *fine-meshed*; → fein III. **~mechanik** f *fine mechanics* pl [sg konstr]; *light engineering precision-tool manufacture* **~mechaniker** m *mechanician*; *precision-tool manufacturer*; *instrument worker* **~mehl** n ⟨mill⟩ *fines* pl **~meßschraube** f ⟨tech⟩ *micrometer-screw* **~messung** f *micrometer measurement* **~metall** n *fine metal* **~passung** f ⟨tech⟩ *medium fit* **~plätterin** f *ironer of fine linen* **~porig** a *fine grained* (*wood*) **~postpapier** n (Kanzleipapier) *bond paper* **~pulverig** a *powdery*, *pulverulent* **~schmecker** m *epicure*; *gastronomer*; *gourmet* (Fr) **~schnitt** m (Tabak) *navy cut* **~schreibpapier** n *superfine writing paper* **~seife** f *fancy soap* **~silber** n *fine silver* **~sinn** m *delicate* (od *refined*, *subtle*) *sense*; *fineness of feeling* (od *taste*); *refinement* **~sinnig 1.** a *fine* (*judge of* . .); *refined* ‖ *ingenious* (*writer*); *clever* (*book*); *fine-drawn* (*argument*) **2.** adv *cleverly*; *ingeniously* **~spinnmaschine** f *spinning-jenny* **~split** m *fine aggregate material* **~stahl** m *refined steel* **~stellen** vt [h] *to adjust* **~struktur** f ⟨phys, glass⟩ *microstructure* **~strumpf** m ⟨com⟩ *fully-fashioned stocking* **~stufenregelung** f *sensitive control* **~vermahlung** f (weitere) *regrinding* **~waage** f *micrometer-balance* **~wäsche** f *fine laundering* | ⟨com⟩ [koll] [konkr] *delicate fabrics* pl **~waschmittel** n ⟨tech⟩ *light-duty detergent* **~zellig** a *fine-celled*; → fein III. **~zerkleinerung** f *fine*(*r*) *reduction* **~zinn** n *grain-tin* **~zucker** m *refined sugar*

Feind m ~(e)s/~e **1.** ⟨mil⟩ **a.** *enemy*; ⟨poet⟩ *foe* ‖ (im Manöver) *aggressor forces*; markierter ~ *skeleton enemy* ‖ der böse ~ *the wicked enemy* **b.** [koll] der ~ (die feindlichen Truppen) *the enemy*; *enemy elements*; starker ~ *power enemy forces* ‖ dem ~e in die Hände fallen *to fall into the hands of the enemy*; (S) *to fall a prey to a p*; → Hand ‖ vom ~e besetzt *enemy-occupied* (*city*) ‖ am ~ bleiben *to engage the e.*; *to keep in touch with* . .; nah am ~ *close to the e.*; ständig am ~ s *to be in constant touch with the enemy* ‖ vor dem ~e fallen *to fall on the field of honour* ‖ zum ~e übergehen *to desert to the enemy* **2.** (persönlicher ~) *enemy*; *foe*; erbitterter ~ *bitter enemy*; → Tod~ ‖ (Gegner) *adversary*, *antagonist*, *opponent*; der (*or* ein) ~ e–r S, ein ~ v e–r S s *to be the enemy of a th*, *to be an enemy of* od *to a th*; *to be a foe to a th*; *to be opposed* (od *averse*, *hostile*) *to a th*; er war ein ~ (v) aller Grausamkeit *he was a foe* (od *he was averse*) *to all cruelty*; *he loathed all c.*; das Buch machte ihm viele ~e *the book made him many enemies* ‖ sich [dat] jdn zum ~e m *to make an enemy of a p*; sich die ganze Familie z ~e m *to bring the house about one's ears*; die Affäre hatte die Leute unter–e–a z ~en gemacht *the affair had set people by the ears* **3.** (of animals, plants) = Schädling **4.** ⟨ec⟩ der böse ~ *the arch-enemy*, *old enemy*, *the Fiend*, *the Evil one*, *the Devil* **5.** [in comp] → Feind-, Feindes- **feind** a [nur pred] jdm ~ s *to bear a p a grudge*, *to have* (od *nurse*, *owe*) *a grudge against a p*; jdm ~ w *to fall out with a p* ‖ e–r S ~ s *to be averse* (od *opposed*) *to a th*; *to be a foe to a th*; *to hate* od *loathe a th* **F·eind-** [in comp] ⟨mst⟩ *enemy* . . **~berührung** f *contact with the e.* ‖ Marschordnung vor ~ *approach march* **~beschuß** m *e. fire* **~bild** n *profile of the e.* **~einbruch** m *e. penetration* **~fahrt** f ⟨mar⟩ *operational cruise* **~flotte** f *e. fleet* **~flug** m ⟨aero⟩(*operational*) *sortie* Fr; *mission*; *raid* **~flugzeug** n *e. plane* od *aircraft* **~frei** a *cleared of* (od *free from*) *e. forces* **~gelände** n *e.-held terrain* **~kräfte** f pl *e. forces* **~lagebericht** m *intelligence report* **~lagebeurteilung** f *intelligence estimate* **~land** n *e. country* **~nachrichten** f pl [koll] *intelligence* | ~abteilung [f] *G-2* N **~sicht** f *detection by the e.*

F·eindes- [in comp] **~hand** f; in ~ fallen *to fall into the e.'s hands*; (S) *to fall a prey to the e.* **~land** n *the hostile* (od *e.*) *country* (od *territory*); in ~ einfallen *to invade the e. c.* **~wärts** adv *in the direction of the e.* **F·eindin** f ~/~nen (vgl Feind 2.) *enemy*, *foe* ‖ *adversary*, *opponent* ‖ sie ist die (*or* e–e) ~ alles Fortschritts *or* e–e ~ vom Fortschritt *she is the* (od *an*) *e. of all progress*, *she is an e. of* (od *to*) *progress* **f·eindlich I.** a **A.** [attr] **1.** *enemy* (*attack*, *country*, *fleet*, *resistance*); *hostile* (*army*, *country*, *race*); die ~en Truppen, das ~e Heer *the e.* ‖ in ~e Hände fallen *to fall into the hands of the e.*; das ~e Feuer *the e.'s fire* ‖ ~e Handlungen [pl] *hostilities* [pl] **2.** [übtr] *adverse* (*critic*; *gale*) ‖ *hostile*, *unfriendly* (*crowd*); *antagonistic* (*influence*) **B.** [pred] jdm ~ s *to be the e. of a p*; *to be hostile towards* (od *inimical to*) *a p*; › feind ‖ e–r S ~ s *to be hostile* (od *inimical*, *antagonistic*) *to a th* **II.** adv *inimically*; sich ~ stellen z jdm, etw; jdm, e–r S ~ gegenübertreten *to oppose a p*, *a th*; *to be averse* od *opposed to a th*; *to antagonize a th* ‖ ~ gesinnt *antagonistically inclined*; *hostile*; jdm, e–r S ~ gesinnt s = feindlich I. B. | **~keit** f, **F·eindschaft** f ~/~en **1.** *enmity*, *hatred* (gegen *of*, *against*); *animosity*, *hostility* (gegen *towards*); *ill will* ‖ in ~ s *or* leben mit *to be at enmity with*; ⟨Am⟩ *to be at outs with*; in ~ geraten mit *to fall out with* ‖ er hegt k–e ~ *he does not bear any enmity* ‖ ~ stiften *to sow the seeds of hatred* ‖ sich jds ~ zuziehen *to bring a p's ill will upon o.s.*; *to incur a p's ill will* ‖ darum k–e ~! *no offence*! *nothing personal meant*! **2.** (Abneigung) *aversion* (gegen *to*, *from*); *antagonism* (zw *between*) **f·eindschaftlich** a *hostile*, *unfriendly* (*crowd*; *demonstration*) **f·eindselig** a *hostile*, *unfriendly* (*crowd*, *demonstration*) ‖ *ill-disposed*, *malignant*, *malevolent* (*p*); *adverse* (*criticism*) | **~keit** f **1.** *enmity*; *hatred*; *hostility* (gegen *to*) **2.** ⟨mil⟩ (feindliche Handlung) [mst pl] ~en *hostilities*; die ~en eröffnen (einstellen) *to open* (*suspend*) *hostilities*

F·eine n (→ Feinheit; fein I. B.) das ~ *the elegance*, *neatness*, *refinement* (in *a p's bearing*, *taste*, etc) **f·einen** vt [h] (Eisen) *to refine*; → verfeinern **F·einheit** f ~/~en (→ fein [a]) **A. 1.** ⟨met⟩ *fineness*; *purity* ‖ ~sgrad [m] *degree of fineness* **2.** *fineness* (*of flour*; *of a structure*); *subtlety* (*of a fluid*) **3.** *delicacy*, *fineness* (*of linen*); *slenderness*, *thinness* (*of a hand*) **4.** *choice*; *excellence*; *exquisiteness*; *superior quality* (*of wine*, etc.) **B.** ⟨übtr &

fig⟩ **1.** *daintiness, elegance* (*of expression*); *delicacy* (*of touch*); *nicety* (*of observation*); *subtlety* (*of thought*); ~ des Gefühls *delicacy, sensitiveness*; ~ der Arbeit *workmanship* ‖ ~en [pl] *delicacies* (*of style*); kl ~en [pl] *niceties* (*of accuracy in a play*) **2.** *elegance, fineness, refinement* (*of manners*, etc.); *politeness* **3.** (äußere ~) *elegance*; *fashionableness*; *showiness*; *splendour*
Feinsl·iebchen n ⟨poet⟩ *darling, sweetheart*
F·einst- ≃**körnig** a *ultrafine-grain(ed)* [attr] **~-mahlung** f *super-fine grinding*

feist a ⟨hunt⟩ *fat and fleshy* (*boar*); *in grease*; ~ s (of deer, etc.) *to be in grease, to be in prime* (od *pride*) *of grease* | ⟨übtr⟩ *fat*; *corpulent, obese*; *plump* (*cheeks*); *stout*; ~e P *fatty* ‖ ~ m *to fatten*; *to fat* **F·eist** n ⟨hunt⟩ *grease* ‖ ⟨übtr⟩ *fat*; *bacon* | ~hirsch [m] *stag in grease* **F·eistling** m ~s/~e (P) ⟨fam⟩ *grampus* **F·eiste** f **1.** = Feist **2.** Hirsch≃ *time* (od *season*) *of grease* **F·eistigkeit** f *state of grease* ‖ *fatness, corpulence, obesity* **F·eisterling** m ⟨bot⟩ (Pilz) *large goat's beard*; *club fungus*; Gattung der ~e *Clavaria* [L]

°**f·eixen** vi [h] ⟨fam⟩ *to grin* (über das ganze Gesicht *from ear to ear*); *to pull faces*; ständig ~ *to be always on the grin*; wir feixten alle *we all had our tongues in our cheeks*; → grinsen

F·elbel m ~s/~ *velveteen, rough plush*
×**F·elber** m, **F·elbinger** m ⟨bot⟩ *willow*
F·elberich m ⟨bot⟩ *loosestrife*
F·elchen m ~s/~ ⟨ich⟩ *white fish*; *vendace*

Feld n ~(e)s/~er **A.** ⟨eig⟩ **1.** *field*, (*tract of*) *open country*; gr ~ *or* weites ~ *plain*; *wide expanse* **2.** (Flur, Acker) *ground*; *arable land*; Korn≃ *corn-f., f. of grain*; Rüben≃ *f. of beet*, Weizen≃ *wheat-f., f. of wheat* **B.** ⟨übtr⟩ **1.** Eis≃ *ice-f.*; Schnee≃ *snow-f.*; *f. of snow* ‖ Gold≃er [pl] *gold-f.s* pl; Kohlen≃ *coal-f.*; Öl≃er [pl] *oil-f.s* ‖ Minen≃ *mine-f.*; Schuß≃ *f. of fire* **2.** ⟨mil⟩ Schlacht≃ *battle-f., f.* (*of battle*) → E. 2. **3.** ⟨sport⟩ (Spiel≃) *field* ‖ → D. **4.** ⟨min⟩ *mining area*; (of coal) *panel* **5.** ⟨phys⟩ (Kraft≃) elektrisches, magnetisches ~ *electric, magnetic f.* **6.** Beobachtungs≃ *f. of observation*; Gesichts≃ *f. of vision* (od *view*) **C.** (**Einzel**≃, **Fach**) **1.** vertieftes viereckiges ~ *panel* (*of a door, wall*); rechteckiges ~ *pane*; (Raum) mit ~ern ausschmükken *to panel* ‖ ⟨arch⟩ geschmücktes ~ (e–r Dekke) *coffer* ‖ (e–r Schüsseltafel) *cell* **2.** (of a flag, shield) *field*; → Wappenschild ‖ *compartment, division, section* ‖ (of a chess board) *square* **3.** (Längs≃ im Geschützrohr) *chase, land* (Ggs Zug [m] *groove*) **4.** ⟨fig⟩ (~ der geistigen Tätigkeit) *field* (*of investigation, research*); *department*; *province, realm*; *scope, sphere* **D.** ⟨sport⟩ das ~ (= Teilnehmer an e–r Jagd, e–m Rennen) *the field* ‖ das übrige ~ *the ruck* **E. Wendungen**: **1.** ⟨fig⟩ das ist ein weites ~ *that subject covers a wide f.* ‖ ⟨min⟩ ein ~ abbauen *to exploit* (od *exhaust*) *a mine* ‖ das ~ bebauen *to till the ground* (od *soil*) ‖ ⟨mil⟩ das ~ behaupten *to hold* (od *maintain*) *the f.* ‖ die ~er durchstreifen *to wander* od *ramble through the f.s*; *to roam about the f.s, to rove* (od *scour, traverse*) *the fields* ‖ ⟨fig⟩ jdm freies ~ l *to give a p full* od *free scope* ‖ ⟨mil⟩ das ~ räumen *to leave the f.*; *to depart*; *to flee*; ⟨fam⟩ *to clear out* **2.** er ist **auf** dem ~e *he is out* (od *at work*) *in the f.* ‖ auf freiem ~e *in the open*; auf f. ~e kampieren *to bivouac* ‖ ⟨mil⟩ auf dem ~e bleiben *to remain upon the f.*; → fallen I. B. 2. ‖ ⟨fig⟩ auf diesem ~e *in this f.* | **aus** dem ~e schlagen *to drive from the f.* | **durch** ~ u Flur *across the f.s* | ⟨mil⟩ **im** ~e *in the f.*; im ~e stehen (of troops) *to be brought together for a campaign*; draußen im ~e stehen (of a p) *to be at the war* (od *front*) ‖ ⟨fig⟩ das ist noch im weiten ~e *that's still a good way off*; . . *still very remote*; . . *still by no means decided* | ⟨fig⟩ (Gründe) **ins ~** führen *to bring forward*; *to put on to the table* ‖ ⟨mil⟩ ins ~ gehen, rücken, ziehen *to go off to the war, to take the f.*; *to battle* (gegen *against*) ‖ ins ~ stellen *to bring together for battle*; *to muster* | **über ~** gehen *to go across country* ‖ ⟨fig⟩ sich über ein weites ~ erstrecken *to cover a wide f.* | zu ~e ziehen = ins ~ ziehen

F·eld- [in comp] **1.** ⟨agr⟩ *field-* . ., *land-* . .; *agricultural* **2.** ⟨mil⟩ *field-* . .; *army-* . .; *camp-* . . **~apotheke** f ⟨mil⟩ *f.-dispensary* **~arbeit** f ⟨agr⟩ *f.* (od *farm*)-*labour* **~arbeiter** m ⟨agr⟩ *f.* (od *farm*)-*labourer* (od *hand*) **~artillerie** f ⟨mil⟩ *f.-artillery* **~arzt** m ⟨mil⟩ *army-surgeon* ≃**·aus**, ≃**·ein** adv *across* (⟨Am⟩ *cross*) *country* **~ausrüstung** f ⟨mil⟩ *f.-equipage* **~bäckerei** f ⟨mil⟩ *f.* od *army bakery* **~bahn** f ⟨rail⟩ *portable* (od *light*) *railway*; *f.* (od *small gauge*) *railway* | ~schiene [f] *light rail* **~bau** m ⟨agr⟩ *farming*; *agriculture*; *tillage* **~becher** m *canteen cup* **~befestigung** f ⟨mil⟩ *f.-work* **~bereinigung** f ⟨agr⟩ *consolidation of landholding(s)* **~bestäubung** f ⟨aero⟩ *dusting crops* **~bestellung** f ⟨agr⟩ *tillage* **~bett** n *army* (od *camp*)-*bed* (⟨Am⟩ a. *cot*); *portable bed* **~binde** f ⟨mil⟩ *sash, scarf*; ⟨mar⟩ *full dress belt*; ⟨aero⟩ *waist-belt* **~blume** f ⟨bot⟩ *f.-flower* **~bluse** f ⟨mil⟩ *service blouse*; *f.-service* od *battle jacket* **~buch** n ⟨surv, etc⟩ *field book* **~champignon** m ⟨bot⟩ *mushroom* **~dieb** m *f. robber* **~diebstahl** m *f. robbery* **~dienst** m *active service* ‖ *f. service* | ≃fähig [a] *fit for active service* ‖ ~ordnung [f] *f.-service regulations*; (Buch) *field manual* ‖ ~stelle [f] *field office* ‖ ~übung [f] *f.-exercise* (od *practice*); ~übungstag [m] ⟨engl⟩ *f.-day* ≃**einwärts** adv *f.wards*; *across the country* (od *fields*) *into the fields*; ein Spaziergang ~ *a cross-country walk*; → –aus **~erbse** f ⟨bot⟩ *f.-pea* **~ersatzbataillon** n *reinforcement battalion* **~fernkabel** n *spiral-four cable* **~flasche** f *water-bottle*, ⟨Am⟩ *canteen* **~flugplatz** m *combat* od *advanced airfield* **~frevel** m ⟨agr⟩ *agrarian crime*; *stealing from the fields*; *mischief done to the fields* (od *crops*) **~frucht** f [koll] *crop* ‖ ≃e [pl] *field-produce* **~funksprecher** m *f. radio*; ⟨fam⟩ *walkie-talkie* **~geistlicher** m ⟨mil⟩ (*army*) *chaplain* **~gemeinschaft** f ⟨agr⟩ *agricultural community* **~gendarmerie** f ⟨mil⟩ *f.-police*; *military police* (MP) **~gepäck** n ⟨mil⟩ *baggage*; ⟨Am⟩ *f. pack, dufflebag* **~gerät** n ⟨agr⟩ *agricultural implement* **~gericht** n *provost court* **~geschrei** n ⟨hist⟩ *password* ‖ ⟨bib⟩ *war cry*; → Losung **~geschütz** n ⟨mil⟩ *f.-gun* (od *piece*); schweres ~ *gun of position* **~glas** n ⟨mil⟩ → –stecher **~gottesdienst** m *camp-service* **~graswirtschaft** f ⟨agr⟩ *rotational system of tilling and pasturing* **~grau 1.** a ⟨mil⟩ *f.-grey* (*uniform*) ‖ der ≃e *the German soldier*; die ≃en ⟨a.⟩ *the f.-greys*, **2.** ≃ n *f.-grey* (*in f.-g.*) **~größe** f ⟨el-phys⟩ *field*, ⟨Am⟩ *f. strength* od *intensity* **~haubitze** f (*f.*) *howitzer* **~hauptmann** m ⟨hist⟩ *commander* (*of mercenaries*) **~heer** n ⟨mil⟩ *f.-troops* pl **~herr** m *commander*; *general* | ~enhalle [f] ⟨Ger⟩ (in München) *Cenotaph* ‖ ~enkunst [f] *generalship*; *strategy* **~hopfen** m ⟨bot⟩ = Hartheu **~huhn** n ⟨orn & hunt⟩ *partridge*; *bird*; (afrikanisches) *francolin*; *bush-partridge* **~hüter** m ⟨agr⟩ *f.-guard* **~instandsetzung** f ⟨mil⟩ *third echelon maintenance* **~jäger** m ⟨mil⟩ *chasseur* Fr **~kabel** n ⟨mil⟩ *assault cable* od *wire* **~kanone** f = Feldgeschütz **~kapazität** f ⟨comp⟩ *card field capacity* **~kessel** m ⟨mil⟩ *dixie* (–*xy*) **~küche** f *canteen*; *cook-house*; *camp* (od *army, field*) *kitchen* ‖ ~ngericht [n] *field-dish* (od *diet*) **~lager** n *camp* **~landeplatz** m ⟨aero⟩ *satellite landing ground* **~lattich** m ⟨bot⟩ = Huflattich **~lazarett** n *ambulance*; *f.-hospital*; *casualty clearing station*, ⟨Am⟩ *dispensary* **~linie** f ⟨phys⟩ *line of flux, line of force* **~magnet** m *f.-magnet* **~mark** f ⟨agr⟩ *all the fields belonging to a village-community* **~marschall** m ⟨mil⟩ *F.-Marshal* (der Herr ~ N. *F.-M. N.*) ‖ ~stab [m]

F.-M.l's baton ≈**marschmäßig** a *in heavy marching order* ‖ ~e Ausrüstung *service marching-order* **~maß** n ⟨agr⟩ *measure of land* ≈**mäßig** a *hasty* (*shelter*) **~maus** f ⟨zoo⟩ *f.-vole*; *harvest-mouse* **~messer** m ⟨surv⟩ *surveyor* **~meßkunst**, **~messung** f *surveying* **~mütze** f ⟨mil⟩ *f.* (od *forage*)-*cap*; *undress cap*; („Schiffchen") *side cap*; ⟨engl a.⟩ *beret* **~ort** m ⟨min⟩ *the end* (od *extremity*) *of a gallery* **~polizei** f ⟨agr⟩ *f.-police*; *rural police* **~post** f ⟨mil⟩ *army postal service* (*for the f. troops*) **|** ~amt [n] *army post office* ‖ ~-brief [m] *letter on active service*; ~nummer [f] *army postal* (⟨Am⟩ *A.P.O.* [*Army Post Office*]) *number*; Kameraden v der andern ~ (Feinde) ⟨hum⟩ *strangers* ‖ ~päckchen [n] *parcel for a soldier in the f.* **~posten** m ⟨mil⟩ *outpost*; *picket* **~-probst** m ⟨mil⟩ *chaplain-general* **~raute** f ⟨bot⟩ *fumitory* **~rüster** f ⟨bot⟩ *common elm* **~salat** m ⟨bot⟩ *corn-salad*; *lamb's lettuce* **~schaden** m ⟨agr⟩ *damage done to the f.* (od *crops*) **~schädling** m ⟨zoo & bot⟩ (*f.-*)*pest* **~schanze** f *f.-work* †**~-scher(er)** m *army surgeon* **~schlacht** f *pitched battle* **|** †**~schlange** f ⟨mil hist⟩ *culverin*, *falconet* **~-schmiede** f *portable* (od *moving*, *travelling*) *forge* **~schnepfe** f ⟨orn⟩ = Brachvogel **~schutz** m ⟨agr⟩ *protection of the f.s* (od *crops*) **~schütz** m = Feldhüter **~schwamm** m ⟨bot⟩ *mushroom* **~soldat** m *soldier of the line*; → feldgrau **~spat** m ⟨min⟩ *fel*(*d*)*spar*; Kali≈ → Orthoklas **|** ~mehl [n] *ground f.r* **~spule** f ⟨el⟩ *field* od *magnet*(*izing*) *coil* **~stärke** f ⟨el⟩ *f.-strength* (od *intensity*) **~stecher** m ⟨opt⟩ (*prismatic*) *binoculars* pl; gr ~ *f.-glass*(*es*) **~stein** m (*rough*) *boulder* (⟨a.⟩ Findling) **|** (Grenzstein) *landmark* **~stiefel** m ⟨mil⟩ *f.-service boot* **~stufe** f (mit Rainböschung) *lynchet* **~-stuhl** m *camp-stool*; *folding-chair* **~telegraph** m ⟨mil⟩ *f.-telegraph* **~truppen** f [pl] ⟨mil⟩ *f.-troops* [pl] **~übung** f ⟨mil⟩ *f.-exercise* (od *practice*) ≈**-verwendungsfähig** a *fit for* (*active service* od) *field duty* **~wache** f *picket* **|** –ndienst [m] *picket-duty* °**~-, Wald- u Wiesen**– ⟨hum⟩ *common* **~webel** m ⟨mil engl⟩ (*company*) *sergeant-major*; ⟨Ger⟩ *sergeant*; Haupt≈ *chief petty officer*; ⟨fig⟩ (auf Bier) "*collar*"; *nick and froth* **~weg** m *f.-path*; *dust* od *dirt road* **~wirtschaft** f *farming*, *agriculture*; *tillage* . . **~zeichen** n *f.-banner*; *flag*, *standard* **~zeugmeister** m ⟨mil hist⟩ General≈ *the Master-General of the Ordnance* **~zug** m **1.** ⟨mil⟩ *campaign* (in e–m ~ *in a c.*), *expedition*; e–n ~ mitmachen *to campaign*; e–n ~ unternehmen *to go on* (od *to organize*) *a campaign* **2.** ⟨fig⟩ *campaign*; ⟨Am⟩ *drive* (gegen *against*) **~zulage** f ⟨mil⟩ *f.-allowance*

F·elge f ~/~n **1.** (Rad≈) *felloe*, *felly*; *rim*; (Rad) mit ~n versehen *to rim* **|** ~nband [n] (Schlauchschoner) ⟨mot, etc⟩ *chafing strip* ‖ ~n-hauer [m] *wheelwright* **2.** ⟨gym⟩ *circle*; → Riesen≈; ~naufschwung [m] *upward circle* **3.** ×⟨agr⟩ *the ploughing of the fallow* **f·elgen** vt [h] **1.** (Rad) *to rim* **2.** ⟨agr⟩ (Land) *to fallow*; *to plough up* **F·elgner** m ~s/~ *wheelwright*

F·ell n ~(e)s/~e **A. 1.** (ungegerbtes ~) a. (behaartes ~ am lebenden T) ⟨allg⟩ *coat* ‖ *fell*; (of sheep) *pelt* ‖ (glatt v gr T) *hide*; *coat* **b.** (mst wertvolles ~ aus kz, weichem Haar) *fur*; Biber≈ *beaver*; → Pelz ‖ [koll] ~e [pl] *peltry* **2.** (abgezogenes, zugerichtetes ~) *skin*: ⟨com⟩ *hide*; → Haut **3.** e–m T das ~ abziehen *to skin an animal* ‖ ⟨fig⟩ er sah s–e ~e fortschwimmen *he found himself at the end of his tether*; ihm waren die ~e fortgeschwommen *he was deeply disappointed*; *his plans had failed* **B.** °(Menschenhaut) *hide*, *skin*, ⟨sl⟩ *bark*; ein dickes ~ h *to have a thick hide* od *skin* ‖ ihm juckte das ~ *he was out of control* (vor . . *with*); *he was in high spirits* ‖ jdm aufs ~ k, jdm das ~ gerben *to tan a p*(*'s hide*); *to give a p a hiding*; *to hide a p*; etw aufs ~ bek *to get a hiding* ‖ ⟨fig⟩ jdm das ~ über die Ohren ziehen *to flay* (od *fleece*, *skin*, *shave*) *a p*; *to pull the wool over a p's eyes*; ⟨sl⟩ *to diddle a p* **C.** ⟨übtr⟩ **1.** (zarte Haut) → Bauch≈, Brust≈, Rippen≈, Trommel≈, Zwerch≈ **2.** unteres ~ *lower head*, *under end* (*of a drum*) **~bereiter** m *hide-dresser*; *skin-dresser* **~händler** m *dealer in peltry* (od *hides*); *skin-dealer* **~messe** f *hide-fair* **~werk** n = Pelzwerk **~zurichter** m = Fellbereiter

Fell·ache m ~n/~n **F·ellah** m ~s/~s (arabisch) *fellah* [pl *fellaheen*]

F·elleisen n *travelling bag*; *valise* [Fr]; *wallet*

Felon·ie f ~/~n *felony*; *heinous crime*

Fels m –sen/–sen [mst nom & acc ~; ⟨poet a.⟩ dat]; → Felsen **1.** (felsiges Gestein) *rock*; *mass of stony matter* **2.** (~block) *block* (od *lump*) *of rock*; *boulder* ‖ (Meeresklippe) *cliff*, *crag*; *reef*; *rock* ‖ [koll] –sen [pl] *rock* (*masses of r.*); *rocks* [pl] ‖ kl ~ *rocklet*; künstlicher ~ *rock* **|** voller –sen *rocky* (*coast*) ‖ auf e–m –sen gebaut *rock-built* (*castle*); aus e–m –sen gehauen *rock-hewn* (*tomb*); v –sen eingeschlossen *rock-bound* (*valley*) **3.** ⟨fig⟩ fest wie ein ~ *as firm as a rock* **|** → Felsen– **~-abhang** m steiler ~ *precipice*; *sheer face of a cliff* ≈**artig** a *rocky*; *rock-like* **~band** n *ledge* **~berg** m *tor* **~block** m *block of rock*; *boulder* **~geröll** n *pebbles* [pl] **~gestein** n *rock*; *stony matter* **~gruppe** f *rocks* [pl]; künstliche ~ *rock-work* **~hügel** m *tor* **~kletterer** m *rock climber* **~klippe** f *cliff*, *crag* **~klotz** m = Felsblock **~kluft** f (*rock-*)*cleft* **~maler** m ⟨praeh⟩ *rock-painter* **~malerei** f = Felszeichnung **~masse** f *masses* [pl] *of rock* **~riß** m *crack* **~ritzzeichnung** f → –zeichnung **~rücken** m *rockridge* **~schlucht** f *rocky defile* **~schutzdach** n ⟨bot praeh⟩ *shelter* **~spalte** f *crevice* **~spitze** f *crag*; *peak of a rock* **~stück** n *rock fragment* **~-sturz** m ⟨geol⟩ *rock-slip* **~tal** n *rock-bound ravine*: tiefes, steiles ~ (in der Sahara) *wadi* (*–dy*) **~wand** f *wall of rock*; steile ~ = Felsabhang **~-werk** n künstliches ~ *rockery*, *rock-work* **~zakken** m *gendarme* **~zeichnung** f ⟨praeh⟩ *petroglyph* ‖ (gemacht) *rock-painting* **F·elsen- ~beere** f ⟨bot⟩ = Brombeere **~bein** n ⟨anat⟩ *internal petrous portion of the temporal bone* **~birne** f ⟨bot⟩ *grape-pear* ≈**fest** a ⟨fig⟩ *firm*, *unshakable* (*conviction*) ‖ [pred] *rock-firm* (*as facts*); das steht ~ *that's as sure as eggs is* (od *are*) *eggs* **~-gebirge** n (in Amerika) *Rocky Mountains* [pl]; ⟨fam⟩ *the Rockies* [pl] **~gehege** n (in Zoologischen Gärten) *rock pit* **~gestade** n; steiles ~ *bluff* **~grab** n *rock-tomb* **~grund** m *rock-bed* **~-höhle** f *rock-cavern* **~insel** f *rocky island*; *skerry* **~keller** m *rock-hewn cellar* **~kirche** f *rock-hewn church* **~kleiber** m ⟨orn⟩ *rock nuthatch* **~malerei** f → Fels– **~mispel** f ⟨bot⟩ = Felsenbirne **~nest** n *rock-built nest*; ⟨fig⟩ *rock-built castle* **~quelle** f *rockspring* **~schönheit** f ⟨ich⟩ *Rock-Beauty* **~taube** f ⟨orn⟩ *rock-pigeon*

F·elsengebirge n *Rocky Mountains* pl

f·elsig a *rocky* (*coast*); *cragged*, *craggy*; *reefy* ‖ ~e Beschaffenheit *rockiness*; *craggedness*, *cragginess*; ~es Gestein *rock* **Fels·it** m ~s/ ⟨minr⟩ *felstone*

Fel·uke f ~/~n ⟨mar⟩ *felucca* [It]

Fem- [in comp] (→ Feme) *Vehmic* **~gericht** n = Feme ‖ das ~ ausüben an jdm *to execute V. justice on a p* **~richter** m *judge presiding over a V. court* **F·eme** f ~/~n **1.** ⟨Ger hist⟩ *the* (*Holy*) *Vehmgericht* (od *Vehme*); *Vehmic jurisdiction* ‖ *the Vehmic court* od *tribunal* **2.** ⟨mod⟩ *jurisdiction in defence of the state*

F·emel m ~s/ ⟨bot⟩ (männlicher Hanf) *fimble*

F·emelbetrieb m *blending-system in forestry*

femin·in a **1.** ⟨eig⟩ = weiblich **2.** ⟨übtr⟩ (of men) *feminine*; *effeminate*, *unmanly*, *womanish*; ~es Wesen *femininism*, *femininity* **Femin·inum** n [L] ~s/-nina ⟨gram⟩ *feminine gender*; *feminine noun* **Femin·ismus** m ⟨pol⟩ *feminism*

F·enchel m ~s/ ⟨bot⟩ *fennel* **~holz** n *sassafras wood* **~kraut** n = Erdrauch **~öl** n *fennel oil*

F·ender m ~s/~ ⟨mar⟩ *fender*

F·en-Distrikt m (in England; → Fenn) *the Fens* pl, *the Fen District*

F·enek m ~s/~s ⟨zoo⟩ (Wüstenfuchs) *fennec*

F·enier [-iə] m [Ir] *Fenian*; Geheimbund der ~ *the Fenian Brotherhood* | ~politik [f] *Fenianism*

ˣ**Fenn** n ~s/~e *fen*; *marshy land*

f·ennosk·andisch a ⟨geol, etc⟩ *fennoscandian*

F·enster n ~s/~ **1.** *window*; mit ~n versehen [a] *windowed*; ein Raum mit niedrigen ~n *a lowwindowed room*; Polstersitz unterhalb des ~s *window-seat* ‖ ohne ~ *windowless* (*room*); [pred] *innocent of windows* | blindes ~ *mock-w.*; Doppel~ *double w.*; Flügel~ *casement* (*w.*); Kipp~, durch Querholz geteiltes ~ *transom* (*w.*); Kirchen~ *church w.*; Teil e–s größeren ~s *light*; Mistbeet~ *frame with lights*; Rück~ ⟨mot⟩ *rear w.*; Schall~ *louvre-w.*; Schalter~ ([*ticket*] *office*) *w.*; (bis auf den Fußboden reichend) *French window* ‖ ⟨engl⟩ Schiebe~ *sash-window*; vorspringendes ~ *oriel* → Seiten~ ‖ **2.** am ~ *at* (od *by*) *the window*; am offenen ~ *at the open w.*; am ~ sitzen *to sit by the w.* ‖ jdm die ~ einwerfen *to break a p's w.s* ‖ mein ~ geht nach der Straße (hinaus) *my w. looks on the street* ‖ ans ~ rennen *to run to the w.* ‖ aus dem ~ sehen, zum ~ hinaus sehen *to look out of the w.* ‖ ⟨fig⟩ etw zum ~ hinauswerfen *to make ducks and drakes of a th, to play ducks and drakes with a th*; sein Geld zum ~ hinauswerfen *to squander* (od *waste*) *one's money* ‖ ⟨fig⟩ er sprach zum ~ hinaus *he spoke without any success* ‖ z ~ hineinklettern *to climb in at the w.* ‖ (etw) z ~ hineinwerfen *to throw in at the w.* **~band** n *hinge* **~bank** f *w.-sill* **~behänge** m pl *w. curtains* **~bekleidung** f *w.-case* **~beschläge** m [pl] *w.-fittings* [pl] **~brett** n *w.-sill* **~brief** m (Umschlag) *w.-envelope* **~brüstung** f *w.-ledge* (od *sill*) **~einfassung** f *w.-case* **~flügel** m *casement* (od *wing*) (*of a w.*) ‖ (nach oben u unten schiebbarer) *sash* **~futter** n *casement* **~giebel** m (*ornamental*) *w.-gable* **~gitter** n *w.-grating*; *lattice*; ⟨prison⟩ *bars* pl; ⟨bank⟩ *grille* **~glas** n *w.-glass* **~griff** m (*w.*) *handle, lock* **~höhle** f ⟨poet⟩ *hollow w.* **~kasten** m (f Blumen) *w.-box* **~kranz** m *circle of w.s* (*round base of dome*) **~kreuz** n *mullion*; *cross-bars* pl (*of a casement-w.*) **~kurbel** f ⟨mot⟩ *w. crank* **~läden** m pl *shutters* pl **~leder** n *wash-leather*; *shammy* **~nische** f *w. recess* **~öffnung** f *w. opening* **~papier** n *vitrified paper* **~pfeiler**, **~pfosten** m *mullion* °**~promenade** f; e–e ~ m *to walk up and down before* (od *beneath*) *a lady's w.* **~putzer** m *w. cleanser* **~rahmen** m *w.-frame*, (am Schiebefenster) *w.-sash* **~riegel** m *w.-bar* ‖ *sash-bolt* **~rose** f (über der Tür) *fan-light*; *Catherine wheel*; ⟨ec arch⟩ *rose-w.* **~scheibe** f *w.-pane*; e–e ~ *a pane* (*of glass*) ‖ die ~n in e–m Hause einschlagen *to break the w.s of a house*; ~n einsetzen *to fit panes in a w.-frame* **~sims** n *w.-sill* **~spiegel** m *w.-mirror* **~sturz** m *lintel* **~tür** f *French w.* **~verkleidung** f *w.-case* **~vertiefung** f *embrasure* **~verzierung** f *w.-tracery*; gitterartige ~ *w.-screen*; *lattice-work* **~vorhang** m *w.-curtain* **~werk** n ⟨ec arch⟩ *lights* **~wirbel** m *bolt* (*of a w.*) **F·ensterchen** n *small window* ‖ (Teil e–s größeren Fensters) *light*

ˣ**f·ensterln** vi [h] *to visit one's sweatheart at* (od *through*) *her window*

°**f·enstern** vt [h] (etw) *to fling, to throw* (in *into*; durch *through*) | (jdn) *to give* (*a p*) *the sack*

-fenstrig a [in comp] *windowed*; groß~ *tall-windowed*; ein zwei~es Zimmer *a room with two windows*

Fenz f [engl] ~/~en *fence*

Ferch m ~[e]s/~e ⟨min⟩ *fire-damp*

F·erge m ~n/~n ⟨bes poet⟩ *ferryman, boatman*; → Schiffer **f·erggen** vt [h] Sw → abfertigen; fortschaffen

F·erien pl **1.** (festgelegte ~ e–r Körperschaft) **a.** ⟨school⟩ *the holidays* [pl]; Oster~ *the Easter holidays*; die gr ~ *the long vacation*; *the summer holidays* **b.** ⟨jur & univ⟩ *vacation* (abbr *vac*); ⟨Am⟩ *recess* (*Easter recess*); die Gr ~ *the long vacation*; ⟨fam⟩ *the long vac, the long* ‖ während der ~ *during vacation* **c.** ⟨parl⟩ *recess*; das Parlament ist in den ~ *Parliament is in recess*; **2.** (jds ~, Freizeit) *holiday*; ⟨Am⟩ *vacation* ‖ ~ h, in den (*or* auf) ~ s *to be on holiday* ‖ in die ~ gehen *to go on holiday*; ⟨univ fam⟩ *to go down* ‖ ~ m ⟨Am⟩ *to vacation* ‖ e–n Monat ~ nehmen *to take a month's holiday* ‖ s–e ~ im Auslande verbringen *to take one's holiday abroad* **~adresse** f *holiday address* **~aufgabe** f *holiday* (od *vacation*) *task* **~heim** n *holiday-home* **~kolonie** f *holiday-camp* (*for children*) **~kurse** m [pl] ⟨univ⟩ *holiday courses* [pl] **~reise** f *holiday trip* **~reisende** [der ~, ein ~r] m ~n/~n *holiday-maker*; ⟨Am⟩ *vacationist* **~richter** m ⟨jur⟩ *Vacation Judge* **~stimmung** f *holiday mood* **~tag** m *holiday* **~zeit** f *vacation-time*

F·erkel n ~s/~ **1.** *young pig*; *piglet*; *shoat*, ⟨Am⟩ *shote*; Mast~ *porker*; → Wurf, werfen **2.** °⟨fig⟩ (P) *dirty p.*; *sloven* °**Ferkel·ei** f ⟨fig⟩ *dirtiness* ‖ *obscenity* **F·erkelkraut** n ⟨bot⟩ *cat's ear* **f·erkeln** vi [h] **1.** *to farrow, to litter, to pig* **2.** °⟨fig⟩ *to be slovenly* ‖ *to behave nastily*; *to use obscene language*

ferm a/adv [österr] = firm, fest, sicher

Ferm·ate f ~/~n ⟨mus⟩ *fermata* [It], *pause*

Ferm·ent n ~s/~e ⟨biol⟩ *ferment, enzyme*, → Diastase *trypsin* | **~ati·on** [*ts*] f *fermentation* **ferment·ieren** vi [h] *to ferment* ‖ ~d a *fermentative*

fern I. a **A.** [attr] **1.** *far* (*country*; *west*); *far-off*; *distant, remote* (*village*) ‖ der ~e Osten *the Far East* ‖ *remote ringing of bells*; *from the remotest parts* ‖ ⟨übtr⟩ → entfernt **2.** (of time) *distant, far-off, remote* (*ages*); die ~e Vergangenheit, Zukunft *the remote past, future* ‖ ~e Zeiten *far-off days*; in ~en Zeiten *far back* (⟨Am⟩ *way-back*) *in the past*; *long ago* ‖ bis in die ~ste Zeit *or* Zukunft *far down into the remotest times* od *future* ‖ in nicht z ~er Zeit *before long* **B.** prep [dat] ~ (v) der Heimat *far* (od *at a distance*; *remote, away*) *from home* ‖ e–r Lösung ~ s *to be far from solution* ‖ die Zeit ist noch nicht ~, als (*or* daß) er hier stand *it is not long since he stood here*; *not so long ago he ..* ‖ das sei ~ (*or* ~e) v mir *far be it from me* (*to do*); das sei ~ v mir! *by no means!, no idea!, far from it!* **II.** adv **1.** *far* (v *from*); *far-off*; *at a distance*; *away* (v *from a p*); ~ in der Straße gehört *heard away in the street* **2.** v ~ (*or* ~e) *from far*; *at* (od *from*) *a distance*; v ~ her *from a distance*; v ~ aus dem Inneren des Landes ⟨Am & Scot⟩ *from way-back* ‖ v ~(e) betrachtet *viewed from a distance*; ⟨fig⟩ *taken detachedly* **3.** nah u ~ *far and near*; v nah u ~ *from far and near*

Fernamb·ukholz n (= P–) *pernambuco wood*

F·ern- ~**·ab** adv *far away, far off*; ⟨Am & Scot⟩ *way-off* **~ablesung** f ⟨el⟩ *remote reading* **~amt** n ⟨telph⟩ *trunk-exchange* od *-office*; ~ bitte! ⟨fam⟩ *give me an orange*; das ~ anrufen *to call up the trunk-e.* | ~sbeamte [der ~, ein ~r] *operator* ~**amtlich 1.** a *telephonic* **2.** adv *by telephone* **~anruf** m *trunk-call* **~artillerie** f ⟨mil⟩ *long-range artillery* **~aufklärung** f ⟨mil⟩ *long-distance reconnaissance* **~aufnahme** f *long-distance view*; ⟨phot⟩ *telephotograph*; Apparat f ~n *telephote* **~bedienung** f *remote control* | ~seinrichtung [f] *r. c. device* ‖ ~staste [f] ⟨typewr⟩ *r. c.* **~betätigung** f *r. c.* **~bewegung** f (v Gegenständen durch ein Medium) *telekinesis* (Gr) ≁|**bleiben** vi [s] *to keep away* (v *from*); *to stay out*; ~ v *to cut* (*a meeting*) || ⟨fig⟩ *to remain aloof* || der Arbeit ~ *to remain off work* | ≁ [n] v Arbeitsplatz *absenteeism* **~erdbeben** n *remote earth-tremors* pl **~fokus** m *telefocus* **~flug** m ⟨aero⟩ *long-distance flight* **~führung** f *remote advance* (*of slides*) od ⟨mil⟩ *air raid* **≁gelenkt** a *distance controlled* (*target ship*) || ~gelenktes Flugzeug *remote-controlled aircraft*; ⟨fam⟩ *drone*; ~es Geschoß, ~er Körper (FK) *guided* od *homing missile* **~gespräch** n ⟨telph⟩ *trunk-call* || ⟨Am⟩ *long-distance call*; ⟨off!⟩ = Orts-, Stadt-, → Weit– || ein ~ anmelden *to put in a l.-d call* (nach *to*); ein ~ führen mit jdm *to call a p by long distance* **~glas** n; gr u kl ~ *binocular*(*s* pl); gr ~ *field* (od *spy*)-*glass*; kl ~ *opera-glass*(*es* pl) ≁|**halten** vt [h] **1.** (Regen, Fremde) *to keep out* || *to hold, warn, fend* (*a p*) *off*; etw ~ v jdm *to withhold a th from a p*; *to shield a p from a th* **2. sich** ~ *to keep away, to absent o.s.* (v *from*); *to stand* (od *keep, hold*) *aloof* (v *from*); *to hold off* (z tun *from doing*); sich ~ v jdm *to keep a p at a distance*; sich behutsam ~ v *to fight shy of* (*a p*) **~handel** m *trade with distant countries* **~heizung** f *distant heating*; *district-heating* **≁h·er** adv; v ~ *from afar* **~h·in** adv *far*; *to a distance* **~hörer** m → Hörer **~kabel** n → -leitung **~kamera** f ⟨el⟩ *telephote* **~kampfgeschütz** n ⟨mil⟩ *long-range gun* **~kontrolle** f *remote audit* od *control* **~kraftübertragung** f ⟨tech⟩ *telemechanics* [pl] [sg konstr]; *transmission of power to a distance* **~kursus** m *correspondence course* **~laster** m *far-wandering freight-car* **~lastfahrer** m *long-distance truck driver* **~lehrinstitut** n *correspondence college* **~leitung** f ⟨telph⟩ *trunk-line* || ⟨tech⟩ ~ v Energie *transmission of energy to a distance* | ~snetz [n] *trunk system* **~lenk-** ~geschoß [n], ~rakete [f] *guided missile*; ~schiff [n] *ship controlled from a distance* || ~sofortzünder [m] ⟨artill⟩ *destructor* || ~system [n] *guidance system* || ~waffe [f] *guided missile* || ~waffenkrieg [m] *press-button war* **~lenkung** f *remote* od *radio control*; *space command* **~licht** n ⟨mot⟩ *main beam headlights* pl, *full h. b.* ≁|**liegen** vi [h] es liegt mir fern z sagen *I am far from saying*; es l. mir fern z behaupten *far be it from me to contend* (*that* . .); dieser Gedanke lag mir ganz fern *this was quite alien to my thoughts* || ~d *distant remote* **~melde-** ~anlage [f] ⟨off!⟩ = Telephon || ~anschlußstelle [f] *signal centre*; ~apparat m *telemeter* || ~aufklärung [f] *signal reconnaissance* || ~auswertung [f] *communication intelligence* || ~bataillon [n] *signal battalion* || ~einrichtung [f] ⟨off⟩ = Telephonanlage || ~netz [n] *signal net* || ~offizier v Dienst *communication watch o.* || ~satellit [m] *communications satellite* || ~technik [f] *telecommunication* || ~trupp [m] ⟨mil⟩ *communication detail* || ~verkehr [m] *signal c.s*; *c. traffic* || ~weitverbindungen [f pl] ⟨Am⟩ *long lines* N || ~wesen [n] *c.s* || ~zentrale f *c. centre* **~meldung** f ⟨telph⟩ *telephonic message* **≁mündlich 1.** a *telephonic* (*talk*); ~e Anfragen *inquiries by telephone* **2.** adv; ~ mitteilen *to communicate by telephone*; ~ sprechen → *telephonieren* **~nachtjagd** f ⟨aero⟩ *long-range night interception* **~nachtjäger** m *l. r. n. fighter* **~objektiv** n ⟨phot⟩ *telephoto lens* **~ost** m *the Far East*; in ~ *in the Far East* **≁östlich** a *Far-Eastern* (*question*) **~photographie** f *telephotography* **~rohr** n **1.** *telescope* **2.** ⟨fig sex⟩ *star-gazer* **3.** [in comp] *telescopic*; ~aufsatz [m] *telescopic sight* || ~sucher [m] ⟨phot⟩ *telescopic* (*view-*)*finder* **~ruf** m **1.** → ~/-gespräch **2.** *telephone*: *Tel. 506* [sprich: *five-o-six*] **~schießen** n ⟨mil⟩ *long-range shooting* **~schreibeempfänger** m (S) *receiver printer* **~schreiben** [h] [nur inf & pp] *to teletype* **~schreiber** m (S) *telautograph*; *teletype*(*writer*); ⟨Am⟩ *teletypesetter*; über ~ (S) leiten *to transmit over wire* || (P & S) *teleprinter* || (P) *teletypist* **~seh-**, **~sehen** → d. **~sein** n *absence* (v *from*); ⟨jur⟩ ~ vom Tatort *alibi* **~sicht** f (*longdistance*) *view, prospect* **≁sichtig** a ⟨med⟩ *farsighted* **~sichtigkeit** f *farsightedness* **~signal** n *distant signal* **~sinn** m (of the blind) *the perception of distant objects* **~sprech-** etc → d. ≁|**stehen** vi [h] ⟨übtr⟩ er steht uns fern *he is a stranger to us*; *we are not in contact with him* ≁|**steuern** vt [h] (Schiff) *to control from a distance* **~steuerung** f *telecontrol*; *telautomatics* [sg konstr]; *radio–* (od *distant, remote*) *control* | ~sapparat *telemotor*; mit ~ *distant controlled* **~straße** f *arterial road*; → u. **~thermometer** n *telethermometer* **~trauung** f *marriage by proxy* **~trieb** m ⟨tech⟩ (Seil≁) *teledynamic transmission gear*; ~seil n *teledynamic cable* **~übertragung** f → Fernkraftübertragung **~unterrichtskursus** m *correspondence* (od *postal*) *course* **~verkehr** m ⟨rail⟩ *long-distance traffic* (od *transport of goods*) | ~sstraße [f] *motorway*; → o. **~wechsel** m = Distanzwechsel **~weh** n *nostalgia* **~wirkung** f *effect transmitted to a distance* || → Telepathie **~zähler** m, **~zählwerk** n *telecounter* **~zielsegeln** n ⟨aero⟩ *long-distance gliding* **~zug** m ⟨rail⟩ *long-distance train* **~zündung** f *remote control ignition*

f·erne [pred a & adv] → fern I. B. II.

F·erne f ~/~n *distance, remoteness*; Entfernung || aus der ~ *from a distance*; *from afar*; *distantly* || Grüße aus der ~ *greetings from abroad* || das klang wie aus weiter ~ *that seemed to be a good way off* || in der ~ *in the distance* || in nicht allzugroßer ~ *in the not-too-distant future* || in weiter ~ *far and wide* || ⟨fig⟩ das ist (*or* liegt) noch in weiter ~ *that is still a good way off*. . . *by no means certain* (od *decided*) || in der ~ liegend *distant*; *remote* (*regions*) || warum denn in die ~ schweifen, wenn das Gute liegt so nah? *you might go further and not fare so well* **f·erner** [compr v fern] **I.** [a] **1.** ⟨eig⟩ = weiter **2.** ⟨übtr⟩ (mst: weiter) *further* (*orders*); → weiter [a] **II.** [adv] **1.** nichts liegt mir ~ *nothing is farther from my thoughts* (als *than*), als Sie z kränken *I am far from offending you* **2.** ~hin, → d. **3.** (außerdem) *further, furthermore*; *besides, moreover* || h Sie ~ etw z sagen? *have you anything further* (od *more*) *to say*? da ist ~ dieser Vorteil *there is this further advantage*; wir h ~ gesehen *we have seen further* (*that* . .) **III.** [conj] *again, then*; ~ liefen . . ⟨*racing*⟩ *also ran* . .; ⟨fig⟩ (*he is an*) *also ran*; (*I'll turn up among the 'also ran'*) „~ liefen"-Artikel pl *also rans* || ~ müssen wir bedenken *again, we must remember* (*that* . .); u ~ *and then* ˣ**F·erner** m = Gletscher **f·ernerhin** adv *henceforth, h.forward*; *from now*

F·ernseh- [in comp] *television-* . ., ⟨Am⟩ *video* . . **~abtaster** m *scanner* **~amateur** m *t.* od *TV fan*, ⟨Am mst⟩ *v. fan, telefan* **~ansager** m *t. announcer*, ⟨Am⟩ *v. a.* **~antenne** f *t.* (⟨Am⟩ *v.*) *antenna* **~apparat** m *t. set, televisor* (aufstellen *to install*); (etw) im ~ sehen *to view on t.*; mit ~ ausgestattet *t.-equipped* (*room*) **~aufnahme** f *t. pick-up*; f ~ geeignet *telegenic* | ~raum [m], ~studio [n] *t.* od *TV studio*; ~wagen [m] *t. reporting van*, ⟨Am⟩ *v. bus* **~bearbeitung** f *t.* (⟨Am⟩ *v.*) *version* **~berichterstattung** f *t. coverage* **~betrachter** m (*t.*) *viewer* **~bild** n *air-picture, t. -picture* (gesendet w *to go on the air*) | ~fläche [f] *field*; ~schirm [m] *screen*; **~dienst** m *t.* (⟨Am⟩ *v.*) *service* **~drehbuch** n *TV* (*shooting*) *script* **~empfänger** m *t.-receiver*; (P) *televiewer*; (S) *t. set*; f Farbaufnahmen *t. colo*(*u*)*r receiving set* **~fassung** f *TV* (⟨fam⟩ *telly*) *version* **~film** m *telefilm* **~gerät** n *t. set*; (f Auto) ⟨Am⟩ *auto-video* **~gesellschaft** f *t. broadcasting station* **~großpro-**

gramm n *spectacular* **~kanal** m *t.* (⟨Am⟩ *v.*) *channel* °**~kiste** f *goggle-box* **~kleinkamera** f ⟨fam⟩ *creepie-peepie* **~koffer** m *portable t. receiver* **~konserve** f *telerecord(ing)* **~lehrgang** m *telecourse* **~-nachrichten** f pl *t. news* **~netz** n *t.* (⟨Am⟩ *v.*) *network* **~programm** n *views*; *t.* (⟨Am⟩ *v.*) *program* od *show* (sehen *to look at, to teleview*) **~reklame** f *commercial t.* **~reportage** f *outside broadcast* **~-reporter** m *o. b.s' commentator* **~röhre** f *t. tube* ‖ *camera tube* **~säuberungsaktion** f *clean-up TV campaign* **~schirm** m *telescreen* **~(seh)er** m *TV--watcher*; *viewer* **~sender** m *t.-transmitter*; *telestation* **~senderecht** n *t. right* **~senderöhre** f *iconoscope* **~sendestelle** f *telestation* **≃senden** vt/i [h] *to televise, telecast* **~sendung** f *t. transmission* od *broadcast(ing)*; *telecast* **~spiegel** m (f Senden u Empfang) *twoway t.* **~spiel** n *teleplay* **~sprecher** m *t. commentator, telecaster* **~steuerung** f ⟨aero⟩ *teleran* **~teilnehmer** m *t.* (⟨Am⟩ *v.*) *viewer, looker--in* | ~kreis [m] *t.* (⟨Am⟩ *v.*) *audience* **~telephon** n *televisiphone* **~übertragung** f *t.* od *TV transmission* **~version** f *t.* (⟨Am *v.*⟩) *version* **~wagen** m *TVmobile* **~zeichen** n *t.* (⟨Am⟩ *v.*) *signal*

f·ern|sehen vi/t [h] *to televise*; *to look in, to watch TV*; *to view* | ≃ n *television* ‖ durch ~ vermitteln *to televise*

F·ernsprech- [in comp] *telephone* **~amt** n *t.--exchange*; *call-office*; Fräulein vom ~ *t.-girl* **~anschluß** m *t. connexion*; ~ h *to be on the t.* (⟨fam⟩ *phone*) **~apparat** m *telephone* **~automat** m *coin-box*, ⟨Am⟩ *pay-phone* **~buch** n *t.-directory* **~dienst** m *t.-service* **~draht** m *t.-flex* **~gebühren** f pl *t. fees* **~netz** n *t. network* **~nummer** f (*t.*-) *call number* **~teilnehmer** m (*t.*) *subscriber* **~-verkehr** m *t. traffic* **~verzeichnis** n = ~buch **~-wagen** m *telemobile* **~wesen** n *telephony*; *telephonic system* **~zelle** f *(tele)phone-booth, call--box*; *kiosk* **~zentrale** f *t.-central (office)*

f·ern|sprechen vi/t [h] → telephonieren

F·ernsprecher m (S) (öffentlicher *public*) *telephone*, ⟨fam⟩ *phone* ‖ am ~ *at the t.*; *on the t.*; am ~ verlangt w *to be wanted on the t.* ‖ durch ~ *on* (od *over*) *the t.*; → fernmündlich, Fernruf | (P) *t. operator*

fernst [sup v fern] **1.** a *farthest, furthest*; *farthermost, furthermost*; *remotest* **2.** adv; am ~en *at (the) farthest*; *farthest*; *furthest*

Ferr·ara n ⟨It⟩ (Stadt u †Staat) *Ferrara*

Ferr·at n (Salz der Sauerstoffsäure des Eisens) *ferrate*

Ferri- [in comp] ⟨chem⟩ *ferric*; *ferri-* **~azet·at** n *ferric acetate* **~chlor·id** n *ferric chloride* **~sulf·at** n *ferric sulphate* **~zyank·alium** n *potassium ferricyanide*; *red potassium prussiate*

Ferr·it 1. n ⟨chem⟩ *ferrite* **2.** m ⟨minr⟩ *ferrite* | ~kernspeicher [m] ⟨comp⟩ *f. core store* **Ferro-** [in comp] ⟨chem⟩ *ferro–*; *ferrous* **~azet·at** n *ferrous acetate* **~chlor·id** n *ferrous chloride* **~-leg·ierung** f *ferro-alloy* **~magn·etisch** a *ferro--magnetic* **~mang·an** n *ferro-manganese* **~sulf·at** n *ferrous sulphate* **~typ·ie** f *ferrotype* **~zyank·alium** n *potassium ferrocyanide*

F·erse f ~/~n **1.** ⟨anat⟩ *heel* **2.** (of a stocking, etc.) *heel*; Socken mit zerrissenen ~n *socks out at h.*; e–n Strumpf mit e–r ~ versehen *to h. a stocking* **3. Wendungen**: die ~ des Achilles *Achilles h., the h. of Achilles* ‖ ⟨fig⟩ die ~n zeigen *to show a clean pair of h.s, to show one's h.s, to take to one's h.s, to give leg-bail* ‖ auf jds ~n *at* (od *on, upon*) *a p's h.s* ‖ jdm dicht *or* direkt auf den ~n *hot on the h.s of a p* ‖ jdm auf den ~n folgen *to follow hard after* (od *behind*) *a p*; die Strafe soll dem Vergehen auf der ~ folgen *the penalty is to follow on the h.s of the offence* ‖ jdm auf den ~n s *to be at a p's h.s*; ⟨fig⟩ *to run a p close*; *to keep close tabs on a p*; . . dicht . . bleiben *to hang close on a p's h.s*; jdm auf die ~n treten *to tread on a p's h.s* ‖ hinter der ~ bleiben (of dog) *to keep to the h.* **F·ersen-** [in comp] *heel* . . **~bein** n ⟨anat⟩ *calcaneum* (L) **~geld** n [nur in:] ~ geben = die Fersen zeigen, → Ferse 3. **~leder** n *quarter (of boots)* **~schoner** m *anti-slip*

f·ertig I. a **A.** [attr] **1.** *complete(d), finished (book)* ‖ ~e Kleider *ready-made* (od *ready-to--wear*) *clothes*; *clothes ready for wearing* (od *for wear*); ~e Kleider ⟨fam⟩ *hand-me-downs*; ein ~er Anzug *a reach-me-down suit* ‖ ~e Speisen *ready-to-eat foods*; *dishes made ready*; *ready--cooked foods* ‖ *ready-built (house, ship)* **2.** (geschickt) *ready (hand, pen; writer)*; *dexterous, skilful*; *fluent (orator)* ‖ *accomplished (pianist)*; *perfect* **B.** [pred] **1. (S)** das Essen ist ~ *dinner is ready* ‖ ~ zum Tragen s *to be ready for wear(ing)* ‖ ~ auf Lager s *to be in stock* ‖ mein Werk ist jetzt ~ *my work is now complete* ‖ der Wagen steht ~ an der Tür *the car is ready at the door* **2. (P) a. jdn ~ m** ⟨fam⟩ *to wade into a p* ‖ sich ~ m *to get ready (g. r.!)* ‖ ~ m! ⟨mil⟩ *make ready!* | ~ s *to be ready*; ⟨Am⟩ *to be through (are you th.?)* ‖ er ist nie zur Zeit ~ *he is never ready in time* ‖ endlich war ich ~ *at last I had done* ‖ ~ zum Abmarsch *ready to march*; ~ zur Reise *r. for the journey* ‖ sich ~ halten *to get ready* ‖ ⟨mil⟩ ~! Legt an! Feuer! *ready, present, fire!* ‖ ⟨sport⟩ ~? los! *are you ready? go!* | ⟨fig⟩ (erledigt) ~ s ⟨fam⟩: *I'm, he's done for, he's had it*, ⟨Am sl⟩ *he is washed up* ‖ (betrunken) ⟨bes Am fam⟩ *tuned* **b. ~ s mit** *to have done* od *finished with (a th, a p)*; ⟨Am⟩ *to be thru with (a th, a p)*; *to be done* od *finished with (a p)*; er war mit den Frauen ~ *he was through with women*; wir waren mit Essen ~ *we had done eating* | er war rasch mit der Antwort ~ *he had a ready answer for any question* ‖ er war schnell mit Entschuldigungen ~ *he was ready at excuses* **c. ~ w** *to get ready*; *to manage (I'll manage)*; *to make both ends meet*; ganz gut ~ w *to manage* (⟨Am⟩ *to make out*) *very well* ‖ (mit der Arbeit) ~ w *to get through (it)*; schnell ~ w mit ⟨fam⟩ *to make short shrift with* | °⟨sex vulg⟩ *to come (off)* ‖ (Mann) *to let go, to shoot*; zus ~ w *to give juice for jelly*; (Frau) ~ w l *to make the chimney smoke* | **~ w mit** jdm *to deal with a p, to get on* (od *along*) *with a p*; *to manage a p*; *to put it across a p* ‖ *to finish a p off* ‖ mit einander ~ w *to hit it off*; *to get on well* | ~ w mit (etw) *to cope with (unemployment)*; *to handle (the traffic)*; *to manage (a boat)*; *to set about (a th)* ‖ *to meet (competition)* ‖ ich kann nicht allein damit ~ w *I cannot manage it alone* ‖ nun laßt ihn sehen, wie er ~ wird *now let him stew in his own juice* **d. ohne** jdn (etw) ~ w *to do* (od *get along*) *without a p (a th)*; *to dispense with (a th)* ‖ er kann mit wenigen Büchern ~ w *he can do with few books* **3. ~ s in** *to be expert* od *skilful at* od *in*; *to be good* (od *a good hand*) *at*; *to be proficient* od *perfect in* **4.** °er ist ~ *he is done* (od *tired out, exhausted*) ‖ *he is done for* (od *ruined*); *it is all over with him* **II.** adv **1.** ein Buch ganz ~ lesen *to read a book quite through* ‖ pack alles ~ *pack everything ready* ‖ ~ angezogen *ready-dressed*; ~ gekocht *ready-cooked (food)*; ~ gepackt *ready-packed*; *packed and ready* **2.** *skilfully, fluently*; *perfectly*; *to prefection*; er spricht ~ Englisch *he speaks English fluently* ‖ er spielt ~ Klavier *he is a perfect pianist*

f·ertig- [in comp] **~|bringen** vt [h] (etw) *to accomplish*; *to bring (a th) about* (od *off*); *to hustle (a th) through*; *to manage*; *to work* ‖ (Komplott) *to engineer* ‖ ein Wunder ~ *to achieve* (od *work*) *a miracle* ‖ du bringst auch alles fertig ⟨Am⟩ *you beat the Dutch* ‖ er bringt es fertig! *he is capable of (doing) it*; *he is impudent enough to do it* | **es** ~ z tun *to contrive* (od *to manage*; ⟨Am⟩ *to make out*) *to do* ‖ es glücklich ~ z tun *to succeed in doing* **~decke** f *precast floor* **≃erzeugnis, ≃fabrikat** n *manufactured article*; *finished product*; *ready-made article*; pl *manufactured* od *finished* *goods* → Fabrikat **≗gericht** n *instant food* **∼geschnitten** a *ready-cut* (*slide mask*) **≗guß** m ⟨met⟩ *finishing-cast* **≗gut** n *finished product*; *finish* | ∼-menge [f] ⟨mill, etc⟩ *output of fine product* **≗haus** n *pre-cut, prefab*(*ricated*) *house*; *prefab* (aus . . *in metal*) Hersteller v ≗ern *prefabricator* **≗industrie** f *finishing industry* **≗kleider** n pl ⟨com⟩ *ready-to-wear clothes* °**∼**|**kriegen** vt [h] = fertigbringen ‖ etw ganz richtig ∼ *to get a th quite right* **∼**|**machen** vt [h] **a.** (etw, jdn) *to get* (od *make*) *ready* ‖ *to execute* ‖ ⟨typ⟩ *to dress* ‖ ⟨phot⟩ *to finish* **b.** jdn ∼ ⟨fam⟩ *to wade into a p*; → erledigen 2. a. ‖ (*of drink*) ⟨bes Am⟩ *to just about fix a p* **c.** sich ∼ *to make o.s. ready* (f, z *for*); *to get* od *make ready* (f, z *for*; z tun *to do*); *to ready o.s.* **≗macher** m ⟨tech⟩ *finisher* **≗montage** f *final assembly* **≗packung** f *prepack* (*vegetables in ∼s*) **≗produkt** n = Fertigerzeugnis **∼**|**stellen** vt [h] (etw) *to finish* (*off*); *to complete*; (Buch) *to make out*; *to get* (od *make*) *ready*; leicht ∼ *to turn off* ‖ (zus–stellen) *to arrange* ‖ → fabrizieren **≗stellung** f *completion*; *finishing execution* (*of a picture*) **≗ware** f, **≗erzeugnis** n ⟨tail⟩ *finished* od *ready-made article*; –waren [pl] ⟨allg⟩ *manufactured goods* → fertig

f·ertigen vt [h] **1.** *to make, manufacture*; → an–, verfertigen; fabrizieren **2.** = ausfertigen

F·ertigkeit f ∼/∼en *dexterity, facility* (z erlernen *in learning*); *proficiency* (in etw *in a th*; z tun *in doing*; *skill* (*in a th*) ‖ *the address* (*of a diplomat*) ‖ ⟨mus⟩ *execution* ‖ (Sprech≗) *fluency* | ∼en [pl] *accomplishments, acquirements, perfections* [pl]; ⟨Am⟩ *skills* [pl]

F·ertigung f ∼/∼en *making, manufacture*; *production* ⟨a. min⟩; *fabrication*; *output, yield*; *finish* | **∼s- ∼auftrag** m *pr. order* **∼fehler** m *m.ring defect* **∼halle** f *workshop*; *finishing shop* **∼industrie** f *m.ring industry* **∼jahr** n *year of m.re* **∼kosten** pl *job costs* **∼maschine** f *processing m.* **∼programm** n *m.ring program* **∼technik** f *technology* **∼teil** n *p.n part* **∼zeit** f *p.n time*

Fes n ∼/∼ ⟨mus⟩ *F flat*; → A-Dur

F·es m & n ∼ & F·esses/∼ & F·esse *fez* [pl *fezes*]; *tarboosh*; der mit rotem ∼ bedeckte Ägypter *the red fez-capped Egyptian*

f·esch a **1.** [attr] *fashionable*; *natty*, ⟨Am⟩ *ritzy* (*suit*); *stylish, spiffy* (*hat*); *dashing* (*rider*), *smart* (*girl*); → elegant **2.** [pred] *nobby, posh*

F·essel[1] f ∼/∼n **1.** ⟨eig⟩ (Fuß≗) *fetter, shackle*; (f Pferd) *trammel*; [mst pl] ∼n *bonds, chains, irons, shackles* [pl]; Hand≗n *darbies, handcuffs* [pl] **2.** ⟨fig⟩ *check, impediment* (f *to*); *restraint* ‖ ∼n [pl] *fetters, shackles* (*of convention*); *trammels* [pl] (*of etiquette*) **3.** Wendungen: **a.** e–e lästige ∼ *a tie* ‖ in ∼n *in bonds* (od *chains, irons*) ‖ in den ∼n der Leidenschaften *under the sway of one's passions*; *in the toils* (*of a passion, spell*) (*to be*) *enslaved by one's p.* **b.** jdm ∼n **anlegen**, jdn in ∼n legen *to clap a p in irons*; *to put a p into irons*; *to fetter* (od (*en*)*chain, iron, pinion, shackle*) *a p*; (Hand≗n) *to handcuff* (od *manacle*) *a p* ‖ ⟨fig⟩ (e–r S) ∼n anlegen *or* (e–e S) in ∼n schlagen *to lay fetters on* (*science*), *to put fetters on* (*the mind*); *to fetter, shackle, trammel*; (die Presse) *to gag, muzzle*; *to grip* (*the imagination*) ‖ die ∼n abschütteln *or* zerbrechen *to break* (od *shake off*) *one's chains*; ⟨poet⟩ *to burst the bonds* ⟨fig⟩ *to shake off the fetters* (*of a treaty*); *to throw off the trammels* (*of a control*) ‖ ⟨fig⟩ sich ∼n anlegen *to give hostages to fortune* (dadurch daß man tut *by doing*) ‖ etw als ∼ empfinden *to feel* (od *realize*) *a th as a check*

F·essel[2] f ∼/∼n ⟨vet⟩ (of a horse) *fetlock, pastern* | ∼gelenk [n] *fetlock joint* | ∼socke [f] *anklet*

F·esselballon m ⟨aero⟩ *captive balloon, sausage* ‖ ⟨mil⟩ *kite-balloon* ‖ ⟨mar⟩ *blimp*

f·esseln vt [h] **A. 1.** ⟨eig⟩ jdn ∼ = jdn in Fesseln legen, → Fessel 3. b. ‖ jdn ∼ an → binden, ketten an **2.** ⟨übtr⟩ **a. jdn ∼ an (etw)** *to confine* (od *tie*) *a p to* (*the bed, house, one's room*); [mst pass] gefesselt s an *to be confined* (*to the house*, etc.); *to be rooted to* (*the soil*); *to be clamped down to* (*the earth*); *to be tied to* (*a wife*); *to be in bondage to*; → binden I. B. 2. b. ‖ **sich ∼ an** *to enslave o.s. to* (*a model*) **b. jdn ∼ an (jdn)** *to attach* (od *attract, draw*) *a p to a p*; er verstand es, die Menschen an sich z ∼ *he knew how to attach people to him* ‖ (jdn) ans Bett (Zimmer) ∼ *to confine . .to one's bed* (*room*) | **sich ∼ an** *to attach o.s. to* (*a p*) **c.** etw ∼ = e–r S Fesseln anlegen, → Fessel 3. b. **B.** ⟨fig⟩ (bannen, bestricken) **1.** (jdn) *to attract, to captivate, to enthral, to fascinate, to intrigue a p* (*his personality intrigued me*) ‖ gefesselt s v *to be taken with* (*a th*); ⟨Am⟩ *to fall for* (*a p*) ‖ (Publikum) *to attract, hold*; *to fetter in chains* (*of wonder*, etc); alles ∼ *to hold the stage* ‖ ⟨parl⟩ das Haus durch e–e Rede ∼ *to hold the floor of the house* **2.** (jds Blick) *to arrest*; (jds Aufmerksamkeit) *to absorb, engage, attract, rivet, engross, fascinate* **3.** (Feind) *to hold, retain*; (Kräfte) *to fix*; *to tie down* **f·esselnd 1.** a *attractive*; *captivating* (*story-teller*); ∼er Redner ⟨Am sl⟩ *spell-binder* ‖ *enthralling, fascinating, stirring, thrilling* (*account, story*); ⟨fam⟩ *taking* (*style*); ⟨Am⟩ *spellbinding* ‖ *absorbing* (*problems*); *arresting, captivating* (*picture* ⟨a. phot⟩); *interesting* (*lecture*) ‖ das ≗ste an . . *the most taking thing about* (*the play is . .*) **2.** adv *attractively*; *vividly* ‖ ∼ erzählen können *to have an admirable knack of story-telling* ‖ ⟨theat⟩ ∼ spielen *to act captivatingly* ‖ ∼ wirken (P) *to draw*

F·esselung f ∼/∼en **1.** *fettering*; *chaining up*; → fesseln | ∼sangriff [m] ⟨mil⟩ *holding attack* **2.** ⟨hors⟩ = Fessel[2]

fest I. a **A.** ⟨**eig**⟩ **1.** ⟨**phys**⟩ (Ggs flüssig etc) **a.** *concrete*; *solid* (*body*; *fuel*) ‖ ≗körperphysik [f] *solid state physics* [sg konstr] ‖ ∼e Nahrung *solid food*; sein Magen kann nichts ≗s behalten *his stomach cannot keep any solid food* ‖ ∼es Fett → Elaidin ‖ ∼ w *to become solid*; *to congeal, freeze*; *solidify*; (of milk) *to be set* **b.** ∼es Land *firm* od *sure ground*; *dry land*; *terra firma* (L); *continent* **2. a.** (Ggs locker) *compact, firm, solid,* (*flesh*) ‖ *close* (*texture, tissue*); *closely knit* ‖ (Ggs weich) ∼er Boden *hard* (od *solid*) *ground*; ∼est, sehr ∼*petrous* **b.** (∼gebaut) *solid* (*house*); *stable* (*foundations*); *substantial* ‖ *safe*; *secure* (*bridge*) ‖ *hard, solid*; *strong* (*muscles*); *sturdy* (*legs, frame*) ‖ ∼es Schuhzeug *stout footwear* (*is recommended*) | (∼gefügt) *tight* (*knot*) ‖ ∼er Schlaf *sound sleep*; er ist in ∼em Sch. *he is fast* (od *sound*; ⟨Am⟩ *tight*) *asleep* ‖ *sound* (*health*) **c.** etw (Haar etc) in ∼e Form bringen *to set a th* **3.** [pred] (Ggs lose) der Nagel ist (*or* sitzt) ∼ in dem Brett *the nail is fast in the board* ‖ die Wurzeln sind *or* sitzen ∼ in der Erde *the roots are firm in the earth* ‖ ∼ auf den Beinen *firm on one's legs*; nicht ∼ auf den B. *groggy, shaky* ‖ → nagel∼ **B.** ⟨**übtr**⟩ **1.** ⟨**tech**⟩ *fixed* (*point, pole*; *circle, coupling*) ‖ *permanent* (*installation*) ‖ ∼er Kran *stationary crane* ‖ ∼e Stange *rigid rod* | ⟨mil⟩ ∼er Ort *fortified post* od *place*; *fort*(*ress*) ‖ ∼e Stellung *fortified* (od *strong*) *position* | ∼er Wohnsitz *permanent residence*; s–n ∼en W. h, ∼ sitzen in . . *to be settled in . .* | ∼e Beschaffenheit = Festigkeit **2. a.** *firm, steady*; ∼e **Beziehungen** h zu *to bear definite relations to* ‖ ∼er **Blick** *firm glance*; *steady look*; *fixed glare* ‖ ∼er Druck *firm pressure* ‖ ∼en Fuß fassen *to gain* (od *get*) *a footing* (in *in*) ‖ ∼er Gewahrsam *close confinement*; *safe custody* ‖ ∼er Griff *firm* (od *tenacious*) *grip* ‖ ∼er Halt *firm hold*; *footing* ‖ ∼e **Hand** *firm* (od *steady*) *hand*; das Gut ist in ∼en Händen *the estate is unsalable*; → besetzt ‖ ∼e Leitung *firm management, steady hand* ‖ ∼er

Schritt, Tritt *firm step, tread* ‖ ~er Zus–halt *cohesion* ‖ ~er w *to tighten* **b.** ~er Schlag *hard* (od *rigorous*) *blow* **3.** (~gefügt) *established; set* (*form*); *settled* (*order*) ‖ ~e **Regel** *hard and fast rule* ‖ ~es System *inelastic* (od *rigid*) *system* ‖ ~e Wendung *set phrase; idiom; idiomatic expression* **4. a.** ~e **Anstellung** *definite appointment* ‖ ohne ~e Beschäftigung *at a loose-end* ‖ ~e Stellung *permanent position* (od *post*) **b.** ⟨**com**⟩ *binding; firm* (*offer, order*); *fixed* (Belastung, Spesen); *standing* (*charges*); ~e Haltung, Stimmung *firm tendency* ‖ ~e Kundschaft *regular customers* [pl] ‖ ~er Markt *firm* (od *steady*) *market* ‖ ~e Währung *stable currency* | (~gesetzt) *fixed* (*date; fee; rate; salary*); ~es **Einkommen** *fixed* (od *safe*) *income* ‖ ~e Preise *fixed prices*; die P. sind ~ *prices are hard*; ~(er) w *to harden, stiffen, firm* ‖ ⟨st exch⟩ ~, mit ~er Tendenz *on a firm note* ‖ **5.** ⟨fig⟩ (charakterlich ~, innerlich ~) *firm* (*conviction, resolve*); *inflexible; steady, steadfast* (*faith, hope*); *fixed* (*principles*); *set, settled* (*opinions*) | *constant; resolute* (*mind*); *steady; strong-minded*; (jdn) ~ m → festigen **b.** ~es Wissen *solid* (od *well-established*) *knowledge*; ~ s in *to be deeply read* od *versed in* (*a th*); → bibel~ **II. adv A.** ⟨**eig**⟩ **1. a.** *closely, compactly* ‖ *fast, firmly; solidly; tightly* ‖ *hard* | **~ anzufassen** *to tighten one's grip* ‖ ~ anliegend *tight* (*jacket*); *tight-fitting; close* (*cap*) ‖ (Schraube etc) ~ anziehen *to tighten* (*a screw*); (Seil) *to tauten* ‖ (etw) ~ binden *to tie tight*; ~er binden *to tie tighter* ‖ ~ eingeschlossen in *closely shut up in* ‖ (etw) ~ fassen *to clutch, to grasp* ‖ er küßte sie ~ auf die Lippen *he kissed her hard on the lips* ‖ ~ sitzen ⟨tech⟩ (of brake) *to be seizing* ‖ ~ im Sattel sitzen *to sit tight*; ⟨fam⟩ *to stick on a horse*; ⟨fig⟩ *to be settled in power*; nicht ~ sitzen (of a hat) *to wobble*; → I. A. 3. ‖ ~ stehen *to stand fast* od *firm* ‖ ~ verschließen *to seal* ‖ ~ verschlossen *fast shut; closely shut up* ‖ ~ versprechen *to promise for certain* ‖ die Tür geht nicht ~ zu *the door won't fasten* ‖ die Tür ~ zumachen *to make the door fast; to fasten* (od *shut*) *the door* **b.** (= zus–) [bei best Verben oft:] *up*: ~ falten *to fold up*; ~ zus–binden *to tie up*; ~-zus–packen *to pack up* **2.** ⟨**übtr**⟩ **a.** (jdn) **~ ansehen** *to look hard at* (*a p*) ‖ jdn ~ in die Augen sehen *to look steadily into a p's eyes*; (jdn) ~ anstellen *to appoint* od *engage definitely*; *to give* (*a p*) *a permanent post*; ⟨mil⟩ ~ angestellt u besoldet *substantive* (*colonel*) ‖ sich ~ behaupten (of prices) *to remain steady* ‖ ~ kaufen *to purchase; to make it a bargain* ‖ ich schlafe sehr ~ *I am a heavy* (od *good*) *sleeper*; er schläft noch ~ *he is still fast asleep* ‖ ~ verankert in *firmly rooted in* . . **3.** ⟨**fig**⟩ *firmly; confidently; definitely; positively* | **~ beharren** bei, auf *to insist on* . .; *to cling* od *stick* (*tight*) *to* . .; ~ bei s–n Grundsätzen beharren *to sit tight* ‖ ~ behaupten *to maintain positively* ‖ ~ bestehen auf etw *to insist* (od *to be insistent*) *on a th*; *to emphasize a th* ‖ Beziehungen ~er binden (*or* schmieden) *to cement the relations* (*between*) ‖ ~ bleiben *to remain firm; to be persistent; to sit tight* ‖ *to stand pat*; . . bei *to persist in* ‖ ~entschlossen [pred a] (P) *resolute; standpat* (*position*) ‖ **~ fassen** *to clinch*; ~ stehen zu jdm *to be solid for a p*; ~ hinter jdm st. *to be solidly behind a p* ‖ ~ überzeugt v etw *to be certain of a th*; ich bin ~ überzeugt, daß . . *I am positive that* . . ‖ ~ umrissen *definite; dried and cut* (*plan*) ‖ er verließ sich ~ auf sie *he pinned his faith on them* ‖ du kannst dich ~ darauf verlassen, daß . . *you may be firmly assured that* . . ‖ ~ zus–schmieden, –schließen *to weld solidly together* **4.** ° ~, ~e *hard* (*to work; to drink hard*); ~(e) drauflos arbeiten *to work away* ‖ °jdn ~e vermöbeln *to give a p a sound thrashing* ‖ °~e! immer ~e druff! *go it; never fear!*; ⟨Am⟩ *atta boy!* ‖ °aber ~e *with a vengeance*; ⟨sl⟩ *with knobs on* **III.** [in comp] → u.

F·est n ~es/~e **1.** ⟨ec⟩ *feast*; (un)bewegliche ~e (*im*)*movable feasts* ‖ das Oster≈ *Easter*, → Pfingst≈, Weihnachts≈ **2.** (weltl. ~) **a.** *festival* bes ⟨mus⟩ *the Mozart Festival* **b.** (~mahl) *banquet, feast* ‖ es war mir ein ~ *it was a picnic* ‖ man muß die ~e feiern wie sie fallen *Christmas comes but once a year*; ⟨Am⟩ *take things as you find them* ‖ ein vergnügtes ~ feiern ⟨Am⟩ *to make whoopee*; → feiern **~abend** m *festive evening; night*; Wagner≈ *a night of Wagner* **~akt** m *ceremony* **~aufführung** f *festival production* **~-ausschuß** m *festival committee* **~chor** m *festival chorus* (od *choir*) **~essen** n *banquet; feast; public dinner*; → ~ | **~gabe** f *gift, present*; ⟨oft⟩ *festive donation* **~geber(in** f) m *host*(*ess*) **~gelage** n *banquet; revelry* **~geläute** n *festive peal of bells* **~-gesang** m *festal* (od *festive*) *song* **~halle** f *hall; banqueting-hall* **~kleid** n *festive garment* (od ⟨poet⟩ *raiment*) **~kommers** m ⟨Ger univ⟩ *students' festive entertainment* **~lied** n = Festgesang **~mahl** n *banquet; feast* **~musik** f *festal music* **~-ordner** m *festival organizer* **~ordnung** f *festival-order; sequence of the different parts* (od *items*) *of a festival* **~programm** n *festival programme* **~rede** f *address; formal speech* **~redner** m *official speaker* **~saal** m = Festhalle **~schrift** f ⟨uni⟩ *Festschrift* [Ger]; ~ f jdn gelegentlich s–s 80. Geburtstages *volume presented to a p on the occasion of his 80th birthday* **~spiel** n *festival* ‖ ⟨hist⟩ *pageant* ‖ die Bayreuther ~e [pl] *the Bayreuth Festival* **~stimmung** f *festivity; gaiety; mirth*; jd, der f die ~ sorgt ⟨Am⟩ *cheer-leader* **~tag** m ⟨ec⟩ *holy-day* ‖ *festival; high-day*, an Fest- u Feiertagen *on highdays and holidays* ‖ die ~e [pl] *the red-letter days* (*of a nation*) **≈täglich** a *festive* ‖ ⟨übtr⟩ *solemn* **~tracht** f *festive robes* [pl] **~wagen** m *display vehicle*, ⟨Am⟩ *float* **~wiese** f *amusement park* **~woche** f *festival week* **~zeit** f *festive season* **~zug** m *procession, pageant; cavalcade*

Festantenne f (→ fest) ⟨wir⟩ *fixed aerial*

f·est|backen vi [h] *to cake together*

f·est|bannen vt [h] *to fascinate*

f·estbesoldet a *salaried* (*classes; official*)

f·est|binden vt [h] **1.** (zus–binden) *to tie up; to truss; to bind* (*a towel*) *in its place* **2.** (jdn, etw) ~ an *to bind* (od *fasten*) *to*; → fesseln, ketten

f·est|bleiben vi [s] *to remain firm, to hold on* ‖ *to stand pat*; in e–r S ~ *to stick to a th*

F·este f ~/~n *castle, stronghold; fastness* → Festung ‖ ⟨übtr⟩ *citadel, fort stronghold* ‖ ⟨bib⟩ die ~ des Himmels *the firmament*

f·este adv → fest II. 4.

f·est|fahren vt [h] **1.** (Wagen im Schlamm etc) ~ ⟨Am⟩ *to stall* ‖ (Schiff) *to run aground* ‖ –ges *to be stalled* ‖ ⟨fig⟩ wir sind gründlich –ge– *we are at the end of our tether*; die S scheint sich –zu– *matters seem to be drifting into a dead-end* | **sich** ~ *to stick* (in . . *in the mud*); *to come to a stop*; ⟨mot a.⟩ *to belly* ‖ ⟨Am⟩ *to stall*

fest- **≈fahrwerk** n ⟨aero⟩ *fixed landing gear, f. under-carriage* | sich **~|fressen** vi [h] ⟨tech⟩ *to seize, jam, stick*; *to get stuck* **~|frieren** vi [s] *to freeze tight* (in .. *key in lock*) **~gebaut** ⟨fig⟩ *transfixed* **~gefahren** a *fast aground* ⟨a. fig⟩ **≈gehalt** m *solid contents* **≈geld** n (⟨a.⟩ ~er [pl]) *cash on deposit* **~gefügt** a *cohesive* (⟨mil⟩ *unit*) **~gesetzt** a *set* (*intervals*) **~gestampft, ~getreten** a *packed* (*earth, snow*) **~gewurzelt** a ⟨fig⟩ (P) *rooted to the spot* ‖ *deep-rooted* (*custom*) ‖ ~ in *rooted in* **≈halteknopf** m *stop knob*

f·est|halten I. vt/i [h] **A. vt 1.** (jdn gewaltsam ~) **a.** ⟨jur⟩ (Dieb) *to arrest, seize; detain* **b.** (jdn, jds Arme) *to hold fast; to pin* (am Boden *to the ground*) ‖ jdn an e–m Orte ~ *to keep a p tied to a place* (*business keeps him* ..) ‖ –ge– w durch *to be pinned* (od *detained*) *by* (*an event*) ‖ ⟨tact⟩ (lähmen) *to immobilize* **c.** (am Knopfloch ~) *to buttonhole* (*a p*) **d.** (stützen) *to hold on* (*will you kindly hold me on?*) **2. a.** (jds Aufmerksamkeit) *to arrest, attract, catch, hold, rivet* ‖ (etw) im Gedächtnis ~ *to hold in one's memory* **b.** (Tatsachen) *to retain* ‖ (die Wirklichkeit) *to pin down*; (etw) im Bilde (etc) ~ *to put on record*; (Eindruck) im Geiste ~ *to register*; *to make a mental note of* ‖ (durch Aufzeichnung) *to record* **3. sich** ~ *to tighten one's grip, to hold on* ‖ *to hold* od *to hold fast* (od *hard*) (an . . *by the rail*); *to hold on* (an . . *to the wall*; mit . . *with one's hands*) ‖ sich an e–a ~ *to clutch at each other* **B. vi 1.** *to hold on*; ~! *hang on*! **2. ~ an** (etw) **a.** *to adhere to* (*a cause, party, school*); *to cling to* (*religion*; *a habit*); *to stick to* (*one's principles, promise, word*); *to abide by* (*a decision*); *to keep to* (*a plan*); *to stand firm to* (*one's conviction*); ⟨mil⟩ am Auftrag ~! *the mission will continue to be carried on*! ‖ am alten ~ ⟨Am sl⟩ *to stand pat* ‖ an s–n Grundsätzen ~ *to sit tight*; *to stick to one's guns* ‖ laß uns an Montag ~ *let us keep to Monday* ‖ innig ~ an etw *to cherish* od *hug a th*; zäh am Leben ~ *to be tenacious of life* **b.** ~ an (jdm) *to adhere* (od *cling, stick*) *to* (*a p*); ⟨sl⟩ *to freeze on to* (*a p*) **II.** ≈ n *adherence, attachment* (an *to*); getreues ~ *fidelity* (an *to*) | starres ~ *stubborn adherence* (an *to*) ⟨a. mil⟩

f·estigen vt [h] mst ⟨übtr⟩ **1.** (Einrichtung) *to compact*; *to make compact* (od *firm, solid*); (Bund, Freundschaft) *to cement*; (Ruf) *to establish*; (Macht) *to consolidate, solidify*; (Währung) *to stabilize* | ⟨mil⟩ (die Front, ⟨a.⟩ sich) ~ *to consolidate* **sich** ~ (of conviction) *to be reinforced* **2.** (jdn, jds Sinn) *to fortify*; *harden*; *settle*; *steady, steel, strengthen*; *stiffen*; gefestigt gegen *steeled against* **F·estigkeit** f ~/ (→ fest I.) **1.** ⟨eig⟩ ⟨phys⟩ *substance, body*; *stability*; *resistance* ‖ *compactness, solidness, solidity* (*of food, flesh*); *strength* (*of a material*); ~ gegen *resistance to*; Dehn≈, Spannungs≈, Zug≈ *tensile strength* ‖ Farb≈ *fastness* (gegen Licht *to light*); *strength*; v höchster ~ *high strength* [attr]; ~sberechnung [f] *stress caculation*; ~sgrenze [f] *structural limit*; ~sprüfung [f] *strength test* ‖ *closeness* (*of a tissue*); *firmness, hardness* (*of ground*); *tightness* ‖ *stability* (*of a bridge, house*) ‖ *fastness, soundness* (*of sleep*) **2.** ⟨übtr⟩ *firmness* (*of a grip*; *friendship, tendency*) ‖ *soundness*; *durability* ‖ *fixedness, fixity* (*of a look*; *prices*); *steadiness* (*of management*) ‖ *stability* (*of currency*) **3.** ⟨fig⟩ *constancy* (*of a feeling, mind*); *firmness* (*of a wife*); *steadiness, steadfastness* ‖ *resoluteness*; innere ~ *inner steadfastness*; *mental ballast*; seelische ~ *fortitude* ‖ Charakter≈ *strength of purpose, willpower* **F·estigung** f *cementation*; *establishment*; *consolidation* (*of peace*) ‖ *fortification*; *strengthening*

F·estival n ~s/~s (Festspiel) *festival*

°**Festivit·ät** f ~/~en *festival*; = Festlichkeit ‖ e–e gr ~ ⟨sl⟩ *a great do*; ⟨Am⟩ *shindig, shindy*

f·est- ~|keilen vt [h] *to key* (auf *on, to*) **~|klemmen** vt [h] (etw) *to lock, jam* (in *in*) ‖ *to pack tight*; *to pin*; –ge–mt [a & adv] *chock-a-block* ‖ sich ~ ⟨mech⟩ *to jam*; *to seize* (*up*) **~|kneten** vt [h] = feststampfen **~komma** n ⟨comp⟩ (*data processing*) *fixed point* **~|kommen** vi [s] (of a ship) *to run aground* **≈körperphysik** f *physics of solid state* **≈land** n *continent*; das ~ Europa *the c. of Europe*; auf dem ~ *on the c.* ‖ das europäische ~ *the Continent* ‖ das amerikanische ~ ⟨Am⟩ *the Continent*; → Kontinent | (Ggs Insel) *mainland* **~ländisch** a *continental* **~|legen** vt [h] **A. (etw)** (unbeweglich m) *to immobilize* **1.** (Grenze, Route, Zeit) *to fix*; (Gebiet) *to mark out* ‖ (Linie, Plan) *to lay down*; *to prescribe* ‖ ⟨aero⟩ (Flug) auf e–r Karte ~ *to schedule* | ⟨übtr⟩ (Reihenfolge) *to adjust, to fix*; (Politik, Ziele) *to define*; (Gesetz, Verfahren, Weg) *to establish*; (Sprache) *to settle* | (etw) durch Vertrag ~ *to stipulate*; gesetzlich ~ *to regularize*; neu ~ *to readjust*; schriftlich ~ *to set* od *write down*; unveränderlich ~ *to stereotype*; zeitlich ~ *to time* ‖ endgültig –ge–gt *definitive* (*edition*) **2.** ⟨com⟩ (Kapital) *to lock up, to sink*; (Marktpreis) ⟨sl⟩ *to peg* ‖ ⟨jur⟩ (Eigentum) durch Bedingungen ~ *to tie up* **B. 1. (jdn)** *to tie* ‖ ⟨mil⟩ (Kräfte) vorzeitig ~ *to tie down* ‖ jdn ~ auf *to tie a p* (*down*), *to pin a p down to* (*a th*); *to commit to* (*a certain policy*) **2. sich** ~ *to bind* od *commit o.s.*; *to tie o.s. down* (auf *to*); *to settle* (auf . . *on a plan*); sich in e–r strittigen S ~ *to go out on a limb* ‖ sich –ge–gt h *to be committed* (*against* . .); *to be fixed*; sich nicht ~ *to keep an open mind*; . . wollen *to hedge* (betreffs *about*); er hat sich ein für allemal –ge–gt *he is bound hand and foot* **≈legung** f ~/~en **1.** *adjustment*; *fixation* (*of frontiers*); neue ~ *readjustment* ‖ *establishment*; gesetzliche ~ *regularization*; vertragliche ~ *stipulation* ‖ *lock-up*; *locking up* (*of capital*) **2.** *committal* (jds auf *of a p to*); → Bindung **3.** ⟨mil⟩ *selection* (*of targets*)

f·estlich 1. a *festive* (*games*; *season*); *festal* (*air, music*); *convivial*; [nur attr] *festival* (*robes*) ‖ ~e Veranstaltung *festivity, conviviality* ‖ = feierlich **2.** adv *festively, festally* ‖ (Tag) ~ begehen *to celebrate, solemnize*; (jdn) ~ bewirten *to feast* (*a p*) *up*; *to entertain* (*a p*) *sumptuously* | **≈keit** f **1.** [abstr] *conviviality, festivity*; *solemnity* **2.** [konkr] *festive entertainment*; *festivity*; *conviviality*; *festival*; gr ~ *fête*, ~ im Freien *fête-champêtre* ‖ [oft pl] ~en *festivities* [pl]; → Feierlichkeit 2.

f·est- ~|liegen [h] *to stick fast*; → festsitzen ‖ ⟨com, st exch⟩ *to be* (*locked up* od) *a hard spot* **~|machen I.** vt/i [h] **A.** vt **1.** (kompakt m) (Masse) *to compact*; *to make compact* (od *firm, solid*); *to fix*; *to solidify* ‖ ⟨tech⟩ (Papier) *to firm* **2.** (befestigen) **a.** (Nagel) *to make fast*; *to clinch, rivet*; (etw) *to fasten, fix* (an *to*) **b.** ⟨mar⟩ (Schiff) *to berth* (an .. *at a quay*); *to moor* ‖ ein Boot ~ *to make a boat fast*; *to fasten a boat* (an *to*) ‖ (Mast) *to ship* ‖ (Tau) *to belay* **3.** ⟨übtr⟩ **a.** e–n Handel ~ *to clinch* od *close a bargain* ‖ ich habe nichts mit ihm –ge–cht *I have arranged nothing with him*; → ausmachen, vereinbaren **b.** ⟨hunt⟩ (Wild = aufspüren) **c.** jdn ~ gegen *to make a p proof against* (od *safe from*) **d.** = festigen **B.** vi ⟨mar⟩ *to moor* (an *at*); (of a ship) *to berth* (*at* . .) **II.** ≈ n *fastening* ‖ ⟨mar⟩ *mooring*

F·estmach- ~stange f (im See, Teich) *ryepeck* **~tonne** f *mooring-buoy*

F·est- ~mark f ⟨Ger⟩ *fixed mark* **~meter** n (abbr fm) ein ~ Holz *1 cbm of wood* (*without interspaces*), *meter of solid timber* **≈|nageln** vt [h] **1.** ⟨eig⟩ (Kiste) *to nail up*; (Deckel) *to nail down*; (etw) *to nail* (auf *on*, an *to*) ‖ er stand wie –ge–lt da *he stood transfixed, .. frozen to the wall* **2.** ⟨fig⟩ eine Lüge (etc) ~ *to nail a lie to the counter* ‖ jdn ~ auf *to nail* od *pin a p down to* (*a statement*) ‖ jdn auf s–e Worte ~ *to tick a p off in his own words* **~nahme** f *apprehension, arrest* (*of a thief*); → Gefangennahme **≈|nehmen** vt [h] (Dieb) *to apprehend, arrest*, ⟨vulg⟩ *pinch*; → gefangen– **~preis** m *fixed price* **~punkt** m *fixed, control* (⟨surv⟩ *reference*) *point* od *mark*; (Höhenmarke) *datum mark*

f·est- ~|rennen vrefl [h] sich ~ *to run o.s. into tangles* **~|schnallen** vt [h] *to strap* (*in*) ⟨a. aero [vrefl]⟩ **~|schrauben** vt [h] (etw) *to screw down* (od *up*) ‖ *to screw* (an *to*) **~|setzen** vt [h] **1.** (jdn) *to confine, immure* (in . . *in prison*); *to imprison* **2.** ⟨übtr⟩ **a.** (Datum etc) *to appoint, fix, set* (f *for*); die Zeit f ein Rennen (etc) ~ *to time a race*; der Beginn des Rennens war auf 3 Uhr –ge–zt *the race was timed to begin at 3* ‖ (*the session is*) *scheduled on Monday* ‖ zur –ge–zten Zeit *at the time appointed, at the set* od *stated time, on time*; zur f. Zeit stattfindend *stated* (*meeting*) ‖ –ge–zter Zeitpunkt *schedule* (*before sch.*) **b.** (Aufgaben) *to appoint*; (Regeln) *to set, to set down* (f *for*) ‖ (Orthographie) *to fix* ‖ *to arrange*; *regulate, settle* ‖ ⟨com⟩ (Preise) *to fix* (auf: *the sum was fixed at 30 marks*; selbst die Preise ~ *to name one's own prices* ‖ (Steuer, Schaden) *to assess* ‖ vertraglich ~ *to stipulate*; → festlegen **2. sich ~ a.** *to establish o.s.*; *to fix*; *settle* (in *in*); ⟨fam⟩ *to come to stay* ‖ ⟨mil & pol⟩ *to get* od *gain a footing* (in *in*); sich ~ in *to occupy* (*a place*) **b.** (of a bullet, etc.) *to lodge* (in . . *in the brain*) ‖ (of a disease) *to settle* (auf, in der Lunge *on the lungs*) **c.** ⟨tech⟩ *to stick* (an *to*) **~̂setzung** f ~/~en **1.** *imprisonment* (*of a p*) **2.** *appointment*; *fixation* (*of a date*, etc.); → Debatte ‖ *arrangement*; *regulation*; *establishment* (*of a text*); *settlement* ‖ *fixation* (*of prices*); *assessment* (*of a tax*) **~̂sitz** m ⟨tech⟩ *snug* od *shrink fit* **~|sitzen** vi [h] **1.** = fest sitzen → fest II. 1. a. **2.** ⟨übtr⟩ **a.** *to be caught* (od *entangled*); *to stick, to stick fast* (in . . *in the snow*); *to be stuck* od *trapped*; ⟨Am⟩ *to be stalled*, ⟨fam⟩ *to be sewed up* **b.** ⟨tech⟩ (S) *to jam, stick*; ⟨Am⟩ *to stall* ‖ *to cling* (an *to*) **c.** (stocken) *to stick* **~|stampfen** vt [h] *to tamp*; *to ram down* **~|stecken** vt [h] *to pin* (an *to*) **~|stehen** vi [h] **1.** = fest stehen → fest II. 1. a. **2.** ⟨übtr⟩ **a.** (S) *to be stable*; (of engines) *to be stationary* **b.** (of a *custom*) *to be established* od *settled*; (of facts) *to be certain*; die S steht fest *this is a positive* (od *certain*) *fact*; soviel steht fest *this much* (od *one thing*) *is certain* (*that* . .); es steht fest, daß . . *it is an understood thing* (od *there is no doubt*) *that* . .; . . einwandfrei . . *it is beyond question*; . . f mich . . *I know for a fact* ‖ sein Entschluß steht fest *his mind is made up*; *he has made up his m.* **~stehend** a *stationary* (*crane*) ‖ *established, settled*; ~er Brauch *custom* ‖ *positive* (*fact*) ‖ *hard and fast* (*rule*) ‖ ⟨phys tech⟩ *fixed* (*force*) **~̂stell-** ~mutter [f] ⟨tech⟩ *locking nut*; ~vorrichtung [f] (z. B. *casement*) *stay* **~stellbar** a *ascertainable*; *detectable*; nicht ~ *unascertainable, undetectable*; schwer ~ *elusive* (*argument*); *evasive* (*meaning*) **~|stellen I.** vt [h] **A.** ⟨eig tech⟩ (Rad etc an e–r Maschine) *to lock*; *fix* **B.** ⟨übtr⟩ **1. a.** (ausfindig m) (etw) *to ascertain, detect, discover, find*; *to find* od *make out, to spot, trace*; (Täter) *to ascertain, trace*; soviel konnte er an dem Ton ~ *he could tell as much by the sound* ‖ *to notice, observe* ‖ es ist schwer, die Tatsachen –zu– *the facts are hard to come by* **b.** (genau, wissenschaftlich ~) *to determine*; *register*; *establish*; *to make sure of* (*a th*); *to prove* ‖ ⟨med⟩ (Krankheit) *to diagnose* (*he diagnosed cancer*) ‖ jds Personalien ~ *to identify a p*; *to establish a p's identy*; jds Stimme ~ *to place a p's voice* **c.** den Tatbestand ~ *to establish* (od *point out, state*) *the facts*; ich stelle nur die Tatsache fest *I am only stating the fact* ‖ (Rechnung) ⟨off⟩ *to certify* **d.** ~, daß . . *to ascertain* (od *discover, make out, make sure*) *that* . .; ~ seitens jds (*or* durch jdn), daß . . *to ascertain from a p that* . .; ich stelle fest (*or* es ist –ge–lt), daß . . *it has been ascertained that* ‖ *to point out* (od *state*, ⟨Am⟩ *claim*) *that* . . **e.** (e–n Vorgang) zeitlich ~ *to time* ‖ (Ort Lage) e–s Feuers (etc) ~ *to locate a fire*; die Lage des Feindes ~ *to locate the enemy's position* **f. sich ~ 1** *to be ascertainable* **2.** (Preis, Schaden) = festsetzen **II.** ~̂ n **1.** ⟨tech⟩ *locking* (*of a machine*); Hebel zum ~ *locking-lever*; Vorrichtung z ~ *locking-device* **2.** = **~̂stellung** f ~/~en ⟨übtr⟩ **1. a.** *ascertainment, detection, discovery* (*of a th*); *ascertainment, tracing* (*of the culprit*); ~en m über *to find out about* (*a th*) ‖ *observation*; *conclusion* | (genaue ~) *determination*; *establishment* (*of a fact, a text*) ‖ ~en [pl] (e–r Kommission) *findings* pl ‖ *diagnosis* (*of a disease*) ‖ die ~ v jds Personalien *the identification of a p* **b.** *statement*; ⟨Am⟩ *claim*; e–e ~ m *to make a statement*; er machte die interessante ~, daß *he made the point that* . . **c.** örtliche ~ *location* (*of a fire*) **2.** = (Festsetzung) *fixation* (*of a price*); *assessment* (*of damages*) | ~sklage [f] ⟨jur⟩ *declaratory action* ‖ ~surteil [n] *decl. judgment* **~stoffgehalt** m *solids content* **~stoffrakete** f *solid-propellant rocket* ⟨a. a-n⟩ **~̂tarif** m *fixed charge* **~verzinslich** a *fixed-interest-bearing* od *fixed yield* (*securities*) **~̂wert** m *fixed value*; *constant* **~̂zeichen** n ⟨radar⟩ *permanent echo* **~̂zeitgespräch** n ⟨telph⟩ *fixed time call*, ⟨Am⟩ *appointment message* **~|ziehen** vt [h] ⟨tech⟩ *to tighten up*, (Schraube) *to screw down* **~|zurren** vt [h] *to lash*; *to make* (*a ship*) *fast to the pier*

Fest·on n [–õ] ~s/~s *festoon* **~stich** m ⟨embr⟩ *whipstitch*

F·estung f ~/~en **1.** *fortress*; *fort*; (of a town) *citadel* ‖ die ~ N. *the fortress of N.* ‖ fliegende ~ ⟨aero⟩ *Flying Fortress*, ⟨fam⟩ *Fort* **2.** (= ~shaft) ⟨Ger⟩ zwei Jahre ~ bek *to be sentenced to two years' confinement in a fortress*

F·estungs- ~artillerie f *siege-artillery* **~bau** m **1.** [abstr] ~, die Kunst des ~s *fortification* **2.** [konkr] *fortifications* [pl] **~graben** m *moat* **~gürtel** m *ring* od *cordon of forts* **~haft** f ⟨Ger⟩ = Festung 2. **~kommandant** m *commandant of a fortress* **~krieg** m *siege-operations* [pl] **~strafe** f = Festungshaft **~wall** m *earthwork, rampart* **~werk** n *fortifications* pl

°**F·ete** f ['fɛtə] [Fr] *fete* (Fr) = Festlichkeit; *jollification*; ⟨sl⟩ *spree*; ⟨Am⟩ *shindy, shindig*

F·etisch m ~(e)s/~e *fetish* ‖ ~anbeter m *fetishist*; ~anbetung f, **Fetisch·ismus** m *fetishism*

f·ett I. [a] **1.** ⟨eig⟩ **a.** (P) *fat* (*man*); *corpulent*; *obese*; *stout* ‖ die ~en Menschen *the obese*; ziemlich ~ *fattish*; → dick ‖ *plump* (*cheeks*) ‖ ~ w *to grow stout*; °dick u ~ w *to put on weight*; *to run to fat* ‖ °davon kann man nicht ~ w *that's not very lucrative, that does not pay* **b.** *fat* (*ox, sow*); → feist ‖ ~ m; ~ w *to fatten, to fat* **2.** *fat* (*soup*); *rich, greasy* (*food*), *lardy* (*bacon*) ‖ sehr ~ *as fat as butter* ‖ °ein ~er Bissen *a dainty bit*; ⟨fig⟩ *a big haul*; *a pretty penny* od *a nice bit of money*; einige ~e Bissen [pl] *some fat pickings* (*for a p*) ‖ °das macht den Kohl nicht ~ *that makes no difference* **3.** ⟨übtr⟩ **a.** *fat, fertile, rich* (*pasture, soil*) ‖ ⟨bot⟩ ~̂e Henne → Fetthenne | *bituminous, fat* (*coal*); ~es Öl *fat* (od *fixed*) *oil* ‖ ~e Masse *fatty matter* ‖ ⟨mot⟩ *rich* (*gas mixture*) | (einträglich) *lucrative, fat* **b.** ⟨typ⟩ (*extra-*) *bold*; ~er Buchstabe *fat-face, fat letter*; ~er Druck → Fettdruck **c.** ~e Pfründe *fat benefice*; ⟨bib⟩ ~e Jahre *years of plenty* **d.** °er ist ~ *he's tipsy* **II.** [adv] sich ~ fressen v *to fatten o.s. on* ‖ ⟨typ⟩ (etw) ~ drucken *to print in bold* (od *full, thick*)-*faced type*; ~ gedruckt *bold* (od *thick*)-*faced*

Fett n ~es/~e **1.** ⟨allg⟩ *fat*; ohne ~ *fatless* ‖ Schinken~̂ *bacon-fat*; Butter~̂ *butter-fat*; Braten~̂ *dripping*(*s* pl), *gravy*; Schweine~̂ *lard*; Nieren~̂ *suet*; ausgelassenes weiches ~ *grease* | ⟨cul⟩ in *or* mit ~ backen, braten *to fry* ‖ ⟨cul⟩ mit ~ begießen *to baste* → Talg ‖ Pflanzen~̂ *vegetable fat* od *tallow* ‖ ⟨anat⟩ = ~gewebe **2.** ⟨tech⟩ Schmier~̂ *grease* **3.** ⟨chem⟩ *fat*; (einfache) ~e [pl] *fats* [pl] **4.** ⟨fig⟩ → abschöpfen ‖ ~ ansetzen *to put on weight, to run to fat*; *to grow stout* ‖ im eigenen ~ schmoren *to stew in one's own juice* ‖ °gehörig sein ~ bek. (*or* kriegen) *to be hauled over the coals*; *to get* od *have one's gruel* od *packet*; er hat sein ~ weg ⟨fam⟩ *he has got* od *caught it hot*; *that will do for him* ‖ er sitzt im ~ *he's on easy street* **~abscheider** m (in Kläranlagen) *grease trap* **~ammer** f ⟨orn & cul⟩ *ortolan* **~ansammlung** f ⟨path⟩ krankhafte ~ *steatosis* [Gr] **~ansatz** m *corpulence* **~̂arm** a *poor in fat*; *of a low fat-content* **~̂artig** a *fatty*; *greasy*; *adipose*; *lardaceous* **~auge** n (auf Suppen) *eye* °**~bauch** m *fat belly* **~baum** m ⟨bot⟩

fat-tree ‖ = Talgbaum **~bestandteil** m *fatty constituent* **≈bildend** a *fat-forming*; ~e Substanz *fat-former* **~bildung** f *fat-formation* **≈dicht** a *grease-proof* **~druck** m ⟨typ⟩ *bold* (od *full, thick*)-*faced type, bold(-face)type*; *heavy type*; *clarendon* **~drüse** f ⟨physiol⟩ *sebaceous gland* **~filter** m *grease trap* **~fleck** m *grease-spot*; *greasy stain* **~-flosse** f ⟨ich⟩ *adipose fin* **~gas** n *oil-gas* **~gehalt** m *fat-content*; ~ der Milch *percentage of butter-fat in milk* **~geruch** m *porky odour* **~geschwulst** f ⟨path⟩ *lipoma* [L] **~gewebe** n ⟨anat⟩ *adipose* od *fatty tissue* **~gewinnung** f *fat-extraction* **~-grieben** f pl *cracklings* **≈haltig** a *adipose, fatty* **~henne** f ⟨bot⟩ *orpine*; *stonecrop*; *Sedum* [L] **~-hering** m *full hering* **~herz** n ⟨path⟩ *fatty heart* **~-kalk** m *fat lime* **~kohle** f *fat* od *bituminous coal* **~körper** m ⟨zoo⟩ (in frogs) *fat-body* ‖ *fatty matter* (od *substance*) **~kraut** n ⟨bot⟩ **1.** *butterwort* **2.** = Fetthenne **≈leibig** a *corpulent, fat, obese*; *stout, pursy* **~leibigkeit** f *corpulence, obesity*; *stoutness*; → Entfettungskur **≈lösend** a *grease solvent* (⟨a.⟩ ~es Mittel) **~mangel** m *fat-shortage* **~masse** f *fat-mass*; *fatty matter* °**~näpfchen** n ⟨fig⟩ ins ~ treten *to drop a brick, to make a faux pas* [Fr]; *to be shocking*; bei jdm ins ~ t. *to put one's foot in it with a p*; *to shock a p*; *to incur a p's displeasure* **~niere** f ⟨path⟩ *fatty kidney* **~papier** n = Pergamentpapier **~pflanze** f *succulent plant* **~polster** n *cushion* (od *pad*) *of fat*, ⟨med⟩ *subcutaneous fatty tissue* **~presse** f ⟨mot⟩ *grease gun* **~räude** f ⟨vet⟩ (in dogs) *red mange* **≈reich** a *adipose, fatty*; *rich in fat* **~säure** f *fatty acid* **~-schabe** f = Fettzünsler **~schmiere** f *lubricant*; (f Leder) *fat-liquor* **~schwanzschaf** n ⟨zoo⟩ *fat-tail* **≈spaltend** a *fat-splitting* **~steiß** m ⟨anthr⟩ *steatopygia* [L] **~steuer** f *tax on fats* **~stift** m *stick of grease paint* **~sucht** f *corpulence, obesity*, ⟨med⟩ *adiposis* **≈undurchlässig** a = –dicht **~verbindung** f *fatty compound* **~wachs** n *adipocere* °**~wanst** m *paunch* **~wirtschaft** f *fat-industry*; *fat-production* **~zünsler** m ⟨ent⟩ Gattung der ~ *Pyralidae* [L]

F·ette f ~/ *fatness*; *corpulence, obesity*; *stoutness*

f·etten I. vt [h] **1.** ⟨cul⟩ (Gericht) *to impregnate with fat*; *to cook with fat* **2.** ⟨tech⟩ *to grease, lubricate*; *to oil* **II.** ≈ n *greasing*; *lubrication*

f·ettig a **1.** *fatty* (*matter, substance*); *greasy* (*wool*); *unctuous*; *smalmy, smarmy* (*hair*); → fett I. **2.** *soiled with grease*; *greasy* (*paper*); ~ v *greasy with*; sich ~ m *to make o.s. greasy* **≈keit** f ~/~en *greasiness* ‖ ~en [pl] *rich food, fat pickings*

F·etzen m ~s/~ **A.** (zerrissene Kleidung) *rags* pl, *tattered clothes* pl ‖ in ~ umhergehen *to go about in rags* ‖ ich habe nur m–n alten ~ *I have nothing but my old rags* **B.** (einzelnes, ein ~ blauen Tuchs *a piece of torn blue cloth* **a.** [mst pl] ~ *rags*; *shreds, tatters*; sein Anzug hing ihm in ~ vom Leibe *his suit was hanging in tatters* **b.** *rag*; er hat nicht e–n ~ auf dem Leibe *he has not a rag to his back* **2.** ⟨übtr⟩ **a.** [mst pl] ~ *tatters, shreds* [pl]; *ribbons, smithers, smithereens* [pl] ‖ (etw) in ~ zerreißen *to tear to shreds* od *tatters*; in ~ gehen *to be reduced to shreds*; *to go to pieces, to be shattered* **b.** ein ~ Papier *a scrap of paper* ‖ ein ~ (*or* der ~ e–r) Wolke *a rag* (od *ribbon, wisp*) *of cloud* ‖ nicht den ~ e–s Beweises *not a shred of evidence* **c.** (. .,) °daß die ~ fliegen . . *that he* od *it made the feathers* od *fur fly*; *with a vengeance*; *like a thousand of bricks*; *with knobs on*; jdn hauen, daß die ~ fliegen *to give a p a thundering good licking*; → tüchtig [adv] **C.** ×(P) *tatterdemalion*; = Lump

feucht a **1.** *damp, moist* (*air, climate, country, place, wind*); *moist, wet* (*weather*); *humid* ‖ *soggy, wet* (*soil*) ‖ *damp* (*bed, cellar, room*) ‖ unangenehm ~, ~ u kalt *dank* (*fog, stone*) ‖ ~ u klebrig *clammy* ‖ warm u ~ *warm and muggy* | ~e Augen *moist eyes*; ~ v (*eyes*) *wet with tears* ‖ ~e Farbe *wet paint* ‖ ~e Packung *wet pack* ‖ ~ m *to moisten, wet*; ~ w *to become moist* od *wet* **2.** ⟨fig⟩ (Trinkerei) ein ~er Abend *a wet night*; ⟨sl⟩ *a binge* ‖ ein Jüngling, der noch ~ hinter den Ohren ist *a green* (od *callow*) *youth*; *a greenhorn* ‖ °ein ~es Mädel *a fast girl* **F·eucht-** [in comp] ⟨typ⟩ oft *wetting* **~apparat** m ⟨typ⟩ *damping-* (od *wetting-*)*machine* **~blatt** n ⟨hunt⟩ = Feigenblatt 2. **~brett** n ⟨typ⟩ *wetting-board* °**≈fr·öhlich** a; ein ~er Abend *a jollification*; ⟨fam⟩ *a spree*; ⟨sl⟩ *a binge*; ein ~es Fest *a drunken frolic* **~haltemittel** n *humectant* **~halter** m *humidor* **~raum** m ⟨typ⟩ *wetting department* **~warze** f = Feigwarze ***F·euchte** f = Feuchtigkeit **f·euchten** vt [h] (etw) leicht ~ *to moisten, to wet*; → anfeuchten, benetzen **F·euchtigkeit** f ~/~en *dampness, humidity, moisture, wetness* ‖ ⟨meteor⟩ absolute, relative ~ *absolute, relative humidity* (*of the atmosphere*) ‖ empfindlich gegen ~ *hygroscopic* ‖ sicher gegen ~ *moisture-proof* **~sanzeiger** m *hygroscope*; *hygrostat*; *humidistat* **≈sbeständig** a *damp proof*; *high-wet-strength* (*paper*) **~sgehalt** m *moisture* (od *water*)-*contents* (*of the air*) **~skorrosion** f *aqueous corrosion* **~smesser** m *hygrometer* **~sregler** m (im Zimmer) *humidifier*

feud·al I. a **1.** ⟨hist⟩ *feudal* **2.** ⟨übtr⟩ *aristocratic* (*leanings*); *distinguished* (*appearance*); *grand* (*building*; *people*) **3.** °(glänzend) *brilliant* (*idea*); *excellent, first-rate, magnificent, tip-top* (*dinner*); ein ~er Kerl ⟨fam⟩ *a brick*, ⟨sl⟩ *a corker*; → famos, Pracht- **II.** adv *capitally, magnificently* ‖ jdn ~ bewirten *to entertain a p sumptuously* ‖ → famos **Feud·al-** [in comp] ⟨hist⟩ *feudal* **~herr** m *f. lord*; *liege* **~herrschaft** f *f.ism*; *f.ity* **~recht** n *f. law* (⟨a.⟩ System des ~s) **~rechte** n [pl] *f. rights* [pl] **~system** n *f. system*; *f.ism* **Feudal·ismus** m ⟨hist⟩ = Feudalsystem

×**F·eudel** m ~s/~ (Scheuerlappen) *mop, swab*

×**f·eudeln** vt [h] *to mop, to swab*

F·euer v ~s/~ **I.** ⟨eig⟩ **A.** (als Naturkraft) [abstr] *fire* [ohne art] ‖ Stämme, die das ~ nicht kennen *tribes ignorant of f.* ‖ mit ~ u Schwert *with f. and sword* **B.** [konkr] das (ein) ~ *the* (*a*) *fire*; die ~ [pl] *the fires* [pl] **1.** (~sbrunst) Groß≈ *fire*; *conflagration*; ~ brach aus (*or* es brach ~ aus) *a fire broke out*; ~! *fire*! **2. a.** (**Ofen**≈ etc) *fire*; im Zimmer ist ~ (= geheizt) *there is f. in the room* ‖ Herd≈ *ingle* ‖ ⟨mar⟩ die ~ [pl] *the fires* pl (*of the boilers*) **b.** ~ z Verbrennen v Gestrüpp, Freuden≈ *bonfire*; *great blazing fire*; Sonnenwend≈ *midsummer bonfire*; *fires* [pl] *of St John*; Oster≈ *Easter fire* **3.** ⟨**mil**⟩ *fire* ‖ ~! *fire*! ~ halt! *hold f.*! ‖ das feindliche ~ *the enemy's f.*; ~ der Atomwaffen *atomic fires*; das ~ der Geschütze *the firing of guns*; langsames, mäßiges ~ *deliberate f.*; lebhaftes ~ *brisk f.*; Artillerie≈ *gun-fire*; ⟨mar⟩ ~ in Längsrichtung über den Bug *end-on f.* ‖ Trommel≈ *drum-f.*; Schnell≈ *running-f.*; zus–gefaßtes ~ *collective f.* | ⟨hist⟩ Griechisches ~ *Greek fire* **4. a.** ⟨**mar, aero**⟩ (Leucht≈, Navigations≈)*light*; feste ~ [pl] *fixed lights*; unterbrochene ~ *intermittent* od *occulting lights* [pl] ‖ ⟨**aero**⟩ Anflugfunk≈ *homing beacon*, Ansteuerungs≈ *location b.*, Flugplatz-Rand≈ *boundary marker b.*, Flugstrecken(leucht)≈ *airway b.*, Funk≈ *radio b.*, Richtfunk≈ *directional radio b.*; Signal≈ *signal b.* | Bengalisches ~ *Bengal light* **b.** Sankt Elms≈ *St. Elmo's fire* **c.** (brennendes Streichholz etc) *light*; darf ich Sie um ~ bitten *give me a light, please* **II.** ⟨**übtr**⟩ **1.** *burning heat* (*of a disease*); kaltes (*or* heiliges) ~, Antonius≈ *St. Antony's fire* **2.** ~ des Weins *fire* (od *ardent spirit*) *of the wine* **3.** *brilliance, -cy* (*of a jewel*) *radiance* **4.** *courage, mettle* (*of a horse*) **III.** ⟨**fig**⟩ *ardour, fervour* (*of patriotism,* *piety), fire* (*of the soul*; *a feeling*; *a passion, a rage*) ‖ *courage, mettle, spirit* (*of a p*); ⟨Scot⟩ *spunk*; ⟨Am⟩ *pep* ‖ *enthusiasm*; (sinnliches ~) *passion*; *passionate eagerness*; *urge* (*of ambition*); weibliches ~ *female urge*; religiöses ~ *religious urge* ‖ *vehemence* (*of eloquence, of passions*) ‖ mit ~ *with a great spirit*; mit ~ tanzen *to dance with an abandon* **IV. 1.** ⟨mil⟩ → ⟨a.⟩ I. B. 3.) ein ~ **anlegen** (im Ofen etc) *to build a f.*; → ~ legen an ‖ ~ (an)machen, anzünden *to make, light* (⟨Am⟩ *fix*) *a f.* ‖ das ~ ausmachen (ersticken) *to put the f. out, to extinguish* (*choke, smother*) *the f.* ‖ das ~ ist ausgegangen *the f. has gone out* ‖ ⟨mil⟩ das ~ **einstellen** *to cease fire*; ~ einstellen! *cease firing*! ‖ ⟨mil⟩ das ~ eröffnen *to open f.* ‖ ⟨mil⟩ das feindliche ~ erwidern *to reply to the enemy's fire* ‖ ~ **fangen** 1. ⟨eig⟩ *to catch* (od *take*) *fire*; *to ignite, to kindle*; (of explosives) *to fire* 2. ⟨fig⟩ *to catch* (*on*) *fire*; *to be thrown into a passion*; ~ fangen an ⟨fig⟩ (P) *to kindle at*; leicht ~ fangen *to be apt to get into enthusiasm*; *to be apt to be captivated* (od *carried away*) ‖ gebrannte Kinder **fürchten** das ~ *a burnt child dreads the f.* ‖ **geben** Sie mir ~? *give me a match, please*; h. Sie ~? *do you have a light*?; ⟨mil⟩ ~ **geben** *to fire* (auf *at*, [*up*]*on*) ‖ ~ an etw legen *to ignite* od *kindle a th*; *to set a th on f.*; *to set f. to a th* ‖ ~ m *to make* (⟨Am⟩ *to build*) *a f.* ‖ ~ hinter e–e S m ⟨fig⟩ *to push* od *urge a th*; *to take decisive steps in a matter* ‖ ~ **schlagen** aus *to strike f. from* (*a stone*) ‖ das ~ schüren *to poke* (od *make up*) *the f.*; ⟨fig⟩ *to blow* od *stir the coals*; → Öl ‖ ~ **speien** (of dragons, guns) *to spit* od *vomit f.* ‖ das ~ unterhalten *to keep up the f.*; ein mörderisches ~ unterhalten *to keep up a murderous f.* ‖ ⟨mil⟩ das ~ vereinigen *to concentrate f.*; das ~ verteilen *to spread* (*the*) *fire*; das ~ vorverlegen *to lift* (*the*) *f.* **2.** ⟨fig⟩ **~ u Flamme s** *to be enthusiastic* (über *at, about*); *to enthuse* (über *about*); gleich ~ u F. s f *to be carried away* (od *captivated*) *by* (*a th*); *to yield to the charms of* (*a p*); ⟨Am sl⟩ *to fall for* (*a p, a th*) ‖ entgegengesetzt wie **~ u Wasser** *diametrically opposed* **3. am ~** *at the fire*; am ~ sitzen *to sit by the fire*; am ~ kochen *to cook over the f.* | Kohlen **auf** das ~ legen *to put coal on the f.* ‖ etw **aufs** ~ setzen *to put* (od *set*) *a th on the fire* | die Kastanien **aus** dem ~ holen *to pull the chestnuts out of the fire* (f jdn *for a p*) | ⟨cul⟩ **bei** langsamem ~ *on a slow fire* | **durch** ~ beleuchtet *firelit*; durch (*or* **mit**) ~ u Schwert *with fire and sword* ‖ f jdn durchs ~ gehen *to go through fire and water for a p* ‖ durchs ~ gegangen s ⟨übtr⟩ *to have been in the war*(*s*); durch das gleiche ~ gegangen s *to have gone through the same mill* | etw **gegen** ~ versichern *to insure a th against fire* ‖ ⟨mil⟩ **im** ~ s *to be under fire*; *to be fired* (od *shot*) *at* (od *upon*); → Eisen ‖ ⟨fig⟩ in ~ (u Flamme) geraten *to be enthusiastic* (bei, über *about*); *to catch* (od *take*) *fire* (über *at*); *to kindle* (*at* ..); *to blaze* (od *flame, fire*) *up* (*at* ..) ‖ → Öl, Hand ‖ ⟨mil⟩ ins ~ k. *to come within the range of the enemy's fire*; er war noch nicht ins ~ gek. *he had not yet been under fire* | ⟨fig⟩ **mit** dem ~ spielen *to play with* (*the*) *fire* od *with edge-tools*; ein Spiel mit dem ~ *a game with the f.* | darf ich Sie **um** ~ bitten? *may I ask you for a light*? ⟨fam⟩ *got a match, please*?; darf ich höflichst .. bitten? *may I trouble you for a light*?; *can you oblige me with a l.*? ‖ ⟨fam⟩ *do you have a l.*?; *hand me a match, please* | ⟨mil⟩ **unter** (schwerem) ~ liegen *or* stehen *to be under f.* (*exposed to heavy f*); nehmen *to fire at*; *to shell* | **von** ~ erfüllt s f *to be ardent for* (*a th*) | ⟨fig⟩ **zw** zwei ~ geraten *to be* (*placed*) *between two fires* od *between the devil and the deep sea* **V.** [in comp] → Feuer-, Feuers- **~abriegelung** f (schießen *to lay down*) *a box-barrage* **~abwehr** f *f.-fighting* [a. attr] **~alarm** m *f.-alarm*; ~übung [f] *f. drill training* **~anbeter** m *f.-worshipper* **~anbetung** f *f.-worship*; *pyrolatry* **~anzünder** m (Holzspäne etc) *f.-lighter*, (f Kohlen) *coal kindler* **~art** f ~en [pl] ⟨mil⟩ *f. tactics* [pl] **~assekuranz** f = Feuerversicherung **~aufnahme** f ⟨mil⟩ *opening f.* **~auftrag** m ⟨mil⟩ *f. mission* **~bake** f *light-beacon* **~ball** m *f.-ball* **~becken** n *brazier* **~befehl** m *order to f., command to open f.*, → –auftrag **~bekämpfung** f *fire-fighting* **~bereich** m *range*; *f.-zone* **≃bereit** a *ready for action*; *in firing position* **~bereitschaft** f *ready-to-f. status* **~beschickung** f ⟨tech⟩ *stoking* **≃beständig** a *fireproof*; *fire-resisting* (*paper, quality*) → feuerfest **~bestattung** f *cremation* **~bock** m (f Holz) *f.-dog, andiron* **~bohne** f ⟨bot⟩ *scarlet runner* **~bohrer** m ⟨praeh⟩ *fire-drill* **~brand** m *f.brand*; ⟨bot-path⟩ *f.-blight* **~brücke** f ⟨met⟩ *fire-bridge* **~büchse** f (in Lok) *f.-box* **~darstellung** f (Manöver) *representation of f.* **~dorn** m ⟨bot⟩ *f.-thorn*; *pyracanth* **~drache** m ⟨myth⟩ *f.-drake* **~eifer** m *ardour*; *ardent zeal*; *passionate eagerness*; mit ~ *with zest and abandon* **~eimer** m *f.-bucket* **~einstellung** f *cessation of f.*; *cease f.* **~erlaubnis** f *permission to f.*; ~! *commence firing*! **~eröffnung** f ⟨mil⟩ *opening of fire* **~erzeugung** f *f.-making* (od *production*) **~esse** f = Schornstein **~esser** m *f.-eater* **~falter** m ⟨ent⟩ (*large, small*) *copper* = Bläuling **≃fangend** a (*in*)*flammable*; *apt to take f.*; nicht ~ *non-flam* (*film*) **≃farben, ≃farbig** a *flame-colo*(*u*)*red* **≃fest** a *f.proof*; *incombustible*; *refractory* (*substance*); *heat-resistant* (*glass*); *f.proof* (*dish*), *oven-table* (*glass*) ~e Erzeugnisse [pl] *f.proof products* [pl]; ~er Stein *f.-stone, f.-brick*; ~er Ton *f.-clay*; ~er Ziegel m *firebrick* ‖ ~ m *to f.proof* **~festigkeit** f *refractoriness* **~fink** m ⟨orn⟩ *f.-finch* **~flechte** f = Muttermal **~fliege** f ⟨ent⟩ *f.-fly* **≃flüssig** a *molten* **~fresser** m = –esser **~funke** m *spark of f.* **~garbe** f *flash* od *cone of f.*, (im Feuerwerk) *girandole* **~gas** n (im Schornstein) *flue gas* **≃gefährlich** a *combustible* (*in*)*flammable*; *fiery* (*district*; *gas*); ~e Güter *combustibles* **~gefährlichkeit** f (*in*)*flammability* **~gefecht** n *f.-engagement* **~geist** m ⟨fig⟩ *fiery spirit*; *live wire* **~gerät** n (f Ofen) *f.-irons* [pl] **~geschwindigkeit** f ⟨mil⟩ *rate of f.* **~gestell** n ⟨for⟩ *f.-lane, f.-line*, ⟨Am⟩ *f.break* **~gitter** n (vor Kamin) *f.-guard* **~glocke** f *alarm-bell, tocsin*; ⟨artill⟩ *box-barrage*, ⟨fam⟩ *umbrella* **~hahn** m *hydrant, f.plug* **~haken** m *poker*; (Feuerwehr) *f.-hook* **≃hemmend** a *f.-resisting* **~herd** m **1.** *hearth*; *f.place*; *f.side* **2.** *f.-centre* **~himmel** m *empyrean* **~höhe** f ⟨artill⟩ *height of axis* od *trunnion* **~hydrant** m = –hahn **~kammer** f *f.-chamber* **~kampf** m *artillery duel*; atomarer ~ *atomic fire fight* **~kanal** m (am Schornstein) *flue* **~kommando** n *firing command* **~kopf** m *hotspur* **~kraft** f *f.-power* **~kraut** n ⟨bot⟩ *willow-herb*; *rose-bay* **~kreuz** n ⟨Scot hist⟩ *fiery cross* **~kröte** f ⟨zoo⟩ = Unke **~kugel** f ⟨meteor⟩ *bolide*; *f.ball, meteor* **~kult** m *f.-worship* **~land** n *Tierra del Fuego* **~länder** m, **~in** f *inhabitant of Tierra del Fuego, Fuegian* **~ländisch** a *of Tierra del Fuego, Fuegian* **~lärm** m *f.-alarm*; ~ schlagen *to cry "f.!"* **~lee** f ⟨mar⟩ *the side* (*of the ship*) *to leeward of the f.* **~leiter** f *f.-ladder*; (Nottreppe) *f.-escape* **~leitgerät** n *gun predictor* **~leitpersonal** n *gunnery personnel* **~leit-Radargerät** n *gun laying radar* **~leitstand** m ⟨mil⟩ *f.-control* od *command* (*tower, post*) **~leitverfahren** *f.-c. method* **~leitung** f ⟨mil⟩ **1.** [abstr] *f.-control* **2.** = Feuerleitstand **~lilie** f ⟨bot⟩ *tiger-lily* **~linie** f ⟨mil⟩ *frontline* **~lösch-**~apparat [m] = Feuerlöscher ‖ ~boot [n] *f.-boat* (od *float*) ‖ ~er [m] (Gerät) *f.-extinguisher* ‖ ~geräte [n pl] *f.-fighting utensils* (od *fittings*) [pl] ‖ ~mannschaft [f] *f.-brigade*;

f.men pl ~mittel [n pl] ⟨chem⟩ *f.-extinguishing compounds* [pl] || ~offizier [m] *f.-prevention officer* || ~teich [m] *static water tank*; (*water reservoir* [*for fire-fighting*]) || ~wesen [n] *organization for the purpose of extinguishing fires* **~mal** n = Muttermal **~masse** f *fiery mass* **~material** n *fuel* **~mauer** f *strong wall* **~meer** n ⟨fig⟩ *sheet of f.* **~melder** m (S) *f. call*, ⟨Am⟩ *f.-alarm box*, selbsttätiger .. *f. detector*; *electric f.-alarm* **~meldestelle** f *f.-station* **~natter** f ⟨zoo⟩ = Kreuzotter **~nelke** f ⟨bot⟩ *scarlet campion, scarlet lychnis*; *Cross of Jerusalem* **~opal** m ⟨minr⟩ *f. opal* **~ordnung** f ⟨mil⟩ *order of f.*; *f.-regulations* pl **~patsche** f (Luftschutz) *f. swatter* **~pause** f ⟨mil⟩ *f. interval*; ~ ! *cease fire*! **~pfanne** f = Feuerbecken **~pflug** m ⟨anthr⟩ *f.-sticks* [pl]; → Feuersäge **~police** f ⟨ins⟩ *f.-policy* **~probe** f ⟨hist⟩ *ordeal by f.* || ⟨fig⟩ *crucial* (od *acid*) *test*; *crucible*; *ordeal*; die ~ bestehen *to stand the test* || (Probealarm) *f.-drill* **~pumpe** f (z Löschen) *f.-pump* **~rad** n (ein Feuerwerk) *Catherine-wheel* **~raum** m *f.-box* **~regelung** f ⟨mil⟩ *f. control* **~regen** m *rain of f.* **~rettungsapparat** m *f.-escape* **~rettungsschlauch** m *canvas-tube* **~riegel** n *box-barrage* **~risiko** n *f. risk* **~rohr** n (am Kessel) *f.-tube*; ⟨mil⟩ *gun* || ~kessel [m] *f.-tube boiler* **~rolle** f ⟨mar⟩ *f.-station*; → Rolle **~rost** m *grate* **≗rot** a *fiery-red* | °**~rüpel** m = Schornsteinfeger **~säge** f ⟨anthr⟩ *f.-sticks* [pl]; → Feuerpflug **~salamander** m ⟨zoo⟩ *spotted* (od *f.-*)*salamender* **~säule** f *column of f.*; *fiery column* **~schaden** m ⟨ins⟩ *f.-damage*; gegen ~ versichern *to insure against f.* **~schale** f = Feuerbecken **~schaufel** f *f.-shovel* **~schein** m *glare*; *glow of fire*; *dazzling light*; ⟨artill⟩ *sky glow* **~schiff** n *lightship* (*the l.* '*Elbe*') || → Brander **~schirm** m ⟨mil⟩ *f.-screen* **~schlag** m ⟨allg mil⟩ *burst*, ⟨artill⟩ *sudden concentration*; *short heavy bombardment* **~schlund** m ⟨poet⟩ = Krater; Kanone **~schutz** m ⟨mil⟩ *protective* od *cover f.* || *f.-protection*; organisierter ~, ~polizei [f] *f.-brigade* || ~farben [f pl] *f.proof paints* [pl] || ~schneise [f] = –gestell **~schwaden** m *f.-damp* **~schwamm** m *corkwood fungus*, *Polyporus* [L]; echter ~ *amadou*; *German tinder* **~schwerpunkt** m ⟨mil⟩ ~ bilden u verlegen *to deliver and shift f. concentration* **≗sicher** a *f.proof* **≗speiend** a *f.-spitting* (od *breathing*); *volcanic*; ~er Berg [m] *volcano*; → Feuerdrache **~spritze** f *f.-engine*; ⟨mot⟩ *motor-engine*; Schlauch f ~ *f.-hose* **≗sprühend** a *f.-darting*; *flashing* **~stahl** m ⟨praeh⟩ *f.-steel* **~stärke** f ⟨mil⟩ *volume of f.* **~stätte** f *scene of a f.* **~steigerung** f *intensivation of f.*, *increased rate of f.* **~stein** m *flint* || ~knolle [f] *flint pebble* **~stelle** f (im Hause etc) *hearth* **~stellung** f *gun emplacement*; in ~ *in firing* od *f.-position*; offene ~ *direct laying position*; verdeckte ~ *defilade position*, in *v.r* ~ *in d.* || (Raketen≗) *launching site* **~stoß** m (MG) *f. burst*; *burst* (⟨a.⟩ Raketen≗) ≗e [pl] *f. by bursts* **~strahl** m *flash of f.* **~taktik** f ⟨mil⟩ *f.-tactics* pl **~taufe** f ⟨fig⟩ *baptism of f.*; die ~ erhalten *to receive one's b. of f.* **~tod** m *death by f.*; den ~ sterben *to die at the stake* **~ton** m *f.-clay* **~tür** f *firing-door*; (im Hochofen) *firing-hole* **~überfall** m ⟨mil⟩ *surprise-f.*, → –schlag **~überlegenheit** f ⟨mil⟩ *f.-superiority* (über *over*); Kampf um die ~ *f.-fight* **~unterstützung** f ⟨mil⟩ *f. support* **~vereinigung** f ⟨mil⟩ *concentration of f.* **≗vergoldet** a *ormolu* **~vergoldung** f *f.* od *hot gilding* **~versicherung** f ⟨ins⟩ *f.-insurance*; Abteilung (e–r Gesellschaft) f ~ *f.-department* || ~sanstalt, ~sgesellschaft [f] *f. insurance company*; *f.-office*; → Feuerpolice **≗verzinkt** a *pot-galvanized* **~verzinnt** a *hot-dipped* **~verzinnung** f *tin-coating* **~vogel** m ⟨orn⟩ *f.-finch* || = Blutfink 2. **~vorbereitung** f ⟨mil⟩ *preparatory f.* **~vorhang** m ⟨mil⟩ *f. screen* **~wache** f **1.** (P) *f.-warden* **2.** *f.-station* **~waffe** f *f.-arm*; *gun* **~walze** f ⟨mil⟩ *rolling barrage* (*gun-f.*); bewegliche ~ *advancing barrage*; langsame ~ *creeping barrage* (*gun-f.*) **~walzen** f [pl] ⟨zoo⟩ *pyrosomes* [pl]; Gattung der ~ *Pyrosomatidae* [L pl] **~wasser** n (Branntwein) *f.-water* **~wehr** f (freiwillige *auxiliary*) *f.-brigade*; ⟨Am⟩ *f.-department* || ~auto [n] *f.-b motor car*, ⟨Am⟩ *f. truck* || ~depot [n], ~wache [f] *f. depot*, *f.-station* || ~fahrzeuge [n pl] *firefighting vehicles* || ~leiter [f] *telescopic ladder*; ⟨Am⟩ *snorkel* → Drehleiter || ~mann [m] *f.man*; ⟨Am⟩ *f. fighter* || ~schlauch [m] *f.-hose*; Vorrichtung z Anschluß des ~schlauches *f.-plug*; *hydrant*; ~übung [f] *fire-drill* **~weihe** f ⟨R. C.⟩ *consecration of the f.* **~werk** n *f.work*; (öffentl. ~ oft) *f.works* [pl] [sg konstr]; *pyrotechnics* [pl]; ein ~ *a f.work*(*s*) || ⟨fig⟩ *f.works* [pl], *pyrotechnics* [pl]; → Feuerwerks- **~werker** m **1.** *pyrotechnist* **2.** ⟨mil⟩ *ordnance technician*; *sergeant artificer* **~werkerei** f *pyrotechnics* [pl] **~werks-** [in comp] *pyrotechnic* || ~körper [m] *f.work*; ~ [pl] *pyrotechnic requisites* [pl] || ~veranstaltung [f] *pyrotechnic display* **~wirkung** f ⟨mil⟩ *f. effect* **~zange** f *f. tongs* [pl]; ich möchte ihn nicht mit der ~ anfassen *wouldn't touch him with a barge-pole* || ~nbowle [f] *love-cup with sugar saturated with rum burning on f.-tongs above the cup* **~zauber** m *f.-magic* **~zeichen** n *beacon*; *signal-light* **~zeug** n *lighter*, → Taschen≗ | ~benzin [n] *lighter fluid* **~zug** m (im Schornstein) *flue* **~zunge** f *dart of f.* **~zusfassung** f → –vereinigung **F·euerling** m ⟨ent⟩ = Bläuling **f·euerlos** a *fireless* **f·euern I.** vt/i [h] **A.** vt **1.** (Ofen) *to fire* | °jdn ~ (fristlos entlassen) ⟨fam⟩ *to sack a p* **2.** ⟨mil⟩ (ab~) e–e Salve ~ *to fire a volley*; Salut ~ *to fire salute* **3.** °⟨fig⟩ (etw) *to fling* od *throw* (in .. *into the corner*) **B.** vi ⟨mil⟩ auf *to fire* (od *shoot*) *at* od (*up*)*on* (*a p*); ⟨Am⟩ *to pull a pistol on* (*a p*); ~ in *to fire into* (*the crowd*) | ⟨biol⟩ (Impulse senden) *to fire* **II.** ≗ n *firing* (*of a furnace*) || *firing* (*of a volley*) || → Feuerung

Feuers- **~brunst** f *conflagration*, *fire* **~gefahr** f *danger of fire* **~glut** f *firelight*; *blazing glow*; *burning heat*; *fire* **~not** f *calamity* (od *distress*) *caused by fire* **F·euerung** f **1.** [abstr] *firing* (*of a furnace*) **2.** [konkr] *fuel*; *firing* **~sanlage** f ⟨tech⟩ *furnace* **~sgerät** n *firing-tool* **~sraum** m ⟨rail⟩ *fire-box* || ⟨tech⟩ *combustion chamber*

F·euilleton ['fœjətɔ̃] n [Fr] ~s/~s *feuilleton*; *light literature* **Feuilleton·ist** m *feuilletonist*

feuilleton·istisch a *feuilletonistic*

f·eurig I. a **1.** ⟨eig⟩ *fiery* (*arrow*; *dragon*); *burning*; *red-hot* (*ashes*) **2.** ⟨übtr & fig⟩ **a.** *fiery* (*sky*); ganz ~ *fiery-red* || *flaming* (*colours*); *flashing* (*eyes*); *strong* (*wine*) **b.** *fiery* (*horse*, *steed*), *mettlesome*, *spirited* **c.** *fiery* (*disposition*); *impetuous*; *volcanic* (*character*) || ⟨fam⟩ [pred] *full of beans* || ~ v *red-hot with* **d.** *ardent*, *burning*, *fervent*, *flaming* (*enthusiasm*, *patriotism*) || *fiery* (*address*), *impassioned*, *passionate*; ~e Worte *words of fire* **II.** [adv] ⟨übtr⟩ *ardently*; *flamingly*; *passionately*; *with a passion*; ~ eintreten f *to be ardent for*

F·eurung f = Feuerung

°**Fex** m ~es & ~en/~e(n) *faddist*; *fop* || Film≗ *film-fan*, *cinemaddict* Fußball≗ *football-fan*; → Berg≗ || Arznei≗ *drug-fiend*

Fez m (= Fes) *fez* °**Fez** m → Feez

°**f. f.** ['ef 'ef] ⟨hum⟩ (statt v. V. für viel Vergnügen) *have a good time*! *have fun*!

°**ff** ['efef] a *first-rate*, *superior* (*quality*); er versteht es aus dem ~ *he knows his world to a T*, *he knows the ins and outs of it*; → Effeff

Fi·aker m [Fr] ~s/~ [österr] **1.** *fiacre* [Fr]; *hackney-carriage* (od *coach*); *cab*; → Droschke **2.** (Kutscher) *hackney-coachman*

Fi·ale f ~/~n ⟨ec arch⟩ (got. Spitztürmchen) (*Gothic*) *spirelet*; *pinnacle*

Fi·asko n [It] ~s/~s ⟨bes Lit, mus & theat⟩ *fiasco*; *complete failure*; *break-down*; ⟨fam⟩ *frost*; ⟨sl⟩ *flop* ‖ ~ m *to fail utterly*; (S) *to break down*; ⟨fam⟩ *to turn out a frost*

F·ibel[1] f ~/~n *primer, speller, spelling-book*; ⟨hist⟩ *horn-book*

F·ibel[2] f ~/-n ⟨praeh⟩ *fibula* [L], *clasp*

F·iber f ~/~en *fibre*; → Faser 1. ‖ er hing an ihr mit jeder ~ s–s Herzens *he was affectionately attached to her* ‖ → Vulkan≃ **fibrill·är** a *fibrillar(y)* **Fibr·ille** f ~/~n ⟨anat⟩ *fibril* **Fibr·in** n ~s/ ⟨physiol⟩ → Faserstoff **Fibro·in** n ~s/ *fibroin* **Fibr·om** n ~s/~e = Fasergeschwulst **fibrös** a *fibrous*

F·ichte f ~/~n ⟨bot⟩ Gemeine ~ *spruce(-fir)*; (*white*) *fir*; *pine* ‖ hohe ~ (auf Neuseeland) *kauri* ‖ Schimmel≃ *Canadian fir* ***f·ichten** a *made of pine-wood*; *pine* (*board*) **F·ichten- ~baum** m = Fichte **~glucke** f ⟨ent⟩ = Fichtenspinner **~hain** m *pine-grove* **~harz** n *galipot*; *pine resin* **~holz** n *pine* (od *spruce*)-*wood*; *fir, pine, spruce* **~nadel** f *pine* (od *fir, spruce*) *needle*; ‖ ~bad [n] *p.-n. bath*; ~extrakt [m] *p.-n. extract*; ~öl [n] *p.-n. oil* **~schwärmer** m ⟨ent⟩ *hawk-moth* **~spargel** m ⟨bot⟩ *pine-sap*; *yellow bird's nest* **~spinner** m ⟨ent⟩ *pine hawk-moth* **~stoff** m ⟨pap⟩ *spruce woodpulp* **~wald** m *pine* (od *fir*)-*wood* **~zapfen** m *pine-cone*

F·ichtelgebirge n ⟨Ger⟩ *Fichtel Mountains*

F·ichteninseln f pl → Pityusen

Fich·u [fiʃ'y] n [Fr] ~s/~s *fichu* [Fr]

°**f·icken** vi/t [h] (= reiben, hin u her bewegen) ‖ (koitieren) vi *to shag, batter, to bate up* | vt *to do, to fuck* **f·ickerig** a ⟨fam⟩ = unruhig; widerspenstig **F·ickfack** m ~(es)/~e ⟨fam⟩ = Ausflucht, Vorwand

Fideikomm·iß n –isses/-isse ⟨jur⟩ (Familien≃) *entail, settlement*; *estate in fee-tail*; Inhaber e–s –isses *tenant in tail*; Übertragung als ~ *entailment* ‖ ein ~ aufheben *to break* (od *cut*) *off an entail*; (etw) in ein ~ verwandeln, als ~ vererben *to entail* (auf *on*)

fid·el 1. a *cheerful, jolly, merry*; ⟨sl⟩ *raughty, rorty* (*time*); °ein ~es Haus *a jolly fellow* ‖ kreuz~ s *to be as merry as a grig* (od *lark, sandboy*) | (gesund) *as fit as a fiddle*; *alive and kicking* | (beschwipst) *funny* 2. adv *cheerfully*; *merrily* **Fidelit·ät** f ⟨univ⟩ *jollification*; *conviviality*; *convivial part of a students' bout*

F·idibus m ~ & –busses/~ & –busse *spill*; *wisp of paper*; *pipe-light*; *lucifer* (*for a p's pipe*)

F·idschi- [in comp] *Fijian* (*character*) **~ausschlag** m ⟨path⟩ = Frambösie **~-Inseln** f [pl] *Fiji Islands* [pl]; Eingeborener der ~ *Fijian* ‖ die Sprache der Eingeborenen *Fijian* (Polynesien)

Fid·uz n ~es/ *confidence* (z *in*); *inclination* (z *to, for*); kein (rechtes) ~ h *to feel no inclination* (*to do*); *to be loath* (*to do*) **fid·uzit** [intj] *yours!*

F·ieber n ~s/ 1. ⟨med⟩ *fever* ‖ hohes ~ *high temperature*; schleichendes ~ *slow fever* ‖ gastrisches ~ *gastric f.*; gelbes ~ *yellow f.* ‖ Tertian≃ *tertian f.*; *tertian*; Wolhynisches ~ *quintan f.* ‖ Wechsel≃ *intermittent f.*; *ague*; ⟨Am⟩ *fever and ague* ‖ Kindbett≃ *puerperal f.*; Scharlach≃ *scarlet f.*; Schnupfen≃ *f. cold* | ~ h *to have a temperature*; *to be f.ish*; immer leichtes ~ h *to run a slight temperature* ‖ .. messen *to take* .. ‖ im ~ phantasieren *to rave*; *to be wandering, delirious* ‖ ~ verursachend *feverish* (*climate*) 2. ⟨fig⟩ *fever*; *intense nervous agitation*; das ~ der Spielwut *the f. of gambling*; er hat das Reise≃ *he is impatient to start on his journey*; *he is afraid he will miss his train*; → fieberhaft **~anfall** m *attack of f.*; *shivering attack* (od *fit*); *ague* **≃artig** a *f.ish*; *febrile* (*state*) **~arz(e)nei** f = Fiebermittel **~baum** m ⟨bot⟩ *fever tree*; (*Australian*) *gum*; *blue Eucalyptus* L **~bläschen** n *f.-blister* **≃frei** a *free from f.* **~frost** m *chill*; *shivering fit* **~hitze** f *f.-heat*; *flush* **≃krank** a *affected by f.*; *f.ish, f.-stricken* od *-ridden* **~kraut** n ⟨bot⟩ *f.few* **~kurve** f *temperature-curve* **≃lindernd**, **≃mildernd** a *antipyretic, antifebrile*; *febrifugal* **~mittel** n *antipyretic, antifebrile*; *febrifuge* **~mücke** f ⟨ent⟩ *anopheles* [Gr] **~reden** n *wanderings* [pl] **~rinde** f ⟨pharm⟩ *cinchona*; *cinchona* (od *Peruvian*) *bark*; *china-bark* **~schauer** m *chilliness*; *shivering attack* od *fit*; *ague* **~tabelle** f *temperature-chart* **~thermometer** n *clinical thermometer* **~traum** m *f.ish dream* **~wahn** m *ravings wanderings* [pl]; *delirium* [L] **~wurzel** f ⟨bot⟩ → Enzian; Galgantwurzel **~zustand** m *feverish condition, febrile state* **f·ieberhaft** ⟨fig⟩ (→ fieberig) 1. [a] a. *feverish* (*desire*); *excited*; *restless*; e–e ~e Erregung *a fever*; *a fever-heat*; in ~e E. versetzen *to set in a fever*; z ~er E. ansteigen *to rise to a fever-heat* ‖ in ~er Erwartung *in a fever of anticipation* ‖ ~e Ungeduld *fever of impatience* b. *intense* (*activity*); *zealous* 2. [adv] *feverishly* (*eager*); *restlessly* ‖ *enormously*; *intensely*; *zealously*; sein Gehirn arbeitete ~ *his brain was working in top-gear* | ≃igkeit f *feverishness*; *nervous excitement* ‖ *intensity*; → Eifer **f·ieb(e)rig**, ***f·ieberisch** a ⟨eig⟩ *feverish* **f·iebern** vi [h] 1. ⟨eig⟩ *to be feverish*; *to have a temperature* 2. ⟨fig⟩ *to be in a fever*; *to get jumpy* (vor *with*); *to be in a state of nervous agitation* ‖ *to rave* ‖ ~ nach *to have a feverish desire for* **f·iebernd** a *feverish* (*hands*); → fieberig ‖ ⟨fig poet⟩ *agitated*; *excited* (*nerve*) ‖ *delirious* ‖ = fieberhaft b.

F·iedel f ~/~n ⟨fam & poet⟩ *fiddle*; (Geige) *violin* ‖ die ~ spielen *to play the fiddle, to fiddle*; (etw) auf der ~ spielen *to play .. upon the f.* **~bogen** m *fiddle-stick* (od *bow*) °**f·iedeln** vi/t [h] 1. vi *to* (*play the*) *fiddle*; *to bow* (auf *on*) ‖ *to scrape on the fiddle*

F·ieder f ~/~n ⟨bot⟩ *pinna* [L]; → Blättchen 2. ‖ = Federchen **f·iedern** vt [h] *to feather*; → gefiedert

***Fiedler** m *fiddler*, ⟨kont⟩ (*gut-*)*scraper*

fiel 1. & 3. sg pret v fallen

f·iepen vi [h] (of a doe) *to whistle* ‖ ⟨hunt⟩ *to whistle on a leaf by way of decoy*

f·ieren vt [h] ⟨mar⟩ (Tau) *to veer away* (od *out*); *to slacken* ‖ (Boot) *to hoist down*; *to lower*

ˣ**fies** a ⟨bes rhein⟩ 1. = ekelhaft, widerwärtig 2. Ekel empfindend; vor etw ~ s = sich vor etw ekeln 3. adv = sehr

Fig·ur f ~/~en I. (Gestalt) A. ⟨eig⟩ 1. → Gestalt 2. (Körper≃) a. *figure*; e–e schlanke ~ *a slim f.*; er hat e–e hübsche ~ *he has a well-developed f.*; er gab e–e imposante ~ ab *he made an imposing f.*; eine gute ~ machen ⟨fam⟩ *to cut a figure*; du machst e–e komische ~ *you look a comical f.*; sie machte e–e lächerliche ~ *she made a f. of fun* (*of herself*); e–e traurige ~ spielen *to cut* od *make a poor f.* b. ⟨übtr⟩ e–e bloße ~, Schach≃ *a mere f.-head, a pawn* B. (dargestellte ~) 1. ⟨arts⟩ *f.* (*of a saint*); *statue* ‖ kl ~ *figurine*; *statuette* ‖ Kinder≃en [pl] *putti* [It] [pl] ‖ Bronze≃en *bronzes* [pl]; Wachs≃ *wax f.* ‖ ein Bild in ganzer ~ *a whole-length picture* ‖ ⟨her⟩ *charge, f.*; gemeine ~en *common charges* [pl]; Herolds≃ *ordinary* ‖ (etw) in e–r ~ darstellen *to f.*; (etw) mit ~en versehen (*or* zieren) *to f.* 2. ⟨Lit, theat⟩ *character*; stehende ~ *stock-f.* 3. Schach≃ *chessman, piece*; → Bauer ‖ ⟨mar⟩ Galions≃ *f.-head* ‖ ⟨mot⟩ Kühler≃ *mascot* II. (Zeichnung) 1. (im Buch etc) *f., illustration* ‖ erläuternde ~ *diagram* ‖ ⟨cards⟩ *court-card, picture-card* 2. ⟨math⟩ *f.*; → einge-, umschrieben 3. mst [pl] ~en *f.s*, (*decorative*) *patterns*; ~en in den Sand malen *to trace patterns in the sand* ‖ ~en laufen *to cut f.s* (*on the ice*); *to skate in f.s* **4.** Tanz≗ *f.* **5.** (graphische ⁓) e–e ⁓, die e–e Acht darstellt *a f. of eight* **III.** ⟨fig⟩ **1.** Rede≗ *rhetorical f.*; *f. of speech*; *metaphorical phrase* **2.** ⟨mus & log⟩ *f.* **≗betonend** a ⟨tail⟩ *figure-flattering*; *emphasizing the figure*

Fig·ura f [L] [nur in:] wie ⁓ zeigt *to all appearances*; *there is every appearance* (*that* ..) **figur·al** a ⟨mus⟩ *florid*; *figural, figurate*; ≗musik f *florid counterpoint* **Figur·ant** m ⁓en/⁓en ⟨theat⟩ *figurant*; → Statist, Statistin **Figurati·on** [ts] [h] ⁓/⁓en ⟨mus⟩ *figuration* **Fig·ürchen** n → Figur·ine **Fig·uren- ~laufen** n *figure-skating* **~tanz** m *f.-dance* **~tänzer** m *f.-dancer* **figur·ieren** vt/i [h] **1.** *vt (mit Figuren zieren) *to figure*; → geblümt **2.** vi **a.** ⟨theat⟩ *to figure* (in *in*) **b.** ⁓ als *to act* (od *pose, posture*) *as* **c.** (S) *to appear, to figure* (in .. *in an account*); ⁓ als *to figure as* .. **Figur·ine** f ⁓/⁓n (kl Figur) *figurine* ⟨a. theat⟩ **fig·ürlich 1.** [a] *figurative* (*sense, use*); *metaphorical*; in ⁓em Sinne *in a figurative sense*; *figuratively* **2.** [adv] *figuratively*

Fikti·on [ts] f ⁓/⁓en *fiction*; *fictitious statement* ‖ ⟨jur⟩ *legal fiction* **fikt·iv** [-f] a *fictive*; *fictitious* ‖ ⁓er Besitz *constructive possession*

Fil-à-Fil- Fr ⁓-Effekt [m] ⟨tex⟩ *pick-and-pick effect*

Fil·ariakrankheit f ⟨med⟩ *filarial disease*

Fil·et [fi'leː] n [Fr] ⁓s/⁓s **1.** *filet* [Fr]; *netting, network*; (in) ⁓ arbeiten *to net* **2.** ⟨cul⟩ *fillet*; *fillet* (*of beef*), *undercut* (*of a sirloin of fillet*; Rinder≗ *fillet* (*of beef*), *undercut* (*of a sirloin of beef*); *fillet* (*of fish*) ‖ (Fisch) in ⁓s teilen *to fillet* **~arbeit** f *netting, network* **~beefsteak** n *fillet of beef* **~braten** m *roast fillet* **~nadel** *netting-needle* **~netz** n (f Haar) *filet-net* **~scheibe** f Sw = Beefsteak **~spitzen** f [pl] *filet-lace* **~steak** n ⟨cul⟩ *fillet* (⟨Am⟩ *porterhouse*) *steak*

F·ilia hospitalis ⁓/ L ⟨stud⟩ *landlord's daughter*

Fili·al- (→ Filiale) [in comp] **~analyse** f *branch analysis* **~bank** f *branch-bank* **~betrieb** m *chain shop* **~bildung** f *filiation* **~generation** f ⟨biol⟩ *filial generation* **~geschäft** n *branch*; *establishment* (od *office*); ⟨Am⟩ *chain-store* **~kirche** f *filial church*; *chapel of ease* **~leiter** m *branch manager* **Fili·ale** f ⁓/⁓n *filiation* (*of a society*) ‖ inst ⟨com⟩ *branch*; *branch-establishment* (od *office*); *office*; *agency*; Unternehmen mit vielen ⁓n *multiple-shop*; ⟨Am⟩ *chain-stores* [pl] **~ngeschäft** n *branch*, ⟨Am⟩ *chain-store* ‖ ⁓e *company shops*, ⟨fam⟩ *multiples* | ⁓sunternehmen [n] ⟨Am⟩ *chain-store* **Filiati·on** [ts] f ⁓/ *filiation*

Filigr·an n ⁓s/⁓e *filigree*; mit ⁓ geschmückt *filigreed* **~arbeit** f *filigree-work* **~glas** n *f.-glass*

Filik·alen pl ⟨bot⟩ = Farngewächse **Filizin·een** [-eːən] [pl] ⟨bot⟩ = Farnkräuter

F·ilm m ⁓(e)s/⁓e **1.** (Häutchen) *film*; *thin coating* (*of oil*) **2.** ⟨phot⟩ *film*; Roll≗ *roll-film* **3.** ⟨theat⟩ (Lauf-, Reihenbild) *the films* [pl]; (stummer ⁓) *moving pictures*, ⟨fam⟩ *the movies* od *pictures* [pl]; *the screen*; *the cinema*, ⟨Am a.⟩ *canned drama* **a. aktueller** ⁓ *topic*; ·Auftrags≗ *sponsored f.*; Dokumentar≗ *documentary f.*; Charakter≗ *feature* (*f.*); erster ⁓ (in Doppelprogramm) *first feature*; Erziehungs≗ = Lehr-; Fernseh≗ *telerecording, kinescope*; Jugend≗ *childrens f.*; Kultur≗ *documentary f.*; Kurz≗ *short* (*f.*); Lehr≗ *educational f.*; Schmal≗ *substandard-size stock*; Spiel≗ *fiction f.*, ⟨Am⟩ *feature*(*-f.*); Stumm≗ *silent f.* od *screen*, .. mit zusätzlicher Radioübertragung *radiovision*; Ton≗ *sound f., talking picture*, ⟨fam⟩ *talkies* pl Trickzeichnungs≗ ⟨Am⟩ *cartoon f.* ‖ Voranzeige, Vorspann aus e–m neuen ⁓ ⟨Am⟩ *trailers* pl ‖ → Wochenschau **b. beim** ⁓, im ⁓ *on the f.s*; *on the screen* ‖ jdn beim ⁓ unterbringen *to get a p on the f.s* ‖ e–n ⁓ ansehen *to see* (⟨tech⟩ *view*) *a f.* ‖ e–n ⁓ drehen *to make, take, shoot a f.* ‖ (etw) f den ⁓ herstellen *to f.*; er eignet sich sehr f den ⁓ *he films well* ‖ spannen *to undershoot* ‖ (etw) im ⁓ zeigen *to screen* ‖ (jdn) im ⁓ zeigen *or* darstellen ⟨Am⟩ *to feature*; ein ⁓ mit N. N. in der Hauptrolle *a f. featuring N. N.* ‖ er will zum ⁓ gehen *he is going to be a f.-actor* **c.** e–n ⁓ v etw drehen *to film a th* ‖ e–n ⁓ inszenieren *or* °drehen *to arrange* (*produce, reel, stage, shoot*) *a f.*; gedreht w *to be on the floor*; der ⁓ ist gut gedreht *the picture is expertly shot* **~akt** m *reel* **~atelier** n *studio*; *live stage* **~aufnahme** f *filming*; *shot*; e–e ⁓ m v etw *to film a th*; sich z e–r ⁓ eignen *to be filmable* **~beruf** m *film-profession* **~besucher** m *f.-goer* **~bewerter** m *cinema manager* **~bildner** m *f.-architect* **~büro** n *f. service* **~darstellung** f *f.ing* ‖ *f.-acting* **~diva, ~göttin** f *screen goddess* od *star* **~drama** n *photoplay* **≗dramatisch** adv (etw) ⁓ aufmachen ⟨Am⟩ *to feature* **~empfindlichkeit** f *f. speed rating* **~festspiele** n pl *f. festival* **~fex** → Fex **~gewaltiger** m *cinemogul* **~größe** f = Filmstar **~halter** m ⟨phot⟩ *film-holder* **~hersteller** m *f. producer*; *moviemaker* **~herstellung** f *cinematographic production*, ⟨fam⟩ *moviemaking* **~industrie** f *film-*(⟨fam⟩ *movie-*)*industry*; *cinematographic industry* **~kamera** f *cine-camera* **~kitt** m *f. cement* **~komödie** f *comic f.* **~kunst** f *cinematics* [sg konstr]; *filmic art*; *filmcraft*; ⟨Am⟩ *features* [pl] **~laufwerk** n *f.-drive mechanism* **~leinwand** f *silver screen* **~lichtschutz** m *photo-packing* **~operette** f *musical* **~packung** f ⟨phot⟩ *filmpack* ⟨Am fam⟩ *cinemactor* **~paradies** n *filmland* (*Hollywood*) **~patrone** f *f. cartridge* **~(probe)fotos** n pl *stills* pl **~produktionsleiter** m *associate producer* **~prüfer** m *f. examiner* **~prüfung** f *f. examination* **~publikum** n *movie audience* **~salat** m *f. jam* **~schauspieler** m *f.* (od *screen, motion-picture*) *actor*, ⟨Am fam⟩ *cinemactor* **~schauspielerin** f *film actress*, ⟨Am fam⟩ *cinemactress* **~spiegel** m ⟨telv⟩ *picture parade* **~spiel, ~stück** n *f.-play* **~spielleiter** m *director*; *film producer* **~spule** f *reel* **~stadt** f *centre of cinematographic industry* **~star** m *f.-star* **~sternchen** n *starlet* **~streifen** m *reel, strip* **~trommel** f *magazine* **~- u Rundfunkstars** m pl *stars of radio and screen* **~verleih, ~vertrieb** m *f. distribution* **~vorführer** m *projectionist* **~vorführung** f *cinematographic reproduction*; *the* (*moving*) *pictures*; *cinema show* | ⁓sgerät [n] *movie projector* **~werbung** f *screen advertising* **~zeit** f *filmic time* **~zeitschrift** f *movie-magazine* **~zensur** f *film-censorship*

f·ilmbar a *filmable* **f·ilmen 1.** vt [h] (etw) *to film*, ⟨Am fam⟩ *to shoot* **2.** ≗ n *filming* **f·ilmisch 1.** a *filmic*; (*as if*) *on film* **2.** adv *filmically* **Filmoth·ek** f ⁓/⁓en *film* (*lending*) *library*

Filo·u [fi'luː] m [Fr] ⁓s/⁓s *schemer*; *carfty fellow*; *diplomatist*; → Spitzbube, Schlauberger

F·ilter m (⟨tech⟩ n) ⁓s/⁓ **1.** (Seihtuch) *filter* **2.** (Filtriergerät) *filter strainer, cleaner* **3.** ⟨phot⟩ *filter* ‖ ·Aufsteck≗ *push-on f.*; Gelb≗ *minus-blue f.*; Luftschutz≗ *safelight f.*; Magenta≗ *minus-green f.*; mehrfarbiges ⁓ *composite f.*; Zy·an≗ *minus-red f.* ‖ ⟨wir⟩ *filter*; *filter-circuit* **~becken** n *filtering-basin* (od *tank*) **~bett** n (Sandfilter) *filter-bed* **~kaffee** m *coffee made in an individual f.* **~masse** f *filter block* **~mundstück** n (an Zigaretten) *filter-tip* **~papier** n = Filtrierpapier **~presse** f *filter-press* **~scheibe** f ⟨theat⟩ *colo(u)r filter* **~stoff** m *filtering material* **~stufe** f ⟨phot⟩ *filter step* **~tuch** n *filter-cloth*

f·iltern 1. vt [h] *to filter*; *strain*; *percolate* = filtrieren **2.** ≗ n = Filtrieren **Filtr·at** n *filtrate* **Filtrati·on** [ts] f *filtration* **Filtr·ier-** (→ filtrieren) [in comp] *filtering* **~apparat** m *filtering-apparatus*; *percolator* **~beutel** m *filtering-bag* **~material**

n filtering-material **~papier** n filter-paper **~trichter** m folding filter; percolator

filtr·ierbar a filt(e)rable || ~es Virus filter-passer

filtr·ieren 1. vt [h] (Flüssigkeit) to filtrate; filter, strain 2. ≗ n filtration, percolation; filtering

F·ilz m ~es/~e 1. a. felt; (Masse) compact mass (of wool, etc.) || mass of twisted hair; ⟨bot⟩ tomentum [L] b. (Stoff aus ~) felt || z ~ m to felt 2. ⟨typ⟩ blanket 3. °⟨fig⟩ (P) miser, niggard; skinflint- → Knicker **≗artig** a felt-like || °**~biene** f ⟨fam⟩ = ~laus **~decke** f felt **~dichtung** f ⟨tech⟩ f. joint **~einlage** f f. lining **≗frei** a: ~e Ausrüstung ⟨tex⟩ antifelting finish **~hut** m f. hat; felt || breitrandiger ~ (f Tropen) terai; runder niederer ~ billycock; steifer ~ bowler; derby (hat); weicher ~ trilby (hat); Homburg hat; soft (f.) hat **~krankheit** f ⟨bot⟩ erineum [L]; erinose **~kraut** n ⟨bot⟩ dodder **~laus** f ⟨ent⟩ crab(-louse) **~macher** m feltmaker **~macherei** f feltmaking **~mütze** f f.-cap **~schreiber** m ⟨bes arts⟩ f.-tip pen **~schuhe** m [pl] f.-slippers [pl] **~sohle** f f. inner sole **~stiefel** m [pl] f.-boots [pl]; (f Damen) f. bootees [pl] **~tuch** n f. cloth; (f Sattel) [AInd] numdah **~unterlage** f f. pad; underfelt **~walze** f ⟨typ⟩ dabber

f·ilzen vt [h] (z Filz m) to felt; → verfilzen

f·ilzig a 1. (verfilzt) twisted; clotted (hair) 2. ⟨fig⟩ = knauserig, knickerig | **≗keit** f ⟨fig⟩ niggardliness, sordidness, stinginess

F·immel[1] m ~s/ ⟨bot⟩ = Femel

F·immel[2] m ~s/~ ⟨†min⟩, iron wedge, gad

°**F·immel**[3] m ~s/~ craze (f for); kink, mania; fad || e–n ~ h to be obsessed, to be a crank; er hat e–n richtigen ~ in bezug auf .. he has a bee in his bonnet about (fresh air) || dieser Humanitäts≗ this humanitarian nonsense; → Dusel, Duselei **f·imm(e)lig** a crazy; ~ s to have a bee in one's bonnet

fin·al a final; ultimate || ⟨gram⟩ final (clause)

Fin·ale n [It] ~s/~n ⟨mus⟩ finale; ⟨sport⟩ final

Fin·anz f ~/~en 1. (Geldwesen) finance; Hoch≗ high finance 2. [konkr] die (Staats-)~en [pl] the finances; the revenue || the finances, pecuniary funds pl (of a p); mit m–n ~en steht es schlecht my finances are low

Fin·anz- ~amt n Revenue-Board (od Office) **~ausgleich** m financial equalization **~ausschuß** m finance committee **~baron** m financial magnate **~beamte** m: der ~ (ein ~r) revenue-officer (od official); ⟨a-engl⟩ fiscal **~gebarung** f management of public finances **~gericht** n finance-court; ⟨engl⟩ Court of Exchequer **~geschäft** n financial transaction **~gesellschaft** f holding company **~gesetz** n Finance Act; ~vorlage finance-bill **~hoheit** f financial sovereignty **~jahr** n financial (od fiscal) year **~kammer** f finance-chamber **~kapital** n (international) financial capital **~kasse** f revenue receiving-office **~kontrolle** f financial control **~kreise** m [pl] financial circles [pl]; die Meinung der ~ financial opinion **~lage** f financial position **~mann** m financier **~mathematik** f commercial arithmetic **~minister** m Finance-Minister, Minister of Finance || ⟨engl⟩ the Chancellor of the Exchequer; ~ e–s indisch. Staates dewan **~ministerium** n the Ministry of Finance; ⟨engl⟩ the Treasury; the Exchequer **~monopol** n State monopoly **~periode** f financial (od fiscal) period **~plan** m the Budget; the Estimates [pl] **~politik** f financial (od monetary) policy **~schuld** f Treasury-debt **~verwaltung** f administration of the finances **~wechsel** m bank-bill; accommodation-bill **~welt** f the moneyed interest; die amer. ~ Wall Street **~wesen** n finance; financial matters od affairs pl **~wirtschaft** f management of public money **~wissenschaft** f science of finance; theory of revenue **~zoll** m financial (od fiscal) duty

finanzi·ell a financial (position); monetary (transaction); pecuniary (difficulties); in ~er Hinsicht, was das ≗e betrifft financially

finanz·ieren vt [h] to finance; to undertake the financing of (a th) **Finanz·ierung** f financing | **~s–** [in comp] finance [attr] (costs) || ~verfahren [n] method of funding

F·indel- ~haus n foundling-hospital **~kind** n foundling

fin de siècle [fɛ̃ də siɛkl] n Fr gay nineties

f·inden vt/i [fand/gefunden] [h] **I.** vt **A.** ⟨eig⟩ 1. (gesuchte S or P) to find (I could not f. it, him); das Buch war nirgends z ~ the book could nowhere be found || er war nirgends z ~ we (they) couldn't find a trace (⟨fam⟩ hide (n)or hair) of him || to come by (a p, a th); Dienstboten sind jetzt schwer z ~ servants are hard to come by now || ⟨bot & zoo⟩ z ~ s to range (in in) || ⟨tech⟩ to locate 2. **(zufällig)** to find; to come across, to meet with; to light (od pitch) on (a th, a p) || ⟨fig⟩ **(stehlen)** to find, earn, win || e–n Gönner ~ to find a patron | ⟨fig⟩ ein Haar in etw ~ to find fault with a th; to disapprove (of) a th; to take offence at a th || es ist so gut wie gefunden it is a bargain; it is dirt-cheap; it is to be had for next to nothing 3. jdn **im Bett**, etc ~ to find a p in bed, at home, at work, .. a p working **B.** ⟨übtr⟩ 1. (durch Suchen feststellen) a. (etw) to discover, find (I f. no sense in it); to find (od make) out || er fand die Lösung the solution came to him || die S ist auf dem Wege, e–e Lösung z ~ the matter is in the way of solution || .. noch nicht gefunden (the causes are) still to seek; leicht z ~ not far to seek | **etw an jdm** ~ to see a th in a p b. → Ausrede || sein Fortkommen ~ to make a living || den Heiland ~ to find Christ || e–n Weg (or e–e Gelegenheit) ~ to see one's way (to do) || s–n Weg ~ to find one's way || Zeit ~ to find time (to do) c. ⟨math⟩ (e–n Punkt) to obtain (by sighting) d. †⟨jur⟩ Urteil ~ to arrive at a legal decision 2. a. **(erhalten)** to meet with; to find || [oft durch pass:] Anerkennung ~ bei .. to be approved of by ..; → Anklang etc || jds Beifall, Bewunderung ~ to command a p's assent, admiration || Erlösung ~ to find (od obtain) salvation || Widerstand ~ to encounter resistance || k–e Worte ~ f to have no words for b. **(erleben)** (Beruhigung, Frieden, Ruhe, Trost) to find (in in); Freude ~ an etw to enjoy a th; to be pleased with a th; → Freude etc || den Tod ~ to catch one's death; to come by one's death; to die (durch .. from a fall); to be killed (bei .. in an accident); .. durch .. he fell 400 meters to his death **C. (dafürhalten, meinen)** 1. [mit Ergänzung] to find; .. langweilig I find the book tedious; .. ausgezeichnet he found the work (to be) excellent; in his opinion the w. was excellent; sie fanden **in ihm** e–n jungen Mann, der .. they found him a young man that .. | ich finde **es** warm hier I find it warm here; I find it impossible to believe || **das** kann ich nicht ~ I disagree; I do not concur (od agree) with you || ich finde nichts dabei I find no harm in it | **es f richtig** (etc) ~ = halten 2. **ich finde, du hast recht** I find (od I am of opinion) you are right; I find you to be right || ich fand, daß .. mißlangen I found other methods fail (od to fail), I f. that other m. failed 3. **[in Fragen]** wie findest du die Zigarre? how do you like the cigar? || findest du nicht, daß ..? don't you think that ..? **D. sich ~** 1. (S) to be found (the book will soon be found) | das Wort findet sich bei Goethe the word occurs (od is found) in G. | das wird sich ~ that remains to be seen; wait and see; I'll see || das wird sich alles schon ~ that will come right 2. (P) er hat **sich** gefunden he has found himself | (= s–n Weg ~) to find one's way (nach to; nach

Hause *home*); ich finde mich schon (zurecht) *I know my way* | *I found myself surrounded by* .. | **sich** [acc] **~ in (etw)** *to reconcile o.s.* (od *to be reconciled*) *to* (*a th*; .. *one's fate*); *to put up with a th*; du mußt dich darein ~ *you must put up with it*; → sich abfinden | **sich** [acc] **zu jdm** ~ *to associate with a p* **3. es ~ sich** Leute, die .. *there are people who* .. || es fand sich, daß er recht hatte *it turned out that he was right*; *he turned out* (od *was found*) *to be right* **II.** vi **1.** er fand nicht **aus** dem Bette *he could not bring himself to get out of bed* **2.** er fand nicht **nach** Hause = fand sich .. → I. C. 2. b. **3.** ich finde da nicht mehr (hin)durch *I am at the end of my tether*; *I am all at sea* **F·inden** n *the finding* **F·inder** m *finder* (*of a th*) | **~-lohn** [m] *finder's reward* **f·indig** a *resourceful*; *ingenious* | **⁓keit** f *resource*; *resourcefulness*; *ingenuity* **F·indling** m ~s/~e *foundling* || ⟨geol⟩ *erratic*; *e. block*

Fin·esse f [Fr] ~/~n *finesse* [Fr], *ingenious artifice* (od *subtelty*); *subtle device*; *acuteness*, *fineness* || ⟨dero⟩ *artfulness*, *cunning*; ~n [pl] *fine points*; ⟨dero⟩ *stratagems*, *tricks*

F·ingalshöhle f (nach ir. Sage) *Fingal's Cave*

F·inger m ~s/~ **1.** *finger*; Gold⁓, Ring⁓ *ring finger*, *third f.*; Mittel⁓ *middle f.*; Zeige⁓ *foref.*; *index*; kl ~ *little f.* ⟨a. sex euphem⟩; mein kl ~ hat's mir gesagt *a little bird told me* (*so*); alle 5 ~ *the bunch of fives* || lange (Diebes-)~ *pickers and stealers*; → 4. | ⟨anat & zoo⟩ *digit* **2.** Handschuh⁓ *f.* **3.** ⟨fig⟩ der ~ Gottes *the f. of God* **4. a.** die (drei) ~ z Schwur **erheben** *to lift up one's hand* || gibst du ihm den kl ~, nimmt *or* will er die ganze Hand *if you give him an inch he takes an ell* || er hat e–n bösen, schlimmen ~ *he has a bad* (od *sore*) *f.* || er hat überall s–e ~ drin (*or* im Spiel) *he has a f. in every pie*, *he has an oar in every boat* || mir jucken die ~ (vor Ungeduld) *my f.s itch*; ihm jucken die ~ danach (*or* er leckt sich alle ~ danach) *his f.s itch to lay hold of it* (od *to get it*) || du brauchst dabei k–n ~ z **krümmen** (*or* krumm z m) du kannst es erreichen, ohne den ~ z k. *you can reach it hands down*; sie hat nie e–n ~ krumm gemacht *she has never lifted a f.* || den ~ auf etw legen *to lay one's f. on a th* || krumme (*or* lange) ~ m *to be light* (od *nimble*)-*fingered*, *to have a long hand*; *to pinch*, ⟨sl⟩ *sneak*; → 1.; die ~ l v etw *not to meddle with a th*; die ~ v e–r [abstr] S l *to leave things alone* || davon würde ich die ~ l *I would not touch that with a pair of tongs* || den ~ **legen** an .. *to lay* (od *put*) *one's finger on*; den ~ auf den Mund legen *to enjoin silence* || k–n ~ **rühren** *not to stir* od *raise a f.* (in *in*); ohne e–n ~ z r. (→ ~ krümmen) (*to win*) *hands down*; || ⟨fig⟩ sich die ~ verbrennen *to burn one's fingers* || sich die ~ **wund** u lahm schreiben *to write o.s. out*; *to work one's fingers to the bone* (*to get a th*) **b.** man kann es sich [dat] **an den (5) ~n** abzählen *you can tell* (od *number*) *it on the f.s*; ⟨fam⟩ *that's as plain as the nose on your face* | jdm **auf** die ~ klopfen *to rap a p's fingers*; *to take a p to task* || jdm auf die ~ sehen *to keep a close* od *sharp eye on a p* || e–n Ring auf den ~ stecken *to slip a r. on to one's f.* | etw nicht **aus** den ~n l *not to let go one's hold of a th* || sich [dat] etw aus den ~n saugen *to garble* (od *fabricate*) *a th* | jdm **durch** die ~ gehen (of criminals) *to give a p the slip*; *to slip a p* || sich [dat] etw durch die ~ gehen l *to let a th slip through one's f.s* || ⟨fig⟩ das Geld rollte ihm durch die ~ *the money slipped through his f.s* || ⟨fig⟩ durch die ~ sehen *to connive* || ⟨fig⟩ jdm durch die ~ sehen *to be lenient towards a p* | er hat mehr Verstand **im kl** ~ als du im ganzen Kopfe *there is more wit in his little f. than in your whole body* || etw in die ~ nehmen *to finger* (od *handle*) *a th* || sich [dat] in den ~ schneiden *to cut one's f.*; ⟨fig⟩ *to be greatly mistaken* | etw **mit** den ~n befühlen, betasten *to finger* (od *handle*) *a th* || mit dem ~ gleiten über .. *to run one's f. over* (*a th*) || ⟨fig⟩ mit dem kl ~ *with a wet f.*, *with a feather*; ich hätte es mit dem kl ~ tun können *I could have done it hands down* || mit dem ~ zeigen *to point with the f.*; mit dem ~ auf jdn zeigen *to point one's f. at a p* | man kann ihn **um** den (kl) ~ wickeln *you can twist* (od *wind*, *turn*) *him round your* (*little*) *finger* | er soll mir nur **unter** die ~ k *let me only get hold of him* || das Geld zerran ihm unter den ~n = das G. rollte .., → o. durch **~abdruck** m *f.-impression* (od *mark*) || (durch Polizei) *f.-print*; *dactylogram*; die –drücke jds nehmen *to f.-print a p*; *to take the f.-prints of a p* || ~verfahren [n] *f.-print system of identification* **~breite** f *f.-breadth*; *f.'s breadth* **~entzündung** f ⟨med⟩ (= böser Finger) *whitlow*; → Finger 4. a. **⁓fertig** a *deft-figered*; *dext*(*e*)*rous* **~fertigkeit** f *dexterity*; ⟨mus⟩ *execution*; *hand* (*whe has a fine h. on the violin*) **⁓förmig** a *f.-like*; ⟨bot⟩ (~ geteilt) *digitale*(*d*) **~gelenk** n ⟨anat⟩ *f.-joint* **~handschuh** m *f.ed glove* **~hirse** f ⟨bot⟩ *f.-grass* **~hut** m **1.** *thimble*; ein ~voll Medizin *a thimbleful of medicine* **2.** ⟨bot⟩ *foxglove*; *digitalis* (L); roter ~ *purple foxglove* **~kraut** n ⟨bot⟩ *Potentilla* (L); (kriechendes ~) *cinquefoil*, Weißes ~ *White Cinquefoil* **~kumme** f *f.-bowl* **~kuppe** f *f.-tip* **~nagel** m *f.-nail* **~ring** m *f.-ring* **~satz** m ⟨mus⟩ *f.ring*; (e–e Stelle) mit bes ~ spielen *to f.*; mit ~ versehen *to f.* **~schale** f *f.-bowl* **~spitze** f *f.-tip*; ⟨fig⟩ bis in die ~n *to one's f.-nails* (od *tips*) | ~ngefühl [n] *delicacy of feeling*, *sensitiveness*; *tact*; ~nschalter [m] ⟨el⟩ *toggle switch* **~sprache** f *f.-language*; *dactylology* **~technik** f *f.-work*; ⟨mus⟩ *execution* **~tier** n ⟨zoo⟩ *aye-aye* **~übung** f *f.-exercise*; ~en [pl] *manual exercises* ⟨vulg a. sex⟩ **~wurm** m = Fingerentzündung **~zeig** m *cue*, *hint* (über *on*); *index* (f *to*); *lead*; *suggestion*; *indication*

F·ingerling m ~(e)s/~e *finger-stall* || ⟨mar⟩ ~e [pl] *pintles* [pl] **f·ingern** vi/t [h] **1.** vi *to play with the fingers* || ⟨fig⟩ ~ nach *to hanker after* (*a th*); *to search for* (*a p*) **2.** vt (etw) *to finger*, → be~ || °⟨fig⟩ *to cope with* (*a th*); wir w das Ding schon ~ *we shall manage it all right*

fing·ieren vt [h] *to feign*, *sham*; *simulate*

fing·iert a *assumed*, *fictitious* (*bill*; *name*), *pro forma* (*account*); *imaginary* (*profit*); *sham* (*sale*)

F·inish n ~s/~s [engl] ⟨sport⟩ = Endkampf || ⟨ind⟩ letzter Schliff; Appretur(mittel)

F·ink m ~en/~en **1.** ⟨orn⟩ *finch*; → Berg⁓; Buch⁓, Edel⁓; Pracht⁓ **2.** ⟨übtr⟩ (P) *bird* (*a gay b.*); *fellow* || → Dreck⁓, Schmutz⁓ || ⟨Ger univ m. m.⟩ ⟨sl⟩ *tosher*

F·ink(e) m ~en/~en Sw. *slipper*

F·inkenschlag m *singing* od *song of finches*

F·inkler m ~s/~ *fowler* || ⟨Ger⟩ (Kaiser) Heinrich (I.) der ~ *Henry the Fowler*

F·inne[1] f ~/~n **1.** ⟨ich, zoo⟩ (Rückenflosse) *fin* **2. a.** ⟨med⟩ (Pustel) *acne*, *pimple* **b.** ⟨vet⟩ ~n [pl] (of pigs) *measles* pl **c.** (Larve des Bandwurms) *bladder worm*

F·inne[2] f ~/~n ⟨tech⟩ (Spitze des Schmiedehammers) *pane*, ⟨dial & Am⟩ *peen*; gespaltene ~ *claw*; Hammer mit gesp. ~ *claw-hammer*

F·inne m ~n/~n ⟨anthr⟩ *Fin*(*n*); → Finnländer

F·innenkrankheit f ⟨med⟩ (→ Finne[1] 2. c.) *cysticercosis* (Gr) (durch den cysticercus)

F·innfisch m ⟨zoo⟩ = Finnwal

f·innig a **1.** ⟨ich⟩ *fin-like* **2. a.** ⟨med⟩ *blotchy*, *pimpled*, *pimply* **b.** (of pigs) *measly*

f·innisch **1.** a *Finnish*, *Finnic* || ~-ugrisch *Finno-Ugrian* (*languages*) || der ⁓e Meerbusen *the Gulf of Finland* **2.** das ⁓e *Finnish*; auf ~ in *F.* **F·innländer** m ~s/~ *Finlander*, → Finne

F·innwal m ~s/~e ⟨zoo⟩ *finner*, *rorqual*

°**F·insel** f ~/~ *particle*; *minute* (od *small*) *part*

°**f·inselig** a *minute* (*work*); *over-elaborate* || ~e Schrift *niggling handwriting*

f·inster A. a **1.** *dark, obscure*; → dunkel || *murky* (*day, night*); bei ~er Nacht *on a dark night* **2.** ⟨übtr⟩ *dark, gloomy* (*face*); *hopeless, melancholy, morose*; *sad, sombre* (*outlook, sky*) || im ~sten Afrika *in the wilds of A.* || *grim, saturnine* (*hermit*); *stern, sullen* (*look*); ~er Blick ⟨a.⟩ *scowl*; ~ anzusehen *grim of aspect* || das ~e Mittelalter *the Dark Ages* [pl] || jdn mit ~en Augen ansehen = ~ ansehen → B. || ~ aussehen *to look grim* || es sieht ~ aus *things look black* (od *hopeless*) || → düster **3.** ⟨fig⟩ *black* (*heart, soul*); *dark* (*thoughts; vice*); *doubtful* (*place*); *racket(t)y* (Lokal); *evil; grim* (*smile*); *sinister* (*deed, instincts, intention, words*); *weird*; e–e ~e Angelegenheit *a grim business* || (P) *sullen-eyed; ghastly, grim* (*figure*); *sombre* (*character*); *shady, rackety* (*fellow*) **B.** adv ⟨übtr & fig⟩ *gloomily, grimly, louringly* || ~ blicken *to look black*; *to gloom, glower, lour, lower* (auf *on*); *to scowl*; jdn ~ ansehen *to glower* (od *scowl*) *at a p* **C.** das ≈e *the darkness, gloominess; hopelesness, sadness* || im ≈en tappen *to be* (od *grope*) *in the dark* **F·insterling** m ~s/~e *obscurant(ist)* **F·instermetten** f pl ⟨ec⟩ *tenebrae* (L) pl **F·insternis** f ~/–nisse *darkness, obscurity* || → Mond≈, Sonnen≈ | ⟨übtr⟩ *darkness, gloominess; sadness; hopelesness* = ⟨fig⟩ *blackness*; die Mächte der ~ *the powers of evil*

F·inte f ~/~n **1.** ⟨fenc, box & mil⟩ *feint; feigned blow*; e–e ~ m *to feint* **2.** ⟨übtr⟩ *feint, pretence, subterfuge; tergiversation*; ⟨Am sl⟩ *stall* || ~n m *to shuffle, tergiversate* || (Kniff) *artifice, stratagem, trick* || (Lüge) *fib*; ~n erzählen *to tell fibs*

°**F·inzel** f = Finsel °**f·inz(e)lig** a = finselig

Fior·ette f ~/~en ⟨mus⟩ *fioritura* It [pl *–ture*]

°**F·ips** m ~es/~e **1.** *fillip* **2.** *tiny little man*; ⟨cont⟩ *Mr. Snip* °**f·ipsen** vi [h] *to fillip*

F·irlefanz m ~es/~e **1.** *frippery; furbelows* pl; *paltry* od *tawdry th; trifle* || *foolish th; nonsense* **2.** (P) *fool, fop; popinjay* || *fidget* **~er·ei** f *frippery*; ~en [pl] ⟨übtr⟩ *nonsense*

firm a [nur pred] *versed, skilled* (in *in*); → beschlagen a 4. **F·irma** f ~/–men ⟨com⟩ *firm* (die ~ N. *the firm of N.*); *concern; house, business* || ⟨engl⟩ die ~ H. *Messrs. H.* || unter der ~ *under the style of*; f e–e ~ zeichnen *to sign for a firm* || Schwindel≈ *long firm*

Firmam·ent n ~s/~e *firmament*; am ~ *in the f.*; das Licht des ~s *the firmamental light* || ⟨fig⟩ *firmament*; am Londoner ~ *in the London f.*

f·irmeln vt [h] ⟨R.C.⟩ *to confirm* **F·irm(el)ung** f ⟨R.C.⟩ *confirmation* **f·irmen** = firmeln

F·irmen- ≈**eigen** a *house* [attr] **~inhaber** m *owner of a firm* **~name** m *firm-name* **~schild** n *fa(s)cia* (L); *sign* (od *fa[s]cia*)*-board of a firm*; ⟨Am⟩ *shingle* **~siegel** n *common seal* **~stempel** m *stamp of a firm* **~wahrheit** f *the genuineness of a firm's style* **~wert** m *goodwill of a firm* **~zeichnung** f *a firm's signature*

firm·ieren vt [h] *to sign on behalf of a firm*

F·irmling m ⟨R.C.⟩ *confirmee*; → Firm(el)ung

F·irn m ~s/~e *firn* [Ger]; *névé* [Fr]; *old, granulated snow of high mountains*; → Gletscher | ~feld [n] *firns* [pl]; *névé* [Fr] ×**f·irn** a *of last year; old* (*wine*) **F·irne** f *old* (od *seasoned*) *condition* (*of wine*) **F·irner** m → Ferner

F·irnis m –nisses/–nisse **1.** *linseed-oil; boiled oil* || mit ~ streichen = firnissen || den letzten ~ bek. *to be varnished* **2.** ⟨fig⟩ *gloss, varnish, veneer(ing), dope* **~baum** m ⟨bot⟩ *varnish-sumach* **~papier** n *oil-paper* **~tag** m ⟨paint⟩ *preview; private view; Vernissage* Fr **f·irnissen** vt [h] *to varnish*; → lackieren

F·irst m ~es/~e (Dach≈) *ridge* || (Berg≈) *ridge; summit, top* || ⟨min⟩ *roof* (*of a pit*) **~balken** m ⟨arch⟩ *ridge-pole* **~haken** m *ridge-hook* **~pfette** f *ridge-purlin* **~stange** f (Zelt≈) *ridge-piece* **~ziegel** m *ridge-* od *crest-tile*

Fis n ~/~ ⟨mus⟩ *F sharp*, → A-Dur

Fisch m ~es/~e → Bd I. *fish* **A. 1.** ⟨ich⟩ **a.** → *fish*; männlicher ~ ⟨sport⟩ *cock*; ~e [pl] *fishes* u *fish* (drei ~e *three fish*); Zoologie der ~e *ichthyology* || jede Art eßbarer ~ ⟨Am⟩ *sea-food* || weiblicher ~ z Laichzeit *spawner* || See≈ *saltwater fish*; Süßwasser≈ *freshwater fish* || fliegender ~ *flying fish* || (ein)gesalzener ~ *salt-fish*; geräucherter ~ *smoked fish* || versteinerter ~ *ichthyolite* || kl ~ *fishlet*; ⟨fig⟩ kl ~e! *small fry; small potatoes!* || ~e fangen *to catch fish*; (im Schleppnetz) *to trawl; to seine* **b.** Wendungen ⟨übtr & fig⟩ → faul A. 2. || gesund *or* munter wie ein ~ (im Wasser) *sound as a roach; as right as rain* || stumm wie ein ~ *mute as a fish* || ⟨fig⟩ es ist weder ~ noch Fleisch *it is neither fish nor flesh*; er .. *he's a half-and-halfer* **2.** ⟨zoo⟩ (fast jedes im Wasser lebende T) *fish*; **3.** ⟨cul⟩ *fish* **B.** ⟨übtr⟩ **1.** ⟨astr⟩ die ~e [pl] *Pisces* (L) pl; das Zeichen der ~e *the constellation Pisces* **2.** (Spielmarke) *fish* **3.** ⟨mar⟩ ~e [pl] = Fischung **4.** ⟨typ⟩ wrong letter **~adler** m ⟨orn⟩ *f.-hawk; osprey* **~angel** f *f.(ing)-hook* ≈**artig** a *f.like; fishy*; das ≈e *the fishiness* **~bällchen** n ⟨cul⟩ *f.ball* **~band** n ⟨tech⟩ → d. **~bauchantenne** f *f.-belly antenna* **~bein** n *baleen, whalebone*; weißes ~ *cuttle-bone*; → Schulpe **~besteck** n *f.-cover* **~blase** f **1.** ⟨ich⟩ *f.-sound; swimming-bladder* **2.** ⟨ec arch⟩ (~nornament) *falchion; the flamboyant; flamboyant style* **~blut** n *f.-blood* || ~ h ⟨fig⟩ *to be f.* (od *cold*)*-blooded* **~brut** f *fry* | ~anstalt [f] *hatchery* **~dampfer** m (mit Schleppnetzen ausgerüsteter) (*f.-ing* od *steam-*)*trawler* **~dünger** m *f.-manure* **~egel** m ⟨zoo⟩ *piscicolous leech* ≈**essend** a *ichthyophagous, piscivorous* **~fang** m *catch of f.; f.ing; haul*; v ~ leben *to earn one's livelihood by f.ing; to f. for a livelihood*; dem ~ nachgehen *to be fond of f.ing* || ~gerät [n] *f.ing-gear* (od *tackle*) ≈**fressend** a *piscivorous* **~frikadelle** f ⟨cul⟩ *f.ball* **~geier** m ⟨orn⟩ *erne* **~gericht** n *f.-course* (od *dish*); → Meeresfrüchte **~geruch** m *f.y smell* **~geschäft** n *f.monger's shop*; im ~ *at the f.monger's* **~geschmack** m *f.y taste; f.iness* **~gift** n *f.-poison* **~glas** n *f.-globe* **~gräte** f *f.bone* | ~nstich [m] *herring-bone stitch* || ~nmuster [n] *h.-b.* || ~nverband [m] ⟨mas⟩ *h.-b. bond* **~haken** m *f.(ing)-hook*; (z Lachsfang) *gaff*; (Lachs) mit e–m ~ fangen *to gaff* **~handel** m *f.ing-trade* **~händler** m *f.monger*; Groß≈ *f.-merchant* **~händlerin** f *f.wife* **~haut** f *f.-skin* || ⟨med⟩ *f.-skin* **~industrie** *f.ing-industry* **~kasten** m *f.-box* (od *tank*) **~kelle** f *f.-slice* **~kessel** m *f.-kettle* **~klops** m ⟨cul⟩ *f.-ball* **~köder** m *f.-bait* **~konserven** [pl] *canned* (od *preserved*) *fish* **~korb** m *f.-basket; creel* **~kultur** f *pisciculture* **~kunde** f *ichthyology* **~laden** m = Fischgeschäft **~laus** f ⟨ent⟩ *f.-louse* **~leder** n *f.-leather; f.-skin* **~leim** m *f.-glue; isinglass* **~logger** m *drifter* **~mahlzeit** f *f.-meal* (od *dinner*) **~markt** m *f.-market*; Londoner ~ *Billingsgate* **~mehl** n *f.-meal* **~meister** m *f.-commissioner* (⟨Am⟩ *warden*) **~messer** n *f.-knife* (od *carver, slice*) **~molch** m → Aalmolch; Riesensalamander **~nahrung** f *f.-diet* **~netz** n *f.ing-net* **~otter** m & f *otter* ≈**reich** a *abounding in f.* || *f.y* (*diet*) **~reuse** f *weir; bow-net* **~rogen** m *roe* **~saurier** m ⟨geol⟩ *ichthyosaurus* (L) **~schuppen** f [pl] *f.-scales* [pl] || ⟨med⟩ ~krankheit [f] *ichthyosis* (Gr); *f.-skin* (*disease*) **~soße** f *f.-sauce* **~speise** f *f.-meal* **~tag** m *f.-day* **~teich** m *f.pond*; *vivarium* (L) **~topf** m *f.-pot* **~tran** m *train-oil, f.-oil* **~treppe** f = Fischweg **~verarbeitungsschiff** n *factory vessel* **~vergiftung** f *f.-poisoning; ichthyism* **~weg** m (f wandernde Fische) *f.-ladder* **~weib** n *f.wife; f.erwife* **~wilderei** f *f.-poaching* **~zucht** f *f.-breeding* (od *hatching*); künstliche ~

pisciculture **~züchter** m *f.-breeder* (od *hatcher*) **~zug** m *haul*; der wunderbare ~ ⟨bib⟩ *the miraculous draught*

F·ischband n (→ Fitsche) ⟨tech⟩ *fish*; *fish-plate* od *-joint*; (*pin hinge and loop hinge*); → Lasche | ~eisen [n] *pin driver* ‖ ~säge [f] *pin hinge saw*

f·ischbar a *fishable* (*stream*) **F·ischchen** n ⟨ent⟩ *silver-fish*; *spring-tail* **f·ischen I.** vi/t [h] **1.** vi **a.** *to fish* (in *in*); *to angle* (*in* ..) ‖ mit Schleppnetz *to trawl* ‖ in e–m Teich ~ *to fish a pond* ‖ ~ nach *to fish for* (*pearls*) **b.** ⟨fig⟩ dabei ist nichts z ~ *there is no profit in it* ‖ im Trüben ~ *to fish in troubled waters* **2.** vt **a.** (Forellen) *to fish* **b.** (jdn) *to draw, fish, pull* (aus *out of*); (etw) *to fish, pick* (*out of, from* ..) **c.** in dem Fluß fischt es sich gut *the river is fishing well* **II.** ≈ n *fishing*; *angling* ‖ durch viel ≈ erschöpft (See) *over-fished* **F·ischer** m ~s/~ **1.** *fisherman*; ⟨poet, bib & †⟩ *fisher*; → Angler ‖ Treibnetz≈, Hochsee≈ *trawler*; *seiner* **2.** = Fischerboot, –fahrzeug **~boot** n *fishing-smack* (od *boat, craft*) **~dorf** n *fishing-village* **~fahrzeug** n *fishing-vessel*; Treibnetz≈, Hochsee≈ *drifter, hooker*; → Fischdampfer **~flotte** f *fishing fleet* **~gerät** n = Fischereigerät **~gilde** f ⟨engl⟩ *Fishmonger's Company* **~hütte** f *fisherman's hut*; *angler's house* **~kahn** m = Fischerboot **~knabe** m *fisherboy* **~netz** n *fishing-net* **~ring** m (the Pope's) *Fisherman's Ring*

Fischer·ei f ~/~en *fishery*, [a. pl] *fisheries*; *fishing* ‖ Binnen≈ *freshwater* (od *river and lake*)-*fishery*; Küsten≈ *coastal f.* ‖ See≈ *sea-fishery*; Hochsee≈ (mit Schleppnetzen) *deep sea fishery*; *trawl-f.*; (*steam-*) *trawling*; *seining* ‖ Perlen≈ *pearl-f.* ‖ Fahrzeug z Schutz der ~ *fishery protection vessel* **~ausstellung** f *fisheries exhibition* **~department** n ⟨engl⟩ (des Wirtschaftsministeriums, → d.) *the Fisheries Division* **~distrikt** m *fishing-ground*; *fishery*; *fishery-district* **~erlaubnis** f *right of fishing*; *fishery* **~gerät** n *fishing-gear* (od *tackle*) **~gesetz** n *fisheries act*

f·ischig a *fishy* **F·ischlein** n *fishlet*; *small fish*

F·ischungen f pl ⟨mar⟩ (am Mast) *partners* [pl]

Fis·ettholz n *young fustic*

°**Fisimat·enten** pl *pretences, subterfuges*; *tergiversations* [pl] ‖ ~ m *to shuffle, tergiversate* ‖ ohne viele ~ *without ceremony* (od *fuss*)

F·isis n ⟨mus⟩ *F double sharp*; → A-Dur

Fisk·al m ~s/~e ⟨a-engl⟩ *fiscal*; *official of the treasury*; *high legal official* | ≈**isch 1.** a ⟨a-engl⟩ *fiscal* (*property*); in ~er Hinsicht *fiscally* ‖ *financial*, ⟨Am⟩ *fiscal* (*year*) ‖ ⟨engl⟩ → *crown* (od *royal*) *property* **2.** adv *fiscally* **F·iskus** m ~/ **1.** ⟨ant⟩ *fisc, fisk*; *the public* (od *Emperor's*) *treasury* **2.** ⟨mod⟩ **a.** ⟨a-engl⟩ *fisc, fisk*; *state-treasury, national treasury* ‖ ⟨übtr⟩ *the state* **b.** ⟨engl⟩ *Exchequer, Treasury* ‖ *the Crown*

×**Fis·ole** f ⟨bot⟩ *bean*; → Fasel[2]

f·ispeln, f·ispern vi [h] = flüstern

fiss·il a *fissile* **Fiss·ur** f ~/~en ⟨path⟩ *fissure*

F·istel f ~/~n **1.** ⟨path⟩ *fistula*; *syrinx* (L) **2.** = ~stimme **3.** [in comp] ⟨path⟩ *fistular, fistulous* ≈**artig** a *fistular* **~gang** m *fistular canal* **~operation** f *syringotomy* **~stimme** f = Falsett

fit a ⟨bes sport⟩ (in Form) *fit* | adv ⟨tail⟩ ~ (angezogen) *fit* (f *for*)

×**F·itsche** f ⟨tech⟩ *fish*; *fish-plate*

F·ittich m ~s/~e *wing*; ⟨poet⟩ *pinion* ‖ auf den ~en des Windes *on the wings of the wind* ‖ unter jds ~en *under a p's wing*; jdn unter s–e ~e nehmen *to take a p under one's wings*

Fitz m *fidget, fuss*; e–n ~ h *to have the fidgets*

F·itzbohne f ⟨bot⟩ = Fasel[3]

Fitzchen n ~s/~ *trifle*; kein ~! *not a bit* ×**F·itze** f ~/~n (of yarn) *skein*; *skeining thread* ×**f·itzen** vt/i [h] **1.** vt **a.** (etw) *to tie into a skein* (od *into skeins*) **b.** (Stirn) *to wrinkle* **2.** vi *to fuss*

fix A. [a] **1.** (fest) *fixed* (*price, salary*); *standard* (*costs*) ‖ ~e Idee *fixed idea*; *singleness of* (*a p's*) *idea*; *monomania* (L) ‖ ⟨chem⟩ *fixed* **2.** ~ u fertig **a.** [pred] (P & S) (*quite*) *ready*; *ready and waiting*; endlich waren wir ~ u fertig *at last we had done* **b.** [attr] ⟨übtr⟩ *cut and dried* (od *dry*); *ready-made* (*ideas, opinions*) **3.** ⟨übtr⟩ (schnell) *alert, deft, quick* (*worker*); *ready* (*writer*); *smart* (*player*; *servant*); → fertig I. A. 2. ‖ ein ~es Kerlchen *a bright* (od *brisk, smart*) *lad*; ein ~es Mundwerk *a deft* (od *ready*) *tongue* ‖ ~ **in** *quick about* (od *smart at*) *one's work*; *quick of perception*; *quick at learning* ‖ ~ **mit** der Feder s *to have a ready pen* **B.** [adv] ⟨übtr⟩ *quickly*; → fertig III. 2. ‖ das geht ganz ~ *that is quickly* (od *easily*) *done* ‖ ~ m ⟨fam⟩ *to look slippy*; mach ~ *do be quick*; jetzt heißt's aber ~ m! *sharp's the word*! **F·ix-** [in comp] *fixed* **~geschäft** n ⟨com⟩ *transaction for delivery at a fixed date* **~punkt** m *fixed point*; *datum mark* **~stern** m *fixed star* **Fixat·iv** n ~s/~e ⟨tech⟩ *fixative* ‖ ⟨cosm⟩ *fixature*; *setting lotion* **f·ixen** vi [h] ⟨st exch⟩ *to bear*; *to speculate for a fall* **F·ixer** m ⟨st exch⟩ *bear* **Fix·ier-** ⟨phot⟩ *fixing-* (*f.-bath, f.-salt*) **~mittel** n *fixative*; *fixer*; ⟨cosm⟩ *fixature* **~natron** n ⟨phot⟩ *sodium thiosulphate* **~prozeß** m *fixative process* **~punkt** m ⟨psych⟩ *fixation-point* **~schraube** f ⟨tech⟩ *lock screw* **fix·ierbar** a *fixable* **fix·ieren A.** vt [h] **1.** (Schreibung etc) *to fix*; *settle*; → festlegen 1. ‖ ⟨chem⟩ *to fix* **2.** (jdn, etw) ~ *to fix* (*a p, a th*) *with one's eyes, to fix one's eyes on* (*a p, a th*); *to fixate* (*a th*) **B.** ≈ n ⟨phot⟩ *fixing* **F–rung** f ~/~en *fixation, fixing*

°**Fixköter** m ⟨bes Am sl⟩ *pooch*

F·ixum n (L) ~s/F·ixa *fixed sum* (od *allowance*)

-fiz·ieren suff [an trans. Verben fremden Ursprungs] *–fy*: quali~ *to qualify*

Fjell n [Norw.] ~s/~e *fjeld*

Fjord m [Norw.] ~s/~e *fiord*

Fla [aus: **Flugzeugabwehr**] ⟨mar⟩ *anti-aircraft* ‖ ~-M.G. n *pom-pom* ‖ durch ~ gesichert *anti-aircraft defended* (*area*) N ‖ ~-Feuerbegrenzungsraum [m] (*a. a.*) *gun fire area* N ‖ ~-Führungsstab [m] *a.-a. artillery operation center* N

×**Fl·abbe** f = Flappe; *wry face* (od *mouth*)

flach I. [a] **A.** ⟨eig⟩ **1.** ~e Hand *flat hand*; *palm*; mit der ~en H. berühren *to palm* ‖ ⟨fig⟩ das liegt auf der ~en H. *that's as plain as plain can be* ‖ die ~e Seite [Klinge] *the flat* (*of a hand* [*sword*]); mit der ~en K. eingreifen *to use the flat of one's sabre* **2.** (eben; → a. Flach-) *even, flat, level* (*ground*), *plane* (*surface*); ~es Land *flat country* od *land*; *flat*; *low-lying marsh* ‖ *flat* (*roof*); (im Orient) *terraced r.* ‖ *flat-bottomed* (*boat*); ~er Kiel *flat bottom* ‖ ~ m *or* w *to flatten* **3.** ⟨math⟩ *plane* (*angle, curve, figure*) **4.** ⟨tech⟩ ~es Schraubengewinde *square thread* ‖ *flattened*; *flat-topped*; *tabulated*; *tabular* ‖ *flat* (*relief*); ⟨paint⟩ *flat* (*tint*) **5.** *shallow, shoal* (*water*); ~e Gewässer [pl] *flats, shallows* [pl]; ~e Stelle *flat*; *shallow*; *shoal*; voll v ~en Stellen *shoaly* ‖ *shallow* (*vessel*); ~er Teller *flat plate* ‖ ~er w *to shallow, shoal* **6.** ⟨min⟩ ~er Gang *or* Zug *flat* **B.** ⟨fig⟩ *dull, flat* (*speech*); *insipid, monotonous, vapid* (*dialogue*); ~ m (*or* w) *to flatten* (*to run shallow*) ‖ *shallow, superficial* (*p*) **II.** [adv] **1.** *flatly* ‖ ~gehendes Schiff *shallow-draught vessel* ‖ das Kornfeld ist ~ niedergelegt *crops are* (*laid flat* od) *flattened* **2.** ⟨fig⟩ *flatly, insipidly* ‖ da kennst du ihn ~ *there you don't know him at all* ‖ °~fallen (nicht stattfinden) *to go off* **Flach** n *flat land*; *flat, shallow, shoal* **~bahngeschütz** n *flat trajectory gun* **~bild** n *low relief* **~boot** n → flach II. 1.; kielloses ~ *punt* **~dach** n *flat-roof* **~draht** m *flat-wire* **~druck** m ⟨typ⟩ *flat-* od *planographic printing* **~eisen** n *flat bar iron* **~feile** f *flat-file* **~feuer** m ⟨mil⟩ *flat trajectory fire*; ~geschütz = Flachbahn- **~fisch**

m ⟨ich⟩ = Plattfisch **~form** f *flattened form* **~gängig** a; ~e Schraube f *square-thread screw* **~gehend** a → flach II. 1. **~geschliffen** a *tabulated* **~gewinde** n *square thread* **~hammer** m *flatter* **~kopf** m *flat-head* ‖ ⟨fig⟩ *shallow person*; *shallow-brained* (od *pated*) *person*; ⟨sl⟩ *flat*; → Dummkopf **~kabel** n ⟨el⟩ *ribbon cable* **~köpfig** a *flat-headed* ‖ ⟨fig⟩ *shallow*; *shallow-brained* (od *pated*) **~küste** f *low-lying coast*; *low* od *alluvial c.* **~land** n *flat land*; *flat*; *plain*; *plain country*; *low-lying* (*marshy*) *land*; Ufer~ ⟨Am⟩ *bench*; *benchlands* [pl] **~meißel** m *flat-chisel* **~profilreifen** m *flat-tread tyre* **~rampe** f *easy gradient* **~rennen** n ⟨sport⟩ *flat-race* (od *racing*) **~schieber** m ⟨tech⟩ *plain slide valve* **~see** f *shallow sea* **~sproß** m ⟨bot⟩ *cladophyll*, *phylloclade* **~stichstickerei** f *flat-stitching* **~wasserräumboot** n *inshore minesweeper* **~zange** f (e–e ~ *a pair of*) *flat pliers* [pl] **~ziegel** m *plain tile*

Fl·äche f ~/~n **1. a.** *flat*, *level* **b.** (äußere ~) *surface*; *superficies*; Heiz~ *heating surface*; Trag~ ⟨aero⟩ *lifting surface*; *wing* ‖ → Ober~ **c.** ⟨geom⟩ *plane*; (*plane*) *surface*; → eben, gekrümmt **d.** ⟨minr⟩ *face*; kl angeschliffene ~n [pl] (of jewels) *facets* [pl] ‖ ⟨geol⟩ Teilungs~n *joints* [pl] ‖ → Ebene **2.** (~raum; Bau~) *area*; *region*; *space*; Mauer~ *space of wall* ‖ absteigende, geneigte ~ *cant*; *ramp*; *slant*, *slope* ‖ ⟨tech⟩ (End~, Ober~, Plan~, Stirn~) *face* ‖ ⟨aero⟩ tragende ~ *bearing area*; → 1. b. **3.** (weite ~) *expanse* (*of field*); *sheet*; Eis~ *sheet of ice*; Schnee~ *sh. of snow*; Wasser~ *sh. of water* ‖ *spread*; e–e zarte gelbe ~ *a tender spread of yellow*; e–e ganze Wand~ nahm ein feiner Teppich ein *along one wall hung a fine spread of tapestry* ‖ ⟨aero⟩ (of a wing) *spread* **4.** dünne ~ (v Holz etc) *plate*; → Platte, Schicht **Fl·ächen-** [in comp] *superficial*; ⟨geom⟩ *plani–* **~abwurf** m ⟨aero⟩ *pattern bombing* **~ausdehnung** f *superficial extent* **~berechnung** f *calculation of area* **~blitz** m *sheet-lightning* **~bomben([ab]wurf** m) n *area* od *pattern bombing* **~druck** m *superficial pressure* **~einheit** f *unit of area* **~endbehälter** m ⟨aero⟩ *tip tank* **~feuer** n ⟨mil⟩ *aera fire* **~größe** f *area*, *extent of area* **~hammer** m *double-faced hammer* **~heizkörper** m ⟨el⟩ *panel heater* **~heizung** f *panel heating* **~inhalt** m *area*; ~ nach Morgen *acreage* | ~sbestimmung [f] ⟨math⟩ *quadrature* **~leuchte** f *surface-lighting unit* **~maß** n *superficial* (od *square*) *measure* **~messer** m (Instrument) *planimeter* **~messung** f *planimetry* **~steuer** f *tax on area under cultivation* **~tank** m ⟨aero⟩ *main wing tank* **~zentriert** a *face-centered* **~ziel** n *area target*

Fl·achheit f ~/~en **1.** *flatness* **2.** ⟨fig⟩ *flatness*, *shallowness*, *vapidness*; *platitude* **fl·ächig** a (⟨a. paint⟩ *colours*) | –~ [suff] *–surfaced*; groß~ *with a large surface*

Flachs m ~chses/~chse ⟨bot⟩ *flax* (brechen *to brake*); → hecheln; ~ raufen, riffeln *to ripple f.*; ~ rösten, rötten *to ret f.*; ~ schwingen *to swingle f.* ‖ Stoff aus ~ *flax* ‖ wie ~ *flaxen* (*hair*) **~artig** a *flaxen*; *flaxy* **~bart** m *flaxen beard* **~bau** m *flax-culture*; *cultivation of flax* **~bereitung** f *flax-dressing* **~blond** a *flaxen* **~breche**, **~brechmaschine** f *flax-brake* **~faden** m *flax-thread*; *harl(e)* **~farben**, **~farbig** a *flaxen* **~faser** f *flax fibre*; *harl(e)* **~haar** n *flaxen hair* **~haarig** a *flaxen-haired* **~hechel** f *flax-comb* (od *hackle*) **~kopf** m *towhead* (*flaxen-haired child*) **~köpfig** a *tow-headed* **~lilie** f ⟨bot⟩ *flax-lily*; *phormium* **~riffel** m *flax-ripple* **~röste** f *retting-process* **~schwinge** f *swingle* **~seide** f ⟨bot⟩ *flax-dodder* **~spinnen** n *flax-spinning* **~spinnerei** f *flax-mill* **~stengel** m *flax-stalk*

°**fl·achsen** vi [h] 1. = ulken 2. = flunkern

***fl·achsen**, **fl·ächse(r)n** a *flaxen*; *flax*; *flaxy*

Fl·ackerfeuer n *flare* ‖ ⟨mar⟩ *flare-up*; *flare-up light* **fl·ack(e)rig** a = flackernd

fl·ackern 1. vi [h] (of fire, etc.) *to flare*, *flicker*, *waver*; hell ~ *to leap*; matt, schwach ~ *to flicker low* ‖ ⟨übtr⟩ (of eyes, hope) *to flicker*; *waver*; es flackerte in s–n Augen *his eyes flickered* **2.** ~ n *flickering*; *flare*, *flicker* ‖ ⟨übtr⟩ *flicker*; das letzte ~ *the last f.* (*of hope*); **fl·ackernd** a *flaring*, *flickering*; ~es Licht *flare*, *flicker* ‖ ⟨übtr⟩ *flickering*; *wavering* (*shadow*)

Fl·addermine f ⟨mil⟩ *small mine*; *fougasse* Fr

Fl·aden m *round flat cake* ‖ ⟨übtr⟩ Kuh~ *clot of cow-dung*

Fl·ader f = Maser, Holzader, Jahresring

ˣ**Flad·use** f *bonnet* ‖ ⟨fig⟩ = Flause

Flagell·ant m ~en/~en ⟨rel & übtr⟩ *flagellant* ‖ ~tum [n] *flagellantism* **Flagell·at** m ~en/~en ⟨zoo⟩ *flagellate*; Gattung der ~en *Euglena* (L) ‖ → Trypanosoma **Flag·elle** f ⟨zoo⟩ *flagellum* (L)

Flageol·ett [–aʒo–] n (Fr) ⟨mus⟩ *flageolet* | ~zug [m] (e–r Orgel) *flute*

Fl·agg- (→ Flagge) *flag* **~leine** f *signal-halyard* **~leutnant** m *flag-lieutenant* **~offizier** m *flag-officer* **~schiff** n *flagship* **~stock** m *flagstaff*

Fl·agge f ~/~n **1.** ⟨mar⟩ **a.** *ensign*; *colours* [pl]; *flag*; Admirals~ *the Admiral's flag*, *the flag* (→ Gösch) ‖ die National~ *or* Landes~ *the national ensign* od *flag* ⟨Am⟩ *colors* pl; ~ der deutschen Kriegsmarine *flag of the German Navy*; die ~ v Großbritannien *the Union Jack*; die amerik. National~ *the star-spangled banner*; *stars and stripes* **b.** Kontor~, Reederei~ *house-flag* ‖ die Not~ aufziehen *to fly* (od *hoist*) *a flag union down* ‖ Quarantäne~ *quarantine-flag*, *yellow flag* **c.** die ~ **dippen** *to dip the flag* ‖ e–e ~ führen (*or* gehißt h) *to fly* (od *show*) *a flag* ‖ die ~ (halb) heißen (*or* hissen) *to hoist the flag* (*at the dip*); heißt ~! *hoist the flag*! ‖ die ~ **setzen** = ~ heißen; ⟨Am⟩ *to make colors*; mit gesetzter ~ *with her colours flying*; die ~ halbstocks setzen *to half-mast the flag*; Topp~n setzen *to fly the mast-head flags* ‖ die ~ streichen *to strike* od *drop one's flag* ‖ ⟨fig⟩ (nachgeben) *to drop one's flag* ‖ die ~ zeigen *to show the flag* | **unter** falscher ~ segeln *to sail under false colours* ‖ unter deutscher ~ fahren *to fly the German flag* **2.** (Fahne → d.) *flag*; *colours* pl; **3.** ⟨fig⟩ *banner*; (*under the b. of freedom*) ‖ die ~ der Revolution *the red flag* ‖ unter falscher ~ segeln → 1. c. **4.** [in comp] → Flagg–, Flaggen–

Fl·aggen- [in comp] **~gruß** m ⟨mar⟩ *salute of the colo(u)rs* **~knopf** m *truck* **~parade** f *hoisting* (*and hauling down*) *of flag*, ⟨mar Am⟩ *colors* pl **~salut** m = –gruß **~signal** n *flag-signal* **~spind** m *flag-locker* **~tuch** n *bunting* **~zeichen** n *flag-signal*; (jdn) durch ~ benachrichtigen *to flag* **fl·aggen** vi [h] (of a ship, etc.) *to fly a flag*; *to hoist one's flag*; halbmast ~ *to hlaf-mast the flag*, *to fly the flag at h.-m.* ‖ jedes Haus hatte geflaggt *every house was flying its flag*

flagr·ant a *flagrant* (*crime*); *glaring* (*contrast*)

Fl·ak [aus **Flug**abwehr**k**anone] f ~/~ ⟨aero⟩ **1.** anti-aircraft (abbr. *A.A.*) *gun*; ⟨sl⟩ *archie*, ⟨mar sl⟩ *Gwennie* **2.** *a.-a. force*; Oberbefehlshaber der ~ *Commander of the A.A. batteries*; leichte ~ *pom-poms* [pl] **~artillerie** f *a.-a. batteries* [pl], *a.-a. artillery* (*A.A.A.*) **~batterie** f *A.A.battery* **~feuer** n *A.A.fire* ~**-geschützt** a *gun-defended* (*area*) **~hochstand** m *a.-a. tower* **~kampfgruppe** *a.-a. combat group* **~kommandeur** m *a.-a. commander* **~posten** m *a.-a. spotter* **~scheinwerfer** m *a. a. search-light* **~schießen** n *A.A. shooting* **~sperrfeuer** n (*a.-a.*) *box barrage* **~sperrgürtel** m (*a.-a.*) *ring fence* **~stellung** f *line of anti-aircraft guns* [pl] **~vierling** m *four-barrel(l)ed a.-a. gun* **~visier** n *A.A. sight* **~zwilling** m *double-barrel(l)ed a.-a. gun*

Flak·on [fla'kɔ̃] m & n (Fr) ~s/~s *flacon* (Fr); *scent* (od *smelling*) *-bottle*

Fl·amberg m ~s/~e ⟨poet⟩ *flamberg*

flamb·ieren vt [h] ⟨cul⟩ *to flamber*; (Huhn) *to singe* ‖ –rt *flambé* Fr (*lit with spirit*)

Flamboy·ant [flɑ̃bwa'jɑ̃] (Fr) **1.** n ~s/ ⟨arch⟩ *the flamboyant* **2.** m ~s/~s ⟨bot⟩ *flamboyant*

Fl·ame m, **Fl·amin** f, **Flamländer** m, **~in** f *Fleming, Flemish* (*wo*)*man, native of Flanders* **fl·ämisch, fl·amländisch** a *Flemish*; das ~e *Fleming*

Flam·ingo m ⟨orn⟩ *flamingo* [pl *-os*] **~blume** f ⟨bot⟩ *Anthurium* (L)

Flamm- **~bogen** m *electric arc* **~bombe** f *oil bomb* **~ofen** m *flame-furnace, reverberatory f.* **~öl** n ⟨mil⟩ *incendiary* s; *flame-thrower fuel* **~punkt** m *flash*(*ing*)*-point* **~rohr** n *flame* (od *boiler*)*-flue* | ~kessel [m] *flue-boiler* ~**rot** a *flame-red*; *flaming* (*flower*) **~schutzsicherung** f *flame arrester* od *trap* ~**sicher** a *fireproof* (*paper*)

Fl·ämmchen n ~s/~n *flamelet*

Fl·amme f ~/~n **A. 1.** ⟨eig⟩ **a.** *flame*; (helle ~) *blaze*; → (nicht)leuchtend ‖ schießende ~ *jet*; → Gas~ **b.** hohe ~n schlagen *to flash* (od *burst*) *into a blaze*; *to be blazing* ‖ (Leiche) den ~n übergeben *to commit to the flames*; *to cremate* ‖ ein Raub der ~n w *to become a prey to the flames* | **in** ~n *ablaze, alight*; *in flames* ‖ in ~n aufgehen *to go up in flames*; *to go alight*; in ~n aufgehen l *to blow* (*a th*) *to blazes* ‖ in ~n ausbrechen *to burst into flames, to spring into a blaze* ‖ (etw) in ~n setzen *to set* (*a th*) *on fire, to set fire to* (*a th*) ‖ (ganz) in ~n stehen *to be* (*all*) *in flames* (od *in a blaze*) **2.** ⟨übtr & fig⟩ *flame* (*of ambition, enthusiasm*); [oft pl] die ~n *the flames* (*of love, passion, wrath*) pl ‖ ganz ~ s *to be all on flame*; → Feuer IV. 2. **3.** ⟨hunt⟩ *tag* (*of a fox's brush* **B.** °(= Geliebte) *love, sweetheart*; ⟨fam & hum⟩ *flame* **C.** [in comp] → Flamm-, Flammen-

fl·ammen vi/t [h] **1.** vi *to flame*; hell ~ *to blaze, to flare* ‖ (of the face) (erröten) *to flush* ‖ ⟨fig⟩ *to flame*; *glow* (v *with*); *to sparkle* ‖ → auf-, entflammen **2.** vt (Stoff) *to water*; → geflammt ‖ (Stahl) *to cloud*; → marmorieren **Fl·ammen-** [in comp] **~blume** f ⟨bot⟩ *phlox* (L) **~eifer** m ⟨fig⟩ *intense* (od *excessive*) *enthusiasm* ~**förmig** a *flame-like*; *flamy, flaming* **~fortpflanzung** f *flame propagation* **~glanz** m *blaze, glare, gleam* **~glut** f *glowing heat*; *glow of flames* **~meer** n *sea of flame*; ein rotes ~ *a red blaze* **~muster** n *wavy* (od *flame-like*) *pattern*; mit ~n schmücken *to water*; mit ~n geschmückt *watered, moiré* (Fr) **~qual** f *the flames* (od *torments*) *of hell* **~rückschlag** m *flare-back, flash-b.* | ~sicherung [f] *flame arrester* od *trap* **~schrift** f ⟨poet⟩ *flaming characters* [pl]; ⟨bib & poet⟩ (Belsazar) *the writing on the wall* **~schwert** n *flaming sword* **~stil** m ⟨arch⟩ *flamboyant* (*style*) **~strahl** m *flame jet* **~tod** m = Feuertod **~werfer** m ⟨mil⟩ *flame-machine* (od *projector, thrower*); *Flammenwerfer* [Ger] **~zeichen** n *flame signal*; durch ~ senden *to flame* ‖ ⟨fig⟩ *oriflamme* **~zündung** f *flame ignition* **fl·ammend 1.** a *flaming*; *blazing* | ⟨fig⟩ *flaming* (*patriotism*); *glowing*; v Begeisterung ~ *enthusiastic* (*address*) ‖ *fulminating* (*protest*) ‖ *scorching* (*sarcasm*); *vehement* **2.** adv ⟨fig⟩ *flamingly*; *fulminatingly*

Fl·ammeri m ~s/~s *flummery, blancmange*

fl·ammig a *flamy, flame-like* ‖ ⟨übtr⟩ (geflammt) *watered* (*silk*); *wavy* (*pattern*)

Fl·andern ⟨geogr⟩ *Flanders* [sg konstr] | ~zaun [m] ⟨mil⟩ *double-apron barbed-wire fence*

fl·andrisch a *Flanders* (*coast*)

Flan·ell m ~s/~e **1.** *flannel* ‖ mit ~ (ab)reiben *to flannel* **2.** [in comp] *flannel* (*shirt*) **~anzug** m *flannels* [pl] ⟨sport a.⟩ *sweat-suit* ‖ in ~ gekleidet *flannelled* **~hose** f *flannels* [pl] **~jakett** n (bunt *or* blau) *blazer* **~imitation** f *flannelette* **~tuch** n *dreieckiges* ~ (über die Windeln gelegt) *pilch* **~übermantel** m ⟨sport⟩ *sweat-suit*

flan·ellen a *flannel* (*shirt*)

Flan·eur [fla'nør] m [Fr] ~s/~e *flaneur* (Fr); → Bummler **flan·ieren** vi [h] *to indulge in flanerie*; *to go gadding about*; → bummeln

Fl·anke f ~/~n **1. a.** ⟨fort & mil⟩ *flank* (*of a bastion*; *regiment*) ‖ die ~n decken *to cover the flanks*; die ~ e–r Festung decken *to flank a fortress*; die feindliche ~ aufrollen, umfassen *to turn the enemy's flank*; → umgehen ‖ in der ~ *in flank*; dem Feinde in die ~ fallen, den F. in der ~ angreifen *to take the enemy in flank* **b.** (of buildings, etc.) *flank, side* **2.** ⟨zoo⟩ (Weiche) *flank* (*of a horse*) **3.** ⟨tech⟩ *flank* (e–s Gewindes *of a thread*); *haunch*; *shoulder* **4.** ⟨gym⟩ *flank-vault* **fl·anken** vt [h] ⟨Ass ftb⟩ (Ball) *to middle* **Fl·anken-** [in comp] *flank* **~angriff** m *f.-attack* **~bewegung** f *f.-movement* **~deckung** f *f.-guard* **~einbruch** m *f.ing penetration* **~feuer** n *f.ing fire* **~marsch** m *f.*(*ing*) *march* **~sicherung** f *f. patrol* **~werk** n ⟨fort⟩ *f.er*

flank·ieren vt [h] *to flank* ‖ –kiert *flanked* (*by two towers*); ~d *flanking* (*attack, fire, turret*)

Flan(t)sch m [engl] ~es/~e; **Fl·an(t)sche** f [engl] ~/~n ⟨tech⟩ *flange*; ~ e–r Kupplung *coupling fl.*; ~ e–s Rohrs *pipe fl.* ‖ dazu: *to flange* | **~en-** [in comp] *flange* **~kupplung** f *f. coupling* **~rohr** n *f.-pipe* **~verbindung** f *f.-joint*

×°**Fl·appe** f = –bbe (ziehen *to make, draw*) *wry face*

°**Flaps** m (P) *cub*; *lout, lubber, oaf*; ein unerzogener ~ *an unlicked cub*, → Flegel, Lümmel

fl·apsig a *loutish, lubberly*; *rough*

Fl·äschchen n *small bottle*; (Riech~) *scent* (od *smelling*)*-bottle* ‖ Arznei~ *phial*

Fl·asche f ~/~n **1.** (mst aus Glas) **a.** *bottle* ‖ kl flache ~, Reise~ *flask*; **b.** (Inhalt e–r ~) *bottle*; e–e ~ Wein *a b. of wine* **c.** e–e ~ mit jdm trinken *to split a b. with a p*; e–r ~ den Hals brechen, e–e ~ zus– trinken *to crack a b. together* | (Bier) auf ~n ziehen *to b.*; ⟨fig⟩ *to b. up* ‖ auf ~n (gezogen) *b.d* ‖ bei e–r ~ (*to discuss a th*) *over a b.* | (**Baby**-Milchgemisch) *formula*; mit der ~ nähren *to bring up on the b.* **2.** ⟨el⟩ Leidener ~ *Leyden jar* **3.** ⟨tech⟩ (Kloben) (*pulley-*)*block* **4.** °= Doofmann, Dämlack; ⟨fam⟩ *nana* **Fl·aschen-** [in comp] bottle– .. **~baum** m ⟨bot⟩ *sweet-sop*; (australischer) *b.-tree* **~bier** n *b. beer* **~blasmaschine** f *b.-blowing machine* **~bürste** f *b.-brush* **~element** n ⟨el⟩ *b. battery* **~etikettiermaschine** f *b. labeller* **~füllapparat** m *b.-filling apparatus* **~glas** n grünes ~ *b.-glass* **~hals** m *narrow neck of a b.* **~halter** m (verschließbarer) *tantalus* (L) **~hülse** f *b. envel*(*l*)*ope* **~kapsel** f *tinfoil cap* (od *capsule*) **~kind** n *b.* (od *b.-fed*) *baby* **~kürbis** m ⟨bot⟩ *b.-gourd* **~leichen** f [pl] (leere ~) ⟨mil sl⟩ *dead marines* od *soldiers* **~milch** f *b.d milk* **~pfand** n *b. deposit* **~post** f *b. post* **~regal** n *wine-bin* ~**reif** a *ready for bottling* ‖ *b.d* **~spülen** n *b.-rinsing* **~spüler** m (⟨a.⟩ –lmaschine) *b.-washer* **~ständer** m *b.-rack* (od *stand*) ‖ = –halter **~verschluß** m *b.-stopper* | ~maschine [f] *b. sealing m.* **~wein** m *wine in b.s* ~**weise** adv *by the b.* **~zug** m ⟨tech⟩ *pulley block*; *tackle block* °**fl·aschig** a = doof, dämlich

×**Fl·aschner** m ~s/~ [swd] *tinman, tinsmith*

Fl·aser f ~/~n ⟨geol⟩ (Ader) *flaser* **fl·aserig** a ⟨geol⟩ *flaser* (*structure*)

Fl·atter- (→ flattern) [in comp] **~geist** m ⟨bib & Lit⟩ = flatterhafte P **~gras** n ⟨bot⟩ *millet-grass* **~hund** m = fliegender Hund; → Hund **~maki** m ⟨zoo⟩ = Pelzflatterer **~mine** f ⟨mil⟩ = Fladdermine **~sinn** m → flatterhaft **~tier** n ⟨zoo⟩ *flying mammal*; Gattung der ~e *Chiroptera* pl; → Fledermaus **fl·atterhaft** a *fickle, flightly, inconstant, volatile* (*p*; *mood*); *skittish, fly* (*little girl*) ‖ ~e P *flibbertigibbet*; *fly-away*; *weather-*

cock ‖ ~er Sinn, ~es Wesen = ≗**igkeit** f ~/ *fickleness, flightiness, inconstancy, volatility* ***fl·att(e)rig** a = flatterhaft **fl·attern 1.** vi [h] (of birds, insects) *to flutter* ⟨a. tech⟩; *flitter; flit* (*from tree to tree*) ‖ ⟨übtr⟩ (of flags) *to float, fly* (auf dem Hause *from the house*); (of hair) *to stream*; (of sails) im Winde ~ *to shiver* ‖ ⟨mot⟩ *to wobble,* ⟨fam⟩ *to shimmy* ([*the weels*] *are not true*) ‖ geräuschvoll ~ *to flap* ‖ etw verführerisch vor jdm ~ l *to dangle a th before a p* **2.** ≗ n *flutter(ing); flit(ting); flap* ‖ *flying; streaming;* ⟨mot fam⟩ *shimmy* **fl·atternd** a *fluttering;* ~e Bewegung *flutter; flit; flap* ‖ *fly-away* (*dress*); *streaming*

flau A. [a] **1.** [attr & pred] **a.** (of colour) *dull; flat, lifeless* ‖ ⟨phot⟩ *thin* (*negative*) **b.** *light* (*breeze*); ~ w (of wind) *to abate; to calm down* **c.** (of drinks) *insipid, stale, weak* (*tea*) **d.** ⟨com⟩ *dull, flat, lifeless* (*money-market*); *slack* (*season*); *stagnant* (*trade*); *weak* (*market*) ‖ *listless* (*assent*) **e.** ~es Gefühl ⟨fam⟩ *droops* pl (*mid-morning d.*) **2.** [nur pred] **a.** (P) ich fühle mich ~, mir ist ganz ~ zumute *I feel quite empty; I feel faint* (*with hunger*) **b.** ⟨com, st exch⟩ *dull;* Tee ~ *tea flat;* Weizen ~ *wheat lifeless* ‖ ~ w *to slacken* **c.** ⟨pol⟩ ~ m *to be a defeatist* (od *pessimist*); *to indulge in defeatism* ‖ ⟨st exch⟩ *to bear* **B.** adv; ~ gehen (of business) *to drag, lag* ‖ mit m–r Kasse steht es ~ *my finances are low* **Fl·aue** f = Flauheit **fl·auen** vi [h] ⟨com⟩ (flau w) *to slacken;* → ab~ **Fl·auheit** f **1.** ⟨mar⟩ *lightness* (*of a wind*); → Flaute ‖ *staleness, weakness* ‖ ⟨com⟩ *dullness, flatness, slackness, stagnancy, stagnation, weakness* **2.** *faintness* (.. vor *with hunger*)

Flaum[1] m ~s/ (on the face, on plants) *down, fluff; flue;* feiner ~ *fuzz* ‖ (on grapes, etc.) *bloom* ‖ mit ~ bedeckt *fluffy* ‖ der erste ~ = ~bart

×**Flaum**[2] m *neutral lard;* → Flom

Fl·aum- ~bart m *fluff; first growth of beard* ‖ ⟨übtr⟩ (P) *stripling* **~feder** f *down* ‖ ~n [pl] *downs* [pl]; = Flaumbart ≗**haarig** a = flaumig

Fl·aumachen n ⟨pol⟩ *defeatism, pessimism*

Fl·aumacher m *defeatist, pessimist* ‖ (Nörgler) *cracker, grouser; wet blanket;* ⟨Am sl⟩ *knocker*

fl·aumig a *downy; fluey, fluffy, fuzzy;* ⟨bot & zoo⟩ *pubescent;* ~e Beschaffenheit *fluffiness*

Flaus m –es/–e; **Flausch** m ~es/~e *pilot-cloth; petersham* (⟨a. Ger univ⟩ –rock)

Fl·ausen f pl *fibs* [pl]; ⟨fam⟩ *tar(r)adiddles* [pl] ‖ ~ m *to tar(r)adiddle; to tell fibs; to spin a yarn;* mach mir k–e ~ vor *don't tell fibs* ‖ (Unsinn) *fudge, humbug, nonsense, trash* ~**macher** m *fibber;* ⟨fam⟩ *tar(r)adiddler* ‖ *humbug* ‖ *prevaricator, quibbler, shuffler*

Fl·aute f ~/~n *calm; lull in the wind;* ⟨mar⟩ *dead calm;* e–e ~ h *to be becalmed* ‖ ⟨com⟩ *slackness, stagnancy, stagnation*

Flav·in n ~s/~e (gelber Farbstoff) *flavine*

Fläz m ~es/~e (Flegel) *ill-bred boor; lout, lubber* °**fl·äzen** vrefl [h] sich ~ *to loll* (in *in*); *to lounge about* (in .. *in a chair*); *to sprawl;* → lümmeln °**fl·äzig 1.** a *boorish, loutish, lubberly* **2.** adv *boorishly, lubberly*

Fl·echse f ~/~n ⟨anat⟩ = Sehne, *tendon* ‖ Knie≗ *hamstring;* die Knie≗n e–s Pferdes zerschneiden *to hamstring a horse* ‖ ⟨bot, cul⟩ *string* **fl·echsig** a = sehnig

Fl·echt- ~arbeit f [konkr] *plaiting* ‖ ⟨arts⟩ *plait-work;* → –werk **~band** n *flat band of plaited straw* (etc) **~ware** f Korb≗n [pl] *wicker-goods* **~werk** n ⟨arts⟩ *plait-, mat-work; matting* ‖ ⟨arch⟩ *lattice(-work), trellis(-work)* ‖ Zierdraht≗ *filigree;* (in carving, etc.) *tracery* ‖ *wattle;* aus ~ herstellen *to wattle;* Korb≗ *wicker-work;* → Faschine **Fl·echte** f ~/~n **1.** (~ aus Haar) *braid, plait;* lange ~ *tress* (*of a girl*) **2.** ⟨path⟩ *herpetic skin-eruption; tetter;* nässende ~ *eczema* (L); fressende ~ *lupus* (L) **3.** ⟨bot⟩ *lichen;* Laub≗ *foliaceous l.* **fl·echten 1.** vt [flocht/geflochten] [h] **a.** (Binse, Stroh) *to plait;* → Hecke ‖ (Seil) *to twist;* (Kränze) *to weave, wreathe* ‖ (die Haare) *to braid, plait, tress* ‖ (Stühle) *to cane* **b.** sich ~ l *to plait* **2.** ≗ n *plaiting* ‖ Korb≗ *basket-making* **Fl·echter** m Korb≗ *basket-maker*

Fl·eck m ~(e)s/~e **A. 1.** (Stück zum Flicken) **a.** (Leder) *patch; vamp* **b.** (Zeug) → flicken **2.** ⟨cul⟩ *boiled tripe* **3. a.** (~ auf Fell, Haut) ⟨zoo & med⟩ *patch, spot; fleck, speck, speckle; blotch* ‖ ein häßlicher ~ *a nasty patch* ‖ → blau I. A. 2. ‖ ein weißer ~ *a patch of white, a white spot; a void* (*in the history of art*) → Kunstlandkarte; weißer Stirn≗ → Blesse; mit ~en versehen *to patch* **b.** dunkler ~ ⟨astr⟩ *macula* (L), *spot* ‖ Licht≗ *patch* (od *fleck*) *of light* **4.** (Schmutz≗) *stain* (*of soup*); *blot, blur; fleck, spot* ‖ voller ~e *covered with stains; stained;* Kaffee≗ *smudge of coffee* **5.** (of a target) schwarzer ~ → Schwarze [n] **6.** ⟨fig⟩ (Schand-≗) *blemish, blot, stain* (auf jds Ehre *on a p's reputation*) **B. 1.** (Stück Land etc) *patch;* ein ~ Land *a p. of land* **2.** (Ortschaft) → Flecken **3.** (Stelle) ein ~ *a spot; a* (*particular*) *place;* es gab einen ~ *there was one spot* (*which* ..); ein schöner ~ Erde *a lovely spot, a beauty-spot* **C.** Wendungen **1.** Wasser macht k–e ~e *water will not stain* ‖ ⟨fig⟩ mach dir nur k–n ~ (ins Hemd) *don't be too finical about it!, go it!* **2.** ⟨fig⟩ **am** falschen ~e *in the wrong place* | (ich stehe schon 1 Stunde) **auf** demselben ~ (..) *on this precise spot* ‖ wir sind noch immer auf dem alten ~e *we are still where we were* ‖ den Nagel auf den rechten ~ treffen *to hit the* (*right*) *nail on the head* ‖ ⟨fig⟩ er hat das Herz auf dem r. ~ *his heart is in the right place* | geh nicht **vom** ~e *don't budge* (od *stir*); das Rad will nicht v ~e gehen *the wheel won't budge* ‖ vom ~e k *to get on* (od *along*) (mit *with*) ‖ nicht v ~e k *to lag, linger* (mit .. *over one's work*); *to stagnate; to mark time;* (of action) *to drag* ‖ vom ~e weg (*to arrest a p*) *on the spot* ‖ (Stoff) v ~en reinigen *to scour* **~entferner** m *spot remover; solvent* **~fieber** n ⟨med⟩ *spotted* od *typhus fever* **~hering** m = Flückhering **~mittel** n = –entferner **~typhus** m *typhus* (*fever*) → Typhus **~wasser** n *scouring-drops* [pl]

Fl·eckchen n **1.** *fleck, speck, speckle; particle;* Staub≗ *fleck* (od *smudge, speck*) *of dust* **2.** ein schönes ~ Erde *a lovely spot of ground; a beauty-spot;* ein schattiges ~ *a shady spot* **fl·ecken** vt/i [h] **I.** vt **1.** (Schuhe) *to patch* **2.** ⟨poet⟩ (Blätter) *to spot;* → gefleckt **3.** → beflecken **II.** vi **1.** (Flecke m) *to make stains; to stain,* → Fleck C. 1.; (of colour) *to come off* **2.** (fleckig w) *to spot* (*easily*); *to stain* **3.** = vom Flecke k → Fleck C. 2. ‖ die Arbeit will heute nicht ~ *today I cannot get on with my work* **Fl·ecken** m ~s/~ **1.** = Fleck A. 1. 2., B. 1. 3. **2.** (→ Fleck B. 2.) *hamlet; village* ‖ Markt≗ *small market-town* **~entfernung** f *removing of stains* **~klee** m ⟨bot⟩ → Geißraute ≗**los** a *unspotted* (*leaves*) ‖ ⟨fig⟩ *speckless, spotless, stainless, unstained* (*reputation*) *without spot* **~mittel** n *spot remover* **~teppich** m *rag rug*

Fl·ecker m ⟨mar⟩ *spotter*

Fl·eckerlsuppe f [österr] *noodle soup*

fl·eckig a *specky, spotted, spotty, stained;* ⟨path⟩ *macular* ‖ ~ m *to spot, stain;* → beflecken ‖ ~ w *to spot, stain;* → flecken II. 2. | ≗**keit** f *patchiness*

fl·eddern vt [h] (Leichen) *to plunder, rob*

Fl·edermaus f ~/–mäuse ⟨zoo⟩ → *bat;* ⟨poet⟩ *flitter-mouse* ‖ gr braune, frühfliegende ~ *noctule* ‖ Zwerg≗ *pipistrel(le)* ‖ Ordnung der –mäuse *Chiroptera* pl; → Bd. I. *bat, serotine* | ~ärmel [m] ⟨tail⟩ *batwing sleeve*

Fl·ederwisch m **1.** *feather-duster*; *Turk's head*; *goose-feather* **2.** ⟨übtr⟩ (P) ein rechter ~ ⟨fam⟩ *a flighty* (od *skittish*) *thing*, *a harum-scarum*

Fleet n ~(e)s/~e [niedd] *ditch*; *channel*, *canal*; *streamlet*

Fl·egel m **1.** (Dresch≃) *flail* **2.** ⟨fig⟩ (P) *ill-bred boor*; *churl*, *clown* ‖ wie ein ~ = ≃haft [adv] **Flegel·ei** f ~/~en *boorishness*, *churlishness*, *rudeness*; *ill-bred* (od *unmannerly*) *conduct* ‖ *act* (od *piece*) *of rudeness*; *rude act*; *impudence*; es war e–e ~ v ihm *it was rude of him* **fl·egelhaft** **1.** a *ill-bred*, *unmannerly*, *unpolished*; *churlish*, *clownish*, *rude*; *impertinent* **2.** adv *boorishly*; *rudely*; sich ~ benehmen *to make a nuisance of o.s.* | **≃igkeit** f *boorishness*, *churlishness*, *rudeness*; → Flegelei **fl·egelig** a & adv = flegelhaft

Fl·egeljahre n [pl] *years of indiscretion*; *hobbledehoy period*; *cubhood*; er ist noch in den ~n *he is still* (*in his teens* od) *an unlicked cub*, *..still without manners* **fl·egeln** vrefl [h] sich ~ = sich fläzen, sich lümmeln

fl·ehen **1.** vi [h] **a.** *to beg*, *implore* ('*let me go*!' *she implored*) **b.** **~ um etw** *to beg* (od *implore*, *plead*, *supplicate*) *for a th*; *to beg* (od *crave*, *implore*, *supplicate*) *a th*; um Frieden ~ *to sue for peace*; um Gnade ~ *to plead for mercy*; um Verzeihung ~ *to crave* (od *supplicate*) *pardon* **c. zu jdm** ~ *to beseech* (od *entreat*, *implore*) *a p* (*to do*; *that*); *to plead with a p* (um *for*); z jdm um Hilfe, Schutz ~ *to implore a p's help*, *protection* **2.** ≃ n *beseeching*, *imploring*, *supplication* (um *for*); *entreaty* **fl·ehend** **1.** a *beseeching*, *imploring* (*look*); *suppliant*, *supplicating* **2.** adv *beseechingly*, *imploringly* **fl·ehentlich** **1.** a; ~e Bitte *entreaty*; *earnest prayer*; (*fervent*) *supplication*; ~er Ton *imploringness* **2.** adv; jdn ~ bitten *to beseech a p* (um *for*; daß .. *that* .. *may* ..; z tun *to do*); *to entreat a p* (*that*; *to do*); *to implore a p* (*to do*); nimm es! bat sie ~ *take it*! *she implored*

Fl·eiperverkehr m = Fleiverkehr

Fl·eisch n ~es/ **A.** (lebendes ~) **1.** ⟨anat, zoo, arts⟩ *flesh* ‖ das lebende ~ *the quick* ‖ steifes ~ ⟨sex⟩ *meat* ‖ bis ins ~ (*to cut*) *to the quick* ‖ ⟨med⟩ wildes ~ *granulations* pl, *proud flesh* ‖ ⟨hunt⟩ e–n Hund ~ kosten l *to flesh a hound* **2.** ⟨bot⟩ *flesh*; (Frucht≃) *pulp*; ⟨Am⟩ *meat* **3.** ⟨bib & fig⟩ **a.** (menschl Körper, Leib) *the flesh* **b.** (sündiger Mensch) *the flesh*; (*the sins' of the f.*) ‖ ⟨bib⟩ *the f. is weak* ‖ ein Pfahl im ~e *a thorn in the f.* **B.** ⟨cul⟩ (*butcher's*) *meat*; ein Pfd ~ *a pound of m.* ‖ Fisch≃ *fish*; Hühner≃ *poultry*, *fowl*; ~ v Hähnchen *chicken* ‖ Pferde≃ *horse-f.* (od *meat*) **C. Wendungen 1.** ~ in Büchsen *canned* (od *tinned*, *potted*) *meat* ‖ Streifen v getrocknetem ~ ⟨SAfr⟩ *biltong* **2.** sein (eigen) ~ **u Blut** *one's own f. and blood* ‖ ⟨fig⟩ v ~ u Blut *racy*; *full of go*; sie sind Menschen v ~ u Blut *they are living f. and blood*; es ist ihm in ~ u Blut übergegangen *it has become nature with him*; sich [dat] in ~ u Blut übergehen l *to engrain into o.s.* | ⟨fig⟩ → Fisch; den Weg alles ~es gehen *to go the way of all f.* **3. ~ ansetzen** *to put on flesh*, *to run to flesh* | ⟨fig⟩ sich ins eigene ~ schneiden *to quarrel with one's bread and butter*; *to cut off one's nose to spite one's face*; *to cook one's own goose* ‖ (Knochen) mit ~ bedecken *to flesh* ‖ (Tierhaut) v ~ befreien *to flesh* **~abfälle** m [pl] *blockers* pl *of meat* **~art** f: ~en [pl] *meats* pl **~auswuchs** m *excrescence* **~bank** f *butcher's stall*; = Schlachtbank **~beschau** f *meat-inspection*; ⟨sex⟩ *skin-show* **~beschauer** m *m.-inspector* **≃bildend** a *f.-forming* **~bilder** m *f.-former* **~bildung** *f.-formation* **~block** m *m.-block* **~blume** f ⟨bot⟩ *ragged robin*; → Lichtnelke **~brühe** f *m.-broth*; *beef-tea*; ⟨cul⟩ *bone stock*; *bouillon* [Fr] **~essen** n *m.-eating* **≃essend** a *m.-eating* **~esser** m *m.-eater* **~extrakt** m *m.-extract* **~farbe** f *f.-colour* (od *tint*); *carnation* **≃farben**, **≃farbig** a *f.-coloured* **~fliege** f ⟨ent⟩ *f.* (od *m.*) *fly*; Gattung der ~n *Sarcophagidae* [L pl] **≃fressend** a *carnivorous* **~fresser** m *carnivore* **~frucht** f *pulpy fruit* **~füllung** f ⟨cul⟩ *stuffing*; ⟨Am⟩ *filling* **~gallerte** f → Aspik **~gang** m ⟨cul⟩ *course* (od *dish*) *of m.*; *main dish* **~gericht** n *dish of m.* **~geschwulst** f ⟨path⟩ *sarcoma* **≃geworden** a ⟨bib⟩ *incarnate* **~hackmaschine** f = –wolf **~halle** f *m.-market* **~handel** m *m.-trade* **~hauer** m *butcher* **~kamm** m *comb* (*of a cock*) **~karte** f *m.-card* **~käse** m ⟨cul⟩ *m.-pie* **~klopfer** m *m.-beater* **~kloß** m *m.-ball*; –klöße [pl] ⟨Scot⟩ *minced collops* [pl] **~klößchen** n *m.-ball*; gebratenes ~ *rissole* **~klumpen** m *mass of flesh* **~konserven** [pl] *preserved* (od *canned*, *potted*, *tinned*) *m.* | ~fabrikation [f] (u –handel) *m. packing* **~konsum** m *m.-consumption* **~kost** f *m.-diet* **~kuchen** m = Fleischkäse **~laberl** n, **~laibchen** n [österr] *rissole*, ⟨Am⟩ *hamburger* **~lauch** m → Zwiebel **~marke** f *m.-coupon* **~markt** m *m.-market* ⟨a. vulg sex⟩ **~masse** f *mass of flesh* **~mehl** n *m.-meal*; (Viehfutter) *dehydrated m.* **~messer** n *carving-knife* **~mürber** m *tenderizer* (dazu: *to tenderize*) **~nahrung** f *m.-diet* **~nelke** f = Fleischblume **~opfer** n *m.-offering* **~pastete** f *m.-pie* **~saft** m *gravy* **~schnitte** f *slice of m.*; (gebratene Rind~) *steak*; *collop* **~speise** f = Fleischgericht **~steuer** f *tax on meat* **~tag** m *m.-day* **~teile** m pl ⟨arts⟩ *flesh* **~ton** m ⟨paint⟩ *flesh-tint*; *flesh* **~topf** m *fleshpot*; ⟨fig⟩ *the fleshpots of* (od *corn in*) *Egypt*; **~verbrauch** m *meat-consumption* **~vergiftung** f *m.* (od *ptomaïne*)-*poisoning* **~versorgung** f *m.-supply* **~vorräte** m [pl] *m.-stock* **~waren** f [pl] *meats* [pl] **~wärzchen** n [pl] ⟨med⟩ *granulations* [pl] **~werdung** f *incarnation* **~wolf** m (*m.-*)*mincer*, *grinder* od *chopper*; *mincing-machine*; ⟨fig⟩ ~! *don't rub it in*! **~wunde** f *soft tissue wound*, *f.-wound*; ~n [pl] *laceration*

fl·eischen vt [h] (Felle) *to flesh*; → Fleisch

Fl·eischer m ~s/~ *butcher*; beim ~ *at the b.'s* **~blume** f ⟨bot⟩ *aspidistra* **~bursche** m *butcher's boy* **~handwerk** n *butcher's trade*; *butchery business* **~hund** m *butcher's dog*; *mastiff* **~laden** m *butcher's shop* **~messer** n *butcher*('*s*)-*knife*

Fleischer·ei f *butchery business*; *butcher's shop*, ⟨Am⟩ *butcher shop*, *meat-market* **fl·eischern** a *fleshy*; (*consisting*) *of flesh* **Fl·eischeslust** f *carnal* (od *fleshly*) *lust* (od *appetite*, *desire*) **fl·eischig** a *fleshy*; *meaty* ‖ ⟨bot⟩ (etc) *pulpous*, *pulpy*; ~er Teil *pulp* ‖ (beleibt) *beefy* (*fellow*), *corpulent*, *fat*, *plump* | **≃keit** f ~/ *fleshiness* ‖ (Beleibtheit) *corpulence* **fl·eischlich** a ⟨fig⟩ *animal*, *carnal*, *fleshly*, *sensual* (*desires*, *lusts*) | **≃keit** f ⟨fig⟩ *fleshliness*, *sensuality*; *carnality* **fl·eischlos** a *fleshless* ‖ *meatless* (*day*, *diet*)

Fleiß m ~es/ *assiduity*, *assiduousness*, *diligence*, *industry*, *sedulity*; eiserner ~ *unflinching* (od *unremitting*, *untiring*) *industry*; → Eifer ‖ s–n ganzen ~ aufbieten *to do one's best endeavours* (od *one's utmost*); *to try one's hardest* ‖ viel ~ verwenden auf etw *to take* (*every*) *pains with a th* | **mit ~** *with diligence*; *assiduously*, *diligently* ‖ (mit Absicht) *on purpose*; *designedly*, *intentionally*, *purposely* ‖ ohne Fleiß k–n Preis *no pains*, *no gains*; *no cross*, *no crown*

fl·eißig **1.** a **a.** *assiduous*, *diligent*, *industrious* (*man*); *hard-working*, *laborious*, *sedulous*, *studious* ‖ *active*, *busy*; *eager*, *keen* ‖ [nur attr] ein ~er Arbeiter *a hard worker*; ein überaus ~er A. *a demon for work*; ~er Mensch *busy bee* ‖ ⟨bot⟩ ≃es Lieschen n ⟨bot⟩ *false mallow* ‖ → arbeit-, betriebsam **b.** *careful* (*investigation*), *painstaking* (*study*) **c.** ein ~er Besucher *a frequent visitor*; → eifrig, emsig **2.** adv **a.** *assiduously*, *diligently*, *sedulously*; überaus ~ *with great assiduity* ‖ ~ arbeiten (etc) *to work hard* **b.** e–e Bibliothek (etc) ~ besuchen *to frequent a library* | ~ spazieren gehen *to take plenty of exercise*

Fl·eiverkehr [= Flugeisenbahn(personen)verkehr] m *combined railway and air service*

flekt·ierbar a ⟨gram⟩ *(in)flexional*; nicht ~ *non-inflexional* **flekt·ieren** vt [h] ⟨gram⟩ (Wort) *to inflect*; flektiert *inflected (word)* ‖ → deklinieren, konjugieren **flekt·ierend** a *flexional, inflexional (language)*; *inflective* **Flekt·ierung** f ~/~en ⟨gram⟩ *(in)flexion* → Deklination, Konjugation

°**fl·ennen** vi [h] *to blubber, whine*; *whimper*; ⟨sl⟩ *to blub*; ⟨fam⟩ *to pipe one's eyes*

Fl·ensburg n (Stadt in Schleswig) *Flensburg, Flensborg* **~er F·örde** f *Flensburg Fjord*

fl·ensen vt [h] (Wal) *to flench, -i-, -nse*

Fl·esche f [Fr] ⟨fort⟩ *fleche* [Fr], *arrow*

Fl·eten m ⟨ich⟩ = Rochen

fl·etschen 1. vt [h] die Zähne ~ *to show one's teeth*; ⟨bib⟩ *to grin* ‖ ⟨vulg fig⟩ *to flash one's ivories* **2.** ≗ n *the show (of one's teeth)*

fl·etschern (nach H. Fletcher, † 1919) ⟨Am⟩ **1.** *to fletcherize* **2.** ≗ n *Fletcherism*

Fl·ettnerruder n ⟨aero⟩ *servo-tab*; *Flettner balance*

†**fleucht** [3. sg prs] (f flieht) v fliehen

†**fleugt** [3. sg prs] (f fliegt) v fliegen

†**fleußt** [3. sg prs] (f fließt) v fließen

flex·ibel a ⟨bookb⟩ *flexible (cover)* **Flexibilit·ät** f *flexibility*; (e–r Einrichtung) ⟨tech⟩ *versatility* ‖ ⟨übtr⟩ (of politics) *mobility, compliance*

Fleur·on [flœ'rõ] n Fr ~s/~s ⟨arch, cul⟩ *fleuron*

Flexi·on f ~/~en ⟨gram⟩ *inflexion, flexion* ‖ [konkr] *inflexion*; *inflexional ending* (od *element*) ~s-Endung [f] *inflexional ending* ~s-lehre [f] *accidence* ≗los [a] *inflexionless* **flex·ivisch** a *inflexional* **Fl·exor** m ~s/–x·oren ⟨anat⟩ *flexor* **Flex·ur** f ~/~en ⟨geol⟩ *flexure*

Flib·ustier m ~s/~ *filibuster*; *buccaneer, freebooter, pirate* ‖ ⟨mod⟩ *exploiter*; *sharper*

Fl·ick- ~gedicht n *cento* L **~kasten** m ⟨mot⟩ *repair outfit* **~lappen** m *patching-cloth*; *patch* **~oper** f ⟨mus⟩ *pastiche* [Fr], *pasticcio* [It] **~schneider** m *jobbing-tailor* **~schuster** m *botcher, cobbler* **~schusterei** f *shoe-repair shop* **~ u Putzzeug** n ⟨mil⟩ *fieldkit* **~werk** n ⟨fig⟩ *patchwork, patchery, patch-up, vamp*; *botching, botchery*; *hodgepodge*; *bungling* **~wort** n *botch, expletive*; *makeshift*; *patch* **~zeug** n ⟨mot⟩ *tyre* ⟨Am⟩ *tire* od *puncture repair outfit*

fl·icken I. vt/i [h] **1.** vt **a.** ⟨allg⟩ *to patch* ‖ (Kleider) *to patch*; *to mend*; *to stitch*; geflickte Stelle *mend* (in *in*) ‖ (Schuhe) *to cobble*; *vamp* ‖ ⟨übtr⟩ (Korb, Hecke) *to patch*; *mend, repair* ‖ ⟨mot, cycl⟩ (Reifen) *to repair* → stopfen ‖ ⟨dero⟩ schlecht *or* stümperhaft ~ *to botch*; *to patch up*, → zus–flicken, Zeug **b.** °⟨übtr⟩ (Wunden) *to sew up, to stitch* **2.** vi *to patch* **II.** ≗ n *patching* ‖ *mending*; *repair* **Fl·icken** m ~s/~ ⟨allg⟩ (auf Tuch, Leder) *patch*; (auf Schuhe) *vamp*; → Fleck(en) ‖ voller ~ *patchy*; e–n ~ aufsetzen *to put a patch on* **~arbeit** f (e–e Näharbeit) *patchwork* **~artig** a *patchwork*; *patchy* **~decke** f *crazy quilt* **~kissen** n *patchwork-cushion* **~teppich** m *rag rug*

Fl·icker m ~s/~ *patcher, patcher up*; *mender*; → Flickschneider, –schuster **Flicker·ei** f ~/~en *patching*; *mending*; → Flickwerk

Fl·ieder m ~s/~ ⟨bot⟩ **1.** (Syringe) *lilac*; **2.** (Schwarzer Holunder) *elder* **~beere** f *elder-berry* **~busch** m *lilac tree* **~tee** m *elder-tea*

Fl·iege f ~/~n **A.** ⟨ent⟩ → Bd. I. *fly* **1.** *fly*; Unterordnung der ~n *Diptera* L pl ‖ v ~n beschmutzt *fly-blown*; v ~n ge-, zerstochen *fly-bitten* **2.** Spanische ~ *Spanish fly*; Gattung der Sp. ~n *cantharides* ⟨a. med⟩ L pl ‖ Stech≗ *stable-fly*; Stuben≗ *house-fly* **3.** Schwarze ~ → Blasenfuß **4.** ⟨angling⟩ ~ als Köder *drake*; künstliche ~ *fly*; mit K.≗n angeln *to fly-fish* **5. Wendungen**: ⟨fig⟩ wie die ~n *(they fell) like flies* ‖ zwei ~n mit e–r Klappe schlagen *to kill two birds with one stone* **B.** ⟨übtr⟩ **1.** (of a sporting gun) *foresight* **2.** (Bärtchen) *imperial* **3.** (kl Schleife) *bow-tie* **4.** (of an apple) *core* **C.** ⟨fig⟩ (P) → Flittchen

fl·iegen vi/t [flog/geflogen] **I. vi [s] A.** (in der Luft ~) **1.** (of birds, etc.) *to fly*; *to take a* (od *one's*) *flight, to wing one's flight* ‖ gut (hoch) ~ *to be a good (high) flyer*; flatternd entlang der Wasseroberfläche ~ (of ducks) *to skitter*; im Schwarm ~ *to flight* ‖ geräuschvoll ~ *to drum* ‖ ~ (bis) nach Berlin (of pigeons) *to fly Berlin*; die Distanz, die ein Vogel fliegt *flight* ‖ Tauben ~ l *to fly pigeons* | (of angels, etc.) *to fly* **2.** ⟨**aero**⟩ (im Flugzeug ~) *to fly* od *voygage* (durch *through*; nach *to*); *to go by air* (nach *to*); *to have a fly*; *to take a* (od *one's*) *flight*; *to travel by air*; ⟨fam⟩ *to take the air* ‖ allein ~ *to solo* ‖ im Verband ~ *to fly in a formation* ‖ mit (*or* in) e–m Flugzeug ~ *to fly an aeroplane* ‖ über das Meer ~ *to fly (over) the ocean, .. the Alps* **B.** ⟨**übtr**⟩ **1. (S) a.** *(of an arrow) to fly* ‖ *flap, skim* (über *over*); *the sparks flew in all directions* ‖ (of dust) *to blow* (um .. *about the car*) **b.** (of flags, clothes, etc.) *to fly*; *flutter*; *stream*; → wehen **c.** (of a ball) zur Seite ~ *to turn aside*; *to twist* **d.** in die Luft ~ (of a building) *to blow up*; *to explode*; in die L. ~ l → sprengen ‖ in kl Stücken ~ *to spray* (über *over*) **2. (P) a.** *to fly, rush*; er flog in s–m Wagen durch .. *he rushed his car through* .. ‖ er fl. mit den Fingern über .. *he flicked with his fingers over* .. ‖ durch ein Buch ~ *to tear through a book*; über die Zeilen ~ *to skim (over) the lines*; er flog im Geiste über .. *his mind rushed over* .. ‖ in die Höhe ~ *to start* **b.** *to be turned out*; *to be sacked*; → hinaus~ **3.** (of time) *to fly* **II. vt [h]** ⟨aero⟩ **1.** (e–e Entfernung, Strecke) *to fly*; *cover*; eine Kurve ~ *to describe a curve* **2.** Aufklärung ~ *to make a reconnaissance flight* ‖ hohe Schule ~ ⟨Am sl⟩ *to stunt* **3.** e–e Maschine ~ *to fly a machine* **III.** ≗ n ⟨aero⟩ *flying (the art of f.)*; *aviation*; Tief≗ *low flying*; Kunst≗ *aerobatics* [pl], ⟨Am sl⟩ *stunt flying* **Fl·iegen-** (→ Fliege) [in comp] **~blume** f ⟨bot⟩ *fly-orchis* (od *orchid*) °**~dreck** m *fly-blow, fly-dung*; *fly-speck*; v ~ beschmutzt *fly-blown* **~fangen** n *fly-catching* **~fänger** m *fly-catcher*; *fly-trap* ‖ ⟨orn⟩ *fly-catcher* **~fenster** n *fly-screen window* **~gewicht** n ⟨box⟩ *fly-weight* (nicht über 113 Pfd; ⟨engl⟩ *126 lbs*) **~gift** n *flybane* **~holz** n ⟨bot⟩ = Quassia **~gitter(fenster)** n *screen* **~klappe ~klatsche** f *fly-flap* (od *swat, whisk*); *flapper, swatter* **~kopf** m ⟨typ⟩ *turned letter* **~leim** m *fly-glue* **~netz** n (f Pferde) *fly-net* **~orche** f ⟨bot⟩ = Fliegenblume **~papier** n *fly-paper* (od *band*) **~pilz** m ⟨bot⟩ *fly-fungus*; *fly agaric* (od *amanita*) **~schimmelpilz** m ⟨bot⟩ *fly-mould* **~schmeiß** m = Fliegendreck **~schnäpper** m ⟨orn⟩ = Fliegenfänger ‖ ⟨Am⟩ *fly-snapper* **~schrank** m *meat-, food-safe* **~schwamm** m ⟨bot⟩ = Fliegenpilz **~stein** m ⟨chem⟩ *fly-stone* **~wedel** m = Fliegenklappe **~zeit** f *fly-time*

fl·iegend A. [prs p] *flying* ‖ ⟨tech⟩ (etw) ~ anordnen *to overhang*; ~ angeordnet *overhung (crank)* **B.** [a] **1.** ⟨eig⟩ *flying*; *volant (angel)*; ⟨her⟩ *volant* | ~er Drache [m] ⟨zoo⟩ *(flying) dragon*; *flying lizard* ‖ ~er Fisch [m] ⟨ich⟩ *flying-fish* ‖ ~er Frosch [m] ⟨zoo⟩ *flying-frog* ‖ ~er Fuchs [m] ⟨zoo⟩ *flying-fox* ‖ ~er Hund [m] ⟨zoo⟩ *flying-fox*; *kalong* **2.** ⟨übtr⟩ *flying*; *floating* ‖ ⟨mil⟩ *flying* | ~es Band *streamer*; ~es Blatt *fly-leaf*; *leaflet* ‖ ⟨Ger⟩ ≗e Blätter [pl] *(a comic paper) Fliegende Blätter*; ~e Brücke *flying-bridge*; ~er Buchhändler *itinerant book-seller*; ⟨mil⟩ *flying (division)* ‖ ~es Dreieck ⟨aero⟩ *flying wing*; ⟨aero⟩ *flying (fortress)*; ~es Geschwader ⟨nav⟩ *flying squadron*; ~e Gicht = Gelenkrheumatismus; *flying, dishevelled (hair)* ‖

~er Händler *kerbstone trader*; ~e Hitze *flush*; *hot fit of fever*; der ≈e Holländer ⟨myth, mus⟩ *the Flying Dutchman* ~e Kolonne ⟨mil⟩ *flying column*; ~es Korps ⟨mil⟩ *flying squad* (od *party*); ~es Lager *flying camp*; ~es Lazarett *flying hospital*; ⟨aero⟩ ~es Personal *flight-echelon*; ~e Polizeikolonne *flying squad*; ~es Rad ⟨tech⟩ *overhung wheel*; ~e Röte *flush*; ~er Start ⟨sport⟩ *flying start* **Fl·ieger** m **A. 1.** (Vogel) *flyer*, ein guter ~ *a good f.* **2.** ⟨**aero**⟩ *airman* ‖ Segel≈ *glider* ‖ ⟨mil⟩ *soldier* (od *member*) *of the air-force* ‖ ⟨Ger⟩ General der ~ *Air Force General* **3.** ⟨**sport**⟩ (Rennpferd) *flyer* ‖ = Kurzstreckenläufer **B. (S) 1.** ⟨**aero**⟩ *aeroplane*, ⟨bes Am⟩ *airplane*; → Aufklärungs≈ ‖ Kampf≈ *bomber, fighter*; Sturzkampf≈ *low dive bomber* **2.** ⟨mar⟩ *middle staysail* **Fl·ieger-** [in comp] ⟨aero⟩ **~abteilung** f *air force section* **~abwehr** f → Flugabwehr **~abzeichen** n *air force badge* (od *decoration*); *airman's* (⟨Am⟩ *aviation*) *badge* [pl *insignia*], ⟨fam⟩ *wings* pl **~alarm** m *air-raid warning*; *alert* ‖ (an Luftschutz) *action warning* ‖ das Zeichen zum ~ geben *to sound an air-raid warning*; → entwarnen **~angriff** m *air-, bombing-raid*; *air-attack* **~aufklärung** f *airplane reconnaissance* **~aufnahme** f, **~bild** n *aerial view*; *air-photo(graph)* °**~benzin** n *aviation petrol* (od ⟨Am⟩ *gasoline* N, *fuel*); ⟨übtr⟩ *aviationspirit* **~beobachtung** f *aircraft spotting* **~beschuß** m *strafing*; unter ~ liegend *strafed* | *anti-aircraft fire* **~bombe** f *air-bomb* **~brille** f *flying goggles* pl **~deckung** f *cover from air-attack* od *-observation* **~einsatz** m *sortie*; erfolgloser ~ *abort* **~erkundung** f = Fliegeraufklärung **~film** m ⟨phot⟩ *aerofilm* **~führer** m *air-force commander* **~geschädigte(r** m) f *bomb damage victim* **~geschwader** n *group* **~handkamera** f *aerial portable c.* **~haube** f *flying-helmet* **~hauptmann** m *flight-captain* **~horst** m *air-port* (od *base* N, *station*) **~jacke** f *flying jacket* **~karte** f *air* od *flight map*; *aeronautical chart* **~kombination** f *flying-suit* **~korps** n *flying corps*; *air force* **~kraftstoff** m *aviation fuel* **~krankheit** f *air-sickness* **~leit- u Flugmelde-** ~dienst [m] *control and reporting*; ~stelle [f] *c.l and r.g post*; ~zentrale [f] *c.l and r.g center* (*SHAPE*) **~leutnant** m *pilot-officer* **~marschbreite** f *dispersed formation in width*; –tiefe [f] .. *in depth* **~notsignal** n *airplane distress signal* **~offizier** m (⟨engl⟩ unter dem *flight-lieutenant*) *flying-officer* **~personal** n *flying personnel* **~schaden** m *air-raid damages* pl | ~anspruch [m] *indemnification for a.-r. d.* **~schule** f *flying-school*; *service flying training school* **~schutz** m *air-raid protection* ⟨fam⟩ *umbrella* ‖ (Jagdschutz) *fighter protection, cover, escort* | ~anzug [m] *flying suit* od *kit* ‖ ~graben [m] *a.-a. trench* **~schütze** m *air-gunner*; *upper turret g.* **~sicht** f *overhead observation* | ~streifen [m] = –tuch **~station** f *air-station* (od *base*) ≈**tauglich** a *fit for flying* **~truppe** f *flying corps*; *pilots and men* [pl] *of the Air Force* **~tuch** n *ground panel* od *strip*; ⟨Am⟩ *marker panel* **~verband** m *air-formation* ‖ (Sonder–) *air task fore* **~visier** n *anti-aircraft sight* **~(vor)warnung** f *alert* **~warnung** f = ~alarm | ~sdienst [m] *air-warning service* **~wetter** n (⟨hum⟩ *un*)*flyable weather* **~zulage** f *flying allowance* od *pay*

Flieger·ei f ~/ *aviation, flying*; *aerial navigation*

Fl·iegerin f *flying woman*; *airwoman*; *aviatress, -trix* **fl·iegerisch** a *aeronautical*; *flying*; ~es Können *flying-efficiency* ‖ *aerodynamic*(*al*); in ~er Hinsicht *aerodynamically*

Fl·iehburg f ⟨hist⟩ *refuge-keep*; *refuge* → Flieh-

fl·iehen vi/t [floh/geflohen] **A.** vi [s] **1.** *to flee* [im prs & prs p ersetzt durch *fly* & *flying*]; *to run away*; *to take wing* ‖ *to seek* (od *take*) *refuge* (in .. *in* od *at a place*); sie floh hinauf in sein Zimmer *she fled up to his room* | aus dem Lande (etc) ~ *to flee from the country*; *to flee one's country*; → B. ‖ in die Wälder ~ *to take to the forests* | vor jdm ~ *to flee from* (od *before*) *a p*; vor dem Feinde ~ *to desert* ‖ vor e–r Gefahr ~ *to flee from a danger*; *to avoid a d.* | z jdm ~ *to seek* (od *take*) *refuge with a p* **2.** ⟨fig⟩ (of days, weeks, etc.) *to fleet*; *to flee* (od *pass*) *away*; *to vanish* ‖ → entfliehen **B.** vt [h] **1.** e–n Ort, jdn ~ *to avoid* (od *shun*) *a place, a p*; die (Gesellschaft der) Menschen ~ *to flee the haunts of men*; (e–e S, Verhältnisse) *to avoid, eschew, shun*; *to keep away from*; die Versuchung ~ *to flee from temptation* ‖ die Welt ~ *to renounce* (od *forsake*) *the world* **fl·iehend** a ⟨übtr⟩ *receding, retreating* (*chin, forehead*) ‖ ≈e [der ≈e, ein ≈er] m ~en/~en *the fugitive* **Fl·ieh-** **~gewicht** n *fly-weight* **~kraft** f **1.** ⟨phys⟩ *centrifugal force* **2.** [in comp] *centrifugal* (*brake* [~bremse]; *clutch* [~kupplung]; *governor* [~regler]; *moment* [~moment n]) | ~kuppelung [f] ⟨aero mot⟩ *centrifugal clutch* ‖ ~zerstäuber [m] ⟨tech⟩ *centrifugal* od *spinning disk atomizer*

Fl·iese f ~/~n *slab*; (Stein≈) *flag*(*stone*); (*floor-*)*tile*; (Wand≈) *wall-tile*; → Kachel ‖ Pflaster aus ~n *flags* [pl] ‖ mit ~n bedecken *to flag*; *to tile*; mit ~n belegt *flagged*; *tessellated* **~nboden** m *flagstone pavement* **~nleger** m *flag dresser* **~nmosaik**, **~npflaster** n *tessellated pavement*

Fl·ieß- (→ fließen) [in comp] **~arbeit** f ⟨tech⟩ *wholesale manufacture on the conveyor-system*; *progressive operations* pl **~band** n ⟨tech⟩ *travelling* od *moving belt*, ⟨Am⟩ (*band*)*conveyer, -or* ‖ vom ~ rollen *to come off the assembly line* | ~montage [f] *progressive assembly* ‖ ~produktion [f] *assembly-belt production* **~fett** n ⟨tech⟩ *semi-fluid grease* **~grenze** f ⟨tech⟩ *yield-point* **~papier** n *blotting-paper* **~pressen** n *extrusion* **~spannung** f *yield-stress*

fl·ießen I. vi [floß/geflossen] [s] **A. 1.** (of liquids) **a.** *to flow, pour, run* (aus *from*; in *into*; über *over*); in ein Zimmer ~ *to flood a room*; (Wasser) ~ l *to run* ‖ (of rivers) ~ in *to flow* (od *run*) *into*, → sich entladen, ergießen ‖ ~ über (of waves) *to wash over*; *to overrun*; Tränen flossen ihr über die Wangen *tears poured down her cheeks* ‖ *perspiration poured from his forehead* **b.** (of *blood*) in Strömen ~ *to run in torrents*; *to run freely*; es wird noch viel Blut ~, ehe .. *blood will flow before ..* ‖ *royal blood flows in his veins* **c.** der Wein floß in Strömen, es fl. viel Wein *there was a lot of wine flowing*; *wine flowed like water* **2.** (of the nose) *to run*; die Wunde floß *blood was running from the wound* **B.** ⟨übtr⟩ **1.** (of sand) *to flow*; *pass* (durch *through*) **2. a.** (of money) *to pour* (in .. *into the Exchequer*) ‖ (*profits*) *go* (*to the endowment fund*) ‖ Gaben flossen reichlich *gifts came in freely*; *it rained gifts* **b.** leicht dahin~ *to flow* (od *glide*) *easily* (od *smoothly*); die Unterhaltung floß nur so dahin *conversation flowed freely* (od *with ease*) ‖ (of time) *to pass away* **c.** die Quellen ~ spärlich *the sourcess are scarce* **d.** ~ **aus** (of actions, etc.) *to come* (od *emerge, flow, proceed, result*) *from* **II.** ≈ n *the flowing* (*of water*); *flow* (*of a brook*); *pour*(*ing*); *fluxion* ‖ ⟨phys⟩ plastisches ≈ *steady* od *viscous flow* **fl·ießend A.** [prs p & pred a] *flowing* ‖ ⟨übtr⟩ *fluid, fluent*; die Grenzen sind ~ *the boundaries are fluid* (od *not fixed*) **B.** [attr a] **1.** ~es Wasser, warm u kalt *running water, hot and cold*; langsam ~es W. *slow-moving w.* **2.** ⟨übtr⟩ *fluent* (*speech*; *English*); *glib*; die Gabe ~er Rede *the gift of the gab*; er besitzt die G. ~er R. *he is a fluent orator* ‖ *easy, smooth* (*style*) **C.** [adv] ~ Englisch sprechen *to speak English fluently*

Fl·iete f ~/~n ⟨vet⟩ *fleam*

Fl·immer m **1.** (flimmerndes Licht) *flicker; glimmer* || °~kiste [f] = Kino; ⟨sl⟩ *flickers* pl; ⟨telv⟩ *goggle-box* || *gleam; glitter* | ⟨übtr⟩ *flicker, gleam* (*of hope*) || → Glimmer, Schimmer **2.** ⟨übtr & fig⟩ = Flitter **3.** ⟨zoo⟩ *cilia* [L]

fl·immern 1. vi [h] (of light) *to flicker; glimmer,* (of stars) *to twinkle* || (of the sun) *to gleam; glitter* || (of the eye) *to waver* || es flimmert mir vor den Augen *I see stars; all swims before my eyes; my head swims* | ⟨film telv⟩ *to scintillate.* **2.** ~̈ n *flickering; glittering; twinkle, twinkling* (*of stars*) || ⟨übtr⟩ *flicker* (*of leaves*) **fl·immernd** a *flickering; twinkling;* ~es Licht *flicker* || *wavering* (*shadow*)

flink 1. a (P) *agile, bright, brisk; slippy; deft, nimble; quick* (*work*[*er*]); *brisk* (*lad*) || (P) *up and coming* || ~ wie ein Wiesel *quick as a flash* **2.** adv *briskly, nimbly* || ~ arbeiten *to be a quick worker* || immer ~ bei der Hand s *to be ready to work* (od *help*) || ~ gehorchen *to be prompt to obey* || ~ lernen *to be quick to learn* || sich ~ u leicht bewegen *to flip* | ~̈heit f *briskness, nimbleness, quickness*

Flint m ~s/~e ⟨minr⟩ *flint* | ~glas [n] *flint--glass* **Fl·inte** f ~/~n ⟨sport⟩ *gun, rifle;* ⟨hist⟩ *musket* || mit der ~ schießen *to gun* (nach *for*); → abfeuern, schultern || Jagd~̈ *sporting-gun;* Schrot~̈ *shot-gun;* Vogel~̈ *fowling-piece;* → Doppel~̈ || ⟨fig⟩ die ~ ins Korn werfen *to throw up the sponge; to give* (od *throw*) *up the game*

Fl·inten- ~kolben m *butt* od *butt-end of a gun* **~kugel** f *bullet* **~schuß** m *rifle-shot*

Flip m [engl] ~s/~s *flip* **fl·irren** vi = flimmern

Flirt [flə:t, flirt] m [engl] ~(e)s/~s *dalliance; flirtation, flirting;* sich in e–n ~ einlassen, e–n ~ anfangen mit *to flirt with* | (P) *flirt;* ⟨fam⟩ *spoon* **fl·irten 1.** vi [h] *to flirt, to gallivant* (mit *with*); ⟨fam⟩ *to fuss, spoon* **2.** ~̈n *flirtation, etc; carryings-on* pl

Fl·ittchen n ~s/~ (Mädchen) *floozie, judy; fly-away*

Fl·itter m ~s/ *spangle, tinsel;* mit ~ besetzen *to spangle, to tinsel;* mit ~ besetzt *spangly* | ⟨fig⟩ *frippery, tinsel; tawdry finery* **~glanz** m *showy* (od *tawdry*) *splendour; tinsel* **~gold** n *tinsel; tombac* **~gras** n ⟨bot⟩ = Zittergras **~kram** m *frippery, tinsel; trinkets* [pl]; *tawdry finery* **~staat** m *tawdry finery* **~werk** n *tinsel;* = Flitterkram || mit ~ schmücken *to tinsel* **~wochen** f [pl] *honeymoon*

***fl·itterhaft**, ***fl·itt(e)rig** a *tinsel; gaudy, showy, tawdry* || †**fl·ittern** vi [h] *to glitter; glisten*

Fl·itzbogen m *boy's bow* °**fl·itzen** vi [s] (P & S) *to flit* (durch *through*); *shoot, breeze, skid, whip, hare, tear, whisk* (aus *out of*; um *round*); ⟨sl⟩ *to nip* || in e–m Ruck ~ *to jerk* °**Fl·itzer** m ~s/~ ⟨mot⟩ = Sportwagen || ⟨sport⟩ (Ball) *fizzer,* (Bodenball) *grounder*

flocht [1. & 3. sg pret] v flechten

Fl·ocke ~/~n **a.** (Woll~̈ etc) *flock; lock* (od *tuft*) *of wool* (etc.) || bes ⟨scient⟩ *floccule, flocculus* [L], *floccus* [L] || Polster~̈n [pl] *flocks* pl **b.** Schnee~̈ *flake of snow* || Schaum~̈ *flake of foam* **c.** Korn~̈n [pl] *corn flakes* pl || Hafer~̈n [pl] *quaker oats* pl | mit Woll~̈n vollstopfen *to flock* || (Papier mit ~n bedecken *to flake* || z ~n w (of snow) *to flake* **d.** Metall~̈n [pl] *metal turnings* pl

fl·ocken vi [h] *to come off in flakes; to descend* (od *fall*) *in flakes*

Fl·ocken- [in comp] *flaky* ~̈**artig** a *flaky* **~bildung** f *flocculation* **~blume** f ⟨bot⟩ *star-thistle; knapweed; sultan; centaurea* [L]; Bisam-~̈ *sweet sultan;* Skabiosen~̈ *Great knapweed* **~muster** a *flock pattern;* mit ~n versehen *to flock* **~papier** n, **~tapete** *flock-paper*

fl·ockig a *flocky, floccose, flocculent, flocculous; fluffy;* → faserig **Fl·ockseide** *floss silk*

Fl·ockwolle f *woolen waste; flock-wool*

flog [1. & 3. sg pret] v fliegen

Fl·ödel m ~s/~ ⟨mus⟩ *purfling*

Floh m ~s/~̈e ⟨ent⟩ *flea* || v Flöhen gebissen *flea-bitten* || ⟨fig⟩ er hört die Flöhe husten *he can see through a millstone* || jdm e–n ~ ins Ohr setzen (scheltend, beunruhigend) ⟨m. m.⟩ *to send a p away with a f. in his ear,* ⟨Am⟩ *to put a bug in a p's ear* || setz ihm k–n ~ ins Ohr *don't put ideas into his head* || lieber e–n Sack ~̈e hüten! *anything rather than that!*

floh [1. & 3. sg pret] v fliehen

Fl·oh- [in comp] *flea-* || °angenehmes **~beißen**! ⟨hum⟩ *sleep tight, mind the fleas don't bite!* **~biß** m *flea-bite* **~braun** a *puce* **~gras** n ⟨bot⟩ *flea-grass* **~hupfspiel** n *tiddly-winks* [pl] **~käfer** m ⟨ent⟩ *flea-beetle* °**~kiste** f (Bett) ⟨fam bes mil⟩ *flea-bag* || (kl Kino, Mietwohnung) *f.-pit* **~kraut** n ⟨bot⟩ *flea-bane* **~krebs** m ⟨zoo⟩ *amphipod* °**~leiter** f (im Strumpf) *Jacob's ladder* °**~markt** m *flea market* od *fair* **~stich** m *flea-bite;* mit ~en bedeckt *flea-bitten*

flöhen vt [h] jdn ~ *to rid a p of fleas* || **sich ~** *to rid o.s. of fleas* **fl·ohig,** ~̈ a *full of fleas*

ˣ**Flom, Fl·omen** m [nordd] = Flaum²

Flor m ~s/~e **1.** (Blüte) **a.** *bloom, flush, heyday, prime;* im schönsten ~ stehen *to be in full bloom* (od *beauty*) **b.** Blumen~̈ *imposing bunch* (od *collection, display*) *of blooming flowers;* Rosen~̈ *bunch of blooming roses* | ⟨übtr⟩ (gew.) Damen~̈ *bevy of ladies; galaxy of beauty* **2.** (zartes Gewebe) **a.** *gauze;* Seiden~̈ *silk g.* || Trauer~̈ *crape;* (als Band) *crape-band* **b.** (haarige Oberfläche) *nap;* (of carpets) *pile* ~̈**artig** a *gauzy* **~band** n (Trauer~̈) *crape-band* **~fliege** f ⟨ent⟩ *lace-wing fly, neuropterous fly;* ⟨Am⟩ *lace-wing* **~schleier** m *veil of crape* **~tuch** n *crape--cloth*

Fl·ora f L ~/–ren ⟨bot⟩ *flora* **flor·al** a = Blumen– (z. B. Muster)

Flor·en m ~s/~e ⟨hist & engl⟩ *florin* (6/8)

Fl·oren- (→ Flora) [in comp] **~gebiet** n *floral zone* **~kunde** f *floristics* [pl]

Florent·iner 1. a *Florentine* || ~ Atlas [m] *Florentine* || ~ Lack [m] *Florentine lake;* ~ Wurzel [f] ⟨bot⟩ *Florentine iris* || das ~ Konzil (1439–1442) *the Council of Florence* **2.** m ~s/~ **a.** (Bew. v Florenz) *Florentine* **b.** (Hut) *flat straw hat with a broad brim* **florent·inisch** a *Florentine*

Flor·enz n It (Stadt) *Florence;* ⟨It⟩ *Firenze*

Floresz·enz f ~/~en *florescence;* = Blüte(zeit)

Flor·ett n ~s/~e *foil* **~fechten** n *foil-fencing*

Flor·ett- ~band n *ferret(-ribbon)* **~garn** n *floss--yarn* **~seide** f *floss-silk* ~̈**seiden** a *flossy*

Fl·orida (abbr. Fla) **1.** *Florida;* Bewohner v ~ *Floridian* **2.** [in comp] *Florida* (*water, wood*)

flor·ieren vi [h] (of artists, etc.) *to flourish; to be in one's heyday* od *prime* || (of trade, etc.) *to prosper, thrive; to be thriving, booming, humming* || die Zeit, in der ein Künstler florierte *the floruit* [L] *of an artist*

Florin m ~s/~s **1.** [Fr] [flɔ'rɛ̃] = Gulden **2.** ⟨engl⟩ ['flɔrin] (Silbermünze, = *2 sh*) *florin*

Flor·ist m ~en/~en *florist* **Flor·istik** f *floristics*

Fl·oskel f ~/~n ⟨rhet⟩ *flourish; florid* (od *flowery*) *expression; rhetorical embellishment;* ⟨fig⟩ ~n [pl] *bouquets* pl

floß [ɔ] [1. & 3. sg pret] v fließen

Fl·oß n [o:] ~es/~̈e **1.** *raft; float*(*ing structure*); → Boje || auf e–m ~ befördern *to raft;* auf e–m ~ fahren *to raft* **2.** ⟨met⟩ *pig* (*of iron*) **~band** n *raft-dog* **~beamte** [der ~, ein ~r] *raft--master* **~brücke** f *floating* (od *raft*)*-bridge* **~führer** m *rafter, raftsman* **~holz** n *raft* **~kragen** m ⟨a–n⟩ (bei der Wasserung der Raumkapsel) *flotation harness* **~sack** m ⟨mil⟩ *rubber boat; pneumatic float* N

fl·ößbar a *floatable;* → Floß

Fl·osse f ~/~n **1.** ⟨ich & zoo⟩ *fin* (*of a fish*); *flipper* (*of a whale*, etc.); *flapper* (*of a seal*) ‖ kl ~ *pinnule* **2.** ⟨übtr aero⟩ *fixed surface*; *fin*; ⟨Am⟩ *stabilizer* → Höhen⁓ **3.** °⟨fig⟩ (= Hand) ⟨sl⟩ *fin, flapper, flipper* ‖ (Fuß, Bein) *leg*

Fl·öße f ~/~n **1.** *the floating* od *rafting* (*of logs*) ‖ *the right of floating* (od *rafting*) **2.** (Schwimmkörper) *float*; *floating appliance* **fl·ö·ßen 1.** vt [h] *to float, raft* **2.** n *floating, rafting*

Fl·ossenfüßer m ⟨zoo⟩ **1.** (Robbe) *pinniped, pinnigrade* **2.** (Flügelschnecke) *pteropod*

Fl·ößer m ~s/~ *rafter, raftsman* **Flößer·ei** f *floating, rafting* (*of logs*)

Flotati·on [ts] f ~/~en ⟨min⟩ *flo(a)tation*; ~sverfahren [n] *flo(a)tation(-process)*

Fl·öte f ~/~n **1. a.** ⟨mus⟩ *flute*; kl ~, Pikkolo⁓ *piccolo* [It]; → Block⁓, Quer⁓, Schnabel⁓ | die ~ spielen, auf der ~ spielen *or* blasen *to flute, to play the flute*; (etw) auf der ~ spielen *to flute, to play on the flute* ‖ ⟨fig⟩ die erste ~ spielen *to play first fiddle* **b.** (Pfeife) *whistle*; Zinn⁓ *tin w.* **2.** ⟨cards⟩ *flush* (lang *straight*) **fl·öten I.** vi/t [h] **1.** vi **a.** (mit den Lippen pfeifen) *to whistle* **b.** (in weichem Ton sprechen) *to flute* ‖ (of birds) *to flute*; *whistle* **2.** [vt] (Melodie) *to whistle* | ⟨fig⟩ °ich werde dir was ~ *I'll see you further first* ‖ °~ gehen (S) (verloren gehen) *to go to the dogs*; *to go west* **II.** ⁓ n *whistling*; *whistle* ‖ *fluting* (*of a bird*) ‖ e–n Hund durch ~ zurückrufen *to whistle a dog back* **Fl·öten- ⁓ähnlich, ⁓artig** a *flutelike* **~bläser** m = Flötenspieler **~register** n *flute*; *flute-stop* (*of an organ*) **~solo** n *flute solo* **~spieler** m *flute-player*; → Flötist **~stimme** f (im Orchester) *flute-part* **~ton** m *flute-note* ‖ *whistle* ‖ ⟨fig⟩ °jdm die –töne beibringen *to put a p through his paces*; *to lecture a p*; *to take a p to task*

fl·öten|gehen vi [s] ⟨fam⟩ = verloren|gehen *to get lost*; *to go to the dogs*

°**fl·ötepiepen**! [intj] *fiddle-de-dee*!, *fiddlesticks*!

Flöt·ist m ~en/~en *flautist, flutist*

ˣ**Flott** n *cream* **flott I.** a **1.** ⟨mar⟩ [nur pred] **a.** *afloat* ‖ (Schiff) ~|machen *to float*; *to set afloat*; wieder ~ m *to refloat* ‖ ~ w (of a ship) *to get afloat*; wieder ~ w *to refloat* **b.** ⟨übtr⟩ *in full swing*; *in activity*; *in cash*; die Firma ist wieder ~ *the firm pays its way again* **2.** ⟨fig⟩ [mst attr] **a.** (lustig) *gay, jolly* (*student*), *merry*; → leichtlebig ‖ *brisk clever, dashing* (*rider*), *smart*; ein ~er Bursche, Spieler *a smart fellow, player*; → flink, schnell **b.** (S) *brisk* (*pace*); *gay* (*feast, life*); *lively* (*dance, tune*); *jaunty* (*manners*) ‖ *excellent*; *smart*; ⟨fam⟩ *jolly*; ⟨sl⟩ *saucy* (*hat, suit, tie*), *slick* (*play*) ‖ ein ~es Leben führen = ~ leben **II.** adv ⟨fig⟩ *gaily*; *briskly*; *nicely*; *smartly*; ⟨Am⟩ *slick*; → flink ‖ **~ gehen** *to go at a good pace*; (S) *to be in full swing*; *to prosper, to thrive*; ~gehend *prosperous* ‖ es ging bei ihm ~ her *he gave us a slick time* ‖ **~ leben** *to go the pace*; *to lead a gay* od *fast life*; *to live in clover* ‖ °~ m = sich beeilen ‖ ~ spielen ⟨Am⟩ *to play slick*; ein Platz, auf dem sich ~ Fußball spielen läßt *a fast football ground*

Fl·otte[1] f ⟨allg⟩ *fleet*; Handels⁓ *mercantile marine* ‖ (Kriegs⁓) ⟨engl⟩ *the Royal Navy*; *the fleet*; Schlacht⁓ *battle fleet*; → Kriegs⁓, Luft⁓ ‖ e–e ~, die durch ihr bloßes Dasein ihren Zweck erfüllt *a fleet in being*

Fl·otte[2] f ⟨spin⟩ (Färbe⁓) *dye-bath*; *wash-liquor*

Fl·otten- (→ Flotte[1]) [in comp] *naval* **~abkommen** n *n. agreement* (bes dtsch-englisches 1937/38) **~arzt** m ⟨nav⟩ *fleet-surgeon* **~bau** m *n. construction*; ~programm [n] *programme of new n. c.* **~begleiter** m (Schiff) *escort sloop* **~chef** m *Commander-in-Chief of the Fleet* **~demonstration** f *n. demonstration* **~einheit** f *n. unit* **~flaggschiff** n *the admiral's flagship* **~kommando** n *n. command* **~manöver** n pl *n. manœuvres* pl **~parade** f *n. review* **~stab** m *the staff of the fleet* **~station** f *n. station* **~stützpunkt** m *n. base* **~verband** m *formation of warships selected from different squadrons* **~verein** m *Navy League* **~vorlage** f *navy bill* **~wesen** n *marine*; das gesamte ~ *the collective shipping* (*of a country*)

flott·ierend a *floating*; ~e Schuld *f. debt*

Flott·ille f ~/~n ⟨nav⟩ *flotilla* [Span] **~nchef** m *leader of a fl.* **~nführer** m *fl. leader*

fl·ottweg adv *offhand, straight away*; *promptly, unhesitatingly*; ⟨Am⟩ *slick*

Fl·otzmaul n ⟨vet⟩ *the wet part of the nose*

Fl·öz n ~es/~e ⟨geol & min⟩ *layer, stratum* [L]; dünnes ~ *seam*, Kohlen⁓ *coal seam* ‖ in ~en auftreten *or* geschichtet s *to be stratified* (od *straticulate*) ⁓**artig** a *stratiform* **~gebirge** n *stratified rock* **~lage, ~schicht** f = Flöz **~schichtung** f *stratification* **~weise** adv *in strata*; ~ gelagert s *to be straticulated* (od *stratified*)

Fluch m ~es/⁓e **1.** *curse, imprecation, malediction*; *anathema* ‖ ⟨ec⟩ *anathema*, → Bann⁓ ‖ ~ dem Mammon! *curse the m.*! ‖ e–n ~ legen auf *to call down* (od *lay*) *a c. upon* (*a country*); ein ~ ruht auf dem Orte *the place is under a c.*; .. *is anathematized* | ⟨fig⟩ dem ~ e–r S ausgesetzt w *or* s *to be doomed to a th*; *to be cursed with a th*; dem ~ der Lächerlichkeit verfallen *to be held up to ridicule* **2.** (Fluchwort) *curse*; *profane oath*; *profanity* (verschleierter ~ *veiled p.*); ⟨fam⟩ *swear-word*; ein kräftiger ~ *a great* od *thumping oath*; e–n ~ tun *to* (*curse and*) *swear* **3.** ⟨übtr⟩ (P *or* S) ⟨poet⟩ *curse* (e–r Gesellschaft *to a society*); *bane* ‖ (Schädling) *pest, plague* (*he was the plague of her life*) ⁓**beladen** a *accursed, under a curse*; *ill-fated, doomed to perdition* **~würdig** a *accursed, execrable*; *abominable, detestable* **fl·uchen I.** vi [h] **1.** jdm ~, ~ auf (jdn, etw) *to curse* (*a p, a th*), *to call down a c. upon, to imprecate c.s* (od *evil*) *upon* (*a p, a th*); *to swear at* (*a th*) **2.** *to c. and sw.*; *to execrate*; ~d (*he went away*) *with an oath* ‖ tüchtig ~ *to sw. lustily*; ⟨fam⟩ *to blast*; wie ein Landsknecht ~ *to sw. like a bargee* (od *trooper, lord*) ~, daß sich die Balken biegen *to make the air blue* **II.** ⁓ n *swearing*; *profane* (od *strong, bad*) *language*; *profanity* ***Fl·ucher** m *curser, swearer*

Fl·ucht f ~/~en **A. 1.** ⟨eig⟩ **a.** ⟨mil⟩ *flight* (vor *from*); *hasty retreat*; *running away*; *run*; ⟨fam⟩ *bunk* ‖ wilde ~ *rout* **b.** *escape* (*of a prisoner*) **c.** (Massen⁓) *rush* (*of a crowd*); panikartige wilde ~ *panic stricken rush*; *stampede* **d.** ⟨hunt⟩ lange ~en *long and high jumps* [pl] (*of deer*) **2.** ⟨übtr⟩ die ~ aufs Land, in die Städte *the flight to the land, to the cities*; die ~ vom Lande *the flight from the land, the rural exodus* (L); ~ in die Sachwerte *the flight to real values* **3. auf** der ~ *flying*; *on the run*; auf der ~ s *to be running away*; *to retreat hastily* ‖ die ~ **ergreifen**, sein Heil in der ~ suchen *to take f.*; *to take to f.* (od *to one's heels*), *to betake o.s. to f.*; ⟨sl⟩ *to bolt, bunk* ‖ **(Feind) in die** ~ schlagen (*or* jagen, treiben) *to put .. to f.*; *to* (*put to*) *rout*; *to make .. run* ‖ sich e–r S **durch die** ~ entziehen *to flee from a th* ‖ in wilder ~ davonlaufen; (jdn) .. vertreiben *to stampede*; *to send* (*a p*) *running for his life* ‖ die ~ in die Öffentlichkeit antreten *to resort to publicity* ‖ ⟨arts⟩ ~ nach Ä. *F. into Egypt* **B.** (→ Flug) ⟨arch⟩ **1.** (zus–hängende Linie) *continuous set* od *series* (S); row; in e–r ~ *in a row*; → Bau⁓ ‖ Treppen⁓ *f. of stairs*; e–e ~ v Zimmern *a suite of apartments* **2.** (Spielraum) (S) *play*; *room for movement* ⁓**artig 1.** a *hurried, sudden* (*departure*); *panic* (*haste*) **2.** adv *with lightning speed*; (Raum) ~ verlassen *to rush out of* (*the room*) **~bau** m (of fox) *refuge-den*; *retreat* **~burg** f = Fliehburg **~gefahr** f *danger* od *risk of escape* **~gerade** f *vanishing line* **~ge-**

schwindigkeit f *escape velocity* | ~sgrenze [f] *escape speed* **~linie** f ⟨arch⟩ *alignment*; *building line* ‖ ⟨opt, arts⟩ *vanishing-line* **~punkt** m ⟨arts⟩ *vanishing-point* **~röhre** f = Fluchtbau **~stab** m, **~stange** f *ranging pole* **≗verdächtig** a: ~ s *to be suspected of escaping* **~versuch** m *attempt to escape*; bei(m) ~ *trying to escape*; e–n ~ m *to make* od *attempt a break*

fl·uchten vi [h] *to* (*be in*) *align*(*ment*); nicht ~d *misaligned* ‖ z ≗ bringen *to align*

fl·üchten vi/t **1.** vi [s] **a.** *to flee, to run away*; *to take* (*to*) *flight*; → fliehen A. 1. ‖ (of a prisoner) *to escape* ‖ ⟨jur⟩ (flüchtig w) *to abscond* **b.** ~ (*or* sich ~ [h]) *to take* (od *seek*) *refuge* (hinter *behind*; in *in*); *to shelter* (*in, under* ..) ‖ *she fled up to his room*; in den Wald ~ *to take to the woods*; .. auf (*the cat*) *took to the tree* od .. *took refuge in the tree*; .. in die Höhle (*the fox*) *took earth*; → sich ~ 2 b .. **c.** ~ mit → ausreißen 2; durchbrennen 2. ‖ ~ vor (etw) *to seek* (od *take*) *refuge from* (*the storm*) ‖ ~ z jdm *to take shelter with a p* **2.** vt [h] **a.** ⟨poet & †⟩ (jdn, etw) *to save*; *rescue*; → bergen **b. sich** ~ → ~ 1. b. ‖ sich in die Öffentlichkeit ~ *to resort to publicity*; sich in e–r S in die Ö. ~ *to give publicity to a th*

fl·üchtend a *fugitive*; *runaway* .. **fl·üchtig I.** [a] **A.** ⟨eig⟩ (P & T) *fugitive* (*prisoner, slave*) ‖ *runaway* (*couple, horse*) ‖ ⟨mot⟩ *hit-and-run* (*driver*) ‖ ~ w *to abscond*; *to run away* **B.** ⟨übtr⟩ **1.** ⟨chem⟩ (of liquids) *volatil*(*izabl*)*e* (*oil*); *non-persistent* (*gas*) ‖ ⟨geol⟩ (of stone) *brittle*; *fragile* **2. a.** *fugitive*; *fugacious* (*life*); *ephemeral, evanescent, fleeting, momentary, passing* (*joys, pleasures*), *transient* (*flush, smile*), *transitory*; *volatile* (*dream*) **b.** *cursory* (*glance, perusal*); *passing* (*remark*) ‖ *hasty*; *sketchy* (*draft*; *knowledge*) ‖ *slight* (*impression*) ‖ *casual* (*acquaintance*); *flying* (*visit*) ‖ *touch-and-go* [attr] ‖ ~er Blick ⟨sl⟩ *look-see*; e–n ~en B. werfen auf *to take a glance at* (*a th*); ~e Prüfung, ~er Überblick ⟨Am sl⟩ *once-over* ‖ jdm mit ~er Feder schreiben *to send a p a hasty line* **B.** ⟨fig⟩ (bes P) *careless* (*work, worker*), *casual*; *desultory*; *frivolous*; *superficial* ‖ *fickle*; *flighty, volatile* **II.** [adv] ⟨übtr⟩ **1.** *transiently* **2.** *cursorily, passingly* ‖ *slightly*; *sketchily* ‖ ~ betrachten *to take a glance at* (*a th*) ‖ (Frage) ~ behandeln, berühren *to skim* ‖ ein Buch ~ durchblättern *to skim* (*over*) *the pages of a book* ‖ ~ entwerfen *to block out* (*plan, work*), *to adumbrate, outline* ‖ ~ erwähnen *to mention passingly* od *in passing* ‖ ~ über e–e Oberfläche gleiten *to skim a surface* ‖ jdn (nur) ~ kennen *to have a bowing acquaintance with a p* ‖ jdn ~ sehen *to have a glimpse of a p*; jdn, etw nur ~ z sehen bek *to get* od *catch a glimpse of a p, a th* ‖ ~ überblicken, prüfen ⟨Am sl⟩ *to once-over* **3.** *carelessly, superficially* **Fl·üchtige** m [der ~, ein ~r] *the runaway*; → Flüchtling **Fl·üchtigkeit** f **1.** ⟨übtr⟩ *fleetingness*; *transience, -cy* (*of pleasures*); *evanescence, transitoriness* (*of life*) **2.** ⟨fig⟩ *carelessness, hastiness*; *superficiality* ‖ *flightiness, volatility* | ~sfehler [m] *oversight, slip* **Fl·üchtling** m ~s/~e *fugitive*; *runaway* ‖ ⟨rel⟩ *refugee*; ⟨pol⟩ *emigrant*; Kinder-~e [pl] *child-refugees* pl | ~spsychose [f] *evacuosis* **Fl·uchtung** f ~/ *co-axiality*; *alignment* | ~sfehler [m] ⟨arch⟩ *error of alignment*; *misalignment*

Fl·ückhering m *eviscerated smoked herring*

Fl·uder m (& n) ~s/~ *wooden channel*

Fl·ug m ~es/≗e **A.** **[abstr] 1.** (of birds) *flight* ‖ .. im ~ (*to shoot a b.*) *in fl., on the wing* **2.** **⟨übtr⟩** (of a ball, bullet, etc) *fl.*; ⟨astronaut⟩ ~ z Mond *ride to the moon* **3.** **⟨aero⟩ a.** *fl.* (v *from*; nach *to*) ‖ antriebsloser ~ *unpowered* od *gliding fl.* ‖ ~ nach oben *or* unten *dive*; überzogener ~ *stall* ‖ auf e–m ~ *on a fl.* ‖ Blind≗ *blind flying*; Gleit≗ *glide* ‖ Kunst≗ ⟨Am sl⟩ *stunt*; Kunstflüge [pl] *aerobatics* pl ‖ Segel≗ *soaring-fl.*; *gliding* ‖ Schwebe≗ *soaring* ‖ Sturz≗ (*nose-*)*dive*; *dive bombing* **b.** (~strecke) *flight* **4.** **⟨fig⟩** *fl.* (*of imagination*); die hohen ≗e der Dichtkunst *the high fl.s of poetry* ‖ der ~ der Zeit *the fl. of time* ‖ **im** ~e *in haste* od *passing*; (die Zeit) verging (wie) im ~e .. *flew* **5. schnellen ~es** *swift of fl.* | **im** ~e *in fl.*; *flying*; *on the wing* (*to shoot a bird on the w.*) ‖ ⟨fig⟩ *in haste*; *in a hurry*; → schnell ‖ im ~e berühren → flüchtig [adv] ‖ wie im ~e vergehen *to pass away quickly* | ⟨aero⟩ e–n ~ m *to have a fly* **B. [konkr] 1.** (zus–fliegende Schar) *flight* (*of starlings*); *flock* (*of gulls*); *swarm*, → Schwarm; Volk ‖ e–n Vogel in e–m ~ schießen *to flight a bird* **2.** ⟨her⟩ *spread* (*eagle*) **C.** [in comp] **~abwehr** f ⟨aero⟩ **1.** *anti-aircraft defence* **2.** [in comp] *anti-aircraft* ‖ ~-artillerie [f] *a.-a. artillery* (abbr *A. A. A.*) ‖ ~-kanone [f] → Flak ‖ ~kreuzer [m] *a.-a. cruiser* ‖ ~maschinengewehr [n] (automatisches) *pom-pom* ‖ ~maschinenwaffe [f] *automatic a.-a. gun* ‖ ~meldeapparat [m] *a.-a. predictor* ‖ ~-rakete [f] *a.-a. missile* od *rocket* ‖ ~waffe [f] *a.-a. force* **~anweisungen** f pl *briefing* **~asche** f *flyash* **~(auf)tanken** n *refuelling in flight* **~bahn** f ⟨phys, ball, astronaut⟩ *trajectory*; ⟨astronaut⟩ *flight* od *orbit path* ‖ ⟨aero⟩ *flight path*; ⟨eig⟩ *track* | ~befeuerung [f] ⟨aero⟩ *navigation light* ‖ ~höhe [f] *ordinate of trajectory* **~ball** m ⟨ten⟩ *volley*; Halb≗ *half volley*; kz ~ *drop-shot* ‖ als ~ spielen *to volley* ‖ ~spieler [m] *volleyer* **~-bedingungen** f pl *flying conditions* **~begeisterung** f *air-mindedness* **~benzin** n *aviation petrol*, ⟨Am⟩ *a. gasoline* **~beratung** *briefing*; ⟨meteor⟩ *information for aviators* **~bereich** m *flying-range*; *r. of flight* **≗bereit** a *ready to fly*; *in flying condition* **~besprechung** f *briefing, dispatch* ‖ ~ nach Landung *debriefing* **~beuteleichhörnchen** n ⟨zoo⟩ *Australian flying squirrel* **~beutler** m ⟨zoo⟩ *petaurist*; *flying phalanger* **~blatt** n *leaflet*; *broadsheet*; *handbill*; zus–faltbares ~ ⟨Am⟩ *folder* ‖ –blätter verteilen, abwerfen *to scatter leaflets* ‖ ⟨Lit hist⟩ *broadsheet, broadside* | ~bombe [f] *leaflet bomb* **~boot** n *flying boat*; (Tragflügelb.) *naviplane* **~brand** m ⟨bot⟩ = Staubbrand **~datenschreiber** m *flight recorder* **~dauer** f *duration of flight* **~deck** n *flying* od *flight* (od *landing*)-*deck* (*on aircraft carrier*) **~dienst** m *air-service* **~-drache** m ⟨zoo⟩ *flying dragon* (od *lizard*) **~drehfeuer** n *revolving airway beacon* **~echse** f ⟨geol zoo⟩ *pterosaur*(*ian*), *pterodactyl*; *flying reptile* **~eichhörnchen** n ⟨zoo⟩ = Flugbeutel– **~eidechse** f ⟨zoo⟩ = Flugdrache **~eigenschaften** f pl *flying characteristics* **~-Eisenbahn-Personenverkehr** m *passenger traffic by rail and air* **~entfernung** f *distance* (*to be*) *flown* **~erfahrung** f *flying experience* **~erprobung** f *flight trial* **~fähre** f ⟨engl⟩ *car air ferry* **~feld** n *airfield*; *air-strip* **≗fest** a *airworthy* (*aero-plane*) **~figur** f *flight manœuvre* **~fisch** m ⟨ich⟩ *flying-fish* **~form(ation)** f *flying formation* (geöffnete *extended*, in Höhe gestaffelte ~ *step formation*) **~fracht** f *air freight* **~-frosch** m ⟨zoo⟩ *flying-frog* **~fuchs** m ⟨zoo⟩ *flying-fox* **~funk(dienst)** m *radio aircraft service* **~gast** m ⟨aero⟩ *air-passenger*; ~ der Touristenklasse *sky tourist* **~gasttreppe** f (⟨a.⟩ selbstfahrende ~) *gangway* **~gelände** n *flying terrain* **~geschwindigkeit** f *flying speed* **~gesellschaft** f *airline* **~gewicht** n ⟨aero⟩ *total* od *flying* od *gross weight*; ⟨fam⟩ *all-up* **~hafen** m ⟨aero⟩ *airport* (angeflogener .. *of call*); *seaplane-station*; ⟨Am⟩ *airdrome*; (auf dem Meer) *floating harbour*; *seadrome* ‖ vor dem ~ landen *to undershoot the airfield* | ~drehfeuer [n] *revolving airport beacon* ‖ ~erkennungszeichen [n] *airport identification sign*(*al*); ~kontrollturm [m] *airport*(*traffic*) *control tower* **~hafer** m ⟨bot⟩ *wild oat* **~hahn** m = Flugfisch **~handbuch** n *aeroplane flight manual* **~haut** f ⟨zoo⟩ *wing*(*-membrane*) **~höhe** f *altitude* of flight; flying od (über Grund) absolute alt. || apex (of the trajectory); höchste ~ ⟨aero⟩ absolute ceiling **~horchgerät** n ⟨aero⟩ sound detector **~hörnchen** n ⟨zoo⟩ flying squirrel **~huhn** n ⟨orn⟩ Sand≈ sand-grouse; ganga; Pterocles (L); → Fausthuhn **~hund** m ⟨zoo⟩ flying-fox (→ fliegender Hund); Gattung der ~e Pteropidae (L) pl **~kapitän** m ⟨aero⟩ flight-captain **~karte** f air-line ticket **≈klar** a ⟨aero⟩ das Flugzeug ist ~ the aeroplane is ready to take off **~körper** m flying object; (mit Raketen- or Luftstrahltriebwerk) missile; gelenkter ~ guided missile **~kraft** f power of flight **~kunststück** n aircraft feat; ⟨sl⟩ stunt; ~e m ⟨sl⟩ to stunt **~lage** f ⟨aero⟩ attitude || flying position; in überzogener ~ s to stall **~lehrer** m flying od flight instructor; instructional pilot **~leistung** f flying od flight performance **~leiter** m airtraffic controller **~leitung** f flying control (centre) | ~seinrichtungen [f pl] f. c. facilities **~linie** f line of flight, → Flugbahn || ⟨aero⟩ e–e ~ benutzen to ride an airline | ~nverkehr [m] air service **~loch** n pigeon hole; entrance to a hive **≈lustig** a airminded (traveller) **~maki** m ⟨zoo⟩ flying lemur; kaguan **~maschine** f flying-machine; → Flugzeug **~meldedienst** m air control service; air traffic control || aircraft reporting service **~meldezentrale** f air raid warning centre (⟨Am⟩ –ter) **~mod·ell** n plane model, flying model; model plane **~motor** m aircraft engine **~objekt** n (unbekannt) unidentified flying object **~ordnung** f: geöffnete ~ extended formation **~personal** n flight personnel **~plan** m air time-table; flight plan od schedule **~platz** m airport, aerodrome (der ~ N. the a. at N.); flying– od aviation-ground od field; ⟨mil⟩ airbase || Not≈ airstrip || kl ~ air-stop || mit ~peilung (blind)fliegen to ride the beam | allgemeine ~beleuchtung general field floodlight system **~post** f air mail; mit der ~ by a. **~prüfung** f flight-test **~rakete** f (f Höhen v rd 150 km) satelloid **~regler** m autopilot; automatic pilot **~sand** m blown sand; drifting sand, sand-drift; quicksand **~saurier** m = Flugechse **~schein** m (flight-)ticket, air ticket, ⟨Am⟩ plane t. | internat. Ausweis f ~e air travel card; → IATA **~schlag** m ⟨ten⟩ = Flugball **~schneise** f (flying) corridor **~schrift** f ⟨Lit⟩ pamphlet; ⟨com⟩ prospectus; folder; ~en schreiben to pamphleteer | ~enschreiber [m] pamphleteer **~schule** f flying-school **~schüler** m pilot-trainee **~sicherheit** f flying safety; aerodynamical safety **~sicherung** f air-traffic control (ATC) | ~sanweisung [f] a.-t. control || ~(sdienst [m]) control centre || ~slotse [m] controller || ~szentrale [f] air traffic control center N **~sicht** f flight visibility **~sommer** m = Altweibersommer **~sport** m = Luftsport **~start** m (senkrechter vertical) take-off **~strecke** f (air) route | ~nbefeuerung [f], ~nbeleuchtung [f] airway beacons pl || ~n(leucht)feuer [n] airway beacon || ~nplan [m] (route) schedule **~stunde** f flying-hour || flight od pilot lesson **~stützpunkt** m ⟨aero⟩ airbase || (auf dem Meer) floating base; seadrome **≈tauglich** a capable of flying **~tätigkeit** f air od flying activity **~taxi** n taxiplane **~technik** f aerodynamics [pl]; aviation **≈technisch** a aerodynamic(al) **~teilstrecke** f leg; (kurze) hop **≈tüchtig** a airworthy **~tüchtigkeit** f airworthiness **~überwachungsinstrumente** n pl flying instruments **~unfall** m plane accident; crash | ~versicherung [f] air insurance **~verbindung** f air connexion **~verbot** n ⟨aero⟩ aircraft grounding **~verkehr** m airtraffic | ~slinie, ~strecke [f] airway; air-line (od route) **~v·orbesprechung** f pre-flight briefing **~vorrichtung** f flying device || ⟨theat⟩ human flying equipment **~wache** f plane spotting post **~wachkommando** n filter center; air traffic control **~weg** m airway; flight path **~weite** f range of flight; flying-range od distance || wing spread **~werk** n airframe **~wesen** n aviation; flying; aeronautics **~wetter** n flying weather | ~dienst [m] airport weather service **~wild** n ⟨hunt⟩ = Federwild **~woche** f aviation week **~zeit** f flying od flight-time; duration of flight **~zeug** n → d. **~zustand** m flight attitude od position

Flügel m ~s/~ **A. 1.** ⟨**orn**⟩ wing; ⟨poet⟩ pinion || kl ~ winglet **2.** ⟨**aero**⟩ (Tragfläche) aerofoil, wing (of an aeroplane); plane; airfoil; fester ~ stationary wing **3.** ⟨**fig poet**⟩ wing (the wings of the wind) **4. a.** e–m Vogel den ~ **beschneiden** to pinion a bird l ⟨fig⟩ jdm die ~ beschneiden to clip the wings of a p || ⟨fig⟩ die ~ über jdn breiten to take a p under one's wings || e–m Huhn die ~ dressieren ⟨cul⟩ to truss a fowl || ⟨hum fam⟩ ihm wachsen schon die ~ he sprouts wings || ⟨**fig**⟩ die ~ hängen l to droop (vor with); to lose heart; to be crestfallen od depressed || ⟨fig⟩ sich [dat] die ~ verbrennen to burn one's fingers || ⟨fig⟩ jdm ~ verleihen (of a feeling) to lend a p wings **b. auf** den ~n des Gesangs winged by the magic of song || auf ~n s–n Weg nehmen to wing one's way || (Vogel; Flugzeug) **in** den ~ treffen to wing || **mit** den ~n schlagen to flap the wings; ⟨fam⟩ to flop || jdn unter s–e ~ nehmen to take a p under one's wings **B.** ⟨**übtr**⟩ **1.** ⟨**bot**⟩ (seitl. Blumenblatt) side-petal; wing || membrane attached to a seed od fruit **2.** ⟨**tech**⟩ blade, vane (of a propeller); fan (of a propeller-screw) || ⟨theat⟩ flipper || sail, vane (of a windmill, etc.) → Anker≈ || flyer, flier (of a spinning-machine) || mudguard, wing (of a motor-car) || feather, wing (of a valve) || hydrometrischer ~ hydrometric vane; screw current meter **3.** ⟨**arch**⟩ (Tür≈) leaf, wing || Fenster≈ casement || wing (of a building); (ein Haus) mit e–m ~ versehen to wing || (Altar-) Seiten≈ side-pieces pl || fold (of a screen) **4.** offene ~ [pl] ⟨**mil**⟩ open flanks || ⟨mil, sport, hunt, pol⟩ rechter ~ right wing || rechter Lungen≈ right lung **C.** ⟨mus⟩ grand piano; grand (am ~ at the g.) **D.** [in comp] wing || ⟨aero⟩ wing **~adjutant** m ⟨mil⟩ high officer attached to a sovereign ruler **~altar** m altar-piece with side-wings; polyptych **~ärmel** m (pl) (bat)wing sleeve, → Fledermaus– **≈artig** a wing-like **~bank** f ⟨spin⟩ flyer **~bombe** f ⟨aero⟩ wing-bomb **~boot** n flying-boat, (Trag≈) naviplane **~bremse** f fan-brake **~decke** f wing-case (od sheath); shard, sherd; elytrum L **~fell** n ⟨path⟩ pterygium L **~fenster** n casement-(-window); (bis z Boden reichend) French window **~fläche** f ⟨aero⟩ wing-area **≈förmig** a wing-shaped; alar, aliform **~fortsatz** m ⟨anat⟩ (am Keilbein) pterygoid process **~frucht** f ⟨bot⟩ smara L **~fruchtbaum** m ⟨bot⟩ Lingoum; Pterocarpus L **≈füßig** a ⟨zoo⟩ aliped (bat) **~gebläse** n ⟨tech⟩ fan-blower; rotary-fan **~geschütz** n outside gun **~holm** m ⟨aero⟩ wing-spar **~horn** n ⟨mus⟩ = Bügelhorn **~kaktus** m ⟨bot⟩ phyllocactus L **~kante** f edge, hintere trailing e. **~klappe** f ⟨aero⟩ wing-flap **~kleid** n ⟨poet⟩ noch im ~e still in one's prime **~knochen** m ⟨orn⟩ wing-bone **~kraft** f wing-power **≈lahm** a with drooping wings; winged by a shot **~mann** m ⟨mil⟩ marker; flank man || file-leader || der rechte ~ the right-hand man (of the rank); der linke ~ the left-hand man (of the rank) || innerer ~ pivot; pivotal man **~mauer** f ⟨fort⟩ wing-wall **~mutter** f ⟨tech⟩ butterfly (od wing, fly)-nut **~nase** f ⟨aero⟩ leading edge **~nuß(baum** m) f ⟨bot⟩ (Caucasian) wing-nut **~pferd** n = Flügelroß **~pumpe** f vane type pump **~rad** n vane-wheel; screw-propeller **~roß** n winged horse; Pegasus L **~samen** m ⟨bot⟩ winged seed **~schlag** m wing-beat (od stroke); ~schläge m to flap **~schnecke** f ⟨zoo⟩ = Flossenfüßer **~schraube** f ⟨tech⟩ wing screw; butterfly bolt **~schuhe** m pl (Merkurs) ⟨myth⟩

heel-wings **~signal** n ⟨rail⟩ *semaphore* **~spanne** f *wing-spread* **~spannweite** f ⟨aero⟩ *wing-spread* **~spitze** f *pinion* **~stärke** f ⟨aero⟩ *wing-thickness* **~tiefe** f ⟨aero⟩ *depth of wing* **~tür** f *folding-doors* [pl] **~welle** f ⟨tech⟩ *vane-spindle*; *propeller-shaft* **~zeichnung** f ⟨orn⟩ *wing-marking*

-flüg(e)lig a [in comp] *winged*; lang~ *long--winged* ‖ e–e zwei~e Tür *a two-leaved door* **fl·ügellos** a *wingless* ‖ ⟨zoo⟩ *apterous* **fl·ügeln** vt [h] ⟨hunt⟩ (im Flügel treffen) (Vogel) *to wing* ‖ → geflügelt **fl·ügge** [mst pred] a *fledged*; ~e Brut *flight*, → Aufflug 2. ‖ ⟨fig⟩ *fledged* | (noch) nicht ~ *unfledged*; ⟨fig a.⟩ *immature* ‖ ~ w *to fledge*; gerade ~ geworden *just fledged*; ~ ge-w–er Vogel, ⟨fig⟩ Mensch *fledgeling* **flugs** adv *forthwith*, *instantly*; *quickly*; (nun aber) ~! *sharp's the word*!

Fl·ugzeug n ~s/~e *aeroplane*, ⟨mil mst⟩ *plane*; *flying-machine*; ⟨Am⟩ *airplane* ‖ ~e [pl] *aircraft*; Luftparade v ~en *fly past* ‖ Rumpf e–s ~s *fuselage* ‖ billiges ~ ⟨Am sl⟩ *flivver*; nicht gemeldetes ~ *itinerant aircraft* | Amphibien~ *amphibian* ‖ Arbeits~ *general service plane* ‖ Bomben~ *bomber*; Jagd~, Kampf~ *fighter-(-plane)*, (gr) *combat* (od *war*) *plane* ‖ Militär~ *military plane*, (gr) *war-plane* ‖ Schleuder~ *catapult-plane* ‖ Schul~ *school-plane* ‖ Schrauben~ *rotating-wing aircraft* ‖ Schwimm~ *sea-plane with floats* ‖ Segel~ *glider* ‖ Sport~ *sports plane* ‖ Torpedo~ *torpedo-bomber* ‖ Übungs~ *training-plane*; Verkehrs~ *air-liner* ‖ Wasser~ *hydroplane*, *seaplane* ‖ → Eindecker, Doppeldecker; Flieger B. 1. | **im ~**, **mit ~**, **per ~** *by air*, *by* (*aero*)*plane*; im ~ fliegen, reisen *to go* od *travel by* (*aero*)*plane*; *to fly* ‖ jdn im ~ befördern *to fly a p* | ein ~ besteigen, in ein ~ (ein)steigen *to emplane* ‖ ein ~ führen *to fly an aeroplane* ‖ ein ~ (durch Schuß) kampfunfähig m *to wing an aeroplane* **~absturz** m *plane crash* **~abwehr** f → Flugabwehr **~bau** m *construction of aeroplanes*; *aircraft-manufacture* od *-industry* **~bauer** m *constructor of aeroplanes* **~beobachter** m *aeroplane--observer* **~besatzung** f *crew of an aeroplane*; *air-crew*, *flight crew*; Boot zur Rettung v in Seenot geratener ~ *mercy-boat* **~fabrik** f *aircraft--factory* **~führer** m (*air-*)*pilot* | ~abzeichen [n] *pilot's badge*, ⟨fam⟩ *wings* pl ‖ ~schein [m] *flying license* **~geschwader** n *squadron* **~halle** f *hangar* **~industrie** f *aircraft-industry* **~kanzel** f *cockpit* **~liegeplatz** m *a. parking platform* **~mechaniker** m *ground mechanic* **~mutterschiff** n *aircraft* (od *seaplane*) *tender* **~rumpf** m *fuselage* **~schiff** n *aircraft depot ship*; → -mutterschiff **~schleuder** f *catapult* | ~schiff [n] *catapult-ship* **~schuppen** m *hangar* **~schwanzflosse** f *empennage* **~schwimmer** m, **~schwimmvorrichtung** f *float* **~sicherungsschiff** n ⟨Am⟩ *aircraft auxiliary* **~stewardeß** f *air hostess*; ⟨Am⟩ *stewardess* **~-stützpunkt** m (auf dem Meer) *seadrome*; *floating harbour* **~torpedo** m = Lufttorpedo **~träger** m *aircraft carrier*, ⟨Am fam⟩ *flattop* | ~kommandobrücke [f] *island* **~waffen** f [pl] *aircraft armament* od *gunnery* **~wart** m *rigger*; ⟨Am⟩ *flight-line attendant* **~zelle** f *air-frame*

ˣ**Fluh** f ~/~e = Felsabhang **Flüh** f = Fluh

Fl·uid- **~extrakt** m *fluid extract* **~kompaß** m ⟨mar⟩ *fluid compass* **Fluid·al-** [in comp] ⟨geol⟩ *fluidal* (*structure*) **Fluidit·ät** f *fluidity* **Fl·uidum** n ~s/–da **1.** *fluid* ‖ ⟨phys⟩ elektrisches (etc) ~ *electric fluid* **2.** ⟨fig⟩ *aura* (L) (*of a p*; *of malevolence*); *atmosphere*, *aura* (*of a room*) ‖ geistiges ~ *fluidic atmosphere* **Fluktuati·on** [ts] f ~/~en *fluctuation* **fluktu·ieren** vi [h] *to fluctuate*

Fl·under m ~s/~; f ~/~n ⟨ich⟩ *flounder*, *fluke*

Flunker·ei f ~/~en *fib*, *fibbing*; ⟨fam⟩ *blarney* **Fl·unkerer** m *fibber*; *story-teller* **fl·unkern** vi [h] **1.** flimmern **2.** (aufschneiden) *to draw the long bow*; *to throw the hatchet* ‖ flunkere nicht! *draw it mild*! → prahlen ‖ *to fib*; *to tell fibs*

°**Flunsch** m ~es~e *mone*, *pout*; e–n ~ m (*or* ziehen) *to pout*; *to hang one's jib*; mit e–m ~ v hier bis Bitterfeld *with one's face at half-past eight*

Flu·or n ~s/ ⟨chem⟩ *fluorine* **~wasserstoff** m *hydrogen fluoride*; ~säure [f] *hydrofluoric acid*

Fluoresze·in [-ei:n] n ⟨chem⟩ *fluorescein*

Fluoresz·enz f ~/ ⟨phys⟩ *fluorescence*; ~schirm [m] *fluorescent screen* | ~-Verstärkerfolie [f] *fl. intensifying sc.* **fluoresz·ieren** vi [h] *to fluoresce* **fluoresz·ierend** a *fluorescent*

Fluor·id n ~s/~e ⟨chem⟩ *fluoride* ‖ (Zähne) mit ~ behandeln *to fluoridize* ‖ (Trinkwasser) mit ~ versetzen *to fluoridate* **Fluor·it** m ~s/~e ⟨chem⟩ *fluorite* **Fluorosk·op** n ⟨med⟩ *fluoroscope*

Fl·ur **1.** m ~s/~e **a.** ⟨hist⟩ *floor*; → Diele **b.** *corridor*; *passage*; ⟨Am⟩ *hallway* ‖ *entrance--hall*; *lobby*, *vestibule*; ⟨Am⟩ *stoop* **2.** f ~/~en *fields* [pl]; *piece of arable land*; *stretch of open grassy country*; *meadow land*; ⟨poet⟩ *lea* ‖ *village lands* [pl] **~bereinigung** → Feld–; *property* (⟨bes Am⟩ *land*) *consolidation*; **~buch** n *field-book*; *ground register*; *r. of village lands* **~fenster** n *staircase* (od *hall*)*-window* **~garderobe** f *hall-stand* **~namen** m [pl] *names* [pl] *of the fields*, *lands* **~platten** f [pl] ⟨mar⟩ (*engine-room*) *floor plates* [pl] **~schaden** m ⟨mil⟩ *damage done to the fields* **~schütz** m *field-guard* **~zwang** m ⟨hist⟩ *compulsory system of common farming* od *tilling*

Fl·use f ~/~n *loose end of thread* (od *fluff*) *on cloth* **~nfrei** a *lint-free* od *non-fluffy* (*cloth*) **fl·usig** a *fluffy*, *fuzzy*

Fluß m –sses/Fl·üsse **A.** **[abstr]** **1.** *flow* (*of a brook*); *the flowing* (*of water*); *run* (*of waves*); *fluxion*; *flow* (*of supplies*) → Abfluß **2.** ⟨med⟩ *flux*(*ion*) (*of blood*, *serum*) ‖ *running*; *catarrh*, *cold* ‖ ⟨path⟩ weißer ~ *leucorrhœa*, *the whites* [pl]; → Schlag~ **3.** ⟨chem & met⟩ *fusion* (*of molten metal*); *melting* **4.** ⟨fig⟩ *flux* (*of words*); *gush* ‖ *cadence* (*of a p's sentences*); *fluency*; *glibness* (*the speech came out with astonishing g.*); *smoothness* **5.** ⟨cards hist⟩ = Flöte 2. **6.** **in ~** ⟨fig⟩ *in flux*, *in a state of flux* (*everything is in a state of f.*) ‖ ⟨mil⟩ in ~ bleiben *to maintain continuous movement*; die Verfolgung in ~ halten *to keep the pursuit in motion*; *to maintain the flow* (*of supply*) ‖ in ~ s (of traditions) *to be fluid*; das In-~-sein *the fluidity* (*of a process*) ‖ in ~ bringen ⟨met⟩ *to flux*; ⟨fig⟩ *to bring into play*; *to start*; in ~ k., geraten *to come into play*; → Gang **B.** **[konkr]** **1.** *river*; *stream* ‖ kl ~ *rivulet*; ⟨Am⟩ *creek*, *run* ‖ an dem ~ *on the river*; das Leben am ~e *the life by the river*; am ~ gelegen *or* wohnend *riverain*, *riverine* ‖ → Fluß– ‖ (den) ~ abwärts *down the river*; .. aufwärts *up the river* **2.** ⟨med⟩ *fluxion* **3.** ⟨met⟩ (Schmelzmasse) *flux*(*ion*); *melt* **4.** (Emailschmelzungsmittel) *flux* **5.** (Neutronen~) ⟨at⟩ *flux* ‖ Versuche mit hohem (N.–) ~ *high flux testing* **6.** ⟨fig⟩ *stream* (*of time*) **~ablagerung** f ⟨geol⟩ *river-drift* (od *deposit*) **~abwärts** adv *downstream*; ~ gelegen *d.* (*village*) **~arm** m *arm* (od *fork*) *of the r.* **~arm** a *poor in r.s*; *r.less* **~-artig** a *r.-like* **~aufwärts** adv *upstream*; ~ gelegen *u.* (*village*) **~bad** n *r.-bath* **~becken** n *r.-basin* **~bett** n *r.-bed* (od *channel*) **~bewohner** m *r.ain* **~bild** n ⟨tech⟩ (Schema) *flow sheet* **~boot** n *r.--boat*; chines. ~ *sampan* **~dampfer** m *r.-steamer*; ⟨fam⟩ *waterbus* **~diagramm** n ⟨comp⟩ *flow charts* **~eisen** n *ingot iron* od *steel*; *mild steel* **~fahrzeug** n, ~e [pl] *r. craft* **~flotte** f *r.ine fleet* **~galle** f ⟨vet⟩ *stifle* **~gebiet** n *r.-basin* **~geschwindigkeit** f ⟨phys⟩ *flux* (*of a fluid*) ‖ ⟨biochem⟩ (des Ab- u. Aufbaus) *flow-rate* **~gott** m *r.-god* **~kanonenboot** n *r.-gunboat* **~krebs** m ⟨zoo⟩ *macruran* *crustacean; crayfish* **~krümmung** f *bend of a r.* **~kunde** f *potamology* **~landschaft** f *r.side*; (∼s-gemälde) *r.-scape* **~lauf** m *r.-course* **~mittel** n ⟨met⟩ *flux* **~mündung** f *mouth of a r.*; (den Gezeiten ausgesetztes ∼sgebiet) *estuary* **~muschel** f ⟨zoo⟩ *r.-mussel; naiad* **~ordnung** f *rule of the r.* **~perlmuschel** f ⟨zoo⟩ *r. pearl-mussel* **~pferd** n ⟨zoo⟩ *hippopotamus* (L); *r.-horse* **~sand** m *r.--sand* **~säure** f ⟨chem⟩ *hydrofluoric acid* **~-schiff** n *r.-boat* **~schiffahrt** f *r.-navigation* **~-schiffer** m *r.-boatman* **~schlauch** m *the lower part of the r.-bed* **~schnelle** f *chute* **~spat** m ⟨minr⟩ *fluor-spar; fluorite* **~stadt** f *r.ain-town* **~stahl** m → Flußeisen **~tal** n *r.-valley* **~ufer** n *(r.-)bank; r.side*; steiles ∼ ⟨poet⟩ *brae* ‖ am ∼ liegend *or* wohnend *r.ine (people)* ‖ ∼land ⟨Am⟩ *bench-land*; tiefliegendes ∼ *r.-bottom* **~-verbesserung** f *r.ine improvement* **~verkehr** m *r.--traffic* **~verunreinigung** f *pollution of the r.* **⁓-wärts** adv *r.ward(s)* **~wasser** n *r.-water* **~windung** f *meander* (od *winding*) *of a r.*

Fl·üßchen n ∼s/∼ *rivulet, runnel, streamlet*; ⟨Am⟩ *creek; run* **fl·üssig I.** a **1.** ⟨eig⟩ *fluid; liquid; fluidible*; → dick∼, streng∼, zäh∼ ‖ ∼er Körper, ∼e Substanz *fluid, liquid* ‖ ∼er Brennstoff *l. fuel*; ∼er Sauerstoff *l. oxygen*, [abbr] *lox*; ⟨mil⟩ ∼es Feuer *l. fire*; ⟨Am hum⟩ *hard liquor*; ∼es Gas *l. gas*; ∼e Kohle, Luft *l. coal, air* ‖ ∼e Nahrung *l. nourishment*; ∼e Krankenkost *sop* ‖ ∼ m *to fluidify, fluidize; liquefy; melt* ‖ ∼ w *to liquefy; to become l.*; *to melt* **2.** ⟨übtr com⟩ *liquid* (Liegenschaften); ∼es Geld, ∼e Gelder *cash; ready money*; die Firma besitzt k–e ∼en Mittel *the firm is short of ready money*; leicht ∼ z machende Posten [pl] *l. assets* [pl] ‖ (Kapital) ∼ m *to convert into cash*; (Papiere) *to realize* **3.** ⟨fig⟩ *liquid (verse); fluent (pronunciation); smooth*; → fließend ‖ → *liquid* **II.** adv ∼ fahren ⟨mot⟩ *to drive steadily; to keep a steady pace* **~gas** n *liquefied gas* | **⁓keit** f ∼/∼en **1.** [abstr] **a.** *fluidity (of air); liquidity; fluid* (od *liquid*) *condition* ‖ ∼, in die etw eingetaucht wird *dip* | ⟨com⟩ *easiness (on the money market)* **b.** ⟨fig⟩ *fluidity (of verse, thought)* **2.** [konkr] *fluid, liquid; liquor*; → Saft **Fl·üssigkeits- ~dichte** f *density of liquid* **~druck** m *hydraulic pressure* **~element** n ⟨el⟩ *one–* od *single--fluid cell* **⁓gekühlt** a ⟨mot⟩ *liquid-cooled (engine)* **~getriebe** n *fluid drive* **~kupplung** f ⟨mot⟩ *fluid clutch* **~maß** n *liquid measure* **~menge** f *amount of fluid* (od *liquid*) **~messer** m *flow-meter* **~reibung** f *fluid friction* **~säule** f *liquid column* **~standanzeiger** m *liquid level indicator* **~stoß-dämpfer** m *hydraulic shock-absorber* **~-treibstoff** m *liquid propellant* **~zähler** m *fluidmeter*

Fl·üssigmachung f ⟨com⟩ *realization (of securities)*; → flüssig I. 2 **fl·ußlos** a *riverless*

Fl·üster- ~galerie f, **~gewölbe** n ⟨arch⟩ *whispering-gallery* **~kneipe** f *whisper joint; speak-easy* **~propaganda** f *underground propaganda*; ⟨fam⟩ *rumo(u)r-mongering* ‖ wie die ∼ meldet ⟨Am⟩ *as the grapevine has it* od *says* **~ton** m *whisper*; im ∼ *in a whisper, in whispers*; im ∼ gehalten *whispered (consultation)*; in s–m halben ∼ *in his side-wing voice* **Fl·üsterer** m *whisperer* **fl·üstern I.** vi/t **A.** vi **1.** (P) *to whisper; to speak in a wh.* (od *under one's breath*); laut ∼ *to stage-wh.* ‖ ∼d *in a wh.* ‖ jdm ins Ohr ∼ *to wh. (to) a p* **2.** ⟨übtr poet⟩ (of leaves, etc.) *to wh.; murmur, rustle* **B.** vt **1.** (Worte) *to wh.*; geflüsterte Worte *wh.(ing)* ‖ jdm etw ins Ohr ∼ *to wh. a th to a p*; jdm ins Ohr ∼ z tun, .. daß *to wh. to a p to do, .. that ..* **2.** ⟨übtr⟩ *to wh.* **II.** ⁓ n **1.** *wh., wh.ing* **2.** *wh.ing (of the sea); rustling; susurration (of trees)* **fl·üsternd 1.** a *whispering* ‖ ⟨übtr⟩ *rustling (leaves); wh.ing (breeze); susurrant, –rous* **2.** adv *in a whisper; whisperingly*

Fl·ut f ∼/∼en **1.** (Wassermasse) *flood*; (gr ∼) *deluge, inundation* ‖ ∼en [pl] *floods* pl ‖ ⟨bib⟩ Sint⁓ *the Flood* (od *Deluge*), *Noah's Flood* ‖ Sturm⁓ *waves agitated by a storm; great tidal wave* **2.** Ebbe u ∼ *ebb and flow*; v Ebbe u ∼ [nicht] beeinflußt *tidal [tideless] (river)* ‖ ∼ *flood(-tide)* ‖ höchster Stand der ∼ *high tide, high water*; niedrigster Stand der ∼ *low tide* ‖ zur Zeit der ∼ *at high tide* ‖ das Eintreten der ∼ *the incoming* od *rise of the tide*; die ∼ kommt, läuft *the tide is coming in*; es ist ∼ *the tide is up, the tide is at the flood*; die ∼ fällt, nimmt ab *the tide is going out*; mit der ∼ treiben, fahren *to tide* ‖ Nipp⁓ *neap-tide*; durch Nipp∼ am Ausfahren gehindert w (of ship) *to be neaped*; Spring⁓ *spring-tide*; (Vor⁓) *in-coming tide* **B.** ⟨fig⟩ **a.** Hoch∼ *the full tide (of a movement; feeling)* ‖ die Sturm⁓ *the tidal waves* pl; die Sturm⁓ der Unruhe *the rising tide of disorder* ‖ die ∼en v Haß *the tides of hate* **b.** *deluge, flood, flow, spate, stream, volley (of petitions, questions, words); crowd (of books); torrent (of orders)*; ⟨Am⟩ *rush* (⟨dial⟩ *rash*) *(of awards)* ‖ e–e ∼ v Schimpfwörtern *a torrent of abuse*; mit e–r ∼ v Flugschriften überschüttet w *to be flooded* (od *deluged*) *with pamphlets* **c.** e–e ∼ v Leuten *a spate of people* **~bett** n *tide-channel* **~gang** m *millrace* **~gatter** n *flood-gate; tide-gate* **~graben** m *waste-pit* **~hafen** m *tidal harbour* **~kanal** m *tidal channel; tideway* **~kraftwerk** n *tidal power--station, tidal generating-station* **~licht** n ⟨el⟩ *floodlight*, ⟨Am fam⟩ *flood* | ∼anlage [f] *fl.l. system* ‖ ∼leuchte [f] ⟨theat⟩ *wide-angle fl. l.* ‖ ∼(schein)werfer [m] *fl.l. projector* ‖ ∼spiel [n] ⟨sport⟩ *fl.l. match* **~messer** m → Wasserstandsmesser, Pegel **~mündung** f *estuary* **~schleuse** f = Freiarche **~strom** m *tide-stream* **~strömung** f *tide--current* **~tide** f *flood-tide* **~tor** n = –gatter **~-ventil** n *tidal valve* **~wasser** n *tide-water* **~welle** f *tidal wave*; brandende ∼ (des *Severn*) *bore*, (des *Trent*) *eagre* **~wende** f *tide-turn* **~zeichen** n *tide--mark* **~zeit** f *tide-time*; Dampfer, Zug, der sich nach der ∼ richtet *tidal steamer, tidal train* **fl·uten I.** vi/t **A.** vi [s] **1.** ⟨eig⟩ *to flow; pour* (in *into*; nach *towards*); *to flood*; über ein Gebiet ∼ *to flood* (od *overflow*) *an area*; über die Ufer ∼ *to overflow the banks* ‖ (of waves) *to surge* **2.** ⟨übtr & fig⟩ **a.** (of air, sand) *to flow* (durch *through*; in *into*) ‖ (of hair) *to stream* (über *over*) ‖ (of light) *to stream, sweep* (*through* ..; unter *below*); **~ in:** *a great brightness flooded the interior* ‖ (of odour) *to billow* (in *into*); (Duft) ∼ l *to waft* (auf *upon*) **b.** (of people) *to crowd* (in *into*); *to pour* (durch *through*); (of bees, etc.) *to swarm* (*into* ..; *out of*; .. *to*) **c.** (of a feeling) *to flow* (durch *through*); *to surge (a relief surged over his face); to sweep (shame swept over him)*; ihre ganze Seele flutete z ihm *all her soul swept towards him* **B.** *vt [h] *to pour; run*; = schwemmen, → d. ‖ ⟨mar⟩ *to flood* **II.** ⁓ n *flow(ing), pour(ing); surging, surge* ‖ *flooding; streaming (of hair, light)* ‖ *surging (of feelings)* **fl·utend** a *flowing; surging (waves)* ‖ *streaming (hair)*

°**fl·utschen** vi [h] *to swish*; ∼d *with a swish* ‖ ⟨fig⟩ (of play, work) *to get on swimmingly* (od *without a hitch*); *to go off very well; to go smoothly*; die Arbeit flutscht heute nur so *I am getting on swimmingly today*; .. nicht recht *I don't get on with my work today*

fluvi·al a *fluvial* **fl·uvioglazi·al** a *fluvio-glacial*

Fluxi·on f ∼/∼en *fluxion*; → Differential

Flysch m ∼s/∼e ⟨geol⟩ *flysh*

F·ock f ∼/∼en ⟨mar⟩ **1.** (Rahsegel⁓) *foresail* **2.** (Stagsegel⁓) *staysail* **3.** Ballon⁓ *balloon jib* ‖ Stag⁓ *forestay sail* ‖ Sturm⁓ *spitfire-jib*; ⟨Am⟩ *spitfire* **~fall** m *jib-halyard* **~hals** m (beim Rahsegel) *fore-tack*; (beim Stagsegel) *jib-tack* **~mast** m *foremast* **~rahe** f *foreyard* **~schot** f *foresheet* **~stag** n *forestay* **~segel** n *foresail; fore(-)course*

F·ocke[1] f = Fock **F·ocke**[2] f = Nachtreiher

föder- **~al** a *federal* **≃al·ismus** m *federalism* **≃al·ist** m ~en/~en *federalist*; ⟨Am⟩ *federal* **≃alistisch** a *federalist* (*party*); ⟨Am⟩ *federal* **≃a-ti·on** [ts] f *federation* **~at·iv** a *federative*; ~er Zus–schluß *confederation* **~·ieren** vt [h] *to* (*con*)-*federate* **~·iert** a *federated*; (*con*)*federate*; der ≃e *the confederate*

F·ohlen n ~s/~ ⟨allg⟩ *foal*; (bis z 4., 5. Jahr) *colt*; weibl. ~ *filly*; → Pony ‖ ~ werfen *to foal* ‖ **f·ohlen** vi [h] (v Pferd u Esel) *to foal*; *to drop a colt*

Föhn m ~s/~e **1.** (warmer, trockener Wind) *föhn, foehn* (= *hot southerly wind blowing down a mountain-side*) [Ger] **2.** → Fön® ⟨el⟩ **f·öhnen** vi [h] es föhnt *the föhn is blowing*

F·öhrde f = Förde

F·öhre f ~/~n ⟨bot⟩ ≐ Kiefer **Föhreneule** f ⟨ent⟩ = Forleule

Fok·al- ⟨phot, opt⟩ **~filter** m *focal-plane filter* **~punkt** m ⟨opt⟩ *isocenter* **~verschluß** m *f.-p. shutter*; → Fokus

F·okker (nach Holl. A. Fokker [†1939]) [in comp] ~-Jagdeinsitzer *single fighter-plane*

F·okus m [L] ~/~ ⟨phys⟩ *focus* [L]

F·olge f ~/~n **1.** **(Aufeinander≃) a.** (natürliche) *sequence* (*of the seasons*); → Erb≃; Sequenz ‖ *order, succession*; in rascher ~ *in rapid succession*; in richtiger ~ *in order* ‖ eine ununterbrochene ~ v *a run of* (*bad luck*); e–e zwangsläufige ~ *a necessity* ‖ Ton≃ *succession of tones* **b.** **[konkr]** (Reihe, Serie) *series*; Neue ~ *New Series* ‖ ~ zus–gehöriger Dinge *set*; ⟨film⟩ *sequence* **c.** [dat] ~ **geben** *to grant* (*a petition*) ‖ ~ **leisten**: (e–m Befehl) *to obey*; (e–r Bitte) *to comply with*; (e–r Einladung) *to accept*; (e–r Vorladung) *to answer* **2.** **(logische ~)** *logical sequence* od *consequence* ‖ ⟨gram⟩ ~ der Zeiten, Zeiten-≃ *s. of tenses* **3.** (zeitliche ~) *sequel* ‖ in der ~ *in the sequel*; *subsequently*; *in course of time* ‖ die ~ wird es lehren *wait and see* **4.** **(kausale) a.** *consequence*; *effect, issue, result*; *sequel, sequence* ‖ als e–e ~ davon *consequently* ‖ natürliche ~ *corollary* (v *of, to*); *natural c.*; als natürliche ~ hiervon *as a corollary to this* | die ~ war, daß .. *the c.e* (od *result*) *was that* ..; die ~ war, daß er abreiste *as a result he left* ‖ die Folge s v (etw) *to be the c.e of, to be consequent on* (*a th*); *to follow* (*this decree follows the murder of* ..) ‖ (etw) zur ~ h (S) *to bring about, call forth, originate*; *bring in its train* od *wake*; *to entail, involve* (*a th*); *to lead to* (*the victory led to the submission of the people*); *to result in* (*a failure*); der Krieg hatte .. z ~ *the war carried with it*; Unheil z ~ h *to spell disaster*; Wiedervergeltung .. *to call forth retaliation* ‖ → in≃, zu≃ **b.** ~n [pl] *consequences* pl; → absehen ‖ bedenke die ~n *mind the c.s* ‖ schwerwiegende ~n h *or* nach sich ziehen, v schwerwiegenden ~n s, nicht ohne sch. ~n s *to result in grave c.s, to be attended with gr. c.s* (f jdn *to a p*) ‖ die ~n tragen *to take the c.s*; *to stand the racket* (f etw *of a th*); die ~n werden nicht ausbleiben, du wirst die ~n z tragen h ⟨fam⟩ *you will hear of it* **~erscheinung** f *sequel* (e–r S *to a th*) ‖ als späte ~ *as an afterthought* **~prämie** f ⟨ins⟩ *renewal* od *subsequent premium* **≃recht**, **≃richtig 1.** a *consequent, consequential*; *consistent*; *coherent, logical*; *straight laced* ‖ –richtig *legitimate* (*result*) **2.** adv *connectedly*; *consistently*; *logically* **~richtigkeit** f *connectedness, consecutiveness, consistency*; *sequence*; *consequentialness* **~satz** m ⟨gram⟩ *consecutive clause* **~-sequenz** f ⟨radar⟩ *recurrence frequency* **≃widrig 1.** a *inconsecutive, inconsequent, inconsistent*; *illogical* **2.** adv *illogically, inconsistently* **~widrigkeit** f *inconsequence, inconsistency* **~zeit** f *sequel*

f·olgen vi [s] **A.** ⟨**eig**⟩ **1.** (P) **a.** jdm ~ *to follow a p* (*we followed them*), *to be at a p's heels*; möchten Sie mir bitte ~ *would you mind coming with me* od *this way* ‖ dicht ~ *to tail after a p*; → Fuß ‖ e–r S ~ *to follow a th* (*I followed the noise*); e–r Route ~ *to follow a route* ‖ (dem Rang nach) *to follow a p* ‖ den Zeilen mit dem Finger ~ *to trace along the lines with the f.* **b.** ⟨**jur**⟩ ~ auf jdn, jdm ~ *to follow a p, to succeed* (*to*) *a p* ‖ auf dem Thron (*or* in der Regierung) ~ *to succeed to the throne*; jdm auf dem T. ~ *to s. a p on the throne* ‖ ⟨com⟩ wir w weitere Zahlungen ~ l *we shall continue our payments*; wir w weitere Notizen ~ l *more items to follow* **2.** **(S)** ~ auf etw, e–r S ~ *to follow a th* (*night follows day*); *to succeed a th* (od *to a th*); es folgte e–e Pause *there was a p.*; dem Sturm folgte Sonnenschein *the storm was succeeded by sunshine*; ein Traum folgte dem anderen *dream followed dream* ‖ *to follow* (*up*)*on, to be consequent on* (*a th*); das einzige, was den Ereignissen folgte, war .. *the only sequel to the events was* .. ‖ ~d auf *consequent* (od *incidental*) *upon* **B.** ⟨**übtr**⟩ **1.** **(dienen)** jdm ~ *to follow a p, to attend on a p* ‖ (gehorchen) *to follow, obey a p*; den Anweisungen ~ *to follow the instructions* ‖ ⟨univ⟩ der Arzt folgte der Berufung, dem Rufe *the doctor responded to the call* ‖ jds Rat ~ *to take a p's advice* ‖ jds Beispiel ~ *to follow in a p's footsteps*; *to follow suit* ‖ er muß immer s–m Kopfe ~ *he will always have his way* ‖ s–n Neigungen ~ *to please o.s.*; → nachgehen | e–m Vorgang ~ *to follow an incident* (*with one's glass*) **2.** **(verstehen)** *to follow* (*a p*; *a lecture*) ‖ (beistimmen) *to go with* (*a p*); ich kann deinen Ansichten (*or* dir in d. A.) nicht ~ *I cannot follow* (od *go with*) *you in your views* ‖ (e–r Erklärung) ~ können *to find plausible* **3.** **(S)** *to be in accordance with*; *to go with* ‖ es folgte .. *this started* .. **4.** ~ **aus** *to follow* (od *ensue, result*) *from*; aus m–n Darlegungen folgt, daß .. *from what I pointed out it follows that* ..; es folgt daraus, daß .. *it follows that* .. **C.** **[abs] 1.** *to follow* (*I followed with the children*) **2.** jds Leiche [dat] ~ *to attend a p's funeral*; ⟨fam⟩ *to follow* **3.** er führte aus wie folgt *he argued as follows*; s–e Vorschläge sind wie folgt *his proposals are as follows* ‖ es folgt der Text .. *following is the text* | ⟨com⟩ Byrons Werke w ~ *Byron's works to follow* ‖ Fortsetzung folgt *to be continued*; Schluß folgt *to be concluded* ‖ was soll dann ~? *what do you want to follow*? ‖ später ~ ⟨fam⟩ *to follow on* **4.** **(gehorchen)** *to comply*; *to come to heel*; *to obey, to be obedient* **f·olgend** a **1.** [attr] *ensuing* (*on the e. days*); *following* (*day, month, week*); am ~en Tage *next day* ‖ *subsequent* (*events*) ‖ er sprach die ~en Worte *his words were as follows*; → Inhalt ‖ jedes ~e Werk *each succeeding work* | (sich ergebend) *consequent, resultant, resulting* **2.** [pred] die Lage ist ~e *this is the situation* ‖ es sind ~e *they* (sc *the wins*) *are as follows* **3.** [abs] **a.** ~es *this* ‖ das ~e ist der Text *following is the text*; *this is the text* ‖ das ≃ *the following* (*the f. was written to him*); ~es ereignete sich *this is what happened*; er führte ~es aus *he pointed out as follows* | **aus** ~em *from the following, from what follows* ‖ **im** ~en *in the following, in the sequel, in what follows*; *below*; im ~en w wir sehen *as we go along we shall see* ‖ er kam **zu** ~em (*or* auf ~es) *he came to this* **b.** die ~en [pl] *the following* pl **f·olgendermaßen** adv *as follows*; *like this*; die Worte lauten ~ *the words are* od *run as follows*; *these are the words*; etwa ~ *something like this* **f·olgenlos** a *without consequences* ‖ *without effect* (od *result*); *resultless* **f·olgenreich** a *effective, resultful* **f·olgenschwer** a *fraught* (od *attended*) *with grave consequences*; *momentous, weighty* **f·olgern 1.** vt [h] (etw) *to conclude, deduce, gather, infer* (aus *from*); z ~(d) *infer*(*r*)*able*; → gefolgert ‖ ~, daß .. *to conclude* od *gather, infer* (aus *from*) *that* ..; daraus läßt sich ~, daß .. *hence we may infer that* .. **2.** ≃ n *inference, inferring* → **F·olgerung** f ~/~en **1.** (Schluß≃) *conclusion*; *deduction, inference* (aus *from*); die ~ ziehen, daß *to draw the deduction that* ..; ~en ziehen *to draw* (*one's*) *inferences* (aus *from*) ‖ durch Schluß≃ *inferentially*; *by way of inference* **2.** stillschweigende ~ *implication*; als natürliche ~ *by implication* **f·olglich** adv *as a consequence*; *consequently, hence, thence, therefore* **f·olgsam** a *obedient*; (of children) *well behaved*; seid ~ *be good*; *behave yourselves*; → artig ‖ → fügsam, gefügig | ≃**keit** f *obedience*

Foli·ant m ~en/~en *folio volume* **F·olie** [–iə] f ~/~n **1. a.** (Metallblättchen) *foil*; *tin-foil, silver-foil* **b.** *foil*; *metallic mixture, quicksilver amalgam* ‖ (Glas etc) mit ~ belegen *to foliate, silver*; Belegen v Glas mit ~ *foliation of glass* **2.** ⟨fig⟩ *foil* (f, z *for, to*); *backing* ‖ e–r S *or* jdm als (*or* zur) ~ dienen *to act* od *serve as a foil to a th* od *a p*; *to form a foil to a th* od *a p* ‖ e–r S ~ geben *to form a foil to a th*; *to set a th off to advantage* **foli·ieren** vt [h] **1.** (Buch) *to foliate, to folio*; → Blatt 2. **2.** (Glas) *to foliate, silver* **Foli·ierung** f ~/~en **1.** *foliation* (*of a book*) **2.** *foliation, silvering* (*of glass*) **F·olio** n [L] ~s/–ien & ~s *folio* [pl *folios*] **~ausgabe** f *folio edition* **~band** m *volume* (*in*) *folio* (*five volumes folio*); *folio-volume*; *foolscap volume* **~blatt** n *folio* **~format** n *folio*; (21 × 33 cm) *foolscap* **~seite** f *foolscap page*; e–e halbe ~ *half a page of foolscap*

Foll·ikel m ~s/~ ⟨anat & bot⟩ *follicle* | [in comp] *follicular* → Bläschen ‖ ~sprung [m] ⟨physiol⟩ *ovulation* **follikul·ar, follikul·är** a *follicular*

F·olter f ~/~n **1.** [**konkr**] ⟨hist⟩ (~bank) *rack*; auf der ~ *on the r.*; jdn auf die ~ spannen *to rack a p, to place a p on the rack* **2.** [**abstr**] **a.** (~strafe) *torture*; ~ am Schnell–, Wippgalgen *strappado* [It]; → foltern **b.** (~qual) ⟨fig⟩ *torture*; *torment* ‖ jdn auf die ~ spannen *to put a p on* od *to the rack* (od *to the torture*); *to rack a p*; ⟨fig⟩ *to tantalize a p* ‖ e–e ~ f jdn s *to be a torture to a p* **~bank** f ⟨hist⟩ *rack* **~gerät**, **~instrument** n *instrument of torture*; *torture instrument* **~kammer** f *torture-chamber* **~knecht** m *torturer, tormentor* **~qual** f *torture*; ⟨fig⟩ *torment, excruciating anguish*; ~en [pl] ⟨sl⟩ *skinners* pl; in ~en *on the rack* **~verhör** n ⟨Am⟩ *third degree* ⟨a. hum⟩ **F·olterer** m *torturer*; *tormentor* **f·oltern** [h] **1.** ⟨hist⟩ *to rack* od *torture*; am Schnellgalgen ~ *to strappado* (*a p*) **2.** ⟨fig⟩ (quälen) *to excruciate, lacerate, rack, torment, torture* (*a p*) ‖ *to put a p on the rack* ‖ jdn mit Fragen ~ *to torment a p with questions*

Fom·ent n ~s/~e ⟨med⟩ *fomentation*; *poultice*

Fön® m ~s/~e ⟨Ger⟩ *hairdryer*

Fond [fɔ̃] m [Fr] ~s/~s **1.** (Grundlage) *foundation*; *groundwork* ‖ er hat e–n guten ~ *he is a good man at heart*; *he is well-grounded* (in .. *in Greek*) | ⟨cul⟩ (Extrakt) *foundation*; (*soup, veal, fish*)*-stock* **2.** *back* (*of a car*) ‖ = Hintergrund

Fond·ant [fɔ̃'dɑ̃] m, [österr] n ~s/~s [Fr] *fondant* [Fr]; *sweetmeat*

F·onds [fɔ̃] m [Fr] ~/~ **1.** (Geld≃) *fund* (f *for*); *stock of money*; Reserve ≃ *reserve fund*; → Tilgungs≃; Unterstützungs≃ ‖ geheime ~ [pl] *secret funds* pl | öffentliche, konsolidierte ~ [pl] *the funds*; *government securities* pl; er hat .. in öffentl. ~ angelegt *he has .. in the funds* **2.** ⟨übtr⟩ (Vorrat) *fund of common sense*; *stock* **~börse** f *Stock Exchange*; → Börse(n–)

Fond·ue [fɔ̃'dy] f [Fr] ~/~s ⟨cul⟩ *fondue*

Fontaineble·au [fɔ̃tɛn'blo:] n ⟨Fr⟩ (Stadt)

Font·äne [fɔ̃–] f [Fr] ~/~n *fountain*

Fontan·elle f [Fr] ~/~n ⟨anat⟩ *fontanel*(*le*)

f·oppen I. vt/i [h] **1.** vt jdn ~ *to banter* (od *chaff, hoax, play up, quiz, rally, tease*) *a p*; ⟨fam⟩ *to pull a p's leg*; ⟨Am⟩ *to needle* **2.** vi *to banter* **II.** ≃ n *bantering, chaffing, teasing* **Fopper·ei** f *banter, chaff, quiz, raillery*

Foraminif·eren pl ⟨bot⟩ *Foraminifera* L pl

F·orce ['fɔ̃rsə] f [Fr] ~/~n **1.** = Kraft; Nachdruck **2.** °jds ~ *a p's forte* (od *strong point*); das ist s–e ~, darin zeigt er gr ~ *that is his strong point* **3.** ⟨cards⟩ *winning card* **forc·ieren** [h] **1.** (etw) *to force* → erzwingen; forciert *forced* (*laugh*) **2.** *to overdo, strain*, → übertreiben | –rt ⟨oft⟩ *over* .. (*oversimplification*)

F·ordauto n (nach H. Ford; †1947) *Ford*; *Ford car*; billiges ~ ⟨Am sl⟩ *flivver*, (*tin-*)*lizzie*

F·örde f ~/~n *fiord, fjord*; *firth, frith* ‖ die Kieler ~ *Kiel Fjord*

F·örder- [in ⟨tech⟩ comp] *conveying*; *hauling*; *winding* **~anlage** f *c. plant* **~apparat** m *c. equipment* **~band** n *c.-belt, conveyer-belt*; *band-conveyor* **~druck** m ⟨mot⟩ *feed pressure* **~gurt** m = –band **~karren** m *truck, troll*(*e*)*y* **~kette** f *chain-conveyor* **~kohle** f *pit-coal*; *run-of-mine coal*; ungereinigte ~ *triping* **~korb** m (*hoisting*) *cage*; *tub* **~kosten** pl *haulage* **~kraft** f *h.-power* **~leistung** f *delivery output* **~leitung** f *feed pipe* **~mann** m ⟨min⟩ *hurrier* **~maschine** f *whim*; *drawing* od *w.-engine* (od *machine*) **~pumpe** f *lifting* od *feed pump* **~quantum** n *output* **~rinne** f *chute* **~schacht** f *shaft*; *working-pit* **~schnecke** f *worm-conveyor* **~seil** n *h.* od *w.-rope* **~strecke** f *h.-road* | je **~tonne** [f] ⟨min⟩ *per ton gotten* **~wagen** m *tram*; *mine car*; (Erz) im ~ fahren *to tram* **~werk** n *pit-head plant*

F·orderer m ~s/~ *claimant*; ⟨fenc⟩ *challenger*

F·örderer m ~s/~ *promoter, supporter*; *patron* (*of science*); *advocate* (*of a cause*) **F·örderin** f *patroness*; *supporter* **f·örderlich** a [mst pred] *beneficial, helpful, useful*; *wholesome*; jdm ~ s *to be beneficial* (od *serviceable, useful*) *to a p* ‖ (e–r S) ~ s *to be beneficial* (od *conducive*); e–m Zwecke ~ s *to subserve* (od *to be subservient to*) *a purpose* ‖ *to make for* (*honesty*) → fördern

f·ordern vt [h] **A.** (**etw** ~) **1.** (**P**) **a.** *to demand, require* (*a th*) ‖ *to postulate* (*for*) (*a th*) ‖ etw als Recht ~ *to claim a th* | (Geld, Preis etc) *to ask* (f *for*), *to charge*; wieviel h Sie z ~? *how much is owing to you*? ‖ e–n z hohen Preis v jdm ~ *to overcharge a p*; er forderte 10 Mark v mir ⟨sl⟩ *he soaked me 10 marks* ‖ behördlich ~ → anfordern **b. v jdm etw** ~ *to demand a th of* (od *from*) *a p, to require a th of a p*; alles, was v e–m K. ge–rt wird, ist .. *all that is required of an artist is* .. ‖ man forderte e–n Eid v ihm *they required an oath of him* ‖ *to exact* (*obedience*) (v *from a p*) ‖ Rechenschaft ~ v jdm *to call a p to account* **c.** ~, **daß** .. *to ask* (od *claim, demand, require that* (.. *should*) ‖ man forderte, daß ich erschiene *they required me* (od *of me*) *to appear, they r. that I should appear*; *they required my appearance* ‖ **v jdm** ~, **daß** .. *to ask of a p that* .., *to demand of* (od *from*) *a p that* .. ‖ v jdm ~ z erscheinen *to require of a p to appear* ‖ ~ unterrichtet z w *to demand to be informed* **2.** (**S**) *to demand, exact, require*; *the emergency requires it*; das fordert die nationale Ehre *that is a precept of national honour*; das f. die Vernunft *that is dictated by reason* ‖ der Sturm forderte 9 Todesopfer *the hurricane took toll of 9 lives* **B.** (**jdn** ~) **1.** ⟨**jur**⟩ jdn vor Gericht ~ *to cite* od *summon a p* **2.** (herausfordern) jdn ~ *to call a p out*; *to challenge a p* (auf Pistolen *to a duel with pistols*) ‖ jdn ~ l *to send a p a challenge* **C.** [**abs**] *to make demands* ‖ ~ Sie! *make it a bargain*! *how much do you charge for it*?

f·ördern vt [h] **A. 1.** (Plan etc) *to* (*help to*) *advance*; *to forward, further*; *to help .. on*; *to promote, support* ‖ (Vorgang) *to assist*; *benefit, to be beneficial* od *conducive to* (*health*); *to improve*; die Verdauung ~ *to aid* (*the*) *digestion*; etw sehr ~ *to be a great aid to a th* ‖ (Funktion, Zweck) *to subserve* ‖ (Handel, Wachstum e–r S etc) *to* *encourage, foster; develop* ‖ → beschleunigen **2.** **(jdn)** ∼ *to assist; to help .. on, to back; support; patronize* | **(etw)** *to promote, support, sponsor; cultivate* (*art, friendship, science*); *patronize*; (Fortschritt) *to develop* ‖ *to refine, perfect* ‖ = förderlich sein **B.** (z Tage ∼) **1.** ⟨min⟩ (Erz) *to mine, raise, work; to bring* (od *draw*) *up to the surface, to bring above ground*; (Kohle) *to haul* **2.** ⟨fig⟩ z Tage ∼ *to bring to light*; (Dokumente) *to unearth; to dig out*; ⟨Am⟩ (Tatsache) *to develop* ‖ z Tage gefördert w *to come to light; to transpire,* ⟨Am⟩ *to develop* **F·ördernis** n –nisses/–nisse *furtherance; help* **f·ördersam** a = förderlich ‖ ⟨poet⟩ = emsig **F·ördertum** n ∼s/ *patronage*

F·orderung f ∼/∼en **1. a.** *demand* (nach *for*; daß *that*); ∼en stellen *to make demands* (an .. *on a p*); → An–, Aufforderung ‖ Schuld≗ *claim* (f *for*) ‖ *requisition*; → Requisition **b.** (Anspruch) *demand* (an .. *on a p*) **c.** ⟨log⟩ *postulate* ‖ (Gebot) *dictate* (*of reason*) **d.** ⟨com⟩ *charge*, → Bedingung, Preis ‖ ungesetzmäßige ∼ *exaction* ‖ ∼en [pl] *unrealized claims* pl, *outstanding debts*; ⟨bal⟩ *debitors* ‖ beitreibbare ∼en *recoverable debts*; uneinbringliche ∼en *claims abandoned* ‖ ⟨jur⟩ gemeinrechtliche ∼en [pl] *legal choses* pl *in action* ‖ e–e ∼ anmelden *to lodge a claim*; wer ∼en z stellen hat, wende sich an .. *claimants should apply to ..* **2.** ⟨fenc⟩ *challenge* (*of a p*); jdm e–e ∼ senden *to send a p a ch.; to challenge a p* ‖ ⟨jur⟩ → Ladung, Vorladung **∼sabtretung** f ⟨jur⟩ *assignment of choses in action* **∼sberechtigter** m *obligee* **∼sklage** f *action for money-judgment* **∼-pfändung** f *garnishment* **∼srecht** n *chose in action* **∼sübergang** m ⟨jur⟩ *transfer of choses in action*; → –abtretung

F·örderung f ∼/∼en **1. a.** *advancement, forwarding, furtherance, promotion* (*of a plan*) ‖ *facilitation* ‖ *aid* (f *to*; in *in*), *assistance; subservience* (f *to*); *support* (*of a cause*); *benefit*, zur ∼ v *for the benefit of* ‖ *encouragement* (*of learning*), *fostering* **b.** *aid, assistance, enc.* (*of a p*); jdm ∼ angedeihen l *to give enc. to a p; to aid a p; to help a p on* ‖ ∼ erfahren *to be aided* od *assisted* **2.** ⟨min⟩ **a.** *haulage, hauling, hoisting* (*of coal*); *mining, winning, drawing; raising* (*of ore*) **b.** *output* = Förderquantum ‖ die ∼ steigern *to increase the output* **∼sgebiet** n *development area*

For·elle f ∼/∼n ⟨ich⟩ *trout*; 5 ∼n *5 trout* ‖ Bach≗, Stein≗ *brook* od *river t.*; Lachs≗, Meer≗ *grey* od *salmon t.*; Regenbogen≗ *rainbow t.*; See≗ *great lake t.*; Zucht≗ *t. bred on t.-farm*; → *trout* **For·ellen-** [in comp] *trout–* **∼-bach** m *t.-brook* **∼barsch** m ⟨ich⟩ *t.-perch*; ⟨Am⟩ *black bass* **∼fang** m *t.-fishing* **∼fischer** m *t.-fisher* **∼fliege** f; künstliche ∼ *t.-fly* **∼stein** m ⟨minr⟩ *troctolite; t.-stone* **∼zucht** f *t.-rearing* **∼züchter** m *t.-breeder*

For·ense m ∼n/∼n *non-resident* ‖ *n.-r. owner of property* (etc.) *in a community* **for·ensisch** a **1.** ⟨jur⟩ *forensic*; → gerichtlich **2.** *n.-r.*

F·orke f ∼/∼n *fork, pitchfork*; → Mistgabel

f·orkeln vt [h] ⟨hunt⟩ (of deer) *to pierce with antlers*

F·orleule f ⟨ent⟩ *pine-bud moth; pine-beauty*

F·orle f ∼/∼n [obd] *pine*

Form f ∼/∼en **I.** **[abstr]** (Gestalt[ung]) **A.** *form* **1.** (als Ausdruck **natürl.** Wachstums) **a.** *form* (*of the face, hand, leg, etc*); Körper≗en [pl] *forms* pl ‖ körperliche ∼ *bodily* (od *material*) *form*; in körperl. ∼ erscheinen (of a spirit) *to materialize* **b.** *form* (*of the leaves, trees; clouds*) **c.** *form* (*of a word*); '*politic*' bildet die Adverbial≗ '*politicly*': *politic makes the adverbial form politicly* ‖ modifizierte ∼ *modification* **2.** **(Gesetzmäßigkeit** in Natur u Kultur) **a.** ⟨**log**⟩ ∼en [pl] des Denkens *forms* [pl] *of reasoning* ‖ Stoff und ∼ *matter and form* ‖ modale ∼ *mode* **b.** ⟨**math**⟩ (→ Funktion) *quantic* **c.** ⟨**gram**⟩ *form; voice*; Tätigkeits∼ *active voice*, Leide≗ *passive v.* ‖ → Modus **d.** ⟨**scient**⟩ Pflanzen≗en [pl] *forms of vegetable life*; Tier∼en *f. of animal l.* ‖ Misch≗ *mixed form* ‖ ⟨biol⟩ abweichende ∼ *aberration* **e.** ⟨**pol, etc**⟩ Regierungs≗ *form of government* | soziale ∼en *forms of social life*; feste ∼ *established* (od *set*) *form* ‖ alte ∼en *ancient forms, old moulds* pl; verträgliche Form des Zus–lebens *modus vivendi* L | gesellschaftliche ∼ *convention; recognized form; manners* pl ‖ gute ∼en *good form; manners* pl; k–e guten ∼en *no manners*; ohne ∼en *without manners* ‖ herkömmliche ∼ *conventionality* ‖ e–e bloße ∼, leere ∼ *a mere form* ‖ nur der ∼ wegen, nur um die ∼ z wahren *for form's sake, as a matter of form; pro forma* L ‖ in aller ∼ *in due form* ‖ sehr auf ∼en halten *to attach great importance to forms, to be a formalist*; .. auf feine ∼en .. *to be a stickler for etiquette* ‖ die ∼ wahren *to comply with form* | ⟨**arts** & **Lit**⟩ (innere, äußere) *pattern* ‖ *form* (*of a drama, a piece of art*) ‖ Farbe u ∼ *colour and form*; Sinn f ∼ *sense of form*; nach Inhalt u ∼ *both in matter and manner* ‖ Gehalt u ∼ *content and form* ‖ Inhalt u ∼ *subject-matter and form* ‖ in bezug auf die ∼ *formally* **3.** ⟨**übtr**⟩ (auf Gegenstände u S jeder Art) → **B. 1. (äußere** ∼) (*outward*) *form* od *shape* (*the tables have the same shape*); *appearance* ‖ in (der) ∼ e–r Kugel *in the form* (od *shape*) *of a globe*; in der ∼ v Tropfen *in the form of drops* ‖ in der ∼ v 5 Mark *in the shape of 5 marks* ‖ in k–r ∼ *not .. in any shape or form* ‖ → Umriß **2.** (die e–m Gegenstand, e–r S **gegebene** ∼) *cast, form, shape*; besondere ∼ *turn* ‖ geprägte ∼ *mould; moulding* ‖ *cut, fashion, make, style* (*of a dress*) **3. a.** die ∼ **annehmen** wie .. *to take form like* (*a pyramid*) ⟨fig⟩ die Dinge nehmen ∼ an *things are shaping up*; endgültige (feste) ∼ annehmen *to set* ‖ runde ∼ annehmen *to round*; die ∼ e–r S annehmen *to take the form of a th* ‖ (feste) ∼ annehmen *to take* (*definite*) *shape* ‖ (etw) in (s–e) endgültige ∼ bringen *to finalize* ‖ e–r S (feste) ∼ geben *to model a th; to put a th into shape; to formalize a th; to give form to a th* (*to a hope*) ‖ (Gedanken) konkrete ∼ geben *to crystallize; embody; incarnate; to make concrete* ‖ (e–m Stein) e–e runde ∼ geben *to round* **b. aus** der ∼ k (of hat, etc) *to get out of shape* ‖ Hose ganz aus der ∼ bringen *to upset the set of trousers* ‖ **in** feste ∼ bringen = ∼ geben → a. ‖ in gebührender ∼ *in due form* ‖ (Absage) in höfliche ∼ kleiden *to couch in polite terms* ‖ ein Mensch mit rauher ∼ *a rough diamond*; ⟨Am⟩ *a man with a bark on* **C.** ⟨**sport** & **übtr**⟩ (Leistungsfähigkeit) *form; fettle* ‖ in ∼ *in form* (f *for*); *in good fettle* od *fig; up to concert-pitch*; nicht in ∼ *out of form; off form; to be below par* ‖ in gr, blendender ∼ *in great form, in fine fettle*; ⟨fam⟩ *in top-notch condition*, ⟨Am sl⟩ *in the groove*; ⟨fam⟩ er ist noch immer mächtig in ∼ *he is still going strong* ‖ an ∼ verlieren *to lose one's form; to strike a bad patch* ‖ in ∼ bleiben *to keep fit* (od *in form*) ‖ jdn wieder in ∼ bringen *to wind a p up*; wieder in ∼ k. *to become wound up; to round into form*; in ∼ bleiben *to keep fit* **II.** **[konkr]** (geformter Gegenstand) ⟨tech⟩ **1. (Modell)** *cast; form; model, pattern, shape* ‖ Hohl≗ *mould, shape*; (Black≗, Kuchen≗) *mould, tin* ‖ ⟨found⟩ *die*; Guß≗ (*casting*) *mould*; in ∼ gießen *to cast, mould*; Guß in verlorener ∼ *lost wax process* | Hut≗ *block; hat shape*; der Hut ist aus der ∼ *the hat is out of shape*; → formen ‖ Schuh≗ → Leisten **2.** ⟨**met**⟩ Wind≗ *tuyère* (Fr) **3.** ⟨typ⟩ *forme, form*; innere (äußere) ∼ *inner* (*outer*) *f.*; geschlossene ∼ *locked-up f.* ‖ Druck≗ *print* **∼änderung** f ⟨phys⟩ *deformation*, ⟨gram⟩ *d.* (*of a word*) **∼art** f *mode of form* **≗bildend** a *formative* (*energy*); ⟨gram⟩ ∼es Element *formative; form-*

ative element **~blatt** n *form; blank;* ein ~ ausfüllen *to fill in* (od *complete*) *a f.*; → Formular **~blech** n *section(al) plate* **~brett** n ⟨tech⟩ *moulding-board* **~draht** m *section(al) wire* **~drehbank** f *shaping lathe* **~eisen** n *section(al) iron* **~erde** f *moulding* (od *modelling*)*-clay* **~fehler** m [konkr] *defect of f.* ‖ [abstr] *informality* ‖ ⟨jur⟩ *error, flaw*; Revisionsbefehl wegen ~s *writ of error* ‖ ⟨off⟩ *lack of statutory f.* **~fräsmaschine** f *form--cutter; profile milling machine* **≈gebend** n *formative; plastic (force)* **~gebung** f *fashioning, forming, modelling, moulding, shaping*; ⟨tech⟩ (*industrial*) *design*; ansprechende ~ *attractive d.*; Rat f ~ *Design Council* **~gefühl** n [f konkr] *design sense*; [f abstr] *sense of order* **~genauigkeit** f ⟨tech⟩ *geometrical precision* **≈gerecht** a *in due form*; ~e Abfassung (v Meldungen) *prescribed rules of format*; → Form I. B. 3. b. **≈getreu** a *true to shape* **≈gewandt** a *finished; polished, urbane (style)* **~gießer** m *moulder* **~kasten** m ⟨tech⟩ *moulding-box* | ~füllsand [m] *body sand* **~mangel** m *defect of form* **~maschine** f *moulding--machine* **~rahmen** m ⟨typ⟩ *chase* **~sache** f *formality; matter of form; merely formal affair*; e–e reine ~ *a mere matter of form* **~sand** m *moulding-sand* **~schneidemaschine** f *shaper* **≈schön** a *attrative (design); distinctively designed; superbly styled* **~schönheit** f *beauty of form* **~stein** m *moulded* (od *shaped*) *brick* **~stück** n (f Rohr) *pipe fitting* **≈veränderlich** a ⟨biol⟩ *metabolous* **~verletzung** f *breach of form* **~verstand** m ⟨mus⟩ *formal understanding* **≈vollendet** n *finished; rounded* **~wechsel** m *change of form* ‖ ⟨com⟩ *accommodation-bill* **≈widrig** a *informal* **~widrigkeit** f *informality* **~wille** m ⟨arts⟩ *will to form; insistence on form* **~wort** n ⟨gram⟩ *form--word*

form·al 1. a *formal (distinction, logic, reasoning)*; ~e Bildung *formal education* 2. [adv] *formally*; inhaltlich wie ~ *with respect to both subject-matter and form* **≈recht** n *adjective law*

F·ormaldehyd m ~s/ ⟨chem⟩ *formaldehyde*

Form·alien [-iən] [pl] *formalities* pl

Formal·in n ⟨chem⟩ *formalin, formol*

formalis·ieren vt [h] *to formalize* **Formal·ismus** m *formalism* **formal·istisch** a *formalistic* **Formali·tät** f -·/-·en *formality*; e–e bloße ~ *a mere f.* ‖ ~en [pl] *formalities* pl; belanglose ~en *formal nothings*; ohne ~en *free and easy* **Formans** n ~/–ntien (sprachl. Bildungselement) *formant*

Form·at n ~s/~e 1. a. *shape, size*; v gr, mittlerem ~ *large-sized, medium-sized*; Zigarre v kl ~ *small-sized cigar* b. (Buch≈) *format* Fr ⟨a. tech⟩; *size* ‖ Zeichnung in kl ~ *thumb-nail*; Skizze in kl ~ *thumb-nail sketch* c. ⟨print⟩ (Stege) *furniture* d. ⟨phot⟩ *size*; ⟨Ger mst⟩ 6×9, 9×12, 15×21 cm; ⟨engl⟩ 4¼×3¼ in. *quarter plate*; 6¼×8½ *in. whole plate* 2. ⟨fig⟩ geistiges ~ *mental* (od *intellectual*) *range* (od *capacity, reach; stature*); ein Mann v ~ *a man of wide mental range* (od *of great ability*); Männer v kleinerem ~ *lesser men* **~festigkeit** f ⟨phys⟩ *dimensional stability*

Formati·on [ts] f ~/~en ⟨mil⟩ *formation*; in geschlossener (geöffneter) ~ *in closed (open) f.*; Gefechts≈ *battle f.*; Marsch≈ *marching f.*; ~ in Linie (neben–e–a) ⟨mil⟩ *line f.*; in ~ fliegen *to formate* | ⟨geol⟩ *formation*; ~skunde [f] *stratigraphy* **f·ormbar** a *plastic, workable (clay)* ‖ *impressionable, pliable (mind)* | **≈keit** f *plasticity* ‖ *pliability* **F·ormel** f ~/~n 1. *formula* [L] [pl *–las, –lae*]; Zauber≈ *charm* ‖ Gebets≈ *form of prayer* ‖ Glaubens≈ *formula (of faith)*; Tauf≈ *baptismal f.* ‖ nach e–r gemeinsamen ~ suchen *to seek a f.*; in e–e ~ fassen, in e–r ~ ausdrücken *to f.rize, f.te* 2. ⟨math & chem⟩ *f.* ‖ auf e–e (einfache) ~ bringen *to express in a brief f.*; *to f.te* **~buch** n ⟨ec⟩ *f.ry* °**~kram** *formulism; formalism* **~sammlung** f ⟨math & chem⟩ *collection of formulas* ‖ → –buch **~wesen** n *system of f.s*; = Formelkram **form·ell** 1. a *formal (permission, visit)*; *stiff (bow)* ‖ *nominal* ‖ (P) *formal, precise, punctilious, prim* 2. adv *in a formal manner; ceremoniously; punctiliously, stiffly*

f·ormen I. vt [h] 1. ⟨eig⟩ a. (etw) *to fashion, form, shape* (aus *out of*; z *into*) ‖ (Teig) z Brot ~ *to mould; to shape into loaves* ‖ (Butter, Ton, Wachs etc) *to mould* (z *into*) ‖ (etw aus Ton etc) *to model, mould* ‖ fein geformte Glieder *delicately modelled limbs* | (profilieren) *to profile* b. (Hut) *to (put on the) block* ‖ (Stein) *to cut, dress; to chisel* (z *into*); (Statue) *to cast* ‖ (in pottery) drehend ~ *to throw* c. (Metall) durch Guß ~ *to found*; (Eisen) *to mould* d. gut geformter Ausdruck *well-turned phrase* 2. ⟨übtr⟩ a. (Gedanken) *to frame; to (put into) shape* ‖ nach dem Muster v .. geformt *patterned along the lines of ..* ‖ (Einrichtung) *to form; to model, mould* (nach *on*) b. sein Leben ~ *to model one's life* (nach *according to; on*) ‖ (jdn, jds Charakter) *to mould* (nach *on*) ‖ (Theorie etc) *to construct* c. **sich ~** *to shape o.s.* ‖ sich ~ nach *to mould o.s. on (a p)* ‖ sich gut ~ 1 *to be shaping well* II. ≈ n 1. *fashioning, forming, shaping* ‖ *moulding, modelling* ‖ Werkzeug z ~ *former* 2. *forming, framing, shaping (of a thought)*, → Formung

F·ormen- (→ Form) **~ausgleich** m ⟨phil⟩ *levelling of forms* **~bildung** f *formation*, → Formung **~lehre** f ⟨scient⟩ *morphology*; ⟨gram⟩ *accidence* **~mensch** m *formalist; stickler for etiquette* **~reichtum** m *abundance* od *variety of forms; wealth of form* **~schließer** m ⟨print⟩ *imposer; stonehand* **~sinn** m *sense of form* **~sprache** f; der Bau zeigt e–e kultivierte ~ *the building expresses a cultivated feeling for design* **~welt** f *world* od *sphere of forms; forms* pl **~wesen** n *formalism, formulism*; → Formelkram

f·ormend n *formative, plastic (force of nature)*

F·ormer m *former* ‖ ⟨tech⟩ *moulder*; (in pottery) *thrower*; → Gießer, Modellierer **Former·ei** f ⟨tech⟩ *founding, moulding* ‖ (Ort) *moulding-shop; foundry* **form·ieren** vt [h] 1. ⟨tech⟩ (Akkumulator, Platten) *to form* ‖ ⟨typ⟩ → umbrechen 2. ⟨mil⟩ (Regiment, Schlachtlinie) *to form*; (Truppen) in e–r Linie ~ *to line up* | **sich ~** *to fall into line, to fall in*; sich in e–r Linie ~ *to form (up) into line* **Form·ierung** f ⟨mil⟩ *falling into line; formation*; → Formation **-förmig** [in comp] *–shaped; –like*; flügel~ *wing-shaped, wing-like* ‖ *–form*, keil~ *cuneiform* **f·örmlich** I. a 1. *formal; ceremonial; ceremonious (unveiling); stiff (reception)* 2. (P) *formal, pedantic; precise, punctilious* 3. °(verblaßt) ein ~er Feiertag *a literal holiday*; e–e ~e Wüste m aus *to make a literal desert of ..*; ein ~er Auflauf *a regular row*; ein ~er Kugelregen *a veritable hail of bullets*; ~er Unsinn *arrant* od *sheer nonsense* ‖ *absolute, downright, outright (swindler), thorough (blackguard)* ‖ → buchstäblich II. adv 1. *formally; ceremoniously (opened)* 2. °(verblaßt) *literally*; ich verhungere ~ *I am literally starving* ‖ *absolutely, downright*; man könnte ~ verzweifeln *you might almost despair*; → sich überschlagen | **≈keit** f ~/~en *formal* od *conventional act; formality; conventionality* ‖ *ceremony* (ohne ~ *without c.*); *ceremoniousness* ‖ der Rede die ~ nehmen ⟨bes Am fam⟩ *to shake the starch out of the prose* **F·ormling** m ~s/~e *molded article; casting, etc* **f·ormlos** I. a 1. *amorphous; formless, shapeless* ‖ *amorphous (mass), ill-designed, unorganized* 2. *informal, unconventional* ‖ *crude, rude, unpolished (manners, style)* II. [adv] *informally; without formality* od *ceremony* | **≈igkeit** f *amorphism; formlessness, shapelessness* ‖ *informality, unconventionality* ‖ *crudity, crudeness; rudeness (of manners)* **Form·ol** n = Formalin **Formul·ar** n ~s/~e (~ z Ausfüllen) *form*, (⟨Am⟩ *printed*) blank ‖ ⟨comp, etc⟩ record form ‖ ein ∼ ausfüllen to fill in a form ‖ Einkommensteuer∸ income tax form; schedule ‖ Versorgung mit ∼en stationery supplies **∼brief** m form letter **∼führungseinheit** f ⟨comp⟩ form guide assembly **∼kopf** m form heading | ∼halter [m] ⟨comp⟩ f. h. holder **∼-schrank** m storage cabinet **formul·ieren** vt [h] (Vorschlag) to formulate; formularize; (Grundsatz) to enunciate, state, word, say (that is well said); neu ∼ to restate, rephrase ‖ etw so ∼ to put a th that way ‖ (Entschließung) to table **Formul·ierung** f ∼/∼en formulation; enunciation, statement; wording ⟨a. gram⟩; turn (of a phrase); (Text∸) framing; neue ∼ restatement **F·ormung** f fashioning; forming, formation, shaping ‖ modelling; moulding ‖ conformation (of a country); figuration (of mysticism); ∼ der Persönlichkeit personality development

Form·osa n (chines. Insel) → T·aiwan

°**forsch 1.** a plucky; energetic, forceful, keen; strong, vigorous ‖ dashing (girl, rider); ⟨Am sl⟩ peppy; ∼er Kerl go-ahead, pushing, spirited fellow; → schneidig; flott **2.** [adv] energetically; dashingly ‖ ∼ auftreten to go it strong °**F·orsche, Forschheit** f dash, energy; go; ⟨sl⟩ hot stuff; ⟨Am sl⟩ pep, peppiness

F·orsch- ∼begierde f, **∼lust** f ardour (od zeal) for research (od learning) **∸begierig** a keen on research od learning **f·örscheln** vi [h] Sw to enquire carefully ‖ → aushorchen, forschen **f·orschen I.** vi [h] **1.** to en–, inquire; ∼ nach etw to inquire (od seek) a th; to inquire (od look, search, seek) for a th; nach den Ursachen ∼ to seek the causes (of a th); eifrig ∼ nach to search out (the truth) ‖ in alten Dokumenten ∼ to examine (od scrutinize) old documents **2.** wissenschaftlich ∼ to research; to carry on research, to do research work **II.** ∸ n **1.** search (nach .. for truth) **2.** (wissenschaftlich) research **f·orschend 1.** [a] inquiring (look), scrutinizing, searching (gaze), studious (glance); ∼er Blick a scrutiny; s–n ∼en Augen entging nichts his probing eyes missed nothing **2.** [adv] inquiringly, scrutinizingly; jdn ∼ ansehen to look intently od inquiringly at a p; to scrutinize od scan a p, to look a p up and down **F·orscher** m ∼s/∼ inquirer, searcher; seeker (nach .. after truth) ‖ mst (wissenschaftlicher ∼) research worker; researcher; learned man; man of science; scholar, student; Rechts∸ student of law ‖ Afrika∸ African explorer ‖ Sh.-∼ Shakespearian student ‖ Chemiker als ∼ research chemist **∼blick** m scholar's eye, scholarly insight (od imagination, intuition, mind); ein Mann mit gr ∼ a man of great penetration **∼geist** m, **∼sinn** m scholarliness; = Forscherblick **∼trieb** m scholarly ardour **F·orscherin** f ∼/∼nen = Forscher **F·orschung** f ∼/∼en (wissenschaftliche) research, investigation; [oft pl] ∼en researches [pl]; ∼en m to make researches ‖ Grundlagenforschung fundamental research ‖ → Erforschung **F·orschungs-** [in comp] research– **∼anstalt** f = –institut **∼arbeit** f r. work, exploration work **∼bemühungen** f pl r. effort **∼gebiet** n field of r.; ∼e [pl] sections of r. **∼gemeinschaft** f: Deutsche ∼ German Society for the Encouragement of Scientific R. **∼institut** n institute for the promotion of scientific and industrial r.; ∼ f Atomenergie Atomic Energy Establishment **∼reise** f voyage of discovery; exploring expedition; e–e ∼ m to go on an exploring e. (nach to) **∼reisende** [der ∼, ein ∼r] m ∼n/∼n explorer **∼satellit** m research satellite **∼stätte** f r. institution **∼trieb** m zeal for r. work **∼weg** m method **∼zwecke** m pl r. work purposes

Forst m ∼es/∼e forest; forest-land, land under forest ‖ ⟨engl⟩ königl. ∼ (royal) forest; ⟨jur⟩ park ‖ Tier∸ deer forest **F·orst-** [in comp] forest(ry) **∼akademie** f school of f.ry **∼akademiker** m (Ggs ⟨tech⟩) student of f.ry **∼amt** n f.(ry) office **∼assessor** m post-graduate of f.ry **∼-aufseher** m keeper of a f.; königl. ∼ ranger **∼-bann** m ⟨hist⟩ royal f.; royal hunting preserve; ⟨jur⟩ park **∼beamte** [der ∼, ein ∼r] m ∼n/∼n f.ry-official; → Förster † **∼beflissene** [der ∼, ein ∼r] m **∼eleve** m = –akademiker **∼fach** n f.ry (he studies f.ry) **∼frevel** m offence against (od under) the f.-laws **∼frevler** m breaker of the f.-laws; trespasser **∼gerechtigkeit** f f.-rights [pl] **∼gesetze** n pl f.-laws, F.ry Acts [pl] **∼haus** n f.er's house (od lodge) **∼mann** m f.er **∼meister** m ⟨m. m.⟩ chief ranger; (head forester) **∼politik** f policy of afforestation **∼recht** n f.-law **∼referendar** m bachelor of f.ry **∼regel** n = –bann **∼revier** n f. district; hunting preserve **∼schädlinge** m pl ⟨zoo & bot⟩ f.-pests [pl] **∼schutz** m protection of f.s | ∼beamter [m] f.-guard **∼verwaltung** f administration of f.s; f.-administration **∼wart** m = Förster f.-warden **∼wesen** n f.ry **∼wirt** m f.-economist **∼wirtschaft** f f.ry; afforestation of land **∸wirtschaftlich** a f.ry (products) **∼wissenschaft** f science of f.ry; Professor der ∼ Professor of F.ry **∸wissenschaftlich** a; ∼er Kursus [m] course in f.ry; ∼es Institut [n] F.ry Institute **F·örster** m ∼s/∼ forester; forest-officer (od official, keeper) ‖ königl. ∼ ranger ‖ Amt e–s ∼s forestership; rangership **Förster·ei** f ∼/∼en forester's district; forester's office ‖ f.'s house (od lodge)

Fors·ythie [–tsiə] f ⟨bot⟩ forsythia (L)

Fort [fo:ə] n ∼s/∼s [Fr] ⟨fort⟩ fort; Panzer∸ armoured fort; Sperr∸ barrier fort ‖ ∼gürtel [m] zone of defence

fort adv **1.** (weg) **a.** away (v .. from home); ∼ v off (the grass, road); nur ∼ v hier! let's go out of this! → fort– A. 1. **b.** [bei Modalverben: ∼ können, etc] ich kann nicht ∼ I cannot go (od get) away ‖ ich muß ∼ I must get along, I must be gone (od off); das muß ∼! that must go!; wir müssen ∼ v hier we must get away from here ‖ Sie wollen doch nicht ∼? you are not going? ‖ du brauchst noch nicht ∼ you need not go yet ‖ das Komma muß ∼ the comma will have to go ‖ sie wollten ihn ∼ h they wanted to get rid of him **c.** ∼! begone! clear out! ⟨sl⟩ hook it! ⟨Am sl⟩ get; schnell ∼! get quick! ‖ ∼ mit dir! marsch ∼! (get) away (od off) with you!, be off!, off you go! ‖ mach dich ∼! be gone!, get you gone! ‖ °∼ mit Schaden! away with it! ‖ ∼ mit dem Feigling! let him go for a coward! **d.** er ist ∼ (= nicht mehr da) he is (od has) gone ‖ er ist ∼ (nicht zu Hause, verreist) he is away; wie lange warst du ∼? how long were you away? ‖ m–e Uhr ist ∼ my watch is gone (od lost); ihr Mut war ∼ their spunk was gone; ∼ ist ∼ over is over, gone is gone **2.** (weiter) (of time) [bei Verben] on; er arbeitete, spielte (etc) ∼ (or weiter ∼) he worked, played on; he went on working, playing; → fort– A. 2. ‖ in einem ∼, ∼ u ∼, immer ∼ continuously, uninterruptedly, without interruption, without stopping (it snowed w. st.) ‖ u so ∼ and so on, and so forth, etcetera [L]

fort- pref (→ weg–; weiter–) **A.** [lebendes, betontes, trennbares pref bei Verben u deren Ableitungen, mst in festen Verbindungen] **1.** (weg) **a.** away, off; ∼gehen to go away, to be off **b.** out; ∼lassen to leave out **c.** jdm etw ∼nehmen to take a th from a p **d.** [oft nicht bes ausgedrückt] ∼gehen to go **2.** (weiter) on; ∼fahren to go on; ∼setzen to carry on ‖ *along, forward **B.** [betontes or unbetontes, untrennbares pref] → ∼an, ∼hin

f·ortan, fort·an adv from this time, forward (⟨Am⟩ forwards); henceforth, henceforward

f·ort- ∼|arbeiten vi = fort arbeiten, → fort 2. **∼|befördern** vt [h] (weg–) (etw) to put away; to remove ‖ jdn eiligst ∼ to hurry a p away **∼|bege-**

ben vrefl [→ geben] [h] (weg–) sich ~ *to depart; to go away* ≈**bestand** m *continuance* ‖ ~ des Tüchtigsten ⟨biol⟩ *survival of the fittest* ~|**bestehen 1.** vi (→ stehen) [h] *to continue, persist; subsist; to be in existence*; → fortdauern ‖ (etw) immer ~ l *to perpetuate* **2.** ≈ n *continuance, persistence (–cy)* ~|**bewegen** vt [h] (etw) *to move; to move on* ‖ sich ~ *to move; to move away* (aus *from*) ‖ sich nicht ~ *not to budge* (od *move*) ‖ sich seitwärts ~ *to sidle* ‖ (sich) ~d *locomotive* ≈**bewegung** f *locomotion*; → Art B. 2.; Pseudopodie ~|**bilden** vt [h] *jdn ~ *to perfect a p's education* ‖ (etw) *to develop, to improve*; → fördern ‖ [mst refl] **sich** ~ *to perfect o.s.* (in *in*); sich künstlerisch ~ *to work at one's art*; → ausbilden ≈**bildung** f *perfecting* ‖ *development; improvement*; berufliche ~ *continuation training*; ~ nach Abschluß der Studienzeit ⟨engl⟩ *postgraduate education*; → Förderung | ~skurse [m] [pl] *refresher courses* (f .. *for teachers*) ‖ ~sschule [f] *continuation-school*; ⟨m. m.⟩ *comprehensive school* ~|**bleiben 1.** vi [→ bleiben] [s] (weg–) *to stay* (od *stop*) *away* ‖ v der Schule ~ *to play truant* ‖ bleiben Sie mir nur fort mit .. *don't bother me with* (*these questions*) **2.** ≈ n *staying away* ‖ (v der Schule) *truancy* ~|**bringen** [→ bringen] vt [h] (weg–) (etw) *to carry away; to convey, to remove; to take away*; bring die Briefe fort nach .. *take the letters to ..* ≈**dauer** f *continuance* (*of fine weather*); *permanence (–cy)*; stete ~ *perpetuance, perpetuation, perpetuity* ‖ → Fortleben ~|**dauern 1.** vi [h] *to continue to exist* (od *last*); *to endure, persist, subsist*; (of impressions) *to linger on* **2.** ≈ n *persistence* ~**dauernd 1.** a *continuous; endless, incessant; lasting; permanent* **2.** adv *continuously; permanently* ‖ ~ schlechte Führung *habitual misconduct* ~|**denken** vt [h] = wegdenken ~|**eilen** vi [s] (weg–) *to hasten* (od *run, scurry*) *away* (od *off*); *to dash* od *make off; to bolt* ~|**entwickeln** vrefl sich ~ *to develop* (z *into*) ~|**erben** vrefl [h] sich ~ *to transmit; to be handed down* (od *passed on*) *by inheritance*; sich ~ auf *to descend* (od *transmit*) *to* (*a p*) ~|**fahren** vi/t **A.** vi [s] **1.** (weg–) *to drive away; to go away* (od *to depart*) *in one's car*; ⟨sl⟩ *to push off* **2.** ⟨übtr⟩ (im Reden etc ~) **a.** *to continue, to go on* (od *ahead*); *to proceed; let's continue where we left off* (.. aufhörten); fahr fort! *go ahead* od *on!*; ~d sagte er *proceeding he said* ‖ eilig ~ *to rush on*; stürmisch ~ *to plunge* (*and then he plunged, 'that's why ..'*) ‖ um –zu– *well, to resume* | unablässig (z reden) ~ *to run on* **b.** ~ in (*or* mit) etw *to continue in a th, to continue a th; to go on* (od *proceed*) *with a th* ‖ beharrlich ~ in *to persist in, to persevere with* (*a th*) ‖ nicht ~ mit etw *to discontinue a th* **c.** ~ z tun *to continue doing* (od *to do*); *to go on doing* (*she went on crying*); *to keep doing* (*he kept asking us*), *to keep on doing*; (beharrlich) *to persist in doing*; nicht ~ z tun *to discontinue doing* **B.** vt [h] (wegfahren) (etw) *to cart away; to convey in a vehicle* ≈**fall** m = Wegfall ~|**fallen** vi = wegfallen ~|**fegen** = wegfegen ~|**fliegen** vi [s] *to fly away* (od *off*); *to take wing* ~|**führen** vt [h] **1.** ⟨übtr⟩ (fortsetzen) **a.** (Linie) *to extend, produce* (v .. bis *from .. to*); *to prolong* **b.** (Erörterung, Geschäft) *to carry on* ‖ (Erzählung) *to continue*, bis auf die Gegenwart ~ *to carry down to the present time*; (Arbeit) *to resume*; wird ~geführt *to be continued* ‖ (e–e Politik) *to pursue; to proceed with* **2.** (weg–) jdn ~ *to walk a p off*; = abführen ≈**führung** f *carrying on; continuation; pursuance* (z ~ e–r Aufgabe *in pursuance of a task*); *resumption* ≈**gang** m **1.** (Ausscheiden) der ~ des Herrn N. *the exit of Mr. N. from the house* (etc.); den ~ jds empfinden → empfinden I. 2. **2.** ⟨übtr⟩ *progress; progression* (*of an action*); s–n ~ nehmen *to be progressing; to proceed; to develop* ‖ guter ~ (*good*) *success*; e–n guten ~ nehmen *to succeed, to be successful* ‖ *continuance, continuation*; → Fortführung ~|**gehen** vi [s] **1.** (weg–) *to go* (*he did not see her go*); *to get along* (*you had better g. along*); *to leave; to take one's departure; to trot along*; ⟨fam⟩ *to toddle*; ⟨Am sl⟩ *to biff off* ‖ unauffällig ~ ⟨fam⟩ *to fade* **2.** ⟨übtr⟩ (weiter–) *to continue; to endure; to go on* (*this cannot go on*); die Zahlungen w ~ *the payments will be continued* ‖ gut *or* glücklich ~ *to* (*make*) *progress; to succeed; to be successful* ~**geschritten** a *advanced* (*ideas, studies*): am meisten in der Zivilisation ~ *most civilized* od *cultivated* (*nations*) ‖ ≈e [pl] *advanced students* pl; Englisch f ≈e *advanced English* ≈**geschrittenen-** *advanced* (*training, trainer, course*) ~**gesetzt** a & adv = fortdauernd ~|**gießen** vt [h] (weg–) (etw) *to pour away* °~|**graulen** vt [h] (weg–) jdn ~ *to worry a p* (aus .. *out of the room*) ~|**heben** vrefl [h] ⟨bib⟩ hebe dich fort *be gone* ~|**helfen** vi [h] (weg–) jdm ~ *to help a p to get away* (od *to escape*) | sich [dat] kümmerlich ~ *to scrape through*; → fristen ~**hin** adv = fortan ~|**jagen** vt/i (weg–) **1.** vt [h] (Fliegen etc) *to drive* od *whisk away* ‖ jdn ~ *to send a p off; to turn away* (od *adrift, out*); *to send a p packing; to give a p the sack, to sack a p*; ⟨Am sl⟩ *to can* ‖ v der Schule ~ → ausschließen **2.** vi [s] *to gallop away* ‖ *to dash off*, → –eilen ~|**kommen I.** vi [s] **1.** (weg–) *to get away* (*we are so busy that I cannot g. a.*); *to get off* (mit .. *by the 5 o'clock train*) ‖ der Beamte wird bald ~ *the official will soon get another appointment* ‖ m Sie, daß Sie ~ *get out; clear off* (od *out*); *leave me alone; I'll see you further first* ‖ m–e Uhr ist mir –ge– *I lost my watch; my w. got lost*; → wegkommen **2.** (weiter–) *to get ahead* (od *along, forward, on*); *to proceed*; ~ mit *to get on with* (*one's work*); ~ in der Welt *to get on in the world* ‖ gut ~ *to do well; to be getting on; to be successful*; (of plants) → gedeihen **II.** ≈ n **1.** *get-away* **2.** ⟨übtr⟩ *living, livelihood*; → Auskommen ‖ kein ~ finden *not to get along* (od *on*) **3.** (z. B. berufliches) *advancement, progress* ~|**lassen** vt [h] (weg–) **1.** jdn ~ *to let a p go, to allow a p to go*; nicht ~ *to detain*; (er wollte fort) aber sie wollten ihn nicht ~ (..) *but they wouldn't let him* **2.** etw ~ *to leave a th out; to omit a th* (aus, v *from*); laß das fort! ⟨Am sl⟩ *give it a miss* ≈**lassung** f *omission* ~|**laufen** vi [s] **1.** (weg–) *to run away*; heimlich ~ *to abscond, to escape* ‖ jdm ~ *to run away from a p* ‖ vor jdm ~ *to run away from a p*; vor sich selbst ~ *to run away from o.s.* **2.** ⟨übtr⟩ (weiter–) die Zahlungen w ~ *the payments will be continued* ‖ (of roads, etc.) *to continue; to extend*; längs der Küste ~ *to extend* (od *run*) *along the coast* ~**laufend 1.** a ⟨übtr⟩ *continuous, running* (*accompaniment*) ‖ *serial* (*pictures*); ~e Nummern *serial numbers*; e–e Erzählung in ~en Nummern *a serial story* **2.** adv (*carried on*) *continuously; without a break* ‖ *in series*; ~ erscheinen *to be published serially* ‖ ~ numerieren *to number serially*; ~ numeriert *consecutively numbered* ~|**leben 1.** vi [h] ⟨übtr⟩ *to live on; to survive* (in *in*) ‖ (of ideas) noch ~ *to linger* **2.** ≈ n *survival* (*of the soul*) ~|**legen** vt [h] (weg–) (etw) *to lay* (od *put*) *aside*; (sorgsam) *to tidy away* ~|**leiten** vt [h] (weiter–) (Wärme etc) *to conduct, to transmit* ‖ °~|**machen** vi **1.** (weg–) *to make off; to depart, to go* (od *get*) *away, to leave* ‖ sich (schleunigst) ~ *to clear out* od *off; to cut and run; to take o.s. off* **2.** ⟨übtr⟩ (weiter–) *to go on; to proceed*; wenn Sie so ~ (dann ..) *if you go on like that* (*you will go far*) **3.** vrfl °**sich** ~ *to get out; to be off*; → 1.; –packen ≈**nahme** f = Wegnahme ~|**nehmen** vt = wegnehmen ~|**packen** vt [h] (weg–) (etw) *to stow away* ‖ °sich ~ *to be gone*; pack dich fort! *get out! be gone!* ~|**pflanzen** vt [h] ⟨übtr⟩ **1.** (Gattung etc) *to* *propagate*; → vererben ‖ ⟨phys⟩ (Wellen) *to propagate*; *transmit*; (Schall, Geruch) *to convey* ‖ (Krankheit etc) *to propagate*, *spread*; → übertragen **2. sich** ~ (of animals, plants) *to propagate o.s.*; *to propagate* ‖ ⟨biol⟩ *to proliferate*, *reproduce* ‖ (of sounds) *to be propagated* od *conveyed*; ⟨phys⟩ (*of light*, *sound*) *to travel* **≗pflanzung** f ⟨scient⟩ ~ der Arten *propagation of species* ‖ ⟨biol⟩ *generation*, *reproduction*; geschlechtliche ~ *sexual reproduction*; *cytogensis*; ungeschlechtliche ~ *monogony* ‖ ⟨phys⟩ *propagation* (*of light*); *transmission* (*of a current*)

F·ortpflanzungs- [in comp] ⟨biol⟩ *reproductive* **≗fähig** a *reproductive* (*bud*, *race*); *procreative* | Alter der **~fähigkeit** f ⟨demog⟩ *reproductive age* **~geschwindigkeit** f *velocity of transmission* **≗-natürliches Paar** ⟨demog⟩ *non-planners* **~organ** n *reproductive* (od *generative*) *organ* **~trieb** m *propagative* (od *procreative*) *instinct* **~verhalten** n *reproductive behavio(u)r* **~zelle** f ⟨biol⟩ *reproductive cell*; geschlechtliche ~ *gamete*

f·ort- ~|raffen vt = wegraffen **~|räumen** vt = wegräumen **F·ortreise** f *departure* **~|reisen** vi *to depart*; *to go away*; *to leave* **~|reißen** vt [h] (weg–) **1.** (etw) *to rip* (v *from*) ‖ (of waves) (Steg) *to sweep away* ‖ (jdn) *to tear* (v *from*); jdm etw ~ *to take a th from a p by force* ‖ die Russen wurden im Gemenge mit –gerissen *the Russians were carried along with them* ‖ sich ~ *to tear o.s. away* ‖ –gerissen *rapt* (aus *out of*; gen, in .. *to*, *into heaven*); → dahin–, hinraffen **2.** ⟨fig⟩ jdn mit sich ~ *to carry a p away*, *to carry a p off his feet*; die Zuhörer mit sich ~ *to carry the audience with one*; *to take the audience by storm*; –gerissen w *to be carried away*, *to be enthralled*; → hinreißen ‖ sich ~ l *to let o.s. be carried away* (z tun *to do*[*ing*]) **~|reiten** vi [s] (weg–) *to ride off* (nach *to*) **~|rennen** vi [s] (weg–) *to dash off*; → –laufen **~|rücken** vt [h] (weg–) (Stuhl) *to push away* (v .. *from the table*) **~|rufen** vt [h] (weg–) (jdn) *to call away* **≗satz** m *continuation*, *extension*, *prolongation* ‖ ⟨bot & zoo⟩ *process*; ~ am Fadenwerk e–r Feder *barbicel*; → Zilie **~|schaffen** vt [h] (weg–) (etw) *to carry away*; *to transport* ‖ *to clear* (od *take*) *away*; *to remove*, *to eliminate* (aus *from*) ‖ (beiseite–) *to stow away* **≗schaffung** f *transportation* ‖ *clearing away*; *removal* ‖ *elimination* (aus *from*) °**~|scheren** vrefl [h] (weg–) scher dich fort *clear off* od *out* **~|-scheuchen** vt [h] (weg–) (Vögel) *to scare* (*away* od *off*); → –jagen **~|schicken** vt [h] (weg–) (jdn) *to send off* (um z tun *to do*); *to pack off* (ins Bett *to bed*) ‖ → entlassen; abschicken **~|schlagen** vt [h] (weg–) (Staub) *to flick* (v *from*); *to flick away* **~|schleichen** vi/refl (weg–) **1.** vi [s] = vrefl **2.** sich ~ [h] *to sneak* (aus *out of*); *to sneak off*; *to steal* od *lurk away* (od *off*); *to wriggle off*; = °sich drücken **~|schleifen**, **~|schleppen** vt [h] **1.** (weg–) (etw, jdn) *to drag* (od *lug*) *off*; (Betrunkenen) *to frog's march off* **2.** (weiter–) ~ *to drag along*; sich ~ *to drag o.s. along*; ich konnte mich kaum ~ *I could scarcely drag one foot after the other* ‖ sich mühsam ~ *to slog along* ‖ sich ~ auf .. (of a coach) *to drag along* (*the road*) **~|schließen** vt [h] (weg–) (etw) *to lock away* **~|schlüpfen** vi [s] (weg–) *to scamper* (od *slither*) *away* **~|schnellen** vt [h] (weg–) (Staub) *to flick* (v *from*); *to flick* (od *fillip*) *away* **~|schreiben** vt ⟨com⟩ *to record current statistical changes* **≗-schreibung** f ⟨com⟩ *the recording of current statistical changes* ‖ ⟨demog-stat⟩ *intercensal estimates* **~|schreiten 1.** vi [s] ⟨übtr⟩ (⟨eig⟩ → ausschreiten) (P) *to advance*, *to go forward* (in .. *into a new world*); *to make progress* (in *in*); ~ mit etw *to proceed with a th* ‖ mit der Zeit ~ *to keep up* (od *to keep pace*) *with the times* | (of events, narrative, etc.) *to move*, *proceed*, *progress*; m–e Kenntnisse in .. schreiten stetig fort *my knowledge of .. progresses steadily* ‖ (das Wetter besserte sich), während der Tag –schritt (..) *as the day wore on* ‖ → fortgeschritten **2.** ≗ n *progress* (*of events*); *progression* ‖ *progress*, *expansion* (*of a movement*) **~schreitend 1.** a *onward* (*movement*), *progressional*; *progressive*; *ever*(-)*increasing* **2.** adv *progressively* **≗schritt** m ~es/~e ⟨übtr⟩ (⟨eig⟩ → fortschreiten) **1. a.** *progress* [engl: nur sg-Form; nie mit unbest. Artikel (→ b.)]; *advancement*; *step forward*; ein entschieden weiterer ~ *a definite step further* ‖ der ~ der Menschheit *the progress of mankind*; *human advancement*; der ~ in der Geschichte *progress in history* **b.** [mst pl] ~e *progress*; *advances* [pl] ‖ die ~e (in) der Medizin *the progress in* (od *of*) *medicine*; die ~e der Technik *technical progress* ‖ einige, geringe, keine ~e *some*, *little*, *no progress* ‖ gr ~e, viele ~e *much progress* | ~e m *to make headway* od *progress* (in *in*); *to advance*, *improve* (*in* ..); *to get* od *come on* od *along*; gr ~e m *to make much headway* od *progress*; gute ~e m ⟨arch, tech, etc⟩ *to continue at a good pace*, ⟨Am sl⟩ *to go strong*; er hat in .. gr ~e gemacht *he has made great progress* [sg!] *in* ..; schnelle (gewaltige) ~e m *to make* od *take rapid* (*giant*) *strides*; die Wissenschaft hat Riesen≗e gemacht *science has made enormous strides* **c. ein** ~ *an advance*, *an improvement* (gegenüber *upon*); das Buch ist ein gr ~ gegenüber s–n Vorgängern *the book is a great improvement upon its predecessors* ‖ ein ~, kein Rückschritt *a progressive step*, *not a retrograde step*; *a progression not retrogression* ‖ kein ~ *not an improvement* (*upon* ..) **2.** ⟨pol⟩ *Liberalism* **≗schrittler** m ⟨pol⟩ *Progressist*, *Progressive Liberal* **~schrittlich 1.** a *forward* (*thinking*) *advance*, *go-ahead* (*views*); *progressive* (*mind*) ‖ ⟨pol⟩ *Progressive*; *Liberal*; *Radical* **2.** adv ~ denkend *forward thinking* (*people*); ~ gesinnt s *to entertain progressive views*

F·ortschritts- ~dusel m *craze* od *mania for progressive reform*; *progressive nonsense* od *craze* **~mann** m *progressist*, *progressive* **~partei** f ⟨Ger hist⟩ die Deutsche ~ *the German Liberal Party*; *the Progressive Party* ‖ ⟨engl⟩ *the Radical* (od *Labour*) *Party*; → liberal

f·ort- ~|schütten vt [h] (weg–) *to pour away* **~|schwemmen** vt [h] (of waves) (etw) *to wash away* **~|sehnen** vrefl [h] sich ~ *to wish o.s. away* **~|setzen** vt [h] **1. a.** = fortführen l. ‖ die Bemühungen in e–r Richtung ~ *to go on to do* (*a th*) ‖ *to carry further*; (Arbeit) *to carry on*, *to continue* ‖ etw weiter ~ *to pursue a th* ‖ (Reise) *to pursue*; s–n Weg ~ *to continue on one's course* od *way* **b. sich** ~ (of a road, condition) *to continue* (*this path continues for miles*) **2.** (weg–) *to put away* **≗setzer** m *continuator* **≗setzung** f ~/~en **1.** [abstr] *carrying on*; *continuation* (*of a discussion*); *resumption* ‖ ~ des Pacht– etc –verhältnisses (mit neuem Eigentümer) ⟨jur⟩ *attornment* **2.** [konkr] (Stück ~) *continuation*; ~ folgt *to be continued* ‖ *sequel* (e–r Erzählung, z e–r E. *of* od *to a story*); ~ v (auf) Seite 9 *continued from* (*on*) *page 9* ‖ in ~en *in numbers*; *serialized drama* ⟨telv⟩; (Roman) in ~en veröffentlichen *to serialize* **~|spinnen** vt [h] ⟨übtr⟩ den Faden e–r Erzählung ~ *to resume* (od *pick up*, *take up*) *the thread of a narrative*; *to continue a narrative* **~|sprengen** vi [s] (weg–) *to gallop away*; *to ride off at full speed* **~|spülen** vt [h] (weg–) (of waves) (etw) *to wash away* **~|stehlen** vrefl [h] (weg–) sich ~ *to sneak* (aus *out of*); *steal away* (od *off*); *to sneak off*; → fortschleichen 2. **~|stellen** vt [h] (weg–) *to put away* **~|stoßen** vt [h] (weg–) (jdn) *to push*, (mit dem Fuße) *to kick* (v .. *off the pavement*); *to push away* (od *back*) ‖ ⟨Rugby ftb⟩ (Gegner) mit der Hand ~ *to hand off* **~|stürmen**, **~|stürzen** vi [s] (weg–) *to dash*, *fling*, *rush* (aus *from*, *out of*); *to dash off*, *to rush away* **~|traben**

vi [s] *to jog off* **~|tragen** vt [h] **1.** (weg–) (etw) *to carry away* **2.** (weiter–) jdn im Schwung ~ *to whisk a p* **~|treiben** vt [h] **1.** (weg–) (jdn) *to drive* (v .. *off the grass*); *to drive* (od *whip, whisk*) *away* **2.** (weiter–) wenn du es so –treibst (..) *if you go on like that* (*you won't go far*) ‖ –getrieben w (of sand, etc.) *to drift* **~|treten** vi [s] (weg–) *to stand away*; er trat fort v der Tür *he stood away from the door* ‖ ⟨mil⟩ *to fall out* **~|wagen** vrefl [h] (weg–) sich ~ *to venture away* (v *from*) **~|währen** vi [h] = fortdauern **~|während 1.** a *constant, continuous, incessant, permanent, perpetual, unceasing* **2.** adv *constantly* (etc.); er lachte ~ *he kept* (*on*) *laughing* ‖ ~ wachsend *ever-growing* (*interest*) **~|wälzen** vt [h] (weg–) (etw) *to roll away* **~|wandern** vi [s] (weg–) *to go away*; → auswandern **~|weisen** vt [h] (weg–) (jdn) *to pack* (od *send*) *off* (aus *out of*); → abweisen **~|werfen** vt [h] *to throw* (od *fling*) *away* ‖ ⟨fig⟩ sich ~ *to make o.s. cheap* **~|wirken** vi [h] (of action, condition) *to continue effective*; *to keep its force*; schwach ~ *to linger on* **~|wischen** vt [h] = wegwischen °**~|wursteln** vi [h] *to muddle* (od *carry, jog*) *on*; *to jog along* **~|ziehen I.** vt/i **1.** vt [h] **a.** (weg–) (etw) *to draw back*; *to withdraw* (v *from*); (Hand) *to remove* **b.** (weiter–) *to carry* od *draw along*; jdn mit sich ~ *to draw* (od *pull*) *a p after one*; er zog sie mit sich fort *he carried them along with him*; → fortreißen; ziehen **2.** vi [s] *to move* (nach *to*); (of birds) *to migrate* (nach *to*); → auswandern ‖ ⟨mil⟩ *to march off* ‖ → fortgehen | (umziehen) *to move, remove* (nach *to*) **II.** ≗ n *migration* (*of birds*) ≗**zug** m *removal* (nach .. *to Berlin*); → fortziehen

f·orte adv (It) ⟨mus⟩ *forte* **F·orte** n *forte* ~s/ ⟨mus⟩ *forte* (It)

Fortepiano n ~s/~s ⟨mus hist⟩ *clavichord*

fortissimo adv (It) ⟨mus⟩ *fortissimo* (It)

Fortissimo n (It) ~s/~s & –mi ⟨mus⟩ *fortissimo*

F·orum n ~s/~s **1.** ⟨ant⟩ (öffentl. Platz) *forum* (L) **2.** ⟨übtr pol⟩ (Stelle u öffentl. Diskussion) (*open*) *forum*; *tribunal* ‖ (Diskussion durch Vertreter verschiedener Richtungen) *panel discussion*; *open forum* ‖ das ~ der Öffentlichkeit *the forum* (od *bar*) *of public opinion*; *publicity*; es gehört vor das ~ der Ö. *it ought to be discussed in public*; vor das ~ der Geschichte *at the bar of history*

forz·ando adv (It) ⟨mus⟩ *forzando* (It)

f·orzen vi [h] [md] *to fart*; → furzen

°**F·ose** f ~/~n ⟨vulg⟩ *whore, bitch, tart*

F·oße f ⟨cards⟩ → Fehlfarbe

Foss·il n ~s/~ien [–iən] *fossil*; ~ien [pl] *fossils* pl, *petrifactions* pl **foss·il** a *fossil* ‖ ~ m, ~ w *to fossilize* **foss·ilienhaltig** a *fossiliferous*

föt·al a *foetal, fetal* ≗**sterblichkeit** f ⟨demog, etc⟩ *stillbirth* **F·ötus** m [L] ~/–ten *f(o)etus*

Foto n ~s/~s = Photographie [f] *snapshot, etc* **~kopiergerät** n *copying apparatus*; kombiniertes ~ *two-step unit* → **~mont·age** [ɑ̃:ʒə] f *photo-mounting* **~narr** m *shutter bug* **~report·age** [ɑ̃:ʒə] f *picture story*

°**F·otze** f ⟨vulg⟩ *crack, slit, fanny, cock-alley* | ~nneid [m] ⟨m. m.⟩ *penis envy*

F·ötzel m ~s/~ Sw (Lump) *scoundrel* ‖ (Taugenichts) *good-for-nothing*

Foul·ard [fu'lɑ̃:r] m ~s/~s [Fr] *foulard*

foulen ['faulən] vi [h] ⟨sport⟩ *to foul*

F·owler- [–au–] ~klappe [f] ⟨aero⟩ (Landehilfe) *Fowler flap*

F·owlersche [au] **Lösung** f ⟨chem⟩ (nach Th. Fowler ['faulə], † 1801) *Fowler's solution*

F·oxterrier m ⟨engl zoo⟩ *fox-terrier* **F·oxtrott** m (amer. Tanz) *fox-trot*; ~ tanzen *to fox-trot*

Foy·er [fwa'je:] n Fr ~s/~s *foyer* [Fr]; ⟨fam⟩ *crush-room* ‖ (Künstler≗) *green-room*

Fr·acht f ~/~en **1.** (~beförderung) (*inland*) *carriage*; ⟨Am⟩ *freight*(*age*) ‖ ⟨mar⟩ *freight*(*age*) ‖ per ~ (*sent*) *by* (od *per*) *rail* ‖ ⟨mar⟩ *by cargo-boat*; *by freight* ‖ → Aus≗, Rück≗; Zeit≗ **2.** (~geld) *carriage* (auf etw *on a th*) 20 Mark ~ *20 marks carriage* (*to buyer's account*); unter Nachnahme der ~ *carriage-forward* ‖ ⟨rail⟩ *freight* (*rates*); ⟨mar⟩ (zuzüglich *exclusive of*) *freight*(*age*); ~ bezahlt *or* franko *freight paid* **3.** (~ladung) *goods* [pl] *sent by goods-train*; ⟨Am⟩ *freight*(*age*) ‖ ⟨mar⟩ *cargo, freight, lading, load* (*of a ship*); → Tonne ‖ ~ führen *to carry freight* **~aufschlag** m *extra* (od *additional*) *carriage*; ⟨mar⟩ *extra* od *additional freight* **~brief** m *consignment-note*; ⟨Am⟩ *bill of freight*; *way-bill* ‖ ⟨mar⟩ *bill of lading* ‖ ⟨aero⟩ *air waybill* (*a. w. b.*) **~dampfer** m *freight* (od *cargo*)-*steamer* **~empfänger** m *consignee* **~ermäßigung** f *reduction of freight* **~flugzeug** n *cargo aircraft*; *freighter* ≗**frei** a [pred] *free of* (*carriage*) *charges*; ~ .. (Ort N. N.) *freight* (*carriage*) *paid* (*to* ..); *carriage-free* (od *paid*) ‖ ⟨mar⟩ *freight-free* **~fuhrmann** m *carrier, carter, freighter, wag*(*g*)*oner* **~geld** n = Fracht 2.; → Fuhrlohn, Rollgeld **~gut** n *goods* [pl] *by goods-train*; (*slow*) *goods traffic*; *P. V.* = Fr (*petite vitesse*); ⟨bes Am⟩ *freight*; als ~ *by freight, by goods train, forwarded as ordinary freight*; als ~ behandeln, befördern *to freight* ‖ ⟨mar⟩ *freight, cargo* | ~beförderung [f] *freight movement* **~kosten** pl = –spesen **~lohn** m = Fracht 2. **~makler** m ⟨mar⟩ *freight-agent* **~-nachnahme** f ⟨allg⟩ *cash on delivery* (abbr *C. O. D.*); *carriage-forward* **~raum** m ⟨mar⟩ *tonnage* ‖ ⟨aero⟩ *goods* od *cargo compartment*; *cargo hoist*; *belly* **~satz** m *carriage-rate*; *freight-rate* **~schein** m = –brief **~schiff** n *cargo-ship, freighter*; ~ f lose Ladungen *bulk carrier*; ~ in Linienschifffahrt *cargo liner*; → –dampfer **~spesen** pl *freight--charges* pl (v .. *amounting to* ..); ⟨rail⟩ *railage*; *railway carriage* **~vertrag** m ⟨mar⟩ *freighting--contract*; (f ganzes Schiff) *charter-party* **~wagen** m *freighter, freight-wag*(*g*)*on* **~zuschlag** m = –aufschlag

fr·achten vt [h] → befrachten; verfrachten

Fr·achter m → Frachtschiff; Be–, Verfrachter ‖ ⟨aero⟩ *cargo plane*

Fr·ack m ~s/≗e *dress-coat, swallow-tail*(*ed*) *coat*, ⟨fam⟩ *swallow-tails* [pl] ‖ ⟨sl⟩ *full waiters* ‖ im ~, in ~ u weißer Binde *in evening-dress*; ⟨fam⟩ *in tails* (*and white tie*) ‖ ~ ist (nicht) vorgeschrieben *evening-dress* (*not*) *obligatory*; ~ oder Smoking? ⟨fam⟩ *black or white*? ~ u weiße Binde *white tie* **~anzug** m = Frack **~hemd** n *dress* (od *evening*)-*shirt*; ~ mit weichem Einsatz *soft--pleated dress-shirt* **~schoß** m *flap* (od *tail*) *of a dress-coat* **~streife** f (der Polizei) *Pansy Patrol*

Fr·age f ~/~n **1. a.** (Ggs Antwort) *question*; *interrogation* **b.** (~satz) ⟨bes gram⟩ *q.*; *interrogative sentence*; indirekte ~ *oblique q.*; rhetorische ~ *rhetorical q.*! **c.** ⟨jur⟩ Suggestiv≗ *leading q.*; Vor≗ *previous q.* ‖ Scherz≗ *conundrum* ‖ unangenehme, unklare ~ *query* ‖ verfängliche ~ *draw* ‖ **2.** (z erörternde *or* z untersuchende S) **a.** (*point in*) *question*; ⟨Am a.⟩ *issue* ‖ die deutsche ~ *the q. of Germany* ‖ e–e prinzipielle ~ *an issue of principle* ‖ e–e ~ der Zeit *a matter* (od *q.*) *of time* ‖ Tages≗n [pl] *q.s of the day*; die soziale (etc) ~ *the social q.* od *problem* ‖ die Alkohol≗ *the Alcohol q.*, die Orient≗ *the Eastern q.* ‖ der ganze ~nkomplex *the whole complex of q.s* od *issues* **b.** einzelne ~ *point*; e–e interessante ~ *a point of interest*; Gewissens≗ *point of conscience* ‖ die ~, Haupt≗, Kern≗ *the point* ‖ Streit≗, entscheidende *issue* ‖ die gr Lebens≗n *the great issues vital to our way of life* **c.** e–e offene ~ *an open q.* ‖ schwierige ~ *problem*; *poser*; *tickler*; die sch. ~ *the puzzle* (*of existence*) **3. a. das ist die** (Haupt-)~ *that is the point* ‖ das ist e–e andere ~ *that's another matter*

|| °dumme ~! °so 'ne ~! *what a q.*! ⟨fam⟩ *ask* (*me*) *another*! || das ist noch sehr die ~ (*or* steht noch .. in ~) *that remains to be seen*; *that's not at all certain* || es ist e–e ~, ob .. *it is a q. whether* .. || die ~ ist, ob .. *the point is whether* .. || die schwierige ~ ist, wie .. *the conundrum is how* .. || die ~, warum .. *the q.* (*as to*) *why* .. || das ist k–e ~ *that is beyond* (od *without*) *q.*; es ist k–e ~, daß .. *there is no q. that* od *but* || ⟨parl⟩ die ~ ist nicht berechtigt *or* zutreffend; die ~ ist belanglos *or* gegenstandslos (geworden) *the q. does not arise* || in ihrem Blick lag e–e ~ *she looked a q.* || die ~ schneidet den ganzen Sachverhalt an *the q. raises the whole issue* || es erhebt sich die ~, ob .. *there arises the q. whether* || e–e ~ kann nichts schaden *there is no harm in asking* **b.** e–e ~ **anschneiden**, aufwerfen *to moot* (od *raise*) *a q.*; e–e neue ~ .. *to raise a new issue* || ⟨univ⟩ alle ~n (in schriftl. Prüfung) beantworten *to floor the paper* || jdm e–e ~ beantworten *to answer a p a q.* || → bejahen || e–e ~ klären *to clear up a q.* || e–e ~ stellen *to ask a q.*; ~n richten (*or* stellen) *to address questions* (an *to a p*) || ~n über ~n stellen; *to launch into a series of q.s*; ~n stellen über etw *to ask* (od *inquire*) *about a th* || jdm e–e ~ stellen, an jdn e–e ~ stellen (*or* richten, °tun) *to ask a p a q.*, *to ask a q. of a p*; *to put a p a q.* od *a q. to a p* || → verneinen || die ~ **stellt sich** *the question arises* (ob *whether*) || jdm die ~ vorlegen *to put a p to the q.* (*whether* ..) || sich die ~ vorlegen, wo .. *to ask o.s. where* .. || sich ständig ~n vorlegen *to heckle o.s.* **c. auf** jds ~ antworten *to answer to a p's q.* || e–e Antwort auf e–e ~ geben *to give an answer to a q.* || auf s–e ~ erwiderte sie .. *in reply* (od *answer*) *to his q. she said* .. | **außer** ~ stehen *to be unquestioned*; *to be out of the q.*; das ist außer ~ *that is not in q.*, ⟨sl⟩ *that's out* | jdn **durch** lästige ~n stören *to heckle a p* | **in** ~ k *to come into q.*; *to be involved*: nicht in ~ k: *this does not apply*, .. *is not applicable* || in ~ k.d *probable*; *potential* (*criminal*) || nicht in ~ k. *to be out of the q.* (od *picture*); *not to arise* (.. *where risk of public disorder did not a.*) || in ~ stellen *to call in q.*; *to question*; *to challenge* (*security*); sehr in ~ .., *to jeopardize* || (Echtheit e–s Dokuments, Wahrhaftigkeit e–s Zeugen) in ~ stellen ⟨jur⟩ *to impeach* | **ohne** ~ *beyond* (od *without*) *q.*; *beyond* od *without controversy* || es ist Herr N. ohne ~ *it is Mr. N. all right* | e–e Kontroverse entstand **über** die ~, was .. *a controversy arose as to what was* .. || wir k. **um** die ~ nicht herum *we cannot evade the question*

Fr·age- [in comp] **~bogen** m *question-form*; *questionary*; *questionnaire* [Fr]; ⟨Am⟩ *question-blank*; ⟨fam⟩ *paper* | ~aktion [f] *survey* **~form** f ⟨gram⟩ *interrogative form*; *question* **~fürwort** n ⟨gram⟩ *interrogative*; *interrogative pronoun* **~satz** m ⟨gram⟩ *interrogative sentence*; *question* **~spiel** n *question-and-answer game*; ⟨fig⟩ *back-chat* **~steller** m *interrogator*, *questioner*, *querist*; ⟨pol⟩ lästiger, störender ~ *heckler* **~stellung** f *questioning*; richtige ~ *useful way of questioning* (od *of putting a question*); *constructive method of proceeding* **~stunde** f ⟨parl⟩ *question period* od *time* **~- und Antwortspiel** ⟨wir⟩ *quiz* **~wort** n ⟨gram⟩ *interrogative particle* **~zeichen** n *note* (od *mark*, *point*) *of interrogation*; *question-mark* (od *stop*) || (~ hinter e–m Wort, zum Zeichen des Zweifels) *query*; ein Wort mit e–m ~ versehen *to query a word* **fr·ägeln** vi/t [h] Sw *to inquire carefully* od *cunningly* **fr·agen I. vi/t** [h] [3. sg prs fragt (frägt) / 1. 3. sg pret fragte (frug) / pp gefragt] **A. vi 1.** *to ask*, *inquire*; *to ask questions* (od *a question*) || wenn ich ~ darf *if I may ask*; frag mich nicht soviel *don't ask so many q.s*; ~ Sie nochmal *ask again* || ohne lange z ~ *unquestioningly* || ohne auch nur z ~ *without asking leave* || da fragst du noch? *how can you question that*?; ⟨prov⟩ wer viel fragt, geht viel irre *if you ask me no questions*, *perhaps I'll tell you no lies*; .. kriegt viel Antwort *many questions*, *many answers* **2. a.** ~ **nach** etw *to ask* (od *inquire*) *for a th* || nach dem Wege ~ *to ask* od *inquire one's way*; nach jds Alter, Namen ~ *to ask a p's age*, *name*; *to ask about* (*a p's profession*) || nach den Ursachen ~ *to inquire into* (od *to seek*) *the causes* || ich fragte nicht danach *I did not inquire* || ~ nach jdm *to ask* (od *inquire*) *for a p*; *to inquire after a patient*; hat jd nach mir gefragt? *has anyone asked for me*? || sie ~ nicht danach, ob *they do not care whether* | **um** Rat ~ *to seek advice* **b.** forschend *or* gebieterisch ~ *to demand* (nach etw *a th*) **c.** nicht ~ nach etw *not to care about a th*; wer fragt danach? *who cares*? °ich frage den Henker (Kuckuck, Teufel) (viel) danach *I don't care a damn* (od *pin*, *rap*, *straw*) **B. vt 1.** **jdn** ~ **a.** *to ask a p* (**nach** *for*; über *about*; um *for*); jdn nach etw ~ *to ask a p* (*for*) *a th*; jdn nach s–m Namen ~ *to ask a p his name*; er fragte mich nach m–m Schneider *he asked me who my t. was*; jdn nach dem Wege ~ *to ask a p the way* || jdn **um** Erlaubnis ~ *to ask a p's permission* (od *a p for permission*); jdn um Rat ~ *to seek a p's advice*, *to consult a p* (⟨a. übtr⟩ ein Buch ..) **b.** Ach, da ~ Sie mich z viel *Ah*, *there you've got me* || jdn die Kreuz u. Quer ~, ⟨fam⟩ jdm ein Loch in'n Bauch ~ *to heckle a p* || → aus–, befragen; so fragt man die Leute aus! ⟨fam⟩ *ask me another*! **c.** ich muß dich etwas ~ *I must ask you something* || dies frage ich dich *this I ask you* || ⟨jur⟩ ich frage Sie, Sie waren also ..? *I put it to you that you were* .. **2. etw** ~ **a.** wie kannst du so etwas ~? *how can you ask a question like that* || immer dasselbe ~ *to keep asking the same question* || ‚Wer ist das'? fragte sie ihn '*Who's that*?' *she asked of him* || da muß man doch ~, warum .. *the question must be asked why* .. **b.** ⟨com⟩ der Artikel ist (sehr) gefragt *the article is in* (*great*) *demand* **3. sich** ~ **a.** *to ask o.s.* (*why* ..) || sich ständig ~ *to heckle o.s.* || sich verwundert ~, warum (etc) *to wonder why* ..; wie kann das s, frage ich mich? *how can that be*, *I wonder*? || ich frage mich auch *I wonder that too* || ich frage mich vergebens, wie .. *I wonder to myself how* .. **b. es fragt sich, ob ..** *it is a question whether* ..; *it is questionable* (od *doubtful*) *whether* || das fragt sich *that is open to question*; *that depends* **II.** ≃ n *asking*; *inquiring*; *questioning* || ≃ kostet nichts *there is no harm in asking* **fr·agend 1.** a *interrogative* (*method*; *pronoun*) || *inquiring* (*look*); → forschend **2.** [adv] *inquiringly at a p* **Fr·agende** [der ~, ein ~r] m **Fr·ager** m *asker*; *inquirer*, *questioner* **fr·aglich** a **1.** [attr] *in question*, *under discussion*; *referred to*; die ~e P *the person in question*; die ~e Periode *the period under discussion* **2.** [pred] *doubtful*, *problematic*(*al*), *questionable*; *open to question*; es ist ~, ob .. *it is questionable whether*; ist es noch ~, wer ..? *is there any question of who* ..? (ob .. *whether* ..); ist sehr ~ *is very problematical* **fr·aglos 1.** [pred a] *indisputable*, *doubtless*, *unquestionable*; *not to be questioned*; *beyond all question* **2.** [adv] *unquestionably*; *decidedly*; *beyond all question*

Fragm·ent n ~s/~e ⟨Lit⟩ *fragment* **fragmen·t·arisch** a *fragmentary*; *incomplete*, *snippy*

fr·agwürdig a *doubtful*, *dubious*, *equivocal* (*success*); *questionable* (*gain*) || *doubtful*, *dubious*, *shady* (*character*); *shady* (*p*)

Frakti·on [ts] f ~/~en **1.** *parliamentary* (*party* od) *group* (*the Liberal p. g. met in caucus* die Liberalen hielten e–e ~ssitzung ab) || ⟨Ger pol⟩ *union* (od *group*) *of politically like-minded members* (*of a representative body*) **2.** ⟨chem⟩ *fraction*; *process of fractionating*, → fraktionieren | **~s- ~anlage** f ⟨chem⟩ *cracking plant* **~disziplin** f *discipline of vote* **~führer** m *leader of a party*, (bei Debatte) *whip*; ⟨Am⟩ *floor leader* **~geist** m *party spirit* **~sitzung** f *group* od *party meeting*; *caucus meeting* **~zwang** m *party-loyalty obligation* **fraktion·ieren** [ts] vt [h] ⟨chem⟩ *to fractionate*; –nierte Destillation [f] *fractional distillation*

Frakt·ur f ~/~en **1.** ⟨surg⟩ *fracture* **2.** ⟨typ, Ger⟩ *fraktur* [Ger]; *the old German type*; *G. script*; ⟨engl⟩ *black-letter*; *Gothic*; *Old English* **~buchstabe** m *Gothic letter* **~schrift** f = Fraktur

Frambös·ie f ~/ ⟨med⟩ *framboesia* L; *yaws* pl

Fr·ame f ⟨archaeol⟩ *framea* [L]

Franc [frɑ̃] m [Fr] ~s/~s → Frank

Franch·ise [frɑ̃'ʃi:zə] f [Fr] ⟨ins⟩ *franchise*

Frangip·an n ~s/~e [–ʒi] *almond-cake*

Frank m ~en/~en (frz. u belg. Münze) *franc* [Fr]; → Franken

frank adv [nur in:] ~ u frei (*quite*) *frankly* od *openly*; um es ~ u frei z sagen *to be* (*quite*) *frank*

Frankat·ur f ~/~en = Freimachung

Fr·anke m, †**Fr·änkin** f **1.** (altdeutsch. Volksstamm) *Frank*, *Frank woman* **2.** (Bezeichnung der Europäer im Orient) *Frank* **3.** ~ m, Fr·ankin f (Bewohner des fränk. Kreises) *Franconian* **4.** ⟨poet⟩ (= Franzose) *Frenchman*

Franken ⟨Ger⟩ **1.** ⟨hist⟩ (Herzogtum) *Franconia* [L] **2.** Ober≗, Mittel≗, Unter≗ *Upper, Middle, Lower Franconia* ‖ ~wald [m] *Frankenwald* [Ger] ‖ ~wein [m] *Franconian wine*

Fr·anken m ~s/~ Schweizer ~ *Swiss franc*

Fr·ankfurt n *Frankfort*; ~ am Main (an der Oder) *Frankfort-on-the-Main* (.. *-Oder*)

Fr·ankfurter **1.** a *Frankfurt* (*merchant*; *sausage*); der ~ Friede *the Peace of Frankfurt* (1871); ~schwarz [n] *Frankfort black* **2.** ~ f *Frankfurt sausage*

Frank·ier- ~maschine f *postage-meter*

frank·ieren **1.** vt = freimachen **2.** ≗ n = Freimachen [n] **frank·iert** a *post-free*; *prepaid* (*letter*); ~er Briefumschlag *stamped envelope* **Frank·ierung** f = Freimachung

fr·änkisch a **1.** (z den Franken gehörig) *Frankish* **2.** (z Franken gehörig) *Franconian*; ≗e Alb [f], ≗er Jura [m] *Franconia Mountains*

fr·anko adv (of letters) *post-free*, *prepaid*; *stamped*; ~ Berlin (of parcels) *post-paid to Berlin* ‖ (of goods) *carriage paid*; ~ Haus *free house*; ~ Berlin *free Berlin, delivered free B.*; → frei **≗stempel** m *stamp*

Frankol·in n ~s/~e ⟨orn⟩ (Feldhuhn in Afrika) *francolin*; *bush-partridge*

frankoph·il a, der ≗e m *francophil*(*e*)

Fr·ankreich *France*; das südliche ~ *Southern F.*; das mittelalterliche ~ *Medieval F.*

Franktir·eur [frɑ̃ti'rœr] m [Fr] ⟨mil⟩ *franc-tireur* [pl *francs-tireurs*]

Fr·äns|chen n *fringelet*; *small fringe* **Fr·anse** f ~/~n *fringe*; *thrum*; *loose thread* ‖ ⟨anat⟩ gezackte ~n [pl] → Fimbrien ‖ mit ~n besetzen *to fringe*, *thrum* **fr·ansen** vrefl [h] sich ~ (of cloth) *to fray*, *frazzle*, *fuzz* **Fr·ansenflügler** m ⟨ent⟩ = Blasenfüßer **fr·ansig** a *fringy* ‖ ⟨bot & zoo⟩ mit ~em, behaartem Saum *fimbriate*(*d*)

Franz n [invar] ⟨school sl⟩ = ~·ösisch

°**Franz** m ⟨aero⟩ (Beobachter) ⟨sl⟩ *shock-absorber*

Fr·anz- ~band m ⟨bookb⟩ *calf-binding*; Buch in ~ gebunden *book bound in calf*, *calf-bound book* ‖ Halb≗ *half-calf binding*; in Halb≗ gebunden *bound in half-calf* **~branntwein** m ⟨med⟩ *pale* (od *commercial*, *industrial*) *brandy*; *alcoholic liniment*; *spiritus vini Gallici* (L) ‖ → Branntwein, Kognak **~brot** n *French roll*

fr·anzen vi [h] ⟨aero sl⟩ *to observe*, *to find one's way*

Fr·anzensbad n (Kurort in Böhmen)

Franzisk·aner m ~s/~ ⟨ec⟩ *Franciscan* **~-kloster** n *Franciscan monastery* **~mönch** m *Franciscan* (od *grey*) *friar*; *Franciscan* **~orden** m *the order of St. Francis*; *the Franciscans* pl

Franz-Joseph-Land n (Inselgruppe im Nördl. Eismeer) *Franz Josef Land*

°**Fr·anzmann** m = Franzose, ⟨engl fam⟩ *frog*

Franz·ose m ~n/~n **1.** *Frenchman*; ⟨hum⟩ *Gaul* ‖ die ~n [pl] *Frenchmen*; *the French* **2.** ⟨tech⟩ (Fahrradschlüssel) *monkey-wrench* **franz·öseln** vi [h] *to imitate French habits*, (etc) **Franz·osen- ~gras** n ⟨bot⟩ *false oat*; → Glatthafer **~holz** n ⟨bot⟩ *guaiacum*; *lignum vitae* (L) **~-krankheit** f ⟨med⟩ = Syphilis ‖ †⟨vet⟩ = Perlsucht **~kraut** n ⟨bot⟩ → Knopf– **französ·ieren** vt [h] *to Frenchify*, *to Gallicize* **Franz·ösin** f ~/~-nen *Frenchwoman* **franz·ösisch** **1.** a *French* ‖ ⟨hum⟩ *Gallic*, *Gaulish* ‖ ⟨ec⟩ *Gallican* ‖ die ≗e Revolution *the French Revolution*; die ~e Sprache *the F. language* ‖ die ~e Kirche [f] *the Gallican Church* ‖ die ~e Literatur, Kunst (etc) *French Literature*, *art* ‖ die ~e Schweiz *the French-speaking part of Switzerland* **2.** ≗, das ≗e *French*; auf ≗ *in F.*; in das ≗e *into F.*; ein Lehrer des ≗en *a French master* **3.** adv sich ~ empfehlen *or* verabschieden *to take French leave*

Franz·ösisch- ⟨teilweise hist⟩ *French* **~-Äquatorialafrika** *Fr. Equatorial A.* **~-Guinea** *Fr. Guinea* **~-Indochina** *Fr. Indo-China* **≗-katholisch** a *Gallican* **~-Somaliland** *Fr. Somaliland* **~-Sudan** *Fr. Sudan* **~-Vorderindien** *Fr. India* **~-Westafrika** *Fr. West Africa*

frapp·ant **1.** a [Fr] *striking* (*likeness*); *remarkable* **2.** adv *strikingly* **frapp·ieren** vt [h] **1.** (jdn) *to strike*; es frappiert mich *it strikes me* (*that* ..) **2.** (Getränk) *to ice*; –rt (*wine*) *frappé* (Fr)

Fr·äse f ~/~n **1.** ⟨met⟩ *milling-cutter* ‖ Bohr≗ *fraise* ‖ ⟨agr⟩ → Boden≗ **2.** → Halskrause

fr·äsen **1.** vt [h] (Holz etc) *to mill* **2.** ≗ n *milling*

Fr·äser **1.** (P) *who works a milling-machine* **2.** (Werkzeug) *milling-cutter*, *–machine*; ~ mit geraden (schraubenförmigen) Schneiden *straight* (*spiral*) *milling-cutter*; Walzen≗ *revolving m.-c.*; Schnitt≗ *edge-trimmer* **Fr·äsmaschine** f ⟨met⟩ *m.-m.*; (f. Holz) *shaper*

°**Fraß** m (*food*:) *tack*; ⟨sl⟩ *grub*, ⟨Am⟩ *slum*; ⟨mar⟩ *slush*; ein erbärmlicher ~ *an abominable food*; ein feiner ~ *a good grub* od *feed*; dort gibt es e–n guten ~ *they do you well there*

fraß [1. & 3. sg pret] v fressen

Fr·ater m [L] ~s/–tres ⟨ec⟩ *brother* (*monk*); ⟨R. C.⟩ *father* **≗nis·ieren** vi [h] ~ mit *to associate* od *fraternize with* (*a p*) **~nit·ät** f ~/~en *fraternity*; *fraternal association* (od *society*)

°**Fr·atz** m ~es/~e (*waggish girl*) kl ~ *little rogue* (*baggage*, *monkey*); hübscher ~ *flyer*; süßer ~! *pretty*! °**Fr·ätzchen** n (→ Fratze 2.) *nice little face* **Fr·atze** f **1.** *grimace*; *wry face* ‖ e–e ~ schneiden *to make a grimace*, *to pull a face*; ~n schneiden *to make grimaces*, *to pull faces*; *to grimace* **2.** °(Gesicht) *face*; e–e ekelhafte ~ *a caricature of a face*, ⟨sl⟩ *an ugly mug* **3.** ⟨fig⟩ (⟨a.⟩ ~nbild [n]) *grotesque figure*; → Zerrbild **~ngesicht** n *mask* **≗nhaft** **1.** a *distorted*, *wry*; *ugly* ‖ ⟨übtr⟩ *bizarre*, *grotesque*; *ludicrous*, *ridiculous* **2.** adv ⟨übtr⟩ *grotesquely* | **~haftigkeit** f ⟨übtr⟩ *grotesqueness* ‖ (etw) zur ~ entstellen *to distort*; *burlesque*, *caricature*, *travesty* **~n-schneider** m *grimacer*

°**Fr·atze** f ~/~n ⟨theat⟩ (Posse) *farce*

Fr·au f ~/~en **A. (Ggs Mann)** **1. a.** *woman*; ⟨sl⟩ *petticoat* ‖ alleinstehende ~ ⟨jur⟩ *feme sole*; (erfolgreich) berufstätige ~ *career woman*; unverheiratete ~ *unmarried woman*, ⟨jur⟩ *feme sole*; verheiratete ~ *married woman*; *matron*, ⟨jur⟩ *feme covert* ‖ ⟨bib, art⟩ die 3 ~en am Grabe (Christi) *the Holy Women at the Tomb* ‖ Mädchenname e–r verheir. ~ *maiden name* ‖ alleinstehende ~ *single woman* ‖ erwachsene ~

woman; Stellung der erw. ~ *womanhood* ‖ die ~en u Mädchen (e–r Familie etc) *the womankind* od *womenfolk* (*of a family*) **b.** (**als Art**) die ~ unterscheidet sich sehr vom Manne *woman differs greatly from man* ‖ die ~ in ihr *the woman in her* ‖ e–e echte ~ *a womanly woman* ‖ die moderne ~ *the woman of today* ‖ Herrschaft der ~ *petticoat government* **c.** ~ vornehmer Geburt *gentlewoman, lady* ‖ Unsere Liebe ~ *Our Lady* **d.** ⟨Ger myth⟩ ~ Holle *Dame Holle* **e.** ⟨cont⟩ *female*; → Weib ‖ e–e ~ mit Vergangenheit *a woman with a past*; e–e ~ v zweifelhaftem Ruf *a demi-rep* | er ist hinter ~en her *he is a lady--killer*, ⟨vulg⟩ .. *after hair* **f.** (**Anrede**) gute ~, liebe ~, ~ Nachbarin *my good woman*; *goody*! **g.** (f ~en bestimmt) ‚~en' [pl] *Ladies* pl, *ladies' cloak-room* **2.** **Ehe≈ a.** *wife*; ⟨jur⟩ *feme covert*; → Gattin, Gemahlin ‖ m–e ~ *my wife*; ⟨engl a.⟩ *Mrs N.*; d–e ~ ⟨vulg⟩ *your good lady* ‖ neuvermählte ~ *bride* **b.** die ~ des Hauses *the mistress of the house*; Herr u ~ *master and mistress* ‖ Haus≈ *housewife* ‖ (Diener:) die ~ ⟨vulg⟩ *the missus* **B.** (**Titel**) **1.** (f verheiratete ~) **a.** ~ N. *Mrs. N., Frau N.*; ~ N., geborene X. *Mrs. N., née X.* ‖ Herr Oberst N. u ~ *Colonel and Mrs. N.* **b.** (~ e–s Pairs) *Lady* (*Lady Mary N.*); (of a *baronet*) *Dame* ‖ (Anrede) ~ Herzogin *Your Grace*; ~ Gräfin *Your Ladyship* ‖ An ~ Gräfin v .. *To the Countess of* .. **c.** **Gnädige** ~ *madam*; ⟨vulg⟩ *missis, missus* ‖ wie geht es Ihrer ~ Gemahlin? *how is Mrs. N.?* ‖ Ihre ~ Mutter, Schwester *your mother, sister* ‖ ~ Dr. N. *Mrs. N.* ‖ die ~ Doktor *the doctor's wife, Mrs. N.* **2.** (f unverheiratete ~) **a.** (Titel f Besitzerin des British Empire Ordens, etc) *Dame*; ~ Marie N. *Dame Mary N.* **b.** (Titel f verdiente ~en) *Mrs.* (*N*) **c.** die ~ Oberin *the matron* **d.** °s–e ~ Braut *his grass-widow* **C.** **Wendungen**: dies war e–e S der ~ *this was a woman's affair* ‖ da steckt e–e ~ dahinter *there's a woman in it* ‖ jdm s–e Tochter zur ~ geben *to give a p one's daughter in marriage* ‖ er hat e–e geborene N. zur ~ *his wife's maiden-name is N.* ‖ e–e ~ nehmen *to take a wife, to get married*; ein Mädchen zur ~ nehmen *to take a woman for one's wife* (od *to wife*), *to marry a woman* ‖ sich mit ~en abgeben (of a married man) *to womanize* ‖ ohne ~en ausgehen ⟨fam⟩ *to go stag* **Fr·auchen** n *little woman*; ⟨fam⟩ *hussy, huzzy* ‖ (to a dog) wo ist ~? *where is your mistress*? | (Anrede f Ehefrau) *dear little wife*; *my dear* **Fr·auen- ~abteil** n ⟨rail⟩ *ladies' compartment* **~amt** n ⟨Ger⟩ *Central Bureau for female labour* **~arbeit** f *women's work*; *female work* **~arzt** m *specialist for women's diseases*; *gynaecologist* **~balsam** m ⟨bot⟩ = Chrysanthemum **~berufe** m pl *occupations of women* **~bewegung** f *woman-movement*; *feminism*; *feminist movement* **~bild** n *lady's portrait* **~bildung** f *female* (od *feminine*) *education* | ~sverein [m] *women's educational association* **~biß** m ⟨bot⟩ = –mantel **~charakter** m *female character* **~college** n ⟨engl⟩ *college for women* **~einfluß** m *petticoat influence* **~eis** n ⟨minr⟩ *selenite*; → Gips **~erziehung** f = **~**bildung **~emanzipation** f *emancipation of women* **~feind** m *woman-hater* **~fisch** m ⟨ich⟩ *whitefish* **~flachs** m ⟨bot⟩ = Leinkraut **~frage** f *woman's rights question*; *questions* pl *concerning the social and political status of women* **~fresser** m = ~hasser **~gemach** n ⟨archaeol⟩ *gynaeceum* **~generation** f *generation of woman* **~geschlecht** n *womankind* **~gestalt** f *female figure*; ⟨dero⟩ in ~ *in petticoats* **~glas** n ⟨minr⟩ = ~eis **~haar** n ⟨bot⟩ *maidenhair* **~haus** n = –gemach; = Bordell **~heim** n *home for women* **~hemd** n *chemise* Fr **~herrschaft** f → ~regiment **~herz** n ⟨bot⟩ *bleeding heart* **~hilfsdienst** m *women's social* (od *welfare*) *work* **~hilfskorps** n ⟨engl⟩ militärisches ~ *Women's Army Auxiliary Corps* (abbr *Waac*) **~kilte** f ⟨bot⟩ = Nachtviole **~kirche** f *Church of Our Lady* **~kleidung** f *women's dress*; ⟨AInd⟩ *sari, saree* ‖ in ~ ⟨dero⟩ *in petticoats* **~kloster** → Nonnenkloster **~krankheiten** f pl *women's diseases*; Lehre v den ~en *gynaecology* **~kraut** n ⟨bot⟩ = ~mantel; Leinkraut **~lehen** n ⟨jur⟩ *mother-string tenure* **~liebe** f *womanly love* **~liebhaber** m *woman-lover* **~mantel** m ⟨bot⟩ *lady's mantle* **~minze** f ⟨bot⟩ *costmary* **~mord** m, **~mörder** m *femicide* **~natur** f *woman-nature* **~putz** m *female finery* **~raub** m *the carrying-away of a woman by force* **~rechte** n pl *women's rights* pl **~rechtler** m *feminist* **~rechtlerin** f *suffragette* **~regiment** n *petticoat--government*; *gynaecocracy* **~rolle** f ⟨theat⟩ *female part* **~schuh** m ⟨bot⟩ *lady's slipper, Venus's slipper, mocassin flower* **~schule** f ⟨Ger⟩ *girls' continuation-school* **~spiegel** m ⟨bot⟩ *Venus's looking-glass* **~sport** m *women's sports* pl **~stift** n *foundation for women* **~stimme** f **1.** *female* od *feminine voice* **2.** ⟨pol⟩ *woman's vote*, [mst pl] ~n *women's votes* pl **~stimmrecht** n ⟨pol⟩ *female* (od *woman, women's*) *suffrage* **~stimmrechtlerin** f *woman-suffragist* **~studium** n *university study of women* **~tag** m ⟨ec⟩ = Marientag **~tracht** f *female dress* **~turnen** n *gymnastics* pl *for women* **~verein** m *ladies association* **~wahlrecht** n = –stimmrecht **~welt** f *womankind*; *women* [pl]; → Damen– **~werk** n ⟨Ger⟩ *German organization for the social and educational concerns of women* °**~zimmer** n ⟨cont⟩ *female*; *woman*; → Weib; ein ~ (P) ⟨vulg⟩ *a bit of skirt* | °~chen [n] ⟨fam⟩ *hussy, huzzy*

Fr·auen- ≈haft a *womanlike, womanly* **~schaft** f ⟨Ger⟩ *Women's Club* °**~sleute** pl ⟨cont⟩ *females* [pl], *women* pl; *womankind, womenfolk* °**~sperson** f ⟨cont⟩ = Frauenzimmer **~tum** n [abstr] *womanhood*; *womanliness*; (in der Ehe) *wifehood* **Fr·äulein** n ~s/~ **1.** (als Titel) **a.** ⟨engl⟩ (f Tochter der Pairs über dem *viscount*) *lady* (*the Lady Mary N.*); Gnädiges ~ *Your Ladyship* **b.** *Miss*; ~ N. *Miss N.*; die ~ Braun [pl] *the Miss Browns* pl ‖ Nein, danke, gnädiges ~ *no thank you, Miss* (*N.*) ‖ Ihr(e) ~ Schwester, Tochter *your sister, daughter*; empfehlen Sie mich bitte Ihrer ~ Tochter *please, remember me to your daughter* od *to Miss* (*N.*) **2.** ***a.** *girl*; *young* (od *unmarried*) *woman* (od *lady*); ⟨fam⟩ *miss*; kl ~ *missy* **b.** (Erzieherin) *governess* ‖ Laden≈ *shop--girl*; Telefon≈ *the telephone-girl*; *operator* | **~chen** n *missy* **fr·aulich** a *womanlike, womanly*; ihre ~e Art *her woman's way* **≈keit** f *wifemanship*

Fr·aunhofersche L·inien f pl (nach J. v. Fraunhofer, † 1826) ⟨phys⟩ *Fraunhofer lines*

frech **1.** a *impudent, pert, saucy*; ⟨Am fam⟩ *sassy* ‖ *brassy*; *brazen*(*-faced*); *impertinent, insolent, rude* ‖ ⟨Am⟩ *cocky*, [pred] *brash, fresh*; ⟨sl⟩ *flossy, gay* (gegenüber .. *with a p*) ‖ ~ wie Dreck *as bold as brass* | ein ~es Bürschchen *a whipper-snapper* ‖ mit ~er Stirn *insolently, with a face of brass* ‖ sei nicht ~ *don't be cheeky*, ⟨Am⟩ *don't get fresh*; ⟨fam⟩ *none of your chat* ‖ °er ist ~ wie Oskar *he is a cool customer*; *he's as bold as brass*; ~ s gegen jdn ⟨fam⟩ *to cheek a p* ‖ ~ aber zugänglich *free of her lips, free of her hips* **2.** adv *impudently* (etc) ‖ ~ auftreten *to brazen it out* ‖ jdn ~ anlügen *to lie in a p's face* °**≈dachs** m *whipper-snapper*; *wiseacre*; *saucy bounder*; *cheeky devil*; (*a*) *fresh one* **≈heit** f ~/~en *impudence, pertness, sauciness* ‖ *brass, effrontery, impertinence, insolence*; *rudeness* ‖ ~en [pl] *impudence*; *impudent remarks* [pl] | °so 'ne ~! *what cheek*! *confound your* (etc) *impudence*! ‖ die ~ h z sagen *to have the cheek to say* ‖ unterlaß d–e ~(en)! *none of your cheek*! ‖ sich jdm gegenüber ~en erlauben *to take liberties with a p*, ⟨Am sl⟩ *to be flossy* od *gay with a p*; erlaub dir k–e ~en! *let me have none of your chat!* **~ling** m ~s/~e = frecher Mensch

Freg·atte f ~/~n ⟨mar hist⟩ *frigate* ‖ ⟨fig⟩ °(Frau) alte ~ *old battleship, old battle-cruiser* **~nkapitän** m ⟨nav⟩ *commander* **Freg·attvogel** m ⟨orn⟩ *frigate* (*–bird* od *–petrel*)

frei a & adv **I. [attr & pred a] A. 1. (mst P** etc) **a.** (nicht in Knechtschaft etc) *free*; auf ~em Fuß *at large* (*he is still at l.*); jdn auf ~en F. setzen *to set a p free*; *to free* od *release a p*; ⟨Am a.⟩ *to enlarge a p* | (ungebunden, ohne Anhang) *unattached* **b.** ⟨**pol**⟩ *free* (*country, people*); *independent* ‖ ein ~er Mann *a f. man,* ⟨jur⟩ *freeman*; ~e Frau *f. woman* ‖ ~e Stadt *free city* ‖ sein ~er Herr s *to be one's own master* ‖ sich ~ schwimmen *to qualify as swimmer* **c.** ~er Ausüber e–r Kunst (etc) *f.-lance*; ~er Beruf *f.-l. profession, liberal profession*; ~er Kunstmaler *f.-l. painter* ‖ die ~en Künste [pl] *the liberal arts* pl **d. (innerlich** ~) *free*; ~er Wille *free will* ‖ aus ~em Willen *of one's own f. will*; °aus ~en Stükken *spontaneously, voluntarily* ‖ ~e Hand h *to have a f. hand*; *to be at liberty* (*to do*); jdm ~e H. l *to give a p a f. hand*; ~e Wahl *liberty* (*to do*); → wahl~ **B.** ⟨**übtr**⟩ **1. a. (unbehindert)** (of actions) *f.* (*gestures*); *easy*; ~ u ungezwungen *f. and easy* (*manners*) ‖ (offen) *open* (*word*); *frank, outspoken* **b. (uneingeschränkt)** *free* (*speech*); *unfettered, unhampered, untrammelled* (*power*) ‖ *free* (*translation*) ‖ ~es Spiel der Kräfte *f. play of one's faculties* ‖ jdm ~en Zutritt z s–m Hause gewähren *to make a p f. of one's house*; ~en Z. h z *to have the freedom* (od *run*) *of* (*a library*) ‖ s–n Gefühlen ~en Lauf l *to give vent to one's feelings, to vent one's f.*; e–r S ~en Spielraum gewähren *to give f. play to a th* ‖ ⟨com, cust⟩ *free*; ~e Verfügung *f. disposal*; ~er Verkehr *f. trade*; *f. movement* (*of goods*); im ~en Verkehr *in the open market* **c.** (unbelastet) [bes in comp, oft pred] gebühren~ *f. of charge*; hypotheken~ *f. and unencumbered*; schulden~ *f.* (od *clear*) *of debt*; zoll~ *f. of duty, duty f.* ‖ sorgen~ *f. from care*; *carefree* ‖ wind~er Tag *day f. from wind* **d.** (⟨**fig**⟩ ungehemmt) *f.* (*views*); *unrestricted*; → willkürlich ‖ ~en Gebrauch m v *to make f. use of* ‖ ~e Übersetzung *f.* (od *loose*) *translation* ‖ ~e Liebe *f. love* **e.** ⟨phys⟩ *f.* (*fall, flow*) ‖ ⟨chem⟩ *free*; *uncombined* (*carbon*); in ~em Zustande *uncombined*; ~ w *to be disengaged* (od *set f.*); ~ werdend *nascent* **2. (ohne Hilfe)** aus ~er Hand (*done*) *by freehand* **3. (unbeschäftigt)** *free* (*I was f. at six*); *disengaged*; Kutscher, sind Sie ~? *driver, are you disengaged?* ‖ ~e Augenblicke *odd moments* ‖ ~e Stunden *leisure* (od *spare, vacant*) *hours* pl ‖ ~er Tag *unoccupied day*; *holiday* (*to-morrow is a h.*); (*my*) *day off*; ~ h *to have a holiday*; heute h wir ~ *this is our day off*; er hat heute ~ (*or* s–n ~en Tag) *today is his day off*; er hat sich e–n ~en T. genommen *he has taken a day off* ‖ ~e Zeit *leisure* (od *off, spare*) *time*; er hat viel ~e Z. *he has a lot of time off* **4. (unentgeltlich)** ~er Eintritt *f. entrance* (od *pass*) ‖ [bes pred] *f.* (f *to*); *gratis, gratuitous* ‖ 100 Mark u ~e Station *100 marks and all found* ‖ 30 Pfd Gepäck ~ h *to be allowed 30 lbs of f. luggage* **5. (unbesetzt) a.** *free* (*seat*); ist dieser Platz ~? *is this seat disengaged?* ‖ *vacant* (*post*); ~e Stelle *vacancy*; die St. ist noch ~ *the post is still open*; ~ w *to fall void* ‖ *unoccupied* (*house,* ⟨mil⟩ *area*), *untenanted* ‖ ⟨telph⟩ (*of line*) *not busy* [pred] ‖ ein Haus ~ m *to vacate a house* ‖ e–n Tag ~ halten *or* l *to keep a day open* (f *for*) **b. (unbeschrieben)** *blank*; (Raum) ~ ‖ l *to leave blank* **6. (~liegend) a.** *open* (*area, field, fire*); ~es Land *clear*; ~e Plätze *open spaces* ‖ ~e Luft *open air*; das ~e Meer *the open sea* ‖ unter ~em Himmel *in the open* (*air*) ‖ das Haus steht ganz ~ *the house is detached* (od *stands alone*) **b.** ⟨**traffic**⟩ *free* (*path, road, way*); ~ f *free for*; *open to* (*talent*); → Bahn 2. ‖ ⟨rail⟩ die Strecke ist ~ *the line is clear* **c.** ⟨**tail**⟩ *open* (*neck*); *bare* (*knee*) **II. [nur pred a] 1.** ~ v *exempt from* (*military service*); ~ v Dienst s *to be off duty,* ⟨Am⟩ *to be off* ‖ *f. from* (*pain*); *free of* (*income-tax*); ~ v Schulden, schulden~ → I. B. 1. c. ‖ *void of* (*fear*); *clear from* (*suspicion*) | (S) *clear of* (*ice, traffic, vessels*); ein Tag ~ v Verabredung ⟨Am⟩ *a dateless day* **2.** ⟨com⟩ **a.** ~ v *f. of* (*charge*) ‖ (fracht~, porto~) *carriage* (*pre*)*paid* od *–free* ‖ → franko ‖ (Lieferung) ~ Bahnhof *f. station, delivered f. at the st.* ‖ ~ Bahnwagen *f. on wag*(*g*)*on* (abbr *f. o. w.*) ‖ ~ Eisenbahn *f. on rail* (abbr *f. o. r.*); ⟨Am⟩ *f. on board* ‖ ~ an Bord ⟨a. Am⟩ *f. on board* (abbr *f. o. b.*); ~ Schiff längsseits *f. alongside ship* (abbr *f. a. s.*) ‖ ~ Berlin *f. Berlin*; ~ Haus *f. house* ‖ ~ durch Ablösung ⟨post Ger hist⟩ *exempt from postage*; ⟨engl⟩ *On Her* (*His*) *Majesty's Service*; ⟨Am⟩ *penalty-envelope* **b.** die Werke Storms sind ~, Storm ist ~ *Storm's works are out of copyright* **3.** ich bin so ~ *I take the liberty* (z tun *of doing*); ⟨fam⟩ *I don't care* (od *mind*) *if I do* ‖ ich bin so ~, Sie z erinnern *permit me to remind you* **4. (of gas,** etc) ~ **w** *to be set free, released* **III. [adv] 1.** *freely*; ~ wachsend *free-growing* ‖ ~ umherlaufen (of dogs, etc) *to be at large* ‖ ~ (im Wasser) s *to be floating* **2.** ⟨übtr⟩ **a.** (unbehindert) *freely*; *easily* **b.** (offen:) (frank u) ~ *frankly, freely, openly*; sprich ~ heraus, °~ v der Leber weg *speak up* (od *quite frankly*) ‖ ~ reden *to come into the open*; ~ mit jdm reden *to be open with a p*; ~ u offen reden über *to be frank and open about* (*a th*) **c.** (ohne Hilfe) er sprach eine Stunde ~ *he spoke without notes for an hour* **d.** (ungehemmt) (*to think*) *freely* ‖ ~ erfunden (*news*) *wholly unfounded in fact* ‖ ~ übersetzen *to translate freely* od *loosely* ‖ ~ verfahren mit *to make free use of* (*a th*); ~ vermittelbar *not rent-controlled*; ~ schalten u walten mit *to be* (od *make*) *free with* (*a th*); ~ umgehen mit etw, etw ~ behandeln *to take liberties with a th* ‖ sich z·u ~ benehmen *to be too free* **e.** ⟨phys & tech⟩ ~ fallend *falling freely*; ~ aufgehängt *freely suspended*; ~ aufliegend *or* gelagert *freely supported*

-frei [lebendes Suffix z Bildung v adj] *non–*: korrosions~ *non-corrosive,* klapper~ *non-chattering* ‖ *–proof*: knitter~ *creaseproof*

Fr·ei- [in comp] **~arche** f *waste-gate* **~bad** n *do* ‖ *open-air* (od *outdoor*) *swimming bath* (od *bathing pool*) **~ballon** m ⟨aero⟩ *free balloon* | ~führer [m] *balloon pilot* **~bank** f (in an abattoir) *cheap-meat department* **~beruflich** a & adv → frei I. A. 1. c. ‖ ~ arbeiten *to work free lanceing* **~betrag** m *tax-free income* **~beuten** vi *to buccaneer, filibuster* **~beuter** m *freebooter*; *buccaneer, filibuster*; bevollmächtigter ~ *captor* **~beuter·ei** f *freebooting* **~beweglich** a ⟨tech⟩ *freely swinging* **~bezirk** m *free zone* **~bier** n es gibt ~ *there are free drinks going* **~billet** n = ~karte **~bleibend 1.** a *free* (*offer*); *non-binding* (*prices*); (*price*) *subject to change without notice* od *engagement* ‖ [mst pred] *without engagement, not binding* **2.** [adv] *without engagement* **~bord** n ⟨mar⟩ *freeboard*; ~marke [f] *load-line mark* **~börse** f *curb market* **~brief** m **1.** ⟨hist⟩ *charter* **2.** ⟨fig⟩ *passport* (f .. *to*) ‖ *patent* (auf .. *for* od *of a th*) ‖ ⟨pol etc⟩ *carte blanche* ‖ *licence,* ⟨Am⟩ *license* ‖ *permit* ‖ *patent* ‖ *privilege* **Fr·eiburg** n ⟨Ger⟩ (Stadt im Breisgau) *Freiburg*; (Stadt in der Französischen Schweiz) *Fribourg* **~bürgschaft** f ⟨hist jur⟩ *frankpledge* **~deck** n ⟨mar⟩ *open-air deck* **~denker** m *freethinker*; *agnostic* **~denkerisch** a *freethinking* **~ding** n ⟨hist⟩ = Femgericht **~exemplar** n *complimentary copy* ‖ *author's copy* ‖ (f Buchhändler) *off c.* ‖ (Besprechungs~)

press od *review c.* **~fahrschein** m ⟨rail, etc⟩ *free--pass* **~fall** m ⟨phys⟩ *free fall* | ~bahn [f] *f.-f. trajectory*; ~schirm m *drop-type parachute* **~fang** m ⟨ftb⟩ *fair catch* **~frau** f, **~fräulein** n *baroness* **~-gabe** f *release*; *emancipation* (*of a slave*); → –lassung ‖ *decontrol* (*of goods*) ‖ *release* (*of a literary work*); (aus Konkursmasse) *disclaimer*; (e–r Vermögenssperre etc) *un–*, *deblocking*; (der Kaution) *release* ‖ ⟨jur⟩ *release*; ~ v Beschlagnahmtem *derequisition* ‖ ⟨aero⟩ *clearance* | ~-bescheid [m] ⟨film⟩ *no-equivalent* (*projection permit*) ‖ ~signal [n] *clear signal* ~|**geben** vt [h] **1.** (jdn) = –lassen **2.** (Ware, Bewirtschaftung) *to decontrol* ‖ (Werk zum Druck, z Aufführung) *to release* ‖ (Vermögen) *to release*; (gesperrtes) *to deblock* ‖ (Beschlagnahmtes) *to derequisition* ‖ (Waren) f den Export ~; (Nachrichten) ~ *to release* ‖ (Flugzeug) f den Anflug ~ ⟨aero⟩ *to clear for approach* ‖ → zurückgeben ‖ [abs] ⟨school⟩ *to give a holiday*; ⟨com⟩ *to give time off* ‖ *to release* (*news*); (nach Zensur) *to pass* ‖ (Straße) *to open* (*to*) ~**gebig** a → d. ~-**geboren** a *free-born* **~gefecht** n *free play*; ⟨fam⟩ *loose play* ~**gegeben** pp (nicht geheim) *unclassified* **~gehege** n (f Tiere im Zoo) *open-air enclosure* **~geist** m = –denker ~**geistig** a *free-thinking*, *latitudinarian* **~gelassene** [der ~, ein ~r] m *freedman* **~geld** n → –wirtschaft **~gepäck** n *free allowance of luggage* (⟨Am⟩ *baggage*) **~-gericht** n = Femgericht ~**gesinnt** a *liberal* **~-grafschaft** f ⟨hist⟩ *countship* (*of Burgundy*) **~-grenze** f *limit of tax-free income* **~gut** n ⟨hist⟩ *allodium* (L), *freehold* ‖ ⟨cust⟩ *free goods* pl **~-hafen** m *free-port*; ~gebiet *free-zone* ~|**halten** vt [h] **1.** (Straße) *to keep clear* (v .. *of civil traffic*) **2.** ⟨übtr⟩ (Angebot) *to keep open* ‖ (etw) *to reserve* ‖ (jdn) *to entertain*; *to treat* (mit .. *to a th*); er hielt uns frei *he stood treat*; alle ~ ⟨Am sl⟩ *to stand Sam*; jdn zu etw ~ ⟨Am fam⟩ *to blow a p to a th* **~handaufnahme** f ⟨phot⟩ *hand-held view*; *view* (*etc*) *with h.-h. camera* **~handel** m *Free Trade*; Anhänger des ~s *Free Trader* | ~s-lehre [f] (*doctrine of*) *Free Trade*; *Cobdenism* ‖ ~spolitik [f] *Free Trade*; ⟨Am⟩ *tariff-reform* ~**händig 1.** a *offhand* (*to shoot o.*); ⟨jur⟩ *by private contract* ‖ ⟨mil⟩ ~er Anschlag *position without support* ‖ ⟨com⟩ ~er Verkauf *open--market sale*; ⟨exch⟩ *direct* (*sale* [*to the public*]) **2.** adv ⟨cycl⟩ ~ fahren *to ride without support* ‖ ⟨arts⟩ *done by free-hand* ‖ ⟨com⟩ *in the open market*; (*to sell*) *offhand* **~handzeichnen** n, –zeichnung [f] *free-hand drawing* ~**hängend** a *suspended* (*nacelle*) ‖ ⟨tech⟩ *overhang*, *overhanging* **~herr** m (abbr Frhr.: Joseph Frhr. v. Eichendorff) ⟨a-engl⟩ *baron* ‖ (Anschrift:) Herrn E. ~ v. Soden; (Anrede:) (norddt.) Herr von Soden, (v Personal:) Herr Baron, (süddt.) Herr Baron ~**herrlich** a *baronial* **~herrschaft** f *barony* **~hieb** m ⟨for⟩ *isolation* ~|**kämpfen** vt *to fight to free* (*a unit*) *in contact* **~karte** f ⟨a. rail⟩ *free ticket* (od *pass*); ⟨theat⟩ *complimentary ticket*, ⟨Am a.⟩ *paper*, *pass* | ~nberechtigter, ~ninhaber [m] ⟨theat⟩ *deadhead* **~kauf** m *redemption* (*of a p*) ~|**kaufen** vt [h] (jdn) *to redeem* (aus *out of*; v *from*); ⟨mil⟩ *to buy off* **~kirche** f *free* (od *not established*) *church* ~|**kommen** vi [s] *to be released* (od *set free*) ‖ *to be acquitted*; *to get off scot-free* ‖ ⟨aero⟩ *to take the air* **~körperkultur** f *nudism*, ⟨euph⟩ *naturism* **~korps** n ⟨mil⟩ *volunteer corps*; ⟨engl⟩ *the Volunteers* [pl] (seit 1908 gehörig z Territorial Army) **~kugel** f *magic bullet*; → Freischütz **~lager** n *night spent in the open air* **~land-** ~pflanzen [f pl] (*wild*) *garden*, (*and agricultural*) *plants* ~|**lassen** vt [h] (jdn) *to free*, *liberate*; *to release* (gegen Kaution *on bail*, ⟨Am *under a $ 100 bond*; z Bewährung *on probation*); *to set free* (od *at liberty*); *to give* (*a p*) *his freedom* ‖ (Sklaven) *to emancipate*, *enfranchise*, *manumit* ‖ (Gefangenen) *to discharge*; *to let .. go* ‖ → frei I. B. 5. 6. **~lassung** f *liberation*, *release* (*of a p*) ‖ *emancipation*, *enfranchisement*, *manumission* (*of a slave*) ‖ vorzeitige bedingungsweise ~ e–s Sträflings *ticket-of-leave*; ⟨Am⟩ *parole* **~lauf** m *free-wheel*(*ing*), ~ mit Rücktrittbremse *f.-w. hub with back-pedal brake* ‖ (mit) ~ fahren *to free-wheel*; ⟨a. mot⟩ *to coast* (den Berg hinunter *down hill*) | ~bremse [f] *back-pedalling brake* | ~nabe [f] *coaster-hub* **~legung** f ⟨arch⟩ *clearing* **~lehen** n ⟨jur⟩ *estate in fee simple* **~leitung** f ⟨el⟩ *overhead* od *open line* | ~sträger [m] *overhead bearer* **~licht-** [in comp] *open-air* (*theatre*) | ~aufnahme [f] *outdoor shot* od *view*; *exterior shooting* ‖ ~bühne [f] *open--air stage* ‖ ~malerei [f] *open-air painting*, *plein-airism* ‖ ~portrait [n] *outdoor portrait* ‖ ~-theater [n] *o.-a. theatre* ‖ ~vorführung [f] ⟨film⟩ *daylight projection* **~los** n *gratuitous ticket*; ⟨ten⟩ (beim Turnier) *bye* **~luft-** [in comp] *open-air* | ~behandlung [f] *open-air treatment* ‖ ~schule [f] *open-air school* ~|**machen** vt [h] **A.** (jdn) *to extricate* (aus *from*); *to get free* ‖ (Weg etc) *to clear* (v *off*) ‖ *to disengage*; den Arm durch e–n Ruck ~ *to jerk* (od *shake*) *one's arm free* ‖ ⟨med⟩ die Brust ~ *to take off one's shirt* ‖ ⟨com⟩ *to clear* (*of debts*) ‖ ⟨phys⟩ *to liberate* (*electrons*) ‖ → befreien **B.** ⟨übtr⟩ **1.** die Bahn ~ f *to pave the way for ..* **2.** (Brief) *to prepay*, *to stamp*; –gemacht *prepaid*, *post-free*; *stamped* (*envelope*) **3.** ⟨phys & chem⟩ (Wärme) *to disengage* **C. sich** ~ *to disengage* (od *extricate*) *o.s.* (v *from*); *to beg off* (*duty*, *obligation*; er kann sich heute nicht ~ *he cannot get away from home* od *work today*; sich durch e–n Ruck ~ *to shake o.s. free* ‖ sich (oben) ~ ⟨med⟩ *to take off one's shirt* ‖ ⟨übtr⟩ *to emancipate o.s.* (v *from*) ‖ ⟨com⟩ sich ~ aus .. *to contract out of a th* ‖ *to get away* (aus *from*) ‖ sich v jdm, v e–m Gefühl ~ *to shake o.s. free from a p*, *from a feeling* ‖ sich e–n Abend ~ *to take a night off* **~machen** n, **~machung** f *extrication* ‖ *clearance* (*of a road*) ‖ *disengagement* (*of heat*) ‖ *prepayment* (*of a letter*) ‖ *emancipation* (v *from*) ‖ *liberation* (*of electrons*) **~-marke** f (*postage-*)*stamp* **~maurer** m **1.** *freemason*, *Mason* **2.** [in comp] *Masonic* (*lodge*) **~maurer·ei** f *freemasonry*; *Masonry* ~**maurerisch** a *Masonic* **~mut** m *candour*, *frankness*, *openness*; *ingenuousness*; mit ~ *candidly*, *openly* ~**mütig** → d. **~plastik** f → Voll– **~platz** m *free place*; ⟨school, etc⟩ *scholarship* ~|**pumpen** vt [h] ⟨min⟩ (Schacht) *to dewater* **~quartier** n *free quarters* [pl] **~-religiös** a *latitudinarian*; *liberal* **~ringen** n ⟨sport⟩ *catch-as-catch-can*; ⟨Am⟩ *all-in-wrestling* **~runde** f (Bier~) ~! *on the house* **~sasse** m *freeholder* ‖ kl ~ *yeoman* ~**schaffend** a *free--lance* [attr] **~schar** f → –korps **~schärler** m **1.** *unauthorized belligerent* ‖ ⟨hist⟩ *free-lance*; *partisan* **2.** *freeshooter*, *sharpshooter*; *franc--tireur* (Fr); ~ [pl] *francs-tireurs*, *irregulars* [pl] **~schein** m → Erlaubnisschein **~schießen** n *shooting-match* (od *competition*) ~|**schneiden** vt [h] ⟨tech⟩ *to back off* **~schule** f *free school* **~schüler** m *boy of a free school* ‖ *free-place scholar* **~-schütz** m ⟨Ger⟩ *Freischütz* [Ger] ~**schwebend** a = –hängend **~sein** n *freedom* (v *from*); (inneres) *detachment* (v *from*) ~|**setzen** vt [h] *to release* (⟨a. at⟩ Energie) **~sinn** m ⟨Ger pol⟩ *Free Thought*; *Liberalism* ~**sinnig** a *broad*, *enlightened*, *liberal*; *latitudinarian* ~|**sprechen** vt [h] ⟨jur⟩ (jdn) *to absolve*; *to acquit* (v *of*); ⟨crim l⟩ den Angeklagten ~ *to find* [vi] *for defendant*; –gesprochen w *to get off*; er wurde v der Anklage des Diebstahls –gesprochen *he was discharged on a charge of theft* ‖ ⟨mst ec⟩ *to absolve* (v *from*) ‖ jdn v e–r Schuld ~ *to exonerate a p* **~sprechung** f *absolution*, *acquittal*, *discharge* (v *from*) ‖ ~ v e–r Schuld *exoneration* **~staat** m *free state*;

republic; der ∼ N. *the Republic of N.* **≗staatlich** a *republican* **∼stadt** f *free city* **∼statt**, **∼stätte** f *asylum, place of refuge*; *sanctuary* (f .. *to a p*) **≗|stehen** vi [h] es steht dir frei *it is left to your discretion*; es steht dir ∼ z tun *it is within your discretion to do*; *you are free* (od *welcome, at liberty*) *to do*; *it is free for you* (od *open to you*) *to do* **≗stehend** a *detached* (*house*) || *self-contained* (*machine*) **∼stein-** *freestone* (*peach*) **∼stelle** f ⟨school⟩ *free-place*; *free scholarship*; ⟨Scot univ⟩ *bursary*; → Stipendium **≗|stellen** vt [h] ⟨übtr⟩ jdm etw ∼ *to leave a th to a p's option*; ich stelle es dir frei *I leave it to you* (*to do*); –gestellt sein *to be optional* **∼stempel** m *stamp* **∼stil** m ⟨swim⟩ *free style*; *rough and tumble* [attr] → Ringen **∼stoß** m ⟨ftb⟩ *free kick*; Elfmeter≗ *penalty-kick* **∼stück** n = –exemplar **∼stunde** f *leisure-hour, play-hour* **∼tisch** m ⟨Ger univ⟩ *free board*; *scholarship* || **∼tod** m *suicide* **≗tragend** a *cantilever* [attr] **∼treppe** f (*outside terraced staircase*:) *flyers*; ⟨Am⟩ *stoop* **∼übungen** f [pl] *gymnastic exercises* [pl], *free standing exercises, Swedish drill*; ⟨Am⟩ *free gymnastics* [pl] **∼umschlag** m ⟨com & post⟩ *stamped envelope* **∼verkehr** m *dealing in the free market*; *inofficial market*; *kerb* (⟨Am⟩ *curb*)-*market* (a. ∼sbörse) **|** ∼skurs [m] *f. m. price* **∼wache** f ⟨mar⟩ *offwatch* **≗|werden** 1. vi [s] *to be set free* ⟨a. chem⟩ || –geworden *active* (*oxygen*) **2.** ≗ n *release* (⟨a. at⟩ *of energy*); *liberation* (*of gases*) **∼wild** n *game* ⟨a. sex⟩ **≗-willig 1.** [a] *free, free-will, unbidden, voluntary* (*service*); *spontaneous* (*act*) || *non-contentious* (*jurisdiction*) **2.** [adv] *freely, spontaneously, voluntarily*; *of one's own accord* (od *free will*) || e–e ∼ auf sich genommene Aufgabe *a self-appointed task*; ∼ dienen *to volunteer*; ∼ tätig s als .. *to volunteer as* ..; e–n Dienst ∼ übernehmen *to volunteer a service* || sich ∼ anbieten *to volunteer* (*to do*); sich ∼ melden f .. *to volunteer for* .. **∼willige** [der ∼, ein ∼r] *the volunteer*; ⟨Ger hist⟩ Einjährig-∼r *citizen who enlisted voluntarily and served only one year* **∼willigkeit** f *spontaneity, voluntariness*; auf ∼ beruhend *voluntary* (Erhebung *inquiry*) **∼wirtschaft** f *doctrine of free economy* **∼zeichen** n ⟨telph⟩ *dial*(*ling*) *tone*; *free-line signal* **∼zeichnung** f ⟨com⟩ *contracting-out* || ∼sklausel [f] *contracting-out clause* **∼zeit** f *leisure* (od *off, spare*) *time*; *vacancy* **|** ∼gestaltung [f] *spare time planning*; *use of leisure*; *l. pursuits*; *recreation*(*al*, ⟨Am⟩ *l. activities*); (*organized*) *recreational programmes* || ∼-hemd [n] *shirt for casual wear*; *leisure shirt* ∼kleidung [f] *clothes for casual wear* **≗zügig** a *freely, without strings*; *free to move about* od *to choose one's domicile* **∼zügigkeit** f *freedom to move about* od *to settle*; *free movement* (*of workers*)

Fr·eie 1. [der ∼, ein ∼r] m ∼n/∼n *the free man*; ⟨jur⟩ *freeman* || ⟨jur⟩ Besitzweise, die z Diensten verpflichtet, die e–s ∼n würdig sind *freehold* **2.** das ∼ (Land) *clear* (*in the clear*); (Ggs bebautes L.) *the country*; *the open air, the open* || im ∼n *in the open* (*air*); *out of doors*; *outdoors*: (*a man who belonged to*) *the out-of-doors* || Bewegung im ∼n *open-air exercise* || Essen im ∼n → Picknick || Lager im ∼n *camp*; im ∼n lagern *to camp* (*out*); die Personen im ∼n lagernd *the camp* || Leben, Spiele im ∼n *outdoor life, games* || Tiere im ∼n beobachten *to do field-work* || ins ∼ gehen *to go into the open*; *to take the air*; jdm ins ∼ folgen *to follow a p out* || im ∼n übernachten (müssen) *to have* od *get the key of the street* **fr·eien 1.** vt/i [h] ⟨liter⟩ (of a man) (um) ein Mädchen ∼ *to woo* od *court a woman* || → heiraten **2.** ≗ n *wooing* (um *of*); *courtship* **Fr·eier** m ∼s/∼ *wooer* (um .. *of a woman*); *suitor* (um *for*) || auf **∼sfüßen** gehen *to go courting* (od *a-wooing*) **∼sman** m = Freier **fr·eigebig 1.** [a] **a.** *generous, liberal* (*man*); *open* (*hand*); *open* (od *free, large*)-*handed, freehearted* (*p*); *munificent* || allzu ∼ *generous to a fault* || ∼ s *to have an open hand* **b.** [pred] ∼ mit *free of* od *with* (*money*), *lavish of* od *in*; *liberal of*; *ungrudging* od *unsparing in* (*praise*) || sich ∼ zeigen *to come down handsomely* **2.** [adv] *generously*, etc **|** **≗keit** f *generosity, liberality, munificence*; *largeness* **Fr·eiheit** f ∼/∼en **A.** [abstr nur sg] **1. a.** *freedom, liberty* (*of a p*; *of a people*); *independence* || bürgerliche ∼ *civil l.*; *franchise*; natürliche ∼ *natural l.* || politische ∼ *political f.* || Freiheit, Gleichheit, Brüderlichkeit! ⟨urspr. Fr.⟩ *Liberty, Equality, Fraternity*! Religions≗, Rede≗, Presse≗ *f. of religion, speech, the press* **|** jdn der ∼ berauben *to deprive a p of his f., to enslave a p* || jdm die ∼ schenken, jdn in ∼ setzen *to give a p his f.*; *to set a p free* (od *at liberty*); ⟨Am⟩ *to enlarge a p*; → freilassen || in ∼ s (of escaped prisoners) *to be at large* || Tiere in ∼ dressiert vorführen *to show trained animals in public*; *to give a show with tr. a.* **b.** ⟨Ger⟩ akademische ∼ *academic f.* (*of speech*, etc) || Bekenntnis≗, Glaubens≗ *f. of faith*; Gedanken≗ *f. of thought*; Gewerbe≗ *f. of trade*; Gewissens≗ *l. of conscience*; Presse≗ *f. of the press*; Religions≗ *religious l.* **2. a.** ∼ der Meere *f. of the seas* **b.** ⟨ec⟩ die Dom≗ *the Close* **3.** ∼ v *exemption* od *f. from*; *immunity from*; Steuer≗ *exemption from taxation* **4.** ⟨übtr⟩ (erlaubte ∼) **a.** (of thought) *f. from narrowness*; *latitude, liberality* (*of interpretation*) || sich die ∼ nehmen *to take the liberty* (z tun *to do* od *of doing*); ich nehme mir die ∼ *permit me* (od *I beg*) (*to remind you* ..) **b.** dichterische ∼ *poetic licence*; *the poet's latitude* **c.** ⟨mot⟩ Bein≗ *legroom*, Kopf≗ *headroom* **5.** innere ∼ *inner f.*; Willens≗ *f. of will* || Handlungs≗ *freedom* (od *liberty*) *of action* **B.** [oft pl ∼en] **1.** *privilege*; → Vorrecht || e–e Stadt mit schrankenlosen ∼en *a wide open town* **2.** (unerlaubte ∼; Willkür) *liberty, licence*; *breadth*; *go-as-you-please*; *individualistic act*; *lack of restraint* || sich ∼en erlauben *or* herausnehmen *to be too free*; *to take freedoms* od *liberties* (gegen [über] .. *with a p*); die Stellen sind mit einiger ∼ behandelt *some liberties have been taken with the passages* **fr·eiheitlich 1.** [a] *free* (*mind, spirit*); *liberal*; *democratic* || *independent*; *individualistic* (*effort*; *thought*); → Freiheits– || *go-as-you-please* || *egoistic* **2.** [adv] *freely*; *with freedom* || etw ∼ behandeln *to take liberties with a th* **Fr·eiheits-∼beraubung** f ⟨jur⟩ *forcible confinement* **∼bewegung** f; die politische ∼ *the struggle for political independence* **∼drang**, **∼durst** m *strong desire* od *thirst for freedom* od *liberty* **∼erhebung** f *liberty-rising* **|** hoher **∼gedanke** *high conception of freedom* **∼glocke** f ⟨Am⟩ *Liberty Bell* (in Philadelphia) **∼kampf** m *war of independence* **∼krieg** m ⟨Ger⟩ die ∼e [pl] *the Wars* [pl] *of Liberation* || ⟨Am⟩ *American War of Independence* (*1775–1783*) **∼liebe** f *love of* (od *for*) *freedom* **≗liebend** a *liberty-loving* **∼strafe** f ⟨jur⟩ (*sentence of*) *imprisonment*; er erhielt e–e ∼ v 3 Jahren *he got three years' imprisonment* **Fr·eiin** f ∼/∼nen = Freifräulein **fr·eilich** adv **1.** (einräumend) *it is true*; *indeed*; *I admit* od *confess*; ∼ er ist Künstler *true* (od *it is true*), *he is an artist*; → allerdings 1. || *though* (*his father, though, seems to have been more enthusiastic*) || da [conj] ∼ .. *since* (*since it is not your own fault, you are* ..) || aber ∼ *but then* **2.** (in Antworten: bejahend) (*why*) *certainly, doubtless, to be sure, by all means* || ja ∼! *oh yes*!, *yes, of course*!, *oh definitely*!, *rather*!, *sure* od *safe thing*!, *indeed I did*!, *I did indeed*! **fr·eimütig 1.** [a] *candid, frank, free-hearted* (od *spoken*), *open*(*-hearted*); *outspoken, plain spoken* **2.** [adv] *candidly, frankly, openly* **|** **≗keit** f = Freimut **Fr·eitag** m *Friday*; → Montag, Kar≗ °**Fr·eite** f *courtship, wooing*; auf die ∼ gehen *to* *go courting* (od *a-wooing*) **Fr·eiwerber** m *matchmaker*

fremd I. [a] **A. 1.** (nicht einheimisch) *foreign* || ⟨übtr⟩ *heterogeneous* (*elements*); *extraneous* (*matter*) **2.** (unbekannt) **a.** [attr] *alien* (*shores, subjects*); *strange* (*face; lands; place; voice*); *unfamiliar* || ein ~er Herr *a stranger; a strange man*; ~e Götter *strange gods*; ~e Leute *strangers* [pl] **b.** [pred] (P) obgleich ~ im Dorfe hatte er beobachtet .. *though a stranger to the village he had noticed that* ..; er ist mir ~ *he is a stranger to me*; er ist mir durchaus nicht ~ *he is no stranger to me*; diese Art Leute sind ihm so ~ *these kind of people are so alien to him* || ich bin ~ hier *I am a stranger here* (od *in these parts*) | (of qualities, subjects, etc) e–r S, jdm ~ s *to be strange to a p* (*the subject is strange to me*); *to be alien* (od *foreign*) *to a th* (.. *to one's feelings*); Furcht ist ihm ~ *he is a stranger to fear* **3.** (Ggs eigen) *not one's own; other*; ⟨com oft⟩ *outside* || ~e Angelegenheit *other people's business* || ~es Gebiet betreten *to trespass upon another's land; to be trespassing* || ~es Geld *outside money* (od *funds* pl) || unter ~em Gesetz lebend *heteronomous* || ~es Gut *other people's property* || in ~e Hand (*or* Hände) fallen *to fall into other hands* || ~e Hilfe *outside help*; (*to accept*) *help from someone else* || ~es Licht abfangen ⟨phot⟩ *to exclude extraneous light* || °mit ~em Kalbe pflügen *to deck o.s. with borrowed plumes* || unter ~em Namen (*to travel*) *incognito* || ~e Rechte *the rights of others* **4.** (fremdartig) *odd, queer, strange*; es kommt mir ~ vor *it seems strange to me* || *bizarre; uncouth* **B.** (ausländisch) **1.** *foreign* (*accent, language, manners*); *outlandish* || ~e Länder [pl] *foreign countries* od *parts* [pl] **2.** ⟨bot⟩ *exotic* (*flowers, fruits*) **II.** [adv] ~ tun, sich ~ stellen gegenüber jdm *to make a stranger of a p; to cut* od *ignore a p* || °~ gehen ⟨sex⟩ *to play the loose*; ⟨vulg⟩ *to mess*; nie ~ gehen *to run straight* || → ~artig 2. **Fr·emd-** [in comp] *foreign* || ⟨scient⟩ *hetero–; xeno–* **~arbeiter** m → Gast– **≈artig 1.** [a] *foreign; heterogeneous* (*elements*) || = fremd A. 4. **2.** [adv] *oddly, strangely* **~artigkeit** f *foreignness; heterogeneity* || *oddness, strangeness* **≈belüftet** a *forced-ventilated* (*motor*) **~bestäubung** f ⟨bot⟩ *xenogamy* **~bezug** m ⟨com⟩ *outside* od *external supply* **≈erregt** a ⟨el⟩ *separately excited* (*generator*), *nonpermanent* (*magnet*), *master-excited* (*transmitter* ⟨wir⟩) **~erregung** f *separate excitation* **~geruch** m *off-odo*(*u*)*r* **~geschmack** m *off-taste* **~gruppe** f ⟨soc⟩ *out-group* **~herrschaft** f *foreign rule; heteronomy* **~herrscher** m *foreign ruler* **~kapital** n *borrowed capital* **~körper** m ⟨anat⟩ *foreign matter* od *substance* (od *body*); *corpus alienum* (L) || [pl] ⟨tech⟩ *impurities* || (P) *outsider; stranger* **~-kraft-** *by means of auxiliary power* **~kühlung** f *induced draught* **≈ländisch** a *foreign* (*accent, language*); *outlandish* || ⟨übtr⟩ *bizarre, strange* **~licht** n ⟨phot⟩ *disturbing* od *stray light* **~peilung** f ⟨aero⟩ *ground-to-air direction finding*; → Rücken– **≈rassig** a *of different race* **~senderreporter** m *monitor* **~sprache** f *foreign language* **≈sprachlich** a *foreign language* (*instruction*) **≈staatlich** a ⟨Am⟩ *foreign* **≈stämmig** a *alien to the race; foreign* || *not native, not genuine* || *exotic* **~stoff** m: ~e [pl] *impurities* [pl] (*in food*, etc) **~strom** m *external* od *outside electricity*; vagabundierender ~ *stray current* **~wort** n *foreign word* **~wörterbuch** n *dictionary of foreign words*

Fr·emde [der ~, ein ~r] ~n/~n **1.** (völlig *total*) *stranger*; jdn wie e–n ~n behandeln *to make a stranger of a p*; → fremd II. **2.** = Ausländer **Fr·emde** f ~/ *another region; district* (od *region*) *away from home* || in die ~ gehen *to take to the road; to go wandering* || in der ~ *away from home; abroad* || → Ausland **Fremdel·ei** f ~/~en = Ausländerei **Fr·emden- ~buch** n *visitors' book; hotelregister* **~führer** m (*tourist*) *guide; cicerone* (It) [pl *–ni*]; → Führer **~haß** m *xenophoby, –bia* (L) **~heim** n *boarding-house; private hotel* **~legion** f *foreign legion* **~liste** f *hotel-register* **~verkehr** m *tourism; tourist traffic*; den ~ heben *to attract tourists* | ~samt [n] *visitors' bureau*; ⟨Am⟩ *tourist board*; ~sgewerbe [n] *tourist trade* **~-zimmer** n *guest* od *spare room* || ~! *rooms* **Fr·emdheit** f *foreignness* || *oddness, strangeness* **Fr·emdling** m ~s/~e *stranger*; er ist kein ~ auf der Bühne *he is no s. to the stage* || = Ausländer

fren·etisch 1. [a] *frantic, frenetic* **2.** [adv] *frantically, frenetically*

frequentat·iv a ⟨gram⟩ *frequentative* **frequen·tieren** vt [h] (Ort etc) *to frequent* **Frequ·enz** f ~/~en **1.** ⟨phys⟩ *frequency*; Hoch≈ *high frequency* **2.** ⟨übtr⟩ *attendance* (*at a meeting*, etc) **3.** Herz≈ *heart rate*; Puls≈ *pulse rate* **~band** n (zugeteiltes) ⟨wir, telv⟩ *channel* **~bereich** m *f. range* **~einstellung** f ⟨wir, telv⟩ *tuning control* **~kurve** f *f.-curve* **~messer** m *f. meter* **≈moduliert** a *f. modulation* (*broadcasting*) (abbr *F. M.*) **~schwankung** f *variation of f.*

Fr·eske f ~/~n ⟨paint⟩ [nur pl] ~n *frescoes* pl [It]; mit ~n bemalen *to fresco* **Fr·eskengemälde** n *fresco; painting in fresco* **Fr·eskenmalerei** f = **Fr·esko** n ~s/–ken *fresco* (It); *painting in fresco, fresco-painting* || (Bild) in ~ malen *to fresco* | m ~s/~s → Kammgarngewebe

Fr·eß- (→ fressen) [in comp] **~begierde** f *gluttony, greediness, voracity* **~beutel** m (for horses) *nose-bag* **~gier** f = –begierde **≈gierig** a *gluttonous, greedy, voracious* || °**~kober**, **~korb** m *lunch-basket; hamper of grub* **~lust** f = –begierde **~-näpfchen** n *bird's trough* **~sack** m **1.** = –beutel **2.** °(P) *glutton*, ⟨vulg⟩ *greedy-guts* **~sucht** f *bulimia* (L) **~trog** m *trough* °**~wanst** m = –sack **~werkzeuge** n pl *biting-apparatus*; ⟨ent⟩ *mouth-organs* [pl] **~zellen** f pl ⟨physiol⟩ *phagocytes* [pl] °**Fress·alien** pl (*food; provisions, victuals* pl); ⟨fam⟩ *eatables* pl, ⟨Am⟩ *eats* pl °**Fr·esse** f ~/~n **1.** (T) *chaps, jaws* pl; *muzzle* **2.** ⟨cont⟩ (P) *chops* pl || °meine ~! *my hat!, my eyes!, my foot!, my aunt!* || °jdm in die ~ schlagen ⟨sl⟩ *to hit a p in the jaw* || die gr ~ h *to talk big; to swagger* od *swank* || halt die ~ ⟨sl⟩ *hold your jaw*; ⟨Am sl⟩ *can it!* → Maul, Schnauze **fr·essen I.** vi/t [fraß/gefressen] [h] **A. vi 1.** (T) *to eat, feed* || e–m Tier z ~ geben *to feed an animal*; dem Vieh Gras z ~ geben *to feed the cattle on grass, to feed* (od *give*) *grass to the cattle* **2.** °(P) *to feed like a glutton; to gobble, gorge, gormandize*, ⟨fam⟩ *guzzle, grub* || °er frißt wie ein Drescher ⟨fam⟩ *he eats his head off* || aus jds Hand ~ *to feed out of a p's hand* || friß Vogel, oder stirb! *make or mar!, do or die!*; ⟨Am⟩ *root, hog, or die!* **3.** ⟨tech⟩ *to corrode* || (Kolben, Lager, etc) *to seize* **4.** ⟨fig⟩ (S) ~ an *to eat* (od *gnaw*) *into* (*a p*); *to corrode* (*a p's life*) || um sich ~ *to fester, rankle* || *spread* (*the fire, disease spread quickly*) **B. vt 1.** (etw) *to eat; devour* || das Pferd frißt mehr als es wert ist *the horse eats its head off* || (*to eat the tree*) *bare*; (*to eat the manger*) *empty* || *to eat a hole in the cloth* **2.** °(P) *to eat voraciously; to gobble* (*up*); *to gorge; to wolf* (*up*); *to consume, devour* || jdn arm ~ *to eat a p out of house and home* || ich werde Sie nicht ~ *I shan't eat you* || er hat die Geschichte glatt ge~ (= geglaubt) *he swallowed the story, hook, line, and sinker* || er hat die Weisheit mit Löffeln ge~ *he thinks himself a know-all* || das freß ich nicht *that won't go down with me* || hast du's ge~? *did you get me?* || etw in sich ~ → hineinfressen || jdn ge~ h *to be down on a p; to have a down on a p; to have* (od *get*) *one's knife into a p* || e–n Narren an jdm ge~ h *to dote on a p; to be mad about .., to be infatuated* (od *smitten*) *with a p* **3.** ⟨fig⟩ (S) *to consume; to swallow* (*the* *business swallows a lot of money*) || ihn frißt der Neid *he is consumed* (od *eaten up*) *with envy* **4.** ⟨tech⟩ (of a piston) *to seize* **5. sich satt** ∼ *to gorge o.s. with food; to eat one's fill* || (S) sich ∼ durch .. *to eat through* .. **II.** ≗ n **1.** [abstr] *gobbling; gorge, guzzle* || jdn zum ∼ lieb h *to dote on a p*; (ich) hab dich zum ∼ gern *darling, I could eat you* || °∼ u Schlafen ⟨sl⟩ *peck and perch* **2.** [konkr] = Fraß || ein gefundenes ∼ *a godsend*, ⟨fam⟩ *a bit of fat*; ⟨Am sl⟩ *a scoop* (*for the newspapers*) || das war ein g. ∼ f ihn *that was grist to his mill*; ⟨sl⟩ *that was jam* od *nuts for him*, ⟨Am⟩ .. *right down his alley* **fr·essend** a ⟨fig⟩ *corroding; corrosive* (*hatred*) || *cancerous; festering* (*sore*), *rankling; mordant* (*disease*); *phagedenic*; ∼es Geschwür *phaged(a)ena* (L); ∼e Flechte → Lupus; ⟨vet⟩ → Fetträude **Fr·esser** m ∼s/∼ *glutton, guzzler*, → Freßsack **Fresser·ei** f ∼/∼en *excessive eating; gluttony; gormandizing*; ⟨sl⟩ *guzzle*

Frett n ∼s/∼e ⟨zoo⟩ = **Fr·ettchen** n ∼s/∼ ⟨zoo⟩ *ferret*; mit ∼ (er)jagen *to ferret*; mit ∼ herausjagen *to ferret away* od *out* **fr·etten** vrefl [h] [österr] sich ∼ = sich einschränken; sich (kümmerlich) forthelfen **frett·ieren** vi [h] *to ferret*

Freud f ⟨mst poet⟩ = Freude 2. **Fr·eude** f ∼/∼n **1. a.** *joy* (an *in*; über *at*); *gladness, rejoicing* (an *in*; über *over*); *glee; happiness*; → Frohsinn, Fröhlichkeit || *delight* (über *at*), *enjoyment, gratification, pleasure* (an *in*; über *in*; f jdn *to a p*) **b.** die ∼n [pl] *the rejoicings* [pl]; die 7 ∼n Mariä *the seven Joys of the Virgin*; die ∼n des Lebens, Amtes *the pleasures* od *sweets* [pl] *of life, of office* **c.** ∼ am Skisport *fondness of skiing* **2.** Grund **für** e–e kl ∼ *some cause for joy, rejoycing, hope, encouragement* || **in** Freud u Leid *in good and evil days; in good and bad times*; F. u L. teilen *to share joy and suffering* || in höchster ∼ *in raptures; enraptured; in an ecstasy of happiness* || herrlich u in ∼n leben *to live in plenty* (od *luxury*) || **mit** ∼n *gladly; with pleasure* || **vor** ∼ hüpfen *to jump for joy*; vor ∼ weinen *to cry with* (od *for*) *joy*; vor ∼ außer sich geraten *to go into transports of joy* (od *into raptures*) || **zu** m–r ∼ *to my joy* (od *glee*); z m–r ∼ höre ich *I am glad to hear* **3. es ist** e–e ∼ .. z sehen (*his skill*) *is a delight to see*; es ist uns e–e gr ∼ *it affords us much pleasure* || **das ist e-e** ∼**, wenn ..** *what joy there is when ..* || es ist (mir) e–e (gr) ∼, mit Ihnen z arbeiten *it is a* (*great*) *pleasure* (*to me*) *to work with you* || es war e–e wahre ∼ *it was a treat* (⟨Am⟩ *a dandy*) || sie tanzte, daß es e–e ∼ war *to see her dancing was a real pleasure* | das Leben ist **nicht eitel** ∼ (u Sonnenschein) *life is not all beer and skittles* od .. *is not all cakes and ale*, ⟨vulg⟩ .. *not all lavender, it ain't all honey* || hämische ∼ *gloat* (über *over*) || helle ∼ *rapture, ravishment; thrill* (od *transports*) *of joy*; er hatte s–e helle ∼ daran *he enjoyed it immensely* || geteilte ∼ ist doppelte ∼ (Goethe) *joy shared is joy doubled* | **der** ∼ **über etw Ausdruck geben** *to express one's satisfaction at a th* || jdm ∼ bereiten *to give a p pleasure; to delight* od *please a p*; jdm e–e kl ∼ bereiten *to give a p a little surprise* || ∼ **finden** (*or* h) an etw *to find pleasure in ..; to get pl. out of ..; to derive* (od *extract*) *pl. from; to take delight in; to delight in; to be pleased with a th; to appreciate* (od *enjoy, relish*) *a th* || **es macht** mir gr ∼ *it gives me great pleasure* (od *much gratification*) (*to hear ..*); s–e Arbeit macht ihm gr ∼ *he derives great pleasure from his work* || mach ihm nicht die ∼ *don't gratify him* || er störte die ∼ des Festes *he was a skeleton at the festivity* || .. teilen → 2. in || jdm die ∼ verderben *to spoil a p's pleasure* **fr·eudelos** a → freudlos **Freuden-** ∼**becher** m *cup of joy*; sein ∼ war voll *the cup of his joy was full* ∼**bezeigung** f *expression of joy*; ∼en [pl] *rejoicings* [pl] ∼**botschaft** f *glad tidings* [pl] ∼**fest** n *rejoicing*, ⟨Am⟩ *whoopee*; ∼e [pl] *rejoicings*; ∼e feiern ⟨Am⟩ *to make whoopee* || *jubilee; feast* ∼**feuer** n *bonfire*; ⟨univ sl⟩ *bonner* ∼**geschrei** n *cries* [pl] *of joy; rapturous cheers* [pl] ∼**haus** n *brothel; disorderly house* || °∼**jäger** m *joy-hog* ∼**leben** n *joyful* od *merry life; life of joy* ≗**los** a = freudlos ∼**mädchen** n *lady of easy virtue, lady of pleasure*; ⟨Am⟩ (*professional*) *daughter of joy* ∼**nachricht** f *gleeful news*; = –botschaft ∼**rausch** m *raptures* [pl]; *ravishment; thrills* [pl] *of joy; transports* [pl] *of joy* ∼**ruf** m *cry of joy*; ∼e ausstoßen *to shout cries of joy* ∼**schauer** m *thrills* [pl] *of joy* ∼**sprung** m *leap for joy*; –sprünge [pl] *capers* [pl]; mein Herz machte e–n ∼ *my heart gave a leap of gladness* ∼**störer** m *kill-joy*; → Störenfried ∼**tag** m *day of joy; day of rejoicing; red-letter day* ∼**taumel** m = –rausch ∼**träne** f *tear of joy* **fr·eudestrahlend 1.** [a] *gleeful; radiant with joy* **2.** [adv] *gleefully* **fr·eudetrunken 1.** [a] *rapturous; flushed* (od *intoxicated*) *with joy; in raptures; enraptured* **2.** [adv] *rapturously; ecstatically* **fr·eudig 1.** [a] *joyful, joyous; cheerful, cheery*; jdn ∼ stimmen *to cheer* od *gladden a p* || ∼er Anlaß *occasion of rejoicing*; → Ereignis; ∼e Erwartung *pleasant* (od *pleasurable*) *anticipation*; ∼e Nachricht *glad tidings* [pl], *gleeful news*; ∼e Stimmung *elation; high spirits* [pl] **2.** [adv] *joyfully; gleefully* || *gladly, readily, willingly*; ∼st *most willingly* | ≗**keit** f *joyfulness, joyousness; cheerfulness* **fr·eudlos** a *mirthless; joyless; without joy; cheerless* || *dismal, gloomy*; → düster

fr·euen vt/refl [h] **1.** vt (nur S): **das freut mich** *I'm glad of that* || dein Erfolg freut mich *I am glad of* (od *am pleased with*) *your success*; es freut mich, **daß** es dir gefällt (*I am*) *glad you like it*; es freut mich, z hören .. *I am glad* (od *happy, pleased*) *to hear ..*; es sollte mich sehr ∼, Sie z treffen *I should be delighted* (od *charmed*) *to meet you* || es würde uns ∼, **wenn** Sie .. kämen *we would like you to have dinner with us*, ⟨Am⟩ *we would like you come to the party* **2.** vrefl **sich** ∼ **a.** *to be glad* od *pleased* (*the less she saw of him the better she was pleased*) || sich ∼ über etw († e–r S) *to be glad of* (od *about, at*) *a th; to be delighted* (od *gratified, rejoiced*) *at* (od *over*) *a th; to rejoice at* (od *over*) *a th*; sich hämisch ∼ über *to gloat on* (od *over*); sich ∼ z hören *to be glad* (od *pleased, rejoiced*) *to hear; to rejoice to hear*; ⟨Am a.⟩ *to admire to hear* || sich königlich (*or* mächtig, wie ein Schneekönig) ∼ *to be charmed* od *enchanted* (*to see ..*); (*he was gay as a cricket*); ⟨Am⟩ *to be tickled* (über *over*) **b. sich** ∼ **an** *to take delight* (od *to delight*) *in, to be pleased with* (*a th*) **c.** sich ∼ **auf** etw *to look forward to a th*; sich darauf ∼ z tun *to look forward to doing*; ich freu(e) mich auf unser Wiedersehen *I'm looking forward to seeing you* **d.** freut euch des Lebens! *get a kick out of living*!

Fr·eund m ∼es/∼e **1.** † = Verwandter **2. a.** *friend*; der ∼ jds *the fr. of a p*; ein ∼ jds *a fr. to* (od *of*) *a p*; ein ∼ v Georg *a fr. of George's*; ein ∼ v mir *a fr. of mine*; er ist mir ein guter ∼ gewesen *he has been a good fr. to me* || intimer ∼ *intimate fr.*; ⟨fam⟩ *chum*; ein treuer ∼ *a true fr.*; *fidus Achates* (L); ∼ im Glück, ∼ in guten Tagen, unzuverlässiger ∼ *fair-weather fr.* || °dicke ∼e *close, intimate friends*; °er u ich sind dicke ∼e ⟨fam⟩ *he and I are very thick*; wir wurden dicke ∼ *we grew fast friends, we grew as 'thick as thieves* || fester ∼ (Liebhaber) ⟨fam⟩ *steady* | jds ∼ bleiben *to keep friends with a p* || sich e–n ∼ gewinnen *to make* (od *win*) *a friend* || e–n ∼ h an jdm *to enjoy a p's friendship* || sich jdn zum ∼e m, jdn z ∼ gewinnen *to make a friend of a p; to make friends with a p* || jdm als ∼ zur Seite stehen *to stand a p's friend* || ⟨prov⟩ in der Not erkennt man s–e ∼e *a friend in need is a* *friend indeed* **b.** ⟨übtr⟩ *friend*; *comrade* ‖ der Hund ist der ~ des Menschen *the dog is the friend of man* **c.** (verblaßt: Bekannter etc) *friend*; *mate*; alter ~ *crony* ‖ gut ~ s mit *to be on friendly terms with* (*a p*) **d.** (in Anrede) *old man* (od *chap*); *laddie*; ⟨Am⟩ *buddy* ‖ lieber ~ *my* (*good*) *friend*; alter ~ *old chap* **e.** ⟨iron⟩ *fellow*; du bist mir ein schöner ~ *you are a nice friend* ‖ ~ Hein *old Nick*, *old Harry* **3.** ⟨übtr⟩ ein ~ s v etw *to be fond of*, *to be partial to a th*; *to like a th*; sind Sie ein ~ v Tanzen *do you like dancing*? ich bin kein ~ v vielen Worten *I am no friend* (od *not a man*) *of many words* ‖ ein ~ v Pferden *a lover of horses*; → Liebhaber ‖ ein ~ der Freiheit *a friend of liberty* **freund** [pred a] jdm ~ s *to be friendly* (od *well-disposed*) *to a p*; *to take kindly to a p* -**freund** [in comp] ein Schach~ s *to be fond of chess* **Fr·eundchen** n (in Anrede) *my good friend*; *old chap* (od *man*); *laddie*; ⟨Am⟩ *buddy* **Freund-** **~-Feind-Kennung** f *identification friend or foe* **~-F.-Kenngerät** n *i. f. or f. equipment* **~gefühle** n pl *positive feelings* **Fr·eundin** f ~/~nen (*woman*, *lady*, *girl*) *friend* **fr·eundlich 1.** [a] *friendly* (*act*; *nod*), *genial* (*man*); *kindly* (*smile*); *accomodating* (*spirit*), *affable* (*manners*); *amiable*, *courteous*, *obliging* (*words*); *pleasant*; mit ~en Grüßen *with kind regards* ‖ *bright*, *fair* (*weather*); *cheerful*, *cheery*, *neat* (*room*) ‖ *generous* (*praise*) ‖ (leutselig) *homy* | [pred] ~ s gegen *or* z jdm *to be friendly* (od *affable*, *kind*) *to a p*; ~ s gegen jedermann *to be hail-fellow-well-met with everybody* ‖ (Raum) ~ m *to brighten* ‖ ~er w *to unbend*; *to relax* ‖ das ist sehr ~ v Ihnen *that is very kind of you* ‖ seien Sie so ~ z tun *be kind enough to do*, *be so kind as to do*; würden Sie so ~ s, mir z sagen *would you kindly tell me*; wollen Sie so ~ s, ihm z sagen *oblige me by telling him* **2.** [adv] *affably*, *courteously*, *obligingly* ‖ jdm ~ gesinnt sein *to be well-disposed to a p*; *to mean well to a p*, *to mean a p well* ‖ ~ antworten *to give a friendly answer* ‖ würden Sie mir ~st sagen .. *would you kindly tell me ..* -**freundlich** [in comp] *pro*–; *–phil*(*e*) ‖ deutsch~ *pro-German*; *Germanophil*(*e*) ‖ *–minded*; er ist Theater~ *he is a lover of the theatre* **Fr·eundlichkeit** f ~/~en *friendliness*, *kindliness*; *affability*, *civility*, *obligingness*; ~en [pl] *civilities* pl; ~en austauschen *to exchange amenities* ‖ h Sie die ~ z tun *have the kindness to do*, *be kind enough to do* ‖ jdm e–e ~ erweisen *to do a p a kindness*; wollen Sie mir die ~ erweisen z antworten *will you do me the kindness to answer*? → Gefälligkeit ‖ (jdm etw) in aller ~ (sagen) .. *without offensiveness* **fr·eundlos** a *friendless* **Fr·eundschaft** f ~/~en **1.** † = Verwandtschaft **2.** *friendship* (mit *with*); *amity*; *friendly relations* [pl] ‖ dicke ~ *close* (od *thick*) *friendship*; *chumminess* ‖ Bande, Beweise der ~ *ties*, *proofs* [pl] *of friendship* ‖ ~ anknüpfen *to strike up a friendship* (*with* ..); ~ halten mit *to keep friends with*; ~ schließen mit jdm *to make friends with*; dicke ~ schl. .. ⟨fam⟩ *to chum up with a p* ‖ in ~ leben *to be on friendly terms* (*with*); ⟨fam⟩ *to keep fair with a p* ‖ in Friede u ~ leben *to live in peace and fr.* (*with* ..) ‖ jdm die ~ aufkündigen *to show a p the door*, ⟨Am fam⟩ *to give a p the gate* **fr·eundschaftlich 1.** [a] *amicable*, *friendly*; als ~er Gruß *by way of amity and salute* **2.** [adv] *in a friendly manner*; ~ gesinnt s gegen *to be friendly to*, *to take kindly to* (*a p*) | **≈keit** f ~/~en *amicability*, *friendliness* **Fr·eundschafts-** **~band** n *bond of friendship* **~bezeigung** f *proof* (od *token*) *of friendship* **~bund** m ⟨pol⟩ *friendly alliance* **~dienst** m *good turn*; nur ein kl ~ *just a friendly office* ‖ ~e [pl] *good offices* [pl]; jdm e–n ~ erweisen *to do a p a good turn* **~inseln** f pl *Friendly Islands*, *Tonga Islands* [pl] **~spiel** n ⟨sport⟩ *exhibition game* **~vertrag** m ⟨pol⟩ *treaty of friendship* od *amity*; *gentleman agreement*

Fr·eundschafts-Inseln f pl Tonga-Inseln

Fr·evel m ~s/~ **1.** ⟨ec & jur⟩ *sacrilege*; *desecration*, *profanation* (an .. *of a th*) ‖ ~ begehen an *to commit sacrilege on a th*; *to desecrate* (od *profane*, *violate*) *a th* (*a temple*) ‖ → Feld≈, Forst≈, Wald≈ **2.** ⟨übtr⟩ *crime*, *misdeed*; *gross offence*; *outrage* (an .. *on a p*, *a th*); ~ begehen an *to outrage* (*a p*, *a th*); → schänden; → ~tat ‖ *sacrilege* (*it would be sacrilege to do*); *wantonness*, *wickedness* ‖ *sin* (*it is a sin to be indoors today*) **~mut**, **~sinn** m *wantonness*; *wickedness* **~tat** f *enormity*, *outrage*, *outrageous crime*, *wicked act*; → Frevel 2. **~wort** n *profane language*; *wicked word* **fr·evelhaft 1.** a ⟨jur⟩ *sacrilegious* (*devastation*) ‖ *atrocious*, *criminal*, *flagrant*, *foul*, *heinous*, *monstrous* (*crime*); *outrageous*, *shameless*, *wicked* (*act*) ‖ ⟨übtr⟩ → freventlich **2.** adv *flagrantly*, *outrageously*, *wickedly* | **≈igkeit** f *flagrancy*, *outrageousness*, *shamelessness*, *wickedness* **fr·eveln** vi [h] *to commit an outrage*; *to do a flagrant wrong* ‖ ~ an jdm *to outrage a p*; ⟨sl⟩ *to do the dirty on a p*; ~ an etw *to outrage a th*; *to violate a th flagrantly*; *to sin* (od *trespass*) *flagrantly against a th* **fr·eventlich 1.** [a] ⟨übtr⟩ *culpable*, *gross* (*carelessness*); *irresponsible*; *mischievous* (*rumour*); *outrageous*, *shameless* (*neglect*, *sale*); *wanton* (*cruelty*); ~er Leichtsinn *wantonness*; → sträflich **2.** [adv] *flagrantly*, *grossly*, *irresponsibly*; *shockingly*; jdn ~ im Stich l ⟨sl⟩ *to go back on a p*; *to leave a p intentionally in the soup* ‖ sich ~ versündigen an jdm ⟨sl⟩ *to do the dirty on a p* **Fr·evler** m ~s/~ *outrager* (an .. *of a p*, *a th*) ‖ *criminal*; *evil-doer*, *malefactor*, *offender*, *sinner*, *transgressor* | **≈isch** a & adv = frevelhaft

Fri·aul n ⟨It⟩ (Prov.) *Friuli*

friderizi·anisch a *relating to* od *concerning Frederick the Great*; die ~e Zeit *the Age of* ..

Fr·iede(n) m ~ns/[pl → ~nsschluß] **1. a.** (Land≈) *the peace*; Königs≈ *the king's peace* **b.** (Waffen≈) *peace*; der ~ v Utrecht *the Peace of Utrecht*; der Westfälische ~ *the P. of Westphalia* (1648) ‖ bewaffneter ~ *armed peace*, *peace in arms*; fauler ~ *foul* (od *unsafe*, *unreliable*) *peace* **2.** (Ruhe) **a.** *peace*, *quiet* **b.** (innerer ~) *peace* (*of mind*); *mental calm*; *tranquillity* **3.** ~ atmen (*of woods*) *to be restful* ‖ e–m Lande den ~ **bringen** *to pacify a country* ‖ ~n finden *to find peace* (in *in*) ‖ ~n h vor *to be safe from* (*a p*) ‖ ~n halten ⟨jur⟩ *to keep the peace* ‖ → herrschen ‖ ~n m *or* schließen *to conclude peace*; *to make peace* (mit .. *with a country*); *to make one's peace* (mit .. *with a p*) ‖ ~n stiften *to pour oil on troubled waters* ‖ den ~n stören ⟨jur⟩ *to break the peace* ‖ ich traue dem ~n nicht *I have no faith in the peace*; *I have my* (⟨vulg⟩ *me*) *doubts*; *I smell a rat* | **im** ~n *in pre-war time*; *in peace-time*(*s*) ‖ in ~n *at peace* (*to live at p. with* ..) ‖ in Ruhe u ~n *in peace and quietness* ‖ jdn in ~n l *to leave a p alone* (od *in peace*); ⟨fam⟩ *to let a p alone*, *to let a p be* ‖ er ruhe in ~n! *peace to his ashes*!, *requiescat in pace* (L) | **um** des lieben ~ns willen *for the love of peace*; steckt es (Beleidigung) ein um des l. ~ns willen ⟨bib⟩ *turn the other cheek* | er ist **zum** ewigen ~n eingegangen *he has gone to his rest* **Fr·iedens-** [in comp] *peace* ..; *of peace*; *pacificatory* ‖ (= vor dem Weltkrieg) *pre-war* [attr] **~aktion** f *steps taken to bring about p.* **~angebot** n *p. offer* **~bedingung** f; ~en [pl] *conditions of p.* **~bewegung** f *p. movement*; → Pazifismus **~bote** m *messenger of p.* **~brecher** m *disturber of the p.* **~diktat** n *dictated p.* **~fahrt** f ⟨SBZ cycl⟩ *p. race* **~flagge** f = Parlamentärflagge **~fürst** m ⟨bib⟩ *the Prince of P.*, *the Saviour* **~fuß** m; auf dem ~e leben mit *to be on a friendly footing* (od *on friendly terms*) *with*; *to be at peace with* (*a p*)

~gliederung f *peacetime order of battle* **~güte** f *pre-war quality* **~kämpfer** m *Partisan of P.* **~konferenz** f *p. conference* **~kongreß** m *p. congress* **~korps** n *Peace Corps* (vgl Entwicklungsdienst) **~lager** n (Ostblock) *p. camp* **≗mäßig** a; ~e Stärke → Friedensstärke **~miete** f *pre-war rent* **~offensive** f *p. offensive* **~parität** f *pre-war parity* **~pfeife** f *pipe of p., p.-pipe* **~politik** f *pacific policy* **~präliminarien** [pl] *peace preliminaries* [pl] **~preis** m *pre-war price* **~richter** m ⟨engl jur⟩ *Justice of the P.* (abbr *J.P.*); ⟨Am⟩ *squire* ‖ besoldeter ~ *stipendiary; stipendiary magistrate* **~schluß** m -sses/-schlüsse *conclusion* od *treaty of p.* **~schwärmer** m *pacifist* **~sicherung** f *guarantee of p.* **~stand** m ⟨mil⟩ *p. footing* **~stärke** f ⟨mil⟩ *p.-establishment* (od *footing*) **~unterhandlungen** [f pl] *p. negotiations* **~vermittler** m *intermediary of p.* **~vermittlung** f *mediation of p.* **~vertrag** m *p.-treaty, treaty of p.* **~vorkämpfer** m → -kämpfer **~wille** f *the will to p.* **~wirtschaft** f *economic conditions in p.-time* **~zeit** f *time of p., p.-time(s)*

Frieden- ~stifter m *peacemaker; pacifier* ‖ ⟨dero⟩ (~ um jeden Preis) *peace-monger* **~stiftung** f *peacemaking; pacification* **~störer** m ⟨pol⟩ *peace-breaker; disturber of the peace* **~störung** f ⟨pol⟩ *breach of the peace; disturbance of the peace* **fr·iedfertig 1.** [a] *peaceable* **2.** [adv] *peaceably* | **≗keit** f *peaceableness; peaceable disposition* **Fr·iedhof** m ⟨allg⟩ *cemetery* (auf dem ~ *in the c.*), ⟨bes Am⟩ *graveyard* ‖ (an der Kirche) *churchyard* °**~(s)jodler** m *churchyard cough* **~(s)säule** f *dead man's lantern* **~tor** n *lichgate* **fr·iedlich 1.** [a] *peaceable* (*p; people*); *pacific; harmonious; well-disposed; amicable* ‖ *irenical* | *peaceful* (*face*); *quiet* (*valley*); *tranquil* (*life*) ‖ sei ~ *be quiet* (od *good*), *don't quarrel*; jdn ~ stimmen *to pacify a p* ‖ ⟨pol⟩ ~e Durchdringung *peaceful penetration* ‖ auf ~em Wege, ~e Weise *peaceably* ‖ ~e Zeiten *or* Tage *halcyon days* **2.** [adv] *peaceably* ‖ *peacefully, quietly* ‖ (*everything was very*) *restful* (*in the woods*) | **≗keit** f *peaceableness; peacefulness* **fried- ~liebend** a *peaceable; peace-loving* **~los** a *troubled* **~sam** a = friedliebend **~selig** a = friedlich 1. a.

°**Fr·iedrich** m ⟨hot⟩ (Hausknecht) *Jack boot(s)* ‖ (Anruf:) *boots*! ‖ setz d-n ~ Wilhelm darunter *sign it*; ⟨fam⟩ *put your John Hancock* od *Henry down* (od *to it*) **~shafen** n ⟨Ger⟩ (Stadt am Bodensee)

fr·ieren vi [fror/gefroren] **I.** (of liquids, etc) **A.** [pers] [s] (= gefrieren) *to freeze; congeal*; das Wasser, der Teich, das Fenster ist gefroren *the water, the pond, the window has* (od *is*) *frozen* | ⟨übtr⟩ → gefrieren 2. **B.** [imps] [h] **es friert** *it freezes*; es friert leicht *there is a light frost*; es hat die Nacht stark gefroren *it froze hard last night* ‖ es hat Eis gefroren *the water is frozen* ‖ es fror Stein u Bein *it was freezing cold* **II.** [imps & pers] (P) [h] mich friert, es fr. mich, ich friere *I am freezing, I feel very cold* ‖ mich friert *or* ich friere an den Füßen *my feet are freezing* (od *very cold*) ‖ ~ wie ein Schneider ⟨fam⟩ *to do a* (*deep*) *freeze* ‖ z Tode ~ *to freeze to death* **Fr·ieren** n *freeze* ‖ *feeling cold*

Fr·ies m ~es/~e **1.** (Stoff) *frieze, frieze-cloth* **2.** ⟨arch⟩ *frieze*; ⟨carp⟩ *moulding(s)* ‖ (Tapeten-≗) *frieze* ‖ ~streifen [m pl] *friezing*

Fr·iese m ~n/~n *Frisian*; die ~n *the Frisians* pl **~nwall** m *moraine*

Fr·iesel m & n ~s/~n = Pustel; ⟨med⟩ ~n [pl] *miliary fever; miliaria* (L) ‖ ~fieber [n] = Frieseln

fr·iesisch 1. a *Frisian, Friesic*; ~e Inseln *Frisian Islands* [pl] **2.** das ≗e *Frisian* (auf ≗ *in F.*)

Fr·iesland *Friesland* **Fr·iesländer** m = Friese

Frigidit·ät f ~/ ⟨sex⟩ *frigidness, frigidity*

Frikad·elle f ⟨cul⟩ *rissole* [Fr] **Frik·andeau** [-do] n [Fr] ⟨cul⟩ *fricandeau* **Frikass·ee** n [Fr] ~s/~s ⟨cul⟩ *white stew; blanquette; fricassee* [Fr] ‖ (Fleisch) z ~ m *to fricassee* **frikass·ieren** vt [h] **1.** (Fleisch) *to fricassee* **2.** °(jdn) ⟨sl⟩ *to beat* (*a p*) *to a mummy*

Frikat·iv m, **-t·ivlaut** m ⟨phon⟩ = Reibelaut

Frikti·on [ts] f ~/~en ⟨phys⟩ *friction* **~sgetriebe** n *friction-gear(ing)* **-skupplung** f *friction-clutch* **-srad** n *friction-wheel* **-sscheibe** f *f.-disc* **-swalze** f ⟨rail⟩ *f.-roller*

frisch I. [a] **A. 1.** (of food, etc) *fresh* (*fruit, vegetable; butter, meat, milk*); nicht ~ *stale*; [pred] *off* (*the meat is a bit o.*) ‖ ~es Brot → II. 1. **2.** (neu) *fresh* (*knife; page*); (nehmen Sie das Handtuch fort u) bringen Sie ein ~es (..) *and bring another* ‖ ~en Tee machen *or* aufgießen *to make new tea* ‖ ~e Wäsche *clean linen*; ~e Kleider, Wäsche anziehen *to change one's clothes, linen* ‖ ⟨fig⟩ e-e ~e Seite anfangen *to turn over a new leaf* **3.** (unverbraucht) *fresh* (*supply, troops*) ‖ ~e Luft *fresh air* (*in the f. air*); ~e Luft schöpfen *to take the air* ‖ mit ~en Kräften *refreshed; with renewed strength* ‖ ~en Mut fassen *to pluck up courage* **B.** ⟨übtr⟩ **1.** ~es Grün *viridity*; ~es Holz *green wood* ‖ ~e Gesichtsfarbe *fresh* (od *healthy, rubicund*) *complexion*; Mädchen mit ~er G. *fresh-faced girl* ‖ *fresh-coloured* od *ruddy* (*cheeks*); ~ aussehend *fresh-looking* **2.** *bright, brisk, gay, lively* (*girl*); ~ u gesund *hale*; ~ u munter *fresh and hearty, as fresh as paint* ‖ sich ganz ~ fühlen *to feel quite fresh*; sich nicht ~ fühlen *to feel rather off*; sich ~ u munter fühlen *to feel wide awake* ‖ (jdn) ~ m *to refresh* **3.** *brisk, cool, fresh* (*breeze, mind*); *crisp* (*air*) ‖ ~(er) w *to be freshing* **4.** *fresh* (*impression*); ich habe es noch ~ im Gedächtnis *it is still fresh in my mind*; (etw) ~ erhalten *to keep fresh* ‖ ⟨hunt⟩ *hot, strong* (*trail*) ‖ ~e Wunde *green wound* ‖ auf ~er Tat *in the very act; red-handed*; jdn auf ~er T. ertappen *to take a p red-handed* **5.** ⟨min⟩ *not brittle* **II.** [adv] **1.** *freshly* (*cleaned floor, gathered peaches, quenched lime*) ‖ ~ gefallen *fresh-fallen* (*snow*); **so**: *fr.-caught* (*fish*), *fr.-killed meat*), *fr.-painted* (*door*), *fr.-ground* (*coffee*) ‖ ~ gelegt *new-laid* (*eggs*); **so**: *new-baked* (*bread*), *new-mown* (*hay*); ~ gemolken *new* (*milk*); ~ gestrichen! *wet paint*! **2.** ~ vom Faß → Faß A. 3. ‖ die Arbeit geht ihm ~ v der Hand *he is a quick worker* ‖ sprich ~ v der Leber weg! *speak up, speak quite frankly* ‖ ⟨prov⟩ ~ gewagt ist halb gewonnen *a good start is half the battle* **3.** nun ~ ans Werk! *now for it! for all you are worth*! ~ ans W. gehen *not to let the grass grow under one's feet; to buckle to* ‖ ~ drauf los! *go it! go ahead! go at it hammer and tongs! keep it up*!; ~ drauf los arbeiten *to work away* **III.** [abs] v frischem *afresh, anew; again; once more* **Fr·isch-** ⟨tech⟩ **~arbeit** f *fining process* **≗·auf**! intj *cheer up! come*! ‖ ~ zur Tat! *go it! play up*! **≗backen** a *new* (*bread*) **~blei** n *refined lead* **~dampf** m *live steam* **~ei** n (Ggs Eipulver) *shell egg* **~eisen** n *refined iron* **~erz** n *raw ore* **~feuer** n (*re*)*fining furnace* od *forge* **~fleisch** n *fresh* od *carcass meat* **≗-fröhlich** a *merry and bright* **~(halte)beutel** m (*cellophane, plastic*) *food bag* ⟨tech⟩ *intake air, inlet air* **~haltekasten** m (f Zigarren) *humidor* **~haltung** f *the preserving* (*of meat*) **~herd** m *refining furnace* od *hearth* **~luft** f *fresh air* | ~fanatiker [m] *fresh-air fiend* **~milch** f *liquid milk* **~obst** n (z Rohessen) *eater* **~ofen** m = -herd **~stahl** m *natural steel* **~wasser** n *fresh water; fresh*

Fr·ische f ⟨allg⟩ *freshness* (→ frisch); *the fresh* (*of the morning*) ‖ grüne ~ *verdancy, verdure* (*of the fields*) | *liveliness, verdure, vigour* (*of youth*); jugendliche ~ *youthful verdancy* ‖ ~ im Alter *a healthy viridity in old age* **Fr·ische Haff,** das (*lagoon in N.-E. Prussia*) *the Frische Haff* (mit Elbing [Stadt]) **Fr·ische N·ehrung,** die (Westpreußen; → vor) *the Frische Nehrung* **fr·ischen** vt/i [h] **1.** vt (Eisen) *to refine*; im Flammofen ~ *to puddle* ‖ (Metall) *to revive, deoxidize, revivify* **2.** vi ⟨hunt⟩ (of a sow) = Junge werfen **Fr·ischling** m ~s/~e ⟨zoo⟩ (*wild boar in its first year*) *squeaker*; ~e [pl] *the young of* ..

Fris·eur [fri'zør] m [Fr] *coiffeur* Fr, *friseur* Fr, *hairdresser*; ⟨fam⟩ *barber* ‖ er ist beim ~ *he is at the hairdresser's* ‖ ~geschäft [n], ~laden [m] *hairdresser's shop*; ⟨Am⟩ *barber-shop* **Fris·euse** [fri'zøzə] f [Fr] *ladies'* (od *woman*) *hairdresser*; *coiffeuse* Fr **Fris·ier-** (→ frisieren) [in comp] **~gehilfe** m *hairdresser's assistant* **~kamm** m *dressing-comb* **~mantel** m (Damen≈) *peignoir* Fr, *dressing-jacket* (od *gown*) **~salon** m *hairdresser's saloon*; ⟨Am⟩ *barber shop*, (*ladies'*) *beauty parlor* **~tisch** m *dressing* (od *toilet*)-*table* **~umhang** m *hairdresser's wrap* ⟨a. tex, com⟩ **fris·ieren** **A.** vt **1.** jdn ~ *to dress* od *do a p's hair*; *to coiffure a p*; frisiert *coiffured* ‖ sich ~ *to dress* (od *do*) *one's hair* **2.** °⟨fig⟩ (Bericht etc) *to cook, doctor, garble, slant*; *to arrange* (*a story*); *to tamper with* (*a th*); ⟨sl⟩ *to fake* ‖ –rt ⟨mot⟩ *souped-up* (Wagen) **B.** ≈ n **1.** *coiffure*; *dressing* (*of a p's hair*) **2.** °⟨fig⟩ *cooking, doctoring* (*of accounts*)

friß imp v fressen

Frist f ~/~en **1.** *limited period*; *given* od *set term* od *time*; *time limit* (*to set a t. l.*) ‖ auf kz ~ *for a short and limited period*; *for a short time* ‖ in bestimmter ~ *within a given period* ‖ in Jahres≈ *in a year's time* ‖ innerhalb e–r ~ v *within a space of* (*2 years*), .. der festgesetzten ~ *within the prescribed period* ‖ in kürzester ~ *at short notice*; *in no time* ‖ z jeder ~ *at a moment's notice* ‖ die ~ ist abgelaufen (*the*) *time is up* **2.** (Aufschub) **a.** ⟨jur⟩ *grace*; e–e ~ v 3 Jahren *3 year's grace*; noch e–e Woche ~ *another week's grace* ‖ Gnaden≈ (f Todeskandidaten) *reprieve, respite*; jdm e–e Gnaden≈ gewähren *to grant a p a reprieve*; *to reprieve* od *respite a p*; e–e ~ v 10 Minuten wurde gewährt *ten minutes' grace was allowed* **b.** ⟨übtr⟩ *law*; jdm e–e ~ v 20 Minuten gewähren *to give a p twenty minutes' law* ‖ ⟨com⟩ kz ~ *reprieve, respite*; e–e kz ~ gewähren *to grant a respite* **~ablauf** m ⟨contr⟩ *expiration of time limit* **~bestimmung** f *fixation of a period* **~erteilung**, **~gewährung** f *respite* **≈gerecht** a *in* (*good*) *time*; nicht ~ *out of t.* | adv jdm ~ kündigen *to give a p* (*his*) (*due*) *notice*; ihm wurde ~ ge–gt *he got his* (*due*) *notice* **~gesuch** n *petition for respite* **~setzung** f *fixing of a term* od *date* **~überschreitung** f *exceeding of t. l.* **~verlängerung** f *temporary postponement*; *prolongation, respite*

fr·isten vt [h] sein Leben ~ *to keep body and soul together*; *to keep the pot boiling*; *to rub along*; *to humdrum*; *vegetate*; ⟨Am⟩ *to beat one's way* ‖ kümmerlich sein L. ~, das nackte L. ~ *to scrape through*; *to scrape a living*; *to eke out a scanty livelihood*; *to keep the wolf from the door*; *to rough it*; → d·urchschlagen I. B. 2. **fr·istlos** a (*dismission*) *without notice* (= *summary dismissal*) | adv ~ **entlassen** *to discharge* od *dismiss w.* (*a moment's*) *n.* ‖ ⟨fam⟩ *to sack on the spot*; ⟨Am⟩ *to fire w. n.* **Fr·istung** f *respite, prolongation*

Fris·ur f ~/~en (*men's*) *haircut*; (*womens'*) *coiffure mode* od *way of dressing the hair*; *head-dress*; ⟨fam⟩ *hair-do*

Frit·euse [–øzə] f ~/~n (*deep fat*) *fryer*

Fr·itfliege f ⟨ent⟩ *frit-fly*

Fr·itte f ~/~n (Glasschmelzmasse) *frit* | ~grund [m] *ground frit* **fr·itten** vt [h] (Masse) *to frit* **≈porzellan** n *fritporcelain*; *soft paste* **Fr·itter** m ⟨wir⟩ *coherer*

Frit·üre f ~/~n *deep fat* **~korb** m *frying basket* **~löffel** m *spider*

friv·ol **1.** [a] *disrespectful*; *impudent*; *shameless*; *cynical* (*p*); ~er Kerl *cynic* | *flippant, frivolous* (*act*); *foul* (*tongue*); *wanton* (*trick*); ~es Spiel *pettifogging* ‖ *indecent, obscene* (*book*) **2.** [adv] *cynically*; *irreverently*; *impudently* ‖ *wantonly* **Frivolit·ät** f ~/~en *disrespectfulness*; *impudence, shamelessness*; *cynicism* | ~en [pl]; ~enarbeit (Schiffchenarbeit) *knotting*; *tat*(*ting*); (etw) mit ~ versehen *to tat*

froh a **1.** (P) *cheerful, gay, joyful, joyous, merry* ‖ ~ s über *to be glad of*, .. *happy at*, .. *pleased with* (*a th*) ‖ sei ~, daß .. *thank God that* ..; ich bin heil~, daß .. *I am very glad that* ..; da kann man (aber) ~ s *one may call* od *count o.s.lucky* ‖ s–s Lebens nicht ~ w *to fret one's life away*; *to worry* **2.** (S) *cheery* (*mood*); *cheerful* (*hope*); sei ~en Mutes *be of good cheer*; *cheer up* ‖ *gay, merry* (*voices*); *happy* (*laughter*); *gay* (*colours*) ‖ *glad, good* (*tidings*); *happy* (*event*); *pleasant* (*anticipation*); ~e Weihnachten! *Merry Christmas*! **~gelaunt** a *in high spirits*; *good-humo*(*u*)*red* **~gemut** a *cheerful* **~wüchsig** a ⟨bot⟩ *thrifty, rank* **fr·öhlich** a *cheerful, frolicsome, gay, gleeful, jovial, joyful, joyous, merry* (*child*) ‖ *gleeful* (*mood*); *gay* (*dances*), *merry* (*voices*); *happy* (*laughter*); ~e Stimmung *high spirits* ‖ ≈e Weihnachten! *Merry Christmas*! ‖ (jdn) ~ stimmen *or* m *to cheer, to exhilarate, to gladden* | **≈keit** f *cheerfulness, gaiety, gladness, glee, hilarity, jollity, joyfulness, merriment, mirth*; ⟨Am sl⟩ *tear* **frohl·ocken** **1.** vi [pp frohlockt] [h] *to be exultant* (od *jubilant*); *to jubilate*; *to shout for joy*; ihr Herz –lockte vor Freude *her heart sang for joy* ‖ *to exult* (über *at, in, over*); *to glory* (über .. *in a victory*) ‖ (hämisch ~) *to gloat* (über .. *over the butchery*); *to triumph* (.. *over a defeated enemy*) ‖ du hast z früh frohlockt *you have triumphed too early* **2.** ≈ n *exultation, jubilation*; *triumph* (über *at*) ‖ mit ~ *exultantly, triumphantly*; (mit hämischem ~) *gloatingly* **frohl·ockend** **1.** [a] *exultant, jubilant, triumphant* ‖ (hämisch ~) *gloating* (*eyes*) **2.** [adv] *exultantly, triumphantly* ‖ (hämisch ~) *gloatingly* **Fr·ohsinn** m *gaiety, good cheer*; *cheerfulness, glee, mirth*; *high spirits* pl; *light-heartedness* **fr·ohsinnig** a *cheerful, gay, joyful*

fromm a **1.** (P) *devout, godly, pious, religious* ‖ ~ erzogen worden s *to be brought up in religion* ‖ ⟨übtr⟩ ~ wie ein Lamm *as meek* od *gentle as a lamb*; *as meek as Moses* ‖ ~ tun *to be mealy-mouthed*; ~ tuend *mealy-mouthed* ‖ ~ w ⟨Am sl⟩ *to get religion* **2.** *gentle, quiet* (*horse*); *meek* **3.** ~er Betrug *pious fraud* **Frömmel·ei** f ~/ *bigotry* ‖ *cant*; *affected* (od *sham*) *piety*; *sanctimony, sanctimoniousness*; *hypocrisy* **fr·ömmeln** vi [h] *to be bigoted* ‖ *to affect piety*; *to cant* ‖ ~der Gefühlsausdruck *cant* ‖ ~d *goody*(*-goody*) **fr·ommen** **1.** vi [h] [nur 3. sg & pl] jdm ~ *to profit a p*; *to be of use to a p*; was frommt es dir, wenn ich absage *what's the use of my declining* **2.** ≈ n; z Nutz u ~ *for the benefit of* (*one's country*); *for the advantage of* (*a p*) **Fr·ommheit**, **Fr·ömmigkeit** f ~/ *piety, devoutness* **Fr·ömmler** m ~s/~; **Fr·ömmling** m ~(e)s/~e *bigot*; *pietist*; *devotee* (*of religion*); *religious zealot*; *religionist* ‖ ⟨dero⟩ *canter, goody, hypocrite*; *Tartuf*(*f*)*e* **Fr·ömmlerin** f ~/~nen = Frömmler; ⟨fam⟩ *holy fowl*

†**Fron** f = Frondienst **Fr·on-**[1] [aus † Adj ≈, heilig] [in comp] *holy* **~altar** m *high* (od *holy*) *altar* **~l·eichnam** m 1. *the Holy Body of Christ* 2. = ~sfest **~l·eichnamsfest** n ⟨R. C.⟩ *Corpus Christi Day* **Fr·on-**[2] [z † fro ‚Herr'] *soc* [in comp] **~arbeit** f ⟨hist⟩ = –dienst ‖ ⟨übtr⟩ *drudge*(*ry*) **~arbeiter** m ⟨hist⟩ *soc*(*c*)*age-tenant*; *villein* ‖ ⟨übtr⟩ *drudge* **~bote** m ⟨hist⟩ *beadle* **~dienst** m ⟨hist⟩ *soc*(*c*)*age* (*service*); *villeinage* ‖ ⟨übtr⟩ *statute-labour* ‖ *drudgery* **~gut** n ⟨hist⟩ *soc*(*c*)*age-tenure* (od *freehold*); *copyhold* **~leute** pl ⟨hist⟩ *soc*(*c*)*age-tenants*; *villeins* pl **~pflicht** f ⟨hist⟩ *soc*(*c*)*age, villeinage*; *soc*(*c*)*age-duty* **~vogt** m *overseer of the soc*(*c*)*age-tenants*

Fr·onde [ˈfrɔ̃də] f (Fr) ⟨pol⟩ *fronde*

fr·onen vi [h] *to do soc(c)age-service*; *to do enforced labour* ‖ ⟨übtr⟩ *to drudge, to toil* **fr·önen** vi [h] ⟨fig⟩ e–r S ~ *to minister to a th*; e–r Leidenschaft ~ *to indulge a passion, to indulge in a passion*; *to pander to a passion*; dem Laster ~ *to addict o.s.* (od *to be addicted*) *to vice*; Rauschgiften ~ *to be a drug-addict*; *to drug*

Fr·ont f ~/~en **1.** ⟨mil⟩ **a.** (Stirnseite) *front* (*of a regiment*) ‖ (Truppen) in breiter ~ aufstellen *to deploy*; sich in br. ~ a., in br. ~ antreten *to deploy* ‖ die ~ abschreiten *to pace down* (*the front*), *to troop the line*; (e–r Ehrenkompanie) *to receive military hono(u)rs, to take the salute* (*of the troops*) ‖ ⟨sport⟩ in ~ gehen *to come to the front* | ~ m *to front* (nach .. *to the left*); ~ m vor jdm *to stand attention, to stand at* (od *to*) *attention*; *to come to attention* ‖ ⟨fig⟩ ~ m gegen etw *to oppose* od *resist a th*; *to offer opposition* od *resistance to a th*; *to protest against a th* **b.** (Kampflinie) *front*; *front-line* ‖ an der ~ *at the front*; an der Ost⁓ *on the Eastern f.* ‖ ein Krieg mit zwei ~en *a war with two fronts* ‖ in vorderster ~ stehen *to be in the front-rank*; ⟨a. übtr⟩ **2.** *front* (*of a house*, etc) ‖ Straßen⁓ *frontage* Inhaber e–s Hauses an der Straßen⁓ *frontager* ‖ ein Haus mit weißer ~ *a white-fronted house*; ein H. mit der ~ nach der Hohen Straße *a house fronting on* (od *to, towards*) *the High Street* ‖ (of house) mit der ~ liegen nach *to front* (*the street*) | die ~ e–s Hauses erneuern *to reface a building* **3.** ⟨meteor⟩ Warm(luft)⁓ etc *warm front, etc* **~abschnitt** m *fr. sector* **~angriff** m *frontal attack* **~antrieb** m ⟨mot⟩ *fr.* (*wheel*) *drive* **~aufwind** m ⟨aero-meteor⟩ *upwash* **~ausbuchtung** f, **~bogen** m ⟨mil⟩ *salient* ‖ –bogen ⟨arch⟩ *frontal arch* **~berichter** m *front-line reporter* **~berichtigung** f (*retrograde*) *correction of the front* **~böe** f *line squall* **~breite** f *width* od *extent of frontage* **~bücherei** f *lending library for combattants at the front* **~dienst** m *service at the fr.* **~einbuchtung** f *re-entrant* **~einsatz** m *combat mission*; ⟨aero⟩ *c. sortie* **~flug** m *war flight* **~flugspange** f *war flight badge* **~flugzeug** n *combat airplane* **~gebiet** n (bis *incl.* rückw. Korpsgrenze) *combat zone* N **~kämpfer** m *combatant* ‖ ~ des ehemal. Weltkrieges *ex-combatant*, ⟨Am⟩ *veteran*; ~bund [m] *union of ex-service men* **~kampftruppen** pl *front line forces* **~koller** m *battle fatigue* **~lader** m ⟨artill etc⟩ *front-end loader* **~lenker** m ⟨mot⟩ *forward control* **~linie** f *front-line* **~mauer** f *frontal wall* **~offizier** m *front-line officer* **~seite** f ⟨arch⟩ *frontispiece* **~soldat** m = –kämpfer **~truppen** f pl *line troops* **~urlaub** m *leave from the front, furlough from the combat zone* **~verkürzung** f *shortening of the fr.* **~verlauf** m *position of the battle fr.* **~wechsel** m *change of front*; ⟨übtr⟩ *volte-face* Fr **~zulage** f *combat pay* od *allowance*

front·al 1. a *frontal* **2.** ⁓ n ~(e)s/~e ⟨ec⟩ (Altar⁓) *frontal* ⁓**angriff** m *head-on* od *frontal attack* od *assault* ⁓**arterie** f ⟨anat⟩ *f. artery* ⁓**-zus-stoß** m *head-on collision* od *clash*

Fr·onten- ~segeln n ⟨aero⟩ *front(al) soaring*

Frontisp·iz n ⟨arch & typ⟩ *frontispiece*

fror 1. & 3. pret v frieren

Fr·osch m ~es/⁓e **1.** ⟨zoo⟩ *frog*; Familie der Frösche *Ranidae, Batrachia* L pl ‖ Laub⁓ *tree-frog*; → quaken ‖ ⟨fig⟩ er hat e–n ~ im Halse *he has a frog in his throat*; er hat e–n ~ im Kopf ⟨sl⟩ *he has a bee in his bonnet* ‖ °sei kein ~! *don't make a fuss*! *come, come*! *come on* od *along*! *be a sport*! **2. a.** (Feuerwerkskörper) *cracker, squib* **b.** ⟨mus⟩ *nut* (*of a violin-bow*) **c.** ⟨typ⟩ *sliding-bar* **3.** ⟨med⟩ = ~geschwulst ‖ ⟨vet⟩ (Gaumenschwellung bei Pferden) *lampas* **4.** ⟨tech⟩ (Knagge) *trip dog* ⁓**artig** a *batrachian* **~biß** m ⟨bot⟩ *frog-bit* **~blut** n ⟨fig⟩ ~ h *to be cold-blooded* **~esser** m (Franzose) *froggy* **~fisch** m ⟨ich⟩ *frog-fish*; *toadfish* **~geschwulst** f ⟨path⟩ *ranula* L **~keule** f = –schenkel **~klemme** f ⟨tech⟩ *wire grip* **~kraut** n ⟨bot⟩ *ranunculus* L **~laich** m *frog-spawn* ‖ °⟨fig⟩ (*Tapiokasuppe* etc) ⟨fam⟩ *fish-eyes* **~löffel** m ⟨bot⟩ *thrumwort, water-plantain* **~lurche** pl *salientia* **~mann** m *frogman* ‖ Bekleidung des ~es *scuba* (= *self-contained underwater breathing apparatus*) *suit* | ~tauchen [n] *scuba diving* **~maul** n ⟨arch⟩ *dormer-window* ‖ ⟨fig⟩ ein ~ m (vor Staunen etc) *to stand agape* **~perspektive** f *bottom view* ‖ ⟨fig⟩ *narrow* (od *parochial, provincial*) *perspective* od *view* ‖ ⟨phot⟩ Aufnahme aus der ~ *ground–* od *low-angle view, worm's eye view*; ⟨film⟩ *tilt shot* | ~sucher [m] *worm's eye finder* **~schenkel** m pl; ⟨cul⟩ *frogs' legs* pl, *froglegs* **~-teich** m *frog-pond* **~tier** n *tailless amphibian*, ⟨scient⟩ *batrachian*

Fr·ost m ~es/⁓e **1.** *frost*; *freeze*; (*severe*) *cold*; trockener ~ *black frost* ‖ (Frucht) durch ~ beschädigen *to frost* ‖ körperliche Schäden durch starken ~ verursacht *frostbite* ‖ durch ~ beschädigt *frostbitten* (*fruit*) **2.** ⟨übtr⟩ *chill, cold(ness)*; vor ~ zittern *to tremble with cold*; *to shiver, to be in a shiver* ‖ (Fieber⁓) *ague*; *chill*; *shivering fit*; *shivering* | ⟨fig⟩ *chill, coldness, coolness, frigidity, frost, frostiness* **~aufbrüche** m pl (*road*) *frost heaving* od *damage* **~ballen** m *chilblain* ⁓**beständig** a *frost resistant*, ⟨tech⟩ *frost-proof* **~beule** f *chilblain*; (offene ~ am Fuß) *kibe* **~blase** f *chilblain* **~brand** m *frostbite* **~fieber** n → Frost 2. **~gefühl** n *chill, chilliness* **~hart** a ⟨for⟩ *frost-hardy* **~riß** m (in Holz) *frost shake* ⁓**rissig** a *frost-cracked* **~salbe** f *ointment for chilblains* **~schaden** m *damage done by frost*; *frostbite* **~schauer** m pl *shivers, shiverings*; *shivering fits* pl **~schutz-** ⟨mot⟩ ~haube [f] *muff* ‖ ~-mittel [n] *anti-freeze* ‖ ~salbe [f] *anti-frostbite ointment* ‖ ~scheibe [f] *screen defroster* ⁓**sicher** a *frost-resistant* **~spanner** m ⟨ent⟩ *winter-moth* **~wetter** n *frosty* (od *cold*) *weather*; *frost* **fr·östeln I.** vi [h] **1.** (P) [imps & pers] es fröstelt mich, mich fröstelt, ich fröstele *I feel chilly, I am shivering* **2.** † (of the weather) es fröstelt *there is a slight frost* **II.** ⁓ n *chill, shiver(ing)* **fr·ostig I.** [a] **1.** *⟨eig⟩ *frigid*; *very cold* **2.** ⟨mst fig⟩ *chilly* (*feeling, manner*), *chill*; *cold, frigid* (*reception*), *frosty* (*smile*); *stiff* ‖ *bleak* (*atmosphere*); *frigid* (*splendour*) **II.** [adv] *frigidly* | ⁓**keit** f ⟨fig⟩ *chilliness, coldness, frigidity, frostiness*

frott·ee a ⟨tex⟩ *towelled*

Frott·ee n [Fr] ~s/~s *friction* (od *sponge*) *cloth*

Frott·ier- [in comp] **~bürste** f *bath* (od *flesh*) *–brush* **~handschuh** m *Turkish square*; *friction* (od *loofah*) *glove* **~handtuch** n *Turkish* (od *bath, rough*) *towel* **~stoff** m = Frottee; ⟨tex⟩ *Turkish towelling* **~tuch** n *terry towel* **frott·ieren 1.** vt [h] (jdn, Haut) *to rub*; (Kopfhaut) *to shampoo* **2.** ⁓ n *friction*; *rub(bing)*; *shampoo(ing)*

×**fr·otzeln** vt [h] = ärgern, necken

Fr·ucht f ~/⁓e **A.** ⟨eig⟩ **1.** ⟨bot⟩ (Feld⁓ etc) *fruit*; ⁓e [pl] *fruits, produce* (*of the fields*), → Feldfrüchte; Getreide, Korn; Ernte ‖ (Baum⁓) *fruit*; ⁓e [pl] *fruits* pl; [koll] *fruit* (*the tree has lost its fruit*); *fruitage* ‖ v Früchten lebend *frugivorous* (*animal*) ‖ ⁓e entwickeln *to set fruit*; ⁓e tragen *to bear* od *yield fruit*; *to fructify, to fruit* ‖ → Balg⁓; Essig⁓; Sammel⁓ **2.** ⟨biol⟩ (Leibes⁓) *f(o)etus*; *offspring* **B.** ⟨fig⟩ *product, profit, result* ‖ [oft pl] ⁓e *fruits* pl, *harvest, offspring, products* pl ‖ reiche ~ ergeben *to yield a rich harvest*; die ersten ⁓e ernten *to reap the first fruits*; die ⁓e e–r S ernten *to reap the reward of a th*; die ⁓e der Arbeit *the benefits of work* **~abtreibung** f ⟨jur⟩ *abortion* **~arten** pl *fruits* pl ⁓**artig** a *fruity* **~auge** n ⟨bot⟩ *fruit-bud* **~becher** m ⟨bot⟩ *cupule* **~bildung** f *fructification* **~blase** f

⟨anat⟩ *amniotic sac* **~blatt** n ⟨bot⟩ *carpel* **~bonbon** m *fruit-lozenge, boiled sweet* **~brei** m ⟨cul⟩ *squash* **≃bringend** a ⟨fig⟩ *fructuous, fruitful, productive, profitable* **~eis** n *fruit-ice; water-ice; sorbet* || ~eiscreme [f] ⟨bes Am⟩ *sundae* **~ernte** f *fruitage* ⟨a. fig⟩ **~essenz** f *fruit-essence* **~fleisch** n *pulp* **~folge** f *shift* .., (3jährig mit Brache) *rotation of crops* **~gehänge** n ⟨arch⟩ *festoon* **~gehäuse** n = –wand **~gelee** n *fruit-jelly* **~handel** m *fruit-trade* **~händler** m *fruiterer* **~handlung** f; Süd~ *Italian warehouse* **~häutchen** n ⟨bot⟩ äußeres ~ *epicarp* **~hülle** f = –wand **~knoten** m ⟨bot⟩ *ovary; pistil* || zus–gewachsener *syncarp* **~kuchen** m = Mutterkuchen **~mus** n *jam* **~presse** f *fruit-press; liquidizer* **≃reich** a ⟨mst fig⟩ *fruitful* = –bringend **~saft** m *fruit* (*apple, orange, etc*) *juice; squash* **~salat** m *fruit salad* **~säure** f *fruit-acid* **~schaumwein** m *sparkling fruit wine* **~schnur** f *festoon* **~stand** m ⟨bot⟩ *fructification* **~stück** n ⟨paint⟩ *fruit-piece* **~torte** f *fruit tart* **≃tragend** a *fructiferous, fruit-bearing*; ~er Baum *fruiter, fruit-bearer* **~wand** f ⟨bot⟩ *seed-vessel; pericarp*; → –häutchen **~wasser** n ⟨anat⟩ *amniotic fluid* **~wechsel** m = –folge **~wein** m *fruit-wine* **~zucker** m *fruit-sugar; fructose*; → Traubenzucker **fr·uchtbar I.** [a] **1.** *fertile* (*soil*), *fruitful, productive, prolific* (*land*); ~ an *fertile in* || (of men, animals) *productive, prolific; fruitful* (*marriage*) **2.** ⟨übtr⟩ *productive* (*intellect*); *prolific* (*writer*); *fecund, pregnant* (*wit*) || *fructuous; fruitful, profitable* (*labours*); ~ an *fruitful* (od *prolific*) *in* **3.** ~ m *to fertilize*; ⟨übtr⟩ *to make profitable* (*f to*); → befruchten **II.** [adv] *fruitfully, productively, prolifically* | **≃keit** f *fertility* (an *of*); *fecundity* || ⟨bes übtr⟩ *fruitfulness, pregnancy* (*of the mind*), *productivity, prolificacy, prolificity* (an *of*) || ⟨demog⟩ natürliche ~ *fertility of non-contracepting couples*; uneheliche ~ *illegitimate fertility*; Index der Gesamt≃ *total fertility* **≃keitsziffer** f ⟨demog⟩ ([un]eheliche) ([*il*]*legitimate*) *fertility rate*; männliche ~ *male f. r.*; gesamte ~ *general f. r.*; ~ nach dem Alter *age-specific f. r.*; ~ nach der Ehedauer *duration specific f. r.* **≃machung** f *fertilization* **Fr·üchtchen** n **1.** *little fruit; fruitlet* **2.** °⟨fig⟩ *young scamp; scapegrace; bad lot* **Fr·üchte- ~kuchen** m *fruit-cake* **fr·uchten** vi [h] ⟨fig⟩ *to avail; to be of use, to be profitable* (jdm *to a p*); → nützen || es fruchtet nichts *it is without avail* od *of no avail, it is useless*; es fr. wenig *it is of little avail*; was fruchtet es? *of what avail is it* od *what avails it* (*to do*)? **fr·uchtig** a *fructed* (*wine*) **fr·uchtlos 1.** [a] *fruitless* || ⟨mst fig⟩ *effectless, fruitless; profitless, useless; ineffective, ineffectual; unavailing, unfruitful, unsuccessful* || *futile* (*endeavo*(*u*)*r*) || ~ s *to be without* (od *of no*) *avail*; alles ~ *all to no avail* || ~es Unternehmen *wild-goose chase* **2.** [adv] *fruitlessly, ineffectually* **Fr·uchtlosigkeit** f *fruitlessness, etc* → fruchtlos

frug·al a *frugal* (*meal*); *simple; unpretentious* **≃lit·ät** f ~/ *frugality; simpleness; unpretentiousness*

früh I. [a] **1.** (Ggs spät) **a.** am ~en Morgen *early in the morning*; Arbeit am ~en M. *early-morning work*; zu ~er Tageszeit *early in the day*; bis in die ~en Morgenstunden *into the small hours of the day* || ~er Ladenschluß *early closing* || z dieser ungewöhnlich ~en Zeit *at this unearthly time* || *prompt, speedy* (*return*) **2.** (früh–, vorzeitig) *early, forward* (*spring; apple*) || *early, premature, untimely* (*death*); (er verlor s–n Vater) in ~em Alter (..) *at an early age* **II.** [adv] ~, *~e **1.** (Ggs spät) *early; in the morning* || recht ~ *bright and early* || ~ am Tage *early in the day*; ~ aufstehen u ~ zu Bett gehen *to keep early hours*; Sie sind schon ~ auf heute morgen *you are early this morning*; ~ auf den Beinen s, ~ tätig s *to be up and doing*; ~ genug ankommen *to be in* (*good*) *time* || gestern ~ *yesterday morning*; heute ~ *this morning*; morgen ~ *tomorrow morning*; übermorgen ~ (*the*) *first thing the day after tomorrow*; am Montag ~ *on Monday morning*; → Frühe || nicht e–e Minute z ~ *not a minute too soon* **2.** (~zeitig) sein Vater starb sehr ~ *his father died before his time* **III.** [abs] ~ u spät *morning and night*; v ~ bis spät *from morning till evening* || → ~er, ~est **Früh- ~apfel** m *early apple; summer apple* **~aufsteher** m *early riser*, ⟨hum⟩ *early bird*; er ist ~ *he is early* **~beet** n *hotbed; forcing* (od *propagating*)*-frame* **≃christlich** a *early Christian* **~druck** m *incunabulum* **~frost** m *early frost* **≃geboren** a *premature* (*baby*) **~geburt** f *premature birth* **~gemüse** n *early vegetable; earlies* pl **~geschichte** f *early history, primitive history* **~geschichtler** m *early historian* **≃geschichtlich** a *primitive* (*church*) **~gottesdienst** m *early service; matins* pl **~herbst** m *early autumn*, ⟨Am⟩ *e. fall* **~jahr** n *spring*; ~smesse [f] *spring fair* **~kartoffel** f *early potato* **~kost** f = –stück **~messe** f ⟨ec⟩ *early mass* **~mette** f ⟨ec C. E.⟩ *matins* pl **≃m·orgens** adv *early in the morning* **~obst** n *primeur* Fr **~reif** m *morning frost* **≃reif** a *early* (*fruit*), *forward* || *forward, precocious* (*boy*); ⟨poet⟩ *rath, rathe* **~reife** f *precocity* (*of a child*) **~romantik** f → Romantik **~schoppen** m ⟨Ger⟩ *morning glass of beer, etc* **≃steinzeitlich** a *eolithic* **~sterblichkeit** f (Säuglings-≃) *neo-natal mortality* **~stück** n *breakfast*; einfaches ~ *continental b.* || das ~ einnehmen *to* (*take*) *breakfast*; als ~ nehmen, zum ~ essen, trinken *to have for b.* || °den eß ich zum ~ ⟨fig⟩ *I'll have him for breakfast* || ~sspeise aus Getreide ⟨Am⟩ *cereal* **≃stücken** vi [h] *to breakfast* || °⟨fig sex⟩ *to get one's eyeful*; sie lädt zum F. ein *she flashes her charms* **~stücks-** ~dose [f] *sandwich box*; ~pause [f] *lunch; elevenses*; ⟨Ger⟩ *second breakfast at nine*; ~ m *to have b.* od *lunch* **~tomate** f *early tomato* **~trunk** m *morning-draught* **~wache** f ⟨mar⟩ *morning watch* **~warnsystem** n **d***istant* **e***arly* **w***arning* (*Dewline*) **~zeit** f *early period; early years* pl; *youth; spring-time* **≃zeitig 1.** a *early; initial; primitive* || *precocious* (*symptom*); *premature, untimely* **2.** adv *in good time* || *soon* || jdn ~ aufmerksam m *to warn a p* (daß *that*, auf *of*) **~zeitigkeit** f *earliness* || *precocity; untimeliness* **~zug** m *early train* **~zündung** f *premature ignition; pre-ignition*; || °⟨sex⟩ mit ~ abkommen *to go off at half-cock*; es gab ~ *it went off at h.-c.* **Fr·ühe** f *early hour* || in der ~ *at an early hour, early in the morning*; heute in der ~ *early this morning*; gleich in der ~ am Montag morgen (*the*) *first thing on Monday morning*; er besuchte uns in aller ~ *he came to see us* (*the*) *first thing in the morning* **fr·üher I.** a **1.** *earlier* **2.** (ehemalig) *former; past* (*errors*); *previous* (*illness*); *late* (*Government*) **II.** adv **1.** *earlier; sooner*; ~ oder später *sooner or later* **2.** *formerly; in the past*; .. anders als ~ .. *to treat a p differently to the old days*; ~ einmal *at some previous time* || Herr N., ~ an der Berliner Oper *Mr. N. late of the Berlin Opera* **fr·üh(e)st** a *earliest*; v s–r ~en Jugend an *from his earliest years* (*it was his ambition* ..) || *primitive* (*form*); *initial* (*stages*) || [abs] am ~en (*at the*) *earliest* od *soonest* **fr·üh(e)stens** adv (*at the*) *earliest* **Fr·ühling** m ⟨a. fig⟩ *spring; spring-time* **Fr·ühlings-** [in comp] *spring; spring-time; vernal* **≃artig** a *springlike; vernal* **~feier** f *celebration in spring; Easter fire* **~großreinemachen** n, **~hausputz** m *spring cleaning* **~knotenblume** f ⟨bot⟩ *snowdrop* **~luft** f *vernal air* **~morgen** m *spring morning* **~regen** m *vernal rain* **~sonne** f *springsun; vernal sun* **~tag** m *spring-day* (→ Herbst-, Sommer-, Wintertag); *day in spring* || **~-Tagundnachtgleiche** f ⟨astr⟩ *the vernal equinox* **~wetter** n *spring-weather*, bei schönem ~ *in fine s.-w.* **~zeit** f *spring-time, spring*

Fruktifikati·on [ts] f ⟨bot⟩ *fructification* **-fiz·ieren** vt [h] *to fructify* **Frukt·ose** f *fructose*

Frustrati·on [–ts–] f ~/~en *frustration*

F·uchs m –ses/F·üchse **A.** ⟨zoo⟩ **1.** *fox*; *old fox*; (über 3 Jahre alt) ⟨hunt⟩ *old f.* Wüsten≈ *fennee* (den ~) umstellen ⟨hunt⟩ (of hounds) *to mark .. to ground*; (e–n ~) aus dem Lager (Bau) treiben *to unkennel* (*unearth*) ‖ dem ~ Standarte, Pfoten etc abschneiden *to break up the fox* ‖ → Füchsin ‖ (in e–r Kleinstadt) wo sich ~ u Hase gute Nacht sagen ⟨Am sl⟩ *in the sticks* **2.** ⟨Lit⟩ Reineke ~, Reinhard der ~ *Reynard* (*the Fox*) **3.** = ~pelz **B.** ⟨übtr⟩ **1.** (Pferd) *sorrel*; *sorrel horse*; *bay, chestnut*; *bright* (od *light*) *bay horse* **2.** ⟨ent⟩ (Gr, Kl *large, small*) ~ *tortoise-shell* (*butterfly*) **3.** (Gold≈) (Geld) *shiner* **4.** °(P) ⟨univ⟩ *freshman*, ⟨sl⟩ *fresher* (krasser ~ *raw f.*); ⟨Am⟩ *flat* ‖ ⟨school⟩ *fag* **5.** ⟨billiards⟩ *fluke* ‖ ⟨cards⟩ (Karo As) *pig's eye* **6.** (Rauchgaskanal) *flue*; *uptake* **C.** °⟨fig⟩ (P) *fox*; → Füchschen; schlauer ~ *crafty dog*; *cunning* (od *sly*) *fox*; *coon*; sich schlau wie ein ~ stellen *to* (*play* [*the*]) *fox* **~balg** m *fox-skin* **~bart** m Mann mit e–m ~ *red-beard* **~bau** m *fox-earth*; e–n ~ verlegen ⟨hunt⟩ *to put to an earth* **~eisen** n, **~falle** f *fox-trap* **~-fährte** *line*; z Bau *drag* (*to hunt the d.*); die ~ rückwärts verfolgen (*of hounds*) *to run heel*(*-way*) **~farbe** f *fox-colour* **≈farben** a *fox-coloured*; *carroty, red* **~höhle** f = –bau **~jagd** f *fox-hunt*(*ing*); Hund z ~ *fox-hound* **~kopf** m *mask* **~lager** n (über d. Erde) *kennel* **~losung** f *billet* **~major** m ⟨Ger univ⟩ *senior man looking after the freshmen* **~pelz(kragen)** m *fox-fur*; *fox* **~röhre** f *drain* **≈-rot** a *fox-coloured* **~schwanz 1.** ⟨zoo⟩ *foxtail* ‖ ⟨hunt⟩ *brush* (*let me put the ~ in her hat*) **2.** ⟨bot⟩ *foxtail*; Roter ~ *love-lies-bleeding* **3.** (Säge) *hand-saw, tenon saw* **≈schwänzeln** vi [h] *to fawn*; ⟨fig⟩ ~ vor jdm *to fawn on a p* **~spur** f; alte ~ *stale line* **~stute** f *sorrel mare* °**≈teufels-w·ild**, **≈w·ild** a; ~ s (w) *to be* (*get*) *furious* (od *infuriated*; *in a wax*), *to be as angry as a wasp, to be red-hot with anger*; (w *to fly off the handle*) ⟨Am⟩ *to be mad* (über *at*), ⟨sl⟩ *burnt-up* **F·üchschen** n *little fox*; ⟨fig⟩ (rothaarige P) ⟨sl⟩ *badger, ginger, Sandy, Rufus* °**f·uchsen** vt [h] S (jdn) *to annoy, irritate, vex*; *worry* ‖ sich [acc] ~ *to be vexed* (über *at*); *to worry* (über *about*); er fuchste sich mächtig *he was mighty vexed* **F·uchsie** [–iə] f ~/~n ⟨bot⟩ *fuchsia* [L] ***f·uchsig** a *foxy* ‖ ⟨fig⟩ *furious* **F·üchsin** f ⟨zoo⟩ *vixen, she-fox*

F·uchtel f **1.** †*broadsword* **2.** ⟨übtr⟩ *control, grip*, (jdn) unter der ~ h *to have* (*a p*) *under one's control* (od *in one's grip, in tow, on toast*); (Massen) unter der ~ h *to sway*; sie hat ihn ganz unter ihrer ~ *she has him in her pocket, she runs him all right* ‖ unter jds ~ stehen *to be in a p's grip* od *under a p's thumb*; *to be swayed by a p* ‖ unter jds ~ bringen *to bring under a p's sway* ‖ unter jds ~ k. *to fall into a p's grip* ‖ jdn unter die ~ nehmen *to keep a tight hand on* (od *over*) *a p, to keep a p under control* (od *well in hand*); *to subject a p to a rigorous discipline* °**f·uchteln** vi [h] ⟨übtr⟩ ~, herum~ *to paw* (auf .. *on the piano*) ‖ ~ mit *to fidget with* (*the hands, pencil*); mit den Armen ~ *to wave* (od *flourish*) *one's arms*; mit den Händen in der Luft ~ *to gesticulate*; er fuchtelte kräftig mit den H. in der Luft *his hands flew expressively in the air* °**f·uchtig** a [mst pred] *furious*; *in a wax*; *as mad as a hatter*; ⟨Am⟩ *mad* (über *at*) ‖ auf jdn ~ s *to be angry* (⟨sl⟩ *waxy*) *at* od *with a p*

F·uder n ~s/~ *cart-load*, (*wag(g)on-*)*load*; ein ~ Heu *a* (*cart-*)*load of hay* ‖ ~weise *by the wag(g)on-load, by wag(g)on-loads*; ⟨übtr⟩ *in heaps* | (of wine) *vat*, → Tonne

Fudschij·ama m (Vulkan in Japan) *Fujiyama*, ⟨fam⟩ *Fuji*

Fug m [nur in:] mit ~ u Recht *with justice*; *by rights, by good* (od *due*) *right*; *legitimately, rightfully*; mit ~ u R. tun *to be justified in doing*; *to be competent to do*; *to have a right to do*

F·uge[1] f ~/~n ⟨arch & carp⟩ *joint*; ~n [pl] *joints*; *seams* (*of a ship*); → Einlegestück, Mörtel; Schlichthobel ‖ (~ aus Nut u Feder) *rabbet--joint*; (Bretter) durch e–e ~ verbinden *to rabbet* ‖ Schwalbenschwanz≈ *dovetail-joint* | in allen Fugen krachen ⟨oft fig⟩ *to be shaken to its foundations* ‖ (etw) aus den ~n bringen *to disjoint, unjoint*; ⟨fig⟩ *to put out of joint*; *to unhinge* ‖ aus den ~n gehen ⟨a. fig⟩ *to be put out of joint, to be unhinged* ‖ die Welt ist aus den ~n *the world is out of joint*

F·uge[2] f ~/~n ⟨mus⟩ *fugue*; kz ~ *fughetta* [It]; e–e ~ spielen *to perform a fugue*

f·ugen vt [h] ⟨carp⟩ *to joint*; (durch Nut u Feder) *to rabbet*; → zus–fügen **F·ugen- 1.** (→ Fuge[1]) **≈dicht** a *joined* **~einlage** f *lining*; *shim* **~kelle** f ⟨mas⟩ *pointing trowel* **≈los** a *jointless*; *without joints* ‖ ⟨übtr⟩ *continuous* **≈maschine** f ⟨tech⟩ *jointing-machine*; *jointer* **~schneider** m *joint-cutter* **~schnitt** m *furrows, groovings* pl **2.** (→ Fuge[2]) **~komponist** m *fuguist* **~stil** m *fugued style*; Komposition im ~ *fugato* [It] **f·ügen** vt [h] **A. 1.** ⟨eig⟩ (etw) *to attach, join* (an *to*); *to add, annex* (an *to*); ein Stück an das andere ~ *to join one piece to another* ‖ *to lay*; *to place, put*; e–n Stein auf den anderen ~ *to lay one stone on another* ‖ → an~, bei~, ein~, hinzu~, ineinander~, zu~, zus-~ **2.** ⟨übtr⟩ (etw) *to decree, to direct, to dispose*; (of God, etc) *to ordain, predestine, will*; es muß s, wie Gott es fügt *it must be as God wills* (od *ordains*) ‖ wie der Zufall es fügte, waren vier Räume da, der Z. fügte es, daß 4 R. da waren *as it happened there were four rooms* **B. sich** ~ **1.** ⟨eig⟩ *to be joined* (an *to*) **2.** ⟨übtr⟩ (passen) *to suit*; *to be convenient* od *suitable* ‖ [imps] wie **es** sich fügt *according to circumstances*; *as it suits you*; es fügte sich, **daß** .. *it chanced* od *happened that* ..; es f. sich, daß ich gerade dort war *I happened to be there* **3.** (P) *to give in* od *way*; *to yield, refrain*; ⟨fam⟩ *to come to heel* ‖ sich ~ lernen *to toe the line* ‖ sich e–r S ~ *to conform to a th*; *to accommmodate* od *adapt o.s. to a th*; sich den Gesetzen ~ *to compromise with the laws*; sich den Regeln ~ *to conform to the rules, to toe the line*; sich jds Plänen ~ *to fall into a p's plans*; sich jdm, jds Meinung ~ *to defer to a p's opinion* ‖ sich ~ **in** etw *to acquiesce in, to put up with, to reconcile o.s. with, to resign o.s.* (od *to submit*) *to a th*; füge dich in das Unabänderliche *resign yourself to irrevocable facts*, ⟨fam⟩ *to sign on the dotted line*; sich darein ~ ⟨Am⟩ *to take the medicine* ‖ sich gut zu etw ~ (bes Farben) *to match a th* **F·ügewort** n ⟨gram⟩ = Bindewort

fug·iert a ⟨mus⟩ *fugued*

f·üglich 1. † a = passend ‖ ~er Weise **2.** adv *conveniently, suitably*; *justly*; (*very*) *well*; du kannst ~ nicht behaupten .. *you can't very well pretend* (*you didn't listen*) **f·ügsam** a (P) *compliant, flexible, pliable, pliant*; *supple*; *docile, ductile, manageable, tractable*; *obedient* | **≈keit** f ~/ *flexibility, pliability, pliancy*; *docility, ductility*

Fügung f ~/~en ⟨gram⟩ *sequence* (*of words*); *construction* ‖ ⟨mst fig⟩ *dispensation*; göttliche ~, ~ Gottes (*or* des Himmels) *heavenly dispensation, dispensation of Providence*; eine seltsame ~ wollte es, daß er genas *his recovery is a special providence*

f·ühlbar 1. a *palpable* (*the swelling is p.*); *tactile, tangible*; *perceptible, sensible* ‖ ⟨übtr⟩ *felt* (*want*); *appreciable, considerable*; *great*; *serious* (*loss*) ‖ sich ~ m *to make itself felt* ‖ → deutlich, merklich **2.** adv ⟨übtr⟩ *perceptibly*; *appreciably, considerably* | **≈keit** f *palpability, tangibility*; *perceptibility, sensibility* ‖ *greatness*; *seriousness* **f·ühlen** vt/i [h] **I.** vt **A. 1.** ⟨eig⟩ (e–n Reiz;

Gegenstand) to feel; to have a sensation of (cold, heat); er fühlte plötzlich Nässe an den Beinen dampness struck his legs || fühle nur, wie kalt ich bin just feel how cold I am || jdm den Puls ~ to feel a p's pulse **2. a.** ich fühle alle meine Glieder I feel wretched, I ache all over; I am quite done up **b.** (Freude, Kummer etc) to feel; jds Tod ~ to feel a p's death **c.** (Gefahr, Unheil) to feel, to sense; er soll m–e Rache z ~ bek. he shall feel my vengeance || in sich ~ → Beruf || Lust ~ to have a mind, to be inclined (to do) || etw wohl ~ to be sensible od aware of a th || jdn etw ~ l to make a p feel a th; jdn s–n Ärger (or s–e schlechte Laune) ~ l to vent one's anger on a p **3.** ich fühlte den Schmerz k. I felt the pain come od coming **4.** ich fühlte, wir hatten Unrecht I felt (that) we were wrong; ich f., daß dies ein Wendepunkt war I felt this to be a turning-point (in ..); jdn etw ~ l to let a p be aware of a th **B. sich ~ 1.** sich warm ~ to feel warm || sich wohl ~ to feel well; to feel at home (in a country); sich wieder ganz im Besitz s–r Kräfte ~, sich wieder ganz wohl ~ to feel quite o.s. again; ich weiß, wie ich mich fühle, wenn .. I know what I feel like if ..; sich danach ~ to feel like it || sich glücklich, beleidigt ~ to feel happy, hurt; sich sicher ~ to feel one's legs (od feet); sich als ein gr Mann ~ to feel o.s. a great man; sich °mies (= miserabel) ~ ⟨fam⟩ to feel lousy; sich unbehaglich ~ to feel out of it; ⟨cosm⟩ sich selbstsicher ~ to feel controlled **2. er fühlte sich** (so recht) he gave himself airs, he thought no small beer of himself; er f. sich ausgeschlossen he felt out of it **II.** vi **1.** to feel; to be sentient || er fühlt sehr fein he is very sensitive || → hören **2. an etw ~** to touch a th; ⟨Am⟩ to feel of a th || ⟨fig⟩ **auf** den Zahn ~ to throw out a feeler; jdm auf den Z. ~ to sound a p out, to put a p through his paces || **mit** jdm ~ to feel for a p, to sympathize with a p || mit den Händen ~ nach to feel for (a th) **F·ühlen** n feeling, feel; → Gefühl || durch ~ feststellen to ascertain by feeling; to feel (ob whether); durch ~ s–n Weg suchen to feel one's way **f·ühlend** a sentient (~e Wesen sentients); feeling (heart); sympathizing; sympathetic (look) **F·ühler** m ⟨zoo⟩ feeler, horn, tentacle; antenna [L] [pl -nae] || ⟨übtr⟩ feeler; draw; ⟨pol⟩ ballon d'essai [Fr]; die or s–e ~ ausstrecken to put (od throw) out feelers **F·ühlhorn** n ⟨zoo⟩ = Fühler **f·ühllos** a senseless, insensible, insentient, unfeeling **F·ühllosigkeit** f senselessness, insensibility **F·ühlung** f ⟨bes mil⟩ contact, touch || ~ h to be in touch (mit with ..); halten to keep in touch (with ..); ~ nehmen, in ~ treten to get into touch, to make contact (with ..); die ~ verlieren to lose (od get out of) touch (with ..) || in enge ~ k. ⟨fig⟩ to come to close quarters (with ..) **~halter** m ⟨tact⟩ tentacle **~nahme** f contact (mit with); approach; communication; understanding || mündliche ~ consultation, discussion

fuhr [1. & 3. pret] v fahren **F·uhr- ~geld** n = -lohn [m] **~gelegenheit** f conveyance **~herr** m livery stable keeper; → Fuhrwerksbesitzer **~knecht** m carter's man **~leute** pl carriers, carters pl **~lohn** m cartage, carriage, wag(g)onage **~mann** [pl ~leute] carrier; carter, wag(g)oner; driver; ein alter ~ an old hand || ⟨astr⟩ Wag(g)oner **|** ~skittel [m] carrier's smock (-frock); ~smantel [m] carter's cloak; ~speitsche [f] cart-whip **~park** m park || ~kolonne [f] ⟨mil⟩ supply (od wagon)-train **~unternehmer** m haulage contractor **~werk** n ⟨allg⟩ conveyance, vehicle; (Pferde≈) v. drawn by horses; → Gespann; Wagen || (f P) carriage || (Last≈) cart; dray; (motor-)lorry || ~sbesitzer, ~svermieter [m] job-master || ~sverkehr [m] vehicular (od wheeled) traffic **~wesen** n conveyance; transport **F·uhre** f ~/~n **1.** [abstr] carriage, conveyance; transport; mit ~ anfahren to carry (od bring) by wag(g)on **2.** [konkr] cart (od wag[g]on)-load; load; e–e ~ Holz a (waggon-)load of timber **f·ühren** vt/i [h] **I. vt A.** *(befördern) [nur in:] (Geld, Waren) aus dem Lande ~ to send out of the country, to export; → aus–, einführen **B. (geleiten) 1. a.** (Blinden) to guide; (jdn) to guide, pilot (durch .. through a forest) || jdn **an** der Hand ~ to lead a p by the hand, to hand a p (nach .. to a seat); (Pferd am Zügel) to lead; (Fahrrad) to wheel; (Braut) **zum** Altar ~ to lead to the altar; (Dame) z Tanz ~ to lead out; z Tisch ~ to take in, ⟨Am⟩ to take out to dinner || jdm die Hand, die Feder ~ to guide a p's hand, pen **b.** ~ Sie mich irgendwohin, wo .. ⟨Am⟩ take me some place where || jdn ~ **durch, nach** .. to take a p through, to (a room); .. **auf- u ab~** to walk a p back and forth; .. **aus, in** to show, usher, walk a p out of, into (the room); er führte die Truppen über .. he marched the troops over (the bridge) || (gewählt:) to conduct (nach to); (zeremoniell) to escort, induct (z .. into a seat) **|** (jdn) **vor** den Richter ~ to carry before the magistrate || vor Herrn N. geführt w to be introduced into the presence of Mr. N. **|** (jdn) **eilig** ~ to hurry (in into); geschäftig ~ to bustle (into ..) || jdn spazieren ~ to take a p for a walk || in Versuchung ~ to lead into temptation **c.** (S) to lead, to take (nach to): the path will lead you to the house; chance led him to Berlin || to bring, to carry; was führt Sie hierher? what brings you here? diese Geschichte führt uns in e–e Zeit .. this story takes (od carries) us to a time .. **d.** (Glas, Speise) **z Munde** ~ to carry to one's mouth, to raise to one's lips **2. (lenken,** leiten) to direct, (he is difficult to d.), to guide **3.** (anführen) (Heer, Expedition) to command, lead; (Truppen) to handle; fight (he fought his troops well) || to control (operations ⟨a. mil⟩) || (Schiff) to fight, pilot, navigate; ein Flugzeug ~ to fly od navigate an aeroplane **C.** ⟨**übtr**⟩ **1. a.** etw bei or mit sich ~ to carry a th with one; Gepäck (etc) ~ to carry luggage **b.** (Wappen) to carry; have; (ein Schwert) to carry || (of a ship) e–e Flagge ~ to fly a flag; (Lichter) to carry; das Schiff führte 10 Geschütze the ship was mounted with 10 guns **c.** (of river) (Geröll) to carry **d.** ⟨com⟩ **(Waren)** to keep, sell, stock; to keep in stock; ⟨Am⟩ to carry || Wolle ~ to deal in wool **2. (Namen,** Titel) to bear; den Titel N. ~ to title o.s. N. || ein Buch, das den T. führt .. a book entitled .. **3.** das **Schwert** ~ (→ o. 1. b.) to wield the sword; to fight; die Feder ~ to wield the pen, to write || das Ruder ~ to handle the oar **4. (Straße)** to construct; to lay down; e–e Mauer ~ um to carry a wall round ..; to wall (a garden); e–e Hecke, e–n Zaun ~ um .. to hedge; to fence (in) || er führte den Draht in .. he inserted the wire into (the hole) **5.** e–n **Schlag** ~ to deal (od strike) a blow (nach at); to strike **6. Buch** (or die Bücher) ~ to keep books (jdm for a p) || Briefwechsel ~ to carry on (od keep up) a correspondence (mit with) || die Kasse ~ to be in charge of the money (⟨cards⟩ .. of the pool); to be the cashier || (Listen) to maintain **7.** ⟨**fig**⟩ jdn an der Nase ~ → nasführen || jdn aufs Glatteis ~ → Eis || → Licht || im Munde ~ to utter; (Sprache) to use; leere Worte im M. ~ to drivel; to talk rot; (den Namen Gottes) unnütz im M. ~ to take in vain || im Schilde ~, im Sinne ~ to design, to plan; to have designs (gegen .. on od against a p) || jdm etw z Gemüte ~ to bring a th home to a p **D. [mit abstr Objekt] 1.** den Beweis or Nachweis ~ f (etw) to prove (a th); to establish, to make good, to verify (a claim) **2. Krieg** ~ gegen to make od wage war against, on (a p); K. ~ mit to be at war with (a p); to fight (a p); e–n K. ~ to fight a war || (Feldzug) to conduct; (Aufruhr) to head **3.** e–n **Prozeß** ~ to go to law, to lay a case; den P. ~ (of a barrister) *to plead* od *try the case* ‖ Klage ~ *to make complaints, to complain* (über *about, of*) **4.** **(Amt)** *to hold* ‖ die Herrschaft ~ *to be at the helm*; *to rule*; die Regierung ~ *to govern*; den Staat ~ *to guide the state* ‖ → Aufsicht ‖ **(Geschäfte)** *to manage, run*; den Haushalt, die Wirtschaft ~ *to keep house* (jdm *for a p*); e–e gute Küche ~ *to keep a good table*; ein gut geführtes Haus *a well-run house* ‖ → Protokoll ‖ die Verhandlungen ~ *to act as the spokesman*; ⟨**parl**⟩ *to lead the House* ‖ den Vorsitz ~ *to take the chair*; den V. ~ in *or* bei *to preside at* od *over* (*a meeting*) **5.** ein **Gespräch** ~ *to have conversation, to converse*; *to talk* (*with*); *to telephone* (mit .. *to a p*) ‖ e–e derbe Sprache ~ *to use strong language* ‖ das Wort ~ *to act as the spokesman* (od *mouthpiece*); das gr W. ~ *to boast, to brag*; *to draw the long bow* **6.** ein glückliches **Leben** ~ *to lead* od *live a happy life*; → Ehe **E. sich** ~ *to bear* od *conduct o.s.* **II. vi 1.** *to lead* ‖ **sich** ~ **l** *to be open to persuasion*; sich nicht ~ l *to refuse to be guided* **2.** (**~d sein**) **a.** *to lead*; *to be in the van*; → ~d **b.** ⟨sport⟩ *to lead*; *to make the running*; er führt um mehrere Längen *he is leading by several lengths* **3.** **(S) a.** die Straße führt nach .. *the road leads to* ..; sein Weg führte durch .. über .. *his way lay* (od *was*) *through* (*a forest*), *over* (*a bridge*); e–e Brücke führt über .. *a bridge leads over* (*the river*) ‖ die Tür führt in den Garten *the door gives into* (od *gives entrance to*) *the garden*; .. in die Halle .. *on to the hall* **b.** ⟨**fig**⟩ alle Wege ~ nach Rom *all roads lead to Rome* ‖ wohin soll das noch ~? *where is that going to lead us?* ‖ **zu etw** ~ *to end* (od *result*) *in, to conduce* (od *lead*) *to*; *to be conducive to a th*; *to bring a th about*; *to work to* (*opposite ends*); *to produce a th*; z nichts ~d *dead end* (*thesis*); z k–m Ergebnis ~ *to come to nothing*; es wird z nichts Gutem *or* z k–m guten Ende ~ *no good will come of it*; *it will come to a bad end* ‖ im weiteren Verlauf z etw ~ *to lead on to* .. ‖ es würde **z weit** ~, wenn ich ausführte *it would take me too long* (od *would be outside my scope*) *to point out* **F·ühren** n *guiding* ‖ *leading*; ⟨hunt⟩ *lead* ‖ ~ v (Lagekarten) *maintenance of* **f·ührend** a **1.** [pred] ~ s *to be leading, to lead*; *to be at the top, to be uppermost* (od *in the van*); als Chirurg ist er sicherlich ~ *as a surgeon he certainly leads*; ~ s unter den Chirurgen *to be in the van* (od *to lead the van*) *of surgeons*; ~ s in .. *to be prominent in* (*one's line*) **2.** [attr] *leading* (*statesman*); *first-rate*; ⟨Am⟩ *banner* (*state of the Union*) ‖ *controlling, directing*; *prominent* ‖ *standard* (Werk); *key* (*personality*) ‖ ~er Dragoman *dragoman in charge* ‖ ~es Pferd (im Viergespann) *leader* ‖ an ~er Stelle stehen = ~ s ‖ hohe ~e Stellung *high directing station, position of primacy*; in ~er Stellung *at the top of the tree*; Mann in ~er St. *leading man*; ⟨Am⟩ *key man* ‖ ⟨theat⟩ ~e Rolle *lead*; ⟨übtr⟩ e–e ~e R. spielen *to be prominent* (*in*) **F·ührer** m ~s/~ **A.** (P) **1.** *guide* (*of the blind*) ‖ *conductor* ‖ ⟨übtr⟩ *guide*; *leader*; die ~ [pl] *the van* (*of civilization*) ‖ geistl. ~ ⟨A Ind⟩ *guru* ‖ jds ~ s *to be a p's guide* (in *in*) ‖ der Instinkt ist ein sicherer ~ *instinct is a safe guide* ‖ ⟨mil⟩ *commander*; *one's superior*; Persönlichkeit e–s ~s *character of a commander* **2.** *driver* (*of a car*); *pilot* (*of a ship*) ‖ Kran⁓ (etc) *craneman*, ⟨Am⟩ *crane operator* ‖ → Lokomotiv⁓, Zug⁓ **3.** (Berg⁓, Stadt⁓) *guide* ‖ ⟨com⟩ → Buch⁓, Rechnungs⁓, Schrift⁓ **4.** (Anführer) **a.** ⟨mil⟩ *commander* ‖ ⟨nav⟩ ~ (der Torpedostreitkräfte) *captain*; (nächsthöher:) *commodore*; (darüber) *admiral* ‖ als ~ fungieren *to be in command* **b.** *chief, head* (*of a clan*); *leader* (*of a party*); *ringleader* (*of a movement*) ‖ die ~ der Industrie *the captains* [pl] *of industry* **c.** ⟨pol⟩ der oberste ~ *the supreme head* (*of the state*) ‖ ⟨Ger hist⟩ der ~ ⟨nazi⟩ *the Führer*; → Duce **B.** **(S)** (Reise⁓) *guide* (durch, für, zu *to*); *guide-book*; ein ~ durch Berlin *a guide to Berlin* ‖ ⟨übtr⟩ (Leitfaden) *guide* (z *to*) **~ausbildung** f *leader-training* **~auslese** f *selection of leaders* ‖ [konkr] *the flower of the leaders* **~besprechung** f *executive meeting*; *conference* **~eigenschaft** f *leadership-quality*; vornehmste ~ *crowing quality of leadership* **~fahrzeug** a ⟨mar⟩ *leader vessel* **~flugzeug** n *command airplane* **~gedanke** m *leadership-idea* **~gehilfe** m → Adjutant, → Bd. I. G-1 etc **~gondel** f ⟨aero⟩ *car* **~grundsatz** m, **~prinzip** n *principle of leadership, leadership-principle* **~hauptquartier** n ⟨nazi⟩ *the Führer's Headquarters* pl **~haus** n ⟨rail, mot⟩ *cab* **~kabine** f *pilot's cabin* **~kanzel** f *pilot's cockpit* **~kompaß** m ⟨aero⟩ *pilot compass* **~kurs** m ⟨mil⟩ *officer training course* **~prinzip** n *principle of authoritarian leadership* **~prüfung** f ⟨mot⟩ *driving-test* **~raum** m ⟨mar aero⟩ *pilot's cabin*; → –sitz **~schein** m ⟨mot⟩ *driving-licence*; ⟨aero sl⟩ *pilot('s) certificate, ticket* | ~entzug [m] *disqualification from driving* (auf .. *for 2 years*), *driving ban* **~schule** f *school for leader-training* **~sitz** m ⟨mot⟩ *driver's seat* ‖ ⟨aero⟩ *cockpit*; → –raum **~staat** m *state based upon the principle of leadership* **~stab** m *command group* **~stand** m ⟨aero⟩ *cabin*; ⟨tech⟩ *control cabin*; ⟨rail⟩ *cab*; (Panzer⁓) *tank commander's position* | ~signal [n] ⟨el⟩ *car* (⟨Am⟩ *cab*) *signal* **F·ührerin** f (*female*) *guide* ‖ *female driver* **f·ührerlos** a *guideless*; *driverless*; ⟨aero⟩ *pilotless, robot* (*plane*) **F·ührerschaft** f ~/ **F·ührertum** n ~s/ **1.** [abstr] *leadership, guidance*; *command* **2.** [konkr] *leaders* pl **F·ührung** ~/~en **A.** [abstr] **1.** ~ durch die Bibliothek *the showing over the library*; ~ durch die Stadt *showing the sights of a town*; *showing round* **2.** *control*; *management* (*of affairs*); *keeping* (*of books*); → Bogen⁓; laufende ~ (v Listen, Karten etc) *maintenance* ‖ *direction, guidance*; *generalship, leadership* (*of a p*) ‖ ⟨mil⟩ *command*; elastische ~ der Versorgung *resilient logistical operations*; straffe ~ *strict control*; die ~ gliedert sich in .. *the command structure is organized into* | die ~ muß ausgehen v .. *the lead must come from* .. ‖ die ~ h *to lead*; *to be uppermost* (od *in the van*) ‖ die ~ an sich reißen ⟨pol⟩ *to usurp the power* ‖ die ~ übernehmen *to take the lead, to take charge*; die ~ in e–r Lage übern. *to take charge of a situation* ‖ unter der ~ v *under the guidance of* ..; ⟨mil⟩ unter der ~ stehen v *to be under the command of*; *to be headed* (od *led*) *by* **3.** ⟨sport⟩ *lead* ‖ die ~ h, in ~ s *to be leading* (od *in the lead*); *to lead* ‖ die ~ übernehmen, in ~ gehen *to lead*; *to take up the running*; (of a horse) *to forge ahead* ‖ e–e 5–1 ~ herausholen *to go into a 5–1 lead, to be leading 5–1.* **4.** (Verhalten) *bearing, behaviour*; *conduct* (*bad, good c.*); Entlassung wegen schlechter ~ *bad conduct discharge* **B.** [konkr] ⟨tech⟩ *guide*; *slide*; Film⁓ *film guide*; Gerad⁓ *guides, guide-bars* pl **F·ührungs- ~akademie** f ⟨mil⟩ *Command College* **~attest** n *testimonial to a p's conduct* **~band** n *driving band* (*of a shell*) **~befehl** m *operation order* **~begriffe** m pl ⟨mil⟩ *command concepts* **~bereich** m *command echelon* **~bogen** m, **~buch** n ⟨mil⟩ *conduct-sheet* (*of a soldier*) **~bügel** m ⟨tech⟩ *guide-ring* **~feder** f = –leiste **~grundlagen** f pl ⟨mil⟩ *bases for operational decisions* **~kabel** n ⟨el⟩ *trailing cable* **~kräfte** f pl *leaders*; Schulung v ~n *leadership training* **~lager** n ⟨tech⟩ *horizontal, vertical neck-journal bearing* **~leine** f, ~seil n *guide-line* ⟨a. a–n⟩ **~leiste** f ⟨tech⟩ *feather* od *wing* (*of a valve*) ‖ (e–r Schiebetür) *tongue* **~lineal** n ⟨tech⟩ *fence* **~nut, ~rille** f *groove* **~panzer** m *key tank* **~ring** m ⟨artill⟩ *driving ring* **~rolle** f ⟨tech⟩ *belt guide*; *g. pulley* od *roller* **~schiene** f ⟨tech⟩ *guide-rail*; ⟨comp⟩ *guiding track* **~schiff** n ⟨mar tact⟩ *headquarters ship* **~schraube** f ⟨tech⟩ *guide-screw* **~schuh** m *guide* od *slide* (*of a cross-head*) **~stab** m (am Geschoß) *guide-rod* || ⟨tact⟩ *operations staff* **~stange** f *guide-rod* **~-trosse** f *tag-line* **~truppen** f pl *command and control troops* **~zapfen** m ⟨tech⟩ *pilot* **~zeugnis** n ⟨mil⟩ *service-record* || ⟨police⟩ *certificate of* (*good*) *conduct, clearance c.*; ⟨a.⟩ *reference* || (f Dienstboten) *character* (*reference*)

Fuk·ose f ⟨chem⟩ *fucose*

F·ulbe pl (hamit. Stamm) *Fula, Fulani*

Fulgur·it m ~s/~e = Blitzröhre

F·üll- (→ füllen) **~ansatz** m ⟨aero⟩ *appendix* [L] **~apparat** m *filling-apparatus* **~artikel** m (Zeitung) *fudge* [abstr] **~blatt** n (Zigarre) *filler leaf* **~bleistift** m *refilling pencil*; *eversharp* **~element** n *inert cell* **~feder** f *fountain-pen, stylograph*; (~halter) *fountain-pen, stylographic pen* **~hahn** m ⟨tech⟩ *feed-cock* **~hebel** m *filling-lever* **~horn** n *horn of plenty, cornucopia* [L] **~körper** m pl *fillings* pl **~maschine** f *filling-machine* **~material** n ⟨typ⟩ *leads* pl **~metall** n *filler metal* **~mittel** n (Streck–) ⟨tech⟩ *filler* **~ofen** m ⟨Ger⟩ *charging--stove* **~ort** m ⟨min⟩ *shaft-station* **~rumpf** m = –trichter **~stab** m ⟨arch⟩ *cabling* **~stein** m *expletive* **~stift** m *filling pencil*; *stylographic pencil* **~stoff** m *filling material*; *fillings* pl **~trichter** m ⟨tech⟩ (*feed*) *hopper* **~vorrichtung** f *filling--device* (od *apparatus*) **~werk** n ⟨arch⟩ *rubble--work* || ⟨arts⟩ *accessories* pl (*of a picture*); *garnishings* pl || ⟨Lit⟩ *padding* **~wort** n ⟨gram⟩ *expletive*

F·ülle f ~/ **1.** (körperliche ~) *corpulence, plumpness, stoutness* || *fullness* (*of the face*) || *richness* (*of a voice*) **2.** (Vorrat) **a.** *plenty* (an *of*) || gr ~, üppige ~ *abundance, wealth* (an, von *of*); verschwenderische ~ *lavish supply*; *profusion* (*of gifts*) || → Hülle **b.** *fullness, richness* (*of colour*); *riches* (*of grace*); *plethora* (*of motives*); *wealth* (*of words, ideas*); die üppige ~ ihrer Locken *the wealth of her showering locks*; die ~ der Einzelheiten *the fullness of detail* **f·üllen** vt [h] **I.** (voll m) **A. 1.** (Gefäß) *to fill* (mit .. *with water*; bis an den Rand *to the brim*) || voll ~ *to fill full, to fill up*; (Glas) *to charge* || (Batterie) *to charge*; (Pfeife) *to load* || die Segel mit Wind ~ *to fill the sails* || sich [dat] die Taschen ~ *to fill one's pockets*; sich den Bauch ~ *to eat one's fill*; *to overeat* (*o.s.*), *to line* (*a p's pockets, one's stomach*) **2.** ⟨cul⟩ (Geflügel) *to stuff* (mit *with*); → gefüllt **3.** ⟨tech⟩ **a.** (hohlen Zahn) *to stop*, ⟨Am⟩ *to fill* **b.** (Ballon, Reifen) *to inflate* **c.** (Bild) mit Farben ~ *to ground*; → grundieren **d.** der Band füllt 300 Seiten *the volume fills* od *covers 300 pages* **4.** (Haus, Kirche) *to fill*; *crowd, throng* (*mit .. with people*) || gefüllt s v *to be crowded with ..* (*books, people*) **5.** (Herz, Seele) *to fill, supply* (*with courage*); ⟨bib⟩ jdn ~ mit etw *to bestow a th on a p, to grant a th to a p* **B. sich ~** (of a glass, room) *to fill* (*with ..*) (*the room filled*) || ihre Augen ~ sich mit Tränen *tears well up to her eyes* **II.** (Flüssigkeit) *to put* od *pour* (in .. *into a glass*); (Bier) auf Fässer ~ *to barrel*; (Wein) auf Flaschen ~ *to bottle* || ⟨übtr⟩ → stopfen **F·üllen**[1] n *filling* (*with ..*); *charging* || *stuffing* (*of fowl*) || *stopping* (*of a tooth*) || *inflating* (*of a ballon*) | ~ v Bier in Fässer *the barrelling of beer*; ~ v Wein auf Flaschen *the bottling of wine* **F·üller** m = Füllfederhalter; Selbst≈ *self-filling fountain pen* || (Tinten≈) *filler* || Zeilen≈ *line-filler*

F·üllen[2] n = Fohlen

F·ullererde f *fuller's earth*

f·üllig a *full* (*face*); mit ~em Gesicht *full in the face, full-faced* (*p*) || *voluminous* (Kleid) **F·üllsel** n ~s/~ ⟨cul⟩ *stuffing*; *force-meat*; → Füllung || (im Ausdruck) *padding*; ~ [pl] *stopgaps* pl **F·üllung** f ~/~en **1.** [abstr] = Füllen[1] **2.** [konkr] **a.** ⟨arch⟩ *bay*; Tür≈ *panel* **b.** (Ladung) *charge* (*of a battery*) || ⟨cul⟩ *stuffing, force-meat* || *filling* (*of a tooth*, etc.) **~sbrett** n ⟨arch⟩ *lining*

fulmin·ant a ⟨übtr⟩ *tremendous*; ⟨fam⟩ *thundering* (*fool*; *lie, mistake*); *thumping* (*dinner*); *whacking, whopping*; → blitzend, drohend

Fumar·ole f [It] ~/~n (vulkan. Gasausstrahlung) *fumarole*; → Mofette

Fum·arsäure f ⟨chem⟩ *fumaric acid*

°**F·ummel** m ~s/~n (altes, schlecht gekleidetes Weib) *frump, dowdy* | *dowdy* (*dress*)

×**F·ummel** f ⟨übtr⟩ *slut*; → Schlampe °**f·ummeln** vt/i [h] vt *to rub and clean* (*one's hands*) | vi ~ an etw *to fumble with*; *to boggle at*; *to paw about a th*; *to paw a th* (*he pawed his beard*) || °⟨sex⟩ *to fumble* °**F·ummler** m ⟨sex⟩ *fumbler, fingerer*

F·und m ~es/~e **1.** [abstr] *finding* **2.** (Gefundenes) *find*; *discovery, invention* || ⟨oft praeh⟩ *find*; ⟨Am⟩ *strike* (*a happy* od *lucky s.*); e–n ~ m *to make a find* **~büro** n *Lost Property Office*, ⟨Am⟩ *Lost and Found* (*Office*) **~diebstahl** m *the keeping of lost property* **~grube** f ⟨min⟩ → –stätte; Grube, Mine || ⟨mst übtr⟩ *mine, source*; ~ der Belehrung *mine* (od *quarry*) *of information*; er ist e–e ~ der Gelehrsamkeit *he is a depository* (od *storehouse*) *of learning* **~gut** n *lost property* **~ort** m ⟨a. biol⟩ *habitat* [L] (*of a plant*, etc.) **~recht** n *law relating to lost property* **~stätte** f ⟨min⟩ (Erz≈) *placer* || *place of finding* (od *discovery*); → –ort **~stelle** f ⟨tech⟩ *source*

Fundam·ent n ~(e)s/~e *base* (*of a mountain*); *bedrock*; *groundwork* || ⟨arch⟩ *foundation*(*s* pl); *substructure* || ⟨typ⟩ *bed* (*of a press*); *form-bed* | ⟨übtr⟩ *basis, foundation*(*s* pl), *groundwork*; → Grundlage || das ~ legen z *to lay the basis* (od *foundation*[*s*]) *of* **fundament·al** a ⟨übtr⟩ *basal*; *fundamental* (*truths*); *bedrock* (*difference*) **Fundamental·ismus** m ⟨Am ec⟩ *fundamentalism* **fund·ieren** vt [h] **1.** = (be)gründen, stiften **2.** (Staatsschuld) *to fund* **3.** ⟨übtr⟩ (Einfluß, Macht) *to consolidate* **fund·iert** a **1.** ⟨com⟩ ~e Anleihe *funded* (od *consolidated*) *loan*; ~e Schuld *funded debt* || ~es Einkommen *unearned income* **2.** ⟨übtr⟩ gut ~ *well-established*; *solid* (*business*); *well-grounded* (*knowledge*); *well-bottomed* (*character*) **Fund·ierung** f *the funding* (*of a loan*) || ⟨übtr⟩ *consolidation*; *establishment*; *foundation*

°**fundig** a (glänzend) *splendid*; ⟨sl⟩ *ripping*; e–e ~e Zeit *a high old time*

f·ündig a ⟨min⟩ = ergiebig || ~ w *to strike*

°**Funds-** [in comp] → °Pfunds-

F·undus m [L] ⟨anat⟩ *fundus* [L]

F·üne m, **F·ünin** f *inhabitant* (od *native*) *of Funen* **F·ünen** n (dän. Insel[gruppe]) *Funen*

f·ünf a **1.** (⟨fam a.⟩ ~e) *five* (*fingers, senses*) || ⟨bib⟩ ~ Bücher Mosis *Pentateuch* || → Pentameter || alle ~ Jahre *every five years*; *quinquennially* || ⟨crick⟩ Schlag f 5 Läufe *five*(*r*) || ~ Prozent, ~ vom Hundert *five per cent, five in the hundred*; Aktien mit ~ Prozent Zinsen *five-per--cents* pl, *fives* pl || ~ Uhr *five o'clock, five* | [abs] die Zahl ~ *the number five* || → acht; zweimal ~ *twice five* || Größe (*or* Nummer) ~ *five* (*three fives* pl) || zu ~en ⟨fam⟩ = zu fünft *in groups of five* || wir waren unser ~ *we were five of us* | → Finger || s–e ~ Sinne nicht bei–e–a h *to have a bee in one's bonnet*; s–e ~ Sinne zus–nehmen *to look alive* || ~ gerade sein l *to stretch a point* || er sieht aus, als könnte er nicht bis ~ zählen → drei **2.** ≈ f *five*; zwei ≈en *two fives*; z ~en *by* od *in fives* || e–e ~ (im Spiel) *a cinq*(*ue*) || Gruppe *or* Satz v ~en *quintuplet* **F·ünf-** ≈**aktig** a; ~es Stück *five-act play* ≈**atomig** a *pentatomic* **~blatt** n = –paß ≈**blätt(e)rig** a *five-leaved* **~c·entstück** n ⟨Am⟩ *five-cent piece*; *nickel* **~d·ollarnote** f ⟨Am⟩ *five-dollar note*; ⟨fam⟩ *fiver* **~eck** n ⟨math⟩ *pentagon* ≈**eckig** a *pentagonal* ≈**fach** a *fivefold, quintuple*; ~er Betrag *quintuple* ‖ um das ≈e *fivefold* **~f·inger-kraut** n ⟨bot⟩ *cinquefoil* **~flach** n ⟨math⟩ *pentahedron* ‖ **≈füßig** a ⟨pros⟩ *of five feet*; reimloser ~er Jambus *blank verse* **≈hundert** a *five hundred* [L: *D*) **≈hundertste** a *five hundredth* **~j·ahresplan** m ⟨Russ⟩ *Five Year Plan* **≈jährig** a *quinquennial* (*office*); ~es Kind *five-year old child* **~kampf** m ⟨sport⟩ *pentathlon* [Gr] **~liber** m ~s/~ Sw *coin of 5 francs* **≈mal** adv *five times*; ⟨parl⟩ ~ unterstrichen *five-lined* (*whip*) **~m·arkstück** n ⟨Ger⟩ *five-mark piece* **~paß** m ⟨arch⟩ (got.) *cinquefoil* **~pf·undnote** f *five-pound note*; ⟨fam⟩ *fiver* **~polröhre** f ⟨wir⟩ *pentode* **≈prozentig** a; ~e Aktien *five-per-cents* pl **≈seitig** a ⟨math⟩ *pentagonal* (*pyramid*) **≈stellig** a *of five digits*; ~e Zahl *five figures* pl; ~e Tafeln [pl] *five-figure tables* pl **≈stöckig** a *five-storied* **~str·omland** n (Ind.) *Punjab*; Bewohner des ~s, Sprache im ~ *Punjabi, -bee* **≈stündig** a; ~e Debatte *five-hour debate* **~t·agefieber** n ⟨med⟩ *quintan fever*; *quintan* **≈tägig** a ~e Tour *five--day tour* **~·uhrtee** m *five o'clock tea* **≈wertig** a ⟨chem⟩ *pentavalent* **~zeiler** m ⟨pros⟩ *quintain, quintet* (mst ababb reimend) **≈zinkig** a: ⟨fig⟩ (Hand) ~e Gabel ⟨fam⟩ *forks* [nur pl], *bunch* of *fives*

F·ünfer m ~s/~ **1.** *number five* ‖ (im Spiel) *cinq*(*ue*) **2.** (Münze) *five pfennig* (*piece*) **≈lei** a; ~ Farben *five kinds of colours*; *five different colours* pl; vgl. dreierlei **F·ünflinge** m pl *quintuplets*, ⟨fam⟩ *quins* pl

f·ünfte a *fifth* ‖ ⟨fig⟩ das ~ Rad am Wagen (*he is*) *the fifth wheel*, .. *super*(*fluous*), .. *de trop* (Fr) ‖ der, die, das ≈ *the fifth*; ~e Kolonne *fifth column*, Mann der .. *fifth columnist* ‖ Karl V. *Charles the fifth*; zu fünft *in groups of five*; → fünf ‖ → achte **F·ünftel** n *fifth*; zwei ~ *two fifths* ‖ ⟨math⟩ / *four fifths*; *four over five* **f·ünftens** adv *fifthly*; *in the fifth place* **f·ünfzehn** a *fifteen* ‖ ≈ (Rugby-Mannschaft) *fifteen* ‖ ⟨Ger⟩ ~ Uhr *3 o'clock p. m.* **f·ünfzehnjährig** a *15 years old*; ≈e [pl] *15 year-old youths* pl **f·ünfzehnte** a *fifteenth* ‖ der, die, das ~ *the fifteenth* **F·ünfzehntel** n *the fifteenth* **f·ünfzig 1.** a *fifty*; vgl achtzig ‖ ~ Pfennig → ≈er **2.** ≈ f *fifty*; unter ≈en *among fifty*; z ≈en *by fifties* ‖ er ist Mitte ≈ *or* Mitte der ≈er *he is half-way between fifty and sixty* ‖ ein Mann in den ≈en *a man in the fifties*

F·ünfziger 1. a. [m] ~s/~; ein ~ *a man of fifty* od *in the fifties, a fifty-year old man* ‖ ⟨Ger⟩ *a fifty pfennig piece, half a mark*; ⟨engl⟩ *sixpence* ‖ °⟨fig⟩ falscher ~ *scoundrel, blackguard* **b.** die ~ (*or* ~jahre) [pl] *the fifties* pl; ein Mann in den ~n (~jahren) *a man in the fifties*; vgl achtzig **2.** ≈ a; die ~ Jahre des 19. Jhs. *the fifties* [pl] *of the 19th century* **f·ünfzigjährig** a *fifty years old*; *fifty-year old* (*p*); ein ≈er → Fünfziger 1. **f·ünfzigste** a *fiftieth* ‖ der, die, das ≈ *the f.* **F·ünfzigstel** n ~s/~ *the fiftieth*

fung·ibel a ⟨jur & st exch⟩ (vertretbar) *fungible* (*articles*) **fung·ieren** vi [h] ~ als *to act as* (*guide*); ⟨mil⟩ als Führer ~ *to be in command* ‖ *to officiate as* (*chairman*); ⟨jur⟩ *to sit as* (*Deputy Chancellor*)

fung·ös a ⟨med⟩ *fungoid, fungous*; *spongy*

F·unk- (f Rundfunk) [in comp] *wireless, radio*; mittels ~ *by* (*means of*) *r.* (*transmission*) **~anlage** f *w. plant* **~ausrüstung** f *r. communication equipment* **~auswertestelle** f *r. evaluation station* **~auswertungsoffizier** m *r. intelligence evaluation officer* **~bake** f = –feuer **~bereitschaft** f *radio alert* **~beschränkung** f *limited r. silence* **~bericht** m *commentary* (über *on*) **~berichter** m (*w.*) *commentator* **~bild** n *w.* od *r. picture*; *wire-photo, telephoto*; *photoradiogram* **~echolot** n *r. altimeter* **~empfang** m *w. reception* **~empfänger** m (Apparat) *w. receiver*; ~ mit Rückkoppelung *heterodyne* (*receiver*) **~-Entfernungsmeßgerät** n *distance measuring equipment* N (*DME*) **~-Entstörung** f *interference suppression* **≈ferngesteuert** a *w.* od *r. controlled* ‖ ~es Flugzeug *r.-c.* (*pilotless*) *plane* ⟨Am⟩ *drone* **~fern-** ~peilung [f] *long-range navigation* (*Loran*); ~schreiber [m] *r. teleprinter* ‖ (tragbarer) ~sprecher [m] (*portable*) *r. telephone* (*set*); über ~ sprechen *to talk by r. t.* ‖ ~steuerung [f] *r. control* **~feuer** n ⟨bes aero⟩ *r.-beacon* **~gast** m = Funker **~gerät** n *w. apparatus* (od *set*) **~hilfsmittel** n *r. aid* **~horchdienst** m *monitoring service* (*to enemy transmissions*) **~-kontakt-Unterbrechung** f *black-out* ⟨a. a–n⟩ **~-landegerät** n *r. landing equipment* **~leit-** | ~sender [m] *r. beacon* ‖ ~stand [m] *radar intelligence collation section* ‖ ~stelle [f] *w. telegraph controlling station* ‖ ~strahl [m] *r. beam*; ⟨aero⟩ *localizer b.*; auf dem ~ fliegen *to fly the b.* **~linie** f *two-station net* **~lot** n ⟨aero⟩ *altimeter* **~-mast** m *r. tower* **~mechaniker** m *r. repairman* **~-meldung** f *w.* od *r. telegram* od *message* **~meß-(verfahren** n) m *radar*; → –ortung | ~gerät [n] *radar*; ~jagd [f] ⟨aero-mil⟩ *ground controlled interception*; ~mann [m] *radar operator*; ~wesen [n] *electronics* [sg konstr] **~mitteilung, ~-nachricht** f *radiogram* | ~nprogramm [n] *r. news program* **~navigationshilfsmittel** n [pl] *r. aids to* (*air*) *navigation* **~offizier** m ⟨mar⟩ *w. officer* **~-ort** m *w. position* **~ortung** f *radiolocation*, ⟨Am⟩ *radar* (= *r. detecting and ranging*) **~peiler** m *direction-finder* **~peilung** f *r. direction-finding*; *r.-bearing*; *r.-goniometry* ‖ Standort nach ~en *r. fix* **~recht** n *law relating to broadcasting in general* **~rufzeichen** n *r. call signal* **~schatten** m *r. shadow* **~schneise** f ⟨aero⟩ *corridor of approach* **~sendung** f *r. transmission* **~sprechgerät** n *field r. set*; *r.phone*; (tragbar) *walkie-talkie* **~-spruch** m *r.* od *w.* (*message*); *radio*(*tele*)*gram, marconigram* ‖ ~ mit offener Anschrift *plain-dress* ‖ durch ~ senden *to wireless* **~station** f *r.* (od *broadcasting, w.*) *station* **~stille** f *broadcasting silence* **~störung** f *r. interference, r. jamming* **~streife** f *squad car* **~telegramm** n = –spruch **≈telegraphisch 1.** a *wireless* **2.** adv *by w.* **~turm** m *r.-tower* **~überwachung** f *r. monitoring* | ~sstelle [f] *net control station* **~verbindung** f *r. contact*; *r. communication* **~verbot** n *r. silence* **~verkehr** m *w.* od *r. service*; *broadcasting* **~wagen** m *r.* (*patrol*) *car* **~wart** m *r. mechanic* ⟨a. aero⟩ **~weg** m *r. channel*; auf dem ~ *by w.* od *r.* **~welle** f *w. wave* **~wesen** n *radiotelegraphy*; *wireless telegraph system*; *broadcasting* **~wetter-**~station [f] *r. weather station* ‖ ~vorhersage [f] *r. w. forecast* **~zeitung** f *r. magazine*

F·ünkchen n ~s/~ *small spark*; *sparklet*

F·unke m ~n/~n **1. a.** *spark*; Feuer≈ *spark of fire*; (Licht≈) *flash* ‖ ~n sprühen *to spark, to give out sparks*; ~n schlagen aus *to strike sparks from* ‖ ⟨fig⟩ °daß die ~n fliegen *like a brick, with a vengeance* | ⟨el⟩ *electric spark*; ⟨mot⟩ (Zünd≈) *spark* **b.** ⟨fig⟩ zündender ~ *spark*; Lebens≈ *spark of life, vital spark* ‖ *flash* (*of hope, inspiration*); ~n [pl] *flashes*; *strokes* (*of humour*); *scintillations* (*of wit*); *spurt* (*of talk*); der letzte ~ *the last flicker* (*of hope*) **2.** ⟨fig⟩ [neg] nicht e–n ~n (v), k–n ~ [acc] (v) *not an atom* (od *a jot, particle, scintilla, vestige*) *of* (*evidence, truth*); *not a scrap* od *spark of* (*imagination, interest*); *not a trace of* (*fear*); *not a grain of* (*pride*); ohne e–n ~n v *without a particle of* (*feeling*); .. v menschlicher Regung *without a grain of humanity* **f·unkeln I.** vi [h] **1.** ⟨eig⟩ (of light, stars, etc) *to sparkle, twinkle*; *coruscate, scintillate* ‖ *glint, glisten*; *glitter* **2.** ⟨übtr⟩ (of the eyes) *to flash*; *to glint*; *glisten*; *scintillate* (vor .. *with anger, excitement*); in hellem Glanze ~ *to shine with a brilliant light* **II.** ≈ n *sparkling, sparkle*; *scintillation, twinkling* (*of the stars*), *twinkle*; *glitter* ‖ ein leichtes ~ *a lambency* ‖ ⟨übtr⟩ *flash*(*ing*); *cor-*

uscation, scintillation **f·unkelnagelneu** a *bran(d)-new*; ⟨übtr⟩ *hot*; *spick and span*; *hard as nails*; *fire-new, mint-new* **f·unkelnd** a *sparkling, twinkling*; *glittering*; *scintillant*; wie Diamanten ~ *diamanté (embroidery)* [Fr] ‖ *coruscating (eyes)*, *lambent (wit)*; *scintillating*

°**funken** vi [h] (= funktionieren) es –kt *it works*

f·unken I. vi/t [h] ⟨wir⟩ **1.** vi *to radio*; *to (broadcast by) wireless*; ⟨fam⟩ *to spark* **2.** vt (Nachricht) *to radio, to wireless*; *to flash* (über .. *over the ocean*); jdm ~ *to radio, to wireless a p (that)*; jdm etw ~ *to radio a p a th* (od *a th to a p*) | vi ⟨mil sl⟩ *to shoot* **II.** ≃ n *sending by wireless* **F·unken-** [in comp] ⟨el⟩ *spark–* ‖ **~bildung** f *sparking* **~entladung** f *spark discharge* **≃erosiv** a *electro-erosive* **~fänger** m *spark-arrester* **~induktor** m *spark* od *induction-coil*; *inductor* **~potential** n *spark potential* **~regen** m *burst of sparks* **~strecke** f ⟨el⟩ *spark gap*; (Apparat) *spark-discharger* | ~nkugel [f] *sparkball* **~telegraphie** f *wireless telegraphy* **~telegraphisch 1.** a *wireless*; ~es Signal *wireless code signal*; (f Schiffe in Seenot) *SOS* **2.** adv *by wireless, by radio* **~telephonie** f *wireless telephony* **~überschlag** m *flash-over* **F·unker** m *wireless operator*; *signalman*, ⟨mar sl⟩ *sparks* pl [sg konstr]

F·unkie [–iə] f ⟨bot⟩ *Funkia* [L]

Funkti·on [ts] f ~/~en **1.** (Tätigkeit) *function*; *activity* ‖ ⟨physiol⟩ *function (of the arteries)*; *action, special activity*; *office (the ear ceased its o.)*; *rôle* [Fr]; die ~, die das Organ ausübt, ist .. *the role the organ plays is ..*; außer ~ setzen *to defunctionalize* ‖ *function, task*; [oft pl] ~en *functions (of a judge)*; die ~ als *the function as (chairman)*; der Ausschuß trat in ~ *the committee started its work* **2.** ⟨math⟩ *function*; ganze ~ *integral f.*; homogene ganze rationale ~ *quantic*; (un)stetige ~ *(dis)continuous function* **~stheorie** f *theory of functions*

Funktion·algleichung [ts] f ⟨math⟩ *functional equation* **–l·ismus** m *functionalism* **Funktion·är** [ts] m ~s/~e *functionary*; *official* **funktion·ell** [ts] **1.** a ⟨physiol⟩ ~es Leiden *functional disease*; in ~er Hinsicht *functionally* ‖ *official*; ~e Pflichten *functionary duties* pl **2.** adv *functionally* **funktion·ieren** [ts] **1.** vi [h] (S) *to act*; *operate*; *work*; ordnungsgemäß ~ ⟨tech⟩ *to run true to form*; die Glocke funktioniert nicht *the bell does not work* ‖ *to function (the office f.s)* ‖ (of the mind) *to operate*; *work* ‖ gut ~d *in good working order* ‖ → fungieren **2.** ≃ n *acting, action, activity*; *operation*; *working* **Funkti·ons-** [ts] [in comp] **~störung** f ⟨med⟩ *malfunction* **~taste** f ⟨comp⟩ *control key* **~unteroffizier** m *Supply* od *Administration N. C. O.* **~verb** n *functional verb* **~zulage** f *rise in* (od *of*) *the salary* ‖ → funktionell

Funt n (russ. Gewicht) *pound* (= *409,51 g*)

F·ünte f ~/~n (Taufbecken) *font*

ˣ**F·unzel** f *poor* (od *wretched*) *lamp*; *insufficient* (od *scanty*) *light*

für I. [prep] **A.** (vor) [nur in formelhaften Wendungen:] Schritt f Schritt *step by step*; Stück f Stück *piece by piece*; Mann f Mann *man by man* ‖ Jahr f Jahr *year by year*; Tag f Tag *day by* od *after day* **B.** [mit acc] **1.** (zugunsten v) **a.** f jdn, etw s *to declare* od *vote for a p, a th*; ich bin f Gehen *I am for walking* **b.** es ist f dich *it is for you* ‖ 2 Mark f ihn *two marks to his credit* ‖ f m–e Rechnung *to my cost*; f mich gibt es nur eine Frage *in my eyes there is but one q.*; dies geht f mich ⟨fam⟩ *this is on me* ‖ f m–e eigene Rechnung *(I work) on my own account* ‖ sie arbeiteten f ihn *they worked on his behalf (14 hours of the day)* ‖ was bedeutet das f dich? *what's that to you?* ‖ sie schwärmt f die Bühne *she is stage-struck*; ich schwärme nun mal f Berlin *Berlin for me* ‖ ich spiele Krickett f mein Leben gern *I am hot on playing cricket*; → essen ‖ v Wichtigkeit f das gesamte Europa *of all-European importance* ‖ °das ist f die Katze *that's nothing* (od *to no purpose*) **c.** f heute, f jetzt *for the present*; Schluß f heute *enough for the present* ‖ f immer *for good* ‖ ein f allemal *once (and) for all* ‖ ~s erste *first of all*; *for the time being, for the present*; ~s erste .. ~s zweite *first .. second* **d.** (um willen) tu es f mich *do it for my sake* **e.** ~ **sich** bleiben ⟨fam⟩ *to keep o.s. to o.s.* ‖ alles f sich h *to have all to o.s.* ‖ er hatte sie ganz f sich *he had her entirely his own* ‖ (allein) f sich leben *to live by o.s.*; er will f sich s *he wants to be alone* ‖ (f eigene Rechnung) *on one's own account* ‖ (ohne Hilfe) f sich studieren *to read on one's own* | e–e Episode ~ sich *an isolated period* ‖ die Katzen sind e–e Rasse f sich *cats are a race to themselves* ‖ an jedem Ort f sich *on any particular place* | dies ist e–e S f sich *this is a separate question* ‖ e–e S f sich allein betrachten *to consider a th on its own merits* ‖ die S hat etw (*or* viel) f sich *there is something* (od *much*) *in that*; das Argument hat viel f sich *there is force in that argument* ‖ an u f sich (betrachtet) *properly* (od *generally*) *speaking*; *in the abstract* **2.** (an Stelle v; statt) **a.** etw tun f *to do a th for (a p)*; Wasser f Wein *water for wine* ‖ als Ersatz f *in return for* ‖ (etw) kaufen f *to buy for (2 sh.)* ‖ ⟨com⟩ f das Hundert *per cent*; f das Pfund *per pound* **b.** (als) f verloren *for lost* ‖ ich halte ihn f e–n Dichter *I think him a poet*; ich h. es f wahrscheinlich *I think it probable*; → halten ‖ → gelten; ungut **c.** (als Lohn f) *for*; büßen f *to suffer for (one's sins)* **3.** (in bezug auf) **a.** ich f m–e P *I for one*; *for my part*; *as for me* **b.** [nach Subst.:] e–e Gefahr f *a danger to (a p)*; Enttäuschung f *a disappointment for* **c.** [nach Adj.:] gut f *good for, a good th for (the health; gout)* ‖ er ist gut f *he is good for (£ 100)* ‖ unmoralisch f *immoral for (a king)* ‖ z teuer f *too expensive for (a p)*; ⟨fig⟩ das ist z hoch f mich ⟨sl⟩ *that beats* (od *licks*) *me* | angenehm f jdn, jdm angenehm *agreeable to a p* ‖ notwendig f *necessary to* **C.** [erstarrt; in Ausruf u Frage nach ‚was'] (vgl. B. 2. b.); was f ein Wein ist dies? *what wine is this?* was f e–e Art Mensch ist er? *what kind* od *manner of man is he?* was f Herren waren dies? *who were these gentlemen?* ‖ was f ein Narr du bist! *what fool you are!* **II.** adv **f u f** *for ever and ever* ‖ ⟨parl⟩ f u gegen *pro and con*; die Stimmen f u gegen, **das Für** u Wider, *the pros and cons* pl

Fur·age [ʒ] f [Fr] ⟨mil⟩ *forage*, → Futter ‖ ~handlung [f] *forage-store* **~vorräte** m pl ⟨mil⟩ *quartermastering stores* **Furag·ier-** [ʒ] [in comp] *foraging (expedition)* **furag·ieren** [ʒ] vi [Fr] [h] *to forage*

†**fürb·aß** adv = weiter

F·ürbitte f ~/~n *intercession*; ~ einlegen *to intercede, plead* (bei .. *with a p*; f .. *for a p*; wegen *for [a th]*) ‖ ⟨ec⟩ *intercession*; *intercessory prayer* ‖ priesterliche ~ *priestly meditation* | **≃n 1.** vi [nur inf & prsp] = Fürbitte einlegen → Fürbitte ‖ ~d *intercessory* **2.** ≃ n *intercession*; *pleading* **~r** m *intercessor*

F·urche f ~/~n (im Acker) *furrow*; kl Saat≃ *drill* ‖ (Rad≃) *rut* ‖ (Gesichts≃) *furrow, wrinkle* ‖ ⟨anat⟩ *sulcus* [L] [pl *–ci*] ‖ → Riefe, Rinne ‖ voll v ~n → furchig ‖ ohne ~n *furrowless* ‖ ~n bilden [vi] *to ridge* ‖ ~n ziehen in *to furrow (land, water)*; *to rut (road)*; *to wrinkle (face)* **f·urchen** vt [h] (Acker) *to furrow* ‖ (of wheels) *to rut* ‖ → durch~; runzeln ‖ → riefen, rillen **~artig** a *furrow-like* **≃rain** m *ridge* **~weise** adv *in furrows* **f·urchig** a *furrowed, furrowy*; *wrinkled, wrinkly (face)*; *rutted, rutty (road)*; ⟨anat⟩ *sulcate*

Furcht f ~/ [pl → Angst, Befürchtung] **1.** *fear* (vor *of*); die ~ vor dem Tode *the fear of death*; ein Anfall v ~ *a spasm of fear*; ein Gefühl der ~ *a fear* (daß *lest*) ‖ gr ~ *dread, fright*; schreckliche ∼ *terror*; → Schreck(en) **2.** nur **keine** ∼! *no fear!*, *never fear!*, k–e Spur v ∼ *no trace of the white feather* ‖ **aus** ∼ vor *for fear of*; aus ∼ daß .. *afraid lest* (.. *should*); aus ∼ überstürzen *or* unüberlegt handeln *to panic* | ∼ **bek.**, in ∼ geraten *to feel fear* ‖ er empfand fast ∼ *he was almost afraid* (*to follow*) ‖ ∼ h = sich fürchten; ∼ h vor jdm *to stand in fear of a p* ‖ k–e ∼ empfinden *to feel no fear* ‖ sie kannte k–e ∼ *she did not know what it was to be afraid* ‖ jdm ∼ einflößen, -jagen; ∼ erwecken in jdm *to strike fear into a p* (od *into a p's heart*); *to daunt a p*; → erfüllen ‖ in ständiger ∼ leben vor .. *to be* od *live in apprehension* od *dread of* (*a th*), *to be disturbed by a thousand fears and surmises* ‖ in ∼ setzen → erschrecken vt **≗bar 1.** a **a.** *frightful*, *ghastly*, *horrible*, *monstrous*, *terrible* (*crime*); *redoutable* (*enemy*); *dreadful* (*monster*) ‖ er ist ∼ in s–r Wut *he is terrible when in a rage* **b.** °(sehr gr) ⟨fam⟩ *dreadful*, *terrible*, *terrific* (*heat*, *pain*); *horrible* (*din*); *tremendous* (*applause*, *fright*); *fierce* (*hatred*); *frightful* (*time*); *awful* (*nonsense*); *unholy* (*row*) | ein ∼er Mensch *a dreadful* (od *horrible*) *bore* | das ist ja ∼ *that's horrible* ‖ der Wein war einfach ∼ *the wine was ghastly* (⟨Am⟩ *fierce*) ‖ die S ist einfach ∼! (*that's*) *a fearful* od *ghastly mess!* **c. das ≗e,** das bevorstand *the impending horror* **2.** adv **a.** *dreadfully*, *frightfully*, *horribly*, *terribly* **b.** °(sehr; sehr gr) ⟨fam⟩ *awfully*, *dreadfully*, *ghastly* (*cold*); *terribly* (*hungry*); *fearfully* (*weary*); ⟨fam⟩ *cruel* (*cold*) ‖ °ich hab dich ∼ doll gerne *I like you ever so* ‖ ∼ elend aussehen *to look perfectly ghastly* ‖ ∼ nett *awfully nice* (*fellow*; .. *of you*) ‖ die S ist ∼ einfach *that's very* (od *awfully*, *quite*) *simple*

f·ürchten vi/t [h] **I.** vi *to feel fear*; *to fear*; fürchte nicht *do not dread* ‖ ∼ für *to fear for* (*a p*, *a th*); *to go in fear of* (*a th*) | ∼, daß: *I fear* (*he might come*) **II.** vt **A. 1.** Gott ∼ *to fear God* **2.** jdn ∼ *to be afraid of*, *to fear a p* ‖ jdn sehr ∼ *to dread a p*; *to be frightened* (od *terrified*) *of a p*; → gefürchtet **3.** etw ∼ *to apprehend* od *fear a th*; *to be afraid of a th*; sehr ∼ *to dread a th*; es ist (*or* steht) z ∼ *it is to be feared* **4. a.** ∼ z tun = sich ∼ z tun, → B. 2. **b.** ∼, daß .. *to fear* (od *dread*, *be afraid*) *that*; ich fürchte, daß wir z spät k. *I am afraid* (*that*) *we shall be late*, *I am afraid lest we should be late*; ich fürchte nicht, daß er das tut *I am not afraid of him doing that* **B. sich** ∼ **1. sich** ∼ vor jdm, etw = jdn, etw ∼, → A. 2. 3. **2. sich ∼ z tun** *to be afraid* (od *fearful*, *shy*) *of doing*; *to fear doing*; *to dread to do* ‖ sie furchtete (= scheute) sich, ihn z treffen *she was afraid to meet* (od *of meeting*) *him* **F·ürchten** n *fearing*; *fear* ‖ er sieht zum ∼ aus *he looks a perfect fright* **f·ürchterlich 1.** a = furchtbar 1. b. **2.** adv er errötete ∼ ⟨sl⟩ *he blushed furiously*; = furchtbar 2. b. **f·urchterregend** a *causing fear*; *alarming*, *fearful*; *panicky* (*speech*) **f·urchtlos 1.** [a] *fearless*; *dauntless*, *intrepid*, *undaunted* ‖ [nur pred] *unafraid* **2.** adv *fearlessly* (etc → 1.) **F·urchtlosigkeit** f *fearlessness*; *freedom from fear*; *dauntlessness*, *intrepidity*, *undauntedness*

f·urchtsam 1. a *faint-hearted*, *timid*, *timorous*; → feig; scheu, schüchtern, zaghaft ‖ [pred] *apprehensive*, *fearful* (z tun *of doing*) **2.** adv *faint-heartedly*, *timidly* | **≗keit** f *faint-heartedness*, *timidity*, *timorousness*

F·urchung f ∼/∼en ⟨biol⟩ *egg-cleavage*; *segmentation* | ∼szelle [f] *blastomere*

f·ürder adv ⟨poet⟩ = künftig; in Zukunft | † = vorwärts, weiter

fürein·ander adv *for one another*, *for each other*

F·urie [–iə] f ∼/∼n ⟨ant myth⟩ *fury*, [mst pl] die ∼n *the Furies*; *dire sisters* pl ‖ ⟨übtr⟩ *fury*; *virago* [L]

Fur·ier m ∼s/∼e ⟨mil⟩ *quartermaster-sergeant*; *Ration N. C. O.* ‖ *forager* | ∼liste [f] *commissary roll*

fürl·ieb|nehmen vi [h] ∼ mit etw *to be content with*, *to make* (*a*) *shift with a th*; *to put up with a th*; .., wenn Sie ∼ mit dem, was es gibt .. *if you will take pot-luck with us*

Furn·ier n ∼s/∼e ⟨carp⟩ *veneer* **∼arbeit** f *v.*(*ing*) **∼hobelmaschine** f *veneer cutting* (od *planing*) *machine* **∼holz** n *v.*(*-wood*); *v.ing* **∼messermaschine** f *veneer slicing machine* **∼presse** f *v.*(*ing*)*-press* **∼säge** f *v.-saw* **furn·ieren** vt [h] (Holzstück) *to veneer* (*with*)

Fur·ore n [It] *furore*; *craze*, *rage*; *sensation* ‖ ∼ m *to make* (od *create*) *a furore*; *to cause a sensation*; *to be a success* (*his speech was a s.*); er macht ∼ *he is a success*

fürs = für das **Fürs·ichsein** n ∼s/ *solitude*, *singleness* **F·ürsorge** f ∼/ *care*; *welfare benefits* pl; für sie u die Kinder würde gebührende ∼ getroffen w *proper provision would be made for her and the children* ‖ individuelle ∼ (*social*) *casework*; soziale ∼ *social welfare*, *welfare work*; Säuglings≗, Kinder≗ *infant welfare*; Mutter- u Kinder≗ *mother and child w.*; Mütter≗ *maternity w.* ‖ der ∼ [gen] bedürftige Familie *problem family* **∼arbeit** f *social assistance*; individuelle ∼ (*social*) *casework* **∼behörde** f *welfare authorities* pl **∼erziehung** f *the bringing up of children under social welfare system* | ∼sheim [n] *remand home* **∼schwester** f = Fürsorgerin **∼stelle** = –behörde **∼wesen** n (*system of*) *social welfare* od *welfare work* **∼zögling** m *child brought up under social welfare system* **F·ürsorger** m ∼s/∼ *social* (*welfare*) *worker* **∼in** f ∼/∼nen (*woman* od *lady*) *social* (*welfare*) *worker* **≗isch** a *welfare* [attr] (*service*); ∼e Leistungen *w. s.s* **f·ürsorglich** *considerate*

F·ürspan m ∼s/∼e ⟨bes praeh⟩ *clasp*

F·ürsprache f ∼/ *intercession*; *mediation* (*through his m.*); ∼ einlegen *to intercede* (bei .. *with a p*; für .. *for a p*) **-sprech** m **1.** ⟨hist⟩ *spokesman* **2.** Sw = Rechtsanwalt **-sprecher** m *intercessor*; *mediator* ‖ = Fürsprech 2.

F·ürst m ∼en/∼en **1.** ⟨a-engl⟩ *prince* (*the Prince of ..*); *sovereign*, *sovereign ruler*; regierender ∼ *reigning prince* ‖ ⟨Ger⟩ die Bundes≗en [pl] *the Princes of the Empire* ‖ kl ∼ *princelet*, *princeling* **2.** (als Titel) ⟨Ger⟩ (Anschrift: Seiner Durchlaucht [reichsunmittelbar: Erlaucht] dem ∼en zu ..), (Anrede: Euer Durchlaucht [Erlaucht]; → fürstlich); ⟨engl⟩ (f dukes & marquises) *Prince* ‖ ⟨a-engl⟩ *Prince*; ∼ Bismarck *Prince Bismarck* ‖ Kirchen≗ *Prince of the Church* ‖ leben wie die ∼en → fürstlich **3.** ⟨übtr⟩ *prince* ‖ Dichter≗ *prince of poets*; der Friedens≗ *the Prince of Peace*; der ∼ der Finsternis *or* dieser Welt *the prince of darkness* od *of this world*; *Satan*; *the Black Prince* **F·ürstbischof** m ⟨Ger⟩ *Prince-Bishop* **F·ürsten- ∼abfindung** f ⟨Ger hist⟩ *redemption of the rights and holdings of the Princes* **∼haus** n *princely house*; *dynasty* **∼hut** m = –krone **∼krone** f ⟨Ger hist⟩ *prince's hat* **∼schule** f *Fürstenschule* [Ger] **∼spiegel** m ⟨Lit⟩ *treatise on statecraft* **∼stand** m *princely rank*; *dignity* od *position of a prince* **F·ürstentum** n ∼s/–tümer *principality* **F·ürstin** f ∼/∼nen ⟨a-engl & übtr⟩ *princess* **f·ürstlich 1.** [a] *princely* ‖ ⟨a-engl⟩ Seine ≗e Durchlaucht *His Serene Highness* ‖ ⟨übtr⟩ *princely*; *magnificent*; *noble*, *royal*, *stately* **2.** [adv] *like a prince* ‖ *magnificently*; *royally*; *sumptuously* ‖ ∼ leben *to live high off the fat* od *on the hog* | **≗keit** f [konkr] ∼en [pl] *royalties* pl, *royalty* (*all r.*)

Furt f ∼/∼en *ford*, *wade* **≗en** vt/i *to pass a ford*

F·ürtuch n [obd] = Brusttuch, Schürze

Fur·unkel m ∼s/∼ *furuncle*; *boil*, *botch* **furunkul·ös** a *furuncular*, *furunculous* **Furunkul·ose** f ⟨med⟩ *furunculosis*

fürw·ahr adv *indeed, in truth; truly;* ⟨iron⟩ *forsooth* ‖ *come* (*come, that's a great deal better*); *I declare*

F·ürwitz m = Vorwitz

F·ürwort n ⟨gram⟩ *pronoun*

°**Furz** m ~es/⁼̃e *fart, wind*; e–n ~ l *to break wind* ‖ °wie ein wildgewordener ~ *like a fart in a bottle, like a pea in a colander*

°**f·urzen** vi [h] *to fart,* ⟨vulg⟩ *poop* ‖ ⟨euph⟩ *to make a noise; to break wind*

Fusa·in n (Bestandteil der Steinkohle) *fusain*

F·usel[1] m ~s/ *bad gin* (od *liquor, spirits*); *potato spirit;* ⟨fam⟩ *hog-wash* ‖ = ~öl **~geruch** m *odour of fusel oil* **~öl** n ⟨chem⟩ *fusel oil; amyl alcohol*

Fusel[2] f ~/~n *flue, fluff, fuzz*

f·uselig[1] a *containing fusel oil* ‖ *intoxicated*

f·uselig[2] a *fluffy, fuzzy* ‖ °sich ~ reden *to dodder;* ⟨Am sl⟩ *to chew the rag*

f·useln[1] vi [h] *to drink bad gin* | *to smell of fusel oil* ‖ = pfuschen

f·useln[2] vi [h] *to fray, frazzle; fuzz*

Füsil·ier m ~s/~e ⟨hist mil⟩ *fusilier* ‖ ⟨Ger⟩ ~e [pl] (bis 1918) *privates* pl; ⟨engl⟩ (als Titel) *Royal Fusiliers* pl ‖ ~regiment [n] *Fusilier Regiment* **füsil·ieren** vt [h] (jdn) *to fusillade; shoot*

Fusi·on f ~/~en ⟨met⟩ *fusion;* → Amalgamierung ‖ ⟨com & pol⟩ *amalgation; consolidation; integration; fusion; merger*

Fus·it m = Fusain

Fuß m ~es/⁼̃e **I.** [pl] ⁼̃e] **A.** (P & T) *foot* ‖ → Pfote, Tatze | ⟨cul⟩ (*calf's*) *foot;* (*pig's, sheep's*) *trotter* **B.** (S) **1.** *foot* (*of a chair, table*) ‖ *leg* (*of a machine*) ‖ *foot* (*of a glass*); Weinglas⁼̃ aus einem Guß mit der Schale *straw-stem* ‖ *base, pedestal* (*of a column*); *base, bottom, foot* (*of a hill*); *heel* (*of a mast*) **2.** *bottom, foot* (*of a list, page*) **3.** *foot* (*of a bed*); *end* ‖ → Ständer, Stütze **II.** (als Maß [ohne pl]; nach Zahlen ~; †⟨Ger⟩; aber lebendig in Engl. [= 30,48 cm]) *foot;* 3 ~ tief *3 feet deep;* 3 ~ tiefes Wasser, ein W. v 3 ~ Tiefe *three feet of water* ‖ er war 6 ~ groß *he stood six feet high* (od *in height*); *he was six f. in height* ‖ 5 ~ u 3 Zoll *five foot* (od *feet*) (*and*) *three* ‖ eine 6 ~ lange Stange *a six-foot pole* ‖ ⟨min⟩ Bezahlung nach ~ *footage* **2.** ⟨pros⟩ (Vers⁼̃) *foot* (*a verse of 6 feet*) **III.** Wendungen **A. 1.** ⟨fig⟩ **fester** ~ *footing, foothold;* festen ~ fassen *to gain* (od *get*) *a footing* (*in*), *to get a toehold* (*in*) ‖ kalte ⁼̃e h (Angst h) ⟨fig fam⟩ *to have cold feet* ‖ sich [dat] **kalte** ⁼̃e holen *to cool one's heels,* (wartend) *to get cold waiting* ‖ kalte ⁼̃e bek. ⟨fig⟩ *to get cold feet* ‖ **leichten** ~es *swiftly, with winged heels* ‖ **stehenden** ~es *on the spot; immediately* ‖ **trokkenen** ~es *dry-shod* **2.** beide ⁼̃e fest auf dem Boden **behalten** *to keep both feet firmly on the ground* ‖ → Hand ‖ (erst einmal) ~ **fassen** *to get a toehold* ⟨a. fig⟩ ‖ jdm den ~ auf den Nacken **setzen** *to set one's foot on the neck of a p; to ride rough-shod over a p* ‖ wir w k–n ~ wieder über d–e Schwelle setzen *we shan't darken your door again* ‖ s–e ⁼̃e unter jds Tisch strecken *to have* od *put one's feet* od *knees under a p's mahogany* ‖ v e–m ~ auf den anderen **treten** *to shift from one foot to the other* | **sich** [dat] den ~ **brechen** *to break one's foot;* → verstauchen ‖ sich die ⁼̃e wund laufen *to chafe one's feet by walking* **B. 1. am** ~e des Hügels *at the foot of the hill* **2. a.** fest **auf** den ⁼̃en *sure-footed* ‖ jdm (*or* e–r S) auf dem ~e folgen *to follow in the wake of a p* (*a th*); die Tat s–n Worten auf dem ~e folgen l *to suit one's action to one's words* ‖ (Heer) auf die ⁼̃e bringen *to collect, to raise;* sich mit Mühe auf die ⁼̃e bringen *to stagger to one's feet* ‖ ⟨fig⟩ auf die ⁼̃e fallen (= immer Glück h) *to fall on one's feet* ‖ jdm auf die ⁼̃e helfen *to help a p to his feet; to help a p up* ‖ sich auf die ⁼̃e m *to set out* (nach *for*); *to start* ‖ auf die ⁼̃e springen *to spring to one's feet* ‖ ⟨fig⟩ jdm auf die ⁼̃e treten *to wound a p's feelings, to hurt a p* **b.** (immer) **auf** die ⁼̃e fallen ⟨fig fam⟩ *to fall on one's feet* ‖ [dat] auf dem ~e folgen *to heel,* ihm auf d. ~ f.d *hard on his heels;* **auf bestem ~e** leben mit *to be on the best* (*of*) *terms with* (*a p*) ‖ auf eigenen ⁼̃en stehen *to stand on one's own legs; to be independent* ‖ jdn auf eigene ⁼̃e stellen *to set a p on his legs;* auf eigene ⁼̃e gestellt w *to come into one's own* | auf freiem ~e *at large;* (jdn) auf freien ~ setzen *to set at liberty* | auf gespanntem ~e leben mit *to be on strained terms* (od *at daggers drawn*) *with* | auf gleichem ~e mit *on a footing with; on terms of equality with* | auf großem ~e leben *to live in great style, to live expensively* | auf gutem (vertraulichem) ~e mit *on good* (*intimate*) *terms with;* auf g. ~e bleiben mit *to keep in with* (*a p*); mit der ganzen Welt auf g. ~e leben *to be square with the world* | ⟨fig⟩ auf schwachen (*or* tönernen) ⁼̃en stehen *to stand on a weak basis; to be ill-founded* **3. bei** ~ bleiben (of dog) *to keep to heel,* bei ~ k *to move to h.* ‖ Gewehr **bei** ~! *order arms!* ⟨fig⟩ G. bei ~ stehen *to wait and see* **4.** sich e–n Nagel **in** den ~ treten *to get a nail in one's foot* **5. a. mit** dem linken ~ zuerst aufstehen *to get up* (*on*) *the wrong side* ‖ mit den ⁼̃en hängen bleiben *to catch one's feet* (in *in*) ‖ ärgerlich mit dem ~e stampfen *to stamp an angry foot* ‖ mit dem ~ stoßen *to kick* ‖ jdn mit ⁼̃en treten *to ride rough-shod over a p, to rough-house a p, to trample upon a p;* etw mit ⁼̃en treten *to override* od *overrule a th;* (das Recht) *to trample* (od *tread*) *under foot;* (Gefühle) *to trample* (*down*); mit ⁼̃en getreten w v *to be trodden underfoot by* (*a p*) ‖ → Hand **b. mit beiden** ⁼̃en auf der Erde stehen *to have both feet on the earth* ‖ mit einem ~e im Grabe ⟨fig⟩ *having one foot in the grave* ‖ **6. unter** den ⁼̃en *under one's feet; under foot* ‖ der Boden brannte ihm unter den ⁼̃en *the place was made too hot for him* ‖ → Boden **7.** den Staub **von** den ⁼̃en schütteln *to shake the dust off one's feet* | v e–m ~ auf den anderen treten *to tread* (od *shift*) *from one foot to the other* **8.** ⟨fig⟩ jdm etw **vor** die ⁼̃e werfen *to throw a th at a p's feet* **9. a. zu ~** *on foot; afoot;* gut z ~ s *to be a good goer* od *walker* ‖ z ~ gehen *to go on foot; walk;* ⟨sl⟩ *foot-slog;* ⟨fam⟩ *to foot it* ‖ lange Strecken z ~ wandern *to tramp* ‖ ich kann v m–r Wohnung die Universität bequem z ~ erreichen *I live within an easy walk of the university* ‖ → Kopf **b.** jdm **zu** ⁼̃**en,** z jds ⁼̃en ⟨a. übtr⟩ *at a p's feet* ‖ jdm z ⁼̃en fallen *to fall at a p's feet* ‖ jdm z ⁼̃en liegen *to be at a p's feet* ‖ z jds ⁼̃en sitzen *to sit at a p's feet* ‖ sich jdm z ⁼̃en werfen *to throw o.s. at a p's feet*

F·uß- [in comp] *foot .., foot-operated* (*brake,* etc) **~abstreicher, ~abtreter** m *door-mat; foot-scraper* **~angel** f *crowsfoot, man-trap* ‖ ⟨mil hist⟩ *crowfoot, caltrop* **~anlasser** m ⟨mot⟩ *foot* ⟨cycl⟩ *kick starter* **~antrieb** m *treadle* (*drive*) **~antritt** m *pedal* **~arbeit** f ⟨sport⟩ *foot-work* **~artillerie** f *foot-artillery* **~bad** n *foot-bath* **~ball** m → d. **~ballen** m *ball of the foot* **~bank** f *foot-stool* **~becken** n *foot-basin* **~bekleidung** f [koll] *footgear, footwear;* orthopädische ~ *surgical shoes, boots* **~beschlag** m (Möbel⁼̃) *shoe* ⁼̃**betätigt** a *foot-operated* (*brake*) **~blatt** n = –sohle **~block** m ⟨mar⟩ *snatch-block* **~boden** m *floor; flooring;* –böden [pl] *flooring* ‖ ~ zw Teppich u Wand *surround* | ~belag [m] *floor covering; flooring* ‖ ~heizung [f] *underfloor heating* ‖ ~-platte [f] *slab* **~breit** m, **~breite** f *foot-breadth* ‖ → weichen **~bremse** f *foot-brake* **~brett** n *foot-board* **~decke** f *mat, rug* **~eisen** n *foot-iron* ‖ ⟨hist⟩ †*foot-trap* **~exerzieren** n *dismounted drill* **~fall** m *prostration* (vor *before*); e–n ~ tun ⟨a. übtr⟩ *to pros-*

trate o.s. (vor *before*) **≃fällig** adv *on one's knees*; jdn ~ bitten *to go on one's knees to a p* **~fehler** m ⟨ten⟩ *foot-fault* **≃fest** a *sure-footed* **~flechte** f *athlete's foot* **≃frei** a; ~er Rock *skirt not reaching down to the feet* **~gänger** m *pedestrian, walker*; *foot-passenger*; ⟨sl⟩ *foot-slogger* ‖ unachtsamer ~ ⟨Am sl⟩ *jay-walker* ‖ Brücke f ~ *foot-bridge*; Weg f ~ → –steig; ~-Kreuz- u Quer-Verkehr [m] *amble scramble* ‖ ~-Schutzinsel [f] *pedestrian island* ‖ ~überführung [f] *foot-bridge* ‖ ~überweg [m] *pedestrian crossing*; *crosswalk* **~gangschaltung** f ⟨mot⟩ *pedal gear-change* **~garde** f ⟨engl⟩ *Foot Guards* pl **~gashebel** m *accelerator* **~gefecht** n ⟨mil⟩ (of cavalry) *fighting on foot* **~gestell** n *base, foot, pedestal*; mit ~ *floor standing* **~gicht** f *podagra*; *gout in the feet* **~grind** m ⟨vet⟩ (bei Vieh) *foot-rot*; ⟨Am⟩ *foot-evil* **~hebel** m *foot-lever*; *pedal* **≃kalt** a *cold at the feet*; *damp under foot* **~kissen** n ⟨ec⟩ *hassock* **~knöchel** m *ankle, ancle*; ⟨anat⟩ *tarsus* L **≃krank** a *footsore*; *having sore feet*; F.–e pl ⟨mil⟩ *march casualties* **~lappen** m pl *foot-bandages* od *rags*; ⟨fam⟩ *toe-rags*, ⟨m. m.⟩ *Prince Alberts* °**~latscher** m ⟨mil fam⟩ *foot-slogger* **~leiste** f ⟨arch⟩ *skirt(ing)-board*, ⟨Am⟩ *baseboard* ‖ *foot-rest*; (im Boot) *stretcher* **~motor** m *foot-mounted motor* **~note** f *footnote* ‖ (etw) mit ~n versehen *to footnote* **~partie** f *walking-tour* **~pfad** m *footpath, footway*; ⟨rail⟩ *attendant path* **~pflege** f *pedicure*; *chiropody* **~pfleger** m *pedicure*; *chiropodist* **~pfund** n ⟨phys⟩ *foot-pound* **~pilzerkrankung** f *athlete's foot* **~punkt** m ⟨astr⟩ *nadir*; ⟨math⟩ → Lot **~rampe** f ⟨theat⟩ *footlights* pl **~raste** f *foot rest* **~räude** f ⟨vet⟩ = –grind **~reise** f *walking-tour*; lange ~ *tramp* **~sack** m *foot-muff* ‖ °⟨fig⟩ (Bart) *door-mat* **~schalter** m ⟨el⟩ *foot switch* **~schaltung** f *pedal control* ⟨mot⟩ *footshifter* **~schemel** m *footstool* **~schweiß** m *sweating of the feet* **~sohle** f *sole of the foot*; ⟨med⟩ *thenar*; ~nreflex [m] *plantar reflex* **~soldat** m *foot-soldier*; *footman*; ~n [koll] *foot* (*5000 f.*) **~spur** f *footmark, footprint*; *track* **~stapfe** f *footstep*; *trace*; → –spur ‖ ⟨fig⟩ in jds ~n treten *to follow* od *tread in a p's footsteps* **~steig** m *pavement*; *causeway*; ⟨Am⟩ *sidewalk, walkway* **~stütze** f *foot-rest*; ⟨cycl⟩ *coaster* **≃tief** a *ankle-deep* **~ton** m ⟨mus⟩ *pitch* (*of an organ*) **~tour** f *walking-tour* **~tritt** m **1.** *step*; *footstep*; ich höre ~e *I hear footsteps*; schwere ~e *the tramp* (*of soldiers*) **2.** (Tritt mit dem Fuß) *kick* ‖ jdm e–n ~ geben *to kick a p* ‖ ⟨fig⟩ *to give a p the sack*; *to reject a p*, ⟨sl⟩ *to pedal a p*; e–n ~ bek. ⟨sl a. fig⟩ *to get the pedal, to get the dirty kick* **3.** (Trittbrett) *footboard*; *pedal*; *treadle*; ~drehbank [f] *foot-lathe* ‖ = –schemel **~tonne** f ⟨phys⟩ *foot-ton* **~truppen** f pl [koll] *foot* (*5000 f.*) **~volk** n *foot-soldiers* pl; *infantry*; → –truppen **~wandern** n *hiking*; *tramping* **~wanderung** f *hike* **~wanne** f *foot-tub* **~wärmer** m *foot-warmer*; ⟨el⟩ *foot stove* **~waschung** f ⟨ec⟩ *maundy*; ⟨arts⟩ *Washing of the Apostles' feet* **~weg** m *footpath, footway*; *pathway*; *lane*; ⟨Am⟩ *walkway* **~winde** f ⟨tech⟩ *foot-winch* **~wurzel-(knochen** pl) f *tarsus* L **~zeug** n = –bekleidung

F·ußball m **1.** *football* **2.** = ~spiel ‖ ~ spielen *to play football* **~elf** f *the eleven* **~feld** n *football field*; ⟨Am⟩ *gridiron* **~hose** f *football shorts* pl; *knickers* pl **~mannschaft** f *football team*; ⟨engl univ⟩ Mitglied der Haupt≃ s *to be a blue*; M. der ~ w *to get one's blue* **~meisterschaft** f *football championship* **~spiel** n *football*; ⟨sl⟩ *footer* ‖ ~ (bei dem der Ball nicht mit der Hand berührt w darf) *Association football*, *Association*; ⟨sl⟩ *socker, soccer* **~spieler** m *footballer* ⟨Am fam⟩ *gridder* (Fußballer) **~-Toto** m *pool* **~wettspiel** n *football* (⟨sl⟩ *footer*) *match*

F·üßchen n *small foot*

F·ussel f ~/~n, F·usselchen n = Fusel[2] | **≃n** vi [h] ⟨tex⟩ *to rub up*; *to pill*

°**f·üßeln** vi [h] *to foot it* ‖ *to make love with one's feet under the table* **f·ußen** vi [h] ⟨übtr⟩ ~ auf *to be based on*; *to rest* (od *rely*) *on*; da war wenig, auf das man ~ konnte *there was little to go upon*; ~d auf gründlicher Kenntnis der .. *basing his conclusions on a mastery of* .. (*he* ..) **-füßer** [in comp] ⟨mst scient⟩ → Bar~; Tausend~, Vier~ **-füßig** [in comp] vier~ *four-footed*; *quadrapedal* **-füßler** [in comp] ⟨pros⟩ Fünf~ *line of five feet*; *pentameter*; → fünffüßig **F·üßling** m *foot* (*of a stocking*); e–n ~ anstricken *to foot a stocking*

Fust·age [fy'sta:ʒə] f [Fr] *cooperage*; *vats* od *tubs* pl; *casks* od *barrels* pl

Fustan·ella f ~/–llen *fustanella*

futsch! adv & pred a [lautnachahmend, vgl ⟨engl⟩ *fut*] *gone*!, *lost*!, *off*!; ⟨mil sl⟩ *napoo*! ‖ ~ gehn *to go to waste*; *to go phut* ‖ ~ ist ~ (*it is*) *no use crying over spilt milk*

F·utter[1] n ~s/ (Vieh≃, Trocken≃) *fodder*, *provender*; *feed, keep*; im Silo konserviertes ~ *silage*, ⟨bes mil⟩ *forage* ‖ (Tier) ~ geben *to feed*; gib dem Pferde ~ *give the horse a feed* ‖ ~ suchen *to forage*; mit ~ versehen *to forage* **2.** °⟨übtr⟩ (P) *food, feed*; *provisions* pl; ⟨fam⟩ *tack, toke, provender*; ⟨sl⟩ *grub* (*a very good g.*); ⟨mil sl⟩ *chow* ‖ (schweres Essen) *stodge* ‖ er ist gut im ~ *he is well fed* ‖ ⟨fig⟩ (f *for*); Kanonen≃ *food for powder, cannon fodder* **~bau** m *cultivation of fodder-plants* **~beutel** m (f Pferd) *nose-bag* **~geld** n *money paid for the keep* (*of an animal*) **~gerste** f *feeding-barley* **~gestell** n (im Stall) *rack* **~getreide** n *coarse grains* pl **~kasten** m *feed-box* **~kosten** pl *keep* (*the horse is not worth its k.*) **~krippe** f *manger* | ⟨übtr Am pol⟩ *spoil* ‖ jd, der nach der ~ trachtet *placeman*, ⟨Am⟩ *spoilsman* | ~nsystem [n] *spoils system* ‖ ~nwirtschaft [f] ⟨pol⟩ *feather-bedding*; *padding* **~lager** n ⟨agr⟩ *silo* °**~luke** f ⟨fig⟩ (Mund) *hatchway*; *grub-shop, rat-trap*; *potato-box*, *–jaw*, *–trap* **~mittel** n *fodder, feed*; ~ [pl] *feeding stuffs* pl **~napf** m *feeding-dish* **~neid** m *envy* **~pflanze** f *fodder-plant* **~rübe** f *feeding-turnip* **~sack** m = –beutel **~schneidemaschine** f *fodder-cutter* **~schütten** n *feeding*; ~! *feed*!, beim ~ °(P) *at* (*one's*) *feed* **~speicher** m ⟨mil⟩ *forage-store* ‖ *silo* **~trog** m *feeding-trough* **~turm** m *silo* **~wert** m ⟨agr⟩ *feeding value*

F·utter[2] n ~s/~ *lining* (*of a furnace*; *coat, pocket*; abknöpfbar *removable*) ‖ ⟨mech⟩ *liner*; *shim*; Metall≃ *metal lining*; *bush* ‖ ⟨tech⟩ (Spann≃) *chuck*; (Fenster≃) *box* ‖ (Reißverschluß≃) *removable lining* ‖ **~mauer** f *prop-wall*; *supporting wall* **~papier** n *liners* pl **~stoff** m, **~tuch** n *lining*; *stuff for lining*

Futter·al n ~s/~e (f Brille etc) (*slip*) *case*; (f Schirm) (*slip*) cover; (f Messer) *sheath* ‖ ⟨tech⟩ *box* ‖ in ein ~ tun *to case*; *to box* | ~kleid [n] ⟨tail⟩ *sh. dress*

f·uttern vi [h] **1.** (T) *to eat, feed* **2.** °(P) *to feed* (*we f. at 7*); ⟨sl⟩ *to grub* **f·üttern**[1] **1.** vt [h] (T) *to feed*; füttere Pferde *give horses a feed* **2.** ≃ n = Fütterung **F·ütterung**[1] f *the feeding*

f·üttern[2] vt [h] (Rock, Tasche etc) *to line* (mit *with*); mit Pelz ~ *to fur*; mit Polster (etc) ~ *to pad* ‖ mit Stoff gefütterter Briefumschlag *cloth-lined envelope* **F·ütterung**[2] f *the lining* (*of a coat*); Pelz≃ *furring*; Polster≃ *padding*

Fut·ur n ~s/~e ⟨gram⟩ *future tense*; *future* **~·ismus** m ⟨arts⟩ *futurism* **~·ist** m ~en/~en ⟨arts⟩ *futurist* **≃·istisch** **1.** a *futurist* (*school*); *futuristic* (*stuff*); ⟨engl⟩ ~e Richtung (seit 1915) *vorticism* **2.** adv *futuristically*

G

G, g [ge:] n ~/~ **1.** (Buchstabe) *G, g* ‖ die 4 gr G = Geist, Geduld, Geld, Glück **2.** ⟨mus⟩ *G*; *sol* [It] ‖ → A-Dur ‖ G-Saite *G-string* ‖ G-Schlüssel = Violinschlüssel ‖ ⟨aero⟩ G-Anzug (gegen Überdruck etc) *G-suit* ‖ ⟨rail⟩ G-Wagen = gedeckter W. ‖ ⟨mil⟩ G-2(-Offizier) (⟨hist⟩ = Ic = Nachrichtendienst ..) *G 2* ⟨bes Am⟩

gab 1. & 3. sg pret v geben

G·abardine [-di:n] m & f Fr *gabardine*

G·abbro m [It] ~s/~s ⟨geol⟩ *gabbro*

G·abe f ~/~n **1.** **(Geschenk)** *gift* (an, f jdn *to a p*; v jdm *from a p*); *offering* (f *for*); *present* ‖ ⟨ec⟩ (Geld≃) *donation* ‖ Liebes≃, milde ~ *alms* [pl & sg konstr]; *charity*; ⟨Am⟩ *hand-out*; um e–e milde ~ bitten *to ask for charity* **2.** **(Begabung)** *gift* (z tun *of doing*) ‖ göttliche ~ ⟨theol⟩ *charisma* ‖ e–e gr ~ h *to have a knack* (z tun *of doing*) ‖ *the g. of song* ‖ ⟨fam⟩ *the g. of the gab* (Rede); *the g. of tongues* (f Sprachen) ‖ *endowment, g., talent*; ein Mann mit vielen ~n *a man of many g.s* **3.** → Geben, Verabreichen **g·äbe** → gang → geben

G·abel f ~/~n **1.** *fork*; ~ mit 3 Zinken *three-pronged f.* ‖ ⟨cul⟩ Dessert≃ *sweet-f.* ‖ *fish-f.*; *crayfish-f.*; *cake-f.*; *snail-f.*; *lobsters-f.*; *oyster-f.* ‖ mit der ~ aufspießen etc *to f.* ‖ ⟨fig fam⟩ 5zinkige ~ *bunch of fives* ‖ (Heu≃, Mist≃) *f., prong*; mit der ~ aufladen *to f.* **2.** ⟨übtr⟩ (≃förmiger Gegenstand) **a.** *f.* (*of a bough, river, road*) ‖ → Stimm≃ **b.** (of a stag) *f.ed antler* **c.** = –deichsel **d.** ⟨tech⟩ (Riemen≃) *belt* (od *strap*)*-f.* **e.** ⟨cycl⟩ *fork* **f.** ⟨telph⟩ (Hörerablage) *cradle*; *fork* od *receiver rest* **3.** ⟨mil & nav⟩ (beim Einschießen) *bracket* (enge, kl *short*, weite, gr *long*); e–e ~ bilden, erschießen *to br.*; ⟨nav⟩ *to straddle* **~antilope** f ⟨zoo⟩ *pronghorn antelope* **~bein** n *wish(ing)-bone* (*of birds*) **~bildung** f *bracketing*; *bracket fire* **~bock** m = –antilope ‖ ⟨hunt⟩ *buck with 2 points* **~deichsel** f *shafts, thills* pl **≃förmig** a *forked, forky*; *bifurcate, furcate*; ⟨ent⟩ *furcal* **~frühstück** n *lunch(eon)*; ⟨Am⟩ *midmorning snack*; ⟨A Ind⟩ *tiffin*; ⟨cul⟩ *déjeuner à la fourchette* Fr; ⟨fam⟩ *elevens(es)*; ein ~ einnehmen *to lunch(eon)* **~geweih** n *forked antlers* pl **~gruppenschießen** n ⟨mar⟩ *ladder* od *searching fire* **~häkelei** f *crochet-work over a metal fork* **~kopf** m ⟨cycl⟩ *fork-head*; ⟨mot⟩ *yoke end* **~kreuz** n ⟨her⟩ *(cross-)pall* **~maß** n ⟨for⟩ *diameter-gauge* **~mücke** f ⟨ent⟩ → Mücke **~pferd** n *thiller* **~rohr** n ⟨tech⟩ *breeches pipe* **~schaltung** f ⟨el⟩ *Y-connection* **~schießen** n = –bildung **~schlüssel** m ⟨tech⟩ *fork-spanner* **~schwanz** m ⟨ent⟩ *puss-moth* **~stapler** m ⟨ind⟩ *fork-lift truck*; ⟨agr⟩ *f.-l.* **~stiel** m ⟨aero⟩ *Y-strut* **~stütze** f *forked stand* od *support*; (MG≃) *bipod* **~weihe** f ⟨orn⟩ *kite* **~zapfen** m ⟨tech⟩ *gudgeon* **g·abeln** vt [h] (etw) → aufgabeln ‖ **sich ~** (of bough, river, road) *to bifurcate, divide, fork* (in *into*) **G·abelung** f ~/~en *bifurcation, forking*; *crotch* (*of a tree*), *embranchment* (*of a river*); (Weg≃) *the parting* (*of the ways*) **G·abler** m ⟨zoo⟩ *stag with forked antlers*

G·ablonz n (Stadt in Böhmen) *Jablonec*

g·ackern **1.** vi [h] *to cackle*, ⟨a. übtr (P)⟩ **2.** ≃ n *cackle, cackling*

G·adem m, **G·aden** m ~s/~ **1.** *small one-roomed house* **2.** ⟨ec arch⟩ Licht≃ *clerestory*

Gadolin·it m ~s/ ⟨minr⟩ *gadolinite*

G·affel f ~/~n ⟨mar⟩ *gaff*; → Besan≃ ‖ Groß≃ *main gaff*; Vor≃ *fore-gaff* **~nock** f *gaff-end* **~schoner** m *fore-and-aft schooner*; *fore-and-after* **~segel** n *gaff-sail*; *spanker*; *spencer, trysail*

g·affen **1.** vi *to gape*; *gaze, stare* (in *into*); *to stand gaping* od *at gaze*; ⟨Am fam⟩ *to rubber* ‖ dumm ~ *to gape like a yokel*; → angaffen **2.** ≃ n *gape, gaping*; *gaze, gazing* **G·affer** m *gaper* **Gaffer·ei** f = Gaffen

G·ag-Spezialist ['gæg–] m ⟨theat⟩ *gag-man*

Gag·at m ~es/~e ⟨minr⟩ *jet*; *hard black lignite*

G·age ['gɑ:ʒə] f ~/~n *remuneration*; *salary*

G·agel m ⟨bot⟩ *wax-berry* (od *myrtle*) **~gewächse** pl ⟨bot⟩ *Myriaceae* L **~strauch** m ⟨bot⟩ *bog-myrtle*; (*sweet*) *gale*

g·ähnen **1.** vi [h] **a.** *to yawn, gape*; er gähnte °fürchterlich *he gave a great yawn, he yawned a huge yawn*; → an~ **b.** ⟨fig⟩ (of an abyss) *to yawn* (*an abyss yawned in front of them*) **2.** ≃ n *yawn(ing)* ‖ ~ steckt an *yawning is catching* **g·ähnend** **1.** a ⟨mst fig⟩ *yawning* (*abyss*) **2.** adv; ~ leer *yawning* (*purse*)

Gaill·arde [ga'jardə] f ~/~n [Fr] ⟨hist⟩ (Tanz) *gaillard*

G·ailtaler Alpen pl (Teil der Karischen Alpen)

G·ala f ~/ **1.** *gala dress*; in ~ *in gala* (od *full*) *dress*; sich in ~ werfen ⟨fam⟩ *to put on one's Sunday best*; ⟨mil sl⟩ *to dag up* ‖ ⟨mar⟩ Flaggen≃ e–s Schiffes *a ship dressed rainbow-fashion* **2.** [in comp] *gala* **~anzug** m *court-dress* ‖ *full* (od *gala*) *dress* **~hut** m ⟨mil⟩ *cocked hat* **~kleid** n *court-dress*; *gown* **~kutsche** f *state carriage* **~uniform** f *full-dress uniform* **~vorstellung** f ⟨theat⟩ *gala-performance*, ⟨Am⟩ *spectacular*

gal·aktisch a *galactic* (*system*) **Galaktom·eter** n *galactometer* **Galal·ith** n ~s/~e *galalith*

Gal·an m ~s/~e *beau* [Fr], *gallant* [gə'lænt], *spark*; *paramour* **gal·ant** a *gallant* [gə'lænt]; *amorous*; *courteous* **Galanter·ie** f ~/~n *gallantry*; *gallant conduct*; *courtesy* **~waren** f pl *fancy-goods* pl

Gal·apagosinseln f pl (am Äquator, im Stillen Ozean) *Galapagos Islands* pl, *Colon Archipelago*

†**G·alater** m, **~in** f (keltisches Volk in Kleinasien) *Galatian* †**Gal·atien** n *Galatia*

G·alaterbrief m *Epistle to the Galatians*

G·alatz n (Hafenstadt Rumäniens) *Galatz*

Galax·ie f [–i:] ~/~n [–i:ən], G·alaxis f *galaxy* ‖ (Milchstraße) *Milky Way, Galaxy*

G·äle m, **G·älin** f *Gael* **g·älisch** a *Gaelic*

Gale·asse f ~/~n ⟨mar⟩ *galleass, -iass*

Gal·eere f ~/~n ⟨mar⟩ *galley*; kl ~ *galliot*

Gal·eeren- [in comp] **~sklave**, **~sträfling** m *galley-slave* **~strafe** f *the galleys* pl; z ~ verurteilt w *to be sent to the g.*; *to be condemned to the hulks*

gal·enisch a (nach röm. Arzt Galen) *Galenic(al)*

Galen·it m ⟨minr⟩ *galena* L

Gale·one f ~/~n ⟨hist mar⟩ *galleon*

Gale·ote f ~/~n ⟨hist mar⟩ *galliot*

Galer·ie f ~/~n **1.** (gedeckter Gang) *gallery*; *loggia* [It] **2.** ⟨arch & theat⟩ *gallery*; ⟨Am⟩ *second balcony*; *bank* ‖ die Zuschauer der ~ *the g., the gods*; f die ~ spielen *to play to the g*; mit ~ *galleried* (*hall*) ‖ ⟨ec arch⟩ säulengetragene ~ *triforium* L **3.** ⟨arts⟩ *g.*; Bilder≃ *picture-g.*

Galg·ant m, **~wurzel** f ⟨bot⟩ *galingale*

G·algen m ~s/~ **1.** (z Hinrichtung) *gallows* pl [sg konstr; ein ~ *a g.s*]; *g.s-tree*; *gibbet* (am ~ *on the g.*) ‖ (es) wird ihn an den ~ bringen (*murder*) *will hang him* ‖ an dem ~ enden *to end on the g.*; (jdn) an den ~ hängen *to gibbet*; an den ~ k *to* *come to the g.* ‖ er gehört an den ~, ist reif f den ~ *he is fit for the g.*; *he is g.-ripe* ‖ Folterstrafe am Schnell~̈, Wipp~̈ *strappado*; dazu: *to strappado* (*a p*) **2.** ⟨übtr tech⟩ *boom*; *crossarms*, *gallows*, *cross-pieces* pl **~frist** f *last respite*, *short shrift* **~gesicht** n *gallows-look*; *hang-dog face* **~humor** m *grim* od *defiant humour* **~miene** f *hanging look* **~strick**, **~vogel** m *gallows-bird*; *hang-dog*; *gaol* (⟨Am⟩ *jail*) *bird*

Gal·icien n [–ts–] ⟨Span⟩ (Prov.) *Galicia* **gal·icisch** *Galician*

Galil·äa n *Galilee* **Galil·äer** m *Galilean* **galil·äisch** a *Galilean*; ~̈es Meer *Sea of Galilee*

Galimath·ias m ~/ *galimatias*

Gali·on n ⟨mar⟩ *cutwater* **~sfigur** f ⟨mar⟩ *figure-head*, ⟨fam⟩ *leddy* **Gali·ote** f = Galeote

g·älisch a (→ Gäle) *Gaelic*, *Goidelic*; das ~̈e, die ~e Sprache *Gaelic*, *Goidelic*

Gal·izien ⟨geogr⟩ (Vor-Karpaten-Landschaft) *Galicia* **Gal·izier** m *Galician* **gal·izisch** a *Galician*

G·alla pl (hamit. Volk in Afrika) *Gallas*

G·allapfel m *gall-nut*; (*oak-*)*apple* od *spangle*

G·alle[1] ~/~n **1.** ⟨physiol⟩ *bile*; (in lower animals) *gall* | ⟨übtr⟩ (Wermut) *wormwood* ‖ *ill temper*; mir kam die ~ hoch, mir lief die ~ über ⟨sl⟩ *I lost my wool* od *hair*; *it got my goat*; → Gift **2.** [in comp] ~̈**treibend** a *cholagogic*, ~es Mittel *cholagogue* → Gallen-

G·alle[2] f ~/~n **1.** ⟨vet⟩ (Schwellung in Gelenken etc) *gall*; *swelling* **2.** ⟨bot⟩ (Mißbildung) *gall* (auf .. *on a plant*, *tree*); → Gallapfel

g·allen vt [h] (→ Galle) **1.** e–n Fisch ~ *to take the gall out of a fish* **2.** (färben) *to gall* **G·allen-** ~̈**artig** a *biliary* ~̈**bitter** a *bitter as gall* **~blase** f *gall-bladder*; Entzündung der ~ *cholecystitis* L **~farbstoff** m *bile-pigment* **~fett** n *cholesterin* **~gang** m = –weg **~leiden** n *bilious complaint* (od *derangement*, *disease*) **~säure** f *gallic acid* **~stauung** f *biliary engorgement* **~stein** m *gall-stone*; *biliary calculus* L ‖ ~kolik [f] *gall-stone colic* ‖ ~leiden [n] *cholelithiasis* [kɔlili'θaiəsis] L ‖ ~operation [f] *cholecystotomy* **~weg** m *bile* (od *gall*)*-duct*; Entzündung der ~e *cholangitis* L ‖ – u Harnwege [pl] *biliary and urinary tracts*

G·allert n ~s/~e **1.** (tierisches ~) *gelatin*(*e*); *glue*; z ~ m, z ~ w *to gelatinize* **2.** ⟨cul⟩ (Nahrung) (Fleisch~̈ etc) *jelly*; z ~ m *to jelly*; ~ bilden, z ~ w *to jelly* ~̈**artig** a *gelatinous*, *gelatinoid*; *jelly-like* (*mass*) ~̈**förmig** a *gelatiniform* **G·allerte** f ~/~n = Gallert

G·allien ⟨hist⟩ *Gaul* **G·allier** m ~s/~ *Gaul*

g·allig a *biliary* ‖ ⟨übtr⟩ *bilious*; *ill-tempered*

gallik·anisch a *Gallican* (*church*, *psalter*)

Gall·ipoli n (Stadt an den → Dardanellen)

g·allisch a *Gallic*, *Gaulish*; *the Gallic War*, *Bellum Gallicum* L; ~e Sprache *Gaulish* **Galliz·ismus** m *Gallicism*; *French idiom* **Gallo-~man·ie** f *Gallomania* ~̈**romanisch** a *Gallo-Roman*

Gall·one f ~/~n ⟨engl⟩ (4,54 [Am 3,78] l) *gallon*

g·allsüchtig a *bilious*, *jaundiced*

G·allup- [–əp] **~-Umfrage** f *Gallup poll*

G·allus m ⟨chem⟩ *nut-gall* **~säure** f *gallic acid*

G·allwespe f ⟨ent⟩ *gall-fly* (od *wasp*)

Galm·ei m ~s/~e ⟨minr⟩ *calamine*

Gal·on m, **Gal·one** f *galloon*; *braid of gold* (etc.)

galon·iert a *galooned*

Gal·opp m ~(e)s/~e **1.** *gallop*; gestreckter ~ *flying* od *full gallop*; kurzer ~ *spin*; im ~ *at a gallop*; Ritt im ~ *gallop* ‖ im ~ reiten *or* rennen *to gallop*; in ~ übergehen *or* fallen *to break into a gallop*; in vollem ~ herank *to come full tilt* (v *from*); in rasendem ~ ⟨sl⟩ (*to ride*) *hell for leather* ‖ kz leichter ~ *canter*, *hand-gallop*; dazu: *to canter* ‖ → Eile **2.** (Tanz) *galop*; ~ tanzen *to galop* **galopp·ieren** vi [s] *to gallop* (durch *through*; über *over*); *to go galloping* ‖ leicht ~ *to tittup* ‖ (Pferd) ~ l *to gallop* **galopp·ierend** a *galloping*; ~er Reiter, ~es Pferd *galloper* ‖ ⟨übtr⟩ ~ *galloping* (*consumption*)

Gal·osche f ~/~n *golosh*, *galosh*; ~n [pl] *goloshes* pl; ⟨Am⟩ *rubbers* pl

Galvanisati·on [-ts-] f *galvanization* **galv·anisch** **1.** a *galvanic* (*battery*, *current*); → Element ‖ *electrolytic* (*bath*); ~e Kette *voltaic couple*; ~er Niederschlag *electro-deposit*; ~e Verzinkung *electro-galvanizing* **2.** adv *galvanically*; *electrolytically*; (etw) ~ versilbern *to electro-plate*; ~ versilberte Ware f *electro-plate*; ⟨fam⟩ *electro* **galvanis·ieren** vt [h] *to galvanize* **Galvanis·ierung** f *galvanizing*; *electro-galvanizing* **Galvan·ismus** m *galvanism* **Galv·ano** n *electrotype*; ⟨fam⟩ *electro* **~kaustik** f *galvanocautery* **~meter** n *galvanometer* **~plastik** f [abstr] *electroforming*, *galvanoplasty* ‖ [konkr] *electrotype* ‖ ~er [m] *electrotyper* ~̈**plastisch** a *galvanoplastic*; *electrotype* ‖ ~e Ätzung *anodic etching* **~skop** n *electroscope* **~technik** f *galvanotechnics*; *electro-plating and electro-forming technology*

Gam·ander m ⟨bot⟩ Gemeiner ~ *germander*

Gam·asche f ~/~n [mst pl] ~n *gaiters*, *leggings* pl; Wickel~̈n *puttees* (*–tties*); in ~n *gaitered* ‖ Schuh~̈n *spats* pl | °⟨fig⟩ ~n h = gr Angst h **~ndienst** m ⟨mil⟩ *pipe-clay*; ⟨Am⟩ *chicken* ~nhose [f] *pull-ups* pl

G·ambe f ~/~n ⟨mus⟩ (Kniegeige) *viola da gamba* [It;] Tenor~̈ *tenor violin* **Gamb·ist** m ~en/~en ⟨a.⟩ *violoncellist*

G·ambia **1.** m (Fluß in Afrika) **2.** n (brit. Kolonie in Afrika) ‖ noch nicht selbständig. Königin Elisabeth II. von England ist Staatsoberhaupt. (Die geringe Größe und mangelnde Wirtschaftskraft machen die Unabhängigkeit problematisch – es wird eine Form der Zusammenarbeit mit Senegal angestrebt); Februar 1965 selbständig

Gamb·it n ~s/~s ⟨chess⟩ *gambit*

Gam·et m ~en/~en ⟨biol⟩ *gamete*

G·amma n ~s/~s [Gr] *gamma* **~eule** f ⟨ent⟩ *g.*(*-moth*) **~strahlen** pl *g. rays* pl

°**g·ammeln** vi *to loaf*, → faulenzen

G·ammelware f *deteriorated fish*, etc °**G·ammler** m ~s/~ *loafer*; ⟨m. m.⟩ *beatnik*; *weirdie*

ˣ**Gams** f ⟨zoo⟩ **1.** = Gemse ‖ ~bart [m] *chamois tufts* od *brush* **2.** [in comp] ⟨bes bot⟩ (~kraut, ~kresse etc) → Gemsen-

Gan·asche f ~/~n ⟨vet⟩ [mst pl] (in horses) *masseteric regions*

°**G·aneff** m = Dieb †**G·anerbe** m ⟨jur⟩ *co-heir*

Gang m ~es/~̈e **A.** [abstr] **1. a.** *go*(*ing*); *walk*(*ing*) | (~art) *gait*, *walk*; elastisch *swing*; *buoyant stride*; gemächlich *stroll*; schlendernd *amble* ‖ *action*, *pace* (*of a horse*) **b.** (S) *action*, *motion*, *hang*, ⟨mach⟩ *action*, *running* ‖ *course* (*of a conversation*); *progress*; → Fort~̈, Lauf, Verlauf ‖ *the run* (S); *the march* (*of events*); *the way* (*of the world*); *the trend* (*of the time*) ‖ der übliche, gewohnheitsmäßige ~ *the routine* (*of business*, *duties*) **2.** regelmäßiger ~ *walk* (mein Lieblings~ *my favourite w.*); kz ~ *turn* ‖ *commission*, *errand*; e–n ~ tun *to go on an errand*; ~̈e besorgen *to run errands*; vergeblicher ~ *fool's errand* ‖ (Arzt~̈) *visit* ‖ ⟨police⟩ *beat*, *round*, auf s–n ~̈en *on his rounds* ‖ → Stuhl~̈ **3.** (Abschnitt, Teil) **a.** ⟨cul⟩ *course*; was wünschen Sie als nächsten ~? *what do you wish to follow?* **b.** ⟨fenc⟩ *pass*; → Waffen~̈ ‖ ⟨sport⟩ *bout*; → Runde **c.** (beim Segeln) *tack* **B.** [konkr] **1.** (Baum~̈) *alley*; *avenue*; langer gedeckter ~ *gallery* ‖ *passage*, *path*, *way*; (unterirdisch) *underground passage* ‖ (Durch~̈, Flur) *corridor* ⟨a. hot⟩; *passage*; (zw Stuhlreihen) *aisle* (⟨a. ec⟩ Mittel~̈ *middle aisle*); ⟨a. rail⟩ *gangway*, ⟨Am⟩ *aisle* ‖ ⟨mar⟩ Planken~̈ *strake*; → Kimm~̈ ‖ (Wasser~̈) *conduit*, *gut* **2. a.** ⟨geol⟩

matrix **b.** ⟨min⟩ 1. *adit, gallery, level, tunnel*; = Erzgang ‖ mächtiger Eruptiv~̈ *dike, dyke* 2. (Gesteinsmasse) *gangue* **3.** ⟨anat⟩ *conduit, duct*; *channel*; *meatus* L **4.** (of a screw) *turn*; → Gewinde **5.** ⟨mot⟩ *gear*; erster ~ *low* (od *bottom, starting*) *gear*; zweiter ~ *second g.*; dritter ~ *top-gear*; Direkt~̈, Normal~̈ *high range*; Berg-, Brems-, Gelände~̈ *low range* | ⟨tech⟩ toter ~ *backlash*; *dead travel*, ⟨mot⟩ *steering play* **C. Wendungen 1.** ⟨mot⟩ e–n anderen ~ einschalten *to change gear* ‖ auf dem 3. ~ fahren *to go on top-gear* | (P) s–n alten ~ gehen ⟨sl⟩ *to carry on* ‖ die S muß ihren ~ gehen *the matter must take its course* | °⟨sex⟩ e–n ~ m ⟨vulg⟩ *to break a lance* (*with a woman*) **2.** jdn **am ~** erkennen *to know a p by his walk* | **im** ~e **(P)** *on the go*; *on foot*; *at work* ‖ (of machines) *in gear*; *working* ‖ im ~ s **(S)** *to be in motion* (od *operation, progress*); *to be on*; *to be afoot* (od *afloat, on foot*); *to be toward*; (of preparations) *to be under way*; (of plans) *to be in the wind* ‖ in vollem ~ s *to be in full blast* (od *swing, stride*) | **in ~ bleiben** *to be kept going* | (etw) in ~ **bringen** *to put* od *set on foot* od *in motion*; *to set* (od *get, start*) *going*; *to bring into play*; *to float, launch, start, work*; ⟨Am⟩ *to operate* ‖ (Motor) *to start up* ‖ ⟨fig⟩ e–e S in ~ br. *to initiate* (*a process*); *to set the ball going* ‖ in geregelten ~ br. *to set in working order* | (etw) in **~ halten** *to keep going*; (Betrieb) *to run*; ⟨Am⟩ *to operate*; (Feuer) *to keep up*; das Gespräch .. *to keep the ball up* od *rolling* | **(P)** recht, richtig in ~ k *to find one's own pace*; *to get going*; *to get into one's stride*; er wird schon in ~ k *he will soon swim all right* ‖ **(S)** (richtig, recht) *to get well into gear*; *to get under way* (*the play got under way very slowly*); *to march*; *to be launched* | (etw) in ~ **setzen** *to set on foot*; *to set going*; = in ~ bringen; (geschickt) *to engineer, manipulate* **gang,** ~̈ [pred a] ~ u gäbe *customary, quite common* od *usual*; *traditional* ‖ *in fashion* od *vogue* ‖ durchaus ~ *nothing out of the ordinary* ‖ ~ u gäbe s *to be in common use*; *to be practiced*; ⟨com⟩ *to pass current* **G·ang- ~art** f ⟨zoo⟩ *locomotory pattern* ‖ ein Pferd alle ~en m l *to put a horse through his paces* **~arten** pl ⟨min⟩ *gangue minerals* **~füllung** f ⟨min⟩ *vein-material* **~gehäuse** n *gear-box* **~gestein** n → Gestein **~höhe** f *pitch of a thread*; ⟨aero⟩ *propeller pitch* **~schaltung** f ⟨mot⟩ *gear-change* **~spill** n ⟨mar⟩ *capstan* **~tiefe** f *depth of a thread* **~züge** pl ⟨min⟩ *shear-zone*; *vein-system* **g·angbar** a **1.** (of roads) *passable, practicable*; ⟨übtr⟩ *possible, practicable* **2.** ⟨com⟩ *current* (*money, value*) ‖ *marketable, merchantable, sal(e)able* (*goods*) | **~̈keit** f **1.** *passableness*, ⟨bes mil⟩ *passability*; *practicability, practicableness* (*of a road*) **2.** *currency* ‖ *sal(e)ability*; *marketability, merchantableness* (*of goods*) **3.** ⟨mach⟩ *right motion* **G·ängelband** n *leading-strings* pl ‖ (jdn) am ~e führen *to conduct in leading-strings*; ⟨fig⟩ *to keep in a state of dependence* od *pupil(l)age*; *to lead* (*a p*) *by the nose* ‖ am ~e geführt w *to be in leading-strings*; ⟨fig⟩ *to be in undue dependence* (v .. *on a p*) **gängeln** vt [h] ⟨fig⟩ (jdn) *to have a p on a string*; *to lead by the nose* ‖ *to keep in a state of dependence* od *pupil(l)age, tutelage*; → bevormunden **G·ängelwagen** m (f Kinder) *go-cart, stroller* **G·ängeviertel** n ⟨Ger⟩ *district in which prostitution is segregated*; ⟨Am⟩ *levee* **G·änger** m *goer, walker* **g·ängig** a *swift* (*horse*); ~ s, Sw ~e Beine h *to be a good walker* ‖ ⟨übtr⟩ *practicable, workable*; = gangbar 2. ‖ allgemein *or* gut ~ *well-established* (*brand*); weniger ~e Artikel [m pl] *also-rans* pl

G·anges m (Fluß in Vorder-Indien)

G·anglien- [-iən] *ganglion* ..; *gangli*(*on*) **~̈förmig** a *gangliform* **G·anglion** n ~s/–lien ⟨path & anat⟩ *ganglion* Gr [pl *–lia*]

Gangr·än f ~/~en ⟨med⟩ *gangrene* **gangrän·ös** a *gangrenous*

G·angster [ˈgæŋstə] m ⟨Am⟩ *gangster*, mit Maschinenpistole ⟨sl⟩ *Tommy gee*; ⟨Am sl⟩ *racketeer* ‖ ~bande [f] *group of gangsters*; *gang of criminals* | **~tum** n (organisiertes) *racketeering*

Gano·ide m ~n/~n ⟨ich⟩ (Schmelzschupper) *ganoid*

°**Gan·ove** [-və] m ~n/~n ⟨sl⟩ *spiv*

Gans f ~/ ~̈e → *goose, sheldrake, shelduck* **1.** ⟨orn⟩ *goose* [pl *geese*]; ~̈e → *goose* ‖ junge ~ *gosling*; → Gänserich ‖ Wilde ~ *greylag* (*goose*), *grey goose* **2.** ⟨fig⟩ *goose, ninny, silly, simpleton*; sie ist e–e dumme ~ *she is a silly*; dumme, eitle ~ ⟨Am⟩ *powder puff* ‖ wie e–e ~ wenn's donnert (*to look*) *like a* (*dying*) *duck in a thunderstorm* **G·änschen** n *gosling*; *goosey* ‖ ⟨fig⟩ (*dummes* ~) *goosey* **G·änse-** [in comp] *goose-* .. **~blume** f, **~blümchen** n ⟨bot⟩ (⟨Am⟩ *English*) *daisy* ‖ mit ~n bedeckt *daisied* (*meadow*) **~braten** m *roast g.* **~brust** f *breast of a g.* ‖ geräucherte ~ *smoked g.-breast* **~distel** f ⟨bot⟩ *sow-thistle* **~ei** n *goose-egg* **~feder** f *g.-feather* (od *quill*) **~fett** n *g.-fat*; *g.-dripping* **~fuß** m ⟨bot⟩ *g.-foot* [pl *–foots*]; *pigweed* **~füßchen** n pl ⟨typ⟩ *inverted commas* pl, *quotation-marks* **~haut** f *g.-skin* ‖ ⟨fig⟩ *g.-flesh, g.-pimples* (~ m *to raise g.-p.*); ⟨fam⟩ *the shivers* pl; es überläuft mich e–e ~, ich krieg *or* hab, bek e–e ~ *my flesh* (od *skin*) *creeps*; *I feel creepy* od *goosey* ‖ jdm e–e ~ über den Rücken jagen *to make a p's flesh creep*; *to make a p's blood run cold* **~hirt** m *g.-herd* **~junge** m *g.-boy* **~kiel** m *g.-quill*; *quill(-pen)* **~klein** n *giblets* pl **~kraut** n ⟨bot⟩ *g.-grass*; *rock-cress* ‖ **~küken** n *gosling* **~leber** f *goose liver* ‖ ~pastete [f] ⟨cul⟩ *g.-l. pie, paté de foie gras* (Fr) **~liesel, ~mädchen** n *g.-girl* **~marsch** m *Indian* (od *single*) *file* (*in I. f.*) **~schmalz** n = –fett **~wein** m ⟨fam⟩ *Adam's ale*; Schluck ~ (Wasser ohne Essen) *duck's breakfast* **G·änserich** m ~s/~e **1.** ⟨orn⟩ *gander* **2.** ⟨bot⟩ *goose-grass*; *tansy* **G·ansljunge(s)** n [österr] = Gänseklein

ˣ**Gant** f ~/~en **1.** Sw = Versteigerung **2.** = Konkurs

ˣ**G·anter** m = Gänserich 1.

ganz I. a [ohne Komparation] **A. 1. (heil)** *whole* (*cup*); *entire* **2. (ungeteilt) a.** [pred] *whole*; (etw) ~ backen *to bake a th whole*; e–e Gans ~ braten *to roast a goose whole* **b.** ~e Figur, Länge *full length* ‖ der ~e Inhalt, Umfang *the whole* (*of morality*); die ~e Frage *the whole question*; *a definite decision* **3. (vollzählig) a.** *complete, entire, full, whole*; der ~e Betrag *the full amount*; *the total*; das Service ist nicht ~ *the service is not entire*; ~ m *to complete* **b.** *whole*; das ~e Haus etc *the whole house, country*; auf der ~en Linie *all down the line*, ⟨übtr fam⟩ *entirely, wholly, totally*; er reiste durch ~ .. *all over Europe, France, the world*; im ~en Lande *all over the country*; über die ~e Erde ⟨Am⟩ *clear around the globe* **c.** *all*; *all Germany, the whole of G.*; *the whole of Protestant G.* ‖ *all the family, world* ‖ *all society* (od *the whole of society*); *all mankind* **d.** ~e Liebe *entire love*; die ~e Wahrheit *the whole truth* ‖ ~e Arbeit m *to go all lengths* ‖ s–e ~e Kraft *all his energy*; Georgs .. *all George's energy* ‖ v ~em Herzen *with all one's heart, with one's whole heart* ‖ der Junge ist der ~e Vater *or* ~ der V. *the boy is a chip of the old block* **4. (in Zeitangaben)** *all*; den ~en M., T. *all the morning, day* (⟨Am⟩ *all m., d.*); das ~e J. *throughout the year*; die ~e Zeit hindurch *throughout* **5.** [bes **nach unbest. Art**: nie *all*!] e–e ~e Stunde *a full hour, fully an hour*; schon e–e ~e Zeit *quite a while* ‖ e–e ~e Zahl *a whole number*; ⟨math⟩ *an integer*; e–e ~e Funktion *an integral function* ‖ er ist ein ~er Kerl ⟨fam⟩ *he's* not half a one ‖ ein ∼er König, Mann every inch a king, man ‖ e–e ∼e Menge quite a lot ‖ e–e ∼e Note a semibreve; ein ∼er Ton a whole tone ‖ ein ∼er Teil a whole **6. [vor pl]** whole; als ∼e Teile as wholes ‖ whole countries, towns ‖ ∼e 10 Jahre 10 whole years, fully 10 years ‖ 3 ∼e Tage 3 clear days ‖ ∼e Stunden hindurch for hours at a time ‖ er blieb ∼e 95 (⟨iron⟩ 20) Sekunden unter Wasser he stayed under the w. for fully 95 (only 20) seconds | °m–e ∼en Bücher all my books **II. adv 1.** completely, entirely, fully, totally, wholly ‖ ∼ bezahlen to pay in full; ∼ übereinstimmen to agree wholly (with) ‖ ∼ das Gegenteil the clear contrary ‖ ∼ oder teilweise in whole or in part ‖ **voll u ∼, ∼ u gar** altogether, fully, quite, throughout, wholly; for good and all; for keeps; ∼ u gar befangen in head over ears in ..; voll u ∼ erfüllen to fulfil up to the hilt ‖ ∼ u gar nicht by no means, not at all, far from that; ∼ u gar nichts nothing whatever **2. a.** ich bin ∼ **Ohr** I am all ears ‖ er war ∼ Flamme he was all flames and raptures ‖ das ist ∼ mein Fall that's just what I like; I like that ‖ das ist ∼ dein Vater that is your father all over ‖ (in Briefen) ∼ der Ihrige Yours (very) truly od sincerely **b. ∼ im Gegenteil** much the reverse ‖ ∼ im Irrtum quite wrong (od mistaken) ‖ ∼ in der Nähe quite close by ‖ soweit ∼ in Ordnung all right in its way ‖ ∼ v neuem all over again **3. [bei Adj. u Adv.] a.** quite (new, old, unexpected); all (covered); perfectly (clear); ∼ kl tiny ‖ aufgeblüht full-blown; ∼ erwachsen quite grown-up ‖ (in Briefen) ∼ ergebenst Yours faithfully; → allerliebst ‖ er ist ein ∼ Großer he is a big bug od wig | ∼ anders quite different; e–e ∼ andere S quite another th ‖ ∼ besonders, weil (more) particularly because ‖ ∼ gehörig good and proper ‖ ∼ gleich (= einerlei) all the same ‖ ∼ gut very well; rigth enough (the material looks r. e.) ‖ ein ∼ herrlicher Anblick quite a wonderful sight ‖ ∼ leidlich well enough; du hast ∼ recht you are quite right; (als Antwort) ∼ recht quite so, just so, that's right **b. es ist ∼ aus mit** it is all over (od up) with (him) ‖ **bis ∼ nach** Afrika hinein right (⟨Am⟩ clear) into Africa ‖ **∼ wie** Sie wollen just as you like **G·anz- ∼fabrikat** n wholly manufactured article **∼franzband** m shagreen binding **∼holz** n unhewn timber; log **≗jährig** a all-season (⟨mot⟩ oil); lasting etc throughout the year **∼leder** [attr] bound entirely in leather **∼leinen** [attr] bound in cloth **∼metall-** [attr] all-metal (plane, construction) **≗seitig** a full-page [attr]; ∼e Reklame ⟨fam⟩ solus **∼stahl-** all-steel (⟨mot⟩ body) **∼stoff** m ⟨pap⟩ pulp **≗tägig** a round-the-clock [attr]; ∼er Arbeiter full-timer **∼tagskleid** n round-the-clock dress **∼ton** m whole tone **∼zeug** n = –stoff ‖ ∼holländer [m] pulper

G·anze 1. das ∼ **a.** the whole (ein ∼s bilden to make a whole); the whole thing; the sum od total (of the gains); totality; → 2. ‖ ⟨mil⟩ das ∼ halt! cease firing! ‖ als ∼s as a whole; at large; in (the) large; in the aggregate; in its entirety; das Publikum als ∼s the public at large ‖ ⟨fig⟩ er übersieht vor lauter Einzelheiten das gr ∼ he does not see the wood for the trees; er verliert das gr ∼ nicht aus den Augen the wood is not lost in the trees **b. aufs ∼ gehen** to go (all out od) the limit (⟨fam⟩ the whole hog, ⟨bes Am⟩ for broke), to go all lengths (od to extremes); to mean business; ⟨fam⟩ to go it (strong), ⟨sex⟩ to go through, ⟨cards⟩ to go nap | **im ≗en** (up)on the whole; altogether; in the lump; im ≗en gut well enough ‖ wir w im ≗en 5 s that will make 5 of us ‖ im ≗en verkaufen to sell by (⟨Am⟩ at) wholesale ‖ (T) im ≗en braten ⟨bes Am⟩ to barbecue; sich im ∼en auf 20 belaufen to number 20 all told, to total 20 ‖ im ≗en genommen taken as a whole, in the aggregate; taking one th with another ‖ im gr ≗en, im großen u ≗en on the whole, ⟨Am⟩ by and large | sich **zu** e–m ∼n formen, zus–fassen to integrate vi **2.** °der ∼ [ein ∼r] the full pint **G·anzheit** f completeness, entirety, integrity, wholeness ‖ ⟨philos⟩ totality; complex unity; ∼stheorie [f] holism | **≗lich** a entire, integral, whole ‖ total **∼sstudie** f general study **g·änzlich 1.** [a] complete, entire (ignorance); total (loss); absolute, utter (tranquillity); ⟨Am a.⟩ all-out **2.** [adv] completely; entirely (forgotten); fully; totally; absolutely, utterly (different); wholly; = ganz u gar, → ganz II. 1. ‖ er ist mir ∼ fremd he is a complete stranger to me; ∼ die Geduld verlieren to lose all patience

×**gapsen** vi [h] to gasp for breath, → japsen

gar I. a **1.** ⟨cul⟩ [mst pred] well-done; (properly) cooked; nicht ∼ not well-done; underdone; eben ∼ just right; → fertig **2.** ⟨tech⟩ [a. attr] purified, refined (metal); ∼ m to refine ‖ dressed (leather); tanned; ∼ m to dress **II.** adv **1.** ∼ gekocht well-done; → stark **2.** (vollständig) → ganz I. 1. ‖ **3.** [als Intensiv; mst unbetont] **a.** ∼ b·ald, ·oft very soon, often ‖ ∼ s·ehr (I know) full well; ⟨sl⟩ not half (he did not half swear) ‖ ich glaube ∼, du hast .. for all I know you have .. ‖ ∼ m·anche Faktoren so many factors; ∼ manches Jahr many and many a year; ∼ mancher Mensch many a man ‖ ∼ z quite too (delightful); → allzu | [betont] ∼ nicht not at all; by no means; never; ∼ nicht übel or schlecht ⟨sl⟩ not half bad; not so dusty; ∼ nicht so leicht not so easy as all that ‖ ∼ nichts not a thing; nothing whatever; etw ist besser als ∼ nichts half a loaf is better than no bread ‖ ∼ kein Zweifel not the least doubt; ∼ k–r none whatever **b.** auch noch ∼, nun ∼ in addition; to crown all (he ..); furthermore, moreover; ⟨Am⟩ too **c.** oder ∼ to say nothing of; let alone; die menschliche Vernunft oder ∼ Gerechtigkeit human reason let alone justice ‖ wenn nicht ∼ not to say ‖ → sogar **4.** (etw) du warst doch nicht ∼ so dumm .. you were never so stupid (as to admit) ‖ ich dächte ∼! warum nicht ∼! I should not think so!; well I never!, no indeed! **G·ar- ∼koch** m keeper of a cook-shop **∼küche** f cook-shop, slap-bang **∼leder** n tanned (od dressed) leather **∼ofen** m ⟨tech⟩ refining furnace **∼probe** f ⟨tech⟩ refining test

G·är- (→ gären) [in comp] fermenting **∼bottich** m f.-tub, fermenter **∼führung** f ⟨brew⟩ method of fermentation **∼futter** n (en)silage **∼kammer** f f.-room **∼keller** m f.-cellar **∼mittel** n ferment

Gar·age [gaˈrɑːʒə] f [Fr] ∼/∼n garage; Turm≗ autosilo; in die ∼ bringen, stellen to garage; ∼nleiter [m] g. manager **Gar·ant** m ∼en/∼en guarantor (f for) ⟨a. bank⟩; bail, guarantee (for ..) **Garant·ie** f ∼/∼n **1.** (full money-back) guarantee, –ty (f etw for a th); security; Anweisungs≗, Zahlungs≗ payment g.; Anzahlungs≗ advance payment g. ‖ ⟨bank⟩ Bietungs≗ tender g., ⟨Am⟩ bid bond; Erfüllungs≗, Liefer≗ performance g., ⟨Am⟩ p. bond; Mangel≗ warranty; ∼ der Unterbringung (e–r Emission) insuring od underwriting (an issue) ‖ bei Beginn der ∼ ⟨contr⟩ at the commencement of the g. period ‖ ∼ ausstellen to issue a g.; e–e ∼ ersetzen to substitute; ∼ übergeben ⟨com⟩ to furnish, submit a g.; ∼ leisten or übernehmen f etw to guarantee a th; wie lange leisten Sie ∼ f den Wagen? how long is the car guaranteed? **2.** [in comp] guarantee .. **∼begünstigter** m beneficiary under a g. **∼ergänzung** f g. amendment **∼datum** n expiration date **∼fonds** m guarantee-fund **∼macht** f ⟨pol⟩ guarantor Power **∼rahmen** m g. od credit ceiling **∼schein** m ⟨jur⟩ guaranty **∼sicherstellung** f g. collateral **∼stempel** m hall-mark | aus e–r **∼verpflichtung** entlassen to *discharge from a g., to release* od *dismiss under a g.* **~zeit** f *duration of g.* (⟨ins⟩ *of cover*) **garant·ieren** vt [h] *to guarantee, warrant* (*a th; that*); *to be bail* od *to vouch for* (*a th*); ich garantiere, daß es echt ist *I warrant it genuine*; → gewährleisten || (Anleihemission) durch Unterzeichnen ~ *to underwrite* || ⟨tech⟩ *to ensure* **Garant·ierung** f *guaranty* (*of a th*)

G·araus m ~/ jdm den ~ m *or* bereiten *to cook a p's goose*; *to give a p his quietus* (od *the works*); *to knock a p on the head*; *to kill*, ⟨fam⟩ *to finish a p*; ⟨sl⟩ *to polish a p off* || *to ruin a p*; ⟨box⟩ *to knock a p out* | e–r S den ~ m *to knock a th on the head*; *to put an end to a th*; jds Plänen den ~ m *to cook a p's goose*

G·arbe f ~/~n *sheaf* [pl *sheaves*]; Haufen [pl] v ~n *stook* (*in st.*) || (Korn) in ~n binden *to sheaf* || ⟨übtr⟩ *bundle, sheaf* (*of rays*); (Feuer~, Schuß≗) ⟨mil⟩ *sheaf of fire*; → Geschoß≗

G·arbe f ~/~n ⟨bot⟩ (Schaf≗) *milfoil, yarrow*; Moschus≗ *musk milfoil* || Sumpf≗ *sneezewort, wild pellitory*

g·ärben vt [h] ⟨tech⟩ = schweißen **G·ärbstahl** m *shear-steel*

Garc·inie f [-iə] ~/~n ⟨bot⟩ *mangosteen*

G·ardasee m ⟨It⟩ *Lake* (*of*) *Garda*

G·arde f ~/ [koll] ⟨mil engl⟩ die ~ *the Guards, the Household troops* || ⟨a-engl⟩ *the Guards* pl; bei der ~ (*to serve*) *in the G.* | ⟨übtr⟩ *battalion, phalanx* || die Alte ~ *the Old Guard* (*of supporters*) **~grenadiere** pl *Grenadiers Guards* pl **~infanterie** f *Foot Guards* pl **~kavallerie** f *Horse-Guards*; → –reiter **~korps** n *the Guards* pl **~leutnant** m *lieutenant of the Guards* **~offizier** m *officer of the Guards* **~regiment** n *regiment of the Guards*; ~ z Fuß *r. of Foot Guards*; 2. Preuß. ~ z Fuß *Second Prussian Foot Guards* **~reiter** pl die (blauen) Königl. ~ *the Blues* pl

Gard·enie f [-iə] ~/~n *gardenia*

Garder·obe f ~/~n **1.** (Kleiderbestand) *wardrobe* (*to renew one's w.*) || ~ständer m *hat-stand*, ⟨Am⟩ *hall-tree* **2.** (Raum f ~) **a.** ⟨theat⟩ *wardrobe*; (Ankleideraum ⟨a. theat⟩) *dressing room* **b.** Publikum≗ *cloak-room*, ⟨Am⟩ *check-room*; s–n Mantel in der ~ abgeben *to check one's coat* || ~nfrau [f] *c.-r. attendant* (⟨Am⟩ *check-*), ⟨Am⟩ *hat check girl*; ~marke [f], ~zettel [m] *c.-r. ticket* od *check* **Garderobi·er** [-bje:] m **Garderobi·ere** [-bjɛrə] f = Garderobenfrau || ⟨theat⟩ (f Kostüme) *wardrobe mistress*

Gard·ine f ~/~n (f Fenster) *curtain*; (Fenster) mit ~n versehen *to curtain* || hinter schwedischen ~n sitzen *to be in goal* **~npredigt** f ⟨fig⟩ *curtain-lecture*, ⟨sl⟩ *pi-jaw*; jdm e–e ~ halten *to give a p a pi-jaw* **~nstange** f *curtain-rod*

Gard·ist m ~en/~en *guardsman*

G·are f ~/~n ⟨agr⟩ *mellowness* (*of the soil*)

g·ären vi [agr, ⟨fig⟩ gärte/gegoren] [h] **1.** ⟨eig⟩ *to ferment* **2.** ⟨übtr⟩ (of the sea) *to rage, work* || ⟨fig⟩ *to be fermenting*; ~d *in a ferment*; es gärt im Volke *the country is in a ferment* (od *in a state of agitation* od *unrest*) || (of feelings) *to simmer*; *effervesce*

G·argel m ~s/~ *croze, groove* || ~kamm [m] *croze*

G·armisch-Partenk·irchen n ⟨Ger⟩ (Kurort in den Bayrischen Alpen)

G·armond f ⟨typ⟩ *garamond*

G·arn n ~s/~e **1. a.** (Spinn≗) *yarn*; Dicke *or* Qualität des ~s *grist*; Roll≗ *reel-yarn* || Woll≗ *woolen yarn*; → Kamm≗ || Strick≗ *knitting-yarn* || ⟨mar⟩ → Schiemanns≗ **b.** (Näh≗) *thread*; → Zwirn **2.** (Netz aus ~) ⟨fig⟩ ins ~ gehen *to be* (*en*)*snared*; → locken **3.** ⟨fig⟩ (Erzählung) *yarn*; ein ~ spinnen *to spin a yarn* **~haspel** f *reel* **~knäuel** n *clew*; *ball of yarn* (od *thread*) **~spule** f *yarn bobbin* **~strähne** f *hank* od *skein of yarn*

Garn·ele f ~/~n ⟨zoo⟩ *shrimp*; gr ~ *prawn* || ~n fangen *to shrimp*; *prawn* || ~nfischer [m] *shrimper*

g·arnicht(s) → gar II. 3. a.

Garn·ier n ~(e)s/~e ⟨mar⟩ *dunnage* **garn·ieren** vt [h] (Hut) *to trim* || ⟨cul⟩ (Fleisch) *to garnish* (mit *with*); Hammelkeule (Rindfleisch) garniert *leg of mutton* (*boiled beef*) *and trimmings* | (Schiff) *to dunnage* **Garn·ierung** f ~/~en **1.** [abstr] *trimming* (*of a hat*) || ⟨cul⟩ *garnishing* **2.** [konkr] *garniture, trimmings* pl || ⟨cul⟩ *garnish, garnishings* pl, *garniture, trimmings* pl; ⟨Am⟩ *fixings* pl | ⟨mar⟩ (Innenbeplankung) *ceiling* **Garnis·on** f ~/~en *garrison*; *army post* || (Stadt) mit e–r ~ versehen, (Truppen) in e–e ~ legen *to garrison*; in ~ liegen, stehen *to be quartered* od *garrisoned* **~dienst** m *garrison-duty* **~lazarett** n *military hospital* **~prediger** m *chaplain* **~stadt** f *garrison-town* **≗verwendungsfähig** a (abbr g.v.) ⟨Ger⟩ *not fit for active service*

Garnit·ur f ~/~en **1.** *garniture, trimmings* pl **2.** *collection*; *set*; Toiletten≗ *toilet set* **3.** ⟨mil⟩ *articles* [pl] *of military uniform*; *military outfit* || zweite ~ *number two dress*, ⟨Am⟩ *second string* **4.** ⟨mod⟩ *accessories* pl

Gar·onne f ⟨Fr⟩ (Fluß)

Garr·otte f [Span] ~/~n ⟨hist⟩ *garrotte* **garrott·ieren** vt [h] (jdn) *to garrotte*

g·arstig 1. a ⟨übtr mst⟩ *nasty*; → übel **a.** (ekelhaft) *nasty* (*smell, taste*); *foul, loathsome* || (anstößig) *foul* (*talk*); *obscene*; *dirty* (*book*) **b.** *inclement* (*weather*); *rough*; *nasty* (*illness*) **c.** (P) *ugly* || *nasty* (gegen *to*); *grouchy, grumpy*; ~er Mensch *curmudgeon* || *naughty* (*child*) **2.** adv *nastily*; *loathsomely* || *roughly*; ~ umgehen mit, behandeln *to rough-house* (*a p*) | ≗**keit** f *nastiness*; *nasty act*

G·ärtchen n *little garden*, → **G·arten** m ~s/≗ *garden*; → Gemüse-, Obst-, Zier≗ || englischer ~ *landscape g.*, französ. ~ *French g.* || jedes Haus hatte s–n eigenen ~ *each house stood in its own g.* || kl ~ hinter dem (*or* am) Hause *g.-plot* (od *ground, spot*); *back yard* (od *garden*), ⟨Am a.⟩ *dooryard* || öffentlicher ~ *public g.*; → ~anlagen || im ~ arbeiten *to g.*, ⟨Am a.⟩ *to make g.* **≗ähnlich** a *gardenesque* **~ammer** f ⟨orn⟩ *ortolan* **~ampfer** m ⟨bot⟩ *patience-dock* **~anlagen** pl *gardens, grounds* pl **~arbeit** f *gardening* **~architekt** m *landscape gardener*; *horticulturist* **~bank** f *g.-seat* **~bau** m **1.** *gardening*; ~ treiben *to g.* **2.** [in comp] *horticultural*; ~ausstellung *h. show*; ~gesellschaft *h. society*; ~schule *h. school*; ~künstler *horticulturist* **~beet** n *bed* **~blume** *g.-flower* **~erde** f *g.-mould* **~fest** n *g.* (⟨Am⟩ *lawn*)*-party* **~gerät** n *g.-tool* **~gewächse** pl *g.-stuff* (od *produce*) **~haus** n *summer-house*; = Hinterhaus **~kunst** f *g. craft*; *horticulture* **~laube** f *arbour* || ⟨Ger⟩ (Wochenschrift) *the Gartenlaube* **~lokal** n *beer-* (od *tea*)*-g.* **~melde** f ⟨bot⟩ *mountain spinach*; *orache* **~messer** n *pruning-knife* **~säge** f *grafting-saw* **~schere** f *pruning-shears* pl; *sécateurs* pl (Fr) **~schirm** m (*garden*) *parasol* **~schnecke** f *g.-snail*; (nackte) *slug* **~siedlung** f *g. city* **~spritze** f *g.-engine* **~stadt** f *g.-city* **~stuhl** m *g.-chair* **~tür** f *g.-door* **~vorstadt** f *g.-suburb* **~walze** f *g.-roller* **~wesen** n *g.ing*; *horticulture* **~wicke** f ⟨bot⟩ *sweet-pea* **~wirtschaft** f = –lokal **~zaun** m *g.-hedge, -fence* **~zimmer** n *g.-room*

G·ärtlein n *little garden* || °⟨fig sex⟩ *orchard*

G·ärtner m ~s/~ *gardener*; Handels≗ *market gardener*; → Landschafts≗ || eingeborener ~ ⟨AInd⟩ *mali* **~bursche** m *under-gardener* **~lehranstalt** f = Gartenbauschule **~säge** f *pruning-saw* **Gärtner·ei** f ~/~en **1.** [abstr] *gardening, horticulture* **2.** [konkr] (Baumschule) *nursery*; *nursery-garden* || Handels≗ *market-garden*

G·ärtnerin f ~/~nen *female gardener* || (Gärtnersfrau) *gardener's wife* **g·ärtnerisch** a *horticultural*; in ~er Beziehung *horticulturally* **g·ärtnern** vi [h] *to garden*

G·ärung f ~/~en **1.** ⟨eig⟩ (kochende *effervescing*) *fermentation* || ⟨med⟩ *zymosis* L || in ~ bringen *to ferment* || ~ verursachend *fermentative* || durch ~ verursacht *fermentative*, ⟨med⟩ *zymotic* **2.** ⟨fig⟩ *ferment(ation)*; *agitation, disaffection, unrest* || in ~ s *to be in a ferment*; *to be up*; *to work* || in ~ bringen *to ferment*; *to stir up*; (Krisis) in ~ halten *to keep on the boil*; in ~ übergehen *to be fermented* **~serregend** a *fermentative*; ⟨med⟩ *zymotic, zymogenic* **~serreger** m *ferment*; ⟨chem⟩ *enzyme* **~sfähig** a *fermentable* **~smittel** n *ferment* **~sprozeß** m *fermentative process*; *fermentation* **~sstoff** m *ferment*; *zymoma*

G·as [a] n G·ases/G·ase [ɑː] **1.** (Heiz~, Leucht~) *gas* [pl *gases*]; ⟨tech⟩ billiges *or* mageres ~ *producer gas* || durch ~ gefeuert *gas-fired* (*furnace*); → Benzin; Edel~ || Apparat z Reinigen v Gasen *wash-bottle* **2.** Gift~ *gas*; *poison* (od *asphyxiating*) *gas* || → Lach~ **3.** → Faulschlamm~ **4.** ~ **abblasen** ⟨mil⟩ *to release gas* || ~ abgeben *to out* od *desorb* od *emit gas* || das ~ abstellen, ausdrehen *to turn the g. down* (od *off, out*) || das ~ andrehen, –zünden *to turn the g. on* || mit ~ angreifen, durch ~ vergiften *to gas* (*he was gassed*) || mit ~ füllen *to gas* || ~ geben ⟨mot⟩ *to accelerate, speed*; ⟨fam⟩ *to open the throttle*; ⟨Am⟩ *to step on the gas, step on it*; gib ~! ⟨sl⟩ *give her the gun*; *let her rip*! || ~ leiten *to pipe gas* (nach *to*) || (Klosettröhre) gegen Gase verschließen, abdichten *to trap* || in ~ verwandeln *to gasify* || ~ wegnehmen ⟨mot⟩ *to release the accelerator*, ⟨aero oft⟩ *to shut off the engine* || ⟨aero⟩ Anflug **mit** ~ *power approach*; Landung **ohne** ~ *power-off landing* **~abführung** f ⟨tech⟩ *g. outlet* **~abscheider** m *g. trap* **~abwehr** f *anti-g. defence* || ~maßnahme [f] *anti-g. precaution* **~alarm** m *g.-alert* **~analyse** f *gas analysis* **~angriff** m *g.-attack* **~anlage** f *g.-fittings* pl **~anlasser** m *g. starter*; ⟨aero⟩ *combustion-type starter* **~anstalt** f *g.-works* pl **~anzünder** m *g.-lighter* **~arm** m *g.-bracket* **~ausstrahlung** f → Fumarole, Mofette **~automat** m *g. slotmachine* **~behälter** m *gasometer*; *gas-holder* **~beleuchtung** f *g.-lighting* **~bombe** f ⟨mil⟩ *g.-bomb* **~bildung** f (⟨a.⟩ aus ungeförderter Kohle) *gasification* **~blase** *bubble of g.* || (im Guß) *blowhole* **~brand** m ⟨med⟩ *g.-gangrene* **~brenner** m *g.-burner* **~brust** f ⟨med⟩ *pneumothorax* **~dämpfe** pl *g.-fumes* pl **~dicht** a *g.-proof*, ⟨Am⟩ *vaportight* **~diffusionsanlage** f ⟨at⟩ *gaseous diffusion plant* **~durchlader** m *g.-operated gun* **~drucklader** m *blowback-operated weapon* **~einschluß** m *occlusion of g.*; *occluded, trapped g.* **~entl·adungslampe** f ⟨el⟩ *gas discharge lamp* **~entwicklung** f *development of gas*; *gas evolution* **~erzeuger** m (g.) *generator* od *producer* **~explosion** f *g.-explosion* **~feuerung** f *g.-firing* **~flamme** f *g.-jet* **~förmig** a *fluid*, (→ *liquid*); *gaseous* (*state*; *fuel*) **~förmigkeit** f *gaseity* **~gemisch** n *gas-mixture* **~generator** m *g. producer* **~geschoß** n ⟨mil⟩ *g.-shell* **~gewinde** n *pipe* od *gas thread* **~glühlicht** n *incandescent* (*g.-*) *light*; ~lampe [f] *incandescent g.-filled lamp* **~granate** f = –geschoß **~hahn** m *g.-cock* **~hebel** m *g.-lever* **~heizung** f *gas-heating* **~herd** m *gas-range* **~installateur** m *g.-fitter* **~kammer** f *g. chamber* **~kampfstoff** m *poison gas* **~kocher** m *g.-cooker*; *g. ring* **~kohle** f *g.-coal*; echte ~ *cannel* **~koks** m *g.-coke* **~krank** a *gassed* **~kranker** m *g. case, g. casualty* **~krieg** m ⟨mil⟩ *gas-war(fare)* **~lampe** f *g.-lamp* **~lanze** f *g.-poker* **~leitung** f *g.* (*pipe-*)*line*; Haupt~ *gas main*; → –installateur **~licht** n *g.-light*; ~papier [n] *gaslight paper* **~mann** m *g.-man*; der ~! ⟨fam⟩ *the gas*! **~maske** f *gas-mask* (od *helmet*); *respirator* **~messer** m *gas-meter* **~motor** m *gas-engine* **~ofen** m *gas-stove* **~öl** n *gas-oil* **~rohr** n *gas-pipe*; → –leitung || ~zange [f] *g. pliers* **~schicht** f → Photosphäre **~schieber** m ⟨mot⟩ *throttle valve* od *slide* **~schleuse** f (im Bunker) *air-lock* **~schutz** m *g.* od *chemical defence* || [attr] *anti-gas* (*equipment*; *mask*); *gas-proof* (*room*) **~schwaden** m *layer of g.* **~schweißbrenner** m *g. torch* **~sicher** a *gas-proof* **~spieß** m *g.-poker* **~strahl** m *g. jet* **~turbine** f *gas-turbine* **~uhr** f = –messer **~vergiftung** f *gas-poisoning* **~wäscher** m *g. scrubber* **~wechsel** m *gas-exchange* **~werfer** m (Apparat) *gas-projector* **~wolke** f *gas-cloud* **~zähler** m = –messer **~zufuhr** f *gas-supply*

×**Gascht, Gäscht** m = Gischt

Gasc·ogne f [-ɔɲə] ⟨Fr⟩ (†Provinz) *Gascony* **Gasc·ogner** m, **~in** f, **gasc·ognisch** a *Gascon*

Gas·el n ~s/~e, **Gas·ele** f ~/~n ⟨Lit⟩ (orient. Gedicht) *ghazel, ghazal*

g·asig a *gaseous, gassy* **Gasol·in** n *gasolene, -line* **Gasom·eter** m *gasometer*; (Behälter) *gas-holder*

G·äßchen n *lane*; *narrow track* (od *passage*)

G·asse f ~/~n **1.** ⟨dero⟩ (enge, dumpfe Straße *alley*; ⟨Am⟩ *alleyway*; ⟨Scot⟩ *gate*; ⟨Ir⟩ *boreen* → Gosse || Sack~ *blind alley* || °⟨fig⟩ hohle ~ (Kehle) *whistle*, (*red*) *gin-lane, peck-alley* || ⟨mil⟩ *gap* **2.** (P) ⟨Rug ftb⟩ *line-out* || → Spalier **~nbube**, **~njunge** m *mudlark*; *street-arab*; ⟨fam⟩ *guttersnipe* **~nhauer** m ⟨hist Lit⟩ → Volksballade || ⟨dero⟩ *street-ballad*; → Schlager **~nkehrer** m *scavenger*

G·ast m ~es/~e **1.** (geladener ~) **a.** *guest* (bei .. *at a meal*); *visitor* (bei .. *to a p*) || seltener ~ *bird of passage*; (*well*) *quite a stranger*! || (jdn) als ~ **aufnehmen** *to entertain*; jdn z ~e bitten *to invite a p*; bei jdm z ~e s *to be a p's guest*; bei jdm abends z ~ s *to be entertained at dinner by a p*; wollen Sie heute Mittag mein ~ s? *will you dine with me as my guest*? || als ~e bei sich h *to entertain* (*a party*); sie h gerade ~e *they have company* od *visitors*; sie h oft ~e *they see much company*; *they entertain a great deal*; sie h nie ~e *they never entertain* || die ~e empfangen *to act as host, to do the honours* **b.** ⟨theat⟩ *guest*; als ~ auftreten *to appear as guest*; (in der Hauptrolle) *to star* **2.** zahlender ~ *paying guest* || (Hotel–, Wirtshaus~) *guest*; *client, customer*; *patron*; ~e [pl] *custom* || ständiger ~ *habitué* Fr (auf den Rennplätzen *of the turf*); → Fahr~, Kur~, Sommer~; Stamm~ **3.** (= Geselle, P) °ein seltsamer ~ *a queer fellow* **4.** [in comp] **a.** → Gast–, Gäste– **b.** ⟨mar⟩ *man*; Signal~ *signalman*; → Backs~, Boots~, Lot~ **~arbeiter** m *immigrant* od *foreign worker* **~dirigent** m ⟨mus⟩ *guest-conductor* **~frei** a *hospitable* (*house, roof*); ~es Haus *liberal table*; ein ~es Haus führen *to keep open house* **~freiheit** f *hospitality* **~freund** m *generous entertainer* || (*welcome*) *guest* **~freundlich** **1.** a *hospitable* (gegen *to*); *hostessy*; *generous* || = –frei **2.** adv *hospitably*; *generously* **~freundschaft** f *hospitality* (gewähren [dat] *to offer*) (gegen *to*); *generosity* || jds ~ genießen *to share a p's bread and salt* **~geber** m *host*; *entertainer, treater* || als ~ fungieren *to act as host* || ~staat [m] *host country* od *nation* **~geberin** f *hostess* **~geschenk** n (*generous*) *gift* **~gewerbe** n *catering industry* od *trade* **~haus** n, **~hof** m *inn, public-house*; ⟨Am⟩ *saloon* || *hotel* || ~besitzer [m] *innkeeper*; *hotel-keeper* **~hörer** m ⟨Ger univ⟩ *auditor* | im **~land** n wohnhaft *resident alien*; → –staat **~mahl** n *banquet* (bei dem ~ *at the b.*), *feast*; ein ~ abhalten *to have a feast* || ~ des Herodes *the Feast of Herod* **~professor** m ⟨Ger univ⟩ *guest-professor* **~recht** n jdm ~ gewähren *to receive a p as guest* **~rolle** f ⟨theat⟩ in e–r ~ auftreten, e–e ~ geben *to* (*appear as*) *guest*; (of a star) *to star*; → gastieren || ⟨übtr⟩ ~n geben *to make* (od *go on*) *a starring-tour* (durch .. *of*

Germany) **~spiel** n ⟨theat⟩ = –rolle ‖ (of a star) *starring*; ~reise, ~tournee [f] (of a star) (*starring-*)*tour* **~stätte** f *restaurant* **~stube** f *tap-room* (*of an inn*) **~wirt** m *caterer*; *restaurant keeper*; *landlord*; *innkeeper*, *publican*; ⟨Am⟩ *saloon-keeper* **~wirtin** f *landlady* **~wirtschaft** f *inn*; *public-house* **~zimmer** n → Fremden–, Gästezimmer **G·äste-** **~buch** n *visitors' book* **~-zimmer** n (of a hotel) *parlour* **gast·ieren** vi [h] ⟨theat⟩ *to appear as guest*; (of a star) *to star, to tour* **g·astlich** a *hospitable* ‖ [adv] jdn ~ empfangen *to offer hospitality to a p*; → gastfrei | **≗keit** f ~/ *hospitality*

Gastr·äa f ⟨biol⟩ *gastraea*; ~lehre [f] *g.-theory* **g·astrisch** a *gastric* (*fever*) **Gastr·itis** f *gastritis* L **Gastromyz·eten** pl ⟨bot⟩ *gast*(*e*)*romycetous fungi* L pl **Gastron·om** m *gastronome*(*r*), *–mist*; *epicure* ‖ **Gastrop·ode** m ⟨zoo⟩ *gast*(*e*)*ropod* **G·astrula** f ~/ ⟨biol⟩ *gastrula* L

G·atchen n ⟨mar⟩ *eyelet* **Gat(t)** n ⟨mar⟩ (Gasse, Rinne) *gat* ‖ (Loch) *hole*

G·atte m ~n/~n *husband* ‖ ⟨liter⟩ *mate, spouse*; → Gattin; Gemahl **†g·atten** vt [h] ⟨übtr⟩ = paaren, ⟨a.⟩ sich ~

G·atter n ~s/~ *lattice*, *trellis*; *grating*; → Gitter, Staket ‖ hohes ~ ⟨hunt⟩ *rasp* ‖ ⟨weav⟩ *creel* **~säge** f *frame-saw* **~tür** f *latticed gate* **~-werk** n *lattice* (od *trellis*)-*work*

°**G·atterich** m ~s/~e ⟨hum⟩ (Gatte) *hubby*(*kins*)

gatt·ieren vt [h] ⟨tech⟩ *to mix*; *calculate a charge*

G·attin f ~/~nen *wife*; wo ist Ihre ~, Herr N.? *where is Mrs. N.?* ‖ ⟨liter⟩ *mate, spouse*

G·attung f ~/~en **1.** ⟨bot & zoo⟩ *genus* L (*a g. consisting of many species* [Arten]); *race*; → Art, Familie **2. a.** ⟨log⟩ *genus, species* **b.** ⟨Lit⟩ *kind*; *genre* ‖ Dichtungs≗ *kind of poetry*; Romane aller ~en *fiction of all kinds* **c.** ⟨übtr⟩ *kind, sort, type*; *description*, *kidney*, ⟨Am⟩ *stripe*; Männer derselben ~ *men of the same kidney* (⟨Am⟩ *stripe*) **G·attungs-** [in comp] *generic* (*character*) **~ausdruck** m *g. term* **~bastard** m ⟨biol⟩ *bigener* **~begriff** m *g. notion* **~bezeichnung** f *g. term* **~kauf** m *sale by description* **~name** m *g. name* ‖ ⟨gram⟩ *appellative*; *common noun* **~-sachen** f pl *unascertained goods* **~schuld** f *obligation in kind* **~waren** f pl *fungible articles*, *fungibles* **~wort** n ⟨gram⟩ *common noun*

Gau m ~(e)s/~e ⟨Ger hist⟩ *Gau* (der ~ Franken *the G. of Franconia*) ‖ *country*; *province*; *district* ‖ ⟨übtr⟩ *region* (*in all regions*) **~leiter** m ⟨nazi⟩ *Gauleiter*; *regional leader*

G·aube f ~/~n → Gaupe

G·auch m ~(e)s≗e ⟨orn⟩ = Kuckuck; Narr, Tropf **~blume** f ⟨bot⟩ *cuckoo-flower* **~heil** n ⟨bot⟩ *self-heal*, *scarlet pimpernel*

G·aucho [–tʃɔ] m [Span] *gaucho*

G·audium n ~s/dien [L] = Freude; Spaß

gaufr·ieren [go–] vt [h] ⟨tech⟩ (Rand) *to goffer, gauffer* **gaufr·iert** a *goffered* (*edges*); *gaufré* Fr

G·aukel- (→ gaukeln) **~bild** n *illusion*, *phantasm*, *phantom*; ~er [pl] *phantasmagoria* **~possen** pl *juggling tricks* pl **~spiel** n *jugglery*, *legerdemain*, *sleight-of-hand* ‖ ⟨fig⟩ *cunning trick*, *imposture*, *trickery* **~werk** n = –spiel **Gaukel·ei** f ~/~en *jugglery* ⟨a. fig⟩; *juggle* **g·aukelhaft** a *juggling* ‖ *deceptive*, *delusive* **g·aukeln** vi [h] **1.** *to juggle* **2.** = flattern **G·aukler** m ~s/~ **1.** *juggler*; *conjurer* ‖ = Possenreißer ‖ ⟨fig⟩ *cheat*, *impostor*, *trickster*; → Scharlatan **2.** ⟨orn⟩ *African buzzard* **~blume** f ⟨bot⟩ *mimulus* L | **≗isch** a = gaukelhaft

G·aul m ~s/≗e alter ~ *hack*, *jade*, *rip*, *screw*; ⟨Am⟩ *plug* | ⟨übtr⟩ = Pferd ‖ e–m geschenkten ~ sieht man nicht ins Maul *beggars must not be choosers* ‖ °mach doch nicht die ≗e scheu! *you don't say so!*, *tell that to the horse-marines!*; ⟨mil⟩ *don't bully the troops!* ‖ der ~ zieht nicht ⟨fig⟩ *that cock won't fight*

G·aumen m ~s/~ **1.** ⟨anat⟩ *palate*; harter ~ *hard p.*; weicher ~ *soft p.*; *velum* L **2.** ⟨fig⟩ ein feiner ~ (*to have*) *a delicate palate*; das ist etw f m–n ~ *I like that*; → kitzeln **3.** [in comp] *palatal*, *palatine*; *palato–* **~kitzel** m *tickle of the palate* **~knochen** pl *palatine bones* pl **~laut** m *palatal* **~segel** n ⟨anat⟩ *velum* L; *soft palate* **~spalte** f ⟨path⟩ *cleft-palate*

G·auner m ~s/~ *knave*, *rascal*, *rogue* ‖ *cheat*, *wangler*; *rook*; ⟨fam⟩ *shark*, *sharp*(*er*), *trickster* ‖ ⟨Am pol⟩ *political man*, *politician* **~bande** f *gang of sharpers* **~herberge** f *thieves' den* **~kneipe** f *flash-house* **~sprache** f *patter*, *thieves' cant*, *flash language* **~streich** m *knavish trick* (*to play a p a k. t.*) **~trick** m *sharper's trick*, *trickster's dodge* **Gauner·ei** f ~/~en *knavery*; *knavish act* (od *conduct*); *sharp practice*; *wangling* = Gaunerstreich ‖ *cheat*, *swindle*; *trickery* **g·aunerhaft** a *knavish*, *roguish*; *trickish* **g·aunern** vi [h] *to cheat*, *rook*, *shark*, *sharp*

G·aupe f ~/~n ⟨arch⟩ (*rectangular*) *dormer-window*

G·autsche f ~/~n [südd] (Schaukel) *swing* | **≗n** vi *to swing*

g·autschen vt [h] ⟨pap⟩ *to couch* **G·autscher** m *coucher*

Gaza-Streifen m *Gaza Strip*

G·aze [ˈgɑːzə] f ~/~n **1.** *gauze*; Draht≗ *wire gauze*; feine ~ *gossamer* **2.** [in comp] *gauze* (*net*) **≗artig** a *gauzy* **~streifen** m ⟨surg⟩ *tampon*

Gaz·elle f ~/~n ⟨zoo⟩ *gazelle* ‖ ~nfluß [m] *Gazelle River*, *Bahr el-Glazal*

Gd·ingen n (poln. Hafen) *Gdynia*

Ge-, ge- pref [untrennbar u unbetont] [⟨engl⟩ geschwunden, doch poet & † erhalten als *a–*; vgl *enough*] **A.** [beim Nomen] **1.** [gemeinschaftsbildend] **a.** Gefährte, Gesell ‖ Gebrüder **b.** Gesang, Geschichte, Gesicht **2.** [kollektivbildend] **a.** (S) [⟨engl⟩ mst durch pl des Grundworts] Gebirge *mountains* pl; Gefieder *feathers* pl **b.** Vorgänge [⟨engl⟩ mst durch Verbalsubst. auf *–ing*] Geschnatter *cackling*; Getrampel *trampling* **B.** [beim Verbum] **1.** [imperfektive (mst intr) Verben perfektiv (oft trans) machend:] frieren – gefrieren; stehen – gestehen **2.** [z Bildg des pp heimischer Verben] **a.** [in einfachen Verben:] bieten – geboten; führen – geführt (aber: logieren – logiert) **b.** [in zus-gesetzten Verben mit einfachem u betontem Präfix:] ·ablaufen – ·abgelaufen; ·ankommen – ·angekommen; ·aufsuchen – ·aufgesucht; d·urchsuchen – d·urchgesucht (**aber:** ·anerkennen – ·anerkannt; ·auferlegen – ·auferlegt; ·einkassieren – ·einkassiert; durchs·uchen – durchs·ucht; untergr·aben – untergr·aben)

Ge- **~·ächtete** [der ~, ein ~r] ~n/~n *outlaw* **~ächze** n ~s/ *groaning*, *moaning* **~·äder** n ~s/ *veins* pl; *streaked appearance*; *veined structure*; *graining*, *marbling*, *veining* **≗·ädert** a *streaky*; *veined* (mit *with*); *veiny* **~·äfter** n ⟨zoo⟩ *dew-claws* pl **≗ge·artet** a (→ arten) **1.** [pred] der Mensch ist so ~, daß er tut .. *it is in the nature of man to do*; = beschaffen [a] **2.** [in comp] .. *natured*; gut~ *good-natured*; *well-bred*, *well-behaved* (*child*) **~·äse** n **1.** *mouth* (*of deer*) **2.** = **~·äß** n *feed*(*ing*), *food* (*of deer*) **~·äst** n *branches* pl; *ramification* **~b·äck** n (feines ~) *pastry*; leichtes ~ *puff*; lockeres ~ *sponge-cake*; → Biskuit, Keks ‖ feines Eier≗ *brioche* Fr ‖ ⟨Am⟩ weiches, nicht süßes, heiß (mit Butter) serviertes ~ *biscuit* ‖ → Süßwaren **~b·ackenes** n *anything baked* **~b·alge** n = Balgerei **~b·älk** n ⟨arch⟩ *beams* pl; *wood-work*; *framework* ‖ ⟨Gr arch⟩ *entablature* ‖ es kracht im ~ ⟨fig⟩ *sth is cracking at the seams* **≗b·ar** 1. & 3. sg pret v gebären **~-b·ärde** f ~/~n *gesture* ‖ lebhafte ~ *gesticulation*; lebhafte ~n m *to gesticulate* ‖ leere ~

empty od *futile gesture* || (etw) durch ~n ausdrücken *to gesticulate*; mit verächtlicher ~ abtun *to pooh-pooh* || nicht durch die leiseste ~ *by no hinted gesture* || e–e verzweifelte ~ m *to throw up one's hands* ≃**b·ärden** vrefl [h] sich ~ *to behave* || sich lebhaft ~ *to gesticulate* || °sich wie wild (*or* wie ein Verrückter) ~ *to act like a madman, to be as mad as a hatter*; *to be furious*; sich ~ wie .. *to assume an air of* .. **~b·ärden-** [in comp] *gesticulative, -tory* | ~spiel [n] *dumb-show, gestures* pl, *pantomime*; → Pantomime || lebhaftes ~ *gesticulation(s* pl) | ~sprache [f] *gesture-language* (od *speech*); *language of gestures* (od *signs*); → -spiel ≃**b·aren 1.** vrefl: sich ~ *to conduct* (od *deport*) *o.s.*; = sich benehmen **2.** ≃ n *conduct, demeanour*; *manner* ≃**b·ären 1.** vt [gebar/geboren] [h] (Kind) *to bear*; *to give birth to* (*she had given b. to triplets*); *to be delivered of* (*a child*); sie gebar ihm 3 Söhne *she bore him 3 sons*; → fehl~, hervorbringen, zeugen || warum sind wir geboren? *why are we born*? || er ist im Jahre 1833 geboren *he was born in 1833* || → geboren **2.** ≃ n *child-bearing*; *parturition* ≃**b·ärend** a *parturient* ≃**b·ärfähig** a *capable of child-bearing* **~bärfähigkeit** f: Periode der ~ *reproductive* od *childbearing period* **~bärmutter** f ⟨anat⟩ **1.** *uterus* L || *matrix* L, *womb* **2.** [in comp] *uterine* (*diseases*); ~senkung [f] *uterine descent* **~b·arung** f ⟨com⟩ *behaviour, conduct*; *ways* pl || ⟨com⟩ *management* °≃**b·auchpinselt** a ⟨m. m. fam⟩ *tickled to death* **~b·äude** n ~s/~ **1.** *building*, (gr ~) *edifice*; → Haus **2.** ⟨übtr⟩ *fabric, structure* (*of the human body*) || ⟨fig⟩ *edifice* (*of his thoughts*); *frame* (*of a system*); → Lehr≃; Gefüge | ~entschuldungssteuer [f] → Mietzinssteuer | ~komplex [m] *group of buildings*; ~steuer [f] *tax on buildings*; *inhabited house duty* ≃**b·aut** a **1.** *built*; ⟨fig⟩ °er ist nun mal so ~ *he is built that way* **2.** [in comp] *built, timbered*; *structured*; gut ~ ⟨a. fig⟩ *well-built* (od *timbered*); (P) *well-made*; ein stark ~er Mann *a man of a strong frame* °**~b·ein** n (= Körper) *body*; der Schreck fuhr ihm ins ~ *the terror shook his whole frame* || jegliches ~ *all and sundry* **~b·eine** pl; jds ~ *a p's bones* pl (*his bones were laid in* ..), *remains* pl **~b·elfer** n *yapping, yelping* || ⟨mst übtr⟩ (P) *bark*; *brawl* **~b·ell** n *bark(ing)*; *baying*

g·eben vt/i [gab/ge~] [h] **I.** vt **A.** [mit **2 Objekten**:] jdm etw ~ *to give a p a th* od *a th to a p* (*it has been given you*) **1. a.** (schenken) *to give* (*he gave him 3 marks*); ihm wurden 3 Mark gegeben *he was given three marks*; → ge~ || jdm etw ungern ~ *to begrudge a p a th* || → schenken, verleihen **b.** (über~) jdm s–e Tochter z Frau ~ → Frau C. || (reichen) *to give, offer*; jdm die Hand ~ *to give a p one's hand*; *to shake hands with a p* || e–m Pferd die Sporen ~ *to put* (od *set*) *spurs to a horse* || → Arm, Brust, Feuer, Finger, Tritt **c.** ⟨übtr⟩ [mit abstr. Sachobjekt] (bieten, übermitteln etc) jdm **Anlaß** ~ *to give a p occasion* (*to do*); was gab dir A. abzulehnen? *what made you refuse? what were your reasons for refusing*? = jdn veranlassen || jdm Aufklärung ~ = jdn aufklären || → Abschied, Auftrag, Ausschlag, Befehl, Beispiel, Bescheid, Frist, Gelegenheit, Genugtuung, Kredit, Laufpaß, Nachricht, Name, Rat, Rechenschaft, Stimme, Unterricht, Verweis, sowie die Verben beauftragen, befehlen etc | ich gebe dir **recht** *I admit you are right*; das gibt dir ein Recht .. *that gives you a right* (*to do*); das gibt dir kein Recht (..) *that is no warrant for you* (*to believe* ..); das Gericht gab ihm unrecht *the court proved him false*; → Schuld **d.** °**es jdm** ~ ⟨fam⟩ *to give it to a p*; ich habe es ihm tüchtig ge~ *I gave it him hot* od *strong, I gave him a piece of my mind*; °gib's ihm! *let him have it*! | gib ihm *eins*! ⟨fam⟩ *jab him one*!; jdm eins über den Kopf ~ ⟨fam⟩ *to conk a p over the head* **2.** sich [dat] ein vornehmes Ansehen ~ → Ansehen || → Blöße, Ehre, Mühe || sich Rechenschaft ~ über *to give o.s. an account of* **3.** jdm z essen, z verstehen ~ *to give a p to eat, to understand*; mir wurde z verstehen ge~ *I was given to understand*; → denken | (Kost u Logis) *they find him in food and lodging* **B.** [mit nur **einem Objekt**] **1.** (etw) **a.** *to give* (f *for*); → bezahlen || sein Leben ~ *to give one's life* || (Geld) auf Zinsen ~ *to put out* (od *lend*) *at interest* || Karten ~ *to deal cards* **b.** *to give, to yield*; Milch ~ (of cows) *to give milk*; schlechtes Licht ~ *to give a bad light* | ich gäbe (et)was drum, wenn ich wüßte, was Sie jetzt denken ⟨fam⟩ *a penny for your thoughts* **2.** mit Ergänzung **a.** (jdn) in die Lehre ~ *to apprentice* (bei *to*) || (jdn) in Kost, Pension ~ *to board out* (bei *with*); (Kind) in Pflege ~ *to put out to nurse* **b.** (etw) auf die Post ~ *to post* || in Druck ~ → Druck II.; → Verwahrung **3.** (veranstalten) (Ball, Essen, Gesellschaft etc) ~ *to give* || ⟨mus & theat⟩ (Konzert, Stück) ~ *to give*; *perform*; ge~ w *to be on* (*what is on tonight*?); *to do* (*we hear it every time it's done*; *to run*; das Stück wurde 40 Abende hinter–e–a ge~ *the play had a run of 40 nights* || etw z besten ~ → Beste 2. b. **4. a.** viel ~ **auf** *to think much of, to set great* od *much store by* (*a th*); ich geb nicht viel darauf *I don't go much on it*; wenig (nichts) ~ auf *to think little* (*nothing*) *of* (*a th*); → beachten || viel auf sich ~ *to be very particular about one's person* **b. (etw) v sich** ~ (Flüssiges) *to ejaculate, to throw up*; er gab das Essen wieder v sich *he vomited* (⟨fam⟩ *shot*) *his dinner* || (Laut etc) *to emit*; *to give* od *let out*; *to make*; (Rede) *to deliver*; (Worte) *to express, utter*; (Flüche etc) *to pour forth* **5.** [mit abstr. Objekt] **a.** Feuer ~ ⟨mil⟩ *to fire*; → Gas, Laut **b.** Anlaß ~ z *to give rise to*; *to cause*; → Achtung, Antwort, Fersengeld, Obacht || das Wort gibt k–n Sinn *the word conveys no sense*; → Versprechen, Wort | **[abs]** ⟨wir, telg⟩ *to key* **6.** etw verloren ~ *to give up as lost*; → frei~ **7.** Gott geb es, daß es so ist! *God grant it may be so*! **C. sich** ~ *to behave*; *to show o.s.* || sich natürlich ~ *to be o.s.* || sich gefangen ~ *to surrender*; *to yield o.s.*; sich geschlagen ~ ⟨parl, etc⟩ *to yield the point*; → erkennen I. B. b, zufrieden || sich offen (etc) ~ *to be open* (*etc*) *in manner* || gib dich drein *put up with it*; → sich fügen || sich als Schöngeist ~ *to play the high-brow* **II.** vimp (erstarrt; vgl I. B. 5. a.) **A. 1. es wird Regen, Schnee** ~ *it will rain, snow*; *there will be* (od *we shall have*) *rain, snow*; → Gewitter || °es wird Skandal ~ *there'll be a row* (od *trouble*) **2. es gab viel z tun** *there was much work to do* (od *on hand*) || °gleich gibt's was! *you'll get it hot in a minute*! || °nun, **was** gibt's? *yes, what is it*?, *what's the matter*?, ⟨fam⟩ *what's* (*doing* od) *the row*?, ⟨Am sl⟩ *what's cooking*?, *what's to pay*? || °was gibt's Neues? *what's the news*?, ⟨fam⟩ *anything doing*? || (reden kann er), °da gibt's nichts (..) *and no mistake* || was gibt's dazu? *what goes with it*? **3. (werden) das** (dieser Stoff) gibt (e–n Rock) *this* (*material*) *will be used for* ..; .. *will make* (*a skirt*) || *this* (*building*) *is* (*going* od *intended*) *to be* od *will be a shop* °**das wird sich schon** ~ *that will soon be over* (od *better*); *that will* (*turn* od *come out* od) *end all right* || °daß sich das gibt! *hold your noise*! *have done*! **B. es gibt e–n Gott** *there is a God* || es gibt Leute, die .. *there are people who* ..; der beste Spieler, den es gibt *the best player alive* (od *living*) || es gibt kein Rotwild in .. *no deer are found in* .. || es gibt k–e gr Leidenschaft mehr *grand passion is a th of the past* || .. gibt es auf Marken *cereals are on points* || es gibt nur das eine *there is nothing for it but one th* || das gibt es nicht mehr *that has ceased to exist* || °sowas gibt es (*or* soll es ~) *there are such things, indeed* **III.** vi *to give*; er gibt mit vollen Händen *he gives generously* od *liberally* ‖ ⟨ten⟩ *to serve*; ⟨cards⟩ *to deal*: du mußt ~ *it's your deal*; wer gibt? *whose deal* bzw *serve is it*? ‖ das gibt z denken *that makes one think* **G·eben** n *giving*; Laune zum ~ *donative mood* ‖ ~ u Nehmen *give and take, giving and taking* **G·eber(in** f) m *giver*; *donor* **G·ebernatur** f *generous nature* od *spirit*

G·ebe- ⟨wir, telg⟩ **~tempo** n *rate of sending* **~übung** f *keying practice*

geb·essert a *stone-strewn* (*path*); → bessern

Geb·et n ~s/~e *prayer* (beim ~ *at p.*); das ~ des Herrn *the Lord's Prayer*; Morgen≃ *morning prayer*, → Frühmette; Abend≃ *evening prayer*; → Tisch≃ ‖ ein ~ emporsenden *to put a prayer* (z Gott *to God*); ein ~ erhören *to answer a prayer*; ein ~ verrichten *to offer a prayer*; ⟨ec⟩ sein ~ verrichten *to say one's prayers*; sein ~ fand Gehör *his prayer found a hearing* ‖ ⟨fig⟩ (jdn) ins ~ nehmen *to catechize*; *to haul .. over the coals*; *to give .. a talking-to*; → Gewissen **~buch** n *prayer-book*; → Brevier, Liturgie **~formel** f *form of prayer* **~glocke** f *prayer-bell* **~mantel** m (jüd.) *prayer-scarf* (od *shawl*) **~mühle** f (buddhist.) *prayer-wheel* **~riemen** m (jüd.) *prayer-thong*; *phylactery* **~teppich** m *prayer-carpet*

geb·eten pp v bitten **Geb·ettel** n ~s/ = Bettelei

ge- ~b·eugt a *stooping*, ⟨Am⟩ *stooped* (*man*) ‖ ~ gehen *to walk with a stoop*; *to slouch*; ~ liegend *recumbent* (*figure*); → gebückt ‖ ⟨fig⟩ schwer ~ *prostrate* (vor *with*) **≃b·ier** imp, **≃b·iert** 3. sg prs v gebären

Geb·iet n ~(e)s/~e **1. a.** ⟨pol⟩ (Hoheits≃, Staats≃) *territory* (auf deutschem ~ *in German t.*) ‖ das Memel≃ *the t. of Memel* ‖ domain ‖ ~ der Gerichtsbarkeit *jurisdiction* **b.** *area*; *district*; *zone* ‖ *ground* → Grenz≃, Nachbar≃; Kriegs≃, Operations≃ ‖ ~ e–r Armee *army area*; ~ des Aufmarsches ⟨tact, etc⟩ *assembly* od *concentration area* ‖ ⟨min⟩ *province* ‖ bebautes ~ *built-up area* **2.** ⟨anat⟩ (Organ≃) *tract* **3.** ⟨übtr⟩ **a.** *area* (*of thought*); *department* (*of learning*); *domain* (*of philosophy*); *field* (*of history, research*); *province*, *sphere*; das ~ der Mineralien *the mineral scene*; Wissens≃ *field of knowledge*; Wissenschafts≃ *domain of science* ‖ *range* (*of interests*); *scope* (*of an inquiry*) ‖ jds ~ *a p's line* od *province*, *sphere*; Spezial≃ *special subject*; *speciality* ‖ → Bereich, Sphäre **b.** neueste Ergebnisse auf dem ~e der Biologie *latest results in biology*; Fachmann auf dem ~e der Philologie *authority on philology*; → beschlagen [a] ‖ auf internationalem ~e *in the international field* ‖ auf dem ~ der Chemie ⟨a.⟩ *in terms of chemistry*; das Buch behandelt ein altes ~ *the book covers old ground* ‖ dies fällt in das ~ der Philosophie *this falls within the province of philosophy* ‖ dies fällt nicht in mein ~ *this is not in my line* (od *is out of my line*), .. *is not within my province* **~shoheit** f *territorial sovereignty* **~skarte** f ⟨rail⟩ *roundabout ticket* **~skörperschaft** f ⟨pol⟩ *political sub-division* **~(s)streifen** m *zone*; schmaler ~ ⟨Am⟩ *panhandle* **~steil** m *sub-area*

geb·ieten vt/i [gebot/geboten] [h] **A.** vt **1.** (P) Ruhe ~ *to impose silence* ‖ jdm etw ~ *to dictate a th to* (od *impose a th on*) *a p*; jdm ~ z tun *to command* od *order a p to do* **2.** (S) (Achtung, Ehrfurcht) *to command* (*his attitude commands respect*) ‖ *to require* (→ fordern A. 2.); das gebietet die nationale Ehre *that is a precept of national honour*; die Klugheit g., vorsichtig z s *let us obey the dictates of prudence*; → geboten **B.** vi ~ **über** *to rule* od *sway over*; *to hold sway over* (ganz Spanien *all Spain*) ‖ ⟨übtr⟩ *to command* (*a rich voice*); *to have at one's disposal*; *to sway* **geb·ietend** a (achtung~) *commanding* **Geb·ieter** m ~s/~ *lord*; *governor*; *master* (*of the house*); *ruler* (über *of, over*) ‖ mein Herr u ~ *my lord and master* **Geb·ieterin** f *mistress* **geb·ieterisch 1.** [a] *authoritative, imperative, commanding, peremptory* (*tone*); mit ~er Stimme *peremptorily* ‖ *dictatorial, imperious* (*ways of a p*), → herrisch, anmaßend **2.** [adv] *imperatively, peremptorily* ‖ ~ auftreten *to have domineering ways*; *to act imperiously* ‖ die Umstände fordern es ~ *circumstances make it imperative* (od *urge it upon us*)

Ge- ~b·ilde n ~s/~ (Geformtes) = Bildung II. 1.; → a. Gefüge **≃b·ildet 1.** a *educated*; (kultiviert) *civilized* ‖ gesellschaftlich ~ *well-bred* ‖ ein ~er Mensch *a gentleman*; *a cultivated man, a person of refinement* | akademisch ~ *university-bred* ‖ wissenschaftlich ~ s *to have had a scientific training* | ~er [compr] *more widely educated* **2.** ≃e [der ~, ein ~r] *the educated man*; die ~n [pl] *the e. classes* pl ‖ ein akademisch ~r *a university man* **~b·immel** n ~s/ *tinkling*; *succession of tinkles* **~b·inde** n ~s/~ **1.** *bundle* ‖ (als Maß) (f Garn) *cut, lea*; (f Baumwolle, Seide etc) *skein* ‖ ~ Heu, Stroh *truss of hay, straw* **2.** (gr Faß) *barrel, cask* **~b·irge** n ~s/~ *mountains* pl; *mountain-range* ‖ *rock formation* ‖ Falten≃ *fold*(*ed*) *mountains*; Block≃ *block mountains*; → Hochland ‖ ins ~ gehen *to go into the m.* **~b·irgig** a *mountainous, mountainy*; *hilly* **~b·irgler** m *mountain dweller*

Geb·irgs- [in comp] mst *mountain-* ..; *mountainous*; ⟨scient⟩ *oro–* **~arten** pl = Gesteine **~artillerie** f *mountain-artillery* **~bewegung** f *orogenic m.* **~bewohner** m = Gebirgler **~bahn** f *mountain railway* **~bildung** f ⟨geol⟩ *mountain-folding*; *orogenesis* L (*–geny*) **~gegend** f *mountainous* (od *hilly*) *country* (od *region*) **~geschütz** n *mountain-gun* **~jäger** m pl ⟨mil⟩ *mountain-infantry* **~joch** n = Einsatt(e)lung **~kamm** m *mountain-ridge* **~kette** f *mountain chain* (od *range*) **~krieg** m *mountaineering warfare* **~kunde** f *orography, orology* **~lage** f waldige ~ *wooded hill-site* **~landschaft** f *mountain-side* **~paß** m *mountain-pass*; ⟨AInd⟩ *gha*(*u*)*t* **~rücken** m *mountain-ridge* **~schlucht** f *canyon*; *gorge* **~strom** m *torrent* **~system** n *mountain system* **~truppen** pl *mountain-troops* pl **~verein** m *mountaineering* (od *climbing*) *club* **~volk** n *mountain-tribe* **~zug** m = –kette

Ge- ~b·iß n –b·isses/–b·isse **1.** (*set of*) *teeth*; ein ~ *a set of t.* ‖ (künstliches) *set of false* (od *artificial*) *teeth*; ⟨dent⟩ *denture* **2.** (am Pferdezaum) *bit*; e–m Pferde das ~ anlegen *to bit a horse* **~bl·äse** n ~s/~ *blower*; *blowing-apparatus*; → Blasebalg ‖ (Flügelrad≃) *fan*(*-blower*); Kreiselrad≃ *turbo-blower*; → Ventilator ‖ ⟨met⟩ *blast* ‖ ⟨mill⟩ *fans* pl ‖ ⟨mot⟩ *supercharger*; Kolben≃ *piston-supercharger* | ~kies [m] *blast grit*; ~maschine [f] *blowing-engine* | ~motor [m] *supercharger engine*; ~ofen [m] *blast-furnace* **~bl·ök(e)** n ~s/ (of sheep) *bleating* ‖ ⟨übtr⟩ (P) *bellowing* **≃bl·ümt** a *figured* (*shawl*), *flowered, flowery*; ⟨com⟩ *sprigged* (*pattern*) **~bl·üt** n ~(e)s/ *blood*; es liegt im ~ = .. im Blut ‖ (ein Mann) aus adligem ~ (..) *of noble birth* (od *descent*); aus fürstlichem ~ *of princely birth*; ein Prinz aus königl. ~ .. *of the blood* **~b·ogen** a [pp v biegen] *bent, curved* (→ Nase) ‖ auswärts ~ *splay* (*foot*) ‖ → gewölbt **≃b·oren** a [pp v gebären] **a.** *born* (in *into* [*a time*]; v *of* [*respectable parents*]); ~ v e–r Zigeunerin *born of a gipsy* ‖ blind ~ *born blind*; (un)ehelich ~ *born in* (*out of*) *wedlock*; → tot~ ‖ als Deutscher ~ (*to be*) *born a German* ‖ ein ~er Künstler *an artist in his every fibre* ‖ ein ~er D. *a German by birth* ‖ ~er Berliner s *to be Berlin born* ‖ ein ~er Australier *a native of Australia*; ein in Italien ~er Maler *an Italian-born painter* **b.** z etw ~ s *to be born to a th*; *to be born to be a th* ‖ ~ s z tun *to be born to do* ‖ er war als Bürger e–r neuen Welt ~ *he was born to be citizen of a new world* ‖

zum Dichter ~ s *to be born a poet*; ein ~er D. s *to be a born poet* || er war zum Juristen ~ *he was born to be a lawyer* || sie sind nun mal z Verbrecher ~ *they can't help being criminals* **c.** Frau N., ~e X. *Mrs. N., née X.* || was f eine ≃e ist sie? *what was her maiden-name?* | ≃e [pl] ⟨demog⟩ *births*; ≃enhäufigkeit [f] *natility*; gesamte ~ *total fertility*; ≃enüberschuß [m] *excess of births over deaths*; ≃enziffer [f] (allg) *total birth rate* **≃b·orgen** a [pp v bergen] *salved* (*ship*) || *sheltered* | ⟨übtr⟩ ~ s *to be safe* od *secure* (vor *from*); *to be in safety* | ≃heit [f], ≃sein [n] ⟨übtr⟩ *safety*; *security* **≃b·orsten** a [pp v bersten] *shaky, shaken* **~b·ot** n ~(e)s/~e **1.** = Angebot **2.** *command*; ⟨mst rel⟩ *commandment*; *precept*; ⟨bib⟩ die Zehn ~e [pl] *the Ten Commandments* pl; ⟨hum⟩ das 11. ~ *the eleventh c.* **3.** (S) ein ~ der Natur, Vernunft *the dictates* [pl] *of nature, reason* || *a precept* (*of honour*); das ~ der Stunde fordert es *the need of the hour requires it* || ⟨prov⟩ → Not || (Schnelligkeit) ist oberstes ~ .. *is the first essential* **4. zu ~e** stehen ⟨com⟩ (of goods) *to be available* | es steht ihm alles **zu ~e** *he is possessing all the attributes, he has everything one could hope for* **≃b·oten** a [pp v (ge)bieten] ⟨ec R.C.⟩ ~er Feiertag *festival to be observed* || [pred] *required*; *indicated*; er hält es für dringend ~, daß wir abreisen *he thinks it most necessary for us to leave*; Rücksicht scheint ~ *consideration seems to be required* **≃br·acht** pp v bringen **≃br·annt** a *baked* (*clay*) || *roast* (*coffee*); ~er Gips *plaster of Paris* | ~markt [a] *marked* (*p*) **~br·äu** n *brew*(*ing*) || ⟨übtr oft dero⟩ *concoction*; *mixture* **≃br·aten** a *roast* (*meat*); richtig ~ *done to a turn* || ≃es [n] *anything roast* **~br·auch** m ~(e)s/≃e **1.** *employment* (*of knives*), *use* (*of arms*; *one's legs*; *a word*) || ~ f *application to* **2.** = Brauch **3.** Wendungen **a. ~ m v etw** *to make use of*; *to resort to*; *to avail o.s. of a th*, ⟨Am⟩ *to avail of a th*; erhöhten ~ m v *to make increased use of*, bestmöglichen ~ m v *to turn .. to full account*; = gebrauchen || schlechten ~ m v *to make a bad use of* (*a th*) || m Sie k–n ~ v .. *don't speak about* (*what I said*) **b. außer ~** *out of use*; *disused*; außer ~ k. *to fall* (od *go, pass*) *out of use*; *to fall into desuetude* od *disuse*; *to be disused* od *discontinued* || außer ~ setzen *to supersede* | **durch ~** *from* od *with use*; durch vielen ~ *by much use* (od *long wear*) | **in ~ k** *to come into play*; **in ~** s *to be in use*; (of customs) *to be in vogue, to obtain*; die Sitte ist nicht mehr in ~ *the custom no longer obtains* || ich habe ihn (sc den Füller) schon Jahre in ~ *I have used it for years, I have had it in use for y.* | **vor** dem ~ z schütteln (of medicine) *to be shaken before taken* | **zum ~** *for use*; z eigenen ~ *for private use* **≃br·auchen** vt [h] **1. a.** (etw, jdn) *to use* (*may I u. your pencil?*); *to make use of*; ~ f *to employ for*; ~ bei *or* in bezug auf, zu *to apply to* (*this term is not applied to ..*) || (Arznei) *to take* || die Beine, s–n Verstand ~ *to use one's legs, one's brains*; Gewalt ~ *to employ force* || nicht mehr gebraucht w *to be disused*; einrosten dadurch, daß etw nicht mehr –braucht wird *to become rusty from disuse* **b.** äußerlich z ~ *for outward application* || ich könnte e–n Mantel ~ *I could do with a coat* || etw (jdn) nicht ~ können *to have no use for a th* (*a p*) || es ist nicht z ~ *it is* (*of*) *no use*; es ist z nichts z ~ *it is no use for anything* || er ist z nichts z ~ *he is no good, he is good for nothing*; er ist z allem z ~ *he can turn his hand to anything* || (S) **sich ~ l z** *to lend itself to* (*a th*); es läßt sich z vielem ~ *it serves* (od *lends itself to*) *many purposes* **2.** *to need, want*; [dafür besser: brauchen, nötig h] **~br·aucher** m *consumer, user* **≃br·äuchlich** a *current* (*word, spelling*); *common*; *customary* (*institution*); *usual*; die ~sten Schlüssel *the most widely used key* [pred] (= in Gebrauch) ~ s *to be in use*; nicht mehr ~ *no longer in use*; → üblich; un~ | ≃keit [f] *currency*; *customariness, usualness* **Ge-br·auchs- ~anmaßung** f ⟨jur⟩ *illicit use of a foreign commodity* **~anweisung** f *directions for use*; ⟨fig⟩ *label* | ~(sheft n) *instruction booklet* od *leaflet* **~artikel** = –gegenstand **≃fähig** a *serviceable, usable*; [pred] **≃fertig** a *ready for use*; [attr] *ready made* **~fahrzeug** n ⟨mot⟩ *utility car* **~gegenstand** m *commodity* **~geschirr** n *utility crockery* **~graphik** f *applied graphics* pl; *advertising art* | ~er[in f] [m] *advertising artist, commercial designer* **~güter** n pl (Inventar) *accountable stores*; *durable goods* **~hook** m ⟨rehab⟩ *utility hook* **~muster** n *functional design*; eingetragenes ~ *registered design* || ~eintragung [f] *d. registration*; ~schutz [m] *registration of designs* od *of trademarks* **~temperatur** f (v Waschmitteln) *working t.* **≃unfähig** a *unserviceable* **~wert** m *value in use*; *use-value* || ~bestimmung [f] (v Waschmitteln) *household performance test* **~zweck** m *practical purpose*

Ge- ≃br·aucht a *second-hand* (*articles*); *old, worn* (*clothes*); *used* || viel ~ *much used* | ≃wagen [m] ⟨mot⟩ *pre-owned* od *second-hand car* **≃br·äunt** a *sunburned* (*-burnt*), *tanned* (*face*) || v der Sonne stark ~ w *to take on a deep sunburn* **~br·aus, -brause** n *raging, surging* (*of the sea*) || *roaring* (*of the wind*); → Brausen **~br·ech** n ~es/~e **1.** ⟨hunt⟩ *ground rooted up by swine* || *snout* (*of a wild boar*) **2.** ⟨min⟩ *brittle rock* **~br·eche** n **1.** ⟨hunt⟩ = Gebrech 1. **2.** °(Erbrechen) *vomiting*; *acts of vomiting* **≃br·echen** v imp [gebrach] [h] ⟨bes bib⟩ es gebricht mir an = es fehlt, mangelt mir an **~br·echen** n ~s/~ (körperliches ~) *bodily weakness*; *infirmity*; die ~ [pl] des Alters *the infirmities of old age*; leichtes ~ *little* od *slight ailment* || ⟨übtr⟩ *frailty* (*of the mind*) **≃br·echlich** a (schwächlich) *frail, invalid, sickly, weak* || (durch Alter) *decrepit, infirm*; *shaky, tottery* || ⟨übtr⟩ (S) *effete* | ≃keit [f] *debility, decrepitude, infirmity*; ⟨a. übtr⟩ **~br·eite** f [koll] = Breiten, → Breite B. †**~br·esten** n = Gebrechen **≃br·ochen** a [pp v brechen] **1.** *splintered* | ⟨übtr⟩ *serrate*(*d*) (*roof*), *broken* (*hues, line*); ~er Akkord *arpeggio* It; ~e Zahl *broken number*; *fraction* **2.** ⟨übtr⟩ *broken* (*voice*); ~ deutsch sprechen *to speak broken German* || ⟨fig⟩ *broken* (*heart*), mit ~em Herzen *broken-hearted* || (nieder~) *broken-down*; schwer ~ *prostrate* (vor Gram *with grief*); (*a man*) *crushed by misfortune* | ≃heit [f] ⟨fig⟩ *exhaustion*; *prostration* **~br·odel** n *boiling, bubbling, simmering* **~br·üder** pl (→ Bruder) *brothers*; die ~ Grimm *the b. Grimm* || ⟨com⟩ *Brothers* (abbr *Bros*); ~ N. *N. Bros* **~br·üll** n *the roaring* (*of lions*); *lowing* (*of cows*) || ⟨übtr⟩ *bellowing*; *bawling, shouting* (*of a p*) || auf ihn mit ~! *up and at him!* **~br·umme** n *buzzing, humming* (*of flies*) || ⟨übtr⟩ *murmuring, muttering* **≃b·ückt** a *bent, stooping*, (*woman*); ~ gehend *slouchy*; → gebeugt || ~e Haltung *slouch* **~b·ühr** f ~/~en **1.** [abstr, nur sg; nur in:] nach ~ *adequately, duly, properly*; *sufficiently*; *deservedly*; nach ~ belohnt *duly rewarded* || über ~ *excessivley*; *immoderately*; *to excess*; *more than is* (*was*) *fit*; jdn über ~ feiern *to praise a p more than is due to him* (od *than he merits*); jds Zeit (etc) über ~ in Anspruch nehmen *to encroach* (od *trespass*) *upon a p's time* **2.** [konkr: pl ~en] **a.** (Abgabe) *duty, toll*; Hafen≃en *harbour dues* pl || (~en der Post) *charges* pl, *postage*; *telegram* (od *-graph*) *ch.s*, *telephone ch.s* pl; e–e ~ erheben *to make a ch.*; → Nachgebühr; Porto **b.** (~en f Schule, Univ., Verein) *fees* pl; Aufnahme≃ *entrance fee*; Immatrikulations≃en *matriculation fees*; Promotions≃en *degree fees* pl **c.** (~en privater P) *fee, remuneration*; e–e ~ berechnen f *to charge a fee for* (*a* visit) **≃b·ühren** vi [h] [nur 3. sg u pl u mit Sachsubjekt] **1.** jdm ∼ to be due to a p; den Eltern gebührt Gehorsam obedience is the parents' due; dem Landesherrn ∼ Gehorsam u Achtung obedience and respect are a sovereign's due ‖ der erste Platz gebührt ihm the first place is due to him; ⟨prov⟩ Ehre, dem Ehre gebührt honour to whom honour is due ‖ jdm geben, was ihm gebührt to give a p his due **2. sich ~** [mst neg] jdm ∼ become (od befit, beseem, suit) a p; **es gebührt sich** nicht f jdn z tun it is not becoming in a p to do; it is not (the) proper (th) for a p to do ‖ wie es sich gebührt as is proper (od due); duly, properly ‖ → sich geziemen, schicken **≃b·ührend 1.** a due (respect); proper (answer); adequate, appropriate; fit; seemly; mit ∼er Sorgfalt with due amount of care **2.** adv duly, properly; sufficiently **Geb·ühren-** [in comp] **~berechnung** f ⟨rail⟩ calculation of charges, ⟨Am⟩ rate od fare c. **~erlaß** m ⟨univ⟩ remission of fees **~ermäßigung** f reduction of fees **~erstattung** f refund of fees **≃frei** a free of charges; exempt from duty | [adv] ∼ (aufgenommen w) .. without fee **~freiheit** f exemption from charges **~marke** f duty stamp **~ordnung** f schedule of fees **≃pflichtig** a subject (od liable) to charges od to a fee; toll [attr] (Autobahn etc) **~sätze** pl rates of charges **~zahler** m dues-payer **geb·ührlich** a becoming (conduct); = gebührend **Geb·ührnisse** f pl ⟨mil⟩ a soldier's pay rations and equipment **geb·unden** a [pp v binden] **1.** ⟨bookb⟩ (hard-) bound; bound (copy of ..); in Leinen ∼ bound in cloth; ganz in Leder ∼ whole-bound **2.** ⟨chem⟩ combined (body); ∼ an combined with ‖ ∼e Wärme latent heat **3.** ⟨mus⟩ ∼es Spiel legato (It) ‖ ⟨pros⟩ ∼e Rede rhythmical language; ∼er Stil poetic diction (od style) **4.** ∼e Marschroute fixed (od prescribed) route (od course) ‖ ⟨com⟩ fixed (price); bonded (traffic) **5.** (P) [mst pred] ⟨fig⟩ ∼ s an to be guided by; to be governed by (firm policies); ∼ s an e–n Ort to be confined to a place; .. an die Zeit to be tied to time; Wirtshaus, das an e–e best. Brauerei ∼ ist tied-house ‖ ∼ s an jdn to be tied to a p; durch sein Wort ∼ bound by his word; sich ∼ fühlen to feel bound (to do); ihm sind .. ∼ his hands are tied; vollkommen ∼ s to be bound hand and foot ‖ kontraktlich ∼er Lehrling bound apprentice | ≃heit [f] ⟨fig⟩ confinement, restraint, restriction; ∼sein [n] ligation an jdn to a p

Geb·urt f ∼/∼en **1.** (∼sakt) birth; ∼en births; bei e–r ∼ at a b.; v jds ∼ an from a p's b. ‖ er ist faul v ∼ he was born lazy; taub v ∼ congenitally deaf ‖ die ∼ Christi the Nativity; nach, vor Christi ∼ → Christus ‖ ⟨euph⟩ interesting event ‖ leichte, schwere ∼ easy, difficult b.; → 3.; unzeitige ∼ abortion ‖ in der ∼ sterben to die in childbed ‖ die ∼ abtreiben to bring about a miscarriage ‖ Frau ohne ∼ nulliparous woman, nullipara **2.** (Abstammung) b., descent, extraction; ein Deutscher v ∼ a German by b.; der Arzt, ein D. v ∼ the German-born physician ‖ v vornehmer ∼ of noble b.; ein Mann v vornehmer ∼ a man of b. **3.** ⟨fig⟩ b., creation (of an idea) das war e–e schwere ∼! that was no easy thing, ⟨sl⟩ that was hell! **4.** [in comp] → Geburten–, Geburts– **Geb·urten- ~abstand** m b. interval **~beschränkung** f planned fertility, (⟨Am a.⟩ pl. motherhood); voluntary parenthood = –regelung **~buch** n b.-roll; register of b. **~planung** f b. spacing | ≃regelnde(s) Paar(e pl) n planners **~regelung** f b.-control; family od fertility planning **~rückgang** m declining b.-rate; decline of the b.-r. | ≃starke Jahrgänge ⟨school⟩ bulge **~überschuß** m surplus of births **~verhütung** f birth control ‖ ∼smittel [n] contraceptive; ∼spille [f] oral contraceptive **~ziffer** f birth-rate; natality ‖ Steigen der ∼ = **~zunahme** f increase od rise in the b.-r. **geb·ürtig** a; aus Bayern ∼ born in Bavaria, a Bavarian by birth **Geb·urts-** [in comp] native ‖ ⟨med⟩ obstetric(al) **~adel** m nobility by birth; noble birth **~anzeige** f notification (od notice) of birth; (in Zeitung:) ∼n [pl] ⟨Am⟩ Blessed Events pl **~beihilfe** f maternity grant **~datum** n date of birth **~eintragung** f entry of birth **~fehler** m congenital defect **~fest** n = –tag **~helfer** m man-midwife, accoucheur Fr, obstetrician ‖ ∼-kröte [f] ⟨zoo⟩ obstetrical toad **~hilfe** f obstetrics pl [sg konstr]; midwifery; Arzt f ∼ maternity doctor **≃hilflich** a obstetric(al) **~jahr** n; jds ∼ the year of a p's birth **~land** n native country **~ort** m b.-place, native place; ⟨Am⟩ home town **~recht** n birth-right **~schein** m birth-certificate, certificate of b. **~schüssel** f b.-plate **~stadt** f native town **~stunde** f; jds ∼ the hour of a p's birth; natal hour **~tag** m **1.** birthday ‖ ich habe am 27. März ∼ my b. is (⟨Am a.⟩ comes on) the 27th of March ‖ ∼skind [n] b. celebrant **2.** ∼s [in comp] birthday (cake, present) **~wehen** pl labo(u)r pains **~zange** f ⟨surg⟩ forceps

Geb·üsch n ∼es/∼e bush, copse, shrubbery, spinney, thicket; brake, brush, scrub; → Gestrüpp, Dickicht ‖ mit ∼ bewachsen bushy, copsy

G·eck m ∼en/∼en beau [Fr], coxcomb, dandy, high-stepper, fop, jackanapes, masher, puppy, prig, swell; ⟨Am a.⟩ dude ‖ ⟨sl⟩ nut, toff **≃enhaft** a coxcombical, foppish, swell(ish); ∼er Mensch = Geck ‖ conceited | ≃igkeit [f] dandyism, foppery, foppishness, puppydom ‖ affectation, conceit **~entum** n [koll] coxcombs pl

G·ecko m ∼s/∼s ⟨zoo⟩ gecko; → Haftzeher

ged·acht [pp v (ge)denken, dachen] **1.** ∼, getan (or getan wie ∼) so said so done **2.** a imaginary (line, number) ‖ ⟨opt⟩ ∼er Brennpunkt virtual focus ‖ ∼er Herr the gentleman in question (od aforementioned; referred to) ‖ das bloß ≃e abstraction

Ged·ächtnis n –nisses/–nisse **1.** (Erinnerungsvermögen) memory (f for); remembrance ‖ ein gutes (schlechtes) ∼ a good od retentive (bad) memory; ein kz ∼ a short m. ‖ °ein ∼ h wie ein Floh or Sieb to have a head like a sieve **2.** (Erinnerung) remembrance (an of), memory; mind; → Andenken, Erinnerung, Gedenken | ⟨übtr comp⟩ store, storage **3. a.** (etw) dem **~ einprägen** to commit to memory ‖ jds ∼ entfallen (S) to escape a p's memory od remembrance ‖ wenn mich mein ∼ nicht im Stich läßt if my memory serves me right ‖ mein ∼ setzte aus my memory went white od blank ‖ das ∼ verläßt mich my memory fails me **b.** soweit ich mich **auf** mein ∼ verlassen kann so far as I can trust my memory | **aus** dem ∼ from momory; by heart ‖ to fade (od pass) from a p's remembrance ‖ (etw) aus dem ∼ verlieren to forget, unlearn | **im** ∼ bewahren: he retained a picture of his father | **in:** fresh in a p's mind ‖ to bear (od keep) in mind; to remember (a th); jdm wieder ins ∼ k (S) to come back (od recur) to a p (od to a p's mind) ‖ (etw) ins ∼ zurückrufen to bring back to mind, to call to mind; jdm etw ins ∼ z. to recall a th to a p's mind od memory: the prosecuter recalled the mass of evidence | sich etw ins ∼ z. to remember a th: he recalled his beautiful evening with her; er versuchte es sich ins ∼ z.–zu– he searched his memory to recall it; → erinnern | **zum ~ an** in memory (od commemoration, remembrance) of; jdm zum ∼, zu jds ∼ to a p's memory **~ausstellung** f commemorative exhibition **~bild** n memory-image **~fehler** m slip of the memory **~feier** f anniversary; commemoration **~gottesdienst** m memorial service **~kirche** f commemorative chapel ‖ °**~kram** m knowledge acquired by cramming **~kunst** f mnemonics, mnemotechnics pl **~künstler** m performer of mnemotechnics **~marke** f ⟨post⟩ commemorative stamp **~rede** f memorial od commemoration speech **~schwäche** f weakness of memory, failing memory ‖ °**~schwund** m; an ∼ leiden to have a short memo-

ry **~stützen** f pl *aids of memory* **~tafel** f = Gedenk- **~tag** m *commemoration-day*; → Jahrestag **~übung** f *memory-training* **~verlust** m *amnesia*

ged·ackt a [† pp v decken] ⟨mus⟩ *closed, gedackt* [Ger] (*organ-pipe*); die °~e *the Gedackt*

ged·ämpft a *hushed* (*footsteps*); *muffled* (*tone*); ~ im Ton *subdued in tone* **1.** *damped* (*sound,* ⟨wir⟩ *wave*); *deadened* ‖ bei, mit ~er Stimme *in an undertone, under one's breath*; (*to sing*) *half-voice* ‖ *dimmed* (*light*) **2.** ⟨cul⟩ *stewed* (*meat*)

Ged·anke m ~ns/~n **1.** (Denken) *thinking, thought* (an *of*; z tun *of doing*) ‖ ~en [koll] *thought* ‖ der wissenschaftliche ~ des 20. Jhs *the scientific thought of the 20th century* **2.** (Denkinhalt) *thought*; *idea* (über, v *of*); ~n [pl] *thoughts* pl ‖ ein guter ~ *a good idea*; originelle ~n *original thoughts* pl; inhaltreiche ~n *aphorisms* pl; kein schlechter ~ *not a bad idea* ‖ der großdeutsche ~ *the idea of Greater Germany*; → Begriff, Idee, Vorstellung **3.** ⟨übtr, Lit & mus⟩ der Leit°~, leitende ~ *the motif*; *the leading thought* (*of a treatise*); → (Leit-)Motiv, Thema ‖ vertiefende ~n [pl] *reflections* pl; ~n u Erinnerungen *Reflections and Reminiscences* (*of Bismarck*) **4.** = Ansicht, Einfall; Sinn etc **5. Wendungen a. kein ~**! *no idea*! *by no means*! *certainly not*! kein ~ daran *nothing of the kind* ‖ **allein** der ~, der bloße ~ ist .. *the very idea of it is* .. ‖ das ist **nur ein** ~ v mir *that is only an idea of mine* ‖ ~n sind **zollfrei** *our thoughts are our own* | jds ~n v etw **ablenken** *to get a p's mind off a th*; zu ~n anregend *thought provoking* ‖ e–n ~n **fassen** *to conceive* (od *form*) *an idea* | den unvernünftigen ~n h *to run away with the idea* ‖ ich **habe** e–n ~n *I have an idea* ‖ er hat k–e eigenen ~n *he has no original thoughts* ‖ ich habe den gleichen ~n wie er *I am of the same opinion as he* ‖ geheime ~n bei e–r S h *to have something at the back of one's mind* ‖ s–e ~n beisammen h *to concentrate one's attention*; *to be attentive*; .. nicht b. h *to go wool-gathering*; *to be inattentive*; ihr Jungen habt **nur einen** ~n (Auto zu fahren) *you young fellow's one idea* (*is to get into a motorcar*) | **es kam mir der** ~, es fiel mir der ~ ein *it occurred to me*; *the idea came to me* (*that* ..); *I came to think of* (*it*); ihnen kam nie der ~ *they never had an idea* ‖ der ~ e–r Täuschung ist ihm nie gek *the idea of a deception has never entered his head* ‖ die besten ~n k hinterher *the best thoughts come too late* | jds ~n **lesen** *to read a p's thoughts* (od *mind*) | **sich** [dat] **~n m** *to worry*; *to wonder* (ob *if*; über *over*); *to worry* (über *about*); sich k–e ~n über etw m *not to care about a th*; mach dir k–e ~n *don't let that trouble you* ‖ sich unnötige ~n m *to trouble* (über *about*) ‖ der ~ machte ihm Freude, Vergnügen *it pleased him to think of it* | s–n ~n nachhängen *to pursue one's thoughts* | .. ordnen *to sort out* .., dem ~n k–n **Raum** (mehr) geben *to refuse to entertain the thought of a th* | der ~ **reifte** in mir *the idea ripened in my mind* ‖ s–e ~n richten auf *to concentrate one's attention on* ‖ der ~ schoß mir durch den Kopf *it flashed upon* (od *across*) *me, it fl. across* (od *into*) *my mind* ‖ e–r S keinen ~n würdigen *to give no thought to a th* ‖ s–e ~n zusnehmen *to collect one's thoughts*; *to concentrate one's attention* **b.** dies bringt mich **auf** den ~ .. *this makes me think*; *that suggests* ‖ jdn auf andere ~n bringen *to divert a p's thoughts* ‖ jdn auf den ~n br. *to give a p the idea* (*of* ..) ‖ auf e–n ~n k *to hit upon an idea* od *a thought* ‖ auf den ~n k *to take it into one's head*; *to conceive the notion* ‖ wie kamst du auf den ~n z glauben ..? *what made you think of believing* ..? ‖ .. damit du auf andere ~n kommst .. *in order to divert you from your thoughts* ‖ auf welche ~n doch die Leute k können *what these people may get into their heads* ‖ auf den ~n verfallen *to run away with the idea* | **beim** Aufbau der ~n *in the reasoning process* | **in ~n** *thoughtful*(*ly*); *preoccupied*; *in thought*; *in* (*the*) *spirit* ‖ in ~n vertieft, versunken *absorbed* (od *rapt, engrossed, wrapped, lost, immersed, buried*) *in thought*; *preoccupied*; *in a brown study* ‖ er sieht sich schon in ~n als .. *he already fancies himself as* (*the ruler*) ‖ in ~n s *to be absent-minded* (od *preoccupied*) ‖ **sich** [dat] in dem ~n gefallen *to like the idea of* (*it*, z tun *of doing*); in ~n verloren *brooding*(*ly*) | ich bin bei dir **mit** m–n ~n *I am with you in* (*the*) *spirit* ‖ mit dem ~n spielen, umgehen, sich mit dem ~n tragen z tun *to consider* (od *contemplate*) *doing*; *to be thinking* od *to have some thoughts* (od *an idea*) *of doing*; *to have it in mind to do* | **sich** [acc] (nicht) mit dem ~n (an etw) abgeben (*not*) *to give a thought* (*to a th*) | **sich** [acc] **von** e–m, dem ~n an etw befreien *to dismiss, discharge, discard a th from one's mind, to get a th out of one's m.*

Ged·anken- **~arbeit** f (rasche *quick*) *reasoning* **°~arm** a *barren of suggestive ideas* **~armut** f *barrenness of ideas* **~austausch** m *interchange of thought*; *exchange of views* (*with* ..) **~blitz** m *brain-wave*; ⟨Am⟩ *brain storm*; ich hab e–n ~ ⟨sl⟩ *I've got a hunch* **~flucht** f *morbid flight of imagination* **~flug** m *high-flying ideas* pl **~folge** f = –gang **~freiheit** f *freedom of thought* **~gang** m *train of thought*; *drift* (*of a speech*) ‖ *drift, reasoning* (*of a p*); ähnliche °~e vortragen *to speak on similar lines* **~gut** n *body of thought*; *ideas, thoughts* pl **~inhalt** m (e–r Metapher, etc) *tenor* (Ggs *image*) **~kreis** m *sphere of ideas*; *ideas* pl **~leere** f *vacancy of mind* **~lesen** n *thought* (od *mind*)-*reading* **~leser** m *thought-reader* **°~los** a *thoughtless, unthinking, unthoughtful*; *unreflecting*; *mechanical*; [adv] *without thinking* **~losigkeit** f *thoughtlessness* **~lyrik** f ⟨Lit⟩ *contemplative lyrics* pl **~prozeß** m *thinking process* **°~reich** a *imaginative* (*general, interpretation*); *thoughtful* (*book*); *fertile in ideas* **~schau** f *vistas* [pl] *of thought* **~splitter** m pl *apercus* [pl Fr]; *aphorisms* pl **~sprünge** [m pl] ~ m *to jump from one th to another* **~strich** m ⟨gram⟩ *dash* **~sünde** f *sin of thought* **~system** n *thought-system* **~übertragung** f *thought-transference*; *telepathy* **~verbindung** f *association of thoughts* od *ideas* **~vermittlung** f (durch Wort u Schrift) *communication* **~verwirrung** f *confusion of thought* **°~voll** a = –reich; adv (*to gaze*) *wistfully* **~vorbehalt** m *mental reservation* **~welt** f *thought*; die griechische ~ *the Greek thought* ‖ *range* (od *scope*) *of ideas*; *ideas* [pl] (*of a p*); in s–r ~ *in his ideas*

Ge- **°~d·anklich 1.** [a] *intellectual, mental*; der ~e Teil *the thoughts* pl (e–s Werkes *in a work*) ‖ rein ~ *abstract, ideal*; *rational, speculative* ‖ ~e Betrachtung *or* Vertiefung *meditation, reflection* **2.** [adv] *intellectually, mentally*; *ideally* **~d·ärm** n ~s/~e [mst pl] ~e *bowels, entrails, intestines* pl; ⟨fam⟩ *guts* pl **~d·eck** n ~s/~e **1.** (Tisch°~) *cover*; zehn ~e auflegen *to lay ten covers*; ein neues ~ auflegen f *to lay an extra place for* (*a p*); e–e Tafel z 20 ~en *a table laid for twenty persons* ‖ → Besteck ‖ (°~betrag) *cover charge* **2.** *menu* [Fr]; trockenes ~ *menu without drinks* **°~d·eckt** a ⟨tact⟩ ~er Raum *dead space*; ~e Stellung *sheltered position* **°~d·ehnt** a ⟨math⟩ *prolate* ‖ ⟨gram⟩ *long* **~d·eih** m [nur in:] auf ~ u Verderb ⟨fig⟩ *for good and evil, for better for worse*; sich auf ~ u V. verbinden mit jdm *to throw in one's lot with a p* **°~d·eihen I.** vi [gedieh/gediehen] [s] **1.** (of plants) *to grow* (⟨fam⟩ *do*) *well*; *to thrive*; ⟨Am a.⟩ *to be thrifty*; Rosen ~ hier nicht ⟨fam⟩ *roses won't do here* ‖ (P) *to prosper, thrive*; *to get on* **2.** ⟨übtr⟩ (S) *to prosper, flourish, thrive* (auf dem Boden der Freiheit *on freedom*); *to blossom* (*the courtship blossomed*); *to succeed* ‖ die Verhandlungen sind schon weit gediehen *the proceedings are far-advanced* (od *well on the way*); wie weit war er (sc der Haß) g.? *how far had it gone*?; es ist soweit g., daß .. *things have come to such a pass that* .. ‖ es gedieh ihm zum Heil *it was for his best*; *things turned out for his best* **II.** ≈ n *prosperous growth*; *thriving* ‖ *prosperity*; *success* **≈d·eihlich** a *prosperous, thriving* (⟨Am a.⟩ *thrifty*); *improving, successful* (*end*)

Ged·enk- [in comp] *memorial*, → Gedächtnis- **~artikel** m (Nachruf) *obituary, o. notice* **~band** m *memorial volume* **~blatt** n *memorial leaf* **~feier** f, **~gottesdienst** m = Gedächtnisfeier, -gottesdienst **~stein** m *memorial stone* **~stück** n *relic* **~tafel** f *memorial tablet*; ⟨Am a.⟩ *marker* **~tag** m *day of remembrance*; Krieger≈ ⟨Am⟩ *Memorial* (od *Decoration*) *Day* (30. März)

Ge- ≈d·enken I. vi/t [gedachte/gedacht] [h] **A.** vi **1.** jds, e–r S ⁓ *to remember a p, a th*; *to think of a p, a th*; *to bring a th back to mind* ‖ *to mention a p, a th*; *to make mention of a p, a th*; jds in Ehren ⁓ *to make honourable mention of a p*; jds im Testament ⁓ *to remember a p in one's will* **2.** ⁓ z tun *to intend, mean, propose to do*; *to think of doing*; ⁓ z s *to hope to be* (*in Berlin in May*) **B.** † vt **jdm etw ~** *to make a p pay for a th*; ich werde es dir ⁓ *you shall smart fot it* **II.** ≈ n *memory* (an *of*); → Andenken ‖ z jds ⁓ *to a p's memory* ‖ jdm ein freundliches ⁓ bewahren *to keep* (*a p*) *in good memory* **≈d·eucht** pp v dünken **~dicht** n ⁓s/⁓e **1.** *poem*; ein ⁓ v N. *a poem by N.* od *of N's*; episches ⁓ *epic poem*; erzählendes ⁓ *narrative p.*; lyrisches ⁓ *lyric*; *lyric poem* ‖ ⁓e [pl] *poems* pl, *poetry*; ⁓e v N. *Poems by N.*, *the Poems of N.*, *N's poetry*; ⁓e schreiben *to write some poetry* **2.** der Hut ist ein ⁓ *the hat is a picture* od *dream*; ein ⁓ v e–m H. *a heart-throb of a h.* | ⁓album [n] *poetry-album*; ⁓form [f]; in ⁓ *in verse*; ⁓sammlung [f] *anthology*; *collection of poems* **≈d·iegen** [† pp v gedeihen] **A.** [a] **1.** *native* (*metal*) ‖ *virgin*; *pure, native* (*gold, silver*); *massive, massy* **2.** ⟨fig⟩ *genuine, true* (*friend*) ‖ *pure* (*style*), *solid* (*worth*), *sterling, superior* (*quality*) ‖ *high-principled, solid* (*man*); *sterling* (*fellow*); *thoroughbred*; *upright* (*character*) ‖ *substantial* (*knowledge*); *thorough* (*knowledge, work*; *worker*) ‖ → gehaltvoll, markig **3.** °das ist ⁓ *that is funny*; °du bist ⁓ *you are funny*; *that's a funny way to behave* **B.** [adv] *solidly* (*built*); *thoroughly* | ≈heit [f] *solidity* ‖ ⟨mst fig⟩ *genuineness*; *purity, solidity*; *sterling quality* (od *worth*); *thoroughness* **≈d·ieh** [pret]; **≈d·iehen** [pp] v gedeihen **≈d·ient** a; ein ⁓er Soldat *an old soldier* ‖ ein ⁓er Artillerist *one who has served with the artillery* ‖ ⁓er Jahrgang *instructed age-class*

Ge- ~d·inge n ⟨min⟩ *contract for job-work*; *tut-bargain*; im ⁓ arbeiten *to work by the job*; *to tut* ‖ *tut-work* | ⁓arbeit [f] *tribute w.*, → Akkord– ‖ ⁓stufe [f] *job mark* **~d·onner** n *thundering*; *repeated rolls of thunder*

Ge- ×**~d·öns** n ⁓es/· *fuss*; mach kein ⁓! *don't fuss!* ‖ °Herr ⁓ *gas-bag, buzz-nagger*, ⟨sl⟩ *hummer* **~dr·änge** n ⁓s/ **1. a.** [abstr] *crowding, thronging*; *ram*; *push*; *press*; *rush, scramble* (nach, um *for*); *squeeze, push* **b.** (Menschenmenge) *crowd, crush, jam, press, throng* ‖ es war ein furchtbares ⁓ *there were enormous crowds of people* ‖ sich im ⁓ verlieren *to lose o.s. in the press* **c.** ⟨fig⟩ = Enge, Klemme ‖ ins ⁓ kommen *to get into a fix* (od *strait*) **2.** ⟨sport⟩ ⟨ftb⟩ *mêlée* (Fr) ‖ ⟨Rugb ftb⟩ *scrummage*, ⟨fam⟩ *scrum*; ein ⁓ bilden *to scrummage* **≈dr·ängt 1.** [a] **a.** *packed closely together*; wir saßen dicht ⁓ *we sat in a tight group* (od *squeeze*) ‖ ⁓e Reihen *serried rows* (⟨mil⟩ *ranks*) **b.** ⟨fig⟩ *potted* (*biography*) ‖ *compact, compressed, concise, sinewy, succinct, terse* (*style*, etc) **2.** [adv] (*to write*) *closely* ‖ ⁓ voll v *crowded* (od *crammed, stuffed*) *with*; *full of* (*events*) | ≈heit [f] ⟨fig⟩ *conciseness, succinctness* **≈dr·echselt** a *turned* | ⟨fig⟩ *elaborate*(*d*), *polished* ‖ *affected, artificial* (*manners*; *style*) **≈dr·eht** a *twisted*; ≈es *twist* **~dr·itt-schein** m ⟨astr⟩ *trine* **≈dr·uckt** a *printed*; *in print* ‖ ≈es *printed matter* ‖ °er lügt wie ⁓ *he lies like a book* **≈dr·ückt** a **1.** ⟨tech⟩ *pressed* ‖ ⟨com⟩ *stringent, tight* (*market*) ‖ *low* (*prices*); ⟨st exch⟩ *depressed* ‖ ⁓e Lage *straitened* od *pinched circumstances* pl **2.** ⟨fig⟩ *depressed* (*mood*); *downhearted, heavy* (*heart*); *low-spirited*; *sick*; *fed up*; ⁓es Aussehen *hang-dog look*; ⁓e Stimmung *low spirits* pl, in ⁓er St. *out of spirits* | ≈heit [f] *depression*; *heaviness* **≈dr·ungen** a [pp v dringen] **1.** *squat, stumpy, thickset* (*p*); *short and thickset*; *square-built* ‖ (of style) = gedrängt 1. b. **2.** sich ⁓ fühlen → dringen B. 3. | ≈heit [f] *compact build* ‖ = Gedrängtheit °**~d·udel** n *strum*(*ming*), *thrum*(*ming*) **~d·uld** f ⁓/ *patience* (mit *with*) ‖ *forbearance, lenience*, → Nachsicht ‖ (Ausdauer) *perseverance* ‖ jds ⁓ sehr **in Anspruch** nehmen *to try a p's patience* ‖ z dieser Arbeit **gehört** gr ⁓ *this work calls for great perseverance* ‖ ⁓ h mit *to have patience with, to be patient with* (*a p*); wir h k–e ⁓ mehr mit ihr *we are out of patience with her*; m–e ⁓ ist ziemlich am Ende *my p. has just about come to an end*; man muß viel ⁓ h *you must have the patience of Job* ‖ mir riß die ⁓ *I was out of patience, I lost all p.* ‖ (nicht) die ⁓ verlieren (*not*) *to lose* (*one's*) *patience* ‖ die ⁓ ist nun zu Ende *the sands of patience have run out* | **in** ⁓ *in patience, patiently*; sich in ⁓ fassen *to compose* (od *posses*) *one's soul in patience* | **mit** ⁓ *with patience*; *patiently* ‖ ° mit ⁓ u Spucke fängt man e–e Mucke *patience and a snare catch many a hare* **≈d·ulden** [vrefl] sich ⁓ *to have patience*; *to wait* (bis *until*); wollen Sie sich bitte e–n Augenblick ⁓ *wait a minute, please* **≈d·uldig 1.** [a] *patient*; ⁓ wie ein Lamm *as meek as a lamb* **2.** [adv] *patiently*; *in* (od *with*) *patience*; *stoically* ‖ ⁓ ertragen *to bear with patience*; *to put up with* (*a th*) **≈d·uldigen** [vrefl] = sich gedulden

Ged·ulds- [in comp] °**~faden** m = Geduld; ⟨fig⟩ da reißt der ⁓ *now I am at the end of my patience* **~probe** f *trial of patience* **~spiel** n *puzzle*; *jig-saw puzzle* ‖ *spillikins* pl ‖ → Patience

ge- ~d·ungen pp v dingen **~d·unsen** a *bloated*; *puffed up*; *puffy* (*face, lids*) **~d·ünstet** a ⟨cul⟩ = gedämpft 2 **~·ehrt** a (in Briefen) Sehr ⁓er Herr ..! (amtlich) *Sir*; ⟨com⟩ *Dear Sir* [pl *D. Sirs*]; Sehr ⁓er Herr N. (vertraulich) *Dear Mr. N.* ‖ ⟨com⟩ Ihr ⁓es Schreiben (*od* Ihr ≈es) vom 10. d. Mts *your favour of the 10th inst.* **~·eignet 1.** [a] ⁓ f *or* z *appropriate* (od *fit, fitting, meet, suitable*) *for, to*; f den Winter ⁓e Kleidung *clothes suitable* (od *adapted*) *for winter wear* ‖ z nichts ⁓ *fit for nothing* | *timely, well-timed*; *favo*(*u*)*rable, opportune*; *expedient, propitious* | [attr] *apt* (*word*); *likely* (*house*); *proper* (*tool*); *suitable* ‖ *available* (Ms) ‖ ein ganz ⁓er Platz f *not a bad place for* .. ‖ in ⁓er Weise *aptly* **2.** [adv] *aptly*; *suitably* **~·eint** a *united* (*nation*)

Geer f ⁓/⁓e ⟨mar⟩ (Haltetau) *vang*

ge·erdet a ⟨el⟩ *grounded*; *earth connected*

Geest f, **~land** n *dry and sandy coastal region*

Ge- ~f·abel n ⟨fig⟩ *fable* (v *of*) **~f·ahr** f ⁓/⁓en *danger* (f .. *to a p, to a th*; e–e ⁓ f den Frieden *a danger to peace*); *peril*, die Gelbe, Rote ⁓ *the yellow, red peril* ‖ e–e ⁓ s *to pose a threat* ‖ drohende ⁓ *menace, threat* (f *to*) ‖ (Wagnis) *hazard, jeopardy, risk* ‖ ⟨ins⟩ (Verlust≈) *risk* ‖ Lebens≈ *d. of one's life* ‖ Minen≈ *d. from mines* ‖ wenn ⁓ **im Anzug** ist *or* droht so (..) *if d. threatens*, (*it is necessary that* ..) ‖ ⁓ im Verzug *imminent d.*; ihm droht ⁓ *d. threatens him* ‖ es besteht ⁓, es ist ⁓ vorhanden, daß *there is a d. that* .. ‖ die ⁓ f .. liegt in .. *the d. to* .. *lies in* .. ‖ ⟨mar⟩ ⁓ in Sicht *breakers ahead* ‖ → Verzug | e–r ⁓ **ins Auge sehen** *to face a d.* | (jdn, etw) der ⁓ **aussetzen** *to expose* (od *lay open*) *to d.* ‖ sich e–r ⁓ aussetzen *to incur a d.*, *to expose o.s. to a d.*; = ⁓ laufen; sich [acc] der ⁓ auss. *to run the d.* (*to do*); sich f jdn e–r ⁓ auss.

to put o.s. in peril for a p ‖ sich ~en aussetzen *to take chances*; sich nicht der ~ e–r S aussetzen *to take no chances with a th*; sich k–n ~en aussetzen *to take no chances* od *risks* | e–e ~ **heraufbeschwören** *to conjure up a d.* ‖ es hat k–e ~ *there is no risk* ‖ ~ **laufen** z verlieren *to run* (od *take*) *the risk of losing*, *to be in d. of l.*; *to run a chance* (z tun *of doing*); .., sich strafbar z m etc *to sail close to the wind*; *he stood at some risk of being smothered*; ~ laufen verhaftet z w *to be liable to arrest* ‖ ~en (auf)suchen *to go in quest of d.* | **auf die ~ hin** z verlieren *at the risk of losing*; selbst auf die ~ hin, verlacht z w *in the face of ridicule* ‖ auf jede ~ hin *neck or nothing* ‖ *at your risk!*; auf eigene ~ *at one's own risk* (od *hazard*); *at one's peril* ‖ auf Rechnung u ~ des Eigentümers *at owner's risk* | **außer** ~ s *to be out of d.* od *out of the wood*; außer ~ vor dem Feuer s *to be clear of the fire* | f Rechnung u ~ v *for account and risk of* | **in** ~ vernichtet z w *in d. of extinction* ‖ in ~ bringen *to bring into d.*; *to expose to d.*; *to endanger*; (jds Ruf) in ~ br. *to compromise* ‖ sich in ~ begeben *to incur d.*, *to expose o.s. to d.*; wer sich in ~ begibt, kommt darin um *he who ventures into d. is likely to perish in it* ‖ in ~ geraten *or* k. *to get into d.*, *to be exposed to d.* ‖ in ~ schweben *or* s *to be in d.* (od *jeopardy*); → Lebens≗ ‖ in ~ s, vergessen z w *to be liable to be forgotten* | **ohne** ~ *without risk* (od *d. of one's life*) ≗**fahrbringend** a *dangerous*; → gefährlich ≗**f·ährden** vt [h] (etw) *to endanger*; *imperil* (*confidence, etc*); (Zukunft) *to jeopardize* (mit *with*); (Ernte) *to menace*; (Stellung) *to compromise*; ⟨chess⟩ *to stalemate* ‖ gefährdete Lage *exposed position* ‖ den Frieden ~d *unlawful* (*assembly*) ‖ wenn .. –det ist *in case of danger for ..* **~f·ährdetenfürsorge** f *welfare work for endangered youth* ≗**f·ahrdrohend** a *menacing, threatening*; *imminent* **~f·ährdung** f ~/~en *endangering, imperilling*; *jeopardy* ‖ wenn es ohne ~ des Verkehrs geschehen kann ⟨mot⟩ *if it does not endanger other traffic* **~f·ahre** n *driving* ‖ *noise of traffic*

Gef·ahren- [in comp] **~anzeige** f ⟨ins⟩ *notice of danger threatening* **~bereich** m *danger-area* **~feuer** n ⟨aero⟩ *hazard beacon* **~gebiet** n *d. zone* **~grenze** f *d. line* **~herd** m *danger-centre* **~klasse** f ⟨ins⟩ *danger-class* **~meldung** f *warning of d.* **~punkt** m *danger-point, d.-spot* **~symbol** n *warning symbol, warning label* **~zone** f *d. zone*; jdn aus der ~ halten *to keep a p out of harm's way* **~zulage** f *danger-allowance*; *incentive* od *d. pay*

Ge- ≗**f·ährlich 1.** [a] *dangerous* (*journey, illness*), *perilous*; *serious* (*crisis*); *critical* (*condition*) ‖ *hazardous, risky*; *stalemate* (*position*) ‖ ~e Dinge *tricky* (od *ticklish*) *things* (*revolvers are t. th.*); ~er Ort ⟨sl⟩ *hot place* ‖ sich auf ~en Bahnen bewegen *to walk upon eggs* ‖ das ~e Alter *the critical years* pl (*of a boy*) | ein ~er Kerl *a dangerous fellow*, *an ugly* od *a rum customer*; ~ aussehen *to look dangerous* | das ist ja nicht (weiter) ~ *that's not very serious*, *that's nothing much* ‖ °hab dich nicht so ~, °tu nicht so ~ *don't make a fuss* **2.** [adv] *dangerously*; *seriously* (*wounded, ill*) | ≗keit [f] *dangerousness* ≗**f·ahrlos** a *riskless*; *without risk*; *involving no risk*; *safe* | ≗igkeit [f] *risklessness*; *safety* **~f·ahrsignal** n ⟨rail⟩ *danger-signal* **~f·ährt** n ~(e)s/~e *conveyance, vehicle* **~f·ährte** ~n/~n m *companion, comrade, fellow*; Leidens≗ *fellow-sufferer*; Reise≗ *travelling companion*; → Lebens≗ **~f·ährtin** f *companion* ≗**f·ahrvoll** a *riskful, risky, involving risk(s), risk-fraught*; *venturesome*; *dangerous*, → gefährlich **~f·alle** m ~n/*~n = Gefallen ‖ das ist mir ein gr ~ *you are doing me a great favour* **~f·älle** n **1.** (of a road, etc.) *falling gradient*, ⟨Am⟩ *grade* ‖ *declivity, descent, slope* ‖ *drop, fall* (*of 10 degrees*); starkes ~ ⟨mot⟩ *steep down gradient* | ⟨tech⟩ *pitch*; nutzbares ~ *effective head* **2.** ⟨fig⟩ °ein gutes ~ h *to drink like a fish* | ~bremse [f] ⟨mot⟩ *holding brake*; ~schmierung [f] *gravity-feed lubrication*

gef·allen vi [→ fallen] [h] **1. a.** jdm ~ *to please* od *suit a p* ‖ *to take* (*a p's*) *fancy* ‖ das Bild gefällt mir *I like that picture*; *the picture strikes my fancy*; es gefällt mir sehr *I am very much pleased with it*; gefällt es dir? *do you like it? is it to your liking* od *taste?* ‖ ich gefiel ihnen nicht *they didn't like me* (od *take to me*) ‖ er hat mir recht gut ~ *I liked the look of him very much*; das gefällt mir an ihr *I like her for it*; es ist unmöglich allen z ~ *it is impossible to suit* (od *please*) *everybody* ‖ das würde ihm so ~ *that would be grist to his mill*, ⟨sl⟩ *that would be nuts to* (od *for*) *him* ‖ die S gefällt mir nicht *I don't like the look of it* ‖ du gefällst mir nicht *you don't look well*; *I don't like the state of your health* ‖ wie hat es dir in Berlin ~? *how did you like Berlin?* ‖ °wie gefällt dir das? ⟨iron⟩ *that's a pretty kettle of fish*, ⟨Am⟩ *that's a fine how-d'ye-do!* ‖ **jdm z ~ suchen** *to* (*shine up to* od) *tickle a p*; (of women) *to set one's cap at a p* **b.** (jds Ohr etc) *to flatter*; *please, suit* **2.** [imps] (belieben) wie es dir gefällt *as you please*; tu, wie es dir g. *do as you like* (od *please*); *please* (od *suit*) *yourself*; ich tue, was mir g. *I do what I please* ‖ wenn es Gott g. *please God*; wie es G. g. *as God wills* **3. sich** [dat] **etw ~ l** *to put up with a th*; *to stand* (od *stomach*) *a th*; ⟨Am a.⟩ *to stand for a th* ‖ ich kann *or* will es mir nicht (so einfach) ~ l *I cannot* od *won't take it lying down* ‖ laß dir nichts ~ *don't let yourself be put upon*; man muß sich nichts ~ l *you must not allow yourself to be put upon*; er ließ sich nichts ~ v ihr *he stood no nonsense from her*; laß es dir nicht v ihm ~ *don't stand it from him*; er ließ sich viel ~ v ihr *he put up with a great deal from her* ‖ er war entschlossen, sich nichts ~ z l *his back was up* | **das lasse ich mir ~** *that is sth like*; *that's to my taste*; (*that's*) *pretty good* (od *useful*), *indeed*; ⟨fam⟩ *not half bad, that's the stuff!* **4. sich ~ in etw** *to indulge* (*o.s.*) *in a th*; *to take pleasure in a th*; er gefiel sich in dem Gedanken, daß .. *he flattered himself that ..* ‖ sich in e–r Rolle ~ *to be pleased with a role*, *to fancy o.s. in a part* (od *in the character of ..*) ‖ sich darin ~ z tun *to take to doing* **Gef·allen** m ~s/*~ (Genuß) *delight, pleasure* (an *in*); *liking, relish* (an *for*); ein ~ am Leben *a zest for life*; je nach jds ~ *to a p's liking* | (Gefälligkeit) *favour, kindness* | jdn **um** e–n ~ **bitten** *to ask a favour of a p* ‖ jds ~ erwecken *to find favour in a p's eyes*; *to please a p* ‖ ~ **finden an** etw *to derive pleasure from*; *to be taken* (*up*) *with a th*; *to take a p's fancy*; *to take delight* (od *pleasure*) *in*; *to take a liking* (od *fancy*) *to a th*; *to feel the better for a th* (*they felt the b. for each other's company*); *to take to a th*; *to be pleased with a th*; *to enjoy* (od *appreciate, relish*) *a th*; ~ daran finden z tun *to enjoy doing*, *to take to doing*; finden Sie ~ am Tanzen *do you like dancing?* | **~ h an** *to have a liking for* ‖ ‖ jdm e–n ~ tun, erweisen *to do a p a favour*; willst du mir den ~ erweisen? *will you do me the kindness?* tu mir den ~, gleich z antworten *do me the f. of answering at once*; *be so kind as to answer ..* | **Ihnen z ~** *to oblige you*; mir z ~ *as a favo(u)r to me* ‖ jds Wünschen z ~ *in deference to a p's wishes* ‖ jdm z ~ reden *to cajole* od *flatter a p*; *to fawn on a p* ‖ tu es mir z ~ *do it to please me, do it for my sake*

Ge- ≗**f·allen** a *fallen* (*angel, woman* Mädchen); e–e ~e Größe (P) *a fallen celebrity*; *a has-been* | ⟨mil⟩ *fallen*, ⟨sl⟩ *cashed-in* | e–e ≗e *a fallen woman* ‖ ≗er *killed soldier*; die ≗en [pl] (im Kriege) *the fallen* pl ≗**engedenktag** m *Remembrance Day* ≗**f·ällig A.** [a] **1.** *accommodating, complaisant*; *attractive, obliging* (*p*); *suave* (*manners*) ‖ um ~e Antwort wird gebeten *the favour of a reply is requested* ‖ wir bitten um ~en Bericht, was .. *please, let us know what ..*; .. um ~e

Zusendung e–s Exemplars *we shall be obliged if you would forward us a copy* ‖ jdm ∼ s *to please* od *accommodate a p*; *to oblige a p* (mit .. *with a th*; dadurch, daß man tut *by doing*); *to assist a p* | °ein ∼es Mädchen *a light woman* **2.** *agreable, attractive* | ⟨com⟩ was ist ∼? *what is it you want*? *what can I do for you*? Bier ∼? (*some*) *beer, please*? **3.** °hier ist etwas ∼ *there is sth special on here*; ⟨sl⟩ *here is an expensive show*; was ist hier ∼? *what's up*? **B.** [adv] **1.** sich jdm ∼ erweisen = jdm ∼ s → A. 1. **2.** **∼**, **∼st** *if you please*; *please*; *pray*; schließ ∼st die Tür *shut the door*, (*if you*) *please*; du wartest ∼st! *if you'll wait*! **Gef·älligkeit** f ∼/∼en **1. a.** (Güte) *complaisance, kindness, obligingness*; *suavity*; die ∼ h z tun *to have the kindness, to be kind enough to do* **b.** (Gefallen) e–e ∼ *a favour, kindness, service*; ∼en [pl] *favours*; *good offices* pl ‖ jdn um e–e ∼bitten *to ask a favour of a p* ‖ jdm e–e ∼ erweisen *to do a p a favour* od *good turn*; *to accommodate a p* (mit .. *with a th*); → Gefallen 2. ‖ aus ∼ gegen Sie *to oblige you* **2.** *agreeableness, attractiveness*; *charm* (*of a tune*) | **∼sakzept** n, **∼swechsel** m *accommodation bill*; ⟨sl⟩ *kite* **∼sdemokratie** f *complacency democracy*

Ge- **≗f·älligst** adv → gefällig B. 2. **∼f·allsucht** f *self-admiration* ‖ *coquetry* (*of a woman*) **≗f·allsüchtig** **1.** [a] *coquettish*; ∼e Frau *coquette, flirt* **2.** [adv] sich ∼ benehmen *to coquet* **∼f·ältel** n = Falten pl, → Falte B. **∼f·änge** n ⟨hunt⟩ = Geweih

gef·angen a [mst pred] **1.** *caught, taken*; *trapped* ‖ *captive, captured*; *imprisoned*; *in prison* ‖ ⟨fig⟩ *captivated*; ⟨fam⟩ *sewed up* ‖ wie in e–m Netz (*I am*) *beset and hemmed in* **2.** [in comp] sich **∼|geben** *to surrender*; *to yield o.s. prisoner* | jdn ∼|halten *to keep a p captive*; (T) *to keep .. a prisoner* ‖ ⟨übtr⟩ (of illness) *to keep a p a prisoner* (im Zimmer *to one's room*) ‖ ⟨fig⟩ *to hold a p*; *to have a p in thrall* | jdn **∼|nehmen** *to capture* od *seize a p*; *to take a p prisoner* (*they were taken prisoners*) ‖ ⟨fig⟩ (of feelings, etc.) *to get hold of a p*; *to captivate* (od *enslave, enthral*[*l*], *hold*) *a p*; jds Einbildungskraft ∼ *to take a p's fancy*; jds Sinne ∼ nehmen *to occupy a p's mind* ‖ –genommen s v, sich ∼ l v *to be captivated, gripped by* (*the play*); *to succumb to* (*the magic of* ..) ‖ das Auge, den Blick ∼d *eye-catching* | jdn **∼|setzen** *to put a p in prison*; *to imprison* (od *lock up*) *a p*; → einlochen; Schutzhaft | ∼|sitzen vi *to be kept captive* (od *a prisoner*); *to be in prison* **Gef·angene** **1.** [der ∼, ein ∼r] *the captive, prisoner*; → Sträfling **2.** die ∼ *the female prisoner*

Gef·angenen- [in comp] **∼arbeit** f *prison-labour* **∼aufseher** m = ∼wärter **∼befreiung** f ⟨jur⟩ *intentional liberation of a prisoner* **∼fürsorge** f *prison welfare-work* **∼haus** n *prison-house*, ⟨oft fig⟩ = Gefängnis **∼kleidung** f *prison-dress* (od *garb*) **∼lager** *prisoners' camp* **∼wagen** m *prison-van*; ⟨sl⟩ *black Maria*; ⟨Am⟩ *patrol-van* **∼wärter** m *gaoler*; ⟨bes Am⟩ *jailer, jailor*; *warder*; *turnkey*; ⟨Am⟩ *guard* **∼wärterin** f *gaoleress* etc.

Gef·angen- **∼haltung** f *detention*; *arrest, confinement* **∼nahme, ∼nehmung** f *arrest*; *caption, seizure* ‖ ⟨mil⟩ *capture*; *taking prisoner* **∼schaft** f *captivity, imprisonment* ‖ in ∼ geraten *to be taken* (od *made*) *prisoner* (*1000 were taken prisoners*)

Gef·ängnis n ∼ses/∼se **1. a.** *gaol, jail, prison*; (Burg≗) *dungeon* ‖ ⟨Am⟩ *jail, prison*; *penitentiary* ‖ ⟨sl⟩ *coop, jug, stir* ‖ Staats≗ *state prison*; Stadt≗ in New York *the Tombs* pl | Ausbruch aus dem ∼ *prison-breaking* ‖ im ∼ *in prison* ‖ (jdn) ins ∼ werfen *to put in p., to send to p.*; *to imprison*; *to run in* **b.** ⟨fig⟩ *prison*(*house*) (*of the London streets*) **2.** (Haft) *hard labour, imprisonment*; z 3 Jahren ∼ verurteilt w *to be sentenced to 3 years' imprisonment*; → Zuchthaus **3.** [in comp] **∼arbeit** f *prison-labour* **∼direktor** m *prison-governor*, ⟨Am⟩ *prison-warden* ‖ °**∼insasse** m *jail-bird* **∼kleidung** f *prison-garb* **∼strafe** f (*sentence of*) *imprisonment*; bei ∼ *under pain of i.* **∼unwesen** n *prison abuses* pl **∼wärter** m = Gefangenenwärter **∼wesen** n *prison-system*

Ge- **≗f·ärbt** a *coloured* (*glasses*; ⟨fig⟩ *account*) **∼f·asel** n *drivel* (⟨Am⟩ *drool*), *gush, raving, rigmarole*; *nonsense*; süßliches ∼ *sillibub, syll–* **∼f·äß** n ∼es/∼e **1.** *container, receptacle, vessel*; *tank*; Zier≗ *vase* **2.** ⟨anat & bot⟩ *vessel*; *canal, duct, tube*; *vas* [L] [pl *vasa*]; Blut≗ *blood-vessel* **3.** (Degengriff) *hilt* **4.** ⟨fig⟩ *vehicle* (f *for*); die ∼e deines Zorns *the vehicle of your resentment* **5.** [in comp] ⟨anat & bot⟩ *vasal*; *vascular*; *angio–* ∼barometer [n] *cistern-barometer* ∼bildung [f] *vascular structure*; *vascularity* ∼bündel [n] pl ⟨bot⟩ (*fibro*)*vascular tissue* ∼geschwulst [f] ⟨path⟩ *angioma* [L]; *vascular tumour* ∼heberbarometer [n] *syphon-barometer* ≗los a ⟨med⟩ *avascular* ∼system [n] *vascular system* ..

gef·aßt **A.** [a] mst [pred] **1.** *collected, composed*; *resigned*; *calm, tranquil*; ∼ bleiben *to remain* (⟨fam⟩ keep) *cool, calm*, ⟨sl⟩ *to keep one's hair* (⟨Am⟩ *shirt*) *on* **2.** ∼ s auf *to be prepared* (od *ready*) *for*; ich bin (*or* mache mich) auf alles ∼ *I am prepared for anything*; darauf ∼ s, daß jd tut *to be prepared for a p to do* ‖ sich ∼ m auf *to prepare* (*o.s.*) *for*; du kannst dich darauf ∼ m *you might as well expect it* **sich** [acc] ∼ m, etw z tun *to brace o.s. to do sth*; °wir können uns auf etw ∼ m ⟨sl⟩ *we are in for it*, ⟨Am⟩ .. *due for the high jumps* **B.** [adv] *composedly, resignedly*; etw ∼ aufnehmen *to take a th composedly* | **≗heit** f *collectedness, composedness, composure* **≗sein** n *preparedness* (auf *for*); *readiness*

Gef·echt n ∼(e)s/∼e **1.** ⟨mil⟩ (Kampf) *action, combat, encounter, engagement, fight*(*ing*) | (kl) *skirmish* ‖ → Schlacht, Treffen; Kampf ‖ hinhaltendes ∼ *delaying* (od *holding-up*) *action* ‖ Schein≗ *sham fight* ‖ ⟨mar⟩ klar z ∼ *ready for action*; Schiff klar z ∼ m *to clear the decks*; *to clear a ship for action* ‖ ein ∼ abbrechen *to break off an action* ‖ ins ∼ k. *to come into action* ‖ ins ∼ werfen *to commit* (*units*); außer ∼ setzen *to put out of action, to incapacitate* **2.** ⟨fig⟩ *encounter, fight* ‖ in der Hitze des ∼s *in the heat of the moment* ‖ (etw) f e–e Behauptung ins ∼ führen *to produce in corroboration of a statement*

Gef·echts- **∼ausbildung** f *combat training, t. for active service* **∼ausrüstung** f *fighting-trim* (*of a ship*) **∼befehl** m *combat order* **∼bereich** m *zone of operations* **≗bereit** a *ready for action*; *in fighting trim* **∼bereitschaft** f *readiness for action* **∼bericht** m *first report on the operations* **∼berührung** f *contact, touch* (*with the enemy*) **∼einheit** f *fighting-unit* **∼feld** n *field of operations* **∼formation** f *tactical f.* **∼fühlung** f *connection, touch* (*with neighbouring units*) **∼führung** f (geplante) *operational planning* **∼gliederung** f *tactical grouping*; *order of battle* **∼handlung** f *operation* **∼kopf** m *war-head* (*of a torpedo*) **∼kraft** f *fighting efficiency* **∼lage** f *state of operations*; *tactical* od *combat situation* **∼landeplatz** m ⟨aero⟩ *combat advanced landing ground* (od *field*) **∼mars** m ⟨mar⟩ *fighting-top* **≗mäßig** a *under* (*simulated*) *combat conditions*; ∼es Schießen *field-shooting*; *battle-practice* **∼munition** f *service ammunition* **∼patrouille** f *combat patrol*; *recon*(*noitring*) *party* **∼schießen** n *field firing* **∼sicherung** f *f. security* **∼stab** m *tactical operations staff* **∼staffel** f *first echelon of supply* **∼stand** m *observation-post of the commanding officer*; *operational* od *battle headquarters* pl, *command post*; Ausweich≗ *alternate C. P.* **∼streifen** m *area allotted to an attacking body* **∼troß** m *first line baggage* **∼turm** m ⟨mar⟩ *turret* **∼übung** f *combat exercise, exercise in military and naval tactics*; ∼en [pl] *manoeuvres* pl; angriffsweise ∼ *offensive-type operations* **∼verbandplatz** m *dressing-station* **∼vorposten** m *ad-*

vanced post by night; [pl] *screening* **~wagen** m *ammunition-wag(g)on* **~ziel** n ⟨mil⟩ *objective of the operations*; *objective point* **~zone** f *zone of operations*

Ge- ≃f·edert a ⟨tech⟩ *spring-mounted*; besonders ∼ *specially sprung*; → gefiedert **~f·ege** n ∼s/ ⟨hunt⟩ *rub, fraying* (*from a stag's horns*) **≃f·ehlt** a (weit ∼) *wide of the mark* → fehlen **≃f·eiert** a ⟨übtr⟩ *celebrated* (*hero*); ∼e Persönlichkeit *celebrity* **~f·eilsche** n *haggling*; *haggle* **~f·eiltheit** f ∼/ *polish* **≃feit** a **1.** [pred] ∼s gegen *to be immune from* (od *against, to*); *to be proof of* od *fortified against*; *to be protected from* od *against*; *to be impervious* od *invulnerable to* (*opposition*) ‖ (jdn) ∼ m *to fortify, to protect* (*against*) **2.** [attr] *charmed* (*life*); *immune* (*p*) **≃f·esselt** a: ans Bett, an den Stuhl ∼ *bed-, chair-ridden*; → fesseln **≃f·estigt** a ⟨übtr⟩ *calm and collected* ‖ ⟨jur⟩ durch Brauch ∼ *prescriptive* (*right*) °**~f·iedel** n *fiddling* **~f·ieder** n *feathers* [pl], *plumage* ‖ †: *fowls* pl **≃f·iedert** a *feathered, feathery*; bunt∼ *gayplumaged* ‖ ⟨bot⟩, (paarig) ∼ (*pari*)*pinnate* (*leaf*) **≃f·iel** [1. & 3. sg pret] v gefallen **~f·ilde** n ∼s/∼ ⟨poet & bib⟩ *fields* [pl], *open country*; die ∼ der Seligen, die Elysischen ∼ *Elysium* [L]; *the Elysian fields* pl **≃f·ingert** a ⟨zoo & bot⟩ *digitate*(*d*) °**~f·itze** n *intricacy, involution* ‖ da gibt's kein ∼! *I brook no contradiction* **~fl·acker** n *flickering* **≃fl·adert** a *streaky* (*wood*) **≃fl·ammt** a *watered* (*silk*); *moiré, chiné* [Fr] **~fl·atter** a *fluttering* **~fl·echt** a ∼(e)s/∼e **1.** *plait, plaiting*; Stroh≃ *plaited straw* ‖ *network, netting*; Zier(draht)≃ *tress*; (*filigree*) ‖ (∼ aus Weiden etc) *hurdle-work*; *wicker-work*; *wattle, wattling*; Rohr≃ *cane-work* **2.** ⟨anat⟩ (Nerven≃) *plexus* L **≃fl·eckt** a *variegated* ‖ *spotted* (*cow, dog*); *speckled* ‖ *freckled* (*skin*) ‖ ∼ mit *patched with*; *maculated with*; → fleckig °**~fl·enn(e)** n ∼es/ *whimpering, whining*; ⟨school⟩ *blubbering* °**~fl·icke** n ∼s/ → Flickwerk **~fl·immer** n ∼s/ *flickering, glittering*; *sparkling*; *twinkling, twinkle*

†**gefl·issen** a = beflissen **~tlich 1.** [a] *deliberate, intentional, premeditated*; *studied* (*insult, display*); *studious*; *wilful* **2.** [adv] *deliberately, designedly, intentionally, purposely, studiedly, studiously*; *to all intents*; jdm ∼ aus dem Wege gehen *to avoid* od *shun a p purposely*

Ge- ≃fl·ochten a [pp v flechten] *braided, plaited* (*band, hair, straw*); *twilled* (*mat*); *twisted*; ∼es Gras *twist of grass* ‖ aus Weidenzweigen ∼ *wicker*; .. ∼er Stuhl *wicker chair*; aus Rohr ∼er Sitz *cane-seat* ‖ ∼er Zaun *hurdle*; → Faschine ‖ ≃es n *twist* **≃fl·ogen** pp v fliegen **≃fl·ohen** pp v fliehen **≃fl·ossen** pp v fließen °**~fl·uche** n *cursing, swearing* **~fl·ügel** n *fowls* pl; ⟨cul⟩ *poultry* | ∼ausstellung [f] *poultry-show* ∼bürzel [m] *parson's* od *Pope's nose* ∼händler [m] *poulterer* ∼handlung [f] *poulterer's shop* ∼keule [f] → Gänse– ∼-zucht [f] *poultry-farming* ∼züchter [m] *poultry-farmer* **≃fl·ügelt** a *winged* (*insect*; *figure*) ‖ ⟨bot⟩ *winged* (*fruit, seed*) ‖ ⟨übtr⟩ ∼es Wort, ∼e Worte [pl] *winged words*; *familiar quotations*; *household words* pl **~fl·unker** m ∼s/ ⟨fig⟩ *fibbing*; *telling lies*; **~fl·üster** n ∼s/ *whisper*(*ing*); *murmur*(*ing*) ‖ ⟨übtr⟩ *rustling, susurration* (*of trees*) **~f·olge** n ∼s/∼ **1.** [abstr, nur sg] im ∼ der Ereignisse *consequent* (*up*)*on the events, as a consequence of the e.* ‖ (etw) im ∼ h = etw zur Folge h → Folge 4. **2.** [konkr] *retinue, suite* (Fr), *train*; *body of attendants* (od *followers, retainers*); im ∼ jds s *to be in a p's suite*; → Gefolgschaft leisten ‖ Trauer≃ *mourners*; es war ein gr ∼ *there were many mourners* **≃f·olgert** a *inferential* ‖ ⟨philos⟩ nur ∼ *ejective*; das nur ∼e *the eject*

Gef·olgs- ~herr m ⟨engl a. hist⟩ *liege*; (*liege*) *lord, overlord*; *the king* **~leute** pl **1.** ⟨hist⟩ = Lehnsleute **2.** *followers, retainers* [pl], *following* ‖ ⟨Am pol⟩ *henchmen* pl | ∼mann [m] **1.** = Lehnsmann **2.** *liege* (*his Majesty's lieges*); *follower, retainer*; ∼wesen [n] ⟨hist⟩ = Lehnsw.

Gef·olgschaft f **1.** [abstr] ⟨a. hist⟩ *allegiance* (jdm gegenüber *to a p*); *devotion, loyalty* (*to a p*); jdm ∼ leisten *to follow a p loyally* **2.** [konkr] *following* (*a large f.*); (*body of*) *adherents, attendants, followers* ‖ ⟨hist⟩ *body of loyal retainers* ‖ (Betriebs≃) *employees* pl; *personnel, staff* ‖ ⟨übtr⟩ diese Theorie verfügt über e–e gr ∼ *this theory has a strong following* | **~smitglied** n *employee*

Ge- ~fr·age n ∼s/ *questionings* pl **≃fr·agt** a ⟨com⟩ (sehr) ∼ s *to be in* (*great*) *demand* **≃fr·äßig** a *ravenous* (*beasts*), *voracious* ‖ *greedy* (*boy*); *gluttonous*; ⟨sl⟩ *gutsy* ‖ ⟨übtr⟩ das ∼e Element *the devouring element*; *the fire* ‖ ⟨fig⟩ *greedy*; °dumm *or* faul u ∼ *stupid* od *lazy and arrogant* ‖ → gierig | ≃keit [f] ∼/ *ravenousness, voracity* ‖ *greediness, gluttony* **~fr·eite** [der ∼, ein ∼er] ∼n/∼n ⟨mil⟩ *lance-corporal* °**~fr·esse** n ∼s/ *gluttony*; *gormandizing*; ⟨sl⟩ *guzzle*

G(e)fr·est n ∼s/ [österr] = Ärger; es ist ein ∼ mit ihm *he is a* (*great*) *nuisance*

Gefr·ier- (→ gefrieren) **~anlage** f *refrigerating-plant*; Schiff mit ∼ *cold vessel* **~apparat** m = –maschine **~fach** n *cold safe* **~fisch** m *frozen fish* **~fleisch** n (*quick-*)*frozen meat*, ⟨fam⟩ *frigo* **~maschine** f *freezer*; *freezing* (od *refrigerating*)-*machine* **~nahrungsmittel** n pl *frozen food* **~pakkungskarton** m *boxboard for frozen foodstuffs* **~punkt** m *freezing-point*; *point of congelation*; *zero* (auf dem ∼ *at z.*; auf den ∼ gesunken *down to z.*) ‖ → Null | ∼messer [m] *cyroscope* ‖ ∼(s)ern·iedrigung [f] *fr.-p. depression* **~salz** n *freezing-salt* **~schutzmittel** n *anti-freezing medium* ⟨fam⟩ *antifreeze* **~trocknung** f *freeze-drying*

Ge- ≃fr·ierbar a *congealable* **≃fr·ieren I.** vi (→ frieren) [s] **1.** *to freeze* (*water freezes at* ..); *to congeal* **≃friertrocknen** vt [h] ⟨tech⟩ *to freeze dry* ‖ gefriergetrocknetes Produkt *freeze-dried product*; das Wasser, der Teich ist **≃froren** *the water, the pond is* (od *has*) *frozen*; die Fenster sind g.n *the windows are frozen* (od *frosted*) **2.** ⟨übtr⟩ das Blut gefror in den Adern *the blood froze in the veins*; bei dem Anblick g.r ihm das B. in den A. *the sight made his blood freeze* (od *run cold*); *the sight froze his blood* ‖ mir sind die Füße steif g.n *my feet are as cold as ice* (od *stiff with cold*) ‖ → gerinnen **3.** ∼ m *to congeal, to freeze* **II.** ≃ n *freezing*; *congelation*; (Kühlhalten) *refrigeration* | ∼es [n] ⟨cul⟩ *ice*; *ice-cream* **~f·üge** n ∼s/∼ *joints* pl (*of beams*) ‖ (of wood, metal, etc.) *grain, texture* | ⟨übtr⟩ *make, makeup*; *texture* (*of snow*) ‖ ⟨fig⟩ *fabric* (*the social f.*), *framework* (*of society*), *structure* (*of a play*); geistiges ∼ *mental make-up* (*of a p*); ⟨Am a.⟩ *set-up* (*of a p's life*) **≃f·ügig** (*≃**f·üge**) a (P) *compliant, flexible, malleable* (*character*), *pliable, pliant, tractable*; *amenable*; *docile*; *submissive*; → fügsam ‖ jdn ∼ m *to bring a p to heel*; *to melt a p* (od *a p's heart*); sich [dat] .. *to bend a p to one's will* | **≃keit** f *malleability, pliability, pliancy, tractability*; *docility*; *submissiveness*

Gef·ühl n ∼(e)s/∼e **1.** (∼ssinn) *sense of feeling* (od *touch*); *touch* **2.** (Empfindung) *feeling, sensation, sense* ‖ ein ∼ des Hungers, Hunger≃ *a sinking in the stomach* ‖ ein ∼ der Wärme, Wärme≃ *a sensation* (od *sense*) *of warmth*; Schmerz≃ *sensation of pain* ‖ kein ∼ in den Fingern h *to habe lost all sensation of feeling in one's fingers* ‖ etw im ∼ h *to sense a th*; *to feel a th instinctively* **3.** (seelisches ∼) ⟨psych⟩ *emotion*; *feeling* (f *for*); *sensation*; *sentiment* ‖ ∼ der Angst *or* Beklommenheit, beängstigendes ∼ *sinking at the heart*; bedrückendes ∼ *mood of oppression*; erhebendes ∼ *feeling of exaltation*; ∼ der Freude *feeling* (od *sense*) *of joy*; ∼ der Furcht *sensation* *of fear, sense of dread* ‖ kein ~ des Hasses *no feeling* (wegen *about*) ‖ ~ der Scham, Scham≗ *shame* | **ausgeprägtes** ~ f *high regard for* ‖ Fingerspitzen≗ → Fingerspitze ‖ deutliches ~ (*she had*) *more than a feeling* ‖ durchdringendes, plötzliches ~ *thrill*; dunkles ~ *indistinct feeling*; ⟨Am sl⟩ *hunch*; → Ahnung ‖ fliegerisches ~ ⟨aero sl⟩ *feel of the stick* ‖ unbehagliches ~ *a feeling of discomfort* ‖ patriotisches, religiöses ~ *patriotic, religious sentiment* ‖ ein Mann v ~ *a man of feeling* (od *sentiment*) | ⟨arts, etc.⟩ *feeling* od *feel* (f *for*); *sense* (f *of*); ~ f das Schöne *feeling for* (od *sense of*) *beauty*; ~ f Anstand, Recht u Unrecht *sense of decency, of right or wrong* ‖ musikalisches ~ → Gehör ‖ Sprach≗ *linguistic feeling* (od *instinct*) **4.** ein ~ **ansprechen** ⟨psych⟩ *to touch a string*; ein ~ beschleicht uns *a feeling creeps over us* ‖ die ~e gingen hoch *or* wurden sehr erregt *feeling went high* ‖ er ist **ganz** ~ *he is very sensitive* ‖ °das ist das **höchste der ~e** *that's as far as we can go*; *that's the utmost concession we can make* | jdm das ~ **geben** f *to make a p feel ..* | **ein ~ h für jdn** *to feel for a p* ‖ ein warmes ~ h für *to have a soft place in one's heart for a p* ‖ ein gewisses ~ h, daß .. *to have a feeling that ..*; ich habe das ~, daß .. *I have the impression, I think that ..* ‖ ich habe das ~, wie .. *it feels to me like ..* ‖ ein sicheres ~ h, daß .. *to feel in one's bones that ..* ‖ kein ~ h *to be without any feeling*(*s*); *to have no sense* (f *of*) ‖ ein zärtliches ~ f jdn h *to feel tenderly for a p* | s–m ~ nachgehen *to follow one's nose* | es geht s–n ~en **nahe** *it comes home to his feelings* | s–e ~e zur Schau tragen *to wear one's heart on one's sleeve* ‖ jds ~e teilen *to feel exactly the same as a p* (*does*) ‖ verhaltene, zurückgestaute ~e *pent-up feelings* ‖ jds ~e verletzen *to hurt a p's feelings* | **an** das ~ appellieren *to appeal to the feelings* (od *emotions*) ‖ es geht **gegen** mein ~ *it goes against the grain* ‖ (etw) **im** ~ h *to feel instinctively*; *to sense* ‖ **mit** ~ *feelingly*; *sensitively*; (*to speak*) *with feeling*; ⟨mus⟩ (*to play*) *with expression* ‖ mit gemischten ~en *with mixed feelings* ‖ dem **~ nach** *to the feel* od *touch* (*it is silk to the f.*)

gef·ühllos a **1.** *insensate, insentient* (*world, nature*); *inaminate* **2.** ⟨übtr⟩ (P) *callous, hard-hearted, remorseless, unfeeling*; *devoid of feeling* | **≗igkeit** f ⟨übtr⟩ *callosity, unfeelingness*

Gef·ühls- [in comp] *emotional* °**~akrobat** m = °Gemütsakrobat **~anwandlung** f *emotion*; ohne ~ *unemotional, -ally* **~art** f *disposition*; *frame of mind* **~ausbruch** m *outburst of emotion*; ⟨Am sl⟩ *splurge* **~ausdruck** m *emotional expression*; *lyricism* **≗betont** a *emotional* (*word*); *emotionally-toned* (*expression*); nicht ~ *unemotional* ‖ °**~duselei** f *sentimentality, sentimentalism*; *emotionalism*; *maudlin, mawkishness* **~kraft** f *intensity* **~lage** f *mood* **~leben** n *feeling-life, emotional life* **~mangel** m *insentience* **≗mäßig 1.** [a] *emotional, emotive*; ~e Beschaffenheit, Natur *emotionality* **2.** [adv] *emotionally, sentimentally* **~mensch** m *emotional* (od *sentimental*) *man* **~philosophie** f *emotional philosophy* **~politik** f *policy determined by sentiment* **~regung** f *emotion*; *sentiment* **≗selig** a *sentimental*; *maudlin, mawkish*; *mushy* **~seligkeit** f = –duselei **~sinn** m *sense of feeling* **~überschwang** m *fervour of emotion*; *hwyl* **~wallung** f *thrill*; *emotional orgasm* **~welt** f *sphere of feeling* **~wert** m *sentimental value*

Ge- **≗f·ühlt** a *felt*; tief~ *deep-felt* (*gratitude*) **≗f·ühlvoll 1.** [a] *feeling, tender*; in ~er Weise *feelingly* ‖ *emotional* (*poetry*); *lyric*(*al*) **2.** [adv] *feelingly*; *with feeling* ‖ ~ differenziert *distinctive in expressiveness* od *emotion* **≗f·üllt** a *filled*; ⟨bot⟩ *double* (*roses*); ~e Schokolade *chocolate cream*; nicht ganz ~ *on ullage* **≗f·unden** a ⟨fig⟩ °~es Fressen → Fressen 2. **≗f·ünft** a *quinary* °**~f·unkel** n = Geflimmer **≗f·urcht** a *farrowed, furrowy*; *wrinkled, wrinkly* (*face*) ‖ *rutted, rutty* (*road*) ‖ ⟨anat & bot⟩ *sulcate*(*d*); *fluted* **≗f·ürchtet** a *dreaded* (*foe, master*); *redoubtable* (*player*) ‖ die ~sten sind .. *the most feared are ..* **≗f·ürstet** a; ~ w *to become possessed of princely rights* **≗g·abelt** a *forked* **~g·acker** a ~s/ *cackling*; *cackles* pl **≗g·angen** pp v gehen **≗g·eben** [pp v geben] **1.** [pred] es war ihm nicht ~ *it was not given to him* (*to do*) ‖ die Fähigkeit war ihm nicht ~ *he was not gifted with the skill* ‖ ⟨a. math⟩ als Grundlage ~ *given* (*given the fact, the change is a consequence of ..*) ‖ (etw) als ~ hinnehmen, voraussetzen *to take for granted* **2.** [attr] *given*; unter den ~en Umständen *under the g. conditions* ‖ die ~e Alternative *the proper alternative* ‖ ~e Größe *given quantity*; ~e Größe, Tatsache (etc) *datum* L [pl *data*]; ~es Niveau *datum-level* ‖ der ~e Ort *the likely place* ‖ zu ~er Zeit *when occasion arises*; *on occasion*; *if need be* **3.** das ≗e *the suitable*; *the* (*only*) *thing*; das ist das ≗e *that is the thing* (f *for*); ⟨fam⟩ *that's the ticket* **≗g·ebenenfalls** adv *in such a case* (od *event*); *when occasion arises*; *possibly*; *in appropriate instances*; ~ sind auch die Namen der .. anzugeben *give also the names of .., if any* od *if indicated, if applicable* ‖ ich hoffe, daß Sie mich ~ rufen w *I do hope that you will consider calling me* **~g·ebenheit** f (*given*) *fact*; *reality* [pl *–ties*]; *situation, condition*; *datum* L; ~en [pl] *data* pl ‖ nehmen wir es als ~ *let's come round to facts*; *let's take it for granted, let's accept* (*that ..*), *let us assume* (*for the sake of argument*)

g·egen I. prep [mit acc] **1.** ⟨eig⟩ **(Richtung)** *against*; *place the bicycle against the wall* ‖ *to hold up to the light* ‖ abstechend ~ *against* (*the background*) ‖ ~ Süden (etc) *towards the south* **2. (wider) a.** *against* ‖ Kampf ~ *fight against* od *with* (⟨Am⟩ *on*); *to fight against* (od *with*); Mann ~ Mann k. *to fight hand to hand* ‖ stoßen ~ *to push against*; schlagen ~ (of waves) *to beat against* **b.** ⟨übtr⟩ *against*; ~ jdn sein *to oppose a p*; ⟨Am a.⟩ *to be on* (absolut .. *dead against*) *a p*; ⟨fam⟩ er hat was ~ mich *he is down on me* ‖ ~ etw s *to be* (od *to set one's face*) *against a th*; *to object to a th* ‖ (jdn) schützen ~ *to defend* od *protect against* od *from* ‖ sicher ~ *safe from*, → gefeit | *contrary to* (*the agreement*); *contrary to human nature, contrary to reason*; *contrary to decency* ‖ → Strich, Strom **c.** ⟨jur⟩ *versus* (abbr *v, vs*); N. ~ X. *N. versus X.* **d.** Heilmittel, Mittel ~ *remedy for* (*gout*); Schloß ~ .. *lock to prevent ..* **3. (Zeit)** *towards*; *towards the end of the 16th c.* ‖ *towards* (od [*somewhere*] *about*; *just on*) *10 o'clock* ‖ etwa ~ Mittag *some time about midday* **4.** ~ 1000 Leute *about a thousand people* **5.** ⟨übtr⟩ **[nach Subst. u Adj]** *towards, to* ‖ Abneigung ~ *aversion to* ‖ *grateful to a p* ‖ → gerecht etc ‖ *kindness to* ‖ *hatred of* od *against* ‖ *severe on, strict with*; → 3. d. **6.** ⟨übtr⟩ **a.** (als Ersatz, Umtausch f) *for*; *in exchange* (od *return*) *for* ‖ *against payment*; ~ B. v *on payment of* ‖ *for prompt* (od *ready*) *cash*; *cash down* ‖ → Bürgschaft ‖ *against receipt* ‖ *to exchange for gold* **b.** 10 ~ 1 wetten *to bet 10 to one* **c.** (im Vergleich z) *in* (od *by*) *comparison with*; *compared with* ‖ es war kein V. (*or* nichts im V.) ~ das .. *it was nothing to* (od *nothing compared with*) *that of the day before*; *it does not compare with that of the d. b.* ‖ die Sitten h sich ~ früher sehr geändert *compared with former days customs have greatly changed* ‖ ~ letztes Jahr (*an increase of £ 300*) *on last year* ‖ eins ~ das andere halten *to compare one th with the other* **II.** adv *contra*, ⟨fam⟩ *con*; für u ~ → für II.

G·egen- [in comp] *counter* (*c.*); *opposite*; *anti-*; *adverse, hostile* ‖ *return*; *in return* **~abzug** m *counter-trace* **~aktion** f *counterblast* (gegen *to*); → –maßnahme **~angebot** n *counter-offer* **~angriff** m ⟨mil⟩ *c.attack* ‖ zum ~ übergehen *to carry the* *war into the enemy's camp* **~anklage** f *counter-charge*; ∼ erheben gegen jdn *to countercharge a p* **~anschlag** m *counterplot*; *countermine*; e–n ∼ m *to counterplot*; (etw) durch ∼ vereiteln *to countermine* **~anspruch** m *counter-claim* **~anstrengung** f *antagonistic effort* **~antrag** m ⟨parl⟩ *c.-motion* **~anzeige** f ⟨med⟩ *contra-indication* **~bedingung** f *counter-stipulation* **~befehl** m *c.-order, countermand* **~bemerkung** f = Erwiderung, Entgegnung **~beschuldigung** f = –anklage **~besuch** m *return-visit* (od *-call*); jdm e–n ∼ m *to return a p's visit* **~bewegung** f *c.-movement*; ⟨fig⟩ *counterblast* (gegen *to*); → Reaktion **~beweis** m *c.-evidence, rebutting ev.* **~bild** n *antitype* **~bogen** m ⟨arch⟩ *counter-arch*; *inverted arch* **~buch** m ⟨com⟩ *bank-book* **~buchung** f ⟨com⟩ *cross-entry* **~bürgschaft** f *counter-security* **~dampf** m *c.-steam* **~deckung** f ⟨st exch⟩ *hedge* **~dienst** m *return-service*; *reciprocal service*; *return*; als ∼ *in return* ‖ jdm e–n ∼ leisten *to return a p's service*; *to do a p a service in return* ‖ ⟨com⟩ z ∼en gern bereit (*to be*) *pleased to reciprocate* **~druck** m *c.-pressure*; ⟨fig⟩ *reaction* ‖ ∼schraube [f] ⟨tech⟩ *thrust(ing)-screw* **≃einander** → d. **~elektrode** f *backing electrode*, ⟨Am⟩ *welding ground* **~erklärung** f *c.-declaration* **~farbe** f *complementary colour* **~feld** n ⟨phys⟩ *opposing field* **~feuer** n (bei Waldbrand) *counter-fire* **~flügel** m *counter-vane* **~forderung** f *c.-claim*; *set-off*; e–e ∼ geltend m *to interpose a counterclaim*; e–e Summe als ∼ beanspruchen *to c.-claim a sum*; etw als ∼ verlangen *to c.-claim for a th* **~frage** f (schärfere) *rebuttal* **~füßler** m pl *antipodes* pl **~geschenk** n *return-gift*; *present in return*; *return* (als ∼ *in r.*) ‖ jdm ein ∼ m *to return a p's present* **~gewicht** n *c.balance*, *b. weight*, *c.-weight* (gegen, zu *to*); ein ∼ in (etw) h *to be c.balanded by*; e–r S das ∼ halten *to c.balance a th*; als ∼ wirken z etw *to c.poise a th* **~gift** n *antivenene, antidote*; ⟨biol⟩ (im Blut) *antitoxin* ‖ ⟨fig⟩ *antidote* (*against*); *remedy* (gegen *for*) **~grund** m *counter-argument*; *counter-reason* **~gruß** m *bow in return*, *r.-greeting*; ⟨mar⟩ *r. salute* **~hieb** m *c.stroke* **~kaiser** m *anti-emperor* **~kandidat** m *rival candidate*; Wahl ohne ∼en *uncontested election* **~keil** m ⟨tech⟩ *gib* **~klage** f ⟨jur⟩ *c.charge* **~kompliment** n *return compliment* **~könig** m *anti-king* **~kopplung** f ⟨el⟩ *negative* od *degenerative feedback* **~kraft** f *antagonistic* (od *opposing*) *force* **~krümmung** f *reverse curve* **~kurs** m ⟨mar⟩ *opposite course*; *reciprocal heading* **~lauf** m *oppositional movement* **≃läufig** a *contrarotating* **~leistung** f *return*; als ∼ *in r.*; e–e ∼ m *to make a r.* (f *for*) ‖ → Entschädigung ‖ Leistung u ∼ *give and take* ‖ ⟨jur, contr⟩ *consideration* **~licht** n *backlight*; ∼aufnahme [f] *against-the-light view*; ∼beleuchtung [f] *rear lighting*; ∼blende [f] *lens-shade* **~liebe** f ⟨fig⟩ *acknowledgement, approval* ‖ der Vorschlag fand (*or* mit diesem V. fand er) k–e ∼ *the proposal was not reciprocated* (od *accepted*) **~logarithmus** m ⟨math⟩ *antilogarithm* **~maßnahme** f *c.-measure* (treffen *to take*); als ∼ *as a c.-m.* ‖ drastische ∼ *counterblast* **~meinung** f *contrary opinion* **~mine** f ⟨mil⟩ *c.mine* **~mittel** n *antidote* (gegen *against, to*) ⟨a. fig⟩; *corrective measures*; *remedy* (gegen *for*) **~molekül** n *antiparticle* **~mutter** f ⟨tech⟩ *lock nut* **~offensive** f ⟨mil⟩ *counter offensive* **~operation** f *c.-move* **~order** f *c.-order*; *c.mand* **~papst** m *antipope* **~part** m = Gegner, Gegenspieler ‖ *c.part*; = Gegenstück **~partei** f *the opposite* (od *other*) *party*; ⟨jur⟩ *the other side* **~pfand** n *c.-pledge* **~pfeiler** m ⟨arch⟩ *c.fort, buttress* **~pol** m *antipole* **~posten** m ⟨com⟩ *cross-entry*; *set-off* **~probe** *c.-* (od *control-*, *check-*)*test* *c.-* (od *control-*)*test* od *-proof* **~prophet** m *antiprophet* **~rechnung** f ⟨com⟩ *c.-account* (od *invoice*) ‖ (z verrechnende Forderung) *set-off*; *offset* **~rede** f *contradiction*; → Entgegnung, Einwendung **~reform** f *counter-reform* **~reformation** f ⟨ec hist⟩ *c.-reformation* (⟨a.⟩ Kunst der ∼) **~reizmittel** n ⟨med⟩ *c.-irritant* **~revolution** f *c.-revolution* **~ruf** m *c.-shout* **~saldo** m ⟨com⟩ *c.balance* **~satz** m → d. **~scheibe** f ⟨mach⟩ *c.-pulley* **~schein** m ⟨astr⟩ *opposition* **~schenkung** f = –geschenk **~schlag** m *c.-* (od *return*)*-blow*, *c.stroke*; zum ∼ ausholen *to prepare for a c.-blow* ‖ ⟨box⟩ *counter*; e–n ∼ tun *to c.* **~schraube** f ⟨tech⟩ *check-bolt* **~schrift** f *written refutation*; → Erwiderung **~schritt** m ⟨fig⟩ *c.-move* (od *measure*) **~see** f ⟨mar⟩ (rollende See gegen den Kurs) *head-sea* **~seite** f *the opposite* (od *other*) *side* (od *opposing party*) **≃seitig** a → d. **~signal** a *c.-signal* **~sonne** f ⟨astr⟩ *c.-glow*; *anti-sun* **~spieler** m ⟨sport⟩ *opposite number* ‖ ⟨Lit & theat⟩ *antagonist* ‖ ⟨übtr⟩ *opponent* **~sprechanlage** f *intercom*(*munication*) *system*, (*wireless*) *intercom* **~(sprech)verkehr** m ⟨wir etc⟩ *duplex communication* **~stand** m → d. **~stimme** f ⟨mus⟩ *c.part* ‖ ⟨parl⟩ *adverse vote*, ⟨Am⟩ *blackball*; die ∼n [pl] *the cons* **~stoß** m *c.stroke*; *counterblast*; ⟨Am⟩ *c.drive* ‖ ⟨mil⟩ *immediate c.attack*; → –angriff **~strom** m ⟨tech⟩ *c.-current*; ∼prinzip [n] *c.-c. principle* **~strömung** f *c.-current* ‖ ⟨fig⟩ *reaction* (gegen *against, from*); → –bewegung **~strophe** f ⟨pros⟩ *antistrophe* **~stück** n *c.part* (z *to*); *opposite number*; *companion-piece*; *mating part*; *equivalent* (z *of*); *fellow* (*the f. is missing*); → Doppelgänger **~stufe** (Treppe) *c.march* **~taktschaltung** f *push-pull connection* **~teil** n → d. **≃über** adv → d. **~verkehr** m *approaching* od *oncoming, opposing traffic*; Straße mit ∼ *two-way street* **~ u Wechselverkehr** ⟨wir⟩ *two-way communication* **~verpflichtung** f *c.-obligation* **~versicherung** f ⟨com⟩ *reciprocal assurance* **~visite** f = –besuch **~vormund** m *c.-guardian, supervising g.* **~vorstellungen** f pl *remonstrances* **~vorschlag** m *c.-proposal*; e–n ∼ m *to advance a c.-p.* **~wall** m ⟨fort⟩ *c.scarp*; *c.work* **~wart** → d. **~wechsel** m ⟨com⟩ *c.-bill* **~wehr** f *defence, resistance*; sich zur ∼ setzen *to offer opposition* od *resistance, to resist* **~wert** m (*equivalent*) *value* (f *for*); *equivalent*; den ∼ f sein Geld erhalten *to get full value for one's money* ‖ ∼mittel [n pl] *c.part funds* **~wind** m ⟨mar⟩ *head-wind*; *contrary wind* **~winkel** m ⟨math⟩ *alternate* (od *opposite*) *angle* **~wirkung** f *c.-action*; *c.check* (gegen *to*); *c.-effect*; *reaction* (auf *to*); ⟨biol⟩ *antagonism*; Wirkung u ∼ *check and c.check* **~zeichen** n ⟨com⟩ *c.mark* **≃|zeichnen** vt [h] *to c.sign* **~zeichnung** f *c.-signature* **~zeuge** m ⟨jur⟩ *c.-witness* **~zeugnis** n *c.-witness* **~zug** m ⟨chess & übtr⟩ *c.-move* ‖ ⟨rail⟩ *same train running in opposite direction*, ⟨Am⟩ *opposing train*

G·egend f ∼/∼en **1.** (Landschaft) *tract of country*; *region*; schöne bewaldete ∼ *fine wooded country*; die Polar≃en [pl] *the Artic regions* pl ‖ die oberen ∼en der Luft *the upper regions of the air*; → Zone **2.** (Distrikt) *district, part, quarter, region*; ⟨Am⟩ *section*; → Himmels≃ ‖ die Rhein≃ *the Rhine district* ‖ aus welcher ∼ stammen Sie? *what part do you come from*? ‖ in dieser ∼ *in these parts*; *about here*; als er in diese ∼ kam *when he came to these parts* ‖ (ich wüßte gern) in welcher ∼ er wohnt (..) *whereabouts he lives* **3.** (Umgegend) *environs* pl, *neighbourhood, surroundings* pl (*of a place*); in der ∼ v Berlin *in the n. of Berlin*; in der ∼ des Schlosses *close by the castle* ‖ die ganze ∼ spricht davon *it is the talk of the neighbourhood* (od *in everybody's mouth*) ‖ (Umgebung) wir wohnen in e–r schönen ∼ *we live in a beautiful neighbourhood* **4.** ⟨med⟩ *region, zone*; die ∼ des Unterleibs, die Unterleibs≃ *the abdominal region*; in der Nieren≃ *in the kidney zone*

g·egen- ~ein·ander adv *against* (od *from*) *one another, against* (od *from*) *each other* ‖ ⟨übtr⟩ (*kind*) *to one another*; *to each other*; gegenseitig ‖

(Dinge) ~|halten, ~|stellen *to compare* | ≃haltung, ~stellung [f] *comparison* **≃satz** m ~es/≃e *oppositeness, contrast* (z *to*); → Gegenteil ‖ Schwarz ist ein ~ z Weiß *black is a c. to white* ‖ *antagonism* (zw *between*); *antithesis* [Gr] (v, z *of, to*); *opposition* (z *to*); → Widerspruch | **im ~ z** *in contrast with*; *contrary to*; *in contradistinction to* od *from*; *in opposition to*; *unlike* (*u. his predecessor*); *diverging* od *differing from* ‖ im ~ zu *unlike* (*a th*); im ~ hierzu *over against this* ‖ im ~ **stehen** *to contradict each other*; im ~ stehen z *to be in contrast to*; *to go contrary to*; *to run counter to*; *to contradict, oppose*; *to be in conflict with* ‖ (etw) in ~ stellen *to place* od *set in contrast*; *to contrast* (mit *with*) *to match* od *set a th against* ‖ e–n ~ konstruieren *to point a contrast* **~sätzlich 1.** [a] *antagonistic* (*force, inclination*); *hostile*; *opposing, oppositional*; ~e Haltung *antagonism*; → entgegengesetzt, feindlich, widrig **2.** [adv] *antagonistically* | ≃keit [f] *antagonism* **≃satzpaar** n *contrasted pair*; in ~en *in c. pairs*

g·egenseitig 1. [a] *mutual* (*friendship*), *reciprocal* (*limitation of ..*); → gemeinsam, reziprok ‖ ~e Abhängigkeit *interdependence*; in ~er Anlehnung ⟨mil⟩ (*to be stationed*) *adjacent to other units*; ~e Beeinflussung *interaction, interplay*; ~e Behinderung *mutual interference*; ~e Beziehung *interrelation, reciprocity* ‖ ~e Durchdringung *interpenetration* ‖ ~e Hilfe *or* Reklame ⟨Am⟩ *log-rolling* ‖ ~es Verhältnis *correlation, interrelation*; in ~em V. stehen *to correlate* (z *to, with*); (Dinge) in ~es V. bringen *to correlate* (*with*) ‖ ~e Verbindung *interconnection*; in ~er V. stehen *to intercommunicate, to interconnect* ‖ ~er Verkehr *intercommunication* ‖ ~e Wirkung *interaction* **2.** [adv] *mutually, reciprocally* ‖ (bei Verben) *one another, each other*; → einander | *inter–*: ~ abhängig *interdependent*; ~ v einander abhängig s ⟨fig⟩ *to be interrelated* ‖ sich ~ beeinflussen *to interact* ‖ sich ~ durchdringen *to interpenetrate* ‖ sie luden sich ~ z Abendessen ein *they dined each other* ‖ sich ~ Anekdoten erzählen ⟨fam⟩ *to swap* (od *swop*) *anecdotes* (od *yarns*) ‖ sich ~ vernichtend *internecine* (*fight*) | **≃keit** f *mutuality, reciprocity* ‖ auf ~ beruhen *to be reciprocal* (*their love is r.*); ⟨ins⟩ auf ~ beruhend *mutual*; Lebensversicherung auf ~ *mutual life insurance*; Versicherungsgesellschaft auf ~ *mutual insurance-company*

G·egenseitigkeits- ~klausel [f] *reciprocity-clause* ~pakt, ~vertrag [m] ⟨pol⟩ *treaty of mutual assistance* ~prinzip [n] *principle of reciprocity* ~verein [m] *mutual benefit society* od *association*; *mutual benevolent society*

G·egen- ~stand m ~(e)s/≃e **A.** ⟨eig⟩ *object*; *material thing*; realer ~ *substance* ‖ fester, runder, spitzer ~ *solid, round, pointed object* ‖ (notwendige, technische) ≃e [pl] (zur Ausrüstung) *paraphernalia* [L pl] **B.** ⟨übtr⟩ **1.** (~ des Denkens, Fühlens) *object* ‖ der ~ s–s Hasses *the object of his hatred*; ~ des Mitleids *object of pity* ‖ er war ihnen ein ~ des Abscheus *he was their* (*pet*) *aversion* ‖ ~ des Arguments *point of issue* (*of discussion*) ‖ ~ des Entsetzens (*object of*) *horror*; ~ der Freude (*object of*) *joy*; der ~ des Gelächters *the laughing-stock*; ~ des Spottes *mockery* (*to make m. of a p*) ‖ er war der ~ begeisterter Kundgebungen *he was the object of enthusiastic demonstrations* ‖ ~ (e–r Verhandlung) *item* **2.** (Versuchs≃) *subject* (*he was made the subject of an experiment*) **3.** (~ der Unterhaltung etc) *subject* | ⟨Lit⟩ *subject* (*of a novel, play*); *theme*; (~sstoff) *subject-matter* | der eigentliche ~ *the point, the main issue*; die Aufmerksamkeit vom (eigentl.) ~ ablenken *to divert attention from the main issue*; v ~ abschweifen *to wander from the point*; *to be wandering*; v ~ abspringen *to fly off from one's word at a tangent*; gerade auf den ~ losgehen *to go straight to the point*; etw zum ~ der Kritik m *to subject a th to criticism*; die S ist z ~ e–s Notenwechsels gemacht worden *the matter has given rise to an exchange of notes* **≃ständig** a ⟨bot⟩ *opposite* (*leaves*) **≃ständlich** a *concrete*; *objective* ‖ *representational* (*picture, painting, art*), ~e Malerei *representationalism* ‖ *objective* (*art*) | ≃keit [f] *objectivity* **≃standslos** a *immaterial, intangible, subtile, illusory, unreal, abstract*; *unsound*; *baseless, groundless* (*fears*), *unfounded* (*rumours*); als ~ erweisen *to prove as unfounded* ‖ *invalid* (*argument, objections*); ⟨arts⟩ *non-representational* | [pred] *settled*; *superfluous, unnecessary, without foundation* ‖ ~ w (of criticism) *to fall to the ground*; (nach s–m Tode) ist der Prozeß ~ geworden *the lawsuit has become unnecessary*; die Frage ist ~ geworden *the question does not arise* **~standstheorie** f ⟨philos⟩ *objectology* **~störmaßnahmen** f pl ⟨mil wir⟩ *anti-jamming* N

Gegen- ~teil n: das ~ *the contrary* (od *opposite, reserve*) ‖ eher zufrieden als das ~ *rather pleased than otherwise* ‖ das genaue ~ z *quite the contrary to*; *the very opposite of* (*he is .. of his brother*); gerade das ~ *just the opposite* ‖ im ~ *on the contrary*; ganz im ~ *quite the contrary* (od *reverse*); nein, im ~ *Oh no we will not* ‖ das ~ davon ist wahr *the reverse of it is true* ‖ wenn nicht das ~ angegeben ist *unless mention is made to the contrary* ‖ ich behaupte das ~ *I maintain the contrary* ‖ (etw) ins ~ verdrehen *to reverse*; *to distort* ‖ ins ~ umschlagen *to turn out to nothing* od *the contrary*; *to fall over backward* **≃teilig** a *contrary* (*opinion*), *opposite* ‖ e–e ~e Antwort *an answer to the contrary*; die ~en Berichte *the reports to the c.* ‖ nichts ≃es *not .. anything* (od *nothing*) *to the contrary*

gegen·über 1. [adv] *opposite*; *over the way*; *vis-a-vis* (v *to*); ⟨typ⟩ *on the facing page*; mir ~, ~ v mir *opposite me, opposite to me, facing me* ‖ der Kirche ~ *opposite the church* ‖ das Haus ~ *the house, the gentleman opposite*; der Herr mir ~ *the g. facing me*; *my vis-a-vis* ‖ ⟨fig⟩ sich e–r harten Wirklichkeit ~ sehen *to find o.s. up against* (od *confronted with*) *a hard reality* **2.** [prep mit dat] **a.** ⟨eig⟩ ~ der Kirche *over against the church, opposite the ch.* ‖ ~ jdm *vis-a-vis a p* **b.** ⟨übtr & fig⟩ ich behaupte dir ~ *I put it to you* (*that*); (*he was very kind*) *to me*; (*obligations, indebtedness*) *to* (*a p*) ‖ *in relation to* (*life*) ‖ *in comparison with*, (*as*) *compared with*; *the attendance was 44 as against 34 last month* ‖ *an increase of £ 50 on last year* ‖ *in the face of these facts* | [bei Adj. u Subst.] *towards, to*; → gegen I. 4. **3.** ≃ n *vis-a-vis* (*my v.*); (jdn) als ~ h *to have for one's v.*

gegen·über- pref [betont, trennbar] **~|liegen** vi [h] e–r S ~ *to be opposite to a th* ‖ ⟨geom⟩ e–r Seite ~ *to be subtended by a side*; (of a side) (e–m Winkel) ~ *to subtend* ‖ ~d *facing*; *opposite, other* (*side*) ‖ in der –den Ecke *in the far corner* **~|sitzen** vi [h] jdm ~ *to sit opposite* (od *vis-a-vis*) *a p* ‖ e–a ~ *to sit vis-a-vis* **~|stehen** [h] vi; e–r S ~ *to face a th*; *to be opposite to a th* ‖ jdm ~ *to be face to face with a p*; *to be in a p's presence*; e–a ~ *to stand face to face*; sich feindlich ~ *to be opposed to each other, to fight* (*against*) *one another* ‖ ⟨fig⟩ Schwierigkeiten ~ *to be up against difficulties*; *to be confronted with d.* **~|stellen** vt [h] (etw) *to oppose* (e–r S *to a th*); e–e S e–r anderen ~ *to contrast one th with another*; *to place* od *set a th over against another* → vergleichen ‖ (jdn) e–r S ~ *to bring up against a th* (*to be brought up against factors which ..*); *to bring a p face-to-face* (od *to confront a p*) *with a th* ‖ jdn e–r P ~ *to pit a p against a p* (*the army had been pitted against superior forces*); sich jdm ~ *to confront a p* ‖ **≃stellung** f *confronting* (mit *with*); *opposition* ‖ *antithesis* ‖ *contrast* ‖ ⟨jur⟩ *confrontation* **~|tre-**

ten vi [s] jdm, e–r S ~ *to confront* od *face a p, a th*; → feindlich

G·egenwart f **1.** (Anwesenheit) *presence*; in jds ~ *in the presence of a p, in a p's presence* || Geistes≈ *presence of mind* **2.** (gegenwärtige Zeit) die ~ *the present; the present time*; in der ~ *in the present day* (od *time*); es verbindet die ~ mit der Vergangenheit *it unites the present with the past* || die Technik der ~ *present-day technics, the t. of the present day* **3.** ⟨gram⟩ *the present; the present tense* **g·egenwärtig** [pred a & adv; a. gegenw·ärtig] **I.** [a] **1.** [attr] *present* (*moment, time*); *actual* (*position*) || *current* (*month*) **2.** [pred] **a.** (anwesend) *present* (bei .. *at a discussion*) **b.** ⟨übtr⟩ jdm ~ s (S) *to be present to a p's mind* (od *in one's memory*); das macht uns .. ~ *that brings us face to face with* .. **II.** [adv] *at present, at the present moment; actually* (*in power*); *nowadays*; (*the greatest*) *living* (*artist*) **G·egenwärtige** n [das ~, ein ~s] durch ~s ⟨com⟩ *by the present*; ⟨jur⟩ *by these presents* || der Schreiber des ~n *the present writer* **G·egenwarts-** [in comp] *present-day* (od *time*) **~geschehen** n *present-day happenings* od *events* pl; *actualities* [pl] *of the present day* **~kunde** f ⟨school⟩ *current affairs* **≈nahe** a *actual; topical* (*subjects*) **~wert** m *present* od *actual value*

ge- **~g·essen** pp v essen **~gl·iedert** a ⟨übtr⟩ *articulate; clear, distinct; systemetically arranged*; → Glieder– **~gl·ückt** a = gelungen **~gl·üht** a *annealed* (*glass, wire*) **≈gn·arre** n ~s/ (Kinder≈) *whining*

G·egner m ~s/~ *enemy* || *adversary, antagonist, opponent*; er ist ein ~ v ihm, sein ~ *he is his opponent* || ~ e–r S *objector to a th*; *opponent of a th*; ~ der Monarchie *antimonarchist*; Impf≈ *objector to vaccination, anti-vaccinist* | grimmiger ~ ⟨sl⟩ *tiger* || er ist kein ernst zu nehmender ~ ⟨Am⟩ *he is easy meat* || sich jdn z ~ m *to alienate* od *antagonize a p* | **≈isch** a *enemy; hostile*, → feindlich || *adverse* (*criticism*); *antagonistic*, → gegensätzlich | **~schaft** f *hostility* (gegen *to*) || *antagonism; opposition, opponency*

geg·oren a [pp v gären] *fermented* **geg·ossen** a *cast* (*rail; hole*); in e–m Stück ~ *cast in one piece*

gegr·illt a (v Rost) ⟨cul⟩ *grilled, broiled*

°**Ge-** **~gröl(e)** n = Gebrüll °**~h·abe** n = Getue **≈h·aben 1.** vrefl [h] sich ~ *to behave* || gehab dich wohl *farewell*; ⟨poet⟩ *fare thee well* | ˣgehab dich nicht so *don't make a fuss* **2.** ≈ n *behaviour, conduct* °**~h·acke** n *chopping, hacking* **≈h·ackt** a *minced* (*meat*); ≈es [n] *hash; minced* (od *sausage*) *meat* °**~h·ader** n = Gezank **~h·alt** **A.** m ~(e)s/~e **1.** (Bestandteile) ~ an Fett, Fett≈ *fat-content*; Zucker≈ *sugar content* || ⟨at⟩ *level* (an *of*) || der ~ e–s Erzkörpers *the tenor of an ore-body*; geringer Metall≈ *a low percentage* (od *proportion*) *of metal* (*in the ore*) || gesetzlicher ~ an Gold, Silber, Fein≈ *standard* || (Raum≈) *volume*; ⟨mar⟩ Tonnen≈ *tonnage* (*of a ship*), Register≈ *register-tonnage*; → Schiffsraum **2.** ⟨übtr⟩ *substance*; (of wine) *body* || *potency; vigour*; ⟨Am⟩ *punch* | ⟨Lit & arts⟩ (Ggs Form) *content* (*of a poem, play*, etc.); geistiger ~ *intellectual content* || *substance; intrinsic value* || *element* (*the ethical e. in* ..); *factor* || ~ u Gestalt *matter and manner, form and matter* || → Bestandteil, Inhalt **B.** n ~(e)s/≈er *salary*; (f Geistliche, Lehrer a.) *stipend*; ⟨Am a.⟩ *compensation* || ~ ist Nebensache *salary is no consideration* || ⟨mil & nav⟩ *pay*; → Einkommen, Lohn **≈h·alten** a [pred] **1.** gut ~ *well-preserved* **2.** ~ s z tun *to be bound* (od *obliged*) *to do* **3.** (of documents) *couched, worded* (*coarsely worded*); der Brief war in scharfen Ausdrücken ~ *the letter was couched in bitter terms* **≈h·altlos** a *empty; empty of meaning; hollow; shallow, superficial, trivial* **Geh·altlosigkeit** f *emptiness; shallowness; superficiality; triviality* **≈h·altreich** a = –voll

Geh·alts- **~abrechnung** f (*salaried*) *payroll* **~abzug** m *deduction from salary* od *pay*; ⟨bes Am⟩ *payroll deduction* **~aufbesserung** f, **~erhöhung** f *increase of salary* **~empfänger** m *salaried worker*; ~ pl *s. class* **~klassen** f pl *grades of salary* **~kürzung** f *cut in salary* **~sätze** m pl *scale of salary* **~verminderung** f *reduction of salary* **~zulage** f *rise* (*to ask for a r.*)

Ge- **≈h·altvoll** a *full-bodied, racy* (*wine*); *substantial* (*meal*) || *full of thought* (od *meat, substance*); ⟨Am⟩ *meaty* (*speech*) **~h·ämmer** n *hammering* | **≈t** a *beaten* (*gold*) **~h·änge** n **1.** ~ v Blumen (z Schmuck) *festoonery; festoons* pl (a. in Stein) || (hängender Schmuck) *hanging ornament; pendant*; Ohr~ *ear-pendant* || ⟨mil⟩ *belt*; Degen≈ *sword-belt* || ⟨tech⟩ *shackle; suspension gear*; Feder≈ *spring-shackle* **2.** = Behang 1. u 2. **3.** = Abhang: ~schutt [m] ⟨geol⟩ *scree* **≈h·arnischt** a **1.** *armed*; (*clad*) *in armour* **2.** ⟨fig⟩ *sharp; sharp(ly)-worded* (*reply*); *strident* (*declaration*) || *severe, vehement, violent* **≈h·ässig 1.** [a] *hateful, malicious, malevolent; spiteful; vengeful* (*glance*); *venomous; waspish* (*nature*); ~es Gerede *backbiting* || (of women) *cattish, catty* **2.** [adv] *maliciously, spitefully*; ~ reden v jdm *to backbite a p* | **≈keit** [f] *malice, spite(fulness)*; *venom* (*with v.*); *waspishness* **≈h·äuft** a *heaped* (Löffel) **~h·äuse** n ~s/~ **1.** ⟨eig⟩ *housing* || *case; casing* ⟨a. typewr⟩; *box* || äußeres, inneres ~ *outer, inner mantle* ⟨mach⟩ || ⟨wir⟩ *cabinet* || mit e–m ~ umgeben, in ein ~ stecken *to case* || (Schnecken≈) *shell* **2.** ⟨bot⟩ (Kern≈) *core*

G·eh- [in comp] → ⟨a.⟩ d. | **≈behindert** a: er ist leicht ~ *he has some difficulty in walking*

Geh·ege n ~s/~ **1.** = Zaun **2.** (eingezäuntes Stück, ⟨a.⟩ im Zoo) *enclosure*; (f Pferde, Vieh) *corral* || ⟨hunt⟩ *preserves* pl; Wild≈ *game preserves*, ⟨jur⟩ *warren* | ⟨übtr⟩ *preserves* pl; *warren* || jdm ins ~ k *to disturb a p's preserves*

geh·eim **I.** [a] **1.** (privat, vertaulich) *confidential* (*communication*); streng ~ ⟨mil⟩ *top secret*; ⟨bes Am⟩ *classified* || *esoteric(al), occult* (*doctrine*) || *private* || ⟨engl⟩ *Privy* (*Council, Counsellor* od *Councillor*); → ≈rat; ≈siegel || ⟨Ger⟩ ≈er Kommerzienrat ⟨m. m.⟩ *knighted industrialist* **2.** (verborgen) **a.** *hidden; secret* (*door; grief; treaty*); [pred] streng ~ *strictly secret, off the record* || *mystic* (*rites, sense*); *occult* **b.** ⟨dero⟩ *clandestine, furtive, secret* (*traffic in* ..); *surreptitious*; ⟨Am⟩ *gum-shoe* (*methods*) || *covert* (*glance, threat*); *deep* (*design*) **c.** ~es Einvernehmen *collusion*; im ~en E. stehen *to be in c.* || ~er Gegenstand *secret matter* || ~e (Presse-)Informationen [pl] ⟨Am sl⟩ *dope* || *ulterior* (*motive*) || ≈e Staatspolizei *State Secret Police*; ⟨nazi⟩ *Gestapo* [Ger]; ⟨Russ⟩ *Ogpu* **II.** [adv] **1.** *confidentially; privately* **2.** *secretly* || *covertly; surreptitiously* || ~ tagen *to sit in secret* **III.** [subst] im ~en (→ insgeheim) *in private; in secret; privately, secretly; sub rosa* [L]; ⟨sl⟩ *on the quiet*, streng im ~en *on the strict quiet* || ⟨theat⟩ s–e im ~en gesprochenen Worte *his aside* (mit *with*) **Geh·eim-** **~agent** m *secret agent* || ⟨Am parl⟩ *lobbyist*; die ~en [pl] *the lobby* **~bote** m *emissary* **~bund** m ⟨mst pol⟩ *secret society* (od *league*) || *know-nothing-party* **~bündelei** f ⟨jur⟩ *connexions with illegal secret societies* **~dienst** m ⟨engl⟩ (staatl.) *the Secret Service*; → Nachrichtendienst **~fach** n (Schublade) *secret drawer* || ⟨fig⟩ ≈er [pl] *recesses* pl (*of the heart*) **~|halten** vt (etw) *to keep private* (od *quiet, secret*); *to make a mystery of; to conceal*; etw ~ vor jdm *to keep a th from a p* **~haltung** f *the keeping secret, concealment* (*of a th*) || ~sbestimmungen [f pl] *security* (⟨bes Am⟩ *classification*) *curtain* || ~sstufe [f] *category of classification; security cl.* || ~svorschrift f *instruction relative to secrecy* **~kabinett** n ⟨engl⟩ (königl) *the Private Secretary's Office* **~konto** n *private account*

~**kräftig** a *sympathetic* ~**lehre** f *esoteric doctrine*; *occultism* ~**mittel** n ⟨med⟩ *nostrum* [L]; *patent* (od *quack*) *medicine* ~**nachricht** f (Presse) *dope* ~**polizei** f *the secret police*; → geheim I. 2. c. ~**polizist** m → Detektiv ~**rat** m ⟨Ger⟩ *Privy Councillor, Counsellor* ~**schloß** n *secret padlock* ~**schreiber** m *private secretary* ~**schrift** f *cryptography* ‖ *writing in cipher*; *cipher*; *secret code* ‖ Schriftstück in ~ *cryptogram, -graph*; *cipher* ‖ in ~ schreiben *to cipher* ‖ ~entzifferung [f] *cryptanalysis* ~**siegel** n ⟨engl⟩ *the Privy Seal*; ~bewahrer *Lord Privy Seal* ~**sitzung** f *secret* (⟨Am⟩ *executive*) *session*; e–e ~ abhalten *to meet in private* (od *in camera*); ⟨Am⟩ *to go into executive session* ~**sprache** f *secret slang* (*of thieves*, etc.), *cant* ~**treppe** f *secret staircase* ~**tuer** m *secretive p* (*he is a s. one*) ~**tuerei** f *secretiveness* ~**tuerisch** 1. [a] *secretive* 2. [adv] *secretively* ~|**tun** vi [h] *to be secretive* ~**vertrag** m *secret treaty* ~**wissenschaft** f *occultism*; *occult science* ~**zimmer** n *secret room*; *closet* **Geh·eimnis** n –nisses/ –nisse *secret* (vor *from*); k–e –nisse vor e–a (*to have*) *no secrets from each other*; ein öffentliches ~ *an open secret* | (tiefes ~; Rätsel) *mystery, deep secret*; *arcanum* [L pl –na] ‖ –nisse [pl] *penetralia* ‖ die –nisse *the mysteries* od *secrets* pl (*of nature*) ‖ die –nisse der Kochkunst *the culinary secrets* | ein ~ **ausplaudern** *or* verraten *to give the game away*; *to let the cat out of the bag*; ⟨sl⟩ *to give away the show, to blow the gaff, to spill the beans*; ⟨Am⟩ *to let on* ‖ es bleibt ein ~ *it remains a mystery* (f *to*) ‖ jdn in ein ~ einweihen *to let a p into a secret*; in ein ~ –ge–ht w *to be taken into a s.* ‖ ein (kein) ~ m aus *to make a* (*no*) *secret of* ..; nicht das geringste ~ m aus der Absicht *not to make the least secret of one's intention* (*to do*); ein ~ verraten *to tell* ~**krämer** m *mystery-monger*; → Geheimtuer ~**krämerei** f *mystery-mongering* ~**voll** a *uncouth*; *mysterious*; *cryptic* (*chuckle*); *dark*; *mystic* (*rites*), *obscure*; das ~e Dunkel, das ihn umgab *the air of mystery which clung about him* ‖ etw mit e–m ~en Schleier umgeben *to throw a cloak of mystery arround a th* | [adv] es ist ~-verführerisch: *its seduction and mystery are* ..

Geh·eiß n ~es/: auf jds ~ *at the behest of a p*

geh·emmt a *shackled*; (P) *self-conscious* ‖ nicht ~ *unshackled*

g·ehen vi/t [ging/gegangen] **I. vi** [s] **A.** (P) **1.** (z Fuß) ⟨a. sport⟩ *to walk* (auf .. entlang *along, down a street*); z Fuß ~ *to go on foot*; *to walk*; „~"! ⟨mot⟩ (Zeichen f Fußgänger) *move!*; ~ lernen *to learn to walk*; ⟨fig⟩ *to find one's feet* ‖ (im) Schritt ~ *to go at a walking pace*; (im) Trab ~ *to trot*; das Pferd geht gut *the horse is a good goer* ‖ gemächlich ~ *to amble, stroll*; gemütlich ~ *to dawdle*; mühsam ~ *to trudge*; nachlässig ~ *to shamble, shuffle*; schnell ~ *to flit, pop, whisk*; schwerfällig ~ *to clump, lumber, plod, tramp*; wankend ~ *to stagger, totter* ‖ nach–e–a ~ *to file* (aus *out of*); aus–e–a ~ *to part* od *separate*; um die Ecke ~ *to turn the corner*; über die Grenze ~ *to stray beyond the boundary* **2. (sich begeben)** *to go* (auf .. *to one's room*; in *into*; *to* [*town*]; nach *to*) ‖ ins Ausland ~ *to go abroad*; → Kirche; Land; Schule; See ‖ betteln ~ *to go begging*; auf die Jagd ~ *to go shooting*; auf Reisen ~ *to go travelling*; baden ~ *to go bathing*; schlafen (*or* z Bett) ~ *to go to bed* (od *rest*); *to turn in*; → spazieren~, verloren~ ‖ über e–e Brücke ~ *to cross a bridge* ‖ unter die Räuber ~ *to join the robbers* ‖ s–r Wege, s–s Weges ~ *to go one's way*; in die Irre ~ *to go wrong* (od *astray*) **3. (fortgehen)** *to go* (nach *to*); *to depart, leave* (nach *for*) ‖ ich muß ~ *I must be off* ‖ daß er ging, konnte .. *his going could* (*do no harm*) ‖ unser Mädchen geht am 1. April *our maid is leaving on April 1st* ‖ **aus** dem Amt ~ *to resign office* ‖ der Offizier muß ~ *the officer must quit the service* od *take his leave* ‖ er ist **v uns** gegangen *he has passed away* (od *departed this life*) ‖ geh!, geh fort!, geh d–r Wege! *clear out!* ‖ woll'n ~!, laß uns ~! *let's go!, let's get going!, let's be off!* **4.** ⟨übtr⟩ er geht gut gekleidet *he is always well dressed*; .. **in Trauer** *he is in mourning*; eingehängt ~ *to go arm in arm* ‖ er geht ins 30. Lebensjahr, ⟨fam⟩ er geht auf die 30 *he is rising 30*, ⟨Am⟩ *he's going on 30* ‖ auf die Universität ~ *to go up to the u.* ‖ ⟨fig⟩ sehr weit ~ *to go to great lengths* ‖ z weit ~ *to go to the extremes* ‖ sicher ~ *to be on the safe side* | **ans** Werk ~ *to go* (od *set about one's* od) *to work*; (e–r S) **auf** den Grund ~ *to get to the bottom of* ‖ ⟨übtr⟩ er geht auf (die) 80 *he is going on 80* ‖ **aufs** Ganze ~ → Ganze 1. b. ‖ jdm **aus** dem Wege ~ *to go out of a p's way*; *to shun a p* ‖ °**durch** die Lappen ~ → Lappen ‖ → ferner Äußere, Bart, Brei, Hund, Leib, Leiche, Leim, Werk ‖ **mit** der Zeit ~ *to go with the times* ‖ mit e–m Mädchen ~ ⟨mil sl⟩ *to square-push* **c.** ~ **Sie (mir) doch mit** Ihren Entschuldigungen *none of your lame excuses* | **zu jdm** ~: *I looked him up*; *to see* (*one's principal*) **5. in sich** ~ *to commune with o.s.*; *to feel remorse*; = sich bessern ‖ mit sich z Rate ~ *to commune with o.s.*; wenn ich mit mir z R. gehe *in my secret councils* **6. jdn** ~ **l** *to let a p go*; (ungestraft) *to let a p off* ‖ laß sie ~ ⟨sl⟩ *let her rip* ‖ das Geschäft ~ l *to let the business slip*; **laß die Dinge** ~ *let well alone*; *let things slide* ‖ **sich** ~ **l** *to let o.s. go*; *to unbend*; *to cut loose*; *to be off one's guard*; ⟨fam⟩ *to wear thin*; Sich–~–Lassen [n] *go-as-you-please* **7. sich müde** ~ *to tire o.s. by walking* **B.** ⟨**übtr**⟩ (S) **1.** (of engines, ships, trains, etc.) *to go* (*the ship, train goes to* ..); *to run, work* (*the engine runs, goes, works perfectly*); die **Uhr** geht nicht *the clock does not go*; die U. geht richtig *the cl. shows the right time* | **(abgehen)** *to leave* (*the train leaves at 10*); das Schiff geht in See *the ship puts out to sea* | *to pass* (*a bottle passed from hand to hand*); die **Kugel** ging durch .. *the bullet passed through* (*the shoulder*) | die **Glocke** geht nicht *the bell does not work* ‖ die Sirenen ~ *the sirens go* ‖ der Teig geht *the dough rises* ‖ die Wellen ~ hoch *the waves are running high, there is a heavy sea on* **2.** die **Tür** geht *somebody is opening the door* ‖ → Gerücht | die **Arbeit** geht flott *the work is progressing briskly* ‖ das **Geschäft** geht gut (schlecht) *the business is doing well* (*badly*); .. *is in smooth* (*low*) *water* ‖ ⟨com⟩ ausgezeichnet ~ (of books, etc.) *to be selling splendidly*; → Abgang ‖ → Melodie **3.** 12 ~ **auf** ein Dutzend *12 go to the dozen*; **in Stücke** ~ *to go to pieces* ‖ *to be divided into* (*equal parts*); 6 geht in 13 zweimal u eins bleibt übrig *6 into 13 goes twice and one over* ‖ (*this cask*) *holds* (*10 pails of water*) ‖ (*this room will*) *hold* (*500 people*) ‖ .. geht in die Tausende (*his profits*) *run* od *amount to thousands* **4. (führen)** der R. g. **bis** zu .. *the skirt reaches down to the ankles*; der Weg geht **durch** .. *the way lies through* (*a wood*); der E. g. durch .. *the entrance* (*to the chapel*) *is by* (*a doorway*); die Gl. g. **in** .. *the bell connects with the kitchen*; das Z. (etc) g. **nach** dem G. *the room looks on to the garden*; die Br. g. **über** .. *the bridge crosses the river*; die Mauer g. **um** .. *the wall goes* od *runs round the whole city*; hier g. es **zu** .. *this way to the Customs* **5. über alles** ~ *to be paramount*; jdm über alles ~ *to think the world of* (*a th*) ‖ **vor sich** ~ *to go on*; *to happen*; *pass*; *proceed*; *to take place*; *to be enacted* (.. *where the crime was e.*) ‖ **in Erfüllung** ~ *to be realized*; *to come true* ‖ jdm **zu Herzen** ~ *to go to a p's heart* **C.** ⟨**fig**⟩ **das** (*or* die S) **geht, es geht 1.** (...,) aber es ging nicht (*he tried to read*) *but it would not do* od *but he could not*; es ging gerade noch (gut) *that was touch and go*; das geht ja bis jetzt ganz gut *that's not so bad after all* ‖ (alles) geht gut .. *is going fine*; *everything went better than*

(*I expected*); → Schnürchen ‖ die S wird schief ~ *the matter will go wrong*; das wird nicht g·ut ~ *no good will come of it*; das hätte ~ können, wenn .. nicht .. *that might have been were it not for* (*your departure*); das geht überhaupt nicht *that won't/doesn't work at all*; ⟨iron⟩ dann wird's auch ohne Sie ~ *thank you for nothing* ‖ das geht zu weit *that's going too far* ‖ das geht so nicht weiter *you can't go on the way you've been* ‖ alles ging drunter u drüber *things were all topsyturvy* **2. es geht** ihm **an** den Kragen *he is in for it* ‖ es g. **auf** Leben u Tod *it is a question of life and death* ‖ es geht auf 10 Uhr *it is getting on for 10 o'clock* ‖ das geht auf dich *that is meant for you* ‖ → Nerv ‖ es g. e–m durch u durch *it gives you a thrill* ‖ das g. **gegen** .. *that goes against* (*my feelings*); → Strich ‖ °das g. **ins** Aschgraue *there is no end to it*; *that's too much of a good th* ‖ wenn es **nach** mir ginge *if I had my way*; wenn es nach dir ginge *for all you care* ‖ es geht nichts **über** die Arbeit *there is nothing like work*; es g. nichts über die gute alte Zeit *give me the good old times*; es g. nichts über (die) Höflichkeit *you can't beat politeness*; das geht über m–n Horizont *that gets me*; (der Streit) geht **um** .. *revolves about* ..; es geht um die Ehre *my h. is concerned* ‖ jeder weiß, **worum** es geht *everybody knows what is at stake* **3.** (wie gefällt es dir?) oh **es geht** (..) *pretty well*; *not bad*; *middling* ‖ das geht *or* wird ~ *that will do* ‖ das g. nicht *that won't do*; *it is no go*; *there is nothing doing*; *that won't wash* **4. wie geht es?** *how are you*?; ⟨bes geh. Spr.⟩ *how are you getting along*? ‖ ⟨fam⟩ wie geht's, (wie steht's)? *how are things* (*going*)? ‖ wie geht es dir? *how are you*?; ⟨fam⟩ *how's the world with you*?; ⟨Am sl⟩ *howdy*(*do*)? ‖ es geht mir **gut** *I am doing well, I am all right*; es geht ihm (pekuniär) gut, sogar sehr gut *he is more than comfortable*; °mir geht's „danke"! ⟨fam⟩ *I'm in my usual*; ⟨Am⟩ *I'm sitting pretty*; es geht mir (gar) **nicht gut** *or* **extra** *I'm feeling out of sorts, I'm far from well* (⟨a⟩ .. **schlecht**); .. schlecht: *he is is a bad way, he is badly off* (..) oder es wird ihm schlecht ~ (..) *or he will be the worse for it* ‖ laß es dir gut ~ *farewell*; → ergehen **5.** es ging sich gut (schlecht) *walking was* (*un*)*pleasant*; *the going was good* (*hard*) **II. vt** [s] **1.** (P) e–n Weg ~ (f andere) *to go on an errand*; Wege ~ *to go on* (od *to run*) *errands* ‖ sie gingen verschiedene Wege *they went their different ways*; ⟨pol⟩ versch. W.e ~ *to walk different sides of the road* ‖ ich muß einige W. ~ *I have several calls to make*; *I have to do some shopping* ‖ *he has gone his own ways* ‖ (S) s–n Gang ~ *to take its course* **2.** °er ist gegangen worden *he has got the sack* **G·ehen** n ⟨sport⟩ *walking*; Wettkampf im ~ *walking-match* | *going, running, working* ‖ (Fort≈) *going*

g·ehend a; glänzend ~ *flourishing* (*practice*)

Geh·enk n ~(e)s/~e = Gehenge, Gehänge

G·ehenlassen n ⟨pol⟩ *laisser-faire* [Fr]

G·eher m ~s/~; ~marathon [n] *walkathon*

geh·euer a [pred] nicht ~ *uncanny, weird*; *eerie, eery* ‖ *precarious, risky* ‖ .. nicht ~ *that ruin is said to be haunted*; .. *gives you the creeps* ‖ die S ist mir nicht ~, das kommt mir nicht ~ vor *that seems to me a risky* od *ticklish matter*; *I feel uneasy about that*; *there is sth mysterious* (⟨sl⟩ *fishy*) *about it*

Geh·eul n ~(e)s/ *howls* pl, *howling*; *ululations* pl, *wailing*; *crying* ‖ *caterwaul*(*ing*); *wail* (*of a cat*) ‖ *scream* (*of sirens*)

Geh·ilfe m ~n/~n **1.** ⟨com⟩ *assistant* (Laden≈ *shop a.*); (Handlungs≈) *clerk* ‖ (Handwerks≈) *journeyman* ‖ ⟨ec⟩ *server* (*of the celebrant*) **2.** ⟨übtr⟩ *helpmate* ‖ *associate*; *attendant* | ⟨fig⟩ *minister* (*of* od *to a p's desires*) ‖ *handmaid*(*en*) (*health and temperance are the handmaidens of* ..) **Geh·ilfin** f *female assistant* od *attendant* ‖ ⟨übtr⟩ *helpmate*; = Gehilfe 2.

Geh·irn n ~(e)s/~e **1.** *brain*; ⟨anat⟩ Groß≈ *cerebrum* [L], Klein≈ *cerebellum* [L]; → Hirn **2.** [in comp] *brain–*; *cerebral, encephalic* °**~akrobat** m *egg-head*, ⟨Am sl⟩ *intellectual heavy-weight* **~arbeit** f = Kopf– **~blutung** f ⟨med⟩ *cerbral h*(*a*)*emorrhage* **~chirurgie** f *psychosurgery* **~entzündung** f *encephalitis* [L]; *brain fever* **~erschütterung** f *concussion of the brain* **~erweichung** f *softening of the brain*; *encephalomalacia* [L] **~geschwulst** f ⟨path⟩ *cerebral tumour* **~haut** f = Hirnhaut **~hautentzündung** f *meningitis* **~kammer** f *ventricle of the brain* **~lähmung** f *cerebral palsy* **~rinde** f *c. cortex* **~schlag** m ⟨med⟩ *apoplexy* **~schwund** m *c. atrophy* °**~(s)kasten** m *cogitation chamber* **~substanz** f: graue ~ *gray matter* **~tätigkeit** f *cerebration* **~wäsche** f ⟨pol⟩ *brainwashing*; *menticide*; sich e–r ~ unterziehen *to brainwash o.s.* **~wassersucht** f *hydrocephalus* **~windungen** f pl *cerebral convolutions*

geh·oben a [pp v heben] ⟨fig⟩ *elate*(*d*) (sich ~ fühlen *to feel e.*); *prideful* (*moment*); ~e Stimmung *elation, high spirits* pl; in ~er St. *elate*(*d*) ‖ *dignified, elegant*; *elevated* (*speech, style*), *lofty* ‖ ~e Stellung, ~er Stand *station in life* (*is a handicap before the Law*)

Geh·öft n ~(e)s/–e *farmstead, farm*

geh·öht a ⟨arts⟩ *heightened* (*drawing*)

Geh·ölz n ~es/~e (*small*) *wood*; → Unterholz

Geh·ör n ~(e)s/ **1.** (Fähigkeit) (*sense of*) *hearing*; *power*(*s*) *of hearing* (od *audition*); das ~ verlieren *to lose the power of hearing, to become deaf*; ohne ~ *deaf* | *ear* (f *for*); fein *correct* od *delicate ear*; scharf *quick ear*; musikalisch *musical ear, ear for music*; nach dem ~ singen, spielen *to sing, play by ear* ‖ (etw) z ~ bringen *to perform, to play*; *to bring out* **2.** (Gehörtwerden; Erhörung) *hearing* ‖ um jds ~ bitten *to ask for* (od *to request*) *a p's attention*; sich [dat] ~ erbitten *to ask, plead to be heard*; darf ich um ~ bitten? *please, give* od *lend me your ear* ‖ ~ finden *to find audience* od *an attentive ear*; .. bei jdm *to gain a p's ear*; *his prayer found a hearing*; sich ~ verschaffen *to gain a h.*; jdm ~ schenken *to give a p a h.*; *to give one's ear to a p*; *to lend an* od *one's ear to a p* od *a th*; e–r S ~ sch. *to listen to a th*; e–r S kein ~ sch. *to turn a deaf ear to a th* **3.** ⟨hunt⟩ *ears* pl (*of a wild-boar*, etc) **~empfindung** f *auditory sensation* **~fehler** m *auditory defect* **~gang** m *acoustic duct* **~knöchelchen** n ⟨anat⟩ eins der 3 ~ *stapes* [L] **~losenschule** f *school for the deaf* **~nerv** m *acoustic* (od *auditory*) *nerve* **~organ** n *auditory organ*; *organ of hearing* **~prüfung** f ⟨mus Am⟩ *audition* **~sinn** m *sense of hearing*

geh·orchen vi [h] (nicht) ~ *to* (*dis*)*obey*; *to be* (*dis*)*obedient*; nicht ~ wollen *to refuse to obey* ‖ jdm (nicht) ~ *to* (*dis*)*obey a p*; ihm wurde (nicht) gehorcht *he was* (*dis*)*obeyed* | (e–r S) *to obey* (*a law*); *to follow* (*directions*); dem Ruder ~ *to answer the helm*

geh·ören vi [h] **I.** [~ + prep] **A. ~ zu 1.** (durch Gesetz, Natur etc ~ z) **a.** *to belong to* (*a class*); *to appertain to* (*the part appertains to the whole*); *to be part of a th*; *to pertain to* (*your remark hardly pertains to the matter*); *to be germane* od *pertinent to* (*a th*) ‖ was Sie sagen, gehört nicht zur S .. *is neither here nor there* (od *is beside the purpose*) ‖ Gefahren ~ nun mal zur Laufbahn des .. *dangers are incidental to* (od *inseparable from*) *the career of* (*a soldier*) **b.** M. gehört z P. *Madeira belongs to Portugal*; *M. is a Portuguese possession* **c.** z dem Hause gehört ein Garten *attached to the house is a garden* ‖ alles, was zum behaglichen Leben gehört *all that contributes to a comfortable life* | **dazu** gehört viel Geld, Geduld *that requires a lot of money, much patience* ‖ das gehört so mit dazu *that's all in the day's work, it's all in the game* ‖ dazu g. nicht viel *it doesn't take much, I could do it hands down* ‖ es g. schon etw dazu, ihn z schlagen *it takes a lot of beating him; he is hard to beat* ‖ es ∼ immer zwei dazu *it takes two to make a bargain* **d.** zeitlich ∼ z *to be contemporary with* **2.** (z e–r Gruppe etc ∼) *to be of* ‖ ich gehöre z s–n Anhängern *I am among his adherents, I am one of his a.* ‖ z denen ∼, die .. *to be of those who* ..; ich g. zu den Leuten, die *I am the sort of man who* ..; mit dazu ∼ *to be in the swim*; er gehört auch dazu *he is one of them*; nicht mehr dazu ∼ *to be out of the swim* ‖ sie ∼ z e–r anderen Welt *they are of another world* ‖ das Buch gehört z den besten s–r Art *the book is one of the best of its kind* ‖ das g. z den Dingen, die .. *this is one of those things which* .. **B. 1. an** das Gericht gehört noch etw Gewürz *the dish wants* (od *requires*) *a little seasoning* | das Buch g. **auf** jenes Bort *the book goes on that shelf* | **~ in** *to fall into* (*a category*); ⟨Am⟩ *to belong in* (*a group*) ‖ Kinder ∼ früh ins Bett *children ought to be in bed early* | **~ unter** *to come* (od *fall*) *under* (*a head*) ‖ ⟨Am⟩ *to belong under*; *to belong among* (*a number*); → zus–∼ **2.** er gehört gehängt z w *he is fit for the gallows* | es g. **hierher** *it belongs here* ‖ wohin g. dies? *where does this go* (od *belong*)? ‖ das g. nicht hierher *that's not to the point, that's beside the purpose*; *that is neither here nor there* **II.** jdm (als Eigentum) ∼ *to belong to a p* ‖ das Gut gehört jetzt Herrn N. *the estate is Mr. N.'s now*; es g. m–m Bruder *it is my brother's*; es g. mir, ihm *it is mine, his*; wem ∼ sie (sc die Bücher)? *whose are they*? ‖ m–e Mußezeit gehört nur mir *my leisure is my own* ‖ m–e Gedanken ∼ ihr *my thoughts turn to her*; dem Tüchtigen g. die Welt *the efficient will win through* ‖ → gebühren **III. es gehört sich** *it is fit* (od *proper, right*; *seemly* [f *in a p*]); es g. sich (nun mal) nicht *it is* (*just*) *not done*; *it's not the thing*; es g. sich durchaus nicht, daß .. *it is not at all fit that* (.. *should*) ‖ es g. sich nicht f jdn *it does not become* od *befit a p*; *it is not becoming to a p* (*to do*) **geh·örig A.** [a] **1.** das ihm ∼e Grundstück *the property belonging to him, his* (*own*) *property*; alle ihm ∼en Sachen *all his belongings* (od *his goods and chattles*) pl; → Zubehör ‖ die z Verwaltung ∼en Beamten *the staff of the administration* ‖ ein der Regierung ∼es Grundstück *a government*(*-owned*) *property* | **zur S ~** *to the point, relevant*; *pertinent* (*remark*); nicht z S ∼ *beside the point, irrelevant* (*remark*) ‖ *necessary, requisite* (f *to, for*); er besitzt nicht die (dazu) ∼en Fähigkeiten f *he has not the qualifications, he is not qualified for* (*the work*) **2. (angemessen)** *adequate, appropriate*; *correct*; *due*; *fit*(*ting*); *proper*; *right* ‖ mit dem ∼en Eifer *with the proper zeal*; mit dem ∼en Respekt *with due respect* **3. (tüchtig)** *sound, thorough*; e–e ∼e Tracht Prügel *a sound thrashing* ‖ *appreciative, generous* (*pull*); ein ∼er Schluck *a gulp, a quaff* ‖ ein ∼er Wirrwarr *a glorious mess* (od *muddle*); → gründlich, tüchtig **B.** [adv] **1.** *adequately*; *duly, properly*; *in due form*; ∼ vorgebildet *qualified* (f *for*) **2.** (tüchtig) *soundly, thoroughly*; *regularly* (*angry*); du wirst es ∼ bek. *you'll catch it*; ich habe es ihm ∼ gegeben ⟨sl⟩ *I have given it him hot*; *I have given him a piece* (od *bit*) *of my mind*; jdn ∼ heruntermachen ⟨sl⟩ *to tick a p off*; ⟨Am sl⟩ *to soak a p*; jdn ∼ schröpfen ⟨sl⟩ *to soak a p* ‖ *good and proper*; *with a vengeance* (*he laid about him with a v.*); ⟨Am sl⟩ *to a fare-you-well* | das rattert ja ∼ *here is a rattling* ‖ es ist ∼ kalt ⟨fam⟩ *it is jolly cold*

Geh·örn n ∼(e)s/∼e *horns* pl; ⟨hunt⟩ *head*; *antlers* pl **geh·örnt** a *horned*; ⟨myth⟩ *Horny* (*Siegfried*)

geh·orsam 1. [a] *obedient*; jdm ∼ s *to be obedient to a p, to obey a p* ‖ (amtlich in Briefen) Ihr ∼er Diener *Your obedient servant* ‖ † ∼er Diener! ⟨iron⟩ *catch me* (*doing that*)! **2.** [adv] *obediently* ‖ ⟨mil †⟩ melde ∼st *I have to report*

Geh·orsam m ∼s/ *obedience* (gegen *to*); freiwilliger ∼ *free-will o.* ‖ (jdn) zum ∼ bringen *to reduce to obedience*; *to bring to heel*; *to break in*; *to bring under*; *to subdue* ‖ ∼ leisten = gehorchen ‖ er verlangt ∼ *he will be obeyed* ‖ sich ∼ verschaffen *to compel* (od *exact, enforce*) *obedience* (v *from*) ‖ den ∼ verweigern *to refuse obedience*; *to act in defiance of orders* **~sverweigerung** f *disobedience* (⟨Ind⟩ *civil d.*); ⟨mil⟩ *defiance of orders, insubordination*

°**Geh·öse** n ∼s/ (Hosen) ⟨sl⟩ *bags*, ⟨Am⟩ *strides*

Gehr- ~dreieck n ⟨carp⟩ *mitre*, ⟨Am⟩ *miter* **~fuge** f *mitre joint*

G·ehre f **1.** (rechtwinkl. Verbindung) *mitre*; *mitre-joint*; ⟨typ⟩ *corner piece* **2.** (Keilstück) *gore, gusset* **g·ehren** vt [h] (→ Gehre 1.) (Bretter) *to mitre*

G·ehrock m *frock-coat*; ⟨Am⟩ *Prince Albert*

G·ehrung f ⟨carp⟩ *bevel* ‖ = Gehre 1. **~shobel** m *m.-plane* **~slade** f *m.-block* **~ssäge** f *m.-box saw*

G·ehstörung f *locomotor disturbance*

°**Geh·udel** n ∼s/ = Hudelei

°**Geh·uste** n *coughing*; *coughs* pl

G·eh- ~verband m *leg-bandage* **~versuch** m *attempt at walking* **~weg** m = Bürgersteig ‖ ∼-platte [f] *quarry tile* **~werk** n *clock* ‖ °∼zeuge [n pl] ⟨hum⟩ *trotters*

Gei f ∼/∼en ⟨mar⟩ *guy*; → ∼tau

G·eier m ∼s/∼ ⟨orn⟩ **1.** *vulture* → d.; dunkler Raben≈ *urubu*; → Aas≈, Lämmer≈ | ⟨fig⟩ *vulture*; wie ein ∼ *ravenous*(*ly*) ‖ °hol dich *or* hol's der ∼! *confound it*! (*the*) *deuce take it*! ‖ °weiß der ∼ *deuce knows* ‖ z ∼ = z Teufel **2.** [in comp] *vulturine*; *vulturous* **~falke** m *gerfalcon*

G·eifer m ∼s/ **1.** *slaver, slobber*; (of horse) *foam* **2.** ⟨fig⟩ *rancour, spite, venom* ‖ s–n ∼ auslassen an ⟨fig⟩ *to vent one's wrath on* (*a p*) **~lätzchen, ~tuch** n *bib* **G·eiferer** m ∼s/∼ *slaverer, slobberer, driveller* **g·eifern I.** vi [h] **1.** *to slaver, slobber*; (of horses) *to foam* **2.** ⟨übtr⟩ (plappern) *to drivel* ‖ ⟨mst fig⟩ *to foam* (*at the mouth*) *with rage*; *to fulminate*; *to rage*; *to spit fire* **II.** ≈ n *slobbering* ‖ *foaming*; *raging*

G·eige f ∼/∼n ⟨mus⟩ *violin*, ⟨fam⟩ *fiddle* ‖ ⟨hist⟩ *viol*; → Baß≈; ∼ spielen *to play the violin* ‖ die erste ∼ *the first violin* ‖ ⟨fig⟩ die erste (zweite) ∼ spielen *to play first* (*second*) *fiddle*; neben jdm die 2. .. *to play second f. to a p* ‖ (Melodie) auf der ∼ spielen *to play* (*on*) *the violin*; ⟨fam⟩ *to fiddle* | ⟨fig⟩ der Himmel hängt ihm voller ∼n *he always looks on the rosy* (od *sunny, bright*) *side of things* **g·eigen** vt/i [h] **1.** vt (etw) *to play* (*on*) *the violin*; ⟨fam⟩ *to fiddle* ‖ ⟨fig⟩ ich werde es ihm schon (*or* ihm schon die Wahrheit) ∼ *I shall give it him hot* (od *give him a piece of my mind*) **2.** vi *to bow, fiddle*; *to play the fiddle* (od *violin*) **G·eigen- ~bau** m *violin-making* **~bauer** m *violin-maker* **~bogen** m *violin* (od *fiddle*)*-bow*; *fiddlestick* **~hals** m *neck of a violin* **~harz** n *colophony, rosin* **~holz** n *fiddlewood* ‖ ∼baum m ⟨bot⟩ *citharexylum* **~kasten** m *violin-case* **~künstler** m *violin-artist*; *great violinist* **~spieler** m *violin-player, violinist*; ⟨fam & dero⟩ *fiddler* **~steg** m *bridge of a violin* **~strich** m *stroke of the violin-bow* **~wirbel** m *peg of a violin*

G·eiger m ∼s/∼ *violin-player, violinist* ‖ ⟨fam & dero⟩ *fiddler* ‖ der erste ∼ *the first violin*

G·eigerzähler m ⟨at⟩ *Geiger counter*

g·eil a **1.** ∼er Boden *luxuriant soil*; ∼e Triebe *luxuriant* od *rank growth* **2.** ⟨sex⟩ *lascivious, lecherous, lustful, salacious, sexy, wanton*; ⟨Am a.⟩ *racy* ‖ *hot*, ⟨sl⟩ *cockish*; ⟨fig⟩ ein ∼er Bock *an old goat* **G·eile** f ∼/∼n ⟨hunt⟩ (Hode) *testicle*

G·eilheit f ∼/ **1.** *luxuriance, rankness* **2.** (Wollust) *lasciviousness, lechery, lust, wantonness*

G·eisel m ∼s/∼n *hostage* ‖ als ∼ behalten *to keep as hostage*; ∼n stellen *to give hostages*

G·eiser m ∼s/∼ (heiße Quelle) *geyser*

G·eison n ∼s/∼s ⟨arch⟩ (Gesims) *corona* L

G·eiß f ~/~en *(she-)goat*; → Ricke **~bart** m ⟨bot⟩ *goat's beard; meadow-sweet; spiraea* L **~blatt** n ⟨bot⟩ *honeysuckle, woodbine* (od *–bind*) ‖ ~gewächse [pl] *Caprifoliaceae* L pl **~bock** m *he* (od *billy*) *-goat* °**~bub** m *young goatherd* **~fuß** m (Stemmeisen) *claw-bar*; V-*shaped gouge* **~klee** m ⟨bot⟩ *broom* **~raute** f ⟨bot⟩ *goat's rue*

G·eißel f ~/~n **1. a.** *lash; scourge* (⟨a. Bußgerät⟩) **b.** ⟨fig⟩ *scourge* (*the scourges of mankind*); *the Scourge of God* (= *Attila*) ‖ *the iron heel* (*of war*); unter der ~ *under the heel* (*of tyranny*) ‖ die ~ schwingen über = geißeln **2.** ⟨zoo & biol⟩ *flagellum* L **~bruder** m = Geißler **~faden** m *flagellum* **~tierchen** n ⟨zoo⟩ *flagellate* ‖ *phytozoon, zoophyte; trypanosome* **g·eißeln** vt [h] **1.** (peitschen) *to lash, scourge* ‖ (als Bußübung) *to flagellate, to scourge*; **sich** ~ *to scourge o.s.* **2.** ⟨fig⟩ (of God) *to chastise, scourge; to castigate; torment* ‖ (in Worten) *to lash* (*with sarcasm*, etc.); *to critize severely*; ⟨fam⟩ *to slate; trounce; vituperate* **G·eißelung** f ~/~en **1.** (Peitschen) *flagellation; lashing; scourging* (*of Christ*) ⟨a. arts⟩ ‖ (als Bußübung) *scourging* **2.** ⟨fig⟩ *castigation, chastisement* ‖ *lashing; severe criticism; vituperation*

G·eißlein n ~s/~ ⟨zoo⟩ *kid*

G·eißler m ⟨hist ec⟩ *flagellant, scourger*

G·eißlersche Röhren f pl ⟨el⟩ *Geissler tubes* pl

G·eist m ~es/~er **A.** [abstr nur sg] **1.** *spirit* (*of God*); reiner ~ *pure spirit* ‖ ⟨philos & psych⟩ *mind*; ~ u Körper *mind and body*; ~ u Materie *mind and matter*; → Gemüt, Herz, Seele, Sinn ‖ ⟨mil⟩ der ~ der Truppe war .. *the morale .. was ..* ‖ führender, überlegener ~ *mastermind*; edler, hoher, reger ~ *noble, lofty, active mind* (od *spirit*); sich [acc] im ~ mit (etw) beschäftigen *to occupy one's mind with ..*; den ~ aufgeben *to give up the ghost; to breathe one's last* **2.** (~esgaben) **a.** *intelligence, mind; spiritual depth, intellectual capacity; mental power; intellect; wits* pl; *brilliance; esprit* Fr; (*his*) *fibre* (*lives on*) ‖ (viel) ~ h *to be* (*highly*) *intelligent*; voller ~ s *to be brilliant* ‖ **ohne** ~ *lacking* (*in*) *intelligence; dull, obtuse, stupid; without originality* **b.** *imagination, spirit* ‖ ich werde **im ~e** bei dir s *I shall be with you in* (*the*) *spirit*; sie sah (ihn, es) im ~e (vor sich) *she had a vision* (od *mental picture*) *of* (*him, it*), *she saw him in imagination*; im ~e versetzt w *to be transported in imagination* (nach *to*); sich [dat] (etw) im ~e vorstellen *to envisage* **c.** *vigour of mind*; **sich** [acc] im ~ mit (etw) beschäftigen *to occupy one's mind with ..*; *mental vitality* (*full of v.*); *fire*; °*fizz* **3. a.** *spirit* (od *character, genius*) *of an age, institution, a language*; im ~e der Freundschaft *in the sp. of friendship* **b.** der gr. ~, der ~ des gr. Volkes *the Greek mind* ‖ der ~ jds *the mind* od *sp. of a p; his m. was filled with ..* ‖ in jds ~e handeln *to act in a p's sp.*, *to follow out the sp. of a p's ideals* ‖ (wir sahen bald), wes ~es Kind er war (..) *what kind of man he was* **c.** (Korps~) *loyalties* pl; *esprit de corps* (*of a corporation*); *spirit* **B.** ⟨theol⟩ **1.** der Heilige ~ *The Holy Ghost* (od *Spirit*); ⟨fig fam⟩ *the devil nobody* (*did it*) **2.** der Böse ~ *the Evil One*, ~ der Finsternis *the Spirit of Darkness* **C.** [konkr, pl ~er] **1.** (P) ein gr ~ *a great mind; man of wit*(*s*); *master-spirit*; gr, führende ~er *great minds, leading spirits; the talent*; e–r der größten ~er s–r Zeit *one of the greatest spirits of his age* ‖ enger ~ *pedant, philistine* ‖ feuriger ~ → Feuer~ ‖ kl ~er *little minds* pl ‖ unruhiger ~ *restless mind; fidget* **2.** dienstbarer ~ *ministering angel* ‖ °⟨fig⟩ = Dienstmädchen; Diener ‖ guter (böser) ~ *good* (*evil*) *genius*; böser ~ *gremlin* ⟨bes aero-sl⟩; böse ~ er *evil spirits* **3.** (~ e–s Verstorbenen) *ghost, spirit*; ~er *spirits*; von ~ern heimgesucht *ghost-ridden* (*house*); ~er gehen im Schlosse um *the castle is haunted* **D.** [in comp] → Geister–, Geistes–

g·eist- ~bildend a *improving* (*book*) **~reich 1.** [a] *bright, intelligent, witty*; ~e Dame *lady of wit*(*s*) ‖ *clever, ingenious; spirited*; ~er Einfall *brain-wave, quip, sally*; spielerisch ~ *lambent* (*wit*) **2.** [adv] *wittily* ≗**reichelei** f *aestheticism; highbrowism* **~reicheln** vi [h] *to play the highbrow* (od *bel esprit*) ‖ ~d *highbrow* (*conversation*) **~sprühend** a *brilliant; sparkling* (*dialogue*); **~tötend** a *deadening; dull; stupefying* **~voll** a *full of spirit* (od *mental vitality*); *brilliant; spirited*

G·eistchen n ~s/~ ⟨ent⟩ Gattung der ~ *Pterophoridae* L pl; *plume-moths* pl

G·eister- [in comp] *ghost–* ‖ **~beschwörer** m *necromancer; sorcerer* ‖ (Austreiber) *exorcist* **~beschwörung** f (Anrufung) *evocation of spirits; necromancy* ‖ (Austreibung) *exorcism* **~erscheinung** f *apparition; ghost; phantom* **~geschichte** f *ghost-story* **~glaube** m *superstition; belief in ghosts* **~hand** f *spirit-hand* **~klopfen** n *spirit-rapping* **~reich** n = –welt **~seher** m *ghostseer; spirit*(*ual*)*ist* ‖ *spirit-monger* **~seherei** f *ghost-seeing; spiritism* **~stunde** f *ghostly hour; the witching-hour of midnight* **~welt** f *the realm of spirits; spirit-world*

g·eisterhaft a *ghostly* (*voice*), *ghostlike* (*to look g.*); (*appearance*); *phantasmal, spectral, supernatural, weird*; ~es Aussehen *ghostliness; unearthly* (*silence*) **g·eistern** vi [h] ⟨fig⟩ *to appear; figure; linger*; ein Vorschlag –rt durchs Land .. *is making its appearance* (od *can be heard*) *here and there*

G·eistes- [in comp] *intellectual, mental* ≗**abwesend** a *absent-minded, absent in mind; preoccupied; wandering* | **G–nheit** [f] *absence of mind; absent-mindedness; abstraction* **~anlage** f *talent*; ~en pl *abilities, aptitudes* **~arbeit** f *brain* (od *head*) *-work* **~arbeiter** m *intellectual worker; black-coat worker*; ⟨Am⟩ *white collar worker* **~aristokratie** f *meritocracy* **~art** f *cast of mind; mentality* **~bildung** f *cultivation of the mind; intellectual culture* **~blitz** m *brain-wave; flash of wit*; ~e [pl] *aphorisms* pl **~erzeugnis** n *mental product*(*ion*) **~freiheit** f *freedom of thought* **~frische** f *mental strength; freshness of mind* **~gabe** f = –anlage **~gegenwart** f *presence of mind* **~geschichte** f *history of mind*; deutsche ~ *history of the German mind* od *of German mentality* od *thought* ≗**gestört** a (*mentally*) *deranged; mentally unsettled* **~gestörtheit** f (*mental*) *derangement* **~größe** f *intellectual greatness* **~haltung** f *spirit; mental attitude* **~held** m; ~en [pl] *great minds, choice spirits; master-spirits* pl **~kraft** f *power of mind; mental strength*; Besitz der ≗e (f Testament) *disposing mind* ≗**krank** a *insane, of unsound mind*; (er ist) anerkannt ~ .. *a certified lunatic* **~kranke** [der ~, ein ~r] *the mental patient* od *case*; Klinik f ~ [pl] *mental hospital* **~krankheit** f *mental disease*; Spezialist f ~en *mental specialist* **~leben** n *intellectual life* **~richtung** f *mentality; turn of mind* **~schärfe** f *sagacity* **~schöpfung** f *conception* ≗**schwach** a *feeble-minded, weak-headed* (od *minded*); *imbecile* **~schwäche** f *feeble-mindedness, weakness of mind; mental deficiency; imbecility* **~schwung** m *flight of imagination* **~stärke** f = –kraft **~störung** f (*mental*) *derangement* **~verfassung** f → geistige V. ≗**verwandt** a *congenial* (mit *with*) **~verwandtschaft** f *congeniality; affinity* **~verwirrung** f *aberration*; → –störung **~welt** f *intellectual* (od *spiritual*) *world* **~wissenschaften** f pl *arts*, [Ger] *do*: *g.* pl **~wissenschaftler** m *man of learning* (od *letters*); *scholar* ≗**wissenschaftlich** a; ~e Abteilung *arts side*; in der ~en A. *on the arts side* ‖ ~e Bildung *scholarship, learning* **~zerrüttung** f *alienation; derangement of the mind* **~zustand** m *mental state*; → –verfassung; geistige V.

g·eistig A. [a] **1.** *spiritual* (*being*); *immaterial* | *intellectual* (*centre, food, needs*), *mental* (*activity, life*), *spiritual* (*growth*) | ∼e **Armut** *intellectual thinness*; ∼e Arbeit = Geistesarbeit; ⟨fig⟩ vor m–m ∼en Auge *in my mind's eye*; ∼e Beschäftigung ⟨Am⟩ *white-collar occupation*; in ∼er Beziehung *spiritually*; *intellectually, mentally*; ∼e Dinge *things of the mind*; ∼e Eigenschaft *spirituality* ‖ ∼es Eigentum *literary property*; → Urheberrecht; ∼e Einstellung [f] *mentality*; ∼er Gehalt *intellectual content*; *spirit* (*of an age*); ∼e Güter *spiritual things*; ∼e Kraft *imagination*; *intuition*; *vision*; ∼es Proletariat *white-collar proletariat*; ∼e Stumpfheit *intellectual torpidity* (od *torpor*); ∼e Überanstrengung *brain-fag*; ∼e Verfassung *mood*; *frame* (od *state, habit*) *of mind*; ∼-seelische V. ⟨mil⟩ *morale*; ∼es Wesen *spirituality*; *mental life, mentality*; *intellectuality* ‖ ∼es Widerstreben *obstinacy of mind* **2.** ∼e Getränke *spirits* pl, *alcoholic* od *spirituous drinks* od *liquors*; → Abstinenz(ler) **B.** [adv] *spiritually* ‖ *intellectually, mentally*; den M. ∼ befreien *to liberate the spirit of man*; ∼ belastet *or* krank *mentally afflicted*; ∼ gerichtet *metaphysical* (*language, mind*) ‖ ein ∼ Anspruchsloser *a low--brow*; ∼ tiefstehend *low-brow* (*man*) **G·eistigkeit** f *spirituality*; *intellectuality* ‖ *mental attitude*; *way of thinking*; französische ∼ *esprit* Fr

g·eistlich a **1.** *spiritual*; *religious* (*lyric*); *sacred* (*music, songs*) | (kirchlich) *ecclesiastical*; *church–* ‖ *clerical* **2.** ∼es Amt *ministerial office* ‖ ∼e Angelegenheit *spiritual* od *religious matters* ‖ ∼er Beruf *clerical profession*; den ∼en B. ergreifen *to enter the church* ‖ ∼e Besitztümer (Einnahmen etc) ⟨hist⟩ *spiritualities* pl ‖ ∼e Fürsten ⟨engl⟩ *Lords spiritual* ‖ ∼e Gerichtsbarkeit, ∼er Gerichtshof *ecclesiastical jurisdiction, e. court* ‖ ∼er Orden *religious order* ‖ ∼es Recht *ecclesiastical law* ‖ ∼e Rechte *ecclesiastical rights*; ⟨hist⟩ *spiritualities* pl ‖ ∼e Schauspiele, Spiele ⟨hist⟩ *mysteries, miracle plays* pl ‖ ∼er Stand [abstr] *holy orders* pl; in den ∼en St. treten *to take h. o.* | [konkr] *the clergy* ‖ ∼e Übungen *rel. exercises*

Geistliche [der ∼, ein ∼r] m ∼n/∼n ⟨C. E.⟩ (ordinierter ∼r) *clergyman*; ⟨fam⟩ *divine*; ⟨High Church⟩ *priest* ‖ ∼ dritten Weihegrades *deacon* (→ Bischof) ‖ die ∼n [koll] *clergymen, the clergy*; 10 ∼ *ten clergy*(*men*); Vorrecht der ∼n, vor dem weltl. Gericht nicht z erscheinen *benefit of clergy* ‖ ∼r w *to take holy orders, to enter the church* | (College⁓, Gefängnis⁓ etc) *chaplain* ‖ ⟨mil⟩ *chaplain*; Schiffs⁓ *ship's chaplain*; ⟨sl⟩ *sky-pilot* | ⟨dissenters⟩ *minister, nonconformist clergyman*; ⟨Am⟩ *clergyman, minister of religion* | ⟨Am sl⟩ *gospel-pusher* **G·eistlichkeit** f ∼/ *clergy* [pl konstr: *the c. are* ..]; diese ∼ *these clergy*

g·eistlos a ⟨übtr⟩ *lacking spirit*; *dull* (*sermon*); *insipid* (*conversation*), *stupid, vapid, watery* ‖ *dull, obtuse, stupid* (*p*) **G·eistlosigkeit** f *dullness, insipidity, vapidity* ‖ *obtuseness, stupidity, stupor* (*of a p*)

G·eitau n ⟨mar⟩ *guy, guy-rope*; *tack*; ∼e [pl] *brails* pl ‖ ∼ des Hauptsegels *clew-garnet*; ∼ der kleineren Segel *clew-line* ‖ dazu: *to guy*

G·eiz m ∼es/ **1.** *avarice, covetousness, cupidity, greed*(*iness*), *stinginess* **2.** ⟨bot⟩ (Seitentrieb) *side-shoot* °**∼hals, ∼hammel, ∼kragen** m *miser, niggard, screw, skinflint*; *codger*; *curmudgeon*; *hunks*; ⟨Am⟩ *skin*; *cheap skate*; *piker* **g·eizen** vi [h] **1.** *to be avaricious* ‖ ⟨mst übtr⟩ ∼ mit etw *to be economical* (od *sparing, stingy*) *of a th*; *to economize* (od *spare*) *in a th*; *to husband a th*; er geizt mit jeder Minute *he is saving every possible minute*; nicht ∼ mit etw *to be lavish of a th, to lavish a th*; *to bring into play* ‖ ∼ nach etw *to aim at a th*; *to be covetous of*; *to aspire to* od *after*; *to hanker after, to strive for a th*; *to covet* od *seek a th* **2.** ⟨hort⟩ *to remove side-shoots* **g·eizig** a *avaricious, covetous, greedy*; *niggardly*; *close*; *stingy* (mit *of*); ⟨fam⟩ *mingy* ‖ ein ∼er Kerl = Geizhals

Ge- ∼j·age n ∼s/ *bustling, hustling* **∼j·ammer** n ∼s/ *lamentation, wailings* pl °**∼j·auchze** n ∼s/ *rejoicings* pl ‖ *exultations, jubilations* °**∼j·odel** n ∼s/ *yode*(*l*)*ling*; = Geschrei **∼j·ohle** n ∼s/ *noisy singing*; = Geschrei °**∼j·ubel** n ∼s/ = Gejauchze °**∼k·eife** n ∼s/ *nagging, scolding*; *worrying* **⁓k·erbt** a *indented, notched* ‖ ⟨bot⟩ *crenate*(*d*) **∼k·icher** n ∼s/ *tittering*; *sniggers, titters* pl °**∼k·itzel** n ∼s/ *tickling*; *tickles* pl °**∼kl·äff(e)** n ∼(e)s/ *yapping, yelping*; *yaps, yelps* pl °**∼kl·apper** n ∼s/ *clattering*; *clatters* pl; *rattles* pl, *rattling sounds* pl °**∼kl·atsch(e)** n ∼es/ **1.** *clapping* (*of hands*) **2.** *chattering*; *gossiping*; *gossip, prattle, tittle-tattle* **gekl·emmt** a (→ klemmen) ([Visier-] Korn) *incorrectly centered* °**∼kl·imper** n ∼s/ *fooling around at* od *drumming on* (*the piano*), *strum*(*ming*), *tink-a-tink* °**∼kl·ingel** n ∼s/ *tintinnabulation*; *jingling, tinkling* (*of bells*); *jingle, tinkle* °**∼kl·irr(e)** n ∼(e)s/ *clanking, clashing*; *clank*; *din*; *clink* (*of glasses*) °**∼kl·öne** n = Geplauder °**∼kl·opfe** n ∼s/ *knocking, rapping*; *knocks, raps* pl **∼kl·üft(e)** n ∼(e)s/ *rifted cliffs* od *cleaved rocks* **∼kn·atter** n ∼s/ *crackling*; *crackle*; (of a machine-gun) *rat-tat-tat* **⁓kn·ickt** a *bent*; ⟨fig⟩ = niedergeschlagen °**∼kn·irsche** n *gnashing, grinding* (*of teeth*) **∼kn·ister** n ∼s/ *crackling*; *crackle* **⁓k·öpert** a *twilled* **⁓k·oppelt** a *geminated* °**∼k·ose** n ∼s/ *billing and cooing* °**∼kr·ächze** n ∼s/ *croaking* ‖ ⟨übtr⟩ *jarring noise* °**∼kr·akel** n ⁓s/ *croaking* **∼kr·änkt** a *grieved*; *wronged*; *hurt, injured, wounded* (*pride*); ⟨Am⟩ *sorry* (über *about*); sich [acc] ∼ fühlen, ∼ s *to feel offended*, etc **∼kränktsein** n *aggrieved feeling, pique* [Fr] **∼kr·ätz** n ∼es/ ⟨met⟩ *dross*; *waste metal*; °**∼kr·eisch(e)** n ∼es/ *screaming, shrieking*; *screams, shrieks* pl; *screeches* pl **∼kr·itzel** n ∼s/ *scrawling, scribbling*; *scrawl, scribble*; → Krähenfüße **∼kr·öpf** n ∼es/ ⟨poet agr⟩ *crops* pl **⁓kr·öpft** a ⟨tech⟩ *cranked*; ∼e Welle *crankshaft*; ∼es Rohr *S-shaped pipe* **∼kr·öse** n ∼s/∼ **1.** ⟨anat⟩ *mesentery* ‖ [in comp] *mesenteric* **2.** ⟨cul⟩ *fry*; *tripe*; (Herz, Leber, Lunge) *pluck*; (Kutteln) *chitterlings* pl **⁓kr·ümmt** a *bent* (*pipe*); *curved* (*surface*) **⁓k·ünstelt** a *affected*; *artificial* **⁓k·uppelt** a ⟨tech⟩ *coupled* °**∼k·üsse** n ∼s/ *kissing and slobbering*

Gel n ∼s/∼e ⟨chem⟩ [abbr v Gelatine] *gel*

ˣ**gel, g·elle, g·ellens** [intj] (→ gelten) = gelt?

Ge- ∼l·ache n ∼s/ *laughing* **∼l·ächter** n ∼s/ *laughter* ‖ brüllendes ∼ *guffaw*; lautes ∼ *broad laugh, gust of laughter*; wieherndes ∼ *horse--laugh*; ein schallendes ∼ *a peal* (⟨Am⟩ *rip*) *of laughter*; *roar*(*s*) ‖ in ein (schallendes) ∼ ausbrechen *to burst out laughing*; *to burst into a shout of laughter*; (*to guffaw*); ∼ auslösen *to excite laughter* ‖ sich dem ∼ aussetzen *to expose o.s. to ridicule*; *to be held up as laughingstock* ‖ jdn z ∼ m *or* dem ∼ preisgeben *to hold a p up to ridicule* ‖ zum ∼ w *to be ridiculed*; er wurde z ∼ in .. *he became the laughing-stock of* (*the town*) °**⁓l·ackmeiert** a *done in the eye*; *sucked in* **⁓l·aden** a **1. a.** *loaded* (*gun*) ‖ ⟨el⟩ *charged*; ∼er Draht *live wire* **b.** ⟨übtr & fig⟩ ∼ mit *pregnant, charged with, full of* (*energy*) ‖ °**∼ s auf jdn** *to be furious with a p* **2.** *invited* (*guest*) **∼l·age** n ∼s/∼ *banquet, feast*; *revelry* ‖ (Zech⁓) *drinking-bout, drunken frolic*; ⟨fam⟩ *spree*; ⟨sl⟩ *binge* (*a cocktail b.*) **⁓l·agert** a **1.** ⟨tech⟩ *fitted* od *hung, mounted* (auf *on*); auf Zapfen ∼ *pivoted* ‖ fliegend ∼ *overhung* **2.** ⟨fig⟩ *circumstanced*; (der Fall) ist anders ∼ .. *is differently circumstanced* **⁓lähmt** a ⟨med⟩ *paralysed* (*limbs*); einseitig ∼ *hemiplegic* ‖ ⟨übtr⟩ ihm war die Zunge wie ∼ *he was tongue-tied* † **⁓l·ahrt** a = gelehrt

Gel·ände n ∼s/∼ **1.** *tract of land, ground*(*s* pl); ⟨bes mil⟩ *terrain*; durchschnittenes ∼ *broken ground*; ∼ ausbauen *to build up an area*; mit dem

~ verwachsen s *to be thoroughly at home on the terrain*; auf freiem ~ *under field conditions*; ~ gewinnen, nehmen *to gain, seize terrain* **2.** [in comp] *cross-country* **~abschnitt** m ⟨bes mil⟩ *sector* (*of terrain*), *terrain compartment* **~antrieb** m *all-wheel drive* **~aufnahme** f *ground survey*; *photo-survey* **~ausbildung** f *field training* **~beschaffenheit** f *ground feature* **~besprechung** f ⟨mil⟩ *staff walk* **~beurteilung** f *terrain analysis* od *appreciation* **~eckpfeiler** m ⟨tact⟩ *t. as an anchor* **~einweisung** f *t. briefing* **~erkundung** f *reconnaissance of position* **~fahren** n *cross-country driving* **~fahrt** f (z –besprechung) *staff ride* **~flugzeug** n *no-airfield aircraft* **~gang** m ⟨mil mot⟩ *underdrive*: *auxiliary gear* **≗gängig** a ⟨mot⟩ *c.-c.* (*lorry*) | **≗keit** [f] *c.-c. capacity* **~lauf** m ⟨sport⟩ *c.-c. race* **~merkmal** n *ground feature* **~punkt** m *landmark* **~reifen** m *c.-c.* od *ground-grip tyre* **~reiten** n *c.-c. riding* **~ritt** m = –lauf **~sprung** m ⟨mil⟩ *break in the ground*; ⟨ski⟩ *gelände jump* **~streifen** m *terrain corridor* **~teile** n pl *terrain*; auffallende ~ *prominent t. features* **~wagen** m *c.-c. car* **~winkel** m ⟨mil⟩ *angle of sight*

Gel·änder n ~s/~ *railing, rails* pl; Treppen≗ *banisters* pl || (Brüstung) *balustrade, parapet* || → Spalier **~docke** f = –stab **~säule** f *baluster* **~stab** m *banister* **~stange** f *hand-rail*

gel·angen vi [s] **1. ~ nach** *to come* od *get to* (*Berlin*); *to arrive at* (*a place*), *in* (*Berlin*); *to reach* (*a place, Berlin*) || ~ **bis** an *or* bis z *to reach* (*the shore*; *the other side*; *a p's car*); ~ in *to gain* od *reach* (*the harbour*); *to come into* (*harbour*) | **an** s–n Bestimmungsort ~ *to reach one's destination* || das Stück ist nicht **auf** uns gelangt *the play has not come down to us* || **in jds Hand** *or* **Hände** ~ *to get into a p's hands*; *to reach a p* (od *a p's hands*); ⟨com⟩ *to come to hand*; Ihr Brief ist in unsere H. gelangt *your letter to hand ..* || nicht in die richtigen H. ~ *to come* (od *get*) *into wrong hands* || **nach Hause** ~ *to get* (od *reach*) *home* || **etw ~ l an** jdn *to address* (od *direct, forward*) *a th to a p* **2.** ⟨übtr⟩ **zu etw** ~ *to attain to a th*; *to attain* od *gain, reach a th* || zur Aufführung ~ *to be performed* || z größerer Klarheit ~ *to attain to a greater clarity* || zur Macht ~ *to attain to* (od *come into*) *power* || z Reichtum ~ *to gain wealth* || z e m Schluß ~ *to reach a conclusion* || z Wohlstand ~ *to attain to prosperity* || zum Ziel ~ *to gain one's ends, object*

°**Gel·ärm** n ~(e)s/ *noisy doings* pl; *noisiness*

Gel·aß n –sses/–sse (~ im Hause) *accommodation* (f *for*); *house-room*; *housing* (*for 20 people*); *room* (viel ~ *plenty of r.*)

gel·assen 1. [a] *collected, composed, resigned*; *placid*; *serene*; *self-possessed*; *poised*; *calm, tranquil*; *cool(headed)*; *imperturbable, unperturbed*; *unruffled* || ~ bleiben *to keep one's temper*; ⟨sl⟩ *to keep one's hair on*; ganz ~ bl. *not to turn a hair* || mit ~er Stimme *in an even* (od *a calm, unhurried*) *voice*; *with composure of one's voice* **2.** [adv] *calmly*; = gefaßt B. || etw ~ aufnehmen *to take a th coolly* **≗heit** f ~/ *collectedness, composedness, composure*; *calmness, imperturbability*; *poise*; *placidity*

gel·ästert a viel ~ *much-maligned*

Gelat·ine [ʒel–] f ~/ **1.** *gelatin(e)* || Spreng≗ *blasting gelatine* **2.** [in comp] *gelatine*; → gallertartig, -förmig | ~dynamit [n] *gelignite* **gelati·n·ieren** [ʒ–] vt/i [h/s] *to gelatinize* **gelatineartig, gelatin·ös** a *gelatinous*

Ge- ~l·äuf n ~(e)s/~e ⟨hunt⟩ (Spur) *scent*; *trail* || ⟨sport⟩ (Boden) *going* °**~l·aufe** n ~s/ *running to and fro*; *running about* **≗l·äufig A.** [a] **1.** [attr] *fluent* (*German*) | *common, current* (*phrase*); *usual* **2.** [pred] ~ s *to be in use*; *to be current* | jdm ~ s *to be familiar to a p*; die S ist mir nicht ~ *I am not familiar with the matter* || Englisch ist ihm ~ *he speaks fluent English* (od *English fluently*) **B.** [adv] *fluently*; ~ Englisch sprechen *to speak English fluently* | **≗keit** [f] ~/ *fluency*; *easiness, facility* **≗l·aunt** a [mst pred] gut ~ *in good humour*; schlecht ~ *in bad humour, out of humour, illhumoured*; wie war er ~? *in what humour was he?* **~l·äut** n ~(e)s/ **1.** *the ringing of bells*; (lautes ~) *peal* **2.** (= die Glocken) *set of bells*; *peal*; → Glockenspiel **3.** ⟨hunt⟩ *bay* (*of dogs* od *hounds*) °**~l·äute** n ~s/ = Geläut 1. **≗l·äutert** a *refined* (*oil*); ⟨übtr⟩ *purified* (*heart*)

gelb I. [a] *yellow*; ~e Farbe *y. colour*; *y.*; ~e Färbung, ~er Ton *y.ness* | (etw) ~ färben *to y.* || ~ w (*turn*) *y.*; ~ u grün w vor Neid *to be green with envy* || ⟨tech⟩ ~ brennen *to dip, to pickle* | ≗e **Acht** f ⟨ent⟩ = Gelbling 3. || ~es Brasilienholz = ≗holz; ~e Rübe *carrot*; ≗es Fieber *y. fever*, ⟨sl⟩ *y. Jack* || ~er Fleck (im Auge) *y. spot* || → Gefahr || ⟨mot⟩ ≗ leuchtet auf *amber shows*; das ~e Licht überfahren, bei ≗ (noch, bereits) aufs Gas steigen *to shoot the amber* || ≗es Meer *Y. Sea* || *y.* (*press, race*); Angehörige der ~en Rassen *the y. men* **II.** ≗ n *yellow*; in ≗ *in yellow*

G·elb- [in comp] *yellow*; *xantho–* **~beeren** f pl chines. ~ *y.* (od *Persian*) *berries* pl **~bleierz** n ⟨minr⟩ *wulfenite* **≗braun** a *y.-brown, titian* **~brennen** n ⟨tech⟩ *dipping*; *pickling* **~buch** n ⟨pol⟩ *Y.-Book* **~eisenerz** n *y. limonite* **~eisenstein** m ⟨minr⟩ *xanthosiderite* **~erde** f *y. ochre* (od *earth*) **~erz** n ⟨minr⟩ *sylvanite* **~färbung** f *y.ing* **~filter** m ⟨phot⟩ *y. filter* **~gießer** m *brassfounder*; *brazier* **~glut** f *y. heat* **≗grün** a *y.-green* **~guß** m *y. brass* **≗haarig** a *y.-haired* **~holz** n *y. wood*; *fustic* **~klee** m ⟨bot⟩ *black* (od *hop*) *medick*; *nonsuch* **~kraut** n ⟨bot⟩ *y. weed* **~kreuz** n (Kampfstoff) *y.-cross gas*; *mustard-gas* **~kupfer** n = –guß **~metall** n *y. metal* **~rand** m ⟨ent⟩ *dytiscus* [L] **~reizker** m ⟨bot⟩ = Ritterling **~rübe** f ⟨bot⟩ *carrot* **~scheibe** f = –filter || **~schnabel** m *greenhorn*; *jackanapes*; *fledgeling*; *whipper-snapper* **~schoten** f pl = –beeren **~schwämmchen** n ⟨bot⟩ = Pfifferling **~stern** m ⟨bot⟩ = Goldstern **~stich** m *yellow tinge* **~sucht** f ⟨med⟩ *jaundice*; ⟨mot⟩ an der ~ leiden *to shoot the amber* **≗süchtig** a *jaundiced*; *icteric* **~veigelein** n ⟨bot⟩ = Goldlack **~weiderich** m ⟨bot⟩ = Weiderich **~wurz** f ⟨bot⟩ *curcuma*; *turmeric* **~wurzel** f *turmeric root*

G·elbe 1. [der ~, ein ~r] m ~n/~n *yellow man*; → gelb **2.** n (im Ei) *yolk* **G·elbe Meer,** das (zw China u Korea) *the Yellow Sea* **g·elben** vt/i [h] *to yellow* **g·elblich** a *yellowish*; *yellowy*; ~es flachsfarbenes Haar *yellowish flaxen hair*; ~grau *beige* **G·elbling** m **1.** ⟨bot⟩ = Pfifferling **2.** ⟨orn⟩ = Goldammer **3.** ⟨ent⟩ *colias, sulphur butterfly*

G·eld n ~es/~er **A. 1.** *money*; ⟨sl⟩ *brass, dough*; ⟨Am sl⟩ *jack, rocks* pl; → Draht, Kies, Moos, Pinke, Zaster || Natural≗ *kind* (*to pay in kind*); Metall≗ *specie*; ⟨Am⟩ *hard cash*; Papier≗ *paper-m.* || kursierendes ~ (e–s Landes) *currency*; gemünztes ~ (e–s Landes) *coinage* || bares ~ *cash*; *ready m.*; Klein≗ *change*; das liebe ~ *lovely m.*; falsches ~ *base* (od *counterfeit, false*) *coin*; sauer verdientes ~ ⟨fam⟩ *kelp*; ⟨com⟩ tägliches ~ *call-m.*; ~ f Finanzierungszwecke ⟨Am⟩ *barrel* | ~er [pl] *moneys*; *funds* pl; *remittances* pl || Staats≗er *State Funds*; Öffentliche ~er *Public Funds* **2.** ⟨st exch⟩ *buyers* pl; mehr ~ als Brief *buyers over* **B. Wendungen 1.** ein schönes **Stück** ~ *a nice bit of m.*; *a pretty penny* (*that will cost a p. p.*); viel ~ *a lot of m.*; *a deep pocket* (*he has a ..*); leicht verdientes ~ *easy m.* | **das** ~ **bleibt** im Lande *the m. remains in the country*; ~ allein macht nicht glücklich *m.'s not everything*; ~ regiert die Welt *m. rules the world*; das ~ rollt *m. rolls*; ⟨com⟩ ~ spielt keine Rolle *m.* (*is*) *no consideration*, ⟨fam⟩ *the sky's the limit*!; Zeit **ist** ~ *time is m.*; ~ ist knapp *m. is scarce*; das ist hinausgeworfenes ~ *that is throwing m. out of the window*; °er ist sein ~ los *he has lost his m.*; *he is* *the loser* | ~ **auftreiben** *to raise* (od *find*) *m.*; °dicke ~er beziehen = ~ verdienen; ~ bringt ~ *m. breeds m.*; das ~ unter die Leute bringen *to make one's m. circulate*; jdm ~ ersparen *to save* (od *spare*) *a p's pocket*; das ~ fliegt nur so davon *m. takes to itself wings*; wenn ich ~ **habe,** werde ich .. *when I have some m.* (⟨Am sl⟩ *when my ship comes in*) *I shall* ..; °er hat ~ wie Heu (*or* dicke ~er) *he has money to burn*; *he is rolling in m.*; ⟨fig⟩ nicht das nötige (Klein-)~ h *to lack the wherewithal* (um z .. *to buy*); → heiraten; ~ herausrücken *to shell out*; das kostet kein ~ *that costs nothing*; bar ~ lacht *m. talks*; **~ m** *to make m.*, ⟨fam⟩ *to line one's pocket*; mit der Kunst ist kein ~ z m *there is no m. in art*; er hat damit viel ~ gemacht *he has made a lot of m. with it*; das ~ reichte ihm länger *he made m. go further*; ~er sammeln f *to make up a purse for*; ~ schlagen aus .. *to trade upon* (*a secret*); auf s–m ~e sitzen *to skin a flint*; ~ stecken in .. *to put money in a business*; ~ verdienen *to earn* (⟨fam⟩ *make*) *m.*; sein ~ ehrlich verd. *to earn an honest penny*; °~ wie Heu verd. *to be coining m.*; sein ~ vertun, verjuxen *to play about, to make it fly*; ~ wechseln *to change money*; sein ~ auf die Straße (*or* z Fenster hinaus) werfen *to throw one's money out of the window*; *to spend m. right and left, to make one's m. fly*; er kann sein ~ nicht z F. hinauswerfen *he has no m. to burn*; jdm das ~ aus der Tasche ziehen *to screw m. out of a p*; ~ zusetzen (*or* verlieren) *to suffer in one's pocket* **2. am** ~e hängen *to be a slave to m.* | **auf** ~ wird nicht gesehen *m.* (*is*) *no consideration* (od *object*) | **bei** ~e s *to be in cash*; *to have m. on hand*; nicht bei ~e s *to be out of cash, to be short of m.* | f sein ~ etw erhalten *to get the worth of one's m.* ‖ nicht f ~ u gute Worte *not for love or m.* | er schwimmt **im** ~e = hat ~ wie Heu ‖ das läuft ins ~ *that runs into m.*; in ~ umsetzen *to convert* (od *turn*) *into m.* | jdm **mit** ~ aushelfen *to lend* (od *advance*) *a p m.*; das ist nicht mit ~ z bezahlen *that is invaluable* ‖ was willst du mit dem ~e m? *what will you do with the m.?*; mit dem ~e knapp s *to be short of money*; mit viel ~ unterstützt *heavily subsidized*; jdn mit ~ern versehen *to put a p in funds*; ⟨Am⟩ *to stake a p*; mit dem ~e um sich werfen *to throw one's m. about* | **ohne** ~ *without m.*; *m.less* | nur **um** des ~es willen arbeiten *to work only in the hope of reward*; jdn um sein ~ bringen → bringen ‖ um sein ~ k *to lose one's m.*; → spielen | **von** s–m ~e leben *to live on one's private income*; jd, der v s–m ~e lebt *a rentier* | (leicht) z ~e k *to come into m.*, (*to coin m.*); (etw) z ~ m *to turn* (od *convert*) *into m.*; *to realize* **~adel** m *the m.ed aristocracy* **~aristokratie** ⟨Am fam⟩ *codfish aristocracy* **~angebot** n ⟨com⟩ *supply of m.* **~angelegenheit** f; ~en pl *m.-matters*; *pecuniary affairs* pl **~anlage** f *investment* **~anleihe** f *m.-loan* **~anweisung** f *remittance, transfer*; telegraphische ~ *cable transfer*; → Postanweisung **~aufnahme** f *the taking up* (od *raising*) *of m.* **~ausgabe** f *disbursement, expense*; gr ~en h *to suffer in one's pocket* **~ausleiher** m = –verleiher **~bedarf** m *pecuniary requirements* **~beihilfe** f (staatl.) *subsidy* **~beitrag** m *subscription*; *contribution in m.* **≃besitzend** a *m.ed* (*classes*) **~bestände** m pl *moneys* **~beutel** m *m.-bag, purse*; → –tasche | ⟨fig⟩ *purse*; ⟨Am⟩ *pocketbook* ‖ jds ~ angreifen *to eat into a p's pocket*; e–n gr ~ h *to have a long purse* (od *deep pocket*); den Daumen auf den ~ halten *to tighten the purse-strings*; den ~ öffnen ⟨Am sl⟩ *to loosen up*; über den ~ verfügen *to hold the purse* (od *the purse-strings*) **~bewilligung** f ⟨parl⟩ *grant of m.* **~börse** f **1.** = –beutel **2.** = –markt **~brief** m *registered letter containing m.* **~büchse** f *m.-box* **~buße** f **1.** ⟨crim l⟩ *compensation* (*in m.*) *given to the injured p* **2.** ⟨tax l⟩ *fine* **3.** ⟨contr⟩ *penal sum* **~durst** m *thirst for* (od *greed of*) *m.* **~einlage** f *m. paid in*; *m. enclosed* **~einnahme** f *takings* pl **~einnehmer** m *collector* **~entschädigung** f *pecuniary compensation*; *indemnity* **~entwertung** f *depreciation of m.* (od *of the currency*) **~ersatz** m *reimbursement*, = –entschädigung ‖ ~mittel [n] *promissory document representing coin* **~ertragstafel** f *m. yield-table* **~erwerb** m *m.-making* **~forderung** f *pecuniary claim* **~frage** f *question of £.s.d.*; es ist k–e ~ *m. is no object* **~geber** m *banker, capitalist, finacier*; *financial backer* **~geschäft** n *m.-transaction*; ⟨sl⟩ *flutter*; ~e m *to engage in financial operations*; ⟨sl⟩ *to have a flutter* (in *in*) **~geschenk** n *gratuity*; *tip*; jdm ein ~ m *to tip a p* **~gier** f *greed of m., m.-grubbing* **≃gierig** a *greedy of* (od *for*) *m.* **~handel** m *m.-trade*; *banking* **~heirat** f *mercenary marriage* **~herrschaft** f *plutocracy, plutarchy* **~hilfe** f *pecuniary aid*; *subsidy* ‖ °**~jäger** m *m.-grubber* (od *shark*) **~kalamität** f = –schwierigkeit **~kasse** f *m.-box* ‖ (Ladenkasse) *till* **~kassette** f *cash-box*; *strong-box* **~katze** f *m.-belt* **~klemme** f = –verlegenheit **~knappheit** f *stringency* od *shortage of m.*; ⟨com fam⟩ *squeeze* **~krise, ~krisis** f *monetary* (od *financial*) *crisis* **~kurs** m *m.-rate*; *rate of exchange* **~leute** pl *m.ed men* od *class*; *capitalists* pl **~makler** m *m.-broker*; *scrivener* **~mangel** m *scarcity of m.*; (a. *monetary pressure*) **~mann** m *m.ed man*; *capitalist* **~markt** f *m.-market* ‖ der engl. ~ *the City* (am ~ *in the C.*); der amerik. ~ *Wall Street* (am ~ *on W. St.*) **~mittel** n pl *means*; *funds* pl; (*pecuniary*) *resources* pl **~not** f *pecuniary distress*; in ~ s *to be in difficulties* **~onkel** m ⟨Am⟩ *sugar daddy* **~opfer** n *financial sacrifice* **~posten** m *sum* (od *item*) *of m.* **~preis** m *rate of exchange*; e–n ~ gewinnen *to win the purse*, **~protz** m ⟨fam⟩ *m.-bags* pl; *plutocrat*; ~en [pl] *plutocracy* **~protzig, ~stolz** a *purse-proud* **~quelle** f *pecuniary source*; → –mittel **~raffer** m *m.-grubber* **~rolle** f *roll of m.*; *rouleau* **~sache** f *m.-matter*; in ~en hört die Gemütlichkeit auf *business is business* **~sack** m *m.-bag* ‖ °⟨fig⟩ (P) ⟨fam⟩ *m.-bags*, ⟨sl⟩ *plute* ‖ ~herrschaft = –herrschaft **~sammlung** f *purse*, ⟨Am fam⟩ *drive*; e–e ~ veranstalten *to make up a purse* (⟨Am⟩ drive) (f *for*) **~schatulle** f *cash-box* **~schiff** n ⟨fig⟩ wenn das ~ ankommt *when my ship comes home* ‖ °**~schneider** m ⟨fig⟩ *extortioner* ‖ °**~schneiderei** f ⟨fig⟩ *extortion*; *robbery, sharping*; ⟨sl⟩ *ramp* **~schrank** m *safe*; → feuerfest ‖ ~knacker *safe-cracker*, ⟨bes Am⟩ *s.-blower* **~schublade** f *till* **~schuld** f *m.-debt* **~schwierigkeit** f ~en [pl] *monetary difficulties*; *pecuniary straits* pl **~sendung** f *remittance* **~sorte** f *coin*; *denomination*; ~en [pl] *coinage*; *currency* **~strafe** f *fine, penalty*; bei e–r ~ v *under p. of* (*£ 5*); (jdn) z e–r ~ verurteilen *to fine a p* (*he was fined 100 marks*); ein Vergehen, auf dem e–e ~ steht *a finable offence*; sich [dat] e–e ~ zuziehen *to incur a fine*; mit e–r hohen ~ belegt w *to be heavily fined* **~stück** n *coin*; *piece of m.* **~stückelungsliste** f ⟨comp⟩ *coinage analysis* **~summe** f *sum of m.* **~tasche** f *m.-bag* ‖ *flat case* (od *purse*); (f Papiergeld) *wallet* **~überfluß** m *abundance of m.* **~umlauf** m *circulation of m.* **~umsatz** m *turnover in m.* **~unterstützung** f = –hilfe **~verdienst** m *m. earned* **~verkehr** m *traffic in m.*; *circulation of m.* **~verlegenheit** f (*pecuniary*) *embarrassment*; in ~ s *to be short* (od *in need*) *of m., to be in low water*; *to be pressed for m.*, in äußerster, schrecklicher ~ *frightfully hard up*, ⟨sl⟩ *down on one's uppers*, ⟨Am sl⟩ *on the rocks* **~verleiher** m *money-lender* **~verlust** m *loss of m.*; *monetary loss* **~verschwendung** f *waste of m.*; *extravagance* **~vorrat** m *cash in hand*; *funds* pl **~vorschuß** m *advance* **~waage** f *m.-balance* **~währung** f *currency* **~wechsel** m *exchange* (*of m.*) **~wechsler** m *m.-changer*; *banker* **~wert** m *m.-value*; *value of* (*in*) *m.* od *currency* **~wesen** n *m. in general*; *m.-matters* pl; *finance* **~wirtschaft** f *monetary system* **~wucher** m *usury* **~zahlung** f *remittance* **~zins** m *interest on m.*

G·eldern n **1.** (holländ. Stadt) *G(u)eldres* **2.** (holländ. Prov.) *G(u)elderland*; Bewohner(in) v ~ *Gueldrian*

G·eldeswert m ~(e)s/~e *value in money, m.'s worth* || Geld u ~ *m. and m.'s worth* **g·eldlich** a *monetary, pecuniary; financial* **g·eldlos** a *moneyless, penniless*

Gel·ee [ʒe'leː] n [Fr] ~s/~s *jelly*; ⟨cul⟩ Aal in ~ *jellied eel*; ~ bilden *to jelly*; ~ Royale f (*bee's*) *royal j.*

Gel·ege n *number of eggs laid; clutch*

gel·egen a [pp v liegen] **1.** ⟨eig⟩ *situated* (an, auf *on*); ~ s *to be situated* (⟨Am a.⟩ *located*); bequem ~ *easy of access* || schön ~ *beautifully-situated* (*hotel*); am Fluß ~ *riverside* (*villa*); an der See ~ *seaside* (*village*), (*village*) *by the sea*; im Westen (etc) ~ *west, western* (*end, part*); hoch ~ *perched* (auf .. *on cliffs*) **2.** ⟨übtr⟩ *convenient, opportune* (*moment*); *proper, suitable*; z ~er Stunde *or* Zeit *at the proper* (od *in due*) *time*; *opportunely* || ~ k *to come in handy*; jdm ~ k (S) *to come opportune to a p; to be convenient to a p; to suit a p*; Sie k mir sehr ~ *you come pat to the occasion*; die S kam ihm gerade ~ *the matter came pat to his purpose*; es kommt mir g. ~ *it suits me perfectly* | **es ist** (mir) nichts **daran** ~ *it is of no consequence* (*to me*); es war ihr nie etw daran ~ *she never cared for it*; es ist mir viel daran ~ *I set great store by it; it is a matter of great consequence to me*; .. an s–r Meinung .. *I am very anxious to know his opinion*; es ist ihm sonst **an nichts** ~ *nothing else matters to him*

Gel·egenheit f ~/~en *occasion* (f *for*; z tun *for doing*) | (gute ~) *chance* || (günstige ~) *opportunity* (f etw *for a th*; z tun *of* [od *for*] *doing; to do*); *facility* (f *for*); e–e günstige ~ ⟨fam⟩ *a good innings*; gute ~en *facilities* (*for*); günstige ~en ⟨fam⟩ *lucky breaks*; ~ öfter z telephonieren *telephone facilities*; e–e sichere ~ (sc Geld z verdienen etc) *a sure snap* | **bei** ~ *on occasion; at one's convenience; when the occasion arises* (od *offers*); *when I get a chance*; bei der ersten (besten) ~ *at one's earliest convenience; on the first opportunity*; bei passender ~ *as occasion serves; at one's leisure*; bei dieser (*or* der) ~ *on this occasion* (*I heard* ..); bei solchen ~en *on such occasions, at such times* | **es bot sich** e–e günstige ~ *a good opportunity presented itself*; .., wie die ~ sich bot .. *as occasion arose*; wenn sich e–e ~ f Sie bieten sollte *should anything come along for you*; .. ihm .. *he was afforded a chance*; mir ist mal wieder e–e ~ in den Schoß gefallen *opp. has once more entered my life*; es gibt noch andere ~en *that's not the only pebble on the beach* | **die ~ abwarten** *to wait one's oppotunity*; e–e ~ benutzen *to avail o.s. of an opportunity*; ~ bieten *or* geben z *to provide an opportunity for; to give occasion to; to give a handle to* (*rumours*); e–e ~ ergreifen *to seize* od *take an opportunity*; die ~ ergreifen *to take occasion* (*to do*) || die ~ beim Schopfe fassen *to take time by the forelock*; jdm ~ z (etw) geben *to give a p the opportunity of* (*a th*); *to give a p occasion to do* (od *the chance of doing*); jdm ~ z (etw) geben *to give a p the opportunity of* (*a th*); *to give a p occasion to do* (od *the chance of doing*); *to put a p in the way of doing*; ~ h z tun *to have* (*an*) *opportunity to do* || ⟨prov⟩ ~ macht Diebe *opportunity makes the thief*; ~ suchen z *to seek occasion for* (*a th*); die ~ verpassen *or* versäumen *to lose* od *miss the opportunity*; ⟨sl⟩ *to miss the bus*; die erste beste ~ wahrnehmen, die sich bietet *to take the best chance going* **Gel·egenheits-** [in comp] *occasional* (*speaker*) **~arbeiten** f pl *odd jobs* **~arbeiter** m *casual; casual labourer* od *hand*; [koll pl] ~ *casual labour* **~bekanntschaft** f *chance acquaintance*; (Mädchen) *pick-up girl* **~dichter** m *occasional writer* **~gedicht** n, **~verse** m pl *occasional verses* pl **~graphik, ~-kunst** f *art for special occasions* **~kauf** m *bargain* || † **~macher(in** f) m = Kuppler(in) **~schrift** f *occasional writing* **~ziel** n *opportunity target*

gel·egentlich 1. [a] *occasional* (*remarks, visits*); *casual, irregular, patchy; odd* (*jobs*), *temporary*; ⟨Am⟩ *transient* **2.** [adv] *occasionally, once in a while, on occasion; at odd moments; off and on*; (*every*) *now and then, at* (*odd*) *times*; ⟨Am⟩ *semi-occasionally, in spots*; nur ~ auftretend *occasional* (*noise*); •er raucht ~ eine Zigarre *he smokes an occasional cigar* || ~ auftretend ⟨a. med⟩ *episodic* (*attack*) | (bei Gelegenheit) *on occasion; at one's convenience* od *leisure* (*I shall do it at my l.*) **3.** [prep (mit gen)] ~ der Feier (*up*)*on the occasion of the festival*

gel·ehrig a *docile, teachable* || *able, apt, clever* || *supple*; → gefügig | **≈keit** f *docility*, (*teach*)*ability*

Gel·ehrsamkeit f ~/ *erudition, learning*; (klassische ~) *scholarship* **gel·ehrt** a *learned, erudite* || ⟨übtr⟩ *learned* (*book; word*); *scholarly* (*work*) || ~e Bildung *erudition* || °⟨fig⟩ ein ~es Haus *a learned man* **Gel·ehrte** [der ~, ein ~r] m ~n/~n *scholar; learned man; man of learning* (od *letters*); gr ~ *savant* [Fr]; Buch≈ *scholiast* **Gel·ehrten-** [in comp] *learned* (*circles, society*); *scholarly* **~republik** f *republic of letters* **~schule** f *Grammar School*; = Gymnasium **~stand** m *learned profession, the learned* pl | nach dem Staub der **~stube** riechen *to smell of the lamp* **Gel·ehrtheit** f *learnedness*; → Gelehrsamkeit

gel·eimt a *sized* (*paper*), °⟨fig⟩ *done in the eye*

Gel·eise n = Gleis

Gel·eit n ~(e)s/~e **A. 1.** [konkr] ⟨jur & mil⟩ *escort*; ~smann *escort*; ~sreiter *mounted e.* || ⟨mar⟩ (~schiffe) *convoy* || → Begleitung 3., Gefolge **2.** freies ~, sicheres ~ *safe-conduct*; jdm freies ~ gewähren *to give a p safe-conduct* | = ~brief **B.** (Begleitung) jdm das ~ geben *to accompany a p*; .. an die Tür *to see a p to the door*; .. an die Bahn *to see a p off*; → geleiten || jdm das letzte ~ geben *to pay a p the last honours* **C. ~boot** n = –fahrzeug **~brief** m *safe-conduct; safeguard* || ⟨übtr⟩ *pass*(*port*) || ⟨com⟩ (Zoll≈) *customs-certificate, permit; transire* **~fahrzeug** n *convoy; sloop*(*-of-war*) **~schein** m ~ f Waren *navicert*; → –brief **~schiff** n *convoy-ship*; ~e [pl] *convoy*; → –fahrzeug **~schutz** m ⟨aero⟩ *escort*, ~ fliegen *to escort* **~zerstörer** m ⟨mar⟩ *convoy destroyer* **~zug** m *convoy*

gel·eiten vt [h] **1.** (schützend ~) ⟨mil⟩ *to escort* || ⟨mar⟩ *to convoy* **2.** ⟨übtr⟩ (aus Höflichkeit begleiten; führen) (jdn) *to conduct, escort* (z *to*); *to show* (*a p from* ... *to* ..); (feierlich) *to induct* od *marshal* (an s–n Platz *into seat*); *to shepherd* (aus *out of*); *to see* (durch *through*); *to walk* (aus *out of*; in .. hinein *into*; nach *to*); → begleiten || Gott geleite dich! *God speed you!* **Gel·eiter** m ~s/~ *guide; conductor*

gel·enk a = gelenkig, → gewandt, flink

Gel·enk n ~(e)s/~e **1.** ⟨anat⟩ (Knochen≈) *joint; articulation*; Hand≈ *wrist*; → Kugel≈; Schuh≈ ⟨tech⟩ *shank* || ⟨bot⟩ *articulation* **2.** ⟨tech⟩ (~band) *joint*; (of a chain) *link* || Kardan≈, Kreuz≈ *Cardan joint*; Universal-≈ *universal joint*; → Feder≈, Sprung≈ **3.** [in comp] *joint–; articular* **~arm** m ⟨tech⟩ *articulated bracket* **~band** n ⟨anat⟩ *ligament* || ⟨tech⟩ *hinge* **~entzündung** f ⟨med⟩ *arthritis* [Gr]; verbildende ~ *a. deformans* [L] **~erguß** m = –wassersucht **~flüssigkeit** f = –schmiere **~gallen** f pl ⟨vet⟩ *galls* pl **~höcker** m ⟨med⟩ *condyle* **~kette** f ⟨tech⟩ *sprocket-chain; link chain* **~knorpel** m *articular cartilage* **~krankheiten** f pl *joint-diseases* pl **~kupplung** f ⟨tech⟩ *joint-coupling* **~lokomotive** f *articulated l.* **~maßstab** m *joint-rule* **~maus** f ⟨path⟩ *joint-mouse* **~punkt** m *fulcrum* **~quarz** m

⟨minr⟩ *itacolumite* **∼rohr** n *joint-pipe* **∼rheumatismus** m *acute rheumatic fever* **∼schleim** m, **∼schmiere** f ⟨anat⟩ *synovia* [L]; ⟨fam⟩ *joint-oil* **∼schmerzen** pl *joint-pains* pl **∼verbindung** f ⟨bot & zoo⟩ *articulation* **∼versteifung** f ⟨path⟩ *anchylosis* [L] **∼wagen-** ⟨rail⟩ *articular* (*structure train*) **∼wassersucht** f ⟨path⟩ *dropsical effusion* **∼zange** f (ausdehnbar) *lazy tongues* pl **∼zapfen** m *joint pin*

ge- ∼l·enkig a *flexible, lissom, pliable, pliant, supple*; → gewandt, flink | ∼̂keit [f] ∼ *flexibility, pliancy, pliability, suppleness* **∼l·ernt** a *skilled* (*worker*); *regular* (*cook*); **∼̂l·ese** n ∼s/ **1.** *excessive and superficial reading* **2.** ⟨weav⟩ *lease* **∼̂l·eucht** n ⟨min⟩ *miner's lamp* **∼̂l·ichter** n ∼s/ = Gesindel, Sippschaft **∼̂l·iebte 1.** die ∼ f ∼n/∼n *the lady-love, love, sweetheart*; ⟨sl⟩ *dona(h)* ‖ *mistress*, → Mätresse **2.** der ∼ [ein ∼r] m ∼n/∼n *the lover, sweetheart*; → Schatz ‖ *paramour* **∼l·iehen** pp v leihen

gel·ieren [ʒe'l–] **1.** vi [h] *to jelly*, ⟨fam⟩ *jell* **2.** ∼̂ n *jellying*; zum ∼ bringen *to jelly*, ⟨fam⟩ *jell*

gel·ind, gel·inde 1. [a] *mild* (*weather, medicine, confusion, surprise*); *gentle* (*breeze, heat*); *light* (*frost*); *moderate* (*appetite*; *demand*); *slow* (*fire*); *soft* (*climate, rain*) | ⟨übtr⟩ *gentle* (*rebuke*); *mild* (*punishment*); *soft* (*sentence*) ‖ ∼ gegen *lenient* od *soft with* (*a p*); ∼re Saiten aufziehen *to come down a peg* od *two*; ∼ w *to relent, to soften* ‖ um es mit e–m ∼n Ausdruck z bezeichnen = ∼ gesagt, → 2. ‖ mit ∼m Grauen *with a touch of horror*; e–e ∼ Wut *a mild fit of rage* **2.** [adv] *gently, mildly* ‖ ∼ abführen *to be mildly laxative* ‖ um es ∼ auszudrücken; ∼ gesagt *to put it mildly, to say the least of it* **Gel·indheit, Gel·indigkeit** f *mildness*; *gentleness, lightness, softness* ‖ *lenience, lenity*

gel·ingen I. vi [gelang/gelungen] [s] **1. jdm** ∼; **es** wird dir ∼ *you will succeed*; es gelang ihm nicht *he failed* ‖ es gelang mir, ihn z überreden *I succeeded in persuading him* ‖ der Plan wird ihm ∼ *he will succeed in his plan, his plan will succeed* od *will be successful*; ihm gelang die Vereinigung der .. *he achieved the union of* ..; es g. ihm gut *he managed to do it* | **jdm nicht** ∼ (S) *to escape a p*; *to elude a p* (*the music of the verse eludes even musical actors*) **2.** (S) *to succeed, to be successful*; *to prosper, to work*; der Plan ist gut gelungen *the plan has worked well* ‖ nicht ∼, °daneben *or* vorbei ∼ *to fail*; gut gelungen *well done* ‖ → gelungen **II.** ∼̂ n *the succeeding*; *success(ful issue)* (*of a plan*)

Gel·ispel n ∼s/ *lisping* ‖ ⟨fig⟩ *murmuring, whispering*

G·elle f ∼/∼n = Jolle

×**g·elle** [intj] = gelt

g·ellen vi [h] (of the voice, etc.) e–e Stimme gellte (*or* es gellte) laut durch das Tal *a shrill voice pervaded the valley* ‖ das Getöse gellt mir in den Ohren *the noise makes my ears ring*; *the n. stuns my ears*; er schrie, daß mir die Ohren gellten *his shouting made my ears ring* ‖ Schreie ∼ durch die Nacht *shrieks ring through* ..

g·ellend a *shrilling* (*cry*); *shrill*

ge- ∼l·oben vt [h] (etw) *to promise* ‖ feierlich (*or* in die Hand) ∼ *to vow* (jdm *to a p*; daß *that*; z tun *to do*); jdm Treue ∼ *to vow loyalty to a p* ‖ **sich** ∼ *to make a vow to o.s.* ‖ gegenseitig ∼ *to covenant* (*to do*; *that*) ‖ ⟨bib⟩ das Gelobte Land *the Promised Land, the L. of Promise* **∼̂l·öbnis** n –nisses/–isse *vow*; (*solemn*) *promise*; ein ∼ ablegen *to make* (od *take*) *a vow*; → Gelübde **∼l·ockt** a *curly* (*hair*) **∼̂l·os** n –ses/ ⟨hunt⟩ *dung, excrement*; *billet* (*of a fox*, etc) **∼̂l·östheit** f ∼/ *abandon*; *relaxation*, → lösen

Gelsenkirchen n ⟨Ger⟩ (Stadt)

gelt a (Ggs melk) *not giving milk*; *barren*

×**gelt** (→ gelten) [intj] (fragender Ausdruck der Zustimmung des Sprechers) das macht nichts, ∼? *that does not matter, does it?* das ist sehr wichtig, ∼? *that is of great consequence, isn't it?* ∼, das schmeckt gut *that's good, eh?*; nur natürlich, ∼? *naturally, don't you think?*

gelten vi [galt/gegolten] [h] **A. (wert sein) 1.** (kosten) was gilt das Meter? *how much is* (od *how much do you charge*) *the metre?* **2. a.** die Mark gilt 100 Pf. *a mark is worth 100 Pf.*; *this note is good for 100 marks* ‖ was gilt die Wette? was gilt's? *how much will you bet?* **b.** ⟨übtr⟩ *to weigh*; (bei *with*) ‖ etwas ∼ *to stand for something*; er gilt etwas *he is a p of consequence*; *his word is held in high esteem*; viel ∼ *to count for much*; *to carry* (*great*) *weight* (bei *with*); nichts ∼ *to stand for nothing* **3.** ∼ **für** *or* **als** *to pass for*; *to be reputed to be* ..; er gilt f e–n reichen Mann (*or* als ein reicher M.) *he passes for a rich man* ‖ *this part is considered the best of the whole* ‖ er gilt nur dafür (*he is not really rich*), *he has only the reputation* (*of being so*) | ⟨med etc⟩ als positiv ∼ *to be called positive* **B. (Gültigkeit h) 1. a.** (of coins, etc) *to be* od *pass current*; *to be valid* (f *for*); der Paß gilt nicht mehr *is no longer valid* (od *in force*) **b.** ⟨übtr⟩ *to hold* (*this holds in German*); *to hold good* (od *true*); *to be valid*; *to prevail*; es **kann** als sicher ∼ *it can safely be assumed*; *these rules will hold good until Easter*; *the law does not run among rebels* ‖ mein Wort gilt *my word goes* (*every time*), ⟨Am⟩ *what I say has to go* ‖ die Wette gilt nicht *the bet is off* ‖ Bangemachen gilt nicht *none of your bluffs*; *bluffing is no go* ‖ bei Gott gilt kein Ansehen der P *God is no respecter of persons* ‖ es ∼! *agreed! done!* ‖ das gilt nicht *that doesn't count*; *that won't do*; *that is not done* od *fair* (*cricket*) **2.** ∼ **von** *or* **für** *to apply* od *refer to, to be applicable to*; *to hold good of*; *what applies to this play, applies as well to the rest* ‖ das gilt auch f dich! ⟨fam⟩ *that goes for you too*; das gilt nicht nur f .. *that covers not only* ..; das gilt f .. *this holds true for* .. **3. jdm** ∼ *to be intended* (od *meant*) *for a p* (*this reproach was intended for you*) ‖ *the challenge is to all mankind*; (*his sympathies*) *were* (*with the Finns*) ‖ er weiß nicht, daß es ihm (s–m Leben) gilt *he does not know that his life is at stake* **4.** ⟨fig⟩ **es gilt**: bei dem Kampf galt es Leben und Tod *in this struggle it was a matter of life and death* ‖ es gilt dem besten v 3 Würfen *it is to be the best of 3 throws* ‖ es gilt e–n Versuch *it depends on a trial* ‖ jetzt gilt es! *be sure now!*, .. nicht den Kopf z verlieren *now it's up to us* (od *it is necessary for us*) *to keep our heads* ‖ *now it became a question of* (*reaching the other side*) ‖ er war tapfer, wo es galt *he was brave in case of need* **5. etw** ∼ **l** *to let a th pass*; *to approve* (*of*) *a th*; *to allow a th*; (Korrektur) *to pass* ‖ etw ∼ l als .. *to pass a th for* ..; .. ohne Frage *or* weiteres ∼ l *to accept* .. *without qu.*; nicht ∼ l *to disallow a th*; nicht ∼ l wollen *to be intolerant of* (*a th*) ‖ das laß ich ∼ *that's something like*; *well done* **g·eltend** a *accepted, acknowledged, established* (*law*), *received* (*pronunciation*); *current, ruling* (*prices*); *valid*; *in force*; die ∼e Bestimmung *the regulation in force, the present r.* ‖ das ∼e Recht in England *the law* ‖ *prevailing* (*opinion*), *prevalent* (*fashion*) | ∼ f *imposed on* .., etc | ∼ m *to assert*; (Anspruch) *to constitute, to make good*; (Einfluß etc) *to bring to bear*; *to exercise, exert*; e–e Entschuldigung (e–n Vorwand) ∼ m können *to have a valid excuse for* ..; (Forderung) *to enforce, press, urge*; *to insit on* ‖ ∼ m, daß .. *to insist* od *maintain that* .. ‖ sich ∼ m (S) (*the prolonged frost begins to make itself felt*) **G·eltendmachung** f ∼/∼en *assertion*; *exercise* (*of an influence*); *enforcement* (*of a th*); *insistence* (e–r S *on a th*); ∼ der eigenen Rechte *self-assertion*

G·eltling m ∼(e)s/∼e (T) **1.** *spade* **2.** *one year old calf* **G·elttier** n ⟨hunt⟩ *yeld* → d., *y. hind*

G·eltstag m Sw *bankruptcy*

G·eltung f ~/~en ⟨übtr⟩ (allgemeine ~) *acceptation, currency* (*of ideas, words*); *prevalence*; *validity* (*of a contract*) || *standing*; *value, worth*; *status* (*of the £*); *weight*; gleiche ~ *equivalence* || *consequence, importance* | sich [acc] z ~ bringen = sich ~ verschaffen; ~ **haben** *to be current*; *to be valid*; *to hold good* (f *for*); *to obtain, to prevail*; *to be in vogue* || keine ~ genießen *to have no standing* || sich ~ verschaffen *to assert* (od *reassert*) *o.s.* (gegen *against*); *to prevail* (*his authority prevailed*) | **an** ~ verlieren *to lose in weight* || **außer** ~ s *to be no longer current* (od *valid, in force*); *to be of no account* || **in** ~ bleiben *to hold good* (bis *until*) || in ~ s = ~ h || **von** ~ s *to be of consequence* || (etw) **zur** ~ bringen *to bring to bear* (bei, auf *on*); *to enhance* = geltend m; .. besser .. *to make a th show to better advantage* || z ~ k *to take effect*; (*to begin*) *to tell*; *to prevail*; *to bob up* (*in a p's talk*); gehörig z ~ k. *to come into one's own*; nicht z ~ k. *to be wasted* (bei, in *on*) **G·eltungs- ~bedürfnis** n *the desire to assert o.s.* (od *to count for something*); *self-assertion* || *sense of importance*; *egotism*; krankhaftes ~ *egomania* || sein ~ z befriedigen suchen *to seek publicity* **~bereich** m ⟨a. jur⟩ *jurisdiction*; *authority, control, power*; *area of application* **~dauer** f *duration of validity*

Ge- ~l·übde n ~s/~ *vow*; *pledge* || ein ~ ablegen, tun *to make* od *take a vow*; ein ~ abgelegt h *to be under a vow* (*to do*); ein ~ ablegen, dem Alkohol z entsagen *to take the pledge*; das ~ brechen (halten) *to break* (*keep*) *the pledge*; e–r S durch ~ verpflichtet w *to be vowed to a th* °**~l·umpe** n = Abfall; Lumpen, Klamotten ≃**l·ungen** a [pp v gelingen] **1.** *successful, perfect* (*work*); *felicitous, happy* (*stroke*) **2.** °⟨fig⟩ *funny*; *queer*, ein ~er Kerl *an odd fish*; ~ aussehen *to look funny* **~l·üste** n ~s/~ *lust* (nach *of, for*); *appetite, desire, longing* (*for*; *to do*) || k–e persönlichen ~ *no personal lusts* pl; ein starkes ~ h *to lust* (nach *after, for*) ≃**l·üsten** vi/imps [h] ~ nach etw *to lust after* od *for*; *to hanker after*; *to long for a th*; *to covet a th* || **es gelüstet mich,** ihn nach .. *I lust, he lusts after, for*; es g. mich, es z tun *I feel a strong desire to do it* || ⟨bib⟩ **sich ~ l** nach etw *to covet a th*

G·elze f ~/~n *castrated* (od *gelded*) *sow*

Ge- ~m·ach n ~(e)s/≃er **1.** [pl ≃er] *apartment chamber, room* || sich in s–e ≃er zurückziehen *to retire* **2.** * [übtr (nur sg)] *comfort*; *quiet* ≃**m·ach 1.** † [a] = gemächlich, ruhig **2.** [adv] *gently, softly*; *slowly*; ~ gehen *to walk slowly*; ~ sprechen *to speak softly* (od *low*) || *gradually*; *by degrees* || nur ~! *come, come! gently does it! hold hard!* ⟨mar⟩ *easy* (*all*)! ≃**m·ächlich 1.** [a] *easy*; *leisurely* (*journey, movements*); *slack, slow*; in ~em Schritt *at a slack pace* || *comfortable* (*to live a comfortable life*) || *easy-going, comfort-seeking* (*gentleman*) **2.** [adv] *easily*; *leisurely*; ~ gehen *to go at a slack pace*; sehr ~ g. *to go at a crawl* || (S) ~ weitergehen, sich ~ entwickeln *to strike a leisurely note* || (P) ~ leben *to live at ease* || ~ eingerichtet *comfortable* (*lodgings*) | ≃keit [f] *easiness*; *leisureliness*; *slackness* || *comfort* ≃**m·acht** a **1.** [pred] ⟨fig⟩ wie ~, geradezu ~ *ripe* (f *for*) || °~! *agreed!* **2.** [attr] *prosperous, thriving*; *well-off* (*p*); ~e Leute *well-to-do people*; so wird er ein ~er Mann *it will be the making of him* || *affected* (*smile*); *artificial* (*flowers*) **~m·achtheit** f ⟨fig⟩ *affectedness, artificiality* **~m·ahl**[1] m ~(e)s/~e **a.** *husband* || (of royalties) *consort*; ~ e–r regierenden Königin *King-Consort*; Prinz≃ *Prince-Consort* **b.** = Gatte; wie geht es Ihrem Herrn ~? *how is Mr. N.*? || †**Gem·ahl**[2] n ~(e)s/~e ⟨poet⟩ = Gemahl[1] & **Gem·ahlin** f ~/~nen **a.** (of royalties) *consort*; ~ des Königs *Queen-Consort* **b.** = Gattin; wie geht es Ihrer Frau ~? *how is your wife* od *Mrs. N.*? || .. u s–e ~ (*Sir Roger*) *and his lady* ≃**m·ahnen** vt/i [h] **1.** [vt] jdn ~ an *to put a p in mind of*; *to remind a p of* (*a th*) **2.** * [vi] ~ an etw *to recall, suggest a th*; *to be reminiscent of a th* **~m·älde** n ~s/~ *painting, picture*; See≃ *sea piece*; → Öl≃ || (Druck) nach e–m ~ v *from a* od *the p. by* | ~ausstellung [f] *exhibition of paintings*; ~galerie [f] *picture-gallery, art gallery*; ⟨Am a.⟩ *museum* **~m·ansche** n ~s/ *dabbling, paddling*; *splashing* **~m·arkung** f ~/~en **1.** *boundary*; ⟨hist⟩ *mark* **2.** ⟨hist⟩ *mark*; *common land held by a village community* ≃**m·asert** a *streaky* (*wood*); *veined* ≃**m·äß 1.** [pred & adv] e–r S ~ *in accordance, compliance, conformity with a th*; *according, conformable to a th*; *in pursuance of a th*; ⟨jur⟩ *pursuant to a th* || ⟨com⟩ Ihren Angaben ~ *to specification* || ihrem Alter ~ (*she dressed*) *to her age* **2.** [prep (mit dat)] ~ e–r S = e–r S ~ → 1. **3.** [als suff] → dem~; erfahrungs~; natur~; pflicht~; standes~; zeit~ | ≃heit [f] ~/ *accordance*; *conformity*; *in* ~ e–r S = e–r S gemäß ≃**m·äßigt** a ⟨pol & rel⟩ *moderate* (*views*); ⟨geog⟩ *temperate* (*zone*) | ≃**er** ⟨pol⟩ *middle-of-the-roader*; *centrist* **~m·äuer** n ~s/~ *walls* pl || altes ~ *ruined* od *decayed walls*; *ruins* pl || es kracht, rieselt im ~ ⟨fig⟩ *sth is cracking at the seams* **~m·ecker** n ~s/ *bleating* (*of goats*) | °⟨fig⟩ *fault-finding*; *nagging*; *nag*

gem·ein I. [a] **A. 1. a.** (allgemein) *universal*; ⟨ec⟩ *catholic* (*faith*) || *common* (*usage, value*; *sense*); das ~e Wohl (*or* Beste) *the common* (od *public*) *weal* (od *good, welfare*) || *man in the street*; *common* od *private* (*soldier* = *private*); = ⟨fam⟩ *Tommy* (*Atkins*); ⟨Am⟩ *G I* (f *Government Issue*) → Gemeine; *the common people* || allen ~ s *to be common to all* **b.** ⟨math⟩ *vulgar* (*fraction*) || ⟨her⟩ *common* (*figures* pl) || ~es Jahr *calendar year* **2.** (alltäglich, gewöhnlich) *common, general, ordinary* **3.** ⟨dero⟩ **a.** °(eklig) *disgusting*; *wretched* (*weather, pain*); *beastly*; ⟨Am⟩ *mean* (*job, weather*) **b.** (niedrig, roh) (P) *low* (*conduct, fellow*), *low-down, mean*; *base, dirty, sordid* (*practices*), *vile* (*phrase*), *gross* (*terms*); *common* (*woman*); *cowardly* (*lie*), *dastardly* (*invention of the Press*); *niddering*; ⟨sl⟩ *scaly*; ⟨Am sl⟩ *lous*(*e*)*y* (*job, weather*) || °es war ~ v dir *it was caddish of you*; °du bist ~ ⟨vulg⟩ *you are a swine* || °~er Kerl *bounder, cad, hog*; ⟨Am a.⟩ *cheap skate*; °~**es** Pack ⟨sl⟩ *scaly lot* || *mean* (*disposition*); *low* (*way of acting*), *foul* (*doings* pl); *filthy* od *foul, vulgar* (*talk*); ~e Witze → Zote || sich ~ m *to make o.s. cheap* **B.** (gemeinsam) etw ~ h mit *to have a th in common with* (*a p*); nichts ~ h (wollen) mit *to have nothing in common with* || sich ~ m mit *to make common cause with* **II.** [adv] ⟨dero⟩ **1.** (*it is*) *beastly* (*cold*); *damned*; *wretchedly* **2.** *lowly, meanly, vilely* || jdn ~ behandeln *to do the dirty on a p, to play it low-down on a p, to play a p foul*; ~ handeln *to do a mean th* **Gem·ein-** [in comp] *common*; *public* **~besitz** m = –gut ≃**deutsch** a *common* (od *peculiar*) *to all Germans* **~eigentum** n *public ownership* ≃**faßlich** a *popular*; = –verständlich ≃**frei** a *free*; der ≃e *the free man* ≃**gefährlich** a *dangerous to the public weal*; er ist ~ *he is a public danger* || *criminal* (*offence*) **~gefühl** n ⟨psych⟩ *sensation caused by bodily conditions* **~geist** m *public spirit* **~gläubiger** m pl *a bankrupt's creditors* pl ≃**gültig** a *generally admitted* **~gut** n *common* od ⟨jur⟩ *community property* || etw zum ~ m f alle *to make a th the c. p. of all* (od *turn a th into c. p.*); *to popularize a th* || ≃haben [n] *public ownership* ≃**hin** adv *commonly, currently, generally, vulgarly* **~kosten** pl *general* od *overhead expenses* od *costs, apportionable costs* **~nutz** m *the public* (od *common*) *weal*; ~ geht vor Eigennutz *Service above Self*; *the public weal comes first* ≃**nützig** a *public-spirited* (*motives*); *conducive to the common welfare*; *non-profit* (*organization*) || ~e Einrichtung *public* *utility*; ~es Unternehmen *public company* **~nützigkeit** f *public-spiritedness*; *non-profit-making* **~platz** m *commonplace, platitude, truism*; ⟨Am sl⟩ *bromide*; ≈e äußern *to platitudinize*; jd, der ≈e äußert *platitudinarian* **~schuldner** m *bankrupt* ‖ ~in [f] *b. firm* **~sinn** m *public spirit* **≈sinnig** a *public-spirited* (od *minded*) **~sprache** f ⟨Lit⟩ *common language* od *tongue*; → Schriftsprache **≈verständlich** a *intelligible to all*; *popular* (*language*); (etw) ~ m *to popularize* **~weide** f *common* **~wesen** n *community, commonwealth* **~wille** m *common* od *public will* **~wirtschaft** f *economic system directed to the common weal* ‖ ≈lich [a] → –nützig **~wohl** n *common* od *public weal* od *welfare*; am ~ interessiert *public-spirited* (*people*)

Gem·einde f ~/~n **1.** ⟨pol⟩ *community*; (Stadt≈) *municipality* (die ~ N. *the m. of N.*); *urban district*; (Bezirks≈) *ward* (*of a city*) ‖ ⟨a-engl, a. Ger⟩ *commune* | *rural district*; (Kirchspiel≈) *parish* **2.** ⟨ec⟩ (in a church) *congregation* **3.** ⟨übtr⟩ *community*; Goethe≈ *community of Goethe's admirers* **4.** [in comp] *municipal*; *parish*; ⟨mst a-engl⟩ *communal*; → Stadt– ‖ ⟨ec⟩ *parochial* **~abgaben** f pl *local rates* pl **~amt** n *rural district offices* pl **~arbeiter** m *municipal* (od *parish*) *labourer* **~beamte** [der ~, ein ~r] m *municipal official* **~betrieb** m *municipal service* ‖ °**~bulle** m = –vorsteher **~gesang** m ⟨ec⟩ *congregational singing* **~glied** n = –mitglied **~haus** n *community centre* **~haushalt** m *municipal* (od *communal*) *budget* **~helfer** m *parish-help* **~kirchenrat** m ⟨ec⟩ *church council* **~land** n *common* **~leben** n *municipal life* **~mitglied** n *citizen*; *parishioner* **~netz** n ⟨el⟩ *secondary distribution network* **~odnung** f *municipal regulations* pl **~pflege** f *municipal welfare-work* ‖ ~r(in [f]) [m] *social welfare officer* **~rat** m *municipal council*; *district-council*; *parish-council*; ⟨ec⟩ → –vertretung **~schreiber** m *parish-clerk* **~schule** f *municipal school*; *parish-school* **~schwester** f *parish-nurse* **~steuern** pl = –abgaben **~tag** m ⟨Ger⟩ *meeting of representatives of the municipalities*; *parish meeting* **~unterstützung** f *parish-relief* **~verband** m *association of municipalities* (⟨Ger⟩ .. *of communes*) **~versammlung** f ⟨ec⟩ *vestry* **~vertreter** m *parish-councillor* ‖ ~ pl ⟨ec⟩ *vestry* ‖ **~vertretung** → –rat **~verwaltung** f *municipal administration* **~vorstand** m *local board* **~vorsteher** m *chairman of the district* (od *parish*)*-council* **~wahl** f *municipal* od *local, council election*

Gem·eine 1. [der ~, ein ~r] m ~n/~n = gemeiner Soldat, → gemein A. 1.; die ~n [pl] *the ranks* pl, *the rank and file* ‖ die ~n [pl] *the commonalty*; ⟨parl⟩ das Haus der ~n *the House of Commons* **2.** †die ~ = Gemeinde | ⟨typ⟩ (kursiv) ~ (*italic*) *lower case* **3.** das ~ *the foul* od *vulgar*; *abjectness, impurity, meanness* ‖ ins ~ herabziehen *to drag down to a low level*; *to foul*; *to vulgarize*; *to pollute*

Gem·einheit f ~/~en **1.** *the lands of a community* **2.** [abstr] *baseness, meanness, sordidness, vulgarity*; *dirty work*; e–e ~ *a mean, vulgar, caddish th*; *a dirty trick, foul play*; ~en *dirty doings* od *things* pl; e–e ~ begehen *to do a mean th* | °*beastliness*; *nuisance*; *wretched thing*; das ist e–e ~ *that's too bad*

†gem·einiglich adv = gewöhnlich

gem·einsam 1. [a] *common* (*interests*); allen ~ *universal*; ~e Bemühungen pl *community effort* ‖ ⟨mil⟩ *joint* (*exercise, planning, staff*) N ‖ ⟨jur⟩ ~er Besitz *joint ownership*; ~es Eigentum an Immobilien *tenancy in common* ‖ ~er Fonds, ~e Kasse (beim Spiel) *pool* ‖ (*our*) *mutual* (*friend*) ‖ ≈er Markt ⟨com pol⟩ *Common Market*; → EWG ‖ ~e S m mit *to make common cause with* (*a p*); laß uns ~e S m ⟨Am fam⟩ *let's put our hand together* ‖ [pred] allen ~ *common to all*; das war alles, was ihnen ~ war *that was all that there was in common between them* (od .. *that they had in common*) ‖ ⟨math⟩ *common* (*denominator, divisor, measure*) | (vereint) *concerted* (*action*), *joint* (*declaration*); *mutual* (*efforts*); *united* (*exertions*) ‖ ⟨Am a.⟩ *get-together* (*dinner*) **2.** [adv] *in company*; *together*; *they appeared t.* (od *in c.*) ‖ ~ in den Tod gehen *to seek death together* ‖ das Haus gehört ihnen ~ *they have the house in joint possession, the house is their common property*; solange sie ~ am Leben sind *during their joint lives* | *jointly, unitedly*; (etw) ~ erlebt h *to have gone through .. together*; ~ handeln *to take concerted* (od *joint*) *action*; (etw) ~ verabreden *to concert* ‖ etw ~ teilen, sich ~ teilen in etw *to share a th* ‖ ~ **mit**: *he was joint guardian to the boy with Mrs. P.* | **≈keit** f *commonness, community* (*of interests*)

Gem·einschaft f ~/~en **1.** ⟨abstr⟩ *community*; *joint ownership*; *partnership* (an *in*); eheliche ~ *conjugal community*; Auflösung der –chen ~ *dissolution of marriage*; Güter≈ *community of goods* ‖ ⟨rel⟩ *communion* (mit .. *with God*) ‖ ⟨übtr⟩ *association, companionship, social communication*; *dealing*(*s*), *fellowship, intercourse* (*with*); mit ihnen wollen wir k–e ~ h *we refuse to have anything to do with them* ‖ *union* (unter *among*) ‖ in ~ mit *in concert* od *alliance with*; *together with*; niemand, mit dem ihn irgend e–e ~ verbindet *no one he has anything in common with* **2.** [konkr] *community*; *body of people*; echte ~ *perfect unity*; *organic union* (od *whole*) ‖ religiöse ~ *religious communion*; die ~ der Heiligen *the Communion of Saints*; ⟨com soc⟩ *unit*; Europäische ~ f Kohle u Stahl → Montanunion | **≈lich 1.** [a] *united*; = gemeinsam **2.** [adv] *in union*; *unitedly*; ~ verlebt (*days we*) *spent together*; ~ zus–halten *to stand together*; *to live in perfect harmony* (od *unity*) **Gem·einschafts- ~anschluß** m ⟨telph⟩ *party-line* **~arbeit** f *co-operation*; *working together to the same end*; *team-work* **~bewegung** f ⟨theol⟩ *evangelicalism* **~ehe** f ⟨anthr⟩ *hetairism* **~empfang** m ⟨wir⟩ *joint reception* (*for the staff*) **~erziehung** f **1.** *social education* (od *pedagogics* pl); *education on social lines*; ⟨engl⟩ *college-training* **2.** ⟨school⟩ *co-education* **~ethik** f *social ethics* pl **~garage** f *pool g.* **~geist** m *community-spirit*; *co-operative spirit* **~gesang** m *community singing* **~hilfe** f ~ der Wirtschaft *subsidy* (od *support*) *from public funds* **~küche** f = Volksküche **~leistung** f *community effort* **~mittel** n pl *public funds* pl **~schule** f *non-denominational school*; *co-educational school* **~schülerin** f ⟨fam⟩ *co-ed* **≈schwierig** a (P) *maladjusted* **~sinn** m = –geist ‖ Mensch mit starkem ~ *good mixer*, ⟨Am⟩ *joiner* **~verpflegung** f *central feeding* **~werbung** f *co-operative advertizing*

Ge- ~m·enge n ~s/ *medley*; (*heterogene*(*ous*) *mixture*; ⟨min⟩ *alligation*; → Hand≈, Gemisch **~m·engesaat** f *mixed cultivation of various fruits* **~m·engsel** n ~s/ = Gemenge **≈m·essen 1.** [a] *measured* (*tread*); in ~em Schritt *at a m. pace* ‖ *regular*; *rhythmical, steady* ‖ (of language) *measured*; *well-weighed*; *deliberate and restrained*; *formal*; *undemonstrative* **2.** [adv] *measuredly*; *regularly* | ~heit [f] ~/ *measuredness*; *deliberation, formality* **~m·etzel** n ~s/ *slaughter*; *butchery, carnage*; *massacre*; *decimation* ‖ Ort des ~s *slaughterhouse* ⟨fig⟩ **≈m·ieden** pp v meiden

Geminati·on [ts] f ⟨gram⟩ *gemination* **gemin·ieren** vt [h] *to geminate* **G·emini-Kapsel** f ⟨a-n⟩ *G. capsule*

Gem·isch n ~es/~e ⟨a. chem⟩ *mixture* ‖ ⟨übtr⟩ *compound, conglomerate, conglomeration*; *medley* (*of emotions*), *mixture*; ⟨dero⟩ *mingle-mangle* (*of ideas*) ‖ buntes ~ *motley* (*of white and grey*); *mottle* ‖ (günstige Brennstoff-)~skala

[f] ⟨aero⟩ *Meadow*; ~regler [m] ⟨mot⟩ *mixture control*

gem·ischt a *mixed*; *medley*; ~e Gesellschaft *medley* ‖ (Herren- u Damengesellschaft) *mixed company* ‖ *joint* (*commission*); ~es Gefühl der Freude u Furcht *mingled pleasure and apprehension*; ~e Gefühle pl *mingled feelings*, → aufnehmen I. B. 1. | ≈- *joint* (*airsport*) **~schmierung** f ⟨mot⟩ *petroil* **≈warenhandlung** f *grocery*; ⟨Am a.⟩ *general merchandise store* **~wirtschaftlich** a ~es Unternehmen *mixed enterprise*

G·emme[1] f ~/~n *gem*; *glyptograph*; vertieft geschnittene ~ *intaglio* [It]; erhaben g. ~ *cameo* **~nschneidekunst** f, **~nschnitt** m *glyptography*, **~nschnitt** m *glyptography*, *glyptics* pl **~nschneider** m *lapidary*

G·emme[2] f ⟨zoo & vet⟩ *gemma* [L] [pl *-mae*]; *gemmule* ‖ Fortpflanzung durch ~n *gemmation*

gem·ocht pp v mögen **g·emolken** pp v melken

°**gem·ollert** a (= gemütlich + mollig) *comfy*

G·ems [in comp] (⟨a.⟩ Gams-) **~bart** m *tuft of bristly hair on the withers of the chamois* **~bock** m **1.** *buck* (od *male*) *of the chamois* **2.** (e-e Antilope) *gemsbok* **~büffel** m ⟨zoo⟩ *anoa* **~jagd** f *chamois-hunt(ing)* **~jäger** m *chamois-hunter* **~kraut** n ⟨bot⟩ *milfoil*; *yarrow* **~kugeln** f pl *bezoar*; *hair-balls* pl **~wurzel** f ⟨bot⟩ *leopard's bane*

G·emse f ~/~n ⟨zoo⟩ *chamois*

G·emsen- [in comp] ~jagd, ~jäger → Gems- ‖ °~eier suchen *to milk the pigeon* (od *bull*, *ram*)

Ge- ~m·üll n ~(e)s/~e *bee-waste* **~m·unkel** n ~s/ *whispers* pl; *whispering*; *rumours* pl (über *of*) **~m·urmel** n ~s/ *murmur(ing)*; *muttur(ing)*; *hubble-bubble* °**~m·urre** n ~s/ *grumbles* pl, *grumbling*; *complaints* pl

Gem·üse n ~s/~ **1.** ⟨cul⟩ *vegetable*; nehmen Sie etw ~ *have some vegetable* **2.** (~arten) *greens*, *v.s* pl (*to sell fruits and v.s*); *garden stuff* od *produce*; ⟨Am a.⟩ *truck* ‖ frisches junges ~ *green v.s* pl ‖ ⟨fig⟩ (Kinder) °junges ~ *small fry* **~arten** pl *v.s* pl **~bau** *cultivation of v.s* **~beet** n *v. bed* **~bude** f = -stand **~garten** m *kitchen-garden*, *v. garden* **~gärtner** m *kitchen* (od *market*)-*gardener*; ⟨Am a.⟩ *truck farmer* **~händler** m *greengrocer*; (auf der Straße) *coster(monger)* **~handlung** f = -laden **~konserven** pl *tinned* (od *canned*) *v.s* **~kost** f *v. diet* **~laden** m *greengrocery*; *greengrocer's shop*; sie ist im ~ *she is at the greengrocer's* **~markt** m *v. garden* **~pflanzen** f pl *v. plants* pl **~platte** f *dish of v.s* **~schüssel** f *v. dish* **~stand** m *green stall* **~suppe** f *v.* od *jardinière* [Fr] *soup* **~waren** f pl *greengrocery*; *green stuffs*, *greens* pl

gem·üßigt a; sich ~ sehen z tun *to feel called upon* (od *compelled*) *to do*

gem·ustert a *figured* (*glass*; *satin*); *fancy* (*waistcoat*); *flowered* (Damast)

Gem·üt n ~(e)s/~er **1.** [abstr nur sg] *mind*; *heart* ‖ *cast of mind*; *disposition*, *nature*; *temper(ament)* ‖ *emotion*, *feeling*, *sentiment* ‖ (*the German*) *temperament*; ein empfängliches ~ *a susceptible mind*; empfindsames, weiches ~ *tender sentiment* (od *feelings*); goldenes ~ *heart of gold*; gutes ~ *good nature*; sonniges ~ *sunny nature*; verträgliches ~ *compatibility of temper* ‖ ein Mann mit ~ *a man of strong emotions* (od *feelings*); er hat kein ~ *he has no feeling(s)* od *heart* ‖ jdm **aufs** ~ gehen *to harp on a p's temper* ‖ jdm etw **z ~e führen** *to bring a th home to a p*; *to impress a th upon a p*; sich etw z ~e führen *to take a th to heart*; °⟨fig⟩ *to appropriate*; *consume*; *drink* (*a bottle of wine*); *to swallow* **2.** [konkr pl ~er] *mind*; ~er *minds* pl; die edelsten ~er *the noblest minds*; ängstliche ~er *fearful people* ‖ die ~er erregen *to excite* od *arouse the* (*people's*) *feelings*; die erregten ~er beschwichtigen *to assuage* (od *calm down*) *the excited feelings* (od *the excitement*); z Zeiten waren die ~er sehr erregt *at times feeling ran high* **≈lich I.** [a] **1.** ~e Aufregung *excited feelings* (*of a p*); *rousing of the feelings*; *mental agitation*; ~e Stimmung *gemütlichkeit*, ⟨Am m. m.⟩ *mellow feeling* **2.** (of things, places, etc.) *comfortable* (*chair*); *cosy* (*cabin*, *corner*), *homely*, *snug* ‖ *hom(e)y* ‖ *leisurely*; *sociable* (*meal*) ‖ **es sich ~ m** *to take it easy*; *to make o.s. at home*; ⟨fam⟩ *to hang up one's hat* ‖ es ist hier sehr ~ *I feel quite at home* (od *quite comfortable*) *here* ‖ ich fühle mich hier sehr ~, ich finde es hier sehr, (°stink)~ *I feel as snug as a bug in a rug* **3.** (P) *easy-going*; *leisurely* ‖ *companionable*, *sociable* (*fellow*); *genial* ‖ nur immer ~ *don't make a fuss*; *easy does it*; *come*, *come* **II.** [adv] *comfortably*; *in comfort*; *cosily*, *snugly* ‖ *at one's ease*; *leisurely* | **~lichkeit** f ~/~en *do*: *g.*; *comfort(ableness)*, *cosiness*, *homeliness*, *snugness*; *ease and comfort* (*of a private house*) ‖ *leisureliness*; *easy-going way* ‖ *companionability*, *sociability*; *geniality*; ⟨Am m. m.⟩ *mellow feeling* ‖ altväterische ~ *old-fashioned cosiness* ‖ in aller ~ *in quiet and comfort*; *composedly* ‖ es geht nichts über die ~ *there is nothing like* (od *give me*) *leisure and comfort* ‖ da hört aber die ~ auf! *that's the limit*! *that beats all*! ‖ in Geldsachen hört die ~ auf *business is business* **≈los** a *unfeeling*; *heartless*, *hard-hearted*; *callous* **~losigkeit** f *unfeelingness*; *callosity*, *callousness*; *heartlessness*

Gem·üts- °**~akrobat** m *extortioner*; *ruthless fellow* **~anlage** f *cast of mind*; *temperamental disposition* (f *for*) **~art** f *cast* (od *turn*) *of mind*, *humour*; *nature*, *temperament* **~bewegung** f *emotion* (stark *strong*, *high*) **~erregung** f *excited feelings* pl; kummervolle ~ *emotional distress* **≈krank** a *heart-sick* (od *sore*); *melancholic*, *-choly* **~krankheit** f *constitutional depression of spirits*; *melancholy* **~leben** n *emotional life*; *feeling-life* **~mensch** m *man of strong emotions* od *feelings*; *emotional* (od *sentimental*) *man* ‖ ⟨iron⟩ = ~akrobat; du bist aber ein ~! *well*, *you've got a mind*, *you have*! **~ruhe** f *composure*; *peace of mind*; *placidity*; in aller ~ *composedly*; s-e ~ bewahren *to keep one's countenance* **~verfassung** f *frame* (od *state*) *of mind*; *humour* **~verstimmung** f *emotional upset*

gem·ütvoll 1. [a] *feeling*, *tender*; *emotional*, *sympathetic* **2.** [adv] *feelingly*; *with feeling*

Gen n ~s/~e ⟨biol⟩ *gene*; ~-Muster [n] ⟨m. m.⟩ *gene complex*; ~-Ort [m] *locus* L; zwei ~-Sätze *two sets of genes*

gen [prep] (aus gegen) ⟨mst bib⟩ ~ Himmel *heavenwards*; ~ Osten *towards the east*

gen·annt a *surnamed*

gen·ant [ʒeˈnant] a *awkward*; *embarrassing*; *delicate*; = heikel, peinlich, Gêne

ge- ~n·arbt a *grained* (*paper*) **~n·as** 1. & 3. pret v genesen **~n·äschig** a = naschhaft

gen·au I. [a] **1.** *accurate*, *correct* (*answer*), *exact* (Waage; *copy*); *precise*; *true* (*weight*) ‖ h Sie (die) ~e Zeit? *have you the right time*? ‖ *close* (*resemblance*); *intimate* (*knowledge*); *nice* (*distinction*); *strict* (*rules*) ‖ *careful*, *meticulous* (*inspection*); *minute* (*investigation*); ~e Beschreibung *detail* ‖ mit ~er Not entkommen *to escape by the skin of one's teeth*, *to have a narrow escape* od *a close shave* ‖ ⟨com⟩ der ~este Preis *the lowest price* **2.** (P) **a.** *careful*; *close*, *strict* (*observer*) ‖ er ist sehr ~ *he is very accurate* **b.** (eigen) [pred] *particular* (in *in*; in bezug auf *about*); *nice* (*in*); *fastidious* ‖ (peinlich ~) *punctilious*; *scrupulous* **c.** (sparsam) *economical*, *sparing* (mit *of*); *close*, *close-fisted*, *parsimonious*, *tight* **II.** [adv] **1.** *accurately*, *exactly* (*the watch goes e.*), *precisely*; *strictly* ‖ *closely*; *carefully*; *minutely*; *nicely* ‖ *in detail*; ⟨fam⟩ *to a T* **2. a.** etw ~ **angeben** *or* erzählen *to give the full particulars of*, *to detail a th* ‖ ~ achten auf *to look carefully after* ‖ ~ bezeichnen, festlegen etc *to pinpoint* ‖ s-e Diät ~ einhalten *to be regular in one's d.* || ~ festgelegt *definite* (*place, time*); *fixed* || etw ~ nehmen, es ~ nehmen mit etw *to take a th seriously*; *to be particular about a th*; er nimmt es sehr ~ *he is very punctilious* (od *scrupulous*), *stands upon points*; es nicht allzu ~ nehmen *to stretch a point, the truth*; er nimmt es mit der Wahrheit nicht so ~ *he is not very scrupulous about telling the truth*; wir nehmen es nicht so ~ *we do not stand on niceties*; ~genommen *strictly speaking*; *when all is said* || ~ gesagt *to be precise* || der Anzug paßt ~ *the suit is a close fit* || ich kann's nicht ~ sagen *I don't know exactly who, why, where*, etc; ⟨Am fam⟩ *I just can't put my finger on it* || es stimmt ~ *it is absolutely accurate* (od *correct*) || ich weiß ~, daß *I am positive that* .. || ⟨fig⟩ wenn man ~ zusieht *if you come to that* **b.** *exactly* (*50 grammes*) || ×~ (z. B.) Bertchen! *the identical!* | **~ auf** die Minute *at the precise moment*; ~ in die Mitte (*to fall*) *plumb in the middle*; ~ ins Zentrum *right in the centre*; *in the very centre*; ~ **um** 10 Uhr *punctually at ten*; *at 10 o'clock sharp*; ~ **zur** Zeit *sharp to time* **c.** ~ **gleich** e–r S *or* P *for all the world like a th, a p* || ~ **derselbe** *exactly the same*; *much the same* || es fühlt sich ~ **so** an *it feels just the same* || *to feel* (denken) *the same* (*way*) *about a th as* ..; er sieht ~ so aus wie .. *he looks for all the world like* (*his father*); ~ **als ob** *for all the world as if*; ~ **so** *that's just it*; ~ **wie** alle Maler *like* (od *in common with*) *all painters* (*he* ..) || ~ wie *just as* (*you advise*); *even as* (*I expected*) || das ist ~, **was** .. *that's precisely what* (*I wanted*) **III.** [abs] aufs ~este *to a nicety, to a T*; *very finely*; ⟨com⟩ aufs ~este berechnet *at the lowest price* || das scheint mir nichts ≃es *that seems to me a somewhat questionable matter*; → geheuer || ⟨dial & hum⟩ nichts ≃es weiß man nicht *that's all I heard about it* **Gen·auigkeit** f ~/~en **1.** *accuracy, exactness, precision* (*of a statement*); Grad der ~ *degree of accuracy*; ~ bis zu 0,1 mg (*result*) *accurate to 0.1 mg* || *closeness* (*of a translation*); *niceness*; *strictness* || *carefulness*; *minuteness* (*of detail*); *particularity*; peinliche ~ *nicety, punctiliousness, scrupulosity*; *fastidiousness* **2.** *economy, parsimoniousness*

Gend·arm [ʒanˈdɑrm] m ~en/~en (Land≃) *country-policeman* (od *constable*); ⟨a-engl⟩ *gendarme* [Fr] **Gendarmer·ie** [ʒandɑrməˈriː] f ~/~n [–iːən] (Land≃) *country-constabulary* (od *police*); ⟨a-engl⟩ *do*: *g.*

Gene [ʒæːn] f [Fr] *awkwardness, uneasiness*

Geneal·oge m ~n/~n *genealogist* **Genealog·ie** f ~/~n *genealogy* **geneal·ogisch** a *genealogical*

°**Ge- ~n·ecke** n ~s/ *teasing*; ⟨Am sl⟩ *kidding* **≃n·ehm** a *acceptable, agreeable, welcome*; *convenient* (*moment*); [pred] jdm ~ s *to suit a p*; es ist mir ~ *I agree* (od *consent*) *to it* **≃n·ehmigen** vt [h] **1.** (etw) *to approve of, to approve*; (Bitte) *to grant*; ~ daß .. *to grant that* ..; jdm etw ~ = erlauben | *to authorize*; (Druck) *to pass*; (amtlich) *to license*; *to sanction* || ⟨com⟩ ~ Sie den Ausdruck m–r vorzüglichen Hochachtung *Yours faithfully* od *truly* (*N. N.*) **2.** sich [dat] etw ~ *to treat o.s. to a th*; °sich (gern) e–n ~ *to indulge in a drink*; ⟨fam⟩ *to indulge* (*to be fond of raising one's elbow*) **~n·ehmigung** f ~/~en *approbation*; *consent*; (vorherige) *authorization*, (nachträgliche) *approval*; *permission* || mit jds – *with a p's approval*; *by authority of a p* || er hatte m–e ~ *he was welcome to it* | (amtliche) *authority*; *licence, sanction*, behördliche ~ erteilen *to give official sanction* (od *the stamp of approval*); e–e ~ besitzen *to hold a licence*; jdm die ~ erteilen *to license a p* (*to do*) || ⟨parl⟩ königl. ~ *Royal assent* (*of a law*) || ⟨typ⟩ (abgedruckt) mit gütiger ~ v *by permission* (od *favour*) *of*; ⟨Am⟩ *by courtesy of* (*Messrs. N.*); die Zeile „mit ~ v" ⟨typ⟩ *credit-line* | ≃spflichtig [a] *subject to a licence*; ~sverweigerung [f] *disavowal* **≃n·eigt** a **1.** [attr] ⟨eig⟩ *inclined* (*plane*); *prone*; *sloping* | ⟨fig⟩ ~es Gehör, Ohr *ready* (od *willing*) *ear*; der ~e Leser *the gentle reader*; ein ~es Publikum *a well-disposed audience* **2.** [pred] ~ s *to be inclined* (od *disposed, prone*) (z *to*; z tun *to do*); *to incline* (*to do*); v Natur ~ s *to be apt* (*to get angry*); → neigen | jdn (s–n eigenen Interessen) ~ m *to bend* od *dispose a p to* .. | **jdm** ~ s *to be well-disposed to a p*; *to wish well to a p*; *to patronize a p* || **e-r S ~ s** *to be disposed towards a th* | ≃heit [f] *inclination, proneness* (z *to*; *to do*); → Neigung

G·enera [L pl] → Genus **Gener·al** m ~s/~e u ≃e ⟨mil⟩ *general Officer, general*; an (den) Herrn ~ N. N. *to General N. N.* || ~ der Infanterie (etc) *General*; kommandierender ~ e–s Armeekorps *General in command of an Army-Corps* || ~ der Flieger ⟨Ger⟩ *Air Force General*; ⟨engl⟩ *Air Chief Marshal* || (das Gehalt e–s ~s *general's pay* **~abrechnung** f ⟨com⟩ *g.-account* **~absolution** f ⟨ec⟩ *g. absolution* **~adjutant** m *adjutant-g.* **~admiral** m ⟨Ger nav⟩ *Admiral of the Fleet* **~agent** m ⟨pol⟩ *agent-g.* **~arzt** m *Director-G. of the Army Medical Services* **~baß** m ⟨mus⟩ *thorough-bass, rough-bass* || ~aussetzung [f] *figured-bass realization* **~bevollmächtigte** m *authorized representative*; der ~ ⟨Ger⟩ *Commissioner-G.* (f *for*) **~-Bundesanwalt** m *Director of the Prosecution* **~direktor** m *Director-G.*; *G. Manager* **~direktorium** n *Board of Directors* **~f·eldmarschall** m *Field-Marshal* **~feldzeugmeister** m *Master G. of the Ordnance* **~fragen** f pl ⟨jur⟩ *g. questions* pl **~gouvernement** n *Polish territory under German rule* (*1939/44*) **~gouverneur** m *Governor-G.* **~handel** m *total foreign trade* **~inspekteur** m *Inspector G.* **~intendant** m ⟨mil⟩ *Commissary-G.* || ⟨theat⟩ *Artistic Director*; *G. Manager* **~kommando** n *the Command of an Army-Corps* **~konsul** m *consul-g.* **~konsulat** n *consulate-g.* **~kosten** pl = Gemeinkosten **~leutnant** m *lieutenant-g.*, ⟨aero⟩ *Air-Marshal* **~major** m *Major-G.* || ⟨aero⟩ *Air Vice-Marshal* **~marsch** m (Alarm) *beat of the drum*; ⟨hist⟩ *general*(*e*) **~nenner** m ⟨math⟩ *common denominator*; unter den ~ bringen *to reduce to a c. d.* **~oberst** m *Colonel-G.* **~oberarzt** m *Surgeon-G.* **~pardon** m *g. pardon* **~pause** *f* ⟨mus⟩ *g. rest* **~police** f ⟨ins⟩ *open* od *floating policy* **~probe** f ⟨theat⟩ *dress-rehearsal* **~quart·iermeister** m *Quartermaster G.* **~quittung** f *receipt in full* **~rat** m ⟨Ger⟩ *G. Economic Council* **~sekretär** m *Secretary General* **~staaten** m pl ⟨a-engl⟩ *States G.* **~staatsanwalt** m *Prosecuter General*; *The King's Proctor* **~stab** m ⟨mil⟩ *the G. Staff* || ~sarzt m *Director-G. of the Army Medical Staff* || –schef m *Chief of the G. St.* || ~skarte f *staff-map*; *ordnance survey map* (*1:100000*) || ~soffizier m *officer in the G. St.* **~stäbler** m ~s/~ *officer in the General Staff* **~stände** m pl ⟨a-engl⟩ = -staaten **~streik** m *general strike*; den ~ ausrufen *to call a g. strike* **~superintend·ent** m ⟨Ger ec⟩ *superintendent-g.* **~synode** ⟨ec⟩ *G. Synod* **~tarif** m *uniform tariff* **~versammlung** f ⟨com⟩ *g. meeting*; (bei UNO) *g. assembly* **~vertreter** m ⟨com⟩ *g. agent* (f *for*) **~-vikar** m ⟨R. C.⟩ *vicar-g.* **~vollmacht** f ⟨jur⟩ *g. power of attorney*

Gener·alin f ~/~nen *wife of a general* **Generalisati·on** [ts] f *generalization* **generalis·ieren** vt [h] *to generalize* †**General·issimus** m ~/-mi *generalissimo* [It] **Generalit·ät** f ~/ ⟨mil⟩ *staff* (od *body*) *of generals* || [koll] *the generals* **Gener·als-~portion** f ⟨cul fam⟩ *general's helping* **~stelle, ~würde** f *generalship*

Generati·on f ~/~en ⟨biol⟩ *generation*; ⟨demog⟩ *cohort* || die junge ~ *the rising g.* **~sdauer** f *length of a g.*, ⟨demog⟩ *mean interval between successive g.s* ~s-Reproduktionsziffer f *g. repro-*

duction rate **~swechsel** m ⟨zoo & bot⟩ *alternation of g.s*; *metagenesis*; *heterogenesis*, *-geny*

Gener·ator m ~s/-t·oren **1.** *generator*; (Ws-) *alternator* **2.** (Gas≈) *producer* **~gas** n *p. gas*, *g. gas* **~kohle** f *p. coal* **~schacht** m *p. body* **Gener·atrix** f ⟨math⟩ *generatrix*

gener·ell a *general*; ⟨com⟩ *blanket* (⟨ins⟩ *policy*) **gen·erisch** a *generic* **generös** [*genə'rø:s*] **1.** [a] [Fr] *generous*, *liberal*, *magnanimous*; *lavish* (mit *in* od *of*) **2.** [adv] *generously*; *lavishly*; ~ umgehen mit *to be lavish in* (*a th*) **Generosit·ät** f ~/ *generosity*

Gen·ese f ~/~n *origin*; *genesis*

gen·esen vi [genas/genesen] [s] *to convalesce*, *mend*, *recover* (v *from*); *to recuperate*; *to regain health* ‖ † die Seele ist ~ *the soul is saved* ‖ †e–s Kindes ~ = gebären ‖ ⟨mil⟩ ≈enkompanie f *convalescent company* **gen·esend** a *convalescent*

G·enesis f **1.** ⟨bib⟩ (1. Buch Moses) *Genesis*; aus der ~ *from G.* **2.** *genesis* (*the g. of* ..); *origin*

Gen·esung f ~/ *convalescence*, *recovery*; der ~ entgegengehen *to approach recuperation*; *to be improving* od *mending* **~sheim** n *conv.* od *nursing home* **~surlaub** m *conv. leave*

Gen·etik f ~/ *genetics* **~er** m *geneticist* **gen·etisch** a *genetic* (*affinity*); *genetical*; in ~er Hinsicht *genetically* **Genet·iv** = Genitiv

Gen·ette [ʒə'net] f [Fr] ~/~n ⟨zoo⟩ (Ginsterkatze) *genet*

Gen·ever [ʒə'ne:və] m [Fr] ~s/~ *gin*, *geneva*

Gen·ezareth, See m ⟨bib⟩ *Lake of Gennesaret*, *Galilean Lake*, *Sea of Galilee*; → galiläisch

Genf n (Stadt u Kanton in der Schweiz) *Geneva*

G·enfer 1. [m] *Genevan*, *Genevese*; die ~ pl *the Genevese* **2.** [a] *Genevan* ‖ *Geneva* (*watch*; *Convention*); ~ Kreuz *the Geneva Cross*; *Red Cross*; ~ See *Lake of Geneva*, ⟨a.⟩ *Lake Leman*

G·engas n *generator gas*; *producer gas*

geni·al 1. [a] ~er Künstler *artist of genius*; ~er Mensch *man of g.*; ~ s *to be a g.*, *to be endowed with g.* ‖ e–e ~e Begabung *a g.* (f *for*); ~e Leistung *stroke of g.* ‖ das ≈e, die ~e Kraft = Genialität | ⟨übtr⟩ *brilliant* (*idea*); *ingenious* (*device*) **2.** [adv] *ingeniously* **~isch** a *with a touch of g.*; *highly gifted* ≈**it·ät** f (*creative*) *g.*; *flash of g.*; *originality* **G·enien** pl (v Genius) *genii*

Gen·ick n ~(e)s/~e *nape*; *back* (od *nape*) *of the neck*; *neck* ‖ Hautfalten am ~ *scruff* (*of the neck*) ‖ (*stiff*) *neck* ‖ *to break one's neck*; jdm das ~ brechen, (of actions) *to bring a p to grief*, *to ruin a p* ‖ jdn am ~ packen *to take a p by the scruff* (*of the neck*) ‖ jdm das ~ umdrehen *to wring a p's neck* **~fang** m ⟨hunt⟩ *stab in the neck* **~fänger** m *hanger*, *cutlass* **~schlag** m ⟨box⟩ *blow in the neck* **~schuß** m *shot in the neck* **~starre** f ⟨med⟩ *cerebro-spinal meningitis* [Gr]

Gen·ie [ʒe'nie:] n ~s/~s **1.** (*creative*) *genius*; *extraordinary imaginative power* ‖ das ~ Goethes *the genius of G.* ‖ er hat ~ *he is a genius* **2.** (P) *genius* [pl *-ses*]; *man of genius*; er ist ein verbummeltes ~ *he has wasted his talents* ‖ verrücktes ~ *mattoid* [It] **3.** Sw *military engineering* **4.** [in comp] **~korps** n ⟨mil⟩ = Ingenieurkorps **~soldat** m ⟨mil⟩ *artificer*; *engineer* **~streich** m *daring achievement* **~truppe** f ⟨mil⟩ = Pioniere

gen·ieren [ʒe'ni:rən] vt [h] **1.** [nur 3. sg & pl] (jdn) *to annoy*, *bother*, *disturb* ‖ [mst fragend *or* verneinend] geniert es Sie, wenn ich rauche? *do you mind* (od *object to*) *my smoking*? ‖ es geniert mich nicht *I don't mind*; es g. mich sehr *Yes, I mind it very much* ‖ es genierte ihn *he felt bothered* ‖ das g. k–n gr Geist *that does not trouble great minds* **2. sich** [acc] ~ *to be* (od *feel*) *embarassed* (od *self-conscious*, *shy*); sich nicht ~ *to be at ease*; sich ~ vor jdm *to be shy of a p*; *not to be at ease with a p*; sich (nicht) ~ z tun *to be shy of doing* (*to make so bold as to do*) ‖ ~ Sie sich nicht *make yourself at home*; *speak quite frankly*; ⟨Am⟩ *feel free* (*to holler*) ‖

gen·ießbar a *eatable*, *edible*; *drinkable* (*wine*); → schmackhaft ‖ ⟨übtr⟩ *enjoyable*; (etw) ~ m *to sugar-coat*; er ist heute wenig ~ *he is difficult to get on with today*; → ungenießbar | ≈**keit** f *edibility* **gen·ießen** vt [genoß/genossen] [h] **1.** ⟨eig⟩ *to eat*, *drink*; *take*; *taste*; *to partake of* (*a meal*); *to have some substenance* (*before leaving*); wollen Sie nicht etw ~? *won't you have something to eat*? danke, ich möchte jetzt lieber nichts ~ *thank you*, *I'd rather not partake just now* ‖ nicht zu ~(d) *uneatable*; *not eatable* od *edible* (*the meat is not e.*) | ⟨übtr⟩ *to taste*, *try* ‖ (e–n Dichter, jds Werke) in Proben ~ *to sample* **2.** (Genuß h an) (Speise) *to enjoy*; recht ~ *to savour*; ⟨fam⟩ *to discusss* | ⟨übtr⟩ (frische Luft, Natur; Kunst; Ruf etc) *to enjoy*, *have*; *to rejoice in* (*good health*) ‖ gr Achtung ~ *to be held in high esteem*; gr Beliebtheit ~ *to be very popular*; er hatte e–e gute Erziehung genossen *he was well brought up* ‖ die Feinheiten e–r S ~ *to savour* od *appreciate the delicacy of a th* ‖ sie ~ das Leben *they are sowing their wild oats*; ⟨Am a.⟩ *they have a pretty colossal time of it* **3.** ~ *to be entitled to* (*safeguards*) **Gen·ießer** m ~s/~ *enjoyer* (*of a th*) ‖ *epicure*, *epicurean*; *sensualist* | ≈**isch** a *enjoying* (*frame of mind*); *free-living*, *epicurean*; ~er Mensch = Genießer

***Genist(e)** n ~(e)s/ *straws*; *twigs* pl ‖ *nest*; *nesting* ‖ = Gestrüpp

Genit·alien pl *genitals* pl **Genit·iv** m ~s/~e ⟨gram⟩ *genitive*; *genitive case* | ≈**isch** a *genitival*

G·enius m ~/–nien *genius* [L pl *genii*]; jds guter ~ *a p's good genius*, *tutelary spirit*, *guardian angel* ‖ *the genius* (*of a language*)

Gen·om n ~(e)s/~e ⟨biol⟩ = Erbmasse

°**Ge- ~n·örgel** n *fault-finding*; *nagging* ≈**n·ormt** a *standardized* (*products*) **~n·oß** m ⟨poet⟩ = **~n·osse** m ~n/~n *associate*, *companion*, *comrade*; *chum*, *mate*; [mst pl] *fellow* (*fellows in misery*) ‖ → Alters≈, Gesinnungs≈, Klassen≈, Partei≈, Standes≈, Volks≈, Waffen≈, Zimmer≈; → Gefährte | *confrère* [Fr]; *partner*, → Kollege ‖ ⟨com⟩ die Herren N. u. ~n *Messrs. N. & Co.* ‖ ⟨dero⟩ *confederate*, → Komplice ≈**n·ossen** pp v gen·ießen **~n·ossenschaft** f ~/~en **1.** [abstr] *association*, *companionship*, *co-operation*, *fellowship*, *partnership* **2.** [konkr] *association*, *company*, *society*; *union* (*credit u.*); Verbraucher-≈ (*retail*) *co-op*(*erative chain*), → eingetragene, Haftung ‖ → Brüderschaft; Gesellschaft; Kartell | ~er [m] *member of a company*; *partner* ‖ *member of a co-operative society* | ≈lich [a] *co-operative* (*society*) **~n·ossenschafts-** ~bank [f] *co-operative bank*; ~wesen [n] *co-op. system*, *consumers' co-operation* **~n·ossin** f ~/~nen (*female-*)*companion* od *comrade*; → Partei≈, Volks≈

G·enotypus m ~/–pen ⟨biol⟩ *genotype*; *genes* pl; identische –pen *identical genetic constitutions*

Genre [ʒɑ̃:r, 'ʒaŋə] n [Fr] ~s/~s *kind*, *style*, *species* ‖ ⟨arts⟩ *genre* **~bild** n *g.-picture* (od *painting*, *piece*), *common life p.* (od *p.*, *p.*) **~maler** m *g.-painter* **~malerei** f *g.-painting*

Gent n (belg. Stadt) *Ghent*

G·entleman [dʒentlmən] m ⟨engl⟩ ~s/–men *gentleman*; ⟨fam⟩ *gent*; ein echter ~ *a real gent* ‖ e–s ~s unwürdig *ungentlemanlike*, *–manly*

G·enua n ⟨It⟩ (Stadt) *Genoa* **Meerbusen v** ~ *Gulf of Genoa* **Genu·ese** m, **Genu·eserin, Genu·esin** f *Genoese* **genu·esisch** a *Genoese*

gen·ug [erstarrtes Adj., ohne Flexion u Komparation] **A.** [a] **1.** *enough*, *sufficient*; ~ Geld, Geld ~ *e.* (od *sufficient*) *m.* (z *for*), *m. e.*; *a sufficiency of m.*; nicht ~ Geld *not e. m.* (um z tun *to do*) ‖ es war Licht ~, (so) daß sie sehen konnten *there was light e. for them to see* **2.** [pred] drei sind

~ *three are e.*; wir sind ~ hier *there are e. of us here*; e–r ist ~ *one will do* ‖ ich denke es ist ~, nun aber ist es ~ *what next*? ‖ laß es ~ s *let it go at that*; *have done with that*; *that will do*; *call it a day*! ‖ nicht ~, daß .. *not e. that* (.., *but* ..) **B.** [abs] **1.** ~ h *to have e.* (⟨vulg⟩ *sufficient*); *to have one's fill*; er hat gerade ~ (sc. getrunken) ⟨fam⟩ *he is just nice, he has had e.* ‖ °der hat ~ *he is done for* (od *played out*) ‖ er hat scheint's noch nicht ~ ⟨Am fam⟩ *he sticks out his chin for more* ‖ ~! *e.* (*of it*)!, *cut it*!, *drop it*!; *get along with you*; ⟨mar⟩ *avast*! ‖ ~ u über~, mehr als ~ *e. and to spare*; (*that will be*) *plently*; *beyond what is sufficient*; wahrhaftig (*or* gerade) ~ *quite enough* **2. ich habe davon** ~ *I am sick of it*; v etw nicht (mehr) ~ h *to run short of a th* ‖ ich habe ~ v ihnen *I have had e. of them*; ~ (davon)! *e. of that*! *no more of this*! → B. 1. ‖ ~ der Worte *done with talking* ‖ er war (nicht) Manns ~ *he was* (*not*) *man e.* (um z tun *to do*) **C.** [adv] *enough*, *sufficiently* **1.** du ißt nicht ~ *you do not eat e.* ‖ → ~tun **2.** [bei Adj. nachgestellt] bist du warm ~? *are you warm e.*; er ist gestraft ~ *he has been punished e.*, *he has his fill of sorrow*; das Boot war nahe ~, (so) daß sie es sehen konnten *the boat was near e. for them to see* **Gen·üge** f ~/ *sufficiency*; jdm ~ tun *to satisfy a p*; *to give satisfaction to a p*; s–r Ehre ist ~ getan *his honour is satisfied* ‖ **zur** ~ *enough*, *sufficiently* (*I know him s.*); er ruhte sich z ~ aus *he had his fill of rest* ‖ selbst als er sich z ~ davon überzeugt hatte, daß .. *even when he was satisfied that she could not be in* .. **gen·ügen** vi [h] **1.** *to suffice*; *to be sufficient*; es wird gerade ~ *it will serve its turn*; Ihr Wort wird ~ *your word will suffice*; e–e kl Summe genügt *a small sum is sufficient* (um z tun *to do*) ‖ das genügt f unseren Zweck *that will do for our purpose* ‖ es genüge z sagen *suffice it to say* **2. a. jdm** ~ *to do for a p* (*any old clothes did for her*); das genügt **mir** *that's enough for me*; *that will do* (*for*) *me*; *that suffices for me*; es g. mir z wissen *it is enough for me to know* ‖ danke, das g. mir! *that's all I wanted to know* ‖ die Antwort g. mir nicht *the answer does not satisfy* (od *suffice*) *me* **b.** (**Anforderungen**) ~ *to meet*, *satisfy*; allen Anforderungen ~ ⟨Am⟩ *to fill the bill* (od *every requirement*); ⟨univ⟩ den A. ~ *to satisfy the examiners*; → entsprechen ‖ **sich** [dat] ~ **l an** *to content o.s.* (od *to be satisfied*) *with* (*he was s. with it*) **gen·ügend 1.** [a] *sufficient* (*income*; *room*) ‖ ~es Auskommen *competency*, *sufficiency*; → befriedigend, zufriedenstellend, *adequate* (Leistungen) **2.** [adv] *sufficiently*; *enough*; ~ (viel) Geld *enough m.* ‖ Prüfung mit ≗ bestehen *to satisfy the examiners fairly well* ‖ *well enough* (*we can hear fairly well here*) **gen·ügsam** a (P) *contented*; *easily satisfied* ‖ ⟨for bot⟩ *little exacting* od *fastidious* → anspruchslos, mäßig | ≗**keit** f ~/ *contentedness* **gen·ug|tun** vi [h] jdm ~ *to satisfy a p*; *to give a p satisfaction* ‖ sich [dat] nicht ~ können in etw, z tun *to spend o.s. in a th*, *in doing*; *to go out of one's way to do* (*he went out of his way to help her*) (aber: genug tun *to do enough*) **Gen·ugtuung** f ~/~en **1.** *satisfaction* ⟨a. theol⟩ (f *for*); *redress*; *reparation*; ~ leisten *to make reparation*; ~ erhalten *to be satisfied*; sich [dat] ~ verschaffen *to obtain redress* ‖ (in Ehrensachen) *s.*; ~ geben *to give s.*; ~ verlangen *to demand s.* **2.** (Befriedigung); *gratification* (über *at*) *to note with g.* ‖ **mit** gr ~ *with great s.*; **es ist mir** e–e gr ~ *it is a great s. to me* (daß *that* ..; z hören *to hear*)

G·enus n [L] ~/G·enera **1.** ⟨biol, zoo & bot⟩ *genus* [pl *genera*] **2.** ⟨gram⟩ *gender*

Gen·uß m –nusses/–nüsse **1. a.** *the consumption* (od *eating*, *taking*) (*of spoiled meat, etc.*); *the partaking* (*of a meal*), lebhafter ~ *discussion* (*of food*) **b.** materieller ~ *indulgence*; übermäßiger ~ alkoholischer Getränke *over-indulgence in alcoholic beverages* ‖ geschlechtlicher ~ *treat* **c.** ~ des h. A. *participation in the Lord's Supper* od *Holy Communion*, *Eucharist* **2.** ⟨übtr⟩ *enjoyment* (*of rights*) ‖ (Nutznießung) *continued enjoyment*; ⟨jur⟩ *use*, *user* (*of property*), *usufruct* ‖ in den ~ e–r S k *to come into the enjoyment of a th* **3.** (innerer ~) *enjoyment* (*of a view*); *fruition*; *luxury* | (Freude) *enjoyment* (an *in*; f jdn *to a p*); *gratification*; *delight*, *pleasure* (an *in*); *gusto*, *relish*, *zest* (an *for*) ‖ ein Hoch≗, ein herzerquickender (*or* wahrer) ~ *a great pl.*, *a great* (od *regular*) *treat*, (⟨Am⟩ *a dandy*) ‖ ~ bringend *pl. giving* (*the opera is a great* od *rare treat*); es ist kaum ein ~, es z lesen *it is almost unreadable* ‖ das war ein gr ~ f ihn ⟨sl⟩ *that was meat and drink to him* ‖ **mit** ~ *with gusto* (od *relish*, *zest*); mit ~ lesen *to read with pl.* ‖ ~ **finden an** *to take pl.* (od *delight*, *enjoyment*) *in*; *to derive pl. from*; *to find relish in* (*a th*) ‖ die Genüsse [pl] *the pl.s* (od *joys*) pl; die G.e des Lebens *the sweets* [pl] *of life* ≗**freudig** a *pleasure-loving* **~mensch** m *sybarite*; *man of pleasure*; *dissipated man*; *voluptuary*; → Genießer **~mittel** n pl *coffee*, *tea*, *chocolate*, *tobacco*, *spirits*; *stimulants*, *beverages*; Nahrungs- u. ~ *provisions and fine foods* ‖ ~-pflanzen [f pl] *stimulant and pseudo-alimentary plants* ≗**reich** a *enjoyable*; *pleasant* **~schein** m ⟨com⟩ (*document giving holder a right to participate in net profit*) "*jouissance*" *share* **~sucht** f *love of pleasure*; *dissipation*; *indulgence* ≗**süchtig** a *pleasure-seeking* **~süchtling** m (alter *old*) *playboy* **Gen·üßling** m ~s/~e = Genußmensch

G·eo ⟨school sl⟩ = Geographie ‖ [in comp] *geo–* **~bot·anik** f *geographical botany* **~däs·ie** f *geodesy* **~d·ät** m ~en/~en *geodesist*; *student of geodesy* ≗**d·ätisch** a *geodetic*(*al*), *geodesic* **~gr·aph** m *geographer* **~graph·ie** f *geography* ≗**gr·aphisch** a *geographic*(*al*); die ~e Lage, ~en Verhältnisse *the geography* (*of a country*); ~e Meile *geographical mile*; in ~er Hinsicht *geographically* **~isoth·ermen** pl *geoisotherms* pl **~l·og(e)** m *geologist* **~log·ie** f *geology* ≗**l·ogisch** a *geologic*; *geological* (*age*, *formation*); der ~e Charakter *the geology* (*of a region*); in ~er Hinsicht *geologically* **~mant·ie** f *geomancy* **~m·eter** m ~s/~ *surveyor* **~metr·ie** f *geometry* ≗**m·etrisch** a *geometric*(*al*); ~es Mittel *geometrical mean*; ~er Ort *locus* [L]; ~e Reihe *geometrical series* ‖ ~e Kunst *geometrical tracery* ‖ **~morpholog·ie** f *geomorphology* **~ph·ag(e)** m *geophagist* **~phag·ie** f *geophagy* **~phys·ik** f *geophysics* pl [sg konstr] **~ph·yten** pl ⟨bot⟩ *geophytes* pl ≗**physik·alisch** a *geophysical* **~politik** f *geopolitics* **~synklinale** pl *geosynclines*, *-clinals* pl **~tekt·onik** f *geotectonics* pl ≗**th·ermisch** a *geothermal*, *-mic* **~trop·ismus** m ⟨bot⟩ *geotropism* ≗**z·entrisch** a *geocentric*

Ge·ode f ~/~n ⟨geol⟩ *geode* **Geo·id** n ~s/~e ⟨geol⟩ *geoid*

ge- ~·ölt a ⟨fig⟩ *oily*; *glib* (*language*); er redet wie ~ *he talks glibly* ‖ (S) wie ~ gehen *to go swimmingly* od *smoothly*; → Blitz ‖ °(P) = gelackmeiert **~·ordnet** a *orderly* (*mind*), *regular* (*life*, *habits*)

G·eorg: ⟨engl⟩ zur Zeit (eines) der ~e gehörig *Georgian* **Ge·orgia** n (Staat der U.S.A.) | **~straße** f (zw der Vancouverinsel u Brit. Columbia) *Strait of Georgia* **Ge·orgien** n ⟨Russ⟩ (Staat südl. des Kaukasus) *Georgia* **Ge·orgier** m ~s/~ (in Transkaukasien) *Georgian* **Georg·ine** f ~/~n ⟨bot⟩ *a kind of dahlia* **ge·orgisch** a (→ Georgier) *Georgian*

Gep·äck n ~(e)s/ **1.** (Passagier≗) *luggage*; ⟨Am⟩ *baggage* ‖ mit leichtem ~ reisen *to travel light* ⟨a. fig⟩; das ~ aufgeben *to book* (od *register*; ⟨Am⟩ *to check*) *one's luggage*; ⟨Am⟩ *to have one's b. checked*; ~ zur Aufbewahrung geben ⟨Am⟩ *to check* **2.** ⟨mil⟩ *baggage*; ~ aufnehmen! *sling* *on packs!* **3.** *belongings* pl; *pack* (*of a pedlar*); ⟨fam⟩ *traps* pl; ⟨Am sl⟩ *plunder*

Gep·äck- [in comp] *luggage*; ⟨Am⟩ *baggage* **~abfertigung, ~annahme, ~aufgabe, ~ausgabe** *l.*– (*b.*–) *office*, ⟨Am a.⟩ *check-room*, *b.-r.* **~aufbewahrung(sstelle)** f *left-luggage office*; *cloak-room*; ⟨Am⟩ *check*(*ing*)-*room* **~beförderungsgesellschaft** f ⟨Am⟩ *b. transfer company*; *moving and express business* **~expedition** f = –abfertigung ‖ †**~droschke** f ⟨engl⟩ *four-wheeler* **~halter** m ⟨mot⟩ (hinten am Auto) *trunk-grid*; ⟨cycl⟩ *carrier* **~karren** m *truck* **~marsch** m ⟨mil⟩ *march with full equipment* **~meister** m ⟨Am⟩ *b.-master* **~netz** n *l.-*, (*b.-*)*rack* **~raum** m *l.-* ⟨Am⟩ *b.-room*; ⟨mot, rail, aero⟩ *l. compartment*, ⟨aero a.⟩ *belly* **~schein** m ⟨Ger⟩ *l.-*, (*b.-*)*ticket* **~sitz** m ⟨mot⟩ *rumble seat* **~stück** n *piece of l.-*, (*b.*) (*3 pieces of l.*) **~träger** m *porter* ‖ ⟨Am⟩ *baggageman*; *redcap* ‖ ⟨cycl⟩ *l. carrier* **~wagen** m ⟨rail⟩ *l,-van*; ⟨Am⟩ *b.-car*

G·epard m ~s/~e ⟨zoo⟩ *hunting leopard*

ge- ~pfändet a ⟨jur⟩ (*cattle*) *distrained* (*up*)*on* | ˊ~e(r [m]) f *distrainee* **~pfeffert** a *peppery*; ⟨fig⟩ *peppered* (*bill*); *salted*, *steep*; ⟨sl⟩ *salt* (*prices*); *stiff* ‖ *coarse*, *fruity* (*jokes*) ‖ → geharnischt 2. °ˊ**~pfeife** n ~s/ *whistling* **~pf·iffen** pp v pfeifen **~pfl·astert** a *paved*; → Schotterstraße **~pfl·egt** a *well-looked after* (od *tended*); *ordered* (*garden*); *cared-for* (*beard*) ‖ (P) *well-groomed*, ⟨cosm⟩ *soigné*(*e*) Fr ‖ *cultivated* (*pronunciation*) **~pfl·ogen** pp v pflegen | ˊ~heit [f] ~/~en *custom*, *practice*, *habit*; gesellschaftl. ~en (e–r Zeit) *conventions* pl

Gep·iden pl ⟨hist⟩ *Gepidae* [L pl], *Gibids* pl

ge- ~pl·agt a *tormented*; ~ v *stricken with* (*gout*); v Neugier ~ *beset by c.* ˊ**~pl·änkel** n ~s/~ ⟨mil⟩ *affray*, *brush* (mit *with*); *skirmish*(*ing*) ‖ *slight quarrel*; *tiff*; ⟨Am⟩ *spat* **~pl·ant** a *planned*; *projected* (*visit*) ˊ**~pl·apper** n ~s/ *babble*, *cackle*, *chatter*, *prattle*, *rattle*, *tattle*; *babbling*, *cackling*; *clacking*; *patter* °ˊ**~pl·ärr** n ~(e)s/ *bawling*, *bleating* ‖ *crying*; *whining*, *whine* ˊ**~pl·ätscher** n ~s/ *babble*, *babbling*; *lap*(*ping*); *plash*; *purl*(*ing*); *splash*(*ing*); *gurgling*; *hubble-bubble*, *murmur* °**~platzt** a *disbanded*, *dissolved* (Unternehmen etc) ˊ**~pl·auder** n ~s/ (*small*) *talk*; *chat*, *chatter*(*ing*); ⟨fam⟩ *gab* °ˊ**~p·oche** n ~s/ = Geklopfe ˊ**~p·olter** n ~s/ *din*; *rumble*, *rumbling noise*; *rumblings* pl ˊ**~pr·äge** ~s/ **A.** [abstr] *coinage*, *coining* ‖ ⟨fig⟩ → Prägen **B.** [konkr] **1.** ⟨eig⟩ *impressed design* od *mark*; (auf Münzen) *coinage*; (auf Wachs etc) *impression* **2.** ⟨fig⟩ *character*; *imprint*; *mark*; *stamp* (*of originality*); das charakteristische ~ *the characteristics* pl; *the characteristic features* pl; *the distinguishing mark*, *the impress* (*of the middle ages*); ein individuelles ~ h *to have individuality* ‖ [dat] das ~ geben *to give a stamp to*, *to set one's stamp upon*; *to leave an impress on*; e–r S sein charakterist. ~ g. *to characterize* (*events*), *to be the keynote of*, *to stamp a th with one's personality* °ˊ**~pr·ahle** n ~s/ *boast*(*ing*); *brag*(*ging*) ˊ**~pr·änge** n ~s/ *flash*, *ostentation*; *ostentatious* (od *flashy*) *display*; *pageant*(*ry*); *parade*; *pomp*; *state* ˊ**~pr·assel** n ~s/ *crackling*, *rattling*; *clatter*; *spatter* **~pr·iesen** pp v preisen **~prüft** a ⟨tech⟩ *proved* °ˊ**~qu·ake** n ~s/ *croaking* °ˊ**~qu·assel** n ~s/ *stupid* (od *trite*) *talk*; *drivel*, *piffle*, *twaddle*; ⟨mil sl⟩ (Offizierbesprechung) *pow-pow*; ⟨Am sl⟩ *ballyhoo* °ˊ**~qu·atsche** n = Gequassel; ⟨sl⟩ *waffle*; hochtrabendes ~ *double talk* °**qu·ieke** n ~s/ *squeaking* **~qu·ollen** pp v quellen

Ger m ~(e)s/~e ⟨hist⟩ *spear*; ⟨sport⟩ → Speer

ger·ade I. [a] **A.** (of numbers) *even* ‖ ~ oder ungerade *odd or even*; ⟨comp⟩ *odd*/*even* (*test*) ‖ ⟨fig⟩ → fünf **B.** (Ggs krumm) **1.** ⟨eig⟩ *straight* (*road*, etc); *straight* od *right* ([*neck*]*line*); in ~er L. *straight* ‖ ~ Strecke *straight*; → Strecke ‖ (*thank God that you still have your*) *sound* (*limbs*) ‖ ⟨math⟩ *right* (*cone*, *cylinder*) **2.** (aufrecht) *erect* (*bearing*); *straight*, *upright* (*tree*) ‖ → ~hängen, ~heraus, ~legen, ~sitzen, ~stehen **3.** ⟨übtr⟩ (direkt) **a.** *direct* (*route*); in ~er Geschlechtslinie *in the direct line* ‖ *exact*, *very*; das ~e Gegenteil *the very* (od *just the*) *opposite*, *quite the reverse* **4.** ⟨fig⟩ (P) (unbeugsam) *undeviating*; *straight* (*look*), *upright* (*character*); *candid*, *downright*, *frank*, *honest*, *straightforward* (*fellow*); ~er Kerl ⟨Am sl⟩ *square shooter* ‖ ⟨prov⟩ der ~ Weg ist der beste *honesty is the best policy* **II.** [adv] **1.** *straight*; ~ aufs Ziel losgehen *to go straight for one's goal* **2.** ⟨übtr⟩ **a.** *exactly*, *directly*, *precisely*; *just*, ⟨bes Am⟩ *right* (*to go right opposite* [entgegengesetzt]) ‖ ~ **10 Meter** *exactly 10 metres* ‖ ~ 10 Uhr (*it is*) *just ten* ‖ ~ so groß wie .. *just as tall as* .. ‖ ~ das **Gegenteil** = das ~ G. → I. B. 3.; es war ~ dies .. *it was*, *in fact this particular* (*measure*); ~ der Mann (*he is*) *just the man* (*for*..) ‖ ~ das Richtige *the very thing*; *just* (od *quite*) *the thing*; *the thing* ‖ dies erwartete ich ~ *I expected as much*; das paßt ~ *that's just right*; das ist es ~ *that is just it* | ~ **dort** *just* (⟨Am⟩ *right*) *there* ‖ ~ **heute** (*he told me*) *only today* ‖ ~ **jetzt** (⟨Am⟩ *right*) *now*; *at that* (*very*) *moment* ‖ das ist ~ **recht** *that is just right* | ~ **in** dem Augenblick *just then*; ~ in der Mitte *right* (⟨Am fam⟩ *r. smack*) *in the middle*; ~ ins Gesicht (*I hit him*) *full in the face* ‖ ~ in die Mitte, ins Zentrum, um 10 Uhr = genau II. 2. b. ‖ ~ zur rechten Zeit *just in time*, *in good t.* | ~ **ablaufend** *being performed*; ~, **als** .. *just as* .. ‖ ~, weil .. *just because* .. **b.** [unbetont] **eben** ~ *just*; *only just*; *just now*; ich erreichte den Zug noch eben ~ *I cut it fine* | **nicht** ~ *not exactly* ‖ er ist nicht ~ dumm *he has brains of a sort* ‖ nicht ~ gut *none too well*, *not too nice* **c. warum** ~ er? *why he of all people*? **2.** [Satz *or* Verb bestimmend] *just*; ich habe ihn ~ **gesehen** *I've just seen him* | ich **war** ~ in Berlin *I happened to be in B. at that time* ‖ ich war ~ im Begriff z gehen *I was about to go*; *I was just going* | er **schläft** ~ *he is sleeping* (od *asleep*) ‖ regnet es ~? *is it raining* (⟨Am⟩ *right*) *now*? ‖ der Gegenstand, der ~ erörtert wird *the subject in hand* **3.** [stark betont] **nun** ~! *all the more!*; *now more than ever*; *with a vengeance* ‖ **nun** ~ **nicht** *not on any account*; *not for the world* **III.** die ˊ~ *the straight line*; ⟨box⟩ linker ~r *jab*; ⟨sport⟩ → Strecke

ger·ade- [in comp] **~·aus** [adv] *right* (od *straight*) *on*; *straight ahead* ‖ ⟨übtr⟩ *peremptorily*; → g.zu, g.heraus ‖ ⟨mil⟩ Augen ~! *eyes front!* ‖ ˊ~richtung [f] ⟨mil⟩ *dressing* | ˊ~anflug [m] *straight-in approach*; ˊ~flug [m] *straight and level flight* **~|halten** vt [h] (etw) *to hold straight* ‖ sich ~ *to stand* (od *walk*) *straight* ˊ**~halter** m (f Kinder) *backboard* **~|hängen** vt [h] (Bild) *to put straight* **~her·aus** adv *candidly*, *frankly*, *outspokenly*; *in plain terms* ‖ *bluntly*; *point-blank*, *roundly*; (*to ask a p*) *outright*; *straight out* ***~hin** adv *bluntly*, *point-blank*, *roundly* **~|legen** vt [h] (etw) *to put straight*, *to straighten* **~|richten** vt [h] *to straighten* **~|setzen** vt [h] (Hut) *to put straight* **~|sitzen** vi [h] *to sit up straight* **~so** adv *just like that*; er ist ~ wie .. *he is just like* ..; ~viel (wie) *just as much* (*as*); ~viele (wie) *just as many* (as) **~|stehen** vi [h] *to stand straight* (od *erect*) ‖ ⟨fig⟩ ~ f (etw) *to answer for*, *to be responsible for*; du hast dafür –zu– *you are in for it* **~wegs** adv *directly*, *straight*; ~ reiten *to ride straight* (*over* ..) ‖ ⟨Am⟩ (*to come*) *clean* (*from*) ‖ (*to run*) *smack* (*into*) **~zu** adv **1.** = geradeaus **2.** *perfectly*, *simply* (*extraordinary*, *lovely*); *nothing short of* (*marvellous*); *downright* (*unpleasant*) ‖ *almost* (*unbearable*); ~ schrecklich ⟨vulg⟩ *something dreadful*; ~ laut aufschreiend *with almost a shriek* ‖ ~ Unsinn *downright* (od *utter*, *sheer*) *nonsense*

|| er überzeugte mich ~ *he went far to convince me* **3.** [**~z·u**] er ist ein wenig ~ *he is a bit blunt* (od *curt, plain-spoken*; *cheeky*)

Ger·adeisen n *spoke-shave* || **ger·adenwegs, ger·adeswegs** adv = geradewegs

Ger·ad- ~flügler pl ⟨ent⟩ *orthoptera* [Gr pl] **~führung** f ⟨tech⟩ *straight-line motion*; → Führung B. **~heit** f ~/ **1.** *evenness*; *straightness* **2.** ⟨fig⟩ (charakterl. ~) *rectitude, straighforwardness, straightness, uprightness* **3.** ⟨Lit⟩ *sincerity* **≛läufig** a *straight* **≛lehnig** a *straight-backed* (*chair*) **≛linig** a *rectilineal, rectilinear* || ein ~er Abkomme *a lineal descendant* **≛schäftig** a ⟨for⟩ *straight(-boled)* **≛sinnig** a = gerade I. B. 4.

ger·ändelt, ger·ändert a ⟨tech⟩ *milled* (*coin*)

Ger·anie [–iə] f ~/~n, **Geranium** n ~s/–nien ⟨bot⟩ *geranium* [L] [pl –s]; *pelargonium* [pl –s]

ge- ~r·ann [1. & 3. sg] v gerinnen **~r·annt** pp v rennen °**~r·appelt** a; ~ voll *chock-full, choke-full* **≛r·assel** n *clank, rattle*; *rattle-rattle*; *clatter*; *din* **~r·astert** a *screened* **≛r·ät** n ~(e)s/~e *implement, tool, utensil* || [oft koll] ~ *implements* pl etc; *apparatus*; *gear, tackle*; *appliances* pl; ⟨Am⟩ *fixings* pl || Garten≛e *gardener's tools*; Ackerbau≛e *agricultural implements*; Angel≛ *fishing-tackle*; Turn≛e *gymnastic apparatus* || → Apparat; Geschirr; Hausrat, Werkzeug

Geräte- ~beschreibung f *item description* **~glas** n *glass* od *apparatus for laboratory use* **~kammer** f *storeroom* **~kasten** m *tool-box* **~prüfung** f ⟨bes wir⟩ *functional testing*; ⟨mil⟩ *service test* od *trial of equipment* **~sammelstelle** f *ordnance collecting point* **~steckdose** f ⟨el⟩ *inlet socket* **~stecker** m ⟨el⟩ *inlet plug* **~turnen** n *heavy gymnastics* pl (*on an apparatus*)

ge- ~r·aten vi [geriet/geraten] [s] **1.** (**zufällig**) *to stumble upon a th*; *to get* (in *into*); *to come, fall* | ⟨mst fig⟩ **an** die falsche Adresse, an den Unrechten ~ *to come to the wrong address*; *to catch a Ta(r)tar* || an e–a ~ *to fall by the ears*; *to come to high words* | **auf** Abwege ~ *to go wrong*; *to get into mischief* || auf den Grund ~ *to run aground* | **aus** dem Häuschen ~, außer sich ~ *to jump out of one's skin*; *to go off one's head*; (vor Wut) *to see red*; (vor Freude) *to be overjoyed* | **in** Eifer ~ *to become heated*; in Gefangenschaft ~ *to be taken prisoner* || sich in die Haare ~ *to fall by the ears* || nicht in die richtigen Hände ~ *to come* (od *get*) *into wrong hands* || in Not ~ *to come to grief* || in Schwierigkeiten ~ *to be landed in* (od *to get into*) *difficulties* || ins Wanken ~ *to totter*; *to reel*; *to sag*; (of conditions) *to tumble out of control* || → Brand, Gefahr, Gesellschaft, Hintertreffen, Klemme, Schulden, Schweiß, Stocken, Vergessenheit, Wut, Zorn | ~ **über** *to come across* (*he came across a book of* ..) | **unter** jds Einfluß ~ *to come under the influence of a p* || unter fremde Herrschaft ~ *to pass under foreign domination* || ⟨bib⟩ unter die Räuber ~ *to fall among thieves* **2.** (**ausfallen, glücken**) *to come off* (*poems that don't come off*); *to turn out*; *to prove*; die Bilder sind schlecht ~ *the photos have turned out* (od *come off*) *badly*; der Kuchen ist ausgezeichnet ~ *the cake is a great success* | s–e Kinder sind gut ~ *his children have turned out well* || nicht ~ *to get into mischief, to go astray* || klein ~ s *to be on the small side* | ~ **s nach jdm** *to take after a p, to resemble a p*; er ist ganz nach dem Vater ~ *he is just like his father*, ⟨sl⟩ *he is the very spit of his f.* | **jdm** ~; alles gerät ihm gut *he is successful in everything, everything succeeds with him* (od *in his hand*) **~r·aten** a [pp v raten] *advantageous, advisable* (*it is not a.* ..); das ~ste wird s *the best th will be* (*to get away*) **≛ratew·ohl** n [nur *in*:] aufs ~ *hit or miss*; *at haphazard* (od *random, a venture*); *indiscriminately*; Antworten aufs ~ *haphazard replies* pl; aufs ~ schießen *to shoot a wild pitch*; wir h ihn aufs ~ aufgesucht *we took a chance of finding him at home* **≛r·ätschaft** f ~/~en [mst pl] ~en *implements* pl, *tools* pl || *apparatus*; ⟨tech⟩ *plant* °**≛r·atter** n ~s/ *chatter*; (*hum and*) *rattle* (*of machines*) **≛r·aufe** n ~s/ *brawl, rough-and-tumble, scuffle*; ⟨fam⟩ *shindy* **~r·äuchert** a *smoke-dried*; *smoked* **~r·auht** a *roughened* (*surface*) **~r·aum** a † *roomy, spacious* | [nur in:] ~e Zeit *a long t.*; *for some considerable time*; noch e–e ~e Weile *quite a while yet*; vor ~er Zeit *long ago, long since*; es wird noch e–e ~e Zeit vergehen, bis .. *it will be* (od *take*) *a long t. before* .. **~r·äumig** a *commodious, roomy, spacious*; *large*; *wide* | **≛**keit [f] ~/ *roominess, spaciousness*; *ampleness*; *capacity*; *largeness*; *wideness, width*; *ful(l)ness* **≛raune** n *murmur* **≛raunze** n [österr] *complaining*

Ger·äusch n ~es/~e *noise*; unangenehmes ~ *jarring n.* || ⟨fig⟩ viel ~ m *to make a fuss* od *stir* || → Lärm, Treiben || ~ v Schritten *footfall*; dumpfes ~ *thud, thump, wump(h)*; klatschendes ~ *smack, slap*; klirrendes ~ *clang*; knisterndes ~ *rustle*; polterndes ~ *rumble*; schwirrendes ~ *swish*; *whirr, whizz*; *zip*; zischendes ~ *fizz* | ⟨med⟩ Atem≛ *murmur*; vesikuläres A. *vesicular m.* **≛arm** a *of low noise level*; *silenced*; *silent* **~boje** f *acoustical b.* **~dämmung** f → Schalldämpfung **≛dämpfend** a ⟨typewr⟩ *absorbing the operating noise*; *antinoise* **~effekt** m *sound effect* **~kulisse** f ⟨theat⟩ *noises-off* **~laut** m ⟨phon⟩ *consonant* **≛los 1.** [a] *noiseless*; *quiet* (*running of a machine*); *silent* (*engine*; *programme* ⟨pap⟩) **2.** [adv] *noiselessly*; *quietly* | **≛**igkeit [f] *noiselessness*; *quiet(ness)* **~messer** m *noise-meter*; *phonometer, audiometer*; *sound-level indicator* **~pegel** m *n. level* **~überprüfung** f *n.-survey* **≛voll 1.** [a] *noisy* (*running of a machine*; *streets*); *clamorous, loud* || ~e Tätigkeit, ~es Treiben *bustle, stir* **2.** [adv] *noisily*

Ger·äusper n ~s/ *general* od *loud clearing of throats* || *humming and hawing, hums and haws*

g·erbbar a *tannable* **g·erben I.** vt/i [h] **A.** vt **1.** (Häute) ~ *to tan* || (weiß ~) *to taw* **2.** (a. gärben) (Metall) *to polish*; Stahl ~ = schweißen **3.** ⟨fig⟩ °jdm das Fell ~, jdn ~ *to give a p a sound hiding* **B.** vi °⟨univ⟩ *to vomit* **II.** ≛ n *tanning*; → *tawing* **G·erber** m ~s/~ (Loh≛) *tanner* || (Weiß≛) *tawer* **~gesell(e)** m *journey-man tanner* **~grube** f *tanpit, -vat* **~handwerk** n *tanner's* (od *tawer's*) *trade* **~lohe** f ⟨gard⟩ (*spent*) *tan*; → Lohe **~messer** n *scraping* (od *fleshing*)*-knife* **~mittel** n *tanning material* od *agent* **~strauch** m ⟨bot⟩ *ink-plant*; *tanner's sumach* (od *tree*) **Gerber·ei** f ~/~en **1.** = Gerben || *trade of tanning* od *tawing* **2.** (Werkstatt) *tannery, tanyard* **G·erb- ~leim** m ⟨pap⟩ *size* **~rinde** f *tan-bark* **≛sauer** [a] ~es Salz *tannate* **~säure** f *tannic acid*; *tannin* || **≛**haltig [a] *tanniferous* **~stoff** m *tannin*; = Gerbsäure **G·erbung** f = Gerben

ger·echt I. [a] **1.** *just, impartial, unbiased* (*judge*); ~ s *to be just* (od *fair*) (gegen .. *to a p*); streng aber ~ *strict but fair* || *just* (*verdict*); *equitable, well-deserved* (*punishment*); das ist s–e ~e Strafe *that serves him right* || *just* (*peace, reward*); *fair* (*account, wages*); e–e ~e S *a rightful cause*; s–e Ansprüche sind ~ *his claims are justified* (od *just, well-founded*) **2. jdm** ~ **w** *to do a p justice*; um Herrn N. ~ z w *in justice* (od *fairness*) *to Mr. N.* || **e–r S** ~ **w** *to do justice to a th*; den Anforderungen ~ w *to meet* (⟨Am⟩ *to fill*) *the requirements*; ⟨Am⟩ *to measure up to the r.* || Bedingungen ~ w *to meet conditions* || e–r S ~ w *to live up to a th, to take a th into consideration*; .. nicht .. *to fall short of, to miss a th* (*he missed an essential part*), *to underplay a th*; dieser Idealismus wird s–m Namen ~ *this idealism lives up to its name* | ⟨fig⟩ er ist **in allen Sätteln** ~ *he is versed in* (od *fit for*) *anything* **II.** [adv] *with justice*; *im-*

partially; *fairly*; *well-deservedly* **III. ≈e** [der ~, ein ~r] m ~n/~n ⟨bib⟩ *the righteous man*; die ~n *the righteous* ‖ er schlief den Schlaf des ~n *he slept the sleep of the just* **~fertigt** a *justifiable, warrantable*; etw ~ erscheinen l *to justify* od *warrant a th* ‖ durch nichts (aber auch gar nichts) ~ *wanton* **≈igkeit** f ~/~en **1.** (P) *justice* (*of a p*; gegen *to*); *equity*; *fairness*; *impartiality* (*of a judge*); *just conduct* ‖ jdm ~ widerfahren l *to do a p justice* **|** (S) *justice, justness, rightfulness* (*of a cause*); *justification* (*of claims*) **2.** ⟨jur⟩ gesetzliche ~ *jurisdiction* (*of claims*) **2.** ⟨jur⟩ gesetzliche ~ *jurisdiction, justice* (strafende ~ *punitive justice*); *the law* ‖ Diener der ~ *servant of the law* ‖ jdn der ~ ausliefern *to bring a p to justice* ‖ der ~ ihren Lauf l *to let justice take its course* **3.** ausgleichende ~ *social j.*; *poetic j.* **≈igkeits-** ~liebe [f] *love of justice*; ~pflege [f] *j.*; *administration of the law*; ~sinn [m] *sense of j.* **≈same** f ~/~n ⟨hist jur⟩ *enjoyment of a right* od *title*; *use, user*; → Servitut ‖ *privilege, prerogative*; aus Regalien (→ d.) abgeleitete ~ *franchise*

Ge- ~r·ede n ~s/ **1.** *chatter* (über *about*); *idle talk*; *gossip*; *groundless rumours*; *tittle-tattle*; *galimatias*; → Geschwätz; Klatsch, Nachrede **2. bloßes** ~ *mere hearsay* ‖ dummes ~ *idle talk*; ich habe genug v diesem .. (*I have had enough of this i. talk*) ‖ irrsinniges ~ *ravings* pl ‖ leeres ~ ⟨sl⟩ *eyewash, rant* ‖ schönes ~ *oratory* (*it's merely o.*) ‖ seichtes ~ ⟨fam⟩ *wish-wash* **|** ein ~ **aufbringen** *to set tongues wagging* ‖ jdn ins ~ bringen *to make a p the talk of the town* ‖ ins ~ k. *to become the talk of the town, to get talked about* ‖ sich in ein langes ~ verlieren *to wander from the point* **≈r·egelt** a *fixed, ordered*; fest ~ *well-ordered* (*conventions*) **≈r·eichen** vi [h] jdm ~ z [nur 3. sg]: **es** gereicht ihm zur Ehre, daß er .. *it does him credit, it redounds* (od *adds*) *to his credit that he* .. es g. mir zu großer Freude *it gives me much pleasure*; .. mir zur größten Genugtuung *it affords me the greatest satisfaction* ‖ **das wird ihm** zum Nutzen, Vorteil ~ *that will be* od *redound to his advantage*; .. z Schaden ~ *that will do him harm*; .. z Schande ~ *that will bring shame upon him*; .. z Verderben ~ *that will bring him to ruin*; .. *will mean his ruin* **≈r·eizt** a *edgy, grumpy, irritable, petulant*; *touchy*; ~ s *to be* od *feel nettled*; s–e Nerven waren ~ *his nerves were on edge* **|** ~heit [f] *grumpiness, irritability, irritation* (über *at, over*), *petulance* °**~r·enne** n *running to and fro*; *bustle* **≈r·euen** vt [h] die Tat gereut mich *I repent* (*of*) *the deed* ‖ [oft imps] **es** wird dich ~ *you will repent* (*of*) *it, you will regret it*; es g. mich, es getan z h *I repent doing it*

G·erhardskraut n ⟨bot⟩ = Giersch

Ger·icht n ~es/~e **A.** ⟨jur & theol⟩ **1.** (Rechtsprechung) *judicature, justice*; *jurisdiction* **2.** (Behörde) *court, court of justice* (od *law*), *law-court*; *bar, forum* [L], *tribunal*; → ~shof ‖ ⟨engl⟩ summarisches ~ v 2 oder mehr Friedensrichtern *petty sessions* pl ‖ ~ f letztwillige Verfügungen *probate-court*; → Amts≈ etc **3.** (Gottes≈) *judg*(*e*)*ment* (über .. *upon a p*); Jüngstes ~ *the Day of Judg*(*e*)*ment*; *the Last Day* (od *Judg*(*e*)*ment*); *the Great Assize*; *judg*(*e*)*ment-day, doomsday* **4.** (Gebäude) *court*; *law-courts* pl **5.** dies wird wohl noch die ~e beschäftigen *this may come into Court* ‖ ~ **halten** = z ~ sitzen ‖ sich freiwillig dem ~ stellen *to give o.s. up to the police* ‖ (jdn) dem ~ überliefern *to bring to justice* **| aufs** ~ gehen *to go to the Court* **|** jdn **beim** ~ verklagen *to have the law of a p*; *to prosecute a p* **|** ⟨fig⟩ mit jdm scharf **ins** ~ gehen *to deal strictly with a p*; *to take a p severely to task*; mit sich selbst .. *to take stock of o.s.* **|** vor (das) ~ bringen *to bring into Court* ‖ vor ~ erscheinen *to appear in Court* ‖ vor ~ gehen *to go to law* ‖ vor ~ k *to come into Court* ‖ jdn vor ~ laden *to cite* od *summon a p* ‖ jdn vor ~ stellen *to bring a p to* ⟨Am *on*⟩ *trial, to put a p on his trial*; *to prosecute a p, to have a p up, to try a p* (wegen *for*); vor ~ gestellt w wegen *to undergo trial for* (*murder*) ‖ vor ~ verhandelt w *to come into Court* **| zu** ~ sitzen über *to sit in judg*(*e*)*ment on a p*; *to try a p* **B.** ⟨cul⟩ *dish*; ~e [pl] ⟨Am a.⟩ *eats* pl ‖ Bohnen≈ *dish of beans*; Fisch≈ *dish of fish*; → Gang ‖ chines. ~ v mixed pickles: *chow-chow* ‖ ⟨Am⟩ ~ aus Fisch, Pökelfleisch u Schiffszwieback *chowden* **ger·ichtet** a **1.** *condemned*; ~ s *to stand c.* **2.** (Richtung h) **a.** *directional* (*radiation*); ~ s *to tend* (nach *to, towards*) **b.** [in comp] *minded, orientated*; diesseits~ *worldly-minded* **ger·ichtlich 1.** [a] *judicial* (*decision, decree*), *judiciary*; *legal* (*procedure*) ‖ ~e Medizin *forensic medicine, medical jurisprudence*; ohne ~e Mitwirkung ⟨contr⟩ *without* (*requiring*) *the consent of any court*; ~e Verfolgung *prosecution* **2.** [adv] *legally*; *by process of law*; *by order of a Court* ‖ jdn ~ belangen *to have a p up, to go to law with a p* ‖ jdn ~ verfolgen, ~ vorgehen gegen jdn *to prosecute a p*; *to take proceedings* (od *an action at law*) *against a p* **Ger·ichts- ~akten** pl *court roll* **~arzt** m *legal medical officer* **~assessor** m ⟨Ger⟩ *senior post-graduate* (*after second examination*) **~beamte** [der ~, ein ~r] *official of a law-court* **~befehl** m *order of the court*; *writ* **~beisitzer** m *assessor*; *assistant to a judge*; *magistrate's clerk* **~beschluß** m *decision*; *order*, bedingter ~ *order nisi* **~bezirk** m *jurisdiction*; *circuit* **~chemiker** m *public analyst* **~diener** m *court-attendant*; *usher* (*of the court*); *apparitor, bailiff*; ⟨hist⟩ *tipstaff* **~entscheid(ung** f) m *judicial ruling*; *decision*; durch Hinweis auf e–e vorhergegangene ~ *by case stated from a decision* **~ferien** pl *vacation of the courts of law*; ⟨Am⟩ *recess* **~gebäude** n *law-courts* pl **~herr** m ⟨hist⟩ *lord of the manor* **~hilfe** f ⟨Ger⟩ *prison relief* (od *welfare*)-*work* **~hof** m (→ Gericht A. 2.) *court*; *court of justice* (od *law*); *law-court*; *judicature, judiciary*; der Hohe ~ *the Court*; Hoher ~! (Anrede des Anwalts) *May it please your Lordship*! ‖ Oberster *or* Höchster ~ *Supreme Court of Judicature* ‖ ~ f Ehesachen *divorce-court*; ~ zur letzten Zuflucht *Court of Last Resort*; → Gericht 2. ‖ Polizei≈ *police-court* **~kanzlei** f *law court offices* pl **~kosten** pl *legal expenses*; *costs* pl **|** ~marke [f] *law stamp* **~medizin** f *forensic medicine* **~offizier** m ⟨Am⟩ *summary court officer* **~ordnung** f *rules* [pl] *of the court* ‖ ⟨Ger hist⟩ Peinliche ~ *first German penal code* (*1532*) **~person** f; ~en [pl] *gentlemen of the robe*; *personnel* od *staff of a court* **~perücke** f ⟨engl⟩ *forensic wig* **~saal** m *court-room* **~schreiber** m *clerk to the court*; *registrar* **~sitzung** f *session*; *hearing*; ⟨engl⟩ vierteljährl. ~en der Friedensrichter *quarter-sessions* pl; kl ~en *petty sessions* pl; → Geschworenengericht; in öffentl. ~ *in open court* **~sporteln** pl *court-fees* pl **~stand** m *domicile*; *jurisdiction* **~tag** m *court-day* **~termin** m *return day* **~verfahren** n ⟨allg⟩ *legal procedure*; *judicial process* ‖ [konkr] *legal proceedings* pl; *trial*; → Prozeß **~verfassung** f *judicial organization* **~verhandlung** f *pleadings*; *legal proceedings* pl; Haupt≈ *trial* **~vollzieher** m *bailiff* **~wesen** n *judicature*; *judiciary*; *judicial system*

Ger·ichtsbarkeit f ~/ *jurisdiction* (über *over*); streitige ~ *contentious j.*, freiwillige ~ *non-contentious j.* ‖ dem Gericht steht die ~ zu über .. *the Court has j. over* ..

ge- ~r·ieben a [pp reiben] ⟨fig⟩ (schlau) *artful, clever, crafty, cunning, dodgy, knowing, tricky*; ⟨sl⟩ *downy*; ein ~er Bursche, ein ganz ≈er *a cunning* (od *knowing*) *one*; ⟨sl⟩ *a downy old bird* ‖ → durchtrieben, gerissen **|** ≈heit [f] *artfulness, craftiness, cunning* **≈r·iesel** n ~s/ *rippling, running, trickling* (*of water*); *babble, bubbling, purl*(*ing*) **~r·iet** [1. & 3. pret] v geraten **~r·ieft,**

~r·iffelt, ~r·illt a *fluted, grooved; channelled; ribbed, ridged*

ger·ing I. [a] **A.** ~ **1.** (klein an Zahl etc) **a.** ⟨eig⟩ *small* (*number, sum; profits*); *little* (*only a l. distance from*) ‖ e–e ~e Anzahl *a paucity* od *fewness* (*of letters*); ⟨com ad⟩ *minimum* (Verschleiß); ⟨st exch⟩ ~es Angebot *few sellers* pl **b.** ⟨übtr⟩ (unbedeutend) *little, small; insignificant, mediocre, poor; scanty* (*means*); *trivial* (*expenses*); *low* (*costs; enrichment* [*of ore*]); *slight* (*curvature*) ‖ nur ~e Ähnlichkeit mit .. *only small resemblance to* (*one another*); ~e Anforderungen stellen an *to ask* (od *require*) *little of a p*; nur ~e Aussichten *but few* od *remote chances*; (*if I had*) *half a chance*; nur ~e Begabung *only moderate* (od *poor*) *ability*; in ~em Grade *little; to a small extent*; sehr ~es Interesse *very little interest*; ~er Umfang *narrowness*; der ~ste Wink *the barest h.* | **nicht** ~ *no little* (*pains*), *no small; no mean* (*ability*); *considerable; great* (*in g. embarrassment*); nicht der ~ste Beweis *not a shred of ev.* kein ~er Erfolg *quite a success*; nicht der ~ste Zweifel *no shadow of doubt* | (jdn) f ~ **halten** *to think little, to have a low opinion of* | ⟨tech⟩ ~e zusätzliche Kraft *touch of power* **2.** (niedrig, dürftig) *inferior* (*stuff, wine*); *low; mean* (*quality, rank*), *poor*; v ~er Herkunft *of low birth*; ~e Leute *persons of the lower classes*; v ~em Stande s *to be of the lower classes* **B.** [compr] **~er** *smaller* (*sum*); *less* (*degree*); *minor* (*artist*) ‖ in ~erem Grade *in a less degree; less* | [pred] ~er als *smaller than; less than; inferior to* (*this quality is inferior to that*) ‖ ~ m, ~ w *to lessen, to diminish* **C.** [sup] **~ste** *smallest; least* ‖ nicht die ~sten Aussichten *not a dog's chance* ‖ es besteht nicht der ~ste Grund dafür *there is no reason in the world for it; the lowest bid* (⟨com⟩ *offer*) ‖ die ~ste Kleinigkeit *the merest trifle* (*puts him out*); bei der ~sten S *at the least word, on the slightest occasion* ‖ v nicht dem ~sten Nutzen *of no earthly use; of no use whatever* ‖ nicht m–e ~ste Sorge *not the least of my troubles* (*is* ..) ‖ *not the slightest doubt* ‖ ohne die ~ste Aussicht *without any chance whatever*; unmöglich, nur die ~ste Vorstellung z vermitteln v *impossible to give any idea of* (*the obscurity*) **II.** [adv] **1.** little; ~ denken v *to think little of, to have a low opinion of, not to think much of* (*a p*); nicht ~ v sich denken *to think no small beer of o.s.* ‖ ~ geschätzt *at a moderate calculation* (*it costs* ..) **2.** [compr] **~er** *less*; nicht ~er v jdm denken, wenn .. *to think none the worse of a p if* .. **III.** [abs] **A. 1.** Vornehme u ⍨e [pl] *high and low* **2. a. ein** ⍨**es** *a small amount; a trifle* (*spare a t. for the waiter*) ‖ es ist nur ein ⍨es f dich *it's a mere trifle for you* (*to do*) ‖ um ein ⍨es erhöhen *to raise* (*by*) *a little* ‖ um ein ⍨es kaufen *to buy cheaply* (od *for a cheap price*) **b. um ein** ⍨es *nearly*; = um ein Haar, → Haar **B.** [comp] **der** ⍨**ere** [ein ~erer] *the inferior; p of lower rank* ‖ kein ~erer als .. *no less a p than* (*Goethe*) ‖ das ~ere v zwei Übeln *the lesser of two evils* ‖ nichts ⍨eres als *nothing short of; nothing less than* (*suicide*) **C.** [sup] **1. der** ⍨**ste** hat e–n Anspruch .. auf .. *even the most lowly have a claim on* .. **2. a. das** ⍨**ste** *the least thing* (*he can do is* ..); *the least bit*; auch das ~ *every little* (*will help him*) ‖ das ~ bringt ihn aus der Fassung *the merest trifle puts him out* | **nicht das** ⍨**ste** *not a thing; not the least bit; nothing what*(*so*)*ever* (od *at all*) ‖ er verdient nicht das ⍨ste *he has no income whatever* ‖ er macht sich nicht das ⍨ste aus .. *he does not care a pin* (od *straw*, ⟨Am⟩ *hoot*) *about* .. **b. am ~sten** *least* (*paid*) ‖ **im** ⍨**sten** treu *honest even in the smallest things* ‖ **nicht im ~sten** *not in the* (*very*) *least; not at all; by no means*

ger·ing- ~|**achten** vt [h] jdn ~ *to look down on a p; to hold a p in low estimation* ‖ etw ~ *to hold a th cheap*; → verachten **Ger·ingachtung** f *disregard; looking down on* (*a p*) ‖ *neglect* (*of a th*); → Verachtung **~fügig** a *unimportant; negligible* (*amount*), *scanty, small* ‖ *insignificant* (*matter*), *little* (*things*), *petty, light, slight, small* (*cares*); *trifling, trivial* (*remark*) | etw ⍨es *nothing to make a song about* | ⍨keit [f] *smallness* ‖ *insignificance, -cy; trifle*; ~en [pl] *trifles* pl **~haltig** a ⟨min⟩ ~es Erz *low-percentage* (od *low-grade*) *ore* ‖ *thin* (*beer*); *watery, weak* ‖ ⟨übtr⟩ *of inferior quality; inferior, poor* **~**|**schätzen** vt [h] jdn ~ *to slight* od *neglect a p*; = geringachten, → d. **~schätzig 1.** [a] *depreciatory; derogatory, disparaging, slighting, supercilious*; → verächtlich **2.** [adv] *disparagingly, slightingly* ‖ jdn ~ behandeln *to give a p the cold shoulder, to slight a p*; etw ~ behandeln *or* betrachten *to disregard* od *neglect a th* ⍨**schätzung** f *superciliousness; disregard* (gegenüber *of, for*); *neglect; slight*; mit ~ behandeln = geringschätzig beh.; (etw) mit ~ zurückweisen *to spurn* **~wertig** a *of small value; inappreciable, negligible*

ge- ~r·ingelt a (→ Ring) *annular* **~r·innbar** a *coagulable* * ⍨**r·inne** n ~s/ **1.** = Rinnen **2.** *artificial channel; race; mill-race, trough*; ⟨Am⟩ *raceway* **~r·innen 1.** vi [gerann/geronnen] [h] (of liquids) *to coagulate; to clot*, (of milk) *to curdle; to turn sour; to congeal* ‖ ⟨fig⟩ (*of blood*) *to curdle* | **(etw)** ~ **l** *or* **m** *to coagulate; to curdle* (⟨a. fig⟩ *to curdle* od *freeze the blood*); *to congeal, to set* **2.** ⍨ n *coagulation; clotting, curdling*; z ⍨ bringen = ~ l ⍨**r·innsel** n ~s/~ **1.** *coagulated mass; coagulum* [L]; Blut⍨ *clot of blood* **2.** = Rinnsal ⍨**r·ippe** n ~s/~ **1.** ⟨eig⟩ **a.** *skeleton*; inneres ~ *endoskeleton*; Haut⍨ (der Gliederfüßer) *exoskeleton* **b.** (P) *scrag, skeleton*; wandelndes ~ *walking skeleton* **2.** ⟨übtr⟩ *skeleton* (*of a leaf*, etc.); *carcass* (*of a ship*); *framework, shell* (*of a building*); *outline* (*of an essay*); → Gerüst **~r·ippt** a *laid, ribbed* (*paper*); *corded* (*cloth, silk*) ‖ ⟨bot⟩ (of leaves) *nerved, nervate* ‖ ⟨arch⟩ *fluted* (*column*) **G(e)r·iß** n [österr] *scramble* (nach *for*) °**~r·issen** a [pp v reißen] ⟨fig⟩ *artful, crafty, cunning, dodgy, sharp, shifty, shrewd, slim, sly* (*fellow*); *smart* (*businessman*); *tricksy, wily; clever*; ⟨sl⟩ *fly* (*little boy*); ein ~er Bursche *an artful dodger, a wily customer*, → gerieben **~r·itten** pp v reiten

G·erm m ~(e)s/~e [bay-österr] *yeast* | ~teig [m] *leavened dough*

Germ·ane m ~n/~n *Teuton*; die ~n [pl] *Teutons* pl, *Germani* [L pl] **Germ·anentum** n *Teutonism* **Germ·anien** *Germania* [L] **germ·anisch** a **1.** *Germanic, Teutonic*; nach frühem ~en Brauch *by early Teutonic custom* **2.** das ⍨e *Germanic, Teutonic*; das Alt⍨e *Old Germanic*; das Ur⍨e *Primitive Germanic* **germanis·ieren** vt [h] *to Teutonize, Germanize* **German·ismus** m ~/–men *Germanism* **German·ist** m *German scholar, student of German*(*ic*) *philology* ‖ ⟨jur⟩ *professor* od *investigator of history of German*(*ic*) *law* **Germ·anium** n ⟨chem⟩ *germanium* [L]

G·ermer m ~s/~ ⟨bot⟩ *hellebore*; Weißer ~ *white h.*; Schwarzer ~ *black h., Christmas rose*

germin·al a *germinal*

gern adv [compr] lieber; [sup] am liebsten **A. (P) 1.** *gladly, readily, willingly; with pleasure* ‖ herzlich ~, v Herzen ~ *with all one's heart* ‖ ~! *right you are!* ‖ (möchten Sie nicht hereinkommen u warten?) Ja, ~ (..?) *Yes, I think, I will,* ⟨fam⟩ *I don't mind if I do* | (Vorschlag) ~ annehmen *to welcome* ‖ ich besehe mir die Bilder ganz ~ *I don't mind having a look at the pictures* ‖ er willigte ~ ein *he agreed freely* (*to do it*) ‖ das glaube ich ~ *I can readily believe it* ‖ das kannst du ~ h *you are welcome to it* ‖ du kannst es ihm ~ zeigen *you can show it him, and perfectly welcome* ‖ so habe ich es ~ *that's what I like*; ⟨iron⟩ *I like that* ‖ sie hilft ~ *she helps willingly* ‖ das hört man ~ *that's welcome news* ‖ nehmen

Sie es ~! *take it, and welcome* || er ist jederzeit ~ gesehen *he is welcome any time* || (es ist) ~ geschehen *don't mention it,* ⟨Am mst⟩ (*you are*) *welcome* || jedes Buch steht Ihnen ~ zur Verfügung *you are welcome to any book* (*of the library*) | ich **antworte** ihm nur **(all)zu** ~ *I am only too willing to answer him*; ~ arbeiten *to fancy working*; spielen Sie ~ T.? *do you go in for tennis?* || er hätte **gut u** ~ das Doppelte leisten können *he could easily have done double as much* || sie tauschten **oft u** ~ Erinnerungen aus *they often liked to exchange recollections* || ich trenne mich **nicht** ~ v ihm *I am loath* (od *I don't like*) *to part with him* | er **möchte** ~ entschlüpfen *he would fain slip away* || ich möchte ~ wissen, ob .. *I should like to know if* ..; das möchte ich ~ wissen! *I wonder!* sie möchte für ihr Leben ~ e–n eigenen Beruf haben *she would dearly like to have a profession of her own* **2. a. ich esse** (*or* trinke) es sehr ~ *I like it very much, I am very fond of it*; ich trinke den Kaffee nicht ~ z süß *I don't like the coffee too sweet* **b.** [betont] das **glaube** ich ~ *I can well believe it*; **jdn ~ h** *or* **mögen** *to like a p, to be fond of a p; to care for a p; to cotton* (od *to take kindly*) *to a p*; ~ oder un~ *whether you like or not!* ob er ihn ~ hatte oder nicht, er schien *like him or not, he seemed* .. || °der kann mich ~ h! *I'll see him further* (⟨sl⟩ *in hell*) *first!* || er hört es ~ *it's music in his ears* || jdn nicht ~ mögen *to dislike a p*; ⟨fam⟩ *to have a down on a p* || etw ~ h *to like* (od *love*) *a th; to be fond of a th* || etw (*or* jdn) ~ sehen *to like a th* (*a p*); etw nicht ~ sehen (*or* h) *to dislike a th, to loathe a th* **3. er tanzt** ~ *he likes dancing, he is fond of dancing*; er arbeitet ~ *he likes work*; (etw) ~ tun *to love to do*; „Sehr ~", (sagte er) "*I'd like to*" .. **B.** °**(S) das ist ~ möglich** *that's quite possible* || der Schlips schiebt sich nur z ~ hoch *the tie is apt to work up*; → leicht

G·ern- ~edichter m *would-be poet* **~egroß** m; ein ~ *a would-be-great man; little tin god*; ⟨fam⟩ *cockalorum*; der kl ~ ⟨sl⟩ *his nibs* pl [sg konstr] || den ~ spielen *to play the great man* **~geschehen!** *don't mention it,* ⟨Am⟩ *welcome* **~gesehen** a *welcome*

Ge- ~r·öchel n ~s/ *rattle* (od *rattling*) *in the throat* **~r·öll(e)** n ~(e)s/~e *pebbles* pl, *rubble*; *boulders* pl | ~abschlag [m] ⟨praehist⟩ *pebble-chopper* || ~formation [f] *boulder-formation* **~r·onnen** a [pp v gerinnen] *coagulated, congealed* (*blood*); *curdled* (*milk*); ~e Milch *curd*; ~e Masse *concretion, congelation* **~r·östet** a *grilled* (*meat*); ~es Fleisch *grill* || *roasted* (*coffee, seeds*) || ~e Kartoffelstreifen [pl] *chipped potatoes* pl, *chips* pl

Gerontol·oge m ~n/~n *geriatrician, –trist* **-log·ie** f *geriatrics*

Gersch[1] m ⟨bot⟩ = Geißfuß

Gersch[2] (türk. Münzeinheit) *piastre* (*–ter*)

G·erste f ~/ ⟨bot⟩ *barley*; [österr] G·erstl ⟨a. cul⟩ = Graupen; Perlen~ *pearl barley* **G·ersten- ~brot** n *b.-bread* **~graupen** f pl → Graupen **~korn** n **1.** ⟨bot⟩ *b.corn* **2.** (am Augenlid) *sty(e), eyesore* **3.** (~leinen) *huckaback* **~kühltrank** m *orgeat* **~mehl** n *b. flour* **~saft** m *b.-water* || ⟨fam⟩ *beer* **~schleim** m *b.-water* **~zucker** m *b.-sugar*

G·erte f ~/~n *switch; rod*; Reit~ *riding-whip* | ~nholz [n] ⟨for⟩ *stake-forest; sapling*

Ger·uch m ~(e)s/~e **A.** (~sinn) [nur sg] *smell, sense of smell* **B.** (Ausdünstung, Duft) **1.** ⟨eig⟩ **a.** *smell, odour; scent* || (Wohl~) *fragrance, perfume; scent* (*of hay, roses*); *pleasant smell; subtle odo(u)r* **b.** schlechter, übler ~ *bad* (od *unpleasant*) *smell* (od *odour*); *stink, stench* || muffiger ~ *fug; reek* (*of the slums*) || schlechte ~e in e–m Raum beseitigen *to deodorize a room* **2.** ⟨fig, mst dero⟩ *odour*; → Ruf || im ~e der Heiligkeit *in the odour of sanctity* || übler ~ *ill fame; bad* (od *ill*) *odour*; in üblem ~ stehen *to be in bad odour, to be of ill report*; in schlechten ~ k *to come into bad repute* **~bes·eitigungsmittel** n *deodorant* **~los** a *odourless; scentless, inodorous* ⟨a. cul⟩ & (gas) *neutral; not smelly; sweet* (*gasoline*) **Ger·uchs-** [in comp] ⟨med⟩ *olfactory* **~nerv** m *olfactory nerve* **~organ** n *olfactory; olfactory organ* **~sinn** m (*sense of*) *smell* **~vermögen** n → Witterungsvermögen **~verschluß** m (an Abortbecken) *stench-trap, trap*

Ger·ücht n ~(e)s/~e *rumour* (über *of*); *report* (*about, of*) || ein bloßes ~ *a mere rumour,* ⟨liter⟩ *merely an on dit* [Fr] || es geht das ~ (*or* das ~ läuft um), daß .. *rumour has it* (od *there are rumours*) *that* ..; *it is rumoured that* ..; es geht allgemein das ~, daß .. *it is all the talk that* ..; es geht das ~, er sei tot *he is rumoured to be dead* || wie das ~ geht *as report has it*; etw als ~ verbreiten *to noise a th*; ~e verbr. *to spread rumours* **~efabrik** f *rumo(u)r mill* **~emacher** m *rumour-monger* **ger·üchtweise** adv *reportedly; as report has it*; ~ verlautet, daß .. = es geht das Gerücht ..; → Gerücht || (nur) ~ ⟨bes Am⟩ *through the grapevine* || ~ verbreitet *rumoured*

Ge- ~r·ufe n ~s/ *repeated calling* (od *shouting*); *shouts* pl **~r·uhen** vi [h] ~ z tun *to condescend* od *deign to do*; ⟨a. iron⟩ || gnädig ~ z tun (of a ruler) *to be pleased to do*; der König hat gnädigst geruht z genehmigen, daß .. *the king has been graciously pleased to approve that* ..; Eure Majestät wollen allergnädigst ~ *may it please Your Majesty* (*to do* ..) **~r·uhig** a *calm, peaceful, quiet; sedate; leisurely; unhurried* (*days*) **~rühmt** a; viel ~ *much-vaunted* **~r·ührt 1.** [a] ~ s *to be moved* (od *touched*) (über *at*; durch, v *by*; vor *with*); → rührselig **2.** [adv] *emotionally* **~r·uhsam** a = geruhig °**~r·umpel** n *bumping, jogging, jolting; rumbling; rumble-tumble; jolts* pl, *rumbles* pl, *rumblings* pl **~r·ümpel** n *junk, lumber, raffle; rubbish, trash*

Gerundi·al- *gerundial* **Gerund·ium** n ~s/–dien *gerund* **Gerund·iv** n *gerundive*; ~isch [a] *gerundial*

ge- ~r·ungen pp v ringen **~r·üst** n ~(e)s/~e **1.** (Bau~) *scaffold(ing)*; ein ~ aufschlagen *to erect a s.*; ein ~ abreißen *to take down a s.* || *rack, stage, stand; trestle*; Balken~ *trestlework* || ~ f e–n Kran *gantry*; ~kran *gantry crane* || ⟨mar⟩ (Reparatur~ f Schiff) *cradle* **2. a.** Knochen~ *skeleton* **b.** ⟨übtr⟩ *frame, framework* (*of society*); *skeleton* (*of a building*) °**~r·üttel** n ~s/ *jogging, jolting; jolts* pl

Ges n ~/~ ⟨mus⟩ *G flat*; ~-Dur *G flat major*

ge- ~s·albt a ⟨fig⟩ *oily, saponaceous, unctuous*; → salbungsvoll **~s·alzen** a *salt* (*butter*), *salted* || ⟨fig⟩ *exorbitant, peppered, stiff* (*price*) **~s·amt** a *entire, total; aggregate; all, whole*; → ganz || der ~e Betrag *the total* (od *full*) *amount*; (*his*) *entire* (*fortune*); die ~e Familie *all the family, the whole family*; das ~e Pr. D. *the whole of Protestant Germany* || ⟨jur⟩ Eigentum zur ~en Hand *joint-property* || ~er Warenaustausch *exchange of all goods* **Ges·amt- ~abmessungen** f pl *overall dim.* **~aufnahme** f ⟨phot⟩ *full* (*general, total*) *view* **~auftrieb** m ⟨aero⟩ *gross lift* **~ausgabe** f *complete edition* od *works* **~befehl** m ⟨mil⟩ *operation order* **~belastung** f ⟨tech⟩ *total load* **~belegschaft** f ⟨ind⟩ *force of men employed* **~betrag** m *total; sum total* **~bremsweg** m ⟨mot⟩ *over-all stopping distance* **~darstellung** f ⟨film⟩ (durch e–e Folge v Bildern) *panorama* **~deutsch** a *all-German* **~druck** m *total pressure* **~eindruck** m *general impression* **~einnahmen** f pl *total receipts* pl **~gewicht** n *total weight* **~gut** n *common property,* (in Ehe) *joint estate* **~haftung** f *joint liability* **~handel** m *total trade* **~hypothek** f *blanket mortgage* **~inhalt** m *total volume* **~interessen** pl *over-all i.* **~katalog** m *general c.* **~kosten** pl (Herstellung u Vertrieb) *over-all marketing charges* **~länge** f *o.-a.* (od *total*) *length* **~leistung** f *t. output* **~preis** m *gross pr.* **~quantum** (an Fleisch, Fisch), das im Jahre verzehrt wird *pack* **~raum-**

bedarf m *t. space required* **~schau** f *comprehensive* (od *synoptic*) *view* **~schuldner** m pl *co-debtors* pl | ≃isch [a] *joint and several* **~strafe** f *t. punishment for concurrent offences* **~summe** f *sum total*; *total* **~tonnengehalt** m *total tonnage* **~unterricht** m *general instruction* **~verband** m *Overall Association* **~verdienst** m *t. earnings* **~versicherungssumme** f *t. premiums in force* **~wille** m *joint will* **~wirkung** f *general effect*

Ges·amtheit f die ~ *the entirety, totality*; *aggregate, whole* (*of* ..) || als ~ *collectively*; das Publ. in der ~ *the public at large*; *the general p.* || ⟨mil⟩ *joint chiefs of staff* N

Gesandte [der ~, ein ~r] m ~n/~n **1.** ⟨dipl⟩ **a.** *envoy*; außerordentlicher ~ *Envoy Extraordinary* || ⟨R. C.⟩ päpstlicher ~ *legate, nuncio* [It] **b.** *envoy*; ⟨R. C.⟩ *internuncio* [It] **c.** ⟨Ind⟩ *resident* (*minister*) **d.** = Geschäftsträger **2.** = Bote

Ges·andtschaft f ~/~en *legation* **~sattaché** m *attaché* [Fr] **~sgebäude** n *legation* **~spersonal** n *the staff of a legation* **~sposten** m *post of an envoy* (od *of a resident*) **~srat** m *counsellor of legation* **~ssekretär** m *secretary of legation*

Ges·ang m ~(e)s/≃e **1.** [abstr] *singing* || (of a bird) *warbling*(*s* pl) **2.** [konkr] **a.** ⟨mus⟩ *song*, → Lied || ⟨ec⟩ *hymn* **b.** ⟨Lit⟩ (Abteilung e–r Dichtung) *passus* L; *canto* It [pl *cantos*] ≃**artig** a *cantabile* (*style*) **~buch** n *song-book*; *book of songs* || ⟨ec⟩ *hymn-book* **~lehrer** m *singing-master* **~lehrerin** f *s.-mistress* ≃**lich 1.** [a] *vocal*; ~er Teil *vocal part, voice-part* || in ~er Hinsicht *vocally* **2.** [adv] *vocally* **~stunde** f *singing-lesson* **~unterricht** m *singing-lessons* pl **~verein** m *singing-club, glee-club, choral union* (od *society*) **~vortrag** m *vocal recital* **Ges·angs- ~einlage** f *inserted song* **~kunst** f *art of singing*

Ge- ~s·äß n ~es/~e *seat* (am ~ *on the s.*); *backside, sit-upon, buttocks* pl, *fundament, hind-quarters* pl, *posterior, rump*; ⟨fam⟩ *bottom* | ~partie [f] *seat* (*of a skirt, etc*); ~tasche [f] *hip* od *back pocket*; ~weite [f] *hip measurement* °**~s·aufe** n ~s/ *carousal, carousing*; *drinking-bout* **~s·ause** n ~s/*humming, buzzing* (*of machines*); *whistling* (*of the wind*) **~s·äusel** n ~s/ *murmuring*, (*gentle*) *rustling, rustle* ≃**sch·acht** a ⟨her⟩ *checky* **~schädigte(r** m) f *harmed, hurt, wronged p*; *aggrieved party*; *loser* ≃**sch·affen** a [pred] ~ s f (P) *to be fitted for* (*a th*); f e–a (wie) ~ *made for one another*; wie ~ f *ripe for*; ein Mann f Abenteuer ~ *a man for adventure*; er ist f diese Arbeit wie ~ *he is cut out for this work* | (S) ~ f *made for*

Gesch·äft n ~(e)s/~e **A.** [abstr] **1.** *affair*; Staats~e [pl] *affairs of* (*the*) *state* || ~e [pl] *duties* pl, *work*; mit ~en überhäuft *overwhelmed with work* **2.** *business, job*; *occupation, trade*; ~e [pl] *pursuits* pl **3.** ⟨com⟩ *b.*; ~e [pl] *business* [sg konstr]; *b. matters* pl; → Detail≃, Engros≃ || ein (einzelnes) ~ *a transaction, deal*; *a piece of business*; ein Profit≃ *a job* || ein gutes ~ *a good stroke of business*; *a bargain*; ein unerlaubtes ~ ⟨Am fam⟩ *a racket*; ein wichtiges ~ *some important business, an important piece of business* || ⟨a. pol⟩ ein zweifelhaftes ~ *a shady transaction*; ⟨Am⟩ *a deal* **4.** °(Bedürfnis) s–e ~e verrichten *to relieve nature, to relieve o.s.*; ⟨fam⟩ *to go somewhere*; ⟨euph⟩ *to wash one's hands*; gr ~e m *to relieve nature* (od *the bowels*), *to defecate*; kl ~e m *to make* (od *pass*) *water* **B.** [konkr] (geschäftl. Einrichtung) *business* (*that's a good b.*), ⟨fam⟩ *biz*; ~e [pl] *businesses* pl || *business-house*; *concern* (ein blühendes ~ a *flourishing c.*); *establishment*; *firm*; *house*; ⟨Am⟩ *proposition* || *shop*; ⟨Am⟩ *store* **C.** ein ~ **abschließen** *to make* (od *strike*) *a bargain*; *to contract* (*to do*) ein ~ aufmachen *to open* (od *start*) *a business* || ein ~ besorgen *to transact a piece of business* || welches ~ betreiben Sie? *what is your trade?* || s–e ~e erledigen *to go about one's business* || die ~e führen *to manage the business* (*of* ..) || die ~e gehen gut *business is doing well*; .. schlecht *business is slack* | **ein** ~ **m mit** *to do a deal with* || er hatte ein gutes ~ gemacht *he had done a good stroke of business*; jeder machte sein ~ dabei *everybody made their bit out of it* || was m die ~e? *how is business* (od *trade*)? || ~e m *to do* (od *transact*) *business*; *to deal* (in *in*; mit *with*) || gr ~e m (→ a. A. 4.), ein gr ~m *to do a great business*; gute ~e m *to do well, to prosper* || s–n ~en nachgehen *to go about one's business* || Freunden ~e in die Hände spielen *to put business in the way of one's friends* || ein ~ übernehmen *to take over a business* || s–e ~e verrichten → A. 4. || sich s–n ~en widmen *to go about one's business* **b.** ~ **ist** ~ *business is business*; *a bargain's a bargain* || **erst das** ~, dann das Vergnügen *business before pleasure* **c. ans** ~! *to* (*our*) *business*! || **aus** dem ~ k *to come away from business* || **ins** (*or* **zum**) ~ gehen *to go to business*; sie geht ins ~ (ist berufstätig) *she goes to business* || sich **vom** ~ zurückziehen *to retire from business*; ⟨fam⟩ *to shut up shop*

ˣ**G(e)sch·aftelhuber** m *Jack of all trades* || *busybody*; ⟨fam⟩ *hummer* | ˣ≃**n** vi [h] ⟨fam⟩ *to throw one's weight about* **Gesch·äftemacher** m *jobber*; *speculator, profiteer*

gesch·äftig 1. [a] *active, busy*; *bustling, stirring*; ~ s *to bustle, stir* || übertrieben ~ *fussy, officious* **2.** [adv] *busily*; *stirringly* || (etw) ~ tun *to busy o.s.* (*with doing a th*) | ≃**keit** f *activity, busyness*; *bustle, stir* || übertriebene ~ *fussiness, officiousness* **gesch·äftlich 1.** [a] *business* (*life, matter*); *commercial* (*speculation*) || in ~en Angelegenheiten *on business*; das ~e Leben geht ungestört weiter *b. as usual*; e–e kl ~e S erledigen *to discharge a small matter of b.*; größeres ~es Unternehmen *transaction*; ~e Verbindungen h mit *to transact b. with* ..; ~e Verhandlungen führen *to talk b.* **2.** [adv] (*he was in Germany*) *on b.*; (*detained*) *by b.* || ~ z tun h mit *to have dealings with* **Geschäfts-** [in comp] mst *business-*, *commercial* **~abgrenzung** f ⟨pol, etc⟩ *delineation of duties* **~abschluß** m ⟨com⟩ *business deal* .. **~anteil** m *share in a b.* **~anzeige** f (in Läden) *show-card* **~aufgabe** f *giving up of b.*; *retirement from b.* **~aufsicht** f; unter ~ stehen *to be under the control of an official receiver* **~ausschuß** m *b.-committee* **~auto** n *b.-car* **~bereich** m; Minister ohne ~ *minister without portfolio* **~bericht** m *b.-report* **~besuch** m *b. call* **~betrieb** m [konkr] *b.* (*operations*); [abstr] *running of a b.*; (Ort) *place of b.*; (Firma) *c. enterprise* || gr ~e *large business* **~brief** m *b.-letter*; *c. letter* || ~papier n *letter-heads* **~buchpapier** n *ledger* od *accountbook paper* ≃**fähig** s *qualified to act and to contract* **~fähigkeit** f ⟨jur a.⟩ *legal capacity, capacity of disposing* **~freund** m *b.-friend* ≃**führend** a *managing* (*director*), ⟨Am⟩ *runner*; erster ~er Beamter ⟨Am⟩ *executive* **~führer** m *b.-manager, general secretary* (*of a club*; ⟨theat⟩ *manager*, ⟨Am⟩ *producer* **~gang** m *course* (od *routine*) *of b.*; im normalen ~ *in the ordinary course of b.* || (Besorgung) *errand* **~gebaren** n *dealing*; (un)anständiges ~ (*un*)*fair d.* || gewinnsüchtiges ~ *rapacious* od *predatory deals* pl **~geheimnis** n *b.-secret* **~geist** m *c. spirit* **~haus** n *b.-house*; *concern, firm* **~herr, ~inhaber** m *principal*; *owner* (*of a b.*); ⟨sl⟩ *boss* **~jahr** n *financial year*; im ~ *during y.* **~karte** f *b.-card* **~kreis** m *b.-circle* **~kunde** f *c. practice*; ⟨school⟩ *b. management* ≃**kundig** a *b.-like*; *versed in b.*, *efficient, experienced* **~lage** f *b.-outlook* **~leiter** m = –führer **~leitung** f *management of a b.*; jdn in die ~ berufen *to make a p a member of the m.* **~leute** pl *b.-people*; *men of b.*; *trades people* **~leben** n *b.-life* **~lokal** n (*place of*) *b.*; *office*(*s* pl); *shop* **~mann** m *b.-man, man of b.*; *tradesman* ≃**mäßig** a → folg. u. **~moral** f *c. morality* **~name** m *firm* **~nummer** f *reference-number* **~ord-**

nung f ⟨parl⟩ (Verfahrensweise) *rules* pl *of procedure*; (feststehende ∼) *standing orders* pl; beantragen, daß zur ∼ gesprochen wird *to rise to (a point of) order*; zur ∼! *may I raise a p. of o.!* **~papiere** n pl *c.* (od *b.*) *papers* pl **~personal** n *the staff* **~raum** m *professional premises* pl; vornehmer ∼ *saloon* ‖ –räume [pl] *b.-premises* pl; amtl. –räume [pl] *House*; ⟨Am⟩ *Building*; –räume f .. ⟨Engl-Am⟩ *Bush House* (London); *Australia House*; –räume des Staates New York ⟨Am⟩ *Empire State Building* **~reise** f *journey on b.*; *b.-trip* **~reisende** [der ∼, ein ∼r] m *c. traveller*; *bagman*; Raum (im Hotel) f ∼ *c. room* **~routine** f *b.-routine* **~rückgang** m ⟨allg⟩ *recession* **~sache** f *matter of b.* **~schluß** m *closing-time* **~sinn** m *b. mind* **~sprache** f *c. language* **~stelle** f *offices* pl, *office*; *bureau*; *agency*; ⟨ins, etc⟩ *field office*; ∼n [pl] ⟨com⟩ *sales offices* **~stille** f *stagnation of b.* (od *trade*) **~straße** f *b.-street* **~stunden** f pl *b.* (od *office*)*-hours* pl, *hours of b.* **~teilhaber** m *partner* **~träger** m ⟨dipl⟩ *chargé d'affaires* [F] **≃tüchtig** a *efficient in b.*; *b.like*; *smart*; ∼er Mann *capable b.man* **~tüchtigkeit** f *b. efficiency* (od *smartness*) **≃unfähig** a ⟨jur-psych⟩ *incompetent* **~untüchtig** a *uncommercial* **~verbindung** f ∼en [pl] *b. relations* pl; mit jdm in ∼ stehen *to transact b. with*; *to deal with*; in ∼ treten *to enter into b. relationship* ‖ ∼en [pl] *trade*; ∼en aufnehmen *to open up a trade* **~verkehr** m *c. intercourse*, *b. dealings* pl; *commerce*, *trade* **~vertreter** m *commercial agent* **~viertel** n (∼ e–r Stadt) *b.-district*; ⟨Am⟩ *downtown*; vom ∼ weg *uptown* **~vorfälle** m pl (sämtl. *total*) *b. activities* **~wagen** m *office car* **~weg** m; auf dem üblichen ∼e *in the way of b.* **~welt** f *b.(-world)* **~wert** m *good will* **~zeit** f = –stunden **~zimmer** n *office*; *bureau*; ⟨mil⟩ *orderly room* ‖ (ab Btl.) *headquarters* pl **~zweig** m *line* od *branch of b.*

gesch·äftslos a **1.** = arbeitslos **2.** *dull* (*season*), *slack* (*time*), *flat*, *lifeless* **≃igkeit** f *dullness*, *lifelessness* **geschäftsmäßig** **1.** [a] *business-like*; ⟨Am fam⟩ *hard-boiled* (*p*); ∼ aussehend *business--looking* ‖ *mechanical*; *perfunctory* **2.** [adv] *in a business-like manner*; *methodically*, *systematically*

ge- ~sch·ah 3. sg pret v geschehen °**≃sch·äker** n *dalliance*, *dallying*, *philandering* **g(e)sch·amig** a [österr] *bashful*, *timid* °**≃sch·arr(e)** n *scraping* **~sch·ätzt** a *valued* (*client*); in Ihrem ∼en Blatte *in your valued columns* ‖ nicht ∼ s *to be disliked*; (S) *to be at a discount* **G(e)sch·au** n [österr] ⟨mst dero⟩ *features* pl, *expression* °**≃sch·aukel** n *rocking* (*of a boat*); *rolling* (*of a ship*); *swaying*; *swinging* **~sch·eckt** a *pied*; *piebald*; → bunt **~sch·ehen I.** vi [geschah/geschehen] [s] [nur 3. sg & pl u mit Sachsubjekt, mst neutralem Fürwort] **1.** *to happen*, *occur*; *to take place*; *to be done*; während dies geschah *whilst this was doing* **a.** ein gr Unglück ist ∼, **es** ist ein gr U. ∼ *a great acc.t has occurred*; etw muß ∼, **es** muß etw ∼ *sth must be done*; wenn k–e W. ∼ .. *unless miracles happen* ..; es geschieht sehr viel f die Jugend *a great deal is done for the young*; ⟨bib⟩ dein W. geschehe! *thy will be done*; nachdem dies ∼ war, schrieb er .. *this done he wrote* ..; → 1. vor a. ‖ **es** geschehe, was wolle *whatever may happen*; **es** kann ∼, daß .. *it may happen that* ..; *sometimes it happens that* .. ‖ es geschehe! *let it be so*! es geschah zur rechten Zeit *it occurred at the right moment*; und schon (*or* damit) ist's ∼! *and there you are*! **b.** die Frage war, was **mit ihm** ∼ sollte .. *what should be done with him*; was soll mit dem ∼, der ..? *what is to happen to him who* ..? **2. es geschieht dir** nichts Böses *no harm will come* (od *will be done*) *to you*; es ist ihm nichts ∼ *he has come to no harm* ‖ es kann dir (dabei) nichts ∼ *nothing can happen to you*; *you can feel quite safe* ‖ es geschieht ihm **recht** (*it*) *serves him right*; ihm g. unrecht *he is wronged* ‖ er wußte nicht, **wie** ihm geschah *he didn't know what happened to him*, *he was quite upset*, *he was at the end of his tether* **3.** es ist **um ihn** ∼ *it is all up* (od *over*) *with him*; *he is done for* **4.** ∼ **ist** ∼ *what is done cannot be undone*; → II. ‖ gern ∼! *don't mention it*! (*you are*) *welcome*! ‖ **so** ∼ [pp] am 1. Mai 1908 *that's what took place on May 1st 1908*; ⟨off⟩ *so done at Kiel this 6th day of May 1967* ‖ es ist so gut wie ∼ *it is as good as done* **5.** ∼ **lassen** *to let pass*; *allow*, *permit*; es ∼ l *to give in*; etw ∼ l *to yield a th to be done*; er ließ es ∼, daß wir *he allowed us to miss the train* **II.** [a] ∼e Dinge *accomplished facts* pl, (unangenehmer Art) *bygones* pl; ∼e Dinge sind nicht z ändern *it's no use crying over spilt milk*; → I. 4. ‖ **≃es** n *accomplished facts* pl; *what is done*; laß einmal ≃es ruhen *let sleeping dogs lie*; *let bygones be bygones* **III.** ≃ n *happenings*, *goings-on* pl; das ∼ der Weltgeschichte *the great events* pl *in history*; Brennpunkt des ∼s *critical point of action*

Gesch·ehnis n –nisses/–nisse *event*, *happening*

Gesch·eide n ∼s/∼ ⟨hunt⟩ *bowels*, *entrails* pl

Gesch·ein n ⟨bot⟩ *inflorescence* (*of vine*)

gesch·eit a *clever*, *intelligent*; *shrewd*, *smart*, *bright* (*fellow*); *prudent*, *sensible*, *wise*; [pred] ⟨fam⟩ *up to snuff* ‖ wir waren um nichts ∼er *we were none the wiser*; ich kann nicht ∼ daraus w *I cannot make head or tail of it*; sei doch ∼ *do be sensible* ‖ ° du bist wohl nicht recht ∼! *what do you mean* (*you are doing*)?, *what is the big idea*?, *you don't seem to be in your right senses* ‖ daraus kann nichts ≃es w *no good can come of it* | **≃heit** f *cleverness*, *shrewdness*, *smartness*; *prudence*

Gesch·enk n ∼(e)s/∼e *gift* (an, für jdn *to a p*; v jdm *from a p*); *present* (an *to*); wie ein ∼ des Himmels *like a gift from heaven* ‖ Weihnachts≃ *Christmas gift* ‖ jdm ein ∼ m *to make a p a present* od *a present to a p*; jdm etw zum ∼ m, jdm ein ∼ mit etw m *to make a p a present of a th* od *a present of a th to a p*; *to present a p with a th*; sich selbst .. *to give a th to o.s.* **~bon** m *promisory note*, *gift coupon* **~buch** n *gift-book* **~paket** n *parcel of presents*, *presentation parcel* **~zweck**: ich wünsche ein Buch z ∼en *I want a book to give as a present*

G(e)sch·erte(r) [ein –r, der –e] m [österr] *yokel*

Gesch·ichtchen n *little story*; *anecdote*

Gesch·ichte f **1.** °(Geschehnis) *event*, *happening*; *adventure* ‖ °(S) *affair*, *business*, *experience*, *story*; e–e **alte** ∼ *an old story*; *Queen Anne is dead*; es ist immer die alte ∼ *it's the old, old story over again*; es ist e–e dumme ∼ *it's a nuisance*; dies ist e–e fatale ∼ *this is a bad job*; *here is a pretty* (od *rum*) *go*; die **ganze** ∼ *the whole thing* (*the whole th. costs 5 marks*); *the whole show* (*he gave the wh. sh. away*); das ist die g. ∼ *that's all about it*; ich will dir die g. ∼ erzählen ⟨sl⟩ *I'll tell you the whole song and dance*; e–e phantastische, unglaubliche ∼ ⟨fam⟩ *a tall story*; ⟨iron⟩ e∼e **schöne** ∼ *a nice state of affairs*, *a pretty mess*; das sind ja schöne ∼n! *fine doings these*! *these are fine doings*!; e–e schwierige ∼ *a difficult business* ‖ mach k–e ∼n *don't be a fool*; *don't make a fuss* ‖ da h wir die ∼! *there you are*! ‖ sie hat ∼n gemacht ⟨sex⟩ *she's been playing tricks*, *she's in trouble* **2.** ⟨**scient**⟩ [nur sg] **a.** *history* (*he studies h.*) ‖ in die ∼ eingehen *to be recorded in the annals of history*, *to pass into history*, ⟨fam⟩ *to go on record*; .. als: *to be placed on record as*, *to go down to posterity as*; *this man* (*deed*) *will go down in history as the greatest rogue* (*knavery*) ‖ er hat sich in das Buch der ∼ eingetragen *his name is enrolled* (od *written*) *in the book of history*; darüber schweigt die ∼ *on that matter history is silent* ‖ das gehört der ∼ an *that belongs to history* ‖ ∼ m *to make history* ‖ in der ∼ bemerkenswert *historic* (*spot*); Sinn f ∼ *historic sense* **b.** die ∼ (e–s Volkes etc) *the history* (*of a people*; *of the French Revolution*); *the story* (*of the Empire*, etc.) ‖ die biblische ∼ *Scripture*, *the Scriptures* pl ‖ ∼ des Altertums, alte ~ *ancient history*; deutsche ~ *German history*; in die deutsche ~ eingehen *to become German h.*; → 2. a. || → Früh≗; Kirchen≗; Kultur≗; Kunst≗; Literatur≗; Natur≗; Vor≗; Welt≗ || jds Lebens≗ *a p's biography, the story of a p's life*; nichts in s–r ~ *nothing in his records* || diese Nadel hat e–e ~ *this pin has a history* **3. (Erzählung) a.** *story, tale; annecdote* || ⟨theat⟩ e–e (improvisierte) lustige, komische ~ *a wheeze* || (Lügen≗) *story* || Klatsch≗ *tale*; (Legende) *legend*; Mord≗ *cock and bull story*; Seemanns≗, Lügen≗ *yarn*; Schauder≗ *horror yarn*; Skandal-≗n pl *scandal* || e–e ~ erzählen *to tell a story, to spin* od *pitch a yarn*; jdm e–e ~ aufbinden *to spin a p a yarn* || u. hiermit ist e–e ~ verknüpft *and thereby hangs a tale* (Shak) **b.** ⟨Lit⟩ *narrative, story*; die ~ v *the story of* ..; Kurz≗ *short story*

Gesch·ichten- ~buch n *story-book* **~erzähler** m *story-teller*

gesch·ichtlich 1. a **a.** *historic* (*building, spot*); ~e Wahrheit *historic truth* **b.** *historical* (*character, method, novel, picture*, etc.); ~er Charakter *historicity*; ~es Drama *historical play, history play*; *history* || ~e Darstellung *history*; ~e Aufzeichnung *record* || in ~er Hinsicht *historically* **2.** adv *historically* (*known, true*); ~ denken lernen *to learn to understand things historically* (od *in the light of history*) || es ist ~ nachgewiesen, daß .. *it is on record that* ..

Gesch·ichts- mst *history, historical* **~buch** n *h. book*; *h.al work* **~forschung** f (*study of*) *h.*; *h.al research* **~gemälde** n *h.-piece*; *h.al painting* **~klitterung** f *falsification* od *slanting of h., bias(s)ed account of h.al events* **~kunde** f (*science of*) *h.* **~maler** m *h.al painter* **~malerei** f *h.al painting* **~philosophie** f *philosophy of h.* **~quellen** f pl *h.al sources* pl **~unterricht** m *instruction in h.* **~werk** n *h.al work* **~wissenschaft** f (*science of*) *h.*

Gesch·icht(s)- ~schreiber m *historian* || (amtlicher) *historiographer* (des Königs *to the king*) **~schreibung** f *history* || (amtliche) *historiography*

Gesch·ick n ~(e)s/~e **A.** *destiny, fate, fortune, lot*; *luck*; *star*; → Schicksal || ein günstiges ~ *a fortunate lot*; *good luck*; *a lucky star*; ein trauriges ~ *a sad fate*; ein widriges ~ *an adverse fate*; *ill luck*; *an unlucky star*, → Miß≗ || s–m ~e danken *to thank one's stars* || jds ~ entscheiden *to decide* (od *seal*) *a p's fate* || er ergab sich in sein ~ *he resigned himself to his fate* || s–e ~e selbst in die Hand nehmen *to take one's fate into one's own hands* **B. 1.** (rechte Gestaltung) das Jackett hat ~ *the jacket is a good fit*; .. hat kein ~ .. *is a bad fit* || etw wieder ins ~ bringen *to put a th in order*; *to right a th* **2.** (Eignung jds) *aptitude* (*he has but little a. for* [f, zu]); *dexterity*; *knack* (z *of*); *skill* (in *in*) || ⟨sport⟩ *science* (*of a player*) || das ~ e–s Staatsmannes *the address of a statesman* || e–e S des ~s (*that's*) *a matter of skill* (od *knack*) || das ~ h z etw (*or* z tun) *to have the knack of a th* (*of doing*); sie hat (gr) ~ f *or* z Handarbeit *she is* (*very*) *clever at needlework* **~lichkeit** f ~/~en *adroitness, cleverness, expertise, dexterity, skill* (in *in*); *skilfulness*; → ~ B. 2. || erfordernd *skilled* (*work*) | ~sspiel [n] *game of skill*

gesch·ickt 1. [a] *adroit* (*orator*), *clever* (*player*; *stroke*); *perfect* (*murder*); *dexterous, skilled, skilful, capable* || ~ s in etw *to be clever* (od *adept, skilful*) *at a th* || ~ z *fit for*; → tauglich **2.** [adv] *cleverly, dexterously* || es ~ anfangen z tun *to contrive* (od *manage*) *to do*; er hatte es sehr ~ angefangen *he had schemed it very cleverly*

Gesch·iebe n ~s/~ ⟨geol⟩ *drift*; *boulder-stones* pl; geritzte ~ [pl] *striated rock-pavements* || glazialer **~mergel, ~lehm** m *boulder-clay*

gesch·ieden a [pp v scheiden] *divorced* (*wife*) || der ≗e *the divorcé* [Fr]; die ~e *the divorcée* [Fr]

gesch·ieht 3. sg prs v geschehen

gesch·ienen pp v scheinen

°**Gesch·ieße** n ~s/ *firing* || °**Gesch·impfe** n ~s/ *cursing, swearing*; (*volley of*) *invectives*; *abusive* (od *strong*) *language*

Gesch·irr n ~(e)s/~e **1. a.** (Haushalts≗) *table-plate* (od *utensils, ware*); Silber≗ *silver-plate*; das Tee≗ *the tea things*; Zinn ≗ *pewter* || *china*; (irdenes ~) *crockery, earthenware*; Küchen≗ *pots and pans, kitchen things* pl; Nacht≗ *chamber-pot*; *chamber*; *night-commode* || Koch≗ *cooking pots* pl; ⟨mil⟩ *mess-tin*, ⟨mar⟩ *mess-traps* pl || das ~ abräumen *to clear the table*; *to clear away*; das ~ abtrocknen *to wipe the dishes* (etc.) **b.** (Geräte) *implements* pl; (*bundle of*) *tools* pl || ⟨spin⟩ *twister* || ⟨aero⟩ Mastfessel≗ *mast mooring-gear* **2.** (Pferde≗) *harness*; (f Zugtiere) *gear*; ~ f 2 Pferde *double harness*; e–m Pferd das ~ anlegen *to harness a horse* || ⟨übtr⟩ (Pferd mit Wagen) *carriage, cart* || sich ins ~ legen (of horses) *to pull hard*; ⟨fig a.⟩ ins ~ gehen *to put forth all one's efforts*; ⟨sl⟩ *to come* (od *go*) *it strong, to come out strong*; ⟨sport⟩ *to extend o.s., to be extended* **~-kammer** f *saddlery* **~raum** m *plate-room* **~-schrank** m *dresser*; *kitchen-sideboard* **~spül-maschine** f *dishwasher* **~tuch** n *dish-cloth*

geschl·agen a ⟨fig⟩ *stricken* (*man*); ein ~er M. s ⟨sl⟩ *to be nowhere* || e–e ~e Stunde (*for*) *a stricken hour*; drei ~e Stunden *three mortal hours*

Geschl·echt n ~(e)s/~er († ~e) **A. 1.** (Gattung) *race*; das menschliche ~, Menschen≗ *the human race, mankind, humankind*; *the species*; → Rasse, Stamm || ⟨bot & zoo⟩ → Art, Familie, Gattung, Rasse **2.** (Generation) *generation*; kommende ~er [pl] *coming* (od *future, later*) *generations* pl **3.** (Familie) *ancestry, descent, family, lineage, race*; *breed, stock, strain*; *birth, extraction*; ein Mann aus berühmtem ~ *a man of illustrious lineage* od *line, a man of family* od *birth*; er stammt aus adligem ~ *he comes of a noble stock* od *strain* **4.** *⟨übtr⟩ (= Art, Klasse) *class, kind, tribe* **B. 1.** (natürl. ~) *sex* || das männliche ~ *the male sex*; das starke ~ *the strong sex*, ⟨sl hum⟩ *the male persuasion* || das weibliche ~ *the female sex*; *petticoats* pl; das schöne, schwache, zarte ~ *the fair, weak, gentle sex* || das andere ~ *the other sex*; Anziehungskraft auf das andere ~ *sex appeal* || beiderlei ~s *of both sexes*; Gleichheit der ~er *sex-equality* **2.** (~ in der Sprache) *gender* **a.** grammatisches ~ *grammatical gender* (*masculine* [z. B. ⟨Ger⟩ der Tisch], *feminine* [die Tür], *neuter g.* [das Buch]) **b.** ⟨engl⟩ natürliches ~ *natural gender* (*he, she* f P, *it* f S); psychologisches ~ *psychological gender* (z. B. *he* [= *the tiger*], *she* [= *the ship*], etc.) **geschl·echtlich 1.** [a] *sexual* (*life*; *organ*); ~e Aufklärung *sexual pedagogics* pl od *education* || ~ Begierde *appetence, lust*; *sexual appetite* od *desire*; ~e Ausschweifung *sexual excess*; ~er Verkehr *sexual intercourse, carnal knowledge*; ~en V. h mit *to have carnal k. of* (*a woman*) || in ~er Hinsicht *sexually* || das ≗e *sex* **2.** [adv] *sexually*; ~ verkehren *to have sexual intercourse* (mit *with*) || ~ interessiert *sexy* | **~keit** f *sexuality*

Geschl·echts- ~akt m *sexual act*; *coition* **~alter** n *generation* **~bestimmung** f *sex-determination* **~charakter** m *sexual character* **~chromosom** f ⟨bot⟩ *sex-chromosome* **~drüse** f ⟨biol⟩ *gonad* **~folge** f *succession of generations*; *lineage* **~genuß** m *sexual pleasure* **~hormon** n *sexual hormone* **~krankheit** f *sexual* od *venereal disease*; Klinik f ~en *lock-hospital* **~leben** n *sexual life* **~lust** f *sexual desire*; die ~ erregend *erogenous* **~name** m *family name* **~organ** n *sexual organ* **~register** n *genealogical register* **≗reif** a *pubescent* **~reife** f *pubescence, puberty* **~tafel** f *genealogical table*; *family tree*; → Stammbaum **~teile** m pl *genitals* pl; *private parts, privates* pl; → Infibulation, Glied, Hoden, Scheide **~trieb** m *sex impulse, sexual instinct* || abnormer ~ des Mannes *satyriasis* **~verhältnis** n ⟨demog⟩ *sex ratio*; primäres ~ *sex ratio* (od *masculinity proportion*) *at conception* **~verkehr** m *sexual intercourse*; *venery*; außerehelicher ~ *criminal conversation*; „zwangloser" ~ *promiscuity* **~wappen** n *family arms* pl **~wort** n ⟨gram⟩ *article* **~zelle** f ⟨biol⟩ *sexual cell*

geschl·echtslos a *sexless* ‖ ⟨gram⟩ *genderless*

Ge- ×**~schl·eck** n = Leckerei ≈**schl·iffen** a [pp v schleifen] *cut* (*glass*; *jewel*; *sharpened* (*knife*) ‖ ⟨übtr⟩ *polished*; *refined*; *acute*; fein ~ *chiselled* (*face*) **~schl·inge** n ~s/ (T) ⟨cul⟩ *pluck*; (of a pig) *ha(r)slet*; *pig's fry* ≈**schlitzt** a (→ schlitzen) *divided* (*skirt Rock*) ≈**schl·ossen** a [pp v schließen] **1.** *closed* (*car*; *syllable*) **2.** ⟨übtr⟩ **a.** ~e Bauweise *row of adjoining buildings* ‖ ⟨el⟩ *complete* (*circuit*) ‖ *crowded* (*forest*) *fully stocked* (*area*); ⟨mil⟩ *serried* (*front*, *ranks*); *close-order* (*drill*); ~e Formation *organized f.*; (Reserven) ~ [adv] einsetzen *to commit .. intact as an entity* ‖ ~e Ordnung *close order* ‖ ~ stehen hinter .. *to be solidly behind* (*a p*); *to be behind* (*a p*) *to a man* ‖ ~e Gesellschaft *private company* (od *circle*); ~e Hauswirtschaft *domestic economy carried on solely by members of the household* | (in **sich**) *integrated* (*services*) **b.** ⟨fig⟩ *tense* (*action*); *compact* (*whole*); *concise*, *terse* **c.** ⟨phon⟩ *close* (*sound*) | ≈heit [f] ⟨fig⟩ *conciseness*, *terseness*; *unity* **~schl·uchze** n ~s/ *sobbings* pl, *sobs* pl ≈**schl·ungen** pp v schlingen

Geschm·ack m ~(e)s/≈e **1.** (~sinn) *taste* ‖ ich habe k–n ~ im Munde *I cannot taste anything* ‖ schlechter ~ (e–r Speise) *unpalatability* **2.** (charakterist. ~ e–r Speise, etc) *t.* (*an unpleasant t.*); *flavour*, *relish*, *savour*; (best. ~) *smack* (*of a th*) ‖ (*the food has no*) *flavour*; es hat e–n süßlichen ~ *it tastes sweet*; *I have a bad t. in my mouth* **B.** ⟨übtr⟩ **1.** (künstlericher, etc ~) *t.* (in *in*); feiner (verwöhnter) ~ *cultivated* od *refined* (*fastidious*) *t.*; er hat ~ *he is a man of t.*; er hat k–n ~ *he has no t.*; .. e–n guten ~ *he has good t.*; sie kleidet sich mit ~ *she dresses in good t.* (od *tastefully*); sie hat k–n ~, sich z kleiden *she dresses in bad t.* | *the t. of the 20th century* ‖ *that does not suit the German t.* ‖ **die** ≈**e(r)** sind verschieden, über den ~ läßt sich nicht streiten *t.s differ*, *there is no accounting* (*for likes and dislikes* od) *for tastes* ‖ dem öffentlichen ~ z gefallen suchen *to tickle popular t.* **2.** (Gefallen, Genuß) *taste* (f *for*); *fancy*, *liking*, *relish* (*for*); *appreciation* (*of*, *for*) ‖ besonderer ~, erhöhter ~ *gusto*, *zest* (*for*); ausgewählter ~ *fastidiousness* | e–r S ~ abgewinnen *to come to like a th*, *to acquire a taste for a th*; ich kann der S nicht den geringsten ~ abg. *it's not at all to my taste* od *in my line* ‖ ~ **finden an** = Gefallen ..; manche f. ~ daran *it is savo(u)ry to some tongues*; k–n ~ f. an *to find no relish in* (*his t. is not for meat*) ‖ den ~ verlieren an *to lose one's taste for* (od *one's interest in*) | **auf** den ~ (*or* in ~) k *to taste blood* ‖ **nach** jds ~ *to a p's liking* (od *taste*); *in a p's line*; das ist ganz nach m–m ~ *that's very much to my taste*; er ist ein Mann nach m–m ~ *he is a man after my own heart*

geschm·acklos **1.** [a] **a.** *tasteless* (*medicine*); ⟨cul⟩ *insipid*, *flavourless* **b.** *tasteless* (*fashion*); *inelegant* ‖ *tactless*; [pred] *in bad taste* **2.** [adv] *tastelessly* ≈**igkeit** f *tastelessness*; das ist e–e ~ *that's bad taste*; → Plattheit; ~en [pl] *lapses into b. t.*

Geschm·acks- **~ausdruck** m *taste* **~muster** n *decorative* od *fancy-design*; → Gebrauchs– **~nerv** m *gustatory nerve* **~probe** f *taste* **~richtung** f *prevailing t.*; *trend* (od *school*) *of t.* **~verirrung** f *lapse of t.*; *perverted t.*; *gross t.lessness*; *bad t.* **~vermögen** n *faculty of tasting*; *gustation* **~zusatz** m *flavour*, *relish*, *savour*; mit e–m ~ v Vanille *vanilla-flavoured*; ohne ~ *unflavoured*

Geschmack(s)- **~sache** f das ist ~ *that's a matter of taste* **~sinn** m (*sense of*) *taste*

geschm·ackvoll **1.** [a] *tasteful*; *elegant*, *smart*, *stylish*; ~e Form *elegance* **2.** [adv] *tastefully*; *in good taste*; sehr ~ ausgestattet *furnished in the best taste*; sehr ~ gekleidet *dressed in absolute taste* **geschm·ackwidrig** a *offensive*

°**Ge-** **~schm·atze** n ~s/ *smacking* °**~schm·ause** n ~s/ *banqueting*, *feasting* ≈**schmaucht** a *fumigated* **~schm·eide** n ~s/~ *jewel(le)ry*; *jewels*, *gems*. pl, *trinkets* pl; *bijouterie* [Fr] ‖ künstlerisches ~ *bibelot* [Fr] ~kästchen [n] *jewel* (od *trinket*) *case* ≈**schm·eidig** a **1.** ⟨eig⟩ *ductile*; *malleable* (*metal*) ‖ *elastic*, *flexible*, *pliable*, *pliant*, *resilient*, *supple* (*leather*); *sleek* (*hair*, *fur*, *skin*); *supple* (*limbs* pl) ‖ (etw) ~ m *to supple*; ~ w *to supple* **2.** ⟨fig⟩ *elastic*; *ductile*, *malleable* (*character*); (Figur) *svelte* [F]; (gewandt) *lissom*, *lithe(some)* (*movements*) ‖ *rangy*; *versatile* (*courtier*, *mind*); *glib*, *voluble* (*tongue*) ‖ ⟨dero⟩ *supple* (*lawyer*); *tricky* | ~keit [f] ~/ *elasticity*, *flexibility*, *pliability*, *pliancy*; *resilience*; *suppleness*, *smoothness* | ⟨fig⟩ *lissomness*, *malleability*; *versatility* ‖ *suppleness*; *ductility* **~schm·eiß** n ~es/ **1.** *dung* (*of birds of prey*); *fly-blow* ‖ (Ungeziefer) *vermin* **2.** ⟨fig⟩ (P) (*low*) *rabble*, *riff-raff*; *vermin*; *the dregs* [pl] (od *scum*) *of society*; → Gesindel **~schm·etter** n ~s/ *blare*, *blaring*, *flourish* ≈**schm·iedet** a *forged*; *wrought* (*nail*); hand~ *hand-wrought* °**~schm·iere** n ~s/ *smearing* ‖ = Gekritzel ≈**schm·iert** a → geölt ≈**schm·inkt** a *rouged* (*woman*) ≈**schm·issen** pp v schmeißen ≈**schmolzen** a *molten*, (*glass*, *gold*, *lava* etc); *melted butter* ≈**schm·ort** a *stewed* (*pears*); ~es Fleisch, ≈es *stew* **~schm·unzel** n ~s/ *smirk(ing)* °**~schm·us**, **~schm·use** n *cuddling*, *hugging* ‖ *cringing* (od *fawning*) *talk* (od *ways*); *cajolery*, *wheedles* pl °**~schn·arche** n ~s/ *snoring* **~schn·atter** n ~s/ *cackling*, *cackle* (*of geese*) ‖ ⟨übtr⟩ *babble*, *cackle*, *chatter(ing)* ≈**schn·iegelt** a *bedizened*, *dapper*, *spruce*; *dandified*; *smartly dressed*; ⟨fam⟩ *spiffy*; ~ u gebügelt *dressed up to the nines*; *spick and span*; → aufgedonnert ≈**schn·itten** a [pp v schneiden] *cut* (*nail*) °**~schnüffel** n ~s/ *sniffings* pl °**~schnurre** n ~s/ *purring* (*of a cat*) ≈**sch·oben** pp v schieben ≈**sch·olten** pp v schelten **~sch·öpf** n ~(e)s/~e *creature* ‖ ‖ °ein liebes ~ *a lovely creature*; *a dear little thing*; ⟨sl⟩ *a peach*, so ein liebes ~! *such a dear*! armes ~! *poor thing*! | ⟨dero⟩ jds ~e [pl] *a p's creatures* pl ≈**sch·oren** pp v *scheren*

Gesch·oß n –sses/–sse **A.** (Abgeschossenes) (Wurf≈) *missile*; → Pfeil, Speer, Stein | (of fire-arms) *projectile*; (f Gewehr, Pistole) *bullet* ‖ → Kugel; Bombe, Granate, Schrapnell ‖ Brand≈ *incendiary projectile*; Leucht≈ *star-shell*; Leuchtspur≈ *tracer(-bullet)* **B.** (in die Höhe Gewachsenes; → Schößling) **1.** ⟨arch⟩ *stor(e)y*; *floor*; → Dach≈, Erd≈; Stock **2.** ⟨bot⟩ *internode* **~aufschlag** m *impact* (*of a projectile*) **~aufzug** m *shell-hoist* **~bahn** f *trajectory* **~boden** m *base of projectile* **~drehung** f = Drall **~einschlag** m = –aufschlag **~fang** m (Schießstand≈) *stop-butt(s)* **~garbe** f *cone of fire* **~geschwindigkeit** f *velocity* (*of a projectile*) **~haube** f *false cap* **~kopf** m *nose* **~mantel** m *jacket*, *shell* **~wagen** m **~zubringer** m *shell bogie*

ge- **~sch·ossen** pp v schießen **Geschr·äge** n ~s/ *paling* **~schr·aubt** a ⟨fig⟩ (of style) *stilted*; *affected*; *laboured*; *stiff*; *unnatural* | ≈heit [f] ~/~en ⟨fig⟩ *stiltedness*; *stiffness* ≈**schr·ei** n ~s/ **1.** *cries* pl, *cry*; *shouts* pl, *shoutings* pl ‖ .. mit gr ~ *shouted* (*ovation*) ‖ lautes *clamour*; *racket*; durchdringendes ~ (a. of birds) *scream*, *screech*, *shriek*, *squall*; jubelndes ~ *loud acclamations* pl; Weh≈ *lamentations* pl, *wailings* pl ‖ wildes, wirres ~ *hullabaloo*; → Zeter≈ ‖ ein lautes ~ erheben *to shout*; *to give* (od *set up*) *a great shout* **2.** (Aufheben) *bother*, *fuss*; mach nicht soviel ~ wegen .. *don't make such a bother about* (*trifles*); → Lärm ‖ ⟨fig⟩ *clamour*, *hue and cry* (gegen *against*; nach *after*); *outcry* (über *at, about*); *racket* (*about*) ‖ viel ~ u wenig Wolle *more squeak than wool*; *much ado about nothing* (Shak) **3.** † = Gerücht °≃**schr·eibe** n ~s/ *writing* °≃**schreibsel** n ~s/ **1.** = Gekritzel **2.** ⟨Lit⟩ *scribble*; *penny-a-lining*; *wish-wash* **~schr·ieben** a [pp v schreiben] *written manuscript* (*notes*); ~e Arbeit *work in manuscript* ‖ ⟨engl⟩ ~es Gesetz *statute*; ~es Recht *statute-law* **~schr·ien** pp v schreien ≃**schr·itt** n ⟨gym⟩ *succession of steps taken as a whole* **~-schr·itten** pp v schreiten ‖ ***geschr·oben** pp v schrauben; → geschraubt ≃**schr·öt** n ~es/ ⟨hunt⟩ *testicles* pl **~sch·ult** a *qualified* (*staff*); *schooled, well-trained, skilled* (*worker*) **~sch·unden** pp v schinden **~sch·uppt** a ⟨bot & zoo⟩ *scaly*; *tegular* ≃**sch·üttel** n ~s/ *shaking*

Gesch·ütz n ~es/~e (einzelnes ~) *gun*; **can-non*; *piece of ordnance* ‖ [koll] ~e [pl] ~ *guns* pl; *ordnance*; **cannon*; schweres ~ *heavy guns* od *ordnance*; (*position-*)*artillery*; **an** die ~e! *action*! schwer(st)es ~ **auffahren** (l) *to draw forth the heaviest artillery* ⟨a. fig⟩; mit schweren ~en ausgerüstet *heavily gunned* (*ship*) ‖ → Bug≃, Draht≃, Eisenbahn≃, Feld≃, Flachfeuer≃, Flugzeugabwehr≃, Haubitze, Mörser, Schiffs≃, Schnellfeuer≃, Steilfeuer≃, Turm≃ ‖ ~ montieren *to mount a gun*; ~ in Stellung bringen *to position a gun*; → richten **~bedienung** f *working* (od *serving*) *of the guns* ‖ [konkr] *gun-crew*; *gunners* **~bettung** f *platform, gun-base* **~bronze** f *gun-metal* **~einschnitt** m *pit* **~exerzieren** n *gun drill* **~fabrik** f *gun-, ordnance-factory* **~feuer** n *gun--fire* **~flugzeug** n *gun-plane* **~führer** m *gun--captain* **~kunst** f *gunnery*; *art of artillery* **~park** m *gun-park* **~pforte** f ⟨mar⟩ *gun-port* **~raum** m (im Unterseeboot) *gun-well* **~rohr** n *gun-barrel* **~stand** m *emplacement*; *platform* (*for a gun*); ⟨nav⟩ *barbette* [Fr] **~turm** m *turret* **~unterstand** m *gun-pit*; kl zementierter ~ *pill-box* ≃**weise** a ~s Feuer *individual gun firing* **~wesen** n *artillery*; *gunnery*

ge- ~sch·ützt a; gesetzlich ~ *registered* (*patent*); → sicher **~schw·ächt** a *enfeebled*; *weakened*

Geschw·ader n ~s/~ ⟨nav⟩ *squadron* ‖ ⟨aero⟩ (*12 aeroplanes*) *squadron*, ⟨Am⟩ *wing*; Verband v drei ~n *wing* ‖ Blockade≃ *blockading sq.*; Bomben≃ ⟨aero⟩ *bombing sq.*; Jagd≃ *fighting sq.* (od *aeroplanes* pl); Schul≃ *training sq.* **~arzt** m ⟨nav⟩ *surgeon-commander* **~chef** m ⟨nav⟩ *commander-in-chief* (od *commodore*) *of a squadron* **~fahrt** f ⟨nav⟩ *squadron-cruise* **~flug** m ⟨aero⟩ *squadron-flight* **~kommodore** m ⟨aero⟩ *squadron--commander* (od *leader*) **~(gefechts)zentrale** f → GCC

°**Geschw·afel** n ~s/ = seichtes Geschwätz ⟨sl⟩ *blether, waffle*, ⟨Am⟩ *boloney*

Geschw·ätz n ~es/ *idle talk, palaver, prate, prattle, tittle-tattle*; (Klatsch) *gossip* (über *about*) ‖ dummes, hohles, leeres, seichtes ~ *balderdash, flummery, gush, nonsense, twaddle, wish-wash*; ⟨fam⟩ *talkee-talkee*; ⟨sl⟩ *hokum, hot air, blether*; ⟨Am sl⟩ *dirt, gas*; *ballyhoo, bunk*(*um*), *fluff*; prahlerisches ~ ⟨fam⟩ *tall talk*

geschwätzig a *garrulous, loquacious, prating, talkative*; *newsy*; *gossipy*; ⟨sl⟩ *blithering*, ⟨Am sl⟩ *gabby* ‖ ~ s *to have a long tongue* | ≃**keit** f ~/ *garrulity, loquacity, talkativeness*

geschw·eift a ⟨tail⟩ *curved, arched*

ge- ~schw·eige adv [erstarrt aus (ich) ~ 1. sg prs v † geschweigen vi] ~ denn *let alone* (*I can't afford to play golf, let alone tennis*); *not to mention* (*.., not to mention all the others who ..*); *to say nothing of*; *much less* (*it has not yet been started much less completed*) ≃**schw·elge** n ~s/ *debauchery, revelry*; *revelling* **~schwellt** a *swelling* **~-schw·iegen** pp v schweigen **~schw·enkt** a ⟨cul⟩ in Butter ~ *sauté* [Fr] **~schw·ind 1.** [a] *fast, quick, swift*; *agile, expeditious, nimble, prompt, rapid, speedy* ‖ mach ~!; ~, ~! *be* (od *come*) *quick*! **2.** [adv] *fast, quickly, swiftly*; ⟨fam⟩ *quick* | ≃schritt [m] im ~ *at the double-quick* ≃**schw·indigkeit** f ~/~en (P) *quickness, speed, swiftness*; *celerity, nimbleness, promptness, rapidity* | (S) (Fahr≃) *speed* (nicht begrenzt *not restricted*); *velocity*; *rate* ‖ Anfangs≃ *initial v.*; Auftreff≃, End≃ ⟨ball⟩ *striking v.*; *v. of impact*; Dauer≃ *permanent sp.*; End≃ *final v.*; Flug≃ *sp. of flight*; Förderungs≃ ⟨min⟩ *extracting* od *hauling sp.*; Fortpflanzungs≃ *sp. of propagation*; Höchst≃ *high sp., top-sp.*; erhöhte ~ ⟨comp ad⟩ *new operating sp.*; Lande≃ ⟨aero⟩ *landing sp.*; mit Licht–, Schall≃ *at* od *with the sp. of light, sound*; Luftdurchlaß≃ *v. of air flow*; Marsch≃, Reise≃ *cruising sp.*; Mündungs≃ *muzzle-v.*; Start≃ *take-off sp.*; Steig≃ ⟨aero⟩ *sp. of climb*; Stunden≃ *sp. per hour*; Überwasser≃ *surface sp.*; Unterwasser≃ *submerged sp.* | die Maschine **arbeitet** mit e–r konstanten ~ v .. *continuous production is at a machine* od *operating speed of ..*; ~ aufnehmen *to gather* od *pick sp.*; die ~ bremsen *to check the sp.* | e–e enorme ~ **entfalten** *to develop an enormous speed*; ~ erhöhen *to put on sp.*; die ~ (e–s Zuges) vermindern *to decelerate* (*a train*); *to slow down* ‖ e–e ~ v 30 Meilen m *or* zurücklegen *to do 30 miles* ‖ ~ **ist** keine Hexerei *dexterity is no sorcery* | **an** ~ abnehmen *to lose speed* (od *way*) ‖ an ~ gewinnen *to take up sp.*; an ~ zunehmen *to gather speed* (od *way*) | **in** *or* **mit** e–r ~ v 30 Meilen in der Stunde *at a speed* (od *rate*) *of 30 miles an hour*, ⟨Am⟩ *at a thirty--mile clip an h.* ‖ mit doppelter ~ (*at*) *twice his* (*her*, etc.) *former speed* ‖ mit gr ~ *with all speed* ‖ mit größter ~ (*at*) *full* (od *top*) *speed*; sich mit größter ~ bewegen (of a car) *to go full speed*; mit größter ~ gehen *to be going all-out* ‖ mit rasender ~ *at full tear* | **~s- ~abnahme** f *decrease of sp.* **~beschränkung** f *sp. limit* **~diagramm** n *v.-diagram* **~einstellung** f ⟨phot⟩ *speed setting* **~grenze** f *sp.--limit* **~kurve** f *v.-curve* **~messer** m *speedometer* ‖ *tachometer* ‖ *sp. indicator* **~überschreitung** f *speeding*; Strafmandat wegen ~ *speeding ticket* **~verhältnis** n *v. ratio* **~zunahme** f *increase of speed*

Geschw·indschritt m ⟨mil⟩ *double*(*-quick*) *time*

Geschwirr n ~(e)s/ *buzz*(*ing*); *ping*(*ing*); *swish*(*ing*); *whirr*(*ing*); *whizz*(*ing*); ⟨fam⟩ *zip*

Geschw·ister pl *brother and sister*; die beiden sind ~ *the two are b. and s.* ‖ *brothers and sisters* pl (*the three are b. and s.*); drei ~ *three brothers and sisters* ‖ s–e ~ *his brother*(*s*) *and sister*(*s*) **~-kind** n *cousin* (*they are cousins*); → Neffe, Nichte **~liebe** f *love between brother*(*s*) *and sister*(*s*); *brotherly* (od *sisterly*) *love* **~paar** n *brother and sister*

ge- ~schw·isterlich a *brotherly*; *sisterly* **~-schw·ollen** a [pp v schwellen] **1.** *swollen* (*veins*); *thick* (*ear*); → angeschwollen **2.** ⟨fig⟩ aufgeblasen **~schw·ommen** pp v schwimmen **~schw·oren** pp v schwören

Geschw·orene [der ~, ein ~r] m ~n/~n *juror, juryman* ‖ [die ~, e–e ~] f ~n/~n *juror, woman juror* ‖ die ~n [pl] *the jury, panel*; meine ~n! *Ladies and Gentlemen of the jury*! ‖ Liste der ~n *panel*; e~e L. der ~n auf–, zus–stellen *to empanel a jury*; die ~n ablehnen *to challenge the array* **~nbank** f *jury-box* **~ngericht** n *jury* (*court*) ‖ periodisches ~ *the Assizes* pl; das ~ abhalten *to hold the a.* **~nliste** → Geschworene

Ge- ~schw·ulst f ~/≃e *bump, swelling*; *wen* ‖ krankhafte ~ *morbid growth*; *tumour*; echte ~ *neoplasm*, unechte ~ *granulation growth* (od *tumour*); → Krebs≃ **~schw·ünge** n ~s/ ⟨gym⟩ *series of swings on the horse* **~schw·ür** n ~(e)s/~e **1.** ⟨path⟩ *abscess, ulcer* ‖ kl ~ *boil*; *pimple, pustule* **2.** ⟨fig⟩ *sore*; → Eiterbeule | ~bildung [f] *ulceration* | geschw·ürig [a] *ulcerated*; *ulcerative*

|| ~ w *to ulcerate* **~s·echstschein** m ⟨astrol⟩ *sextile* (*aspect*) **≚s·egnet** a *blessed*; *peaceful*, *lush* (*countryside*); *prosperous* (*new year*) || ~e Mahlzeit! *I hope you'll make* (od *you made*) *a good meal* (od *you'll enjoy your meal*) || ein v Schicksal ~er *one of the blessed* °**~seich** n ~es/ *wish-wash*, *wishy-washy talk*; ⟨Am sl⟩ *ballyhoo* || langes ~ *rigmarole* °**~s·eire** n ~s/ *blarney*, *eyewash* **~s·ell** m, **~s·elle** m ~n/~n **1.** ⟨poet⟩ *chap*, *fellow*; ⟨sl⟩ = Gefährte || → fahrend; ein lustiger ~ ⟨fam⟩ *a gay bird* (od *blade*); *a gay young dog*; die jungen ~n *the young blades* pl | ⟨dero⟩ *bird*, *dog*, *fish*; ⟨fam⟩ *bloke*; ⟨Am sl⟩ *gink*, *guy* || roher ~ *rowdy*, *ruffian*; ⟨Am sl⟩ *bohunk* || ⟨iron⟩ ein schöner ~ *a nasty fellow* || ein schweigsamer ~ *a dumb dog* || ein verschlagener ~ *a sly dog*, *a sly one* **2.** (Handwerks≚) *journeyman*, *journey-worker*; Schneider≚ *journeyman tailor* **~s·ellen-** **~arbeit** f *journey-work* **~herberge** f *journeymen's lodging-house* **~jahre** f pl = –zeit **~prüfung** f *journeymen's test* **~stand** m *state of a journeyman* **~zeit** f *journeyman's years* [pl] *of service* **≚s·ellen** vt/refl [h] **1.** [*vt] = vereinigen, -binden **2.** [refl] **sich** ~ z jdm *to join a p*, *to associate with a p*; *to range up beside a p*; sich wieder ~ z jdm *to rejoin a p*; z ihnen gesellte sich Herr N. (*or* Herr N. g. sich ihnen zu) *they were joined by Mr. N.* || gleich u gleich gesellt sich gern *birds of a feather flock together*; *like attracts like* **≚s·ellig 1.** [a] (umgänglich) *sociable*; *companionable*, *convivial*; *social*; ein ~er Mensch *a* (*good*) *joiner*, *mixer* || (~ lebend) *gregarious* (*animal*); *social* (*man is a social being*) || ~er Abend *sociable* od *social evening*; ~es Leben *social life*; ~er Verein *social club*; *society*; ~e Vereinigung *sociable* od *convivial meeting*; ~e Zus–kunft ⟨fam⟩ *social*; ⟨Am⟩ *sociable*; → Beisammensein **2.** [adv] *sociably*; *socially* | **≚keit** f ~/~en **1.** *companionableness*; *sociability*; *sociality* **2.** (gesellschaftl. Leben) *company*; die ~ lieben *to be fond of company*; sie h viel ~ *they see* od *have much company* || ~en [pl] *company*; *socialities* pl

Ges·ellschaft f ~/~en **I.** [abstr] **A.** **(Zus–leben) 1.** *company*, (*–panionship*); (sittlich) gute, schlechte ~ *good*, *bad c.* || → Gemeinschaft || (~ besserer Art) *society*; passende ~ *suitable s.* | jds ~ **genießen,** suchen, meiden *to enjoy*, *seek*, *avoid a p's s.* || jdm ~ leisten *to bear* (od *keep*) *a p c.*; *to join a p* (*in a walk*) || der ~ wegen, um ~ z leisten *for fellowship's sake* | **in** ~ *in c.* (mit *with*) || er ist oft in ~ v 2 Damen *he is often seen in the c. of two ladies* || ⟨fig⟩ ich befinde mich (hierbei) in guter ~ *I sin* (od *err*) *in good c.* || in schlechte ~ geraten *to get into bad c.* || **zur** ~ mitweinen *to weep for c.* **2.** *⟨übtr⟩ (S) Bücher sind s–e liebste ~ *books are his best companions* || (dieses Metall) findet sich oft in ~ v (..) *is often found in combination with ..* **B.** **(soziale Form)** *s.*; die menschl. ~ *human s.*; *the social fabric* || (Standes≚) *s.*; die bürgerl. ~ *civil s.*; die gute ~ *good* s.; die vornehme ~ *fashionable* (od *elegant*) *s.*; Damen der ~ *s. ladies* pl; Spitzen der ~ *leaders of s.* || ⟨Lit⟩ Treffpunkt der ~ *salon* [Fr] **II.** [konkr] **A.** **1.** *association*, *s.*; → Brüderschaft; Klub; Körperschaft; Verein || ⟨com⟩ Handels≚ (*trading*) *c.*; *s.*; ⟨Am⟩ *public utility* || offene Handels≚ *partnership*; ~ mit beschränkter Haftung *Limited Liability C.* || ⟨SBZ⟩ ~ f Sport u Technik *S. for Sports and Technique* | ⟨ec⟩ die ~ Jesu *the S. of Jesus*; *the Jesuits* pl | ⟨arts, Lit etc⟩ *s.*; gelehrte, literarische ~ *learned*, *literary s.* (etc); ⟨engl⟩ die ~ der Wissenschaften *the Royal S.*; ⟨Ger⟩ *the Academy of Sciences* || (polit. ~) *association*; Bau≚ *building society*; die ~ f *the S*, *for ..* **2.** **(Unterhaltung) a.** *party*; ⟨Am a.⟩ *bee* || e–e ~ v .. *a party of* (*mountaineers*); Jagd≚ *hunting party* || sie bildeten e–e ~ v 10 Leuten *they formed a party of ten* || → sich anschließen I. B. **b.** *party*, *social gathering*; Herren- u Damen≚ *mixed c.*; in gr Stil ~en geben *to entertain largely*; auf e–r ~ *at a party*, ⟨Am a.⟩ *on*; *we want one good girl on this party*; e–e ~ geben *to give* (⟨Am fam⟩ *throw*) *a party*; sie gaben nie ~en *they never entertained*; sie h viele ~en *they see much company*, er geht viel in ~ *he goes a great deal into society* **B.** ⟨**dero**⟩ bunte ~ *varied lot*; e–e sehr gemischte ~ *a very mixed company* od *crowd*; e–e seltsame ~ *an odd assortment* || (Clique) *bunch* (*he is the best of the b.*); *clique*, *crowd*, *set*; ⟨Am⟩ *lay-out*; e–e spaßige ~ *a funny lot*; die ganze ~ *the whole lot* (⟨sl⟩ *caboodle*)

Ges·ellschafter m ~s/~ **1.** *companion*; *associate*; er ist ein guter ~ *he is good company*, *he is a* (*good*) *mixer* **2.** ⟨com⟩ *associate*; *partner* (e–s Unternehmens *in* od *of a concern*); stiller ~ *sleeping partner* | **~in** f ~/~nen (*lady-*)*companion* || ⟨com⟩ *female partner*

ges·ellschaftlich 1. [a] *social* (*position*, *reform*, *relations*); ~e Konvention *convention*; ~es Leben *social life*, *society*; ~er Schliff *good breeding*, *society manners* pl; ~e Stellung *caste*; *level*; *social status* || in ~er Hinsicht *socially* || → gesellig **2.** [adv] *socially* || sich ~ unmöglich m *to make o.s. impossible in society* || ~ weit unter jdm stehen *to be far beneath the social level of a p* || auf ~ niedere Stufe herabsinken *to lose caste* | **≚keit** f ~/ *sociality*

Ges·ellschafts- **~anzug** m *evening-dress*; ⟨fam⟩ *tails*; ⟨mil⟩ kl ~ *ordinary dress uniform* **~dame** f *society-lady* || *lady-companion* **~demographie** f *social demography* **≚fähig** a *upper class* [attr], ⟨fam⟩ *U* (nicht ~ *non-U*) **~fahrt** f ⟨rail⟩ *party travel* **~gliederung** f *social stratification* **~gruppe** f *s. status group* **~inseln** f pl *Society Islands*, *Tahiti Islands* pl **~kapital** n *joint stock*; *registered capital* (*of a company*) **~klasse** f *social class*; (*his*, *her*) *world*; exklusive ~ *caste* **~klatsch** m *society gossip* **~kleid** n *gown* **~kleidung** f *dress--clothes* pl **~kreis** m *circle of acquaintances* (od *friends*); in hohen u niederen ~en *in high and low places* **≚kritisch** a *criticizing the society ..* | adv *.. as a social critic* **~kunst** f *social art* **~lehre** f *social theory*; *theory of society* **~leute** pl *society--people* **~lied** n *social song* **~manieren** f pl *social manners*; *company-manners* **~mitglied** n *member of a society* **~ordnung** f *social order* **~raum** m *drawing-room*; *lounge* || *society-room* **~reise** f *personally conducted tour* **~scherz** m *parlour trick* **~spiel** n *social game*; *round game* || °~ z zweit ⟨sex⟩ *the national indoor game*, *the first game ever played*; das ~ z zw. spielen ⟨sex⟩ *to play tiddlywinks*, ⟨vulg⟩ *to play at lift-leg* **~stat·ut** n *articles of association* **~steuer** f *corporation-tax* **~stück** n ⟨paint⟩ = Genrebild; ⟨theat⟩ *social drama* **~stufe** f *social rank*; → Stufe || jdn auf eine höhere ~ heben *to bring social elevation to a p* **~tanz** m *ballroom* od *social dancing* **~ton** m *society tone* **~trieb** m *social instinct* **~vertrag** m (*Rousseau's*) *social contract* || *deed of association* (od *partnership*) **~wagen** m *char-a-banc* [Fr] **~wissenschaft** f *social science* | **≚lich** [a] *of s. sc.s*; ≚liches Grundstudium ⟨SBZ⟩ *study of Marxism and Leninism* **~zimmer** n *drawing* (od *reception*)*-room*; ⟨a-engl⟩ *salon* [Fr]

Ge- **~s·enk** n ~s/~e **1.** *die*; *swage*; (Metall) in ~en bearbeiten *to swage* **2.** ⟨min⟩ *sump* | ~-hammer [m] *drop h.* ~klotz, ~stock [m] *swage--block* ~schmieden [n] *swaging* **≚s·essen** pp v sitzen **~s·etz** n ~es/~e **1.** ⟨jur⟩ *law* || die ~e [pl] *the l.s* pl, *the l.* (*of England*) || ⟨engl⟩ geschriebenes ~ *statute* || Reichs≚ etc, Parlaments≚ *act*; ~ f Erziehungswesen *education act* || ~ w *to become l.*, *to pass into l.*; ~ w l *to pass* (*a bill*) *into l.*; (ein) ~ ist in Kraft *law stands*; e–m ~ unterwerfen *to put under* (*federal*) *l.* | **Auge** des ~es *limb of the l.* || der B. des ~es *the letter of the l.* || die ~e achtend *l.-abiding*; dem ~ ins Gesicht schlagen *to cheat the l.* ‖ **auf dem Boden** des ~es stehen *to take one's stand on the wording of the l.*; *to be based on the l.* ‖ auf **Grund** des ~es, nach dem ~e *under the l.* (*hundreds were arrested*) ‖ **im Namen** des ~es *in the name of the l.*; ⟨engl a.⟩ *in the queen's name* ‖ in den Augen des ~es, nach dem ~e *in the eye of the l.* ‖ **mit** dem ~ in Konflikt k *to fall foul of the l.*; Gefahr laufen, mit dem ~ in K. z k *to skirt the outer fringe of the l.*, *to sail close to the wind*; nicht mit dem ~ in K. k *to keep o.s. on the right side of the l.* ‖ Achtung h **vor** dem ~ *to be l.-abiding* | das ~ **anrufen** *to appeal to the l.*; auf ein ~ bezughabend *statutory*; ein ~ erlassen *or* geben *to enact* od *make a l.*; ~e geben *to legislate*; ein ~ in Kraft setzen (*or* treten l) *to put a l. into force*; ein ~ tritt in K. *a l. comes into force*; kraft ~es *by act of l.*; ein ~ verabschieden *to pass a bill* **2.** ⟨rel⟩ die göttlichen ~e [pl] *the laws of God* ‖ ⟨bib⟩ das ~ (*or* ~ Mose) *the law of Moses* **3.** ⟨scient⟩ *law*; Natur≈ *l. of nature*; *the l. of gravity* ‖ alles bewegt sich nach ~en *everything moves in accordance with l.* ‖ *the l.s of painting* ‖ oberstes ~ der Staatsmannskunst *the supreme l. of statesmanship*; (*economy is*) *the overriding factor* **4.** ⟨übtr⟩ *the l. of self-preservation* ‖ das ~ des Handelns *the initiative, the power of action*; das ~ des H. an sich reißen *to usurp the initiative*; das ~ des H. bestimmen, diktieren, vorschreiben *to have* od *possess the i.*; er ließ sich v niemand das ~ des H. vorschreiben *he allowed nobody to take the i. from him* ‖ ~ der großen Zahl *law of the big number*

Ges·etz- (→ a. ~es–) **~antrag** m ⟨parl⟩ *bill*; ~ e–s Abgeordneten *private* (⟨Am⟩ *special*) *bill* **~auslegung** f *interpretation of the law* **~blatt** n *official gazette announcing new laws* **~buch** n *code* (*of laws*); → bürgerlich **~entwurf** m *bill*; → G.es-vorlage **≈gebend** a *legislative* (*assembly*) ‖ ~e Gewalt *legislature*; *legislative body* **~geber** m *legislator*; *lawgiver* **~gebung** f *legislation* **~konkurrenz** f *merger* **~kraftverleihung** f *enactment* (*of a l.*) **≈mäßig 1.** [a] *lawful, legal, legitimate* (*ruler*); → legitim ‖ *natural* (*development*) **2.** [adv] *lawfully*; *legally* ‖ *in conformity with the course of nature* **~mäßigkeit** f *lawfulness, legality, legitimacy* ‖ *conformity with natural law*; sittliche ~ *morality* **~sammlung** f *body of laws*; *statute-book* **~tafel** f ⟨bib⟩ die ~n [pl] *the tables of the law*; → Dekalog, Gebot **≈widrig** a *illegal, unlawful*; ~e Handlungen [pl] *malpractices* pl **~widrigkeit** f *illegality, unlawfulness, lawlessness*

Ges·etzes- (→ a. Gesetz–) **~annahme** f *enactment* (*of a l.*) **~kraft** f *legal force*; ~ erlangen *to become law*; *to pass into l.*; ~ h *to be valid* **~lücke** f *loophole* **~recht** n ⟨engl⟩ (geschrieb. Recht) *statute-l.* **~übergabe** f (an Petrus) ⟨arts⟩ *Delivery of the L.-scroll* **~vorlage** f *bill*; e–e ~ annehmen (verwerfen) *to pass* (*to throw out*) *a bill*; die ~ ist v Parlament angenommen worden *the bill has passed the house*; → Einzelberatung

ges·etzlich 1. [a] *lawful* (*age*); *legal* (*tender, liability*); *statutory*, ~e Meile *statute mile*; ~e Verfügung *enactment* ‖ ~e Erbfolge *intestate succession* ‖ (etw) f ~ erklären *to legitimate* (od *legitimatize, legitimize*); als ~ anerkennen *to legalize* **2.** [adv] *legally*; ~ anerkannt *Imperial* (*bushel*); ~ geschützt *registered*; ~ unerlaubt *unlawful* (*gain*); ~ (vorgeschrieben) ⟨com⟩ *statutory* (Rücklagen) | **≈keit** f *lawfulness*; *legality*; *legitimacy*

ges·etzlos a *lawless*; *anarchic*(*al*) **≈igkeit** f *lawlessness*; *anarchy, chaos*

ges·etzt a **1.** *composed, demure, grave*; *sedate, steady*; *sober* ‖ *staid* (*for his age*) ‖ ~es Alter *the age* od *years of discretion*; in ~eren Jahren *of mature age* **2.** in wohl~er Rede *in set phrases* ‖ ⟨mus⟩ weit (eng) ~ *in open* (*closed*) *harmony* **3.** ~, daß .. *granted* od *given that* ..; ~, dies wäre wahr *granting this to be true*; ~, er wäre in England geboren *suppose* od *supposing him born in England*; ~ es war so *suppose it was so* ‖ ~, daß .. *assuming that* .. ~ den Fall, daß .. *put the case that* ..; ~ (den Fall), daß s–e Papiere nicht in Ordnung wären *in case his papers were not all right* | **≈heit** f ~/ *composedness, demureness*; *sedateness, soberness, staidness*; *steadiness*

°**Ges·eufze** n ~s/ *sighings* pl, *sighs* pl; *groan*(*ing*)

ges·ichert a *assured* (*position*), *safe, secured, sheltered*; (s–e Zukunft) war ~ .. *was assured*

Ges·icht n ~(e)s/~er [doch vgl A. 3. b.] **A.** [abstr, nur sg] **1.** (Sehvermögen) *sight, vision*; *eyesight*; das ~ verlieren *to lose one's sight* **2.** (Anblicken, Blick) *sight*; etw aus dem ~ verlieren *to lose sight of a th*; etw z ~ bek *to get sight of, to come in sight of, to set* od *clap eyes on a th*; *to sight a th*; etw kam mir z ~ *something caught my eye* **3.** (geistiges Auge) **a.** *sight*; inneres ~ *mind's eye* ‖ zweites ~ *second sight* **b.** (Vision) *vision*; ~e [pl] *visions* pl; ~e h *to see visions* od ⟨fam⟩ *things* **B.** [konkr] (Angesicht) [pl ~er] **1. a.** *face*; *countenance*; ⟨liter⟩ *visage*; → Miene ‖ ⟨sl⟩ *dial, mazzard, mug* | (aufgeschwommen) *pudding f.*; länglich *longish f.*; scharfgeschnitten *hatchet*(*y*) *f.* ‖ schmal *thin f.*; mit schmalem ~ *thin of face* ‖ (ein) volles ~ h *to be full in the f.* ‖ *brown of f.* ‖ ein aggressives ~ h *to wear an agg. f.* Fräulein N., mit strahlendem ~, .. *Miss N., her face beaming* .. **b.** (P) lauter neue ~er [pl] *so many unfamiliar faces* od *people*; furchtbare ~er *dreadful shapes* pl | ein offizielles ~ **annehmen** *to assume an official mien*; ein anderes ~ aufsetzen *to assume a different expression* ‖ ein ernstes ~ bewahren *to keep a straight f.*; die S hat ein doppeltes ~ *there are two sides to it*; ein (böses) ~ m *to put on a f.*; ein verdutztes (etc) ~ m *to look puzzled* (*etc*); mach kein so trauriges ~! *cheer up*!; auf sein ehrliches ~ hin anschreiben l *to travel on one's f.* ‖ ein (langes) ~ m (*or* schneiden, ziehen) *to make or pull a* (*long*) *f.* (über *over*); ~er m *or* schneiden *to make* od *pull faces*; ein dummes (*or* verstimmtes) ~ m *to look down one's nose*; sie machte ein langes ~ *her face fell*; .. ein ~ wie 7 Tage Regenwetter *her face was at half past eight*; er macht ein ~ wie ein Topf voller Mäuse *he's a sour-puss*; *he looks like a wet Sunday*; jdm ~er schneiden *to make faces at a p*; dein ~ verrät d–e Gedanken *yours is a tell-tale f.*; sein ~ verstellen *to disguise one's f.*; das ~ verziehen, ein schiefes ~ m *to make a wry f.*; .. z Weinen .. ⟨fam⟩ *to laugh on the wrong side of the mouth*; sein wahres ~ zeigen *to show one's colours* | jdm etw **am** ~ absehen, → absehen | die Not schaut ihm **aus** dem ~ *want is written in his f.* ‖ er ist s–m Vater wie aus dem ~ geschnitten *he is the very spit of his father* (*his perfect image, living picture, dead ringer*) | wir hatten die Sonne **im** ~ *we had the sun in our eyes*; .. den Wind im ~ .. *the wind in our face* ‖ ein Schlag **ins** ~ *a facer*, ⟨fig⟩ *a smack* (⟨Am *sock*) *in the eye*; *a rebuff*; jdm mit der Kerze **ins** ~ leuchten *to flare a candle at a p*; jdm ins ~ *to a p's f., in the teeth of a p*; jdm etw direkt ins ~ sagen *to say a th to a p's f.* ‖ jdm ins ~ lachen *to laugh in a p's f.* ‖ jdm ins ~ schlagen *to smack a p in the f.* ‖ (S) ⟨fig⟩ e–r S direkt ins ~ schlagen *to be an outrage to .., to contradict a th flatly, to be at variance with*; *to clash* (od *conflict*) *with a th* ‖ jdm (direkt) ins ~ sehen *to look a p* (*straight*) *in the f. to meet a p's eyes squarely, to face a p*; .. forschend .. *to search a p's f.*; e–r S ins ~ sehen *to face a th*; *you must look the facts in the f.*, ⟨Am⟩ *you must face the music* | er saß **mit** dem ~ nach dem Fenster *he was facing the window* | komm mir nicht wieder **vors** ~ *don't let me see you again* | der Hut steht ihr nicht **zu** ~ *the hat does not suit her*; es steht ihm schlecht z ~ *it ill becomes him* (*to do*); (jdn) z

~ bek *to set eyes upon* .., .. nur wenig .. *to see little of* .. **C.** ⟨fig⟩ (S) *appearance, face*; *physiognomy* (*of a country*); *aspect, look* ‖ das geistige ~ e–r Epoche *the mental physiognomy* (od *aspect*) *of an era*; das wahre ~ e–s Landes *the true character of* .. ‖ e–r S ein anderes ~ geben *to put a new f.* (od *a different complexion*) *on a th* ‖ dadurch bekommt die S ein anderes ~ *that makes all the difference* ‖ e–r S ein ganz bes ~ verleihen *to make all the difference to a th* ‖ das ~ verlieren ⟨fig⟩ *to lose face* **Ges·ichtchen** n ~s/~ *little f.*; ein hübsches ~ *a pretty f.* **Ges·ichts-** *face, facial* **~achse** f *visual axis* **~ausdruck** m *f. expression, expression of f.*; *physiognomy*; *brow* **~behandlung** = ~massage **~bildung** f *features* pl; *physiognomy* **~drüse** f *f. gland* **~emulsion** f (hydratisierend) *fluid* °**~erker** m (Nase) *beacon* **~falte** f *f. wrinkle* **~farbe** f *complexion*; v frischer ~ *fresh-complexioned*, v dunkler ~ *black-a-vised* **~feld** n *field of vision* (od *view*); *visual field*; ⟨phot⟩ *coverage* ‖ ~ausfall [m] ⟨psych⟩ *scotoma*; ~messung [f] *perimetry* **~index** m ⟨anthr⟩ *f.l index* **~konturenemulsion** *contour-lift film* ® **~kreis** m *sight*; *range of vision* ‖ ⟨übtr⟩ *ken* (*within, outside one's k.*); *orbit* ‖ geistiger ~ *horizon* (*mental, political h.*); *purview, range, scope*; gr ~ *wide outlook* (od *range*); → erweitern **~kunde** f *physiognomy* **~linien** f pl *f.-lines* pl **~maske** f (⟨cosm⟩ *f.l*) *mask*; *film* **~massage** f *f.-massage*; ⟨Am⟩ *f.l treatment* od *massage*, ⟨fam⟩ *f.l* **~muskel** m *f.l muscle* **~nerv** m *visual nerve* **~puder** m *f. powder* **~punkt** m *point of view* (pl *points of view*) ‖ *angle*; *outlook*; ⟨Am⟩ *slant* (*many new s.s* ‖ v diesem ~e aus *from this p. of v.*; sich v rein ideellen ~en leiten l *to be guided by purely ideal motives*; vom rassischen ~ *from the racial angle* **~raffung** f (Beseitigung v Falten) *face lifting* **~rose** f → Rose **~schmerz** m *f.-ache* **~schönheitspflege** f *f.-lifting*, → ~massage **~sinn** m *vision*; *visual faculty* od *power* **~spannung** f ⟨cosm⟩ *f.-lifting* **~straffung** f *build-up* **~tau** m *skin dew* **~täuschung** f *optical illusion* **~urne** f ⟨praeh⟩ *f.-urn* **~wasser** n *f.-lotion, f. tonic* **~weite** f *line of sight*; *range of vision* **~winkel** m ⟨phys⟩ *visual angle* ‖ ⟨anthr⟩ *facial angle* **~züge** m pl *features, lineaments* pl; mit hübschen ~n *well-featured*

Ge- ~s·ims n –ses/–se ⟨arch⟩ *cornice*; ⟨carp⟩ *moulding*(*s* pl); → Sims **~s·inde** n ~s/~ **1.** (Haus~̽) *domestics, servants, menials* pl ‖ ⟨agr⟩ *labourers* pl **2.** [in comp] *servants'*; ~ball, ~lohn, ~stube, ~wohnungen *servants' ball, wages, hall, quarters*; ~bureau [n] *registery-office for servants*; ~ordnung [f] *regulations for servants* **~s·indel** n ~s/ *mob, rabble, riff-raff*; ⟨Am sl⟩ *scalawags* pl **~s·ingen** n ~s/ *singing*; *sing-song*

ges·innt a **1.** [pred] wie ist er ~? *what are his views* (od *opinions*)? ‖ ich bin anders ~ *I am of a different opinion*, .. anders ~ als ihr *I have different views to* (od *from, than*) *you*; → gesonnen **2.** [in comp] .. *disposed*, .. *minded* **a. feindlich** ~, freundlich ~ → feindlich, freundlich ‖ gütig ~ *kindly disposed, of a kind disposition* ‖ irdisch ~ *worldly-minded*; er ist christlich ~ *he is a Christian* | wie ist er politisch ~? *what are his politics*? ‖ ein treu ~er Anhänger *a trueblue adherent*; imperialistisch ~ *imperialist*(*ic*) ‖ er ist kaiserlich ~, königlich ~, monarchisch ~ *he is an imperialist, a royalist, a monarchist* ‖ er ist (durchaus) sozialistisch ~ *he is a* (*thoroughgoing*) *socialist*; kommunistisch ~ *red* | **wohl~** *well--disposed* (jdm *to a p*); *friendly* (*nation*); → gleich~, gut~, übel~

Ges·innung f ~/~en *characteristic way of thinking*; *spirit*; *mental attitude*; *opinions, views* pl; → Anlage, Charakter ‖ s–e politische ~ *his political attitude, his politics* pl [pl konstr] | *sentiment* (*not the deed but the sentiment* ..); *feelings* (*no fine f.*), *sentiments, impulses* pl ‖ edle ~ *noblesness of mind, nobility*; echte ~ *genuine feelings*; kriecherische ~ *servility*; schmutzige ~ *meanness*; treue ~ *faithfulness, loyalty* (gegen *to*); vaterländische ~ *public-spiritedness*; *patriotism*; *national feelings* **~sakrobat** m *time-server* **~sgenosse** m *mind-mate*; *man of like leanings* (od *propensities*; *adherent* od *supporter of the same cause*; ⟨pol⟩ *political friend, fellow-traveller* ‖ treuer ~ *faithful companion* **~̽slos 1.** [a] *fickle*; *without character*; *irresponsible, unprincipled, unreliable, unscrupulous* **2.** [adv] *unscrupulously* **~slosigkeit** f *lack of character*; *fickleness*; *irresponsibility*; *unprincipled conduct* **~̽streu** a *faithful, loyal, staunch* **~̽stüchtig** a *stalwart, staunch* ‖ ⟨dero⟩ *cringing, fawning, sycophantic, fickle*; ein ~er Mensch *an opportunist*, ⟨pol⟩ *a trimmer* **~stüchtigkeit** f *stalwartness* ‖ ⟨dero⟩ *opportunism*; *time-serving*; *trimming* **~sumschwung, ~swechsel** m *change of opinion* ‖ ⟨pol⟩ *volte-face*

Ge- ~̽s·ittet a *polished, refined, urbane* (*manners*) ‖ *civilized* (*condition, people*); *cultivated*; *well-bred, -mannered*; ~ m *to civilize, cultivate* **~s·ittung** f ~/~en *civilization, civilized condition*; *culture*; *cultivation* **~̽smokt** a → smoken °**~s·öff** n ~(e)s/ *slop, wash*; ⟨sl⟩ *tiff, swill*, ⟨Am⟩ *rotgut swill* **~̽s·ogen** pp v saugen **~̽s·onnen** a [pp v sinnen] [nur pred] ~ s z tun: *I intend* (od *propose*), *it is my intention to do*; *to have a mind, to be* (od *feel*) *disposed* (od *inclined, willing*) *to do*; ich bin nicht ~ *I do not intend* (od *propose*), *I am not inclined* (*to do*); *I'm not going* (*to pay more*) ‖ er ist anders ~ als du → gesinnt **~̽s·otten** pp v sieden **~̽sp·alten** a *cloven* (*hoof*); *split* ‖ *forked* (*tongue*) ‖ ⟨fig⟩ *divided* (*soul*) **~sp·an** [a:] m (in Ungarn) *the chief* od *head of a district* †**~sp·an** m = Gefährte, Genosse **~sp·ann** n ~(e)s/~e **1.** *team*; ein ~ Pferde *a t.* (⟨Am a.⟩ *a span*) *of horses*; in ~en *teamwise* ‖ ~führer [m] *teamster*; ~gefährte [m] *team mate* **2.** (Fuhrwerk) *horse*(*s*) *and carriage*; *turn-out*; ⟨Am⟩ *rig* **3.** ~fuhrwerk [n] *vehicle drawn by animals* **~̽sp·annt I.** [a] **A.** [attr] **1.** *tightly stretched*; *tense*; *tight*; *taut* (*muscle*); straff ~ *highly tensioned* (*rope*) **2.** ⟨übtr⟩ *intense, restless, tense* (*expectation*) ‖ *close* (*attention*); *intentness*; (*with close* od *rapt a.*); in ~ester Erwartung *on the tiptoe of expectation* **3.** ⟨fig⟩ *strained, tense*; ~es Verhältnis *tension*; ~e Verhältnisse *strained relations*; auf ~em Fuße → Fuß III. B. 2.; aufs äußerste ~e Nerven *nerves strained to breaking point* **B.** [pred] ich bin ~, ob .. *I am anxious to know if* .., *I wonder if* (od *whether*) .. ‖ ~ s auf *to be agog for* (*news*); *to be on edge for* (*a th*) ‖ aufs höchste ~ s vor Erwartung *to be on tiptoe with expectation* ‖ ~ vor *tense with* ‖ °ich bin ~ wie ein Regenschirm *or* Flitzebogen *I'm as keen as mustard, all keyed up* ‖ ~ w (of relations) *to become strained*; → Spannung **II.** [adv] *attentively*; *eagerly*; *with close attention*; (*to look*) *intently* (*at a th*); ~ beobachten *to watch* .. *intently*; ~ lauschen *to strain to listen* | **~̽heit** [f] ⟨übtr & fig⟩ *intentness*; *tenseness* ‖ *tension*; *strained relations* pl; → gespannt I. A. 3. **~sp·anschaft** [a:] f *district under the control of a* 'Gespan' **~spärre** n ⟨arch⟩ *rafters* pl **~sp·aße** n ~s/ *jesting, joking* **~̽'spaßig** a *funny* **~sp·eie** n ~s/ *spitting, vomiting* **~sp·enst** n ~es/~er **1.** *apparition, ghost, phantom, spectre*; *wraith*; ⟨hum⟩ *spook* ‖ an ~er glauben *to believe in ghosts*; v ~ern heimgesucht, verfolgt *haunted*; in dem Schlosse geht ein ~um *the castle is haunted* ‖ ⟨übtr⟩ er sieht aus wie ein ~ *he looks like a ghost* ‖ *phantom, phantasm*; ~er sehen *to see phantoms* **2.** ⟨fig⟩ *haunting fear*; *nightmare* (*of famine*); *spectre* **3.** [in comp] als Name f best. Tiere, → ~heuschrecke

Gesp·enster- [in comp] *spectral* **~erscheinung** f *apparition* **~furcht** f *fear of ghosts* **~geschichte** f *ghost-story* **~glaube** m *belief in ghosts* **~schiff** n *spectral ship* **~spuk** m *spookiness, spookery* **~-stunde** f *ghostly hour of midnight*

gesp·ensterartig, gesp·ensterhaft, gesp·enstig, gesp·enstisch a *spectre-like*; *spectral*; *ghostly* || ⟨fig⟩ *ghastly, lurid, unearthly*

Gesp·enst- ~heuschrecke f ⟨ent⟩ *spectre-insect, stick-insect* **~maki** m, **~tier** n ⟨zoo⟩ *spectre--lemur*; *tarsier*

Ge- ~sp·err n ⟨hunt⟩ *brood, covey* || ⟨tech⟩ = **~sp·erre** n ⟨tech⟩ *stop*; *locking-gear* **≚sperrt** a *barred, closed*; *shut* od *blocked* (*up*); ⟨typ⟩ *spaced*; ⟨com⟩ *blocked, frozen* (*account*); ⟨mil⟩ *out of bounds*, ⟨Am⟩ *off limits* **≚sp·ickt** a *larded meat*; ⟨fig⟩ *interlarded* (*with*) || gut ~ *well-lined* (*purse*) **~sp·iele** m ~n/~n **~sp·ielin** f ~/~nen *playmate* **≚sp·ien** pp v speien **~sp·inst** n ~es/~e **1.** *fabric*; *spun yarn*; Seiden≚ *spun silk*; → Kokon || loses ~ *rove*; Vor≚ *roving*; (Fasern) z ~en verarbeiten *to rove* || → Gewebe **2.** ⟨fig⟩ *web* (*a web of lies*) || → Hirn≚ | ~faser [f] *textile fibre* ~pflanze [f] *fibre-plant* **≚sp·onnen** a [pp v spinnen] *spun*; fein ~ ⟨a. fig⟩ *flimsy, tenuous* || ⟨prov⟩ es ist nichts so fein ~, es kommt doch an das Licht der Sonnen *truth will out* † **~spons** -ses/-se **1.** m = Bräutigam; Gatte **2.** n = Braut; Gattin **~-sp·ött** n ~(e)s/ *jeers* [pl], *jeerings* pl, *mockery* (über *of*), *mockeries* pl; *derision, ridicule* || sein ~ treiben mit jdm *to make a mockery of a p* || jdn z ~ m *to hold a p up* (od *to expose a p*) *to ridicule*; sich z ~ m *to make an exhibition of o.s. to be exposed to ridicule* || z ~ w *to become a laughing--stock* **~sp·öttel** n ~s/ *jeering, scoffing*; *railing* **~spr·äch** n ~(e)s/~e *conversation, talk*; *discourse*; → Unterhaltung; Zwiegespräch | Telefon≚ *c. by telephone* || ~ mit Gebühren ⟨telph⟩ *collect call* || R-~ *reversed call* || ein dienstliches, wissenschaftliches ~ *an official, scientific c.* || ins ~ eingeflochten *interlocutory* (*remark*) || es war das ~ der ganzen Stadt *it was the t. of the town* || ein ~ mit jdm anknüpfen, sich in ein ~ mit jdm einlassen *to enter into c.* (od *to argue*) *with a p* || ⟨telph⟩ ein ~ anmelden nach .. *to put a call through to ..* || das ~ bringen auf .. *to turn the c.n to .., to bring the c.n round to a th* || ein ~ führen mit *to have a t.* (od *c.n*) *with*; das ~ nicht versickern l *not to let the c.n flag* **≚spr·ächig** a *communicative, conversational, talkative*; (sehr ~) *voluble* || jdn ~ m *to lubricate a p's tongue*; *to draw a p out*; ~ w → aufgeschlossen, zugängig | ≚keit [f] ~/ *c.ness, t.-tiveness*; *volubility*

Gespr·ächs- ~basis f *basis of discussion* **~form** f *conversational form* || *interlocutory form* **~gegenstand** m *subject of conversation, topic* **~partner** m *interlocutor*; *telephonee* **~stoff** m *talking point(s)*; *conversation* (*his c. was limited*) || *topics* pl (*the t. of the day*) **~thema** n = -gegenstand; ein ~ h *to have sth to talk about* **~ton** m *conversational tone*; in gewöhnlichem ~ *in the tone of ordinary conversation* **≚weise** adv *in conversation* (od *talk*); *in the course of* (*the*) *conversation*; *conversationally*

Ge- ≚sprayt a ⟨cosm⟩ *sprayed* **≚spr·eizt** a **1.** mit ~en Beinen (*with legs*) *astride*; *straddle--legged*; *with legs straddling*; *unfolded* (Lafette) **2.** ⟨fig dero⟩ *bombastic, florid* (*language*), *pompous, stilted*; *turgid* (*style*); *sprawly* (*letters*) | ≚-heit [f] ~/~en ⟨fig⟩ *floridity, floridness*; *pomposity, stiltedness* **~spreng** n ~(e)s/~e *crowning* (*of a reredos*) **≚spr·enkelt** a *mottled* (*cloth*); *speckled, dappled, piebald* °**~spr·itze** n ~s/ *squirting, spouting* **~'spritzter** m [österr] *wine soda* **≚spr·ochen** a [pp v sprechen] *spoken* (*language*) **~spr·udel** n ~s/ *bubbling, spouting*; *sputter* **≚spr·ungen** a [pp v springen] *cracked* (*glass*) **~'spusi** n ⟨invar⟩ [österr] *love affair* **~st·ade** n ~s/ ⟨poet⟩ = Ufer, Küste

Gest·alt f ~/~en † **A.** [**abstr**] (Zustand; Art u Weise) *condition*; ⟨Am a.⟩ *shape* || *kind, manner, way* || nach ~ der Dinge *according to circumstances* || ⟨philos⟩ *configuration, gestalt* || solcher-≚ *in this way*; ⟨Am⟩ *in such shape* (*that* ..); → der≚ **B.** [**konkr**] **1.** (äußere ~) *outward form*; *shape*; *appearance*; → Form B. 1. || die ~ des Kopfes, Schiffes *the shape of the head, ship* || in menschlicher ~ *in human shape*; in der ~ v *in the shape* (od *guise*) *of ..* || in der ~ e-r Kugel *in the shape* (od *form*) *of a globe*; in ~ v 20 Mark *in the shape of 20 marks* || ⟨R. C.⟩ Abendmahl in beiderlei ~ *communion in both kinds* || ⟨übtr⟩ *form, frame* (*of a system*) | (Körper≚) *figure, stature*; e-e hohe, schlanke, schöne ~ *a tall, slim, handsome figure* || v imposanter ~ *of imposing stature*; v mittlerer ~ *of middle height*; er war v untersetzter ~ *in person, he had a dumpy figure* || → Figur I. A. 2. | feste ~ **annehmen** (of plans) *to take definite shape* || e-r S ~ geben *to give shape to a th*; *to put* (od *get*) *a th into shape* || ~ finden in *to find a shape in ..* **2.** (innere ~) ⟨philos⟩ (*characteristic*) *form*; *mould* **3.** (P) *figure*; eine der größten ~en s-r Zeit *one of the greatest figures of his age* || ⟨Lit⟩ *character*; ⟨arts⟩ Kinder~en [pl] *putti* [It pl] || geheimnisvolle ~en *mysterious shapes* pl **~psychologie** f *gestalt-ps.*

-gestalt [in comp] → Gestalt A.; Miß≚, Un≚

ge- ~st·alten vt [h] **1. a.** ⟨eig⟩ *to fashion* (aus *from, out of*; in *into*; nach *after*; z *to*); *to form* (nach *after, by, from, upon*; z *into*); (Garten, Stadt) *to model* (nach *after, on*); *to mould* (z *into, to*); *to shape*; im Bilde ~ *to figure* **b.** ⟨übtr⟩ (Charakter, Geist) *to form, mould* (nach dem Muster v *on*); (Gedanken) *to frame* (nach e-m Grundsatz *on a principle*); *to shape*; → formen || (Unternehmen) *to organize* || (e-e Lehre etc) *to construct* || (ein Kunstwerk) *to create* || s-e Geschicke nach eigenen Grundsätzen ~ *to work out one's destinies along one's own lines* || (Gegenstand) lebendig ~ *to vitalize* || e-e Rolle originell ~ *to create a part* || (Gegenstand) dramatisch ~ *to dramatize* **2. sich** ~ *to form, shape, frame* || (of events) *to go*; *to turn out* (f *to*); *to work out*, ⟨Am a.⟩ *to shape up* || es gestaltete sich z s-m Besten *it turned out to his best*; s-e Gesundheit gestaltet sich immer besser *his health is improving steadily* || (of a play) *to settle down* (*to one's satisfaction*) **~st·altend** a *constitutive, constructive, formative* (*energy*) **≚st·alter** m *designer*; *organizer*; *shaper*; Schaufenster~ *window-dresser* || ⟨arts & Lit⟩ *creator* || *constructor*; → Erbauer **~st·alterisch** a = gestaltend **~st·altet** a *fashioned, formed, modelled, moulded* || schön ~, wohl ~ *well--shaped, well-shapen* (*woman*); *well-made* (*th*) || bei so ~en Verhältnissen *under such circumstances* **~st·altig** a [in comp] → viel~ **~st·altlos** a *shapeless* || ⟨fig⟩ *vague* **≚st·altung** f ~/~en **1.** [abstr] *the fashioning, forming, moulding, shaping* || *formation* || bildliche ~ *figuration, representation* || ⟨arts & Lit, theat⟩ (of a part) *creation*; *production*; dramatische ~ *dramatization, dramatic representation* | (Art der ~) *arrangement*; *make-up* (S) || *formation*; *structure* (*of rocks*) || äußere ~ *configuration* (*of a room*) || planmäßige ~ *organization*; *scheme* **2.** [konkr] (Gestaltetes) *form* || *condition, state*

Gest·altungs- ~art f *style*; ~ im Wohnhausbau *style of domestic architecture* **≚fähig** a *shap(e)able*; *plastic* **~fähigkeit** f *plasticity* **~kraft** f *creative power* **~kunst** f *art of creation* **~prozeß** m *formative process* **~technik** f *method of design*

°**Ge- ~st·ammel** n ~s/ *stammering*; *stammers* pl; = Gestotter °**~st·ampfe** n ~s/ *stamping*; *stamps* pl **≚st·and** 1. & 3. sg pret v gestehen **~st·ände** n ~s/~ ⟨hunt⟩ *aerie, aery* (*of falcons, hawks*) **≚-st·anden** pp v stehen & gestehen **≚st·ändig** a *confessing*; ~ s *to confess, to make a confession*; → bekennen, eingestehen **~st·ändnis** n -nisses/-nisse *confession*; ein ∼ ablegen, erzwingen *to make, to force a confession*; → Zwangsmaßnahme ‖ (Eingeständnis) *admission* (*his a. about having heard* [.. gehört z h]); *avowal, confession* ‖ °zum ∼ zwiebeln ⟨Am sl⟩ *to sweat* **∼st·änge** n ∼s/∼ **1.** *poles, rods, rails, stakes* pl; *linkage* ⟨a. mot⟩ ‖ ⟨mech⟩ *leverage*; *system of levers* **2.** = Geweih **∼st·ank** m ∼(e)s/ *offensive smell*; *stench*; *reek* (*of the slums*); (stark) *stink* ‖ ⟨mil sl⟩ *niffy*

G·estapo [ɑː] f ⟨nazi⟩ (aus: *Ge*heime *Sta*atspolizei) *secret police*

Gestati·onsbericht m [österr] Geschäftsbericht

gest·atten vt [h] (formell = erlauben) **1.** etw ∼ *to allow* (od *admit, permit*) *a th*; ich gestatte k–n Skandal hier *I do not permit noise here*; Rauchen ist hier nicht gestattet *smoking is not allowed here* | **(S)** *to admit* (od *allow, permit*) *of a th*; die S gestattet k–n Verzug *the matter admits of no delay* ‖ soweit es die Gesundheit g. *so far as health permits*; nicht –tet *off-limits* (*area*) **2. jdm** ∼ z tun *or* ∼, daß jd tut, jdm etw ∼ *to allow* (od *permit*) *a p to do*; ich werde ihm nicht ∼ dorthinzugehen, ich werde nicht ∼, daß er dorthin geht *I shall not allow him to go there*; ich werde es ihm nicht ∼ *I shan't permit* (*him to do*) *it* ‖ ∼ Sie mir z bemerken *permit me to remark* | ⟨com⟩ ∼ Sie (mir) die Anfrage *I beg to ask you*; ∼ Sie mir, Ihnen mitzuteilen, *I beg to inform you* **gestattend** a *permissive* **Gest·attung** f *permission*

G·este f ∼/∼n *gesture*; e–e leere ∼ *an empty g.*; höfliche ∼ *act of courtesy*; e–e noble, vornehme ∼ *a generous g.*; nur die ∼ m v .. *to go through the motions of* ..

ge- ∼st·ehen vt [gestand/gestanden] [h] **1.** s–e Schuld (etc) ∼ *to confess* (⟨Am fam⟩ *to fess*) *one's fault*; alles ∼ ⟨Am⟩ *to come clear*; ∼, daß .. *to confess that* **2.** ⟨übtr⟩ ∼, daß .. *to admit* (jdm gegenüber *to a p*) od *own*, ⟨fam⟩ *confess that* ..; ich muß ∼, daß ich d–e Ansicht nicht teile *I must admit that I do not share your opinion*; ich gestehe, daß es wahr ist *I admit it to be true*; ich g., ich wunderte mich *I confess I was surprised* ‖ ich gestehe es getan z h *I admit* od *own doing* (od *having done*) *it*, *I confess to doing it* ‖ die Wahrheit z ∼, ich habe es vergessen *to tell the truth* (od *truth to tell*; *the truth is*) *I forgot about it*; offen gestanden *candidly, honestly* (*h., I forgot it*) **≃st·ehungskosten** pl ⟨com⟩ *cost price*; *prime* od *first cost*; *all-in cost*; *cost of production* **∼st·eigert** a *added* (*interest, solicitude*); *enhanced, intensified* **≃st·ein** n ⟨geol⟩ *rock* ‖ klastisches ∼ *clastic rock*; geschichtete ∼e *stratified rocks*, Sediment≃e *sedimentary rocks* pl ‖ Gang≃e *dyke rocks*; Tiefen≃e *plutonic rocks*; → Gabbro; Erguß≃, Eruptiv≃ ‖ Hohlraum im ∼ → Druse; taubes ∼ (z Ausfüllen der Hohlräume) *waste-rock*; *gob*(*bing*) ‖ → Mineralien **Gest·ein(s)-** [in comp] ⟨geol⟩ **∼art** f *type of rock* pl **∼bildung** f *the forming of rock* **∼formation** f *formation*; ∼, die v e–r darüberliegenden Schicht ganz bedeckt ist *inlier* **∼kunde** f *petrology*; *petrography* **∼magma** f *rock-magma* **∼masse** f *mass of rock*; *rock* **∼-schlacke** f *scoria* **∼schmelze** f *liquid rock* **∼schicht** f ⟨min⟩ *layer* **∼schutt** m *detritus* L **∼stücke** pl *fragments of rock*

Ge- ∼st·ell n ∼s/∼e **1.** (Ständer) *stand*; *stage*; *stillage*; (Bock≃) *trestle* ‖ Flaschen≃ *bin*; Wäschetrocken≃ *clothes-horse* ‖ *rack*; Futter≃ *rack for fodder*; *crib* | ⟨for⟩ *line, ride* **2.** (Gerippe) *frame* (*of an umbrella*); *framework*; *skeleton* (Stahl≃ *steel s.*) **3.** °⟨fig⟩ (P) dürres ∼ *skeleton*; sie ist das reinste ∼ *she is as thin as a hop-pole* **≃stellen** vt [h] ⟨cust⟩ (Koffer) *to present* **≃stellt** a: auf sich (selbst) ∼ (*to fight*) *independently*

Gest·ellung f ∼/ ⟨mil⟩ *reporting for service* ⟨cust⟩ *presentation* | **∼s- ∼befehl** m ⟨mil⟩ *induction order*; erhalten *to be ordered to report for service* **≃frei** a ⟨cust⟩ *exempt from presentation* **∼pflicht** f *obligation of pr.* **≃pflichtig** a *subject to pr.*

g·estern A. adv **1.** *yesterday* ‖ ∼ vor 8, 14 Tagen *yesterday week, yesterday fortnight* ‖ v ∼ *of yesterday* ‖ ∼ abend *yesterday evening*; *last night*; ⟨Scot⟩ *yestreen* ‖ ∼ früh *early yesterday* ‖ ∼ morgen *yesterday morning* **2.** v ∼ s *to be of yesterday*; ⟨fig⟩ *to be out of date* ‖ °ich bin nicht v ∼ *I am no fool, I know what's what, I wasn't born yesterday*; ⟨mar⟩ *I didn't come up in the last bucket* **B.** ≃ n *yesterday*; vergiß das leidige ≃ *forget the troubles of yesterday*

°**Ge- ∼st·ichel** n ∼s/ *gibing, girding, jeering, sneering*; *gibes* pl, *jeers* pl, *sneers* pl **≃st·iefelt** a *booted*; *in boots* ‖ ∼ u gespornt *booted and spurred*; → an∼ ‖ ⟨Lit⟩ der ≃e Kater *Puss in Boots* **≃st·ielt** a ⟨bot & zoo⟩ *stalked*

Gestikulati·on [ts] f ∼/∼en *gesticulation*; (etw) durch ∼en ausdrücken *to gesticulate* **gestikul·ieren** vi [h] *to gesticulate* **gestikul·ierend** a *gesticulatory*

ge- ∼st·immt a [pred] ∼ s auf *keyed to* (*a tone*); ⟨fig⟩ *to be attuned to* ‖ gut ∼, schlecht ∼ *good--tempered, bad-tempered* **≃st·irn** n ∼(e)s/∼e (Sternbild) *constellation* ‖ *star* | ∼höhe [f] *celestial altitude* | ∼kult [m] *star-worship*; *Sabaism* **∼st·irnt** a *starred*; ∼er Himmel *starry sky, spangled heavens* pl **∼st·oben** pp v stieben **≃st·öber** n ∼s/ Schnee≃ *flurry of snow*; *driving snow*; *snow-storm*; *squall* **∼st·ochen** a [pp v stechen] ⟨hunt⟩ [pred] (Gewehr) *on hair trigger*; ⟨phot⟩ ∼ scharf *needle sharp* **∼st·ohlen** pp v stehlen ‖ °der kann mir ∼ bleiben *I'll see him further first*; das kann mir ∼ bl. *I loathe it* °**≃st·öhn(e)** n ∼(e)s/ *groaning, moaning*; *groans* pl, *moans* pl °**≃st·olper** n ∼s/ *stumbling* **∼st·orben** pp v sterben ‖ tafelmäßig ≃e pl ⟨demog⟩ *death function* **∼st·ört** a → geistes∼ **∼st·oßen** a *pounded* (*sugar*) ‖ *abrupt, disconnected*; *staccato* (*tones*) °**≃st·otter** n ∼s/ *stuttering*; *stutters* pl; = Bestammel ˣ**∼st·owt** a ⟨cul⟩ *stewed* °**≃str·ampel** n ∼s/ *moving restlessly*; *fidgeting* (*with the legs*) **≃-str·äuch** n ∼(e)s/∼e *shrubbery*; *bushes* pl, *shrubs* pl **∼str·eckt** a; ∼ am Boden liegend *procumbent* **∼str·eift** a *striped* (*shirt*; *trousers*); *laid* (*paper*); *with* (*black and white*) *stripes* **∼str·eng** a **1.** = streng ‖ den ∼en V. herauskehren *to do the heavy father* ‖ ∼e Herren [pl] *harsh rulers* pl; ⟨fig⟩ die ≃en Herren *three usually cold days in May* (*11th–13th*) **2.** † (in Anrede) *gracious*; ∼ Herr! *Gracious Master*! *Your Worship*! **∼str·i-chelt** a *broken* (*line*); *shot*; *dashed* (*line*) **∼str·ichen** a [pp v streichen] **1.** *painted*; frisch ∼! (z Warnung) *wet paint*! **2.** ∼ voll *striked* (*measure*), *level* (*spoon*) ‖ ∼es Papier *glazed paper* **3.** ⟨typ⟩ *deleted*

g·estrig a *of yesterday, yesterday's* ‖ die ∼e Post, Zeitung *yesterday's post, paper* ‖ die ∼e Nacht *last night* ‖ den ganzen ∼en Tag *the whole of y.* | ⟨com⟩ unser ≃es *our letter of y.*

ge- ∼str·itten pp v streiten **≃str·üpp** n ∼(e)s/∼e *scrub, spinney*; *brake*; *copsewood, unterwood*; ⟨Am⟩ *brush*; ⟨fig⟩ *jungle* **≃st·ühl** n ⟨ec⟩ *pews* pl, *seats* pl ‖ (f Chorherren) *stalls* pl °**≃st·ümper** n ∼s/ *bungling*; *bungle* **∼st·unken** pp v stinken **≃st·üt** n ∼(e)s/∼e ⟨hors⟩ *stud* | ∼buch [n] *stud--book*; ∼hengst [m] *stud-horse*; *stallion*; ∼s-brandzeichen [n] *stud-brand*; ∼stute [f] *stud--mare* **≃s·uch** n ∼(e)s/∼e *application* (an jdn *to a p*; um etw *for a th*); auf das ∼ v *on the app. of* (*15th inst.*); ein ∼ bei jdm einreichen *to submit* od *file an app. with* od *to a p*; ein ∼ richten an *to make an app. to* (*a p*) ‖ (Bittschrift) *petition, formal request, suit* (an *to*); ein ∼ richten an *to petition* (*a court*) | ∼steller [m] *applicant*; *petitioner* **∼s·ucht A.** [a] **1.** ⟨com⟩ [nur pred] *in demand*; (sehr) ∼ s *to be in* (*great*) *demand*; nicht ∼ s (of stocks) *to be easy*; → begehrt, gefragt ‖ (in Inseraten) *wanted* ‖ v der Polizei ∼ *wanted by the* *police* **2.** ⟨übtr⟩ *required* (*quantity*) ‖ (weit hergeholt) *far-fetched* ‖ (wohl überlegt) *studied* (*politeness*) ‖ (geziert) *affected* **B.** [adv] ⟨übtr⟩ *studiedly* (*polite*) **|** ≃heit [f] ⟨übtr⟩ *studiedness* ‖ *affectation* **≃s·udel** n ~s/ *scrawl*(*ing*); *scribble, scribbling* ‖ → Sudelei °**≃s·umm(e), Ges·ums** n ~es/ *buzzing, humming*

ges·und A. [a] **1.** (Ggs krank) *healthy* (*p;body; appetite, mind, skin*); *ruddy* (*complexion*); *sound* (*heart, lungs*) ‖ geistig ~ *sane*; körperlich u geistig ~ *s. and h.*; der ~e Menschenverstand *common sense* ‖ ~ s *to be well* ‖ er ist (nicht) ~ *he is in good* (*bad*) *health*; dein Herz ist ganz ~ *your heart is perfectly sound*; sein ~er Arm (sc der andere ist verletzt) *his good arm*; ~ an Gliedern *sound in limb*; ~ aussehend *rosy about the gills*; ~ wie ein Fisch *as sound as a bell, as fit as a fiddle* ‖ frisch u ~ *hale*; ~ u munter *safe and sound* ‖ sich [acc] ~ erhalten *to keep fit*; wieder ~ w *to recover*; *to be restored to health* **|** **(S)** k–e ~e Situation *no wholesome sit.* **2. a.** (der Gesundheit dienlich) *healthy* (*mode of life*); *wholesome* (*food; climate, exercise, laugh*); Obst ist ~ *fruit is good for you*; *salubrious* (*air*) **b.** (moralisch~) *salutary* (*lesson*); *healthy, wholesome* ‖ das ist ihm ganz ~ *that will be a good lesson for him*; *that serves him right* **c.** °⟨fig com⟩ **sich ~ m** *to save one's* (⟨Am⟩ *to bring home the*) *bacon*; ⟨Am sl⟩ *to make it, to clean up*; sich ~ m an etw *to profit a good deal by a th* ‖ durch den Verkauf hätte er sich wieder ~ m können *the sale might have put him on his feet again* **3.** ⟨übtr⟩ (S) *sound* (*conditions, judgement, opinions*, etc.); *common-sense* (*judgement*) **B.** [adv] *healthily*; ~ leben *to live a healthy life* **Ges·und- ~beten** n *faith-healing* (od *care*) **~beter** m *faith-healer* **~brunnen** m = Heilquelle **ges·unden** vi [s] *to recover, recuperate*; *to recover* (od *regain*) *one's health* **Ges·undheit** f ~/ **1.** *health*; der ~ dienlich *wholesome, salubrious* ‖ körperliche u geistige ~ *h. of body and mind* ‖ geistige ~ *sanity* ‖ gute ~ *soundness of h., good* (od *sound*) *h.*; ⟨mil & sport⟩ *fitness*; bei guter ~ *in good h.*; bei bester ~ *in the best* (od *pink*) *of h.*; *alive and kicking* ‖ aus Rücksicht auf die ~, ≃shalber *for the sake of h.* ‖ wie steht es mit der ~? *how is your h.*? er ist die verkörperte ~ *he looks the very picture of h.*; es geht mit s–r ~ abwärts *his h. is failing* ‖ → angreifen I. B. 3.; wüsten **2.** *wholesomeness* (*of food*); *salubrity* ‖ *soundness* (*of conditions, opinions*, etc.) **3.** auf Ihre ~! *your health*! auf jds ~ trinken *to drink a p's health* ‖ viele ~en ausbringen *to propose many toasts* ‖ ⟨Ger⟩ (beim Niesen) (zur) ~! *God bless you*! **|** **≃lich 1.** [a] *sanitary*; ~er Schaden *injury to h.*; ~er Zustand *physical condition*; *state of h.* (*of a p*); *sanitary conditions* pl (*of a country*); in ~er Hinsicht *sanitarily*; ~e Überwachung *sanitation* **2.** [adv] *sanitarily*

Ges·undheits- [in comp] *sanitary* **~amt** n *sanitary board*; ⟨Ger hist⟩ Reichs≃, etc *Public Health Administration* **~apostel** m = –prediger **~appell** m ⟨mil⟩ *physical inspection* **~attest** n *certificate of h.* ‖ ⟨mil⟩ *c. of fitness* **~behörde** f *board of public h.* **~beratungsstelle** f *h. unit* **~buch** n ⟨mil⟩ *h. record book* **~dienst** m (staatl.) *National H. Service*; *socialized medicine* **~fanatiker** m *h. faddist* **≃fördernd** a *healthy, wholesome* **≃gemäß 1.** [a] ~e Lebensweise *regimen* **2.** [adv] ~ leben *to live a h.y life* **~lehre** f *hygiene, hygienics* pl **~minister** m ⟨engl⟩ *M. of H.* **~ministerium** n ⟨engl⟩ *Ministry of H.* **~nachweis** m *credentials of good h.* **~paß** m ⟨mar⟩ *bill of h.* (*clean, foul B. H.*) **~pflege** f *sanitation*; Öffentl. ~ *H. Public Welfare*; → –wesen **~polizei** f *sanitary police* **~prediger** m *sanitarian* **~problem** n *public h. pr.* **~regel** f *rule of h.* (od *diet*) **~rücksichten** f pl: aus ~ *for reasons* (od *for the sake*) *of h.* **≃schädlich** a *insanitary, unh.y* (*place*), *unwholesome* (*climate*) **~schutz** m bei der Arbeit *industrial hygiene* **~vorschriften** f pl *sanitary regulations* pl **~wesen** n *sanitation*; *public hygiene* od *health* **~zeugnis** n = –attest **~zustand** m = gesundheitlicher Zust.

Ge- ~s·undung f ~/ *recovery, recuperation* **≃s·ungen** pp v singen **≃s·unken** pp v sinken **~-t·äfel** n ~s/ *wainscot*; *inlaying, panelling* **≃t·an** a [pp v tun] gesagt, ~ *so said so done* ‖ nach ~er Arbeit *when work is finished*; *after work* **~t·ändel** n ~s/ *dalliance, flirting, philandering, toying*; *trifling* **≃t·eilt** a *divided*; *split* ‖ *shared* (*joys*) **~t·ier** n ~(e)s/ *animals* pl; *animal kingdom* ‖ (schädliches) *vermin* **≃t·igert** a *brindled, streaked*; *striped* (*like a tiger*) ‖ ~e Katze *tabby*; *tabby cat* ‖ → geflammt °**~t·ön** n ~(e)s/ *ringing, sounding, clanging, clangour* **≃t·önt** a *coloured, tinted* (*paper*); leicht ~ *off-white* **~t·ose, ~t·öse** n ~s/ *confused noise*; *din*; (Kriegs≃) *hubbub*; *racket*; *thud*; *crash, peal* (*of thunder*); *uproar* °**~tr·abe** n ~s/ *trotting* **≃tragen** a ⟨mus⟩ *slow*(*ly*) °**~tr·ampel** n ~s/ *stamping, trampling*; *tramples* pl **~-tr·änk** n ~(e)s/~e *drink* (weich *soft*, hart *hard*); *beverage*; (of medicine *or* poison) *potion* ‖ destilliertes ~ *liquor* ‖ geistige ~e [pl] *spirits* pl, *spirituous liquors* pl ‖ alkoholfreies ~ *soft drink*; starkes ~ *strong drink* ‖ kl „~efabrik" [f] (Automat) *flomatic drink dispenser*, ~eindustrie [f] *b. industries* pl; ~karte [f] *price-list*; ~steuer [f] *b. tax* **~tr·appel** n ~s/ *tripping, trotting*; *tramping, tramp-tramp, pit-a-pat*; Pferde≃ *chop-clop* °**~tr·atsch(e)** n ~es/ *silly talk*; *gossip*, ⟨fam⟩ *jaw*; → Geseich, Geseire, Gewäsch **~tr·auen** vrefl [h] sich ~ z tun: ich getraue mich (*or* mir), es z tun *I dare do it, I venture to do it*; ich getraue mich (mir) nicht, es z tun *I dared* (od *durst*) *not do it, I did not dare* (od *venture*) *to do it* ‖ ich hätte mich (mir) nicht getraut .. *I dare not have done it* **|** ich getraue mich (!) nicht hinaus *I dare not go out* ‖ ich getraute mir (!) das nicht *I did not dare* (od *risk venture*) *it* ‖ → erdreisten *°**~tr·eibe** n ~s/ *bustle* (*of life*)

Getr·eide n *corn*; ⟨bes Am⟩ *grain* ‖ [in comp] (→ a. Korn–) *corn* ..; *grain* .. **~älchen** n Gruppe der ~ = Fadenwürmer **≃arm** a *lacking* (od *poor*) *in corn* **~art** f *kind* (od *sort*) *of corn* ‖ ~en [pl] *cereals* pl **~bau** m *cultivation of corn*; *corn--growing* **~boden** m = –land **~börse** f *corn-exchange* **~brand** m ⟨bot⟩ *smut*; → Brand **~ernte** f *corn-harvest* **~feld** n *corn-field, field of corn* **~handel** m *corn-trade* **~kleinhändler** m *corn-chandler* **~kümmel** m ⟨Ger⟩ *spirituous liquor from corn* **~lager** n *silo* **~land** n *corn-land* **~laubkäfer** m ⟨ent⟩ *corn-weevil* **~magazin** n *granary* **~mähmaschine** f *corn-cutter* **~makler** m *corn-factor*; ⟨Am⟩ *grain-broker* **~mangel** m *shortage of corn* **~mehl** n *corn-flour* **~motte** f ⟨ent⟩ *corn-moth* **~pflanzen** f pl *cereals* pl **≃reich** a *rich in corn* **~speicher** m *granary*; *silo* **~sperre** f *embargo on export of corn* **~trockenanlage** f *grain-drying plant* **~wucher** m *profiteering in corn* **~wurm** m ⟨ent⟩ *corn-moth* **~zins** m *corn-rent* **~zoll** m *corn-duty*

getr·ennt a *separate* (*parts*); ~ v *separate from*; ⟨jur⟩ *seperated* (Ehegatten *couple*[*s*]); ~ leben *to live separate*; ~ schlafen (of parents) *to occupy separate bedrooms* **≃leben** n (of married persons) ⟨jur⟩ *separation*

getr·eu 1. [a] = treu **a.** ein ~er Diener *a faithful* (od *trusty*) *servant* ‖ ⟨Ger hist⟩ der ~e Eckart *the faithful Eckhardt*; ⟨engl⟩ *St. George* **|** ⟨fig⟩ *accurate, close, faithful* (*translation*), *true* (*copy*) **b.** [pred] ~ s–m König *true to his king* ‖ s–n Grundsätzen ~ (*or* ~ s–n G.) *true to his principles* **2.** [adv] *faithfully*; *truly* **3.** ≃e [der ≃e, ein ≃er] *the trusty follower*; *henchman*; s–e ≃en ⟨Am pol⟩ *his henchmen* **|** **~lich** adv *faithfully, loyally, truly*

Getr·iebe n ~s/~ **1.** ⟨tech⟩ (Zahntrieb) *gear unit*; (Triebwerk) *drive mechanism*; hydraulisches ~ ⟨mot⟩ *fluid drive*; Reduktions≃ *speed reducer*; Reib≃ *friction-gear*; synchronisiertes ≃ *syncro-mesh gear*; Zahnrad≃ *gearing* (~ mit Außenverzahnung *external g.*, mit Innen- *internal g.*) ‖ *works* pl (*of a watch*) **2.** ⟨übtr⟩ *machinery* (*of the state*); *mechanism, workings* pl (*of a system*) ‖ *bustle*; *hurly-burly*; *hurry and bustle* (*of the City*) **~bremse** f *gear brake* **~fett** n *glar grease* **~lehre** f *kinematics* pl [sg konstr] **~motor** m *geared m.* **~turbine** f *geared turbine*

ge- ~tr·ieben a [pp v treiben] ⟨arts⟩ ~e Arbeit *embossed work*; Kunst der ~en A. *empaestic art*; mit ~er A. geschmückt *chased* (*metal*); *raised* (*gold*) °≃**tr·ippel** n ~s/ *tripping*; *pit-a-pat* °≃**tr·ödel** n ~s/ *dawdling, loitering* **~tr·offen** a [pp treffen] sich ~ fühlen *to find that the cap fits*; *to stand abashed*; er fühlte sich ~ *they had caught him, he was caught*; *he looked offended* ‖ ⟨phot⟩ gut ~ *come out well* **~tr·ost 1.** [a, mst pred] *confident*; *courageous* ‖ sei ~ *be of good hope, cheer up* ‖ °du bist wohl nicht (recht) ~ *you seem to have taken leave of your senses*; *you are mad* **2.** [adv] *confidently*; *safely* ‖ Sie können ihm ~ glauben *you are safe in trusting him* ‖ das kannst du ~ tun *that you can well do*; *you can do that without hesitation* †**~tr·östen** vrefl [h] ⟨bibl⟩ sich ~ *to hope confidently* (od *patiently*); *to be confident* ‖ sich e–r S ~ *to trust in a th*; *to expect a th confidently* **~tr·übt** a *muddy, turbid* ‖ ⟨fig⟩ *clouded, cloudy* (v *with*); *darkened* (durch *by*); nicht ~ *unshadowed* (*by*) **~tr·unken** pp v trinken

G·etter m, n ~s/~ (Fangstoff) *getter*

G·etto n ~s/~s *ghetto* [It], *Jews' quarter*

°**Ge- ~t·ue** n ~s/ *ado*; *circumstance* (*without c.*); *fuss* ‖ *affectation* (*this is mere a.*), *affectedness* ‖ vornehmes ~ *airs* (*and graces*) ‖ *farce, pretence*; kein leeres ~ mit *no great pretence of* (*historical accuracy*) ‖ schmeichlerisches ~ ⟨Am sl⟩ *ballyhoo* **~t·ümmel** n ~s/ *bustle*; *hurly-burly*; *turmoil*; *uproar, tumult*; → Gewimmel, Gewirr ≃**t·üpfelt** a *dotted, speckled, spotted* **~t·uschel** n (–flüster) ⟨Am⟩ *grapevine* °**~t·ute** n ~s/ *tooting, tootling*

ge·übt a *experienced, practised* (*orator*), *skilled* (*artist*); *scientific* (*boxer*); *knowing* (*with a k. hand*) ‖ ~ in *versed* (od *practised, skilled*) *in* | ≃**heit** f ~/ *experience, skill*

Gev·atter m ~s/~ ⟨poet⟩ **1.** = Pate **2.** (in Anrede) *gaffer*; ⟨dial⟩ *neighbour* **3.** ⟨dero⟩ = Spießbürger ‖ ~ Schneider u Handschuhmacher *tradesfolk, tradespeople* | **~in** f ~/~nen = Patin; ⟨fam⟩ *gammer* **~schaft** f = Patenschaft **~schnaus** m *christening-feast*

gev·iert 1. [a] *quartered, squared*; *square* ‖ ⟨her⟩ *quartered* (*shield*) **2.** ≃ n ~s/~e *square*; 3 Fuß im ~ *three feet square* ‖ ⟨her⟩ *quarter*; die 4 ~e *the four quarters* [pl] (sc: *dexter chief*; *sinister chief*; *dexter base*; *sinister base*) ‖ ⟨typ⟩ *em* (*a page of 24 ems*) **~eilt** a *quartered* ≃**fuß** m *square foot* ≃**maß** n *square measure* | ≃**schein** m ⟨astr⟩ *quartile aspect*

Gew·ächs n –ses/–se **1.** ⟨bot⟩ *growth* (*this tree is a miraculous g.*); *product*; die Tomaten sind fremdes ~ *the tomatoes are of foreign growth*; → Kraut, Pflanze ‖ Weine v edelstem ~ *first growth wines*; → Jahrgang ‖ ausländisches ~ *exotic plant*; *exotic* | ⟨fig⟩ dies ist nicht Ihr eigenes ~ *this is not of your own growth* **2.** ⟨path⟩ *excrescence, growth, wen*; → Geschwulst **~haus** n ⟨hort⟩ *greenhouse, conservatory* ‖ *hothouse*

ge- ~w·achsen a [pp v wachsen] *grown* (*soil*) ‖ ⟨fig⟩ jdm (nicht) ~ s (*not*) *to be up to a p*; er ist dir nicht ~ *he is no match for you*; *you are too much for him* ‖ e–r S (nicht) ~ s (*not*) *to be up to a th*; e–m Posten ~ s *to be adequate to a post, to fill a post*; der Aufgabe (nicht) ~ s *to be* (*un*)*equal to the task*; *to be found wanting to one's t.*; der Lage war er nicht ~ *the situation was beyond* (od *out of*) *his depth* ‖ sich jdm, e–r S ~ zeigen *to cope with a p, a th*; *to rise to* (*the occasion*) **~w·agt** a *bold* (*step*); *hazardous, risky* (*experiment*); *off-colo*(*u*)*r* (*remark*); ~e S (*it was*) *touch-and-go* ≃**waff** n ~(e)s/~e ⟨hunt⟩ (*boar's*) *tushes* **~w·ählt** a *elegant* (*style*) ‖ gut ~ *well-chosen*; *felicitous* (*expression*) ‖ sich ~ ausdrücken *to use genteelisms* **~w·ahr** a [pred] e–r S (*or* e–e S) ~ w *to become aware of* (od *alive to*) *a th*; ⟨Am⟩ *to get wise to a th* ‖ *to notice*, → bemerken, entdecken, erkennen ‖ °etw ~ w *to notice a th*; ~ w, daß .. *to n. that* ≃**w·ähr** f ~/ *guaranty, guarantee* (f *for*), *security* (*for*) ‖ ohne ~ *without guarantee*; *subject to correction* ⟨jur⟩ (f Sachmängel) *as is* ‖ ~ leisten f etw, die ~ übernehmen f etw = gewährleisten ‖ → Garantie, Sicherheit; Bürgschaft ‖ wir müssen die ~ h, daß .. *we must have the guaranty* | ~klassen [pl] *grade standards* **~w·ahren** vt [h] (gewählt f beobachten) *to notice, observe, perceive, descry* **~w·ähren** vt [h] **1.** (P) (Bitte, Frist) *to grant*; Rabatt ~ *to allow a discount* ‖ jdm etw ~ *to grant* (od *allow, yield*; ⟨liter⟩ *accord*) *a p a th* (od *a th to a p*) ‖ jdm e–e Bitte ~ *to grant a p's request*; jdm e–n Wunsch ~ *to fulfil a p's desire* ‖ jdm 200 Mark monatlich ~ *to allow a p 200 marks a month* ‖ jdm Schutz, Zuflucht ~ *to give shelter* od *protection to a p*; *to shelter* od *protect a p* ‖ jdm gütigst e–e Unterredung ~ *to vouchsafe a p an interview* ‖ → bewilligen **b.** (S) *to afford* (*the tree affords a pleasant shade*); *to offer*; die Bestimmung gewährt uns viele Vorteile *the decree offers us many advantages* **2.** jdn ~ l *to give a p rope*; *to give a p his head*; *to let a p have his own way*; laß ihn ~ *let him* (*do as he likes*) ‖ = jdn in Ruhe l **3.** Erziehung des ≃**währenlassens** *nonfrustration*; E. d. Nicht~ *frustration*

gew·ähr- ~leisten vt [h] (etw) *to en-, in-, assure*; *guarantee, warrant* (*a th*); *to vouch for* (*a th*); ~, daß .. *to guarantee* od *warrant that ..*; ~, daß etw echt ist *to w. a th genuine* ‖ jdm etw ~ *to guarantee a p a th* (od *a th to a p*); jedem B. wird A. –stet *every citizen is guaranteed work* ≃**leister** m *guarantee, guarantor* ≃**leistung** f *guaranty, guarantee* (f etw *of* od *for a th*) ‖ ⟨jur⟩ *warranty*; ~ f Rechtsmängel *warrant of title*

Gew·ahrsam m ~s/ **1.** *care, charge*; *safe keeping*; etw in ~ h *to be in charge of a th, to have the care of a th*; *to have a th in safe keeping*; etw in ~ nehmen *to take charge of a th* **2.** ⟨jur⟩ *custody*; *imprisonment*; sicheres ~ *safe keeping* (od *custody*) ‖ (Ort des ~s) *lock-up* ‖ (jdn) in ~ halten ⟨Am⟩ *to hold* ‖ jdn in ~ nehmen *to take a p into custody, to arrest* od *imprison a p* ‖ sich in polizeilichem *or* sicherem ~ befinden *to be in safe keeping* **Gew·ährs- ~mann** m *authority*; Beda ist ~ dafür, daß .. *we have it on the authority of Bede that* (*the Anglo-Saxons ..*) ‖ (f Gerücht etc) *informant* (*my i. is ..*) **~leute** pl ⟨a.⟩ *brain*(*s*) *trust*; (f „Briefkasten" e–r Zeitung) *brains trust* **Gew·ährung** f ~/~en *grant*; *the granting* (*of a request*); *allowing* (*of a discount*); *fulfilment* (*of a desire*); er erreichte die ~ s–s Wunsches *his desire was fulfilled*

Gew·alt f ~/~en **A. 1.** (Macht, Herrschaft) *power* (über *over*; *of*); *command* (*of*), *control* (*of*), *dominion* (*over*); *grip* (*on*), *hold, influence, mastery, sway* (*over*) ‖ ~ über Leben u Tod *power over life and death* ‖ **höhere** ~ *Act of God*; *force majeure* Fr; *vis major* L (a. Krieg, Streik etc) ‖ die höheren ~en *the higher powers* ‖ ausübende ~ (im Staate) *executive*; Ausübung öffentl. ~ *exercise of public authority*; gesetzgebende ~ *legislature*; gesetzmäßige ~ *authority*; höchste ~ *supremacy* (über *over*); souveräne ~ *sovereignty*; ⟨Am⟩ (über Land) *Eminent Domain* ‖ elterliche, väterliche ~ *parental, fatherly authority* **2.** (Kraft) *force*; *might*; *power* (*of the waves*; *of eloquence, passion*); die ~ des Windes *the violence of the wind*; Natur≃en [pl] *natural forces* pl ‖ die ~ (etw) z tun *the power to do* (*a th*); mit nackter ~ *by sheer force* **3.** (unrechtmäßige ~) *force, violence*; brutale ~ *brute* (od *brutal*) *force* **B. 1.** jdm, e–r S ~ **antun** *to do violence to a p, a th*; *to offend against a th*; *to outrage a th*; → vergewaltigen; (dem Sinn) ~ antun *to distort, pervert*; ohne der S ~ -zu- *fairly*; **sich** [dat] ~ antun *to lay hands on o.s.* ‖ ~ anwenden *to employ force*; *to use violence*; brachiale ~ anw. *to use the strong arm*, ⟨Am fam⟩ *to slug it out*; *to strong-arm* ‖ ~ erleiden müssen *to be exposed to violence* ‖ ~**geht** vor Recht *might makes* (od *is*) *right* ‖ ~ h über jdn, etw *to have authority* (od *power*) *over*; *to control, sway a p, a th*; darüber h wir k–e ~, das entzieht sich unserer ~ *that is beyond our control* ‖ die ~ verlieren über *to lose control of* (*o.s.*); .. *one's grip on* (*a p*) ‖ der ~ weichen *to yield to force* **2. durch** bloße ~ *by sheer force* **|** (Land) wirtschaftlich ganz **in** s–e ~ bek *to obtain an economic hold on a country* ‖ **in** s–e ~ bringen *to bring under one's sway*; *to conquer, subdue*; (jdn) *to overrule, overwhelm* ‖ in jds ~ geraten *to fall into a p's grip* ‖ (jdn) in der ~ h *to have a p in one's power* (od *in one's pocket, in tow*; ⟨sl⟩ *on toast*); *to have a grip on a p*; → beherrschen ‖ sie hat ihn ganz in ihrer ~ *she runs him all right* ‖ die Furcht hatte ihn in ihrer ~ *fear had him in its grip* ‖ **sich in der ~ h** *to keep o.s. under control*; *to have command of o.s.*, .. ganz .. *to be completely self-possessed* ‖ in der ~ jds (e–r S) s *to be in the power* (od *grip*) *of a p* (*a th*); *to be at the mercy of a p* ‖ in jds ~ stehen *to be in a p's power* (*to do*) **| mit** (roher) ~ *by* (*sheer*) *force*; *forcibly*; *by foul means*; *with violence*; (etw) mit ~ erzwingen *to force* (*an entry*; *a confession*); (Tür) mit ~ öffnen *to force open*; mit offener ~ *by open force* ‖ mit (aller) ~ *with all one's might, with might and main*; ⟨fig⟩ *by hook or by crook, at all costs*; *absolutely*; er wollte mit aller ~ hinein *he insisted* (od *was very keen*) *on getting in*; er wollte mit ~ nichts davon wissen *he refused to hear of it* ‖ es wird mit ~ Winter *winter sets in with great severity* **| unter** der ~ stehen v *to be in the power* (od *under the heel*) *of* .. ‖ unter Androhung v ~ *under the threat of violence* **~akt** m = -tat **~friede** m *peace dictated by armed force* **~haber** m = Machthaber **~herrschaft** f *despotism*; *tyranny* **~herrscher** m *despot*; *tyrant* **~-losigkeit** f *non-violence* **~marsch** m *forced march* **~maßregel** f *violent* od *strong measure*, ⟨Am sl⟩ *strong-arm method* **~mensch** m *brute*; *rowdy* **~streich** m *coup de main* [Fr]; ⟨pol⟩ *coup d'état* [Fr] **~tat** f *act of violence*; (*act of*) *outrage* (an on); *foul play*; ~en [pl] (*acts of*) *violence* **≃tätig** a *violent* (*methods*), *outrageous* (*crime*) ‖ *brutal*; ~er Mensch *brute*; *man of brutal instincts* **~tätigkeit** f *violence*, (*act of*) *outrage* **~verbrecher** m *violent criminal*; *gangster, racketeer*; *thug*; *cut-throat*

Gew·altenteilung f (im Staate) *sharing of power*; *distribution of the functions of power*
gew·altig A. [a] **1.** (mächtig) *violent* (*blow*); *vehement* (*desire*); die ~e Hand Gottes *the almighty power of God*; *powerful* (*ruler*); = mächtig **2.** ⟨übtr⟩ **a.** (heftig) *violent* (gale); *vehement* (*wind*) **b.** (ungeheuer) *enormous, huge, immense, mighty, portentous, prodigious, tremendous* (*building, rock*; ⟨a. übtr⟩ *cold, delight, strength*); *vast* (*quantities*; *sum of money*); *stupendous* (*height*); *mammoth* (*shoulders*) **c.** *violent* (*blow*; *efforts*) ‖ *egregious, stupendous, tremendous*; *vast* (*difference*); *powerful* (*voice*) ‖ ⟨fam⟩ *roaring*; *thundering* (*mistake*); *thumping*, ⟨sl⟩ *whacking* (*lie*) ‖ → enorm, riesig **B.** [adv] **1.** [vor Adj.] *enormously* (*rich*); *immensely, stupendously, tremendously* ‖ ⟨fam⟩ *thumping* (*great*); *whacking* (*big* [*horse*]); *mighty* (*interesting*) **2.** °da irrst du dich ~ *you are very much mistaken*, .. *wide* od *quite off the mark*; (jdn) ~ loben *to praise hugely* ‖ *with a vengeance*; er schlug ~ um sich *he laid about him hammer and tongs* ‖ ⟨fam⟩ *smartish* (*it hurt s.*) ‖ ⟨Am fam⟩ *plenty* **C.** [abs] die ≃en *the rulers*; *magnates* [pl] ‖ etw ≃es ⟨fam⟩ *a thumper* **gew·altsam 1.** [a] *forcible* (*entry*); *high-handed* (*ruler*); (*reconnaissance*) *in force*; *violent* (*deed*); ~er Tod *violent* od *unnatural death* (~en Todes sterben *to die a v. d.*) **2.** [adv] *by* (*sheer*) *force*; *forcibly*; *with violence* ‖ ~ in Besitz nehmen *to usurp* (*the throne*) ‖ (jdn) ~ entführen *to kidnap*; (Frau) *to ravish* (*away*) ‖ (etw) ~ erzwingen *to force* (*an entry*) ‖ (Türe) ~ öffnen *to force open* **| ≃keit** f *forcibleness*; *violence*; *violent deed*

gew·alzt a *rolled* (*plate*; *wire*)
Gew·and n ~(e)s/≃er **1.** ⟨eig⟩ *garb* (*in the g. of* ..); *garment* ‖ (Damen≃) *dress*; (langes, in e–m Stück) *robe*; (lose fallendes) *gown* **|** (amtl. ~) *gown*; *robe*; akademische ≃er *academic robes* pl ‖ ⟨ec⟩ *vestment*; Meß≃ *chasuble* ‖ im schlichten ~ des Bürgers *in civvies* pl **|** ⟨arts⟩ malerische Anordnung v ≃ern *drapery* **2.** ⟨fig⟩ *attire, dress, garb, garment*; der Erde grünes ~ *the earth's garment of green*; Frühlings≃ *spring-dress*; *attire of spring* ‖ *guise* (*in new g.*); *get-up* (*of a book*) **~haus** n ⟨engl⟩ *Clothworkers' Hall* ‖ ⟨Ger⟩ (z Leipzig) *Gewandhaus*; ~konzerte [pl] *G.-concerts* pl **~meister** m ⟨film⟩ *costume expert* **~nadel, ~schließe** f ⟨bes praeh⟩ *clasp* **~ung** f ~/~en *drapery*
Gew·ände n ~s/~ ⟨arch⟩ *jamb door-post*(*s*) **~säule** f *jamb*(*-shaft*)
gew·andt 1. [a] *deft, lissom, nimble, quick*; *adroit* (*workman*); *clever* (*diplomatist, player*) ‖ *fluent* (*orator*); *apt*; *ready, versatile* (*writer*); *smart* (*businessman*), *businesslike* ‖ rede~ *glib, voluble*; ein in allen Dingen ~er Mann *an all-round man*; → geschickt; geübt **|** ~es Auftreten, ~e Umgangsformen *good manners* pl (od *breeding*) ‖ *polished, urbane*; *elegant* (*style*) **2.** [adv] *adroitly*; *cleverly*; *readily* **| ≃heit** f *deftness, nimbleness* ‖ *adroitness*; *address*; *cleverness*; *readiness*; *versatility*; *facility* ‖ ~ im Auftreten *good manners* pl
gew·ann [1. & **3.** pret] v gewinnen **Gew·ann(e)** n ~(e)s/~e ⟨agr⟩ *square plot*; *strip of land*
gew·ärtig a [nur pred] e–r S ~ s *to be expectant of a th, to expect a th*; *to be prepared* (od *ready*) *for a th*; er muß ~ s, daß er .. *he has to reckon with being dismissed* **| ~en** vt [h] etw z ~ h *to have to reckon with a th*; *to have to face* od *encounter a th*; schwere Bestrafung z ~ h *to incur severe punishment*; wir werden Schwierigkeiten z ~ h *we must be prepared for difficulties*; du wirst Strafe z ~ h *you'll be in for it* ‖ → gewärtig s
°**Gew·äsch** n ~(e)s/ *chatter*; *jabber*; *palaver, rant, twaddle*; leeres ~ *flummery, slip-slop, wish-wash, talkee-talkee*; ⟨sl⟩ *eye-wash*; ⟨Am sl⟩ *fluff*
Gew·ässer n ~s/~: das ~, die ~ [pl] *the waters* pl (*of a lake*, etc.); die Quell≃, Einzugs≃ *the head-waters* pl; Kampf um ~ *combat at river lines, r. crossing operations* **~kunde** f *hydrography* **~schutz** m *pollution control* od *abatement*
gew·ässert a *watered* (*wine*) ‖ *watered* (*silk*); *moiré, chiné* [Fr]; ~er Stoff *moire* (!) [Fr]
Gew·ebe n ~s/~ **1.** *woven fabric*; *textile*; *web, weft* ‖ *stuff* ‖ Leinen≃ *linen fabric*; Woll≃ *woollen fabric* ‖ sehr dünnes ~ *cobweb*; feines ~ *tissue* **|** (Webart) *fabric, texture*; feines ~ *fine texture*, grobes ~ *coarse t.* ‖ → Kett-, Schußfäden; Spinn≃ **2.** ⟨anat & biol⟩ *tissue*; Zell≃ *cellular tissue, cell-tissue* ‖ ⟨bot⟩ Bildungs≃, Teilungs≃ *meristem* [Gr] **3.** ⟨fig⟩ verschlungenes ~ *warp and woof* ‖ Lügen≃ *web* (od *tissue*) *of*

lies; ∼ v Lüge u Verleumdungen *web of lies and calumnies* **~einlage** f ⟨mot⟩ (Reifen≃) *plies* pl *of fabric* **~inkrustierung** f *loading of fabrics* **~papier** n *reinforced paper* **~(strahlungs)dosis** f ⟨at⟩ *tissue dose* **~schaden** m *t. injury*

Gewebs- [in comp] ⟨biol⟩ *histo–* **~lehre** f *histology* **~tod** m; lokaler ∼ *gangrene, necrosis* [Gr] **~trennung** f spaltförmige ∼ *fissure* **~zerfall** m *histolysis* [Gr]

gew·ebt a *woven* (*fabric*); → weben

gew·eckt a ⟨fig⟩ *alert, clever, quick-witted*; *bright*; *sharp, shrewd, smart*; ganz ∼ s ⟨sl⟩ *to be all there*; er ist ein ∼er Bursche *his head is screwed on the right way*

Gew·ehr n ∼(e)s/∼e **A.** ⟨mil⟩ **1.** *rifle*; (*hand-*) *gun*; → Büchse; Flinte; Maschinen≃ ‖ † (frühere Arten:) *musket*; *firelock*; → Muskete, Steinschloß≃ ‖ → Feuerwaffe; Seiten≃; Waffe **2. a.** ein ∼ anlegen, sichern *to level, to secure a rifle* ‖ ∼e schultern *to shoulder arms*; ∼e rechts am Riemen tragen *to trail arms*; ∼e zus–stellen, zus–setzen *to pile arms* ‖ dieses Bataillon zählt 800 ∼e *this battalion has a strenght of 800 men* ‖ ∼ bei Fuß stehen *to stand at ease*; ⟨fig⟩ *to wait and see* **b. an** die ∼e! (⟨mil a.⟩ ins ∼!) *to arms! stand to!*; ⟨fig⟩ *now for it!* ‖ das ∼ **über**! 1. *shoulder arms!* 2. *slope arms!* ‖ °⟨fig⟩ mit ∼ über ⟨sex⟩ *hard-on* ‖ ∼ **ab**! ∼ bei Fuß! *order arms!* ‖ präsentiert das ∼! *present arms!* **B.** ⟨hunt⟩ *fangs* pl (*of a wild boar*) **~fabrik** f *rifle-factory*; *small--arms factory* **~feuer** n *rifle-fire*; *fusillade* **~gestell** n *r. rack* **~granate** f *rifle-grenade* **~granatgerät** n *grenade launcher* **~griffe** m pl *manual exercise* od *drill* **~kammer** f *bolt* **~kolben** m *butt*(*end*) *of a rifle, r. butt* **~lauf** m (*rifle-*)*barrel* **~magazin** n (*rifle-*)*magazine* **~pyramide** f *pile of arms, gun stack* **~reinigen** n *r. cleaning* **~riemen** m *rifle* od *gun sling* **~schaft** m *stock* **~schein** m ⟨hunt⟩ *gun--licence* **~schlitten** m *machine-gun carriage* **~schuh** m *scabbard* **~schuß** m *rifle bullet* **~stand** m *stand of arms* **~ständer** m *rifle-rack*

Gew·eih n ∼(e)s/∼e *antlers, horns* [pl]; Hirsch ohne ∼ ⟨Scot⟩ *hummel* ‖ das ∼ fegen *to rub one's antlers* ‖ Sprosse am ∼ *antler* ‖ ⟨fig⟩ dem Ehemann ein ∼ aufsetzen *to cuckold one's husband* **~baum** m ⟨bot⟩ *kentucky coffee-tree* **geweiht** a ⟨hunt⟩ *with antlers*

ge- ~w·eiht a *consecrate*(*d*); *dedicated* ‖ dem Tode ∼ *devoted* (*head*) °**≃w·eine** n ∼s/ *weeping*; *crying* **~w·ellt** a ⟨tech⟩ *corrugated* ‖ *wavy* (*hair*)

Gew·erbe n ∼s/∼ **1.** *trade*; *business*; *occupation*; → Beruf 3. d. ‖ Wander≃ *hawking trade* ‖ Kunst≃ *handicrafts* pl; Kunst u Kunst≃ *arts and crafts* pl ‖ Fabrik≃ *industry* ‖ die Händler e–s best. ∼s *the trade* **|** ein dunkles schmutziges ∼ *a shady, dirty business* ‖ ein ehrliches ∼ *an honest trade* ‖ ein ∼ ausüben, beitreiben *to carry on* (od *to follow*) *a trade* ‖ ein ∼ m aus *to make a trade of*; *to traffic in* (*a th*) ‖ was ist Ihr ∼? *what is your trade?* ‖ im ∼ tätig s *to be in the trade* **2.** [in comp] *trade ..*; *industrial* **~aufsicht(samt** n) f *t.-board* **~bank** f ⟨Ger⟩ *t.-bank*; *ind. bank* **~freiheit** f *freedom of t.* **~gericht** n ⟨Ger⟩ *ind. court* **~gesetz** n *t.-law, ind. law*; ∼gebung [f] *ind. legislation* **~hygiene** f *ind. hygiene* **~krankheit** f *t. disease* **~kunde** f *technology* **~lehrer** m *teacher at a t.-school* **~ordnung** f *t. regulations* pl **~politik** f *ind. policy* **~rat** m *t.-board* ‖ *member of the t.--board* **~schein** m *t.sman's* (od *hawker's*) *licence* **~schule** f *t.-school*; *ind.* (od *technical*) *school* **~steuer** f *t. tax* **≃tätig** a *industrial* **≃treibend** a *trading*; *ind.* (*classes*) ‖ der ≃e *the t.sman*; ≃er s *to be in the t.* ‖ die ≃en *the t.sfolk, t.speople* **~verband** m *t.-association* **~verein** m *t.smen's club*

Gew·erbfleiß m *industry* **gew·erbfleißig** a *industrious* **gew·erblich 1.** [a] *industrial* (*interests*); im ∼en Leben tätig sein *to be in in the trade* ‖ → gewerbsmäßig **2.** [adv] *industrially* **Gewerbs- ~leute** pl *tradespeople, tradesfolk* **~mann** m *tradesman*; ∼ sein *to be in the trade* **≃mäßig 1.** a ⟨übtr⟩ *habitual*; *professional* (*thief*; *prostitution*); *making a trade of* (*a th*) **2.** *professionally* **~zweig** m *branch* (od *line*) *of trade*

Ge- ~w·erf n ∼(e)s/∼e ⟨hunt⟩ = Gewehr B. **~w·erk** n ∼(e)s/∼e *trade* ‖ *corporation*; *guild* **~w·erke** m ∼n/∼n ⟨min⟩ *member of a cost-book company* **~w·erkschaft** f ∼/∼en **1.** ⟨min⟩ *cost--book company*; *mining company*; ⟨Am⟩ *labor union* **2.** ⟨com & pol⟩ *trade-union* (pl *t.-unions*); in e–e ∼ zwingen, in e–r ∼ zus-zwingen *to unionize* ‖ Mitglied e–r ∼ (*trade-*)*unionist*; Arbeitnehmer, der k–r ∼ angehört *non-unionist*; *non-union workman*; Vertragsverpflichtung des Arbeitnehmers, k–r ∼ beizutreten ⟨Am⟩ *yellow--dog contract* **| ~(l)er** m (*trade-*)*unionist*; Nicht≃ *non-unionist* ‖ ⟨Am⟩ Geschäft, in dem nur ∼ tätig sind *closed shop*; G., in dem a. Nicht≃ tätig sind *open shop* **|≃lich** a *trade-unionist*; *unionist* **~w·erkschafts-** [in comp] (*trade-*)*unionist*; ∼bund m ⟨SBZ⟩ *association of t. unions*; ∼bewegung [f], ∼wesen [n] *trade-unionism* **~w·erkverein** m = Gewerkschaft 2. ×**~w·ese** n *fuss* ‖ → Anwesen **≃w·esen** pp v sein ‖ ∼e [pl] *has-beens* pl, ∼e [f] = geborene *née*, (*Miss G. that was*)

Gew·icht n ∼(e)s/∼e **A. 1.** [abstr, nur sg] *weight* (*of a p, a th*); ⟨Am a.⟩ *heft* ‖ ∼ bei d. Geburt *birth weight* ‖ volles ∼ *full w.*; etw, um das ∼ voll z m *a make-up w.* ⟨a. fig⟩ ‖ leicht an ∼ *light in w.*; nach ∼ verkaufen *to sell by w.* ‖ *what is your w.?* ‖ das ∼ jds *or* e–r S feststellen *to find the w. of a p, a th* ‖ ein ∼ h v *to weigh* (*20 stones*); nicht das volle ∼ h *to be short in w.* ‖ ∼ ansetzen, an ∼ zunehmen *to put on w.* ‖ Eigen≃, totes ∼ *dead-weight*; Lebend≃ *live weight* **2.** ⟨phys⟩ spezifisches ∼ *specific gravity*; *density* **3.** (∼smaß) → Apotherker≃, Handels≃, Troy≃; → Karat ‖ indisches ∼ *ser, seer* (ca. *1 kilo*); (f Gold, Silber) *tola* (*180 grains*) **4.** (Last) *weight*; *burden*; *heaviness* **5.** ⟨fig⟩ **a.** *weight*; *consequence, importance*; *pith*; ⟨fam⟩ *punch* ‖ v gr ∼ *of great moment*, v k–m ∼ *of no m.* **b.** e–r S gr ∼ **beilegen** *to attach great importance* (od *w.*) *to a th*; *to set great store by a th* ‖ ∼ erhalten: *the question was brought to a point*; .. durch .. *to get point from ..* ‖ nicht ins ∼ fallen *to effect little or nothing*, ⟨sl⟩ *to cut no ice*; sehr ins ∼ fallen bei .. *to have much w. with ..*; e–r S mehr ∼ geben *to add w. to a th* ‖ ∼ h *to weigh* (bei *with*); gr ∼ h *to carry w.* (*with*); kein ∼ h *to have no w.* (*with*); jedes Wort sollte ∼ h *every word had to tell* ‖ gr ∼ legen auf etw = e–r S ∼ beilegen *to lay stress on*; (zu) wenig ∼ legen auf .. *to slight* (*too easily*) ‖ e–r S besonderes ∼ verleihen *to lend great w. to, to give point to a th* ‖ sein ganzes ∼ in die Waagschale werfen *to throw one's influence into the scale*; → Lanze **| an** ∼ abnehmen (P) *to reduce one's w.*; an ∼ gewinnen (S) *to gather momentum* ‖ an ∼ verlieren *to lose in w.* ‖ **ins** ∼ fallen *to count* (*that does not c.*); *to matter*; sehr ins ∼ .. *to be of great consequence*; noch mehr ins ∼ .. *to be much more important*; nicht ins ∼ .. *to be of no importance* od *moment*; nicht ins ∼ fallend *negligible* **B.** [konkr, pl ∼e] **1.** (∼sstück) *weight*; *lump of metal*; (des Pendels) *bob* **2.** (∼ z Belasten) *weight* **~heben** n ⟨gym⟩ *weight-lifting* **| ≃ig** a ⟨fig⟩ *important* (*decision*), *momentous*; *paramount* (*reasons*), *pregnant* (*words*); *significant*; *weighty* ‖ ∼es Argument *arg. carrying w.*; *strong* (*evidence*) ‖ *authoritative, influential* (*p*); ∼e P ⟨fam⟩ *bigwig*, ⟨Am fam⟩ *big noise* **|** ∼keit [f] ⟨a.⟩ *impact* **Gew·ichts- ~abgang** m *short w.*; *under--weight* **~abnahme** f *decrease of w., loss in* od *of w.* **~analyse** f ⟨phys⟩ *gravimetric analysis* **~aräometer** n ⟨phys⟩ *gravimeter* **~ausfall** m = –abgang **~ausgleich** m ⟨racing⟩ *handicap* **~einheit** f *unit of w.* **~hebel** m *w.ed lever* **~klassen** f pl ⟨box⟩ *w.-*

-classes pl ≃**los** a *weightless* **~losigkeit** f *weightlessness* **~maß** n *w.* **~regler** m *w.ed governor* **~satz** m *set of w.s* **~schale** f *weight-scale; scale-pan* **~stück** n *w.* **~system** n *system of w.s* **~verlust** m *loss in* od *of w.* **~zoll** m *duty by weight*

ge- **~w·ickelt** a ⟨fig⟩ °schief ~ s *to be on the wrong tack, .. in the wrong box; to be very much mistaken* °**~w·ieft** a = gewiegt ‖ *cunning* °**~w·iegt** a *experienced, shrewd, smart;* ⟨sl⟩ *salted (journalist);* ~er Bursche *old bird* °≃**w·ieher** n *neigh(ing)* ‖ ⟨übtr⟩ → Gelächter **~w·iesen** pp v weisen **~w·illt** a [nur pred] ~ s z tun *to be willing* (od *inclined, prepared, ready*) *to do;* nicht ~ s *to be unwilling* (*to do*), *to refuse* (*to do*); ~ s, etw z erreichen *to be bent on a th* ≃**w·immel** n ~s/ *jumble; skein;* → Durcheinander ‖ *swarm; crowd, throng* °**~w·immer** n ~s/ *whimper(ing), whine; whinings, wails, wailings; moanings* [pl]; *snivel*

Gew·inde n ~s/~ **A.** [abstr] = Windung(en) **B.** [konkr] **1. a.** (Schrauben≃) *(screw-)thread; worm;* Außen≃ *external thread,* Innen≃ *internal thr.;* linksgängiges, rechtsgängiges ~ *left-hand, right-hand thread;* Flach≃ *square thread* | Außen≃ schneiden *to cut an external thread;* Innen≃ schn. *to tap,* → ~loch **b.** ⟨anat⟩ *coils, turns, whorls* [pl] (*of a spiral shell,* etc.) **2.** *skein* (*of yarn*) **3.** (Blumen≃) *garland; wreath* **~anschluß** m ⟨tech⟩ *threaded (pipe) connection* **~bohrer** m *screw-tap* **~bohrung** f *screwed hole* **~buchse** f *threaded bush* **~drehbank** f *screw-cutting lathe* **~durchmesser** m: äußerer ~ *diameter of a bolt* (od *screw*); innerer ~ *diameter at bottom of a thread* **~gang** m *screw thread* | ~zahl [f] *number of threads* **~kupplung** f *screw-coupling* **~lehre** f *(screw-)thread gauge* **~loch** n *screwed hole* **~schneiden** n *screw-cutting; threading* **~steigung** f *thread pitch* **~stift** m *threaded pin*

Gew·inn m ~s/~e **A.** [abstr] **1.** *the winning* (*of a battle*) ‖ ⟨sport⟩ *success; victory; win* (*he had four wins*); e–n ~ buchen können *to score a success;* ein leichter ~ ⟨sl⟩ *a sitter* **2.** (Lotterie≃) *winner;* jedes zweite Los ist ein ~ *every second ticket will be a winner* **3.** ⟨übtr⟩ **a.** (Nutzen) *advantage; benefit; gain* (aus etw *from a th;* f .. *for a p; to a th*); *profit* ‖ (P) (*he is a great*) *asset* (*for our staff*) ‖ ~ an *margin of* (*leisure, time*); ein ~ f die Gesundheit *a gain to one's health* ‖ geistiger ~ *intellectual gain* **b.** mit ~ lesen *to read to advantage;* mit ~ verkaufen *to sell at a profit* ‖ jdm ~ bringen *to profit a p* ‖ es bringt kaum ~ es z lesen *it is almost unreadable* ‖ ~ h v, ~ ziehen aus etw *to make a profit on a th; to profit by a th* **B.** [konkr] (Geld≃) **1.** *gain, profit,* mst *profits; gains, gainings, proceeds* pl; *yield;* ⟨sl⟩ *plunder;* gr ~ ⟨Am sl⟩ *scoop* ‖ reiner ~ *net profit* (od *proceeds*); Anteil≃ ⟨Am sl⟩ *rake-off* ‖ schnöder ~ *filthy lucre* ‖ ~ abwerfen *to leave* (od *yield*) *a profit;* ⟨Am⟩ *to come out of the red;* k–n ~ abwerfend *nonprofit (organization)* ‖ ⟨ins⟩ *benefit* **2.** (Wett≃) *winnings* pl **3.** (Lotterie≃) *prize;* die ~e austeilen *to distribute the prizes* ‖ das Los kam mit gr ~ heraus *the ticket was drawn with a big prize* **~abschöpfung** f *ax(e) of the treasury* **~anteil** m *share in the profits; dividend; bonus;* → Dividenden–; Coupon ‖ ⟨ins⟩ Police mit (ohne) ~ *(non-)participating policy* ‖ *bonus; author's royalty* ≃**berechtigt,** ≃**beteiligt** a ⟨ins⟩ *participating (policy)* **~beteiligung** f *profitsharing, participation in profits* | ~srecht [n] *participating right* ≃**bringend** a *paying, profitable; lucrative;* nicht ~ *unprofitable* **~chance** f *show of winning* **~liste** f *list of winners* ‖ (Lotterie≃) *prize-list* **~marge** [-ʒe] f *margin of profit* **~nummer** f *winning number* **~rechnung** f *profit-account* **~steuer** f *profits-tax* **~streben** n, **~sucht** f *covetousness, greed; lucre;* aus ~ *for lucre* ≃**süchtig** a *greedy; mercenary (motive)* **~überschuß** m *margin of profit* **~- u Verlustkonto** n *profit and loss account;* ~ u V.rechnung *pr. and l. statement* **~vortrag** m *balance carried forward;* ⟨bal⟩ *undistributed net pr., accumulated earnings* pl

gew·innen vt/i [gewann/gewonnen] [h] **I.** vt **1.** (erringen) **a.** e–e Schlacht, e–n Sieg ~ *to gain* od *win a battle, a victory;* den Sieg ~ *to win the day* od *field; to be victorious* ‖ die Oberhand ~ *to gain mastery* (od *the upper hand*) (über *over*); *to prevail* ‖ → wagen ‖ (e–n Preis) *to carry off; to gain; land; obtain* ‖ *to win* (*a race*) ‖ ⟨jur⟩ *to win* (*a case*) **b.** er konnte es nicht **über sich** ~ *he could not face it; he could not bring himself; he could not find it in his heart* od *make up his mind* (*to do*) **2.** ⟨übtr⟩ **a.** (Geld etc) *to gain* (durch *by;* v *from*); (Reichtum) *to acquire* ‖ das gr Los ~ *to draw the first prize* ‖ an dem Geschäft gewann er 2000 Mark *he made 2000 marks on the transaction* ‖ °hier ist nicht viel z ~ *there is not much doing here;* was ist damit **gewonnen**? *what does it profit us? what's the use of it?* ‖ so gut wie gew. *all over but the shouting* ‖ ⟨prov⟩ wie gew. so zerronnen *lightly come, lightly go; soon got, soon gone; easy come, easy go* **b.** (Bedeutung, Einfluß, Kraft, Zeit etc) *to gain, win; get, obtain* ‖ Boden *or* Raum ~ *to gain ground;* Kenntnis über etw ~ aus *to derive knowledge of a th from* (*a th*); e–e Vorstellung v etw ~ aus *to derive* (od *get*) *an idea of a th from* ‖ Interesse ~ an *to become interested in* **c.** es gewinnt den Anschein, als ob .. *it looks as if ..* ‖ dadurch gewinnt die S ein ganz anderes Gesicht *that makes all the difference* **3.** jdn (*or* jds Gunst) ~ *to gain* (od *win*) *a p over* (f *to*); *to rope a p in;* jdn f sich ~ *to win a p* (od *a p's support*); *to win a p over to one's side* (*to do*) ‖ (e–e Frau) *to make a conquest of;* die Hand e–r Dame ~ *to win a lady's hand* ‖ (e–n Mann) *to capture* ‖ jdm viele Freunde ~ *to win a p many friends;* → Freund 2. a. ‖ die öffentl. Meinung ~ *to carry public opinion* ‖ ⟨theat⟩ das Publikum ~ ⟨sl⟩ *to put it over* ‖ jds Hilfe, Sympathie ~ *to enlist a p's help, sympathies;* jds Interesse ~ *to interest a p* (f *in*) ‖ als Vortragender war Herr Prof. N. gewonnen worden *Prof. N. had been retained* od *secured as lecturer* **4.** (erreichen) *to gain, reach, win; to gain distance, the shore* **5.** ⟨min & com⟩ (Erze, Mineral) *to win; to mine;* → fördern B. 1. ‖ (Öl) *to derive* od *extract, win* (aus *from*) **II.** vi **1.** ⟨mil⟩ *to be victorious* ‖ ⟨sport⟩ *to win* (um 2 Längen *by two lengths*); bestimmt ~ *to be a sure winner;* als erstes ~ (of a horse) *to come in* (od *to land*) *first* ‖ leicht ~ *to walk over;* (of horse) *to romp home* ‖ spielend ~ *to win hands down* **2.** (in Lotterie) jedes zweite Los gewinnt .. *wins, will be a winner;* Nummer 58 hat gewonnen *the prize has fallen to number 58* ‖ (beim Spiel) *to win* **3.** ⟨übtr⟩ *to gain; to win through* ‖ er gewinnt bei näherer Bekanntschaft *he improves on acquaintance* ‖ ~ **an** *to gain* (od *win*) *in;* an Boden ~ *to gain ground;* an Kraft ~ *to gather force,* (of efforts) *to gather momentum;* an Wärme ~ (of the voice) *to gather ardour* ‖ **durch** den Rahmen hat das Bild sehr gewonnen *the frame greatly improves the effect of the picture* **gew·innend** a ⟨übtr⟩ *engaging, winning,* = einnehmend **Gew·inner** m ~s/~ *winner; gainer* ‖ der Name des ~s *the winning name* **Gew·innung** f ~/~en ⟨übtr⟩ *acquisition* (*of money*); *conquest* (*of land, a p*); *extraction* (*of information*) | ⟨min⟩ *extraction* (*of oil*); ~ aus *extraction from ..* ‖ *mining, raising, winning* (*of minerals, coal*)

Ge- **~w·insel** n ~s/ *whimpering, whining* †**~w·inst** m ~es/~e = Gewinn B. ‖ ~partie [f] ⟨cards⟩ (Tour v 2–3 ~en) *rubber* ≃**w·irkt** a (→ Wirker, wirken) *warp-knitted* **~w·irr(e)** n ~(e)s/ **1.** [abstr] *confusion; confused mass* (*of people*); *criss-cross* (*of streets*); *jumble; maze; tangle* (*of the traffic*); *topsy-turvydom; tumble; welter* (*of ideas*); *whirl, whirligig* (*of time*); *wilder-*

ness (*of houses*); ein tolles ~ *a bedlam* (*of traffic*) || (Stimmen≈) *confusion of voices*; *blur* (*of whispers*); *buzz*; *hubbub* **2.** ⟨tech⟩ (Inneres e–s Schlosses) *ward*

gew·iß I. [a] [ohne Komparation] **A.** [pred] **1.** [subjektiv] e–r S ~ s *to be sure* (od *certain, confident*) *of a th*; ich bin s–r Zustimmung ~ *I am sure of his assent* || s–r S ~ s *to be sure of one's ground*; ich bin m–r S ~ *I am quite certain* (od *absolutely positive*) || des *or* das bin ich ~ *I am sure of it* || ich bin ~, daß .. *I am* (od *feel*) *sure that* .. **2.** [objektiv] *certain*; die S ist ~ *the fact is certain*; soviel ist ~ *this* (od *so*) *much is certain* || ich halte s–e Rückkehr f ~ *I look upon his return as a certainty* || eine Belohnung ist ihm ~ *he is sure of a reward* **B.** [attr] **1.** *[objektiv] **a.** dem –ssen Tode entgegengehen *to face certain death*; mst = sicher **b.** = bestimmt **C.** [pronominal] *certain* || ein –sses Etwas *a certain sth* || –sse Fälle *certain cases*; unter –ssen Bedingungen *under c. conditions* || bis z e–r –ssen Grenze *to a c. limit*; in –sser Beziehung, Hinsicht, bis z e–m –ssen Grade *to a certain extent* od *degree*; in –ssem Sinne *in a sense* || e–e –sse Bescheidenheit *sth of modesty*; es ist ein –sser Fortschritt *there is progress of a kind* | –sse Leute *certain people*; ein –sser Georg Braun *a certain G. B.*; ein –sser N. *a certain Mr. N.* **II.** [adv] **1.** [subjektiv] **a.** *surely, to be sure*; es wird ~ noch regnen *it will still rain, I'm sure*; du hast ~ nichts dagegen *surely you have no objection*; Sie müssen es ~ bewundern *you must be sure to admire it* **b.** (in Antworten) ‚darf ich Sie sprechen?' ‚≈' '*May I speak to you*?' '*You may*'; (hast du ihm geschrieben?) ‚≈' (..) (*Of course* od *indeed*) *I have* (u ä.) || *certainly*! *of course*! *sure*! *sure* (od *safe*) *thing*! *rather*! *by all means*! **2.** [objektiv] *certainly*; *surely*; = sicher **III.** [abs] das ist nichts ≈sses *that is no certainty*; *that is nothing definite* || °was ≈sses weiß man nicht *nothing definite is known*

Gew·issen n ~s/*~ **1.** *conscience* **2.** Wendungen **a.** abgestumpftes ~ *seared c.*; ein gutes, böses *or* schlechtes ~ *a good, bad c.*; mit ruhigem ~ *with a good* (od *safe*) *c.* || ein reines, ruhiges ~ *a clear, peaceful c.* || schuldbeladenes ~ *guilty c.* || feinfühlendes *or* zartes ~ *sensitive c.* || enges, weites ~ *narrow, elastic c.*; ein weites ~ h *not to be over-scrupulous* || ein wissenschaftliches ~ *a scientific c.* **b. gegen** Recht u ~ *contrary to right and morals* || **nach** bestem Wissen u ~ *conscientiously* || ein Mensch **ohne** ~ *a man with no c.*; → ≈los || **wider** besseres Wissen u ~ *contrary to the dictates of c.* **c.** mein ~ **quält** mich *my c. torments me* || das ~ schlug ihm, sein ~ regte sich *his c. was roused* || ⟨prov⟩ ein gut ~ ist ein sanftes Ruhekissen *a quiet c. sleeps in thunder* **d.** sein ~ **beruhigen** *to pacify* od *soothe one's c.*, ⟨fam⟩ *to square one's c.*; um das ~ z beruhigen *for conscience(') sake* || sein ~ erforschen *to search one's c.*; das ~ erleichtern *to ease* (od *relieve*) *one's c.* || der Stimme des ~s folgen *to follow* (od *obey*) *the voice* (od *promptings*) *of c.* || sich ein (kein) ~ m aus (*or* über) etw, sich ein (kein) ~ m, etw z tun *to have* (*no*) *scruples about doing a th*; sich ein ~ m z tun *to scruple to do*; *to be scrupulous about doing* od *to do*; sich ein ~ daraus m z tun *to make it a matter of c. to do* **e.** ein Mann mit 5 Morden **auf dem** ~ *a man with 5 murders to his credit*; jdm schwer aufs ~ fallen *to weigh heavily upon one's c.* || auf dem ~ h *to have* (*a p, a th*) *on one's c.* | gegen sein ~ handeln *to act against the dictates of c.* | jdm **ins** ~ reden *to appeal to a p's c.*; *to give a p a talking-to*; *to have a p on the carpet*; (gehörig) *to give a p a thorough gruelling* | sich **mit** s–m ~ abfinden *to compound one's c.*

gew·issenhaft 1. [a] *conscientious*; *scrupulous* (in .. *in a th*); *nice* (in bezug auf *about*) || *painstaking* (*work*) || nicht sehr ~ *not over-nice, not over-scrupulous* (in *in*) **2.** [adv] *conscientiously*; *scrupulously* | ≈**igkeit** f *conscientiousness*, etc

gew·issenlos 1. [a] *conscienceless, unconscientious, unprincipled* (*conduct*), *unscrupulous* || *reckless* **2.** [adv] *unconscientiously, unscrupulously* ≈**igkeit** f ~/ *unconscientiousness*, etc.

Gew·issens- ~angst f *anguish, anxiety*; *pangs* od *qualms* [pl] *of c.* **~biß** m *prick* (od *sting, twinge*) *of c.*; [mst pl] –bisse *compunction*; *qualms* [pl]; *remorse* (über *at*; wegen *for*); –bisse h (*or* sich .. m) *to feel remorse*; mach dir k–e –bisse deswegen *don't trouble your head about that* **~ehe** f *cohabitation*; *concubinage*; → wilde Ehe **~frage** f *question of c.*; → –sache **~freiheit** f *freedom of c.* **~klausel** f ⟨engl⟩ *c.-clause* **~konflikt** m *conflict of c.* **~not** f = –angst, –bisse **~pflicht** f *dictate* od *commands of c.*; → Pflicht **~ruhe** f *tranquillity of c.* **~sache** f *matter* (od *case, point*) *of c.* **~zwang** m *restraint of c.*; unter ~ handeln *to act under a r. of c.* **~zweifel** n *conscientious scruple*

gewisserm·aßen adv *in some measure*; *to a certain extent*; *so to speak, as it were* || ⟨fam⟩ (*I'm*) *sort of* (*hurt*) **Gew·ißheit** f ~/~en *certainty*; e–e unumstößliche ~ *an established c.*; mit ~ *with certainty* || innere ~ *certitude*; *conviction* || → Sicherheit || sich ~ über etw verschaffen *to make sure of a th*

gew·ißlich adv *certainly, surely*; *assuredly*

Gew·itter n ~s/~ *thunderstorm*; → Sturm; Wetterleuchten || ein schweres ~ ist im Anzuge (*or* zieht auf) *a severe* (od *violent*) *thunderstorm is brewing* || es wird ein ~ geben, wir w noch ein ~ bek. *there will be a th., we shall have a th.* | ⟨fig⟩ *storm*; *tempest* || *kick-up, row*; *trouble*; (*domestic*) *thunderstorm* ≈**artig** a *thundery* ≈**drohend** a *threatening* (*sky*) **~flug** m ⟨aero⟩ *gliding-flight before a thunder-storm* **~gefahr** f; es ist ~ *there is a thunderstorm threatening* **~himmel** m *thundery sky* **~kopf** m ⟨meteor⟩ *thunderhead* **~luft** f *thundery* (od *sultry*) *air* ⟨a. fig⟩ **~regen** m, **~schauer** m *thundershower* **~schutz** m *lightning arrester* ≈**schwanger,** ≈**schwül** a *thunderous* (*day*), *thundery* (*air*) **~schwüle** f *thundery state*; *sultriness* **~wolke** f *thunder-cloud*

gew·itt(e)rig a *thunderous*; *thundery*

gew·ittern vi/imps [h] es gewittert *there is a thunderstorm*; *it thunders* || ⟨fig⟩ *to thunder*; es gewittert in der Luft *the air is thundery*

gew·itzigt a *wiser than before* || *clever, knowing* || ~ s *to have learnt better*

Gew·oge n ⟨fig⟩ *rush, swirl* (*of the City*); *whirl, whirligig* (*of time*) || ~ des Kampfes, Kampf≈ *mêlée* Fr; im ~ *in the thick of the battle*

gew·ogen a [pp wiegen] [mst pred] jdm ~ (= freundlich gesinnt) s → freundlich 2. || er ist mir nicht ~ *he is ill-disposed towards me* || bleiben Sie mir ~! *keep me in good remembrance* || °Sie können mir ~ bleiben *thank you for nothing*!; °der kann mir ~ bl. *I'll see him further first* | [attr] *affectionate* | ≈**heit** f ~/ *affection*; *goodwill* || h Sie die ~ *have the kindness* (*to step this way*)

gew·öhnen vt [h] **1. a.** (P, T) ~ an .. *to accustom* (od *habituate, inure*) *to* (*order, discipline*); *to familiarize a p with* (*a th*); jdn an den Gedanken ~, daß .. *to bring a p round to the idea that* .. || an häusliches Leben ~ *to domesticate*; e–n Hund ans Haus ~ *to domesticate a dog* **b.** (abrichten) (T) *to break in*; *to train* (*to do*) **2. sich ~ an** *to accustom* (od *habituate, harden, season*) *o.s. to*; *to get into the habit of* (*a p, a th*); *to acclimatize o.s. to*; *to get accustomed* (od *used*) *to* (*a th*); ich gewöhnte mich daran *I got used to it*; sie hatte sich daran gewöhnt z .. tragen *she had taken to wearing* (*a brooch*); sich an die Schiffsbewegungen ~ *to find* od *get one's sea-legs* **3. gewöhnt s an** *to be accustomed* od *used to*; *to be inured* od *seasoned to* (*cold*, etc.) || gewöhnt sein z tun *to be accustomed to do, to be in the habit of doing*; ich bin es gewöhnt, früh aufzustehen *I have got accustomed to getting up early*

Gew·ohnheit f ~/~en **1.** *habit* (z tun *of doing*); *custom, practice, wont* | die Macht der ~, das macht die ~! *the force of habit* || ein Mensch v festen ~en *a man of regular habits* || diese ~, die er hatte *this habit of his* || es ist s–e ~ *it is his wont* (*to do*); es ist nicht m–e ~ *it is not my way* (*to do*); wie es s–e ~ war *as was his custom* | **aus** (alter) ~ *from* (od *out of*) *habit* || aus der ~ k *to get out of the habit* || nach s–r ~ *according to his wont* || v s–n ~en abweichen *to go out of one's way* || jdm z ~ w *to grow on a p*; es ist ihm z ~ geworden *it has become a habit with him* || sich etw z ~ m, etw z ~ w l *to make a practice of a th* | e–e ~ **annehmen** *to develop a habit*; *to take to* (*drinking*, etc); schlechte ~en annehmen *to drop into bad habits* || die ~ an sich h *to be in the habit, to be wont* (*to do*) **2.** (Brauch) *custom, usage*

Gew·ohnheits- [in comp] *habitual* **≃mäßig 1.** [a] *customary, habitual*; *mechanical*; *routine* (*work*); ~er Brauch *routine*; rein ~ *formal* (*call*) **2.** [adv] *habitually*; *from habit*; *by force of habit* **~mensch** m *a slave to custom* (od *routine*); *a creature of habit* **~recht** n *prescriptive right* | ⟨engl⟩ *Common Law* || *customary* (*of a manor*) **~sünde** f *besetting sin* || °**~tier** n = –mensch **~trinker** m *habitual drunkard*; *tosspot* **~verbrecher** m *habitual* (od *professional*) *criminal*; *gaol-bird*

gew·öhnlich I. [a] **1.** (üblich) *common* (*event*), *customary* (*occupation*); *habitual* (*his h. seat*), *ordinary*; *usual* (*the u. questions*); ein ~er Anblick *a familiar sight*; ein ganz ~es Gemüse *a common* od *garden vegetable*; im ~en Leben *in everyday* (od *ordinary*) *life* || → abgedroschen | der ~e Mann *the common* (od *ordinary*) *man, the man in the street*; der ~e Sterbliche *the ordinary mortal* **2.** ⟨dero⟩ (unfein) (of people, manners) *common, vulgar*; er sieht sehr ~ aus *he looks very common*; → gemein **II.** [adv] **1.** *commonly, usually*; *generally* || komm wie ~ *come as usual* (od *at the usual time*); er sagte weniger als ~ *he said less than usual*; etw ~ tun *to be in the habit of doing*; die Läden schließen ~ um .. *it is usual for shops to close at* (*7 o'clock*) **2.** *vulgarly* (*to behave v.*); *in a vulgar manner* | **≃keit** f ⟨dero⟩ *commonness*; *vulgarity*

gew·ohnt a **1.** [pred] ~ s z tun *to be accustomed* (od *wont*) *to do*; *to be in the habit of doing* || er war ~, daß man gegen ihn höflich war *he was accustomed* od *used to polite treatment from everybody* od *to being politely spoken to* || etw ~ sein = gewöhnt sein an etw, → gewöhnen 3.; sie müssen es ~ sein *they must be used to it* || etw ~ w *to get accustomed to a th* || ⟨prov⟩ jung ~ ist alt getan *just as the twig is bent the tree's inclined* (*Pope*) **2.** [attr] *habitual* (*actions*; *manner*); *wonted*; er kam zur ~en Stunde *he came at his wonted hour*; → gewöhnlich || das ~e Geleise *the rut*; in das ~e G. k. *to get into a rut*

Gew·öhnung f ~/~en *getting used* (an *to a th*) *habituation* (an *to*); durch ~ der Augen an *by accustoming one's eyes to ..*; ~ an Klima, Verhältnisse *acclimatization* || ~ (e–s Tiers) ans Haus *domestication* (*of an animal*) | *breaking in*; *training* (*of an animal, a p*)

Gew·ölbe n ~s/~ **1.** *arched roof* (od *ceiling*); *vault*; *vaulting*; *dome* || → Fächer≃; Kreuz(grat)≃ *groined v.*; –(rippen)≃ *cross-ribbed v.*; Spitzbogentonnen≃ *pointed tunnel v.*; Stalaktiten≃ *stalactite v.*; Stern≃ *star v.*; Tonnen≃ *barrel v., tunnel v.* || ~ des Himmels *vault of heaven* **2.** (Raum mit ~) *vault* || sicheres feuerfestes ~ *safety-vault, strong-room*; Grab≃ *vault* || Keller≃ *cellar(s* pl) **≃artig** a *vaultlike* **~bau** m *vaulting* **~kappe** f *vaulting cell* **~pfeiler** m *vaulting-pillar*; → Strebepfeiler **~schlußstein** m *keystone* **~stein** m keilförmiger ~ *voussoir* Fr

ge- ~w·ölbt a *arched, vaulted* || ⟨tech⟩ *concave, dished, domed* (Uhrglas); *barrel* (*road*) **≃wölk** n ~(e)s/ (*body of*) *clouds* pl **≃w·ölle** n ⟨hunt⟩ (ausgespienes) *casting(s* pl) **~w·onnen** a [pp v gewinnen] → gewinnen || wir h ~es Spiel *the game is as good as won* **~w·orben** pp v werben **~w·orden** pp v werden **~w·orfen** pp v werfen **≃w·ühl(e)** n ~(e)s/ *concourse, crowd, swarm, throng* || *hurly-burly*; *hurry and bustle* (*of life*); ⟨Am a.⟩ *shuffle*; im ~ der Menge *in the bustle of the crowd* || ~ des Kampfes *mêlée* Fr; im ~ der Schlacht *in the thick of the battle* || → Getümmel, Wühlerei **~w·unden** a [pp v winden] **1.** *coiled* (*mat*) || ⟨tech⟩ *spiral, twisted* || *circuitous, devious, sinuous* (*river, road*); *winding, meandering* (*streets*) **2.** ⟨fig⟩ *crooked, devious*; *sinuous*; *tortuous* (*phrases*); ~e Erklärung *evasion* **~wünscht** a *most desirable*; meist ~ *mostly asked for* || das ≃e (*did you get*) *what you wanted*? **~w·ürfelt** a [pp] *chequered*; ~es Muster *chequer* °**≃w·ürge** n ~s/ **1.** *gulping, swallowing*; *gulps* pl **2.** (Gemetzel) *slaughter(ing)* **3.** °⟨fig⟩ *drudgery* **≃w·ürm** n ~(e)s/~e *reptiles, worms* pl; *vermin*

Gew·ürz n ~(e)s/~e ⟨cul⟩ *spice*; *condiment*; *seasoning(s* pl); ~e [pl] *spices* pl; *spicery* | ⟨fig⟩ *spice*; e–r S ~ verleihen *to give spice to a th* **≃artig** a *aromatic, spicy* **~auszug** m = –extrakt **~büchse** f *spice-box* **~essig** m *aromatic vinegar* **~extrakt** m *spice-extract* **~händler** m *dealer in spice*; *grocer* **~inseln** f pl *Spice Islands*; *Moluccas* pl **~kasten** m *spice-box* **~körner** n pl *pimento* **~krämer** m = –händler **~laden** m *grocer's shop* **~nägelein, ~nelke** f *clove*; ~nbaum [m] ⟨bot⟩ *clove-tree*; ~nöl [n] *clove-oil* **≃reich** a *aromatic, spicy* **~salz** n *spice-salt* **~strauch** m ⟨bot⟩ *spice-bush* **~waren** f pl *groceries* pl **~wein** m *spiced wine*

ge- ~w·ürzig a = würzig **~würzt** [a] (gut, scharf ~) ⟨cul⟩ *highly seasoned*; *devilled*; [adv] ~ grillen *to devil* **~w·ußt** pp v wissen **~z·ackt** a ⟨bes bot⟩ *jagged, serrate(d), serriform*; *toothed*; fein ~ *serrulate*; → zackig **≃z·äh(e)** n *miner's tools* pl | ~trommel [f] *tool chest* **~z·ähnelt, ~z·ahnt, ~z·ähnt** a ⟨bot⟩ *dentate(d), denticulate(d), indented* || ⟨tech⟩ *cogged*; *toothed*; *tooth-shaped* (*grinding ring*); ~es Schwungrad *gear-flywheel* **≃z·änk** n ~(e)s/, °**≃z·anke** n ~s/ *squabbling, squabble*; *quarrel(ling)*; *wrangle* **≃z·appel** n ~s/ *fidgeting, fidgets* pl (*of a boy*); *kicking* (*of a baby*); *struggling* || (im Wasser) *flounder(ing)* **≃z·eiten** f pl; die ~ *the tide* (*the tides, ebb and flow*) | ~hub [m] *tidal range*; ~kraftwerk [n] *tidal power plant* ~signal [n] *tide-signal*; ~strom [m] *tidal water*; ⟨Am⟩ *tide-water*; ~tafeln [f pl] *tide-tables* pl; || ~theorie [f] ⟨astr⟩ *tidal theory* || ~wechsel [m] *turn of the tide* **≃z·elt** n ~(e)s/~e = Zelt **≃z·err(e)** n ~(e)s/ *tug(ging)*; *violent pull(s* pl) **≃z·eter** n ~s/ *squall(ing)*, (*yelling*) *clamour* || ⟨übtr⟩ *bother, fuss* || → Geschrei, Zetergeschrei °**≃z·eug** n ~(e)s/ *workman's tools* pl **≃z·iefer** n ~s/~ *insects* pl, *vermin* **~zielt** a *pinpointed* (*attack*) ⟨a. fig⟩ **~z·iemen** vi/refl [h] jdm ~ *or* sich f jdn ~ *to become* (od *befit, behove* [⟨Am⟩ *behoove*], *beseem*) *a p*; dieser Ton geziemt dir nicht (*or* geziemt sich nicht für dich) *this tone does not become you* | **es –mt sich,** daß man ihn grüßt *it is the proper thing to bow to him, it is fitting that you should bow to him* || er weiß, was sich geziemt *he knows what is fit and proper* || wie es sich geziemt *as is fitting* **~z·iemend 1.** [a] *due* (*respect*); *proper*; mit s–m Rang ~er Würde *with dignity proper to his rank* || *convenient, decent, fitting, seemly* **2.** [adv] *decently*; *properly* (*to behave p.*) || *in suitable words* **~zinkt** a ⟨tech⟩ *pronged* °**≃z·iere** n ~s/ = Geziertheit **~z·iert 1.** [a] (P, manners) *affected*; *finical, finicking, foppisch*; (⟨Am⟩ *finicky* ⟨fam⟩ *prissy*); *mincing, niminy-piminy*; *prim, prudish, demure* || (of style) *mannered, studied* || ~e Ausdrucksweise ⟨engl

Lit⟩ *euphuism* **2.** *affectedly, mincingly, primly* **|** ∸heit [f] ~/~en *affectation; finicality; primness; prudery* °∸**z·irp** n ~(e)s/ *chirp(ing)* ∸-**z·isch(e)** n ~(e)s/ *hiss(ing), whizz(ing)* °∸**z·ischel** n ~s/ *whisper(ing)* **~z·ogen** a [pp v *ziehen*] **1.** *towed (artillery)*; ⟨tech⟩ *drawn (wire)*; fein ~ *thin drawn (wire)*; hart ~ *unannealed* (od *hard drawn*); ~es Rohr *solid drawn pipe* ‖ ~er Lauf (am Gewehr etc) *rifled barrel* ‖ *dipped (candle)* **2.** ⟨com⟩ *drawn (cheque)* ∸**z·ücht** n ~(e)s/ ⟨fig dero⟩ (Gesindel); mob, *rabble, riff-raff; vermin* ‖ → Brut, Sippschaft ∸**zw·eig** n ~s/ *branches* pl, *boughs* pl **~zw·eit** a *bipartite*; → binär **~zwieselt** a ⟨for⟩ *forked* ∸**zw·itscher** n ~s/ (of birds) *chirping, twitter; chatter* ⟨a. übtr⟩

gezw·ungen [pp v zwingen] **1.** [a] *constrained, forced, strained (laugh); stiff, unnatural*, → geziert **2.** (adv] *constrainedly, forcedly, perforce* **~ermaßen** adv *perforce* **|** ∸**heit** f *constraint, unnaturalness*

Ghats pl (ind. Bergzüge) *Ghats* **gh·anisch** a *Ghanaian*

Ghas·el n → Gasel **Gh·asi, ghazi** (Türk.) *Ghazi*

Gh·etto = Getto **Ghibell·ine** = Gibelline

gib imp v geben **gibt** 3. sg prs v geben

G·ibbon m ⟨zoo⟩ (Menschenaffe) *gibbon*

Gibell·ine m ~n/~n, **gibell·inisch** a *Ghibelline*

Gibr·altar *Gibraltar; the Rock* ‖ die Straße v ~ *the Strait of G.* **~fieber** n = Maltafieber

G·icht[1] f **1.** ⟨path⟩ *gout*; (oft:) *the gout*; (~ in den Füßen) *podagra* ‖ ~ h *to have the g.* ‖ durch ~ verursacht *gouty* ‖ fliegende ~ Gelenkrheumatismus **2.** ⟨bot⟩ (Weizenkrankheit) *gout* ∸-**artig** a *gouty* **~beere** f ⟨bot⟩ *black currant* †∸-**brüchig** a ⟨bib⟩ *palsied, paralytic* ‖ der ∸e *the paralytic*, ⟨bib⟩ *one having the palsy* **~knoten** m *gouty concretion; tophus* L ∸**krank** a *gouty* **~-kraut** n ⟨bot⟩ = Gänseblume, Gnadenkraut etc **~mittel** n pl *antiarthritics* **~morchel** f ⟨bot⟩ = Stinkmorchel **~rose** f ⟨bot⟩ = Päonie **~schmerzen** m pl *gouty pains* pl

G·icht[2] f ~/~en ⟨met⟩ (am Hochofen) *throat* ‖ *charge, burden* **~gas** n *blast-furnace gas* **~-schwamm** m *tutty* **~staub** m *flue-dust*

g·ichtisch a *gouty (pains)* ‖ ~ veranlagt *gouty*

°**G·ickgack** n (Kinderspr.) *cackle (of geese)*

°**gicks** adv = kicks ‖ °**g·icksen** vi = kicksen

G·iebel m ~s/~ *gable(-end)*; abgetreppter ~ recessed gable; → ~feld **~dach** n *g.-roof* **~feld** n ⟨ant arch⟩ *pediment, tympan(um)* **~fenster** n *g.-window* ∸**förmig** a *g.-shaped* **~haus** n *g.d house* **~schenkel** m, **~schräge** f *slope* **~seite** f *(gable-)-front* **~wand** f *gable-end* **g·ieb(e)lig** a *gabled*

G·ien n ~s/~e ⟨mar⟩ *winding-tackle*

Gier[1] f ~/ ⟨übtr⟩ *greed* (nach *for, of*); *cupidity, avidity; greediness; rage (for ..), voracity (of ..)* ‖ **|** ∸**en** vi [h] ~ *to hunger, thirst, yearn* (nach *for*), *to covet (a th)* ‖ ⟨aero⟩ *(of plane) to yaw*

Gier[2] f ~/~en ⟨mar⟩ *sheer, yaw* **~brücke** f *swing bridge* **~fähre** f *trail ferry* **| ~en 1.** vi [h] ⟨mar, aero⟩ *to sheer, yaw* **2.** ∸ n *sheer, yaw(ing)*

g·ierig 1. [a] *greedy (eagle); voracious* ‖ ⟨übtr⟩ *covetous (eyes, glances); grasping, greedy, voracious (man)* **| ~ nach** *covetous* (od *greedy, ravenous) of; avid of* od *for; eager for; intent* (od *sharp-set) upon*; ~ s nach *to be a glutton for; to long for (news)* **2.** [adv] *(read) avidly; covetously; (drink) greedily; (look at a p) hungrily*; (etw) ~ an sich reißen, ~erledigen *to mop up* **|** ∸**keit** f ~/ *greediness, voracity* ‖ = Gier[1]

Giersch m ⟨bot⟩ *gout-weed, bishopweed*

G·ieß- (→ gießen) **~bach** m *(mountain) torrent*, ⟨fig⟩ *torrent* **~becken** n *basin, ewer* ‖ *sink* **~fieber** m *smelter's fever* **~flasche** f ⟨met⟩ *ingot mould* **~form** f *mould* ⟨a. print⟩; (f Roheisen) *sow* **~haus** n *casting-house; foundry* **~hütte** f = –haus **~kanne** f *watering-can; sprinkler*; ⟨Am⟩ *sprinkling-can* ‖ ihre Stimme klingt wie e–e ~ .. *bites like an emery wheel* **|** ~nbrause [f] *rose* **~loch** n *hole (of a mould); funnel (of a furnace)* **~löffel** m *casting-ladle* **~maschine** f *casting-machine* **~modell** n *casting-mould* **~ofen** m *founding-furnace* **~pfanne** f *ladle; melting-pot* **~topf** m ⟨typ⟩ *metal pot* **~trichter** m ⟨found⟩ *gate* **~zettel** m ⟨typ⟩ *bill of found* (od *type*)

g·ießbar a ⟨tech⟩ *capable of being cast* **G·ieße** f ~/~n (e–r Schale) *lip* **g·ießen I.** vt/i [goß/gegossen] [h] **A.** vt **1. a.** (Flüssigkeit) *to pour* (auf *on*; aus *from, out of*; in *into*); *to pass* (durch *through*); *to put, run* (in *into*) ‖ *to dash water in a p's face* ‖ *the coffee was spilled on the cloth* ‖ *to pour oil into the lamp*; ⟨fig⟩ → Öl **b.** °einen auf die Lampe (*or* hinter die Binde) ~ → Binde 2. **c.** ⟨übtr poet⟩ (Licht, Segen etc) *to shed; diffuse* ‖ (of the sun) (Strahlen) *to pour* (in .. *into*) **2.** ⟨hort⟩ (begießen) *to water* **3.** ⟨met⟩ *to cast, found; fuse* ‖ (geschmolzenen Stahl) *to teem* (in *into*) ‖ (Kugeln) *to mould*; (Wachs) *to mould* (in *into*) ‖ (Glocke) *to found* ‖ er goß die Figur aus Erz *he cast the figure in metal* **|** ⟨typ⟩ (Schrift) *to found, cast* **4. es gießt sich** schlecht aus diesem Krug *it is awkward to pour from this jug* **B.** vi [mst imps] **es gießt** (in Strömen) *it is raining hard, it is pouring (with rain); it is raining* (od *coming down) in torrents*; es goß wie mit Mulden *it rained cats and dogs*, ⟨Am⟩ .. *pitch-forks* **II.** ∸ n *watering (of plants)* ‖ ⟨tech⟩ *pour(ing) (of metal)* **G·ießer** m ~s/~ *(type-) founder; moulder* ‖ (Likör∸) *bottle pourer* **Gießer·ei** f ~/~en [abstr & konkr] *found(e)ry*

G·ift n ~(e)s/~e **1.** *poison* (schleichendes ~ *slow p.*; schnell wirkendes ~ *rapid p.*); *toxicant* ‖ tierisches ~, bes Schlangen∸ *venom* **|** ⟨path⟩ (Bakterien∸) *virus* L; *toxin*; → Ptomaine **|** ~ legen *to put out poison*; ° ich könnte ~ darauf nehmen *I will be bound (that)*; darauf kannst du ~ n. *you can bet your shirt on that; you can* od *may gamble on it, you can kiss the book on that* **2.** ⟨übtr⟩ **a.** ~ f jdn s *to be poison to a p (lenience is p. to many people)* ‖ *baneful* (od *noxious) influence; poison (of jealousy); virus (of a doctrine)* ‖ das reinste ~ s *to be very poisonous* **3.** ⟨fig⟩ *malice, malignity, spite; spleen; venom*; voll v ~ u Galle s *to be bursting with malice*; ~ u G. speien *to vent one's spleen; to be mad with rage* **4.** [in compl] *poison(ous); toxic(al)* **~baum** m ⟨bot⟩ *p.-tree*; der ~ *the Upas tree* **~becher** m *p.-cup* **~beere** f ⟨bot⟩ *p.-berry* **~blase** f (of snakes) *p.-bag* **~buch** n ⟨pharm⟩ *p.-book* **~drüse** f ⟨zoo⟩ *p.-gland* **~eiche** f *Poison Oak* **~efeu** m *Poison Ivy* ∸**fest** a *proof against p.* **~flunder** m ⟨ich⟩ *sting-ray* **~gas** n ⟨mil⟩ *poison-gas* **~getreide** n *poisoned cereals* ∸**grün** a *bright gr.* **~handel** m *trade in p.* **~kammer** f ⟨pharm⟩ *p.-cabinet* **~kies** m ⟨minr⟩ *arsenopyrite, mispickel* **~lehre** f = Toxikologie **~mehl** n (arsenige Säure) *p.-flour* **~mischer** m *p.er*; °⟨hum⟩ = Apotheker **~mischerei** f *p.ing* **~morchel** m ⟨bot⟩ = Stinkmorchel **~mord** m *(murder by) p.ing* **~mörder** m *p.er* ‖ °**~nudel** f *cigar* **~pflanze** f *p.ous plant* **~pilz** m ⟨bot⟩ *p.ous fungus; toadstool* **~saft** m ⟨zoo⟩ *p.ous fluid* **~schein** m ⟨pharm⟩ *purchasing warrant for p.s* **~schlange** f *p.ous* (od *venomous) snake*; kl ~ *krait* **~schrank** m ⟨pharm⟩ *p.-cupboard* **~schwamm** m = –pilz **~stachel** m *p.-sting* **~stoff** m *poison; toxin* ‖ ⟨med⟩ *virus* L ⟨a. fig⟩ ‖ v ~en reinigen *to decontaminate* **~trank** f *p.ed draught* **~turm** m *p.-tower*; → –kies **~weizen** m (gegen Ratten) *p.ed wheat* **~wirkung** f *p.ous effect* **~zahn** m *p.-fang* (od *tooth*)

g·iftig A. [a] **1. a.** *poisonous (fluid; snake); venomous (snake)*; nicht ~ *non-poisonous (snake)* ‖ *toxic (condition, drug)*; ~e Substanz *toxicant*; ~e Wirkung *toxical effect* **b.** ⟨fig⟩ (zersetzend) *baneful; deleterious (thoughts); poisonous (influence), pernicious (doctrine); ruinous; virulent (disease)* **2.** ⟨fig⟩ (boshaft) *edgy; envenomed* (*words*); *malicious, malevolent, malignant, scathing, shrewish*; *spiteful* (*speech*); *venomed, vicious* (*tongue*); *virulent* ‖ *cantankerous*; ⟨fam⟩ *rumbustious*, ⟨Am⟩ *rambunctious* (*woman*); °e–e ~e Kröte *a spiteful little toad*; → wütend | er ist sehr ~ in s–n Reden *he has a malicious tongue, his speech is full of spite* ‖ ein „giftiger" Brief *a poison-pen letter* **B.** [adv] ⟨fig⟩ *maliciously, viciously*; *cantankerously* ‖ ~ wirkend *toxicant* ‖ er starrte sie ~ an *he glared at her venomously* | **≗keit** f *venomousness*; *toxicity*; *virulence*; *toxic* od *poisonous nature* od *condition* ⟨fig⟩ *banefulness, perniciousness* ‖ *maliciousness, malice, viciousness, virulence* (*of speech*)

Gig f ~/~s **1.** ⟨mar⟩ *gig* ‖ *clinker-built boat*; *skiff* **2.** n (2rädr. Wagen) *gig*

gig·ampfen vi/t [h] Sw = schaukeln

Gig·ant m ~en/~en ⟨ant myth⟩ *giant* | **≗isch** a *gigantean*; *gigantic* (*fight*; *height*) **~enkampf** m, **Gigantomach·ie** f ⟨ant myth⟩ *gigantomachy*

G·igerl m ~s/~ *dandy, fop*; ⟨sl⟩ *masher*; ⟨Am sl⟩ *dude* | **≗haft** a *dandy*(*ish*), *foppish*

G·igolo [ʒi–] m = Eintänzer

Gigue [ʒi:g] f Fr ~/~s ⟨mus⟩ **1.** (Viola) *gigue* Fr **2.** ⟨mus⟩ *gigue*; ⟨engl⟩ (Tanz) *jig*

G·ilatier n ⟨zoo⟩ *gila monster*

Gilb m ~(e)s/ (in Wäsche) *the devil "Yellow"* **~blume** f ⟨bot⟩ *yellow camomile*

G·ilbertinseln f pl (Koralleninseln im Stillen Ozean) *Gilbert Islands*

G·ilde f ~/~n ⟨hist⟩ **1.** *g*(*u*)*ild*; *corporation* ‖ ⟨engl⟩ die (78) jahrhundertealten mächtigen ~n der City v London *the Livery Companies*; Amtskleidung, –tracht der ~n *livery*; Zugehörigkeit z e–r der ~n *livery* **2.** [in comp] **~bruder** m *member of a guild* **~meister** m *head of a guild*

G·ilden- [in comp] **~halle** f, **~haus** n *guild-hall* **~sozialismus** m *guild socialism*

G·illing, G·illung f ⟨mar⟩ **1.** (e–s Rahsegels) *roach* **2.** (des Hinterschiffs) *tuck*

G·impe f *gimp, gymp* | ~nspitze [f] *gimp*

G·impel m ~s/~ **1.** ⟨orn⟩ *bullfinch*; → *grosbeak*; Blutfink, Dompfaff **2.** ⟨fig⟩ *dunce, dupe, simpleton*; ⟨sl⟩ *cully, pigeon*; ⟨Am⟩ *sucker*, ⟨fam⟩ *pushover* ‖ auf den ~fang ausgehen ⟨fig⟩ *to work the confidence trick*

ging 1. & 3. sg pret v gehen

G·ingam m (Baumwollstoff) *gingham*

Ging·ellisamen m = Nigersamen

G·inster m ~s/ ⟨bot⟩ *broom*; Besen≗ *Scotch br.*; niedriger ~ *dwarf br.*, Sand≗ *hairy green weed*; Stech≗ *furze, gorse*; → *broom* | ~katze [f] ⟨zoo⟩ *Genette*

G·ipfel m ~s/~ **1.** *summit, top*; (spitzer) *peak, pinnacle* **2.** ⟨fig⟩ *acme, climax, culmination, culminating-point, height, peak, pinnacle, pitch, summit, top*; das ist der ~! *that's the* (*dizzy* od *frozen*) *limit*; (Höhe, Höhepunkt) auf dem ~ der Macht *at the pinnacle of power*, .. des Glücks *on the crest of the wave*; .. des Ruhmes *at the zenith of one's fame*; der ~ der Vollkommenheit *the pink of perfection*; der ~ der Frechheit *the height of impudence* **~höhe** f ⟨ball⟩ *ordinate*; ⟨aero⟩ (*absolute*) *ceiling* **~leistung** f ⟨tech⟩ *peak-achievement* ‖ ⟨sport⟩ *record* **~knospe** f *end-bud* **~konferenz** f ⟨pol⟩ *summit c.* **~punkt** m *culminating point* **≗ständig** a ⟨bot⟩ *terminal, apical* **~trieb** m ⟨for⟩ *top-shot*; *leader* **~wert** m *peak value*

g·ipf(e)lig a [in comp] *peaked*; zwei~ *two-peaked* **g·ipfeln** vi ⟨fig⟩ ~ in *to culminate in*; *to reach the climax* od *zenith* (od *one's peak*) *in* ..; *to attain one's height in*

G·ips m –ses/–se ⟨minr⟩ *gypsum*; *hydrous sulphate of calcium* ‖ gebrannter ~ *plaster of Paris, gesso* ‖ kristallisierter ~ *selenite* ‖ in ~-(verband) *in plaster*, ⟨Am⟩ *in cast* **~abdruck, ~abguß** m *plaster-cast* **~arbeiter** m *plasterer* **≗artig** a *chalky* **~bett** n *plaster-jacket* **~bewurf** m *plastering* **~bild** n *plaster figure* **~binde** f *plaster of Paris bandage* **~figur** f *plaster figure*; ~enhändler [m] *dealer in plaster-figures* **≗haltig** a *gyps*(*e*)*ous* **~kraut** n ⟨bot⟩ *gypsophila* **~mehl** n *flower of gypsum, powdered gypsum* **~modell** n *plaster-model* **~mörtel** m *plaster, stucco* **~verband** m ⟨surg⟩ *plaster* (*of Paris*) *dressing*; *to put a p's leg in plaster* (*of P.*) (⟨Am⟩ *in cast*)

g·ipsen vt [h] *to plaster* **G·ipser** m ~s/~ *plasterer*

Gip·ürarbeit f *gimp-work* **Gip·üre** f *gimp*

Gir·affe f ~/~n ⟨zoo⟩ *giraffe*; → Okapi

Gir·ant [ʒi:–] m ~en/~en ⟨com⟩ *in–, endorser*

Gir·at, Girat·ar m ~s/~e ⟨com⟩ *in–, endorsee*

gir·ierbar a *endorsable, in–* **gir·ieren** vt [h] ⟨com⟩ (Scheck, Wechsel) *to endorse, in–* (auf jdn *in favour of a p*); *to circulate*

Girl·ande f ~/~n *garland*; *festoon* ‖ mit ~en schmücken *to festoon, garland*

G·irlitz m ~es/~e ⟨orn⟩ *serin*

G·iro [ʒi:–] n ~s/~s ⟨bank⟩ *in–, endorsement*; ausgefülltes ~ *special e.*; unausgefülltes ~ *blank e.* ‖ (etw) mit s–m ~ versehen, (e–r S) sein ~ geben *to endorse* **~abteilung** f *cheque department* (*of a bank*) **~bank** f ⟨Ger⟩ *transfer-bank* **~geschäft** n ⟨Ger⟩ *transfer-business* **~guthaben** n ⟨Ger⟩ *balance in a tr.-b.* **~kasse** f ⟨Ger⟩ *communal bank* (etc.) *connected with the tr.-bu.* **~konto** n ⟨Ger⟩ *drawing* od *current account* **~kunde** m ⟨Ger⟩ *customer of a tr.-ba.* **~·obligo** n *endorser's liability* **~überweisung** f ⟨Ger⟩ *ba.-tr.* **~verband** m ⟨Ger⟩ *Clearing House of the Association of Bankers* **~verkehr** m ⟨Ger⟩ *tr.* (od *clearing*)*-bu.* **~zahlung** f ⟨Ger⟩ *payment by ba.-tr.* **~zentrale** f ⟨Ger⟩ *clearinghouse* (*of communal banks*)

Gir·onde f [ʒi'rɔ̃d] ⟨Fr⟩ (Fluß u Departement)

g·irren vi [h] ⟨orn⟩ *to coo* ‖ ⟨fig⟩ (P) *to* (*bill and*) *coo*

Gis n ~/~ ⟨mus⟩ *G sharp* ‖ ~-Moll *g sharp minor*

g·ischen vi [h] *to foam, froth* ‖ *bubble, effervesce*

G·ischt m ~es/~e *spindrift, spray*; *foam*; *froth*

g·issen vt [h] ⟨mar⟩ (etw) *to estimate*; → Besteck **G·issung** f ⟨mar⟩ *dead reckoning*

G·itarre f ~/~n *guitar*; ~ spielen *to play the g.* ‖ hawaiische viersaitige ~ *akulele*; japan. dreisaitige ~ *samisen* **~nspieler** m *guitar-player*

G·itter n ~s/~ **1. a.** *lattice, trellis* (Draht≗ *wire-lattice* [od *trellis*]); *grating* (Fenster≗ *window-g.*); *fence*; *railing*; ⟨zoo⟩ *railings* ‖ mit e–m ~ versehen *to lattice, trellis*; hinter ~n sitzen *to sit behind bars* ‖ Feuer≗ *fire-guard*; Kamin≗ *grate* ‖ ~ in e–r Tür *grill*(*e*) Fr **b.** ⟨arch bes ec⟩ *screen*; Altar≗ *parclose*; → Lettner **c.** ⟨wir⟩ *grid* **2.** ⟨übtr geog⟩ (~netz) *grid* **3.** ⟨opt⟩ *grating*; ⟨mar⟩ *graticule*; Beugung am ~ *diffraction grating* **≗artig** a *latticed*; *lattice-like* **~bett** n *latticed bedstead*; *bed with* (*cord*) *netting* **~brücke** f *lattice bridge* **~draht** m *wire-netting* **~durchgriff** m ⟨phys⟩ *grid penetration factor* **~fenster** n *barred window*; *lattice-window* **≗förmig** *n latticed*; *cross-barred*; *trellised*; *grid-form* (*signal nets*) **~gleichrichter** m *grid* od *bias rectifier* **~kennlinie** f *grid characteristic* **~kreis** m ⟨wir⟩ *grid-circuit* **~mast** m *lattice tower*; *trellis-mast* **~netz** n ⟨geog⟩ *grid* | ~karte [f] *coordinate map* **~pflanze** f ⟨bot⟩ *Cape pondweed* **~rumpf** m ⟨aero⟩ *truss type fuselage* **~schlange** f ⟨zoo⟩ *python* **~spektrum** n *grating spectrum* **~stoff** m *canvas* **~tor** n *trellis*(*ed*)*-gate* **~verzierung** f *lattice-ornament* **~vorspannbatterien** pl ⟨el⟩ *grid bias batteries* pl **~werk** n *lattice-work*; *trellis-work*; *grating*; geflochtenes ~ *fret* **~widerstand** m ⟨wir⟩ (f Netzempfänger) *grid-leak*; (f Batterieanschluß) *grid-resistance* **~zaun** m *railed fence*; *trellis-work fence* **~zeichnung** f *cross-hatching*

g·ittern vt [h] *to lattice, rail*

Glac·é [gla'se:] n (Fr) ~s/~s *glacé fabric* **~handschuh** m *kid-glove* || °⟨fig⟩ (jdn) mit ~en anfassen *to featherbed* **~karton** m *enamel* od *glazed board* **~leder** n *glacé-kid* **~papier** n *enamel paper, enamels* pl

glac·ieren [-si:-] vt [h] ⟨cul⟩ (Früchte) *to frost, to ice* **glac·iert** a ⟨cul⟩ *glazed; glacé* Fr; *frosted, iced*; ~er Überzug *frosting, icing*

Glac·is [gla'si:] n (Fr) ~/~ ⟨fort⟩ *glacis* Fr

Gladi·ator m ~s/-at·oren ⟨ant⟩ *gladiator*

Gladi·ole f ~/~n ⟨bot⟩ *gladiolus* L

Gl·anz m ~es/ **A.** [abstr, nur sg] **1.** *brightness* (*of the stars*), *brilliance* (*of the sky*), *brilliancy*; *sparkle* (*of eyes*); *glory* (*of the morning*), *radiance, splendour*; Farben≗ *brightness of colour*; Regenbogen≗ *iridescence* || *glitter, sparkle*; blendender ~ *glare*; heller ~ *blaze, resplendence* (*of candles*) **2.** (an Gegenständen) *lustre* (*of gold*); *polish*; Glas≗, Metall≗ *lustre* || *brilliance* (*of jewels*); wasserartiger ~ *water* || *gloss* (*of a stuff*); *sheen* (auf Seide *on silk*); schillernder ~ *water*; e–m Gewebe atlasartigen ~ verleihen *to beetle a fabric* || *glaze*; Schuh≗ *polish*; ⟨Am⟩ *shine* **3.** ⟨übtr⟩ **a.** *splendour* (*of society*; *of a p's achievements*); *brilliance* (*of the court*); *glitter*; *glory, lustre, magnificence, pomp*; → Blüte ⟨fig⟩ || *perfection, polish* || äußerer ~ *gilt, gloss*; täuschender ~ *tinsel* **b. etw s–s ~es berauben** *to take the bloom off a th* || e–r S neuen ~ verleihen *to give new lustre to a th* | **sich in** s–m vollen ~ zeigen *to show great form*; *to show to perfection* || (Prüfung) **mit** ~ bestehen *to pass with distinction*; °mit ~ durchfallen *to fail miserably* || °er flog mit ~ hinaus ⟨fam⟩ *they turned him out with a vengeance* (od *like a hundred of bricks*) || °sich mit ~ aus der Affäre ziehen *to back out cleverly* **B.** [konkr] ⟨chem⟩ ~e [pl] *lustrous ores* pl; [nur in comp] .. *glance*; Blei≗ *lead glance*, etc. **~bürste** f *polishing brush* **~fäden** m pl *metallic threads* ⟨a. weav⟩ **~fasan** m ⟨orn⟩ (Königs≗) *Impeyan pheasant* **~farbe** f *brilliant* od *glossy colo(u)r*; *gloss ink* **~firnis** m *brilliant* (od *glazing*) *varnish* **~fisch** m = Schmelzschupper **~gold** n *brilliant gold; gold-foil* **~gras** n ⟨bot⟩ *phalaris* L **~haut** f ⟨path⟩ *glossy skin* **~jahr** n ⟨com⟩ *peak-year*, ⟨Am⟩ *banner-year*; ~e [pl] *boom-years* pl **~käfer** m ⟨ent⟩ ⟨Am⟩ *gold-beetle* **~karton** m = -pappe **~kattun** n *glazed calico* **~kobalt** m *cobalt-glance*; *cobaltite* **~kohle** f *glance-coal*; *anthracite* **~lack** m *brilliant varnish* **~leder** n *patent leather* **~leinwand** f *glazed linen* **~leistung** f *peak-achievement*; *splendid achievement*; ~en [pl] *splendours* pl **~lichter** n pl ⟨phot & fig⟩ *high-lights* ≗**los** a *lustreless*; *lack-lustre* (*eyes*); *dim, dull* **~mittel** n *brightener* **~papier** n *glazed* (od *enamel*) *paper* **~pappe** f *glazed board* **~periode** f = -zeit **~presse** f *glazing calender* **~punkt** m ⟨fig⟩ *clou* Fr; *chief attraction*; (of a revue) *high-light*; → Höhepunkt **~ruß** m *shining soot* **~seide** f *lustrine, lustring* **~seite** f ⟨a. fig⟩ *bright side* **~silber** n *silver glance* **~stärke** f *gloss starch* **~stelle** f ⟨fig⟩ die ~n *the purple patches* (*in an essay*); *plums* pl **~stoff** m = Kunstseide **~stück** n ⟨fig⟩ *gem* ≗**voll** a *brilliant*; *gorgeous, grand, magnificent*; *splendid* (*period, scene*); *bright* (*future*) **~wichse** f *boot-polish* **~zeit** f *palmy days* pl; *prime* **~zwirn** m *glacé thread*

gl·änzen vi [h] **1.** ⟨eig⟩ (of jewels, stars) *to coruscate, glisten, glitter, shine, sparkle* (*with*); *to be brilliant* (*with gold*) || → Gold **2.** ⟨übtr⟩ **a.** (of eyes) *to blaze*; *glitter* (vor .. *with excitement*); *his face shone with happiness* **b.** (P) *to be conspicuous*; *to shine, scintillate* (als .. *as a teacher*); er glänzte durch .. *he was conspicuous for* (*his knowledge*); .. °durch Abwesenheit .. *by his absence* || (of wit) *to coruscate* (v *with*); *to glitter*; *sparkle* **gl·änzend A.** [a] **1.** ⟨eig⟩ **a.** *bright, brilliant, resplendent, glittering* (*armour*), *lustrous* (*hair*); *radiant* (*stars*), *shining*; *sparkling* (*jewels*) **b.** *brilliant, glorious* (*day*); *radiant* (*morning*) **c.** (blank) *glossy, shiny* **2.** ⟨übtr⟩ *gorgeous, grand, magnificent, splendid* (*scene*); ~e Versammlung *gallaxy* || *admirable, bright* (*future*); *brilliant* (*scholar*); *first-rate*; *glorious* (*achievement*; *victory*); *magnificent* (*rider*); *shining* (*example*); *splendid, striking* (*essay*); ein ~er Flieger *an ace* || ⟨fam⟩ *nailing* (*play*); ⟨sl⟩ *top-hole* **3.** °⟨fig⟩ **a.** *brilliant, excellent, splendid* (*idea*); *grand* (*weather*) || *showy* (*career*) || ⟨fam⟩ *clinking, rattling* (*success*); *ripping*; *roaring* (*health*); *topping*; *a ripping good story*; in ~er Verfassung *in the pink of condition*; *a high old time*, ⟨Am⟩ *a slick time* **b.** er ist einfach ~ als .. *he is perfectly gorgeous as* (*Hamlet*) || ⟨sport⟩ ~ s in *to be a whale at* (*football*); er ist ~ ⟨Am sl⟩ *he is mustard* **c.** ~! *good egg*! *fine*! wie geht es dir? ≗! *how are you*? *Full of beans*! **d.** ein ~er Reinfall *a grand failure* || das -e Elend *the shabby genteel* **B.** [adv] **1.** *brightly, brilliantly* (*lighted*); *radiantly* **2.** ⟨übtr & fig⟩ *admirably*; *brilliantly* (*to write b.*); *magnificently, splendidly*; ⟨fam⟩ *famously* || °~ dastehen *to be on velvet* || ⟨com⟩ ~ gehen *to go off like a house on fire* || das paßt mir ~ *that suits me down to the bottom* od *ground* || ~ vorwärtskommen ⟨fam⟩ *to get on famously* (*with* ..), *to get on like a house on fire* || ~ wirken *to work to perfection*

Gl·arner m, **~in** f *inhabitant of Glarus* **Gl·arner Alpen** pl (Teil der Westalpen) *Glarus Alps* **Gl·arus** n (schweiz. Kanton)

Gl·as n ~es/≗er **A. 1.** (Stoff) **a.** *glass*; feines Flach≗, Spiegel≗ *plate-g.*; Jenaer ~ *Jena g.*; nicht springendes ~ ⟨mot⟩ *non-shattering* (od *triplex*) *g.*; *splinter proof g.* || (plan)geschliffen (*flat*)*ground* || buntes ~ *stained g.* || unter ~ *under g.*; unter ~ u Rahmen *glazed and framed* || ~ blasen *to blow g.*; ~ m *to make g.* || °du bist doch nicht aus ~? *is your father a glazier*? || mit ~ bedecken, versehen *to glaze* **b.** ⟨geol⟩ *glass*; natürliches ~ *natural g.* **2.** [koll] **a.** = Fenster-(scheiben) pl (etc) **b.** (~waren) *glass* (*glass and china*) **3.** (Gegenstand aus ~) **a.** (Gefäß) *glass*; ≗er *glasses* pl || geschliffenes ~ *ground* od *cut g.*; plan- *optical flat g.* || Trink≗ *drinking-g.*; Wein≗ *wineg.*; ~ ohne Fuß u Henkel *tumbler* || volles ~ *bumper*; ein ~ voll Wein *a glassful of wine*; ein halbes ~ .. *half a g.* (*of wine*); ⟨sl⟩ *a split of brandy* (etc) || zwei ~ Bier *two g.es of beer*; ⟨engl⟩ *two stouts* | ein ~ Kognak nach dem anderen trinken *to drink g. after g. of brandy* || bot ihnen ein ~ W. an *offered them vermouths* || beim ~e Wein *over a bottle* || °er hat z tief ins ~ geguckt *he has had a g.* (od *drop*) *too much* **b.** (Brille) *g.es* pl, *spectacles* pl **c.** = Sanduhr **d.** ⟨poet⟩ = Spiegel **B.** ⟨mar⟩ -ses/-sen (= $^1/_2$ Stunde Wache) *bell*; *half-hour of the watch*; ~en *eight bells* (= *midnight*) **~arbeit** f (Gefäße) *g.-work* ≗**artig** a *vitreous, g.y*; *g.* (od *vitreous*)*-like* **~auge** n ⟨anat⟩ *g. eye* || ⟨vet⟩ (of a horse) *wall-eye* ≗**äugig** a ⟨vet⟩ *wall-eyed* **~baustein** m *g.-brick* **~behälter** m *g. case* || *g.-tank* (*for seals*) **~bildner** m *glass-former* **~blasen** n *g.-blowing* **~bläser** m *g.-blower* **~boot** m ⟨zoo⟩ *cephalopod*; *Argonauta Argo* L || †~-**brenner** m = -macher **~bruch** m *g. breakage* **~bürste** f *g.-brush* **~deckel** m *g.-cap* (od *cover*) **~erz** n *silver glance* **~fabrikation** f *g.-manufacture* **~faden** m *g.-thread* ≗**faserverstärkt** a *glass-reinforced* **~fenster** n *g. window* **~flasche** f *g. bottle* **~flügler** m ⟨ent⟩ (Schmetterling) *g.-wing* **~fluß** m = -paste **~galle** f *g.-gall, sandiver* **~gefäß** n *g.-vessel* **~gemälde** f *stained-g. window* **~gespinst** n *g. thread*; = ~watte **~glanz** m *lustre* **~glocke** f *g.-globe*; *g.-cover*; *g.-shade*; ⟨hort⟩ *bell-g.* **~handel** m *g.-trade* **~händler** m *dealer in g.*, *g.-man* **~harmonika** f (*g.-*)*harmonica*

~haus n *g.-house* = Gewächshaus ‖ wer im ~ sitzt, sollte nicht mit Steinen werfen *people in g.--houses shouldn't throw stones* **~hütte** f *g.-factory* (od *works* pl) **~industrie** f *g.-industry* **~kasten** m *g.-case* **~kopf** m ⟨geol⟩ brauner ~ = Brauneisenerz; roter ~ = Roteisenstein; schwarzer ~ *psilomelane* **~koralle** f *g.-bead*; (schwarze) *bugle* **~korb** m (f Glas) *crate* **~körper** m (im Auge) *vitreous humour* (od *body*) **~kraut** n ⟨bot⟩ *g.--wort*; *pellitory* **~kugel** f *g.-globe* od *-head* **~-kühlofen** m *leer* **~kuppel** f (der Kanzel) ⟨aero⟩ *canopy* **~lava** f *volcanic g.*; *obsidian* **~leinwand** f *g.-cloth* **~macher** m *g.-founder* **~maler** m *g.--stainier* **~malerei** f *g.-painting* (od *staining*); *stained g.* **~masse** f *vitreous mass* **~mehl** n *g.-meal* (od *powder*) **~opal** m *hyalite* **~papier** n *g.--paper* **~paste** f *g.-paste*; *enamel* **~perle** f *bead* **~platte** f *g.-plate* (od *sheet*); Tisch mit ~ *g.-topped table* **~porzellan** n *vitreous porcelain* **~rahmen** m *g. frame* **~rohr** n (am Destillierapparat) *delivery-tube* **~röhre** f *g.-tube* **~salz** n = –galle **~scheibe** f *g.-pane* (od *sheet*); *windowpane* **~scherbe** f *piece of broken g.*; ~n [pl] *cullet*; *broken g.* **~schirm** m *g. shade* **~schlange** f ⟨zoo⟩ (Echse) *g.-snake* **~schleifen** n *g.-grinding* **~schleifer** m *g.-grinder* **~schmalz** m ⟨bot⟩ *g.wort*; *marsh samphire* **~schmelz** m *enamel* ‖ ~masse [f] *frit* **~schnecke** f ⟨zoo⟩ *g.-snail* **~schneiden** n *g.--cutting* **~schneider** m *g.-cutter* **~schrank** m *g.-cupboard*; *display cabinet*; → –vitrine **~schüssel** f *g. dish* **~schwamm** m ⟨zoo⟩ *g.-sponge*; Ordnung der ~̈e *hexactillenida* L **~seide** f *g.-silk* **~seife** f *g.-soap* **~splitter** m *shiver of g.* **~stein** m *axinite* **~tafel** f *g.-plate* (od *sheet*) **~tränen** f pl *g.-drops*, *Prince Rupert's drops* pl **~veranda** f *sun parlour* **~versicherung** f *g.-insurance* **~vitrine** f *showcase* **~wand** f *g.-partition* **~waren** f pl *g.ware*; Verkäufer v ~ *g.man* **~watte, ~wolle** f *fibre g.*; *g. wool*

Gl·äschen n *small glass*; (Schnaps) *peg*; *tot* (*two tots of whisky*) ‖ °er hat ein ~ über den Durst getrunken *he has had a glass* (od *drop*) *too much*

Gl·aser m ~s/~ *glazier*; ⟨fig⟩ ist dein Vater ~? *is your f. a g.?* **~diamant** m *g.'s diamond* **~gesell(e)** m *journeyman-g.* **~handwerk** n *g.'s trade* **~kitt** m *putty* **~meister** m *glazier*

Glaser·ei f ~/~en *glaziery*; *glazier's trade* (od *work* ‖ (Laden) *glazier's* (*work*)*shop*

Gl·äserklang m, **~klingen** n *clinking of glasses*

gl·äsern 1. [a] *glass* (*instrument*); *of glass*; *glassy*, *vitreous* ‖ ⟨übtr⟩ *glassy* (*look*); mit ~en Augen *glassily*; ~ w *to glaze* **2.** [adv] *glassily* **glas·ieren 1.** vt [h] (Steingut) *to glaze*; *to varnish*; glasierte Ofenkachel *Dutch tile* ‖ (Papier) *to enamel* ‖ → glacieren **2.** ~̈ n *glazing* **gl·asig** a ⟨geol⟩ *vitreous* (*lustre*) ‖ ⟨übtr⟩ *glassy* (*eyes*), *glazed*; *lifeless*; → gläsern **Glast** m ~es/ [obd] = Glanz ~̈**ig** a = glänzend **Glas·ur** f ~/~en *glaze*, *glazing*; *varnish*; geflammte ~ *furnace transmutation glaze*; (Schmelz) *enamel* ‖ ⟨cul⟩ *frosting*, *icing* | ~brand [m] *glaze baking*

gl·att A. [a] compr ~er, ~̈er; sup ~est, ~̈est] **1. a.** *smooth* (*floor*, *surface*; *face*); *satiny* (*paper*) ‖ einseitig ~ *machine glazed* (*paper*); *flush* (*door*, *without panels*); ⟨mot⟩ *good going* (*road*); *fine--grained* (*flour for rolls*, etc); (of the sea) *glassy*, *smooth*; *unruffled* ‖ ⟨typ⟩ ~er Satz *running-on matter* ‖ Gewehr mit ~em Lauf *smooth-bore* | (of style) *flowing*, *round*, *smooth* **b.** *glossy*, *polished*; *sleek* (*hair*, *skin*); *smooth* **c.** (schlicht) *plain* (*material*) ‖ (nicht lockig) *lank* (*hair*) ‖ (unbehaart) *glabrous* **2.** (glitschig) **a.** *slippery* (*deck*; *floor*; *eel*); es ist hier sehr ~ z gehen *it is very slippery walking here* **b.** ⟨übtr⟩ *sleek*, *slippery*; *smooth* (*tongue*, *words*); *suave*; *bland*; *oily*; → Aal; ~e Art *suave manners pl*; ~e Zunge *glib tongue* **3.** ⟨übtr⟩ *smooth* (*development*, *landing*); *straight forward* (*business*); *unobstructed*; e–e ~e S *a straightforward matter*; *uneventful* (*journey*; *recovery*) **4.** °⟨fig⟩ *absolute*; *blunt*; *downright*; *flat* (*contradiction*, *denial*); ⟨Am⟩ *slick* ‖ e–e ~e Lüge *a pure* (*simple*, *flat*) *lie*, *a plumper*; ein ~es Nein *a plump no*; ~e Unmöglichkeit *sheer impossibility*; ~er Unsinn *downright nonsense* **B.** [adv] **1.** *smoothly*; ~ anliegen *or* sitzen *to fit close* ‖ ~ geschoren *closely cropped*; ~ rasiert *clean* (od *smooth*)*-shaven* **2.** ⟨übtr⟩ *smoothly* (*to land s.*); *without a hitch*; *without ado*; es ging ~ *it was plain sailing* ⟨fig⟩; ~ ab-, verlaufen *to go off well*, *to go with a swing*; ~ (vonstatten) gehen *to go* (od *run*) *smoothly*; *to go swimmingly* ‖ jdm ~ eingehen *to go down well with a p* ‖ ~ gewinnen *to win hands down* **3.** °⟨fig⟩ **a.** *absolutely*; *bluntly*, (*to deny*) *downright*, *flatly*; *roundly* ‖ *clean* (*impossible*) ‖ s–e Bitte wurde ~ abgelehnt *his request was refused point blank* ‖ ich schlug es ihm ~ ab *I gave him a flat denial* ‖ ~ erfunden *cut out of* (*the*) *whole cloth* ‖ ~ 50 Mark gewinnen ⟨Am sl⟩ *to win 50 marks cold* ‖ jdm etw ~ ins Gesicht sagen *to say a th straight in a p's face* ‖ ich will nicht ~ Nein sagen *I won't say No off-hand* ‖ er sprang ~ aus .. *he jumped bang out of* (*the window*) ‖ (im Spiel) ~ 100 Mark verlieren ⟨fam⟩ *to lose a cool hundred* ‖ *he flatly refused to obey* ‖ → glattweg **b.** *completely*, *entirely*; ich hatte es ~ vergessen *I had completely* (⟨Am⟩ *plumb*) *forgotten about it* **~|bürsten** vt [h] *to brush up* ~̈**butt** m ⟨ich⟩ *rhombus laevis* L ~̈**deck** n *flush deck*; ~schiff [n] *flush-decked ship* **~|drücken** vt [h] *to flatten out* ~̈**eis** n *glazed frost*; *slippery ice*, *silver thaw*; *glazed ice*; es ist ~ *it is* (od *the streets are*) *very slippery* (od *glazed*) *with ice*; Bei Frost ~gefahr ⟨mot⟩ *Slippery when frosty* ‖ jdn aufs ~ führen *to lead a p astray* (od *by the nose*); *to dupe* od *trick a p* ~̈**feile** f *smoothing file* **~gehend** a ⟨sl⟩ *slick* (*play*) **~gestrickt** a (→ glatt; stricken) *plain-knit* **~haarig** a *smooth-haired* ~̈**hafer** m ⟨bot⟩ *false-oat*; *oat-grass* ~̈**hai** m ⟨ich⟩ *tope* **~|hobeln** vt [h] *to plane* **~|kämmen** vt [h] (Haar) *to sleek*; glattgekämmt *slicked-back* (*hair*) **~|machen** vt [h] *to smooth*, *polish*; *even*; *flush*; (Haar) *to slick* ‖ ⟨übtr com⟩ *to pay up*; *to settle*; *to square* (*up*); *to even up* **~schnitt** n ⟨phot⟩ *straight edge* **~|stellen** vt [h] ⟨übtr com⟩ = –machen ~̈**stellung** f ⟨com⟩ *evening up*; *paying up*; *liquidation*; *realization*; *settlement* **~|streichen** vt [h] *to flatten out*; *to smooth down* ~̈**wal** m ⟨zoo⟩ *Greenland whale* **~w·eg** adv *downright*; *flatly*; *plump* (*he lied p.*); *point-blank*; = glatt B. 3. **~|ziehen** vt [h] *to straighten*; *flatten* **~züngig** a *smooth-tongued* (od *faced*); *glib*; *plausible* (*person*)

Gl·ätt- [in comp] (→ glätten) **~ahle** f *round broach* **~bein** n *burnisher* **~eisen** n *smoothing-iron* **~gerät** n *burnisher*; *glazer* **~holz** n *burnisher*; *sleeker*; *slicker* **~maschine** f *glazing machine*; *planing-machine*; *rolling-machine* **~presse** f *smoothing-press*; ⟨typ⟩ *standing-press* **~werkzeug** n *burnisher*, *polishing* (od *smoothing*) *-tool* **~zahn** m = –werkzeug

Gl·ätte f ~/ **1. a.** *smoothness*; *evenness* ‖ *glassiness* **b.** *glossiness*; *gloss*; *polish* (*of a mirror*); *sleekness* **2. a.** *slipperiness* (*of the ice*) **b.** ⟨übtr⟩ *sleekness* (*of manners*); *slipperiness*; *smoothness*; *suavity* **3.** (of style) *finish*; *polish*; *smoothness*

gl·ätten A. vt [h] **1. a.** (etw) *to smooth*, *surface*, *even*; *to give* (*a th*) *a smooth* ‖ (Haar) *to set*, *to sleek* ‖ (polieren) (Metall) *to burnish*, *furbish*, *polish*; *planish*; *plane*; (Stein) *to face* | ⟨tech⟩ (Papier) *to glaze*, *to satin* ‖ (Tuch) *to calender*, *to press* ‖ (Leder etc) *to supple*; ⟨pap⟩ *to flatten*; *to straighten* (*prints*) **b.** ⟨fig⟩ (Stil) *to file*; *finish* ‖ (wissensch. Werk) *to chisel* ‖ *to supple*; *to tone down* **2. sich ~** (of the sea, conditions, etc) *to calm* *down*; *to smooth down* **B.** ≃ n *smooth*(*ing*); *sleeking* ‖ *glazing*; *polishing*

Gl·ätter m *smoother* **Gl·attheit** f = Glätte 1. 2.

Glatz n (Stadt in Niederschlesien) **Gl·atzer Bergland** n (Teil der Sudeten) *Glatz Mountains*

Gl·atze f ∼/∼n *baldness*; *bald-head* (od *pate*); ⟨fam⟩ *disc* **Gl·atzflechte** f ⟨vet⟩ *herpes tonsurans* L **gl·atzig** a *bald*; = glatzköpfig **Gl·atzkopf** m *bald-head*; *bald-headed p.*; *shaveling* **gl·atzköpfig** a *bald-headed* (od *pated*); *shaveling*

Gl·aube(n) m ∼ns/ **1.** *belief* (an Gott *in God*; an sich selbst *in o.s.*); *faith* (*in*); der ∼, daß .. *the b. that* .. ‖ ⟨rel & pol⟩ *creed* ‖ ⟨theol⟩ *faith* (*his f. is strong*); *religious b.*; *persuasion*; der christliche ∼ *the Christian f.*; katholischen ∼ns s *to be of the Roman Catholic p.* | **blinder** ∼ *unquestioning* od *implicit f.* ‖ fester ∼ *firm b.*; *p.* ‖ unerschütterlicher ∼ *unswerving f.* | s–n ∼n **abschwören** *to abjure one's f.*; s–n ∼n bekennen *to avow* (od *profess*) *one's f.*; s–n ∼ verleugnen *to renounce one's f.* ‖ am ∼n festhalten *to abide by one's f.* ‖ der ∼ allein macht selig *f. alone makes happy*; °⟨iron⟩ ∼ macht selig! *don't believe it*! *never*! **2.** ⟨übtr⟩ *belief* **a.** ∼n **finden** *to find credit*; (S) ∼ f. bei *to go down with* (*a p*) ‖ nicht viel ∼n f. bei jdm *not to cut much ice with a p* ‖ jdm ∼ schenken *to believe* (od *credit*, *trust*) *a p*; *to give credence* od *credit to a p*, .. darin, daß .. *to take a p's word for it that*; .. k–n ∼ sch. *to doubt* (*a p's words*); e–r S ∼n sch. *to believe a th*; *to give* (od *attach*) *credence* (od *credit*) *to a th* ‖ des ∼ns s, daß .. *to believe* od *hold that* ..; jdm den ∼n versagen *to disbelieve a p*; den ∼n an etw verstärken *to give further credence to a th* **b. auf** Treu u ∼n hinnehmen *to take* (*a th*) *on trust* ‖ laß ihn **bei** s–m ∼n *let him believe what he likes* ‖ **in** gutem ∼n *in* (*all*) *good f.* ‖ es bestärkte ihn in dem ∼n, daß .. *it made him all the more believe that* .. ‖ ich war im ∼n, dich dort z finden *I thought* (od *expected*) *to find you there* **c. des ∼ns s, daß ..** *to believe* od *hold that* .. **gl·auben** vt/i **A.** vt **1.** (etw; [mst pron:] es, das) *to believe*; nicht ∼ *to disbelieve*; es wird allg ge–bt *it is common belief*; (beweisen läßt sich das nicht), das muß man ∼ (..), *that is a matter of faith*; er glaubt nicht, was .. *he does not believe what* (*he preaches*) ‖ ⟨mst übtr⟩ das will ich (gerne) ∼ *I should think so*, (*I'm sure of it*); ja, das glaube ich *yes*, *I b.* (od *think*) *so*; das glaube ich nicht, das kann ich nicht ∼ *that won't go down with me*; könnt ihr's ∼? *would you b. it*? ihr mögt es ∼ oder nicht *b. it or not*; das glaubst du doch *or* wohl selbst nicht! *tell me another*!; das ist kaum z ∼ *that is past belief*; nicht z ∼ *incredible* ‖ ich glaube nur e–n Teil v .. *I discount a great deal of* (*what I hear*) ‖ er glaubt alles, was .. *he swallows everything that* (*is told him*) | ich **glaube es ihm** nicht *I do not b. what he says*; du kannst es mir ∼ *you can take it from me*; *you may b. me*; ⟨Am⟩ *b. me*; ich glaub's Dir ⟨iron⟩ *well I never*! **2. ∼, daß .. a.** *to b. that* (*there is a God*) ‖ zuversichtlich ∼, daß .. *to trust that* .. **b.** ⟨übtr⟩ (vermuten) *to b.* (od *hold*, *think*; *suppose*; ⟨Am⟩ *to allow*) *that* ..; *to be of the belief that* ..; ich glaube (wohl), ich werde bald zurück s *I dare say I shall soon be back*; er wird k, gl. ich *I think* (⟨Am a.⟩ *calculate*, *guess*, *reckon*) *he will come*; man glaubte, daß er .. gestohlen habe *he was thought* (od *supposed*) *to have stolen* ..; ich glaube, daß er ein Dichter ist *I think* (od *b.*) *him to be a poet* ‖ ich **gl. gar,** du hast es ihm gesagt *I even think* (od *for all I know*) *you have told him* ‖ ich **möchte** ∼, daß .. *I should say that* .. **3. er glaubt, recht z h** *he b.s himself to be right*; er gl., berechtigt z s *he thinks he is authorized* ..; er glaubte, ihn z kennen *he thought he knew him* ‖ ich glaubte, dich dort z finden *I thought* (od *expected*) *to find you there* ‖ sich geborgen ∼ *to think o.s. safe* ‖ wir glaubten dich in Berlin *we thought you were in B.*; ∼, es m z müssen *to feel obliged to do it* **4.** [**abs**] ich glaube *I think so* ‖ glaubst du wirklich? *are you sure*? ‖ ich glaube gar! *I should think not*! *impossible*! *nonsense*! **B.** vi **1.** ⟨rel⟩ *to believe*; *to have faith* ‖ → A. 4. **2.** ⟨übtr⟩ **jdm** ∼ *to b.* (od *trust*; *credit*) *a p*; *to give credence* (od *credit*) *to a p*; jdm nicht ∼ *to disb. a p*; du kannst mir ∼ *you can take it from me*; ich glaube Ihnen aufs Wort *I take your word for it* ‖ e–r S ∼ *to b.* od *trust a th*; *to give* od *attach credence* od *credit to a th*; → trauen **3. a. an** Gott ∼ *to b.* (od *have faith*) *in God* ‖ ∼ an jdn *to b. in a p*, *to trust a p*; *to have confidence in a p* **b.** ∼ an (etw) *to b. in* (*a th*); *to indulge in* (*witchcraft*) ‖ er hat **daran** ∼ **müssen** *he has gone to his fate*; *he has met his fate* **4. jdn** ∼ **m** *to make a p b.*; er ist nicht so alt, wie er uns ∼ m möchte *he is not so old as he would have us b.*; er will ∼ m, daß er nichts davon weiß *he wants us to b. he knows nothing about it* **Gl·aubens-** [in comp] .. *of faith* **∼abfall** m *apostasy* **∼artikel** m *article of f.* **∼bekenntnis** n *confession of f.*; *creed*; *credo* L; das Apostolische ∼ *the* (*Apostles'*) *Creed* ‖ Anhänger e–s best. –nisses *confessionist* **∼bewegung** f ⟨Ger⟩ *F. Movement* **∼bote** m *apostle*; *missionary* **∼eifer** m *religious zeal* od *enthusiasm* **∼freiheit** f *religious liberty* **∼gemeinschaft** f *denomination* **∼genosse** m *co-religionist*; *fellow-believer* **∼lehre** f *creed*; *religious doctrine* od *belief*; *dogmatics* pl **∼regel** f *rule of f.*, *dogma* **∼sache** f *matter of f.* od *religion* **∼satz** m *dogma* **∼spaltung** f *schism* **∼streit** m *religious controversy* **≃streng** a *orthodox* **∼wut** f *religious fanaticism* **∼zeuge** m *martyr* **∼zwang** m *constraint* od *coercion in matters of f.*

Gl·aubersalz n ⟨chem⟩ *Glauber's salt*

gl·aubhaft 1. [a] *believable*, *credible*, *plausible*; *faithful*, *veracious*; *authentic*; ⟨jur⟩ (m *to give*) *prima facie* (*evidence*) ‖ das klingt sehr ∼ *that sounds quite credible*, .. wenig ∼ .. *hardly credible*; kaum ∼ *hardly credible*; *extravagant*, *tall* (*story*) ‖ etw ∼ m *to make a th appear credible* **2.** [adv] *credibly* | **≃igkeit** f ∼/ *credibility*; *authenticity* **≃machung** f *the making credible* od *likely* (*of a fact*); die ∼ der Behauptung war ihm nicht gelungen *he had not succeeded in making the statement credible* **gl·äubig 1.** [a] *believing* (*Christian*); *pious*, *religious*; recht∼, streng∼ *orthodox*; leicht∼ *credulous* **2.** [adv] *b.ly* ‖ er hörte ganz ∼ zu *he listened as if he believed everything* **Gl·äubige** [der ∼, ein ∼r] m *the* (*true*) *believer* ‖ die ∼n [pl] *the faithful* **Gl·äubiger** m ∼s/∼ ⟨com⟩ *creditor*; drängender ∼ *dun* ‖ ∼staat *cr.-state*; ∼versammlung *meeting of cr.s* **gl·aublich** a *believable*, *credible*; → glaubhaft ‖ *likely* | **≃keit** f ∼/ *credibility*

gl·aubwürdig a **a.** (P) *credible*, *veracious*; (*witness*) *worthy of credit*; *trustworthy* **b.** (S) = glaubhaft | **≃keit** f ∼/ *credibility*, *veracity* (*of a p*); *credence*; *authority* ‖ [dat] die ∼ absprechen *or* nehmen *to discredit* (*a th*, *documents*)

Glauk·om n ∼s/∼e ⟨med⟩ *glaucoma*

Glaukon·it m ∼s/∼e ⟨minr⟩ *green sand*

glazi·al a ⟨geol⟩ *glacial* **≃bildung** f *glacial deposit* **≃periode** f *glacial epoch* (od *era*, *period*)

gleich I. [a] **A.** [attr] **1.** ⟨math⟩ *equal*; 2 ∼e Seiten, Winkel *two e. sides*, *angles* ‖ in ∼em Abstand v e–a *equidistant* (od *in e. distance*) *from each other* **2.** ⟨übtr⟩ **a.** *equal*; *the same* ‖ v ∼er Größe, Höhe *of e. size*, *height* ‖ ∼e Rechte f alle *e. rights for all* ‖ in ∼em Maße, z ∼en Teilen *e.ly* ‖ ∼er Lohn f ∼e Arbeit *the same wages for the s. work*; am ∼en Orte *in the s. place*; zum ∼en Preise *at the s. price*; zur ∼en Zeit *at the s. time* **b.** *like*; ∼e Freiheit f sich *a like liberty for himself*; v ∼en Leidenschaften wie *of l. passions with*; in ∼er Weise *in l. manner* (od *sort*, *wise*); *in the s. way*; *l.wise* ‖ ∼e Vorzeichen ⟨math⟩ *l. signs* pl **c.** ⟨com⟩ *even* (*quantities*) ‖ ∼en Datums *of even* *date*; v ~em Inhalt *of even tenor* **d.** auf ~er Stufe stehen mit *to be on an equality with*; (jdn) auf ~e Stufe stellen mit *to equate with* ‖ v den ~en Voraussetzungen ausgehen wie jd *to be on common ground with a p* ‖ *a neck and neck race*; die ~e Zahl Punkte *or* Stimmen h wie jd *to tie with a p*; ⟨golf⟩ wir h die ~e Zahl Schläge *like as we lie* **B.** [pred] **1.** ⟨math⟩ *equal*; a ist ~ b *a is e. to b*; 3 × 3 ist ~ 9 *thrice three is* (*e. to*) *nine* **2.** ⟨übtr⟩ **a.** *equal*; wir sind alle ~ vor dem Gesetz *we 're all e. before the law*; ~ an *e. in* (*strength*); e–r S ~ s *to be e. to a th* **b.** *like, alike* ‖ jdm ~ s *to be l. a p*; er ist genau ~ s–m Vater *he is for all the world l. his father* ‖ er ist ihm ~ (an Rang etc) *he is on a par with him*; *he is e.* (od *peer*) ‖ die Fälle sind nicht ganz ~ *the cases are not on all fours* ‖ sie sind alle ~ *they are all tarred with the same brush*; .. total ~ .. *cast in the same mould*; nicht zwei sind ~ gewesen *no two have been alike* **3. es ist ganz** ~ *it is a case of six of one and half a dozen of the other* ‖ es ist mir ganz ~ *it is all one* (od *all the same*) *to me* | ~, was er denkt *no matter what he thinks* .. **4.** [abs] ~ s–m Vater sagte er .. *l. his father he said* **II.** [adv] **A. 1.** *e.ly* (*to divide e.*); *even* (*the two run e.*); → ~mäßig ‖ *alike, in l. manner* ‖ ~ alt, groß s *to be the s. age, size* ‖ ~ gut s *to be equally good, to be as good as* .. ‖ ~ klug *level in intelligence*; ~ temperiert *isothermal*; ~ tüchtig *equal in abilities* ‖ (zwei Sprachen) ~ gewandt sprechen *to speak .. e.ly fluently* ‖ ~ weit entfernt *equidistant* **2.** ~ **als ob** (*or* wenn) *just as if* **3. a.** ~ bei (*or* nach) s–r Ankunft *on his arrival*; ~ darauf *presently*; *before long*; ~ nachdem er .. *as soon as he* ..; ⟨fam⟩ *directly he* .. ‖ ~ morgen früh *first thing in the morning* **b.** ~ um die Ecke *just round the corner*; ~ auf der ersten Seite *on the very first page* ‖ ~ hier *here and now*; *right here* ‖ ~ dahinter kam .. *on the heels of that came* (*a reaction*) **B. 1.** *directly, immediately*; *at once*; *right away*; *in a moment* ‖ ich komme ~ *I'm coming in a moment*; ich bin ~ wieder da *I shan't be a minute*; ~ nach jdm k *to run a close second to a p*; er kommt ~ *he is on his way*; ~! *coming, Sir* ‖ °~ setzt's was *you'll get it hot in a minute* ‖ es muß ja nicht ~ s *it needn't be at once* ‖ (*you must not condemn him*) *out of hand* ‖ ich dachte es ~ *I thought as much* ‖ wie ist doch ~ sein Name? *I say, what's his name?* **C. wenn** .. ~ = wenngleich; **ob** .. ~ = obgleich **III.** [subst] **1.** → ihres~en, m–s~en, s–s~en; der~en, des~en; ohne~en, sonder~en **2. a.** der ~e *the same man*; er ist seit .. nicht der ~e *he is not the s. man since* (*his illness*) **b.** das ~e *the s.*; ein ≗es besorgen etc *to match a th*; ich wünsche dir das ~e (*I wish*) *the s. to you*; das ~e galt f .. *the s. applied to* (*her*) ‖ ein ≗es tun *to do the s. thing*; ich werde ein ≗es tun für ihn *I'll do as much for him* ‖ ≗es erzeugt ≗es *like begets l.* ‖ jdm ≗es mit ≗em vergelten *to give a p tit for tat* ‖ ~ u ~ .. → gesellen ‖ das kommt **aufs** ≗e hinaus *it comes to the s. th* ‖ **ins** ≗e bringen *to make even*; *to settle*; ins ≗e k. *to get even* **~alt(e)rig** a *of the same age*; sie sind ~ *they are the same age* **~artig** a *homogeneous*; *of the same kind* **≗artigkeit** f *homogeneity, homogeneousness* **~atomig** a *homatomic* **~bedeutend** a *synonymous* (*words*); *interchangeable* (*terms*); → Synonym ‖ ~ mit *synonymous* (od *equipollent*) *with*; *equivalent* (od *tantamount*) *to*; ~ s mit *to amount to* **~berechtigt** a *enjoying equal rights*; ~ mit *on an equality with* **≗berechtigung** f *equality, parity*; politische ~ *equality of status* **~|bleiben** vi [s] sich ~ *to remain the same*; *to remain stationary*; es bleibt sich gleich, ob .. *it's all the same whether*; das bleibt sich gleich *that makes no difference* **~bleibend** a; (sich) ~ *static*; *constant* (*force, risk, pressure*); *invariable, unvarying*; *uniform*; *level* (*premium*)

gl·eichen vi [glich/geglichen] [h] jdm (e–r S) ~ *to be like, to resemble* od *match a p* (*a th*); sie ~ e–a wie ein Ei dem andern *they are alike as two peas* **gleichen** [in comp] → gleich III. 1. **Gl·eicher** m *equator* **≗maßen, ≗weise** adv *in like manner*; *likewise* **gl·eichfalls** adv *also, likewise*; *as well*; *too* (*she too looked up*); → auch 1. a.; desgleichen 2.; ebenfalls ‖ Herr N. ist tot u s–e Frau ~ *Mr. N. is dead and so is his wife* ‖ (in Erwiderung e–s Wunsches) danke, ~! *thanks, the same to you!*; ⟨iron⟩ ~! *ditto!* **gl·eich-** **~farbig** a *of the same colour*; sie sind ~ *they are the same colour* **~förmig 1.** [a] *equable, equal*; *uniform* (*twist*); ⟨phot⟩ *even* (*illumination*) → einförmig ‖ ~ m *to coordinate* **2.** [adv] *equably, equally*; *uniformly* **≗förmigkeit** f *equality*; *uniformity*; *conformity* **~geachtet** a *equally-esteemed* **~gerichtet** a *acting in the same direction*; *rectified* (*current*); ⟨fig⟩ *acting in unison* **~geschlagen** a ⟨tech⟩ ~es Drahtseil *long-lay wire rope* **~geschlechtlich** a → homosexuell **~gesinnt** a *of like mind*; *like-minded* | ≗e [pl] *kindred souls* **~gestaltet** a *of the same shape* **~gestimmt** a ⟨mus⟩ *equally tuned*; *tuned alike* ‖ ⟨fig⟩ *congenial*; *sympathetic* | ≗heit [f] ⟨Lit⟩ *consistancy*

Gl·eichgewicht n ~s/ **1. a.** ⟨eig⟩ *balance, equilibrium, poise*; *equilibration* (mit *with*; z *to*) **b.** ⟨fig⟩ *b., e.rium*; *poising*, (*equi*)*poise*; → Unausgeglichenheit ‖ ⟨pol⟩ politisches ~ *political e.rium*; ~ der Kräfte *b. of power* ‖ seelisches ~ *mental e.rium, poise of mind* **2.** das ~ **behalten** *to maintain one's e.rium*; *to keep* (od *preserve*) *the b.*; das ~ halten *to hold the b.* (zw *between*); sich das ~ halten *to be in e.rium*; *to b.*; das ~ herstellen *to adjust the b.*; ⟨fig⟩ ein ~ herstellen *to strike a b.*; das ~ wiederherstellen *to redress the b.* ‖ das ~ stören *to disturb the e.rium* ‖ das ~ verlieren *to lose one's b.*; *to overbalance*; das seelische ~ .. *to go off the deep end* | jdn **aus** dem ~ bringen *to throw a p off his b.*; *to sweep a p off his feet*; *to unbalance* (od *unsettle, upset*) *a p*; *to unhinge a p's mind* ‖ aus dem ~ k = das ~ verlieren ‖ (etw) **im** ~ halten *to b.*; *to equilibrate, to equipoise*; sich im ~ halten, im ~ s *to be in e.rium* (od *poise*); (of scales) *to b.* ‖ im ~ schweben *to be poised* ‖ **ins** ~ bringen *to equilibrate, to poise*; .. mit .. *to bring a th in balance with* ..; den Etat ins ~ .. *to balance the budget* **~sfehler** m *lack of e.rium* **~skonstante** ⟨chem⟩ *constant of e.rium* **~slage** f *position of equilibrium* **~slehre** f = Statik **~ssinn** m *static sense* **~sstörung** f *disturbance of the e.rium*; *unbalancing*; ⟨aero⟩ *vertigo*; ⟨med⟩ *imbalance* (*of eyes*, etc); ⟨fig⟩ *disequilibrium* **~szustand** m *state of e.rium*; *static condition*

gleich- **~gültig A.** [a] **1.** [pred] **a. er** ist mir ~ *I am indifferent to him*; **es** ist ~ *it is immaterial* (od *irrelevant*; *of no consequence*); *it makes no difference*; *it's all the same* (.. mir .. *to me*); es ist mir ~ *it is all the s. to me*; .. wenn ich höre *it does not mean anything to me to hear, I don't care if I hear* ..; wie du es ausdrückst, ist mir total ~ *I don't care a pin how you word it*; Politik ist mir ~ *I am not interested in politics, I am unconcerned with p.*; d–e Gefühle sind mir ~ .. *are indifferent to me*; die Mitteilung ist mir ~ *I set no store by the information*; .. ist mir durchaus nicht ~ *I set great store by the i.* **b.** °[abs] ~, ob .. *regardless of whether*; ~, wer .. *no matter who* ..; ~, was du tust *whatever you do* **c.** (P) ~ s *to be indifferent* (gegen *to*) ‖ *to be casual* (od *careless, nonchalant*) **2.** [attr] *careless, casual, negligent* (*worker*); *impassive*; *indolent, listless* (*p*); *nonchalant* (*face*); *cold* (*glance*) ‖ *phlegmatic, stolid* **B.** [adv] *indifferently*; *unconcernedly*; *uninterestedly*; *halfheartedly* ‖ *carelessly, casually*; *nonchalantly* **≗gültigkeit** f *indifference* (gegen *to*); *lethargy*; *unconcern* ‖ *carelessness*; *nonchalance* **≗heit** f ~/ *identity, likeness, sameness*; *uniformity* ‖ *equality* (jds mit *of a p with*; zw *between*); (an Rang etc) *parity*; ∼ vor dem Gesetz *equality before the law* ‖ Verfechter der ∼, ∼sapostel *egalitarian*; ∼slehre *egalitarian doctrine* ‖ ∼szeichen ⟨math⟩ *sign of equation* **∼kernig** a ⟨at⟩ *equinuclear* **≈klang** m ∼s/≈e *unison*; *unisonance*; *consonance* **∼|kommen** vi [s] jdm ∼ *to equal a p* (an *in*); *to be up to a p*; jdm in etw –zu– suchen *to rival a p in a th* ‖ e–r S ∼ *to equal a th*; *to be equal* (od *to come up*) *to a th*; es kam e–m Schmerz ∼ *it was like pain*; nicht ∼ *to fall short of* **≈lauf** m ⟨tech⟩ *synchromesh*; ⟨comp⟩ nicht im ∼ *(cards) out of step*, aus dem ∼ k *to get out of step* **∼laufend, ∼läufig** a *parallel* **∼lautend** a *unisonant*; *consonant*, *homophonic* (*words*); ∼es Wort *homophone* ‖ (of letter, etc.) *of even* (od *the same*) *tenor*; *to the same effect* **∼|machen** vt [h] (etw) *to equalize* (mit *to*, *with*); (Dinge) *to level*; e–e Linie e–r anderen ∼ *to make a line equal to another* ‖ (Stadt) dem Boden ∼ *to make* (od *lay*) *even with the ground*, *to raze to the g.*, *to level to* od *with the g.*, ⟨fam⟩ *to clear down* ‖ jdn ∼ mit .. *to level a p with* (*a p*); *to put a p on an equality with* **≈macher** m ⟨pol⟩ *leveller*; *egalitarian*, *equalitarian* **≈macherei** f (*process of*) *levelling*; *equalitarianism*, ⟨soc⟩ *egalitarianism*; *schematism* **∼machung** f *equalization*; *levelling* **∼maß** n = Ebenmaß **∼mäßig 1.** [a] *even* (*voice*; *beat of the heart*, *speed*); *regular*, *rhythmical*; *uniform* (*distribution*, *heat*), *of the same uniformity* ‖ *proportionate*; *symmetrical* (*build*) **|** *equable* (*temper*); *equal* (*ease*); *steady* (*speed*) ‖ ⟨fig⟩ *level* **2.** [adv] *equally*; *evenly*; *regularly*; *uniformly* ‖ ∼ stetige Bewegung *sweep* (*of the tide*; a. übtr) **|** **≈mäßigkeit** f *evenness*; *regularity*; *uniformity* ‖ *equability* **≈mut** m *equanimity* (*with e.*); *calmness*; *imperturbability*; *indifference*; stoischer ∼ *stoic indifference*, *stoicism*; s–n ∼ wiedergewinnen *to recover one's temper* **∼mütig** a *equable*; *equal* (*mind*); *even*, *even-tempered*; *calm* **∼namig** a *homonymous* (*words*); *having the same name* ‖ ⟨math⟩ *correspondent*; ⟨phys⟩ *analogous* (*poles*)

Gl·eichnis n –nisses/–nisse ⟨rhet⟩ *simile*; *image*; *allegory*; → Bild; Metapher ‖ ⟨bib⟩ *parable* **≈artig** a *allegoric*(*al*), *parabolic*(*al*) **∼rede** f *parable*; *allegory* **≈weise** adv *allegorically*, *parabolically*; *by way of parable*

gleich- ∼|richten 1. vt [h] ⟨wir⟩ *to rectify*; ∼ mit *to bring in line with* **2.** ≈ n ⟨radar⟩ *detection* **≈richter** m ⟨el⟩ *commutator* ‖ ⟨wir⟩ *rectifier*; ⟨telg⟩ Hochfrequenz≈ *detector* **≈richtung** f ⟨wir⟩ *rectification* **∼sam** adv **1.** *as it were*, *so to speak*; ∼ ein H. *a kind of heaven*; ∼ eine Ungerechtigkeit *in the nature of an injustice*; *sth in the n. of a vision* ‖ ⟨vulg⟩ *like*; er zitterte ∼ am ganzen Körper *he was all of a tremble like* **2.** ∼ als ob (*or* wenn) (*just*) *as if*; es war ihm ∼ als erwachte er aus .. *it was for him like passing out of* (*a dream*) ‖ er sah sie ∼ wie in e–r Vision *he saw her as in a v.* **∼|schalten** vt [h] *to synchronize* ‖ ⟨bes pol⟩ *to co-ordinate*, *unify*; jdn ∼ *to make a p toe the line*; *to bring .. into a line* (mit *with*) ‖ sich ∼ *to toe the line*; ⟨übtr⟩ sich ∼ mit .. *to throw in one's lot with* **≈schaltung** f *synchronization* ‖ ⟨bes pol⟩ *equalization*; *co-ordination*; *unification* **∼schenk(e)lig** a ⟨math⟩ *isosceles* [L] (*triangle*); ∼es Winkeleisen *equal angles* pl **∼schritt** m ⟨a, mil⟩ *equal step* ‖ *measured tread* (im ∼ *with a m. t.*); im ∼! *quick time–march*! **∼seitig** a ⟨math⟩ *equilateral* (*triangle*) **∼|setzen** vt [h] etw ∼ mit *to equate a th with* ‖ etw unterschiedslos ∼ mit *to lump a th together with* **∼silbig** a *parisyllabic* **∼sinnig** a *equidirectional* **≈spannungs-** ⟨phys⟩ *equipotential* (*field*) **≈stand** m ⟨sport⟩ *tie*; ⟨ten⟩ → Einstand **∼|stehen** vi [h] jdm ∼ *to equal a p*, *to be on a par* (od *an equality*) *with a p* ‖ ⟨sport⟩ ∼ mit jdm *to tie with a p* ‖ ⟨golf⟩ wir stehen gleich *like as we lie*; ∼d *all square* **∼|stellen** vt [h] *to reset* (*a clock*) ⟨el⟩; etw e–r S (*or* mit e–r S) ∼ *to equalize* od *equate a th with a th*; jdn jdm (*or* mit jdm) ∼ *to bracket* od *level a p with a p*; *to put a p on a par with a p*; –gestellt w mit *to get in the same class with* ‖ sich jdm (*or* mit jdm) ∼ *to put o.s. on a par with a p* **≈stellung** f *equalization* (*of children*); *levelling*; *emancipation* **∼stimmig** a *unisonant*, *unisonous*; *in unison*; → gleichgestimmt, einstimmig **≈strom** m ⟨el⟩ (Ggs Wechselstrom) *continuous current* (abbr *C. C.*), *direct current* (*D. C.*); (Wechselstrom) in ∼ umwandeln *to rectify* ‖ ∼-dynamo *continuous current generator*; ∼motor *continuous current motor* **≈taktfeuer** n *intermittent light* **∼teilig** a *of equal parts* **∼|tun** vi [h] es jdm ∼ *to equal*, *copy*, *imitate*, *match a p*, *to follow a p's example*, *to come up to a p*; es jdm ∼ wollen *to compete*, *vie with a p* **Gl·eichung** f ∼/∼en ⟨math⟩ *equation*; ∼ ersten Grades *or* lineare ∼ *equation of the 1st degree* od *linear e.*; ∼ zweiten Gr. *or* quadratische ∼ *e. of the 2nd degree* od *quadratic e.*; ∼ dritten Gr. *or* kubische ∼ *e. of the 3rd degree* od *cubic e.*; ∼ vierten Gr. *or* biquadratische ∼ *e. of the 4th degree* od *biquadratic e.*; ∼ fünften Gr. *quintic e.* ‖ identische ∼ *identical e.* ‖ zweigliedrige *or* binomische ∼ *binomial e.*; dreigliedrige ∼ *trinomial e.* **gleich- ≈verteilung** f *equipartition* **∼viel** adv **1.** [mst –'–] *all the same*, *all one* ‖ ∼! *no matter*; ∼, wer (wo, etc) .. *no matter who* (*where*) ..; ∼, ob .. *no matter if* .. **2.** [attr] ['––] *just as much* (*water*); *the same amount of* (*money*); *the equal number of* (*strokes*); → gleich I. ‖ ∼fache Größe *equimultiple* **·∼wertig** a *equivalent* (mit *to*); *equipollent* (mit *with*); ∼ s mit *to be on a par with*, *to be in the same class with* **|** ∼keit [f] *equivalence* **·∼wie** adv (*just*) as ‖ *like* (*I cannot work l. you*) **·∼wink(e)lig** a *equiangular* **·∼wirkend** a *equipotential* **∼·wohl 1.** [adv] *all the same*; *nevertheless*, *notwithstanding*; *yet* **2.** ×[conj] = obgleich **∼zeitig 1.** [a] *contemporaneous*; *contemporary*; *coincident*(*al*); *simultaneous*; *synchronous* (mit *with*); *concurrent* (*application*); ∼ s mit *to coincide with* **2.** [adv] *contemporaneously*, *simultaneously* (mit *with*), *along* (*with*); ∼ auftretend *coincident*(*al*) **|** ≈keit [f] *coincidence* (mit *with*); *contemporaneity*, *contemporaneousness*, *simultaneity*, *synchronism*

Gleis n ∼es/∼e **1.** ⟨eig⟩ **a.** (Wagenspur) *track*; *rut* **b.** ⟨rail⟩ *rails* pl; *line*; *permanent way*; ⟨Am⟩ *track*(*s* pl) ‖ einfaches ∼ *single l.*; doppeltes ∼ *double l.* ‖ Abfahrts≈ *down l.* (od *side*), Ankunfts≈, ∼ nach London, *up l.* ‖ ∼ frei *line* (⟨Am⟩ *normal*) *clear* ‖ Anschluß≈, Ausweich≈, Rangier≈ *siding* ‖ (Zug) **auf** ein anderes ∼ fahren *to shunt* ‖ auf ∼en laufen *to run on rails* ‖ **aus** dem ∼e springen *to get off the l.*; *to run off the metals* (od *rails*); ⟨Am⟩ *to jump* (od *leave*) *the track*(*s*) **2.** ⟨**fig**⟩ (gewohntes) *groove*, *rut*, *track* ‖ das **alte**, ausgetretene ∼ *the beaten track*, *the old groove*; im alten ∼e *in the same old rut* ‖ enges ∼ *narrow groove*; festes ∼ *groove*, *routine* **| auf** ein falsches ∼ geraten *to get on the wrong track* ‖ (etw) auf ein totes ∼ schieben *to shelve*, *to put on the shelf*; ⟨Am⟩ *to table*; *to sidetrack*, *sideline* (*politician*, *idea*, *move*) **| aus** dem ∼e *off the rails*; (jdn) aus dem ∼e bringen *to lift out of the groove*; *to put out* ‖ **im** alten –se bleiben *to keep in the old groove* ‖ (etw) wieder **ins** ∼ bringen *to put right again*; .. k .. *things come back to normal*, *things take care of themselves* **∼anschluß** m (*own*) *siding* **∼bildstellwerk** n (*signal box with*) *push button geographical circuitry*; *geogr. panel* **∼dreieck** n *triangular set of rails* **∼freimelderelais** n *track release* (⟨Am⟩ *control*) *relay* **∼kette** f *creeper track* **|** ∼nfahrzeug [n] *full-track vehicle* **≈los** a *untracked* **∼strecke** f *track* **∼tafel** f *track diagram*, ⟨Am⟩ *tr. indicator chart* **∼verlegung** f *track laying* **∼waage** f *weigh-bridge*

Gleisch m ∼es/∼e (Feuer≈) *glow of fire*

Gl·eisner m *dissembler, hypocrite; Pharisee* | **~·ei** f *hypocrisy; simulation* | **⁓isch** a *hypocritical; Pharisaic(al)*

gl·eißen vi [h] *to glitter; to shine*

Gl·eit- *gliding, sliding, glide, slide* **~aar** m ⟨orn⟩ *black-winged kite* **~anflug** m *gl.g approach* **~bahn** f ⟨mar-aero⟩ *slipway,* ⟨mar⟩ *shipway;* (beim Stapellauf) *sl.-ways* pl ‖ ⟨tech⟩ *guides* pl, *sleigh; slide* (od *guide*)*-bars* pl, ⟨Am⟩ *chute* **~bestimmung** f; ~en [pl] *escalator clauses* pl (*of an agreement*) **~bewegung** f *sl.g motion* **~boot** n *hydroplane; hydroglider* **~bügel** m ⟨el⟩ *collector* **~fläche** f *guide-surface* ‖ *tread* (*of a tyre*) **~flieger** m *glider* **~flosse** f ⟨aero⟩ *planing fin* **~flug** m ⟨aero⟩ *glide; gl.g flight;* e–n ~ m *to glide;* den Kanal im ~ überqueren *to glide the Channel* ‖ langer, steiler ~ *volplane;* in langem, steilem ~ niedergehen *to volplane* | ~kurve [f] *gl.g turn;* ~zeug [n] *glider,* ⟨Am a.⟩ *sailplane* **~flüssigkeit** f (f Fräser) *coolant* **~hang** m (v Fluß, Berg) *slip-off slope,* → Prall– **~klausel** f ⟨contr, wages, etc⟩ *escalation clause* **~klotz** m ⟨tech⟩ *guide* (od *slide*)*-block; slipper* **~kontakt** m *sl.g contact* **~lafette** f ⟨rail⟩ *sl.g mount* **~lager** n ⟨tech⟩ *plain bearing* **~landung** f *glide landing* **~laut** m ⟨phon⟩ *glide* **~schiene** f *guide-rail; skid* **~schuh** m = –klotz **~schutz** m ⟨mot⟩ *non-skid* | ~kette [f] *n.-s. chain;* ~profil [n] *n.-s. tread;* ~reifen *n.-s. tyre* **~sitz** m ⟨tech⟩ *free fit* **~spiralflug** m ⟨aero⟩ *spiral glide* **~weg** m ⟨aero⟩ *gl. path* **~winkel** m *gl.g angle* **~zahl** f *gl.g ratio*

gl·eiten I. vi [glitt/geglitten] [s] **A. 1.** (durch Wasser, Luft ~) (of *ships, birds,* etc.) ⟨a. aero⟩ *to glide* (durch *through;* in *into;* über *across, over*) ‖ (of a boat) *to float* (*over* ..); leicht ~ *to slip* (*through; over* ..) | (of water) *to flow* ‖ (of dust, etc.) *to swim* (in *in; into*) **2. ~ über** (of hands) *to glide* (od *pass*) *over;* (of eyes) *to go* (od *run, travel*) *over; her glance passed, sweeped over* ..; *a smile passed over her face;* (of an ice-sheet) *to override;* (of feelings, the mind) *to travel* (*through; over* ..) **3.** (**P**) *to glide* (*over the ice*); schnell ~ über *to slide, skim over;* **mit** dem Auge, den Fingern ~ über .. *to run one's eye, one's fingers over* .. ‖ mit etw ~ durch *to pass a th through* .. **B.** (**aus~**) *to slide, slip, slither; his foot slipped;* **aus** der Hand ~ *to slip from one's hand, grasp, power, control;* .. **durch** .. *to slip through one's fingers;* .. **von** .. *the book slid off my knees* ‖ unversehens ~ *to slide* (*into* ..) **C. etw ~ l** *to slide* (od *slip*) *a th* (in *into*); *to pass a th* (durch *through*) ‖ das Auge ~ l *to run one's eye* (*over* ..) ‖ etw heimlich ~ l *to slip a th* (*into* ..); etw durch die Hände ~ l *to let a th dribble through one's hands;* den Blick über das Z. ~ l *to sweep the room with a look* **II.** ⁓ n **1.** *glide, gliding* **2.** (Aus⁓) *slide, sliding; slither;* (Seitwärts⁓) *skid* ‖ ins ~ k *to slide, slip, skid; slither;* er war mit den Füßen ins ~ gek *his feet had slipped from under him* **gl·eitend** a; ~e Reime *gliding* (od *dactylic*) *rhymes* ‖ ~e Skala *sliding scale* (*of prices*) **Gl·eiter** m ~s/~ → Gleitflugzeug

Gl·eiwitz n ⟨†Ger⟩ (Stadt in Oberschlesien)

Gl·etscher m ~s/~ *glacier, glacial* **~bildung** f *g–l formation* **~brand** m = Sonnenbrand **~eis** n *g–r ice* **~floh** m ⟨ent⟩ *g–r-flea* **~forscher** m *g–list* **~kunde** f *glaciology* **~mühle** f *moulin* [Fr] **~mulde** f *rock-basin* **~periode** f *g–l period* **~schlamm** m *g–r-mud* **~schliff** m *glaciated rock* **~spalte** f *crevasse* [Fr] **~tal** n *g–r-valley* **~tisch** m *g–r-table* **~wind** m *glacier freeze*

glich 1. & 3. sg pret v gleichen

Gl·ied n ~(e)s/~er **A.** (of living beings) **1.** (Körper⁓) **a.** *limb* (künstl. *artificial*); Rumpf u ~er *body and limbs; member* (*the hand is a m. of the arm*) ‖ Geschlechts⁓ *sexual member;* ⟨anat⟩ männliches ~ *penis* [L]; ⟨vulg⟩ *cock, it, little finger, Sir Thomas* **b.** (Gelenk) *joint;* Finger⁓er *joints of the finger* **c.** s–e **gesunden** ~er h *to be sound in life and l.* ‖ ein Mann v starken ~ern *strong-l.ed man* ‖kein ~ **rühren** können *not to be able to stir a l.* ‖ s–e ~er strecken *to stretch one's l.s* | **an** allen ~ern beben(d), zittern(d) *to tremble all over* (*with every l. trembling*) ‖ die Nachricht fuhr mir **in die** ~er *the news gave me a bit of a jar;* der Schreck fuhr mir in alle ~er *I felt the shock in every l.;* ich hatte Schmerzen in allen –ern, ich fühlte alle m–e ~er *I had pains all over* ‖ er hatte e–e Krankheit in den ~ern *he was sickening for a disease* **2.** ⟨zoo⟩ ~ e–s Bandwurms *proglottis* **3.** ⟨übtr⟩ *m.* (*of the family, of society*); verbindendes ~ *link* (zw *between*) ‖ bis ins 7. ~ ⟨bib⟩ *unto the 7th generation* ‖ ein ~ bilden v *to make one of* .. **4.** ⟨mil⟩ (~er neben–e–a) *rank;* das erste ~ *the front rank,* das letzte ~ *the rear rank* ‖ (~er hinter–e–a) *file* ‖ in Reih u ~ *in rank and file;* ~ f ~ *in files* ‖ aus dem ~ treten *to break ranks, to fall out;* ins ~ treten *to fall in;* in e–r Linie z 3 ~ern antreten *to fall in three deep* **B.** ⟨übtr⟩ (S) **1.** (of a chain) *link* ‖ ~er e–r Röhre *joints of a pipe* **1.** *member* (*the village is the m. of a parish*) ‖ *division, part; section; article; paragraph* ‖ Satz⁓ *clause* (od *division*) *of sentence; member* ‖ ⟨math⟩ *member* (*of an equation,* etc) ‖ ⟨log⟩ *term* (*of a syllogism*) ‖ ⟨mus⟩ charakterist. ~ e–s Werkes *motif* **~ersatz** m ⟨surg⟩ *prosthesis* [Gr] **~maß** n, **~maße** f: [mst pl] –ßen *limbs, extremities* pl; → Glied A. 1. c. **~staat** m *member-state* (od *nation*)

Gl·ieder- ~bau m *articular structure;* ⟨arch⟩ *panel frame* **~fahrzeug** n *articulated v.* **~frucht** f ⟨bot⟩ *loment* **~füßer** m ⟨zoo⟩ *arthropod* **~kette** f *link--chain* **~maßstab** m *folding rule* **~puppe** f *jointed doll* ‖ ⟨arts⟩ *lay figure; manikin; mannequin* Fr **~reißen** n *rheumatic pain* **~starre** f *Little's disease* **~tier** n ⟨zoo⟩ *articulate* **~werk** n *linkage; link-work* **~zollstock** m *folding rule*

-glied(e)rig gerad~ *straightlimbed* ‖ vier~ *four-membered* **gl·iedern** vt [h] **1.** *to articulate;* gegliedert *articulate* ‖ ⟨tact⟩ *to distribute* ‖ ⟨arch⟩ *to divide;* 3 Bogen ~ das Schiff *the aisle is divided by 3 arches* ‖ (Satz) *to analyse;* (Gedanken) *arrange; dispose; to put together* ‖ gegliedert s *to be divided* (in *into*); kunstvoll geg. *artistically proportioned* **2. sich ~ in** *to be divided into* (*parts, paragraphs*); *to consist of* **Gl·iederung** f ~/~en **1.** ⟨bot & zoo⟩ *articulation* ‖ ⟨arch & Lit⟩ *arrangement; disposition* ‖ *division* (in *into*) **2.** [konkr] die ~en *the formations* (od *sections*) (*of an organization*) **~sübersicht** f ⟨allg⟩ *organization chart*

Gl·imm ~entladung f ⟨el⟩ *glow-discharge* **~lampe** f *glow-lamp* **~licht** n *glow-light* °**~stengel** m (Zigarre, –arette) *fag* **gl·immen A.** vi [glomm & glimmte/geglommen & geglimmt] **1. a.** *to burn faintly; to glow; smoulder;* ~de Kohlen *embers* pl **b.** ⟨fig⟩ (of feelings) *to smoulder* **2.** *to glimmer; to shine faintly* **B.** ⁓ n **1.** *smoulder(ing)* ⟨a. fig⟩ **2.** *glimmer; faint gleam* **Gl·immer** m ~s/ **1.** *glimmer; faint gleam* **2.** ⟨minr⟩ *mica* [L] **⁓artig, ⁓haltig** a ⟨minr⟩ *micaceous* **~blättchen** n pl *shiners* **~schiefer** m *mica-schist* **gl·immerig** a ⟨minr⟩ *micaceous*

Glimpf m ~(e)s/ ⟨übtr⟩ *gentleness, mildness; softness* ‖ mit ~ *gently, mildly* **gl·impflich 1.** [a] *gentle, mild; forbearing* (gegen), *indulgent* (*to a p*) **2.** [adv] *gently, mildly* ‖ das ging noch einmal ~ ab *that went off pretty well* (od *without injury, punishment,* etc) ‖ ~ davonk *to come* (od *get*) *off lightly* (od *easily*) ‖ jdn ~ behandeln *to let a p down gently* (od *easily*); nicht gerade ~ *his treatment could hardly be called gentle*

Gl·itschbahn f ˣ**Gl·itsche** f *slide* °**gl·itschen A.** vi [s] **1.** (P) *to glide* (über .. *over*) **2.** (aus~) *to slide, slip, slither; skid* **B.** ⁓ n **1.** *glide, gliding* **2.** *slide, sliding; slither* ***gl·itsch(e)rig, gl·itschig** a *greasy, slippery* (*road, slope*); *slithery* **glitt** 1. & 3. sg pret v gleiten

gl·itzern 1. vi [h] *to glint, glisten, glister, glitter; sparkle; twinkle* || ~d fallen auf *to glint on* **2.** ≃ n *glisten, glister, glitter; sparkle; twinkle*
gl·itzernd a *glistening,* etc; *sparkling; spangly (dew)* **Gl·itzerschmuck** m *spangle, tinsel*
glob·al a *global* | *across-the-board (tax cut); world's eye* (Sicht ⟨fig⟩) | ≃transport [m] ⟨mil aero⟩ *full lift* **Gl·obetrotter** m *globetrotter*
Globiger·inen pl ⟨zoo⟩ *Globigerinae* L pl; ~-schlamm [m] *globigerina-mud* (od *ooze*)
globul·ar a *globular* | ≃- *gl. (projection)*
Globul·in n (Eiweißkörper) *globulin; actin*
Gl·obus m ~/–ben ⟨geog⟩ *globe;* Erd≃ *terrestrial g.,* Himmel≃ *celestial g.*
Glock → Glocke **Gl·öckchen** n ~s/~ *small bell*
Gl·ocke f ~/~n **A. 1.** *bell;* (Satz abgestimmter) ~n *chime* || ° = Uhr **2.** = Klingel **3. a.** die ~n [nom] **läuten** *the bells are ringing;* er hatte nur die ~n läuten hören *he knew nothing definite about it* || °**die** ~ hat voll geschlagen *the clock has struck the hour;* °die ~ schlägt zehn *it is striking ten (o'clock);* °Glock 10 *ten o'clock* || ⟨übtr⟩ ich sagte ihm (wir wußten), was die ~ geschlagen hatte *I told him where to get off (we knew what it meant to us* od ⟨sl⟩ .. *what was up)* || was ist die ~? *what o'clock* (od *time*) *is it?* **b.** e–e ~ **gießen** *to found* od *cast a bell* || e–e ~ läuten *to ring a bell;* die ~n aller Kirchen sollen geläutet werden *all the churches are to peal their bells;* die ~ ziehen *to ring the bell* || (etw) an die gr ~ bringen *or* hängen *to blaze* od *blazon .. abroad; to make .. public; to promulgate, advertize* **B.** ⟨übtr⟩ **1.** ⟨bot⟩ *bell, cup* **2.** (Glas≃) ⟨hort⟩ *bell-glass* (od *jar*); *globe; glass-shade;* Taucher≃ *diving-bell* || ⟨cul⟩ *cloche* Fr; *dish (butter-dish)* **3.** ⟨fenc⟩ *bell-guard* **4.** *receiver (of an air-pump)* **5.** → ~nhut **Gl·ocken-** *bell–* **~becher** m ⟨praeh⟩ *b.-shaped cup* **~blume** f ⟨bot⟩ *b.-flower; harebell, campanula* [L] || ⟨Scot⟩ *bluebell* || (gr weiße *or* rote ~) *Canterbury bell* **~blumengewächse** pl *lobelia* **~boje** f *b.-buoy* **~-~bronze** r *b.-metall* ≃**förmig** a *b.-shaped;* ⟨bot⟩ *campanulate* **~geläut** n *peal of b.s;* unter ~ *to the pealing of bells* **~gerüst** n *b.-frame* **~giebel** m *b.-gable* **~gießer** m *b.-founder* **~guß** m *b.-founding* **~hammer** m *clapper* **~haus** n *b.house* **~heide** f ⟨bot⟩ → Heide **~hut** m *cloche* Fr **~klang** m *ring of bells* ≃**klar** a *clear as a b.* **~klöppel** m *clapper* **~kurve** f ⟨math⟩ *normal distribution curve* **~läuten** n *b.-ringing* **~metall** n *b.-metal* **~rock** m *flared skirt* **~schlag** m *stroke;* pünktlich auf den ~ *on the stroke,* od *second; on the stroke of (eight);* er geht mit dem ~ *he goes to the second* **~schlegel** m *clapper* **~speise** f *b.-metal* **~spiel** n *chimes* pl; *chime of bells; carillon; glockenspiel* [Ger] **~stuhl** m *belfry* **~tierchen** n pl *Ciliata* L pl **~turm** m *belfry* **~vogel** m ⟨orn⟩ *b.-bird* **~zeichen** n ⟨telph⟩ *telephone-b.;* → Zeichen **~zug** m *b.-rope* **gl·ockig** a *b.-bottomed (skirt)* **Gl·öckner** m **1.** *b.-ringer; sexton* **2.** ⟨orn⟩ *b.-bird*
Gl·ogau ⟨†Ger⟩ (Stadt an der Oder)
glomm 1. & 3. sg pret v glimmen
Gl·oria n [L] ~s/ ⟨ec⟩ das kl ~ *Gloria Patri,* etc. || das gr ~ *Gloria in excelsis* **Gl·orie** [–iə] f *glory; magnificence; pomp; splendour;* → ~n-schein [m] *aureole, gloriole, glory, halo; nimbus* L **Glori·ette** f ⟨arch⟩ *gloriette* **glorifiz·ieren** vt [h] *to glorify* **glori·os 1.** [a] *glorious, magnificent, splendid* || °⟨fig⟩ → famos, glänzend **gl·orreich 1.** [a] *glorious; illustrious; triumphant* **2.** [adv] *gloriously; in great glory*
Gloss·ar n ~(e)s/~e ⟨Lit⟩ *glossary* **Gloss·ator** m ~s/–at·oren *glossator* || *commentator* **Gl·osse** f ~/~n **1. a.** ⟨Lit⟩ *gloss* || *annotation; interpretation* **b.** *comment* (z *on*) **1.** ⟨übtr, dero⟩ ~n [pl] *sneers* pl; *sneering remarks* pl; *flouts, gibes, jeers, scoffs* pl; ~n m über *to sneer* (od *carp, mock, scoff*) *at ..; to make mock of ..,* ~ m z .. *to find fault with (a th)* **~nmacher** m ⟨dero⟩ *faultfinder* **~nschreiber** m *glossographer* **gloss·ieren 1.** vt [h] (Text) *to gloss (glossed edition)* || *to annotate* **2.** ≃ n *glossing; annotation* **Gl·ottis** f [Gr] ⟨anat⟩ *glottis* Gr
Gl·otzauge n **1.** ⟨med⟩ (~nkrankheit) *exophthalmus* L **2.** °⟨fam⟩ ~n [pl] *goggle* (od *saucer, pop*) *eyes; eyes like saucers* pl **gl·otzäugig** a *g.* (od *s., p.*)*-eyed* **gl·otzen 1.** vi [h] *to gape, stare;* (finster ~) *to glower;* ⟨Am⟩ *to be pop-eyed* (vor *with*) || °⟨fam⟩ = blicken **2.** ≃ n *gape, stare; glower*
Glox·inie [–iə] f ~/~n f ⟨bot⟩ *gloxinia* [L]
Glück n ~(e)s/ **A. 1.** *(good) luck, (good) fortune* || *success; prosperity; sunshine* || *happiness; felicity* || vom ~ begünstigt *fortunate, lucky* **2.** (~szufall) *chance, fortune, luck* || Kriegs≃ *fortune of war* **B. 1.** ⟨aero⟩ ~ **ab**! *good luck* (od *speed, trip*)! || ~ **auf**! ⟨mst min⟩, **viel** ~! *good luck!* || viel ~ auf den Weg! *good journey!* **2.** ein K. des ~s *a child of fortune* || F.e im ~ *fair-weather friends* || ~ im Un≃ *a blessing in disguise* || ⟨prov⟩ jeder ist s–s ~es Schmied *everyone is the maker* od *architect of his own fate;* ~ u Glas, wie leicht bricht das *glasses and lasses are brittle ware* **3. das** ~ **ist** ihm hold *luck is with him; fortune smiles on him* || das ist ein ~! *that is a blessing* (od *mercy*) || *that was your luck; you were lucky in that* || es ist ein ~, daß sie dich nicht sah *luckily for you she did not see you* || es war ein gr (*or* wahres) ~, daß .. *it was a happy chance that; it was most fortunate that ..;* [abs] ein ~! *thank goodness!;* ein wahres ~! *how fortunate!;* .., daß .. *quite a mercy that ..;* diese Frau wird sein ~ s *this wife will be the making of him, .. will be his luck* || wie es das ~ wollte *as (good) luck would have it;* **was** f ein ~, daß er .. *what a good th he ..* **4. jdm** ~ **wünschen** *to wish a p good luck;* z etw *to congratulate* od *felicitate a p on a th* || ich wünsche dir viel ~ zum Neuen Jahr *I wish you a Happy New Year;* .. zum Geburtstage *I wish you many happy returns of the day* || jds ~ im Wege stehen *to stand in a p's way* **5.** ~ oder Un≃ **bringen** *to make or mar* || sein höchstes ~ erleben *to have the time of one's life* | ~ **haben** *to be lucky* (od *in luck*); *to have a stroke of luck; to score (we rather scored);* diesmal h Sie noch ~ gehabt *you have come off lucky this time;* anhaltendes ~ h *to be in bonanza* || wenn man ~ hat *with luck* || er hat immer ~ *he always turns up trumps* || du hast ~ gehabt, daß alles gut abging *luckily for you everything went off smoothly* || viele v ihnen h ~ dabei *many of them are getting away with it* || das ~ h .. *to have the luck* (z s *to be ..*) || er hat mehr ~ als Verstand *some have more by hit than by wit, he's a lucky dog* || ~ h mit etw *to be fortunate* od *lucky in a th* || kein ~ h *to have no luck;* ⟨Am sl⟩ *to fall down* (in *in;* mit *on*) | **sein** ~ **m** *to make one's fortune* od ⟨sl⟩ *pile;* wenn ich mein ~ mache *when my ship comes home* ⟨fig⟩; jds ~ s *to be the making of a p;* sein ~ **suchen** *to seek one's fortune* || sein ~ versuchen *to try one's fortune* od *luck* (mit .. *at a th; with a p*) || das ~ hat sich **gewendet** *the tide has turned* **6. auf gut** ~ *hit or miss; at random; at a venture,* ⟨Am⟩ *on an off-chance* || auf gut ~ hin, daß man ihn trifft *on the chance of seeing him* || auf gut ~ versuchen *to take one's chance;* etw auf gut ~ .. *to take one's chance of doing a th; to chance a th (I'll chance it)* || **mit** wechselndem ~ *with changing fortunes* | da kann man **von** ~ **sagen**! *this was a piece of good luck, indeed!* || er kann v ~ s. *he can congratulate h.s.;* daß .. *it was a piece of good luck that he ..; luckily for him he ..;* du kannst v ~ s.! *bless your stars!;* **vom** ~ begünstigt *favoured by fortune; fortunate; lucky (p)* | **zum** ~ *as good luck would have it; fortunately; luckily;* z s–m ~ *luckily for him* **Glück-** **·~auf** n *cheer,* ⟨fam⟩ *cheerio; hurrah (a hurrah for the winner!);* ein ~ unseren F.en! *here's to our old friends!* ≃**bringend** a *auspicious, fortunate, propitious; lucky;* → ≃-haft, etc

Gl·uck- ~henne [f] = Glucke, ~ruf [m] *cluck* **Gl·ucke 1.** f ~/~n *clucking-hen; broody hen* **2.** (Pilz) *goat's beard* **3.** ⟨ent⟩ *egger;* ~n [pl] *Lasiocampidae* L pl **gl·ucken** vi [h] (of a hen) *to cluck* ‖ ⟨übtr⟩ (of water) = gluckern, glucksen

gl·ücken vi [s] **1.** (of actions, etc) *to come off* (*this bluff came off*); *to succeed* (bei jdm *with a p*); *to be successful; to turn out well; to work* (bei *with*); der Plan glückte **ihm** *his plan succeeded;* ihm glückt alles *he is successful in everything; he always turns up trumps* **2.** [imps] .., daß **es ihm** nicht glückte (*he regrets*) *that he did not succeed;* → mißlingen; **es mag** ~ **mit** d. Pl. *the plan may succeed* ‖ es glückte ihm nicht .. z tun *he did not succeed in doing ..; he failed to do ..*

gl·uckern vi [h] (of water) *to guggle, gurgle*

Gl·ück- **≗haft** a *happy* (*ending*) **≗lich A.** [a] **1.** (P) *happy* (*man*); e–e ~e Natur *a h. n.* ‖ ~ s, sich ~ fühlen *to be* od *feel h.;* überaus ~ *jubilant* ‖ ~ s, etw z besitzen *to be fortunate in a th* ‖ sich ~ schätzen *to think o.s.f.* (wenn .. *when* ..); du kannst dich ~ sch. *bless your stars!, you can congratulate yourself* ‖ jdn ~ m *to make a p* (*feel*) *h.* ‖ ⟨prov⟩ ~ ist, wer vergißt, was nicht mehr z ändern ist *what can't be cured must be endured* ‖ w Sie ~ mit ihr! *I wish you joy of her;* am ~sten s (zeitl.) *to be at one's happiest* **2.** *h.* (*event*) ‖ *f.* (*circumstances*) ‖ *prosperous* (*issue; land; time*); *successful* ‖ *good, pleasant* (*journey*) ‖ (~ gewählt) *felicitous* (*illustration*); *h.* (*thought*); ~er Ausdruck (*or* Gedanke, Griff) *felicity;* e–e ~e Hand h z tun *to have a lucky* (od *skilful*) *hand in doing* ‖ e–e ~e Fügung s *to be providential for* (*a p*) **B.** [adv] **1.** (*to live*) *happily* **2.** *well* (*chosen*); ~ v statten gehen *to come off well* ‖ ~ ank *to arrive safe*(*ly*); ~ zurück *safe back* ‖ ° und nun hat er sich ~ auch das noch verscherzt ⟨fam⟩ *and now he has gone and blundered that* **C.** [abs] **1.** wer ist **der ≗e**? *who is the lucky one?, .. the bridegroom?* ‖ ⟨prov⟩ dem ≗en schlägt keine Stunde *no hour strikes to the h. man* **2.** er war **am ~sten** *he was happiest* **≗lichenfalls** adv *with luck* **≗licherweise** adv *fortunately, happily, luckily, mercifully* **~lichkeit** f *happiness* | ~sapostel [m] *Utopia-maker* (od *monger*)

Gl·ücks- ⟨mst⟩ *fortune, luck*(*y*) **~beutel** m *lucky-bag, grab-bag;* → –topf **~fall** m *f., l.; l.y chance; a stroke of good l.;* unerwarteter ~ *windfall; manna from heaven* **~gefühl** n *happiness, blissfulness; rapture; thrill of joy* **~göttin** f *F.* **~güter** pl *gifts* pl *of f.; riches* pl, *wealth* **~hafen** m = –topf **~händchen** n ⟨bot⟩ *terrestrian orchid; Gymnadenia* L **~haube** f ⟨biol⟩ (Eihäute) *caul* **~jäger** m *f.-hunter* **~kästchen** n *good-l. casket* **~kind** n *child of f.;* ⟨fam⟩ *l.y dog* **~klee** m ⟨bot⟩ *four-leaved clover* **~pfennig** m *l.-money* (od *penny*); *l.y penny* ‖ °**~pilz** m ⟨fig⟩ *l.y fellow* (od ⟨fam⟩ *dog*) **~rad** n *f.'s wheel* ‖ *lottery-wheel* **~ritter** m *soldier of f.; adventurer* **~spiel** n *game of chance; gambling* **~spinne** f ⟨ent⟩ *money-spinner* **~stern** m *l.y star* **~strähne** f *stroke* (⟨Am⟩ *run*) *of luck, lucky strike, luck in streaks* °**~topf** m *l.y-bag* (od *tub*); in den ~ greifen *to try one's l.;* er hat in den ~ gegriffen *he has come into a windfall* **~treffer** m *piece of good f.* **~umstände** pl *fortunate circumstances* ‖ °**~vogel** m *l.y dog* **~wechsel** m *change of f.* **~wurf** m *l.y throw* (od *hit*) **~zufall** m = Glück A. 2.

Gl·ück- **~sache** f; das ist ~ *that's a matter of luck* **≗selig 1.** [a] *blissful; blessed, happy; rapturous* **2.** [adv] *blissfully,* etc. **~seligkeit** f *bliss, blissfulness, happiness; felicity; euphoria* **≗strahlend** a *beaming, beatific* (*smile*); *blissful, rapturous; radiant* **≗verheißend** a *auspicious, propitious; promising; happy* (*omen*) **~wunsch** m **1.** *congratulation, felicitation* (z *on*) ‖ mit besten –wünschen f das Fest *with the compliments of the season;* herzlichen ~ u alles Gute! *I give you joy, health, happiness, every blessing;* mit herzlichen –wünschen f .. *with all good wishes for ..* ‖ jdm s–n ~ aussprechen *to congratulate* od *felicitate a p* (z *on*); ⟨Am⟩ *to offer a p one's congratulations* **2.** [in comp] *congratulatory;* ~adresse [f] *c. address*

gl·ucksen vi [h] (P) *to gurgle; to hiccup; to hum and haw* ‖ etw ~d äußern *to gurgle a th* ‖ ~der Laut *or* Ton *gurgle* ‖ → glucken, gluckern | **~d** ⟨fig⟩ *effervescent* (*gaiety*)

Gl·üh- **~bad** n ⟨tech⟩ *annealing bath* **~birne** f ⟨el⟩ *bulb* **~faden** m *filament* **~kathode** f ⟨el⟩ *hot cathode* **~kerze** f ⟨mot⟩ *heater plug* **~kopf** m ⟨tech⟩ *hot bulb;* ~motor *h.-b. engine* **~lampe** f *incandescent lamp; glow-l.; filament-l.* | ~nfaden [m] *filament* **~licht** n *incandescent light* **~ofen** m *annealing furnace; forge* **~rohr** n *ignition tube* **~span** m = Hammerschlag **~strumpf** m (Gas≗) *gas-mantle* **~topf** m *annealing pot* **~wein** m *mulled claret* **~würmchen** n ⟨ent⟩ *glow-worm* **~zündung** f *incandescent explosion; spontaneous ignition; glow-ignition*

gl·ühen I. vi/t [h] **A.** [vi] **1.** *to glow; to be in a glow* od *blaze; to be red-hot* ‖ die Sonne glüht sehr *the sky is all aglow* **2.** ⟨übtr⟩ (of the face, etc.) *to burn;* s–e Hand glühte *his hand was burning;* (*his cheeks*) *go hot;* ~ v *to be aglow with* **3.** ⟨fig⟩ *to burn* od *glow, to be ablaze* od *aglow* (vor .. *with anger, enthusiasm*); er glüht fürs Vaterland *he is aglow with patriotism* ‖ s–e Augen ~ vor .. *his eyes flash* (od *glow*) *with* (*delight*) ‖ (of colours) *to flame, to glow* **B.** [vt] etw ~ *to make a th red-hot; to cause a th to glow* ‖ (Erze) *to calcine;* (Metall) *to anneal* **II.** ≗ n *glow*(*ing*); etw z ~ bringen *to cause a th to glow;* z ~ erhitzt w *to glow* ⟨a. fig⟩ **gl·ühend A.** [a] **1.** *glowing, live* (*embers*); *incandescent* (*gas*); *red-hot* ‖ [pred] *in a glow; aglow, ablaze,* ⟨sl⟩ *hot as blazes* **2.** ⟨übtr⟩ *burning* (*face*); *glowing; hot* **3.** ⟨fig⟩ *ardent; burning* (*zeal*); *fervent* (*hatred*), *fervid* (*love*); *glowing* (*admiration; patriot*); *hot; passionate* (*enthusiasm*) **B.** [adv] **1.** ~ heiß *glowing; in a glow* od *blaze;* ⟨sl⟩ *hot as blazes;* ~ rot *glowing; red-hot* **2.** ⟨fig⟩ *fervently, fervidly* (*to love f.*); *passionately*

Gluk·ose f ⟨chem⟩ *glucose* **–s·urie** f *–suria*

×°**gl·upen** [u:] **1.** vi [h] (finster blicken) *to glower; lour, lower* **2.** ≗ n *glower*(*ing*)

Gl·ut f ~/~en **1.** *blaze* (*she warmed her hands at the b.*); *glowing fire;* in ~ *in a blaze* od *glow; ablaze, aglow* ‖ *heat* (*of the sun*) ‖ → Rot≗, Weiß≗ **2.** ⟨übtr⟩ *glow;* die ~ des Abendhimmels *the glow of sunset* ‖ (of cheeks) *glow, red* **3.** ⟨fig⟩ *ardour; fervour* (*of patriotism*); *fire* (*in a p's eyes*); *flames* pl (*of love, zeal*); *flush; glow* (*of enthusiasm*); *heat; violence* (*of passion*) ‖ Farben≗ *blaze* od *glow of colo*(*u*)*r*[*s* pl] **~asche** f *embers* pl **~esse** f *blast forge* **≗flüssig** a *molten* **~gefühl** n *glow; sense of intense warmth* **≗heiß** a *glowing; in a glow* (od *blaze*) **~meer** n *sea of fire* (od *flame*); *blaze* **≗rot** a *fiery red*

Glut·en n ~s/ *gluten* **Glut·in** n ~s/ *glutin*

Glyko- (Süß-) *glyco-* **~ch·olsäure** f *glycocholic acid* **~g·en** n *glycogen* **~k·oll** n *glycocoll* **Glyk·ol** n ~s/~e ⟨chem⟩ *glycol* **Glyk·ose** f = Glukose **Glykosur·ie** f = Gluko–

Gl·yphe f ~/~n ⟨arch⟩ *glyph* **Gl·ypte** f ~/~n *engraved gem* **Gl·yptik** f *glyptics* pl **Gl·yptodon** n ⟨zoo⟩ *glyptodon* **Glyptoth·ek** f *collection of glyptographs; collection* (od *museum*) *of works of sculpture*

Glyzer·id n ~s/~e *glyceride* **–r·in** n ~s/~e *–rine; glycerol* **Glyz·inie** f ~/~n *wistaria* L

Gn·ade f ~/~n **A.** ⟨rel⟩ **1.** (*divine*) *grace* ‖ dank der ~ Gottes, durch G. ~ *by the grace of God;* das Königtum v G. ~n *the divine right of kings;* ein Künstler v G. ~n *a heaven-born artist* ‖ das ist e–e ~ des Himmels (*or* v Gott) *that is a dispensation of Providence* (od *an unmerited favour of God*) **2.** *mercy* **B.** (P)

1. a. *favour, goodwill, kindness* b. Ew. ~n! *Your Grace* (od *Honour, Worship*)! 2. *clemency, forgiveness, mercy, pardon; bounty, charity* || ⟨mil⟩ *quarter*; k–e ~ *no quarter* || ~! ⟨school⟩ *fains!, fain I!, fain it!* 3. jdm e–e ~ **erweisen** *to show* (od *grant*) *a p a favour* || jdm ~ erweisen, jdm ~ widerfahren l *to have mercy on a p, to show a p m.; to pardon a p* || ~ finden *to be pardoned*; ⟨mil⟩ k–e ~ finden *to find no quarter* || ~ finden vor jdm *to find favour with a p* (od *in a p's eyes*); *to be in a p's good graces* || ~ f Recht ergehen l *to temper j. with m.; to show m.; to be merciful* 2. **auf** ~ u Un~ ausgeliefert *at the m.* (*of*) **sich auf** ~ u Un≈ ergeben ⟨mil⟩ *to surrender* (*at discretion* od) *unconditionally*; sich jdm auf ~ .. *to throw o.s. on a p's m.* || auf d–e ~ verzichte ich *I refuse to depend on your favour* od *bounty* | **aus** ~ u Barmherzigkeit *for charity's sake*; ⟨übtr⟩ etw aus ~ u B. tun *to do a th condescendingly* (od *with a show of condescension*) || jdn **in** ~(n) aufnehmen *to receive a p graciously*, .. wieder .. *to take a p into favour again* || jdn in ~n entlassen *to dismiss a p graciously* | **ohne** ~ *without m.*; *mercilessly*; ⟨mil⟩ *no quarter* | **um** ~ bitten, flehen *to sue for m.*; *to beg for pardon*; ⟨mil⟩ *to cry* (od *sue for*) *quarter*; → B. 2. | **von** jds ~ leben (*or* abhängig s) *to live on a p's charity*; *to depend on a p's bounty* **gn·aden** vi [h] jdm ~, [nur in:] gnade [3. subj] Gott! gnade dir G.! gnade dir! *God have mercy upon you! God help you!* || (wenn ..,) dann gnade Gott (...,) *what will become of us then*

Gn·aden- ~akt m *act of grace* **~bezeigung** f *favour; grace* **~bezüge** m pl; ~ f e–n Monat *a month's allowance by special favour* **~bild** n ⟨RC⟩ *miraculous image* **~brief** m *letters of privilege* **~brot** n ⟨fig⟩ *charity*; das ~ essen *to live on ch.* **~erweis** m ⟨jur⟩ *Act* (od *Bill*) *of Oblivion; act of grace; amnesty* **~frist** f *grace* (e–e ~ v e–m Jahr *a year's grace*); ⟨jur⟩ *respite* **~gabe** f ⟨theol⟩ *charism* **~gehalt** n, **~geld** n *pension; allowance* **~geschenk** n *present given as an act of grace* **~gesuch** n *clemency plea* (ablehnen *to refuse*) **~kirche** f *church of grace* **~kraut** n ⟨bot⟩ *hedge hyssop* **~lehre** f ⟨theol⟩ *doctrine of grace* **~lohn** m *allowance* **~madonna** f *Virgin of Mercy* **~mittel** n ⟨theol⟩ *means of grace* **~ordnung** f ⟨Ger⟩ *regulations for the granting of pardons* **~ort** m *place of religious veneration* **~recht** n ⟨Ger⟩ *law relating to pardons* (od *amnesties*) **~schuß** m ⟨hunt⟩ e–m Tier den ~ geben *to put down* **~stoß** m *finishing stroke; coup de grâce* Fr; **~stuhl** m ⟨theol⟩ *mercy-seat* (*of God*), ⟨arts⟩ *the Holy Trinity* **~tod** (P) *euthanasia*; (T) *mercy killing* **~wahl** f ⟨theol⟩ *election, predestination* **~weg** m; (Strafe) auf dem (*or* im) ~e erlassen *to remit by an act of grace* (od *pardon*); .. *by amnesty* || (Pension) auf dem ~e gewähren *to grant by way of grace* **~zeit** f = –frist

gn·ädig A. [a] 1. (of God) *gracious; merciful*; jdm ~ s *to be m. to a p, to have mercy* (*up*)*on a p*; Gott sei uns ~! *Lord have mercy* (*up*)*on us!* || ⟨übtr⟩ Gott sei mir ~! ~er Gott! *gr. me! good gr.!* | (P) *gr.; clement, lenient* (gegen *to, towards*); *condescending*; aller~st *most gr.* || °du bist aber ~ ⟨iron⟩ *you are very gr., indeed* c. (in Anrede) ≈er Herr ⟨engl⟩ *my lord; your lordship* || ≈e Frau ⟨engl⟩ *my lady*; ⟨Ger⟩ *madam*, (fam) *ma'am, 'm*; ≈es Fräulein *madam* 2. (S) *favourable, propitious*; das Schicksal möge uns ~ s *may the fates* (od *gods*) *be propitious to us* || *lenient* (*judgement; sentence*); *mild* **B.** [adv] *condescendingly; gr.ly*; (P) ~st geruhen z tun *to be pleased to do* || *indulgently, leniently*; du bist noch ~ davongek *you have got off* (*pretty*) *eas*(*il*)*y*; ~gst annehmen *to make it favo*(*u*)*r to accept* **C.** [abs] m–e ≈e, m–e ≈ste *madam* || (Diener:) °die ≈e *the missus*; (Putzfrau:) °m–e ≈e *the lady I oblige*

°**Gnatz** m ~es/~e 1. = Grind 2. ⟨fig⟩ *curmudgeon; ill-tempered fellow* || *miser* **gn·atzig** a 1. = grindig 2. ⟨fig⟩ *grumpy; ill-tempered* || *tight*

Gneis m –ses/–se ⟨minr⟩ *gneiss*

Gn·esen ⟨†Ger⟩ (Stadt) Provinz Posen

Gn·itte, Gnitze f [niedd] ~/~n *gnat*

Gn·om m ~en/~en ⟨myth⟩ *gnome; goblin; sprite* ≈**enhaft** a *gnomish, gnomelike*

Gn·ome f ~/~n *gnome; maxim* **Gn·omiker** m *gnomic poet* **gn·omisch** a *gnomic*

Gn·omon m ~s/–m·one ⟨astr & math⟩ *gnomon* (Gr) **Gnom·onik** f ~/ *gnomonics* pl

Gn·osis f [Gr] ~/ ⟨ec⟩ *gnosis* **Gn·ostiker** m ~s/~ **Gnostiz·ismus** m ~/ *gnosticism*

Gnu n ~s/~s ⟨zoo⟩ *gnu, wildebeest*

Gobelin [gɔ'blɛ̃] m (Fr) ~s/~s *Gobelin* (*tapestry*)

G·ockel, G·ockelhahn m *cock, rooster*

ˣ**G·ode** m & f = Pate, Patin

G·odesberg, Bad n (1969 in → Bonn eingemeindet)

G·öhrde f ⟨Ger⟩ (Wald in Prov. Hannover)

God·etie [-iə] f ~/~n ⟨bot⟩ *godetia* L

Goethe- **~forscher** *student of G.* **~forschung** f *research-work on G.; studies in G.* **~gesellschaft** f *G. Gesellschaft* [Ger] **~jahrbuch** n *G. Jahrbuch* [Ger] **~zeitalter** n *the Age of G.* **Goethisch** a *Goethian* (*style*) **Goeth·it** m (nach Goethe) ⟨minr⟩ *Goethite*

Gold n ~(e)s/ 1. gold, ⟨chem⟩ *aurum* L; 20 Karat ~ *20 carat g.*; aus ~ *of g.* || ⟨arts⟩ (etw) mit ~ auslegen *to inlay with g., to damascene*; mit ~ überziehen *to gild* || die Bilder w mit ~ aufgewogen *the pictures are worth their weight in g.* 2. [koll] ~ (= Münzen aus ~) *g.*; in ~ bezahlen *to pay in g.*; nicht mit ~ z bezahlen *worth its weight in gold; priceless* (*service*); eine Stange ~ *a lot of money* 3. ⟨übtr⟩ a. *gold, mammon, money*; Gier nach dem ~ *greed of g.* || es ist nicht alles ~, was glänzt *all is not g. that glitters, the grey mare is the better horse* b. (Farbe v ~) *g.*; *the g. of her hair, her hair is like g.* 4. ⟨fig⟩ ein Herz v (*or* wie) ~ *a heart of g.*; lauter wie ~ *pure as g.* || treu wie ~ *true as steel* || °er ist noch ~ gegen .. *he is an angel compared with ..* **~abgabe** f ⟨Ger⟩ (1916) *compulsory surrender of g. to the state* **~arbeit** f *g.smith's work* **~ader** f *vein of g.* **~adler** m ⟨orn⟩ *g.en eagle* **~after** n ⟨ent⟩ *gold-tail moth* **~agio** n ⟨com⟩ *premium on g.* **~ammer** f ⟨orn⟩ *g.-hammer* **~anleihe** f *g.-loan* **~arbeiter** m *g.smith, jeweller* **~auge** n ⟨ent⟩ *g.en-eyed fly* **~ausfuhr** f *export of g.*; ~punkt *upper g.-point* **~bad** n ⟨phot⟩ *g.-bath* **~barren** m *bullion; ingot of g.* **~barsch** m ⟨ich⟩ *ruff* **~behandlung** f ⟨med⟩ *g.-injection* **~bergwerk** n *g.-mine* **~bestand** m *g.-reserves* pl **~bilanz** f *balance-sheet on g.-basis* **~blatt** n ⟨bot⟩ *star apple* (*-tree*) **~blättchen** n *g.-foil* (od *leaf*) **~blech** n *plate of g.* **~brasse** f ⟨ich⟩ *dorado* ≈**braun** a *auburn; titian; golden-brown* **~brokat** m *samite* **~bronze** f *shell g.*; (f Möbel) *ormolu* **~butt** m ⟨ich⟩ = Scholle **~chlorid** n ⟨chem⟩ *auric chloride* **~chlorür** n ⟨chem⟩ *aurous chloride* **~deckung** f ⟨com⟩ *g.-cover* **~distel** f ⟨bot⟩ *g.en thistle* **~draht** m *g.-wire* **~drossel** f ⟨orn⟩ *oriole* **~elfenbeinkunst** f ⟨arts⟩ *sculpture in ivory and g.* **~erz** n *g.-ore* **~faden** m *g.-thread* **~falter** m ⟨ent⟩ *lycaenid* **~farbe** f *g.-colour; orpiment* ≈**farben,** ≈**farbig** a *g.-coloured; g.en* **~fasan** m ⟨orn⟩ *g.en pheasant*; °⟨fig⟩ (schöne Frau) *silver pheasant* **~feld** n *g.-field* **~fieber** n *g.-fever* **~finger** m *ring--finger* **~fink** m ⟨orn⟩ = Stieglitz **~fisch** m *g.fish*; (angeln, bek *to catch*); °⟨fig⟩ (reiche Erbin) *heiress*; ~glas [n] *g.fish-globe* || **~flitter** m *g. spangle* **~fuchs** m *bay* (*horse*) || °= Goldstück ≈**führend** a ⟨min⟩ *g.-bearing*; ~er Quarzgang *reef* **~gehalt** m *g.-content; percentage of g.* **~geier** m ⟨orn⟩ *g.en vulture* ≈**gelb** a *g.en yellow; g.--coloured, g.en* (*beard*); ~ w *to turn g.en*; →

Hahnenfuß **~geld** n *g.* (*to pay in g.*) **~gewicht** n *g.-weight*; → Troygewicht **~gewinnung** f *the obtaining* (od *production*) *of g.* **~glanz** m *g.en lustre* **~glätte** f ⟨chem⟩ *g. litharge* **~gräber** m *g.-digger* **~grube** f *g.-mine* ‖ ⟨fig⟩ *bonanza* (f *to*); *g.-mine, mint of money* **~grund** m ⟨arts⟩ *g.-size* **~gulden** m ⟨engl hist⟩ *florin* (*of Edward III*; = *6/8*) **~haar** n *g.en hair* **∼̽haarig** a *g.-haired* **~hähnchen** n ⟨orn⟩ *g.-crest*; *g.en-crested wren* **∼̽haltig** a *auriferous*; *g.-bearing*; ∼e Erde ° ⟨Am⟩ *pay-dirt* **~handel** m *g.-trade* **~hase** m ⟨zoo⟩ = Aguti **~henne** f ⟨ent⟩ → –laufkäfer **~inflation** f *g.-inflation* ‖ °**~junge** m *darling* (*son*) **~käfer** m ⟨ent Am⟩ *g.-beetle* (od *bug*) **~kernwährung** f *g. exchange standard* **~kies** m *auriferous gravel* **~kind** n *darling*; *love* **~klausel** f ⟨Ger⟩ *g.-clause*; *clause stipulating that payment is to be made in gold* **~klee** m ⟨bot⟩ *yellow trefoil* **~klumpen** m *lump of gold, nugget*; → –barren **~könig** m ⟨min⟩ *g. regulus* **~körnchen** n *small grain of g.* **~kraut** n ⟨bot⟩ *groundsel* **~krone** f *g. crown* **~kurs** m *g.-rate* **~küste** f *G. Coast* **~lack** m **1.** ⟨bot⟩ *gilly flower, wall flower* **2.** *g. varnish*; *aventurine* **~lahn** m *g. tinsel*; *flattened g.-wire* **~laufkäfer** m ⟨ent⟩ *carabid* **~legierung** f *g.-alloy* **~leiste** f *gilt cornice* **~lilie** f *g.-lily* **∼̽lockig** a *g.en-locked* **~macher** m *alchemist*; ∼kunst [f] *alchemy* **~mark** f ⟨Ger⟩ *g. mark* **~mine** f *g.-mine*; ⟨fig⟩ = –grube **~mull** m ⟨zoo⟩ *g.en mole* **~münze** f *g. coin, g. piece* **~nest** n ⟨min⟩ *pocket* **~note** f *banknote covered by g.* **~orfe** f ⟨ich⟩ *orfe* **~papier** n *g.-paper* **~parität** f ⟨com⟩ *g.-parity* **~platte** f *g.-plate* **~plattierung** f *g. plating* **~plombe** f *g.-filling* **~probe** f *g.-assay* **~punkt** m ⟨com⟩ *g.-point*; oberer (unterer) ∼ *upper* (*lower*) *g.-p.* **~purpur** m ⟨chem⟩ *purple of Cassius* **~regen** m ⟨bot⟩ *laburnum* L **~regenpfeifer** m ⟨orn⟩ *g.en plover* **∼̽reich** a *rich in g.*; *auriferous* **~rute** f ⟨bot⟩ *g.en rod* **~salz** n ⟨chem⟩ = –chlorid **~schaum** m *Dutch foil* (od *g. leaf*) **~scheider** m *g.-refiner* **~schläger** m *g.-beater*; ∼haut [f] *g.-beater's skin* **~schmied** m *g.smith*; ∼earbeit *g.'s work*; ∼ekunst [f] *g.'s art* **~schnitt** m *gilt edge*; mit ∼ *g.-edged* (*book*) **~seife** f ⟨min⟩ *g.-deposit* **~silber(legierung** f) n *electrum* **~standard** m *g. standard*; mit ∼ *on g.*; den ∼ aufgeben *to go off g.* **~staub** m *g.-dust* **~stein** m ⟨minr⟩ *chrysolite* **~stern** m ⟨bot⟩ *yellow gagea* L; *yellow star of Bethlehem* **~stickerei** f *g.-embroidery* **~stoff** m *g. brocade* (od *material*) **~stück** n *g. coin* **~tresse** f *orris*; *g. lace* **~überzug** m *g.-coating* **~umlauf** m *g. circulation*; ∼swährung [f] *g. exchange standard* **∼̽umrandet** *g.-edged* **~verbindung** f *g.-compound* **~waage** f *g.-balance* (od *scales* pl) ‖ ⟨fig⟩ jedes Wort (*or* alles) auf die ∼ legen *to weigh one's words* (od *every word*); *to pick and choose one's words* **~währung** f *g. standard* od *currency* **~wäsche** f *g.-washing* **~wäscher** m *g.-washer* **~wert** m *g.-value* **~wespe** f ⟨ent⟩ *chrysid*; *ruby-wasp* **~wirker** m *g.-weaver* **~wolf** m ⟨zoo⟩ = Schakal **~wurz** f ⟨bot⟩ *celandine* **~wurzel** f ⟨bot⟩ *g.en thistle* ‖ = –wurz **~zertifikat** n ⟨Am⟩ *g.-certificate* **~zieher** m *g.-wire drawer*

°**Goldchen** n *darling*; *goldilocks* sg

g·olden a **1.** ⟨fig⟩ *gold*; ∼e Kette, Uhr *g. chain, watch*; ∼es Tafelgeschirr *g.-plate*; *table-ware of g.*; ∼e Brille *g.-rimmed glasses* pl ‖ [pred] (*made*) *of g.* **2.** ⟨übtr⟩ (goldgelb) *g.en* (*apple, hair, tinge*) **3.** ⟨fig⟩ **a.** *g.en* (*humour*); ∼es Herz *heart of g.*; ∼e Stimme *voice of g.* **b.** *excellent, g.en* (*days*), *happy* (*time*); *precious*; ∼e Worte *a g.en saying, g.en words* pl ‖ °er ist noch ∼ gegen .. → Gold 4. ‖ → goldig 1. ⟨übtr & fig⟩ a. ‖ ∼̽e Acht f ⟨ent⟩ = Gelbling 3. ‖ ∼e Ader f *haemorrhoidal vein* ‖ ∼̽e Aue f ⟨Ger geog⟩ *the Golden Aue* (*in Thuringia*) ‖ ∼̽e **Bulle** f ⟨hist⟩ *the G.en Bull* (*1356*) ‖ ∼̽e **Hochzeit** f *the g.en wedding* ‖ ∼̽e Horde f ⟨hist⟩ *the G.en Horde* (*of Tartars*) ‖ ∼̽es Horn ⟨geog⟩ 1. (in Konstantinopel) *G.en Horn* 2. *G.en Horn* (*S. Francisco*) ‖ ∼̽es **Kalb** n ⟨bib⟩ *the Golden Calf* ‖ ∼e **Mitte,** Mittelstraße *f the golden mean* ‖ ∼e **Rose** f ⟨R. C.⟩ *the Golden Rose* ‖ ∼er **Schnitt** m ⟨math⟩ *the golden section* ‖ ∼er **Sonntag** m ⟨ec⟩ *Trinity Sunday* ‖ ∼̽es **Vlies** n *the Golden Fleece*; Orden vom ∼̽en V. *the Order of the G. F.* ‖ ∼e **zahl** f ⟨astr⟩ *the golden number* ‖ ∼̽es **Zeitalter** n *the Golden Age* **b.** jdm ∼e **Berge** versprechen *to feed a p with extravagant hopes* ‖ ⟨prov⟩ Handwerk hat e–n ∼en **Boden** *handicraft is a source of prosperity* ‖ jdm ∼e **Brücken** bauen *to build* (od *lay*) *a golden bridge for a p*

g·oldig a ⟨übtr & fig⟩ **1.** *golden* (*hair, sunshine*) **2.** *capital, excellent*; *glorious* (*weather*); ⟨fam⟩ *divine* ‖ e–e ∼e Stimme *a voice of gold* ‖ *darling* (*child*); *pretty* ‖ *buoyant, cheerful* (*optimism, spirits*); *light-hearted* ‖ *radiant, warm* (*smile*) **3.** °das ist ja ∼ *that's ripping*; ⟨iron⟩ *that's a pretty mess*

Golf[1] m ∼s/∼e *gulf* **~kraut** n ⟨bot⟩ *Gulf-weed* **~strom** m (warme Meeresströmung im Atlantik) *Gulf-stream*

G·olf[2] n ∼s/ ⟨sport⟩ *golf* ‖ ∼ spielen *to* (*play*) *g.* **~junge** m *caddie* **~platz** m *g.-course*; (*g.-*)*links* [sg konstr] **~schläger** m *g.-club* **~spiel** n *golf* **~spieler** m *golfer* **~tasche** f *golf bag*

Goli·arden m pl ⟨Lit⟩ *Goliards* pl

G·oliath m ∼s/∼s (riesiger Mensch) ⟨bib⟩ *Goliath* **~gewinde** n ⟨el, bes theat⟩ *G. Edison screw*, ⟨Am⟩ *Mogul base sc.* **~käfer** m *G. beetle*

G·olkvogel m ⟨orn⟩ = Mandelkrähe

Gon·ade f ∼/∼n → Keimdrüse

G·ondel f ∼/∼n **1.** ⟨mar⟩ *gondola* It **2.** ⟨aero⟩ *airship car*; *g.*; *nacelle* Fr **~führer** m *gondolier*

g·ondeln vi [s] **1.** *to row* (od *go*) *in a g.*; *to row a g.* **2.** °⟨fig⟩ *to drive* (durch *through*) ‖ *to saunter, stroll* **Gondol·iere** m ∼/–ri *gondolier*

G·ong n & m ∼s/∼s **1.** *gong*; *tomtom*; *tam-tam* **2.** (europäisch.) *gong*; das ∼ geht → gongen **~schlag** m *sound of the gong* ‖ ⟨wir⟩ (es ist) mit dem ∼ 20 Uhr ⟨engl⟩ (*it's*) *eight o'clock* **~signal** n ⟨sport⟩ → stoppen

g·ongen vi [h] *to hit* od *strike the gong* ‖ es gongt zum Essen *the gong is sounding for dinner*

Gon·idien [–iən] pl ⟨bot⟩ *gonidia* L pl

Goniom·eter n *goniometer* **Goniometr·ie** f *goniometry* **goniom·etrisch** a *goniometric*

g·önnen vt [h] **1. a.** jdm etw ∼ *to allow* (od *give, grant*) *a p a th*; *grant* (*me a few more hours of rest*); *do me the honour* (*of a visit*) ‖ jdm das Wort ∼ *to grant a p the h. of speaking* **b.** *not to envy* od (*be-*)*grudge a p a th*; ich gönne ihm .. *I do not grudge him* (*these pleasures*) ‖ ich gönne es ihm v Herzen *I wish him every joy with it* | °den Reinfall gönne ich ihm *I am glad he had this piece of ill luck* **c. sich** [dat] etw ∼ *to allow* (od *permit*) *o.s. a th*; *to give o.s. some rest* **2. jdm etw nicht** ∼ *to* (*be*)*grudge* od *envy a p a th*; ich gönne es ihm nicht *I gr. it him* ‖ sie ∼ uns nicht das liebe Brot *they gr. us the very food we eat*; .. die Luft .. *the air we breathe* ‖ der Erfolg war mir v ihnen nicht gegönnt *they gr.d me my success* ‖ das ist die Einstellung: einer gönnt dem anderen nichts *that is a dog-in-the-manger policy* **G·önner** m ∼s/∼ *patron, protector*; *benefactor, well-wisher* **∼̽haft 1.** [a] *condescending*; *patronizing*; ∼es Verhalten *patronage* **2.** [adv] *condescendingly*; *patronizingly*; (jdn) ∼ behandeln *to patronize* | **~in** f *patroness, protectress* **~miene** f *patronizing air* **~schaft** f *patronage* ‖ [konkr] *patrons* pl

Gonok·okkus m ∼/–kken ⟨med⟩ *gonococcus*

Gonorrh·öe f [Gr] / n ⟨med⟩ *gonorrhoea*

G·öpel m ∼s/∼ *windlass* ‖ ⟨min & tech⟩ *gin*; *whim*; (v Pferden gedreht) *horse-whim* (od *gin*) **~stange** f *whim-shaft* **~triebwerk** n *gear*

gor 1. & 3. sg pret v gären

°**G·ör** n ∼s/∼en, **~e** f *little thing*; ⟨cont⟩ *brat*

G·ording f ~/~s ⟨mar⟩ (Nock~̈) *earing*
g·ordisch a (*to cut the*) *Gordian* (*knot*)
G·orgo f ~/–g·onen ⟨Gr myth⟩ *Gorgon* **Gor-g·onen-** *Gorgonian* ‖ ~haupt [n] *Gorgon's head*
G·orki n ⟨Russ⟩ (Wolga-Stadt) → N. Nowgorod
G·örlitz n (Stadt an der Lausitzer Neiße)
G·orlspitze f (z Besatz) *guipure*; *gimp*
G·ösch f ~/~en ⟨mar⟩ *jack* ‖ *inset* (*in a flag*)
ˣ**G·osche** f = Gusche
G·ose f *Gose* [Ger]; *pale and light beer*
G·osen, das Land ~ ⟨bib⟩ *the land of Goshen*
g·oß 1. & 3. sg pret v gießen °**G·osse** f ~/~n *gutter*; *kennel* ‖ ⟨fig⟩ *gutter*; *slums* pl; jdn aus der ~ ziehen *to take a p out of the gutter*; jdn durch die ~ ziehen *to drag a p's name through the mud*; *to fling* (od *throw*) *mud at a p*
ˣ**G·össel** n ~s/~ *little goose* °⟨a. fig⟩
G·öta-Elf m (schwed. Fluß) → **Gotland**
ˣ**G·ote** m ~n/~n = Pate & f ~/~n = Patin
G·ote m ~n/~n ⟨hist⟩ *Goth*; die ~n *the Goths pl*; Ost~̈n *East Goths, Ostrogoths* West~̈n *West G.* pl
G·öteborg n (Stadt in Schweden)
G·othien, G·othland n → Gotland
G·otik f ~/ *Gothic style*; *G. architecture* ‖ Früh~̈ *early G., E. English Style*; Hoch~̈ *Decorated St.*; Spät~̈ *florid G.*, ⟨engl⟩ *Perpendicular St.* **g·otisch** a **1.** *Gothic* ‖ ~e Schrift ⟨typ⟩ *blackletter type, G. type* ‖ die ~e Sprache *G.*; → 2. ‖ ~er Stil *G.* (*style*); (e–r S) ~es Aussehen geben *to Gothicize* ‖ v ~em Aussehen *G. in character* **2.** [abs] **das** ~̈**e** *G.*; *the G. language*
G·otland, G·ottland n *Gothland, Got*(*t*)*land*
g·otländisch a *of Gothland, of Got*(*t*)*land*
G·ott m ~es/~̈er **A. 1.** *god*; *deity* ‖ Liebes~̈ *god of love*; *Cupid* ‖ ein Anblick, Mahl f ~̈er *a sight, feast for the gods* ‖ wann er kommt, das wissen die ~̈er *God knows when he comes* **2.** ⟨fig⟩ *god*; ihr ~ ist ihr Geldbeutel *their god is their money* **B.** [one pl] **1.** *God* ‖ der Dreieinige ~ *the triune God* ‖ ~, der Herr *the Lord*; ~ Vater → ~vater; → ~essohn ‖ die Mutter ~es *the Virgin* (*Mary*) ‖ der Allmächtige ~, ~ der Allmächtige *Almighty God*; *the Almighty*; der liebe ~ *God*; *the Lord* ‖ das Reich ~es *the kingdom of heaven* ‖ ~es freie Natur *the realms of Nature* **2. a. ach** ~! **o** ~! *O Gid*! *O Lord*! ⟨vulg⟩ (*by*) *golly*!, ⟨Am⟩ *O Lordy*! ‖ gerechter ~! *Lord have mercy*!, ⟨vulg⟩ *Lor-a-mussy*! ‖ **gr** ~! **mein** ~! gnädiger ~! *my God*! *good God* od *Lord*! *good Gracious*! *Gracious me*! ⟨fam⟩ *dear me*! *my eye*! *my word*! ‖ ~ ja, den kenne ich *good heavens, I know him* ‖ wahrhaftigen ~! *by God*! **b. bei** ~ *by God*! ⟨vulg⟩ *by golly* od *gum*! ‖ ich möchte bei ~ es ..! (*I*) *would to Got it* ..!; (beim) wahrhaftigen ~! *as there is God above*! ‖ **in** ~ *in God* (*here rests in G.*) ‖ **mit** ~! *God be with you*! geh' mit ~ *adieu* ‖ **von** ~ gesandt *god-given*; *heaven-sent* (*message*) ‖ v ~ verlassen *god-forsaken*; °du bist wohl ganz v ~ v. *you seem to be out of your senses* ‖ **vor** ~ *before God* ‖ **zu** ~ beten *to pray to God* (od *Heaven*); ich hoffe z ~, es .. (*I*) *would to Got it* .. ‖ in ~es **Namen** *in God's name*; °⟨fig⟩ *I don't care* ‖ um ~es willen *for God's* od *goodness' sake* (*don't do it*)! ‖ → Gnade A. 1. **c. leider ~es** *sad to say*; *unfortunately* **d.** ~ **befohlen**! *good-bye*! ‖ ~ behüte dich! *God protect you*! → ~̈bewahre ‖ sein Gesicht sah aus, daß (sich) ~ erbarm! *his face was a perfect sight* ‖ °~ erbarm! ⟨vulg⟩ *bly me*! ‖ ~ gebe (*or* gebe ~) (*I*) *would to God* (*that* ..); ~ gebe dir Frieden! *God bless you*! ‖ → gnaden ‖ grüß' ~! *good day*! ⟨Am⟩ *adios*! ‖ ~ grüß' .. *God bless* (*the trade*) ‖ ~ hab' ihn selig! *may his soul rest in peace*! ‖ so wahr mir ~ helfe! *so help me God*! ‖ ~ ist mein Zeuge! *I call God to witness*! *as God is my judge*! ‖ ~ sei Dank! *thank God* (od *goodness, Heaven*!) ~ (sei) Lob u D.! *heaven* od *God be praised* (*and thanked*) ‖ ~ sei mit Euch! *God be with you*! ‖ da sei ~ vor! *God forbid*! ‖ ~ verdamm mich (..) *dam* (*it* [*all*])!; *I'll be damned* (*if* ..) ‖ ~ vergelt's, v.'s ~! *God reward*! ‖ das walte ~! *God grant it*! ‖ weiß ~, ~ weiß (..,) *God* od *goodness knows* (*where* ..); u ~ weiß wer sonst noch *and I don't know who all*; das wissen die ~̈er *God knows, not I*!; sie träumte ~ weiß (nicht) was *she was dreaming of God knew what* ‖ ich bin, weiß ~, nicht kleinlich *God knows, I am not particular*; *I'm not p., by God*! ‖ so ~ will! will's ~! *please God*! *God willing*! ‖ wollte ~, daß .. *would to God that* .. **e.** °~ **u alle Welt** kennen *to know everybody* (od *all and sundry*; ⟨Am sl⟩ *the whole show*), ⟨fam⟩ .. *all the world and his wife* ‖ °wie ~ in Frankreich leben *to live like a fighting cock* od *like a king*; *to live in clover* od *on* (⟨Am⟩ *off*) *the fat of the land* ‖ (..), wie ihn ~ geschaffen hat (..) *as God made him* ‖ den lieben ~ e–n guten Mann s l *to let things slide*; *not to worry*; *to loaf* ‖ alle Tage, die ~ w läßt *every day that God makes* ~̈**ähnlich** a *godlike, divine* ~̈**begnadet** a *heaven-born, h.-inspired* (*artist*); *divne* (*talent*) ~̈**be-w·ahre**! intj *God forbid*; °I ~! *by no means*! *certainly not*! ~̈**ergeben** a *devout, pious*; *resigned to the will of God* ~̈**gefällig** a *pleasing to God*; ein ~es Leben führen *to lead a pious life* ~̈**gläubig** a ⟨Ger⟩ *free-thinking* ~̈**gleich** a *divine, godlike* **~l·ob**! intj *thank God*! *God be praised*! ~̈**los 1.** [a] *godless, impious, ungodly, unrighteous* ‖ °~ *naughty, wicked* **2.** [adv] *impiously*; ~ leben *to lead a godless life* **~losen 1.** die ~ [pl] *the godless* ‖ *the wicked* **2.** [in comp] ⟨russ⟩ ~bewegung [f] *Godless League*; ~feldzug [m] *anti-god campaign* **~losigkeit** f *godlessness, impiety, ungodlines* ‖ °~ *naughtiness, wickedness* **~mensch** m ⟨theol⟩ *the incarnate Son*; *God-man* ‖ ~natur [f], ~-menschl. Einheit [f] *hypostatic union* ~̈**-mensch-liche** Einheit (Christi) *hypostatic union* °**~seib·ei-uns** m *Old Nick* (*the devil*) ~̈**selig 1.** a *godly, pious*; *religious* **2.** adv *piously* **~seligkeit** f *godliness, piety, r.ness* **~sucher** m *God-seeker* **~v·ater** m *G. the Father* ~̈**verflucht** a *cursed, damned* **~-vergeß** m, **~vergessen** n ⟨bot⟩ *white horehound*; *black horehound* ~̈**vergessen** a *reprobate*; *impious, ungodly* ~̈**verlassen** a *god-forsaken* (*man*) ‖ *desolate, wretched* (*place*) **~vertrauen** n *belief* (od *confidence, faith*) *in God, religion* ~̈**voll** a ⟨fig⟩ *divine, delightful, lovely* (*sight*) ‖ *capital, ripping, splendid* ‖ °⟨iron⟩ du bist ja ~, das ist ja ~ *that's the limit*; *that takes the cake*; *that's a funny way to behave* **~wesen** n *deity, godhead*
G·ötter- ~baum m ⟨bot⟩ *tree of heaven* **~bild** n *idol*; *image of a god* **~bote** m *messenger of the gods*; ⟨ant myth⟩ *Mercury* **~dämmerung** f ⟨myth⟩ *Twilight of the Gods* **~dreiheit** f *triad* **~funke** m *divine spark* **~gestalt** f *deity*; *god* ‖ ⟨fig⟩ *divine form* **~glaube** m *belief in* (od *worship of*) *gods* ~̈**gleich** a *godlike* **~leben** n °ein ~ führen → Gott B. 2. b. **~lehre** f *mythology* **~mahl** n ⟨Gr myth⟩ *banquet of the gods* ‖ °⟨fig⟩ ein ~ *a feast for the gods* **~pflaume** f ⟨bot⟩ *ebony-tree*; *date plum*; *lotus* L **~sage** f *myth* **~sitz** m ⟨Gr myth⟩ *Olympus* L; *celestial abode* **~speise** f ⟨Gr myth⟩ *ambrosia*; *food of the gods* ‖ ⟨fig⟩ → –mahl **~spruch** m ⟨Gr myth⟩ *oracle* **~trank** m ⟨Gr myth⟩ *nectar*; *drink of the gods* **~trias** f *triad* **~verehrung** f *worship of gods* **~welt** f ⟨Gr myth⟩ *Olympus* L
G·ottes- ~acker m *churchyard, graveyard*; *God's acre* **~anbeterin** f ⟨ent⟩ *praying mantis* L **~beweis** m *argument* (od *proof*) *for the existence of God* **~dienst** m ⟨allg⟩ *public worship* ‖ ⟨C. E.⟩ *divine service*; ⟨Am a.⟩ *meeting* ‖ e–n ~ abhalten *to conduct* (od *take*) *a service* ‖ Abend~ *evening service* ‖ ~ordnung [f] *ritual*; → Liturgie ~̈**-dienstlich** a *ritual*; *religious* **~friede** m ⟨hist⟩ *truce of God* **~furcht** m *fear* (od *awe*) *of God*; *piety* ~̈**-fürchtig** a *godfearing, pious, religious* **~gabe** f *bles-*

sing; *gift of God*; *divine gift* **~gedanke** m *God-idea* **~geißel** f ⟨hist⟩ *the Scourge of God* (= Attila) **~gelehrtheit** (†–lahrt–) f *divinity, theology* **~gericht** n = –urteil **~geschenk** n °⟨fig⟩ *godsend, mercy* (f *to*) **~glaube** m *belief in God*; *faith*; *theism* **~gnade** f *blessing*; *grace*; → Gnade ‖ *godsend, mercy* (f *to*) **~gnadenkraut** n ⟨bot⟩ = Gnaden– **~gnadentum** n (*the theory of*) *the divine right of kings* **~haus** n *house of God*; *place of worship*; *church* **~kasten** m *collecting-, poor-box* **~lästerer** m *blasphemer* **~̈lästerlich** a *blasphemous* **~lästerung** f *blasphemy* **~lehre** f *divinity, theology* **~leugner** m *atheist* **~leugnung** f *atheism* **~lohn** m *God's reward, heavenly r.d* **~mord** m *deicide* **~mörder** m *deicide* **~pfennig** m *earnest-money* **~reich** n (*kingdom of*) *heaven*; **~sohn** m *son of God*; *the Son* **~tisch** m ⟨ec⟩ *the Lord's Table*; *communion-table* **~urteil** n ⟨hist⟩ *ordeal* **~verächter** m *flouter of God* **~verehrung** f *worship of God* **~wort** n *the Bible, the Book*

G·ottestum n *deity, divinity* (*of Christ*), *godhead, godhood, godship* **G·ottheit** f ~/~en **1.** [abstr] = Gottestum **2.** [konkr] *deity, divinity* **G·öttin** f ~/~nen *goddess* **G·öttingen** n ⟨Ger⟩ (Universität) *Go(e)ttingen* **g·öttlich A.** [a] **1.** *divine* (*mercy, revelation*); *godly, godlike*; *celestial, heavenly* ‖ ⟨übtr⟩ *divine* (*talent*); *heavenly* (*thought*); *pious* (*life*) **2.** °⟨fig⟩ *capital, delicious, delightful, heavenly, divine* (S), *lovely* (*sight*); °ein ~er Fraß *a feast for the gods*; ⟨Am sl⟩ *a splendid blow-out* **B.** [adv] °⟨fig⟩ *deliciously*; *splendidly* **C.** [abs] **das ~̈e** *the divine*; *divine things* pl **| ~̈keit** f ~/ *divinity*; *godliness* °**g·ottserbärmlich,** °**g·ottsjämmerlich 1.** [a] *piteous*; *pitiable, pitiful* ‖ *detestable, execrable* (*food*); *miserable*; *wretched* **2.** [adv] *piteously* (*to cry p.*) ‖ *miserably, wretchedly* **G·ötze** m ~n/~n **1.** *idol*; *false god*; ein ~ aus Holz *an idol in wood* **2.** ⟨fig⟩ *idol*; e–n ~n m aus *to idolize*; *to make an idol of* **G·ötzen- ~bild** n *idol*; (*graven*) *image* **~diener** m *idolater* **~dienerin** f *idolatress* **~dienst** m *idolatry* ‖ ~ treiben mit etw *to idolize a th* **~tempel** m *heathen place of worship*

Gou·ache- [gu'aʃ] → Guasch–

goutieren [gu–] vt [h] (etw) *to enjoy*; *to delight in*; *to be pleased with*

Gouver- ~n·ante [gu–] f ~/~n *governess* **~nement** [guvɛrn'mɑ̃] n [Fr] ~s/~s ⟨a-engl, bes Russ⟩ *government* ‖ ⟨Ger⟩ das General~̈ *the General Government* **~neur** [guvɛr'nør] m [Fr] ~s/~e *governor* ‖ ⟨Am⟩ ~ e–s Staates *State Governor*; Residenz des ~s *the Executive Mansion*

Gr·ab[1] n ~(e)s/~̈er **1.** (Erdloch) *grave* (*of a p*); *tomb* ‖ (~hügel) *g.* ‖ ⟨praeh⟩ Hügel~̈ *barrow, tumulus* L [pl *–li*]; *cairn* **|** (Fels~̈, Stein~̈) *sepulchre*; (unterird. ~) *tomb*; das Heilige ~ *the Holy S.* **2.** ⟨fig⟩ *death*; *g.* (*of a p's freedom*) **3.** **feuchtes** ~ *d. by drowning* ‖ verschwiegen wie das ~ *secret as the g.* ‖ sein eigenes ~ **graben** *to dig one's own g.* ‖ sein ~ **finden** *to meet one's d.*; *to be killed, to fall* (*in battle*); → Wellen; er wird sein ~ dort finden *he'll leave his bones there* **|** Gebet **am** ~e *committal prayer*; Worte am ~e *c. service* ‖ der Gottesdienst am ~e wurde .. *the service at the graveside was* (*conducted by* ..) ‖ ⟨prov⟩ am Grabe noch pflanzt man *or* er die Hoffnung auf *he hopes against hope* ‖ ⟨fig⟩ am Rande des ~es *on the brink of the g.*; mit e–m Fuß im ~e stehen *to have one foot in the g.* ‖ sich im ~e umdrehen *to turn in one's g.* ‖ **ins** ~ *into the g.*; bis ins ~ *till d.* ‖ jdn ins ~ bringen *to be the cause of a p's d.*; das wird ihn ins ~ br. *that will be the d. of him* **| über's** ~ hinaus *beyond the g.* **|** jdn **zu** ~e geleiten *to attend a p's funeral* ‖ (Einrichtung) z ~e läuten *to sound the knell of* (*a th*) ‖ (jdn; ⟨fig⟩ etw) z ~e tragen *to bury* **4.** *sepulchral* **~̈ähnlich, ~̈artig** a *s.* **~denkmal** n *tomb* **~einfassung** f *enclosure of a g.* **~geläut(e)** n *knell, toll* **~gesang** m *dirge*; *funeral song* **~gewölbe** n (*sepulchral*) *vault*; *familyvault*: *tomb* **~hügel** m *g.*; *g.-mound*; ⟨praeh⟩ *tumulus* L **~kreuz** n *g. marker* **~legung** f *burial, interment* **~lied** n ~ –gesang **~mal** n *sepulchre, tomb*(*stone*); *monument*; ~ des Unbekannten Soldaten *Unknown Warrior's g., Cenotaph* **~platte** f *g. brass* od *slab* **|** ~nabdruck [m] *brass rubbing* **~rede** f *funeral oration* od *sermon* **~schändung** f *outrage* (*od sacrilege*) *on a g.* **~schaufel** f (*sexton's*) *spade* **~schrift** f *epitaph* **~stätte** f *burial* (od *burying*)-*-place*; *g., tomb* **~stein** m, **~tafel** f *g.stone, headstone, tombstone* **|** ~bildhauer [m] *monumental mason* **~urne** f *funeral urn*

Gr·ab-[2] (→ graben) **~scheit** n *spade*; *shovel* **~stichel** m ⟨engr⟩ *burin, graver*; *graving-tool*; *die* **~stock** m *digging-spade* (od *stick*) **~wespe** f ⟨ent⟩ *digger-wasp*; *fossorial wasp*

°**gr·abbeln** vi [h] *to grabble, grope*; *fumble* (nach *for*)

gr·aben I. vt/i [grub/ge~] **A.** vt **1.** (Grab, Loch) *to dig*, (Höhle) *to excavate* ‖ e–n Schacht ~ *to sink a shaft* ‖ ⟨bes mil⟩ e–n Graben ~ *to dig a trench* ‖ ⟨prov⟩ → Grube **2.** Kartoffeln ~ *to dig potatoes* **3.** *to dig one's spurs into his horse* ‖ ⟨fig⟩ (of grief) *to cut deep furrows* (in .. *in a p's brow*) **4.** sich in den Boden ~ (T) *to make a burrow in the ground* ‖ *the aeroplane buried its nose in the sand* ‖ ⟨fig⟩ sich ~ in .. *to delve into* (*a p's heart*) **B.** vi **1.** ⟨agr⟩ *to dig* **2.** ~ **nach** .. *to dig for* (*gold, ore*; *treasures*) **II.** ~̈ n *digging* **Gr·aben** m ~s/~̈ **1. a.** *ditch*; Abzugs~̈ *sewer* ‖ (Wasser~̈, Stadtwasser~̈) *moat* ‖ ⟨fort⟩ *fosse*; ⟨mil⟩ *trench*; erster ~ *fire-trench*; zweiter ~ *support t.*; dritter ~ *reserve t.*; letzter ~ *communication t.* **b.** e–n ~ ziehen *to* (*make a*) *ditch*; aus dem ~ herausz. *to unditch*; (etw) mit e–m ~ umgeben *to ditch* ‖ (Boden) mit ~̈ durchziehen ⟨mil⟩ durch ~̈ befestigen *to* (*en*)*trench* **2.** ⟨geol⟩ *fault trough*; *rift valley*; *graben* [Ger]; ⟨mar⟩ *Japan Trench*; *Tonga T.*; *Aleutian T.* **~bagger** m *trencher, ditcher* **~bestreichung** f ⟨fort⟩ *enfilade* **~böschung** f ⟨fort⟩ äußere ~ *counter-scarp*; innere ~ *escarp* **~bruch** m ⟨geol⟩ *fault-block depression* **~geschütz** n *t.-mortar*; ~e [pl] *t. artillery* **~kampf** m ⟨mil⟩ *t.-fighting* **~krieg** m ⟨mil⟩ *t.-warfare* **~schere** f ⟨fort⟩ (kl Wall) *tenail(le)* Fr **~sohle** f *t.-bottom* **~spiegel** m *t.scope* **~streiche** f ⟨fort⟩ *caponier* Fr **~wehr** f ⟨fort⟩ = –streiche ‖ *parapet*

Gr·äber m ~s/~ *digger* **~**[1](→ Grab)dienst [m] *graves registration* (*service*) ‖ ~feld [n] ⟨praeh⟩ *barrows* pl, *urn-field* **Gr·abes**[1] *sepulchral* **~dunkel** n *s. darkness* **~rand** m *brink of the g.* **~stille** f *s.* (od *deadly*) *silence* **~stimme** f *s. voice* **Gr·abung** f ~/~en ⟨praeh⟩ *dig*

Gr·ad m ~es/~e **A. 1.** ⟨scient⟩ **a.** ⟨math & phys⟩ (abbr °; [pl] nach Zahlen ° sprich ~) *degree* ‖ 20° Celsius, Réaumur, Fahrenheit 20 degrees (*20°*) centigrade (*20° C*) *Réaumur, Fahrenheit*; 20° Kälte *20° of frost, 20° below zero*; einige ~ unter Null *some points below zero*; 20° Wärme (*or* über Null) *20° above zero*; bei 30° Wärme *at a temperature of 30 degrees* ‖ in ~e abteilen, staffeln *to graduate* **|** ⟨arith⟩ → Gleichung **b.** ⟨geog⟩ Breiten~̈ *degree of latitude*; Längen~̈ *d. of longitude* **c.** ⟨gram⟩ Steigerungs~̈ *degree of comparison* **d.** Verwandtschafts~̈ *degree of consanguinity*; Vetter ersten, zweiten ~es *cousin of the first, second d.* **2.** ⟨univ⟩ akademischer ~ *d.* ‖ ⟨engl⟩ ~ höherer Ordnung *honours d.*; einfacher *or* gewöhnlicher ~ *pass, pass d.*; Student, der den höheren (einfachen) ~ erwirbt *honours-man* (*passman*) ‖ e–n ~ erlangen, erwerben *to take one's d.* **B.** (~ in Rang, Qualität etc) **1.** *degree*; *grade*; *pitch*; *standard*; *step*; → Rang, Stufe ‖ Dienst~ *grade*; *rank* **2. a.** Beamte **aller ~e** *officials of all g.s* ‖ ein hoher ~ v .. *a high g. of* (*prudence, civilization*) ‖ Schulen höheren ~es *higher g. schools* ‖ der höchste ~ *the perfection*; der höchste ~ der Dummheit *the height of folly*;

die Beschießung erreichte ihren höchsten ~ *the bombardment rose to its maximum pitch* ‖ du bist e–n ~ in m–r Achtung **gestiegen** *you have risen a step in my estimation* | **bis z** e–m gewissen ~e *to a certain d.* (od *extent*), *up to a point, as* (od *so*) *far as it goes* ‖ (..,) bis z welchem ~e er .. (*I do not know*) *to what extent he ..* ‖ **in** dem ~e, wie *or* als *much* od *intensely as*; in außerordentlichem ~ *in an extraordinary d.* ‖ in äußerstem ~e *exceedingly, extremely* ‖ in geringem ~e *in a small d.*; *little*; in nicht g. ~e *in no small d.* ‖ in gewissem ~ *to a certain d.* ‖ in hohem ~e *to a high d.*; *highly*; *singularly* ‖ in höchstem ~e *in the highest d.* ‖ in solchem ~e *to such a d.* | dem ~e **nach** *in d.* | sich **um** 180° ändern, um 180° umschwenken *to about-face* vi, ⟨pol⟩ *to turn double*; um 180° umschlagen *to change course through 180 d.s* **~bezeichnung** f *graduation* **~bogen** m ⟨geom & surv⟩ *protractor* **~einteilung** f *graduation*; mit ~ *divided into degrees* | ~ssystem [n] ⟨geog⟩ *earth reference s.* **~kreis** m *graduated circle* **~messer** m ⟨fig⟩ *criterion, standard*; *index* **~messung** f ⟨geog⟩ *astronomical measurement*; *m. of the earth's surface*; (Dreiecks≈) *triangulation* **~netz** n *network of parallels and meridians*; ⟨mil cart⟩ *grid*(*iron*) | ~entwurf [m] *map projection* **~skala** f *graduated scale*; mit ~ versehen *to graduate* ‖ **~strich** m *mark* **≈weise 1.** [adv] *gradually*; *by degrees* **2.** [a] *gradual* **~zahl** f (Kraftstoff≈ etc) *grading*

Grad- [in comp] → Gerad– **≈e** = gerade **~flügler** m pl (*order of*) *orthoptera* **~heit** f = Geradheit

Gradi·ent m ~en/~en ⟨phys⟩ *gradient*

Grad·ier- **~haus** n = –werk **~verfahren** n *graduation method* **~waage** f *areometer, hydrometer* **~werk** n *graduation-works* pl; *thorn-house*; *cooling stack* **grad·ieren** vt [h] ⟨chem & tech⟩ *to graduate* **Grad·ierung** f *graduation*

Gr·adlaufapparat m ⟨mar⟩ *gyroscopic apparatus*; *gyroscope* **gr·adlinig** = gerad– **-gradig** [in comp] → erst~, zweit–; hoch~

Gradu·ale n ~s/–lien *gradual* **Gradu·alpsalmen** f pl ⟨bib⟩ *Gradual Psalms, Songs of Degrees*

gradu·ell 1. [a] *gradual* **2.** [adv] *gradually*

gradu·ieren vt/i [h] **1.** vt (e–e Skala) *to graduate* ‖ ⟨univ⟩ jdn ~ *to admit a p to a degree*; ⟨Am⟩ *to graduate a p* **2.** vi ⟨univ⟩ *to graduate*

Gradu·ierte m [der ~, ein ~r] ~n/~n *the graduate* **Gradu·ierung** f ~/~en ⟨univ⟩ *graduation*

Gr·af m ~en/~en ⟨engl⟩ (Adelsrang zw marquis u viscount) *earl* (*the Right Honourable the Earl of ..*) ‖ ⟨a-engl⟩ *count* (*Count Bülow*) ‖ → Pfalz≈ (⟨Ger⟩ Anrede: (Herr) ~; unter Adligen: Herr von B.; Anschrift Herrn Otto ~ B. *or* Herrn ~ v. B. **Gr·afen-** **~krone** f *coronet* **~stand** m, **~würde** f *earldom* **Gr·äfin** f ~/~nen ⟨engl & a-engl⟩ *countess* ‖ e–e ~ aus eigenem Recht, durch Geburt *a c. in her own right* **gr·äflich** a *belonging to an earl* (od *a count*) ‖ *like an earl* (od *a count*) **Gr·afschaft** f ~/~en **a.** *county*; die ~ Surrey *S. County, the C. of S.*; in der ~ S. *in* (*the C. of*) *S.*, ⟨Am⟩ *in S. C.*; ⟨Ir⟩ die ~ Dublin *C.D.* ‖ Hauptstadt e–r ~ *county-town* **b.** ⟨engl hist⟩ *earldom* **Gr·afschafts-** **~beamter** m: höchster jurist. ~ ⟨Am⟩ *sheriff* **~bezirk** m (6 Meilen im Quadrat) ⟨Am⟩ *township* **~gericht** n *County Court* **~richter** m oberster ~ ⟨Scot⟩ *sheriff*(*-deputy*; Bezirk e–s ~s *sheriffship* **~(stadt)rat** m ⟨engl⟩ *C.* (*borough*) *Council*

gr·afisch a etc → graphisch etc

Gral m ~(e)s/ ⟨hist⟩ *the Holy Grail* **~suche** f *the quest for the grail*

gram a [pred] jdm ~ s *to have a grievance* (od *grudge, spite*) *against a p*; man kann ihm nicht ~ s *one cannot take a dislike to him* ‖ jdm ~ w *to come to dislike a p* **Gram** m ~(e)s/ *grief* (über *at*), *sorrow*; *affliction, trouble* ‖ der ~ nagt an ihr *g. preys upon her mind* ‖ aus ~ sterben *to die of g.* ‖ vom ~ gebeugt *bowed down by* (od *with*) *g.*; *g.-stricken* ‖ vor ~ vergehen, –schmachten *to pine* (od *fret one's life*) *away*; ⟨fam⟩ *to take on* **gr·ämen** vt [h] **1.** (jdn) *to grieve*; *worry* ‖ es grämt mich *it frets* od *g.s me* (*to see ..*) ‖ °das soll mich wenig ~ *that won't trouble me*; *that's all the same to me* **2. sich** ~ *to fret*; *to g.*; (über *at, over*; um *for*); *to worry* (über *about*); sich z Tode ~ *to fret o.s. to d.*; *to fret one's life away* **grämlich** a *gloomy*; *morose, sully, sullen*; *fretful*; *peevish* **gr·amverz·errt** a *distorted with grief* **gramvoll** a *grief-stricken, sad, careworn, melancholy*; [pred] *full of g.*

Gramin·een [-e:ən] pl ⟨bot⟩ *gramineous plants* pl; *grasses* pl; *Gramineae* L pl

Gramm n ~(e)s/~e (nach Zahlen ~) **1.** *gram*(*me*); 100 ~ *a hundred grams*; ein ~ Wasser *one gram of water*; 50 ~ Reis *50 grammes of rice* **2.** [in comp] *gramme*; *g.-atom* ‖ *g.-calory*

Gramm·atik f ~/~en *grammar* **≈·alisch** a = grammatisch **~ker** m *grammarian* **gramm·atisch 1.** [a] *grammatical* (*gender*) ‖ ~er Wechsel *g. change, Verner's Law* **2.** [adv] *g.ly*; ~ korrekt *g.ly correct*; *g.ly* ‖ der Satz ist ~ korrekt *the sentence is g.*

Gr·ammel f ~/~[n] [bay, österr] = Griebe

Grammoph·on n ~s/~e *gramophone*; ~ an Radio angeschlossen *radio-g.* ‖ ein Lied etc im ~ festhalten *to record a song* ‖ nach dem ~ tanzen *to dance to the g.* **~anschluß** m ⟨wir⟩ *g. pick-up* **~nadel** f *g.-needle* **~platte** f *g.-record*; ein Lied auf e–e ~ übertragen *to record a song for the g.* **~scheibe** f *g.-disk*

Gr·ampiangebirge n ⟨Scot⟩ *The Grampians* pl

Gran n ~s/~e (nach Zahlen ~) ⟨engl pharm⟩ *grain* (= *0,065 g*); 12 ~ Kalomel *12 g.s of c.*

Gran·ada n ⟨Span⟩ (Stadt)

Gran·at[1] m ~s/~e ⟨minr⟩ *garnet*; → Pyrop

Granat[2] m ~s/~e ⟨zoo⟩ = Garnele

Gran·at- (→ Granat[1] u Granate) ⟨bot⟩ *pomegranate*; ⟨mil⟩ *shell* **~apfel** m *p.*; ~baum [m] *p.* (*tree*); ~muster [n] *p. pattern*; ~sirup [m] *p. syrup, grenadine* Fr **~baum** m *p.* (*tree*) **~einschlag** m *sh. hit* **~feuer** n *sh.-fire*, sicher gegen ~ *sh.-proof* **~füllung** f *bursting charge* **~hülle** f *sh.-wall* **~kammer** f *sh.-room* **~kopf** m *nose* **~splitter** m *sh.-splinter, sh-fragment* **~trichter** m *sh.-crater* (od *hole*) **~werfer** m (Geschütz) *trench-mortar* | ~nest [n] *m. pit*

Gran·ate f ~/~n ⟨mil⟩ *shell*; schwere ~ ⟨sl⟩ *crump*; *coal-box*; (leichter Ratscher) ⟨sl⟩ *whiz*(*z*)*-bang* ‖ Brisanz≈ *high-explosive sh.* ‖ Leucht≈ *star-sh.* ‖ Leuchtspur≈ *tracer* | Hand≈ (*hand-*) *grenade*; *small bomb*; Gewehr≈ *rifle-grenade*; Eierhand≈ ⟨sl⟩ *egg-bomb* | Platzen v. ~n *sh.-burst* ‖ °Bomben u ~n! = Donnerwetter!

Gran Canaria f (Insel) *Grand Canary*

Gran Cañon m (des Colorado) *Grand Canyon*

Gran Chaco [tʃ–] m (südamerik. Landschaft)

Grand [grɑ̃] m [Fr] ~s/~s ⟨cards⟩ *grand*; ~ Solo *solo grand*; ~ aus der Hand *open g.*

Gr·ande m ~n/~n [Span] *grandee* **Grand·ezza** ~/ f *grandeur* ‖ *formal gravity*

×**gr·andig** a *gravelly*; → grantig

grandi·os a [It] *grand* (*days*); *magnificent* (*view*), *splendid*; *grandiose, pompous*

gran·ieren vt [h] *to grain, granulate*

Gran·it m ~s/~e ⟨minr⟩ *granite* ‖ hart wie ~ *as hard as g.* ‖ °auf ~ beißen *to bite a file* **≈artig** a *granitic* **~felsen** m *granitic rock* **~gebirge** n *granite mountains* pl **~marmor** m *g. marble* **~porphyr** m *g. porphyry*

gran·iten a *granite, granitic*; ⟨a. fig⟩

Gr·anne f ~/~n ⟨bot⟩ *awn, beard* ‖ ⟨zoo⟩ *whiskers* pl (*of a cat*); ⟨furriery⟩ *top hair*

×**gr·antig** a *cantankerous*; *cross*; = mürrisch

granul·är a granular **Granulati·on** [ts] f [abstr & konkr] granulation **granul·ieren** 1. vt [h] to granulate; to grain || granuliert granulated 2. ≃ n granulation **Granul·it** m ∼s/∼e ⟨minr⟩ granulite **Granul·ose** f granulose

-graph·ie suff -graphy (z. B. geography)

Gr·aphik f ∼/∼en the graphic arts pl (⟨Ger⟩ painting being excluded); graphics pl **Gr·aphiker** graphic (od commercial, designing) artist; illustrator **gr·aphisch** 1. [a] graphic (art; symbol); ∼e Anstalt art printers pl | ⟨scient⟩ g. (method; solution); ∼es Rechnen g. algebra || ∼e Darstellung diagram, graph | ⟨fig⟩ graphic, vivid (description); ∼e Gestaltung artwork, layout; ∼e Virtuosität extraordinary draftsmanship 2. [adv] g.ally **Graph·it** m ∼(e)s/∼e ⟨minr⟩ 1. black-lead, graphite, plumbago || mit ∼ schwärzen to black-lead 2. [in comp] graphite (oil) **graphit·ieren** vt [h] to black-lead **graph·itisch** a graphitic

Grapho- [in comp] grapho- **∼l·it** m grapholite **∼l·oge** m grapho-analyst **∼log·ie** f graphology **∼st·atik** f graphical statics pl

×°**gr·apschen** vi [h] = grapsen °**gr·apsen** vi/t [h] 1. [vi] ∼ nach etw to grab (od snatch) at a th; to grab (od snatch) a th 2. [vt] etw ∼ = ∼ nach etw

Graptol·ith m ∼s/∼en ⟨pal, zoo⟩ graptolite

Gr·as n ∼es/≃er 1. grass; [koll] herbage || (Rasen) (Land) mit ∼ bebauen to (lay down in) g.; mit ∼ bewachsen g.-grown (courtyard); g.ed (walk); overgrown with g. 2. ⟨fig⟩ darüber ist lange ∼ gewachsen that's a th of the past; that has long od clean been forgotten, it is dead and buried || das ∼ wachsen hören to hear the g. grow; to see through a millstone; er denkt er hört das ∼ w. he thinks he's the cat's whiskers || wo er hinhaut, da wächst kein ∼ wieder if he strikes he strikes thoroughly || in's ∼ beißen to bite the dust, to kick the bucket, (to die) 3. [in comp] grass- ..; graminaceous, gramineous °**∼affe** m uppish boy od girl, Miss Pert **≃artig** a graminaceous, gramineous; grassy **∼baum** m ⟨bot⟩ g.-tree **∼büschel** m g.-tuft **∼butter** f g.-butter **∼decke** f = -matte **∼ebene** f → Pampa, Prärie, Savanne **∼eule** f ⟨ent⟩ g.-moth **∼faser** f g.-fibre **∼feldbau** m g.-growing (od farming); pasture-farming **∼fleck** m g.-stain **≃fressend** a graminivorous **∼futter** n g.; pasture **∼fütterung** f g.-feeding **≃grün** a g.-green **∼halm** m g.-blade; blade of g. **∼hecht** m ⟨ich⟩ young pike **∼hüpfer** m ⟨ent⟩ g.hopper **∼land** n g.-land; pasture **∼lauch** m ⟨bot⟩ = Schnittlauch **∼leinen** n g.-cloth **∼lilie** f ⟨bot⟩ asphodel **∼matte** f matting of g.; ⟨AInd⟩ tatty **∼milbe** f ⟨ent⟩ harvest-mite **∼mücke** f ⟨orn⟩ white throat (→ d., warbler); black cap **∼narbe** f (piece of) turf, sward **∼nelke** f ⟨bot⟩ thrift **∼nutzung** f g.-cutting **∼öl** n g.-oil **∼pferdchen** n = -hüpfer **∼pflanze** f graminaceous plant **≃reich** a g.y **∼samen** m g.-seed, hay-seed **∼schneidemaschine** f, **∼schneider** m g.-cutter **∼sichel** f g.-hook **∼sittich** m ⟨orn⟩ budgerigar **∼stengel** n g.-stalk; trockener ∼ windlestraw **∼topf** m ⟨bot⟩ club-rush **∼webe** f = Altweibersommer **∼weide** f pasture(-ground) **∼wirtschaft** f = -feldbau **∼wuchs** m growth of g.; mit üppigem ∼ abounding in g.; g.y **∼wurzel** f ⟨bot⟩ couch-g. **Gr·äschen** n small grass-blade **gr·asen** 1. vi [h] (T) to graze || Vieh ∼ l to graze cattle 2. ≃ n grazing **Gr·aser** m ⟨hunt⟩ tongue (of a stag, etc.) **Gr·äser** pl Gramineae L pl; grasses pl **gr·asig** a grassy; grass-like **Gr·äsling** m ⟨ich⟩ = Äsche; Gründling

grass·ieren vi [h] (of diseases, vices, etc.) to be rampant, rife, prevalent; to prevail; → wüten | **∼d** a prevalent; epidemic

gr·äßlich A. [a] 1. dreadful, frightful, ghastly, grisly, gruesome; heinous, hideous, horrible, monstrous (crime), shocking (story); abject (poverty) 2. °⟨fig⟩ abominable, detestable (p); miserable (dinner); wretched (cold; place); ⟨fam⟩ awful, beastly (weather); cruel, fearful, ghastly, horrible, terrible; ⟨Am a.⟩ fierce; jdn in e–e ∼e Verlegenheit bringen to put a p in an awkward position || hier ist ja °e–e ∼e Wirtschaft here's a ghastly mess B. [adv] horribly, terribly (distorted) || ⟨mst °fig⟩ ∼ aufgeregt awfully excited; ⟨fam⟩ beastly (tough) || ein ∼ dummer Kerl a ghastly fool; ein ∼ langweiliger M. a terrible (od fearful) bore || mir war ∼ zumute I felt miserable | **≃keit** f ghastliness, hideousness

Grat m ∼(e)s/∼e 1. (scharfe Kante) burr; edge, fin, beard; (an e–r Schneide) wire-edge 2. ⟨arch⟩ a. (Dach≃) arris b. (Schnittlinie zweier Gewölbe) groin; ∼e [pl] groins pl; → Rippe 3. (of mountain, rock) ridge; (scharfer) arête Fr; chine; Gorner ∼ Gorner Grat [Ger] **Gr·äte** f ∼/∼n (Fisch≃) fish-bone; bone; die ∼n herausnehmen aus e–m Fisch to bone a fish **gr·äten** vt [h] (Fisch) to bone **Gr·äten- ∼muster, ∼ornament** n herring-bone pattern **∼schritt** m ⟨ski-ing⟩ herring-bone **∼sparren** m ⟨arch⟩ hip **∼stich** m herring-bone (stitch); mit ∼ nähen to herring-bone **∼ziegel** m hip tile **gr·ätig** bony (fish); full of fish bones || ⟨fig⟩ irritable; angry

Gratifikati·on [ts] f ∼/∼en bonus L; gratuity

gr·ätig a bony (fish) | ⟨fig⟩ irritable; = grantig

Gr·äting f [engl] ∼/∼e ⟨mar⟩ (∼fußboden) grating

gratin·ieren vt [h] ⟨cul⟩ (Fleisch) to gratinate

grat·is adv gratis L; free of charge **≃aktie** f bonus-share **≃beilage** f free supplement **≃exemplar** n complimentary copy **∼muster** n free sample

Gr·ätsche f ⟨gym⟩ splits pl (an .. on the horse; über over); e–e ∼ m = **gr·ätschen** vi [h] to do the splits || → spreizen **Gr·ätschstellung** f splits pl; ∼ einnehmen to do the sp.

Gratul·ant m ∼en/∼en congratulator; -lant -**l·antin** f ∼/∼nen = Gratulant -**lati·on** [ts] f ∼/∼en -lation (z etw on a th) || ∼sschreiben [n] -latory letter **gratul·ieren** vi [h] jdm ∼ to -late od felicitate a p (z etw on a th); schriftlich ∼ to send written -lations; darf man ∼? may I -late you? | **sich** ∼ to -late o.s. (that ..) || (wenn ..) da kannst du dir ∼ (if I catch you,) you'll be sorry for y.s.

grau I. [a] 1. ⟨eig⟩ grey, ⟨bes Am⟩ gray (colour; hair, eyes; coat); etw ∼ greyish || ∼e Farbe grey(ness); sein Gesicht nahm e–e unheimlich ∼e F. an his face turned a ghastly grey || ⟨fig⟩ darüber brauchst du dir k–e ∼en Haare wachsen z l you need not trouble your head about that || in ∼er Kleidung in grey || ∼er Kopf grey (od hoary) head | ∼er Bär grizzly bear || ⟨ec⟩ ≃e Brüder Grey Friars pl || ⟨med⟩ ∼e Salbe grey ointment || ⟨med⟩ ∼er Star grey cataract || ∼e Substanz grey matter (of the brain) | ∼ m to (make) grey; ∼ färben to paint grey; sich ∼ färben to become grey || ∼ w to grey, (P) grizzle; to become grey | colourless (sky) || grey, livid; pale (vor with) 2. ⟨übtr⟩ (of time) distant, remote; ∼es Altertum remote antiquity; in ∼er Vorzeit from time immemorial || dim (ideas); dull; vague 3. ⟨fig⟩ gloomy, monotonous, sombre || ∼es Elend = °Kater || ∼ ist alle Theorie all theorizing is unproductive **II.** *[adv] greyly **III.** [abs] ≃ n grey; in ≃ in g.; ein dunkles ≃ a dark g. || ≃ in ≃ ⟨paint⟩ grisaille Fr || ⟨fig⟩ etw ≃ in ≃ malen to paint .. in the darkest colours **≃bart** m g.beard; ⟨fig⟩ veteran **∼bärtig** a grey-bearded **∼blau** a g.-blue **∼braun** a taupe Fr **≃brot** n g. bread, brown b. **≃buch** n ⟨pol⟩ g.-book **∼bünden** n Sw (Kanton) Grisons Fr pl **∼farbig** a g.-coloured **≃fäule** f g.ish discolo(u)ration produced by the -schimmel **≃fuchs** m ⟨zoo⟩ g. fox **≃giltigerz** n ⟨minr⟩ g. copper ore **∼grün** a g.(ish)-green; glaucous **≃guß** m g. (cast) iron **∼haarig** a g.-haired; grizzled; hoary **≃hörnchen** n ⟨zoo⟩ g. squirrel **≃kappe** f = Röhrling **≃kehlchen** n ⟨orn⟩ hedge-sparrow **≃kopf** m g. head **∼köpfig** a g.-headed **≃papagei** m ⟨orn⟩ g. parrot;

jako ≃**rock** m *g.-coat* **~scheibe** f ⟨telv⟩ *ambient light filter* ≃**schimmel** m **1.** ⟨zoo⟩ *grey; grey horse* **2.** ⟨bot⟩ *botrytis,* → –fäule **~schwarz** a *g.(ish)--black* ≃**spießglanz** m ⟨chem⟩ *stibnite; antimony glance* | ~erz [n] *antimonite; grey antimony ore* ≃**tier** n = Esel ≃**wacke** f ⟨geol⟩ *greywacke* ≃**-werk** n → Feh, ⟨bes her⟩ *vair* °**Gr·auchen** n *small donkey* **gr·auen**[1] **1.** vi [h] *to become* (od *grow, turn*) *grey; to grey* ‖ (of the day) *to dawn*; der Morgen graut *it begins to dawn*; der Tag beginnt z ~ *the day is breaking* **2.** ≃ n → Morgengrauen ***grau-lich**[1], **gräulich**[1] a *greyish,* ⟨bes Am⟩ *grayish; dusky* ‖ ~ blau *greyish-blue* ‖ (aber) → greulich

gr·auen[2] **1.** vimps [h] **es graut mir** vor etw *I dread* (od *fear*) *a th; I am afraid of a th* ‖ es g. mir bei dem Gedanken *I shudder at the thought* (an *of*); *I sh. to think* (daß *that* ..) **2.** vrefl [h] **sich ~ vor** etw *to dread* (od *fear*) *a th; to be afraid of a th*; er graut sich vor .. *he dreads* (*the long journey*) **Gr·auen** n ~s/ **1.** *dread* (vor etw *of a th*; z tun *of doing*); *horror* (vor *of*); ein leises ~ *a slight feeling of dread* ‖ ein ~ empfinden bei dem Gedanken *to shudder at the thought* (*of* ..), *to sh. to think* (*that* ..) ‖ ~ empfinden vor etw = sich grauen vor ‖ es erfaßte (*or* überlief) ihn ein ~ *he was filled* (od *seized, struck*) *with horror* ‖ ~ erregen *to inspire* od *provoke h.*; ~ erregend [a] *gruesome* (*sight*); *grim, sinister* (*look*); = grauenhaft ‖ jdm ~ einflößen *to fill* (od *strike*) *a p with h.*; *to shock a p; to make a p shudder* **2. a.** das ~ in .. *shocking misery in* (*the slums*) **b.** das ~ ⟨fam⟩ *the horrors* pl ≃**haft 1.** [a] *ghastly, hideous, horrible, monstrous; shocking*; → gräßlich **2.** [adv] *horribly, terribly* ≃**voll** a *gruesome* (*sight*); → grauenhaft **gr·aulen** vimp & refl es grault mir (*or* ich graule mich) bei dem Gedanken *I shudder at the thought* (an *of*); *I sh. to think* (daß *that* ..) ***gr·aulich**[2] a *gruesome*; = gruselig ‖ → graulig

Gr·aupe f ~/~n [mst pl:] ~n *pot-barley*; Perl≃en *pearl barley*; ⟨Ger⟩ ~nsuppe [f] *soup of pearl barley* **Gr·aupel** f ~/~n [mst pl:] ~n *sleet* (*soft hail*) **gr·aupeln** vimps [h]: es graupelt *it is sleeting* **Gr·aupelschauer** m *snow-pellet* –**wetter** n *sleety weather*

Graus[1] m ~es/ *horror, dread*; → Grauen, Schrecken ***graus** a *horrible*; → grauenhaft, schrecklich **gr·ausam 1.** [a] *cruel* (*man*); *brutal; fierce; remorseless; ferocious, atrocious; truculent* ‖ ~ gegen *cruel to; hard on* (*a p*) ‖ *cruel* (*fate*); *hard; inhuman* (*punishment*); → hart ‖ °(verblaßt) es ist ~ v dir *it is cruel of you*; *sick* (*joke*, etc) **2.** [adv] *cruelly*; jdn ~ behandeln *to inflict cruelty on a p* ‖ °~ kalt *cruel cold,* ⟨sl⟩ *beastly cold* | ≃**-keit** f ~/~en *cruelty* (gegen *to*) ‖ *ferocity; truculence; brutality* (*of circumstance*); *cruelty* (*of fate*); seelische ~ in der Ehe *incompatibility of temper-(ament)* **gr·ausen 1.** vimps [h] mir graust *or* es graust mir (*ich grause mich) bei dem Gedanken *I shudder at the thought* (an *of*); *I sh. to think* (daß *that* ..); ihr grauste, als .. *she shuddered when she* .. **2.** ≃ n *horror*; → Grauen ‖ kaltes ~ *the creeps* pl; *the jim-jams* pl; ihn packte ein k. ~ *it made his flesh creep* **gr·ausig** a (a. grauslich *grooly*) *grisly; lurid; uncanny, weird* ‖ = gräßlich A. 1.

Grav·amen n [L] ~s/–mina = Beschwerde

Gr·avelingen n ⟨Fr⟩ (Ort bei Calais) *Gravelines*

Gr·avensteiner [–f–] m (Apfelsorte v Gravenstein in S.-Jütland)

Grav·eur [gravør] m Fr ~s/~e *engraver* **Grav·ier- ~anstalt** f *e.r's establishment* **~instrument** n *graver* **~kunst** f (*art of*) *e.ving* **~maschine** f *e.ving m.* **~zeug** n *e.ving-tools* pl **grav·ieren**[1] **1.** vt [h] *to e.ve* ‖ *to enchase* (auf *on*) ‖ graviert *e.ved* **2.** ≃ n *e.ving* **Gravierung** f ~/~en *e.ving*

grav·ieren[2] vt [h] *to aggravate; to add to* | **~d** a *a.ting; incriminating, –natory* **Gr·avis** m [L] ⟨pros⟩ *grave; grave accent* (*à*) **Gravit·ät** f ~/ *gravity* **Gravitati·on** [ts] f ~/ *gravitation* **gravi-t·ätisch** a *grave, solemn; pompous* **gravit·ieren** vi [h] *to gravitate* (nach *to, towards*)

Grav·üre f ~/~n *engraving*; → Helio-, Photo≃

Graz n (Stadt in der Steiermark)

Gr·azie f ~/ **1.** [abstr] *grace; gracefulness* ‖ *beauty; charm; elegance* ‖ sie hat viel ~ *she is very graceful*; beim Tanz zeigt sie ihre ganze ~ *her dancing exhibits all her charm* ‖ mit ~ *with grace; gracefully*; °⟨übtr⟩ *dexterously, skilfully* **2.** [konkr] ⟨ant⟩ die (drei) ~n [pl] *the* (*three*) *Graces* ‖ ° sie ist nicht gerade e–e ~ *she's not exactly a beauty* **grazi·ös 1.** [a] *graceful* (*figure, step*); ~e Haltung *gracefulness* ‖ (of a woman) *gracile* **2.** [adv] *gracefully; with grace*

Gräz·ismus m ~s/–men *Graecism, Gre-*

Greenwich ['grinidʒ] n ⟨England⟩

Gregori·anisch a *Gregorian* ‖ ~er Gesang ⟨R. C.⟩ (nach Gregorius d. Gr.) *Gregorian* (*chant*); *plainsong* ‖ ~er Kalender [m] (nach G. XIII.) *G. Calendar* (1582; Engl: *1752*)

Greif m ~(e)s & ~en/~e & ~en ⟨her⟩ (Fabeltier) *griffin, griffon, gryphon*

Gr·eif- *prehensile* **~arm** m ⟨zoo⟩ *tentacle*; ⟨rehab⟩ *crochet-hook* **~backe** f = Greifer **~fuß** m ⟨zoo⟩ *pr. foot* **~haken** m ⟨rehab⟩ *crochet-hook* **~klaue, ~kralle** f *claw, talon* ‖ ⟨fig⟩ die gierigen ~n [pl] *the vulture-talons* pl **~kraft** f *pr. power; prehensility* **~rad** n = Handrad **~schwanz** m ⟨zoo⟩ *pr. tail*; mit ~ *pr.-tailed* **~spiel** n (Kinder-≃) *tag, tig* **~stachler** m ⟨zoo⟩ *pr.-tailed porcupine* **~vorrichtung** f = Greifer **~zehe** f ⟨zoo⟩ *pr. toe* **~zirkel** m *callipers* pl, ein ~ *a pair of c.*

gr·eifbar A. [a] **1.** ⟨eig⟩ *seizable; palpable, tactile, tangible*; nicht ~ *impalpable* **2.** ⟨übtr⟩ (leicht erreichbar) *handy*; ⟨mst com⟩ *available, ready* (*source of revenue*); *on hand; in stock* ‖ ~e Waren [pl] *spot goods* **3.** ⟨fig⟩ (deutlich) *evident; obvious* (*advantages*); *palpable* (*truth*); *tangible* (*distinction*) ‖ ~e Gestalt *or* Form annehmen (of plan, wish) *to be realized, to materialize*; die Erfüllung .. ist in ~e Nähe gerückt *the fulfilment .. is approaching realization* **B.** [adv] die Erfüllung ist ~ nahe → A. 3. | ≃**keit** f *palpability*, etc **gr·eifen** vi/t [griff/gegriffen] [h] **I.** vi **A.** [mit prep] **1. ~ an** etw *to touch a th*; er griff mit der Hand (*or* s–e Hand griff) an den Hut *his hand went to his hat* ‖ ⟨fig⟩ *he attacks my honour* ‖ das g. mir ans Herz *that grips my heart, goes to my h.*; .. *touches me to the quick* **2.** er griff **hinter** sich *he reached behind him* **3. in** die Luft ~ *to clutch at the air* ‖ in die Saiten ~ *to strike* (od *sweep, touch*) *the strings; to run one's fingers over the st.* ‖ in die Tasche ~ *to dip* (od *dive*) *into one's pocket* ‖ in ein Wespennest ~ *to stir up a wasp's nest* **4.** ~ **nach** (etw) *to catch at* (*straws*), *to grasp* (od *clutch*) *at, to make a clutch* (od *grab, grip*) *at* (*a th*); *to reach* (od *grab*) *for, to make a reach for* (*a th*); *to grip* (*a th*); hastig ~ nach *to snatch at, to make a snatch at* (*a th*); tastend ~ nach *to feel* (od *grope*) *for* (*a th*) ‖ sie griff **mit** der Hand (*or* ihre H. griff) nach .. *her hand went out to, strayed to* (*the rope*) | ⟨fig⟩ *to seize upon* (*a chance, pretext*); (of the heart, mind) *to reach after* (*happiness*) ‖ mit Freuden ~ nach *to take* (*a th*) *up with pleasure* ‖ mit beiden Händen ~ nach *to jump at* (*an offer*) **5.** ⟨fig⟩ **um sich** ~ *to gain ground; to gather way; to increase, spread*; (of vices) *to be rampant*; schnell um sich ~ *to mushroom*; um sich ~d *rampant, rife* **6.** ⟨fig⟩ jdm **unter** die Arme ~ *to give a p a helping hand; to help a p* (mit *with*) **7.** ⟨mst fig⟩ **zu** (etw) ~ *to have recourse to, to resort to* (*base means*); *to draw on* (*a th*) ‖ zum Äußersten ~ *to go to extremes* ‖ zur Feder ~ *to take pen in hand; to take to writing* ‖ zur Flasche ~ *to take to drink* ‖ ohne zur Gewalt z ~ *without resort to force* ‖ zu den Waffen ~ *to rise in arms; to take up arms* ‖ → ein~, hinein~, ineinander~ **B.** z hoch ~ *to put an estimate too high* ‖ ⟨mus⟩ falsch ~ *to strike a wrong chord*;

→ fehl∼ **C.** der Fuß konnte nicht ∼ *it was impossible to gain a firm footing*; das Schloß will nicht ∼ *the lock won't catch* **II.** vt **1.** (etw) *to grasp, seize*; fest ∼ *to clinch, clutch* ‖ (Tasten) *to touch*; e–n Akkord ∼ *to strike a chord* | ⟨übtr & fig⟩ etw z hoch ∼ *to put* (od *estimate, reckon*) *a th too high* ‖ Platz ∼ *to gain ground* ‖ es ist mit Händen z ∼, man kann es mit H. ∼ *it is as clear as noonday*; *it is quite obvious* ‖ (etw) aus der Luft ∼ *to concoct, fabricate, invent*; es ist rein aus der L. gegriffen *it is cut out of whole cloth*; *it's pure invention* **2.** (jdn) *to catch*; *seize*; er griff ihn an den Arm *he seized him by the arm* **Gr·eifen** n *clutch, grasp, grip* ‖ ∼ spielen *to play tag* (od *tig*) ‖ zum ∼ eingerichtet *prehensile* (*toe*) ‖ z ∼ nahe *palpably near*; *quite near* ‖ die friedvolle Stimmung war beinahe zum ∼ *peacefulness was almost a touchable th* **Gr·eifer** m ⟨tech⟩ **1.** (Greifvorrichtung) *grab* ‖ *grapnel, grapple*; (Bagger≗) *excavator* **2.** [in comp] *grab* ∼bagger [m] *g.-bucket, g.-excavator* **∼seil** n *g.-rope* **∼system** n *claw feed s.*

gr·einen 1. vi [h] *to whine*; *blubber, cry* ‖ † = knurren **2.** ≗ n *whine, whining* †**Gr·einer** m *cantankerous* (od *quarrelsome*) *p*

greis a *hoary* (*head*); *grey-haired with age*; greiser Mann *hoary old man*; *man of advanced age* **Greis** m ∼es/∼e = greiser Mann; die ∼e der Apokalypse *the 24 Ancient Elders* **Gr·eisen- ∼alter** n *senility*; *old age* **∼bart** m ⟨bot⟩ *Florida moss* **∼blödsinn** m *senile dementia* **∼bogen** m ⟨med⟩ (am Auge) *arcus senilis* L **≗haft** a *senile* **∼haftigkeit** f *senility* **∼haupt** n, ⟨bot⟩ *old-man cactus* **Gr·eisin** f ∼/∼nen *old woman* od *lady* **Gr·eiskraut** n ⟨bot⟩ *groundsel*

grell A. [a] **1.** *dazzling*; *fierce glaring* (*light*) **2.** *crude, eager, loud, glaring* (*colo*[*u*]*r*); *lurid* (*sky*) ‖ *garish, gaudy* (*dress*) *loud* (*suit*); *ostentatious, showy*; nicht ∼ *unostentatious* **3.** *shrill, strident* (*voice*); *harsh*; *grating* (*sound*); ∼es Klirren *screech* **4.** ⟨fig⟩ *harsh* (*contrast*); *striking*; *violent* **B.** [adv] *dazzlingly*; ∼ erleuchtet *garish* (*shop*) ‖ *glaringly* ‖ *harshly* ‖ ∼ abstechen gegen *to form a striking contrast to ..* | **≗e, ≗heit** f *dazzle* ‖ *crudeness, glare*; *gaudiness* ‖ *harshness*; *shrillness, stridency*

Gremi·ale n ∼s/∼n ⟨R. C.⟩ *gremial* **Gr·emium** n ∼s/–mien [–iən] *body*; *committee*; *panel*; ständiges ∼ *standing body*

Grenad·ier m **1.** ⟨hist⟩ *grenadier* **2.** ⟨mod engl⟩ *guardsman*; die ∼e [pl] *Grenadier Guards* pl ‖ ⟨Ger⟩ *infantryman, private*; ∼e [pl] *storm* (od *assault*) *troop* **Grenad·in** [–'dɛ̃] m [Fr] ∼s/∼s ⟨cul⟩ *grenadine* **Grenad·ine** f ∼/ (Gewebe) *grenadine*

Gr·endel m ∼s/ ⟨agr⟩ *share-beam*

Gr·enz- *border*(*land*), *boundary, frontier*, ⟨biol⟩ *liminal* **∼abfertigung** f *customs clearance* **∼alter** n ⟨ins⟩ *limiting age* **∼ball** m ⟨Ger sport⟩ *b.dary ballgame* **∼baron** m ⟨engl hist⟩ *b.-baron* **∼befestigung** f *f.-fortification* **∼begriff** m *b.land-term* **∼bewohner** m *b.er, f.s-man* **∼bezirk** m *b.-district*; *f.-area* **∼daten** pl *ratings* **∼fall** m *b.line case* ‖ *limiting case* **∼fälschung** f *falsification of the b.dary* (od *f.*) **∼festung** f *f.-fortress* **∼gänger** m *East Berliners who worked in West Berlin*, etc, *f. worker*; ⟨Am⟩ *international commuter* **∼gebiet** n = –bezirk **∼geschwindigkeit** f *limiting speed* **∼jäger** m *armed revenue-officer* **∼kämpfe** pl *b.-fighting* **∼kohlenwasserstoffe** pl = Paraffine **∼kommission** f *delimination commission* **∼land** n *b.land* ⟨a. fig⟩; ⟨engl⟩ (zw Engl. u Schottld) *the B.*; ⟨hist⟩ *the Marches* pl ‖ ∼deutsche [pl] *b.land Germans*; *German b.ers* pl **∼last** f ⟨el⟩ *maximum load* **∼lehre** f (Instrument) *limit-gauge* **∼linie** f *b.* (*od b.dary*)*-line* ‖ *line of demarcation*; ⟨jur⟩ *metes and bounds* **∼mal** n *landmark* **∼mark** f *b.-land*; *f.-district*; ⟨Ger hist⟩ *the Mark* **∼maß** n ⟨tech⟩ *tolerance*; *allowance* **∼nachbar** m *neighbour* **∼nutzen** m *marginal utility* **∼pfahl** m *b.dary-post* **∼posten** m *f. station* **∼schichtzäune** m pl ⟨aero⟩ *speed fences* **∼schutz** m *protection of the f.s*; *f.-defence* ‖ [konkr] *f.-guards* pl | ∼truppen [f pl] *f. guard forces* **∼soldat** m *f.-soldier* **∼sperre** f *embargo on b.-traffic* **∼spiel** n ⟨tech⟩ *maximum tolerance* **∼staat** m *b.* (od *f.*)*-state* **∼stadt** f *b.* (od *f.*)*-town* **∼station** f *f.-station* **∼stein** m *b.darystone*; ⟨for⟩ *merestone* **∼strang** m ⟨anat⟩ *sympathetic chain* **∼streit** m *b.dary-dispute* **∼streitigkeiten** pl *f.-hostilities* (od *troubles*) pl **∼übergang** *f.-crossing*; [konkr] *f. station* **∼verkehr** m *b.-traffic* **∼wache** f *f.-guard*; *b.dary-man* **∼wall** m *f.-wall* **∼wert** m *marginal* od *limiting value*; ⟨math⟩ *limit* **∼widerstand** m ⟨el⟩ *critical resistance* **∼winkel** m ⟨opt⟩ *critical angle* **∼zeichen** n *b.dary mark* **∼ziehung** f *f. demarcation* **∼zoll** m *customs* pl

Gr·enze f ∼/∼n **1. a.** (natürl. ∼) *boundary* (*a brook forms the b.*) **b.** (Landes≗) *border*; *frontier*; ⟨engl⟩ ∼ zw England u Schottland *the Border* ‖ ⟨pol⟩ *frontier*; Staats≗n ⟨Am a.⟩ *state-lines* pl ‖ die ∼n im Gelände festlegen *to pinpoint the boundaries on the ground* | **an** der ∼ *on the f.*; hart an der ∼ liegen *to straddle the b.*; **über** die grüne ∼ gehen *to cross the b. illegally*; *to steal away over the f.*; die ∼ überschreiten *to cross the f.*; sie sind längst über die ∼ *they have left the f. far behind* **2.** [**v abstr**] (End≗) *limit* (*of a p's credit, exertion, patience*) ‖ *verge*; bis an die ∼ e–r S *to the v. of a th*; an der ∼ des Krieges *on the v. of war* ‖ Alters≗ *limit of age*; obere (untere) ∼ *superior* (*inferior*) *l.* ‖ es gibt k–e ∼n *the sky's the l.* ‖ die äußerste ∼ *the extreme*, (*to a maximum*); die äußerste ∼ des Erträglichen *the last straw* ‖ e–e Erhöhung der Preise in mäßigen ∼n *a reasonable rise in prices* ‖ ⟨Am a.⟩ *deadline* (*by the d. of May 1st*) **3. ∼n [pl]** ⟨**übtr & fig**⟩ **a.** *bounds, confines, limits* pl ‖ bis an die äußersten ∼n *to the utmost bounds* (*of ..*); innerhalb der ∼n *within the confines, marks* (*of ..*); außerhalb der erlaubten ∼n ⟨school⟩ *out of bounds*; sich in den ∼n halten, die ∼n einhalten *to keep within bounds* ‖ jenseits der Grenzen (des Anstandes, etc) *beyond the pale* ‖ alles muß s–e ∼n h *we must draw the line somewhere, there must be a limit to everything*; *one must draw the line somewhere* ‖ alle ∼n übersteigen *to exceed all bounds*; erlaubte ∼n überschreiten *to go over the line*; das überschreitet alle ∼n *that's the limit* ‖ k–e ∼n kennen *to know no bounds*; k–e ∼n kennend *wide-open* ‖ hier sind s–r Machtbefugnis feste ∼n gezogen *here is a limit to his authority* **b.** die ∼n der Erkenntnis *the boundaries* od *limits of knowledge, science* ‖ (e–r S) ∼n setzen *to limit*; *to put a ceiling on ..*; die erlaubte ∼ überschreiten ⟨fig⟩ *to get out of line* → begrenzen **gr·enzen** vi [h] **∼an 1.** ⟨eig⟩ *to border on* (*Scotland borders on England*); *to adjoin* (*a th*); *to be coterminous with* (⟨a.⟩ an–e–a∼) od *to be adjacent* od *adjoining* (*a th*) **2.** ⟨fig⟩ *to border on*; das grenzt ans Lächerliche *that borders on the ridiculous*; *that's nothing short of r.* ‖ *to verge on*; das g. an Wahnsinn (ein Wunder) *that verges on madness* (*falls short of a m.*) | **∼d an** *bording on* (*frenzy*), *all but* (*frenetic*) ‖ sein an Unverschämtheit ∼es Benehmen *his behavio*(*u*)*r bordering on insolence*, *his almost impudent b.*

gr·enzenlos 1. [a] *boundless* (*ocean*), *unlimited*; *vast* ‖ ⟨mst °fig⟩ *boundless, limitless* (*ambition*), *unbounded* (*joy*), *illimitable* (*wealth*); *unlimited* (*impudence*); *excessive*; → ungeheuer **2.** [adv] *exceedingly, excessively* (*tired*); *absurdly*; *hopelessly*; *very* **≗igkeit** f *boundlessness*; *unboundedness*; *excessiveness* **Gr·enzer** m ∼s/∼ *frontiersman*

Gr·euel m ∼s/∼ **1. a.** *abomination, horror* (vor *of*); ∼ empfinden vor *to have a horror of ..* **b.** (∼tat) *atrocity*; ∼ [pl] begehen *to commit atroc-*

ities **c.** (Schrecken) *the horrors of war* **2.** °⟨fig⟩ (Gegenstand *or* P des Entsetzens) er ist ein ~ *he is a perfect horror*; er ist mir ein ~ *he is my chief aversion*; blaue Krawatten sind mir ein ~ ⟨fam⟩ *blue ties are my pet aversion*; *I detest* (od *loathe*) *bl. t.* **~erzählungen, ~geschichten** pl *horrors* pl **~märchen** pl, **~propaganda** f *atrocity mongering* (od *propaganda*) **~tat** f *atrocity*; *atrocious* od *heinous crime* od *deed*

gr·eulich a & adv = gräßlich

Gr·iebe f ~/~n: [mst pl] ~n *greaves, graves*

ˣ**Gr·ieben** m ~s/~ †**Griebs** m ~es/~e (*apple-*) *core*

Gr·ieche m ~n/~n *Greek* **Gr·iechenland** *Greece*

Gr·iechin f ~/~nen *Greek* **gr·iechisch 1.** a *Greek* (*art*; *literature, history, fire*) ‖ ⟨arch⟩ *Grecian* (*architecture*; *nose*; *slippers*) **2.** das ≃e *Greek, the G. language*; ~es Idiom *Graecism* **3.** [in comp] *Greek Orthodox* (*Church*); *Greco--Roman*

ˣ**gr·ienen** vi [h] = grinsen

Gr·iesgram m ~(e)s/~e (P) *curmudgeon*; *grumbler*; *crab, groucher, croaker* **gr·iesgrämig** a *grouchy, grumpy*; *morose, peevish, soggy, sullen*

Gr·ieß m ~es/~e **1.** (Sand) *gravel*; *coarse sand* ‖ (Metallkörper) *grit* ‖ ⟨tech mill⟩ (Stein≃ etc) *middlings, tailings, grits* pl ‖ (Harn≃) *gravel* ‖ (Grus) *small coal* **2.** ⟨cul⟩ *grits, groats* pl; ⟨engl⟩ *semolina*; | ~brei [m] *gruel*; ~mehl [n] *semolina*; ~suppe [f] *semolina-soup*; ~trichter [m] ⟨tech mill⟩ *grits channel* **gr·ießig** a *gritty*

Gr·iff m ~(e)s/~e **A.** [abstr] **1. a.** *clutch* (nach *at*), schneller ~ *snatch* (nach *at*) ‖ *grasp* (*of the hand*); (*firm*) *grip*; ⟨com⟩ *touch*; ⟨tex⟩ → e. **b.** ⟨gym⟩ Rist≃ *ordinary grasp*; Kamm≃ *reverse g.* ‖ ⟨wrestling⟩ *clinch, grip, hold*; erdrosselnder ~ *stranglehold*; Ringkampf, bei dem jeder ~ erlaubt ist *catch-as-catch-can* **c.** ~e [pl] am Gewehr *manual drill* od *exercises* ‖ ~e m *or* °kloppen *to do rifle exercises* **d.** ⟨mus⟩ *touch*; gr ~e *long spans* pl ‖ Kunst≃ *trick, dodge* **e.** ⟨tex⟩ *handle*; *feel* (fest *firm*; kernig *crisp*; rauh *harsh*; seidig *silky, scroopy*) **2. a. ein ~ noch** u .. *another moment and* .. ‖ ein glücklicher ~ *a happy touch, a hit*; mit **sicherem** ~ *with a sure t., with a sureness of t.* ‖ ein kühner ~ *a daring trick* **b.** e–n ~ **tun** in .. *to dive* (od *dip*) *into* ..; e–n ~ tun nach = greifen nach ‖ e–n guten ~ tun *to make a lucky hit* (mit *with*) ‖ etw **im** ~ h, den richtigen ~ e–r S kennen *to have the knack of a th* **B.** [konkr] **1.** (Hand≃) *haft, handle* (*of a pan*); *handhold* ‖ *helve* (*of a hammer*); *shaft* (*of an axe*); etw mit e–m ~ versehen *to helve a th* ‖ *grip, hilt* (*of a sword*); ein Messer mit knöchernem ~ *a bonehandled knife* ‖ *knob* (*of a door*) ‖ *stop* (*of a violin*) **2.** ⟨tech⟩ *clutch, purchase* **3.** ⟨fig⟩ → Klaue, Kralle ≃**bereit** a *within hand-reach* **~brett** n (of a violin); *finger-board* **~kurbel** f *hand-crank* ≃**technisch** adv ~ gut ⟨mach⟩ *within easy reach* **~übungen** pl *manual exercises* pl **~zapfen** m *tang* (*of a knife*) **griff** 1. & 3. sg pret v greifen **gr·iffig** a *handy* (*tool*) ‖ das Tuch ist sehr ~ *the cloth has a good feel* ‖ *course-grained, granulated* (*flour*) ‖ ⟨mot⟩ *road-holding* (*tire*) | **~keit** f ⟨mot⟩ *grip*(*ping power*)

Gr·iffel m ~s/~ **1.** (Schieferstift) *slate-pencil* **2.** ⟨bot⟩ (of a pistil) *style* → Pistill **~förmig** a *styloid* **~fortsatz** m ⟨anat⟩ *styloid process*

Griffon [grifɔ̃] m [Fr] ⟨zoo⟩ (~hund) *griffon*

Gr·ille f ~/~n **1.** ⟨ent⟩ *cricket* **2.** ⟨fig⟩ *caprice, freak, maggot, whim, whimsy*; *crochet, fad* ‖ ~n fangen *to be in the blues*; *to mope* (*by o.s.*) ‖ er hat immer ~n im Kopf *his head is full of fads and fancies* ‖ ich werde dir d–e ~n schon austreiben *I'll soon drive these whims out of your head* **~nfänger** m *mope, crank* **~nfängerei** f *the mopes* ≃**nhaft, *grillig** a *freaky, whimsical*; *crotchety* ‖ *grumpy, morose*

Gr·ill(er) m ~s/~e(r) ⟨cul⟩ *grill*(*er*) **gr·illen** vt [h] *to grill, broil*

Grim·asse f ~/~n *grimace*; *wry face*, ⟨sl⟩ *mug*; e–e ~ schneiden *to make a wry face* ‖ ~n *grimaces*; *mops and mows* pl; ~n sch. *to make grimaces*; *to mop and mow*; *to pull faces* **grimm 1.** [a] *grim*; *fierce, furious* **2.** [adv] *grimly* **Gr·imm** m ~(e)s/ *fury, rage, wrath* ‖ s–n ~ auslassen *to vent one's fury* (an *on*) **~darm** m ⟨anat⟩ *colon*

Gr·immen n ~s/~ *griping pains*; *gripes* pl

gr·immig 1. [a] *grim*; *fierce, furious, truculent*; *vehement* (*opponent*); ~ aussehen *to look like thunder* ‖ ⟨übtr & fig⟩ *fierce* (*cold*), *hard* (*winter*), *intense*; *raging, severe*; *vehement* (*hatred, strife*), *violent*; *wild* (*sea*) **2.** [adv] *fiercely, furiously* ‖ *intensely, severely*; *vehemently*; ~ kalt *cruel cold* | ≃**keit** f *fierceness, fury* ‖ ⟨fig⟩ *intensity, severity, vehemence*

Grind m ~(e)s/~e **A. 1.** (Schorf auf Wunden) *crust, scab* **2.** (Kopfschuppen) *scurf* **B. 1.** ⟨path⟩ (am Kopf) *favus* L; *porrigo* L ‖ (.. der Haut) *impetigo* L **2.** ⟨vet⟩ (Räude) *scab*; *mange* **3.** ⟨bot⟩ *dodder* **gr·indig** a **1.** *scabby, scabbed* ‖ *scurfy* **2.** *porriginous* ‖ ⟨vet⟩ *scabbed, scabby*

gr·insen 1. vi [h] *to grin* (über *at*; übers ganze Gesicht *from ear to ear*; wie ein Honigkuchenpferd etc *like a Cheshire cat*); ständig ~ *to be always on the grin*; (boshaft) *to leer*; (lächelnd) *to sport one's ivory* **2.** ≃ n *grin*; *grinning*; *leer* ‖ ein ~ aufsetzen *to grin a grin*

Gr·ippe f ⟨med⟩ *influenza*; ⟨fam⟩ *flu*(*e*)

°**Grips**[1] m ~es/ (Verstand) *common sense*; ⟨fam⟩ *gumption*; ⟨sl⟩ *savvy*; ⟨hum-anat⟩ *grey matter* ‖ °~kasten [m] ⟨fam⟩ *sconce, nut*; *knowing-box*

°**Grips**[2] m ~es/ (Griebs = Kehlkopf) [nur in:] jdn am ~ (u Kragen) packen *to take a p by the scruff of his neck* (od *by the throat*)

Gr·iqua pl (Mischlingsvolk in Afrika) **Gr·iqualand** n (in Südafrika)

gr·ob I. [a] **A.** ⟨eig & übtr⟩ **1.** † = massig, groß **2.** (of fabric, texture) *coarse* (*sieve, thread, wire*; *flour, sand*; *bread, food*) ‖ ~es Geschütz *heavy artillery* (od *guns*); ~e Schrift *broad writing, thick script* **3.** *gross* (*features*) ‖ *coarse* (*hands*); *common* (*clothes, furniture*); *crude* (*interpretation, manners, methods*) ‖ *rough* (*voice*) **4.** ⟨übtr⟩ *rough* (*work, sea, sketch, outlines*) **B.** ⟨fig⟩ **1.** *crass* (*stupidity, ignorance*); *gross* (*blunder, insult, misuse, negligence*; *egregious* (*error*); ~er Schnitzer ⟨sl⟩ *howler* ‖ *coarse* (*jokes*); *flagrant* od *bouncing* (*lie*); *flagrant* od *great* (*sinner*) **2.** (**unhöflich**) *bluff, blunt*; *downright*; *uncouth* ‖ *coarse, rough, rude*; *ill-mannered, impolite, unpolished* ‖ ~er Kerl *tough customer*; *coarse* (od *rough*) *fellow*; *bully, rough, ruffian*; ~er aber gutartiger Mensch *rough diamond* ‖ *snorty* (*letter*) ‖ mit ~en Worten *in strong terms* (od *language*) | ~ gegen *rough with, rude to* (*a p*) ‖ °~ wie Bohnenstroh *or* Sackleinwand *most abusive*; *as gruff as a bear* ‖ ~ w *to become abusive* **II.** [adv] **1.** *coarsely* ‖ *broadly* (*the pen writes b.*) ‖ ⟨cul⟩ ~ hacken *to dice* **2.** *bluntly*; etw ~ heraussagen *to speak one's mind* **3.** *brusquely, roughly*; *rudely*; jdn ~ behandeln *to treat a p rough*(*ly*); *to ride rough-shod over a p*; °**jdm** ~ k *to fly at a p*; *to be uncivil to a p* **4.** ~ lügen *to tell a flagrant lie* **III.** [abs] im ~en (*to plan out*) *in the rough*; (etw) aus dem ~en herausarbeiten, im ~en bearbeiten *to rough-cast*; *to rough-hew*; *to rough in* (od *out*); im ~en bearbeitet *rough-hewn*; *rough and ready* ‖ er ist aus dem gröbsten heraus *he has broken the back of the difficult job* ≃**abstimmung** f ⟨wir⟩ *coarse tuning*, ⟨phot⟩ *c. adjustment* od *focusing* ≃**brot** n *coarse bread* ≃**einstellung** f ⟨wir⟩ *frequency selection*; ⟨phot⟩ *rough focusing* **~fädig** a *c.-spun*; *c.-threaded* **~faserig** a *c.-fibred* ≃**feile** f *c.* (od *rough*) *file* ≃**filter** m *roughing filter* °≃**futter** n ⟨cul⟩ *roughage* ≃**gefüge** n *gross structure* **~gemahlen** a *c.ly ground* ≗**gewicht** n *gross weight* ≗**kohle** f *lump coal* ~**körnig** a *c.-grained* (*sand*) ≗**mahlung** f ⟨tech⟩ *crushing* ~**maschig** a *c.-meshed* ≗**mörtel** m *concrete* ≗**passung** f = –sitz ≗**schliff** m *snagging* ≗**schmied** m *blacksmith, farrier* ~**schlächtig** a *coarse* ~**schnäuzig** a ⟨fig⟩ *hardmouthed* ≗**-schnitt** m *coarse cut* ~**sinnlich** a *grossly sensual* ≗**-sitz** m *loose fit* ~**strähnig** a *c.-stranded* (*rope*) ≗**-waren** pl *c. goods* ≗**wäsche** f *heavy laundering* ≗**waschmittel** n *h. duty detergent* **Gr·obheit** f ~/~en (→ grob) **A. 1.** *coarseness* **2.** *grossness; crudeness, crudity* ‖ *roughness* **B.** ⟨fig⟩ *bluntness; uncouthness* ‖ *roughness, rudeness* (*of a p*) ‖ ~en [pl] *abuse; abusive* od *strong language; rude things* pl; jdm ~en sagen *to abuse a p* ‖ (*you may have it explained with*) *a little more roughness and a little less delicacy* **Gr·obian** m ~(e)s/~e *boor, lout* ‖ *bargee*; ein richtiger ~ *a regular b.*; so'n ~! *what a churl,* ⟨Am⟩ *roughneck*! **gr·öblich 1.** [a] (→ grob I. B. 1) *gross* (*insult, negligence*); *crass* (*ignorance*); *flagrant* (*offence*); *shameless* **2.** [adv] *grossly* ‖ jdn ~ beleidigen *to insult* (od *abuse*) *a p grossly* ‖ (sich) ~ irren *to be greatly mistaken* ‖ sich ~ vergehen gegen etw, etw ~ verletzen *to offend grossly against a th*

Gr·öfaz m [invar] ⟨anti-nazi⟩ „größte(r) Feldherr aller Zeiten" (Hitler) *itma* (*it's that man again*)

Grog m ~s/~s *grog* ‖ e–e Art ~ *toddy*

°**gr·ö(h)len** vi [h] *to bawl, squall* ‖ über's ganze Haus ~ *to bawl about the house* **Gr·ö(h)ler** m *bawler*

Groll m ~(e)s/ *grievance; grudge, ill-feeling, -will; bitterness; malice, pique* (über *at*); *rancour* (über .. *of a defeat*); *resentment* (gegen *against*; über *at*); *spite* (*against*) ‖ ohne ~ *without animosity* (od *ill-will*) ‖ jds ~ erregen *to pique a p* ‖ e–n ~ auf jdn h, ~ hegen gegen jdn *to bear a p a grudge; to have* od *harbour a grudge* (od *grievance, spite*) *against* | ⟨Am⟩ *to h. an edge on a p* ‖ s–n ~ nicht merken l *not to betray one's r.* **gr·ollen 1.** vi [h] **a.** jdm ~, mit jdm ~ → Groll hegen gegen **b.** *to frown, lour; to be sullen* | ~d *grumbling, resentful* **c.** ⟨übtr⟩ (of thunder, etc.) *to roar; rumble* **2.** ≗ n *anger; sullenness* ‖ ⟨übtr⟩ *roar, rumble, rumbling* (*of guns, thunder*)

Gr·oningen n (holländ. Prov. u Stadt)

Gr·önland n ⟨geog⟩ *Greenland* ~**fahrer** m (Schiff) *G.man; G. whaler* ~**wal** m ⟨zoo⟩ *G. whale* **Gr·önländer** m ~/~ **1.** *Greenlander* **2.** ⟨sport⟩ (Paddelboot) *kayak* **gr·önländisch 1.** a *Greenland; Greenlandish* ‖ *Greenlandic* (*language*) **2.** das ≗e *Greenlandic*

Gros[1] [gro:] n [Fr] ~/~ **1.** ⟨mil⟩ *bulk; main forces* pl od *body* **2.** ⟨weav⟩ *gros de Naples*

Gros[2] [grɔs] n [Fr] ~ses/~se (nach Zahlen ~) *gross; twelve dozen*; 3 ~ *three gross* (Bleistifte *of pencils*) ‖ ≗weise *by the gross*

Gr·oschen m ~s/~ ⟨Ger⟩ **1.** ⟨hist⟩ (a. guter ~, = ($^1/_{30}$ Taler) *groschen* **2.** ⟨mod⟩ *ten-pfennig piece* | ⟨übtr⟩ ein paar ~ *a few pence* ‖ e–n schönen ~ verdienen *to earn a pretty penny* ‖ den ~ 5mal herumdrehen, bevor man ihn ausgibt *to flay* od *skin a flint* ‖ s–e paar ~ zus–halten *to economize* (*we must e.*) ‖ jetzt (endlich) ist der ~ gefallen *at last the penny drops*; (*it took you a long time to understand*); (verstehe ich) *that rings the bell* ~**automat** m *penny-in-the-slot machine* ~**blatt** n *penny press* ~**grammophon,** ~**orchestrion** n ⟨Am fam⟩ *juke-box*

groß I. [a] **A. 1. (räumlich)** [Ggs *small*] **a.** ⟨eig⟩ *big* (*body, lump*), *large* (*house, rock, room; cigar*) ‖ ~e Augen, Ohren *large eyes, ears* ‖ ~e Bohnen *broad beans* ‖ die ~e Zehe *the big toe*; so ~ wie e–e Hand *the size of a hand*; ein hand~er Stein *a stone the size of a fist* ‖ wie ~ ist es? *what size is it?* | *big* (*girl*); mein ~er Bruder *my big brother* ‖ *tall* (*man*) ‖ ich bin ~ genug *I am big enough* (*to do*) | *he was tall for his age*; er war 5 Fuß ~ *his height was 5 feet; he was 5 feet tall*; er ist etw über 5 F. ~ *he tops 5 feet* ‖ sie schienen so ~ wie er *they seemed of his own height* ‖ der Hund ist etwa so ~ wie ein Fuchs *the dog stands about as high as a fox* ‖ die Säulen sind 9 m ~ *the pillars stand 30 feet high* ‖ ein wenig (z) ~ geraten s *to be on the large side* ‖ ~ w (of children) *to grow big*; z ~ w f *to outgrow* (*a house*) **b.** ⟨übtr⟩ *large* (*fortune, income, property, supply*), *major* (*effects*), *broad* (*age-group*); *big* (*noise*) ‖ ~er (Anfangs–) **Buchstabe** *capital; capital letter*; → Großbuchstabe ‖ auf ~e Fahrt gehen *to go on a long tour* ‖ ~e Ferien *long vacation* ‖ ~es Format *large size* ‖ ~es Geld *large money* (~ oder klein? ⟨fam⟩ *long or short?*) ‖ ~es Geschäftchen m, ≗ m ⟨Ammenspr.⟩ *to do number two* ‖ mit ~er Geschwindigkeit *with high speed* ‖ ≗es Hauptquartier *General Headquarters* pl ‖ ~e Havarie *general average* ‖ die ~e Masse *the masses* pl ‖ der ≗e Ozean *the Pacific* ‖ in ~em Umfange, zum ~en Teil *largely* ‖ ⟨mus⟩ ~e Terz *major third* ‖ die Produktion ist dreimal so ~ wie die v Italien *the production is three times that of Italy* ‖ sehr ~ *bulky; huge; immense; spacious; vast* **2.** [**gefühlsbetont**: auffällig, unangenehm ~ (Ggs *little*)] **a.** *great; formidable*; (*with your g. foot*) ‖ *g.* (*fly, wasp; drops*) ‖ jener ~e Mann *that great tall man; towering* (*figure*); ein ~er Stock *a great big stick*; ein ~er Erfolg *quite a record* **b.** ⟨astr⟩ **der** ≗**e Bär** *the Great Bear; Charles's Wain*; die ~e **Pyramide** *the Great Pyramid* ‖ ~e Dogge *great dane*; ~e Halle *great hall* ‖ e–e ~e **Menge, Zahl** Leute *a great many people* ‖ in ~em Umfange *to a great extent* **c.** (vornehm, wichtig) *grand* (*question*); ~e **Herren,** Leute *grand* (od *great*) *people; swells* pl, ~e Dame *grand* (od *great*) *lady* ‖ ~es Geschworenengericht *grand jury*; ≗es Hindernisrennen (z *Aintree*) *the Grand-National* ‖ (einflußreich) °~es Tier (P) *big bug* (od *gun, swell, wig*) **3.** ⟨fig⟩ zur ~en **Armee** abgehen *to join the majority* ‖ gr **Augen** m *to open one's eyes; to stare* ‖ auf ~em **Fuße** leben *to live in grand style* ‖ den ~en **Herrn** spielen *to play the fine gentleman; to do the swell* ‖ das ~e **Los** *the first prize* ‖ *grand* (*old man*) ‖ °ein ~es **Maul** h (*or* riskieren) *to have a loose tongue; to boast, to swagger* ‖ °~e **Rosinen** im Kopfe h *to have high-flying ideas* (od *a swelled head*) ‖ ~e **Stücke** auf jdn halten *to think higly of a p* ‖ °~e **Töne** reden *to draw the long bow; to rant; to swagger* ‖ in ~er Uniform *in full dress; in gala uniform* **B.** ⟨fig⟩ **1.** (of qualities, feelings, etc.) *great* (*height, kindness, patience, pleasure, success*) ‖ *grand, lofty, noble* (*thoughts*) ‖ ~e **Liebe** *grand love* ‖ die ~en **Vier** ⟨biol⟩ *the four great rulers* (*hunger, love, flight, aggression*) ‖ ~en **Wert** legen auf .. *to set great store by*; ~e **Zeiten** *great times* ‖ *bad* (*drought*); *intense* (*cold, heat*); *stark* (*horror*); ~e **Verluste** *heavy losses* ‖ äußerst *dire* (*danger*); sehr ~e **Sorgen** *no end of troubles* ‖ ~er **Unterschied** *vast* (od *wide*) *difference* **2.** (P) **a.** *great* (*artist, builder; composer, poet*); *eminent* ‖ ~er **Charakter** *grand character*; ~es **Licht** *shining light*; er ist nicht gerade ein ~es L. *he does not exactly shine* ‖ ⟨Ger⟩ der ≗e **Kurfürst** *the Great Elector* (*of Brandenburg*) ‖ *desperate* (*fool*) ‖ ich bin kein ~er **Redner** *I am no good as a speaker*; .. kein ~er Spaziergänger *I am not much of a walker* ‖ °ein ~er **Tänzer** vor dem Herrn *a great dancer* ‖ ein ~er Quacksalber *no end of a quack* **b.** ~ s *to be great* (im .. *at golf, at cooking*); *to be a swell* (*at cricket*); ~ im Schwindeln *a master of deception* ‖ er war ganz ~ *he was great* (*when he spoke*) ‖ °die Tage waren ganz ~ *we had a tall time of it* ‖ → größer, größt **II.** [adv] **1.** ~ schreiben *to write large* ‖ jdn ~ ansehen *to look at a p in amazement, to stare at a p* ‖ ~ auftreten *to put on airs; to swagger; to do the swell* ‖ ~ v jdm denken *to have* *a high opinion of a p* || ~ u edel denken *to think nobly* || ~ drehen *to turn up* (*flames*) || (etw) ganz ~ schreiben ⟨fig⟩ *to emphasize* **2.** °(verblaßt) nicht ~ *not much*; das braucht dich nicht ~ aufzuregen *you need not much trouble about that*; was ist da noch ~ z tun? *there is not much to be done* **III.** [abs] **1.** (in Titeln) Karl der ≈e *Charles the Great, Charlemagne*; Friedrich der ≈e *Frederic(k) the Great*; → Grande || die ≈en *the Great*; *great* (od *grand*) *people* || *older people*; *elders* pl || ein ≈er *a great man* || ~ u kl *great and small* **2. das** ≈**e** *the great*; das g.e Ganze *the matter as a whole*; etw ≈es *great things* pl || das ≈e an ihm *what is great in him*; alles ~e *all that is great* (an *in*) || im ~en *in* (*the*) *large*; im ~en u ganzen *on the whole*; im ~en u ganzen betrachtet *taken by and large*; *generally speaking*; (*to designate an area*) *as to its general trace*; im ~en festlegen *to establish roughly* || im ≈en wie im Kleinen *in great as in little things* || ⟨prov⟩ wer das Geringe nicht ehrt, ist das ≈e nicht wert *take care of the pence and the pounds will take care of themselves*

Gr·oß- [in comp] *large-scale* (*attack*; *fighting*; *photograph*; *employment of forces*); *Great–*; *Grand–* || ⟨scient⟩ *mega–*; *megalo–* **~admiral** m ⟨Ger⟩ *First Lord of the Admiralty*; → Generaladmiral **~angriff** m *major* od *l.-sc. attack* ≈**-artig 1.** [a] *beautiful, excellent, first-rate, glorious* (*day*); *grand* (*fight, sight*); *grandiose, phenomenal, remarkable*; *spectacular*; *swell* (*plan*); *woderful* (*scenery*) || e–e ~e S *or* P ⟨sl⟩ *a knocker, knock--out, scorcher*; ⟨Am⟩ *proud*, ⟨sl⟩ *wow* || er war ~ *he was gorgeous, terrific*, ⟨Am sl⟩ *mustard* || ~! ⟨Am sl⟩ *wow* | ⟨iron⟩ *egregious* (*folly*) **2.** [adv] *greatly, splendidly, wonderfully* **~artigkeit** f *grandeur, magnificence, splendour* **~aufnahme(n** pl) f ⟨film⟩ *close-up*(*s* pl) ≈**äugig** a *large-eyed* **~baum** m ⟨mar⟩ *main boom* **~betrieb** m *wholesale business*; *large*(*-scale*) *concern, plant* || °heute herrscht ~ auf .. *today there are great events on* (*the race--course*) **~brand** m *conflagration* **~brit·annien** *Great Britain* || ~ u die Kolonien *Greater Britain* **~brit·annisch** a *British*; die ≈e Regierung *Her* (*His*) *Majesty's Government*; *the Court of St. James's*, Ihre ≈e Majestät *Her Britannic Majesty* **~buchstabe** m *capital*; Name in ~n *name in block capitals* ≈**denkend** a *high* (od *large*)*-minded* ≈**-deutsch** a *including all Germans* || ≈es Reich ⟨hist⟩ = † **~deutschland** *Greater Germany* **~einsatz** m ⟨mil⟩ *l.-sc. operation* **~eltern** pl *grand-parents* pl **~enkel** m *great-grandson* **~enkelin** f *great-granddaughter* **~fahndung** f *dragnet raid*, ⟨Am⟩ *police round-up*, (*inter*)*national hunt* **~fall** m ⟨mar⟩ *main halyard* **~familie** f *family-group* **~feuer** n = –brand **~finanz** f *high finance* ≈**flächig** a: *extensive area* (*effects*) **~flosser** m ⟨ich⟩ *labyrinth--fish* **~flug-** ~hafen [m] *airterminal*; ~zeug [n] *giant aeroplane* **~format** n ⟨pap⟩ *foolscap*; ⟨phot⟩ *large-size* (*camera*) **~funk-** ~stelle [f] ⟨wir⟩ *high-power wireless* (abbr *W. T.*) *station* ≈**fürst** m ⟨Russ⟩ *Grand-Duke* **~fürstentum** n ⟨Russ⟩ *Grand-Duchy* **~fürstin** f ⟨Russ⟩ *G.--Duchess* **~fußhuhn** n *megapode* **~gaffel** f ⟨mar⟩ *main gaff* **~gr·undbesitz** m *large landed property* **~gr·undbesitzer** m *large landed proprietor* (od *landowner*) **~gut** n *large estate* **~handel** m *wholesale trade* (od *business*); *commerce* || ~sgeschäft [n] *wholesale business* (od *firm*); ~sindex [m] *index-number of wholesale prices* **~händler** m *wholesaler, wholesale merchant* (od *dealer*) **~-handlung** f *wholesale firm* ≈**herzig** a *generous--hearted*; *high* (od *large*)*-minded*; *magnanimous* **~herzigkeit** f *magnanimity* **~herzog** m ⟨Ger⟩ *Grand Duke* **~herzogin** f ⟨Ger⟩ *Grand Duchess* ≈**herzoglich** a ⟨Ger⟩ *Grand-ducal* **~herzogtum** n ⟨Ger⟩ *Grand Duchy* **~hirn** n ⟨anat⟩ *cerebrum* L; ~rinde [f] (*cerebral*) *cortex* **~industrie** f *heavy industry*; ⟨Am⟩ *big business* || [konkr] *big industrialists* pl **~industrielle** → Industrielle **~inquisitor** m ⟨ec⟩ *grand-inquisitor* ≈**jährig** a *of* (*full*) *age*; ~ w *to come of age*; → majorenn || der ≈e *the major* **~jährigkeit** f *majority, full age* **~kampf-flugzeug** → Flugzeug **~kampfschiff** n ⟨mar⟩ *super-Dreadnought*; *capital ship*; *battleship* **~-kampftag** m *great battle day* **~kanzler** m ⟨engl⟩ *the Lord* (*High*) *Chancellor* **~kapital** n *high finance* **~kapitalist** m *big capitalist*; *tycoon*; die ~en ⟨sl⟩ *the heavy metal* **~katzen** pl *great cats pl* **~kaufhaus** n *supermarket* **~kaufmann** m *wholesale merchant* **~kind** n *grandchild* **~knecht** m *head-servant, foreman* || die °**~kopfeten** pl ⟨sl⟩ *the tops, high-ups, bigwigs, mugwumps* ≈**köpfig** a *megacephalic, -cephalous*; *big* (od *large*)*-headed* °≈**kotzig** a ⟨Am fam⟩ *snooty* **~kreuz** n *Grand Cross* **~kundgebung** f *mammoth demonstration* **~loge** [ʒ] f *Grand Lodge* **~luftlage** f *over-all air situation* **~macht** f *Great* (od *Big*) *Power*; die ≈e *the Great Powers* pl ≈**m·ächtig** a *all-powerful*; ~st *most potent* (*king*); (*high and*) *mighty* **~mama** f *grandma, grandmam*(*m*)*a* **~mannssucht** f *boastful manner*; *rodomontade*; *swagger*; ⟨sl⟩ *swank* **~mars** m ⟨mar⟩ *main-top* || ~stange [f] *main topmast* ≈**maschig** a *large-meshed* **~mast** m ⟨mar⟩ *mainmast* || °**~maul** n ⟨fig⟩ *blusterer*; *boaster*; *braggart*; *show-off*; *swashbuckler* || °≈**mäulig** a ⟨fig⟩ *bragging*; *loud-mouthed*; *swaggering*; ⟨sl⟩ *tall, swank* || ~ auftreten *to ruffle it*; *to swagger* || °**~mäuligkeit** f *swagger*; ⟨sl⟩ *swank* **~meister** m *Grand Master* **~mogul** m *Great Mogul*; ⟨übtr⟩ *the Great Panjandrum* **~mut** f *bounty*; *breadth of mind*; *magnanimity*; *generosity* ≈**mütig** a *great* (*soul*); *magnanimous*; *generous* **~mütigkeit** f = –mut **~mutter** f *grandmother*; *grandparent* ≈**mütterlich** a *grandmotherly* **~-oheim, ~onkel** m *grand-uncle* **~oktav(format)** n *large octavo* **~packung** f *outsize box*, etc; *magnum* **~papa** m *grandpapa* ⟨fam⟩ *grandpa*; *gran*(*d*)*-dad* **~photo** n *photomural* **~pönitenziar** m ⟨R. C.⟩ *Grand Penitentiary* **~produzent** m *large producer* **~quart(format)** n *large quarto* **~rat** m Sw *member of a Kanton-Parliament* **~raum-** ~büro [n] *typing pool*; ~-Plattenspeicher [m] ⟨comp⟩ *data disc file*; ~speicher(ung [f]) [m] *file storage*, ~speicher mit Schnellzugriff *large capacity high-speed store*; ~strategie [f] *world-wide str.*; ~wirtschaft [f] *l.-sc. political economy* ≈**räumig** a *area* (*effects*) **~rechenanlage** f *electronic computer* **~reeder** m *large shipowner* **~reinemachen** n *big clean* **~russen** pl *Great Russians* pl **~schaden** m ⟨ins⟩ *heavy damage* od *loss* **~schiffahrtsweg** m *ship-canal* **~schlagzeile** f *banner headline* **~schmelze** f *large foundry* °≈**schnauzig** a *swaggering, swell*; ⟨sl⟩ *swank* **~schot** m ⟨mar⟩ *main-sheet* **~segel** n *mainsail* **~siegelbewahrer** m ⟨engl⟩ *the Keeper of the Great Seal* (jetzt: *the Lord Chancellor*) **~sortiment** n *wholesale book-trade* ≈|**sprechen** vi [h] *to talk big* (od *large, tall*); *to draw the long bow* **~sprecher** m *boaster, braggart, swaggerer, wind--bag* **~sprecher·ei** f *boasting, grandiloquence*; *big talk*; *swagger* ≈**sprecherisch 1.** [a] *boastful, grandiloquent, swaggering, vainglorious* **2.** [adv] *boastfully, grandiloquently* || °≈**spurig** a *grand* (*he was too g. to* ..); *ruffling*; *tall* (*talk*); *uppish*; *arrogant, pompous, vain* **~staat** m = –macht **~stadt** f *large town* (od *city*) || ~jugend [f] *youth of a large town* || ~kind [n] *city-bred child*; ~randgebiete [n pl] *subtopia* ≈**städtisch** a *characteristic of* (od *pertaining to*) *a large town* **~städter** m *man about town* **~steingräber** pl ⟨praeh⟩ *megalithic circles* od *structures*; *dolmen* **~sultan** m *Grand Sultan* **~tante** f *grandaunt* **~tat** f *exploit, feat*; *great* (od *noble*) *deed* **~teil** m: der ~ *the bulk* **~tuer** m *boaster, braggart*; ⟨fam⟩ *squirt* **~tuer·ei** f *vainglory, vaingloriousness*; → –sprecherei ≈**tuerisch** a = –sprecherisch, –spurig ≈|**tun** vi/refl ~, sich ~ *to boast*; *to show off*; *to* *swagger*; ⟨sl⟩ *to swank* ‖ gern ~ *to be fond of show* ‖ (sich) ~ mit etw *to boast* (od *brag*) *of a th*; *to parade a th*; *to show a th off* **~unternehmer** m *large industrialist* **~vater** m *grandfather*; ~-*corny*; ~stuhl [m] *grandfather's chair* **~väterchen** n = -papa **≗väterlich** a *grandfatherly* **~veranstaltung** f ⟨a. sport⟩ *major event* **~verband** m *major formation* **~verbraucher** m *bulk* od *l.-sc. consumer* **~verkauf** m *b. sale* **~versuch** m *l.-sc. experiment* **~vieh** n *great cattle* **~wesir** m (moham.) *grand vizier* **~wild** n *big game*; ~jäger *b. g. hunter* **~wirtschaft** f *large scale economy* **~w·ürdenträger** m *high dignitary* **≗|ziehen** vt [h] (Kind) *to breed*; *to bring up* (mit *on*), (Familie) *to raise*, *to rear* ‖ (Vieh) *to breed*, *to raise*, *to rear* **≗zügig 1.** [a] *broad* (*outlook*), *broad-minded*; *liberal*, *charitable*, *responsive* (*p*); in ~er Weise *liberally* ‖ ~ s *to come down handsome* | *grand*, *noble* (*achievement*) ‖ *bold* (*design*) | ⟨tail, tex⟩ *flamboyant* **2.** [adv] *generously*, *handsomely* (*rewarded*); *liberally*; sich ~ verhalten gegen jdn *to do the handsome thing by a p* ‖ *boldly*; *on a grand scale*; *g.-sc.* od *imaginative* (*program*) **~zügigkeit** f *breadth of mind*; *handsomeness*

Gr·öße f ~/~n **A.** [abstr, nur sg] **1.** (räumlich) **a.** *bigness*, *largeness*; *bulk*; *extent*; *range*; *size*; *volume*; *dimensions*, *proportions* pl; *extent*, *scope* ‖ an ~ *in size*; v der ~ e–r Hand *the size of a hand* ‖ °v anständiger ~ *good-sized* **b.** (Höhe) *height*; *tallness* ‖ ein Mann v mittlerer ~ *a man of medium height* ‖ in natürlicher ~ *full-scale* [attr]; → Lebens≗ **2.** ⟨fig⟩ **a.** *greatness* (*of a task*); *largeness* (*of a power*); *magnitude* (*of a force*) ‖ die ~ des Betrages *the total amount* ‖ *volume* (*of trade*) **b.** *greatness* (*of a p*; *a mind*); *grandeur*; *height* (*of a p's genius*); erhabene ~ *sublimity*; moral. ~ *moral size* ‖ Seelen≗ *greatness of soul* ‖ sich der ~ der Stunde bewußt s *to be alive to the greatness of the hour* **c.** *hugeness*, *vastness*, *enormity*, *immensity* **B.** [e–e best. ~; pl ~n] **1.** ⟨math⟩ *quantity*; (un)bekannte ~ (*un*)*known q.*; gegebene, gesuchte ~ *given*, *required q.* ‖ *entity*, → Faktor ‖ unberechenbare ~n [pl] *imponderables* **2.** [abstr] ein Stern erster ~ *a star of the first magnitude* **3.** ⟨com⟩ (Nummer) *size* ‖ verschiedene ~n v Handschuhen *different sizes of gloves*; Scheren verschiedener ~en *different-sized scissors*; v mittlerer ~ *mediumsized*; (je) nach ~ *according to size* ‖ welche Kragen≗ *what size collar* (*do you take*)? ich habe ~ 40 *I take size 40* (*in collars*); (Dinge) nach der ~ ordnen (etc) *to size* **4.** ⟨fig⟩ (P) e–e bekannte ~ *a well-known personality*; *a celebrity*; ⟨theat⟩ *a star* ‖ e–e geistige ~ *a luminary*; *a shining light* ‖ Finanz≗ *financial magnate*; ⟨fam⟩ *big gun* ‖ °alle ~n sind sich darüber einig ⟨fam⟩ *all nibs are agreed on that*

großent·eils adv *largely*; *in a great measure*; *to a great extent* **Gr·ößen- ~bestimmung** f ⟨tech⟩ *rating* **~ordnung** f *scale*; *order of magnitude* | einheitliche **~regelung** f *standardization of sizes* **~verhältnis** n *proportion*; *ratio of size* (od *dimensions*); *scale*; -nisse [pl] *proportions* pl ‖ → Maßstab **~wahn** m *delusion of grandeur*; *megalomania* ‖ °⟨übtr⟩ *swelled head*; °(P) *would-be poet*, *etc*; er leidet an ~ *he suffers from a swelled head* ‖ ≗sinnig [a] *top lofty*; ⟨psych⟩ *grandiose* ‖ ~vorstellungen [pl] *delusions* [pl] *of greatness*

gr·ößer compr a **1.** *bigger*, *larger*; nicht ~ s als (of units) *to bulk no larger than ..* ‖ *taller*; er ist e–n halben Kopf ~ als ich *he is half a head taller than I*; *he tops me by half a head* **2.** ⟨fig⟩ *greater* (*care*); *more intense*; *worse*; *heavier* ‖ immer ~ *greater and greater* (*distance*); immer ~ werdend *ever-increasing* ‖ jeder ~e Krieg *any major war* ‖ er ist nicht ~ als ich *he does not stand any higher than I do* ‖ ~ s als (S) *to be paramount to ..* ‖ der ~e Teil *the best part* **Gross·ist** m ~en/~en *wholesale merchant* (od *dealer*); *wholesaler*; ⟨Am⟩ *jobber wholesaler* **Gr·ossobuchhandel** m = Groß-sortiment **gr·ößte** sup **A.** [a] **1.** *biggest*, *largest* **2.** *greatest* (*care*; *poet*) ‖ *prime* (*importance*); der ~ Teil *most part* (*of the year*); *the greater* od *major part*; *the majority* (*of the people*); während des ~n Teils des 15. Jhs *for the best part of the 15th c.* ‖ die ~ Aufmerksamkeit *the closest attention* ‖ zur ~n Belustigung *greatly to the edification* (*of*); v ~em Interesse *of paramount interest* ‖ im ~n Regen *in a downpour of rain* ‖ mit ~er Geschwindigkeit *with all speed*; mit ~er Vorsicht *with superlative* (od *the utmost*) *care* ‖ der ~ Schurke *the veriest rascal* **B.** [abs] am ~n *biggest*, *largest*; *greatest* **gr·ößtenteils** adv *for the most* od *best part*; *mostly*; *chiefly*, *mainly* **Gr·ößtmaß** n *maximum measure* **gr·ößtmöglich** a *maximum potential* (*density*); die ~e Sorgfalt *the greatest possible care* od *the g. c. p.* | ([falsch!] ~st) **Gr·ößtwert** m *maximum value*

grot·esk 1. [a] *grotesque* (*figure*, *gestures*); *fantastic* ‖ ~e Gestalten [pl] *g.s.* pl ‖ ⟨übtr⟩ *g.* (*mistake*) **2.** [adv] *g.ly* **3.** ≗ f ⟨typ⟩ *sanserif* | ≗e f ⟨arts & Lit⟩ *grotesque*

Gr·otte f ~/~n *grotto* ‖ ⟨übtr⟩ *cave*; *hole* **~nwerk** n *shell-work*

gr·ub 1. & 3. pret v graben **Gr·übchen** n ~s/~ *dimple* (*in the face*, *on the cheek*) ‖ ⟨scient⟩ *fossula* L **Gr·ube** f ~/~n **1.** *cavity*, *hole*, *pit* ‖ ⟨min⟩ *mine*, *pit*; *working*(*s* pl); *quarry* | ⟨fig⟩ = Grab; in die ~ fahren ⟨fig⟩ *to die*; *to go down* (*in*) *to the grave* ‖ wer anderen e–e ~ gräbt, fällt selbst hinein *harm watch*, *h. catch*; ⟨m. m.⟩ *the biter bit* [pp], *For 'tis a sport to have the engineer Hoist with his own petar* (*Shak*) **2.** ⟨anat⟩ *pit*; Herz≗, Magen≗ *pit of the stomach* **Grübel·ei** f ~/~en *brown study*; *musing* [*s* pl]; *contemplation*, *meditation*, *speculation*, *pondering* **gr·übeln 1.** vi [h] *to contemplate*, *meditate*, *muse*, *ponder* ‖ ~ über etw *to muse* od *ponder on* od *over*; *to speculate* (*on*, *about*); *to ruminate upon* od *about*; *to contemplate a th*; ⟨Am⟩ *to mull over a th*; → brüten **2.** ≗ n = Grübelei **Gr·uben- ~anlage** f *working*[*s* pl] **~arbeiter** m *miner*; *collier*, *pitman* **~bau** m *mining* **~blende** f *miner's lantern* **~brand** m *underground fire* **~gas** n *fire-damp*; *marsh-gas*; *methane* **~holz** n *pit-props* pl **~kopf** m *pit-head* **~lampe** f *Davy*(-*-lamp*) **~lokomotive** f *mining l.* **~sand** m *pit-sand* **~schiene** f *tram* **~schmelz** m (Emailmalerei) *champlevé* Fr (*enamel*) **~unglück** n *mine-disaster* **~wetter** n = -gas **~wurm** m ⟨zoo⟩ *hookworm* **Gr·übler** m ~s/~ *ponderer*; *introvert*; *p given to introspection* (od *deep musing*) **≗isch** a *meditative*, *speculative*; *musing*, *pondering*

Gr·ude f ~/ **1.** *hot ashes*; *embers* pl **2.** *coke-breeze* **3.** ~, ~herd *coke-breeze stove*

Gruft f ~/≗e *sepulchre*, *tomb*; *vault*; *grave* ‖ (künstlerische) *mausoleum* ‖ → Höhle

×**Gr·umbiern** f pl; → Grundbirne

Gr·um(me)t n ~(e)s/ ⟨agr⟩ *after-grass*; *after-math*, ⟨Am⟩ *rowen* **grün** a **A. 1. a.** *green*; ⟨her⟩ *vert*; ~e Farbe *g.*, *g.ness*; dunkel~ *dark g.*, *bottle-g.*; *apple-*, *moss-g.* ‖ oliven~ *olive-g.*; smaragd-~ *emerald-g.* ‖ ~e Erde ⟨minr⟩ *celadonite*, *glauconite* ‖ „~e Minna" *Black Maria* ‖ ~e Seife *green soap* ‖ ~e Welle bek ⟨traffic⟩ *to get the go-ahead* **b.** (frisch) *fresh*, *green* (*food*); *verdant* (*avenues*; *grass*), *verdurous*; ~e Vegetation *verdure* ‖ ~e Heringe *white herring* ‖ die ≗e Insel (sc Irland) *the Emerald Isle* ‖ ⟨bib⟩ am ~en Holz *in the green tree*; → ≗donnerstag ‖ ~e Weihnachten *green Christmas* **c.** ~ färben *to paint green*; *to green* **2. a.** (unreif) *green* (*apples*), *unripe* (*fruit*) ‖ *unseasoned* (*wood*); *undressed* (*skin*) **b.** ⟨fig⟩ *green*; *inexperienced* ‖ °~er Junge *greenhorn*; *jackanapes*; *whipper-snapper*; als ich noch ein ~er J. war *in my salad days* **B.** ⟨fig⟩ Wendungen ‖ °komm an m–e ~e Seite *come* (od *sit*) *close to me* ‖ °auf k–n ~en Zweig k *to* *be doomed to constant failure*; *to fail to prosper* || °jdn über den ~en Klee loben *to praise a p to the skies* || am ~en Tisch gefaßt *bureaucratic, red-tape* (*decision*) || jdm nicht ~ s *to get one's knife into a p*; er ist ihm nicht ~ *he can't stand him* || es wurde ihm ~ u gelb vor den Augen *he saw stars* || ~ u gelb vor Neid *green with envy* || jdn ~ u blau *or* gelb schlagen *to beat a p black and blue* **C.** [als Subst.] **Grün** n **1.** (grüne Farbe) *green*; Schweinfurter ≃ *Paris g.*; ein sattes, tiefes ~ *a rich, deep g.*; die Dame in ~ *the lady in g.* || *g.ness* || °es ist dasselbe in ~ *it's twelve of one and a dozen of the other* (*makes no difference*) **2.** (gr. Vegetation) *green* (*the fresh g. of the meadows*); frisches ~ *verdancy, verdure, viridity* || [koll] *g.ery* || *grassy spot*; ⟨golf⟩ (gr. Rasen) *g.*; das ein Loch umgebende ~ *putting-g.* || °bei Mutter ~ schlafen *to sleep in the open* **~auge** n ⟨ent⟩ *gout-fly* **~baum** m ⟨bot⟩ *privet* **~bein** n ⟨orn⟩ *sandpiper* **~berger** m → Surius (aus Schlesien) *Silesian wine* **~bleierz** n ⟨minr⟩ *green load ore* **~buch** n ⟨pol Ind⟩ *g.-book* **~d·onnerstag** m ⟨ec⟩ *Maundy* (⟨Am⟩ *Holy*) *Thursday* **~dung** m *g.-manure* **~düngung** f *g. manuring* **~erde** f → grün A. 1. a. **~fäule** f *mildewed wood* **~feuer** n (Feuerwerk) *g. fire* **~fink** m ⟨orn⟩ *g.finch* **~fläche** f *lawn, greens* pl **~futter** n ⟨agr⟩ *g. fodder*; im Silo konserviertes ~ *silage* | ~lader [m] *g. crop loader* **≃gelb** a *g.ish yellow* **~gürtel** m (e–r Stadt) *g. belt* **~holz** n (der Bebeerurinde) *g.heart* **~kern** m ⟨cul⟩ ⟨Ger⟩ *g. spelt*(*-corn*) **~knochen** m ⟨ich⟩ *garfish* **~kohl** m *kale, kail*; *colewort* **~kram** m *g.-grocery, g.stuff*; *fresh vegetables* pl; *g.*[*s* pl] || ~händler [m] *g.grocer* || ~handlung [f], ~laden [m] *g.grocery* **~kreuz** n ⟨mil⟩ (Kampfstoff) *g.cross*; *asphyxiating gas* **~land** n *pasture-land* **~sand** m ⟨geol⟩ *g.sand*; *glauconite* || °**~schnabel** m → Gelb– **~span** m ⟨a. chem⟩ *verdigris*; v ~ überzogen *verdigrised* **~specht** m ⟨orn⟩ *g. woodpecker* **~stein** m *g.stone* **≃stichig** a ⟨phot⟩ *g. tinged* **~streifen** m *planting strip*, → Mittel– **~waren** pl = –kram **~zeug** n = –kram

Grund m ~es/ ≃e **I.** ⟨eig & übtr⟩ **A. 1.** (Meeres-~) *bottom*; die tiefen ≃e *the depths* pl (*of the ocean*) || ⟨übtr⟩ (Bodensatz) *dregs, grounds, lees* pl **2.** (Erd≃) [mst Boden] der ~ u B. *the ground*[*s* pl] (*of a hospital*); *territory*; *premises* (*of a factory*); ⟨Am⟩ *lot* || auf dem ~ u B. *in the g.s*; auf eigenem ~ u B. *in its own g.* **3.** Tal≃ *valley*; Wiesen≃ *meadow-land* || Jagd≃ *hunting-g.*; liegende ≃e *bottom-lands* pl; *landed property* **4.** ⟨übtr⟩ **a.** (Fundament) *basis, foundation*; *g.* || ⟨fig⟩ die ersten ≃e, Anfangs≃e [pl] *the elements, first principles, rudiments* [pl] (*of a th*) **b.** *base, root, bottom* (e–s Gewindes *of a thread*) **c.** (Farben≃) *g.*; (rotes Kreuz) auf weißem ~e (..) *on a white g.*; ⟨paint⟩ *background* **B. 1.** ⟨mar⟩ ~ **bek.** *to strike soundings*; ~ h *to be in s.s*; k–n ~ h *to be out of s.s* || den ~ legen z etw *to lay the foundation(s) of a th* || ⟨mar⟩ ~ **suchen** *to try to find bo.* || den ~ unter den Füßen verlieren *to get out of one's depth* **2. auf** dem ~ *aground* || ⟨fig⟩ e–r S auf den ~ gehen *to go to the bo.* (od *root*) *of a th*; *to probe a question to the bo.*; *to get down to bedrock* || ⟨mar⟩ auf ~ geraten, auf ~ k (of ship) *to run aground*; *to* (*take*) *g.* || e–r S auf den ~ k *to get to the bo. of a th* || (Schiff) auf ~ setzen *to run aground*; *to g.*; *to beach* || auf ~ sitzen *to be aground* | ⟨fig⟩ **aus** dem ~ = v ~ aus || aus dem ~e des Herzens *from the bo. of one's heart* | **bis auf** den ~ ⟨a. fig⟩ *to the dregs*; *to the last drop* || bis auf den ~ niederreißen *to level to the g.* || **bis in** den ~ erschüttern *to shake* (*a house*) *to its f.s* | **im ~e** *at* (*the*) *bo.*; *in reality* (od *truth*); *after all*; *basically*; *at bo.*; *in the main*; *as good as* || im ~e genommen *fundamentally*; *properly speaking*; *properly*; *virtually*; *when all is said and done* || im ~e s–s Herzens *at the bo. of his soul*, ..; ein guter Kerl *a good man at bo.* || (Schiff) in den ~ bohren *to sink, founder* || ⟨fig⟩ in ~ u Boden *radically* | ⟨fig⟩ **von ~ auf** od **aus** *profoundly, fundamentally, radically*; *thoroughly, from the very base* ⟨a. cosm⟩; v ~ aus anfangen *to start from rockbo.* || sich v ~ aus bessern *to turn over a new leaf* | **zu ~e gehen** ⟨fig⟩ (P) *to go under, to go to the wall* (od *the dogs*); *to perish* (an *of*); allmählich z ~e gehen *to peter out* || (etw) e–r S z ~e legen *to take as a basis for a th*; *to model on a th* || e–r S z ~e liegen *to be at the bo. of a th*; *to underlie a th*; *to form the basis of a th* || z ~e richten *to destroy, to ruin* **II.** ⟨**fig**⟩ **A. 1.** (**Anlaß**) *cause*; ~ zur Klage *c. for complaint* || *occasion* (*to do*) **2.** (**Ursache**) *g.s* pl; *reason* (f *for* od *of*; warum *why*; z tun *for doing, to do*); ≃e f s–e Enttäuschung *g.s for his disappointment* || ein berechtigter ~ *a case* (*for*); s–e ≃e f *his c. for* .. **3. Beweg≃** *motive* **4. Beweis≃** *argument*; ≃e f u wider *a.s for and against*; *the pros and cons* pl **B. 1.** ich **habe** ~ **zur** Annahme *I have good reason* (od *g.s*) *for thinking*; jeden, k–n ~ h *to have every, no r.* (*to do*); das hat s–n ~ *there is a good r. for it* || ⟨prov⟩ willst du e–n ~ h, mußt du e–n Hund graben ⟨m. m.⟩ *an easy th to find a stick to beat a dog* || ich sehe k–n vernünftigen ~ dafür *I do not see the fun of it* || das ist der ~ *that is why* || ein um so triftigerer ~ *all the more r.* (*that* ..); um so mehr ~, weshalb .. *an added r. why* ..; ein weiterer ~ *an additional r.* (*for* ..) || kein dringender ~, daß wir ihn belästigen *no need for us to worry him* || es war kein triftiger ~ vorhanden z tun *there was no point in doing*; es gibt gewichtige ≃e z sagen *there is a strong case for saying* **2. auf** ~ [+ *gen*] *on* (od *under*) *the authority of, on the basis of* || auf ~ Ihres guten Rufes *on the strength* (od *by* [od *in*] *virtue*) *of your reputation*; auf ~ e–s Artikels *prodded by an a.*; auf ~ aller Zeugnisse .. *on all evidence* (*that is available*) || auf ~ aller R. *in the light of all the results* .. || auf ~ des V. *under the treaty* || auf ~ dessen, daß *on the g.s that* .. || nicht auf ≃e hören *not to listen to argument* | **aus** demselben ~e *for the same r.*; (ebenfalls) *by the same token* || aus diesen ≃en *on these g.s* || aus dem einfachen ~e, weil .. *for the simple r. that* .., *on the g. that* .. || aus welchem ~e? *for what r.? with what object?* || aus religiösen ≃en *on religious g.s* || aus sittlichen ≃en *on ethical g.s* || aus ≃en der Religion *on religious g.s* | **mit** (gutem) ~ *with r.*; *justly*; (etw) mit ~ behaupten *to have good r. for asserting* | er fragte **nach** ~ u Ursach *he asked for the whys and wherefores* | **ohne** jeden ~ *without rhyme* od *r.* || ganz ohne ~ *quite unreasonably*; nicht ohne ~ *not without some cause*; *reasonably*; nicht ganz ohne ~ *not unreasonably* **III.** [in comp] *ground–* || *basic* || *chief, main, principal*; *original*; *fundamental*; *landed* **~adel** m *l. aristocracy* **~angel** f *drail, g.-line* **~angeln** n *g.-angling* **~anker** m ⟨aero⟩ *g. anchor* **~anschauung** f; v solchen ~en ausgehend *so g.ed* (*he* ..) **~anstrich** m *priming*; *prime* od *first coat*(*ing*) *of paint* **~ausbildung** f *b. training* **~ausstattung** f *initial outfit* **~baß** m ⟨mus⟩ *g.-bass* **~bau** m *foundation*(*s* pl) **~bedeutung** f *b.* (od *o.*) *meaning* **~bedingung** f *main condition* **~begriff** m *basic* (od *fundamental*) *idea*; ~e [pl] *f.s* pl, *principles*; ~e der Technik *general technical terms* pl **~berührung** f ⟨mar⟩ ~ h *to be in soundings*; *to touch g.* **~besitz** m *real estate* (od *property*); *l. property* || kl ~ *small holding* **~besitzer** m *l. proprietor*; *landowner, -lord* **~bestandteil** m *element* °×**~birne** = Kartoffel **~buch** n ⟨Ger⟩ *real register of property*; (f Land) *land* od *g. register*; ⟨engl hist⟩ (1086) *Domesday* (*Book*) || ~amt *Registry* (⟨Am⟩ *Land*) *Office for real estate*; ~auszug [m] *abstract of title*, ~eintragung [f] *entry in the* .. **~daten** pl ⟨comp⟩ *b. data* **~deutsch** n *b. G.* **~dienst** m ⟨hist⟩ *servitude to the lord of the manor* **~dienstbarkeit** f *real servitude*

~eigentum n *realty*; zeitlich unbeschränktes ~ *estate in fee simple*; → –besitz ‖ ~smakler [m] ⟨Am⟩ *realtor* **~eigentümer** m = –besitzer **~einstellung** f *b. attitude* (od *outlook*) **~eis** n *g.-ice*, (im Fluß) ⟨Am⟩ *frazil* ‖ °ihm ging manches mit ~ *he was in a blue funk* **~erwerbssteuer** f ⟨Ger⟩ *land transfer tax* **~farbe** f *g.-colour*; *primary c.* ‖ = –anstrich **~fehler** m *cardinal fault*; *radical error* **~feste** f: die ~n [pl] *the foundations* pl; in den ~n *in its very f.*; in s–n ~n erschüttern *to shake to its* (*very*) *f.* ‖ an den ~n rütteln *to undermine the f.* **~fläche** f *base* **~form** f *simple* (od *elementary*) *form*; *b. form* **~funktion** f *b. function* **~gänger** m ⟨mar⟩ *sunken torpedo* **~gebirge** n ⟨geol⟩ *primitive rock*; *basement* **~gebühr** f *b. fee*; ⟨telph⟩ *subscription* **~gedanke** m *b.* (od *f.*, *general*, *leading*) *thought* od *idea*; *motif* **~gefüge** n ⟨min⟩ *matrix* **~gehalt** n ⟨Ger⟩ *b. salary* od *fee* **~geschirr** n ⟨mar⟩ *g.-tackle* **~geschwindigkeit** f ⟨aero⟩ *g. spaed* (*G/S*) **~gesetz** n *b. law* **~gewebe** n ⟨biol⟩ *stroma* **~heil** n ⟨bot⟩ *bugle* **~helligkeit** f ⟨telv⟩ *brightness* **~herr** m *lord of the manor*; ⟨a-engl⟩ *seignior, seigneur* | ~lich [a] *manorial*; ~schaft [f] *manor*; *territorial domain* **~kapital** n *authorized* od *o. capital* **~karte** f ⟨Ger⟩ *historical map* **~kenntnisse** pl *f.* od *b. knowledge* **~konstruktion** f *b. design* | in e–r **~konzeption** ⟨tech⟩ *f.ly* **~kredit** m ⟨Ger⟩ *long-dated credit on real property* **~lack** m ⟨tech⟩ *priming lacquer, priming varnish* ‖ ⟨cosm⟩ *satinbase* **~lage** f *basis, groundwork* ‖ ⟨mst fig⟩ *basis*; *bedrock*; *groundwork*; *keystone*; *foundation*(*s* pl); *fundamentals* pl (*of religion*); *fundamental principles*; = erste Gründe, → Grund A. 4. a. ‖ ⟨philos⟩ *substratum* L; wesentl. ~ *hypostasis* | die ~ v etw bilden *to underlie a th* ‖ jeder ~ entbehren *to be without foundation* ‖ auf breiterer ~ (*to treat*) *on broader lines*; ‖ auf e–e neue ~ stellen *to put on a new basis* ‖ sich auf die ~n besinnen *to get down to bedrock*; auf der ~ der Gemeinnützigkeit *on a non-profit-making basis*; auf der ~ entwickelt v .. *a development of* .. **~lagenforschung** f ⟨math⟩ = Axiomatik; *basic* od *fundamental research*; *fundament research* **~last** f *first charge on property* | ~enenergie [f] (in 24 Stdn) ⟨el⟩ *base-load power* **~legend** **1.** [a] *b.* (*fact*); *f.* (*truth*); ~ f *f. to* ‖ *constitutive* (*factor*); *sweeping* (*character*); ⟨Am⟩ *bo.* (*facts*) **2.** [adv] *b.ally*; *f.ly*; **~legung** f *foundation*; *establishment* **~leiden** n *underlying cause of death* **~linie** f *base* (*-line*); *g.-line*; *guiding l.*; ⟨pol⟩ *line* **~luft** f *g. air* **~mauer** f *g.-course*; *basement*; verstärkte ~ *footing basement* **~metall** n *base, basis* **~mine** f ⟨mar⟩ *g.-mine* **~pfandrecht** n *law of mortgage* **~pfeiler** m *supporting pillar*; ⟨fig⟩ *bedrock, keystone*; *warp and woof* **~plan** m ⟨arch⟩ *g.-plan* **~platte** f *g.-plate*; *base, pedestal*; ⟨mar⟩ *bed-plate* **~preis** m *base-rate*; *basic price* **~prinzip** n *b.* (od *f.*) *principle*; *keystone* **~rechnungsarten** pl *f. rules of arithmetic* **~rechte** pl *b. rights of the citizen* **~regel** f *b. rule* **~rente** f *g.-rent* **~richtung** f ⟨mil⟩ *basis for side-firing* | ~slinie [f] ⟨artill⟩ *zero line*; ~swinkel [m] *base angle* **~riß** m *g.-plan, plan view* (*of a building*) ‖ ⟨übtr⟩ *compendium* L ‖ die –risse [pl] *the outlines* pl (*of a history*) ‖ im ~ *in outline* **~satz** m ⟨math⟩ *axiom*; *maxim* ‖ *principle*; *slogan*; (Partei~) *tenet*; *gospel* (*of temperance*) ‖ es ist sein ~ (*or* ein ~ bei ihm), .. *his p.le is* (*to do*) ‖ sein ~ war, Menschen z führen *he believed in leading people* ‖ nach dem ~ (..) *upon the p.le* (..); (etw) nach gesunden ~en einrichten *to organize on sound lines* ‖ ein Mann v hohen ~en *a man of high p.le*; *a high-p.led man*; v moralischen ~en geleitet *p.led* ‖ e–n ~ befolgen *to proceed upon a p.le* ‖ e–n ~ h *to hold a p.le* ‖ es sich z ~ m *to make it a rule* | **~satzerklärung** f *declaration of intent*; ⟨pol⟩ (*formal*) *statement of policy* **~satzdebatte** f ⟨parl, etc⟩ *principle debate* **~sätzlich** a *f.*; *b.*; ⟨jur⟩ *leading* (*decision*); e–e S v ~er Bdtg *a matter of policy*; aus ~en Erwägungen *as a. m. of p.* | adv *on p.le*; *in general*; *as a general p.le* ‖ ~ enthalten s in .. *to be axiomatic in* .. **~schleppnetz** n ⟨mar⟩ *trawl(-net)* **~schuld** f *land charge* **~schule** f ⟨Ger⟩ *junior school for the first four years*; ⟨Am⟩ *b. track* **~schwelle** f ⟨arch⟩ *g.sel* **~see** d ⟨mar⟩ *g.-sea* (od *swell*) **~soll** n *b. quota* **~ständig** a ⟨bot⟩ ~es Blatt *g.-leaf* **~stein** m *foundation-stone* ‖ ⟨fig⟩ *foundation* (od *corner*)*-stone*; *foundations* pl; *bedrock, keystone* ‖ den ~ e–s Gebäudes legen *to lay the foundations of a building*; ⟨fig⟩ den ~ legen z etw *to lay the foundations* (*of England*) **~steinlegung** f *laying of the first stone*; *corner-st. laying ceremony* **~stellung** f ⟨gym, mil⟩ *normal position* ⟨a. tech⟩; *standing at* (od *to*) *attention* **~steuer** f *real tax* **~stimme** f ⟨mus⟩ *bass* **~stimmung** f ⟨fig⟩ *keynote*; *general tone* **~stock** m *basis*; *foundation*(*s* pl); *stock*; *basic arsenal*; *fund*; *general stock* (*of human knowledge*) **~stoff** m ⟨a. chem⟩ *element base, radical, base* od *raw material* | ~industrie [f] *basic industries* pl **~strich** m (beim Schreiben) *down-stroke* **~stück** n *real property* (od *estate*) ‖ *premises*; auf dem ~ *on the p.*; bebaute u unbeb. ~e pl ⟨bal⟩ *property, plant, and equipment*, ⟨com-bal⟩ *freehold and leasehold*; ⟨Am⟩ *land and buildings*; ⟨bal⟩ *real property* | ~smakler [m] *real estate broker* od *agent*, ⟨Am⟩ *realtor* | ~skosten [pl] *cost of land* ‖ ~smarkt [m] *property* (od *estate*)*-market* ‖ ~ssachen → Testament ‖ ~sübereignungsurkunde [f] ⟨jur⟩ *warrant* (od *full covenant*) *deed* ‖ ~sverkäufer [m] *grantor* **~stufe** f ⟨school⟩ *basic track* **~tatsache** f *fundamental* (od *basic*) *fact*; *ground-fact* **~taxe** f *basic tariff* **~teilung** f ⟨agr⟩ *dismemberment* **~text** m *original text* **~thema** n ⟨mus⟩ *basic theme* **~ton** m ⟨mus⟩ *keynote, tonic* ‖ ⟨fig⟩ *general tone, keynote* | ~art [f] *fundamental key* **~trieb** m *primary instinct* **~typ** m *basic type* **~übel** n *basic evil*; *the root* (od *source*) *of evil* **~überholung** f *major* od *complete overhaul* **~umsatz** m (Stoffwechsel~) *basal metabolism* **~ursache** f *prime cause* **~vermögen** n *capital stock* ‖ = –besitz **~wahrheit** *f. truth*; ~en [pl] *f.s* pl; *verities* pl (*of the Christian faith*) **~wasser** n *g.-water*; ~spiegel *w.-level, w.-table* **~wert** m *b. value* **~wort** n *radical word* **~zahl** f *cardinal number* ‖ (of a logarithm) *base* **~zeit** f (Wort~) ⟨comp⟩ *word-time*; ⟨phys⟩ *b. t.* **~zins** m *ground-rent* **~zug** m ⟨fig⟩ *chief* (od *principal*) *feature*; *distinctive mark*

gr·und- [in comp] [verstärkend vor Adj, pred mit schwebender Betonung: ~ehrlich] *downright*; *entirely*; *extremely*; *most*; *out and out*; *radically*; *thoroughly*; *very* **~anständig, ~ehrlich** a; °ein ~er Kerl *a downright sort of man*, ⟨fam⟩ *a jolly good fellow* **~falsch** a *entirely wrong* **~gelehrt** a *most erudite* od *scholarly* **~häßlich** a (*very*) *ugly* **~sätzlich** → ~satz **~verschieden** a *very unlike* (*v a th*); *heterogeneous, dissimilar*

Gr·undel f ~/~n ⟨ich⟩ *goby*; → Gründling

gr·ündeln vi [h] (*ducks*) *are on the feed*

gr·ünden vt [h] **1.** (Kirche, Stadt etc) *to found, plant* (nach dem Muster v *on the pattern of* ..) ‖ (Reich) *to build up*; *to create*; *to lay the foundations of* ‖ (Gemeinschaft) *to constitute*; (Religion) *to establish* ‖ e–e Professur ~ *to endow a professorship* **2.** (Geschäft) *to establish, to set up, to start* ‖ ⟨com⟩ (Gesellschaft etc) *to float, launch, promote*; .. wurde 1923 ge–det (*the organization*) *had its inception in 1923* **3.** etw (Hoffnung etc) ~ **auf** *to base* od *found a th on* ..; (Argument) *to ground on*; *to predicate a statement on* .. ‖ ge–det s auf .. *to be based* (od *founded, grounded*; *bottomed*) *on* **4. sich** ~ **auf** *to rest on*; = gegründet s auf, → 3.

Gr·ünder m ~s/ **1.** *founder* ‖ ⟨übtr⟩ *builder, creator*; *originator* **2.** ⟨com⟩ *founder, promoter* ‖ ⟨dero⟩ *promoter*; *speculator*; *jobber* **~aktien** pl *founders' shares* pl **~jahre** pl, **~zeit** f ⟨Ger⟩ (nach 1871) ⟨com⟩ *promotion period*; *time of wild speculation* | ~stil [m] *Wilhelminien style*

grund·ieren 1. vt [h] ⟨tech⟩ (Holz, Leinwand) *to ground*; *prime*; *size*; *stain* **2.** ≈ n = Grundierung **Grund·ierer** m *grounder* **Grund·ierung** f ⟨paint⟩ *grounding*; *priming* [a. konkr]; *undercoat*; ⟨cosm⟩ *foundation*

gr·ündlich A. [a] **1.** (S) *complete*; *thorough* (*rest*); *all-round* (*knowledge*); *close* (*examination*); ~e Kenntnisse h *to have a good grounding*; *to be well-grounded* (in *in*) ‖ *careful*, *painstaking* (*investigation*) ‖ *sweeping*, *radical*, *thorough-going* (*reform*) **2.** (P) *efficient* (*worker*); *deep*, *profound* (*scholar*); *solid*; *accomplished* (*philosopher*) **B.** [adv] *carefully* ‖ *completely*; *thoroughly*; *down to the ground*; *out and out*; *radically*; *root and branch* ‖ aber ~! *with a vengeance*! ‖ (etw) ~ erklären *to thrash out* ‖ etw ~ kennen *or* können *to have a th at one's finger's ends*; *to have the knack of a th*; ~ gezeichnet *thoroughly* od *well-charted* (*map*) | jdm ~ die Meinung sagen *to give a p a piece of one's mind*; °jdn ~ vornehmen *to bring a p to book*; *to haul a p over the coals* ‖ °da hast du dich ~ getäuscht! *you're all wrong*! *catch me doing that*! ‖ °ich werde es ihm ~ besorgen ⟨fam⟩ *I'll give it him hot* **≈keit** f *thoroughness* ‖ *carefulness*; *profundity*, *solidity*, etc.

Gr·ündling m ⟨ich⟩ *groundling*, *gudgeon*

gr·undlos A. [a] **1.** ⟨eig⟩ *bottomless* (*abyss*), *unfathomable* (*depth*, *sea*) ‖ *impassable*; *sloppy*, *soppy* (*road*) **2.** ⟨fig⟩ *bottomless* (*ignorance*); *boundless* **3.** (unbegründet) *groundless*; *gratuitous*; *immaterial*, *unreal*, → gegenstandslos; *unfounded* (*suspicion*); [pred] *without foundation* **B.** [adv] *without reason*; *unreasonably*

Gr·undlosigkeit f *bottomlessness*, etc

Gr·ündung f ~/~en **1.** [abstr] *foundation*; *founding* ‖ *creation* ‖ *establishment*; *starting* ‖ ⟨com⟩ *flo(a)tation*, *formation*, *promotion* (*of a company*) **2.** [konkr] *foundation*; → Gesellschaft; Niederlassung ‖ *establishment* ‖ schwindelhafte ~ *bubble-company* **~saktienemission** f *flo(a)tation* **~sbank** f *promoter bank*, *issuing house* **~sfonds** m ⟨univ⟩ *foundation* **~skapital** n *original* od *initial capital* **~skosten** pl ⟨com⟩ *preliminary expenses* **~smächte** f pl (der UNO) *charter members* pl **~smitglied** n *ch. m.* **~surkunde** f *foundation-charter* ‖ ⟨com⟩ *memorandum of association*

Gr·üne 1. (= Grün 2.) [~s, das ~] *the fresh green*; *verdure* ‖ *fr. vegetables*; *g.s* pl | *g.ness*, die Farbe spielt ins ~ *the colour has a g.ish hue* od *tint* **2.** das ~: im ~n *in the open*, *in the fields* (od *country*); e–e Fahrt ins ~ *a trip into the country* ‖ Konzert im ~n *open-air concert* **3.** °[der ~, ein ~r] (Polizist) ⟨fam⟩ *cop*, *bobby*; ⟨Am⟩ *bluecoat*

gr·ünen vi [h] *to green*; *to become* (od *grow*, *turn*) *g.*; *to be g.* ‖ ⟨übtr, poet⟩ = blühen **Gr·ünes** n → Grüne 1. **gr·ünlich** a *greenish* ‖ ins ≈e spielen *to have a greenish hue* od *tint* **Gr·ünling** m ~s/~e **1.** ⟨orn⟩ *greenfinch* **2.** ⟨bot⟩ *green white-spored agaric*; *Tricholoma* L **3.** °⟨fig⟩ = Grünschnabel

gr·unzen 1. vi [h] *to grunt* ‖ °(etw) ~d äußern *to g.*; er grüßte ~d *he g.ed a greeting* **2.** ≈ n *g.(ing)*; mit e–m ~ *with a g.* **Gr·unzer** m **1.** *grunter* **2.** ⟨ich⟩ *g.(er)* **Gr·unzochse** m ⟨zoo⟩ *yak*

Gr·uppe f ~/~n **1. a.** (P) *group*; *cluster* (*of spectators*); *section*; *set*; kl ~ *knot*, *band*, *squad*; gr ~ *squadron*; ~ v Sachverständigen *panel*; in ~n *in groups* ‖ ⟨Am a.⟩ *crowd*, *gang* (*of boys*) **b.** ⟨mil engl⟩ (4. Teil e–s Zuges) *section*; (kl zus-geschlossene ~) *squad* ‖ ⟨Ger pol⟩ *section* **c.** in ~n anordnen, einteilen *to group*; ⟨mil⟩ *to squad* ‖ sie bildeten e–e ~ um .. *they grouped themselves round* .. **2.** *group* (*of houses*, *languages*); *cluster* (*of hills*); *clump* (*of trees*); ~ v Unglücksfällen *series* (od *chapter*) *of accidents* **3.** ⟨artill⟩ *volley* **4.** ⟨aero⟩ *wing*

Gr·uppen- *group-*, *section-*; *collective* (*migration*, *insurance*) **~addition** f ⟨comp⟩ *cross-addition* **~bild** n *g.-piece* **~bildung** f *g.-formation*; ⟨demog⟩ *g.ing* **~ehe** f ⟨anthr⟩ *g.-marriage* **~feuer** n ⟨mil⟩ *g.-firing*; *firing by s.s* od *volleys* **~flug** m ⟨mst aero-mil⟩ *group flight* **~führer** m ⟨mil & pol⟩ *s.-leader* **~gespräch** n *panel-discussion* **~gewohnheiten** f pl *institutions* **~kommandeur** m ⟨aero engl⟩ (Oberst) *g.-captain* ‖ ⟨Ger⟩ (Major) *squadron-leader* **~multiplikation** f *g. m.* **~reise** f *common interest g. travel* **~schalter** m ⟨el⟩ *gang switch* **~sex(us)** m *group sex* **~summen** f pl ⟨comp⟩ *departmental totals* **~unterricht** m *g.-instruction* **≈weise** adv *in g.s*; *by squads* **~wirtschaft** f ⟨for⟩ *g. system*

grupp·ieren 1. vt [h] (S, P) *to group*; *to arrange in* (od *form into*) *g.s* (od *a g.*) | **sich** ~ *to cluster* od *gather* (um *round*); wir gruppierten uns um .. *we g.ed ourselves round* .. **2.** ≈ n *g.ing* **Grupp·ierung** f *g.ing*; *arrangement* (*in a g.*) ‖ [konkr] ~en [pl] ⟨pol⟩ = Gruppen

Grus m –es/–e **1.** ⟨geol⟩ *fine gravel*; *fine granular material* **2.** *small coal*

gr·uselig a (*creepy-*)*crawly*; *hair raising* (*story*); *uncanny*, *weird*; *spooky* **gr·useln 1.** vrefl/vi [imps] ich gruselte mich *or* es g. mir (*or* mich), mir (mich) g. es *I felt creepy*; *my flesh* (od *skin*) *crept*; *a c. feeling came over me* ‖ jdn ~ m = mit ≈ erfüllen **2.** ≈ n *creeps* pl; *c.(-c.) feeling*; ⟨sl⟩ *jim--jams* pl ‖ ein ~ befiel mich = es gruselte mich ‖ jdm ~ verursachen, jdn mit ~ erfüllen *to give a p the creeps*, *to make a p's flesh creep*

Gr·uß m ~es/≈e **1.** (~ durch Worte etc) *greeting* (an *to*, v *from*); *salutation*; ⟨bib⟩ der Englische ~ *the Angelic S.*; Willkommens≈ (*words of*) *welcome* ‖ dem Schiff zum ~ *in g. to the ship* ‖ ≈e erwidern, senden *to return*, *send g.s* ‖ er reichte mir die Hand z ~ *he held out his hand to greet me* **2.** ⟨mil, mar & pol⟩ (Ehren≈) *salute*; (*military*) *s.* ‖ den Arm zum ~ erheben *to raise one's arm in s.* (od *to the s.*), ⟨nazi⟩ z deutschen ~ *in the G. s.* **3.** (~ an e–n, v e–m Dritten) [oft pl] ≈e *compliments*; *regards* pl ‖ mit besten ≈en v Herrn N. *with Mr. N's c.s*; mit herzlichen ≈en an .. *with kindest r.s to* (*your mother*) ‖ ich soll e–n ~ (*or* ≈e) ausrichten v Herrn N. *Mr. N. sends his c.s*; bestelle d–m Gatten e–n herzl. ~ *give my kindest r.s to your husband*; *remember me to your h.* **4.** ⟨fig⟩ ≈e des Frühlings *g.s of spring* **~bekanntschaft** f *nodding acquaintance*; er ist e–e ~ v mir *we are on bowing terms* **~form** f *mode of g.*, *salute* **~formel** f (*formula of*) *s.* **~pflicht** f ⟨mil & mar⟩ *obligation to salute* **~zeichen** n *salutation* **gr·üßen** vt/i [h] **A.** vt **1.** jdn ~ *to greet*, (⟨mil, etc⟩ *salute*, ⟨fam⟩ *cap*) *a p* (mit *with*); als erster ~ *to be the first to greet*, *to bow first* ‖ *his uncle's man touched his hat to the young gentleman* ‖ (durch Verbeugung etc) *to bow* (od *nod*) *to a p*; *to raise one's hat to a p* ‖ grüße bitte d–n Bruder v mir *please*, *remember me to your b.*; g. ihn herzlich v mir *give my kindest r.s to him*; m–e Frau läßt d–e Mutter herzlich ~ *my wife sends her love to your mother*; jdn ~ l *to give* od *send a p one's r.*; wir l ihn ~ *remember us to him*; er läßt Euch alle ~ *he sends g.s to you all*; *he desires to be remembered to you all* **2.** ⟨mil, mar & pol⟩ (jdn) *to salute* **3.** Gott grüß dich! *God be with you* ‖ Gott grüße das (..) *God bless the* (*honest handicraft*) **B.** vi **1.** *to salute*; *to raise one's hat* ‖ flüchtig ~ *to give a perfunctory salutation* ‖ nach Art der Mohamedaner ~ *to salaam* ‖ Herr N. läßt ~ *Mr. N. sends his c.s* **2.** ⟨mil & mar⟩ *to salute* (*properly*) **3.** Grüß Gott! *Good day* (*to you*)! **4.** ⟨übtr⟩ Burgen ~ v den Höhen *castles greet us from the heights* **Gr·üßfuß** m: mit jdm auf dem ~e stehen *to be on bowing terms with a p*

Gr·ütz- ~beutel m ⟨path⟩ *atheroma* Gr; *sebaceous cyst* **~brei** m *gruel*; *groat-gruel* °**~kasten** m (Kopf) ⟨sl⟩ *sconce. pannikin, knowledge--box* °**~kopf** m = Dummkopf **~wurst** f ⟨Ger⟩ *sausage with an addition of groats* **Gr·ütze** f ~/ **1.** ⟨Ger⟩ *coarsely ground barley* (*oats, buckwheat*; *groats* pl) ‖ Rote ~ *groats cooked with red fruit--juice* **2.** °(Verstand) *brains, wits* pl; ⟨fam⟩ *gumption*; ⟨sl⟩ *savvy*

×°**Gsch·aftlhuber** m ~s/~ *busybody* ×°**Gscherte(r)** m *country bumpkin*, ⟨Am⟩ *hillybilly*

×°**Gsp·usi** n *sweetheart*, ⟨vulg⟩ *bit* ‖ *love-affair*

Guadalaj·ara n (Stadt in Mexiko)

Guadalquiv·ir m ⟨Span⟩ (Fluß)

Guadel·oupe [–u:p] f (die größte Insel der Kleinen Antillen) *Guadaloupe*

Guaj·akholz n *guaiacum*; ~öl *g. wood oil*

Guan·ako n ~s/~s ⟨zoo⟩ *guanaco*

Gu·ano m ~s/ ⟨agr⟩ mit ~ düngen *to guano*

Gu·aschmalerei f *guache* ‖ Bild in ~ *guache*

Guatemala n (mittelamer. Republik) | **-lteke** m, **-ltekin** f; **g-ltekisch** a *Guatemalan*

Gu·ave f ⟨cul⟩, **~nbaum** m ⟨bot⟩ *guava*

Guay·ana, Guai·ana n *Guiana*

G·uben ⟨†Ger⟩ (Stadt) → Neisse

G·uck- °**~auge,** °**~äuglein** n ⟨sl⟩ *peeper* °**~glas** n *transparent glass* °**~indiewelt** f *pert youngster*; = Grünschnabel **~kasten** m *peep-* (od *raree*)--*show*; ⟨fam⟩ *goggle-box* | ~bühne [f] ⟨theat⟩ *picture-frame stage* **~loch** n *peep* (od *spy, eye*)--*hole*

°**g·ucken 1.** vi [h] *to look, peep* (*out of*; *through*; *into*); *peer*; *peek* ‖ laß mich mal ~ *let me have a peep* (od *look*) ‖ in alle Ecken ~ *to poke into every corner* ‖ °guck nicht so dumm *you look a perfect fool* | °⟨fig⟩ er hat z tief ins Glas geguckt *he has taken a drop too much* ‖ °in den Mond ~ *to be the loser*; *to whistle for one's money*; ⟨sl⟩ *to be the pigeon* ‖ der Schelm guckt ihm aus den Augen *he is a slyboots* **2.** ≗ n *peep*(*ing*); *peek*(*ing*) **G·ucker** m *peeper*; *opera glass*(*es*) °×**G·ucker(le** n) m pl (Augen) *winkers, blinks* **g·uck-guck – da!** *peep–oh!* ≗**spiel** n *bo-peep, peek-a-boo*

G·udschar m ~en/~en ⟨Ind⟩ *Gujar*

Gu·elfe [gw-] m ⟨hist⟩ *Guelph, Guelf*

Guer·eza m ~s/~s ⟨zoo⟩ (Stummelaffe) *guereza*

Guer·illa [ge'rilja-] f [Span] ~/~s *guer*(*r*)*illa*

G·ugel f ⟨hist ec⟩ *cowl* | ~hupf [m] *pound-cake*

Guill·oche [gi'jɔʃə] f Fr ~/~n ⟨arch⟩ *guilloche*; *wave* **guilloch·ieren** [gijɔ'ʃ-] vt *to guilloche*; *wave*

Guillot·ine [gi(l)jo'ti:nə] f ~/~n *guillotine*

guillotin·ieren [gi(l)jo-] vt [h] *to guillotine*

Guin·ea [gi'nea] n *Guinea*; Bewohner(in) v ~ *G.n*; Busen von ~ *Gulf of G.* **~körner** pl, **~pfeffer** m *guinea grains* pl **~wurm** m ⟨zoo⟩ *guinea-worm*

Guin·ee [gi'ne:] f ~/~n ⟨engl⟩ = (21 sh) *guinea*

Guirl·ande f = Girlande **Guit·arre** f = Gitarre

G·ulasch m & n ~(e)s/ ⟨cul⟩ *goulash*; *stewed beef* °**~kanone** f ⟨mil⟩ *bean-gun*

G·ulden m ~s/~ **1.** ⟨hist⟩ (Goldmünze) *florin* ‖ (Silber–) *gulden* **2.** ⟨mod⟩ (holländ. Silber≗; = 100 Cent) *guilder, gulden* **g·ülden** a ⟨poet⟩ = golden **G·uldenbaum** m ⟨bot⟩ *liquidambar*

G·ülle f ~/~n = Jauche, Pfütze

×**Gült, G·ülte** f *yield* ‖ = Abgabe, Zins

g·ültig a **1.** (rechts~) *valid* (*contract, marriage*; *digit*); dauernd ~ *standing* (*order*); (Wahl) f ~ erklären *to validate* ‖ als ~ anerkannt *received* (*pronunciation*); als allgemein ~ angesehen *orthodox* ‖ ⟨rail⟩ Billet f 3 Tage ~ *ticket available for 3 days*; ⟨Am⟩ (*ticket*) *good* (*on different lines*) **2.** *good, legal* (*money*); *current*; *lawful* **3.** ~ s *to be in force, to be valid*; (of a law, etc) *to hold*; nicht ~ s f *not to hold for* ‖ (of a verdict) *to stand*; ⟨Am fam⟩ *to go* | ≗**keit** f **1.** ⟨contr⟩ *validity*; *force* (*of an agreement*); in ~ *in force* ‖ v allgemeiner ~ *orthodox*; *universal* (*rule*) ‖ ein Billet mit dreitägiger ~ *a ticket available for 3 days* **2.** *currency, legality* (*of money*); *lawfulness* | ~sdauer [f] *validity* (*of a ticket*); *term* (*of a guarantee*); *life* (*of a letter of credit*); ~serklärung [f] *validation* (*of an election*)

G·ummi 1. n ~s/~s ⟨bot⟩ *gum*; ~ absondern (of trees) *to* (*exude*) *gum* ‖ (Klebstoff) *gum* **2.** m ~s/~s *rubber*; (Hart≗) = Ebonit; Alt≗ *used rubber* (*to regenerate used r.*); ‖ Radier≗ m *india-rubber* ‖ auf ~ fahren *to run on rubber-tyres* (⟨Am⟩ *–tires*) ‖ elastisch wie ~ *as elastic as rubber* **3.** ⟨sex-med⟩ *French letter* | → Schaum≗ **~apfel** m ⟨bot⟩ *poon*; *tamenu* **~ar·abikum** n *gum arabic* ≗**artig** a (klebrig) *gummy* **~artikel** m pl *r.-goods* pl ‖ ⟨sex-med⟩ *preventives* pl **~badewanne** f *bathinette* **~ball** m *r.-ball* **~ballon** m (an mediz. Apparaten) *r.-bulb* **~band** n *elastic* (*band*) | ≗chen [n] (z Verpacken) *r. band* **~bande** f (am Billard) *r.-cushion* **~baum** m ⟨bot⟩ **1.** *gum*(*-tree*); blauer, roter, weißer ~ *blue, red, white gum* **2.** *r.-plant* (od *tree*) **~beine** n pl: ~ h ⟨fig⟩ *to have r. legs* **~belag** m *r. flooring* **~bereifung** f *tyring* ‖ [konkr] *tyres, tires* pl **~beutel** m *r.-bag* **~bezug** m *r.oid covering* **~bonbon** m *gum--drop* **~boot** n ⟨mar⟩ *r.-boat* **~druck** m ⟨typ⟩ (~verfahren) *offset* **~el·astikum** n *gum-elastic* **~fluß** m ⟨bot⟩ *gummosis* **~-Gew·ebe-Kombinati·on** f ⟨mot, tech⟩ *r. fabric combination* **~gutt** n ⟨chem⟩ *gamboge* **~handschuh** m *r.-glove* **~harz** n *gum-resin* **~kabel** n *r.-insulated wire* **~knüppel** m (*r.-*)*truncheon*, ⟨Am⟩ *billy* ‖ 50 Schläge mit dem ~ *50 blows from the r.-t.* **~lack** m (*gum-*)*lac* **~linse** f ⟨phot, telv⟩ (*super-*)*zoom lens* **~lösung** f *r. solution* **~mantel** m *mackintosh*; *waterproof* **~membran** f *r.-diaphragm* **~pedal** n *r.-pedal* **~pfropfen** m *r.-stopper* **~regenerierung** f *regeneration of used rubber* **~reifen** m *tyre*; (bes ⟨Am⟩) *tire* **~riemen** m *r.-belt* **~ring** m *r.-ring*; ⟨tech⟩ *r. gasket, r. washer* **~schlauch** m *r.-hose*, ⟨mot, cycl⟩ *inner tube* **~schuhe** m pl *galoshes, goloshes* pl; ⟨Am⟩ *r.s* pl; ⟨sl⟩ *gums* ‖ hohe ~ *r.-boots* pl **~stempel** m *r.-stamp* **~stoff** m *r.-cloth*; *waterproof cloth* **~strumpf** m ⟨med⟩ *r.-stocking* **~waren** pl *r.-goods* ~fabrik [f] *india-r. works* pl **~wasser** n *gum-water* **~werke** pl *india-r. works* pl **~zelle** f *padded cell* (od *room*) **~zug** m (an Stiefeln) *elastic*(*-side*); mit ~ *elastic*(*ated*) (*stocking*) **gumm·ieren** vt [h] *to gum*; *to rubber*; gummiert *rubberized, gummed*; *adhesive* (*envelope*) **Gumm·osis** f = Gummifluß

G·umpe f ~/~n (Rühr≗) ⟨tech⟩ *dolly*

G·undelrebe f, **G·undermann** m ⟨bot⟩ *ground-ivy*; *Glecoma* L **G·ünsel** m ~s/ ⟨bot⟩ *bugle*

G·unst f ~/ **A. 1.** *favo*(*u*)*r, goodwill*; *grace*; **2.** *partiality*; *favo*(*u*)*r* ‖ nach ~ (*to treat*) *with partiality*; (*to be appointed*) *by f.itism* (od *f.*) **3.** = Erlaubnis **4.** *f.able* (od *suitable*) *condition*; *f.ableness* (*of the weather, the moment*) **B. 1.** jdm e–e ~ **erweisen** *to do* od *show a p a f.*; → gewähren ‖ jds ~ gewinnen, erlangen *to win a p's f.* ‖ die ~ verloren h *to be out of f.* **2. in jds** ~ bleiben *to keep in with a p* ‖ in jds ~ (*or* in ~en bei jdm) stehen *to be in a p's good graces* (od *books*); in jds besonderer ~ st. *to be high in a p's f., to be the* (od *a great*) *f.ite of* (od *with*) *a p* ‖ sich in jds ~ setzen *to ingratiate o.s. with a p* | **mit** ~ *by* od *with your permission*; *by your leave* | alles geht dort **nach** ~ *f.itism is rampant there* | sich **um** jds ~ bemühen, um jds ~ buhlen *to court a p's f.*; *to curry f. with a p* | **zu jds~en** *in a p's f.*; *to a p's credit*; ein Saldo v .. z Ihren ~en *a balance of .. in your f.* (od *to your credit*) ‖ z ~en Frankreichs handeln *to play the French game* ‖ ⟨sport⟩ der nächste Lauf fiel aus z ~en Schwedens *the next heat went to Sweden* **~bezeigung,** –bezeugung f *mark of f.*; *kindness*; *kindly act* **g·ünstig A.** [a] [attr] (of actions, things) *favo*(*u*)*rable* (*answer,* *terms*) ‖ *convenient* (*time*); *fair* (*weather, wind*); *propitious* (*moment*); *auspicious* (*beginning*) | ~e Beleuchtung *good light*; ~e Gelegenheit *opportunity*; *facility* (f *for*); *low* (*costs*); in ~em Lichte *in a f.able* (od *good*) *light*; in ~stem Falle *at* (*the*) *best*; unter ~en V. *under f.able circumstances* **2.** [pred] (S) jdm ~ s (of the weather) *to be f.able to a p* ‖ e–r S ~ s *to f. a th* ‖ ~ s f etw *to be f.able for a th*; *to be propitious for* (od *to*) *a th*; *to f. a th*; *to make for a th* **B.** [adv] *f.ably* ‖ ~ abschneiden (vi) *to come off well* ‖ sich ~ aussprechen über .. *to speak well of ..* ‖ e–r S ~ gegenüberstehen *to f. a th* ‖ jdm ~ gesinnt sein *to be well-disposed to a p* ‖ jdn ~ stimmen *to influence a p f.ably*; *to propitiate a p* **G·ünstling** m ~s/~e *favo(u)rite* ‖ ⟨dero⟩ *minion* (*of a king*) ‖ ⟨pol⟩ *follower*; ⟨Am⟩ *henchman* **~swesen** n, **~swirtschaft** f *favo(u)ritism*

G·unterskala f †⟨mar⟩ *gunter*; *Gunter's scale*

Gur f ⟨minr⟩ *guhr* [Ger]; → Kiesel≃

G·urgel f ~/~n ⟨anat⟩ *throat*; *gullet* ‖ jdm an (*or* bei) der ~ packen *to take a p by the th.*; jdm an die ~ springen *to fly at a p's th.* ‖ jdm die ~ zuschnüren *to strangle a p*; die ~ netzen *to moist one's clay* ‖ → Hals, Kehle **g·urgeln A.** vi [h] **1.** (P, ⟨übtr⟩ of a brook) *to gurgle* **2.** ⟨med⟩ *to gargle* **B.** ≃ n **1.** *gurgle*; *gurgling sound* **2.** *gargling* **G·urgelwasser** n *gargle*; *throat-wash* ‖ °(Trunk) *gargle*

G·urke f ~/~n **1.** ⟨bot⟩ *cucumber*; eingelegte ~n *preserved cucumbers* pl; sauere ~, Salz≃ *pickled cucumber, salted c.* ‖ kl ~ (z Einlegen in Essig) *gherkin* **2.** °⟨fig⟩ **a.** (Nase) ⟨sl⟩ *boko, conk* ‖ (Branntwein≃) *bottle-nose* **b.** e–e ulkige ~ *a queer bird* (od *customer*) **G·urken- ~baum** m ⟨bot⟩ *c.-tree* **~beet** n *c.-bed* **~hobel** m *c.-slicer* **~kraut** n ⟨bot⟩ *borage* ‖ *dill* **~salat** m *c. salad* ‖ °was versteht der Bauer v ~ *a country bumpkin is a country bumpkin* **~zeit** f °⟨fig⟩ die saure ~ *the dead* (od *dull, silly*) *season*

g·urren 1. vi [h] (of doves, ⟨übtr⟩ infants) *to coo* **2.** ≃ n *coo*; *cooing*

G·urt m ~(e)s/–e (Leder≃) **a.** (Leib≃) *belt, girdle* ‖ ⟨mil⟩ (f Waffen) *b.*; Anschnall≃ ⟨mar, aero⟩ *safety-b.*; Patronen≃ *cartridge-b.*; MG-Patronen≃ *feed b.* ‖ Trag≃ *strap*; → Riemen ‖ mit e–m ~ befestigen, umgeben *to gird, girdle*; *belt* **b.** Sattel≃ *girth*; die ~e anziehen *to tighten the g.s* **~band** n *g.-web*; *webbing* **~bogen** m ⟨arch⟩ *wall arch* **~förderer** m *b.-conveyer* **~riemen** m *g.-strap* **~sims** m ⟨arch⟩ *fascia* L **~trommel** f *b. drum* **~zeug** n *b.ing*; (Fallschirm≃) *harness* **~zuführung** f (*c.-*)*b. feed* **G·ürtel** m ~s/~ **1.** *belt, waist-b.*; *waist-band*; *girdle* ‖ den ~ enger m *to tighten one's b.*; unter den ~ boxen *to hit below the b.* **2.** ⟨übtr⟩ (Streifen) *b.* (*of gardens*); (Erd≃) *zone*; Tropen≃ *tropic* (od *torrid*) *z.*; Festungs≃ *b. of fortifications* ‖ mit e–m ~ umgeben *to b.*; *to z.*; → gürten; Verkehrs≃ *b.* **~bahn** f = Ring– **~flechte** f = –rose **~kraut** n ⟨bot⟩ *club-moss* **~panzer** m ⟨mar⟩ *b.-armour* **~rose** f ⟨med⟩ *shingles* pl **~schnalle** f *b.-buckle* **~straße** f *transversal route* **~tier** n ⟨zoo⟩ *armadillo, dasypod*; ausgestorbenes Riesen≃ *glyptodon* **g·urten 1.** vi [h] ⟨mil⟩ *to load* (od *charge, pack*) *the b.* **2.** ≃ n *the filling* (*of the b.*) **g·ürten** vt [h] **1.** (jds Leib; jdn; ein Kleid) *to gird*; → umgürten ‖ ⟨poet⟩ die Lenden ~ = sich ~ ‖ (Pferd) *to girth* **2.** ⟨poet⟩ **sich ~ zu tun** *to gird o.s., to gird one's loins to do*; *to buckle to do* ‖ sich mit dem Schwert ~ *to buckle* od *gird* (*on*) *one's sword*

G·ürtler m ~s/~ = Gelbgießer

°**G·usche** f ~/~n *chops* pl; → Fresse, Schnauze

G·uß m G·usses/G·üsse **A.** [abstr] (Gießen) *casting* (*of metal*; *of a bell*), *founding*; durch ~ formen *to found* ‖ aus e–m ~ *homogeneous, uniform*; ⟨fig⟩ *accomplished, perfect*; *highly finished* **B.** [konkr] (Gegossenes) **1.** ⟨tech⟩ **a.** *cast, casting*; *pour* ‖ blasiger ~ *honeycombed casting* **b.** ⟨typ⟩ (Schrift≃) *fount* **2. a.** (of water) *gush*; *jet* ‖ (of rain) *downpour, pour*; *shower* **b.** ⟨cul⟩ *icing*; Zucker≃ *sugar icing* (dazu: *to ice*) **~abdruck** m *cast* **~asphalt** m *melted asphalt* **~blase** f ⟨met⟩ *blow-hole*; *flaw* **~block** m *ingot* **~eisen** n *cast iron* **≃eisern** a *c.-iron* (*fence, pipe*) **~fehler** m *pouring defect*; *flaw in the casting* **~form** f (*c.ing*) *mould*; *c.* **~loch** n *gate, gutter*; ⟨hist-fort⟩ *murder-hole* **~mauerwerk** n *rubble-work* **~messing** m *c. brass* **~modell** n *c.g pattern* **~naht** f *fin* **~regen** m *sudden shower of rain* **~stahl** m *c. steel* **~stein** m *drain, sink* **~stück** n *c.ing*; *c. work* **~waren** f [pl] *c.ings* pl; *foundry goods* pl **~zapfen** m ⟨typ⟩ *jet* **~zwieback** m *iced biscuit*

G·usto m It ~s/~s *taste*; nach s–m ~ *to his t.*

gut 1. [a] [compr: besser; sup: best] **A.** (S) **1. a. (haltbar; nützlich)** *good* (*cloth*; *knife*; *pen*); *serviceable, useful*; (*the coat is still*) *wearable*; (*the cake will soon be*) *ready* ‖ (ertragreich) *fertile, g.* (*year*); *rich* (*soil*) **b. (kräftig)** *g.* (*lungs*; *blow*); *sound*; *strong* (*voice*); bei ~er Gesundheit *in g. health*; nicht sonderlich ~ *indifferent* ‖ *g., substantial* (*meal*); *able* (*leadership*); *g.* (*memory*); *happy* (*idea*) **c. (rechtsgültig; zuverlässig)** *good* (*money*); *reliable* (*source*) **d. (frisch, bekömmlich)** *good* (*egg, meat*); *fresh* **2. a. (günstig, angenehm)** *good* (*weather, wind*; *end, news, opportunity*; *sign*); *agreeable*; *fair, fine, pleasant* ‖ ⟨com⟩ ~er Absatz *ready sale* ‖ ~e Besserung! *a speedy recovery*! ‖ ~er Eindruck *g. impression* ‖ e–n ~en Verlauf nehmen *to come off* (od *turn out*) *well* ‖ *in good circumstances* ‖ ein ~er Witz *a g. joke*; *a g.'un* ‖ wozu soll das ~ s? *what is the good of it*? **b. (befriedigend)** *good* (*wages*; *position*) ‖ ~e Geschäfte m *to do g. business* ‖ *good* (od *correct, idiomatic, standard*) *English*; kein ~es E. *not English* **c. (geneigt, freundlich)** *fair*; *friendly* (*relations*), *g.* (*humour*), *kind* (*act*) ‖ mit ~em Willen *with g.will* ‖ ~e Magie *white magic* **3. (reichlich)** *a g. mile*; *a g. hour*, *fully* (od *quite*) *an hour*; ~ 8 Tage *fully a week*; das hat noch e–e ~e Weile Zeit *there's plenty of time for that* ‖ ein ~es Stück *a g. deal* (*of this success*); ein ~es St. Geld *a pretty penny*; ‖ ein ~er (*or* ~) Teil der Schuld lag an ihm *it was mostly his fault, he was mostly to blame for it* **4. (auserlesen, wertvoll) a.** ~er Anzug *Sunday's best, Sunday clothes* ‖ ins ~e (Heft) schreiben *to write out in fair copy* ‖ ~e Stube *parlour*; *drawing-room* ‖ ein ~er Tropfen *a g. wine* **b. (gehaltvoll)** *good* (*book, literature*; *sermon*); *sterling* (*quality*) **5. (sittlich ~) a.** *good* (*example*); ~e Manieren, ~er Ton *g. manners* ‖ ~e Sitten *g. standards of morality*; *decency, propriety* ‖ ein ~er Geist *a spirit of g. fellowship* **b.** ein ~es Leben führen *to lead a g. life* ‖ ~e Werke *g. works* ‖ e–e ~e S *a g. cause* ‖ ein ~es Gewissen *a g. conscience* **B. (P) 1. a. (tüchtig)** *good* (*tailor*; *lawyer*; *artist*); *competent, efficient* (*worker*); er war ein ganz *or* recht ~er Soldat *he was a soldier all right*; nicht sonderlich ~ *indifferent* (*player*) ‖ *bright, clever* ‖ (überzeugt) ein ~er Deutscher *a g. G.* **b. (angesehen)** *good*; *respectable*; aus ~er Familie s *to be of a g. family*; aus ~em alten Haus stammen *to spring from an ancient house* **2. a. (geneigt)** *good, friendly*; *kind* (*master*); *kind-hearted*; (Anrede) ~er Herr *my dear Sir* ‖ °[verblaßt] der ~e Mann *that g. man* ‖ e–es ~en Tages *one day* **b. (ergeben)** *good* (*comrade, friend*); °ein ~er Kerl, °e–e ~e Haut *a jolly g. fellow*; ⟨fam⟩ *a regular brick* **3. (sittlich ~)** *good* (*father, husband*; *king*); *conscientious, dutiful* **C. Wendungen 1. a.** ~e **Absichten** h *to be well-meaning* ‖ ~e Aufnahme finden *to have a g. press* ‖ sein ~es Auskommen h *to be well off* ‖ ~e Aussichten h *to be in a fair way* (*to succeed*); *to be in the running* (*for ..*) ‖ fröhlich u ~er **Dinge** s *to be in g.*

humour (od *in high spirits*) || auf ~em **Fuße** stehen mit *to be on g.* (od *friendly*) *terms with* (*a p*) || es kostet mich mein ~es **Geld** *I must pay dearly for it* || ~en Glaubens (*or* in ~em Glauben) *in g. faith*; in ~em Gl. handeln *to act in g. f.* (od *bona fide* L) || → Glück || es ist kein ~es **Haar** an ihm ⟨sl⟩ *he is a bad egg* || °kein ~es Haar an jdm l *to pick* od *pull a p to pieces* || ~er Hoffnung s → schwanger || ~en Muts, ~er **Laune** s *to be of good cheer* || **Mann** → Gott B. 2. e. || ~e Miene zu bösem Spiel m *to grin and bear it*; *to make the best of a bad job* || ~e Nachbarschaft halten *to be neighbourly* || alles v der ~en **Seite** sehen *to look on the bright* (od *sunny*) *side of things* || das hat s–n ~en Sinn *there is g. reason for it* || gegen die ~en Sitten verstoßen *to offend against the proprieties* od *against accepted moral standards* || sich e–n ~en **Tag** m, ~e Tage verleben *to have a g. time of it*; → b. || das hat noch ~e **Wege** (*or* Weile) *that is still a long way off* || ⟨prov⟩ ein ~es Wort findet e–n ~en Ort *a g. word never comes amiss* (od *is never misplaced*) || jdm ~e Worte geben *to give g. words to a p* || **zu ~er Letzt** *in conclusion*; *finally, lastly*; *as a g. finish* **b.** (in **Begrüßungen**) ≗en Tag! *How do you do*? *How are you*? *Good morning*! *Good afternoon*! *Good evening*! || *Good night*! **2. [pred] ~ sein**: (S) ganz ~ s *to be not bad*; *to be well enough*; ⟨fam⟩ *to be not so dusty* || ~ s f jdn *to be g. for a p*; *to do a p g.*; nicht ~ s f jdn *to do a p no g.* || ~ s gegen *to be g. for* (*headache*) || die Äpfel sind ~ zum Kochen .. *are good cookers* || wozu ist das ~? *what's comfortable here* || laß es ~ s *let it be enough*; *let it pass*; *that will do*; *never mind* || **so ~ s wie ..** *to be as g. as ..*; so ~ wie nur einer *with the best* || es ist so gut wie fertig *or* gewonnen (*it's*) *all over bar* (*the*) *shouting*; *the lawsuit is as g. as won*; so ~ wie getan *pretty well done*; es ist so ~ wie unmöglich *it is practically impossible* || Ende ~, Alles ~ *All's Well that Ends Well* (Shak) **|** (P) ~ **s in** *to be g.* (od *quick*; *a g. hand*) *at* (*languages*); ⟨sl⟩ *to be a whale* od *a nut* (⟨Am⟩ *shark*) *at* (*football*) || ~ **s mit jdm** *to be on friendly terms with a p*; sie sind sich wieder ~ *they are friends again* || jdm (*or* mit, z jdm; gegen jdn) ~ s *to be g.* (od *kind*) *to a p*; *to take kindly to a p*; *to like* od *love a p* || jdm nicht ~ genug s *not to be up to a p's standard* || sie ist doch so ~ ⟨iron⟩ *she's goody-goody* || z ~ s f *to be too g. for ..* || es ist z ~ um wahr z s *it's too good by half* || **sei so ~**! *there's a dear*! || sei so ~ u schreib ihm (*or* ihm z schreiben) *be so g. as to write him, be g. enough* (od *have the kindness*) *to write him*; *please, write him* **| es ist ~**! *all right*! || ⟨iron⟩ das ist ja ~ *that's very g.* || es ist alles **ganz schön u ~**, aber .. *it's all very well* (od [*well and*] *good*; *fine*) *but ..* || es ist (ganz) ~, daß .. *it is all to the g. that ..* || es war auch ~, daß .. *it was as well that ..* || es ist schon ~ *it is all right, Sir*; *never mind*; *that'll do* || **schon ~, aber** .. *quite right but ..* || es wird ~ s **z tun** *it will be well to do*; es ist nicht ~, daran z rühren *let sleeping dogs lie* **| mir ist nicht ~** *I don't feel well* (od *up to the mark*) **| es ~ h** *to be well off*; *to have a g. time* || der hat's ~! ⟨Am fam⟩ *pretty soft for him*! || es f ~ halten *to think fit* (od *g., proper*) (*to do*) **| ~ aussehen** *to look g.* (od *smart*) || ~ riechen, schmecken *to smell, to taste g.* || ~ **werden** (S) *to be to the g., to turn out well*; es wird schon ~ w *it will turn out all right*; °das kann ja ~ w *that's a nice beginning* || ich weiß es noch so ~! *I remember it so well*! **|** im Zeichnen **hat er ≗ bek** *in drawing he gained a g. mark* **| ~! ~ so**! ~, **der Mann**! *good!, well done*!; *all right*! ⟨sl⟩ *righto*!; *good show*!, ⟨Am⟩ *nice going*; nun ~ (denn) ⟨sl⟩ *okay*! *O. K.*! **II. [adv] A. [bei Verben] 1.** *well*; ⟨Am a.⟩ *good* || recht ~ *all right*; *well enough* || er schreibt ~ *he writes a g. hand* || etw ~ können *to do a th well*; *to have the knack of a th*; ~ lernen *to learn easily* || mach d–e S ~ *do your job thoroughly* **|** das Schiff fährt ~ .. *is a g. sailer* || er schläft ~ *he is a g. sleeper* || die Äpfel kochen sich ~ .. *are good cookers* || das Instrument spielt sich ~ *the i. plays well* || jdm ~ bek (of food) *to agree with a p*; laß es dir ~ b. *I hope you'll enjoy it* **2. so ~ wie** *as well as*; → sowohl || so ~ ich konnte (kann) *for all I was* (*am*) *worth* || ebenso ~, geradeso ~ *just as well*; wir können ebenso ~ gleich fahren *we may as well start at once* || er hat so ~ wie abgelehnt *he has as g. as declined* **3. a. das fängt ja ~ an** *that's a nice beginning* || da kam er ~ an *he met with a snub* || das ging nochmal ~ aus *that turned out luckily once more* || **es geht mir ~** *I am doing well*; *things are going well with me* || wenn's ~ geht *with luck* || es sich zu ~ gehen l *to do o.s. too well* || alles steht ~ mit .. *all is well with ..* || sich ~ stehen mit *to stand fair* (od *well*) *with*; *to be on friendly terms with ..* || sich ~ stellen mit *to put o.s. right with* (*a p*) || **das trifft sich ~**! *well met*! || das kannst du ~ **tun** *you can do that without risk* **b.** du hast es ihm ~ **gegeben** *you gave him the right answer* || es ~ meinen mit jdm *to mean a p well*; die Sonne meint es ~ *the sun is rather hot* || **du hast ~ lachen**, reden *it is easy* (od *all right*) *for you to laugh, to talk* || hier ist ~ wohnen, hier wohnt sich's ~ *it's pleasant to live here* || er **täte ~ daran**, sofort z reisen *he would be wise* [od *well advised*] (*it would be well for him*) *to start at once*; er hat ~ daran getan .. *he has done well* (*to apply to ..*); **das mag ihm** nur ~ tun *that mightn't be a bad th for him* **c. ~ u gern** *at least*; ~ u g. drei Meter *fully 3 metres* || **kz u ~** *in short* **d. für ~** (= f immer behalten, schenken) ⟨fam⟩ *for g.*, ⟨sl⟩ *for keeps* **B. 1. [vor Adj.]** ~ angeschrieben s bei *to be in a p's g. books* || ein ~ bürgerliches Haus *a g.(-class) family hotel*; ~ bürgerliche Küche *g. plain cooking* || auf ~ deutsch *in plain German*; ~ deutsch mit jdm reden *to give a p a piece of one's mind* || ~ gebaut *well-set* (*p*) || ~ haltbar s *to keep well* || ~ kirchlich gesinnt *devoted to the church*; ⟨fam⟩ *churchy* || ~ d(a)ran s = es ~ h → I. C. 2. b. **2.** ~ 3 Meilen v *3 g. miles from* (*here*); ~ 3 Meter *fully 3 metres*, → II. A. c.

G·ut n ~(e)s/≗er **A.** ⟨scient & philos⟩ [abstr] **1.** *good*; ein kostbares ~ *a precious g.*; *a treasure* || das höchste ~ *the supreme g.* || ideelle ≗er *ideal g.s*; irdische ≗er *worldly g.s* pl || → Gute; zugute **2.** ⟨übtr⟩ *store*; *treasure* (of songs) || Kulturgüter *cultural g.s* pl **B.** [konkr] (S) **1.** (jds Habe) **a.** *belongings, g.s* pl; *property*; Geld u ~, Hab u ~ *g.s and chattels* pl; *bag and baggage* || bewegliche (liegende) ≗er *movable* (*real*) *property*; ~ u Blut *life and property*; *everything* || nicht um alle ≗er der Welt *not for the world* || ⟨prov⟩ unrecht ~ gedeihet nicht *ill-gotten gains never prosper* **b.** *endowments* pl (*of an institution*) **2.** ⟨com, scient⟩ **a.** ≗er *g.s*; Genuß≗er, Konsum≗er, ≗er erster Ordnung *consumption-g.s* pl, *g.s of the first order* **b.** Handels≗ *commodity*; [mst pl] ≗er *commodities* pl, *g.s* pl; *merchandise*; irdenes ~ → Steingut || schwimmendes ~ *venture* **3.** ⟨rail⟩ ≗er *g.s*; ⟨Am⟩ *freight*; → Eil≗, Expreß≗, Fracht≗, Stück≗ **4.** ⟨mar⟩ *gear* (*and tackle*); laufendes, stehendes ~ *running, standing gear* || (bei Gefahr) über Bord geworfene ≗er *jetsam*; das Ü.b.w.n der ≗er *jettison* || treibendes ~ *flotsam* **5.** ⟨tech⟩ *material, stuff* **C.** (Land≗) *estate*; *country-seat* || Bauern≗ *farm*; selbst bewirtschaftetes ~ *home-farm* || auf dem ~e des Fürsten N. *at Prince N's*; er lebt auf s–n ≗ern .. *on his estates* **g·ut-≗achten** n (*expert*) *judgement* (od *evidence, testimonial, opinion*) (über *on*); *expert o.*; *expertise*; medizinisches ~ *medical* od *advisory opinion*; Rechts≗ (durch Anwalt) *counsel's o.* || ein ~ einfordern *to take expert o.*; ein zweites ~ einholen ⟨med⟩ *to get another o.* ≃**achter** m *expert*; ⟨Am a.⟩ *sharp* ‖ ~fähigkeit, ~tätigkeit [f] *expertise* **~achtlich 1.** [a] *expert* (*o.*) **2.** [adv] sich ~ äußern *to give an expert o.* (*on* ..) **~artig** a *good-tempered, harmless, inoffensive* (*animal*) ‖ ⟨med⟩ *benign* (*tumour*); ~ verlaufen (of disease) *to be benign* ≃**artigkeit** f *harmlessness* ≃**dünken** n *discretion*; mst: nach ~ *at d.*; *as one sees proper*; nach ~ handeln *to use one's own d.*; es ist Ihrem ~ überlassen *it is within your d.*; *it is left to your judgement*; er konnte nach ~ verfahren mit .. *he could dispose of it as he pleased*; *he had it all his own way with it* ≃**edel** m (Traubensorte) *chasselas* Fr **~erhalten** a *well-preserved* **~gearted** a = –mütig **~gebaut** a *well-made* **~gehend** a ⟨fig⟩ *prospering, flourishing, thriving* (*business*) **~gelaunt** a *good-humoured* **~gemeint** a *well-meant* **~gesinnt** a *of a good disposition*; *well-intentioned*; jdm ~ s *to be well-disposed to a p* ≃**gewicht** n *allowance*; *tret* **~gläubig** a *credulous*; *gullible*; *bona fide* L (*owner, purchase*) | adv *in* (*all*) *good faith* ≃**gläubigkeit** f *credulity* **~|haben** vt [h] (etw) *to have to one's credit* ‖ ich habe noch 5 Mark ~ *I have still 5 marks to my credit* (bei .. *with you*) ≃**haben** n (ausreichend *sufficient*) *balance* (*in one's favour*); sein ~ war 50 M. *his b. stood at 50 marks* ‖ kein ~ *no funds* **~|heißen** vt [h] (etw) *to approve, to approve of*; *to countenance*; *sanction*; *applaud*; ⟨Am a.⟩ *to stand for*; nicht ~ *to disapprove of, to frown upon*; *to take a dim view of*; (endgültig) *to turn thumbs down on* **~herzig** a *good* (od *kind*) ≃**leuthaus** n *almshouse*, ⟨Am⟩ *poorhouse* **~|machen** vt [h] etw ~, wieder ~ *to compensate* (od *to make up* od *amends*) *for a th*; *to make a th good*; (Fehler) *to repair*; *to redeem* (*errors*); (Unrecht) *to right, undo* ‖ ⟨hort⟩ → veredeln **~mütig** a *genial*; *good* (od *kindly*)*-natured*; → gütig ≃**mütigkeit** f *good nature*; *bonhomie* Fr, *geniality, kindness* **~|sagen** vi [h] ~ f etw *or* jdn *to answer* (od *vouch*; *be surety*) *for a th* od *a p*; → bürgen ≃**schein** *gift coupon*; ⟨com⟩ *c.* Fr; *credit-note* (f *for*); *voucher*; ⟨Am a.⟩ *trading stamp* | ~-system [n] *stamp program* **~|schreiben** vt [h] jdm e–n Betrag ~ *to enter* (od *place, put, pass*) *a sum to a p's credit*; *to credit a sum to a p* (od *a p's account*); *to c. a p with* (od *for*) *a sum* ‖ jdm die Waren ~ *to trust a p for the goods* ≃**schrift** f *credit-entry* (od *item*); *allowance, discount* | ~anzeige [f] *c. advice* **~|tun** vi [h] **1.** (of children, etc.) *to obey, to be obedient*; *to toe the line*; er tut nicht gut *he is a good-for-nothing* **2. a.** das tut gut *that is soothing*; etw Ruhe tut gut ⟨Am⟩ *a rest comes good* **b.** dies tut nicht gut *this comes to no g.* **c.** jdm ~ *to do a p g.*; die Pillen taten mir sehr gut *the pills did me a lot of g.* ‖ es tut e–m gut *it does one's heart g.* (*to see*); es tut mir in der Seele ~ *it warms the cockles of my heart* (*to see* ..) **~unterrichtet** a *well-informed* (*circles*) **~willig 1.** a *affable, complaisant, obliging* (*man*); *willing* **2.** adv *willingly*; *peacefully* ‖ → bereit–, freiwillig ≃**willigkeit** f *complaisance*; *willingness* **G·ütchen** n *small estate*; → gütlich tun **G·ute**: **A.** [der ~, ein ~r] *the good man* ‖ (Anrede) mein ~r *my g. man* ‖ die ~ *the g. woman* ‖ die ~n [pl] *the g.*; *the righteous*; ~e u Böse *g. and bad*; *sheep and goats* **B.** ~s [das ~, ein ~s] **1.** *good*; *g. thing*; *what is g.* ‖ ich habe v ihm nur ~s empfangen *I have had nothing but g. at his hands*; man hat mir so viel ~es v ihm erzählt *I heard* od *had such g. reports of him* ‖ an das ~ glauben *to believe in what is g.* ‖ alles ~ *everything g.*; alles denkbar ~ *all the g. in the world* ‖ etw ~s *something g.*; etwas ~s ist doch daran *there's something in that* ‖ nichts ~s *no g.* ‖ ~s tun *to do g.* (*to a p*; *with*) **2.** °**das** ~ an der Geschichte **ist** .. *the fun of it* (od *the best of the joke*) *is* .. ‖ das **bedeutet** nichts ~s (f ihn) *this bodes* (*him*) *no g.* ‖ °was bringst du ~s? *what's the latest news*? ‖ das ~ empfiehlt sich selbst *a g. wine needs no bush* ‖ die S hat auch ihr ~s *there is also a bright side to the question* ‖ ~s mit Bösem vergelten *to return g. for evil* ‖ jdm ~s wünschen *to wish a p well* (od *well to a p*) ‖ das ist **des ~n z viel** *that's too much of a good thing* ‖ des ~n z viel tun *to overshoot* (od *overstep*) *the mark*; *to overshoot o.s.*; *to overdo it* ‖ **im** ≃**n, in ~m** *amicably*; *gently*; *in a friendly manner* (od *spirit, tone*); *on frinedly terms* ‖ im ≃n vorangehen *to give a good example* ‖ im ~n wie im Schlimmen zus–stehen *to stand by one another through thick and thin* | e–e Kraft **zum ~n** *a power for the g.* ‖ zum ~n ausschlagen *to be to the g.* ‖ z nichts ~m führen *to come to no g.* ‖ (etw) zum ~n lenken *to direct for the best* ‖ zum ~n raten *to advise for the best* ‖ sich zum ~n wenden *to take a turn for the better* **G·üte** f ~/ **1.** (**P**) *benignity, goodness, good nature*; *kindliness, kindness* ‖ die ~ Gottes *the grace of God* | er ist die ~ selbst *he is the pattern of g.ness* ‖ jds ~ ausnützen *to take advantage of a p's g. n.* ‖ wenn Sie die ~ h wollen, z .. *if you will be so kind as to* ..; *would you have the kindness to* .. ‖ durch die ≃ v *by favour of* .. **2.** ⟨übtr⟩ (gütliche Regelung) den Weg der ~ beschreiten *to settle a matter amicably* ‖ durch ~ *by fair means* ‖ in ~ *amicably*; *in a friendly way*; in ~ geht alles *everything can be settled amicably*; mit jdm in ~ fertig w *to keep on the right side of a p* ‖ ein Vorschlag zur ~ *a conciliatory proposal* **3.** (**S**) **a.** *g.ness* **b.** *quality*; *excellence* ‖ die ~ [+ gen] zeigt sich bei .. *the proof of the pudding, apple is in the eating* ‖ erster, zweiter ~ *first, second class*; v ausgezeichneter ~ *of first-class quality*; *excellent, superior* ‖ mittlere ~ *average quality level* (*AQL*) ‖ °e–e Dummheit erster ~ *a folly of the first magnitude* ‖ °⟨rail⟩ erster ~ fahren *to travel first class* **4.** (im Ausruf) °(ach, o) du m–e ~! *good heavens*! *good*(*ness*) *gracious*! *gracious me*! *bless my soul*! *oh my*! ⟨vulg⟩ *Lor'-a-mussy* (f: *Lord have mercy*), *my eye*(*s*)! **~antrag** m *petition for amicable settlement* **~grad** m, **~klasse** f *grade* **~kontrolle** f, **~prüfung** f *quality control* od *test* **~verfahren** n *amicable settlement* **~vorschrift** f *qu. specification* **~zeichen** n ⟨com⟩ *quality-mark*; *brand*

G·üter- *goods* ..; ⟨Am⟩ *freight* **~abfertigung** f ⟨rail⟩ (~stelle) *g.* (od *forwarding*) *department* od *office* **~annahme** f ⟨rail⟩ *receiving office* **~bahnhof** m *g. station*; ⟨Am⟩ *f.-depot* **~erzeuger** m *producer of g.*; *producer of wealth* **~expedition** f = –abfertigung **~fernverkehr** m ⟨mot⟩ *long-distance lorry-traffic* **~gemeinschaft** f eheliche ~ *matrimonial joint ownership of property* **~kraftverkehr** m *road haulage industry* **~makler** m *estate-agent*; *land-jobber* **~markt** m *commodity-market* **~recht** n *law of property*; eheliches ~ *legal p. relations of married parties*, (vertragl., ehel., gesetzlich *contractual, matrimonial, statutory*) *régime* Fr | ehel. ~sverzeichnis [n] *marriage p. register* °**~schlächter** m *land-jobber* **~schuppen** m ⟨rail⟩ *g. shed, warehouse* **~tarif** m *g. tariff*; ⟨Am⟩ *f.-t.* **~tausch** m *exchange of g.*; *traffic in g.* **~transport** m *g. traffic, transport of g.* **~trennung** f (in Ehe) *seperation of property*; *separate ownership of p.* **~umlauf** m *circulation of g.* **~verbrauch** m *consumption of g.* **~verkehr** m ⟨rail⟩ *g. traffic*; ⟨Am⟩ *f.-t.* **~verteilung** f *distribution of g.* **~wagen** m ⟨rail⟩ offener ~ *platform-car*, (*open*) *g.-truck* (od *wag*[*g*]*on*); ⟨Am⟩ *f.-car* ‖ gedeckter ~ (*covered*) *g. w.*; *g.-van*; ⟨Am⟩ *f.-car* **~zug** m ⟨rail⟩ *g.-train*; ⟨Am⟩ *f.-t.* ‖ ~verkehr [m] *g.-t. traffic* **g·ütig 1.** [a] *good, kind* (*father*; *heart*), *kindhearted* ‖ *gracious* (*God*); ~ gegen *good* od *kind to* ‖ *benevolent, benignant, charitable*; *gracious* (*God*) | ⟨übtr⟩ *kind* (*attention*; *fate*; *permission*); mit ~er Genehmigung v *by favour of* ‖ °~er Himmel! *good heavens*! **2.** [adv] ~, ~st *kindly*; erlauben Sie mir .. *will you kindly*

permit me ..; wie ~ v dir! ⟨iron⟩ *how good of you!*
G·ütler m *small landowner*; *farmer* **g·ütlich 1.** [a] *amicable* (*settlement*), *friendly*; auf dem Wege ~er Verständigung *a.ly*; *by fair means* **2.** [adv] *a.ly* || (etw) ~ beilegen *to settle a.ly* || sich ~ einigen *to come to an a.le arrangement* || sich ~ tun an .. *to do o.s. well on*; *to regale o.s. on* (od *with*); *to indulge in* (*a glass of wine*) **G·uts- ~beamter** m *estate-official* **~besitzer** m *landed proprietor*; *gentleman farmer*; *landowner* **~besitzerin** f *landed proprietress* **~haus** n *farmhouse* **~herr** m *lord of the manor* || *landlord* **~herrschaft** f ⟨Ger⟩ *manorial domain* **~́herrschaftlich** a *manorial* (*church*); *domanial* **~hof** m *farm-yard* **~pächter** m *tenant-farmer* **~verwalter** m *estate agent*; *bailiff* **~verwaltung** f *estate-administration* od *management*

G·utsche f ⟨sculp⟩ = Stecheisen

×**G·uts|chen** n pl, **G·utsel** n pl (*boiled*) *sweets*

Guttap·ercha f ~/ *gutta-percha* (⟨a. golf⟩ .. *-ball*)

G·uttemplerorden m *Independent Order of Good Templars*

guttur·al 1. [a] ⟨phon⟩ *guttural* (*sound*); *throaty* (*voice*) || ~ aussprechen *or* m *to gutturalize* **2.** ~́ m ⟨phon⟩ *guttural*; *guttural* (od *velar*) *sound* **Guttur·alis** m L, **Guttur·allaut** m = Guttural

Gw·alior n (vorderindische Provinz)

Gymnasi·al- ~bildung f *classical* od *humanistic education* **~direktor, ~lehrer, ~schüler** m ⟨Ger⟩ *headmaster, master, scholar of a 'gymnasium'*

Gymnasi·ast m ~en/~en = Gymnasialschüler

Gymn·asium n ~s/-sien **1.** ⟨Ger⟩ *high-class secondary school providing humanistic education*; *h.-sch.*, *gymnasium* || musisches ~ *g. providing musical training* **2.** ⟨engl⟩ *grammar-school*, ⟨Am⟩ *high school* **Gymn·astik** f ~/ **1.** ⟨eig⟩ *gymnastics* pl [pl konstr]; *physical drill*; ~ treiben *to do ph. d.*; Schwedische ~ *Swedish drill* od *exercises* pl ~apparat [m] *body exerciser* | ~schule [f] *school of g.s* **2.** ⟨übtr⟩ *gymnastic* **gymn·astisch** a *gymnastic*; ~e Übungen *physical drill*

Gymnosp·erme f ~/~n ⟨bot⟩ *gymnosperm*

Gynäko- [in comp] ⟨med⟩ **~l·oge** m ~n/~n *gynaecologist* **~l·ogisch** a *gynaecological*; ~er Kalender *pregnancy record* od *history*

Gynok·ardiaöl n *Chaulmugra oil*

Gyro- [in comp] **~r·ektor** m ~s/-t·oren ⟨aero⟩ *gyrorector* **~sk·op** n ~s/~e *gyroscope*

H

H, h [hɑː] n ~/~ **1.** *H, h* || mit ~ aussprechen *to aspirate* **2.** ⟨mus⟩ *B, b*; → A-Dur | H-Bombe [f] *hydrogen bomb*; H-Linie [f] ⟨tail⟩ *H-line*

Haag m; der ~ *the Hague* || im ~, in den ~ [dat] *in the H.* || ~er Abkommen [n] *Hague Convention*; ~er Fr. K. *Hague Peace Conference*

Haar n ~(e)s/~e **A. 1.** (P & T) **a.** (Einzel~́) *hair*; ein ~ ausreißen *to pull out a h.*; mehrere ~e *several hairs* pl **b.** [koll] das ~, die ~e [pl] *the hair*; man wird das ~ wieder lang tragen (*long*) *hair will come in again* || ⟨zoo⟩ *pelage*; mit gesträubtem ~ (of hounds) *with their hackles up*; lockiges ~ *curly h.*; langes offenes ~ (of women) *long tresses* pl || Kopf~́ *h. of the head* || kz u wolliges ~, Neger~́ *wool*; volles ~ *thick h.*; kz geschnittenes ~ (of women) *Eton crop* || was f ~(e) hat sie *what colour is her h.?* || sie hatte brünettes ~ *she had h. the colour of chestnuts* || graues ~, graue ~e [pl] *grey h.*; ⟨fig⟩ *grey hairs* pl || feines ~ *pile*; wirres ~ *mat*(*ted hair*) | Bogen~́ ⟨mus⟩ *bowhair* **2.** ⟨übtr⟩ *hair*; *filament*; ⟨bot⟩ ~e *hairs*; *trichomes* pl (*of a plant*) || (on velvet) *pile* **B. 1.** die ~e **brennen** *to curl the h.* || die ~e fallem ihm aus *he is losing his h.* || (jdn) an *or* bei den ~en fassen *to take by the h.* || die ~e hochstecken *to put one's h. up*; die ~e losmachen *to let* (od *put*) *one's h. down* || sich das ~ *or* die ~e m *to do one's h.* || jdm die ~e schneiden *to give a p a h.cut*; sich die ~e sch. l *to have one's h. cut*; *to have a h.cut* || die ~e verlieren *to lose one's h.* || s-e ~e (lang) wachsen l *to grow one's h.* (*long*) | kurze ~e sind bald gebürstet ⟨prov⟩ *a short horse is soon curried* **2.** ⟨fig⟩ → gut I. C. 1. || die ~e standen ihm **z Berge** *his h. stood on end*; jdm die ~e z Berge stehen l *to be h.-raising* (*a h.-r. trick*) | sich die ~e **ausraufen** *to tear one's h.*; ein ~ in etw **finden** *to find a h. in the soup*; ihr ~ fliegt *her h. is blowing* (*in the wind*); sie **frißt** mir die ~e vom Kopf *she eats my head off*; ihm wurde kein ~ **gekrümmt** *not a h. of his head was touched* (od *hurt*); er mußte ~e l *he got fleeced*; ~e l müssen *not to escape unscathed*; kein gutes ~ an jdm l *not to have a good word to say about a p*; er hat mehr **Schulden** als ~e auf dem Kopfe *he is up to the ears in debt*; darum brauchst du dir k-e grauen ~e **wachsen** z l *you need not bother* od *trouble about that*; er hat ~e auf den **Zähnen** *he has plenty of fight in him*; *he has plenty of pluck*; *he's a tough customer*; sie .. *she's a spit-fire, hell-cat* | es hängt **an** e-m ~ *it's touch-and-go* (ob *wether*, mit *with*); sein Leben hing **an** e-m ~ *his life hung by a thread* || (etw) an den ~en herbeiziehen *to drag in by the head and shoulders*; an den ~en herbeigezogen *far-fetched* | **aufs** ~, auf das ~ genau *to a h., nicety, fit, T*; *minutely*; *exactly*; *in detail*; → gleichen | sich **in** die ~e geraten, kriegen *to fall by the ears* || sich in den ~en liegen *or* bei den ~en h *to be at loggerheads* (mit *with*); *to wrangle* (über *over*); *to be quarrelling* | **mit** → Haut; mit schneeweißem ~ *snowy-h.ed* | **um ein** ~, ums ~ *by the fraction of an inch*; *by a shave*; *a trifle* (*wider*) || wir wären um ein ~ getötet *we were within an ace of being killed*; .. ertrunken *we had a hairbreadth escape from drowning* || (*that*) *just about* (*took our paint off*); (*she*) *pretty near* (*fainted*) || ums ~! *close th* od *shave!* **nicht um ein** ~ *not* (*by*) *a hair's breadth*, *by no hairbreadth*; *not an inch* (od *a whit*); **um kein** ~ *not a jot*; → ~esbreite **~́ähnlich** a *h.-like* **~ansatz** m *h.line* **~ausfall** m = -schwund **~balg** m ⟨anat⟩ *h.-follicle*; ~milbe [f] ⟨zoo⟩ *face mite* **~ballen** m ⟨vet⟩ *h.ball* **~band** n *fillet*; *ribbon* **~besen** m *h.-broom* **~beutel** m ⟨hist⟩ *bag* (od *tie*)-*wig* **~boden** m = Kopfhaut **~breit** n; nicht um ~e = um kein Haar **~bürste** f *h.brush* **~busch** m ⟨mil⟩ *horse-h. plume* **~büschel** m *tuft of h.* **~entfernungsmittel** n ⟨cosm⟩ *h.-remover, depilatory* **~ersatz** m *h. used in h.dressing* **~farbe** f *colour of h.* **~färbemittel** n *h.-dye* **~farn** m ⟨bot⟩ *maiden-h. fern* **~faser** f *filament* **~́fein** a *h.-fine*; *capillary*; *thin as a h.* || ⟨fig⟩ *fine*; *nice*; *subtle* **~festiger** m ⟨cosm⟩ *setting lotion* **~filz** m *h.-felt* **~flechte** f *braid* od *plait of h.* **~follikel** m = -balg **~́förmig** a *capillary* **~frisur** f *head-dress*; *coiffure* Fr; ⟨bes Am⟩ *h.do* **~garn** n *worsted thread*; *pile*; ~teppich [m] (*velvet*) *pile carpet* **~gefäß** n ⟨anat⟩ *capillary*(*-tube*) **~́genau** a = -scharf 2. **~gras** n ⟨bot⟩ *lyme-grass* **~holz** n *buckthorn wood* **~kamm** m *h.-comb*; (z Festhalten) *h.-slide* **~kl·ein** adv = auf's Haar **~kräftigungsmittel** n *h.-restorer* **~krankheit** f *disease of h.* **~krem** m *pomatum* L **~krone** f ⟨bot⟩ *pappus* L **~künstler** m *coiffeur* Fr **~locke** f *lock*; (gerollte) *curl* **~́los** a *hairless* **~mit-**

tel n *h.-restorer* **~moos** n ⟨bot⟩ *h.-moss*; *Golden Maidenhair* **~nadel** f *h.pin*; ~kurve [f] *h.p.* (*bend*) **~netz** n *h.-net*; flüssiges ~ *spray net, h. sp.* **~öl** n *h.-oil* **~pfeil** m *h.-slide* **~pflege** f *careful treatment of the h.* **~pinsel** m ⟨paint⟩ (*camel's*) *h. brush* **~pomade** f ⟨cosm⟩ *pomatum* L **~riß** m ⟨tech⟩ *micro-crack, h. c.* **~röhrchen** n *capillary*; ~wirkung *capillarity* **~salbe** f = –krem **~salz** n ⟨chem⟩ *h.-salt* **≃scharf 1.** [a] **a.** *extremely sharp*; *as sharp as a razor, razor--sharp* **b.** ⟨fig⟩ *clear-cut* (*lines*); *subtle* **2.** [adv] ⟨fig⟩ *precisely*; da heißt es ~ aufpassen *this requires the utmost attention*; ~ bezeichnen *to pinpoint*; sich [dat] ~ bewußt *acutely conscious* **~schleife** f *bow* (od *ribbon*) *for the h.* **~schmuck** m *h. ornament*; *head-dress* **~schneidemaschine** f *clippers* pl; e–e ~ *a pair of c.* **~schneiden** n *h.cutting* **~schneider** m *h.dresser*; beim ~ *at the h.dresser's* **~schneidesalon** m *h.dressing saloon* **~schnitt** m *h.cut*, ⟨fam⟩ *h.do* **~schopf** m *tuft* od *shock of h.*; ⟨bot⟩ *thitledown, etc* **~schuppen** pl *scurf* **~schwund** m *loss of h.*; ⟨med⟩ *alopecia* L **~seil** n *twist of horse-h.s*; ⟨surg⟩ *seton* **~sieb** n *h.-sieve* **~spalter** m ⟨fig⟩ *h.-splitter* **~spalter·ei** f ⟨fig⟩ *quibbling*; *h.-splitting*; ~ treiben *to split h.s* **~spange** f *slide*(*-fastener*); kl ~ *bobby pin, clip* Schmuck≃ *barrette* **~spatium** [ts] n ⟨typ⟩ *h.-space* **~stern** m **1.** ⟨zoo⟩ *crinoid* **2.** ⟨astr⟩ = Komet **~strang** m ⟨bot⟩ *sulphur wort* ‖ *dropwort* **≃sträubend 1.** [a] ⟨fig⟩ (abscheulich) *burning* (*shame*); *ghastly, monstrous, outrageous, rotten, scandalous*; *shocking* ‖ *egregious, gross, incredible* (*folly*) **2.** [adv] *outrageously* ‖ *incredibly* **~strich** m *h.-line* (od *stroke*), *upstroke*; ⟨typ⟩ *serif, ceriph* **~teil** n ⟨cosm⟩ (zur Frisur gekauft) *hairpiece* **~tracht** f *style of wearing one's h.*; *h.dressing* **~trockengerät** n *h.-dryer* **~tuch** n *h.-cloth* **~ver**[1] **lust** m = –schwund **~wasser** n *h.-lotion, h.-restorer* **~wickel** m *curl-paper* **~wild** n ⟨zoo⟩ *quadrupedal game* **~wuchs** m *growth of h.* **~wulst** m *h.-pad*; *bun* **~wurm** m ⟨zoo⟩ *h.-worm* (od *eel*) **~wurzel** f *root of the h.* **~wust** m *mop* **~zange** f *tweezers*, e–e ~ *a pair of t.* **~zirkel** m *h.-compasses*; ein ~ *a pair of h.-c.* **~zopf** m *braid of h.*; *pigtail*

Haardt f → Hardt

h·aaren vt/refl [h] ⟨tech⟩ (Fell) *to depilate*; = sich ~ (T) *to lose one's hair*; er haart sich *his hair is coming out* **H·aaresbreite** f *h.breadth* | um ~ *by the skin of one's teeth*; nicht um ~ *not* (*by*) *a h.b.*; auch nicht um ~ *not by so much as a h.'s b.* †**h·aaricht** a = **h·aarig A.** [a] **1.** *hairy, hirsute* ‖ ⟨bot & zoo⟩ *pilose, pilous* ‖ die ~e Seite (of cloth) *the nap*; *pile* ‖ (Anzug) ~ m (of dog) *to cover with hairs* **2.** °⟨fig fam⟩ *awful, beastly*; *curious*; *incredible*; das war e–e ~e Geschichte *that was an awful business* ‖ e–e ~e S (hübsches Mädchen) *a hairy bit*; ⟨sex⟩ *a bit of rough* **B.** [adv] °⟨fig⟩ *awfully, beastly* (*cold*); da ist es ~ zugegangen *there was a rough time of it* **C.** [in comp] *haired*; schwarz~ *blackhaired* | ≃**keit** f *hairiness*

H·aarlem, H·arlem n (holländ. Stadt) *Haarlem, Haerlem, Harlem*

Hab n (= Habe), [nur in:] ~ u Gut, → Gut

Hab·ana → Havanna

H·abe f ~/ jds ~ *a p's belongings, effects, goods* pl; *property*; bewegliche ~ *chattel*; (un)-bew. ~ (*im*)*movable property*; (*im*)*movables* pl

habeat sibi L *let him have his own way*

h·aben vt/aux [hatte/gehabt] [h] **I.** vt **A. 1.** (**besitzen**) **a.** *to have* ⟨a. sex⟩, *to have got*; *hold*; *possess*; *he has* (*got*) *a car, a house, child, many friends*; er hat nichts *he has* (*got*) *nothing*; ~ Sie ..? ⟨com⟩ *can I have ..?*; ich habe den Hut schon 3 Jahre *I've worn the hat* (*for* od *these*) *3 years* ‖ hat sie blaue Augen? *has she* (⟨Am⟩ *does she have*) *blue eyes*? ‖ die Gicht ~ *to have* (*got*) *the gout*; → Durst, Hunger | (als Eigenschaft ~) schlechte Laune ~ *to have a bad temper* ‖ *her eyes wore their old expression* ‖ → Achtung, etc, recht, unrecht ‖ er hat k–n guten Charakter *he has no good character*; ⟨Am⟩ *he does not have a g. ch.* **b.** (**S**) *to have*; die Stadt hat 10000 Einwohner *the town has* (*a population of*) *10000 inhabitants* ‖ *the room has 4 windows* ‖ *there are two roots to the plant*; *there are 60 minutes in an hour*; ein Dutzend hat 12 Stück *twelve go to the dozen* | ⟨tech⟩ *to be fitted with* **2.** (**bek.**) *to have, get*; ich habe es v m–r Tante *I have* (od *I got*) *it from*; ich habe es aus .., v .. *I have taken it from Goethe* ‖ sonst hatten Sie nichts? *you have had nothing else*? ‖ er hat viel v s–r Mutter *he has many traits of his m., he resembles his m. closely* ‖ woher hast du das? *where did you come by it* (od *pick it up*)? ‖ das hab ich noch nicht gehabt *that's something I have not yet learned* ‖ hattet ihr euer Frühstück um 8 Uhr? *did you have breakfast at 8*? **3. a. etw ~ wollen** *to want a th*; *to wish for a th*; er will alles ~, was (..) *he wants everything* (*he sees*); (wie ein Schwein) (alles) f sich ~ wollen ⟨Am⟩ *to hog .. for o.s.*; wenn er mich ~ will, (..) *if he wants me* (*he ..*) ‖ was will er dafür ~? *what does he want for it*? ‖ (Frage des Kellners) was wollen Sie dann ~? *what do you want to follow*? | [neg] °⟨fig⟩ ich will es **nicht** ~! *I won't have it*! ich will nicht ~, daß du .. sagst *I will not have you say such things*; ich möchte nicht ~, daß es erörtert wird *I would not have it discussed* ‖ ich möchte dich nicht gekränkt ~ *I did not wish to offend you* **4.** [mit Ergänzung] **a.** etw **bereit** ~ *to be ready with a th* ‖ sie hatte ihn ganz **nahe** bei sich *she had him quite near to her* ‖ kaum hatte ich den Koffer glücklich **oben,** so .. *scarcely had I succeeded in lifting the trunk when ..* ‖ Goethes Werke **vollständig** ~ *to have Goethe's works complete*; *to have a complete set of G.'s w.*; → vorrätig ‖ → fertig~, gern~, lieb-~, nötig~ **b.** Geld **auf der Bank** ~ *to have money at the bank*; → liegen ‖ (jdn) **zum Freunde** ~ *to have for a friend* **c.** °hast du die Suppe **auf**? *have you finished your soup*? ich habe das Buch **durch** *I have read the book through*; → an~, auf~ **d.** (**zu tun h**) ich hatte e–n Brief zu schreiben *I had to write a letter, I had a l. to w.*; ich habe viel z tun *I have much work to do* ‖ (in Verträgen etc) sie ~ z tun *they will do*; er hat sich z melden bei *he will report to ..* ‖ er hatte den Wagen dort den ganzen Tag stehen *he had the car standing there all day* ‖ °(×~ = hawwe) Sie ~ nich z ~, was Sie gehabt ~; Sie ~ z ~, was Sie z ~ ~! *never mind what you did, better mind what you should have done*! **e.** °er hat gut **lachen, reden** → gut II. A. 3. b. **5. zu ~ a.** es ist noch z ~ *it is still to be had*; *it is still for sale, still obtainable* ‖ bei allen Buchhändlern z ~ *to be had of all booksellers* ‖ ist Roastbeef noch z ~? *is roast beef still going* (od *on*)? **b.** (**P**) °sie ist noch z ~ *she is still open for an offer* ‖ wen glaubst du vor dir z ~? *whom do you think you are speaking to*? ‖ °er ist dafür z ~ *he will be ready to do it*; dafür bin ich nicht z ~ *nothing doing*! **B.** °**sich** [acc] ~ (P) *to get excited* (od *nervous*); °hab dich nur nicht *don't put on airs, don't make a fuss* | °**es hat sich** [dat] **was** *nothing doing*; *catch me* (*doing that*) **C. bes Wendungen 1.** seltsame **Ansichten** ~ *to hold strange views* ‖ ein Auge ~ auf jdn (bes Kind) *to keep an eye on a p* ‖ ⟨bes sex⟩ *to make up to a p*; *to make eyes at a p* ‖ hab **Dank** *thanks* ‖ °wir ~ nur noch 3 Minuten *we have only another 3 minutes* ‖ wir ~ noch e–n Monat bis O. *Easter is four weeks off* ‖ e–n **Piek** ~ auf jdn *to have a grudge against a p* ‖ e–n guten Ruf ~ *to bear a good character* (unter *among*) ‖ er hat die **Schuld** *the fault is his*; *it is his f.* ‖ → Wahl **2.** °da *or* jetzt hab ich dich! *I've got you there*! *now I have caught you*! ⟨fam⟩ *I've got your number now*! ‖ **Familie** ~ *to have a f.* ‖ nicht seinesgleichen ~ *to have no equal* ‖ jdn zum Narren, zum besten ~ → beste ‖

† Gott hab ihn selig! †*God rest his soul!* **3. a.** (Namen etc) °**am Schnürchen** ~ *to have at one's finger's ends* || → Gewissen, Hals || → Auge, Gewalt, Hand **b.** °e–e S **satt** ~ *to be tired* (od *sick*) *of a th*; *to be fed up with a p* || **zu eigen** ~ *to own, to posses* **4.** ⟨**fig**⟩ **a.** °er h·at **etwas** *there's something the matter with him*; was hat er nur? *what's the matter* (od *wrong*) *with him*? || °er hat etwas gegen dich *he bears you a grudge*; ⟨fam⟩ *he has a down on you* **b. an sich** [dat] ~; er hat etw Bescheidenes an sich *there is sth modest in him*; wie es Männer an sich ~ *as men go*; (..) *as men have a way of doing*; er hat e–e furchtbare Art an sich *he has a terrible way with him*; etw v e–m Genie .. *to be touched with genius*; sein Wesen hat etw v Unverschämtheit an sich *his manner partakes of impudence* | **bei sich** ~ *to carry* (*he carried no luggage*); ich hatte k–n Pfennig bei mir *I had not a penny about* (od *on, with*) *me* | er hatte viele Strapazen **hinter sich** *he had undergone many fatigues* | der Mann, den er gern **um sich** hatte, war .. *the man he liked to have about him was* .. | (etw) **unter sich** ~ *to be in* (od *to have*) *control of* (*a th*); *to control* (*a th*); *to command* (*a regiment*) **c.** was ~ wir **davon**? *what is the good of it*?; *what does it profit us*?; *what good would it do any of us*? || °das hat man nun davon *and all for nothing* || viel v etw ~ *to profit by a th*; *to derive great profit from a th* || → dagegen~, voraus~ **5.** °**das hat s–e Zeit** (*or* gute Weile) *there's plenty of time for that* || es hat s–e Richtigkeit *it is all right*; ⟨sl⟩ *it is okay* (od *O. K.*) || °das hat nichts **auf sich,** das hat nichts **z sagen** *that makes no difference*; *that does not matter* (od *is of no consequence* od *importance*) || °das hat etwas **f sich** *there's s.th in that*, ⟨fam⟩ *you've got s.th there* **6. es** ~ **a.** °**wir haben's ja** *we have money in plenty* || ja, hier hab ich's schon (was wir suchen) *yes, here we are* || °**da hast du's** (was du wünschst) *here you are* | ⟨fig⟩ (Ausruf) jetzt hab' ich's! *I've got it*! || °da hast du's! da ~ wir's (wieder)! was hab ich dir gesagt! *there*! *there you are*! *there now*! *so there*!, ⟨Am fam⟩ *there it goes again*! || °da hatte er's *so there it was* | °**wir ~'s** noch weit bis nach Hause *it's still a long way home* || °ich hab es am weitesten *I have the longest way home* | °was hat's denn f Not? *what's the trouble*? **b.** es gut ~ → gut I. C. 2. b. || es auf der **Brust** ~ *to have a cold on the chest* || sie wollte es nicht **Wort** ~ *she refused to own* (od *admit*) *it* || die Aufgabe **hat es in sich** *the problem teems with difficulties* **7.** °er ist **haste** (= hast du) **was kannste** davongelaufen *he ran hell for leather* **II. v/aux** [zur Bildung des Perfekts] **1.** ich habe ihn nicht gesehen *I have not seen him* || ich hörte, er hätte es gefunden *I heard he had found it* || ich habe ihm gestern geschrieben *I wrote* (*to*) *him yesterday* || °ich hatte es ganz vergessen gehabt *I had all forgotten about it* **2.** ich habe ihn singen hören *I've heard him sing* || ich h. ihn ausreden l *I've heard him out* || er hätte uns helfen können *he might have helped us* || wir hatten ihn sprechen müssen *we had had* (od *had been obliged*) *to see him* || wir hatten ihn sprechen wollen *we had wanted to see him*

H·aben n ⟨com⟩ *credit*; das Soll u ~ *the debit and credit*; → Aktiva, Gut≈, Saldo

H·abenichts m *have-not*; –se [pl] *havenots*

H·abenseite f ⟨com⟩ *credit-side, creditor*

H·abenzinsen pl *creditor interest rates* | –sabkommen [n] *Agreement on C. I. R.*

×**H·aber** m = Hafer

°**H·aberecht** ~s/~e m = Rechthaber

H·abgier f ~/ *avarice, covetousness, graspingness, greed(iness)*; diese ~ *this grab and keep* | *money-grubbing* | ≈**ig 1.** [a] *avaricious* || ~ auf *or* nach .. *covetous* od *greedy of* ..; *grasping at* .. || ~er Mensch ⟨Am⟩ *go-getter* **2.** [adv] *avariciously*, etc

h·abhaft a [nur pred:] [gen] ~ w *to get hold of* (*a th, a p*); *to lay hands on* (*a th*)

H·abicht m ~(e)s/~e ⟨orn⟩ *hawk*; gr ~ *goshawk* | **~s- ~auge** n ⟨fig⟩ *hawk's eye*; mit ~en *hawk-eyed* (*p*) **~kraut** n ⟨bot⟩ *hawk weed* **~nase** f ⟨fig⟩ *aquiline nose, hook-nose*; mit e–r ~ *hawk-nosed* (*p*) **~pilz** m ⟨bot⟩ *Hydnum imbricatum* L

Habilitati·on [ts] f ~/~en ⟨Ger univ⟩ *qualifying o.s. for lecturing*; *habilitation* [Ger] || ~sschrift [f] *thesis for the h.* **habilit·ieren** vrefl [h] sich ~ *to qualify* (*o.s.*) *for lecturing*; *to habilitate* [Ger]; –tiert *qualified*; ~er Doktor (Dr. habil) (*degree of*) *doctor habilitatus*

***Hab·it** n [Fr] ~s/~e ⟨ec⟩ *habit*; *dress, garment*

H·abitat n ~s/~s (Behausung, Heimat) *habitat* (a. f Menschen unter Wasser)

Habitué [–ty'e:] m [Fr] ~s/~s *habitué* Fr; ~ auf, in *h. of* (*the turf*; *the opera*) **habitu·ell** a *habitual* (*actions*) **H·abitus** m (L) ~/ *bearing, deportment* || ⟨biol & med⟩ *habit*; geistiger ~ *habit of mind* || Kristall≈ *crystal shape*

h·ablich a Sw *wealthy, well-to-do*

°**H·abschaft** f, **H·abseligkeit** f = Hab u Gut; all s–e ~ [~en pl] ⟨fam⟩ *all his things, traps* pl

h·absüchtig a = habgierig

H·achse [ks] f ~/~n ⟨vet⟩ *hock, hough* || ⟨cul⟩ *heel, hock*; *knuckle* (*of veal*); *hough* od *shin* (*of beef*)

Hack n *chopped, minced meat* || ⟨fig⟩ ~ u Pack [n] *ragtag*; *ragtag and bobtail*; *riff-raff* **~bank** f *chopping-block* **~bau** m ⟨agr⟩ *working with the hoe*; ⟨bes praeh⟩ *hoeing* **~beil** n *chopper*; *chopping-knife*; (schweres ~) *cleaver* **~block** m = –bank **~braten** m ⟨Ger⟩ *chopped meat steak*; *Hamburg steak* **~brett** n **1.** *chopping-board* **2.** ⟨mus hist⟩ *dulcimer*; → Zimbal **~fleisch** *chopped* od *minced meat* **~frucht** f *root-crop* | ~bau [m] *cultivation of hoed vegetables* **~gerät** n *hoeing-tool* **~klotz** m = –bank **~maschine** f *mincing-machine* **~messer** n = –beil **~ordnung** f ⟨eth⟩ *pecking oder*

H·acke[1] f ~/~n = Hacken

H·acke[2] f ⟨agr & gard⟩ *hoe*; *mattock*; Spitz≈ *pick, pickax(e)*; mit Spaten u ~ *with pick and shovel* || (Boden) mit der ~ bearbeiten *to hoe*

H·acke- [in comp] **~bank** f etc = Hackbank etc °**~peter** m *dish of roast minced meat*

H·acken m ~s/~ **a.** ⟨anat⟩ = Ferse **b.** (Strumpf≈) *heel*; verstärkte ~ *lisle h.s* pl **c.** (Schuh≈) *heel* (*to wear high h.s*) || die ~ zus–klappen *to click* od *clap one's h.s* || ⟨fig⟩ → ablaufen; jdm auf die ~ treten *to tread on a p's h.s*; °sich auf die ~ m *to take to one's h.s*

h·acken vt/i [h] **A.** vt **1.** ⟨agr⟩ (Boden, Pflanzen) *to hoe*; *hack* **2.** (Holz, Fleisch) *to chop* || (Fleisch) fein ~ *to mince*; gehacktes Fleisch *chopped* od *minced meat* || °lieber Holz ~ als .. *I'd rather chop wood than* .. **3.** (of birds) *to peck* ([*at*] *a p*) **B.** vi **nach** jdm ~ = jdn ~ || °⟨fig⟩ **auf jdn** ~ *to fall upon a p*

H·acker m ⟨agr⟩ *hoer* || *chopper* (*of wood*, etc.)

×°**H·ackerle** n pl (Zähne) *peggies*

H·äckerling m ~s/ = **H·äcksel** m & n ~s/ *chaff*; (Stroh etc) z ~ schneiden *to chaff* **~bank, ~maschine** f *chaff-cutter*

H·ad(d)schi m ~s/~s [moham.] *hadji*

H·ader[1] m ~s/ (Zank, Streit) *bickering*[*s pl*]; *dispute*; Lärm u ~ *brawl, wrangle* || ⟨soc⟩ *enmity, feud*; in ~ leben mit *to be at feud with* || Zank u ~ *feuds* pl ⟨a. pol⟩ **H·ad(e)rer** m *quarreller* **h·adern** vi [h] *to bicker*; *quarrel, squabble* (mit *with*); (laut) *to brawl*; mit G. ~ *to rail against God*

×***H·ader**[2] m ~s/~n *rag, tatter*; ⟨pap⟩ ~n (*or* ~lumpen) pl *rags* pl | ~lump [m] ⟨fig⟩ (P) *ragamuffin*

H·adern- ~drescher m *willow for rags* **~krankheit** f *wool-sorter's disease*; *anthrax* L **~papier** n *rag-paper* **~schneider** m *rag-cutter*

H·ades m ⟨ant⟩ *Hades* Gr

†**H·äduer** m pl (gall. Völkerschaft) *Ædui*

ˣ**H·äfele** n = kl Hafen, → Ringele

ˣ**H·afen**¹, **H·äfen** m ~s/~ = Topf; → Häfele

H·afen² m ~s/≃ **1.** ⟨mar⟩ (for shelter) *haven*; (offering accomodation) *harbo(u)r*; (as a town frequented by ships) *port*; kl ~ *marina* It ‖ (mit Zollstation) *(sea)port*; der ~ v .. *the port of (Kiel)* | Binnen≃ *inland h.r* ‖ Flug≃, Luft≃ *airport*; Seeflug≃ *naval aerodrome* ‖ Frei≃ *free port* ‖ (See–) Handels≃ *(sea)port* ‖ Heimat≃ *home port* ‖ Kriegs≃ *naval port* (od *station*) ‖ Umschlags≃ *tran(s)shipment h.r* ‖ Zufluchts≃ *h.r of refuge* | im ~ anlegen *to h.r* ‖ in den ~ einlaufen *to make port*; in e–n ~ einlaufen *to enter* (od *put into*) *a h.r* **2.** ⟨fig⟩ *haven, port, refuge, shelter* ‖ in den ~ der Ehe einlaufen *to marry* **~abgaben** pl = –gebühren **~amt** n *port-office* **~anlagen** pl *h.r-docks* pl **~arbeiter** m *docker*; *longshoreman* **~becken** n *basin*; (abgeschlossenes) *dock* **~behörde** f *h.r* (od *port*) *authorities* pl **~damm** m *jetty, mole*; *quay, pier*; *breakwater* **~dieb** m ⟨Am⟩ *wharf-rat* **~gebiet** n (e–r Stadt) *waterfront* **~gebühren** f pl, **~gelder** n pl *h.r-dues* pl **~kapitän** m ⟨nav⟩ *h.r-master* **~kommandant** m ⟨nav⟩ *h.r-admiral* (od *captain*) **~kosten** pl *anchorage* **~meister** m *h.r-master*; ⟨Am⟩ *port-warden* **~ordnung** f *port-regulations* pl **~platz** m *(sea)port* **~polizei** f *h.r-police* **~sperre** f *fortified barrier* (od *barrage*) *of h.r* (od *port*) **~stadt** f *seaport* (*town*) **~telegramm** n ⟨telg⟩ *port-warning* **~verwaltung** f *h.r-administration*

H·afer m ~s/ ⟨bot⟩ *oats* pl ‖ (Korn) *oats* pl; ⟨Scot & Ir⟩ *corn* ‖ Flug≃, Wild≃ *wild oat*; Wiesen≃ *false oat* | °⟨fig⟩ ihn sticht der ~ *he feels his oats*; ⟨fam⟩ *he puts on dog* **~bau** m *cultivation of oats* **~bier** n *oat-beer* **~blume** f ⟨bot⟩ = Goldstern **~brei** m *porridge*; ⟨Am⟩ *oatmeal* **~brot** n = –kuchen **~ernte** f *crop of oats*; *oat-harvest* **~fliege** f ⟨ent⟩ *frit-fly* **~flocken** f pl *flaked* (⟨Am⟩ *ground, rolled*) *oats* pl; ⟨engl⟩ *Quaker oats* **~grütze** f *grits* pl, *groats* pl, ⟨cul⟩ (Brei) *porridge* **~halm** m *oat stalk* **~kakao** m *oat-cocoa* **~kuchen** m *oatcake* **~mehl** n *oatmeal* **~pflanze** f ⟨bot⟩ *oat(-plant)* **~sack** m *oat-bag* **~schlehe** f ⟨bot⟩ *bullace* **~schleim** m *gruel* **~spreu** f *oat-chaff* **~stroh** n *oat-straw* **~suppe** f *skilly* **~wurz(el)** f ⟨bot⟩ → Bocksbart

Hafer·ei f ~/~en = Havarie

Haff n ⟨Ger⟩ (an Ostsee) *lagoon*; *haff* [Ger]; Frisches ~ *Frisches Haff* [Ger]

ˣ**H·afner** m ~s/~ [südd] = Töpfer

†**Haft** m ~(e)s/~e *holdfast*; = Halt; Haken

Haft f ~/ *arrest, confinement, imprisonment*; Schutz≃ *protective custody* ‖ strenge ~ *close confinement* ‖ (jdn) aus der ~ entlassen *to discharge* (*from prison*); aus der ~ entweichen *to break out of pr.*; in ~ *under arrest* ‖ (jdn) in ~ behalten *to detain* ‖ (jdn) in ~ nehmen (*or* setzen) *to place under confinement*; *to take into custody* (od *in charge*); *to arrest* ‖ z 3 Tagen ~ verurteilt *condemned to 3 days' imprisonment* | ⟨fig⟩ = Fessel **~befehl** m ⟨jur⟩ *warrant of arrest* (f Entwichenen *escape w.*); *writ of attachment*; ⟨jur⟩ *capias*; *mittimus* L **~dolde** f ⟨bot⟩ *burparsley*; *Caucalis* L **≃fähig** a *adhesive* **~fähigkeit** f *adhesiveness, adhesion*; (v Klebband) *tackiness* **~grund** m (Farbe) *wash primer*; *etch pr.* **~kraft** f *adh. power* **~ladung** f ⟨artill⟩ *hollow* (od *magnetic anti-tank*) *charge*; gerichtete ~ *shaped ch.* **~organ** n ⟨zoo⟩ *suctorial organ*; *o. of attachment* **~pflicht** f (*third party* od *common law*) *liability*; beschränkte ~ *limited l.* → Haftung | ~anspruch [m] *l. claim*; ~gesetz [n] *Employers' L. Act*; *Workmen's Compensation Act* (1897–1906) ‖ ~versicherung [f] *l.y* (od *third-party*) *insurance* **≃pflichtig** a *liable*; *under l.y* **~prüfungsverfahren** n *remand procedure*; im ~ vorgeführt *appeared on r.* **~schale** f ⟨opt⟩ *adhesive* od *contact lens* **~scheibe** f *adhesive disk*; ⟨zoo⟩ *suctorial pad*; ⟨bot⟩ (of algae) *holdfast* **~sitz** m ⟨tech⟩ *wringing od keying fit* **~summe** f *liabilities* pl **~vergehen** n *breach of arrest* **~vermögen** n = –fähigkeit **~verschonung** f *exemption from arrest* **~vollzug** m ⟨jur⟩ *arrest, imprisonment* **~zeher** m ⟨zoo⟩ *gecko*; Gattung der ~ *Geckotians*; *Geccotidae* L pl

-haft suff [z Bildung v Adj] **1.** [aus Subst. im Sinne v] **a.** 'habend': dauer~, ekel~, herz~ **b.** 'nach der Art v': jungen~, märchen~, stümper~ **2.** [aus Verben im Sinne v] 'neigend z': flatter~, schwatz~

h·aftbar a *answerable, liable, responsible* (f etw *for a th*); jdn ~ m *to make* (od *hold*) *a p liable* (*for* ..) | **≃keit** f *liability* (f *for*)

h·aften I. vi [h] [abs] → A. 2. a. **A.** ⟨eig⟩ **1.** ~ an **a.** *to adhere* (od *cling, stick*) *to* (*mud clung to his clothes*) ‖ ⟨übtr⟩ *to attach* (od *cling*) *to*; an Macht haftet gr Verantwortung *great responsibilities attach to power*; all sein Denken haftet an materiellen Dingen *all his thoughts are centred* od *fixed on material things*; s–e Hoffnungen hafteten an .. *his hopes centred in* (*the young monarch*) **b.** er haftet an Kleinigkeiten *he attaches great importance to trifling details* **2. a.** *to stick* (**an** *to*); *the stamp stuck to* (*his fingers*) ‖ *his eyes were fixed upon* (*a picture*); *the nickname stuck to him*; etwas wird ~ bl. *some of it will stick* ‖ im Gedächtnis ~ bleiben *to be remembered*; die Szene wird mir ewig im G. ~ (bleiben) .. *will for ever be imprinted on my mind* | [abs] nur kurz ~ *in at one ear and out at the other* → Ohr; bei dir haftet auch gar nichts *you can never remember anything* **b.** *to be caught, get entangled* (in *in*); *his foot was caught in* (*a net*) **B.** ⟨**jur**⟩ ~ f etw *to be liable* (od *answerable*) *for a th*; *to guarantee a th*; → bürgen **II.** ≃ n **das** ~ **an** ⟨übtr⟩ *the attachment* od *clinging, sticking*) *to* **H·äftling** m *prisoner, detainee*

H·aftung f ~/ *liability* ‖ Gesellschaft mit beschränkter ~ *limited* (*liability*) *company* | ⟨tech⟩ (— Haften) *adhesion, adherence*; (Beton an Eisen) *bond*

H·ag m ~(e)s/~e **1.** (Zaun) *fence, hedge*; *enclosure* **2.** (Umzäuntes) *enclosure*; *fenced pasture*

H·age- ~buche f ⟨bot⟩ *hornbeam*; *carpinus* L **≃büchen** a → hahnebüchen **~butte** f ⟨bot⟩ *hip, hep* **~buttenstrauch** m ⟨bot⟩ *brier, briar*; *dogrose, eglantine* **~dorn** m ⟨bot⟩ *hawthorn*; *whitethorn*; *may*; Frucht des ~s *haw* **~stolz** m (*old*) *bachelor*, ⟨fam⟩ *old maid in pants*

H·agel m ~s/ **1.** ⟨eig⟩ *hail*; es fiel ~ *it hailed*; *h. fell* **2.** ⟨übtr⟩ *h.* (*of stones, bullets*); *flight* (*of arrows, missiles*); *fusillade*; *volley*; ein ~ v Geschossen *a h. of shot and shell*; *a rain* (*of blows*); der ~ des Sperrfeuers *the blizzard of the barrage* ‖ *shower* (*of letters, gifts*) **3.** ⟨fig⟩ *flood* (*of threats*); *hailstorm*; *shower* (*of invitations*); *volley* (*of reproaches*); e–m ~ v Fragen ausgesetzt w *to be subject to a barrage of questions* **≃dicht** a; ~ fallen *to fall as thick as h.* ‖ ~e Hiebe *a h. of blows* **~korn** n *h.stone* ‖ ⟨med⟩ (am Augenlid) *chalazion*; → Gerstenkorn **~schaden, ~schlag** m *damage* (*caused*) *by h.* **~schauer** m *h.storm*; *shower of h.* **~schnur** f ⟨zoo⟩ (im Ei) *chalaza* L **~versicherung** f *h.-insurance* **~wetter** n *h.storm*

h·ageln vimps [h] **1.** ⟨eig⟩ es hagelt *it hails* ‖ es hagelte gr Schloßen *there was a shower of large hailstones* **2.** ⟨übtr⟩ es hagelte Steine *stones fell in showers* ‖ (*charges*) *flow thick and fast*; *it rained blows, curses* ‖ es hagelte Verwünschungen um ihn her *imprecations rattled about his head*

h·ager a *gaunt* (*figure*), *haggard, lank*(*y*), *lean*; *spare*; *scraggy, skinny, thin*; ⟨Am⟩ *scrawny* ‖

~e P *scrag* | ≗**keit** f *gauntness, h.ness, lank(i)ness* etc

Hagg·ada f ⟨theol⟩ *haggadah* **Hagio- ~graphen** pl ⟨bib⟩ *hagiographa* Gr pl **~graph·ie** f *hagiography*

hah·a 1. intj ~! *ha ha!* **2.** ≗ n *ha ha*

H·äher m ~s/~ ⟨orn⟩ *jay*; → *cuckoo*

H·ahn m ~s/≗e **A.** ⟨orn⟩ **1. a.** *cock*; junger ~ *cockerel* ‖ Haus≗ *dunghill cock*; ⟨Am⟩ *rooster* ‖ Kampf≗ *fighting c.* **b.** der welsche ~ *the Gallic c.* ‖ roter ~ (= Feuer): jdm den roten ~ aufs Dach setzen *to set a p's house on fire* **c.** kein ~ kräht danach *nobody will care a straw* (od *damn, pin*); *n. will give a hoot about it* ‖ der Haupt≗ ⟨school⟩ (of boys) *the c. of the school* ‖ der ~ im Korbe *the c. of the roost* ‖ er stolziert einher wie der ~ auf dem Mist *he struts about like a c. on a dunghill* **2.** ⟨orn⟩ *cock*; → Männchen **B.** ⟨übtr⟩ **1.** (an Faß, Leitung) *cock, tap*; ⟨Am⟩ *faucet* ‖ Gas≗ *gas-tap*; *switch*; Wasser ≗ *water-tap* ‖ ⟨tech⟩ *cock*; Abblase≗ *blow-off cock*; Ablaß≗, Ablauf≗ *bib-c.*; Absperr≗ *stop-c.*; Durchgangs≗ *passage c.*; Entwässerungs≗ *drain-c.* ‖ Dreiwege≗ *three-way c.*; Misch≗ *mixed c.* **2.** (am Gewehr) *cock*; ~ in Ruh *at half c.*; ~ gespannt *at full c.* ‖ den ~ e–s Gewehrs spannen *to c. a gun* **3.** → Wetter≗ **~balken** m ⟨arch⟩ *topbeam, purlin* **~gehäuse** n ⟨tech⟩ *chamber of a cock* **~kegel** m, **~küken** n, **~schlüssel, ~wirbel** m ⟨tech⟩ *plug*; *turning-piece* **~rei** m *cuckold*; (e–n Mann) z ~ m *to cuckold*

H·ähnchen n ~s/~ *cockerel*

°**h·a(h)nebüchen** (f hagebüchen) **1.** [a] ⟨fam⟩ *awful (nonsense)*; *impossible, incredible*; *intolerable*; *scandalous*; = haarsträubend ‖ das ist ja ~ *that's the limit* **2.** [adv] *incredibly, etc*

H·ahnen- ~balken m → Hahnbalken ‖ *roost*; *perch* **~feder** *cock's plume* **~fuß** m *cock's foot* ‖ ⟨bot⟩ Gelber ~ *crowfoot*; *Ranunculus* L; goldgelber ~ *goldilocks* **~kamm** m ⟨eig & bot⟩ *cockscomb* **~kampf** m *cock-fight(ing)* | ~platz [m] *pit* **~schlagen** n *cock-shy* **~schrei** m *cock-crow* **~sporn** m ⟨bot⟩ *Plectranthus fruticosus* L **~tritt** m **1.** (im Ei) *cicatricle, tread* **2.** ⟨vet⟩ (of a horse) *stringhalt*; *springhalt*

H·ai m ~(e)s/~e ⟨ich⟩ *shark*; Blau≗, Menschen≗ *blue-sh.*; Glatt≗ *tope*; Hammer≗ *hammer-head*; Herings≗ *porbeagle*; Hunds≗ *dogfish*, → d.; Wal≗ *whale sh.* | auf ~e jagen *to sh.-hunt* **~fang** m *sh.-fishing* **~fisch** m *sh.* | ~haut [f] *shark-skin*; ~lebertran [m] *sh.-liver oil*

Haidarab·ad n (Stadt u Provinz) *Hyderabad*

Ha·idar Pasch·a n ⟨Turk⟩ (Stadt am Ostufer des Bosporus, Vorort von → Istanbul)

H·ain m ~(e)s/~e *grove, wood* **~ampfer** m *blood-wort*; *wood-sorrel* **~buche** f ⟨bot⟩ → Hage– **~bund** m ⟨Ger Lit⟩ *Hainbund* **~butte** f = Hage– **~simse** f *woodrush*

Ha·iti (westind. Insel) *Haiti*; Bewohner v ~ *Haitian* **ha·itisch** a *Haitian*

H·äkchen n ~s/~ *(small) hook*; *hooklet* ‖ ~ (V) vor e–m Wort *tick* (*to tick a word*) ‖ → Apostroph ‖ ⟨prov⟩ was ein ~ w will, krümmt sich beizeiten *just as the twig is bent, the tree's inclined* (A. Pope) **H·äkel-** *crochet* **~arbeit** f *c.-work* **~garn** n *c.-thread*; *c.-wool* (od *silk, cotton*) **~kante** f *purls* pl **~nadel** f *c.-hook* (od *needle*) **~naht** f ⟨tail⟩ *edging seam*

Häkel·ei f ~/~en **1.** (Handarbeit) *c.(-work)* **2.** ⟨fig⟩ *banter*; *chaff*; *teasing* ***h·äk(e)lig** a ⟨fig⟩ *delicate, ticklish*; *critical* **h·äkeln A.** vi/t [h] **1.** (mit der Häkelnadel arbeiten) **a.** vi *to crochet*; *to work with a c.-needle* **b.** vt (e–e Decke, Spitze) *to (work in) c.*; gehäkelt *c.ed* [ˈkrouʃeid] **2. sich ~ mit jdm** *to chaff* od *tease a p* **B.** ≗ n *crocheting* [ˈkrouʃeiiŋ] **H·aken** m ~s/~ **1.** ⟨eig⟩ (aus Metall, Holz) **a.** *hook*; Feuer≗ *fire-h.*; Fleisch≗ *meat-h.* ‖ Boots≗ *boat-h.*; → Enter≗; Wirbel≗ ‖ Hut≗ *hat-h., hat-peg*; Kleider≗ *clothes peg*; *hanger* ‖ Karabiner≗ *spring* (od *snap*)*-h.* ‖ → Kant≗ **b.** (Klammer) *clamp, clasp, holdfast* ‖ ~ u Ösen [pl] *hooks and eyes* pl **c.** ⟨tech⟩ (z Greifen) *catch*; *clutch* ‖ ⟨met⟩ *rabble* **d.** (etw) an e–n ~ hängen *to hang on a peg* (od *h.*); *to hang up*; ⟨fig⟩ .. den .. h. *to throw to the dogs* ‖ (etw) mit e–m ~ befestigen, fangen, fassen, mit e–m ~ versehen *to hook* **e.** (of hare) > *90 turn*; < *90° wrench*; (→ 2. *to w., t.*) **2.** ⟨übtr⟩ (*in moving, writing*) *sharp bend*; *hook*; *twist*; schwungvoller ~ (am Buchstaben) *curlicue* ‖ ⟨box⟩ *hook*; jdm e–n ~ versetzen *to h. a p*; jdm e–n linken ~ versetzen *to land a p a left(-hand) h.* ‖ ~ schlagen, e–n ~ m (in der Flucht) *to double*; ⟨hunt⟩ → 1. e. **3.** ⟨fig⟩ (Hindernis) *hitch, snag*; *trouble*; *drawback*; *obstacle* ‖ der ~ dabei ist (*or* es hat den ~), daß .. *the t. is that ..*; hier ist (*or* da sitzt) der ~ *here is the t.*; *there's the rub* (Shak); das ist der ~ *that's the t.*; gewöhnlich ist irgendwo ein ~ dabei *there is usually a snag* od *hitch about it somewhere*, ⟨Am sl⟩ *there are usually some strings attached to it* ‖ die S hat e–n ~ *there's a catch to it* **h·aken** vt/i [h] **1.** vt (etw) *to hook* (an *on to*; *to*; in *in*); → ein~, zu~ | sich ~ *to hook* (an .. *on a p's arm*) ‖ sich ~ l *to hook*; sich hinten ~ l (of a dress) *to hook up the back* **2.** vi *to be caught, to get entangled* (in *in*) **H·aken-~blatt** n *hook-butt* (od *scarf*) **~büchse** f ⟨hist⟩ *(h)arquebus* Fr ≗**förmig** a *h.ed*; *h.-like* (od *shaped*); ⟨scient⟩ *unciform*; *uncinate*; ~er Ansatz *h.* **~gimpel** m ⟨orn⟩ *pine-grosbeak* **~kette** f *h.-link chain* **~kreuz** n *h.ed cross* ‖ (Symbol) *fylfot*; *swastika* | ~fahne [f] *swastika flag* **~leiter** f *h.-ladder*; (Feuerwehr≗) *pompier's ladder*; ⟨Am⟩ *h.-and-ladder* **~lilie** f ⟨bot⟩ *crinum* L **~nagel** m *h.ed* (od *clasp*) *nail* **~nase** f *h.-nose*; *h.ed nose* **~schlüssel** m *h.-spanner* **~schnabel** m *h.ed beak* **~schraube** f *h.-bolt* **~stange** f *h.ed pole* **~schütze** m ⟨hist⟩ *(h)arquebusier* Fr **~wurm** m ⟨zoo⟩ *h.worm*; *ankylostoma* Gr; ~krankheit [f] *ankylostomiasis* Gr; *h.worm* (od *tunnel*) *disease* **~zange** f ⟨surg⟩ *long forceps* **h·akig** a *hooked*; *aquiline* (*nose*) ‖ ⟨minr⟩ *hackly* (*fracture, surface*); ~e Stacheln tragend *uncinate*

Halal·i n ~s/~s ⟨hunt⟩ *hallali*; *bugle-call*; *(view-)halloo*; *mort* Fr ‖ das ~ blasen *to sound the hallali*; *to give a (view-)halloo*; *to blow a mort*; beim ~ dabei s *to be in at the kill*

halb I. [a] **1.** ⟨eig⟩ **a.** [mst mit indef art] *half*; ein ~es Dutzend *half a dozen*, ⟨Am⟩ *a h. dozen* ‖ ~er Penny *h.penny* ‖ e–e ~e Stunde *h. an hour*, ⟨Am⟩ *a h. hour* ‖ mit ~er Fahrt ⟨mar⟩ fahren *to sail at h.-speed* ‖ zum ~en Preise *at h. the price*; Kinder z ~en Pr. *children h.-price* ‖ alle ~en Stunden *every h. hour* ‖ ein ~er Ton *a semitone, h.-tone* ‖ auf ~em Wege *h.-way*; ein auf ~em W. gelegenes Haus *a h.-way house* ‖ zwei u e–e ~e Meile *two and a h. miles, two miles and a h.*; *two and a h. per cent (interest)*; → andert~; dritte~ **b.** ⟨com⟩ ein ~er Anteil *a h. share*; der ~e Betrag *h. the amount*; *to meet a p h.way* ‖ e–e ~e Länge *a h. length* **2.** ⟨übtr⟩ (ein gr Teil v) *half* ‖ *you can see it with h. an eye* ‖ sein ~er Einfluß *h. his influence* ‖ er war nur mit ~em Herzen dabei *he was h.-hearted about it* ‖ ~e Maßnahmen [pl] *h.-measures, h.-and-h. measures* pl ‖ nach s–r Krankheit ist er nur noch ein ~er Mensch *after his illness he is not h. the man he was* ‖ bis in den ~en Mittag schlafen *to sleep nearly the whole morning* ‖ nur mit ~em Ohre zuhören *to listen only with one ear* ‖ die ~e Stadt spricht davon *it's the talk of the town* ‖ e–e ~e Wahrheit *a h.-truth* ‖ auf ~em Wege *half-way, mid-w.*; ‖ jdm auf ~em Wege entgegenk. *to meet a p h.-w.* ⟨a. fig⟩ **II.** [adv] *half* **1. a.** [bei Adj, Adv] ~ **gar** *or* **durch** *h. cooked*; *medium*; ~ besinnungslos ⟨box fam⟩ *punch* ‖ durchdacht *h. thought-out*; ~gebildet *semi-educated*; ⟨cont⟩ *demi-semi-educated*; ~ hinüber (beschwipst) *h.-gone, h.-seas-over*; ~ reif h.-ripe (apples); ~ tot h. dead; ~ so gr wie .. h. as large as ..; ~ soviel h. as much; nicht ~ soviel not h. of it; ein ~mal soviel(e) h. as much (many) again; die Wartezeit ist schon ~ um the period of waiting is h. over; °es ist ~ so wild it isn't as bad as that **2.** [bei Verben] er **aß** den Apfel nur ~ he only ate h. the apple || bevor er die Zigarre ~ aufgeraucht hatte before he was h.-way through his cigar (he saw) || ~ heißen ⟨mar⟩ to dip the flag || als er den Weg ~ hinuntergegangen war half-way down the lane (he saw); nur ~ bei der S s to be h.-hearted about a th || ~ im Schlaf h. asleep || man darf nichts ~ tun you must not do things by halves || nur ~ z·uhören to listen only with one ear **3.** ~ .. ~ .. h. .. h.; h. kneeling h. sitting || ~ **u** ~ h. and h.; ⟨Am⟩ fifty-fifty; (etw) ~ u ~ mit jdm teilen to divide (a th) with a p fifty-fifty || ich habe mich ~ u ~ entschlossen I have h. a mind (to leave) || ich versprach es ~ u ~ ⟨fam⟩ I kind of promised **4.** ~ **vier** h. past three; ⟨Am a.⟩ h. after three; ⟨Scot⟩ h. four; um vier ein ~ at h. past four || es ist schon ~ it is h. past already || es schlug ~ the clock struck the h. hour; it was striking the h. hour || die Uhr schlägt voll u ~ the clock strikes the hours and h. hours **III.** [abs] **1.** [der ≃e, ein ≃er] h. a glass od pint; zwei ≃e Helles, two halves of ale **2.** [die ≃e, e–e ≃e] = Hälfte; [südd] e–e ≃e ([nordd] e–n ≃en) trinken to drink a pint || ×= Seite; ×geh auf die ≃e keep out of the way; über die ≃e bringen to do for a p **3.** das ist **nichts ≃es** u nichts Ganzes that is neither fish, flesh nor fowl || etw ≃es a h.-measure; an imperfection, insufficiency **H·alb-** [in comp] half; ⟨scient⟩ hemi–; semi– **~achse** f s.-axis **~affe** m ⟨zoo⟩ lemur **~analphabet** m s.-literate **~amerikaner** m hyphened American **≃amtlich 1.** [a] s.-official; officious **2.** [adv] s.-officially **~atlas** m satinet(te) **~bauer** m small farmer **≃-betrunken,** °**~-besoffen** h.-gone, h.-seas-over **~bildung** f sciolism, superficial knowledge; quackery; smattering (in .. in, of a th) **~-bitter** a bitter sweet; ~e Schokolade b.-sw. chocolate **~blut** n h.-blood, h.-breed, h.-caste || ⟨engl⟩ ~ (Pferderasse) cob **≃blütig** a h.-blooded; h.-bred; h.-caste **~brillanten** pl s.-precious stones pl **~bruder** m sibling; = Stiefbruder **≃bürtig** a h.-bred; h.-caste **~distanz** f ⟨film⟩ angle shot(s) **≃dunkel** a penumbral **~dunkel** n half-light; ⟨paint⟩ chiaroscuro It **≃durchlässig** a s.permeable **~edelstein** m s.-precious stone **~erhaben** a: ~e Arbeit ⟨arts⟩ basso-relievo It **~fabrikat** n s.-manufactured article od product **≃fertig** a h.-finished (product); ~e Erzeugnisse unfinished goods | adv ~ s mit to be h.way through doing od with a th | ~fabrikat [n] = Halbfabrikat **≃fett** a ⟨typ⟩ s.-bold; s.-bituminous (coal) **~flottille** f h. flotilla **~flügel** m ⟨theat⟩ book (⟨Am⟩ two-fold) wing **~flügler** pl ⟨ent⟩ Gattung der ~ h.ptera Gr pl **~flugschlag, ~flugball** m ⟨ten⟩ h.-volley **~franzband** m h.-calf; in ~ gebunden h.-bound **≃gar** a h.-cooked; underdone **~gas** n ⟨mot⟩ h. throttle **≃gebildet** a h.-educated **~gefrorene(s)** n sorbet **≃geschichtlich** a s.-historical **~geschoß** n ⟨arch⟩ entresol Fr **~geschwister** pl siblings; = Stiefge- **~geviert** n ⟨typ⟩ en **~gezeit** h.-tide **≃glänzend** a ⟨phot⟩ s.glossy **~gott** m demigod; hero **~holz** n h.-timber **~hufner** m = –bauer **~insel** f peninsula L; die ~ N. the p. of N. | ~bewohner [m] p.r; ≃förmig [a] p.r; ~krieg [m] the P.r War (1808–14) **~invalide** m s.-invalid **~jahr** n h.-year; six-months pl **≃jährig** a s. m. old; of six m. **≃jährlich 1.** [a] h.-yearly; ⟨Am⟩ s.-annual **2.** [adv] each h.-year; every six m.; s.-annually **~konsonant** m s.-consonant **~körper** m ⟨phys⟩ h.-body **~kreis** m h.-cycle; s.circle || ≃förmig [a] s.circular || ~transporteur [m] s.c. protractor **~kugel** f h.sphere || ≃förmig [a] h.spheric(al) **~lang** a: machs °~! ⟨fam⟩ draw it mild!; ~er Ärmel half-sleeve, ~e Socke half-hose, ~es Unterkleid demi-slip **~kuppel** f s.-dome **≃laut 1.** [a] low, subdued (voice) **2.** [adv] in an undertone; under one's breath **~lederband** m h.-leather binding **~leinen** n h.-cloth; in ~ gebunden h.-cloth **~leiter** m ⟨el⟩ s.conductor **~-mantelgeschoß** n = Dumdumgeschoß **~maske** f half-mask; domino **≃mast 1.** [adv] ~, auf ≃ at h.-mast; ⟨Am a.⟩ at h.-staff; ⟨mar, comm⟩ at the dip; → flaggen || Fahne auf ~ setzen to h.-mast the flag; ⟨Am a.⟩ to haul the flag to h.-staff **≃matt** ⟨phot⟩ s.mat(t) †**~meister** m = Abdecker **~mensch** m s.-human being; centaur **≃menschlich** a s.-human **~messer** m s.-diameter; radius **~metall** n s.-metal **≃monatlich 1.** [a] s.-monthly, fortnightly || ~e Zeitschrift s.-monthly **2.** [adv] s.-monthly; every fortnight **~mond** m h.-moon, crescent || ⟨her & pol⟩ the Crescent | ≃förmig [a] crescent **~muschelglas** n ⟨opt⟩ meniscus L **≃n·ackt** a h.-naked **≃offen** ajar, h.-open **~pacht** f share farming **≃part** adv; mit jdm ~ m to go halves (⟨Am⟩ fifty-fifty) with a p **~profil** n h.-sideface **~rechte** m (der ~, ein ~r) ⟨ftb⟩ inside right **~rock** m demi-slip **≃roh** a rare; very underdone **≃rund** a h.-round (file, iron); s.circular **~säule** f respond **~schatten** m **1.** shadowy light; ⟨paint⟩ h.-shade; penumbra L **2.** [in comp] penumbral **~scheidwirtschaft** f share-tenancy **~schlaf** m dog-sleep; twilight sleep; s.-trance **~schlichtfeile** f second cut file **~schlummer** m drowse **~schluß** m ⟨mus⟩ imperfect cadence; h. close **~schnepfe** f ⟨orn⟩ h.-snipe; lesser snipe; becassine **~schuh** m (low) shoe; Oxford shoe, ~e [pl] Oxfords; (zweifarbiger ~) saddle-shoe **~schwache** f → –zarte **~schwester** f = Stiefschwester **~seide** f h.-silk; poplin; ⟨bes Am⟩ near-silk **~seite** f ⟨print⟩ h.-sheet **~seitenblindheit** f hemianopsia L **~seitenlähmung** f hemiplegia L **~sold** m ⟨mil & nav⟩ h.-pay || auf ~ gesetzt s to be put on h.-pay **≃selbständig** a s.-active (Zielflug homing) **~spänner** m = Halbbauer **~starke[r]** m teddy boy **≃starr** a ⟨aero⟩ s.-rigid **≃steif** a (Kragen) s.-stiff **~stiefel** m pl h.-boots pl; → Kothurn **≃stocks** adv = halbmast **~stoff** m h.-stuff || ⟨pap⟩ rag pulp **≃stündig** a h. an hour's (talk); lasting h. an hour; ⟨Am⟩ a h. hour's (talk) **≃stündlich 1.** [a] h.-hourly **2.** [adv] every h.-hour **~stürmer** m ~s/~ ⟨ftb⟩ inside forward **≃-tägig** a s.-diurnal **~tags-** ~arbeit [f] part-time job; ~kraft [f] (P) part-timer **~teil** m = Hälfte **~ton** m ⟨mus⟩ s.tone || ⟨arts⟩ h.-tone; undertone || ~zeichnung [f] washdrawing **≃t·ot** a h.-dead, dead-and-alive || er lachte sich ~ he split his sides; ⟨Am⟩ he laughed like everything **~trauer** f h.-mourning **~tuch** n kersey **~tür** f ⟨agr⟩ Dutch door **~- u Fertigfabrikate** pl finished stores and products in process **~vers** m ⟨pros⟩ h.-line hemistich **~vokal** m s.vowel **≃voll** a h.-full **≃w·ach** a h.-awake; somnolent; ~er Zustand [m] somnolence, -cy **~waise** f fatherless od motherless child **~waren** pl (z. B. Zwirne) = –fabrikate **~wassergas** n s.-water-gas; Dowson gas °**≃wege** adv; mach es nur ~ draw it mild! **≃wegs** adv h.(-way) (he met us h.-w.) || (ziemlich) middling; tolerably || [pred] (leidlich) middling (I felt m.); so-so; nur ~ gut etc it could be worse; ⟨Am sl⟩ it's not so hot; (jdn, etw) ~ wiederherstellen to h.-mend **~welt** f h.-world; demi-monde Fr || Dame der ~ cocotte Fr; demi-mondaine; ⟨fam⟩ demi-rep **~wertszeit** f radioactive period; h.-life (period) **~wissen** n, **~wisser·ei** f sciolism; superficial knowledge; quackery; smattering (in in, of a th) **~wisser** m quack; sciolist; smatterer **≃wöchentlich** a h.-, s.-weekly **~wolle** f h.-wool, ⟨Am⟩ near wool **≃wollen** a h.-woollen || ~es Zeug linsey-woolsey **~-wollstoff** m; starker ~ wincey **≃wüchsig** a half-grown || ≃e[r] m hobbledehoy, ⟨Am⟩ teenager **~zarte** f teddy girl **~zeile** f ⟨pros⟩ h.-line; hemistich; erste ~ first half-line, on-verse; zweite ~

off-verse **~zeit** f ⟨ftb⟩ *h.-time* **~zelt** n *lean-to tent* **~zeug** n *s.-(manufactured) product*; ⟨pap⟩ *h. stuff* | ~-Holländer [m] *breaker*

-halb 1. → andert~, dritte~ **2.** (= Seite) → außer~, inner~; ober~, unter~ **3.** (= wegen) [nach *gen* des Fürworts] → des~, wes~

Halbe-H·albe [nur in ~ m *to go*] *fifty-fifty*

-halben prep [nach Fürwort u Adj] **a.** (Ort) → allent~ **b.** (= wegen) → deinet~, meinet~

-halber prep (= wegen) [mit vorgestelltem *gen* des Hauptworts]: alters~ *on account of age*; beispiels~ *by way of example*; ehren~ *honoris causa*; *honorary* (*degree*); krankheits~ *on account of* (od *owing to*) *illness*; sicherheits~ *for safety('s) sake*; *for the sake of safety*

H·albheit f ~/~en *imperfection, incompleteness, insufficiency*; er ist nur e–e ~ *there is no wholeness about him* ‖ ~en [pl] *half-measures* pl

halb·ieren vt [h] (Größe, Fläche) *to bisect, to halve*; *to cut in two*; (Summe) ~ mit jdm *to divide a sum with a p fifty-fifty*; *to halve a sum with a p* ‖ ⟨golf⟩ ein Loch mit jdm ~ *to halve a hole with a p*

Halb·ierung f ~/~en *bisection* | ~slinie [f] *bisecting line*; *bisector*; *bisectrix*

H·alde f ~/~n *hill-side*; *slope*; *slag pile*; ⟨min⟩ *waste-heap*; *tailings, tumbles* pl

H·aleb n (= Aleppo in Nordsyrien) *Aleppo*

half 1. & 3. pret sg v helfen

H·alfa f ⟨bot⟩ *esparto*

H·älfte f ~/~n *half* ‖ ⟨bes jur & scient⟩ *moiety* | die ~ v 10 ist 5 *h. of ten is five* ‖ er gab jedem e–e ~ *he gave each of the two one h.* | die ~ + gen *h. the men*; *h. of these words*; *h. your time*; *h. his fortune* ‖ die absteigende ~ *the down* (*of life*) ‖ die ~ davon ist faul *h. of it is rotten, half of them are rotten* | d–e ~ ist kleiner als s–e *your h. is smaller than his*; die größere ~ *the larger h.* ‖ ⟨fig⟩ m–e bessere ~ (Frau) *my better h.* | eine in ~n zahlbare Summe *a sum payable in moieties* ‖ (Gebiet) in 2 ~en teilen *to divide into two halves* ‖ (Summe) z gleichen ~n teilen mit jdm *to halve a sum with a p* ‖ ihr kennt ihn nur zur ~ *you don't h. know him* ‖ **auf** der ~ der Strecke machte er schlapp *he became limp before he had covered h. the distance* ‖ auf die ~ verringern *to cut in h.*; auf die ~ zurückgehen, sich um die ~ verringern *to fall by half*; mit etw **zur** ~ fertig s → halbf. s

H·alfter[1] f ~/~n (Pistolentasche) *holster*

H·alfter[2] f ~/~n; m & n ~s/~n *halter, stable-collar* ‖ ein Pferd an ein ~ legen *to h. a horse*; an das ~ gewöhnen *t. h.-break a h.* **~geld** n *the groom's gratuity from the purchaser* **~kette** f *h.-chain* **~riemen** m *h.-strap* **h·alftern** vt [h] (ein Pferd) *to h.* (*a horse*); *to put a h. upon* (*a horse*)

halky·onisch a *halcyon* (*calmness*)

***H·all** m ~(e)s/~e *sound, peal*; *clang, clangour*

H·alle n ⟨Ger⟩ (Stadt) → Hall·enser, Hall·ore

H·alle f ~/~n (gr Raum, Saal f Empfang etc) *hall* ‖ gr ~ ⟨Am⟩ *auditorium* L | ⟨ec⟩ *porch*; *vestibule*; → Bahnhofs≚; ⟨hot⟩ *lobby*; *lounge* ‖ ⟨parl⟩ (Säulen≚) *porch*; *pillared arcade*; *portico* It ‖ Kur≚, Trink≚ *pump-room* | Turn≚ *gymnasium* L ‖ Flugzeug≚, Luftschiff≚ *hangar*; *shed* ‖ → Markt≚

hallel·uja intj & ≚ n ~s/~s *hallelujah*

h·allen vi [h] *to sound*; (wider~) *to resound*; (of the voice) *to reverberate*; *to thrill* (durch .. *through the room*); *to clang*; ~d *ringing* (*voice*)

H·allen- *indoor* [attr] (*championships*; *game*; *range*; *riding tournament*; *swimming pool*; *sports*) | ~bad [n] *indoor swimming-bath*, ⟨Am⟩ *i. s.-pool*; ~deck [n] *hangar deck*; ~kirche [f] *church with aisles of equal height*; ~turnen [n] *gymnastics* pl; ~vorfeld [n] ⟨aero⟩ *apron*

Hall·enser m ⟨Ger⟩ *inhabitant of* (od *p born in*) *Halle on the Saale*

H·alligen pl; die ~ ⟨Ger⟩ *the Halligen* pl Ger

H·allimasch m ~s/~e ⟨bot⟩ *honey-fungus*

H·alljahr n ~s/~e ⟨bib⟩ *year of jubilee*

hall·o 1. intj *hallo(a) there*! *hullo(a)*! ‖ ⟨hunt⟩ *halloo*; *tally-ho*! **2.** ≚ n *h.*, *h.*; ⟨hunt⟩ *h.*, *t.-ho* ‖ *uproar*; es erhob sich ein ~, als .. *there was a regular hallo when* .. ‖ ~ rufen (⟨a.⟩ ~en) *to h.*, *hallo(a)*, *hullo(a)*; ⟨hunt⟩ *to halloo*; *tally-ho*

Hall·ore m ~n/~n *salt-maker* (bes *at Halle*)

H·allstattzeit f [österr] ⟨praeh⟩ *Hallstatt Period*

H·allsteindoktrin f *Hallstein-Doctrine*

Halluzinati·on [ts] f ~/~en *hallucination* ‖ ~en h *to see things* | h–t·orisch [a] *hallucinatory*

H·alm m ~(e)s/~e (Gras≚) *blade*; (Getreide≚) *stalk*; *stem*; das Getreide auf dem ~ *the crop*; (Stroh≚) *straw*; in die ~e schießen *to run to straw* ‖ ⟨cul⟩ *drinking-straw* **~fliege** f *gout-fly* **~frucht** f *cereal* **~knoten** m *joint*

H·alma n ~s/ (Spiel) *halma* [= Gr „springe!"]

Halmah·era n (größte Insel der Molukken)

H·älmchen n ~s/~ *small blade* (od *stalk* etc)

Halo- ⟨chem⟩ **~g·en** n ~s/~e *halogen* | ≚·ieren [vt] *to halogenize* **~gen·id** n ~s/~e *haloid* | ~salz [n] *h. salt*; ~e *halides* pl **~m·eter** n *halometer* **~ph·yte** f ⟨bot⟩ *halophyte*

Hals m ~es/ **A.** [pl ≚e] **1.** (Nacken) *neck*; kz, schlanker, steifer ~ *short, thin, stiff neck* **2.** (Kehle) *throat*; schlimmer ~ *bad th.* **3.** ⟨übtr⟩ **a.** ⟨tail⟩ *throat* (*open at the th.*) **b.** *neck* (of a bottle, violin) ‖ *stem* (of a wine-glass); *tail* (of a note) ‖ Säulen≚ *neck-mould* **B.** [pl H·alsen] ⟨mar⟩ (Haltetau) *tack* **C. 1.** jdm den ~ **abschneiden** *to cut a p's th.* ‖ sich den ~ ausspülen *to gargle one's th.* (mit *with*) ‖ den ~ ausrecken, e–n langen ~ m *to stretch* od *crane one's n.*; *to crane* (nach *at* od *for*) ‖ den ~ brechen *to break one's n.*; → ~ u Beinbruch ‖ das bricht ihm den ~ *that will ruin him* ‖ wir h mancher Flasche den ~ gebrochen *we have cracked many a bottle* ‖ ⟨hunt⟩ (of dog) ~ geben *to give tongue*; mit hellem ~e *in full cry* ‖ sich [dat] den ~ spülen (= trinken) ⟨vulg⟩ *to wash one's ivories* ‖ jdm den ~ umdrehen *to screw* (od *twist*) *a p's neck round*; ⟨fig⟩ *to break a p's n.*; ⟨sl⟩ *to scrag a p* ‖ es kann ihm den ~ kosten *that may cost him his life* ‖ °er kann den ~ nicht voll genug kriegen *he can never get enough* ‖ sich den ~ verdrehen *to rubber around* ‖ den ~ aus der Schlinge ziehen *to slip one's n. out of the collar* **2. ~ über Kopf** *head over heels*; *headlong*; *helter-skelter* **3.** °**am** Halse h *to have on one's back* ‖ bis an den ~ *up to the ears* (*in water*) ‖ (an e–m Band) am Halse getragen *worn on a neckband* ‖ °sich die Schwindsucht an den ~ ärgern *to worry o.s. to death* ‖ °es ging ihm an den ~ *his life was at stake* ‖ °sich jdm an den ~ werfen (of a girl) *to throw o.s. at* (*a man*); *to throw o.s. away upon a p* ‖ °jdm etw an den ~ werfen *to shoot a th at a p* | °du wirst die Polizei **auf** den ~ bek *you'll have the police down on you* ‖ °sich etw auf den ~ laden; etw auf dem ~e h *to be saddled with a th*; *she had two children on her hands* (od *back*) ‖ °sich die ganze Familie auf den ~ bringen *to bring the house about one's ears* | °wir schrieen **aus** vollem ~e *whe shouted at the top of our voices*; °wir sch. uns die Lunge aus dem ~e *we nearly screamed our lungs out* ‖ °aus vollem ~e lachen *to have a good laugh* | °sein Hab u Gut **durch** den ~ jagen *to waste one's substance in drink* | °es **im** ~e h *to have a sore throat*; der ~ tut mir weh, es tut mir im ~e weh *my throat pains me* ‖ *the words stuck in his throat* ‖ **in** (*or* **mit**) bloßem ~e (*to go*) *with one's th. exposed*; ⟨hunt⟩ → C. 1. | **um:** *to fall on a p's neck*; sich um den ~ fallen *to embrace* (*each other*) ‖ es geht um den ~ *it is a question of life and death* | °sich etw **vom** ~e schaffen *to get a th off one's mind* ‖ °bleib mir vom ~e *keep out of my way*; *stay away from me*; *leave me alone*! ‖ bleib mir mit deinem Klatsch v ~e *don't pester me with your gossip* | °die Zunge hing ihm **zum** ~e heraus *his tongue was out* || °es hängt mir zum ~e heraus; die S steht mir bis zum ~e *I am fed up* (*to the teeth*) *with it*; *I am sick* (*and tired*) *of it*; .. nachgerade .. *I'm getting a bit sick of it* || °jdm zum ~e herauswachsen (S) *to make a p sick* (*and tired*) | bis zum ~ (in Arbeit etc) *up to the chin, eyes* **~abschneider** m *cut-throat*; → Erpresser | ⁓isch [a] *cutthroat* [attr] **~ader** f *cervical vein*; (Kehlader) *jugular vein* **~band** n *necklace, dog--collar* | ~fink [m] ⟨orn⟩ = Prachtfink **~berge** f ⟨hist⟩ *gorget* **~binde** f *neck-tie*, ⟨mil⟩ *neckband* || ⟨fenc⟩ *neck bandage* || lederne ~ ⟨dial⟩ *stock* **~bräune** f ⟨path⟩ *diphtheria* L **⁓brechend, ⁓brecherisch** a *breakneck* (*speed*); *hair-raising* (*tricks*); *back-breaking* (*load*) **~bund** n *neckband* (*of a shirt*) **~drüse** f *jugular gland* **~eisen** n *iron collar*; ⟨Scot⟩ *jougs* pl **~entzündung** f *inflamed th.*; *inflammation of the th.*; eitrige ~ *angina* L **~gericht** n ⟨jur⟩ *criminal court* **~geschmeide** n *necklace* **~geschwulst** f *swelling* od *tumour in the n.* od *th.* **~geschwür** n *ulcer in the n.* **~kette** f *collar*; *neck chain*; *necklace-collar* **~kragen** m ⟨es & jur⟩ (aus Pelz) *tippet* || (Umhang) *cape* || (Leinen⁓) *collar* **~krankheit** f *th. disease* **~krause** f *ruff*; *frill* **~lappen** m (of a cow) → Triel **~muskel** m ⟨anat⟩ *cervical muscle* **~nerv** m *cervical nerve* **~priese** f *neckband* **~reif** m (gallisch, gewunden) *torque* **~riemen** m *neck strap* **~schlagader** f ⟨anat⟩ *carotid* **~schleife** f *neck-tie* **~schmerzen** m pl *sore throat* **~schmuck** m *necklace* **⁓starrig** a *headstrong, obstinate, stubborn*; *contumacious* **~starrigkeit** f *obstinacy, stubbornness*; *perversity*; *wilfulness*; ⟨jur⟩ *contumacy* **~stück** n *neck-piece* || (of beef) *neck beef* || (of mutton) dünnes ~ *scrag* **~tracht** f *neck-gear* **~tuch** n *neckcloth, neckerchief, scarf*; wollenes ~ *comforter, muffler* **~tüchlein** n *choker scarf* °~- **u Beinbruch**! ⟨fig⟩ *good luck*! ⟨Am⟩ *mud in the eye*! **~wärmer** m (wollener) *comforter* **~weh** n *sore th.* **~wirbel** m ⟨anat⟩ oberster ~ *atlas*

h·alsen A. vt/i [h] **1.** vt **a.** *to embrace*; *hug*; ⟨Scot⟩ *to halse* **b.** (Schiff) *to wear*; *veer* **2.** vi ⟨mar⟩ *to tack, wear* **B.** ⁓ n *tacking, wearing* **-halsig** [in comp] kurz~ *short-necked* → wag~

×**halt** adv: er ist ~ ein Bummler *he is a regular loafer*; *he is nothing but a l.* || er wird ~ nicht k *he won't come, I'm sure* || da muß man ~ arbeiten *there is nothing for it but to work* || es ist ~ so *it is just so*; das ist ~ so u nicht anders *that's exactly how it is*

halt intj *hold*!; *stop*! ⟨a. mot⟩ || (nicht z fest) *that will do*! || *hold hard*!; ~!, ~ an! ⟨mar⟩ *avast*! || *wait a minute*! || ~! das Geld her! *stand and deliver*! || ~! *hi you*! (od *you there*! *here*!) *what are you doing there*? || ⟨mil⟩ ~! wer da? *halt*! *who goes there*?; Batterie ~! *stand fast*! das Ganze ~! *cease firing* || ⟨sport⟩ ~! die Zeit ist um! *Time*!

Halt m ~es/~e **A. 1.** (Griff etc) *footing*; *hold*; ~ suchen *to seek support*; k–n ~ bieten f *to afford no hold for* (*foot or hand*); e–n festen ~ bek *to get a purchase* (*with one's feet*); den ~ verlieren *to lose one's footing*; den ~ wiedergewinnen *to recover one's footing* **2.** ⟨fig⟩ **a.** (Stütze) *support*; dies gibt ~ *this lends steadiness*; k–n ~ finden *or* h an jdm *to find no support* (od *backing*) *from a p*; sie fand an ihm e–n festen ~ *she found in him her mainstay* **b.** (innerer ~) *stay*; *religion is the stay of thousands* || er ist ein Mensch ohne inneren ~ *he has no* (*moral*) *backbone*; *he is lacking in fixity* (od *strength*) *of purpose* || den inneren ~ verlieren *to go off the deep end* || s–s ~es beraubt w *to have the ground cut from under one* || geistiger, moralischer ~ *mental, moral ballast*; *morale* (*of the troops*) **c.** (Einfluß, Macht) *grip, hold* (über *on, over*); *purchase* (über *over*); s–n ~ über jdn verlieren *to lose one's grip on a p* || festen ~ gewinnen in .. *to be firmly fastened upon* (*a country*) || k–n festen ~ h *to be of no standing*; *to have no permanency* **B. 1.** (Ruhe, Stillstand) *halt*; *temporary stoppage* || ~ gebieten *to call a halt*; e–r S ~ g. *to cry a halt to a th*; *to stop a th* **2.** ⟨rail⟩ *stop* **haltmachen** *to make* (od *call*) *a halt*; *to halt*; *rest*; (plötzlich) *to pull up short*; (of a rider) *to alight, stop*; *to stop over* (⟨Am⟩ *off*); *to put in* (*for lunch*) || die Truppen ~ l *to halt the troops* | ⟨fig⟩ ~ bei *to draw the line at* || nicht davor ~ z tun *not to recoil* od *shrink from doing*; *not to stop at doing* || vor nichts ~ *to stick* (od *stop*) *at nothing*

h·altbar a *solid, stable, strong* || (dauerhaft) *durable* (*goods*); *serviceable, holeproof* (*cloth*); sehr ~ s *to wear well* | *valid* (*reason*), *tenable* (*theory*) || ⟨mil⟩ (z halten) *defensible*; *tenable* (*fortress*; *position*) | **⁓keit** f *consistence, –cy*; *solidity, stability*; *durability*; *wear, wearing*; *life*; sehr gr ~ *very good wearing*; *keeping quality*; *shelf* (od *storage, service*) *life* (⟨a.⟩ ~sdauer) **⁓machung** f (*food*) *conservation*

H·alte- ~bügel m ⟨tech⟩ *bracket* **~feder** f ⟨tech⟩ *retainer spring* **~kind** n = Pflegekind **~linie** f ⟨mot⟩ *stop line* **~mannschaft** f ⟨aero⟩ *landing party*; *handling crew* **~platz** m Taxi⁓ *rank*, ⟨Am⟩ *stand* **~punkt** m **1.** = Stützpunkt **2.** = Haltestelle **3.** ⟨aero⟩ *taxi holding position* **4.** ⟨mil⟩ *stopping place* **~seil** n *tether* **~signal** n ⟨rail⟩ *block-signal*, ⟨mot⟩ "*Halt*" *sign* **~stelle** f *resting* od *stopping place*; (*bus*) *stop*; ⟨el⟩ *tram-*(*way*), od ⟨Am⟩ *streetcar* (*line*) *stop pedestrian loading island* **~tau** n *handling guy*; ~ (des Segels) *tack*; ⟨aero⟩ *anchor cable, guide-rope* **~verbot** n "*No Waiting* od *Stopping*" (sign); "*Waiting Prohibited*"; "*Clearway*" **~vorrichtung** f; ~en [pl] (beim Stapellauf) *blocks* pl **~zeichen** n = Haltesignal **~zeit** f ⟨mot⟩ *Waiting* (begrenzt *limited*)

h·alten vt/i [hielt/gehalten] [h] **I.** vt **A.** (**S, ein T** ~) **1. a.** (unterhalten) *to keep* (*a car, horses, servants*) || (Zeitung) *to take in a paper* || *to hold* (*the bank*) **b.** (**besitzen**) auf Lager ~ *to* (*keep in*) *stock* || in Gewahrsam ~ *to take care of*; *to keep* (*a th*) **2.** (**fest**~) **a.** ([etw] in der Hand) ~ *to carry* gehalten w in ..: *the glass is supported in ..* || sie hielt sich stützend an .. *she held on to* (*his right arm*) || (*the patient could not*) *hold* (*his water*) || *hold* (*my hat a moment*) || (in) *to hold in one's hand* **b.** *to hold* (*a fortress*); (Stadt) ~ gegen *to make good* (od *to keep*) *against* **3.** (in e–e best. Lage, Richtung bringen) **etw ~ an** .. *to hold* (od *put up*) *a th to one's mouth*; .. gegen das Licht *to the light*; (die Hände in) *to keep ..* (*in one's pockets*); das Ohr an die Tür ~ *to apply one's ear to the door* | (nimm diese Tatsachen) u halte sie **gegen** .. (..) *and set them against the fact that ..* **4. a. Andacht** ~ *to attend to one's devotions* || (**Fest**) *to keep*; **Frieden** ~ *to keep one's peace* || (**Gesetze**) ~ *to observe, keep* || (e–e **Hochzeit**) ~ *to celebrate* **Schule** ~ *to keep* (*school*) || **Schritt** ~ mit .. *to keep abreast of* (*a p*); **Takt** ~ *to keep time* || *to keep* (*one's word* od *promise*); sein Wort nicht ~ *to go back on one's word*; *to back out of one's promises* || die **Zunge** ~ *to hold one's tongue* **b.** (**ab**~) e–e **Ansprache** ~ *to give* (od *deliver*) *an address* || die **Predigt** ~ *to preach the sermon* || e–e **Rede** ~ *to make a speech*; (Versammlung) *to hold*; e–n **Vortrag** ~ *to give* (od *deliver*) *a lecture* **5.** (**S in e–m Zustand** ~) (Fleisch) **frisch** ~ *to keep fresh*; ein gut ge~es Wirtshaus *a well kept inn* || rein ~ *to keep clean* | etw **im Gang** ~ *to keep a th going* || im Gleichgewicht ~ *to balance* || das Zimmer war ganz in Weiß ge~ *the room was decorated entirely in white* || in Grenzen ~ *to keep within limits* || *to keep* (*in order*) || im Zaume ~ *to keep under control* | (**Preise**) auf der Höhe ~ *to keep up*; niedrig ~ *to keep down* || den Marktpreis ~ ⟨sl⟩

to peg the prices || jeden **Einsatz** ∼ (beim Spiel) *to take any stakes* | → **Ohren** || die **Zügel** locker (stramm) ∼ *to keep the reins loose* (*tight*) **B. (P) 1.** jdn gefangen ∼ *to keep a p prisoner* || → Schach, Zaum, Schranken | jdn **auf dem laufenden** ∼ *to keep a p informed* (od *up-to-date*; *up to the mark*) || jdn frei∼ *to treat a p* (z etw *to a th*); *to pay a p's expenses*; wir ∼ dich frei *it's* (od *have this one*) *on us* || Kinder streng ∼ *to be strict with the children* || (die Zuhörer) in Spannung ∼ *to hold* || jdn beim Wort ∼ *to hold a p to his word* || jdn zum besten ∼ *to make fun of a p*; *to mock a p*; *to hold a p up to ridicule* **b. (zurück∼)** *to detain*; *keep*; es hält mich nicht mehr *I can sit it no longer*; halt mich nicht *don't keep me* || (e–n Strauchelnden) *to hold up* **c. (an∼)** er ist ge∼, den Schaden z ersetzen *he is pledged to make good the damage* **C.** ∼ **für** (= **glauben**) **1. a. (P)** ich halte ihn f m–n Freund *I hold* (od *believe, consider, think*) *him to be my friend* || für wie alt ∼ Sie ihn? *what age do you suppose him to be?*, ⟨Am⟩ *how old do you take him to be?* || jdn irrig ∼ f *to take a p for*; *what do you take me for?* || *to be counted a gentleman* **b. (S)** das Leben f e–n Fluch ∼ *to count life a curse* || ich halte es f m–e Pflicht *I deem it my duty* || ich h. die Lage f ernst *I regard the situation as serious* || ich h. es f möglich *I think it possible* || man hielt es f passend *it was felt proper* || es f richtig ∼ z tun *to think fit* (od *good, proper*) *to do*; etw f richtig ∼ *to approve of a th* || jdm etw zugute ∼ *to give a p credit for a th* **2. es mit jdm** ∼ *to hold* od *side, join with, to back a p*; es mit beiden Parteien ∼ *to run with the hare and hunt with the hounds* **3. viel** *or* **gr Stücke** ∼ **von** *to think highly* (od *much* od *the world*) *of*; sehr viel ∼ v *to set great store by*; *to believe in*; *to be a believer in* (*iodine*); nicht viel ∼ v *to think poorly of ..*; *to have no opinion of*; nichts .. *not to believe in a th* || was hältst du davon? *how does this seem to you?*; *what's your view of the matter?*; *how do you feel about it?*; *what do you make of it?* || Sie wissen, was sie v Ärzten hielt *you know what she was like about doctors* || Wunder was ∼ v *to think the world of* **II. sich** ∼ ⟨mil⟩ *to maintain one's defense* **A. (P) 1.** sich **aufrecht** ∼ *to go upright*; *to hold up one's head* || brav = wacker || sich gerade ∼ *to hold one's back up* || sich abseits ∼ *to hold o.s. aloof*; *to keep aloof*; *to keep to o.s.* | sich ∼ *to carry o.s.* (*with dignity*); sich gut *or* wacker ∼ *to stand one's ground*; ⟨Am, fam⟩ *to take it on the chin* || sich gut ∼ *to keep up well*; *to do well* || sich wacker ∼ *to play the man, to come out well* || du hast dich wunderbar ge∼ *you are wonderfully preserved* | **(sich stützen)** *to steady o.s.*; um sich z ∼ .. *for support* (*she grasped a chair*) || sich im Gleichgewicht ∼ *to keep in equipoise* || sich über Wasser ∼ *to keep afloat* || sich in e–r Stellung ∼ ⟨Am sl⟩ *to hold down a job* **2. (zurück∼)** er ließ sich nicht ∼ *there was no holding him*; er konnte sich nicht ∼ vor L. *he had to hold his sides with laughter* **3. ich halte mich an ihn** *I cling* od *stick to him*; *I keep friends with him*; *I keep to* (*that plan*) || sich dicht an der Küste ∼ *to hug the coast* || sich **ans** Gesetz ∼ *to abide by the law* || *to adhere to* (*rules*); sich (streng) an die Regeln ∼ *to follow the rules*; *to toe the line* (*to stick closely to the r.*) | sich **in** den Grenzen der Vorschriften ∼ *to keep within the rules* (*of the House*) | sich ∼ **mit** *to carry on with* (*a woman*) | sich **bereit** ∼ *to keep ready* || sich etw gegenwärtig ∼ *to be aware of a th*; *to be alive to a th* | sich **ran** *or* **dazu∼** *to make haste*; *to look sharp, to put* od *keep one's nose to the grindstone* || sich **rechts, links** ∼ *to keep* (od *strike, bear*) *to the r., l.* | sich schadlos ∼ *to indemnify o.s.* **4.** sich [dat] den Bauch ∼ *to hold one's sides* (vor *with laughter*) **5.** sich **f klug,** unwiderstehlich ∼ *to consider* (od *think*) *o.s. clever, irresistible* **B. (S)** *to keep*; (of colour) *to last* || sich gut ∼ (of cloth) *to wear well*; (*of flowers*) *to last well* || die F. kann sich nicht länger ∼ *the fortress cannot hold out any longer*; sich hartnäckig ∼ (*rumours will*) *persist a long time* || die Forderung hielt sich in mäßigen Grenzen *the demand kept within reasonable limits* || die Kurse ∼ sich *the exchange remains firm* || das Stück wird sich nicht lange ∼ *the play will not run much longer* **III.** vi **A. (haltmachen)** *to halt*; *to* (*come to a*) *stop* || kurz(e Zeit) ∼ *to stop off* || er hielt an der S. der St. *he drew up at the side of the road* || der Zug hält an (*or* auf) allen St. *the train stops* (⟨Am⟩ *is held*) *at all stations* | **∼d** *stationary* (*vehicle*) **B. 1. (Druck aushalten)** *the cord holds*; *the rope is safe* || (of an anchor) *to bite* || (of the ice) *to hold, bear* || länger ∼ als etw *to outwear a th* || der Stoff hält gut *the material wears well* || er schuftet, was das Zeug hält *he works with might and main*; *he works hammer and tongs* **2.** mit s–r Meinung nicht **hinter dem Berge** ∼ *to express one's opinion openly* **3. an sich** ∼ *to hold one's hand*; *to control, check, contain o.s.*; *to keep o.s. well in hand*; er konnte nicht an sich ∼ *he could not help himself*; er mußte an sich ∼, sie nicht z küssen *it went hard with him not to kiss her* **4.** ∼ **auf** *to stand upon* (*ceremony*); *to respect* (*one's status*); *to observe* (*good manners*) || **auf sich** ∼ *to be self-respecting*; sehr auf sich, auf s–e Kleidung ∼ *to think a lot of one's p, of one's clothing*; auf sich ∼d *self-respecting*; jeder, der etw auf sich hält *any s.-r. p* **5. es hält schwer,** sich auf der Karte zurechtzufinden *it is difficult to see one's way on the map* || °**dicht** ∼ (nichts ausplaudern) → dicht∼ **IV. H·alten** n **1.** *halt*; *stop*(*ping*); (Wagen) zum ∼ bringen *to bring to a halt*; *to stop*; ⟨Am⟩ *to halt* **2.** *the keeping* (*of servants*; *of a feast*); *retaining* (*terrain*) || *observation* (*of laws*) || *the making* (*of a speech*) || *holding* (*of meetings*) || ⟨sport⟩ *holding* (*of an opponent*) **3.** (sie lief), da war kein ∼ mehr (..) *there was no holding her* **H·alter** m ∼s/∼ **1.** (Stütze) *hold*; ∼ [pl] f Füße u Hände *foot and hand holds* pl || *handle*; *holdfast*; *hook*; *rest*; *support* || U-förmiger ∼ *stirrup* || (f Briefschaften) *rack* **2.** (Haltvorrichtung) *holder* (*for a bottle*); *support hook* || Feder∼ *penholder* **H·älterteich** m *wintering pond* **H·alterung** f ∼/∼en *holding, holder*; *mounting, m. support*; *supporting facility* **-haltig,** [österr] **-hältig** [in comp] *containing*; *bearing*; *holding*; *-ferous*; s·ilber∼ *argentiferous* || r·eich∼ *rich* **h·altlos** a **1.** *limp*; *unstable, unsteady*; *boneless*; *without backbone*; *invertebrate, irresolute*; *unprincipled*; *aimless* (*youth*); ∼er Mensch ⟨sl⟩ *loose fish*; ∼ s *to be off one's oats* || *lax* (*conduct*) **2.** (unhaltbar) *untenable* (*theory*) || *baseless*; *unfounded, unsubstantial* (*rumour*) **3.** (grundlos) *gratuitous* **H·altlosigkeit** f ∼/∼en **1.** (P) *unsteadiness, irresoluteness, spinelessness* **2.** *untenableness* (*of a theory*) || *baselessness* (*of a statement*); *unfoundedness* **H·altung** f ∼/∼en **1.** **(Körper∼)** *bearing* (*a good, military, self-confident b.*); *carriage* (*of a p's head*; aufrechte ∼ *erect c.*); *deportment* (laxe ∼ *careless d.*); *gait* (*a stiff g.*) || *posture* || *comportment* (*of a stag*) || ⟨arts⟩ *action* || ⟨phot⟩ *attitude, pose* (un)gezwungen (*un*)*affected*; *self-conscious*) *action* (*of a player, horse*) || ⟨golf⟩ *stance* || sich e–e bessere ∼ angewöhnen *to accustom o.s. to a better carriage* || in militärischer ∼ *at attention*; milit. ∼ annehmen *to stand* (*at*) *attention*; *to come to a.* || stramme ∼ annehmen *to spring to attention* **2. (geistige** ∼) *attitude* (gegen, z *towards, to*; an-, einnehmen *to assume*); Geistes∼ *attitude of mind* || *approach* (gegenüber jdm *to a p*) || ∼ bewahren *to maintain one's upright bearing*; *to keep one's countenance, to save one's face* || abwartende ∼ *waiting* od *wait-and-see attitude* || abweichende ∼ einnehmen gegenüber .. *to join issue with a p's* *conclusions*; → ablehnend || e–e energische (theatralische) ~ einnehmen *to take a strong line* (*to strike an attitude*) || ohne innere ~ *meek in spirit* || ⟨Am⟩ *slant* **3.** (e–s **Briefes** etc) *tone* || ~ der **Börse** *the tone on Change*; matte ~ *flatness* || der Markt schloß in ruhiger aber fester ~ *at the close the market was quiet but firm* || fremde Werte zeigten feste ~ *foreign stocks were firm* **4. sittliche** ~ *moral outlook* od *will-power*; *principle* (*a man of high p.*)

Hal·unke m ~n/~n *blackguard*; *rascal*; *scoundrel*; *scum*; die ~n [pl] *the scum*; *riff-raff* || ⟨hum⟩ *rascal*; *rogue* **~ngesicht** n *gallows-look* **~nstreich** m *scurvy trick*

Hamam·elis f ⟨bot⟩ *witch hazel*

Häma- ~t·it m ~s/~e ⟨minr⟩ *haematite* **~t·om** n ⟨path⟩ *haematoma* **~tur·ie** f *haematuria*

H·amburg n ⟨Ger⟩ (Freie u Hansestadt) Hafen: „Das Tor zur Welt"

H·ameln n ⟨Ger⟩ (Stadt) *Hamelin*; → Rattenfänger

H·amen[1] m ~s/~ *purse* (od *draw*)*-net*; Kescher

H·amen[2] m ~s/~ = Angelhaken

h·ämisch 1. [a] *crafty*; *gloating* (*smile*); *malicious* (*grin, pleasure*); *sneering* (*remark*) || *spiteful*; *ironical*; *sardonic* || ~es Gesicht, Bemerkung *sneer*; ein ~es G., e–e ~e B. m *to sneer* (über *at*) **2.** [adv] *maliciously* (*to grin m.*); *sneeringly* || sich ~ freuen *to gloat* (über [*up*]*on, over*) || ~ kichern *to snigger, snicker* (*at*) || ~ spötteln *to sneer* (*at*)

Ham·it m ~en/~en ⟨bib⟩ *Hamite*; die ~en *the Hamites* **ham·itisch** a *Hamitic* (*language*)

H·ämling m *eunuch* **H·ammel** m ~s/~ & ⁓ ⟨zoo⟩ *wether* || ⟨cul⟩ *mutton* || nach e–m ~ mit 5 Beinen suchen ⟨fam⟩ *to look for maidenheads* || ⟨fig⟩ (Rekrut) *joskin, rustic*; ⟨sl⟩ *rooky*, ⟨aero⟩ *erk* **~braten** m *roast mutton* **~fleisch** n *mutton* || ⟨cul⟩ ~, Kohl u Kartoffeln *Irish stew* **~keule** *leg of m.* **~möhre** f ⟨bot⟩ *parsnip* **~reis** m *pilaff* **~rippchen** n *muttonchop* **~rücken** m *saddle of m.* **~sprung** m ⟨parl⟩ *division*

H·ammer m ~s/⁓ **A.** (Werkzeug) **1.** *hammer* || ⟨min⟩ *mattock*; ~ u Schlägel *h. and wedge* || Schmiede⁓ *smith's h.*; *sledge h.* || Splitt⁓, Klau⁓, Finn⁓, ~ mit gespaltener Finne *claw-h.* || ~ mit Kugelfinne *ball pane h.* || ~ mit zwei Bahnen *double-faced h.* || Preßluftbohr⁓ *pneumatic drill* || Vorschlag⁓ *forehammer* | Schlacht⁓ *slaughter-h.* || ~ zum Steinhauen *scutch* | mit dem ~ **schlagen** *to* (*knock* od *hit with the*) *h.* || den ~ zerschlagen auf .. *to break the h. on ..* | ~ **u Amboß** *hammer and anvil*; ⟨fig⟩ zw ~ u A. s *to strike and to be struck*; *to bear the brunt*; ~ oder A. s *to dominate or be d.d* **2. Holz**⁓ *mallet* || ⟨parl & **Auktions**⁓⟩ *gavel* || ⟨fig⟩ unter den ~ bringen (k) *to bring* (*come*) *under the h.* **3.** ⟨übtr⟩ **a.** *sport h.* **b.** (Glocken⁓, Klavier⁓) *hammer* **c.** ⟨anat⟩ (im Ohr) *malleus* L **B.** (Eisenwerk) *forge* **~bahn** f *h.-face* **~bär** m *tup* **~eisen** n *h.-wrought iron* **~fallwerk** n *drop-h.*; *drop-press* **~finne** f *pane of a h.* **⁓gar** a *tough-pitch* (*copper*) **~glocke** f *clock-bell* **~hai** m ⟨ich⟩ *h.-shark* **~klavier** n ⟨mus hist⟩ *clavichord*; *h.-clavier* [Ger] **~kopf** m *h.-head*; *tup* | ~schraube [f] *T headed bolt* **~schlag** m **1.** *h.-blow* (od *stroke*); *blow of the h.*; *stroke with a h.* || (drei) ⁓e tun *to tap the stone* **2.** ⟨met⟩ *h.-* (od *forge*)*-scale* **~schmied** m *h.-smith* **~schmiedestück** n *drop-forging* **~stiel** m *helve*; *haft*; *handle* (*of a h.*) **~werfen** n ⟨sport⟩ *h.-throw*(*ing*); *throwing the h.* **~werk** n *ironworks, forge* || *striking mechanism* **~wurz** f ⟨bot⟩ Weiße ~ *white hellebore* **h·ämmerbar** a (kalt) *malleable*; (warm) *forgeable* | ⁓keit [f] ~/ *malleability*

h·ämmern A. vi/t [h] **1.** vi **a.** (des Spechts) *to rap, tap* **b.** *to h.*; drauflos~ *to h. away* (an *at*) || ~ an *to h.* (od *knock, rap*) *at* (*the door*) || ~ auf etw *to h. on a th*; *to h.* (od *rap, tap*) *a th* || auf dem Klavier ~ *to pound the piano* **c.** ⟨fig⟩ (of the heart, etc.) *to beat*; *throb* (vor *with*); *to work* **2.** vt **a.** (Metall) *to h.* (z *into*); glatt ~ *to planish* **b.** ⟨fig⟩ jdm etw ins Gewissen ~ *to h. a th into, to impress a th upon a p* (od *a p's mind*) **B.** ⁓ n *h.ing*; *knocking, rapping* (an *at*); *rap, tap* (an .. *at the door*)

Hämo- [in comp] (Blut–) *haemo–*, ⟨Am⟩ *hemo–* **~glob·in** n *h–globin* **~l·yse** f *h–lysis* Gr **⁓l·ytisch** a *h–lytic* **~phil·ie** f *h–philia* L **~pt·yse** f *h–ptysis* Gr **~rrhag·ie** f *h–rrhage* **~rrhoid·al** [–ridɑ:l] a *h–rrhoidal*; ⁓knoten [pl] *h. excrescences* pl; *piles* pl **~rrho·iden** [–ri:dən] pl ⟨path⟩ *h–rrhoids, piles* pl **~spor·idium** n ⟨zoo⟩ *h–sporidium* L [pl] *–dia*] **~st·ase** d *h–stasis* Gr

H·ampelmann m *dancing* (*supple-*)*jack* ⟨a. fig⟩

°**h·ampeln** vi [h] = zappeln || ~ nach etw *to make a grab at a th*

H·amster m ~s/~ ⟨zoo⟩ *hamster*; *German marmot* || *greedy as a h.* | ~backen [f pl] *cheeks like a h.*; ~fell [n] *h.'s skin* **~·ei** f ⟨fig⟩ *hoarding*; *grabbing* | **~er** m ⟨fig⟩ *hoarder*; *grabber* **h·amstern A.** vi/t [h] ⟨fig⟩ *to hoard, grab*, ⟨Am sl⟩ *sock* **B.** ⁓ n *hoarding*

Hand f ~/⁓e **I. 1.** ⟨anat⟩ *hand* || durch Aufheben, Hochheben der ⁓e *by show of h.s* || er hat alle ⁓e voll z tun *his work is cut out for him* || flache, hohle ~ *palm*; (etw) mit der fl. ~ berühren, in der ho. ~ verbergen *to palm* **2.** ⟨fig⟩ **a.** (**Schutz**) in Gottes ~ *in the h.s of God*; *in God's keeping* || Gunstbezeigungen aus jds ~ *favours at a p's h.* || die schützende ~ v jdm abziehen *to withdraw one's protecting h. from a p* || e–e offene ~ h *to be open-h.ed* || ihm fehlt die väterliche ~ *he lacks the guiding h. of a father* | (**Fügung**) Gottes ~ sehen in .. *to see the h. of God in* (*history*) **b.** (**Macht**) *hand*[*s* pl]; *grasp*; *grip*; *sway* || ich bin ganz in Ihrer ~ *I am entirely in your h.s* || er hat sein Leben ganz in s–r ~ *he has the ball at his feet* || wir h die Situation ganz in unserer ~ *we have the situation in our h.s*; *the situation is well in h.* || das Heft fest in der ~ h *to hold all the strings in one's h.* || es lag in m–r ~ *it was* (od *lay*) *in my h.s* || es liegt in d–r ~ *it lies with you* (*to do*); **3.** (**Geschick**) e–e leichte ~ *a light h.*; e–e glückliche ~ *a lucky h.*; ⟨gard bes Am⟩ *green thumb* || e–e bessernde ~ legen an etw *to improve a th* || °e–e lockere ~ h *to be ready with a blow* || mit geschickter, kluger ~ *with a skilful h.*; *skilfully*; jds g. ~ im Spiel vermuten *to suspect a p's deft complicity in a th* || mit starker ~ lenkte er .. *with a strong h. he ruled* (*the country*) **4. a.** (**Handschrift**) *hand*; e–e gute, leserliche ~ schreiben *to write a good, legible h.* **b.** ⟨cards⟩ e–e gute ~ *a good h.*; ⟨fig⟩ er hat etw hinter der ~ *he is a man with a background* **5.** (**Träger der** ~) in **guten** ⁓en (*the book is*) *in good h.s*; in den **besten** ⁓en *in the best of h.s*; der Wein wurde v **zarter** ~ dargeboten *the wine was presented by dainty h.s* (od *by ladies*) || das Buch war schon in **vielen** ⁓en *the book has passed through many h.s* || das Haus ist in **festen** ⁓en *the house is unsal*(*e*)*able* || er ist in f. ⁓en ⟨fam⟩ *he's hooked* (*up*); sie ist in f. ⁓en *she's private property*; ⟨Am fam⟩ *she's been going steady* || aus **erster** ~ *at the best h.*, (*to learn, buy a th*) *at first h.*; aus zweiter ~ *at second h.*; *second-h.*; Informationen aus erster ~ *first-h. information* || aus **sicherer** ~ *on good authority* || die **rechte** ~ (jds) (*a p's*) *right hand*; ⟨hors⟩ *whip h.*; linke ~ *bridle h.* || *right-h. man* || die „schöne" ~ *the right h.* || er hat 2 linke ⁓e *his fingers are all thumbs*; ich habe .. *I feel all th.s* || von verbrecherischer ~ (*done*) *by criminal h.s* **6.** ⟨**jur**⟩ **öffentliche** ~ *authoritative power* od *corporation*; *the State*; *public funds* pl; Unterstützung aus ö. ~ *the dole*; U. aus ö. ~ beziehen *to be on the dole* || Tote ~ *mortmain*; an die T. ~ veräußern *to amortize*; Veräußerung an die T. ~ *amortization* **II. bes Wendungen A.** [**sg** ~] **1.** ~ aufs Herz *hand on heart* || ~ in ~ (*to go, work*) *h. in h.* (mit *with*) ||

~ in ~ gehen ⟨sex⟩ *to hold h.s,* ⟨vulg⟩ *to play at handy* ‖ ~ über ~ (*to climb, swim*) *h. over h.*; ~-über-~ Schwimmen *trudgen stroke* ‖ **~ u Fuß h** *to be solidly built*; die S hat ~ u F. *there is sth in that*; sein Vorschlag hatte ~ u F. .. *was very much to the point*; alles, was er sagt. hat ~ u F. *there is reason in all he says* ‖ weder ~ noch F. *neither rhyme nor reason* ‖ °~ v der Butter *h.s off*! **2. ~ anlegen** *to lend a h.*; *to play one's part* ‖ ~ anl. an etw *to put a h. to a th*; letzte ~ anl. *to put the finishing touches* (an *on*) ‖ an jdn ~ anl. *to do a p harm* ‖ jdm die ~ **bieten** *to hold out* (od *offer*) *one's h. to a p*; jdm die ~ der Versöhnung b. *to reconcile a p* ‖ jdm kräftig die ~ **drücken** *to give a p a firm h.shake*; *to wring a p by the h.* ‖ die ~ warnend erheben *to hold up a warning h.* ‖ die ~ erheben gegen .. *to lift one's h. against a p* ‖ jdm die ~ **geben** *to give a p the h.*; *to shake h.s with a p*; ich kann Ihnen k–e ~ g. *I can't shake h.s*; sich [dat] die ~ geben *to shake h.s* (auf etw *on a th*) ‖ er gab ihm die ~ s–r T. *he gave him his daughter in marriage* ‖ (immer *or* überall) die ~ im Spiele h *to have a h. in*; *to have a finger in the pie* (*in every pie*); *to have an oar in another's boat* (*in every man's boat*) ‖ jds ~ **halten** (u drücken) *to hold h.s with a p*, ⟨vulg⟩ *to play at handy* ‖ die ~ auf dem Beutel halten *to be tightfisted* ‖ jdm die ~ küssen *to kiss a p's h.* ‖ schnell die ~ von etw l *to drop a th like a hot potato* ‖ ~ **legen** an jdn *to lay h.s on a p*; *to attempt a p's life*; ~ an sich legen *to lay h.s on o.s.* ‖ die ~ an (*or* auf) etw legen *to lay h.s on a th*; *to appropriate a th* ‖ die ~ für etw ins Feuer legen *to be full of enthusiasm for a th, to guarantee a th*; .. f jdn .. *to go bail* (od *to vouch*) *for a p*; .. dafür, daß .. *to guarantee that* ..; dafür lege ich m–e ~ ins Feuer *I'll go bail for that*, ⟨fam⟩ *I would give my ears* ‖ ~ ans Werk legen *to go* od *set to work* ‖ die letzte ~ legen an etw *to give the finishing touch(es) to a th*; *to put the finishing h. to a th* ‖ jdm die ~ **reichen** *to offer one's h. to a p* ‖ er reichte ihm widerstrebend die ~ *he gave him a reluctant h.* ‖ ⟨übtr⟩ jdm die ~ reichen *to offer a p one's h. in marriage* ‖ jdm die ~ **schütteln** *to shake a p by the h.* ‖ man konnte nicht die ~ vor den Augen **sehen** *you could not see beyond your noses* ‖ ⟨prov⟩ eine ~ **wäscht** die andere *one good turn deserves another*, ⟨fam⟩ *roll my log and I'll roll yours* **3.** die Politik der **freien** ~ *the policy of the free h.* ‖ *to have a free h.*; *to be free* (od *at liberty*) (*to do*); jdm freie ~ l *to give a p a free h.* ‖ gib ihm den kl Finger, so will er gleich die **ganze** ~ *give him an inch and he'll take an ell* ‖ jdm die **schöne** ~ geben *to give a p the right h.* ‖ e–e **sichere** ~ h *to have a firm h.* **4. an ~ e–r S** (*to judge*) *by* od *from a th*; *in the light of* (*the latest results*); **an der ~** (*to lead a p*) *by the h.* ‖ jdm etw an ~ geben *to give a p the refusal of a th*; jdm ein Haus an ~ g. *to give a p an option on a house* ‖ jdm etw an die ~ g. *to furnish* od *supply a p with a th* ‖ jdm an die ~ gehen *to lend a p a h.* ‖ etw an ~ h *to have the refusal of a th* ‖ etw an der ~ h *to have a th at h.* (od *in readiness*; *available*) | es liegt (klar) **auf** der ~ *it is* (*quite*) *obvious* (*that* ..); (*the reason*) *isn't far to see* | °⟨fig⟩ **aus** der ~ fressen *to feed out of a p's h.* ‖ ⟨fig⟩ etw aus der ~ geben, verlieren *to lose control of a th*; *to loosen one's grip on a th*; *to lose the grip of* (*a subject*); *to let a th slip out of one's h.s* ‖ aus der ~ in den Mund leben *to live from hand to mouth* ‖ der Tod hat ihm die Feder aus der ~ genommen *death has struck the pen from his h.* ‖ jdm etw aus der ~ reißen *to snatch* od *jerk a th out of a p's h.* ‖ jdm etw aus der ~ schlagen ⟨fig⟩ *to tear a th from a p* ‖ jdm die Waffen aus der ~ schlagen *to strike the weapons from a p's h.s*; ⟨fig⟩ *to steal a p's thunder* ‖ aus freier ~ zeichnen *to draw by free-hand* | **bei der ~** *at* (⟨Am⟩ *on*) *h.*; *to have a th at h.* (od *in readiness*; *available*) ‖ jdn bei der ~ nehmen *to take a p by the h.* ‖ schnell bei der ~ s *to be ready* (od *very obliging*) (mit *with* [*a gun*]) | mit dem Stock **in der** ~ trat er ein .. *he entered, stick in hand*; mit .. in der ~ *holding* ..; °nicht in die ~! *by no means, on no account*! ‖ °in die ~ gespuckt! *take off the gloves*!, *beef up*! ‖ °besser als in die hohle ~ geschissen ⟨vulg⟩ *better than a kick in the pants* ‖ etw fest in der ~ behalten *to keep hold of a th* ‖ jdm etw in die ~ drücken *to thrust a th into a p's h.* ‖ jdm etw in die ~ geben *to put a th into a p's h.s* ‖ etw in die ~ geloben *to promise a th solemnly* ‖ ⟨übtr⟩ jdn fest in der ~ h *to have a p well in h.*; (etw) .. *to have firm control of*; → I. 2. b. ‖ muß in einer ~ liegen *must be undivided* ‖ (etw) in die ~ bek *to gain control* (*of events*); (etw) in die ~ nehmen *to take in h.*; *to take up* (od *on*); e–e Aufgabe in die ~ n. *to set one's h.s to a task* | **mit einer** ~ *one-h.* [attr]; **mit der** ~ (gemacht) *by h.*; .. hergestellt *h.-made*; .. gewebt *h.-woven* ‖ Griff mit der ~ *handgrip* ‖ (Gegner) mit der ~ fortstoßen ⟨Rugb ftb⟩ *to hand off* ‖ mit der ~ gleiten über .. *to pass* (od *run*) *one's h. over* (*a surface*) ‖ er winkte mir mit der ~ *he waved his h. to me* ‖ mit der linken ~ schlagen ⟨baseball⟩ *to southpaw* | **um** die ~ e–r Dame anhalten *to ask the h. of a lady in marriage* | **unter** der ~ ⟨fig⟩ *underhand*; (*to sell*) *secretly* (od *by private contract*); *privately*; ⟨sl⟩ *on the sly, crook, quiet* (abbr *q.t.*); *under the table*; sich [dat] etw unter der ~ beschaffen ⟨sl⟩ *to wangle a th* | (etw) **von** der ~ weisen *to refuse* od *reject a th*; *to decline doing a th*; es läßt sich nicht v der ~ w. *it cannot be denied* ‖ ihm geht die Arbeit flott v der ~ *he is a quick worker* ‖ v ~ z ~ gehen *to go from h. to h.*; *to pass through many h.s* ‖ v ~ *manually*; v langer ~ vorbereitet *prepared long in advance* | **vor der** ~ *first*; *first of all*; *for the present*; *just now* | **zur** ~ h *to have at* (⟨Am⟩ *on*) *h.*; *to have to one's h.*; *to have* (*a th*) *handy* od *pat* ‖ (nicht) z ~ s (*not*) *to be handy* ‖ zur rechten ~ *on the right-h. side* **B. [pl ~̈e] 1.** ~̈e hoch! *h.s up*!, ⟨Am fam⟩ *put 'em up*! ‖ ~̈e weg! *h.s off*! die ~̈e **auflegen** *to lay on one's h.s* (*in blessing*) ‖ jdm die ~̈e **binden** *to force a p's h.s*; ihm sind die ~̈e gebunden *his h.s are bound* ‖ etw den ~̈en jds entreißen *to strip a th from a p's h.s* ‖ die ~̈e falten *to fold one's h.s*; *to join h.s* ‖ die ~̈e v etw l *to let a th alone* ‖ die ~̈e in den Schoß legen *to twiddle one's fingers* (od *thumbs*); *to fold one's h.s*; *to idle one's time away*; *to take it easy* ‖ sich die ~̈e **reichen** *to shake h.s*; .. fürs Leben *to join h.s for life* ‖ alle ~̈e voll z tun h *to have one's h.s full* ‖ sich die ~̈e **waschen** *to wash one's h.s*; (z Damen) wollen Sie sich die ~̈e waschen? *do you want to powder your nose*?; sich wegen e–r S die ~̈e in Unschuld waschen *to wash one's h.s of a th* ‖ die ~̈e über dem Kopf zus–schlagen *to be struck with amazement* **2.** er lebte **von s–r ~̈e Arbeit** *he lived by his h.s* **3. an ~̈en u Füßen** gebunden s *to be bound h. and foot* | (jdn) **auf** (den) ~̈en tragen *to make much of* (*a p*); er trug sie auf ~̈en *he did everything he could for her*; (Kind zu zweit) auf verschränkten ~ tr. *to chair* | jdm .. **aus den ~̈en** reißen *to tear* (*a th*) *from a p* | jdm **in die ~̈e** arbeiten (*or* spielen) *to play into a p's h.s* ‖ etw in die ~̈e bek *to be placed in control, to get hold of a th* ‖ in jds ~̈e fallen, jdm in die ~̈e fallen *to fall into the h.s of a p*; *they got their h.s on him*; (S) *to fall in with a p* ‖ dein Brief ist in m–e ~̈e gelangt *your letter has come to h.* ‖ etw in ~̈en h *to have hold of a th* ‖ wieviele h den Brief schon in ~̈en gehabt! *how many have handled the letter*? ‖ wir h noch etw Geld v Ihnen in ~̈en *we have still some of your money in h.* ‖ in die ~̈e klatschen *to clap one's h.s*; *to applaud* ‖ (etw) in jds ~̈e legen *to lay into a p's h.s* ‖ in den ~̈en jds liegen (S) *to be vested in a p* ‖ die Beine in die ~̈e nehmen *to put one's best foot foremost* ‖ jdm etw in die ~̈e spielen *to arrange for a th to fall into a p's h.s* ‖ das Buch hat ihm der

Zufall in die ⁓e gespielt *the book came into his h.s by accident* ‖ → in die ∼ sp. ‖ in andere ⁓e übergehen *to change hands* ‖ in amerik. ⁓e über-*to pass into American h.* ‖ → I. 5. | **mit den ⁓en** in den Taschen, auf den Knien *his h.s in his p.s, h.s on k.s* ‖ mit beiden ⁓en ⟨fig⟩ *with both h.s* ‖ mit rauhen, harten ⁓en *roughhanded* ‖ (etw) mit den ⁓en anfassen *to handle* ‖ mit den ⁓en befördern, tragen *to manhandle* ‖ mit ⁓en z greifen (*it is*) *quite obvious* ‖ mit den ⁓en reden *to gesticulate* ‖ sich mit ⁓en u Füßen gegen etw sträuben *or* wehren *to fight* (*against*) *a th h. and foot* (od *with might and main*), *to oppose a th tooth and nail* ‖ mit beiden ⁓en z·ugreifen ⟨fig⟩ *to grasp eagerly* ‖ gleich geschickt mit beiden ⁓en *ambidex-t(e)rous* ‖ (etw) mit bloßen ⁓en anfassen *to grasp in one's bare h.s* ‖ etw mit eigenen ⁓en m *to do a th for o.s.* ‖ mit leeren ⁓en weggehen *to go empty-handed* | (etw) **unter** den ⁓en h *to have in h.* (od *on one's h.s*) ‖ unter den ⁓en zerrinnen *to melt away in one's h.s* | **zu ⁓en v Herrn N.** (als Bearbeiter) (*for* od *to the*) *attention of Mr. N.*; Gebr. N. N. z ⁓en des Verkaufsleiters *The Sales Manager, N. N. Bros.* ‖ (etw) z ⁓en jds übersenden *to deliver to a p* ‖ z treuen ⁓en *in trust* **III.** [in comp] → Hand-; Hände-

H·and- [in comp] *hand-*; *manual* **∼anlegen** n → Hand; Grüßen durch ∼ an die Kopfbedeckung ⟨mil⟩ *h. salute* **∼antrieb** m *h.-drive*; *h.-driving* **∼apparat** m ⟨scient⟩ *handy* (od *working*) *collection* ‖ ⟨telph⟩ *h.set* **∼arbeit** f **1.** (Ggs Maschinen-) *h.-labour*; *m. labour*; *h.-work*; kunstvolle ∼ *h.icraft*; ∼sschule *h.work classes* pl **2.** (weibl) *needlework*; feine ∼ *fancy-work* **∼arbeiter** m *m. labourer* **∼atlas** m *school-atlas* **∼auf** n ⟨ftb⟩ *touch-down* **∼auflegung** f ⟨ec⟩ *imposition of the h.s* **∼ausgabe** f *medium-sized reference book* **∼ball** m, **∼ballspiel** n ⟨bes Ger sport⟩ *h.ball* **∼ballen** m *ball of the thumb* **∼beil** n *hatchet* **∼besen** m *h.-broom*; *brush* **∼betrieb** m *m. power*; mit ∼ *h.-driven, h.-operated* **∼bewegung** f *wave of the* (od *one's*) *h.*; ⟨comp⟩ *h. travel*; mit e–r schwungvollen ∼ *with a sweep of the h.* **∼bibliothek** f *reference library* **∼bohrer** m *gimlet* (dazu: *to g.*) **∼breite** f *h.breadth*; *h.* (= *4 inches*) **∼bremse** f *h.-brake* ‖ ⟨mot a⟩ *parking b.* **∼buch** n *h.book*; *m.* [s]; *text-book*; *guide* **∼deutungslehre** f *chiromancy* **∼eimer** m *pail* **∼eisen** n *h.cuff* **∼eule** f, **∼feger** m (Besen) *whisk*; *h.-broom* **∼exemplar** n *reference-book, copy in use* **⁓fertig** a *h.y* **∼fertigkeit** f *h.iness*; *h.*; *m. skill* ‖ ∼sunterricht [m] *m. training* **∼fessel** f *h.cuff* ‖ jdm ∼n anlegen *to h.cuff a p* **⁓fest** a *stalwart, stout*; *robust, strong, sturdy*; *strapping* (*girl*); ⟨Am⟩ *rugged* | (S) *strong* (*branch*; *position*) ‖ *downright* (*lie*); *rank* **∼feuerlöscher** m *h.-extinguisher* **∼feuerwaffen** f pl *small-arms* pl **∼fläche** f *palm* **∼flügler** m ⟨zoo⟩ → Fledermaus **⁓förmig** a ⟨scient⟩ *palmate(d)* **∼galopp** m *canter* **⁓gearbeitet** a *h.-made* **∼gebrauch** m *h.-use* **⁓gefertigt** a *h.-made* **∼geld** n ⟨com⟩ *earnest(-money)*; *han(d)sel* ‖ ⟨mil⟩ *bounty* ‖ jdm ein ∼ geben *to han(d)sel a p* **∼gelenk** n *wrist* (am ∼ *on the w.*) ‖ ⟨fig⟩ °er hat ein lockeres ∼ *he has a ready h.* ‖ ⟨fig⟩ °aus dem ∼ *with the greatest ease*; *without any preparation*; *offhand*; etw aus dem ∼ m *to swing a matter over one's head*; (etw) aus dem ∼ einrichten *to improvise* ‖ ⟨mus⟩ Anschlag aus dem ∼ *w.-touch* ‖ Schlag aus dem ∼ *w.-stroke* ‖ ⟨crick⟩ schnellende Wendung des ∼s *flick* | ∼slähmung *w.-drop* **⁓gemein** a: ∼ w *to come to blows* (od *grips*; *close quarters*); ∼ w mit jdm *to close with a p* **∼gemenge** n *scuffle* (im ∼, beim ∼ *in the sc.*); *rough-and-tumble*; *close fight* (od *quarters*); *dog-fight*; *mix-up*; ⟨Am⟩ *rough-house* ‖ ⟨sport ftb⟩ *scrimmage*; ⟨Am school⟩ *rush* ‖ ⟨mil⟩ *affray*; *skirmish*; *h.-to-h. fighting*; ins ∼ k mit *to close with* **⁓genäht** a *h.-sewn* **∼gepäck** n *small luggage* ‖ ⟨rail⟩, ∼aufbewahrungsstelle *left luggage office*; *cloak-room*, ⟨Am⟩ *parcel room, baggage to hand check-room*; (Gepäck) im ∼raum abgeben *to cloak-room*, ⟨Am⟩ *to have one's h.-baggage checked* **⁓gerecht** a *h.y*; *dext(e)rous*; *skilful* **⁓gesteuert** a *manual* **⁓geschmiedet,** **⁓gewirkt** a *h.-wrought* **∼gewindebohrer** m *h.-tap* **∼gießmaschine** f *h.-casting machine* **∼glocke** f *h.bell* **∼granate** f ⟨mil⟩ *h.-grenade* ‖ ovale ∼ *Mill's bomb* | ∼nwurfstand [m] *gr. court* **∼greiflich 1.** [a] **a.** *clear, evident, manifest, obvious, plain*; *palpable, tangible* (*advantage*); *rank* (*nonsense*) **b.** ∼ w *to cut up rough* **2.** [adv] ∼ vor Augen führen → ad oculos ‖ hier zeigt sich Verrat am ∼sten *that is treason at its baldest* **∼griff** m **1.** [abstr] *grasp* ‖ ∼e [pl] ⟨mil⟩ *m. exercises* **2.** [konkr] *grip-handle* (*of a knife*); *haft* (*of a tool*); *h.hold*; *handle*; sich am ∼ festhalten (im Bus) *to strap-hang* ‖ ⟨telph⟩ *h.set* **3.** ⟨fig⟩ (Kniff) *knack*; *manipulation* **∼guß** m ⟨typ⟩ (Lettern) *h.-cast* **∼habe** f *device*; *dodge* (z *for*) ‖ *chance, possibility* ‖ e–e schnelle ∼ *a rough-and-ready method* (*of administration*) ‖ e–e ∼ bieten z *to give a handle to* (*rumours*); e–e ∼ schaffen f .. *to make provision for ..* **⁓haben** vt [h] (Waffe, Werkzeug) *to handle, wield*; *to use* (*tools*); (Maschine) *to operate, work* ‖ (Boot) *to manage*; (Segel) *to manipulate*; (Geschäft) *to run*; (Recht) *to administer* ‖ jdn ∼ *to deal with*; *to manage, manipulate* ‖ sich leicht ∼ l *to handle easily* ‖ l. z ∼(d) *feasible, manageable, tractable*; schwer z ∼(d) *unmanageable, unwieldy* **∼habung** f *management*; *manipulation* ‖ ⟨tech⟩ *handling* ‖ *administration* (*of justice*); (feder)leichte ∼ *finger-tip operation*; mit 2 ⁓en z ∼ *two-h.ed* **⁓haft** a: auf ∼er Tat *in the very act* **∼harmonika** f ⟨mus⟩ *accordion, concertina* **∼hebel** m *h.-lever* **∼hochheben** n → Hand I. 1. **∼karren** m *h.-cart*; *truck*; → Schiebkarren **∼kasse** f *till-money* **∼kauf** m *purchase in the lump* ‖ *first purchase on a day* **∼klapper** f; Spanische ∼ *castanets* pl **∼kloben** m ⟨tech⟩ *h.-vice* **∼koffer** m *attaché-case*; (*suit*)*-case*; *portmanteau*; ⟨Am⟩ *valise* Fr **∼korb** m, **∼körbchen** n *h.-basket* **∼kurbel** f *h.-crank* **∼krem** f *h. cream* **∼kurbel** f *cranking handle* **∼kuß** m; jdm e–n ∼ geben *to kiss a p's h.* **∼lampe** f *h.-lamp*; *inspection l.* **∼langer** m **1.** (P) *hack*; *hodman*; *navvy*; *devil*; ⟨Am sl⟩ *stooge* ‖ bloße ∼dienste tun *to do mere navvy's work*; *to devil* (f *for*) ‖ ⟨cont⟩ *underling*; *understrapper* **2.** ⟨fig⟩ *handmaiden* (*of politics*) **∼lauf** m *h.-rail* **∼läufereisen** n *h.-rail iron* **∼lesekunst** f *h.-reading*; *palmistry*; *chiromancy* **∼leser(in** f) m *h.-reader*; *palmist* **∼leuchte** f *portable* od *inspection lamp* **∼leuchter** m *h.y candlestick* **∼loch** n *h.-hole* **∼mal** n = Muttermal **∼mehr** n ∼s/ Sw *majority by show of h.s* **∼mühle** f *h.-mill*; *quern* **∼naht** f *h.-seam* **∼papier** n = Büttenpapier **∼pferd** n *near horse*; *led-horse* **∼pflege** f *manicure* **∼presse** f *h.-press* **∼pumpe** f *h.-pump* **∼puppe** f *Punch*; ∼ntheater [n] *Punch and Judy show* **∼rad** n *h.-wheel*; ⟨cul⟩ *rotary beater* **∼reichung** f *assistance*; *help*; *service* **∼rücken** m *back of the hand* **∼ruder** n (Steuer⁓) *h.-rudder* **∼säge** f *h.saw* **∼satz** m *h.-set type* | ∼type [f] *founder's type* **∼schaltung** f *m. switching*; ⟨mot⟩ *finger-tip gearshift* **∼schein** m *promissory note* **∼schelle** f *manacle, h.cuff*; ∼n [pl] *darbies* pl, ⟨fam⟩ *chinkers* **∼schlag** m *blow with the h.* ‖ *joining of h.s, h.shake* ‖ sich durch *or* mit ∼ verbinden *to join h.s* ‖ ⟨übtr⟩ *stroke of work*; *h.'s turn* (*he has not done a ..*) **∼schreiben** n *autograph* **∼schrift** f *h.* (fließende ∼ *running h.*); → Hand I. 4. a. ‖ *h.writing*; ⟨Am⟩ *h.write* ‖ in ∼ geschrieben *in manuscript* ‖ ⟨typ⟩ *round h.* ‖ ⟨hist⟩ *manuscript* | ∼enkunde [f] *palaeography*; → Paläograph **⁓schriftlich 1.** [a] (*h.*)*written*; *manuscript* (*notes*); ∼es Ms, ∼er Text *h.-lettered* od *illuminated m-t* **2.** [adv] *in writing* **∼schuh** m *glove*; Glacé∼ *kid-glove* ‖ ⟨hist⟩ Panzer⁓ *gauntlet* ‖ Fehde⁓ *glove* ‖ die ∼e ab-, ausziehen *to* draw off one's gloves ‖ mit e–m ~ (or mit ~en) bedecken to glove; in ~en gloved (h.s) ‖ ⟨fig⟩ jdm den ~ hinwerfen to fling (od throw) down the gauntlet od glove to a p ‖ möchte ihn nicht mit ~n anfassen wouldn't touch him with a (barge-)pole ‖ ~(aus)weiter [m] glove stretcher; ~fabrik [f] glove-factory; ~fach [n] ⟨mot⟩ glovebox; ~-knöpfer [m] buttonhook; ~laden [m] gloveshop; ~leder [n] kid-leather; ~macher [m] glover **~-schutz** m ⟨tech⟩ h.-guard **~serviette** f waiter's cloth **~setzer** m ⟨typ⟩ compositor **~siegel** n one's own signet **≗signiert** a autographed; ~e Ausgabe au.d copy **~spiegel** m h.-glass (od mirror) **~-spritze** f syringe **~stand** m ⟨gym⟩ h.stand **~staubsauger** m dustette **~steuerorgan** n m. control **~-streich** m ⟨mil⟩ surprise attack **~täschchen** n (f Damen) vanity-bag, reticule **~tasche** f h.-bag, ⟨Am⟩ valise, satchel, grip, purse pocketbook (for women); gr ~ carry-all **~teller** m = –fläche **~-tuch** n towel; auf Rollen laufendes ~ roller-t.; jack-t. ‖ (jdn) mit e–m ~ abtrocknen, trocken reiben to t.; sich mit ~ abtrocknen to dry o.s. on a t.; to t. o.s. | ~halter, ~ständer [m] t.-horse od rail **~umdrehen** n; °im ~ ⟨fam⟩ in a jiff(y), shake, trice; in (next to) no time; in the turning of a h.; in three shakes of a duck's tail; before you know (knew) where you are (were); like winking; before you can (could) say Jack Robinson; (etw) im ~ einrichten to improvise **~umschaltung** f = –schaltung **~verkauf** m ⟨pharm⟩ open sale **~verletzung** f injury to one's h. **~vermittlung** f ⟨telph⟩ m. service od exchange **~voll** f h.ful; e–e ~ Salz a h.f. of salt; e–e ~ Schriftstücke a bundle of papers; einige ~ Sand some h.fuls of sand; ganze Hände voll v .. whole clutches of .. **~vorlage** f ⟨tech⟩ rest for a h.-tool **~waffen** pl small arms pl | ~munition [f] sm. calibre amm. **~wagen** m truck **~wahrsager(in** f) m = –leser **~walze** f h.-roller **~weberei** f h.-loom weaving **~webstuhl** m h.-loom **~wechsel** m ⟨com⟩ note of h. **~werk** etc → d. **~winde** f ⟨tech⟩ h. winch **~wörterbuch** n school (od pocket)-dictionary **~wurzel** f ⟨anat⟩ **1.** wrist; carpus L **2.** [in comp] carpal; ~band [n] transverse carpal ligament ‖ ~knochen [m] = Erbsenbein **~zeichen** n ⟨typ⟩ ☞ index **~zeichnen** n free--h. drawing **~zeichnung** f free-h. drawing **~zettel** m h.bill

H·ändchen n ~s/~ small (od little) hand | ~halten [n] ⟨sex⟩ holding hands

H·ände- **~druck** m grasp of the h.; h.-grip (a firm h.-g.); h.shake; etw durch ~ besiegeln to shake h.s on a th **~heben** n show of h.s **~klatschen** n clapping of h.s; applause, cheer ‖ jdn durch ~ herbeirufen to clap one's h.s for a p **~ringen** n wringing one's h.s **≗ringend** adv despairingly; fervently; imploringly; urgently; jdn ~ bitten to implore (od supplicate) a p despairingly **~schutzvorrichtung** f ⟨tech⟩ h.-guard **~spiel** n gesticulation **~waschen** n washing one's h.s

H·andel m ~s/ **A.** *__1.__ [abstr] business; dealings pl ‖ † = Angelegenheit **2.** [mst] pl ≗ → d. **B.** ⟨com⟩ **1.** (einzelner ~; ~sgeschäft) bargain, business (a good stroke of b.); deal; transaction; → Geschäft; Tausch ‖ e–n ~ abschließen to strike (od make) a bargain; to come to terms; to do a deal (with a p) ‖ °Kuh≗ = Schiebung **2.** (~sverkehr) **a.** ⟨allg⟩ (~ jeder Art; Klein≗ u Groß≗) trade (in etw in a th) ‖ [abstr] (~ gr Stils, bes mit Ausland) commerce ‖ Tausch≗ barter; T. treiben to barter ‖ Einzel≗ retail trade; Klein≗ trade; Groß≗ wholesale t. ‖ Hausier≗ peddling **b.** ~ **u Gewerbe** c. and t.; ~ u Industrie c. (od t.) and industry ‖ ~ u Wandel t. and traffic; business in general ‖ ~ zur See oceanic (od seaborne) c. | ~ treiben to carry on c.; to t. (od deal, traffic) (in or mit etw in a th; mit jdm with a p) **c.** ⟨übtr & dero⟩ traffic (mit etw in a th); weißer Sklaven≗ white slave traffic; Seelen≗ traffic in souls ‖ Schleich≗ smuggling; S. treiben to smuggle ‖ ~ mit Rauschgiften drug-peddling ‖ ~ mit Ämtern traffic in appointments **H·ändel** m pl (→ Handel A. 2.) quarrel ‖ ~ h to be at odds; to have a squabble (mit with) ‖ ~ suchen (or anfangen) to pick (od seek) a q. (with a p) **~suchen** n picking a q. **≗süchtig** a q.some ‖ ⟨jur⟩ litigious **h·andeln** vi/t [h] **I.** vi **A. 1.** to act; eigenmächtig ~ to act arbitrarily od arrogantly; entschlossen ~ to act (in a resolute manner od) with decision od determination; klug ~ to act wisely ‖ auf eigene Faust ~ to act on one's own ‖ sofort ~ to take immediate action; laßt uns ~ let us be up and doing; jetzt ist Zeit z ~ the time to press the button is now ‖ er handelt wie er predigt he practises what he preaches ‖ grausam **an** jdm ~ to act cruelly by, to deal cruelly by od with a p; an jdm schlecht ~ to do a p a bad turn; er handelte recht an .. he did what was right by (the child); unehrlich ~ an .. to palter with a p ‖ er handelte an ihm wie ein Bruder he treated him like a brother | s–m Befehle **gemäß** wurde gehandelt his command was acted upon; ~ im Einvernehmen mit .. to act in concert with; to work in with a p; ~ **nach** to act up to (a p's advice); to go upon ‖ ~ **gegen** to act contrary to; to infringe od violate (God's law) **2.** (S) ~ **von,** ~ **über** to deal with; to treat of; to be concerned with; worüber handelt der Artikel? what is the subject of the article? **3. es handelt sich um** e–n Mann in dunklem Anzug the man in question wore a dark suit; the house in q. is .. ‖ es h. sich darum, ob .. the question is, whether; .. darum, z tun it is a question of doing .. ‖ darum handelt es sich gerade that's just the moot q. ‖ es h. sich um folgendes here is the point ‖ hier h. es sich um Leben u Tod this is a case of life and death ‖ es h. sich um einfache Sachen it is a matter of simple things ‖ .., bes wo es sich um Liebe h. particularly where love is concerned ‖ worum h. es sich eigentlich? what is the point in q. (od at issue)? ‖ es handelte sich bei Weizenbau um die Unterscheidung v .. in wheat-growing one had to differentiate between .. ‖ wenn es sich darum handelte, den Frauen z schmeicheln, war er .. when it came to flattering women he was ..; wenn es sich um Fr. h.t when women are concerned **B.** ⟨com⟩ **1. a.** to bargain, haggle; bei festen Preisen wird nicht gehandelt with fixed prices there can be no b.ing ‖ ~ um to b. about; to chaffer over; to h. about, over; ~ mit jdm um etw to b. with a p for a th **b. mit sich ~ l** to be open to an offer; ⟨fig⟩ to think it over, to be open to conviction **2. mit etw** ~ to deal (od trade, traffic) in a th; ⟨Am⟩ to handle a th **II.** vt **1.** ⟨com⟩ **gehandelt w** to be dealt in; to be quoted; nicht g. w (of foreign notes) to be prohibited ‖ (Wechsel) to negotiate; ⟨Am⟩ to handle †**2.** = kaufen **H·andeln** n action; doings pl ‖ durch schnelles ~ by swift action ‖ sittliches ~ moral conduct ‖ verwegenes ~ derring-do ‖ ein Wille zum ~ a will to act; jdn z ~ treiben to stir a p to action **h·andelnd 1.** [a] active ‖ ⟨übtr Lit⟩ leading, principal; die ~en Personen e–s Dramas the principal characters in a drama; ~e P ⟨ant⟩ protagonist **2.** [adv] actively; ~ eingreifen to be active, to take an active part (in in) **H·andels-** [in comp] commercial; trade(-) **~abkommen** n c. agreement **~adreßbuch** n t. directory **~agent** m t. agent **~akademie** f c. academy **~akzept** n = –wechsel **~amt** n (f Lohnfragen) t.-board **~artikel** m article; commodity **~attaché** m (Fr) c. attaché **~bank** f c. bank **~beflissene** [der ~, ein ~r] c. clerk **~bericht** m market (od c.) report, City article **~beschränkung** f restriction on t. **~betriebslehre** f science of c. and industrial organization **~beziehungen** pl c. relations pl **~bilanz** f balance of t. | ~defizit [n] t. deficit **~blockade** f blockade of commerce **~branche** f = –fach **~brauch** m t.--custom; usage; custom of od in t. **~brief** m c. letter **~buch** n account-book; ledger **~chemiker** m c.

chemist **~dampfer** m *merchant steamer* **~drang** m *trade drive* **≃einig, ≃eins** [pred a] ∼ w *to come to terms*; ∼ s *to be agreed* **~erlaubnis** f *trading licence* **~fach** n *branch* od *line* (*of business* od *t.*) **~firma** f *c. firm* **~flagge** f *merchant flag* **~flotte** f *merchant fleet*; *mercantile marine* **~frau** f *tradeswoman* **~freiheit** f *freedom* (od *liberty*) *of t.* **~-freund** m *business friend* **~gärtner** m *market--gardener* **~gärtnerei** f *market-gardening* **~geist** m *c. spirit* **~genosse** m *partner* **~genossenschaft** f [abstr & konkr] *partnership*; → –gesellschaft **~geographie** f *c. geography* **~gericht** n *court of trade*; *c. court* ‖ beim ∼ eingetragen *registered* **~geschäft** n **1.** [abstr] *business, transaction* **2.** [konkr] *business*; *establishment*; *firm* **~gesellschaft** f *t. association* ‖ *trading company*; ⟨Am⟩ (*business*) *corporation*; offene ∼ *unlimited mercantile partnership*; → (öffentl.) Körperschaft **~gesellschafter** m *partner* **~gesetz** n *c. law* ‖ ∼buch (abbr HGB) n *Code of C. Law* ‖ ∼gebung [f] *c. legislation* **~gewächs** n ⟨hort⟩ *cash-crop* **~gewerbe** n *trade* **~gewicht** n *avoirdupois* → Bd. I, S. 1112ff. **~gewinn** m *trading profit* **~güter** n pl *goods* pl; *merchandise* **~hafen** m *trading-port, c. port* **~haus** n *c.* (od *trading*) *house*; *concern* **~herr** m **1.** gr ∼ *c. magnate*; *merchant-prince* **2.** *head* od *principal* (*of a firm*) **~hochschule** *academy of commerce*; *c. college* **~interessen** n pl *c. interest* pl **~jude** m *trading jew* **~kammer** f *Chamber of Commerce*; ⟨Am⟩ *Board of Trade* **~kapital** n *trading capital* **~kapitän** m *merchant captain* † **~kollegium** n = –kammer **~kompa(g)nie** f *trading-company* **~korrespondenz** f *c. correspondence* **~krieg** m *economic* od *c. war*(*fare*) **~krisis** f *c. crisis* **~kunde** f *c. science* **~lehranstalt** f = –schule **~lehre** f = –kunde **~lehrer** m *teacher at a c. college* **~leute** pl *tradespeople* **~makler** m *mercantile broker* **~mann** m *tradesman, trader*; *shopkeeper* **~marine** f *mercantile marine*; ⟨engl⟩ Flagge der ∼ *Red Ensign* **~marke** f *t.-mark* **~minister** m ⟨Ger⟩ *Minister for T.*; ⟨engl⟩ *President of the Board of T.*; ⟨Am⟩ *Secretary of Commerce* **~ministerium** n ⟨Ger⟩ *Ministry of Commerce*; ⟨engl⟩ *Board of T.*; ⟨Am⟩ *Department of Commerce* **~monopol** n *c. monopoly* **~museum** n *museum of t.* **~nachrichten** f pl *c. news*; *City news* **~name** m *t.-name* **~niederlassung** f *factory*; *trading settlement* **~organisation** f (HO) ⟨SBZ⟩ *state retail store* **~platz** m *trading-post*; *staple*; ‖ Haupt≃ *emporium* L; befestigter ∼ *fort* Fr **~politik** f *c. policy* **~preis** m (des Großhändlers f den Kleinhändler) *t.-price* **~recht** n *c.* (od *mercantile*) *law* **~register** n *register of firms* **~reisende** [der ∼, ein ∼r] m *c. traveller* ‖ ⟨sl⟩ *bagman*; ⟨Am⟩ *drummer* **~richter** m *lay assessor for the decision of c. suits* **~sache** f *c. matter* **~schiff** n *trading--vessel, merchant-ship*; *merchantman* **~schiffahrt** f *mercantile shipping*; *merchant service* **~schule** f *c. college* od *school* **~schulwesen** n *c. schools in general* **~spanne** f *margin*; *difference between the buying and selling prices* **~sperre** f *embargo* (*on goods*) **~staat** m *c. state* **~stadt** f *c. town*; *trading city* (od *town*) **~stand** m *trading* (od *merchant*) *class*; *merchants* pl **~statistik** f *c. statistics* pl **~straße** f *t.-route*; *highway of commerce* **~strom** m *current of exch.* **~system** n *mercantile system* **~tag** m → Industrietag **~teil** m (in a newspaper) *c. column*; *t. section* **~theorie** f *mercantile doctrine* (od *theory*) **≃üblich** a *in accordance with c. usage*; *usual in* (*the*) *t.*; ∼e Bezeichnung *t.-name*; ∼e Qualität *c. quality* od *grade* | [adv] ∼ gefärbt ⟨m. m.⟩ *certified food colo*(*u*)*r* **~unternehmen** n, **~unternehmung** f *c. enterprise* **~verbindungen** f pl *c. connexions*; *business-connexions* **~verbot** n *prohibition of trade* **~verkehr** m *t., c. exch.* od *intercourse*; *traffic* | ∼swert [m] *t. value* **~vertrag** m *c. treaty* **~vertreter** m *mercantile agent* **~volk** n *c. nation* **~volumen** n *volume of exch.* **~waren** f pl *t. goods*; *merchandise*; e–e ∼ware *an article of m.* **~wechsel** m *t.-bill* (od *acceptance*) **~weg** m = –straße **~welt** f *trade* **~wert** m *market* (od *trade*) *value* **~wesen** m *commerce in general* **~wissenschaft** f *science of commerce* **~wörterbuch** n *c. dictionary* **~zeichen** n *brand*; → –marke **~zeitung** f *c. paper* (od *news* pl) **~zentrum** n *emporium* L **~zuschlag** m *conventional allowance* **~zweig** m *branch of trade*

h·andeltreibend a *trading* (*classes*); *commercial* ‖ ein ≃er *a trader*

-händig a *–handed*; zwei∼ *double-handed*

H·andikap [ˈhændikæp] n [engl] *handicap* °≃**-pen** [–ən] vt [h] *to handicap* **~per** m [–ər] m *handicapper* **~rennen** n *handicap*

H·ändler m ∼s/∼ **1.** *dealer* (mit [*or* *in] etw *in a th*); *trader*; → Vertreibung ‖ ⟨dero & übtr⟩ *trafficker* (mit .. *in drugs*; *votes*) **2.** [in comp] **a.** Groß≃ *merchant*; *wholesaler* ‖ Klein≃ *tradesman*; Einzel≃ *retailer*; ⟨Scot & Am⟩ *merchant* ‖ Straßen≃ → Hausierer, Höker **b.** *–monger*; (*ironmonger*; *cheesemonger*) ‖ *tea-dealer* (od *merchant*); *wine-merchant* ‖ Öl≃ *oilman*; → Lumpen≃ ‖ Zeitungs≃ *newsvendor*; *news-agent* | **~in** f ∼/∼nen *tradeswoman* **~tum** n *tradespeople*; *trading people* **h·andlich** a *handy* (*tool*); *workable*; *easy to handle*; → handhaben | ≃**keit** f *handiness* **H·andlung** f ∼/∼en **1.** *act* (*the first a. of the day was ..*); *action*; *deed* ‖ edle ∼ *noble deed*; gemeine ∼ *mean act*(*ion*) ‖ f s–e ∼en verantwortlich *responsible for one's acts* ‖ ⟨ec⟩ heilige ∼ *religious act, sacred rite*; *sacrament* ‖ ⟨eth⟩ action | ⟨Lit⟩ (in a novel, play) *action, story*; innere ∼ (Aristote's) *praxis*; steigende ∼ *complication, epitasis*; fallende ∼ *reversal*; .. macht sich e–r strafbaren ∼ schuldig *shall be guilty of offence* ‖ (Plan der ∼) *plot* ‖ der Ort der ∼ *the scene of the action* ‖ es ist sehr wenig ∼ in .. *there is very little story in ..*; ein Stück ohne ∼, *a plotless play* ‖ die ∼ spielt in .. *the action is laid in* (*York*) **2.** †(= Geschäft) *trade*; *business*; *shop* ‖ die ∼ erlernen *to learn a trade* **H·andlungs- ~art** f = –weise **~bevollmächtigte** m [der ∼, ein ∼r] *attorney*; *proxy*; *authorized agent* **~fähigkeit** f *competence to perform legal acts* **~freiheit** f *liberty of action*; ⟨fam⟩ *green light* **~gehilfe** m (Verkäufer) *shop--assistant* ‖ (Schreiber) *office-clerk* **~gehilfin** f *female sh.-a.* **~kette** f ⟨eth⟩ *chain of actions* **~lehrling** m *learning sh.-a., learning-clerk* **~reisende**(**r**) m = Handelsreisende **~weise** f *procedure*; *mode* (od *way, line, course*) *of dealing* (od *acting*); *tack* ‖ *behaviour*; *dealing* ‖ allg. ∼ *general pattern of conduct*

H·andmehr n ∼s/ Sw *majority by a show of hands*

H·andwerk n ∼(e)s/∼e **1.** *trade*; das Schlachter≃ *the t. of a butcher* ‖ *craft*; Goldschmiede≃ *goldsmith's craft* ‖ Kunst≃ *handicraft* ‖ ein ehrliches ∼ *an honest trade* (treiben *to practice* [*a craft*]); sich auf sein ∼ verstehen (*or* sein ∼ kennen) *to be a handy man with one's tools*; *to be a good hand at one's trade* ‖ ⟨prov⟩ ∼ hat e–n goldenen Boden *a trade in hand finds gold in every land* | ⟨fig⟩ jdm das ∼ legen *to put a stop to a p's plans*; ‖ ⟨fig⟩ jdm ins ∼ pfuschen *to encroach upon a p's province*; *to put one's nose into a p's business* **2.** das ∼ *the trade*; *the craft*; *the guilds* pl ‖ das deutsche ∼ *the German handicrafts* pl **H·andwerker** m ∼s/∼ (gelernter ∼) *craftsman*; *tradesman*; ⟨mach⟩ *mechanic*; wir h die ∼ im Haus *we've got the plumbers* (*etc*) *in* ‖ ⟨Ger mil⟩ ⟨hum⟩ *peace-time soldier* **~werker- ~Fachabgrenzung** f ⟨engl⟩ *demarcation* **~gilde** f **1.** ⟨engl⟩ *Livery-Company*; ⟨hist⟩ (*crafts* od *trade-*) *g*(*u*)*ild* ‖ Mitglieder der ∼ *liveryman* ‖ oberstes Gericht der ∼ *the court of the master* **2.** ⟨Ger⟩ *corporation*; *g*(*u*)*ild* **~innung** f = –gilde **h·andwerklich** a *manual* (*work*) ‖ *mechanical* **H·andwerks- ~bur-**

sche, **~geselle** m *itinerant journeyman* **~gruß** m *j.'s salute* **~kammer** f ⟨Ger⟩ *chamber of (craftsmen's) trade* **~lade** f ⟨hist⟩ *box containing the statutes* (etc) *of a corporation* **~leute** pl *craftsmen, mechanics* pl **~mann** m *craftsman, mechanic; handicraftsman; artisan* **~̈mäßig 1.** [a] *workmanlike* ‖ ⟨bes fig⟩ *mechanical* **2.** [adv] *mechanically* **~meister** m *master of a trade; handicraftsman* **~technik** f *technique of craftsmanship* **~zeug** n *implements, tools* pl; ⟨Am⟩ *findings* pl ‖ ⟨a. übtr⟩ *kit;* ~ des Jägers *hunting-kit* ‖ ~ e–s Gelehrten *a scholar's stock-in-trade* **~zunft** f = Handwerkergilde

h·anebüchen (f hagebüchen) → hahnebüchen

H·anf m ~(e)s/ ⟨bot⟩ *hemp* ‖ aus ~ (gemacht) *h.en* ‖ Bengal~̈, Madras~̈, Sunn~̈ *sunn, sunn h.; Indian h.* ‖ Faser~̈ *fibre h.;* Haschisch~̈ *hashish h.;* Sisal~̈ *Sisal h.* ‖ getrockneter ~ (als Narkotikum) ⟨Ind⟩ *b(h)ang* ‖ ~ brechen *to break h.;* → hecheln, raufen, rösten, schwingen **~bau** m *h. growing* **~breche** f *h.-brake* **~darre** f *h.-kiln* **~dichtung** f ⟨tech⟩ *gasket* **~faser** f *h.-fibre* **~garn** n *h.-thread* **~hechler** m *h.-dresser* **~kraut** n ⟨bot⟩ *h.-agrimony* **~nessel** f ⟨bot⟩ *h.-nettle; Galecopsis* L **~öl** n *h.-oil* **~papier** n *Manila paper* **~rose** f ⟨bot⟩ ostind. ~ *hibiscus* L **~samen** m *h.-seed* **~seil** n, **~strick** m *h.(en) cord* **~tod** m ⟨bot⟩ *orobanche* **~zwirn** m *h.-thread* **h·anfen, h·änfen** a *h.(en) (cord); of h.* **H·änfling** m ~(e)s/~e ⟨orn⟩ *linnet*

Hang m ~(e)s/~̈e **1.** [konkr] (of ground) *slope;* grüne ~̈e *grassy slopes* pl ‖ *declivity, incline, inclination; inclined plane; pitch; slant* ‖ ⟨arch⟩ *pitch (of a roof)* ‖ steiler ~ *acclivity* **2.** [abstr, nur sg] *bent (a natural bent for music); inclination* (z *to, for*); *leaning, tendency; addiction* (z *to*); *passion* (z *for*); *penchant (for)* | ein angeborener ~ z *a disposition to; a strain of (melancholy, superstition)* ‖ ⟨dero⟩ *proclivity* (z .. *to idleness, extravagance;* z tun *to do*); *propensity* (z *to; for gambling; to do, for doing*) **~aufwind** m *up-current due to a slope* **~bau** m ⟨agr⟩ *irrigation applied to sloping surfaces* **~eisen** n (Glocke) *clap-hanger* **~ende** n ⟨min⟩ *overlying stratum* **~segeln** n ⟨aero⟩ *ridge-soaring* **~stellung** f ⟨tact⟩ *slope position* **~wind** m ⟨aero⟩ *upslope-wind* **~winkel** m *gradient of slope*

Hangar ['ãgaːr] m [Fr] ~s/~s ⟨aero⟩ *hangar*

H·änge- °**~backen** f pl *flabby cheeks* pl **~bahn** f *aerial ropeway;* elektr. ~ *telpher-line* | ~laufkatze [f] *overhead conveyor trolley* °**~bauch** m *pendulous abdomen;* ⟨fam⟩ *paunch* **~birke** f *weeping birch* **~bock** m = –werk **~boden** m *hanging-floor* **~brücke** f *suspension* (od *hanging*) *bridge* °**~busen** m *pendulous* od *pendant breasts* pl **~dekoration** f ⟨theat⟩ *flown set* **~fähre** f (am Seil) *flying* (od *floating*) *bridge* **~kommission** f ⟨paint⟩ *hanging-committee* **~kühler** m ⟨aero⟩ *underslung radiator* **~lager** n ⟨tech⟩ *hanger* **~lampe** f *hanging-lamp; pendant-l.* **~matte** f *hammock* **~ohren** n pl *lop-ears; flapping* od *pendant ears;* mit ~ *flap-eared* **~plan** m ⟨theat⟩ *fly-plot,* ⟨Am⟩ *hanging chart* **~pfosten** m, **~säule** f *suspension post* **~schloß** n *padlock* **~wand** f ⟨min⟩ *hanging-wall* **~werk** n ⟨arch⟩ *truss; truss-frame* **~zapfen** m ⟨arch⟩ *pendant, -dent* **h·angeln** vi [h] ⟨gym⟩ *to climb a rope* od *travel along a bar hand over hand* **H·angelseil, -tau** n *climbing rope* **h·angen A.** vi [3. sg prs hängt, ˣhangt hing/gehangen] [h] [verdrängt durch hängen vi → d. II.] **B.** ~̈ n mit ~ u Bangen *with anxious suspense* od *misgivings, with great anxiety* **h·ängen** vt/i [h] **I. vt** [hängte/gehängt] **A.** (etw) **1.** an e–n Haken ~ *to hang from* (od *to*) *a hook, to h. up;* er hängte den Hut an .. *he hung his hat on a peg* **2.** ⟨fig⟩ sein Herz an etw ~ *to set one's h. on a th; to be very fond of a th, to be much attached to a th* ‖ (Gemeinheiten) niedriger ~ *to expose, unmask* **B. 1.** jdn ~ *to h. a p;* gehängt w *to be h.ed; to come to the gallows; to h. (he deserves to h.);* ⟨jur⟩ *to he h.ed by the neck* **2. sich** ~ **a.** *to h. o.s.* **b. sich** ~ **an** .. *to h. on* (od *to hook on to*) *a p's (arms);* sich an jdn ~ *to run after a p;* = ~ an → II. A. 1. **3.** °**ich will mich** ~ **l** *I'll be bothered* od *h.ed; I'll eat my head (if ..)* **II. vi** [hing/gehangen] **A. (S) 1. a.** (befestigt s) ~ an *to h. from (the ceiling)* od *to (a hook); the hat h.s on a peg* ‖ (of door) ~ in *to h. on (hinges)* **b. (lose)** ~ an *to h. by;* das Siegel hängt an e–m Bande *the seal is suspended by a ribbon* ‖ ⟨fig⟩ an e–m Faden ~ *to h. by a thread* ‖ (of clothes) an jdm ~ *to h. about* od *on a p* **c.** (haften) ~ an *to adhere* (od *cling, stick*) *to* ‖ an jds Arm ~ *to h. on a p's arm* ‖ ⟨übtr⟩ sein Auge hing an ihrem Munde *his eyes hung upon her lips* ‖ u alles, was daran hängt *and all that pertains to it* **2. (schweben) a.** in der Luft ~ *to h.* (od *dangle*) *in the air* ‖ Regenwolken ~ am Himmel *there is rain h.ing about* **b. (drohend)** ~ über .. *the sword h.s over his head; the cliff overhangs the river* **c.** ⟨fig⟩ der Prozeß hängt *the law suit is going on* od *is pending* ‖ die Partie h. noch *the game h.s in the balance; .. is still undecided* **3.** ~ **nach** .. *to incline towards;* der Wagen hängt nach der e–n Seite *the carriage h.s on* (od *leans towards*) *one side* **4.** voller Früchte, Mäntel ~ *the trees are loaded with fruit, the wardrobe is packed with coats* ‖ ⟨fig⟩ der Himmel hängt ihm voller Geigen *he has a cheerful temper* (od *disposition*) **B. (P)** [ell] ⟨fig⟩ °er hängt! ⟨fam⟩ *he's booked; he's done for* ‖ °hier hängt er! *here I am* **1.** ~ **an a.** am Galgen ~ *to h. on the gallows* | **b.** ⟨übtr⟩ *to h. on (a p's arms);* ⟨fig⟩ an jdm ~ *to be attached to a p;* fest ~ an .. *to cling to a p* ‖ an etw ~ *to be much attached to, very fond of a th;* zäh am Leben ~ *to have a tenacious hold on life* **2.** °er hängt **bei** s–m Wirt *he owes money to his landlord* ‖ †°⟨Ger univ⟩ er h. **mit** ihm *he will fight with him* **C. ~**|**bleiben** vi [s] **1.** *to adhere* (od *cling, stick*) (an *to*); *to catch* (an *on;* in *in*); *to jam; to be caught* (in *in*); *to hitch* od *hook* (auf *on to;* in *in*) ‖ mit dem Fuß ~bleiben *to catch one's foot* (in *in*); ich bin mit dem Kleid daran ~geblieben *I have caught my dress on it* ‖ ·etwas bleibt immer ~ *something always sticks* | °⟨fig⟩ (P) ⟨school⟩ *not to get one's remove* ‖ in e–r Stadt ~bleiben *to stay* (od *linger*) *on* **D. ~**|**l 1.** ich habe m–n Hut ~|l *I've left my hat (at ..)* **2.** die Flügel ~|l *to let droop the wings* **3.** ⟨fig⟩ den Kopf ~|l *to h. the head; to droop* (vor *with*); *to be down in the mouth;* den K. nicht ~|l *to come up smiling* ‖ °den Mund (*or* das Maul) ~|l *to mope; pout* **H·ängen** n *the hanging (of a p)* ‖ °mit ~ u Würgen *by* (od *with*) *the skin of one's teeth* **h·ängend** a *hanging; pendant, -dent; suspended;* lose ~ *flowing (tie)* ‖ *inverted (valve)* ‖ ~er Gegenstand *hanger; hanging (gardens);* ~e Ohren = Hängeohren ‖ frei (*or* lose) ~ *flowing (sleeves);* ~es Stück, ~er Teil *flap (of a garment)* | ~e Felswand *overhanging cliffs* pl **H·angende** n [das ~, ein ~s] ⟨min⟩ *hanger; roof* **H·anger** m ~s/~ ⟨mar⟩ (kz Tau) *hanger;* doppelter ~ *span* **H·änger** m ~s/~ *shift (dress); topcoat, topper; swagger-coat* ‖ *housecoat* **h·ängig** a *declivitous, sloping* ‖ ⟨jur⟩ *pending (suit)* **H·ängsel** n ~s/~ *hook(let)* ‖ (of clothes) *loop; tab*

Hangtschou [–tʃau] n (Stadt, China) *Hang-chow*

H·ankou, H·ankau n (Stadt in China) *Hankow*

Hanke f ~/~n (of a horse) *haunch*

H·annemann, geh du voran ..! *you will have to bell the cat*

Hann·over n [–f–] ~s/ *Hanover* **~·aner** m [–v–], **h–·oversch** [–f–] a *Hanoverian*

Hanomag m [inv] = Auto der H.-overschen Maschinenbau A. G.

Hans A. 1. (P) a. *John;* ⟨fam⟩ *Jack* **b.** Meister ~ (der Henker) *Jack Ketch* ‖ ~ Guck-in-die-Luft *John-a-Dreams;* (pedestrian) *jaywalker;* ~ G.! *get your eyes chalked!* ‖ ~ Dampf in allen

Gassen *Jack of all trades, lad of the village*; *Paul Pry* ‖ ~ u Grete *Jack and Gill* od *Jill* ‖ ich will ~ heißen, wenn das anders ist *that's the truth as sure as my name is Jack Robinson* ‖ *I'm a Dutchman if I do!*; ~ im Glück s *to kill the goose for* od *with the golden eggs* **2.** **(T)** *Jack* ‖ ~ Huckebein ⟨Lit⟩ *boding raven* ‖ Lachender ~ ⟨orn⟩ = Riesenfischer **3.** **(S)** der blanke ~ *Davy-Jones's locker* (*the sea*) ‖ der Gelbe ~ (= gelbes Fieber) *Yellow Jack* **B.** [in comp] **1.** → ~narr, ~wurst **2.** Fasel-⩪ *driveller* **⩪chen** n ~s/ *Johnny* ‖ was ~ nicht lernt, lernt Hans nimmermehr *you can't teach an old dog new tricks*

Hansa, H·anse f ~/ ⟨Ger hist⟩ (*the*) *Hanse, Hanseatic League* | ~stadt [f] *Hanseatic town* **Hanse·at** m ~en/~en **1.** *native of a Hanseatic town* **2.** ⟨hist⟩ *member of the Hanse* **⩪isch, h·ansisch** a *Hanseatic*

Hänsel·ei f ~/~en *hoaxing*; *teasing*; *leg--pulling*; ⟨Am⟩ *ribbing* **h·änseln 1.** vt [h] jdn ~ *to chaff* (od *hoax, rag, tease,* ⟨Am⟩ *needle*) *a p*; *to pull a p's leg*; ⟨sl⟩ *to bosh* (⟨Am⟩ *jolly,* ⟨sl⟩ *spoof*) *a p* **2.** ⩪ n = Hänselei **Hans-** **~n·arr** m *tomfool*; *fool* **~w·urst** m ~es/ ⟨theat & Lit⟩ *buffoon*; *clown*; *merry-andrew*; ⟨hist⟩ *pickle-herring, zany* ‖ ~-streiche [pl] *buffoonery* | ⟨übtr⟩ *buffoon*; *merry--andrew, zany*

H·antel f ~/~n ⟨gym⟩ [mst pl] ~n (*pair of*) *dumb-bells* pl; ~übungen m *to do dumb-bell exercises*; *to dumb-bell* | ⟨athl⟩ *bar-bell* **h·anteln** vi [h] *to dumb-bell*

°**hant·ieren** vi/t [h] **1.** vi **a.** *to gesticulate, gesture* ‖ ~ mit etw *to handle* (od *manage*) *a th*; *to work with a th*; mit dem Messer ~ *to fidget* od *gesture with a knife* **b.** (geschäftig s) *to bustle* (od *fidget, fuss*) (*about*) **2.** † vt = (be)treiben; handhaben **Hant·ierung** f **a.** *gesticulation, gesture* ‖ *management* ‖ *occupation* ‖ *fidgeting* (*with*) **b.** *bustle, bustling*; *fidgeting*; *fuss* ‖ ~en [pl] *doings* pl

H·apag (aus: **H**amburg-**A**merikanische **P**aketfahrt-**A**ktien**g**esellschaft) *Hamburg-America Line*

°**h·aperig 1.** [a] *scanty*; *poor* ‖ *embarrassing*; *knotty* **2.** [adv] *poorly, stammeringly* °**h·apern** v/imps [h] **a.** es hapert *there is a hitch* ‖ am Geld hat es immer gehapert *money has always been short* ‖ es h. an allem *we are short of everything* ‖ es h. an etwas *sth is amiss* ‖ (..) haperte es bei ihm an allen Enden (*in the other subjects*) *his knowledge was very poor* ‖ im L. hapert es bei ihm (*or* es h. mit s–m L.) *Latin is his weak point* **b.** an dieser Stelle hapert es stets *at this point you always stick fast* ‖ es hapert mit den Verhandlungen *there is a hitch in the negotiations*

°**H·äppchen** n ~s/~ *little bit*; *morsel*; *tot* **H·appen** m ~s/~ *bit, bite, morsel, piece, nibble, mouthful*; ein ~ Brot *a morsel of bread* ‖ ein gr ~ *a hunch* ‖ ein guter (*or* fetter) ~ *a fine morsel* | ⟨übtr⟩ °sie nimmt k–n ~ Brot v ihm *she won't accept anything from him* ‖ °er wird sich diesen ~ nicht entgehen l *he won't let this opportunity slip* **h·appig** a (P) *greedy*; *insatiate* ‖ ⟨übtr⟩ (of a demand) °ein bißchen ~, etwas ~ *a bit thick*

H·appy ·End n [–æ–] ~s/~s *happy ending*

Harak·iri n ~s/~s *hara-kiri*; *happy dispatch*

H·araß m –sses/–sse (Lattenkiste) *crate*

H·ärchen n ~s/~ *little hair*; ⟨bot⟩ feines ~ *villus* L [pl *villi*] ‖ man hat ihm kein ~ gekrümmt *not a hair of his head was touched*

Hardt f, **~gebirge** n ⟨Ger⟩ *Hardt Mountains* pl

H·arem m ~s/~s [Turk] *harem*

h·ären a *made of hair, h.y*; ~es Gewand *h.-shirt*

Häres·ie f ~/~n [–ˈiːən] *heresy* **Här·etiker** m ~s/~ *heretic* **här·etisch** a *heretical*

H·arfe f ~/~n **1.** ⟨mus⟩ *harp* ‖ auf der ~ (die ~) spielen *to* (*play* [*upon*] *the*) *harp* **2.** ⟨übtr agr⟩ *screen for grain* (etc.); ⟨Scot⟩ *harp* **h·arfen** vi [h] *to* (*play* [*upon*] *the*) *harp* **⩪begleitung** f *h.-accompaniment* **~klang** m *h.ing*; *sound of the h.* **~-schläger** m = –spieler **~schnecke** f ⟨zoo⟩ *h.*(*-shell*) **~spiel** n *h.ing* **~spieler** m, **Harfen·ist(in** f ~/~-nen) m ~en/~en, **H·arfner(in** f) m (*female*) *h.er, h.ist*

H·arke f ~/~n ⟨agr⟩ *rake* ‖ °ich werde ihm zeigen, was 'ne ~ ist *I'll tell him what's what,* .. *a thing* od *two*; ⟨Am⟩ .. *where he gets off* **h·arken** vt/i [h] **1.** vt (Feld) *to rake*; glatt ~ *to rake up* (od *over*) **2.** vi *to rake*

H·arlekin m ~s/~e **1.** ⟨theat⟩ *harlequin*; ⟨übtr⟩ *buffoon* **2.** ⟨ent⟩ *h.* (od *magpie*) *moth*; *gooseberry-moth* **~·ade** f ~/~n *h.ade* **~karo** n *h. check*

Harm m ~s/ ⟨bes poet⟩ *grief, sorrow* **h·ärmen** vrefl [h] sich ~ *to grieve* (über *at, over*; um *for*) ‖ *to chafe*; *fret*; *languish, pine*; *worry* (über *about*) ‖ härm dich nicht darum *don't worry about that* ‖ sich z Tode ~ *to fret one's life away* (od *out*); *to worry o.s. to death* **h·armlos 1.** [a] *harmless* (*onlooker*); *innocent*; ~ wie ein Kind *as simple as a child*; ~ aussehend *h.-looking*; ~ tun *to put on an i. air* | (S) *h., i.* (*pleasures*); *s.* (*intention*) ‖ *innocuous, inoffensive, mild* (*medicine*), *unoffending* ‖ *insignificant*; e–e ~e S *small fry* **2.** [adv] *h.ly* **⩪igkeit** f ~/~en *h.ness*; *innocence*; *innocuousness*, etc.

Harmon·ie f ~/~n ⟨mus⟩ *harmony*; *concord* | ⟨übtr⟩ *h.* (*to live in h. with*) ‖ ~ der Sphären *h. of the spheres* | ~lehre [f] *theory of h.*; ~lehrer [m] *harmonist* **⩪ren A.** vi [h] **1.** ⟨mus⟩ *to harmonize* **2.** ⟨fig⟩ **a.** (S) *to chime, to h.* (mit *with*); *to be in keeping* (*with*); die Farben ~ nicht *the colours do not h.*; *the c. clash*; schlecht ~ *to chime ill* (*with* ..) **b.** (P) *to agree*; *to pull together*; gut mit–e–a ~ *to get on well together*; *to hit it off*; *to click*; in gewissen Punkten nicht ~ *to differ on certain points* **B.** ⩪ n **1.** ⟨mus⟩ *harmonization* **2.** *agreement*; *concord* **Harm·onik** f ⟨mus⟩ *harmonics* pl **Harm·onika** f ~/~s **1.** ⟨mus⟩ Glas⩪ *harmonica*; Mund⩪ *mouth-organ* ‖ Hand⩪, Zieh⩪ *accordion* **2.** chemische ~ *chemical harmonicon* **3.** ⟨rail⟩ *movable covered gangway with accordion walls* **harm·onisch A.** [a] **1.** ⟨mus⟩ *harmonic*; *harmonious, melodious*; ~ m *to harmonize* ‖ ⟨math & phys⟩ *harmonic*; ~e Reihe *h. progression*; ~e Teilung *h. division*; → Mittel **2.** ⟨übtr⟩ *harmonious* (*arrangement*; *meeting*; *family*) **B.** [adv] *harmoniously*; ~ angeordnet *or* wirkend *harmonious* (*room*) **Harmon·istik** f ⟨bib⟩ *harmonistic* **Harm·onium** n (L) ~s/–nien [–iən] ⟨mus⟩ *harmonium* L ‖ ⟨hist⟩ Vorstufe des ~s *seraphine*

H·arn m ~(e)s/ *urine* ‖ ~ l = harnen **~abfluß** m: unwillkürlicher ~ (*urinary*) *incontinence* **~apparat** m *urinary organs* pl **~beschwerden** f pl *urinary troubles* pl **~blase** f ⟨anat⟩ *urinary bladder*; → Blasen- **~drang** m *urge to void,* ⟨med⟩ *urgency* (*of micturition*); krankhafter ~ *micturition*; → –zwang **~entleerung** f; übermäßige ~ *diuresis* Gr **~fluß** m → –abfluß **~grieß** m *gravel* **~krankheit** f *urinary disease* **~kraut** n ⟨bot⟩ *yellow seed* **~lassen** n *urination*; (häufiges) *micturition* **~leiter** m *ureter*; Entzündung der ~ *ureteritis* L **~messer** m *urinometer* **~organ** n *urinary organ* **~röhre** f ⟨anat⟩ *urethra* L; hintere ~ *posterior part of the urethra* ‖ Instrument z Untersuchung der ~ *urethroscope* **~röhren-** *urethral*; ~katarrh [m] *urethritis* Gr; ~verengerung [f] *stricture of the urethra* **~ruhr** f ⟨path⟩ **1.** *polyuria* L **2.** Wasser⩪ *diabetes insipidus* L; → Zucker⩪ **3.** ⟨vet⟩ = Lauterstall **~sack** m ⟨anat⟩ *allantois*; → –strang **~sand** m = –grieß **~säure** f ⟨chem⟩ *uric acid* | ~salz [n] *urate* **~sediment** n *urinary sediment* od *deposit* **~stein** m → Blasen-, Nierenstein **~stoff** m **1.** *urea*; ⟨chem⟩ *carbamide* **2.** [in comp] *ureal* **~strang** m ⟨anat⟩ *urachus* L **~strenge** f = –zwang **⩪treibend** a (*di*)*uretic* ‖ ~es Mittel *diuretic* **~untersuchung** f; chemische

~ *uroscopy* **~vergiftung** f *urema* L **~verhaltung** f **1.** *anury* **2.** *ischuria* L **~wege** m pl = –apparat **~winde** f ⟨vet⟩ Schwarze ~ *haemoglobinaemia* L **~zwang** m ⟨path⟩ *strangury* **h·arnen 1.** vi [h] *to micturate, urinate*; *to make* od *pass water*; → pissen **2.** ≗ n *urination*; *micturition* ‖ Blut≗ ⟨path⟩ *haemoglobinuria* L

H·arnisch m ~es/~e **1. a.** ⟨hist⟩ *armour*; *harness*; *hauberk* **b.** ⟨fig⟩ jdn in ~ bringen *to enrage* od *exasperate a p*; *to get a p's back* od *dander up* ‖ in ~ geraten *to fly into a passion* (über *about*); *to get upon one's legs* ‖ im ~ s *to be in a passion*; .. *off at a deep end*, .. *up in arms* **2.** ⟨übtr⟩ **a.** ⟨geol⟩ *slickenside* **b.** ⟨weav⟩ *harness*; ~stuhl [m] *h.ing loom*

Harp·une f ~/~n *harpoon* | ~ngeschütz [n] *whale-gun* **Harpun·ier** m ~s/~e *h.er* **h.en** vt [h] *to h.*

Harp·yie [yiə] f **1.** ⟨ant⟩ *Harpy* **2.** ⟨orn⟩ *h.eagle*

h·arren vi [h] **1.** [gen +] ~ **a.** (S) *to await a th*; *the problem still awaits solution*; ein furchtbarer Anblick harrte ihrer *a terrible sight awaited her* **b.** sie ~ der Dinge, die da k sollen *they wait and see* **2. auf etw** ~ *to wait* od *hope confidently for*; *to look forward to*; *to trust to a th* ‖ auf **jdn** ~ *to have hope in a p*; *to trust a p* **3.** jds ~ *to be in store for a p*

harsch 1. [a] (S) *harsh* (*colour, voice*); *coarse, crude*; *rough* ‖ (P) *harsh*; *cruel* (gegen *to*); *hard* (*on a p*); *severe* (*with* ..) **2.** [adv] *harshly*, etc **3.** ≗ m ~(e)s/ *caked snow*

hart A. [a] **1.** (Ggs weich) **a.** ⟨**eig**⟩ *hard* (*stone*; *wood*; *mattress*; *pencil*); *firm, solid*; ≗er als *harder than* ..; ~ wie Stein *adamantine*; *as hard as a brick* ‖ *hard-boiled* (*egg*); *I like my egg h.-b.* ‖ *hard* (*ground, water*) **b.** ⟨**fig**⟩ e–n ~en Kopf h *to be headstrong* od *stubborn* ‖ e–n ~en Leib h *to be constipated* ‖ e–e ~e Nuß *a hard nut to crack* **2.** ⟨**übtr**⟩ (Ggs mild) **a.** *hard* (*winter*; *fight*; *words*); *heavy* (*blow*); *bitter* (*words*); *severe* (*loss*); *grim* (*death*); *sore* (*trial*); *strong, vehement* ‖ sein Gesicht nahm ~e Züge an *his face hardened*; ~e Gesichtszüge h *to be hard-featured* ‖ ~e Prüfungen *great trials* pl ‖ ein ~er Wettkampf *a close thing*; es war ein ~er W. ⟨Am⟩ *it was nip and tuck* (zw *between* ..) ‖ *difficult, hard* (*work*); *heavy*; *stiff* (*climb*); er wird e–n ~en Stand h *he will have much to contend with* **b.** *hard* (*heart*; *fate, punishment, times*); *Draconian* od *Draconic* (*laws*); *harsh* (*judgement*); *rigid, rigorous* ‖ ~e Tatsachen *hard* (⟨Am⟩ *frozen*) *facts*; T. sind ~ u unerbittlich *facts are stubborn things* ‖ ~e Linien *hard contours* ‖ mit ~en Gesichtszügen *hard-featured*; sein Antlitz nahm ~e Züge an *his face hardened* **c. (P)** *tough-minded*; *harsh* (*tyrant*) ‖ du kannst nie ~ s *you never can be stiff in the neck* ‖ ~ s gegen *to be hard* (od *down*) *on, to be severe* od *strict with* (*a p*) ‖ es ist ~ f ihn *it is hard on him* (*to yield*) ‖ der Boxer ist ~ im Nehmen v Schlägen *the boxer can take severe punishment* ‖ ~ bleiben *to keep a stiff* (*upper*) *lip*, .. *a stiff face*; *to harden one's heart* ‖ (jdn) ~ m *to harden*; (Herz) ~ m *to indurate* ‖ ~ w *to harden, indurate*; *to become inflexible* **3.** ⟨phon⟩ *hard* (*accent*; *consonant*) **B.** [adv] **1.** *hard*; (etw) ~ **backen** (kochen) *to bake* (*boil*) *hard* ‖ die Wege sind ~ gefahren *the roads have been trampled hard* ‖ ⟨aero⟩ ~ landen *to land with a bump* **2.** ⟨**fig**⟩ *hard*(*ly*); ~ **bedrängt** *hard pressed*; *hard-up* ‖ ~ bestrafen *to punish hard* (od *severely*) ‖ jdn ~ mitnehmen *to exhaust a p greatly*; *to pull a p down*; *to shake a p severely* ‖ wenn es ~ auf ~ geht *if the worst comes to the worst*; es ging ~ auf ~ *it was a matter of life and death* ‖ es ging ~ her *there was a stiff fight* ‖ es wird ihm ~ ergehen *it will go hard with him* ‖ jdm ~ ank *to come hard to a p*; es kommt mir ~ an *I find it hard* (*to do*) **3.** ~ **am Wege** *hard* (od *close*) *by the road* ‖ ~ am Feind *hard upon the enemy*; *in close contact with the enemy* ‖ ~ am Wind *close to the wind*; *close-hauled* ‖ ⟨mar⟩ ~ Backbord! *hard a-port*! **H·art-** *hard* **~blei** n *h. lead* **~brandstein** m *h. burnt brick* **~brot** n *h.-bread*; ⟨mar⟩ *ship's biscuit* **~erz** n *h. ore* **~faser** f ⟨tex⟩ *durable fibre*; ⟨Am⟩ *durable fiber* | ~pappe [f] *hardboard*, ~platte [f] *wallboard* **~futter** n *corn*; (Roggen u Weizen) *h.-corn* ≗**gekocht** a *h.-boiled* **~geld** n *coin*; *h. cash*; *specie* ≗**gesinnt** a = –herzig ≗**gesotten** a *h.-boiled* ‖ ⟨fig⟩ (*case-*)*h.ened* (*scoundrel, sinner*); *callous, h.-headed* **~gewebe** n *laminated fabric*; *laminate fabric base* **~gummi** m → Gummi 2. **~guß** m ⟨tech⟩ *chilled casting* | ~walze [f] *chilled iron roll* **~harz** n *h. resin* ≗**herzig** a *h.-hearted, heartless*; *unfeeling*; er ist ~ genug *he has the h.* (z tun *to do*) **~herzigkeit** f *h.ness*; *h.-heartedness* **~heu** n ⟨bot⟩ *St. John's wort*; *Hypericum perforatum* L **~holz** n *h. wood* ≗**hörig** a = schwerhörig **~käse** m *h. cheese* ≗**köpfig** a *headstrong*; *stubborn*; → –näckig **~köpfigkeit** f *st.ness* **~lage** f ⟨mot⟩ (des Steuers) *steering lock* ≗**leibig** a *constipated, costive* **~leibigkeit** f *constipation, c.ness* **~lot** n *h.-solder* ≗**löten 1.** vt [h] *to braze* **2.** ≗ n *h.-soldering*; *brazing* **~lötstelle** f *braze* **~manganerz** n ⟨minr⟩ *psilomelane* ≗**mäulig** a (of horses) *h.-mouthed* **~metall** n *h. metal*; *sintered hard carbide* ≗**näckig 1.** [a] (P) *dogged, headstrong, obstinate, persistent, pertinacious, stubborn, unyielding* ‖ (S) *obstinate, stubborn* (*resistance*); *persistent*; *obstinate* od *refractory* (*disease*) **2.** [adv] *obstinately, stubbornly*; *strongly* (*defended*) **~näckigkeit** f *doggedness*; *obstinacy, persistence* (*-cy*); *pertinacity*; *stubbornness wilfulness* **~papier** n *laminated* od *h. paper* **~paraffin** n *h. paraffin* **~porzellan** n *h. paste* **~puder(etui** n) m ⟨cosm⟩ *compact* **~riegel** m ⟨bot⟩ *dogwood*; *cornel* ~**säufer** m *heavy* od *hard drinker* ≗**schalig** a *h.shell*(*ed*); *testaceous* **~spiritus** m *solid spirit* **~stahl** m *h. steel* **~traber** m (Pferd) *trotter* **~wurst** f *h. sausage* **h·ärtbar** a *capable of being hardened*; *hardenable*; (Kunststoff) *thermosetting* | ≗**keit** *hardening quality*

H·ärte f ~/~n **1.** *hardness* (*of iron, water*) **2.** ⟨übtr⟩ **a.** *h.* (*of winter*; *work*); *harshness*; *hardship*; *heaviness*; *roughness* ‖ *rigidity, rigour* (*of the law*); *severity*; ~n [pl] *hardships*; *rigours* pl; zu unbilligen ~n führen *to lead to undue hardship*; mit rücksichtsloser ~ *with unfeeling rigour*; er hat ~ gegen sich selbst *he can be tough with h.s.* **b.** *hard disposition*; *cruelty*; ~ des Herzens *hard-heartedness* **~bad** n ⟨phot⟩ *hardener* **~beihilfe** f *hardship allowance* **~fall** m *extreme case* **~fonds** m ⟨soc⟩ *hardship fund* **~grad** m *degree of hardness* ‖ *h.* (*of steel*); ⟨phot⟩ *grade* (*of contrast*) **~messer** m *scleroscope*; ⟨x-ray⟩ *penetrometer* **~mittel** n *hardening agent*; ⟨phot⟩ *hardener* **~probe, ~prüfung** f, **~versuch** m *hardness test* **h·ärten 1.** vt *to harden*; *to indurate*; (Metall) *to temper*; (Eisen, Stahl) *to chill*; gehärtet *watered* (Stahl) ‖ ⟨fig⟩ (jdn) *to harden, indurate* (gegen *against, to*) **2.** ≗ n = Härtung **H·artmann** m, ≗chen [n] *billy-cock, hard-hitter, bowler*(*hat*) **H·artung** m ~s/ = Januar **H·ärtung** f ~/~en *hardening* (*of fat*); *tempering* **~sbad** n *hardening bath* ≗**sfähig** = härtbar

Harz[1] m ⟨geog Ger⟩ *the Harz Mountains* pl

H·arz[2] n ~es/~e **1.** *resin*; (bes Terpentin) *rosin*; Geigen≗ *colophony* ‖ versteinertes ~ → Bernstein ‖ mit ~ einreiben = harzen ‖ Kunst≗ *artificial* od *synthetic r.* **2.** [in comp] *r.* ..; *r.ous* **~elektrizität** f *r.ous electricity* **~gas** n *r. gas* **~geruch** m *r.ous odour* ≗**haltig** a *r.ous, r.iferous* **~kitt** m *r.ous cement* **~lack** m *r. lac* **~nutzung** f *r. tapping* **~öl** n *r. oil* **~säure** f *r. acid* | ~salz [n] *r.ate* **h·arzen 1.** vt [h] *to resin*; (Geigenbogen) *to rosin* **2.** vi ⟨for⟩ *to tap* **3.** ≗ ⟨for⟩ *bleeding*

H·arzer (→ Harz[1]) **1.** a *of the Harz Mountains*; ~ Käse *cheese made in the H. M.* **2.** m **a.** *inhabitant* od *native of the H. M.* **b.** = ~ Käse

***h·arzicht** a = harzig **h·arzig** a *resinous*

H·asa, El n (arabische Landschaft)

Has·ard n ~s/ *gambling game with dice; hazard* ‖ ~ spielen *to play a game of hazard* **~̽·ieren** vt [h] *to hazard; risk; venture; stake* **~spiel** n **a.** *game of chance; gambling* ‖ Karten~̽ *gambling game of cards* **b.** ⟨fig⟩ *gamble; venture; risky undertaking*

Hasch·ee n ~s/~s ⟨cul⟩ *hash*

h·aschen A. vt/i [h] **1.** vt **a.** (Dieb) *to catch* ‖ jdn (im Spiel) ~ *to tag* od *tig a p* ‖ (Schmetterling) *to catch; seize* ‖ (etw) *to catch; seize; snatch* **b. sich** ~ *to play touch-and-run; to play tag* od *tig* **2.** vi ~ **nach a.** *to snatch* od *snap at; to make a snatch at (a th)* **b.** ⟨übtr⟩ *to aim at; to fish for (compliments); to strain* od *run after; to strive for (recognition); to try to gain* od *win (a smile); to court (applause)*; nach Effekt ~ *to strain after effect* **B.** ~̽ n **1.** *catching*; (Spiel) *tag, tig; touch--and-run*; ~ spielen *to play tag* od *tig* **2.** ~ **nach a.** *snatch(ing) at* **b.** ⟨übtr⟩ *aiming at; fishing for; straining after; striving for* **‖ C.** °~ → Haschisch

H·äs/chen n *little* od *young hare; leveret* ‖ °(unerfahrener) ⟨aero⟩ *pup* ‖ ⟨sex⟩ *bunny*

†**H·äscher** m *bailiff; catchpoll, -pole* ‖ ⟨fig⟩ *myrmidon (the myrmidons of the law)*

H·ascher(l n [österr]) m ~s/~ = armes Kind; armer Kerl

hasch·ieren vt [h] ⟨cul⟩ *to hash; to mince*

Hasch(·isch) n ~/ (Rauschgift) *hashish, -sheesh*

H·ase m ~n/~n **1.** ⟨zoo⟩ **a.** → *hare*; gr amer. ~ *jack rabbit* ‖ junger ~ *leveret*; männlicher ~ *buck* od *male hare*; → Häsin ‖ ~n jagen *to course hares* ‖ ⟨cul⟩ falscher ~ *meat loaf* **b.** ⟨übtr⟩ °alter ~ *old hand*, ⟨aero sl⟩ *split-arse pilot*, ⟨Am⟩ *sweet* od *hot pilot* od *birdman* → Häschen; er ist kein heuriger ~ *he was not born yesterday* **c.** °⟨fig⟩ da liegt der ~ im Pfeffer *there's the rub* ‖ wir w sehen, wie der ~ läuft *we shall see how things go*; wollen sehen wie der ~ läuft *let's see how the cat jumps*; wir wissen, wie der ~ läuft *we know the way the cat is jumping; we know which way the wind blows* **2.** ⟨übtr⟩ °mein Name ist ~, ich weiß v nichts *I know, of course, nothing whatever about it*

H·asel f ~/~n ⟨bot⟩ **1.** = ~nuß **2.** *witch--hazel* **~busch** m *h.(-bush)* **~̽farben** a *h.-nut brown* **~huhn** n ⟨orn⟩ *h.-grouse* (od *hen*) **~maus** f ⟨zoo⟩ *dormouse* **~nuß** f ⟨bot⟩ *h.; h.-tree* ‖ (Frucht) *filbert, h.-nut* | ~öl [n] *h.-n. oil* **~rüsselkäfer** m → Rüsselkäfer **~rute** f *h.-wand* **~schwamm** m ⟨bot⟩ *polyporoid fungus* **~strauch** m = –busch

H·asen- ~ampfer m ⟨bot⟩ *wood* (od *clover*)--*sorrel* **~balg** m *h.-skin* **~braten** m *roast h.* **~brot** n **1.** ⟨bot⟩ *field wood-rush* **2.** °⟨hunt⟩ *spare sandwiches brought home* **~fell** n *h.-skin* **~fuß** m ⟨fig⟩ *coward, poltroon*; ⟨sl⟩ *funker*; ein ~ s *to be yellow* **~̽füßig** a ⟨fig⟩ *cowardly*; ⟨sl⟩ *funky* **~glöckchen** n ⟨bot⟩ *light-blue Spanish Scilla* **~hacke** f ⟨vet⟩ (on a horse's hind leg) *curb* **~herz** n ⟨poet⟩ = –fuß **~̽herzig** a *pigeon-livered* **~jagd** f *h.--hunting* (od *coursing*) ‖ °⟨fig⟩ *hurry (there is no h.)* **~klee** m ⟨bot⟩ *hare's foot (trefoil)* **~klein** n ⟨cul⟩ = –pfeffer **~kohl** m = –ampfer **~kopf** m (= Esparsette) ⟨bot⟩ *sainfoin* **~lattich** m ⟨bot⟩ *wall-lettuce* **~lippe** f ⟨path⟩ = –scharte **~maus** f ⟨zoo⟩ *chinchilla* **~ohr** n ⟨bot⟩ *h.'s ear; thorough--wax; buplever* °**~panier** n: das ~ ergreifen *to run like a h.; to show the white feather* (od *a clean pair of heels*); *to take to one's heels* **~pfeffer** m ⟨cul⟩ *jugged h.* **~pfötchen** n ⟨bot⟩ = –klee **~pilz** m ⟨bot⟩ = Röhrling **~̽rein** a ⟨hunt⟩ *well-trained (hound)* ‖ ⟨fig⟩ nicht ganz ~ ⟨pol⟩ *not reliable*, ⟨sex⟩ *an easy mark* **~rücken** m *saddle of h.* **~scharte** f ⟨path⟩ *h.-lip* **~schwanz** m *tail of h.* ‖ ⟨bot⟩ *h.'s tail grass*

häs·ieren vt/i *to cross-hatch*; → stricheln

H·äsin f ~/~nen *female hare; doe*

H·aspe f ~/~n *hasp; staple; clamp; hinge* ‖ (etw) mit e–r ~ befestigen *to hasp, staple*

H·aspel f ~/~n ⟨tech⟩ **1.** (Förder~̽) *winch windlass* **2.** (Garn~̽) *reel*; (Seiden~̽) *filature*

h·aspeln A. vt [h] ⟨tech⟩ **1.** (etw) *to windlass* **2.** (Garn, Seide) *to reel (off)* **3.** ⟨fig⟩ *to fidget* **B.** ~̽ n **1.** *windlassing* **2.** *reeling*

H·aß m Hasses/ *hatred* (gegen *of; against; for*); *strong dislike; spite*; ⟨poet⟩ *hate* ‖ eingefleischter ~ *rancour; inveterate spite* ‖ ein ~ *a feeling of hatred; an aversion, a dislike* | tödlicher, unversöhnlicher ~ *deadly, implacable h.* ‖ aus ~ *out of spite* ‖ ~ ausdrücken *to speak daggers* ‖ e–n ~ auf jdn h *to have an av. to a p; to hate* (od *dislike*) *a p* ‖ ~ hegen gegen jdn *to entertain feelings of h. for a p* ‖ ~ säen *to sow the seeds of h.* ‖ ~ im Herzen tragen *to be filled with feelings of h.* ‖ sich jds ~ zuziehen *to incur a p's enmity* **~̽erfüllt** a *spiteful; filled with feelings of h.*; ⟨Am⟩ *yellow*; ~er Blick *look of hatred*; ~e Reden halten *to speak daggers* **~̽erregend** a *hateful; odious* **~gefühle** n pl *feelings of h.* **hassen I.** vt [h] **1.** (jdn) ~ *to hate; to have a strong aversion to (a p)*; jdn tödlich ~ *to hate .. like sin* (od *with a deadly hate*); sie ~ sich tödlich *they hate each other like poison* **2.** ⟨übtr⟩ **(etw)** ~ *to hate, loathe; detest, abhor (he loathed socialism; fish; early rising)* ‖ ~ z tun *to hate doing* od *to do; to detest* (od *abhor*) *doing* ‖ bestgehaßt *loathed* **II.** vi ⟨hunt⟩ ~ **auf** (of crows) *to mob* **~swert, ~swürdig** a *hatable, hateful, hateworthy, odious* **H·asser** m ~s/ *hater*

h·äßlich A. [a] **1.** ⟨eig⟩ **a.** *plain (girl) (plain almost to homeliness)*; *ill-favo(u)red*; ⟨Am⟩ *homely* ‖ abstoßend ~ *ugly (p)*; ~ wie die Nacht (*or* Sünde) *as ugly as sin* **b.** *uncomely, unhandsome (house); ugly; unsightly (country)* ‖ ein ~er Anblick *or* Zug *an eye-sore* **2.** ⟨**übtr**⟩ (S) *inconvenient; unpleasant; untoward (event; injury)* ‖ *bad, dirty; nasty; ugly (weather); hateful (night)*; ⟨sl⟩ *beastly* ‖ *bad (conduct, humour); nasty (expression, look, words; cough; book, play)* ‖ *loathsome, offensive (smell, taste)* ‖ *ugly (rumours); vicious (habits, thoughts)* ‖ ~e Beschaffenheit *nastiness; ugliness; viciousness* ‖ e–e ~e S *a nasty* od *ugly affair* **3.** ⟨übtr⟩ (P) *nasty, unkind* (gegen *to*); ~es Wesen *nastiness* ‖ es ist ~ v dir *it is horrid of you* **B.** [adv] **1.** ~ gekleidet *plainly clothed* **2.** *nastily; unkindly* | **~̽keit** f **1.** *plainness* ‖ (abstoßende ~) *ugliness (of a p)* **2.** ⟨übtr⟩ *badness; nastiness; ugliness*; ~en [pl] *nasty remarks*

hast 2. sg prs v haben °**h·aste** = hast du? ‖ ~ 'ne Zigarette *got a fag?* ‖ ~ was kannste *all one knows; (to ride) hell-for-leather*

Hast m ~/ *haste, hurry; press (of modern life)*; (Überstürzung) *precipitance, -cy; precipitation* ‖ in wilder ~ *(in) h.-scurry; in hot haste* **h·asten 1.** vi [h] *to hasten, h.; sc.; to be in a h.(-sc.)* ‖ ~d *in a h.-sc.* **2.** ~̽ n *hurry, scurry* **h·astig 1.** [a] *hasty (glance; steps), hurried (speaker); precipitate (rush)*; ⟨fam⟩ *slap-dash (work)* ‖ *abrupt (departure); sudden* **2.** [adv] *hastily, hurriedly; precipitately; in haste; in a hurry; (in) h.-sc.; slap-dash* ‖ *abruptly, suddenly* | ~ greifen nach *to snatch, snap at (a th)* ‖ ~ essen [vi] *to gobble*, [vt] *to wolf down*; Essen ~ hinterschlingen *to bolt one's dinner* ‖ ~ ausbrechen in *to burst into*; (etw) ~ äußern *to blurt out* | **~̽keit** f *hastiness*; = Hast

hat 3. sg prs v haben

h·ätscheln vt [h] (jdn) *to caress, fondle, pet*

h·atsch·i ⟨hum intj⟩ (niesend) *a-tissue*

Ha(r)tsch·ier m ~s/~e ⟨hist⟩ *mounted halberdier; soldier of the Imperial life-guard*

h·ätte 1. & 3. sg pret subj v haben

Hatz f ~/ **1.** ⟨hunt⟩ **a.** *coursing; hunt with hounds* **b.** *pack of hounds* | ~laut [m] ⟨hunt⟩ *cry* **2.** ⟨übtr⟩ *merry-making*

Hau m **1. a.** † = Hauen; Hieb **b.** °~e [pl] *beating, flogging, thrashing, whipping*; ~e bek *to get a beating; to be flogged* **2.** *place where wood* *is felled* ≃**bar** a *fellable, ripe* (*tree*) **~degen** m **1.** ⟨hist⟩ *broadsword* **2.** ⟨übtr⟩ (P) *swordsman*; alter ~ *veteran*, ⟨sl⟩ *old sweat* **~hechel** f ⟨bot⟩ *rest harrow* **~klotz** m *chopping-block* **~krankheit** ⟨vet⟩ *lead poisoning* **~messer** n *cutting knife* **~stein** m *ashlar* **~zahn** m *fang, tusk*

H·aube f ~/~n **A.** (P etc) **1. a.** (of women) *cap*; Bade≃ *bathing-cap*; (mit Bändern) *bonnet*; ⟨hist⟩ *coif* ‖ ein Mädchen unter die ~ bringen *to get* od *marry a girl off*; unter die ~ k *to get off*; *to manage it* | Schwestern~ *cornet* **b.** ⟨ec⟩ (Kapuze) *hood*; Mönchs~ *cowl* **c.** ⟨mil⟩ *conical helmet*; ⟨Ger hist⟩ Pickel~ *spiked helmet* ‖ ⟨hist⟩ (Hirn≃) *casque, coif*; Kessel≃ *basinet*; Sturm≃ *morion* | Fecht≃ *fencing cap* **2.** ⟨scient, bes orn⟩ *crest*; *tuft of feathers* (od *hair*) | ⟨zoo⟩ *second stomach* (*of ruminants*) | ⟨bot⟩ *helmet*; *crest*; *tuft of hair* **B.** ⟨übtr⟩ (S) **1.** ⟨math⟩ *spherical cap* (*of a globe*) **2.** ⟨arch⟩ *crest*; *crown*; *cupula* L; *dome*; → Kappe **3.** *cap*; *cover*(*ing*) (*of a valve*); *hood*; *lid*; *top* ‖ ~ f Tee-, Kaffeekanne *cosy* ‖ ⟨mot⟩ (Kühler≃) *bonnet*; ⟨Am⟩ *hood* ‖ ⟨mar⟩ Turm≃ *turret-hood* | *eye* (*of a hammer*, etc.) **H·auben- 1.** ~geschoß [n] *capped shell* **2.** ⟨orn⟩ *crested*; *tufted*; ~huhn [n] *crested fowl*; ~lerche [f] *crested lark* ‖ kl ~reiher [m] *squacco* ‖ ~wachtel [f] → Schopfwachtel **3.** teils † (→ Haube A. 1. a.) ~kopf, ~stock [m] *milliner's block*; ~macherin [f] *milliner*; ~verschluß [m] ⟨mot⟩ *bonnet fastener*

H·aubert m ~s/–e ⟨hist⟩ *hauberk, haw–*

Haub·itze f ~/~n ⟨mil⟩ *howitzer* **Haub·itzen-** [in comp] *howitzer* (*horse-battery*)

H·auch m ~s/~e **1.** (Atem) *breath*; bis zum letzten ~ *to the last b.* ‖ ⟨phon⟩ (Laut) mit e–m ~ aussprechen *to aspirate* **2.** (Luft≃) *whiff* (*of fresh air*) ‖ *waft, whiff* (*of odour*); *breathing* **3.** (dünne Schicht) *bloom* (*on plums*, etc) **4.** ⟨fig⟩ (Spur) *shade* ‖ rosiger ~ *bloom* (*on cheeks*); *glow* (*of youth*) ‖ zarter ~ *waft* (*of peace*) ‖ der leiseste ~ e–r Verstimmung *the slighest trace of a misunderstanding*; ein ~ v *a tinge* od *touch of*; → Anflug **~bild** n *pictured gelatine* ≃**d·ünn** a *paper-, wafer-thin*; (Strumpf) *sheer, filmy* **~laut** m ⟨gram⟩ *aspirate*; mit ~ aussprechen *to aspirate* ≃**z·art** a *delicate* **h·auchen 1.** vi/t [h] **a.** vi *to breathe*; *respire* **b.** vt (~d äußern) (Gebet) *to br.* ‖ ⟨gram⟩ *to aspirate* **2.** ≃ n ⟨gram⟩ *aspiration*

H·audah f [invar] ([Baldachin]sänfte) *howdah*

H·audegen m **1.** ⟨hist⟩ *broadsword* **2.** ⟨übtr⟩ (P) *swordsman*; *warhorse*; ein alter ~ *a veteran*, ⟨sl⟩ *an old sweat*

H·auderer m ~s/~ (Miet-Kutscher) [nwd] *cabman*

H·aue f ~/~n **1.** ⟨agr⟩ *hoe*; *mattock*; *axe* **2.** (Prügel) *larrup* **h·auen I.** vi/t [hieb, haute/gehauen] [h] **A.** vi **1.** *to strike* (mit *with*); mit e–r Axt ~ *to cut* (od *strike, work*) *with an axe*; *to use an axe*; mit dem Schwert ~ *to thrust the sword* (durch *through*; in *into*) ‖ ~ auf etw *to hit, strike a th*; ~ gegen *to hit, strike against* (*a th*); ~ nach *to strike at* | er haute um sich *he laid about him* ‖ jdm ins Gesicht ~ *to hit, strike a p in the face* **2. ~ u stechen** *to cut and thrust* ‖ ⟨fig⟩ das ist nicht ge~ u nicht gestochen *that is neither fish, flesh nor fowl*; *that's quite ineffective* ‖ *that's not cricket* ‖ hier weiß man nicht, was ge~ u gestochen ist *you don't know which is which* (od *how things stand*) ‖ ⟨fig⟩ mit jdm in dieselbe Kerbe ~ *to concur entirely with a p* ‖ ⟨fig⟩ über die Schnur ~ *to kick over the traces*; *to overstep the mark* **B.** vt **1.** (Erz, Kohle) *to hew*; *cut*; (Steine) → klopfen ‖ *to cut* (*files*) ‖ *to break* (*the ground*) *with a hoe* ‖ ×(Fleisch, Holz) *to chop*, → hacken ‖ ×(Gras, Wiese) *to cut*; → mähen **2.** ein Loch ~ *to cut a hole* (in .. *in the ice*) ‖ Stufen ~ *to cut* (od *hew out*) *steps* (*in the rock*); *to cut* (*a road*) (*through* ..) ‖ (e–e Figur) in Marmor ~ *to hew out in marble* **3.** (etw) aus Stein ~ *to carve* .. *out of stone*; (etw) in Stücke ~ *to cut, hew to pieces* ‖ jdn hinter die Ohren ~ *to box a p's ears* ‖ ⟨fig⟩ jdn über's Ohr ~ *to cheat* (od *do*; ⟨fam⟩ *best*) *a p* **4.** (mit der Peitsche, Rute ~) (= prügeln) *to beat, flog, lash, thrash, whip*; hau hin! ⟨fam⟩ *make it snappy* °haut ihn! *give it him!* °haut dem Kerl eins drauf *punch the beggar's head* ‖ (Pferd) *to cut* .. (*with a switch*) ‖ °jdn zum Krüppel (*or* krumm u lahm) ~ *to break every bone in a p's body* **5. sich** ~ *to fight* (über *about*; um *for*); *to have a fight* (*they are having a f.*); *to scuffle* **II.** ≃ n *striking* (*with*); *thrusting* ‖ *cut*(*ting*) ‖ *beating, flogging*, etc **H·auer** m ~s/~ **1.** (P) *hewer*; → Bild≃ etc **2.** (Zahn) *fang, tusk* (*of a wild boar*); mit ~n versehen [a] *tusked*; (jdn) mit dem ~ durchbohren *to tusk* **3.** ⟨hunt⟩ *wild boar* **H·äuer** m ~s/~ ⟨min⟩ *hewer, coalface worker* **Hauer·ei** f ~/~en *fight*; *scuffle*; allgemeine ~ *free fight*; ⟨Am⟩ *free-for-all*

†**Hauf** m = Haufe **~werk** n *won minerals*

H·äufchen n *small heap* (*of earth*) ‖ (P) *little band* od *group* ‖ ⟨fig⟩ °sie saß da wie ein ~ Unglück *she sat there, a picture of misery* **H·auf**(**e**) m ~(e)s/~e **1.** ⟨mil⟩ (Trupp) ein ~ Krieger *a body of warriors*; *a troop* **2.** der gr ~ *the common herd* od *people*; *the crowd*; *the masses* pl; *the multitude* (od *populace, ruck*) ‖ mit dem gr ~n gehen *to go with* (od *to follow*) *the crowd* ‖ lärmender ~ *rabble* ‖ e–n verlorenen ~en führen *to lead a forlorn-hope* **3.** * → Haufen 3. **h·äufeln** vt [h] (Kartoffeln) *to earth* (od *mould*) *up*; (Erdbeeren) *to hill* **H·aufen** m ~s/~ **1.** (of earth, etc.) *heap*; *mass*; ~ Erde, Erd≃ *heap of earth*; Sand≃ *h. of sand*; → Hügel; Mist≃ ‖ Getreide≃ *mow*; → Heu≃ **2.** (S) *heap, mass, pile*; ein ~ Steine etc *a pile of stones*; *pack* (*of cards*); *a swarm* (*of bills*) → Partie, Satz, Stoß ‖ ein gr ~ *a large quantity* od *amount* (*of corn, money*); *a crowd* (*of books*) ‖ *a lot, sight* (*of money*); ~ [pl] v ⟨fam⟩ *lots* (*and lots*) *of* (*cigars*); *heaps, oodles* [pl] *of* (*money*) **3.** (a. *Haufe) (P) *crowd, multitude, number* (*of children*); *ruck* (*of opponents*); ein ~ Leute *or* Menschen *a stream* (⟨fam⟩ *a lot*) *of people*; *a crowd* od *multitude, throng* ‖ *a band* (*of robbers*); *gang* (*of workmen*) ‖ ~ [pl] v Leuten *crowds* (⟨fam⟩ *heaps* od *lots*) *of people* ‖ kl dichte ~ [pl] *knots, clusters* pl (*of sightseers*) ‖ in hellen ~ *in crowds, in heaps* ‖ → Haufe; Schar **4.** [**abstr**] ~ v *reams* (*and r.*) *of*; ein ~ Arbeit *a heap* (od *lot*) *of work*; ich habe e–n ~ A. mit der S *the matter gives me a lot of w.* ‖ *a pack* (*of lies*); .. Unsinn *a lot of rubbish* **5.** alles **auf** e–n ~ legen, werfen *to lay* od *throw everything on to a heap*; (etw) auf e–n ~ legen *to heap* .. *on a pile, to pile* .. *up* | Holz **in** ~ aufschichten *to pile up timber* ‖ (Heu) in ~ setzen *to cock*; *to pile into cocks* ‖ die Leute strömten in ~ aus .. *people came trooping out of* (*the theatre*) ‖ (Erde) in ~ zus–häufen *to mound* ‖ in kl ~ zus–stehen *to stand about in knots* | (Pflanze) **mit** e–m ~ Erde umgeben *to hill* | °jdn **über** den ~ fahren, rennen *to run over* [prep] *a p*; *to run a p down*; *to knock a p over* ‖ °über den ~ schießen *to shoot down* ‖ ⟨fig⟩ (etw) über den ~ werfen *to cast* (od *throw*) *to the winds*; (Plan) *to throw over, to throw overboard*; *to upset*; (die Tradition) *to make hay of* (*tradition*) **~sand** m ⟨found⟩ *black sand* ≃**weise** adv *in crowds, in heaps*; ~! *heaps!* **~wolke** f *piled* od *heap cloud*; *cumulus* L **h·äufen** vt [h] **1.** *(e–n Tisch) *to heap* (mit *with*) ‖ (Gefäß) *to heap*; gr gehäufter Löffel voll *heaped spoonful*; ganz voll ~ *to heap full high* **2.** (sammeln) **a.** → an~, auf~, zus–~ **b.** (Wirkungen) *to accumulate*; *pile* ‖ Verbrechen auf V. ~ *to commit one crime after another*; *to add c. to c.*; *to heap c. upon c.* **4. sich** ~ **a.** (of sand) *to accumulate*; *to bank up* **b.** ⟨übtr⟩ *to accumulate*;

to gather head; to increase, multiply (*complaints multiplied*); *to be cumulative* (od *rampant*); die Verbrechen ~ sich *crime is spreading* ‖ sich ~d *cumulative* (*evidence*); *accumulative* **h·äufig 1.** [a] **a.** *frequent* (*headache; attacks; visits*); ~er Besuch *frequentation* (*of a place*); ~es Vorkommen *frequency* ‖ sehr ~ *continual* (*shouting*) **b.** *abundant; much* (*rain, snow*); (P) *frequent* (*visitor*); ~er Besucher *frequenter* (*of a place*) **c.** [pred] ~ s *to be frequent* (in *in*); *to be abundant, copious, numerous* **2.** [adv] *frequently*; nicht ~ *infrequently*; sehr ~ *continually*; *often* ‖ (Ort) ~ besuchen *to frequent*; (of ghosts) *to haunt* ‖ ~ auftreten *to be frequent* (in *in*); *to be abundant* (od *copious*) | ~̈**keit** f *frequency*; ⟨demog⟩ absolute ~ *class fr.*; *ratio* (*attendance r.*); *recurrence; repetition* | ~ziffer [f] ⟨demog⟩ *rate* **H·äuflein** n ~s/~ (P) *little band* (*of a few veterans*) **H·äufler** m ~s/~ ⟨gard⟩ *cultivator* **H·äufung** f ~/~en **1.** *accumulation* (*of wealth*); *heaping, piling* **2.** ⟨fig⟩ *acc.; multiplication* ‖ *increase; spreading* (*of crime*) **H·aufwerk** n ⟨geol⟩ *heap of debris*; → Hauf-

H·aupt n ~es/~̈er (vgl z ~̈en 1. a.) **1.** [gewählt & ⟨poet⟩ f Kopf] **a.** (P & T) *head* ‖ jdm das ~ abschlagen *to behead a p* ‖ sein ~ beugen vor jdm *to bow to* (od *before*) *a p* ‖ das ~ entblößen *to uncover* od *bare one's head* ‖ ⟨fig⟩ (*discord raised its*) *h.* | feurige Kohlen auf jds ~ sammeln *to heap coals of fire on a p's h.* ‖ den Feind aufs ~ schlagen *to inflict a defeat on the enemy; to defeat the e. decisively* ‖ mit erhobenem ~ *with h. erect* ‖ mit gesenktem ~e *with bowed h.* ‖ er ragte um ~es Länge über die anderen empor *he stood* (od *was*) *head and shoulders above the others* ‖ **zu** ~̈**en (jds)** *at* (od *above*) *a p's h.; on high; overhead* **b.** gekrönte ~̈er *crowned h.s* pl ‖ die greisen ~̈er der Stadt *the hoary City Fathers* pl ‖ ⟨univ⟩ bemoostes ~ *veteran student; old boy* **2.** (Führer) *head* (*of the family*); *chief, leader* (*of a party*) ‖ das ~ der engl. Kirche *the Supreme H. of the Church of England*; die Reformation der Kirche an ~ u Gliedern *the root and branch reformation of the church* **3.** ⟨poet⟩ (of mountains) *head, summit, top* **4.** [in comp] *head; ch(ief); top; cardinal, central, main, pr(incipal); leading*; ⟨com⟩ *general* **~abschnitt** m *ch. section* **~absicht** f *main* (od *pr.*) *intention* **~(absperr)ventil** n *main* (*stop*) *valve* **~achse** f *pr. axis* **~agent** m *ch. agent* **~(angriffs)-ziel** n *primary target* N **~anlage** f ⟨comp⟩ *main unit*; v der ~ getrennt *off line*; mit der ~ verbunden *on line* **~anliegen** n *major concern* **~-anschluß** m ⟨wir⟩ *main set* **~argument** n; jds ~ *a p's case* **~artikel** m ⟨com⟩ *ch. article; staple* **~attraktion** f *clou* Fr **~aufenthaltsort** m *headquarters* pl **~augenmerk** n *special attention*; sein ~ richten auf *to focus one's attention on ..* **~ausschuß** m *steering committee* **~bahnhof** m *central station* **~bedeutung** f *primary meaning* **~beruf** m *ch. occupation* **~bestandteil** m *ch. ingredient* od *constituent*; ~e [pl] *major components* **~beteiligte** pl *pr. persons* **~betrag** m *total amount; sum total* **~bewaffnung** f *main armament* **~buch** n ⟨com⟩ *ledger*; ~̈er [pl] *all l.s* **~büro** n → –sitz **~darsteller** m ⟨theat⟩ *leading actor; principal; protagonist*; ⟨Am a.⟩ *headliner* **~darstellerin** f ⟨theat⟩ *leading lady*; als 2. ~ auftreten *to co-star* **~deck** n ⟨mar⟩ *main deck* **~delegierte** pl *ch. delegates* **~depot** n *base depot* N **~dynamo** f *pr. dynamo* **~eigenschaft** f *pr. quality* **~einflugzeichen** n ⟨aero⟩ *boundary beacon* **~eingang** m *ch.* od *main entrance* od *approach* **~erbe** m *ch. heir* **~ereignisse** n pl *pr. events* pl **~erfolg** m ⟨theat⟩ (*the play was a*) *good draw* **~erfordernis** n *prerequisite; ch. requisite* **~fach** n *pr.* (od *major, main*) *subject*; ⟨Am⟩ erstes ~ *major*, zweites ~ *minor*; sein ~ m in *to major in ..* ‖ [konkr] *principal drawer* **~faktor** m *major factor* **~fehler** m *main defect* ‖ der ~ an dem Stück *the ch. drawback in .., the ch. objection to the play* (*is ..*) **~feind** m *ch. enemy* **~feldwebel** m *sergeant major*, ⟨Am⟩ *first s.*, ⟨sl⟩ *topkick* **~figur** f *main figure*; ⟨theat⟩ *principal; central* (od *pr.*) *figure* **~film** m *feature film*, ⟨fam⟩ *features* pl **~fluß** m *main river* **~frage** f *ch. question*; ⟨mst⟩ *point* **~führer** m *principal; ringleader* **~funkstelle** f *net control station* **~gangster** m *big shot* **~gebäude** n *main building* **~gebirgskette** f *main range* **~gedanke** m *cardinal* (od *fundamental*) *idea; ch. thought*; ⟨fig⟩ *keynote; keystone; burden* **~gefreite(r)** m *private first class* **~gegenstand** m *pr. subject* **~geschäfts-** ~stunden [f pl] *rush hours*; ~sviertel [n] *shopping centre* **~gesprächsgegenstand** m *staple of a conversation*; ~̈e [pl] *leading topics* pl (*of the day*) **~gericht** n *main course* od *dish* **~gestalt** f (in a play) *hero*; → –person **~gewicht** n; das ~ auf Fleisch legen *to emphasize meat* **~gewinn** m *first prize* **~gläubiger** m *pr. creditor* **~gleis** n *main* od *through line* od *track* **~grund** m *ch. reason* **~grundsatz** m *leading principle* **~gruppe** f *main group* **~haar** n *hair of the head* **~hahn** m ⟨tech⟩ *main cock*; den ~ abstellen *to turn off* (*the gas*) *at the mains* ‖ °⟨fig⟩ *cock of the roost; topliner* **~halle** f *great hall* **~handelsartikel** m *staple* **~handelsplatz** m *emporium* L; *centre of commercial activity* **~handrad** n *master* (⟨theat⟩ *m. dimmer*) *wheel* (⟨Am⟩ *handle*) **~herausgeber** m *editor(-in-chief)* **~industrie** f *staple industry* **~inhalt** m *substance* (*of a speech*); *sum* **~instinkt** m *major i.* **~inhaber** m *senior partner* **~kampffeld** n *defensive area main fighting area* (od *zone*) **~kampflinie** f (H. K. L.) *main line of resistence* **~kanal** m *artery* **~kartei** f *master file* **~kasse** f ⟨com⟩ *ch. paydepartment* °**~k·erl** m *brick*; → Prachtkerl **~kontor** n *head-office* **~ladung** f *base charge* **~lager** n ⟨tech⟩ *main bearing* **~landstraße** f *trunk-road* **~lehrer** m *headmaster* (*of an elementary school*) ‖ °**~leidtragende** [der ~, ein ~r] *the loser* **~leiter** m *principal* (*of a business*); ⟨Am⟩ *executive* **~leitung** f (Gas~̈) *main*; ⟨el⟩ *power line* **~leute** pl (→ Hauptmann) ⟨mil⟩ *captains* pl **~linie** f ⟨el & rail⟩ *main line, trunk-line* **~macht** f *main striking force* **~mahlzeit** f *ch.* (od *pr.*, ⟨Am a.⟩ *biggest*) *meal* (*dinner* ⟨mst⟩ abends) **~mangel** m = –fehler; ⟨agr com⟩ (T) *defects for which vendor is liable only within a certain period* **~mann** m ~s/–leute ⟨mil⟩ *captain*; ~ bei *c. in the infantry*; ~ (Ing.) *c. in the engineer corps*; *e. c. in other arms*; ~ v Köpenick *copper c.* ‖ Rang, Stelle e–s ~s *c.cy, c.ship* **~maschine** f *pr. dynamo* **~masse, ~menge** f *bulk* **~mast** m *mainmast* **~merkmal** n *ch. mark; characteristic feature* **~nachweis** m → Schlüsselliste **~nenner** m ⟨math⟩ *common denominator* ‖ ⟨fig⟩ *the fundamentals* pl **~niederlage** f ⟨com⟩ *main depot* od *stores*; → –handelsplatz **~nummer** f (im Programm) *ch. turn*; ⟨Am⟩ *head-liner* **~ort** m *pr. place; country town* **~packer** m *head-packer* **~person** f *pr. person; chief*, ⟨iron⟩ *Number One* ‖ ⟨Lit⟩ *pr.* od *leading character*; → –darsteller, –figur; –hahn, –nummer **~pfeiler** m *main pillar* **~pleuellager** n ⟨mot⟩ *master rod bearing* **~portal** n *front-door*, → –eingang **~post(amt** n) f *the General Post Office* **~probe** f ⟨theat⟩ *dress-rehearsal* **~programm** n ⟨film⟩ *feature*, ⟨rad, telv⟩ *Home Service* **~punkt** m; ~e [pl] *main* od *ch. points* pl **~quartier** n *headquarters* pl [sg konstr]; ~ des Obersten Befehlshabers *General Headquarters* (abbr *G. H. Q.*) **~quell(e** f) m *headspring* **~quittung** f ⟨com⟩ *general receipt* **~rechnung** f *general account* **~-richtung** f ⟨fig⟩ ~en [pl] *trend; main tendencies* pl **~rohr** n *main*; ~ der Wasserleitung *water-main* **~rolle** f ⟨theat⟩ *ch. part; leading rôle*; → –darsteller, –figur ‖ jdm e–e ~ geben *to star a p*; in der ~ gastieren *to star it* ‖ (jdn) in der ~ aufweisen ⟨film *to feature*; ein Film mit N. N. in der ~ *a film featuring N. N.* ‖ ⟨fig⟩ die ~ spielen *to play first fiddle* **~sache** f *main thing* od *point; main issue*;

substance; *pivotal question*; ⟨Am fam⟩ *lowdown* ‖ in der ~ *on the whole, in the main* ‖ das ist die ~ *that is the point*; ⟨fam⟩ *that is everything* ‖ s–e Arbeit ist ihm immer die ~ gewesen *his work has always been pre-eminent with him* **~̊sächlich** **1.** [a] *ch., main, pr.* **2.** [adv] *ch.ly, mainly, pr.ly* **~sammler** m *main* od *trunk sewer* **~satz** m ⟨gram⟩ *pr. clause* **~schalter** m ⟨el⟩ *main switch*, ⟨theat⟩ *grand master* **~schaltraum** m ⟨theat⟩ *intake room*, ⟨Am⟩ *electrical vault* **~schlacht** f *main battle* **~schlagader** f ⟨anat⟩ *aorta* L ‖ °**~schlager** m ⟨theat⟩ *good* od *box-office draw*; *hit* ‖ ⟨Lit⟩ *best seller* ‖ ⟨film⟩ *theme-song* **~schluß-** [in comp] ⟨el⟩ *series* (*wound*); ~dynamo [f & m] *s.* (*w.*) *dynamo*; ~motor [m] *s. motor* **~schlüssel** m *master* (od *pass*)*-key* **~schriftleiter** m *editor*(*-in-chief*) **~schuld** f *pr. fault*; du hast die ~ *it is mainly your fault* **~schuldige** [der ~, ein ~r] m ⟨jur⟩ *the principal* **~schuldner** m *pr. deb*(*i*)*tor* **~schule** f ⟨Ger⟩ *the upper classes* (*of an elementary school*) **~schwein** n ⟨hunt⟩ *wild boar after fifth year* **~segel** n *mainsail*; Geitau des ~s *clew-garnet* **~sicherheit** f ⟨com⟩ *primary security* **~sicherung** f ⟨el⟩ *mains fuse* **~signal** n ⟨rail⟩ *home-signal* **~sitz** m *headquarters* pl [sg-konstr] ‖ ⟨fig⟩ *focus* (*of a sedition*) ‖ ⟨com⟩ *home office, head-o.* **~sorge** f *ch. concern*; die ~ muß s *all the concern must be* (*that..*) **~spant** n ⟨mar⟩ *main frame* **~spaß** m *capital joke*; ⟨sl⟩ *scream* **~spieler** m ⟨theat⟩ *protagonist*; → –darsteller **~stadt** f *capital*; *metropolis*; ~ e–r Grafschaft *county town* (⟨Am⟩ *seat*) **~̊städtisch** a *metropolitan* **~star** m → –darsteller **~stelle** f *main office* **~sternbild** n ⟨astr⟩ ~er [pl] *cardinal signs* pl **~steuer-** ~amt [n] n *Receiver-General's Office* ‖ ~kompaß [m] ⟨mar⟩ *pelorus* **~stimme** f *leading part*; *pr. voice* **~straße** f *pr. street*; *artery*; (Landstraße) *highway*; *main* (od *arterial*) *road* **~strecke** = –linie **~streich** m = –spaß **~strom** m **1.** *main stream* ‖ ⟨el⟩ *main current* **2.** [in comp] ⟨el⟩ *series* (*wound*); ~dynamo [m] *s.* (*w.*) *dynamo*; ~kreis [m] *main* od *power circuit*; ~leitung [f] *main*; ~motor [m] *s. motor* **~strömung** f ⟨fig⟩ ~en [pl] *main tendencies* pl **~stück** n *pr. piece* ‖ ⟨ec⟩ *article* (*of faith*) **~stütze** f *mainstay* (*of a theory*); die ~n weltlicher Macht *the sinews of temporal power* **~stützpunkt** m *main base* **~summe** f *sum total* **~täter** m ⟨jur⟩ *principal* **~tau** n ⟨mar⟩ *shroud* **~teil** m *main*; *body*; *main* (od *major*) *part* **~thema** n ⟨m. m.⟩ *underlying theme* **~ton** m ⟨gram⟩ *stress accent*; *stress*; der ~ liegt auf *the st. is on ..* **~treffer** m *first prize*; ⟨Am fam⟩ *jackpot* **~triebfeder** f *mainspring* **~triebkraft** f ⟨fig⟩ *prime mover* **~triebwerk** n ⟨tech, a. a-n⟩ *service module* **~trupp** m ⟨mil⟩ *main body*; *support proper*; (*rear-guard*) *reserve* **~tugend** f *cardinal virtue* **~typ** m ~s/~en *main type* **~übel** n *pr. evil* **~übertragungsleitung** f ⟨el⟩ *trunk transmission line* **~uhr** f *master clock* **~umstand** m *pr. circumstance* **~- und Staatsaktionen** f pl ⟨Ger Lit⟩ *drama of sensational contemporary incident* **~ursache** f *main* (od *pr., leading*) *cause*; *chief contributor* (*to accidents*) **~verbandplatz** m ⟨mil⟩ *ch. dressing station* **~verfahren** n ⟨jur⟩ *trial* **~vergnügen** n *ch. delight*; *great fun* **~verhandlung** f = –verfahren **~verkehrs-** ~adern [pl] *main arteries* pl (*of a town*) ‖ ~straße [f] *arterial* (*main, major*) *road*; *highway* ‖ ~stunden [pl], ~zeit [f] *rush* od *peak hour*(*s*) **~versammlung** f ⟨com⟩ *general meeting* **~verteidigungslinie** f *main line of defence* **~vorstand** m *executive committee* **~wache** f ⟨mil⟩ *main-guard* **~wachtmeister** m = –feldwebel **~welle** f ⟨tech⟩ *main shaft* **~werk** n *pr.* (od *ch.*) *work*; *masterpiece* **~widerstandslinie** f *main line of resistance* **~wort** n *noun, substantive*; begriffliches ~ *abstract noun* **~wurzel** f *taproot* ⟨a. fig⟩ **~zeit** f ⟨mach⟩ *productive time*; ⟨gram⟩ ~en [pl] *primary tenses* pl **~zeuge** m *pr. witness* **~ziel** n *pr.* (od *major*) *object* **~zollamt** n *general custom-house* **~zug** m *pr. trait, characteristic* (od *main, salient*) *feature*; die ~̊e jds (*or* e–r S) schildern *to feature a p* (*a th*) **~zweck** m *ch. object*; *main end* **~zweig** m *main branch*; ⟨bot⟩ *leader*

H·äuptling m ~(e)s/~e *chief*(*tain*); *head* (*of a clan*); *headman*; *leader* ‖ *chieftain* (*of brigands*)

hau-ruck intj ⟨mar⟩ *yo*(*-heave*)*-to*

Haus n ~es/~̊er **A. 1.** (Wohn~̊) (*dwelling-*)*-house*; Einfamilien~̊ ⟨Am⟩ *home* ‖ dreistöckiges ~ *three-storied h.*; kl einstöckiges ~ *bungalow* kl Neben~̊ *outh.*; Klein~̊ mit Garten ⟨Am⟩ *homestead* ‖ (Wohnung) *home*; *quarters* pl ‖ ~ u Hof *h. and home* **2.** (= ~bewohner) **a.** (Familie) *h., home*; *family*; *h.hold* ‖ Herr, Frau, Sohn des –ses *master, mistress, son of the h.* **b.** Pensions~̊ *boarding-h.* ‖ ⟨school⟩ *h.*; ⟨univ⟩ *college* **c.** (Fürsten~̊) *h.*; *dynasty*; das ~ Coburg, York *the H. of Coburg, York* **d.** Armen~̊ *workh.*; ⟨sl⟩ *the h.* **e.** Gottes~̊ *the H. of God* **B. 1.** (Beratungs~̊ etc) ⟨parl⟩ **a.** die ~̊er des Parlaments *the H.s of Parliament* **b.** (= Mitglieder) *the H.*; das ~ der Gemeinen, Unter~̊ *the* (*H. of*) *Commons* (Vorsitzer: *the Speaker*); ~ der Lords, Ober~̊ *the* (*H. of*) *Lords* (Vorsitzer: *the Lord Chancellor*); → eröffnen ‖ ⟨Am⟩ ~ der Abgeordneten *the H. of Representatives* (Vorsitzer: *the Speaker*) ‖ das ~ ist nicht beschlußfähig! *no h.! the H. has not a quorum*; ein b.es ~ bilden *to constitute a h.* **2.** (Geschäfts~̊, Verwaltungs~̊) *h.*; ⟨Am mst⟩ *building* (*the Empire State Building*) ‖ ⟨pol⟩ ~ z Pflege engl.-amer. Beziehungen *Bush H.* (*London*) ‖ ⟨com⟩ *business, establishment, firm*; *trading-h.* ‖ ~ nebst Grund u Boden *the premises* pl **3.** ⟨theat⟩ *h.*; volles ~ *full h., capacity audience*, ⟨fam⟩ *bumper, sellout*; das ganze ~ fesseln *to hold the stage* **4.** öffentl. ~ *h. of ill fame*; *brothel* **C.** ⟨übtr⟩ **1.** ⟨zoo⟩ Schnecken~̊ *shell*; *snail-sh.* **2.** ⟨astr⟩ die 12 ~̊er [pl] des Himmels *the h.s* pl **3.** *eye* (*of a hammer*) **D.** °⟨fig⟩ (P) ein gelehrtes ~ *a great scholar*; *a scholarly mind* ‖ fideles ~ *jolly fellow* ‖ altes ~ ⟨sl⟩ *old bean* od *egg* ‖ **E. Wendungen** (→ bes A. B.) **1.** ‖ °er hat Einfälle wie ein altes ~ *he has all sorts of funny ideas*; °auf ihn kann man ~̊er **bauen** *you may rely confidently on him* ‖ ⟨fig⟩ das ~ bestellen *to set one's h. in order*; *to put one's affairs in order* ‖ °jdm das ~ einlaufen *to besiege a p* (mit *with*) ‖ ⟨parl⟩ das ~ durch e–e Rede fesseln *to hold the floor of the H.* ‖ frei ~ ⟨com⟩ *delivered free domicile* ‖ ein gr ~ führen *to live in great style* ‖ jdm das ~ führen *to keep h. for a p* ‖ ein offenes ~ halten *to keep open h.* ‖ das ~ hüten *to keep the h.*; *to stay at home* ‖ jdm das ~ verbieten *to forbid a p the h.* ‖ ich befahl ihm, das ~ z verlassen *I ordered him out of the h.* **2.** ~ **an**~ wohnen *to be next-door neighbours* | **aus** gutem ~ (*to be*) *of* (*a*) *good family* ‖ (Wäsche) aus dem ~ geben *to put out* ‖ jdn aus dem ~ weisen *to show a p the door*; *to turn a p out of doors* | **außer** –se s *to be away from home* **d. im** ~e ⟨com⟩ *on the premises* ‖ im ~e des Herrn N. *at Mr. N's*; ⟨Am⟩ *at the N. home* ‖ im ~e Schmidt *at the Smith's* ‖ er ist im ~e *he is indoors* (od *within doors*) ‖ sie half im ~e (‚als ..) *she helped about the h.* (*when*) ‖ ⟨theat⟩ stürmischen Beifall im ~e finden *to bring down the house* ‖ (nicht mehr) Herr im ~e s *to be* (*no longer*) *master in one's own h.* | jdn **ins** ~ aufnehmen *to receive a p into one's h.* ‖ sie brachte e–e gute Mitgift ins ~ *she brought a good dowry with her* | nach ~e *home* jdn nach ~e begleiten *to see a p home* ‖ nach ~e k *to come in* (od *home*) ‖ nach ~e zurückkehren *to set out for home*; ⟨engl jur a.⟩ *he went back to chambers* ‖ die Rückkehr nach ~e *the return home* | **von** ~e *from home* ‖ v ~e aus ist er Mediziner *he started* (*his career*) *in medicine* ‖ v ~e aus ist er sehr reich *he is born rich*; *he is of a wealthy family* ‖ v

~e aus träge *naturally indolent*; *indolent by nature*; v ~ aus Gelehrte [pl] *scholars in their own right* ‖ v ~ z ~ *from h. to h.*; Werbung v ~ z ~ *h.-to-h. canvassing* ‖ beste Grüße v ~ z ~ *with kindest regards to you all* | ein Garten **vor** dem ~e *a front garden* ‖ ⟨theat⟩ vor ersten ≈ern spielen *to play to record h.s*; vor leeren (vollen) H. spielen *to play to empty (full) h.s* | sie ritt **zum** ~e des Herrn N. *she rode to Mr. N's* ‖ **zu** ~e *at home*; *in* (*to be in*); nicht z ~e *out*; ⟨engl jur⟩ (Gerichtsferien) *nobody is in chambers now* ‖ z ~e gemacht *home-made*; .. gesponnen *homespun* ‖ z ~e bleiben *to stay at home*; ⟨Am a.⟩ *to stay home*; z ~e bleibend (*or* sitzend) *home-keeping*; jdn z ~e finden *to find a p in* ‖ er freute sich, wieder z ~e z s *he was glad to be home again* | bei Ihnen fühle ich mich wie z ~e *with you I always feel at home* (od *at ease*) ‖ tun Sie, als ob Sie z ~e wären *make yourself at home* ‖ er ist in Hamburg z ~e *he is a native of Hamburg* ‖ ⟨fig⟩ er ist in der Politik sehr z ~e *he is familiar with* (od *at home*, *well up*, *well-versed in*) *politics* **Haus-** [in comp] *house*; *h.hold*; *d(omestic)*; *f(amily)*; *private* **~abbruchunternehmer** m *h.breaker* **~anzug** m (bes für Damenpartys) *hostess suit* **~altar** m *h.hold altar* **~andacht** f *f. prayers* pl **~angestellte** f *d. servant*; *maid* | **~(r)** m *d. servant*; ⟨Am⟩ *h.worker* **~anschluß** m *service pipe* ‖ *residence telephone* | ~kasten [m] ⟨el⟩ *service board*, ⟨Am⟩ *s. equipment* **~apotheke** f *medicine chest*; ⟨Am⟩ *first-aid kit* **~arbeit** f *h.-work*, *d. work*; (tägl.) *char(e)*, ⟨Am⟩ *chores* pl ‖ ⟨school⟩ *home-work*, *h.-w. assignment* **~arrest** m *confinement at one's h.* **~arzt** m *f. doctor* ‖ unser ~ *our medical man*, *our doctor* **≈backen** a *home-baked*; *home-made* ‖ ⟨fig⟩ *homely*, *plain*, *simple*; *humdrum* **~bau** m *building of h.(s)* **~bedarf** m *necessaries* pl *wanted in a h.*, *h.hold requisites* pl ‖ für den ~ *for the h.* **~besitz** m *ownership of h.s*; *h. property*; *housing property* **~besitzer** m *proprietor of a h.*, *h.-owner*; *landlord*; ~verein [m] *association of house-owners* **~besorger** m [österr] → –mann, –wart, Portier **~besuch** m *home visit* **~bettelei** f *begging from door to door*; *mendicancy* **~bewohner** m *h.mate*, *inmate*; die ~ [pl] *the h.(hold)*; *the f.* **~bibliothek** f *private library* **~bock** m ⟨ent⟩ = Bockkäfer **~boot** n *h.-boat* **~brand** m *d. fuel* od *coal* **~bursche** m *footboy* ‖ °⟨fig⟩ *h.mate* **~dame** f *châtelaine*; *hostess*; *h.keeper* **~diener** m *male servant*; *man-s.t*; Hotel≈ *porter*; *boots* pl [sg konstr] ‖ °**~drache** m *shrew*; *vixen*; *she-dragon* **~eigentümer** m = –besitzer **~flagge** f ⟨mar⟩ *h.-flag* **~fleiß** m = –industrie **~fliege** f ⟨ent⟩ *h.-fly* **~flur** m *entrance--hall*; *vestibule* **~frau** f *mistress of the h.*; *h.wife*; *hausfrau*; sparsame ~ *thrifty h.keeper*; nach ~enart *home-cooked*; ≈liche Instinkte *home-wifely i.s* **~freund** m *f. friend* ‖ ⟨dero⟩ (Liebhaber) *cicisbeo* (It) **~frieden** m *d. peace* **~friedensbruch** m *breach of d. peace*; ⟨jur Scot⟩ *hamesucken* **~gebrauch** m *d. use*; f den ~ *for the h.(hold)* **~geflügel** n *poultry* **~gehilfin** f = –angestellte **~geld** n ⟨Ger⟩ *insurance-benefit* (*for a sick p staying at his home*) **~gemeinschaft** f *h.-community*; *the h.* **~genosse** m *h.mate, inmate*; ~n [pl] *inhabitants of a h.* **~gerät** n *h.hold gear* (od *goods* pl); → –rat **~gericht** n ⟨hot⟩ *chef's special(ity)* **~gesetz** n *f. law* (*of a dynasty*, etc) **~gesinde** n *d. servants*, *d.s* pl **~gewerbetreibende** [der ~] m = Heimarbeiter **~glocke** f *h.-bell* **~gott** m *h.hold god* **~grille** f ⟨ent⟩ *h.-cricket*; *cricket on the hearth* **~hahn** m *d. cock* **~halt** m **1.** *h.hold*; *family*; *hearth* ‖ ⟨demog⟩ gemischter ~ *composite h.hold* ‖ getrennter ~ *separate establishment* ‖ gewöhnl. ~ *private* od *f. h.hold* ‖ jdm den ~ besorgen *or* führen *to keep h.* (od *to manage*, ⟨fam⟩ *to do*) *for a p* ‖ e–n ~ gründen *to set up h.*; *to settle down* ‖ e–n ~ leiten *to manage a h.hold* **2.** (Staats≈) *budget* **3.** [in comp] ~seife [f] *d. hard soap*; ~tarif [m] ⟨el⟩ *h.hold tariff* **≈halten A.** vi [h] **1.** jdm ~, f jdn ~ *to keep h.* (od *to manage*, ⟨fam⟩ *to do*) *for a p* **2.** ~ mit etw *to economize*, *spare* od *husband a th*; ~ mit s–n Kräften *to reserve one's strength* **B.** ≈ n *h.keeping*; sparsames ~ *d. economy* **~halter, ~hälter** m *h.holder* ⟨bes bib & übtr⟩ **~hälterin** f *h.keeper* **≈hälterisch 1.** [a] *economical*; *thrifty* (mit *of*); nicht ~ *thriftless*, *unthrifty* **2.** [adv] ~ umgehen mit etw = haushalten mit **~halts-** | ~bogen [m] *h.hold schedule*; ~gegenstände [pl] *furnishings* pl; *furniture*; ~geld [n] *h.keeping allowance*; ~geschäfte [pl] *h.hold avocations* pl; ~hilfe [f] (P) *home-help*; ~jahr [n] *financial* (od *fiscal*) *year*; ~kühlschrank [m] *d. r.*; ~kunde [f] *home-making* ‖ ~plan [m] ⟨parl⟩ *budget*; den ~plan vorlegen *to bring in the b.*; im ~ unterbringen *to b.*; ~tiefkühltruhe [f] *home freezer*; ~voranschlag [m] ⟨parl⟩ *the Estimates* pl; ~vorstand [m] *head* (od *master*) *of a h.hold*; *h.holder*; ~waschmittel [n] *h.hold detergent* **~haltung** f **1.** *management of a h.hold*; *h.keeping*; *h.wifery*; Kunst der ~ *d. economy* **2.** = Haushalt **~haltungs-** [in comp] ~liste [f] ⟨Ger⟩ *list of families and inhabitants of a h.*; ~vorstand [m] = Haushaltsvorstand **~-Haus-verkehrsdienst** m *door-to-door service* **~herr** m *master of the h.*; *h.holder*; *host*; → Hausbesitzer | ~nherrlichkeit [f] ⟨fam⟩ *landlordism* **≈hoch** [a. ˈ–ˈ–] **1.** [a] *as high as a h.* **2.** [adv] *ace high* (od *head and shoulders*, *several cuts*, *by a long chalk*) (*above*); jdm ~ überlegen s ⟨Am a.⟩ *to put it all over a p* | –hoher Favorit ⟨racing⟩ *hundred-to--one shot* **~hofmeister** m *steward* ‖ *major-domo* (*of a princely h.hold*) **~huhn** n ⟨orn⟩ *d. fowl*; ≈er [pl] *poultry* **~hund** m *h.-dog* **~industrie** f *home* (od *village*, *cottage*)-*industry* **~installation** f *plumbing work* **~kapelle** f *private chapel*; Geistlicher e–r ~ *chaplain* ‖ ⟨mus⟩ *private band* **~kaplan** m; ~ des Königs *d. chaplain to the king* **~katze** f *d. cat* **~kauf** m *purchase of h.* **~kleid** n *h.* (od *morning*)-*gown*; *h.-dress* **~knecht** m **1.** (in Gasthöfen) *boots* pl [sg konstr]; *ostler* **2.** °⟨fig⟩ = –schlüssel °**~knochen** m = –schlüssel **~konzert** n *private c.* **~kost** f *h.hold* (od *homely*, *simple*) *fare* ‖ †**~kreuz** n ⟨fig⟩ *d. calamities* pl, *f. grief* ‖ (Ehefrau) *shrew*, *scold* **~laub** n, **~lauch** m ⟨bot⟩ *h.leek* **~lehrer** m *private tutor* **~lehrerin** f *governess* **~leinen** n, **~leinwand** f *homespun linen* **~liste** f *list of h.mates* **~macher-** m *home-made* (*sausage*); *our own make*; *home-spun* (*linen*) **~macht** f *dynastic power* **~mädchen** n, **~magd** f *h.-maid*; *d. servant*; *hired girl*; ⟨Am⟩ *chambermaid*, *waitress* **~mann** m *h.-porter*; → –meister **~mannskost** f *good plain* (od *homely*) *fare*, *plain cooking* **~marder** m ⟨zoo⟩ *h.-marten* **~marke** f *f. mark*; *written symbol* (od *sign*) **~maus** f *h.-mouse*; *common m.* **~meier** m ⟨hist⟩ *major-domo*; *seneschal* **~meister** m *h.-steward*; *janitor*; *care-taker* ‖ = –mann **~miete** f *h.-rent* **~mittel** n *home medicine* **~musik** f *d. music* **~mutter** f ⟨übtr⟩ *matron* **≈mütterlich** a *matronly* **~nummer** f *number of a h.* **~orden** m *f.-badge* (od *insignia*) **~ordnung** f *rules* [pl] *of a h.*; *h.(hold)-regulations* pl **~pflege** f (of insured sick p) *home-treatment* ‖ *out(-door) relief* **~plage** f *d. trouble* ‖ †**~postille** f *book of devotions* (od *sermons*) *for f. use* **~rat** m *h.hold effects* pl (od *furniture*); alter ~ *old h.hold goods* pl | ~sentschädigung [f] *h.hold compensation*; ~sversicherung [f] *insurance of contents* **~recht** n *d. authority*; v s–m ~ Gebrauch m *to turn a p out of doors* **~regiment** n ⟨hist⟩ *h.hold regiment* **~reinigung** f; gründliche ~ *h.-cleaning* **~rock** m *ordinary dress*; *undress* (*jacket*) **~schabe** f ⟨ent⟩ *cockroach* **~schlachtung** f *slaughtering on the premises* **~schlüssel** m *h.-key*; (Drücker) *latch-key* **~schuh** m *slipper*; ~e ohne Absätze *flat-heeled slippers* pl **~schwalbe** f ⟨orn⟩ *h.-swallow* **~schwamm** m ⟨bot⟩ *wood-fungus*; *dry-rot* **~spinne** f ⟨ent⟩ *h. spi-*

der **~stand** m *h.hold* || sich e–n eigenen ~ gründen *to set up for o.s.*; *to settle down* **~steuer** f = Gebäudesteuer **~suchung** f *domiciliary visitation*; *searching of a h.*; allgemeine ~ *h.-to-h. search*; bei ihm wurde e–e ~ vorgenommen *his h. was searched*; ~en m *to make searches from h. to h.* **~suchungsbefehl** m ⟨jur⟩ *search-warrant* **~taube** f ⟨orn⟩ *h.-pigeon* **~taufe** f *private baptism* **~telephon** n *intercommunication*; ~ im Krankenhaus *intrahospital telephone* **~tier** n *d. animal* | ~beförderung [f] *pet transport* (od *service, flight*) **~tochter** f *h.hold trainee, companion h.maid* **~trauung** f *private wedding* **~truppen** f pl ⟨hist⟩ *h.hold-troops* pl; *life-guards* pl (*of a prince*) **~tür** f *front-door*; Verkauf an der ~ *d.-to-d. selling* **~unke** f ⟨zoo⟩ *rushtoad*; ⟨fig⟩ *home-bird* **~vater** m *father of* (*the*) *f.*; *master of h.*; *pater familias* L **~verwalter,** **~vogt** m *h.-steward*; ⟨theat⟩ *h. manager* **~wappen** n *f.-arms* pl **~wart** m *porter*; ⟨Am⟩ *janitor* **~werk** n = –fleiß **~wesen** n *d. concerns* pl; *h.hold affairs* pl **~wirt** m = –besitzer **~wirtin** f *proprietress of h.* **~wirtschaft** f *h.keeping, h.-wifery*; (Fach) *home economics* | ~skunde [f] *d. science* **≗wirtschaftlich** a *h.hold*; *h.keeping*; *d.* **~wurz** f ⟨bot⟩ = –lauch **~zentrale** f ⟨telph⟩ *private branch exchange* **~zins** m *h.-rent* | ~steuer [f] *h.(-rent) tax* **H·äus|chen** n ~s/~ *small house* || (Abort) ⟨hum⟩ *parliament*; Fischer≗ *fishing-box*; Jagd≗ *hunting-box* || °⟨fig⟩ jdn aus dem ~ bringen ⟨sl⟩ *to get a p's goat*, ⟨Am⟩ *to get a p's shirt out*; (ganz) aus dem ~ geraten (sein) *to fly off the handle, to go off the deep end*, (*to be beside o.s.*; ⟨sl⟩ *to be all of a dither*) **h·ausen** vi [h] **1.** (wohnen) *to dwell, live* (*in caverns*); *reside*; wir ~ schon lange hier *we have resided here for a long time*; ~ **in** .. *to inhabit* (*a place*); in verfallenen Wohnungen ~ *to live in tumble-down dwellings* | wie Schweine zus–~ *to herd together like pigs*; *to pig* (mit *with*); *to pig it* **2.** ⟨fig⟩ (of criminals, storms) schlimm *or* übel ~ *to play havoc* (in *in*; unter *among*); übel ~ in e–m Land *to devastate* (od *lay waste*; *ravage*) *a country*; *to work havoc throughout a c.*

H·ausen m ~s/~ ⟨ich⟩ *hausen* [Ger]; (*largest species of*) *sturgeon* **~blase** f; (Klärmittel) *ichthyocolla, isinglass*

H·äuser- **~anbau** m entlang e–r Landstraße *ribbon-building, ribbon development* **~block,** **~-komplex** m *block of houses*; viereckiger ~ *square* **~makler** m *house-agent*; ⟨Am⟩ *realtor* || ⟨dero⟩ *h.-monger* **~reihe** f; ~ auf ansteigendem Gelände *terrace* **haus·ieren 1.** vi [h] *to peddle* || ~ mit Waren *to peddle* od *hawk goods* || ⟨fig⟩ ~ gehen mit *to peddle* (*new ideas*) || °sie geht mit ihren Reizen ~ ⟨vulg⟩ *she flashes her charms* || er muß mit s–n Fähigkeiten förmlich ~ gehen *he must actually go begging with his accomplishments*; er geht mit s–m Wissen ~ *he has* od *puts all his kn. in the window* **2.** ≗ n *hawking, peddling*; *pedlary* || Betteln u ~ verboten *begging and hawking prohibited* **Haus·ierhandel** m *hawking, peddling, pedlary* **Haus·ierer** m ~s/~ *pedlar, hawker*; ⟨Am⟩ *peddler*; ⟨a. fig⟩ (Bücher≗) *colporteur* Fr **Haus·ierwaren** pl *pedlary* **H·äusler** m ~s/~ *cottager* **h·auslich** a [bay, österr] = sparsam **h·äuslich A.** [a] **1.** (**S**) *domestic* (*happiness, life, work*; *sewage*); ~e Angelegenheiten *domesticities* pl; *household affairs* pl || ⟨school⟩ ~e Aufgaben [pl] *home-work* || *family* (*peace, row*) || ~er Herd *fireside*; im ~en Kreise *by the fireside* || (jdn) an ~es Leben gewöhnen *to domesticate* **2.** (**P**) *family* (*man*); *home-keeping*; *thrifty* (*girl*); ~ w *to settle down* (*to domesticity*) **B.** [**adv**] sich ~ einrichten *to make o.s. at home*; sich bei jdm f lange Zeit ~ einrichten *to settle down for a long stay with a p* | **≗keit** f ~/ **1.** *domesticity*; *family life*; *fireside* **2.** (Sparsamkeit) *economy, thriftiness* **3.** [konkr] = Haushalt

H·ausse ['ho:sə] f Fr ⟨com⟩ *boom*; *sudden activity of commercial and industrial life* || *rise in prices*; ~ u Bankrott ⟨bes Am⟩ *boom and bust* || ⟨st exch⟩ auf ~ spekulieren *to deal* od *speculate for a rise*; ⟨fam⟩ *to bull* **Hauss·ier** [ho:'sje:] m Fr ⟨st exch fam⟩ *bull* **hauss·ieren** [ho:'s–] vi [h] (of prices) *to rise*; *to boom*

Haut f ~/~≗e **A. 1. a.** ⟨anat⟩ *skin*; *integument*; ⟨sl⟩ *bark* || Leder≗ *corium* L; oberste Schicht der ~, Ober≗ *epidermis* Gr; *cuticle* || innere ~ (unter der Ober≗) *cutis* L, *derma* Gr || durch die ~ wirkend *percutaneous*; unter der ~ angebracht *hypodermic* (*injection*); *subcutaneous* **b.** (of horse, ox) *hide*; *pelt*; (of calf) *kip*; → Balg, Fell || abgeworfene ~ *slough* (*of a snake*) || ⟨com⟩ ≗e [pl] *hides* pl, *skins pl*; 10 ≗e *a dicker*; ≗ebearbeiter *hide-dresser* **2.** nichts als ~ **u Knochen** *mere s. and bones*; *s.ny* || die ~ v (etw) **abschälen,** –schürfen *to excoriate* (*a limb*); sich die ~ abschürfen *to graze one's s.* || (e–m T) die ~ abziehen *to s.* || e–e ~ bilden (of wounds) *to s.* (*over*) | ⟨fig⟩ er mußte s–e ~ z Markte tragen *he had to risk his own life*; ⟨sl⟩ *it's ·your funeral!*; er verstand es, sich s–r ~ z wehren *he knew how to save his s.* | (etw) **auf** der bloßen ~ tragen *to wear next to one's s.* || bis auf die ~ *to the skin* || ⟨fig⟩ sich auf die faule ~ legen *to idle away one's time* | ⟨**fig**⟩ **aus** der ~ fahren *to lose one's wool* od *hair*; *to jump out of one's skin*; das ist um aus der ~ z fahren *that's enough to drive one mad*; er kann aus s–r ~ nicht heraus *he can't shake off his nature*; ich möchte nicht **in** s–r ~ stecken *I should not like to stand in his shoes*; er steckt in k–r gesunden ~ *he his a sickly sort of p*; **mit ~ u Haar** *out and out*; *root and branch*; *altogether*; *thoroughly*; mit heiler ~ *by the s. of one's teeth*; *with life and limb*; .. davonk *to save one's bacon*; mit s–r ~ bezahlen *to pay for* (*a th*) *with one's life* **B.** ⟨**übtr**⟩ **1.** (dünne Schicht) *coating*; *film* (*of the eye*); *membrane*; *pellicle*; *skin* (*on milk*) **2.** *peel* (*of fruit*) **3.** ⟨mar⟩ (of ship) *skin*; *outer layer of planks* || ⟨tech bes a-n⟩ *skin*, (äußere) *outer shell* **C.** °⟨fig⟩ (P) e–e gute alte ~ *a good old skin* (od *soul, body*); e–e ehrliche ~ *an honest fellow* → **C.** [in comp] *s*(*kin*), *c*(*utaneous*), *d*(*erma–*) **~abschürfung** f *excoriation* **~arzt** m *d.tologist* **~ausdünstung** f *perspiration* **~ausschlag** m *c. eruption*; *rash* **~blüte** f ⟨path⟩ *pimple* **~drüse** f → Talgdrüse **≗eng** a ⟨tail⟩ *skin-tight*; (bequem) (*comfort-*), ganz ~ *power-stretch* (*bra*) **~entfettung** f *defatting of the skin* **~entgiftungssalbe** f *decontamination ointment* **~entzündung** f ⟨path⟩ *d.titis* L **~falte** f *pucker, wrinkle*; tiefe ~ *furrow* **~farbe** f *colour of* (*the*) *s.*; (natürliche) ⟨cosm bes Am⟩ *colo(u)r on the naked side*; (of the face) *complexion* **~finne** f ⟨path⟩ *acne* **~flügler** m ⟨ent⟩ *hymenopterous insect*; Gattung der ~ *Hymenoptera* Gr pl **~furche** f = ~falte **~grieß** m ⟨path⟩ *milium* L **~jucken** n ⟨med⟩ *itching of the s.*; *pruritus* L **~knötchen** n ⟨path⟩ *papule, -la* L **~krankheit** f ⟨med⟩ *s. disease*; → Flechte || Arzt f ~en *d.tologist*; Lehre v den ~en *d.tology* **~krem** f *s. cream*, kühlende ~ *cold cr.* **≗nah** a *skintight*; *with a clingy fit* **~öl** n ⟨a.⟩ *sun-tan lotion* **~pflege** f *care* (od *improvement*) *of the s.*; *cosmetics* pl | ~mittel [n] *cosmetic*; *skin food* **~pilz** m ⟨bot⟩ *hymenomycete* **~polyp** m ⟨path⟩ *c. pendulous tumour*; *polypus* [L] **~reflex** m *s. reflex* **~reinigungsmittel** n *s. cleaner* **~reiz** m *c. irritant* **~riß** m *crack in the s.* **~rötung** f *erythema* L **~schutzmittel** n *s. protecting agent* **~sinnesorgane** pl *s.-sensory apparatus* **~skelett** n ⟨zoo⟩ *exoskeleton* **≗sympathisch** a ⟨tex⟩ *agreeable to the skin* **~tau** m ⟨cosm⟩ *s. dew* **~tuberkulose** f ⟨path⟩ *lupus* L **~übertragung** f *s.-grafting* **~verbrennung** f *scald* **~verletzung** f *s. wound*; *c. lesion* **~wassersucht** f ⟨path⟩ *anasarca*; *subcutaneous dropsy* **~wirkung** f ⟨el⟩ *s. effect* **~wolf** m ⟨path⟩ *intertrigo* L **~wunde** f *s.-wound* **~wurm** m ⟨vet⟩ *s.-worm* **H·äutchen** n

~s/ ~ *coating, film* || ⟨anat, bot & zoo⟩ *membrane, pellicle, tegument, tunic*; Jungfern≈ *hymen* || e–m ~ähnlich, v e–m ~ umgeben *membran(e)-ous* **h·äuten** vt [h] **1.** (T) *to skin*; *flay* **2. sich** ~ *to cast* (od *shed*) *one's skin* || (of a snake) *to slough* (*its skin*) **-häuter** [in comp] D·ick~ ⟨zoo⟩ *pachyderm* **h·äutig** a *cutaneous*; *membranous* (*bag*); *skinny* || dick~ *thick-skinned*; *pachydermatous*; dünn~ *thin-skinned*

°**H·autevol·aute** f [invar] ⟨hum⟩, **Hautevol·ee** [o:tvɔ'le:] f Fr ~/ die ~ *the upper ten*; *the cream of society*; Mitglied der ~ ⟨bes Am⟩ *socialite* **Hautgout** [o:'gu:] m Fr ~s/ *haut-goût* Fr; *high flavour* (*of game*) || ~ h (of meat) *to be high* od *gamy* **Hautreli·ef** [o:rə'ljef] [n] [Fr] ~s/ ⟨arts⟩ *high relief*; *haut-relief* [Fr]

H·äutung f **1.** *skinning* (*of an animal*) **2.** (Sichhäuten) *shedding* **H·äutungs-** ~apparat [m] *skinning apparatus*; ~stadium [n] *shedding stage*; Tier im ~ *shedder* || ~zeit [f] *shedding season*

Hav·anna(zigarre) [invar] f *Havana* (*cigar*)

Havar·ie f ~/~n [–i:ən] ⟨mar⟩ *average*; *sea-damage*; *break-down* || gr (kl) ~ *general* (*petty*) *a.* || ~ aufm *to adjust, settle a.*; Ersatz f ~ erhalten *to recover a.*; ~ erleiden *to suffer s.-d.* **~dispacheur** m [–pɑ'ʃør] *a.-adjuster* **~fall** m *case of a.* **~rechnung** f *a.-bill* **havar·ieren** vi/t [h] **1.** vi *to suffer s.-d.* **2.** vt (Schiff) *to damage* || havar·iert [a] *s.-d.d* (*goods*)

H·avelland [–f–] n ⟨Ger⟩ *Havelland, country watered by the Havel*

H·avre, Le ['ɑ:vr] n ⟨Fr⟩ (Hafenstadt)

Haw·aii- ~-Insel *Hawaiian Island*

×**H·axe** f ~/~n [südd] = Hachse ⟨cul⟩ *heel* || ⟨übtr⟩ (P) (Beine) ~n *stumps*

he [intj] **1.** (*here*) *hi*! *hi, you there*! *hallo*(*a*), *you there*! *ho there*! *I say*! || ⟨mar⟩ *ahoy*! **2.** [interr] was meinst du, he? *don't you think, eh*?

H·ebamme f ~/~n ⟨med⟩ *midwife* | ~ngesetz [n] *Midwives Act*; ~nkunst [f] *midwifery*

H·ebe- **~arm** m *lifting arm*; *lever* **~baum** m *heaver*; *long lever* **~bock** m *gin, jack* **~bühne** f *lifting platform*; ⟨mot⟩ *car lift*; ⟨theat⟩ *lifting* (⟨Am⟩ *elevator*) *stage*; ⟨a-n⟩ *rising floor* **~daumen** m *wiper* (*lifting a hammer*) **~kolben** m *lifting piston* **~kraft** f *lifting power* **~kran** m *winch* **~lade** f *lever jack* **~maschine** f *hoist*; *hoisting engine* **~muskel** m ⟨anat⟩ *elevator* **~rolle** f *tax-list* **~schiff** n *salvor* **~stange** f *crow-bar* **~stelle** f *collecting-office*; *receiver's office* **~vorrichtung** f *lifting tackle* od *device*; *haulage* **~werk** n *elevator*; *haulage* **~zeug** n = –maschine || (aus Eisenkrampen) *slingdogs* pl **~zylinder** m *lifting cylinder* **H·ebel** m ~s/~ ⟨tech⟩ *lever* (an .. *on a machine*); (an e–r Welle) *tappet* || *crank*; *handle* || ⟨mil⟩ Abzugs≈ *firing-l.*; Anlaß≈ *starting-l.*, Einrück≈ *coupling-l.*; → Schalt≈ etc | e–n ~ **ansetzen** *to apply a l.*; *to l.*; ⟨fig⟩ hier muß der ~ angesetzt w *this is where you must make your big effort* (od .. *employ your chief influence*) || ⟨fig⟩ alle ~ in Bewegung setzen *to set every spring in motion*; *to leave no stone unturned*; *to pull endless strings* (*to catch*; *to get* ..) **~anwendung** f *leverage* **~arm** m *l. arm* **~bremse** f *l.-brake* **~(dreh)punkt** m *fulcrum* **~fangvorrichtung** f *arresting l.* **~kraft** f *l.age* **~presse** f *l.-press* **~mechanismus** m *l. mechanism*, ⟨Am⟩ *l. machine* **~schalter** m *l.-switch* **~schwung** m ⟨phot⟩ *stroke on the l.* **~stützpunkt** m *fulcrum* L **~übersetzung** f *l.age* **~werk** n *l.age*; *system of l.s* **~wirkung** f *l.age* **h·eben** vt/i [hob/gehoben] [h] **I.** vt **A. 1.** (hoch~) (Gewicht) *to lift*; *to raise* || mühsam ~ *to heave* || (mit Flaschenzug) *to hoist* || die Arme, Hände ~ *to raise one's arms, hands* || (zum Schwur) *to lift up one's hand* || er hat sich e–n Bruch gehoben *he has got a rupture* || °⟨fig⟩ e–n ~ *to raise one's elbow* (*he is fond of his drops*) || °wollen wir (schnell) e–n ~? *d'you feel like a small spot*?, *what about a quick one*? **2.** (jdn, etw) *to lift*, (auf *on to*; in *into*; über *over*); *to heave, hoist, raise* || **(auf)** *we raised him to his feet*; *lifted him to the shoulders*; *on to the horse* | (e–e Tür) **aus** den Angeln ~ *to unhinge*; ⟨fig⟩ (etw) *to unbalance, unhinge, upset* || (Gegner) aus dem Sattel ~ *to unhorse*; ⟨fig⟩ *to supplant, supersede* || (Kind) aus der Taufe ~ *to stand sponsor to* | (jdn) **in** den Adelstand ~ *to raise to the peerage* || in den Himmel ~ *to belaud, exalt, praise to the skies* | **(von)** *to lift the lid off a vessel* || (jdn) vom Pferde ~ *to lift down from the horse* **3.** e–n Schatz ~ *to raise a treasure* || die St. ~ *to raise, elevate one's voice* | ⟨**übtr**⟩ (mehren) (Ansehen, Stimmung) *to add to*; *to enhance, improve, increase, lift, raise*; *to ameliorate* (*conditions, etc*); auf e–e höhere Stufe ~ *to lift* (od *raise*) *to a higher plane* || moralisch ~ *to elevate* || gehobene Stellung *leading, prominent position* **5.** ⟨math⟩ (Brüche) *to reduce* **B. sich** ~ **1.** (of waves) *to lift*; *rise*; sich ~ u senken *to heave*; *to rise and fall*; s–e Hand hob sich zum Gruß *his hand rose in salute* || (of a lid) *to raise itself*; sich ~ l *to lift* || er hob sich mühsam auf die Füße *he heaved himself to his feet* **2.** (of a fraction) drei hebt sich gegen drei *three cancels three* **3.** ⟨**übtr**⟩ *to improve, increase*; *thrive* || (of feelings) *to soar* **4.** hebe dich weg! *clear out*! ⟨bib⟩ *get thee hence* (*Satan*)! **II.** vi ⟨math⟩ *to cancel out* **H·eben** n **1.** *heave*; *lift* (*of the eyebrow*); *lifting, raising* || ⟨math⟩ *reduction* **H·eber** m ~s/~ *siphon, syphon* | ~barometer [n] *s.-barometer* || ~leitung [f] *siphon piping* od *conduit* **h·ebern** vt/i *to siphon*

Hebr·äer m ~s/~ *Hebrew* **hebr·äisch** a *Hebraic*; *Hebrew* || das ≈e *Hebrew*; auf ~ *in H.*

Hebr·iden pl **1.** (Inseln an der Westküste Schottlands) *Western Islands*; *Hebrides* (auf .. *in* ..) **2.** (melanesische Inselgruppe) → Neue Hebriden

H·ebung f ~/~en **1.** = Heben **2. a.** *raising* (*of a ship*) || (of ground) *elevation* **b.** ⟨übtr⟩ *enhancement, improvement*; *increase* (*of power*) | sittl. ~ *uplift*; *uplifting* (*of mankind*) | ⟨pros⟩ *arsis* Gr; *stressed part*; *stress* (*4 stresses*)

H·echel f ~/~n ⟨spin⟩ *hackle*; *flax-comb* || ⟨fig⟩ (jdn) durch die ~ ziehen *to haul over the coals* | ~bank [f], ~bock [m] *hackling-bench*; ~hanf [m] *hackled hemp*; ~kraut [n] ⟨bot⟩ *rest harrow*; ~maschine [f] *porcupine* **Hechel·ei** f ~/~en ⟨fig⟩ *severe criticism* (od *censure*); *slating* **h·echeln** vt/i [h] **1.** vt (Flachs, Hanf) *to hackle*; *comb*; *tease* **2.** vi; mit–e–a ~ *to quarrel with each other* **H·echler** m *hackler* °**Hecht**[1] m *dense clouds* pl *of tobacco smoke*; *smoky air* **H·echt**[2] m ~(e)s/~e *pike*; ~e [pl] *pike* (*a few pike*) || junger, kl ~ *jack, pickerel, pikelet* || ausgewachsener ~ *luce* || See≈ *hake* || ⟨fig⟩ wie ein ~ im Karpfenteiche *like a pike in a fishpond* | ~barsch [m] *pike-perch*; ~dorsch [m] *hake*; ~sprung [m] ⟨gym⟩ *dive*; e–n ~ m *to dive*; *to plunge head foremost into the water* **h·echten** vi [h] = e–n Hechtsprung m

H·eck[1] n ~(e)s/~e ⟨mar⟩ *stern*; *poop*; am ~ *at her st., astern* ⟨a. a-n⟩; ⟨aero⟩ *tail* **~anker** m *st.-anchor* **~bord** n *tafferel* **~fallschirm** m ⟨aero⟩ *para-brake* (dazu: *to p.-b.*) **~flagge** f *st.-flag* **~form** f *the shape of the st.* **~gallerie** f *st.-gallery* **~geschütz** n *st.-chaser*; ⟨aero⟩ *rear-gun* **~kran** m *st.-crane* ≈**lastig** a *st.-heavy* **~laterne** f *st.-lamp*; *poop-lantern* **~leine** f *st.-rope* **~licht** n (weiß) ⟨aero⟩ *st.* (⟨Am⟩ *tail*) *light* **~motor** m ⟨mot⟩ *rear-engine* **~rad** n ⟨Am⟩ *st.-wheel* | ~dampfer [m] *st.-wheeler* **~reling** f *taffrail* **~schütze** m ⟨aero⟩ *rear-gunner* **~see** f *st. sea* **~spill** n *aft capstan* **~stand** m ⟨aero⟩ *r.-g.'s turret* **~tau** n *st.-fast* **~waffe** f ⟨aero⟩ *tail gun*

H·eck-[2] (→ hecken) **~bauer** n & m (Käfig) *breeding-cage* **~pfennig** m *luck-penny* (od *money*); *nest-egg* **~zeit** f *breeding-time*

H·ecke[1] f ~/~n *hedge*; (mst lebend) *quickset hedge*; ~ aus Büschen *hedgerow*; Dornen≈ *thorn-hedge* (ausbessern *to plash*) ‖ ⟨racing⟩ ~ mit Graben *bullfinch* ‖ (Garten) mit e–r ~ umgeben *to hedge* ‖ ⟨prov⟩ niemand sucht e–n hinter der ~, der nicht selbst dahinter gelegen hat *the pot calls the kettle black* ‖ → Zaun | tote ~ *dead hedge*

H·ecke[2] f ~/ (Brut) *brood*; *hatch* **2.** (Brutstätte) *breeding-place* ‖ *b.-cage* **h·ecken A.** vi/t [h] **1.** vi *to breed, hatch* (*out*) ‖ ⟨fig⟩ *to increase* **2.** vt (Junge) *to hatch* **B.** ≈ n *breeding*; *hatch*(*ing*)

H·ecken- (→ Hecke[2]) **~braunelle** f ⟨orn⟩ *dunnock* **~bruder** m (P) *hedge-bird* **~gang** m *lane between hedges* **~hüpfen** vi ⟨aero sl⟩ *to h.hop* **~kirsche** f ⟨bot⟩ *honeysuckle* **~landschaft** f *bocage* **~rose** f ⟨bot⟩ *brier-* (od *briar*)*-rose*; *dog-rose* **~schere** f *hedge-shears* pl **~schneider** m *hedger* **~schütze** m *sniper*, ⟨Am⟩ *bush-whacker* **~springer** m ⟨aero sl⟩ *sky-hog, grasshopper*

H·eckerling m = Häcksel

h·eda [intj] *hi! hallo!* ‖ = he

H·ede f ~/~n [niedd] = Werg *tow*; *oakum*

H·ederich m ~(e)s/ ⟨bot⟩ **1.** (Ackerrettich) *jointed charlock*; *wild radish* **2.** (Ackersenf) *wild* (od *field*) *mustard*; *charlock*

Hed·onik f ⟨ant philos⟩ = Hedonismus

hed·onisch a *hedonic* **Hedon·ismus** m *hedonism*

H·edschas [Arab] *Hejaz* **~bahn** f *Hejaz Railway*

H·edschra f [Arab] *hegira, hejira*

Heer n ~(e)s/~e **1.** ⟨mil⟩ *army*; → Miliz≈, Reserve, Söldner≈ ‖ stehendes ~ *standig army*; aktives stehendes ~ *regular army* ‖ ~, Flotte u Luftstreitkräfte → Wehrmacht ‖ im ~ dienen *to serve with the colours* ‖ ins ~ eintreten *to enter* (od *join*) *the a.*, ⟨bes Am⟩ *to join the ranks*; *to go into the a.*; *to enlist*; *to join up* | ⟨myth⟩ das Wilde ~ *the Wild Hunt, the Furious Host* ‖ → ~schar **2.** ⟨fig⟩ *rank* (*of workers*); *a.* (*of ants, workmen*); *host* (*of servants*); *great multitude* (*of troubles*); *large number* **~bann** m *arrière-ban* **~fahrt** f *military expedition* **~folge** f ⟨hist⟩ *feudal* (od *military*) *service* **~führer** m *commander-in-chief*; *general*; der oberste ~ *the supreme head of the fighting services* **~lager** n (*army-*)*camp* **~schar** f ⟨poet⟩ *host*; ⟨bib⟩ himmlische ~en [pl] *heavenly hosts* pl; Herr der H. ~en *the Lord of Hosts* **~schau** f *military review* **~straße** f ⟨hist⟩ *spacious country road* **~wesen** n *military system*; *military matters* **~wurm** m ⟨ent⟩ *army-worm* **~zug** m *campaign*; *expedition* **H·eeres- ~abteilung** f *division*; *corps* **~archiv** n *a. archives* pl **~bedarf** m *a.-requirements* (od *supplies*) pl **~bericht** m = Wehrmachtbericht **~dienst** m *military* (⟨engl⟩ *national*) *service* ‖ jdn z ~ einberufen *to call a p up*; *to summon a p to the colours* ‖ sich zum ~ melden *to enlist in the a.*; *to join up* | ~pflicht [f] *conscription*; ~vorschrift [f] (HDV) *Army Regulation* N **~feldzeugmeisterei** f ⟨engl⟩ *Royal A. Ordnance Corps* **~flieger-** ~bataillon [n] *army aviation battalion* ‖ ~staffel [f] *a. a. company* ‖ ~truppe [f] *Army Air Force* N **~gebiet** n: rückwärtiges ~ *communications zone* **~gefolge** n = Heerfolge **~gruppe** f *a.-group*; ~ Mitte *Central A. G.*, ~ Nord *Northern A. G.* **~industrie** f *armaments industry* **~kartenstelle** f *Army Map Service* N **~leitung** f *a. command*; die Oberste ~ *the Supreme Command*; *the A. Council*; Chef der ~ *Commander-in-Chief of the A.* **~lieferant** m *a.-contractor* (od *broker*) **~lieferung** f; ~en [pl] *a. supplies* pl **~macht** f *army* **~sanitätsinspektion** f *a. sanitary inspection* **~sanitätswesen** n *a. medical service* N **~verwaltung** f *a. administration* **~zug** m = Heerzug

H·eerrauch m = Höhenrauch

H·eerschnepfe f ⟨orn⟩ = Halbschnepfe

H·efe f ~/~n **1.** (Bier≈) *yeast*; *barm*; (~ geben *to pitch*); die ~ kommt an *fermentation comes through*; Ober≈ *top y.*, Unter≈ *bottom y.*; Extrakt aus frischer Bier≈ *marmite* ‖ (Back≈) *y.* **2.** (Bodensatz) **a.** *dregs, lees* [pl]; °*sediment* **b.** ⟨fig⟩ *dregs, lees* pl; *refuse*; den Kelch bis auf die ~ leeren *to drink the cup to the lees*; die ~ der Gesellschaft *the dregs* od *scum of society* **~apparat** m ⟨brew⟩ *y. propagator* **~gabe** f *quantity of y. for pitching* **~gebäck** n *buns, scones* pl, **~kuchen** m *raised cake* **~nahrung** f ⟨brew⟩ *nutrients* pl **~pilz** m *y.-fungus* **~reinkultur** f *y.-culture* **~stück** n *y.-cake moistened* **~teig** m *dough made with y.*

h·efig a *barmy*; *full of lees*; *sedimentous*; *mothery*

H·efnerkerze f *Hefner candle*; → Bd. I, S. 1120

Heft[1] n ~(e)s/~e (Griff) **1.** ⟨eig⟩ *haft* (*of a knife*); *handle* (*of a chisel, hatchet*) ‖ *hilt* (*of a sword*); bis ans ~ *up to the hilt* ‖ (Messer) mit e–m ~ versehen *to haft*; (Schwert) *to hilt* **2.** ⟨fig⟩ das ~ in der Hand h *to keep the reins in one's own hands*; *to be at the helm* ‖ das ~ aus der Hand geben, l *to let the reins slip out of one's hands, to drop the reins* ‖ jdm das ~ aus der H. nehmen *to wrest the power out of a p's hands* **3.** ⟨dial⟩ *hamlet* **~eisen** n ⟨glass⟩ *punty*

Heft[2] n ~(e)s/~e (Geheftetes) **1.** (Schreib≈) *exercise-book* **2.** *small book, booklet in paper covers*; *book* (*of stamps*; *of tickets*); Noten≈ *music-book*; Akten≈ *file* ‖ das Buch erscheint in einzelnen ~en *the book will be published in numbers* (od *serial parts*); → Lieferung **3.** °⟨fig⟩ (P) ein fideles ~ *a gay bird*; ein verrücktes ~ *a queer sort of fellow*

H·eft- (→ heften) **~draht** m *stitch wire* **~faden** m, **~garn** n *basting* (od *stitching*)*-thread*; *whipcord* **~haken** m *hook* **~klammer** f *wire paper clip*; *clip* (*paper-*)*fastener* ‖ (of a book) *staple*; dazu: *to staple* **~lade** f ⟨bookb⟩ *sewing-frame* **~mappe** f *file* **~maschine** f *stitching-machine*; ⟨bookb⟩ *stapler* **~nadel** f *stitching-needle* **~niet** n *dummy rivet* **~pflaster** n *adhesive plaster*; *court-plaster*; *sticking-plaster* **~schnur** f *sewing-cord* **~stich** m ⟨tail⟩ ~e [pl] *tacking* (*stitches*); ⟨bookb⟩ *tack* **~zapfen** m *tang* (*of a knife*) **~zwecke** f *drawing-pin*; *tack*; ⟨Am⟩ *thumb-tack* **~zwirn** m = –faden

H·eftchen n *small copy-, note-book*

***H·eftel** m & n ~s/~ *clasp*; *fastening*; *hook*; → Spange ***h·efteln** vt [h] (etw) *to clasp*; *to fasten with hooks and eyes* **H·eftelmacher** m *clasper* ‖ °aufpassen wie ein ~ *to look out like a lynx* **h·eften A.** vt [h] **1.** (Naht, Saum) *to tack* ‖ (Akten, Buch) *to sew*; *stitch*; mit Draht ~ *to staple, wire* ‖ (Buchteile) *to tape*; *baste* **2.** (befestigen) **a.** ~ **an** *to affix* (od *attach, fasten, pin*) *to*; mit Zwecken ~ an *to tack to*; ~ auf *to tack on to* **b.** ⟨übtr⟩ die Augen, Blicke ~ auf .. *to fasten* (od *fix, glue, rivet*) *one's eyes on* ..; *his eyes were glued to* .. ‖ ein V. an jds Namen ~ *to fasten a crime on a p* **3. sich ~ an a.** s–e Augen hefteten sich auf .. *his eyes were glued to* .. **b.** *to attach to* (*responsibilities attach to power*); *to cling to* (*a th*) ‖ der V. heftete sich an s–e Sohlen *or* Fersen *the criminal followed close at his heels*; .. *dogged his footsteps* ‖ ein Fluch heftet sich an s–e Fersen *he lies under a curse* **B.** ≈ n **1.** *sewing*; ⟨bookb⟩ (*wire-, thread-*)*stitching*; *tacking* **2.** *fastening, pinning* (an *to*) **H·efter** m (Werkzeug) *fastener*; *stapler*

h·eftig A. [a] **1. (S)** *hard* (*blow*); *heavy* (*rain*); *keen* (*frost, hunger*); *severe, violent* (*pain, storm*); *sharp, vehement* (*wind*); *rough-and-tumble* (*fight*); *bitter* (*struggle*); *fierce* (*hostility*); *acute* (*jealousy*); *furious* (*anger*); *intense* (*hatred*); *strong* (*words*); ⟨fam⟩ *tearing* (*rage*); ~e Erkältung *bad cold* ‖ *violent* (*propaganda*); *virulent* (*press campaign*) **2. (P)** *impetuous, passionate, violent*; ~ w *to lose one's temper*; er wird leicht ~ *he is of a violent temper* ‖ *fanatical, rabid* (*partisan*); *vehement* (*opponent*) **B. [adv]** *heavily, severely, vehemently* ‖ *furiously*; *intensely*; (*it froze*) *hard*; (*the wind blew*) *high* || mein Fuß schmerzt ~ *I have a violent pain in the foot* || ~ fallen *to come down with a run* || ~ fluchen, schimpfen *to swear terribly*; *to use strong words* || ~ toben *to fret and fume* || ~ weinen *to cry bitterly* || ~ aneinandergeraten *to come to a heated dispute* | ≃**keit** f *heaviness, keenness; severity, vehemence, violence* || *impetuosity; intensity; virulence* (*of the attacks*); die ganze ~ *the brunt* (*of war*)

H·eftung f ~/~en *tacking* || *sewing, stitching*; Draht≃ *stapling; wire-stitching*

H·ege f ~/ ⟨for⟩ *nusery; close*(*d* ⟨Am⟩) *season*

Hegeli·aner m (nach G. W. F. Hegel) *Hegelian*

Hegeli·anisch, H·egelsch a *Hegelian* (*philosophy*) || ~es System der Philosophie *Hegelianism*

H·egemeister m *senior forester* → hegen

Hegemon·ie f ~/~n *hegemony, supremacy* (in *in*); *political predominance* od *preponderance*

h·egen A. vt [h] **1.** † = einhegen **2.** ⟨übtr⟩ **a.** (schonen) (Wild) schützen u ~ *to preserve* **b.** (pflegen) (Garten etc) *to cultivate; tend* || (jdn) ~ u pflegen *to foster, tend; to nurse tenderly* || *(Beziehungen, Zustände) *to cultivate* **3.** * = enthalten; bergen **4.** ⟨mst fig⟩ (Gedanken, Gefühle) **a.** (Hoffnungen, Meinungen, Verdacht, Zweifel) *to entertain, have; cherish, foster; nurse, nourish* || Besorgnisse, Befürchtungen ~ *to have misgivings* (*that* ..) || → Groll || Haß ~ *to nourish* od *nurse feelings of hatred* || e–n Wunsch ~ *to foster* od *have a desire* **b.** (böse Absichten [etc], Rache) *to harbour* **B.** *≃ n **1.** *cultivation; tending* **2.** *entertainment; having; cherishing* || *harbouring* (*hopes*, etc.) **H·eger** m ~s/~ (*game*)*keeper*

H·ehl n (*m) ~(e)s/ [nur in:] aus e–r S kein ~ m, *e–r S kein ~ h *to make no secret of a th; to make no bones about a th*; er macht kein ~ daraus *he makes no bones about it* (*about saying so*) || → Bedenken; ohne ~ *quite frankly; outspokenly; without reserve*; sich ohne ~ aussprechen über etw *to make no secret of a th* || ***h·ehlen A.** vt/i [h] **1.** vt (etw) *to conceal* (vor jdm *from a p*); → ver~ **2.** vi *to receive stolen goods*; ⟨sl⟩ *to fence* **B.** ≃ n = Hehlerei **H·ehler** m *concealer* || *receiver of* (od *dealer in*) *stolen goods*; ⟨sl⟩ *fence* **Hehler·ei** f *receiving of* (od *dealing in*) *stolen goods*; ⟨sl⟩ *fencing* **H·ehlernest** n ⟨sl⟩ *fence; fencing-ken*; ⟨Am⟩ *plant*

hehr a *august, exalted, majestic, noble* (*personage*) || *exalted* (*diction*); *grand* (*view*); *sublime* (*beauty, moment*); *sacred* (*songs, writings*)

hei [intj] *hey! hurra*(*h*)!

°**H·eia** f (Bett) in die ~ gehn *to go to bye-byes*

H·eide[1] m ~n/~n **1.** ⟨ec⟩ *heathen, pagan; non-Christian* || ~n [pl] *heathens* pl; [koll] die ~n *the heathen* **2.** ⟨bib⟩ (A. T.) (Nichtjude) *gentile* **3.** ⟨übtr⟩ *heathen, pagan* **4.** → Heiden-

H·eide[2] f ~/~n **1.** (unbewohntes, -bebautes Land) *heath; moor; moors* pl; *moorland* || Lüneburger ~ *the Lüneburg Moor* od *Heide* **2.** ⟨bot⟩ (~kraut, Besen≃) *heath*(*er*); *ling; Erica* L || Baum≃ *tree h.*; Glocken≃, Sumpf≃ *bell-h.*; Schnee≃ *winter h.* **~bauer** m *German settler between the Danube and Neusiedler-See* **~boden** m *moor*(*-land*); *heath* **~busch** m ⟨bot⟩ *gorse; furze* **~grütze** f *buckwheat* **~honig** m *heather-honey* **~korn** n = –grütze **~kraut** n ⟨bot⟩ = Heide[2] 2. **~land** n, **~landschaft** f = Heide[2] 1. **~mehl** n *buckwheat flour* **~moor** n → Hoch- **~röschen** n, **~rose** f = Sonnenröschen

H·eidel- ~beere f ⟨bot⟩ *bilberry*, ⟨bes Scot⟩ *blaeberry, whortleberry* **~beerstrauch** m *bilberry* od *blaeberry, whortleberry* (*bush*) **~berger** (aus: Heidelberg) *Heidelberg* (*Catechism*) || ~ Faß [n] *the Great Tun of Heidelberg* **~bergmensch** m ⟨anthr⟩ *the Heidelberg man; Homo Heidelbergensis* L

H·eiden- (→ Heide[1]) **A.** ⟨ec⟩ **~apostel** m ⟨ec hist⟩ *apostle of gentiles* **~bekehrung** f *conversion of heathens to Christianity* **~christ** m ⟨ec hist⟩ *heathen proselyte to Christianity* **~korn** m = Buchweizen (aus heidnischen Ländern, aber → Heidekorn) **~mission** f *foreign mission* **~tempel** m *pagan temple* **~welt** f *heathen world; heathendom* **B.** [**Intensivum** = riesig, Höllen-, Mords-]; [Betonung: ·–·–] °**~·angst** f *mortal fear* (od *fright*); ⟨sl⟩ *blue funk*; ~ h *to be frightened to death* (vor *of*), *to be in a b. f.* **~arbeit** f *the devil of a job* °**~g·eld** n; ein ~ ⟨fam⟩ *a gr. lot of m.*; .. verdienen ⟨Am sl⟩ *to clean up*; das kostet ein ~ *that is a devil of a sum to pay* ≃**mäßig 1.** [a] *enormous, outrageous, stupendous; terrible* **2.** [adv] ~ viel Geld *an enormous lot of m.*; .. verdienen ⟨Am sl⟩ *to clean up* °**~l·ärm,** °**~skandal** m = Höllenlärm **~schrecken** m = Höllen- °**~spaß** m *capital fun; high jinks*; es macht mir e–n ~ *I think it c. f.* **H·eidentum** n **1.** [abstr] *heathenism, paganism; heathenry; heathen religion* (od *character*) **2.** [konkr] [koll] *heathendom; the heathen* pl

h·eid·i 1. [intj] *hey! hey-day! hurra*(*h*)! *ho!* **2.** [adv] ~ gehen *to get lost*; mein Geld ist alles ~ *my money has all gone*

H·eidin f ~/~nen *pagan* → Heide[1] **h·eidnisch** a *heathen* (*customs; temple*) || ⟨übtr⟩ *barbarous; heathenish* || ~ m *to heathenize*

H·eidschnucke f ~/~n *sheep in the Lüneburg Heide* | ~nwolle [f] *estridge wool*

Heid·uck m ~en/~en *heyduck; Hungarian mercenary foot-soldier* od *man-servant*; (Ungarn) *liveried retainer*

h·eik(e)l a **1.** *delicate, ticklish* (*affair*); *nice, thorny* (*question*); *kittle, pernickety, trappy* || h.e Lage *tight corner; subtle, tender* (*point*); den ~en P. berühren ⟨fig⟩ *to put the finger on the sensitive spot*; heikles Thema *scabrous, sore, tender* (*subject*), ⟨Am sl⟩ *hot potato* **2.** (P) *fastidious; squeamish*; = wählerisch

heil A. [a] **1.** (unversehrt) *whole; uninjured* || mit ~er Haut *unscathed*; → Haut || (gesund) *sound* (*limbs*) || ~ w *to heal*; der Arm wird bald wieder ~ s *the arm will soon be all right again* **2.** (S) *whole; unbroken; unmended; without holes* od *patches*; der Topf ist noch ~ *the pot is still whole* || (wieder) ~ m *to mend, repair* **3.** ×(= groß) ~e Angst = Heidenangst **B.** [adv] → heilfroh **Heil** n ~(e)s/ **A. 1. (Rettung)** ⟨ec⟩ (Seelen) *salvation*; das ~ der Welt *Christ, the Saviour* || das Jahr des ~s *the year of grace*; im Jahre des ~s 1967 *in the year of our Lord 1967* od *in the year 1967 A. D.* **2. (Nutzen)** *benefit, good, welfare, well-being* || zum ~ jds *for the good* (od *benefit*) *of a p*; es wird z ~ ausschlagen *it will be to the good* || jdm ~ u Segen wünschen *to wish a p the best of luck* || ~ v e–r S (*or* jdm) erwarten *to expect great benefit from a th* (*a p*) || auf jds ~ bedacht s, f jds ~ sorgen *to look tenderly after* (od *to watch over*) *a p*('*s welfare*) | (Glück) *happiness* || sein ~ versuchen *to try one's luck* od *fortune*, ⟨fam⟩ *to have a go at it* **B.** (in Grußformeln) **1.** ~! *hurra*(*h*)! ⟨poet⟩ *hail!* ⟨sl⟩ *cheerio!* || *Heil!* [Ger]; Gut ~! *Good Luck!*; Sieg ~! *Heil* [Ger] *Victory!* || ~ rufen *to cheer, to hurra*(*h*); dreimal ~ rufen *to give three cheers* od *hurras*; jdn mit ~ begrüßen *to greet a p with hurra* **2.** ~ dem Sieger, Könige! *cheers* od *hurra for the v, k.!*; ⟨poet⟩ *hail to the victor*, etc **C.** [in comp] *th*(*erapeutic*), *m*(*edical*) **~anstalt** f *m. sanatorium; hospital; clinic* **~anzeige** f ⟨med⟩ *indication* **~bad** n **1.** *th. bath* **2.** (Ort) *health resort; spa* **~behandlung** f *mechano-therapy* ≃**bringend** a *beneficial* (*effect*); = heilsam **~brunnen** m = –quelle **~durchblutung** f *curative hyperemia* **~erde** f ⟨med⟩ *th. clay and moorland soil* **~erfolg** m *th. success; successful th. result* **~erziehung** f ⟨med⟩ *medico-pedagogic treatment; p. therapy* **~faktor** m *th. factor* **~fieber** n ⟨med⟩ *fever applied to th. ends* **~fürsorge** f *medical care* **~gehilfe** m = Krankenpfleger **~gymnastik** f *physiotherapy; mechano-*

-therapy **~gymnastin** f *physiotherapist* **~impfung** f *inoculation with a serum* **~kostbehandlung** f *dietary treatment* **~kraft** f *healing* (od *curative*) *power*; ≗e [pl] *healing properties* pl **≗kräftig** a *curative, healing, th.(al)*; *medicinal* **~kraut** n: ≗er [pl] *officinal herbs* pl; Berg-~ *sheep's-bit* **~kunde** f *medicine*; *medical science*; *th.s* [sg konstr] **≗kundig** a *skilled in medicine* **~kundige** [der ~, ein ~r] m *trained layman in medicine* **~kunst** f *art of healing*; *m. art* **~magnetiseur** m *magnetizer* **~magnetismus** m *animal magnetism* **~magnetopathie** f *magnetotherapy* **~methode** f *cure*; *method of treatment* **~mittel** n *medicament*; *medicine*; *drug*; *remedy* (gegen Gicht *for gout*); spezifisches ~ *specific (drug)* ‖ ⟨übtr⟩ *cure, remedy* (gegen *for*) ‖ soziales *or* politisches ~ *nostrum* L | ~lehre [f] *pharmacology* **~pädagogik** f = -erziehung **~pädagog(in** f) m *child-guidance worker* **~pflanze** f = -kraut **~praktiker** m *lay m. practitioner* ‖ ⟨dero⟩ *quack* **~prozeß** m *healing process* **~quell(e** f) m *mineral spring*; *spa*; ~n [pl] *waters* pl **~serum** **~stätte** f *sanatorium* L; *home* (f *for*) **~therapie** f *therapy* **~trank** m *medicine*; *medicinal drink*; *potion* **~verfahren** n *cure*; *medical treatment*; *therapy*; Radium≗ *radio-therapy* **~wert** m *th. value* **~wirkung** f *th. effect* **~zweck** m *th. object* od *purpose*; z ~en verwandt *applied to th. ends* **H·eiland** m ~(e)s/~e ⟨ec⟩ *Christ*; *the Saviour* **h·eilbar** a *curable, healable* | **≗keit** f *curability* **H·eilbutt** m ⟨ich⟩ *halibut* **h·eilen** vt/i [h] **1.** vt (jdn) *to heal, cure* (v *of*); ⟨a. fig⟩ ‖ (Krankheit) *to cure*; (Wunde) *to heal* ‖ ⟨fig⟩ (Übel) *to cure, heal*; *remedy*; *salve* **2.** vi (of wounds) *to heal* (*up* od *over*); die Wunde heilt v selbst *the wound is healing up by itself*; die W. ist *or* hat gut geheilt *the wound has closed well* **h·eilfroh** a [pred] *extremely* (od *very*) *glad* **h·eilig A.** [a] **1.** (P) ⟨ec⟩ **a.** *holy*; der ≗e Geist *the Holy Ghost* od *Spirit*; die ≗e Mutter *the Blessed Virgin*; die ≗en Drei Könige *the (Three) Magi* L pl; ⟨R. C.⟩ der ≗e Vater *the Holy Father* **b.** (vor Eigennamen) *Saint*; der ~e Augustinus *Saint Augustine*; die ~e Elisabeth *Saint Elizabeth* **c.** ⟨übtr⟩ *saintly* (*man*) **2.** (S) **a.** ⟨ec⟩ *holy*; die ≗e Schrift *Holy Scriptures* (od *Writ*); das ≗e Abendmahl *Holy Communion*; *the Blessed Sacrament*; der ≗e Gral *the Holy Grail*; das ≗e Land *the Holy Land*; ⟨R. C.⟩ ~e Handlung *sacrament*; der ≗ Stuhl *the Holy See*; der ≗ Abend *Christmas Eve*; die ≗e Allianz *The Holy Alliance*; das ≗e Römische Reich Deutscher Nation *the Holy Roman Empire of the German Nation* **b.** ⟨übtr⟩ *holy, pious, saintlike, saintly* (*life*); ~e Stille *divine peace*; *heavenly* (*thoughts*); es ist mein ~er Ernst *I am absolutely earnest*; *sacred* (*duty*); ~e Scheu vor *great dread of* **c.** (geheiligt) *sacred* (*edifice, writings*); *inviolable* (*treaty*); *sacrosanct*; *solemn*; *venerable* | [pred] ~ s *to be sacred* (jdm *to a p*); sein Wort ist uns ~ *his word is inviolable* (od *sacrosanct*) **3.** °~er Bimbam! *Great Scott!*, *Dear me!* ‖ °da soll doch gleich ein ~es Donnerwetter dreinschlagen! *damn it all!* **B.** [abs] mein ≗stes *my holy of holies* (sc *my work* ..); → Aller~st; → ≗e **C.** [adv] hoch u ~ schwören *to swear by all that's holy* ‖ (hoch u) ~ versprechen *to promise (most) solemnly* (⟨fam⟩ *faithfully*) ‖ °du kannst dich ~ darauf verlassen *you may rely on it with absolute certainty* **≗·abend** m *Christmas Eve* **~|halten** vt [h] (etw) *to hold sacred*; *to reverence* **≗haltung** f *venerable observance*; *veneration*; *worship* **~|sprechen** vt [h] ⟨ec⟩ (jdn) *to canonize* **≗sprechung** f ⟨ec⟩ *canonization* **~tuend** a *sanctimonious*; *sanctified* °**≗tuerei** f *sanctimoniousness* **H·eilige 1.** [der ~, ein ~r] m ~n/~n; [die ~, e-e ~] f ~n/~n **a.** ⟨ec⟩ *the Saint* (pl *Saints*) **b.** ⟨übtr⟩ *saintly man* od *woman*; °ein wunderlicher ~r *a queer customer* (⟨sl⟩ *bird*) **2.** das ~ *the holy quality*; *the sacred character*; *holiness*; *sacredness*; → heilig

h·eiligen vt [h] **1.** ⟨ec⟩ (etw) *to hallow*; *make holy*; *sanctify* **2.** ⟨übtr⟩ *to sanctify*; *justify, sanction*; der Zweck heiligt die Mittel *the end sanctifies the means* **H·eiligen- ~bild** n *image of a saint*; ⟨ec⟩ *icon* Gr; *charm* **~figur** f *sacred figure* **~holz** n = Guajakholz **~kalender** m *Calendar of Saints* **~-pflanze** f *lavender-cotton, Santolina* **~schein** m ⟨ec⟩ *aureole, gloriole, glory, halo, nimbus* ‖ ⟨übtr⟩ sich mit e-m ~ umgeben *to give o.s. sanctified airs*; *to affect holiness* **~schrein** m ⟨ec⟩ *shrine* **~tag** m *saint's day* **~verehrung** f *saint-worship* **H·eiligkeit** f **1.** ⟨ec⟩ *holiness*; *sacredness*; *saintliness*; *sanctity*; im Geruch der ~ stehen *to be in the odour of sanctity* ‖ ⟨übtr⟩ *sacredness, sanctity* (*of an oath*); *inviolability* **2.** ⟨R. C.⟩ Seine ~ *His Holiness* **H·eiligtum** n ~s/≗er **1.** *sacred edifice*; (als bes Teil e-r Kirche etc) *sanctuary, shrine*; Entweihung, Raub e-s ~s *sacrilege* ‖ ⟨übtr⟩ *sanctum* L (*his particular s.*); ureigenstes ~ *sacred privateness* **2.** *relic* **H·eiligung** f *sanctification* ‖ *consecration* **h·eillos 1.** a ⟨übtr⟩ (S) *desperate* (*state of affairs*); *hopeless* (*confusion*); *incredible, terrible* (*disorder*); *unbearable* ‖ ⟨fam⟩ *awful* ‖ in -loser Angst ⟨sl⟩ *in a blue funk*; *unmitigated* (*nuisance*) **2.** adv *hopelessly*; *incredibly*; ~ verfahren [a] *hopelessly muddled* | **≗igkeit** f *desperateness*; etc **H·eilruf** m (*exclamation of*) *greeting* ‖ *hurra(h)*; drei ~e ausbringen *to give three cheers* (auf *for*) **H·eils- ~armee** f *Salvation Army* (gegr. 1877); Mitglied der ~ *Salvationist* **~geschichte** f *the Story of the life and sufferings of Christ* **~lehre** f *doctrine of salvation* **~ordnung** f christliche ~ *Christian dispensation* **~wahrheit** f christliche ~en [pl] *Christian truths* pl **h·eilsam 1.** [a] *curative* (*medicine*); *healing* (*ointment*) ‖ ⟨übtr⟩ *salubrious* (*climate*); *beneficial, salutary* (*effect*); *wholesome* (*punishment*) ‖ ~ s f jdn, etw *to be beneficial to a p, to a th* **2.** [adv] *beneficially, usefully* ‖ ~ wirken *to effect a cure*; *to cure*; ⟨übtr⟩ *to be beneficial* (auf *to*) | **≗keit** f ~ *salubrity, salutariness, wholesomeness* **H·eiltum** n ~s/≗er ⟨R. C.⟩ *collection of relics* **~sbuch** n *list of relics* **H·eilung** f ~/~en *curing, healing* (*of a disease, wound*); *cure* (*of a p*); ~ bewirken, herbeiführen *to effect a cure* ‖ ⟨übtr⟩ *healing* **~s-kosten** pl *medical expenses* **~sprozeß** m *healing process*

Heim A. [n] ~(e)s/~e **1.** (Wohnung) *home*; *dwelling, house*; *residence* ‖ ein eigenes ~ *a house of one's own*; im eigenen ~ wohnen *to live in one's own home* ‖ ein ~ gründen *to settle down* ‖ ein ~ finden *to find a home* (in *in*) **2.** (Anstalt) *home*; (*convalescent*) *home* od *hospital*; *home* (*for invalids*); ⟨med⟩ *asylum* **B.** ≗ [adv] *home*; *towards home*; *homeward* **~arbeit** f *home-work, out-work*; *cottage-work* **~arbeiter(in** f) m *h.-, out-worker* **~bastelkasten,** -satz m *Do it Yourself Kit* **≗|begeben** vrefl [h] sich ~ *to go h.*; *to set out for h.* **≗|bringen** vt [h] (etw) *to bring h.*; (jdn) *to bring back* **≗|eilen** vi [s] *to hasten h.* **≗|fahren** vi [s] *to drive h.*; *to return h.* **~fahrt** f *return* (od *journey*) *h.*; *drive h.* **~fall** m ⟨jur⟩ **1.** ⟨bes hist⟩ ~ eines Lehens an den Lehnsherrn *escheat*; ⟨jur⟩ *reversion* | ~sgut [n] *escheat*; (Lehen) als ~sgut einziehen *to escheat* **2.** ⟨med⟩ → Rückfall **≗|fallen** vi [s] **1.** ⟨hist⟩ *to revert by escheat* (an *to*) **2.** *to devolve* (an *on*); *to revert* (an *to*) **≗fällig** a *reversionary, revertible* (an *to*) **≗|finden** vrefl [h] sich ~ *to find one's way h.* **~|fliegen** vi [s] *to fly h.*; (of birds) *to h.* **~fracht** f *h.-freight*; *freight home* **≗|führen** vt [h] (jdn) *to lead h.*; (Braut) *to take h.* **~fürsorge** f *h. care* **~gang** m *going h.* ‖ ⟨mst fig⟩ *decease* **≗|gehen** vi [s] *go h.* (a. ⟨fig⟩: sterben) ‖ ⟨fig⟩ *to decease*; *to depart this life* °**≗|geigen** vi [h] = -leuchten **~gestaltung** f *h.-furnishing*; *furnishing of the h.* **≗gesucht** a v Unglück ~ *stricken* (*areas, city*); v Fieber ~ *fever-haunted* (*regions*) **~industrie** f *h., cottage-industry* **~kehr** f (bes nach der Hochzeitsreise) *h.-coming* || *return h.*; ⟨pol⟩ *repatriation* ≗|**kehren** vi [s] *to return h.*; *to set out for h.* **~kehrende** [der ~] m, **~kehrer** m *h.-comer*, ⟨mil⟩ *returnee*; *returned p*; ⟨pol⟩ *repatriate(d PW)* | ~verband [m] *association of repatriates* **~kino** n *h.-cinema* ≗|**k** vi [s] *to come in*; *to come* od *return h.* **~kunft** f *return h.* ≗|**leuchten** *vi* [h] ⟨fig⟩ jdm ~ *to give a p a piece of one's mind*; *to see a p h.*; *to send a p about his business*; ⟨Am⟩ *to tell a p where to get off*; ⟨parl⟩ jdm in der Debatte gehörig ~ *to wipe the floor with a p* **~reise** f *h.ward* od *return journey*; *journey h.*; *return* || (of ship) *h.ward voyage* || auf der ~ *h.wards*; auf der ~ befindlich *h.ward-bound* (*ship*) ≗|**reisen** vi [s] *to travel h.ward*; *to return* ≗|**reiten** vi [s] *to ride h.* ≗|**schaffen** vt [h] *to take h.*; *to bring back* ≗|**schicken** vt [h] *to send h.* || ⟨fig⟩ (Feind) gehörig ~ *to beat* od *drive back*; *to repulse* || (jdn) *to give a rough welcome*; ⟨sport⟩ *to punish*; ⟨pol⟩ *to repatriate* **~schule** f ⟨Ger⟩ *boarding-school* ≗|**sehnen** vrefl [h] sich ~ *to long for h.*; *to be h.-sick* ≗|**senden** vt [h] = –schicken **~spiel** n ⟨ftb⟩ *h. game* **~stätte** f ~/~n **1.** (Heim) *home* (f *for*); *h.stead* **2.** [urspr. Am] (staatl. ~) *h.stead* | ~nbewegung [f] *h.stead-movement*; ~ngesetz [n] *H.stead Act* ≗|**suchen** vt [h] **1.** (of famine, etc.) (Land etc) *to visit*; *afflict*; *trouble*; *to try*, *obsess* (*a p*) || plötzlich ~ *to overtake* || die Sünden der Väter ~ *to visit the sins of the parents* (an *on*) || –gesucht s v *to be stricken with*; *to be visited with* (*doubts*); durch ein Erdbeben ~gesucht *smitten by an e.* **2. a.** (of enemy) (Land) *to overrun*, *ravage* **b.** (of ghosts) (Ort) *to haunt*; (of robbers, vermin) *to infest* **c.** (of demons) (jdn) *to haunt*, *obsess* **d.** °jdn ~ *to pay a surprise visit to a p* **~suchung** f **1.** *visitation*; *affliction*; *trial*; *trouble*; *ordeal* **2.** *haunting*; *infestation* **3.** *obsession* **4.** (= Besuch) ⟨R. C.⟩ Mariä ~ *the Visitation* (2. Juli) **~textilien** pl ⟨com⟩ *domestic textiles* pl **~tücke** f *insidiousness*; *malice*; *treachery*; *foul* od *underhand wiles* pl ≗**tückisch 1.** [a] **a.** *foul*, *insidious*, *malicious*, *perfidious*; *treacherous*; *underhand* (*practices*); *cowardly* (*attack*), *dastardly* (*inventions of the Press*); in ~er Weise *foully* **b.** *insidious* (*disease*); *subtle* (*drug*) **2.** [adv] *foully* (*murdered*); *insidiously*, *maliciously* || jdn ~ an-, überfallen *to get one's claws into a p* **~weg** m *way* (od *return*) *h.*; auf dem ~e *on my way h.* (*I* ..) **~weh** n *h.-sickness*; *nostalgia* L || brennendes ~ *a thrill of h.-s.* || aus ~ *from nostalgia*; ~ h *to be h.sick*; jdm ~ m *to make a p feel h.sick* || v ~ geplagt *nostalgic* (*p*) ≗|**zahlen** vt [h] ⟨fig⟩ (etw) *to requite*, *return* || jdm ~ *to give a p a change*, jdm etw ~ *to requite a p for a th*; es jdm ~ ⟨Am sl⟩ *to get back on a p* || das werde ich ihm aber ~ *I shall pay him back for that*; *I'll make him pay for that*; *I'll be quits with him* || jdm mit gleicher Münze ~ *to pay a p back in his own coin*; *to give a p tit for tat* **~zahlung** f ⟨fig⟩ *requital*; *retaliation* ≗|**ziehen** vi [s] = –gehen, –fahren **H·eimat** f ~/~en **1.** *native place* (od *town, land*); *residence*, *home* || *n. country*, *h.land*; ⟨mil sl⟩ (= England) *Blighty* || m–e zweite ~ *my second h.* || v Indien in die ~ fahren *to leave India for h.* || Dienst in der ~ *h.-service* || → Herberge **2.** ⟨zoo & bot⟩ *habitat* L; ⟨com⟩ *country of origin* **~dresse, ~anschrift** f *h.-address* **~auskunftstelle** f *information office for the lost territories* ≗**berechtigt** a *native* **~boden** m *n. soil* **~dichter** m *vernacular poet* **~dichtung** f *v. poetry* **~dienst** m ⟨mil⟩ *h. defence* **~flughafen** m ⟨aero⟩ *h.-station* **~gebiet** n *h. area* **~gefühl** n *h.-feeling*; → Heimweh **~hafen** m *h. port*; *port of registry* **~horst** m ⟨aero⟩ *h. station* **~kunde** f *knowledge of* (od *instruction in*) *the nature, geography, and folklore of one's n. country* **~kunst** f *art of n. origin and growth* || *vernacular literature*; *regionalism* (Th. Hardy, G. Hauptmann) **~land** n *h.land*; *n. country* (od *land, soil*) || ⟨com⟩ (S) *country of origin* ≗**liebend** a *h.-loving* **~ort** m *n. place* (od *town*) **~recht** n *right of domicile* od *settlement* **~schein** m *certificate of origin* od *domicile* °**~schuß** m ⟨mil sl⟩ (a) *Blighty one* (→ Heimat 1.) **~schutz** m **1.** *protection of the countryside against the effects of industrialism*; → Naturschutz **2.** ⟨mil⟩ *h. defence* | ~luftflotte [f] *h. defence air force* **3.** ⟨pol⟩ (Österr.) *h. defence force* **~sinn** m (of pigeons) *homing instinct* **~staat** m *country of origin* **~stadt** f *n. town*; ⟨Am⟩ *h.-town* **~urlaub** m *h.-leave* **~vertriebene(r)** m *expellee* **~wimpel** m *paying-off pennant* **h·eimatlich 1.** [a] **a.** *native* (*woods*); ~er Boden *n. soil*; *h.land*; s–e ~e Welt *his world at h.* **b.** *vernacular* (*language*; *poetry*) **c.** *h.-like*, *h.ly*; ~es Gefühl *h.liness*; *h.feeling*; ~e Klänge *sounds of home* **2.** [adv] *like home*; ~ anmutend *h.ly*, *h.like*; ⟨fam⟩ *homy*; alles mutet mich hier ~ an *all seems to me h.like* (od *like h.*) *here* **h·eimatlos** a *homeless*; *without home* || ~es Tier *waif* || verlassener, –loser Mensch *waif*; –lose u verwahrloste Kinder *waifs and strays* pl **H·eimatlose** [ein ~r, der ~] *a p without h.* (od *nationality*); ⟨Am⟩ *maverick* **H·eimats-** ~hafen etc → Heimat– **H·eimatvertriebene** m [der ~, ein ~r] *expatriate* **H·eimchen** n ~s/~ ⟨ent⟩ *cricket*; ⟨fig⟩ (Frau) *h.-maker* **h·eimelig** a → anheimelnd, gemütlich **h·eimisch** a **1.** → ein~ **2.** (heimatlich) *home*; ⟨mst com⟩ ~e Gewässer *h. waters* pl; ~e Industrie *h. industries* pl **3.** ⟨übtr⟩ **a.** *h.like*, *h.ly* || [pred] ~ s in etw *to be at h. in* (od *familiar with*) *a th* || ~ w in *to become acclimatized in* (*a country*) || sich (nicht) ~ fühlen *to feel at h.*; ⟨Am⟩ *to acclimatize* (*to f. out of it*) **b.** (Tier etc) ~ m *to acc.*; *to domesticate*; *to naturalize* || es jdm ~ m *to make a p feel at h.*; es sich ~ m *to make o.s. at h.* **h·eimlich A.** [a] **1.** *concealed, hidden* (*paths*), *secret* (*love*); = geheim **2.** ⟨mst dero⟩ *clandestine* (*tryst*), *furtive* (*blow, glance, wish*); *secret* (*sale, traffic*), *stealthy* (*glances*); *surreptitious*; *underhand* (*intrigues*); *covert* (*threat, warfare*); ⟨Am⟩ *sneaking, gum-shoe* (*methods*) **B.** [adv] *clandestinely*; *furtively*; *secretly*; *in secret*; *stealthily*; *by stealth*; ⟨sl⟩ *on the quiet* od *sly* || ~ anzetteln *to frame* (*a plot*); ~ ausgeführt, getan *furtive* (*act*); ~ wirkend *insidious, subtle* (*drug*); (Unrecht) ~ dulden *to wink at*; jdm ~ entwischen *to give a p the slip*; (jdn) ~ ermorden *to burke*; °sich ~ aus dem Staube m *to bolt*; *to make a bolt for it*; *to steal away*; *to take French leave* || ~ schleichen ⟨Am⟩ *to pussyfoot*; sich ~ schl. in .. *to steal into* .. || jdm ~ e–n Blick zuwerfen *to steal a glance at a p* **~tuend** a *furtive* (*p*); *secretive*; *mysterious*; ⟨Am⟩ *pussyfooting* ≗**tuer** m *furtive p*; ⟨Am⟩ *pussyfooter* ≗**tuerei** f *air of secrecy* (od *m.ness*); *hush-hush*; ⟨pol⟩ *hush-hush policy* || ⟨Am⟩ *p.ing* **~|tun** vi [h] *to affect an air of m.ness*; *to behave m.ly*; ⟨Am⟩ *to pussyfoot* (über *on*) **H·eimlichkeit** f **1.** *furtiveness*; *secrecy*, *secretiveness*; *stealthiness*; in aller ~ *in all secrecy* **2.** (Geheimnis) *secret*; k–e ~en unter e–a h *to have no secrets between each other* **h·eimwärts** adv *home*; *towards h.*, *h.wards*; s–e Schritte ~ lenken *to set one's face toward h.* **H·eimwesen** n ~s/~ Sw = Anwesen

Hein ⟨Lit⟩ Freund ~ *Death* || ⟨mar⟩ *Jack tar* **H·einrich** m ~s/~e **1.** ⟨Ger hist⟩ ~ der Vogler *Henry the Fowler* (*919–36*) **2.** ⟨bot⟩ Blauer ~ = Natternkopf || Großer ~ = Alant || Guter ~, Roter ~ *Good King Henry*; *mercury goose-foot* **H·einzelmännchen** n ⟨myth⟩ *brownie*; *goblin*; die ~ [pl] *the little people*

H·eirat f ~/~en *marriage* (mit jdm *to a p*) || mit (*or* nach) der ~ *on m.* (*the estate passed to the husband*) || Liebes≗ *love-match* **h·eiraten** vi/t [h] **1.** vi *to marry* (spät *late*, jung *young*); *to settle down* || unter–e–a ~ (of tribes) *to intermarry* || aus Liebe ~ *to m. for love*; (nach) Geld ~ *to m.* (*for*) *money* || in e–e Familie ~ *to m. into a* *family*; immer in verwandte Familien ~ *to breed in and in* ‖ nach Amerika ~ *to m. and settle in America* **2.** vt (jdn) *to marry*; *to take in marriage* ‖ → 1. **H·eirats-** *m(arria)ge*, *m(arr)ying* **~alter** n *m.ge* od *m.ying age*; Mindest≃ *minimum m.ge age* (16 Jahre) **~antrag** m *offer* (od *proposal*) *of m.ge*; *suit*; e–n ~ m *to propose m.ge*; jdm e–n ~ m *to propose to a p* **~anzeige** f *notice* od *announcement of marriage* **~büro** n *m.ge-agency* **~erlaubnis** f *m.ge-licence* **≃fähig** a *m.geable* (*p*; *age*); *eligible* (*p*) ‖ (of woman) *nubile* ‖ in ~em Alter s *to be of an age* (od *old enough*) *to marry* **~fähigkeit** f *m.geable age*; *nubility* **~gut** n *dowry*; *m.age--portion* **~kandidat** m *m.ying man*; *suitor* **~kontrakt** m *m.age-contract* (od *articles* pl; *settlement*) **≃lustig** a *matrimonially inclined*; *keen on m.ying* **~markt** m *m.ge-market* **~stifter** m ⟨dero⟩ *match--maker* **~urkunde** f *m.ge-certificate* **~vermittler(in** f) m *m.ge-agent*; *professional match-maker*; ⟨Am⟩ *m.ge counselor* **~vermittlung** f *match--making* | ~sinstitut [n] *matrimonial agency*; ~sprovision [f] *m.ge brok(er)age* **~vertrag** m = –kontrakt **~ziffer** f der Verwitweten etc *re-m.ge rate*, ~ der Ledigen *first m.ge rate*

h·eisa, heißa intj *hey*!; = hei

***h·eischen** vt [h] ⟨poet⟩ = erbitten, fordern

h·eiser a *hoarse* (*voice*), *husky*, *raucous*, *thick* ‖ ~ s *to have a frog in the throat*, *to have lost one's voice* | **≃keit** f *hoarseness*, *huskiness*, *raucousness*

heiß A. [a] **1.** ⟨**eig**⟩ *hot* (*fire*; *iron*; *water*; *springs*; *steam*); *warm* ‖ glühend ~ *red-hot*; kochend ~ *boiling(-hot)*; *scalding(-hot)* ‖ noch ganz ~ (of food) *hot and hot*; *the food came hot to the table*; etw ~ essen (halten) *to eat* (*keep*) *a th hot* ‖ ich finde es ziemlich ~ hier *I find it rather warm here* ‖ (Tuch) ~ pressen, plätten *to hot--press* ‖ sich ~ laufen (of machine) *to run hot*; *to heat* **2.** ⟨**übtr**⟩ **a.** *hot* (*day*, *summer*; *forehead*); brennend ~ *burning* od *piping hot* (*day*) ‖ ~e Chemie *hot chemistry*, *hot-atom chemistry* ‖ ~ u feucht *sultry* (*wind*) ‖ ~e Zone *torrid zone* **b.** ~e Tränen *scalding* (od *bitter*) *tears* ‖ **(P)** [pred] ~ s *v to be aglow with* (*the exercises*); glühend ~ s *to be sweltering*; mir ist ganz ~ *I feel quite hot* od *warm* ‖ es überläuft mich ~ *it makes me go hot all over* ‖ jdn ~ m *to make a p warm* od *hot* **3.** ⟨**fig**⟩ **a.** *hot* (*battle*, *contest*); *keen*; ⟨sl⟩ *gruelling* (*combat*); am ~esten *at the hottest* ‖ *warm* (*work*) **b.** *ardent* (*love*), *burning*, *fervent* (*prayer*; *desire*), *fervid*, *passionate*, *vehement*; ~er Dank *perfervid gratitude*; ~e Vaterlandsliebe *flaming patriotism*; ~e Wallungen *thrills*, *throbs* pl ‖ ~es Blut h *to be hot-tempered* **c. (P)** *ardent* (*admirer*), *passionate*, *vehement*; ⟨vulg sex⟩ *hot*, *on heat* **4.** ⟨**fig**⟩ → Eisen, Hölle etc; der Boden wurde ihm zu ~ unter den Füßen *the place was getting too hot for him* (od .. *too hot to hold him*) ‖ es wird nichts so ~ gegessen, wie es gekocht wird *never trouble till trouble troubles you* ‖ ganz ~ (= nahe daran) s *to be getting hot* **B.** **[adv]** *hotly* ‖ ⟨mst fig⟩ (*to love*) *ardently*, *fervently*, *keenly*, *passionately*; *vehemently* ‖ da ging es ~ her *the feeling went high there*; *there was hot work there*; *it was a rough-and-tumble fight* **~blütig** a ⟨fig⟩ *hot--blooded*, *hot-tempered*; *passionate* **≃dampf** m *superheated steam* | ~maschine [f] *engine worked with superheated steam* **~gelaufen** a *heated* (*bearing*) **~geliebt** a *dearly beloved* **≃hunger** m *voracity*; *voracious* (od *insatiable*, *ravenous*) *appetite*; ⟨med⟩ *bulimia* L | ⟨fig⟩ *craving*, *thirst* (nach *for*) ‖ ⟨dero⟩ *greed*, *greediness* (nach *of*); *voracity* (*of*) **~hungrig A.** [a] **1.** [pred] *excessively hungry*; *voracious*; *ravenous* **2.** ⟨fig⟩ *voracious* (*reader*); *thirsting* (*eyes*); ~ s nach *to thirst for* ‖ ⟨dero⟩ *greedy* (nach *of*) **B.** [adv] *thirstily* ‖ *greedily* **~kühlung** f *glycol* od *chemical cooling* **≃laufen** n ⟨tech⟩ *running hot*; *heating* **≃luft** f *hot air* | ~bad [n] *hot-air bath*; ~dusche [f] *electric hair dryer*; ~maschine [f] *hot-air engine*; ~ventilator [m] *h.-a. blower*; ~zufluß [m] *h.-a. inlet* **≃sporn** m ~s/~e *hotspur*; *hothead*; (nach Shak: *Henry H.r*); *rash* (*p*) **~siegelung** f *heat sealing* **~spornig** a *impetuous*; *rash* **~strahltriebwerk** n ⟨aero⟩ *thermal jet engine* **~umkämpft** a *hard disputed* (*place*) **≃w·asser-** ~gerät [n] *hot-water apparatus*; ~heizung [f] *hot-water heating*; ~speicher [m] *hot-water container*; *geyser*; ⟨el⟩ *thermal storage water heater*; ~spender [m] *immersion heater*; *geyser*; ~versorgung [f] *hot-water supply*

h·eißa(ssa) intj = heisa

h·eißen[1] vt/i [hieß/geheißen] [h] **I. vt A. (befehlen) 1.** ***etw** ~ *to order a th* (*the retreat*); ich habe es ge~ *I ordered* (od *caused*) *it to be done* **2. jdn** ~ **a.** wie er sie ge~ hatte *as he had told them* | tu wie dir ge~ ist *do as you are bid* od *told* **b.** jdn **willkommen** ~ *to bid* od *make a p welcome*; *to welcome a p* **c.** jdn ~ **z tun** *to command* (od *order*, *tell*) *a p to do*; *to bid a p do* ‖ jdn *or* jdm ~, etw z tun *to order* (etc) *a p to do a th* **3.** jdn (*or* jdm) etw [nur: **es, dies, was** etc] ~; wer hat es dich ge~? *who bade you do it*? *who told you to do it*? was habe ich dich ge~? *what did I tell you to do*? **4. a. jdn tun** ~ *to bid a p do*; *to command* (od *order*, *tell*) *a p to do*; ich hieß ihn eintreten *I bade him enter*; wer hat dich das tun ~? *who told you to do that*? **b.** *etw tun ~ *to order a th to be done* **B. (nennen) 1.** jdn ~ *to call* od *name a p* (nach *after*); sie hießen ihn Fritz *they called him Frederick* (od *by the name of F.*); er hieß mich e–n Narren *he called me a fool* **2.** °das heiße ich e–n festen Schlaf! *that's what I call a sound sleep*! **II. vi 1.** *to be called* (nach *after*), *to be named*; er heißt Fritz *he is called Frederick*, *his name is F.* ‖ wie heißt du? *what is your name*? ‖ ⟨mil⟩ wie heißt der Mann? *take his name*, *sergeant-major*! ‖ wie heißt der Ort? *what is the name of the place*? ‖ ‚Herr N.?' ‚So heiße ich' '*Mr. N.*?' '*That is my name*' ‖ er heißt mit Spitznamen N. *he is nicknamed N.* ‖ ich will ein Schuft ~, wenn .. *I'm a Dutchman if* ..; oder ich will nicht N. ~ *or I'm a Dutchman* **2. (bedeuten) a.** *to mean*, *signify* ‖ (Text) **soll** ~: *is amended to read*: .. ‖ **was** (*or* **wie**) **heißt** ‚turnen' auf Englisch? *what is* (od *is called*) 'turnen' *in English*; *what do you call* 'turnen' *in E.*; *what is the English for* 'turnen?' ‖ **was heißt hier** „spät"?! *never mind about* "*late*"! Herr .. wie heißt er doch gleich? *Mr .. what's his name*? **b. das will etw** (*or* **viel**) ~ *that is saying* (od *that means*) *a great deal* (od *a lot*, *a long word*) ‖ was soll das ~? *what does that mean*? *what is the meaning of that*? ‖ das will nichts ~ *that does not matter*; es heißt nicht viel *it isn't up to much* ‖ **soll das ~, daß** .. *does that mean that* (*you won't come*); *am I to understand* (*you did it*)? ‖ das soll so etwas ~ *that's intended to create an impression* **c. jetzt heißt es arbeiten** (sich eilen)! *business before pleasure now*; *sharp's the word*! ‖ da heißt es aufgepaßt! *so now be careful*!, *now look out*! ‖ hier heißt es ‚entweder .. oder' *it must be the one thing or the other* **d. das heißt** *that is*; *that is to say*; *to wit*; d. h. vorausgesetzt, daß (..) *that is presuming* (*I am allowed*) **3. es heißt** *it is said*; *they say*; es h., er sei entk *he is said to have escaped* ‖ .., damit es nicht heiße .. *that it may not be said* (*that* ..) ‖ es heißt in der Bibel *it says in the Bible*; wie es bei Goethe h. *as Goethe has it*; heißt es nicht in dem A., daß ..? *does it not say in the Agreement that* ..? ‖ (er selbst wird k,) **wenigstens heißt es so** (...) *at least that's what they say*

h·eißen[2] vt [heißte/geheißt] [h] ⟨mar⟩ (= hissen) (Fahne, Boot) *to hoist*; heiß Flagge! *hoist the flag*! ‖ (Boot) halb ~ *to hoist in dip* (= *at the dip*) **H·eißstropp** m *sling*; *hoist--rope*

-heit suff **1.** [abstr] *-hood*; Falsch~ *falsehood*; Kind~ *childhood* ‖ *-ness*; Keck~ *sauciness* ‖ *-ty*; Gleich~ *equity*; Schön~ *beauty* **2.** [konkr] **a.** [koll] → Christen~, Mensch~ **b.** → Hoheit

h·eiter A. [a] **1.** **(hell)** *bright, cheerful* (*day*); *clear, fair* (*weather*), *serene, clear* (*sky*); ~ scheinen (of the moon) *to shine serene*; ~ w *to brighten* (*up*); *to clear up* ‖ *gay*; *smiling* (*landscape*) ‖ er betrachtete die S v der ~en Seite *he saw the funny* od *sunny side of it* ‖ ⟨fig⟩ wie ein Blitz aus ~em Himmel *like a bolt from the blue* **2.** **(P) a.** *cheerful* (*fellow*); *bright*; *buoyant, blithe*; *bright* (*smile*) ‖ *gay, happy, hilarious, jolly* (*company*), *jovial, airy, jauntry*; *merry* ‖ *calm, quiet, serene, unruffled*; ~e Ruhe *serenity* ‖ ~ w *to expand*; *to warm* od *cheer up, to brighten*; ~ bleiben *to keep up one's spirits* **|** ~es **Gemüt,** ~er Sinn *cheerful nature* od *disposition* ‖ ~e Laune, ~e Stimmung *high spirits* pl; in sehr ~er St. s *to be elevated* od *merry* ‖ *sanguine* (*temperament*) = *sanguineness* **b.** *gay* (*laugh, song, voice*); die ~e **Welt** M.s *the gaiety of Mozart's music* **3.** °⟨iron⟩ das ist ja ~ ⟨fam⟩ *that's funny*; .. *a nice state of affairs*; .. *the limit*; das kann ja ~ w *that can turn out a nice mess* **B.** **[adv] (P)** *brightly*; *cheerfully*; *gaily* ‖ *serenely* **|** ≃**keit** f **1.** *brightness*; *clearness*; *serenity* **2.** (P) *cheerfulness*; *gaiety, glee, hilarity, merriment, mirth* ‖ *calmness* ‖ allg ~ erwecken *to set everyone laughing*; ungetrübte ~ *undisturbed serenity* **3.** gr ~ erwecken *to cause great amusement* ‖ allgemeine ~ erwecken *to excite much amusement, to raise a laugh*; unter der wachsenden ~ der Zuhörer *to the growing amusement of the audience*

H·eiz- *heating* **~anlage** f *h. plant* (od *facilities, installations* pl) **~apparat** m ⟨el⟩ *h. apparatus*; *heater*; *radiator* **~batterie** f ⟨el⟩ *A-battery*; ⟨wir⟩ *filament-b.* **~dampf** m *h.-steam* **~effekt** m *h. effect* **~energie** f *filament e.* **~faden** m ⟨el⟩ *filament* **~fläche** f *h. surface* **~gas** n *fuel gas* **~kanal** m *flue* **~kessel** m *h. boiler* **~kissen** n ⟨mst el⟩ *heating pad* **~körper** m *heater, radiator* **~kraft** f *h.* (od *calorific*) *power* **~lüfter** m *fan convector* **~material** n *fuel* **~ofen** m; elektrischer ~ *electric* (*h.*) *stove* **~öl** n *fuel oil*; *oil fuel* **~platte** f = Kochplatte **~raum** m **1.** ⟨mar⟩ *stoke-hold* **2.** *h.-room*; (f Zentralheizung) *furnace* **~regler** *filament resistor* **~rohrkessel** m *fire tube boiler* **~schlange** f ⟨tech⟩ *h. coil* **~sonne** f ⟨el⟩ *reflector bowl fire* **~stoff** m *fuel* **~strom** m ⟨wir⟩ *filament current*; ⟨el⟩ *h.-current* (*circuit*) **~stunde** f *firing hour* **~trockner** m *heat drying machine* **~tür** f *fire-door*; *stoke-hole* **~vorrichtung** f *h. device* **~wert** m *heat-value*; *calorific* (od *thermal*) *v.*; oberer ~ *gross c. v.* **~zweck** m; f ~e *for h. purposes* **h·eizbar** a *capable of being heated*; *heatable* ‖ *provided with a stove*; *stove-heated* (*room*) **h·eizen A.** vt/i [h] **1.** vt (Ofen) *to heat*; (Kessel) *to fire*; (Maschinen) *to stoke* ‖ (Raum) *to heat*; ⟨el⟩ *to heat electrically*; mit Warmwasser ~ *to heat by hot-water*; gut geheizt *wellheated* (*room*) **2.** vi **a.** *to make a fire* ‖ ⟨tech⟩ *to fire*; *stoke* **b.** ~ **mit** .. *to heat with* (*coals*, etc.); *to burn* (*wood*); *to fire* (*oil*) **c.** der Ofen heizt gut *the stove heats well* ‖ das Zimmer heizt sich gut *the room is easily heated* **B.** ≃ n *heating*; *firing* (*of a boiler*); *stoking* **H·eizer** m *fireman, stoker* ‖ ⟨rail⟩ *fireman*; Stand des ~s *footplate*

H·eizung f ~/~en **1.** [abstr] *heating* (*of a room, house*); Boden≃ *panel h.*; Dampf≃ *steam h.*; Ofen≃ *h. by stoves*; Strahlungs≃ *radiant h.*; ⟨mot⟩ Wagen≃ *h. system*; Warmluft≃ *hot-air h.*; Warmwasser≃ *hot-water h.* ‖ Fern≃ *long-distance h.* ‖ Zentral≃ *central h.*; ~sanlage *c. h. system* **|** *firing* (*of a boiler*; *of an engine*); Öl≃ *oil-firing* **2.** [konkr] **a.** = ~sanlage ‖ die ~ abstellen *to turn off the radiators* **b.** (Heizstoff) *fuel* **c.** = Heizraum 2. **H·eizungs- ~anlage** f *h. plant* (od *installation*); *radiators* pl; *furnace*; *stoking plant* **~methode** f *method of h.* **~rohr** n *h. pipe*

Hekat·ombe f ~/~n *hecatomb*; *massacre*

H·ekla m (isländ. Vulkan) (*Mount*) *Hecla*

H·ektar n (abbr ha; = 100 Ar) ~(e)s/~ *hectare*

h·ektisch a *hectic*; *consumptive*

H·ekto- (= 100) **~gramm** n *hectogram*(*me*) **~gr·aph** m *hectograph* **~graph·ie** f *hectography* ≃**graph·ieren** vt [h] *to hectograph* **~gr·aphisch** a *hectographic* **~liter** n (abbr hl) *hectolitre*

H·ektor ⟨übtr⟩ (Hund) °wie ~ an die Buletten *with a vengeance, like old boots*

H·ekuba ⟨Gr ant⟩: Was ist ihm ~? *What's Hecuba to him*? (Shak); *it's all the same to him*

Hel·anka ® f ~/ *Helanca* (*texturing process*)

Held m ~en/~en **1.** ⟨myth⟩ *hero*; die 9 guten ~en *the Nine Worthies* (*of the World*); ~ der Arbeit ⟨SBZ⟩ *h. of labo*(*u*)*r*; National≃ *national h.* ‖ ⟨mil⟩ *h.*; Flieger≃ *ace* **2.** ⟨Lit⟩ *h.* ‖ ⟨theat⟩ *leading man* ‖ den ~en spielen *to play the* (*part of the*) *h.* **3.** ⟨übtr⟩ **a.** *of note*; *celebrity* ‖ der ~ des Tages *the lion* (*of the day*); jdn zum ~en des T. m *to make a lion of a p*; *to lionize a p* **b.** °er ist kein ~ im Gr. ⟨fam⟩ *he is not much in Greek* ‖ ⟨iron⟩ °du bist mir ein schöner ~ *you're a nice sort of a fellow*; ⟨sl⟩ *a funker you are* **H·eldbock** m ⟨ent⟩ *longicorn* **H·elden- ~buch** n *late medieval collection of rewritten German epics* **~dichtung** f *epic* od *h.ic poetry* **~epos** n *epic poem*; *epic* **~gedenktag** m ⟨Ger hist⟩ (16. März) *H.es' Day*; ⟨engl⟩ *Remembrance*; (⟨Am⟩ 11. Nov.); ⟨Am hist⟩ (30. Mai) *Memorial D.* **~gedicht** n = -epos **~geist** m *h.ism* **~geschlecht** n *h.ic race*; *race of h.es* °**~keller** m *funk-hole* **~leistung** f *h.ic* od *epic achievement* **~lied** n ⟨Lit⟩ *h.ic epic lay, epic song* **~mut** m *valo*(*u*)*r, prowess, bravery*; *h.ism* **~rolle** f ⟨theat⟩ *leading character*; *chief part* **~ruhm** m *h.ic renown* **~sage** f *h.ic legend* od *saga, story* **~sinn** m *h.ism* °**~stück** n; ein echtes ~ *a regular feat* **~tat** f *exploit, feat*; *prowess*; *valiant deed*; *deed of valour*; ⟨Lit⟩ *geste* **~tod** m *h.ic death* ‖ ⟨mil⟩ *death in action* (od *battle*); *death in the field of honour*; den ~ sterben *to die a h.'s death*; *to fall in the field of honour* (od *in action*) **~verehrung** f *h.-worship* **~zeitalter** n *h.ic age* **h·eldenhaft, heldenmütig 1.** [a] *heroic, valiant* (*deed*); → heroisch **2.** [adv] *h.ally*; *valiantly* **H·eldentum** n *heroism* **H·eldin** f *heroine*; *amazon* ‖ ⟨theat⟩ *leading lady* **h·eldisch** a & adv = heldenhaft

H·elder m ~s/~ *undiked fen-land*

Hel·enenkraut n ⟨bot⟩ = Alant

H·elfe f ⟨weav⟩ (Stützfaden) *heddle* **h·elfen** vi [half/geholfen] [h] **A.** **(P)** **1.** **jdm** ~ **a.** *to help* (od *assist, befriend*; ⟨liter⟩ *abet, succour*) *a p*; *to back a p up*; *to give help to a p*; *to give a p a hand* ‖ [ell] hilf Himmel! ⟨vulg⟩ *bly* (*me*)! ‖ hilf ihm aus dem M. *help him off with his coat* ‖ ich half ihr es suchen *I helped her* (*to*) *find it* ‖ ihm wurde geholfen *he was helped* ‖ jdm in der Not ~ *to relieve a p in need*; *to help a lame dog over a stile* **|** ⟨jur⟩ so wahr mir Gott helfe! *so help me God*! ‖ °⟨iron⟩ warte, ich werde dir ~ ⟨fam⟩ *I am just going to give it to you* **b.** **sich** selbst ~ *to shift for o.s.* ‖ °.. aber helf' er sich .. *but I could not help myself*; .. *but it could not be helped* ‖ sich z ~ **wissen** *to be full of resource*, ⟨fam⟩ *to know the ropes*; sich nicht mehr z ~ wissen *to be at the end of one's tether* (od *at one's wit's end*) **|** **[neg]** das half gar **nichts (wenig)** *that didn't do at all* (*that was all to small purpose*); ich **kann mir nicht** ~ *I cannot help it, I cannot help m.s.*; sich [dat] nicht mehr z ~ wissen *to be upon one's last legs*; das hilft mit nichts *that won't meet my case* **c.** jdm ~ **auf, aus, bei, in, über** etw *to help* (od *assist*) *a p on* (*a horse*), *out of* (*a car, a difficulty*), *with* (*his work*), *into* (*the shoes*), *over* (*an obstacle*) ‖ ⟨fig⟩ jdm auf die Beine (*or* über den Berg) ~ *to give a p a leg up*; .. auf die Sprünge ~ *to jog a p's memory* ‖ jdm beim Aussteigen ~ *to help* (od *aid, assist*) *a p in getting out* **d. jdm ~ z tun**

to help od *aid a p to do* od *in doing, to assist a p in doing*; ⟨fam⟩ *to help a p do (a th)* ‖ ich habe ihm den Mantel anziehen (ausziehen) ~ *I've helped him on (off) with his coat*; ich hab' ihm die Pakete tragen ~ *I helped him (to) carry the parcels*; er hat sich ~ l bei .. *he has had help in (his work)*; sich v jdm ~ l *to get a p to help one (to do)* **2.** **[abs]** *to help (in the shop)*; kann ich ~? *can I lend a hand*? ‖ ~ **bei** *to help with (the harvest)* **B. (S) 1.** e–r S ~ *to assist a th (rest assists the process)*; *to help a th*; ⟨Am sl⟩ *to boost a th* **2.** [neg & interr] **a. jdm** ~ *to avail* od *profit a p*; was hilft uns das? *what good is that to us*? ‖ ⟨bib⟩ was hülfe es dem Menschen, wenn .. *what is a man profited, if* .. ? ‖ es hilft ihnen nichts *it does them no good*; *they are not the better for it*; das Leugnen half ihm nichts *his denial availed him nothing*; es hilft uns nicht viel *that's not much help* **b.** [abs] **es hilft nichts** *it is no good*; *it is of no use*; es half alles nichts *all was of no avail* ‖ da h. kein Sträuben *willy-nilly (we ..)* ‖ das hilft (alles) nichts *I cannot help it*; es h. (alles) nichts, er .. *there is no (other) alternative, he (must leave)* ‖ was hilft's? *how can I help it*? **3.** [abs] **a.** das Mittel hilft glänzend *this is an excellent remedy* (gegen *for*); es hilft gegen Gicht *it is good for the gout* ‖ die Arznei hat (nicht) geholfen *the medicine has done much (no) good* **b.** ~**, etw z tun** *to help* od *go to do a th*; ~ etw z bilden, ~ bei der Bildung v etw *to go to form a th*; *to go to the formation of a th*; *to promote a th* **H·elfer** m ~s/~ *helper*; *assistant* **H·elferin** f ~/~nen *helpmate* ‖ Fürsorge≈ *social worker* **H·elfershelfer** m ⟨jur⟩ *abettor (-er)* (~ s *to abet*); *accomplice, confederate*; (Diebes≈) *stall*; *tout*; ⟨sl⟩ *bonnet*; → Handlanger

×**H·elge** f ~/~n, **H·elgen** m ~/~ ⟨mar⟩ = Helling

H·elgoland ⟨Ger geog⟩ *Heligoland* ≈**er(in** f) m *inhabitant of H.* ≈**er-, h≈isch** [a] *H. (fishing, Bight)*

H·elikon[1] m ~s/ ⟨ant⟩ *Helicon*

H·elikon[2] n ~s/~s (Baßtuba) *helicon*

Helik·opter m ~s/~ → Hubschrauber

Helio- (Sonnen-) ~**gr·aph** m ~en/~en *heliograph* ~**graph·ie** f *h.y* ≈**graph·ieren** vt [h] *to h.* ≈**gr·aphisch** a *h.ic* ~**grav·üre** f *heliogravure* ~**m·eter** n ~s/~ *heliometer* ~**sk·op** n ~s/~e *helioscope* ~**st·at** m ~s/~e *heliostat* ~**tr·op 1.** n ~s/~e **a.** ⟨bot⟩ *heliotrope*; *cherry-pie* **b.** ⟨astr⟩ *heliotrope* **2.** m ~s/~e ⟨minr⟩ *heliotrope* ~**trop·ismus** m *heliotropism* ≈**z·entrisch** a *heliocentric*

H·elium n *h.* (verstrahlen *to emit*) | ~-Ionenstoß [m] *h.-ion collision*

hell A. [a] **1.** (Ggs **dumpf**) (of sound) *clear (tone)*; *resonant, ringing*; *clear-toned (bells)* ‖ *acute, high, shrill*; e–e ~e Stimme *a clear high voice* **2. a.** (Ggs **dunkel**) am ~en (*or* ~-lichten [→ hellicht]) Tage *in the face of day, in broad* od *full daylight*; es war schon ~ *it was quite light*; ein schöner ~er Raum *a nice light room* ‖ es ist mir nicht (mehr) ~ genug zum Lesen *I can't see to read* ‖ *light (colour; beer)*; *light-coloured (clothing, dress)*; ~st *flaming (colours)*; ⟨engl⟩ ~es Bier v Faß *bitter* ‖ *fair (hair)*; v ~er Gesichtsfarbe *fair in complexion, f.-skinned* **b.** (~ strahlend) *bright (sun)*; *glittering (stars)*; *luminous*; *serene (sky)*; *shining (rays)*; *lustrous (splendour)*; in ~en Flammen stehen *to be in a blaze, to be fiercely burning*; ~er Schein, ~e Masse *blaze* ‖ ~ w *to brighten* ‖ *bright (day), cheerful, fine* **3.** ⟨**fig**⟩ **a. (laut)** *loud, ringing (laughter, cheer)*; ~er Jubel *jubilations* pl; ~e Entrüstung *disgust, revolt* ‖ → Haufe(n) **b. (rein)** s–e ~e Freude h an *to take intense* (od *keen, real*) *delight in* ‖ ~e Tränen weinen *to weep bitterly* ‖ in ~er Verzweiflung *in deep despair* ‖ °~er Unsinn *downright* (od *sheer, screaming*) *nonsense* **4.** ⟨**fig**⟩ **(P)** *bright (lad), clear (mind)*; *clear-headed*; *discerning*; *intelligent*; *lucid*; *shrewd*; → helle **B.** **[adv] 1.** *clearly*; *loud(ly)*; *resonantly*; ~ beleuchtet *brightly lit*; ~ klingend *clear-toned* ‖ ~ auflachen *to burst out laughing* **2.** (→ A. 2. b.) *brightly, luminously*; ~ scheinen *to blaze*; (of the moon) *to shine serene* *~**·auf** adv; sei ~! *cheer up*! ~**blau** a *light-blue* ~**blond** a *fair* ~**braun** a *light-brown*; *auburn*; *fawn*; *hazel (eyes)*; ~e Farbe *buff* ≈**dunkel** n ⟨paint⟩ *chiaroscuro* Ir, *clair-obscure* Fr ‖ ⟨übtr⟩ *twilight* | ~-nuance [f] ⟨paint⟩ *tonal value* ~**erleuchtet** a ⟨theat etc⟩ *brillant* ~**farbig** a *light-coloured*; *fair (hair)* ≈**feld** n ⟨microscope⟩ *bright field* ~**gelb** a *l.-yellow* ~**grau** a *l.-grey* ~**grün** a *l.-green* ~**hörig** a (P) *quick of hearing*; (Wand) *not sound-proof* ‖ ⟨scient⟩ *clairaudient* ≈**hörigkeit** f ⟨scient⟩ *clairaudience* ~**klingend** a *clear, resonant, sonorous* ~**leuchtend** a → helleuchtend ~**(l)odernd** a *blating, flaming* ~**rot** a *l.-red*; *nacarat* | ~glühend [a] *bright red hot*; ~glut [f] *b. red heat* ≈**sehen** n *clairvoyance* Fr; *second sight* ~**sehend** a *clear-headed*; *shrewd*; →–seherisch ≈**seher·ei** f ⟨dero⟩ = Hellsehen ≈**seher** m *clairvoyant* Fr ‖ *visionary* ≈**seherin** f *clairvoyante* Fr ~**seherisch** a *clairvoyant* ‖ *visionary* ‖ *extrasensory (conception)* ~**sichtig** a = –sehend ≈**sichtigkeit** f *clear-headedness*; *shrewdness* ~**strahlend** a *beaming*; *radiant (face)* ~**tönend** a *highpitched (voice)*; *shrill* ~**wach** a *wide-awake*

H·ellas n *Hellas, Greece*; → Hellene

°**H·elle** [das ~, ein ~s] n (Bier) *light beer*; ⟨engl⟩ *bitter*; drei ~! *three bitter*! ‖ °munteres ~s ⟨sl⟩ *bevvy*; → heben I. A. 1.

°**h·elle** a *shrewd*; ⟨fam⟩ *cute*; *up to snuff*

***H·elle**[1] f = Helligkeit ×**H·elle**[2] f → Hölle 3. b.

Helleb·arde f ~/~n *halberd* –**d·ier** m *-dier*

H·ellegatt n ~s/~e ⟨mar⟩ *store-room*

Hell·ene m ~n/~n ⟨ant⟩ *Hellene*; die ~n [pl] *the Hellenes* pl **hell·enisch** a *Hellenic* **Hellen·ismus** m *hellenism* **hellen·istisch** a *Hellenistic*

H·eller m *farthing* | ⟨fig⟩ *penny, rap*; *bean* ‖ k–n ~ wert *not worth a rap, button, etc*; er besitzt k–n roten ~ *he has not a p. to his name* (od .. *to bless himself with*); ⟨sl⟩ *he has not got a red bean*; ich gebe k–n roten ~ dafür *I don't give a brass farthing for it*; auf ~ u Pfennig *to the last p.*; *exactly* ‖ → Bohne, Deut **H·ellerkraut** n ⟨bot⟩ *penny-cress*

Hellesp·ont m ⟨ant⟩ *Hellespont* → Dardanellen

h·elleuchtend a *bright (light, sky)*; *shining* **h·ellicht** a (hell + licht) [nur in:] ~er Tag *daylight*; am ~en Tage *in broad daylight* **H·elligkeit** f (→ hell A. 2.) **1.** *lightness (of a room)*; *brightness, brilliance (of the sky)*; *luminosity* **2.** ⟨phys⟩ *intensity of light* ⟨a. theat⟩ | ~sgrad, ~swert [m] *brilliancy, -ce*; ⟨paint⟩ *tonal value*; ~smesser [m] *photometer*; ~smessung [f] *photometry*

H·elling f [~/~en] & m [~s/~e] ⟨mar⟩ *slip, slipway, launching-ways* pl; Bau≈ *building slip*

***Helm**[1] m ⟨mar⟩ *helm*; *steering gear*

Helm[2] m (of an axe, etc) *handle, helve*

Helm[3] m ~(e)s/~e **A.** ⟨eig⟩ **1.** ⟨mil⟩ *helmet* (~ ab! *off h.*); ⟨poet⟩ *helm* ‖ (of firemen, etc.) *(protective) headpiece* ‖ → Stahl≈ etc **2.** ⟨her⟩ (Figur) *helmet* **B.** ⟨übtr⟩ **1.** ⟨arch⟩ = ~dach [n] **2.** *head (of a retort)* ~**biene** f = Drohne ~**bohne** f ⟨bot⟩ *hyacinth bean* ~**busch** m *aigrette* ~**dach** n ⟨arch⟩ *pyramidal roof (of a spire)* ~**figur** f *helmet* ≈**förmig** a *h.-shaped*; *h.-like* ~**kleinod** n ⟨her⟩ *crest* ~**kraut** n ⟨bot⟩ *h.-flower*; *skull-cap* ~**schmuck** m ⟨her⟩ *crest* ~**sturz** m *visor*; *movable face-guard* ~**wachtel** f ⟨orn⟩ *h.-quail* ~**zier** f ⟨her⟩ *crest*

Helm·inthe f ~/~n ⟨zoo⟩ (Wurm) *helminth*

Hel·obien [–iən] pl ⟨bot⟩ *Helobiae, Najadales*

Hel·ot(e) m ~en/~en ⟨Gr ant⟩ *helot*

H·elsingfors, Helsingf·ors n, **H·elsinki** n ⟨finn⟩ *Helsingfors*; *Helsinki*

H·elsingör n (dän. Hafenstadt) *Elsinore*

Helv·etien [ts] ⟨hist⟩ *Helvetia* L = Schweiz

Helv·etier [ts] m ⟨hist⟩ *Helvetian* = Schweizer

helv·etisch a ⟨hist⟩ *Helvetian* ‖ ⟨rel⟩ *Helvetic*
Hemd n ~(e)s/~en **1. a.** (Ober≃ f Männer) *shirt*; buntes ~ *coloured sh.*, gestreiftes ~ *striped sh.*; Ober≃ mit steifem Einsatz *white starched sh.*, ⟨Am⟩ *boiled sh.* ‖ (~ f Damen) *chemise* Fr; † *shift* ‖ (Spitzen≃) *camisole* ‖ → Nacht≃, Unter≃ **b.** Wendungen: das ~ ist mir näher als der Rock *near is my shirt, but nearer is my skin* ‖ er würde dir sein letztes ~ geben *he'd give you the sh. off his back* ‖ kein ~ auf dem Leibe h *not to have a sh. to one's back* ‖ bis aufs ~ ⟨a. fig⟩ *stripped to one's sh., to the skin*; sich bis aufs ~ ausziehen *to strip to one's sh.*; ⟨fig⟩ jdn bis aufs ~ ausziehen *to fleece a p* ‖ im bloßen ~e *in one's sh.* ‖ (wo ist er, sie?) °Im ~! ⟨hum⟩ .. *In his, her skin*! ‖ ohne ~ *shirtless* **2.** (Bluse) **a.** f Frauen, Kinder → ~bluse **b.** (f Männer) *shirt*; → Kittel ‖ ⟨pol⟩ Braun≃ *brown sh.*; Schwarz≃ *black sh.* **~ärmel** = Hemds- **~bluse** f (f Frauen) *shirt*; *sh.-blouse* | ~n– ~ärmel *sh.-bl. sleeve*; ~kleid *sh.waister* **~einsatz** m *sh.-front* **~hose** f (f Herren) *cami-boxers* pl; (f Frauen) *combinations* pl (e–e ~ *a pair of c.*); *cami-knickers* pl ⟨Am⟩ *union-suit* **~knopf** m = Hemden- **~kragen** m *sh.-collar* **~krause** f *frill* **~rock** m *shirtwaister* **~röckchen** n *short slip* °**H·emdchen** n *little shirt* ˣ**H·emde** n = Hemd **H·emden- ~fabrikant** m *shirt-maker* **~industrie** f *sh.-making industry* **~knopf** m *sh.-button* **~macher** m *sh.-maker* °**~matz** m *a child in its sh.* **~stoff** m *shirting* **~tuch** n (weißes) *shirting* **H·emdsärmel** m *shirt-sleeve*; in ~n *in one's sh.-sleeves*; (*to sit*) *sh.-sleeved*
Hemeralop·ie f ⟨med⟩ *hemeralopia* [L]
Hemi- (Halb-) **~anops·ie** f ⟨path⟩ *hemianopsia* L **~pt·eren** pl ⟨ent⟩ *hemiptera* Gr pl **~sphäre** f *hemisphere* ≃**sph·ärisch** a *hemispheric*(*al*)
H·emm- ~keil m *scotch*; → –schuh **~kette** f *drag-chain* **~klotz** m = **~schuh** m *brake-shoe*; *drag*; *scotch*, *skid*; *trig*; (Rad) durch ~ hemmen *to scotch*; *trig* | ⟨fig⟩ *drag* (f etw *on a th*); *spoke*: jds Plänen e–n ~ anlegen *to put a spoke in a p's wheel*; ein wesentlicher ~ im sozialen Leben der Hindus *a principal spoke in the Hindu wheel* **~stoff** m ⟨biol⟩ *inhibitor* **~vorrichtung, H·emme** f ~/~n *stop*; *braking* (od *checking*) *device* **h·emmen** vt [h] **1.** (Lauf e–s Rades etc) *to check*, *hamper*, *retard*, *slacken*; (durch Hemmschuh) *to scotch* ‖ (Gang e–r Maschine) *to choke*, *clog*, *embarrass* ‖ (Fließen v Wasser) *to stem*; (v Blut) *to sta*(*u*)*nch* **2.** ⟨**übtr**⟩ (Fortschritt) *to check*, *delay*, *hinder*, *impede*, *obstruct*, *retard*; *to be obstructive of* od *to*; (Ausdrucksweise) *to cram* (*a p's style*); (Entwicklung, Wachstum) *to stunt*; (Handel) *to cramp*; (Verkehr) *to hold up*, ⟨Am⟩ *to tie up* ‖ (Gefühl) *to curb*, *repress*, *restain*; ⟨mil⟩ *to check*, *impede* **3. jdn** ~ *to ba*(*u*)*lk*, *hamper*, *hinder*, *impede*, *shackle*, *trammel a p* ‖ auf Schritt u Tritt gehemmt s, sich g. fühlen *to be hampered at every step*, *to be ill at ease*; g. s durch *to be hidebound* (od *hampered*, *hamstrung*) *by* (*tradition*) **4. [abs]** *to be a hindrance*; *to be obstructive* od *retardatory* **h·emmend 1.** [a] *hampering*, *hindering*, *impeding*, *slackening*; *obstructive*; *inhibitive* **2.** [adv] ~ wirken auf etw, e–r S ~ in den Weg treten = hemmen 2. **H·emmnis** n –nisses/–nisse *barrier*, *hindrance*, *impediment*; *obstacle*, *obstruction* (f *to*) ‖ ein ~s f (etw) = hemmen ‖ die –nisse aus dem Wege räumen *to remove the obstacles* **H·emmung** f ~/~en **A. [abstr] 1.** → Lade≃; *retardation* (*of growth*); *slackening* (*of a movement*); *delay*; *obstruction* (*of progress*) ‖ *repression* (*of feelings*); *stoppage* **2.** ⟨psych⟩ *inhibition* ‖ (k–e) ~en h *to feel* (*no*) *i.s*, an ~en leiden *to suffer under i.*; präventive, (repressive) ~ *preventive* (*positive*) *check* ‖ s–e Einbildung kennt k–e ~en *he has no bubble in his trumpet* **B. [konkr]** ⟨tech⟩ (in der Uhr) *escapement* **H·emmungs-** [in comp] *checking*; *retarding*, *retardatory*; ⟨physiol⟩ *inhibitory*; → hemmend **~bildung** f ⟨biol⟩ *abnormal formation* ≃**los 1.** [a] *uninhibited*, *unrestrained*; *unconscionable*, *unscrupulous*; *desperate* **2.** [adv] *unscrupulously* **~mechanismus** m ⟨eth⟩ *inhibitive m.* **~rad** n (in Uhr) *escape*(*ment*)-*wheel*
ˣ**hen** adv = hin ‖ ˣ**hend·al** adv = hinab
H·endel n ~s/~ [österr] ⟨cul⟩ *cockerel*, *hendel*; verrückt wie ein ~ *mad as a March-hare*
H·endiady·oin n Gr („1 durch 2“) *hendiadys*
Hengst m ~es/~e ⟨zoo⟩ (Zucht≃) *stallion*; *sire* ‖ ~ u Stute *sire and dam* | ⟨übtr⟩ (of an ass, etc.) *male* ‖ ⟨dero⟩ = Kerl
H·enkel m ~s/~ *handle* (*of a pot*); *ear* (*of a cup*); ⟨tech⟩ *lug* ‖ (z Aufhängen) *hanger*; *coat-hanger* **~korb** m *market basket* **~kreuz** n *cross of St. Anthony* **~krug** m *jug* **~topf** m *pot with a h.*
***h·enken** (mst hängen) vt [h] jdn ~ *to hang a p* | ~swert [a] *fit to be hanged* **H·enker** m ~s/~ *executioner*, *hangman*; ⟨fam⟩ *Jack Ketch* ‖ Amt des öffentl. ~ *hangmanship* | °⟨fig⟩ zum ~! *hang it* (*all*)! *the deuce*! *the devil*! *confound*!; zum ~ nochmal! *dash it* (*all*)! zum ~ mit .. *hang the expense*, *reform be damned*! der ~ hol' das Zeug! *the devil take it*! ⟨sl⟩ *rot the stuff*! ‖ der ~ soll mich holen, wenn ..! *I'll be hanged* od *blowed if* ..! ‖ scher dich zum ~! *go to Jericho*!, *go to blazes*!, → Teufel **~beil** n *executioner's axe* **~lohn** m *hangman's fee* **H·enkers- ~beil** n = Henker– **~frist** f = Galgenfrist **~knecht** m *hangman's assistant* ‖ ⟨fig⟩ *hired ruffian*; *myrmidon*; *satellite* **~lohn** = Henker– **~mahl** n, **~mahlzeit** f (*a p's*) *last meal*
H·enna f (Farbstoff) *henna* **~blätter** n [pl] *h.-leaves* pl **~strauch** m *h.*(-*tree*)
H·enne f ~/~n **1.** ⟨orn⟩ *hen*; junge ~ *pullet* ‖ ⟨prov⟩ → Ei **2.** ⟨bot⟩ fette ~ → Fetthenne
H·ennegatt n ⟨mar⟩ (f das Steuerruder) *helmport*
H·ennegau m (belg. Prov.) *Hainau*(*l*)*t*
Henriqu·atre [ɑ̃ri'katr] m [Fr] ⟨übtr⟩ *the Henri Quatre beard*
Heortolog·ie f (Kalenderforschung) *heortology*
H·eppe f ~/~n ⟨for⟩ *brush-hook*, *bill*(-*hook*)
Hepta- (Sieben-) *hepta-* **~ch·ord** m *heptachord* **~·eder** n ⟨math⟩ *heptahedron* **~g·on** n ⟨math⟩ *heptagon* **~meter** [hep'ta-] m ⟨pros⟩ *heptameter* **~t·euch** m ⟨bib⟩ *heptateuch*
her adv **1.** (zum Sprechenden hin) **a.** [mit Verben] *here*, *hither*; *along* → her- 1. | das Buch ~! *out with the book*! *give me the book*; ~ damit! *out with it*!; ich mußte ~ *I had to come here* **b.** (Ausgangspunkt betonend) v .. ~ *from*; v Osten ~ *from the east* ‖ v oben (unten) ~ *from above* (*below*); v weit ~ *from* (*a-*) *far* ‖ wo~? *whence*? *from where*? wo~ hast du das? wo hast du das ~? *how did you come by it*? *where did you get it* (*from*)? ‖ wo ist er ~? *what* (*part of the*) *country does he come from*? *where does he hail from*? **2.** (Richtung, Bewegung) **a.** hinter jdm ~ s *to be after a p*; *to follow a p about*; *to run at a p's heels*; hinter e–r S ~ s *to be after a th* ‖ um uns ~ war Ruhe *around us all was quiet* **b.** hin u ~ → hin **3.** ⟨übtr⟩ es geht hoch ~ *things are* (*getting good* od) *going well*, → ~gehen; das ist nicht weit ~ *that is not up to much*; *that is second-rate*; es ist nicht weit ~ mit ihm ⟨sl⟩ *he is no great shakes*; .. mit ihnen *they are small fry* **4. (zeitlich)** es ist schon 50 Jahre ~, seit (*or* daß) es passierte *it is now 50 years since* (od *that*) *it happened*; es ist zwei J. ~, daß .. *it is two years ago that*, .. *2 y. since* (*he died*) ‖ es ist e–e Ewigkeit ~ *it is an age* (*since* ..) ‖ es ist lange ~ *it is long ago*; wie lange ist es ~? *how long ago is it*? ‖ von alters ~ *from of old*; → jeher
her- pref [betont, trennbar] → her 1. a. **1.** (zum Sprechenden hin) **a.** → ~bringen, ~eilen etc | [vor pp] → ~gebracht, ~gelaufen **b.** (Ausgangspunkt betonend) ~kommen etc **2.** ⟨übtr⟩ [mst

nur Richtung oder Bewegung bezeichnend] **a.** → ~gehen, ~richten etc **b.** → ~beten, ~leiern etc **c.** → ~fallen, ~halten, ~machen **3.** [f pref hin-] → ~geben, ~gehen, ~halten

her·ab adv **a.** [mst pref → herab–] **b.** den Berg ~ *down the m.*; ins Tal ~ *downhill* ‖ vom Himmel ~ *from h.* ‖ v oben ~ *from above*; ⟨fig⟩ *with a superior air*; er benahm sich sehr v oben ~ *he behaved very condescendingly* ‖ ~ mit ..! *down with ..!* → herunter ‖ (= hinab) bis ~ zu der Zeit v .. *down to the time of* **her·ab-** pref [betont, bei Verben trennbar] mst: *down, downward(s)*, oft ⟨übtr & fig⟩ → herunter– **~|bemühen** vt [h] (jdn) = herunter– **~|beschwören** vt [h] (Fluch) *to draw down* **~|bitten** vt [h] (Gottes Segen) *to call down* **~|blicken** vi [h] ⟨fig⟩ (verächtlich) ~ auf .. *to look* (od *gaze*) *down upon* (*a p, a th*) **~|bringen** vt [h] ⟨fig⟩ (etw) ~ auf *to bring down upon* (*a p*) **~|drücken** vt [h] ⟨com⟩ (Preise) *to beat* (od *force*) *down*; *to depress* ‖ (jdn) = –setzen **~|fahren** vi [s] *to descend* **~|fallen 1.** vi [s] *to fall down*; *to drop* (v *from, off*) ‖ ~ v (of light) *to fall from above* (*the gallery*) ‖ (of ground) *to sink*; *to fall away* (*in long slopes*) ‖ lose ~ (of garment) *to flow* (v *from*) **2.** ≈ n *downfall* **~|fließen** vi [s] *to flow* (od *pour, run*) *down*; *to pour* (*out*) (v *from*) **~|führen** vt [h] *to lead down* **~|gehen** vi [s] *to descend*; *to go down* **~|hageln** vi [h] ⟨fig⟩ Hiebe, Flüche hagelten auf sie herab *blows, curses fell in showers on them* ‖ Flüche ~ l auf *to hail* (od *rain*) *curses on* (*a p*); Steine ~ *to hurl stones* (*on a p*) **~|hangen** vi = **~|hängen** vi [h] *to hang down*; *to dangle, to swing* (v *from*); *to droop* (über *over*); lose ~ (of a garment) *to flow* (v *from*) **~hängend** a *flowing* (*garment*); *slack* (*rope*) **~|k** vi [s] *to come down*; *to descend* **~|l** vt [h] **1.** *to let down*; (Boot) *to lower*; *to haul down* ‖ (Fahne) *to dip* ‖ etw vom Preise ~ *to reduce the price* **2. sich** ~ **a.** *to descend* (an *on*); *to drop* (v .. in *from .. into*) **b.** ⟨fig⟩ *to condescend, deign, vouchsafe* (z *to*; z tun *to do*); sich ~ z e r Antwort *to deign* od *vouchsafe an answer* ‖ ⟨dero⟩ *to condescend* od *stoop* (*to*; *to do*) **~lassend 1.** [a] *condescending*; *affable* ‖ ⟨dero⟩ *c., patronizing, supercilious* ‖ ~es Wesen *c.ness*; *s.ness* **2.** [adv] *c.ly*; *with condescension*; jdn ~ behandeln *to look down upon a p*; ⟨Am⟩ *to high-hat a p* **≈lassung** f ⟨fig⟩ *condescension* **~|mindern** vt [h] *to decrease*; *diminish*; *lessen*; *impair*; → –setzen **~|regnen** vi [s] ⟨fig⟩ ~ auf *to rain* od *splash* (*up*)*on* .. **~|schießen** vt/i [h] (Vogel) aus der Luft ~ *to bring down*; *to drop* **2.** vi **a.** ⟨aero⟩ mit dem M-G ~ auf jdn *to shoot down on a p with one's m. g.* **b.** (of an eagle) ~ auf .. *to pounce* od *swoop upon* ‖ (of water) vom Felsen ~ *to shoot* (od *rush, sweep*) *down the rock* **~|sehen** vi [h] *to look down* | ⟨mst fig⟩ geringschätzig auf etw ~ *to disregard* od *neglect a th* ‖ .. auf jdn ~ *to look down upon, to l. d. one's nose at a p* ‖ ~d auf jdn *supercilious* **~|setzen** vt [h] **1.** ⟨eig⟩ (etw) *to take down* ‖ ⟨arch⟩ (Dach, Decke) *to lower* **2.** ⟨übtr & fig⟩ **a.** (Preis etc) *to cut, lower*; *to put, mark* (⟨fam⟩ *knock*) *down*; *to reduce*; (allmählich) *to shade*; z –gesetzten Preisen *at reduced* od *markdown prices* ‖ (Bestände) *to run down* ‖ ~ um .. *to take down a hole*, etc ‖ (Buchpreis) *to remainder* ‖ (Gehälter) *to reduce*; ⟨Am⟩ *to slash* (auf *to*) ‖ (Steuern, Unkosten) *to cut down* **b.** (Forderung) *to narrow down* (auf *to*) ‖ (Tempo) *to tone down* ‖ (Freude) *to allay* **c.** ⟨dero⟩ (jdn, etw) *to belittle, decry, depreciate, disparage*; *to run* (od *cry, let*) *down* (*a p, a th*); ⟨Lit⟩ *to write down* ‖ *to detract* (od *derogate*) *from* (*a th*) ‖ ⟨Am sl⟩ *to knock* **~setzend 1.** [a] *derogatory, disparaging* **2.** [adv] *d.ly*; *in disparagement* **≈setzung** f *reduction* (*of salary*; der Löhne *in wages*); *lowering*; *cutting-down* ‖ *belittlement, depreciation* (*of a p*); *disparagement* e–r S (*of a th*); *derogation*; *detraction* (e~r S *from a th*); *reflection* (*on a th*) **~|sinken** vi [s] ⟨übtr⟩ (S) *to descend*; (of the night) *to close down* (auf *on*); (of sounds) *to sink* (z .. *to a whisper*); auf Null ~ *to dwindle* (od *sink*) *to nothing*; auf e–e gesellschaftlich niedere Stufe ~ *to lose caste*; in e–n Zustand der Ohnmacht ~ *to fall to a low level of incompetence* **~|springen** vi [s] *to drop* (v .. in .. *from .. into the garden*); *to spring* (v *from*) **~|steigen** vi [s] *to step off* (*a chair*, etc), *to descend* (v .. *from a hill*), *to alight*; *to drop* (od *get*) *down* (v .. *from the chaise*); vom Pferde ~ *to alight* (od *get down*) *from the horse*; *to dismount* **~|stimmen** vt [h] ⟨übtr⟩ *to lower*; *to tune down*; *to depress* **~|stoßen** vi [s] = –schießen **~|strömen** vi [s] ~ auf .. (of water) *to pour in upon ..*; ~ v *to pour* (*out*) *from* **~|stufen** vt [h] *to downgrade* **~|stürzen** vi [s] (of a bird) *to come down*; → –schießen etc **~|tröpfeln** vi [s] ~ an (*or* v) der Wand *to trickle down the wall* **~|wünschen** vt [h] Unglück ~ auf .. *to imprecate evil upon* (*a p*); → –beschwören, –bitten **~|würdigen** vt [h] jdn ~ (of actions) *to degrade, abase a p* ‖ sich ~ *to demean* (od *degrade*) *o.s.* (durch *by*) **≈würdigung** f *degradation, abasement* **~|ziehen** vt [h] *to pull* (od *draw*) *down* ‖ ⟨fig⟩ etw auf sich ~ *to bring a th down upon o.s.* ‖ jdn zu sich ~ *to drag a p down to one's own level*

Her·aldik f ~/ *heraldry*; *armory* | **~er** m ~s/~ *heraldist*; *p versed in heraldry*

her·aldisch 1. [a] *heraldic* ‖ ~e Kunst *blazonry* ‖ in ~er Hinsicht *heraldically* **2.** [adv] *heraldically* ‖ (etw) ~ ausmalen, erklären *to blazon*

her·an adv (°ran) **a.** [mst als pref] → heran– **b.** ~ z mir! *come up here!* immer ~! *come on! come along!* **her·an**[1] pref [betont, bei Verben trennbar] *on, up*; *near* **~|bilden** vt [h] (jdn) *to breed, train*; *to bring up* (z *to*); *to educate*; z guten Bürgern –gebildet w *to be bred* (od *brought up*) *good citizens* **≈bildung** f *upbringing*; *training* **~|bringen** vt [h] (Stuhl) *to bring up*; ~ an *to bring* (*a chair*) *to* (*the table*); ⟨übtr⟩ → vorbringen ‖ (Truppen) *to bring* (od *move*) *up*; (eilig) *to hurry up*; bring ihn heran *bring him along*; jdn v der Hauptstadt ~ *to bring a p down* **~|drücken** vt [h]: er drückte es an sich heran *he pressed it towards him* **~|eilen** vi [s] *to draw near in haste* **~|fahren** vi [s]: Autos k –ge– *motor cars come rolling up* ‖ ~ an *to draw up to* (*the gate*); *to pull in to* (*the shore*) **~|führen 1.** vt [h] (Truppen) → –bringen ‖ ⟨übtr⟩ (jdn) ~ an *to make .. familiar with* **2.** ≈ n *forward movement* (*of reserves*) **~|gehen A.** vi [s] **1.** gehen Sie etw näher heran *walk* (od *step*) *somewhat nearer* ‖ ~ an (etw) *to draw to* (*the table*); *to walk* (*up*) *to* (*a th*); *to approach* (*a th*) ‖ ~ an jdn *to step up to a p*; heimlich ~ an jdn *to sidle up to a p* ‖ ⟨box⟩ scharf ~ an jdn *to press a p closely* **2.** ⟨übtr⟩ ~ an (e–e S) *to embark upon, to set about* (*a task*); *to get down to* (*work*); *to start, tackle* (*a th*); .. planlos (nachlässig) .. *to make a hit-and-miss* (*bits-and-pieces*) *approach to*; man ging an das Problem heran *the p. was approached* (ernstlich *attacked*); wieder ~ an *to return to* (*one's task*) ‖ gehen Sie tüchtig heran (*or* °ran)! *go ahead! go at it hammer and tongs!, go it!* **B.** ≈ n *approach* (an *to*) **≈halten** n: nahes ~ ⟨mil⟩ *close-in location* (*of the reserve*) **~|holen** vt [h] (jdn) *to get along*; jdn ~ an *to bring a p to* (*the phone*) **~|jagen** vi [s] (of a car) *to scurry up* **~|k A.** vi [s] **1.** **(P) a.** *to advance*; *to come on* (od *up*; *along*); *to draw near*; langsam u einzeln ~ *to straggle up*; v allen Seiten ~ *to close in* ‖ (of ship) nahe ~ *to come alongside*; (P) (an jdn) *to run a p close* ⟨a. fig⟩ **b.** ~ an jdn *to get to a p*; *to come* (od *draw*) *up to a p*; man kann an ihn nicht ~ *he is unapproachable*; *he's a hard man to see*; ⟨übtr⟩ *he is elusive*; näher ~ an .. *to gain on a p* ‖ ~ an (etw) *to get near* (*a place*); auf einige Meter an jds Tisch ~ *to come to within a few meters of a p's* *table* ‖ ∼ an etw *to come by* (od *to get at*) *a th*; *to get down to a th*; an ein Ideal ∼ ⟨Am⟩ *to measure up to an ideal*; → –reichen ‖ ⟨mar⟩ an den Wind ∼ *to close the wind* ‖ er kommt jährlich an 10000 Mark heran *he touches 10000 marks a year* **2.** (**S**) *to advance*; *to come up* (v *from*); *to come on* (*her illness came on suddenly*); *to draw on*; die Nacht kam heran *night closed in* **F** (of events, time) *to come* (od *roll*) *round* (*when his birthday came round*) ‖ nahe an e–e Zahl ∼ *to equal a number* ‖ die Dinge an sich ∼ l *to let what's coming to one come* ‖ laß doch die S an dich ∼ *don't worry*; *wait for sth to turn up* **B.** ≈ n *approach* °∼|**kriegen** vt [h] jdn ∼ *to get a p to work*; *to buttonhole a p* °∼|**lotsen** vt [h] ⟨fam⟩ *to give* (*the salt*) *a fair wind* °∼|**m** vrefl [h] sich ∼ an (etw) *to apply o.s. to* (*a meal*); *to set one's hand to* (*a task*); *to get* (od *settle*, *sit*) *down to* (*one's work*); *to set* (od *go*) *about*, *to set to work on* (*a problem*); *to start* (od *venture*) *on* (*a th*) | sich ∼ an jdn *to approach* od *accost* ⟨a. pol⟩, *to make up to*, (v der Seite) *to edge up to a p* ‖ ⟨dero⟩ *to force o.s. upon a p* ∼|**nahen 1.** vi [s] *to approach*; *to draw near* **2.** ≈ n *approach* °∼|**nehmen** vt [h] ⟨school & sport⟩ jdn ∼ *to put a p on* ∼|**pirschen** vrefl [h] ⟨hunt⟩ sich ∼ an *to stalk* (*a stag*) ∼|**reichen** vi [h] **a.** ∼ bis an *to come up to*; *to reach to* .. (*the ceiling*); *to touch* ‖ *to reach down to* (*the canal*) **b.** ⟨übtr⟩ ∼ an *to equal* od *touch* (*a th*, *a p*); an das Niveau ∼ *to be up to the level*; nicht ∼ an .. *not to be in the same street with*, ⟨Am sl⟩ *to have nothing on a p* ‖ er reicht an s–n Vater als .. nicht heran *he is not up to his father as a scholar*; niemand kann an ihn ∼ *nobody can touch him* ∼|**reifen** vi [s] = –wachsen ∼|**reiten** vi [s] an jdn ∼ *to ride up to a p* ∼|**rollen** vi [s] (of cars) *to come along*; *to roll up* ∼|**rücken** vt/i **1.** vt [h] (Stuhl) *to draw* (od *hitch*, *move*) *up* (an *to*) **2.** vi [s] *to advance*; *to approach*; *to draw near* ∼|**rufen** vt [h] (jdn; ein Auto) *to hail* ∼|**schaffen** vt [h] (etw) = herbei– ∼|**schlängeln** vrefl [h] sich ∼ *to sidle up* (an *to*) ∼|**schleichen** vi [s] (sich) ∼ an jdn *to steal upon*; *to slip* od *sidle up to*; ⟨Am⟩ *to creep up on a p* ∼|**setzen** vrefl [h] sich z jdm an e–n Tisch ∼ *to join a p at table* ∼|**springen** vi [s] *to rush along*; er kam –gesprungen *he came rushing along* ∼|**strömen** vi [s] ⟨fig⟩ *to flock* (*to do sth*); v allen Seiten ∼ *to be pouring from every side* ∼|**tasten** vrefl [h] sich ∼ an *to grope* od *feel one's way to*(*wards*) .. ∼|**treten** vi [s] *to advance* ‖ ∼ an jdn *to approach a p*, *a purchaser*; *to get on to*; *to step* (od *march*) *up to a p*; (um Hilfe) *to resort to a p* ∼|**wachsen** vi [s] *to adolesce* ‖ ∼ z *to grow to* (*be*[*come*] *a great man*); sie wuchsen z gesunden Knaben heran *they grew up* (od *they grew to be*) *healthy boys* ∼**wachsend** a *adolescent*; *rising* (*generation*) ∼|**wagen** vrefl [h] sich ∼ an *to venture near* .. ∼|**ziehen** vt/i **1.** vt [h] **a.** (Stuhl) *to draw* (⟨Am fam⟩ *pull*) *up* od *nearer* (an *to*; f *for*); *to bring closer* (*to*) ‖ (etw) mühsam ∼ *to drag*; *lug*; *trail* **b.** ⟨übtr⟩ *to consult* (*a doctor*; *a book*); *to go back to*; *to draw upon* (*a source*); *to have recourse to* (*means*) ‖ jdn ∼ *to engage* (od *enlist*) *a p*; *to ask a p in* (als .. *as a consultant*); *to summon a p* (z etw *to a th*); weibliche Hilfe ∼ *to draw upon female labour*; (Kräfte) *to mobilize* ‖ (Worte jds) *to quote* (*much-appropriated remark*) **2.** vi [s] *to draw near* ≈**ziehung** f *consultation*; *enlistment* (*of a p*) ‖ unter ∼ s–r Erfahrungen *in the light of his experiences*

H·erauch m ∼(e)s/ *haze*, *peat-smoke*

her·auf adv: die Treppe ∼ *up the stairs*, *upstairs* ‖ ∼ mit euch! *come upstairs at once*! ‖ v unten ∼ *from below* **her·auf-** pref [betont, bei Verben trennbar] *up* (*here*); *upwards*; *upstairs*; ⟨bes fig⟩ (f hinauf–) ∼|**arbeiten** vrefl [h] ⟨fig⟩ sich ∼ *to work* od *fight one's way up* (z *to*); *to rise from the ranks* ∼|**bemühen** vt [h] (jdn) ∼ *to trouble of coming up* ‖ sich ∼ *to trouble to come up*; wollen Sie sich nicht ∼? *won't you please come up*? ∼|**beschwören** vt [h] **1.** (Geister) *to conjure up* **2.** ⟨fig⟩ (im Geiste) *to conjure up* ‖ *to bring about* (od *on*), *to suggest*; (e–e Krise) *to precipitate*; (Streit) *to work up*; sein Unglück ∼ *to ride for a fall*; den Zorn jds ∼ *to bring a p's wrath down* (auf *upon*) °∼|**bitten** vt [h]: jdn ∼ (l) *to ask a p* (*to come*) *up* (*to one's room*) ∼|**bringen** vt [h] *to bring up* ∼|**dämmern** vi [s] ⟨fig⟩ *to dawn* ∼|**dringen** vi [s] (of sounds) *to arise*; *to come* (aus *from*); v unten ∼ *to come from below* ∼|**führen** vt [h] (jdn) *to lead up* ∼|**k** vi [s] *to come up*(*stairs*) ‖ den Berg ∼ *to come up the hill*; die Treppe ∼ *to c. up the stairs* ‖ die Straße ∼ *to come along* (od *up*) *the street* ‖ jdn ∼ l *to show* od *have a p up* | ⟨übtr⟩ (of storm) = –steigen ∼|**rasen** vi [s] –gerast k *to come dashing up here* ∼**rufen** vt [h] *to call up* (⟨a. fig⟩ *old memories*) ∼|**reichen** vt [h] (Teller bei Tisch) *to pass up* ∼|**schnellen** vi [s] (of speed) ∼ z *to run up to* ∼|**schwanken** vi [s]: die Treppe ∼ *to stagger up the stairs* ∼|**setzen** vt [h]: er wurde zwei Plätze –gesetzt *he went up two places* ‖ (Preise) *to raise*; *to advance* ∼|**steigen** vi [s] **1.** (Berg, Treppe) *to come up*; *to mount*; *ascent* **2.** ⟨fig⟩ (of storm) *to approach*; *to come on*; *to draw near*; (of clouds) *to stalk up*; ∼ aus *to come* (od *emanate*, *emerge*) *from* ‖ (of dangers) *to spring up* ‖ ein neuer Tag stieg herauf *a new day dawned* ∼|**stimmen** vt [h] ⟨mus⟩ *to raise the pitch of* .. ‖ ⟨fig⟩ (stärken) *to tone up* ∼|**stolpern** vi [s] die Treppe ∼ *to stumble up the stairs* ∼|**ziehen A.** vt/i **1.** vt [h] (etw) *to pull up* ‖ er zog ihn z sich herauf *he drew him up to him* ‖ ⟨fig⟩ jdn z sich ∼ *to lift a p up to one's own level* **2.** vi [s] ⟨fig⟩ *to approach*; ein Unwetter zieht herauf *a storm is brewing* **B.** ≈ n *approach* (*of a storm*)

her·aus adv (°raus) **a.** *out*; der Splitter ist ∼ *the splinter is out*; das Buch (Gesetz) ist ∼ *the book* (*law*) *has come out* ‖ ob er .. gesehen hatte oder nicht, war noch nicht ∼ *whether or no he had seen .. was not yet established* | °ich muß hier ∼ *I must get out of here* ‖ ⟨fig⟩ °fein ∼ s *to be in clover* (od *on velvet*); *to be well off* **b.** gerade ∼, frei ∼ *right out*, *outright*; *openly*, *bluntly*; ⟨fam⟩ *flat* **c.** aus dem Fenster ∼ *from* (od *out of*) *the window* ‖ es ist ein Stück aus dem Glase ∼ *there is a chip out of the glass* ‖ aus dem Hafen ∼ s *to be free of the harbour* ‖ aus dem Innern des Landes ∼ *from within the country*; aus den Reihen des Adels ∼ *from within the nobility* ‖ aus der Tiefe e–s Gefühls ∼ *from the depth of a feeling* ‖ aus sich ∼ (*to do sth*) *on one's own* ‖ die Haltung, aus der ∼ man der Situation Herr wurde *the attitude which mastered the situation* | nach vorn ∼ *in front*; Zimmer im 3. Stock nach vorn ∼ *three-pair front*; .. nach hinten ∼ *three-pair back* | v innen ∼ *from within* **d.** ∼! *out*! ∼ mit ..! *out with* ..! ∼ mit der Sprache! ∼ damit! *speak out*!, *come across* (*with it*)!; ⟨fam⟩ *spit it out*!, ⟨Am fam⟩ *own up*!; ∼ mit dir! *get* (*the hell*) *out of here*! **her·aus-** pref [betont, bei Verben trennbar] *out*; [oft ⟨übtr & fig⟩ f hinaus–] ∼|**arbeiten** vt [h] **1.** (Figur) ∼ aus .. *to carve out of* (*the rock*); *to hew out in* (*the rock*) ‖ (das Gerippe an Tieren) *to skeletonize* | ⟨fig⟩ (Gedanken, etc) *to beat* (od *knock*, *thrash*, *work*) *out*; (Methode) *to hammer out* ‖ mühsam ∼ *to evolve*, *elaborate*; *enucleate*; *quarry* (aus *out of* ..) **2. sich** ∼ **aus** *to work one's way out of*; *to work out of* ..; (mühsam) *to extricate o.s. from* (*the snow*); *to disentangle from* .. ∼|**beißen** vt [h] **1.** ⟨eig⟩ (Stück) *to bite out*; ∼ aus .. *to bite out of* .. **2.** °⟨fig⟩ jdn ∼ *to get a p cleverly out of a scrape* ‖ er beißt z sehr den Vorgesetzten heraus *he comes the superior too much*; *he is too bossy*; er beißt gern den V. heraus *he likes to play the principal* **3. sich** ∼ *to fight bravely*; er hat sich –gebissen *he has worked his way out of the mess* ∼|**bek** vt [h]

1. ⟨eig⟩ (Nagel) *to get out*; ~ aus *to draw out of* (*the wood*) ‖ Geld ~ *to get money back in exchange*; *to get one's change*; wir bek eine Mark heraus *we get a mark change*; hier ist das Geld, das Sie ~ *here is your change* **2.** ⟨übtr⟩ **a.** (schwierige Aufgabe) *to puzzle out*; *to solve* ‖ (entziffern) *to spell .. out* ‖ *to find* (od *make*) *out*; *to get to the bottom* (od *in the way*) *of*; *to trace*; ~, daß etw ist *to find a th to be* **b.** etw ~ aus jdm *to elicit a th from a p*; ein Geheimnis aus jdm ~ *to worm a secret out of a p*; nichts aus jdm ~ *to get no change out of a p*; ich kann aus dem Kind nichts ~ *I can't get anything out of the child* **~|bemühen** vt [h] jdn ~ *to trouble a p to come out*; sich ~ *to take the trouble to come out* **~|bilden** vt [h] ⟨arts⟩ *to form, shape* **~|bitten** vt [h] jdn ~ *to ask a p to come out* **~|bringen** vt [h] **1.** ⟨eig⟩ (jdn) *to bring out*; (an die frische Luft ~) *to take out* ‖ (Tier aus dem Lager) ⟨Am⟩ *to bolt* | er brachte alles wieder heraus, was .. *he brought back* (od *up*) *all* (*he had eaten*) ‖ (Nagel) = –bek ‖ (Flecke) *to remove*; *to take out* **2.** ⟨übtr com⟩ (Handelsartikel) *to market*; *to turn out* ‖ ⟨theat⟩ (Stück) *to bring* (⟨Am a.⟩ *put*) *out*; *to produce*; wieder ~ ⟨film⟩ *to reissue*; hervorragend –gebracht *fittingly featured* ⟨a. typ⟩ ‖ (Buch) *to bring out*; *to give* (od *put*) *forth*; *to publish* ‖ (Worte) *to utter, to express*; (hastig) *to bolt*; donnernd ~ *to thunder* ‖ ich bring's nur nicht heraus ⟨Am⟩ *I just can't put it across* ‖ (Tatsachen) *to bring* (od *get, sift*, [mühsam] *work*) *out*; *to elicit, extract* (aus jdm *from a p*) **3.** ≃ n (neuer Typen) ⟨bes mot⟩ *styling* **~|drängen** vt [h] (jdn) *to shoulder .. out*; *to oust* (aus *from*) **~|drücken** vt [h] (die Brust) *to stick out* °**~|ekeln** vt [h] jdn ~ aus .. *to worry a p out of* (*the room*) ‖ ⟨Am⟩ *to freeze out* **~|fahren** vi [s] **1.** *to come out* (im Omnibus *by bus*); *to drive, sail out* (aus *of*) **2.** ⟨fig⟩ das Wort war ihm nur so –ge– *the word has escaped him*; *he had blurted out the word*; *it was a slip of the tongue* **~|fallen** vi [s] *to fall out*; ~ aus *to fall out of ..* **~|finden** vt [h] **1.** (etw) *to ascertain*; *discover*; *to find* (od *make, pick*) *out*; *to spot, trace*; ⟨Am sl⟩ *tab*; ⟨math etc⟩ *to figure out*; ~, daß .. *to ascertain that*; ~, daß etw ist *to find a th to be* ‖ den Sinn e–r S ~ *to get the hang of a th*; man kann es nicht ~ *there is no way of telling* **2. sich** ~ *to find one's way out*; sich ~ aus *to f. one's w. out of*; = –winden ≃**forderer** m *challenger* **~|fordern** vt [h] **1.** (jdn) *to challenge, defy, provoke* (z *to*) ‖ jdn zum Kampf, Zweikampf ~ *to challenge a p*; *to call a p out*; *to square up to a p*; *to throw down the glove to a p*; ich fordere dich deswegen z K. heraus *I'll fight you for this* **2.** ⟨übtr⟩ (Kritik) *to invite*; Theorie, die z Kritik –fordert *theory open to much criticism* ‖ das Schicksal, die Vorsehung ~ *to defy Providence, to fly in the face of P.* ‖ die Welt ~ *to cry defiance to the world* ‖ *to ask* (od *look*) *for* (*trouble*), ⟨Am sl⟩ *to ask for it* ‖ *to tempt, court* (*disaster, trouble, fate*) **3.** [abs] zum Widerspruch ~ *to be provocative* **~fordernd 1.** [a] *defiant*; *provocative*; in ~er Art *p.ly* ‖ z Widerspruch ~ *p.* (*speech*) ‖ e–e ~e Haltung einnehmen ⟨Am sl⟩ *to have a chip on one's shoulder* **2.** [adv] *defiantly*; *p.ly*; jdn ~ ansehen *to quiz a p* ‖ ~ auftreten *to ask for trouble*; *to trail one's coat* ‖ jdn ~ fragen *to demand of a p* ‖ es wirkt ~ *it is asking for trouble* (*to do*) ≃**forderung** f **1.** (jds ~) *challenge* (z *to*); *defiance, provocation* (*to*); ohne ~ *unprovoked* (*insult*) ‖ ~ zum Zweikampf *ch.*; die ~ annehmen *to take up the gauntlet* od *glove*; *to accept the ch.* ‖ (Frechheit) *effrontery* **2.** *ch., irritant* (e–r S *to a th*); *defiance* (*of fate*) **~|fühlen** vt [h] (etw) *to feel, sense*; *twig* **~füttern** vt [h] *to feed up* ≃**gabe** f **1.** *delivering, –ry*; → Rückgabe **2.** *editing* (*of a book*) ‖ ⟨com⟩ *bringing out*; *publication* (*of a book*); → Ausgabe **~|geben** vt/i [h] **A.** vt **1.** (etw) *to deliver, hand* (jdm *to a p*); → zurückgeben **2.** (Zeitung) *to run*; (Buch) *to edit*; *publish* ⟨a. com⟩ **B.** vi: er konnte nicht ~ *he could not give any change*; *he had no small ch.*; geben Sie mir auf 10 Mark heraus *give me ch. for 10 marks* ≃**geber** m *editor* (*of a book, etc*); als ~ e–r Zeitschrift fungieren *to edit a periodical*; Amt e–s ~s *editorship* ‖ → Verleger ≃**geberin** f *editress* **~|gehen** vi [s] ⟨übtr⟩ **a.** (of *stains*) *to come out* **b.** (P) aus sich ~ *to come out of one's shell*; *to expand, thaw, unbend*; ⟨Am⟩ *to loosen up* **~|greifen** vt [h] ⟨übtr⟩ (Beispiele) *to choose*; *to take* (v *from*); um nur ein Beispiel –zu– *to cite but one instance* **~|gucken** vi [h] *to peer out*; ⟨Am a.⟩ *to peek out* **~|h** vt [h] (Aufgabe) *to have got out*; → –bek ‖ °⟨übtr⟩ er hatte es endlich heraus *he had got the idea*; *he had got the hang of it* ‖ den Kniff (*or* e–e S, etc) ~ *to have got the knack of a th*; *to have a th at one's finger's ends* **~|hängen** vt/i [h] **1.** vt (Fahne) *to hang* (od *put*) *out* **2.** vi; es hängen viele Fahnen heraus *flags fly from many houses* ‖ °es hängt mir z Halse heraus *I am disgusted with it, I am sick of it* **~|hauen** vt [h] **1.** (Figur) ~ aus *to carve out of* (*the rock*); *to hew out in* (*the rock*) **2.** °jdn ~ aus *to extricate* (od *disentangle*) *a p out of ..* **~|heben** vt [h] **1.** ⟨eig⟩ (etw) *to lift out*; ~ aus *to lift out of ..* ‖ (jdn) *to hand* (od *help*) *out*; ~ aus *to help out of* (*the car*) **2.** ⟨übtr⟩ (etw) *to bring out in relief*; *to relieve*; *to set off* (auf .. *against a background*) ‖ ⟨fig⟩ *to single out* (als *as*); ~ aus *to lift* (od *raise, single*) *out of* (*a phere, a company*); → hervor– | **sich** ~ *stand out* (als *as*; auf .. *against a background*); sich ~ aus *to stand out among*; sich aus der Masse ~ *to rise out of the ruck* **~|helfen** vi [h] (jdm) *to help out*; ~ aus *to help* (od *hand*) *out of* (*a car*); jdm aus e–r Schwierigkeit ~ *to pull a p through* **~|holen** vt [h] **1.** ⟨eig⟩ (etw) *to draw* (od *get*) *out*; *to extract*; ~ aus *to get from* (od *out of*); *to draw* (od *fish*) *out from* (*one's pockets*) ‖ (of dogs) (Fuchs aus dem Bau) *to bolt* **2.** ⟨übtr⟩ **a.** (etw) *to extract*; *to get* od *pick out* (aus e–r S *from a th*); (mühsam) *to quarry* (*out of ..*); den vollen Gehalt aus etw ~ *to get* (*the*) *full value out of a th* ‖ ⟨ten⟩ e–e 5–1-Führung ~ *to go into a 5–1 lead* **b.** *to educe*; *extract, elicit, get* (aus jdm *out of a p*); (auf Umwegen) *to worm* (*out of a p*); das Äußerste *or* Letzte aus jdm ~ *to get the utmost* (od *best*) *out of a p* **~|hören** vt [h] ⟨a. fig⟩ *to be receptive to* (*a tone, etc*) °**~|kehren** vt [h] den Vorgesetzten ~ → –beißen 2. **~klappbar** a *folded* (*crank, page*) °**~|knobeln** vt [h] ⟨sl⟩ *to nut out* **~|k** vi [s] **1.** (mst P) *to come out*; *to emerge* (*from*); *to get out* (od *away*) ‖ ~ aus *to come out from* (*the gate*); *to come out of* (*the room*); er freute sich aus London –zu– *he was glad to get out of L.* ‖ ⟨übtr⟩ es kam h., daß *it developed that* **2.** ⟨übtr⟩ **a. aus** e–r Schw. ~ *to get out of a difficulty*; → Lachen ‖ **mit** etw ~ *to come out with a th* ‖ aus sich ~ = –gehen ‖ °wir sind (in der Lotterie) wieder nicht –ge– *once more, our ticket has not been drawn* **b.** (of a book, secret) *to come out*; neu –ge– *just published* ‖ (of facts) *to emerge* ‖ ⟨math⟩ es kommt immer dasselbe heraus *the result is always the same* **3.** ⟨fig⟩ was kommt **dabei** heraus? *what's the unse of it?* ‖ es kam nichts dabei heraus *nothing came* (*out*) *of it*; bei diesen Erörterungen kommt nichts heraus *these discussions don't lead anywhere*; nichts kam bei diesen Bemühungen heraus *nothing came of these efforts* ‖ bei dem Geschäft kommt nichts heraus *the transaction will not pay* ‖ das kommt alles **auf** eins heraus *that comes to exactly the same th*; *it is all the same* (*in the end*) ‖ (P) ~ auf: *the child threw back to his grandparents* °**~|kriegen** vt [h] (Flecke) *to remove* (aus *from*) ‖ ⟨übtr⟩ etw ~ *to find a th out*; (Wahrheit) *to elicit* (aus *from*) ‖ (Tönung) *to hit off* (*the right shade*) **~|l** vt [h] (etw, jdn) *to let out*; (jdn) ~ aus *to let out of*

(*prison*) **~|kristallisieren** vrfl [h] ⟨fig⟩ sich ~ *to become clear* **~|lesen** vt [h] *to read* (Erwünschtes *the desired conclusions*); (Sinn) *to deduce, obtain* **~|locken** vt [h] (jdn) ~ aus *to allure* (od *draw, entice*) *from* (od *out of*) ‖ (etw) *to elicit* (od *worm*) *from* od *out of* (*a p*); *to get out of* (*a p*) **~|lösen** vt [h] (Knochen) ⟨cul⟩ *to remove, free*; *to bone* (*meat*) **~|lügen** vrefl [h] sich ~ aus .. *to lie o.s. out of* .. **~|m** vt [h] (Flecke) *to remove* (aus *from*) | °**sich** ~ (nach Krankheit) *to pick up, to recover* ‖ er hat sich sehr –gemacht *he has come on tremendously*; .. *developed wonderfully*; .. *done splendidly* **~|manövrieren** vt [h] ⟨a. fig⟩ (jdn) *to manoeuvre out of* .. **≈nahme** f ⟨surg⟩ *enucleation* (*of a tumour*) **~|nehmen** vt [h] **1.** ⟨eig⟩ (etw) *to extract*; *to take out*; *unload*; ~ aus *to extract from*; *to take from* od *out of* (*a trunk*) ‖ ⟨surg⟩ (Mandeln) *to enucleate*; s–e M. wurden –genommen *his tonsils came out*; **sich** [dat] die Mandeln ~ l *to have one's tonsils out* ‖ du kannst dir zwei ~ *you may take two for yourself* (od *your own*) **2.** ⟨übtr⟩ **sich** [dat] etw ~ *to assume a th*, sich Freiheiten ~ gegenüber jdm *to make* (od *be*) *free with a p*; *to take liberties with a p*; sich zuviel ~ auf Grund e–r S *to presume on a th* ‖ sich ~ z tun *to make* (od *be*) *bold to do*; *to presume to do* **3.** ≈ n *unloading* (d. Films) **~|platzen** vi [s] **1.** ~ mit (etw) *to burst* od *come out with* (*a th*) ‖ mit der Wahrheit ~ *to blurt out the truth*; *to shoot out* (*a question*); *to rap out* (*an oath*) **2.** [abs] *to burst* (od *rap, rattle*) *out*; *to explode, flare* ‖ ‚Eine dumme S', platzte er heraus. '*Silly business', he exploded* ‖ vor Lachen ~ *to burst out laughing, to burst with l.* °**~|poltern** vi/t **1.** vi [s] ⟨übtr⟩ (of words) *to tumble out*; = –platzen **2.** vt [h] (Sätze) *to bark* (od *rap, rattle*) *out*; → –platzen mit **~|posaunen** vt [h] (Worte) *to roll out* **~|pressen** vt [h] (Saft) *to squeeze* (*out*); ~ aus *to press* (od *squeeze*) *from* (od *out of*) ‖ ⟨übtr⟩ (Geständnis, Versprechen) ~ aus .. *to extort* (od *extract, force, screw, wrest, wring*) *from* (od *out of*) *a p*; *to force out* **~|putzen** vt [h] **1.** (jdn) *to bedizen*; *to turn out*; *to dress up to the nines*; *to doll* (od *get*) *up*; *to deck* (od *trick*) *out*; *to prink*; *to smarten up*; *to tit(t)ivate*; ⟨sl⟩ *to tog* ‖ (etw) *to deck*; *decorate*; *to smarten up* **2. sich** ~ *to get o.s. up, to bedizen* (*preen, prink, tit*[*t*]*ivate*) *o.s.*; *to doll* od *smarten up*; *to put on frills* ‖ sich aufs äußerste ~ *to dandify o.s. up to a pitch of completeness* ‖ –ge–zt ⟨Am fam⟩ *fussed up* **~|ragen** vi [h] *to project* (über *over*); = hervorragen **~|reden** vrefl [h] sich ~ *to invent excuses*; = Ausreden m **~|reißen** vt [h] **1.** (etw) *to pull* (od *rip*) *out*; (Blatt) *to tear out*; ~ aus *to tear from* (od *out of*) ‖ (of bombs) (Fensterrahmen) *to wrench out* ‖ ⟨mar⟩ die Feuer ~ *to draw the fires* ‖ (Land) ~ aus *to jerk out of* **2.** (Pflanze) mit der Wurzel ~ *to root up*; *to tear up by the roots*; *to uproot* ‖ jdn aus dem heimatlichen Boden ~ *to uproot a p from his soil* ‖ ⟨fig⟩ das hat ihn –gerissen *that* (*has*) *saved him* °**~|rücken** vi/t **1.** vi [s] ~ aus *to move out of* .. ‖ ⟨übtr⟩ ~ mit *to come out with* (*the truth*); *to disclose* ‖ mit der Sprache ~ *to speak one's mind*; *to sp. out*; ⟨sl⟩ *to come clean*; nicht mit der Sp. ~ *to withhold one's opinion*; *to beat about the bush*; ⟨dero⟩ *to hedge* ‖ mit dem Gelde ~ *to come down with the m.*; ⟨sl⟩ *to shell out* (od *peel off*) *one's m.*; ⟨sl⟩ *to shell* (od *fork*) *out* **2.** vt [h] sein Geld ~ = mit dem G. ~ ‖ widerwillig e–n Dollar ~ *to screw out a d.* ‖ den letzten Pfennig ~ ⟨sl⟩ *to fork out one's last 'pfennig'* **~|rufen** vt [h] ⟨mil⟩ *to turn out* (*the guard*) ‖ ⟨theat⟩ (Schauspieler) *to call for*; *to summon* (od *call*) *before the curtain*; er wurde sechsmal –ge– ⟨fam⟩ *he took six curtains*; (Schüler) *to call* .. *to the front* °**~|rutschen** vi [s] → entfahren **~|sagen** vt [h] (etw) glatt ~ *to tell bluntly*; s–e Meinung offen ~ *to speak one's mind freely, to have ths straight out*; sag es frei heraus ⟨sl⟩ *spit it out* ‖ rund –gesagt, ich kann nicht .. *to speak plainly, I cannot* ..; das ist rund –gesagt *that is flat* **~|schälen** vt [h] ⟨übtr surg⟩ (Geschwulst) *to enucleate* ‖ ⟨fig⟩ (Sinn) *to enucleate*; *to lay bare* (od *open*) (aus *from*); *to clear up* **~|schauen** vi [h] **1.** = –sehen **2.** ⟨fig⟩ °es schaut nichts dabei heraus = es kommt nichts .., → –k °**~|schießen** vi [s] ⟨fig⟩ (P) ~ aus *to pop* (od *rush, tear*) *out of* (*a door*) **~|schlagen** vt/i **1.** vt [h] (Funken) ~ aus .. *to strike from* (*the stone*) | ⟨übtr⟩ Geld, Gewinn ~ aus .. *to make m. by*; *to profit by a th*; *to make a profit on a th* ‖ ⟨sl⟩ *to wangle* ‖ möglichst viel ~ aus .. *to make the most of a th*; .. wollen *to be looking for a big penny for a little ha'penny* ‖ die Kosten ~ *to get paid for one's expenses* ‖ (Vorteile) *to gain*; *get, obtain* (f *for*); möglichst viel ~ f jdn *to get the best possible terms for a p* **2.** vi [s] die Flammen schlugen zum Dach heraus *the flames burst throught the roof* **~|schmeißen** vt [h] ⟨eig⟩ hinaus– *to throw* od *cast out*; aus e–m Lokal –ge–missen w ⟨sl⟩ *to hit the pavement* ‖ jdn (fristlos entlassen) ⟨fam⟩ *to fire a p* **~|schmettern** vt [h] (of an organ) (Töne) *to roll forth* ‖ (Worte) *to roll* (od *shoot*) *out*; → –poltern **~|schneiden** vt [h] ⟨surg⟩ (Gewächs) *to snip out* (aus *of*) **~|sehen** vi [h] aus dem Fenster ~ *to look out of the w.* °**~|setzen** vt [h] (jdn) = hinaus– **~|springen** vi [s] **1.** *to jump out* (aus *of*) **2.** (S) **a.** = hervorspringen **b.** °⟨fig⟩ nichts Gutes wird dabei ~ *no good will come of it*; es springt nichts dabei heraus *there is not much* (od *no profit*) *in it*; *it will not pay* **~|sprudeln** vt [h] ⟨übtr⟩ (Worte) *to spit forth* (od *out*) (gegen *at*); *to sputter* **~|stammeln** vt [h] (Worte) *to stutter out* **~|stecken** vt [h] (Kopf) *to put out* (aus *of*); (schnell) *to pop out of* (*the window*); –gesteckt w *to pop* (aus *out of*) (*heads were popping out of the w.*) ‖ (Zunge) *to put* (od *shoot, stick*) *out* (jdm *at a p*) **~|stehen** vi [h] = hervor– **~|stellen** vt [h] **1.** ⟨eig⟩ = hinaus– **2.** ⟨übtr⟩ **a.** ⟨sport⟩ (Spieler) *to turn out* ‖ (etw) gr ~ *to play up, dramatize, highlight*; *to make* .. *a feature*; (in Zeitung) *to headline* ⟨a. fig⟩, *to give publicity to* .. **b.** (Gedanken etc) *to bring* (od *pick, point*) *out*; *to emphasize*; *to set forth* od *off* (gegen *against*); klar ~ *to bring to prominence*; *to hit off* **3.** ⟨fig⟩ **sich** ~ (of remarks, events) *to prove*; *to turn out*; *to become clear*; die Behauptung stellte sich als wahr, als ein Irrtum heraus *the statement proved* od *turned out* (*to be*) *true, a mistake*; es stellte sich heraus, daß er recht hatte *it turned out that he was right*; *he proved* (od *turned out*) *to be right*; *he was proved right*; wie sich später –stellte *in the sequence* **~|stöhnen** vt [h] *to groan* vt **~|stoßen** vt [h] ⟨übtr⟩ (Worte wütend) *to come out with* (*an oath*); (ärgerlich) *to say harshly, to hiss*; *to puff out*; (Fluch) *to rap* (od *whip*) *out*; → –poltern, –schmettern, –sprudeln **~|strecken** vt [h] (Zunge) = –stecken **~|streichen** vt [h] ⟨übtr⟩ (jdn, etw) *to extol, praise*; (*be*)*hand*; *to make much of*; ⟨Lit⟩ *to write up* ‖ ⟨fam⟩ *to crack up* ‖ sich selbst ~ *to blow one's own trumpet* | ⟨mst com⟩ *to boom*; *puff*; ⟨Am sl⟩ *to boost* **~|strömen** vi [s] *to pour out* ‖ ⟨übtr⟩ (of people) ~ aus *to pour forth from* (*the church*) **~|stürzen** vi [s] *to rush out* ‖ ~ aus *to fall from* (*the window*); *to pop* (od *rush, whip*) *out of* (*a door*) **~|suchen** vt [h] (etw) *to pick out* (v *from*) **~|treiben** vt [h] = hinaus– **~|treten** **A.** vi [s] **1.** *to come* od *step out*; ~ aus *to come out from* (*a gate*); *to emerge from*; *to step out of* ‖ ⟨fig⟩ aus s–r Zurückhaltung ~ *to burst out of one's shell* **2.** *to protrude*; *to stick out*; (of eyes) *to be staring*; → hervor– ‖ (of stars) *to come out*; (of the moon) *to sail out* **B.** ≈ n *emergence* **~tüfteln** vt [h] *to puzzle out* °**~|tun** vt [h] ⟨übtr⟩ (jdn) = –setzen **~|wachsen** vi [s] ~ aus *to grow from* (*the axil*) ‖ aus s–n Kleidern ~ *to grow out of one's clothes*; *to outgrow one's cl.* ‖ ⟨übtr⟩ *to develop* (aus *from*); *to grow* (*out of* ..); aus armen Verhältnissen ~ *to rise from poor surroundings* ‖ °jdm zum Halse ∼ = –hängen **∼|wagen** vrefl [h] sich ∼ *to venture out* **∼|winden** mst vrefl [h] ⟨übtr⟩ sich ∼ aus *to extricate o.s. from*; *to wriggle, weasel out of* (*a bargain*) **∼wirtschaften** vt [h] (P) *to get .. out* (aus *of*) ‖ (S) sich ∼ l *to yield* **∼|wollen** vi [h] *to want to get out* ‖ nicht mit der Sprache ∼ ⟨fig⟩ *to beat about the bush*; *to withhold one's opinion*; ⟨dero⟩ *to dodge*; *hedge* **∼|ziehen I.** vt [h] **1.** (etw) *to remove*; *to draw* (od *pull*) *out* (aus *from*); (Kork, Zahn) *to extract* ‖ (Nägel) ∼ aus *to draw from* (*the wood*) ‖ (Schlüssel) aus der Tasche ∼ *to take out*; (Messer) *to pull* (od *whip*) *out*; → hervorziehen ‖ (S) (Fleck) *to take out* **2.** (jdn) *to disengage, disentangle, extricate* (aus *from*) **| sich** ∼ **aus** *to e. o.s.* (od *to d., d.*) *from*; *to back out of*; *to wriggle out of* (*a difficulty*); ⟨Am sl⟩ *to crawfish out of* (*a transaction*); sich möglichst gut aus e–r S ∼ *to make the best of a bad bargain* **II.** vi [s] aus Bonn ∼ *to move out of B.*

h·erb(e) A. [a] **1.** (of taste) *harsh, sharp, tart* ‖ *dry* (*wine*) **2.** ⟨übtr⟩ **a.** *bitter, rough* (*wind*); *unpleasant* **b.** *harsh* (*colour*; *odour*) ; *rough* (*voice*); *sour* (*smell*); *grim* (*smile*) **c.** *acrimonious*; *bitter* (*disappointment*; *fate*); *dry* (*facts*); *harsh* (*feelings*; *words*; *punishment*; *system*); *hard, sour* (*time*) ‖ (of style) *austere, plain, severe* **B.** [adv] *harshly*; *bitterly*; *severely* **| ∸heit** f ∼/∼en **1.** *harshness*; *dryness* (*of wine*) **2.** ⟨übtr⟩ *bitterness, roughness*; *sourness*; *hardness, harshness*; *austerity*; *severity* **∼süß** a *bitter-sweet*

Herb·arium n (L) ∼s/–rien [–iən] ⟨bot⟩ *herbarium* L; *herbary*

H·erbe f ⟨poet⟩ = Herbheit

h·er|begeben vrefl [h] sich ∼ *to betake o.s. here*

herb·ei adv ∼, ihr Männer! *come here* (od *on*), *my men*! ‖ schnell ∼ mit dem Wasser! schnell das W. ∼! *bring the water, quick*! ‖ das Geld muß wieder ∼ *the money must be got back* **herb·ei-** pref [betont, bei Verben trennbar] *here, hither*; *near*; *on*; *up* **∼|bringen** vt [h] *to bring*; (jdn) *to bring along* ‖ ⟨übtr⟩ → bei-, vorbringen **∼|eilen** vi [s] *to come* (*up*), *approach in haste*; ⟨Am sl⟩ *to skin up* ‖ zu jds Schutz ∼ *to fly to a p's protection* **∼|führen** vt [h] **1.** (jdn) *to bring, lead up* (od *forward*) **2.** ⟨mst übtr⟩ (etw) *to effect*; *to bring* (*punishment*); *to bring to pass*; *to cause*; *contrive*; (Wechsel) *to engineer*; (Krankheit) *to induce*; *to motivate*; *occasion*; (Krise) *to precipitate*; *produce*; e–e Krise durch etw ∼ *to make a crisis of a th* ‖ *to bring about* (od *on*) ‖ (Einschränkung) *to arrange, provide for*; (Komplikationen) *to make for*; *to work up for* ‖ (Haltung) *to conduce to, to be conducive to*; *to contribute to*; (Entwicklung) *to lead to*; *to give rise* od *occasion to* **∼|holen** vt [h] (jdn) *to bring in* (od *up*); *to fetch*; *to get along*; *to send for* ‖ (jds Hilfe) *to enlist* **∼|k** vi [s] (P) *to advance*; *to come along* (od *on, up*); (schnell) *to brisk* (*up*); *to draw near*; langsam u einzeln ∼ *to straggle up*; v allen Seiten ∼ *to close in*; → heran– **∼|l** vt [h] **1.** (jdn) *to permit to come near* **2.** ⟨mst übtr⟩ sich ∼ z tun *to condescend, deign to do*; sich nicht ∼ z tun *to loathe, refuse, scorn to do*; er konnte sich nicht dazu ∼ .. *he could not find it in his heart to do* **∼|laufen** vi [s] er kam mit .. –ge– *he came running with* (*roses*) **∼|locken** vt [h] → locken, ⟨Am sl⟩ *to rope* (*a p*) *in* **∼|rasen, ∼|rennen** vi [h] *to rush up, scurry up* **∼|rufen** vt [h] jdn ∼ *to call for* (od *to*) *a p*; (Auto) *to hail*; (Arzt) *to summon*; jdn durch Händeklatschen ∼ *to clap one's hands for a p*; e–n Hund durch die Pfeife ∼ *to whistle to a dog* **∼|schaffen** vt [h] (etw) *to bring forward*; *to produce* ‖ (Geld) *to find* (f *for*); *to procure*; das Nötige ∼ f *to forage for* (*a meal*) **∼|sehnen** vt [h] *to yearn to a p*; *wish for a th* **∼|strömen** vi [s] ⟨übtr⟩ in Scharen –ge–mt k *to come together in crowds* ‖ ∼ z *to crowd* (od *flock*) *to* (*a meeting*); ∼ um .. z hören *to flock to hear* .. **∼|winken** vt [h] (jdn) *to beckon, wave*; *signal* **∼|wünschen** vt [h] (etw) *to wish for* **∼|ziehen** vt [h] ⟨fig⟩ e–n Streit an (*or* bei) den Haaren ∼ *to want a pretext to quarrel* ‖ an den H. –gezogen (Beispiel) *far-fetched*

h·er|bek vt [h] [interr & neg] *to get*; *obtain*

h·er|bemühen vt [h] (jdn) ∼ *to trouble a p to come round* ‖ sich ∼ *to trouble to come round*; *to take the trouble of coming round*

H·erberge f ∼/∼n **1.** [konkr] †*inn* ‖ ⟨com⟩ *house of call*; *travellers' rest-house* ‖ ∼ zur Heimat *doss*(*-house*); ⟨Am⟩ *flophouse* **|** Jugend∸ *youth hostel* **2.** ⟨übtr⟩ *refuge, shelter*; *accomodation*; *lodging*; jdm ∼ geben *to accommodate, lodge, shelter a p*; e–r Volksmenge ∼ geben *to house a population* †**h·erbergen** vi/t [h] **1.** vi *to lodge*; *to put up* **2.** vt = beherbergen **H·erbergsmutter** f *housekeeper of a hostel* (etc); *hostess* **H·erbergsvater** m *housekeeper*; *host*

h·er- ∼|bestellen vt [h] jdn ∼ *to bid, ask, order a p round* **∼|beten** vt [h] ⟨ec⟩ *to drone out*; *to gabble*; (Gebet) *to say over monotonously* **∼|bitten** vt [h] jdn ∼ *to ask a p round* **∼|bringen** vt [h] (jdn, etw) *to bring round*; *to bring here* (*what brings you here?*); (v der Hauptstadt her) *to bring down* **|** hergebracht *conventional, customary* ‖ althergebracht *ancient, old*(*-time* [attr]); *time-honoured*; *traditional* (*custom*); *vested* (*privileges*); *well--established*

Herbiz·id n ∼s/∼e *herbicide*; *weed killer*

Herbst m ∼es/∼e **1.** *autumn*; ⟨Am⟩ *fall*; im ∼ *in* (*the*) *a.* ‖ ⟨fig⟩ der ∼ des Lebens *the a. of life* **2.** ⟨× & poet⟩ = Ernte; Weinlese **3.** [in comp] *a.al* (*rains*) **∼abend** m *a. evening* **∼anfang** m *beginning of a.* **∼faden** m = Altweibersommer **∼färbung** f *a. tints* pl ‖ ‖ erste ∼ zeigen (*the leaves, hardly turned as yet, were just promising colour*) **∼ferien** pl ⟨Ger⟩ *a.-holidays* pl **∼laub** n *a. leaves* **|** ∼-farben [f pl] *a. hues* pl **∼luft** f *a.al air* **∼messe** f *a.al fair* **∼monat** m ⟨poet⟩ *harvest-month*; *September* **∼mond** m ⟨poet⟩ *h.-moon* **∼morgen** m *a. morning* **∼nachmittag** m *a. afternoon* **∼rose** f ⟨bot⟩ *a. rose*; *hollyhock* **∼rübe** f ⟨bot⟩ *common turnip* **∼saat** f *sowing of winter corn* **∼semester** n ⟨engl⟩ (Okt. bis Mitte Dez.) *Michaelmas term*; ⟨Am⟩ *fall term* **∼tag** m *a. day* **∼wetter** n, **∼witterung** f *a.*(*al*) *weather* **∼zeit** f *a.*(*-tide*) **∼zeitlose** f ⟨bot⟩ *meadow-saffron*; *a. crocus* L; *colchicum* L **h·erbsten** vi/t [h] **1.** vi es herbstet *a. is approaching* **2.** ×vt = ernten **h·erbstlich** a *autumnal* **H·erbstling** m ⟨bot⟩ *a. fruit*; *a. fungus*

H·erd m ∼(e)s/∼e **1.** ⟨eig⟩ **a.** *hearth*; *fireplace* ‖ Koch∸ *range*; *cooking-stove*, ⟨Am a.⟩ *cook--stove* ‖ Heimchen am ∼ *cricket on the h.* **b.** ⟨hist hunt⟩ Vogel∸ *decoy* **2.** ⟨übtr⟩ *h., home*; *fireside*; *home-life*; am heimischen (*or* häuslichen) ∼ *by the fireside*; *round the family hearth* ‖ e–n eigenen ∼ gründen *to settle down* ‖ ⟨prov⟩ eigener ∼ ist Goldes wert *there is no place like home*; *my house is my castle* **3.** ⟨fig⟩ **a.** ⟨scient, biol & bot⟩ *matrix* **b.** *centre* (*of earth-quake, fire*, etc); *focus* (*of disease, in kidney*); *seat* **∼besen** m *h.-broom* **∼eisen** n *h.-plate* ‖ *poker* **∼feuer** n *ingle* **∼frischarbeit** f ⟨met⟩ *refinery* (od *h.*) *process* **∼frischeisen** n *h. refined iron* **∼frischen** n *open h. refining* **∼frischstahl** m *h. refined steel* **∼geld** n ⟨hist⟩ *h.-money* **∼glühofen** m ⟨met⟩ *nozzle-end of the blower* **∼guß** m *open sand casting* **∼infektion** f ⟨med⟩ *focal infection* **∼ofen** m *h. furnace* **∼rost** m *firegrate* **∼schlacke** f *clinker* **∼stein** m *h.stone* **∼steuer** f ⟨hist⟩ *h.-money*

H·erd- ∼buch n (Rind, Schwein) *herd-book*, ⟨hors⟩ *stud-b.*, (*sheep*) *flock-b.* **H·erde** f ∼/∼n **1.** ⟨allg⟩ *herd* (*of cattle, deer*, etc.); *drove*; *flock* (*of sheep, geese*); e∸e ∼ Rinder *a h. of cattle* ‖ in ∼n gehen *to walk in droves*; *to h.* **2.** ⟨übtr⟩ (P) mst ⟨dero⟩ *crowd, flock, h., mass, multitude, rabble*; (Horde) *raffle*; die gr ∼ *the h., the multitude* ‖ in ∼n gehen *to h. together* ‖ der ∼ folgen *to follow* *the leader* **H·erden-** *herd, gregarious* **≚artig** a *g.* **~geist** m *h.-mind; h.-instinct* **~mensch** m *g. p*; → –tier **~tier** n *g. animal* **~trieb** m *h.-instinct*; *g.ness* **≚weise** adv *in droves* od *herds*; *g.ly*

heredit·är a (erblich) *hereditary*

h·er|eilen vi [s] *to come up in haste*; *to rush up*

her·ein adv (°rein) ∼! *come in*!, ⟨Am⟩ *come*!, *step in*! ‖ immer ∼, m–e Herrschaften! *step up, step up, Ladies and Gentlemen*! ‖ hier ∼ *this way, please* ‖ von außen ∼, v draußen ∼ *from without*; *from out-of-doors*; *from outside* ‖ er durfte nicht ∼ *he was not allowed to enter*; er wollte ∼ *he wanted to come in* **her·ein-** pref [betont, bei Verben trennbar] *in* **~|bek** vt [h] (Gelder) *to get* (od *take*) *in*, (Artikel) *we have just had some in* **~|bemühen** vt [h] jdn ∼ *to trouble a p to come in* ‖ sich ∼ *to trouble to come in*; *to take the trouble of coming in*; wollen Sie sich nicht ∼? *won't you, please, step in*? **~|bitten** vt [h] jdn ∼ (l) *to ask* (od *invite*) *a p* (*to come*) *in* **~|brechen 1.** vi [s] ⟨fig⟩ (of the night, of misery) **a.** *to close in, to draw on*; *to fall* (*night is falling*); (of a storm) *to come on*; *to set in* **b.** ∼ über jdn *to break* (od *close*) *in upon a p*; *to break* (od *burst, come, descend*) *upon a p*; *to sweep over a p*; *to befall* (od *overtake*) *a p*; der Regen brach über uns herein *the rain caught us*; *we were caught in the rain*; *the spendour of the Renaissance had broken upon Italy* ‖ → einbrechen **2.** ≚ n *closing-in*; *coming-on*; ∼ der Nacht *nightfall* **~|bringen 1.** vt [h] (etw, jdn) *to bring in* **2.** ≚ n *the bringing-in* (*of the luggage*) **~|dringen** vi [s] ⟨übtr⟩ (of odour) *to float in* (durch *through*) **~|fallen** vi [s] **1.** ⟨übtr⟩ (of rays) seitwärts ∼ *to slant in* (durch *through* ..) **2.** °⟨fig⟩ *to be done* (od *taken in*; *sold*); *to put one's foot in it*; *to be the loser*; tüchtig ∼ *to get it in the neck*; –ge– s *to be bitten, to have been caught* ‖ glaub nicht, daß sie so leicht –fällt *don't mistake her for an easy mark* ‖ ∼ **auf** .. *to be taken in by*; *to fall* (*blindly*) *into* (*a p's plans*), ⟨Am⟩ *to fall for* (*an idea*); ∼ auf etw *to swallow the bait*; ⟨Am sl⟩ *to fall for* (*a th, a p*); er fiel glänzend darauf herein *he rose at* od *to the bait* (od *he fell for it*) *beautifully* ‖ darauf fall ich nicht herein *that cock won't fight with me* ‖ → Reinfall **~|fluten** vi [s] ⟨a. übtr⟩ (of light) *to flow* (od *pour*) *in*; ⟨fig⟩ → –strömen **~|führen** vt [h] (jdn) *to show* (od *take, usher*) *in*; ∼ in .. *to show into* **≚gabe** f ⟨st exch⟩ *contango, continuation* **~|geben** vt [h] ⟨st exch⟩ (Papiere) *to contango*; *continue*; *to give on* **≚geber** m ⟨st exch⟩ *lender* °**~|hauen** vi [h] tüchtig ∼ *to fall to* [adv]; *to play a good knife and fork* **~|holen** vt [h] jdn ∼ *to have a p in* ‖ ⟨com⟩ Aufträge ∼ *to solicit orders*; *to canvass* **~|k** vi [s] **1.** *to come* (od *get, step, walk*) *in*; ∼ in .. *to come into* ..; ∼ z jdm *to come in to a p*; zur Tür ∼ *to come in at the door* ‖ auf e–n Sprung ∼ *to drop* (od *look, pop*) *in*; ⟨Am a.⟩ *to come by* ‖ nach–e–a ∼ *to file in* ‖ unbemerkt ∼ *to edge* od *slip in* **2.** ⟨übtr⟩ (S) *to come in*; *to come to hand*; *to roll in* ‖ der Zug ist gerade –ge– *the train is just in* **~|l** vt [h] jdn ∼ *to admit a p*; *to let a p in*; (etw, jdn) nicht ∼ *to keep .. out*; sich ∼ (sc ins Haus) *to let o.s. in* ‖ (Luft) *to let in* ‖ °**~|latschen** [aː] vi [s] *to lurch in* **~|laufen** vi [s] *to run in*; –ge– k *to come running in* ‖ herein- u herauslaufen *to pop in and out* °**~|legen** vt [h] ⟨fig⟩ jdn ∼ *to do* (od *jockey, hood-wink, dupe, sell*) *a p*; *to let* (od *take*) *a p in* **~|locken** vt [h] *to rope .. in* °**~|lotsen** vt [h] (jdn) *to entice into coming in*; *to induce to come in* **~|marschieren** vi [s] *to march* od *troop in*; nach-e–a ∼ *to file in*; –rt k *to come trooping in* **≚nahme** f *taking-in*; *discounting* (*of bills*) ‖ ⟨st exch⟩ *backwardation* **~|nehmen** vt [h] *to take in*; *to admit* ‖ (Wechsel) *to discount* ‖ ⟨st exch⟩ (Papiere) *to accept in continuation* **≚nehmer** m *bear, borrower* ‖ **~platzen** vi [s] ⟨fig⟩ *to burst* (od *butt, pop*) *in*; ∼ auf *to barge in on* (*a p*); in *to burst, pop into* (*a room*) ‖ bei jdm ∼ *to burst upon a p* (mit etw *with a th*) **~|regnen 1.** v/imps [h] es regnet herein *it rains in* **2.** vi [h] ⟨fig⟩ *invitations rained in* °**~|reiten** vi [s] jdn ∼ *to let a p down*; *to bring a p to grief*; *to get a p into trouble* ‖ sich ∼ *to come to grief*; *to get o.s. into trouble*; *to ride for a fall* **~|schauen** vi [h] ⟨fig⟩ *to drop* (od *look, pop*) *in* (bei jdm *at a p*); zum Fenster ∼ *to look in at the window* **~|scheinen** vi [h] z Fenster ∼ (of the sun) *to shine in at* od *through the w.* **~|schicken** vt [h] (jdn) *to send in* **~|schneien** vi [h] **1.** v/imps es schneite zum Fenster herein *it snowed in at the w.* **2.** ⟨fig⟩ (⟨a.⟩ –ge–it k) *invitations came snowing in*; *it snowed invitations*; → –strömen, –regnen ‖ (P) ∼, –ge–it k *to blow* (od *butt, pop, breeze, happen, drift, roll*) *in* **~|spazieren** vi [s] ⟨fair⟩ immer –rt! *walk up*! **~|stolzieren** vi [s] *to stalk, march in* **~|strömen** vi [s] *to flow, pour in*; ∼ in *to pour, stream into*; ⟨übtr⟩ (of people) *to crowd, flock, pour into* ..; –ge–mt k *to come pouring in* ‖ zum Fenster ∼ (of light) *to pour, stream in at the w.*; *to roll in*; (of music) *to drift in* ‖ ⟨fig⟩ ∼ auf jdn *to pour in upon a p*; *decorations poured in upon him*; *decorations rained upon him* **~|stürmen** vi [s] ⟨mil⟩ *to charge in*; –ge–mt k *to come charging in* ‖ ⟨fig⟩ ∼ auf jdn (of feelings) *to crowd in upon a p* (*thick and fast*); → –brechen auf **~|stürzen** vi [s] *to pounce* (od *hurtle, rush, shoot*) *in* (aus *from*) **~|treten** vi [s] *to enter*; stolz ∼ *to sail in* °**~|türmen** vi [s] *to amble in* **~|ziehen** vt/i **1.** vt [h] (jdn) zur Tür ∼ *to draw in by* od *through the door* **2.** vi [s] zum Tor ∼ *to march in through the gate*

h·er- ~|erzählen vt [h] (etw) *to rehearse*; *to relate in detail*; *to drone*; *to tell droningly* **~|fahren** vi [s] ich bin –ge– *I drove here*; *I came* od *got here* ‖ °⟨übtr⟩ ∼ über .. = herfallen **≚fahrt** f *journey back* **~|fallen** vi [s] **1.** ∼ über jdn **a.** *to fall* (*descend, pounce, rush, spring, set*) *upon*; *to fall foul of*; *to swoop down upon*; *to pitch into*; ⟨fam⟩ *to set about a p* **b.** ⟨übtr⟩ (heruntermachen) *to come down upon*; *to fall* (od *jump*; *pounce*) *upon*; *to fly at*; *to go for*; *to round on*; *to pitch* (⟨sl⟩ *to walk*) *into a p* **2.** über ein Land ∼ *to overrun a country* **3.** über sein Frühstück ∼ *to fall upon one's b.*; ⟨sl⟩ *to walk into one's b.*; er fiel über das Essen her *he fell* (od *set*) *to* [adv] *with a good appetite* **~|finden** vi & vrefl [h] (sich) ∼ *to find one's way* (*he could not find his w.*) **≚fracht** f *home* (od *inward*) *freight* **~|führen** vt [h] (jdn) *to bring here* (⟨poet & bib⟩ *hither*) **≚gang** m *the circumstances* pl ‖ *happening, occurance*; erzähle mir den ∼ *tell me what happened*; *give me an account of it*; im einzelnen *tell me the details* **~|geben** vt [h] (etw) *to give* (*away*); *to give up* (*two sons*); *to part with* (*a th*); *to surrender* ‖ wieder ∼ *to give back*; *to return* ‖ *to lend* (*one's name*) (zu *to*) ‖ der Stoff gibt nicht mehr her als e–e Bluse *the m. is only sufficient for a bl.* | etw f e–e S ∼ *to exchange a* od *one th for another* | **sich** ∼ z etw *to lend o.s. to a th* **~gebracht** a → –bringen **~|gehen** vi [s] **1.** ˣ°geh her *come here*; *come along* ‖ ˣwo wollen wir ∼? *which way shall we go*? ‖ er ging neben s–r Mutter her *he walked at his mother's side*; hinter jdm ∼ *to walk behind a p*; *to follow a p's steps*; *to follow in a p's rear*; vor jdm ∼ *to walk ahead of a p* **2.** °⟨übtr⟩ *to happen* ‖ [mst imps] wie es in Hotels –zu– pflegt *as hotels go*; auf dem Feste ging es viel besser her als .. *the festival went much better than* (*we expected*) ‖ so geht es her in der Welt *that's the way of the world*; *such is life* ‖ da ging es heiß her, → heiß B. ‖ es ging hoch, lustig her *there was plenty of life* (od *gaiety*) → her; es ging toll her *the feeling went high*; *we had a high time of it*; *there were wild goings on* **3.** °∼ über jdn, etw = –fallen über ‖ es ging über ihn her ⟨sl⟩ *they walked into him* **~|gehören** vi → hierher °**~gelaufen** a *alien, foreign*; *from nowhere*; *homeless*; *unknown* ‖ *insignificant*; *nondescript*; *vagabond*; ein ∼er Kerl *a vagabond* (*kind of fellow*); *a p of no account*; irgendein ∼er

Zigeuner *some yellow dog of a gipsy* **~|h** vt → her **~|halten** vt/i [h] **1.** vt (die Hand) *to hold out*; *to stretch forth* ‖ ⟨fig⟩ den Kopf ~ *to suffer*; *to die* **2.** vi, °~ müssen *to have to suffer*; °sein Beutel mußte ~ *he had to foot the bill, he had to pay the piper*; er mußte schon wieder ~ *he served as a butt again* **~|holen** vt [h] (jdn, etw) *to fetch* (aus *from*) ‖ hol ihn her *bring him here*; *get him to come here* ‖ (jdn) ~ l *to send for* ‖ ⟨fig⟩ der Gedanke ist weit –ge–lt *the idea is rather far-fetched* **~|hören** vi [h] *to listen*; *to pay attention* ‖ e–n Augenblick bitte alle ~! *one moment please, everybody*!

H·erero pl (Gruppe der Bantuneger)

H·ering m ~s/~e **1.** ⟨ich⟩ *herring* ‖ grüner ~ *white* od *fresh herring* (gebacken *fried*) ‖ Räucher-≃, geräucherter ~ *red* od *smoked h.* ‖ gesalzener u geräucherter (*or* gedörrter) ~ *kipper*; (.. leicht geräucherter) *bloater* ‖ marinierter, saurer ~ *soused, pickled h.*; Salz≃ *salted h.* ‖ → Brat≃; Matjes≃ ‖ eingepfercht wie (gepökelte) ~e *packed* od *jammed like sardines* od *h.s*; **2.** ⟨übtr⟩ **a.** (Zeltpflock) *tent-peg, deadman* **b.** °(P) er ist der reine ~ *he is as thin as a lath* ‖ wie ein ausgenommener ~ (*lean as* od) *like a shotten h.* od *skinned rabbit* **H·erings-** °**~bändiger** m *counterjumper* **~fang** m *h.-fishery* **~fisch** m → Menhaden **~fischer** m *h.-fisher* **~fischerei** f = –fang **~gräte** f *h.-bone* **~könig** m ⟨ich⟩ (*John*) *dory* **~lake** f *h.-pickle* **~logger** m *h.-drifter* **~schwarm** m *shoal of h.s* **~tonne** f *h.-barrel*

h·er- ~|jagen vi [s] hinter jdm ~ *to run* (⟨fam⟩ *to tear*) *after a p*; *to give chase to a p* **h·er|k** vi [s] **1. a.** (P) komm mal her *come here* (⟨poet & bib⟩ *hither*) **b.** *to come along* (auf der Straße *the road*) **c.** ⟨übtr⟩ ~ v = stammen v **2.** ⟨übtr⟩ (S) ~ v **a.** *to come from*; er wußte nicht, wo das Geld herkam (*or* woher das G. kam) *he did not know where the m. came from* ‖ ⟨telph⟩ *he had no knowledge of the source* od *origin ot the call* **b.** *to arise* (od *spring, derive*) *from* ‖ *to originate in*; *to be due to* (od *caused by*) (*to our negligence*) **| ≃k** n *routine* **1.** (P) = Herkunft 1. **2.** (Brauch) *custom*; *observance*; *tradition*; *usage* **~kömmlich 1.** [a] *c.ary*; *t.al*; *usual*; *conventional* (*weapons*); *normal*; ~er Brauch *observance* **2.** [adv] *t.ally, by convention*

H·erkules ⟨Gr myth⟩ *Hercules* ⟨a. astr⟩; die Arbeiten des ~ *the labours of H.*; ~ am Scheidewege *H.' choice* ‖ ⟨fig⟩ der reine ~ *a regular H.* **~arbeit** f ⟨übtr⟩ e–e ~ *a H–lean labour* od *task* **~käfer** m ⟨ent⟩ *H. beetle* **~keule** f ⟨bot⟩ *H.' club* **~kraut** n ⟨bot⟩ *cow-parsnip*; *Heracleum* L **~pulver** n *H. powder* **~säulen** pl ⟨übtr⟩ (Straße v Gibraltar) *Pillars* pl *of H.* **~staude** f = –kraut **~taten** f pl *Deeds of H.*

herk·ulisch a *Herculean*; *Hercules-like*

H·erkunft f ~/≃e **1.** (P) *birth, descent, extraction, origin*; *source* (*of news*) ‖ er war deutscher ~ *he was of German extraction* ‖ v guter ~ (*quite*) *well born*; v niederer ~ *of humble* od *low ex.* (od *o.*) **2.** (S) *derivation*; *o.*; *provenance*; v zweifelhafter ~ *of doubtful pr.* ‖ Land der ~ *country of o.* ‖ fremder ~ *ecdemic* ‖ die ~ läßt sich nicht verleugnen (P, T) *blood will tell* **~sbescheinigung** f *certificate of o.* **~sbezeichnung** f *place* (od *country*) *of o.*; *o. brand*

h·er- ~|langen vt [h] (etw) = herreichen **~|lassen** vt [h] jdn ~ *to allow* od *suffer a p to come*; er wurde –ge– *he was let* (*to*) *come here* **~|laufen** vi [s] *to run here*; → hereilen; –ge– ‖ hinter jdm ~ *to run after a p*; ⟨fig⟩ *to toady to a p* ‖ er lief direkt hinter ihnen her *he ran at their heels* ‖ vor jdm ~ *to run before a p* **~|legen** vt [h] leg es her *lay* od *put it near*; .. hierher *lay it here*; → hinlegen °**~|leiern** vt [h] (Gebet etc) *to drone* (*out*); *to gabble*; *to recite droningly* **~|leiten** vt [h] **1.** sie mußten das W. weit ~ *they had to bring* (od *fetch*) *the water a long distance* **2.** ⟨übtr⟩ **a.** (Wort) *to derive* (v *from*) **b.** ⟨log⟩ (Schluß) *to deduce* (v *from*) **c.** sich ~ v *to derive* (od *to be derived*) *from* ‖ (zeitlich) *to date from* ‖ sein Geschlecht leitet sich her v .. *his family is descended from* .. **≃leitung** f *derivation* (v *from*); *deduction*

H·erling m ~s/~e *unripe grape*

H·erlitze f ~/~n ⟨bot⟩ *cornel*; *dogwood*

h·er- ~|locken vt [h] (jdn) *to* (*al*)*lure, entice* **~|m** vrefl [h] ⟨fig⟩ sich ~ über (etw) *to attack, tackle* (*a problem*); *to grapple with*; *to set about* (*a th*) ‖ *to fall* (od *set to work*) *upon*, ⟨sl⟩ *to walk into* (*one's meal*) → herfallen (P)

H·ermannstadt n (Stadt in Siebenbürgen)

Hermaphrod·it m ~en/~en *hermaphrodite* **~·ismus** m *h.ditism* **H·erme** f ~/~n ⟨sculp⟩ *terminal figure*

H·ermarsch m *march back* (od *home*)

Hermel·in 1. n ~s/~e ⟨zoo⟩ (weißes) *ermine*; (bes braunes) *stoat* **2.** m ~s/~e (~pelz) *ermine* **~fell** n *ermine* **~mantel** m *ermine-mantle* **~pelz** m *ermine* **~spinner** m ⟨ent⟩ *ermine-moth*

Hermen·eutik f *hermeneutics* pl [sg konstr] ‖ h–tisch [a] *hermeneutic* **herm·etisch 1.** [a] *hermetic*; *air-tight* **2.** [adv] *hermetically*

h·er- ~|murmeln vt [h] (etw) *to murmur* **~|müssen** vi → her **~n·ach** [adv] *after*(*wards*); *hereafter*; *later*(*on*), *subsequently*; kurz ~ *shortly after* **~|nehmen** vt [h] (etw) *to get, take* (aus, v *from*); wo soll ich es ~? *where am I to get it*? ‖ → vornehmen ‖ es nimmt arg her *it is very wearing*

H·ernie [–iə] f ~/~n ⟨med⟩ *hernia* L; *rupture*

hern·ieder adv *down*; [mst pref bei Verben]

hern·ieder- pref [betont, bei Verben trennbar] *down*; → herab–, herunter–; nieder– **~|blicken** vi [h] *to look* (od *gaze*) *down* (auf *upon*) **~|fahren** vi [s] *to descend* **~|gehen** vi [s] *to descend* ‖ ⟨übtr⟩ ~ bis .. an *to reach down to* .. **~|hageln** vi = herab– **~|neigen** vrefl [h] sich ~ z *to bow* (od *bend*) *down towards* **~|prasseln** vi [s] (of rain) *to come down* (*in floods*) **~|regnen** vi → herab– **~|rieseln** vi [s] (of rain) *to drizzle down* **~|steigen** vi [s] = herab– **~|strömen** vi [s] Ehrungen strömten auf ihn hernieder *honours rained upon him* **~|stürzen** vi [s] = herunterstürzen **~|ziehen** [h] ⟨fig⟩ (etw) auf sich ~ *to bring down upon o.s.*

Her·oe m [–o:ə] ~n/~n *hero* **~nkultus** m *heroworship* **~ntum** n *heroism* ‖ *heroic age* **Hero·in** n ~s/ (Rauschgift) *heroin*, ⟨sl⟩ *snow* **Hero·ine** f ~/~n ⟨theat⟩ *heroine*; *leading female character, leading lady* **her·oisch 1.** [a] *heroic* (*age*); *epic* (*poetry*); *chivalrous* (*bearing*); *grand* (*language*); *valiant* (*deeds*) ‖ ⟨pros⟩ ~es Versmaß, ~er Vers (= Hexameter) *heroic verse, h. metre*; ~es Reimpaar *h. couplet* **2.** [adv] *h.ally*; *v.ly*; *ch.ly* **Hero·ismus** m *heroism*

H·erold m ~s/~e **1.** ⟨her & hist⟩ *herald* **2.** ⟨übtr⟩ *forerunner, harbinger, herald, precursor* **~s|amt** n ⟨engl⟩ *H.s' Office* **~sbild** n, **~sfigur** f = Heroldstück **~klasse** f ⟨engl⟩ die 3 ~n → Wappenkönig **~skollegium** n ⟨engl⟩ *H.s' College*; *C. of Arms* **~skunst** f *h.ry* **~rock** m *tabard* **~stab** m *h.'s staff* (od *rod, wand*) **~stück** n ⟨her⟩ *charge*

H·eros m ~/Her·oen *hero*; National≃ *n. h.*

Herostr·atentum n (nach Herostratos) *wanton destructiveness* **herostr·atisch** a *destructive*

H·erpes f ~/ ⟨path⟩ *herpes*

h·er|plappern vt [h] (Gebet) *to drone, gabble*; *to reel* (od *rattle*) *off*

Herr m ~n/~en **A. 1. (Gebieter) a.** Gott der ~ *the Lord*; der ~ der Heerscharen *the Lord of hosts* ‖ unser ~ *our Lord* (*Jesus*); *the Master*; *Christ* ‖ ~ der Finsternis *prince of darkness* ‖ das Haus des ~n *the House of God*; der Tag des ~n *the Lord's Day* **b.** *lord, master, ruler* (über *of, over*); *monarch* (*she was the m.*) ‖ der ~ des Hauses, Haus≃ *the master of the h.* ‖ ~ u Diener *master and servant* ‖ *master* (od *owner*) *of a dog* ‖ Guts≃ *squire*; → Landes≃ ‖ oberster ~ *sovereign*;

supreme lord; unser ~ u König *our sovereign lord* ‖ Lehns~ *liege, liege lord*; → Grund~ ‖ → Dom~, Stifts~ **c.** ⟨com⟩ *governor, principal*; ⟨sl⟩ *boss* ‖ aufsichtführender ~ *shop-walker* **2. a. adliger** ~ *nobleman*; Standes~ *lord, peer*; †⟨hist⟩ *gentleman* ‖ ~ von N. ⟨Ger⟩ *Herr von N.*; Herr (General) Richard von Feist (*General*) *Herr R. v. F.*; ⟨engl⟩ (*General*) *Sir R. F.* (Anrede: *Sir R.*, bzw *General*); → Adel, Lord **b. geistlicher** ~ *clergyman* ‖ ⟨engl parl⟩ höhere geistliche ~en *Lords Spiritual* **c. (Mann)** *gentleman*; spanischer ~ *hidalgo* ‖ ~ ohne Dame (in einer Gesellschaft, bei einer Party) ⟨Am sl⟩ *stag* ‖ feiner ~ *fine gentleman*; ⟨sl⟩ *nob*; *toff*; vornehmer ~ *swell*, ⟨Am sl⟩ *high-roller* **3. Alter** ~ **a.** °mein alter ~ (Vater) *my father*, ⟨fam⟩ *governor*, ⟨sl⟩ *old man*; *the pater* L **b.** ⟨univ⟩ *old* od *College graduate*; ⟨Am⟩ *alumnus* L ‖ (of a club) *old boy* | °⟨hum⟩ der hohe ~ *his nibs* **4. (Titel) a.** (vor Eigennamen) ~ Feist *Mr Feist*; ⟨AInd⟩ *Feist Sahib* ‖ der junge ~ Richard *Master R.* **b.** Ihr ~ Vater (Bruder) *your father* (*brother*) ‖ (der) ~ Doktor (*the*) *Doctor*; ~ Doktor (Professor, Oberst) N. *Doctor* (*Professor*, *Colonel*) *N.* ‖ der ~ Präsident *Mr President*; ⟨engl parl⟩ *Mr Speaker* **5. (Briefadresse)** ~n Richard Feist *R. F., Esq.*; *Mr R. F.* ‖ ~n Doktor N. *Doctor N.* ‖ ⟨com⟩ die ~en Heinemann *Messrs H.* **6. (Anrede) a.** mein ~ *Sir*; m–e ~en [pl] *Gentlemen*; → a. A. 2. a. **b.** Sehr geehrter ~! *Sir*, (vertraulich) *Dear Sir* ‖ Sehr g. ~ N.! *Dear Mr N.* ‖ Sehr g. ~ Professor N.! *Dear Professor N.* ‖ ⟨com⟩ Sehr geehrte ~en! *Gentlemen*, (*Dear*) *Sirs*; ⟨mil⟩ m–e ~en, ich melde *gentlemen, the commanding officer* **c.** Gnädiger ~ *My lord*; ⟨AInd⟩ *Sahib*; (malaiisch) *Tuan* ‖ Gnädigster König u ~ *most gracious Majesty* ‖ ⟨hum⟩ mein ~ u Gebieter *my lord and master* **c.** °bester ~! *man alive*! ‖ °mein lieber ~ *my good man* **B. Wendungen 1.** im Jahre des ~n 1918 *in the year of our Lord 1918* ‖ Geliebte im ~n *My beloved brethren* ‖ °~ du m–e Güte! ~ je! (*O*) *Lord*! *good Lord*! *good heavens*! *goodness gracious*! | ~ der Schöpfung (= Mensch) *lord of creation* ([pl] ⟨a. hum⟩); *man*; in (aus) aller ~en Länder(n) (*from*) *all over the world* ‖ ein gr Schütze vor dem ~n *a great shot* ‖ vor den hohen ~n geführt w *to be ushered into the Presence* ‖ ⟨prov⟩ wie der ~ so der Knecht (⟨fam⟩ so's Gscherr) *like master like man* ‖ ein besserer ~ *a gentleman moving in upper circles* **2.** jdn mit ~ **anreden** *to call a p* ~ ‖ den gr ~n spielen *to play the gentleman*; strenge ~en regieren nicht lange ⟨fig⟩ *blow the wind ever so fast, it will lower*; °den vornehmen ~n markieren *to do the swell* **3. a.** sein **eigener** ~ *one's own master*; (*to paddle one's own canoe*) ‖ wir wollen sehen, wer v uns ~ ist *we'll se which of us is m.* ‖ s–r Sinne ~ s *to be in one's* (*right*) *senses*; *to have one's wits about one* ‖ ~ der Lage (*or* Situation) *m. of the s.*, .. s *to rule the roast* (⟨fam⟩ *roost*); *to have the game in one's hands* **b.** ~ **s in** *to be supreme in* (od *over*) ‖ ~ im eigenen Hause s *to be m. in one's own h.*; ⟨fam⟩ *to be cock on one's own midden* od *dunghill*; Frankreich ist ~ im eigenen H. *Fr. is mistress in her own h.* ‖ ~ s über etw *to be master* (od *in control*) *of a th*; *to be supreme* (od *to rule*) *over a th*; *to control a th* **4.** e–r S (*or* über e–e S) ~ **w** *to master a th*; *to bring a th under control* ‖ ~ der Lage w *to come out on top* (od .. *out top-dog*) ‖ über jdn ~ w, jds ~ w *to get the better of a p*; *to master* od *rule a p* ‖ ~ w über s–e Leidenschaften (etc) *to conquer* (od *overcome*, *master*) *one's passions* ‖ die Depression wurde ~ über sie *depression had its way with her* ‖ sich zum ~n m über etw *to bring a th under control* **H·errchen** n ⟨cont⟩ *petty master*; *lordling* ‖ *little man*; mein ~ *little man* ‖ feines ~ *beau, fop* ‖ *master* (*of a dog*)

h·er- ~|**rasen** vi [s] hinter jdm ~ *to race in pursuit of a p*; → –jagen ~|**rechnen** vt [h] *to enumerate* ~|**reichen** vt [h] (etw) *to reach* (v .. *from the shelf*) ‖ jdm etw ~ *to hand* (od *pass*, *reach*) *a p a th* (*pass me the salt, please*) ~**reise** f *journey home* od *here*; *homeward* (od *return*) *journey* ~|**reisen** vi [s] *to travel* (od *come*) *here*

H·erren- ~**abend** m *gentlemen's social gathering*, *all-male dinner* ‖ ⟨fam⟩ *gander-party*, ⟨Am⟩ *stag party*, *smoker* ~**anzug** m *gentlemen's suit* ~**anzugsstoff** m (⟨a.⟩ ~e [pl]) (*gentle*)*men's suiting* ~**artikel** m pl *gentlemen's articles* pl; *haberdashery* ~**ausstattungsgeschäft** n *the outfitter's* (od *hosier's*, *haberdasher's*) (*shop*) ~**doppel(spiel)** n ⟨ten⟩ *men's doubles* pl ~**einzel(spiel)** n *men's singles* pl ~**fahrer** m **1.** *private* od *owner-driver* **2.** *amateur-motorist* ~**gesellschaft** f → ~abend ~**gut** n *domain* ~**handschuhe** m pl *gentleman's gloves* ~**haus** n **1.** ⟨engl⟩ *manor* (od *mansion*)-*house*; *hall* **2.** ⟨Ger hist⟩ *the Prussian Upper House* ~**hemd** n *man's shirt* ~**hof** m = –sitz ~**kleidung** f *men's wear* ~**konfektion** f *gentlemen's outfitting* | ~sgeschäft [n] *outfitter's* ~**leben** n ⟨fig⟩ ein ~ führen *to live like a lord*; *to live in clover* ~**los** a *derelict*; *masterless*; *unappropriated*, *unclaimed* (*goods*); *unowned*; *unidentified* (*dog*), *abandoned* (*cat*) ‖ ~es Gut ⟨mar⟩ *derelict*; ~e S *waif*; ~es T *waif*, ⟨Am⟩ *maverick* ~**mensch** m *masterful*, *racy*, *strong type of man* ~**moden** f pl = –konfektion ~**moral** f ⟨Ger philos⟩ *morality of the strong* ~**partie** f → ~abend ~**pilz** m ⟨bot⟩ → Steinpilz ~**reiter** m *amateur* (od *gentleman*) *rider* ~**sattel** m *saddle*; im ~ reiten (of a lady) *to ride astride* ~**schneider** m *tailor*; *suitmaker* ~**schnitt** m (of ladies) *Eton crop* ~**sitz** m **1.** *manor-house* **2.** = ~sattel ~**sporthemd** n ~ mit weichem Kragen *tunic shirt* ~**- u Knaben-Oberkleidung** f *men's and boys' outerwear* ~**volk** n *racy*, *strong nation* ~**wäschegeschäft** n = –ausstattungs– ~**zimmer** n *study*; ⟨fam & hum⟩ *den*

H·errgott m *the Lord*; *God* ‖ °er lebt wie der ~ in Frankreich → Gott in Fr. **H·errgotts-** ~**frühe** f: in aller ~ *at cock-crow*; *at an unearthly hour*; *first thing* (*in the morning*) ~**käferchen**, ~**schäfchen** n ⟨ent⟩ *lady-bird* ~**schnitzer** m *carver of crucifixes*

h·er|richten vt [h] *to put into shape*; (Zimmer) *to do* od *fit up*; *to tidy* ‖ *to put* (od *set*) *in order*; *to set out* ‖ (Leder) *to dress*; (Hecke) *to trim*; (Möbel) *to touch up* ‖ ~ z *to make up into* .. ‖ (Stück) f die Bühne ~ *to arrange for the stage* ‖ *to prepare*; *to get ready*

H·errin f ~/~nen *mistress*; fürstliche, königliche ~ *Sovereign M.* ‖ ⟨übtr⟩ *female ruler*; *m.* (über *of*) **h·errisch 1.** [a] *arrogant*, *dictatorial*, *domineering*, *haughty*, *imperious*, *masterful*, *overbearing*, *peremptory*; *dogmatic*; *magisterial*; *bossy*; *offhand* ‖ ~es Auftreten, Wesen *arrogance*, *overbearingness* **2.** [adv] *arr.ly*, etc. ‖ ~ auftreten *to be arr.* (etc.); *to act haughtily*; *to lay down the law* ‖ ~ auftreten gegenüber jdm *to domineer* (od *lord it*) *over a p* **herrj·e(min·e)** intj → Herr du m–e Güte **h·errlich 1.** [a] ⟨fig⟩ *charming* (*material*); *delightful*, *glorious* (*weather*); *lovely*; ⟨Scot⟩ *bonny*; ⟨Am a.⟩ *proud* ‖ *capital*, *excellent*, *grand*, *magnificent* (*music*); *splendid*; *superb*; *sumptuous* ‖ ein ~er Tag *a day of days* | ⟨iron⟩ *fine*, *jolly*, *pretty* ‖ e–e ~e Kritik! *criticism indeed*! ‖ das ist ja ~! *I like that*! du bist wirklich ~! *you really are the limit*! **2.** [adv] *excellently*, *magnificently* ‖ ~ warm *lovely and warm* ‖ ~ u in Freuden leben *to live on* (⟨Am⟩ *off*) *the fat of the land* | ~**keit** f ~/~en **1.** *excellence*, *magnificence*, (*the splendours of the world*) ‖ (*Solomon in all his glory*); *grandeur*, *majesty* (*of scenery*, etc.); ~en [pl] *magnificent features* (*of a work*) ‖ °da war es mit der ~ vorbei *that was the end of the pomp* (od *show*) **2.** † (als Titel) Seine ~ *His Lordship*

3. [konkr] (= Herrschaft 2. a.) ⟨hist⟩ *domain, lordship* **H·errnhuter** m ~s/~ **1.** *Moravian* **2.** [in comp] *Moravian*; ~brüdergemeine (*sect of*) *Moravians* **H·errschaft** f ~/~en **A.** [abstr, mst nur sg] **1.** *authority*; *control* (über *of, over*); *command* (*over the forces of nature*); *dominion* (*under the d. of prejudices*); *grip* (*on*); *headship*; *mastery* (*of, over*); *power* (*over*) | ⟨pol⟩ *domination* (*over*), *rule*; *sway* (*over*); *sovereignty*; ⟨AInd⟩ *raj* (*the British r. in India*) ‖ ~ zur See *naval supremacy*; ~ durch Diktatur *dictatorial* (od *totalitarian*) *rule* ‖ unter Britischer ~ *under British domination* (od *rule*) ‖ → Gewalt, Macht, Regierung | (S) *control(ling influence)*; *control*; *sway* (*of fashion*) ‖ ~ der Technik *technocracy* **2. a.** die ~ **ausüben** *to exercise sov.* ‖ sich der ~ bemächtigen *to usurp the throne*; *to seize the reins of power* ‖ die ~ führen *to be in power*; ⟨fig⟩ *to rule the roast* ‖ ~ über *supremacy of, over*; die ~ gewinnen über *to gain the mastery over ..*; *to prevail over*; *to overrule* (*a th*); = Herr w über ‖ die ~ **h über** *to have power over*; *to hold sway over ..*; *to rule* (od *sway*) *over*; *to predominate over*; *to control, to dominate* ‖ die ~ an sich **reißen** = sich der ~ bemächtigen ‖ (etw, jdn) s–r ~ unterwerfen *to subject to one's rule*; *to subdue* ‖ die ~ über sich verlieren *to lose control over o.s.* **b.** sich **unter** jds ~ beugen *to submit to a p's rule* ‖ (etw, jdn) unter s–e ~ bringen *to bring under one's r.* (od *control*); *to subject to one's r.* ‖ unter jds ~ fallen *to fall under a p's control* (od *sway*) ‖ unter jds ~ k *to come under a p's r.* ‖ zur ~ k *to come into power*; *to rise to ascendancy* **B.** [konkr, pl ~en] **1.** (~sgebiet) *domain, demesne*; *lordship*; *sovereignty*; *estate, manor*; die ~ N. *the N. domain* **2.** (P) **a.** (of domestics) *master and mistress*; *employers*; *rulers* pl **b.** die ~, die ~en *Mr and Mrs N.*; *Dr. N. and Mrs N.*; *Sir George* (*N.*) *and Lady N.* ‖ °m–e ~en *Ladies and Gentlemen* **c.** m–e alten ~en *my old folks at home*; er wurde vor die hohen ~en geführt *he was ushered into the Presence* ‖ hohe u höchste ~en *persons of high and the highest rank*; *illustrious p.s* pl **d.** °~! ~ noch einm·al! *Lord! good heavens!* **h·errschaftlich** **1.** [a] **a.** *manorial* (*lands, woods*); ~es Gut *manor*; *estate*; ~es Haus *manor-house, mansion(-h.)*; ~er Sitz *manor(-h.)* ‖ ~er Wagen *private car* **b.** *elegant* (*flat*); *fashionable*; *first-class* (*hotel*) **2.** [adv] *elegantly* **H·errschafts-** ~antritt [m] *accession*; ~bereich, ~bezirk [m] *jurisdiction*; ~dekret [n] *instrument of rule*; ~recht [n] ~e [pl] *sovereign rights* pl **h·errschen** vi [h] **1. (P)** *to be master*; *to dominate* (*she wanted to d.*); *to rule* (nach e–m Grundsatz *by a principle*); *to wield the sceptre*; allein ~ *to be supreme* | ~ **über** *to be master* (od *in control*) *of*; *to be supreme over* (od *in*); *to reign* (od *rule, sway*) *over*; *to control, rule, sway* ‖ despotisch ~ über *to domineer over*; *to lord it over* ‖ uneingeschränkt ~ .. *to reign supreme over* ‖ ⟨fig⟩ souverän ~ .. *to ride supreme on* (*the air, waves*) **2.** ⟨**übtr**⟩ **(S)** *to prevail*; *to be prevalent*; *to reign* (*silence reigned*); (bestehen) (of a custom) *to be in vogue* (unter *among*); (of disease, vice) *to be rife* (od *rampant*) ‖ es herrschte Friede *there was peace* (*between ..*); *p. prevailed*; es h. F. im Lande *p. ruled the c.* ‖ Frost h. im Tal *frost held the v.* ‖ °hier herrscht Ordnung! *my word is law here! no answer-back!* ‖ *distress is riding among the people* **h·errschend** a **1.** *dominant* (*will*); *ruling* (*class*); das ~e Geschlecht *the dom. sex*; die ~e Schicht *the ruling section* **2.** (vor~) *predominant, prevailing* (*opinion, conditions*), *prevalent*; die ~e Mode *the vogue, the fashion*; abweichend v der ~en Meinung *contrary to the general opinion* **H·errscher** m ~s/~ *ruler, sovereign*; *monarch*; *potentate*; ⟨a. übtr⟩ *prince* ‖ ⟨Am pol⟩ *boss* ‖ alleiniger, unumschränkter ~ *autocrat*; unumschränkter ~ s in *to reign supreme in ..* ‖ jdn zum ~ m in *to make a p supreme in ..* ‖ → Selbst≈ **~blick** m ⟨übtr⟩ *commanding look* **~familie** f *reigning* (od *ruling*) *family*; *dynasty* **~geschlecht** n *dynasty* **~gestalt** f *ruler*; *dynast, monarch, prince* **~gewalt** f *sovereign power* **~haus** n *dynasty*; *reigning house* **≈los** a; –lose Zeit *interregnum* [L] **~miene** f ⟨übtr⟩ *c.ding air*; *air of c.d* **~stab** m *sceptre* **~stuhl** m *throne* **~talent** n *king-craft* **~wort** n ⟨übtr⟩ *word of command* **H·errscherin** f ~/~nen *sovereign*; die königliche ~ *the S. Lady* ‖ ⟨übtr⟩ *mistress*; *queen* (*of the seas*) **H·errschsucht** f *thirst for power* ‖ *domineeringness, imperiousness, overbearingness* **herrschsüchtig** a *thirsty for p.* ‖ *d.ing, imperious, o.ing*

h·er- **~**|**rücken** vt/i **1.** vt [h] (Stuhl) *to move up* (an *to*) **2.** vi [s] *to move up* (an *to*); *to draw near* **~**|**rufen** vt [h] (jdn) *to ask round*; *to call here* ‖ er rief hinter ihm her *he called after him* **~**|**rühren** vi [h] ⟨fig⟩ (S) v (etw) ~ *to come* (od *arise, derive, emanate, flow, proceed, spring*; ⟨Am a.⟩ *stem*) *from*; *to be derived from*; *to originate in*; *to be due* (od *owing*) *to*; *to be attributed to* (*a th*) ‖ (of idea) ~ v jdm *to originate with* (od *from*) *a p* ‖ *to be spawned from*: der v Kuba ~de Umsturz *the Cuba-spawned subversion* **~**|**sagen** vt [h] (etw) *to say* (od *repeat*) *by rote*; *to recite, rehearse*; Aufgabe(n), Gebet ~ *to say one's lessons, one's prayers* **~**|**schaffen** vt [h] (etw) *to bring* (od *get*) *here*; *to bring round* **~**|**schauen** vi = –sehen **~**|**schicken** vt [h] (jdn, etw) *to send along* (od *round*) **~**|**schleichen** vi [s] ~, sich ~ *to steal round*; *to sneak here* **~**|**schleppen** vt [h] (etw) *to drag* (od *lug*) *along* ‖ sich ~ *to plod one's way* (nach *to*) °**~**|**schnattern** vt [h] (Worte) *to gabble*; *to reel* (od *rattle*) *off* **~**|**schreiben** vrefl [h] ⟨fig⟩ sich ~ v = herrühren v **~**|**sehen** vi [h] *to look*; sie glaubte, er sähe her *she thought he was looking*; er sah zufällig her *he happened to look* **~**|**senden** vt = –schicken **~**|**setzen** vt [h] (etw) *to put* (od *place*) *here* (od *near*) ‖ setz dich her *sit down beside me* **~**|**singen** vt [h] *to sing monotonously* od *droningly* °**~spionieren** vi [h] hinter jdm ~ *to spy* (*up*)*on a p* **~**|**springen** vi [s] vor jdm ~ *to frisk before a p* **~**|**stammen** vi [nur prs & pret] ~ v **1.** (P) = (ab)stammen v **2.** (S) = herkommen 2.; herrühren **≈stammung** f = Abstammung **~**|**stellen** **I.** vt [h] **A.** ⟨eig⟩ (etw) = –setzen ‖ stell dich hier her *stand here* ‖ ⟨mil⟩ † herstellt euch! *as you were!* **B.** ⟨übtr⟩ **1.** (Brücke, Haus) *to build*; (Karte) *to construct*; *make* ‖ (Getränk, Medizin) *to concoct, make, prepare* | ⟨tech⟩ (Buch, Stahl) *to make, manufacture, produce*; (Waren) *to be a manufacturer of*; *to turn out*; billig –ge–te Waren *sweated articles* ‖ *to do* (*3 copies*) **2.** ⟨übtr⟩ **a.** (Zustand) *to bring about* (od *off*); *create*; (Ordnung) *establish*; (Frieden) *make*; (Vertrauen) *produce* ‖ *arrange* (f *for*); *make up*; ⟨telph⟩ (Verbindung) *to put through* **b.** (= wieder~) er war v s–m Unfall –ge–t *he had recovered from ..* **c.** wieder~ (Bild, Text) *to restore*; *renovate, repair* ‖ (Frieden) *to re-establish*; jds G. wieder~ *to restore a p to health*; er ist wieder –ge–t *he is recovered* **II.** ≈ n → I. ‖ ~ der Verbindung *connection establishment* **≈steller** m ⟨tech⟩ *maker, manufacturer, producer, processor* ‖ *constructor* (*of a map*) **≈stellung** f ~/~en **1.** *building, construction* ‖ *making-up, preparation* (*of a drink*) | ⟨tech⟩ *making, manufature, fabrication, processing, production* **2.** ⟨übtr⟩ **a.** *bringing about*; *creation*; *establishment* (*of order*); *production* **b.** Wieder≈ *restoration, renovation* ‖ *re-establishment*; ⟨med⟩ (P) *recovery* | ~sbedingungen f pl *conditions of preparation*; ~skosten [pl] *cost of production*; *labo*(*u*)*r content*; ~sleiter [m] ⟨film⟩ *producer*; ~smethode [f] *manufacturing m.* od *process*; ~spreis [m] *price of production*; ~sverfahren [n] *manufacturing process*;

~sweise [f] *manner* (od *method*) *of production* °~|**stottern** vt [h] (Worte) *to stammer* (od *stutter*) *out* ~|**stürzen** vi [s] ⟨fig⟩ *to run* (od *dash, rush*) *here* || (sich) ~ über = herfallen ~|**tragen** vt [h] (etw) *to carry round* od *here*; vor sich ~ *to carry before one* ~|**treiben** vt [h] °was trieb dich her? *what made you come here*? || er trieb alles vor sich her *he drove all before him* || vor sich ~ *to chase* || ⟨ftb⟩ (Ball) sachte vor sich ~ *to dribble* ~|**treten** vi [s] *to step here* od *near*

H·ertz [invar] n *cycles per second*; v 30 ~ (Hz) bis 20 Kilo-~ (kHz) ⟨wir⟩ *30 to 20000 vibrations in frequency* || ~sche Wellen *Hertzian waves*

her·über adv (°rüber) *across* (z *to* ..); *hither* || nicht über den Graben ~ *not beyond that ditch* || nach hinten ~ *over backwards*; v drüben ~ *from over there* || bis in unsere Zeit ~ *down to our time* || ~ u hinüber *hither and thither* **her·über-** pref [betont, bei Verben trennbar] *across, over* ~|**bemühen** vt [h] (jdn) *to trouble a p to come over* || sich ~ *to trouble to c. o.* ~|**bitten** vt [h] (jdn) *to ask over* (od *round*) ~|**bringen** vt [h] (jdn) *to bring over* (od *round*) °~|**bugsieren** vt [h] *to give* (*the salt*) *a fair wind* ~|**eilen** vi [s] *to come over in haste* ~|**gelangen** vi [s] *to get across* ~|**holen** vt [h] (jdn) *to fetch round* ~|**k** vi [s] **a.** (v der anderen Seite) *to come across* (z jdm *to a p*) **b.** *to come over* (od *round*) (*to a p*); *to step round* (*to a p*); z e–m Besuch ~ *to come over on a visit*; ich werde sofort in Ihr Büro ~ *I'll come along to your office immediately* || –ge– s *to be over* || → blechen ~|**nehmen** vt [h] ⟨mar⟩ *to take off* ~|**reichen** vt/i [h] **1.** vt (etw) = her– **2.** vi, ~ in unsere Zeit *to reach into our t.* ~|**rufen** vt [h] (jdn) *to ask* (od *call*) *round* ~|**schicken** vt [h] (jdn) *to send round* od *over* ~**tragen** vt [h] ein Geräusch z jdm ~ *to carry a noise towards a p*

her·um adv (°rum) [nicht ersetzbar durch: umher] **A.** (in **best.** Richtung) **1.** ⟨**eig**⟩ **a.** um .. ~, ~ um .. *round*; ⟨Am⟩ *around* || *a rope r. a tree*; immer um das Haus ~ *r. and r. the h.*; gleich um die Ecke ~ *just r. the corner* **b.** ganz ~ *all* (*a*)*r.* || im Kreise ~, rings~ (*a*)*r.*; *r. about*; im Kreise um ihn ~ *r. about him*; alle rings um mich ~, ihr Jungens! *r. me, all of you boys*! || falsch ~ *the wrong way round* || so ~ *this way r.* || hinten (vorn) ~ *by the back* (*front*) *door* (od *entrance*); → hinten || oben ~ *along the top side* (od *road*) || rechts (links) ~ *to*(*wards*) *the right* (*the left*) || die Reihe ~ *all in turn*; bis die R. ~ ist *till we come full circle* **2.** ⟨übtr⟩ das Gerücht ist in der ganzen Stadt ~ *the r. has spread all over the t.*; *the r. went the r. of the t.* || das Jahr ist (noch nicht) ~ *the y. is* (*not yet*) *over* **B.** (in **unbest.** Richtung) **1.** ⟨eig⟩ hier~ *hereabout*(*s*); *somewhere r. here*; da~, dort~ *thereabouts* **2.** ⟨**übtr**⟩ **a.** um jdn ~ s *to make up to a p*; sie ist immer um ihn ~ *she is always hanging about him* || *(Maß, Wert) um 50 Mark ~ *about 50 marks* **b.** (**zeitlich**) *about*; ⟨Am a.⟩ *around*; um das Jahr 1500 ~ *about the year 1500* || um Weihnachten ~ *somewhere about Ch. time*; um 5 Uhr ~ *about 5 o'clock* **her·um-** pref [betont, bei Verben trennbar] **1.** [nicht ersetzbar durch: umher–] *round*; → ~bringen, ~drehen, ~k etc **2.** [ersetzbar durch: umher–] *about*; → ~gehen in, ~liegen, ~lungern etc °~|**albern** vi (a. umher–) [h] *to fool* (od *monkey*) *ab.* (⟨Am⟩ *ar.*) (mit jdm *with a p*); *to act up* °~|**ärgern** vrefl (a. umher–) [h] sich ~ mit *to squabble* (od *wrangle, wrestle*) *with* || °~|**balgen** vrefl (a. umher–) [h] sich ~ mit *to scuffle* (od *wrestle, wrangle*) *with* °~|**basteln** vi [h] ~ an *to busy o.s.* (od *to fumble, muddle*) *with* °~|**biestern** vi (a. umher–) [h] *to behave boisterously*; *to fuss ab.* °~|**bek** vt [h] ⟨fig⟩ (jdn) = –bringen 2. ~|**bessern** vi [h] ~ an etw *to correct* od *mend a th here and there* (od *now and again*) ~|**betteln** vi (a. umher–) [h] *to go ab. begging*; *to beg from door to door* ~|**blättern** vi (a. umher–) [h] in e–m Buche ~ *to skim through a b.* ~|**bringen** vt [h] **1.** (etw) *to bring r.* (od *over*) || → –tragen; –wenden **2.** ⟨fig⟩ (jdn) *to bring* (od *talk*) *r.* (od *over*); → –kriegen (Zeit) *to pass, spend*; *idle away* ~|**bummeln** vi (a. umher–) *to loaf* (od *gad, loiter, moon*; ⟨sl⟩ *mess, mooch, mouch*) *ab.*; ⟨fam⟩ *to trapes, trapse* || in der Stadt – *to knock ab. t.* °~|**doktern** vi [h] an jdm (sich) ~ *to physic a p* (*o.s.*) ~|**drehen** vt/i [h] **A.** vt **1.** (etw) *to turn r.* || zw den F. ~ *to roll between one's fingers*; er drehte es herum u wieder herum in .. *he turned it r. and r. in his hands*; jeden Fünfer etc erst zweimal ~ (bevor man ihn ausgibt) *to skin* od *flay a flint* || (Mast) *to slew, slue* müßig ~ *to twiddle* || um die Achse ~ *to roll*; im Kreise ~ *to wheel r.* | ⟨fig⟩ er dreht mir die Worte im Munde h. *he twists* (od *misconstrues*) *every word I say* **2.** **sich** ~ *to turn r.*; (im Bett) *to roll* (od *turn*) *over* || (of the mast) *to slew* || sich blitzschnell ~ *to spin* (od *flash*) *r.* || sich im Kreise ~ um *to wheel r.* ..; → drehen **B.** vi; ~ an etw *to twiddle at, to fumble with a th* ~|**drücken** vi/refl [h] ~ an etw *to pinch a th* | °⟨übtr⟩ **sich** ~ **in** *to sneak ab.*; *to hang ab.* (*a place*); *to frequent* || ⟨fig⟩ sich ~ um *to back* od *sneak out of* (*a difficulty*); *to dodge* od *evade, shirk* (*a duty*) °~|**drucksen** vi [h] **1.** *to potter ab.* **2.** *to hem and haw* ~|**erzählen** vt [h] *to pass the word around* (*that*) ~|**fahren** vi [s] **1.** *to drive r.* || ~ um *to drive* (od *go*) *r.* (*a corner*); *to r.* (*a corner*) **2.** (a. umher–) *to drive ab.*; *to go* (od *move*) *ab.*; auf der St. ~ *to drive up and down the street* || ⟨mar⟩ *to sail ab., to cruise*; auf dem M. ~ *to sail* (od *navigate, roam*) *the sea*; in der ganzen W. ~ *to travel* (od *roam*) *the whole world* || mit den Händen in der Luft ~ *to gesticulate* °~|**flanieren,** ~|**flankieren** vi (a. umher–) [h] *to rove ab.*; auf den St. ~ *to parade the streets* ~|**flattern** vi (a. umher–) [s] *to flit* (od *flutter*) *ab.* ~|**fliegen** vi [s] **1.** ~ um *to fly r.* (*a place*) **2.** (a. umher–) *to fly ab.* ~|**fragen** vi (a. umher–) [h] *to make inquiries* (bei jdm *of a p*) ~|**fuchteln** vi (a. umher–) [h] ~ mit *to rollick* (*blades*); mit den Händen ~ *to work with one's hands*; (verzweifelt) *to make desparing gestures with one's hands*; (in der Luft ~) *to gesticulate* || ihre Hände fuchtelten herum vor .. *her hands flashed ab. before* (*her eyes*) ~|**führen** vt [h] (jdn) *to conduct* (od *show*) *r.*; *to play the guide to a p, to take a p about*; jdn ~ auf, in .. *to show a p over* (od *r.*) (*a ship*); *to take a p over* (*a library*) || eiligst ~ um .. *to hurry* (*a p*) *r.* || ⟨fig⟩ → Nase °~|**fuhrwerken** vi [h] † = –fuchteln °~|**furzen** vi [h] ⟨fig⟩ (faulenzen) *to fart ab.* °~|**fummeln** vi (a. umher–) [h] *to fumble ab.*; ~ an *to fumble* vt ~|**geben** vt = –reichen ~|**gehen** vi [s] **1.** *to go r.*; immer im Kreise ~ *to go r. and r. in a circle* || ~ um .. *to walk r.* (*the corner*); *to r.* (*the c.*); seitlich ~ um *to flank* (*a th*) || ein B. ging um das ganze Haus herum *a balcony ran the entire way r. the h.* | ⟨fig⟩ der Gedanke ging mir den ganzen Tag im Kopfe h. *the thought was running in my head all day* | etw ~ l *to hand* (od *pass*) *r.*; (Flasche) *to circulate* **2.** (a. umher–) *to walk* (od *move*) *ab.* || auf der Straße ~ *to walk up and down the st.*; *to walk the st.*; im Zimmer ~ *to walk ab. the room* || °~|**hacken** vi [h] ~ auf *to chop away at* (*a th*) ⟨fig⟩ ~ auf jdm *to peck at, to pick on*; ⟨Am sl⟩ *to chew the rag at a p* ~|**hämmern** vi [h] *to bang away* (auf *at* [*the piano*]) °~|**hantieren** vi (a. umher–) [h] *to bustle* od *fumble, potter, tinker*) *ab.* °~|**hetzen** vt/i (a. umher–) **1.** vt [h] (jdn) *to rush ab.* **2.** vi [s] *to dart* (od *fly, rush*) *about* ~|**holen** vt [h] (jdn) *to bring* (od *fetch*) ~|**horchen** vi (a. umher–) [h] *to scout ab.* °~|**humpeln** vi (a. umher–) [s] *to hobble ab.* (*with a stick*) ~|**hüpfen** vi (a. umher–) [s] *to frisk* (od *hop, skip*) *ab.* ≚**huren** n *promiscuous copulation* ~|**irren** vi (a. umher–) [s] *to stray ab.* ~|**jagen** vi (a. umher–) [s]

⟨übtr⟩ *to scamper* (*od rush*) *ab.* °~|**jockeln** vi (a. umher–) [s] *to racket ab.* °~|**kalbern** vi = –albern ~|**klettern** vi (a. umher–) [h] *to climb ab.* ~|**kommandieren** vt [h] *to order*, ⟨sl⟩ *boss* (*a p*) *ab.* (⟨Am⟩ *ar.*) ~|**k** vi [s] **1.** *to c. r.* (z *to*); → herüber–; ~ um .. *to c. r.* (*a corner*); *to r.* (*a c.*) | ⟨fig⟩ ~ um etw *to avoid* (od *dodge, evade*) *a th*; *to keep away from a th*; wir k nicht um die Tatsache h., daß *we cannot get away from the fact that* ..; *there is no way to get around it* ⟨a. fig⟩; man kommt nicht um den Verdacht h. *you cannot help suspecting*; .. um die Wahrheit h. *you cannot help facing the truth* **2.** (a. umher–) **a.** er war in der Welt –ge– *he had been ab. in the w., he had seen much of the w.*; ein viel –ge–er Mann *a far-travelled man* **b.** (of rumours, etc.) *to get ab.*; *to leak* (od *ooze*) *out*; *to transpire* °~|**kramen** vi (a. umher–) [h] *to grub* (od *rout*) *ab.* (in *in*) ~|**kratzen** vi [h] auf der Geige ~ *to scrape the fiddle* ~|**kriechen** vi [s] **1.** ~ um *to crawl* (od *creep*) *r.* .. **2.** (a. umher–) *to creep ab.*; (of invalids) *to crawl ab.* °~|**kriegen** vt [h] **1.** (etw) *to get r.* **2.** ⟨fig⟩ jdn ~ *to bring* (od *coax, talk*) *a p r.*; *to win* (od *talk*) *a p over*; *to come* od *get r. a p*; *to get at a p* ~|**laufen** vi [s] **1.** *to run r.*; ~ um .. *to run r.* .. ‖ ⟨übtr⟩ *to go* (od *move*) *r.* ‖ der Balkon lief um .. ~ → –gehen **2.** (a. umher–) *to rove, ramble, stroll, trapse*; *to move ab.*; → –streichen ~|**legen** vt [h] ~ um .. *to lay* (od *put*) *r.* .. ~|**liegen** vi (a. umher–) [h] *to lie about* ‖ unordentlich am Boden ~ *to lie littered ab. the floor*; .. auf dem Tische, im Zimmer ~ *to litter the table, the room* ‖ etw ~ l *to leave a th ab.* ‖ °~|**ludern** vi (a. umher–) [h] *to knock ab.*; ⟨sl⟩ *to be out on the tiles* ≈**lungerer** m ~s/~ *layabout*; ~ [pl] *layabouts* pl °~|**lungern** vi (a. umher–) [h] *to idle, loaf, loiter, maroon*; *to hang* (od *loaf, loiter, loll, moon, muck, potter, prowl*; ⟨sl⟩ *mooch, mouch*) *about*; *to scull, stick around*; ⟨Am sl⟩ *to bum* ‖ im G. ~ *to hang ab. the garden*; auf den Straßen ~ *to prowl the streets* °~|**meckern** vi [h] meckere nicht herum *don't find fault with everything* ‖ ~ an ⟨bes Am sl⟩ *to chew the rag at* °~|**pfuschen** vi [h] *to mess ab*; ~ an *to fudge* (*a th*); *to fumble* (od *muddle*) *with*; *to monkey* (od *tamper, tinker*) *with* (*a th*) °~|**poltern** vi (a. umher–) [h] *to racket* od *barge ab.* °~|**püttjern** vi [h] *to mess* (od *muddle, tool, potter,* ⟨vulg⟩ *sod*) *ab.* (an .. *with a th*) ~|**rasen** vi (a. umher–) [s] *to dash* (od *race, rush*) *ab.*; im Zimmer ~ *to dash ab. the room* °~|**raten** vi [h] *to guess* ~|**reden** vi/t [h] **1.** vi; um etw ~ *to argue r. and r. a th*; *to talk r. a th* **2.** vt (etw) = –sprechen ~|**reichen** vt [h] (etw) *to hand* (od *pass, send*) (*a*)*r.*; (Flasche) *to circulate*; *to help* (*the potatoes*) ~|**reisen** vi (a. umher–) [s] *to travel ab.*; in e–m Lande ~ *to travel* (*ab.*) *a c.* ~|**reißen** vt [h] (etw, jdn) *to pull* (od *swing*) *r.* ⟨a. fig⟩ ~|**reiten** vi (a. umher–) [s] **1.** ~ um .. *to ride r.* .. **2.** *to ride ab.* ‖ ⟨fig⟩ ~ auf etw *to be harping on*; *to insist on a th*; *to ring the changes on a th*; *to belabour the point*; auf jdm ~ *to plague, worry a p* ~|**rennen** vi (a. umher–) [s] *to bustle* (od *tear*) *ab.* ~|**rücken** vt/i **1.** vt [h] (Möbel) *to move ab.* **2.** vi [s] *to jig ab.* (auf *on*); → –zappeln °~|**saufen** vi (a. umher–) [h] ⟨sl⟩ *to booze*; *to go on the booze* °~|**scharwenzeln** vi [h] *to bustle* (od *wriggle*) *about*; *to gallivant*; um jdn ~ *to fawn upon a p*; → –tanzen ~|**schaukeln** vi (a. umher–) [h] *to jig ab.* (auf *on*) ~|**schicken** vt [h] (etw) *to send r.* [a. abs] ~|**schiffen** vi [s] ~ um .. *to sail r.* ..; ~ um .. *to double, round* (*a cape*) °~|**schlagen** vrefl [h] sich ~ mit .. *to fight* (od *squabble*) *with a p*; ⟨übtr⟩ *to grapple with* (*a th*); *to battle it out with a p* (um .. *for a th*) ~|**schleichen** vi (a. umher–) [s] *to sneak* (od *prowl*; ⟨Am sl⟩ *snoop*) *ab., to gumshoe*; ~ in *to sneak ab.* (*the house*) ~|**schlendern** vi (a. umher–) [s] *to saunter* (od *laze, moon, stroll*) *ab.*; im Garten ~ *to potter ab. the g.*; ⟨Am⟩ *to tool* ~|**schleppen** (a. umher–) [h] *to drag ab.*; sich ~ *to drag o.s. ab.*

~|**schleudern** vt [h] *to fling* (od *spin*) *r.* °~|**schnüffeln** vi (a. umher–) [h] *to sneak* (od *poke, scout*; *to poke and pry*; ⟨Am sl⟩ *snoop, nose*) *ab.*; im Hause ~ *to sneak ab. the h.* °~|**schwänzeln** vi [s] = –scharwenzeln ~|**schwärmen** vi (a. umher–) [s] *to moon ab.* ~|**schweifen** vi = –schwärmen ~|**schwenken** vi [s] *to turn r.*; *to veer r.* (z *to*) ~|**sehen** vi = umher– ×~|**sielen** vrefl [h] sich ~ *to roll, wallow* (in *in*) ~|**sitzen** vi [h] ~ um *to sit* (*a*)*r.* (*the camp-fire*) ‖ ⟨übtr⟩ *to idle* (od *loaf, loiter*) *about* ~|**spazieren** vi (a. umher–) [s] *to stroll* od *walk ab.* ~|**spielen** vi [h] *to monkey ab.* ‖ ⟨mst übtr⟩ ~ mit .. *to fool* (od *fumble, meddle, monkey, trifle, fiddle*) *with*; *to play about with* (*a gun*); ~ an etw (u beschädigen) *to maul a th ab.* ~|**sprechen** vt [h] ⟨übtr⟩ (etw) *to divulge*; *spread* ‖ sich ~ (of news) *to get ab.* od *wind*; *to leak out*; *to filter through* ~|**springen** vi (a. umher–) [s] *to jump* (od *leap, scamper*) *ab.*; *to kick up one's heels*; die Hunde sprangen um sie h. *the dogs jumped about her* ~|**spritzen** vt/i (a. umher–) **1.** vt [h] (etw) *to spill*; *sprinkle* **2.** vi [s] *to splash ab.* ~|**stehen** vi [h] **1.** *to stand r.*; ~ um .. *to stand r.* ..; *to surround* (*a bed*) **2.** (a. umher–) *to stand about*; überall standen Autos herum *there were cars all ab.* ~|**stellen** vt [h] ~ um .. *to stand* (od *place, put*) *r.* .. ‖ sich ~ um .. *to stand r.* .. ~|**stöbern** vi (a. umher~) [h] *to fuss* od *rummage*) *about* (in *in*) ~|**stochern** vi (a. umher–) ~ in .. *to dig into* .. ~|**strampeln** vi [h] *to kick ab.*; mit den B. ~ *to fling one's legs ab.* ~|**streichen** vi (a. umher–) [s] *to rove ab.*; → –bummeln; in den Wäldern ~ *to rove the woods*; auf den St. ~ *to tramp, prowl the streets* ~|**streichend** a *roving*; *vagabond* ≈**streicher** m *rover, tramp*; *vagabond* ~|**streifen** vi (a. umher–) [s] *to gad, roam, rove, wander ab.*; im Lande ~ *to roam* (*ab.*) *the c.*; auf den M. ~ *to roam* (*travel*) *the seas*; in der Welt ~ *to roam the w.* ~|**streiten** vrefl [h] sich ~ mit *to argue with*; *to join* (od *take*) *issue with* (*a p*) ~|**streuen** vt (a. umher–) [h] (etw) *to scatter* °~|**strolchen** vi (a. umher–) [s] *to prowl, rove ab.*; in der Stadt ~ *to knock ab. t.* ~|**suchen** vi (a. umher–) [h] ~ in .. *to forage, fumble, rake in* (*one's pockets*); *to ferret, grope, grub about in* (*a drawer*); in dem ganzen Orte ~ *to sleuth ab. all over the place*; ⟨übtr⟩ ~ nach .. *to beat* (od *grope*) *ab. for* (*a solution*) °~|**sumpfen** vi (a. umher–) [h] ⟨sl⟩ *to* (*go on the*) *booze*; *to be out on the tiles* ~**tändeln** vi [h] *to potter* (*ab.*) ~|**tanzen** vi [h] ~ um .. *to dance r.* .. ‖ ⟨übtr⟩ ~ um jdn *to dance attendance* (*to fawn*) *upon a p*; ‖ ⟨fig⟩ jdm auf der Nase ~ *to treat a p like dirt*; er läßt sich nicht auf der N. ~ *he does not allow h.s. to be put upon* ‖ du darfst dir in der S nicht auf der N ~ l *you must not take it lying down* ~|**tasten** vi (a. umher–) [h] ~ nach .. *to feel, grope ab. for* .. ~|**toben** vi (a. umher–) [h] wie wild ~ *to rage, to ramp*(*age*) ~|**tollen** vi (a. umher–) [s] *to lark, romp, fool ab.*; *to kick up one's heels* °~|**torkeln** vi (a. umher–) [s] *to barge* od *totter ab.* ~|**tragen** vt [h] **1.** ~ um *to carry r.* .. ‖ ⟨fig⟩ (Gerücht) *to circulate*; *divulge* **2.** (a. umher–) er trug es mit sich h. *he carried it ab. with him* ‖ ⟨fig⟩ (Gefühl, Kummer etc) mit sich ~ *to nurse* ~|**trampeln** vi (a. umher–) [h] *to trample ab.* ‖ auf dem Grase ~ *to tr. the grass down* | ⟨fig⟩ auf jdm ~ *to tr. upon a p*; auf jds Gefühlen ~ *to tr. down a p's feelings* ~|**treiben** vrefl (a. umher–) [h] sich ~ ⟨fig⟩ *to gad, hang, hover, muck, knock ab.*; *to be* (*up*)*on the gad*; sich in e–m Ort ~ *to gallivant ab. a place* (mit .. *with a girl*) ≈**treiber** m *loafer*; → –streicher ~**trommeln** vi [h] auf *to pummel* vt ~|**tummeln** vrefl [h] sich ~ *to bustle ab.*; = –hantieren; –tollen ~|**wälzen** vt [h] ⟨fig⟩ (etw) im Geiste ~ *to roll in one's mind* | sich ~ *to roll* (in *in*); °sich im Bette ~ *to roll over in bed* ~|**wandern** vi (a. umher–) [s] *to wander ab.*; → –streifen ‖ in e–m Land ~ *to wander about a c.* ~|**wenden** vt [h] (etw) *to turn* (od *bring, get*) *r.*

(*with a sweep*) || sich ~ *to turn r.*; sich plötzlich ~ nach jdm *to flash r. on a p* ~|**werfen** vt [h] **1.** ⟨übtr⟩ (Boot, Körper) *to slew*; → –reißen; den Kopf ~ *to toss one's head* **2.** (a. umher–) *to toss ab.*; ⟨fig⟩ mit dem Gelde ~ *to chuck m. about*; er wurde im Leben –geworfen *he was tossed ab. in life* || sich im Schlaf ~ *to toss (ab.) in one's sleep* ~|**wickeln** vt [h] (Tuch etc) ~ um *to twist* (od *wind, wrap, wreathe*) *r.* .. ~|**winden** vt [h] ~ um = –wickeln || sich ~ um *to wind (itself) r.* .. ~|**wirbeln** vt [h] (etw, jdn) *to spin, whirl, fling r.*; *to toss ab.* ~|**wühlen** vi (a. umher–) [h] *to root(le)* (in *in*) || ⟨fig⟩ *to grub, poke, root, rout, rummage ab.* (in *in*; unter *among*) °~|**wursteln** vi [h] = –püttjern °~|**wüten** vi (a. umher–) [h] *to rage, ramp(age)* °~|**zanken** vi [h] *to scold* || sich ~ *to quarrel, squabble* (*with* ..) °~|**zappeln** vi [h] *to fidget (ab.)* ~|**zerren** vt/i [h] **1.** vt (etw) *to lug, tug ab.* **2.** vi; ~ an .. *to tug away at (a th)* ~|**ziehen** vt/i **1.** vt [h] e–n Zaun ~ um L. *to fence land*; *to surround l. with a fence*; –gezogen ⟨tech⟩ *wrap-around (bumper)* **2.** vi (a. umher~) [s] *to move, rove, wander ab.*; *to nomadize* ~**ziehend** a *nomadic (tribes)*; *wandering*; *itinerant, strolling (players)* ~**zigeunern** vi [h] *to roam the world like a gipsy*

her·unter adv (°runter) **1.** *down*; z mir ~ *d. to me*; die Tr. ~ *d. the stairs*; *d.stairs* || ich muß jetzt ~ *I must get d. now* || ~ mit der Fahne! *d. with the flag!*; → nieder || ~ vom Baume! *come* (od *get*) *d. from the tree!* || den Hut ~! *off with the hat! hats off!* **2.** °~ s *to be* (od *feel*) *poorly, to be in poor health* || *to be tired* (od *worn out*) || er ist mit s–n Nerven ganz ~ *his nerves have completely broken d.* **her·unter-** pref [betont, bei Verben trennbar] *down*; → herab–; hinunter– ~|**bemühen** vt [h] jdn ~ *to trouble a p to come d.* || sich ~ *to trouble* (od *take the trouble*) *to come d.* ~|**blicken** vi [h] *to look d.* (aus, v *from*) || ~ auf = herab– ~|**bringen** vt [h] **1.** bring es (v B.) herunter *get it d. (from the atticks), (clear the atticks of it)* **2.** ⟨übtr⟩ *to bring d.*; *to lower*; (Preise, Temperatur) ~ auf *to reduce to* || (den Himmel) auf die Erde ~ *to bring d. to earth* | ⟨fig⟩ (ein Geschäft) *to mismanage, ruin*; *to let d.* || jdn ~ *to ruin a p*; (gesundheitlich) *to weaken a p, to pull a p down* ~|**drücken** vt [h] (etw) *to press, force d.* || ⟨übtr⟩ (Preise) = herab– || ⟨com⟩ (Papiere, den Markt) *to bear* ~|**fallen** vi [s] *to fall d.*; *to fall off (the horse)* || **(S)** *to come (tumbling) d. (with a crash)*; (of fruit) *to drop off (the tree)*; (of hair) *to flow d. (the back)*; → herab– ~|**fieren** vt [h] ⟨mar⟩ (Boot) *to lower (away)* ~|**flattern** vi [s] ~ v *to flutter off (the table)* ~|**fliegen** vi [s] *to fly d.*; ⟨aero⟩ im Zickzack ~ *to zigzag d.* ~|**fließen** vi [s] *to flow, pour d.*; (of water) *to pour d. (the stairs)* ~|**führen** vt [h] ⟨übtr⟩ (Bericht) ~ bis auf *to bring d. (the present time)* ~|**gehen** vi [s] *to descend, to go d.*; ⟨aero⟩ *to drop* | ⟨übtr⟩ (of quality, etc.) *to go d.*; *to decline, fall*; *to recede* || ~ auf .. *to come d. to (a time)* || ~ mit (etw) *to abate (the price)*; *to reduce*; *slacken (speed)* || –gegangen s *to be d.* ~**gek** a [pred] **a.** *run-d. (farm)* || (in Kleidung etc) *d. at heel*; *out at elbows*; gänzlich ~ *d. and out, d. on one's uppers* || °Mensch, bist du ~ *that's quite a comedown for you* **b.** (gesundheitlich) ~ s *to be reduced* (durch .. *by famine*) °~|**gießen** vt [h] (Getränk) *to knock back*; *to whip, quaff off* ~|**gleiten** vi [s] ~ an *to slither d. (a wall)* ~|**handeln** vi [h] v Preise ~ *to haggle over the price*; *to try to cut the price d.* | vt [h] (Preis) *to beat d.* ~|**hangen** vi [h] *to hang d.* (v *from*) ~|**hängen** vi [h] *to droop* (über *over*); *to hang d.* (v *from*) || (of chin) *to sag* || (auf) (of hair) *to hang d. (one's back)* °~|**haspeln** vt [h] ⟨übtr⟩ (etw) *to reel off* ~|**hauen** vt [h] (Zweig) *to cut off* || °jdm eine ~ *to slap a p's face, to box a p's ears*; *to fetch, give a p a box on the ears* ~|**heben** vt [h] (jdn) *to lift d.* (v *from*) ~|**helfen** vi [h] jdm ~ *to help a p d.* (v *from*) ~|**holen** vt [h] (etw) *to get d.* || (Flugzeug, Vogel durch Schuß) *to bring d.*; er hatte mit dem ersten Schuß zwei Vögel –geholt *he had two birds d. to his first shot* ~|**jagen** vi [s] die Straße –gejagt k *to come tearing along the road* | vt [h] *to chase, drive, shoo off (a tree)* ~|**kippen** = –gießen ~|**klappen** vt [h] *to turn d.* || ~|**k** vi [s] **1.** *to come d.*; *to come d.stairs*; *to descend*; *to get d.* (an .. *to the entrance*) || schwungvoll die Straße ~ *to c. swinging d. the street* **2.** ⟨fig⟩ *to come d. in the world*; *to sink* (od *be brought*) *low*; °einen ~ ⟨school⟩ *to go d. one* || (gesundheitlich) er ist sehr –ge– *he has run to seed*; *he is greatly reduced (by his illness)*; dabei kommt man h. *that tells upon you in the long run* || ~ l *to let* od *run d. (a farm)* || das ≚ *the letting d. process*; → –gek °~|**kriegen,** ~|**langen** vt [h] (etw) *to hand* (od *pass, reach*) *d.* (v *from*) || °jdm eine ~ = –hauen ~|**l** vt [h] (Vorhang) *to let d.*; (Boot) *to lower*; (Fahne) *to dip* ~|**laufen** vi [s] er kam den Pfad –ge– *he came running d. the path* °~|**leiern** vt [h] ⟨mus⟩ (Stück) *to rattle* || (Gebet) *to drone*; *gabble*; *patter*; *to rattle off* ~|**lesen** vt [h] *to read d. (the numbers)* ~|**m** vt [h] (jdn, etw) *to abuse*; *crab*; *decry*; *flay*; *maul*; *trounce*; *slate*; *to dress, run d.*; *to pitch* (⟨sl⟩ *walk*) *into* ..; (Buch) *to pull* od *tear to pieces*; *to scarify* || ⟨sl⟩ *to blow up*; *to slang*; *to tick off* || ⟨Am⟩ *to bawl out*; *to salt, cry d.*; *to score, soak*; ⟨fam⟩ *to knock*; *to jump upon (a p)* → abkanzeln; herfallen über ~|**müssen** vi → herunter ~|**nehmen** vt [h] (etw) *to take d.* || (hängenden Gegenstand) *to unhang*; ~ v *to remove from* ~|**plappern** vt [h] (Gebet) *to gabble, patter* ~|**prasseln** vi [s] ⟨fig⟩ (auf) (of blows) *to rain (upon a p)*; → –regnen °~|**putzen** vt [h] (jdn) *to haul .. over the coals*; *to take .. to task*; *to snub, rebuff*, ⟨fam⟩ *trim*, ⟨Am⟩ *razz*; → –machen ~|**rasen** vi [s] –gerast k *to c. tearing d. (the stairs)* °~|**rasseln** vi/t **1.** vi [s] (of a storm) *to rattle d.* **2.** vt [h] ⟨mus⟩ *to rattle off*; (Rede) *to run, reel off* °~|**rattern** vt [h] = –rasseln ~|**reden** vt [h] das Blaue vom Himmel ~ *to talk nineteen to the dozen* ~**regnen** vi [h] ⟨fig⟩ ~ auf .. *to rain (up)on*; → –prasseln || (Bomben) ~ l auf *to hurl d.* (od *to rain*) *upon* ~|**reichen** vt/i [h] **1.** vt (etw) = langen **2.** vi; ~ bis an (*or* z) *to reach to* .. ~|**reißen** vt [h] **1.** (Plakat) *to tear* (od *pull*) *d.*; (Fensterläden) *to force d.*; ~ v *to whip (a cloth) off (the table)*; .. vom Körper ~ *to snatch off* || (etw) mit sich ~ *to bring d.* **2.** °⟨fig⟩ (Buch, Stück) *to pull* od *tear to pieces*; *to excoriate, scarify*; *to run, write d.* **3.** ≚ n ⟨a.⟩ *pounce* ~|**rücken** vi [s] *to move d.* ~|**rutschen** vi [s] auf *to slide d. (the banisters)* || → Buckel ~|**sausen** vi [s] ~ auf (of eagles) *to pounce upon, to swoop (d.) upon* .. ~|**schießen** vt/i **1.** vt [h] = herab– **2.** vi [s] = –sausen ~|**schlagen** vt [h] ⟨übtr⟩ = –klappen °~|**schliddern** vi [s] *to slip (down, in the mud)* °~|**schlingen** vt [h] (Speise) ⟨fam⟩ *to bolt*; *lower*; *to wolf d.* ~|**schlucken** vt [h] **1.** (etw) *to swallow* **2.** ⟨fig⟩ (Wort) *to keep back* || (Beleidigung) *to stomach*; *to put up with* .. °~|**schnattern** vt [h] = –plappern ~**schrauben** vt [h] ⟨fig⟩ *to scale d. (wages)* ~|**schreiben** vt [h] (Brief) *to write off* ~|**schütteln** vt [h] (Äpfel) *to shake d.* ~|**sehen** vi [h] *to look d.* || ⟨fig⟩ ~ auf .. = herab– ~|**setzen** vt [h] (etw) *to put d., to lower* || ⟨fig⟩ = herab– 2. ~|**sinken** vi [s] *to sink d.*; → herab– ~|**spielen** vt [h] (Stück) *to rattle (off)* ~|**streifen** vt [h] *to strip, peel off* ~|**stürzen** vi [s] = herab– || °~|**trinken** vt [h] (gierig) *to swill* ~|**tröpfeln** vi [s] die Backen ~ (of tears) *to trickle d. the cheeks* ~**wehen** vt/i [h/s] *to blow off* ~|**werfen** vt [h] *to cast* od *throw d.* (aus v *from*) ~|**wirtschaften** vt [h] (etw) *to deteriorate*; *dilapidate*; *ruin*; (Gut, Schule) *to let, run d.* ~|**zählen** vt [h] (an) *to check (names on the fingers)* °~|**würgen** vt [h] = –schlucken ~|**ziehen** vt/i

1. vt [h] (etw) *to draw, pull d.*; tief –gezogen über .. (*a hat*) *pulled low d. over* (*the eyes*) **2.** vi [s] = hinunter– ‖ → (Buch) –m

H·ervey-Inseln f pl → Cook-Inseln

her·vor adv **1.** *forth* ‖ aus den Bäumen ~ *out of the trees* ‖ unter dem Sofa ~ *from under the sofa*; → heraus **herv·or-** pref [betont, bei Verben trennbar] *forth*; *forward*; *out* **~|blicken** vi [h] *to peep out* (aus *of*) **~|brechen A.** vi [s] **1.** ⟨eig mil⟩ ~ aus .. *to sally* od *rush from* (*an ambush*); aus e–m Engpaß (etc) ~ *to debouch* ‖ (of deer) ~ aus *to dart forth* (od *out*) *from* ..; aus dem Lager ~ *to break cover* **2. a.** ⟨übtr⟩ (of water) *to burst forth* ‖ (of light, sun) *to burst* (*forth, out*) (aus *from*); *to emerge* (*from* ..); *to come out*; aus den Wolken ~ *to burst through the clouds* **b.** ⟨fig⟩ (of a smile) *to flash out* ‖ (of feelings) *to arise*; *to break forth* (od *out*); *to burst out* ‖ (nach ..) brach es aus ihm hervor .. (*after a long silence*) *he broke out* .. **B.** ≃ n **1.** ⟨mil⟩ *sally*; *rush* (*from* ..) **2.** ⟨übtr⟩ *burst*; *breaking forth*; *outburst* **~|bringen A.** vt [h] **1.** ⟨eig⟩ **a.** ⟨biol⟩ (Nachkommen) *to bring forth, to generate*; *to give birth to*; *to procreate, produce*; *to throw up* (od *off*); (of females) *to bear*; (of males) *to beget*; (of fish) *to spawn* **b.** (of soil) (Früchte) *to produce*; (of plants) (Blätter) *to throw out* **2.** ⟨übtr⟩ **a. (P)** (Worte) *to utter*; *to throw out* ‖ (Gedanken) *to conceive* ‖ ⟨arts & Lit⟩ (schaffen) *to produce*; *create*; schnell ~ *to throw off* **b. (S)** ⟨phys⟩ (Hitze) *to generate*; *produce* ‖ (Elend, Unheil) *to beget*; *breed, cause*; *to bring about*; (Gefühl) *to engender*; *generate*; *produce*; *to make* (*noise*); *to spring* (*a surprise*); *to give rise to*; die Zeit brachte viele Genies hervor *the age was productive of men of genius* **B.** ≃ n = ≃**bringung** f **1.** *bringing forth*; *generation, procreation, production* **2.** ⟨übtr⟩ **a.** *utterance* (*of words*) ‖ *production*; *creation* (*of poetry, etc*) **b.** *generation* (*of heat*) ‖ *breeding* (*of crime*) **~|dringen** vi [s] ⟨übtr⟩ (of sounds) ~ aus *to come, arise from*; = –brechen **~|gehen** vi [s] **1.** (P) ~ aus .. *to arise, emerge from* (*mean surroundings*); Dr. N., der aus der Berliner Universität –gegangen ist *Dr. N. a product of Berlin University* ‖ als Sieger, Erster aus dem Kampfe ~ *to come out victor, winner*; *to come out on top*; *to be victorious*; als Preisträger *he emerged a prizeman* **2.** ⟨übtr⟩ **a.** (of sounds, etc.) *to arise, issue, proceed* (aus, v *from*) **b.** (als log. Folge) *to follow, result* (aus *from*); *it is apparent from this fact that* ..; aus dem, was du sagst, geht hervor, daß .. *from what you say it follows, results that* ..; es geht eindeutig h. aus .. *it is clearly shown by* .. **~|gucken** vi [h] *to peep* (aus *from, out of*); hinter der Mauer ~ *to peep from behind the wall* **~|heben** vt [h] **1.** ⟨arts⟩ (etw) *to make* (*a th*) *stand out*; *to pick out* (durch *by*); *to relieve* (gegen *against*); *to set off* (auf .. *against* [*a background*]); (etw) im Druck ~ ⟨print⟩ *to display* (*headlines*); etw plastisch (*or* lebendig) ~ *to bring* (od *place, throw*) *a th in* (od *into*) *full* (od *strong*) *relief*; *to highlight* **2.** (Gedanken) *to accentuate*; *to bring to prominence*; *to give prominence to* ‖ (etw in Worten ~) *to emphasize highlight, stress*; *to insist on* ..; *to lay* (od *place*) *emphasis on* ..; *to point out*; *to lay stress on* ..; (Unterschiede) *to bring out* (*details*); wert –gehoben z w *worthy of emphasis*; *worth mentioning* ‖ e–n moralischen Standpunkt ~ *to point a moral* ‖ ~, daß .. *to insist* (od *point out*; *urge*) *that* ..; *to make the point that* ..; was –zu– ist, ist dies, daß .. *the points to be made are that* .. ≃**hebung** f **1.** *relief* **2.** *accentuation* ‖ *emphasis*; *insistence*; → Betonung; Nachdruck **~|holen** vt [h] (etw) *to fish out* (aus *from*; *out of*); *to grub up* (od *out*); (s–e Schlüssel) *to produce*; *to take out*; *to reach for* (*a th*) ‖ (jdn) ~ aus *to fetch from* ‖ → heraus– **~|k** vi [s] *to come forth* (aus *from*); nach–e–a ~ hinter .. *to file out from behind the* (*wardrobe*) ‖ ⟨übtr⟩ (of the moon, etc.) *to come out*; *to emerge* (*from* ..); *to show* ‖ (of qualities) *to peep out*; *to crop up* ‖ allmählich ~ (of news) *to filter* **~|kriechen** vi [s] *to creep forth* (aus .. *from*; hinter .. *from behind*) **~|leuchten** vi [h] (of lightning) *to flash out* (aus *from*); *to shine forth* od *out* ‖ ⟨fig⟩ (of qualities) *to flash out*; *to come forth*; *to emerge* (*from* ..) **~|locken** vt [h] (etw) heraus– ‖ (Tränen) *to fetch* ‖ ⟨fig⟩ Hund **~|lugen** vi [h] unter dem Bett ~ *to peep from under the bed*; = –gucken **~|quellen** vi [s] (of water) *to spring* (aus *from*) ‖ ⟨übtr⟩ *to proceed* (*out of* ..) **~|ragen A.** vi [h] **1.** (S) *to jut forth* od *out*; *to project* (über *over*); *to protrude*; *emerge* (v *from*); (of cliffs) *to beetle* (*over* ..) **2.** ⟨übtr⟩ (P) **a.** *to distinguish o.s.*; *to excel* (an *in*); *be conspicuous, pre-eminent, prominent* (unter *among*); *to stand out* **b.** ~ über jdn *to rise* (od *tower*) *above a p*; *to overtop a p* (um .. *by several inches*) ‖ ⟨übtr⟩ *to exceed* (od *excel, overtop, surpass*) *a p* (an *in*) **B.** ≃ n *projection*; *prominence*; *protrusion* **~ragend A.** [a] **1.** ⟨eig⟩ = –stehend ‖ (of a surface) ~e Stelle *prominence* **2.** ⟨fig⟩ *conspicuous*; *excellent*; *eminent*; *first-rate, f.-class*; *prominent, salient*; *commanding* (*influence*), *exceeding* (*beauty*), *outstanding*; *exceptional*; *distinguished, marked*; *brilliant*; *tremendous, stupendous*; *great* (*it's g.*); *flashy* (*names*) ‖ ~er Zug, ~e Bedeutung *salience, -cy* ‖ ⟨fam⟩ *crack* (*shot*); *roaring, topping* (*dinner*); *splendid* (*man*); ~er Flieger *ace* ‖ ⟨Am sl⟩ *swell* (*plan*) ‖ → famos **B.** [adv] *conspicuously*; *prominently*; *most successfully*; *superlatively* ‖ ⟨fam⟩ *ripping, thundering* (*good*) ≃**ruf** m ⟨theat⟩ *recall*; *summons to come back* **~|rufen** vt [h] **1.** ⟨theat⟩ jdn ~ = heraus– **2.** (etw ~) **a.** im Geiste ~ *to call* (od *conjure*) *up, to suggest* **b.** ⟨phys⟩ (Hitze) *to generate, produce, engender* (Schwingungen) in der Luft ~ *to set up in the air*; (Feuer) *to start* ‖ (Tränen) *to call forth*; Blasen auf der Haut ~ *to blister the skin* **c.** (= –bringen) *to beget, breed*; *to bring on* od *about, bring to pass*; *to occasion*; (Sympathie) *to call forth*; (Übelkeit) *to cause*; (e–n Eindruck) *to create*; (Gefühle) *to engender, elicit, evoke*; (Begeisterung) *to generate* (in *in*); *to produce*; *to give rise* ‖ Glück ~ *to make for happiness*; *to originate* (*a war*); ~ *to raise* (*a laugh, a storm of protest*); der Gedanke rief in ihm ein Verständnis f .. hervor *the thought brought to him a sense of* ..; (Müdigkeit) –ge– durch .. (..) *bred of* (*a long ride*); dies war –ge– durch die Tatsache, daß *this was due to the fact that* .. | ~d *evocative* ≃**rufung** f *breeding*; *evocation* (*of an atmosphere*); *generation*; *production* **~|schauen** vi [h] → sichtbar s **~|schießen** vi [s] ⟨fig⟩ *to dart forth* od *out*; (of flames) *to leap*; (of buds) *to shoot* **~|schimmern** vi [h] *to shine forth* **~|schnellen** vi [s] *to leap up* **~|sprießen** vi [s] *to sprout* (aus *from*) **~|springen** vi [s] **1.** *to bound*; *leap* (aus *from*) **2.** ⟨übtr⟩ = –ragen, –stehen **~springend** a *protrusive* (*chin*); *protuberant* **~|spritzen** vi [s] *to shoot, spout* (aus *from*); *to spirt up* (*out of* ..) **~|sprudeln** vi/t **1.** vi [s] *to bubble*; *to to pour forth*; *to spring* (aus *from*) **2.** vt [h] (Worte) *to splutter* (*out*) **~|stechen** vi [h] ⟨übtr⟩ *to stand out*; *to be conspicuous*; *to shine* **~stechend** a *conspicuous*; *outstanding*; *paramount* (*facts*); *predominant*; *prominent* (*quality*); *salient* (*features*); *striking*; der ~e Zug *the dominant note* (*in his character*) **~|stehen** vi [h] (of eyes, etc.) *to bulge*; *to jut* (*forth* od *out*); *to project, protrude*; (of ears) *to stick out* | ~d [a] *bulging* (*eyes*); *protrusive, protuberant* **~|stottern** vt [h] *to stumble out* **~|strecken** vt [h] → vorstrecken **~|strömen** vi [s] ~ aus *to pour* (od *gush, spring, stream*) *from* **~|suchen** vt [h] (etw) *to search out*; *to seek*; *to pick out* (aus *from*) **~|tauchen** vi [s] plötzlich ~ aus *to dart* (od *leap, spring*) *from*; → –k **~|treiben**

vt [h] (Sproß) *to push out* **~|treten A.** vi [s] **1. (P) a.** ⟨eig⟩ *to come forward*; *to steep forth* (od *forward, up*); ~ aus .. *to emerge* (od *to step out*) *from* .. **b.** ⟨**übtr**⟩ *to come into prominence*; *to c. to the fore* (od *front*); *to be conspicuous*; *to be in evidence*; *to shine* (*as a writer*); *to show o.s.*; *to make o.s. a name* (*as* ..); politisch ~ *to play a part in politics* **2. (S) a.** ⟨eig⟩ = –stehen **b.** ⟨übtr⟩ *to come out*; (Frage) *to loom up* ‖ *to stand out* (aus *from*); klarer ~ *to emerge more clearly*; scharf ~ *to stand out in relief*; .. gegen *to tell against* (*a background*); plastisch ~ *to come into bold relief* ‖ (of impressions) *to tell* **c.** ~ l (= –heben) *to relieve*; *to set off*; *to throw up*; (Eigenschaft) *to accentuate*; (Unterschiede) *to bring out*; *to make .. more striking* **B.** ≗ n *projection*; *protrusion*; *protuberance* ‖ ⟨übtr⟩ *emergence* (aus *from*); *outcrop* **~tretend** a = –stehend ‖ ⟨geol⟩ ~e Teile [pl] *outcroppings* pl (*of a rock*) ‖ ⟨übtr⟩ *outstanding*; → stehend **~|tun** vrefl [h] ⟨fig⟩ sich ~ *to distinguish, signalize o.s.*; *to put o.s. forward*; *to be* (od *make o.s.*) *prominent* (unter *among*); *to excel* (als *as*; in *in, at*); *to shine* (*as* ..); → –treten 1 b. **~|zaubern** vt [h] ⟨übtr⟩ (etw) *to call, conjure up* ‖ aus dem Boden ~ *to improvise* **~|ziehen** vt [h] (etw) *to extract*; *produce*; (Messer) *to take out*; schnell ~ *to whip* (aus *out of*) ‖ unter .. *to drag* od *haul a p from beneath* (od *under*) *the bed*

h·er- ~|wagen vrefl [h] sich ~ *to venture to come round* (od *here*) **~wärts** adv *on the way here*; *on the return journey* **≗weg** m *the way back*; *journey back* **~|wehen** vt [h] (etw) *to blow here* (od *this way*) **~|weisen** vt [h] jdn ~ *to show a p the way here* **~|winken** vt [h] (jdn) *to beckon*; *to signal* **~|wünschen** vt [h] (jdn) *to wish* (*a p*) *to come here*

Herz n ~ens ⟨med a.⟩ ~es/~en **A.** ⟨anat⟩ **1.** *heart* ‖ Fett≗ *fatty h.*; Raucher≗ *smoker's h.*; Sport≗ *athletic h.* ‖ ⟨scient⟩ die Lehre vom ~en *cardiology* ‖ ~ alter Menschen ⟨fam⟩ *old pump* od *ticker* ‖ (~gegend) *h.*; *bosom*; *breast* **2.** ⟨fig⟩ *h.*; *soul*; *feeling*; *sympathy* ‖ *h.*; *courage*; *energy*; *will* ‖ *h.*; *mind*; *spirit* ‖ Frauen≗en [pl] *women's h.s* pl; Mutter≗, Vater≗ *mother's h., father's h.*; ~ u Verstand *brains and feeling*; ein ~ u e–e Seele *h. and soul united*, .. s mit *to be hand in glove with* (*a p*) **B.** ⟨**übtr**⟩ **(S)** *h.* (*of a cabbage*); *centre*; *central* (od *innermost*) *part*; *core*; ein ~ bilden *to h. up* ‖ *central area*; *interior*; im ~en Berlins *in the h. of Berlin* ‖ *essence*; *essential* (od *vital*) *part*; *marrow*; *pith* **C.** ⟨**übtr**⟩ **(P)** *darling, dear*; *ducky*; *pet*; *sweetheart* ‖ mein ~ *my love*; *darling*; *dearest h.* **D.** (Figur e–s ~ens) **a.** ein ~ aus .. *a h. of* (*gingerbread*) **b.** ⟨cards⟩ *heart* (*he hadn't a h.*) ‖ (~farbe) *h.s* pl; ~ ist Trumpf *h.s are trumps*; → ~as, ~dame, ~könig, ~neun **c.** ⟨bot⟩ Flammendes (*or* Hängendes, Tränendes) ~ *bleeding h.* **E. Wendungen** ⟨mst fig⟩ **1. hartes ~** *hard h.*; (heiß *eager*); eisernes ~ *h. of steel*; steinernes ~, ~ v Stein *stony h., h. of stone* od *flint* ‖ ~ wie Gold, lauteres ~ *h. of gold* ‖ betrübtes ~ *heavy h.* ‖ gebrochenes ~ *broken h.*; gebrochenen ~ens *h.-broken*; warmes ~ *warm h.* (f *for*) ‖ leichten ~ens *with a light h.*; *light-heartedly*; *without hesitation*; schweren ~ens, mit schwerem ~en *with a heavy heart*; *reluctently*; blutenden ~ens *with a bleeding* (od *an aching*) *h.* ‖ im Innersten (*or* im Grunde) s–s ~ens *in one's h.* (*of h.s*) ‖ in den heimlichsten Falten s–s ~ens *in the innermost recesses of his h.* ‖ mit allen Fasern s–s ~ens *with every fibre of his h.* ‖ sie sind ein ~ u e–e Seele *they are close friends*; *they are as thick as thieves* **2. a.** das ~ **schlägt** *the h. beats* od *pulsates*; das ~ klopfte *or* pochte stark *the h. palpitated, throbbed* **|** es geht e–m dabei das ~ auf *it makes one's h. rejoice*; es frißt ihm das ~ ab *it eats into his h.*; das ~ **blutete** mir bei .. *my h. bled at the sight*; blutenden ~ens unterschreiben *to sign with a heavy h.* ‖ mir brannte das ~ vor .. *I burned with* .. ‖ °ihm fiel, sank, °rutschte das ~ in die Hose *his h. went down to his heels, pants, boots*; .. *was in his b.*, ⟨sl⟩ *he got into a* (*blue*) *funk* ‖ ihm gehört unser ganzes ~ *we love him with h. and soul* ‖ das ~ lachte ihm im Leibe, das ~ lief ihm über (*or* schlug ihm höher) vor Freude *his h. leaped up* (od *glowed*) *with joy*; *his h. was thrilled* ‖ mir schlug das ~ bis zum Halse hinauf, das ~ stand mir still *I had my h. in my mouth*; *my h. leaped into my m.* ‖ die ~en schlugen ihm entgegen *their h.s went out* (*in affection*) *to him* ‖ die ~en höher schlagen l *to make the h.s leap with joy* ‖ das ~ tut mir weh, wenn .. *my h. is heavy when I see* .. ‖ ⟨bib⟩ Wes das ~ voll ist, des gehet der Mund über *for out of the abundance of the h. the m. speaketh* (Matt. 12, 34) **b. s-m ~en Luft m** *to give vent to one's feelings*, *to relieve one's f.* ‖ jds ~en nahestehen *to be near a p's h.* ‖ s–m ~en e–n Stoß geben *to come down a peg or two*; *to give way* ‖ es tut m–m ~en gut *it does my h. good* **3. a.** ein (weiches) ~ **haben** *to have a soft* od *sore spot in one's h.* (f .. *for a p*); *to be tender-hearted*; er hat kein ~ (im Leibe) *he has no h.*; *he is* (*perfectly*) *h.less*; viel ~ h *to have plenty of h.* ‖ das ~ h z etw = übers ~ bringen ‖ (nicht) das ~ h z tun (*not*) *to have the h. to do* ‖ das ~ auf dem rechten Flecke h *to have one's h. in the right place* ‖ das ~ auf der Zunge h (*or* tragen) *to wear one's h. on one's sleeve* **b. jds ~ aufwühlen** *to tear at a p's h.* ‖ jds ~ besitzen (S) *to have a p's h.* ‖ sein religiöses ~ entdecken *to get to religion* ‖ sein ~ erleichtern *to get it off one's chest* ‖ jds ~ gewinnen, stehlen *to win, steal a p's h.* ‖ sein ~ hängen an .. *to set one's h. on a th*; *to give one's h. to a p* ‖ sein ~ in die *or* beide Hände nehmen *to get a grip on o.s.*; *to take one's courage in both hands*; sein ~ verlieren an .. *to lose one's h. to a p* **c. sein ~ ausschütten** *to talk it out*; *to unbosom o.s.*; jdm .. *to pour out* (od *to open*) *one's h. to a p* ‖ sein ~ befreien, erleichtern *to unburden one's mind, soul* ‖ jdm das ~ brechen *to break a p's h.* ‖ das ~ ergreifen *to pull at the h.strings* ‖ jdm sein ~ erschließen, entdecken *to open* (*to lay bare*) *one's h. to a p* ‖ jdm sein ~ schenken *to give one's h. to a p* ‖ jdm das ~ schwer m (of grief) *to weigh upon a p*; *to weigh a p down* ‖ jdm das ~ zerreißen *to pull at a p's heart-strings* **| sich** [dat] **ein ~ fassen** *to pluck up* (od *to take*) *h.* (od *courage*); *to take h. of grace* ‖ sich das ~ aus dem Leibe reden (weinen) *to talk o.s. hoarse* (od *to death*) (*to cry one's eyes* od *h. out*) **4. a.** komm **an** mein ~ *come to my h.* ‖ °er hat's am ~ ⟨fam⟩ *he has a h.* ‖ die S liegt mir sehr am ~en *I have the matter very much at h.*; *it sticks in my h.*; .. einzig .. *my only h.'s desire is* ..; .. sehr .. *the m. is very near to my h.*; *I attach great importance to the m.* ‖ die Sorge nagt an s–m ~en *grief is preying on his mind* ‖ jdn **ans** ~ drücken *to press a p to one's bosom* ‖ ⟨fig⟩ jdm ans ~ greifen *to cut a p to the h.*; *to pull at a p's h.-strings*; *to tear at a p's h.* ‖ sie (es) wuchs ihm ans ~ *he grew very fond of her* (*it grew on him*); jdm ans ~ gewachsen s (*or* am ~en liegen) *to be near*(*est*) *a p's h.*; *to be very dear to a p* ‖ jdm etw (eindringlich) ans ~ legen *to urge a th upon a p* ‖ kühl bis ans ~ *as cold as ice*; (der Ort) ist ihm ans ~ gewachsen *he is very fond of* .. **b.** ⟨fig⟩ jdm **auf** dem ~en brennen = ins ~ schneiden, am ~en liegen ‖ etw auf dem ~en h *to have a th on one's mind* ‖ jdn auf ~ u Nieren prüfen *to put a p through his paces*, ⟨Am a.⟩ *to put a p to the acid test* ‖ Hand aufs ~! *speak frankly*! **c. aus** tiefstem ~en (*or* dem Innersten s–s ~ens) *from the depth of his h.* ‖ aus vollem ~en *cordially, h.ily*; *out of the buoyancy of one's h.*; = v ganzem ~en ‖ °aus s–m ~en k–e Mördergrube m *to wear one's h. upon one's sleeve*; *to be very outspoken*; *to speak one's mind* ‖ jdm aus dem ~en sprechen *to echo a p's sentiments*; die Worte waren ihm ganz aus dem ~en gesprochen *these words were just after his own h.* **d. im ~en** *at h.*; tief betrübt im ~en *heavy at h.* || im ~en bewahren *to cherish* (*a p's memory*) || (Worte) im ~en tragen *to carry in one's h.* || sie schlossen sie in ihr ~ *they took her to their h.s* || ⟨fig⟩ jdm ins ~ schneiden (*or* e–n Stich ins ~ geben) *to cut a p to the h.* od *quick*; *to pierce a p's h.* || sich etw ins ~ schreiben *to take* (od *lay*) *a th to h.* || man kann nicht ins ~ sehen *you cannot search the h.*. || jdm e–n Dolch ins ~ stoßen *to thrust a dagger through a p's h.* || die Kugel traf ihn mitten ins ~ *the bullet passed right through his h.* **e. mit dem ~en** an die Arbeit gehen *to put one's h. into one's work*; sich mit dem ganzen ~en in die A. werfen *to throw o.s. h. and soul into one's w.*; °mit dem ~ in der Hose ⟨sl⟩ *in a dither*; mit ganzem ~en bei (der S) s *to lend .. h. and soul*; er ist mit dem ~en bei der A. *his h. is in his w.* || er hat (es) mit dem ~en z tun *he has a* (*weak*) *h.* (od *a h.-trouble*) || etw nur mit halbem ~en tun *to do a th with half a h.* (od *half-h.edly*) **f.** ganz **nach** m–m ~en *quite after my own h.* **g.** ich konnte es nicht **übers ~ bringen** *I could not find it in my h.*; *I had not the h.*; *I could not prevail on m.s.* (*to do*) **h.** sprechen, wie e–m **ums** ~ ist *to speak* (*out*) *one's mind*; nicht wissen, wie e–m ums ~ ist *not to know how one feels* || es wird mir weh ums ~, wenn .. *I become heavy at h. when I see ..* **i.** ein Kind **unter dem ~en** tragen *to be with child, to be in the family way* **k. von ~en** *cordially*; *h.ily*; *from one's h.*; v ~en dankbar *sincerely grateful*; v ~en froh *very* (⟨fam⟩ *awfully*) *glad*; v ~en gern *very* (od *most*) *willingly* || v ganzem ~en *with all one's h., with one's whole h.*; *whole-h.edly* || v ~en k *to come from one's h.* || etw v ~en wünschen *to have a th at h.* || jdn v ganzem ~en lieben, jdm v ~en zugetan s *to love a p dearly, deeply* | mir fiel ein Stein **vom ~en** *a weight was taken off my mind* || sich etw vom ~en reden *to get a th off one's chest* || sprich frisch vom ~en weg *speak your mind freely* | **zu ~en gehen** *to touch the feelings*; (*their sufferings worked* [*wrought*] *upon our feelings*); jdm z ~en g. *to go* (od *appeal*) *to a p's h.*; *to stir a p's h.*; *to strike a p to the h.*; *to touch a p*; z ~en gehend *h.-stirring* || sich etw (sehr, schwer) z ~en nehmen *to take a th* (*grievously*) *to h.*; *to take on about a th*; nimm es dir wohl z ~en *lay it to h.* || z ~en sprechen *to speak to the h.* || Zugang z jds ~en finden *to win one's way to a p's h.* **F.** [in comp] (→ ⟨a.⟩ Herzens–) *h*(*eart*), *c*(*ardiac*), *cordial* **~ader** f ⟨anat⟩ *aorta* L °**≈allerl·iebst** a = allerliebst **~allerl·iebste**: die ~ *the beloved*; *sweetheart* **~·as** n ⟨cards⟩ *ace of h.s* **≈beklemmend** a *h.-stirring, h.-diseasy* (*moment*); [pred] *wringing to the h.* **~beklemmung** f ⟨med⟩ = –bräune || ⟨fig⟩ ~en [pl] *h.-searchings* pl **~beschaffenheit** f *c. condition* **~beschwerde** f, ~n [pl] *h.-trouble* **~beutel** m ⟨anat⟩ *pericardium* L | ~entzündung [f] *pericarditis* Gr **≈bewegend** a = –ergreifend **~bewegung** f = graphische Darstellung v ~en *cardiogram* **~blatt** n **1.** ⟨bot⟩ *Parnassus grass* **2.** °⟨**fig**⟩ = Herz C; ⟨sex⟩ *bunny*; °du bist mein ~ *you are the apple of my eye* °**~blättchen** n ⟨fig⟩ = –blatt 2. **~block** m ⟨path⟩ *h. block* **~blume** f ⟨bot⟩ *bleeding h.* **~blut** n ⟨fig⟩ *h.'s blood* (*of genius*); *life-blood* **~bräune** f ⟨med⟩ *angina pectoris* L **~b·ube** m ⟨cards⟩ *knave of h.s* **~d·ame** f ⟨cards⟩ *queen of h.s* **~dampf** m ⟨hors-vet⟩ *broken wind* ×**~drücken** n: er starb nicht an (*or* am) ~ *he was very outspoken* **≈erfreuend** a = –erquikkend **≈erfrischend** a *refreshing to the h.* **≈ergreifend 1.** [a] *h.-stirring*; *moving*; *pathetic, piteous* **2.** [adv] *pitiably*; *pathetically* **≈erhebend** a *h.-stirring*; *cheering* **≈erleichternd** a *h.-easing* **~erneuerung** f ⟨theol⟩ *regeneration of the h.* **≈erquikkend** a *h.-warming, h.-whole* (*laugh*); es ist ~ *it is h.ening* (*to see ..*) **≈erschütternd** a *h.-stirring* **≈erwärmend** a *h.-warming* **~erweiterung** f ⟨path⟩ *athlete' h.*; *c. dilatation*; an ~ leiden *to suffer from a dilated h.* **~fehler** m *c. defect*; *h.-trouble, -disease* **~fell** n = –beutel **≈förmig** a *h.-shaped*; *cordiform*; ⟨bot⟩ *cordate* (*leaves*); verkehrt ~ *obcordate*; ~er Gegenstand *h.* **~gegend** f *c. region* **~geräusch** n ⟨med⟩ ~e [pl] *c. murmurs* pl **≈gewinnend** a *winning*; *winsome* **~grube** f ⟨anat⟩ *pit of the stomach* **~hälfte** f; die linke (rechte) ~ *the left* (*right*) *h.* **~(innen)haut** f ⟨anat⟩ *endocardium* L; Entzündung der ~ *endocarditis* **~infarkt** *c. infarction*, ⟨mst⟩ *h. attack* **≈·innig, ≈·inniglich** a *h.-felt*; *h.y* **~insuffizienz** f *c. insufficiency* **~kammer** f ⟨anat⟩ *ventricle* **~kirsche** f ⟨bot⟩ *h.-cherry* **~klappe** f *c. valve* | ~nentzündung [f] *valvulitis*; ~nfehler [m] *valvular disease of the h.* **~klopfen** n ⟨med⟩ *palpitation*; er hatte starkes ~ *his h. was palpitating*; ich bekam ~, als .. *my h. leaped into my mouth when ..*; mit entsetzlichem ~ *with his* (*her*) *h. in his* (*her*) *throat*; ~ verursachen *to bring one's h. into one's thr.* **~kohl** m *savoy* **~k·önig** m ⟨cards⟩ *king of h.s* **~krampf** m; ≈e [pl] *angina pectoris* L **≈krank** a; ~ s *to suffer from* (od *be afflicted with*) *a diseased, disordered h.* **~krankheit** f *h. disease* **~kranzgefäß** n ~e [pl] *coronary vessels of the heart* | Mittel gegen ~leiden *anticoronary agent* **~lähmung** f *c. paralysis* **~leiden** n *h. trouble*; *h.-disease* **~messer** m *cardiometer* **~mittel** n *h.* od *cardiac stimulant* **~muschel** f ⟨zoo⟩ *h.-cockle* **~muskel** m ⟨anat⟩ *myocardium* L | ~entzündung [f] *myocarditis* Gr; ~infarkt [m] *myocardial infarction* || ~schwäche = –insuffizienz **~n·eun** f ⟨cards⟩ *nine of h.s* **~neurose** f *neurosis of the h.* **~ohr** n ⟨anat⟩ *auricle* **~pause** f ⟨med⟩ *perisystole* **~schlag** m **1.** *h.-beat* (od *throb*); *pulsation*; beschleunigter ~ *palpitation*(*s* pl); *tachycardia* L **2.** *apoplexy of the h.*; *h. attack*; *h. failure*; *c. paralysis* || ⟨fig⟩ *pulse* (*of a large town*) **≈schlechtig** a ⟨vet⟩ *broken-winded* **~schlechtigkeit** f ⟨bet⟩ *broken wind* **~schwäche** f *c. weakness* (od *insufficiency*); *h. failure* **~spezialist** m *h. specialist* **~spitze** f ⟨anat⟩ *apex* (L) *of the h.* **≈stärkend** a *cordial*; ~es Mittel *cordial* **~stärkung** f *stimulation of the h.* || [konkr] = –mittel **~stolpern** n ⟨path⟩ *arhythmia* L **~stoß** m *h. stroke*; *c. beat* **~stück** n ⟨rail⟩ *frog* **~tätigkeit** f *action, activity of the h.*; beschleunigte ~ *tachycardia* L **~ton** m; ≈e [pl] *h. sounds* pl **~transplantation** f ⟨surg⟩ *transplantation of ..* **~trieb** m ⟨bot⟩ *principal shoot* od *sprout* **~verfettung** f ⟨path⟩ *fatty degeneration of the h.*; an ~ leiden *to suffer from a fatty h.* **~vergrößerung** f ⟨path⟩ *hypertrophy of the h.* **~verkalkung** f *calcification of the h.* **~verpflanzung** f → Herztransplantation [f] **~weh** n ⟨fig⟩ *h.-ache*; *grief*; ~ h *to be h.-sick* **~wurm** m ⟨ent⟩ *caterpillar of the cabbage moth* **~wurz** f ⟨bot⟩ (= Alant) *elecampane* **~wurzel** f ⟨bot⟩ *tap-root* **~z·ehn** f ⟨cards⟩ *ten of h.s* **≈zerbrechend** a *h.-breaking* (*sight*) **≈zermürbend** a *h.-stirring* (od *tearing*) **≈zerreißend** a *h.-breaking*; *h.-rending* (od *tearing*); *blood-curdling* (*cry*); *piteous* (*aspect*)

h·er- ~|zählen vt [h] *to enumerate*; an *to check names on one's fingers* **≈zählung** f *enumeration* **~|zaubern** vt [h] = hervor–

H·erzchen 1. *little heart* (*of chocolate*) **2.** ⟨fig⟩ = Herz C. °**H·erze**! n (*my*) *love*!

Herzeg·owina, die *Herzegovina*

h·er|zeigen vt [h] (etw) *to show*; nun zeigt her, was .. *now show us what ..*; *now let me see what ..*

H·erzeleid n *heart-break, –burnings, –searchings* pl; *affliction*; *sorrow*; ~ h *to be heart-sick*

h·erzen vt [h] (jdn) *to caress, cuddle, fondle, hug, snuggle* || sich ~ u küssen *to bill and coo*

H·erzenbrecher m *lady-killer*; *lady's man* || ⟨sl⟩ *masher*, ⟨Am a.⟩ *sheik*(*h*); → Schwerenöter

H·erzens- ~andacht f *fervent devotion* **~angelegenheit** f *matter of the h.* **~angst** f *anguish of mind* **~bildung** f *inward culture* **~bund** m *h.-bond* **~ein-**

falt f *simplicity of h., simple* (od *single*)*-h.edness* **~ergießung** f ⟨mst⟩ ~en [pl] *effusions* pl; *outpourings* (*of a p's mind*) [pl] **~freude** f *h.'s joy* (f *to*) **~freund** m *very dear fr., p close to one's h., intimate fr.* **≁fr·oh** a [mst pred] *very* od *extremely glad* **~geheimnis** n *bosom-secret* **~grund** m [nur in:] aus ~ *with all one's h.* **≁gut** a *very kind; kind-h.ed* **~güte** f *kind-h.edness; kindness of h.; loving kindness* **~kind** n *darling, sweetheart* **~kummer** m *h.-burnings* pl **~kündiger** m ⟨poet⟩ (= Gott) *searcher of* (*men's*) *h.s* **~lust** f [nur in:] nach ~ *to one's h.'s content*; nach ~ essen *to play a good knife and fork*; sie narrte ihn nach ~ *she fooled him to the top of her bent* ‖ Regen, Hagel u .. tobten nach ~ *rain, hail .. had it all their own way* **~meinung** f *candid* (od *frank, sincere*) *opinion* **~sache** f = –angelegenheit **~töne** m pl: echte ~ *notes of genuine feeling* **~wunsch** m *h.s desire*

ˣ**H·erzerl** n = Herzchen 2. **h·erzhaft 1.** [a] *bold, courageous, stout*(*-h.ed*) (*fellow*) ‖ *h.y* (*pull, meal*); *vigorous; vehement* ‖ *firm* (*measures, resolution*); *resolute* **2.** [adv] *boldly, courageously; h.ily*; er schlug ihm ~ auf die Schulter *he gave him a h.y smack on the sh.* ‖ ~ schmecken ⟨cul⟩ *to be appetizing* od *tasty* | **≁igkeit** f ~ *boldness; courage, courageousness, h.iness; vigorousness* ‖ *firmness; resoluteness*

h·er|ziehen vt/i **1.** vt [h] (etw) *to draw* (od *pull*) *near*; (etw) ~ z jdm *to move .. towards a p* ‖ etw hinter sich ~ *to drag along the floor; to trail; sweep* (*one's skirt*); jdn hinter sich ~ *to drag a p after one* ‖ was hat dich –gezogen? *what made you come here*? **2.** vi [s] **a.** ⟨mil⟩ *to march here*; auf der Str. ~ *to march along the road* ‖ ich bin vor 2 Monaten –gezogen *I moved* (od *came to live*) *here 2 months ago* **b.** ⟨fig⟩ ~ über .. *to inveigh* (od *rail, thunder*) *against* (*a p*); *to rail at* (*a p*); *to pick* (*a p*) *to pieces*

h·erzig a *lovable; charming, pretty*; ein ~es Kindchen *a little love of a child* **-herzig** [in comp] *–hearted*; hart~ *hard-h.*; weich~ *soft* (od *tender*)*-h.* ‖ *–minded; –souled*; hoch~ *high-minded*

h·erzlich A. [a] *c*(*ordial*) (*tone*); *h*(*eart*)*y* (*thanks*); *warm* (*welcome*); *h.felt* (*congratulations*); *affectionate; deeply felt; effusive; sincere; tender* (*love*) ‖ ~e Aussprache *h.-to-h. talk*; ~es Beileid *sincere sympathy*; ~e Bitte (*urgent*) *entreaty*; ~es Einvernehmen *whole-h.ed understanding*; ein ~es Lachen *a h.-whole laugh* ‖ (in Briefen) ~e Grüße, mit ~en Grüßen *with kindest regards* (an *to*) ‖ in der ~sten Weise *in the most c. of ways* **B.** [adv] **1.** *affectionately; c.ly; h.ily; sincerely, warmly* ‖ (jdn) ~ begrüßen *to welcome c.ly*; ~ lachen *to laugh h.ily*; (jdn) ~ umarmen *to embrace effusively* ‖ grüße ihn ~ v mir *give him my kindest regards* **2.** °[verblaßt als Intensivum] (*she detested him*) *c.ly; h.ily* (*tired of a th*) ‖ *exceedingly, extremely* (*bad*); *completely, perfectly* (*indifferent*); *thoroughly; very*; ⟨fam⟩ *jolly, awfully* ‖ ~ dankbar *sincerely grateful* ‖ er war ~ dumm *he was an awful fool* ‖ ~ gern *most* (od *very*) *willingly; with great pleasure* ‖ ~ wenig ⟨sl⟩ *a fat lot* ⟨iron⟩ ‖ ich wußte ~ wenig davon ⟨fam⟩ *I knew precious little about it* | **≁keit** f *c.ity; h.iness; warmth*; mit bes ~ *affectionately*

Herzlichst Dein N. *Very best Yours N.*

h·erzlos 1. [a] *heartless; callous; cruel; unfeeling* **2.** [adv] *h.ly* **≁igkeit** f *h.ness; c.sness; c.lty*

H·erzog m ~(e)s/≁e *duke* (Anrede: *My Lord Duke; Your Grace*; Anschrift: *To His Grace the Duke of* ..); (königl. Prinz) *royal duke* | **~in** f ~/~nen *duchess* (Anrede: *Your Grace*) ‖ ~-witwe [f] *dowager duchess* **≁lich** a *ducal* **~swürde** f *dukedom* **~tum** n *duchy; dukedom*; das ~ N. *the Duchy* (od *Dukedom*) *of N.*; ⟨engl⟩ die ≁er des Königl. Hauses *the Duchies of Cornwall and Lancaster*

herz·u- pref [betont, bei Verben trennbar] *here; up*; → heran-, herbei- **~|eilen** vi [s] *to come up in haste; to hasten to the spot* **~|holen** vt [h] (jdn) *to fetch here* **~|kommen** vi [s] ⟨eig⟩ (P) *to come along; to arrive on the scene*; → hinzu- **~|treten** vi [s] *to step up; to approach*; → hinzu-

herz·ynisch a *Hercynian, Thuringian*

Heses n ⟨mus⟩ *B double flat*

Hesper·iden pl **1.** ⟨Gr myth⟩ *Hesperides* L pl **2.** ⟨ent⟩ (Kleinschmetterling) *Hesperiidae* L pl

H·esse m, **H·essin** f *Hessian* ‖ blinder Hesse! *stupid*! [subst] **H·essen** n *Hesse, Hessia*; †Großherzogtum ~, ~-Darmstadt *Duchy of Hesse-Darmstadt*; †~-Homburg *Hesse-Homburg*; †Kurfürstentum ~, ~-Kassel *electorate of Hesse* (*-Cassel*); ~-Nassau *Hesse-Nassau* **h·essisch** a *Hessian,* (*of*) *Hesse* **H·essische Bergland,** das *The Hessian Hills*

Het·äre f ⟨Gr ant⟩ *courtesan, -zan; hetaira* Gr

hetero- [in comp] (fremd-, verschieden-) *hetero–* **~d·ont** a *–dont* (*dentition*) **~d·ox** a ⟨ec⟩ *–dox* **≁dox·ie** f *–doxy* **≁gam·ie** f *–gamy* **~g·amisch** a *–gamous* **~g·en** a *–geneous* **≁g·enesis** f *–genesis* **≁genit·ät** f *–geneity* **≁gon·ie** f *–gony* **~m·orph** a *–morphic, –morphous* **≁morph·ie** f *–morphy* **≁morph·ismus** m *–morphism* **~n·om** a *–nomous* **≁nom·ie** f *–nomy* **~ph·on** a ⟨mus⟩ *–phonic* **≁-phyll·ie** f ⟨bot⟩ *–phylly* **~pl·astisch** a *–plastic* **≁pt·eren** pl ⟨ent⟩ *–ptera* L pl **~zyklisch** a *–cyclic*

Heth·iter, Hett·iter m ~s/~ ⟨ant⟩ *Hittite*

H·etz- ~artikel m *inflammatory* (od *sensational*) *article* **~blatt** n ⟨Am⟩ *yellow* (od *sensation-mongering*) *newspaper* **~feldzug** m ⟨Am⟩ *yellow press campaign* **~hund** m ⟨hunt⟩ *hound*: Führer der ~e *huntsman* ‖ ⟨hist⟩ (bei Stierhetze) *bulldog* **~jagd** f **1.** *chase* (*of boars, foxes*); *course* (*of hares*); *coursing; hunting with hounds; run with the hounds* ‖ ⟨hist⟩ *baiting* (*of bears, bulls*) **2.** °⟨übtr⟩ *bustle; great hurry; rush* (*of modern life*); es war die reinste ~ *it was a regular race* **3.** ⟨fig⟩ = Hetze **~-kampagne** f = –Feldzug **~peitsche** f *hunting-whip* **~presse** f ⟨Am⟩ *yellow press* **~rede** f *inflammatory speech* **~redner** m *agitator; demagogue* **~ruf** m *taunting clamour* **~schrift** f *sensational pamphlet*

H·etze f ~/~n **1.** ⟨hunt⟩ = Hetzjagd 1.; → a. Hatz ‖ ⟨hist sport⟩ Bären≁ *bear-baiting* **2.** ⟨übtr⟩ = Hetzjagd 2. **3.** ⟨fig⟩ *chase* (auf jdn *after a p*); *baiting*; (mit lautem Geschrei) *hue and cry*; e–e ~ beginnen *to start a hue and cry* (auf *on*); *to make a dead set* (auf jdn *at a p*) ‖ *vehement agitation* (gegen *against*) **4.** Zeitungs≁ *press campaign*

h·etzen vt/i **I.** vt [h] **A. 1.** (Wild) *to hunt with hounds*; (Füchse etc) *to chase*; (Hasen) *to course; run* **2.** ⟨übtr⟩ (jdn) *to chase; chevy; chivy; hound*; (v Ort z Ort *from place to place*) ‖ (of misfortune) *to dog, harass, pursue; worry* ‖ (jdn) z Tode ~ *to hound* (od *hunt*) *to death; to hunt* (od *run*) *down* (*to d.*); (Redensart etc) z T. ~ *to ride to d.* ‖ mit allen Hunden gehetzt (*to be*) *up to all the tricks of the trade; thoroughly trained; thorough-paced* (*rascal*) ‖ ich kam mir vor wie ein gehetztes Wild *I felt harassed to death* **3.** ⟨fig⟩ (schnell befördern) (jdn) *to hurry; race* (durch *through*); *to rush* (über *over*) ‖ ich wünsche nicht gehetzt z w *I refuse to be rushed, I won't be rushed* **B.** (reizen; antreiben) **1.** ⟨hist sport⟩ (Bären etc) *to bait* (mit *with*) **2.** e–n Hund ~ auf *to set* (od *hound*) *a dog at* (*a p*) **3.** (jdn) ~ auf *to hound on* (*a p*); ~ gegen *to set* (od *pit*) *against*; → auf~ ‖ Leute gegen–e–a ~ *to set people by the ears* **II.** vi **A.** [h] **1.** = jagen **2.** ⟨fig⟩ *to excite the feelings; to make mischief*; ~ gegen *to agitate against*; ~ zw *to cause discord between* **B.** [s] (rasen) *to chevy; race; rush*; ⟨mot⟩ *to scorch*; nur nicht ~ *I won't be rushed, please*

H·etzen n **1.** *chasing, coursing* (*of hares*) ‖ ⟨übtr⟩ *harassing; worry* **2.** ⟨fig⟩ *great hurry; rush* **3.** *agitation* (gegen *against*) **4.** ⟨eth⟩ *inciting movement* **h·etzend** a = hetzerisch **H·etzer** m ⟨fig⟩ *inciter, instigator* ‖ ⟨pol⟩ *political agitator; dem-*

agogue; *mischief-maker*; ⟨Am⟩ *rabble-rouser* **Hetzer·ei** f ~/~en ⟨fig⟩ **1.** = Hetzjagd 2. **2.** *harassing*; *worry* **3.** ⟨pol⟩ *agitation*; *demagogy*; *mischief-making* **h·etzerisch** a ⟨pol⟩ *inflammatory* (*article*); *sensational*; ⟨Am⟩ *yellow* (*press*) ‖ *demagogic*; *mischief-making*

H·eu n ~(e)s/ *hay*; ein Bund ~ *a bundle* (od *truss*) *of hay*; ein Fuder ~ *a* (*cart-*)*load of hay* ‖ ~ m *to* (*make*) *hay*; ins ~ fahren *to go haying*; ~ wenden, trocknen *to ted hay* ‖ °⟨fig⟩ → Geld ‖ er hat sein ~ im Trocknen *he has got his hay in*; ⟨fig⟩ *he has made his bit*; °nur ~ u Stroh im Kopf h *to have no milk in the coco-nut* **~asthma** n *hay-asthma*; → –fieber **~barg** m (in Friesland) *hay-shed* **~baum** m *hay-beam*, *-pole* **~bazillus** m ⟨med⟩ *hay-bacillus* L **~boden** m, Sw **~bühne, ~diele** f *hayloft* **~bündel** n *hay-bundle* **~ernte** f *hay-harvest*, *-crop*; *hay-making time* **~falter** m ⟨ent⟩ (*large*, *small*) *heath* **~feim(en)** m *haystack* **~fieber** n *hay fever* **~fuhre** f *hay-cart* **~gabel** f *hay-fork* **~haufen** m *haycock*; *haymow*; → –schober **~hütte** f *haystack stand* **~macher** m *haymaker* **~markt** m *hay-market* **~miete** = –schober **~monat** m *July* °**~ochse** m *blockhead*; *idiot* **~pferd** n **1.** ⟨ent⟩ *grasshopper* **2.** °⟨fig⟩ = –ochse **~raufe** f *hay-rack* **~rechen** m *hay-rake* **~reiter** m *haycock stand* **~schnupfen** m = –fieber **~schober** m *hayrick*, *haystack* **~schrecke** f ⟨ent⟩ *grasshopper*; *locust*; Fang≃ *mantis* L; Wander≃ *migratory locust* | ~nkrebs [m] ⟨zoo⟩ *mantis-shrimp*; *squill*; ~nschwarm [m] *swarm of locusts* **~stadel** m *hay-barn* ‖ *hayrick* **~tee** m *hay-tea* **~wagen** m *hay-cart* **~wender** m *tedder*; *tedding-machine* **~wurm** m ⟨ent⟩ *hay-worm*

Heuchel·ei f ~/~en *dissimulation*; *dissembling*; ⟨ec⟩ (salbungsvolle) *cant*; *hypocrisy*; *sham*; *snivel*(*ling*) **h·eucheln A.** vi/t [h] **1.** vi *to dissemble*; *dissimulate*; *feign*; *snivel*; *to play the hypocrite* **2.** vt (Gefühl) *to affect*; *counterfeit*; *fake*; *feign*; *simulate*; Frömmigkeit ~ *to cant* **B.** ≃ n *dissembling*; *dissimulation*; *simulation*

H·euchler m ~s/~ *hypocrite*; *pharisee*; *pious fraud*; *counterfeiter*; geschickter ~ *profound dissembler* | ≃**isch 1.** [a] *hypocritical*; *deceitful*; *double-faced* (*man*); *feigning* (*p*); *dissembling* (*face*) **2.** [adv] *h.ly*; ~ reden *or* tun *to cant*

h·euen 1. vi [h] *to make hay* **2.** ≃ n *haying*

h·euer adv (*in*) *this year*; *this season*

H·euer f ~/~n *hire*; *rent*; ⟨mar⟩ *wages* pl °**~baas** m ⟨mar⟩ *shipping-master* **~brief** m = –vertrag **~lohn** m *wages* pl **~vertrag** m **1.** (Fracht-) *charter-party* **2.** (Arbeits-) *shipping-articles* pl | **~ling** m *hired labourer*; *tenant working for pay* **h·euern** vt [h] **1.** (Schiff) *to charter* **2.** (jdn) *to engage*, *hire* ‖ ⟨mar⟩ (Besatzung, Seemann) *to sign on*; *to ship*

H·eul- ~boje f ⟨mar⟩ *whistling buoy* **~bombe** f ⟨aero⟩ *screaming bomb* **~ton** m ⟨aero⟩ *warble*; (of siren) *scream*, *signal* (*at varying pitch*) **~vorrichtung** f *screaming device* **h·eulen I.** vi [h] **A. 1.** (of wolves) *to howl*; (of owls) *to hoot* **2.** ⟨übtr⟩ (of wind) *to scream*, *howl*; *roar*; *whistle*; das Meer heulte *it blew great guns* ‖ (of siren) *to hoot*; *scream* **B.** °(P) **1.** (weinen) *to blubber*, *cry*; ⟨fam⟩ *to turn on the waterworks*; *to blub* ‖ (jammern) *to snivel*; *ululate*; *whimper*, *whine* **2.** (schreien) *to bawl*, *howl*; *squall*; (etw) ~d äußern *to howl* **II.** ≃ n **1.** *howl*, *howling*; *hoot*(*ing*); *scream* ‖ °es ist zum ~! *it's great fun*! **2. a.** *blubbering*, *crying* ‖ *snivel*(*ling*); *whimper*(*ing*); *whine*; ⟨bib⟩ (Matt. 8, 12) da wird s ≃ u Z. *there shall be weeping and gnashing of teeth* **b.** *bawl*(*ing*); *howl*(*ing*) **h·eulend** a *howling*, *ululant* (etc) °**Heuler·ei** f = Heulen 2. a.

Heune ⟨poet⟩ → Hunne

h·eurig a *this year's*; *of this year*; *this season's* (*vintage*) ‖ der ≃e *new wine*; er ist kein ~er Hase *he wasn't born yesterday*; ≃e pl *new potatoes*

Heur·istik f ⟨scient⟩ *heuristics* pl

h·eute adv **1.** *today*, *this day* ‖ noch ~ *this very day*; ~ in den frühen Morgenstunden *during the early hours of today* ‖ ~ abend *this evening*; *tonight*; ~ nacht *tonight* ‖ ~ früh *early this morning*; ~ morgen *this morning* ‖ ~ in 8 Tagen, ~ über 8 Tage *today week*, *this day week*; ~ in 6 Jahren *6 years hence* ‖ ~ vor 8 Tagen *today week*; *a week ago*; es ist ~ (gerade) 8 Tage her *it is* (*just*) *a week today* ‖ was du ~ kannst besorgen, das verschiebe nicht auf morgen *don't put off till tomorrow what you can do today*; *do it now*! | bis ~ *to this day*; *to date* ‖ für ~ *for the present* ‖ v ~ *from today*; v ~ ab *commencing from today*; ⟨com⟩ 6 Monate nach dato v ~ *six months after date* ‖ ⟨prov⟩ ~ rot morgen tot ⟨prov⟩ *tomorrow we die* ‖ ⟨fig⟩ nicht v gestern u ~ *nothing new* ‖ v ~ auf morgen *between now* (od *this*) *and tomorrow*; ⟨fig⟩ *in a trice*; *quickly* ‖ lieber ~ als morgen *sooner today than tomorrow* **2.** (= heutzutage) *nowadays*, *today*; das Deutschland v ~ *the Germany of today*; *presentday G.*; die Frau v ~ *the woman of today*; *the modern w.* **h·eutig A.** [a] **1.** *of this day*; *today's*, *this day's*; ⟨com⟩ *of this date* ‖ der ~e Tag *this day*, *today*; die ~e Nummer der ‚Welt' *today's* '*Welt*'; mit der ~en Post *by today's mail* (od *post*); vom ~en Tage, Datum *of this day*, *date* ‖ an e–m Nachmittag wie dem ~en *on an afternoon like today's* ‖ bis auf den ~en Tag *up to the present day*; *to date* **2.** (gegenwärtig) *present*; *modern*, *contemporary* ‖ die ~e Jugend *the youth of the present day* ‖ die ~e Zeit *the present time* (od *age*, *day*); *today* ‖ das ~e England *the E. of today*; *present-day E.* ‖ auf dem ~en Stand der Forschung *up to date* **B.** [abs] ⟨com⟩ **Ihr ≃es** *your favour of today*; unter ≃em *under today's date* **h·eutigestags, h·eutigentags, h·eutzutage** adv *nowadays*; *today*; (*at*) *the present day*; *these days*; *in our day* od *times*

Hexa- [in comp] (Sechs-) *hexa-* **~ch·ord** m ⟨mus⟩ *–chord* **~·eder** n ⟨minr⟩ *–hedron* **≃·edrisch** a *–hedral* **~g·on** n ⟨math⟩ *–gon* **≃gon·al** a *–gonal* **~gr·amm** n *–gram* **Hex·ameter** m ⟨pros⟩ *–meter* **Hex·an** n ⟨chem⟩ *–ne* **H·exapla** f *–pla* **–p·oden** pl ⟨ent⟩ *–pods* pl **~t·euch** m ⟨bib⟩ *Hexateuch*

H·exe f ~/~n **1.** ⟨myth⟩ *witch*; *sorceress* **2.** ⟨übtr⟩ (altes Weib) *hag*; *old witch*; *crone*; *henwife*; *beldame* ⟨cont⟩ ‖ (böses) *hellcat*; *vixen* ‖ (häßliches) *lemon* ‖ ⟨hum⟩ kl ~ *gipsy*; *minx*; *flirt*; *hussy* | ≃**n** vi [h] ⟨myth⟩ *to practise sorcery* (od *witchcraft*) ‖ *to juggle*; *to perform conjuring tricks* ‖ er kann ~ *he is a sorcerer*; *he is a conjurer* (od *juggler*) ‖ °ich kann nicht ~ *I am no conjurer*; *my name's Simpson*, *not Samson* ‖ das geht wie gehext *it works like magic* **H·exen- ~besen** m **1.** ⟨myth⟩ *w.es' broomstick* **2.** ⟨bot⟩ *w.es' broom* **~finger** m ⟨geol⟩ *belemnite* **~jagd** f ⟨pol⟩ *w.-hunt* **~kessel** m *w.'s cauldron* ‖ ⟨fig⟩ *jam*, *mess*; *pot of trouble* ‖ *pandemonium* L **~kraut** n ⟨bot⟩ *mandragora*; *mandrake*; *enchanter's nightshade* **~kreis** m *magic circle* **~kunst** f *w.craft*; *sorcery*; *wizardry*; *black art* **~mehl** n ⟨bot⟩ *w.-meal*; *lycopodium* L **~meister** m *sorcerer*; *wizard* **~milch** f ⟨bot⟩ = Wolfsmilch **~pilz** m ⟨bot⟩ → Röhrling **~probe** f *w.es' ordeal* **~prozeß** m *witch*(*craft*)*-trial* **~ring** m ⟨bot⟩ *w.es' ring* **~sabbath** m *w.es' sabbath* ‖ ⟨fig⟩ *pandemonium* **~stich** m ⟨weav⟩ *herringbone stitch* **~schuß** m ⟨med⟩ *crick in one's back*; *lumbago* L **~trank** m *hellbroth* **~verfolgung** f *w.-hunt* ⟨a. pol bes Am⟩ **~versammlung** f ⟨Scot⟩ *coven* **~werk** n *w.ery*, *w.work* **~zwirn** m ⟨bot⟩ *dodder* **H·exer** m ~s/~ *ringer* (*who rings the changes on himself*)

Hexer·ei f ~/~en *sorcery*, *witchcraft*, *witchery*; (unter Negern in Westind. u Am.) *voodoo* ‖ (Taschenspielerei) *conjuring*; *jugglery* ‖ → Geschwindigkeit ‖ °das ist k–e ~ ⟨fam⟩ *that's easy enough*; ⟨fam⟩ *you can do that easy*

Hi·atus m ~/~ ⟨gram⟩ *hiatus* L

Hib·ernien n (röm. Name Irlands) *Hibernia*
Hib·iskus m (L) = Eibisch *hibiscus*
H·ickelhäuschen n (Spiel) *hopscotch*
H·ickory m ⟨bot⟩ *hickory* **~holz** n *hickory*
hie adv **1.** [nur in einigen Wendungen f hier:] ~ u da *here and there*; → hier **2.** ×= hier ⟨Ger hist⟩ ~ Welf! ~ Waiblingen! *Hie W.! Hie W.!*
hieb 1. & 3. sg pret v hauen **H·ieb** m ~(e)s/~e **A.** [abstr] **1.** ⟨eig⟩ **a.** *blow, cut, stroke* (*of a mower*); *hit* (auf, nach *at*); ⟨fam⟩ *whack, knock, rap, swack, clout; dig* ⟨a. fig⟩ ‖ ⟨fenc⟩ *cut* ‖ Axt~ *stroke of the axe*; ~ mit der P. *cut with a whip*; *lash* ‖ Sch.t~ *sword-cut*; *blow from a sword*; (heftiger) *slash* ‖ ⟨crick⟩ leichter ~ flick | ⟨fig⟩ auf den ersten ~ *at the first attempt* ‖ mit e–m ~ *at one* (od *a single*) *blow* ‖ der ~ sitzt *the hit tells* (od *goes home*); jdm e–n ~ versetzen *to deal a p a blow*; *to strike a p*; z e–m ~ ausholen *to lift one's arm to strike* (nach *at*) **b.** °~e [pl] *beating, flogging, thrashing, whipping*; ~e austeilen *to deliver blows*; ~e bek *to get a thr.*; gleich setzt es ~e *you'll be getting a thr.* **2.** ⟨fig⟩ **a.** *cut*; *hit* (auf *at*); *fling*; *lash* ‖ ein gut sitzender ~ *a home thrust* ‖ der ~ galt mir *that was a hit at me* ‖ jdm e–n ~ versetzen *to have a fling at a p* **b.** °= Rausch; e–n ~ h *to be elevated* **B.** [konkr] **1.** (Schramme) *cut*; *gash*; *scar*; (tiefer) *slash* **2.** (of a file) *cut*; einfacher (zweifacher, feiner, grober) ~ *single* (*double, fine, coarse*) *cut* **3.** ⟨forest⟩ *cut of timber* **~fechten** n *cut-fencing* ‖ ~- u Stoßfechten *cut-and-thrust* ‖ ~- u stichfest [a] *water tight*; *realistic* (Dialog); *iron-clad* (Alibi); ~ s: (*this story doesn't*) *hold water* **~waffe** f *slashing weapon* ‖ ~ u Stoßwaffe *cutting and thrusting weapon* **~wunde** f *cut*; *gash*; *scar*; *slash*
hielt 1. & 3. sg pret v halten
hien·ieden adv *here below* **hier** adv **1.** *here*; (auf Briefen) *local* ‖ ~ auf Erden *here below* ‖ → ~-zulande ‖ ~ in Amerika (etc) *over here* ‖ ~ am Ort *in this place, city* ‖ ~ an dieser Stelle *on this spot here* | ~ draußen (drinnen) *out* (*in*) *here* ‖ ~ durch *through here* ‖ ~ nahebei *near here*; *near* (*to*) *this place* ‖ ~ oben (unten) *up* (*down*) *here* ‖ mein Freund ~ *my friend here*; diese Bücher ~ ⟨vulg⟩ *these here books* | ~ ruht in Gott .. *here rests in peace* .. ‖ ~, nimm dies *here, take this* ‖ er ist nicht ~ *he is not here* (od *present*); ~! *here! present!* ‖ ⟨telph⟩ ~ ist Georg N. *this is George N., George N.* (*is*) *speaking* (*here*); (‚Könnte ich Herrn N. sprechen?') ‚Der ist ~ am Apparat' (..) *speaking* ‖ ⟨wir⟩ ~ ist Berlin (*this is*) (*Radio*) *B. calling*; ⟨Am-Ger⟩ *this is AFN* ‖ ~ sind wir schon *there you are* ‖ ~ ist es (sc was wir suchen)! *here you are!* ‖ die Polizei wird gleich ~ s *the police will be round immediately* | v hier *from here* ‖ ich bin nicht v ~ *I am a stranger* (od *not a resident*) *here* ‖ °du bist wohl nicht v ~ *you are out of your senses*; *are you mad?* **2.** ⟨übtr⟩ (an dieser Stelle [sc e–s Buches etc]) *here* (*he looked at me*); *this* (od *here*) *is where* ‖ *at that*; *at these words* ‖ den wirst du ~ aus dem Spiel l *you will leave him out of this* ‖ °es steht mir bis ~ *I am fed up* (od *sick of it*) ‖ ~ u da → gelegentlich **h·ieran** [a. –·–] adv *about this* (*there was something ludicrous a. th.*); (*I had not thought*) *of this*; (*he could not believe*) *in this*; (*he attached a cord*) *to this* ‖ ~ ist nichts z ändern *this can't be helped*; *I cannot help it* ‖ ~ ist kein wahres Wort *there is no thruth in this*
Hier·arch m ~en/~en *hierarch* **Hierarch·ie** f ~/~n *hierarchy* **hier·archisch** a *hierarchic*(*al*)
hier- **~auf** adv **1.** ~ (sc auf e–m Stück Papier) war geschrieben *on this was written* **2.** ⟨übtr⟩ (*you may be proud*) *of this* ‖ (*I must insist*; *you can rely*) *on this*; (*I must persist*) *in this* ‖ *to this* (*he replied* ..) **3.** (zeitlich) *hereupon, thereupon*; *upon, after this, that*; *then* **~aufhin** adv *upon this, hereupon* **~aus** adv **1.** *from this* (od *these*) (*came* ..); *out of this* (*you won't get much*); *by* (od *from*) *this* (*we won't profit much*) ‖ ~ wurde nichts *this never came to anything*; ~ wird nichts Gutes w *no good will come of it* **2.** (als Folge) *from this* (*it follows that* ..); *hence* (*we infer that* ..) **~|behalten** vt [h] *to keep here*; *to keep back* **~bei** adv **1.** *at this, that*; *on this occasion* **2.** (inliegend) *herewith*; *with this*; *annexed, enclosed* **~|bleiben** vi [s] *to remain* (od *stay*) *here*; (*can't you*) *stay on?* **~durch** **1.** [–·–] (örtlich) *through here*; *through this place* **2.** [·–] *by this*; *by this* (od *these*) *means*; *hereby*; ich erlaube mir, Ihnen ~ mitzuteilen *I beg to inform you that* .. **~ein** adv *into this* (*place*) ‖ *to this* (*he could not consent*) **~für** [a. –·–] adv **1.** *for this, for it*; der Grund ~ war *the reason for this was* .. ‖ er hatte k–n Sinn ~ *he had no sense of it* ‖ ich wünschte e–n Zeugen ~ *I wanted a witness to this* **2.** *for this*; *instead of it* **~gegen** adv *against this* od *it* ‖ ~ ist nichts z m *this can't be helped* ‖ ~ ist nichts einzuwenden *there is no objection to this* **~her** adv **1.** *here*; *this way* ‖ bitte ~ *this way, please*; *right over here* ‖ bis ~ *to this point*; bis ~ u nicht weiter *I draw the line at this*; (zeitlich) *hitherto*; bis ~ u nicht weiter *so far and no farther* **2.** [in comp] (a. hierh·er) ~|bitten vt (jdn) *to ask* (*a p*) *round* ‖ ~|bringen vt *to bring along* (*here*) ‖ ~|gehen vi: geh ~ *step this way* ‖ ~|gehören vi: er (es) gehört nicht ~ *he* (*it*) *does not belong here*; (nicht) ~gehörend (*not*) *to the point, purpose*; (*not*) *relevant* ‖ ~|kommen vi *to come* (*along*) *here*; *to come along* (od *round*); k Sie ~, bitte, wollen Sie ~ k, bitte *come this way, Sir* **~herauf** adv *up here*; komm ~ *come up here* **~heraus** adv *out here* **~herein** adv *in here* **~herum** adv *this way round* ‖ *hereabout*(*s*); *about here* **~herunter** adv *down here* **~hin** adv *here*; *this way* **~hinauf** adv *up here* **~hinaus** adv *out here* **~hinein** adv *in here* **~hinter** adv *behind this*; *at the back of this* **~hinunter** adv *down here* **~in** adv *herein*; *in this*; ~ war er wie .. *in this he was like his father* ***~lands** adv *in this country*; *over here* **~mit** adv *herewith*; (*along*) *with this* ‖ *to this* (*he joined another piece*); ~ ich bin einverstanden *to this I agree* (od *I give my consent*) ‖ ~ beschäftigte er sich .. *in this he engaged for a time* ‖ ⟨com⟩ wir bringen Ihnen ~ zur Kenntnis .. *we beg to advise you* (*that* ..) ‖ ~ wird bescheinigt, daß .. *this is to certify that* .. **~nach** adv **1.** *after this* (*it was his turn*); *after that* ‖ (zeitlich) *hereafter*; gleich ~ *hereupon*; *upon this* **2.** ⟨übtr⟩ (demzufolge) *according to this*; *by* (od *from*) *this* (*you cannot judge him*); ~ z urteilen *at this rate* (*it will take him 3 years to get there* ***~nächst** adv *next to this* **~neben** adv *next door to us*; *close by*
Hiero- [in comp] *hiero-* **~gl·yphe** f **1.** ⟨ant⟩ *-glyph* ‖ ~n [pl] *-glyph*(*ic*)*s* pl; Schrift in ~n *-glyphics* pl; *writing in -glyphs*; *-glyphic writing* ‖ ein-, zwei-, dreikonsonantige ~n [pl] *uni-, bi-, triliterals* **2.** ⟨übtr⟩ °d–e ~n *your* -glyphs (*I cannot read*) **~gl·yphisch** a *-glyphic*(*al*) **~krat·ie** f *-cracy* **~mant·ie** f *-mancy* **~ph·ant** m ⟨ant⟩ (Weihepriester) *-phant* **~skop·ie** f *-scopy*
h·ier- **~orts** adv *in this place* (od *country*); *in these parts* **~sein** n ~s/ *presence* ‖ *visit*; während m–s ~s *during my stay here* **~s·elbst** adv *here*; *in this place* **~über** adv **1.** ⟨eig⟩ *over here*; *over this place* ‖ ~ geht nichts *there is nothing like it*; *you cannot beat it* **2.** ⟨übtr⟩ *in this connection*; *in* (od *concerning*) *this matter* ‖ *at* (od *about*) *this* (*he was angry*); (*we were glad*) *of this*; (*I shall write you*) *on this* **~um** adv ⟨übtr⟩ *about this*; *on this account*; ~ wurde viel gekämpft *for this there was much fighting* **-unter** adv **1.** *under this*; *below this* ‖ (in documents) *hereunder*; wie ~ angegeben *as under* **2.** (unter ihnen) *among these* **3.** ⟨übtr⟩ was soll man ~ verstehen *what are we to understand by this?* **~von** adv ⟨übtr⟩ *of this* (*you cannot be relieved*); *hereof* ‖ ~ kann ich mich nicht trennen

I cannot part with it || ~ hängt alles ab *on this everything depends* **~vor** adv ⟨übtr⟩ ~ graut es mich *I shudder at this* || ~ ekelte es ihn *he was disgusted with this* ***~wider** adv ⟨übtr⟩ *against this* **~zu** adv ⟨übtr⟩ ~ kommt noch (*or* ~ zähle man) *add to this* || Wissen ist nichts im Vergleich ~ *knowledge is nothing to it*; im Gegensatz ~ *over against this* || ~ kann ich nichts sagen *to this I can't say anything*; er hatte ~ k–e Vorschläge z m *he had no s. to make on this score* **~zulande** adv *in this country*; *in these parts* od *quarters*; *over here* **~zwischen** adv *between these*

h·iesig a *of this place*; *of this country*; *local*

hieß 1. & 3. sg pret v heißen

h·ieven vt [h] ⟨mar⟩ (etw) *to heave*

H·ift- ~horn n *bugle(r)* **~stoß** m *mort*

H·ildesheim n ⟨Ger⟩ (Stadt)

H·ilfe f ~/~n **A.** [abstr] **1.** *help*; *aid* (f *to*); *assistance*; *support* (*of a Power*); *sustainment* || (~ in Not) *relief, succour* || er ist e–e gr ~ *he is a great help* || erste ~ *first aid* || ⟨pol⟩ gegenseitige ~ ⟨Am⟩ *log-rolling*; Ausschuß für g. ~ *inter-aid committee* || → Mithilfe **2. a.** jdm alle ~ **abschneiden** *to deprive a p of all h.*; jdm ~ angedeihen *or* zuk l *to give aid to a p*; *to bring a p h.* || ⟨sport⟩ ~e geben *to render aid* || es gibt k–e ~ mehr f ihn *he is past remedy* (od *cure*) || e–r S ~ gewähren *to afford assistance* (od *support*) *to a th*; *to support a th* || ~ leisten *to bear a hand*; ~ u Beistand leisten *to lend one's aid and assistance* || jdm ~ leisten *to assist* (od *back, help*) *a p* || ~ suchen *to seek h.* **b. mit** ~ **jds** *with the h.* (od *support*) *of a p* || mit ~ v *with* (od *by*) *the aid of* (*sedatives*); *by means of*; *by dint of* (*knocking*); mit ~ ihres Wissens *in the light of their knowledge* | **ohne** s–e ~ (*I succeeded*) *no thanks to him* || ohne ~ anfangen *to start from scratch* || ohne ~ s *to stand alone*; → ~smädchen | jdn **um** ~ bitten *to ask a p's h.* || um ~ flehen *to pray for h.*; um jds ~ flehen *to implore a p's h.* || um ~ rufen *to cry for h.* | **zu** ~! *h. h.*! || jdm z ~ eilen *to rush to a p's assistance*; e–r Stadt .. *to hasten to the relief of a town* || jdm z ~ k *to come* (⟨mil⟩ *to march*) *to a p's aid*; e–r S z ~ k *to come to the aid of a th*; jds Gedächtnis z ~ k *to assist a p's memory* || etw z ~ nehmen *to make use of*; *to draw upon*; *to resort to a th* || jdn z ~ rufen *to call in a p's assistance* || einem Heer Truppen z ~ schicken *to send troops for the relief of an army* **B.** [konkr] **1.** (P) *h.*; *h.ing hand*; *woman-h.*; → Stütze **2.** (P & S) *asset* (f *to*) || verläßliche ~ *stand-by* || ~n [pl] *subsidiaries* pl **≃bittend** a = –flehend **≃bringend** a *affording h.*; *h.ful* **≃flehend** [prs p] sie k ~ z ihm *they implore his h.* || [a] *suppliant* **~leistung** f *aid, assistance, h.*; *relief* **~ruf** m *cry* (od *call*) *for aid*; ⟨mar⟩ *distress-call*) || ⟨übtr⟩ *entreaty*; *appeal*; *imploration*; *urgent request* **≃rufend** a = –flehend **h·ilflos 1.** [a] **a.** *defenceless, destitute, forlorn, h.less*; *stranded*; *wretched* **b.** (untauglich) *h.less*; *feckless, inefficient, shiftless* || *blank* (*look*) || ~er Mensch *stick-in-the-mud*; *poor stick* || ~ dastehen (*or* s) vor .. *to be lost before* (*the intrigues of* ..) **c.** der Hilflose; die ≃en *the destitutes* pl **2.** [adv] *h.lessly*; jdn ~ ansehen *to look blankly at a p* **≃igkeit** f *defencelessness*; *h.lessness*; *shiftlessness* **h·ilfreich 1.** [a] *h.ful* (*p*); *h.ing* (*hand*); *expansive* **2.** [adv] *h.fully* **H·ilfs-** *ass*(*istant*); *aux*(*iliary*); *subs*(*idiary*); *anc*(*illary*); *supplementary*; *p*(*art*)-*t*(*ime*); *accessory*; *under-* **~aktion** f *work of relief* **~angestellte**: [der ~, ein ~r] *supernumerary* **~anleihe** f *relief-loan* **~antenne** f *artificial aerial* **~anzeigegerät** n *anc. indicator* **~arbeiter** m (*minder's*) *ass.*; *p.-t. worker*; *h.er*; *subs.*; → –angestellte **~ausbilder** m *assistant instructor* **≃bedürftig** a *requiring h.*; *needy, indigent* **~bedürftigkeit** f *indigence* **~beleuchtung** f = Not- **≃bereit** a *ready to h.*; *h.ful*; → hilfreich **~bereitschaft** f *h.fulness* **~bischof** m *suffragan*; *suf. bishop* od *bishop-suf.* **~buch** n *compendium*; *handbook, manual* (f *to*) **~denkschrift** f ⟨dipl⟩ *aide-memoire* Fr **~dienst** m *voluntary service for one's country* || ~e [pl] ⟨tech⟩ *anc. services* **~expedition** f *expedition in relief* **~felge** f *extra rim* **~flughafen** m *supplementary aerodrome* **~frequenz** f ⟨wir⟩ *back-up fre.* **~geistliche** [der ~, ein ~r] *curate*; *ass. priest* **~gelder** n pl *subsidies* pl; mit ~n versehen *to subsidize* **~größe** f *aux. aid* od *factor* **~heer** n *aux. army*; *aux.ries* pl **~industrien** f pl *subs. industries* pl **~kasse** f *provident fund* (od *society*) **~kellner** m ⟨Am⟩ *bus-boy* **~kirche** f *chapel-of-ease* **~kolonne** f, **~kommando** n ⟨rail⟩ *breakdown gang*; ⟨Am⟩ *wrecking crew* **~kondensator** m *aux. condenser* **~korps** n *aux. troops* pl **~kraft** f *h.er*; *h.ing hand*; *temporary ass.*; ⟨univ⟩ *famulus* L **~kreuzer** m *armed merchant cruiser* **~lehrer** m *u.-teacher*; *p.-t. te.*; *supply t.*; ⟨dero⟩ *usher* **~linie** f ⟨math⟩ *subs. line* **~mädchen** n (*lady's*) *h.* **~mannschaft** f = –kolonne **~maschine** f *aux. engine*; ⟨mar⟩ kl ~ *donkey-engine* **~maßstab** m *aux. ruler device*; *vernier* Fr **~mittel** n *aid*; *contrivance, device*; *expedient, resort* (z *to*), *resource*; *vehicle* (f *for* od *of*); (*orthopaedic*) *appliance*; Methode mit (ohne) ~ (*non-*) *app. m.*; ⟨mil⟩ *asset* (*in battle*); ein gutes ~ z .. ⟨fam⟩ *a good dodge for* (*learning a language*); → –quelle || (Heilmittel) ~ *remedy*; als ~ gegen Arbeitslosigkeit *as a r. for unemployment* **~motor** m ⟨tech⟩ *aux. motor*; *servo-m.* **~posten** m ⟨med⟩ *first-aid station* **~prediger** m = –geistliche **~quelle** f *resource*; [mst pl] ~n *r.s* pl; → –mittel || reich an ~n *r.ful*; ohne ~n *r.less*; Summen der noch nicht eingesetzten ~n *potential*; ~n an Menschen u Material *resources and manpower* **~rakete** f *Jato* **~redakteur** m *ass. editor* **~ruder** n ⟨aero⟩ *Flettner balance*; *tab* **~schiff** n *aux. vessel* **~schule** f *school for backward children* **~schwester** f *junior n.* **~telefonist** m *p.-t. telephonist* **~truppen** pl *aux. troops*; *aux.ies* pl **~- u Wiedergutmachungsabkommen** n *United Nations Relief and Rehabilitation Administration* (*UNRRA*) **~ventil** n *aux. valve* **~vorrichtung** f *servo-booster, s.-mechanism* **~wagen** m ⟨mot⟩ *service car* **~welle** f ⟨tech⟩ *subs. shaft* **~werk** n *relief work* **~wissenschaft** f *aux. science* **~zeitwort** n ⟨gram⟩ *aux. verb* **~ziel** n ⟨artill; aero-phot⟩ *reference point* **~zug** m ⟨rail⟩ *breakdown* (⟨Am⟩ *wrecking*) *train*

hilfst 2. sg pres; **hilft** 3. sg pres v helfen

Him·alaja m *Himalaya* (*Mountains*), *Himalayas* pl

H·imbeer- *raspberry–* **~gelee** n *r.-jam* °**~-Heini** m *cissie* **~saft** n *r.-juice* **~sirup** m *r.-syrup*; *r.-vinegar* **~steckling** m *r.-cane* **~strauch** m *r.-bush*

H·imbeere f ~/~n ⟨bot⟩ *raspberry*

H·immel m ~s/~ **A. 1. (sichtbarer) a.** (*the*) *sky*; *firmament*; ⟨poet⟩ *heaven* || bedeckter ~ *clouded* od *overcast sky*; gestirnter ~ *starry sky*; *spangled h.s*; (mit Schäfchenwolken) gestreifter ~ *mackerel-sky* || am ~ *in the sky*; hoch am ~ *high in the h.s*; die Sonne stieg am ~ auf *the sun rose in the sky* || gegen den ~ sich abzeichnende Silhouette *sky-line* || ⟨fig⟩ vom ~ gesandt *h.-sent*; v ~ stammend *h.-born* || der ~ strahlte in e–m hellen Blau *the sky was a bright blue* **b.** (Klima) *h.*; *skies* pl; *climate, clime* **c.** ⟨fig⟩ *horizon*; *sphere*; am literarischen ~ *in the realm of letters* **2. (unsichtb.) a.** *h.* [ohne art] ⟨a. fig⟩; ⟨poet⟩ *sky* **b.** ⟨fig⟩ *h.*; *state of happiness* **3.** ⟨übtr⟩ **a.** Bett≃ *canopy, tester*; Thron≃ *baldachin* **b.** ⟨theat⟩ Bühnen≃ *h.*; *canopy* **c.** ⟨min⟩ = First **B. 1. a.** der ~ **hängt** ihm voller Geigen *he looks on the sunny side of things* || er glaubte, der ~ würde einstürzen, wenn .. *he thought the sky would fall if* ..; ein Getöse, als fiele der ~ ein *a noise like the racking of h.* || soweit der ~ **reicht** *as far as the eye can reach* || die Schleusen des ~s öffneten sich *it was pouring with rain* || dem ~ sei Dank *thanks be* *to God; thank goodness* (od *H.*) || ~ **u Erde** in Bewegung setzen *to move h. and earth; to leave no stone unturned* (*to get* ..); den (*or* e–n) ~ auf E. h *to have a h. on earth; to have the time of one's life; to live in clover* || ~ **u Hölle** in Bewegung setzen *to raise Cain* (*to get* ..); *to move h. and earth*; ~ u Hölle z Zeugen anrufen *to call h. and earth to witness*; ~ u Hölle-(Kinder-)Spiel *hopscotch* **b.** der ~ **sei** mein Zeuge! *God be my witness*! || der ~ **weiß**, wo ..; weiß der ~, wo .. *h.* (od *goodness, God, the Lord*) *knows where* .. (*I don't*) || der ~ **behüte** uns vor .. *may h. preserve us from* .. || der ~ verhüte ..!, das verhüte der ~! *God forbid* || wollte der ~ ..! gebe es der ~ ..! *would to H.* ..! *I wish to goodness* ..! **c.** °**Herr des** ~**s**! Gütiger ~!, Mein ~! Ach du lieber ~! *good h.s*! *good(ness) gracious*! *dear me*! *H. help me*! || °Gerechter ~! *dear heart alive*! || °~ noch einmal! ~ Donnerwetter! *damn it*! *the deuce take it*! || um (des) ~s willen! *for h.s sake*! *for goodness' sake*! *in h.s name*! **2.** wie **aus** allen ~n gefallen s *to be dumbfounded* (od ⟨fam⟩ *flabbergasted*) || (es kam) aus heiterem ~ .. *right out of the blue* || wie ein Blitz aus heiterem ~ *like a bolt from the blue* | **beim** ~! *by God*! | **gen** ~ *h.ward(s)*; gen ~ stehend *turned-up* (*nose*) | **im** ~ *in h.*; hoch oben im ~ *on high*; im ~ u auf Erden *in h. and earth* || wie im ~ leben = den ~ auf Erden h || im siebenten ~ ⟨theol⟩ *in the seventh h.*; *in the h. of h.s* || ⟨fig⟩ im 7. ~ s *to be in the seventh h. of delight*; *to walk upon air* | **in** den ~ eingehen *to go to h.* || in den ~ entrückt *carried up to h.* || (jdn) in den ~ heben *to belaud* (od *extol, praise*; *cry up*) *to the skies* || in den ~ k *to go* (od *get*) *to h.*; *to join the angels* || der Berg reicht in den ~ *the mountain reaches into the clouds* || die Bäume wachsen nicht in den ~ *no tree goes on growing until it reaches the sky*; es ist dafür gesorgt, daß die B. nicht in den ~ w. *everything has a limit to its growth*; *there is a limit to everything* | **unter** freiem ~ *under the open sky*; *in the open* (*air*); unter fr. ~ liegen *to be open to the sky* | **vom** ~ her *from on high*; ein Zeichen vom ~ *a sign from H.* || ⟨fig⟩ wie v ~ gefallen *quite suddenly* || ⟨prov⟩ es ist noch kein Meister v ~ gefallen *no man is born master* || das Blaue v ~ herunterlügen *to lie in one's throat* | **zum** ~ hinauf *h.ward(s)* || es schreit z ~ *it is a sin and shame*; das Elend schreit z ~ *the misery is a disgrace to humanity*; .. *is perfectly scandalous*; es stinkt z ~ *it smells to high h.*; z ~ strebend *lofty* | **zw** ~ u Erde schweben *to hover between h. and earth* **^~an** adv *h.ward(s)* **^~·angst** a es ist mir ~ → Angst **^~anstrebend** a *sky-scraping*; *h.-aspiring* (*tower*) **~bett** n *fourposter* **^~blau** a *azure*; *sky-blue* || (etw) ~ färben *to azure* °**~donnerwetter**! → Donnerw. **~fahrt** f ⟨ec⟩ Christi ~ *the Ascension*; Mariä ~ *the* (*Feast of*) *Assumption* (15. Aug.) **~fahrts-** ~blume [f] ⟨bot⟩ *cat's foot*; *cudweed*; ~fest [n] *Ascension-Day*; ~insel [f] *Ascension Island* (brit. seit 1815) || ~tag [m] = –fest **~hoch 1.** [a] *sky-scraping*; *towering* **2.** [adv] *sky-high* || (jdn) ~ bitten *to implore*; ~ jauchzen *to exult, jubilate* **~hüpfen** n (Kinderspiel) *hopscotch* **~reich** n (*kingdom of*) *h.*; *kingdom-come* || des Menschen Wille ist sein ~ *man will have his own way, man is fond of his own w.* **~schlüssel** m, **~schlüsselchen** n ⟨bot⟩ *primrose*; *Primula* [L] **^~schreiend** a *crying* (*shame*); *disgraceful*; *flagrant*; *infamous*; *scandalous*; *shameful* (*wrong*) || *crass* (*ignorance*); *utter* || *idiotic* (*nonsense*) **~strich** m *region, climate, clime*; *zone* **^~stürmend** a ⟨fig⟩ *sky-aspiring* (od *scraping*); *titanic*; *audacious*; *revolutionizing* (*invention*) **^~wärts** adv *h.ward(s)*; *sky-ward(s)* **^~weit 1.** [a] ⟨fig⟩ *enormous* (*difference*); *very great*; *huge*; *immense*; *vast* **2.** [adv] *enormously*; *immensely*; ~ (v–e–a) entfernt (*or* verschieden) s *to be poles asunder* od *apart*; ~ verschieden s *to be diametrically opposed*; *to differ from each other as wide as east from west* °**Himmel·ei** f *affected emotion*; *gush* ***h·immeln** vi [h] *to be effusive*; *to gush* **H·immels-** *cel(estial)* **~achse** f *cel. axis*; *axis of the world* **~äquator** m *cel. equator*; *equinoctial* **~bahn** f *path* (od *track*) *of the h.ly bodies* **~berg** m ⟨poet⟩ *sky, h.s* **~beschreibung** f *uranography* **~blau** n *azure*; *sky-blue* **~bote** m *h.ly messenger* **~botschaft** f *h.-sent message* **~braut** f ⟨poet⟩ = Nonne **~brot** n ⟨bot⟩ *manna-ash* **~dom** m *dome* (od *vault*) *of the sky* **~erscheinung** f *phenomenon* (od *sign*) *in the h.s*; *cel. apparition* **~gegend** f *quarter* || aus allen ~en *from all quarters* || die vier ~en des Kompasses *the four cardinal points* (*of the compass*) **~gewölbe** n *cel. sphere*; *firmament* **~karte** f *celestial map* **~körper** m *celestial body* **~kreis** m *circle of heavens* **~kugel** f *cel. globe*; *orb* **~kunde** f *astronomy*; → –beschreibung **~landschaft** f ⟨paint⟩ *sky-scape* **~lauf** m *movement of the h.ly bodies* **~leiter** f ⟨bot⟩ *Jacob's ladder* **~licht** n *cel. light* **~mechanik** f *celestial mechanics* **~raum** m *expanse of the h.s* **~richtung** f = –gegend **~ringglobus** m *armillary sphere* **~schlüssel(chen)** = Himmel– **~schrift** f (Reklame) *sky-writing, aerial advertising* **~schwertel** n ⟨bot⟩ = Schwertlilie **~strich** m = Himmel– **~tau** m ⟨bot⟩ *sundew*; –brot **~wagen** m ⟨astr⟩ = Großer Bär **~zelt** n *canopy* od *vault of heaven* **h·immlisch A.** [a] **1.** ⟨mst bib & theol⟩ *h.ly*; ⟨poet⟩ *supernal* || euer ~er Vater *your Father in H.* || die ~en Mächte *the powers above* || ~es Reich = Himmelreich || die ~e Stadt *the H.ly City*; *Paradise*; → Heerschar || dazu gehört e–e ~e Geduld *that would try the patience of Job* || °~er Vater! = du lieber Himmel! → B. 1. c. **2.** ⟨übtr⟩ *celestial, divine* (*music*), *h.ly* (*beauty*) **3.** °⟨fig⟩ *delicious*; *gorgeous* (*she was g. as Ophelia*); *h.ly* (*peaches*); *lovely* (*picture, poem*) || *glorious, magnificent* (*weather*); ~! *divine*! **B.** [**adv**] °⟨fig⟩ *d.ly*; *gl.ly*; *go.ly*; *mag.ly* **C.** [**abs**] die ^~en ⟨poet⟩ = Götter

hin adv **1.** (v Sprechenden fort) **a.** [mit Verben] *there*; *thither*; → hin– 1. **b.** ⟨bes rail⟩ ~ u zurück *there and back*; ⟨mar⟩ *out and home* || zwei Fahrkarten 2. Klasse ~ u zurück *two second-class returns* || ich mußte ~ *I had to go there*; er wollte ~ *he wanted to go there* || sie sind schon ~ *they are on their way* || °also ~! *so here goes*! **2.** (Richtung) **a.** *along*; an der Küste ~ *along the shore*; auf der Straße ~ *along the road* || auf dem Wege nach Berlin ~ *on the way to B.* || nach dieser Richtung ~ *this way*; *in this direction*; nach dem Osten ~ *to* (od *towards*) *the east* || über die ganze Welt ~ *all over the world* || vor sich ~ *to o.s.*; *silently* || z ihm ~ *towards him*; bis zur Mauer ~ *up to the wall* || → wo ~ || wo ist er ~? *where has he gone*?; wo willst du ~? *where are you going to*? **b.** °Geld ~, Geld her *hang the cost, man*! || °das ist nicht ~ u nicht her *there is not much in that* || → ~ und her || ~ u wieder *off and on, here and there*; *now and then* (od *again*); *occasionally*; ~ u wieder auftretend *occasional* **3.** ⟨**übtr**⟩ **a.** (**zeitlich**) es sind noch 3 Wochen ~ *it's another three weeks* || es kann nicht mehr lange ~ s *it cannot be long now* **b.** wo denkst du ~? *what is the idea*? || *what do you mean* (*you are doing*)? || wo will das noch ~? *what will this end in*? || auf diesen Entschluß ~ *on the strength* (od *in the light*) *of this resolution*; auf die Gefahr ~ z verlieren *at the risk of losing* || nach außen ~ ruhig *outwardly quiet* **4.** °⟨fig⟩ ~ s *to be gone, ruined, lost, tired*; ~ ist ~ *there* od *it is no use crying over spilt milk*; *gone is gone, lost is lost*; alles ist ~! *it's all up*! | (P) ganz ~ s *to be quite done up* (od *worn out, gone*) || = ~gerissen

hin- pref [betont, bei Verben trennbar] → hin 1. a. **1.** (v Sprechenden weg) **a.** *there*; *thither*; → ~bringen, ~geben, (etw) ~halten, ~k, ~reisen

b. (= nieder) down; → ~fallen, ~stellen, ~werfen etc 2. ⟨übtr⟩ (Richtung) → ~deuten, ~nehmen, ~reißen, ~schlängeln etc 3. ⟨fig⟩ → (Zeit) ~bringen, (jdn) ~halten; ~reichen, (jdn) ~richten, ~ziehen

hin·ab 1. adv d(own) den Berg ~ d. the mountain; d.-stream; ins Tal ~ d.hill; etw weiter ~ a little farther d. ‖ bis ~ z even to ..; bis ~ z der Zeit [+ gen] d. to the time of Caesar ‖ ~ mit ihm! d. with him 2. **~-** pref [betont, bei Verben trennbar] down, d.(ward[s]); → hinunter– **~|blicken** vi [h] ⟨eig⟩ (→ herab–) ~ auf jdn to look (od gaze) d. at a p; → hinunter~ **~|fahren** vi [s] die Straße ~ to drive d. the road; ⟨cycl⟩ den Berg mit Freilauf ~ to coast; ⟨mount⟩ den Bergabhang ~ to glissade **~|fließen** vi [s] to flow (od pour) d. **~|gehen** vi [s] to descend; to walk (od go) d. (nach, z to); den Berg ~ to descend the hill; to walk (od go) d. the hill; die Straße ~ to walk (od go) d. the street ‖ (of ground) to slope; es ging steil den Berg hinab the road led steeply d. the mountain-side **~|gießen** vt [h] to pour d. **~|gleiten** vi [s] ⟨übtr⟩ ~ in to glide (od slide, slip) into .. **~|lassen** vt [h] to let d. ‖ sich ~ to let o.s. d.; to drop (into ..) **~|reichen** vi [h] ~ bis z to reach d. to .. **~|rollen** vt/i den Hügel ~ to roll d. the hill **~|schauen, ~|sehen** vi [h] = –blicken **~|sinken** vi [s] ins Grab ~ to sink into the grave ‖ ⟨fig⟩ ~ z to degrade into **~|steigen** vi [s] ins Erdgeschoß ~ to descend to the g.-f.; → –gehen **~|stürzen** vi [s] ~ aus to drop (od fall) from .. ‖ ~ in (of water) to fall into (the sea); → ab–, hinunter–; herabschießen **~|ziehen** vt [h] (jdn) ~ in to drag into

hin·an- pref [betont, bei Verben trennbar] A. ⟨eig⟩ [fast ganz zurückgedrängt durch heran–] up; → a. hinauf **~|gehen** vi [s] den Hügel ~ to ascend (od go up) the hill ‖ es ging hier etwas h. the path ascended here a little **~|steigen** vi [s] den Berg ~ to ascend (od mount) the hill B. ⟨übtr & fig⟩ → heran–

hin|arbeiten 1. vi [h] ⟨übtr⟩ ~ auf etw to drive od aim at, be out for, make for a th; to further a th; darauf ~ z erlangen to tend (od strive) to get ‖ vor sich ~ to work away by o.s. 2. vrefl; sich ~ nach to work one's way to(wards)

hin·auf adv a. [mst nur als pref] → hinauf– b. die Treppe ~ up the stairs, upstairs; die andere Seite ~ up the other side; den Rhein ~ up the R. ‖ dort ~ up there; hier ~ up here, up this way; etw weiter ~ a little farther up ‖ ~ auf on to (the balcony); ~ in up into (the sky); ~ nach up to (Scotland); ~ z up to (God); bis ~ z up to ‖ er wollte ~ he wanted to get up(stairs)

hin·auf- pref [betont, bei Verben trennbar] up; upwards; upstairs; → herauf– **~|arbeiten** vrefl [h] sich ~ to work one's way up(wards); to toil (od work) up; sich auf den Felsen, Hügel ~ to toil up to the rock, hill ‖ → herauf– **~|befördern** vt [h] (jdn) im Fahrstuhl schnell ~ to shoot up; to whisk up(wards) **~|blicken** vi [h] ~ an or z to look (od gaze) up at (a building; a p); zum Himmel ~ to glance up at the sky, to lift one's eyes towards the sky; scheu z jdm ~ to cast a shy look up at a p ‖ ⟨übtr⟩ z (or an) jdm ~ to look up to a p (als .. as one's leader) **~|bringen** vt [h] to bring up; (jdn) in sein Zimmer ~ to get up to his room ‖ (Motor) ~ bis z to bring (od get) up to (90) **~|fahren** vi/t 1. vi [s] to drive (od run) up; den H., die Str. ~ to drive (cycle) up the hill, street ‖ (den Fluß) to mount 2. vt [h] (jdn) = –befördern **~|fallen** vi [s] °⟨fig⟩ die Treppe ~ to drift up the ladder of promotion; er fiel die T. hinauf u wurde .. he was kicked upstairs and became .. **~|führen** vt [h] (jdn) to lead (od take) up; jdn auf das Deck ~ to walk a p up the deck ‖ ⟨übtr⟩ (etw) ~ z to bring up to (highest tension) **~|gehen** vi [s] to walk (od go) up (z to); ⟨fam⟩ to slip up ‖ to ascend od go up; walk up; mount (the stairs) ‖ to walk od go up (the street) ‖ es ging steil den Berg hinauf the road led steeply up the hill ‖ ⟨übtr⟩ ~ bis z .. to go as high as (5000 marks) **~|geleiten** vt [h] (jdn) to show (od walk) up **~|heben** vt [h] to hoist up; ~ auf to lift on to **~|helfen** vi [h] jdm ~ to give a p a leg up; ~ auf to help a p on to .. **~|klettern** vi [s] ~ an e–m B., S. to climb a tree, a rope; to clamber (od shin, swarm) up a tree, a rope ‖ ⟨übtr⟩ ~ z to climb to °**~|langen** vi [h] = –reichen **~|laufen** vi [s] to run up(stairs) **~|limitieren** vt [h] (at auctions) to repeat bids **~|marschieren** vi [s] to march along (od up) (the street) **~|rasen** vi [s] to tear up (the stairs) **~|reichen** vt/i [h] 1. vt (etw) to reach (od hand, pass) up (z .. to a p) 2. vi; er kann nicht ~ he cannot reach up to it ‖ ~ bis z, an to reach to the top (of a th); to come to **~|rücken** vi [s] to move up **~|schicken** vt [h] to send up **~|schleppen** vt [h] to drag (od lug) up (the stairs) ‖ sich die T. ~ to plod up the stairs **≈schnellen** n (steep) jump (of price) **~|schrauben** vt [h] ⟨übtr⟩ (Preise) to screw up ‖ (Leistungen) to tune up **~|schreiten** vi [s] (majestätisch) to sweep up (the street) **~|schwingen** vrefl [h] sich ~ to rise; sich ~ auf .. to jump on to (a carriage) with a swing **~|sehen** vi [h] = –blicken **~|setzen** vt [h] (jdn) → herauf– ‖ ⟨übtr⟩ (Summe) to boost; ⟨Am⟩ to whoop (auf to); (Preis) to mark up; (Miete) to screw up; to raise **~|springen** vi [s] ~ an (of a dog) to fuss up to, to jump up against (a p) ‖ ~ auf to jump on to; to hop up to (a carriage) **~|steigen** vi [s] to ascend (z to); to ascend, climb, mount; go up (the stairs) ‖ ⟨übtr⟩ z hoher Stellung ~ to rise to the top of the tree **~|strömen** vi [s] ⟨übtr⟩ to pour up; in Scharen ~ nach to come pouring up to .. **~|tragen** vt [h] (etw) to take up **~|treiben** vt [h] den Schaum ~ auf .. to blow the spray to the top-deck ‖ ⟨übtr⟩ (Preise) to boost; to force (od push, send) up **~|wagen** vrefl [h] sich ~ to venture up **~|winden** vt [h] to wind up ‖ sich ~ (of path) to wind up (a hill) **~|ziehen** vt/i 1. vt [h] to pull up ‖ sich ~ to pull o.s. up; → Hose 2. vi [s] ~ z to troop up (to his study)

hin·aus adv a. out ‖ er wollte ~ he wanted to get out ‖ ~ auf out on to (the balcony); ~ aufs offene Meer (fahren to sail) out on the high seas; ins Freie ~ out into the open ‖ dort, hier ~ out there, here; nach vorn (hinten) ~ → heraus ‖ über .. ~ beyond (the river); past (the gate); ~ s über (or aus) .. to be free of (the harbour) ‖ ~! out!, out here!, clear (od get) out! ~ mit euch! out with you! out you go (od get)! ~ mit dem Kerl! out [vt] that man! b. ⟨übtr⟩ (zeitlich) auf Jahre ~ for years (to come) ‖ über die Zeit ~ beyond the hour; über die 60 ~ (he is) on the shady side of 60; bis über 2 Uhr ~ till past two o'clock | weit über sein Eink ~ (to live) far in excess of one's income ‖ darüber ~, über dieses ~ beyond this (he knew little); in addition; what is more (he had ..) ‖ darüber bin ich (längst) ~ I am above that ‖ °hoch ~ wollen to aim (od fly) high; to be very ambitious ‖ (es ist nicht abzusehen), wo das ~ soll there is no saying what all this will end in ‖ worauf wollen sie nur ~? what are they driving at? **hin·aus-** pref [betont, bei Verben trennbar] out ‖ ~ .. über over; **~|befördern** vt [h] to chuck (od turn, hustle, chase) .. out; to expel **~|begeben** vrefl [h] sich ~ to make one's way out **~|begleiten** vt [h] (jdn) to see (od show) out **~|blicken** vi [h] to look (od gaze) out **~|bringen** vt [h] to bring (od take) out °**~|bugsieren** vt [h] (jdn) to eject, expel; to turn (od shove, hustle) out **~|drängen** vt [h] (jdn) to drive od elbow .. out; ⟨Am⟩ to crowd out ‖ ~ aus to squeeze out of; eiligst ~ aus to hustle out of (the room); ⟨soc sl⟩ to freeze a p out **~|eilen** vi [s] to hurry (od rush) out °**~|ekeln** vt [h] = heraus- **~|fahren** vi [s] to drive (od run) out; ⟨mot⟩ to motor out (nach to) ‖ im Bogen ~ aus to swing out at (a gate) ‖ aufs Meer ~ to put (od stand) out *to sea* || ~ über *to overshoot* (*a limit*) °~|**feuern** vt [h] (jdn) = –werfen °~|**fliegen** vi [s] ⟨fig⟩ sofort ~ *to get the sack*; *to be sacked* ~|**führen** vt [h] (jdn) *to bring* (od *lead*) *out* (in .. *into the open*) || (etw) über sich selbst ~ *to carry beyond its own limits* ~|**gehen** vi [s] **1.** ⟨eig⟩ *to go outside*; *to go* (od *walk, pass*) *out* (auf .. *to the street*; *on to the deck*; aus *out of*; in *into*); auf den Fußspitzen ~ *to tiptoe out*; zur Tür ~ *to pass out through* (od *out of*) *the door*; z Hintertür ~ *to go out at the back-door* **2.** ⟨fig⟩ (S) **a.** (of windows, etc.) ~ nach, auf .. *to look out on* (*to*) ..; *to give upon* (*the street*); *to face* (*the garden*) **b.** ~ über *to go beyond* (*the loss*); *to exceed*; *to be in excess of*; *to overrun* (*the time*); *to overleap*; *to pass*; *to top* (*the price*); (of numbers) *to total over* (*300*) **c.** ⟨fig⟩ worauf ging s–e Bemerkung nur hinaus? *what was he driving at*? ~|**gelangen** vi [s] ~ über .. *to get beyond* .. ~|**geleiten** vt [h] (jdn) *to show* (od *see, usher, walk*) *out* ~|**greifen** vi [h] ⟨übtr⟩ ~ über *to reach beyond* ~|**jagen** vt [h] (jdn) *to drive out* ~|**k** vi [s] ⟨übtr⟩ ~ auf = –laufen 2. || ~ über *to get over* ~|**komplimentieren** vt [h] *to bow .. out* ~|**l** vt [h] (jdn) *to let out* ~|**laufen** vi [s] **1.** *to run out* (in *into*) || zur Hintertür ~ *to run out at the back-door* **2.** ⟨fig⟩ (of remarks) ~ auf .. *to amount* (od *come, tend*) *to*; *to be tantamount to*; *to result in*; ⟨Am⟩ *to come up* od *down to*; darauf läuft alles h. *that is the main point*; es läuft (sich) auf dasselbe (*or* eins) h. *it comes to the same th*; *it's six of one and half a dozen of the other*; worauf läuft das alles h.? *what does it all add up to*? ~|**leben** vi [h] über e–e Zeit *to survive an era* (bis *into*) ~|**lehnen** vrefl [h] sich ~ *to lean out* ~|**marschieren** vi [s] *to march out* || hinter–e–a ~ *to file out* ~|**ragen** vi [h] ~ über *to project beyond* .. || ⟨fig⟩ *to tower above* (*a p*); *to dominate* (*a th*) ~|**reichen** vi [h] ~ über *to extend* (od *go, reach, stretch*) *beyond*; *to exceed, surpass* ~|**reiten** vi [s] aufs Land ~ *to ride out into the country* ~|**schaffen** vt [h] *to get* (od *take*) *out* ~|**schauen** vi [h] *to gaze* (od *peer*) *out* (auf *on*; über *across*) ~|**schicken** vt [h] (jdn) *to send out* (od *forth*); durch Handbewegung ~ *to motion out* ~|**schieben** vt [h] ⟨fig⟩ (etw) *to defer, delay, postpone, prolong, protract*; *to put off*; s e Meinung ~ bis .. *to reserve one's opinion until* .. ~|**schießen** vi [s] ⟨fig⟩ ~ über .. *to overshoot* (*a th*); übers Ziel ~ *to overshoot the mark*; *to overshoot* (od *overreach*) *o.s.* ~|**schleichen** vi [s] *to creep* (od *slink, sneak, steal*) *out*; ~ aus *to creep* (etc) *out of* || sich ~ [h] = ~ | ~|**schleppen** vt [h] *to drag* (od *haul, lug*) *out* °~**schmeißen** vt = –werfen; *to sling* od *hurl* (*a p*) *out* (*of the room*) °≈**schmeißer** m (in Bars) ⟨sl⟩ *chucker-out* → Raus- ~|**sehen** vi [h] *to look* (od *glance*) *out* (nach .. *at*; *towards*); aufs Meer ~ *to look out to sea* ~|**setzen** vt [h] **1.** (etw) = –stellen **2.** °(jdn) *to put* (od *turn*) *out*; *to put out of doors* || ⟨jur⟩ (Pächter) *to evict* || ⟨fam⟩ *to chuck out*; *to out* ~|**stellen** vt [h] (etw) *to put out* (od *outside*; *out-of-doors*) ~|**stoßen** vt [h] (jdn) *to thrust out*; in die Welt ~ *to throw upon the world* ~|**streben** vi [h] über sich selbst ~ *to strive beyond one's limits* ~|**strömen** vi [s] ⟨übtr⟩ (of people) *to pour out* (auf .. *into the road*); *to flock out* (nach *to*) ~|**stürzen** vi [s] *to dart* (od *dash, rush, shoot, tear*) *out* ~|**tragen** vt [h] *to carry out* ~|**treiben** vt [h] (jdn) *to drive out* (in *into*); *to eject, evict, expel*; (Vieh) *to run out* || ~ aus *to drive* (od *whip*) *out of*; *to evict, expel from* .. || (Korken) *to blow off* (aus *from*) ~|**treten** vi [s] *to come, pass, step out* (auf .. *on to the terrace*); ~ aus *to emerge from* ..; in die Sonne ~ *to come out into the sunlight* °~|**tun** vt [h] (jdn) = –setzen, –werfen ~|**wachsen** vi [s] ~ über etw *to outgrow* od *overgrow a th* || ~ über jdn *to grow beyond a p* || über sich ~ *to overgrow o.s.* ~|**wandern** vi [s] *to flock out* (nach *to*) ~|**weisen** vt [h] jdn ~ *to show a p the door*, .. *a p out*; *to turn a p out* (od *out of doors*) ~|**werfen** vt [h] **1.** (etw) *to cast* (od *throw*) *out*; ~ aus *to throw out of* .. || ⟨fig⟩ sein Geld zum Fenster ~ *to play ducks and drakes with* (od *to make d. and d. of*) *one's m.*; *to squander one's m.* **2.** (jdn) *to clean* (od *clear, put, throw, turn*) *out*; *to eject* ⟨fam⟩ *to chuck* (od *kick, sling*) *out*; *to pack off*: *to send* (*a p*) *packing*; zur Tür ~ *to turn out of doors*; jdn beim Kragen ~ *to throw a p out neck and crop* || (entlassen) ⟨fam & sl⟩ *to boot* (od *fire*) *out*; *to sack*; *to give a p the sack* (⟨sl⟩ *the bird*) ~|**wollen** vi [h] **1.** *to want* (od *wish*) *to go* (od *get*) *out* **2.** ⟨fig⟩ hoch ~ *to aim* (od *fly, soar*) *high*; *to fly at high game*; höher ~ *to fly at higher game* || ~ auf .. *to aim at, to be driving at* ..; worauf ich h. will, ist *my point is*; wissen, wohin .. h.will *to know one's way about*; worauf wollte er hinaus? *what was he driving at*? wo will das noch hinaus? *what will this end in*? || höher ~ *to want to rise in the world*; zu hoch ~ *to set one's sight too high*; ~ über .. *to strive beyond* (*a th*); *to try to surpass* (*a th*) ≈**wurf** m ⟨sl⟩ *brush-off* ~|**ziehen** vi/t **1.** [s] *to go* (od *flock, march, troop*) *out*; in den Krieg ~ *to go to the war* **2.** vt [h] ⟨mst fig⟩ (Debatte) *to draw out*; *to extend, protract* || sich ~ (of actions) *to drag along* (od *on*); *to draw out*; *to extend*; *to be drawn out*

h·in- ~|**begeben** vrefl [h] sich ~ *to betake o.s. there*; sich ~ nach .. *to go* (od *repair, resort*) *to* ~|**bemühen** vrefl [h] sich ~ *to trouble to go there* ~|**bestellen** vt [h] jdn ~ *to order a p to appear* (od *to go*) *there* ~|**bewegen** vrefl [h] sich ~ nach *to go* (od *move*) *towards* (*the door*) ≈**blick** m [nur in:] in (*or* im) ~ auf *in the face of* ..; *in the light of* (*his experience*); *in view of* (*his youth*); *with regard* (od *respect*) *to* ~|**blicken** vi [h] ~ nach *to look towards* || er blickte vor sich hin *he gazed before him* ~|**bringen** vt [h] **1.** bring es hin *take* (od *carry*) *it there*; ich werde Sie z ihm ~ *I'll take you along to him* **2.** ⟨fig⟩ (Zeit) *to consume, pass, spend*; müßig ~ *to idle* (od *pass, waste*) *away* ~|**brüten** vi [h] vor sich ~ *to brood over one's misfortunes*; *to be in a brown study* ~|**denken** vi → hin

H·indenburg n ⟨†Ger⟩ (Stadt)

h·inderlich a **1.** *cumbersome, cumbrous*; *embarrassing, inconvenient* (f *to*); *obstructive* (f *of, to*) **2.** jdm ~ s *to encumber* (od *discommode, embarrass, inconvenience*) *a p*; = hindern 1. || [dat] ~ s = hindern 2. **h·indern** vt [h] **A.** (jdn ~) **1.** (= jdm hinderlich s) *to hamper* (od *handicap, hinder, impede*) *a p*; gehindert w durch *to be hampered* (od *handicapped*) *by* ..; → hinderlich 2. || jdn ~ **bei** (*or* **in**) etw *to hamper* (od *handicap, hinder, obstruct*) *a p in a th* (od *in the execution of a th*); dies hinderte ihn beim Üben *this hampered him in his exercises*; .. ihn in s–n Bewegungen *this hampered his movements* **2.** jdn ~ **an** etw, jdn ~ **z tun** *to hinder a p from doing* (*a th*); *to prevent* (od *stop*) *a p from doing* (⟨fam⟩ *a p doing*) (*a th*); ich hinderte ihn am Eintreten (*or* einzutreten) *I prevented him from entering*; *I prevented his* (⟨fam⟩ *him*) *entering* **B. etw** ~ *to hinder* (od *abrogate, check, obstruct, prevent, thwart*) *a th*; *to stand in the way of* .., *to interfere with a th*; → hinderlich 2. || etw z ~ suchen *to discountenance* || (Entwicklung) im Wachstum ~ *to dwarf, stunt* **H·indernis** n ~ses/~se **1.** [abstr & ⟨übtr⟩ konkr] **a.** *hindrance* (f *to*), *impediment, obstruction*; *check*; *handicap*; *barrier, obstacle* (*to* ..) (⟨mil⟩ an ~se angelehnt *with their flanks based on o.s*; durch ~se einengen *to canalize by o.s*); *stumbling--block* (f *to*); (Draht≈) *entanglement* || ein ~ nehmen ⟨hors⟩ *to jump over an obstacle*, ⟨fig⟩ *to take the jump*; ~se [pl] ⟨fam⟩ *difficulties* pl || gr ~ *drag* (f etw *on a th*); unerwartetes ~ *snag* **b.** e–e Reise **mit** ~sen *a j. beset with di.s* || **ohne** ~ *without a hitch* || sie war ihm (*or* f ihn) ein gr ~ *she was a drag on him* || das Haupt≈ im sozialen

Leben der Hindus war .. *the principal spoke in the Hindu wheel was ..* ‖ jdm ~se **in den Weg** legen *to put obstacles in a p's way* ‖ sich gr ~sen **gegenübersehen** *to be up against a brick-wall* ‖ auf ~se stoßen *to meet with di.s* ‖ ein ~ **überwinden** *to negotiate an obstacle*; ~se überw. *to overcome di.s*; alle ~se überw. *to carry all before one* **2.** ⟨sport⟩ [konkr] **a.** *obstacle*; ~ aus Reisig *hurdle*; → Hecke; Graben ‖ Rennen mit ~sen → ~rennen **b.** [in comp] **~bau** m *construction of obstacles* **~feuer** n ⟨aero⟩ *obstruction light* **~lauf** m *obstacle-race*; *steeple-chase*; ⟨univ sl⟩ *grind* ‖ Schneeschuh≈ *slalom* **~läufer** m *steeplechaser* **~rennen** n *steeplechase* ‖ [abstr] *steeplechasing* **~sprengtrupp** m *obstacle demolition squad* **H·inderung** f *hindrance, obstruction* ‖ ohne ~ *without let* od *hindrance*; er duldete k–e ~ *he tolerated neither let nor h.* **~sgrund** m *obstacle*

h·in|deuten vi [h] ~ auf **1.** ⟨eig⟩ *to point to* od *at* (*a p, a th*) **2.** ⟨fig⟩ ~ auf etw *to point* (od *refer*) *to a th*; *to hint* (⟨Am⟩ *squint*) *at a th*; *to indicate* (od *intimate, suggest*) *a th*; *to be indicative* (od *suggestive*) *of a th* ‖ darauf ~, daß .. *to indicate* od *intimate that ..*; alles deutet darauf hin, daß er ermordet worden ist *everything points to his having been murdered*; *all the indications are* (od *there is every indication*) *that he was murdered* **H·indeutung** f ⟨fig⟩ ~ auf etw *hint* (*indication, intimation*) *of a th*

H·indin f ~/~nen ⟨zoo⟩ *hind*

H·indi n ~/ Ind *Hindi* **H·indost·an** n *Hindostan, Hindustan* **H·indostani** n [Ind] das ~ *Hindustani, Hindoostanee* **h·indost·anisch** a *Hindustani* **H·indu** m ~s/~s *Hindu, -doo* ‖ ~ der niedrigsten Klasse *untouchable* **≈·anisch** a *Hindu, Hindoo* **~·ismus** m *Hinduism* **~kusch** m *Hindu-Kush, Hindoo--Koosh* **~stan** n → Hindostan

hind·urch adv ⟨mst⟩ *thr(ough)* **1.** (räumlich) [mst nur als pref] → hindurch- **2.** (zeitlich) den ganzen Abend ~ *all thr. the evening*; die ganze Nacht ~ *all night* (*long*), *the whole night thr.*; *all* (*the year*) *round*; *thr.out* (*the y.*); *thr.out* (*the Middle Ages*); all die langen Jahre ~ *thr. all the long years*; ein Jahrhundert ~ *over a century* ‖ sein ganzes Leben ~ *thr. all* (od *all thr.*) *his life* ‖ die ganzen Menschenalter ~ .. *all down the ages* (*men have been ..*) die ganze Zeit ~ *thr.out* ‖ er schlief den ganzen Tag ~ *he slept the clock round* **hind·urch-** pref [betont, bei Verben trennbar] **1.** [mst bei intr. *or* reflex. Verben u in Verbindung mit prep]: ~gehen durch .., nach ..; zwischen .. ‖ → sich **2.** *[bei trans. Verben verstärkend f durch-]: ~lassen = durchlassen **~|arbeiten** vrefl [h] sich ~ durch .. *to work one's way thr.* (od *across*) (*a country*); (mühsam) *to scramble thr. ..*; ⟨übtr⟩ *to work* (*one's way*) *thr.* (*a work*) ‖ sich nach *or* zu *to work round to ..* **~|blitzen** vi [h] ⟨fig⟩ ~ zw (of a lake) *to peep out between* (*the gaps*) °**~|bugsieren** vt [h] (jdn) ~ durch .. *to push* (od *shove, thrust*) *thr. ..* **~|drängen** vrefl [h] sich ~ durch *to press thr.* (*a crowd*); *to shoulder one's way thr.* **~|fahren** vi [s] °er fuhr mit der Hand h. *he ran* (od *slipped, thrust*) *his hand thr. it* **~|finden** vrefl [h] °ich finde mich nicht mehr h. *I am all at sea*; *I am at the end of my tether* **~|gehen** vi [s] ~ durch *to go* (od *pass*) *thr.* (*a door*) **~|k** vi [s] ~ durch .. *to come thr. ..*; ~ zw .. ⟨übtr⟩ *to appear* od *emerge from among the trees* **~|ringen** vrefl [h] sich ~ z *to win thr. to ..* **~|schlängeln** vrefl [h] sich ~ *to thread one's way through* **~|schleusen** vt [h] *to slip* ⟨a. mil⟩ **~|winden** vrefl [h] sich ~ *to wangle one's way through*; .. durch .. *to wind thr. ..* **~|ziehen** vrefl [h] ⟨fig⟩ sich ~ durch .. (of a thought) *to run thr.*; *to pervade* (*a poem*)

hin·ein adv *in*; wir fanden e–n Weg ~ *we found some way in* ‖ rechts ~ bitte! *enter to* (od *on*) *the right, please*! ‖ nur ~! *walk* (od *step*) *in*! ‖ er wollte ~ *he wanted to get in* | in .. ~ *into*; bis in (*or* mitten in) die K. ~ *right into the* (*middle of the*) *church* ‖ bis in den frühen Morgen ~ (*to talk*) *into the small hours* ‖ bis tief in die N. ~ *far into the night* **hin·ein-** pref [betont, bei Verben trennbar] *in*; *inside* ‖ ~ .. in .. *into ..* ‖ → sich ‖ → herein- **~|arbeiten 1.** vt [h] (etw) *to work in*; *to incorporate* (*facts*) **2.** vrefl [h] sich ~ *to w. in*; sich ~ in .. *to w. o.s.* (od *one's way*) *into ..* (so sehr *so deeply*) | jdm **~|befehlen** *to interject orders into a p's responsibility* **~|beißen** vi [h] ~ in .. *to bite into ..* **~|blicken** vi [h] ~ in .. *to look into ..* **~|bringen** (→ herein-) vt [h] (etw) *to take in*; ~ in *to take into ..* ‖ ⟨fig⟩ (etw) unbemerkt ~ in .. *to insinuate into ..*, *to smuggle a th in through the backdoor* °**~|bugsieren** vt [h] (jdn) durch Schiebung ~ in .. *to job into* (*an office*) **~|denken** vrefl [h] sich ~ in .. *to think o.s. into ..*; *to enter into a p's ideas* **~|drängen** vt [h] (jdn) ~ in *to press* (od *to squeeze*) *into* ‖ sich ~ *to crowd* (od *nip*) *in*; sich ~ in .. *to press* (od *squeeze o.s.*) *into ..*; *to shoulder one's way into ..* **~|dringen** vi [s] ~ in .. *to crowd into ..*; → eindringen **~|eilen** vi [s] *to hurry in*; (schnell) *to fly* (od *rush*) *in*; ~ in .. *to hurry into ..* **~|fahren** vi [s] mit dem B. ~ *to go in by bus* ‖ ⟨fig⟩ mit den F. ~ *to slip one's fingers inside* **~|fallen** vi [s] *to fall in*; ~ in *to fall into ..*; (plötzlich) *to slump into ..*; → herein- **~|fassen** vi [h] ~ in *to dip* (od *delve*) *into ..* (*a pocket*) **~|finden** vrefl [h] sich ~ ⟨fig⟩ *to find one's feet* (od *legs*); sich ~ in .. *to get used to ..*; *to settle down in*; → sich finden in **~|flechten** vt [h] ⟨fig⟩ (Gedanken) *to weave in* **~|fluten** vi [s] *to pour in*; (of air) *to drift in* ‖ ⟨übtr⟩ (of people) *to crowd in*; ~ in .. *to pour* (od *stream*) *into* (*the church*) **~|fressen** vt [h] ⟨fig⟩ (etw) in sich ~ *to gulp down*; *to put up with*; s–n Ärger in sich ~ *to hide one's anger, to swallow one's vexation* ‖ sich ~ in (of feelings) *to eat into* (*a p*) **~|führen** vt [h] (jdn) *to lead* (od *show, walk*) *in* ‖ ~ in .. *to lead into .* **~geboren** [pp]: ~ s in .. *to be born into* (*a world of ..*) **~|geheimnissen** vt [h] zuviel ~ in etw *to mystify a th* **~|gehen** vi [s] **1.** *to walk* (od *go*) *in* (z jdm *to a p*); *to pass inside*; ~ in .. *to go into ..* **2.** ⟨übtr⟩ in den Krug g. 2 L. h. *the jug will contain* (od *hold*) *2 litres*; in den Saal g. 2000 M. h. *the hall will seat 2000 people* ‖ ⟨tech⟩ *to fit in* [adv], gerade ~: *it's a tight fit* ‖ (*can we all*) *fit in*? **~|geleiten** vt [h] (jdn) *to hand* (od *show*) *in* **~|geraten** vi [s] ~ in *to get o.s. into ..* **≈grätschen** n ⟨ftb⟩ *sliding tackling* **~|gucken** vi [h] *to peer* (*with*)*in*; ⟨übtr fam⟩ *to drop in* ‖ ~ in .. *to peer into ..* **~|heiraten** vi [h] ~ in .. *to marry into* (*a family*) **~|helfen** vi [h] jdm ~ *to help a p in*; ~ in .. *to help into ..* **~|jagen** vi [s] ⟨übtr⟩ ~ in (of a car) *to buck into* **~|kichern** vi [h] in sich ~ *to chuckle to o.s.* **~|knie(e)n** vrefl [h] ⟨fig⟩ sich ~ in *to work o.s.* (od *one's way*) *into ..*; *to apply o.s. to* (*a th*) ‖ knie dich richtig h.! *put* od *keep your nose to the grindstone* **~|lachen** vi [h] in sich ~ *to laugh to o.s.* **~|langen** vi [h] ~ in *to reach in* **~|l** vt [h] (jdn *to let in* **~|leben** vi [h] in den Tag ~ *to idle away one's time*; *to live in a happy-go-lucky fashion* **~|legen** vt [h] **1.** (etw) *to put inside*; ~ in .. *to put in ..* **2.** °⟨fig⟩ (jdn) → herein- **~|lesen** vt [h] (etw) ~ in .. *to read into ..* ‖ sich in e–n Autor ~ *to get used to an author's diction* **~|manövrieren** vt [h] jdn in e–e Verlegenheit ~ *to have a p nonplussed* **~|marschieren** vi [s] hinter–e–a ~ *to file in* **~|mischen** vrefl [h] sich ~ in .. *to interfere* (od *meddle*) *with* (od *in*) ..; Sie h sich nicht –zu– *mind your own business* °**~|pfuschen** vi [h] ~ in .. *to tamper with*; *to dabble in* (*politics*) °**~|platzen** vi [s] ⟨fig⟩ *to burst* (od *butt*) *in*; ~ in .. *to burst into ..*; ⟨sl⟩ *to barge into* (*a room*) **~|ragen** vi [h] ~ in .. *to lap* (od *project*) *into ..* ‖ °**~|rasen** vi [s] → –jagen **~|reden** vi [h] **1.** ins Blaue (*or* in den Tag) ~ *to talk at random*; *to t. rubbish* ‖ in jdn ~ *to keep t.ing to a p*; → einreden auf ..; Gewissen ‖ ⟨übtr⟩ ~ in etw *to interfere* (od *meddle*) *with a th*; Sie h hier nichts –zu– *mind your own* *business*; er hat hier nichts -zu- *he has no voice in this matter* || °jdm ~ *to interfere with a p* **2.** sich ~ in .. *to t. o.s. into* (*a passion*) **~|reißen** vt [h] (jdn) *to let .. in for* **~|reiten** vi/t **1.** vi [s] *to ride in*; ~ in .. *to ride into* **2.** vt [h] °jdn ~ → hereinreiten **~|rennen** vi [s] ~ in *to run* (od *rush*) *into*; *to buck into* (*a river*); ⟨sl⟩ *to barge into* ..; (mit Wucht) *to run full tilt into* .. °**~|sausen** vi [s] = hereinfallen **~|schaffen** vt [h] *to carry* (od *get*) *in*; ~ in .. *to carry into* .. **~|schieben** vt [h] (etw) *to shove* (od *thrust*) *in*; ~ in .. *to shove into* ..; (Schublade) *to close*; °sich ~ *to nip in* **~|schleichen** vi [s] *to creep* (od *steal*) *in*; ~ in *to creep* (od *sneak, steal, wriggle*) *into* .. || sich ~ [h] = ~ °**~|schlittern** vi [s] ⟨fig⟩ ~ in .. *to* (*s*)*tumble* (od *blunder*) *into* (*war*) || (jdn) ~ l in *to let .. in for* **~|schmuggeln** vt [h] (etw) *to smuggle in* (z .. *to a p*); ~ in .. *to smuggle into* .. **~|schreiten** vi [s] stolz ~ *to stalk in* **~|schütten** vt [h] (etw) *to pour in*; ~ in .. *to pour into* .. **~|segeln** vi [s] (P) *to sail in* (°→ hereinfallen) **~|sehen** vt [h] ⟨fig⟩ in jdn *to see the inside of of a p's mind* **~|springen** vi [s] *to hop* (od *jump*) *in* **~|stechen** vi [h] er stach mit dem Stocke h. *he thrust his stick into it* **~|stecken** vt [h] (etw) *to put* (od *thrust*) *in*; den Kopf zur Tür ~ *to put in one's head at the door* || (Schlüssel) ~ in .. *to insert into* .. || ⟨fig⟩ die N. ~ in .. *to poke one's nose into* ..; er steckt überall die N. h. *he will interfere with other people's business* || ⟨übtr⟩ Geld ~ in *to put m. into* ..; *to invest m. in* .. **~|steigen** vi [s] *to get* (od *climb*) *in*; ~ in .. *to get into* .. **~|stopfen** vt [h] (etw) ~ in .. *to cram* (od *pack, ram, thrust*) *into* .. **~|stoßen** vt [h] *to push* (od *poke, force*) in; ~ in *to push* (od *thrust*) *into* .. **~|strömen** vi [s] *to flow* (od *pour*) *in*; (of smoke) *to drift* (od *float*) *in* || ~ in *to flow* (od *pour, stream*) *into* ..; (of people) *to crowd* (od *flock, pour, stream*) *into* .. **~|stürzen** vi [s] *to dart* (od *dash, rush*) *in*; ~ in .. *to dart into* .. **~|tragen** vt [h] *to carry in* || ⟨übtr⟩ *to introduce*; ~ in .. *to introduce into* ..; *to impart to* .. **~|treiben** vt [h] *to drive* od *force in*; ~ in .. *to drive into* ..; (jdn mit Gewalt) *to terrorize* (od *whip*) *into* ..; -getrieben w in .. *to drift into* (*war*) **~|treten** vi [s] *to go in*; *to enter*; ~ in .. *to enter* (*a room*) **~|tun** vt [h] (etw) *to put in*; ~ in .. *to put in* (*one's pocket*); °e-n flüchtigen Blick ~ in .. *to glance into* .. **~|versetzen** vrefl [h] sich ~ in jdn *to enter into a p's feelings*; *to place o.s. in spirit in a p's mind*; *to put o.s. in a p's place* **~|wachsen** vi [s] in e-e Rolle ~ *to grow to a part* **~|wagen** vrefl [h] sich ~ *to venture in* **~|werfen** vt [h] (etw) *to throw* (od ⟨fam⟩ *chuck*) *in*; zum Fenster ~ *to throw in at the window* || ⟨fig⟩ e-n flüchtigen Blick ~ in *to* (*throw a*) *glance into* || ⟨fig⟩ sich mit Inbrunst ~ in .. *to throw one's soul* (od *heart*) *into* .. **~|wollen** vi [h] → hinein || °das will nicht in m-n (*or* mir nicht in den) Kopf h. *that's beyond me*; *that beats me* **~|ziehen** vt [h] (etw) *to drag* (od *haul*) in | ⟨übtr⟩ (etw) in die Unterhaltung ~ *to drag in*; (jdn) *to get* (*a p*) *into trouble*, ~ in .. *to drag* (od *bring, draw*) *into* ..; *to implicate* (od *involve*) *in* ..; *to rope into* .. || (etw) unnötig in die Debatte ~ *to lug in* || (die Polizei) *to call in* **~|zwängen** vt [h] *to squeeze* od *force in*; ~ in .. *to sq. into* .. || sich ~ in .. *to nip into*

h·in- **~|fahren** vi/t **A.** vi [s] **1.** ⟨eig⟩ ich werde ~ *I'll drive* (od *go*) *there*; ~ nach, zu *to drive* (od *go*) *to* .. || an der K. ~ *to sail along the shore* **2.** ⟨übtr⟩ **a.** mit der H. ~ über .. *to pass* (od *run*) *one's hand over* **b.** *to pass away*; *to die* **c.** fahre hin! *farewell*, (*dear friend*)! || *farewell to* (*true love*)! || *away with you*, (*foul assassin*) **B.** vt [h] (etw) ~ nach *to convey* (od *take*) *to* .. || ich werde Sie ~ *I'll drive you there* **≗fahrt** f *journey* (od *way*) *out*; ⟨mar⟩ *passage* (od *voyage*) *out*; die ~ nach .. *the journey to*; auf der ~ *on my way out*; → -reise **~|fallen** vi [s] *to fall* (od *drop*) *down*; *to fall, drop* || lang ~ auf .. *to f. flat on* ..; *to come down full length on* .. || heftig u plötzlich ~ *to dump, plump* **~fällig** a **1.** (P) *decrepit, frail, infirm, invalid* ['invəli:d], *weak* **2.** (S) *futile* (*argument*), *invalid* [in'vælid], *ineffective, untenable, weak*; ~ w *or* s *to be anulled*; *to fall to the ground*; *to pass into the realm of limbo* **≗fälligkeit** f *decrepitude, frailty, infirmity, weakness* (*of a p*) || *futility*; *weakness* (*of a th*) **~|finden** vi refl [h] (sich) ~: ich werde (mich) schon ~ *I'll find my way there all right*; ~ nach, zu *to find one's way to* .. **~|fläzen** vrefl [h] sich ~ *to loll back* (in *in*) **~|fließen** vi [s] *to flow* (od *pass*) *along* || (of time) *to pass* **≗f·ort** adv *henceforth, henceforward*; *from this time on* (od *forward*); *in the future* **≗fracht** f *outward freight, freight outward*(*s*) **~|führen** vt/i **1.** vt [h] (jdn): ich werde Sie ~ *I'll lead* (od *take*) *you there*; ~ nach, zu *to lead* (od *take*) *to* .. **2.** vi [h] → wohin

hing 1. & 3. sg pret v hangen; hängen

h·in- **≗gabe** f ⟨fig⟩ (innere ~) *abandon*(*ment*); *devotion*; selbstlose ~ *selflessness*; mit gänzlicher ~ *with heart and soul*; mit ~ tanzen *to dance with an a.*; mit wahrer ~ (*to work*) *with real a.* || ~ an *addiction to*; *devotion to* (*sport*); *surrender to* (*materialism*) || ⟨sex⟩ (bes weiblich) völlige ~ *total abandon* **≗gang** m ⟨fig⟩ (Tod) *decease, demise*; ⟨lit⟩ *departure* **~|geben** vt [h] **1.** (etw) *to give* (*away*); *sacrifice*; *surrender*; (Zeit, Geld) *devote*; *give up* (e-e S *to a th*); sein L. ~ f *to give up* (od *lay down*) *one's life for*; *to sacrifice o.s. for*; → opfern **2.** sich (e-r S) ~ *to abandon o.s. to* (*a vice*); *to give way to* (*despair*); *to apply* od *devote o.s. to* (*literature*); *to give o.s. up to* (*business*); *to give one's mind* (od *life*) *to* (*study*); *to indulge in* (*card-playing*); *to surrender o.s. to* (*despair*); sich (e-r S) besonders ~ *to make a speciality of* (*a subject*) || sich H. ~ *to cherish* (od *entertain*) *hopes*; sich e-r L. ~ *to indulge a passion*; sich e~r T. ~ *to be* od *labour under a delusion* | sich jdm ~ *to devote one's life to a p* **~gebend** a *adoring* (*glance, love*) || *attached*; *devoted* (*mother*); *enthusiastic*; *faithful* **≗gebung** f ⟨fig⟩ (innere) = Hingabe **~gebungsvoll** **1.** [a] = hingebend **2.** [adv] *faithfully, loyally* **~g·egen** conj *but*; *however*; *on the other hand*; *whereas*; ~ glaubten wir (*or*: wir gl. ~) nicht, daß .. *however, we did not think that* .. **~gegossen** pp (v hingießen): °sie lag da wie ~ *she lay there quite negligently stretched out* **~|gehen** vi [s] **1.** ⟨eig⟩ *to go* od *get along*; (schnell) *to trot along* || ich werde ~ *I'll go there*; ~ nach, zu *to go to* ..; geh mal oben hin *just go upstairs*; er mußte 2mal ~ *it took him two visits* **2.** ⟨übtr⟩ **a.** (of time) *to elapse, pass, run* **b.** (of actions) *to p.*; es mag ~ *it may p.* || etw ~ l *to let a th p.*; *to countenance* (od *overlook*) *a th*; *to p. a th over*; → dulden I. A. 2. **c.** mit der Hand ~ über *to p. over* || leicht ~ über etw *to skim over a th* **~|gehören** vi [h] das g-rt dort nicht hin *that does not belong there*; jdm zeigen, wo er h.g-rt *to teach a p his place* **~|gelangen** vi [s] als wir dort h-gten *when we arrived* od *got there* || ~ nach, zu etw *to reach a th* **~|geraten** vi [s] wo mag er nur ~ s? *where can he be, I wonder*? || ⟨iron⟩ wo sind wir ~! *what has become of us*! **~gerissen** pp (v hinreißen) [& pred a] *carried away*; *enraptured* (durch, v *by*); *overcome* (v *with*); *rapt* (*by, with*) || *enthusiastic* | H-sein [n] *entrancement, rapture*; *pathos* **~gestreckt** pp, lang ~ liegen *to lie prone* (od *prostrate*; *stretched out*) °**h·ingeworfen** a (→ hinwerfen) ⟨fig⟩ (flüchtig *or* schnell) ~ *sketchy* (*lines*); *slapdash* (*style*) **~gezogen** pp (v hinziehen) sich ~ fühlen z *to feel* (*o.s.*) *drawn to*; *to yearn towards*; (of the heart) *to go to* ..; *to take to* (*a p*) **~|gleiten** vi [s] ⟨übtr⟩ ~ über .. *to run over* ..; schnell ~ .. *to skim over* (*a th*) **~|halten** vt [h] **1.** ⟨eig⟩ jdm etw ~ *to hold a th out to a p* **2.** ⟨fig⟩ (jdn) ~ *to keep .. in the air*; *to put .. off* (durch .. *with excuses*; bis z .. *till next day*); *to temporize with* ..; mit eitlen Versprechungen *to* *hold a p in hand* || ⟨bes Am⟩ *to stall (off)* || (etw) *to delay*; (Prozeß) *to dodge* | ~d [a] ⟨mil⟩ *delaying (action, defence)* **~|hängen** vt [h] *to hang up* || °(etw) ~ l ⟨fig⟩ *to delay; hang up; put off*; man ließ die S ~ *the matter was hung up* °**~|hauen** vt/i [h] **1.** vt ⟨fig⟩ (Arbeit) *to knock off*; –ge–e Arbeit *slap-dash work* || sich ~ *to throw o.s. down*; = hinfläzen; ⟨mil⟩ (schlafen gehn) *to kip down; to hit the sack, hay, roost, tick, feathers,* ⟨Am fam⟩ *to flop* **2.** vi *to get a move on,* ⟨mar⟩ *to smack it about* || lang ~ *to come down full length* (auf *on*) || hau hin! *look sharp; get cracking!* ⟨bes Am⟩ *make it snappy!* ⟨bes mar⟩ *smack it about!*; ⟨mil⟩ *there's a war on!* || das haut hin *that will do nicely* °**~|helfen** vi [h] ich werde ihm ~ *I'll help him to get there* || sich ~ ⟨fig⟩ *to make both ends meet* **~|hören** vi [s] *to listen*

h·inken A. vi [h] **1.** (P) *to (walk with a) limp; to be lame* (auf *in a leg*) **2.** ⟨übtr⟩ (of argument, verse, etc.) *to halt; be defective* (od *lame, unsatisfactory*) **B.** ≃ n *limp; limping* | ~d a **1.** *lame, limping*; ~er Gang *limp* **2.** ⟨übtr⟩ *defective, halting, lame (verse; argument)* || ⟨fig⟩ *lagging behind; lingering; behind time*; ⟨poet⟩ der ~e Bote *bad news*

h·in- ~|knien vi [s] *to kneel down* **~|k** vi [s] *to come along* (od *round, up*); ich werde gleich ~ *I'll be round in a minute* || ⟨übtr⟩ wo sollten wir ~? *what should we come to?* || °nirgends ~ *to keep to o.s.; to see no company* | °wo ist mein Schirm –ge–? *where has my umbrella got to?* || der Stein kam nicht ganz hin *the stone fell short* °**~|kriegen** vt [h] (etw) *to manage* **~|kritzeln** vt [h] (etw) *to scrawl*; eilig –ge–lte Worte *hasty scrawls* pl **~|langen** vt/i [h] **1.** [vt] jdm etw ~ *to hand* (od *reach*) *a p a th* (od *a th to a p*) **2.** [vi] **a.** ~ nach etw *to reach a th* **b.** °⟨fig⟩ *to suffice* (f *for*); *to be sufficient*; das wird ~ *that will do*; °das langt nicht hin u nicht her *that won't do at all* **~länglich 1.** [a] *sufficient; satisfying; adequate* **2.** [adv] *sufficiently; enough* **~|l** vt [h] ich werde ihn nicht ~ *I shall not allow him to go (there)* °**~|laufen** vi [s] lauf mal hin *just run* (od *go quickly*) *there* **~|legen** vt [h] **1.** (etw) *to lay* (od *put*) *down*; (Geld) ⟨sl⟩ *to plank down* || °⟨theat⟩ (Rolle) *to play well* || wieder ~ *to replace* || ⟨com⟩ sich [dat] ein z gr Lager ~ *to overstock o.s. with goods* || (etw) ~ vor jdn *to lay before a p* **2. sich** ~ *to lie down* **~|leiten** vt [h] (S) (Wasser) *to convey* (v .. nach *from .. to*); *to lead* **~|lenken** vt [h] (etw) ~ auf *to direct* (od *turn*) *to ..* **~|lesen** vi [h] vor sich ~ *to read to o.s.* °**~|m** vt/i [h] **1.** [vt] °(töten) *to do away with,* ⟨sl⟩ *to finish, scupper (a p); to bump off* || etw schnell ~ = hinwerfen || etw ~ → 2. b. **2.** [vi] **a.** ×wo macht ihr hin? *where are you going to?* || °mach hin! *be quick, look sharp* **b.** da hat der Hund schon wieder –gemacht *the dog has misbehaved itself again* ≃**marsch** m *march out*; der ~ nach *the march to ..* **~|marschieren** vi [s] ~ nach *to march to ..* **~|morden** vt [h] (Menschen) *to butcher, massacre, slaughter* **~|murmeln** vi [h] vor sich ~ *to mutter to o.s.* **~|müssen** vi [h] → hin **~|nehmen** vt [h] **1.** (etw) *to accept; take* || ⟨übtr⟩ etw als selbstverständlich ~ *to take a th for granted*; (gelassen) *to face up to ..*; auf Treu u Glauben ~ *to take on trust*; mit Vorsicht ~ *to discount* **2.** ⟨fig⟩ [mst neg] (dulden) *to countenance, endure* (v jdm *from a p*); *tolerate* || viel ~ müssen *to have to forbear a lot* || etw ruhig ~ *to put up with a th*; ⟨sl⟩ *to stand the gaff*; ⟨Am sl⟩ *to stand for a th* || e–e B. ruhig ~ *to pocket* (od *swallow*) *an insult; to sit down under an i.*; e–e D. einfach (*or* ohne weiteres) ~ *to take a threat lying down* **~|neigen** vi [h] ~ z *to gravitate* (od *lean*) *to(wards); to incline to (an opinion)*

h·innen adv ⟨poet⟩ v ~ *away from here*

h·in- ~|opfern vt [h] *to sacrifice recklessly* (od *uselessly*) °**~|pflanzen** vrefl [h] ⟨fig⟩ sich ~ *to plant o.s.* °**~|plumpsen** vi [s] *to dump, flop, plump* **~|raffen** vt [h] (of death etc.) (jdn) *to cut off; sweep* (od *snatch*) *away*; hingerafft *rapt* (aus *out of; from* [*our midst*]); f immer –gerafft *rapt away for ever* **~|reden** vi/t [h] vor sich ~ *to talk to o.s.* **~|reichen** vt/i [h] **1.** [vt] jdm die Hand ~ *to hold* (od *put*) *out one's hand to a p; to offer one's h. to a p* **2.** [vi] °es reicht nicht hin u nicht her *it is quite insufficient* **~|reichend 1.** [a] *ample; sufficient; adequate*; ~es Auskommen *sufficiency*; e–e ~e Menge v *a sufficiency of* **2.** [adv] *sufficiently; enough* ≃**reise** f *journey* (od *way*) *out; outward journey*; ⟨mar⟩ *voyage out*; auf der ~ *on my way out*; auf der ~ über N. fahren *to travel outward via N.* **~|reisen** vi [s] ich werde ~ *I'll travel* (od *go*) *there*; ~ nach, z *to go to ..* **~|reißen** vt [h] jdn ~ *to carry* od *sweep a p away,* ⟨fam⟩ *off his feet; to enrapture, entrance, overpower, ravish, thrill, transport a p*; jdn ~ z *to inspire a p with* || [mst pass] –gerissen w *or* s *to be carried away,* etc. (durch, von *by*; vor *with*); –g. w z .. *to be moved to (ovations)*; –g. s *to be in raptures* || sich ~ l *to allow o.s. to be carried away*; sich ~ l v s–n G. *to indulge one's feelings, to yield to one's f.*; sich ~ l z (etw) *to commit o.s. to (a th); to surrender to the length of doing*; → hingerissen **~reißend** a *captivating; enchanting; inspiring (oratory); overpowering; ravishing; thrilling; marvellous* **~|richten** vt [h] **1.** *(etw) ~ nach *to direct to ..* **2.** (jdn) *to behead, execute*; ⟨Am⟩ *to put .. to the sword*; ⟨el⟩ *to electrocute* ≃**richtung** f *execution*; ⟨el⟩ *electrocution* | ~sbefehl [m] *death-warrant* **~|rücken** vt [h] (etw) ~ an, nach *to move to* (od *towards*) °**~|sagen** vt [h] er hat es nur so –gesagt *he has said it without thinking* °**~|sausen** vi [s] ~ nach, z *to dash* (od *rush*) *to ..* **~|schaffen** vt [h] (etw) ~ nach *to convey* (od *transport*) *to ..* **~|scheiden 1.** vi [s] *to decease; depart from life; pass away* **2.** ≃ n *decease, demise; departure; passing* **~|schicken** vt [h] ich werde es (ihn) ~ *I'll send it (him) there* (od *round*) **~|schieben** vt [h] jdm etw ~ (*or* etw ~ z jdm) *to push* (od *slide*) *a th to* (od *towards*) *a p* **~|schießen** vi **1.** [h] ~ auf *to shoot at* (od *towards*) **2.** °⟨fig⟩ [s] = hinsausen **~|schlachten** vt [h] ⟨übtr⟩ = hinmorden **~|schlagen** vi [s] lang ~ *to fall* (od *come down*) *full length* (auf *on*) || °da schlag einer lang hin! *that's a tall order! that's the limit!* || zum ≃ *smashing* **~schlängeln** vrefl [h] sich ~ *to meander; wind along*; sich ~ durch .. *wind through* **~|schleichen** vi [s] & refl [h] (sich) ~ nach, z *to creep* (od *steal*) *to ..* || ⟨übtr⟩ (of time) ~ *to pass slowly* **~|schlendern** vi [s] *to saunter along* **~|schleppen** vt [h] ⟨übtr⟩ (ausdehnen) (etw) *to drag on* (od *out*) || sich mühsam ~ *to toil along* **~|schleudern** vt [h] *to fling down* || ~ nach .. hin *to fl. towards ..* °**~|schmeißen** vt [h] = hinwerfen °**~|schmieren** vt [h] ⟨fig⟩ (Brief) *to scrawl, scibble* **~|schreiben** vt [h] *to put* (od *write*) *down* || ⟨arith⟩ (beim Addieren) die Einer ~ u die Zehner übertragen *to dot and carry* **h·in|schütten** vt [h] (etw) ~ auf .. *to pour* (od *shed, spill*) *on ..* **~|schwinden** vi [s] *to evanesce; pass away*; → verschwinden **~|sehen** vi [h] *to look; be looking; have a look; watch*; er sah jetzt hin *he was looking now* || er sah vor sich hin *he gazed before him* **~|sehnen** vrefl [h] sich ~ nach *to long* (od *pine*) *for* **~|setzen** vt [h] (etw) *to put* (od *set*) *down* || sich ~ *to sit down*; sich ~ zur Arbeit (*or* um z arbeiten) *to sit down to work* || sich gerade ~ *to sit up straight* ≃**sicht** f [nur nach prep in] **1. a. in anderer** ~ *in other respects; otherwise* || in der ~ *in that point* (od *respect*); *on that head* || in dieser ~ *in this regard* (od *respect*); *on this head* || in e–r ~, in gewisser ~ *in a way* (od *sense*); *in some respects* pl od *manner; in certain ways*; (P) *(bright) in spots* || in jeder ~ *in every regard* (od *respect, way*); *in all respects; on all grounds; at all points; down to the ground; all the way through* || in jeder ~ das große Werk e–s großen Meisters *no mean achievement by any standard* || in mancher(lei) ~ *in some ways* || in vieler(lei) ~ *in many respects* (od *ways*; *points*); *in a lot of ways* || in welcher ~? *in what way*? **b. in ~ auf** etw *in respect* (od *point*) *of*; *in regard of* (od *to*); *with regard to*; *as to*; *concerning* **2.** [in + Adj + ~ = engl adv] in geldlicher etc ~ *monetarily*; *climatically*; *militarily*; *politically*; in stimmlicher (*or* gesanglicher) ~ *vocally* || in ~ auf *in terms of* (*business, policy*); (*details*) *on* .. **~sichtlich** prep [mit gen] ~ e–r S = in Hinsicht auf **~|siechen** vi [s] *to die off* || ⟨fig⟩ *languish* (unter *under*); *pine away* **~|sinken** vi [s] *to drop*; *to fall* (od *sink*) *down* °**~|springen** vi [s] = hinlaufen **~|starren** vi [h] er starrte vor sich hin *he stared before* (od *ahead of*) *him* **~|stellen** vt [h] **1.** ⟨eig⟩ **a.** (Dinge) *to place* (od *put, set*) *down* (auf *on*); (der Reihe nach) *set out* || jdm e–n Stuhl ~ *place* (od *set*) *a chair for a p* || wieder ~ *replace* || jdn ~ *to place* od *appoint a p* **b. sich** ~ *to stand* (gegenüber) *opposite*) **2.** ⟨übtr⟩ (im Geiste ~) **a.** die Pn w in ihrer ganzen Natürlichkeit vor uns –ge–llt *the p.s are brought before us in all their truth* **b. etw ~ als** *to pose* od *represent, describe a th as* .. || als glaubwürdig ~ *to make* (*a th*) *out*; als Tatsache ~, daß .. *to aver that* ..; *to give it as a fact that* .. || das Buch wird als Mißerfolg –g. *the book is written down a failure*; .. als ausgezeichnet –g. .. *is voted excellent* **| jdn ~ als** .. *to hold a p up as* (*a model*); jdn als Lügner ~ *to make a p out* (od *to write a p down*) *a liar*; *to give a p the lie* **c. es so ~, als ob** .. *to make believe that* .. **d. sich** breitbeinig ~ *to plant one's feet firmly to the ground*; sich breitbeinig ~ vor jdn *to square up to a p* || **sich ~ als** .. *to give o.s. out as* ..; *to pose as* .. °**~|sterben** vi [s] = dahin- **~|streben** vi [h] ~ nach *to strive to reach* (*the shore*) || ⟨übtr⟩ *to aspire to* (*honours, rule*); *to strive for* od *after*; *to tend towards* .. **~|strecken** vt [h] (die Hand) *to hold out* (jdm *to a p*) || ⟨übtr⟩ °(jdn) *to knock down*; *to stretch on the ground* **| sich** ~ *to loll*; sich lang ~ *to stretch o.s.*; *to lie down full length*; *to loll back* **~|streichen** vi [s] (of time) = hingehen 2. **~|stürzen** vi [s] **1.** *to fall* (*the horse fell*); *to fall* (od *tumble*) *down* **2.** °~ nach, z *to dash* (od *rush*) *to* ..

hint·an- pref [betont, bei Verben trennbar] **~|bleiben** vi [s] *to lag behind*; *to linger* **~|halten** vt [h] (etw) *to hold back*; *to withhold*; (Gefühle) *to restrain* || sich ~ *to hold back*; *to withhold one's hand* **~|setzen, ~|stellen** vt [h] (etw) *to disregard*; *neglect*; *overlook*; *set aside*; = verschieben || (jdn) *to neglect*; *ignore, slight*; –gesetzt w *to go to the wall*; *to be put on the shelf* **~setzung** f *disregard, neglect* (*of duties*); mit *or* unter ~ s–r S. *with disregard of* (od *for*) *his own safety*

h·inten adv **1. a.** *behind*; *at the back*; *at* (od *in*) *the rear* || ~ im Schiff *aft* || weit ~ *far in the rear* od *distance*; *far away out* (*in* ..); ⟨theat⟩ *upstage*, ~ Mitte *up centre* (⟨Am⟩ *center*) **b. (etw) ~ anfügen** *to annex, to append* (an *to*) || ~ anstehen, sich ~ anstellen *to line up behind the queue* || ~ aufsitzen, sich ~ aufsetzen ⟨cycl⟩ *to ride pillon* || ~ ausschlagen (of horse) *to lash out*; *to kick*; ⟨übtr⟩ *to be wanton* || .. ~ herab *her hair fell down behind* || die ~ Laufenden (sc Tiere e–r Herde) *the tail ones* || ~ sitzen (sc im Wagen) *to sit in the rear* **c. ~ u vorn** *everywhere*; ⟨mar⟩ *fore and aft* || °es reichte bei ihm nicht ~ u nicht vorn *he was in great straits* || °lieber Georg ~ u lieber G. vorn *George here and G. there, G. everywhere* **2. a. nach** ~ (*to go*) *to the rear* (od *back*); *backward(s)*, *rearward(s)*; ⟨mar⟩ *aft, towards the stern* || ein Blick nach ~ *a backward glance* || nach ~ (hinaus)gehen zu (*of rooms*) *to back on to* (*the park*); nach ~ hinaus wohnen *to live at the back* || Zimmer im II. Stock nach ~ (hinaus) *two pair back* || nach ~ k ⟨Am⟩ *to come back* || lauf mal nach ~ *run along to the back* || der Stuhl fiel nach ~ über *the chair fell over backwards* **b. von** ~ *from behind*; *from the rear*; v ganz ~ *from far back* || ⟨mar⟩ v vorn bis ~ *from stem to stern* || (jdn) v ~ erdolchen *to stab a p in the back* || den Feind v ~ fassen *to take the enemy in rear* **·~·an** adv *behind*; *at the back*; *in the rear* **|** ~setzen, etc → hintan- || ~stehen → hinten 1. b. **·~dr·ein** adv = hinterdrein **·~her·um** adv; ~, v ~ **1.** *from behind*; *from the rear*; ~ k *to come by* (od *through*) *the back-door* **2.** ⟨fig⟩ **a.** *by a roundabout way*; *indirectly*; ~ getan *done in a corner*; ~ z verstehen geben *to air* .. *on the side*; etw ~ versuchen *to beat about the bush* **b.** *illegally, illicitly*; *by dubious* (od *illicit*) *means*; ⟨sl⟩ *on the quiet*; sich etw ~ be-, verschaffen ⟨sl⟩ *to wangle a th* **·~hin** adv *behind*; *to* (od *towards*) *the back* (od *rear*); *backward(s)*, *rearward(s)* **·~n·ach** adv = hinterdrein **·~·über** adv *backwards*; .. fiel ~ *the chair fell over backwards*; er fiel ~ *he went over on to his back*

h·inter prep **A. [mit dat] 1.** ⟨eig⟩ ~ dem H. *behind the house*; *at the back* od *rear of the h.*; ⟨Am a.⟩ *back of* ..; ~ dem V. hervor *from behind the curtain* || ~ jdm *behind a p*; *in* (od *at*) *the rear of a p*; *in a p's rear* (od *wake*) || (nächst Fritz saß mein Vater) mit Georg ~ ihm (..) *with George beyond him* || dicht (*or* gleich) hinter jdm *at* (od *on*) *a p's heels* || e–r ~ dem anderen *in file* || er kam ~ mir her *he came after me*; → hergehen || dauernd ~ jdm her s *to dog a p* || wir ließen .. ~ uns *we got clear of* (*the suburbs*) || er .. ~ sich *he shut the door behind him* || die Tür .. ~ ihm *the door closed upon him* || ~ jdm zurückbleiben *to lag behind a p* **2.** ⟨übtr & fig⟩ *behind* (*a th*; *a p*); *at the back* (od *bottom*) *of* (*a th*); *in the wake of* (*a th*); ⟨Am⟩ *back of* (*a th*) || ~ dem Kampf stand der Glaube .. *at the back of the contest was the belief* (*that* ..) || er hat das ganze Volk ~ sich *he has the whole nation at his back* || e–e K. ~ sich h *to have gone through a disease*; er hat e–e schwere K. ~ sich *he has just recovered from a serious illness* || nun hab ich's beinahe ~ mir *I'm very nearly over it* **3.** ⟨fig⟩ mit etw ~ dem Berge halten, *etw ~ dem B. h. *to keep a th secret*; *to be reticent about a th*; *to conceal a th* || °es (faustdick) ~ den Ohren h *to be more smart than honest*; → trocken || ~ jds Rücken *behind a p's back* || ~ etw her s *to be after a th*; *to strive for* od *after a th*; *to be a demon for* (*money*) || er steckt ~ der ganzen S *he is at the bottom of the whole th*; *he is the wire--puller*; ~ der S steckt nicht viel *there is not much in that* || ~ der Zeit zurücksein *to be behind the times* **|** °**~ jdm herlaufen** *to run after a p*; *to importune* od *molest a p* || ~ jdm (etw) her s *to be after* (od *on the track of*) *a p*; (*to go in for* [*money*]) || ~ jdm stehen *to back a p up*; *to stand by a p* || °das hätte ich nicht ~ ihm gesucht *I should not have thought that of him* || → zurückbleiben || er stand (nicht) ~ ihnen zurück *he was behind them* (an *in*); (*he kept on the level with them*) **|** etw ~ sich h ⟨fig⟩ (zeitl.) *to be past a th* || er hatte kein Geld ~ **sich** *he had no m. at his back* || (etw) ~ sich l *to leave behind* || jdn weit ~ sich l *to leave a p far behind*; *to put a p into the shade* || (etw) ~ sich (gelassen) h *to be past a th* ⟨a. fig⟩ **B. [mit acc] 1.** ⟨eig⟩ ~ das Haus *behind the house* || *to the back* (od *rear*) *of* .. || er sah ~ sich *he looked behind him*; *he l. back* **2.** ⟨übtr & fig⟩ *behind*; *to the bottom of* .. **3.** ⟨fig⟩ (jdn) ~'s Licht führen *to deceive, dupe*; *to take in*; ⟨sl⟩ *to dope* || ~ etw k *to get behind* (od *to the bottom of*) *a th*; *to get the hang of a th*; *to begin to realize a th*; ⟨Am⟩ *to get on to a th*; ~ jds Schliche (*or* jdm ~ die) Schliche k *to spot a p's artful practices* || °jdm eins ~ die O. geben *to box a p's ears* || °das schreib dir ~ die Ohren *take particular note of that*; *that's what I recommend you* || °sich ~ etw m *to apply* od *devote o.s. to a th*; *to inquire into a th* || sich ~ jdn stecken *to use a p as a tool* || (etw) ~ sich bringen *to get over .., to go through with*; das Schwerste e–r S ~ sich br. *to break the back* od *neck of a th*

h·inter- pref [betont] **1.** [untrennbar, z Bildung v Subst., Adj. u Adv. (≗fuß; ≗halt; ~listig)] *back-*; *hind-*; *rear-* **2.** [trennbar, z Bildung v Verben) **a.** *to the back*; → h·interbringen, -laufen etc **b.** *down*; → h·intergießen

hinter- pref [unbetont, untrennbar] **1.** [z Bildung v Verben] → hinterbr·ingen, –g·ehen **2.** [z Bildung v Adv.] → hinterdr·ein, hinterh·er **~-achs-** ≗bremse [f] *rear brake* ·≗**achse** f *rear axle*; (of a locomotive) *trailing-axle* ·≗**ansicht** f *back-view* ·**~ausgang** m *back way out* **~arbeiten** (drehen, fräsen) vt [h] *to back off* ·≗**backe** f *buttock*; ~n [pl] = Hinterteil ·≗**bänkler** m ⟨pol⟩ *back bencher* ·≗**bein** n *hind leg* || auf den ~en stehen (T) *to ramp*; auf den ~en stehend *rampant* (*lion*) || ⟨fig⟩ sich auf die ~e stellen *to stand on one's hind legs*; *to show fight* || (e–s Stuhls) *backleg* **~bl·eiben** vi [s] *to remain behind*; *to be left behind* ≗**bl·iebene** [der ~, ein ~r] *surviving dependent*; (in Todesanzeigen) (*the*) *bereaved*; die (trauernden) ~n [pl] *the bereaved* pl | ~nfürsorge [f] *care for widows and orphans*; ~nkasse [f] *W.s' and O.s' Fund*; ~nversicherung [f] *W.s' and O.s' Insurance* || ~nversorgung [f] = –fürsorge ·~|**bringen** vt [pp –gebracht] [h] **1.** (etw) *to take* (od *carry*) *to the back* (od *rear*); .. *backwards*, *rearwards* **2.** ⟨fig⟩ ich konnte k–n Bissen ~ *I could not eat a morsel* **~br·ingen** [pp –bracht] [h] (mst heimlich ~) jdm etw ~ *to inform a p of a th*; *to tell a p a th* (od *a th to a p*); wer hat es dir –bracht? *who has told you*? das war ihm –bracht worden *he had notice of that*; man –brachte ihm, daß .. *he was told that ..*; ich verspreche, nichts z ~ *I promise not to tell* || e–r Behörde etw über jdn ~ *to inform against a p*; *to tell on a p* ≗**br·inger** m *informer*; *tell-tale* ≗**br·ingung** f *communication, impacting* ·≗**deck** n ⟨mar⟩ *poop*; → Achterdeck ·~|**drehen** vt ⟨tech⟩ *to back off* **~dr·ein** adv **1.** (örtlich) [in Verbindung mit Verben] = hinterher **2.** (zeitlich) *afterwards*; *subsequently*; ~ hat man gut reden *it's easy to prophesy after the event* **h·intere** a **1.** *hinder, posterior* (*parts*); *back, rear* (*platform*); die ~n Bänke *the back benches*; die ~n Glieder *the rear ranks*; in den ~n Teilen *in the back parts* (*of the town*) || am ~n Ende .. *at the far end of the hall, at the far edge of the wood* || das ~e Ende *the tail* (*of the procession*); *the heel* (*of a hunt*) **2.** *hind* (*leg, wheel*); → Hinterbein, –rad; –teil °**H·intere** m –r(e)n/ *backside, rump*; *bum*; *buttocks, posteriors, hind quarters* pl; ⟨fam⟩ *behind, bottom, cheeks* pl, *stern*; ⟨hum⟩ *latter end* || (der Hose) *slack* | ein Tritt in den ~rn *a kick in the pants*; jdm in den –rn treten *to kick a p's behind* || jdm den –rn versohlen *to give a p a good hiding* od *licking*; er schlug ihn auf den bloßen –rn *he whipped his bare skin* **h·inter- ~ein·ander** adv → Gänsemarsch || *one after another* (od *the other*); ⟨tech⟩ (*to operate*) *in series* || *in file* (~ fahren *to ride in f.*); z zweien ~ *in double file*; (schnell) ~ *in* (*rapid*) *succession* || (of 2 horses) ~ gespannt *tandem* || zehnmal ~ *ten times running*; *ten times over* (od *together*) || 2 Tage ~ *two day* (*at a time* od) *in succession* || wochenlang ~ *for weeks on end*; .. *at a stretch*; .. *together* || etw ~ tun (P) *to do a th in turns* || kz (*or* dicht) ~ k (S) *to come one on top of the other* || rasch ~, ~ weg *without interruption* (od *a break*); *uninterruptedly*; *right off the reel* || ein Paar Pferde ~ gespannt *tandem*; ⟨cycl⟩ ein Fahrrad mit 2 Sitzen ~ *a tandem* ≗**-e-a-fahren** n *riding in file* **~-e-a-|schalten** vt [h] ⟨el⟩ *to connect in series* ≗**-e-a-schaltung** f ⟨el⟩ *series connection* **h·inter-** °**~fotzig** a = –listig ·≗**frucht** f = –korn ·~|**führen** vt [h] (jdn) *to lead* (od *take*) *to the back* od *rear* ·≗**fuß** m *hind foot*; ≗e [pl] *hind feet*; *heels* pl ·≗**gäßchen** n, ·≗**gasse** f *back alley* ·≗**gaumen** m ⟨anat⟩ *soft palate* || ~laut ⟨phon⟩ *back vowel*; *back consonant* ·≗**gebäude** n *back building*; *outhouse* ·≗**-gedanke** m *mental reservation*; *arrière pensée* Fr; ~n [pl] *arrière pensée*; *ulterior motives* pl || ~n h *to have sth at the back of one's mind* || das mögen ihre ~n s *that may be at the back of their minds* || ohne ~n *guileless*(*ly*) °·~|**gehen** vi [pp –gegangen] [s] geh mal hinter *just go* (*along*) *to the back*; *go behind and look* **~g·ehen** vt [pp –gangen] [h] (jdn) ~ *to cheat* (od *circumvent, deceive*); *to impose* (od *practise*) *upon*; *to palter with*; ⟨Am⟩ *to doublecross* || er hat mich –gangen *he did not act square with me*; wir wurden –gangen *we were imposed upon* ≗**g·ehung** f *deception*; *fraud* ·≗**gelände** n *back country*; *terrain at the back* ·≗**gestell** n **1.** *back* (od *rear*) *portion* **2.** °⟨fig⟩ = Hinterteil °·~|**gießen** vt [h] (Getränk) *to gulp* (*down*); *to knock back*; *to pour down one's throat*; *to toss off*; ⟨sl⟩ *to lower, swig*; *down* (*a drink*) || in gr Zügen ~ *to quaff* ·≗**gl·asmalerei** f ⟨arts⟩ *glass-picture*; *églomisé* Fr; [a. konkr] (Bild) ·≗**glied** n ⟨mil⟩ *rear rank* || ⟨log & math⟩ *consequent* ·≗**grund** m ~(e)s/≗e **1.** ⟨eig⟩ **a.** *background*; ⟨phot⟩ (un)ruhiger ~ (*busy*) *plain b.*, störender ~ *obtrusive b.* || ein Kopf auf e–m ~e *a head against a b.* || im ~e *in the b., in the rear*; im ~e der Kirche *at the back of the church* **b.** ⟨theat⟩ *back* (*scene*); (Vorhang) *backdrop* **2.** ⟨fig⟩ **a.** *background* (*political b.*); *setting* **b.** (etw) **als ~ benutzen** f *to use .. as b. for* (od: *as the b. of ..*) || den ~ bilden z (S) *to be the b. of ..*; den ~ e–r Feier bilden *to underlie a ceremony* || e–n ~ bilden z *to form a b. to ..* || als ~ dienen z *to serve as a b. to ..* || die S hat e–n ~ *there is a mystery lurking at the back of it* | **(P) im ~ bleiben,** sich im ~ halten *to keep* (od *remain*) *in the b.*; *to efface o.s.*; *to make o.s. scarce* ⟨fam⟩ *to take a backseat*; das Sich-im ~-h. *self-obliteration* || im ~ stehen *to be in eclipse* || in den ~ gedrängt w *to undergo eclipse* || in den ~ geraten *to recede into the b.* || (jdn) in den ~ schieben, verweisen *to reduce* (*a p*) *to the b.*; (etw) *to relegate* (*a th*) *to the b.* || in den ~ treten *to recede into the b.*; ⟨fig⟩ *to fade out*; ⟨Am fam⟩ *to take a back seat* ·**~gründig** a *subtle, problematic enigmatic*; *puzzling*; *difficult to fathom*; *esoteric* || *inscrutable, enigmatic, crytic* (*style*) || das ist e–e ~e Frage (*or* S) *there is more in this question* (*in it*) *than meets the eye* ·≗**halt** m ~(e)s/~e **1.** *ambush*; ⟨mil⟩ *ambuscade* || jdm e–n ~ legen *to lay an a.h* (od *a trap*) *for a p* || aus dem ~ angreifen *to* (*spring an*) *a.de*; (jdn) *to a.de, a.h* || im ~ lauern, liegen *to lie in a.h*; *to lie perdu*(*e*) || (jdn) im ~ verbergen *to a.de, to a.h* || sich in den ~ legen *to lie down in a.h* || (jdn) in e–n ~ locken *to decoy a p into an a.h* (od *a trap*) **2.** ⟨fig⟩ *reserve*; (etw) im ~ h *to have in r.* || ohne ~ *without guile*; *guileless*(*ly*) *†**~h·alten** vt [h] (etw) *to hold* (od *keep*) *back*; *to withhold* (jdm *from a p*) ·**~hältig 1.** [a] *furtive* (*glance*); *hole-and-corner* (*methods*); *sly, wily*; *foul, insidious, perfidious, underhand*; es war nichts ≗es dabei *there was nothing underhand about it*; → –listig, heimtückisch **2.** [adv] *f.ly*; *i.ly, p.ly* | ≗keit [f] *f.ness*; *i.ness*; *p.ness*; *perfidy* ·≗**hand** f **1.** (of horse) *breech*; *hind quarters* pl; *haunches* pl **2.** ⟨cards⟩ *the youngest hand*; in der ~ s *to be the y. h.*; *to play last* ·≗**hangstellung** ⟨tact⟩ (*reserve-*)*slope position* ·≗**haupt** n ⟨anat⟩ *occiput*; *back of the head* | ~s– *occipital* ~bein [n] *o. bone* | ~höcker [m] *o. protuberance* ·≗**haus** n *back-building*; *back-house* || ~ zwei Treppen *back second floor* | ~garten [m] *back garden* **~h·er** adv *behind* || (zeitlich) *after*; *afterwards*; *subsequently*; → hinterdrein **hinterh·er-** pref [betont, bei Verben trennbar] *behind*; *after* **~|gehen** vi [s] *to walk behind*; *to follow in the rear*;

wir wollen ~ *we will bring up the rear* ~|k vi [s] *to come* (*up*) (od *to follow*) *behind*; *to bring up the rear* ~|laufen vi [s] er kam –gelaufen *he came running behind*, (jdm) ~ ⟨sl⟩ *to tail* ~|rasen vi [s] er kam –gerast *he came tumbling behind* ~|reiten vi [s] *to ride behind* ~|schreiten vi [s] *to stride behind* ~|trotten, ~|ziehen vi [s] *to lumber behind* ~|zuckeln vi [s] *to trot behind*

h·inter- ·~́hirn n ⟨anat⟩ *hind-brain* ·~́hof m *backyard* ·~́indien ⟨geog⟩ *Farther* (od *Further*) *India*; *Indo-China*; *Indo-Chinese peninsula* °~|-kippen vt = –gießen °~|klemmen vrefl sich ~ = sich hinterlegen ·~́kopf m *back of the head* | ~-zuwenden [n] ⟨orn-eth⟩ *head flagging*; → –haupt ·~́korn n *corn of inferior quality* ·~́lader m *breech-loader*; *breech-loading gun* ·~́ladung f *breech-loading* | ~sgeschütz *b.-l.ing gun* ~́lage f Sw = Faustpfand ·~́land n *country district*; (Küsten-) *hinterland* [Ger]; *interior*; ⟨col⟩ *backward territory*; ⟨Am⟩ *backcountry* (od *district*); ⟨Austr⟩ (entferntes unbewohntes) *back blocks* pl; das hinterste ~ *the back of beyond* °·~|l vt [pp -gel-] [h] jdn ~ *to allow a p to go behind* (od *to the back*); *to admit a p*; laß mich mal hinter *let me pass to the back* ~l·assen vt [pp ~] [h] **1.** (zurücklassen) (Notiz, Spuren) *to leave* (*behind*); s–e Arbeit –ließ allmählich ihre Sp. *his w. began to tell on him*; er –ließ kein Testament *he left no will behind* (*him*); er –ließ nichts als Schulden *he left nothing* (*behind* [*him*]) *but debts* ‖ ⟨übtr⟩ er hat nichts ~ *he left no message* od *word* **2.** (of a deceased p) (Land, Geld) *to leave*; jdm etw ~ *to l. a p a th* (od *a th to a p*); jdm etw als Erbschaft ~ ⟨oft übtr⟩ *to hand a th down to a p* ~l·assen a *posthumous* (*works*) | ~́schaft [f] ⟨jur⟩ *estate* ~́l·assung f = Vermächtnis; → Testament ·~-lastig a ⟨aero⟩ *tail-heavy* ·~́lauf m ⟨hunt⟩ *hind leg* (*of a dog*) ·~|legen vt [pp –gelegt] [h] *to place at the back* | sich tüchtig ~ *to go thoroughly* (od *to throw o.s.*) *into it* ~l·egen vt [–legt] [h] (Geld etc) *to put up* ..; bei der Bank ~ *to deposit* (od *consign, lodge*) *m. in a b.* (f jdn *to a p's credit*); *to b. m.* (*for a p*); –legtes Geld *deposit*; → deponieren ‖ (Pfand) *to lodge as security* ‖ (Testament) *to deposit* ~́l·eger m *depositor* ~́l·egung f *c.ment*; *d.ing*, *lodging*; ⟨jur⟩ *lodg*(*e*)*ment* (*of m.*) | ~s-schein [m] *certificate of d.*; ~ssumme [f] ⟨st exch⟩ *margin* ·~́leib m ⟨zoo⟩ *hind quarters* pl ·~́linse f *rear lense* ·~́list f *cattiness*, *furtiveness*, *insidiousness*; *underhandedness*; *underhand conduct* ~llstig **1.** [a] *cattish*, *catty*; *foul*; *furtive* (*conduct*); *hole-and-corner*; *insidious*; *underhand*; → hinterhältig, heimtückisch **2.** [adv] *foully*; *furtively*; *insidiously* | ~́keit [f] = –list ·~́mann m **1.** ⟨mil⟩ *rear-rank man*; *coverer* **2.** ⟨übtr⟩ **a.** ⟨mar⟩ (Schiff) *ship next astern* **b.** ⟨com⟩ *subsequent endorser* **c.** *backer*, *supporter* | ~schaft [f] ⟨ftb⟩ *rear-guard formation* **d.** ⟨cards⟩ jds ~ s *to play after a p* ·~́mast m ⟨mar⟩ *mizzen-mast* ~pausche f (Sattel~́) *cantle* ·~́pforte f *back-gate*; ⟨mar⟩ *stern-port* ·~́pfote f ⟨zoo⟩ *hind foot* ·~́-pommern n *Further Pomerania* ·~́rad n *back* (od *hind*)-*wheel*, *rear-wheel*; *trailing wheel* (*of a locomotive*) | ~achse [f] *rear axle*; ~antrieb [m] *back-wheel drive* ·~́rhein m *Hinter-Rhein* [Ger] ·~rücks adv *from behind*; jdn ~ anfallen *to stab a p in the back* ‖ ⟨übtr⟩ *behind a p's back*; *insidiously*; → hinterlistig 2. ·~́saß, -sasse m *copyholder*; *small farmer* ·~́satz m ⟨log & gram⟩ *concluding* (od *consequent*) *clause*; *apodosis* ·~́schiff n ⟨mar⟩ *stern*; *hind part of ship*; → Heck ·~́-schliffwinkel m ⟨tech⟩ *relief angle* °·~|schlingen vt [–geschlungen] [h] (Speise) *to gulp*, *to swallow*; ⟨sl⟩ *to lower*; hastig ~ ⟨sl⟩ *to bolt*; *to wolf* (*down*) ‖ (Getränk) = –gießen ·~|schlucken vt [pp –geschluckt] [h] **1.** *to swallow*; *to gulp* (*down*) **2.** ⟨fig⟩ *to swallow*; = hinnehmen 2. ·~́segel n ⟨mar⟩ ~ [pl] *after-sails* pl ·~́seite f *back* (*of a door*); *hinder part* *·~sinnig a bes Sw = schwermütig ·~́sitz m ⟨cycl & mot⟩ *pillion* °·~|spülen vt = hinunter- ·~ste [sup v hinter] **1.** [a] *hindmost*; ⟨mar⟩ *aftermost*; → zuhinterst **2.** °~́ m = Hintere ·~́steven m ⟨mar⟩ *stern* (od *main*)-*post* ·~́stube f *back-room* ·~́stück n *hinder piece* ·~́-tasche f *hind-pocket* ·~́teil n **1.** *back* (od *rear*) *part*; *hinder part* ‖ (of a ship) *after-part*; *poop*; *stern* **2.** *breech*; *hams* pl; *hind-quarters* pl (of a horse); *backside*; → Hintere ·~́treffen n [nur in:] **a. im** ~ **s** *to be at a disadvantage*; *to be handicapped*; wir sind in dem Kampf im ~ *our back is to the wall in the struggle* **b. ins** ~ geraten *or* k *to drop back*; *to fall behind*; *to fall* (od *recede*) *into the background*; ⟨sport⟩ *to be out of the running* (od *out of the swim*); ⟨sl⟩ *to be put in the cart* ‖ jdm gegenüber ins ~ g. *to be outdistanced by a p* ·~|-treiben vt [–getrieben] [h] *to drive to the back* ~tr·eiben vt [–tr·ieben] [h] (etw) *to circumvent*; *counteract*; *frustrate*; ⟨parl⟩ *to obstruct*; *thwart*; → vereiteln, hindern ~́tr·eibung f *circumvention*; *frustration*; *obstruction* (*of a bill*) ·~́treppe f *backstairs*; *service stairs* pl; *back staircase* (od *steps* pl) °·~́treppen- ⟨fig⟩ *backstairs* (*plot*); *backdoor*; *gumshoe* (*methods*); *underhand*; *yellow* | ~gutachten [n] *curbstone opinion*; ~roman [m] *cheap sensational novel*; *shilling shocker*; *thriller*; *lovey-dovey stuff* °·~|trinken vt [–getrunken] [h] = –gießen ·~́tür f **1.** *backdoor*; durch die ~ entweichen *to escape by the backdoor* **2.** ⟨fig⟩ *backdoor*; *loophole*; *outlet* ‖ e–e ~ offen l *to leave a loophole for escape*; (etw) durch die ~ (wieder) einführen *to introduce underhand* (od *in an underhand way*) | ~klausel [f] ⟨Am sl⟩ *joker* °·~́viertel n *hind quarters* pl ‖ °= Hintere ·~́wäldler m *backwoodsman*; ⟨Am⟩ *hillbilly* ·~́wand f *back-wall* °·~|würgen vt = –schlucken ·~́zahn m ⟨zoo⟩ *back tooth* ·~́zeug n (f Pferd) *breeching*; *crupper* ·~|ziehen vt [–gezogen] [h] (etw) *to drag to the back* ~z·iehen vt [–zogen] [h] ⟨fig⟩ Steuern, Zölle ~ *to defraud the revenue* ·~́z·iehung f *defrauding*, *defraudation* ·~́zwiesel m *hind-bow*; *cantle*

h·in- ~|tragen vt [h] trag es hin *carry it there*; (nach *to*) ~|träumen vt [h] (Zeit) *to dream away* ‖ vor sich ~ *to be in a state of reverie*; *to be musing* ~|treiben vt [h] treib sie (sc Schafe) hin *drive them there*; ~ nach, z *to drive to ..* ~|treten vt [h] treten Sie dorthin *stand over there*; .. hierhin *step this way*; ~ z *to step up to ..* °~|tun vt [h] *to place*; *to put* (*down*); tu es dorthin *put it there* ‖ ⟨fig⟩ .. aber ich weiß nicht genau, wo ich ihn ~ soll .. *but I cannot quite place him*

hin·über adv **a.** *over*; quer ~ *across*; er konnte nicht ~ *he could not get over* ‖ über .. ~ *over*, *across* (*the fields*, *river*) ‖ ~ nach, z *over to*; bis ~ z *away to* **b.** °⟨fig⟩ °~ s *to be no longer of use*; °das Glas ist ~ *the glass is broken*; °der Schirm ist ~ *the umbrella has served its time* (od *has seen better days*) ‖ °er ist ~ *it's all over with him*; *he is dead* ‖ (zeitlich) = vorüber **hin·über-** pref [betont, bei Verben trennbar] *over-* ~|blicken vi [h] = –sehen ~|bringen vt [h] (jdn) *to take over* (z *to*) ~|eilen vi [s] *to hasten* (od *hurry*, *rush*) *over* (nach, z *to*); *to run along* (z *to*) ~|fahren vi/t **1.** vi [s] *to drive* (od *run*) *over* (z *to*); (im Schiff) *to cross* (od *sail*) *over*; (in der Fähre) *to ferry across* ‖ ~ über *to cross* (*the Channel*); ⟨mot⟩ (nach l., r.) scharf ~ *to change lanes abruptly*; → fahren **2.** vt [h] jdn ~ *to drive* (od *run*) *a p over* ‖ (Gepäck) *to convey* od *transport* ~|fallen vi [s] *to fall* (od *go*) *over* (in *into ..*) ~|führen vt [h] vt/i **1.** vt (Pferd) *to lead across* (*the river*); (schwimmend) ~ über *to swim across ..* **2.** vi [h] (of thoughts) ~ z *to lead on to ..* ~|gehen vi [s] *to go* (od *amble*, *pass*, *step*, *walk*) *over* (nach, z *to*); er ging auf die andere Seite hinüber *he crossed* (*over*) *to the other side* ‖ ⟨fig⟩

(sterben) *to go west* **~|gelangen** vi [s] *to get over* **~|helfen** vi [h] jdm ~ *to help a p over* **~|klettern** vi [s] *to climb over* (in .. *into the garden*) **~|k** vi [s] *to get over*; zu jdm *to come and see a p* || °ich komme gleich hinüber *I'll be along shortly* **~|l** vt [h] jdn ~ *to allow a p to go over* **~|laufen** vi [s] *to run over* (z *to*) **~|lehnen** vrefl [h] sich ~ *to lean over* (*don't l. over too far*); sich ~ über .. *to lean over* (*the table*) **~|neigen** vi [h] ⟨fig⟩ ~ z *to veer to* .. **~|ragen** vi [h] *to lap over* (in .. *into*); ~ über etw *to overlap a th*; → –reichen **~|reichen** vt/i [h] **1.** vt (etw) *to hold out* (z .. *to a p*); *to pass on* (z jdm *to a p*) **2.** vi *to reach* (bis an .. *the hall*; ~ bis ins .. *into the 20th c.*); *to reach across* (nach *for*) **~|reiten** vi [s] *to ride over* (z *to*) **~|schaffen** vt [h] (etw) *to get over*; → –fahren **~|schicken** vt [h] *to send over* (z *to*) **~|schieben** vt [h] (etw) *to shove over* (z jdm *to a p*) **~|schlagen** vt [h] (Brücke) *to construct* (nach *to*) **~|schlummern** vi [s] ⟨fig⟩ in die Ewigkeit ~ *to pass away softly* **~|schweifen** vi [s] (of eyes) *to go* (z *to*); (of thoughts) *to drift away* (nach *to*) **~|schwenken** vi [h] ⟨fig⟩ ~ nach, z *to veer round to* **~|sehen** vi [h] *to see over* (in .. *into the garden*); z jdm ~ *to gaze over* (od *glance along*) *at a p*; *to look across to a p*, *to look towards a p*; *to look a p's way* **~|springen** vi [s] *to leap over* **~|steigen** vi [s] *to climb* (od *step*) *over* **~|tragen** vt [h] (jdn) *to carry over* || den Kampf ~ nach .. *to shift the scene of fighting to* .. **~|wechseln** vi [s] ⟨fig⟩ ~ z *to shift to* ..; *to veer round to* ..; *to go over* (od *to secede*) *to* (*a party*); ~ v .. z *to shift* (od *veer*) *from .. to* **~|werfen** vt [h] (etw) ~ über *to fling* (od *throw*) *across* (*the table*) **~|ziehen** vt/i **1.** vt [h] (etw) *to draw across* (od *over*) || (jdn) z sich ~ *to draw* od *attract a p*; *to win a p over to one's side* **2.** vi [s] ~ nach, z *to march* (od *move*) *to* ..

h·in und h·er adv *backwards and forwards*; *to and fro*; *up and down*; *hither and thither*; *about*; *from place to place*; *from side to side*; ⟨Am⟩ *back and forth*, *hither and yon* || e–e Bewegung ~ *a movement to and fro* || → hin 2. b.

Hin und Her n ~/ (*the to-and-fro* [pl *tos and fros*]; *seesaw*; *ebb and flow*; *up-and-down* [pl *ups and downs*] || *swing* (*of a pendulum*) | ⟨übtr⟩ *vacillation* || das scharfe ~ des D. *the cut and thrust of dialogue* || ein ewiges ~ *an everlasting coming and going*; nach längerem (*or* vielem) ~ *after tedious discussions* (od *correspondence*) **h·in- und h·er-** pref [betont, bei Verben trennbar] *backwards and forwards*; *to and fro*; *about* **~|bewegen** vt [h] *to move to and fro* || sich ~ (S) *to swing* (*in the wind*); ⟨mech⟩ *to reciprocate* **~|fahren** vi [s] *to drive to and fro* (od *up and down*); *to drive about* || ⟨mar⟩ *to sail about*; *to cruise* **~|flattern** vi [s] *to flit to and fro* **~|gehen** vi [s] *to walk about*; *to pass to and fro*; im Zimmer ~ *to traverse the room*; auf der Straße ~ *to walk the street* || ⟨mech⟩ (S) *to reciprocate* **~gerissen** a *torn* (zwischen .. *between* [*hope and fear*]); *racked* (v .. *by* ..) **~|laufen** vi [s] *to run to and fro*; wütend (*or* wie wild) ~ *to run amok* **~|pendeln** vi [s] ⟨fig⟩ ~ zw *to gravitate* (od *oscillate*) *between* || °**~|rasen** vi [s] *to rush about*; = –laufen **~|reißen** vt [h] ⟨fig⟩ *to distract* (*a p*) **~|schlagen** vi [h] mit etw ~ *to flick a th back and forth* **~|schwanken** vi [h] ⟨fig⟩ *to oscillate*; *vacillate*; *to sway* od *wobble from side to s.* **~|schwingen** vt/i [h] **1.** vt; etw ~ *to swing a th to and fro* (od *from side to side*) **2.** vi *to oscillate*; mit etw ~ = etw ~ | **~|überlegen** vt [h] etw ~ *to rack one's brains about a th*; *to turn a th over in one's mind* **~|werfen** vt [h] ⟨übtr⟩ (of the sea) (Schiff) *to toss* || ⟨fig⟩ –geworfen w *to be t.ed about*; *to t.* || sich ~ *to t. about*

Hinundh·er- ~bewegung f *motion backwards and forwards*; ⟨mech⟩ *reciprocating motion*; *reciprocation* (*of a spring*) **~fahren** n ⟨mar⟩ *cruise* **~fahrt** f *the journey* (⟨mar⟩ *passage*) *out and back* **≃schieben** vt [h] (P) *to order .. around* od *about* **≃schusseln** vi [s] *to squirrel* **~schwanken 1.** n ⟨fig⟩ *oscillation*; *vacillation* **2.** ≃ vi [h] ⟨fig⟩ (P) *to chop* (*and change*) **~schwingen** n *swing*; *oscillation* **~weg** m *the way out and back* **~wogen** n *back-and-forth surge* (*of a battle, etc*)

hin·unter adv *down*(*wards*) || die Straße ~ *down the street*; in die Stadt ~ *d. town* || die Treppe ~ *d. the stairs*, *d.stairs*; ins Tal ~, den Berg ~ *d. the hill*, *downhill*; den Fluß ~ *d. stream* || bis ~ z *or* an (*right*) *d. to* (*the sea*); ich kann den Lärm bis ~ zur Halle hören ⟨Am⟩ *I can hear the noise way d. the hall* || nach unten ~ *d.ward* || ~ mit ..! *d. with* || °ich muß ~ *I must get d.* || → hinab **~|bemühen** vrefl; sich ~ *to trouble to go d.* **~|beugen** vt; den Kopf ~ *to bend one's head d.* (bis z *to*) || sich ~ *to stoop* (z *to*) **~|blicken** vi [h] *to look* (od *gaze*) *d.* (auf jdn *at a p*; in *into* ..); ⟨fig⟩ → herab- **~|eilen** vi [s] *to hurry* (od *rush*) *d.* (nach *to*); die Treppe ~ *to hurry d. the stairs* **~|fahren** vi [s] *to drive d.*; *to go* (od *pass*, *roll*) *down*; ⟨rail⟩ *to ride d.* (nach *to*); schnell ~ *to rush d.* (*to* ..) || die Straße ~ *to drive d.* (od *along*) *the street* || ⟨mount⟩ den Berg ~ *to glissade*; ⟨cycl⟩ den B. mit Freilauf ~ *to freewheel d. the hill*; *to coast* || ⟨mar⟩ an der Küste *to sail* (langsam: *to drop*) *d. the coast* **~|fallen** vi [s] die Treppe ~ *to fall d. the stairs*; *to have a fall d. the st.*; kopfüber die T. ~ *to go* (od *pitch*) *headlong d. the st.* °**~|fegen** vi [s] die Straße ~ *to rush* (od *tear*) *d. the road* **~|fliegen** vi [s] kopfüber ~ *to go d. headlong* (od *head foremost*); die Treppe ~ *to go headlong d. the stairs* || (S) ~ *to flutter d.* **~|fließen** vi [s] *to flow* (od *pour*) *d.*; die Treppe ~ *to flow d. the stairs* **~|führen** vt/i [h] **1.** vt (jdn) *to lead* (od *take*) *d.* (in *into* ..) **2.** vi (of a road) *to lead* (od *run*) *d. to* .. || → herunter- **~|gehen** vi [s] *to walk* (od *go*) *d.* (nach, z *to*); → hinab- || (of food) die Kehle ~ *to slip d. the throat*; *to go d.* **~|geleiten** vt [h] (jdn) *to hand d.* (nach, z *to*) **~|gießen** vt [h] *to pour d.* || ° = hintergießen **~|gleiten** vi [s] ⟨eig⟩ *to slide* (od *slip*) *d.*; an *or* in etw ~ *to slide* (od *slither*) *d.* (*a rope*, *a well*); → hinab- **~|helfen** vi [h] jdm ~ *to help a p d.* °**~|kippen** vt [h] (Getränk) = hinter- **~|klettern** vi [s] *to climb* (od *scramble*) *d.* (in *into* ..); an e–m Baum ~ *to climb* (od *shin*) *d. a tree* **~|lassen** vt [h] *to let d.*; *to lower* || sich ~ *to let o.s. d.* **~|laufen** vi [s] *to run* (schnell: *to rush*) *d.*; die .. ~ *to run d.* (od *along*) *the street* **~|purzeln** vi [s] *to come tumbling down* **~|rasen** vi [s] die .. ~ *to dash* (od *fly*, *rush*, *shoot*, *tear*) *d.* (od *along*) *the street*; *to rattle* (od *spin*) *along the road*; (rücksichtslos) ⟨sl⟩ *to blind along the r.*; → –sausen **~|reichen** vi [h] (S) ~ bis auf .. *to reach to the bottom of the sea*; ~ bis z *to reach d. to* **~|reiten** vi [s] die .. nach .. ~ *to ride d. the road towards* .. **~|rennen** vi [s] die .. ~ *to fly* (od *rush*) *d. the street* **~|rollen** = hinab- **~|rücken** vi [s] rück ein wenig hinunter *move d. a little* **~|rutschen** vi [s] *to slip d.*; an (*or* auf) etw ~ *to slide* (od *slither*) *d. a th* || die Str. waren ihm über die Knöchel –gerutscht *his stockings were d. over his ankles* **~|sausen** vi [s] = –rasen || (of stones) die Klippe ~ *to hurtle d. the cliff* **~|schauen** vi [h] = –blicken **~|schicken** vt [h] *to send d.* **~|schleichen** vi [s] die .. ~ *to slip d. the street* °**~|schlingen** vt [h] (Speise etc) = hinterschlingen, –gießen **~|schlucken** vt [h] = hinterschlucken | ⟨übtr⟩ (Worte) *to gulp d.*; (Beleidigung) *to pocket*; *swallow* (*a lot*) || ich will es lieber ~ *I prefer to keep quiet* **~|schreiten** vi [s] die Treppe ~ *to step* (stolz: *to stalk*) *d. the stairs* **~|sehen** vi [h] *to look d.* (in *into* ..); das Tal (*or* im Tal) ~ *to look d. the valley* **~|springen** vi [s] die Treppe ~ *to bound d. the stairs* **~|spülen** vt [h] (Pille etc) *to wash d.* (mit *with*) || °(Getränk) = hintergießen **~|steigen** vi [s] *to go* (od *step*) *d.*; in e–e Grube ~ *to go d. a mine*; → hinab- **~|stürzen** vi/t **1.** vi [s] **a.** (fallen) *to fall* (od *tumble*) *down*; → hinab- **b.** (eilen) = –rennen, –rasen, –sausen **2.** °vt [h] = hintergießen **~|tragen** vt [h] *to carry d.* || °**~|trinken** vt = hintergießen **~|werfen** vt [h] *to throw d.* (in *into* ..); jdn die Treppe ~ *to kick a p d.stairs* °**~|würgen** vt [h] (etw) = hinterschlingen, –schlucken **~|ziehen** vt/i **1.** vt [h] (jdn) *to drag d.(ward)* || sich ~ bis an .. (of a park) *to reach as far as* (*the shore*) **2.** vi [s] ~ nach *to march d. to* **~|zwingen** vt [h] *to force down*

h·in- **~|wagen** vrefl [h] sich ~ auf *to venture on*; .. nach *to v. to*; ich wage mich nicht hin *I do not v.* (*to go*) *there* **~wärts** adv *on the way out* ´~-**weg** m *the way out*; auf dem ~ *on my way*

hinw·eg adv **a.** mst ⟨poet⟩ (= weg) *away*; *off* || ~ in den Krieg *off to the wars* || ~! *get away with you!*, *go away!*, *off you go!* ~ mit ihm! *away with him* **b.** über .. ~ *over*; *across*; *beyond*; über die Baumwipfel ~ öffneten sich .. *away over the crests .. opened out* || ⟨fig⟩ über jds Kopf ~ *over a p's head*; über ihre Köpfe ~ (*he talked*) *over their heads*; über alle Hindernisse ~ *in the face* (od *in spite*) *of all obstacles* || °darüber bin ich lange ~ *I have done with that ever so long*; *I have got over that ever so long* **~|brausen** vi [s] mst ⟨fig⟩ (S) ~ über .. *to sweep* (od *rush*) *across* **~|bringen** vt [h] jdn ~ über .. *to carry a p over* (*troubles*); *to help a p to tide over* (*a bad time*) °**~|denken** vt [h] es war nicht –zu– *it could not be dispensed with*; *we could not do* (od *go*) *without it*; er war nicht –zu– *we could not dispense with his services* **~|fegen** vt [h] ⟨fig⟩ (jdn, etw) (of death, etc) *to sweep away* || ~ über (of storm, etc) *to sweep across* od *over*; über das Land ~ *to sweep* (*over*) *the country* **~|feuern** vi [h] ~ über jdn *to fire over a p* **~|führen** vt [h] (jdn) *to march off* **~gehen** vi [s] **1.** (P) **a.** eilig ~ über *to hurry* (od *hasten*) *over* **b.** leicht ~ über etw *to make light of*; *to pass lightly over a th* **c.** ~ über etw *to pass* (od *gloss, gloze*) *a th over*; *to slide* (od *slur*) *over a th*; *to dismiss* (od *ignore, overlook*) *a th*; .. mit Achselzucken .. *to shrug a th off*; man kann ruhig darüber ~ *it can safely be ignored* **2.** (of storm, etc.) *to sweep across* od *over*; → –fegen **~|heben** vrefl [h] ⟨bib⟩ hebe dich hinweg .. † *get thee hence, satan* **~|helfen** vi [h] jdm ~ über .. *to tide a p over* (*a loss*) **~|k** vi [s] ~ über .. *to negotiate* (*a hill*) || ⟨fig⟩ ~ über .. *to get* (od *tide*) *over* (*a loss*), *to live it down*; → Berg 3. a. **~|raffen** vt [h] = hinraffen **~|räumen** vt = weg- **~|rauschen** vi [s] ~ über (of time) *to sweep over* **~|reden** vi [h] über die Köpfe der Hörer ~ *to talk over the heads of the audience* **~|reißen** vt [h] = –raffen **~|reiten** vi [s] über alle Hindernisse ~ *to ride straight* **~|schreiten** vi [s] ~ über *to pass beyond* (*a th*); *to pass* (*a th*) **~|sehen** vi [h] ~ über .. **a.** ⟨eig⟩ *to overlook* (*a word*) **b.** ⟨fig⟩ = –gehen 1. c. **~|setzen** vi/refl [h] **1.** [vi] ~ über .. *to jump* (od *leap*) *over* ..; ~ über e–e H. *to clear* (od *negotiate, rush, vault*) *a hedge*; → –springen **2.** [vrefl] sich ~ über (etw) *to brush* (*a th*) *aside* od *away*; *to put* (*a th*) *aside*; *to dismiss* (od *disregard, ignore, override*) (*arguments*; *claims*); *to make light of* (*discomfort*); *to infringe* (od *offend against*) (*custom, rules*); *to throw* (*a th*) *to the winds*; (lachend, leichthin) *to laugh .. off* || sich über alles ~der Ehrgeiz *vaulting ambition* (Shak) **~|springen** vi [s] ~ über e–n Fluß *to jump, leap* (*over*) *a river*; → –setzen || hoch über jdn ~ *to leap high over a p* **~|stehlen** vrefl [h] sich ~ *to steal away* **~|täuschen** vt/i [h] **1.** [vt] jdn ~ über etw *to delude a p as to a th*; sich ~ über .. *to delude o.s. as to* ..; *to make light of* .. **2.** [vi] ~ über etw *to gloss over a th*; *to varnish a th* (durch *or* mit .. *with*) **~|wenden** vrefl [h] sich ~ *to turn away* **~|ziehen** vi [s] *to move away*

h·in- ´~**weis** m –es/–e **a.** *information*; *allusion* (auf *to*); *hint* (auf *at*); *index* (*to*); *reference* (*to*); –e m *to make references*; (Buch) mit –en versehen *to reference* (*a book*) || (kein) ~, daß .. (*no*) *indication that* .. **b.** nachdrücklicher ~ auf *insistence on* || *hint, suggestion*; wichtiger ~ *point*, ⟨Am⟩ *pointer* (auf *to*) **c. unter ~ auf** *by reference to*; *making references to*; *referring to* || ⟨jur⟩ e–e Berufung zulassen unter ~ auf e–e vorhergehende Gerichtsentscheidung *to allow an appeal by case stated from a decision* | ~schild [n] *direction sign* ~zeichen [n pl] *marks of reference* (*, →, etc) **~|weisen** vi/t [h] **1.** [vi] (P) ~ auf etw (*or* jdn) **a.** ⟨eig⟩ *to motion to a th*; *to indicate a th* (*a p*) **b.** mst ⟨übtr⟩ *to allude* (od *advert, refer*) *to*; *to hint* (⟨Am⟩ *squint*) *at*; *to comment on a th*; *to indicate* (od *intimate, suggest*) *a th*; *to point a th out*; (S) *to point to*; → hindeuten 2. || darauf ~, daß .. *to point out that* ..; (nachdrücklich) *to insist that*; alles wies darauf hin *everything pointed to it, there was every indication* (*that* ..) **2.** [vt] jdn ~ auf .. *to refer a p to*; *to call* (od *draw*) *a p's attention to* (*a th*); *to point* (*a th*) *out to a p* || jdn warnend ~ auf .. *to warn a p of a th* **~weisend** a ⟨gram⟩ *demonstrative* (*pronoun*); ~es Fürwort *demonstrative* **~|welken** vi [s] *to fade away* **~|wenden** vt [h] (etw) ~ nach, z *to turn* (od *direct*) *to*(*wards*); (den Geist) *to bend to* || s–e Augen waren nach ihr –gewandt *his eyes were bent towards her*; z ihm –g. begann sie .. *with her face turned in his direction she began* .. || **sich** ~ nach, z *to turn to*(*wards*) ´~**wendung** f *approach* (z *to*) **~|werfen** vt [h] **1. a.** (etw) *to throw* (od *fling*) *down*; → niederwerfen || (Korn) *to t. out* || sich ~ *to t. o.s. d.*, *to prostrate o.s.* (vor *before*) **b.** ⟨cards⟩ die Karten ~ *to t. up the cards* || die Arbeit ~ *to down tools* **2.** jdm etw ~ *to t. a p a th* (od *a th to a p*); jdm den Fehdehandschuh ~ *to fling* (od *t.*) *d. the gauntlet to a p* **3.** ⟨fig⟩ (Worte) *to t. out*; *to drop, to utter*; gesprächsweise ~ *to t. out* (od *let fly*) *in talk*; e–e Bemerkung ~ *to make a casual remark*; –geworfene Bemerkung *casual remark*; leicht –geworfen *uttered at random* || jdm s–n Posten ~ *to chuck one's job back to a p* || (Gedanken) schnell ~ *to dash off*; *to jot d.* || (Zeichnung) *to sketch*; (schnell) *to dash off* **~w·ieder(um)** adv *again, but*; *once more* || *on the other hand*; *in return* **~|wirken** vi [h] ~ auf .. *to make for* (*the making of nations*); *to tend towards* ..; *to conduce to* **~|wollen** → hin

°**Hinz** u Kunz *Tom, Dick, and Harry* || ~ u K. nicht nachstehen *to keep up with the Joneses*

h·in- **~|zählen** vt [h] (Summe) *to count out*; *to pay down* od *out* **~|zaubern** vt [h] ⟨fig⟩ (etw) *to improvise* **~|zeigen** vt/i [h] **1.** [vt] (etw) *to show* **2.** [vi] ~ auf jdn *to indicate a p* **~|ziehen** vt/i **A.** vt [h] **1.** (Vorgang) *to draw out*; *lengthen*; *protract*; *prolong*; (Urteil) *to wiredraw* **2.** (jdn) z sich ~ *to attract*; [mst pass] = gezogen w z *to be drawn* (od *attracted*) *to a p*; instinktiv –gezogen w z *to gravitate to*; → hingezogen **3.** sich ~ **a.** (of land) *to extend, stretch* (an .. entlang *along*; bis *to*; v .. bis, *from .. to*); (of roads) *to lengthen out*; sich seitwärts ~ um .. *to flank* (*a meadow*) **b.** (of events) *to drag on* (od *out*); *to linger, wear* **B.** vi [s] ~ nach *to go* (od *march*; *move*) *to*; *to* (*re*)*move to* .. **~|zielen** vi [h] **a.** ~ nach *to aim at*; *to aim* (od *level, point*) *a weapon at* **b.** ⟨fig⟩ ~ auf *to drive* (od *aim*) *at* || (S) *to tend in the direction of*; *to tend to*; ~ auf Erreichung e–r S *to make for a th*

hinz·u- → herzu- **~|denken** vt [h] (etw) *to add in thought* (od *in the mind*) **~|eilen** vi = herzu- **~|fügen** vt [h] (etw) *to add* (*some water*); (beigeben) *to annex* (z *to*), *to append*, (*sub*)*join* || etw e–r S (*or* *z e–r S) ~ *to add a th to a th* (*some water to the coffee*); weiter ~ *to superadd*; e–m Schriftstück s–n Namen ~ *to put one's name to a d.* || er fügte hinzu, daß .. *he added that* .. ´~**fügung** f *addition* (z *to*); ⟨Lit⟩ spätere ~ *accretion*; *secondary addition* **~|gehören** vi [h] (*this word does not*) *belong to it*; er gehört mit hinzu *he is included in it* (od *among them*); *he is one of them* **~|gesellen** vrefl [h] sich ~ (z) jdm *to join a p*; es gesellten sich noch drei hinzu *they* (od *we*) *were* *joined by three more* **~gezogen** a *consulted* (*doctor*) **~|k 1.** vi [s] ⟨übtr⟩ (of diseases) *to supervene* (z *on, upon*); Bronchitis kam hinzu *b. supervened*; → herzu- ‖ es kommt noch hinzu, daß .. *add to this that* ..; es kam noch hinzu (*or* hinzukam noch), daß die Mehrzahl .. *added to this the majority was absent* **2.** ≗ n *supervention* | ~d [a] *additional* ‖ *supervening* **~|nehmen** vt [h] *to add* (z *to*); *to include* (z *among*) **~|rechnen** vt [h] = –nehmen **~|setzen** vt [h] (etw) *to add* (e–r S *or* z e–r S *to a th*); → –fügen **~|treten 1.** vi [s] ⟨übtr⟩ *to supervene*, → –kommen **2.** ≗ n = –kommen °**~|tun** vt [h] (etw) *to add* (z *to*) **~|zählen** vt [h] (Zahl) *to add* (z *to*) **~|ziehen** vt [h] (Arzt) *to call in, to consult*; e–n anderen Arzt ~ *to get another opinion* ‖ (die Polizei) *to call in* ≗**ziehung** f *calling-in*; *consultation*

H·iob ⟨bib⟩ *Job* **H·iobs- ~bote** m *bringer of bad news* **~botschaft** f *Job's news* **~geduld** f *Job's patience* **~post** f = –botschaft

hip-hip-hurra [intj] *hip hip hurra*(*h*)

H·ippe f ~/~n **1.** ⟨hort⟩ *curved pruning-knife* ‖ *scythe* (⟨a.⟩ *of Death*) **2.** ×⟨zoo⟩ *she-goat*

H·ippie m ~s/~s *hippie* pl *hippies*

Hippo- ([Gr] Pferd-) [in comp] *hippo-* **~dr·om** m *hippodrome* **~gr·yph** m *hippogriff, -gryph*

Hipp·ursäure f ⟨chem⟩ *hippuric acid*

Hirn n ~(e)s/~e **1.** ⟨anat⟩ **a.** *brain*; (~substanz) *b.s* pl; → Gehirn ‖ Groß≗ *b. proper*; *cerebrum* [L]; Klein≗ *little b.*; *cerebellum* [L] **b.** ⟨cul⟩ *b.s* pl **2.** ⟨übtr & fig⟩ (= Kopf; Verstand) *b.s* pl; (gewählt:) *b.* (*a clear b.*); *mind*; das ~ e–s Laien *a lay mind*; das Werk menschlicher ~e u Hände *the b.s and hands of man*; → Kopf ‖ das (*or* sein) ~ anstrengen *to exert one's b.* ‖ sich das ~ zermartern *to cudgel* (od *rack*) *one's b.s* **3.** [in comp] *cerebral* | → a. Gehirn- **~anhang** m *hypophysis*; *pituitary gland* **~forschung** f *b.-research* **~gespinst** n ⟨fig⟩ *chimera*; *phantasm, phantom*; *utopia*; *vagaries* pl ‖ *crochet*; *fancy, whim* ‖ bloße ~e [pl] *mere fancies*; z ~en neigen *to have a bee in one's bonnet* **~haut** f *meninx* L; ≗e [pl] *meninges* L pl; harte ~ *pachymeninx*; weiche ~ *leptomeninx* | ~entzündung [f] *meningitis*; *b.-fever* **~höhle** f *cavity of the b.* **~holz** n ⟨carp⟩ *grain-cut timber*; *cross-grained wood* °**~kasten** m *skull*; ⟨sl⟩ *nut, knowledge-box* **~kraut** n ⟨bot⟩ *basil* ≗**los** a ⟨fig⟩ *b.less*; *stupid* **~mantel** m *pallium* L **~masse** f *cerebral substance* **~nervenpaar** n; das 10. ~ *vagus* L ≗**organisch** a *brain* (*syndrome*) **~quese** f ⟨zoo & vet⟩ *coenurus cerebralis* L **~schale** f *skull*; *b.-pan*; *cranium* L **~schlag** m ⟨med⟩ *apoplexy* °≗**verbrannt** a ⟨fig⟩ *crazy* (*idea*); *mad*; *crack-b.ed* ‖ *b.less, foolish, stupid* **~wellenbild** n ⟨psych⟩ *electro-encephalogram*

Hirsch m ~es/~e **1.** ⟨zoo⟩ *stag*, ⟨hunt⟩ *antlered stag*; → röhren ‖ Edel≗, Rot≗ *red deer* ‖ Dam≗ *fallow deer* ‖ ~ im 1. Jahre → ~kalb; ~ im 2. J. *brocket, pricket*; ~ im 4. J. *staggard*; ~ im 5. J. *stag*; ~ nach dem 5. J. *hart*; → Hangul, Maral, Pudu, Wapiti **2.** ⟨fig⟩ alter ~ ⟨aerosl⟩ *crack flyer* ‖ ⟨übtr⟩ f Bohrer; Heugabel u. a. ‖ ‚Zum Goldenen Hirsch' *Inn to the Golden Stag* **3.** [in comp] *cervine* **~antilope** f *pronghorn* **~bock** m *buck, stag* **~braten** m *venison* **~brunft** f *rutting season of stags* **~brunst** f **1.** ⟨zoo⟩ = –brunft **2.** ⟨bot⟩ = –trüffel **~dorn** m = Kreuzdorn **~eber** m ⟨zoo⟩ *babiroussa*; *Indian hog* **~fänger** m ⟨hunt⟩ *misericord* ‖ ⟨mar fam⟩ *cutlass* ‖ *case-knife* ≗**farben** a *fawn*(*-coloured*); *fallow* **~ferkel** n ⟨zoo⟩ *chevrotain* **~geweih** n *antlers* pl; ~e [pl] *stags' antlers* **~haken** m ~ [pl] *canine-tooth in upper jaw in stags* ≗**halsig** a ⟨hors⟩ *ewe-necked* **~horn** n **1.** *staghorn*(*s* pl) **2.** ⟨chem⟩ *hartshorn*; ~geist [m] *spirit of h.*; ~knopf [m] ⟨m. m.⟩ *elkhorn button*; ~salz [n] *salt of h.*; *sal volatile*; *ammonium carbonate* **~jagd** f *stag-hunt*(*ing*) **~käfer** m ⟨ent⟩ *stag-beetle* **~kalb** n *fawn*; *young deer* **~keule** f ⟨cul⟩ *haunch of venison*; *braised deer steak* **~klee** m ⟨bot⟩ *hemp-agrimony*; = Leberblume **~kolben** m ⟨bot⟩ *sumac*(*h*) **~kuh** f *hind* ‖ ~antilope f ⟨zoo⟩ = Kuhantilope **~leder** n *buckskin* **~rücken** n *saddle of venison* **~schwamm** m ⟨bot⟩ = Ziegenbart **~sprung** m ⟨hors⟩ *capriole* **~streuling** m ⟨bot⟩ = –trüffel **~talg** m *deer-suet* **~trüffel** f ⟨bot⟩ *stag-truffle* **~wurz** f *sulphur-wort* **~zunge** f ⟨bot⟩ *h.'s t.*

H·irschling m ⟨bot⟩ = Reizker

H·irse f ~/ ⟨bot⟩ *millet*; Blut≗ *fingered panicum*; Kolben≗, italien. ~ *panic*; *Italian m.*; Mohren≗ *sorghum* ‖ Indische ~ *d*(*h*)*urra*; Ind.-afrik. ~ *Eleusine coracana* **~brei** m *m.-pap* **~fink** m ⟨orn⟩ = Grün- **~gras** n *m.-grass* **~korn** n *m.-seed* | ≗förmig [a] *miliary* **~pilz** m = Röhrling

H·irt m ~en/~en, (Vieh≗) *herdsman*; (Schaf≗) *shepherd* ‖ Seelen≗ *pastor*; *shepherd*; → **H·irte** m ~n/~n ⟨bib⟩ = Hirt; der Gute ~ *the Good Shepherd*; *Jesus Christ* **h·irten** vt [h] Sw = Vieh hüten **H·irten- ~amt** n ⟨ec⟩ *parson's* (od *parson's* (od *pastor's*) *office*; *pastoral office*; *pastorate* **~brief** m ⟨ec⟩ *pastoral* ‖ ⟨bib⟩ *pastoral epistle* **~dichtung** f ⟨Lit⟩ *pastoral poetry* **~flöte** f *shepherd's pipe*; *reed-pipe*; ⟨hist⟩ *syrinx*; ⟨myth⟩ *pan-pipe* **~gedicht** n ⟨Lit⟩ *pastoral* (*poem*); ⟨ant⟩ *eclogue, bucolic* **~gott** m *god of shepherds*; *Pan* **~idylle** f *pastorale* **~knabe** m *shepherd-boy* **~könig** m *shepherd king* **~leben** n *pastoral* (od *shepherd*) *life* **~mädchen** n *shepherd-girl* **~spiel** n ⟨Lit⟩ *pastoral play* **~stab** m *shepherd's crook* (od *staff*) ‖ ⟨ec⟩ *pastoral staff*; *crosier, crozier* **~täschel** n ⟨bot⟩ *sh.d's purse* **~volk** n *pastoral* od *nomad tribe* od *people* **H·irtin** f ~/~nen *sh.dess*

His n ~/ ⟨mus⟩ *B sharp*

Hisp·anien n ⟨poet⟩ = Spanien

h·issen 1. vt [h] ⟨mar⟩ (Flagge) *to fly, hoist* (auf e–m H. *from a house*); die Flagge wurde auf dem Schiff gehißt *the ensign was broken on board the ship*; → heißen **2.** ≗ n *hoist*(*ing*) **H·iß-** *hoisting* (*machine*) **~tau** n ⟨mar⟩ *hoist-rope*; *halyard*

Histo- ([Gr] Gewebs-) [in comp] ⟨med⟩ *histo-* **~gen·ese** f *histogenesis* **~log·ie** f *histology*

°**Hist·örchen** n ~s/~ *little story* od *tale*; *anecdote*

*__Hist·orie__ [–iə] f *history* ‖ *story*; *tale* | ~nbild [n] *history-piece*; *historical picture*; ~nmaler [m] *historical painter* *__Hist·orik__ f *science of history* | ~er [m] ~s/~ *historian* **Historiogr·aph** m *historiographer* **hist·orisch A.** [a] **1.** *historic*: **a.** (Geschichte ausmachend; durch G. ausgezeichnet) *h.* (*building, spot*; *times*; *sense, truth*); *a*(*n*) *h. church* **b.** ⟨gram⟩ *h.* (*tenses*) **2.** *h.al*: **a.** (geschichtlich) *h.al* (*development*; *interest*); *h.al mission, debt* ‖ der ~e Falstaff *the h.al Falstaff* **b.** (geschichtswissenschaftlich) *h.al* (*method, principles*; *treatment*) **c.** (Geschichte behandelnd) *h.al* (*work*; *novel, play*; *picture*; *geography*) **d.** *(v geschichtlicher Bdtg) *h.al* (*event*); *h.al* (*personage*); er ist ~ *he has passed into history* **3.** ~er Charakter, Wert *historicity* ‖ auf ~em Wege, vom ~en Gesichtspunkt *historically* **B.** [adv] *h.ally* (*known*) **Histor·ismus** m ⟨Ger⟩ *overestimation of historical development* od *treatment*; *historicism*

H·itler (Adolf): ⟨nazi⟩ Anhänger A. ~s *Hitlerite*; Weltanschauung ~s *Hitlerism* ‖ ~jugend [f] (abbr HJ) *Hitler Youth* (*Organisation*); ~junge *H. Youth lad*

×**H·itsche** f ~/~n = Fußbank; kl Schlitten

H·itz- ~bläschen n, **~blase** f *heat-rash, heat-spot* **~blattern** f pl = –pocken **~drahtinstrument** n ⟨el⟩ *hot wire instrument* **~kopf** m *hothead*; *hotspur* (Shak); *spitfire*; *Tartar* ≗**köpfig** a *hot-headed* (od *brained*); *choleric*; ~es Wesen = **~köpfigkeit** f *hot temper*; *hot-headedness* **~pickel** m = –bläschen **~pocken** f pl ⟨med⟩ *prickly heat* **~schlag** m ⟨med⟩ *h.-stroke*; *h.-apoplexy* **H·itze** f **1.** *heat* (*of* *the fire, sun*); Weißglüh⁓ *white h.*; ~ ausstrahlen *to radiate h.* | *h.*; *hot weather*; drückende ~ *sweltering h., swelter*; ~ z Ersticken *stifling h.*; tropische ~ *tropical h.*; bei der ~ *in the h.* ‖ vor ~ umkommen *to swelter* **2. a.** (*state of feeling hot*) *heat*; in ~ geraten *to get into a h.*; *to become hot* **b.** ⟨med⟩ *high temperature*; *heat*; Fieber⁓ *febrile h., fever-h.* ‖ (T) *oestrum* → Laufzeit **3.** ⟨fig⟩ **a.** *h.* (*of passion*); *anger*; *passion*; *rage*; *transport*; in ~ geraten *to fly into a passion*; *to get excited* ‖ sich in ~ reden *to talk o.s. into a h.* **b.** *h.* (*of an attack*; *of a debate*); *ardour, fervour* ‖ °in der ~ des Gefechts *in the h. of the moment* **4.** ⟨tech⟩ e–e ~ v *a set of* (*20 strokes*) **~barriere** f ⟨aero⟩ *h.* od *thermal barrier* **⁓beständig** a (of colour) *h.-proof* | ⁓keit [f] *heat resistance, thermal stability* **~blitz** m ⟨at⟩ *h. flash* **⁓frei** a [pred] ⟨school⟩ ~ h *to have the afternoon off* **~grad** m *temperature*; hoher ~ *high temperature* ‖ ⟨fig⟩ *heat* **⁓härtbar** a *thermosetting* (Plastik) **~mauer** f → –barriere **~messer** m *pyrometer* **~periode** f *hot-weather spell, heat wave* **~schild** m → Wärme– ⟨a–n⟩ **~welle** f *heat wave*

h·itzig A. [a] **1. a.** (P & of disposition) *choleric, fiery, hasty* (*words*), *heady, hot* (*temper*), *hot-tempered, hot-headed* (*p*); *impetuous*; *irascible, irritable* (*p*); *passionate*; *peppery*; *red-hot*; *spirited* (*horse*); *testy*; *violent*; sie ist e–e ~e Natur *she has a hasty temper*; → Hitzkopf ‖ ~ w *to bridle up*; *to lose one's hair*; *fierce* (*argument*) **b.** *hot* (*contest*); *excited* (*debate*); → heiß **2.** (T) ~ s (w) *to be* (*go*) *on heat* **3.** *acute* (*disease*); *high* (*fever*) **B.** [adv] *excitedly*; *heatedly*; *with some heat*; ~ über etw her s *to be hot upon a th* | **⁓keit** f = Hitze 3.

hm [intj] *hum*(*ph*)! *ahem*! ‖ ~ m *to humph*

h·o, Rüd', h·o! ⟨hunt⟩ *soho*!

hob 1. & 3. sg pret v heben

H·obel m ~s/~ *plane* ‖ Falz⁓ *rabbet-pl.*; Kehl⁓ *moulding-pl.*; Lang⁓ *trying-pl.*; Schlicht⁓ *smoothing-pl.*; Schrupp⁓ *jack-pl.* ‖ ⟨cul⟩ *mandoline* **~bank** f *joiner's bench*; *planing-b.* **~eisen** n *plane-iron* (od *bit, cutter*) **~kasten** m *plane-stock* **~messer** n = –eisen **~schlitten** m ⟨met⟩ *planer-slide* **~späne** m [pl] *shavings* pl; *chippings* pl; weiche ~ (z Polstern) ⟨Am⟩ *excelsior* **~werk** n *planning plant* **h·obeln 1.** vt/i [h] **a.** vt (Brett) *to plane* ‖ (Bohnen, Kohl) *to shred* **b.** vi *to pl.* ‖ ⟨fig⟩ wo gehobelt wird, da fallen Späne *you can't make an omelet without breaking eggs* **2.** ⁓ n *planing* **H·obler** m ~s/~ *planer*

Hob·oe f ~/~n ⟨mus⟩ *hautboy, oboe* **Hobo·ist** m ~en/~en *hautboy-player*; *oboist*

hoch I. [a] [hohe(r, -s)/compr höher/sup höchst] **A.** [attr & pred] **1.** ⟨eig⟩ **a.** (S) *high* (*house, mountain, tower*); *tall* (*mast, steeple, tree*); sehr ~ *lofty*; ein 5 Stockwerke hohes Gebäude *a building of 5 storeys*; *a b. 5 st. high* (od *in height*) ‖ Stuhl mit hoher Lehne *high-backed chair* | (of stature) *tall*; *lofty* (*stature*); → groß ‖ er ist v hohem Wuchs *he is a tall man* **b.** (~ oben) *on high*; *above, aloft*; die hohen Sterne *the stars on high* ‖ *high* (*flight*) ‖ im hohen Norden *in the arctic regions, in the far north* **c.** (Geld) °auf die **hohe Kante** legen *to save*; *to put by*; °auf dem hohen **Roß** sitzen, sich aufs hohe R. setzen *to ride the high horse*; *to lord it over*; ⟨Am⟩ *to get high-hat* ‖ die Hohe **See** *the high seas* [pl]; auf der hohen See *in the open sea*; auf die hohe See fahren *to sail out to sea* ‖ in hohem **Winkel** *at a high angle* ‖ v hoher **Warte** herab *condescendingly* **2.** ⟨übtr⟩ **a.** hohes **Alter** *antiquity*; (P) *old* (od *great*) *age* ‖ ein hoher Siebziger *a man far* (od *well on*) *in the seventies* ‖ es ist hohe Zeit *it is high time* **b.** ⟨mus⟩ *high* (*voice*); das hohe C *the high C* ‖ in hohen **Tönen** *loudly*; in h. T. reden *to be high-falutin*(*g*); *to boast* **3.** ⟨fig⟩ **a.** (im Rang) *high* (*officer, official*) ‖ der hohe **Adel** *the aristocracy*; ⟨engl⟩ *the nobility* od *peerage* ‖ hohes Amt *high office* ‖ hohe Geburt *high* (od *exalted*) *birth*; v hoher G. *high-bred* (od *born*) ‖ das hohe Haus ⟨engl parl⟩ *the House* ‖ der Hohe Herr *the presence*; °⟨iron⟩ *his nibs* ‖ die Hohen Herrschaften *the presence* ‖ die Hohe Obrigkeit *the authorities* pl, *the government* ‖ hohe Persönlichkeit *exalted personage* ‖ die hohe Politik *high politics* ‖ die Hohe Schule *horsemanship*; *the art of riding* ‖ °hohes Tier *big bug* (od *pot, wig*); *great gun*; ⟨Am sl⟩ *big noise*; *mugwump* **b.** ⟨ec⟩ *high* (*festival*; *Mass*) ‖ das Hohe Neujahr *the feast of Epiphany* **c.** [abstr] **(groß)** *high* (*fever*; *percentage*; *play*; *price*; *speed*; *temperature*); *extreme* (*cold*); *great* (*importance*); *exalted* (*mission*); in hohem **Grade** *to a great extent* ‖ *big* (*income, sum*); *heavy* (*costs* [pl]; *penalty*); *stiff* (*demand, price*) | z hohe Forderungen *overcharge*; z hohe Schätzung *over-estimate* | *high* (*culture*); *lofty* (*aims*); *noble* (*task*); *sublime*; in hohem Ansehen *in high repute*; in hoher **Blüte** *in full bloom* ‖ e–e hohe **Meinung** h v *to have a high opinion* (od *to think highly*) *of ..* ‖ hoher **Mut** *high mettle*; h. Sinn *lofty mind* ‖ e–e hohe **Stellung** *a position of eminence* **B.** [pred] **1.** (die Pfeiler) sind 5 Meter ~ .. *stand 5 metres high* ‖ 4 Stock ~ (*the house is*) *four storeys high* (od *in height*) **2.** 2 Treppen hoch *second floor*; *up two pair of stairs*; er wohnt 3 Treppen ~ *he lives 3 floors up* ‖ der Vorhang ist ~ *the curtain is up* ‖ ⟨artill⟩ (Schuß) (zu) ~! *up*! **3.** ⟨übtr⟩ es ist ~ an der Zeit *it is high time* ‖ ~ an Jahren s *to be advanced* (od *up*) *in years*; ~ in den Siebzig *late* od *far in the seventies* ‖ wie ~ ist die Summe? *what is the amount*? ‖ ~ im Preis stehen *to be high* od *expensive* ‖ 3 Meter ~ u 4 M. breit *3 metres high by 4 metres wide* ‖ das Klavier ist e–n Ton z ~ *the piano is up a tone* ‖ 10 Mann ~ *no less than 10 men*; wir waren 10 M. ~ *we were ten all of us* ‖ ⟨fig⟩ das ist mir (etw) z ~ *that's beyond me* od *a cut above me* **II. [adv] 1.** ⟨eig & übtr⟩ *aloft*; *high* **a.** jdm etw ~ anrechnen *to appreciate a th highly in a p*; ~ fliegen *to fly high*; → ~fliegen | ~ gehen → ~gehen | (Bild) ~ hängen *to sky* | ~ liegen (of land) *to lie high* ‖ das Haar ~ m *to put up one's hair* | die Sonne steht ~ *the sun is high*; .. *stands high in the sky* ‖ die Aktien stehen ~ *the shares are up* ‖ er steht uns viel z ~, als daß wir (..) *we think much too highly of him* (*to imagine him capable of ..*) | ~ steigen *to go up*; *to climb high* ‖ ⟨fig⟩ *to rise high*; (of feelings) *to run high*; so ~ (war .. gestiegen) *to such a pitch* (..) | den Kopf ~ tragen ⟨a. fig⟩ *to hold one's head high* | Hände ~! *hands up*! Kopf ~! *head up*! *cheer up*! **b.** ~ **am** Himmel *high in the sky* ‖ ~ **oben** im Himmel *on high*; ~ oben in der Luft (⟨Am⟩ *way*) *up in the air*; ~ oben im Norden *in the far north* **c.** (*to sing*) *high* ‖ ⟨cards⟩ (*to play*) *high* **d. z ~ singen** *to sing sharp* | z ~ (+ Verb) *over-*; (jdn) z ~ besteuern *to overtax*; (etw) z ~ (ein)schätzen *to overvalue, overrate* **2.** ⟨fig⟩ *highly* (*important, welcome*); ~ denken v *to think highly of ..* ‖ ~ gestellt *highly placed* (*official*); → hoch- ‖ jdm etw ~ anrechnen *to give a p credit for a th* ‖ (der Brief) kam ihm ~ z stehen *cost him dear* ‖ ~ hinauswollen → hinaus 2. b. ‖ ~ u heilig, → heilig C. **3.** dreimal ~ rufen *to give 3 cheers* ‖ dreimal ~ u ein Tusch ⟨Am⟩ *3 cheers and a tiger* **4.** ⟨math⟩ fünf ~ drei (5^3) *five cubed*; *five raised to the third power*, ⟨fam⟩ *five to the third*, drei ~ n (3^n) *three to the nth*; → Quadrat **III.** [abs] **~ u niedrig** *high and low*; *rich and poor*

Hoch[1] n ~s/~s **a.** *cheer*; ein (drei) ~ ausbringen *to give a cheer* (*three cheers*) (auf jdn *for a p*) **b.** (Trinkspruch) *toast*; ein ~ auf jdn ausbringen *to propose* (od *give, submit*) *the toast of a p*; *to drink a p's health*; *to toast a p*; → leben **Hoch**[2] n ~s/~s ⟨meteor⟩ *high* [*highs*]; *high area*; *anticyclone* **H·och-** [in comp] [in Subst. u. Verben betont; in Adj. attr betont, pred unbetont] *high*;

highly ‖ ⟨fam⟩ f hinauf-, herauf- **~achse** f *vertical axis* **~·achtbar** a *honourable, respectable, worthy* **~|achten** vt [h] (jdn) *to esteem* (od *respect, value*) *highly* **~achtend** adv = –achtungsvoll **~achtung** f **a.** *esteem, respect*; bei aller ~ vor .. *with all due deference to* ‖ ~ empfinden für *to have the highest esteem for*; jdm ~ zollen *to render tribute to a p*; alle ~ vor dir! *I take off my hat to you* **b.** (im Briefschluß) mit ~, mit größter (*or* vorzüglicher) ~, mit dem Ausdruck der größten ~ → **~achtungsvoll 1.** [a] *deferential, respectful* **2.** [adv] (Briefschluß) ~ *Yours faithfully* od *very truly*; (formell) *Your obedient servant* **~adel** m (Grafen – Herzöge) *high nobility* **~alpen** pl *High Alps* **~altar** m ⟨ec⟩ *high altar* **~amt** n ⟨R. C.⟩ *High Mass* **~angesehen** a *of high repute* od *standing* **~ansehnlich** a = –achtbar **~antenne** f ⟨wir⟩ *roof aerial* **~|arbeiten** vrefl [h] sich ~ *to work o.s.* (od *one's way*) *up* (z *to*) **~aufnahme** f ⟨phot⟩ *vertical-shape picture* **~bahn** f *overhead* (od *high-level*) *railway*; ⟨Am⟩ *elevated railroad* (El, L) **~bau** m *surface building* od *engineering* ‖ *architectural construction*; *superstructure work*; *overground works* ‖ Leitungs~ *overhead construction* | ~amt [n] *Building* od *Surveyor's Office* **~beanspruchbar** a *high-duty* [attr] **~begabt** a *highly gifted*; *brilliant*; (*man*) *of parts* od *talents* **~begeistert** a *wildly* od *highly enthusiastic*; ⟨Am a.⟩ *proud* **~beglückt** a *highly elated*; *thrice blessed*; ⟨Am a.⟩ *proud* **~behälter** m *elevated* od *overhead tank* **~beinig** a *high-standing* (*dog*); *long-legged*; ⟨fam⟩ *weedy* **~bejahrt** a *advanced in years, well up in years, stricken in years* od *age*; *of advanced age* **~bekümmert** a *deeply grieved* **~beladen** a *loaded high* **~berühmt** a *highly renowned* **~besteuert** a *high-taxed* **~betagt** a = –bejahrt °**~betrieb** m *hustle and bustle*; *intense activity*; ⟨com⟩ *peak-time*; *rush*(*-hours*); *pressure of business* ‖ ~ h *to do a roaring trade*; *things are going strong* ‖ (Spaß) ⟨sl⟩ *burst*; *sprees* pl ‖ es herrscht ~ *things are running at high* od *fever pitch* **~bild** n ⟨phot, film⟩ *vertical picture*; ⟨geol⟩ *relief* | ~karte [f] *relief-map* **~blatt** n ⟨bot⟩ *bracteole*; ~er [pl] *involucre* **~blüte** f ⟨fig⟩ *bloom*; *peak* **~|bringen** vt [h] (Speise) aus dem Magen ~ *to throw up* ‖ ⟨fig⟩ *to enhance*; *raise*; °jdn ~ *to throw a p into a tizzy, to key .. up* **~brüstig** a *high-breasted* **~bunker** m *tower shelter* **~burg** f ⟨fig⟩ *centre*; *citadel*; *nursery*; *stronghold* (*of socialism*) **~chlorung** f ⟨chem⟩ *superchlorination* **~dampf** m → Volldampf **~decker** m ⟨aero⟩ *high-wing* (*monoplane*) **~deutsch** a *High-German*; °auf ~ *in plain German* **~druck** m **1.** ⟨print⟩ *letterpress-*(od *relief-*)*printing* **2. a.** ⟨tech⟩ *high-pressure* (a. fig) **b.** ⟨fig a.⟩ *rush* ‖ mit ~ arbeiten *to work at h. p.*; bei uns herrscht ~ *we are working at h. p.* **c.** (Druck) *pressure*; unter ~ *under* (*full*) *pressure* **d.** [in comp] *h.-p.* (*engine, steam*) ‖ ~gebiet [n] ⟨meteor⟩ = Hoch² ‖ ~krankheit [f] *hypertonia* ‖ ~rücken [m] ⟨meteor⟩ *ridge of high pressure* ‖ ~welle [f] ⟨at⟩ *blast wave* **~ebene** f (*high*) *tableland*; *plateau* Fr [pl –x, –s] **~·ehrwürden** ⟨ec⟩ *Reverend*; Ew ~ *Reverend Sir*; ⟨Ir⟩ *Your Reverence* **~empfindlich** a *very sensitive*; ⟨tech⟩ *highly responsive*; *high-speed* (*film*); *fast* (*emulsion*) **~entwickelt** a *subtle* (*sense*) **~entzückt** a *in ecstasies*; *enraptured* **~erfreut** a *in great joy*; *highly pleased* od *delighted*; *overjoyed* (über *at*); ⟨Am a.⟩ *proud* **~explosiv** a; ~er Stoff *high explosive* **~|fahren** vi [s] aus dem Schlaf ~ *to wake with a start* ‖ ⟨fig⟩ *to flare up*; *to burst* od *fly into a rage*; –gehen ‖ *to rear one's head* **~fahrend** a *haughty*; *overbearing*; in ~em Tone reden *to ride the high horse*; ~es Wesen *haughtiness* °**~fein** a *superfine*; *exquisite, superior*; *A 1*; *first-class*; *tiptop*; ⟨Am⟩ *dandy* **~finanz** f *high finance*; ⟨Am⟩ *Wall Street* **~fläche** f = –ebene **~|fliegen** vi [s] *to soar* ‖ ⟨aero⟩ (steil) *to zoom* **~fliegend** a ⟨fig⟩ *soaring, vaulting* (*ambition*); *high-falutin*(*g*); *high-flown* (*problems*); ~e Pläne, Ziele h *to fly high*; *to fly at high game* **~flieger** m ⟨aero⟩ *high flying machine* **~flut** f *high tide* ‖ ⟨fig⟩ *full* (od *liberal*) *tide*; *flood-tide*; *excessive supply, large quantity* (v *of*) **~format** n *upright size, portrait shape* **~frequ·ent** a ⟨wir⟩ *high-frequent* **~frequenz** f ⟨tech⟩ **1.** *high frequency* **2.** [in comp] *h.-f.* (*current*); *electronics* (*warfare*) **~frisur** f *upswept hair-style*; *upsweep*; ⟨Am⟩ *upswept hairdo*; e–e ~ tragen *to wear one's hair in an u.* (*h.*) **~gang** m → –hub **~garage** f *parking garage* **~geachtet** a *highly respected*; überall ~ s *to stand high in popular esteem* **~gebildet** a *highly educated* **~gebirge** n *high mountains* pl **~gebirgs-** [in comp] *Alpine* (*flora*) **~geboren** a *high-born*; *highly descended* ‖ (Titel) ⟨engl⟩ (of barons, etc.) *Right Honourable* **~geehrt** a (in Briefen) ~er Herr! *Sir* **~gefühl** n *elation*; *exaltation*; *exultant feelings* pl; *ecstasy, rapture*; im ~ des Sieges *elated by the victory* **~|gehen A.** vi [s] **1.** (of the sea) *to run high*; (of a river) *to be in spate* ‖ (of the curtain) *to rise*; der Vorhang war –gegangen *the c. was up* ‖ (of mist) *to lift* ‖ ⟨übtr⟩ (of price) *to go up, to rise*; rapide ~ *to sky-rocket* **2.** ⟨fig⟩ **a.** (of feelings) *to run high* **b.** (P) *to be up in arms*; = –fahren; ⟨sl⟩ *to go through the roof*; da ging ich h. *that got my goat* ‖ *to see red*; ⟨Am⟩ *to blow up* ‖ vor Wut die Wände ~ *to be beside o.s. with rage*, (vor Schmerz) *to writhe with pain* ‖ °er ging h. ⟨police⟩ *they nabbed him* **B.** ~ n *rise*; *lift* **~gehend** a *proud* (*waters*), ~e Wogen *heavy sea* ‖ *intense* **~geglättet** a ⟨pap⟩ *super-calendered* **~gelegen** a *high-lying* **~gel·ehrt** a *erudite*; *very learned* **~gemut** a *cheerfully confident*; *sanguine, optimistic* **~genuß** m; ein ~ *an exquisite* (od *a great*) *delight* od *enjoyment*; *a* (*great* od *rare*) *treat* (f *to*); ⟨Am⟩ *a dandy* ‖ ein ~ f jdn s *to be meat and drink to a p* ***~gericht** n *high court of Justice* ‖ *place of execution* **~gerüstet** a ⟨mil⟩ *fully armed*; *ready for war* **~gesch·ätzt** a *highly esteemed, much-valued* **~geschlagen** a (*his collar was*) *up* **~geschlossen** a ⟨tail⟩ *button-up* [attr] (*golfer*); *turtle-neck* (*sweater*) **~geschraubt** a ⟨fig⟩ *screwed-up*; *exorbitant* **~geschwollen** a *proud* (*flood*) **~gesinnt** a *high-, noble-minded* **~gespannt** a ⟨fig⟩ *high-pitched* (*emotions*); *high-strung* (*patriotism*); *high, sanguine* (*expectations*); *highly concentrated* (*musicianship*) **~gestreckt** a ⟨fig⟩ *high-pitched* (*aim*) **~gestellt** a (P) *of high rank, highly placed* (*official*) **~gestimmt** a *high-strung*; *elate*(*d*); *intense* (*p*); *sanguine, optimistic*; *in high spirits* **~gestochen** a ⟨fam⟩ *putting on airs, giving o.s. airs* **~gewachsen** a *lanky*; ⟨Am fam⟩ *gangling* **~glanz** m ⟨tech⟩ *burnishing*; *polish*; *bright* od (*high-*)*mirror finish*; *brilliant polish*; auf ~ bringen (satinieren) *to glaze* ⟨a. phot⟩; (etw) in ~ polieren *to burnish*; | ~papier [n] *friction glazed paper*; ~poliert *burnished*; ~politur [f] *brillant polish* **~glut** f *white heat*; ⟨a. fig⟩ **~gotik** f *decorated style* **~grab** n *table-tomb* **~gradig 1.** [a] [vor Abstr.] *intense* (*cold, heat*), *extreme, great* (*excitement*); *intense* (*stupidity*); *sublime* (*impudence*); *towering* (*rage*); *violent* **2.** [adv] *to* od *in a high degree*; *extremely* (*nervous*); *singularly, unusually*; *very*; *seriously ill*; ~ schwindsüchtig *far gone in consumption* **~|halten** vt [h] **1.** (Glas) *to hold up* | ⟨fig⟩ die Fahne ~ *to keep the flag flying*; das Banner der Freiheit ~ *to hold high the b. of f.* ‖ *to hold up* (*one's head*) **2. a.** ⟨übtr⟩ (jdn) *to uphold*; *support* ‖ ⟨com⟩ (Markt) *to peg* **b.** *to* (*hold in*) *honour*; *to think highly of* (*a p*); = –achten ‖ jds Andenken etc ~ *to cherish a p's m., etc* **~haltig** a ⟨min⟩ *rich*; *high-grade* (*ore*) **~haus** n *high building*; ⟨Am⟩ *sky-scraper* **~|heben 1.** vt [h] **a.** (Schweres) *to heave*; *to hoist up*; *to lift* (*up*); *to give* (*a th*) *a lift* ‖ (Kleid) *to hold up*; (Deckel) mit Gewalt ~ *to prize up* od *open*; *to pry* **b.** die

Hände ~ *to hold up* (od *raise*) *one's hands*; (sich ergeben) *to throw up one's hands* **2.** ~ n ⟨parl⟩ durch ~ der Hände *by show of hands* °~**h·eilig** a = hoch u heilig, → heilig ~**herzig** a *generous*; *high-, noble-minded*; *magnanimous* **~heim** n ⟨Ger⟩ (Weinort am Main) | ~er [m] → *hock* **~herzigkeit** f *generosity*; *magnanimity* **~hub** m ⟨tech⟩ *upstroke* ~|**hüpfen** vi [h] vor Freude ~ *to jump for joy* ~**interessant** a *most interesting* **~jagd** f *deer-hunt(ing)* ~**jagen** vt [h] ⟨aero-mot⟩ *to rev up*, → *rev*, *to race* ~**kant** adv *on edge*; *on end*; *edgeways*, *–wise*; ~ stehen (stellen) *to stand* (*set*) *on edge* **~kanten** n *edge raising* ~**kantig** adv = –kant || ⟨fig fam⟩ jdn ~ hinauswerfen *to fire a p* ~|**kippen** vt [h] *to tip up* **~kirche** f ⟨engl ec⟩ *High Church* **~kirchler** m ⟨engl⟩ *High--Churchman*; *ritualist* ~**kirchlich** a ⟨engl⟩ *High Church*; *ritualistic* **~klapp-** ~bar [a] *tip-up* [attr], *tiltable*; ~bett [n] ⟨Am⟩ *murphy bed* ~|**klappen** vt [h] (Kragen) *to pull up*; mit –geklapptem Kragen *with collar up*; (Spiegel) *to raise* ~**klingend** a ⟨fig⟩ *high-sounding* (*titles*); *high-flown*; *pompous* ~|**k A.** vi [s] **1. a.** *to mount up* (*he felt the anger mounting up within him*) || (of food) *to be thrown up* **b.** (P) °die Treppe ~ = heraufkommen || ⟨fig⟩ *to get on*; *prosper*, *rise*; jdn ~ l *to let a p up*; wieder ~ *to pick up* || wenn es hochkommt (sind es 50) *at most* (..) **B.** ~ n ⟨fig⟩ *rise* **~konjunktur** f ⟨com⟩ *intense activity*; *boom* ~|**krempeln** vt [h] (Ärmel etc) *to tuck* (od *roll*) *up* **~kurzzeiterhitzung** f (f Milch) *short time high temperature pasteurization* **~land** n **1.** *highland*, *upland*; das schottische ~ *the Highlands* pl; ⟨Russ⟩ *Kazakh Uplands*; *Plateau of Tibet* **2.** [in comp] → ~s- **~länder** m *highlander*; (Schotte) *Highlander* || Überwurf der ~ *tartan* ~**ländisch** a *highland*; *High-* **~lands-** *highland* (*district*); *Highland* (*plaid*) ~|**leben** vi [h] [nur in:] er soll ~! er lebe hoch! *three cheers to him*! *Long live* (*the king*)! || jdn ~ l *to drink a p's health*; *to toast a p*; *to give 3 cheers for a p* ~**legen** vt [h] *to put up* (*one's feet*) **~leistungs-** *high power* (od *efficiency*) (*motor*); *heavy-duty* (*engine*, *oil*); ⟨phot⟩ *high-output* (*lamp*) ~**liegend** a *elevated* (*district*) **~meister** m ⟨Ger hist⟩ *Grand Master* (*of the Teutonic Order*) **~meistertum** n ⟨Ger hist⟩ *Grand Mastership* **~messe** f = –amt ~**mod·ern** a *up-to-date*; ⟨sl⟩ [pred] *all the kick* ~**molekular** a ⟨chem⟩ *of high molecular weight* **~moor** n ⟨geol⟩ *raised* od *domed bog* **~mut** m *arrogance*; *haughtiness*; *superciliousness*; *pride* || ~ kommt vor dem Fall *p. goes before a f.*; jdm den ~steufel austreiben *to cure a p of his pride* od *conceit* ~**mütig** **1.** [a] *arrogant*, *haughty*, *overweening*; *proud*; *supercilious*; ⟨bib⟩ *high*; → –näsig **2.** [adv] *arrogantly*; *haughtily*; *proudly* ~**näsig** [a] *bumptious*, *cocky*, *stuck-up*; *high-nosed*; *uppish*; *lofty*, *superior* || ⟨sl⟩ *snooty*; ⟨vulg⟩ *tossy*, *pursy*; ⟨Am sl⟩ *high hat*; ~er Geselle *h.h.* **2.** [adv] *loftily*; sich ~ benehmen ⟨Am⟩ *to wear a h. h.* || (jdn) ~ behandeln *to h.-h.*; ~ dreinschauen *to look down* (*one's nose*) (auf [*up*]*on*); ~ s ⟨fam⟩ *to be high in the instep* **~näsigkeit** f *loftiness*; *superciliousness*; ⟨Am⟩ *h.-h. attitude* ~|**nehmen** vt [h] **1.** = –heben 1. a. **2.** ⟨fig⟩ (jdn) *to hoax*; *to pull* (*a p's*) *leg* || *reprimand*; *haul over the coals* || *bleed*; *fleece* || *bully* ~**notpeinlich** a ⟨hist⟩ *penal*, *criminal* (*code*) **~ofen** m ⟨tech⟩ **1.** *blast-furnace* (anblasen *to blow in* ..; abstechen *to tap*) **2.** [in comp] *b.-f.* (*gas*) ~**päppeln** vt [h] *to take great pains in bringing up* (*a child*, *dog*) **~parterre** n *entresol* Fr **~plateau** [–to:] n Fr *elevated plateau*; felsiges ~ (Norwegens) *fjeld* ~**preisen** vt [h] (jdn) *to extol to the skies* ~**prozentig** a *of a high percentage* || ⟨übtr⟩ *high-grade* (*ore*); *superior*; *hard* (*liquor*) **~punkt** m ⟨meteor⟩ *high point* **~quart** f ⟨fenc⟩ *high carte* (od *quarte*) **~rad** n ⟨cycl⟩ *high bicycle* ~**ragend** a *lofty* **~rechnung** f *computer prediction* ⟨a. bei Wahlen⟩ ~|**reißen** vt [h] (etw) *to rip away* || *to hoi(c)k*, *zoom* (*a plane*) || ⟨fig⟩ (jdn) *to rouse* (od *stir*) *up* || ⟨sl⟩ *to zoom* **~relief** [–ljef] n *bold relief* ~**rent·abel** a *highly profitable* **~reservoir** n *elevated tank* ~|**richten** vt [h] = aufrichten || sich ~ *to straighten one's back*; *to st. o.s. up* ~**r·ot** a *bright red*; *scarlet*; *ruddy* **~ruf** m *cheer*; jdn mit ~en begrüßen *to cheer a p* **~saison** [–sɛ:'zɔ̃] f *height of the season*, ⟨bes Am⟩ *peak s.* ~**satiniert** a ⟨pap⟩ *super-calendered* ~|**schätzen** vt [h] *to esteem highly*; *to appreciate* **~schätzung** f *high esteem* ~|**schieben** vt [h] (Fenster) *to put up* || sich ~ (of ties) *to ride up* ~|**schießen** vi [s] ⟨fig⟩ (P) (Temperatur) *to shoot up* || (of flames) *to leap* (v *from*); (wachsen) *to run up* ~|**schlagen** vt [h] *to strike up*; (Ball) *to sky* || (Kragen) *to turn up* ~**schnellen** vi [s] *to bounce* ~**schottisch** a *Gaelic*; *Erse* ~|**schrauben** vt [h] ⟨fig⟩ (Preise) *to screw up* || (Miete) *to rack* || ⟨fig⟩ *to pitch* (*one's expectations*) *high* **~schul-** *higher* od *university* (*education*); *academical* **~schule** f ~/~n **1.** *university*; *university college*; *Alma Mater* L; Technische ~ *College of Science and Technology*; *the Polytechnic*; Tierärztliche ~ *Veterinary College*; Forstliche ~ *School of Forestry*; *Forestry Institute* **2.** Handels~ *Commercial Academy* (od *College*); Landwirtschaftliche ~ *College of Agriculture*; ~ f Musik *College* (od *Academy*) *of Music*; ~ f Politik *Academy of Politics* **3.** ~ f Lehrerbildung *training college for elementary teachers* || → Volks~ **~schüler** m *student* **~schul-** ~lehrer [m] *teacher at a university* od *college* || *professor*; *reader*; *lecturer*; ~reife [f] ⟨Ger⟩ *university qualification*; *matriculation level* || ⟨engl⟩ *qualification by higher school certificate*; die ~ erwerben *to pass the matriculation examination*; ~stufe [f] *higher education*; ~wesen [n] *universities in general*; *organization of higher education* **~schutzeinrichtungen** f pl ⟨at⟩ *extra--protective devices* od *measures* ~**schwanger** a *far advanced in pregnancy* ~|**schweben** vi [h] *to hover* od *tower aloft* **~see** f **1.** *high sea*[*s* pl]; *main* (od *open*) *sea* **2.** [in comp] *sea-going*, *ocean-going* (*ship*); *ocean* (*escort*); *deep-sea* (*fishery*, *fishing*); *High Seas* (*Fleet*); *sea* (*tug*); *deep-sea* (*yacht*) ~|**seilen** vt [h] ⟨mount⟩ (jdn, sich) ~ *to rope up* ~**selig** a *late*; der ~e Fürst *the l. prince*, *of blessed memory* ~|**setzen** vt [h] *to set upright* || sich ~ *to sit up* (*in bed*) ~**sinnig** a = –gesinnt **~sitz** m ⟨hunt⟩ = –stand || ⟨engl univ⟩ *high table* **~sommer** m *midsummer* ~|**spannen** vt [h] ⟨fig⟩ (Ideal) *to string* **~spannung** f **1.** ⟨el⟩ *high tension* (od *voltage*; *pressure*); diese Leitung ist mit ~ geladen *this line carries high-voltage* **2.** ⟨fig⟩ *extreme anxiety*; es herrschte ~ in .. *there ruled a feeling of anxious suspense in* .. **~spannungs-** *high-tension*; ~leitung [f] *h.-t. line*; *power line*; ~motor [m] *h.-t. motor*; ~strom [m] *h.-t. current*; ~mast [m] *pylon*; ~zündung [f] *h.-v. ignition* ~**spielen** vt [h] *to place undue emphasis on*, *to put u. importance to*, *to play up* (*a th*) **~sprache** f *Received Standard*; die Deutsche ~ *St. German* ~|**springen** **1.** vi [s] *to jump* od *leap* (*up*) **2.** ~ n ⟨sport⟩ *high-jumping* **~sprung** m ⟨sport⟩ *high jump*; ~ Champion *h.-j.er* || ~ mit Anlauf *running h. j.* ~**stämmig** a ⟨hort⟩ *standard* (*rose*, *tree*) || ⟨übtr⟩ *tall* **~stand** m ⟨hunt⟩ *high stand* || *raised platform* (od *stage*); ⟨mil⟩ *elevated position* || ⟨fig⟩ *acme*, *peak* **~stapel·ei** f *professional swindling*; *confidence trick* **~stapler** m *conf.-man*; *crook*; *fraud*; *sharper*; *swindler*; ⟨sl⟩ *high-flyer*; *spiv*; *four-flusher*; ausgemachter ~ *super-c. man* || ~welt [f] ⟨fam⟩ *swell mob* ~|**stecken** vt [h] (Haare) *to put up* ~|**stehen** vi → hoch II. 1. a. **~stehend** a *upright*; *upstanding* (*pile*) || ⟨fig⟩ *highly placed*; *high* (*people*); *distinguished*; *highminded*; ⟨print⟩ *superior* **~stift** n ⟨Ger hist⟩ (bis 1806) *bishopric*; *diocese* ~|**stimmen** vt [h] ⟨fig⟩ (Hoffnungen) *to raise high* **~straße** f (auf Pfeilern etc) *aerial highway* ~**strebend** a *aspiring*, *towering* (*ambition*); *vaulting* (Shak) ≗|**streifen** vt [h] (Ärmel) *to tuck up* **~tal** n ⟨Am⟩ *park* **~ton** m ⟨gram⟩ *principal accent* ≗**tönend** a ⟨fig⟩ *bombastic, high-falutin(g)*; *h.-flown*; *h.-sounding*; *pompous*; ~e Redensarten *claptrap* ≗**tonig** a ⟨gram⟩ *stressed*; ~ s *to have the chief accent* **~tour** f *mountain tour* || ⟨tech⟩ auf ~en *in top gear* ≗**tourig** a *high-speed* (*engine, rotation*) **~tourist** m *mountaineer* **~touristik** f *m.ing* ≗**trabend 1.** [a] *grandiloquent, ranting*; *high-sounding, high-flown, flowery, florid* || *high-falutin(g)* (*stuff*) || ~er Schwätzer *ranter*; ~e Dinge [pl] *high-fly*; = –tönend; *high-flown* (*poems*) **2.** [adv] *gr.ly*; ~ predigen, reden *to rant* **~traber** m (Pferd) *high-stepper* ≗|**tragen** vt [h] ⟨fig⟩ den Kopf (*or* die Nase) ~ *to perk up*; *to perk up one's head*; ⟨Am sl⟩ *to wear a high hat* ≗|**treiben** vt [h] *to push up* || ⟨fig⟩ (Preise) *to force* (od *send*) *up*; *to inflate*; *raise*, ⟨Am fam⟩ *to jack up*; (bei Auktionen) *to bid up*; (Papiere) ⟨Am⟩ *to balloon*; *to bull* (od ⟨sl⟩ *stag*) (*the market*) **~ufer** n *upland* **~- u Tiefangriffe** ⟨aero⟩ *low and high attacks* **~- u Tiefbau** m (*firm of*) *superstructure and underground engineering* **~- u Tiefstellen** n *rising and lowering* (*of projector, etc*) **~vakuumröhre** f *hard tube* ≗**verehrt** a → –geehrt **~verrat** m *high treason*; *treason-felony* **~verräter** m *person guilty of h. t.*; *traitor* ≗**verräterisch** a *t.able* ≗**verzinslich** a *bearing high rates of interest* **~wald** m *timber* (⟨Am⟩ *rain*) *forest* **~wasser** n **1.** *high water*; (of a river *or* the sea) *floods* pl; *freshet, spate*; ~ führen *to be in flood*; die Bahnlinie steht unter ~ *the floods are out along the railway line* || v ~ ab-, eingeschlossen *floodbound* (*town*) **2.** [in comp] *high-water*; ~damm [m] *flood-protection dam*; °~hose [f] *h.-w. pants*; ~schaden [m] *damage caused by the floods*; ~stand [m] *h.-* od *flood-w. level*; ~standzeichen [n] *h.-w. mark* **~weide** f *mountain* (od *Alpine*) *pasture* °≗**w·eise** a *very wise*; ⟨iron⟩ *sapient* ≗|**werfen** vt [h] *to throw up*; (Münze) *to toss* || ⟨fig⟩ den Kopf ~ *to toss the head* **~wert** m ⟨cart⟩ *northing of map-grid, coordinate number* *≗**wert** a = –verehrt ≗**wertig** a *of high value* od *quality*; *valuable*; *high-grade* (*ore*); *first-class* (od *rate*) ≗**wichtig** a *vital* **~wild** n *big game*; *red deer* ≗|**winden** vt [h] ⟨tech⟩ *to wind* (*up*); *to hoist up*; (Anker) *to purchase*; (Auto) *jack* (*her*) *up* ***~-wohlgeboren** (Titel: im Brief) Euer ~! *Sir,* || Euer ~ ergebenster N. N. *Yours truly N. N.* | (auf Briefen) Herrn N. N. ~ *N. N., Esq.* ≗**wohllöblich** a *worshipful* ≗**wüchsig** a *tall*; *high of stature* **~würden** ⟨ec⟩ (Titel) S–e ~ Herr Dekan *the Very Reverend the Dean* (*of* ..) **~würdigst** ⟨R. C.⟩ (Anrede) *Right Reverend* **~zahl** f ⟨math⟩ *exponent* **~zeit** f ⟨fig⟩ *high time*; *festivity* || *acme* od *peak* (*of a th*) || → Hochzeit ≗|**ziehen** vt [h] *to pull up*; *to draw* (*one's legs*) *up*; (Hose etc.) *to hitch* od *pull up* || ⟨theat⟩ *to tie off* || in e–r Schlinge ~ *to sling*; sich ~ *to sling o.s. up* || ruckartig ~ ⟨sl⟩ *to hoi(c)k* ⟨a. aero⟩; *to yank* || ⟨engl⟩ Fenster ~ → hochschieben **~ziel** n *principal* (od *salient*) *aim*; *ideal* **~zucht** f (of cattle, etc.) *high-grade stock* ≗|**züchten** vt [h] ⟨hort⟩ (Pflanze) *to force* || ⟨übtr⟩ (Industrien) *to spoon-feed* **~zuverehrend** a *highly esteemed*; → (sehr) verehrt

h·öchlich adv *highly*; *greatly*; *to a high degree*

höchst adv **A. 1.** *highly* (*amusing, important*); *greatly*; *ultra-*; ~ lichtstark ⟨opt⟩ *u. high-speed* (Objektiv); ⟨phot⟩ *u.-rapid*; jdn ~ erfreuen *to gratify a p h.* od *g.* || *most* (*kind*; *advanced* [*country*]); *very*; es ist ~ wahrscheinlich, daß er kommt *he is most likely to come* || *abysmally*; *acutely* (*jealous*); *blatantly* (*uneconomic*); *crucially*; *frightfully*; *singularly* (*unattractive*); *supremely* (*improbable*) || ~ ärgerliche S *exasperating matter*; ~ vortrefflich *superexcellent* || ⟨fam⟩ *jolly* (*difficult*); *pretty* (*cold*); *mighty* (*interesting*); es war ~ harmlos *it was all harmless enough*; e–e ~ unangenehme Zeit *a frightful time*; ~ wenig *devilish little* | ~zulässige Grenze *ceiling*; ~zulässige Personalstärke *personnel c.* **2.** [vor Adj. oft engl sup des Adj.:] ~ seltsame Geräusche *the strangest* (od *the most extraordinary*) *noises*; °es ist ~ abscheulich v dir *it is the most abominable th of you* **H·öchst-** *top-, ceiling-*; ⟨tech⟩ *maximum* L ~ädt [n] ⟨Ger⟩ (an der Donau in Bayern); Schlacht bei ~ *battle of Blenheim* **~alter** n *m. age*; *life span* **~belastung** f ⟨tech⟩ *peak-load*; *m. load* ≗**besteuert** a *most heavily taxed* **~betrag** m *m.* **~bietende** [der ~, ein ~r] *the highest bidder* ≗**eigen** a; der König in ~er P *the king himself* ≗**empfindlich** a *ultrafast, u.rapid, u.sensitive* **~gebot** n *the highest bid* od *offer* **~geschwindigkeit** f *m.* od *top speed*; erlaubte ~ *sp.-limit* **~gewicht** n *m. weight* **~kommandierende** m ⟨mil⟩ *the General Officer Commanding in Chief* **~last** f *m. load* **~leistung** f *culminating achievement*; *m. productivity*; *m. effort*; ⟨sport⟩ *record* (oft [pl] *records*) || ⟨tech⟩ *m. capacity*; *m. output* (*of a mine*); Jahr der ~ *peak-year* | ~(sfähigkeit [f]) *target* **~lohn** m *m. wage(s)* **~maß** n *m.* (an .. *of liberty*) **~preis** m *m.* od *outside price*; *peak-price*; *pr. ceiling*; ~e [pl] *c. prices* **~satz** m *m. rate*; *m.* **~stand** m *peak*; Jahr des ~es *p.-year* **~temperatur** f *peak t.* ≗**wahrscheinlich** adv *most likely* od *probably*; *as likely as not*; *quite likely* **~wert** m *m. value*; neue ~e ⟨st exch⟩ *new peaks* **~zahl** f *highest number*; *m.*; *peak figure* ≗**zulässig** a *m. permissible* (*load*)

h·öchste a [attr] **1.** ⟨eig⟩ *highest* (*mountain*); *tallest* || ~r Stand der Flut *high tide* **2.** ⟨übtr & fig⟩ **a.** *highest* (*conditions*; *offer*); *maximum*; ~er Preis *peak* od *top price* || *crowning*; *first*; *ideal*; *perfect*; *primary*; *uppermost*; *entire* || *extreme*; *intense*; *utmost*; *utter*; *prime* (*importance*); ~ Vortrefflichkeit *superexcellence*; ~r Wasserstand *maximum flood water level* **b.** ~ **Anforderungen** stellen an jdn *to require a great deal* (⟨fam⟩ *a lot*) *of a p* || der ~ Augenblick *the top moment* (*of the day*) || in ~r Erregung *at white heat*; *in a white h. of passion* || *most sanguine* (*expectations, hopes*) || im ~n Falle *at the utmost* || ~ Gefühle *superlatives* pl || ~ Geheimhaltungsstufe *cosmic* N || der ~ der Genüsse *the ideal enjoyment*; → Hochgenuß || ~ Gewalt *sovereign power*; *supreme rule*; *sovereignty*; ⟨engl⟩ (im Staate) *the Crown* || das ~ Glück *the utmost pleasure* || der ~ **Grad** *the pinnacle* (*of freedom*) || in ~m (*or* im ~n) Grade *in the highest degree*; *in the extreme*; *flagrantly, grossly*, → höchst; im ~n Gr. höflich *nothing if not polite* || das ~ Gut *the sovereign good* || die denkbar ~n Komplimente *the highest possible compliments* || ~ Leidenschaft *white heat* || in ~m Maße = im ~n Grade || ~e **Not** *utter misery*; in der ~n N. *in the last extremity* || ~r Punkt *height, peak*; Befehl v ~r Stelle *top level order*; ~ Stufe *top*; in ~r Stellung, auf ~r Stufe *at the top of the tree*; ⟨univ⟩ *first class*; ~ Steuerklasse *top bracket* || in ~n Tönen *in superlatives* || im ~n Unwillen *in a blaze of indignation* || im Zustand ~r Verwirrung *in a state of the utmost confusion* || ~ Vollkommenheit *high watermark of perfection* || v ~r Wichtigkeit *of the utmost* (od *last*; *most crucial*) *importance*; *of cardinal* (od *primary*) *i.* || ~ **Wut** *white heat* || ~ Zahl *peak* || es ist ~ Zeit *it is high time* (*that .. should*) || z m–r ~n Zufriedenheit *to my utter contentment* **H·öchste 1.** [das ~, ein ~s] *the ideal*; *the sublime*; *the highest* (od *loftiest*) *aim*; nach dem ~n streben *to aspire to the h. excellence* (od *perfection*) || sein ~s leisten *to do one's utmost* || das ~, was man erwarten kann *the most you can expect*; das ~ in der Welt ist die Kunst *art is the greatest th in the w.* **2.** (verblaßt) **auf das** ≗, aufs ≗ *in the h. degree*; *in the extreme*; *ex-*

tremely; down to the ground || aufs ~̈ angespannt *intense (life)* || am ~̈n *highest* **h·öchstenfalls** adv; **h·öchstens** adv *at best; at most; at the outside; at the (very) utmost; if any;* ~ die Grenzen abstecken .. *to mark off the frontiers, if any* .. **H·ochzeit** [ˈhɔxtsait] f ~/~en *wedding; nuptials* pl; *marriage ceremony* || die grüne ~ *the wedding day* || silberne (nach 25), goldene (50), diamantene (60), eiserne (65 Jahren) ~ *silver, golden, diamond, iron wedding* || ~ m *to celebrate one's w.; to solemnize one's nuptials; to get married; to marry* || wann soll die ~ s? *when shall it be?* || ~ zu Kana ⟨a. paint⟩ *Wedding at Cana* || ⟨prov⟩ man kann nicht auf zwei ~en zugleich tanzen *you can't eat your cake and have it* **h·ochzeiten** vi [h] *to marry; to get married* ˣ**H·ochzeiter** m = Bräutigam ˣ**H·ochzeiterin** f = Braut **h·ochzeitlich** a *nuptial; bridal;* ⟨bib⟩ ~es Kleid *wedding-garment* || ⟨übtr⟩ *festive* **H·ochzeits-** **~bett** n *nuptial* od *bridal bed; marriage-bed* **~bitter** m *inviter to a wedding* **~bräuche** m pl *m. customs* pl **~feier** f *m. ceremony* || *w. celebration* **~feierlichkeiten** pl *w. festivities* **~fest** n *m.-feast; w. feast* (od *festival*); *n. feast* **~gast** m *w.-guest* **~gedicht** n ⟨Lit⟩ *epithalamium* L **~geschenk** n *w.-gift* (od *present*) **~kleid** n *w.-dress* || ⟨orn & zoo⟩ *n. plumage* **~kuchen** m *w.-cake* **~leute** pl *w.-guests* pl **~mahl** n *w.-dinner* (od *banquet*); *bridal banquet* **~marsch** m ⟨mus⟩ *w.-march* **~nacht** f *w.-night* **~reise** f *w. tour; honeymoon-trip* (od *tour*) **~schmaus** m = –mahl **~tag** m *w.-day* **~tracht** f *w.-garment* **~truhe** f *m.-coffer* **~zerem·onie** f *w. ceremony* **~zug** m *w.-procession*

H·ock m ~s/~̈e Sw *social gathering* **H·ocke** f ~/~n **1.** ⟨agr⟩ *shock* **2.** ⟨gym⟩ *squat* **h·ocken I.** vi/t [h] **A.** [vi] **1.** (geduckt sitzen) *to crouch (on the ground), to squat; cower* || bei–e–a ~, zus- ~ *to huddle up to one another; to huddle together* || (sitzen) *to sit;* (of birds) *to perch, roost* || wir hockten e–r auf dem anderen *we sat on the top of each other* **2.** °⟨cont⟩ (sich aufhalten) *to stay;* ⟨fam⟩ *stop* || immer zu Hause ~ *to stick at home; to be a stay-at home* || ⟨fig⟩ sie ~ dauernd zus– *they are on very intimate terms* **B.** *[vt] (Getreide) *to shock* **II.** ~̈ n *crouch(ing); squat(ting)* **h·ockend** a *crouching; cowering (position)* || ~ sitzen *to sit hunched up;* sich ~ setzen *to hunch o.s. up* **H·okker** m ~s/~ *(small) stool; tabouret* | ~grab [n] ⟨praeh⟩ *grave with bodies crouching;* ~stellung [f] *crouched position* **H·öcker** m ~s/~ **a.** ⟨allg⟩ *protuberance, projection* || ⟨geog⟩ *roche moutonnée* Fr; ⟨bot & zoo⟩ *process;* kl ~ *tubercle* **b.** ⟨zoo⟩ (of a camel, etc.) *hump;* Kamel mit e–m (2) ~(n) *one- (two-)humped c.* **c.** ⟨path⟩ (dafür mst: Buckel, → d.) *hump, hunch;* ein Rücken *or* Mensch mit e–m ~ *a humpback, hunchback;* er hatte e–n ~ *he was humpbacked* (od *hunch-*) **d.** → Gelenk~̈ | ~landschaft [f] *region characterized by r.s m.s* || ~sperre [f] ⟨mil⟩ *anti-tank teeth* pl **H·öckerchen** n = kl Höcker †**h·öckericht** a ⟨bib⟩ = **h·öckerig** a **a.** *bumpy; humpy (road); ragged, rough, rugged; uneven;* → knorrig, knotig **b.** *humpy (back);* → buckelig

H·ockey [ˈhɔki] n [engl] **1.** ⟨sport⟩ *(field-)-hockey* [Ggs *(ice-)h.*] **2.** [in comp] *hockey (ball, club);* ~schläger *h. stick; bandy*

H·ocko- → Hokko-

H·ode m [~n/~n] & f [~/~n] ⟨anat⟩ *testicle,* [mst pl] ~n *testicles;* → Neben~̈n **H·oden** m ~s/~ = Hode || °→ Ei **H·oden-** ⟨med⟩ *testicular* **~bruch** m *scrotal hernia* **~entzündung** f *orchitis* L **~sack** m ⟨anat⟩ *scrotum* L; [in comp] *scrotal* **~wassersucht** f → Wasserbruch

H·of m ~(e)s/~̈e **1.** (eingehegt) **a.** *court(yard);* (Wirtschafts~̈) *yard* || ~ hinter dem Hause *back-yard,* ⟨Am⟩ *dooryard* || ⟨univ⟩ viereckiger ~ *court, quad(rangle)* || Haus u ~ *house and home* || auf dem ~e *in the courtyard* **b.** Gast~̈ *inn* || Burg~̈, Schloß~̈ *bailey* || → Kasernen~̈, Kirch~̈, Kloster~̈, Schul~̈, Bahn~̈, Gerichts~̈, Schlacht~̈, Vor~̈ **2. a.** (Bauerngut) *farmstead, steading; freehold,* → Gut || Edel~̈ *country-seat; manor* **b.** Guts~̈ *farm-yard;* ~ mit Schobern *rick-yard* **3. a.** (Fürsten~̈) *(royal etc) court* || am ~e (des ..) *at the c. (of ..);* am englischen ~e *at the C. of St. James's;* bei ~e, z ~e *at c.* || ~ halten *to keep c.* **b.** = ~staat || e–n ~ abhalten *to hold a c.* **c.** ⟨übtr⟩ Hotel zum Bayrischen ~ *Hotel Bavaria;* Restaurant z B. ~ *Bavaria R.* **d.** (~dienst) ⟨fig⟩ jdm den ~ m *to c. a p; to pay one's c. to a p; to dance attendance upon a p; to make up to a p;* e–r Dame den ~ m *to court, woo (to pay one's addresses to) a lady* **4.** ⟨übtr⟩ **a.** (of the moon, etc) *corona* L, *halo* **b.** ⟨anat⟩ (Warzen~̈) *areola* L; *halo* **c.** *dark circle round the eyes* **5.** [in comp] → Hof-; Höfe- **~adel** m *c.-nobility* **~amt** n *c.-office* **~arzt** m *c.-physician* **~bäcker** m *baker to the c.* **~ball** m *c.-ball* **~beamte** [der ~, ein ~r] *c.-official* **~besitzer** m *farmer; freeholder* **~buchhändler** m *bookseller to her Majesty the Queen* **~bühne** f = –theater **~burg** f ⟨Ger⟩ *the Imperial Palace; Hofburg* **~charge** [–ʃarʒə] f = –amt **~dame** f *maid of honour; lady-in-waiting; Lady of the Bedchamber* **~dichter** m *poet to the court;* ⟨engl⟩ *Poet Laureate* **~dienst** m *attendance at the c.;* ⟨hist⟩ *socage* **~etikette** f *c.-etiquette* ~̈**fähig** a *suitable for presentation at c.* **~fähigkeit** f *right of presentation at c.* **~fest** n *gala; gala day* **~fräulein** n *maid of honour* **~gänger** m *subsidiary agricultural labourer* **~gericht** n ⟨hist⟩ *manorial c.; c.-baron* **~gesellschaft** f *c.-society* **~gesinde** n *farm-labourers* pl (od *servants*) **~gunst** f *c.-favour* **~günstling** m *c.-favourite, c.-minion* **~gut** n *(crown-)domain; royal demesne* ~̈|**halten** vi [h] *to keep c.* **~haltung** f die Königl. ~ *the (Royal) Household* **~hund** m *house* (od *yard*)*-dog, watch-dog* **~jagd** f *hunt held at c.* **~kanzlei** f *c.-chancery* **~kapelle** f **1.** ⟨ec⟩ *chapel royal; royal ch.* **2.** ⟨mus⟩ *musicians* (od *children*) *of the ch. royal* **~kaplan** m *c.-chaplain* **~kirche** f = –kapelle **~kleid** n *c.-dress* **~kreise** m pl *c.-circles* pl **~lakai** m *c. footman* **~leben** n *c.-life* **~leute** pl *c.iers, c.men* pl **~lieferant** m; Königl. ~ *purveyor to the royal household* **~loge** [ʒ] f ⟨theat⟩ *royal box* **~maler** m *c.-painter* **~mann** m = Höfling ~̈**männisch** a *c.like; courtly* **~marke** f = Hausmarke **~marschall** m *marshal of a prince's household;* ⟨engl⟩ (Ober~̈) *Lord Chamberlain* **~meister** m **1.** *steward;* (Ober~̈) *Lord Steward* **2.** *tutor* ~̈**meistern** vi/t [h] ~ an jdm *or* jdn ~ *to domineer* (od *lord it*) *over a p; to find fault with a p; to jaw a p* **~nachrichten** f pl *c. circular* **~narr** m *fool at c.; c.-fool* **~oper** f *Royal* (od *State*) *Opera;* ⟨engl⟩ *Covent Garden (Theatre)* **~organist** m ⟨engl⟩ *organist to his Majesty's Chapel Royal* **~poet** m → –dichter **~prediger** m *c.-chaplain* **~rat** m ⟨österr⟩ (Titel) *Hofrat* | ~s|ecken, –s|winkel [pl] *receding hairline at the temples* **~raum** m *(c.-)yard* **~recht** n ⟨hist⟩ *manorial law* **~reite** f ⟨agr⟩ *farm-yard* **~schatzmeister** m *the Treasurer of the Household* **~schauspieler** m *actor at the royal* (od *state*) *theatre* **~schneider** m *c.-tailor; tailor to the king* **~schranze** m ~n/~n ⟨cont⟩ *petty* (od *fawning*) *c.ier* || ~ntum [n] *c.iers' arts* pl **~seite** f *yard-side* **~sitte**[n pl] f *c.-etiquette* **~staat** m **1.** *(royal) household; c.;* gr ~ halten *to keep great state* **2.** *c.-dress;* im ~ s *to be dressed up to the nines* **~tag** m *c.-day* **~theater** n *c.* (od *state*) *theatre* **~tor** n *yard-gate* **~tracht** f *c.-dress* **~trauer** f *c.mourning* || ⟨fig⟩ (an Fingernägeln) *mourning-bands;* du hast ~ *you're mourning for the cat* od *for the whole family* **~tür** f *yard-door* **~wesen** n *c. life; c. affairs* pl **~wirtschaft** f *farm-system* **~zeremoniell** n *c.-etiquette* **~zug** m ⟨rail⟩ königl. ~ *royal train* **~zwang** m *compulsory attendance at c.* || (Etikette) *c.-etiquette*

H·öfe- **~bank** f *land-bank*; *agricultural bank* **~buch** n *farm register* **~rolle** f ⟨Ger⟩ *roll of 'Erbhöfe'*

H·offart [ɔ] f ~/ *vainglory, -gloriousness*; *inordinate pride*, → Hochmut **h·offärtig** [ɔ] a *vainglorious*; → hochmütig

h·offen I. vi/t [h] **A.** vi **1.** *to hope*; *entertain hope*; laß uns weiter ~ *let us hope on*; *don't let us lose hope* ‖ ⟨com⟩ *we trust* (*you will be satisfied*) **2.** [in Antwort] (hat er ..?) Ich hoffe (..) *I hope so*; oh ja, ich h. *oh yes, rather* ‖ ich h. nicht *I hope not* **3.** ~ auf etw *to hope for a th*; wir ~ auf dein Kommen *we hope you will come* **B.** vt **1.** [nur mit neutr. Pron. *or* Adj. als Objekt] *to hope* **a.** ~ wir's *let's hope so*; °~ wir das Beste, lieber Leser *let us hope for the best* ‖ ich hoffe v s–m Einfluß das Beste *I trust he will be a power for good* ‖ er hat nichts z ~ *he has nothing to hope for* ‖ es ist sehr z ~ *it is much to be hoped* **b.** [in Antwort] (Glaubst du, daß er ..?) Ich hoffe es *I hope so* ‖ das will ich nicht ~ *I trust it is not so*; *I hope not* **2. a.** ich hoffe k z können *I hope to be able to come* **b.** ~, daß .. *to hope that ..*; zuversichtlich ~, daß .. *to trust* (od *be confident*) *that ..* ‖ ich hoffe, daß sie k *I hope* (*that*) *they will* (od *may*) *come*; er hoffte, daß etw eintreten würde *he hoped for sth to turn up* ‖ er hoffte, daß der Schlüssel gefunden würde *he hoped for the key to be found*; *he h. that the k. would be f.* ‖ [parenth.] (.. ein Kursus), der, so hofft man, am .. (*.. a course*) *which, it is hoped, will begin on May 1st* **II.** ≗ n *hoping*; *hope*; so langes ~ *so much hoping* ‖ ~ u Harren macht manchen zum Narren *hope deferred maketh the heart sick* **h·offentlich** adv **a.** [in Antwort] *I hope so*; *let us hope so* **b.** er wird ~ k *I hope he will come*; *it is to be hoped that he will c.* ‖ ein Kursus, der ~ am .. beginnen wird *a course which, it is hoped*, (od *which as I hope*) *will ..* **-höffig** [suff] ⟨min⟩ (z. B. erdöl~), ***h·öfflich** a ⟨min⟩ *promising*

H·offnung f ~/~en **1. a.** *hope* (geringe *slim*) ‖ (nicht) ein Schimmer v ~ (*not*) *a gleam* (od *ray*) *of h.* ‖ aufkeimende ~ *budding h.*; e–e schwache ~! *what a h.!* ‖ ⟨bib⟩ Glaube, Liebe, ~ *Faith, H., Charity* | *expectation*; *promise* ‖ die ~ auf etw *the h. of a th*; k–e ~ auf Beilegung *no promise of settlement* **b.** ⟨übtr⟩ (P & S) er war die ~ s–s Landes *he was the h. of his country* ‖ ich bin ihre einzige ~ *I'm all she's got to look to* ‖ Die letzte ~ ⟨bes Am jur⟩ *Court of Last Resort* **2. a. es ist noch** ~ *there is h. still*; es ist k–e ~ mehr *there is no h. left*; es ist k–e ~ mehr f ihn *he is past h.* ‖ guter ~ s *to be full of h.*; (of a woman) *to be expecting* od *confined, in the family way* ‖ s–r ~ Ausdruck geben *to give expression to one's h.* **b. wenig ~ bieten** *to hold out little h.* ‖ die ~ schien sich z erfüllen *this h. seemed close to fulfilment*; ~en erwecken *to raise h.s*; neue ~en er- *to give rise to new h.s* ‖ ~ **haben** *to entertain h.*; *to be h.ful*; *to h.* (*that ..*); k–e ~ h *to be h.less*; berechtigte ~ h *to have good h.s* (*that*); jds ~ beflügeln *to inspire a p's h.s*; eitle ~en nähren *to cherish vain h.s*; wenig (*or* schwache) ~ h *to h. against h.* (*that ..*) ‖ jdm ~en m *to give a p grounds for hoping*; *to hold out h.s to a p* (*that ..*); jdm (sich) unbegründete ~en m *to flatter a p* (*o.s.*); jdm ~en auf etw m *to hold out to a p the prospect of a th*; sich ~en m *to be h.ful* (od *full of h.*); sich k–e ~en m *to be h.less*; sich ~en m auf .. = s–e ~ **setzen** auf .. *to place* (od *set*) *one's h.s* (*up*)*on ..*; *to pin one's faith on*; *to bank* (*up*)*on*; auf ihn setzt man die größte ~ *he is the great h.*; m–e einzige ~ setze ich auf ihn *my only h. is in him* ‖ jdn mit leeren/falschen ~en speisen *to tantalize a p* ‖ s–e ~en z Grabe tragen *to bury one's h.s* ‖ ~ versprechen = ~ bieten ‖ jds ~en zerstören, zunichte m *to dash a p's h.s* **c.** sich **an** die letzte ~ klammern *to catch* (od *grasp*) *at a straw* ‖ **in** der ~, Sie z treffen *in the h. of meeting you*; in der leisen ~, ihn z t. *on the chance of m. him* ‖ in der süßen ~ *in the fond h.* ‖ jdn **mit** leeren ~en (ab)speisen *to delude a p with vain h.s* ‖ **zu** den besten ~en berechtigen *to justify most brilliant prospects*; ein junger Mann, der z gr ~en berechtigt *a young man of* (*great*) *promise*; *a young h.hul* **H·offnungs-** **~anker** m *firm basis of a p's h.s* **~freude** f *h.fulness* **≗freudig** a *hopeful* **≗los 1.** [a] *h.less* (*situation*); *desperate, grey, gloomy*; *forlorn*; *gone*; *hard* (*case* [a. ⟨fig⟩ P]); *desperate* (*fool*); [pred] *without h.* ‖ ~! *no*(*t an*) *earthly!* (P & S) *past recovery* **2.** [adv] *h.lessly*; *helplessly*; *shatteringly*; er ist ~ krank *he is past h.* ‖ °er (*or* es) ist ein –loser Fall *he's* (od *it's*) *too far gone* **~losigkeit** f *h.lessness*; *despair* **~strahl** m *flash* (od *gleam*) *of h.* **≗voll** a *h.ful*; *encouraging*; *promising full of h.*

hof·ieren A. vi [h] **1.** jdm ~ = den Hof m, → Hof 3. d. **2.** *to keep* od *hold court* ‖ *to live like a lord*

h·öfisch a ⟨hist & Lit⟩ *courtly*; ~e Lebensart *c. breeding*; *c. manners* pl ‖ ~e Dichtung *c. poetry*; ~es Epos *court epic*; ~e Lyrik *c.ly lyrics* pl | *polished, refined* **h·öflich 1.** [a] *courteous*; *affable*; *civil*; *polite*; *polished, suave* (*manners*); *urbane*; immer hübsch ~ bleiben *to keep a civil tongue in one's head* **2.** [adv] *civilly*; *politely, suavely, urbanely* | ~st *most obligingly* (od *accommodatingly*); (etw) ~ ablehnen *to decline with thanks*; darf ich Sie ~st bitten, das Fenster z schließen? *will you please close the window? oblige me by closing the w.*; ~ sprechend *fair-spoken* **3.** [abs] den ≗en spielen *to do the polite*; *to do the polite* (od *civil*) *thing* | **~keit** f ~/~en *courtesy*; (⟨traffic⟩ *road c.*); *civility, politeness*; *suavity, urbanity* ‖ ~en austauschen *to exchange civilities*; jdm e–e ~ erweisen, sagen *to pay a p a compliment* ‖ aus ~ *by courtesy*; aus ~ beigelegter Titel *courtesy title* ‖ aus ~ gegen ihn *in compliment to him*; *to oblige him* | ~sbesuch [m] *courtesy call*; ~sbezeigungen [f pl] *attentions* pl; ~sschlußformel [f] (Brief≗) *complimentary close* **Höfling** m ~(e)s/~e *fawning courtier*

H·öft n ~(e)s/~e [niedd] (Haupt) *groyne*; *promontory*

h·ohe a → hoch ‖ das ≗ u Edle *the sublime*

H·öhe f ~/~n **A.** [abstr] **1.** *height* (*of a mountain, tree*); *altitude* (gr *high*); *elevation* (über NN *above sea-level*); ⟨aero⟩ ~ über dem Boden *absolute hight* ‖ (als Maß) ⟨astr, geog & geom⟩ *altitude* (*of a star*); *height* (*of 2000 metres*); ⟨Am a.⟩ *high* ‖ negative ~ *depression* (*of a star*) | ⟨mar⟩ *bearings* pl ‖ ⟨arch⟩ ~ unter e–m Bogen (etc) *headway, headroom*; lichte ~ *clearance* ‖ ⟨mus & tech⟩ *pitch* (*of a tone*) | *amount* (*of a bill*); *extent* (*of profits*); *level* (*of prices*); ~ des Zinsfußes *rate of interest* ‖ die ungewöhnliche ~ *the highness* (*of the rates*) **2.** ⟨fig⟩ *height* (*of genius*); *loftiness* **B. 1.** (hoher Ort) *high place* (od *point, region*); *altitude, height*; dort oben in der ~ *up there in the h.*; in sehr gr ~n *at very high altitudes* ‖ ⟨aero⟩ Gipfel-≗; größte erreichbare ~ *ceiling*; in gr ~ fliegend, operierend *high-level* (*bomber*) **2.** (Gipfel) **a.** *peak, summit, top* (*of a mountain*) **b.** ⟨fig⟩ (= ~punkt) *acme, height*; *peak, pinnacle*; *pink* (*of perfection*); *pitch* (*of greatness*) **C.** [konkr] (Anhöhe) *elevation*; *height, hill* (*h. 60*); *mound*; *ridge* **D. Wendungen 1.** die ~ des Berges beträgt 800 Meter *the hill has a height of 800 meters*; ⟨bes a. mot⟩ *brow* (*of a hill*) ‖ e–e gr ~ erreichen *to reach* (od *come to*) *a great height* ‖ ⟨mar⟩ die ~ nehmen *to take the bearings* ‖ °das ist (denn doch) die ~ (⟨hum⟩ 'h')! *that is the* (*lurid, ruddy, frozen, dizzy*) *limit!*, ⟨fam⟩ *that takes the cake!* ⟨sl⟩ *that licks everything!* ⟨Am sl⟩ *that beats all!* **2. auf** der ~ des Meeres ⟨mar⟩ *on the open sea* ‖ auf der ~ v Suez *off Suez* | ⟨fig⟩ auf der ~ *at the height* (od *peak*) (*of his fame*) | auf der ~ s *to be up-to-date*; *to be up to concert-pitch*; (of police, etc) *to be well to the fore*; auf der ~ s in .. *to be up in ..* ‖ *to be* (od *feel*) *up to the mark*; nicht (ganz) auf der ~ s *to be* od *feel* (*a bit*) *below par* ‖ auf der ~ der Wissenschaft *up-to-date with modern science* (od *research*) ‖ auf (*or* in) gleicher ~

mit *on a level with*; *level* (od *up, flush*) *with*; *abreast of*; in unerreichten ~n wandeln *to walk with one's head among the stars* | auf die ~ steigen *to climb to the summit*; ⟨fig⟩ auf e–e unerträgliche ~ st. (of feelings) *to rise to a height past endurance* | **aus** der ~ *from above* ‖ aus niedriger ~ *low-level* (*attack*); aus gr ~ *high-level* (*aiming*) | **bis zur** ~ **v** *up to the level of*; (Beitrag) bis z ~ v (..) *to the amount of ..* | **in der** ~ *above, aloft*; *on high*; ⟨bib⟩ *in the heights* ‖ in der ~ des Magens *stomach-height* ‖ (Rechnung) in ~ v *to the amount of* ‖ ein Beitrag in ~ v *an amount of, a sum amounting to, a sum to the tune* (od *value*) *of* (£ *50*); *an a. equal to a month's wages* ‖ in gleicher ~ *in the same altitude* ‖ in gl. ~ ruhen auf .. *to rest flush on ..* ‖ in voller ~ (*to pay*) *in full* | **in die** ~ *up*(*ward*); *aloft* | [in Verbdg mit Verben] (→ a. hoch-): ⟨fig⟩ sich in die ~ arbeiten → hocharbeiten ‖ (etw) in die ~ bringen *to build* od *work up*; *to strengthen*; → hochbr- ‖ sich in gr ~n erheben *to mount up to great heights* ‖ ⟨fig⟩ in die ~ fahren *to start*; *to bounce* od *flare up*; → hochfahren ‖ in die ~ fliegen → hochfl- ‖ etw in die ~ f. l *to bounce a th* ‖ in die ~ gehen → hochgehen, hochfahren; (of prices) ⟨bes Am⟩ *to boom* ‖ (Hand) in die ~ halten *to hold aloft* (od *up*), → hochh- ‖ in die ~ k *to rise*; ⟨fig⟩ *to get on*; *to prosper* ‖ in die ~ krempeln → hochk- ‖ in die ~ reißen → hochr- ‖ in die ~ schießen (of plants) *to spring up rapidly*; → hochsch-, hochgehen ‖ in die ~ schnellen (*of prices*) *to* (*sky-*)*rocket* vi ‖ in die ~ springen *to jerk up*; → hochsp- ‖ in schwindelnde ~n steigen (of prices) *to go up to astronomic heights*; *to run mountains high* ‖ (jdn) in die ~ tragen *to bear aloft* ‖ in die ~ treiben → hochtr- ‖ in die ~ ziehen *to pull up* | sich **zu** s–r vollen ~ aufrichten *to draw o.s. up to one's full height* **H·oheit** f ~/~en **A. 1.** [abstr] *high dignity* (od *position, rank*) **2.** ⟨pol⟩ *sovereign authority* od *power*; *sovereignty*; unter deutscher ~ *under G. s.* **3.** ⟨fig⟩ *highness* (*of a p's character*), *loftiness, nobleness*; *grandeur, majesty*; erhabene ~ *sublimity* (*of nature*) **B.** (Titel) Seine (Königl.) ~ ⟨a. a-engl⟩ *His* (⟨engl⟩ *Royal*) *Highness*; K. ~ h geruht (..) *Your R. H. has been pleased* (*to ..*) ‖ ⟨übtr hum⟩ S–e ~ *his nibs* **h·oheitlich** a *sovereign (right, state)* **H·oheits-** [in comp] *sovereign*; *territorial* **~abzeichen** n ⟨mil⟩ *nationality mark* (*of the cap*); ⟨aero engl⟩ *roundel* **~gebiet** n *dominion*; *s. territory* **~gewalt** f *jurisdiction* **~gewässer** n pl *t.l waters* pl **~grenzen** f pl *boundaries* pl **~rechte** n pl *s.* od *t.l rights*; königl. ~ *regalities* **~träger** m *sovereign* ‖ ⟨pol⟩ *leading functionary* **≈voll** a *august, dignified, majestic* **~zeichen** n *s.* od *national emblem* (⟨her engl⟩ *the Lion and the Unicorn*; ⟨Ger⟩ *the Eagle*) ‖ Königl. ~ pl *regalia* L pl → –abzeichen **Hohel·ied** n H.enl.(e)s/ ⟨bib⟩ das ~ *the Song of Songs* od *of Solomon* **H·öhen- ~angabe** f ⟨cart⟩ *spot elevation* od *height* **~angriff** m *high level raid* **~angst** f *acrophobia* **~atmer** m ⟨aero⟩ (Gerät) *breathing* od *oxygen apparatus*; *respirator*; *mask* **~aufgabe** f *descent* ⟨a. aero⟩ **~darstellung** f ⟨mil⟩ *relief*; *representation of varying levels* **~druckkabine** f ⟨aero⟩ *pressure cabin* **~flora** f *Alpine flora* **~flosse** f ⟨aero⟩ *tailplane*, ⟨Am⟩ *stabilizer* | ~neinstellung [f] *t., st. adjustment* **~flug** m *altitude flight*; ⟨fig⟩ *fl. of fancy* | ~zeug [n] *stratoplane*, (f Gäste) *stratocruiser* **~forschungsrakete** f *sounding rocket* **~gelände** n *hilly ground* **~gewinn** m *gain in altitude* **≈gleich** a *level* (⟨rail⟩ *crossing*) **~kabine** f *pressure cabin* **~kaltfront** f ⟨meteor⟩ *upper cold front* **~klima** n *mountain climate* **~krankheit** f *high altitude nausea*; *vertigo*; *anoxia*; *aeroembolism* **~kreis** m ⟨astr⟩ *vertical* od *azimuth circle* **~kurort** m *mountain health resort* **~kurve** f *contour line*; Karte mit ~n *c. map* **~lage** f *altitude* (*of a place*); *elevation, level*, in gr ~n *in high levels* **~l·angstreckenflugzeug** n *stratoliner* **~leitwerk** n ⟨aero⟩ *elevator unit* **~linie** f → –kurve **~luft** f *mountain air* **~marke** f ⟨surv⟩ *bench-mark* **~messer** m *altimeter*; *hypsometer*; (mit Echolot) *sound-ranging a.r*; (mit Funkmeß) *radar a.r*; ⟨a-n⟩ *stratoscope* **~meßplan** m ⟨mil⟩ *vertical plotting board* **~messung** f *altimetry*; *hypsometry* **~rauch** m → Herauch **~richt-** [in comp] ⟨mil⟩ *elevating*; ~bogen [m] *e. arc*; ~kanonier [m] *e. setter*; ~maschine [f] *e. gear* **~richtung** f ⟨mil⟩ *elevation* **~rücken** m *dominating range* **~ruder** n ⟨aero⟩ *elevator* **~schicht-** ~linie [f] ⟨cart⟩ *contour* ‖ ~plan [m] *c. map* **~schreiber** m *altigraph* **~schutzanzug** m *scaphander* **~sonne** f ⟨med⟩ *mountain sun*; künstl. ~ *artificial sunrays* pl; *a. insolation*; Behandlung mit ~ *ray therapy* ‖ (Gerät) (Wz) *mercury vapour lamp* **~stellung** f ⟨mil⟩ *commanding position*; *height*; ⟨phot⟩ *tilt adjustment* **~steuer** n ⟨aero⟩ *elevator* **~steuerung** f *altitude control* **~strahlung** f *cosmic radiation* (od *rays* pl) **~streuung** f ⟨mil⟩ *vertical dispersion* **~tafeln** f pl *hypsometric*(*al*) *tables* pl **~unterschied** m *difference of level*; *d. in elevation*; *rise*/*fall* **~verlust** m *loss in height* **~wind** m ⟨meteor⟩ *upper-wind* **~winkel** m *angle of elevation* od *sight*; negativer ~ *a. of depression* **~zeiger** m *indicator of altitude* od *elevation* **~zug** m *ridge of hills*

Hohenst·aufe m ~n/~n ⟨Ger hist⟩ *member of the dynasty of H.n*; die ~n [pl] *the H.n*

Hohenz·oller m ~n/~n ⟨Ger hist⟩ *member of the dynasty of H.n*; die ~n [pl] *the H.n*

Hohepr·iester: [der ~, ein H.rp.] m H.np.s/ H.np. ⟨bib⟩ *high-priest*; einige ~ *some high-priests* **hohepr·iesterlich** a *high-priestly*; *pontifical* **H·öhepunkt** m ~(e)s/~e ⟨übtr & fig⟩ **1.** *culminating point*; *culmination* (*of a fever, fashion, movement*); *climax* (*of a drama*); ~e [pl] *dramatic high lights* ‖ *meridian* (*of a career*); *pinnacle* (*of life*) ‖ *height*; *high tide*; *high-watermark* (*of literature*); ⟨Am a.⟩ *high point* ‖ *acme* (*of perfection*); *apex* L; *apogee* (*of trade*); *maximum* (*of temperature*); *peak, pinnacle, pitch*; *sum*; *summit* (*of fame*); *zenith* **2. Wendungen a.** das Jahr des ~s *the peak-year* (f *for*) ‖ der ~ des Tages *the chief thrill of the day* ‖ dies war der ~ [gen] *this was the climax to a series of events* | e–n ~ **ausmachen** *or* bilden *to make a peak* (in *in*) ‖ den ~ erreichen *or* finden *to reach* (od *find*) *one's culmination* (od *climax, high-watermark, peak, zenith*) (in *in*); *to culminate* (bei *with*; in *in*); e–n ~ erreichen *to run at records*; den ~ nicht err. ⟨fig⟩ *to slide off* (od *fall short of*) *the peak*; den ~ überschreiten *to cap the climax* **b. auf** dem ~ *at the pinnacle* (od *pitch*) (*of ..*); auf dem ~ s–r Macht *at the zenith of his powers*; auf dem ~ der Schlacht *in the height of battle* ‖ auf den ~ bringen *to bring to a climax* ([Not] *to a crisis*) ‖ auf dem ~ s *or* stehen *to be at high tide* (od *at one's zenith*; *in one's heyday*) ‖ langsam auf den ~ steigen (of a cold) *to creep towards its peak* **h·oher** a → hoch **h·öher** [compr v hoch] **A.** [a] **1.** [attr] **a.** *higher* (*house*; *rank*); *superior* (*position*); in e–m ~en Stockwerk *on an upper storey* | ⟨übtr⟩ *greater*; *superior* (*law*); *spiritual*; *divine*; *supernatural* (*power*) ‖ ⟨theol⟩ *dynamical* (*inspiration*) **b.** [feste Verbindungen:] ~e **Beamte** pl *higher officials* ‖ ~er Beruf *learned profession* ‖ ~e Bildung *higher education* ‖ °~er Blödsinn *sheer nonsense* ‖ ~e Forschungsarbeiten [f pl] *advaneed research* ‖ ~e **Gewalt** *Act of God*; *force majeure* Fr; durch ~e G. *by* (*an*) *Act of G.* ‖ ~e Klassen = ~e Schichten ‖ e–e ~e **Macht** *the powers* pl *above*; *God* ‖ ~e M. *higher mathematics* ‖ ~en Ortes *by authority*; *by the authorities*; *by the powers that be*; ⟨mil⟩ *at headquarters* ‖ ~er O. *superior officer*; ~re O.e [pl] *top o.s* ‖ in ~en Regionen schweben *to float* (od *live*) *in higher regions* ‖ ~e Säugetiere *higher mammals* ‖ die ~en Schichten *the upper classes* ‖ ~e **Schule** *secondary sch. for boys*; ~e Mädchenschule *high school*; ~e Schulen [pl] *institutions of higher learning* || °er ist ein ~er Schüler *he attends a secondary school* || auf e–r ~en Warte *on a higher plane* (od *level*) || ~e Ziele *higher ends* **2.** [pred] *higher* (im Rang *in rank*) || ~ als *higher than*; die Einnahmen sind £ 70 ~ als im Jahre 1970 *the receipts are £ 70 up on those in 1970* **B.** [adv] *higher*, ⟨artill⟩ ~! *up!*; immer ~ *h.r and h.r*; *up and up* || ⟨übtr⟩ *more highly* | ~ entwickelt *higher* (*mammals*) || das Fieber ging ~ *the fever went higher* || → Brotkorb || der Ort liegt etw ~ *the place lies somewhat higher up* (*than ..*); ~ gelegen *higher* (*plane*) || das Herz schlug ihm ~ → Herz E. || sie stehen ~ als er *they are superior to him*; ~stehend *superior* **~stufen** vt [h] (im Gehalt etc) *to upgrade* **h·ohes** → hoch

hohl I. [a] **A.** (Ggs massiv, ⟨fig⟩ echt) **1.** (ausgehöhlt) *hollow* (*tree*; *tooth*) || (leer) *hollow* (*ball*; *square*); ~er Raum *hollow*; *vacuum* || e–n ~en Magen h *to feel hollow, to feel a vacuum in the lower regions* || (etw) ~ m *to hollow* **2.** ⟨übtr⟩ (*of sound*) *hollow*; *dull, muffled* || mit ~er Stimme *in a hollow voice* || ⟨tech⟩ ~e Welle *hollow shaft* **3.** ⟨fig⟩ **a.** *hollow* (*joys, pleasures*); *empty* (*phrases, words*); *unsubstantial* (*hopes*); *vain* (*splendour*) || *idle, vacuous* (*life*) **b.** *shallow, shallow-minded* (*p*); *feather* (od *empty*)*-headed* (od *-brained*) || ~er Kopf *rattle-brain, r.-pate, feather-head, f.-brain*; ⟨sl⟩ *saphead*; ⟨Am sl⟩ *bromide* || ~er Schwätzer ⟨sl⟩ *blank*(*y*) *orator* **B.** (rund vertieft) *hollow*; *concave*; *depressed*; sunken; ~e Fläche *concave* || auf beiden Seiten ~ *concavo-concave* || ~e Augen, Wangen *hollow* (od *cavernous*) *eyes, cheeks* || → Gasse, ≗weg || → Hand; (etw) in der ~en H. verbergen *to palm* || ~er Raum *hollow*; *depression* **II.** *⟨adv⟩ ~ klingen *to ring hollow*; *to sound h.* || ~ husten *to have a hollow cough* **H·ohl-** *hollow* **~ader** f ⟨anat⟩ *vena cava* L **≗äugig** a *h.-eyed* **≗backig** a *h.-cheeked* **~bau** m ⟨fort⟩ *reduit* Fr; ~ten [pl] *casemates* pl **~beitel** m = –meißel **~bohrer** m *h. drill* **≗brüstig** a *h.-chested* **~dechsel** m *h. adze* **~eisen** n (Werkzeug) *gouge* **≗erh·aben** a *concavo-convex* **~fläche** f *concave surface*; *concave* **~gebiß** n (hors) *curb*(*-bit*) **≗geschliffen** a *h.-ground* (*razor*); *concave* **~geschoß** n *h. projectile* **~geschwür** n = Fistel **~gewebe** n *tubular fabric* **~glas** n *h. glass-ware*; *concave glass* **~guß** m *h. casting* **~hering** m *shotten herring* **~hörner** n pl = Horntiere **~kehle** f ⟨arch⟩ *h. moulding*; *cavetto*; *cyma recta* L; *scotia* || *flute, groove, hollow* **~keil** m *h. key* **~klinge** f *h.-ground blade* °**~kopf** m = hohler Kopf °**~köpfig** a *empty-headed* **~körper** m *h. body* (od *piece*); ⟨aero⟩ *float* **~kugel** f *h. ball* (od *globe, sphere*) **~ladung** f *h. charge*; N *base detonator* **~leiste** f *h.* (*moulding*) **~linse** f *concave lens* **~masche** f *h. stitch* **~maß** n *measure of capacity* **~mauer** f *h. wall* **~meißel** m *gouge* **~münze** f ⟨hist⟩ *bracteate* **~nadel** f ⟨med⟩ *cannula* L **~naht** f *hemmed seam* **~organ** n *h. organ* **~pfennig** m ⟨hist⟩ = –münze **~platten-Brückengerät** n *hollow-deck bridging equipment* **≗prägen** vt [h] *to emboss* **~rad** n *annular wheel* **~raum** m *h.* od *empty space*; *chamber*; *vacuum* L; *cavity* || ⟨min⟩ durch Abbau entstandener ~ *gob* | ~bildung [f] *cavitation*; ~strahlung [f] ⟨at phys⟩ *black-body radiation* **≗round** a *concave* **~saum** m *hemstitch*; (etw) mit e–m ~ nähen *to hemstitch*; ~arbeit [f] *drawn work* **~schleifmaschine** f *internal grinder* **~schliff** m *h. moulding* **~spat** m ⟨minr⟩ *h. spar*; *chiastolite* **~schraube** f *h. bolt* **~spiegel** m *concave mirror* **~steg** m ⟨print⟩ *furniture* **~stelle** f ⟨radiology⟩ *gas pocket* **~taube** f ⟨orn⟩ *wild pigeon* **~tier** n ⟨zoo⟩ *coelenterate*; die ~e [pl] *Coelenterata, Hydrozoa* pl **~vene** f = –ader **~walze** f *h. cylinder* **~wand** f *h. wall* **≗wangig** a = –backig **~waren** f pl *h.-ware* **~weg** m *defile*; *narrow pass*; *gorge*; ⟨Am a.⟩ *notch* **~welle** f ⟨tech⟩ *h. shaft* **~wurz** f ⟨bot⟩ *fumitory*; *Corydalis* L **~zahn** m ⟨bot⟩ *hempnettle*; *Galeopsis* L; ~rad [n] ⟨tech⟩ = Hohlrad **~ziegel** m *air-brick* || *concave tile* **~zirkel** m *inside callipers* pl **~zylinder** m *h. cylinder* **H·öhle** f ~/~n **1.** (unterird. Gesteins≗) *cave, cavern*; Tropfstein≗ *stalactite c.* || *cavity*; *hole*; *hollow*; → Grube || kl ~ *grotto*; → Grotte **2.** (of wild beasts) *den, lair*; (of badger, etc.) *hole*; (of rabbits, etc.) *burrow*; in die ~ des Löwen gehen *to beard the l. in his den* **3.** ⟨anat & bot⟩ *cavity*; *pit*; *antrum* L; *sinus* L || Arm≗ *armpit*; Bauch≗ *abdominal cavity*; Magen≗ *pit of the stomach*; Mund≗ *mouth-cavity*; Stirn≗ *sinus* L **4.** ⟨übtr dero⟩ *den, hole, hovel* ***h·öhlen** vt [h] *to hollow*; → aus~ || ⟨prov⟩ steter Tropfen höhlt den Stein *constant dropping wears the stone* **H·öhlen-** [in comp] *cave-* ⟨a. praeh⟩; *spelaean, speleological* **~bär** m ⟨zoo⟩ *c.-bear* **~bewohner** m *c.-dweller*; *troglodyte* **~bilder** n pl *c.-paintings* pl **~fauna** f *c.-fauna* **~fisch** m *c.-fish* **~flora** f *c.-flora* **~forscher** m *spel*(*a*)*eologist, spelunker*, ⟨fam⟩ *potholer* **~forschung** f *c.-research*; → –kunde **~funde** m pl ⟨praeh⟩ *c.-remains* pl **~gans** f = Brandente **~hyäne** f ⟨zoo⟩ *c. hyena* **~kunde** f *spel*(*a*)*eology* **≗kundlich** a *spel*(*a*)*eological* **~malerei** f *c.-painting* **~mensch** m *c.man*; ~en [pl] *spelaean people* **~tempel** m ⟨Ind⟩ *c.-temple* **~tiere** n pl *c.-animals* pl **~wohnung** f *c.-dwelling* **H·ohlheit** f ~/~en **1.** *⟨eig⟩ *hollowness* (*of a tooth, voice*) **2.** mst ⟨fig⟩ *emptiness, hollowness*; *shallowness*; *vanity*; ~en [pl] *vain gauds* pl **H·öhlung** f ~/~en **1.** *excavation*; → Aus≗ || [fast konkr] *hollow*; *chamber*; → Höhle **2.** (Wölbung) *concavity, depression*; *dent, dip, indent*

Hohn m ~(e)s/ **1.** *mockery* (über *of*); *scorn*; *derision*; *disdain*; *flout, gibe* (od *jibe*), *jeer, scoff* (über *at*), *sneer, taunt*; bitterer ~ *biting sarcasm* **2. a.** das ist der **reine** ~ *that is sheer mockery*; *that's ridiculous* || **ein** ~ **auf** die Freiheit *a mockery of freedom*; ein wahrer ~ auf .. *an absolute libel on* (*national independence*) || er war allen ein **Gegenstand des ~s** *he was the scorn of* (od *a scorn to*) *all* | *jdm ~ **sprechen** = jdn verhöhnen || e–r S ~ sprechen *to defy* (od *disregard, override*) *a th*; *to set a th at defiance* (od *nought*); *to throw a th to the winds*; das spricht der Gerechtigkeit ~ *that flies in the face of justice, that is a libel on justice* **b.** jdn **mit** Spott u ~ überschütten *to heap jeers and mockeries upon a p* | **zum** Spott u ~ w *to become a mockery* || jdm z ~e *in defiance of a p*; sie taten es uns z ~ *they did it to spite us* || e–r S z ~ *in the face of a th* ×**h·ohnakeln** vi [h], °**h·ohnecken** vi [h] = **h·öhnen** vt/i [h] **1.** vt (jdn) *to deride, mock*; = verhöhnen **2.** vi *to flout, gibe, jeer, mock, scoff, sneer* (über *at*) °**h·ohnepipeln** vi [h] = höhnen; ulken **H·ohngelächter** n *scornful laughter*; *mockery* **h·öhnisch 1.** [a] *derisive* (*laughter*); *gibing*; *mocking, scornful, sneering, taunting*; *ironic, sardonic* (*laugh*), *satirical* (*laughter*); *cynical, sarcastic* || ~e Anspielung *taunting reference*; ~e Bemerkung *flout, gibe, jeer, sneer* **2.** [adv] *derisively, gibingly, mockingly, scornfully, sneeringly, tauntingly*; *ironically, sardonically*; *cynically, sarcastically* || jdn ~ aufziehen, jdm ~ antworten *to twit a p*; ~ fragen *to ask quizzically* || ~ lächeln = **h·ohnlächeln 1.** vi [h] *to smile derisively* **2.** ≗ n = Hohnlachen **h·ohnlachen 1.** vi [h] *to laugh derisively* od *scornfully*; *to sneer* (über *at*); ~ über etw *to deride* (od *flout, sneer*) *a th* **2.** ≗ n *derisive laughter*; *sneer* (über *at*) || jdn mit ~ behandeln *to laugh a p to scorn*; = verhöhnen

hoh·o! intj *oho*! *ah*!

Höker m ~s/~ **1.** (herumziehend) **a.** = Hausierer **b.** (mit Wagen) *hawker*; *intinerant vendor* **c.** (mit Marktwaren) *coster*(*monger*) **2.** (mit eigenem Laden) *huckster*; *retail dealer* || sie ist beim ~ *she is at the huckster's* **3.** ⟨fig⟩ *huckster*; *pedlar* **~frau** f *huckst*(*e*)*ress*; *huckster*, = Höker **~kram** m *pedlar's* od *small wares*; *pedlary* **~laden** m *huckster's shop*; *retail-shop* **~weib** n = –frau **Höker·ei** f ~/~en **1.** [abstr] *pedlary, pedlaring* ||

huckstering **2.** [konkr] *huckster's shop* **H·ökerin** f ~/~nen = Hökerfrau **h·ökern A.** vi [h] **1.** *to go hawking; to huckster;* ~ mit etw *to hawk* od *huckster a th* **2.** ⟨fig⟩ = hausieren ⟨fig⟩ **B.** ≗ n *hawking; huckstering*

H·okkovogel m ⟨orn⟩ *Penelopine bird; guan*

H·okuspokus m ~/ **1.** (Formel) *hocus-pocus* ‖ *mumbo-jumbo* ‖ ~! *hey presto!* **2.** ⟨übtr⟩ *hokey--pokey; hanky-panky; jugglery; trickery* ‖ *humbug;* ⟨Am sl⟩ *ballyhoo* (über *about*) ‖ ~ m *to hocus-pocus; to humbug; to play tricks*

hold A. [a] **1.** [pred] *kind, propitious* (jdm *to a p*); *gracious* ‖ jdm ~ s (P) *to be attached to a p; to have a liking for a p; to love* od *like a p* ‖ (of fortune, etc.) *to smile upon a p;* das Glück war ihm ~ *his luck held good;* das G. war ihm nicht ~ *his l. was against him;* möge das G. dir ~ s! *may good luck attend you!* ‖ e–m Vorschlage ~ s *to favour a proposal* **2.** [attr] ⟨übtr⟩ *charming, lovely, sweet (girl)* ‖ *lovely, sweet (face, song; evening; spring);* ⟨poet⟩ *gracious (rain)* **B.** [adv] *(to smile) graciously,* etc.

H·olda ⟨Ger myth⟩ *Holda; Frau Holle* [Ger]

H·oldchen n (Anrede) *love, sweet(heart)*

H·olde 1. a. m [der ~, ein ~r] *beloved, love* **b.** f [die ~] *lovely* (od *sweet*) *girl* ‖ *sweetheart* **2.** die ~n [pl] ⟨Ger myth⟩ *the host of the dead*

ˣ**H·older** m = Holunder **H·oldin** f → Holde

h·old- ~lächelnd a *sweetly smiling* **~selig 1.** [a] *graceful; lovely, sweet (woman)* ‖ *gracious (old man)* **2.** [adv] *(to smile) graciously, sweetly* | **~seligkeit** f *gracefulness; loveliness,* etc.

°**holdri·o**! intj *hey-day! tol-de-rol! tra-la-la!* | ≗ m ~(s)/~(s) *harum-scarum*

h·olen vt [h] **A. 1. jdn** ~ *to fetch a p, to go* od *come for a p;* hol ihn *(go and) fetch him;* jdn ~ l *to send for a p* ‖ hol ihn **ans** Telephon *get him on the phone* ‖ jdn **zur** Hilfe ~ *to seek a p's help* ‖ hol' ihn der **Teufel**!, ihn soll der T. ~! *he may go to the devil!* **2. etw** ~ **a.** *to fetch a th; to go* od *come for a th;* (Gehalt) *collect; to retrieve (he r.d his hat)* ‖ bei ihm ist nicht viel z ~ *there's not much to be got out of him;* °hier ist nichts z ~ *nothing doing!* ‖ hol's der Teufel! *confound it!* **b. Atem** *or* Luft ~ *to take* (od *draw*) *breath,* → Kastanie **c.** (S) ⟨wir⟩ *to pick up* **3. a. jdm etw** ~ *to get* od *find a p a th* (od *a th for a p*); *to collect a th for a p;* hol es mir bitte *do get it for me;* ~ Sie mir ein Auto *please, find me a car* **b. sich** [dat] etw ~ *to get o.s. a th,* sich **Rat** (*or* Rats), Trost ~ bei *or* v jdm *to seek advice, comfort from a p; to apply to a p for a., c.* **c.** °⟨fig⟩ **sich e-e Krankheit** ~ *to catch* (od *contract, develop*) *a disease; to be infected with a d.* ‖ sich e–e Erkältung, kalte Füße ~ *to catch a cold, cold feet;* sich e–n Rausch ~ *to get over the line;* sich Schläge ~ *to get a licking* od *hiding* **B.** ⟨mar⟩ (ziehen) *to haul*

H·olfter m = Halfter **H·olk** m → Hulk

°**h·olla**! intj *hollo! holla! holloa! hallo! halloa!* ‖ u damit ~! = basta! ‖ ~ rufen *to hollo, hallo*

H·olland *the Netherlands* (od *Low Countries*) pl; *Holland;* ganz ~ *the whole of the Netherlands* ‖ ⟨prov⟩ da war ~ in Not *now they were in a pretty mess* ‖ Nord≗ *North H.;* Süd≗ *South H.* ‖ aus ~ kommend, stammend *Dutch* **H·olländer A.** *Dutchman* [pl *-men*]; er ist ~ *he is a D.* ‖ die ~ [pl] *Dutchmen; the Dutch* pl **B.** ⟨übtr⟩ **1.** der Fliegende ~ (Geisterschiff; ⟨mus⟩ Oper v Wagner) *the Flying D.* **2.** ˣ*manager of a dairy-farm* **3.** ⟨pap⟩ *Hollander; pulp* od *beating-engine, beater* | = ~-käse **C.** [in comp] **a.** ~bl·au [n] *Holland blue* ‖ ~eintrag [m] *b. filling* ‖ ~geschirr [n] *b. tub* ‖ ~k·äse [m] *Dutch cheese* ‖ ~m·ühle [f] = Holländer B. 3. ‖ ~müller [m] ⟨pap⟩ *beaterman* **b.** (~zig·arre) e–e ~ *a Dutch cigar* ˣ**Holländer·ei** f *dairy-farm* **H·olländerin** f ~/~nen *Dutch woman; D. girl* **h·olländern** vt/i [h] **1.** vt ⟨tech⟩ (Lumpen) *to pulp* (od *beat*) *in a Hollander* (→ Holländer B. 3. a.) **2. a.** vi *to skate in the Dutch style, on the outside edge* **b.** ≗ n *skating on the o. e.* **h·olländisch 1.** [a] *Dutch (language, literature);* → niederländisch ‖ ~e Tunke, Sauce *Hollandaise; Dutch sauce* ‖ (Gebiet) ~ m *to Dutchify* **2.** [abs] das ≗e *Dutch;* auf ≗, im ≗en *in Dutch*

H·olle[1] f ~/~n *crest; tuft of hair* od *feathers*

H·olle[2] → Holda; ⟨fig⟩ Frau ~ schüttelt die Betten (es schneit) *the old woman is picking her geese* ‖ ~s Federn *Mother Carey's chickens*

H·ölle f ~/ **1.** (Unterwelt) *hell* [ohne best. Art, a. unter 2. 3.]; ⟨ant⟩ *Hades* Gr; *Orcus* L, *Tartarus* L; ⟨bib⟩ *Sheol* [ʃi:oul] **2.** ⟨ec⟩ **a.** *h.; place of damnation; inferno* It; *pandemonium* L; *infernal regions* pl ‖ der Fürst der ~ *the Prince of Darkness* ‖ in der ~ *in h.* **b.** ⟨fig⟩ *h.; place of misery;* ⟨sl⟩ *blazes* pl ‖ die Qualen der ~ *the tortures of H.* **3.** ⟨übtr⟩ **a.** (in games) *den, h.* **b.** *vicious haunt;* → Spiel≗ **c.** ˣ*chimney corner* **4. Wendungen a.** die reine ~ auf Erden *a regular h. on earth* ‖ es war die ~ los *there was a h. of a noise* od *racket; pandemonium reigned (in the hall)* → Himmel B. 1. a. ‖ ⟨fig⟩ Qualen der ~ erleiden *to suffer h.* ‖ jdm die ~ heiß m *to give a p h.; to make it* od *things warm for a p; to give it a p hot* **b. in die** ~ **k** *to be doomed to h.* (od *damnation*); *to be damned* ‖ jdm das Leben **zur** ~ **m** *to make a p's life a perfect h.; to lead a p a dreadful dance* (od *a dog's life*); das ganze Haus zur ~ m *to raise h. generally in the house* ‖ zur ~ niederfahren (of Christ) *to descend into h.;* → Teufel; der Weg zur ~ ist mit guten Vorsätzen gepflastert *h. is paved with good intentions* **H·öllen-** [in comp] **A.** *hellish, infernal;* *(a) hell of a ..; (the) devil* (od *deuce*) *of a ..;* → höllisch **~brand** m *hell-fire* °**~braten** m *scoundrel* **~brut** f *hellish crew; vicious lot* **~fahrt** f ⟨bib⟩ *(Christ's) descent to hell* **~fürst** m → Hölle 2. **~hund** m **1.** ⟨ant⟩ *hell-hound; Cerberus* L **2.** ⟨fig⟩ *hell-hound; fiend* °**~leben** n: ein ~ *a hell of a life;* ein ~ h *to suffer a hell on earth* **~maschine** f *infernal machine* **~pfuhl** m *fiery pit* **~pein, ~qual** f *torments of hell* ‖ *agonizing* (od *excruciating*) *pain* **~schlund** m *jaws of hell; bottomless pit* **~stein** m ⟨chem⟩ *lunar caustic (nitrate of silver)* **B.** °[verblaßt; als Intensivum] [mit zweitem Ton: H·öllen·angst] *(a) hell of a ..;* → Heiden-, Mords- **~·angst** f = Heiden- **~l·arm** m *(a) hell of a noise; (the) deuce* (od *devil*) *of a row; hullabaloo; pandemonium* L; ein ~ brach los *a p. broke loose;* ~ m *to raise hell; to make* (od *kick up*) *hell's* (od *the devil's*) *own noise* (od *din*) **~schr·eck(en)** m; er hatte e–n ~ *he had the devil of a fright* **~skand·al, ~spekt·akel** m = –lärm; e–n ~ m ⟨sl⟩ *to raise the roof*

ˣ**Holler(busch)** m = Holunder

h·öllisch A. [a] **1.** *⟨bib⟩ *hellish (damnation, fire); infernal* ‖ *devilish (plot); fiendish; vicious; heathenish;* → Höllen-, Hölle **2.** ⟨mst °fig fam⟩ *hellish (heat, speed); mighty; awful, horrible, terrible;* → enorm, riesig ‖ ~e Angst → Heidenangst; e–n ~en Appetit h *to have a hell of an appetite* ‖ ein ~er Kerl *a devil of a fellow* **B.** [adv] ⟨fig fam⟩ *devilish (little); hellishly (long way); infernally (cold); ruinously;* ~ heiß *as hot as hell;* ~ viel ⟨Am sl⟩ *a helluva (= hell of a) lot*

Holler·ith- ~maschine f → Lochkartenmaschine **~system** n *punch-card s.*

ˣ**höllsch** a = höllisch: 'n ~en Kerl [nom]

Holm[1] m ~(e)s/~e (Flußinsel) *holm(e); islet* ‖ ~gang ⟨hist⟩ *duel to the death; holmgang* [Ger]

Holm[2] m ~(e)s/~e ⟨tech⟩ *cross-beam; transom* ‖ ⟨aero⟩ Trag≗ *spar* ‖ (am Barren, etc) *bar; pole*

Holo- (Gr) [in comp] *holo-* **~·eder** n ⟨minr⟩ *holohedral form* **~edr·ie** f ⟨minr⟩ *holohedrism* **~graph·ie** f ⟨a. phot-cart⟩ (mit Laser) *holography* **~z·än** n ~(e)s/ (Gr: ganz neu) ⟨geol⟩ (obere

Abt. des Quartärs einschließlich Gegenwart) *holocene*; → -zän

holp(e)rig 1. [a] *bumpy, humpy (road); jolting, jolty; rugged (ground)* ‖ *bad; rough, uneven* ‖ ~e Beschaffenheit *bumpiness, ruggedness* | ⟨fig⟩ *jolting, rugged (verses); unpolished* ‖ *clumsy (style)* **2.** [adv] ⟨fig⟩ *joltingly* ‖ die Lektion ~ aufsagen *to stumbly through one's lesson* **h·olpern 1.** vi [h] (of vehicles) *to jolt; jounce; lumber* (über *across*); *rumble* ‖ ~de Bewegung *jolt, rumble* **2.** ⍨ n *jolt(ing); rumble, rumbling*

H·olschuld f ⟨jur⟩ *debt bound to be collected*

^×^**Holst** (= Hulst) ⟨bot⟩ *holly(-tree)*

H·olste m ~n/~n ⟨Ger⟩ *inhabitant of Holstein*

H·olstein ⟨Ger⟩ *Holstein* **H·olsteiner** m = Holste **h·olsteinisch** a *Holstein* ‖ ~es Rindvieh ⟨Am⟩ *holsteins* pl

h·olter(die)polter adv *helter-skelter; slap-bang, slap-dash; headlong*

Hol·under m ~s/~ ⟨bot⟩ **1.** Schwarzer ~ *elder*; ⟨Scot⟩ *bourtree*; *Sambucus* L; → Holder ‖ Zwerg⍨ → Attich **2.** Blauer ~ *lilac*; *Syringa* L **~beere** f *e.berry* **~markkugel** f ⟨el⟩ *pith ball* **~suppe** f *e.berry soup* **~tee** *e.-tea* **~wein** m *e.-b. wine*

H·olz n ~es/⍨er **A. 1.** *wood (of a tree)*; ⍨er *woods*; → Unter⍨, Eichen⍨ ‖ frisches ~ *green wood*; dürres ~ *dead wood*; Jung⍨ *young wood*; *sap-wood* ‖ (etw) in ~ verwandeln *to lignify* ‖ eingelegte Arbeit in ~ *intarsio, -sia*; auf ~ eingelegte Schildpattarbeit *buhl* (Fr: nach A.-C. Boul[l]e) **2.** ⟨com⟩ **a.** (Nutz⍨, Bau⍨) *timber*; ~ auf dem Stamme *standing t.*; gesägtes *or* zugerichtetes ~ ⟨Am⟩ *lumber* ‖ Rund⍨ *round t.*; Schnitt⍨ *sawed t.* **b.** ein (Stück) ~ *a t.*; *piece of wood*; Stückchen ~ *chip* ‖ ⟨cul⟩ Nudel⍨ *rolling-pin*; ⟨sport⟩ Schlag⍨ *bat* ‖ Klein⍨, Spalt⍨, ~ z Anbrennen *kindling(-wood)*; Brenn⍨ *firewood*; → Streich⍨ ‖ (Dach) durch ein Stück ~ stützen *to timber* **3. a.** er saß da **wie ein Stück** ~ *he sat there like a block of wood* ‖ ~ anfassen! *touch w.!*, ⟨Am⟩ *knock on w.!* ‖ **~ hacken,** klein m *to chop wood*; ~ hauen, schlagen *to cut timber*; *to fell trees* ‖ wo ~ gehauen wird, da fallen Späne *there is no smoke without fire* ‖ °^×^sie hat ~ bei der Wand *or* vor der Tür *or* ^×^Hütt'n *she's got an ample bosom* ‖ °viel ~ werfen (beim Kegeln) *to knock down a good many pins* **b.** (→ A. 1.) **aus** ~ *made of wood*; *wooden*; ein Gegenstand aus ~ *a wooden piece*; (..) aus ~ *(all walls were) wooden*; → hölzern ‖ ⟨fig⟩ das ~, aus dem Helden geschnitzt sind *the stuff that heroes are made of*; (P) aus demselben ~ geschnitzt *cut from the same bolt*; *of the same stamp*; *cast in the same mould*; er ist aus ganz anderem ~ geschnitzt *he is of quite a different cut*; er ist dazu aus dem richtigen ~ geschnitzt *he's got what it takes*; aus ~ gezimmert *timbered* ‖ **ins** ~ schießen (of a tree) *to run to leaves and wood* **B.** (Wald) *wood, woods* pl; *forest* → Wald **C.** [in comp] *wood-*; *timber-*; *ligni-*; *xylo-* | (= aus ~ gemacht) *w.en* **~abfall** m *waste w.* **⍨ähnlich** a *w.-like* **~alkohol** m ⟨chem⟩ *w.-alcohol* (od *spirit*) **~apfel** m ⟨bot⟩ *crab-apple*; *wilding* **~arbeit** f ~, ~en [pl] *w.work* **~arbeiter** m *w.worker*; *worker in w.* **~arm** a *scantily w.ed* **~art** f *kind of w.*; ~en *w.s* pl; *kinds* pl *of w.* **~artig** a *ligneous, w.y* **~asbest** m ⟨minr⟩ *l. asbestos*; *rock-cork* **~asche** f *w.ashes* pl **~äther** m *methyl ether* **~auktion** f *public sale of w.* od *t.* **~axt** f *(w.-)felling-axe* **~bank** f; lange ~ mit hoher Lehne *settle* **~baracke** f *w.en hut* **~bau** m *w.en structure*; *t.-work* **~bearbeitung** f *w.-working* ‖ ~smaschine [f] *w.-working machine* **~bein** n *w.en leg*; *peg* (od *pin*)*-leg*; ⟨fam⟩ *t.-toe(s)* **~beize** f *w.-mordant* **~bekleidung** f *w. covering*; *skin (of ship)* **~biene** f ⟨ent⟩ *carpenter* (od *w.*)*-bee* **~bild** n ⟨arts⟩ *sculpture in w.* **~bildhauer** m ⟨arts⟩ *carver in w.*, *w.-carver* **~bildhauerei** f ⟨arts⟩ *w.-carving*; *sculpture in w.* **~birne** f ⟨bot⟩ *wild pear* **~bläser** m pl (P) ⟨mus⟩ *the w.(s)*, [koll] *the w.-wind* **~blasinstrument** n ⟨mus⟩ *w.en wind-instrument*; die ~e [pl] *the w.-wind*; *the w.(s)* **~block** m *log of w.* **~bock** m **1.** ⟨eig⟩ *sawing-block* (od *trestle*) **2.** ⟨ent⟩ *w.-tick* ‖ = Bockkäfer **3.** (P) *obstinate brat*; *clumsy fellow* **~boden** m **1.** *w.en floor* (od *bottom*) **2.** *wood-loft* **~bohrer** m **1.** ⟨eig⟩ *auger* **2.** ⟨ent⟩ *borer* **~brandmalerei** f *pyrography*; *poker-work* **~bündel** n *bundle of sticks*; *fag(g)ot* **~destillation** f *w.-distillation* **~dieb** m *stealer of w.* **~draht** m *w.-wire* **~drehbank** f *w.-turning lathe* **~essig** m *pyroligneous acid*; *w.-vinegar* **~fällen** n *w.-cutting* ⟨bes Am⟩ *lumbering* **~fäller** m *lumberman*; *w.-cutter*; ⟨Am⟩ *lumberer, logger* **~faser** f *w.-fibre* ‖ (v Gemüse) *roughage* | ~garn [n] ⟨tex⟩ *wood fibre yarn*; ~stoff [m] *lignin(e)* **~fäule** f *dry-rot* **~feuer** n *w.* (od *log*) *fire* **~floß** n *w.-float* (⟨Am⟩ *flat*); *raft* **⍨frei** a ⟨pap⟩ *free from w.*, *w.-free* **~frevel** m = Wald- **~fuhre** f *cartload of w.* **~fußboden** n = Holzboden 1. **~futter** n ⟨tech⟩ *w.en lining* **~gas** n *w.-gas* **~gefälle** n *income from w.* od *a forest* **~geist** m = -alkohol **~geräte** n pl = -waren **~gerechtigkeit** f *right to cut or collect w.* **~gewächs** n ⟨bot⟩ *ligneous plant* **~gewebe** n *tissue of w. and cotton* **~gummi** n *w. resin* **~hacker** m *w.-cutter* **~haltig** a *(paper) containing mechanical w.* **~häher** m ⟨orn⟩ = Eichel- **~hammer** m *mallet*; schwerer ~ *maul*; °jdm eins mit dem ~ versetzen ⟨fam⟩ *to knock a cold* | ~methode(n pl) [f] ⟨fig⟩ *sledge hammer methods* **~handel** m *timber* (od *w.*)*-trade* **~händler** m *t.* (od *w.*)*-merchant* **~harmonika** f = Xylophon **~hauer** m = -hacker **~haufen** m *pile* (od *stack*) *of w.* **~haus** n *t.-house*; ⟨Am⟩ *frame-house* **~hof** m = -platz | (eiserne) **~hunde** pl (im Kamin) *fire dogs* **~imprägnierung** f *w.-impregnation* **~käfer** m *w.-beetle*; = -bohrer 2. **~kasten** m *w.en box* **~kauf** m *purchase of w.* **~kirche** f *frame-church* **~kirsche** f ⟨bot⟩ *wild cherry* **~kiste** f *w.en chest* **~klotz** m *w.en block*, → -scheit **~knüppel** m *cudgel*; dicker ~ *round t.* **~kohle** f *charcoal* **~konservierung** f *w.-preserving* **~kopf** m ⟨fig⟩ *w.en-head*; ⟨Am⟩ *bonehead* **~krähe** = Schwarzspecht **~latte** f *lath*; *batten*; ~nverschlag [m] *w.en packing boards* **~laus** f ⟨ent⟩ *psocid* **~löffel** m *w.en spoon* **~malerei** f *panel-painting* **~mangel** m *dearth* (od *shortage*) *of w.* **~markt** m *w.-* (⟨Am⟩ *lumber-*) *market* **~masse** f → -stoff **~mehl** n *w.-meal*; *w.-flour* **~mosaik** n *intarsia, -sio*; *marquet(e)ry* **~nagel** m *(w.en) peg*; langer ~ *tre(e)nail* **~obst** n *wild fruit* **~öl** n *w.-oil*; (chines. ~) *gurjun balsam* **~opal** m ⟨minr⟩ *w.-opal* **~pantoffel,** °**~pantine** f *clog* **~papier** n *w.-paper* **~pappe** f *w.-pulp board* **~pfahl** m *w.en pile*; *picket* **~pflanze** f *ligneous plant* **~pflaster** n *w. pavement* (od *paving*) **~pflock** m *peg*; mit e-m ~ befestigen *to peg* **~pilz** m *dry-rot* **~platte** f → -stock **~platz** m *t.* (od *w.*, ⟨Am⟩ *lumber*)*-yard* **⍨reich** a *rich in w.*; *(well-)w.ed*; *w.y* **~reifen** m *w.en hoop* **~rot** n *red-w. extract* **~säge** f *w.-saw* **~säure** f ⟨chem⟩ = -essig **⍨saures Eisen** n *iron liquor* **~schachtel** f *w.en box* **~scheibe** f *w.en disk*; (Schieß-) *w. target* **~scheit** n *billet* (od *log, chunk*) *of w.* **~schiff** n *w.en ship* **~schlag** m **1.** *w.-cutting* **2.** (Ort) *clearing* **~schläger** m = -fäller **~schleifer** m ⟨pap⟩ *pulp grinder* **~schleiferei** f *pulp factory* **~schliff** m *(mechanical) w.-pulp* **~-schneidekunst** f *xylography* **~schneider** m **1.** *sawyer* **2.** ⟨arts⟩ *xylographer*; *w.-engraver* **~schnitt** m ⟨arts⟩ *w.-cut* | ~blatt [n] *w.cut print (black line)*, → -stich ‖ ~künstler [m] *w.-designer* **~schnitzel** n pl *whittling w.* **~schnitzer** m ⟨arts⟩ *w.-carver* **~schnitzerei** f ⟨arts⟩ *w.-carving* **~schraube** f *w.-screw* **~schuh** m (ganz aus Holz) *w.en shoe*; *sabot* ‖ (mit Oberleder) *clog* ‖ (auf e-m Eisenring) *patten* **~schuppen** m *w.-house* (od *shed*) **~schwamm** m *dry-rot*; *w.-fungus* **~schwarte** f *slab* **~sohle** f *w.en sole* **~sorte** f *kind of w.*; → -art **~span** m *chip*; ⍨e [pl] *w.-shavings* pl | ~platte [f] *chip-board* **~spiritus** m = -alkohol **~splitter** m *chip, sliver, splinter (of w.)*; ~ [pl] *matchwood*, ⟨Am⟩ *kindling* *w.* **~stab** m *w.en bar*; *slat* **~-Stahl-Karosserie** f ⟨mot⟩ *composite* (*metal-w.*) *body* °**~stall** m = –schuppen **~stapel** m *pile of w.* **~stein** m *fossil w.* **~stich** m *w.-engraving* (*white line*) **~stift** m *peg*; → –nagel **~stock** m ⟨arts⟩ *plate* **~stoff** m *lignin*(*e*); = –schliff **~stoß** m *pile* (od *stack*) *of w.* **~streifen** m *slat* **~stück** n *log*; *timber* **~taube** f ⟨orn⟩ *w.-pigeon*; kl ~ *stockdove* **~tee** m *blood-purifying tea* **~teer** m *w.-tar* **~teller** m *trencher* **~verarbeitung** f = –bearbeitung **~verband** m, **~verbindung** f *w.-joint*(*ing*); (*method of*) *jointing or fastening timbers*; *bond*; → Zapfen **~verkleidung** f *planks* pl; *w. lining*; *weather boarding* **~verkohlung** f = –destillation **~verschalung, ~vertäfelung** f = –verkleidung **~verschlag** m *w.en partition* **~verzierung** f *w.-work*; → –brandmalerei, –mosaik **~verzuckerung** f *w. saccharification* **~wagen** m *w.* (od *t.*) *cart* **~wand** f *w.en partition* **~waren** f pl *w.en-wares* (od *articles*) **~watte** f *w. wool mixed with cotton* **~weg** m *logging road* ‖ ⟨fig⟩ auf dem ~e *off the track* od *beam*; auf dem ~ s *to be in the wrong box*; *to bark up the wrong tree*; *to back the wrong horse* **~werk** n *w.work* **~wespe** f ⟨ent⟩ *horntail* **~wirtschaft** f *t.-trade* **~wolle** f *w.-wool*; ⟨Am⟩ *excelsior* **~wurm** m ⟨zoo⟩ *w.-worm*; → –bohrer **~zahn** m *cog of w.* **~zaun** m *hoarding* **~zellstoff** m *lignocellulose*; *chemical w.-pulp* **~zucker** m ⟨chem⟩ *xylose* **H·ölzchen** n *small plinter*; *small piece of wood* **h·olzen** vi/t [h] **1.** vi **a.** *to cut wood*; *to collect* (od *gather*) *w.* **b.** °⟨sport⟩ *to play unfairly* ‖ sich ~ *to use the cudgels*; *to fight, quarrel* **2.** vt **a.** *to cover* (od *supply*) *with w.* **b.** dies Stück Wald wurde geholzt *the trees of this part of the forest were cut down* **c.** ⟨fig ftb⟩ (jdn) *to foul* ‖ → verholzen °**Holzer·ei** f *free fight*; *fighting with cudgels*; *brawl*; *scuffle* **h·ölzern A.** [a] **1.** ⟨eig⟩ [nur attr] (→ Holz A. 3. b.) *wooden* (*box, spoon*, etc.) **2.** ⟨übtr⟩ (of sound) *dead, dull*; *wooden* **3.** ⟨fig⟩ (P) *wooden* (*fingers*); *awkward, sticky, clumsy* (*fellow*); *gauche*; *stiff* (*style*); ~e Art *or* Beschaffenheit *woodenness*; er hat ein ~es Benehmen *his manners are clumsy* **B.** [adv] (*to behave*) *awkwardly*; *stiffly* | ≗**heit** f ⟨fig⟩ *awkwardness*; *clumsiness*; *woodenness*; *stiffness* **h·olzig** a *ligneous* (*substance*); *woody* (*flavour*) ‖ ⟨übtr⟩ (of food) *stringy* (*meat*); *tough*; *woody*; *hard* ‖ ~e Beschaffenheit *woodiness* **H·olzung** f ~/~en *wood, forest*

H·omburg n ~s/ ⟨Ger⟩ (Badeort) | ~hut [m] *homburg hat*

hom·erisch a *Homeric* (*age, laughter*)

H·omespun [ˈhoumspʌn] n ⟨engl⟩ *homespun*

Homil·et m ~en/~en *homilete, -list* | **~ik** f ⟨theol⟩ *-letics* pl | ≗**isch** a *-letic* **Homil·ie** f ~/~n *homily*

Homo- Gr (Gleich-) *homo-* **~gamie** f ~/ *h.gamy* ≗**g·amisch** a *h.gamous* ≗**g·en** a *h.geneous* **~gen(e)it·ät** f *h.geneity* ≗**genis·ieren** vt *to h.genize* ≗**l·og** a *h.logous* **~n·ym** n *h.nym* ≗**n·ym** a *h.-nymous* **~nym·ie** f ~/~n [-iːən] ⟨gram⟩ *homonymy*; *zero-derivation* (*e.g. squirrel/to sq.*) ≗**ph·on** a ⟨mus⟩ *h.phonous* **~phon·ie** f *h.phony* **~sexualit·ät** f *h.sexuality* ≗**sexu·ell** a *h.sexual* **~zyg·ot** m ⟨biol⟩ (a. ≗er Organismus) *h.zygote* ≗**zyg·ot** a *h.zygous*

Homöo- Gr [in comp] (ähnlich) *homoeo-* **~p·ath** m *h.path, –pathist* **~path·ie** f *h.pathy* ≗**p·athisch** a *h.pathic*

Hom·unkulus m L *homunculus* L

H·onanseide f *Honan silk*

H·ondo n (japan. Insel)

Hondur·aner m ~s/~, **h.-nisch** a *Honduran*

Hond·uras n (mittelamer. Republik) *H.*

h·onen vt [h] (feinschleifen) *to hone*

***hon·ett** a Fr *decent*; *respectable*

H·ongkong n (Insel vor Kanton, China)

H·onig m ~s/ *honey*; Bienen≗ *h.*; Heide≗ *heather-h.* ‖ Scheiben≗, Waben≗ *h. in the comb*; *comb-h.*; Jungfernscheiben≗ *virgin h.* ‖ Schleuder≗ *extracted h.*; Seim≗ *strained h.* ‖ Kunst≗ *artificial h.* | ⟨fig⟩ jdm ~ um den Mund (°ums Maul) schmieren *to butter a p up*; ⟨Am fam⟩ *to h.-fug*(*g*)*le* od *softsoap a p* **~ameise** f ⟨ent⟩ *h.-ant* **~anzeiger** m ⟨orn⟩ = –kuckuck **~bär** m ⟨zoo⟩ *h.-bear*; → Kinkaju **~bau** m *h. culture* **~biene** f *h.-bee* **~blume** f *h.-flower* **~dachs** m ⟨zoo⟩ *h.-badger* **~drüse** f ⟨bot⟩ (of flowers) *nectary*; Saft der ~ *nectar* **~falke** m ⟨orn⟩ *h.-buzzard* **~farbe** f *h.-colour* ≗**farben** a *amber*(*-coloured*) **~fresser** m ⟨orn⟩ *h.-eater*; *poëbird* **~gefäß** n = –drüse **~gras** n ⟨bot⟩ *soft Holcus* [L] **~kelch** m = –drüse **~klee** m ⟨bot⟩ *melilot*(*e*) **~kuchen** m *gingerbread* ‖ °grinsen wie ein ~pferd *to grin like a Cheshire cat* **~kuckuck** m ⟨orn⟩ *h.-guide* **~magen** m (of bees) *h.-bag* ***~mond** m ⟨poet⟩ = Flitterwochen **~motte** f ⟨ent⟩ *h.comb moth* **~palme** f ⟨bot⟩ *coquito* **~pilz** m ⟨bot⟩ *h.-fungus* **~saft** m ⟨bot⟩ *nectar* **~sauger** m = –fresser **~säure** f *oxymel* **~schleuder** f *h. extractor* **~stein** m ⟨minr⟩ *h.stone*; *mellite* ≗**süß** a *h.-sweet*; *sweet as h.*; *h.ed* ‖ ⟨fig⟩ *h.ed*; *mellifluous* (*words*); *sweet* **~tau** m ⟨bot⟩ *h.-dew* ≗**tragend** a *melliferous* **~trank** m ⟨poet⟩ *mead* **~wabe** f ~/~n [pl] *h.comb* **~waben-** [in comp] *h.comb*; ~arbeit [f] *h.c. work*; ~muster [n] *h.c. pattern*; ~spule [f] *h.c. coil* **~werkzeuge** n pl ⟨bot⟩ *nectaries* pl ≗**wochen** pl ⟨poet⟩ = Flitterwochen **~zelle** f *h.c. cell*

H·onnef n, Bad n (Stadt am Rhein)

Honneurs [ɔˈnœrs] pl [Fr] **1.** *honours* pl; die ~ m *to do the h.* **2.** ⟨cards⟩ *h.*; die ~ sind gleich verteilt *the h. are easy* **honor·abel** a *honourable* **Honor·ant** m ⟨com⟩ *acceptor* (*of a bill*) **Honor·ar** n ~s/~e *fee* (f *for*); *honorarium* L; *remuneration* | ≗frei [a] *without obligation* ‖ ~professor [m] ⟨Ger univ⟩ *honorary title granted to associate professors*; *h.y pr.* ‖ ~rückvergütung [f] (geheim) ⟨med⟩) *kickback* **Honorati·oren** [ts] pl *local people of rank* **honor·ieren** vt [h] (Arzt) *to fee*; *remunerate* (f *for*) ‖ ⟨com⟩ (Wechsel) *to honour, meet*; *accept*; *pay*; honoriert w *to find due protection* ‖ nicht ~ *to dishonour* **Honor·ierung** f *remuneration* (*of a doctor*); *payment* ‖ ⟨com⟩ *acceptance, payment, protection* (*of a bill*) °**hon·orig** a *honourable, respectable*; ~er Mann *man of honour*

Honol·ulu n (Stadt auf Hawaii)

H·onved f **1.** (ungar. Landwehr, Wehrmacht) die ~ *the Honved*(*s* pl) **2.** (P) der ~ *the Honved*

Ho(o)rn, Kap n *Cape Horn*

H·opfen m **1.** ⟨bot⟩ *hop* **2.** ⟨com⟩ *hops* pl **3.** ⟨fig⟩ °an ihm ist ~ u Malz verloren *he is a hopeless case*; *he is hopeless* **4.** [in comp] **~ballen** m *hop-pocket* **~bau** m *hop-culture* **~bier** n *hopped beer* **~bitter** m *hop-bitters* pl **~buche** f ⟨bot⟩ *hop-hornbeam* **~darre** f *hop-kiln*; *oast* **~dolde** f *umbel* **~gabe** f (*rate of*) *hopping* **~garten** m *hop-garden* (od *yard*) **~klee** m ⟨bot⟩ *yellow clover* **~mehl** n *lupulin* **~pflanze** f *hop-plant* **~pflücker** m *hop-picker*; *hopper* **~stamm** m *hop-bine* **~stange** f *hop-pole* ‖ °⟨fig⟩ dünn wie e–e ~ *as thin as a lath* **~strauch** m ⟨bot⟩ *hoptree* **~zapfen**: reife ~ [pl] *hops* pl

h·opfen vt [h] stark gehopft *dry* (Bier)

Hopl·it m ~en/~en ⟨Gr ant⟩ *hoplite*

°**hopp**! [intj] *quick*(*ly*)! ‖ ~ ~! **1.** *be off*! ⟨sl⟩ *hop it*! **2.** *fire away*! ‖ °aber etw ~! *without answering back*! *look sharp*! ⟨sl⟩ *make it snappy*!

h·oppeln vi [s] *to hop, to jump*

°**H·oppelpoppel** m **1.** *punch*; *egg-flip* **2.** *fried potatoes mixed with ham and eggs*

°**h·oppla**! [intj] *houp-la*! *hullo*! *ugh*!

°**Hops** m H·opses/H·opse *hop*; *jump*

°**h·opsa**! [intj] *hullo*! *hey*! °**h·opsassa**! [intj] *hey-day*! *hullo*! °**h·opsen** vi [s] **1.** (P) *to hop*; *jump*; *skip*; (etw) ~ l *to hop* ‖ (tanzen) ⟨sl⟩ *to hop* **2.** (of vehicles) *to jolt*; *jounce* **H·opser** m **1.** *hopper* **2.** (Sprung) *hop*; *jump* ‖ (Tanz) ⟨sl⟩ *hop*(*ping*); *galop*; ~ tanzen *to galop* °**h·ops|gehen** vi [s] *to go pop*; ⟨sl⟩ (S) *to go to pot*, (P) *to peg out*

H·ör- (→ hören) ⟨physiol⟩ *auditory* **~apparat** = –rohr **~bereich** m = –weite **~bericht** m ⟨wir⟩ *running commentary* (über *on*); *eye-witness account* **~brille** f *hearing-aid* [attr] od *ear-glasses* pl **~empfindung** f *au. sensation* **~fehler** m *au. defect* **~fläche** f ⟨ac⟩ *sensation area* **~folge** f ⟨wir⟩ *feature program* **~frequenz** f *audio frequency* **~funk** m *sound broadcasting* **~gerät** n *hearing-aid* ([attr] *h.-a. battery*) **~kapsel** f = –muschel **~kraft** f *hearing-power* **~maschine** f = –rohr 1. **~meßapparat** m *audiometer* **~muschel** f ⟨telph⟩ *receiver* **~nerv** m *au. nerve* **~raum** = –saal **~rohr** n **1.** (f Schwerhörige) *ear-trumpet* **2.** ⟨med⟩ **a.** *stethoscope* || mit ~ untersuchen *to stethoscope*; ~untersuchung [f] *stethoscopy* **b.** [in comp] *stethoscopic* (*examination*) **~saal** m *auditorium* L; *auditory*; *lecture-room*; *class* **~schärfe** f *hearing acuity* **~schlauch** m = –rohr 1. **~schwelle** f *au. threshold* **~spiel** n ⟨wir⟩ *sound* od *radio-drama* (od *play*); *wireless-play* | ~schreiber [m] *scripter* **~trichter** m = –rohr 1. **~verlust** m *hearing loss* **~vermögen** n *audition*; *faculty* (od *power*) *of hearing* **~weite** f *range of audibility*; in ~ *within hearing, within ear-shot*; ⟨bes mar⟩ *within hail*; außer ~ *out of hearing* (od *ear-shot*); *out of hail* **~werkzeug** n *au. organ*; *organ of hearing*

hor·azisch a ⟨ant⟩ *Horatian* (*ode*)

h·örbar 1. [a] *audible, hearable*; ⟨physiol⟩ *audile* || kaum ~ *subaudible*; die Töne waren deutlich ~ *sounds came clearly* || ~ w *to meet the ear*; *to come* (*through*); vom Dorf her wurde Lachen ~ *from the village came the sound of laughter* || sich ~ m *to make o.s. heard* **2.** [adv] *audibly* | **≚keit** f *audibility*

H·orbel f ~/~n ⟨orn⟩ = Bläßente

H·orch- (→ horchen) [in comp] ⟨bes mil⟩ *listening* **~apparat** n = –gerät **~empfänger** m ⟨wir⟩ *interceptor* **~funk** m *radio interception* **~gang** m ⟨fort⟩ *l.-gallery* **~gerät** n ⟨bes mil⟩ *sound-detector* (od *indicator, locator*) || ⟨mar⟩ (Unterwasser≚) *hydrophone* **~posten** m ⟨mil⟩ **1.** (Ort) *l.-post* **2.** (P) *l.-sentry*; ~ [pl] **~stelle** f ⟨wir⟩ *interception station* **~trupp** m *l.-patrol* **~vorrichtung** f *l.-device*

h·orchen A. vi [h] **1.** (lauschen) *to listen*; ⟨liter⟩ *to hearken*; horch! *hark*! || °horch mal *just listen* (*a minute*); *look here* || ~ auf *to listen to* (*a p, a th*); *to pay attention to*; → gehorchen **2.** ⟨dero⟩ (heimlich) *to eavesdrop* (an .. *at the door*) **B.** ≚ n *eavesdropping* **H·orcher** m *eavesdropper* || *listener* || ⟨prov⟩ der ~ an der Wand hört s–e eigne Schand *listeners never hear any good of themselves*

×**H·orde**[1] f ~/~n *hurdle*(*-wall*) || *grating*; *latticed screen* || *floor* (*of a kiln*) | (T) (a. ~nlager) *corral*; *pen*

H·orde[2] f ~/~n **1.** *horde*; *crowd, tribe, troop* (*of nomads*) || *horde*; *pack* (*of wolves*) **2.** ⟨cont⟩ *band, gang, horde* (*of robbers*); *pack*; *rabble* **h·ordenweise** adv *in hordes*

H·ore f ~/~n ⟨R. C.⟩ *canonical hour*; *hora canonica* L | ~n [pl] ⟨ant⟩ *Horae* L pl

h·ören vt/i [h] **I.** vt **A.** ⟨eig⟩ **1.** (etw, jdn) *to hear*; zufällig ~ *to overhear* || (etw) nicht ~ (können) *to miss* (*a good deal of the speech*); man konnte vor Lärm sein eigenes Wort nicht ~ *you could not hear your own words for noise* || man hört überall Gerüchte *the air is filled with rumours* || man hörte ein Scharren *there came a scraping* || es wurde gesagt, so daß ich es hörte *it was said in my hearing* || die Stimme wurde durch die Tür gehört *the voice came through the door* || (ungeduldig) hast du's gehört? *are you listening*? **b. ich höre ihn k** *I hear him coming* (od *come*); man hörte ihn k *he was heard to come* || ich hörte ihn nie derartiges erwähnen *I never heard him mention anything like that* || sie hatte ihn oft e–n gr Maler nennen ~ *she had often heard him called a great painter* || → Gras || ich habe es sagen ~ *I have heard it said* (*that* ..); *I have heard tell of it* || ich habe sagen (munkeln) ~, er käme *I've heard a sort of rumor he might be coming* **2. a.** er hört sich gern (reden) *he likes to hear himself* (*talk*) **b. sich ~ l** (→ B. 4.) (P) *to let o.s. be heard*; die öffentl. Meinung hat sich ~ l *public opinion has become vocal* || (sich produzieren) *to perform* (vor *before*) **B.** ⟨übtr⟩ **1. e-e Deputation** ~ *to hear a d.*; beide Seiten ~ *to hear both sides* || jdn zuende ~ *to hear a p out* **2. a. die Messe** ~ *to hear Mass* **b.** ⟨mus & theat⟩ *to hear* (*an opera*; *a pianist*); *to listen to* (*a concert*) | ⟨wir⟩ Rundfunk, Radio ~ *to listen in* || ein Konzert im R. ~ *to listen-in to a concert* || ich kann China ~ *I can get China* **c.** bes ⟨univ⟩ *to attend, hear*; ein Kolleg ~ über .. *to hear a course of lectures on* (*Sh*); er hörte Philosophie *he attended philosophical classes*; ich hörte Sh bei ihm *I heard his lectures on Sh.* || e–n Professor ~ *to hear a prof.* **3. (erfahren) a.** *to hear, learn*; ⟨fam⟩ *to have*; er hörte es vom Briefträger *he had it from the postman*; wenn ich nichts anderes v Ihnen höre .. *unless I hear from you to the contrary* ..; dies habe ich v ihm (*or* durch ihn) gehört *I have the news from him* (od *through him*); das hört man gern *that's welcome news* || nach allem, was man hört, muß er .. *from all one hears he must be ill*; soviel ich höre .. *as far as I hear* (*he is away*) | ~, **daß** .. *to hear* (od *learn, understand*) *that* ..; ich höre, er ist krank *I hear* (*that*) *he is ill*; er war fremd hier, höre ich (*or* wie ich h.) *he was a stranger here, I understand* | **am** Schritt hörte ich, **daß** du es warst *I recognized you by your step*; *I knew it was you from your step* || **aus** dem Jubel höre ich, **daß** .. *from the acclamations I infer* **II.** vi **A.** ⟨eig⟩ **1.** *to hear* || er hört nur auf e–m Ohr, er kann auf e–m O. nicht ~ *he is deaf in one ear* (od *of an ear*); er h. schwer *or* schlecht *his hearing is bad, he is dull* od *hard of hearing*; er h. sehr gut *he has a quick ear* **2. sagen ~ v** *to hear say* (od *tell*) *of* (*a th*); wir h **sagen** (munkeln) ~, er käme (vielleicht) *we've heard a sort of rumor he might be coming* **B.** ⟨übtr⟩ **1. (zuhören) a.** ⟨parl⟩ hört! hört! *hear*! *hear*!; ⟨Am⟩ *that's right*! **b.** ~ **Sie**! *look here*! *mind you*! ⟨Am sl⟩ *I'm telling you*; ~ Sie, Herr N. *come, Mr. N.* || hör mal! *look here*!, *here*! aber h. mal! *I say*! || ~ Sie mal! *I say*!, *Here*! ⟨Am⟩ *Say*! || aber ~ Sie mal! *well, I never*! *well, I must say*! **c.** [mst neg] er will **nicht** ~ *he refuses to take advice* (od *to listen to reason*) || °er hört (aber auch) gar nicht *he is very naughty* || ⟨prov⟩ wer nicht ~ will, muß fühlen *he who will not listen to reason must suffer* **2.** ~ **auf** (jdn, etw) *to listen to*; *to give ear* (od *to lend an ear*) *to* (*a p, a th*); hör auf d–e Mutter! *mind your m.*!; alles hört auf sein Kommando *everybody obeys his orders* || er (der Hund) hört auf den Namen Beppo *he answers to the name* (*of*) *B.* || ~ Sie nicht auf ihn! *don't pay any attention to him*! **b.** ⟨univ⟩ **bei** e–m Professor ~ *to hear a professor*; *to attend the lectures and classes of a pr.* **c.** ~ **von jdm,** v seiten jds (vgl. B. 3. b.) *to hear from a p* || laß mal v dir ~ *let me hear from you now and then*; er hat lange nicht(s) v **sich** ~ **l** *he has not written for a long time*; ich lasse v mir ~ *I'll let you know* **3. (erfahren) a.** ich höre aus Indien ab u zu *I hear from India now and then* **b.** ~ **v jdm, über jdn** (vgl. B. 2. c.) *to hear of* (od *about*) *a p* (*I have just heard of him*); was wir da v dir ~, gefällt uns gar nicht *we don't like the sound of this at all* || ~ v, über etw *to hear* od *learn of a th*; *to get wind of a th*; er will nichts davon ~ *he won't hear of* (⟨Am a.⟩ *to*) *it* **4. das läßt sich** ~ *that is quite plausible*; *there is something in that*; *that sounds well*; ⟨fam⟩ *that is something like*; ⟨Am⟩ *that listens to me, now you're talking* || (Witz) *that's a good un*! || das läßt sich eher ~ *that's more like it* **H·ören** n: beim ~ der Musik .. *when* od *while listening to the m. he fell asleep* || da verging ihm ~ u Sehen *he was stunned* od *flabbergasted* || °er raste .., daß e–m ~ u S. verging *he tore along the road that I received the* *surprise of my life*; ich werde es ihm geben, daß ihm ∼ u. S. vergeht *I'll make him see stars* | Rundfunk∼̈ *listening-in* **H·örensagen** n *hearsay* ‖ v ∼ *by hearsay*; dies beruht nur auf ∼ *this is mere hearsay* ‖ ⟨jur⟩ auf Grund v ∼ *hearsay* (*evidence*) **H·örer** m ∼s/∼ **1.** (P) **a.** *hearer*; *listener*; *auditor* **b.** ⟨univ⟩ *student* ‖ Gast∼̈ *non-matriculated student*; *auditor* **c.** ⟨wir⟩ Rundfunk∼̈ *listener-in listener*; Schwarz∼̈ *pirate-listener* **2.** ⟨telph⟩ (Hörmuschel) *receiver*; *ear-piece*; Kopf∼̈ *headphones*; *ear-phones* pl ‖ den ∼ abnehmen *to answer the telephone* ‖ den ∼ auflegen *or* anhängen *to ring off*; *to hang up* **∼gabel** f ⟨telph⟩ *rest* | **∼in** f ∼/∼nen = Hörer 1. **∼meinungsforschung** f *audience* od *listener research* **∼schaft** f *audience, auditory*; ⟨mst univ⟩ *hearers, students* pl **h·örig** a *dependent*; *subordinate*; *subject*; [pred] *in bondage* od *serfdom* ‖ ⟨oft cont⟩ *submissive*; *complaisant, obsequious* ‖ der dem Könige ∼e Minister *the m. submissive to the k.*; die e–m fremden Lande ∼e Presse *the press under the political influence of a foreign country* | ⟨sex⟩ *masochist*, ⟨fam⟩ *pussy-struck* **-hörig** [in comp] f·ein∼ *quick-eared*; schw·er∼ *hard of hearing*; → hell∼ **H·örige 1.** [der ∼, ein ∼r] m *attendant, dependent, retainer, subordinate, vassal* ‖ *bond(s)man, serf, thrall* ‖ ⟨übtr⟩ *slave* (*the slave of, a slave to a th*), *thrall* ‖ ⟨sex⟩ *masochist* **2.** (die) ∼ *bond(s)woman*; *slave* **H·örigkeit** f *dependence, subordination* ‖ ⟨hist & übtr⟩ *bondage*; *serfdom, servitude, slavery, thraldom* ‖ ⟨sex⟩ *masochism* ‖ in ∼ geraten *to get into thraldom*; in die ∼ jds, e–r S g. *to become dependent on a p*; *to become slave to a th*

Horiz·ont m **1.** *horizon* (künstlicher *artificial h.*; ⟨aero⟩ *gyro h.*; am ∼ *on the h.*); *skyline*; Depression des ∼s *dip of the h.* ‖ ⟨theat⟩ Rund∼̈ *stage h.*; *cyclorama* ‖ → Gesichtskreis **2.** ⟨fig⟩ geistiger ∼ *mental h.*; *outlook*; *scope* ‖ er hat e–n engen ∼ *he has a narrow mind*; e–n ∼ h wie ein Kompotteller *not to see beyond one's nose*; .. e–n weiten ∼ *he is a man of broad views* ‖ s–n ∼ erweitern *to widen one's mental h.* ‖ am politischen *on the political h.* ‖ das geht über m–n ∼ *that is above* (od *beyond*) *me*; ⟨Am sl⟩ *it gets me* **horizont·al 1.** [a] *horizontal* (*direction, line, position*); *level* (z *with*) ‖ ∼e Lage *horizontality*; *horizontal* (aus der ∼en L. *out of the h.*); → ∼̈-; ∼̈e **2.** [adv] *horizontally* **Horizont·al-** *horizontal* **∼bewegung** f *h. movement* **∼ebene** f *h. plane* **∼entfernung** f *ground range* **∼flug** m ⟨aero⟩ *h.* (od *level*) *flight* **∼pendel** n *tromometer* **∼reichweite** f = –entfernung **Horizont·ale** f *horizontal line*; *horizontal*

Horm·on n ∼s/∼e ⟨physiol⟩ *hormone*; *internal secretion* ‖ ∼drüsen [pl] *glands of internal secretion*; *ductless* (od *endocrine*) *glands*; *endocrine* pl ‖ ∼forschung [f] *endocrinology*

H·orn n ∼(e)s/∼̈er **A.** [pl ∼̈er] **1.** ⟨zoo⟩ **a.** (of cattle, etc.) *horn* ‖ ohne ∼̈er *h.less* ‖ → Ein∼̈ **b.** ⟨ent⟩ *feeler, antenna* L, *h.* **2.** ⟨übtr⟩ ∼̈er (of the devil) *h.s* pl **3. a.** (e–m Tier) die ∼̈er abnehmen *to h.* ‖ ∼̈er tragen *to have h.s*; ∼̈er tragend *h.ed* ‖ mit den ∼̈ern stoßen (of a bull) *to use the h.s* ‖ (jdn) mit den ∼̈ern aufspießen, durchbohren *to gore up*; *to gore with the h.s* **b.** ⟨fig⟩ sich die ∼̈er ablaufen, -stoßen *to sow one's wild oats* ‖ jdm ∼̈er aufsetzen *to cuckold* od *graft a p* ‖ die ∼̈er einziehen *to draw in one's h.s* ‖ jdm die ∼̈er zeigen *to show a p one's teeth*; *to offer stubborn resistance to a p* ‖ den Stier bei den ∼̈ern packen *to take the bull by the h.s* **B.** [ohne pl] (∼substanz) *horn*; *keratin* **C.** [pl] ∼̈er] (Gegenstand aus ∼ [→ B.]; *or* in Gestalt e–s ∼s [→ A.]) **1.** Trink∼̈ *drinking-h.* **2.** Pulver∼̈ *powder-h.* ‖ → Füll∼̈ **3. a.** Jagd∼̈ *hunting-h.*; *huntsman's h.* ‖ ⟨bes mil⟩ (Signal∼̈; Post∼̈) *bugle*(*-h.*); *h.*; → Krumm∼̈ **b.** ⟨mus⟩ (Ventil∼̈; Wald∼̈; Bügel∼̈) *French h.*; *saxh.*; → Tuba ‖ Englisch ∼ = Oboe ‖ kl ∼ *cornet*; → Kornett **c.** **das ∼ blasen, ins ∼ stoßen** *to blow* (od *wind*) *the h.*; *to give a blast on the h.* ‖ ⟨fig⟩ in dasselbe ∼ stoßen *to sing the same song*; in jds ∼ blasen *to echo a p*; sie bläst mit ihm in dasselbe ∼ *she is merely his echo, she always chimes in with him* **4.** ⟨el⟩ Nebel∼̈ *fog-h.* ‖ ⟨mot & aero⟩ Signal∼̈ *motor-h.*; (lautes) *klaxon*(*-h.*) **5.** (of the moon) *h.*; *crescent* ‖ (of the anvil) *h.* **6.** = ∼schwiele **D.** [in comp] → Horn-; Hörner- *h.*(*ed*); *h.y*; *corneous*; *kerato-*, *cerato-* **∼arbeit** f *h.work* **∼̈artig** a *h.-like, h.y* **∼baum** m ⟨bot⟩ *h.beam* **∼berger** a °wie das ∼ Schießen ausgehen *to misfire, to come to nothing*; *to go up like smoke* **∼bläser** m *h.-player*; *h.er* **∼blatt** n ⟨bot⟩ *h.wort*; *ceratophylium* L **∼blende** f ⟨minr⟩ **1.** *h.-blende*; → Amphibol **2.** [in comp] *h.b.*; ∼asbest [m] *h.b. asbestos*; ∼fels [m] *amphibolite*; ∼schiefer [m] *h.b. schist* **∼brille** f *h. spectacles* (e–e ∼ *a pair of h.-s.*); *h.-rims* pl; *h.-rimmed glasses* pl **∼drechsler** m *h.-turner* **∼erz** n ⟨minr⟩ *h. silver*; *s. chloride* = –silber **∼eule** f ⟨orn⟩ *h.*(*ed*) *owl* **∼farbe** f *h. colour* **∼fasan** m ⟨orn⟩ *tragopan* **∼fels** m ⟨geol⟩ *h.fels* [Ger]; *cornubianite* **∼fessel** f **a.** ⟨hist⟩ *bandoleer*; *cord for the hunting-h.* **b.** *ornamental cord* **∼fisch** m ⟨ich⟩ *file* (od *trigger*)*-fish*; Gattung der ∼e [pl] *Balistidae* [L pl] **∼̈förmig** a *h.-shaped*; *h.-like* **∼frosch** m ⟨zoo⟩ *h.-frog* **∼griff** m *h. handle* **∼haut** f **1.** (of the epidermis) **a.** *h.y layer*; *corn* **b.** [in comp] *h.y*; *callous* **2. a.** (of the eye) *cornea* L **b.** [in comp] *corneal*; *kerato-* ‖ ∼entzündung [f] *keratitis* [L] ‖ ∼kegel [m] *keratokonus* L ‖ ∼transplantation [f] *corneal graft* (*operation*) **∼̈häutig** a = Hornhaut 1. b. **∼hecht** m ⟨ich⟩ *h.beak* **∼kirsche** f ⟨bot⟩ = –strauch **∼klee** m ⟨bot⟩ *bird's foot trefoil*; *Lotus* L **∼kluft** f ⟨vet⟩ *transverse fissure in the hoof* **∼knopf** m *h. button* **∼koralle** f ⟨zoo⟩ *h.y coral* **∼kraut** n ⟨bot⟩ *mouse-ear*; *cerastium* L **∼krebs** m ⟨path⟩ *h.y cancroid* **∼löffel** m *h. spoon* **∼macher** m *h.-maker*; *h.er* **∼mehl** n = –späne **∼mohn** m ⟨bot⟩ *h.-poppy*; *Glaucium* L ‖ °**∼ochse** m ⟨fig⟩ (P) (*old*) *ass*; *blockhead*; *mutton-head*, ⟨sl⟩ *moke*; ⟨Am sl⟩ *mutt* **∼pfeife** f *h.pipe* **∼rabe** m ⟨orn⟩ *rhinoceros h.bill*; → –vogel **∼ring** m *h. ring* **∼schicht** f *h.y layer* **∼schlange** f ⟨zoo⟩ = –viper **∼schnabel** m ⟨orn⟩ *beak* **∼schwiele** f *corn* **∼signal** n ⟨mil⟩ *bugle-call* **∼silber** n ⟨minr⟩ *h. silver*; *silver chloride*; = –erz **∼spalte** ⟨vet⟩ *longitudinal fissure in the hoof*; → –kluft **∼späne** m pl *h. shavings* pl **∼stein** m ⟨minr⟩ *h.stone* **∼stoff** m *h.*; *keratin* **∼strahl** m ⟨vet⟩ *bar* (*of the hoof*) **∼strauch** m ⟨bot⟩ *cornel*; *dogwood*; *Cornus* L **∼substanz** f *h.y substance* **∼tier** n *h.ed animal*; Gattung der ∼e *Bovidae, Cavicornia* L pl **∼vieh** n **1.** *h.ed cattle* **2.** °⟨fig⟩ (P) = –ochse **∼viper** f ⟨zoo⟩ *h.ed viper*; *cerastes cornutus* L **∼vogel** m ⟨orn⟩ *hornbill*; Gattung der ∼̈ *Bucerotidae* L pl **∼wand** f ⟨vet⟩ *crust* od *wall* (*of the hoof*) **∼waren** f [pl] *h. ware*; *h. goods* pl **∼werk** n ⟨hist fort⟩ *h.work* **H·örnchen** n **1.** *small h.* ‖ ⟨zoo⟩ *cornicle*; *antenna* **2.** (Gebäck) *crescent roll* od *bun*; ⟨Am⟩ *crescent* **3.** (f Suppe) *elbow macaroni* **h·örnen** a *horn*; (*made*) *of h.*; *h.y* ‖ ⟨Ger Lit⟩ ∼̈ Siegfried *or* Hürnen Seyfried *H.y S.* **h·örnen** vt/i [h] **1.** vt (mit Hörnern versehen) *to h.* ‖ ⟨sex⟩ *to graft* **2.** vi (of stag) *to shed its antlers*

H·örner- **∼klang, ∼schall** m *sound of bugles* (od *h.s*); *bugle-sound* **∼schlitten** m *sledge* od *sleigh with long h.-shaped runners* **∼träger** m ⟨zoo⟩ *h.ed animal* **h·örnern** a = hörnen ***h·ornicht** a = **h·ornig** a *corneous, h.y*; *callous*; *ceratose* ‖ ∼e Beschaffenheit *h.iness* **-hörnig** [in comp] *-h.ed*; ein∼ *one-h.ed*; zwei∼ *two-h.ed*

Horn·isse f ∼/∼n ⟨ent⟩ *hornet* **∼nnest** n *h.s' nest* **∼nschwärmer** m ⟨ent⟩ *h.-moth* **∼stich** m *h.-sting*

Horn·ist m ∼en/∼en ⟨mil⟩ *bugler*; Bataillons∼̈ *drum-major* ‖ ⟨mus⟩ *hornist, horn-player*

***H·ornung** m ∼s/ = Februar *February*

Horosk·op n ~(e)s/~e ⟨astrol⟩ *horoscope*; *nativity* (errichten *to cast*, deuten *to read*); jdm das ~ stellen *to cast a p's h.* od *n.*

°**horr·end** **1.** [a] *dreadful* (*pain*); *horrible*; *stupendous* (*mistake*); *terrible* (*heat*); ⟨fam⟩ *awful* (*nonsense*) ‖ *enormous* (*expenses*), *exorbitant* (*prices*); *extravagant, immoderate* **2.** [adv] *dreadfully*; *terribly*; *enormously*; ⟨fam⟩ *awfully*

Horrid·o n ⟨hunt⟩ *halloo, soho*; → Joho

°**H·orror** m L ~s/ *horror*; e–n ~ h vor etw *to have a h. of a th*; *to loathe a th* ‖ → Abscheu

H·örselberg m ⟨Ger⟩ (bei Eisenach) *Mountain of Venus*

Horst m ~es/~e **1. a.** (of eagles, etc.) *eyrie*; *aerie* **b.** ⟨fig aero⟩ (Flieger~̂) *aerodrome, air-port* | ~kommandantur [f] *station headquarters* **2.** *hurst*; *copse*; = Gebüsch **3.** ⟨geol⟩ *horst* [Ger] **h·orsten** vi [h] *to nest*

H·ort m ~(e)s/~e **1.** (Schatz) **a.** ⟨poet⟩ *hoard*; Nibelungen~̂ *h. of the N.ngs* **b.** ⟨mod⟩ *accumulation* (*of gold*) **2.** (Schutz) **a.** [abstr] *protection, safeguard*; *refuge, shelter*; ein starker ~ *a tower of strength*; *bulwark* (*of civilization*); *stronghold* (*of protestantism*) **b.** [konkr] (Ort) *refuge, shelter* ‖ sicherer ~ *a safe retreat* | (Heim) *asylum*; *home* (*for children*); Kinder~̂ *day-nursery* | (P) *protector, supporter* **~geld** n *h.ed money* **h·orten** vt [h] (Geld; ⟨mod⟩ Gold) *to hoard, accumulate* ‖ ⟨com⟩ *to stockpile*

Hort·ensie [iə] f ⟨bot⟩ *hydrangea*; *Hortensia*

H·ortnerin f ~/~nen *directress of a d.-n.* → o.

Hortol·og m *horticulturist* **~·ie** f *horticulture*

H·ortung f *hoarding, accumulation* (*of money*)

H·ös|chen n **1.** *small breeches* pl ‖ (f Mädchen) *drawers knickers, panties* pl ‖ ein ~ *a pair of small b.s, d.s* **2.** ⟨übtr⟩ (of bees) *wax covering on the hind legs* **H·ose** f ~/~n **A.** ⟨eig⟩ **1.** **(f Männer)** **a.** *trousers* pl; ⟨Am a.⟩ *pants*; ⟨fam⟩ *bags, breeches* **b.** **(eng anliegend)** *tights* pl; ⟨Scot⟩ *trews* pl ⟨a. mil⟩ | lange weiße ~ (aus Segeltuch) *white ducks*; (Arbeits~̂) *slacks* pl ⟨a. mil⟩; (in Glockenform) *bell-bottoms* pl | ⟨mil⟩ Gala~̂ *full-dress trousers* **c.** (kz, Knie~̂) (*knee-*)*breeches* pl; *shorts* pl; Buckskin~̂ *buckskins* pl ‖ weite Knie~̂ *knicker*(*bocker*)*s* pl; (ganz kz) *shorts*; (aus Leder) *chaparejos, -rajos* [Span], ⟨fam⟩ *chaps* pl ‖ Reit~̂ *riding-b.s*; *leathers* pl ‖ Golf~̂ *plus-fours* pl ‖ **d.** dunkle ~ *dark*(*-coloured*) *trousers*; helle ~ *light-coloured t.*; → gestreift **2.** **(f Damen)** **a.** (Schlupf~̂) *drawers, pantalet*(*te*)*s*; ⟨fam⟩ *knickers* pl **b.** ⟨hist⟩ lange weiße ~ *trousers* **3.** → Bade~̂ etc **4.** **Wendungen** **a.** e–e ~ (*ein Paar ~n) *a pair of trousers* (etc); drei ~n *three pair of t.* **b.** ⟨fig⟩ das ist ~ **wir Jacke** *that is much of a muchness*; *it's as long as it is broad*; *it's six of one and half-a-dozen of the other*; es war f sie ~ wie J. *to them it was all tweedledum and tweedledee* | °⟨fig⟩ die Frau hat die ~n an ⟨prov⟩ *the grey mare is the better horse*; sie hat die ~n an *she wears the breeches* ‖ sich e–e ~ **anmessen l** *to be measured for a pair of trousers* ‖ °jdm die ~n ausziehen ⟨fam⟩ *to make a p pay through his nose* ‖ .. bauschen sich *bag* (*at the knee*) ‖ er hat gestern die ersten ~n bek *he was put into* (*long*) *t.s yesterday* ‖ die ~ durchsitzen *to wear out the seat of one's t.s* ‖ die ~ bis an die Knie hoch-, umkrempeln *to roll one's t.s to one's knees*; sich [dat] die ~ hochziehen *to hitch one's t.s up* ‖ °e–m die ~n stramm ziehen *to dust a p's coat for him*; jdm die ~ herunterziehen *to unbreech* ‖ °⟨fig⟩ er hat die ~n **voll** *he is in a blue funk*; *he has the jitters* **c.** °⟨fig⟩ sich **auf** die ~n setzen *to work hard* ‖ ⟨fig⟩ das Herz fiel ihm **in die ~(n)** *his heart sank* (*within him*); *his h. was in his boots* ‖ °⟨fig⟩ vor Angst in die ~n m *to have got the scatters*, ⟨mil⟩ *to shit blue lights, to shit bricks* **B.** ⟨übtr⟩ (of horses) *the lower thigh* ‖ ⟨orn⟩ *thick feathers on the legs* ‖ → Wasser~̂; Wind~̂ **H·osen-** *breeches-*; *trouser-* [doch → ~tasche] **~anzug** m *tr. suit* **~aufschlag** m → –umschlag **~band** n *tr.-band* ‖ ⟨hist⟩ (Strumpf-) *garter* | ~orden [m] (*Order of the*) *Garter* (höchster engl. Orden, gegr. 1350) **~bein** n *tr.-leg*; mein eines ~ *the leg of my tr.* | ~schoner [m] *protective facing* od *edging* **~biese** f *piping* **~boden** m *seat of the tr.s* **~boje** f ⟨mar⟩ *br.es-buoy* **~bügelfalter** m = –strecker **~bund** m *waist-band* **~gurt** m = –bund **~klammern** f pl ⟨cycl⟩ *tr.-clips* pl **~klappe** f *fly*; ⟨hist⟩ *braguette* Fr **~knopf** m *tr.-button* **~latz** m = –klappe °**~matz** m *new-br.ed boy* **~rock** m *divided* od *tr. skirt* **~rohr** n ⟨tech⟩ *br.es-pipe* **~rolle** f ⟨theat⟩ *br.es-part* **~schlitz** m *slit of the tr.s* °**~stall** m; dein ~ ist offen *your shop-door is open* **~steg** m *tr.-strap* **~stoff** m *tr.ing* **~strecker** m *tr.-press* (od *stretcher*) **~tasche** f *br.es-pocket*; *tr.*(*s*)*-pocket* **~träger** m ~s/~ *braces*, ⟨Am⟩ *suspenders* pl; ein ~, ein Paar ~ *a pair of braces*, etc. **~tuch**, **~umschlag** m (⟨a.⟩ –auf–) *turn-up, upturn* **~zeug** n = –stoff ‖ ×°**~türl** n → ~stall

Hosi·anna n ⟨bib⟩ *hosanna* (rufen *to shout*)

Hospit·al n ~(e)s/~e u ~̂er *hospital*; ~bruder = **~·iter** m ~s/–ten (*knight*) *hospital*(*l*)*er*; die –ten *the brotherhood of h.s* **~·iterin** f (a. **~schwester**) die ~nen [pl] *the sisterhood of h.s* **~schiff** n *hospital-ship* **Hospit·ant** m ~en/~en ⟨univ⟩ *auditor*; ~ bei .. *attendant on the lectures* (od *classes, exercices*) *of* ‖ ⟨school⟩ *candidate under the instruction of a senior master* **hospit·ieren** vi [h] ⟨univ⟩ ~ bei .. *to attend the lectures* od *exercises of*; ⟨school⟩ (of a candidate) *to attend the classes for methodical instruction* **Hosp·iz** n ~es/~e **1.** *hospice* ‖ *asylum*; *home* **2.** *boarding* (od *lodging*)*-house*; Christliches ~ *Christian Private Hotel* ‖ ⟨univ⟩ *hostel*

H·ostie [–iə] f ~/~n ⟨R. C.⟩ *host*; *consecrated bread* (od *wafer*) **~nteller** m *paten*, ⟨Am⟩ *patene*

Hot·el n ~s/~s **1.** *hotel*; Schloß~̂ *Castle Hotel*; Strand~̂ *Beach H.*; ~ Wien *Vienna H.* [mit Eigennamen oft ausgelassen]: *the Ritz, the Savoy* ‖ *Court, Hall*, etc. (*Lincoln Hall Hotel*) ‖ ⟨Am⟩ *hotel, house* (Adler~̂ *the Eagle House*) ‖ → Gasthof; Hospiz; Hof | ein ~ *a* od *an hotel* ‖ die ~s am Orte *the local h.s* **2.** (~pension) *residential h.*; *private h.*; (ohne Alkoholkonzession) *temperance h.* **3.** ~ garni Fr *lodging house, h. garni* Fr **~besitzer** m *h.-keeper*; *h.ier* Fr **~dieb** m ⟨fam⟩ *snoozer*, ⟨Am⟩ *prowler* **~diener** m ⟨fam⟩ *boots* pl [sg konstr] **~fach** n *h. trade* **~fremdenbuch** n *h.-register* **~gast** m *h.-guest* **~gewerbe** n *h. industry* od *business* **~leitung** f *h. management* **~page** [–pɑ:ʒə] m *bell-boy*; ⟨Am fam⟩ *bell-hop* **~portier** m *porter* **~wagen** m ⟨fam⟩ *h.-bus* **~wesen** n *h.s in general*

Hotelier [hɔtel'je:] m Fr *hotel-keeper*; *hotelier*

°**hott**! intj *gee*! *gee-ho*! *gee-up*! → hü

H·otte f ~/~n (Wein~̂) = Kiepe

hottehü **1.** intj = hott **2.** ~̂ n (Kinderspr. = Pferdchen) *gee*(*-gee*) ⟨a.⟩ **H·otto, H·ottopferd** n

H·ottentott(e) m –totten/–totten *Hottentot*

H·ottentotten- [in comp] *Hottentot* **~brot** n *H. bread* **~sprache** f *language of the Hottentots*

hottent·ottisch a *Hottentot*(*ic*)

h·overn vi [s] ⟨mar⟩ *to hover*

hu! intj *ugh*! *whew*! ⟨Am⟩ *gee*! ‖ °**hü** = hot

H·ub m ~(e)s/~̂e **1.** ⟨abstr⟩ *heave*; *lift* ‖ ⟨tech⟩ *stroke* (*of a piston*); *throw* (*of a crank*) **2.** (~höhe) (*height of*) *lift*; *lifting height* (*of a crane*) ‖ (~länge) *length of stroke* ‖ (~strecke) *stroke* od *travel* (*of a piston*) | [in comp] ⟨tech⟩ *hoisting* (*chain, rope*); *lifting* (*bridge, pump*); *lifting gear* (*piston*) **~höhe** → Hub 2. **~inhalt** m ⟨mot⟩ *cubic capacity* **~kraft** f *lifting capacity* (od *force*); *buoyancy* **~motor** m *hoist motor* **~pumpe** f *lift-pump* **~raum** m *piston displacement, swept volume* **~schrauber** m ⟨aero⟩ *helicopter*, ~ im Nahverkehr *helibus* | ~landestelle [f] *helistop*; *heliport* **~spiegel** m ⟨phot⟩ *flap mirror* **~stapler** m ⟨agr⟩ *fork-lift* **~ventil** n *lift-*

-valve **~volumen** n ⟨mot⟩ *cylinder capacity; piston displacement* **~wagen** m *lift truck* **~zähler** m *stroke counter*

h·üben adv *on this side*; ~ u drüben *on this s. and on the other s.; on either s.*

ˣ**H·uber** m = Hüfner (Besitzer e–r Hufe)

Hubertus- (nach St. Hubertus, † 727) **~kraut** n ⟨bot⟩ *yellow rocket; wintercress* **~orden** m *Order of St. Hubert* (bayr. Orden)

hübsch A. [a] **1. a.** † *or* ˣ (hofmäßig; feingesittet) *nice*; ˣ~e Leute *nice* (od *kind*) *people* **b.** [pred] *fair, kind, nice*; es war (nicht) ~ v dir *it was* (*not*) *nice of you* **2.** (~ aussehend; anmutig) **a.** (P) *comely, good* (od *nice*)*-looking; handsome* (*girl*); *nice; pretty* (*child*); ⟨Scot⟩ *bonny, -nie* ‖ ⟨Am fam⟩ *crummy, cunning*; ~e Frau, ~es Mädchen *looker*; ~er Mensch *good-looker* ‖ e–e ~e Blondine *a beautiful fair girl* **b.** (S) *fine* (*head*); *handsome* (*dress*); *neat* (*building*); *picturesque* (*scene*); *pretty* (*house; voice*) | *pleasant* (*weather*) ‖ °e–e ~e Summe, ein ~es Stück Geld ⟨fam⟩ *a tidy sum, a pretty pot of money, a pretty penny*; ein ~es Vermögen *a handsome* (od *nice, tidy*) *fortune* ‖ (der Ort liegt) e–e ~e Strecke v hier (..) *a good distance from here* ‖ ganz ~ *decent* (*house*) **c.** ⟨iron⟩ *nice, pretty*; das ist ja e–e ~e Geschichte *that's a pretty kettle of fish* (od *a pretty mess*) **d. sich ~ m** *to dress up*; *to smarten o.s.* **B.** [adv] **1. a.** *nicely*; °bitte ~ um Verzeihung *apologize nicely* ‖ ~ gewachsen *well-set* ‖ °sei ~ artig *behave yourself*; °sitz ~ ruhig *don't fidget* ‖ ~ m (of a dog) *to beg* **b.** (verblaßt) bleib ~ gesund *take care of yourself* od *of your health* ‖ nur immer ~ langsam *take your time, please* ‖ °das will ich ~ bleiben l! *catch me* (*doing that*)! *Not I*! ‖ ~ warm *lovely* od *nice and warm* ‖ es tut ganz ~ weh *it hurts quite a bit* **2.** *nicely, prettily*; ~ geputzt *prettily dressed up*

huch intj = hu

H·uch m ~s/~e, **H·uchen** m ~s/~ (Donaulachs) *huchen* [Ger]

H·ucke f (→ Hocke) **1.** *heap; stack* **2.** *bundle, pack* **3.** °⟨fig⟩ *back*; jdm die ~ vollhauen *to give a p a baker's dozen* od *a sound licking*; sich die ~ vollachen *to sit gloating by o.s.*; jdm die ~ volllügen *to tell a p a pack of lies* °**~bein** m ⟨Ger⟩ Hans ~ *limping* od *lame Jack*

h·ucken vi/t [h] **1.** vi = hocken **2.** vt (jdn) *to carry on one's back*

°**h·uckepack** adv (*to carry, ride*) *pick-a-back* | ≗beförderung [f], ≗dienst [m] ⟨rail-mot⟩ *car baggage service*; ⟨fam⟩ *piggy-back* ‖ ≗flugzeug [n] *p.-a-b. plane* ‖ *piggy-back* (*riding*) ‖ ≗verkehr [m] ⟨rail-mot⟩ = –dienst

ˣ**H·udel** m *mop; rag* **Hudel·ei** f *bungle; bungling work* ‖ *slatternliness; slipshod work* | = Schererei

H·ud(e)ler m *botcher, bungler, dabbler*; ⟨fam⟩ *muff* **h·udeln** vi/t [h] **1.** vi *to be slipshod* od *slovenly* ‖ *to work carelessly* **2.** vt **a.** (etw) *to bungle; to do* (*a th*) *badly; to huddle* (od *slur*) *over* (*a th*) **b.** (jdn) *to annoy, vex*

ˣ**h·udern** vt (of a hen) (Küken) *to brood* | **sich ~** *to wallow in the sand*

H·udsonbai [ˈhʌdsn–] f ⟨geogr⟩ *Hudson Bay* **Huds·onien** *area to the West of H. B.*

H·uf m ~(e)s/~e ⟨vet⟩ *hoof* ⟨a. vulg fig = Fuß⟩ [pl *hoofs*, **hooves*]; Spalt≗ *cloven hoof* ‖ (of horse) (jdn) mit dem ~ schlagen *to* (*strike with the*) *hoof* **~bein** n ⟨vet anat⟩ *coffin-bone; phalanx tertia* L **~beschlag** m [abstr] *farriery; shoeing* ‖ [konkr] *shoes* pl **~blatt** n ⟨bot⟩ → –lattich **~eisen** n **1.** (*horse*)*shoe* ‖ e–m Pferd die ~ abnehmen *to unshoe a horse*; sich [dat] in die ~ hauen *to interfere*; ein ~ verlieren (of horse) *to cast a shoe* **2.** [in comp] ~ausschnitt [m] ⟨tail⟩ *horseshoe neckline* ~form [f] *h. shape*; in ~ *in the form of a h.*; ≗förmig [a] *h.-shaped* od *-like* ‖ ~kurve [f] *h. bend h.* ‖ ~magnet [m] *h.-magnet*; ~niere [f] *h.-kidney*; ~tisch [m] *h. table* **~gelenklahmheit** f *lameness caused by an inflammation of the frog; podotrochilitis* L **~geschwür** n *hoof-abscess* **~hammer** m *shoeing-hammer* **~kratzer** m *hoof-pick* **~krebs** m ⟨vet path⟩ *canker; pododermatitis* L **~lattich** m ⟨bot⟩ **1.** *coltsfoot, foolfoot* **2.** gr ~ *butter-bur*; → Pestwurz **~messer** n *hoof-paring knife* **~nagel** m *horseshoe-nail* **~polster** n *hoof-pad* **~rehe** f = Rehe **~schlag** m **1.** *hoof-beat; horse's kick* **2.** (Spur im Boden) *beaten track* **~schmied** *farrier*; ⟨Am⟩ *horseshoer* **~schmiede** f *shoeing forge* | ~handwerk [n] *farriery* **~spalte** f = Hornspalte **~spat** m *bone spavin* **~tier** n *hoofed* od *ungulate animal; ungulate*; fossiles ~ *dinoceras* ‖ Gattung der **~e** *Ungulata* L pl **~tritt** m = –schlag 1.

H·ufe f ~/~n ⟨hist agr⟩ (*60–100 acres*) *hide*

-hufer m ⟨zoo⟩ → Ein~, Unpaar~ *soliped, solidungulate*; Zwei~, Paar~ *artiodactyl*(*e*)

-hufig a *hoofed*; breit~ *broad-hoofed*; ein~ *soliped, solidungulate*; zwei~es Tier *artiodactyl*(*e*)

H·ufner, H·üf- m ~s/~ ⟨agr⟩ *possessor of a hide of land; farmer*

H·üft- (→ Hüfte) *hip-; coxal* **~bein** n *hip-bone; ilium* L **~bild** n *hip-length portrait* **~gehänge** n → Beintasche **~gelenk** n *hip-joint* | ~entzündung [f] *coxitis*; ~verrenkung [f] *dislocation of the h.-j.* **~halter** m *girdle* **~horn** n = Hifthorn **~krankheit** f, **~leiden** *hip-disease* ≗**lahm** a *lame in the hip; hipshot* **~nerv** m *sciatic nerve* **~pfanne** f *socket of the hip-bone* **~polster** n *dress-improver; bustle* **~schmerz** m *hip-pain; sciatic pain; coxalgia* L **~stück** n ⟨cul⟩ *haunch* **~weh** n *hip-gout; sciatica* L

H·üfte f ~/~n ⟨anat⟩ *hip; haunch; coxa* L ‖ ⟨zoo⟩ *haunch* ‖ bis an die ~n reichend *hip-deep; up to the hips* | ~nhoch [a] *waist-high*; ~nstück [n] ⟨cul⟩ *rump*

H·ügel m ~s/~ *hill, mound*; steiler ~ ⟨Am⟩ *butte* ‖ spitzer felsiger ~ *tor* ‖ Kreidekalk≗ [pl] *Downs* pl | kl ~ *hillock, hump*; ⟨SAfr⟩ *kopje*; kl runder ~ *mamelon* ‖ niedriger ~ *knoll* ‖ kl Erd≗ *hummock*; Grab≗ *mound* ‖ Stein≗ *cairn* ‖ ⟨fort⟩ Befestigungs≗ *rideau* Fr | Spitze des ~s *hill-top*; die Sp. des ~s erreichen *to top the hill* ‖ mit e–m ~ umgeben *to hill* **~abhang** m *hill-slope* (od *-side*); steiler ~ *brow* **~festung** f *hill-fort*(*ress*) **~grab** n ⟨hist⟩ *cairn*; ⟨praeh⟩ *tumulus* L [pl *-li*] **~kette** f *chain of hills* **~land** n *hill-country; hilly* (od *rolling, elevated*) *country; wold* **~landschaft** f *hilly landscape* ***hüg(e)licht, hüg(e)lig** a *hilly; billowy, undulating*; ~e Beschaffenheit *hilliness*

Hugen·otte m ~n/~n ⟨hist⟩ *Huguenot*

h·uh intj = hu **h·üh** intj = hü

H·uhn n ~(e)s/≗er ⟨orn⟩ **1. a.** Haus≗ (~ u Hahn) (*domestic* od *barndoor*) *fowl*; ⟨Am a.⟩ *chicken* ‖ (weibliches ~) *hen*(*-bird*); junges ~ *chicken* ‖ → gackern; glucken **b.** ⟨hunt⟩ Feld≗, Flug≗ (*game*) *bird*; → Birk≗ etc **c.** ⟨cul⟩ → Geflügel ‖ Fleisch v ~ *fowl* **d.** Auslauf f ≗er *fowl-run*; ⟨Am⟩ *chicken-yard* ‖ ≗er halten *to keep fowls* ‖ mit den ≗ern aufstehen *to rise with the lark*; .. z Bett gehen *to go to bed with the sun* ‖ °da lachen ja die ≗er! *it's enough to make a cat laugh*! **2.** ⟨fig⟩ (P) krankes (*or* lahmes) ~ *lame duck* ‖ °ein unsolides ~ *a loose fish*; °ein verrücktes ~ *a crazy bird; a queer fish* ‖ wie ein ~, das ein Ei legen will *like having kittens* ‖ ein blindes ~ findet auch mal ein Korn *every dog has his day* **3.** ≗er(vögel) **H·ühnchen** n *pullet; chicken* ‖ (noch) ein ~ mit jdm zu rupfen h *to have a bone to pick with a p; to have a rod in pickle for a p* **H·ühner-** (→ Huhn) ≗**artig** a *gallinacean, gallinaceous* **~auge** n (am Fuß) **1.** *corn* ‖ °jdm die ~n schneiden *to cut a p's corns* ‖ ⟨mst fig⟩ °jdm auf die ~n treten *to tread* (od *step*) *on a p's corns* (od *toes*) **2.** [in comp] **~n-** *corn-*; ~operateur [m] *chiropodist; corn-cutter*; ~pflaster [n] *corn-plaster* **~auslauf** m → Huhn 1. d. **~bein** n ⟨cul⟩ *drumstick* **~biß** m ⟨bot⟩ *chickweed* **~blindheit** f = Nachtblindheit **~brust** f

⟨fig⟩ *pigeon-breast*; mit e–r ~ *pigeon* (od *chicken*)-*breasted* | ~cholera [f] ⟨vet⟩ *chicken-cholera* **~darm** m ⟨bot⟩ *chickweed* **~dieb** m *poultry-stealer* **~ei** n *hen's egg* **~falk** m = Habicht **~farm** f *poultry-farm, hen-run* **~feder** f *feather of a hen* **~frikassee** n ⟨cul⟩ *fricassee of fowl* **~futter** n *food for poultry* **~grind** m ⟨vet⟩ *comb-disease*; *favus* L **~haltung** f *the keeping of fowls* **~händler** m *poulterer* **~haus** n *hen-house* (od *roost*) **~hof** m *poultry-yard* **~hund** m *pointer*; *setter*; *spaniel*; ⟨Am⟩ *bird--dog* **~korb** m *hen-coop* **~krankheiten** f pl = Geflügel- **~leiter** f *hen-roost* ‖ °⟨fig⟩ das Leben ist e–e ~ *life is full of besetting troubles* **~markt** m *poultry-market* **~milbe** f ⟨ent⟩ *itch-mite* **~myrthe** f ⟨bot⟩ *chickweed* **~pastete** f *chicken-pie* **~pest** f ⟨vet⟩ *chicken-pest* **~schwarm** m ⟨bot⟩ *bog pimpernel* **~stall** m = –haus **~stange, ~steige** f, **~steg** m = –leiter **~suppe** f *chicken-broth*; (mit Lauch) *cocky-leekie* **~tod** m ⟨bot⟩ *henbane*; *Hyoscyamus* L **~vieh** n *poultry* **~vögel** m pl *gallinaceous* (*game-*) *-birds* pl; → *partridge, ptarmigan,* (*sand*)*grouse* **~zucht** f *poultry-farming*; *breeding and rearing of chickens*

°**hu-h·upp**! intj ⟨mar⟩ *heave-ho*! *heave ahoy*!

°**h·ui 1.** [intj] **a.** ~! *ho*! *huzza* **b.** *whew*!; *quick*! *like a shot*! **2.** [a pred] oben ~, unten pfui *beau--nasty*; (*to be*) *starched and ironed before one is washed* **3.** ≗ [m]; in e–m ~! *in a trice* od *jiffy*!

H·uka f ~/~s (orient. Wasserpfeife) *hooka*(*h*)

H·uker m ~s/~ ⟨mar⟩ *hooker*

H·uld f ~/ *grace*; *divine clemency*; Gottes (*or* des Himmels) ~ *the grace of God* ‖ *favour, goodwill, grace*; *graciousness* (*of the king*); *kindness* ‖ in jds ~ stehen *to be* (od *stand*) *in a p's favour* (od *good graces*) **~göttin** f ~/~nen ⟨ant⟩ die drei ~nen *the three Graces* pl **h·uldigen** vi [h] **1.** (jdm) **a.** ⟨bes hist & übtr⟩ *to pay* (od *do, render*) *homage to* (*the liege lord*; *sovereign*); *to do* (od *make, pay*) *obeisance to* (*a p*) ‖ ⟨hist⟩ sich v jdm ~ l *to receive a p's oath* (od *declaration*) *of allegiance* **b.** e–r Dame ~ *to pay one's addresses* (od *attentions,* od *one's court*) *to a lady*; *to court a l.* **2.** ⟨übtr⟩ (e–r S ~) **a.** *to adopt*; *embrace, espouse* (*a cause*); *subscribe to* (*a doctrine*); (e–r Mode) *follow*; e–r Ansicht ~ *to embrace* (od *entertain, hold*) *an opinion*; *to be wedded to an opinion*; der A. ~, daß .. *to claim that* .. ‖ *to be an advocate of* (*reform*); *to advocate* (*progress*) ‖ *to be an adherent of* (*a theory*); der Nützlichkeit ~d *utilitarian* **b.** *to addict o.s. to, to be addicted to* (*drink*; *wine*); *to indulge in* (*gambling*); dem Rauschgift ~der *drug addict* **H·uldigung** f ~/~en **a.** ⟨bes hist⟩ *homage* (*of Princes*), *obeisance* **b.** ⟨jur⟩ *oath of allegiance* **c.** ⟨übtr⟩ *expression of adoration* (od *love, affection*); *ovation*; *enthusiastic reception*; *spontaneous applause* ‖ jdm e–e ~ darbringen *to pay* (*do, render*) *homage to a p*; .. zuteil w l *to give a p an ovation* **d.** (f e–e Dame) *courting*; e–r D. s–e ~ m = e–r D. huldigen **~sakt** m *solemn act of h.* **~seid** m *oath of all.* **~s-feier** f = –akt **H·uldin** f ⟨myth⟩ *graceful woman* ‖ *goddess* **h·uldreich, huldvoll 1.** [a] *gracious, merciful*; *benevolent, kind* **2.** [adv] *graciously*; *kindly*

H·ülfe f = Hilfe **h·ülflos** a = hilflos

Hulk f ~/~e(n) & m ~(e)s/~e(n) ⟨mar⟩ *hulk*; ~ mit Scherenkran *sheer-hulk* ‖ = Holk

H·üll- [in comp] (→ hüllen) ~blatt [n] ⟨bot⟩ *spathe*; ~kelch [m] ⟨bot⟩ *calyx*; ~wort [n] *euphemism* **H·ülle** f ~/~n **1.** (of the body) **a.** *cover*(*ing*); *integument* ‖ ⟨a-n⟩ *skin*; (*outer*) *shell* ‖ ~n [pl] ⟨pap-com⟩ *shells* ‖ ⟨zoo⟩ *shell* **b.** ⟨fig⟩ die belastende ~ *the encumbering husk* ‖ die irdische (*or sterbliche*) ~ *the mortal remains* pl ‖ ⟨prov⟩ im Jenseits fallen alle ~n *beyond the grave the mask falls* ‖ °die ~ u Hülle (*or*: in ~ u F.) *in abundance, in profusion, in plenty*; *abundantly*; *enough and to spare*; ⟨Am⟩ *with* (*fortune*) *aplenty* ‖ °hier ist Arbeit die ~ u F. *here is plenty of work*; (etw) in ~ u F. h *to have heaps* (*of time*); *to have* (*money*) *to burn*; *to roll in* (*money*) **2.** ⟨übtr⟩ **a.** ⟨bot⟩ (Hochblätter) *involucre, -crum* L ‖ (Samen≗) *capsule*; *hull*; *husk*; → Hülse **b.** *case* (*of a shell, an umbrella*); *protective* (od *outer*) *cover*(*ing*) (*of a statue*); *envelope, envelopment*; *sheath*; *wrapper* (*of leather*); *wrapping* ‖ Papier≗ *jacket* (*of a book*) ‖ Finger≗ ⟨med⟩ *stall* ‖ ⟨aero⟩ (*balloon-*) *-envelope* ‖ die ~ fiel *the covering fell* **c.** ⟨fig⟩ *veil* (*of mist*; *of a mystery*) ‖ äußere ~ *shell* **h·üllen** vt [h] **1. a.** ⟨eig & übtr⟩ (etw, jdn) ~ in *to envelop* (od *fold, wrap*) *in* ..; *to wrap up in* ..; dicht ~ in *to smother in* ..; er hüllte sie in s–n Mantel, er h. s–n M. um sie *he folded* (od *wrapped*) *his cloak about her* ‖ [oft pass] gehüllt s in *to be enveloped* (od *swathed, wrapped*) *in* (*a cloak*); .. *shrouded in* (*mist*); dicht g. in .. *smothered in* (*foliage*); *the house was enveloped in flames* **b.** (Worte) ~ in .. *to couch* (od *wrap up*; *disguise*) *in* ..; gehüllt s in .. *to be couched in* ..; *the affair is shrouded in darkness* (od *mystery*) **2. sich ~ in** .. *to envelop* (od *wrap*) *o.s. in* ..; *to wrap up in* .. ‖ ⟨fig⟩ *to wrap o.s. in* (*reserve*); sich in Stillschweigen ~ *to be wrapped in silence*; *to maintain silence*; *to be silent* (über *about*) **H·üllenbahn** f Ballon≗ *fabric panel*

H·ulman m ~s/~s ⟨zoo⟩ (Stummelaffe) *langur*

H·ulock m ~s/~s ⟨zoo⟩ (Gibbonaffe) *hoolock*

H·ülse[1] f ⟨bot⟩ (Stechpalme) *holly*

H·ülse[2] f ~/~n **1.** ⟨bot⟩ (of beans, pease, etc.) *hull, husk, pod, shuck, shell*; *rind* **2.** ⟨übtr⟩ **a.** *protective cover*(*ing*); (Geschoß≗) *case*; Patronen≗ *cartridge-case*; Granat≗ *shell* **b.** ⟨tech⟩ *sleeve*; ⟨sl⟩ (Steck≗) *socket* ‖ leere ~n [pl] *empties* pl *__h·ülsen__ vt/i [h] ⟨bot⟩ **1.** vt = ent-, aushülsen **2.** vi *to pod* **H·ülsen-** ≗**artig** a *leguminous* **~boden** m *base of a cartridge-case* **~fänger** m ⟨mil⟩ *easel-bag* **~frucht** f *legume*; ≗e [pl] *legumes* pl; [koll] *pulse* [sg konstr] **~früchtler** pl ⟨bot⟩ Gattung der ~ *leguminous plants*; *Leguminosae* L pl **~gewächse** n pl = –früchtler **~kegel, ~keil** m ⟨tech⟩ *cone-key* **~kupplung** f ⟨tech⟩ *sleeve-coupling* **~schlüssel** m *angle box spanner* **~sperre** f ⟨artill⟩ *cartridge-case detent* ≗**tragend** a ⟨bot⟩ *leguminous* **~wurm** m ⟨zoo⟩ *hydatid*; *taenia echinococcus* L **h·ülsig** a *husky*; *shelled*; *shelly*

ˣ**Hulst** m, Hülst m ~es/~e ⟨bot⟩ = Hülse[1]

Hultsch·iner Ländchen n ⟨†Ger⟩ (zw Oppa u Oder)

hum·an 1. [a] *humane* **2.** [adv] *humanely*; ~ denken *to be h. disposed* | ~psychologie [f] *human ps.* **Humani·ora** L pl *literae humaniores* L pl; *humane learning* **humanis·ieren** vt [h] (Volk) *to humanize* **Human·ismus** m ~/ ⟨hist⟩ der ~ *Humanism*; *the Revival of Learning* **Human·ist** m ~en/~en **1.** ⟨hist⟩ *humanist*; *adherent of the doctrines of Humanism* **2.** ⟨mod⟩ *man with a classical education* **human·istisch A.** [a] **1.** ⟨hist⟩ *humanistic* **2.** ⟨mod⟩ *classical*; ~e Bildung *classical education*; *humane learning*; *scholarship* **B.** [adv] ⟨mod⟩ ~ gebildet *classical* (*student, teacher*); ~ gebildeter Mann = Humanist 2. **humanit·är** a *humanitarian*; *philanthropic* **Humanit·ät** f ~/ *humanity*; es ist ein Akt der ~ *it is an act of h.* (*to help him*) | °~sapostel [m] ⟨cont⟩ *dogooder, humanitarian*; °~sduselei [f] ⟨cont⟩ *sentimental h.ism*; *h. nonsense*; ~sidee [f] ⟨philos⟩ *idea of humanity*

H·umboldt- (nach A. von H.; † 1859) *Humboldt* | **~-Bai** f *H. Bay* ~fluß [m] *H. River*; ~kette [f] *H. Range*; ~strom [m] *H. current*; *Peruvian current*

°**H·umbug** m [engl] ~s/ *humbug*; *flummery*; *nonsense*; *swindle* ‖ so ein ~! *what h.*!; er redet lauter ~ *he talks nothing but n.*; → Schwindel

Humer·ale n ~s/–lien [–iən] ⟨R. C.⟩ *humeral*

Hum·in n ⟨chem⟩ *humin* **~säure** f *humic acid* **~stoffe** m pl *humates* pl **Hum·it** m ⟨minr⟩ *humite*

H·ummel f ~/~n **1.** ⟨ent⟩ *humble-bee*; *bumble--bee* ‖ ⟨fig⟩ °er hat ~n in der Hose *he has got the*

fidgets **2.** ⟨fig⟩ (P) °e–e wilde ~ *a romp*; *a regular tomboy* **~fliege** f *bee-fly*

H·ummer m ~s/~(n) ⟨zoo⟩ **1.** *lobster*; weibl. ~ *hen-l.* ‖ ⟨cul⟩ *l.*, ⟨Am a.⟩ *l. meat* **2.** [in comp] *lobster* **~fang** m *l.ing*; *l.-catch(ing)* **~krabbe** f *prawn* **~salat** m *l.-salad*

Hum·or m ~s/ *humour* ‖ der ~ Shakespeares *the h. of Sh.* ‖ ausgelassener *or* sprudelnder ~ *exuberant* (od *overflowing*) *h.*; derber ~ *broad* od *rough h.*; feiner ~ *subtle h.*; goldener ~ *golden h.*; heiterer ~ *gay* od *sprightly h.* ‖ ein Mann mit ~ *a man of h.*; er hat (Sinn f) ~ *he is a man of h.*, *he can see a joke*; .. k–n ~ *he has no sense* od *gift of h.* ‖ ~ der Verzweiflung *grim h.* ‖ sich mit ~ in e–e mißliche Lage finden *to keep one's h. under trying conditions* ‖ k–e Szene, die ~ aufweist *no humorous scene* **humor·al** a, **Humor·al-** [in comp] ⟨med⟩ *humoral* **Humor·eske** f **1.** ⟨Lit⟩ *humorous sketch* od *story* **2.** ⟨mus⟩ *humoresque* ***hum·orisch** a = humoristisch **Humor·ist** m ~en/~en *man of h.*; *comical p* ‖ ⟨Lit⟩ *h.ist*; *humorous writer* (od *talker*); *comic strip artist* **humor·istisch** **1.** [a] *humoristic*; *humorous* (*character*, *writer*); derb ~ *broadly h.*, *Rabelaisian*; ~er Schriftsteller (etc) *h.ist* ‖ *comic strip* (*artist*) ‖ *droll*, *facetious*, *funny*; → humorvoll ‖ (in newspapers) ~e Ecke, ~er Teil *comic strips* pl; *funny column*; ~e Pointe ⟨theat⟩ *gag* **2.** [adv] *humorously*; *facetiously*; **hum·orvoll** **1.** [a] *full of h.*; *humorous* (*characterization*); ~er Mensch *h.ist*; ~e Einfälle, Regungen *strokes* [pl] *of h.*; ~es Wesen *h.ousness*; → humoristisch **2.** [adv] *humorously*

hum·os a (→ Humus) *humous*

ˣ**H·ümpel** m = Haufen

h·ump(e)lig **1.** [a] (of gait) *hobbling*, *limping*; *stumbling*; *lame*; ~er Gang *hobble*, *limp* **2.** [adv] (*to walk*) *with a l.* **h·umpeln** vi [h] *to hobble*, *limp* (auf 2 Stöcken *on two sticks*); *to stumble*

H·umpen m ~s/~ *beaker*; *tankard*; (Deckel≈) *jug*; ein ~ Ale *a t. of ale*; ein voller ~ *a bumper*

H·umus m (L) ~/ ⟨agr⟩ *humus* L; *vegetable mould*; *topsoil* **≈artig** a *mouldy*; *humus* [a] **~boden** m, **~erde** f *humus soil*; *mould* **~pflanze** f *saprophyte* **~säure** f *humus acid*

Hund m ~(e)s/~e **A.** ⟨zoo⟩ **1.** Gattung der ~e *Canidae* L pl **2.** a. Haus≈ *domestic dog*; junger ~ *puppy* ‖ Jagd≈, Spür≈ *hunting-dog*; *hound*; Koppel ~e (*leash* od *pack of*) *hounds*; in der Parforcejagd z Pferde den ~en folgen *to ride to hounds*; *to follow the hounds* ‖ → Blut≈ etc ‖ Polizei≈ *police-dog*; Schäfer≈ *sheep-dog*; Deutscher Sch. *Alsatian*; *German shepherd* Wind≈ *greyhound* ‖ kl walisisch. ~ *corgi*; irisch. Wolfs≈ *Irish wolf-hound*; Eskimo≈, Schlitten≈ *husky* **b.** ‖ die ~e **antreiben** ⟨eng hunt⟩ *to tally-ho* ‖ °**dicker** Hund (S) *tall order*, *story*, *talk*; (P) *hard-boiled egg*; ⟨jur⟩ *serious case* ‖ der getroffene ~ bellt *if the cap fits wear it* ‖ (sich) e–n ~ **halten** *to keep a dog* ‖ ⟨fig⟩ °er ist **bekannt** wie ein bunter ~ *he is well-known all over the place* ‖ ~e, die viel bellen, beißen nicht *barking dog seldom bites*, *great barkers are no biters* ‖ schlafende ~e soll man nicht wecken ⟨prov⟩ *let sleeping dogs lie* ‖ tote ~e beißen nicht *dead men tell no tales* ‖ den letzten beißen die ~e *the devil take the hindmost*; *last man out*! ‖ °bei dem Wetter jagt man k–n ~ vor die Tür *in weather like that you wouldn't turn out a dog* ‖ °das kann e–n ~ jammern *that's a pitiable affair* ‖ °ihn pißt kein ~ an *he is beneath contempt* ‖ °**wie** ein beschneiter ~ ⟨fam⟩ *dumbfounded*; °**wie** ~ u Katze leben *to lead a cat and dog life*; wie ~ u K. s *to be at daggers drawn* ‖ °da liegt der ~ begraben *that is the sore point*; .. *the devil of it*, .. *the root of the trouble* ‖ kein ~ nimmt ein Stück Brot v ihm *no one will have anything to do with him* ‖ ein ~ schilt den andern Kläffer *the pot calls the kettle black* (*-arse*) ‖ °damit lockt man k–n ~ hinterm Ofen hervor *that won't* (*go down* od) *wash*; *that will answer no purpose* ‖ viele ~e sind des Hasen Tod *many hounds soon catch the hare* ‖ °**auf den** ~ **k** *to go to the dogs* od *devil*; auf den ~ gek *down and out*; ⟨fam⟩ *gone a holy mucker* ‖ °da liegt der Knüppel **beim** ~e *it is a case of Hobson's choice*; **mit** allen ~en gehetzt *artful*, *dodgy*, *tricky*; *thorough-paced* (*rascal*); *out-and-out* ‖ °kommt man **über** den ~, kommt man auch über den Schwanz *when the main work is done*, *the rest is a mere trifle* ‖ °das ist **unter** dem ~, unter allem ~ *that's about as bad as bad can be* ‖ **vor** die ~e gehen → auf den ~ k **2.** ⟨übtr⟩ **a.** ⟨zoo⟩ Fliegender ~ *kalong*; *flying fox* **b.** laufender ~ *Vitruvian scroll* ‖ weiße ~e *white-crested waves*; *white-caps*; *white horses* pl **3.** ⟨astr⟩ der Gr ~ *Sirius*; *Canis major* L; *dog-star* ‖ der Kl ~ *Canis minor* L **4.** °⟨fig⟩ *cad*; *dog*, *hound*; ein gemeiner ~! *a dirty dog*!, so ein ~! *what a cad*! ‖ ein schlauer ~ *a sly dog* ‖ Blut≈ *blood-thirsty blackguard*; Himmel≈ *hell-hound* **B.** ⟨min⟩ *car*; *tub*; *dog*; *trolley* **C.** [in comp] → Hunde-; Hunds-

H·ündchen n ~s/~ *doggy*, *-gie*; *puppy* **H·unde-** **A.** ⟨zoo⟩ *dog-*; *canine* **~abteil** n ⟨rail⟩ *dog-box* **~art** f **1.** *breed* od *variety of dogs* **2.** *habit*; nach ~ *as dogs go* **≈artig** a *doglike* **~ausstellung** f *dog-show*; ⟨Am a.⟩ *bench-show* **~bandwurm** m ⟨zoo⟩ *taenia echinococcus* L; → Hülsenswurm **~biskuit** n *dog-biscuit* **~biß** m *dog-bite* **~blume** f ⟨bot⟩ *dandelion*; *lion's tooth* **~fahrkarte** f *dog-ticket* **~fleisch** n *dog's flesh*; *dog-meat* **~floh** m ⟨ent⟩ *dog-flea* **~führer** m *dog-handler* **~futter** n *pet foods* pl **~gebell** n *barking of dogs* **~geschlecht** n *canine world* **~halsband** n *dog-collar* **~haus** n, **~hütte** f *kennel*; in der H. liegen *to kennel*; sich in der ~ verkriechen *to kennel up* **~krankheiten** f pl *diseases in dogs* **~kuchen** m = –biskuit **~leine** f *dog-lead*; Hunde sind an der L. zu führen *dogs must be kept on leads* **≈lieb** a (P) *doggy* **~liebhaber** m *dog-fancier* **~loch** n *miserable hut* **~natur** f *doggy nature* **~peitsche** f *dog-whip* **~rennen** n *dog-race*; *dog-racing* °**~schnauze** f *dog's nose* od *muzzle* ‖ °kalt wie 'ne ~ *as cool as a cucumber* **~schule** f *dog training school* **~sperre** f *muzzling order for dogs*, *quarantine* **~stall** m *kennel*; im ~ unterbringen *to kennel* **~steuer** f *dog-licence* (od *tax*) **~wache** f ⟨mar⟩ *dog-watch* **~wärter** m *dog-keeper*, *dog-feeder* **~zucht** f *dog-breeding* **~züchter** m *dog-fancier* **~zwinger** m = –hütte ‖ **B.** °⟨übtr⟩ (→ Hunds- B.) & ⟨dero⟩ [als Intensivum] *dreadful*, *nasty*; ⟨sl⟩ *beastly*; *blooming*; → Mords- **~arbeit** f *drudgery*; *fag*; so 'ne ~! *what a fag*! **≈elend** a *rotten*, *dog-tired*; sich ~ fühlen *to feel as sick as a dog* °**~fraß** m ⟨sl⟩ *beastly meal* °**~geld** n *mere trifle*; → –lohn; f ein ~ *dirt-cheap* °**~kälte** f *bitter cold*; ⟨sl⟩ *blooming cold* °**~leben** n: jdm ein ~ bereiten *to lead a p a dog's life* ‖ °**~loch** n *mean hovel*; *kennel* °**~lohn** m *wretched pay* °**≈mäßig** a *miserable*; *wretched*; ⟨sl⟩ *beastly* °**≈müde** a *dead-*, *dog-* (⟨Am⟩ *bone-*)*tired* **~übel** a = –elend °**~wetter** n *beastly weather*

H·undert **1.** [n] ~(e)s/~e *hundred* **a.** [nach Zahlbegriffen] ~ [pl] *h.* [pl konstr]; *five score*; fünf ~ v .. *five h. of* (*them*); mehrere *several h.*; einige ~ *some h.* ‖ eins vom ~ *one in a h.*; *one per cent.*; fünf vom ~ (*or* auf das ~) *5 per cent.*; ⟨com a.⟩ *a shilling in the pound*; ⟨Am⟩ *5 cents on the dollar* ‖ ~ u eins *a h. and one* ‖ gr ~ *long h.* (= *120* [*eggs*]) **b.** ~e [pl] *h.s* (*of people*) pl; ~ u aber ~ *h.s and h.s* ‖ z ~en *by the h.* **2.** ≈ [a] *hundred* ‖ ~ Soldaten *a* (od *one*) *h. soldiers*; mehrere ~ Mann *several h. men*; ein paar ~ Menschen *some five h. people* ‖ der ~ u erste *the h. and first*; der sechs~vierzigste *the six h. and fortieth* ‖ Zeit *or* Alter v ~ Jahren *centenary*; ~ Jahre alt w *to live to a h.* ‖ einmal in ~ Jahren vorkommend *centennial* ‖ ~ Pfund (Gewicht) *centner* [Ger]; ⟨Am⟩ *h.weight* (engl = 112 Pfd); (Geld) *a h. pounds* **H·undert-** **~dollar(note** f) ⟨Am sl⟩ *yard*

~~fach, ~~fältig a *h.fold* ~**fünfundsiebziger** m ⟨jur §⟩ *Oscar, pansy* ~~**gradig** a *centigrade* ~**guldenblatt** n ⟨arts⟩ *H. Guilder Print* ~**jahrfeier** f, ~**jahrtag** m *centenary*; ⟨bes Am⟩ *centennial*; *h.th anniversary*; Zwei~~jahrfeier [f] *bicentenary*; ⟨bes Am⟩ *bicentennial* ~~**jährig** a *centenary*; ⟨bes Am⟩ *centennial* ‖ *a hundred years old* ‖ ⟨engl⟩ der ~~e Krieg *the H. Years' War* (*1337–1453*) ~**jährige** [der ~, ein ~r] m, die ~ [f] ~n/~n *centenarian* ~~**jährlich** a *centennial* ~~**karätig** a ⟨fig⟩ *of impeccable character* ~~**köpfig** a *h.-headed*; *centicipitous* ~~**mal** adv *a h. times*; viel~ *many h.s of times* ~~**malig** a *repeated a h. times* ~~**prozentig 1.** [a] *cent per cent*; *a h. per cent* (*American*); *quintessential* (*toryism*); *purest*; *undiluted* ‖ *complete*; *out-and-out*; *thorough-paced*; ~ sicher *or* zuverlässig *perfectly good* **2.** [adv] *a h. per cent*; *quintessentially* ~**prozentige(r)** m (P) ⟨fig⟩ *h.-per-center* ~**satz** m *percentage* ~**tausend** n *a h. thousand*; ~e [pl] *h.s of thousands* ‖ es geht in die ~e *it runs into six figures* ~~**weise** adv *by the h.*; *by h.s* **H·underter** m ~s/~ **1.** ⟨math⟩ *hundred*; die ~ [pl] *the h.s* pl **2.** *a h. mark note* **h·underterl·ei** a *of a h. different sorts*; *of a h. and one kinds* **H·undertschaft** f ~/~en ⟨hist⟩ *hundred* **h·undertste** a; das ~ *the h.th*; *centesimal* ‖ das weiß nicht der ~~ *not one in a h. knows that* ‖ das ~~ ins Tausendste reden, vom ~~n ins Tausendste k *to wander off into details* od *trivialities*; *to talk nineteen to the dozen*, *to jump from one subject to another* **H·undertstel** n ~s/~ *h.th* ‖ ~ Gramm *centigramme*; ~ Liter *centilitre*; ~ Meter *centimetre* **h·undertstens** adv *in the h.th place*

H·ündin f ~/~nen *bitch*, *she-dog* **h·ündisch** f **A.** [a] **1.** ⟨eig⟩ *doggy*; *doggish*; *canine* **2.** ⟨mst fig⟩ (P) **a.** (kriecherisch) *cringing*, *fawning*, *obsequious*, *servile*, *toadying*; ~es Benehmen *fawningness* **b.** [pred] *dirty*, *impudent*; er ist ~ *he is a dirty fellow*; das ist ~ *that's dirty* **B.** [adv] ⟨fig⟩ *fawningly* **H·unds-** [in comp] **A.** ⟨mst übtr, bes bot & astr⟩ *dog-* ~**baum** m ⟨bot⟩ *spindle-tree* ~**beere** f ⟨bot⟩ *dogberry* ~**dill** m, ~**dolde** f ⟨bot⟩ = –petersilie °~**fott** m *dirty dog*; *low fellow*; *mean blackguard* (od *scoundrel*) ‖ ⟨prov⟩ ein ~ gibt mehr als er kann *you cannot expect a man to give more than he has* ~~**föttisch** a *dirty*; *mean*; *low-down* ~**giftgewächse** n pl ⟨bot⟩ *apocynaceous plants* pl ~**gleiße** f ⟨bot⟩ = –petersilie ~**gras** n ⟨bot⟩ *dog's grass* ~**hai** m ⟨ich⟩ *dogfish* ~**hirse** f ⟨bot⟩ = –zahn 1. ~**kamille** f ⟨bot⟩ *dog's* od *stinking camomile* ~**kirsche** f ⟨bot⟩ *white bryony* ~**kohl** m ⟨bot⟩ *dog's bane* ~**kraut** n ⟨bot⟩ *bitter-sweet*; *woody nightshade* ~**nelke** f ⟨bot⟩ *soap-wort* ~**petersilie** f *dog's poison*; *fool's parsley* ~**rose** f ⟨bot⟩ *dogrose* ~**stern** m ⟨astr⟩ = Gr Hund, → Hund A. 3. ~**tage** m pl ⟨astr⟩ *dog-days* (*24/7–24/8*) ~**tagshitze** f *canicular heat* ~**veilchen** n ⟨bot⟩ *dog-violet* ~**wut** f ⟨vet⟩ = Tollwut ~**zahn** m ⟨bot⟩ **1.** *Bermuda grass*; *Cynodon* L **2.** *dog's tooth violet*; *Erythronium* L **3.** *dandelion* ‖ ~ornament [n] *dog-tooth ornament*; *dog-teeth* pl ~**zähne** m pl ⟨vet⟩ *dog-teeth*; *canine teeth* ~**zecke** f ⟨ent⟩ *acarid*; *tick* ~**zunge** f ⟨bot⟩ *dog's tongue* **B.** °⟨übtr (→ Hunde- B.) & dero⟩ ~~**gem·ein 1.** [a] *dirty*; *mean*; *scurvy* ‖ ⟨sl⟩ *beastly* (*weather*); ⟨fam⟩ *infernial* **2.** [adv] *dirtily*; *meanly*; jdn ~ behandeln *to do the dirty on a p* ~**gem·einheit** f *dirty act*; *dirtiness*; *meanness* ~**miser·abel 1.** [a] *abominable*; *execrable*; *miserable* (*achievement*); *very poor* (*wine*) ‖ mir ist ~, ich fühle mich ~ *I am feeling perfectly rotten* **2.** [adv] *miserably*; *badly*

H·üne m ~n/~n **1.** ⟨hist & praeh⟩ *giant* **2.** ⟨mst übtr⟩ *g.*; *huge man* ‖ ein ~ v Gestalt *a regular g.* (od *a man of Herculean build*; *a colossus*) **H·ünen-** ~**gestalt** f *colossus*; *giant*; *Hercules* ~**grab** n ⟨praeh⟩ *barrow*, *cairn* ~~**mäßig** a = hünenhaft ~**stein** m ⟨praeh⟩ *megalith*; *menhir*; *monolith* ~**weib** n *g.ess*; *huge woman* **h·ünenhaft** a *gigantic*; *herculean*; *colossal*; *giant* [attr] ‖ *enormous*, *huge*

H·unger m ~s/ **1. a.** *hunger* ‖ er hatte e–n entsetzlichen ~ *he was terribly hungry*, ⟨vulg⟩ *his appetite was sth frightful* ‖ krankhafter ~ *bulimia* L; *morbid h.* ‖ Heiß~~, °Bären~~ *ravenous h.* | (~snot → d.) *famine*; *starvation*, ⟨Am fig⟩ *the wolf at the door* **b.** ⟨prov⟩ ~ ist der beste Koch *h. is the best sauce* ‖ ~ bek *to get hungry* ‖ ~ h *to be h.y*; °ich habe ~ wie ein Wolf, ich habe e–n Bären~~ *I am h.y as a wolf* od *a hunter*; *I am ravenously h.y*; *I am famishing*; ⟨Am fam⟩ *I am wolfish* ‖ ~ leiden *to suffer* (*from*) *h.*; *to starve* ‖ ihn plagt der ~ *he is starving* ‖ ~s sterben, vor ~ st. *to die of h.* (od *famine*); *to starve to death*; jdn ~s st. l *to starve a p* ‖ s–n ~ stillen *to satisfy* od *still one's h.* (mit *with*) ‖ jdn durch ~ zwingen z (etw) *to starve a p into* (*submission*) ‖ vor ~ umk *to starve* **2.** ⟨fig⟩ ~ nach *h.* (od *thirst*) *for* od *after* (*knowledge*); Heiß~~ nach *bulimia* od *voracity for* (*books*) ‖ ~ nach Land, Land~~ *h. for land*; ~ h nach *to h.* (od *thirst*) *for* od *after* (*kindness*); → hungern A. 2. **3.** ~**blockade** f ⟨mil⟩ *h.-blockade* ~**blume** f ⟨bot⟩ **1.** *draba* L; *whitlow grass* **2.** *corn marigold* ~**diät** f = –kur ~**gebiet** n; ~e [pl] *famine-affected areas* pl ~**gefühl** n *sensation* od *pangs* [pl] *of h.*; ein ~ h *to feel empty* ~**korn** n = Mutterkorn ~**krankheit** f *disease resulting from scanty nourishment* ~**kur** f *h.* od *fasting cure* od *diet* °~**leben** n *starvation* °~**leider** m *poor wretch*; *starveling* ‖ *miserly wretch* °~**lohn** m *starvation-wage(s)*; ein reiner ~ *a mere pittance* ~**marsch** m ⟨pol⟩ *h.-march* ~**öd·em** n ⟨path⟩ *oedema resulting from scanty nourishment* °~**pfote** f: °(an den) ~n saugen = am Hungertuch nagen ~**stein** m *salt pan scale* ~**streik** m ⟨pol⟩ *h.-strike*; in den ~ treten *to* (*go on*) *h.-st.* ~**tod** m *death from starvation*; den grausigen ~ sterben *to die the gruesome death by st.* ~**tuch** n *Lenten-veil*; ⟨fig⟩ °am ~ nagen *to suffer* (*from*) *h.*, *to keep the wolf from the door* ~**typhus** m = Fleckfieber ~**zustand** m (*state of*) *h.*; *inanition* **h·ungern A.** vi [h] **1. a.** [imps] mich hungert, es hungert mich *I am* (od *feel*) *hungry*; mich hungert sehr ⟨fam⟩ *I am famishing* (od *starving*) **b.** [pers] *to hunger* (*for days*); *to go h.y*; *to be without food* ‖ jdn ~ l *to starve a p* **c. sich** z Tode ~ *to starve o.s. to death* **2.** ⟨fig⟩ ~ nach .. *to be desirous of*; *to crave* (od *long*) *for*; er *or* ihn hungerte nach Frieden *he h.ed* od *thirsted for* od *after peace*; *he was h.y for peace*; wir ~ nach Mozart *we lust for Mozart* **B.** ~~ n *hungering* **H·ungersnot** f *famine*; *dearth of food* ‖ *in allen* Gebieten herrschte ~ *all districts were affected by f.*; Behebung der ~ *f. relief* **h·ungrig** a **1.** *hungry* (*children*; *stomach*); sehr ~ *starved*, *sharp-set*; ~ s *to feel empty* od *h.y* ‖ ⟨prov⟩ e–m ~en Magen ist nicht gut predigen *a h.y belly has no ears* **2.** ⟨fig *h.y*; ~e Blicke werfen nach .. *to cast h.y eyes at* (*a th*) ‖ ~ s nach .. *to be h.y for* (*land*)

H·unne m ~n/~n ⟨hist⟩ *Hun*; die ~n *the Huns* pl; ~nschlacht *Battle on the Catalaunian Plain* (451 n. Chr.) | ⟨fig⟩ *Hun*; *barbarian* **h·unnisch** a *Hunnish* (*hordes*) ‖ ⟨fig⟩ *barbarous*

H·unsrück m ⟨Ger⟩ (Gebirge) *Hun(d)srück*

Hunt m ~s/~e ⟨min⟩ = Hund B. *trolley*

H·upe f ~/~n ⟨mot⟩ *motor-horn*; *hooter*; *honker*; Ball~~ *bulb-horn*; laute elektr. ~ *klaxon*; nicht v der ~ heruntersteigen ⟨fam⟩ *to drive on the horn*; die ~ ertönen l *to honk one's klaxon*; → **h·upen 1.** vi [h] *to honk*; *hoot*; wiederholt ~ *to tootle* **2.** ~~ n *honking*; *hooting* ~~**signal**, ~~**zeichen** n *honk* ‖ ein ~ geben *to blow one's horn*; *to honk*; (lautes) *to blow a blast on one's horn*

*__Hupf__ m ~es/~e *hop* ⟨a. aero⟩; *skip* ‖ *caper*, *frisk*, *gambol* ×**h·upfen** vi [s] = hüpfen ; (tanzen) ⟨sl⟩ *to hop* ‖ ° das ist gehupft wie gesprungen = Hose wie Jacke **h·üpfen A.** vi [s] **1. a.** ⟨mst P⟩ *to hop*; *jump* (vor Freude *for joy*); *to leap*; *skip*, *bound*, *tittup* ‖ vor Freude ~, ~ u springen *to* caper; *frisk, gambol*; *skip* ‖ ~ über (etw) *to hop* (od *jump*) *over* (*a ditch*); *to hop* (od *jump, skip*) (*a ditch*) **b.** (of a boat) *to bob* ‖ *jig* ‖ das Herz hüpfte ihm im Leibe *his heart leapt for joy*; *his h. gave a leap*; *his h. jumped* ‖ gehüpft → hupfen **B.** ≗ n *hop, skip* ‖ *caper, frisk, gambol* ‖ *bob* **h·üpfend** a *hopping*; *skipping* ‖ ~es Insekt *hopper* ‖ ~er Puls *jumping pulse* ˣ**H·upfer** m ~s/~ (Sprung, Satz) *bound*; *hop*; *leap*; *jump*; in weiten ~n *with long strides* **H·üpfer** m ~s/~ *hopper, jumper, skipper* ‖ *hopping animal*; *hopper* ˣ**H·upferling** m ⟨bot⟩ = Springkraut **H·üpferling** m ⟨zoo⟩ *cyclops* **H·üpf- ~maus** f → Springnager **~spiel** n (Kinderspiel) *hopscotch* **~spinne** f ⟨ent⟩ = Spring– ˣ**h·uppen** vi [s] = hüpfen

H·ürde f ~/~n **1. a.** ⟨hors⟩ *hurdle* (mit Graben *bullfinch*); die ~ verweigern ⟨hors⟩ *to shag back* **b.** ⟨sport⟩ *fence*; *grating* ‖ ⟨mil⟩ *wattled h.*; *wattle* (*-work*) ‖ ~ aus Eisen *iron h.* ‖ (Platz) durch ~n einschließen *to h.* **2.** (eingehegter Platz) **a.** *enclosure, pen* **b.** (f Schafe) *sheepfold*; *pen* ‖ die Schafe in der ~ *the fold* ‖ (Schafe) in der ~ einpferchen *to pen, fold* **c.** (f Pferde, Vieh) *corral*; → Koppel ‖ in e–r ~ einkoppeln *to corral* **d.** (Pfandstall f verirrtes Vieh) *pound* **h·ürden** vt [h] (Schafe) *to pen* **H·ürden- ~aufseher** m (→ Hürde 2. d.) *pound-keeper* **~lager** n *sheepfold* **~lauf** m *h.-race*; *h.s* pl; an e–m ~ teilnehmen *to run a h.-race*; *to h.* **~läufer** m *h.s racer* **~rennen** n *h.-race*; ein ~ reiten *to ride a h.-r.* **~schlag** m *movable sheepfolds* pl **~werk** n *h.-work*; *w.-work*

H·ure f ~/~n *prostitute*; *bitch, harlot, street--walker, strumpet, trollop, whore*; ⟨Am a.⟩ *bag* ‖ *loose* (od *common*) *woman*; *woman of easy virtue*; alte ~! ⟨vulg⟩ *old rip*! Die ~ v Babylon ⟨arts⟩ *The Courtesan of B.* | ⟨fig⟩ die ~ Erfolg *the bitch--goddess success* **h·uren** vi [h] (of a man) *to whore*; *fornicate*; *indulge in fornication*; ~ mit .. *to practise fornication with ..* ‖ (of women) *to prostitute o.s.*; *to be a prostitute*; *to be on the streets*; *to prowl* ‖ ⟨vulg⟩ *to bitch* ‖ → Erpel **H·uren-** °**~balg** m = –kind °**~bock** m *fornicator*, ⟨vulg⟩ *punker* **~haus** n *house of ill fame*; *brothel* °**~jäger** m *fornicator* **~kind** n *bastard child* **~leben** n *dissolute* od *loose life* **~nest** n *haunt of prostitutes* **~pack** n *lewd rabble* **~sohn** m *bastard son*, ⟨vulg⟩ *son of a gun* od *bitch* **~weib** n = Hure **~wesen** n *prostitution* **~wirt** m *pimp* **~wirtin** f *brothel-keeper* **~wirtschaft** f *fornication*; *harlotry* ‖ das ist die reine ~ *that's a haunt of pr.tion* **H·urer** m ~s/~ *fornicator, debauchee, lecher*; †*whoremonger* **Hurer·ei** f ~/ *fo.tion*; *harlotry*; *whoring* **h·urerisch** a *whorish*; *lecherous*; *lewd*

H·uri f ~/~s [Arab] *houri*

Hur·one m ~n/~n *Huron* **H·uronsee** m (in Kanada) *Lake Huron*

***hurr**! intj *whir* ‖ in e–m ≗ *whirring* **hurr·a**! **1.** intj *hurra(h)*! *huzza*! *cheers*! ‖ ~ rufen *to give a cheer*; *to shout hurra(h)*; *to hurra(h)*; dreimal ~ rufen *to give three ch.s* **2.** ≗ n ~s/~s *hurra(h)*; *shout of hurra(h)*; ein dreifaches ~ auf .. *three ch.s for ..*! ≗**patriot** m *jingo(ist)*; *chauvinist* **~patriotisch** a *jingo(istic)*; *chauvinistic*; ⟨Am⟩ *spread--eagle* (*article*) ≗**patriotismus** m *jingoism*; *ultra--patriotism* ≗**ruf** m = Hurra ‖ jdn mit ~en empfangen *to cheer a p* ‖ .. unter den ~en der Menge *.. to the ch.s of the crowd* (od *ch.ed by the c.*) ‖ nicht enden wollende ~e [pl] *round after r. of ch.s* **~schreier** m = –patriot ˣ**h·urren** vi [s] *to hurry*; *flit, whisk*; *fly* **h·urtig 1.** [a] *agile, alert, nimble*; *prompt*; *quick, speedy*; *swift* **2.** [adv] *in a hurry*; *promptly*; *quickly* ‖ °etwas ~! *hurry up*! *look alive*! ⟨fam⟩ *get a move on*! ⟨sl⟩ *make it snappy*! ⟨Am sl⟩ *step on it* | ≗**keit** f *agility*; *promptness*; *speediness, swiftness*

Hus·ar m ~en/~en ⟨a. hist⟩ *hussar* **Hus·aren- ~affe** m ⟨zoo⟩ *guenon*; *cercopithecus* L **~cape** n, **~jacke** f *dolman* °**~fieber** n ⟨hum m. m.⟩ *scarlet--fever* **~mütze** f *busby* **~regiment** n *h. regiment*; Königl. Leib≗ *the King's Own H.s* pl **~ritt** m ⟨fig⟩ ~e [pl] *capers, escapades* pl **~streich** m, **~stückchen** n *coup de main* Fr **~tasche** f *sabretache* **~uniform** f *hussar uniform*

°**husch**! intj **a.** ~! *shoo*! ~, fort! *shoo, get out*! ‖ ~ rufen *to shoo* **b.** *quick*! *all of a sudden*; *in a hurry* od *trice*; *in an instant*; ~! weg war sie (sc die Maus)! *in a trice it was off*! *and off it went*! ‖ ~, ~! *look alive*! *°**Husch** m ~es/~e *sudden movement*; *whisk* ‖ im ~ *with* od *in a whisk*; *in a hurry* od *trice* ‖ jdn auf e–n ~ besuchen *to drop* (od *look*) *in on a p*; ich war auf e–n ~ bei ihm *I paid him a flying visit* ˣ°**H·usche** f ~/~n **1.** *light shower* (*of rain*) **2.** ˣ*licking, thrashing*; → Prügel ‖ = Ohrfeige ˣ**h·usch(e)lig 1.** [a] *hasty*; *hurried*; *bungling, superficial* ‖ *fidgety* ‖ *fickle*; *flighty* **2.** [adv] *in haste*; *hurriedly*; *superficially* ˣ**h·uschen** vi/refl [h] **1.** vi **a.** *to hurry* ‖ *to fidget* **b.** *to work hastily*; *to bungle, muddle* **2. sich** ~ *to wrap* (*o.s.*) *up* (in *in*) **h·uschen 1.** vi [s] (of mice, etc.) *to scurry, scuttle*; *whisk* (in .. *into*); hinundher~ *to flit to and fro* ‖ ⟨übtr⟩ ~ über etw *to slur over ..*; *to do .. badly*; *to bungly a th* | (of shadows, etc) *to glide* (od *pass*) *furtively* (*over*), *to steal* (über *across*); *his eyes flew off to ..*; *a shadow of grief crossed his face*; vorbei~ *to flash* (od *flit*) *past* **2.** ≗ n *scurrying, whisking*; *scurry, whisk* ˣ**H·uscher** m = Husche 1. ˣ**h·uschig** a = husch(e)lig

H·üsing f **1.** ˣ(= Wohnung) *housing*; *home, house* **2.** ⟨mar⟩ (geteerte Leine) *housing*

h·ussa! intj *huzza*! ‖ ~ rufen *to huzza* ‖ ~-ho! ⟨hunt⟩ *yoicks*; → horrido, joho

Huss·it m ~en/~en ⟨ec hist⟩ *Hussite*; die ~en [pl] *the Hussites* pl ‖ ~enkriege [pl] *the War of Hussites* (*1419–36*) **huss·itisch** a *Hussite*

h·üsteln 1. vi [h] *to cough slightly*; *to hem*; *to give a short* od *slight cough*; trocken ~ *to hack* **2.** ≗ n ~s/ *slight cough*; *hem* **h·usten I.** vi/t [h] **A.** vi **1.** *to* (*give a*) *cough* ‖ leicht ~ *to give a slight* (⟨iron⟩ *little*) *c.* ‖ heftig *or* stark ~ *to c. loudly*; ‖ ⟨sl⟩ *to bark*; er hustet heftig *he has a bad c.* ‖ trocken ~ *to hack* **2.** °⟨fig⟩ °ich huste darauf ⟨sl⟩ *I don't care a damn for it* **B.** vt (aus~) *to c. up*; Blut ~ *to spit blood* (*from the lungs*) ‖ °jdm die Ohren voll ~ *to worry a p by c.ing* ‖ °ich werde dir was ~! *I'll see you further first*; *you may whistle for it*!, *catch me* (*doing that*)!, *not I*! **II.** ≗ n *cough(ing)* ‖ durch ~ zum Schweigen bringen *to c. down* **H·usten** m ~s/ ~ *cough* (leichter *slight*) ‖ starker (*or* heftiger) ~ *a bad* (od *nasty*) *c.* ‖ kz trockener ~ *dry c.*; *hack*; *hacking c.*; hohler ~ *hollow c.*; schwindsüchtiger ~ *churchyard c.* **~anfall** m *attack* (od *bout, fit*) *of c.ing* **~bonbon** m *c.-drop*; *c.-lozenge*; *pectoral l.* **~kitzel** m: ich habe e–n ~ *I have a sensation of tickling in my throat* **~krampf** m *spasm of c.ing* **~lindernd** a *c.--easing* (od *relieving*; *loosening*) **~mittel** n, **~mixt·ur** f *c.-mixture*; *pectoral* **~reiz** m *irritating c.* **~saft** m *cough-mixture*

Hut[1] m ~(e)s/≗e **A.** (Herren≗) **1.** *hat*; Filz≗ *felt hat* | Schlapp≗ *slouch* (od *squash*) *hat* ‖ (breitrandiger ~) *wide-awake*; *sombrero* [Span]; (der engl. Geistlichen) *shovel hat* ‖ (~ mit schmalem Rand) *Homburg* (*hat*); *trilby* | steifer ~ *bowler* (*hat*); ⟨fam⟩ *billycock*; ⟨Am⟩ *derby(-hat)* | dreieckiger ~, Gala≗ *cocked hat* ‖ Kardinals≗ *cardinal's hat*; *red hat* **2.** Damen≗ *lady's hat*; (ohne Rand) *bonnet*; (runder enganliegender ~) *toque* ‖ gr breitrandiger ~ auf Porträts der 18. Jhs. *picture-hat* **3. a.** da **geht** mir (e–m) der ~ **hoch** (vor Wut)! *that blows my stack*; *that gets my goat up*; *my tail's out*! (*it's enough to take the roof of your head off, it's fit to send you wild*); ihm ging der ~ hoch *he flew off the handle*; sein ~ sitzt auf 7 Schoppen *he has a drop in his eye* **b.** ~ **ab**! *hats off*! ‖ ⟨fig⟩ ~ **ab vor** ..! *hats off* od *I take off my hat to* (*this man*)! ‖ ohne ~, k–n ~ tragend *hatless*; sich dafür einsetzen, k–n ~ z tragen *to advocate hatlessness* ‖ den ~ abnehmen *to remove* (od *take off*) *one's hat*; *to raise* od *touch one's hat* (vor jdm *to a p*) ‖ den ~ aufsetzen *to put one's hat on* (verkehrt *backwards*); *to cover one's head*; den ~ keck (*or* schief) auf– *to cock one's hat*; °jdm den ~ eintreiben *to bonnet a p* ‖ °er trägt den ~ im Genick *he wears his hat at the back of his head* ‖ den ~ ins Gesicht ziehen *to pull* od *squash one's hat down over one's eyes* **c.** °wenn .., gibts was **auf** den Hut *if you do not follow my directions, there will be trouble* ‖ er bekam (°kriegte) eins auf den ~ *he got it in the neck, he got a smack in the eye* ‖ **mit** dem ~ auf dem Kopfe *with one's hat on* ‖ mit dem ~ in der Hand .. *hat in hand*; mit dem ~ in der H. kommt man durchs ganze Land *fair and softly goes far in a day* ‖ divergierende Meinungen **unter** e–n ~ bringen *to reconcile conflicting opinions* **B.** ⟨übtr⟩ **1.** Zucker≈ *sugarloaf*; ein ~ Zucker *a loaf sugar* **2.** *cap*; *cap-like structure*; ⟨bot⟩ (of a fungus) *pileus* L

Hut[2] f ~/ **A. 1.** (Obhut, Schutz) *care, keeping*; *custody*; *guardianship, protection* ‖ **in guter** ~ *in good hands* ‖ in jds ~s, unter jds ~ stehen *to be in a p's k.*; *to be in* (od *under*) *a p's c.*; wir sind in Gottes ~ *we are in God's k.* (od *in the hands of God*); das Ansehen des Landes ist in Ihrer ~ *the prestige of the country is in your k.* ‖ (jdn) in s–e ~ nehmen *to take under* od *into one's c.* **2.** (Wachsamkeit) *guard*; *vigilance* ‖ **auf der** ~ **s** *to be on one's g.*; *to be on the alert* (od *watch*), ⟨sl⟩ *to have one's eyes skinned*; *to look* (⟨Am⟩ *watch*) *out*; *to keep a good look-out*; *to mind one's P's and Q's*; *to take no chances*; *to be cautious* ‖ sehr (*or* wohl) auf der ~ s *to be very g.ed*; ⟨fam⟩ *to keep one's weather-eye open* ‖ nicht auf der ~ s *to be off one's g.* ‖ auf der ~ bleiben *not to drop one's g.* ‖ auf der ~ s gegen *to g. against*; *to be g.ed against*; vor jdm auf der ~ s *to beware of a p* ‖ auf der ~ s z tun → sich hüten ‖ auf der ~ bleiben *to keep on the watch* **B.** ⟨agr⟩ **1.** (Hüten) *herding, tending* (*of a flock*) **2.** die ~ Schafe *the flock* od *herd of sheep* **3.** (Weide) *pasture, pasturage*

H·ut-[1] **~affe** m ⟨zoo⟩ *bonnet-macaque* **~band** n *hat-band* **~besatz** m *hat trimming* **~bürste** f *hat--brush*; weiche ~ *hat-pad* **~fabrik** f *hat-manufactory* **~fabrikant** m = –macher **~form** f *hat-shape* (od *form*) ‖ (f Hutmacher) *hat-block* (od *mould*) **≈förmig** a *cap* (od *hat*)*-like*; ⟨bot⟩ *pileate* **~futter** n *hat-lining* **~futteral** n = –schachtel **~geschäft** n = –laden **~größe** f: welche ~ h Sie? *what size do you take in hats?* **~haken** m *hat-peg* (od *hook*); Gestell (etc) mit ~ *hat-rack* **~krempe** f *hat-brim* **~laden** m *hat-shop*; (Damen≈) *milliner's* **~macher** m *hatter*; *hat-maker*; er ist beim ~ *he is at the hatter's*; (Damen≈) *milliner* **~nadel** f *hat-pin* **~pilz** m ⟨bot⟩ *pileate fungus* **~rand** m *hat-brim* **~schachtel** f *hat-box*; *bandbox* **~schlange** f ⟨zoo⟩ *naja* **~schnur** f *hat-string* ‖ ⟨fig⟩ °das geht mir denn doch über die ~! *well, if that doesn't beat everything! that's a tall order! that's the limit!* **~ständer** m *hat-stand* **~steife** f *hat-stiffening* **~zucker** m *loaf-sugar*

H·ut-[2] **~haus** n ⟨min⟩ *miners' meeting-room*; *miners' tool room* **~mann** m ⟨min⟩ *overseer* **~recht** n ⟨hist⟩ *right of pasture* **~weide** f *pasture*; *meadow kept for grazing only*

H·ütchen n ~s/~ *small* (od *little*) *hat*

h·üten I. vt [h] **A. 1. a.** (Vieh) *to herd*; *tend*; *to watch over*; *to watch* **b.** (Kind) *to tend*; das Feuer ~ *to nurse the fire* **c.** Sch. l sich leichter ~ (*or* ~ sich leichter) als G. *sheep are more easily tended than geese*; (Kleinod) *to cherish* **2.** ⟨übtr⟩ (etw ~) **a.** (schützen) *to guard*; *look after*; *protect*; die Geschicke e–s Volkes ~ *to watch over the destinies of a nation* ‖ *to guard* (*life and property*); *to keep* (*a secret*) ‖ ängstlich gehütet *jealously guarded* (*balance*) **b.** das H. ~ *to keep house* ‖ das B. ~ *to keep one's bed*; *to be confined to one's bed*; *to stay in bed*; *to lay up* ‖ das Z. ~ *to keep* (od *be confined to*) *one's room* **B. sich** ~ **a.** sich ~ z tun *to be wary of doing*; *to guard o.s. from doing*; *to be careful not to do*; °ich werde mich schwer *or* schön ~, es wieder z tun *I shall take jolly good care not to do that again* ‖ °ich werde mich schön ~! *I do not see the fun of it*! .. *see the idea*! *catch me doing that*! **b. sich** ~ **vor** *to beware of*; *to fight shy of* (*a p*; *bad company*) ‖ *to guard against* (*infection, temptation*); *to be guarded* (od *on one's guard*) *against*; → auf der Hut s **II.** ≈ n *herding, tending* (*of sheep*) ‖ *guarding*, etc. **H·üter** m ~s/~ **1.** (Vieh≈) *herdsman*; *keeper* (*my brother's k.*); (Wald≈) *warden* **2.** ⟨übtr⟩ *guardian* (e–r S *over a th*); *protector* (*of a th*); ~ der Kultur *warden of culture* **~lohn** m *h.'s wages* pl

×**H·utsche,** ≈ f ~/~n **1.** *footstool* **2.** (Schaukel) *swing* ×**h·utschen** vt [h] **1.** *to glide, slip* **2.** *to rock*

H·üttchen n ~s/~ *small hut* **H·ütte** f ~/~n **1.** (Wohn≈) *cottage*; *hut*; *poor dwelling*; ⟨bib⟩ *tabernacle* ‖ (Indianer≈) *wickiup* ‖ kl ~ *cabin, cot*; ⟨fam⟩ *hutch*; kl armselige ~ *hovel*; *shanty*; ⟨Am sl⟩ *shack* ‖ kl Schutz≈ *temporary shelter* ‖ Senn≈ *chalet* ‖ Jagd≈ *hunting-box*; Fischer≈ *fishing-box* ‖ ⟨mil⟩ Feld≈ *hut*; in Feld≈n hausen *to hut* | (Schuppen) *outhouse*; *shed* ‖ Tier≈ *cote* | ⟨prov⟩ Raum ist in der kleinsten ~ *there is room enough in the smallest hut* **2.** ⟨mar⟩ *poop* **3.** ⟨tech⟩ *forge*; *foundry*; *smelting-house*; *metallurgical works*; *mill* **H·ütten- ~arbeiter** m *smelter*; *foundry-man* **~bau** m = –wesen **~besitzer** m *owner of a foundry*; *smelter* **~bewohner** m *cottager*; *dweller in the hut* **~chemiker** m *ore assayer* **~deck** n ⟨mar⟩ *poop-deck* **~industrie** f *smelting*; = –wesen **~jagd** f ⟨hunt⟩ *decoy-shooting from a hut* **~koks** m *foundry* (od *mine*)*-coke* **~kunde** f *metallurgy* **~mann** m *metallurgist* **≈männisch** m *metallurgical* **~meister** m *overseer of m. works* **~rauch** m *smelter's fume* **~werk** n *smelting* od *m. works* pl; *foundry*; *smeltery* **~wesen** n *metallurgy*; *-gic engineering* **~zink** n *spelter*

H·utung f ~/~en (→ Hut[2] B.) *pasture* ‖ = Hutrecht **H·ütung** f = Hüten [n]

×**H·utzel** f ~/~n *dried pear, etc*; *shrivelled woman*

Hy·aden pl ⟨ant & astr⟩ *Hyades* L pl

hyal·in a *hyaline* **Hyal·it** m ⟨minr⟩ *hyalite*

Hyalo- *hyalo-*; **~ph·an** m ⟨minr⟩ *hyalophane*

Hy·äne f ~/~n ⟨zoo⟩ *hy*(*a*)*ena*; Streifen≈ *striped h.*; gefleckte ~ *spotted h.* ‖ ⟨fig⟩ *hy*(*a*)*ena*; *vulture* **~nhund** m ⟨zoo⟩ *hy*(*a*)*ena-dog*

Hyaz·inth m ~(e)s/~e ⟨minr⟩ *jacinth, hyacinth*

Hyaz·inthe f ⟨bot⟩ *hyacinth*; ⟨engl⟩ (blaue) *bluebell* ‖ Wilde ~ *harebell*

Hybr·id m ~en/~en ⟨biol⟩ *hybrid* **hybr·id** a *hybrid*; ~e Bildung, ~es Wort *hybrid* **Hybr·idenzüchter** m *hybridist, hybridizer* **hybr·idisch** a = hybrid **H·ybris** f Gr *hybris*

Hydath·ode f ⟨bot⟩ *hydathode* **Hydat·ide** f ⟨zoo⟩ *hydatid* **H·ydra** f ~/–dren ⟨ant, astr⟩ *Hydra*; ⟨zoo⟩ *h.* L **Hydräm·ie** f ⟨path⟩ *hydraemia* L **Hydr·ant** m ~en/~en *hydrant*; *fire-plug* **Hydrargill·it** m ~en/~en ⟨minr⟩ *hydrargillite* **H·ydrasystem** n ⟨com⟩ = Schneeballsystem **Hydr·at** n ~s/~e ⟨chem⟩ *hydrate* | ~kalk [m] *h. lime* ‖ ~wasser [n] *water of hydration* **Hydr·aulik** f ~/ *hydraulics* pl [sg konstr] **hydr·aulisch 1.** [a] *hydraulic* (*brake, lift, motor*; *cement*; *drive*; *pressure*; *system*; *press*; *ram*) **2.** [adv] *hydraulically* **Hydraz·in** n ~s/~e ⟨chem⟩ *hydrazine* **Hydr·id** n *hydride* **Hydr·ier-** ~anlage [f] *hydrogenation plant* ‖ ~benzin [n] *hydrogenated gasoline* **hydr·ieren 1.** vt [h] *to hydrogenize, hydrate* **2.** ≈ n **Hydr·ierung** f *hydrogenation* **H·ydro-** [Gr] (Wasser-) [in comp] *hydro-* **~biologie** f *h.biology* **~chin·on** n ⟨chem⟩ *h.quinone* **~dyn·amik** f *h.dynamics* pl [sg konstr] **≈dyn·amisch** a *h.dynamic* **≈el·ektrisch** a *h.-electric* **~-**

gr·aph m *h.grapher* **~graph·ie** f *h.graphy* **≚gr·aphisch** a *h.graphic(al)* **~log·ie** f *h.logy* **≚l·ogisch** a *h.logic(al)* **~l·yse** f ⟨chem⟩ *h.lysis* L **~l·yt** n ~s/~e ⟨minr⟩ *h.lyte* **~-Make-up** n (mattleuchtend) ⟨cosm⟩ *coverfluid* **~mech·anik** f *h.mechanics* pl [sg konstr] **~m·eter** n *h.meter* **≚m·etrisch** a *h.metric* **~nephr·ose** f ⟨path⟩ *h.nephrosis* L **≚p·athisch** a *h.pathic* **~ph·an** m ~s/~e ⟨minr⟩ *h.phane* **~ph·yten** pl ⟨bot⟩ *h.phytes* pl **~pneumatikfederung** f ⟨mot⟩ *air-oil suspension* **~sph·äre** f ⟨phys⟩ *h.sphere* **~st·atik** f ⟨phys⟩ *h.statics* pl [sg konstr] **≚st·atisch** a *h.static* (*balance*; *pressure*) **~sulf·it** n ⟨chem⟩ *hyposulphite* **~t·echnik** f *hydrotechny* **~therap·ie** f ⟨med⟩ *h.therapy* **~x·id** n ~s/~e ⟨chem⟩ *h.xide* **~xylam·in** n ⟨chem⟩ *h.-xylamine* **~z·ele** f ⟨med⟩ *h.cele* **~z·oon** n ~s/–z·oen ⟨zoo⟩ *h.zoan*; Gattung der –zoen *h.zoa* L pl

Hygi·ene f ~/ *hygiene*; *hygienics* pl; *hygienic conditions* pl; psychische ~ *mental health*; → Gesundheit | ~slip [m] *sanitary pants* pl **Hygi·eniker** m *hygienist* **hygi·enisch 1.** [a] *hygienic*; *sanitary*; ~ m *to sanitate*; in ~er Hinsicht *hygienically* **2.** [adv] *hygienically*

H·ygro- [Gr] (Feuchtigkeits-) *hygro-* **~gr·aph** m *h.graph* **~m·eter** n *h.meter* **~phyt** m *h.phyte* **~sk·op** n *h.scope* **~sk·opisch** a *h.scopic*; ~e Eigenschaft *h.scopicity* **~skopizit·ät** f *h.scopicity*

Hygr·om n ~s/~e ⟨path⟩ *hygroma* [L]

H·ylo- (Stoff-) *hylo-* **~zo·ismus** m ⟨philos⟩ *h.zoism*

H·ymen m ⟨ant⟩, n ⟨anat⟩ *hymen* Gr **~omyz·et** m ⟨bot⟩ *h.omycete* **~opt·ere** f ~/~n *h.opter*; *h.opterous insect*; Gattung der ~n *H.optera* pl

H·ymne f ~/~n ⟨rel⟩ *hymn*; ~n singen *to h.*, *to sing h.s*; (Gott) in ~n preisen *to h.* | ⟨pol⟩ *anthem*; National≚ *national a.*; → Hymnus **H·ymnen-** **~dichter** m *h.ologist*; *h.odist*; *h.ist*; *lyric poet* **~dichtung** f *h.ology*; *h.ody*; *lyric poetry* **~gesang** m *m singing of h.s*; *h.ody* **~sammlung** f *h.al* **h·ymnisch** a *h.al*; *h.ic* **Hymnol·og** m *h.ologist* **Hymnolog·ie** f *h.ology* **hymnol·ogisch** a *h.ologic(al)*; in ~er Hinsicht *h.ologically* **H·ymnus** m ~/–nen = Hymne || ⟨fig⟩ –nen singen auf .. *to praise .. to the skies*

H·yper- [Gr] (über .. hinaus) *hyper-*; → über- **~äm·ie** f ⟨med⟩ *h.aemia* [L] **≚b·olisch** a ⟨math⟩ *h.bolic* (*cylinder*; *logarithm*; *spiral*) || ⟨rhet⟩ *h.bolic(al)* **~bolo·id** n ~s/~e ⟨math⟩ *hyperboloid* (ein-[zwei]schaliges *of one* [*two*] *sheet*[*s*]) **~bor·eer** m, **≚bor·eisch** a *h.borean* **~dul·ie** f ⟨R. C.⟩ *h.-dulia* [L] °**≚klug** a *overwise* **≚kritisch** a *over-critical*, *h.critical* **≚mangansauer** a ⟨chem⟩ –saures Kali [n] *potassium permanganate* **~metrop·ie** f ⟨med⟩ *h.metropia* [L] **~nephr·om** [o:] n ~s/~e ⟨path⟩ *h.nephroma* [L] **~ost·ose** f ⟨med⟩ *h.ostosis* [L] **~sth·en** m ⟨minr⟩ *h.sthene* **~ton·ie** f ⟨path⟩ *h.-tonia* [L]; *h.tonus* L **~t·oniker** m ~s/~ *h.tonic patient* **~trich·ose** f *h.trichosis* [L] **~troph·ie** f ~/~n ⟨path⟩ *h.trophy* **Hyp·erbel** f ~/~n **1.** ⟨rhet⟩ *hyperbole* || in ~n sprechen *to employ* od *use hyperbole*; *to exaggerate*; (etw) in ~n ausdrücken *to express hyperbolically* **2.** ⟨math⟩ *hyperbola* L || ~funktion [f] *hyberbolic function* || ~verfahren [n] ⟨aero⟩ *SHORAN*, → d.

h·ypno- [Gr] (Schlaf-) *hypno-* **hypno·id** a *hypnoid* **Hypn·ose** f ~/~n **1.** *h.sis* L; *h.tic state* || durch ~ (*to produce*) *h.tically* || jdn durch ~ bringen z *to h.tize a p into*; (jdn) in ~ versetzen *to h.tize* || die Lehre v der ~, die Erscheinungen der ~ *h.-tism* **2.** ⟨vet⟩ *catalepsy* **hypn·otisch 1.** [a] *h.tic* (*sleep*) || ~es Mittel *h.tic* || ~er Zustand *h.tic state*; *h.tism*; *trance* || durch ~e Mittel; auf ~em Wege *h.tically* **2.** [adv] *h.tically* **Hypnotis·eur** [–'zør] m ~s/~e *h.tist*; *h.tizer* **hypnotis·ierbar** a *h.tizable*; *susceptible to h.tism* **hypnotis·ieren 1.** vt [h] (jdn) *to h.tize*; *mesmerize* || ⟨fig⟩ *to h.tize*; *fascinate* **2.** ≚ n *h.tizing*; *h.tization*; *h.tism*; *mesmerism* || ⟨fig⟩ *power of suggestion*; *fascination* **Hypnotis·ierte** [der ~, ein ~r] *the p h.tized*; *the h.tic*; → Medium **-tis·ierung** f ~/~en = Hypnotisieren [n] **-t·ismus** m *h.tism*; *mesmerism*

H·ypo- Gr (unter) *hypo-* **~chlor·it** n ⟨chem⟩ *h.chlorite* **~ch·onder** m *h.chondriac* **~chondr·ie** f ~/ *h.chondria* [L]; ⟨path⟩ *h.chondriasis* [L] **≚ch·ondrisch** a *h.chondriac(al)* **≚chondr·ist** m ~en/~en *h.chondriac* **≚derm·atisch** a *h.dermic* (*injection*; *syringe*) **≚g·yn** a ⟨bot⟩ *h.gynous* (plant) **~k·austum** n ⟨ant⟩ *h.caust* **~ph·yse** f ⟨physiol⟩ *h.physis*; *pituitary gland* **~plas·ie** f ⟨path⟩ *h.-plasia* L **~p·yon** n ⟨path⟩ *h.pyon* **~st·ase** f ⟨philos & med⟩ *h.stasis* [L] **≚stasieren** vt [h] (Gedanken) *to h.statize* **~st·ylos** m ~/–len ⟨arch⟩ *h.style* **~-sulfit** n ⟨chem⟩ *h.sulphite* **~t·aktisch** a ⟨gram⟩ *h.tactic* **~t·axe** f ⟨gram⟩ *h.taxis* [L] **~ten·use** f ~/~n ⟨math⟩ *h.tenuse* **~th·ek** f, → d. **~th·ese** f ~/~n *h.thesis* [pl *–ses*]; Arbeits≚ *working h.* || als ~ *by way of* (*an*) *h.* || e–e reine ~ *a pure h.*; *a mere assumption* || e–e ~ aufstellen *to frame* (od *make*) *an h.*; *to h.thesize* **~th·etisch 1.** [a] *h.thetic(al)*; e–e ~e Annahme m *to h.thesize* **2.** [adv] *h.thetically* **~trich·ose** f *h.trichosis* L **~xanth·in** n ⟨chem⟩ *h.xanthine*

Hypoth·ek f ~/~en (Grundstücks≚) *real estate mortgage* (auf *on*); ⟨Scot⟩ *hypothec* || die erste ~ *the first m.* || e–e ~ aufnehmen auf ein Haus *or* ein H. mit e–r ~ belasten *to m. a house* || das H. ist über u über mit ~en belastet *the h. is m.d to the hilt* || Bestellung e–r ~ *hypothecation* || auf dem H. stehen zwei ~en *the h. has two m.s on it*; m–e ~ steht an erster Stelle *I have the first m.*; *my m. takes priority over the subsequent ones* || Geld ausleihen auf ~en *to lend money on m.* || ein Darlehen als ~ eintragen l *to have a loan registered as a m.* || e–e ~ zurückzahlen *to redeem a m.* || e–e ~ kündigen *to call in a m.* || die Zurückzahlung e–r ~ verlangen *to foreclose a m.* || durch Eintragung e–r ~ gesichert *secured by m.* **≚a·risch 1.** [a] *hypothecary* (*loan*; *debt*; *security*); ~er Gläubiger *mortgagee*; ~e Verpfändung *hypothecation* **2.** [adv] *by mortgage*; ~ belastet *encumbered with a mortgage* od *with mortgages* **Hypoth·eken-** **~aufwertung** f ⟨Ger⟩ *revalorization of m.s* **~bank** f ⟨Ger⟩ *land m.-bank* **~brief** m *m.-deed* (od *bond*) || *m. debenture-bond* **~buch** n ⟨Ger⟩ *register of m.s* **~darlehen** n *m.-loan*; *hypothecary loan* **~forderung** f *hypothecary claim* **~gewinnabgabe** f *m. gain levy* **~gläubiger** m *m.e-holder*, *mortgagee* **~pfandbrief** m *m.-debenture* **~schein** m *m.-deed* (od *bond*) **~schuld** f *m.-debt* **~schuldner** m *mortgagor*

H·ypso- Gr (Höhen-) *hypso-* **~graph·ie** f *h.-graphy* **~m·eter** n *h.meter* **~metrie** f *h.metry* **≚m·etrisch** a *h.metric*

Hyr·are f ~/~n ⟨zoo⟩ *hyrax* [L]; *rock-badger*

Hyst·eresis [Gr], **Hyster·ese** f ⟨phys⟩ *hysteresis*

Hyster·ie f ⟨med⟩ *hysteria* [L]; *hysterics* pl; Anfall v ~ *fit of hysteria* **Hyst·eriker** m ~s/~ *person subject to hysteria* **hyst·erisch** a *hysteric(al)*; *vapouring* || ~e Anfälle, Zustände *hysterics* pl; *hysterical fits* pl; ~e Anfälle bek, in ~e Krämpfe fallen *to go* (*off*) *into hysterics*

Hysterotom·ie f ⟨surg⟩ *hysterotomy*

I

I, i n ~/~ *I, i*; der Punkt, das Tüpfelchen auf dem ~ *the dot on the i* ‖ I-Profil [n] *I-beam section*; → i-Punkt, i-Tupfel

°**i** [i:] [intj] **1.** ~ *faugh! ugh!* = igitt **2.** [verblaßt] ~ bew·ahre! ~ w·as! ~ **w·o**! *not in the least! not at all! no idea! certainly not! I should think not! nonsense! God forbid!* ‖ ~ freilich! *of course! to be sure!* ‖ ~ zum Donnerwetter! *confound it! damn it!* ~ z Kuckuck was .. ? *what on earth .. ?*

·**i·ah** ['i:'ɑ:] **1.** [intj] *hee-haw!* ~ schreien *to hee-haw* **2.** ≈ n *hee-haw*; *bray of an ass* | ⟨übtr⟩ m (Esel) *hee-haw* ·**i·ahen** vi [h] *to hee-haw*

I·ambe m = **I·ambus** m L ~/–ben ⟨pros⟩ (·–) *iamb, iambus* L [pl *iambuses*]; (Vers) *iambic* [mst pl –ben *iambics*]; fünffüßiger ~ *five-foot iambic*; → Blankvers **i·ambisch** a *iambic* (*foot, metre, verse*); ~er Vers ⟨a.⟩ *iambic*

Ibad·an n (Handelsort in Süd-Nigerien)

Ib·erer m ⟨hist⟩ *Iberian* **Ib·erien** *Iberia* **ib·erisch** a *Iberian* ‖ die ≈e Halbinsel *the Iberian Peninsula* ‖ die ~e Sprache, das ≈e *Iberian* **Ibero-Amerika** *Ibero-America* **ib·ero-amerikanisch** a *Ibero-American*

·**Ibis** m ·Ibisses/·Ibisse ⟨orn⟩ *ibis* [pl *ibes*]

ich pron pers *I*; (~ selbst) *I myself*; ~ z. B. *take me, for an example* ‖ ⟨fam⟩ *me*; *myself*; ⟨com⟩ *self* ‖ Herr N., mein Bruder u ~ *Mr. N., my friend, and myself* ‖ ~ Unglücklicher! *poor* od *wretched me!* ‖ ~ bin es ⟨fam⟩ *it is me*; ⟨fam⟩ *it's yours truly* **Ich** n ~s/~e; das ~ *the I*; ⟨philos⟩ *the ego* L; ⟨fam⟩ *the me* ‖ das eigene ~ *the own self*; das liebe ~ *the dear self*; mein zweites ~ *my second self* **~bedingt, ~betont, ~bezogen** a *egocentric*; *self-centred*; *egoistic* ≈**bewußtsein** n *individual consciousness* od *thinking*; *individual character*; *individuality* ≈**erzählung** f *tale told in the first p* ≈**heit** f *ego, individuality*; *self* ≈**kult** m: ~ treiben *to cultivate egotism*

Ichn·eumon m & n [~/~e & ~s] ⟨zoo⟩ *ichneumon*; *Pharaoh's rat* ‖ e–e Art ~ *meerkat*

Ichno- Gr (Fußspur-) **~log·ie** f *ichnology*

·**Ich-Roman** m ⟨Lit⟩ *novel told in the first p*

·**Ichsel** n ~s/~ ⟨arch⟩ *re-entering angle*

·**Ichsucht** f *egoism*; *egotism*; *self-interest* (od *love*); *selfishness* ·**ichsüchtig** a *ego(t)istic(al)*; *self-centred*; *self-interested*; *selfish*

–**icht** suff [z Bildung v] **1.** Adj.: töricht → Tor [m] ‖ ⟨obs⟩ haaricht → Haar; hornicht → Horn; nervicht → Nerv; = -ig **2.** Subst: Dickicht, Röhricht

Ichthyo- Gr (Fisch-) *ichthyo-* **~d·ont** m ~en/~en ⟨pal⟩ *i.dont* **~l·og(e)** m *i.logist* **~log·ie** f *i.logy* **~ph·ag(e)** m ⟨pal⟩ *i.phagist* **~phthalm** m ⟨minr⟩ *i.phthalmite* **~saurus** ~/–rier ⟨pal⟩ *i.-saurus* **Ichthy·ol** n ⟨chem⟩ *ichthyol*

·**Idaho** n (Staat der U.S.A.)

Ide·al n ~(e)s/~e **1.** (Vollkommenheit, höchstes Ziel) *ideal* ‖ ein ~ an Schönheit *an ideal of physical beauty*; das muß das ~ s *that must be the ideal*; er hat k–e ~e mehr *he has abandoned* od *lost his ideals*; ein Mensch mit hohen ~en *a man of lofty ideals* **2.** (Muster) (*beau*) *ideal*; *model*; *standard* ‖ sie ist das ~ e–r Hausfrau *she is the* (*very*) *ideal of a housewife* (od *the ideal h.*) ‖ → °Schwarm **ide·al A.** [a] **1.** *ideal* (*perfection*); ⟨fam⟩ *first-rate* (*actor*); *born* (*teacher*) ‖ °[verblaßt] *ideal* (*place*); *excellent, perfect, splendid*; ⟨sl⟩ *ripping*, → famos **2.** = ideell **B.** [adv] *ideally*; *perfectly* ‖ ~ veranlagt *ideal, idealistic*; ~ veranlagter Mensch *idealist* **Ide·al- ~bild** n *ideal image* ≈**is·ieren** vt/i [h] *to idealize* **~·ismus** m ⟨philos⟩ (Ggs Realismus), ⟨Lit⟩ (Ggs Materialismus) *idealism* ⟨a. übtr⟩ **Ideal·ist** m ~en/~en *idealist* ‖ ⟨dero⟩ *idealist, visionary*; kein bloßer ~ *no mere idealist* ≈**isch 1.** [a] *idealistic*; *ideal* ‖ ⟨dero⟩ *Utopian*; *visionary*; *unpractical* **2.** [adv] *idealistically* **Ide·al-konkurrenz** f ⟨jur⟩ *nominal coincidence* (*of offences*) **~typ** m *ideal type* **Id·ee** f ~/~n **1.** ⟨philos⟩ **a.** ⟨Gr⟩ *idea*; *ideal form*; *mental image*; *pattern* **b.** ⟨mod⟩ *idea*; *subjective notion*; *object of thought*; *mental perception* **2.** [verblaßt] *conception, idea, notion* ‖ *way of thinking*; *imagination* ‖ *vague belief*; *fancy* ‖ ein Mann mit ~n *a man* (*full*) *of i.s*; *an i.'d man*; ohne ~n *unidea'd* ‖ e–e gute ~ *a good i.* (od *hit*) ‖ falsche ~ *delusion*; fixe ~ *fixed i.*; *idée fixe* Fr; *obsession, monomania* L **3.** °⟨fig⟩ (Spur) e–e ~ (..) *a small amount, a trifle* (*of sugar*); *a pinch* (*of salt*); *a tinge* (*of sarcasm*); nur e–e ~ Rum *just a suspicion* od *drop of rum*; (um) e–e ~ höher, z lang *just a trifle higher, too long* **4.** °**keine** ~! *no i.!* ‖ °e–e leise ~ h v *to have an inkling of* (*a th*) ‖ °k–e blasse ~ h *to have not the faintest* od *slightest i.* (*of* ..) ‖ °das ist e–e ~! *that's a good i.* (v dir *of yours*)!, ⟨Am fam⟩ *you've got sth there* ‖ °das ist nicht 'ne ~ besser *that is not a bit better*; e–e geistreiche, gute ~ *a brain-wave* ‖ sich e–e ~ m v *to form an i. of* .. ‖ der ~ Fleisch u Blut verleihen *to put flesh and blood on the i.* ‖ jdn **auf** die ~ bringen *to give a p the i.*; auf e–e ~ k *to hit on an i.*; °er kam auf die ~ z klingeln *he got the i. into his head* (od *it occurred to him*) *that he might ring the bell* ‖ **von** e–r ~ Bessene(r) *ideologue*

ide·ell 1. [a] *ideal* (*representation*); *existing only in idea*; *imaginary*; in ~er Hinsicht *ideally* **2.** [adv] *ideally* **Id·een-** [–e:ən] *ideal* ≈**arm** a *poor in i.s*; *without imagination* **~assoziation** f *association of i.s* **~austausch** m *interchange of i.s* **~flucht** f = Gedankenflucht **~gemeinschaft** f *community of i.s* od *interests* **~geschichte** f = Geistesgeschichte **~-kreis** m *range of thought* **~lehre** f ⟨Gr philos⟩ *theory of i.s* ≈**reich** a *full of i.s*; *i.'d* **~verbindung** f = –assoziation **~welt** f *world of i.s*

·**Iden** m pl ⟨ant⟩ *ides* L pl (der 13. [im März, Mai, Juli, Oktober der 15.] Tag des Monats); die ~ des März *the ides of March*

identifiz·ieren vt [h] jdn ~ *to identify a p*; *to prove a p's identity*; *to place a p* (*I could not place him*) ‖ sich ~ mit jdm (etw) *to i.fy o.s. with a p* (*a th*) **Identifiz·ierung** f *i.fication* ‖ ⟨com⟩ ~szeichen (auf Kisten) *tally* **id·entisch** a *identical* ‖ ⟨math⟩ ~e Gleichung *i.cal equation*; ⟨dipl⟩ ~e Note *i.c note* ‖ ~ s mit .. *to be i.cal* od *i.fied with* ..; sich ~ erklären mit .. *to i.fy o.s. with*; *to throw in one's lot with* (*a p*) **Identit·ät** f ~/ *i.ty* ‖ ⟨log⟩ Satz v der ~ *law* (od *principle*) *of i.ty* ‖ die ~ jds, e–r S nachweisen *to prove the i.ty of a p* (*a th*) **Identit·äts- ~-ausweis** m *identification papers* **~nachweis** m *proof of i.ty* **~philosophie** f *philosophy of i.ty*

Ideo- Gr (Gedanken-) *ideo-* **~gr·amm** n *i.gram, i.graph* **~graph·ie** f *i.graphy* **~l·og(e)** m *i.logist, i.logue* ‖ ⟨übtr⟩ *visionary theorist*; *sophisticated p*; ⟨Am sl⟩ *highbrow*, ⟨hum⟩ *screwball* **~log·ie** f *i.logy* ‖ ⟨übtr⟩ *pure theory*; *sophistication*; ⟨Am sl⟩ *highbrowism* ≈**l·ogisch 1.** [a] *i.logical* ‖ ⟨übtr⟩ *visionary*; ⟨Am sl⟩ *highbrow* **2.** [adv] *i.logically*

Idio- [Gr] (Eigen-) *idio-* **~blast** m ⟨bot⟩ *i.blast* ≈**gr·aphisch** a *i.graphic* **~latr·ie** f *i.latry* ≈**m·orph** a *i.morphic, -phous* ≈**p·athisch** a ⟨med⟩ *i.pathic* **~pl·asma** n ⟨biol⟩ *i.plasm* **~synkras·ie** f *i.syncrasy*; ⟨med⟩ → Allergie ≈**synkr·atisch** a *i.syncratic* **Idi·om** n ~s/~e ⟨gram⟩ **1.** *idiom*; → Mundart ‖ *form* od *turn of expression* **2.** *i., language* (*of a* *country*); fremdes ~*foreign i.* **idiom·atisch** ⟨gram⟩ **1.** [a] *i.atic* (*English*; *expression*); ~e Wendung *i.*; *i.atic usage*; in ~er Hinsicht *i.atically* **2.** [adv] (*to write*) *i.atically* **Idiom·atik** f ~/ *study of i.atic expressions* ‖ *sum total of i.atic expr. in a language* **Idi·ot** m ~en/~en **1.** ⟨path⟩ *idiot*; *imbecile*; *natural*; ⟨Am⟩ *moron*; → Kretin **2.** °⟨fig⟩ *blockhead*, (*blithering*) *fool*, *i.*, *noodle* **|** °~enkringel [m] ([Menschen im] Foyer) *crush-room*; °≃ensicher [a] *foolproof* **Idiot·ie** f ~/~n ⟨path⟩ *idiocy*; *imbecility*; mongolische ~ *mongolism* **Idi·otikon** n [Gr] ⟨gram⟩ *idioticon* **idi·otisch 1.** [a] ⟨path⟩ *idiotic*; *half-witted*, *imbecile* ‖ °⟨fig⟩ *foolish*; *idiotic* **2.** [adv] *idiotically* ***Idiot·ismus** m ~/–men ⟨gram⟩ *idiom*, *idiotism*

·Ido n ~/ (Weltsprache) *Ido*

Idokr·as m ⟨minr⟩ *idocrase*

Id·ol n ~(e)s/~e *idol* **Idolatr·ie** f *idolatry*

Id·yll n ~s/~e *idyl(l)*; *peaceful pastoral* (od *rural*) *life* (od *scene*, *spot*); *secluded spot* **Id·ylle** f ~/~n **1.** = Idyll **2.** ⟨Lit⟩ *idyl(l)*; *bucolic*, *pastoral*; ~ in Prosa *prose idyl(l)* **|** ~ndichter *idyllist*; *idyllic poet* **id·yllisch 1.** [a] *idyllic* (*scene*, *place*); *bucolic*, *pastoral*; *picturesque* ‖ *piping* (*times of peace*) **2.** [adv] *idyllically* (*situated*)

-ig suff [z Bildung v Adj.] **1.** [aus Subst.] (= besitzend; versehen mit): buckelig, goldig, herzig [vgl herzlich], mutig **2.** [aus Verben] (= die Fähigkeit des Verbs besitzend): findig, säumig, wendig

·Igel m ~s/~ **1.** ⟨zoo⟩ *hedgehog*; *urchin* ‖ See≃ (*sea-*)*urchin*; *echinus* L ‖ er paßt dazu wie der ≃ z Halstuch *he is a square peg in a round hole* ‖ „~" (Bummelstreik 1962) ⟨Ger post⟩ *working to rule* **2.** ⟨agr⟩ = Hackgerät **3.** ⟨hist mil⟩; ⟨tact⟩ *all-round defence* **|** ~bildung, ~stellung [f] *h.* (*defence*) *position* **4.** °⟨fig⟩ *spiky p*; *cantankerous fellow*; *h.* **5.** ≃**artig** a *h.-like*; *bristly*; *spiky* **~fisch** m ⟨ich⟩ *prickly globe-fish* **~kaktus** m ⟨bot⟩ *h.-cactus* **~kolben** m ⟨bot⟩ *bur-reed*; *Sparganium* L **~schwamm** m ⟨bot⟩ *h.-mushroom* **~stellung** f ⟨mil⟩ *h.-position*

°**ig·itt**! intj; ~ ~! *faugh*! *foh*! *ugh*! *Good* (od *Goodness*) *Gracious*! → i!

·Iglu m ~s/~s (Schneehütte) *igloo*, *iglu*

Ignor·ant m ~en/~en *ignoramus* L; *ignorant p*; *duffer*; ⟨sl⟩ *nitwit* **Ignor·anz** f ~/ *ignorance* (*of a p*); → Unwissenheit **ignor·ieren** vt [h] jdn ~ *to ignore* (od *cut*, *slight*) *a p*; *to take no notice of a p*; *to give a p the cold shoulder*, *to cold-shoulder a p*; *to give a p the go-by*; jdn vollkommen ~ *to cut a p dead* ‖ etw ~ *to i.* (od *pass by*) *a th*; *to take no n.* (od *heed*) *of a th*; e–e Tatsache ~ *to blink a fact*

Igu·anodon n ~s/~s ⟨zoo⟩ *iguanodon*

ihm pron pers [dat sg v 'er'] **A. 1. a.** (P & T) *him* [engl stets vor dem Akk.]; ich erzählte ~ die Geschichte *I told him the story* ‖ ~ selbst *himself* **b.** (S & T) *it*; ich gab ~ (sc dem Hunde) z trinken *I gave it* (od *him*, → d.) *a drink* **c.** *(of countries, ships, etc.) *her*; der Gesandte schickte ~ (sc Italien) die Urkunde *the amb. sent her the deed* **2. a.** *to him*; es gehört ~ *it belongs to him*; *it is his* ‖ [engl mst hinter dem Akk.] sie erklärte es ~ *she explained it to him* **b.** (S etc) *to it*; er schrieb ~ (sc dem Einfluß) den Erfolg z *he ascribed the success to it* **c.** *to her*; er widmete ~ (sc dem Schiffe) *he devoted .. to her* **3. a.** *for him*; *she bought a book for him* **b.** (T & S) *for it* **c.** (of countries, etc.) *for her* **4.** es war ~, als wenn er erwachte aus .. *it was for him like passing out of ..* ‖ mit der ~ eigenen sanften Stimme *with that soft voice of his* **B.** [nach best prep] **1.** (P & T) *him*; mit ~ *with him*; v ~ *by him* ‖ er hatte kein Bild v ~ *he had no photo of him* ‖ e–e Schwester v ~ *a sister of his* **2.** (S & T) *it*; v ~ (sc dem Hund) *by it* (od *him*, → 1.) **3.** (of countries, etc.) *her*; mit ~ (sc Italien) *with her* **C.** [dativus ethicus] der Diener wurde ihm krank *the s. went ill on him* **ihn** pron pers [acc sg v 'er'] **1.** (P & T) *him*; sie streichelte ~ (sc den Hund) *she stroked him* **2.** (S & T) *it* **3.** (of the moon, etc.) *her* **ihnen** pron pers [dat pl v 'sie' pl] (vgl ihm) **A. 1.** (P, T, S) *them* [engl stets vor dem Akk.]; *I told them the story* ‖ ~ selbst *themselves* **2.** *to them*; *it belongs to them*; *it is theirs* ‖ [engl mst hinter dem Akk.] *he communicated the news to them* **3.** *for them*; *he bought a book for them* **4.** mit der ~ eigenen Genauigkeit *with that exactitude of theirs* **B.** [nach best prep] *them*; mit ~ *with them*; v ~ *by them* ‖ er hatte kein Bild v ~ *he had no photo of them* ‖ ein Freund v ~ *a friend of theirs* **·Ihnen** pron pers dat v 'Sie' [sg & pl] **A. 1.** *you* [engl stets vor dem Akk.]; *I must tell you the truth* **2.** *to you* [engl mst hinter dem Akk.]; *I will explain it to you* **3.** *for you*; *I bought these books for you* **B.** [nach best prep] *you*; mit ~ *with you* ‖ *.. no photo of you* ‖ ein Freund v ~ *a fr. of yours* **ihr**[1] pron pers [nom pl v 'du'] *you*; ~ übrigen *the rest of you* ‖ ~ selbst *yourselves* ‖ ~ hattet das tapfere Herz *yours was the brave heart* **ihr**[2] pron pers [dat sg v 'sie'] (vgl ihm) **A. 1. a.** (of P & ships) *her*; ~ selbst *herself* **b.** (S & T) *it* (*I gave it* [*the cat*] *a drink*) **c.** (T, of the sun) *him* (*I caught him* [sc *the mouse*] *a smack*) **2. a.** *to her*; *it belongs to her*; *it is hers* ‖ [engl mst hinter dem Akk.] *he suggested it to her* **b.** (S & T) *to it* (*he ascribed the success to it*) **c.** (T, of the sun) *to him* (*it is due to him* [sc *the sun*]) **3. a.** *for her* (*he bought the book for her*) **b.** (T & S) *for it* **c.** (of animals, the sun) *for him* **4.** mit der ~ eigenen sanften Stimme *with that soft voice of hers* **B.** [nach best prep] **1.** (P) *her*; mit ~ *with her*; v ~ *by her* ‖ e–e Schwester v ~ *a sister of hers* ‖ *he had no picture of her* **2.** (S & T) *it*; v ~ (sc der Spinne) *by it* **3.** (T, of the sun) *him*; mit ihr (sc der Ratte) *with him*

ihr[3] pron poss (→ sie, sg fem) **A.** [a] **1.** (P, ⟨fam⟩ of ships) *her*; *her dress*; *her hats*; einige ~er Londoner Freunde *some London friends of hers* **2.** (S & T) *its* **3.** (T, of the sun) *his*; ihr (sc der Ratte) Schwanz *his tail* **B.** [abs] [~e(r)/~es/ [pl] ~e] *hers*; (mein Schirm u) nicht ~er (..) *not hers* **ihr**[4] pron poss (→ sie, pl) **A.** [a] *their*; ~ Bruder *their brother*; ~e Brüder *their brothers*; einige ~er Freunde *some friends of theirs* **B.** [abs] [~e(r)/~es/[pl] ~e] *theirs*; mein Hut u nicht ~er *my hat and not theirs* **Ihr** [pron poss] (→ Sie) **1.** [a] *your*; ~ Herr Vater *your father*; ~e Bücher *your books* ‖ mein Mann u ~ Gatte *my husband and yours* ‖ e–r ~er Freunde *a friend of yours* ‖ → dein **2.** [abs] [~e(r)/~es/[pl] ~e] *yours*; mein Messer u nicht ~es *my knife and not yours* **·Ihre**[1] pron poss (→ ihr[3]) **1.** [a] ~ Majestät *Her Majesty* **2.** [abs] der, die, das ~, [pl] die ~n *hers*; es war der ~ (sc Schirm) *it was hers* **·Ihre**[2] pron poss (→ ihr[4]) **1.** [a] ~ Majestäten *Their Majesties* pl **2.** [abs] der, die, das ~, [pl] die ~n *theirs*; es ist das ~ (sc Haus) *it is theirs*; es waren die ~n (sc Schuhe) *they were theirs* **·Ihre**[3] pron poss [abs] (→ Ihr) der, die, das ~, [pl] die ~n *yours* ‖ (in Briefen) Stets der ~ *ever Yours*; ganz der ~ *Yours* (*very*) *truly* ‖ es ist das ~ (sc Messer) *it is yours* ‖ tun Sie das ~ *do your best* ‖ Schöne Grüße an Sie u die ~n *kind regards to you and yours* **·ihrer** pron pers [gen] **1.** [v 'sie' fem] *of her* **|** *of it* **|** *of him*; → ihr[2] **2.** v 'sie' [pl] *of them*; sie waren ~ sechs *they were six*; *there were six of them*; ~ w viele s *they will be many*; er wird sich ~ erinnern *he will remember them* **·Ihrer** pron pers [gen v 'Sie'] *of you*; sind Sie nicht ~ sechs? *are there not six of you*? ‖ ich werde ~ gedenken *I shall remember you* **·ihrerseits** adv **1.** (z 'ihrer' 1.) *for* od *on her part*; *on her side*; *in her turn*; die Türkei ~ *Turkey for her part* **|** *for its part*; *on its part* od *side* **|** (S, etc.) *for his part*; *on his part* od *side*; die Spinne ~ *the spider, for his part ..* **2.** (z 'ihrer' 2.) *for their part*; *on their part* od *side*: die Regierung ~ *the Government for their part* (*are prepared*) **·Ihrerseits** adv *for your part*; *on your part* od *side* **·ihresgl·eichen** adv [erstarrter gen] **1.** (→ ihr[3]) *her like*; ⟨fam⟩ *the like of her* **2.** (→ ihr[4]) *their like*(*s*); ⟨fam⟩ *the* *like(s) of them* ·**Ihresgleichen** adv (→ Ihr) *your like*; ⟨fam⟩ *the like of you* ‖ [pl] *your like(s)*; ⟨fam⟩ *the like(s) of you* ·**ihrethalben, ·ihretwegen** adv **1.** (→ ihr³) *on her account*; *for her sake*; *on* (od *in*) *her behalf*; *for all* od *aught she cares* **2.** (→ihr⁴) *on their account*; *for their sake*; *on* od *in their behalf*; *for all* od *aught they care* ·**Ihrethalben, ·Ihretwegen** adv (→ Ihr) *on your account*; *for your sake*; *on* od *in your behalf*; *for all you care* ·**ihretwillen, ·Ihretwillen** adv [nur in:] um ∼ = ihret-, Ihrethalben ·**Ihrige** pron poss [abs] = Ihre¹, ², ³ †·**Ihro** pron poss = Euer 2. *·**ihrzen** vt [h] (jdn) *to address a p as* 'ihr'

Ik·on(e) f ∼/∼(e)n *icon* Gr **ik·onisch** a *iconic*

Ikono- Gr (Bilder-, Bild-) *icono-* **∼gr·aph** m *i.-graph* **∼graph·ie** f *i.graphy* **∼kl·ast** m *i.clast* **∼kl·astisch** a *i.clastic* **∼latr·ie** f *i.latry* **∼log·ie** f *i.logy* **∼mach·ie** f *i.machy* **∼st·ase** f ∼/–staten *i.stasis* Gr

Ikosa·eder n ∼s/∼ ⟨math⟩ *icosahedron*

·**Ikositetraeder** n ∼s/∼ ⟨math⟩ *icositetrahedron*

·**Iktus** m L ∼/∼ ⟨pros⟩ *ictus* | ⟨path⟩ *ictus*

-ikum suff ⟨chem & med⟩ [f Fachausdrücke] *-ic*; Anästhet∼ *anaesthetic* °**-ikus** L suff [z Bezeichnung v P] Med∼ *medical man* ‖ ein Pfiff∼ *a sly one*; *a slyboots*; Schwachmat∼ *weakling*

·**Ilang-·Ilang** n ∼s/ ⟨bot⟩ *ilang-ilang* (⟨a.⟩ Öl)

ˣ·**Ilge** f ⟨bot⟩ *flag*

Ili·ade f, ·**Ilias** f *Iliad* ·**Ilion** Gr, ·**Ilium** L ⟨ant⟩ *ancient Ilium* L; Bewohner v ∼ *Ilian*

·**illegal 1.** [a] *illegal* **2.** [adv] *illegally* **∼it·ät** f ∼/∼en *illegality* ·**illegitim** a (unrechtmäßig) *illegitimate* (*candidate*) ‖ (unehelich) *illegitimate* (*child*) **∼it·ät** f *illegitimacy*

ˣ·**illern** vi [h] *to peep* (in *into*; um *round* ..)

illimit·iert a ⟨com⟩ *unlimited* (*order*)

Illinois [ili'nɔi] ⟨Am⟩ **1.** *Illinois*; Bewohner v ∼ *I.(i)an* **2.** [in comp] *I.an*; ⟨geol⟩ *Illinoian*

illiquid a ⟨com⟩ *illiquid* **∼it·ät** f *illiquidity*

illoy·al 1. [a] *disloyal*; *unfair* **2.** [adv] *disloyally*

Illoyalit·ät f *disloyalty*

Illumin·at m [L] ∼en/∼en: [mst pl] ∼en **1.** ⟨hist⟩ *illuminati* L pl **2.** ⟨ec hist⟩ = ∼enorden [m] ⟨ec hist⟩ (1776–84/85) *illuminati* **Illuminati·on** [ts] f ∼/∼en **1.** (Beleuchtung) (*artificial*) *illumination*, [oft pl] ∼en *i.s* pl **2.** ⟨hist paint⟩ (in Mss) *i.*; *miniature* **Illumin·ator** m ⟨hist paint⟩ *illuminator* **illumin·ieren** vt [h] **1.** (Stadt) *to illuminate*; *to light up brilliantly*; [a. abs] **2.** ⟨hist paint⟨ (Manuskript) *to illuminate*, *miniate*

Illusi·on f ∼/∼en *illusion*; *misleading impression*; *delusion* ‖ sich [acc] ∼en hingeben, sich [dat] ∼en m *to delude o.s.* (betreffs, über *as to*); sich der ∼ hingeben *to be under an ill.* (*that* ..); ich mache mir k–e ∼en über .. *I have no ill. about* .. ‖ jdm s–e ∼en rauben (*or* zerstören), jdn aus allen ∼en reißen *to disill.(ize)* (od *disabuse*, *disenchant*, *undeceive*) *a p* **Illusion·ismus** m *ill.ism* **Illusion·ist** m ∼en/∼en *ill.ist* **illusion·istisch** a *ill.nal*; *ill.ary* **illus·orisch** a *illusory*, *illusive*; *deceptive*; → gegenstandslos

ill·uster a *illustrious* (*lineage*); *distinguished*, *famous*; *noble* **Illustrati·on** [ts] f ∼/∼en (Bild) *illustration*; ganzseitige ∼ *plate* | ∼sgraphik [f] *pictorial art* **Illustr·ator** m ∼s/–at·oren *illustrator* **illustr·ieren** vt [h] **1.** (erläutern) *to illustrate*; *to be illustrative of* (*a th*); *to make clear* **2.** (mit Bildern schmücken) *to ill.*; *to ornament*; (Buch) übermäßig ∼ u den Text vernachlässigen *to grangerize*; reichlich –rt *lavishly illustrated* ‖ –rte Zeitung, **Illustrierte** f *picture magazine*; *pictorial* | ∼nschönheit [f] *pin-up girl* **Illustr·ierung** f *illustration* (z *to*); *picture* ‖ zur ∼ *in* od *as i.*

†**Ill·yrien** n (Küstenland am Adriatischen Meer) *Illyria* †**Ill·yrier** m, **∼in** f *Illyrian* †**ill·yrisch** a *Illyrian* †**∼e Halbinsel** f → Balkanhalbinsel †**∼es Gebirge** n → Dinarische Alpen ∼e Sprache, das ∼e *Illyrian*

ˣ·**Ilme** f ∼/∼n ⟨bot⟩ = Ulme

·**Ilmensee** m [Russ] *Ilmen Lake*; *L. I.*

·**Iltis** m ∼ses/∼se ⟨zoo⟩ *polecat*; *fitchet*, *fitchew*, *foumart*; → Frettchen, Marder, Wiesel

im ⟨fam⟩ = in dem **1.** ∼ (*or* in dem) *in the* (*garden*, *house*); niemand ∼ Hause *nobody about* (⟨Am⟩ *around*) *the h.*; weiter unten ∼ Tal *farther down the v.*; ⟨rail⟩ ∼ Zuge *on the train* **2.** [nur ∼] **a.** ∼ Hemd(e) s *to be in one's shirt* ‖ ∼ Hut(e), Mantel *with one's hat*, *coat on*; ∼ H., M. s *to be covered* (od *to wear a hat*); *to wear a coat* **b.** ∼ Schlaf(e) (hörte ich ..) *in my sleep* (..); (*when*) *sleeping* (..); ∼ Traum *in one's dream*; *dreaming* ‖ ∼ Sommer *in* (*the*) *summer*; ∼ Mai *in May* ‖ ∼ Osten *in the east* **c.** [vor Abstr.] ∼ Auftrag(e) v *by order of* .. ‖ → Begriff ‖ ∼ Bilde s → Bild C. 1. a. ‖ → Durchschnitt etc; Grund I. B. 4. d.; Hinblick etc; Namen ‖ s–e Hände ∼ Spiel h *to have one's finger in the pie* ‖ → Vergleich etc; **d.** [vor neutr. subst. Adj.] ∼ allgemeinen *in general*; *generally* (*speaking*) ‖ → Besondere; einzelne; freie; gering III. C. 2. b.; groß III. 2. ‖ ich bin ganz ∼ klaren *I am quite positive* (über *about*); *I quite understand* ‖ im reinen s mit *to have come to terms with*; *to be quits with* ‖ ∼ übrigen *for the rest*; *in other respects*; *otherwise* ‖ wir sind noch ∼ unklaren *we are still in the dark* (über *about*); *we are still undecided* | ∼ Deutschen *in German* | ∼ Fallen *or* Sinken s *to be on the decline*; *to sink* ‖ ∼ Steigen s *to rise*; ⟨fig⟩ *to be in the ascendant*

imagin·är a ⟨math⟩ *imaginary* (*number*)

***Imaginati·on** [ts] *imagination* **Imag·ismus** m ⟨engl & Am poet⟩ *imagism*, → d. **Im·ago** f (L) ∼/∼s *or* –gines ⟨scient ent⟩ *imago* L

·**Imbergans** f ⟨orn⟩ = Eistaucher

imbez·ill a ⟨med⟩ *imbecile* **∼it·ät** f *imbecility*

·**Imbiß** m –sses/–sse: kl ∼ *light meal* (od *repast*); *refreshment*; *snack*; ⟨Am⟩ *light lunch*(*eon*); ⟨liter⟩ *collation* ‖ e–n kl ∼ (ein)nehmen (*or* z sich nehmen) *to have a snack*; ⟨Am⟩ *to* (*take a light*) *lunch*(*eon*) **∼halle, ∼stube** f *snack-bar*; *luncheonette*; ein Glas in der ∼ trinken *to have a drink at the bar* **∼-stand** m *buffet*

Imitati·on [ts] f [L] ∼/∼en ⟨mus⟩ *imitation* | ⟨mst com⟩ *i.*; e–e ∼ v Marmor, Marmor∼ *an i. of marble* ‖ *counterfeit*, *fake*, *sham*; die Tassen sind ∼ *the cups are a fake*; die Perlen sind sämtlich ∼ *the pearls are all shams* **Imitati·ons-** *imitation*; *artificial*; *counterfeit*; *sham* **imit·ieren** vt [h] **1.** (jdn; jds Bewegungen) *to imitate*; *mimic*; → karikieren, parodieren **2.** ⟨com⟩ (Perlen etc) *to i.*; *counterfeit*, *fake*, *sham* **imit·iert** a *i.* (*pearls*); *f.* (*pewter*); → künstlich, unecht

·**Imker** m ∼s/∼ *bee-keeper*, *-master*; *apiarist*, *apiarian* **∼·ei** f ∼/∼en *apiculture*; *bee-culture*, ⟨Am⟩ *-yard*

imman·ent a ⟨philos & theol⟩ *immanent*; *immanental* **Imman·enz** f ∼/ *immanence*

·**immateriell** a *immaterial* (*goods*; *values*)

Immatrikulati·on [ts] f ∼/∼en *matriculation* **∼sbestimmungen** pl *regulations for the m.* **∼sprüfung** f ⟨engl⟩ *m.* (*-examination*) **immatrikul·ieren** vt [h] (jdn) *to matriculate*; –liert w *to be m.d* (in .. *at a College*); *to be entered* (*as*) *a student of* (..) ‖ sich ∼ l *to m.* (an .. *in a university*) **immatrikul·iert** a *m.d*; nicht ∼ *non-m.d*

ˣ·**Imme** f ∼/∼n *wasp* ‖ = Biene; → Wespe

Immedi·at- *immediate*; *direct* **∼eingabe** f, **∼gesuch** n *i. petition*; *petition made direct to the sovereign* (etc)

imm·ens a *immense* (*wealth*) **∼it·ät** f *immensity* | ∼ur·abel [a] *immensurable*; *immeasurable*

·**immer** adv **I.** ⟨eig⟩ **A. 1.** *always*; *constantly*; *continuously*; *permanently*, *perpetually* ‖ *water always holds a quantity of* ..; er will ∼ etw Besonderes *he always wants sth special*; ∼ müssen wir fragen *always we have to ask questions*; so ist es ∼ mit dir *that's always the way with you*; er war fröhlich wie ∼ *he was his old cheery self*; → immerfort | ⟨Am a.⟩ *all the time* **2.** [nur in best Verbindungen:] *ever*,

→ B. 2. b. c. 4. 6. **B.** [best. Verbindungen] **1.** er war ~ nur eine Freude f mich *he was never anything but a pleasure to me* || ~ etw tun *to keep doing a th*; er rauchte ~ *he kept smoking* || er spart ~ *he saves and saves* (*but* ..) **2.** [vor compr] **a.** ~ **besser** *better and b.*; ~ größer *greater and gr.* || ~ leichter u leichter *easier and easier* || ~ weiter gehen *to walk on and on*; er schrie ~ weiter *he went on crying* || ~ widerstrebender *more and more reluctant* || ~ breiter u tiefer w (S) *to go on widening and deepening* **b.** e–e ~ größere Menge *an ever bigger crowd*; ~ schnellere Folge *ever quicker succession*; ~ wiederkehrend *ever recurrent* (*noise*) **c.** ~ **mehr** *they hated each other increasingly* || ~ mehr wachsendes Entsetzen *ever increasing horror* || Köpfe u ~ mehr Köpfe *heads and more heads and more* **3.** (im Briefschluß) ≗ **der Ihrige** .. *ever Yours* ..; *Yours truly* .. **4.** ~ **noch, noch** ~ *still* || ~ **wieder** *ever and again* od *anon*; *again* (od *often, time*) *and again*; *constantly*; *time after t.*; ⟨Am⟩ *time without number*; e–e S ~ wieder berühren *to return to a th again and again*; ~ u ~ wieder *over and over again*; ab u zu ~ wieder *every once and again* **5.** ~, **wenn** er kann .. *whenever he came we* .. **6. f** ~, **auf** ~ *for ever*; *for good*; *for evermore*; *as a permanency*; f ~ u ~ *for ever and ever*; *for ever and aye* od *anon*; *for ever and a day*; ⟨Am a.⟩ *for keeps* **II.** [verblaßt] **1. wie auch** ~ *however*; Leute, wie reich sie auch ~ s mögen, w .. *people, however rich, will be* (*excluded*); wie einfach auch ~ *how simple soever* || **was (auch)** ~ eintreten mag *what*(*so*)*ever* (od *no matter what*) *may happen*; was f Gründe du auch ~ hast *what*(*so*)*ever reasons you have* || wer auch ~ *whoever*; wen ~ du erkennst .. *whomever* (od *no matter whom*) *you recognize* || **wo auch** ~ *whereever*; *no matter where* .. **2.** °**laß ihn nur** ~ **k** *let him come, though*; *let him come when he likes* || °wir wollen ~ anfangen *we will begin anyway* || er ist ~ dein Vorgesetzter *he is your superior after all* **~d·ar** adv ⟨bib & poet⟩ *evermore*; *for ever*; = f immer **~fort** adv *always*; *from first to last*; *eternally*; = immer I. A. 1. || er sah sich ~ um *he kept turning round*; *he turned round and round* **~grün 1.** a *evergreen* (*shrub*); ~e Eiche *live oak* **2.** ≗ n ⟨bot⟩ *evergreen*; *periwinkle*; gr ~ *larger p.*; kl ~ *common p.*; rundblättriges ~ *wintergreen* **~h·in** adv *after all* (*it might have been worse*); *anyhow, anyway* (*they were learning the language*); *somehow* || *all the same*; *nevertheless*; *still*; *yet* (*the Great War has made it plain that* ..); [stets am Ende des Satzes:] *though* (*she must have been attached to him, though*) **~während 1.** [a] *everlasting*; *perennial endless, eternal, perpetual*; *unceasing* **2.** [adv] *everlastingly*; *perpetually*; *unceasingly* **~z·u** adv *from first to last*; *endlessly*; *perpetually, uninterruptedly, unceasingly*; = immer I. A. 1. || ~! *go on*! ⟨fig⟩ *go it*! *keep it up*!

Immersi·on f ~/~en ⟨astr & opt⟩ *immersion*

Immigr·ant m ~en/~en *immigrant* **Immissi·on** f **1.** *appointment* (in .. *to an office*); *installation* **2.** ⟨jur⟩ *immission* || ⟨Ger⟩ *penetration of smoke, gas, etc. from one building to another*

immob·il a *immobile*; *immovable*; *stationary* || (Truppen) ~ m *to immobilize* **Immobili·ar- ~klage** f ⟨jur⟩ *real action* **~kredit** m *mortgage credit* **~vermögen** n *real property* (od *estate*); *realty*; *things* [pl] *real* **~versicherung** f *insurance of r. p.* **Immob·ilien** pl *real estate* od *property*; *realty*; *immovables* pl **~gesellschaft** f *property company* **~handel** m *dealing in r. e.*; *r. e. business* **immobilis·ieren** vt [h] *to immobilize*

Immoral·ismus m *immoralism* **-lit·ät** f ~/ *immorality*

Immortalit·ät f *immortality* **Immort·elle** f ~/~n ⟨bot⟩ *everlasting flower*; *everlasting*; (Sand≗) *immortelle*

imm·un a *immune* (gegen *from*); (jdn) ~ m *to i.nize*; *to render i.ne* || ⟨übtr⟩ *insusceptible* (gegen *to*); *proof* (*against*); → gefeit **~is·ieren** vt [h] (jdn) *to immunize*; *render immune* **≗is·ierung** f *i.nization*; *opsonic action* **≗it·ät** f ~/ **1.** ⟨jur⟩ *i.nity*; → Freiheit || ⟨ec⟩ [pl] *i.nities, privileges* pl **2.** ⟨med⟩ *i.nity* (gegen *from*); natürliche ~ *natural i.*; erworbene ~ *artificial i.*; ~ verleihen *to confer i.* **≗-chemie** f *i.no-chemistry* **≗körper, ≗stoff** m, **≗substanz** f *antibody*; *i.nity-conferring substance*; (vgl Antitoxin, Opsonin)

·Impaß m –sses/–sse ⟨cards⟩ *finesse*

Impast·ierung f, **Imp·asto** n ⟨paint⟩ *impasto* It

Imped·anz f ~/ ⟨el⟩ *impedance*

·Imperativ m ~s/~e ⟨gram⟩ *imperative*; *i. mood* || ⟨philos⟩ kategorischer ~ *categorical i.* **imperat·ivisch** a *i.* **Imper·ator** m L ~s/–rat·oren ⟨ant⟩ *imperator* || ⟨mod⟩ *emperor*; *imperator* **imperi·al** a *imperial* **≗·ismus** m ~/ *i.ism* || Geld≗ *plutocracy* **≗·ist** m ~en/~en *i.ist* **~·istisch** a *i.-istic* (*age*); *i.ist* (*policy, theory*); *jingo*; ~e Einstellung *i.ist leanings* pl **Imp·erium** n (L) ~s/–rien ⟨ant⟩ *imperium* L || ⟨mod⟩ *empire*; *imperium* L

·Imperfekt(um ~s/–ta) n ~s/~e ⟨gram⟩ *imperfect*; *i. tense*; → Vergangenheit

Imperson·ale n ~s/–lien *impersonal verb*

impertin·ent a *impertinent*; *impudent, insolent, saucy* **Impertin·enz** f ~/ *impertinence*; *impudence*

·Impetus m L *impetus* L; *impulse*; *stimulus* L

·Impf- (→ impfen) **~arzt** m *inoculator, vaccinator* **~gegner** m *anti-v.nist*; *opponent of v.ation*; *conscientious objector* **~gesetz** n *v.ation-Act* **~-messer** n *v.ator* **~narbe** f *v.ation scar* **≗pflichtig** a *subject to* (*compulsory*) *v.ation* **~pflichtige** [der ~, ein ~r] m *p subject to v.ation* **~schein** m *certificate of v.ation*; ⟨Am⟩ *immunization register* **~stoff** m *vaccine* (*matter*) | → Lymphe, Serum **~zwang** m *compulsory v.ation* **·impfen** vt [h] **1.** ⟨scient⟩ (P, T) *to inoculate* (mit *with*); sich ~ *to i. o.s.* (*with*) || (Kind, etc) gegen Pocken ~ *to i. with cow-pox against small-pox*; *to v.ate* [a. abs]; wieder~, nach~ *to rev.ate*; ein Kind ~ l *to have a child v.ated* **2.** ⟨hort⟩ → (ein)-pfropfen **3.** ⟨fig⟩ jdm etw ins Herz ~ *to engraft* od *implant a th* (*deep*) *in a p's heart* od *mind*; *to instil*(*l*) *a th into a p's mind*; *to imbue a p with a th* **·Impfling** m ~s/~e **1.** *child, p subject to vaccination*; *v.ated subject* **2.** ⟨hort⟩ = Pfropfreis **Impfung** f ~/~en ⟨scient⟩ (Schutz≗) *inoculation* (gegen *against*, mit *with*) || ~ gegen Pocken *v.ation*; Wieder≗, Nach≗ *rev.ation* || e–e ~ m *or* vornehmen = impfen

Implantati·on [ts] f ~/~en ⟨med⟩ *implantation*

impliz·ieren vt [h] (etw) *to imply* **impl·izit** a ⟨log⟩ *implicit* **impl·izite** adv L *implicitly*

Implos·ion f ~/~en *implosion*; → Explosion

imponder·abel a ⟨übtr⟩ *imponderable* **I-r·abile** n L ~/ [mst pl] **I-rab·ilien** pl **1.** †⟨phys⟩ *i.ables* pl **2.** ⟨fig⟩ *i.able matters* pl; *i.abilia* L pl **I-rabilität** f *i.ability*

Impon·ier- ~gehabe n ⟨eth⟩ *display* **impon·ieren I.** vi [h] **1.** *to be imposing*; *to be of an i. character* od *appearance*; *to impose* (durch *through*) **2.** jdm ~ *to impress a p deeply* od *strongly*; *to strike a p forcibly*; *to appeal to a p strongly* || jdm z ~ suchen *to put on airs with a p*; *to bluff a p* || jdm nicht ~ ⟨sl⟩ *to cut no ice with a p* || sich ~ l *to be deeply affected* od *impressed*; ich lasse mir nicht durch Drohungen ~ *I am not impressed by threats* || imponierend [a] *imposing*; *marvellous* (Leistung); ~e Art *i.ness* **II.** ≗**(wollen)** n ⟨eth⟩ *display*

Imp·ort m ~(e)s/~e = Einfuhr 1. **Imp·orte** f ~/~n **1.** *Havana* (*cigar*); ~n [pl] *Havanas* pl, *Havana cigars* pl **2.** *imports* pl; *import*(*ed*) *goods* pl **-t·eur** [–'tør] m ~s/~e *importer* **import·ieren** vt [h] (Waren) *to import*

impos·ant 1. [a] *commanding, compelling* (*personality*); *imposing* (*magnitude*); *impressive*; *majestic, stately*; *striking*; ~es Auftreten *command-*

ing presence; ~e Gestalt *c. figure* **2.** [adv] *imposingly*; *strikingly*

·impotent a ⟨med⟩ *impotent* **I-nz** f ~/ *i.nce*; ⟨physiol⟩ *infertility*, *infecundity*

Imprägn·ier- [in comp] *impregnating* (*oil*, *substance*) || *impregnation* (*vessel*) **i-en 1.** vt [h] (Holz) *to impregnate* (mit *with*); (Tuch) *to waterproof* **2.** ≈ n *impregnation* **i-t** a *impregnated*; *rotproof*; *waterproof* (*coat*); ⟨theat⟩ *fireproof* **I-ung** f ~/ ~en *impregnation* **~smittel** n *impregnating agent*; *impregnant*; *water-*, *fireproofing liquid*

impraktik·abel a *impracticable*

Impres·ario m (It) ~s/~s *impresario* [pl *-rios*]

Impressi·on f ~/~en *impression* **~·ismus** m ~/ ⟨arts, mus & Lit⟩ *i.ism* **~·ist** m ~en/~en *i.ist* **≈·istisch 1.** [a] *i.istic* (*painting*; *painter*; *poems*) **2.** [adv] *i.istically* **Impr·essum** n ~s/–ssen ⟨typ⟩ *imprint* **Imprim·atur** n (L) ~s/ ⟨print⟩ *imprimatur* L

Impr·omptu [a.: ɛ̃prɔ̃'ty] n [Fr] ~s/~s ⟨mus & Lit⟩ *impromptu* Fr

Improvisati·on [ts] f ~/~en *improvisation*; *extemporization*; → Stegreif || ⟨theat sl⟩ ad lib; komische ~ *gag* **-s·ator** m ~s/–sat·oren *improvisator*, *extemporizer*; ⟨theat⟩ *ad libber* **i-s·ieren** vt [h] ⟨mus & Lit⟩ (Melodie, Verse) *to improvise*, *extemporize*; *to produce extempore*; *to vamp*; (Mahl) *to knock .. up* ⟨fam⟩; ⟨theat⟩ *to ad-lib*, ⟨sl⟩ *to gag* **i-s·iert** a *improvised*, *extemporized*; *impromptu*; *extempore*; ~e Begleitung *vamp* || ~e Komödie → Stegreifkomödie

Imp·uls m L ~es/~e ⟨phys⟩ *impulse*; *impulsion*; ⟨el⟩ *pulse*; spezif. ~ (Raketentriebwerk) *specific thrust*; ⟨übtr⟩ *impulse* ⟨a. path⟩; *impetus*; *stimulus* L; jdm (e–r S) e–n ~ geben *to give an impulse to a p* (*a th*); *to impel a p*; *to stimulate a p* (*a th*) || unter dem ~ des Augenblicks *on the impulse* od *spur of the moment*; *done on i.* **Imp·uls-** ⟨wir⟩ *impulse* (*amplitude*, *modification*) **|** ~änderung [f] *change of momentum*; ~folgefrequenz [f] *pulse recurrence frequency*; ~geber [m] ⟨comp⟩ (*electronic*) *emitter*; ~meter [m] ⟨tech⟩ *impulse meter* **impuls·iv 1.** [a] *impulsive* (*act*); *impulsive* (*man*; *man*) *of impulse* **2.** [adv] *impulsively*; **~ handeln** *to act on impulse* **Impulsivit·ät** f ~/ *impulsiveness*

imst·ande adv **1.** er ist gut ~ f sein Alter *he is well preserved for his age* **2. a.** ~ s z tun *to be capable of doing*, *to be able to do*; *to be equal to doing*; nicht ~ .. *to be incapable of doing*, *to be unable* od *impotent to do*; nicht ~ z sprechen *incapable of speech* **b.** ⟨dero⟩ ~ s z (etw) *to be capable of* (*every wickedness*), *to be wicked enough for ..*; ~ s z tun *to be capable of doing*; *to go* (*to*) *the length of doing*

in prep **I. [mit dat]** (vgl im) **A.** ⟨**eig**⟩ **1.** (**Raum**; **Ort**) **a.** *in* (*Europe*, *Germany*); ~ der Stadt *in* (*the*) *town* **b. vor Städtenamen**: [vor Großstadt u Wohnsitz] *in*, [sonst] *at*; ~ Berlin *in Berlin*; ich wohne schon jahrelang ~ Lübeck *I have lived in L. for years* || er studierte in Kiel *he studied* od *was at Kiel* || die Leute ~ Hamburg *the Hamburg people* || *at the battle of W.* **|** [⟨engl⟩ andere Auffassung:] ich bin nie ~ London gewesen *I have never been to London* **c.** ~ **der Kirche, Schule** at (od *in*) *church*, *school* || drinnen ~ der K. *within the church* || ~ allen **Hotels** *at all hotels*; ~ **dem Hause** m–s Onkels *at my uncle's* || in e–r Mannschaft .. (*to play*) *in* (⟨Am⟩ *on*) *a team*; ~ der dritten Strophe *in the third strophe* **|** ~ der Hohen **Straße** wohnen *to live in* (⟨Am⟩ *on*) *High Street* **|** ~ den Straßen herumgehen *to walk* (*about*) *the streets* || ~ der ganzen Stadt *all over the town*; *throughout the t.* **|** ⟨übtr⟩ ~ den **Grenzen** s–s Einkommens leben *to live within one's income* || ~ den **Reihen** des Adels *within the nobility* || ~ e–m **Umkreis** v nicht über 2 Meilen v B. *within two miles of Berlin* **2.** (**Zeit**) **a.** *in* || ~ unserer Z. *in our age*; ~ dieser Z. *in this period* || ~ der Frühe *early in the morning* od *day* || ~ der Gegenwart *in* od *at the present day*; ~ der Jugendzeit *in early life*; ~ s–m ganzen L. *all through his life* **|** ~ e–r M. *in a minute*; ~ Zukunft *in the future* || ~ 5 Jahren *in 5 years*; *5 years hence*; ~ den nächsten 20 J. *within 20 years from now* || gleich ~ den ersten M. s–r Ehe *within a few months of his marriage* || ~ einigen T. *a few days hence* || ~ Kürze, ~ kurzem *in a short time*; *shortly* **b.** (**Zeitpunkt**) ~ diesem Alter *at this age*; im A. v *at the age of ..* **|** (Zeitraum) → innerhalb **B.** ⟨**übtr**⟩ **1.** (**Zustand**) **a.** ~ Schwarz *in black* || ~ Hemdsärmeln *in one's shirt-sleeves* || ~ U. *in uniform* || ~ Fahrt, ~ vollem Lauf *under way* || ~ Hörweite *within hearing* **|** ~ ihrer **Angst** *in her anxiety* (*she ..*); ~ Freud u Leid *in good and evil days*; ~ Trauer *in mourning*, *in black*; → Grad etc. || ~ eigener P *personally* **b.** *under* || ~ **Behandlung** s *to be under treatment*; sich ~ e–m Irrtum befinden *to be mistaken*; ~ Narkose *under chloroform*; ~ Reparatur *under repair*; ~ Übereinstimmung mit den Bestimmungen *under the regulations*; ~ dem Wahn leben *to be under the delusion* (*that ..*); in gutem baulichen Zustand *in* (*good*) *repair* **c.** *with* || ~ der besten Absicht *with the best intensions*; ~ aller Eile *with all speed* **2. a. gut s ~ etw** *to be good* (od *quick*; *a good hand*) *at a th* || bewandert *or* geschickt ~ *clever* (od *adept*, *skilful*) *at*; *skilled* od *versed in*; *familiar with* (*a th*) **b. handeln** ~ *to deal* (od *traffic*) *in* (*a th*) **|** ⟨fig⟩ er bekämpfte es mit allem, was ~ **ihm** war *he fought it hammer and tongs* (od *tooth and nail*); ⟨Am⟩ .. *with all there was to him* || die Ursachen liegen ~ ihm *the causes are within* (od *inside*) *him* || sich ~ jdm täuschen *to be disappointed in a p* **|** °er hat's ~ **sich** *he has it in him*; *there's sth in him* || °das hat es ~ sich *that's a hard nut to crack*, ⟨Am⟩ *it's got a kick to it* **3.** (**erstarrt**) → Betracht etc; Hinsicht **II. [mit acc]** (vgl ins) **A.** ⟨**eig**⟩ **1.** (**Richtung**: **Raum**) **a.** *into* (*the house*, *room*) || ~ die St. *into* (*the*) *town* || ~ die K., Sch. *into the church*, *school*; *to ch.*, *sch.* → K., Sch. || ~ See stechen *to put* (*out*) *to sea* **b.** [⟨engl⟩ andere Auffassung, bes bei *to place*, *put*] *in* || ~ den Ofen stellen *to place in the oven*; den Finger ~ das Wasser stecken *to put one's finger in the water*; sich ~ jds Lage versetzen *to put o.s. in a p's place* || ~ den Torweg einbiegen *to turn in at the gateway*; vgl durch I. A. 2. b. **2.** (**Zeit**) *into*; bis ~ das nächste J. *into the coming year* || °in die Jahre k (P) ⟨sl⟩ *to be getting on* || bis ~ die frühen Morgenstunden *into the small hours*; u weiter bis ~ unsere Zeit *and on to our own day*; → bis I. A. || es ging ~ die H. *it ran into the hundreds* || (etw) in die Länge ziehen *to protract*; *to spin out*; sich ~ die L. ziehen *to be protracted*; (of roads) *to lengthen out* **B.** ⟨**übtr**⟩ **1.** *into*; *to sink into oblivion*; *to fly into a passion*; → Erscheinung || **teilen** ~ *to divide into*; verwandeln ~ *to convert into* **|** *to*; in Musik setzen *to set to m.*; (Kind) ~ den Schlaf singen *to sing to sleep* || ~ Ordnung bringen *to reduce to order*; (jdn) in gr Schwierigkeiten br. *to put to great inconvenience*

-in [lebendes suff z Bildung weibl. Wesen u Berufe z Maskulinen auf –er etc] [Wiedergabe des Stichworts im Engl.] **1.** [durch bes Wort:] Damenschneider~ *dressmaker*; Putzmacher~ *milliner* || Hünd~ *bitch* **2.** [durch Hinzufügung von] **a.** *female*, *girl*, *lady*, *woman*: Ärzt~ *woman-doctor* [pl *woman* (od *women*)-*doctors*]; Begleiter~ *female companion*; Sänger~ *lady singer* [pl *lady singers*] || Häs~ *female hare*; Hünd~ *lady dog* **b.** (T) *she*: Hünd~ *she-dog* **3.** [durch bes Endung] **a.** *-ess*: Dichter~ *poetess*; Löw~ *lioness* **b.** *-trix* [z masc *-tor*]: Verwalter~ *administratrix*

in- L = nicht **~adäqu·at 1.** [a] *inadequate*; *not adequate* **2.** [adv] *inadequately* **~akkur·at 1.** [a] *inaccurate*; *not accurate* **2.** [adv] *inaccurately* **~-akt·iv** a **1.** *inactive* (*soldier*; *member*); *indolent* || *unoccupied*; ~ s *not to take an active part*; *not to be an active member* **2.** ⟨chem⟩ ~es Gas *inert gas* **|** ≈vit·ät [f] ~/ *inactivity*

In- [→ in II. B.] **~·angriffnahme** f ~/ *beginning, starting; tackling (of problems); undertaking (of a th); coping, grappling (with); embarking, entering ([up]on) (a th)* **~·anspruchnahme** f ~/ **1.** die ~ e–r S *the employment* od *use of a th*; ⟨com⟩ *implementation* (e–r Garantie) ‖ ~ v Raum *occupancy of space* ‖ ohne ~ v Waffen *without resort to arms* ‖ unrechtmäßige ~ *encroachment* (od *infringement, inroad*) ([gen] *on a th*) **2.** ~ jds f *or* durch .. *absorption of a p's mind in ..; engrossment* od *preoccupation of a p's mind with (a th)* ‖ infolge starker ~ *owing to pressure of work* **3.** ~ der Zeit jds (*or* v jds Zeit) *absorption of a p's time; call* (od *demand*) *upon a p's time* ‖ ohne ~ s–r Einbildungskraft *without drawing on his imagination* ‖ e–e starke ~ m–r Börse *a drain* (od *strain*) *on my purse* ‖ übermäßige ~ m–r Zeit *encroachment* (od *infringement, inroad*) *on my time*

Inaugur·al- L *inaugural* ‖ ~dissertation [f] ⟨univ⟩ *dissertation; i. treatise*; ~rede [f] *i. speech*; *i.* [s] **-rati·on** [ts] f ~/~en *inauguration* **i-r·ieren** vt [h] (etw) *to inaugurate*

In·aussichtstellung f ~/ *promise (of a th)*; ~ v Hoffnungen *the holding forth of hopes* (auf *of*)

·Inbegriff m ~(e)s/~e *essence, quintessence; sum; embodiment, incarnation (of health)*

·inbegriffen adv → einbegriffen, einbegreifen

Inbetr·ieb- **~nahme** f ~/~n *initiation; opening (of a railway-line); starting (of a works)* ‖ *exploitation; utilization*; ⟨comp⟩ *implementation; commissioning* (e–s Werks etc) **~setzung** f [gen] *starting of (a th); putting .. in operation; setting .. going* ‖ *initiation; opening*

·Inbild n ~(e)s/~er → Ideal

·Inbrunst f ~/ *ardour, ardours* pl *(of passion); fervour, fervency; passion; unction; (religious) urge*; mit ~ *with fervour; fervently* **·inbrünstig** **1.** [a] *ardent (love); fervent, fervid; deep; passionate* **2.** [adv] *ardently; fervently*; = mit Inbrunst | **≈keit** f ~/ = Inbrunst

Indam·in n ~s/ ⟨chem⟩ *indamine*

Indanthr·en n ~s/~e ⟨com⟩ **1.** *indanthrene* **2.** ~blau [n] *i. blue*

indefin·it a *indefinite* **Indefinitpronomen** n ⟨gram⟩ *indefinite pronoun*

indeklin·abel a ⟨gram⟩ *indeclinable (noun)*

ind·em **A.** [adv] (* = indes) **B.** [conj] **1.** (Gleichzeitigkeit) *as*; ~ er vorüberging, bemerkte ich .. *as he passed I noticed ..* ‖ ~ er dies sagte, hob er .. *saying this he lifted ..*; → während **2.** (= dadurch daß) man befestigt die Feder, ~ man sie befeuchtet *you fix the feather by moistening it* ‖ ~ er dies schilderte, schrieb er e–e Satire *in describing this he was writing a satire* ‖ *(= da, weil) *as; since*

Indemnit·ät f ~/~en ⟨pol⟩ *indemnity*; jdm ~ erteilen *to give an i. to a p; to indemnify a p* (f *for*) **~sgesetz** n ⟨engl hist⟩ *Act of Indemnity (1660)*

Ind·en n ~s/~e ⟨chem⟩ *indene*

Ind·ent n & m, **~geschäft** n ⟨com⟩ *indent*; (etw) durch ein ~ bestellen *to indent*

Independ·ent m ~en/~en ⟨engl ec hist⟩ (seit ca. 1644) *Independent* | **≈** [a] ⟨ec⟩ *independent* **Independant·ismus** m ⟨ec hist⟩ *Independency*

·Inder m, **~in** f *Indian, Indian woman*; eingerener ~ *Hindoo, Hindu*

ind·es(sen) **A.** [adv] *meantime, meanwhile; in the meantime; by that time* ‖ *at that moment (a girl had entered)* **B.** [conj] **1.** [beiordnend: jedoch] *however*; → aber ‖ *after all; all the same; nevertheless; still; yet (it was so)* ‖ *though* [stets am Ende des Satzes] (*I wish you had told me, though*) **2.** [unterordnend: während] *while; whereas*

·Index m L ~es/~e *or* Indizes **1.** ⟨math⟩ *index* **2.** (Verzeichnis) ⟨bank⟩ *(shares) i.*; *i.*; (Buch) mit e–m ~ versehen *to i.* ‖ ⟨R. C.⟩ der ~ *the I. (of Prohibited Books) (to put on the I.)*; (Buch) auf den ~ setzen *to ban; interdict* ‖ ⟨stat⟩ *index number* ‖ ⟨comp⟩ *subscript* **~klausel** f *escalator clause* **~lohn** m *escalator* **~- u Verteilerlisten** pl *register and distribution lists*

·indezent **1.** [a] *indecent (story); improper; unbecoming* **2.** [adv] *indecently*

·Indiafaser f ⟨com⟩ *crin végétal* Fr

Indi·ana n (Staat der U.S.A.)

Indi·aner m ~s/~ (*Red* od *American*) *Indian*; die ~ [pl] ⟨a.⟩ *the redskins* pl, ⟨fam⟩ *the Reds* pl ‖ *(honest) Injun; Amerind(ian)* ‖ südamerik. ~ *Indio* | ⟨übtr⟩ (feindliche Flieger) ⟨aero⟩ *strangers* pl | [in comp] *Indian*; ⟨Am fam⟩ *Amerind(ian)* **~frau** f *squaw* **~hütte** f *wigwam* **~reich** n *I. state* **~sommer** m *I. summer* **~sprache** f *language of the American I.s* **~stamm** m *I. tribe*; die 5 **≈e** *the Five Nations* pl **~territorium** n *I. Territory* **Indi·anerin** f ~/~nen *American I. woman; squaw*; Weißer, der mit e–r ~ verheiratet ist *squaw-man* **indi·anisch** **1.** [a] *Indian*; ⟨Am fam⟩ *Amerind(ian)*; ~e Frau *squaw*; ~e Sprache → 2. **2.** das **≈e** *Indian*

·Indien ⟨geog⟩ *India*; (*the East Indies* pl) ‖ Brit. Reichsamt f ~ *I. Office* ‖ Stern v ~ (Orden) *Order of the Star of I.* ‖ Selbstverwaltung f ~ ⟨Ind⟩ *Swaraj*; Verfechter der Selbstverwaltung f ~ *Swarajist* ‖ Europäer, der lange in ~ gelebt hat ⟨AInd⟩ *Qui h(a)i* **Indienfahrer** m (Schiff) *Indiaman*

Ind·ienst- **~haltung** f (of a warship) *keeping in commission* **~nahme** f feierliche ~ → Einweihung **~stellung** f ⟨nav⟩ *commissioning (of a warship)*

·indifferent **1.** [a] **a.** (P) *indifferent* (gegen *to*) **b.** ⟨phys⟩ ~es Gleichgewicht *indifferent* od *neutral equilibrium* ‖ ⟨chem⟩ *neutral; indifferent (waters); inert (gas)* **2.** [adv] *indifferently* **Indiffer·enz** f *indifference* (gegen *to*); *unconcern; neutrality* | ~punkt [m], ~zone [f] ⟨phys⟩ *i. point; point of i.*

·Indig- [in comp] (= Indigo-) *indigo-*

indig·en a *indigenous* **Indigen·at** n *legal indigenous status, right of a native*

Indigesti·on f ~/~en *indigestion*

Indignati·on [ts] *indignation* **indign·iert** **1.** [a] *indignant* **2.** [adv] *indignantly* **Indignit·ät** f *indignity; insult*

·Indigo m ~s/~s **1.** ⟨bot⟩ (~strauch) *indigo; i. plant; anil; I.fera* L **2.** ⟨com⟩ (Farbstoff) *i.; a.* **3.** (Farbe) *i.* [pl *i.s*] **4.** [in comp] *i.* **≈ähnlich** a *i.tic*

Indikati·on [ts] f ~/~en ⟨med⟩ *indication*

·Indikativ m ~s/~e ⟨gram⟩ *indicative; i. mood*

indikat·ivisch a *i.* **Indik·ator** m ~s/–kat·oren **1.** ⟨phys & chem⟩ *indicator* L [in comp] *i.* ‖ ~diagramm [n] *i. diagram* **Indik·atrix** f ~/ ⟨geom⟩ *indicatrix* L

Indikti·on [ts] f ~/~en ⟨ec⟩ *indiction*

·indirekt **1.** [a] *indirect (method; result; tax)* ⟨gram⟩ ~e Rede *i.* (od *oblique, reported*) *speech*; (etw) in ~er Rede zitieren *to quote i.ly* ‖ ⟨mil⟩ *i.* (*fire, laying* Richten); ~e Leistung etc *aside* ‖ ~e Ursache *collateral* od *secondary cause* ‖ auf ~em Wege *i.ly, mediately* **2.** [adv] *i.ly; by i.ion*

·indisch a **1.** *Indian (flora; language; life)* ‖ ~er Flachs *jute* ‖ ~er Feigenbaum *banian-tree* ‖ ~es Korn → Sorghum ‖ ~er Kaufmann *banian, banyan* ‖ der **≈e** Ozean *the I. Ocean* ‖ das ~e Kaiserreich *the I. Empire* ‖ die einheimische ~e Regierung ⟨AInd⟩ *the Sirkar* od *Sircar* ‖ die ~e Literatur, Kunst *I. literature, art* **2.** [in comp] *I.*

·indiskret **1.** [a] *indiscreet; tactless*; in ~er Weise *i.tly* **2.** [adv] *indiscreetly; tactlessly* **I-ti·on** [ts] f ~/~en *indiscretion*; e–e ~ begehen *to commit an i.; to be indiscreet*; ⟨sl⟩ *to drop a brick*

indiskut·abel a *indiscussible*; [pred] *out of court*

·indisponibel a ⟨com⟩ *not capable of being disposed of* **·indisponiert** a [mst pred] *indisposed; out of sorts; seedy; unwell*; ⟨Am a.⟩ *mean*; → unpäßlich | **≈heit** f *ailing; ill health*, etc

Individu·al- [in comp] *individual* ‖ ~eigentum [n] *private* od *personal property* ‖ ~psychologie [f] *i. psychology*; ~versicherung [f] *i. insurance* **≈isieren** vt [h] *to individualize; individuate* ‖ *partic-*

ularize, specify **~is·ierung** f ~/~en *i.lization* **~·ismus** m *i.lism* ‖ *self-centred conduct*

Individual·ist m ~en/~en *i.list* **individual·istisch 1.** [a] *i.listic*; *i.list* (*development*); in ~er Weise *i.listically* **2.** [adv] *i.listically* **~it·ät** f ~/~en *i.lity*; *individual character*; *distinct personality* ‖ e–r S ~ verleihen *to i.lize a th* **individu·ell 1.** [a] *individual* (*difference*); *particular* ‖ ~e Behandlung *i.lization*; in ~er Hinsicht, vom ~en Standpunkt aus *i.lly* **2.** [adv] *i.lly* (*different*); ~ behandeln, darstellen *to i.lize* **Indiv·iduum** n ~s/–duen **1.** *individual*; *i. person* ‖ *human being*; *p.* **2.** ⟨cont⟩ *fellow*; *man*; ⟨sl⟩ *bloke*, ⟨Am sl⟩ *guy*

Ind·iz n ~es/~ien [iən] ⟨jur⟩ *indicium* L; *evidence*; [mst pl] ~ien *indicia* | ·Indizes [pl] v Index [m] *circumstantial* od *presumptive evidence* **≃·ieren** vt [h] *to indicate* ‖ –rt *indicated* (*work*); –rte Leistung *indicated power*; es f–rt halten *to consider proper* (od *advisable*)

·Indo- [in comp] *Indo-* **~·arier** m (*I.-*)*Aryan* **~·ch·ina** *I.china* **≃chin·esisch** a *I.-Chinese* **~europ·äer** m *I.-European* **≃europ·äisch** a *I.-European* **~germ·ane** m *Aryan*; *I.-European* **≃germanisch 1.** [a] *I.-Germanic* **2.** ≃; das ~e *I.-Germanic* **~log(e)** m *indologist* **~log·ie** f *Indology* **≃sk·ythisch** a *I.-Scythian* (od *Scythic*) **~n·esien** [–iən] *Indonesia* **~n·esier** m ~s/~ *Indonesian* **≃n·esisch** a *Indonesian*

indol·ent a *indolent*; *inactive*; *idle* ‖ (schmerzlos) *indolent* (*tumour*) **Indol·enz** f ~/ *indolence*

indoss- **~·abel** a ⟨com⟩ [pred] *endorsable* **≃·am·ent** n ~(e)s/~e ⟨com⟩ *endorsement*, *ind-*; *transference* **≃·ant** m ~en/~en *endorser*, *ind-*; *transferrer*, *transferor* **≃·at** m ~en/~en; **≃·at·ar** m ~s/~e ⟨com⟩ *endorsee*, *ind-*; *transferee* **~·ieren 1.** vt [h] ⟨com⟩ (e–n Wechsel) *to endorse*, *ind-* **2.** ≃ n *endorsation*; ⟨a.⟩ *backing* **≃·ierung** f **Ind·osso** n ~s/~s = Indossament

Indox·yl n ~s/~e ⟨chem⟩ *indoxyl* **~säure** f *indoxylic acid*

Indri m ~s/~s ⟨zoo⟩ *indri*

in dubio pro reo L ⟨jur⟩ (*to*) *give a p the benefit of the doubt*; *in dubio pro reo*

Indukt·anz f ⟨phys⟩ *inductance* **Indukti·on** [ts] f ~/~en **1.** ⟨philos⟩ *induction*; *inductive reasoning*; (etw) durch ~ ableiten, schließen *to induce*; auf dem Wege der ~ *inductively* **2.** ⟨phys el⟩ *induction*; wechselseitige ~ *mutual i.*; durch ~ erzeugen *to induce* **Indukti·ons-** ⟨el⟩ *induction-* **~apparat** m *inductor* **~elektrizität** f *i.-electricity* **≃frei** a *non-inductive* (*circuit*) **~gesetz** n *Faraday's Law of electromagnetic inductance* **~ofen** m *i.-furnace* **~spule** f *induction coil* **~strom** m *i.-current*; *induced current* **indukt·iv 1.** [a] *inductive* (*method*); auf ~em Wege *i.ly*, *by i. reasoning* **2.** [adv] *i.ly* **Induktivit·ät** f *inductivity*; *inductance* **Ind·uktor** m ~s/–ukt·oren ⟨el⟩ *inductor* | ~spule [f] *induction-coil*

in dulci jubilo L (in süßem Jubel) ⟨fam⟩ = → herrlich u in Freuden

indulg·ent 1. [a] *indulgent* **2.** [adv] *indulgently* **Indulg·enz** f *indulgence*; *remission*

·Indus m (Strom in Vorderindien) *Indus*

industrialis·ieren 1. vt [h] (ein Land) *to industrialize* **2.** ≃ n = **I-s·ierung** f ~/~en *i.zation* **Industr·ie** f *industry*; Handel u ~ *commerce and industry* ‖ chemische ~ *chemical i.ries* pl ‖ Baumwoll≃ *cotton industry*; Eisen≃ *iron industry* ‖ in der ~ beschäftigt *or* verwandt, f die ~ eingerichtet *industrial* (*classes*; *alcohol*) ‖ in bezug auf die ~ *i.ly* ‖ die Einführung der ~ in e–m Lande *the i.ization of a country* ‖ ~n in e–m L. gründen *to i.ize a country* **Industr·ie-** *industrial* **~aktie** f *i. share*; ~n [pl] *i.s* pl **~anlage** f; ~n [pl] *i. fixtures* pl; *plant* **~arbeit** f *i. labour* od *work*; *factorywork*; Heimschule f ~ (f gefährdete Kinder) *i. school* **~arbeiter** m *i. worker*; *factory-worker*; *mill-hand* **~ausstellung** f *i. exhibition* **~bahn** f ⟨Am⟩ *industrial track* **~bank** f *i. bank* **~baron** m *captain of industry*, ⟨Am fam⟩ *tycoon* **~belastung** f ⟨Ger⟩ *charge on industry under the Dawes Plan* (*1924*) **~betrieb** m *i. establishment* **~bezirk** m *i.* od *manufacturing district* **~dunst** m *smog* **~erzeugnis** n *i. product* **~gebiet** n *i. region*; ⟨Ger⟩ (Westfäl. ~) *the Black Country* **~gelände** n *i. area* **~gericht** n *i. court* **~gesellschaft** f *i. company* **~kammer**: Industrie- u Handelskammer *Chamber of Com. & Ind.* **~land** n *i. country* **~magnat** m = –baron **~messe** f: Britische ~ *the British Industries Fair* **~nation** f *industrialized nation* **~obligation** f *i. bond* **~papier** n; ~e [pl] *i. securities* pl; *i.s* pl °**~ritter** m *swindler*; *exploiter* **~staat** m *i. state*; ein Land z e–m ~ m *to i.ize a country* **~stadt** f *i.* od *manufacturing town* **~tag** m: Industrie u Handelstag → Spitzenverband **~unternehmen** n *i. undertaking* od *enterprise* **~zeitalter** n *i. age*; *age of industry* **~zweig** m (*branch of*) *industry* **industri·ell 1.** [a] *industrial* (*occupation*; *wealth*); ⟨engl hist⟩ ~e Umwälzung *I. Revolution* ‖ in ~er Hinsicht *i.lly* **2.** [adv] *i.lly* **Industri·elle** m [der ~, ein ~r] ~n/~n *industrial*(*ist*); *manufacturer*; der Groß≃ *the industrial magnate*; *captain of industry*

induz·ieren vt [h] ⟨philos & el⟩ *to induce*

inein·ander 1. [adv] *into each other*; *into one another* **2.** [in comp] *or* [bei Verben betontes, trennbares pref]: **~|arbeiten** vi [h] *to interact*; *co-operate*; *to play into each other's* (od *one another's*) *hands* **≃arbeiten** n *interacting*, *interaction* **~|flechten** vt [h] (Dinge) *to interlace*, *-twine*, *-twist*, *-weave* **~|fließen** vi [s] *to interflow* **≃fließen** n *interflow* | ~d *interfluent*; (Farbe) ⟨paint⟩ *fondu* Fr **~|fügen** vt [h] (Dinge) *to weld*; *to join into a whole* ‖ ⟨übtr⟩ *to couple*; *unite* **≃fügung** f *jointing* **~|greifen** vi [h] **1.** ⟨tech⟩ (of cogs) *to gear together*; *to g. into each other*; *to match*; *interlock*; *tooth*; (of wheels) *to lock*, *mesh* **2.** ⟨fig⟩ *to work together*, *co-operate* **≃greifen** n *gearing* ‖ ⟨fig⟩ *interplay* (*of forces*) | ~d *interdependent*; ⟨tech⟩ *interlocked* **~|legen** vt [h] *to clasp*; die Hände –gelegt hörte er zu *he listened, with one hand clasped in the other* **~|packen** vt [h]: *to pack into each other*; –gepackt s *to be packed one inside another*; *to be nested* **~|passen** vi [h] die Becher p. in–e–a *the cups are nested* **~|schieben** vt [h] (Dinge) *to telescope* ‖ sich ~ *to telescope* ⟨a. rail⟩ **~|schlingen** vt [h] *to twist* **≃spielen** n ⟨fig⟩ *interplay* (*of forces*) **~|stecken** vt [h] (Rohre) *to fit into each other*; *to stick one within another* **~|stricken** vt [h] grüne u blaue Wolle ~ *to knit in the green with the blue wool* **~|übergehen** vi [s] *to blend* | ~d *transilient* (*rock*) **~|weben** vt ⟨fig⟩ [h] *to wind into each other*; *to interpenetrate* ‖ sich ~ *to i.*

Inempf·angnahme f *reception*

Inersch·einungtreten n *appearance*; *emergence*

·inexakt 1. [a] *inexact*; *inaccurate*; *not exact* **2.** [adv] *inexactly*

in ext·enso L *in full*; *in extenso*

infall·ibel a [mst pred] *infallible* **Infallibilit·ät** f ~/ *infallibility* (*of the pope*)

inf·am 1. [a] *infamous* (*crime*); *atrocious*; *cowardly* (*lie*); *detestable*; *dirty* (*practices*); *foul* (*rogue*); *shameless* (*liar*) ‖ ~er Kerl ⟨Am⟩ *heel* ‖ in ~er Weise *shamelessly*; → gemein | [verblaßt:] *confounded*; *infernal* (*nuisance*); *beastly* (*cold*); ⟨Am⟩ *pesky* **2.** [adv] *atrociously*; *detestably*, etc ‖ [verblaßt:] *confoundedly*; *deucedly* **Infam·ie** f ~/~n *infamy*; *disgrace*; *shamefulness*

Inf·ant m ~en/~en *infante* [Span] **·Infant(e)r·ie** f ~/~n ⟨mil⟩ **1.** *infantry*; *foot*; *foot soldiers* pl ‖ Hauptmann der ~ *captain of foot* ‖ ~ u Kavallerie *foot and horse* ‖ → Schütze **2.** [in comp] *infantry* (*brigade*, *division*) **~attacke** f *i. charge* **~begleitgeschütz** n *i. support gun* **~führer** m *officer commanding the i. of a division*, etc. **~geschütz** n *trench-gun* **~kolonne** f *i.supply column* **~regiment** n *i. regiment*; *regiment of foot*; *Rifle regiment*; *Rifles* pl; das fünfte ~ *the fifth foot* **~schule** f *I.*

School **~spitze** f *i. point* **~taktik** f *i. tactics* pl **~-verband** m; ∸e [pl] *i. units* pl **~werk** n ⟨fort⟩ *entrenchment* **·Infant(e)r·ist** m ~en/~en *i.man*; *foot* od *i. soldier* ‖ 3000 ~en *3000 foot* od *infantry* **infant·il** a *childish*; *retarded* **Infantil·ismus** m *infantilism* **Inf·antin** f ~/~nen *infanta* [Span]

Inf·arkt m ~s/~e ⟨path⟩ *infarct*

°**Infaul·enzia** f *lazyitis* ‖ ~ h *to slumber in*

Infekti·on [ts] f ~/~en ⟨med⟩ *infection*; (~ durch Berührung) *contagion* **~skrankheit** f *infective* od *infectious disease*; (durch Berührung verursacht) *contagious d.* **~smodus** m *mode of infection* **~smöglichkeit** f *susceptibility to infections* **infekti·ös** [ts] a *infectious*; *infective*; ~e Beschaffenheit *infectiousness*

·Infel f ~/~n ⟨R. C.⟩ → Inful

inferi·or a ⟨dero⟩ *inferior*; *mediocre*; *poor* (*player*); *second-rate*; ~er Geist *mediocrity*; in ~er Weise *inferiorly* **∸it·ät** f ~/~en *inferiority*; *mediocrity* | ~skomplex [m] *i. complex*

infern·al(isch) a ⟨mst übtr⟩ *infernal* (*smell*); *devilish*, *hellish*; *outrageous*

Infibulati·on [ts] f ~/~en ⟨ant⟩ *infibulation*

Infiltrati·on [ts] f ~/~en *infiltration* **i-tr·ieren** vt [h] *to infiltrate*; ⟨übtr⟩ (Land) *to i.* (mit *with*)

infinitesim·al a *infinitesimal* **∸rechnung** f *i. calculus* **·Infinitiv** m ~s/~e ⟨gram⟩ *infinitive* (*form* od *mood*) **infinit·ivisch** a *infinitive* **Infinit·ivus** m L = Infinitiv **Infin·itum** n L *infinity*, *infinitude*; *the infinite* ‖ ad ~ L *to infinity*

infiz·ieren vt [h] ⟨med⟩ (jdn) *to infect* (mit *with*) ⟨a. fig⟩ ‖ sich ~ *to become* od *get infected*

in flagr·anti L *in flagrante delicto* L

inflat·ieren vt [h] (Währung) *to inflate*; –flatiert *inflated* **Inflati·on** [ts] [h] ~/~en ⟨com⟩ *inflation*, ⟨Am⟩ *depression* (1929 ff.) **i-(al)·istisch** a *inflationary* **Inflations-** *inflationary* (*effects*); ~erscheinung [f]; ~en [pl] *inflationary symptoms* pl; ~politik f *inflationism*

Influ·enz f ~/ ⟨el⟩ *induction*; **influence*; ~maschine [f] *influence machine*

Influ·enza f It –/ ⟨med & vet⟩ *influenza* ‖ *grippe* Fr; ⟨fam⟩ *flu*(*e*); ~ h *to have* (*the*) *flu* ‖ (T) → Staupe **influ·ieren** vi [s] *to flow in*

inf·olge 1. [prep] [gen] *on account of*, *in consequence of*, *as the* (od *a*) *result of*, *on the strength of*; *consequent* od *subsequent* (*up*)*on*; *owing to* ‖ *from*; → wegen ‖ ~ vieler Proteste (..) *as a result of many protests*; ~ e–s Unfalls *owing to an accident* **2.** [adv] ~ v [vor Abstrakten ohne Art.] = 1. ‖ ~ v Anziehung *as the result of attraction*; ~ v Mißverständnissen *owing to misunderstandings* **~d·essen** [adv] *consequently*; *as a consequence* od *result*; *in consequence* (*he was sacked*); *accordingly*; → daher; deshalb, folglich

Inform·ant m ~en/~en *informant* | ~ennetz [n] *i. net* –**mati·on** [ts] f ~/~en **a.** *information* (über *about*, *on*); e–e ~ *a piece of i.*; diese ~ *this piece of i.* ‖ zur ~ *for i.* **b.** ~en [pl] *i.* [sg]; *communications*; *particulars* pl, ⟨comp⟩ *data* pl; k–e ~en *no i.*; ~en waren notwendig *i. was necessary*; ~en einziehen *to gather i.*; die neuesten ~en geben *to bring a p up to date* ‖ geheime ~en ⟨sl⟩ *dope* ‖ → Erkundigung **Informati·ons-** *information*; *informative* **~besuch** m *exploratory visit* **~büro** n *inquiry office*; *information bureau* od *department* **~dichte** f ⟨comp⟩ *packing density* **~einheit** f *item* (*of information*) ⟨a. comp⟩ **~gehalt** m ⟨commun⟩ *selective i. content*; mittlerer ~ *s. i. rate* **~ministerium** n ⟨engl⟩ *Ministry of I.* **~speicher** m ⟨comp⟩ *memory* **~- u Systemtheorie** ⟨cyb⟩ *i. theory* **~verarbeitung** f *i. processing* **informat·orisch** a *informative* (*account*); *informatory*; *exploratory* (*visit*) **inform·ieren** vt [h] (jdn) *to inform* (über *of*; *about*, *on*); *to instruct*, *orient*; jdn ~ über .. *to make a p acquainted with* ‖ **sich ~ über** .. *to gather information about* ..; *to make o.s. acquainted with* (*a th*) | **~d** a = informatorisch **Inform·ierung** f ~/~en *information*; z d–r ~ *for your i.* ‖ zur ~ *for reference*; es dient nur der (*or* zur) ~ *it is for reference only*

infra- L [in comp] *infra-* **~rot** a *infra-red* (*radiation*; *ray lamp*) | ∸-strahler [m] *infra-red heater*; *radiant heater* **∸schall** m *infrasonics* [sg konstr] **∸struktur** f *infrastructure*

·Inful f ~/~n ⟨ec⟩ **1.** *infula* [L] ‖ ~n [pl] (–hängende Bänder) *infulae* **2.** = Bischofsmütze

Inf·us n ~es/~a = Infusum **Infusi·on** f ~/~en ⟨med⟩ *infusion* | ~stierchen [n pl] = **Infus·orien** [–iən] pl v Infusorium ⟨zoo⟩ **1.** *Infusoria* L pl **2.** [in comp] *infusorial*; *infusorian* | ~erde [f] ⟨geol⟩ *infusorial earth*; *diatomite* → Kieselgur **Infus·orium** n ~s/–rien ⟨zoo⟩ *infusorian*, *infusory*; → Infusorien **Inf·usum** n ~s/–sa = (Tee-)Aufguß

Ing·angsetzung f *beginning*, *starting*; *start*

Ingäv·onen m pl ⟨Ger hist⟩ *Ingaevones* L pl

Ingeni·eur [inʒen'jø:r] m ~s/~e *engineer*; leitender ~ ⟨nav⟩ *chief engineer*; Schiffs– *ship's engineer*; Zivil∸ *civil engineer*; → Betriebs∸; Diplom∸; **~bauten** m [pl] *civil engineering works* (od *buildings*) pl **~schule** f *e.ing school*; *technical college*

·Ingermanland n ⟨Russ⟩ *Ingria*, *Ingra*

·Ingesinde n ~s/ = Dienerschaft

Ingredi·ens, -z n ~/–di·enz(i)en *ingredient*

Ingr·eß m –esses/–esse ⟨R. C.⟩ *ingress*

·Ingrimm m ~s/ *fury*, *rage*, *wrath*; *intense anger* **∸ig 1.** [a] *furious* (*sea*), *raging* (*storm*); *violent* (*struggle*); *deep*, *fervent*, *fierce*, *intense* (*hatred*); ⟨fam⟩ *wild* **2.** [adv] *furiously*, etc

·Ingrün n = Immergrün

·Ingvä·onen = Ingävonen

·Ingwer m ~s/ **1.** ⟨bot⟩ (Pflanze) *ginger*(*-plant*), *Zingiber* L **2.** ⟨pharm⟩ *g.*; (etw) mit ~ würzen *to g.* **3.** °~ (~schnaps) *g.-brandy* **4. ~bier** n *g.-ale*; → –limonade **~gewächse** n pl ⟨bot⟩ *zingiberaceous plants* pl **~keks** n *g.bread-nut*; *g.-snap* **~likör** m *g.-oil* **~pflanze** f *g.-plant* **~schnaps** m ⟨Am sl⟩ *jake*

·Inhaber m ~s/~ **1.** (Besitzer) *owner*, *possessor*, ~ v Übersetzungsrecht *o. of the right of tr.n*; *proprietor* (*of a firm*); *keeper* (*of a shop*), Laden∸ *shop-keeper* ‖ ⟨jur⟩ *tenant* (*of real property*); *holder* (*of a licence*); (*record*)*holder* ‖ ⟨ec⟩ ~ e–r Pfründe *incumbent*; → Pfarrer **2.** *occupant* (*of a room*); *occupier*; *tenant*; Amts∸ ⟨bes Am⟩ *office-holder* **3.** *bearer* (*of a certificate*, *title*); ~ e–s Patents *patentee* ‖ ⟨com⟩ *bearer*; *holder* (*of a ticket*) ‖ (e–s Wechsels) *holder* ‖ (*bond*)*holder* ‖ auf den ~ lautend *payable to bearer* **4.** ⟨sport⟩ *holder* (*of a cup*, *record*); ~ e–s Pokals s *to hold a cup* **~aktie** f *bearer-share* **~papier** n ⟨com⟩ ~e [pl] *bearer securities* pl ‖ etc

inhaft·ieren vt [j] (jdn) *to imprison*, *incarcerate*; *arrest*; *to put .. in prison*; *to commit .. to p.* **Inhaft·ierung** f, **Inh·aftnahme** f *imprisonment*, *incarceration*

Inhalati·on [ts] f ~/~en *inhalation* ‖ ~sapparat [m] **-l·ierapparat** m *inhaler*; *inhaling-apparatus*; *spray-apparatus*; *throat-spray* **inhal·ieren 1.** vt [h] *to inhale* **2.** ∸ n *inhaling*

·Inhalt m ~(e)s/~e **1.** (stofflicher ~) *contents* pl (*of a bottle*; *parcel*; *play*; *book*); der ~ .. ist verschieden *the contents .. vary* **2.** ⟨math⟩ Flächen∸ *superficial area* (od *space*); *area of surface* ‖ körperlicher ~, Raum∸ (*solid*) *content*; *volume*; *capacity* **3.** ⟨übtr⟩ (geistiger etc ~) *content* (*of a statement*); *c.s* (*of an order*); *essence*; *purport*; *substance*; *tenor* (*of a speech*) ‖ ~ u Form *s. and form*; → Buchstabe ‖ Vorstellungs∸ *content* ‖ wesentlicher ~ *meat* (*of an agreement*) ‖ der ~ ihres Lebens *the centre of her liefe* ‖ → Gehalt **4. des ~s** *to that effect*; Berichte des ~s *reports to the e.*; desselben ~s *to the same e.*; oder Worte dieses ~s *or words to this e.* ‖ e–e Erklärung etwa folgenden ~s *a declaration approximately to this e.*; v gleichem ~ *of even tenor*; der Brief **hatte folgenden ~** *the letter ran as follows*; *the letter was to the* *following e.* || **dem ~e nach** *virtually; virtual (promise)* **≃leer** a *blank (expression); empty (words); hollow; idle (life); shallow, superficial; trivial; vain (delight)* **≃lich 1.** [a] (*wesentlich*) *substantial* || in ~er Beziehung *with regard to content* od *substance; substantially; in substance* **2.** [adv] *substantially; in substance* **≃los** a *insignificant; meaningless, unmeaning; unsubstantial (hopes); unreal, visionary* = i–leer || → gegenstandslos, leer, nichtssagend **≃reich** a *substantial; full of substance* (od *meat*); *pregnant (words); purposeful; weighty* || *comprehensive; voluminous* **Inhalts- ~-angabe** f (of a novel, story) *abstract, argument; epitome; summary;* kz ~ *recapitulation;* → Abriß, Auszug || e–e ~ v e–r S geben *to epitomize* od *summarize a th; to recapitulate a th* **~berechnung** f → Kubikinhalt **≃leer** etc a = inhaltleer etc **~reichtum** m *comprehensiveness;* → inhaltschwer **~übersicht** f = –verzeichnis; → a. –angabe **~vermerk** m ⟨jur⟩ *docket;* (Akten) mit ~ versehen *to docket* **~verzeichnis** n *table of contents; index;* ⟨jur⟩ *docket;* → –angabe **~voll** a *expressive, meaning (look)* || *substantial; full of meat* (od *substance*); *momentous (day); pregnant (words); purposeful; significant; weighty* **·inhaltschwer** a *momentous (day); pregnant; weighty; profound* (Bemerkung)

inhär·ent 1. [a] *inherent;* jdm *or* e–r S ~ *inherent in a p, in a th* **2.** [adv] *inherently* **Inhärenz** f ~/ *inherence* **inhär·ieren** vi [h] *to inhere;* jdm *or* e–r S ~ *to inhere in a p, in a th*

inhib·ieren vt [h] ⟨jur⟩ (etw) *to inhibit; prevent; stay* **Inhibiti·on** [ts] f ~/~en *inhibition*

·Inholz n ⟨mar⟩ (Schiffsrippe) *rib; timber;* → Spant || über die ≃er genagelte Latte *ribband*

inhomog·en a *unhomogeneous; heterogeneous*

inhum·an a *inhuman; brutal, cruel* **≃it·ät** f *inhumanity; brutality*

Iniquit·ät f *inequity; unfairness*

Initi·al [ts] n ~s/~e **~buchstabe** m = Initiale **~kurzwort** n *acronym* (z.B. *Care*) **~sklerose** f ⟨med⟩ *i. sclerosis* **~zündung** f *priming* **Initi·ale** [ts] f ~/~n *initial;* ⟨paint⟩ *illuminated letter* **Initiati·on** [ts] f *initiation* **Initiat·ive** [ts] f ~/ *initiative; energy, go, push; activity* || Unternehmer≃ *business enterprise* || ~ liegt bei wenigen (*or* wenige h ~) *few have i.* || v wem ging die ~ aus? *whose i. was it? who had the i.?* || die ~ ergreifen *to take the i.* (od *the lead*) || k–e ~ h *to lack i.* || auf Ihre ~ hin *on your i.* || aus eigener ~ *on one's own i.* od *accord; independently* || durch s–e ~ *through his own energy* (od *activities*) **Initiativrecht** [ts] n *initiative;* das ~ besitzen *to have* (od *possess*) *the i.* **initi·ieren** [ts] vt [h] (jdn) *to initiate* (in *into*)

Injekti·on [ts] f ~/~en ⟨med⟩ *injection* | ~s-spritze [f] *hypodermic needle,* ⟨fam⟩ *hypo* **Inj·ektor** m ~s/–·oren ⟨tech⟩ *injector* **injiz·ieren** vt [h] (etw) *to inject;* –zierte Flüssigkeit *injection*

Inj·urie [–iə] f ~/~n *insult; libel; outrage; defamation, slander* || ~n [pl] *abuse; abusive language* **~nklage** f ⟨jur⟩ *action for libel* **injur·ieren** vt [h] (jdn) *to insult; outrage*

·Inka m ~s/~s ⟨hist⟩ (in Peru) *Inca* **~bein** n, **~knochen** m ⟨anat⟩ *I. bone* **~reich** n *I. State*

inkarn·at 1. a ⟨arts⟩ *flesh-coloured, incarnadine; pink, rosy* **2.** ≃ n ⟨arts⟩ *carnation; flesh colour* (od *tints* pl) **Inkarnati·on** [ts] f ~/~en ⟨theol⟩ *incarnation* || ⟨fig⟩ *embodiment, incarnation*

Inkarzerati·on [ts] f ~/~en ⟨path⟩ *incarceration (of a hernia)* **i-r·iert** a *incarcerated*

Ink·asso n ~s/~s *or* –ssi ⟨com⟩ **1.** *cashing, collection, encashment;* das ~ e–s Wechsels besorgen *to undertake the coll. of a bill;* (etw) zum ~ übernehmen *to receive for coll.;* zum ~ vorzeigen *to present for c.* **2.** [in comp] *collecting* **~geschäft** n *c.ing business* **~kosten** pl *c.ing expenses* **~provision** f *c.ing provision*

Inklinati·on f ~/~en ⟨astr & phys⟩ *inclination* || ~ der Magnetnadel *dip* od *i. of the needle* **~s-nadel** f *dipping-needle* **~swinkel** m *angle of i.* **i-nieren** vi [h] ⟨fig⟩ *to incline* (z *to;* z tun *to do*); ~ f etw *to i. toward a th; to be i.d to a th; to feel drawn to a th; to have a bias towards a th*

inklus·ive 1. [adv] *inclusive;* die Seiten 10 bis 15 ~ *pages 10 to 15 i.;* von Montag bis ~ Freitag *from Monday till Friday i.(ly)* **2.** [prep] [mit Genitiv] = einschließlich 2.

ink·ognito 1. [adv] *incognito,* ⟨fam⟩ *incog (to travel i.)* **1.** ≃ n ~s/~s *incognito* [pl *-tos*]; das ~ lüften, wahren *to drop, keep up one's i.*

inkohär·ent a *incoherent* **I-r·enz** f *incoherence*

·Inkohlung f ~/~en ⟨geol⟩ *carbonization*

·in- L (= nicht) **~kommensur·abel** a ⟨math⟩ *incommensurable* **~komm·entmäßig** [–ˈmɑ̃] *inconsistent with student convention* || *inappropriate; incorrect (behaviour)* || [pred] *out of place* **~kommod·ieren** vt [h] (jdn) *to incommode; annoy, disturb, inconvenience* **~kompar·abel** a *incomparable; matchless, unique* **~kompat·ibel** a ⟨scient⟩ *incompatible; discordant* **≃kompatibilit·ät** f *incompatibility* **~kompetent** a ⟨jur⟩ *incompetent* **≃kompetenz** f *incompetence, -cy* **~komplett** a *incomplete* **~kongruent** a *incongruous* **≃kongruenz** f *incongruity* **~konsequent 1.** [a] *inconsequent, inconsequential; incoherent; inconsistent* **2.** [adv] *inconsequentially, inconsequently* **≃konsequenz** f *inconsequence; incoherence; inconsistency* **~konsistent** a *inconsistent* **≃konsistenz** f *inconsistency* **~konstant** [a] *inconstant* **~konstitutionell** a *unconstitutional* **≃kontinenz** f ⟨path⟩ *incontinence (of urine)* **~konven·abel, ~konvenient** a *inconvenient* **≃konvenienz** f *inconvenience*

Inkorporati·on [ts] f ~/~en *incorporation* (in *into*) **inkorpor·ieren** vt [h] (Land) *to incorporate*

·inkorrekt a *incorrect; inaccurate; inappropriate* | **≃heit** f ~/~en *incorrectness; inaccuracy*

·In- (→ in) **~kr·afttreten** n ~s/ *the passing,* ⟨bes Am⟩ *passage (of a bill); the coming* od *entry into force (of a treaty); commencement (of an act);* Tag des ~s *effective date* || die Zeit des ~s *the effective date (of a decree);* vor dem ~ *before* (od *prior to*) *the effective date (of a law)* **~kreis** m ⟨math⟩ *inscribed circle* **~krem·ent** n ~s/~e ⟨math⟩ *increment (of velocity)* **~kr·et** n ~s/~e ⟨med⟩ *endocrine;* = Hormon | ≃·orisch [a] *endocrine (gland)* **≃krimin·ieren** vt [h] (jdn) *to incriminate* | ~d a *incriminating; incriminatory* **~krustati·on** [ts] f ~/~en *incrustation* **~kubati·on** [ts] f ~/~en ⟨med & biol⟩ **1.** *incubation* **2.** [in comp] ~s- = *i.* | ~szeit [f] *i. period* **~kub·ator** m (Brütapparat) *incubator* **·~kubus** m [L] *incubus* L

·inkulant a ⟨com⟩ *disobliging; impolite; unaccomodating* **·Inkulanz** f *disobligingness*

Inkun·abel f ~/~n ⟨print⟩ *incunabulum* [*–la* pl] L; *early printed book; black-letter edition*

·Inland n ~(e)s/ **1.** (Ggs Ausland) **a.** *native country; homeland; home;* „~" ⟨aero⟩ "*Domestic*"; im ~ geboren *native born;* → Ausland **b.** [in comp] → Inlands- **2. a.** = Binnenland, Landinnere **b. [in comp]** → Inlands-; ~beschaffung [f] *domestic procurement;* ~düne [f] *inland-dune;* ~eis [n] ⟨geogr⟩ *inland-ice;* ~funk [m] ⟨m. m.⟩ *Home Service;* ~(s)wechsel [m] *domestic bill;* ~(s)zoll [m] *i. duty* **·Inländer** m (Ggs Ausländer) *native* || → Binnenländer **·inländisch** a (Ggs ausländisch) *indigenous, native* || ⟨com⟩ *internal;* ⟨bes Am⟩ *domestic; home (market, produce; industry);* ~er Handel *home* od *inland trade;* ~es Porto *home postage;* ~e Steuer → Einnahme; ~er Wechsel *inland bill of exchange;* ~es Brot *home--made bread;* ~e Seide *h.-m. silk* || ~es Getreide *h.-grown grain* **·Inlands-** = inländisch || → a. Inland- | ~anleihe [f] *domestic loan;* ~markt [m] *home market;* ~modell [n] ⟨com⟩ *local pattern;* ~porto [n] *inland* od *domestic postage*

·**Inlaut** m ⟨gram⟩ *medial sound* ‖ im ~ *medially*, im ~ stehend *medial* (*consonant*) ·**inlautend 1.** [a] *medial* **2.** [adv] *medially*

·**Inlett** n ~s/~e **1.** (Stoff aus rotem Köper) *tick*; *ticking* **2.** (Hülle hieraus) (*bed-*)*tick*

·**inliegend** a [pred] *enclosed*

inm·itten prep [gen] ~ e–r S *in the midst* od *middle of a th*; *amid*(*st*) *a th*; ~ der E. *amidst the events*; *a. the splendour*; ~ Afrikas *in the heart of Africa*; ~ der Menge *amidst* od *among the crowd*

Inn m (Nebenfluß der Donau)

·**inne-** pref [betont, bei Verben trennbar] ~|**behalten** vt [h] (etw) *to keep back*, *to withhold*; sie behielten ihm s–n Lohn inne *they kept back his wages*, *they withheld the wages from him* ~|**haben 1.** vt [h] (Land) *to hold*; *own*, *possess*; → besitzen ‖ (e–n Raum) *to occupy*; (Laden, Geschäft) *to keep* ‖ (Amt, Stellung) *to hold*; ⟨Am a.⟩ *to hold down* ‖ ⟨fig⟩ → beherrschen **2.** ≙ n *holding* (*of land*); *tenure* (*of an office*) ~|**halten** vt/i [h] **I.** vt (Gesetz, Regel) *to keep*, *observe*; die Vorschriften ~ *to toe the line* ‖ *to adhere* od *keep to* (*a plan*); den Kurs ~ *to hold on* [prep] *one's course* ‖ = einhalten I. 3. **II.** vi *to halt*, *pause* (um z tun *to do*); *to stop*; halt inne! *hold on*! *stop there*! ⟨fam⟩ *shut up*! ‖ mit Lesen (etc) ~ *to cease* (od *leave off*; *stop*) *reading*; *to desist from reading*; jdn ~ l *to give pause to a p* ≙**haltung** f *observance* (*of a fixed time*) *~|**sein 1.** vi [s] ⟨philos⟩ jdm ~ *to be inherent in a p*; *to inhere in a p*; *to indwell* od *infuse a p* ‖ ⟨übtr⟩ diesem Verhalten wohnt wahrer Mut inne *in such conduct resides true courage* **2.** ≙ n *inherence*, *-cy*; *indwelling* ~|**werden** vi [s] e–r S ~ *to become aware* od *conscious of a th*; *to become alive to a th*; *to awake to a th* ‖ *to perceive*, *sense a th* ~|**wohnen 1.** vi [h] = innesein; es wohnt ihnen selbst k–e Schönheit inne *they are not beautiful in themselves*; der ihm ~de Zustand *the inherence in him* **2.** ≙ n = Innesein

·**innen** adv *within*, *inside*; *on* od *in the inside*; *within doors* ‖ *in here* ‖ ~ u außen *inside and out*; *within and without*; ⟨fig⟩ *very thoroughly*; ~ im Hause *within the house*, *within doors*; → drinnen ‖ *internally*; *inwardly*; ~ befindlich *inner*, *inward*, *internal*, *interior* | ⟨racing⟩ ~ liegen *to have the pole* | **nach** ~ *towards the inside*; *inwards*, *inwardly* ‖ nach ~ aufgehen (of a door) *to open inwards*; *to open into the room* ‖ nach ~ k *to come in*(*side*) ‖ ⟨med⟩ nach ~ schlagen *to retrocede*; nach ~ schlagend *retrocedent* (*gout*) ‖ die Füße nach ~ setzen *to turn in one's toes* | **von** ~ *from within*; *from the inside* ‖ v ~ heraus erfolgend *spontaneous* (*growth*); *instinctive*; *automatic* ‖ der zweite Ring v ~ *the inner ring but one* ‖ v ~ öffnen *to open from* (*the*) *inside* ‖ °sich v ~ betrachten *to listen to o.s.*

·**Innen-** [in comp] *inner*; *inside*; *interior*; *internal*; *inward*; ⟨scient⟩ *endo-*; → Binnen- ~**antenne** f ⟨wir⟩ *inside aerial* ~**architekt** m *indoor* od *interior decorator* ~**architektur** f *interior architecture* ~**aufnahme** f ⟨phot⟩ *interior*, ⟨film⟩ *i. shooting* ~**ausstattung** f = –dekoration ~**bahn** f ⟨sport⟩ *inside track* ~**ballast** m ⟨mar⟩ *internal ballast* ~**beleuchtung** f *indoor lighting* ≙**bords** adv ⟨mar⟩ *inboard*; *inside the ship* ~**dekoration** f *interior decoration*; *furniture* ~**dienst** m ⟨mil⟩ *home* od *interior service* ‖ *home civil service* | ~personal [n] ⟨ins⟩ *inside staff* ~**durchmesser** m *inside* od *internal diameter* ~**einrichtung** f *interior accommodation* ~**fläche** f *inside*; *inner surface* ~**getriebe** n ⟨tech⟩ *internal gearing* ~**gewinde** n *internal* od *female screw thread* ~**graben** m ⟨fort⟩ *inner moat* ~**handel** m = Binnenhandel ~**haut** f ⟨bot⟩ *endocarp* ~**kabine** f ⟨mar⟩ *inside cabin* ~**kammer** f ⟨mar⟩ *inner cabin* ~**kante** f *inner edge* ~**lampe** f ⟨mot⟩ *courtesy light* ~**leben** n *inner life*; jds ~ *a p's mind* ~**lenker** m ⟨mot⟩ *sedan* ~**markt** m = Binnenmarkt ~**mauer** f *inner* od *interior wall* ~**minister** m ⟨engl⟩ *Secretary of State for the Home Department*; ⟨fam⟩ *Home Secretary*; ⟨Am⟩ *Secretary of the Interior* ‖ ⟨a-engl⟩ *Minister of the Interior* ~**ministerium** n *Home Office*; ⟨Am⟩ *Department of the Interior* ‖ ⟨a-engl⟩ *Ministry of the Interior* ~**passagier** m *inside passenger*; *inside* ~**politik** f *home* od *domestic policy*; *home affairs* od *politics* pl ~**raum** m (*the*) *interior*, *inside* ~**schau** f *introspection* ~**schicht** f *inner layer* ~**schraube** f ⟨mar⟩ *inner screw* ~**seite** f *inner side*; *inside*, auf der ~ *on the i.* ~**sitz** m *inside seat* ~**stadt** f *city*, ⟨Am⟩ *downtown district* ~**tasche** f *inside breast pocket* ~**taster** m *inside calliper* ~**verzahnung** f *internal teeth* pl ~**wache** f *inner guard* ~**wand** f *inner wall* ~**welt** f *internal* od *inner world*; (*the*) *inside* ~**winkel** m ⟨math⟩ *interior* od *internal angle* ~**zünder** m *internal fuse*

·**inner-** [in comp] ~**artlich** a ⟨bot; zoo, eth⟩ *intraspecific* ≙**asien** *Central Asia* ~**ballistisch** a *interior ballistic* (*factor*) ~**deutsch** a *internal*; ~e Angelegenheit *internal affair* ~**dienstlich** a *internal* ~**islamisch** a *inter-Islamic* ≙**kiel** m *inner* od *inside keel* ~**parteilich** a *intra-party* ~**politisch** a *internal* (*feuds*); *home* (*affairs* pl); *civil* (*convulsions* pl) ~**staatlich** a *domestic* ‖ *intrastate*

·**innere** a [nur attr] **1. a.** *inner*, *interior* (*wall*); *internal* (*layer*) ‖ *inside* (*diameter*) | ⟨anat & path⟩ *internal* (*organ*); *intrinsic* (*muscle*); *intestine* (*motion*) | ~ Beschaffenheit *internality* (*of an institution*) ‖ ~r Dienst ⟨mil⟩ *duty in barracks* ‖ ~ Krankheit *internal disease* od *complaint*; ~ Abteilung ⟨med⟩ *i. ward*; Arzt f ~ Krankheiten *i. specialist*; ⟨Am a.⟩ *interne*, *internist* ‖ ~ Linie *inner* od *interior line* ‖ ~ Sammlung *recollection* ‖ ~e Sekretion *internal secretion* ‖ ~ Unruhen [pl] *domestic disturbances* pl ‖ ~ Verletzungen *internal injuries* pl ‖ die ~ Stadt *the centre of the town*; *the City* | die ~ Abhängigkeit zweier Organisationen v e–a *the interdependence of two organizations* **b.** ⟨übtr⟩ *intrinsic* (*rottenness*; *value*); *inner*, *internal* (*forces*); *inside* (*help*) ‖ wesentliche ~ Eigenschaften [pl] *internals* pl **2.** (Inlands-) *civil* (*struggles*), *domestic* (*problems*); *internal* (*administration*, *crisis*, *relations*); *intestine* (*war*); *home* od *inner* (*mission*); *home* od *domestic* (*policy*); *inner* (*politics* pl); → Innen- **3.** ⟨gram⟩ *cognate* (*object*) (z. B. *to live a virtuous life*) **4.** (seelisch) *inner* (*life*); *interior*; *inward* (*desire*, *experience*); *spiritual* (*eye*); *mental* ‖ ~ Disziplin → Halt ‖ der ~e Mensch *the inner man*; *the soul*; *the mind* ‖ ~e Zweifel [pl] *introspective questionings* pl ·**Innere** n ~n/ **A. 1.** (*the*) *interior*, *inside* (*of a house*, etc.) ‖ (*the*) *bowels* pl (*of the earth*, *of Paris*); das ~ des Landes *the interior* od *inside of the country*; *the upcountry* ‖ das ~ e–r Kirche (etc) *the body* od *inside of a church* | (≙ Teile) *the gizzard*, *inside* (*of a bird*) **2.** ⟨pol⟩ Minister(ium) des ~n → Innenminister(ium) **3.** *inner* od *spiritual part* (*of man*); (*the*) *mind*, *soul* **B. 1. das** ~ **nach außen** (*to turn*) *the inside out*; *the wrong side out* ‖ sich um Äußerlichkeiten aufregen u das ~ vernachlässigen ⟨bib⟩ *to strain at a gnat and swallow a camel* (Matth. 23, 24) **2. im** ~**n a.** *within*; *inside*; im ~n des Hauses *within* od *inside the house*; *within doors*; aus dem ~n des Hauses *from within* ‖ Beerdigung im ~n der Kirche *intramural burial* **b.** *internally*; Spannungen im ~n *internal tensions*; tief im ~n des Landes *in the depth* od *heart of the country* **c.** *inwardly* (*she smiled i.*); *at heart*; *in* (*the*) *spirit*; *in one's spirit* **3. in s-m** ~**n** *in his own bosom*; *in his spirit*; *within* od *inside himself*; sie wußte, was in s–m ~n vorging *she knew what passed through his mind* **4. ins** ~ verlagern *to locate within the mind*; *to interiorize* **5. mit s-m ganzen** ~**n** (*he was*) *heart and soul* (bei der Arbeit *in his work*) **Inner·eien** pl ⟨cul⟩ *offal*(*s*), *innard*(*s*); ⟨bes Am⟩ *variety meats*; (of poultry) *giblets* ·**innerhalb 1.** * [adv] [dafür mst (dr)innen] ‖ nach ~ *towards the inside* od *the interior* **2.** [prep] **a.** [mit gen] ~ der Kirche, Stadt *within* od *inside the church, the town* || ~ der 4 Wände *within the walls* || *within the limits* | ⟨übtr⟩ ~ der Grenzen des Gesetzes *within the meaning of the act* || ~ der Machtbefugnis jds *within a p's powers* | (Zeit) ~ zweier Stunden [gen] *within two hours*; ⟨Am⟩ *inside of two hours* || *in a matter of* (*a few days*) **b.** ~ v vier Tagen *within* (⟨Am⟩ *inside of*) *4 days* **·innerlich A.** [a] **1.** ⟨eig⟩ [dafür mst: inner] *inner, internal* (*injuries*) || ⟨übtr⟩ *intrinsic* (*qualities*) **2.** ⟨fig⟩ *intimate* (*relation, sense*) || *mental, spiritual*; *inward*; *introspective*; ~e Veranlagung *introspectiveness* || (innig) *deeply felt*; *fervent* **B.** [adv] **1.** ⟨eig⟩ *internally*; ~ anzuwenden *to be taken internally* **2.** ⟨fig⟩ *intimately*; *inwardly*; ~ veranlagt *introspective* (*p*) | **≗keit** f *inner nature* od *feeling*; *inwardness* || ⟨mus a.⟩ *pensiveness* (e.g. Brahms, 1. Klav.-Konz.) **·innerste A.** [a; nur attr] *innermost* (*court*) || ⟨fig⟩ *in*(*ner*)*most* (*thoughts*); *most inward*; *deepest*; *intimate* (*feelings*) || der ~ Kern *the root* (*of a matter*) **B. das** ≗ *the in*(*ner*)*most*; **aus** dem ~n der Erde *from* (*the*) *earth's deepest bosom* || *the in*(*ner*)*most heart* od *self* (*of a matter*); *the very heart* || → Inneres | **aus** s–m ≗n *from the very centre/center of his being* | **im** ≗**n** *at the core*; *at the heart* (*of the family*) || *in the depths* (*of the country*) || *at the bottom* (*of his soul*); er fühlte sich im ≗n s–r Seele hingezogen *he was drawn to it heart and soul*; ich wußte im ≗n *I knew in my bones*; in Ihrem ≗n *in your heart of hearts* || es erschütterte sie bis ins ≗ *it shook her to the heart, foundations,* (*very marrow of the*) *bones*; es drang W. bis ins ≗e *it pierced to the very core of William*

Innervati·on [ts] f ⟨med⟩ *innervation* **innerv·ieren** vt [h] (Organ) *to innervate*

·innig A. [a] **1.** ⟨übtr⟩ *close, intimate* (*friendship*); ~e Vertrautheit mit .. *an intimate knowledge of* (od *acquaintance with*); *a thorough familiarity with* (*a th*); ~e Zus–arbeit *zealous co-operation* **2.** ⟨fig⟩ *ardent, fervent* (*desire*); *fervid*; *intense*; *perfervid* (*adherent*) || *affectionate, cordial*; *deep* (*gratitude*); *heartfelt* (*thanks*); *hearty* (*welcome*); *passionate* (*love*); *sincere*; ~st *in*(*ner*)*most, sincerest* **B.** [adv] **1.** *closely* (*connected*); *intimately*; *thoroughly*; ~ vermischen *to interblend* **2.** ⟨fig⟩ *deeply*; *fervently*; *heartily*; *passionately*; *sincerely*; *from full heart*; *from one's heart* || ~ mit jdm empfinden *to feel warm towards a p*; sie liebte ihn ~ *she loved him* (*very*) *dearly* | **≗keit** f **1.** *intimacy* ⟨a. arts⟩; *thoroughness* **2.** ⟨fig⟩ *ardour, fervour*; *heartiness*; *passionateness*; *sincerity* || → Inbrunst | **~lich** adv *deeply*; *fervently*; *from full heart*; *passionately*; = innig B. 2. **·Innung** f ~/~en *g*(*u*)*ild*; *corporation, company*; → Gilde, Zunft **~sbrief** m *guild's charter* **~sverband** m *association of g.s* **~swesen** n *g.-system*

·Innsbruck n (Stadt in Tirol)

·in- L (= nicht) **~offiziell 1.** [a] *unofficial*; *informal*; *off the record* **2.** [adv] *unofficially* **~offiziös** a **1.** ⟨jur⟩ *inofficious* **2.** *not having a semi-official character*; *not officially authorized* || *informal* **~opportun 1.** [a] *inopportune, unseasonable* **2.** [adv] *inopportunely*

in petto It *secretly*; *in contemplation*; *in readiness* || °etw ~ h *to contemplate* (od *to plan*) *a th*; ⟨fam⟩ *to have sth up one's sleeve*; ~ h f (jdn) *to have a th in store for*

inquir·ieren vt [h] etw ~ *to inquire into a th*; *to examine* (*into*) *a th*; *to investigate a th* || → verhören **Inquisiti·on** [ts] f ~/~en ⟨hist ec⟩ *inquisition* **Inquis·itor** m ~s/–sit·oren *inquisitor* **inquisit·orisch** a *inquisitorial*

°**ins 1.** = in das; ~ Fenster (hinein)werfen *to throw in at the window*; ~ Gefängnis stecken *or* werfen *to put in jail* od *prison*; ~ Haus *inside* || sich ~ Benehmen setzen mit .. *to communicate with a p*; ⟨Am⟩ *to contact a p*; ~ Leben rufen *to create, found* (*a th*); jdn ~ Vertrauen ziehen *to take a p into one's confidence* || bis ~ nächste Jahr *into the coming year* **2.** = in des; ~ Teufels Namen! *confound it! damned!*

·Insasse m ~n/~n *inhabitant, inmate* (*of a house, town*); die ~n [pl] *the house* || *resident* (*of a town*) || *lodger* (*of a room*); *occupant* (*of a bus, a plane, a room*); [pl] *passengers* (*of the train*) || ⟨übtr & fig⟩ *denizen* (*of the wood*); *tenant*

insbes·ondere adv *especially, particularly*; *principally*; *in particular* || jeder T. ~ *each several part*

·Inschrift f ~/~en (auf Stein etc) *inscription*; *epigraph*; ⟨num⟩ *i.*; *legend*; ⟨cart⟩ *l.* | **~en-** *i.al*; *e.ic* **~kunde** f *e.y*

Ins·ekt n ~(e)s/~en **1.** ⟨ent⟩ *insect*; ⟨Am a.⟩ *bug* || vollentwickeltes ~ *imago* L; Ur≗en [pl] → Apterygoten **2.** °⟨fig⟩ *insect* **Ins·ekten-** *insect*; *entomo-* **≗artig** a *i.-like*; *entomic* **≗blütig** a ⟨bot⟩ *entomophilous* (*plant*) **~fraß** m ⟨for⟩ *devastation* **≗fressend** a *i.ivorous* **~fresser** m *i.ivore*, Ordnung der ~ *I.ivora* L pl **~kenner** m *e.logist* **~kunde** f *e.logy*; praktische ~ *i.ology* **~plage** f *i.-pest* **~pulver** n *i.icide*; *i.-powder* **~sammler** m *i.t-collector*; ⟨Am⟩ *bug-hunter* **~sammlung** f *collection of i.s* **~spritze** f *gun* **~stich** m *i.-sting* **Insektiz·id** n ~s/~e *insecticide*

·Insel f ~/~n **1. a.** *island*; die ~ N. *the i. of N.* || auf der ~ *in* od *on the i.* || (etw) z e–r ~ m *to i.* **b.** ⟨nur in festen Verbindungen & poet⟩ *isle*; die Britischen ~n *the British I.s*; die Grüne ~ (Irland) *the Emerald I.* || die ~ Wight *the I. of Wight* **c.** ⟨geog⟩ ~n über dem Winde (in Westindien) *Leeward I.ds*; ~n unter dem Winde *Windward I.ds* pl **d.** kl ~ *islet*; → Inselchen **2.** ⟨übtr⟩ Verkehrs≗ *i.d*; *refuge* || ⟨aero⟩ Flug≗ *floating base* od *airport* **3. [in comp]** *insular* **≗artig** a *i.r* **~bewohner** m *islander*; Gewohnheiten der ~ *i.r habits* pl **~brite** m *i.r Briton* **~germane** m *i.r Teuton* **~gruppe** f *archipelago*; *group of i.ds*; *i.d-group* **~heimat** f ⟨poet⟩ *i.d-home* **~kette** f *string of i.s* **~klima** n *i.r climate* **~kontinent** m *i.d-continent* **~lage** f *i.rity* **~land** n *i.r country* (od *land*) **~meer** n → Archipel **~reich** n *i.r country*; ⟨poet⟩ *i.d-kingdom* **~schwarm** m = –gruppe; ≗e pl *archipelago* L **~staat** m = –reich **~stadt** f *i.d town* **~volk** n *i.ders* pl **~welt** f = –schwarm **·Inselchen** n ~s/~ *islet* || ~ im Flusse *holm* || flaches ~, Felsen≗ *rocky island*

Inser·at n ~(e)s/~e ⟨com⟩ *advertisement* || ein ~ aufgeben *to insert an ad.t*; *to advertise* (in *in*); durch ~ suchen *to ad.se for* .. **Inser·aten-** [in comp] ⟨com⟩ *advertising*; ~büro [n] *ad.sing agency*; ~setzer [m] *advertisement compositor*; ~wesen [n] *ad.sing* **Inser·ent** m ~en/~en ⟨com⟩ *advertiser* **inser·ieren A.** vt/i [h] ⟨com⟩ **1.** (etw) *to advertise* **2.** vi *to ad.* (in *in*); *to put an ad in the paper* **B.** ≗ n *advertising* **Inserti·on** [ts] f **1.** ⟨com⟩ *ad.sing* || *ad.sement* **2.** ⟨anat & bot⟩ *insertion*

insgeh·eim adv = im geheimen, → geheim III.

†**insgem·ein** adv *commonly*; *generally*; *usually*

insges·amt adv *altogether* || alle ~ *one and all*; (*to be received*) *in a body*; *in corpore* L || etwa ~ 150 Personen (*or* 150 P ~) *about 150 persons all told*; die Partei erhielt ~ 200 Sitze *the party all told got 200 seats* || Handelsschiffe mit ~ 50 000 Tonnen *merchant men totalling 50 000 tons* || das sind ~ .. *this makes a total sum* (*of 40 hours*)

·Insichgeschäft n ⟨com⟩ *transaction which an agent* (etc.) *concludes by entering in himself*

·Insiegel n ~s/~ (*official*) *seal*

Ins·ignien pl *insignia* L pl; *badges* [pl] *of office* || königliche ~ *regalia* L pl

Insinuati·on [ts] f *insinuation* **insinu·ieren** vt [h] *to insinuate* (daß .. *that*); *to suggest*

inskrib·ieren vt [h] (jds Namen) *to inscribe* || sich ~ l *to be inscribed* (in *on* [*a list*]); ⟨univ⟩ *to enter one's name* **Inskripti·on** [ts] f *inscription*

insof·ern 1. [adv] *so far*; *thus far*; *to that extent* (*he is right*) **2.** [conj] ~ (als) *as far as*; *so far as* || *kein Hinweis, ~ ich sehen kann *no reference that*

I can see || (*these speeches have symbolical value*) *in that they* (*remind us of*..)

Insolati·on [ts] f *insolation* → insolieren

insol·ent a *insolent* **Insol·enz** f ~/~en *insolence*

insol·ieren vt [h] (etw) *to insolate* → Insolation

insolv·ent a *insolvent*; *bankrupt* || ~ w *to become i.*; *to go b.* **Insolv·enz** f ~/~en *i.ency*; *b.cy*; ~ anmelden *to file one's petition in b.cy* **~anzeige** f *declaration of insolvency*

ins·onderheit adv = insbesondere

Inspekt·eur [–'tør] m ~s/~e ⟨mil⟩ *Chief* (*of Engineers, Ordnance, Transportation*); ⟨mar & aero⟩ *Inspector*; General≈ *I.-General* || *director* **Inspekti·on** [ts] f ~/~en **1.** [abstr] *inspection*; ⟨aero⟩ ~ nach demFlug *post-flight i.*; → Besichtigung; Aufsicht **2.** [konkr] (P) *inspectorate* || (Amt) *inspectorate*; *inspectorship* || General≈ *I.ate-General* **Inspekti·ons-** [in comp] *inspection*(-*-district*) **~reise** f *tour of i.*; jährliche ~ *perambulation* **Insp·ektor** m ~s/–ekt·oren **1.** *inspector*; Polizei≈ *police-i.*; Schul≈ *i. of schools* || *bailiff* (*of a manor*) || *overseer* **2.** [in comp] (a. ~en-) *i.al*; *i.ial* **Inspektor·at** n, **Insp·ektorstelle** f *i.ship*

Inspirati·on [ts] f ~/~en *inspiration*; → Eingebung **inspir·ieren** vt [h] (jdn) *to inspire* || ⟨übtr⟩ (Presse) *to i.*; –riert *i.d*

Inspiz·ient m ~en/~en *superintendent*; *director* || ⟨theat⟩ *stage manager* **inspiz·ieren** vt [h] (Schule etc) *to inspect*; *to superintend* || (Distrikt, Gut) *to perambulate* || → besichtigen

Installat·eur [–'tør] m ~s/~e *fitter*; ⟨el⟩ *electrical fitter*; *gas-fitter*; (f Wasser) *plumber*; Heizungs≈ *steam-fitter* **Installati·on** [ts] f ~/~en *installation* | ~sanlagen [pl] *plumbing*; *fittings* **install·ieren** vt [h] **1.** ⟨el-tech⟩ *to install*; (Leitung) *to fit* (in *in*) || (Apparat) *to fix*; ⟨telph⟩ *to put in* **2.** (jdn) *to install* **install·iert** a *piped* (*for water and gas*); ⟨el⟩ *wired*

inst·and|halten vt [h] (Straßen etc) *to keep up*; *to keep in* (*good* od *decent*) *repair*; .. *in trim*; *to maintain* **I-haltung** f ~/~en *upkeep*; *keeping in* (*good*) *repair* od *trim*; *maintenance* **~sarbeiten** pl *m.-work*; *conditioning-w.* **~skosten** pl *upkeep*; *cost of upkeep* **·inständig 1.** [a] *earnest* (*request*); *instant*; *urgent* || ~e Bitte *instance*; auf jds ~e B. (hin) *at a p's i.* (od *urgent request*) **2.** [adv] *particularly*; *urgently*; jdn ~ bitten *to beseech* od *implore a p* (*to do*); jdn ~ um etw bitten *to urge a th upon a p*; jdn ~ um Hilfe bitten *to implore a p's help*; ~ um Gnade bitten *to supplicate for mercy*; ~bitten, daß .. *to s. that* **3.** auf das ~ste *most urgently* | ≈**keit** f *earnestness*; *instancy*; *urgency* **inst·and|setzen** vt [h] **(etw)** *to put in* (*good*) *condition*; *to restore to a proper c.*; wieder ~ *to restore*, *recondition*; *reestablish*; *repair*, *mend* || **(jdn)** *to enable* **I-setzung** f ~/~en *reconditioning*; *repair*; *restoring*, *restoration* || ~sarbeiten [pl] *repairs* pl (an .. *to a building*); *repairing operations* pl | ~s-u Nachschubverbände u -einheiten [pl] *supply and maintenance formations and units*; ~swerkstatt [f] *repair shop*

·instant a *instant* (Kaffee)

Inst·anz f ~/~en ⟨jur⟩ *instance* || Gericht der ersten ~ *court of first i.* || in der ersten (zweiten) ~ *in the first* (*second*) *i.* || e–e höhere ~ *a superior court* || Gericht der letzten ~ *court of last i.* od *resort* || in letzter ~ *without further appeal*; ⟨übtr⟩ *in the last resort*; *in the ultimate contingency* **~enweg** m ⟨jur⟩ *stages* [pl] *of appeal* || ⟨übtr Ger⟩ *the usual* (od *prescribed*) *channels*; s–e Beschwerde ging den ~ *his complaint went through the u. ch.s* **~enzug** m *successive* (*stages of*) *appeal*

·Inste m ~n/~n ⟨agr Ger⟩ [nod, nordd] *agricultural labourer receiving his wages partly in money partly in kind*; → Instleute, Instmann

·instehend a *herein*; *in this writing*; *inside*

Instellung- ~bringen, ~gehen n ⟨mil⟩ *going into the line*; *taking up a position*; ⟨artill a.⟩ *forming-up*

Inst·inkt [st] m ~(e)s/~e *instinct* (f *for*); *innate impulse* || aus ~ *on instinct* || feiner ~ *flair* (f *for*); *selective in.*; gesunder ~ ⟨fam⟩ *horse sense* || es weckt die niederen ≈e *it awakens lower in.s* | ~bewegung [f] ⟨biol, eth⟩ *fixed motor pattern*; ~handlung [f] *instinct* | ≈**haft** a *in.ive*; ⟨phys⟩ *inborn, unconditioned* (*reflex*) **instinkt·iv 1.** a *in.ive* **2.** adv *in.ively*; ~ handeln *to act on in., to act in.ively* **inst·inktmäßig** a & adv = instinktiv || ~es Verhalten *in.ive behaviour*

institu·ieren vt [h] (etw) *to institute*; *establish*; *to set up* **Instit·ut** n ~(e)s/~e *institute* || (Anstalt) *establishment*; *institute*; *institution*; (*educational in.tion*) **Instituti·on** [ts] f ~/~en *established custom*; *institution*; zur ~ m *to i.alize* || die ~en [pl] ⟨jur⟩ *the Institutes* pl (*of Justinian*) || (Anstalt) → Institut **institution·ell** a *institutional* **Instit·uts-** [in comp] *in.tional* (*life*)

·Instleute pl *agricultural labourers* pl; → Inste

·Instmann m = Inste; [pl] Instleute

instru·ieren vt [h] jdn ~ *to instruct a p*; *to give a p instruction* (in *in*) || *to inform* (über *of, about*); *to give a p i.tions*; *to coach, teach a p* (was .. *what to do*) || **sich ~ über etw** *to inquire* (*about* od *into*) *a th*; *to make inquiries* (über *about* od *on*) **Instrukti·on** [ts] f ~/~en *instruction* || ⟨jur⟩ ~ des Solicitors über Rechtsfall *brief* || ~en [pl] *i.s* pl; *directions* pl; ⟨mil a.⟩ *orders* pl; nach den ~en *on the i.s* **instrukt·iv** [*f*] a *instructive* **Instrukti·ons-** [in comp] *instructional* (*cruise*) | ~stunde [f] (*instructive*) *lesson*; *hour of instruction*; ≈mäßig [a & adv] *according to i.s* od *regulations*; ≈widrig [a & adv] *contrary to i.s* **Instr·uktor** m ~s/–·oren *instructor*; *tutor*

Instrum·ent n ~s/~e **1.** (Werkzeug, Gerät) *instrument* ⟨a. mus⟩ (*musical i., stringed i., wind i.*) || *tool, implement* **2.** ⟨jur⟩ (Urkunde) *legal i.*; *document*; *deed* **3.** ⟨fig⟩ sie sind nur s–e ~e *they are merely his i.s* **Instrument·al-** [in comp] *i.al* | ~begleitung [f] ⟨mus⟩ *accompaniment on a musical i.* ~musik [f] *i.al music* ~verein [m] *orchestral society* **Instrum·enten-** ~anflug [m] *instrument approach*; ~anordnung [f] *i. layout*; ~brett [n] ⟨mot⟩ *dash-board*; *instrument panel*; ~macher [m] (*musical*) *i. maker*; ~handlung [f] *music shop*, ~kasten [m] ⟨surg⟩ *case of i.s*; ~leuchte [f] *d.-b. light*; ~öl [n] *meter oil*; ~ring [m] *instrument ring* ⟨bes a. a–n⟩ **instrument·ieren 1.** vt ⟨mus⟩ *to i.*; *to score*; *orchestrate* **2.** ≈ n & **Instrument·ierung** f *i.ation, orchestration* || *arrangement of music* || ⟨tech⟩ *i. work*

Insubordinati·on f ~/~en *insubordination*; *disobedience* || ~ & ~svergehen *act of i.tion*

Insul·aner m ~s/~, **~in** f *islander*; *inhabitant* (od *native*) *of an island*; ⟨fig hum pol⟩ = West-Berliner [pl] **insul·ar** a *insular* (*position, narrow-mindedness*)

insult·ieren vt [h] **1.** *to insult* **2.** ≈ n & **Insult·ierung** f ~/~en *insulting*; *insult, i.s* pl (*offered to a p*); *affront* || *insulting speech* od *action*

Insurg·ent m ~en/~en *insurgent*; *rebel* **Insurrekti·on** f ~/~en *insurrection*; *rebellion*

Ins-W·erk-setzen n ~s/ *setting in operation* || *contrivance*; *act of contriving* || *management* || (e–s Betrugs) *contrivance*; *deceitful practice*

inszen·ieren vt [h] ⟨theat⟩ *to produce*; *to get up*; *to stage*; *to put* (*play*) *on stage* || das Stück läßt sich schwer ~ *the play does not stage well* || gut inszeniert *well got up* **Inszen·ierung** f ~/~en ⟨theat⟩ *production*; *setting*; *staging*; *get*(*ting*)-*up* (*of a play*)

Int·aglio [–aljo] n ~s/–lien *engraved gem*

int·akt a *intact*; *unhurt*

Int·arsienmalerei f ⟨paint⟩ *tarsia*; *t. style*

integr·al 1. [a] *integral, whole* **2.** ≈ n ~s/~e ⟨math⟩ *i.* (*value*) | ≈rechnung [f] ⟨math⟩ *i. calculus* **Integration** f *integration* **integr·ierend** *integrant* (*parts*) **integriert** a ⟨psych⟩ nach außen ~ *out-going* (*child*) **Integrit·ät** f ~/ *integrity*, wholeness, soundness || (Moral) uprightness; honesty

Intell·ekt m ~s/ intellect **~ual·ismus** m intellectualism **i-u·ell** a intellectual; enlightened | ≃e [m] [der ~, ein ~r] ~n/~n intellectual; the intellectuals [pl] (of a country) || ⟨fam⟩ highbrow, ⟨Am a.⟩ egghead **intellig·ent** a intelligent || ⟨fam⟩ sharp **Intellig·enz** f ~/~en **1.** intelligence || ⟨fam⟩ sharpness **2.** the intellectuals [pl], intelligentsia (of a country) **3.** [in comp] ~alter [n] ⟨psych⟩ mental age; °~bestie [f] highbrow ⟨fam⟩; ~blatt [n] advertiser; intelligencer; ~quotient [m] index of i.ce; i.ce quotient (I. Q.)

Intend·ant m ~en/~en superintendent || ⟨theat⟩ director || ⟨mil⟩ commissary **-dant·ur, -d·anz** f ~/~en board of management || ⟨mil⟩ commissariat **-dant·ur-** commissary N; ~rat [m] ⟨mil⟩ commissary; ~truppe [f] Finance Corps N

Intensit·ät f ~/~en intensity, -siveness | ~s-einstellung [f] ⟨radar⟩ i. control; ~messer [m] level recorder ⟨a. at⟩ **intens·iv** a intensive (methods, agriculture); intense || violent; vehement || (Arbeit) eager; intense; ardent (feeling) | ~kultur [f] ⟨agr⟩ high farming **Intenti·on** [ts] f ~/~en intention; ~en [pl] i.s pl; purpose

·inter- ~alli·iert a interallied; ⟨mil⟩ combined ≃**block(leerstelle** [f]) m ⟨comp⟩ interblock (gape) **~d·ikt** n ~(e)s/~e **1.** (Verbot) (authoritative) prohibition **2.** ⟨ec⟩ interdict || jdn mit dem ~ belegen ⟨ec⟩ to i. a p; to lay a p under an i. **~ess·ant** a interesting (book, p, head), attractive (p) || sie will sich ~ m she wants to make herself i. || juicy (news) **Inter·esse** n ~s/~n interest (an [dat], für in) || v ~ f den Zeitungsleser newsworthy || voll lebhaften ~s on fire with i. (f in) || ich kann der S mein ~ nicht versagen I cannot disinterest myself from it; ein Mann v allseitigem (einseitigem) ~ a catholic-minded man (⟨bes Am⟩ a one-track mind) || sein eigenes ~ im Auge h to study one's own i. || er hatte ein persönliches ~ daran his personal concerns were in question; es liegt in s–m eigenen ~ zu it is to his own i. to || jds ~ in Anspruch nehmen to hold a p's i. || er nimmt an nichts ~ he takes no i. in anything; ~ erweckend evocative (book) || ~n [pl] (Zinsen) interest ≃**los** a uninterested; indifferent; listless, dull, sluggish **~ngemeinschaft** f community od union of i.; pool **~ngruppe** f ⟨bes Am⟩ pressure group **~nkonflikt** m conflict of i. **~nrechnung** (Zinsrechnung) i.-account **~nsphäre** f ⟨pol⟩ sphere of influence; domain **Interess·ent** m ~en/~en interested p od party **interess·ieren 1.** vt [h] to interest || jdn f etw ~ to i. a p in a th; an etw –rt w to get i.ed in a th, to warm up to a th **2.** vrfl **sich** f jdn ~ to interest o.s. (od to take an interest) in a p, to have a p's interest at heart **3.** er, das –iert mich I am i.ed in him, it; that intrigues me (to know); .. nicht that is not my line || sich lebhaft ~ f to take a lively i. in; to throw o.s. into || das –iert dich that concerns you **interess·iert 1.** [a] covetous, selfinterested; small-minded || ~ s an [dat] to be i.ed in || innerlich ~ s an to warm (up) to (one's work), to feel keen about **2.** [adv] i.edly: they walked i.edly round the exhibition || ~ mit dem Finger zeigen to point an i.ed finger; er blickte ~ he cast an i.ed eye

inter- ≃fer·enz f ~/ ⟨phys⟩ interference || ~-bild [n] ⟨wir⟩ i. figure; ~farben [pl] interfering colours pl **~glazi·al** a interglacial (period)

Interi·eur [interi'ør] n ~s/ ⟨arts⟩ interior

interim·istisch a temporary, provisional (state)

·Interims- ~aktie f scrip; ~aktien [pl] scrip [koll] **~anleiheschein** m scrip **~bescheid** ⟨jur⟩ provisional sentence **~lösung** f "stopgap" measure **~nachlaßverwalter** m temporary administrator **~jacke** f, **~rock** m ⟨mil⟩ fatigue-jacket **~regierung** f prov. od care-taker government **~schein** m interim certificate; prov. scrip **~uniform** f ⟨mil⟩ undress (uniform, clothes, suit); in ~ in undress

inter- ≃jekti·on [ts] f ~/~en ⟨gram⟩ interjection **~koloni·al** a intercolonial **~konfessionell** interdenominational **~kontinent·al** a intercontinental (rocket) ≃**laken** n Sw (Kurort im Kanton Bern) ≃**line·ar-** ~übers·etzung [f], ~version [f] interlinear translation ≃**m·ezzo** n ~s/~s & –zzi interlude, intermezzo; → Werbefernsehen-Kurzfilm **~ministeri·ell** a interministerial (committee) **~mitt·ierend** a ⟨scient⟩ intermittent

int·ern a internal (questions) **Intern·at** n ~s/~e boarding-school

inter- ~nation·al [ts] **1.** a international (fame) || ≃e Arbeiterbindung I. (Association) || ~e(r) Charakter i.ity; I–e Zivilluftfahrt-Organisation I. Civilian Aviation Organization (ICAO); ~er Sportler, der ≃e ⟨fam⟩ internatter **2.** die ≃e f (Sozialistenhymne) the i.e Fr | ≃**ne** m [ein ~r, der ~] ~n/~n resident pupil, boarder **~n·ieren** vt [h] to intern; detain; to keep in confinement; to confine (with)in a fortress, etc. ≃**n·ierte** m [der ~, ein ~r] & f ~n/~n internee; (political) prisoner; p. confined in a fortress, etc. ≃**n·ierung** f ~/~en internment; ⟨Ind⟩ detention; deportation | ~s-lager [n] internment camp; ⟨mil⟩ detention camp ≃**n·ist** m ~en/~en ⟨med⟩ internal specialist || ~enkongreß [m] Congress of Chemical Medicine ≃**pellati·on** f ~/~en ⟨engl parl⟩ question (to a minister) || ⟨a-engl⟩ interpellation **~pell·ieren** vt [h] ⟨engl parl⟩ to ask od address a question || ⟨a-engl⟩ to interpellate **~person·ell** a interpersonal (relations) **~planetarisch** a interplanetary (space) ≃**pol·ieren** vt [h] to interpolate ≃**pr·et** m ~en/~en interpreter; expounder || ⟨mus & fig⟩ exponent ≃**pretati·on** f ~/~en interpretation (of a text) || reading (of facts) | **~s-** interpretative (i. art) ≃**pretativ-Code** m (z Programmierung mathem. Programme) i. mathematical auto-code **~pret·ieren** vt [h] to interpret **~pung·ieren, ~punkt·ieren** vt [h] to ≃**pung·ierung,** ≃**punkti·on** f ~/~en punctuation | ~szeichen [n] p.n-sign od -mark; stop ≃**r·egnum** n ~s/ interregnum || interval ≃**-rogat·ivum** n ~s/–t·iva ⟨gram⟩ interrogative pronoun od particle ≃**v·all** [v] n ~(e)s/~e ⟨a. mus⟩ interval; in ~en v 25 Jahren at quarter-century intervals | ~sprung [m] sudden i. transition **~-ven·ieren** vi [h] to intervene; to -pose ≃**venti·on** f ~/~en intervention; -position ≃**v·iew** [–'vju:] n ~(s)/~s interview || ein ~ gewähren to give an i.; der Presse gewährtes ~ press-i. **~v·iewen** [–'vju:ən] vt [h] to i. a p; to arrange (od have) an i, with a p; to give a p an i.; der –te the interviewee ≃**z·onenhandel** m interzonal trade

Intest·at m ~en/~en ⟨jur⟩ intestate | ~erbe [m], ~erbin [f] intestate (od ab intestato) heir(ess), heir(ess)-at-law | ~erbfolge [f] succession by the next of kin; ⟨jur⟩ intestacy

Inthronisati·on, Inthronis·ierung f enthronement **inthronis·ieren** vt to enthrone

int·im I. [a] **1.** [pred] intimate (mit with) || ganz ~ s mit to be matey od hand in (od and) glove with; ~ w to get matey; man darf mit ihr nicht ~ w it does not do to be too i. with her **2.** [attr] i. (friend, circle, stories, liberties); ~er Freund firm friend; i.; bosom-friend, ⟨fam⟩ (great) pal **II.** [adv] ~ verkehren or s mit to be i. od familiar with a p, ⟨fam⟩ to be cheek by jowl with a p || ~ tun to hob-nob with a p || to be hail-fellow-well-met with a p **Intimit·ät** f ~/~en intimacy || (unerlaubte) ~en familiarities **·Intimus** m ~/–mi L familiar od intimate friend || ⟨fam⟩ chum

intoler·ant a intolerant **Intoler·anz** f ~/ intolerance

Intonati·on f ~/~en ⟨phon⟩ intonation **inton·ieren** vt [h] ⟨mus⟩ (anstimmen) to tune up || (in singender Sprache vortragen) to intone

·intra- ~muskul·är a intramuscular (injection) **~uter·in** a intra-uterine (mortality); foetal (deaths)

intransit·iv [–f] a ⟨gram⟩ *intransitive* **≃um** [–v–] n ∼s/–tiva *intransitive verb; verb neuter*

intraven·ös [–v–] a *intravenous (injection)*

Intrig·ant 1. [m] ∼en/∼en *intriguer, schemer, plotter, twister;* ⟨theat⟩ *villain;* ⟨pol⟩ *wire-puller* **2.** ≃ [a] *intriguing, designing, scheming, plotting* **∼in** f ∼/∼nen *designing woman* **Intr·ige** f ∼/∼n *intrigue; scheme, scheming* ‖ er versteht sich auf Intrigen *he knows how to make i.s* **intrig·ieren** vi [h] *to intrigue, to (plot and) scheme; to hatch plots*

Intr·ittfallen n *coming into step* ⟨a. mach⟩

Intro- ∼duktion f *introduction* **≃vertiert** a *withdrawn* ‖ ∼e(r) (m) f *introvert*

Intuiti·on [ts] f ∼/ *intuition* **i-t·iv** [–f] a *intuitive*

°**·intus** L; etw ∼ h *to have sth in one's head (stomach)*; etw nicht ∼ kriegen können *not to get the hang of a th*; wenn ich was ∼ habe *when I've got the liquor on board me*

In·umlaufsetzen n *circulation* ‖ *emission*

Inundati·on [-ts-] f ∼/∼en → Überschwemmung

In- u Auslandspatente pl *patents at home and abroad,* ⟨engl⟩ *U. K. and Overseas patents*

Inval·ide m [der ∼, ein ∼r] ∼n/∼n *invalid; disabled worker, soldier* od *sailor* ‖ ⟨mil⟩ als ∼ entlassen w *to be invalided out of the army* **∼n-∼dank** *Society for the care of Disabled Soldiers* **∼haus** n *hospital for disabled soldiers* **∼sold** m, **∼pension** f, **∼rente** f *old-age pension; disability benefit* **∼versicherung** f *old-age* (od *invalidity, disability) insurance* **Invalidit·ät** f ∼/ *invalidity;* (Arbeitsunfähigkeit) *disablement (from earning)*

Invasi·on f ∼/∼en *invasion*

Invent·ar n ∼(e)s/∼e, **∼ium** n ∼(s)/–tarien *inventory stock;* ⟨bal⟩ *accountable stores* ‖ geistiges ∼ *plant* ‖ ein ∼ aufnehmen *to draw up an inventory, to take stock* ‖ lebendes u totes ∼ *live and dead stock* | ⟨fig fam⟩ (P) altes ∼(ium) *old furniture* **∼buch** n *balance book* **∼errichtung** f *filing of inventory* **≃mäßig** a *inventorially* **∼stück** n *article of the inventory;* ⟨jur⟩ (im Laden) *fixture* **∼verzeichnis** n ⟨bal⟩ *land and buildings, furniture and fixtures* **inventaris·ieren, invent·ieren** vt [h] *to inventory, to draw up an inv. of;* (bei Versteigerungen) *to catalogue; to take stock of* **Invent·ur** f ∼/∼en *inventory, stock-taking* ‖ ∼ m *to take stock* **∼ausverkauf** m *stock-taking sale*

Inversi·on f ∼/∼en *inversion*

Inverk·ehrbringen n *commercialization*

invest·ieren vt [h] *to invest* ‖ jdn mit etw ∼ *to invest a p with a th* ‖ –rtes Geld *money invested* **Investierung, Investition** f ∼/∼en *investment* | ∼sfeld [n] *outlet for i. funds;* ∼sgüter [pl] *capital goods;* ∼squote [f] *rate of i.*

Investit·ur f ∼/∼en *investiture* **∼streit** m *investitive contest, dispute about investiture*

·in- (→ in[nen]) **∼wärts** adv *inward(s)* **∼wendig 1.** [a] *inward, interior, internal, inner* **2.** [adv] *within, inside* ‖ ich weiß, wie das Haus ∼ aussieht *I know what the inside of the house looks like* ‖ ich kenne es in- u auswendig *I know it thoroughly* od *out and out* od *by heart; I know all about it, I know all the ins and outs of it* **∼wief·ern, ∼wiew·eit** adv *(in) how far; to what extent* ‖ ∼ es mir möglich war *the extent to which I have been able* ‖ (Frage) ∼? *how so?, in what way?* **∼wohnend** a ⟨scient⟩ *immanent* **·≃wohner** m ∼s/∼ *inhabitant* **·≃zucht** f ∼/ (P & T) *inbreeding, breeding in and in* ‖ durch ∼ verdorben *inbred* **∼zw·ischen** adv *meantime, meanwhile; in the meantime; by that time, by then, by this*

I·on n ∼s/∼en ⟨phys⟩ *ion;* negatives ∼ *anion* | ∼enaustauscher [m] *ion exchange resin (filter)* ≃enbeheizt [a] *ion-heated (cathode);* ∼engitter [n] *i. lattice;* ∼enröhre [f] *ion(ic) tube;* ∼en(stärke)messer [m] *ionometer;* ∼enwolke [f] *ion cloud* | ∼entheorie [f] *ionic theory* **≃is·ieren** vt *to ionize* **∼is·ierung** (Spaltung v Molekülen u Atomen in Ionen) *ionization* ‖ Verlust durch ∼ *i. loss* | ∼selektrode [f] *ionizing electrode*

I·onier m, **∼in** f *Ionian* **i·onisch** a *Ionian, Ionic* ‖ ≃e Inseln [f pl] *Ionian Islands* ‖ das ≃e Meer (zw Griechenland & Unteritalien) *the Ionian Sea;* ∼e Säulenordnung *Ionic order*

ionog·en a (nicht)∼ *(non-)ionic* ⟨a. tex⟩

I·ota n ∼s/∼s *iota;* nicht ein ∼ *not the least bit;* ⟨theol⟩ *not a jot* od *a tittle*

I·owa [ai'o:va] n (Staat der U.S.A.)

·I-Punkt m *dot;* ⟨fig⟩ auf den ∼ *on the dot* ‖ mit ∼ versehen *to dot*

Ir·ak m *Irak, Iraq*

Ir·an n ∼s/ *Iran* **∼ier(in** f) m, **≃isch** a *Iranian*

Iraw·adi m (Strom in Hinterindien)

·Irbis m ∼ses/∼se ⟨zoo⟩ *ounce; snow leopard*

·irden a *earthen; fictile;* ∼es Geschirr *earthenware, crockery; earthen pots* od *vessels* pl

·irdisch 1. [a] *earthly, terrestrial;* (zeitlich) *temporal;* (weltlich) *worldly, mundane (pleasures);* (menschlich) *human* ‖ die ∼en Dinge [pl] *things (of* od *on this earth,* od *here below);* an ∼en D.en hängend *earthbound* **2. ≃e(r)** m, **≃e** f, **≃e(s)** n *earthly being, mortal man, woman;* **das ≃e** *(the things of) this world; earthly things* od *concerns* pl

·Ire m *Irishman,* (**·Irin** f *Irishwomen)* ‖ die Iren [pl] *the Irish* ‖ (gewählt) *Milesian, Hibernian, Son of Erin;* ⟨iron⟩ nur m *Pad(dy), Pat, bog-trotter;* ⟨Am sl⟩ *Mick(y)* **·irisch** a *Irish;* (gewählt) *Milesian;* der ≃e Freistaat *The Irish Free State,* [Ir] *Saorstat Eireann;* (seit 29. 7. 1937) *Eire* ‖ die ∼e Mundart *Erse;* der ∼e Akzent, das ∼e Englisch *brogue*

·irgend adv; wenn ich ∼ kann *if I possibly can;* was ich ∼ kann *whatever* od *anything I can do* ‖ wann (wo) es ∼ geht *whenever (wherever) it may be possible* ‖ wenn es ∼ geht *if ever possible;* so schnell wie ∼ möglich *as soon as ever possible;* wenn ∼ daran gedacht w kann *if the matter can be at all thought of;* wer nur ∼ anständig ist *any respectable p, anybody (who is) commonly* (od *at all) decent* **∼·ein(e** f) [pron] m, n *some(one);* ⟨allg⟩ *any(one)* ‖ [pl] –welche *some, any* ‖ ∼e Tasse *some cup (or other), any cup;* ∼ anderer *some one else, anybody else;* [negativ stets] *any;* ohne irgendwelche Kosten (Hilfe) *without any expense, assistance (whatever)* ‖ auf ∼e Weise (schlecht oder recht) *by hook or by crook* ‖ ist hier im Dorfe ∼ Platz, wo ..? ⟨fam⟩ *is there anywhere in the village where ..?;* in ∼em Grade *in one degree or another;* ∼ Anwesender *any of those present* ‖ ∼ (z. B. Zivilist) *a nondescript (e.g. civilian)* **∼-einer, ·∼jemand, ·∼wer** [abs] *somebody, someone;* [allg *or* neg] *anybody, anyone;* ∼ muß es getan h *somebody must have done it;* ∼ hat gesagt *somebody (or other) has said;* wenn ∼ wüßte *if any p* (stärker: *anybody in the whole world) knew* ‖ ⟨fam⟩ [pl konstr] *if anybody comes down here with their own car;* ∼ von zweien: *either,* wenn ∼ von beiden *if either side (refuses to meet the other)* **∼einmal** *(at) some time or other;* ⟨allg⟩ *at any time* **∼etwas** *something;* [allg *or* neg] *anything,* ⟨fam⟩ *any mortal thing,* gibt es ∼ Reizenderes? *can there be anything more delightful?* noch ∼? *anything else?, there is sth I saw; is there anything you saw?* **∼wann** = –einmal, *anywhen* **∼wie** = auf –eine Art (u Weise) *somehow (or other), in some way (or other), one way or another,* [allg] *anyhow;* [stärker:] *by hook or by crook;* wer ∼(wie) kann *anybody who possibly can* od *who is at all able (to)* **∼wo** *somewhere (or other), in some place (or other);* ⟨allg⟩ *anywhere;* ∼anders *somewhere else;* ist er hier ∼ (im Hause etc) *is he about (the place)?,* ist N. (hier) ∼? *is N. anywhere about?* **∼woher** *from somewhere, from some place (or other);* [allg] *from anywhere* **∼wohin** *somewhere (or other), to some place or other;* [allg] *anywhere, to any place (what-*

soever); gehst du ~? *are you going somewhere*?; wenn du ~ gehst *if you go anywhere*

Iridaz·een pl ⟨bot⟩ *iridaceous plants*

·Iris f ~/ **1.** ⟨myth⟩ (Regenbogen, Götterbotin) *Iris* ⟨a. astr⟩ **2.** ⟨bot & anat⟩ *iris* **3.** ~blende [f] ⟨phot⟩ *diaphragm*, ⟨Am⟩ *iris*; ~bogen [m] *rainbow*; ~druck [m] *irisated print*; ~farbe [f] *iridescent colour* **iris·ieren 1.** vi (schillern) *to be iridescent, to iridesce* **2.** ⁓ n *iridescence*

·Irische See, die *the Irish Sea*

·Irland n ~s/ *Ireland, Erin, the Emerald Isle*; ⟨iron⟩ *Patland* **·Irländer(in** f) m → Ire, Irin **·irländisch** a = irisch; ~es Moos ⟨bot⟩ *carrageen*

Irok·esen pl (Indianerstämme in U.S.A.), *Iroquoians* **irok·esisch** a *Iroquois, Iroquoian*

Iron·ie f ~/ *irony, satire*; die ~ des Schicksals *ironic fate, the irony of fate* (Th. Hardy); romantische ~ ⟨Ger⟩ *romantic irony* (F. Schlegel); tragische ~ *dramatic irony* **Ir·oniker** m ~s/~ *a p given to irony, ironist* **ir·onisch** a *ironic(al)*; er meinte es ~ *he said it with his tongue in his cheek*; ~er Zug um den Mund *sneer* **ironis·ieren** vt *to treat* (*with irony* od) *ironically*

·Irr- [in comp] (→ irre[n]) **~fahrt** f *wandering(s* pl), *vagaries* pl ‖ ⟨fig⟩ *errantry* (*of knights*), *odyssey* (*of a man's soul*) **~gang** m **1.** *erratic journey, round-about way, wrong way* **2.** (Labyrinth) *labyrinth, maze* **~garten** m, **~gebäude, ~gewinde** n *labyrinth, maze, crinkum-crankum* ⟨a. fig⟩ **~glaube** m *erroneous belief, heterodoxy*; (Ketzerei) *heresy* **⁓gläubig** a *heterodox*; *heretical* **~gläubige(r** m) f *heretic* **~gläubigkeit** f *heresy* **~läufer** m (Brief) *misrouted letter* **~lehre** f *false doctrine, heterodoxy* ‖ ⟨ec⟩ *heresy* **~lehrer** m *heretic, teacher of heretical doctrine* **~licht** n *ignis fatuus, will-o'-the-wisp, jack-o'-lantern* ⟨a. fig⟩ **~sinn** m **1.** *madness, mental derangement* od *alienation*; *distraction, insanity, lunacy, delirium* **2.** ⟨fig⟩ *absurdity* **⁓sinnig** a **1.** *lunatic, insane*, (*mentally*) *deranged* **2.** ⟨fig⟩ *absurd* **~stern** m *comet* **~wahn** m *delusion* **~weg** m *wrong track* od *way, path* ‖ auf ~e geraten *to miss* od *lose one's way* ⟨a. fig⟩; *to go astray* **~wisch** m a) = ~licht; b) (Kobold) (*malicious* od *mischievous*) *imp*

irration·al a ⟨math⟩ *irrational, surd*; ~e Größe *surd* **irration·ell** a *unreasonable, irrational*

·Irre f ~/; in der ~ *astray, out of the way* ‖ in die ~ führen *to lead astray* ‖ ⟨fig⟩ *to deceive, to lead by the nose* **·irre** a & adv *astray, off the road, off the right way, on the wrong track* ⟨a. fig⟩, *lost*, ⟨fig⟩ *wrong* ‖ (verwirrt) *wrong, perplexed, confused* ‖ ⟨med⟩ (*mentally*) *deranged*; *out of one's mind* od *wits*; *mad, insane* ‖ ⟨jur⟩ *non compos* (*mentis*) ‖ *he has a confused* od *wild look*; *he held mad speeches* ‖ du bist wohl ein bißchen ~ im Kopf *I think you are a bit crazy*; er war ganz ~ (irrte sich) *he was completely puzzled* ‖ ~ sein = *irresein* **~|fahren, ~|gehen** vi [s] *to go wrong* od *astray*; (Brief) *to miscarry* **~|führen, ~|leiten 1.** vt [h] *to misdirect, misguide*; *to take* od *send* (*a p*) *wrong, to lead .. astray, to take .. out of his way* ‖ ⟨fig⟩ *to mislead, to lead astray, to put on the wrong scent*; *to delude, dupe*, ⟨sl⟩ *dope*; *to impose upon, to mystify, deceive*; ⟨sl⟩ *to lead .. up the garden path*; ⟨ftb⟩ (beim Weitergeben des Balles) *to sell the dummy* ‖ *a misguided child* ‖ **sich durch etw ~ l** *to be misled*, ⟨fam⟩ *to be taken in* **2.** vi *to deceive*, ⟨fig⟩ *to draw a red-herring across the path* od *trail* | ~d *deceptive*; ~de Bezeichnung *misbranding* **⁓führung** f *mystification*; *deception*; *misleading statement* od *information* **⁓leitung** f *misguidance* **~|machen** vt [h] *to confound, puzzle, bewilder, perplex, confuse* ‖ er läßt sich durch nichts ~ *nothing can put him out, .. divert him from his purpose*; er wird mich nicht ~ *he will not disconcert me*; laß dich nicht ~ *don't let yourself be put off* **~|reden** vi [h] *to wander in mind*; *to rave*; *to talk incoherently*; *to be delirious* **~|reiten** = ~fahren **~|sein** vi [s] *to be mistaken* od *confused, puzzled* ‖ (im Kopfe) *to be off one's head*, ⟨fam⟩ *off one's chump, to be crazy* od *delirious* **⁓sein** n *bewilderment, distraction, perplexity*; (stärker:) *delirious state, mental alienation*; manisch depressives ~ *manic-depressive psychosis* **~|werden** vi [s] *to grow* od *get confused* od *puzzled* ‖ ~ an [dat] *not to know what to make of*; *to be mistaken in* (*a p*); *to go astray in* (*one's belief*) **·Irre** m [der ~, ein ~r] ~n/~n *madman*; *lunatic*; *insane p, mental patient*; ⟨scient⟩ *psychopath(ic)* **·Irre** f ~n/~n *mad woman*; *lunatic*, etc.

ir- (nicht) **⁓realit·ät** f *unreality* **~regul·är** a *irregular* (*forces*); ~e Truppen *irregulars* pl ‖ *unconventional* (*warfare*) **⁓regularit·ät** f ~/~en *irregularity* **~relev·ant** a *irrelevant, trifling* **~religi·ös** a *irreligious* **⁓religiosit·ät** f ~/ *irreligion, irreligiousness, lack of religion*

·irren A. vi [h, bei Ortsveränderung: s] **1.** (körperlich) *to go astray*; *to rove, ramble, stray* (*from one place to another*); *to wander*; sie irrte durch e–n Wald *she was wandering* (*roaming*) *about* (*through*) *a wood* (nicht *to err*!) ‖ ~der Ritter *knight-errant* **2.** (geistig) *to be* od *go wrong* (*about*); *we cannot go far wrong in doing it*; *to be mistaken* od *deluded, to suffer from illusions* od *delusions*; *to be deceived* ‖ hier irrt Goethe ⟨fam, hum⟩ *here G. is beside the mark*; wenn ich nicht irre *or* [eingeschoben] .., irr' ich nicht, .. *if I am not mistaken*; darin darf man sich nicht ~ *no mistake*! **3.** ⟨rel⟩ (milder als sündigen) *to stray from the right path*; ⟨bibl⟩ *to offend against the law*; ⟨prov⟩ **Irren** ist menschlich *to err is human*; *we are all liable to error* **B.** fast † vt [h] = irreführen; die Umstände irrten mich *I was deluded by the circumstances* **C. sich** ~ vrefl *to make a mistake*; *to be mistaken* od *amiss*; *to be in error*; *to commit an error*; *to be* od *go wrong* ‖ **sich sehr** ~ *to be very much mistaken*, (od *far out*) (in *in*), ⟨fam⟩ *to be quite wrong* (od *beside the mark*); sich vollkommen ~ *to get it all wrong*; sich gröblich ~ *to blunder* ‖ **sich in etw** ~ *to misjudge* od *misunderstand a th*; sich in jdm ~ *to mistake a p's character*; *to be mistaken in a p*; sich in der P ~ *to mistake a p for somebody else* ‖ ich irre mich nicht *I am not mistaken, I am positive*; ich **muß** mich geirrt h *I must have been mistaken, I must have made a mistake*; du hast dich geirrt ⟨fam⟩ *you've got it wrong*; ich weiß, ich **kann** mich ~ *I speak under correction* **·Irren-** ~anstalt [f] (*Private*) *Mental Home*; ~arzt [m] *alienist*, ⟨fam⟩ *mad-doctor*; *mental specialist*; ⟨scient⟩ *psychopathist*; ~haus [n] *lunatic asylum, madhouse*; ⟨engl a.⟩ *Bedlam*; ⟨Am sl⟩ *bughouse* ‖ wie im ~ *like Bedlam*; ~häusler [m] *lunatic, madman*; ⟨engl⟩ *Bedlamite*; ~heilkunde [f] *psychotherapeutics, psychotherapy* **·irrig** a *erroneous, wrong, false*; (ungenau) *inexact, incorrect*; (erdichtet) *ficticious* ‖ e–e S ~ auffassen ⟨fam⟩ *to get the wrong end of the stick* **~erw·eise** adv *erroneously, wrongly, by* (*a*) *mistake, through an error* **⁓keit** f *erroneousness, falseness*; *incorrecteness*; *fallacy, fallability*

Irrig·ator m ~s/–at·oren *irrigator* **irrit·ieren** vt [h] (ärgern) *to irritate, provoke, worry* (*the light worries my eyes*) ‖ (beirren) *to puzzle*

·Irr- ~sal n ~(e)s/~e *error, going astray, wandering* **~tum** m ~(e)s/⁓er *error, grave error, mistake, fault*, ⟨sl⟩ *bloomer*, ⟨Am⟩ *slip-up*, (beim Reden) *slip of the tongue*; (Mißverständnis) *misunderstanding, misconception*; ⟨jur⟩ Rechts⁓ *mistake of law*, Tatsachen⁓ *m. of fact*; ~ in den Angaben *misreporting*; ~ in der Einreihung *tabulating error* | aufgrund e–s ~s *under a mistake*; e–n ~ begehen *to commit a slight error, to make a tremendous mistake*; *to blunder*; in gefährlichem ~ befangen über *dangerously deluded as to ..*; *im ~ s to be in error, to be mistaken, to deceive o.s. to be in the wrong* (⟨fam⟩ *wr. box*); da sind Sie im ~

you're wrong there; im ∼ verstrickt *error-stricken* (*souls*) ‖ ∼ vorbehalten *errors* (*and omissions*) *excepted* (abbr *E. & O. E.*) ‖ e–n ∼ berichtigen *to rectify an error*; *to correct a mistake*; in e–n ∼ verfallen *to fall into an error* ‖ in e–m ∼ befangen *mistaken* ‖ jdm den ∼ nehmen *to undeceive* od *disabuse a p*; in jds ∼ verfallen *to fall into the fallacy of a p* ‖ Sie sind sehr im ∼! *you are altogether mistaken*; *you are quite out*; Sie befinden sich in e–m ∼ *you are* od *labour under a misapprehension* od *delusion* **≗tümlich 1.** [a] *erroneous* **2.** [adv] = **≗tümlicherweise** adv *erroneously, by mistake* **~ung** f ∼/∼en **1.** = Irrtum *error, mistake* | ∼szeichen [n] ⟨wir, telg⟩ *erase signal* **2.** (Streit) *difference* **~wahn** m → Wahn **~weg** m *wrong track*; auf dem ∼ *on the wrong track*; sich in ∼e verwickeln *to lead o.s. astray*

Isab·ell- ~farbe f *Isabel(-colour), cream-colour, Isabella* **≗farben, ≗farbig** a *isabelline, cream-coloured* ‖ *fallow-dun* (*horse*)

°·**Ische** f ∼/∼n ⟨teens⟩ (Mädchen) flotte, schaue ∼ *slick chick*

·**Ischias** m ∼/ ⟨med⟩ *sciatica*; ⟨scient⟩ *ischiagra* **~nerv** m *sciatic nerve*

·**Isegrim** m ∼(e)s/∼e *Isengrim, the wolf* ‖ ⟨fig⟩ *morose fellow, grumbler*; ⟨fam⟩ *bear*

Isfah·an n → Ispahan

Isl·am m ∼s/ *Islam*(*ism*) **≗is·ieren** vt *to Islamize* **≗·itisch** a *Islamic, Islamitic*

·**Island** n *Iceland* **≗er(in** f) m *Icelander* ·**isländisch 1.** [a] *Icelandic* **2.** ≗ [n] das ∼e *Icelandic*; auf ∼ *in Icelandic*

Isle de France [il də frɑ̃s] f (Kernland Frankreichs im Pariser Becken)

·**iso-** Gr (gleich) **≗g·one** f *isogon*(*ic line*) | ∼nkarte [f] *isogonic chart*

Isol·ator m ∼s/–at·oren ⟨el⟩ *insulator* **Isol·ier-** [in comp] *insulating* **~band** n *i. tape* od *band* **~kleidung** f: biologische ∼ *biological isolation garment* (*big*); ⟨a–n⟩ Zubringer der ∼en *big swimmer* **~masse** f *i.g substance*; ⟨bes theat⟩ *mica* **~schemel** m ⟨el⟩ *insulator, i.g-stool* **~schicht** f *i.g-layer* **~schutz** m *insulation* **~station** f ⟨med⟩ *isolation ward* **~stoff** m *insulator* **~überzug** m *insulating covering* **~zelle** f *cell for single confinement* **isol·ieren 1.** vt [h] ⟨el⟩ *to insulate*; gegen Hitze ∼ *to heat-i.* ‖ ∼d *insulating* (*material*) ‖ ⟨fig⟩ *to isolate*; ganz –rt s *or* stehen *to stand all alone* ⟨a. fig⟩ **2. sich** ∼ vrefl *to isolate* (*o.s.*) **isol·iert** a *insulated* (*wire*); nicht ∼ *bare* (*wire*) **Isol·ierung** f ∼/∼en ⟨el⟩ *insulation* ‖ ⟨fig⟩ *isolation* ‖ ⟨med⟩ ∼ v Krankheitsverdächtigen *quarantine*

iso- Gr (gleich) **~m·etrisch** a ⟨scient⟩ *isometrical* **≗th·erme** f ∼/∼n *isotherm*(*al line*) **~th·ermisch** a *isothermal* **≗t·op** n ∼s/∼e ⟨at⟩ *isotope* | *deuterium and tritium are i.s of hydrogen* | ∼nindikator [m] ⟨at, med⟩ *tracer*; ∼ntrenn(ungs)-anlage [f] *i. separation plant*

Ispah·an n (Stadt im Iran)

Isra·eli m ∼s/∼s *Israeli* [invar] **Israel·it** m ∼en/∼en *Israelite, Jew, Hebrew*

·**iß**! imp; ·**ißt** 2. & 3. p sg pres ind v essen

ist 3. p sg pres ind v sein ·**Ist-** *actual* **~-Ausgabe** f *a. issue* **~-Bestand** (Ggs Soll- ..) m *a. amount, quantity, stock*; ⟨bank⟩ *a. balance*; ⟨mil⟩ *a. state* (*of equipment*) **~-Einnahme** f *net receipts* **~maß** n *a. size* **~-Stärke** f ⟨mil⟩ *a. numbers* pl | ∼meldung [f] *daily strength report* **~wert** m *true* od *actual value*

Istanb·ul n ⟨türk⟩ [Gr] (= Konstantinopel)

†**Istäw·onen** pl (germ. Volksstamm) *Istævones*

·**Isthmus** m ∼/·Isthmen *isthmus*

·**Istrien** n *Istria*

†·**Italer** pl (Volksstamm) *Itali* L pl

It·alien n *Italy*

Itali·ener(in f) m *Italian* **i-nisch** a *Italian* ‖ ∼e Nacht f *illumination* ‖ (Sprache) auf ≗ *in Italian*

Iterati·on [ts] f ∼/∼en ⟨comp⟩ *iteration*

·**Ithaka** n (e–e der Ionischen Inseln) *Ithaca*

Itiner·arium n ∼s/–rien *itinerary, traveller's guide*

°**Iw·an,** ⟨Ger mst⟩ ·Iwan ∼s/∼e *Russian*

J

J, j [jɔt] n ∼/∼ *J, j*

ja 1. [adv] [betont] *yes*; ⟨rhet⟩ *yea*; ⟨Am fam⟩ *yeah* ‖ ∼ sagen, *to say yes, to consent*; mit ∼ antworten *to say yes, to answer in the affirmative*; zu allem ∼ (u amen) sagen *to say yes* (od *to consent*) *to everything*; jd, der zu allem ∼ (u amen) sagt *a yes-man*; er sagte nicht ∼ u nicht nein *he didn't commit himself*; (ich war da.) – Ja? *Were you*?; (Richard!) – Ja? *Yes*?, *Well*? ‖ **aber** ·ja!, **~ doch**! *to be sure*! *surely*! *yes, I did*! **~ fr·eilich**! *to be sure*! *certainly*! (*yes,*) *indeed*! ⟨fam⟩ *sure thing*! **~ nicht** *not as much as* .. **~w·ohl,** ⟨fam⟩ **~w·oll**! (*yes,*) *certainly*! *I do* (*did*), .. *I was* ‖ ⟨Am fam⟩ *yep*! **wenn ~** *if so, in that case* **2.** [intj] [unbetont] *well* ..; ja, sie ·ist so *she* (*certainly*) *is so to be sure* ∼, wissen Sie denn nicht? *why, don't you know*? | ich tat es ∼ nur dir zu Gefallen *well, I did it only to please you*; mich beseelt ∼ der Wunsch *be sure that I personally am inspired by the desire*; ich will es dir ∼ geben, aber gern tu ich's nicht *well, I will give it you but not very willingly*; ich freu' mich ∼, aber *it's not that I'm not delighted, but* | ⟨emph⟩ ich sagte es dir ∼ *I told you so, didn't I tell you so*? na, da haben wir es ∼! *there now*! | ⟨emph⟩ Hunderte, ∼ Tausende *hundreds, nay thousands*; er ist arm, ∼ bettelarm *he is poor or, what is more, a pauper*; (*his attitude is improper,*) *if not* (*monstrous*); ich schätze, ∼ verehre ihn *I appreciate him, nay I almost venerate him* | (rückbezüglich) das ist ∼ zum Verrücktwerden! *that* (*really*) *drives me mad*; er hat es ∼ absichtlich getan *why, he did it on purpose*; da bist du ∼ endlich *well, you've come at last*; ∼, das waren glückliche Stunden *those were happy hours indeed*; ∼, das wird kaum möglich s *well, that will hardly be possible*; du weißt es ∼ *you surely know it* | [betont u lang] [beim imp]: tu es j·a nicht *be sure not to do it*; *don't do it under any circumstances*; erzähl' es ihm j·a nicht! *don't go telling him*; das soll er mir j·a lassen *whatever happens, he should leave that alone*; sieh es dir j·a an! *don't fail to have a look at it*; daß du's ihm j·a sagst! *be sure and tell him*! | (Verwunderung ausdrückend) es schneit ja *I say, it's snowing* ·**Ja** n ∼s/∼s *yes*, ⟨parl⟩ *aye*; mit lautem ∼ *with a loud yes*; (eine Frage) mit ∼ beantworten *to answer .. in the affirmative* ‖ sie war sein ∼ u Amen *she was alpha and omega to him, he swore by her* ‖ ich gebe mein ∼ u Amen dazu *I give my consent to it* **~bruder** m *time-server*, ⟨fam⟩ *yes-man* ‖ die **~stimmen** pl *the affirmative votes* pl, *the ayes* pl; die ∼ sind in der Mehrheit ⟨parl⟩ *the ayes have it* **~wort** n; das ∼ geben *to consent*; (e–m Freier) *to accept a suitor, to accept a p's offer of marriage*

J·abo m ∼s/∼s ⟨mil sl⟩ = Jagdbomber

j·ach a = jäh(e) **≗taufe** f = Not-

J·acht f ∼/∼en *yacht*; –klub [m] *yachting club*

°×**jäck** a *batty* ‖ ∼ s auf *to have .. on the brain*

J·äckchen n ∼s/∼ (*short*) *jacket*; *coatee*; kz enges wollenes Ärmel≗ *spencer* **J·acke** f ∼/∼n *jacket*; *top* (*pyjama t.*); (eng anliegend, mst aus Leder) *jerkin*; (aus Wolle) *jersey, guernsey* || Ärmel-≈ *sleeved waistcoat,* (Kittel f Knaben) *tunic* || Bord≈ ⟨mar⟩ *pea-jacket*; Matrosen≈ *monkey--jacket* || ⟨mil⟩ *coatee* | jdm die ∼ vollhauen ⟨fam⟩ *to dust a p's jacket* ⟨fig⟩ || das ist e–e alte ∼ (Geschichte) *that's stale news*; das ist ∼ wie Hose ⟨vulg⟩ → Hose wie ∼ | ∼nhemd [n] *shirt-coat*; ∼nkleid [n] *twosome*; *ensemble* Fr **Jack·ett** [ja–] n ∼(e)s/∼e (Herren-) *short coat*; (*sack-*)*coat* || (Damen-) *jacket* **∼anzug** m *lounge suit*

J·affa n (Hafenstadt in Palästina, Israel)

J·agd f ∼/∼en **1. a.** (Hetzjagd auf Fuchs, Hirsch) *hunt, hunting* **b.** (auf Schalwild, Vögel) *shooting* **c.** *coursing hare* (*by greyhounds*) **d.** (Pirsch≈) *stalking* **2.** (Revier) (*place-*)*sh.g, sh.*(*--ground*) **3.** ⟨poet⟩ *chase* || ⟨fig⟩ (nach) *pursuit* (*of*) || das ist e–e ∼! (Hetzerei) *that is a rush*; ∼ nach Ämtern u Gold *place-h.g, the race for gold, h. after fortune* || *Wotan's wild chase* **4. hohe** (niedere) ∼ *big* (*small*) *game sh.g*; *he stayed there for the sh.g* || ∼ im Dickicht *cover-sh.g*; auf Schmetterlinge *catching butterflies, butterflying,* auf Walfische *whaling* || die ∼ ist **auf (zu)** *the season is open* (*close*) || ⟨aero⟩ freie ∼ *free-lancing, f.-lance fighter patrol* || **auf die ∼ gehen** *to go on a h., to go h.g*; *to go sh.g*; ⟨Am⟩ *to gun* || auf die ∼ reiten *to ride to hounds* || die ∼ geht auf (fängt an) *the sh.g* (*h.g*) *season begins* || die ∼ soll um 6 beginnen *the shoot is timed to start at six* || auf der ∼ s *to be at the chase, to be out sh.g, to be h.g* || (mit dem Gewehr) *to go sh.g* || e–e ∼ pachten *to lease game preserves* || an der Parforce≈ teilnehmen *to ride to hounds, to follow the h.s* || in voller ∼ *in full cry* || ⟨praehist & geogr⟩ v der ∼ leben *to live by h.g* **5. ∼ m auf** [acc] *to give chase to*; *to chase, pursue* (*a thief*); *to persecute*; *to hunt after*; ∼ auf *a man--hunt for* (*a p*) || ⟨fig⟩ die ∼ aufgeben *to give up the chase* || ⟨fig⟩ ∼ nach *scramble for* (*place, wealth*) || auf der ∼ nach jdm *on a p's track* **6.** (Weidmannskunst) *huntsmanship, huntsman's craft* **7.** [koll] (Jäger, Treiber, Hunde) *the meet, the field, the hunt* **8.** *h.g-.., sh.g-..* **∼abwehr** f ⟨aero⟩ starke ∼ *strong fighter defence* **∼anzug** m *h.g--dress* od *-suit* **∼ausdruck** m *h.g-term* **∼aufseher** m *game-keeper* **∼berechtigung** f *sh.g-license* **∼beute** f ⟨hunt⟩ *game, battue, kill* (*the total kill*) || gute ∼ m *to make a good bag*; geringe .. *he had very poor sport* **∼bezirk** m *sh.g* od *h.g-ground* **∼bomber** m *fighter-bomber* | ∼geschwader [n] *f.-b. wing* **∼büchse** f, **∼flinte** f (*sporting-*)*gun, shotgun,* (leichte) *fowling-piece* **∼einsitzer** m ⟨aero⟩ *single--seat fighter* **∼expedition** f *safari* **∼fieber** n *buck--fever* **∼flieger** ⟨aero⟩ *pursuit* od *fighter pilot,* (*aerial*) *fighter* **∼flugzeug** n *fighter* **∼freund** m = ∼liebhaber **∼frevel** m *poaching* **∼frevler** m *poacher* **∼gefilde** n pl; selige ∼ *happy h.g-grounds* **∼gehege** n *preserve* **∼geleit** n ⟨aero⟩ *fighter escort* **∼genossenschaft** f *shooting syndicate* ≈**gerecht** a *sportsmanlike, huntsmanlike, sporting* **∼gerechtigkeit** f *right of h.g* od *sh.g* **∼geschichte** f a) *huntsman's yarn* b) *hunting-story* **∼geschwader** n ⟨aero⟩ *fighter-squadron* od *wing*; *fighter aeroplanes* pl **∼gesellschaft** f *h.g-* od *sh.g-party* od *-field*; *hunt, chase* **∼gesetz** n *game-law* **∼gewehr** n = ∼büchse **∼gründe** f pl = ∼gefilde || in die ewigen J. eingehen (in's Jenseits) *to go to the happy h.g-grounds*; jdn in die ewigen J. schicken *launch a p into eternity* **∼gruppe** f ⟨aero⟩ *pursuit group* **∼haus** n *h.g-box, sh.g-box* **∼häuschen** n *lodge* **∼horn** n *bugle*(*-horn*), *h.g-horn* **∼hund** m (*fox*)*hound*; *hunting* od *sporting dog*; *(in hare-h.g) *beagle*; *pointer, setter*; *retriever* → Hund A. 1. || die Koppel ∼e *the hounds* pl, *the pack* **∼hündin** f *bitch hound, brach* **∼hüter** m (*game*) *keeper* **∼hütte** f *sh.g.-lodge* **∼kanzel** f *screened sh.g-stand* **∼kalender** m *sporting-almanac* **∼karte** f *sh.g licence* **∼kleid** n, **∼kleidung** f *sh.g.-clothes* pl; *h.g-dress* od *-garb* **∼liebhaber** m *sportsman*; ⟨sl⟩ *h.g fan* **∼lust** f (*huntsman's*) *sport* **∼machen** n *chase* **∼messer** n *h.g-knife, hanger,* ⟨Am⟩ *bowie-knife* **∼mütze** f *deerstalker* **∼netz** n *h.g-net* **∼ordnung** f *rules* [pl] *of the chase, regulations* [pl] *for sportsmen, forest-laws* pl **∼pächter** m *lessee of a shoot* **∼partie** f *h.g-* od *sh.g-party* **∼peitsche** f *h.g-crop* od *-whip* **∼personal** n *h.g-train* **∼pferd** n *hunter* **∼rakete** f *air-to-air missile*; ferngelenkt *guided aircraft rocket* (*GAR*) **∼recht** n *sh.g-license* **∼reiten** n *hunt-race* **∼rennen** n *steeple--chase* **∼revier** n *h.g-ground, preserve, sh.g* **∼rock** m **a.** (*fox-hunter's*) *pink, pink* od *scarlet coat, pink h.g-coat* **b.** *huntsman's coat, sh.g-jacket, Norfolk jacket* **∼ruf** m *h.g-call, tally-ho* **∼schein** m *sh.g* od *game-license* od *permit*; e–n ∼ erwerben *to take out a l.* **∼schiff** n *chaser* **∼schlitten** m *h.g-sledge* **∼schloß** n *h.g-seat* od *-lodge* **∼schutz** m ⟨aero⟩ *fighter escort* N, ⟨fam⟩ *umbrella* **∼sperre** f ⟨aero⟩ *fighter screen* **∼springen** n *hunter trial*(*s*) **∼staffel** f ⟨aero⟩ *fighter squadron* **∼stock** m *sh.g-stick* **∼stück** n ⟨arts⟩ *game-piece*; *h.ing picture* **∼stuhl** m *seat-stick* **∼tag** m *h.ing day* **∼tasche** f *sportsman's* od *game-bag* **∼tiere** n pl *beasts* [pl] *of the chase, game* **∼uhr** f *h.g-watch* **∼verbände** pl ⟨aero⟩ *fighter formations* pl **∼vergnügen** n *sport*; *pleasures* [pl] *of the chase* **∼vogel** m, **∼geflügel** n *game-bird* **∼wagen** m *trap, dog-cart,* (mst großer, vierspänniger) *drag*; *surrey* ⟨a. mot⟩ **∼wesen** n *sport*; *h.g affairs* pl **∼zeit** f *open* od *sh.g-, h.g-season* **∼zeug** n *h.g-equipage, h.g-apparel* **∼zug** m (Gespann) *carriage-and-four, four-in-hand* || (Teilnehmer [pl]) *h.g train, sh.g party*; *h.g expedition*; *hunt* **∼zweisitzer** m ⟨aero⟩ *two-seater fighter* **j·agdbar** a *warrantable* (*stag*); ∼es Wild *fair game*; ∼e Tiere [pl] *beasts* pl *of chase* **j·agen A.** vt [h] **1.** ⟨allg⟩ *to drive* (*quickly*), *to chase, pursue* (*a thief*); *the enemy was driven out of the country, the wind drives the clouds*; *the children chased each other* **2.** ⟨hunt⟩ *to chase*; (Löwe, Fuchs, Hirsch) *to hunt*; (auf der Pirsch) *to stalk*; (Hühner) *to shoot*; (Hasen mit Hunden) *to course* **3.** ⟨fig a.⟩ *to chevy, chivy*; (wie) mit Hunden: *to hound*; *to rush* (*a p over the countryside*); e–n Wagen *or* mit e–m W. ∼ (durch) *to send a car shooting* (*through the countryside*); *we raced our horses* (*over the plain*); müde ∼ *to tire out*; (ein Pferd) zu Tode ∼ *to ride to death* **4.** ein **Ereignis** jagte das andere, ein **Witz** jagte den anderen *the events* (*jokes*) *came in rapid succession* | **aus** dem Bett ∼ *to rout* od *rouse a p out of* (*his*) *bed*; aus dem Hause ∼ *to turn* (⟨fam⟩ *kick*) *out* (*of doors*); aus dem Dienste ∼ *to send .. away,* ⟨fam⟩ *to give .. the sack*; aus–e–a–∼ *to scatter, disperse* || er hat sein ganzes Geld **durch** die Kehle gejagt *he has wasted his whole fortune in drink* || **in** die Flucht ∼ *to put to flight*; *to rout*; in Furcht ∼ *to frighten*; *to strike with terror*; es jagte mir das Blut in den Kopf *it made the blood rush to my head*; jdm (sich [dat]) eine Kugel in (durch) den Kopf ∼ *to blow out a p's* (*one's*) *brains*; jdm ein Messer in den Leib ∼ *to run a knife into a p*; er läßt sich nicht ins Bockshorn ∼ *he won't let be intimidated* od *bullied*; ein Volk in e–n Krieg hinein ∼ *to stampede a people into a war* || **von** Haus u Hof ∼ *to turn out of house and home* || zum Teufel (Kuckuck, Henker) ∼ ⟨fam⟩ *to send to the devil, to hell* **B. vi** [h] [bei gr Ortsveränderung: s] **1.** [h] *to go* od *to be* (*out*) *hunting, to ride to hounds,* etc. (→ A. 2.) **2.** (mit Schnelligkeit) *to rush, run, dash* (*ride, gallop, drive*) (⟨fam⟩ *to pelt*) *along* od *ahead* (*at full speed*) || (P) *to tear*; (Wolken) *to scud* (⟨a. nav⟩ Schiff vor dem Winde); (Wind) *to race* (*over the moor*); (Maus) *to scurry*; (T., Kind, zu Pferde) *to scamper*; (Menschen) *to scramble* (*for the pennies*); (Enten beim Einfallen, Fisch an der Angel) *to skitter*; (plötzlich davon∼) *to whip* (*out, away, off*) || (T) (= Beute m) *to prey upon animals*; (*of cars*) das Auto jagte .. über .. gegen .. *the car darted* od *scorched across the bridge and went smash into a brick wall* **3.** ⟨fig⟩ **nach etw** ∼ *to hunt, run, tear* *after* (*wealth*); *to be in pursuit of* **J·agen** n ~s/ *hunting, shooting*, etc. ‖ *forest section* → jagen **J·äger** m ~s/~ **1.** *hunter, huntsman, sportsman*; die ~ [pl] *the field*, ⟨sl⟩ *the guns* pl ‖ die ~ brachen früh zur Jagd auf *the shooting-party started early* ‖ (Förster) (*wood-*)*ranger* ‖ (Heger) *keeper* ‖ (Wildhüter) *gamekeeper*; der Wilde ~ *the Wild Huntsman*; eifriger ~ *Nimrod* **2.** ⟨mil⟩ *rifleman, sharpshooter*; ~ zu Pferde *mounted r.*, er wurde zu den ~n (Waffengattung) eingezogen *he was called up to the rifles* **3.** ⟨aero⟩ ~ = Jagdflugzeug **~art** f ⟨cul⟩ nach ~ *chasseur* Fr; *huntsman style* **~bataillon** n ⟨mil⟩ *battalion of riflemen* od *sh.s* **~bursch(e)** m *huntsman's boy, young huntsman* **~garn** n *hunting-net* **≗grün** a *hunting green* **~haus** n *keeper's cottage* od *lodge* **~horn** n *huntsman's* (*bugle-*)*horn* **~hut** m *deerstalker* (*hat*) **~joppe** f *shooting-jacket* **~hemd** (nach G. Jäger geb. 1832) n *Jaeger shirt* **~kunst** f *huntsmanship* **~latein** n ⟨fam⟩ **a.** *sportsman's slang* **b.** *huntsman's tough yarns* pl **~leitzentrale** f ⟨aero⟩ → GCI-Verfahren **~meister** m *master of the chase* od *hunt, Master hunter*; Reichs≗ *Controller of the Hunt* **~messer** n *hunting-knife* **~recht** n *huntsman's fee* (*right*) ‖ (für die Hunde) *quarry* **~sprache** f *sportsman's language, hunting terms* **~steig** m *hunters' footpath* **~tasche** f *shooting-pocket, gamebag* **Jäger·ei** f ~/ *hunting, huntsmanship, woodcraft* **J·ägerin** f ~/~nen *huntress, sportswoman* **J·ägersmann** m *forester, huntsman*

J·aguar m ~(e)s/~e ⟨zoo⟩ *jaguar*

j·äh(e) **I.** [a] **1.** (steil) *sheer* (*cliff*), *steep* (*rock*), *precipitous* (*declivity*); *rapid* (*descent*); ~er Abhang *precipice*; ~er Sturz *precipitation* **2.** (hastig) *sudden* (*fall, drop, pain, fright, jump, death*); *rapid* (*fall*) ‖ ~e Flucht *precipitate* od *headlong flight* **3.** [pred] (*vorschnell*) *he is all too hasty, rash*; (barsch) *abrupt, impetuous* **II.** [adv] ~ innehalten *to stop with a jerk* **J·ähe** f ~/ *steepness*, etc. → jäh 1. ‖ *suddenness*, etc. → jäh 2. ‖ *hastiness*, etc. → jäh 3. **j·äh(lings)** adv **1.** (steil) *abruptly, precipitately, precipitously*; ~ fallen v *to fall precipitate from*; *precipitantly*; ~ herabstürzend *precipitant* ‖ etw ~ herabstürzen *to precipitate* **2.** (hastig) *suddenly*; (*all*) *of a sudden*; *hastily* ‖ ~ vorwärtsstürzen [vi] *to rush* (*on*) *headlong*

J·ahr n ~(e)s/~e **A.** **(Abschnitt)** **1.** ⟨allg⟩ *year*; das ganze ~ dauernd *perennial*; mehr als 2 ~e dauernd ⟨bot⟩ *perennial*; ein volles ~ *a* (*whole*) *twelvemonth, a full y.*; ein rundes ~ *about a y.* ‖ ein halbes ~ ⟨mst⟩ *six months*; ein Viertel≗ *three m.s*; dreiviertel ~e *nine m.s*; anderthalb ~e *eighteen m.s* **2. das bürgerliche ~** *the civil y.*; ein gesegnetes ~ *a good y.*; ein reiches ~ *a y. of plenty*; die 7 fetten u die 7 mageren ~e *the 7 y.s of great plenty and the 7 y.s of famine* ‖ das 63. ~ *the grand climacteric* ‖ sein freiwilliges ~ abdienen *to serve one's y. in the army as volunteer* ‖ jdm ein gutes u gesundes ~ wünschen *to wish a p health and happiness during the coming y.* **3. das laufende ~** *the current y., this y.*; das vorige (vergangene), kommende (künftige, nächste) ~ *the last y., the coming* od *next y.*; k.de ~e *years ahead* ‖ alle ~e *every y.* **4. ~ für ~** *y. by y.* ‖ **in diesem ~** *this y.*; im vergangenen (vorigen) ~ (*or* voriges ~) *last y.*; im nächsten (kommenden) ~ *or* nächstes ~ *coming* od *next y.* ‖ **(Datum) im** ~e 1939 *in* (*the year*) *1939*; im ~e des Heils 1400 *in the y. of grace* od *A. D.* (= anno Domini) *1400* ‖ schon im ~e 1600 *as early as 1600*; 1911 ausgestellt, aber im ~e zuvor gemalt *exhibited in 1911, but painted the previous y.* ‖ vom 1. Mai dieses ~es *of May 1st* ‖ das geschah im *or* zu Anfang der 30er ~e *that happened at the beginning of the thirties* od *in the early thirties* ‖ heute in 6 ~en *6 years hence* ‖ Weihnachten in e–m ~ *a y. come Christmas* ‖ in diesem Mai w *or* sind es 40 ~e, daß sie sich trafen *it is 40 years this May since they met* ‖ in jungen ~en *at an early age*; in den letzten ~en *of late*; *of recent years* ‖ **mit** den ~en .. *with y.s he became a socialist*; mit den ~en wurde er weiser *he became wiser as he grew older* ‖ **nach** ~en *after many y.s*; **nach** ~ u Tag *after a month of Sundays* ‖ **ohne** ~ (abbr o. J.) (Buch & fig: Frau) *no date* (abbr *n. d.*) ‖ **seit** (einigen) ~en *for* (*some*) *y.s past, of late y.s*; seit ~ und Tag *for a long time past, for many a long day*; ⟨fam⟩ *for ages* ‖ **übers** ~ *today twelvemonth, a y. hence* ‖ ~ **um** ~ *every y.* ‖ ein ~ ums andere *every other y.* ‖ **vor** e–m ~e *a y. ago* ‖ vor ~ und Tag *many y.s ago*; vor vielen, vielen ~en *y.s and y.s ago* **5. (Dauer)** das ganze ~ über *or* hindurch *all the y. round* ‖ nach einer Arbeit von 10 ~en *after 10 y.s' work* ‖ über 20 ~e lang *for more than 20 y.s* ‖ für e–e Zeit von 2 ~en *for a two-y. term* ‖ für einige ~e *for the space of some y.s* **B. (Alter)** **1.** ein Kind von 8 ~en *a child of eight y.s*; *a 14 y. old boy, a boy aged 14* ‖ er ist 30 ~e alt *he is 30 y.s old* od *of age*; sie ist über 20 ~e alt *she is turned 20* ‖ noch nicht 40 [über 40] ~e alt *on the right* od *sunny* [*wrong* od *shady*] *side of 40* ‖ er soll mit 9 ~en .. *he is said to have composed well at 9 y.s old* ‖ er hat 30 ~e auf dem Rücken *he is turned 30* ‖ u wenn ich 100 ~ alt werde! *though I live to be a hundred*! **2. in die ~e k** *to grow in y.s, to come to age* ‖ bei ~en s *to be advanced in y.s* ‖ in den besten ~n s *to be in the prime of life*; er ist in der Blüte der ~e *he is in his prime* ‖ in jüngeren ~en *in earlier days*; in reiferen ~en *in riper y.s* ‖ man sieht ihm s–e ~e nicht an *he carries his y.s well* ‖ ich spüre m–e ~e *I begin to feel my age* ‖ er ist schon bei ~en *he is getting on in y.s* ‖ bei s–n (hohen) ~en *at his age* ‖ vor s–n ~en sterben *to die before one's time* | → **Jahres-** **J·ahr-** **~buch** n *annual register, y.-book, almanac* ‖ (*of colleges*) *calendar*; ⟨Am⟩ *catalogue* **~bücher** n [pl] *annals pl* **~gang** m *annual set*, (einer Zeitschrift etc) *y.*; ⟨allg⟩ *age group*; ⟨school, mil⟩ *class* (*the 1914 class*); ⟨univ⟩ demselben ~ angehören *to be in the same class*; jdm e–n ~ voraus s *to be a class ahead of a p*; ⟨mil⟩ der jüngste ~ *the youngest levy* ‖ (Wein) *vintage* (a. fig: P); die besten ≗ [pl] *the best vintages* pl; *he has a choice y.'s vintage in his cellars* ‖ mit 4 ≗en *four-y.* (*medical school*) **~gehalt** n *annual salary* **~geld** n *y.ly allowance, pension* **~h·undert** n *century*; das ~ der Aufklärung *the age of enlightenment* ‖ in der Mitte des 20. ~s *in the mid-twentieth c.* ‖ von ~ zu ~ *from age to age*; im Laufe der ~e *in the lapse of ages* | ~wende [f] *turn of the c.*; ~e alt *c.ries-old*; ≗ealt, ≗elang [a] *secular* **~markt** m *fair*; es war ~ *there was a f. on, there was the annual f.*; der ~ wird abgehalten w *the f. will be held* ‖ der ~ des Lebens "*Vanity F.*" | ~sbude (*f.*) *stall*, (*f.*) *booth*; ⟨Am fam⟩ *spot-joint*; ⟨Scot⟩ ~n [pl] *the shows*; ~sgeschenk [n] *fairing* **~t·ausend** n *millennium* | ~-Weltendeglaube [m] *adventism* **≗weise** adv *annually, y.ly* **~wuchs** m *y.'s growth* **~zahl** f ⟨num⟩ *date* **~z·ehnt** n *decade, decennium* **jahr·aus, jahr·ein** adv *y. in, y. out, every y., from y.'s end to y.'s end* **j·ahrelang** **1.** [adv] *for y.s*, ⟨fam⟩ *for ages* ‖ *through the y.s* **2.** [a] *lasting* (*for y.s*); *permanent*; *y.s of* (*experience, privation*) **j·ähren:** sich ~ [h] *to be a y. old* od *ago* ‖ *to come round*: *on March 5th the day of his death comes round* **J·ahres-** **~abonnement** n *annual subscription* **~abschluß** m ⟨com⟩ *a.l balance* (*sheet*) (per *as at*) ‖ (Vertrag) *contract for one y.* **~bericht** m *a.l report*, ⟨school⟩ *school prospectus*, ⟨Am⟩ *catalogue* **~bezug** m = ~abonnement **~bilanz** f *a.l balance* (*sheet*) **~dauer** f *a y.'s time* **~einkommen** n *a.l income* **~ende** n *y.'s end* **~erhebung** f *A.l Review* (⟨a.⟩ N) **~ertrag** m *purchase* **~fahrkarte** f ⟨rail⟩ *season-* od *a.l ticket* **~feier** f *anniversary* **~folge** f *succession of y.s* **~frist** f *space of a y., a y.'s time* ‖ in ~ *within a y.* **~gehalt** n *annuity* ein ~ v .. aussetzen für *to settle an a.ty* *of .. upon a p* **~kommun·alsteuer** f (Schätzwert) *a.l rateable value* **~konferenz** *a.l conference* **~lauf** m *course of the y.* **~rechnung** f *a.l account* **~reingewinn** m *net income for the y.* **~rente** f *a.ty* → ~gehalt **~ringe** m pl (eines Baumes) *a.l rings* **~schluß** m *close of the y.* **~tag** m *anniversary, commemorationday*; 500ster ~ *quincentenary*; → Bestehen **~umsatz** ⟨com⟩ *a.l turnover* **~versammlung** f *a.l meeting* **~wechsel** m, **~wende** f *turn of the y.* ‖ (Fest) *New Y.*; Glückwünsche zum ~ *wishes on the occasion of the New Y., compliments of the season* **~wind** m *Etesian wind* **~zahl** f (*date of the*) *y.* **~zeit** f *season*; zu (in) dieser ~ *at this time of y.*; → Saison; nicht der ~ entsprechend *unseasonable* **~ziffer** f *a.l rate* **j·ährig** [a] *a* od *one y. old* ‖ [in comp] (zehn- etc) (*ten*) *y.s old*, (*ten-*)*y.*; s–e siebenjährige Regierung *his seven-y. reign*; (10 Jahre dauernd) *lasting ten y.s* **j·ährlich** 1. [a] *yearly, annual*; ~es Einkommen *a.l income*; ~e Rente *annuity* 2. [adv] *a.lly, every y., by the y.*; *per annum* **J·ährling** m ~(e)s/~e *yearling*

J·ähzorn m ~(e)s/ 1. (Ausbruch) *sudden anger, violent passion* (*he flew into a v. p.*) 2. (Eigenschaft) *irascibility*, zum ~ neigen *to have an evil temper* ‖ ⟨poet⟩ *choler* **j·ähzornig** a *irascible, choleric, warm-blooded, hot-* od *quick-tempered, passionate*; ~ s *to have an evil temper, to be liable to explode*

J·ako m ⟨orn⟩ *jako*; *grey parrot*

J·akob m ~s/ *James*; ⟨bib⟩ *Jacob* ‖ billiger ~ *cheap Jack* ‖ der wahre ~ (P & S) ⟨sl⟩ *the real Simon Pure*, ⟨Am sl⟩ *the* (*real*) *Mc Coy* **~sleiter** f ⟨allg⟩ *Jacob's ladder* **~sstab** m ⟨astr⟩ (Meßinstrument) *Jacob's staff* **~stag** m *St. James's day* **Jakob·iner** m ~s/~ *Jacobin* **~mönch** m ⟨ec⟩ *Dominican* **~mütze** f *Phrygian cap* **jakob·inisch** a *Jacobinic*(*al*)

Jak·ute m, **Jak·utin** f (türk.-tatar. Volk in Sibirien) *Yak*(*o*)*ut* **Jak·utsk** n *Yakootsk*

Jal·apa f ~/ ⟨bot⟩ *jalap*; falsche ~ *four o'clock, marvel of Peru*

Jalousie [ʒalu:'zi:] f ~/~n [–ən] *blind* | ~blech [n] *louvre sheet*; ~tür [f] *shutter door*; ~verschluß [m] ⟨phot⟩ *louvre shutter*

Jam·aika n (e–e der Großen Antillen) *Jamaica* **jamaik·anisch** a *Jamaican* **Jamaika- ~pfeffer** m (Nelken-) *allspice* **~rum** m *Jamaica*

J·ambus m ~/–ben *iambus, iambic* (*foot*)

j·ambisch a *iambic*; ~e Verse *iambics*

J·ammer m ~s/ 1. (Klage) *lamentation, distress, woe* 2. (Elend) *misery, distress*; *wretchedness, calamity*; in ~ und Not *in want and despair* 3. (Mitleid erweckendes Elend) ‖ es ist ein ~ *it is a pity*, (schwächer) *it is a bore*; es ist wirklich ein ~, das Elend mit ansehen z müssen *it is really pitiable to see such misery*, etc. (vgl. 2.) ‖ es ist ein ~ ihn anzusehen *he looks the picture of wretchedness* 4. ⟨fam⟩ *seediness* → Katzen≈ 5. ⟨fig⟩ das ist der alte ~ (die alte Geschichte, Sache) *that is the old wretched tale over again* **~bild** n *piteous* od *woeful sight* **~blick** m *woeful look* **~geschrei** n *doleful cry*; *lamentation* **~gestalt** f *miserable* od *piteous figure* °**~lappen,** österr **~pepi** m *crybaby, milksop* ≈**schade** a es ist ~ *it is a thousand pities* od *a sad pity* **~tal** n *vale of tears* (*and woe*) **~ton** m *doleful accent* ≈**voll** a *lamentable, doleful, deplorable, miserable*; (*to look*) *woebegone*; *woebegone* (*face*) **j·ämmerlich** 1. [a] *deplorable, lamentable, woeful, sorry* (*sight*), *miserable* (*existence, life, salary*), *wretched* (*clothing*), *piteous* (*death*) ‖ (verächtlich) *pitiable, pitiful* (*screaming, weeping*); e–n ~en Eindruck m *to make a poor appearance*; .. ~es Machwerk (*this piece is*) *a clumsy bungle* 2. [adv] *deplorably*, etc.; er sah ~ aus *he presented a piteous spectacle* ‖ sich ~ fühlen *to be* od *feel miserable, to be under the weather* ‖ er heulte ~ *he cried fit to break his heart* ‖ ~ durchprügeln *to thrash unmercifully* **j·ammern** 1. vi [h] (über [acc]) *to lament*; *wail, moan, yammer, whine*; *mourn* (um *for*; über *over*) ‖ ~d bitten um *to whine for*; ~d sprechen zu *to whine at a p*; über die Vergangenheit ~ *to bemoan the past* ‖ (wimmern) *to wail* 2. vt & imps [h] *to move to pity* ‖ er jammert mich, mich jammert seiner *I pity him*

Jangtsekiang m (chin. Fluß) *Yangtzekiang*

J·anhagel m ~s/ ⟨fam⟩ *mob*; *tagrag and bobtail*; *rabble*; *riff-raff*; *the low classes* pl

Janitsch·ar m ~en/~en *janissary, janizary* | ~|enmusik [f] ⟨mil⟩ *Turkish music*

J·anker m ~s/~ [südd] 1. *longing* 2. *jacket*

J·änner ⟨poet & österr⟩ m ~s/~, **J·anuar** m ~(e)s/~e *January*; im ~ *in J.*; → April

J·apan n *Japan* **Japanische Meer,** das *the Japan Sea, the Sea of Japan*

j·appen, ⟨fam⟩ **j·apsen** vi [h] *to gasp, sob, pant* (nach Luft *for breath*); er konnte ja kaum noch ~, so entkräftet war er *he could hardly gasp from exhaustion*

°**J·aps** m –ses/–sen (Japaner) *Jap*; *Nips* pl

Jarg·on [ʒɑr'gɔ̃:] m ~s/~s *jargon*

Jasm·in m ~s/~e ⟨bot⟩ *jessamin*(*e*), *jasmine* ‖ wilder ~ *white lilac* | ~laube [f] *jessamine bower*

J·aspis m ~ & –sses/~ & –sse ⟨minr⟩ *jasper* | ~ach·at [m] ⟨minr⟩ *jaspagate*; ~porzell·an [n] *jasper-ware, Wedgwood ware*

J·assy n (Stadt in Rumänien)

j·äten vt/i [h] ⟨agr, hort⟩ *to weed* **J·äter** m ~s/~ (P) *weeder* **J·äthacke** f ~/–n *weeding-hoe*

J·auche f ~/–n 1. *dung-water* 2. ⟨allg⟩ *sullage, sewage* 3. ⟨fig⟩ (Gesöff) (a. Dividenden≈) *swipes, swills* 4. ⟨med⟩ *ichor* | ~(n)grube [f] *cesspool, sink* **j·auchig** a ⟨med⟩ *ichorous, ichory*

j·auchzen I. 1. vi [h] *to shout with* od *for joy*; *to exult, jubilate, cheer* 2. vt [h] jdm Beifall ~ *to applaud a p*; die Menge jauchzte B. *the crowd cheered lustily* ‖ sein Herz –zte vor Freude *his h. thrilled in him with joy* II. ≈ n ~s/ *shout*(*ing*), *exultation* **J·auchzer** m ~s/~ (P) *shouter* ‖ (Laut) *shout, cheer*

j·aulen vi [h] *to whine*, ⟨Am⟩ *to yip*

J·ause f ~/~n [österr] → Vesperbrot

J·ava n (e–e der Sunda-Inseln) **Jav·ane** m, **Jav·anin** f *Javanese* **J·avamensch** m ~en/~en *pithecanthropus*

jaw·ohl adv 1. (Antwort) *yes* (*indeed*) ⟨mil⟩ *yes, sir*; (*have you got a pencil?*) *here you are*! (*may I speak to you?*) *yes, you may* 2. (Zustimmung) *that's right*, (*sir*); *right you are*; *that's so*; *just so*; *exactly, precisely*; *all right*! ⟨sl⟩ *right-o* 3. (eigene Meinung bekräftigend) *I mean it, positively*; (*you don't say so*) jawohl, es ist so *yes, I do say so*; es ist .., ~ ..! *it is unfair, that's what it is* ‖ ⟨Am fam⟩ *yeah*; *I might as well*; vgl ja

J·azz m ~/ *jazz* | ~fanatiker [m] *j.-fan*; ⟨Am sl⟩ *hepcat*; ~kapelle [f] *j.-band*; ~musik [f] ⟨Am sl⟩ *hepcat*; ~(musik)platte [f] *j.record*

j·e intj → Oje!, ⟨vulg⟩ *Law* (f *Lord*); (*no, sir*)! ~ n·un! ⟨fam⟩ *why*!, *well* (*now*)!

j·e adv 1. (jedesmal) je 3 *three at a time* ‖ je 2 u 2 *two by two*; *by twos, in pairs* ‖ .. je e–n *Penny*, (*they cost, he gave them*) *a penny each*; je Meter (= à M.) *the metre* ‖ ⟨med⟩ *ana* (*grams 50*) ‖ nach je 4 Tagen (*after*) *every four days* ‖ je 10 in e–r Schachtel *ten pieces in each box*; je 6 Stück bilden e–n Satz *every six pieces form a set* ‖ je im 5ten Jahre *every five years* ‖ je der dritte *every third man* 2. [bei compr] **je .. je ..; je .. umso ..; je .. desto ..**: je länger (eher), je lieber *the longer* (*sooner*) *the better*; je älter er wird, umso (*or* desto) bescheidener wird er *the older he gets the more modest his pretensions become* 3. **je nach ..** *according to* (*the*) *circumstances* od *with circumstances*; je nach Bestimmung der Behörden *as the authorities may determine* ‖ **je nachdem** ⟨fam⟩ [abs] *it depends*; *as it* (od *the case*) *may*/*might be*;

(*that's*) *according*; **je nachdem, wie ..** *in proportion as, according as* || .. **je nachdem, ob ..** (*nouns are masculine or feminine*) *according as* (*the objects they denote are male or female*) **4.** (jemals, irgendeinmal) hast du das je gesehen? *have you ever seen that*; wer hätte das je gedacht? *who would ever have thought of that* || ohne je davon gehört zu h *without ever having heard of it* || ~ dagewesen (*one of the biggest*)-*ever* (*Xmas gifts*) **5.** (immer) *always, ever* || **von je her** *from times immemorial*; *at all t.s*; *t. out of mind* || **je und je** *on and on for ever*; ich habe dich je und je geliebt *I loved you always*

Jeans [dʒi:nz] pl (Texas-, Nietenhose) *jeans*

×**Jeck** m → Geck | ≗ [a] *mad, foolish*

j·edenfalls adv *at all events, at any rate, in any case, altogether* || *by all means*; *anyhow, anyway* || (so oder so) *somehow or other* || *certainly, doubtless, undoubtedly*; (.. *has*) *if anything* (*a mitigating effect*); es wäre ~ besser, wenn *it would be undoubtedly better if* || (wahrscheinlich) *very likely* **jed·ennoch** conj *nevertheless* **j·ede(r** m, **-s** n) f pron [als attr a] (~ e–r Gattung) *every* (*man must die*) | (aus e–r Reihe) *each* (*pupil of the third form*) | (von zweien) *either* (*spelling is correct*) | (~ beliebige) *any* (*at any rate*) | ~n Tag *or* mit ~m Tage *every day*; ~ zweite P *every other p* || *he wrote to whomever he invited* || *his every action* || ~r geringste Fehler *the slightest mistake, ever so slight a mistake* | *each word should be repeated twice* | .. ~ Art .. *public opinion deprecated any cruelty towards them*; *any message was welcome*; *I expect him back any minute*; zu ~r beliebigen Stunde *at no matter what hour*; ~ einzelne Mannschaft *any one team*; ~r andere, der *any other man that*; *at any time given*; ~ Überraschung kann mißlingen *surprise can always fail* (*of success*) **2.** [als Subst.] (vgl. 1.) *every* (*each*) *one, everybody, every* (*each*) *man* od *woman, everything* (*each thing*) || *like every one who has travelled much, I am* .. || *everyone says so* || *everybody knows* || *everyone seated themselves*; *everybody had done their bit* | ein ~r v uns *each of us* | *either of them was mistaken* || *each of them held fans in their hands* | so, daß es ~r sehen kann *for any one to see* | **all und ~r** *all and sundry, each and all* **3.** ⟨prov⟩ ~r ist sich selbst der nächste *charity begins at home*; es kehre ~r vor s–r eigenen Türe *let each mind his own business*; ~r für sich und Gott für uns alle *every man for h.s., and* .. **j·ederlei** a *of every sort* (*kind*), *of each sort* (*kind*); *of every description* **~mann** pron (vgl. jeder) *everyone, everybody*; *each one*; *anyone, anybody* || *every man*; *every mother's son* || das ist nicht ~s S *that's not a thing everybody would care about, it's not every one's taste*; vor ~ *in the face of all the world* **~zeit** adv *always, at all times, at any time*; ⟨hot⟩ *in and out of season*

j·edes- ~mal adv (*at*) *every time*, (*at*) *each time, always* || ~ wenn *whenever* **~malig** a *actual* (*state of the market*), *existing* (*circumstances*), *in* (*for*) *each special case* || nach der ~en Lage *according to circumstances* **jed·och** conj *yet, still, however* || *nevertheless* || *notwithstanding, for all that* || *only*; ~ Peter fürchtete sich nicht *only P. was not afraid* || *though*, ⟨Am⟩ *tho* [in Endstellung] er verlor jedoch den Kopf *he lost his head, though* **j·edweder,** –de, –des [pron] *each, every, any, any and all* (vgl. jeder) **j·eglicher,** –che, –ches [pron] *every, each*; ein ~ *every* (*each*) *one, all* || u jedermann ging, daß er sich schätzen ließe, ein ~ in s–e Stadt *and all went to be taxed, every one into his own city* **jeher** adv: seit ~ *always*; v ~ *at all times, from times immemorial, ever* **Jel·ängerjel·ieber** n ~s/~ ⟨bot⟩ *honeysuckle, woodbine* **j·emals** adv *ever* (vgl. je) **j·emand** pron **1.** *somebody, someone*; jemand will Sie sprechen *there is somebody to see you* || (bei Ungewißheit) *anybody, anyone* || ist ~ da? *anybody about*?; *unless there had been anybody* || wenn ~ v uns fragte *if any of us asked* || er sah, daß ~ da war *he saw that there was company* || irgend ~ hat es mir erzählt *someone or other told it me* || **~ anderer** *or* **anders, sonst ~** *some* (*any*) *other p, someone* (*anyone*) *else* || als ob ~ sagen wollte *as though someone would say* **2.** [als Subst.] ein gewisser ~ *a certain p*; dieser ~ *this p* **3.** [als a] ⟨fam⟩ ~ Fremdes *some stranger*, ~ Hohes *some great personage*; ⟨fam sl⟩ *some big bug*

J·emen, Jem·en n (arab. Staat) *Yemen*

×**j·emers, j·emersch, j·emine**; ach ~! *dear me*! *good gracious*! (vgl. oj·e) || ⟨vulg⟩ *cheese and crust* (f *Jesus Christ*); *crimes*! *cripes*! *criming*!

J·ena n ⟨Ger⟩ (Universitätsstadt) | ~er Glas® n *Jena glass*

j·ene(r m, **~s** n) f & pl pron **1.** [als a] *that* [pl *those*], *the former* || (hinweisend) ⟨† & poet⟩ *yon, yonder* [nur attr] || auf ~r Seite des Gebirges *on the other side of the mountains*; in ~m Leben *in the life to come, in the other world* || in ~n Tagen (Vergangenheit) *in those days, in days of yore*; (Zukunft) *in future days* **2.** [als subst, abs] *that one* [pl *those ones*] dieses und ~s *this and that*; von diesem und ~m sprechen *to speak of one th and another* || dieser *the latter*, ~r *the former* || das soll dieser und ~r holen! *the devil* od *deuce may take it*! **j·enseit(s) 1.** [prep] [mit gen] *on the other* (*further*) *side of* (*the Rhine*), *beyond, over*; ~ des Grabes *beyond the grave, hereafter, in the world to come*; ~ des Wassers *across the water* (od *sea, channel*), ~ der Fünfzig ⟨fam⟩ *on the wrong* (*shady*) *side of fifty* || ~ v G. u B. *beyond good and evil* **2.** [adv] *on the other side, yonder* **j·enseitig** a *further, opposite*; *on the other side*; auf dem ~en Ufer *on the opposite bank* || *otherwordly* **J·enseits** n ~/ (*the*) *other world*, (*the*) *beyond*, (*the*) *life to come*, (*the*) *next life*; das bessere ~ *the brighter world* || ins ~ befördern *to launch into eternity, to send to glory*; ins ~ abgehen ⟨fam⟩ *to go to kingdom-come*

Jeni(s)s·ei [–e:i], der (Sibirien-Fluß) *the Yenisei*

Jeremi·ade f ~/~n *jeremiad, lamentation, woeful tale*

J·erezwein [ˈce:res] m ~s/~e *sherry*

J·erichorose f ⟨bot⟩ *rose of Jericho*

J·ersey [ˈdʒə:zi] n (engl. Kanal-Insel) || ⟨tail⟩ (Stoff) *Jersey* | ~vieh [n] *J. cattle*

j·erum intj; o ~!, ⟨fam⟩ *dear me*!

Jer·usalemsblume f ⟨bot⟩ *cross of Jerusalem*

×**J·essas**! intj ⟨fam⟩ *Jeese*! *Jeez*! (f *Jesus*)

Jesu·it m ~en/~en *Jesuit* **Jesu·iten- ~general** m *general of the J.s* **~moral** f *J.ical doctrine* **~orden** m *order of the J.s* **~priester** m *J. priest* **~schule** f *J. school, J. college* **Jesuiter·ei** f ~/~en *Jesuitism, Jesuitry* **jesu·itisch** a → *Jesuitic*(*al*) **Jesuit·ismus** m *Jesuitism* **J·esus** m [gen, dat J·esu, acc J·esum] *Jesus*; ~ Christus *Jesus Christ*; im Namen Jesu *in the name of Jesus*; der Herr ~ *the Lord Jesus* **~kind** n *the infant* od *child Jesus*

Jet m ~s/~s, ~flugzeug [n] *jet*

Jet·on [ʒəˈtõ] m ~s/~s Fr (Spielmarke) *chip*

j·etzig a *present* (*time*), *existing* (*circumstances*), *actual* (*state of things*), *modern, prevailing* (*fashion, way of thinking*); ⟨com⟩ (Kurs, Preise) *actual, current* || in der ~en Zeit *nowadays, in our times* (*days*); der ~e König *the reigning king*; der ~e Herzog v York *the now* od *present Duke of Y.* **j·etzt** adv **1.** *now, at present, at this time*; ⟨Am fam⟩ *here is where* || **eben ~** *just now, this* (*very*) *moment* || **gleich ~** *instantly, immediately, at once* || **erst ~** *only* od *but now* || **selbst ~** *even now* || **noch ~** *even now, to this very moment* (*day*) **2.** [nach prep] **für**: genug f ~! *so much for the present* || **bis ~** *hitherto, until now, as yet, for the time being* || **v ~ an** *or* **ab** *from this time, henceforth* **3.** **~ u allezeit** *now and evermore* || gerade ~ bedeutsam *topical* (*interest*) || und ~ die Arbeit *now for* *work* || nicht gerade ~ *not for the moment* || ~ oder nie *now or never* **≗zeit** f *the present time* (*day*), *modern times* pl, *those days* pl *of ours*; in der ~ *in these days, in modern times* → heutzutage

j·eweilig a *for the time being, specific* (*situation*) || (*p*) *in office* od *charge*; *p on duty* **j·eweils** adv *at a time*; man trifft ~ e–n v beiden an *one meets one of the two every time*; die ~ höhere Stelle *the next higher command*; die ~ .. *each containing* ..

J·iddisch n ~/ (Judendeutsch) *Yiddish*

°**J·immyschuhe** m pl *winklepickers*

J·iu-J·itsu n ~/ [Japan] *j(i)u-jitsu*

J·och n ~(e)s/~e **1.** ⟨eig⟩ *yoke*; ins ~ spannen *to* (*put to the*) *yoke*; (e–m Ochsen) das ~ abnehmen *to unyoke* **2.** ⟨fig⟩ jdm ein ~ auferlegen *to impose a y. on a p, to bring a p under one's y.*; das ~ abschütteln *to shake off one's y.*; an einem ~e ziehen *to bear the y. together*; unter das ~ geraten, k *to pass under the yoke* || (*the*) *iron heel* (*of modern civilization*) **3.** ein ~ Ochsen *a y. of oxen* **4.** (Berg~) *col* (*depression in mountain-chain*) **5.** ⟨arch, tech⟩ *bay*; Brücken~ *girder, span* **6.** Joch- ⟨scient⟩ *zygo-, zygomatic* **~bein** n ⟨anat⟩ *y.-bone, cheek-bone* **~brücke** f *pile-bridge* **~feld** n ⟨tech⟩ *bay of a bridge, bridge-bay* **~pfahl** m ⟨tech⟩ *pile* (*of a bridge*) **~spannung** f *span* (*of a bridge-bay*) **~träger** m ⟨arch⟩ *arch top piece* **~weite** f ⟨tech⟩ *width of the bay*(*s*) (*of a bridge*)

J·ockei ['ʒɔkai] m ~s/~s *jockey* | ~gewicht *riding-weight*

°**j·ockeln** vi *to totter* (*up to*); im Wagen *to jolt*; im Bus *to wobble, wabble*; ⟨rail⟩ *to hurtle*

J·od n ~(e)s/ ⟨chem⟩ *iodine* **≗haltig** a *iodureted* **~·id** n *iodide* **≗ig** a *iodous* **~of·orm** n ~s/ *iodoform* **~kalium** n *iodide of potassium* **~metall** n *metallic iodide* **~quecksilber** n *iodide of mercury* **~säure** f *iodic acid* **~silber** n *iodide of silver* **~tinktur** f ⟨med⟩ *tincture of iodine* **~vergiftung** f *iodine poisoning*; *iodism* **~zahl** f *iodine number*

j·odeln vt/i [h] *to yodel* **J·odler** m ~s/~ (P) *yodler* || (Schrei) *yodel*

J·oga m ~(s)/ *yoga*

J·oghurt m & n ~s/ *yogurt, yoghourt*

Joh·annesburg n (Stadt in Transvaal)

Joh·anni(s) = Johannistag **Joh·annis-** ~beere [f] (*red*)*currant*, schwarze ~ *blackc.* ~beersaft [m] (*red*)*c. juice* ~beerstrauch [m] ⟨bot⟩ *c.-bush* ~brot [n] *carob, St. John's bread*; ~brotbaum [m] ⟨bot⟩ *carob* ~fest [n], ~tag [m] *St. John's day, Midsummerday* ~feuer [n] *St. John's fire* ~kraut [n] ⟨bot⟩ *St. John's wort*; ~trieb [m] ⟨fig⟩ *Indian Summer* || ~würmchen [n] *glow-worm* **Johann·iter** m ~s/~ *knight of St. John of Jerusalem* | ~orden [m] *order of* (*the knights of*) *St. John of J.* ~ritter [m] *knight of St. John of Jerusalem*

j·ohlen vi [h] ⟨fam⟩ *to bawl, catcall, maffick, howl, yowl, yell* **Joh·o**! ⟨hunt⟩ *tally-ho*!, *soho*!

°**J·öhre** f = kl Kind, mst Mädchen → Gör

°**J·okel** m ~s/~ ⟨fam⟩ *clod-hopper*; *jake*

Jokoh·ama n *Yokohama* (Japan)

Jokos·uka n *Yokosuka* (Japan)

J·okus m ~/ [L] *joke*; *fun, practical joke*

J·olle f ~/~n ⟨mar⟩ *jolly-boat*; *yawl*

Jongl·eur [ʒɔŋ'gløə] m ~s/~e *juggler* **jonglieren** [ʒɔŋ'gli:rən] vt/i (mit etw) ~ *to juggle* (*with*)

Jonqu·ille [ʒɔŋ'ki:je] f ⟨bot⟩ *jonquil*

J·oppe f ~/~n *short coat*; *jacket*; *jerkin*

J·oppe n [Gr] → Jaffa

×°**J·ör** n = Gör, kl Kind, mst Mädchen

J·ordan m (Fluß in Palästina) *Jordan River*

J·osef, J·oseph, keusch wie ~ *pure as Joseph*; keuscher ~ *immaculate J.*, ⟨fam⟩ *bashful Joe*

J·ota n ~(s)/~s *jot, iota*, kein ~ *not an iota, a jot, a whit*; (*not to give in*) *an inch*

Joule n ~(s)/~ *joule*

Journ·al [ʒur–] n ~(e)s/~e *diary, journal* || ⟨hot⟩ *tabular ledger*, ⟨fam⟩ *tab*, ~führer [m] *bill clerk* || (Zeitung) *paper, magazine* || ⟨com⟩ *day-book* || ins ~ eintragen = **≗is·ieren** *to enter in the day-book*, etc **~·ismus** m ~/ *j.ism* **~·ist** m ~en/~en *news*(*paper*)*man*; *pressman, correspondent*; (Zeilenschinder) *space-writer* | ~entribüne [f] *reporters' gallery* **~·istik** f ~ *j.ism* **~istin** f ⟨Am sl⟩ *newshen* **≗·istisch** a *j.istic*

jovi·al a *jovial, merry, convivial, cheerful*; ⟨fam⟩ *jolly* (*fellow*) || ~er Kerl ⟨Am a.⟩ *backslapper* **≗it·ät** f ~/ *joviality, jovialness*, etc

Juan-Fern·andez (Inseln im Stillen Ozean)

J·ubel m ~s/ *jubilation, exultation, merry-making*; *mirth, public joy*; allgemeiner ~ *universal rejoicings* pl; *cheers* (*of welcome*) *round* od *for a p* **~braut** f, **~bräutigam** m *bride-jubilant, bridegroom-j.t*; *jubilee bride, j. bridegroom*; *wife* (*husband*) *celebrating her* (*his*) *silver* (*golden*) *wedding* **~feier** f, **~fest** n *j.ee, rejoicings* pl **~gesang** m *song of joy* || *j.ee-song* od *-hymn* **~geschrei** n *shout of rejoicing, yell of triumph* **~greis** m *old man celebrating his j.lee* **~hochzeit** f *silver* (*golden, diamond*) *w.* **~jahr** n *jubilee-year* || (nur) alle -jahre *once in a way*, ⟨fam⟩ *once in a blue moon*

j·ubeln vi [h] *to rejoice, exult, maffick, shout with joy* (über [acc] *about*); *to triumph* || jubele nicht zu früh, es kann noch anders k *don't crow too soon, things may turn out differently*; du hast zu früh gejubelt *you boasted too soon* **Jubil·ar(in** f) m ~(e)s/~e *celebratee* **Jubil·äum** n ~s/–läen (50-jähriges) *silver j.* **jubil·ieren** vi [h] *to celebrate a jubilee* || (jubeln) *to exult, to shout with joy*

j·uch! **juchh·e**! intj *hurra*!, *huzza*!, *hey-day*!

J·uchten m ~s/; ~leder [n] *yuft*(*en*)

j·uchzen vi [h] ⟨fam⟩ *to shout, warble, yodel*

J·uck ~flechte, ~krankheit ⟨med⟩ *prurigo* L

J·ucken n ~s/ *itching, itch*; ⟨med⟩ *prurigo* || ich fühle ein ~ in der Haut *my skin itches* **j·ucken 1.** vt [h] es juckt mich *my skin itches*, .. am Arm *my arm itches* || (kratzen) *to scratch, rub*; sich blutig ~ *to scratch o.s. till the blood comes* **2.** vi [h] *to itch, prickle*; ~d *itching, itchy*; ⟨med⟩ *prurient* || ⟨fam⟩ ihm juckt der Buckel *or* das Fell *he is itching for a drubbing* || ⟨fam⟩ ihm ~ die Finger danach *his fingers itch to take it*; ⟨fam⟩ ihr ~ die F., ihm e–e Ohrfeige zu geben *her fingers itch to give him a* .. **J·ucker** m ~s/~ *small, quick coachhorse*

Jud·äa n *Judea, Judæa*

judais·ieren vi/t [h] *to judaize* **J·udas-** ~baum [m] (*European*) *Judas-tree* ~haar [n] *carroty hair* ~kuß [m] *traitor's kiss, Judas-kiss* ~ohr [n] ⟨bot⟩ *Jew's-ear* **J·ude** m ~n/~n *Jew*, ⟨sl⟩ *Jid*; ⟨Am⟩ *Hebrew*, ⟨Am sl cont⟩ *kike* || der Ewige ~ *the Wandering Jew* | haust du m–n ~n, hau ich d–n ~n *measure for measure, tit for tat* || für das Gewesene gibt der ~ nichts *for the past the Jew does not care a fig* **j·üdeln** vi [h] *to speak like a Jew*

J·uden- ~bart m ⟨bot⟩ *old man's beard* **~deutsch** n *Yiddish* **~frage** f; die ~ *the Jewish question* **~-gasse** f *Jew's street* °**~helm** m *bowler*(*-hat*), *billy-cock* **~hetze** f *Jew-baiting* **~kirsche** f ⟨bot⟩ **1.** *wintercherry* **2.** = Eberesche **~pech** n *Jew's pitch, bitumen, asphaltum* **~schaft** f ~/ *Jews* [pl], *Jewry* **~schule** f **1.** *Jewish school* **2.** ⟨fig⟩ *hullaballoo*; *confused hubbub*; hier geht es zu wie in einer ~ *here you might be in bedlam* **~tempel** m *synagogue* **~stadt** f *Jewish town* || (Viertel) *Jewish quarter* **~tum** n *Hebrewism, Semitism, Judaism, Jewry* **~verfolgung** f *pogrom, Jew-baiting* **~viertel** n *ghetto, Jewry* **J·üdin** f ~/~nen *Jewess* **j·üdisch 1.** [a] *Jewish, Judaic*; ⟨Am⟩ *Hebrew*; ~e Gedankenwelt *Hebraism* **2.** [adv] *like a Jew, Jewishly*

J·udo n ~(s)/ ⟨sport⟩ *Jiu-Jitsu* → d.

J·ugend f ~/ **1.** *youth, early years* pl || v ~ auf *from a child* (.. *boy*, .. *girl*), *from one's y.*, *from early childhood*; sorglose ~ *y. without care*; in früher ~ *in early childhood, in old days* pl; in der Blüte der ~ *in the prime* (*flush, bloom*) *of y.*; in m–r ~ *when I was young* **2.** [koll] *young people, (the) youth*; moderne ~ *(the) modern y.*, die reifere ~ *mature y.*; die ~ v heute *the rising generation*, die deutsche ~ *German y., young Germany*; die studentische ~ *academical y.s* ‖ ~ hat k–e Tugend ⟨prov⟩ *boys have toys; boys will be boys; you cannot put old heads on young shoulders* **~alter** n *(days of) y.*; *y.ful age, juvenile years* od *days* pl **~amt** n *Y. Welfare Office* **~anmut** f *gracefulness of y.* **~arbeit** f *early* od *j. work* ‖ *work among the young* **~betreuer** m → –leiter **~bewegung** f *y. movement* **~blüte** f *flower* od *prime* od *bloom of y.* **~buch** n ⟨com⟩ *juvenile* **~bund** m *y.-club* **~burg** f *children's castle; castle used as y. centre* **~dorf** n *ch.'s village* **~erinnerung** f *y.ful remembrance, recollection from childhood* ‖ *memory of one's y.* **~eselei** f *y.ful escapade* **~fehler** m *boyish (girlish) fault* **~feuer** n *y.ful ardour, heat, fire* **~freund** m *childhood's friend* **~frische** f *fresh bloom of y., y.fulness, bloom* **~fürsorge** f *welfare work for the young* | ~heim [n] *approved school* **~̈gefährdend** a *harmful for y.s* **~gefährdung** [f] durch schamlose Veröffentlichungen *corruption of j.s by immodest publications* **~gefährte, ~genosse** m; mein ~ *the companion* od *comrade of my y.* **~gericht** n *j. court* **~herberge** f *(y.) hostel* **~herbergs-** ~vater [m] *(y.) hosteller*; ~wanderer [m] *hosteller* **~irresein** n ⟨med⟩ *hebephrenia*; mit ~ behaftet *hebephreni(a)c* **~jahre** n pl *early years* **~kraft** f *y.ful vigour* od *strength* ‖ in der ~ *in the green* **~kriminalität** f *teen-age crime*; *j. deliquency* **~leiter(in** f) m *y. leader* od *worker* **~liebe** f *boy and girl love, early attachment, calf-love* ‖ (Mädchen) *old flame* **~organisation** f *y.* od *j. organization* **~periode** f *the early period (in Sh's dramatic work)* **~pflege** f *y. work* **~pfleger(in** f) m *Child Welfare Officer*; *Y. Worker* **~psychiatrie** f *child guidance* **~schriften** f pl *books* [pl] *for the young, j. literature* **~stil** m ⟨arts⟩ *"art nouveau" movement* Fr **~streich** m *boy's trick, youthful prank* **~sünde** f *sin of one's y.* **~torheit** *y.ful escapade*; er hat s–e ~en hinter sich *he has sown his wild oats* **~traum** m *y.ful dream* **~treffen** n *y. rally* **~verbrechen** n *juvenile crime* **~verbrecher** m *j. offender, y.ful criminal* **~verwahrlosung** f *j. delinquency* **~wanderer** m *y. hosteller* **~weihe** f *y. initiation ceremony* **~werk** n ⟨arts⟩ *early work*; *juvenilia* pl **~zeit** *early life* **j·ugendlich** a *j., y.ful* ‖ *youngminded* ‖ ~es Alter *adolescence* (m.: 14–18; f: 12–16); ~e Begeisterung *enthusiasm of youth*; ein ~er Greis *a hale and hearty old man* ‖ ~er Leichtsinn, der zum Tode führt ⟨Am⟩ *teenicide* ‖ ~er Übermut *y.ful wantonness* od *high spirits* pl **J·ugendliche** m [der ~, ein ~r; die ~, e–e ~] ~n/~n *juvenile*, ⟨Am a.⟩ *teenager (13–19)* ‖ ~ [pl] h k–n Zutritt *no admission for the young* **J·ugendlichkeit** f ~/ *y.fulness, youngmindedness*

Jugosl·awe m *Yugoslav* –**sl·awien** n *Yugoslavia* („Südslawien")

°**j·üh!** intj *gee! gee-ho!* **j·uhu!** *yoo hoo!*

J·ukon m (Nordamerika-Fluß) *Yukon River*

J·ulfest n ~(e)s/~e *yule*

J·uli m ~(s)~s *July*; im ~ *in July*; → April

J·ülich n (†Herzogtum im Rheinland) *Juliers*

Julienne [ʒyl'jen] f ~/ ⟨cul⟩ *julienne*

J·ulische Alpen pl *Julian Alps*

J·umbo n ~s/~s (Dickerchen) *jumbo*

J·umper(kleid n) ['dʒʌmpə] m ~s/~s *jumper (suit)*

j·ung [~̈er, am ~̈sten] a *young, youthful* ‖ ~er **Mann** *youth, young man*; ~e **Dame** *y. lady, p*; ~e **Frau** *y. wife, bride*; ~es **Mädchen** *y. lady, woman*; L. war zu .. Mädchen herangewachsen *Laura had grown to be a fine young stripling*; ~e **Leute** *youths*; ~ **u alt** *old and young alike*; die ~̈en *the young people*; der ~e Goethe *the young G.* | ⟨fig⟩ *new (shares, etc.)*; *fresh (blood, foliage, etc.)*; *recent (times)*; *early (morning)*; *under-developed (Land)* ‖ ~ **u frisch** *young and brisk*; sein ~̈stes Werk *his latest work* ‖ die ~̈sten Ereignisse *the latest events*; die Geschehnisse der ~̈sten Vergangenheit *the occurrences in recent times* ‖ der ~̈ste Tag, das ~̈ste Gericht *Doomsday, the last day of judgement* ‖ er hat ~̈ere Beine *he is lighter of foot* ‖ ein ~es Ehepaar *a newly married couple* ‖ *green (peas)*; ~es Gemüse *fresh vegetables* ⟨fig⟩ (= ~es Volk) *raw youths*; ~e Gans *green* od *silly goose* ‖ *green, new (wine)* ‖ *fresh (beer)* ‖ in ~en Jahren *in one's young* od *green days* | ⟨prov⟩ ~ gewohnt, alt getan *the child is father of the man; what is bred in the bone, won't out of the flesh; once a use, and ever a custom* ‖ ~ gefreit hat noch niemanden gereut *happy the wooing that is not long a-doing* **J·ung-** **~arbeiter** *young worker* **~bier** n *fresh beer* od *ale* **~brunnen** m *fountain of youth, well of juvenescence* **~frau** f **1.** ⟨eig⟩ *maid, virgin*; (ledige) *spinster*; zur ~ herangewachsen *grown up (od ripened) to womanhood* ‖ die heilige ~ *the Holy (od Blessed) Virgin, Our Lady*; ⟨bib, arts⟩ *the wise and the foolish virgins* ‖ die ~ v Orleans *the Maid of Orleans*; bei Shaw: *Saint Joan* **2.** ⟨astr⟩ *Virgo* **~̈fräulich** a **1.** *virginal, immaculate* **2.** *virginlike, maiden(ly)* **3.** ⟨fig⟩ *virgin (soil, territory)* **~frauschaft, ~fräulichkeit** f *virginity, maidenhood* ‖ *chastity* (Symbol der ~ *unicorn*) **~gesell(e)** m *bachelor, celibate, single man*; ⟨Am⟩ *bach* ‖ (bei Handwerkern) *youngest journeyman* ‖ eingefleischter ~ *confirmed bachelor*, ⟨fam⟩ *old bach* **~gesellenhaushalt** (*or* –leben) führen ⟨sl⟩ *to bach* **~gesellenleben** n, **~gesellenstand** m *bachelorship, bachelorhood; single life* **~gesellin** f *bachelor girl* **~henne** f *pullet* **~mann** m *youngster, boy-scout*; ⟨mar⟩ *ordinary seaman* **~meister** m *last master received into a guild* **~sein** n *youngness, youthfulness, youth, youthful state, freshness (of youth)* **~̈steinzeitlich** a *neolithic* **~student** m *freshman* **~tier** n ⟨hunt⟩ *young doe* **~türken** pl *etc Young Turks, etc* **~̈verheiratet** a *newly wed*; ~es Paar *newly weds* **~vieh** n *young cattle* **~volk** n ⟨engl⟩ *(wolf-) -cubs* pl; (Mädchen) *brownies* pl **J·unge A.** m ~n/~n **1.** *boy, lad; youngster*, ⟨fam⟩ *young 'un*; kl ~ *kid* ‖ ein lebhafter ~ *a lively young sprig*; ein heller ~ *a bright lad*; ein grüner, dummer ~ *an unlicked cub, a snotty (od saucy) stripling*; ein ~ (Ggs: Mädchen) *a male child* **2.** (Anrede) *sonnie!* ⟨fam⟩ *old chap!, old fellow!* ~ns! ⟨fam⟩ *lads!* **3.** (Lehr~̈) *apprentice* **4.** ⟨cards⟩ *knave* **5.** ⟨fig⟩ ein schwerer ~ *a bad lot*, ⟨Am sl⟩ *a tough*; ein ausgekochter ~ *a cunning bird* **B.** n [das ~, ein ~s] ~n/~n *young animal; young; young one*; (Raubtier) *cub, whelp*, (Hund) *puppy*, (Katze) *kitten*; *calf; baby* ([attr] *elephant, kangaroo, rhinoceros, camel, giraffe, hippopotamus*); (Hase, Kaninchen) *young*; (Rotwild) *fawn* ‖ ~ [pl] werfen *to bring forth young; to cub, whelp, puppy, kitten, calve, fawn* **J·üngelchen** n ~s/~ [dim] z Junge *laddie*

j·ungen vi [h] *to bring forth young* (→ Junge B.) ‖ die kl Arten jungen sehr oft *the small species have young very frequently* **J·ungen-** **~̈haft, ~̈mäßig** a *boyish* ‖ *ill-behaved* **~streich** m *boyish trick* **J·ünger** m ~s/~ *disciple* (Christi *of Christ*), *apostle; follower* ‖ *a disciple of Nietzsche* ‖ ⟨fig⟩ *devotee, votary (of art, science), adherent, adherer, son* ‖ ein ~ der Wissenschaft *a man of science* ‖ ⟨arts⟩ die ~ in Emaus *the Supper at E.* | ~schaft [f] *(the) following of the disciples; (obedience is the mark of the true) disciple (of Christ)* **j·ünger** a compr (→ jung) *younger, junior; newer (forms)* ‖ er ist 5 Jahre jünger als ich *he is (by) five years my junior*; sie heiratete e–n ~en Sohn aus .. *she married a younger son of good family* **J·unges** n [ein ~, das –ge] (T) *baby (elephant* → Junge B.) **J·ungfer** f ~/~n **1.** †(Titel) *Miss*, ~ Neugier *Miss Curiosity*, ~ Naseweis *Miss Pert* ‖ alte ~ *old maid, elderly spinster*; ⟨fam⟩ *tabby* ‖ e–e zimperliche alte ~ *a prudish old maid* **2.** ⟨fam⟩ = Jungfrau *virgin*; sie war schon vor ihrer Ehe k–e ~ mehr·*even before her marriage she had lost her virginity* **3.** (Kammer≗, Zofe) (*lady's*) *maid* **4.** ⟨tech⟩ (Handramme) *beetle, paving-ram* **5.** ⟨bot⟩ ~ im Grün *ragged-lady* **6.** ⟨mar⟩ (~block) *dead-eye, uphroe* **j·üngferlich** a *virginal, maidenly, maidenish, maidenlike* ‖ (spröde) *coy* ‖ (geziert) *prim* ‖ (zurückhaltend) *reserved, shy* **J·ungfern-** **~fahrt** f ⟨mar⟩ *virgin voyage* **~flug** m ⟨aero⟩ *maiden flight* od *hop* **~glas** n ⟨minr⟩ *mica* **~-häutchen** n ⟨anat⟩ *hymen, virgin(al) membrane*; ⟨vulg⟩ *maid's ring* **~honig** m *virgin honey* **~kranich** ⟨orn⟩ *Numidian crane, demoiselle* **~kranz** m *bridal wreath* **~milch** f ⟨pharm⟩ *benzoin(e)* **~öl** n (kaltgepreßt) *virgin oil* **~raub** m *rape, ravishment* (*of maidens*) **~räuber** m *ravisher* **~rede** f *maiden speech* **~reise** ⟨mar, etc⟩ *maiden trip* od *voyage* **~schaft** f, **~stand** m *virginity, maidenhood*; *spinsterhood* **~zeugung** f *parthenogenesis* **J·üngling** m ~(e)s/~e *young man, youth* [pl *-s*], *lad*; *adolescent*; *young fellow, youngster, sprig, stripling*; ⟨fam⟩ *kid* ‖ ein gr, blonder ~ *a tall blond youthful fellow* **J·ünglings-** **~alter** n *youth, adolescence* **~brigade** *lads brigade* **~feuer** n *juvenile ardour* **~jahre** n pl *years* pl *of one's youth* **~verein** m *young men's* (*Christian*) *association* **j·üngst(hin)** adv *of late, lately, newly, recently*; ich sah ihn ~ *I saw him quite recently, the other day* **j·üngste** a *youngest*; (Zeit) *last*; → jung, jünger; ⟨fig⟩ *latest* (*fashion, speech*) ‖ *the most recent* (*events*) ‖ (*the*) *lowest ranking* (*soldier*) ‖ mein ≗r *my youngest* ‖ sie gehört nicht mehr zu den ≗n, sie ist auch nicht mehr die ~ *she's no chicken* ‖ der ≗ Tag, das ≗ Gericht *Doomsday, the day of reckoning, the Last Judgement* ‖ in der ~n Zeit *of late*; bis in die ~ Zeit *until quite recently*

J·uni m ~(s)/~s *June* **~käfer** m *June-bug*

j·unior a *junior* (abbr jun. Ggs: senior)

J·unker m ~s/~ *young nobleman* ‖ (Land-) *squire* ‖ ⟨Ger⟩ *junker, younker*; ~ „Flaumbart“ *j. beardy* **≗haft** a *squirelike, aristocratic* (*appearance*) ‖ *haughty and arrogant* **~herrschaft** f *squirearchy* **≗mäßig** a *squirelike* **~tum** n (Stand) *squirearchy*; (Sitten) *manners* pl *of country squires*

jun·onisch a *Junonian* (*appearance*)

Jupe [ʒyp] f Fr *skirt*

J·upiterlampe f ⟨film⟩ *klieg light*

J·ura **1.** m *Jura Mountains* ‖ Fränkischer ~ *Franconian Jura* **2.** n ⟨geol⟩ ~, ~ Formation [f] *Jurassic formation* **jur·assisch** a *jurassic*

J·ura n pl L *law* ‖ ~ studieren *to read law, to study laws, to prepare for the bar* **jur·idisch** a →juristisch **Jurisdikti·on** f ~/ *jurisdiction* ‖ ⟨hist engl⟩ *soccage* **Jurisprud·enz** f ~/ *jurisprudence* **Jur·ist** m ~en/~en *lawyer, jurisconsult*, ⟨bes Am⟩ *jurist* ‖ (Student) *jurist, law-student, student of law* ‖ er ist ~ v Beruf *he is a lawyer by profession* **Juri-ster·ei** f ~/ ⟨fam⟩ *law*; ⟨dero⟩ *lawyer's trickery* od (*sharp*) *practice* **jur·istisch** a *juridical, legal* ‖ ~e Fakultät *faculty of law* ‖ die ~e Laufbahn verfolgen *to practise at the bar* ‖ ~e P *legal p* od *entity*; *artificial p, body corporate, corporate body* ‖ jede ~e P des öffentlichen u privaten Rechts *any entity under public and private law* **J·uror** m ~s/–·oren ⟨arts⟩ *juror*; *member of a jury* **J·ury** f ~/~s **1.** ⟨jur⟩ *jury* ‖ gr ~ *grand jury* ‖ kl ~ *petty jury* ‖ ⟨engl⟩ Frauen≗ *jury of matrons*; deren Mitglied *jury-woman* **2.** ⟨übtr art⟩ *jury*; *panel of judges* **j·ust** adv *just now, even now, but just* ‖ das ist ~ das Richtige *that is just the right th* ‖ ~ nicht *not quite, not exactly* ‖ er ist ~ kein Tugendbold *he is not exactly a pattern of virtue* **Just·ier-** *adjusting-*(*crew, balance, scales*) **|** ~schiene [f] ⟨comp etc⟩ *aligner bar* **just·ieren** vt [h] ⟨tech⟩ *to adjust, standard*; (Gewehr, Geschütz) *to zero in* ‖ *to align* (auf .. *in the axis*) ‖ ⟨typ⟩ *to justify, to fit up* (*the matrix*) **Just·ierung** f ~/~en *adjustment* **justifiz·ieren** vt [h] *to justify* ‖ (berichtigen) *to rectify* **Just·iz** f ~/ *law* (*and its application*) **~beamte(r)** m *officer of justice* **~gewalt** f *judicature*, ⟨engl⟩ *judiciary* **~irrtum** m *miscarriage of justice* **~minister** m ⟨Ger⟩ *Minister of Justice* ‖ ⟨m. m.⟩ *Lord* (*High*) *Chanceller* ‖ ⟨Am⟩ *Attorney General* **~ministerium** n ⟨Ger⟩ *ministry of justice*; ⟨engl⟩ [gibt es nicht]; ⟨Am etwa⟩ *Department of Justice*; Staatssekretär des ~s ⟨Am etwa⟩ *Solicitor General* **~mord** m *judicial murder* **~palast** m *law-courts* pl, *courts of justice* **~pflege** f *administration of justice* **~rat** m ⟨Ger⟩ *Counseller of Justice*; ⟨engl⟩ *King's* (*Queen's*) *Counsel* (*K. C., Q. C.*) **~verwaltung** f = ~pflege **~wesen** n *the law*; *justice*; *law-affairs* pl ‖ Chef des Militär≗s *Judge Advocate General*

J·ute f ~/ *jute* ‖ ~faserbündel [n] *batch* (*of jute*) **|** ~doppelleinen [n] *tarpaulin*

J·üten pl (Bewohner Jütlands) *Jutes* **J·ütland** n *Jutland*; †*Cimbric Chersonese* **J·ütländer** m (= Jüte), **~in** f *Jutlander* **j·ütländisch** a *Jutish, Jutlandish, of Jutland*

Juw·el n ~(e)s/~en *jewel, gem* ‖ ~en [pl] *jewel(le)ry* ‖ *costly, rare jewel*; ein landschaftliches ~ *a marvellous site* od *view* ‖ (*our servant is a*) *perfect jewel* ‖ mit ~en besetzt *jewelled* (*neck-lace*) ‖ von ~en glitzernd *jewelled* (*lady*) ‖ mit ~en schmücken *to jewel* **Juw·elen-** **~handel** m *jeweller's trade* **~händler** m *jeweller* **~kästchen** n *jewel-box* od *-case, casket* **~schmuck** m *set of jewels* **Juwel·ier** m ~s/~e *jeweller* **|** ~geschäft, ~laden *jeweller's* (*shop*)

J·ux m ~es/~e *joke, lark, great fun*; *spree*; ⟨sl⟩ *wheeze* ‖ *harmless little boyish frolic* ‖ sich e–n ~ m *to have a good time*, ⟨fam⟩ .. *a lark* od *spree*; *to go on the spree* ‖ er macht sich gern e–n ~ *he likes a joke*, etc.; *that was only a joke*

K

K, k [kɑː] n ~/~ *K, k*

K·aama n ~s/~s ⟨SAfr⟩ (Ochsenantilope) ⟨zoo⟩ *kaama, hart(e)beest*

Kab·ale f ~/~n ⟨hebr⟩ (rabbinisch *kabbala* = Geheimlehre) *cabal, intrigue, plot*; Schillers „~ u Liebe“ “*Intrigue and Love*” ‖ ~n schmieden *to hatch plots, to cabal, to intrigue*

Kabar·ett n ~(e)s/~e *cabaret* **|** *hors-d'œuvre dish*

K·abbala f ~/ *cab(b)ala* **Kabbal·ist** m ~en/~en *cab(b)alist* **| ~ik** f ~/ *cab(b)alism, cab(b)alistic art*

Kabbel·ei ⟨fam⟩ f ~/~en *squabble, squabbling*; ⟨Am sl⟩ *rhubarb* **k·abbeln** **1.** vi [h] ⟨mar⟩ die See kabbelt, geht kabbel *the sea is choppy* **2.** °**sich** ~ vrefl *to quarrel, squabble*; ⟨fam⟩ *argufy* **k·abbelig** a *gusty, whiffling* (*wind*); *choppy, rippling* (*sea*)

K·abel n ~s/~ *cable* ‖ doppeladriges ~ *twin wire*; dreiadriges ~ *three-core c.* ‖ Erd≗ *underground c.*; See≗ *submarine c.*; Blei≗ *lead-covered c.* ‖ Haupt≗ *omnibus wire*; Zünd≗ ⟨mot⟩ *high tension c.* ‖ ein ~ legen *to lay a c.* **~abzweigung** f *c. tap* **~anschluß** m *cable connection* **~armierung** f *c. armour(ing)* **~bahn** *c.-tram(way)* **~bautrupp** m ⟨telph⟩ *c.-laying party* **~brunnen, ~-schacht** m ⟨el⟩ *jointing chamber* **~bericht** m, **~depesche** f, **~(tele)gramm** n *cable(gram), c.-message* **~graben** m ⟨mil⟩ *wire trench* **~kanal** m ⟨el⟩ *cable duct* **~mantel** m *c. sheath* **~rinne** f ⟨el⟩ *troughing* **~rohr** n ⟨el⟩ *duct, pipe, tube*; (Gemeinde≗) *trunk* *line conduit* | ~strang [m] *multiple duct*, 〈Am〉 *conduit run* **~rolle** f *c.-coil* **~schiff** n *c.-ship* **~-schloß** n *c.-shackle* **~schuh** m 〈el〉 *lug*; 〈mot〉 (f Zündung) *cable socket* (f Licht) *connector* **~tau** n 〈mar〉 *hawser* **~verbindung** f 〈bes mil〉 *routing* **~verzweiger** m *terminal block* **~winde** f *windlass*; 〈mar〉 (f See~) *paying-out gear* **~zug** m *c.-troop*

Kabel·ar n ~s/~e 〈mar〉 (Anholtau) *messenger*

K·abeljau m ~s/~e & ~s 〈ich〉 *cod, codfish*

k·abeln vi [h] *to cable, to send a cablegram*

K·abestan m ~s/~e 〈mar〉 *capstan*

Kab·ine f ~/~n *cabin* | ~nenteisung [f] 〈aero〉 *wind-shield defroster*; ~nkoffer [m] *c. trunk*; ~-luftmotor [m] *c. supercharger*; ~roller [m] *cycle car* **-·ett** n ~(e)s/~e **1.** (Raum) *c.et, small room, closet* ‖ aufs ~ (Klosett) gehen *to go to the WC* **2.** (Schränkchen) *c.et* **3.** (Ministerium) *c.et, government*, 〈Am〉 *administration* ‖ ein ~ bilden *to form a c.*; ~ stürzen *to overthrow a c.* **~bild** n, **~photographie** f *c.et-photograph* **Kabin·etts-** *cabinet* **~befehl** m *Order in Council* **~frage** f *c. question*; 〈fig〉 *vital q.* **~minister** m *C. Minister* **~mitglied** n 〈pol〉 *c. member* **~rat** m (P) *Privy Councillor* ‖ (Sitzung) *C. Council, c. meeting*; 〈engl〉 *Privy Council* **~stück** n 〈arts〉 *c. piece* od *picture*

Kabriol·ett n ~(e)s/~e *cabriolet, gig, trap*; 〈mot〉 *convertible*

K·abul n (Hauptstadt Afghanistans) *Kabul*

Kab·use f ~/~n **1.** (Kombüse) 〈mar〉 *caboose* **2. ~, Kab·uff** n (*windowless*) *attic-room*

Kab·yle m, **Kab·ylin** f (Berberstamm N.-Afrikas) *Kabyle*; → Rîf

K·achel f ~/~n *glazed tile* (*for stoves*); (farbige) *Dutch tile* | ~ofen [m] *German* (〈Am〉 *porcelain*) *stove* **k·acheln** vt [h] *to tile*

°**K·acke** f ~/ *cack(y)*; *shit* 〈a. fig〉 **~n** vi [h] *to c.*

°**K·aczmarek** m ~s/~s 〈mil sl〉 *bad bargain*

Kad·aver m ~s/~ *dead body*; *corpse*; 〈cont & zoo〉 *carcass* **~gehorsam** m *mechanical drill, m. discipline*; *blind obedience* **~verwertung** f *carcass conversion*

Kad·enz f ~/~en 〈mus〉 *cadence*

K·ader m ~s/~ 〈bes SBZ mil〉 *skeleton, *cadre* | ~abteilung [f] *staff department*; ~ausbildung [f] *cadre training*; ~übung [f] (mst Rahmenübung) *cadre manœuvre*

Kad·ett m ~en/~en *cadet* ‖ 〈fig〉 ihr seid mir schöne ~en *you're a nice lot* **Kad·etten- ~anstalt, ~haus** n *milirary school* od *college* **~korps** n *cadet-corps* **~schiff** n *training-ship, school-ship*

K·adi m ~s/~s *cadi* ‖ z ~ laufen *to run to the c.*; vor den ~ schleppen *to drag before the c.*

K·admium n 〈chem〉 *cadmium* | ~gelb [n] *c.-yellow* ‖ ~oxid [n] 〈chem〉 *cadmic oxide*

K·äfer m ~s/~ *beetle* (→ d. u *weevil*); 〈Am〉 *bug*; 〈scient〉 *coleopter* ‖ 〈fig, fam〉 (Mädchen) *sweet little th*; °ulkiger kl ~ *funny little bug*; ein netter kl draller ~ *a nice buxom little wench, a pretty little flapper* ‖ 〈mot fig hum〉 „Käfer" (〈Ger〉 Volkswagen) "*bug*" **~sammler** m 〈scient〉 *coleopterist* **~sammlung** f *collection of b.s* °**k·äfern** vi [h] herum| ~ *to potter about*

K·aff n ~(e)s/ **1.** (Spreu) *chaff* **2.** 〈fig〉 *nonsense, rubbish* **3.** ~(e)s/~s & ~e („Nest") *poor, miserable village* od *town, awful hole*; 〈bes Am〉 *one-horse* od *tank town*; der Ort ist ein entsetzliches ~ *the place is terribly slow*

Kaff·ee [〈vulg〉 ˈkafə] m ~s/~s *coffee* ‖ gemahlener (gebrannter) ~ *ground* (*roasted*) *c.* ‖ ~ mit Milch *c. and milk* ‖ ~ verkehrt *white c., café au lait* Fr ‖ Tasse ~ *cup of c.* ‖ kalter ~ 〈fig〉 *twice-told story* ‖ sich ~ brauen *to brew o.s. c.* ‖ das ist ein anderer ~! (etw ganz anderes) [österr] 〈fig〉 *that' a different cup of tea!* **~bau** m *cultivation of c.* **~baum** m *c.-tree* od *shrub* ‖ großes Café in Leipzig **~bohne** f *c.-bean, c.-berry* **~brenner** m *c.-roaster* **~brett** n *c.-tray* **~eis** n *iced c.* **~ersatz** m *c.-substitute* **~filter** m *percolator* **~garten** m *c.-garden* **~gebäck** n 〈engl〉 *tea-cake* **~geschirr** n *c.-things* pl **~gesellschaft** f; e–e ~ geben *to give a c.-party* **~kanne** f *c.-pot* **~klatsch** m 〈engl, mm fam〉 *cat-, hen-, tabby-party*: *a meal of tea, cakes, and scandal* (*Thackeray*) **~löffel** m 〈engl〉 *tea-spoon* **~maschine** f *c.-machine, percolator* **~mühle** f *c.-grinder* **~mütze** f *cosy* **~pause** f *c. break* **~pflanzung** f *c.-plantation* **~röster(ei** [f]) m *c.-roaster* **~satz** m *c.-grounds* pl **~schlacht** f 〈fig hum〉 *coffee* (〈m. m.〉 *tea*) *fight* **~schwester** f *lover of c.*; (Klatsche) *gossip, scandalmonger* **~sorten** pl *coffees* **~tasse** f *c.-cup* **~tisch** m *c.-table* **~topf** m *c.-pot* **~trommel** f *c.-roaster* **~vergiftung** f *caffeinism* **~wirt** m *keeper of a c.-house* od *café* **~zeug** n *c.-service, c.-things* pl **Kaffe·in** [eːˈiːn] n ~(e)s/ 〈chem〉 *caffeine* **Kaff·eetscherl** n [–tʃəl] → –tscherl; [österr] das ist ein ~! *that is some coffee!*

K·affer m ~n/~n (Gruppe der Bantuneger) *Caffre, Kaf(f)ir* ‖ 〈fig, fam〉 *duffer, blockhead* | ~hirse [f] *sorghum* | ~nland [n] *Kaffraria*

K·äfig m ~(e)s/~e *cage*; in e–n ~ sperren *to c.*

K·aftan m ~(e)s/~e *caftan*

K·äfterchen m ~s/~ *closet, small chamber* ‖ (Fach) *pigeonhole, compartment*

k·ahl a (Kopf) *bald, shorn* ‖ (Baum) *bare, leafless*; die Raupen h alles ~ gefressen *the caterpillars have stripped all the leaves off* ‖ (Wand) *bare, blank* ‖ (Vogel) *callow* ‖ (Gegend) *barren, bleak* ‖ 〈fig〉 *bare, naked, poor, paltry, empty, sorry, plain* ‖ ~ geschoren *close-shaven* od *-cropped* **K·ahl- ~frost** m *black frost* **~gehauen** a 〈for〉 *clear-cut* **~hauen** vt [h] *to clear* **~hirsch** m *hummel* **~kopf** m **1.** *baldhead, -plate* **2.** *baldheaded p* **~köpfig** a *bald(headed)* **~köpfigkeit** f *bald(headed)ness* **~schlag** m 〈for〉 *clear felling* **~stelle** f 〈for〉 *clearing* **K·ahlheit** f ~/ (→ kahl) *baldness* ‖ *bareness* ‖ *callowness* ‖ *barrenness* ‖ 〈fig〉 *bareness, bleakness*

K·ahm m ~(e)s/~e *mould* **k·ahmen** vi [h] *to become* (*grow, turn*) *mouldy, fusty* **k·ahmig** a *mouldy, fusty* (*beer, wine, wine-cask*)

K·ahn m ~(e)s/~e *boat, skiff* ‖ (Lichter) *lighter* ‖ (Last-) *barge* ‖ (Flach~) *punt* ‖ (gr Flach~) *pontoon* ‖ ~ fahren *to go boating, punting*; 〈fam〉 *to take a row* **~bein** n 〈anat〉 *navicular bone* **~fähre** f *ferry boat* **~fahren** n, **~fahrt** f *boating(-trip)*, 〈fam〉 *punting turn on the river* **~führer** m *ferryman, bargee* **~ladung** f *boatful*

K·ai m ~s/~s & ~e *quay, pier, wharf*; *jetty, mole*; *landing-place* ‖ ab ~ *ex quay* ‖ (Schiff) am ~ festmachen *to wharf* **~anlage** f *wharfage, quay* **~arbeiter** m *wharfman, docker* **~gebühr** f, **~geld** n *quayage, quay dues* pl, *pierage, wharfage* **~mauer** f *seawall* **~meister** m *wharfinger*

K·aiman m ~s/~e 〈zoo〉 (Panzerechse) *caiman, cayman, alligator*

Kain·it m ~s/ 〈minr, agr〉 *kainite*

K·ainsmal n *mark of Cain*; 〈allg〉 *stigma*

K·airo n *Cairo* **K·airo-, K·airoer(in** f) m *Cairene*

K·aiser m ~s/~ *emperor*; der Deutsche ~ *the German E., the Kaiser* ‖ sich um des ~s Bart streiten 〈fig〉 *to quarrel about nothing*; wir wollen nicht um's ~s Bart streiten *don't let's split hairs* ‖ wo nichts ist, hat der ~ sein Recht verloren *where nought's to be got, kings lose their scot* (= *tax*) ‖ ~! *first!, tops!* (wie im Abzählvers: „~, König, Edelmann; Bürger, Bauer, Bettelmann") **~baum** m 〈bot〉 *Paulownia* **~burg** f *imperial palace* **~(gebirge** n) (Gruppe der Nordtiroler Kalkalpen) **~haus** n *i. family* **~krone** f *i. crown* ‖ 〈bot〉 *fritillaria* **~manöver** n 〈Ger mil〉 *grand manœuvres* pl **~mantel** m 〈ent〉 *fritillary* **~quartett** n [österr] *Emperor Quartet* (Haydn) **~reich** n *empire* **~schmarrn** m 〈cul〉 *scrambled pancake* **~schnitt** m 〈med〉 *cæsarean section* od *operation* ‖ e–n ~ m 〈fam〉 *to do a cæsarean* **~stadt** f *imperial town* **~wahl** f *election of an e.* **~walzer** m *Emper-*

or's Waltz (*by Joh. Strauss jr.*) **~wetter** n ⟨Ger⟩ ⟨mm engl⟩ *king's weather* **~-W·ilhelm-Kan·al** m *Kiel canal* **~würde** f *e.ship, i. dignity* | **~in** f ∼/∼-nen *empress* ‖ ∼-Mutter *empress-dowager* **~́lich** a *imperial*, ⟨hist⟩ *Cæsarean* ‖ er war gut ∼ gesinnt *he was a true imperialist*; die ~́en [pl] ⟨pol⟩ *the I.s* ‖ ⟨mil⟩ *the Imperial troops* pl **~tum** n ∼(e)s/–tümer *empire* ‖ *imperial dignity*

ˣ**K·aje** f ∼/∼n [niedd] *embankment, dam*

Kaj·üte f ∼/∼n *cabin* ‖ erste ∼ *saloon*; *stateroom* **~nbett** n *berth* **~nkappe** f ⟨mar⟩ *companion(-hatch)* **~nkoffer** m *cabin-trunk* **~npassagier** m *cabin passenger* **~treppe** f *companion-way, -stairs*

K·akadu m ∼s/∼s ⟨orn⟩ *cockatoo*

Kak·ao m ∼s/ *cocoa* ‖ °⟨fig⟩ jdn durch den ∼ ziehen *to poke fun at a p, to pull a p's leg*; *to throw dirt on a p, to drag a p through the mire*; ⟨Am⟩ *to kid* (*the pants off*) *a p* **~baum** m *c.-tree* **~bohne** f *c.-bean* **~butter** f *c.-butter* **~dose** f *c.-tin* **~krug** m *chocolate-pot* **~masse** f *c.-paste, baking ch.* **~pulver** n *nibs* pl **~schale** f *c.-shell*

K·akerlak m ∼(e)s & ∼en/∼en **1.** *albino* **2.** (Insekt) *cockroach, black-beetle*

K·aki m ∼s/ *khaki* | ∼pflaume [f] *persimmon*

K·aktus m ∼/Kakt·een ⟨bot⟩ *cactus*; Säulen~́, Kerzen~́ *columnar c.* ‖ °⟨vulg⟩ *turd, shit*: °e–n ∼ pflanzen ⟨fig fam⟩ *to post a letter* (→ Kacke) **~́-artig** a ⟨scient⟩ *cactaceous* **~feige** f *fruit of the opuntia* **~schildlaus** f ⟨zoo⟩ *cochineal*

Kalab·asse = Kalebasse **~nbaum** m *crescentia*

Kalabr·eser m ∼s/∼; **~hut** m *sombrero* **Ka·l·abrien** n (Halbinsel Italiens) *Calabria*

Kalah·ari f (Wüstensteppe in S.-Afrika)

Kalamit·ät f ∼/∼en *calamity*; *misfortune, –hap*

Kal·ander m ∼s/∼ *calender, rolling-machine*

kal·andern vt [h] ⟨tech⟩ *to calender, roll* ⟨pap⟩

°**K·alauer** m ∼s/∼ ⟨fam⟩ (*stale* od *bad pun* od *joke*; *sorry jest*) "*chestnut*", "*Joe Miller*" | **~́n** vi [h] *to crack stale jokes, to pun*

K·alb n ∼(e)s/~́er **1.** *calf*; weibl. ∼ *cow-c.*, männl. ∼ *bull-c.* ‖ (Reh- *or* Hirsch∼) *fawn* ‖ Tanz ums goldene ∼ *dance round the golden c.*; das g. ∼ anbeten *to worship the golden c.*; mit fremdem ∼e pflügen *to plough with another p's heifer*; Augen wie ein gestochenes ∼ *eyes like a stuck pig*; ein ∼ absetzen *to wean a c.*; das gemästete ∼ schlachten *to kill the fatted c.* **2.** ⟨fig⟩ *calf, colt, tomfool* **~fell** n *calfskin* ‖ ⟨mil⟩ *drum* **~fleisch** n *veal* °**~fleischliebhaber** m ⟨Am sex sl⟩ *cradle snatcher* **~fleischpastete** f *veal-pie* **~leder** n *calf*(*-leather*) ‖ in ∼ gebunden *calf-bound* **~lederband** m *volume* (*bound*) *in calf* **~ledereinband** m *calf-binding* **K·älbchen** n ∼s/∼ *little calf, young c.* **K·albe** f ∼/∼n *heifer* **k·alben** vi [h] *to calve* **K·älber-** **~braten** m *roast veal* **~lab** n, **~magen** m *rennet* **~milch** f *sweetbread* **~zahn** m *calf's tooth* ‖ ⟨arch⟩ *denticle* **Kalber·ei,** ~́ f ∼/∼en ⟨fam⟩ *friskiness*; *wanton sport*; *tomfoolery*; *playfulness* **k·älb(e)rig** a ⟨fam⟩ *frisky, frolicsome, playful, foolish* **k·albe(r)n,** ~́ vi [h] **1.** *to calve* **2.** °⟨fig fam⟩ *to frisk* od *fool about*; *to frolic, gambol* **K·albs-** **~braten** m *roast veal* **~bregen** m *calf's brains* pl **~bröschen** n *sweetbread* **~brust** f: gefüllte ∼ *stuffed breast of v.*; ⟨fig⟩ (Spiel) *consequences* **~frikassee** n *blanquette* **~fuß** m *calf's foot* **~fußsülze** f *c.'s foot jelly* **~gekröse, ~geschlinge** n *c.'s tripe, c.'s pluck* **~hachse** f ⟨cul⟩ *c.'s foot, knuckle of v.* **~karbonade** f, **~kotelett** n *v. cutlet* **~keule** f *leg of v.* **~kopf** m *c.'s head* ‖ °⟨fig fam⟩ *great fool, dunce* **~milch** f *sweetbread* **~nierenbraten** m *loin of v.* **~nuß** f *kernel of v.*; gedämpfte ∼ *fricandeau* Fr **~rippenstück** n *ribs of v.* **~roulade** f *fillet of v.* **~schnitte** f, **~schnitzel** n *v.-cutlet*

Kald·aunen f pl *intestines* pl; ⟨cul⟩ *tripe*

Kaleb·asse f ∼/∼ ⟨bot⟩ *calabash, gourd*

†**Kaled·onien** n *Caledonia* ⟨† & poet⟩ (= Schottland) ‖ kaledonisch [a] *Caledonian*

Kaleidosk·op n ∼(e)s/∼e *kaleidoscope, show-glass*

Kal·enden pl (Monatserster) *calends* ‖ → Iden

Kal·ender m ∼s/∼ *calendar, almanac*; Julianischer, Gregorianischer ∼ *Julian, Gregorian C.* ‖ das müssen wir im ∼ rot anstreichen *this day must be chalked up* **~berechnung** f *computation of the almanac*

Kal·esche f ∼/∼n *chaise, fly*; *barouche*

Kal·eu [ka'lɔi] m ⟨mar⟩ → Kapitänleutnant

Kalf·akter m ∼s/∼ *fireman, fire-lighter* ‖ ⟨fig⟩ (Schwindler, Schmeichler) *toady*; (Aushorcher) *spy*; (Anschwärzer) *backbite*

Kalf·aterer m ∼s/∼ ⟨mar⟩ *caulker* **kalf·atern** vt/i [h] ⟨mar⟩ *to caulk* od *grave* (*a ship*)

K·ali n ∼s/ ⟨chem⟩ *kali, potash* ‖ chlorsaures, kohlensaures, übermangansaures ∼ → Kalium– **~bergwerk** n *potash-mine* **~feldspat** m ⟨minr⟩ *orthoclase* **~lauge** f *caustic* od *potash lye* ‖ *lye* **~rohsalz** n *abraum salt, waste salt* **~seife** f *potash-soap*

Kal·iber n ∼s/∼ *calibre, bore* (*of a gun*) ‖ ⟨allg⟩ *gauge*, ⟨Am⟩ *gage* ‖ Bombe schweren ∼s *heavy calibre bomb* ‖ ⟨fig⟩ vom selben ∼ *of the same sort* od (*mental*) *calibre*, (⟨Am⟩ .. *timber*) **kalibr·ieren** **1.** vt [h] ⟨tech⟩ *to graduate, size, gauge, calibrate* **2.** ~́ n *calibration* **-kal·ibrig** a [in comp] 12-∼e Flinte *twelve-bore shot-gun*

Kal·if m ∼en/∼en *caliph, calif* **Kalif·at** n ∼(e)s/∼e *caliphate*

Kalif·ornien n (Staat der U.S.A.) *California*

K·aliko m ∼s/∼s *calico* ‖ ⟨bookb⟩ *cloth* ‖ in ∼ *in cloth*(*-binding*) ‖ grober ∼ *dowlas* **~papier** n *imitation c.*

Kalisch (Stadt u Provinz in Polen)

K·alium n ∼s/ ⟨chem⟩ *potassium* | ∼chlor·at [n] *chlorate of potash*; ∼k·arbonat [n] *carbonate of p.*; ∼permanganat [n] *potassium permanganate*; ∼zyanid [n] (Zyankali) *potassium cyanide*

K·alk m ∼(e)s/∼e *lime* ‖ gebrannter, ungelöschter ∼ *burnt l., quicklime*; gelöschter ∼ *slaked l.* ‖ ∼ brennen *to burn l.* ‖ mit ∼ bewerfen ⟨tech⟩ *to roughcast, to plaster* ‖ mit ∼ tünchen *to whitewash* **~ablagerung** f ⟨geol⟩ *calcareous deposit* **~anstrich** m *whitewash* **~́arm** a *deficient in l.* **~́artig** a *calcareous* **~berge** m pl *chalkdowns* pl **~bewurf** m (*coat of*) *plaster*(*ing*), *roughcast* **~bindungsvermögen** n *calcium chelating power* **~boden** m *l. soil* **~brennen** n *l.-burning* **~brenner** m *l.-burner* **~bruch** m *l.stone quarry* **~brühe** f *milk of l.* **~ei** n *waterglass egg* **~düngung** f *liming* **~erde** f *c. earth* **~faß** n *mortar-trough, l.-tub* **~́fliehend** a ⟨bot⟩ *calcifugous* **~gebirge** n *c. mountains* pl **~glimmer** m ⟨minr⟩ *margarite* **~grube** f *l.*(*stone*) *pit* **~́haltig** a *calcareous* **~konkretion** f, eiförmige K.en [pl] ⟨geol⟩ *ovoids* **~́liebend** a ⟨bot⟩ *calcicolous* **~löschen** n *slaking of l.* **~maler·ei** f *fresco-painting* **~mangel** m *deficiency of l.* **~mergel** m *l. marl* **~milch** f *lime wash* **~mörtel** m *l. mortar* **~niederschlag** m *l. preciptate* **~ofen** m *l.-kiln* **~́reich** a *hard* (*water*) **~salpeter** m *calcium nitrate* **~sinter** m *calcareous sinter* **~spat** m *calcite* **~stein** m *l.stone* **~(stein)bruch** m *l.stone quarry* **~tuff** m *travertin*(*e*) It **~tünche** f *l.-wash* **~wasser** n *l.-water* **k·alken** **1.** vt [h] *to whitewash* ‖ ⟨agr⟩ *to lime* **2.** vi [h] *to slake* od *temper lime* **k·alkig** a *chalky, limy*; ⟨scient⟩ *calcareous, calciferous*

Kalk·ul, Kalk·ül m ∼s/, **Kalkulati·on** f ∼/∼en *calculation, computation* (sorgfältig *scrupulous*); etw in den Kalkül ziehen *to calculate* **Kalkul·ator** m ∼s/–lat·oren *accountant, calculator, reckoner* **kalkul·ieren** vt/i [h] *to calculate, estimate, compute* ‖ niedrig kalkuliert *calculated at a low rate* od *with a narrow margin*

Kalk·utta n *Calcutta*

K·alla f ∼/∼s ⟨bot⟩ *calla*

Kalligr·aph m ~en/~en *calligrapher* **-graph·ie** f ~/~n [–i:ən] *calligraphy, penmanship* **k.·aphisch** a *calligraphic(al)*

°**Kalm·äuser** m ~s/~ ⟨fam⟩ *moping fellow, dreamer* ‖ (Duckmäuser) *sneak* ‖ (Geizhals) *skinflint, miser* **kalm·äusern** vi [h] ⟨fam⟩ *to mope*

K·alme f ~/~en ⟨mar⟩ (Zeit) *calm* ‖ (Ort) *c. latitude* od *region* | ≈**n** vi [h] ⟨mar⟩ *to be still, to become c.* **~nzone** f *doldrums* pl

Kalm·uck m ~(e)s/ (Zeug) *bearskin, kalmuck*

Kalm·ücke m, **Kalm·ückin** f ⟨Russ⟩ *Calmuck, Kalmuck (woman)*

K·almus m ~/ **1.** (echter) *(sweet) calamus, sweet-flag* **2.** (unechter) *sword-flag*

K·alomel n ~s/ *calomel*

Kalori- ~meter n ⟨phys⟩ *calorimeter* **~metr·ie** f *calorimetry* ≈**m·etrisch** a *calorimetric(al)* **Kalor·ie** f ~/~n [–i:ən] ⟨phys⟩ *calorie; heat unit*; gr ~ *large c.*; ohne ~n ⟨Am ad⟩ *no cal* [attr] *(to keep fit)* | ~ngehalt [m] *c. value*; ~verbrauch [m] *c. expenditure* **Kal·orik** f ~/ *calories* pl [sg konstr] **kal·orisch** a *caloric (engine)*

Kal·otte f ~/~n *calotte*; ⟨R. C.⟩ *skull cap*

K·alpak m ~s/~s ⟨mil⟩ *kalpac, busby*

kalt a & adv **1.** ⟨**eig**⟩ *cold (wind, water, colo(u)r,* etc.); *chilly (night, air)*; *frigid (zone)*; *severe (winter)*; *bleak (house, day)* ‖ eis~, eisig ~ *icy (icily) c., frosty, glacial*; naß~es Wetter *raw weather* ‖ empfindlich, bitter ~ *painfully, bitterly c.* ‖ es ist sehr ~ geworden *there is a nip in the air* ‖ ~er Schlag (Blitz) *harmless flash (of lightning)* **im** ≈**en sitzen** *to sit in the c.* | ⟨med⟩ ~es Fieber *ague*; ~er Brand *gangrene*; ~er Schweiß *c. sweat* ‖ **mir ist** ~ *I feel c.* od *chilly, I am c., I feel a chill, I am chilled (to the bones)* ‖ es **überläuft** mich (dabei) eis~ *I go c. all over*, ⟨fam⟩ *it gives me the creeps* od *shivers* od *a fit of shivers, it makes my flesh creep*; es überläuft mich heiß u ~ *it makes me go hot and c. all over* ‖ ~ **w** *to grow c., to cool down*; mir **wird** ~ *I am getting c.* ‖ ⟨fig fam⟩ °**jdn** ~ **m** *to do for a p; to silence a p; to do a p in; to do a p's job for him*; ⟨Am⟩ *to bump a p off* | ⟨prov⟩ **~e Hände,** warmes Herz *c. hands, a warm heart* | ⟨cul⟩ **~e Speisen** *c. dishes*; ~er Aufschnitt *c. slices of meat and sausage*; ~e Küche *c. meal, collation*; °~e Mamsell ⟨Ger⟩ ⟨hot⟩ *larder cook*; ~e Ente *(love-, claret-)cup* ‖ ~ [adv] rauchen *to suck at a c. pipe,* etc. ‖ **etw** ~ **m** *to cool (down), to chill,* ⟨scient⟩ *to refrigerate*; ~ aufbewahren *to keep c.*; ~ stellen *to cool (down); to (put on) ice* (→ 2.); ~ gestellter Sekt *champagne frappé* | ⟨tech⟩ **e-n Ofen** ~ **legen** *to blow out a furnace* **2.** ⟨**fig**⟩ *callous*; **das läßt mich** ~ *that leaves me c.* od *unmoved; that does not trouble* od *affect* od *touch me*; ⟨fam⟩ *I don't care a rap, I wouldn't care less* | **er läßt mich** ~ *he is indifferent to me* | ⟨sex⟩ *frigid*; °sie ist nicht ~ *she's oncoming* | ~ **bleiben** *to keep cool, to keep one's temper* ‖ **~en Blutes** *in cold blood, callously (he callously killed him)*; er bewahrte ~es Blut ⟨fam⟩ *he took it coolly* | **~er Verstand** *cool and collected reason*; ein ~er u besonnener Mensch *a cool hand* ‖ (teilnahmslos) *unconcerned, insensible, unimpassioned* ‖ ~ wie eine Hundeschnauze *as cool as a cucumber* | **~es Benehmen** *chill* od *coldness of manners*; sie empfing ihn ~ *she gave him a very cool reception*; sie zeigte ihm die ~e Schulter *she gave him the cold shoulder* | jdn ~ stellen [h] *to put a p on the shelf, to shelve, shunt*; *to boycott a p,* ⟨Am⟩ *to side-track a p*; ~ gestellt w *to be left out in the cold* ‖ e–e sehr ~e Rede *a glacial speech* ‖ er ist weder ~ noch warm (unentschlossen) *he is neither hot nor cold, he is lukewarm about it* ‖ sich ~ stellen *to affect indifference* | **~e Farben** pl *cold colours (blue,* etc.) ‖ **~e Fährte** f ⟨hunt⟩ *cold* od *stale scent* **K·alt-** ≈**berechnend** a *hardboiled* ≈|**biegen** vt [h] *to bend cold* **~blut** n *strong draught-horse* **~blüter** m ⟨zoo⟩ *cold-blooded* (⟨scient⟩ *poikilothermic) animal* ≈**blütig** a **1.** ⟨eig zoo⟩ *cold-blooded, with* od *having c. blood (fish, reptiles)* **2.** ⟨fig⟩ *cold-blooded, cool, cool-headed, cold-livered, as cool as a cucumber*; *nervy*; ⟨bes Am sl⟩ *hardboiled (swindler)*; ~er Mensch ⟨a.⟩ *cool hand* **3.** [adv] *coolly, deliberately, in cold blood* **~blütigkeit** f *cold blood(edness), coolness* ⟨a. fig⟩ ‖ ⟨fig⟩ *calmness, presence of mind, deliberateness, composedness* ‖ *nerve* ‖ ⟨mil⟩ ~ der Führung *firmness on the part of the leader* **~bruch** m (of metal) *cold shortness* ≈**brüchig** a *cold-short (metal)* **~gepreßt** a *virgin* (Öl) **~gerührt** a ⟨cosm⟩ *c. (cream)* ≈|**hämmern** vt [h] ⟨tech⟩ *to c.-hammer* **~haus** n ⟨hort⟩ *c. glass-house* (Ggs *hothouse*) ≈**herzig** a *c.(hearted); frigid; frosty* **~herzigkeit** f *c.ness, frostiness, frigidness, frigidity, c.-heartedness* **~leim** m *c. glue* **~luft-** ⟨meteor⟩ ~front [f] *arctic front*; ~keil [m] *wedge of c. air* **~mamsell** f ⟨hot⟩ *larder cook* **~-n·adelradierung** f *engraving* ≈|**pressen** vt [h] *to c.press* **~schale** f *sweet beer-, wine-* od *fruit-soup served c.* **~schmied** m *brazier* ≈**schmiedbar** a *malleable* ≈**schnäuzig** a *impertinent, impudent* | adv *with the greatest coolness*; er hat mich ~schnäuzig abgefertigt *he gave me a cool set-down* **~sinn** m *frigidness, frigidity, coldness, frostyness, callousness* ≈**sinnig** a *frigid, cold, frosty, callous* **~start** m ⟨mot⟩ *c. start* **~stellen** n *cold-shouldering*; ⟨Am fam⟩ *freezing .. out* (→ kalt) **~strecken** n ⟨tech⟩ *stretching of metals* [pl], *cold working* ‖ ~gestreckt (Geschützrohr) *c.-worked, self-hooped* **~walzwerk** n *c. rolling mill* **~wasserheilanstalt** f *hydropathic (establishment)* **~wasserkur** f *c.-water cure, cold hydropathic treatment* **~wasserumschlag** m *c.-water compress* od *bandage* **~-welle** f ⟨cosm⟩ *c. wave* **K·älte** f ~/ **1.** ⟨eig⟩ *cold(ness), chilliness, frost, frostiness* ‖ beißende, eisige, schneidende, starke, wahnsinnige ~ *biting, icy, cutting, severe, incredible c.* ‖ die ~ läßt nach *the weather is getting mild* ‖ vor ~ zittern *to shiver with c.* ‖ 10 Grad ~ *10 degrees of frost* od *below zero* ‖ er brachte e–n ganzen Wagen voll ~ herein *he brought a gust of c. air in with him* **2.** ⟨fig⟩ *coolness, coldness; callousness*; ⟨sex⟩ *frigidity; bleakness (of a church)* **~anlage** f *refrigerating plant* ≈**beständig** a *low-temperature* od *frost resistant, anti-freezing* .. **~einbruch** m *sudden (spell of) frost,* ⟨Am⟩ *cold-snap* ≈**erzeugend** a ⟨scient⟩ *frigorific* **~erzeuger** m *freezing machine* od *apparatus, refrigerator, compressor* **~grad** m *degree of frost* od *below zero* **~isol·iermittel** n *c. insulator* **~lagerraum** m *chill room* **~leistung** f *refrigerating capacity* **~mischung** f *freezing-mixture* **~mittel** n *refr. agent* **~welle** f *c. spell,* ⟨Am a.⟩ *c.-snap* **k·älten** vt [h] *to chill, to cool (with ice), to ice*; ⟨scient⟩ *to refrigerate* **k·ältlich** a *somewhat cool, chilly, coldish*

K·alterer S·ee m (bei Bozen, Südtirol) **1.** *Lake Kaltern* **2.** *Kaltern wine* (bitte 1/4 Kalterer!)

Kalv·arienberg m ⟨bib, ec⟩ *(Mount) Calvary*

Kalvin·ismus m ~/ *Calvinism* **Kalvin·ist** m ~en/~en *Calvinist* **kalvin·istisch** a *Calvinistic(al)*

kalzin·ieren 1. vt [h] ⟨chem⟩ *to calcine* **2.** ≈ n *calcination* **K-rofen** m *calcining kiln*

Kalz·it m ~(e)s/~ *calcite*

K·alzium n ⟨chem⟩ *calcium* **~chlor·id** [–kl–] n *calcium chloride* **~karb·id** n *calcium carbide* **~-komplexbildungsvermögen** n *calcium sequestering power*

k·am 1. & 3. sg pret v kommen *to come*

K·ama m ~s/~s ⟨zoo⟩ *kaama, hart(e)beest*

Kamar·illa f ~/–rillen & ~s *camarilla*

K·ambalholz n (⟨W.-Afr⟩ Rotholz) *camwood*

Kamb·odscha n (in Indochina) *Cambodia*

K·ambrik(leinwand f) m ~s/ *cambric*

Kamb·üse f ~/~n ⟨mar⟩ → Kombüse

k·äme 1. & 3. sg subj. pret v kommen

Kam·ee [e:(ə)] f ~/~n [e:ən] *cameo*

Kam·el [e:] n ~(e)s/~e **1.** ⟨zoo⟩ *camel*, weibl. *she-c.* ‖ einhöckerig *dromedary* ‖ auf dem ~ (reiten) (*to go*) *on c.-back* **2.** ⟨fig⟩ °~! ⟨fam⟩ *mutton-head*! ⟨Am sl⟩ *mutt*!; *silly ass*! (→ Esel, etc) **3.** °~ ⟨univ hist⟩ ⟨sl⟩ *tosher* **4.** ⟨mar⟩ *c.* (*floating machine*) **~führer** m → –treiber **~garn** n *mohair(-yarn)* **~haar** n *c.'s hair*; (Stoff) *camlet* **~haardecke** f *c. hair rug* od *cover* **~haarimitat** n ⟨tex⟩ *imitation camelhair* **~hengst** m *male c.* **~heu** n *c.-grass* **~kuh** f, **~stute** f *she-c.*, *female c.* **~reiter** pl *c.ry* **~schaf** n *l(l)ama* **~treiber** m *c.-driver*, *c.eer* **~ziege** f *Angora-goat*

Kam·elie [–iə] f ~/~n ⟨bot⟩ *camellia*

°**Kam·elle** f ~/~n ⟨urspr dial⟩ olle (= alte) ~n *friends of old*; *old stories* od *stuff*; *chestnuts* pl

K·amera f ~/~s ⟨phot⟩ *camera*; Blitz≃, Mikro≃, Geheim≃ *candid c.* **~assistent** m ⟨film⟩ *assistant c.man* **~einstellung** f *c. adjustment* **~-Erdsatellit** m *Satellite and Missile Observation System* (*Samos*) **~fahrgestell** n *c. truck* **~gehäuse** n ⟨Tonfilm⟩ *blimp* **~mann** m ⟨film⟩ *operator* **~neiger** m *tilt(ing) head* **~objektiv** n *c. lens* **~-wagen** m ⟨film⟩ *rotumbulator*, *dolly*

Kamer·ad m ~en/~en, **~in** f ~/~nen *comrade*, *companion*, *fellow*, *mate*, *matey*; ⟨mil⟩ *f. soldier*; ⟨hum⟩ ~ v der anderen Feldpostnummer („Feind") ⟨sl⟩ *stranger* ‖ ⟨fam⟩ *chum*, *pal*, *crony*; ⟨mar, mil sl⟩ *swaddy* ‖ ⟨Am sl⟩ *buddy* | *school-fellow*; *f.-student*, *f.-soldier* ‖ *brother officer* | alte ~en *old comrades*, *old friends*; s–e Frau war ihm ein guter ~ *his wife was his faithful companion*; ein treuer ~ *a true* od *tried friend* **~schaft** f ~/~en **1.** *comradeship*, *good fellowship* od *companionship* ‖ ⟨mil⟩ echte ~ *esprit de corps* Fr ‖ er hielt gute ~ *he practised good f.* **2.** [koll] *set of chums*, *society of friends*, etc., ⟨Am sl⟩ *gang* | ~sabend [m] ⟨Ger⟩ *party* (od *informal meeting*) *of friends*, *fellow-soldiers*, etc; *free-and-easy*; ~s-ehe [f] *companionate* od *-able marriage*; ~sgeist [m] *team-spirit*; *esprit de corps*; *loyalty* **≃schaftlich 1.** [a] *companionable*; *chummy*, *matey*, *pally* ‖ *fellow* [attr] (*feeling*) ‖ in ~em Ton *with a note of camaraderie* ‖ *friendly* (*tap*, *intercourse*); etw auf ~e Weise anstreben *to work on the old boys' net* **2.** [adv] *friendly*, *comradely* | ≃keit [f] *camaraderie*, *mateyness*

Kamer·al- ~wesen n *finances* pl; *fiscal affairs* **~ien** pl, **~wissenschaft** f *fiscal science*, *political economy*, *science of finance*, *cameralistics* pl **Kameral·ist** m ~en/~en *financier*

Kamer·un n *Cameroon*, *the Cameroons* pl

Kam·ille f ~/~n *camomile* ‖ (römische ~ *Roman*) *c.* ‖ echte ~ *Hungarian* od *German c.* ‖ Hunds≃ *stinking* od *dog's c.* ‖ falsche ~ *scentless c.* ‖ stinkende ~ *may-weed*, *dog-fennel* **~ntee** m *c.-tea*

Kam·in m & n ~(e)s/~e **1.** (Schornstein) *chimney(-pot)* **2.** (offen im Zimmer) *fireplace*, *fireside*; Öfen u ~e erhalten ihren Zug durch Schornsteine *stoves and f.p.s obtain their draught by ch.s*; am ~ *by the f.s.*; sie saßen alle um den ~ herum *they all sat round the f.s.* **3.** ⟨geol & mount⟩ *chimney*; e–n ~ durchklettern *to climb a ch.* **~absatz, ~rand** m *hob*, *sidecasing of the f.p.* **~anzug** m ⟨tail⟩ *hostess suit* **~aufsatz** m *overmantel*, *mantlepiece ornament* **~bauer** m *steeplejack* **~-besen** m *hearth-broom* **~bock** m *fire-dogs* **~ecke** f *ingle-nook*, *ch.-corner* **~feger** m *ch.-sweep(er)* **~feuer** n *ch.fire*, *ingle* **~gerät** n (*set of*) *fire-irons* pl **~kleid** n ⟨tail⟩ *hostess gown* **~loch** n (mit Rost) *purgatory* **~rohr** n, **~röhre** f *stove*, *smoke-pipe*, *ch. flue* **~rost** m *f.p.-grate* **~schirm** m *fire-screen* **~sims** m *mantelpiece* **~teppich** m *hearthrug* **~vorsteher** m *fender* **~zange** f *fire-tongs* pl **~zug** m *ch. draught*

†**Kamis·ol** n ~(e)s/~e *jacket*, *doublet*

K·amm m ~(e)s/≃e **1.** ⟨eig⟩ *comb*; Galanterie≃ *fancy comb*; Elfenbein-, Schildpatt- etc *ivory*, *tortoise shell*, etc. *c.*; Steck≃ *Spanish back c.*; Staub~ *small-tooth c.* od *dandruff-c.* ‖ ⟨fig⟩ sie sind alle über e–n ~ geschoren .. *tarred with the same brush*; alle(s) über e–n ~ scheren *to treat everybody* (*everything*) *alike* **2.** ⟨zoo & anat⟩ (des Hahns) *crest*, (*cock's*) *comb* ‖ (des Pferdes) *crest*, *edge of neck* ‖ (des ~molches) *back crest* | ⟨cul⟩ (vom Schlachtvieh) *spare-rib*, *neck*, *scrag* ‖ ⟨fig⟩ ihm schwillt der ~ (vor Übermut) *he is on his high horse*, *he is growing arrogant* od *wanton*, *he has got a swollen head*, (vor Zorn) *his blood is up* **3.** (Gebirgs-, Dünen-, Wellen-~) *crest*, *ridge*; (e–s Deiches) *summit*, *top*, *superior surface* **4.** ⟨mech⟩ (Weber~) *reed*, *slay*, *comb* ‖ (am Zahnrad) *cog* (*of a wheel*), *cam* **~abfall** m ⟨spin⟩ *c.ings* pl **≃artig** a → ≃förmig **~baumwolle** f *carded cotton* **~braten** m *roasted neck of beef* **~bürste** f *c.-brush* **~eidechse** f ⟨zoo⟩ *iguana* **≃förmig** a *c.-shaped*, *pectinate* **~futteral** n *c.-case* **~garn** n *worsted* (*yarn*) **~garnfärberei** f *w. dyeing* **~garnspinner** m *w.-spinner* **~garnspinner·ei** *w. spinning-(-mill)*; *w.-manufacture* **~garnstoff** m *w. yarn cloth*, gerippter .. *whipcord* **~garnweber** m *w. weaver* **~gras** n ⟨bot⟩ *coxcomb-grass*, *dog's-tail-grass* **~-griff** m ⟨gym⟩ *undergrasp* **~grind** m ⟨vet⟩ *mange in horse's mane* **~haar** n (*horse's*) *mane* **~hornwespe** f ⟨ent⟩ *pine-saw-fly* **~lade** f ⟨tech⟩ *c.-tray* **~lerche** f ⟨orn⟩ *crested lark* **~linie** (eines Gebirges) *ridge line* **~-Macher** m *c.-maker* **~-Molch** m ⟨zoo⟩ *great water-newt* **~-Muschel** f ⟨zoo⟩ *pecten*, (*e*)*scallop*, *scale* **~-Muskel** m ⟨anat⟩ *pectinate muscle* **~rad** n ⟨tech⟩ *cog-wheel* **~schneidemaschine** f ⟨tech⟩ *comb-cutting machine* **~setzer** m ⟨tech⟩ *carder* **~stück** n ⟨cul⟩ *neck*, *scrag*; (v Schwein) *collar*, *spare-rib* **~tolle** f *forelock* **~-wolle** f *worsted* od *carded wool* **~wollgespinst, ~-wollenzeug** n *w. goods* od *stuffs* od *fabrics* pl **~-zapfen** m ⟨tech⟩ *thrust-journal* **~zug** m ⟨weav⟩ *sliver*, *top*, *combed material* **k·ämmen 1.** vt [h] *to comb* ‖ (Flachs) *to riffle* ‖ (Wolle) *to card* od *comb* **2.** vrefl **sich** ~ [h] *to comb one's hair*

K·ammer f ~/~n **1.** (Stube) *apartment*, (*small*) *room*; kl ~ *closet* ‖ (Schlaf≃) *bedroom* ‖ ⟨anat, tech, zoo⟩ *chamber* ‖ ⟨mar⟩ *cabin* ‖ ⟨hist⟩ Folter≃ *torture-chamber* ‖ (Gewehr≃) *ch.* ‖ ⟨mil⟩ (Waffen-, Geräte- etc ~) *depot*, *unit stores* pl; auf ~ empfangen *to receive from unit d.* ‖ (Herz≃) f ⟨anat⟩ *ventricle* ‖ ⟨min⟩ *excavation*, (erzhaltige ~) *lode* ‖ (Schleusen≃) *lock ch.* **2.** (Behörde) *board* ‖ ⟨pol⟩ *ch.*; ⟨engl⟩ Erste ~ *House of Lords*, *Upper House*; Zweite ~ *House of Commons*, *Lower House* ‖ die einzelnen ~n des Gerichts *the different courts of justice* ‖ die beiden ~n (des Parlaments) traten zu e–r Sitzung zus *the two ch.s assembled for a sitting*; die französische ~ wurde aufgelöst *the French Ch. was dissolved* **~auflösung** f ⟨parl⟩ *dissolution of P.* **~bau** m ⟨min⟩ *excavation* °**~bulle** m = –unteroffizier **~diener** m *valet*; königlicher ~ *groom of the ch.*, *body guard* **~frau** f *ch. maid*, *lady's-maid*, *waiting-woman*, königliche ~ *lady-in-waiting*; oberste ~ *Mistress of the Robes* **~fräulein** n *maid of honour*, *lady of the bedchamber* **~gericht** n ⟨Ger⟩ *Supreme Court of Justice*, *highest court of appeal* **~gut** n *domain*, *demesne*, *crown land* **~herr** m *ch.lain*, *Gentleman of the Bedchamber* **~herrnschlüssel** m *gold key of a ch.lain* **~herrnwürde** f *ch.lainship* **~jäger** m *royal huntsman* ‖ (für Ungeziefer) *rat-catcher* **~jungfer** f *lady's-maid*, *ch.-maid*; jdm als ~ dienen *to lady's maid a p* **~junker** m *gentleman of the bed-ch.* **~kätzchen, ~mädchen** n *waiting-* od *ch.-maid* **~konzert** n *ch.-concert* **~mädchen** n = ~jungfer **~musik** f *ch. music* **~page** m *ch.-page* **~präsident** m [Fr] *President of the Ch. of Deputies*; ⟨engl⟩ *Speaker of the House of Commons* **~rat** m ⟨engl hist⟩ *Councillor of the Exchequer* **~richter** m ⟨Ger⟩ *Judge of the Supreme Court* **~sänger(in** f) m ⟨Ger⟩ (*royal*, etc) *concert singer* **~schreiber** m *store clerk* **~sekretär** m ⟨hist⟩ *Secretary of the Exchequer, clerk to the Exchequer* **~spiele** [pl] ⟨Ger theat⟩ *kammerspiele* **~ton** m ⟨mus⟩ *concert-* od *standard pitch* **~tuch** n ⟨tex⟩ *cotton cambric* **~tür** f *door of the ch.* **~unteroffizier** m ⟨mil⟩ *non-commissioned officer* (abbr *N.C.O.*) *storeman* **~wesen** n *finances* pl **~wissenschaft** f *science of f.s* **~zofe** f = ~jungfer **K·ämmerchen, ~lein** n ~s/~ *little chamber*, ⟨fam⟩ *cubby*; *little bedroom*; im stillen ~ *alone in your little bed-room* ‖ ~ vermieten (Kinderspiel) *puss-in--the-corner*

Kämmer·ei[1] f ~/~en (Woll-) *woolcombing*

Kämmer·ei[2] f ~/~en (Behörde, → Kammer) *board of domains* od *finances*; städtische ~ *municipal b. of f.*‖⟨engl⟩, *Exchequer, Treasury (Board)* **~kasse** f *municipal treasure* **~verwaltung** f *municipal administration of finances* **K·ämmerer** m ~s/~ (Kammerherr) *Chamberlain* ‖ (Stadt-) (*city* od *municipal*) *treasurer*

K·ämmling m ~s/ [mst] **~e** [pl] *combings* pl

K·amp m ~(e)s/~e **1.** ⟨agr⟩ *enclosure, enclosed field* **2.** ⟨hort⟩ *nursery(-garden), plantation*

Kamp·agne [-ˈpanjə] f ~/~n **1.** ⟨mil⟩ (Feldzug) *campaign* **2.** ⟨tech & agr⟩ *working season* od *period*; *c.* **3.** ⟨pol⟩ (Wahl¨~) ⟨bes Am⟩ *c.*

Kamp·anien n ⟨It⟩ (Landschaft) *Campania*

Kamp·anje f ~/~n ⟨naut⟩ *poop*

K·ämpe m ~n/~n ⟨poet & hist⟩ *champion* (*of damsels in distress*), *knight* (*at arms*); *jouster*; ⟨fam⟩ *warhorse* **k·ampeln** vi & sich ~ [h] ⟨fam⟩ *to bicker, brawl, quarrel; to be at loggerheads*

Kamp·escheholz n *campeachy-* (od *log*)*wood*

K·ampf m ~(e)s/¨~e **A.** ⟨mil⟩ **1.** *fighting* (um *for*) [mst imperfektiv]; *fight* (*for*) [mst perfektiv] ‖ *combat* (mst Zwei¨~ ⟨a. fig⟩) ‖ (Schlacht) *battle*; heißer ~ *b. royal* ‖ (Gefecht) *action, engagement*; *struggle* (um .. *for a bridge*) **2.** der **Brennpunkt** des ~es *the brunt of the battle*; die Hauptlast des ~es tragen *to bear the brunt of the fighting*, etc. **3. blutiger** ~ *sanguinary battle* (um *for*) ‖ erbitterte ¨~e [pl] *grim fighting, fierce battles* pl ‖ heftiger ~ bei erster Feindberührung *violent encounter* ‖ heißer ~ *hot fight(ing), dog fight* ‖ kz scharfer ~ ⟨fam⟩ *brush* (*with*) ‖ örtliche ¨~e [pl] *local engagements* pl; regelrechter ~ *stand-up f.* ‖ schwere ¨~e *heavy fighting*; die schweren ¨~ bei Arras *the agony of A.* ‖ verdeckter ~ *covered war* od *action* ‖ wogende, wechselvolle ¨~e *tug-of-war* (um *for*) **4. End**¨~ *final f.* ‖ Groß¨~ *first class battle* ‖ Häuser- u Straßen¨~ *house-to-house and street f.ing* **5. ein** ~ **auf Leben u Tod** *a life and death struggle, a f. to the death*; ~ bis aufs Messer *f. to the bitter end* ⟨a. fig⟩; ~ bis zum letzten Graben *f. to the last trench*; ~ Mann gegen Mann *hand--to-hand f.*; ~ im eigenen Land *fighting in one's native country*; in den ¨~en in Flandern *in the f.ing in Flanders* **6.** die ¨~e in .. sind **abgeschlossen** *f.ing in .. is finished*; den ~ aufnehmen *to open hostilities*; *to engage the target* (*at great distances*); ⟨übtr⟩ *to set to*; .. mit ⟨übtr⟩ *to tackle*; e–n ~ bestehen *to f. an action*; den ~ einstellen *to break off an engagement*; schwere ¨~e [pl] sind im Gange *heavy f.ing is* (*in progress* od) *going on*; es fanden erbitterte ¨~e statt *fierce battles were fought* **7. am** ~ teilnehmen *to see action*; sich **im** ~ messen mit *to do battle with*; sich **in** den ~ stürzen *to fling o.s. into the fray*; nachhaltig in den ~ eingreifen *effectively influence the course of the b.*; Truppen in den ~ werfen *to hurl in troops*; in den ~ ziehen *to march to battle*; sich **zum** ~ stellen *to accept the combat*; Feind zum ~ zwingen *to force an action* **B.** ⟨allg⟩ *struggle, battle* ‖ der ~ **ums Dasein,** um die Macht, **für** die Freiheit *the struggle for existence, for the ascendency, for freedom, the battle of life* **C.** ⟨fig⟩ **1.** der ~ **der Geister** *the intellectual conflict*; der lebendige ~ des Dialogs *the cut and thrust of dialogue*; regelrechter ~ *stand-up fight*; etw in ehrlichem ~ davontragen *to carry a th in open warfare*; ~ bis aufs Messer *skin game* **2.** jdm den ~ **ansagen** *to stand up to a p*; den ~ bis zur Entscheidung ausfechten *to fight it out*; e–n ~ bestehen *to hold one's own* (*against*); im ~ liegen *to be at variance*; sie liegen in ewigem ~ mit–e–a (wie Kampfhähne) *they are always sparring at each other* (*like game-* od *sparring cocks*) **3.** ~ **dem Verderb** *salvage campaign*; ~ dem Verbrechertum *war to criminals*; ..! *down with, away with ..!* **4.** ~ **gegen** die Arbeitslosigkeit *war on unemployment*; ~ gegen den Schmutz *anti-filth c.*; ~ gegen die Malaria *bout with m.*; *c. against cancer* **5. im** rauhen ~ .. *in the rough and tumble* (*of political life*); .. im ~ mit .. (*ambition*) *warring against* (*duty*) **D.** ⟨gym, athl, etc⟩ *athletic contest*; Ring¨~ *wrestling*; (Schlägerei) *fight, fisticuffs* pl **~abschnitt** m (zeitl.) *stage of combat* **~anlage** f ⟨mil⟩ *battle position* **~ansage** f *challenge* (an *to*), *revolt* (*against*); es sah aus wie e–e ~ *it looked like throwing out a ch.* **~anzug** m ⟨mil⟩ (⟨Ger⟩ aller Waffengattungen & Truppenteile) *batlle-suit* (⟨a. aero⟩ Springeranzug = *jump suit* N) **~arten** pl *forms of combat* **~aufgabe** f, **~auftrag** m *c. task* **~ausrüstung** f *b. order* **~bahn** f ⟨sport⟩ *arena, stadium, track* **~begierde** f, **~eslust** f, **~esmut** m *lust* od *love of battle, combat* od *f.ing*; *f.ing mood*; *eagerness to f., readiness for action, combativeness, warlike* od *martial ardour* ¨~**begierig,** ¨~**esmutig** a *eager to f., eager for battle*; *bellicose, pugnacious, combative*; *courageous* ¨~**bereit** a *ready to f., ready for battle*; ⟨fam⟩ *game*; sich ~ zeigen *to show f.* **~bereitschaft** f *readiness for b., state of mobilization* **~brüderschaft** f *brotherhood in arms* **~bund** m *militant league*; *armed* od *f.ing formation* **~einheit** f ⟨mil⟩ *tactical* od *f.ing unit* **~einsatz** m *f.ing* **~erfolg** m *success in battle* ¨~**erprobt** a (*fire-*) *seasoned, war-trained, battle-tried*; *veteran* (Truppe) ¨~**fähig** a *able, capable, effective* (*troops*) **~feld** n = ~platz **~flieger** m *bomber-pilot*; erfolgreicher ~ *star-turn pilot* | ~verband [m] *bomber formation, b. aircraft* **~flugzeug** n *tactical aircraft*; *combat* od *f.ing plane*, (*f.ing*) *bomber, f.er* (*plane*), *battle-* od *war-plane, raider*; ~ (mit Kanone) *gun-plane*; schwere, leichte ~e *heavy, light bomber aircraft*; gr ~ *aerial dreadnought*; 4-motoriges ~ ⟨Am⟩ *flying fortress* **~freude** f *pugnaciousness, pugnacity, combativeness* ¨~**freudig** a *full of f., war-like* **~front** f *firing-line, fire line* **~führung** f *f.ing*; bewegliche ~ *elastic tactics* pl; einheitliche ~ *centralized direction of the* (*combat*) *operations*; psychologische ~ *psychological warfare* | ~s- u Versorgungsanlagen [pl] *command and supply installations* **~gas** n *poison gas, noxious* od *poisonous gas* → ~stoff **~gebiet** n *f.ing zone* **~gefährte, ~genosse** m *companion* od *brother in arms, fellow combatant* **~geist** m *militancy, combative spirit, fighting spirit* od *quality*; er hat k–n Funken ~ mehr *he has not an ounce of f. left in him*; jdm neuen ~ einflößen *or* wecken *to put a new f. into a p* **~gelände** n *f.ing* od *battle area* od *ground, f.ing zone* **~gemeinschaft** f *f.ing team* **~gerät** n ⟨mil⟩ *utensils, tools, engines* pl **~geschehen** n *combat operations* **~geschwader** n, Gruppe e–s ~s *bomber squadron group* **~gewohnt** a *trained for f.ing, accustomed to f., trained in war, war-hardened* **~gewühl** n *turmoil* (*of battle*); im ~ *in the fray* od *thick of the battle* **~gruppe** f *f.ing cadre*; *regimental combat team* N, (Stab) *combat command*, (Sonderverband) *task force* **~hahn** m *game-, fighting-, sparring-cock*; ⟨fig⟩ *quarrelsome fellow*; *squabbler*; (Raufbold) *brawler* **~handlung** f *f.ing*; *tactical operation*; (*combat*) *action*; *engagement* ⟨a. mar⟩; ~en [pl] *combat operations*; ~ melden *to report f.ing*; es fanden k–e ~en statt *no f.ing took place* **~handschuh** m *gauntlet* **~kraft** f *combat effectiveness*; *f.ing strength* od *value*; ¨~e

[pl] (*f.ing*) *forces* **≃kräftig** a *combat-fit*; (*troops*) *possessing a combat potential* **~läufer** m ⟨orn⟩ *ruff*, (Weibchen) *reeve, ree* **~linie** f *f.ing line*; vorderste ~ *spearhead*; Haupt≃ [f] *main f.ing line* **≃los** a *peaceful* | adv (*to win*) *hands down* **~lust** f, **~mut** m = ~begierde, ~geist; ~ zeigen *to show one's teeth* **~lustig** a, **~mutig** a = ~begierig **~organisation** f ⟨pol⟩ *f.ing organ* **~platz** m *field of battle, battle-field, scene of action*; ⟨sport⟩ *arena, ring*; ⟨hist⟩ (Turnier≃) *the lists* pl; den ~ betreten *to enter the lists*; ⟨fig⟩ *cockpit* (*of discords*) **~preis** m *prize* **~rede** f *f.ing speech* **~richter** m *umpire* **~roß** n *charger, war-horse* **~ruf** m, **~geschrei** n *war-cry, battle-cry*; ⟨fig⟩ *slogan*, ⟨Am univ⟩ *yell* **~schiff** n, Groß≃ *capital ship, dreadnought* **~schwimmer** m *undersea diver*; *frogman* | ~trupp [m] *underwater demolition team* **~spiel** n *prize-f.ing, athletic contest*; ⟨hist⟩ (ritterliches Turnier) *tournament, tilt*(*ing*), *joust*(*ing*) **~stand** m *f.ing position* **≃stark** a *combat capable* **~stellung** f, Haupt≃ *main f.ing line* **~stoff** m; flüchtiger *nonpersistent chemical agent*; → seßhaft *persistent*; flüssig *ch. warfare fluid agent*; ätzend *blister gases*; erstickend *choking gases* (→ -gas) | ~bombe [f] *gas bomb*; ~sperre [f] *chemical barrier* **~tätigkeit** f *active combat*; *c. activity*; örtliche ~ *local* (*f.ing*) *activity*; die ~ einstellen *to cease firing* **~truppe** f *combat troops* pl, *close c. elements*; ~n [pl] *line troops*; *front-line forces* **≃tüchtig** a *f.ing fit* **~unfähig** a *disabled, invalid*(*ed*); ~ m ⟨mil⟩ *to disable, incapacitate*; *to render* (*a unit*) *incapable of combat*; ⟨mar⟩ *to put out of action*; ⟨fig⟩ *to put out* (*of the running*); ⟨sport⟩ *to knock out* **~verband** m *combat team* N; als (gemischter) ~ (eingesetzt) *for task force* N **~wagen** m ⟨hist⟩ *f.ing vehicle*; ⟨mil⟩ *tank, armoured car*; Zweimann≃ ⟨sl⟩ *honeymoon*; leichter ~ (mit M.G.) *light tank*, ⟨sl⟩ *female t.*; mittlerer ~ *medium t.*; schwerer ~ *heavy t., land cruiser*; ~ mit Geschütz ⟨sl⟩ *male t.* | ~abwehr [f] *anti-tank defence*; ~artillerie [f], ~geschütz [n] *a.-t. artillery, .. gun* (→ Panzerwagen) **~weise** f *tactics and f.ing methods* **~wert** m *combat*(*ive*) *value* od *capability, efficiency* **~wille** m (unbeugsamer *invincible*) *f.ing spirit* **~zeuge** m *second* **~zone** f *combat zone* **k·ämpfen** vi [h] *to combat, battle, fight*; *strive, contend, struggle* (um *for, about*), (gegen *with, against*) (verzeifelt *desperately*); *to struggle against imperialism, difficulties*; *to fight about ideals*; *to contend for the inviolability of* .. || sie ~ gegen das Feuer an *they fight the fire*; er kämpfte gegen die Wellen, Schwierigkeiten an *he battled the waves, the difficulties*; *to combat a tendency* || für e-e S ~ gegen *to fight a cause against* | ⟨fig⟩ gegen Vorurteile ~ *to battle with prejudice*; *ambition warring against duty* || tüchtig ~ *to make a fight of it*; bis zum letzten, äußersten ~ *to fight to the last, to the bitter end*; bis zur Entscheidung ~ *to fight to a finish* || zu ~ h mit *to labour under* (*difficulties*); mit ehrlichen Mitteln ~ *to play the game*; schwer z ~ h *to be hard up*; ~ oder untergehen *do or die*; ~ für *to stand up for*; ~ gegen *to antagonize* (*a theory*); geg. Windmühlen ~ *to tilt at windmills* || mit dem Tode ~ *to struggle with death* || jdn zu Boden ~ *to floor a p* || sie kämpfte mit e–m Lächeln, mit Tränen *she suppressed a smile, a tear* | **~de** Truppe *combat troops* pl

K·ampfer m ~s/ *camphor* **~baum** m *c.-tree* **~essig** m *c.ated vinegar* **~geist** m *c.ated spirits* pl **~säure** f ⟨chem⟩ *c.ic acid* **~spiritus** m *spirits* [pl] *of c.* **k·ampfern** vt [h] *to c.ate*

K·ämpfer m ~s/~ *combatant, warrior*; *battler, fighter, champion* (für gegen *for againt*); *defender* (f *of*); Faust≃, Ring≃ *prize-fighter*; ⟨a. nazi⟩ alter ~ *old stalwart, old pioneer*; alte ~ [pl] ⟨nazi⟩ *old guard* | ⟨arch⟩ *impost, abutment*; *springing-stone*; (am Fenster) *transom* **k·ämpferisch** a *militant, combative, pugnacious*; ~e Haltung *heroic fight*; ~e Atmosphäre *embattled atmosphere*

kamp·ieren vi [h] *to* (*en*)*camp, to be encamped, to camp out*; *to bivouac* (*in the open*) || ⟨fig⟩ auf dem Sofa ~ *to spend the night on the sofa*

Kamtsch·atka n (Halbinsel NO-Asiens) *Kam*(*ts*)*chatka* **-schad·ale** m **-lin** f *Kamchatkan*

†**K·ana** n ⟨bib⟩, Simon v ~ *Simon the Canaanite* †**K·anaan** n ⟨bib⟩ *Canaan*

K·anada n *Canada*

Kan·adier m ~s/~ *Canadian* || ⟨fam⟩ *Canuck*

°**Kanaille** [kan'aljə] ~/~n **1.** *rascal, scoundrel* **2.** [koll] *rabble, pack*

Kan·ake m ~n/~n **1.** (Hawaier) *Kanaka* **2.** °⟨fig⟩ *blockhead, duffer*

Kan·al m ~(e)s/≃e (natürlicher) *channel*; der Englische ~ *the* (*English*) *Ch.*; über den ~ *across the Ch.* || (künstlicher) *canal, waterway*; enger ~ *narrow passage*, ⟨Ger⟩ Mittelland≃ *Midland canal*; ⟨Am⟩ *Florida waterway*; der Bau von ≃en *the making of c.s* || Abzugs≃ [m] *sewer, drain, pipe, conduit, duct* || ⟨comp, rec, etc⟩ *channel*; ~-kapazität [f] *limiting capacity of a communication ch.* | ⟨fig⟩ *ch., conduit*; ohne ~ ⟨med⟩ *ductless* (*gland*); die unterirdischen ≃e *the subways* (*of trade*) || ⟨anat⟩ *meatus* L; ⟨fam⟩ ich habe den ~ voll davon *I'm* (*completely*) *fed up with it* **~arbeiter** m *navvy*; *sewerman* **~bau** m *c.-making, c.-ization* **~boot** n *c.-boat* **~flieger** m *cross-ch. pilot* **~gas** n *sewer gas* **~inseln** f pl *Ch. Islands* **~netz** n *drainage* (od *collecting, sewerage*) *system* **~schifffahrt** f *c.-navigation* **~schleuse** f *c.-lock* **≃ikulär** a ⟨med⟩ *canalicular* **~isati·on** f ~/~en (e–r Stadt) *sewerage, drains* [pl], *drainage* || (e–s Flusses) *canalization* **≃isieren** vt [h] *to canalize* || (Straßen) *to drain by means of sewers* || (Stadt) *to sewer*

K·anapee n ~s/~s *sofa, settee*

Kan·ar(i)en (n) pl | –ienvogel [m] *canary* (*bird*); Kanarische Inseln [f pl] *Canary Islands, Canaries* pl

°**Kan·aster, Kn·aster** m ~s/ (*bad*) *tobacco*; ein elender ~ *tobacco of a kind*

Kand·are f ~/~n ⟨hors⟩ *curb*(*-bit*), *bridle-bit*; die ~ scharf anziehen *to tighten the curb*; auf die ~ beißen *to champ the bit*; er ritt das Pferd auf ~ *he rode the horse on the curb*; ein Pferd an die ~ legen *or* nehmen *to curb a horse* | ⟨fig⟩ jdn an die ~ nehmen *to take a p in hand strongly, to put the curb on a p*; jdn an der ~ halten *to keep a p in check* **~nstange** f *curb-bit* **~zügel** m *curb rein*

K·andel f ~/~n *gutter*; *spout, gutter-pipe*

Kandel·aber m ~s/~ *candelabrum*; *chandelier*

K·andelzucker m *sugar-candy*; → Kandis

K·andia f ⟨It⟩ *Candia*, → ⟨a.⟩ Kreta

Kandid·at m ~en/~en *candidate, claimant, applicant* (*for*); geistlicher ~ *probationer*, (Presbyter) *licentiate*; ⟨pol⟩ *nominee*; e–n ~en aufstellen *to nominate* od *run a candidate*; sich als ~ aufst. l → kandidieren; ⟨parl⟩ als ~ auftreten *to come forward as a c.* || unbekannter ~ ⟨Am fam⟩ *dark horse* **~enliste** f ⟨fam⟩ *ticket*, ⟨Am⟩ *slate*

Kandidat·ur f ~/~en *candidature*, ⟨Am⟩ *candidacy* (*of a p for*) **kandid·ieren** vi [h] *to be a candidate* (f *for*), *to stand* (*for*), ⟨Am⟩ *to run* (*for*) || ⟨parl⟩ *to contest* (*a seat*) (*in Parliament*); *to put one's name down* (*for*)

kand·ieren vt [h] *to candy, crystallize*; kandiert *candied* (*fruit*); *iced* **Kand·ierung** f ~/ *candying, icing* **K·andis** m ~/ ~zucker, Zucker≃ [m] ~/ (*sugar-*)*candy*

Kan·eel [ka'ne:l] m ~(e)s/ *cinnamon*

K·anevas [–was] m ~/~ *canvas*; ~stickerei *tapestry*

K·ängeruh n ~s/~e & ~s *kangaroo*

Kan·in n ~(e)s/–e *rabbit* (*used to indicate mock furs*) **Kan·inchen** n –s/~ *rabbit, cony* || männl. ~ *buck*, weibl. ~ *doe* || ~ jagen *to* *rabbit* **~bau** m (*r.-*)*burrow* **~futter** n *rabbit food* ⟨a. hum cul⟩ **~gehege** n *r.-warren* **~hecke** f, **~wurf** m *r.'s nest* **~klein, ~ragout** n ⟨cul⟩ *stewed rabbit* **~stall** m *r.-hutch*

Kan·ister m *canister*; ⟨mot⟩ *motorcar can*

K·anker m ~s/~ ⟨hort⟩ *canker* | ⟨zoo⟩ *harvest spider*; *daddy-long-legs*

k·ann 1. & 3. p sg pres v können

K·ännchen n ~s/~ *cannikin, small jug* **K·anne** f ~/~n *can* (*of coffee*), *jug* (*of cream*), *pot, tankard*; ⟨Am⟩ *pitcher*; (Bier≈) *pot*; (Wein≈) *quart* ‖ ⟨fig⟩ es gießt mit ~n *it's raining in torrents* ‖ er hat zu tief in die ~ geguckt *he has taken a drop too much* ‖ ⟨stud sl⟩ in die ~ steigen *to drink by order* (*at a student's feast*); er wurde in die ~ geschickt *he was ordered to drink*; in die ~! *drink*! **~gießer** m ⟨fam⟩ *pot-house* (od *would-be*) *politician*; *quidnunc* **~gießer·ei** f ⟨fam⟩ *pothouse politics* pl, *political twaddle* **≈gießern** vi [h] ⟨fam⟩ *to rant* od *twaddle about politics*

kannel·ieren vi [h] *to channel, chamfer* **K-rung** f ~/–en *chamfering, channelling* **-l·üre** f ~/~n *chamfer*; geschweifte ~ *spiral fluting*

K·annen- ~maß n *measure of a pot* od *quart* **~milch** f *milk in cans* **~pflanze** f ⟨bot⟩ *nepenthe*(*s*), *pitcherplant* **~wärmer** m *cosy* **≈weise** adv *by pots, by quarts*

Kannib·ale m ~n/~n *cannibal* **kannib·alisch 1.** a *cannibal* ‖ ⟨fig⟩ *savage, brutal* (*act*), *cruel*; ⟨sl⟩ *tremendous* (*heat, hunger*) **2.** [adv] ⟨fam⟩ *enormously, awfully*

K·anoe n ~s/~s = Kanu *canoe*

K·anon m ~s/~s ⟨ec⟩ *canon* ‖ ⟨mus⟩ *round*; ⟨engl hist⟩ *catch*; → unter aller Kanone

Kanon·ade f ~/~n *cannonade, bombardment*

Kan·one f ~/~n **1.** *gun, piece* (*of ordnance*), **cannon* ‖ die ~n [koll pl] *the cannon*; Feuer der ~n *gunfire* | Maschinen≈ *automatic gun*; Revolver≈ ⟨engl⟩ *hotchkiss-gun* | ~n **auffahren** (festmachen) *to bring up* od *mount* (*to house*) *the guns*; ~ richten *to point a g.*; ~ vernageln *to spike a g.* **2.** ⟨fig⟩ ⟨iron⟩ *stove* ‖ (⟨fam⟩ P) *great* od *big gun*; *big one* od *un*; *ace*; ⟨sl⟩ *nailer*; ⟨Am sl a.⟩ *Big Noise*; ⟨sport⟩ *crack* (*hand*) **3.** ⟨fig⟩ **mit ~n** auf Spatzen schießen *to break a butterfly on the wheel* ‖ °sie spielt **unter** aller „~" (urspr. [L] *sub omni canone*) *she plays execrably, below contempt* **Kan·onen- ~bereich** m *c.-range* **~bohrer** m *tube bit* **~boot** n ⟨mar⟩ *gunboat, sloop* (*of war*) **~bürste** f *c.-brush* **~donner** m *roar, peal, boom of guns* od *of c.* **≈fest** a *c.-proof* **~feuer** n *artillery-fire, c.ade* **~fieber** n *funk, bullet-fever* **~flugzeug** n *c.-fighter* **~futter** n *food for powder, c. fodder* **~gießerei** f *gun-foundry* **~haubitze** f *c.-howitzer* **~lafette** f *gun mounting* **~metall** n *gun-metal* **~motor** m ⟨aero-mot⟩ *c. engine* **~pforte** f ⟨mar hist⟩ *port* **~schlag** m *puff, bursting-charge*; (Feuerwerk) *maroon* **~schuß** m *c.-shot* **~schußweite** f *c.-shot range* **~stand** m: hinterer ~ ⟨aero⟩ *tail turret* **~stiefel** m [pl] *jack-boots* pl **~wischer** m *sponge* **Kanon·ier** m ~(e)s/~e *gunner, artilleryman*; Richt≈ *gun-layer* | **≈en** vt/i [h] *to c.ade*

Kanonik·at n ~(e)s/~e ⟨ec⟩ *canonry, prebend* **Kan·oniker** m ~s/~, **-kus** m ~/–ker *canon, prebendary* **kan·onisch** a *canonic*(*al*) ‖ ~es Recht *canon law* **kanonis·ieren** vt [h] *to canonize* **K-s·ierung** f ~/~en *canonization*

Kanon·issin f ~/~nen *canoness* **-·ist** m ~en/~en *canonist*

Känoz·oikum n ~s/ ⟨geol⟩ *Cenozoic*

K·ansas n (Staat der U.S.A.), K·ansas City

Kansu n (Prov. Chinas)

Kant·abrische Gebirge, das ⟨It⟩ *the Cantabrian Chain* od *Mountains*

K·ant- ~beitel m ~s/~ *cant* od *corner chisel* **~haken** m *grapple, -ling-iron, cant-hook*; ⟨fam⟩ beim ~ fassen *to collar* **~holz** n *squared timber*

Kant·ate f ~/~n ⟨mus⟩ *cantata* ‖ Sonntag ~ *fourth Sunday after Easter*

K·ante f ~/~n *edge* | (Rand) *brim, border, margin* | (Leiste) *ledge* | (Mauer≈) *crest* ‖ abgeschrägte ~ *chamfer* ‖ hohe ~ (eines Brettes) *edge*; *narrow side* (*of a board*); auf der hohen ~ *on edge*; *on the narrow side*; *to stand tiles on their sides* ‖ abgerundete, scharfe, stumpfe ~ *rounded, sharp, blunt edge* ‖ schräge ~ *bezel* (*of a gem*) | ⟨arch⟩ scharfe ~ *arris* | Bord≈ *kerb* | ⟨embr⟩ *lace* ‖ (Tuch-) *list, selvage, selvedge* | (Trimmung) ⟨aero⟩ *tab* | ⟨fig⟩ auf die hohe ~ legen *to put by, to save*, ⟨fam⟩ *to salt away* od *down*; ⟨Am a.⟩ *to put down south*; das kommt auf d. h. ~ *that goes down south* ‖ ⟨fig⟩ an allen Ecken u ~n *in every corner* **K·antel** n ~s/~ *square ruler* **K·anten** m ~s/~ (Brot-) *top* od *bottom crust*, **k·anten** vt [h] *to cant, tilt, turn up, set on edge* ‖ (Stein) *to square* ‖ schräg ~ *to bevel* ‖ (randen) *to border, to edge* **K·anten- ~ansicht** f *profile* **~brett** n *shelf for mugs*, etc. **~eingriff** m (Zahnrad) *edge interference* **~fräsmaschine** f *edge milling machine* **~kleid** n *dress trimmed with lace* **~schärfe** f *edge sharpness* **~schiene** f ⟨rail⟩ *edged rail* **~tuch** n *lace-trimmed neckerchief*

K·anter m ~s/ ⟨hors⟩ *canter* | **≈n** vi/t *to c.*

Kanthar·ide f ~/~n ⟨ent & med⟩ *Spanish fly* **~npflaster** n ⟨med⟩ *blister*

Kanti·aner m ~s/~ ⟨philos⟩ *disciple of Kant*

k·antig 1. [a] *angular, edged*; *having sharp edges* **2.** [adv] ~ behauen [a] *squared*

Kantil·ene f ~/~n ⟨mus⟩ *cantilena*

Kant·ine f ~/~n ⟨mil⟩ *canteen, soldiers' bar*; ⟨mar⟩ *galley*; ⟨Am⟩ *post-exchange* (abbr. *P.X.*); e–e ~ führen *to run a c.* **~nwirt** m *c.-keeper*

K·anton, Kwangtschou (Prov. Chinas) *Canton*

Kant·on m ~(e)s/~e (Sw: Einzelstaat; Fr: Kreis) *canton* **≈·ieren** vt [h] (Truppen) *to quarter, canton* | vi *to be quartered* **~·ierung** f ~/~en *quartering, cantonment*

Kanton·ist m ~en/~en; unsicherer ~ ⟨fam⟩ *wobbler*; *unreliable, shifty fellow, who cannot be trusted*; *not a safe card* **K·antor** m ~s/Kant·oren *precentor* ‖ *parish schoolmaster and organist* **K·antus** m ~/ ⟨univ⟩ e–n ~ anstimmen (*or* steigen l) *to sing a jolly song*

K·anu n ~s/~s *canoe*; *dugout* ‖ (f eine P mit Doppelpaddel) *Rob Roy c.* ‖ (mittelamerikan. Rindenboot) *pitpan* ‖ (im) ~ fahren *to c.* **Kan·ute** m ~n/~n *canoeist*

Kan·üle f ~/~n ⟨med⟩ *tubule, canula* L

K·anzel f ~/~n **1.** ⟨ec⟩ *pulpit*; ⟨hist⟩ *ambo*; die ~ besteigen *to mount the p.*; auf der ~ *in the p.*; v der ~ herab *from the p.*; sich v der ~ ablesen (⟨dial⟩ werfen) l *to have one's banns published* **2.** ⟨univ⟩ (mst österr) (*professorial*) *chair* **3.** ⟨hunt⟩ *elevated cover* (*like a pulpit*) **4.** ⟨aero mil⟩ *turret, nose compartment*, ⟨fam⟩ *p.* (in *in*) **5.** ⟨met⟩ *p.* **~beredsamkeit** f *p.-eloquence* od *-oratory* **~brüstung** f *p.-rail* **~dach** n, **~haube** f, **~himmel** m *sound-boards* pl, *canopy* **~lied** n *hymn before the sermon* **~mißbrauch** m ⟨jur⟩ *abuse of the p.* °**~pauker, ~trommler** m ⟨sl⟩ *tub-thumper, -banger*; ⟨sl⟩ *devil dodger* **~rede** f *p.-oration, sermon* **~redner** m *p. orator*, (*eloquent*) *preacher, clergyman* **~ton** m *sermonizing* **Kanzl·ei** f ~/~en (*government*) *office, secretariate*, ⟨jur⟩ *chambers* pl (*to be in ch.*); *chancellery*, ⟨Ger⟩ *chancery*; *German ch. type* ‖ ⟨mil⟩ *orderly room* ‖ [koll] *personnel of these offices, staff of ministerial department* **~amt** n *chancery-office* **~beamte(r)** m *official of a ch.* **~bedarf** m *office needs, o. appliances* **~diener** m *office-attendant* **~direktor** m *head of the office* **~gericht** n *Court of Chancery* **~handschrift** f *chancery-hand* **~papier** n *foolscap* **~personal** n *staff* (*of a public office*) **~rat** m *Chancery-Conncillor* **~schreiber** m *Chancery-clerk* **~schrift** f *court-hand, engrossing hand* **~stil** m *official style* ‖ ⟨jur⟩ *legal style, law-style* **~vorsteher** m *head clerk of a* *chancery* **K·anzler** m ~s/~ (a. Bundes≗) *Chancellor*; Reichs≗ ⟨hist⟩ *Ch. of the Reich*; der Eiserne ~ (Bismarck) *the Iron Ch.* || ⟨univ⟩ (Kurator) *Ch.* **~krise** f *ch.-crisis* **~würde** f *ch.ship* **Kanzl·ist** m ~en/~en (*chancery-*)*clerk, copying clerk*

kanzerog·en a ⟨path med⟩ *cancerogenic*

Kanz·one f ~/~n ⟨poet⟩ *canzona*

Kaol·in n [in der Fachsprache nur: m] ~s/ (*raw*) *kaolin* **~grube** f *china clay pit*

K·ap n ~s/~s ⟨geogr⟩ *cape, promontory; headland* || ~ Ho(o)rn *C. Horn*, das ~ der Guten Hoffnung *C. of Good Hope, the C.* | ~branntwein [m] ⟨SAfr⟩ *C. smoke*; ~ Breton-Insel [f] (kanad. Insel) *Cape Breton, Cape Breton Islands*; ~holländisch [n] *Afrikaans*; ~kolonie [f], ~land [n] *Cape Colony*, ⟨a.⟩ *the Cape*; ~-Mulde f (S.-Afrika) ⟨mar⟩ *Cape Basin*: ~stadt f *Cape Town, Capetown*; ~ Verde [n] *Cape Verd(e)*; ~verdische Inseln [f pl] *Cape Verd(e) Islands* pl

Kap·aun m ~(e)s/~e *capon* | ≗**en** vt [h] *to c.*

Kapazit·ät [ts] f ~/~en **1.** ⟨eig⟩ (Fähigkeit) *capacity* || ⟨el⟩ *c.y*, ~ eines Sammlers *charge c.ty* od *c.tance* || (Brückenbau) *water way* || (Fassungsvermögen) *capaciousness*; e–e ~ h v .. *to make available a capacity of* .. **2.** ⟨fig⟩ (Fachgröße, Berühmtheit) *celebrity*; *eminent specialist*; *authority*; *man of great ability*; *one of the first authorities in the field of* .. **~sausweitung** f ⟨el⟩ *expansion in c.ty* „**~überschreitung**" f ⟨comp⟩ "*tape entry exceeds programmed c.ty*"

°**Kap·ee** n: schwer v ~ s *to be slow-witted* od a *slow-coach*; ⟨Am⟩ *slow on the up-take*, ⟨sl⟩ *doughy*

Kap·elle[1] f ~/~n ⟨ec⟩ *chapel*, ~ der Dissenters *bethel* | (Musikkorps) (*musical*) *band*; *choir*; kl ~ *orchestra*; e–e ~ v 3 Mann *a three-piece orchestra* || die ~ setzte ein *the band struck up*

Kap·elle[2] f ~/~n ⟨met, chem⟩ (Tiegel) *cupel, test* **~nofen** m ⟨met⟩ *assay* od *c.ling* od *muffle furnace* **~nprobe** f *c. test* od *assay* **~nraub** m ⟨met⟩ *loss by c.lation* **~nsilber** n *fine silver* **~nzange** f ⟨met⟩ *c.-tongs* pl **kapell·ieren** vt [h] ⟨chem, met⟩ *to c., refine*

Kap·ellmeister m (→ Kapelle[1]) *band-master, conductor*; *musical director*

K·aper[1] f ~/~n ⟨bot⟩ *caper* || → ~n-

K·aper[2] m ~s/~ ⟨mar hist⟩ (Pirat[enschiff]) *private*(*er*), *corsair, freebooter, captor* | ⟨mod⟩ durch gültigen Kaperbrief legalisiert **~brief** m *letter of marque* **~fahrt** f *naval raid* **~gasten** m pl *crew of a pirate* (*ship*) **~schiff** n *privateer, pirate* (*ship*), *corsair, raider* **Kaper·ei** f ~/~en *privateering*

k·apern 1. vi [h] *to cruise as a pirate, to carry on piracy* **2.** vt [h] *to capture, seize*; ge–rtes Schiff *prize* || ⟨fig⟩ *to capture, catch, seize, collar*; sie kaperte sich e–n Mann *she captured a man* || ⟨fam⟩ *to bag, collect*

K·apern- (→ Kaper[1]) **~sauce, ~soße** f *caper-sauce* **~staude** f, **~strauch** m *caper-bush*

Kap·ernaum n ⟨bib⟩ der Hauptmann v ~ *the centurion at Capernaum*

°**kap·ieren** vi/t [h] ⟨fam⟩ *to take in, to grasp* (*understand*) || hast du –rt? ⟨fam⟩ *do you get me*?; ich –re nicht, daß ⟨fam⟩ *I don't quite twig* (*that*); –rst du denn das nicht? *why, don't you see that*?; –rt? ⟨sl⟩ *savvy*? || er –rt schwer ⟨Am⟩ *he's slow on the up-take*, ⟨sl⟩ *he's doughy*

Kapill·ar- ~aszension f *capillary rise* **~depression** *c. depression* **~gefäß** n ⟨anat⟩ *c.* (*vessel*) **~kraft** f *c. action* **~it·ät** f ~/ *capillarity, capillary attraction* || soziale ~ ⟨demog⟩ *intergenerational social mobility*

Kapit·al n ~(e)s/~ien *capital, substance, fund(s), means, stock*; *money*; angelegtes ~ *invested c.*; flüssiges ~ *available funds* || ~ u Zinsen *principal and interest* || arbeitendes, totes ~ *working, dead c.*; brachliegendes ~ *loose c.*; hinlängliches ~ *ample means*; eingefrorenes ~ *frozen c.* || ~ schlagen aus ⟨fig⟩ *to make c. out of, to turn .. to account, to cash in on .., to capitalize on ..*; ~ aufnehmen *to raise c.* od *money*; ~ kündigen *to call in c.*; (fast) ohne ~ (anfangen) ⟨Am sl⟩ .. *on a shoestring*; ~ in ein Geschäft stecken *to put money in a business*; vom ~ leben *to live on one's c.*; die Zinsen z ~ schlagen *to add the interest to c.*; geistiges ~ *intellectual c.*; Gesundheit ist das beste ~ *health is the best investment* | ⟨übtr⟩ *capital owing classes* **kapit·al** a *capital, royal* (*stag*) || *chief, principal* (*question*) **Kapit·al- ~abgabe** f *c. levy* **~abwanderung** f *migration of c. to foreign markets* **~anlage** f *investment* | ~gesellschaft [f] *i. trust* **~anleger** m *investor* **~aufwand** m *i. of c.*; *c. cost*; Analyse des ~s *c. expenditure analysis* **~einlage** f *c. paid* od *brought in* **~erhöhung** f *increase of c.* **~ertrag** m *rent, revenue*; *yield on investment funds* | ~ssteuer [f] *c. gains tax* **~flucht** f *c. flight* **~güter** n pl *durable goods* **~hirsch** m *royal stag* **~junge, ~kerl** m ⟨fam⟩ *brick, ripper* **~konto** n *stock-account* ≗**kräftig** a *moneyed, wealthy, wellfounded, well provided with c., having ample means* **~mangel** m *want of funds* **~markt** m *money market* **~schwund** m *dwindling of assets* **~steuer** f *property-tax* **~verbrechen** n *crime*; (*it is not a*) *criminal offence* (*to do that*) **~verbrecher** m *capital criminal* **~verkehr** m *movement of c.* **~verlust** m *total loss* **~vermögen** n *funded property* **~wirtschaft** f *management of c.* **~zufluß** m *increase of c.* **~zuwachssteuer** f *c. gains tax*

Kapit·äl n ~s/~n ⟨arch⟩ → Kapitell

Kapitälchen n ~s/~ **1.** ⟨typ⟩ [pl] *small capitals* od *initials* **2.** ⟨com⟩ *small capital* **kapitalis·ieren** vt [h] (mit Geld versehen) *to capitalize, fund, finance* || (Geld flüssig m) *to turn into money, to realize, to convert into capital, to capitalize* **K-rung** f *accumulation on interest* **Kapital·ist** m ~en/~en *capitalist, plutocrat, financier*, ⟨fam⟩ *moneyed man*; '*Man of Property*' | ≗**isch** a *capitalist* (*the c. powers*) **Kapit·än** m ~(e)s/~e *captain, shipmaster*; ⟨com-mar⟩ *master*(*-mariner*), *skipper*; ⟨mil-mar⟩ ~ zur See ⟨engl⟩ *captain R.N.* = *captain of the Royal Navy* **~leutnant** m *lieutenent-commander, senior lieutenant* **Kap·itel** n ~s/~ (Buch≗ & ⟨ec⟩) *chapter* || *budget* N || ⟨übtr⟩ *topic*; ⟨comp⟩ *section* || jdm das ~ lesen ⟨fam⟩ *to read a p a lecture, to reprimand* (⟨fam⟩ *lecture*) *a p* || in das ~ gehören *to come under the head*; das ist ein ~ f sich *that is quite a special* (od *different*) *matter*, ⟨Am sl⟩ *that is a horse of a different color* ≗**fest** a *well-versed, well-read* (*in*) ≗**weise** adv *by chapters* **Kapit·ell** n ~s/~e ⟨arch⟩ *chapiter* (*of column*), *capital*; → *capitals* **kap·iteln** vt [h] **1.** *to divide into chapters* **2.** ⟨fig⟩ *to reprimand, scold* (⟨fam⟩ *lecture*) *a p* **Kapit·ol(ium)** n; das ~ *the Capitol* (in Rom) **Kapitul·ant** m ~en/~en *capitulant* || (Soldat) *re-enlisted man* **Kapitul·ar** m ~(e)s/~e *capitular* **Kapitulati·on** f ~/~en (Festung etc) *capitulation*, (bedingungslos *unconditional*) *surrender* || (Soldat) *re-enlistment*, → **kapitul·ieren** vi [h] *to capitulate* || (freiwillig weiter dienen) *to re-enlist* || ⟨fig⟩ ~ vor (etw *or* jdm) *to bow to* (*the storm*); *to capitulate* od *submit to* (*a p*)

Kapl·an m ~(e)s/≗e *chaplain*; ⟨mil sl⟩ *padre*

K·apok m ~s/ *kapok* | ~(schwimm)weste *k. vest*

°**kap·ores** a [hebr] = kaputt

†**Kap·otte** f ~/~n *hood* (od *cloak*) **K·äppchen** n ~s/~ *small skullcap* || ⟨ec⟩ *calotte* **K·appe** f ~/~n **A. 1.** *cap*; Bade≗ *bathing-cap*; Isolator≗ *insulator cap*; **Sturz**≗ *crash helmet*; Kugel≗ *spherical cap*; **Staub**≗ *dust-cap*; Narren≗ *fool's cap*; Mönchs≗ *skullcap* **2.** (Kapuze, a. ⟨tech⟩) *hood*, Mönchs≗ *cowl, hood*; Falken≗ *hood* **3.** (oberer Teil) *top-piece, top* (*of a dike*), Schuh≗ *toe-cap, toe-piece*; mit breiter ~ *square-toed*

(*boot*) ‖ (Brückenbau) *top* od *ridge beam* ‖ ~ e–s Kohlenmeilers *top of a coalpile* **4.** ⟨arch⟩ (Gewölbe≃) *vault* ‖ *caping, coping, cowl* **5.** ⟨mar⟩ (Luken≃, Kajüts≃) *companion hood* **B.** ⟨fig fam⟩ jdm etw auf die ~ geben *to take a p down*; ⟨prov⟩ gleiche Brüder, gleiche ~n *like pot, like cover*; *birds of a feather flock together*; jedem Narren gefällt s–e ~ *every man has his hobby*; (etw) auf s–e nehmen ⟨fig⟩ *to undertake the responsibility* od *risk of*; *to be answerable for*; *to make o.s. responsible for*; *to shoulder* (*a th*)

†**Kappad·okien** n (in Kleinasien) *Cappadocia*

K·app- **~fenster** n **1.** *window in a vaulting-cell* **2.** *dormer-window, attic-window* **~hahn** m *capon* **~laken** n ⟨mar⟩ *primage* **~messer** n *cleaver* **~naht** f *lap-seam, flat seam* | ~ärmel [m] *fl.-s. sleeve*

k·appen vt [h] (Bäume) *to lop, poll, top*; gekappter Baum *pollard* | (Hähne etc) *to capon* | (Schuhe) *to (toe-)cap, to tip* ‖ (Strümpfe) *to heel* | (Tau, Mast) *to cut*

°**K·appes** m ~/~ **1.** (Kohlkopf) *white cabbage* **2.** ⟨fig⟩ ~! *nonsense!*

K·äppi n ~s/~s *military cap, kepi*

Kapr·iccio [–'pritʃo:] n ~s/~s ⟨mus⟩ *capriccio* **-·ice** [–sə] f ~/~n *whim, caprice, fancy* **-i·ole** f ~/~n ⟨hors⟩ *caper, leap* ‖ ⟨fig⟩ *mad trick, gambado* ‖ ~n m *to cut capers, caperings*; *to caper* (*about*) **kapriz·ieren,** sich ~ [h] (auf [acc]) *to set one's heart* (*on*), *to take* (*a th*) *into one's head, to be keen* (*on*), *to fancy* (*a th*) **kaprizi·ös** a *capricious, whimsical*

K·apsel f ~/~n ⟨bot, etc⟩ *capsule*; ⟨a–n⟩ abwerfbare ~ *ejection capsule* ‖ (Büchse) *box, case*; Flaschen≃ *bottle cap* ‖ ⟨pharm; a-n⟩ *capsule* ‖ ⟨tech, ceram⟩ *saggar*; (Gieß≃) *shell of mould* ‖ mit ~(n) versehen *to cap* **~ankupplung** f ⟨a-n⟩ *link-up* (an *with*) **~blitz** m ⟨phot⟩ *capsular flash* **~gebläse** n ⟨mot⟩ *valve compressor* **~maschine** f *bottle capping machine* **~mutter** f *capped nut* **k·apseln** vt/refl [h] *to cap* | sich ein|~ *or* ab|~ *to seclude, isolate o.s.*; er hat sich eingekapselt *he lives in seclusion*

°**kap·utt** a (S) *broken, in two*; *battered* (*mirror*), *smashed* (*glass*) ‖ (P) *ruined*; *done for*; ⟨fam⟩ *busted*; *down and out*; *shot*; *fagged out* ‖ ~ gehen ⟨sl⟩ *to go nuts* od *fut*, ⟨sl⟩ *to go to pot*; (mit Knall) *to go bang*; (verderben) *to spoil* ‖ (T) *to die* ‖ ~ m (zerbrechen) *to break* (~ gehen *to b. down*, ⟨mach, fam⟩ *to conk out*) ‖ (ruinieren) *to ruin*; sich ~ m *to wear o.s. out*; sich ~ arbeiten *to work one's head off*; ich bin völlig ~ *I'm done for*

Kap·uze f ~/~n *cap, hood* ‖ (Mönchs≃) ⟨ec⟩ *cowl, hood* **-z·iner** m ~s/~ *Capuchin* (*friar*) ‖ ⟨fig⟩ *cup of coffee with but a drop of milk* **~affe** m ⟨zoo⟩ *c.(-monkey)* **~kloster** n *C. convent* **~kraut** n ⟨bot⟩ *love-in-a-mist* **~kresse** f ⟨bot⟩ *nasturtium, Indian cress* **~mönch** m *C. monk* **~nonne** f *C. nun* **~orden** m *order of C.s* **~predigt** f *burlesque sermon*, ⟨fam⟩ *long lecture*

K·ar n ~s/~e ⟨bes Scot⟩ *corrie*; *cirque* Fr | ~see [m] *tarn*

K·ar- **~freitag** m *Good-Friday* **~samstag** m *Holy Saturday* **~woche** f *Passion* od *Holy Week*

Karab·iner m ~s/~ *car(a)bine* **~haken** m *snap-* od *spring-hook, swivel* **~schuh** m *c. bucket* **Karabin·ier** [karabin'je:] m ~s/~s *car(a)bineer*

Kar·affe f ~/~n *carafe, decanter, water-bottle*

Karak·orum-Kette f *Karakorum Rang*

Karambol·age [–'lɑ:ʒə] f ~/~n ⟨bill⟩ *cannon* ‖ ⟨fig⟩ *collision*; (P) *unfriendly encounter* **karambol·ieren** vi [h] (Billard) *to cannon*, ⟨Am⟩ *carom, carambole* ‖ ⟨fig⟩ *to collide* ‖ mit jdm ~ *to run against a p*

Karam·el m ~s/~e *cramel* | ~le [f] *toffee*

Kar·at n ~(e)s/~e *carat* **~gold** n *alloyed gold*

Kar·ate n ~s/~ *karate* (*self-defense*) **karat·ieren** vt [h] *to alloy* (*gold*) *with other metals*

-kar·ätig a [in comp] .. *carat* (*gold*, etc.); zwölf~ *twelve carats fine*

Kar·atschi n (Stadt an der Indusmündung) *Karachi, Currachee*

Kar·ausche f ~/~n ⟨ich⟩ *crucian*

Karaw·ane f ~/~n *caravan, safari* **~nstraße** f *c.-route* **Karawanser·ei** f ~/~en *c.sary*, (*c.*)*-serai*

Karaw·anken pl (südl. Ostalpenkette)

Karb·atsche f ~/~n *koorbash, leather scourge* ‖ ⟨hunt⟩ *hunting-crop*; *horse-whip* | ≃**n** vt [h] *to horse-whip, lash*

Karb·id n ~s/ *carbide* ‖ Kalzium≃ *calcium carbide* **~lampe** f *carbide lamp, acetylene lamp*

Karbolin·eum n ~s/ ⟨chem⟩ *carbolineum*

Karb·olsäure f ⟨chem⟩ *carbolic acid* ‖ mit ~ tränken *to carbolize*

Karb·on n ~s/ ⟨geol⟩ *carboniferous formation* | ~papier [n] (= Kohle–) [österr] *carbon* (⟨Am a.⟩ *copy*) *paper*

Karbon·ade f ~/~n *cutlet, chop*

Karbonis·ier-Ofen m ⟨met⟩ *carburizing furnace*; ⟨spin⟩ *carbonizing stove* **k-s·ieren** vt [h] ⟨spin⟩ *to carbonize* **K-s·ierung** f ~/ v Wollgeweben *wool cloth carbonizing*

Karb·unkel m ~s/~ ⟨med⟩ *carbuncle*

Kardam·om n ~s/ (ind. Gewürz) *cardamom*

Kard·an- **~achse** f *cardan shaft* **~antrieb** m ⟨tech⟩ *c. drive*; ⟨mot⟩ *shaft drive transmission* **~gelenk** n *c. joint*; *Hooke's joint* **~übertragung** f *system of transmission by c.* **~welle** f *c. shaft* | **k-nisch** a: ~e Aufhängung [f] *c.ic suspension, gimbals* pl; ~er Bügel [m] *gimbal*

Kard·ätsche f ~/~n *horse-brush, curry-comb* ‖ ⟨spin⟩ *card* | ~nführer [m] (Spannrahmen) *card tenter* | ≃**n** vt [h] (Pferd) *to curry* ‖ ⟨spin⟩ *to card, teasel* **K·arde** f ~/~n ⟨bot & tech⟩ *teasel, teazel, teazle* **~ndistel** f ⟨bot⟩ *teasel, card-thistle*; *shepherd's rod* od *staff* **k·arden, kard·ieren** vt [h] ⟨spin⟩ *to card, teasel*, etc. (→ Karde)

Kardin·al m ~(e)s/≃e *cardinal* ‖ ⟨orn⟩ *c.-bird* **~blume** f *Lobelia cardinalis* **~fehler** m *c. error* **~punkt** m *c.* (od *chief, salient*) *point* **~tugend** f *c. virtue* **~zahl** f *c. number* **~züge** m pl *salient features* **Kardinal·at** n ~(e)s/, **Kardin·alswürde** f *c.ship* **Kardin·als-** **~hut** m *c.'s hat* **~kollegium** n *college of c.s*

Kardio·ide f ⟨math⟩ (Herzkurve) *cardioid*

Kard·one f ~/~n (Artischocke) ⟨bot⟩ *cardoon*

Kar·elien n (Finnland & UdSSR) *Carelia* **Kar·elier** m *Carelian*

Kar·enz- **~frist** f ⟨ins⟩ *qualifying period* **~zeit** f ⟨com, ins⟩ *waiting time*; ⟨med⟩ *latent period*; *safety p.* ⟨a. at⟩

†**karess·ieren** vt [h] *to caress* ‖ *to flatter*

Karfi·ol m ~s/~e [sdd] ⟨bot⟩ *cauliflower*

Karf·unkel m ~s/~ ⟨med⟩ *carbuncle* ‖ ⟨minr⟩ (*garnet*) *carbuncle, almandine, pyrope*

k·arg a (sparsam) *parsimonious* ‖ (knauserig) *close, niggardly, stingy* ‖ (ärmlich) *scanty, paltry, poor* (*wages*); *spare* (*meal*); *slender* (*remains*); *sterile* (*soil*) ‖ ⟨fig⟩ ~ mit .. *sparing of* (*thanks*); nicht ~ mit *ungrudging in* (*praise*) | **~en** vi [h] (mit) *to be economical, parsimonious*; *spare, niggardly* od *stingy* (*with money*); *to be sparing* (*of words, thanks*) ‖ nicht ~ *to be lavish* (*with one's thanks*); *to be unsparing* (*in* od *of praise*; *in efforts*); er –gte nicht mit s–m Lob *his praise was generous* | ≃**heit** f ~/ *parsimony, stinginess, scantiness, sterility* ≃**lich** a & adv *sparing, scanty* [*-tily*], *poor, piteous, paltry* ‖ *slender* (*means*) ‖ *scanty, frugal, scrimpy, skimpy* (*meal*) ‖ *poverty-stricken* (*conditions*) | *he is wretchedly paid* ‖ etw ~ erhalten *to be starved of a th*

Kar·iben, kar·ibisch → Kar·aiben, kar·aibisch

kar·ieren vt [h] *to chequer* **kar·iert** a *checked, chequered*; *cross-lined*; ~es Muster *checker*; ~es Papier *squared* (od *quadrille ruled*) *paper* ‖ rot-weiß ~es Tuch *a red-and-white check* *cloth*; bunt (schottisch) ~er Stoff, ~es Muster *tartan*

Karikat·ur f ~/~en *caricature*; (Witzblatt≈) *cartoon* **~enreihe** f (Zeitung) *comic-strip*, ⟨fam⟩ *funnies* pl **~enzeichner** m *caricaturist*; *cartoonist* **karik·ieren** vt [h] *to caricature* ‖ (nachmachen) *to take off*

kari·ös a ⟨scient⟩ *carious* (*teeth*)

K·arische Meer, das (Teil des Nördl. Eismeers) *Sea of Kara*

karitat·iv [–f] a *eleemosynary*

Karlsruhe n ⟨Ger⟩ (Stadt in Baden)

K·armel m, Berg ~ (Palästina) *Mount Carmel*

Karmel·iter m ~s/~ ⟨ec⟩ *Carmelite* (*friar*)

karmes·in, karmois·in [–mwa–] a *crimson*

Karm·in n ~(e)s/ *carmine* **~blau** n *indigo-c.*

Karnati·on [–ts–] f ~/ ⟨paint⟩ *flesh-colour*

Karne·ol m ~(e)s/~e ⟨minr⟩ *cornelian*

K·arner m ~s/~ *ossuary*; *charnel-house*

K·arneval m ~s/~ (Fastnacht) *carnival*

°**Karn·ickel** n ~s/~ [niedd] ⟨zoo⟩ *rabbit* ‖ fruchtbar s wie die ~ *to breed like rabbits* ‖ °wer war das ~? *who began the quarrel?*; das ~ hat angefangen *the cat has done it* ‖ wer ist das ~ (der Sündenbock)? *who is the* (*scape*)*goat* ‖ °er ist ein ganzes ~ *he is quite an artful dodger*

Karn·ies [i:s] n ~es/~e [–zə] ⟨arch⟩ *cornice*, *ogee* ‖ verkehrt steigendes ~ *reversed o.* **~eisen** n ⟨carp⟩ *quirk o. iron* **~hobel** m *o.-plane*

K·arnische Alpen pl *Carnic Alps*

K·ärnten n *Carinthia* **K·ärntner** m, **~in** f, **kärntnerisch** a *Carinthian*

K·aro n ~s/~s *check*, *square* ‖ ⟨cards⟩ *diamonds* pl; ~-Sieben, ~-As *seven*, *ace of d.*; ~ ist Trumpf *d. are trumps* **~muster** n *chequers* pl

Kar·obe f ~/~n ⟨bot⟩ → Karube

Karol·inen pl (in Mikronesien) *Caroline Islands*, *Carolinas* pl

Kar·osse f ~/~n *state coach* **~r·ie** [–i:] f ~/~n [–i:ən] ⟨mot⟩ *car* od *carriage body*; *coach-work* ‖ Ganzstahl≈ *all-steel b.* ‖ geschlossene, offene ~ *enclosed*, *open b.* | ~bauer [m] *coach-builder*; ~blech [n] *b. sheet*; ~form [f] *body design* ~gerippe [n] *framework of b.*; ~werk [n] *car b. works* [sg konstr]

Karot·in n ~s/ *carotene* **Kar·otte** f ~/~n *carrot*

Karp·athen pl, **~gebirge** n (in SO.-Europa) *Carpathians* pl, *Carpathian Mountains* pl

K·arpfen m ~s/~ ⟨ich⟩ *carp* (⟨cul⟩ blau *dashed with vinegar*) | ~brut [f] *c.'s fry* ~teich [m] *c.-pond*

K·arre f ~/~n (→ Karren) *cart*; (Munitions- etc ≈) *dolly* ‖ °m–e ~ ⟨mot⟩ *my car*, ⟨cycl⟩ *my grid*; e–e entsetzliche ~ ⟨sl⟩ *an awful rattletrap*, *rattler*, *jigger*, *bike*; ⟨Am sl⟩ *flivver* ‖ (Schub≈) (*wheel*)*barrow*; e–e ~ schieben *to push a barrow*; (Hand≈) mit 2 Rädern *hand truck* od *cart*; elektrische ~ *electric t.* ‖ ⟨fig⟩ die ~ einfach laufen l *to let things slide*; die ~ war verfahren *we* (*they*) *were deep in the mud*, *things were completely muddled up*; die ~ in den Dreck fahren ⟨fam⟩ *to make a mess of it all*; die ~ aus dem Dreck ziehen *to clear up the m.*; sich vor die ~ spannen l v *to be used as tools*

Karr·ee n ~s/~s ⟨mil⟩ (*hollow*) *square* ‖ Tanz≈) *set* ‖ ein ~ formieren ⟨mil⟩ *to form* (*a*) *sq.*; ein ~ durchbrechen *to break through a sq.* ‖ ⟨cul⟩ *best end*; *sparerib* (*of pork*)

K·arren pl ⟨geol⟩ *clefts* (*in limestone*)

k·arren vi/t [h] *to cart*, *wheel*; *to remove .. on a cart*, etc. ‖ ⟨fam⟩ vi [h] *to drive slowly* ‖ vrfl; sich tot ~ *to tire o.s. with carting*, etc. **K·arren** m ~s/~ (→ Karre) (stark, mst 2rädrig) *c.*, *dray*(*-c.*); Dung-, Schutt≈ *tumbrel*, *-bril*; Milch≈, Fastnachts- *or* Faschings≈ etc *float* ‖ °⟨fig⟩ wir ziehen ja alle am selben ~ *we are all in one boat* ‖ °⟨fig⟩ der ~ steckt im Dreck ⟨fam⟩ *all the fat's in the fire* **~förderung** f *wheeling* **~gaul** m *c.-horse*; alter ~ *nag*, *old jade* **~gleise** n *c.-rut* **~kasten** m *body of the c.* **~ladung** f *c.-load* **~schieber** m *barrow-man* **~strafe** f *hard labour* **~zähler** m ⟨min⟩ *truck counter* **K·arrer** m ~s/~ Sw = Kärrner

°**Karr·ete** f ~/~n *rattletrap*; (*dear*) *old push-bike*

Karri·ere [–rj'e:rə] f ~/~n; in voller ~ *at full gallop*, *at a rattling pace* ‖ (Laufbahn) *career*; ~ m *to get on* (*in life*), *to work one's way up*, *to be successful*; darauf aus s bes schnell ~ z m *to be bent on advancement* ‖ jd, der ~ macht **~macher** m *careerist* | auf **~machen** versessen *career-minded* °**Karri·ole** f ~/~n *gig*, *fly*, *dog-cart* | °≈n vi [h] [bei Zielangabe: s] *to drive* od *race* **K·ärrner** m ~s/~ *carter*, *drayman*; *carrier*

K·arst[1] m ~(e)s/~e ⟨hort⟩ *mattock*, (*prong*) *hoe* | ≈en *to hoe*

Karst[2] m ~(e)s/ *karst* (*in Istria*, etc.).

Kart·ätsche f ~/~n *grape-shot* | ≈n vt/i [h] *to shoot with g.-s.* **K-n-** ~feuer [n] *g.-s. fire* ~kugel [f] *ball for g.-s.*; ~schuß [m] *g.-s.*

Kart·aune f ~/~n ⟨mil hist⟩ *cannon-royal*

Kart·ause f ~/~n *Carthusian monastery* | ≈r m ~s/~ *C.* (*friar*) ‖ ~likör [m] **1.** (Angehöriger des ~ordens) *Carthusian* **2.** (~likör) *chartreuse*; ~nelke [f] ⟨bot⟩ *C. pink*; ~pulver [n] *C. powder*

K·arte f ~/~n **A.** *card* **1.** (Ausweis-, Eintritts-≈) (*admission-*, *theatre-*) *ticket* ‖ Bahnsteig≈ *platform ticket*; Fahr≈ *railway ticket* **2.** (Wand- *wall-*, Land≈) *map* ‖ Generalstabs≈ *ordnance map*; Luftbild≈ *air survey map*, ⟨Am⟩ *aerial map* | (See-, Stern-, Wetter≈) *chart* ‖ ⟨rail⟩ Übersichts≈ *rough railway map* ‖ *motoring map* **3.** Tanz≈ *programme*, *card* ‖ (Besuchs-, Visiten≈) *visiting card* | Speise≈ *bill of fare*, *menu* (*card*); Tages≈ (*list of*) *day's specials*; Wein≈ *wine-list*; nach der ~ *à la carte* Fr **4.** Paket≈ *parcel form*; Post≈ *post-card*; Glückwunsch≈ *greeting-card*; ~ mit Rückantwort *reply-card* | Kartei≈ *index card* **5.** ⟨cards⟩ *playing card* **B. 1.** ~ abbestellen *to cancel a booking*; **e-e ~ lösen,** knipsen *to book*, *to punch a ticket* **2. e-e ~ aufziehen** *to mount a map*, (auf Leinwand -gezogen) *linen map*; e–e ~ anlegen v *to map* (*a district*); auf k–r ~ verzeichnet *unchartered*, *unmapped*; der ~ nach *by the map* (*this road seems to be shorter*); es durch ~n darstellen *to map it* **3.** er **gab s-e Besuchs≈ ab** *he left his card*; sie schickten zu ihrer Verlobung k–e ~n *they sent out no engagement-cards* | wir essen nach der ~ *we lunch à la carte*; Herr Ober, die ~ bitte! *waiter, give me the bill of fare, please* **4.** ⟨cards⟩ **ein Spiel ~n** *a pack of cards*; ~ spielen *to play* (*at*) *cards*; (~n) abheben (mischen, geben) *to cut* (*shuffle*, *deal*) (*the cards*); wer gibt ~n? *whose deal is it?* e–e hohe, niedrige ~ ausspielen *to play a high*, *low card*; e–e Grand≈ [etwa] *a nap hand*; e–e Grand≈ aus der Hand spielen [etwa] *to go nap* ⟨a. fig⟩; schlechte ~n bek *to get a bad hand*; er behielt alle guten ~n in der Hand *he kept all the trumps in his hand*; die ~n hinlegen *to put all one's cards on the table*, ⟨fam⟩ *to show down*; sich nicht in die ~n gucken l *to hide one's hand*; auf e–e ~ setzen *to back a card* | ⟨**fig**⟩ auf die falsche ~ **setzen** *to bet on the wrong horse*; alles auf e–e ~ setzen *to stake all in one venture* od *on one throw*, *to have all one's eggs in one basket*; die ~n durchschauen *to see through a th*; jdm in die ~n sehen *to s. thr. a p's game*; die ~n aufdecken *to show* od *expose one's hand* (*prematurely*); mit offenen ~n spielen *to put one's cards on the table*, *to play with open cards* | die ~n **legen** *or* **schlagen** *to tell fortunes*; jdm die ~ legen *to tell a p's fortune from the cards* **Kart·ei** f ~/~en *card-register*, *-catalogue*, *-index*, *-file* ‖ *filing cabinet* ‖ Haupt≈ *master file* | ~karte [f] *i. card*; ~karton [m] *i. c.-board*; ~kasten [m] *c. index box*; ~kenngruppe [f] *records control symbol* **Kart·ell** n ~(e)s/~e **1.** ⟨com⟩ *cartel*, ⟨bes Am⟩ (Kontrollgesellschaft) *trust*, (vorübergehender Zus–schluß) *pool*, (Absatzorganisation) *syndicate*, ⟨Am⟩ *ring*, ~mitglied *ringster* **2.** (Forderung) *challenge*; ~ tragen *to bear* od *deliver a challenge* | ~bruder [m] ⟨Ger univ⟩ *member of an allied students' corps*; ~träger [m] *second who delivers a challenge*; ~verband [m] *federation of student's corps*; ~system, ~wesen [n] *cartelism* **kartellis·ieren** vt [h] *to cartelize, concentrate* **K·arten-** **~ablage** f ⟨comp⟩ *being ejected from the machine* **~art** f ⟨comp etc⟩ *class of card* **~ausgabe** f *booking-office*, ⟨Am⟩ *ticket-window* **~ausrüstung** f *map outfit, chart equipment* **~ausschnitt** m *map section* **~auswahl** f ⟨comp⟩ *card selection* **~auswerfer** m ⟨typ⟩ *card-dropper* **~bild** n *figure on a card* | ~anzeiger [m] ⟨radar⟩ *plan position indicator* (*PPI*) **~blatt** n (*single*) *card, map*, etc, *chart sheet* **~brief** m *card-letter, l.-c.* **~durchgang** m ⟨comp⟩ *card passage* **~entfernung** f *map range* **~entwurf** m ⟨comp⟩ *form and card design* **~folie** f (transparent z Ablesen) *overlay* **~halter** m *map holder* **~haus** n; s–e Pläne stürzten zus wie ein ~ *his plans collapsed like a house of cards*; ⟨fig⟩ *castles* pl *in Spain, castle in the air* ‖ ⟨mar⟩ *chart-house* **~könig** m ⟨cards⟩ *king* ‖ ⟨fig⟩ *mock* od *trumpery king* **~künstler** m *c.-juggler* **~kunststück** n *c.-trick* **~legekunst** f *cartomancy* **~lese-** u Stanzeinheit f ⟨comp⟩ *card reader and punched card output* **~locher** m *card punch* (*control unit*) **~lochung** f (direkt) ⟨comp⟩ "*direct to card*" | ~s-Steuereinheit [f] *c. p. control unit* **~macher** m *c.-maker* ‖ (Zeichner) *m.-maker*, ⟨scient⟩ *cartographer* **~magazin** n ⟨comp⟩ (⟨a.⟩ –zuführung) *hopper* **~maler** m *c.painter* **~maßstab** m *scale of the m.* **~material** n *maps and charts* **~mischen** n *shuffling* (*of c.s*) **~mischer** m *collator* **~paket** n (⟨a.⟩ –satz [m]) ⟨comp⟩ *card deck* **~papier** n *c.-paper, thin c.board* **~pappe** f *c.board* **~reiter** m (*card*) *index tab* **~satz** m *set of cards* **~schlagen** n *fortune-telling from c.s* **~schläger** m ⟨weav⟩ *c. cutter* **~schlägerin** f *fortune-teller from c.s* **~schlagmaschine** f ⟨weav⟩ *c. punching machine* **~signatur** f (~zeichen [pl]) *conventional signs* **~spiel** n *game of c.s* ‖ (die Karten) *pack of c.s* ‖ (das Spielen) *c.-playing*; beim ~ *over c.s* **~ständer** m *c. rack* **~stanzer** m *monitor printer*, ⟨comp⟩ *card punch* (*output operates at a speed of 100 cards per minute*) **~stapel** m *batch*; mischt 2 ~ *merges two sets of cards* **~stecher** m *geographical engraver, engraver of maps and charts* **~stelle** f *map section*; *mapping office* **~takt** m ⟨comp⟩ *normal machine card cycle* **~tasche** f ⟨mil, etc.⟩ *m.-case, m.-holder*; (für Besuchs~) *c.-case* **~verkauf** m beginnt um 7 Uhr *the booking office opens at 7 o'clock* **~vordruck** m *map blank* **~winkelmesser** m *m. protractor* **~zähler** m (S) ⟨comp⟩ *card counting feature* **~zeichen** n *map symbol* **~zeichnen** n *m. drawing, cartography* **~zeichner** n *cartographer* **~zufuhr** f ⟨comp⟩ *being fed into the machine*; k–e ~ *cards not ready for punching* **~zuführung** f (S) ⟨comp⟩ *hopper* **kart·ieren** vt [h] *to plot a map*; *to enter on a map*

kartesi·anisch a *Cartesian* (*philosophy*; ⟨math⟩ *methods*); ~er Taucher *bottle-imp*

†**Karth·ager** m, **~in** f, **karth·agisch** a *Carthaginian*

Karth·ago n *Carthago, Carthage*

Kart·offel f ~/~n *potato*, ⟨sl⟩ *murphy*; Früh~n *early p.es*; mehlige, glasige ~n *mealy, glassy p.es*; Pell~n, ~n in der Schale *p.es* pl *in their jackets*; Röst~n *roast p.es* ‖ ~n schälen *to peel p.es* | °⟨fig⟩ ~ (= Taschenuhr) *turnip*; er hat e–e ~ im Gesicht *he has a nose like a boiled turnip* ‖ °(Loch im Strumpf) *potato* ‖ °'rin in die ~n, 'raus aus den ~n! *he* (etc) *is blowing hot and cold* **~ausgraber** m *p. grubber* od *digger* **~aushebepflug** m *p. digger* **~bau** m *cultivation of p.es* **~bauer** m *p. grower, cultivator of p.es* **~branntwein** m *p.-brandy* **~brei** m = ~mus **~brennerei** f *starch spirit distillery* **~käfer** m *p.-beetle* **~kloß** m *p.-dumpling* **~krankheit** f *p.-rot* **~kraut-** u Knollenfäule f *late blight* **~krebs** m *p. cancer* **~legemaschine** f *p. planting machine* **~löffel** m *Parisian spoon* **~mehl** n *p.-flour* **~miete** f *clamp* **~motte** f ⟨ent⟩ *tuber-worm* **~mus** n *mashed p.es* pl **~presse** f *ricer* **~puffer** m *p.-pancake* **~pür·ee** n = ~mus **~salat** m *p.-salad* **~schälmaschine** f *p. peeler* **~schlempe** f *distiller's wash* **~schnitten,** geröstete ~ (*pommes frites*) *crisps* pl, (*pommes soufflées*) *chips* **~schorf** m *p. scab* **~sort·iermaschine** f *p. sorter* **~suppe** f *p.-soup* **~stärke** f *p. starch*

Karto- **~gr·amm** n ~s/~e ⟨stat⟩ *map* **~gr·aph** m ~en/~en *map-maker, cartographer* **~graph·ie** f ~/ *cartography, mapmaking* **~gr·aphisch** a *cartographic*(*al*); ~e Abteilung [f] *map-department* **Kart·on** [–'tɔŋ] m ~s/~s (Pappe) *cardboard, pasteboard* ‖ (Schachtel) *cardboard box* ‖ ⟨arts⟩ *cartoon* ‖ ⟨bookb⟩ *boards* pl | ~fabrik [f] *board mill* | ~gerahmt [a] ⟨phot⟩ *card-mounted* (Dia); ~papier [n] *card*; ~pappe [f] *box-board* **Karto·n·age** [–'na:ʒə] f ~/~n *cardboard* ‖ ~n [pl] *c. boxes* | ~nfabrik [f] *c.* (*box*) *factory, board mill*; *cardbox manufacturing*; ~nmaschine [f] *cardboard* od *cardbox machine*; ~npappe [f] *box board*; ~nwaren [f pl] *cardboard articles* pl **karto·n·ieren** vt [h] *to bind in boards, to board* ‖ –rt *in boards*; in Leinen –rt *in cloth boards*; flexibel –rtes Buch *paperback* **Kartoth·ek** f ~/~en = Kartei **Kart·usch-** ~beutel [m] *cartridge-bag*; ~hülse [f] *cartridge case*; ~raum [m] *powder room*; *cartridge chamber*; ~vorlage [f] ⟨artill⟩ *flash reducer* **Kart·usche** f ~/~n (Patrone) *cartridge* | ~nornament [n] ⟨arch⟩ *cartouche* Fr

Kar·ube f ~/~n ⟨bot⟩ *carob*

Karuss·ell n ~(e)s/~s & ~e *merry-go-round, roundabout*; ⟨Am⟩ *carousal, carrousel* Fr

Karyat·ide f ~/~n ⟨arts⟩ *caryatid*

K·arzer m ~s/~ *students' prison, lock-up*; 3 Tage ~ *three days of detention*

Karzin·om n ~s/~e ⟨path⟩ *carcinoma* L

ˣ**Kas** [a:] m *cheese* | ⟨fig sl⟩ *rot*; *damn th*

K·asack m ~(e)s/~e ⟨tail⟩ *house smock* | ~schürze [f] *shortie overall*

Kas·an, K·asan n (an der Wolga) *Kazan, Kasan*

Kaschel·ott m ~(e)s/~e *cachalot, sperm whale*

ˣ°**Kasch·emme** f ~/~n, *thieves' den* ‖ *low pub*; *ale-, pot-, mug-house*; ⟨Am⟩ *joint, dive*

K·äscher m ~s/~ → Kescher

kasch·ieren vt [h] ⟨phot⟩ *to mount*; –rt *coated with paper*, etc ‖ ~e Folie *backed foil* | ⟨tail⟩ *to bond, back*

K·aschmir **1.** n (vorderind. Provinz) *Cashmere* **2.** m ~s/ (Stoff) *cashmere*

K·aschu- **~nuß** f *cashew-nut*

Kasch·ube m ~n/~n ⟨geog⟩ *Kashoub, Kashoob*

K·äse m ~s/~ *cheese* ‖ weißer ~ = Quark; Mager~, Fett~ *lean, rich ch.*; Streich~ *ch. spread* ‖ Backstein-, Holländer~, Schweizer~, Rahm~ *baked, Dutch, Swiss, cream ch.* ‖ der ~ ist durch .. *ripe*; Butterbrot u ~ *ch. and bread and butter* | ⟨fig fam⟩ mach' *or* red' nicht solchen ~ *don't talk such rot*; ~! *nonsense*! ‖ drei~hoch ⟨fam⟩ *not bigger than twopenny loaves* ‖ °⟨fig⟩ (Uhr) *kettle, turnip* **~artig** a *caseous* **~auflauf** m ⟨cul⟩ *ch.-soufflé* **~bäcker** m *ch. baker* **~bildung** f *caseation* **~blatt** n (Zeitung) ⟨dero⟩ *rag paper*; *pulp* **~bohrer** m *ch.-taster* **~butter** f *ch.-curds* pl **~fliege** f *ch.-fly* **~form** f *ch.-mould* **~glocke** f *ch.-(plate) cover* **~händler(in** f) m *ch.monger* **~hürde** f *ch.-crate* **~kammer** f *ch.-room, dairy* **~kuchen** m *ch.-cake* **~lab** n *rennet* **~laib** m *whole ch.* **~made** f *ch.-hopper*, (bes in Gorgonzola) *maggot* **~messer** n *ch.-knife* ‖ ⟨mil hum⟩ *dagger, poniard, bayonet*; ⟨hum⟩ *pig-sticker ch.-toaster* **~milbe** f *ch.-mite* **~napf** m *ch.-bowl, ch.-vat* **~platte** f *ch.-tray* **~rinde** f *ch.-paring, rind of ch.* **~schimmel** m *blue-mould* **~schnitte** f, geröstete ~ *Welsh rarebit* od *rabbit* **~stange** f *ch.-straw* **~teller** m *ch.-plate*

~törtchen n *ch.-tartlet* **≃weiß** a ⟨fig⟩ *deadly pale,* (*as*) *white as a sheet* od *ghost* **~wirtschaft** f *ch.-dairy* **Kase·in** n ~s/ *casein* **k·äsen** vi/t [(P) h & (S) s] *to curd, curdle*; die Milch käst .. *curdles* | Milch ~ *to turn milk into cheese* **Käser·ei** f ~/~en *ch.-dairy* | *ch. making* **k·äsig** a *ch.-like, cheesy; caseous* ‖ ⟨fig⟩ *deadly pale; cheesy* (*complexion*)

Kasem·atte f ~/~n *casemate* **Kas·erne** f ~/~n *barracks* pl ‖ ⟨fig⟩ (*rabbit-*)*warren, barrack* **Ka-s·ernen-** **~arrest** m *confinement to* od *detention in b.s* **≃artig** a *b.-like* (*building*); ~es Haus *a b. of a house* **~dienst** m *b.-service* **~hof** m *b.s-square* | ~blüten [f pl] ⟨fig⟩ *drill-sergeants' jokes* od *bulls; Tommy Atkins's choice expressions, sayings* od *language* **~inspektor** m *b. master* **~stube** f *b. room* **kasern·ieren** vt [h] *to put into b.s*; **-iert** *quartered in b.s* **Kas·ino** n ~s/~s *club*(*-house*), *casino* ‖ ⟨mil⟩ *mess* ‖ (in Bädern) (*assembly-*)*rooms* pl

Kask·ade f ~/~n *cascade* | ~ngebirge [n] (U.S.A.) *Cascade Range* ~nschaltung [f] ⟨el⟩ *c. connection*; ~numformer [m] *c. converter*

K·asko m ~s/~s ⟨mar⟩ *hull* | ~versicherung [f] ⟨mar, aero⟩ *hull insurance*; ⟨mot⟩ *collision coverage*

K·asperle n ~s/~s *Punch* ‖ ~ u Käthchen *P. and Judy* | ~theater [n] *P.-and-J.* (*show*) ‖ ⟨Am⟩ *puppet theater*

K·aspische Meer, das *the Caspian Sea*

k·assa adv (*to buy*) *cash down* **K·assa** f ~/ ⟨com⟩ *cash; ready money*; per ~ *for* od *in cash* ‖ ~ gegen (Verladungs-)Dokumente *cash against* (*shipping*) *documents* **~geschäft** n *cash-* od *ready-money business*; *dealings for c.* od *m.* **~lieferung** f *spot delivery* **~preis** m *cash-price* **~scheck** m *cash order*

Kassati·on f ~/~en ⟨jur⟩ *annullation, cassation* ‖ (Entlassung) *discharge, dismissal* **~shof** m ⟨jur⟩ *Court of C.* **~gesuch** n *petition of appeal*

Kass·awa f ~/ ⟨bot⟩ *cassava, manioc*

K·asse f ~/~n *money-, cash-, strong-box*; (*money-*)*chest, safe* ‖ (Ort) *pay-* od *cash-office* od *-desk* ‖ (Schalter) ⟨rail⟩ *ticket-o.*, ⟨theat, film⟩ *booking o.* ‖ (im Restaurant) an der ~ *at the desk* ‖ (Laden, Schublade) *till* ‖ (Spiel) *pool* ‖ Gemeinde-(Unterstützungs)≃ *community chest* ‖ (Geld) *cash; ready money*; sofortige ~ ⟨bes Am⟩ *spot cash* | Bitte **zur** ~! *pay at the desk, please*; (im Laden, Aufschrift: ~) *pay here*! (Bank) **an** der ~ *over the counter* ‖ per ~ *prompt cash*; **bei** ~ s *to be in cash* od *in funds, to be flush of money*; immer b. ~ s ⟨sl⟩ *to be oofy*; wie ist er bei ~? *how is he off for money*?; nicht *or* schlecht bei ~ s *to be out of* od *short of cash*; ⟨fam⟩ .. *in low water* od .. *hard up,* .. *stumped,* .. *broke* | die ~ **führen** *to act as cashier, to keep the cash* (*accounts*) ‖ ~ m *to make up the cash-account* ‖ gemeinschaftliche ~ *common purse* ‖ ⟨theat⟩ volle ~n m *to fill* (⟨fam⟩ *to sell out*) *the house* **K·assen-** **~abschluß** m *closing of* (*cash-*)*accounts, c.-balance* **~anweisung** f *c. order*; (Schatzanweisung) *treasury bill* **~arzt** m *panel-doctor*; zum ~ gehen ⟨fam⟩ *to go on the p.* ‖ amtliche Liste der ≃e *panel* **~beamte(r)** m *c.ier, teller* **~beleg** m *c. voucher* **~bericht** m *balance sheet* **~-bestand** m *c.* od *b. in hand, c. b., b. in c.* **~betrug** m *embezzlement* **~bilanz** f *b. of c.*; ~ m *to b. the c.* †**~billett** n = ~schein, ~anweisung **~block** m ⟨com⟩ *cash pad* **~bote** m *bank messenger* **~buch** n *c. book* **~darlehen** n *money loan* **~defizit** n *deficit of money* **~dieb** m *peculator, embezzler* **~diebstahl** m *peculation, embezzlement* **~erfolg** m ⟨theat⟩ (*she got a big*) *box-office* **~führer** m *c.ier, treasurer* **~führung** f *c.-keeping* **~kladde** f *c. diary* **~konto** n *c. account* **~kontrollapparat** m *c. register* **~patient** m *panel-patient, panelite* **~posten** m *c. entry* ‖ zur **~praxis** zugelassen *on the panel* **~preis** m *c. price* **~quittung** f *receipt* **~rechnung** f *c. account* **~revision** f (*c.-*)*audit*(*ing*) **~revisor** m (*official*) *auditor* **~schein** m = -anweisung **~schlager** m *bestseller* **~schrank** m *safe, strong-box* **~stück** n ⟨theat⟩ *stock-piece, play drawing full houses* **~sturz** m *audit,* ~ m *make up the c.* **~verwaltung** f ⟨mil⟩ *paymaster's office* **~wart** m *treasurer* **~zettel** m *coupon*

K·assel n ⟨Ger⟩ (Stadt) *Cassel*

Kasser·olle f ~/~n *stew-pan, saucepan*

Kass·ette f ~/~n *deed-, cash-, strong-box* ‖ (für Wertsachen) *casket* ‖ ⟨arch⟩ *coffer* (*of a ceiling*) ‖ ⟨phot⟩ *plate-holder, dark-slide*; *film magazine*; (*film-pack*) *adapter* **Kass·etten-** **~decke** f *coffered ceiling* **~schleuse** f ⟨phot⟩ *pass box* **~schlitten** m ⟨phot⟩ *dark-slide carriage* **Kass·ier(er)** m ~s/~e (~) *cashier*; ⟨bank⟩ *teller*; *treasurer*; *booking clerk* **≃en**[1] vt/i [h] *to collect,* (*en*)*cash*

kass·ieren[2] vt [h] (entlassen) *to cashier* (*officers*), *dismiss, discharge* ‖ (ungültig erklären) *to annul* ‖ (Urteil) *to rescind, quash, to set aside* **Kass·ierung** f ~/~en (Ungültigkeitserkärung) *annulment, cassation* ‖ (Entlassung) *discharge*

Kass·uben m pl = Kasch·uben

Kastagn·ette [kastan'jetə] f ~/~n; [pl] *castanets* **Kast·anie** f ~/~n *chestnut* ‖ wilde ~ *horse-ch.* ‖ Edel≃ *edible ch.*; gebratene ~n, ganz heiß! *roasted ch.s*! ‖ ⟨fig⟩ die ~n für jdn aus dem Feuer holen *to pull the chestnuts out of the fire for a p*; *to be a p's cat's paw*; *to do a p's dirty work* **Ka-st·anien-** **~baum** m ⟨bot⟩ *ch.*(*-tree*); Edel≃ *sweet* od *Spanish ch.*; Roß≃ *horse ch.* **~braun** n *ch.*(*-colour*) **≃braun** a *auburn* (*hair*), *ch.* (*hair, horse*) **~reis** m ⟨cul⟩ *pudding of puréed ch.s and whipped cream* **~schale** f *ch.-skin* **~wald** m *ch.-grove*

K·ästchen n ~s/~ *little chest* od *box* ‖ (für Wertsachen) *casket*

K·aste f ~/~n *caste* **~ndünkel, ~ngeist** m *caste-feeling, exclusiveness, spirit of caste*

kast·eien vt [h] *to chastise, mortify* ‖ **sich** ~ *to mortify one's flesh,* ⟨fig⟩ *to deny o.s. everything, to macerate o.s.* **Kast·eiung** f ~/~en *chastisement, maceration, mortification, self-castigation*; *austerity*; *severe self-discipline*

×**K·äste** [mst -ʃte] f ~/~n = Kastanie

Kast·ell n ~(e)s/~e *citadel, castle, castellet*; (*Roman*) *fortification*; *stronghold* ‖ ⟨naut hist⟩ (Vorder≃, Hinter≃) *forecastle, aftcastle* **Kastel-l·an** m ~s/~e *castellan* ‖ (Haushofmeister) *steward, majordomo* | **~in** [f] ~/~nen *chatelaine*

°**Kastelmacher** m (Italiener) *Ity,* ⟨Am⟩ *dago*

K·asten m ~s/~ & ≃ **1.** *box, case* ‖ *crate* (*of beer*) ‖ (Schrank) *chest, cabinet, cupboard, wardrobe* ‖ (Truhe) *trunk* ‖ (f Musikinstrumente) *case* ‖ ⟨typ⟩ *case* ‖ (f Kleintiere) *hutch* ‖ (einer Trommel) *barrel* ‖ (Futterkiste) *bin* ‖ (Gehäuse) *housing, case* ‖ ⟨min⟩ *timbering* ‖ (Schub≃) *drawer* **2.** ⟨fig fam⟩ alter ~ (Haus) *wretched hovel* ‖ Noahs ~ *Noah's Ark* ‖ er hat Kisten u ~ voll *he has more than he knows what to do with* ‖ er bekam 3 Tage ~ *he got 3 days arrest* ‖ °(dicke Frau) *strapping wench* **3.** °etw (Grips) auf dem ~ h ⟨fam⟩ *to have gumption,* ⟨Am⟩ *to h. it on the ball* **·Abfall**≃ *refuse box*; Armen≃ *poor-box*; Asch≃ *dustbin, ash-pan* **B·au**≃ *box of bricks* **B·ienen**≃ *wooden beehive* **Bl·umen**≃ *window box* **Br·ief**≃ *letter-, pillar-,* (⟨Am⟩ *mail-*) *b.*; e-n Brief in den ~ werfen *to post* (⟨Am⟩ *mail*) *a l.* **Br·unnen**≃ *water-cistern* **F·arb**≃ *colour* od *paint-box, box of water-colours* **F·orm**≃ *casting box* **G·eld**≃ *strong-box, money-box, safe, coffer* **H·obel**≃ *plane stock* **Kar-t·ei**≃ *card-index drawer* od *cabinet* **K·eim**≃ *malting floor* **Klav·ier**≃ *case of a piano* **K·ohlen(einfüll)-**≃ *coal-box,* (*scuttle*) **K·utsch**≃ *boot of a coach* **La-f·etten**≃ ⟨mil⟩ *trail-box* **N·ummern**≃ (f die Klingel) *annunciator, call-bells* pl **·Öl**≃ *oil bath* **·Orgel-**≃ *organ-case* **Patr·onen**≃ *cartridge* od *ammunition box* **R·ing**≃ (Fassung) *bezel, collet* **Sch·all**≃ *resonance box, sound-body, resonating body* od *chamber* ‖ Schmuck≃ *coffer*; in .. legen *to coffer* ‖ Schau≃ *show-case* ‖ Schr·ift≃, S·etz≃ ⟨typ⟩

letter-case || Souffl·eur≗ *prompter's box* || Sp·ül≗ *flush-box* **Verband**≗ (*medical and surgical*) *pannier, ambulance box* || W·asser≗ *water tank, water basin* || Zig·arren≗ *cigar-box* || Z·irkel≗ *compass case, drawing instrument case* **K·asten-** **~aufsatz** m *box* **~balken** ⟨nav⟩ *box-beam* **~bett** n *box-form bed* **~biegepresse** f *body forming machine* **~damm** m *coffer dam* **~deckel** m *lid of a box* **~drachen** m *box-kite* **~form** f *flask mould* **~fußrampe** f ⟨theat⟩ *magazine footlights* **~gebläse** n *chest blowing machine* **~gehänge** n *bucket hanger*; ~ mit Boden-(Seiten)entleerung *bottom-(side-)dump b.* **~geist** m → Kaste **~gestell** n *stand of boxes* **~glühung** f ⟨met⟩ *close annealing* **~guß** m *flask* od *box casting* **~herrschaft** f → Kaste **~kamera** f *box-camera* **~karren** m *trunk barrow* **~kette** f *bucket chain* **~kipper** m *dump tip box wagon* **~lafette** f *box-trail carriage* **~lautsprecher** m *cabinet loudspeaker* **~magazin** n (*rifle*) *magazine* **≗mäßig** a → Kaste **~oberlicht** n *battens* **~reflektor** m ⟨theat⟩ *open footlight* **~schloß** n *case* od *box lock* **~wagen** m *box cart*; *trolly, drag*; ⟨rail⟩ *lorry* **~werk** n ⟨arch⟩ *coffer-work* **~zimmerung** f ⟨min⟩ die ~ schlagen *to jam props and stalls* pl

K·äste(nbaum m) f [südd] = Kastanie(nbaum)

Kastili·aner m, **~in** f ⟨Span⟩ *Castilian* (*woman*) **kastili·anisch, kast·ilisch** a *Castilian* **Kast·ilien** n *Castile* **Kast·ilier** m → Kastilianer

K·astor m ~s/ ⟨zoo⟩ *castor, beaver* || ⟨astr⟩ *C.* **~hut** m *beaver-hat, c.* **~öl** n ⟨med⟩ *castor-oil*

Kastr·at m ~en/~en *castrate*; *eunuch* **kastr·ieren** vt [h] *to castrate, emasculate*

Kasu·alien pl *extra-duties* pl || *casual fees* pl

Kasu·ar m ~(e)s/~e ⟨orn⟩ *cassowary* → Emu

Kasu·ist m ~en/~en *casuist* | **~ik** f *casuistry* | **≗isch** a *casuistic*(*al*)

K·asus m ~/~ *case*; ~ Nominativus *or* Rektus ⟨gram⟩ *nominative c.*; obliquer ~ *oblique c.* | ~endung [f] *c.-termination*; ~regeln [f pl] *rules* pl *about c.s*

Kata- **~f·alk** m ~(e)s/~e *catafalque* **~k·austik** f ~/~en ⟨phys⟩ (Brennlinie) *catacaustic curve* **~k·omben** f pl *catacombs* pl **≗l·ektisch** a ⟨pros⟩ *catalectic* **~l·og** m ~(e)s/~e *catalogue*, ⟨Am⟩ *catalog* || e–n ~ aufstellen v *to catalogue* (*a library*) **≗logis·ieren** vt [h] *to catalogue* **~lys·ator** m ~s/–sat·oren ⟨chem⟩ *catalysator, catalyser, catalyst, activator* **~l·yse** f ~/~n ⟨chem⟩ *catalysis* **~phor·ese** f ~/~n *cataphoresis* **~p·ult** m ~s/~e ⟨ant, aero⟩ *catapult* || *launching rail* || preßluftgetriebener (pulvergetriebener) ~ *compressed air* (*powder*) *impulse c.* || mit dem ~ abschießen *or* starten *to catapult, to launch by c.* | ~flugzeug [n] ⟨mar⟩ (auf Fl.z.trägern) *catafighter*; ~sitz [m] ⟨aero⟩ *ejector seat*; ~start [m] *c. launch* **≗pult·ieren** vt [h] ⟨aero, etc⟩ *to launch* **~r·akt** m ~(e)s/~e *cataract, water-fall* || ⟨path⟩ (grauer Star) *cataract* **Kat·arrh** m ~(e)s/~e *catarrh* || Bronchial≗ *a cold on the chest, bronchitis*; (Schnupfen) *a cold in the head* **katarrh·alisch** a ⟨scient⟩ *catarrhal* **Kata-** **≗stroph·al** a & adv *catastrophic* (*situation*); *diastrous* (*result*) || ⟨übtr⟩ *devastating, overwhelming* || ⟨fam⟩ *awful* **~str·ophe** f ~/~n *catastrophe, disaster* || ⟨theat Lit⟩ *dénouement* Fr | ~nbekämpfung [f] *disaster control*; ~nflucht [f] *exodus*; ~nhilfe [f] *d. unit* od *crew*; *d. relief* [abstr]; ~nschutz [m] *incident* od *damage control* N

Katal·ane m → Katalonier

Katal·aunische Felder n pl (bei *Châlons-sur-Marne*) *Catalaunian Fields*

Katal·onien n *Catalonia* **Katal·onier** m, **~in** f, **katal·onisch** a *Catalan, Catalonian*

Kat·aster m & n ~s/~ ⟨engl⟩ [gibt es nicht]; etwa: *land-register* || ⟨engl⟩ (Steuerregister) *register of assessment* | ~amt [n] *l.-r. office*; ~auszug [m] *extract from the l.-r.*

K·ate f ~/~n *cottage, cot*, → Kätner || ⟨dero⟩ *hovel*

Kat- **~ech·ese** [–ç–] f ~/~n *catechizing* **~tech·et** [–ç–] m ~en/~en *catechist* | **≗isch** [a] *catechetic* **~echisati·on** [ts] f ~/~en *catechization* **≗echis·ieren** vt [h] *to catechize* **~ech·ismus** m ~/–men *catechism* **~echum·en(e)** m ~en/~en *catechumen* **~egor·ie** [i:] f ~/~n [–i:ən] *category, order* || ~n [pl] ⟨philos⟩ *categories, predicaments* || das gehört nicht in diese *or* zu dieser ~ *that does not belong in this category*; unter e–e ~ bringen *to blanket* **≗eg·orisch** a ⟨philos⟩ *categorical* (*imperative*) || e–m Vorschlag ein ~es „Nein“ entgegensetzen *to veto a proposal categorically* || ~ fordern *to demand imperatively*

K·atechu n ~s/ ⟨pharm⟩ *catechu* || ~pastille, ~pille [f] *cachou*

K·ater m ~s/~ *male* (od *tom-*)*cat* || gestiefelter ~ *Puss-in-Boots* | ⟨fig⟩ (P) *growling bear* | ⟨fig fam⟩ *crapulence, headache from last night's carouse*, ⟨Am⟩ *hangover*; e–n ~ h *to be blue* (*green, yellow*) *about the gills*; *to feel seedy* od *cheap* (od *like the morning after the night before*) || moralischer ~ *dejection*; *dejected state of mind*; *self-reproach* **~frühstück** n *breakfast after the night before*; ⟨Am⟩ *hangover b.* **~idee** f *rum, mad* od *foolish idea*; *absurdity*

Kath·arsis f ~/ ⟨Lit⟩ *catharsis*; *purgation*

Kath- **~·eder** m & n ~s/~ (*professor's*) *lecturing-desk, pulpit* || ⟨fig⟩ *professorial chair* || vom ~ *ex cathedra* | ~blüte [f] *pulpit flower of rhetoric, professor's unintentional funny statement*; ~held [m] *learned disputant*; ~sozialismus [m] *academic socialism, socialism of the chair*; ~weisheit [f] *theorism, theoretical knowledge, professorial wisdom* **~edr·ale** f ~/~n, **~edr·al-** *cathedral* [s & a] **~·ete** f ~/~ ⟨geom⟩ *one of the two small sides of a rectangular triangle* **~·eter** m ~s/~ ⟨med⟩ *catheter* **≗·etern** vt [h] ⟨med⟩ *to catheterize* **~·ode** f ~/~n ⟨el⟩ *negative electrode*; *cathode*; flüssige ~ ⟨el⟩ *pool c.* | ~nstrahlröhre [f] *cathode ray tube* **~ol·ik** m ~en/~en, **~in** f ~/~nen **≗·olisch** a (*Roman*) *Catholic* || ~ w *to turn* (*R.*) *C.* **≗olis·ieren** vi [h] *to incline to the R. C. church, to catholize* **~oliz·ismus** m ~/ *Catholicism* || ⟨cont⟩ *Popery*

katilin·arisch a *Catilinarian*; *revolutionary*

K·ätner m ~s/~ *cottager*, → Kate

Kat·ode f ~/~n ⟨tech⟩ → Kathode

Kat·optrik f ~/ ⟨opt⟩ *catoptrics* pl

Katsch n (vorderind. Provinz) *Cutsh*

K·att f ~/ ⟨mar⟩ *cat-o'-nine-tails* || (Pfahl) *mooring-stamp*; ein Boot vor e–e ~ legen *to moor a boat* || (Schiffsflaschenzug) *tackle* **~anker** m ⟨mar⟩ *cat, kedge-anchor, backing anchor* **~block** m ⟨mar⟩ *cat block* **~takel** n *cat tackle*

ˣ**Katt·eiker** m ~s/~ *squirrel*

k·atten vt [h] *to cat* (*the anchor*), → Katt

K·attowitz n † ⟨Ger⟩ (Stadt in Oberschlesien) *Katowice*

Katt·un m ~(e)s/~e *calico, cotton*(*-cloth*); ⟨Am⟩ *muslin* || (Möbel-) *chintz* || (bedruckter) *print* | B·ett≗ *bed ticking*; Buchbinder≗ *embossed calico*; F·utter≗ *calico for lining* || Gl·anz≗ *glazed calico* **~bindung** f *calico weave* **~druck** m *c. printing* **~drucker** m *cotton-printer* **~druckerei, ~fabrik** f *c.o-printing works* sg konstr **~kleid** n *print*(*-dress*) **~papier** n *chintz-paper* **~weberei** f *manufactory of calico, c. weaving mill* **~zeug** n (indisches) *dungaree*

K·atz f [invar] → ~e °**≗balgen,** sich [h] *to scuffle, wrangle, bicker*; *to bandy words* (*with*) **~balger·ei** f ~/~en *scuffle, quarrel, wranglings* pl **≗buckeln** vi [h] *to boot-lick*; *to bow and scrape*; *to cringe*; *to play up* (vor *to*) **~fahren** n ⟨tech⟩ *traversing* **K·ätzchen** n ~s/~ *kitten, pussy-cat*; wie ein ~ *kitten-like* || ⟨bot⟩ [pl] *catkins* pl **K·atze** f ~/~n **1.** *cat*, ⟨fam⟩ *puss*; → Kater;

weibliche ~ *(lady-)cat*; getigerte ~ *tabby(-cat)*; die ~ schnurrt .. *purrs*, faucht *spits*, macht e–n Buckel *puts up its back*; so naß wie e–e ~ *as wet as a drowned rat* | neunschwänzige ~ *cat(-o'-nine-tails)* | (Geld≈) *pouch* | ⟨fig⟩ sie ist e–e falsche ~ *she is a she-cat* od *a nasty cat* ‖ sie spielt mit ihm wie die ~ mit der Maus *she plays cat-and-mouse with him* **2.** ⟨fig⟩ die ~ im Sack kaufen *to buy a pig in a poke* ‖ die ~ aus dem Sack l (Geheimnis verraten) *to let the cat out of the bag, to spill the beans*; die ~ ist aus dem S. *the murder is out* ‖ mir ist e–e ~ über den Weg gelaufen *a black cat has crossed my path* ‖ der ~ die Schelle umhängen *to bell the cat* ‖ °für die Katz' *for the birds* ‖ Katz' u Maus spielen *to play loose and fast* ‖ wie Hund u ~ stehen *to be at daggers drawn*, wie .. leben *to lead a cat-and-dog life* ‖ er geht drum herum wie die ~ um den heißen Brei *he is beating about the bush* ‖ geh' nicht wie die ~ um d. h. B. *stop beating around the bush* ‖ das trägt die ~ auf dem Schwanze weg *it is as light as a feather* **3.** ⟨prov⟩ die ~ läßt das Mausen nicht *cat will after kind, cats will catch mice*; *what is bred in the bone will out in the flesh*; bei Nacht sind alle ~n grau *when candles are out all cats are grey* ‖ ist die ~ nicht zu Hause, tanzen die Mäuse *when the cat's away the mice will play* °**K·atzelmacher** m = Kastelmacher **K·atzen-≈artig** [a] *catlike, feline*; mit ~er Behendigkeit *with the quiet motion of a cat* | [adv] *like a cat* **~-auge** n ⟨minr⟩ *cat's eye* ‖ ⟨mot, cycl⟩ *reflector*; *rear reflector* ‖ ~n h *to have eyes like a cat* **~-balg** m *cat's skin* **~brei** m ⟨fig⟩ *trifle*, ⟨Am sl⟩ *snap* **~buckel** m *raised back of a cat, humped back* ‖ **e–n** ~ m = **≈buckeln** vi [h] (vor [dat]) *to cringe, crouch (to)* **~darmfiedler** m *gut-scraper* **~fell** n *cat's skin, catskin* **≈freundlich** a & adv [etwa] *with a dissembling smile, with malicious suavity*; *cringing(ly)* **~geschlecht** n *feline kind, family of cats* **~geschrei** n *caterwauling, mewing of cats* **~gold** n *yellow glimmer, cat gold* **≈haft** a = –artig **~hai** m ⟨ich⟩ *nurse hound* **~jammer** m ⟨fig⟩ (→ Kater) *crapulence, seediness*; ich hab 'nen gewaltigen ~ *I've got a hang-over that will make history* **≈jämmerlich** a *seedy, low-spirited, all--overish* **~klee** m ⟨bot⟩ *kidney-vetch* **~kopf** m ⟨fig⟩ *box on the ear* ‖ *round paving* od *head stone* ‖ (Schiffbau) *chain toggel*; ≈e [pl] (Pflaster) *cobblestone* **~kopfschloß** n *box lock* **~kraut** n (Baldrian) *valerian* **~minze** f ⟨bot⟩ *cat-mint* **~musik** f *cat-calls* pl; *tin-kettle serenade, caterwauling* **~-pfötchen** n *cat's paw* ‖ ⟨bot⟩ *cat's foot* ‖ ~ geben *or* m *to cringe* **~silber** n ⟨minr⟩ *white glimmer* **~-sprung** m ⟨fam⟩ es ist nur ein ~ bis dorthin *it is but a stone's throw distant* **~steg** m, **~steig** m *narrow path* **~tisch** m *little folks' side-table*; am ~ essen müssen *to have to eat alone at a side--table (as punishment for children)* **~wäsche** f ⟨fig⟩ heute m wir ~ *today we shall only give ourselves a cat's lick* **~wels** m ⟨ich⟩ *cat-fish* °**k·atzig** a ⟨sl⟩ *catty (manners)*; sei nicht so ~ *don't be a cat*

K·au- ~fläche f *masticating surface* **~gummi** m *chewing-gum* | ~rest [m] *cud* **~magen** m ⟨zoo⟩ *gizzard* **~muskel** m *masticatory muscle* **~tabak** m *chewing-tobacco*, (Stück) *quid*, (Rolle) *twist* **~-werkzeuge** n pl *masticators* pl, → kauen

K·auderwelsch n ~es/ *jargon, lingo, gibberish, shyster-language*; *scientese*; ⟨fam⟩ *double Dutch, talkee-talkee* | **≈en** vi [h] *to gibber, jabber*; *to talk gibberish* od *Dutch*, etc

kaud·inisch a; das ≈e Joch *the Caudine Forks*

k·auen vt/i [h] *to chew, masticate* ‖ (hörbar) *to munch*; (of a horse) am Gebiß ~ *to champ the bit* ‖ (mümmeln) *to mumble* ‖ am Bleistift(ende) ~ *to nibble the end of a p.*; an den Nägeln ~ *to bite one's nails* ‖ ⟨vulg⟩ *to chaw (a quid of tobacco)* | (Worte) *to mumble*; *to drawl out (one's words)* ‖ an etw z ~ h *to pore over, to plod at (one's lessons)* ‖ das gab ihm etw z ~ *that gave him a hard nut to crack* ‖ → wiederkäuen

k·auern vi & sich ~ [h] *to cower*; *to squat (down)*; sich ~ *to crouch, to be crouched* ‖ *to huddle (a few sheep huddled near)* | ⟨her⟩ ~d *couchant*

K·auf m ~(e)s/≈e **1.** (das Kaufen) *purchase, buying*; durch ~ *by purchase* **2.** (das Gekaufte) *purchase* **3.** (guter ~) *bargain*; vorbeugende ≈e ⟨bes Am⟩ *hedging*; **in den** ~ (geben *to give*) *into the b.* ‖ z ~ anbieten *to offer for sale* ‖ e–n ~ m *or* abschließen *to make* od *strike* od *close a b.* ‖ Anzahlung auf den ~ m *to give earnest, to pay .. on account* ‖ billigen ~es abgeben *to sell at a moderate price* ‖ **mit in** den ~ nehmen *to take into the b.*; Sie w es in ~ n. müssen *there is nothing for it*; (etw) in ~ nehmen *to chance*; die Nachteile mit in (den) ~ n. *to take the bad with the good* **4.** ⟨fig⟩ das muß man mit in den ~ nehmen *that's all in the day's work, you must put up with it, you must make the best of it* ‖ leichten ~es davonkommen *to get off fairly well* od *cheaply* od *easily* **~ab-schluß** m *(completion of a) purchase* **~anlaß** m *buying motive* **~anschlag** m *valuation* **~auftrag** m *order to buy, buying* od *p. order* **~bedingungen** f [pl] *conditions* pl *of p.* **~bereich** m *shopping area* **~brief** m ⟨com⟩ *bill of sale, p.-deed, sale note* **~-buch** n *p. book* **~fahrer** m (Schiff) *trading-* od *merchant-vessel, trader, m.-craft* od *-man* ‖ (Reeder) *shipowner, owner of a m.-vessel*, etc. **~-fahrtei** f ⟨mar⟩ *maritime trade* **~fahrt·eiflotte** f *merchant-fleet, convoy of m.-men* **~fahrt·eischiff** n = –fahrer **~geld** n *p.-money* **~gesuch** n *offer to buy*; (in Anzeigen) *Wanted* od *Required* **~glätte** f *litharge for sale, commercial litharge* **~gut** n *merchandise* **~halle** f *market-hall, salesroom* **~-haus** n *trading-* od *staple-house, commercial h.*; (Warenhaus) *warehouse, store(s* pl*)*; ⟨Am⟩ *department store*; Groß≈ *supermarket, emporium* | ~kette [f] *department store chain* **~herr** m *merchant* **~hof** m *emporium*, → –haus **~-kontrakt** m *contract of sale* od *purchase, purchasing-contract* **~kraft** f *purchasing* od *buying power*; früher hatte 1 DM die ~ v 2 jetzigen *formerly 1 m. went as far as 2 now* **≈kräftig** a *able to buy* **~laden** m *store (house)*, *(grocer's* od *retail) shop*, ⟨Am⟩ *merchandising store* **~leute** pl *merchants* pl **~liebhaber** m *bidder*; *intending buyer* **~lust** f *demand*; *inclination* od *disposition to buy* **≈lustig** a *inclined to buy* | K–ge(r) *would-be* od *prospective buyer* **~mann** m; [pl] Kaufleute (→ Kofmich) (→ Groß≈, Kleinhändler) ⟨allg⟩ *business-man* ‖ (Groß≈) *wholesale-dealer, trader, merchant* ‖ [in Zus–setzungen mst] *dealer in ..* ‖ ich gehe zum ~ *I go to the grocer's* ‖ (Ladeninhaber) *tradesman*, (kl) *shopkeeper, retailer* ‖ (Büroangestellter) *clerk* ‖ (Verkäufer[in]) *salesman (saleswoman)* ‖ ~ w *to go into business, to become a b.-man* ‖ °⟨fam⟩ ~ lernen *to learn a b.* ‖ gerissener ~ *smart b.-man* **≈männisch 1.** [a] *mercantile, commercial (enterprise)* ‖ ~er Angestellter *c. employee* ‖ ~er Beruf *business* ‖ (praktisch) *b.like* ‖ ~e Beziehungen [f pl] *b.-connexions* pl; ~er Stil *c. style* **2.** [adv] ~ geschult *c.ly trained* **~mannschaft** f *the merchants, the c. world, body of m.s* **~manns-** ~akzept [n] *trade acceptance*; ~frau [f] *m.'s*, etc *wife*; ~gilde [f] *m. guild, corporation of traders*; ~gut [n] *merchandise, c. articles* pl; ~klasse [f] *m. class*; ~kreise [m pl] *c. circles*; ~laden [m] → Kaufladen; ~stand [m] *profession of commerce, mercantile calling* ‖ [koll] *mercantile class, c. world*; ~stil [m] *commercialese*; ~ware [f] *merchandise, c. goods* pl **~objekt** n *purchase* **~-preis** m *(buying* od *p.-)price, prime cost* **~schilling** m *earnest-money* **~summe** f *p. money* **~unlust** f *disinclination to buy, consumer* od *sales resistance* **~vertrag** m = ~kontrakt **≈weise** adv *by (way of) p.* **~wert** m *marketable value* **~wut** f *speculating-*

-mania **~zettel** m *note of p.* **k·aufen** vt/refl **sich** [dat] [h] *to buy, purchase* (v *from*); sie –fte ihm ein B. *she bought a book for him* || aus zweiter Hand ~ *to buy at second hand*, ⟨fam⟩ *to pick up second-hand* || preiswert ~ *to get good value for one's money* || wo ~ Sie? *where do you (generally) get your supply*? || ist dies zu ~? *is this purchasable*? | ⟨fig fam⟩ ich werde ihn mir ~! *I shall give him a piece of my mind!, I'll call him to account*, ⟨fam⟩ *I'll let him have it*! °was kaufe ich **mir** wohl dafür! *what's that to me!, that won't help me!*, ⟨fam⟩ *I get no change out of it* | **sich** v etw **frei** ~ *to free o.s. from .. by paying ..* | jdn ~ (bestechen) *to bribe a p* | gekauft w *to be in demand* **K·äufer** m ~s/~ *purchaser, buyer*; (Kunde) *customer*; ⟨jur⟩ *vendee*; *bidder, demander* || ~ finden *to meet with buyers*; willigen .. *with ready purchasers*; (of merchandise) *to move* | ~in [f] ~/~nen *woman buyer*, ~nen [pl] *women buyers* pl | ~schaft, ~schicht [f] *purchasing public* **k·äuflich 1.** [a] *marketable* (*goods*), *purchasable, for sale, to be sold*; ⟨fam⟩ *to be had* od *got for money* || *purchasable* (*love*); ~es Mädchen *a girl of easy virtue* || (bestechlich) *bribable, open to bribery*; *venal*; *mercenary* **2.** [adv] ~ erwerben *to buy* || ~ überlassen *to sell* | **≗keit** f ~/ *being for sale* || ⟨fig⟩ (Bestechlichkeit) *venality, corruptibility*

Kauk·asien n *Caucasia* **Kauk·asier** m, **~in** f, **kauk·asisch** a *Caucasian* **K·aukasus** m, **~gebirge** n (*Mount*) *Caucasus*

K·aulbarsch m ⟨ich⟩ *blacktail, ruff*

K·aulquappe f ~/~n ⟨zoo⟩ *tadpole*

k·aum 1. [adv] *scarcely, hardly*; ich glaube ~, daß .. *I don't know that* (*I should like it*); ~ glaublich *hard to believe*; ~ merklich *subtle*; er dachte ~, daß *he little thought that* ..; ~ sichtbar *sub-visible*; ich kann ~ *I cannot well*; ~ etliche Hundert *but a few hundreds*; sie war noch ~ zur Frau gereift *she was scarcely a woman as yet*; sie hatte ihn ~ erwartet *she had only half expected him* | **wie** ~ ein anderer *few* (*have* ..) *as thoroughly as he* | **wohl** ~ [abs] kannst du das? – Kaum! (= ich glaube es ~) .. *I shouldn't think so, I should think not*; ⟨fam⟩ *not* (⟨sl⟩ *not bloody*) *likely!, not much*! **2.** [conj] ~ hatte er .., als *he no sooner had .. than*; *he had hardly* od *scarcely gone when she came in*; ⟨fam⟩ *directly he was alone* (*he did it*)

K·auri m & f *cowry*(*-shell*) | ~fichte [f] *kauri*

kaus·al a *causal, causative* || ~er Nebensatz *adverbial clause denoting cause* **Kaus·al- ~gesetz** n *law of causation* **~nexus, ~zusammenhang** m, **~prinzip** n *causality*; *chain of causation, connection between* (od *interdependence of*) *cause and effect*; die Fähigkeit, die ~zus–hänge festzustellen *the causativeness of the human mind* **~partikel** f ⟨gram⟩ *causative particle* **Kausalit·ät** f ~/ *causality* **Kausat·ivum** n ~s/–va ⟨gram⟩ *causative* (*verb*)

K·ausch(e) f ~/~n (Metallring) ⟨mar⟩ *thimble, gutter ring, cord eye*

K·austik f ~/ (*art of*) *etching* | **~um** n ~s/–ka ⟨med⟩ *caustic* (*substance*) **k·austisch** a *caustic*; ⟨fig⟩ (beißend) *cutting* (*remark*)

Kaut·el f ~/~en ⟨jur⟩ (*pre*)*caution, reservation*

kauteris·ieren vt [h] (ätzen) *to cauterize*

Kauti·on f ~/~en *surety, security*; *guarantee deposit* || ⟨jur⟩ *bail, surety* || ⟨com⟩ *caution money* || ~ zahlen *to pay sec.*; ~ fallen l *to jump b.*; gegen ~ (aus der Haft) entlassen *out on b.*; ~ stellen *to give b., to provide sec.* **≗sfähig** a *b.able*; *able to give b.* **≗spflichtig** a *liable to give b.*, etc. **~shöhe** f, **~ssumme** f *amount of sec.* **~sversicherung** f *guarantee insurance* **~swechsel** m ⟨com⟩ = Depotw.

Kautsch f ~/~s (Langliege, Liegesofa) *couch*

K·autschuk m ~(e)s/~e *caoutchouc, India-rubber* **~baum** m *rubber-tree* **~lösung** f (*r.*) *solution* **~masse** f *c. paste* **~milch** f *c. milk* **~pflaster** n *r. surgical plaster* **~stempel** m *r. stamp* **~stopfen** m *r. stopper* **~walzwerk** n *r. rolling machine* **~waren** f pl *India-r. goods*

K·auz m ~es/≗e **1.** ⟨orn⟩ *screech-owl* **2.** (Knotenfrisur) *top-knot*, (am Hinterkopf) *chignon, bun* **3.** ⟨fig⟩ närrischer ~ *queer* od ⟨fam⟩ *rum customer, strange fellow* || ⟨fam⟩ *odd stick*; *strange fish, queer bird* || wunderlicher ~ *oddity of a fellow*; *curiosity*; *freak*; *misfit*; *quite a character*; ⟨Am fam⟩ *screwball*; ⟨sl⟩ *geezer* || reicher ~ *rich fellow*; komischer ~ *crank*; absonderlicher ~ *freak* | es muß auch solche Käuze geben *it takes people of all sorts to make up a world, there must be some of all sorts* **≗chen, ≗lein** n ~s/~ *little* (*screech-*) *-owl*; *owlet*

Kaval·ier m ~(e)s/~e (ritterlicher Mann) *gentleman*, ein vollendeter ~ *a complete g.*, den ~ spielen *to play* od *ape the g.* || (Begleiter der Dame) *cavalier*; ⟨fam⟩ *squire of dames*, ihr ~ *her admirer* || ⟨hist⟩ *courtier, knight, nobleman, cavalier* | ⟨arch⟩ (Firstziegel) *ridge plate* **≗mäßig** a *g.like, g.ly* | adv ⟨a.⟩ *cavalierly* **~start** m ⟨aero⟩ *zoom*; den ~ m *to zoom off*

Kavalk·ade f ~/~n *cavalcade, company of riders* **Kavaller·ie** f ~/~n [i:ən] *cavalry, horsemen* pl; *horse* [koll] **~angriff** m *c. charge* od *attack* **~draht** m *field-wire for c.* **~gefecht** n *c. engagement* **~kaserne** f *horse-barracks* **~offizier** m *c. officer, officer of c.* od *of horse* **~pferd** n *c.-, troop-horse, trooper* **~posten** m *horseguard, mounted sentinel, vedette* **~regiment** n *regiment of horse, c. regiment* **~schleier** m *c. screen* **~sendegerät** n *transmitter for c.* **~stiefel** m *jack-boot, top-boot* **Kavaller·ist** m ~en/~en *c.-man, trooper, horse-soldier* || **sabre* || *rough-rider*

Kavi·ar m ~(e)s/ *caviar*(*e*) || ⟨fig⟩ ~ fürs Volk *c. to the general* (Shak) **~brötchen** n *sandwich* od (*French*) *roll with c.*

Kavitati·on [–ts–] f ~/~en (Hohlraumbildung) *cavitation*

K·ebs- ~ehe f *concubinage* **~frau** f, –weib [n] *concubine* **~kind** n *bastard, natural child*

k·eck 1. [a] *bold, daring* || *plucky, jaunty*; *flippant* || (frech) *impertinent, impudent, audacious, forward, pert*; ⟨fam⟩ *cheeky, saucy* || ⟨sl⟩ *cocky* || *saucy* od *perky* (*little hat*) || er log mit ~er Stirn *he lied with audacity* || *pert* (*little pug-nose*) **2.** [adv] ⟨a.⟩ *acock* || sag's nur ~ heraus! *out with it*! | **≗heit** f ~/~en *boldness, daring*; *pluck* || *pertness, impudence* || ⟨fam⟩ *sauciness* || ⟨sl⟩ *cockiness* | **~lich** adv *boldly, pluckily*

k·eckern vi [h] (of fox) *to bark*

Kees n ~es/~e [bayr, österr] = Gletscher

K·efirpilz m *kefir, kephir*; *k. fungus*

K·egel m ~s/~ **1.** [pl] (*nine*)*pins, skittles*; ⟨Am a.⟩ *tenpins* pl || ~ schieben *to play* (*at*) *ninepins*, etc; die ~ aufstellen *to put up* **2.** ⟨geom⟩ *cone*; gerader ~ *right c.*, schiefer ~ *oblique c.*; steiler ~ *short taper*; Schrift≗ ⟨typ⟩ *shank* od *depth of a letter* || ⟨geogr⟩ *cone, peak* **3.** *natural child, squat little p* || Kind u ~ *the whole tribe* || weder Kind noch ~ *neither chick nor child* || mit Kind u ~ *with bag and baggage* **4.** ⟨hunt⟩ der Hase macht ~ *the hare sits up* **~achse** f ⟨geom⟩ *axis of the c.* **~auslaß** m ⟨tech⟩ *exhaust valve c.* **~bahn** f *skittle-* od *ninepin-alley*; automatische ~ *spotter* **~fläche** f *conical surface* **~form** f *c.l shape* **≗förmig** a *c.l, coneshaped, tapering* **~getriebe** n *bevel gear* **~gewinde** n *taper thread* **~junge** m *thrower-up, marker*; ⟨Am⟩ *pin-boy* **~kugel** f *skittle-ball* **~kupplung** f *cone type clutch* **~lehre** f (S) *taper gauge* **~linie** f *conic line* **~palast** m ⟨Am⟩ *bowling alleys* pl **~projektion** f *c. projection* **~rad** n *angular* od *bevel* od *c.l wheel* | ~antrieb [m] *bevel gear drive*; ~verzahnung [f] *bevel* **~schieber** m *skittle-player* **~schnitt** m ⟨geom⟩ *conic section* | ~lehre [f] ⟨geom⟩ *conics* pl, *conic sections* pl **~schub** m *game of ninepins* || = ~bahn **~spiel** n *n.s, skittles* pl **~spieler** m *skittle-player* **~stärke** f ⟨typ⟩ *point* od *type size* **~stift** m *tapered pin* **~stumpf** m *obtuse c., truncated c.* **~ventil** n *c.l valve* **k·eg(e)lig** a *conical* **k·egeln** vi [h] *to play* (*at*) *n.s* od *sk.s* ‖ ⟨allg⟩ *to bowl* **K·egler** m ~s/~ *sk.-player*

K·ehl- **~abschneider** m *cutthroat, throat-slitter* ‖ ⟨fam fig⟩ *usurer* **~ader** f *jugular vein* **~balken** m ⟨arch⟩ *valley-beam; collar b.* **~blech** n (Dach≗) *gutter-lead, flashing* **~brett** n *valley-board* **~dach** n *valley roof* **~deckel** m ⟨anat⟩ *throat-flap, epiglottis* **~hobel** m *chamfering-, moulding-plane* **~kopf** m ⟨anat⟩ *larynx*; am ~ *on the l.* | ~bänder [n pl] ⟨anat⟩ *laryngeal ligaments* pl; ~entzündung [f] ⟨med⟩ *laryngitis*; ~krebs [m] *cancer in the throat*; ~mikrophon [n] *throat* od *necklace microphone*; *laryngophone*; ~schwindsucht [f] ⟨med⟩ *laryngeal phthisis*; ~spiegel [m] *laryngoscope*; ~verschlußlaut [m] ⟨phon⟩ *glottal stop* **~lappen** m ⟨orn⟩ *wattle* **~laut** m ⟨gram⟩ *guttural* (*sound*) **~leiste** f *channel, talon, ogee, moulding* **~messer** n *moulding cutter* **~riemen** m *throat lash* **~rinne** f *hollow gutter* **~ziegel** m *gutter-tile* **K·ehle** f ~/~n **A. 1.** *throat*; *throttle, swallow*; → hohle Gasse ‖ ⟨rhetor⟩ *gorge* ‖ (Luftröhre) *windpipe, voice* **2.** ⟨übtr tech⟩ *chamfer, channel* ‖ ⟨fort⟩ *gorge* **B.** es geht ihm **an** die ~ *he is in great difficulties* ‖ jdm das Messer an die ~ setzen ⟨fig⟩ *to hold a knife to a p's throat* ‖ sie saßen sich an der ~ *they were at each other's t.ts* ‖ sie sprangen e–a an die ~ *they flew at each other's t.ts* ‖ **aus** voller ~ *full-throated*; *at the top of one's voice, of their voices*, .. lachen *to laugh heartily, to shout with laughter* ‖ sein Geld **durch** die ~ jagen *to waste one's money in drink* ‖ **in** die unrechte, falsche ~ k *to go down the wrong way* ⟨a. fig⟩ | **sich** [dat] die ~ **abschneiden** *to cut one's own t.t* ‖ sich die ~ **anfeuchten** *or* spülen (trinken) *to rinse* od *moisten one's t.t*, ⟨fam⟩ *to wet one's whistle, to gargle* ‖ sich die ~ ausschreien ⟨sl⟩ *to shout one's head off* ‖ Angst **schnürte** ihm die ~ zu *fear gave him a choking sensation*; *sobbing choked her* ‖ es schnürt mir die ~ zu *I feel choking*; .. wie –ge–rt (*her throat was*) *tight*; ..–rte sich zu .. *closed up* **k·ehlen** vt [h] **1.** ⟨tech⟩ *to chamfer, channel, groove, flute* **2.** (Fische aus|~) *to gut* **3.** °**sich** aus|~ *to scream* od *shout from one's t.t* **K·ehlung** f ~/~en *chamfer, channel, flute, moulding*

K·ehr- (→ Kehricht-) **~aus** m (*concluding* od *last dance*) '*Sir Roger*'; die Kapelle spielte den ~ *the band played for the break-up*, ⟨sl⟩ *chucker out* ‖ den ~ tanzen *to dance Home Sweet Home* od *Good Night Ladies* **~bild** n *inverted image*; ⟨opt⟩ *back-to-back display* **~blech** n *dust pan* **~frau** f *charwoman* **~gleis** n *Y-track* **~maschine** f *sweeping machine, street cleansing machine*; *carpet cl. m.* **~pflug** m *turn wrest plough* **~reim** m *refrain, burden* **~scheibe** f *revolving target* **~seite** f *reverse, back* ‖ ⟨fig⟩ *seamy side* ‖ jedes Ding hat s–e ~ *there is a reverse for every medal*; *no rose without a thorn*; die ~ nach oben (*to turn*) ..*face down* **~wert** m *reciprocal value* **~wisch** m *mop, whisk* **K·ehre** (des Weges) f ~/~n *turn*(*ing*), *bend*; *winding* ‖ ⟨el-rail⟩ *loop* ‖ ⟨gym⟩ *turn, rear-vault* ‖ ⟨aero⟩ *turn* **k·ehren** vt/refl [h] **1.** *to sweep, dust, brush*; neue Besen ~ gut *a new broom sweeps clean* ‖ (Straße) *to scavenge, sweep*; (Kamin) *sweep* ‖ kehre vor d–r eigenen Tür! *mind your own business*! **2.** ⟨fig⟩ (drehen, wenden) *to turn* (*over*) ‖ alles zum besten ~ *to turn everything to advantage* ‖ das Oberste z unterst ~ *to turn* (*everything*) *upside down* ‖ das Äußere nach innen ~ *to turn a th outside in* ‖ s–e beste Seite nach außen ~ *to show o.s. to the best advantage* ‖ s–e rauhe Seite nach außen ~ *to show one's rough side*, ⟨fam⟩ *to cut up rough* ‖ [dat] den Rücken ~ *to turn one's back* (*up*)*on* **3. sich** ~ [h] *to turn round* ‖ (rechtsum) kehrt (sc euch)! (*right*) *about turn* od *face*; → ~machen ‖ kehre (sc dich) in dich! *repent*!; sich **an** etw [acc] ~ [mst negativ] *to care* od *trouble about*; *to pay attention to*; *to regard, heed, mind* (*a th, a p*) ‖ **in sich** ge–rt *abstracted*; *lost* od *withdrawn in thought*; ich habe mich **in** mich gekehrt *I have* (*am*) *retired into myself* ‖ sie saß in sich gekehrt *she sat engrossed in her own thoughts* od *wrapt in meditation*; in sich ge–rte P *introvert*, nach außen g. P *extrovert* ‖ sich **zur** Buße ~ *to become penitent* **K·ehrer** m ~s/~ *sweep*(*er*), ⟨allg⟩ *cleaner* **K·ehricht** m & n ~(e)s/ *sweepings* ‖ *garbage* ‖ *dirt, dust, rubbish* ‖ ⟨sl⟩ *junk, muck* **~abfuhr** f *removal of r.* **~eimer** m, **~faß** n, **~kasten, ~kübel** m *r.-box, d.-bin* **~haufen** m *d.-heap*, ⟨fam⟩ *muck-, junk-heap* ⟨a. fig⟩ **~schaufel** f *d.-pan*, (gr) *d.-shovel* **~wisch** m *d.er* **kehrt|machen** vi [h] ⟨mil⟩ *to face about, to wheel* ‖ ⟨allg⟩ *to turn round* od *back*; → kehren 3. | ≗ [n] verboten! *No U Turn*! **K·ehrtwendung** f *about-face* ⟨a. fig⟩; ⟨fig⟩ e–e ~ m *to revoke o.s.*

Keib m ~en/~en [südd] = Aas, Lump, Kerl

k·eifen vi [h] *to scold*; *bicker, squabble, swear*; *bark, yelp* **K·eiferin** f ~/~nen *scold, shrew*

K·eil m ~(e)s/~e **1.** *wedge* ‖ e–n ~ treiben zw *to drive in a w. between*; ⟨fig⟩ *to estrange* (*two friends*) ‖ durch e–n ~ befestigen, spalten *to w.* ‖ ⟨prov⟩ ein ~ treibt den andern *one nail drives the other* (*out*) **2.** ⟨typ⟩ *quoin* **3.** ⟨arch⟩ *keystone* **4.** (Donner≗) (*thunder-*)*bolt* (schleudern *to hurl*) **5.** (z Festmachen) *chock*; mit ~en befestigen, z Stehen bringen *to ch.* **6.** (Brems≗) *sprag* **7.** ⟨tech⟩ *coin, gib, key* **8.** ⟨mil⟩ *coin* ‖ (Angriffs≗) *spearhead, arrow-head* **9.** (Stück) *hunk* (*of bread*), *w.* (*of cheese*) **10.** (Näherei) *gore, gusset*; mit e–m ~ versehen *to gore, gusset* **11.** °~e [pl] *blows* pl ‖ ~e kriegen *to get a good thrashing, licking* ‖ da hat's gehörige ~e gesetzt *hard blows were struck* **~bein** n ⟨anat⟩ *nape-bone*, ⟨scient⟩ *sphenoid*(*al*) *bone* **~bolzen** m *cotter bolt* **~fäustel** n ⟨min⟩ *w.-driver* **~feder** f ⟨tech⟩ *coiled spring* **~ferse** f (Strumpf≗) *pouch heel*; ⟨tex⟩ *gusset type heel* **~form** f ⟨aero⟩ *Vee* od *wedge formation* **≗förmig** a *w.-shaped* ‖ (Schrift) *cuneiform*, ⟨scient⟩ *sphenoid* **~hacke, ~haue** f *pick*(*axe*) **~hose** f ⟨tex⟩ *stretch pants* pl **~kissen** n *padded wedge* **~klemme** f ⟨rail⟩ *w. rail anchor* **~loch** n ⟨mil⟩ *slot for key*, ⟨tech⟩ *cotter slot* **~lochhammer** m *slotting hammer, stone splitting h.* **~nut** f *keyway, groove* **~rahmen** m ⟨typ⟩ *quoin-chase*; ⟨paint⟩ *stretcher* **~rad** n *w.-friction wheel* **~riemen** m ⟨tech⟩ *V-belt* | ~scheibe [f] *Vee-pulley* **~rillenkranz** m ⟨mach⟩ *grooved V-belt rim* **~ring** m *conical ring* **~robe** f *gored dress* **~schrift** f *cuneiform*; in ~ *in c.* **~stein** m *voussoir* Fr **~stift** m *taper pin* **~stück** n (Näherei) *gore, gusset*; mit e–m ~ versehen *to gore, gusset* **~verbindung** f *keying* **~verschluß** m ⟨artill⟩ *wedge breech, sliding w.* **k·eilen** vt [h] *to wedge* ‖ *to fasten with wedges, to chock* | °(jdn) *to thrash*; sie w sich ~ *they will come to blows*; sie keilten sich darum *they tussled for it* | ~ zu *to invite to join* (*a society, corporation*, etc.), ⟨Ger univ⟩ *to canvass*, ⟨sl⟩ *to rope in* **K·eiler** m ~s/~ *tusker* °**Keiler·ei** f ~/~en *free fight, brawl, scuffle, tussle* (um *for*) ‖ ⟨sl⟩ *roughhouse*

K·eim m ~(e)s/~e **1.** ⟨bot⟩ *germ, sprout, seed*; (*s.-*)*bud* ⟨a. fig⟩ ‖ ⟨minr⟩ *crystal nucleus* ‖ ⟨physiol⟩ *ovum*; befruchteter ~ *embryo* **2.** ⟨fig⟩ *g.s* pl *of a disease*; *s.s of patriotism*; *g.s of future conflicts*; im ~e befindlich *g.inal*; *in the bud* ‖ im ~e ersticken ⟨fig⟩ *to nip in the bud* **~bildung** f ⟨chem⟩ *nucleus formation* **~blatt** n ⟨bot⟩ *s.-leaf, cotyledon* ‖ ⟨biol⟩ (äußeres) *ectoblast, ectoderm*; (inneres) *entoderm, hypoblast* **~drüse** f ⟨biol⟩ *gonad, g.-gland* **~faden** m ⟨bot⟩ *g.-tube* **≗fähig** a *capable of g.inating* **~fähigkeit** f *g.inative faculty* **≗frei** a *g.-proof, sterile, free from bacilli* ‖ ~ m *to pasteurize, sterilize* **~haut** f *g.-membrane, blastoderm* **~hülle** f *perisperm* **~kapsel** f *spore* **~kern** m *g.inal nucleus* **~korn** n (befruchtetes) (*oo*)*spore* **~kraft** f *vitality* **~ling** m *embryo*, (*small*) *g.* **~material** n,

~stoff m *blastema* **~plasma** n *protoplasma, g.-plasma* **~saal** m (Mälzerei) *malting floor* **~sack** m *embryo-sac* **~stoff** m *blastema* **≈tötend** a *g.icidal, g.icide* **~töter** m (Mittel) *g.-killer, g.icide* **~träger** m ⟨med⟩ *(g.-)carrier* **~wurzel** f ⟨bes for⟩ *radicle* **~zahl** f ⟨bact⟩ *bacterial count* **~zeit** f *period of g.ination* **~zelle** f *g.-cell, bud-c.*; *reproductive c.*

k·eimen 1. vi [h] *to germinate*, (of seed) *sprout*; (of potatoes) *to grow out* || (of tree, horn) *to bud* || ⟨allg⟩ *to come up, show* || *shoot* || (of plant) *to grow* | ⟨fig⟩ *germinate*; *spring forth*; *grow*; ~de Liebe, Leidenschaft *growing love, rising passion*; ~des Leben *nascent life* **2.** vt *to bring to germination* || ⟨brew⟩ *to soak* (*the barley*) **K·eimung** f ⟨biol⟩ *germination*

k·ein(e f) m, n pron **1.** [als adj] *no, not a, not one, not any* || er hat ~ Geld *he has no m.*; er gab mir ~ Geld *he didn't give me any m.* || er hat ~e eigenen (sc Bücher) *he has none of his own* || er ist ~ E. *he isn't an Englishman*; ~ Tag verging, es verging ~ Tag *not a day passed* || *no new pictures could be hung* || er ist ~ Schütze ⟨sl⟩ *he can't shoot for toffee*; er hat absolut ~e Chancen ⟨sl⟩ *he has not an earthly* || ich kann mir denken, daß ~ J. .. *I cannot think how any boy could stand it* || ~ J. *no boy*; ~ Mensch *no one, not a single p* || I bewahre! ~ Gedanke! *Nonsense! It's not to be thought of* || sie würdigte ihn ~es Blickes *she did not so much as look at him* | du bist ~ Kind **mehr** *you are no longer a child*; ~ Wort mehr! *not another word!* es besteht ~e Gefahr mehr *there is no danger now* || er hat **gar** ~e Verwandten mehr *he has no relations left to him whatever* || es ist **noch** ~ halbes Jahr her *it is not six months ago* || es ist ~ **so** grober F. *it is not so bad a mistake* || **Nur** ~e Vorträge! *Here, here, no lectures!* || Gewinn **oder** ~ G.! *profit* od *no profit!* er las fast überhaupt ~e Gedichte *he read next to no poetry* | ich gehe **auf ~en Fall** mit *I shan't go with you under any circumstances*; das geht auf ~en Fall *that will never do* (→ Fall) || **in ~er Weise** (⟨mil sl⟩ [⟨hum⟩ sup] in ~ster Weise) *not in any way, in no wise*; es nützte der S in ~er Weise *it did not help matters at all*, ⟨Am⟩ .. *h. m. any*; in ~er Weise befriedigend *anything but satisfactory* || **unter ~en Umständen** *on no account* **2.** **[als subst] ~er** [m]; **~e** [f] *none, no one, not (any) one, nobody, not .. anybody*; *he is none of the wisest*; ~er war da *nobody was there*; ~er v ihnen *not one of them*; er, sie steht ~em nach *he, she is inferior to none* || **~(e)s** [n] *nothing, not one, not .. anything* || ~s d–r Bücher gefällt mir *I don't like any of your books* || **fast** ~er v ihnen *hardly any(body) of them* || ~er v **beiden** *neither of them, neither the one nor the other* || (Wein oder Bier?) ≈s v beiden! ..? *Neither* || ~ **anderer** als *none other but* || ~er will vom andern etw wissen *neither will have anything to do with the other* **keinenfalls** = keinesfalls **keinerlei** a *no*; *not of any sort, kind, description*; *of no sort*, etc.; *not any .. whatever*; es ist ~ Raum f *there is no scope whatever for* || auf ~ Weise *by no means*; *in no way, manner, wise* **k·einerseits** adv *on neither side, in neither direction* **keinesfalls** adv *not anyway*; *on no account* od *condition*; es würde ~ e–n guten Eindruck m *it would create anything but a good impression*; (.. –) ≈! (*perhaps his brother will continue the grant*, –) *Not he!* **k·eineswegs** adv *not in the least, by no means, on no account, nowise, in no way, in no wise, not at all*; *never*; *not a bit (of it)*; *far from it*; *nothing of the sort* || .. ~ schwerer *this table is not any heavier than that one*; es nützte der S ~ *it didn't help matters at all*, ⟨Am⟩ .. *h. m. any*; er war ~ glücklich *he was not altogether a happy man* || er ist ~ gesund *he is far from well* || ~ **zu** gut *none too good*; ⟨Am⟩ *he didn't speak any too low*; ~ **so** hoch *none so high*; ~ **allzu** leicht *none too easy* || (in **Antworten**) (*You should have been a man.* –) Oh nein ~! *Indeed I should not! I guess not!*; (*you will leave that alone!* –) Oh nein, ~ *Oh no, we will not* **k·einmal** adv *not once, never (once)*; *not a single time* || ⟨prov⟩ einmal ist ~ *once does not count, the exception proves the rule*

K·eks m –es/–e *biscuit*; ⟨Am⟩ *cracker, cooky*

K·elch m ~(e)s/~e *cup, goblet* || ⟨ec⟩ *chalice communion-cup* | ⟨fig⟩ der bittere ~ der Leiden *the bitter cup of sorrow*; zw Lipp' u ~es Rand schwebt der finstern Mächte Hand *there's many a slip 'twixt cup and lip* | ⟨bot⟩ *calyx* **~blatt** n ⟨bot⟩ *sepal* **~blüte** f *calycinal flower* **≈blütig** a *calycifloral* **~decke** f ⟨ec⟩ *chalice-veil* **~deckel** m ⟨ec⟩ *paten, chalice-lid* **≈förmig** a *cup-shaped*, ⟨scient⟩ *calyciform* **~glas** n *chalice*; *(large) glass cup, crystal goblet* || (f Champagner) *tall (champagne-)glass* **~hülle** f ⟨bot⟩ *calycle* **≈los** a ⟨bot⟩ *acalycinous* **~narbe** f ⟨bot⟩ *umbril* **≈ständig** a ⟨bot⟩ *calycinal* **~tellerchen** n ⟨ec⟩ *paten* **~tuch** n ⟨ec⟩ *purificatory* **~weihe** f *consecration of the communion-cup*

K·elle f ~/~n (Maurer≈) *trowel*; mit der ~ auftragen *to t.* || (Gieß≈) *(hand) ladle* || (Suppen≈) *(soup-)ladle* || (hölzerne ~) *wooden spoon* || (Schöpf≈) *scoop* || (Fisch≈) *(fish-)slice* || (Küchen≈) *basting spoon* | essen, was die ~ gibt *to take pot-luck*

K·eller m ~s/~ *cellar (c.)*; *cave* || ⟨minr⟩ *enlargement* || (Flaschen≈) *bottle shop* || (Gär≈) *fermentation room, tun* od *vat r.* || (Gewölbe) *vault, warehouse* || (Wein≈) *wine c.age* || *underground wine restaurant (in almost every German & Austrian town)*: Auerbachs ~ (Leipzig), Rat(hau)s≈: im tiefen ~ sitz ich hier *my voice is in my boots* **~assel** f *wood-louse, sow-bug* **~fenster** n *c.-window* od *-skylight* **~geschoß** n ⟨arch⟩ *basement*; (Raum) *underground floor* **~gewölbe** n *(u.g.) vault, c. vault* **~hals** m *mouth, opening, neck of a c.* || ⟨bot⟩ *daphne*, echter ~ *mezereon* **~laden** m *u.g. shop* **~lager** n *cask-stand, stillion* **~loch** n *air-hole of a c., vent-hole* **~meister** m *(head) c.man, butler*; *wine--steward* **~meisteramt** n *butlership* **~miete** f *c.age* **~schabe** f = ~assel **~sinkkasten** m ⟨arch⟩ *c. sink water trap* **~treppe** f *c. stairs* pl **~wirt** m *keeper of a (wine-)c.*, etc., *tavern-keeper* **~wirtschaft** f *u.g. restaurant*, etc **~wohnung** f *u.g. dwelling* od *apartments* od *lodgings* pl **~wurm** m = ~assel **~zins** m *c.age* **Keller·ei** f ~/~en *cellar(age)* **K·ellner** m ~s/~ *waiter, barman*; *butler, tapster* | ~in [f] *waitress, barmaid*; ⟨fam⟩ *nippy* **~junge,** ~lehrling [m] *(bus-* od *pot-)boy, boy-waiter, waiting-boy*

Kelp m ~(e)s/~e (Tangasche) *kelp*

Kelt m ~(e)s/~e ⟨praeh⟩ (Beil) *celt*

K·elte m ~n/~n; **K·eltin** f ~/~nen *Celt*, **Kelt* || Gaele [m], -lin [f] *Gael*

K·eltenstamm m *Celtic tribe* (od **Keltic*) *nation* od *tribe*

K·elter f ~/~n *wine-press*, ~ Christi ⟨rel, arts⟩ *mystic w.-p.*; die ~ treten *to tread the grapes* **~bütte** f *p.-vat* **~haus** n *p.-shed* **~mantel** m *(wine)p. cloak* od *mantle* | **~er** m ~s/~ *wine-presser* | **≈n** vt [h] *to tread (the grapes), to press (out)* | ≈ n *vinification*

Keltib·erer m, **~in** f; **k·erisch** a *Celtiberian* **K·erien** n *Celtiberia* **k·eltisch** a *Celtic*; die ~en Randvölker *the Celtic fringe*

K·elvin npr *Kelvin*; ⟨therm⟩ *kelvin*; null Grad ~ = –273,16°C (abs. Nullpunkt); + 273,16° ~ = 0°C (Wassergefrierpunkt); + 373,16° ~ = 100°C (Wassersiedepunkt)

Kem(e)n·ate f ~/~n ⟨hist poet⟩ *ladies' bower (with a fireplace)*; ⟨übtr⟩ *ladies' room*

K·enia 1. m (Berg in O.-Afrika) *Kenya* **2.** n (Kenialand) *Kenya*

k·enn- *characteristic* **≈bake** f *landmark beacon* **~bar** a *knowable, distinguishable, distinct* **≈buchstabe** m *ch. letter* **≈daten** pl *characteristics, characteristic values* **≈feuer** n *identification beacon* **≈frequenz** f *assigned frequency* **~gruppe** f ⟨wir⟩ *identification group* **≈karte** f *identity-card* **≈leit-**

wert m ⟨el⟩ *indicial admittance* **≈licht** n *navigation light* **≈linie** f *ch. line* **≈lochung** f ⟨comp⟩ *special designation*; *punching of d.s* **≈marke** f *identification mark* **≈melodie** f ⟨wir⟩ *signature tune*; *theme* **~nummer** f ⟨mil⟩ f Spezialausbildung *specification serial number* N; ⟨aero⟩ *air movement designation number* N **≈ruf** m *recognition call* **≈satz** m ⟨comp⟩ *label* **≈wert** m *ch. value*; ⟨aero⟩ ~e [pl] *nomenclature* [koll] **≈wort** n ⟨mil⟩ (*pass*)*word* **≈zahlen** f pl (des Absatzes) *standard figures* (*of distribution*), (*d.*) *indices* **≈zeichen** n *sign, distinguishing attribute, ch. mark, hall-mark, mark of distinction, token* || ⟨med⟩ *symptom* || ⟨agr⟩ *ear-mark* || ⟨mach⟩ *identification plate* || ⟨fig⟩ *note*; das ~ dieser Religion *the note of this religion* | ~tafel [f] ⟨mot⟩ *licence plate, number plate* **~zeichnen** vt [h] *to mark, define, distinguish, characterize* || sich ~ *to distinguish o.s.* | ≈ [n] ⟨comp⟩ *punching of designations* **~zeichnenderweise** adv *symptomatically, significantly, in a ch. manner*; ~ kam sie zu spät *she was late as could have been expected* **≈zeichnung** f *marking* **≈ziffer** f ⟨math⟩ *characteristic*; *key*; ⟨comp⟩ *department number* **≈zug** m *characteristic feature* **k·ennen** vt/refl [kannte/gekannt] [h] *to know* (*a p*), *to be acquainted with* (*a th*) || wir ~ **ihn** oberflächlich, von Ansehen *we k. him slightly, by sight*; .. nur vom Hörensagen .. *only from hearsay*, mit Namen *by name* || ⟨fam⟩ .. durch u durch *we k. him every inch*, .. ganz genau ⟨sl⟩ *we've got him taped* || soweit wir ihn ~ *from our k.ledge of him* || seit wann ~ Sie ihn? *since when have you k.n him?* | wir ~ **es** gründlich *we k. it thoroughly*, .. v vorn u hinten, in- u auswendig *we k. the ins and outs of it*; .. *it inside out* || das ~ wir wohl *we are not ignorant of it*; etw genau ~ ⟨fam⟩ *to have a th at one's fingers' ends*; etw nicht ~ *to be unaware* od *ignorant of a th* || das kennt man schon! *Well, well, we k.* (*all about*) *that!* | wir ~ **ihn als** zuverlässigen Menschen *we k. him as a reliable p*; .. *for an unwelcome visitor* | (beim Vorstellen) ~ Sie Herrn N.? *have you met Mr. N.?* Wir ~ **uns** noch nicht lange *we have not k.n each other long*; wir ~ uns vom Theater *we k. each other from the theatre* | er kennt s–n Goethe *he is quite at home in his G.* | **~lernen** *to* (*get* od *come to*) *k.*; *to learn to k.* (*the bases of* ..); ⟨bes Am⟩ (P) *to meet first*; *to hear* (*an answer*) || ich möchte sie ~ l. *I should like to get to k.* od *meet her*; es freut mich, Sie ~ gelernt z h (*I am*) *glad to have met you, to k. you*; damals erst habe ich ihn ~ l. *I got to k. him then for the first time* || wir sind so **im ersten ≈lernen** [n] *we're just beginning to k. each other* | ⟨fig⟩ ich lernte ihn v e–r ganz neuen Seite ~ *I got an insight into another side of his character* || du wirst mich noch ~ l.! (drohend) *you will find me an awkward customer to deal with!* | **zufällig ~ l.** *to meet* (*with*), *to fall in with*, ⟨fam⟩ *to pick up* || **besser ~ l.** *to form* od *make a p's acquaintance, to become* (*better*) *a.ted with a th* || ich hoffe wir w sie **näher ~ l.** *I hope we shall make their a.ance* od .. *we shall k. them better* || jdn nicht ~ **wollen** *to cut a p* | **er kennt sich** hier aus *he knows all about this place* || er kennt sich vor Stolz selbst nicht mehr *pride has turned his head* **k·ennenswert** a *worth knowing* **K·enner** m ~s/~; (**~in** f ~/~nen) *connoisseur, expert, judge, specialist* (*of a th*); ⟨Am sl⟩ *crackerjack* || ~ v Blumen, Vögeln *flower-, bird-fancier*, ~ v Sprachen *linguist*, ~ des Lateinischen *Latin scholar*, ~ des Pflanzen-, Tierreichs *botanist, zoologist* || die ~ [pl] *the knowing*, ⟨Am⟩ *those in the know* || er ist ein ~ v Teppichen ⟨fam⟩ *he knows all about carpets* **~auge** n *eye of a judge* **~blick** m *look* od *glance of a connoisseur* **≈isch** a *appreciative* **~miene** f *air of a c.* **~schaft** f ~/ *c.ship, expertness, thorough knowledge* **K·enning** f ~/~ar *kenning* → d. in Bd. I **k·enntlich** a (an [dat]) *distinguishable* (*by*); *easy to know* od *recognize* || ~ gemacht *marked* || ~ m *to mark, to make known* || (bemerkbar) *conspicuous* | **≈keit** f ~/ *c.ness*; *cognoscibility, discernibleness* | **≈machung** f ~/ (*hall-*), (*ear-*)*marking, labelling* **K·enntnis** f ~/~se *knowledge*; *intelligence*; *information, notice, cognizance*; ⟨bes Am⟩ *skill* (v *in*) || geringe, oberflächliche ~ v *a smattering of* od *in*; gründliche ~ *mastery of* | **~se** [pl] *attainments, acquirements, accomplishments* pl; *knowledge* (in *of*), *information*; *culture, education* || mit guten engl. ~sen *proficient in English* || ~se über den Feind *enemy information* || ~se u Fähigkeiten *skill*; Fach≈se, Spezial≈se ⟨fam⟩ (*manufacturing*, etc) *know-how* || ~se sammeln *to acquire a large range of knowledge*; gute ~se h in .. *to have a good* od *an excellent k. of mathematics* || gründliche ~se des Englischen *an all-round k. of E.* | jdm v e–r S ~ **geben**, etw zu j–s ~ bringen, jdn in ~ setzen v *or* über *to notify* od *apprise* od *inform a p of*; jdn davon in ~ setzen, daß *to let a p know that*; etw **zur ~ bringen** *to give notice of*; *to notify for information* || jdm etw zur ~ bringen *to bring .. to the n. of a p*; mir wurde dies zur ~ gebracht *this fact was brought to my n., I have been informed of it* | ~ **h v** *to have k. of*; *to be aware of* || ~ **erhalten** *or* gewinnen aus *to derive k.* (*of Shak.'s life*) *from* (*his sonnets*) || v e–r S ~ erhalten *to be informed of a th* || **(jdm) zur** ~ k, zu j–s ~ k, daß *to come to a p's k., under* (*a p's*) *n.* || (gebührende) ~ **nehmen** v, etw (gebührend) zur ~ nehmen *to take* (*due*) *cognizance* od *n.* od (*calm*) *note of, to make o.s. acquainted with a th, to note a th* || z ~ u Beachtung! *for your information and guidance* || sich v etw ~ **verschaffen** *to obtain information about a th* | **das entzieht sich m-r** ~ *that baffles me* **K·enntnis-** **≈los** a *ignorant, lacking in knowledge* **~nahme** f *cognizance*; zur ~ *for information*; bei genauer ~ *on further examination* **≈reich** a *learned, well-informed*; *knowledgeable*; *experienced, versed* **K·ennung** f ~/~en *identification code*

Kent·aur m ~en/~en *centaur*; → Zentaur

K·enterhaken m ⟨mar⟩ *cant-hook, grappling-iron* **k·entern** **1.** vi [s] ⟨mar⟩ (*of ship*) *to capsize, overset, overturn*, ⟨naut sl⟩ *to turn turtle* || er –rte mit s–m B. *he overturned his boat* **2.** vt [h] ⟨tech⟩ (e–n Balken) ~ *to cant* (*up*), *turn up, overturn* **3.** ≈ n ~s/ ⟨mar⟩ *turn* (*of the tide*)

Kent·ucky n (Staat der U.S.A.)

Ker·amik f ~/ *ceramics* pl; *ceramic* (od *potter's*) *art* || Grob≈ *heavy clay industry*, Grob- u Fein≈ *heavy and fine c. works* [sg konstr]

Kerat·in n ~s/ *keratin* **Kerat·om** n ~s/ *keratoma*

K·erb- **~bolzen** m *groove-stud* **~haue** f ⟨min⟩ *pick*(*axe*) **~hauer** m ⟨min⟩ *cutter* **~holz** n *tolly, tally, score* || (jdm) aufs ~ schreiben *or* setzen *to tally, score*, ⟨fig⟩ *to chalk up, to set down* (*to a p's debit*) || er hat bei mir etw auf dem ~ *he is in my black* od *bad books* || er hat manches auf dem ~ *he has a lot to answer for* **~messer** n *notching-knife* **~säge** f *rip* (od *pit, notching*) *saw* **~schnitt** m, **~schnitzerei** f *chip carving* **~schnittarbeit** f *chip carved ware* **~schnitzer** m *chip-carver* **~stift** m *grooved pin* **~tier** n *insect* **~tierkunde** f *entomology* **~zahn** m *crenature* **K·erbe** f ~/~n *jag, nick, notch, recess*; *dent*; (*flat*) *indent*; *incision* || Scharf≈ [f] *V-*(*shaped*) *notch* || Z·ahn≈ [f] *dental notch* **k·erben** vt [h] *to notch, indent*; (Nadeln) *to groove, channel*; (Kohle) *to cut, kerve*; (Münzen) *to mill* || gekerbt ⟨bot⟩ *crenate*(*d*) **K·erbung** f ~/~en *notching, indentation* || ⟨bot⟩ *crenature*; ⟨bot, zoo⟩ *serration*

K·erbel m ~s/ ⟨bot⟩; ~kraut [n] *chervil*

K·erf m ~s/~e ⟨ent⟩ = Kerbtier

Kergu·elenland n (subantarktische Inselgruppe im Indischen Ozean) *Kerguelen Land*

K·erker m ~s/~ *prison, jail, gaol* || ⟨hist⟩ (Burg≈) *dungeon* || schwerer ~ *penal servitude* || in den ~ werfen *to throw* (*a p*) *into prison* || zu ~-

(strafe) verurteilen *to sentence to gaol* ‖ Ausbruch aus dem ~ ⟨Am⟩ *jail-delivery* **~fieber** n *jail-fever* **~haft** f *imprisonment, gaol* → vor. **~meister** m *jailer, turnkey*

K·erl m ~s/~e *fellow* (⟨vulg⟩ *feller*); *customer*; *boy* ‖ ⟨sex⟩ *bugger* ‖ ⟨fam⟩ *chap(pie)*; ⟨sl⟩ *bloke, cove, bird, dog, egg, fish*; ⟨sl⟩ *hepcat*; ⟨mil & sl⟩ *wallah*, ⟨Am sl⟩ *character, duck, gink, guy* ‖ *individual* ‖ der ~ Jones *that Jones man*; *that professor chap, that American chap* | **alter** ~ *old boy* | anständiger ~ ⟨sl⟩ *loyal baggage* ‖ armer ~ *poor fellow*; ⟨fam⟩ *poor devil*, der arme, alte ~ ⟨sl⟩ *that poor old egg*; **dummer** ~ *geezer, duffer*; durchtriebener ~ ⟨sl⟩ *sly dog*, ⟨fam⟩ *(artful) dodger*; **einfältiger** ~ *silly f., blockhead*; ⟨Am sl⟩ *galoot* ‖ ein echter ~ ⟨sl⟩ *a true Trojan, a regular f.*, ⟨Am sl⟩ *a real gent* ‖ ehrlicher ~ *honest f.*; bist du ein ~ oder ein Waschlappen? *are you man or mouse*?; ekelhafter ~ ⟨vulg dero⟩ *bugger* ‖ elender ~ *villain, wretch, beggar*; **famoser** ~ *fine f.*; ⟨fam⟩ *a trump, a regular brick, a sound egg*, ⟨Am⟩ *a r. guy*; fauler ~ *johnny*; fremder ~ ⟨univ⟩ *outsider*; furchtbarer ~ ⟨sl⟩ *a holy terror*; **ganzer** ~ *a splendid* od *fine f.* ‖ gemeiner ~ *blackguard; low* od *common f.*; *perisher; hog, swine*; ⟨sl⟩ *dirty dog* ‖ geriebener ~ *a cunning sort of f.* ‖ glücklicher ~ *lucky dog* ‖ grober ~ *ruffian; rough* od *rude f.*; *churl* ‖ großer ~ *big f.* ‖ guter ~ *good-natured f.*, ⟨sl⟩ *good egg* ‖ ganz guter ~ ⟨sl⟩ *not half a bad sport*; *he is a good* (od *the right*) *sort* ‖ **langer** ~ *long, lanky f.*; die langen Kerls (Friedrich Wilhelms I.) *the tall guards* ‖ brutaler ~ ⟨Am sl⟩ *gorilla*; liederlicher ~ *rake, gay* od *fast f.*; lustiger ~ ⟨sl⟩ *jolly dog* od *chap, gay blade*; du bist mir ein **netter** ~ ⟨iron⟩ *you are a nice sort of a f.*; *you are a beauty*!; **prächtiger,** prachtvoller ~ ⟨fam⟩ *a regular brick, a jolly sound f.* ‖ **schlechter** ~ *rogue, scoundrel, a bad character*, ⟨fam⟩ *a bad lot* od *egg* ‖ seltsamer ~ *a queer specimen, a funny fish*; **übler** ~ ⟨sl⟩ *pill, a bad egg* ‖ ungeschickter, tölpelhafter ~ ⟨naut sl⟩ *swab*; **widerlicher** ~ *son of a gun*; ⟨Am sl⟩ *kike* **K·erlchen** n ~s/~ *little man, fellow, chap*; *nice little beggar* ‖ schmuckes ~ *dapper little man* (Thackeray); ⟨fam⟩ *hop-o'-my-thumb, manikin* ×°**K·erle**! (= Kerl) *laddy*!, *laddie*!

K·ermes *m* ~/~ *scarlet-dye*, → Kirmes

K·ern *m* ~(e)s/~e **1.** ⟨eig⟩ *kernel*, ⟨scient⟩ *nucleus* ‖ (Apfel≃ etc) *pip* ‖ (Kirsch≃, Pflaumen≃ etc) *stone* ‖ (Haselnuß≃) *kernel* ‖ (Getreide≃) *grain* ‖ (olive) *pit* ‖ mit festem ~ *clingstone* [attr] **2.** (Innerstes, Herz etc) *heart, core* ‖ (Holz≃) *woodheart, woodcore* ‖ (Flachs≃) *boon of flax* ‖ *heart (of salad)* ‖ (Mark) (Holunder≃ etc) *pith* **3.** ⟨tech⟩ (Kanonen≃) *bore* ‖ (Gieß≃) *mould core* ‖ (Marmor≃) *hard grain* ‖ (Tau≃) *(hempen) core of a rope* **4.** ⟨chem, astr⟩ *nucleus* (e–s Kometen); g–g– ~e [pl] (mit derselben Protonen- u. ders. Neutronenzahl) *even-even nuclei* **5.** ⟨fig⟩ (Wesens≃) *(the) pith of a matter* ‖ *main substance, quintessence, heart*; *best part*; *essence*; *grist, nub, pith*; *merits of the question*; *meat of the agreement*; *core, kernel, central* (od *most vital*) *point*, ⟨Am⟩ *nub (of a matter)* ‖ *bedrock (of reality)* ‖ *gist (of a conversation)* ‖ *core (of a drama)* ‖ der ~ des Heeres etc *the flower of the army*; *of society* | *the elite of the nation*; ⟨mil⟩ *core (of fire support)* | **am** ~ e–r S vorbeireden *to talk about the egg without considering the yolk*; **im** ~ .. *at bottom he is a* .. ; **bis zum** ~ e–r S dringen *to get to the very core* od *bottom of a th*; z ~ e–r S k *to get down to brasstacks* | **das ist** der ~ der ganzen Frage *that is the main point* od *main issue of the problem* ‖ der ~ der S ist .. *the point I wish to make is* .. ‖ edler ~ in rauher Schale *rough diamond* ‖ in dem Jungen steckt **ein guter** ~ *there is sth good in the young fellow* ‖ **des Pudels** ~ *the gist of the matter* ‖ das also war des Pudels ~! *so that's what it meant really*! **K·ern-** [in comp] ⟨chem, at, phys⟩ *nuclear* **~abstand** m *internuclear distance* **~apfel** m *calville* **≃artig** a *kernel-like*, ⟨scient⟩ *nucleoid* **~ausdruck** m *pithy expression* **~beißer** *m* ⟨orn⟩ *grosbeak*; (gemeiner) *hawfinch, cherry-finch* **~beschuß** m *n. bombardment* **~bildung** f (natürliche) *nucleogenesis* **≃br·av** [–f] a *honest to the backbone* **~brennstoff** m *atomic fuel* **~chemie** f *n. chemistry* **≃deutsch** a *German to the backbone* **~drehbank** f *core turning lathe, core-frame* **~durchmesser** m *minor diameter* **≃elastisch** a ⟨tex⟩ *core-spun* **~energie** f ⟨chem⟩ *n. energy* | ~kraftwerk [n] *n. power station*; ~risiko [n] ⟨ins⟩ *n. risk* **≃faul** a *fox(e)y (timber), rotten at the core* **~fäule** f ⟨for⟩ *stem-rot* **≃fern** a ⟨at⟩ *planetary* (Elektron) **≃fest** a *very firm, thoroughly* od *very solid, robust* **~feuer** n *central fire* **~flachs** m *heckled flax* **~fleisch** n *solid meat* **≃förmig** a *in shape of a kernel*, etc. **~forscher** m *n. scientist* **~frage** f *central problem, pivotal question*; *point*; ⟨Am⟩ *nub question* **~forschungszwecke** pl *n. research purpose* **≃fremd** a *extranuclear (field)* **~frucht** f *kernel-fruit* **~fusion** f *n. fusion* **~gehäuse** n ⟨bot⟩ *core* **~geschoß** n *armo(u)r-piercing shell* **≃ges·und** a *thoroughly sound*; *as sound as a bell*; *fresh as a daisy* od *rose*, ⟨hum⟩ *as paint*; *in the pink of health* **~guß** m *cored work* ‖ *cored casting* **≃g·ut** a *thoroughly good* **~holz** n *heart-wood* **~kabel** n *central quad of a cable* **~kasten** m ⟨found⟩ *core box* **~kettenreaktion** f *n. chain reaction* **~ladungszahl** f *atomic number* **~leder** n *bend leather* **~linse** f ⟨opt⟩ *n. lens* **~los** a *seedless (raisins)* **~mehl** n *prime* od *fine flour* **~mensch** m *man of sterling character* **~moment** n ⟨mech⟩ *moment of normal force* ‖ *nuclear m.*; magnetisches ~ *n. magnetic m.* **≃nah** a *fixed (electron)* **~nährstoffe** m pl ⟨agr⟩ *basic nutrients* **~obst** n *pome fruit* **~physik** f *nuclear physics* [pl; sg konstr] angewandte ~ *nucleonics* **≃physikalisch** a *nucleic* **~punkt** m ⟨fig⟩ *core, kernel*; *central* od *essential, crucial point*; ⟨Am⟩ *nub (of a question)*; wir wollen zum ~ der S k *let us get at the hard nub of the business*; den ~ treffen *to hit the mark* **~reaktion** *f nuclear reaction*; durch thermische ~ ausgelöst *thermo-n.* (Spaltung) **~reaktor** m *nuclear reactor, atomic pile* **~riß** m ⟨tech⟩ *internal crack*, ⟨for⟩ *heart-shake* **~rohr** n ⟨mil⟩ *(inner) tube, barrel* **~schacht** m (Hochofen) *shaft, body* **~schatten** m *inmost deepest shadow* **~schleife** f ⟨bot⟩ *chromosome* **~schuß** m *point-blank shot* **~seife** f *grained, laundry, hard soap* **~spaltung** f *n. fission* ~s-explosion [f] *fission burst* **~speicher** m ⟨comp⟩ *core store* **~spindel** f ⟨tech⟩ ⟨found⟩ *core-spindle* **~spruch** m *aphorism*; *pithy sentence, expressive saying* **~spur** f ⟨at⟩ *n. particle track* **~stahl** m *first-rate steel* **~stück** n ⟨arts⟩ *pièce de résistance* Fr; ⟨tech⟩ *major unit* **~technik** f *n. engineering* **~truppen** f pl *choice troops* pl **~verschmelzung** f *nuclear fusion* **~waffen** f pl *n. weapons* | ~krieg [m] *n. war* **≃w·eich** a (Eier) *soft-boiled* **~werk** n ⟨fort⟩ *main work*; ~fäden [m pl] pro cm ⟨tex⟩ *ends pl per inch* **~wolle** f *finest back* od *spine wool, prime wool* **~wort** n *word coming from the heart*; *expressive w.*; *saying of deep meaning*; *expressive term* **~zerfall** m ⟨chem⟩ *n. disintegration* **k·ernen**[1] vt [h] *to pip, to stone* **k·ernenhaft, k·ernig** a ⟨fig⟩ *full of pep*; (markig) *pithy* ‖ (derb) *strong*

k·ernen[2] vt [h] → kirnen ‖ **Kerner** → Karner

Kertsch n (Hafenstadt der Krim) *Kerch*

K·erze f ~/~n **1.** ⟨allg⟩ *candle*; (Wachs≃) *wax c.*; dünn .. *taper*; (Talg≃) *tallow c.*; ⟨Harrow sl⟩ *tolly* **2.** ⟨mot⟩ *(spark) plug* **3.** ⟨gym⟩ *shoulder stand on floor*; ⟨ftb⟩ *sky-ball* **K·erzen- ~docht** m *wick of a c., c. wick* **≃ger·ade 1.** [a] *bolt upright, stiff and erect, (as) straight as a flag-pole* od *as a dart* **2.** [adv] *sheer (into)*; *(to go, walk, sit) bolt-upright*; ~ abstürzen ⟨aero⟩ *to plummet*; ~ in die Höhe springen *to spring erect*

~gewinde n ⟨mot⟩ *spark-plug thread* **~gießer** m *c. maker* **~gießmaschine** f *c. moulding machine* **~halter** m, **~leuchter** m *c.-stick* **~licht** n, **~schein** m *c.-light* ‖ bei ~ *by c.-light* **~stummel** m, **~stumpf** m *c.-stub* **~weihe** f ⟨ec⟩ *C.mas* **~ziehmaschine** f *c.-dipper, c. manufacturing machinery*

K·erzel n ~s/~ [österr] *small candle* | °~-schlicker [m] ("*candle swallower*") ⟨sl⟩ *RC self--righteous church-goer* (cf *twicer*) ⟨Am sl⟩ *knee--bender*

°**k·esch** a *jaunty, sprightly*

K·escher m ~s/~ (Fisch≃) *landing-net* ‖ (Schmetterlings≃) *butterfly-* od *ring-net* **k·eschern** vt [h] *to catch with ring-net* ‖ ich –rte ihn auf *I stirred him up, I encouraged him, I bucked him up*

k·eß a (→ fesch) *dashing, jaunty, smart*

K·essel m ~s/~ **A. 1.** *kettle, heater, boiler* ‖ Dampf≃ *(steam-)b.* ⟨a. rail⟩; Tee≃ *tea-k.* ‖ Wasch≃ *wash-b.* ‖ F·isch≃ *tin pannier* ‖ M·aisch-≃ *mash copper* ‖ Koch≃ *boiler* ‖ Hopfen≃ *wort copper* ‖ Druckluft≃ *air compression plant* ‖ P·ech≃ *waxer* ‖ L·eim≃ *glue-pot* ‖ W·ind≃ *air chamber* ‖ Sch·iffs≃ *marine boiler*; H·ochdruck-≃ *high pressure b.*; H·öchstdruck≃ *super high p. b.* ‖ verzinnter ~ *tinned k.* od *copper* ‖ W·eihwasser≃ ⟨ec⟩ *holy water pot* od *font* **2.** (Becken) *basin* ‖ (Behälter f Flüssigkeiten) *tank* **3.** ⟨geog⟩ (Tal~) *valley, gorge* ‖ ⟨mil⟩ *excavation* ‖ ⟨allg⟩ *hollow* ‖ (Vulkan≃) *crater* **4.** ⟨hunt⟩ *(badger's) kennel* ‖ *(boar's) couch* ‖ → ~treiben **5.** ⟨tact⟩ *pocket* **B.** ein ~ **voll** *a k.-ful* ‖ den ~ aufs Feuer setzen *to put the k. on* ‖ ~ **flicken** *to mend pots and pans* ‖ ~ abpicken ⟨mar⟩ (= abklopfen) *to scale a b.* ‖ ~ abblasen *to blow off ..* ‖ ~ speisen *to feed ..* ‖ ⟨fig⟩ alles in e–n ~ werfen *to treat all alike* **~asche** f *potash* **~·ausbesserung** f *repair to a b.* **~blech** n *b. plate* **~explosi·on** f *b. explosion* **~-flicker** m *tinker* **~fundament** n *b.-seating* **~haken** m *pot-hook, pot-hanger* **~haube** f *basinet* **~haus** n *b. room* od *house* **~jagd** f → ~treiben **~mantel** m *b. shell* **~pauke** f ⟨mus⟩ *k.-drum* **~probe** f ⟨tech⟩ *b.-test* **~schlacke** f *b. slag* **~schmied** m *brazier, coppersmith*; *k.-maker, b.-maker* **~schmiede** f *brazier's forge* od *shop* **~stein** m *fur, grounds, b.-scale, (water-)incrustation*; viel ~ h *to be furred up*; v ~ befreien *to descale* | ~ablagerung [f] *scale deposit*; ~beseitigung [f] *descaling* **~treiben** n ⟨hunt⟩ *drive, battue(-shooting)*; *circular beat* ‖ ⟨fig⟩ *dead set*, (Razzia) *dragnet raid* **~wagen** m ⟨rail⟩ *tank wagon*, ⟨Am⟩ *t. car* **~wand** f *b. shell* **~waren** f pl *pots and pans* **K·eßler** m ~s/~ *brazier, tinker*

Ketch·up [–'ʌp] m, n *catchup*

Ket·on n ~s/ *ketone*

K·etsch f ~/~en ⟨mar⟩ (Zweimaster) *ketch*

K·etscher m = Kescher *landing-net*, etc.

K·ett- ~baum [m] ⟨weav⟩ *warp beam*; ~fäden [m pl] pro cm ⟨tex⟩ *ends* pl *per inch* **K·ettchen** n *small* od *little chain*; *ch.let* **K·ette** f ~/~n **A. 1.** *chain* ‖ Steg≃ *stud link ch.*; steglose ~ *plain link ch.*; ⟨tech⟩ endlose ~ *endless ch.* | ·Uhr≃ *watch--ch.* ‖ H·als≃ *necklace*; enge ~ (gleichgroßer Perlen) *choker*, → Verlauf≃ ‖ K·inn≃ ⟨hors⟩ *curb-ch.* ‖ ·Arm≃ *ch. bracelet* ‖ Fräs≃ *moulding ch.* ‖ Z·ug≃ *pull-ch.* ‖ Schn·ee≃ *non-skid ch.* ‖ ·Ordens≃ *collar* od *neck-ch. of the order* ‖ R·aupen≃ *creeper chain* **2.** ⟨geog⟩ (Gebirgs≃) *range*; *mountain ch.*: *Aling Kangri R.* (*Tibet*): *Karakorum R.*; *Cantabrian Ch.* **3.** ⟨weav⟩ *warp*; *ch. course* ‖ ~ u Schuß *warp and woof* **4.** ⟨mil⟩ Schützen≃ *skirmishing line* ‖ Posten≃ *cordon, line of outposts, ch. of sentries* od *posts* ‖ Melde≃ *relay* **5.** ⟨hunt⟩ *covey* (*of partridges*) **6.** ⟨aero⟩ ~ v ⟨Ger⟩ 3, ⟨engl⟩ 5–6 Flugzeugen *flight, patrol* **B.** e–n Hund an die ~ legen *to ch. up a dog* ‖ jdn in ~n legen *to shackle a p, to put a p into ch.s* od *fetters* ‖ v der ~ losmachen *to unchain* | ⟨fig⟩ ~ bilden *to form a ch.*; ⟨police⟩ *to link hands* ‖ in ~n geboren *born in bondage*; die ~n zerreißen *to strike away* od *off the ch.s* **C.** ⟨fig⟩ ~ v .. *string of* (*vehicles*), v Ereignissen *series of events* ‖ e–e endlose ~ v *no end of* ‖ (*a link in the*) *ch. of generations* **K·ettel** n ~s/~ (eisernes Verbindungsband) *hook* **k·etteln** vt [h] *to fasten with a chain, to link* **k·etten** vt [h] (an [acc]) *to chain* (*to*), *to fasten with a ch.* ‖ ⟨fig⟩ gekettet an *attached, bound, wedded, rooted, yoked to* ‖ es gelang ihr, ihn völlig an sich zu ~ *she succeeded in getting him completely under her influence* **K·etten-** **~antrieb** m *ch. drive* **~armband** n *ch. bracelet* **~aufhängung** f ⟨tech⟩ *catenary suspension* **~bahn** f *ch. railway* **~baum** m *roller* od *warp* od *yarn beam* **~b·echerwerk** n *ch. elevator* **~brief** m *ch.-letter* **~bruch** m ⟨math⟩ *continued fraction* **~brücke** f *suspension bridge* **~dr·uckmaschine** f *ch. printing mill* **~einziehen** n ⟨weav⟩ *warp-drawing-in* **~elevator** m *ch. elevator* **~faden** m *warp-thread* **~fahrzeug** n *track-type vehicle* **~feier** (Petri) f ⟨ec⟩ *Lammas(-day)* (1. August) **~flieger** m (Karussel) *flying boats, airship ride* **~f·örderer** m *ch.* od *bucket conveyer* **~förderung** f ⟨min⟩ *ch. haulage* **≃förmig** a *ch.like* ‖ ⟨chem⟩ *forming a ch.* **~fräse** f *ch. cutter mortising machine* **~garn** n ⟨weav⟩ *warp thread* **~gebirge** n *mountain ch.* **~gelenk, ~glied** n *link of a ch.* **~getriebe** n *ch. drive* od *gear* **~handel** m "*chain-trade*", *trade in which there are too many middlemen* (→ Schieber) **~heber** m ⟨weav⟩ *lifting cord* **~hemd** n *byrnie*; *coat of mail* **~hund** m *bandog, mastiff, watchdog* **~karuss·ell** n *chairoplanes* pl **~kasten** ⟨mar⟩ *ch. locker* **~kugel** f *ch.-shot* **~kuppelung** f ⟨rail⟩ *ch.-coupling* **~laden** m *ch.-store* **~länge** f ⟨mar⟩ *cable's length, ch.-length* **~isolator** m *ch. insulator* **~naht** f, **~stich** m *ch.-stitch seam* **~panzer** m *(ch.-)mail* **~pumpe** f *ch.-pump* **~rad** n *chain wheel, sprocket wheel* **~raucher** m *ch.-smoker*; ~ s *to ch.smoke* **~reaktion** f (*nuclear*) *ch. reaction* | ~smaschine [f] *pile* **~rechnung** f, ~regel [f] ⟨math⟩ *double* od *compound rule of three*; ⟨comp⟩ ~en [pl] *calculating with a common multiplier or divisor* **~reflex** m ⟨eth⟩ *reflex ch.* **~reim** f *ch.ed rhyme* **~ring** m *shackle* **~rost** m *ch. grate* **~scherer** m *warper* **~schlepper** m *crawler tractor* **~schloß** n *ch.-lock* **~schluß** m *poly-syllogism* **~schutz** m ⟨cycl⟩ *ch.-guard, ch.-cover*; ⟨mot⟩ *track guard* **~seide** f (2mal gezwirnt) *thrown silk* **~spanner** m ⟨cycl⟩ *ch. adjuster* **~spule** f ⟨weav⟩ *warp bobbin* **~stich** m (beim Nähen) *ch.-stitch* ‖ ⟨mar⟩ *ch.-knot* | ~durchnähmaschine [f] (f Schuster) *ch.-stitch sole sewing machine* **~strafe** f *confinement in irons* **~strang** m ⟨weav⟩ *warp* **~stuhl** m ⟨weav⟩ *warp loom* **~tau** n ⟨mar⟩ *ch.-cable* **~trieb** m ⟨cycl⟩ *ch. gear(ing)* **~triebrad** n ⟨mech⟩ *ch.-pulley* **~werk** n *ch.-work* **~wicklung** f ⟨el⟩ *basket winding* **~winde** f ⟨mar⟩ *ch.-jack* **~wirkware** f ⟨tex⟩ *warpknitted fabric* **~zus-stoß** ⟨mot⟩ *multiple crack-up*

K·etzer m ~s/~ (**~in** f ~/~nen) *heretic* ⟨a. fig⟩ **~gericht** n *inquisition* **~geschichte** f *history of heresy* **~haupt** n ⟨hist⟩ *heresiarch* **~verbrennung** f *auto-da-fe, burning of heretics* **Ketzer·ei** f ~/~en *heresy, heterodoxy* **k·etzerisch** a *heretical, heterodox* ‖ ~e Ansichten, Meinungen *heretical views, opinions*

k·euchen vi [h] *to pant* (unter *under*), *puff, gasp* (*for breath*); *to breathe hard* od *with difficulty, to wheeze* ‖ ~ vor .. *to blow*, etc. *with* (*exertions*) ‖ die Treppe hinauf~ *to puff up the stairs* **K·euchhusten** m (*w*)*hooping cough*

K·eule f ~/~n **1.** (Waffe) *club* ‖ ⟨allg⟩ *cudgel, bludgeon* ‖ mit ~n (er)schlagen *to club* od *cudgel* (*to death*) **2.** ⟨gym⟩ *Indian club*; → schwingen **3.** ⟨cul⟩ *leg, round, joint* od *shoulder* (*of mutton*, etc.); (Gans≃ etc) *thigh*; ⟨hunt⟩ *haunch* (*of venison*) **K·eulen-** **~ärmel** m *leg-of-mutton* od *melon sleeve* **≃förmig** a *club-shaped* ‖ ⟨scient⟩ *claviform* ‖ ⟨ent⟩ mit ~en Fühlern *clavicorn*; .. Tastern *clavipalp*

~schlag m *blow with a club* **~schwingen** n *Indian club exercise* **~träger** m *clubman*

K·euper(mergel) m ~s/ ⟨geol⟩ *red marl, keuper*

k·eusch a *chaste* ‖ (unbefleckt) *maidenly, innocent, pure*; ⟨rel⟩ *immaculate* ‖ ⟨allg⟩ das ~este Mädchen *the most respectable (modest, virtuous, innocent) girl*; *virgin (modesty)* ‖ die ~e S. *virtuous Susanna* **~baum** m, **~lamm** n *chaste tree* | **≗heit** f ~/ *chastity* ‖ *innocence, purity* ‖ ⟨allg⟩ *modesty, virtue*

Key-Inseln f pl (bei Florida) *Key-Islands*

Kh·aiberpaß, Khyberpaß m (zw Afghanistan u Pakistan) *Khyber Pass*

Kh·aki n ~/ **1.** (Farbe) *khaki* **2.** m ~/ (Stoff) *khaki* | ~zeug [n] *kh.s* pl

Khart·um n (Stadt im Sudan) *Chartum*

Khed·ive m ~n/~n *khedive*

Khyberpass ['kai–] m → Khaiberpass

Kiangsi n (Prov. Chinas)

Kiangsu n (Prov. Chinas)

Kiautschou [–au] n ⟨†Ger⟩ *Kiaochow*

K·ichererbse f ⟨bot⟩ *chick-pea* **K·ichern** n ~s/ *titter(ing), giggle* ‖ ⟨fam⟩ *snigger(ing), sniggers* pl (→ Gekicher) ‖ in ~ ausbrechen *to get the giggles*

k·ichern vi [h] *to titter, giggle, chuckle* ‖ ⟨fam⟩ *snicker, snigger, sniggle* (über *at*) ‖ sie kicherte in sich hinein *she chuckled to herself*

k·icken vt [h] ⟨sport bes ftb⟩ *to kick* °**K·icks** m ~es/~e (Billard) *false stroke, miss, mis-cue* ‖ ⟨fig⟩ *blunder* °**k·icksen** vi [h] *to make a miss, to mis-cue* ‖ ⟨fig⟩ *to blunder* **K·ickstarter** m ~s/~ ⟨mot cycl⟩ *kickstarter*

K·iebitz m ~es/~e ⟨orn⟩ *lapwing, peewit* ‖ Gold≗ ⟨orn⟩ *golden plover* ‖ ~e [pl] → *plover* | ⟨fig⟩ (Zuschauer) ⟨bes cards⟩ (**~er** m ~s/~) *looker-on*, ⟨Am⟩ *kibitzer* | **≗en** vi ⟨fig⟩ *to look on*; *to listen* **~blume** f ⟨bot⟩ *checkered daffodil*

K·iefer[1] f ~/~n ⟨bot⟩ *pine(-tree)*, (gemeine) *Scotch fir* od *pine, pinus sylvestris* L ‖ Berg≗ *mountain pine*; Weimuts≗ *white p.*; Zirbel≗ *cembran p.*; → Latsche; Kiefern-

K·iefer[2] m ~s/~ ⟨anat⟩ *jaw(-bone)* ‖ ⟨scient⟩ *maxilla* ‖ Ober-, Unter≗ *upper, lower jaw* ‖ ⟨ent scient⟩ *mandible* **~eiterung** f *ulceration of the jaw* **~höhle** f ⟨med⟩ *maxillary sinus* | ~neiterung [f] ⟨path, med⟩ *suppuration of the maxillary sinus* **~klemme** f ⟨med⟩ *lock-jaw* **≗los** a *without a jaw* od *mandible* **~muskel** m ⟨anat⟩ *masseter*, ⟨scient⟩ *maxillary (muscle)* **~orthopäde** m *orthodontist* **~taster** m ⟨ent⟩ *maxillary palp* **~zungenmuskel** m ⟨anat⟩ *genio-glossus*

k·iefern a *(of) pine, (made in) fir* **K·iefer(n)-**[1] **~blasenrost** m ⟨bot⟩ *p. blister* **~blattwespe** f ⟨ent⟩ *p. saw-fly*; Larve der ~ *p. worm* **~bohle** f *p. plank, deal board* **~eule** f ⟨ent⟩ *p.-beauty* **~gehölz** n *p.-wood* **~harz** n *p.-resin* **~holz** *p.-timber, p.-wood, (red) deal*; Tisch aus ~ *deal table* **~kreuzschnabel** m ⟨orn⟨ *parrot-crossbill* **~nadelöl** n *fir* od *p. needle oil* **~rüsselkäfer** m *p.-weevil* **~schwärmer** m ⟨ent⟩ *p. hawk-moth* **~spanner** m *p. looper* **~spinner** m *p. moth* **~zapfen** m *p.-cone*

K·iek-in-die-Welt m ~/~ *greenhorn, mannikin, little chap* (→ kieken)

ˣ**K·iek(e)** f ~/~en *warming-pan, foot-warmer*

°**k·ieken** vi [h] ⟨dial & fam⟩ *to peep* **K·ieker** m ~s/~ ⟨phot⟩ *viewer* ‖ ° jdn auf dem ~ h *to have it in for a p*

Kiel n ⟨Ger⟩ (Stadt) **K·ieler Bucht** f *Kiel Bight, Bay of Kiel* **K·ieler Woche** f *Kiel Regatta*

K·iel m ~(e)s/~e **1.** (Feder≗) *quill* **2.** ⟨mar⟩ *keel* ‖ Flach≗ *flat bottom* ‖ Schlinger≗ *bilge k.* ‖ auf eigenem ~ *on her own b.*; auf ebenem ~ *on an even k.* **3.** ⟨zoo & bot⟩ *k.* ⟨scient⟩ *carina* L **~blätter** n pl ⟨bot⟩ *k.-petals* pl **~block** m ⟨mar⟩ *k.-block* **~bogen** m ⟨arch⟩ *k.-arch* **~feder** f *quill(-pen)* **~flosse** f ⟨aero⟩ *(b.) fin* **~flügel** m = ~klavier **≗förmig** a *k.-shaped*, ⟨scient⟩ *carinate(d)* **~fuge** f (Schiffbau) *rabbet* **~gang** m ⟨mar⟩ *garboard strakes* pl **~geld** n ⟨mar⟩ *k.age* **~holen** n ⟨mar⟩ a) *careening*; b) *k.hauling* **≗holen** vt [h] ⟨mar⟩ a) *to careen (a ship), to heave (a ship) down*; b) (Strafe) *to k. haul* **~jacht** f *k. yacht, k.er* **~klavier** n *harpsichord, cembalo* **~legung** f ⟨mar⟩ *laying down* **~linie** f ⟨mar⟩ *line ahead* **≗·oben** a, adv *k. upwards, upturned* **~planke** f ⟨mar⟩ *garboard plank* **~platte** f ⟨mar⟩ *garboard plate* **~raum** m ⟨mar⟩ *ship's hold* **~schwein** n ⟨mar⟩ *ke(e)lson* **~schwertjacht** f ⟨mar⟩ *k. and centre-board y.* **~sponung** f = ~fuge **~wasser** n ⟨mar⟩ *wake*; *eddy* (od *dead, bilge*) *water*; im ~ folgen *to follow in the wake* ⟨a. fig⟩

K·ieme f ~/~n *gill (of a fish)*; [mst pl] *gills*, ⟨scient⟩ *branchiae* pl L **K·iemen- ~atmer** ⟨ich⟩ *g.-breather* **~bogen** m ⟨arch⟩ *g.-arch* **~deckel** m ⟨ich⟩ *g.-cover*, ⟨scient⟩ *operculum* **~faser** f ⟨ich⟩ *g.-filament* **≗förmig** a ⟨scient⟩ *branchiform* **~fuß** m *b.ireme* **~füßler** m pl *water fleas*, ⟨scient⟩ *b.i-pods* pl **~haut** f *g.-flap* **~höhle** f *g.-chamber, -cavity* **~öffnung** f *g.-opening*

K·ien m ~(e)s/ *resinous pinewood, kindling* ‖ °⟨fig⟩ rede doch nicht solchen ~ *don't talk such rubbish* ‖ °er ist mächtig auf dem ~ *he's up to snuff* **~apfel** m *pine-cone* **~bohrer** m ⟨ent⟩ *p.-weevil* **~fackel** f *p.-wood torch* **~föhre** f ⟨bot⟩ *fir, p.* → Kiefer[1] **~harz** n *p. resin* **~holz** n *resinous p.-wood* **~öl** n *p.-oil* **~ruß** m *p.-soot, smoke-black, lampblack* **~span** m *p.-splinter* | **≗ig** a *resinous*

°**K·ientopp** m ~s/~e ⟨sl⟩ *movies* pl, → Kino

K·iepe f ~/~n *back-basket, dosser*

K·ies m ~es/~e **1.** (Geröll) *gravel, grit*; grober Strand≗ *shingle* ‖ mit ~ bestreuen *to grit, to gravel*; mit ~ beschottern *to ballast (roads)* **2.** ⟨min⟩ *pyrites* | ~ baggern *to draw out gravel* ‖ Eisen≗ ⟨minr⟩ *marcasite, pyrites* ‖ Filter≗ *filtering gravel* **3.** °(Geld) ⟨sl⟩ *dust, dirt, brass*, ⟨Am⟩ *dough* **~ader** f ⟨min⟩ *streak of pyrites* **~allee** f *gravelwalk* **≗artig** a *gritty, gravelly* **~bank** f *g.l bank* **~beton** m *g.l concrete* **~bett** n (Fluß≗) *pebbly bed* **~bettung** f *gravel ballast* **~boden** m *g.ly soil, gravel ground* **~brenner** m ⟨tech⟩ *pyrites-kiln* **~filter** m ⟨tech⟩ *rubble* od *gravel filter* **~grube** f *gravel pit* od *extraction* **~sand** m *gravel* **~schüttung** f *ballasting* **~weg** m *g.led path*

K·iesel m ~s/~ *pebble* ‖ ⟨min⟩ *flint(-stone)*; ⟨scient⟩ *silex* L **~ader** f ⟨min⟩ *vein of f.* **~alge** f ⟨bot⟩ *diatom* **≗artig** a *f.y*, ⟨scient⟩ *silicious* **~erde** f *silica, silicious earth, f.y earth* **≗erdehaltig** a *s.s, siliciferous* **~fels** m *f.y rock* **~fluß** m *s.s flux* **~flußsäure** f *fluo-silicic acid* **~gestein** n *s.s rock* **~glas** n *flint-glass* **~gur** f ⟨geol Ger⟩ *diatomite, kieselguhr* [Ger] **≗hart** a *as hard as fl., fl.y* **~herz** n ⟨fig⟩ *heart of fl.* **~kalk** m ⟨geol⟩ *s.s limestone* **~kupfer** n *silicated copper* **~lunge** f ⟨med⟩ *silicosis* **~mangan** n *s.s manganese* **~sand** m *pebbly sand* **≗sauer** a ⟨chem⟩ *silicic* **~säure** f *s.c acid* **~schiefer** m *cherts* pl, *s.s schist, f.y slate* **~sinter** m *s.s sinter* **~stein** m *f. pebble(-stone), pebble-f.* **~tuff** m *s.s sinter of the Geyser* **~zinkerz** n *hemimorphite*

***k·iesen** vt [kieste & kor/gekiest & gekoren] [h] *to choose* ˣ°**k·iesetig** a *dainty, fastidious, (easily disgusted by food)*

k·iesig a *gravelly, gritty* → Kies

Ki·ew n ⟨Russ⟩ (Hptst der Ukraine) *Kiev, Kief(f)*

K·ikelkakel n ~s/ *chit-chat, tittle-tattle*

kikerik·i intj & ≗ n *cock-a-doodle-doo* **~n** ['iːən] vi [h] *to crow (like a cock)*

K·ilbi f ~/–benen Sw → Kirchweih; dazu: ~tanz [m]

Kilimandsch·aro m (Afrikan. Berg) *Kilimanjaro*

k·lle, k·ille! *tickle, tickle*! ‖ °~ ~ übern Sonntag ⟨sex⟩ *week-ender*; *week-end outing*

k·illen vi [h] *(of sails) to shiver, flap*; → umbringen

K·ilo n ~s/~s; **~gr·amm** n *kilogram(me)*; ~kalorie [f] *kilocalorie* **~amp·ere** n *kilo-ampere* **~kalor·ie** f *k.-calorie* **~h·ertz** n *k.-hertz (per second)* **~m·eter** n *k.metre, k.meter* **~m·eter-**

fresser m ⟨mot fam⟩ *road-hog*, ⟨sl⟩ *speed merchant, speedster* **∼m·eterstein** m *milestone* **∼m·eterzähler** m *cyclometer, (h)odometer, mileage recorder* od *indicator, mileometer* **∼w·att** ⟨el⟩ *k.watt* **∼w·attstunde** f ⟨el⟩ *k.watt hour*

K·imberley [–li] n (Stadt in S.-Afrika)

†**K·imbern** m pl (german. Volksstamm) *Cimbri*

†**k·imbrische Halbinsel** f *Cimbric Chersonese*

K·imm[1] f ∼/ (Schiffbau) *bilge* **∼gang** m *b. strake*

K·imm[2] f ∼/ ⟨naut⟩ (*visible*) *horizon* **∼tiefe** f *dip of the h.*; *dip angle*

K·imme f ∼/∼n **1.** (Visier≗) (*notch of the*) *backsight*; (*V of*) *rear-sight*; ∼ u Korn *notch and head-sight* **2.** (Rand) *edge, border* **3.** (Faßrand) *chime, chimb, croze* **4.** (Schiffbau) *bilge* **5.** ⟨allg⟩ (Kerbe) *notch* (a. ⟨sex vulg⟩); *V-shaped incision* | ≗n vt [h] (Fässer) ∼ *to chime*

kimm·erisch a ⟨fig⟩ (fern, dunkel) *Cimmerian*

K·imming mst **Kimmung** f **1.** = Kimm[2] *horizon* **2.** (Luftspiegelung) *mirage* **3.** → Kimm[1] *bilge* **∼sglocke** f *bilge strake*

Kim·ono m (⟨a.⟩ ['...] ∼s/∼s [Jap] *kimono* | ∼ärmel [m] *k. sleeve*; ∼bluse [f] *k. blouse*; ∼kragen [m] *k. collar*

K·ind n ∼(e)s/∼er **1.** *child*: *he/she*; vor der Geburt: Es, es *it* (→ Baby); (unmündiges ∼) *infant* || kl ∼ *babe, baby*; *toddler* || totgeborenes ∼ *still-born ch.* || eheliches ∼ *ch. born in wedlock* || uneheliches ∼ *bastard, natural* od *illegitimate ch.*; ∼ der Liebe *love-ch.* | ⟨übtr⟩ ein liebes ∼ *a dear little girl*; liebes ∼! *darling*! | **Kinder** [pl] *ch.ren offspring, progeny, issue, family*; ⟨fam⟩ *kids*; *little ones*; *chicks* pl || Fest der Unschuldigen ∼er (28. Dez.) *Innocents' Day* | sind ∼er da? *is there any family*? ihre ∼er *her ch.ren* od *family* || heimatlose, verwahrloste ∼er *waifs and strays* pl | ein ∼ bek (*to be going*) *to have a ch., to be with ch., to be having a baby* || sie wird im November wieder ein ∼ bek *she will be lying in again in November* || er hörte, es würde ein ∼ **k** *he heard that there was to be a ch.* || es sind ∼er gek (in der Ehe) *there have been ch.ren* || ein ∼ v ihm *a ch. by him*; er bekam .. *he got a ch. by her* | ∼er in die W. **setzen** *to bring* od *put ch.ren into the world* || ein ∼ **zeugen** *to beget a ch.* || ein ∼ **gebären** *to give birth to a ch.* || ein ∼ unter dem Herzen **tragen** *to be with ch., to be expecting* od *in the family way* || eines ∼es **genesen** *to be delivered of a ch.* | ein ∼ **abtreiben** *to procure abortion* || ein ∼ **trocken legen** *to change a ch.'s diaper* | an ∼es Statt **annehmen** *to adopt* || **braver Leute** ∼ *the son of honest parents* || er hat ∼er wie die **Orgelpfeifen** *he has ch.ren in regular steps* || ein ∼ aus der **Taufe heben** *to stand sponsor to a ch.* | du bist selbst nicht ∼ **genug** *you are not enough of a ch. yourself* kein ∼ **mehr** s *to be no longer a ch., to be past ch.-hood*; ⟨fam⟩ *she is no chicken* || als ich **noch** ein ∼ war *when I was a kid* || **v** ∼ **auf** *from a ch., from one's infancy, from* (*early*) *ch.hood* || wie sage ich es meinem ∼e? *how can I enlighten my ch.*? || mit ∼ u **Kegel** (*with*) *bag and baggage*; weder ∼ noch Kegel h *to have neither chick nor child*; mit ∼ u Kegel spazierengehn *to go for a walk with the whole tribe* **2.** ⟨**übtr**⟩ die ∼er Israel, Gottes, des Teufels, der Finsternis *the Ch.ren of Israel, of God* [od *the pious*], *of satan, of darkness* || ein ∼ des Todes *a dead man* || wes Geistes ∼ er ist *what kind of a man he is* || ein ∼ des 19. Jhs *a ch. of the 19th century* || ein Berliner ∼ *a true* od *real Berliner*; ein ∼ dieser Stadt *a native* (*son*) *of this town* || ein dralles ∼ v Lande *a pink, healthy, bouncing country lass* || ∼ des Glücks *minion of fortune, lucky fellow*, ⟨fam⟩ *l. dog* || ein ∼ s–r M. *an offspring of his muse* || jedes ∼ weiß (daß) *it is common knowledge* (*that*); *any fool knows* (*that*) **3.** (**Anrede**) mein liebes ∼ *my dear ch.* || schönes ∼ *fair lady, beloved girl* || ihr Kinder! *you people*! *chaps*! **4.** ⟨**fig**⟩ sie ist **unschuldig wie** ein neugeborenes ∼ *she is as innocent as a new-born baby*; ist **noch ganz** ∼ *she is still quite a ch.* || er ist noch ein rechtes ∼ *he is still a regular ch., a mere babe* (*in the ways of the world*) || sei doch kein ∼! ⟨fam⟩ *now don't be silly* || wir w das ∼ schon **schaukeln** *we'll manage* od *swing it somehow, we'll push the matter through*; ⟨Am⟩ *we'll do the trick* || der Vorschlag war v Anfang an ein **totgeborenes** ∼ *from the very beginning it was an abortive scheme* || er ist **lieb** ∼ bei *he is a favorite with*; sich [acc] bei jdm l. ∼ m *to get under a p's skin*; er versucht sich l. ∼ bei mir z m *he is always trying to get into my good books, to ingratiate h.s. with, to endear h.s. to, to make h.s. pleasant to me* || wir wollen das ∼ beim rechten **Namen** nennen *I call a spade a spade*, ⟨vulg⟩ .., *some call it a bloody shovel* || das ∼ mit dem **Bade** ausschütten *to throw out the ch. with the bath-water* (Observer) || °den h sie als ∼ zu heiß gebadet *he got a knock in the cradle* **5.** ⟨**prov**⟩ gebranntes ∼ scheut das Feuer *once bitten twice shy* || aus ∼ern w Leute [etwa:] *the ch. is father of the man* || ∼er sind ∼er *boys will be boys*; *one cannot put old heads on young shoulders* || ∼er u Narren sprechen die Wahrheit *ch.ren and fools speak the truth* || wenn das ∼ ertrunken ist, wird der Brunnen zugedeckt *after death the doctor* **∼bett** n *ch.bed, confinement* || im ∼ liegen *to lie in, to be confined* || ins ∼ k *to be brought to bed* **∼bettfieber** n *puerperal fever* **∼bettzeit** f *lying-in time* **∼bewachen** n *baby sitting* **∼taufe** f *baptism*; *christening(-feast)* **K·indchen** n ∼s/∼ *baby, little child, infant* ×**K·indelbier** n *christening-dinner* od *-feast* **K·inder-** **∼abteilung** f ⟨med univ sl⟩ *the kids* **∼amme** f (*wet-*)*nurse* **∼arbeit** f *ch.-labo(u)r* **∼art** f *ch.ren's way* od *manner* **∼arzt** m *p(a)editrician* (*Am*) **∼augen** n pl °⟨fig sl⟩ *saucer-eyes*, mit erstaunten ∼ *pop-eyed* **∼ball** m *ch.ren's ball* **∼beihilfe** d *ch.ren's allowance* **∼bekleidung** f ⟨com, ad⟩ *children's clothing* **∼brei** m *spoon-food, pap* **∼buch** n *book for the young*; ≗er *juveniles* ⟨sl⟩ **∼dieb** m *kidnapper* **∼feind** m *ch.-hater* **∼flasche** f *baby bottle* **∼frau** f (*ch.ren's*) *nurse* **∼fräulein** n *mother's help, nursery governess* **∼freund** m *lover of ch.ren, ch.-lover* **∼fürsorge** f *ch. welfare* **∼garten** m *kindergarten, nursery-school*, ⟨Am⟩ *pre-sch.* **∼gärtnerin** f. *ki. teacher* **∼gebären** n *ch.bearing* **∼geld** n *family allowance* **∼gesellschaft** f *ch.ren's party* **∼gesicht** n *a ch.'s face* **∼glaube** m *faith of a ch.* **∼heilkunde** f *p(a)ediatrics* **∼hort** m *day-nursery* **∼jäckchen** n *child's jacket* od *cardigan* ⟨a. com, ad⟩ **∼jahre** n pl *infancy, ch.hood*; aus den ∼n s *to be out of ch.h.* **∼klapper** f *ch.'s rattle* **∼kleid** n *ch.'s frock* **∼kleidung** f *ch.ren's clothes* **∼krankheiten** f pl *ch.ren's complaints*; ⟨fig⟩ *teething troubles, growing pains* **∼lähmung** f *infantile paralysis*; spinale ∼ *poliomyelitis* ⟨fam⟩ *polio* **∼lätzchen** n *bib* **∼lehre** f *Sunday-school* (*teaching*) **∼leichen** f pl *corpses of ch.ren* **≗l·eicht** a: das ist ∼ *nothing is easier than that*; ⟨fam⟩ *that's as easy as pie*; ⟨Am sl⟩ *that's kidstuff* || ⟨fam⟩ *dead easy, as easy as ABC*, ⟨Am⟩ .. *as falling off a log* **≗lieb** a *fond of ch.ren* **∼liebe** f **1.** *love of ch.ren, parental affection, l. for one's ch.ren* **2.** *ch.ren's l., filial aff.* **∼lied** n *nursery-rhyme* od *-song* **∼literatur** f *juvenile literature* **∼löffel** m *dessertspoon* **≗los** a *ch.less*; ≗loses Ehepaar *ch.less married couple*; sie sind k. *they have no family* **∼losigkeit** f *failure of issue*; *ch.lessness* **∼mädchen** n, **∼magd** f *nurse-maid, n.ry-governess* **∼märchen** n *fairy-tale, n.rytale* **∼mord** m *ch.-murder, infanticide* || der Bethlehemitische ∼ *the M.* od *Massacre of the Innocents* **∼mörder(in** f) m *infanticide* **∼nahrung** f *infant food* **∼narr** m, **∼närrin** f *one who dotes on ch.ren* **∼pflegerin** f *nanny* **∼pocken** f pl ⟨med⟩ *small-pox* || °glatt wie ein **∼popo** *like a baby's bottom* **∼possen** f pl *ch.ish tricks* pl **∼psychologie** f *ch. psychology* **∼raub** m *kidnapping* **∼räuber** m *kidnapper*, ⟨Am sl⟩ *snatch(er)* ≃**reich** a *prolific* (*couple*); ~reiche Familie *large family*; Bund der K–en ⟨nazi⟩ *The Rich in Ch.ren Families Association* (Times) ~**schänder** m *ravisher of ch.ren* ~**schar** f *small fry* ~**schlafzimmer** n *night nursery* ~**schriften** f pl *juvenile literature, juveniles* pl ~**schuhe** m pl *ch.ren's shoes* pl; noch in den ~en stecken *to be still in one's teens* od *one's swaddling--clothes* ‖ die ~ ausgezogen h *to be no longer a baby, to be out of leading-strings*; in den –en stekken (S) *to be in its infancy* od *initial stages* ~**schule** f *infant sch.* ~**schürze** f *ch.'s pinafore* ~**segen** m *a quiver full of children* ~**sessel** m *high chair* ~**spiel** n *ch.'s play* ‖ ⟨fig⟩ *trifle, walk-over*; ⟨Am sl⟩ *pipe, pushover*; kein ~ *no picnic, quite a business*, (*it takes*) *a bit of doing* ‖ das ist ein ~ dagegen *that's ch.'s play to it*; es war mir ein ~ *I took it in my stride* | ~zeug [n] *toys, playthings* pl ~**sprache** f *ch.'s language, infant's prattle* ~**sterblichkeit** f *infant mortality* ~**stimmen** f pl *ch.ren's voices* pl, *infant voices* pl ~**stube** f *nursery*; der ~stube entwachsen *to emerge from n.y guidance* ‖ *raising* (*if you'd had any r.*) ‖ gute ~ *good bringing up, good manners, mannerliness*; k–e ~ *or* e–e schlechte ~ *no manners* ‖ er hat e–e gute ~ gehabt *he has been well brought up* ‖ v guter ~ *well bred*; v wenig guter ~ *underbred* ~**streiche** m pl = ~possen ~**stuhl** m *high chair* ~**taufe** f *christening of infants* ~**trage** f *carry-cot* ~**- u Hausmärchen** ⟨Ger⟩ *Household Tales* ~**wagen** m ⟨sport⟩ *go-, push-, mail-cart*; (für Säuglinge) *perambulator* ‖ ⟨fam⟩ *pram*; *baby-carriage*, (leichter) *stroller*; den ~ .. schieben *to wheel the p.* ~**wärterin** f (*part-time*) *ch.-nurse, ch.ren's nurse*; farbige ~ *mammy* ~**welt** f *young people, the young* pl ~**zähne** m pl *milk-teeth* ~**zeit** f *ch.hood* ~**zucht** f *education, government of ch.ren* ~**zulage** f *family allowance* **Kinder·ei** f ~/~en *juvenility, ch.ishness*; ~en [pl] *ch.ish things* pl ‖ (Streich) *ch.ish trick* ‖ (Kleinigkeit) *trifle*, ⟨Am⟩ *kidstuff* **K·indes-** ~**alter** n *infancy, ch.'s age*; im ~ *of tender age* ~**beine** n pl; v ~n an ⟨fig⟩ *from infancy, f. a ch., f. ch.hood* ~**kind** n *grandch.* ~**kinder** pl ⟨allg⟩ *great grandch.ren* ~**liebe** f *filial love* ~**mord** m *ch.-murder* ~**mörder** m *infanticide* ~**nöte** f pl *labour* ‖ in ~n s *to be in travail* od *labour, to labour with ch.*; ⟨fig⟩ *to be in a pickle* od *mess* ~**pflicht** f *filial duty* ~**teil** m *ch.'s portion* **K·indheit** f /~ *ch.hood, infancy*; frühe ~ *babyhood*; das erinnert mich an s–e ~ *that reminds me of him as a ch.* ‖ v ~ an *from a ch.*; die Schätze ihrer ~ *her ch.hood treasures*; ein Freund aus der ~ *a ch.h. friend*; ~serinnerungen *ch.h. memories* od *recollections*; *reminiscences of ch.h.*; ~serlebnisse *ch.h. experiences* **k·indisch** a ⟨dero⟩ *ch.ish, ch.like, puerile*; ≃werden [n] *dotage, second ch.hood*; ~ w *to enter one's second ch.hood, to dote* ‖ ~es Wesen [n] *ch.ishness, puerility* **K·indlein** = Kindchen, Fest der Unschuldigen ~ (28. 12.) *Childermas-day* **k·indlich** a **1.** *ch.like, ch.ish* (*face, age, pleasures*) ‖ e–e ~e Leidenschaft *a ch.'s passion* **2.** *simple, innocent* (*of soul*); ~es Lächeln *a ch.'s smile*; s–e ~e Seele *his ch.'s soul* **3.** (gegenüber den Eltern) *filial* | sich ~ [adv] freuen *to be pleased as a ch.* (od *as Punch*) | ≃**keit** f *innocence, simple-mindedness* **K·indschaft** f *relation of a ch. to its parents*, ⟨scient⟩ *filiation* °**K·indskopf** m ⟨fig⟩ *baby, puck*; *simpleminded fellow*; sei kein ~! *be your age!* **K·indspech** n ⟨med⟩ *meconium* L

K·inediapositiv n *cine-diapositive* od *-slide* **Kinem·atik** f *cinematics* [sg konstr] **Kinematogr·aph** m ~en/~en *cinematograph* | ≃**isch** a *cinematographic* **Kin·etik** f ~/ *kinetics* pl [sg konstr] **kin·etisch** a *kinetic*

K·ingston n (Hauptstadt v Jamaika)

Kingtehtschen n (Stadt in China)

Kingtschou [–au] n (Stadt in der Mandschurei) *Kinchow, Chinchow*

K·ink f ~/~en ⟨mar⟩ *kink, squirm*

K·inkaju m ~s/~ ⟨zoo⟩ *kinkajou*

K·inkerlitzchen pl *useless finery, fal-lal*; *fallals, gewgaws*; ⟨fig⟩ *trifles, fads, vagaries* pl

K·inn n ~(e)s/~e *chin* (energisch *energetic*); das ~ in die Hand geschmiegt *the ch. cupped in one's h.*; Doppel≃ *double chin*; Fleisch unter dem ~ (Wamme) *gills*; sich das ~ streichen *to stroke one's chin* ‖ mit markantem ~ *square-jawed*; er hat ein energisches ~ *he's a man behind a chin*, ⟨Am hum⟩ *he has a ch. like a cowcatcher* ~**backen** m, ~**backe,** ~**lade** f ⟨anat⟩ *jaw(-bone), cheek-bone* ‖ ⟨zoo⟩ *mandible* ‖ unter den ~n befindlich *submaxillary* (*gland*) | ~ndrüse [f] (*sub*)*maxillary gland*; ~nkrampf [m] ⟨med⟩ *lock-jaw*, ⟨scient⟩ *trismus* L; e–n ~ bek *to contract a l.-j.* ~**band** n *chin-piece* ~**bart** m *imperial, goatee* ~**binde,** ~**-haube** f *wimple* ~**grübchen** n *dimple in the chin* ~**haken** m ⟨box⟩ *upper cut*; *hook* ~**halter** m (Geigen≃) *chin rest* ~**kette** f ⟨hors⟩ *curb(-chain)* ‖ e–m Pf. die ~ einhängen *to curb a horse* ~**lade** f → ~backen ~**riemen** m ⟨mil & hors⟩ *chin-strap*

°**K·innings**! = Kinder! ⟨fam⟩ *chaps*!

K·ino n ~/~s ⟨fam⟩ *cinema*; (*the*) *pictures* pl; ⟨Am⟩ *movies, talkies* pl; ⟨Am a.⟩ *theater*; im ~ *at the c.* ~**besitzer** m *exhibitor* ~**besucher** m *movie-, film-goer*, ⟨sl⟩ *cine-goer* ~**freund** m *movie fan* ~**gesellschaft** f *movie company* ~**narr** m *movie fan*, ⟨Am⟩ *cinemaddict* ~**orgel** f *wurlitzer* ~**reklame,** ~**werbung** f *screen advertising* ~**vernarrtheit** f *cinemania* ~**vorführapparat** m *motion picture projector*, ⟨fam⟩ *cine-projector* ~**vorstellung** f *cinemashow, the* (*moving*) *pictures* pl ~**wand** f *screen* °**K·intopp** m ~s/~s = ⟨sl⟩ Kientopp

Ki·osk m ~(e)s/~e *kiosk*; ⟨Am⟩ *newsstand*

Ki·oto n (japan. Stadt)

K·ipf(el n) m ~s/~ ⟨cul⟩ *roll*; *crescent* | [österr] du bist ein ~ *you are a silly*

K·ipp- ~**achse** f *hingepin* ~**anlage** *tipping plant*; Spül≃anlage *discharge rinsing plant* ≃**bar** a *arranged for being tipped* ~**becher** m *tipping bucket* ~**becherwerk** n *elevator with bucket-tipping device* ~**bewegung** f *tilting movement* ~**frequenz** f *relaxation frequency* ~**hebel** m *rocking lever* ~**karren** m *tipping cart* ~**lampe** f *dipping lamp* ~**lore** f *tilting lorry, truck tipper* ~**moment** n *overturning* od *tilting moment*; ⟨aero⟩ *pitching m.* ~**mulde** f *tipping trough* od *hopper* ~**ofen** m *tilting furnace* ~**pfanne** f *swing pan* ~**schalter** m ⟨el⟩ *tumbler* od *toggle switch* ~**ständer** m ⟨mot-cycl⟩ ~**vorrichtung** f *hinge fitting, tipping device* (*for trucks and cars*); Lkw mit ~ *dump truck* ~**wagen** m *tipper*; *tip* od *tilting wagon, dump-cart* ~**wäsche** f *swing sieve* **K·ippe** f ~/~n **1.** auf der ~ stehen *to stand atilt* ‖ ⟨fig⟩ *to be on the verge of bankruptcy* od *on the brink of ruin*; (*it*) *was touch-and-go* **2.** (Wippschaukel) *seesaw* **3.** ⟨gym⟩ *upstart*; ⟨Am fam⟩ *kip* **4.** ⟨tech⟩ *hinge*; *tipping plant* **5.** *fag-end, butt(--end)* (*of a cigarette*), ⟨sl⟩ *nicky* | ~ntabak [m] *hard-up* °**k·ipp(e)lig** a = wackelig *dangerous*; *doubtful* °**k·ippeln** vi [h & s] **1.** *to be on the tilt* **2.** *to* (*play at*) *seesaw* **3.** *to trawl, wrangle* **k·ippen I. 1.** vi [h] (um) ~ *to lose one's balance* ‖ ⟨mar⟩ (*of a ship*) *to careen* ‖ *to* (*play at*) *seesaw* | [s] *to tip* od *topple over* od *up* **2.** vt [h] *to put on the edge, to tilt* (*up*), *to cant* ‖ ⟨mar⟩ ein Boot ~ *to careen* .. ‖ ein Faß ~ *to set .. atilt* nach hinten ~ *to recline* (dazu: *reclination*) | °e–n (sc. Humpen etc) ~: °wir wollen e–n ~ *let's have a drink, take a drop* ‖ etw ~ *to tip a th* (in *into*; aus *out of*); den Inhalt e–r Schachtel .. *to tip* .. (*on to the table*) **II.** ≃n ⟨phot⟩ *inclining, inclination* (e–s Bildes) | ~**d** *tipping*; nach beiden Seiten ~der Wagen *wagon for tipping towards either side* **3.** *to cut* (*the edges*) *off, to clip* (→ kappen) ‖ ~ **u wippen** *to clip and weigh* (*coins*) **K·ipper** m ~s/~ ⟨tech⟩ *tipper, wipper* ‖ ⟨min⟩ *tipping device for rubbish* ‖ einseitiger Kasten≃ *side dump tip box wagon*; *dumper* ‖ Stirn≃ *end tip* *wagon* | ~ **u Wipper** *money-clipper, counterfeiter of coin, (false) coiner* **Kippungswinkel** m ⟨aero⟩ *angle of inclination*

K·irbe f ~/~n bayr → Kirchweih

K·irch- ~**dorf** n *village with a church* ~**gang** m *going to ch., ch.-going* ‖ (nach dem Wochenbette) *ch.ing* ‖ sie hat ihren ~ gehalten *she has been ch.ed* ~**gänger** m *ch.-goer*; er ist kein ~ *he doesn't practise his religion* ~**hof** m *ch.yard* ‖ (→ Friedhof) *cemetery* ~**spiel** n *parish*; ⟨Am⟩ *town*; das ~ N. *the parish of N.* ~**sprengel** m *diocese* ~**tag** m = ~weih(e) ~**tür** f *ch.-door* ~**turm** m *steeple* | ~-politik [f] *parochial politics, p.ism; narrow-minded policy*; ~politiker [m] *parish pump politician*; optimistischer ⟨Am sl⟩ *booster*; ~-spitze [f] *spire* ~**weih(e)** f *consecration* od *dedication of a ch.* ‖ (Kirmes) ⟨Ger⟩.*parish fair; kermis, ch.-ale* **K·irche** f ~/~n **1.** *church; place of worship* ‖ ⟨allg⟩ *the Lord's House, the H. of God* ‖ die ~ [abstr] *the Ch.* [f] ‖ die Christus≈ *Christ Ch.* ‖ ~ der Dissenters: *chapel* | anglikanische ~ *Anglican Ch., Ch. of England* ‖ (National≈ Schottlands) *the Presbyterian Ch., Established Ch. of Scotland* | die (mit dem Bösen) kämpfende ~ *the Ch.-militant* ‖ (oberste ~nbehörde) ⟨engl⟩ *Ch. Assembly* | Landes≈ *national place of worship* (z. B. engl. ~ in Wiesbaden) **2.** (Gottesdienst) *(divine) service*; ~ halten *to hold the s.* ‖ in die ~, zur ~ gehen *to go to ch.* ‖ in der ~ ⟨arch⟩ (Gebäude) *in(side) the ch.*, ⟨rel⟩ *at ch.* ‖ nach der ~ *after ch.* od *after the s., when the s. was over* ‖ jdn zur ~ anhalten *to exhort a p to attend ch.* **K·irchen-** *ecclesiastical, church-* ~**älteste(r)** m *ch.-warden* ‖ (Presbyter) *elder* ~**amt** n *ec. function* od *duties* pl; *ch.-office, eldership* ~**bann** m *excommunication*; (gegen Stadt, Land) *interdict*; in den ~ tun *to excommunicate* ~**bau** m *ch.-building* ~**besuch** m *attendance at ch.* ~**besucher** m *ch.goer* ~**buch** m *parochial* od *parish-register* ~**buße** f ⟨ec⟩ *(ch.) penance* ~**chor** m *choir* ~**dieb** m *ch.-robber* ~**diebstahl** m *ch.-robbery* ~**diener** m *sexton, sacristan*; ⟨Am⟩ *usher* ~**dienst** m *ministration, ch.-service* ~**fahne** f *banner* ~**fest** n *ch.-festival* ~-**fluch** m *anathema* ~**fürst** m *prince* od *high dignitary of the ch., ec. prince, prelate* ~**fürsten** pl *lords spiritual* ~**gebet** n ⟨ec⟩ *common prayer* | ~buch [n] (Ch. of Engl.) *Book of Common Prayer* ~**gebrauch** m *ec. observance* od *rite* ~**gemeinde** f *parish* ~**gemeinschaft** f *ch. membership* ~**gerät** n *ch.-plate, sacred vessels*, etc. ~**gericht** n *spiritual court* ~**gesang** m (Lied) *hymn, (Gregorian) chant; canticle; psalm* ‖ (Singen) *congregational singing* ~**geschichte** f *ec. history* ~**gesetz** n *canon-law* ~-**gewalt** f *ec. power* ~**gut** n *ch.-property* ~**jahr** n *ec. year* ~**kalender** m *ch.-almanac; ch.-calendar* ~-**konzert** n *sacred concert* ~**lehen** n *ec. fief* ~**lehre** f *ch. doctrine* ~**lehrer** m *teacher* od *father of the ch.* ~**licht** n ⟨fig⟩ *a (shining) light of the ch.* ‖ er ist kein ~ *he is no sh. l., no great genius*, ⟨sl⟩ *he's short-weight* ~**lied** n *hymn, psalm* ~**maus** f; arm wie e–e ~ *as poor as a ch.mouse* ~**musik** f *ch.-music, sacred music* ~**ordnung** f *ritual* ~**ornat** n *vestments* pl ~**patron** m *patron* od *saint of a ch.* ~**pfleger** m *ch.warden* ~**postille** f *collection of sermons* ~**rat** m *consistory*, (P) *member of a c.* ~**raub** m *ch.-robbing, spoliation of a ch.* ~**räuber** m *ch.-robber, spoliator of a ch.* ~**recht** n ⟨engl⟩ *canon(ical) law; law spiritual* ⟨Ger⟩ *ec. law* ≈-**rechtlich** a *canonical* ~**regiment** n *ch.-government* ~**sache** f *ec. matter* ~**satzung** f *ordinance of the ch.* ~**schiff** n ⟨arch⟩ *nave* ~**schmuck** m *ch.-decoration* ~**sitz** m *pew, seat in a ch.* ~**spaltung** f *schism* ~**staat** m ⟨hist⟩ *Pontifical State, Papal States* pl ~**steuer** f *ch.-tax, ch.-rate* ~**strafe** f *ec. punishment* ~**streitigkeit** f *religious controversy* ~**stuhl** m *pew* ~**vater** m *Father of the Ch.* ~**verbesserer** m *reformer* ~**verbesserung** f *reformation* ~**versammlung** f *synod*, ⟨engl⟩ *the Ch. Assembly* ~**vorstand** m *board of ch.wardens* ‖ (P) (⟨a.⟩ -vorsteher [m]) *ch.warden* ~**zehnt** m *tithe charge* ~**zucht** f *ec.* od *ch. discipline* **K·irchentum** n *ecclesiasticism* **K·irchlein** n ~s/~ *small church, chapel* **k·irchlich 1.** a *churchly (faith), ecclesiastical, ritual, clerical, canonical*; ~ gesinnt *religious, churchy*; ~e Gesinnung *ch.manship*; ~e Ländereien *Ch. lands* pl ‖ ~es Leben *ecclesiasticism*; ~er Mann *strict churchman* **2.** ≈e n: das ~ *spirituality* | ≈**keit** f ~/ *religiosity, conformity* od *attachment to the church, ecclesiasticism*

Kirg·ise m ~n/~n, **kirg·isisch** a *Kirghiz*

Kirg·isien n, **Kirgisist·an** n *Kirghiz Republic*

K·irmes f ~/~(s)en = Kirchweihe

k·irnen vt [h] *to churn* → kernen

k·irr(e) a *tame* ‖ ⟨fig⟩ *tractable* ‖ ~ m *to make (a p) t.* (durch *by*), *to bring round* **k·irren** vt [h] **1.** *to tame*, etc. **2.** ⟨hunt⟩ (ködern) *to bait, allure, decoy* **K·irrung** f *baiting*, etc. ‖ *bait*

K·irsch m ~es/ ⟨Ger⟩ *(not-sweetened) cherry-brandy, kirsch* [Ger] ~**baum** m *ch.-tree* ~**blüte** f *ch.-blossom* ‖ *blossoming of ch.-trees* ~**branntwein** m → Kirsch ~**fliege** f *ch.-fruitfly* ~**kern** m *ch.-stone* ~**kuchen** m *ch.-cake* ~**lorbeer** m ⟨bot⟩ *ch.-laurel* ≈**rot** a *ch.-coloured* ~**saft** m *ch.-juice* ~**wasser** n → Kirsch **K·irsche** f ~/~n *cherry* ‖ saure ~ *morel(lo)* ‖ Herz≈ *(white) heart-ch.* ‖ schwarze Wild≈ *merry*; mit ihm ist nicht gut ~n essen *he is not a nice customer to deal with, it's bad to get on with him* **k·irschen** a *of ch.-wood*

Kischin·ew n (Hptst. Bessarabiens) *Kishinev*

Kis·il-Irm·ak m (Fluß in Kleinasien)

K·issen n ~s/~ *cushion* ‖ Kopf≈ *pillow* ‖ Heiz≈ *electric warming pad* ‖ Sitz≈ ⟨mil⟩ *c.* ‖ Sattel≈ *pad* ‖ Keil≈ *padded wedge* ‖ Stempel≈ *ink pad* ‖ Nadel≈ *pin c.* ‖ Klöppel≈ *lace pillow* ‖ Kumt≈ *horse-collar pad* ‖ Schwimm≈ *water-wings* ‖ Ordens≈ *c. with the orders* ~**bezug** m *pillow-case, p.-slip* ~**tanz** m *c. dance*

K·issingen n ⟨Ger⟩ (Badeort)

K·iste f ~/~n **1.** *box, chest, case*; (Truhe) *coffer* ‖ Latten≈ *crate* ‖ Arznei≈ ⟨mil⟩ *medicine chest* ‖ Futter≈ *bin* ‖ Pack≈ *packing case* ‖ Zigarren≈ *cigar box* **2.** °⟨hum aero, mot⟩ *jalopy, rattle-trap, old tub* ⟨aero⟩ *crate, kite, bus*; ⟨hum⟩ *flivver* **3.** °~ (S, Angelegenheit) ⟨sl⟩ schwierige ~ *(a) bad business*; faule ~ *mess*; die ganze ~ *the whole caboodle* **K·isten-** ~**ausmaße** n pl *case dimensions* ~**beschläge** m pl *box fittings* ~**boden** m *bottom of ..* ~**brennstempelapparat** m *box branding apparatus* ~**brett** n *box board* ~**deckel** m *lid of ..* ~**holz** n *wood for ..* ~**nagelmaschine** f *case nailing machine* ~**nagler** m *box nailer* ~**öffner** m *nail wrench* ~**verschluß** m *locking device for ..* ~**zucker** m *cask-sugar*

K·itsch m *shoddy, trash*, ⟨sl⟩ *tripe, slush*; ⟨paint⟩ *daub*; ⟨sl⟩ *hokum*, ⟨bes theat⟩ *sob-stuff* | ~roman [m] *trashy novel* | ≈**ig** a *meretricious; shoddy, trashy, cheaply sentimental, slipslop, sloppy, slushy, wishy-washy; mawkish*

Kitt[1] m ~s/ der ganze ~ *the whole lot*

K·itt[2] m ~(e)s/~e *cement, mastic* ‖ (Glaser~) *putty*; ⟨chem⟩ *lute* | Asbest≈ *asbestos putty* ‖ feuerfester ~ *fireproof cement* ‖ Harz≈ *rosin mastic* ‖ Isolier≈ *insulating cement* ~**erde** f *c.-clay* ~**messer** n *p.-knife* ~**verglasung** f *p.-glazing*

°**K·ittchen** n ~s/~ (Gefängnis) *prison, gaol; jug (in j.)*; ⟨Am sl⟩ *hoosegow*

K·ittel m ~s/~ *frock, smock*; Maler≈ *white s.*; (Knaben≈) *tunic* ‖ *(workman's) blouse*, (Frauen≈) *overall*; ⟨Am⟩ *overalls* pl; (Spiel≈) *romper* (Labor≈) *(white) overall* | ~kleid [n] *smock dress*

k·itten vt [h] *to cement* ‖ (Glaserei) *to putty* ⟨chem⟩ *to lute* (mit *with*); → Kitt[2]

K·itz n ~es/~e **1.** *fawn, kid* **2.** *kitten*

K·itzbühler Alpen pl *Kitzbühl Alps* pl

K·itzel m ~s **1.** *tickling, titillation, itching* ‖ (Gefühl) *titillation* ⟨fig⟩ *gratification (of one's* *senses), pleasant sensation* **2.** ⟨fig⟩ (Verlangen) *desire, sensual appetite,* ⟨scient⟩ *prurience, -cy* (nach *after)* **~husten** m *tickling cough* | **≗ig** = kitzlig **k·itzeln** vt [h] *to tickle, titillate* ‖ es kitzelt mich *I am itching, I have a tickling sensation* ‖ jds Gaumen ~ *to tickle a p's palate, to please a p* ‖ (Gefühle) ~ *to titillate* **K·itzler** m ~s/~ ⟨anat⟩ *clitoris* **k·itzlig** a *ticklish, sensitive* ‖ ⟨fig⟩ *nice, ticklish, delicate*; *tender (spot)* ⟨fig⟩

Kiuschiu n (japan. Insel) *Kyushu*

K·iwi m ~s/~s ⟨orn⟩ *kiwi,* ⟨scient⟩ *apteryx*

°**klab·astern** vi [s] *to potter about, to toddle along, to clatter along* od *about*

Klab·autermann m *hobgoblin (in a ship)*

°**Klacks** m ~es/~e *(but a) bit, trifle*

kl·ack(s) intj *bang!, slap-bang!*

Kl·adde f ~/~n *rough sketch* od *copy*; ⟨Am⟩ *scratch-pad draft* ‖ *rough book*; *(scribbling) pad*

kladderad·atsch 1. intj *bang!* **2.** ≗ m ~es/ der ganze ≗ *the whole caboodle* od *lot* ‖ da haben wir den ~! *now there's a mess!* ‖ der große ~ *the great collapse* | ⟨Ger⟩ *satirical magazine*

kl·affen vi [h] *to gape, yawn, be ajar* ‖ ~d *gaping (wound)* ‖ zwischen Wort und Tat klafft bei ihm ein Widerspruch *with him deeds and words are not in keeping* **kl·äffen** vi [h] *to yelp, bark, yap, yip* ‖ ⟨fig⟩ *to brawl*; er kläfft nur *his bark is worse than his bite* ‖ er muß immer erst ~ *he must always grumble first* **Kl·äffer** m ~s/~ *yelping dog* ‖ ⟨fig⟩ *brawler*

Kl·after f ~/~n *fathom* ‖ (Holz) *cord* **~holz** n *stackwood, c.-wood* **~maß** n *f.*; *c.-measure* **≗-weise** adv *by the f., by f.s* ‖ *by the c.* **-kl·afterig** a [in comp] *..f.s long* **kl·aftern** vt [h] *to f.* ‖ (Holz) *to c. up* ‖ der Adler klaftert fast 2 m *the eagle has a span of nearly two metres* ‖ breit ~d *wide spread (wings)*

Kl·ag- ~antrag m *plaint* **~artikel** m ⟨jur⟩ *grievance, pl.* **~erhebung** f *making a charge* **~geschrei** n *wailing, pl.ive crying* **≗los** *uncomplaining* **≗lustig** a *litigious, quarrelsome* **~schrift** f *bill of compl.* **≗süchtig** a *querulous* **kl·agbar** a *actionable*; ~e Mißstände *indictable nuisances*; (Außenstände) *recoverable (by process of law)* ‖ ~ w (gegen jdn) *to sue (a p) at law, to enter* od *bring in an action (against a p), to go to law* **Kl·age** f ~/~n **1. a.** (mit Worten) *complaint* **b.** (Jammerlaute) *wailing*; *lament(ation)* ‖ (Stöhnen) *moaning* ‖ es wurde ~ geführt, daß *it was complained that* ‖ es w ~n laut *there are c.s* ‖ laute ~ erheben gegen *to clamour against* ‖ über etw ~ führen *to complain of a th* ‖ Grund zur ~ geben *to give just cause for c.* **2.** ⟨**jur**⟩ **a.** (Ursache, Gegenstand) *grievance, matter* od *cause of c.t* **b.** (gerichtliche ~) *charge, suit, action, law-suit* **c.** (~schrift) *writ*; ~ abfassen *to draw up an indictment* | Beleidigungs≗ *libel action* ‖ Ehescheidungs≗ *petition* **d.** die ~ **abweisen** (der ~ stattgeben) *to find* [vi] *for defendant (for plaintiff)*; e–e ~ beantworten *to interpose an answer* **~ erheben,** eingeben, anstrengen, einreichen, anstellen *to file suit*; *to institute legal proceedings* (gegen *against*), *to go to law*; Erhebung e–r öffentlichen ~ *filing of information*; etw z **Gegenstand** e–r ~ m *to make a gr. of a matter* ‖ **gegen jdn** e–e ~ anhängig m auf .. *to bring an ac. for .. against a p, to sue a p for* ‖ ihre ~ war, daß *her case was that,* ⟨Am⟩ *she charged that* ‖ gegen die Krone kann k-e ~ angestrengt w *no ac. will lie against the Crown* ‖ mit e–r ~ abgewiesen w *to be non-suited* ‖ e–e ~ zurückziehen *to withdraw a ch.* ‖ e–e ~ entscheiden *to give judgement* **~abweisung** f *non-suit* (dazu: *to n.-s.* [vt/i]) **~antrag** m ⟨jur⟩ *prayer in complaint*; ~ stellen *to pray in c.t* **~beantwortung** f *answer to a ch., statement of the defendant, plea, refutation of a ch.* **~erhebung** f unterlassen *to forbear* **~figur** f ⟨arts⟩ *weeper, mourner* **~gedicht** n *elegy* **~geschrei** n *cries*; *loud lament(ation)* **~grund** m *cause* od *matter of c.t*; *gr.* **~häufung** f *consolidation (of actions)* **~laut** m *accent of grief, plaintive note* **~lied** n *dirge, l.ation*; *plaintive song*; ⟨fig⟩ *jeremiad (against)* (anstimmen *to raise*) | (bes Toten≗) *elegy* (oft in allg. Bedeutung v ~) **~mauer** f (Jerusalem) *Wailing Wall* **~punkt** m *head of a ch.* od *ind.* **~recht** n *right of ac.* **~sache** f *lawsuit* **~schrift** f *writ, plaint, bill of c.t, statement of claim, legal action* **~sucht** f *litigiousness, querulousness* **≗süchtig** a *litigious, querulous* **~ton** m *plaintive accent, doleful sound* od *tone* **~unterlassung** f *forbearance* **~weib** n ⟨hist⟩ *(hired female) mourner* **≗weise** adv *by way of c.t* **kl·agen 1.** vi [h] (T) *to cry* | (P) *to complain, lament* (um *for*, über [acc] *over)* ‖ jdm gegenüber ~ *to c. to a p (that)*; .. heftig .. *to groan to a p (of a th)* ‖ (jammern) *to wail* ‖ um e–n Todesfall ~ *to grieve for a death*; ~ über *to bemoan (the past)*; (unzufrieden) *to fret (about), to repine (at, against)* ‖ *to utter one's c.ts* (über [acc] *of)*; ⟨med⟩ worüber ..? *what does he c. of?* ‖ ohne zu ~ *uncomplaining(ly)* | ⟨jur⟩ *to bring* od *take ac., to go to law, to sue (at law)* (auf etw *for ..)* ‖ der ≗de *the plaintiff* **2.** vt **jdm etw** ~, jdm sein Leid ~ *to c. to a p, to pour out one's troubles (of* od *about a th)* | † ×⟨bib⟩ (= beklagen) *to mourn (the dead)* **3.** vrefl sich heiser ~ *to make o.s. hoarse with wailing* **Kl·äger** m ~s/~ ⟨jur⟩ *plaintiff, complainant*; ⟨Scot⟩ *complainer* ‖ öffentliche(r) ~ *(public) prosecutor* ‖ (auf Ehescheidung) *petitioner* **kl·ägerisch** a ⟨jur⟩ *the pl.'s*; *of the pl., refering to the pl.* **~erseits** adv *on the part of the pl.* **kl·äglich I.** [a] **1.** *woeful, deplorable, lamentable* **2.** (Stimme) *plaintive* **3.** (jämmerlich) *doleful, piteous, pitiable, pitiful, deplorable (condition)*; *abject*; *week, poor*; *wretched (voice, education)*; *sorry (sight)*; e–e ~e Darstellung *a poor account*; *miserable, lamentable (end)* **II.** [adv] *woefully (small, neglected)*; *(to weep) piteously* ‖ s–e Bemühungen sind ~ gescheitert *his efforts have failed miserably* | **≗keit** f ~/~en *woefulness, deplorableness* ‖ *plaintiveness* ‖ *piteousness*, etc

°**Klam·auk** m ~s/~e *hubbub, hullabaloo*; ⟨sl⟩ *paint, row-de-dow, ruction* (über, um *about*); um dies Stück wurde viel ~ (Reklame) gemacht *there has been a lot of puffing up for this play* ‖ °~ m *or* schlagen ⟨sl⟩ *to paint the town red*

Kl·amm f ~/~en *gorge, glen, ravine, canyon*

kl·amm a (eng) *tight, narrow, close* | (knapp) *scarce, short* ‖ das Wasser wird ~ *water is running short* ‖ das Geld ist ~ *funds are low,* ⟨fam⟩ *I'm hard up* od *(stoney) broke* | (erstarrt) *numb, clammy (hand)*; *damp (room)*

Kl·ammer f ~/~n **1.** ⟨tech arch⟩ *cramp(-iron), staple, brace, clamp, clincher,* ⟨carp⟩ *hold-fast, dog* ‖ Wäsche≗ *(clothes'-)peg* ‖ Heft-, Büro-, Papier≗ *clip*; Muster≗ *paper-fastener* ‖ ⟨chem⟩ *clamp* ‖ ⟨dent⟩ *clasp* ‖ (eines Buches etc) *clasp, hook* ‖ ~n einsetzen *to fix the cramps*, etc.; mit ~n befestigen *to clamp, staple* ‖ Balken w mit ~n verbunden *beams are fixed together with clamps, staples* ‖ e–e starke ~ erhalten ⟨übtr⟩ *to be held together, to be unified* (durch *by*) **2.** ⟨typ gram⟩ *parenthesis,* ⟨math⟩ *bracket* ‖ runde ( ) *round*, eckige [ ] ~ *square brackets* pl ‖ zus-fassende ~n ¦ ¦ *brace* [sg] ‖ ⟨mus⟩ ¦ *accolade, brace* ‖ in ~n setzen *to include in parenthesis* ‖ ⟨math⟩ die ~n auflösen *to remove the brackets* ‖ in ~n setzen *to put in b.s*; in ~n *within b.s* **≗affe** m ⟨zoo⟩ *sapajou* **~beutel** m *bag for* od *with pegs* **~eisen** n ⟨tech⟩ *grappling-* od *cramp-iron* **~haken** m ⟨arch⟩ *square clincher, dog hook* ‖ ⟨carp⟩ *hold-fast* **~hefter** m *clipbinder,* ⟨Am⟩ *stapler* °**~mäuschen** n *pillion girl* | ~sitz [m] *flapper-bracket* **~satz** m *sentence in parenthesis* **kl·ammern** vt [h] *to fasten, clamp, clinch, brace, clasp* | vrefl: **sich** ~ [h] (an [acc]) *to cling* (od *hold on, hang on*) *(to)* ‖ sich ~ an *to grasp at (the main theme)* ‖ sich an jdn ~ *to keep to a p*; *to clutch at* ‖ ⟨fig⟩ *to hitch o.s. to (hopes)* ‖ sich an ein Wort, etc ~ *to cling to a word*, etc

Klam·otte f ∼/∼n ⟨mas⟩ *broken brick* ‖ ⟨fig⟩ **∼n** pl (Siebensachen etc) *kit*, (*glad*) *rags*, (*belongings*); *togs*, *toggery*, *duds*; ⟨Am mil sl *monkey suit* | ⟨theat⟩ *wheezes* pl; gute ∼n *gags* ‖ (billiger Film) *B-picture* ‖ (Geld) ⟨sl⟩ *boodle*, → Kies, Moos

Kl·ampe f ∼/∼n *clasp*, *hasp*, ⟨mar⟩ *cleat*, *chock* ‖ (Klammer) *cramp*; U-förmige *stirrup*

Kl·ampfe f ∼/∼n *guitar* | ≈n vi/t [h] *to play* (.. *on*) *the g.*

klam·üsern vi [h] = kalmäusern

Kl·ang m ∼(e)s/≈e *sound* ‖ *boom* (*of the ocean*) ‖ scharfer ∼ *twang* (*of a fiddle*) ‖ *clang*(*our*) (*of a large bell*) ‖ *ring*(*ing*), er hat e–n hohlen ∼ *it rings* (*his words ring*) *hollow*; *chime*, *chiming*, *tinkle*, *tinkling* (*of bells*) ‖ *strains*, *notes* (*of music*); unter den ≈en [+ *gen*] *to the strains* (*of the national hymn*) ‖ (**Ton**) (Ggs *noise*) *note*, *tone* (*of a voice*) ‖ (**Melodie**) *tune* ‖ (melodisch, rhythmisch) *lilt* ‖ (**∼fülle**) *sonority* ‖ (des Geldes) *ring*(*ing*), *chink*(*ing*) ‖ (der Gläser) *clinking* ‖ (der Schwerter) *clash* ‖ ein verdächtiger ∼ *a catch* (*in a p's voice*) ‖ (**∼farbe**) *timbre*, *ring* (*of a voice*) ‖ dem ∼ nach *by the sound of it* | **mit Sang u** ∼ *with singing and bands playing* ‖ ohne Sang u ∼ *silently*, *without a sound*; *clandestinely*, *secretly*; *unceremoniously*, *without military honours* ‖ °ohne Sang u ∼ verduften (= weggehen) *to sneak off* | ⟨**fig**⟩ *ring*: *the word has a peculiar r. about it* ‖ dieser Gedanke hat e–n sehr modernen ∼ .. *has a very modern r.* ‖ e–n (k–n) guten ∼ h *to be in good repute*, *to be held in high esteem* (*in ill repute*) **kl·ang**[1] 3. p sg pret v klingen **kl·ang**[2] intj kling-klang! *ding-dong*! **Kl·ang-** **∼boden** m *sound-board* **∼dichtung** f *poésie pure*(*Baudelaire*) **∼farbe** f *accent*, *timbre*, *tone-colour*, *tonality* | ∼nregelung [f] ⟨wir⟩ *tone control* **∼figuren** f pl ⟨phys⟩ *acoustic figures* pl **∼film** m *sound* od *talking film*; *talkie* **∼fülle** f *sonority*, *volume*, *resonance*, *ful*(*l*)*ness* **∼körper** m ⟨übtr mus⟩ *band*, *orchestra*; *instrumental ensemble* **∼lehre** f *acoustics* [sg konstr] ≈**los** a *soundless*, *tuneless*, *mute*; *flat-toned* (*voice*) ‖ ∼ verschwinden *to slip away unceremoniously*, *to drop out unconspicuously* **∼messer** m *phonometer* **∼motorik** f ⟨poet⟩ *impulse of sound* (*controlling the timbre of the voice*) ≈**nachahmend** a *onomatopoeic*, *onomatopoetic* **∼nachahmung** f *onomatopoeia* ≈**reich**, ≈**voll** a *sonorous*, *musical*, *full-sounding*, *tuneful*; *fruity*, *orotund* (*voice*) **∼reinheit** f *clarity* **∼sinn** m ⟨mus⟩ *sensitivity to sound* **∼stufe** f ⟨mus⟩ *interval* **∼wort** n *sonorous word*, *onomatopoetic word*

Kl·app m ∼(e)s/∼e *clasp*, *clash*, *blow* **kl·app**! *bang*! *clash*! (→ klipp-∼) **Kl·app-** *tip-up* [attr] ≈**bar** a *hinged* **∼bett** n *folding bed* **∼blende** f (Scheinwerfer≈) ⟨mil⟩ *dropshutter*, *blindage lid* **∼boden** m *hinged bottom* **∼brücke** f *bascule bridge*, *lever-draw b.* **∼deckel** m *snap*(*-lid*); (am Schreibtisch) *drop front* **∼fenster** n *drop-*, *trap-window* **∼flügel** m ⟨tech⟩ *folding wing* **∼form** f ⟨tech⟩ *f.g mould* **∼horde** f ⟨tech⟩ *dumping kiln* **∼horn** n ⟨mus⟩ *cornet*, *key-bugle* | ∼vers ⟨m. m.⟩ *limerick* **∼hut** m *opera hat* **∼kamera** f *folding camera* **∼kamerad** m (Scheibe) ⟨mil sl⟩ *bobbing bastard* **∼korn** n ⟨mil⟩ *moveable foresight* **∼kragen** m *turndown collar* **∼kübel** m *hinged* od *tipping bucket* **∼kulisse** f ⟨theat⟩ *book-flat*, ⟨Am⟩ *two-fold flat* **∼laden** m ⟨arch⟩ *folding-shutter*, *venetian blind* **∼leiter** f *f.g-ladder* **∼luke** f *hinged hatch* **∼madonna** f ⟨arts⟩ *opening virgin* **∼maßstab** m *pliant rule* **∼messer** n *jack knife*, *clasp-*, *spring-k.* **∼mütze** f *cap with flaps* **∼-Plafond** m ⟨theat⟩ *book-ceiling* **∼prahm** m *hopper* **∼pult** n *folding desk* **∼rad** n ⟨mil⟩ *f.g wheel*, *f.g bicycle* **∼scheibe** f *bobbing-target* **∼schild** m ⟨mil⟩ *hinged shield* **∼schirm** m *f.g-screen* **∼sessel** m = ∼stuhl **∼sitz** m *let-down seat* (*in a car*), *tip-up seat*, *folding-*, *flap-seat*; ⟨fam⟩ *dicky*; ⟨aero, mot⟩ (runder) *bucket-seat* **∼sporn** m ⟨mil⟩ *f.g trail-spade* **∼stoß** m ⟨bill⟩ *peculiar stroke*, *massée-stroke* **∼stuhl** m *joint-*, *camp-stool*; *reclining* od *folding chair* **∼stulle** f ⟨m. m.⟩ *sandwich* **∼sucher** m ⟨phot⟩ *folding finder* **∼tisch** m *f.g* od *dropleaf* od *tip-up* od *gate-leg table* **∼trompete** f *key-trumpet* **∼tür** f *trapdoor* **∼ventil** *clack-* od *flapper valve* **∼verdeck** n *collapsible* od *folding hood* od *roof* od *top* **∼visier** n ⟨mil⟩ *folding* od *leaf sight* **∼ziel** n ⟨mil⟩ *collapsible target* **∼zylinder** m *opera-hat* **Kl·appe** f ∼/∼n **1.** ⟨tech, anat, zoo, bot⟩ *valve* ‖ ⟨tech⟩ *flap*, *trap*, *damper*, *spring*, *clack* | Anruf≈ ⟨telph⟩ (*calling*) *drop*, *indicator*, *annunciator* ‖ Aschfall≈ *ash-damper*, *-door* ‖ Auspuff≈ *exhaust cut out* ‖ Backofen≈ *damper* ‖ Boden≈ ⟨rail⟩ *bottom flap*, *hinged bottom* ‖ Drossel≈ *throttle valve* ‖ Fenster≈ *radiator shutters* ‖ Fernsprech≈ = Anruf≈ ‖ Fliegen≈ *fly-killer*, *flap*; ⟨fig⟩ zwei Fliegen mit einer ∼ schlagen *to kill two birds with one stone* ‖ Herz≈ *valve* (*of the heart*) ‖ Hosen≈ (Hosenlatz) *fly* ‖ Luft≈ *ventilator*, ⟨mus⟩ *key*, *piston*, *stop*; (Orgel≈) *stopple* ‖ Ofen≈ *flap-door*, *damper* ‖ Ohren≈ *ear tab* ‖ Rauch≈ *smoke ventilator* ‖ Scheu≈ ⟨hors⟩ *blinker*, *winker*, *eye-flap*, *blinder* ‖ Schulter≈ *shoulder strap* ‖ Sicherheits≈ *safety valve* ‖ Taschen≈ *flap* ‖ Tisch≈ *flap* ‖ Umschlag≈ *envelope flap* ‖ Ventil≈ *valve* ‖ Verschluß≈ *shutter* **2. a.** ⟨fam⟩ (= Mund) *trap*; die ∼ halten ⟨bes Am⟩ *to keep one's trap shut*; °halt' die ∼! *hold your tongue*, ⟨fam⟩ *stop your jaw*! *shut up*; *shut your trap*! ‖ er hat e–e große ∼ *he is always bragging* ‖ jdm eins auf die ∼ geben *to hit a p in the mouth* **b.** ⟨fam⟩ (= Bett) °in die ∼ gehen *to turn in* (*between the sheets*), ⟨bes Am sl⟩ *to hit the hay* **kl·appen 1.** vt [h] *to clap*; *to strike together*; *to flap*, *clack*, *clash* | in die Höhe ∼ *to tip up* **2.** vi [h] *to flap*, *clap* (mit etw .. *a th*) ‖ er klappte zus *he collapsed*, *he had a breakdown of mental energy* ‖ (klappern, wiederholt ∼) *to rattle*, *clatter* | ⟨fig fam⟩ es klappt (stimmt) *it fits* (*properly*), *tallies*, *squares*, *works well* (*together*), *it is all right* ‖ *it is a success*, *comes off* (*well*), ⟨fam⟩ *it's O.K.* od *okay* ‖ es klappt nicht *it fails*, *does not work*, *does not come off*, *is not possible*; *there must be sth wrong* (*with it*); es –pte tadellos *it went very well*; es –pt nicht, da –pt was nicht ⟨fam⟩ *there is* (od *must be*) *a hitch* **3.** vrefl: **es klappt sich** hoch *or* in die Höhe *it springs up*, *starts up*, *jerks up* **Kl·appen** n ∼s/ *clapping*, etc ‖ ⟨fig⟩ wenn es zum ∼ kommt *if things come to a head*, *to a show-down*, *to the point*, ⟨fam⟩ *to the push* ≈**artig**, ≈**förmig** a *valvular*, *valviform*, *valvar*, *valvate* **∼betätigung** f ⟨aero⟩ *flap control* **∼brücke** f *bascule bridge* **∼feder** f ⟨mus⟩ *key-*, *stop-spring* **∼fehler** m ⟨path⟩ *valvular defect* **∼horn** n ⟨mus⟩ *key-bugle*, *cornet* **∼instrument** n ⟨mus⟩ *keyed instr.* **∼loch** ⟨allg, tech, mus⟩ *vent* **∼öffnung** f; selbsttätige ∼ ⟨tech⟩ *selfopening flap* **∼öler** m *flapcovered oil cup* **∼schrank** ⟨telph⟩ *magnetoboard*, (*drop*) *switchboard*; ∼ für Reihenanlagen *s.b. for intercommunication sets*; schnurloser ∼ *cordless s.b.* **∼tasche** f *flap pocket* **∼ventil** n *clack-*, *flap-*, *leaf-valve*, *hanging valve*, *clapper* **∼verschluß** m *hinged cover*; ⟨phot⟩ *flap shutter* **∼visier** n ⟨mil⟩ *folding sight* **∼wehr** n *leverweir*

Kl·apper f ∼/∼n (Vogelscheuche) *rattle*, *flapper* ‖ (Mühlen≈) *clapper* ‖ ⟨weav⟩ *flier* **∼apfel** m *calville* °**∼bein** n ⟨fam⟩ *rattlebones*; *skeleton* ‖ ⟨fig⟩ *Death* ≈**dürr** a *bony*, *weedy*; (*as*) *thin as a lath*, (*as*) *lean as a rake* ≈**frei** a ⟨tech⟩ *non-chattering* °**∼gestell** n (P) *bag of bones* **∼hülse** f ⟨bot⟩ *rattlebox* **∼karre** f ⟨cycl⟩ *bone-shaker* °**∼kasten** m (Klavier) *tin-kettle* ‖ (Wagen) *rattle-trap*; *rattler*; *knockmobile* **∼mühle** f *mill with a clack*, ⟨fig fam⟩ *chatterbox* ‖ ihre Zunge geht wie e–e ∼ *she talks nineteen to the dozen* **∼schlange** f *rattlesnake*, *rattler*; ⟨fig, hum, sl⟩ *typist* **∼storch** m ⟨hum⟩ *stork* **∼topf** m ⟨bot⟩ (*yellow-*)*rattle* **Klapper·ei** f ∼/∼en *rattling*, *clacking* **Kl·äpper-Ei** n ⟨bes Am⟩ *nog* **kl·app(e)rig** a *rattling* | ⟨fam & fig⟩ *shaky*, *rickety*, *decrepit* (*bicycle*), *ramshackle*, *dilapidated* (*car*) || °⟨mot⟩ er fängt an ~ z w *he's beginning to go a bit wonky* || (P) *weak, deficient; seedy, weedy, shaky* **kl·appern 1.** vi [h] *to rattle(-rattle)* || (mit den Z.) *to chatter (one's teeth)* || (mit den Füßen) *to patter* || (mit den Sch.) *to rattle (one's keys)* || (Storch) *to clatter* || ⟨typewr⟩ *to tap, click* **|** ⟨fig⟩ **a.** (schwatzen) *to chatter, prattle* **b.** (Reklame m) ⟨fam⟩ *to puff one's trade* **2.** ˆ~ n; ~ gehört zum Handwerk *advertising* od ⟨fam⟩ *puffing is part of the trade*

kl·appig a ⟨bot⟩ *valvar, valvate* || 2~ *bivalve*

Kl·aps 1. m –es/–e *pat, flap, smack, slap, rap;* ⟨Am⟩ *spat* || *spanks* od *smacks (on the buttocks)* || jdm tüchtig ~e geben *to spank a p hard* **|** ⟨fig⟩ °**e-n** ~ h *to be a bit dotty* od *daty; to have a screw loose, .. a bee in one's bonnet* **2.** intj *flap! smack! bang! crash! pat!* **kl·apsen** vt *to flap, smack, clap, slap, pat, tap*

kl·ar A. [a] **I.** ⟨eig⟩ **1.** *clear (well, water, sky; voice)* **2.** (rein) *pure (air)* || der ~e Spiegel des Sees *the smooth surface of the lake* **3.** (durchsichtig) *transparent, pellucid, limpid (cristals, glass, liquids,* etc) || ⟨fig⟩ e–m ~en Wein einschenken *to tell a p the plain truth* **4.** (strahlend) *bright (sky, eyes);* (Wetter) *serene* **5.** (v Grau freie Farben) *clear, bright* **6.** (gut sichtbar) *distinct, clearly perceptible, bold (outlines)* **7.** (fein, klein, gemahlen) ⟨dial⟩ ~er Zucker *pounded sugar* || Holz ~ m *to chop wood* **8.** ⟨mar⟩ (im vorschriftsmäßigen Zustand) ~ Schiff (a. ˆ~schiff) *quarters;* ~ Schiff anschlagen *to beat to quarters* (→ Klar-) || (v Gerät) *clear (rope, hawse)* || *clear (coast)* || ~ voraus, achteraus! *clear ahead, astern!* || ~ z Wenden (Segel) *ready about!* ~ z Gefecht *ready for action* || ~ m nach *to clear for* || .. ~ m *to get the machines, a boat ready* || alles ~ soweit *all plain sailing so far* || sich ~ m *or* halten *to get ready* || (Rettungsboote) ~ m *to clear* || die Riemen ~ m *to ship the oars* **II.** ⟨fig⟩ (unverkennbar, unmißverständlich) *intelligible (facts); decided (answer); limpid, transparent, (pel)lucid, perspicuous, terse (style); clear-cut* (Auftrag) || (leicht faßbar) *plain* || ⟨fam⟩ so ~ wie Kloßbrühe, wie dicke Tinte, wie der Tag *as plain as a pikestaff, clear as ditch-water* od *ink, mud, day(-light)* || ~ u deutlich *clear and distinct* || (offenkundig) *obvious, manifest, evident* **|** .. das war **doch** ~ *she liked him, that was plain;* .. ganz ~ .. *self-evident, obvious, certain;* ganz ~ w *to become patently clear;* du mußt nachgeben, das ist doch ~ ⟨fam⟩ .. *that's flat;* es ist (f jeden vernünftig denkenden) **ja** ~, daß .. *it stands to reason that ..* **|** bald wird es allen ~ **sein** *they will all soon see* od *understand it;* plötzlich stand mir alles ~ vor Augen *I suddenly saw it all so clearly* || die Dinge w **allmählich** ~ *the situation grows clearer, things are straightening out* || ich bin nicht ganz ~ über .. *I'm not quite positive about (one point)* || **es wurde ihm endlich** ~ (daß) *it began to impress itself upon him (that);* .. **plötzlich** .. *it struck home to him;* .. **langsam** .. *it dawned upon him;* .. mir ganz ~ *I came to see quite clearly* **| sich** [dat] **über etw** ~ **w** *to grasp, understand, comprehend, realize a th* od *that; to take stock of (a p's character)* || darüber muß man sich ~ w *that should be clearly understood* || es wurde mir ~ *it was borne in upon me, the truth came to me that* || sich ~ w *to make up one's mind;* .. ob .. *to make sure whether* || .. über .. ⟨Am⟩ *to get wise to a th* || ich bin mir jetzt ~ darüber *now I've got to the bottom of it* **| jdm etw ~ m** *or* w l *to explain a th, to make a p understand a th, to make a th clear* od *plain to a p;* .. überzeugend .. *to bring a th home to a p, to put a th across a p* || .. ~ legen .. *to lay a th out (for a p);* .. ~ stellen .. *to unfold, reveal, to point out, to argue (the advisability of), to set forth; to straighten up ..;* l Sie mich das ~ stellen *let's get that right* (⟨Am⟩ *straight*), *let's get the facts clear* || .. überzeugend .. *to urge a th upon a p* || .. augenscheinlich .. *to demonstrate a th to a p* || ich werde ihm den Standpunkt gehörig ~ m *I shall give him a piece of my mind* || habe ich es ~ gemacht? *do I make myself clear?* || **sich etw ~ m** *to realize a th* || sich e–n ~en Kopf schaffen *to clear the cob-webs from one's brain* **B.** [adv] **etw ~ aussprechen** *to be explicit about ..* || ~ hervorheben, z Ausdruck bringen, daß *to make it clear that* || ~ denken *to have a clear understanding* || s–e Schuld lag ~ zu Tage *his guilt was proved up to the hilt* || habe ich mich ~ ausgedrückt? *have I made myself clear?* ~ sprechen *to speak clear(ly);* ~ sehen *to see day-light, to see one's way clear, to be all awake* || endlich ~ sehen *to come down from the clouds* || jdn klipp u ~ fragen *to ask a p a question point-blank* **|** ⟨fam⟩ (gewiß) ist das wahr? – Na klar! .. *certainly!* **C.** n **das** ˆ~**(e)** ⟨dial⟩ (Weiß v Ei) *the white of the egg* || der ˆ~e ⟨dial⟩ *pure starch spirit (as a drink);* ein ˆ~er *a glass of it* || **die Kläre** ⟨dial⟩ *starch* || ⟨poet⟩ = Klarheit || ⟨min⟩ *coal dust* **|** ⟨fig⟩ (sich) **im** k–en s über *to be aware of a th;* .. ganz im k–en s über *to know (a th) precisely, to have no question in one's own mind about a th; to see, understand a th clearly;* .. **nicht** .. *to be in two minds on a th* (→ im) **|** die Dinge **ins** kl–e **bringen** *to settle things, to find out the truth about things* || (mit sich) über etw ins kl–e k *to make up one's mind about a th*

kl·ar- ~äugig a *bright-eyed* **~blickend** a *clear-sighted, sagacious* **~denkend** a *lucid* ˆ~**eis** n *transparent ice* ˆ~**gasanlage** f *clear gas plant* ˆ~**glasglocke** f *clear-glass globe* ˆ~**lack** m *varnish* **~|legen** vt *to clear up* → klar A. II. || *to clear (a rope)* **~|m** vt → klar A. II. **~|schleifen** (Glas) *to grind, smooth* **~sicht-** ~bluse [f] *see-through blouse;* ~folie [f] *antidim foil;* ~scheibe [f] ⟨bes mot⟩ *clear vision screen;* ⟨mot a.⟩ *non-clouding screen;* ~tuch [n] *anti-mist cloth* ⟨a. mot⟩ **~|stellen** vt = klären *to clear up* ˆ~**stellung** f *clearing up of a matter, elucidation* ˆ~**text** m ⟨wir⟩ *plaintext;* in ~ *in the clear* **Kl·är- ~anlage** f *sewerage (purification plant)* **~apparat** m *waste paper purifier* **~becken** n *filter-bed, settling sump; clarifier* **~faß** n *s.g cask, settler* **~gefäß** n (f Zucker) *clarifier* **~meister** m ⟨brew⟩ *clarifierman* **~mittel** n ⟨brew⟩ *beer finings* pl, *clarifier* **~pfanne** f *clearing pan* **~schlamm, ~rückstand** m *sewage sludge*

kl·aren vi [h] → auf|klaren **kl·ären 1.** vt [h] *to clear, clarify;* (reinigen) *defecate, purify; fine (down);* ⟨chem⟩ *filter, decant* **|** ⟨fig⟩ *to clear up (a point of a dissension)* **2.** vrefl: **sich** ~ *to become clear, to clarify, purify; settle, fine (down)* **3.** ˆ~ n *clearing, purifying, purification, fining,* etc. **|** *clearing up* **Kl·arheit** f ~/ (→ klar) **1.** *clearness, brightness; serenity; transparency, limpidity;* ⟨phot⟩ *distinctness (of details)* **2.** ⟨fig⟩ *lucidity, clarity; distinctness; obviousness, plainness, evidence;* sich [dat] ~ verschaffen *to find out* (über *about*) **3.** (Helligkeit, Glanz, Licht) *brightness; bright light, broad daylight*

klar·ieren vt [h] ⟨com, mar⟩ *to clear (a ship at the custom-house)* (nach *for*) **Klar·ierung** f *(ship's) clearing, clearance* **~sbrief** m *ship's manifest, bill of clearance* **~sspesen** pl *charges for clearance, clearing charges*

Klarin·ette f ~/~n *clari(o)net* **K-tt·ist** m ~en/~en *clarinet-player*

Kl·ärsel n ~s/ (Zuckersaft) *clarified syrup*

Kl·ärung f ~/~en *clarification* ⟨a. fig⟩; ⟨fig⟩ *elucidation, clearing up (of a situation, of a text)* || die Aussprache hat viel zur ~ beigetragen .. *helped greatly in clearing up misunderstandings*

Kl·asse f ~/~n (→ erst C) **1.** ⟨allg⟩ *class* (⟨mar⟩ erste ~ *cabin cl.*); *order, division, rating;* Menschen zweiter ~ *second raters* **2.** ⟨bot, zoo, minr⟩ *class;* e–e ~ besteht aus mehreren Ordnungen *a class consists of many orders;* → Art,

Gattung, Ordnung ‖ in ~n ordnen *to classify* **3.** ⟨school⟩ ⟨Ger⟩ *klasse*; ⟨engl⟩ (Altersstufe) *form* ‖ in der 4. ~ sitzen *to be in the fourth form, to be a fourth-former* ‖ oberste ~ *head form, sixth form* ‖ (~nzimmer) *class room* **4.** ⟨rail, etc.⟩ Fahrkarte 1. ~ *first-class ticket* **5.** (Wertgruppe) ein Künstler erster ~ *or* v ~ *an artist of the first rank*; Lügner erster ~ *a born liar*; °er ist ~! ⟨fam⟩ *he's cl. enough*! er ist schon hohe, gr ~ *there's a good deal of cl. about him*; °das ist ~ *that's high-cl.*; ganz große ~ *tip-top*; e–e ~ für sich *a select cl.*; [abs] ~! *posh* (*varsity sl is p.*) **6.** (Lotterie~̇) *cl.* **7.** ⟨soc⟩ *cl.*; die höheren u niederen ~n *the higher and the lower cl.s* ‖ die gehobene ~ der Bürger *the upper middle cl.* ‖ die niederen ~n ⟨fig⟩ *the rank and file*; *the masses* **Kl·assen- ~älteste(r)** m *monitor, senior pupil, top* (*boy*) *of a form*, ⟨Am⟩ *cl. president* **~arbeit** f (*written*) *class-exercise* **~aufseher** m *monitor* **~̇-bewußt** a *cl.-conscious* **~bewußtsein** n *cl.-feeling, cl.-consciousness* **~blindheit** f *caste-blindness* **~-buch** n *cl.-book, list of absence, roll* **~dünkel** m *cl.-conceit* **~einteilung** f *classification, categorization* **~erste(r** m) f *head boy* (*girl*) **~geist** m *caste-feeling* **~genosse** m *cl.-mate* **~haß** m *cl.-hatred* **~herrschaft** f *cl.-rule* **~kamerad** m *class-, form-mate*; mein ~ N *N who was in the same form with me* **~kampf** m *cl.-struggle, -warfare, -conflict* **~-lehrer** m *formmaster*, ⟨Can⟩ *home room teacher* **~̇-los** a *cl.less* (*society*) **~spiegel** m (Sitzordnung) *cl. plan, form layout* **~sprecher** = –ältester **~steuer** f *graduated tax* **~wahlsystem** n *system of cl. voting* **~zimmer** n *schoolroom, form-* od *cl.-room* **klas·s·ieren** vt [h] *to class, classify, screen, grade* **Klassifikati·on** [ts] f ~/~en *classification, break-down* **klassifiz·ieren** [ts] vt [h] *to classify, rank, assort*; schwer z ~ (*or* –rbar) *borderline* [attr] **-kl·assig** a [in comp] .. *-class* ‖ vier~ *four-class* ‖ erst~ *first-rate, A 1* [ei wʌn] → eins A, prima **Kl·assik** f ~/ *classicism*; (Goethezeit) *German c.* | ⟨mus⟩ Wiener ~ *Viennese classical period* (1780–1830) **Kl·assiker** m ~s/~ *classic, classical author* | ~ausgabe [f] *edition of classical authors* **kl·assisch** a **1.** (hervorragend) *classic*(*al*); das ~e Altertum *the cl.cal ages*; antik ~ *ancient cl.c* (*poets*) ‖ ~e Bildung, ~er Stil *cl.cism* ‖ ~es Werk *standard work* **2.** ⟨fig⟩ ist das nicht ~? *isn't that topping*?, *that beats all*!, *that's the limit*! | *typical* (*example*); *conventional* (*power sources*) **Klassiz·ismus** m ~/ *classicism* **Klassiz·ist** m *student of the classics, classicist, classical scholar* **~̇isch** a *semi-classical* (*buildings*)

kl·astisch a ⟨geol⟩ *clastic, fragmental* (*rocks*)
×**Kl·ater** m **1.** *filth, dirt*; *rag*: k–e ~n auf dem Leibe *not a rag to one's back*; **2.** *slut* **kl·at(e)rig** a ⟨fam⟩ **1.** *dirty* **2.** *slovenly*; *ragged* **3.** *precarious* (*matter*) **4.** (of mood) *out of sorts*

Kl·atsch I. m ~es/~e **1.** *smack*(*ing*), *clash*(*ing*); (→ Knall) **2.** (Geschwätz) *talebearing*; (*idle*) *gossip, tales* pl, *gadabout, tittle-tattle*, viel ~ *gossip in plenty* ‖ (üble Nachrede) *scandal* **II.** ~̇! intj *flap*! *pop*! *smack*! *slap*! *crack*! *smash*! **Kl·atsch-~base,** ~liese f, **~bruder** m = ~schwester **~geschichte** f *scandal*; *idle tale*; *gossip* **~gesellschaft** f **a.** *g.ing party* **b.** *company of scandalmongers*, "*school for scandal*" (Sheridan) **~̇haft** a *loving scandal*; *g.y, g.ing, tattling* ‖ *chatty, talkative, indiscreet* **~haftigkeit** f *g.ing disposition* **~-Journalist** m *g.-writer* **~maul** n *g., scandalmonger, chatterbox, telltale, talebearer, -teller* **~mohn** m ⟨bot⟩ = ~rose **~̇naß** a *dripping wet, soaked to the bones* **~nest** n *place abounding in gossip*, "*Chattery*" (*Thackeray*) **~rose** f ⟨bot⟩ *common red* (od *corn-*)*poppy* **~schwester, ~tante** f, **~weib** n *tattler*; *news-, scandal-monger*; *talebearer gossip*; ⟨fam⟩ *tabby* **~sucht** f *gossiping disposition* **~̇-süchtig** = ~haft **Kl·atsche** f ~/~n **1.** *flap, fly--flap* ‖ → Peitsche **2.** ⟨fam⟩ *tattler, gossip, tale--teller, -bearer, scandal-monger*; ⟨school-fam⟩ *sneak* **3.** ⟨school⟩ (verbotene Übersetzung) *crib* **kl·atschen** vi/t [h] **1.** ⟨eig⟩ *to clack, pop, flap, smack*; (*of water*) *to splash*; (*of brooklet*) *babble*; (in Badewanne) *gurgle*; (of waves) (*s*)*wash, slap* ‖ schweig' oder ich klatsch' dir e–e (sc. Ohrfeige) *shut up, or you'll get a slap* ‖ *to crack* (*a whip*) ‖ (*of rain*) *to splash, patter*; es klatscht nur so *it's pouring cats and dogs* ‖ mit den Händen *or* in die Hände ~ *to clap* (*one's*) *hands*; es wurde geklatscht *hands clapped* ‖ jdm Beifall ~ *to applaud a p, to clap applause to a p* **2.** ⟨fig⟩ vi (schwatzen) *to gossip, tattle, chat*(*ter*) (über jdn *about a p*) ‖ *to talk scandal* **Kl·atscher** m ~s/~ *gossip, scandal--monger, tell-tale, blabber* ‖ *informer*; ⟨school--fam⟩ *sneak* ‖ (Beifall~̇) *applauder, clapper* **Klatscher·ei** f ~/~en *gossip*(*ing*), *blabbing*, etc.; → Klatsch ‖ (Verleumdung) *slander, scandal--mongering, backbiting* **kl·atschhaft** a *gossiping, gossipy* **~̇igkeit** f ~/ *gossiping disposition, talkativeness*

Kl·au f ~/~en ⟨mar⟩ *throat* (*of main sail*) | ~fall [n] ⟨mar⟩ *throat-halliard, -ha*(*u*)*lyard*

kl·auben vt [h] **1.** ⟨fam⟩ *to pick* (*out*) (*peas, berries, vegetables*); *to lift* (*potatoes*); ⟨tech⟩ *to sift*; ⟨min⟩ *to select* ‖ *to pick to pieces* ‖ aus den einzelnen Wörtern klaubte er sich mühsam den Sinn zus *brooding* od *pondering over the single words he found out the meaning of the sentence* **2.** ⟨fig⟩ *to quibble, cavil* (an .. *at a th*) **3.** [österr] = sammeln: *to gather* (*pine-cones*; *firewood*) **Kl·auber** m ~s/~ *picker, sifter* ‖ ⟨fig⟩ *caviller* **Klauber·ei** f *picking, sifting* ‖ ⟨fig⟩ *quibbling, hair-splitting*; *cavilling* **Kl·aubetisch** m *picker table*

Kl·aue f ~/~n **1.** *claw* ‖ (Raubvogel~̇) *talon, fang* ‖ (Raubtier) *claw* ‖ (Pfote) *paw, foot* ‖ (Gift-~̇) *claw-joint* (*of spiders*); jdn den ~n des Todes entreißen *to snatch a p from the jaws of death* **2.** ⟨fig⟩ (Hand) *clutch, grappler*; in den ~n jds s *to be in a p's clutches* ‖ *to save from the grip of death* ‖ ⟨übtr⟩ (Handschrift) *paw*; °er schreibt e–e entsetzliche ~ *he writes an ugly fist, an awful scrawl* **3.** (Huf) *cloven foot* **4.** ⟨tech⟩ = Greifer; ⟨mot⟩ ~ der Kurbelwelle *crankshaft starting jaw* ‖ *claw* (*of a hammer*) ‖ Kuppel~̇ ⟨rail⟩ *coupler jaw* ‖ Nagel~̇ *spike drawer* ‖ ~ f unmittelbaren Gang *direct driving clutch* **kl·auen** vt [h] **1.** ⟨dial⟩ (kratzen) *to claw, paw, scratch* **2.** °⟨fig sl⟩ *to pinch, filch, snaffle, nip, scrounge, bone, sneak*, ⟨Am a.⟩ *snitch* ([v] jdm *from a p*); (Äpfel) ⟨school sl⟩ *to slog* | ⟨school sl⟩ (abschreiben) *to crib* (bei, v *from one's neighbour*) **Kl·auen- ~fett** n *cattle-* od *neat's-foot oil* **~̇förmig** a *claw-shaped*, ⟨scient⟩ *unguiform* **~̇-füßig** a *claw-footed* **~hammer** m *claw hammer* **~-hand** ⟨med⟩ *claw hand* **~körper** m ⟨tech⟩ *dog* **~-kupplung** f ⟨tech⟩ *claw* od *dog, jaw coupling*, ~ f unmittelbaren Gang *high speed clutch* **~kurbel** f *forked lever* **~seuche** f *black-leg, foot-rot, claw--disease* ‖ (der Schafe) *whitlow* **~winde** f ⟨tech⟩ *jack with claw* **kl·auig** a *clawed, fanged, pawed*

Kl·ause f ~/~n **1.** *cell, hermitage* **2.** *gorge, narrow valley, defile* **3.** ⟨fig fam⟩ (*small secluded dwelling*) *den, hole*; *closet*; ⟨sl⟩ *digs* **4.** ⟨dial⟩ *sluice, lock* **Kl·ausel** f ~/~n ⟨jur parl⟩ *clause* ‖ ⟨jur⟩ *rider* ‖ ⟨Am pol⟩ (heimlich eingeschobene ~, die Gesetz illusorisch macht) *joker* ‖ ⟨com⟩ *proviso, stipulation, condition* ‖ ohne ~n *with no strings attached* **Kl·ausner** m ~s/~ *hermit, anchorite, recluse* **~leben** n *life of a recluse, hermit's life* ‖ ⟨fig⟩ *solitary existence* **Kl·ausur** f ~/~en *seclusion*; ⟨ec⟩ (Gebiet) *enclosure* **~arbeit** f *examination-paper, unseen translation*, etc

Klaviat·ur f ~/~en *key-board* ⟨a. print⟩; *keys* pl ‖ (Orgel~̇) *manual* ‖ stumme ~ *chirogymnast* **Kl·avier** n ~(e)s/~e *piano*(*forte*) ‖ ~ spielen (können) *to play the p.*; er spielt gerade ~ *he is playing on the p.*; er übt ~ *he practises the p.*; er lernt ~ spielen *he learns the p.*; er paukt auf dem ~ herum *he strums on the p.*; sich ans ~ setzen *to sit down at the p.* || elektrisches ~ *player-p.* **~auszug** m *p.f.-arrangement, p.-score* **~band** n (Scharnier) *p. hinge* **~bearbeitung** f *music arranged for the p.* **~begleitung** f *p.-accompaniment* **~lehrer** m *p.-teacher, teacher of the p.* **~leuchter** m (*p.*) *sconce* **~mechanik** f *p.-mechanism* od *action* **~saitendraht** m *p. wire* **~schule** f **1.** *manual* od *exercises for the p.* **2.** *p.-classes* **~sessel** m *music-stool* **~sonate** f *sonata for p.f.* **~spiel** n *p.-playing* **~spieler** m *pianist* **~stimmer** m (*p.-*)*tuner* **~stück** n *piece of p.-music* **~stuhl** m *music-stool* **~stunde** f *p.-lesson* **~tasten** f pl *keys* **~transport** m *p. removing* **~unterricht** m *p.-lessons, l.s on the p.* **~virtuose** m *p.-virtuoso* **Klavik·ord** n ~s/~e *virginal* **Klaviz·imbel** n ~s/~ ⟨mus⟩ *harpsichord; manichord*

Kl·eb(e)- ~band n = –streifen **~bild** n ⟨arts⟩ *collage* **~ecken** f pl ⟨phot⟩ *mounting corners* pl **~folie** f *m. tissue* **~kraut** n ⟨bot⟩ *goose-grass* **~marke** f *sticker* **~mittel** n *gum, glue, adhesive substance*; ⟨scient⟩ *agglutinant* **~nelke** f ⟨bot⟩ *catch-fly* **~papier** n *paster, catch-fly* **~pflaster** n *court-plaster, adhesive plaster* **~plakat** n *poster* **~presse** f *joiner, splicer* ⟨a. film⟩ **~ranft** m (v 2 Broten) *kissing crust* **~samen** m ⟨bot⟩ Chinesischer ~ *Japanese Pittosporum Tobira* **~stelle** f *join, splice* ⟨a. film⟩ **~stoff** m *gum, adh.*; ⟨Am⟩ *mucilage* || ⟨phot⟩ *mountant* || ⟨chem⟩ *gluten* **~streifen** m *adh. tape* **~zettel** m *adh. label, sticker* **kl·eben I. 1.** vt [h] *to paste, stick, glue; to gum* (an *to*, auf *on*, in *in*) || ⟨allg⟩ *to fasten, attach* || ich klebte ihm e–e (Ohrfeige) *I gave him a box on the ear*, ⟨Am sl⟩ *I pasted him one* **2.** vi [h] (an [dat]) *to stick, adhere, cling* (*to*); wie Pech ~ *to stick like glue*; *his wet clothes cling to his body; burs stick to his trousers* || der Leim klebt gut, schlecht *the glue sticks fast, badly* | ⟨fig⟩ es klebt Blut an s–n Fingern *his fingers are stained with blood* || vor Durst klebt ihm die Zunge am Gaumen *his tongue is so parched that it sticks to the roof of his mouth* || er klebt zu sehr am Äußerlichen *he clings too much to mere formalities* || zu Hause ~ *to stick at home* || die Fliegen bleiben am Leim ~ *the flies stick fast in the glue* || °der Schüler ist ~geblieben *the pupil has not been promoted* || mein Pferd klebt *my horse is nappy* **II.** ≈ n ⟨rec⟩ *editing* (*the tape*) **Kl·eber** m ~s/~ **1.** *one who pastes on; a sticker of bills* || ⟨fig fam⟩ *sticker-on, bore* **2.** ⟨chem⟩ *gluten* **3.** *nappy horse* **kl·eb(e)rig** a *sticky, adhesive, glutinous, viscid, gummy, viscous*; (Hände) *clammy* | **≈keit** f ~/ *stickiness, gl.ness, adh.ness*; ⟨scient⟩ *viscosity* || *clamminess*

kl·ecken vi [h] = klecksen **Kl·ecker- ~fritze** m, **~liese** f [etwa] *slobber-John, mud-lark* **kl·eckern** vi [h] *to slobber* || wie geht's Geschäft? – Es kleckert .. *it just drags along* | vrefl **sich** voll~ *to beslobber o.s. in eating* **Kl·ecks** m –ses/–se (*ink-*) *-blot, blotch, blur; splash* °**Kl·ecksel** m ~s/~ (Maler) *brother of the brush*; ⟨fam⟩ *daub* **kl·ecksen** vt/i [h] *to blot, blotch, blur; to smudge; to make* (*ink-*)*blots* | ⟨fig dero⟩ (malen) *to daub* || (schreiben) *scrawl, scribble* **Kl·eckser** m ~s/~ *scrawler, scribbler* || ⟨fam⟩ *ink-spiller* | ⟨fig dero fam⟩ (Maler) *daub*(*er*) **Kleckser·ei** f ~/~en *blotting*, ⟨fam⟩ *ink-spilling* || ⟨fig⟩ *scribbling; daubing* **kl·ecksig** a *blotchy, blotted*

°**Kled·asche** f ~/~n → Kleidung

Kl·ee m ~s/ ⟨bot⟩ *clover, trefoil* || ⟨Ir⟩ *shamrock* || ⟨fig⟩ jdn über den grünen ~ loben *to praise a p up to the skies*; ⟨fam⟩ *to crack up* **~acker** m *c.-field* **~blatt** n (*leaf of*) *t.*; ⟨Ir⟩ *shamrock* || vierblättriges ~ *four-leaved c.* || ⟨fig⟩ nettes ~ *triplet, trio; nice set of fellows*, ⟨fam⟩ *three of a kidney*; (*autobahn junction*) *c.leaf*, ⟨Am fam⟩ *pretzels* | ~bogen [m] ⟨arch⟩ *t.-arch*; ~kreuzung [f] ⟨mot⟩ *c.leaf* **~blüte** f *c.-blossom* **~feld** n *c.-field* **~salz** n ⟨chem⟩ *sorrel-salt* **~säure** f ⟨chem⟩ *oxalic acid*

Kl·ei- ~acker m *clay field* **~boden** m *c.ey soil*

Kl·eiber m ~s/~ ⟨orn⟩ *nuthatch*

Kl·eid n ~(e)s/~er **1.** (~ungsstück bes = *gown* od *cloak*) *garment* || (ganze ~ung) *garments, clothing, clothes* pl, *dress* || (Amts~ & ⟨poet⟩) *garb* || ⟨ec⟩ *habit, frock* || ⟨poet & rhet⟩ *raiment, vestment* | **Damen≈** (→ d.) ⟨allg⟩ *dress*; ⟨sport & mod⟩ *frock* || elegantes ~ (*dinner-, tea-*)*gown*; schwarzes ~ *black*, schwarze ~er *blacks* pl; Reit≈ *habit, riding-dress* od *-gown* | **fertig gekaufte** ~er *ready-made clothes* pl, ⟨fam⟩ *hand-me-downs* pl ⟨Am⟩ *store-clothes* | alte ~er *duds, rags* | ein ~ **an-, ausziehen** *to put on, take off a dress*; s–e ~er .. *one's clothes*; er fiel mit allen ~ern ins W. *he fell into the water with all his c.s on* || ⟨prov⟩ ~er m Leute *fine feathers make fine birds, cl.s make* od *the tailor makes the man* **2.** ⟨fig mst⟩ *garb* (*of virtue*, etc.) || die Stadt hatte ein festliches ~ angelegt *the town had assumed a festive garb* **Kleidchen** n ~s/~ *child's garment* **kl·eiden 1.** vt/refl (sich) ~ *to clothe, dress* (*o.s.*) || (gehobene Spr.) *to attire, array, apparel* (*o.s.*) ⟨a. fig⟩ || (mit Kleidern versehen) *to clothe, rig up, pay for someone's clothes* | sich gut, schlecht, bunt, schwarz ~ *to dress well, badly, in colours, in black* | er kleidet sich vornehm *he is elegantly dressed*, .. auffällig *he dresses showily* || gut, tadellos gekleidet *well dressed, faultlessly tailored* || sorgfältig gekl. *smart, spruce; neat in dress* || faszinierend gekl. *dressed up to kill* || gekl. in *garbed in, swathed in* (*a white apron*) || zu leicht gekl. *too lightly clad* **2.** vt; **das kleidet** dich gut *that suits you well, that becomes you* | [abs] das kleidet (gut) *that's very becoming* **3.** ⟨fig⟩ (Gefühle, Gedanken etc) in Worte ~ *to clothe* od *express in words, to put into words, couch in words, word, phrase* || die Wiesen h sich in neues Grün gekl. *the meadows have put on fresh green* || *all this was* clothed *and* couched *in expressions .. and* cast *in the most graceful and becoming forms* || er kleidete sich in .. *he girded himself in* (*a new humanity*) **Kl·eider- ~ablage** f *cloak-room* **~aufwand** m *sumptuous*(*ness of*) *dressing, expensive* od *costly style of dressing, stylishness* **~bestand** m *wardrobe* **~bügel** m (*coat-, dress-*)*hanger*, (*clothes-*)*suspender* **~bügler** m *tailor's presser* **~bürste** f *c.s brush* **~büste** f *dummy* **~fabrik** f *clothing factory* **~fex** m (P) *c.s-horse* ⟨hum fig⟩ **~geld** n *allowance for dressing, c.g allowance* **~geschäft** n *ready-made-c.s-shop, c.g establishment, warehouse for gentlemen's outfit* **~gestell** n → ~ständer **~haken** m *c.s peg* od *pin, coat-rack* od *-stand* **~handel** m *dealing in c.s, old c.s trade* **~händler** m *dealer in* (*old*) *c.s, second-hand c.s-dealer, wardrobe dealer* || *merchant-tailor, clothier, outfitter* **~handlung** f *c.s-shop* **~hefter** m *coat baster* **~kammer** f ⟨mar⟩ *c.g-room, wardrobe* **~karte** f *c.g book* od *card* **~kartenabschnitt** m *c.s coupon* ×**~kasten** = –schrank **~klopfer** m *c.s-beater* **~laus** f ⟨zoo⟩ *body-louse*, ⟨mil sl⟩ *cootie* **~leiste** f *c.s rack* **~macher** m (*ladies'*) *tailor* **~macherin** f *dress-maker* **~magazin** n = ~geschäft **~markt** m *market for second-hand-c.s, old-c.s market*, ⟨fam⟩ *rag-fair* **~mode** f *fashion in c.s* **~motte** f ⟨ent⟩ (*c.s-*)*moth* **~musterung** f ⟨mar⟩ *mustering bags* **~narr** m *dandy, fop* **~närrin** f *woman overfond of finery* **~ordnung** f *dress regulations* pl || *sumptuary laws* pl || gegen jede ~ ⟨fig fam⟩ *quite unwarrantable* **~posamenten** [pl] *tailor's trimming* **~pracht** f *luxuriousness in c.s, splendour* od *gorgeousness in dress*(*ing*) **~presse** f *ironing press* ⟨a. el⟩ **~puppe** f *dummy* **~rechen, ~riegel** m *peg-board* **~reiniger** m *c.s cleaner* **~sack** m ⟨mar⟩ *sailor's bag*, ⟨mil⟩ *kit*, (*kit-*)*bag*, ⟨bes Am⟩ *duffel bag* **~schmuck** m *finery, fine c.s, gorgeous attire*, ⟨fam⟩ *adornments* pl **~schrank** m *cupboard* (*for c.s*), *wardrobe*, ⟨Am⟩ *c.s closet* **~ständer** m *c.s-* od *coat-stand, c.s-tree; hall-*

-stand, rack **~stoff** m *c.g material; suiting; dress fabric* || leichter Damenwollstoff *delaine* || *dress--material* **~tracht** f *costume, fashion in dress(ing)* **~trödler** m *old-c.s-man; fripperer; slop-seller* **~verleih(anstalt** f) m ⟨fam⟩ *costume place* **~-verleiher** m ⟨theat⟩ *costumier* Fr **~verwahrerin** f *wardrobe keeper* **~vorrat** m *wardrobe; stock of c.s* **~wenden** n *c.s-turning* **kl·eidsam** a *becoming, fitting (well)*, nicht ~ *unbecoming, fitting badly* **Kl·eidung** f ~/~en **1.** (~s-stücke) *clothing, clothes* pl; *wear; vestment(s); wardrobe* **2.** (Bekleidung, Tracht) *c.s, c.g, dress, (wearing-)apparel, attire, costume, habiliment, garments* pl || ⟨poet, rhet⟩ *raiment* || ⟨arts⟩ *drapery* || ⟨school⟩ College≗ *garb* || vorgeschriebene ~ aus Zelluloseleinen *regulation viscose linen uniform* || ländliche ~ *rough country things; covering* || (Berufs≗) ⟨fam⟩ *togs, toggery;* ⟨mar⟩ *long togs* od *shore-c.s* || ⟨mil⟩ *equipment, accoutrement* || bürgerliche ~ *plain* od *civilian's c.s* || er trug schwarze ~ *he wore black, he was dressed in black* **3.** (Kleiden) *c.g, dressing* || jdm Kost u ~ geben *to find a p in food and c.g* **| ~s-** *sartorial* **~s-stück** n *piece* od *article of dress;* ⟨com⟩ *item of clothing; garment* || ~e [pl] *c.s, wearing-apparel, garment*

Kl·eie f ~/~n *bran;* (Mehl≗) *poll(ard)* || feine, grobe ~ *small, broad bran* || (Grützen≗) *bran of grit* || (Getreide) v ~ befreien *to unbran* **Kl·eien-~beize** f *bran-maceration* **~brot** n *bread mixed with bran, bran-bread* **~mehl** n *poll(ard), grit* **kleiig**[1] a (→ Kleie) *branny*

kl·eiig[2] a (→ Klei) *clayey*

Klein n ~s/~e; Gänse-, Hasen≗ *the giblets of a goose, hare* | °(Ammenspr.) ~ m *to do number one* **kl·ein I. [a] A. 1. (v Gattung)** *little* [compr *less, lesser;* sup. *least*]; ⟨zoo, ent⟩ *lesser (stable--fly),* ⟨astr⟩ (Bär); der ~e Finger *the little finger* || (gefühlsbetont) der (liebe) ~ Kerl *the little fellow; a little lane* || *she was still rather little when it came to affairs of the spirit* **2. (v Art)** *small,* ~ f s–e Jahre *small* od *short for his years* (→ u.) **3. (winzig)** *minute, diminutive, tiny, wee;* ~ aber oho! *(he is) cockalorum;* winzig ~ *tiny little, wee little, pin-point* → klitze~ || ein ~ wenig *(a) very little, just a little, a wee little (bit of)* || ein ~ wenig Butter *a little butter* || es ist ein ganz ~ wenig *or* ~es bißchen zu groß *it is the tiniest bit too big* **4. (v Wuchs)** *small, short (in* od *of stature)* || *so short alongside his tall father* || ein ~er Kerl *a short man* **5. (untersetzt u ~)** *short and stout; stocky, podgy, pudgy, dumpy, squat* **6. (unbedeutend)** *petty (troubles, minds); insignificant, trifling (mistake)* (→ u.) **7.** ⟨math⟩ unendlich ~ *infinitesimal, evanescent* **8. (niedrig)** *mean (spirit); despicable, contemptible (stinginess)* **9. [im Ggs z e-m Größeren]** der ≗e Bär ⟨astr⟩ *the Lesser* od *Little Bear* || ein ~es Glas Bier *a small glass of beer* || die ~en Propheten ⟨bib⟩ *the minor prophets* || ~e Terz ⟨mus⟩ *minor* od *lesser third* || ⟨jur⟩ ~er Diebstahl *petty larcency* || *petty (debts, cash* Beträge, *charges, average, troubles,* ⟨jur⟩ *jury)* || die ~eren Übel [pl] *the lesser evil (of life): of two evils choose the less* **B. [mit Subst] 1. (P) a.** ~es (= junges) **Kind** *little child; toddler;* ⟨Am⟩ *kid;* ~e Kinder *little folks,* ⟨fam⟩ *small fry;* ~es Baby ⟨Am a.⟩ *pickaninny* || m–e ~e Schwester *my kid sister* || der ~ere, ~ste Bruder *the younger, youngest br.* || ~er Schelm *little rogue* || (Anrede) ~er Mann *little man* **b.** ~e **Familie** *small family* || nette ~e Teegesellschaft *little tea-party* | ⟨übtr⟩ ~e **Leute** *small* od *common people;* ~er Bäcker *back-street baker;* ganz ~er Eisenhändler *ironmonger in quite a small way;* ~e Bauern, Sparer *small land--owners, investors;* Auto des ~en Mannes *motor--car for the man of modest means;* ~er **Schwindler** *small-scale crook;* ~er (= großer) Gauner *(a bit* od*) somewhat of a swindler;* ~e **Geister** *small* od *narrow minds, small wits, narrow-minded people* **2. (T)** ⟨hunt⟩ ~es Wild *small game;* ~e Fische *small fry* **3. (S) a.** ~er **Anker** ⟨mar⟩ *grapnel;* ~e glänzende Augen *small beady eyes;* ~e Anzeigen *small* od *classified advertisements,* ⟨fam⟩ *smalls* pl, ⟨Am⟩ *small ads;* ~er Buchstabe *small letter,* ⟨typ⟩ *lower case;* ~e Versalie ⟨typ⟩ *small capital;* in ~en Dingen *in small things;* ~e Eier *small eggs;* ~es Geld *(small) change, small coin;* die dritt~ste Grafschaft *the third smallest of the counties;* (Wolken:) *little light silver clouds* [ohne Komma], ~es Zimmer *small room* **b.** ⟨übtr⟩ ~er Dienstanzug *shell jacket, undress uniform;* ~e Weine *cheap wines* **4. [abstr]** .. nach den ~sten **Anstrengungen** *(a weak heart troubled him) after the slightest* (od *after any strenuous) effort;* s–e armselig ~en Anstrengungen *his poor little efforts;* (nachsichtig) s–e ~en Eigenschaften *his little ways;* ~e Anzahl, ~es Vermögen *small number, fortune;* ~e Freuden *modest pleasures;* ~e Geschichte *short story;* ~e Meile *short mile;* ohne die ~ste Mühe *without the slightest* od *least trouble;* (schwach) ⟨med⟩ *small* od *feeble pulse;* ~es Schläfchen *nap, doze,* ⟨fam⟩ *snooze, forty winks;* ~e Stimme *small voice;* ~e Stunde *less than an hour;* in ~em Umfange *in a small way;* ~er Unterschied, Irrtum etc *slight difference, mistake, progress;* e–e ~e Weile *a little while, a short time;* ~es Zeichen .. *small token (of my gratitude)* **C. [mit Verb] ~ geraten** (P, S) *to be (etc) on the small side* || **~ m, hacken, hauen,** schneiden *to chop up* od *small;* Holz ~ m *to chop* od *whittle wood;* Speisen ~ m, schneiden, hacken *to mince;* ⟨fig⟩ (jdn) ~ m *to take the starch out of;* ~ schneiden, reißen *to shred* || ~er m *to shorten, to reduce in size* || kurz u ~ schlagen, hacken etc *to knock, dash, cut to pieces* ⟨fam⟩ *to smithereens* **| sich** ~ m *to make o.s. small,* ⟨fig⟩ *to humble* od *degrade, efface o.s.* **| als ~ hinstellen** *to minimize* | ~er **werden** *to grow less; to diminish, shrink, decrease;* allmählich .. ⟨fam⟩ *to tail off* || ~ w ⟨fig⟩ *to pocket one's pride, to come down* **| ~kriegen** *to master* || ⟨fig⟩ °ich kann es nicht ~ kriegen *I can't get over it, I can't make it out* || °nicht ~ z kriegen s *to persevere unflinchingly, to be indefatigable* | ~ geblieben *stunted, undergrown* **II. [adv]** ~ **schreiben** *to write small* || ⟨fig⟩ Gehälter w ~ geschrieben *salaries are minuscule* || **~ denken** *to have narrow views, to be narrow-minded* || v jdm ~ denken *not to think much of a p* || **~ anfangen** *to begin in a small* od *modest way* || es **geht** bei ihm ~ her *he lives in a small* od *poor way, in strained circumstances, he is badly off* || **~ beigeben** ⟨cards⟩ *to play low;* ⟨fig⟩ [abs] ⟨fam⟩ *to give in, to sing small, to draw in one's horns, to come off the high horse; to put one's pride in the pocket;* ⟨Am⟩ *to back* od *pipe down,* ⟨pol⟩ *to climb down;* nicht ~ b. *to show fight* **III. ≗e(r)** m (~r! *little one!*), **≗e** f, **≗e(s) [oft klein geschrieben** → 2. u 3.] **1.** der ≗e *the little boy, man;* die ≗e *the little girl, woman;* m–e ≗e *my sweetheart;* die ≗en *the little ones* pl || ein ≗er (sc Schnaps) ⟨fam⟩ *a drop of sth,* sie erwartet etw ≗es *she is expecting (a baby), she is with child* (→ Kind) | ≗er, ≗e, ≗es! *little one!,* ⟨sl⟩ *tit!* || die ≗sten ⟨fam⟩ *the littlest ones* **| etw ≗es** *a small th, a trifle* || es ist ihm ein ~es *it's child's play* od *a mere trifle to him* || ⟨prov⟩ wer das ≗e nicht ehrt, ist des Großen nicht wert *who will not keep a penny, shall never have many; take care of the pence, and the pounds will take care of themselves* **2.** [invar a als n] °~ m (urinieren) ⟨fam⟩ *to flower* || **groß u ~** *old and young, (both) great and small, children and grown up persons; high and low* || **von** ~ an *or* auf *from a child, from one's childhood, from an early age* **3.** [mit prep] **bei** ~em *step by step* **| im** ~en *in a small compass* od *way, in detail, on a small scale* || ⟨arts⟩ *in miniature* || im ~en verkaufen *to (sell by* ⟨Am⟩

at) retail || im ~en sparsam, im großen verschwenderisch *penny-wise and pound-foolish* | bis **ins** ~ste gehend *minute* (*inquiry*), *subtle* (*efficiency*) | **über** ein ~es (sc Weilchen) *in a short time, after a little while* | **um** ein ~es *very nearly, by* od *within a hair-breadth* || um ein ~es war ich verloren *I had a narrow escape* **Kl·ein-** *small, petty, miniature* **~aktie** f *people's share* **~anzeigen** f pl *classified advertisements*; ⟨fam⟩ *smalls*, ⟨Am⟩ *want ads* → klein I. B. 3. **~arbeit** f *minute* od *petty work*, ⟨pol⟩ *fence-mending* **~·asien** ⟨geogr⟩ *Asia Minor, Lesser Asia* **≗äugig** a *s.-eyed*, ⟨scient⟩ *microphthalmic* **~auto** n *m. car, s.* (*motor-*)*car, runabout, baby* od *light car*, ⟨engl a.⟩ *baby Austin*; ⟨Am sl⟩ *flivver* **~bahn** f *light railway, narrow gauge r., branch-line* (*r.*) | ~hof [m] ⟨Am⟩ *way-station*; ~lok(omotive) [f] *n.-g. locomotive*; ~material [n] *l.-r. material* **~bauer** m ⟨agr⟩ *s. farmer, crofter*; *tenant peasant*; ⟨engl⟩ *p. f., s.-holder* (bis 50 *acres*) **~bedarf** m *packets in s. quantities* **~bessemerei** f *baby Bessemer steel plant* **~betrieb** m *s.-scale plant*; ⟨agr⟩ *s. farm* **~bild-** ~film m *min. film*; ~kamera [f] *min. camera*, ⟨fam⟩ *minicam*; ~radiographie [f] *miniature film r.* **≗blätt(e)rig** a ⟨bot⟩ *s.-leaved* **~blütig** a *with s. flowers* od *blossom* **~brenner** m (Gas) *by pass* **~bürger** m *s. man, humble citizen* **≗bürgerlich** a (*lower*) *middle class, plebeian* **~bus** m (–autobus) ⟨mot⟩ *microbus* **chirurgie** f *minor surgery* **≗denkend** a *narrow-minded* **~eisen** n *light-section iron* **~eisenindustrie** f *s. iron trade* **~eisenerzeugnis** n *s. iron trade ware* **~elektromotor** m *s. power electromotor* **~format** n ⟨film⟩ *min. size* **~format-** *miniaturization of* .. | ~zeitung [f] *tabloid* **~flugzeug** n *light plane, baby avionette* Fr **≗flüßig** a *s.-footed* **~garten** m (*kind of*) *allotment garden* | ~siedlung [f] *all. settlement* **~gärtner** m *all.* od *amateur gardener* **≗gedruckt** a (*line*) *in small print* **~geist** m *mean spirit* **~geisterei** f *narrow-mindedness* **≗geistig** a *p.-minded, of a narrow mind, of a mean* od *p. mind* od *spirit* **~geld** n *loose money* od *cash*, ⟨Am sl⟩ *chicken-feed*; (*small*) *change, s. coin*; das nötige ~ *the needful* **≗gewachsen** a *undersized* **~geschäft** n, → ~handel **~gewehr** n *m. rifle*; ~e [pl] *s. arms* pl **~gewehrfeuer** n ⟨mil⟩ *musketry-fire*, unregelmäßiges ~ *dropping-fire* **~gewerbe(betrieb)** m *s. industry* **≗gläubig** a *of little faith, faint-hearted* **~gläubigkeit** f *lack of* od *lacking in faith* od *confidence*; *faint-heartedness* **~golf** n *clock* od *mini-golf* | ~platz [m] *putting green* **~grundbesitzer** m *s.-holder* **~handel** m *retail business, s. trade*; ~handel treiben *to retail* **~handelsgeschäft** n *retail enterprise* od *firm* **~händler** m *petty tradesman, p. shopkeeper*; *retailer*; *huckster* **~hauskolonie** f ⟨Am⟩ (an Autostraßen) *cabin colony* **~herd** m *rangette* **≗herzig** a *faint-hearted*, → ≗mütig **~hirn** n ⟨anat⟩ *cerebellum* L **~holz** n *sticks* pl, *firewood, kindling*; ⟨aero sl⟩ ~ m *to crash*; aus (etw) ~ m *to smash .. to matchwood, to make mincemeat of* .. **~hörer** m ⟨rec⟩ *earphone* **~kaliber-** ~gewehr [n] *m. rifle*; ~schießen [n] *m. rifle shooting, s. calibre practice, gallery practice*; ~schießstand [m] *s.-bore target range*; ~waffe [f] *s.-calibre arm, s.-b. rifle, subcalibre* **≗kalibrig** a *of small bore* **~kampfwagen** m ⟨mil⟩ *Baby tank, tankette* **~kapazitätsmesser** m *s.-capacity meter* **~kaufmann** m *retail shopkeeper* **~kind** n *infant*; *pre-school child*; (3–6 Jahre); beaufsichtigtes ~ *sittee*; Kleinstkind *baby* (0–3 Jahre) **~kinder-** ~bewahranstalt [f] *day-nursery*; unentgeltliche: *crèche* Fr; ~kleidung [f] ⟨com, ad⟩ *infant wear*; ~schule [f] *infant-school*; –(st)k.-wäsche [f] *baby-linen* **~kopf** m ⟨ich⟩ *morris* **≗köpfig** *s.-headed*, ⟨scient⟩ *microcephalous* **≗körnig** a *s.-grained* **~kram** m *s. shop* || ⟨fig⟩ *trifles, oddments*; *details, minutiae* pl **~krieg** m *guer(r)illa war(fare)* **~küche** f *kitchenette*; elektrische ~ *portable electric stove* **~kunst-** ~bühne [f] *cabaret*, → Brettl; ~möbel [n pl] *s. art furniture* **~landbesitz** m *s.-holding* (⟨engl⟩ bis 50 *acres*) **~lastwagen** m *light truck* **≗laut 1.** [a] ⟨fig⟩ *shame-faced, downcast, dejected, subdued, low-spirited*, ⟨fam⟩ *down in the mouth* || e–n ~ m *to put a p down, to take a p down a peg or two* || ≗ w *to assume a more modest tone*, ⟨fam⟩ *to sing s., to come d. a p. or t., to draw in one's horns* **2.** [adv] *faintly, shamefacedly* **~lichtbildkunst** f *photomicrography* **~lok** f *light rail motor tractor* **~luftschiff** n *s. airship, blimp*; ⟨Am⟩ *rubber cow* **~|machen** vt [h] (Holz) *to chop* (*up*) **~malerei** f *m. painting*; ⟨fig⟩ *attention to detail* **~meister** m *s. craftsman*; ~ pl ⟨arts⟩ *lesser Masters* pl **~möbel** n [sg & pl] *occasional furniture* **~mut** m *pettiness*; *despondency, pusillanimity* **≗mütig** a *faint-hearted, despondent*; *pusillanimous*; *of little spirit*; ~ w *to lose heart* od *confidence* **~mütigkeit** f = ~mut **~offsetdruck** m *s. offset printing* **~oktav** n *s. octavo* **~preisgeschäft** n *limited price store* **~quart** *n s. quarto* **≗räumig** a *s.-roomed* **~russe** m, **~russin** f *Little Russian* **~rußland** n *Little Russia* **~schaden** m ⟨ins⟩ *minor loss* **~schalter** m ⟨el⟩ *installation switch* **~schlag** m (Straßenbau) *broken stone*; *chippings* pl **~schmied** m *toolmaker* **~seher** m (Mikroskop) *microscope* **~staat** m *minor* od *s. state* **~staaterei** f *particularism* **~stadt** f *s.* od *provincial town*; ⟨Am sl⟩ *hick town*; (ohne Theater) *fit-up-town* **~städter(in** f) m *provincial*; *inhabitant of a s.* od *provincial* od *country-town* **≗städtisch** a *provincial, s.-town* [attr] (*businessman*) **~städterei** f *provincialism* **~station** f (Funk) *s. power station* **~steller** m (Gas) *by pass* **~transformator, ~umspanner** m ⟨el⟩ *toy transformer* **~verkauf, ~verkäufer** m = ~handel, ~händler **~vieh** n *s. cattle*; °⟨prov⟩ ~ macht auch Mist *many drops make a water*; *all is grist to our mill*; *'every little helps', as the old woman said when she pissed in the sea* **~waffenfeuer** n *s. arms fire* **~wagen** m *compact car, minicar* **~welt** f *microcosm*; ⟨fig⟩ *the nether regions*; bürgerliche ~ *bourgeoisie, middle class* **~wild** n ⟨hunt⟩ *s. game*; *beasts and fowls of warren* **≗winzig** a *weeny* **~wohnung** f *s.-sized flat*; *s. apartment*; *flatlet* **≗zähnig** a *s.-toothed* ⟨a. tech⟩; ⟨zoo, anat, scient⟩ *microdont* **Kl·einchen** n ~s/~ *little baby, little one* (a. Anrede) **Kl·eine(r)** f (m) → klein III. **kl·einerenteils** adv *to a smaller extent* **Kl·einerwerden** n *diminution, shrinkage*; *growing less, decrease* **Kl·einheit** f ~/ *littleness, smallness*; (Winzigkeit) *minuteness, tininess*, etc. (vgl. klein) **Kl·einigkeit** f ~/~en *trifle*; *it's a mere trifle*; *little* [s] || es ist k e ~ *it is no small thing, no light matter* || jede ~ *every little irrelevancy* || unbedeutende ~ *insignificant* od *petty matter* || f e–e ~ ⟨fam⟩ *for a song* || wir wollen e–e ~ essen *let's have a bite* || ⟨dero⟩ *paltry thing* || *a mere flea-bite* || *head-wounds are no joke* || wegen der geringsten ~ *on the slightest provocation* || ⟨iron⟩ die ~ v 10000 Mark *the tidy sum of 10000 marks* || dies ist durchaus k–e ~ (= Leichtigkeit) ⟨fig⟩ *this is never plain sailing*; ⟨Am⟩ *it's no cinch* | **~en** [pl] *toys*; *odds and ends*; *bits and pieces*; *minor details*; *petty matters* pl || *minutiae, nugae* pl L || sich mit ~en befassen *to busy o.s. with trifles* od *details, to peddle, to trifle away one's time* || aus ~en Staatsaffären m *to magnify minor crises* **~skrämer(in** f) m *pedant(ic fellow), peddler, potterer, hair-splitter, fussy fellow* || er ist ein ~ *he is very punctilious, he is a square-toes* pl [sg konstr] **~skrämerei** *f* ~/~en *fussiness, peddling, pedantry*; *trifling*; *punctiliousness* **kl·einlich** a (P) *narrow(-minded), pedantic, little-minded, petty, niggling* || *mean, base, shabby* || (sehr genau) *fussy, punctilious, pernickety* | (S) *petty* (*quarrels*), *poky* (*room, occupation*), *paltry* (*things*); ⟨Am⟩ *picayune*; *picayunish* (*idea*) | sich in ~er Weise befassen mit *to peddle with, to fuss about* **≗keit** d *narrow-mindedness, pettiness* ||

paltriness || *shabbiness, meanness* **Kl·einod** n ~s/~e & Klein·odien *jewel, gem* ⟨a. fig⟩ | königliche ~ien *insignia* od *emblems* od *ensigns* pl *of royalty, crown-jewels* pl || ⟨fig⟩ *treasure, precious th* od *possession* | ⟨her⟩ *ornament* **Kleinst-** ~bildkamera [f] *midget camera*; ~empfänger [m] ⟨wir⟩ *midget receiver*; ~film [m] *microfilm*; ~gefügebild [n] ⟨met⟩ *micrograph*; ~hörer [m] ⟨wir⟩ *insert earphone*; ~kind [n] → Klein-; ~maß [n] *minimum*; ~mikrophon [n] *midget microphone*; ≈möglich [a] *minimum* (*speed*); ~spiel [n] *min. clearance*; ~übermaß [n] *min. interference*; ~wagen [m] ⟨mot⟩ *midget car, mini*(*car*), ⟨Am⟩ *Econo car, fam bubble-car, pick-up* (*truck*)

Kl·eister m ~s/~ (*starch*)*paste*; ⟨bookb⟩ *size* | ⟨fig hum⟩ (Mehlspeise) *pap* || er arbeitet (als Journalist) mit Schere u ~ *he works with pastepot and scissors* **~pinsel** m *p.-brush* **~topf** m *p.-pot* **kl·eistern** vt [h] *to paste, to size* **kl·eistrig** a *sticky, pasty*

Kl·emm- ⟨tech⟩ *clamping* .. **~bolzen** m *cl.-bolt*; *binder plug* **~eisen** n *vice-cheek, horse-bit* **~futter** n *cl. chuck* **~haken** m ⟨carp⟩ *holdfast* **~isolator** m *cleat insulator* **~leiste** f ⟨telph⟩ *screw terminal* **~-Mutter** f *tightening nut* **~notizbuch** n *spring-back notebook* **~platte** f ⟨rail⟩ *clip, cl. plate* **~ring** m *cl.* od *locking ring* **~rolle** f ⟨el⟩ *clamp roller* **~rücken** m ⟨bookb⟩ *spring clasp* **~schraube** f *attachment screw*; ⟨el⟩ *binding post* od *screw, terminal* **~sitz** m ⟨tech⟩ *force fit* **~verbindung** f *screw fastening, clamps connection* **Kl·emme** f ~/~n **1.** ⟨tech⟩ *instrument for squeezing*; *clamp, fix, holdfast*; ⟨el⟩ *terminal*, ⟨Am⟩ *binding screw* od *post* || ·Abzweig≈ ⟨el⟩ *branch terminal*; ~ des Netzschalters *power switch terminal* || Art·erien≈ ⟨surg⟩ *artery forceps* pl || Einheits≈ ⟨rail⟩ *universal rail anchor* || T·uch≈ ⟨surg⟩ *towel clip* **2.** ⟨fig⟩ (Verlegenheit) *dilemma, difficulty, quandary, embarrassment, trouble*; ⟨fam⟩ *scrape, mess, jam* (*I got into a j.*; *you shall get me into no more sc.s*; *he would get into no end of sc.s*) | (Enge) ⟨fam⟩ *straits* [pl], *pinch, fix,* (*tight*) *corner* || in e–r schönen *or* in der ~ sitzen, stecken *to be bunkered, in a tight corner, fix, tight* od ⟨iron⟩ *fine hole, tough spot*; ⟨sl⟩ *to be up the pole, up a stump* od *tree*; *to be treed, in the soup,* ⟨iron⟩ *in a nice soup* || in die ~ geraten *to get into a sc.* od *hot water*; *to be thrown into a dilemma* || ich hab' dich in der ~ *I've got you in a cleft stick* || jdm aus der ~ helfen *to help a p out of a scrape, tight hole,* etc. || sich aus der ~ ziehen *to get out of a tight hole*; in der ~ ⟨fam a.⟩ *in the wrong box* **kl·emmen A.** vt [h] **1.** ⟨eig⟩ *to jam, cramp, squeeze a th* (*between* ..) || er klemmte sich e–e Z. in den Mund *he jammed a cigar into his mouth* || *to pinch, press, nip* || (zuspferchen) *to tuck* **2.** ⟨fig⟩ °(stehlen) ⟨fam⟩ *to pinch, filch, pilfer* **B.** vi/refl (**sich**) ~: die Tür klemmt (sich) *the door sticks, catches* || ich habe mich geklemmt *I've got jammed* (*in* ..) || die Maschine klemmte (sich) *the machine got jammed* || °~ Sie sich dahinter! *put* od *keep your nose to the grindstone* **C.** ≈ n *jam, squeeze*; *pressure,* etc **Kl·emmen-** ~anschluß [m] ⟨el⟩ *terminal connection*; ~spannung [f] ⟨el⟩ *terminal voltage*

Kl·emmer m ~s/~ **1.** *pince-nez* Fr, *eyeglasses, folders* pl **2.** ⟨fig⟩ → klemmen A. 2. ⟨fam⟩ *pincher, pilferer*

Kl·empner m ~s/~ *plumber* ⟨a. aero, hum⟩; *tinker, tinman, tinsmith*; Gas≈ *gas fitter* **~anzug** m, **~hose** f *blue jeans* pl **~arbeit** f *tinman's work* **~handwerk** n *tinsmith's craft* **~waren** f pl *tinware* **Klempner·ei** f ~/~en **1.** [abstr] *tinman's trade* **2.** [konkr] *tinman's workshop, plumbery*

kl·engen, kl·enken vt [h] (Nadelholzsamen) *to detach from the cone* (*by warming*)

°**Kl·epper** m ~s/~ ⟨hum cont⟩ *nag, screw, hack*(*ney*), *jade, rip*; ⟨Am sl⟩ *plug*

Kl·epper-® ~boot [n] ⟨Ger⟩ *collapsible boat*; ~mantel [m] *waterproof* (*cloak*); *mackintosh*

Klepto- *klepto* **~m·ane** m ~n/~n *k.maniac* **~man·ie** f ~/ *kleptomania*

klerik·al a *clerical* ≈**e(r)** m ~n/~n *clerical*(*ist*); *churchman* ≈**·ismus** m ~/ *clericalism* **Kl·eriker** m ~s/~ *clergyman*; ⟨fam⟩ *cleric* **Kleris·ei** f ~/ *clergy*; *clerical set* **Kl·erus** m ~/ *clergy*

Kl·ette f ~/~n ⟨bot⟩ *bur*(*dock*) || ⟨fig⟩ er klebt wie e–e ~ *he sticks like a bur,* ⟨fam⟩ *he's a bore* od *sticker-on* od *barnacle* || er hängt sich wie e–e ~ an e–n *he sticks to you like glue* **kl·etten** vt [h] *to pick, card, cull* (*wool*) **Kl·etten-** ≈**artig** a *burry* **~distel** f *bur-thistle* **~samen-, (wurzel-)öl** n *bur-*(*dock-*)(*root*)*oil* **~wolf** m ⟨spin⟩ *burring-willow*

Kl·etter- *climbing* **~eisen** n pl *cl.-irons,* → Steig- **~fähigkeit** f *cl. power* **~farn** m ⟨bot⟩ *cl. fern* **~fisch** m ⟨ich⟩ *cl. perch* **~fuß** m ⟨orn scient⟩ *scansorial foot* **~pflanze** f *climber, creeper* **~rose** f ⟨bot⟩ (rote) *rose-creeper,* (*crimson*) *rambler* **~schuh** m ⟨el⟩ *climber* **~seil, ~tau** n ⟨gym⟩ *cl. rope* **~stange** f ⟨gym⟩ *cl.-pole,* (*greasy*) *pole* **~turnen** n *jungle gym* **~vögel** m pl ⟨orn⟩ *climbers,* ⟨scient⟩ *scansores* pl **Kletter·ei** f ~/~en *climbing* **Kl·etterer** m ~s/~ *climber*

kl·ettern vi [h & s] *to climb,* (mühsam) *to clamber, scamper, scramble,* (schnell) *swarm* (ein *or* an e–m Seil hinauf .. *up a rope,* aus dem Bett *out of bed,* auf e–n Balkon *to a balcony,* auf e–n Baum (*up*) *a tree*; *to scale* (*a mountain*), *to mount* (*a peak*) || ~d ⟨bot⟩ *creeping*; ⟨orn⟩ *climbing,* ⟨scient⟩ *scansorious* | ⟨fam fig⟩ das ist ja um auf die Bäume zu ~ *that's enough to make one jump out of his skin, that does beat my grandmother*

Kl·eve n ⟨Ger⟩ (Stadt) *Cleves*

kl·ick intj *click*! ≈**er** m *marble* (*m.s is played by children,* ⟨fam⟩ *bonce*

Kl·icke f ~/~n (→ Clique, Klique)

Kli·ent m ~en/~en *client* **~·el** f ~/~en; **~schaft** f ~/ *clientele, clients, customers* pl

Kl·iff n ~s/~e *cliff*; Rotes ~ (Sylt) *Red Cl.*

Kl·ima n ~s/~te *climate* || mildes, rauhes, heißes, gemäßigtes, kaltes ~ *mild, rough, torrid, temperate, frigid cl.* || Binnen≈ *continental cl.*; Höhen≈ *high altitude cl.* || in jedem ~ *in any cl.* || Klein≈ *microcl.* || See≈ *ocean cl.* || sich an ein ~ gewöhnen *to acclimatize* (*o.s.*) **~anlage** f *air conditioning* (*plant*); mit ~ *air-conditioned* **~lehre** f *climatology* **~wechsel** m *change of climate* **klimak·t·erisch** a ⟨scient⟩ *climateric*(*al*), *menopause* (Jahre *period, change*) **klimatis·ieren** vt [h] *to air-condition* **klim·atisch 1.** [a] *climatic* || ~er Kurort [m] *climatic health resort* || ~e Verhältnisse [n pl] *cl. conditions* **2.** [adv] *cl.ally* **klimatol·ogisch** a *climatological*

°**Klimb·im** m & n ~s/ *humbug, nonsense* | *tricks* pl *of the trade* || mit gr ~ *with great pomp* (→ °Tamtam), viel ~ für .. *to make a great fuss about a th* | der ganze ~ *the whole concern* od ⟨sl⟩ *caboodle* | ~ m *to have a jollification* || .. großer ~ *last night there was a big do*

kl·immen vi [klomm/geklommen] [s] (auf [acc]) *to climb* (*up*) | ⟨fig⟩ *to aspire* (nach *to*), *to rise* (bis *to*) **Kl·immzug** m ⟨gym⟩ *chinning the bar*; 10 ≈e m *to chin the b. 10 times*; *pull-up* (*8 p.-ups*) ⟨fig mil⟩ na, wer macht noch e–n ~ (will noch e–n Napf voll)? *seconds up*!

Klimper·ei f ~/~en *jingling, tinkling* || (auf Instrumenten) *strumming* **Kl·imperkasten** m ⟨fam⟩ *tin-kettle, music-box*

kl·impern vi [h] ~ mit .. *to jingle, tinkle* vt; mit dem Gelde ~ *to chink one's m.* | auf e–m Klavier ~ *to strum* (*on*) *a p.*; .. *to twang on a guitar* | ⟨fig⟩ ich lasse mir nicht an den Wimpern ~ *I won't be done in the eye*

kl·ing intj kling-klang → d.

Kl·inge f ~/~n *blade*; *sword, sabre* || vor die ~ fordern *to challenge* || über die ~ springen l ⟨fig⟩ *to put to the sword* || e–e gute ~ schlagen *to be a* *good swordsman*; (⟨fam⟩ beim Essen) *to play a good knife and fork* ‖ die ~n kreuzen mit *to measure* od *cross swords with* ‖ mit der flachen ~ eingreifen *to use the flat of one's sabre* od *sword* ‖ etw mit der ~ ausmachen, ausfechten *to fight it out* ⟨a. fig⟩ | ~n·abziehapparat [m] *sharpener for razor blades*; ~nausstoßer [m] *blade dispenser*

Kl·ingel f ~/~n (*small*) *bell, hand-bell*; ⟨hot⟩ *call-bell* ‖ ~ (= ~knopf) *bell(-push)*; ⟨fam⟩ (*press-*)*button* **~bahn** f *loop-line* **~beutel** m *alms-bag, collection-bag* **~fee** f ⟨hum⟩ (Telefonfräulein) *hello girl* **~knopf** m *bell(-push)*, (*press-*) *button* | ~krieg [m] *p.-b. war* **~schnur** f, **~zug** m *bell-rope, bell-pull* **~zeichen** n *ring*: *in response to the ring* ‖ ⟨telph⟩ *tinkle, trill* **kl·ingeln** vi [h] (P) *to ring the bell* (nach jdm ~ *for* ..) | (v der Glocke) *to ring* ‖ (Schelle) *to tinkle* ‖ es klingelt *the bell rings, there is a ring* | (of motors) *to knock, pink* **kl·ingen** **1.** vi [klang/geklungen] [h] ⟨allg⟩ *to sound, ring*, ⟨a. fig⟩; *that rings true* ‖ (v Metallen, Glas) *to ring, clink, tinkle, jingle* ‖ *the musical clinking of glasses* (Thack); die Gläser klangen, sie ließen die Gl. ~ *they touched the glasses* ‖ ⟨telph⟩ *to ring, tinkle* ‖ (*of bells*) *to chime* ‖ (v den Ohren) *to tingle* (a.: *didn't your ears burn? it still rings in my ears*) ‖ ~de Münze *specie*, ⟨fam⟩ *hard cash* ‖ ~der Name *reputation* ‖ ~de Schelle ⟨bib⟩ *tinkling cymbal* ‖ mit ~dem Spiel *with drums beating, with fifes and drums* ‖ es –gt wie Unsinn *it sounds nonsense*; .. gut *it sounds well*; .. wahr *it rings true* **2.** ≈ n *ting, clang* (*of a bell*) ‖ (Glocke) z ≈ bringen *to clang*

-kl·ingig a [in comp] zwei~ *two-bladed*

Kl·ingklang m *jingle, ring, ding-dong, jingle-jangle* **kl·ingling**! *ding-dong*!, → kling! **Kl·ingstein** m ⟨minr⟩ *phonolite, clink-stone*

Kl·inik f ~/~en *clinic(al hospital)* (in der ~ *at th c.*); *infirmary, nursing-home* ‖ ~ f ansteckende Krankheiten *isolation hospital* ‖ P·oli≈ *dispensary* (*and surgery*) | *clinical lectures* pl | [abstr] die ~ der T. *our knowledge of tuberculosis*; *clinical knowledge* | ~assistent [m] = Krankenpfleger; ~packung [f] ⟨pharm⟩ *hospital pack* **~er** m ~s/~ *clinician* **kl·inisch** a *clinical*; *in* (Patient), *in-patient* (*treatment*) ‖ ~e Semester durchmachen *to walk the hospitals* pl

Kl·inke f ~/~n **1.** (Griff, Drücker) *door-handle* **2.** ⟨dial⟩ (= Türfalle) *latch*; ⟨bes Scot⟩ *sneck* **3.** ⟨dial⟩ (= Schnäpper) *catch*, ⟨Scot⟩ *snib* ‖ ⟨mar⟩ (Sperr≈) *pawl* **4.** ⟨el⟩ *jack* **kl·inken** vt [h] (Tür, Schloß) ·auf~ *to unlatch* (etc); *to open*; z·u~ *to latch*, etc., *to shut*

Kl·inker m ~s/~ (*Dutch*) *clinker, Dutch brick*; *cinder block* **~bau** m ⟨arch, mar⟩ *clinch-building* **~boot** n ⟨mar⟩ *clincher-built boat, funny* **~verkleidung** f; mit ~ *faced with clinkers*

Kl·inse, Kl·inze f ~/~n *cleft, crevice*; *crevasse*

Klipp m ~s/~s ⟨mod⟩ *clip*

kl·ipp[1] intj. ~-klapp *click-clack, pit-(a)-pat*

kl·ipp[2]; ~ u klar [a & adv] *as clear as daylight, evident(ly), distinct(ly)* ‖ (*to prove*) *convincingly* ‖ *point-blank* (*refusal*) ‖ (*I told him*) *point-blank*

Kl·ipp- ~dachs, ~schliefer m *rock-badger*; *hyrax* **~fisch** m ⟨ich⟩ *clipfish, haberdine*; *cured and dried cod* °**~schule** f *ABC-school* °**~schüler** m *abecedarian* **Kl·ippe** f ~/~n **1.** ⟨eig⟩ *rock*; *sea stack*; *klippe*; blinde ~ ⟨mar⟩ *rock awash* ‖ zackige ~ *crag* **2.** (steiler Küstenabfall, Kliff) *cliff* **3.** ⟨fig⟩ *this is the rock on which the undertaking will be wrecked*

Kl·ipper m ~s/~ (Segler) ⟨mar⟩ *clipper*

kl·ippig a *rocky, craggy*, → Klippe

kl·ippklapp! (Hände) *flip-flap*! ‖ (Füße) *pit-(a-)pat* ‖ (Mühle) *click-clack*

Kl·ique f ~/~n *clique*; *gang*; *coterie* Fr ‖ *confraternity* ‖ ~nwirtschaft [f] *partisanship*

kl·irr! intj *smash*! *crash*! *clash*! **kl·irren** vi [h] ~ mit *to clink, chink, click* (*glasses*); *clatter* (*plates*); *rattle* (*windows*); *to clash* (*weapons*); *clank* (*chains*); *jingle* (*small chain*) | ≈ n *the chink*, etc. (*of money, cups*); *clang* | **~d** fallen auf *to clatter*, etc *upon* ‖ ~d zerbrechen *to break with a clatter*

Klisch·ee n ~s/~s ⟨typ⟩ (*stereotype*) *plate*; *printing block, galvano, cut, electro(type), cliché* ‖ Farb≈ *colour block*, ⟨Am⟩ *color engraving* **~abzug** m *block pull*, ⟨Am⟩ *engraver's proof* **klisch·ieren** vt [h] *to electrotype* | ≈ n *stereotyping, block making* **Klisch·iermaschine** f ⟨print⟩ *dabbing m.*

Klist·ier n ~(e)s/~e ⟨med⟩ *injection, enema*, **clyster* ‖ jdm ein ~ geben *to administer* od *apply an enema to a p* **~spritze** f *rectal syringe, enema*

°**Kl·itsche** f ~/~n (*small*) *estate, farm*, etc

kl·itschig a (Brot) *slack-baked, doughy*

°**kl·itschnaß** a ⟨fam⟩ *soaked to the bones*

°**kl·itzekl·ein** a *tiny*; ⟨Scot⟩ *wee*, ⟨Am⟩ *weeny*

°**Kl·o** n ⟨fam⟩ (f Klosett) *lav, loo* **~papier** n *bumf*

Klo·ake f ~/~n **1.** *sewer, drain, cesspool, cloaca* **2.** ⟨zoo⟩ *cloaca* **~nanlage** f *sewerage* **~nwasser** n *drainage, sewage*

Kl·öbeisen n *riving knife, river* **Kl·oben** m ~s/~ (Holz) *log* ‖ ⟨tech⟩ *block, pulley* ‖ ⟨carp⟩ *holdfast* ‖ ~ f Flaschenzug *block for tackles* **~arbeit** f *work done by the pulley* **~holz** n *logwood*; *split firewood* **~säge** f *large saw, frame-saw* **~seil** n *pulley-rope* **kl·obig** a *massive, chunky*; *awkward, rude, clumsy* (*fellow*) ‖ *clumping, heavy* (*boots*) ‖ *plump, broad, big* (*nose*) ‖ *boorish* (*appearance*) | [adv] ~-ge- *or* behauen *rough-hewn*; sich ~ ausdrücken *to express o.s. clumsily*

kl·omm 1. & 3. p sg pret v klimmen

°**kl·ö(h)nen** vi [h] **1.** *to lament* **2.** *to spin yarns, to* (*have a*) *chat*; *to gossip*

Klon m ~s/~e ⟨bot⟩ *clone* → vol. I.

Kl·opf- ~bremse f *knock suppressor* **~brett** n ⟨print⟩ *planer* **~bürste** f ⟨print⟩ *beating brush* **~fechter** m *pugilist, boxer, bully* ‖ ⟨fig⟩ *wrangler, polemic writer* **~fechter·ei** f *pugilism* **≈fechterisch** a *pugilistic* **≈fest** a ⟨tech⟩ *knockproof*; ~er Brennstoff *anti-knock fuel* **~festigkeit** f *knock-resistance*; *knock rating, anti-knock quality* **~garn** n *yarn for wicks* **~geist** m *noisy ghost* **~gestänge** n ⟨min⟩ *signal wire* **~hengst** m *gelding* **~holz** n ⟨print⟩ *planer* | ~abzug [m] ⟨print⟩ *p. proof* **~käfer** m ⟨ent⟩ *death-tick* **~keule** f *beetle, mallet* **~maschine** f ⟨tech⟩ *beating machine* **~schall** m ⟨med⟩ *percussion sound* **~schlägel** m (Wagenbau) *hollowing hammer* **~stange** f (Teppich-) ⟨a-engl⟩ *cross-bar, carpet rod* **~wolf** m ⟨spin⟩ *beating opener* **kl·öpfeln** vt/i [h] *to knock* od *tap gently and repeatedly* **kl·opfen** vt/i [h] **1.** vt *to knock, beat, rap* ‖ leise *to tap* ‖ (Teppiche) *beat* ‖ (Steine) *break* ‖ (Fleisch) *make* (*meat*) *tender by beating* (*it*) ‖ *to beat* (*meat, flax*) ‖ *to beat the dust out of the clothes* ‖ *to knock a nail into a wall* ‖ Griffe ~ (⟨mil sl⟩ kloppen) *to make rifle exercise* ‖ Skat ~ (⟨fam⟩ kloppen) *to play cards* ‖ (Form) ⟨typ⟩ *to plane down* ‖ jdm auf die Finger ~ *to give a p a rap* (od *to rap a p*) *on the knuckles* ‖ *to tap* od *pat a p on the shoulder*; *to slap a p's back*; *he patted her understandingly on the sh.* **2.** vi [h] an die Tür ~ *to knock* od (leise) *tap at the door* ‖ es klopft *somebody is knocking at the door, there's a knock* od *a quick tap at* od *on the door* ‖ es klopfte *a knock came to the door, there was a kn.* ‖ gegen, an etw ~ *to tap a th* ‖ der Specht klopft (am Baume) .. *taps* ([*on*] *the tree*) ‖ er klopfte ans Glas, auf den Tisch *he rapped* (*on*) *his glass*, (*on*) *the table*; auf Holz ~ ⟨fig⟩ *to touch wood* ‖ *my heart is throbbing for expectation* ‖ mit (ängstlich) klopfendem H. *with a beating heart* ‖ heftig ~ (of heart) *to palpitate* ‖ (of petrol, engine, motor) *to pink, knock, hammer* ‖ ~des Geräusch ⟨mot⟩ *knocking* | ⟨fig⟩ auf den Busch ~ *to take soundings*; bei jdm .. *to sound a p's opinion* **3.** ≈ n *knocking*, leises *tap(ping)*, lautes *banging* ‖ durch ≈ wecken *to knock up* ‖ → Massieren ‖ (Herz) *palpitation*,

(Puls) *pulsation* || ⟨mot⟩ *knocking, pinking* **Kl·opfer** m ~s/~ *beater* || (Tür~̈) *knocker, rapper, click*; der ~ ertönte *there was the sound of a rat-tat* || ⟨el⟩ *tapper* || ⟨telg⟩ *sounder* || (Schlegel) *beetle* | ⟨übtr⟩ [österr] e–n ~ h *to be* (*mildly*) *cracked* °**Kl·oppe** f ~/ *beating, licking, thrashing* **Kl·öppel** m ~s/~ (Klopfholz) *beetle, mallet* || (Glocke) *tongue, clapper* || (Trommel) *drum-stick* || (z Klöppelei) *bobbin, lace-bone* **~arbeit** f *b.-work, pillow-l.* **~arbeiterin** f *l.-maker* **~garn** n *l.-yarn* **~kissen** n *l.-cushion* od *-pillow* **~maschine** f *b.-* od *braiding machine, spindle-loom* **~muster** n *l.-pattern* **~seide** f *blond-silk* **~spitze** f *bone-* od *pillow-l.* **~zwirn** m *l.-yarn* **kl·öppeln** vt [h] *to make* (*bone-*)*lace* **Kl·öppler** m ~s/~ *lace-maker* **Kl·ops** m ~es/~e ⟨Ger⟩ *force-* od *mince-meat ball* || Königsberger ~ *minced liver balls* pl *with caper-sauce* || Klopse [pl] ⟨Scotch cul⟩ *collops* pl

Klos·ett n ~(e)s/~e ⟨fam⟩ **Kl·o** n ~s/~s (→ Toilette, Latrine) (*water-*)*closet*, (abbr *W.C.*) || *convenience, lavatory* || ⟨sl⟩ *rear* || ⟨Am⟩ *toilet* || Str·eu~̈ *earth-closet* **~anlage** f *l. installation* **~bürste** f *balai* Fr **~papier** n *toilet-, sanitary paper*; Rolle ~ *t.-roll* **~schüssel** f *flush pan* **~sitz** m *t. seat* **~spüler** m *flush cistern*

Kl·oß m ~es/~̈e, ⟨dim⟩ ~̈chen (v Erde) *clod, ball* od (*c*)*lump of earth* || ⟨fig⟩ *lump* (*in the throat*) || ⟨cul⟩ *dumpling* (*of meat, rice*); Kartoffel-, Mehlklöße [pl] *potato, flour dumplings* pl || Korinthen~ (im Schlafrock) *dog in a blanket* || ⟨Engl⟩ **~brühe** f *gravy with dumplings* || ⟨fig⟩ → °klar || er spricht als hätte er e–n ~ im Munde *he speaks as if he had a hot potato in his mouth* **~gesicht** n *pudding-face* **kl·oßig** a *cloddy, pasty, sticky*

Kl·oster n ~s/~̈ *monastery, convent, cloister* || (f Nonnen) *nunnery* || ins ~ gehen *to enter* (*to go into*) *a m.*, etc., *to turn monk*; (v Nonnen) *to take the veil* || ins ~ gehen wollen *to mean to be a monk* od *nun* || jdn ins ~ stecken *to shut a girl up with the sisters*, °⟨fig fam⟩ aufs ~ gehen *to go a little journey* (*to the W. C.*) **~brauch** m *monastic custom* od *rule* **~bruder** m *friar*; *lay-brother* **~frau** n *nun* **~gang** m *cloisters* pl **~garten** m (im Kreuzgang) *quadrangle* **~geistliche(r)** m *friar, monk* **~gelehrsamkeit** f *m.c learning* **~gelübde** n *m.c vow, profession* **~gemeinde** f **1.** *community* (*fraternity, sisterhood*) *of monks* od *nuns* **2.** *parish connected with a convent* **~gewand** n *m.c garb* od *dress* **~gewölbe** n *cloister vaulting* **~gut** n *estate belonging to a convent* **~hof** m *manor* **~kirche** f *monastery-church* **~leben** n *m.c life* **~leute** pl *conventuals* pl **~ordnung, ~regel** f *m.c discipline* od *regulations* pl **~schule** f *convent-school* **~schwester** f *nun*; *lay-sister* **~zucht** f *m.c discipline* **~zwang** m *claustral confinement* **kl·österlich** a *monastic, conventual*; *cloistral, cloistered*

Kl·österreich n ⟨hum⟩ (Österreich) *priest-ridden Austria* (*rich in monasteries*)

°**Kl·öten** f pl ⟨sex vulg⟩ *testicles*, → Hoden

Kl·otz m ~es/~̈e *block*; (Stamm) *trunk*; *stump*; *chunk* || (Holz) in ~̈e sägen, schneiden *to log* || e–n ~ Holz spalten, kleinmachen *to split a block of wood, to chop up a log* || ~ zum Holzhacken *chopping block* || (*he slept like a*) *log* od *top* || s–e Armut ist ihm ein ~ am Bein .. *a great hindrance to him*, ⟨fam⟩ .. *a drag on him* || taub wie ein ~ *as deaf as a post* | ⟨fig⟩ (P) *hulk, clod, lout* || (~kopf) *blockhead*; *poker face* **~bremse** f *block brake* °**~kopf** m *blockhead* **~pflaster** n *block pavement* **~wagen** m (Sägewerk) *drag* **kl·otzen I.** vi [h] **1.** *to spend a great deal of money* || ~ müssen *to pay through the nose* **2.** ⟨mil⟩ *to mass troops* od *fire* **3.** ⟨ftb⟩ *to kick a p's shins* **II.** ~̈ n ⟨mil⟩ *concentration* **kl·otzig 1.** [a] *cloddy* || (sehr groß) *mighty* || *clumping* (*shoes*) || ⟨fig⟩ *blockish, clumsy, rude* **2.** [adv] ~ viel G. *enormous lots of money*; *enormously* od *awfully, disgustingly* (*rich*, dazu: *to stink of m.*); ~ viel zu tun *an awful lot to do*

Kl·ownskomödie f [–au–] *knock-about comedy*

Kl·ub m ~s/~s *club* || e–n ~ bilden *to corporate o.s. into a club* ~̈**fähig** a (gesellig) *clubbable* **~hütte** f *Alpine Club chalet* **~jacke** f *blazer* **~mitglied** n *member of a club, clubman* || jd, der das ~leben liebt *clubman, clubbist, clubster, habitué of clubs* **~sessel** m *lounge-chair*

Kl·ucke f ~/~n = Glucke **kl·ucken** = glucken

°**Kl·uft**[1] f ~/~en (→ Kleidung) *clothes, dress*, etc. || ⟨fam⟩ *duds* pl || ⟨mil⟩ *kit, togs* pl; *uniform*

Kl·uft[2] f ~/~̈e **1.** *gap, cleft, fissure, rift* || (im Gebirge) *crevice, cleft* || (Abgrund) *abyss, gulf, chasm* ⟨a. fig⟩ || ⟨fig⟩ *hiatus, gap* (*of events*), *rift* (*between two people*) || e–e tiefe ~ trennt diese beiden A. *there is a wide gulf between these two views* || *gulf* (*of caste-feeling*) **2.** ⟨min⟩ *fissure, crevasse, cleavage, cleft, chasm* || ⟨geol⟩ *joint* **3.** ⟨tech⟩ (Maßstab) *folding rule* **4.** ⟨met⟩ *tongs* pl **5.** (Holz) *split timber, log wood* **kl·üften** vt [h] ⟨dial⟩ *to cleave* **kl·üftig** a *full of clefts*, etc. → Kluft

kl·ug I. [a] **1.** **(vernünftig)** *intelligent* (*man, fellow*), *clever* (*head*), *sensible* (*compromise*) || (~ u schlagfertig) ⟨fam⟩ *bright* || **(weise)** *wise, sage*; ⟨Am⟩ *brainy*; *a wise man, a man of sense*; *as wise as an owl*; er wird nie ~ w *he will never grow wise*; es wäre ~ v ihm *it would be wise of him*; der ~̈ste gibt nach *the wiser head gives in*; um nichts ~̈er s *to be none the wiser* (jetzt *for it*); er hätte ~̈er s sollen *he ought to have known better* || er ist sehr ~ *he has plenty of brains* | **(vorsichtig)** *prudent* (*behaviour*), *cautious* (*deliberation*); wir hielten es für ~̈er .. *we thought it more prudent* (*to defer the case*) || **(scharf unterscheidend)** *discerning* (*and keen of perception*), *judicious* | **(scharfsinnig)** *acute* (*intellect*), *sagacious* (*dog, policy*); ⟨fam hum⟩ *judgmatical* (*chap*) | **(praktisch gescheit)** *shrewd, hard-headed*, ⟨fam⟩ *sharp* || **(zweckdienlich)** *politic* || **(geschickt)** *skilled*, (*workman*), *skilful, ingenious* (*contriving*), *clever* (*horse, thing*; *at doing*); *able, talented, competent* (*to do a th*), *dexterous* (= *neat-handed* u *mentally adroit*), ⟨fam⟩ *smart* (*talker, retort*) | **(schlau)** *cunning, artful, subtle, sly*; ein ganz ~̈er ⟨sl⟩ *a deep one* || **(gewitzigt)** *knowing* | **(gebildet)** *clever* || **(gelehrt)** *learned* **2.** was für ein ~er Einfall *what a bright* od *good idea*, .. ~er Gedanke .. *a happy thought* || ~e Bemerkung, ~er Ausspruch ⟨Am⟩ *wise-crack* **3.** ~ w *to learn wit* || ⟨prov⟩ durch Schaden wird man ~ *one learns by experience*; *live and learn*! *bought wit is best*; *wit once bought is worth twice taught* || er ist nicht recht ~ *he is* (*not in his right senses* od) *out of his s.s* || laß dir raten, wenn du ~ bist *a word to the wise* (*don't*!) || ich kann **daraus** nicht ~ w *I can't make it out, I can m. nothing of it, I can't make head or tail of it* || ich kann aus ihm nicht recht ~ w *he puzzles me, I can't make anything* od *much of him*; ⟨fam⟩ *I can't make him out* || durch bittere Erfahrung ~ geworden *taught by bitter experience* || daraus mag der Teufel ~ w *the devil h.s. could not understand that* **II.** [adv] ~ berechnend etc *diplomatic* || ~ handeln *to act prudently* || er tat ~ daran, es nicht zu tun *he was wise in not doing it* || ~ reden, schwatzen, ⟨fam⟩ schnacken, °scheißen *to think o.s. very smart, to wisecrack*; ⟨Am sl⟩ *to be a smart-aleck*, ⟨engl⟩ .. *a wiseacre*; Sie h ~ reden! *it is easy for you to say so* **Kl·ug-**~̈**schnacken** vi [h] *to wise-crack* **~schnacker, ~schwätzer**, °**~scheißer** m *wise-crack, smarty, wiseacre*; ⟨Am sl⟩ *smart-aleck, wiseguy* **Klügel·ei** f ~/~en *sophistry, subtilization, subtle tomfoolery, affected wisdom* || *refinement* **kl·ügeln** vi [h] *to subtilize, sophisticate*; *to affect wisdom* **kl·ugerweise** adv → klug II. **Kl·ugheit** f ~/ *prudence, judiciousness, knowingness, good sense, wit, wisdom* || *cunning, slyness, shrewdness, cleverness*, etc. → klug **~sregel** f *policy, worldly maxim*; *prudentials* pl **Kl·ügler** m ~s/~ *wiseacre, sophist* **kl·üglich** adv *prudently, wisely, judiciously* || *cun-*

ningly, cleverly, etc→klug **K-ling** m ~(e)s/~e *prig*

Kl·ump m ~s/ (= Klumpen) °in ~ hauen *to smash to smithereens, to strike* .. (*all*) *of a heap* | ~fisch [m] ⟨ich⟩ *sun-fish*; ~fuß [m] *club-foot*, ⟨scient⟩ *talipes* L; (P) *taliped*; ˜füßig [a] *club-footed*; ~füßigkeit [f] *clubfootedness* ×**Kl·ümpchen** n ~s/~ (*boiled*) *sweets* **Kl·umpen** m ~s/~ (*c*)*lump* (*of sugar*); *mass*, ⟨Am⟩ *gob* (*of ash*) ‖ (Blut) *dot* ‖ *dab* (*of butter*) ‖ (Gold) *ingot, bar*; ⟨min⟩ *nugget* ‖ ⟨met⟩ *lump, bloom, ball* ‖ (Erde) *clod* ‖ (Haufen) *heap, bulk* ‖ alles auf e–m (e–n) ~ *all of a heap* ˜**frei** a *nonclotting* (*glue*) **kl·ümp(e)-rig** a *cloddy* **kl·umpig** a *lumpy, cloddish*; *clotted, cloddy, grumous* (*blood*) ‖ ~ w *to clot*

Kl·üngel m ~s/~ *clique, set, gang, coterie* Fr

Kluniaz·enser m pl *Cluniacs* pl

Kl·unker m ~s/~ **1.** *breloque, appendage* **2.** *tassel, bob* **3.** °⟨fam⟩ *lump of muck* | ~wolle [f] *clotted wool, breechings* pl °**kl·unkern** vi [h] *to dangle* **Kl·unse** = Klinse

Kl·uppe f ~/~n ⟨tech⟩ (Zange: e–e ~ *a pair of*) *pincers* ‖ Meß˜ *slide-gauge* ‖ (Schrauben˜) *die-stock* ‖ ⟨el⟩ *jointing clamp* ‖ ⟨weav⟩ *clip, tenter-hook* [bayer-österr] *clothes-peg* | ⟨fig⟩ (Hand) *clutch*

Klus f ~/~en Sw = Engpaß, Schlucht **Kl·üse** f ~/~n; ~nloch [n] ⟨mar⟩ *hawse*(*-hole*) ~n-deckel [m] *hawse plug*

°**Kl·utentramper** m *clodhopper* ‖ (Ire) *Bog-trotter*

Kl·üver m ~s/~ ⟨mar⟩ *jib*; ·Außen˜ *flying jib* | ~baum [m] ⟨mar⟩ *jib-boom* | ~fall [n] *jib halliard* | ~schot [f] *jib sheet*

Klyst·ier n ~s/~e → Klistier etc *enema*

kn·abbern vt/i [h] *to nibble, mumble*; *gnaw* (an [*at*]); *horses nibble the bark from the trees*; *squirrels nibble at beechnuts* ‖ *the child nibbles its chocolate* ‖ nichts zu ~ *nothing to eat* ‖ *to crackle* (*biscuits*) ‖ an den N. *to bite one's nails*

Kn·abe m ~n/~n *boy, lad* ‖ *male child* ‖ *youngster, stripling* ‖ *youth* ‖ ⟨fam⟩ alter ~! *oldie*! *old boy* (od *lad, chap*)! °ein alter ~ *an old bird* **Kn·aben-** ~**alter** n *boyhood* ‖ im ~ *when a boy* ~**anteil** n der Geborenen *masculinity proportion at birth* ~**bekleidung** f ⟨com, ad⟩ *small boy's clothing* ˜**haft** a *boyish*, ⟨dero⟩ *puerile*; (unreif) *crude*; ~es Lachen *a boy's laugh* ~**haftigkeit** f *boyishness* ‖ *crudeness* ~**hort** m *boys' home* ~**kraut** n ⟨bot⟩ *orchis*, → d. ~**schänder** m *sodomite* ~**schänderei** f *sodomy* ~**schauspieler** m *boy-actor* ~**schule** f *boys' school* ~**stimme** f *boy's voice* ~**streich** m *boyish trick* ~**zeit** f (*years of*) *boyhood* **Knäblein** n ~s/~ *baby-boy* ‖ ei, ei! u siehe es war ein ~ *twig and berries*!

kn·ack(s)! intj *snap*! *crack*! **Kn·ack-** ~**laut** m ⟨phon⟩ *glottal stop* ~**mandel** f *shell-almond* ~**wurst** f (Zervelat-) *saveloy*, ⟨Am⟩ *knockwurst* **Kn·acke** f ~/~n ⟨theat⟩ *tie-off* (⟨Am⟩ *lash*) *screw* **Kn·äckebrot** n *rye wafer* **kn·acken**[1] vi/t [h] *to crack* ‖ (Gewehrschloß) *to click* ‖ (~d brechen) *to snap* | vt *to crack* (*open*), *to crack* (*nuts*); ⟨mil sl⟩ (Panzer) *to bust* ‖ *to break* (*a safe*) *open* | ⟨fig⟩ an dem Kerl knackt doch alles *he is always spick and span*; → Nuß **kn·acken**[2] vi [h] ⟨univ sl⟩ mit dem Biere ~ *to drink little, slowly, niggardly* **Kn·äckente** f ⟨orn⟩ *garganey* **Kn·acker** m ~s/~ **1.** *cracker*(*s* pl) **2.** alter ~ *old niggard* ‖ *old-timer, old man* **Kn·acks** m ~es/~e *cracking, crack, snap* ‖ die Tasse hat e–n ~ bek *the cup* (*is*) *cracked* ‖ ⟨fig⟩ s–e Gesundheit hat durch den Unfall e–n ~ bek *this accident has injured his health*; *his health is shaken* .., *his health suffered* (*in the war*) ‖ er hat s–n ~ weg *he has a weak spot* (*from his accident*); ⟨fig⟩ *springs have been broken in him* ‖ °er hat e–n ~ *he is crazy* °**kn·ackig** a *spick and span*, → knacken[1] **kn·acksen** vt/i [h] = knacken

Kn·agge f ~/~n **1.** (Holzknorren) *knot, knag*; ⟨tech⟩ *stop* **2.** ⟨tech⟩ *cam, catch* ‖ ⟨mot⟩ *tappet*

Kn·all m ~(e)s/~e & ˜e (bes Donner) *clap* ‖ (Tür) *bang* ‖ (Aufschlag) *thud* ‖ (Platzen e–s Luftballons) *phut*, ⟨Am⟩ *chug*; ⟨aero⟩ (Überschall˜) *boom* ‖ (Peitsche, Schuß) *crack* ‖ (Explosion, Schuß) *crash, sharp report, explosion, detonation*, ⟨fam⟩ *pop* ‖ er warf die Tür mit e–m ~ zu *he slammed* od *banged the door* ‖ der Kork sprang mit e–m ~ heraus *the cork came out* (*with a*) *pop* ‖ ein ~ ertönte *a report rang out* ‖ mit e–m ~ öffnen *or* schließen *to snap* | °⟨fig⟩ ich glaube du hast 'nen ~ *you must be crazy* (od *cracked, tapped*; *a bit dotty*) | ~ u Fall (*all*) *of a sudden, suddenly*; *unexpectedly*; *on the spot, then and there, without much ado, without notice* od *warning, at a moment's notice*; er wurde ~ u Fall entlassen *he was given the sack* ~**bonbon** m & n *cracker* ~**büchse** f *pop-gun* °˜**bunt** a *gaudy, gay*, (*tastelessly*) *showy* ~**effekt** m ⟨theat⟩ → –körper; *stage-effect*; *clap-trap, sensation, spectacular effect*; ⟨sl⟩ *gimmick*; ⟨Am⟩ *punch line*; mit e–m ~ enden *to have a spectacular finish* ~**erbse** f (*toy-*)*torpedo* ~**frosch** m *thunder-flash* ~**gas** n *detonating gas* ~**gasgebläse** n *oxyhydrogen blow pipe* ~**glas** n *Prince Rupert's drop*; *candle-bomb* ~**gold**, ~**silber** n *fulminating gold* od *silver* ~**kapsel** f, ~**kapselsignal** n ⟨rail⟩ *detonator* ~**(kau)gummi** m *bubble gum* ~**korken** m → –frosch ~**körper** m *maroon* °~**protz** m ⟨sl⟩ *oof-bird*; *bounder plute* (= *plutocrat*) ‖ ~en [pl] ⟨Am fam⟩ *codfish aristocracy* ~**pulver** n *fulminating powder* ~**quecksilber** n *fulminate of mercury* ˜**rot** a *scarlet*, (*of a*) *glaring* od *rakish red*; *pink* (*coat*) ~**säure** f ⟨chem⟩ *fulminic acid* ~**signal** n ⟨rail⟩ *fog-signal* ~**zucker** m ⟨chem⟩ *nitrosaccharose* ~**zündsatz** m *flash compound* **kn·allen 1.** vi [h] (Kork) *to pop* ‖ (Schuß) *to crack* ‖ (Motor, durch Fehlzündung) *to misfire, chug* ‖ (Donner) *to clap* ‖ ⟨chem⟩ *to detonate, fulminate*; *to explode* (*with a report*) ‖ es knallte *there was a report* ‖ gleich knallt's! *you'll get a box on the ear*! ‖ drauf los| ~ *to bang away* | (mit der Peitsche) *to crack* od *smack* (*a whip*) ‖ (mit dem Gewehr) *to shoot off* (*one's gun*) | [s] der Topf ist in die Luft geknallt *the pot blew up* od *was blown up* **2.** vt [h] er hat sich e–e Kugel in den Kopf geknallt *he blew out his brains* ‖ er knallte die Türe (zu) *he slammed the door* ‖ er knallte ihm eine (Ohrfeige) *he gave him a box on the ear* °**Kn·äller** m ~s/~ ⟨sl⟩ *gimmick* **kn·allig** a ⟨fig⟩ *blatant, aggressive, crude*; (of colour) *loud, gaudy*; *jazzy* ‖ (auffallend) *slangy* → knallbunt

kn·app a **1.** (**eng, dicht**) das Kleid sitzt ~ [adv] *or* ist ~ [a] *the dress is tight, fits tightly, fits closely to the body* ‖ (Bett) *narrow* ‖ (Schuh) *tight* ‖ ⟨fig⟩ *succient, curt*; *concise, terse* (*style*); (aber treffend etc) *pithy, trenchant, pointed, crisp, laconic*; *brief* (*formulation*); *thumbnail* (*sketch*) **2.** (**beschränkt, dürftig, ärmlich**) *scarce, scanty* (*meal, income, money*), *insufficient* (*for the demand, need*), *barely sufficient* ‖ *short* (*measure*), *stinted* (*rations*) ‖ ~e Kost, Diät *short commons* pl, *low regimen* ‖ meine Zeit ist ~, ich bin ~ an Zeit *my time is limited, I am pressed for time* ‖ ~e Zeiten *hard times* ‖ *meagre, poor*; *shabby, mean* (*circumstances*) ‖ ich bin ~ an Geld, das Geld ist mir ~ *or* ist ~ bei mir *I am short of money* od *low in cash*, ⟨fam⟩ *I am hard up* ‖ an etw ~ w *to run short of a th* ‖ die Vorräte w uns ~ *we are running short* od *out of provisions* ‖ *money is tight*; G. ~ halten ⟨com⟩ *to tighten m.*; *butter is in short supply* ‖ ein ~es Auskommen *a bare living* ‖ Butter ist nach wie vor ~ *butter remains short*; .. wird ~ *runs short* ‖ u nicht z ~ *enough and to spare* | [**adv**] der Gewinn ist so ~ berechnet, daß *the profits are cut so fine that* ‖ sie hält ihn ~ *she keeps him closely* od *short*; *she pinches, stints, scrimps, skimps him* ‖ sie mißt sehr ~ *she gives very short measure* ‖ es geht ~ zu bei ihm *he lives in poor, mean, straitened circumstances*; *he has barely enough to live on* ‖ dann wurde getrunken, aber nicht zu ~! *then followed a jolly good drinking-bout; and we made a night of it* || (als Antwort) ja, und nicht zu ~! *and how! Rather! with a vengeance! I should think so!* (→ ob: und ob!) **3. (gerade noch zureichend)** e–e ~e Mehrheit *a small, narrow, bare majority* || mit ~er Not *with difficulty, barely; just: he just caught his train* || mit ~er Not davonk *to have a narrow* od *hair-breadth escape* || das war ein ~es Entkommen *that was a close shave, a narrow escape* od *squeak, a near th*; er kam mit verdammt ~er Not davon *he had a dev'lish narrow squeak of it* (Thack.) | **[adv]** *scarcely*; ~ bestehen *to scrape through the exam* || ~ 200 m von *a bare 200 metres from* || ~(e [a]) 100 Mark *barely 100 marks; a short 5 minutes* || e–e Pause v ~ e–r Stunde *or* v e–r ~en [a] Stunde *an interval of close upon an hour* || ~ e–e Meile *a short mile* || es geht ~ aus *it is a tight fit* || er bestand die Prüfung ~ *he scraped through the examination, his was a mere pass* **kn·appen** vi [h] er knappt mit s–m Gelde *he keeps his money short* | er knappt *he stints*

Kn·appheit f ~/ *narrowness, stringency, tightness* || *shortness, shortage, meagreness* || *scarcity, scantiness* || *conciseness* || *hardness*, etc. → knapp

Kn·app- ~eisen n *mattock* **~sack** m *knapsack*

Kn·appe m ~n/~n (Schild≈) *(e)squire, shield bearer* || *page* || ⟨min⟩ *miner, pitman* || *miller's journey-man* **Kn·appschaft** f ~/~en *miners' union* **~skasse** f *miners' box* od *benefit fund* **~sverband** m *miners' union* **~sverein** m *Miners' Friendly Society*

kn·apsen vt [h] **1.** *to pinch off* **2.** er knapst sich manches ab *he stints himself of many a th*

Kn·arre f ~/~n *rattle* || °⟨mil⟩ *gun, rifle*, ⟨hum⟩ *blunderbuss*; ⟨sl⟩ *barker; gruelstick*, ⟨Am⟩ *rod* | **≈n** vi [h] (Tür, Bett) *to creak, squawk*; (Stimme) *to squeak, grate; rattle* | mit etw ~ *to rattle a th* || mit dem Stuhl ~ *to creak the chair*

Kn·ast m ~es/~e (im Holz) *knot, knag, snag, nob* || °~ schieben (Strafe absitzen) *to do time* | ⟨fig⟩ reicher alter ~ *rich old niggard, rich old-timer* | °~bruder [m] *jail-bird* **kn·ästig** a *knotty*, etc

Kn·aster = Kanaster, *tobaccy* || ~bart [m] *(old) fogey, old grumbler* | **≈n** vi [h] **1.** °*to smoke* **2.** = knistern

kn·attern 1. vi [h] (Brand) *to crackle* || (Gewehrfeuer) *to rattle* || (Motorrad) *to chug* || (Fahne) *to flap* **2.** ≈ n *rattling* od *rattle (of musketry)* || *clack and clatter (of iron wheels)* || ⟨el⟩ *sizzle*

Kn·äuel m & n ~s/~ *clew, ball (of tread); hank skein* ⟨a. fig⟩ || Garn in ein ~ wickeln *to wind up thread into a ball* || ein Woll≈ entwirren *to disentangle a skein of wool* | ⟨fig⟩ *skein, tangle, entanglement* || *conglomeration; heap* || *crowd, throng (of people)* || *maze (of thought)* || ein ~ bilden *to crowd together, to cluster* **~wickelmaschine** f *balling machine* **~wickler** m *ball-winder, baller*

Kn·auf m ~(e)s/≈e *head, button, stud* || (Tür≈) *knob* || (des Degens) *pommel* || ⟨arch⟩ *capital*

Kn·aulgras n ⟨bot⟩ *cock's-foot (grass)*

kn·aupeln vt [h] *to gnaw*; → knabbern

Kn·auser m ~s/~ *niggard(ly p), miser*; ⟨fam⟩ *meanie; skinflint*, ⟨Am⟩ *tightwad* → Knicker **~·ei** f ~/~en *niggardliness, stinginess, meanness, cheese-paring* || (knauserige Sparsamkeit) *parsimony, penuriousness* | **≈ig** a *tight(-* od) *close(--fisted), stingy, cheese-paring, mean (about money); sordid, niggardly* (mit *of*); *miserly*; ⟨fam⟩ *constipated; penny-pinching* | jdn ~ behandeln *to scant a p* | **≈n** vi [h] *to be niggardly; to be stingy* (mit *of*), *to scrimp, pinch, scant*

Kn·autsch m ~(e)s/~e *crease* | °f ~/~e ⟨hum⟩ *couch* **kn·autschen** vt [h] *to crumple, ruffle*

Kn·ebel m ~s/~ **1.** (Knüttel) *cudgel; short stick* **2.** ⟨tech⟩ *crossbar* || (zum Spannen der Säge) *tongue* **3.** ⟨mar⟩ *toggle* **4.** (Hals≈) *clog (about a dog's neck)* **5.** (Trage≈) *packingstick* **6.** (Mund≈) *gag* **~bart** m a) *twisted* od *waxed* od *turned-up moustache, Vandyke beard* b) *imperial, tuft, goatee beard* **~holz** n *packing-stick* **~schalter** m *toggle switch* **~schraube** f *tommy screw* **~spieß** m ⟨hunt⟩ *hog-spear* **~gelenk** n ⟨tech⟩ *toggle(-joint)* **~trense** f *snaffle, gagbit* **kn·ebeln** vt [h] *to tie, bind, fasten (with a short stick)* || (im Munde) *to gag* ⟨a. fig⟩ || *to muzzle (the press), to suppress, fetter* **Kn·ebelung** f ~/~en ⟨fig⟩ *throttling, muzzling, fettering*

Kn·echt m ~(e)s/~e **1.** *servant, menial, drudge* || ⟨mar⟩ *knight* || ⟨agr⟩ *farmer's man, farm-servant, -labourer, -hand, plough-boy* | Groß≈ ⟨agr⟩ *head labourer* || Handwerks≈ *journeyman* || Haus≈ *boots* || Holz≈ *lumberman, lumberer* || Lands≈ *free lance, lansquenet, lance-knight* || Pferde≈ *footman, lackey, groom, attendant* || Spieß≈ *pikeman, lansquenet* || Stadt≈ *town-beadle* || Stall≈ *stable-man* od *-boy* || Stück≈ *bombardier* | ~ Rupprecht *Santa Claus, Father Christmas* | ⟨fig⟩ ~ Gottes *servant of God* **2.** (Unfreier) *slave, thrall* || ⟨fig⟩ ~ der Sünde *slave to sin* || ⟨hist⟩ *villein, feudal serf, bondsman* **3.** ⟨fig tech⟩ *horse, jack* || Stiefel≈ *boot-jack* || ⟨carp⟩ *trestle* || *(joiner's) support stock; standing vice* **kn·echten** vt [h] *to enslave*, ⟨poet, rhet⟩ *to enthral* **kn·echtisch** a *slavish, servile, obsequious, submissive* **Kn·echts- ~arbeit** f *menial work, drudgery* **~dienst** m (Frondienst) *villeinage, villainage, menial* od *hard service* **~gestalt** f ⟨bib⟩ *form of a servant* **~sinn** m *servility, servile disposition* od *spirit, flunkeydom, flunkeyism* **Kn·echtschaft** f ~/ *servitude, slavery* || ⟨hist⟩ *serfdom, bondage*; ⟨poet, rhet⟩ *thraldom* | ⟨fig⟩ *thraldom, vassalage, serfdom* || jd in die ~ führen *to reduce a p to servitude* **Kn·echtung** f ~/~en *enslaving, enslavement, subjugation, oppression*

Kn·eif m ~(e)s/~e *clasp-knife* || ⟨hort⟩ *hedgingbill* || (Schuhmacher≈) *paring-knife* | **≈en 1.** vt [kniff/gekniffen] [h] *to pinch, squeeze, nip; to twitch, tweak* | mit gekniffenen Augen *with blinking eyes* | ⟨mar⟩ den Wind ~ *to hug the wind, to keep close to the wind* **2.** vi [h] °⟨fam⟩ *to show the white feather; to funk (it), to back out; to shirk (fighting, responsibility)*; ⟨Am⟩ *to back down* || er kniff aus *he ran away, bolted* **Kn·eifer** m ~s/~ **1.** (ein ~ *a pair of*) *(clip* od *spring) eye-glasses* pl; *pince-nez* Fr **2.** ⟨fam⟩ (P = Drückeberger) *funk(er), quitter* **Kn·eifzange** f ~/~n (e–e ~ *a pair of*) *(cutting) nippers; cutting pliers; pincers* pl

Kn·eip- ~abend m *free-and-easy, (students') drinking-bout* od *carousal* **~bruder** m ⟨fam⟩ *old boozer, tippler* **~lied** n *drinking-song* **~name** m *student's nickname* **~schenke** f = Kneipe 2. **~tag** m ⟨univ⟩ *student's drinking-day* **~wart** m ⟨Ger univ⟩ *student who superintends the supply of beer* **~wirt(in** f) m *inn-keeper, publican*; ⟨fam⟩ *mine host* **~zange** f = Kneifzange **Kn·eipe** f ~/~n **1.** (Zange) *pincers* pl (→ Kneifzange) **2.** (Ausschank, Wirtshaus) °~ *pot-house, peg-house, pub; ale-* od *beer-house* od *-shop*; ⟨sl⟩ *boozer, jerry-shop*; ⟨Am⟩ *saloon*; verbotene ~ ⟨Am sl⟩ *speak-easy* || finstere ~ *low dive* | ~nviertel [n] ⟨Am sl⟩ *Skid Row* **3.** *students' club-house* **4.** *drinking-hall* (in 3.) **5.** [abstr] ⟨Ger univ⟩ *drinking-bout, jollification, jolly* || große ~ *festival drinking-bout* || Spiel≈ *free-and-easy with playing cards, ninepins* etc. **kn·eipen 1.** vt [h] *to pinch, squeeze, nip* || [imps] es kneipt mich im Magen, Bauche, Leibe *I feel a griping pain in my stomach, bowels, belly*; ⟨fam⟩ *I have the gripes* **2.** vi [h] *to tipple (beer), to booze, carouse* || mit jdm ~ *to hobnob with a p* **Kneiper·ei** f ~/~en *drinking-bout, jollification, carousal, tippling*, ⟨fam⟩ *boozing* **Kneipi·er** ['pje:] m ~s/~s *inn-keeper, publican*

Kn·eller m ~s/ *very bad tobacco*

×°**Kn·eppchen**: weeß ~! [etwa:] *gonnows*

Kn·et- ~holz n ⟨carp⟩ *plastic wood* **~kur** f *massage(-treatment)* **~maschine** f *(dough-, clay-)*

-kneading machine, dough mixer **~scheit** n *kneading-beetle* **~tisch** m ⟨bak⟩ *kneading board* **~trog** m ⟨bak⟩ *kneading-trough* **kn·eten** vt [h] *to knead (dough)* || *to temper (loam)* || *to mould (wax)* || ⟨med⟩ *to massage, shampoo (the body)* || ⟨fig⟩ zu etw ~ *to knead, mould (into a nation)* **Kn·eter** m ~s/~ *kneader*; (Margarine≃) *worker*; ⟨tech⟩ *pugging machine*

kn·ick intj *click*! **Kn·ick** m ~(e)s/~e **1.** *crack, flaw* || *crease, fold* || *bend, break* || *breach, bruise* **2.** ⟨arch⟩ *angle, break (of a wall)* **3.** *quickset hedge* **~beine** pl *turned-in legs* pl **~ei** n *cracked egg*; ~er [pl] *cracks* **≃fest** a *unkinkable* (Draht) **~festigkeit** f *buckling strength* **~flügel** m ⟨aero⟩ *gull wing* **~hebel** m *articulated lever* **~holz** n *brushwood* **~plattfuß** m *skew foot* **~pyramide** f ⟨Eg⟩ *bent p.* **~spantboot** n ⟨mar⟩ *sharpie* **~stag** n ⟨mar⟩ *top-stay* **~stütz** m ⟨gym⟩ *bent-armrest* **Kn·ickebein** m ~s/ **1.** *weak-kneed p* **2.** *egg-flip* od *-liqueur* | **≃ig** a *knock-* od *weak-kneed* **kn·icken 1.** vt [h] *to crack, break; flaw, burst* || (Draht, etc) *to kink* || *to snap off (twigs)* || *to fold (paper)* || ⟨mech⟩ *to crank* || *to crack (fleas,* etc) || ⟨fig⟩ *to discourage, dishearten (a p)* | geknickt [pp] *blasted (hopes)*; *blighted (existence)* || .. wie e–e Lilie *like the last rose of summer* || er ist ganz g. *he is completely crushed, limp, broken-down* od ⟨fam⟩ *quite down in the mouth* od *done for* **2.** vi [h] *to crack, flaw, break, burst, split*; die starken Balken knickten wie Strohhalme *the strong beams split like straws* | sie knickte in den Knien *or* ihre Knie knickten *her knees began to buckle, her knees gave way* °**Kn·ikker** m ~s/~ **1.** *niggard*, ⟨fam⟩ *hunks, skinflint* (→ Knauser) **2.** = Kl·icker | ~bocker [m] *knickerbockers* pl °**Knicker·ei** f ~/~en *niggardliness, stinginess*, etc (→ Knauserei) °**kn·ikk(e)rig** a *niggardly, stingy; mean*, etc °**kn·ickern** vi [h] *to be niggardly*, etc || (beim Kaufen) *to haggle* **Kn·ickung** f ~/~en ⟨tech⟩ *buckling*

Kn·icks m ~es/~e *curts(e)y*, e–n ~ machen vor *to (make* od *drop a) curtsy to* | **≃en** vi [h] *to curts(e)y, bow* || sie verließen ~d das Z. *they bowed themselves out of the room*

Kn·ie n ~s/~ **1.** *knee*; ein rundes, spitzes ~ *a well-rounded, a sharp k.* || *the k.s of one's trousers* || das ~ beugen *to bend a k.* || **auf** die ~ fallen vor *to k.l to* || sie fielen vor ihm auf die Knie *they went down on their k.s before him* || auf den ~n (liegen *to be) on one's k.s* || auf die ~! *to your k.s!* || jdn **in, auf** die ~ zwingen *to force* od *bring a p to his k.s* || sich auf die ~ werfen *to fling o.s. on one's k.s* || sie lagen auf den ~n u beteten *they knelt down in prayer* || die ~ schlotterten ihm *his k.s shook* || **in** den ~n zittern *to slake in one's shoes*; weich in den ~n *on one's k.s* ⟨fig⟩ || **mit** schlotternden ~n *with shaking k.s* || e–n Jungen **übers** ~ legen *to put* od *have a boy across one's k. for a good thrashing* | ⟨fig⟩ etw übers ~ brechen *to hurry a th (through, over), to make short work of it, to act precipitately* **2.** (Wege-, Fluß≃) *bend* **3.** ⟨tech mech⟩ *knee, joint, angle, bend, elbow, crank*; (Siphon) *drain trap* **~band** n *garter* **~beuge, ~beugung** f *genuflexion* || ⟨gym⟩ *(deep) k. bend; k.-benders* pl; *k.-bending*, in der ~beuge *at the k.-b.* **~bewegung** f ⟨tech⟩ *toggle motion* **~buckel** m (Rüstung) *k.-cap, -piece* **~bundhose** f ⟨m. m.⟩ *knickerbockers* pl **~fall** m *genuflexion, prostration*; e–n ~ tun *to prostrate o.s.* **≃fällig** adv *upon one's k.s, on bended k.s* **~flechse** f ⟨anat, vet⟩ *ham-string* || jdm die ~ durchschneiden *to hamstring a p* **≃frei** a *(skirt) leaving the k.s uncovered* **~gamasche** f *legging* **~geige** f *violoncello*; ⟨hist⟩ *bass-viol* **~gelenk** n *k.-joint* || *(of horses) stifle(-joint)*; ⟨tech⟩ *toggle-joint* **≃halftern** vt [h] (T) *to hamshackle* **~hebel** m ⟨tech⟩ *joint* od *bent lever* **~hebelbremse** f ⟨tech⟩ *toggle-joint brake* **≃hoch** a *k.-deep, up to the k.s* **~holz** n *k. timber* || ⟨bot⟩ *k.-pine* **~hose(n** pl) f (e–e ~ *a pair of) breeches* (= Reithose, Hofkostümhose) || *knee-length trousers* pl, ⟨fam⟩ *knickers* pl; *plusfours* pl || kurze ~ *shorts* pl (→ Hose) **~kehle** f *k.-hollow, ham* od *arch (of the knee)* || ⟨vet⟩ *hough* **~kehlenmuskel** m *hamstring*, ⟨scient⟩ *poplitic muscle* **~kissen** n ⟨ec⟩ *hassock* || ⟨sport⟩ *pad, legging* **≃lange Socke** f *knee-length sock* **~leder** n *apron*; *k.-strap* **~polster** = ~kissen **~riem** m ⟨fam⟩ Meister ~ *Master Cobbler* **~riemen** m *shoemaker's stirrup* **~rohr** n *pipe bend, p. elbow*; *e. p.* **~scheibe** f *k.-cap, -pan*, ⟨anat⟩ *patella* L **~schiene** f *k.-piece, k.-guard* **~schnackler** m *k.-trembling* **~schnalle** f *k.-buckle* **~schützer** = ~kissen *or* ~wärmer **~schwamm** m ⟨med⟩ *white swelling* **≃steif** a *stiff in the k.-joints* **~strümpfe** pl *knee-length stockings* pl; *golf-hose, turn-over socks* **~stück** n ⟨tech⟩ *k., elbow, angle* || ⟨arts⟩ *k.- (od three quarter) portrait* **≃tief** a *k.-deep* **~verbindung** f *elbow joint* **~wärmer** m *k. cap* **≃weich** a *weakk.d* ⟨a. fig⟩ **~welle** f ⟨gym⟩ *k.-grinder* **kn·ien** ['kniːən] vi [h] *to kneel* (vor *before*) | er kniete nieder, er ist niedergekniet *he knelt down, he went down on his knees*; ⟨ec⟩ *he genuflected* | ~d *on his knees*

°**Knies** m ~es/ = Dreck || = Streit | **≃en** vi [h] knoß/geknossen = feige kneifen | **~er** m = Feigling

°**knif** intj (abbr f:) kommt nicht in Frage

Kn·iff m ~(e)s/~e **1.** *pinch, twitch* **2.** (Kneifmal) *bruise, pinching-mark* **3.** *fold, crease, wrinkle* || (~ der Hose) *crease*; der Rock hat mehrere ~e bek *the skirt got creased* **4.** ⟨fig⟩ *trick, dodge, art, wile, artifice, fetch, knack, ruse, stratagem, rig, trap*; ⟨sl⟩ *fake, flim-flam, racket*, ⟨com sl⟩ *gimmick* || jdm ~e beibringen *to put a p up to the ropes* || ~e [pl] *sharp practices* || etw durch ~e durchführen *to wangle a th*; wieder dieselben ~e m *to be at one's tricks again*; den ~ (e–r S) heraushaben *to have the knack (of a th), to know the ropes*; ~e anwenden *to play tricks*; geh' mir nur mit d–n ~en! *none of your monkey business*; ich konnte nicht hinter s–e ~e k *I could not get behind his underhand work, sly manœuvres*

kn·iff 1. & 3. p sg pret v kneifen **kn·iffen** vt [h] *to fold (down), crease, wrinkle; to make creases in* || (Buchseite) *to dog's-ear* **kn·iff(e)lig** a **1.** *difficult, intricate, scabrous; trappy* **2.** = kniffig | **≃keit** f *intricacy* **kn·iffeln** vi [h] *to intrigue, manœuvre* **kn·iffig** a *tricky, wily, intriguing, full of tricks*; ⟨sl⟩ *gimmicky* **Kn·iffler** m ~s/~ **1.** *trickster*, etc. **2.** *p who knows how to manage difficult and intricate things*

Kn·igge: kennen Sie ~ nicht? ⟨m. m.⟩ *have you read Emily Post*?

Kn·ilch m ~es/~e ⟨urspr⟩ *bumpkin*; *cad*

Kn·ips m ~es/~e *fillip; jerk, rap; click* **~zange** f *ticket nippers* pl; ⟨engl⟩ *bell-punch* **kn·ipsen 1.** vi [h] *to fillip, to snap one's fingers* || (schnellen) *to flick* || (mit der Schere etc) *to snip* **2.** vt [h] (Billette) *to clip, punch* || ⟨phot⟩ *to snapshot* | ⟨phot⟩ jdn ~ *to snap a p*; ⟨el⟩ sie knipste den Schalter an *she flipped the switch* **Kn·ipser** m → Knipszange

Kn·irps m ~es/~e *pigmy, whipper-snapper, urchin, midget, shrimp, chip, spud, hop-o'-my-thumb, Jack Sprat* || (kl Junge) *little man, tiny tot* || ® *folding* od *pocket* od *travelling umbrella*; ⟨fam⟩ *stubby* || kl ~ *undersized boy*

kn·irschen 1. vi [h] (Schnee, Kies) *to creak, crunch* || (Türangel, Rad) *to grate, creak* || *to grind (over the rails, against the curb)* || ~d halten *to grind to a stop* | vor Wut ~ *to foam with rage*, mit den Zähnen ~ *to gnash one's teeth* || das Pferd knirscht am Zügel *the horse champs (on) the bit* | laut ~d *strident* **2.** ≃ n *creak, (s)crunch*

Kn·ister- ~gold n *tinsel* **~rasseln** n ⟨path⟩ *crepitus (of lungs)* **kn·isterig** a *rustling (leaves, silk)*; *crackling (fire), creaking (boots,* etc.) **kn·istern** vi [h] (Feuer, Papier) *to crackle* || (Balken) *creak,* *crack* || (*snow*) *to creak, crunch* || (*silk*) *rustle* || ⟨chem⟩ *to crepitate* | ~d *crisp* (*bills*)

°**Kn·itter** m ~s/~ (*c*)*rumple, crease* | ~̈arm [a] *crease-resistant*, ~festigkeit [f] *creasing resistance*; ~̈frei [a] *creaseproof*; ~probe [f] *crumpling proof* ~̈**ig** a **1.** (*c*)*rumpled, ruffled, creased, wrinkled* **2.** *grumbling* || *irritable* | ~̈**n** vi [h] *to rumple, wrinkle* || *crackle*, etc (→ knistern) | vt *to crumple, crease, ruffle*

Kn·obelbecher m *dice-box* || ⟨mil sl⟩ *jack-boot* **kn·obeln** vi [h] *to* (*play with*) *dice* || wollen ~! *head*(*s*) *or tail*(*s*)? (→ Kopf)

Kn·oblauch m ~(e)s/ ⟨bot⟩ *garlic* | **~-** ⟨cul⟩ *bourguignon*(*ne*) Fr **~geruch** m *smell of g., g.ky odour* **~hederich** m, **~rauke** f ⟨bot⟩ *crow g., hedge g., moly* **~zehe** f *clove of g.*

Kn·öchel m ~s/~ **1.** ⟨anat⟩ (Finger~̈) *knuckle* || (Gelenk) *joint* || (Ellbogen~̈) *knuckle of the elbow* || (Fußgelenk) *ankle*(*-bone*), ⟨scient⟩ *tarsus* || bis über die ~ *a.-deep* **2.** (Spiel~̈ pl) *bones* **~gelenk** n *a.-joint* **~socken** pl *anklet socks, anklets* pl **~spiel** n *game of knuckle-bones* pl **Kn·öchelchen** n ⟨anat⟩ *small bone*; ⟨scient⟩ *ossicle*

Kn·ochen m ~s/~ *bone* || nur Haut u ~ *all but skin and b.* || ⟨fig⟩ ein Haufen ~ (dürrer Mensch) *a bag of b.s*; gekreuzte ~ *cross-b.s* || starke, zarte ~ [pl] *strong, weak b.s* pl || Pf. Fl. mit ~ *pound of meat with the b.* || ihm taten alle ~ [pl] weh *every b. in his body ached* || naß bis auf die ~ *wet to the skin* || ⟨fig⟩ bis auf die ~ (national) *to the core*; *thoroughly* (*national*) || sich auf die ~ blamieren *to make an utter fool of o.s.* || er hat kein Mark in den ~ *there is no go in him* || sie h Disziplin in den ~ *discipline has become a second nature with them* || die Nachricht fuhr ihm in die ~ *the news startled him*; es ist mir in die ~ gefahren ⟨fam⟩ *it got under my skin* || nimm die ~ zus! ⟨mil⟩ *attention!*, "*Shun!*" || du bist ein elender ~ *you're a regular rotter* || °⟨mil⟩ alter ~ *old vet*(*eran*) || °~ (= Hausschlüssel) *latch-key* ~̈**artig** a *bony*, ⟨scient⟩ *osseous, ossiform* **~asche** f *bone-ashes* pl **~auswuchs** m ⟨path⟩ *exostosis* **~band** n *ligament* **~bau** m *bony frame*, ⟨scient⟩ *osseous structure* **~beschreibung** f *osteography* ~̈**bildend** a *b.-forming*, ⟨scient⟩ *osteoplastic* **~bildung** f *b.-formation, ossification* **~brand** m ⟨path⟩ *phosphorus necrosis*, ⟨fam⟩ *phossy jaw* **~bruch** m ⟨surg⟩ *fracture* (*of a b.*) **~drechsler** m *b.-turner* **~dünger** m *b.-manure* **~düngung** f *manuring with b.-dust* ~̈**dürr** a *dry as a b., all skin and b.s, like a bag of b.s* **~einrichter** m *b.-setter* **~entzündung** f ⟨path⟩ *inflammation of a b., ostitis* **~erweichung** f ⟨path⟩ *softening of the b.s*, ⟨scient⟩ *osteomalacia* od *malacosteon* **~feile** f ⟨surg⟩ *raspatory, b.-file* **~fleisch** n → -koch- **~fraß** m ⟨path⟩ *caries* L **~fuge** f *juncture of the b.s* **~fügung** f *articulation of the b.s, symphysis* **~gebäude, ~gerüst** n *skeleton* ⟨a. fig⟩, *system of b.s, osseous frame, scaffold* **~geschwulst** f ⟨path⟩ *osteoma* **~gewebe** n *b.-tissue* ~̈**hart** a *as hard as b., ossified*; ~ w *to ossify* **~hauer** m ⟨hist⟩ *butcher* **~haus** n *charnel-house* **~haut** f ⟨anat⟩ *periosteum* **~hautentzündung** f ⟨path⟩ *periostitis* **~kochfleisch** n *knuckle-b.s* **~kohle** f *b.-black, animal black* (od *b. charcoal*) **~kunde** f, **~lehre** f *osteology* **~leim** m *b.-glue* ~̈**los** a *b.less* **~mann** m *skeleton* || ⟨fig⟩ *Death* **~mark** n *marrow* (*of a b.*) **~mehl** n *b.-meal* od *-dust*; mit ~ düngen *to b.* **~mühle** f *b.-mill*; ⟨crem⟩ *cremulator* **~naht** f ⟨anat⟩ *suture* **~öl** n *neat's foot oil, b.-oil* **~pfanne** f *articular cavity, cotyla* **~porzellan** n *frit-porcelain* **~säge** f *b.-saw* **~säure** f *phosphoric acid* **~schildchen** n *b.-label* **~schmerz** m ⟨path⟩ *b.-ache*, ⟨scient⟩ *osteocope* **~schwarz** n = ~kohle **~schwund** m *osteoporosis* **~splitter** m *splinter* od *sliver of b.* **~substanz** f *osseine* **~s·uperphosph·at** n *b. superphosphate* **~system** n ⟨anat⟩ *osseous system* **~tafelleim** m *b.-glue in blocks* **~teeröl** n *b. oil* ~̈**tr·ocken** a *dry as dust* ⟨a. fig⟩ **~verarbeitungsanlage** f *b. working plant* **~verb·indungs-** ~bänder [pl] *syndesmosis* ~schiene [f] *bone plate* **~wucherung** f ⟨path⟩ *hyperostosis* L **~zange** f ⟨surg⟩ *b.-nippers* pl **kn·öcherig** a *bony* (*hand*) **kn·öchern** a (*made of*) *bone* || ⟨anat⟩ *osseous* **kn·ochig** a *bony* (*hand*), *scraggy, scrawny, angular* (*body*), ⟨scient⟩ *osseous* || [in comp] st·ark~ *raw-boned, strong-, large-limbed*; z·art~ *having delicate bones*

Kn·ödel m ~s/~ (südd = Kloß) ⟨cul⟩ *dumpling* | °~̈n vi *to speak like having a potato in one's mouth*

Kn·olle f ~/~n *node*; ⟨bot⟩ (Zwiebel) *bulb* || (Kartoffel~̈) *tuber*, kl ~ *tubercle, nodule* || ~n bilden *to bulb* **~nbl·ätterpilz** m *death-cup, bulbous* od *poisonous agaric* **~ngewächs** n *tuberous, bulbous* od *bulbed plant* **~nsellerie** m ⟨bot⟩ *celeriac* **~ziest** m *Japanese artichoke* **Kn·ollen** m ~s/~ *lump, knob, clod* || = Knolle || ⟨fig⟩ *rustic*; *rude fellow, churl*; *peasant* | ~nase [f] *potato nose* **kn·ollig** a *knobby, cloddy, knotty* || ⟨bot⟩ *tuberous, bulbous* (nierenförmig) *drusy*

Kn·opf m ~(e)s/~̈e **1.** *button* || Blüten~̈ ⟨bot⟩ *tuft*, (Knospe) *bud* || Doppel~̈ *link*(*-b.*) || Dreh~̈ *turning knob* || ⟨tech⟩ *rotating b.* || Dr·uck~̈ ⟨el⟩ = Klingel~̈; ⟨tail⟩ *press stud, patent* od *snap fastener* || Dr·uck~̈st·euerung ⟨mar⟩ *p.-b. steering gear* || F·enster~̈ *knob, handle* (*to twiddle the knobs*) || Fl·aggen~̈ ⟨mar⟩ *truck* (*of the flagstaff*) || Flor·ett~̈ *b., pommel* || Klingel~̈ (*bell-*)*b., push-b.* || Kr·agen~̈ (*collar*) *stud* || L·ogleinen~̈ ⟨mar⟩ *knot* || Mansch·etten~̈ *stud, sleeve-link* || Perlm·utter~̈ *pearl b.* || Reg·ister~̈ ⟨mus⟩ *stop-*(*knob*) || S·attel~̈ *pommel* || ⟨mus⟩ (Mandoline) *tail-piece* || Schw·ert~̈ *pommel* || mit Seide überzogener ~ *silk b.* || St·ecknadel~̈ *head* || St·ock~̈ *head pommel* || T·urm~̈ *top, ball, pommel* || übersponnener ~ *b. spun over* || überzogener ~ *covered b.* || W·äsche~̈ *linen b.* | ⟨fig⟩ netter ~ *nice chap* || alter ~! ⟨sl⟩ *old fog*(*e*)*y!* || ~̈e [pl] ⟨fam⟩ (⟨vulg⟩ Knöppe) *funds, tin, brass, chink, dust* || heraus mit den Knöppen *pay up!* ⟨fam⟩ *fork out the chink!* || mit zwei Reihen Knöpfen *double-breasted* || mit Knöpfen versehen [vt] *to b.* || ⟨mil sl⟩ die ~̈e (⟨vulg⟩ Knöppe) bek *to be promoted lance corporal* od (*artillery*) *lance bombardier* (→ Gefreiter) || an den ~̈en drehen *to twiddle with one's b.s* || auf den ~ drücken (Klingel) *to press the b.* || ein ~ ist ab *there's a b. off* **2.** [südd] = Knoten *knot* (*in a piece of string*) **~binse** f *common* od *bog rush* **~draht** m (f Stecknadeln) *head-wire* **~dreher** m *b. turner* **~druck** m: auf e–n ~ *at the touch of a b.* **~dübel** m *knob dowel* **~fabrik** f *b.-manufactory* **~form** f *b.-mould* **~gabel** f ⟨tech⟩ *b. stick* || ⟨mil hist⟩ *b.-cleaner* || wie auf der ~ geputzt *clean as a b.-stick* **~gießer** m *b.-founder* **~klette** f ⟨bot⟩ *b.-bur* **~kraut** n *field scabious, galinsoga* **~leiste** f *button panel* **~loch** *b.-hole*; ~̈er nähen *to b.h.*; ~blume [f] *b.-hole*; mit e–r ~ *wearing a flower*; ~mikrophon [n] *lapel m.*; ~näher [m] *b.-hole worker*; ~nähmaschine [f] *b.-hole sewing machine*; ~schere [f] (e–e ~ *a pair of*) *b.-hole scissors* ~̈**los** a ⟨tail⟩ *no-b.* (Hänger) **~öhr** n, **~öse** f *b.-shank* **~reihe** f *row of b.s* pl || mit zwei ~n *double-breasted* **~sonde** f ⟨med⟩ *blunt sound* **~spindel** f (f Stecknadeln) *header* **~stopper** m ⟨mar⟩ *rope stopper* **~zieher** m *b.-hook* **Kn·öpfchen** n *small button, ball* od *knob* || Kragen~̈ *stud* ⟨fig⟩ (→ Knopf) °~! *chappie!* || ~stiefel, ~schuhe [m pl] *button*(*ed*) *boots, shoes* pl **kn·öpfen** vt [h] *to button* **Kn·öpfer** m ~s/~ *button-hook* **Kn·öpfrock** m *button-through skirt* °**Kn·opp** m ~s/~e (W. Busch) (*old*) *sober-sides* °~̈**chen** n *whipper-snapper*, → Knirps

Kn·opper f ~/~n ⟨bot⟩ *gall*(*-nut*), *drillet*

°**kn·orke** a *topping, swell, toff*; ⟨Am⟩ *bully*

Kn·orpel m ∼s/∼ ⟨anat & cul⟩ *cartilage, gristle,* ⟨scient⟩ *chondrus* **∼bildung** f *chondrosis* **∼fische** m pl ⟨ich⟩ *cartilaginous* od *clasmobranch fishes* pl **∼flosser** m ⟨ich⟩ *chondropterygian* **∼gerüst** (des Rückgrats) ⟨anat⟩ *notochord* **∼haut** f *perichondrium* **∼leim** m *chondrin* **∼lehre** f *chondrology* **∼werk** n ⟨arts⟩ (*baroque ornamental motif*) "*gnarling*" **kn·orp(e)lig** a *cartilaginous, gristly*; ⟨scient⟩ *cartilaginiform*

Kn·orren m ∼s/∼ **1.** (Holz≈) *knot, knar, knag, snag, gnarl* **2.** (Auswuchs) (*hard*) *excrescence, hump* ‖ ⟨anat & bot⟩ *exostosis, tuberosity* **kn·orrig** a *knotty, knaggy, knobby*; *gnarled, gnarly* (*hands*) **Kn·ospe** f ∼/∼n (v Blatt, Blüte *leaf-, flower-*)*bud, button*; kl ∼ *eye*; Blatt≈ ⟨scient⟩ *gemma*; ∼ treiben *to bud, shoot, gemmate* | ⟨fig⟩ *tender shoot,* "*sweet seventeen*"; → ∼nball | ≈n vi [h] *to bud, burgeon*; *shoot, sprout* **∼n- ∼ball** m *cinderella* (*dance*), ⟨fam⟩ *foal and filly dance* **∼-bildung** f ⟨scient⟩ *gemmation* ≈**haft** a *bud-like* **∼hülle** f ⟨bot⟩ *cap,* ⟨scient⟩ *hymen* **∼zeit** f *budding-season* **kn·ospig** a *bud-like* ‖ (voller Knospen) *full of buds*

Kn·ötchen n ∼s/∼ *small knot,* ⟨scient⟩ *nodule* ‖ ⟨med & bot⟩ *tubercle, papula, papule* ≈**artig** a *nodular* **∼flechte** f ⟨bot⟩ *lichen* °**Kn·ote(n)** m ∼n/∼n **1.** *journeyman* **2.** ⟨fam⟩ *bounder, rough, rowdy, hooligan, lout, bully, ruffian, boor, cad*; ⟨Am sl⟩ *bohunk, hoodlum* ‖ so ein ∼! *what a cad*! **kn·öteln, kn·oten** vt/i [h] *to knot, to make* od *form a k.* **Kn·oten** m ∼s/∼ **1.** *knot*; einfacher ∼ *overhand k.*; Weber≈ *weaver's k.*; Kreuz≈, viereckiger Doppel≈ *reef-k.*; falscher Doppel≈, Altweiber≈ *granny('s k.)*; ∼ mit Schleife *slip-k.* | ⟨mar⟩ Tau≈ (verschiedener Art) *bend, hitch, fisherman's bend*; Acht(er)≈ *half hitch, figure of eight k., German k.*; Doppelverschlingungs≈ *loop k.*; Rundtörn≈ *round turn and half hitch*; Fallreeps≈ *wall k.*; (im Tau) *kink*; Woll≈ *burl* | e–n ∼ binden, knüpfen, schlagen, schlingen *to tie a k.*; .. lösen *to undo,* od *unravel a k.* ‖ durch ∼ [pl] zus–binden *to k. together* ‖ e–n ∼ ins Taschentuch m *to tie a k. in one's handkerchief* ‖ die ∼ m (an e–m Paket) *to fasten the k.s* **2.** ⟨mar⟩ das Schiff läuft 14 ∼ die Stunde *the ship does* od *makes 14 k.s an hour* ‖ ∼ der Logleine *k. of the logline* **3.** ⟨tail⟩ (Schlips) *bow, tie*; seidener Doppel≈, Künstler≈ ⟨Am⟩ *Windsor tie, string-tie* **4.** Haar≈ *k., chignon, bob* (→ Kauz); griechischer ∼ *Psyche k.* **5.** ⟨astr⟩ auf-, absteigender ∼ (Schnittpunkt der Planeten- usw. bahnen) *ascending, descending node* **6.** ⟨bot med⟩ *node* ⟨bot⟩ (Stengel-≈) *joint* ‖ ⟨bot⟩ (Holzknorren) *knag,* etc → Knorren ‖ ⟨bot⟩ Frucht≈ *ovary* ‖ ⟨anat⟩ (Schwellung) *tuber,* kl ∼ *tubercle* ‖ ⟨med⟩ (im Gesicht) *papule, nodule*; Gicht≈ *k., node* ‖ ⟨min⟩ *nodule, k.s* [pl] (*in slate*) **7.** ⟨fig⟩ *k., k.ty point, rub, difficulty, problem* (*of fate*); er fand e–n ∼ darin, *he met with an obstacle* (*when* ..) ‖ hier hat es e–n ∼ *there's a hitch somewhere, something is* od *seems wrong about it* ‖ den (Gordischen) ∼ zerhauen *to cut the* (*Gordian*) *k.* ‖ e–n ∼ lösen *to solve a difficulty* **8.** ⟨liter⟩ (Drama etc) *plot, intrigue, nodus of the plot, entanglement*; Schürzung des ∼s *working up the plot, epitasis*; der ∼ verdichtet sich *the plot thickens*; Lösung des ∼s *unravelling of the plot, development, denouement* Fr, tragischer ∼ *catastrophe*; *final solution* **∼amt** n ⟨telph⟩ *tandem office* ≈**artig** a *knotty* **∼bildung** f ⟨scient⟩ *nodulation*; ⟨path⟩ *tuberculization* **∼fänger** m (Sieb) ⟨pap⟩ *pulp strainer* ‖ ⟨weav⟩ *knot catcher* ≈**haft** = knotig **∼holz** n *k.ted, gnarled wood* → Knorren ≈**los** a *k.less*; ⟨bot⟩ *jointless* (*stem*) **∼lösung** f ⟨liter⟩ → Knoten 8. **∼punkt** m ⟨scient, math⟩ *point of junction,* ⟨fig⟩ *converging point, ganglion* ‖ ⟨astr⟩ *node* ‖ ⟨phys⟩ *nodal* od *focal point* ‖ ⟨rail⟩ *junction* (*point*), *point of intersection*; *branching--off* od *central station, centre* | ∼belastung [f] *k. load* **∼punktelast** f *load in the joints* **∼schrift** (der alten Peruaner) *quipu* **∼schürzung** f ⟨liter⟩ → Knoten 8. **∼stich** m ⟨embr⟩ *k.-stich* **∼stock** m *thorn-stick* **∼tau** n *k.ted rope* **∼verbindung** f ⟨el⟩ *T-joint* **Kn·öterich** m ⟨bot⟩ *knot-grass*; *spurry, -ey* **kn·otig**[1] a **1.** *knotty, knaggy, knobby*; *gnarled* (*branches, fingers*) **2.** ⟨bot⟩ *jointed*; ⟨scient⟩ *nodose, nodular* ‖ ⟨path⟩ *tuberculous* | ≈**keit** f *knottiness*; *nodosity* **kn·otig**[2] *coarse, rude, vulgar*; *like a bounder, boorish, caddish* | ≈**keit** *coarseness,* etc. **Kn·ubbel, Knubben** m ∼s/∼ *knot, gnarl, knob*

Kn·udel f → Nudel | ≈**n** vt [h] *to canoodle, to hug and kiss*

Kn·uff m ∼(e)s/≈e *buffet, cuff, poke, thump, punch* | ≈**en** vt [h] *to cuff, thump, buffet, poke, pommel* (*in the ribs*) **kn·uffig** a adv ⟨eig⟩ *rude, coarse, vulgar* ‖ ⟨fig⟩ *immense*(*ly*), *awful*(*ly*), ⟨fam⟩ *tremendous* (*heat*), *-ly* (*hot*)

Kn·ülch m → Knilch

°**kn·üll(e)** [pred a] ⟨fam⟩ *tipsy*; *tight,* (*drunk*) | **∼en** vt [h] *to crumple, ruffle, crease* | °≈**er** m ∼s/∼ (S) ⟨sl⟩ *smasher, screamer* | *stunt*

Kn·üpf- ∼arbeit [f] *knotwork, knotted work* od *lace*; ∼maschine [f] (Netz≈) *netting machine* **∼-teppich** m *knot-carpet* **kn·üpfen** vt [h] *to tie* (*a knot*), *to knit, to knot* (*a shawl*) ‖ *to join, unite, attach* ‖ *to net* (*a purse*) ‖ *to weave* (*carpets*) ‖ an den Galgen ∼ *to hang* (*a p*); *to string* (*a p*) *up* | ⟨fig⟩ *to form* (*a friendship, an attachment* [*for*]) ‖ gr Hoffnungen an etw ∼ *to have great hopes in a th* ‖ enger ∼ *to tighten* (od *draw closer*) (*the bonds of friendship*) ‖ e–e Bedingung an etw ∼ *to add a condition to a matter, to make a th dependent on*; an die Geschenke waren Bed.en ge–ft *the pr.s were given with reservations* | **sich an etw ∼** *to be connected* od *tied up with*; *to attach* (*o.s.*) *to*; *associations which attach to it*; u daran .. *and thereby hangs a tale* (Shak, As You Like It; II.7.28)

Kn·üppel m ∼s/∼ (*short*) *stick*; *cudgel, club,* ⟨Am⟩ (Polizei≈) *espantoon, bludgeon*; ⟨sl⟩ *cosh* ‖ *log of wood,* ⟨for⟩ *billet* ‖ Gummi≈ ⟨Am sl⟩ *billy* ‖ (Hunde≈) *clog* ‖ ⟨met⟩ *billet* ‖ (Seil) *winch, lever* ‖ ⟨aero⟩ (Steuer≈) *control-column,* ⟨sl⟩ *joy--stick* | ⟨übtr cul⟩ (Brötchen) (*small*) *roll* | ⟨fig⟩ der ∼ liegt beim Hunde *there's no choice* od ⟨fam⟩ *it's Hobson's choice* ‖ jdm e–n ∼ zw die Beine werfen *to put a spoke in a p's wheel* ‖ Politik des gr ∼s *big stick policy* **∼band** n (Seil) *winch(--handle)rope* **∼brücke** f *bridge of bare poles* od *round sticks, pole-bridge* **∼damm** m *log-road,* ⟨Am⟩ *corduroy-road* ≈**dick** a ⟨fig⟩ *not single spies, but in battalions* (Shak, Hamlet IV. 5.) ‖ ich hab's ≈dick (satt) *I'm fed-up with it* **∼herrschaft** f, **∼regiment** n *club law* **∼holz** n (*round*) *billet-wood, fagots* pl **∼steuerung** f ⟨aero, tech⟩ *stick control* **∼walzwerk** n ⟨met⟩ *billet mill* **∼weg** m [österr] = –damm

kn·urren 1. vi [h] (über [acc]) *to grunt, gnarl, snarl, growl* ‖ ⟨fig⟩ (P) *to growl, grumble, quarrel, snap* ‖ er hat immer etw zu ∼ *he has always sth to grumble at* ‖ (v Magen) *to rumble* **2.** ≈ n *grunting,* etc. ‖ (im Leibe) *rumbling* **Kn·urr- ∼hahn** m ⟨orn⟩ *black-cock* ‖ ⟨ich⟩ *gurnard* ‖ ⟨fig⟩ *growler, grumbler* **∼kater** m *growling* od *spitting tom-cat*; ⟨fig⟩ → o. **kn·urrig** a *grumbling, growling, snarling* (a. P)

Kn·usper- ∼chen n ∼s/∼ *biscuit,* ⟨Am⟩ *cookie* **∼flocken** f pl *corn-flakes* ×**∼le** n pl ⟨cul⟩ *crispies* **∼schwarte** f ⟨cul⟩ *crackling* **kn·usp(e)rig** a *crisp*(*y*), *short* ‖ ⟨fig⟩ ein ∼es Mädchen *a bonnie girl* ‖ als ich noch jung und ∼ war *in my heydays* **kn·uspern** vt [h] *to nibble*

Kn·ust m [uː] ∼(e)s/∼e **1.** *crust* (*of bread*) **2.** = Knorren **3.** *core* (*of apple*)

Kn·ute f ∼/∼n *knout* ‖ jdm die ∼ geben, jdn mit der ∼ schlagen *to knout a p* ‖ türkische ∼ *Turkish knout* od *harrow* ‖ mit eiserner ∼ regieren *to rule with a rod of iron*

°**kn·utschen** [u:] vt [h] *to crush* (*a th*) ‖ *to fondle, squeeze* (*a p*); ⟨Am⟩ *to pet, neck,* → *necking-party*

Kn·üttel m ~s/~ = Knüppel **~holz** n *billet-wood* **~vers** m *doggerel rhyme* od *verse*

°**Kö** f invar = Königsstraße in Düsseldorf

koalis·ieren vrefl: sich ~ *to form a coalition*

Koaliti·on [ts] f ~/~en *coalition, combination* **~sfreiheit** f *rights of free collective bargaining* **~s-recht** n *right of combining, freedom to organize, freedom of association* ‖ *law as to trade unions* **~s-regierung** f *coalition government* **~sverbot** n *prohibition to combine*

ko·axen vi [h] *to croak*

K·obalt n ~(e)s/~e ⟨chem⟩ (→ Kobold) *cobalt* ‖ arseniksaurer ~ *c. bloom, arseniate of c.* **~arsenikkies** m *glaucodot(e)* **~beschlag** m *c. crust* **~blau** n *c. blue, smalt* **~blüte** f *c. bloom* **~bombe** f *C-bomb* **~chlor·ür** n *chloride of c.* **~erz** n *c. ore* **~glanz** m *c.-glance* **~haltig** a *c.iferous, c.ic* **~kies** m *linn(a)eite* **~oxid·uloxid** n *China blue* **~speise** f *c. speiss*

K·obel m [österr] ~s/~ (Verschlag) *partition* ‖ (Kiste) *box*; (Lattenkiste) *crate* ‖ (Tauben~) *dovecot(e)*

K·oben m ~s/~ *pigsty* ‖ ⟨fig⟩ *hovel, pen*

K·ober m ~s/~ *back-basket, hamper*

K·öbes m ~/ [Kurzform v Jakob(us)] *Jamie*

K·oblenz n ⟨Ger⟩ (Stadt an Rhein u Mosel)

K·obold m ~(e)s/~e (→ Kobalt) (*hob)goblin, spirit, imp* ‖ ⟨fig⟩ *imp, flibbertigibbet*: sie ist ein lustiger kl~ *she's a merry little imp* **~maki** m (Halbaffe) ⟨zoo⟩ *spectre-lemur* **~streich** m *impish trick*

Kob·olz m: ~ schießen *to* (*turn a*) *somersault*

K·obra f ~/~s (Brillenschlange) ⟨zoo⟩ *cobra*

K·oburg n → Coburg

Koch [–o:–] n [österr] ~s/ ⟨cul⟩ (Brei) *pudding, porridge*

K·och m ~(e)s/~e (*man-*)*cook* (→ Köchin); ~ f *à-la-carte*-Gerichte *short-order c.* ‖ (Küchenchef) *chef*: *the chef at Bays's, that renowned cook* (Thack.) ‖ Hilfs~ ⟨Am⟩ *flunkey* ‖ ⟨prov⟩ viele ~e verderben den Brei *too many cooks spoil the broth* (→ Hunger) **K·och-** mst *cooking* (→ kochen) **~anlage** f *c. plant* **~apfel** m *c.-apple, codlin(g), beefing* **~apparat** m *c. apparatus*; ⟨mil⟩ *camp-kitchen*; ⟨Am⟩ *chafing dish* **~beständig** a ⟨chem⟩ *stable when boiling* **~birne** f *stewing-* od *c.-pear* **~brigade** f ⟨hot⟩ *kitchen-staff* **~buch** n *cookery-book*, ⟨Am⟩ *cook-book* **~echt** a *boilfast* (Stoff) **~festigkeit** f *resistance at the boil* **~fertig** a *ready-to-cook* **~feuer** n *fire for c.* **~gefäß** n *cooker, c.-vessel* **~gelegenheit** f *c.-range*; Zimmer mit ~ ⟨Am⟩ *room with light housekeeping* **~gerät** n *c. apparatus* **~geschirr** n *hollow ware, kitchen-utensils* od *things* pl ‖ ⟨mil⟩ *mess-tin, m.-gear*; *canteen* **~herd** m *kitchener,* (*c.-* od *kitchen-*)*range* **~käse** m *cook cheese* **~kelle** f *basting ladle* **~kessel** m *copper, boiler* ‖ ⟨mil⟩ *camp kettle,* ⟨sl⟩ *dixie* ‖ ⟨pap-ind⟩ *pulp boiler* **~kiste** f *hay-, c.-box, self-cooker* **~kunst** f *cookery, culinary art, art of c.* **~künstler(in** f) m *clever cook* **~loch** n ⟨mil⟩ *c.-pit* od *-hole* **~löffel** m (*pot-*)*ladle* **~maschine** f *c.-apparatus, tin-kitchen, kitchener* **~nische** f *kitchenette* **~ofen** m *c.-stove, range*; ⟨Am⟩ *cook-stove* **~pfanne** f (*sauce-*)*pan* **~platte** f ⟨el⟩ *stove-, c.-plate, hotplate* **~probe** f *boiling test* **~salat** m ⟨cul⟩ *boiled lettuce* (*in a thick sauce*) **~salz** n *common salt, kitchen salt,* (*sodium chloride*) **~salzlösung** f *brine, salt solution* **~schrank** m *cabinet cooker* **~schule** f *c. school* **~stelle** f *c. range* **~stück** n ⟨cul⟩ *piece of meat for boiling* **~topf** m *saucepan, cooker, pot* ‖ elektrischer ~ *electric pan* ‖ °(Stahlhelm) ⟨mil sl⟩ *panic bowler* **~wein** m *c.-wine* **~zucker** m *brown sugar, lump sugar* **K·ochen** n ~s/ *cookery, cooking* ‖ beim ~ .. *in the cooking* (*add sugar*) ‖ °das Wasser ist am ~ .. *near the boiling point,* ⟨fam⟩ *near the boil* ‖ er setzte den Kessel zum ~ aufs Feuer *he placed the kettle upon the fire to boil* ‖ leicht z ~ bringen *to bring to a simmer* ‖ in gelindem ~ halten *to simmer* ‖ ⟨fig⟩ die Volksseele zum ~ bringen *to bring the public feeling to the boiling point*; jdn z ~ bringen *to make a p's blood boil* **k·ochen 1.** vt [h] (zubereiten) ~ (lassen) *to cook, boil,* ⟨fam⟩ *do* ‖ *to boil eggs, vegetables, potatoes*; *to cook meat, a meal* ‖ Leim ~ *to heat the glue* ‖ weich ~ *to boil tender*; halbgar ~ *to parboil* ‖ Kaffee, Tee ~ *to make coffee, tea* ‖ gekochtes .. *boiled beef, mutton*; .. Obst *stewed fruit* ‖ richtig *or* tadellos gekocht *done to a turn* **2.** vi [h] *to be cooking*: *the meal is c.* ‖ (Flüssigkeiten) *to boil, to seethe* ‖ gelinde ~ *to simmer,* stark *to wallop* ‖ das Wasser kocht *the water is boiling* ‖ *the peas must boil longer* ‖ das Wasser kocht auf (nahezu) .. ⟨fam⟩ .. *is near the boil* | ⟨fig⟩ es kocht in ihm, er kocht vor Wut *he is boiling* od *seething* od *mad with passion* od *rage, his blood is up* ‖ die ~de Brandung *the foaming surf* **3.** [abs] *to cook, to do* (od *attend to*) *the cooking* ‖ sie kocht gut *she's a good cook*; sie versteht gut zu ~ *she understands the culinary art* **4.** vrefl **sich** ~: diese Erbsen ~ sich schlecht *these peas are bad cookers,* sie ~ sich nicht gar .. *they don't get tender in ever so long boiling* **K·ocher** m ~s/~ (Kessel) *boiler* ‖ ‖ (Gerät) *cooker* ‖ (Gips~) *calciner* ‖ ⟨tech⟩ *digester* **Kocher·ei** f ~/~en *cookery, cooking* **K·öchin** f ~/~nen (*female*) *cook*

K·öchel npr [österr] | ~verzeichnis [n] *Köchel* (Mozart) *catalogue*

K·öcher m ~s/~ *quiver* ‖ (Golf) *bag* **~fliege, ~jungfer** f ⟨ent⟩ *caddis-fly*; Larve der ~ *caddis(-worm), straw-worm*

K·odak m ~s/~s *kodak*

°**k·oddrig** a *loose, impudent* ‖ e–e ~e Schnauze .. *a loose* od *noisy tongue* ‖ [adv] ich fühle mich ~ *I feel sick,* ⟨Am⟩ .. *like throwing up*

K·öder m ~s/~ *bait, lure* ‖ mit e–m ~ versehen [vt] *to bait* ‖ künstlicher ~ *fly, squid* ‖ am *or* auf den ~ anbeißen *to nibble* od *take the bait* ‖ ~ auslegen *to scatter bait* | ⟨fig⟩ *inducement, attraction, enticement, decoy, stool-pigeon*; etw als ~ benutzen f *to dangle a th before* (*a p*) **~fisch, ~wurm** m *live bait* **~nadel** f *baiting needle* **ködern** vt [h] *to bait,* (*al*)*lure, to decoy* ‖ ⟨fig⟩ *to entice, allure*; *he tried to entice her*; sich ~ l *to rise at* od *to bait*; sie ließ sich nicht ~ *she would not let herself be caught*

K·odex m ~es/~e & K·odizes *codex, old manuscript* ‖ ⟨jur⟩ *code* ‖ ⟨telg⟩ *code* **K·ode(x)- ~schlüssel** m ⟨telg⟩ *code* **~telegramm** n *code telegramm* **~wort** n *code word* **Kodifikati·on** [ts] f ~/~en *codification* **kodifiz·ieren** vt [h] *to codify*

Kodiz·ill n ~(e)s/~e ⟨jur⟩ *codicil*

Koedukati·on [–'tsio:n] f ~/ *coeducation* (*of boys and girls*) ‖ Schüler e–r ~sschule ⟨Am⟩ *co-ed*

K·ofel m ~s/~ [bayer-tirol] Bergkuppe

Koexist·enz f ~/: friedliche ~ *peaceful coexistence*

Koffe·in n ~s/ = Kaffein **~frei** a *c.-free*; *de-caffeined* (*coffee*)

K·offer m ~s/~ **1.** (Straßenbau) *layer of broken stones* **2.** *box, trunk* ‖ (kl) *portmanteau* ‖ (Hand~) *hand bag, suit-case* ‖ (Stadt~) *attaché case* ‖ gr ~ [pl] ⟨mil, aero sl⟩ *big stuff*; ⟨typewr⟩ *carrying case* ‖ die ~ packen *to pack one's baggage* **~apparat** m ⟨wir⟩ *portable wireless set,* ⟨fam⟩ *walkie-talkie* **~beschläge** m [pl] *trunk fittings* pl **~brücke** f ⟨mot⟩ *luggage grid* **~damm** m *cofferdam*; dazu: *to coffer* **~empfänger** m ⟨wir⟩ *portable set* **~griff** m *trunk handle* **~pappe** f *tr.-board* **~raum** m ⟨mot⟩ *luggage-hold, boot*; ⟨Am⟩ *trunk* **~riemen** m *tr. strap* **~schließfach** n ⟨rail⟩ *l.-locker,* ⟨Am⟩ *self service b. l.* **~schloß** n *tr. lock* **~träger** m *porter*

°**K·ofmich** m ~s/~e ⟨dero⟩ (= Kaufmann) *trafficker*

K·og [o:] m ~(e)s/~e *polder*

K·ogel m ~s/~ *dome-shaped hill*

K·ognak [kɔŋak] m ~s/~s *cognac, French brandy* | ~schwenker [m] *br.-balloon*

Kogn·at [kɔg'na:t] m ~en/~en *relative having the same parents or grandparents* | (Ggs Agnat) *relative on the mother's side*

kohär·ent a ⟨phys⟩ *coherent* **Kohär·enz** f ~/~en *coherence* **Koh·ärer** m ~s/~ ⟨el, wir⟩ *coherer* **kohär·ieren** vi [h] *to cohere* **Kohäsi·on** f ~/~en *cohesion, coherence, -cy*

K·ohl[1] m ~(e)s/ *cabbage* ‖ Rot, Weiß~̽ *red, white c.* ‖ Blumen~̽ *cauliflower*; Grün~̽ *kale*; Kraus~̽ *curly c.*; Meer~̽, See~̽ *sea-k.*; Rosen~̽ *Brussels sprouts*; Wirsing~̽ *savoy (c.)* ‖ ~ bauen *to grow cabbages* | ⟨fam fig⟩ (Unsinn) *twaddle, rubbish*; er redete fürchterlichen ~ *he talked awful rot*; das ist ja alles ~ *that's all rubbish*; schwatze k–n ~! *don't talk nonsense*!; aufgewärmter ~ *raked-up story* ‖ das macht den ~ nicht fett *fine words butter no parsnips* **~arten** f pl *cabbage-tribe* [sg], ⟨scient⟩ *brassicaceous plants* **~blatt** n *c.-leaf* ‖ °**~dampf** m ⟨mil sl⟩ *twist, (hunger)*; ich habe *or* schiebe ~ *I have a tremendous twist* **~eule** f ⟨ent⟩ *c.-moth* **~fliege** f ⟨ent⟩ *c.-fly* **~floh** m ⟨ent⟩ *c.-flea* **~garten** m *kitchen-garden* **~gemüse** n *cabbage* **~kopf** m *c.-head, (head of) c.* **~lauch** m ⟨bot⟩ *c.-garlic* **~markt** m *vegetable-market* **~palme** f ⟨bot⟩ *c.-tree* **~pflanze** f *(young) c.-plant*; ~n [pl] = ~arten **~r·abi** m ⟨bot⟩ *kale-, c.-turnip, kohlrabi* **~raps** m = ~saat **~rapsöl** n *rape-seed oil* **~raupe** f ⟨ent⟩ (v ~weißling) *c.-caterpillar* **~röschen** n ⟨bot⟩ *bugle* **~roulade** f *rolled cabbage-leaves stuffed with minced meat* **~rübe** f ⟨agr⟩ *turnip, swede* **~rübenwinter** m ⟨Ger⟩ *the turnip-winter 1916/17* **~saat** f, **~same** m ⟨bot⟩ (Sommerraps) *colza, cole-, rape-seed* **~salat** m ⟨Am⟩ *cole slaw* **~sprossen** m [pl] ⟨agr⟩ *Brussels sprouts* pl **~stiel, ~strunk** m *c.-stalk* **~wanze** f ⟨ent⟩ *c.-bug* **~w·eißling** m *c.-butterfly, c.-white*

K·ohl-[2] (→ Kohle) **~amsel** f ⟨orn⟩ = Amsel **~meise** f ⟨orn⟩ *great titmouse, coal-tit*; ⟨Am⟩ *chickadee* ~̽**(pech)rabenschwarz** a ⟨fam⟩ = ~schwarz **~rappe** m *black horse* ~̽**schwarz** a *(as) black as coal* (od *pitch, soot, ink*), *jet-black* **K·ohle** f ~/~n **A.** ⟨allg⟩ *coal* ‖ ⟨el⟩ *carbon* ‖ aufbereitete ~ *dressed c.*; Braun~̽ *brown c.*; *lignite*; Erbs~̽ *pea c.*; Eß~̽ *forge c.*; Fein~̽ *small c.*; Fett~̽ *fat c., rich c.*; rohe Förder~̽ *rough c.*; Gas~̽ *gas c.*; glimmende ~n [pl] *embers* pl; glühende ~n [pl] *red-hot* od *live coals* pl; Graphit~̽ *graphitic carbon*; Holz~̽ *charcoal*; Licht~̽ *electric lighting carbon*; Mager~̽ *semibituminous c.*; medizinische ~ *medical charcoal*; minderwertige ~ *poor c.*; Perl~̽ *pea c.*; Schiefer~̽ *slaty c.*; schlackende ~ *clinkering c.*; schlackenreine ~ *c. free of slag*; Schmiede~̽ *smithy c., forge c.*; Stein~̽ *pit c.*; tierische ~ *animal charcoal*; Torf~̽ *peat c.*; Zechen~̽ *pit c.*; Zeichen~̽ *carbon* | ⟨fig⟩ weiße ~ (Wasserkraft) *white c.* **~papier** n *carbon paper* **B.** ~n [pl] *coal*; einzelne ~stücke *coals* pl; ein Sack ~n *a sack of coal* ‖ °⟨fig⟩ (= Geld) (Hauptsache: die ~n stimmen) **C.** ~ fördern *to raise coal*; ~ hauen *to pick c.*; (Holz)~ brennen *to burn coal, to make charcoal*; mit ~ heizen *to heat with c.*; ~(n) anfahren *to deliver c.*; Ersatz der schwarzen ~ als Kraftquelle durch die weiße (= Wasserkraft) *substitution of waterpower for c.*; ⟨mar⟩ ~n nehmen *to coal*; Schiffe mit ~ versorgen *to coal ships*; in ~ verwandeln *to carbonize*; sich in ~ verwandeln *to turn to coal, to become carbonized*; mit ~ zeichnen *to draw with carbon* | ⟨fig⟩ wie auf glühenden ~n sitzen *to be on hot bricks*, ⟨Am⟩ *to be on the anxious seat*; über glühende ~ gehen *to fire-walk*

k·ohlen[1] **1.** vi [h] *to burn badly, to char*; der Docht kohlt *the wick burns with a sooty flame* | ⟨mar⟩ (= Kohlen einnehmen) *to coal* **2.** vt [h] *to char, to carbonize (wood)*; *to make charcoal* | *to draw with carbon* **3.** ~̽ n *charring*, ⟨scient⟩ *carbonization, carburization*

°**k·ohlen**[2] vi [h] **1.** *to talk bosh* od *rubbish* **2.** *to tell fibs*; ohne ~ zu wollen! *no kidding*!

K·ohlen- ~abladeplatz m *c. tip* od *hoist* **~abraum** m *coal waste* **~ader** f *c.-vein* **~aktien** f [pl] *shares* [pl] *in a c.-mine* **~anleihe** f '*c.-loan*' *based on the price of c. as a standard of value in the* ⟨Ger⟩ *inflation period* **~an·ode** f *carbon anode* **~arbeiter** m *collier, coal-miner*; *pitman* **~aufbereitung** f *c. dressing* **~becken** n *c.-, fire-pan*; *brazier* ‖ ⟨min⟩ *c. field* ‖ ⟨geol⟩ *c.-basin* **~behälter** m *c.-bin* **~bergmann** m *c. miner, collier* **~bergwerk** n *colliery, coal-mine* od *-pit* **~bestand** m *amount of c.* **~bohrer** m (P) *c. borer* ‖ (S) *c. drill* **~brenner** m *charcoal-burner* **~brenner·ei** f *ch. burning* ‖ *ch.-kiln* od *-works* [sg] **~bunker** m ⟨mar⟩ *c. bunker* **~bürste** f *carbon-brush* **~dampf, ~dunst** m *smoke of burning c., c.-smoke* **~dampfer** m *(steam-)collier* **~dioxid** n *carbon dioxide* **~druck** m *car. print* **~eimer** m *c.-scuttle* **~fadenlampe** f *carbon filament lamp* **~feld** n *c. field* **~feuer** n *c.-fire* **~feuerung** f *c. firing, heating with c.*; ⟨tech⟩ *combustion of c.* **~flöz** n *c. seam* od *vein*; ⟨geol⟩ *layer* od *bed of c.* **~förder-** ~anlage [f] *c. conveying plant* ~maschine [f] *colliery winding* od *hauling machine* ~ung [f] *output of c.* **~formation** f ⟨geol⟩ *carboniferous formation* **~gas** n *c. gas* **~gebiet** n *c. field* **~gebirge** n *carbonaceous rocks* pl **~glut** f *live c.s* pl **~grieß** m *small c.* **~großhändler** m *wholesale c. merchant* **~grube** f *c. mine* od *pit, colliery* **~grubenbesitzer** m *c.-owner* **~grus** m *slack* **~handel** m *c.-trade* **~händler** m (gr) *c. merchant*; (kl) *c.-man* **~handlung** f *c. merchant's business* **~hydrat** n *carbohydrate* **~hydrierung** f *hydrogenation of c.* **~kasten** m *c.-box*, eiserner *c.-scuttle* **~kammer** f *c.-room, -cellar, -hole* **~klein** n *slack*; *c.-dust*; *small c.*; (beim Ziegelbrennen) *breeze* **~korb** m *c.-scuttle, c.-skip, c.-basket* **~ladung** f *c.-cargo* **~lager** n *c. stores* pl; ⟨mar⟩ *c. depot*; ⟨geol⟩ *c.-bed, c.-seam* **~leichter** m ⟨mar⟩ *c.-lighter* **~magn·at** m *rich c.-owner, owner of c. mines* **~mahlanlage** f *c. grinding plant* **~mangel** m *c. famine* od *shortage* **~mann** m *c.-man* **~meiler** m *charcoal pile* **~meßfahrt** f *c. consumption trial* **~(mon)oxid** n *carbon monoxide* **~nebel** m *smog* **~niederlage** f *c. stores* **~oxid** n ⟨chem⟩ *carbon(ic) (mon)oxide* **~ox·idgas** n *carbon oxide gas* **~päckchen** n *c.ing rig* **~pier** f *c.ing pier* °**~pott** m *Black Country*; *(coal) mining towns* pl **~prahm** m ⟨mar⟩ *c. lighter* ~̽**sauer** a *carbonic*; ~̽saures Ammoni·ak *ammonium carbonate*; ~̽saurer Kalk *carbonate of lime*; (doppelt) ~̽saures Salz *(bi)carbonate*; ~̽saures Natron *carbonate of soda*; ~̽saures Wasser *aërated water* **~säure** f ⟨chem⟩ *carbonic acid*; (→ a.) Kohlendioxid | ~schnee [m] (feste ~) *carbon dioxide snow* **~schacht** m *c.-pit* **~schaufel** f *c.-shovel* **~schicht** f ⟨geol⟩ *layer of c.* **~schiefer** m *carbonaceous* od *bituminous shale* **~schiff** n *collier, c.-barge* od *-boat* **~schippe** f = ~schaufel **~schlamm** m *c. washings* pl **~station** f ⟨mar⟩ *c.ing station* **~staub** m *c.-dust* | ~feuerung [f] *pulverised c. firing, c. dust firing*; *c. d. furnace*; ~lunge [f] ⟨path⟩ *miner's lung*; *anthracosis* Gr **~stift** m *charcoal-crayon* **~stoff** m ⟨chem⟩ *carbon* | ~element [n] ⟨el⟩ *carbon-combustion cell*; ~̽haltig [a] *carbonaceous*; ⟨biochem⟩ *organic carbonycle*; ~kette [f] ⟨chem⟩ *carbon chain*; ~stahl [m] (weicher *low*) *carbon steel*; ~verbindung [f] ⟨chem⟩ *carbon compound*; *carburet* **~syndik·at** n *c.-syndicate, association of the whole German c.-mining industry* [Times] **~teer** m *c. tar* **~tender** m ⟨mar⟩ *coaler* **~träger** m *c.-heaver* **~trimmer** m *c. trimmer* **~übernahme** f ⟨mar⟩ *c.ing* **~verbrauch** m *c. consumption* **~versorgung** f *c. supply*; ⟨mar⟩ *the c.ing (of a fleet)* **~vorkommen** n *c. deposits* **~vorrat** m *c. supply* **~wagen** m *coal-waggon* ‖ ⟨min⟩ *c. hutch* ‖

⟨rail⟩ *tender* **~wasserstoff** m *hydrocarbon* **~zeche** f *colliery*; *c. mine*, *c. pit* **~zeichnung** f *charcoal--drawing* **K·öhler** m ~s/~ *charcoal-burner* ‖ ⟨fig⟩ *coalfish* **~glaube** m *blind* od *simple faith* **~hütte** f *charcoal-burner's hovel* **k·ohlig** a *coaly*

Koh·orte f ~/~n *cohort*; ⟨übtr⟩ = Generation

koit·ieren [o:i] vi [h] ⟨eig⟩ *to copulate*, ⟨allg⟩ *cohabit*; *have intercourse* (mit *with*) **K·oitus** [o:i] m ~/~ ⟨eig⟩ *coition*, *close hug*; *sexual intercourse* ‖ ⟨allg⟩ *cohabition*

K·oje f ~/~n **1.** ⟨mar⟩ (Schlaf≗) *bunk* (dazu: *to b.*); ⟨mar, aero⟩ (*sleeping-*)*berth* ‖ *cabin* **2.** *cabin*, *box*, *booth* (*on exhibitions*) **3.** ⟨fam, mil sl⟩ °rin in die ~! *let's turn in*! (Kind) *beddy-gosy*!

Koka·in [a'i:n] ~s/ ⟨chem⟩ *cocaine*; ⟨sl⟩ *coke*, *snow* ‖ ~vergiftung [f] *cocainism*

Kok·arde f ~/~n ⟨mil⟩ *cockade*, *rings* ‖ ~n-blume [f] ⟨bot⟩ *gaillardia*

K·oker m ~s/~ **1.** (Töpferbrennkapsel) *saggar* **2.** ⟨mar⟩ (Öffnung f Ruderschaft) *helm-port* ‖ *case for mast*

Koker·ei f ~/~en *coke works* pl [sg konstr]; (Anlage) *coking plant* **K·okerkohle** f *c.g coal*

kok·ett a *coquettish* (*gait*, *behaviour*); *flirtatious* | ≗**e** *coquette*, *flirt*, *jilt*, *light-o'-love* **Koketter·ie** f ~/~n *coquetry*, *coquettishness*, **kokett·ieren 1.** vi [h] *to flirt*, *coquet*, *ogle* (mit *with*) | ⟨fig⟩ er –rte mit e–m Hauskauf *he had a fancy to buy a h.* **2.** ≗ n *flirting*

Kok·ille ['i:jə] f ~/~n *cast iron mould*

Kok·on [kɔ'kɔ:ŋ] m ~s/~s *cocoon* (m *to make*)

K·okos- ~baum m *coco(a)nut tree* **~faser** f *coir* **~fett** n *c. butter* **~läufer** m *c. matting* **~milch** f *c. milk* **~nuß** f *coco(a-)nut* **~nußöl** n *coco(a-)nut oil*

Kok·otte f ~/~n *prostitute*, *drab*; ⟨fam⟩ *perfect lady* ‖ geldgierige ~ ⟨Am sl⟩ *gold-digger*

K·oks m ~es/~e **1.** *coke* **2.** (Geld) *pelf* **3.** (→ Kokain) **4.** *nonsense* **5.** *bowler*, *billycock* **~ofen** m *brazier*, *coke-furnace*, *c.-kiln*, *c. oven* | °≗**en** vi [h] **1.** *to take cocaine* **2.** *to sleep*, *snore*

K·ola (Halbinsel im nordwestl. Rußland)

K·olanuß f ⟨bot⟩ *cola-nut*, *bissy nut*

Kol·atsche f ~/~n ⟨österr cul⟩ *pastry envelope* (*filled with jam* od [Topfen–] *white cheese*)

K·olben I. m ~s/~ **1.** (Keule) *club*, *mace* ‖ (Gewehr~) *stock-*, *butt-end*; mit dem ~ dreinschlagen *to butt-end* **2.** ⟨bot⟩ *spike* (*of reeds*, *maize*, etc.), ⟨scient⟩ *spadix*; ⟨Am⟩ *cob* **3.** ⟨tech⟩ Dampf≗ *steam-piston*; eingeschliffener ~ *ground-in piston*; der ~ frißt *the piston grinds* ‖ Brenn≗, Löt≗ *burning-*, *soldering-iron* ‖ Druck≗ *plunger*, *forcer*, *piston* (*of a pump*) ‖ Vergaser≗ *carburetter p.* ‖ Stufen≗ *differential p.* ‖ Dreh≗ *rotary p.* ‖ durchbrochener ~ *valve-p.* **4.** ⟨chem⟩ Glas≗ *alembic*, *flask*, *retort* ‖ Absauge≗ *suction flask* ‖ ⟨el⟩ (Glühlampe) *bulb* **II** ≗ vi [h] der Mais kolbt *the maize is putting on its spikes* **K·olben- ~achse** f *piston pin* ≗**artig** a ⟨scient⟩ *spadiceous* **~aufgabe-vorrichtung** f *p. feeder* **~blitz** m ⟨phot⟩ *flashbulb* **~bolzen** m ⟨mot⟩ *p. pin* **~buchse** f *p. boss bushing* **~gebläse** n *p. blower* **~hals** m *small of the* (*rifle-*) *-stock* **~hebel** m *beamlever* **~hirse** f ⟨bot⟩ *Italian millet* **~h·ingang** m *p. forward stroke* **~hub** m *p. stroke* **~liderung** f *p. packing* **~lokomotive** f *reciprocating locomotive* **~maschine** f *p.-engined plane* (Ggs *jet pl.*) **~moos** n ⟨bot⟩ *club-moss* **~motor** m *p. engine* **~n·iedergang** m *p. down stroke* **~ring** m *p. packing* **~rohr** n ⟨tech⟩ *barrel* **~r·ückgang** m *p. return*; *p. backward stroke* **~scheibe** f *p.-head* **~-schieber** m *p. valve* **~schlackern** n *p. slack* **~schlag** m ⟨mil⟩ *blow*, etc. *with the butt-end of a rifle* **~-schlüssel** m *p. wrench* **~spiel** n *p. clearance* od *play* ‖ *p. up-and-down stroke* od *p. forward-and-backward stroke* **~stange** f *p. rod*, *pump spear* **~stangenbruch** m *break-down of the p. rod* **~stoß** m ⟨mil⟩ *thrust with the buttend of a rifle* **~stulp** m *p. packing leather* ≗**tragend** a ⟨bot scient⟩ *spadiceous* **~-ventil** n *p. slide valve* **~verdrängung** f *p. displacement* **~wasserkäfer** m ⟨ent⟩ *hydrophilus* **~weg** m *p. travel* **~zirkel** m *bullet-dividers* pl **k·olbig** a *club--like*, *knobby* ‖ ⟨bot scient⟩ *spadiceous*

†**K·olchier** m, **~in** f *Colchian* †**K·olchis** n (Landschaft am Schwarzen Meer) *Colchis*

K·olchos m, n ~/–'ose, **Kolch·ose** f ~/~n ⟨Russ agr⟩ *kolkhoz*; *collective farm*

K·older- ~gatt n ⟨mar⟩ *whip-staff hole* **~stock** m (Arm des Steuerruders) *whip-staff*

Kolhapur n (vorderind. Bezirk)

K·olibri m ~s/~s ⟨orn⟩ *humming-bird*, *colibri*

K·olik f ~/ *colic*, *gripes* pl, *griping pains* pl

K·olk m ~(e)s/~ *pool* (*in a river*); *pothole* | ~bildung [f] *scour*, *erosion*, *undermining*

°**k·olken** vi [h] *to talk rot*; dazwischen ~ *to barge in* **K·olkrabe** m ⟨orn⟩ *common raven*

Kol- ~laborati·on [ts] f ~/~en *collaboration* | ~ist [m] *quisling*, → d. ≗**labor·ator** m ~s/–at·oren *collaborator* ≗**labor·ieren** vi [h] *to collaborate* ≗**later·al** a *collateral*; ≗erbschaft [f] *c. succession*; ≗steuer [f] *tax on estate inherited by c. descendants*; ≗verwandte(r [m]) [f] *collateral relation* ≗**lation·ieren** vt [h] *to collate*, *compare* ‖ *check off*

Koll·age [–ɑ:ʒə] f ⟨arts⟩ (Klebebild) *collage* Fr

Koll·eg n ~s/~ien ⟨univ⟩ *course of lectures*; ein 3stündiges ~ über [acc] *a c. of three l.s a week on* ..; ~ abhalten, lesen, hören *to deliver*, *read*, *attend* (*a c. of*) *l.s*; das ~ schwänzen *to shirk* od *miss* od *cut a l.*; ein ~ schinden *to attend l.s on the cheap*; ein ~ belegen *to enter one's name for a c. of l.s*; ~ien lesen (über [acc]) *to lecture* (*on*) | ~-gelder [n pl] (der Studenten) *inscription-fee*; (der Professoren) (*amount of*) *students' fees*; ~heft [n] (*student's*) *note-book*; ~mappe [f] *folio case* **-l·ege** m ~n/~n *colleague* (Sehr verehrter Herr ~ *My respected c.*) ‖ *fellow-minister*, *-driver*, *-waiter*, *-worker* ‖ ⟨fam⟩ *mate*, *chum*, *pal* ‖ ⟨Ger hum⟩ *brother-officer* ‖ ⟨parl⟩ mein verehrter Herr ~ ⟨engl⟩ *my right honourable friend*, *my noble f.*; die Herren ~en ⟨engl⟩ *the h. gentlemen*, ⟨Am⟩ *the g.* **k-legi·al** a **1.** *like a colleague*; mit ~em (Gewerkschafts-)Gruß *fraternally yours* ‖ [adv] ~ handeln *to act as a good c.*, *mate*, etc **2.** ~e Meinung *opinion of the board*, etc (→ Kollegium) **-legiali·t·ät** f *comradeship*, *community spirit*, *loyalty to one's c.s*, etc **-l·egin** f ~/~nen *lady c.*, etc (→ Kollege) **-legi·at-** m ~(e)s/~e *collegiate*, *collegian* ‖ ~kirche [f] *collegiate-church* **-l·egium** n ~s/–gien **1.** = Kolleg **2.** *staff of professors*, *teachers* ‖ *council* ‖ *board* ‖ *body* (*of persons*) ‖ *committee* ‖ *assembly* (*of judges*); *court* ‖ *College* (*of physicians*, etc) **-lekt·aneenbuch** n *scrap-book*, *commonplace-book*, *book for cuttings*, *extracts*, etc **-l·ekte** f ~/~n (Sammlung) *collection* ‖ ⟨ec⟩ *offertory*; (Gebet) *collect*; [konkr] ⟨fam⟩ *plate* **-lekteur** [kɔlek'tø:ə] m ~(e)s/~e *collector* **-lekti·on** [ts] f ~/~en ⟨com⟩ *range*, *set* **k-lekt·iv** a *collective* (*security*, *punishment*) | ≗um [n] ~s/–va ⟨gram⟩ *c. noun* **Kollekt·iv- ~anklage** f ⟨jur⟩ *blanket indictment* **~ausstellung** f ⟨m. m.⟩ *retrospective* s; Nolde-~ *exhibition of N.'s collective works* **~begriff** m *collective* **~eigentum** n *c. ownership* **~gesellschaft** f *partnership* ‖ *joint-stock company* **~interesse** n *public interest* **~linse** f *positive lens* **~schuld** f ⟨com⟩ *c. liabilities* ‖ ⟨pol⟩ *c. offence* **~strafe** f *c. fine* **~verhandlungen** f pl *c. bargaining* **~versicherung** f *group-insurance* **~vertrag** m *multilateral treaty*; *c. agreement* ⟨a. com⟩ ≗**ieren** vt [h] *to collectivize* **~·ierung** f *collectivization* **Koll·ektor** m ~s/–ekt·oren ⟨el⟩ *commutator*

Koller[1] n ~s/~ *collar*, *cape* ‖ *buff-coat* ‖ *pea jacket* ‖ ⟨Ger univ⟩ *white leather-breeches* od *ducks*; in ~ u Kanonen *in w. d. and top-boots* pl

K·oller[2] m ~s/ **1.** ⟨vet⟩ *staggers* pl, *megrim*, *vertigo* **2.** (P) *megrim*, *temper*, *staggers* pl; ⟨fig⟩ *rage*, *fury*; *craze*, *frenzy* ‖ den ~ bek *to fly into a passion*; den ~ h *to be in the tantrums*, *to have a*

wild fit of passion; ⟨fam⟩ *to have a mad fit* **~gang** m *grinding mill, edge-runner* **~mühle** f *edge-mill* **~stoff** m ⟨pap⟩ *broke* **k·ollerig** a *staggery, giddy* || ⟨fig⟩ *crazy, raving* **k·ollern**[1] vt/i [h & s] *to roll* | vi [h] (v Truthahn) *to gobble* || (v Eingeweiden) *to rumble* **k·ollern**[2] vi ⟨vet⟩ *to have the staggers* | ⟨fig⟩ *to be in the tantrums*, etc. (→ Koller[2])

Kollier [kɔl'jeː] n ~s/~s *collar* (*of pearls*, etc)

Kol- ≗lid·ieren vi [h] *to collide, clash* (mit *with*) | ⟨fig⟩ die beiden Vorlesungen ~ (zeitlich) *the two lectures take place at the same time* || mit den Gesetzen ~ *to be in conflict with the law* || unsere Ansichten ~ *our views clash* **~lim·ator** m ~s/–a-t·oren ⟨opt⟩ *collimator* **~lisi·on** f ~/–en *collision, conflict, clash* | ~skurs [m] (Rakete) *collision course*

*__K·ollo__ n ~s/~s & K·olli *bale, package, parcel*

Koll- ~·odium n ~s/ ⟨chem⟩ *collodion*; mit ~ bestreichen *to collodion* | ~(baum)wolle, ~emulsi·on [f] etc. *c. cotton, c. emulsion*, etc **~o·id** n [–lo'iːt] n ~(e)s/ *colloid* **≗oid·al** a *colloidal* (*silver, substance, state*)

Kol- ~l·oquium n ~s/–quien *colloquy*; *oral exam*(*ination*) **~lusion** f ⟨jur⟩ *covin*

Köln n (Stadt) *Cologne* (*on the Rhine*) **K·ölner 1.** [m] ~s/~ *inhabitant of Cologne* **2.** der ~ [a] Dom *the C. Cathedral* **k·ölnisch** a (*of*) *C.* || ≗(es) Wasser *eau-de-C.*, ⟨Am⟩ *cologne*; dazu: *to cologne* (*o.s.*)

Kolomb·ine [iː] npr f ~/~n ⟨theat⟩ *Columbine*

K·olon n ~s/~s **1.** *colon, two dots* **2.** ⟨anat⟩ *colon*

Kolon·el f ~/ ⟨typ⟩ *minion*

Koloni·al- ~amt n *Colonial Office* **~bund** m Reichs≗ ⟨nazi⟩ *Reichs C. League* **~forschung** f *c. research* **~helm** m *c. helmet* **~handel** m *c. trade* **~macht** f *colonizing power* **~minister** m ⟨engl⟩ *Secretary of state for the Colonies* **~politik** f *c. policy* **≗pol·itisch** a *c.-political* (*problems*) **~probl·em** n *problem of colonies* **~reich** n *Empire* **~-system** n (*British*) *colonialism* **~verein** m ⟨engl⟩ *the C. League* **~völker** n [pl] *c. peoples* pl **~waren** f [pl] *c. goods* od *produce, groceries* pl | ~händler [m] *grocer*; *provision-merchant*; ⟨Am⟩ *corner grocer*; beim ~ *at the grocer's* ~handlung [f] *grocer's shop, grocery*; ⟨Am⟩ *corner g., g.-store* **~wesen** n *colonial affairs* pl; Anhänger, Verfechter des ~s *colonialist* ⟨mod derog⟩ **~werte** m [pl] *c. shares* **~wirtschaft** f *c. commerce* od *trade* **Kolon·ie** f ~/~n ['iːən] *colony, settlement* || ~n gründen *to found colonies, to make settlements* || Bakterien≗ *bacteria colony* **nisati·on** f ~/~en *colonization* **-nis·ator** m ~s/–at·oren *colonizer, colonist* **k-nisat·orisch** a *colonizing* **k-nis·ieren** vt [h] *to colonize* **-n·ist** m ~en/~en *colonist, settler*; *planter* || unrechtmäßiger ~ ⟨Am⟩ *squatter*

Kolonn·ade f ~/~n *colonnade* **Kolonne** f ~/~n ⟨typ⟩ *column* || (*vehicle*) *c.*; *convoy* || leichte ~ *regimental baggage* | (P) (Arbeits≗) *gang* | Nachschub≗ *supply c.* || Munitions≗ *ammunition c.*; ⟨mil sl⟩ ~ brr! *transport c.* || ⟨fig⟩ °das war vielleicht 'ne ~! *they were a nice lot*! || 5. ~ *fifth c.*; Angehöriger der 5. ~ *fifth c.ist* | in geschlossenen ~n ⟨mil⟩ *in close c.s* **~nbrücke** f *bridge for all arms* **~ndurchmarschzeit(en)** f *time length*(*s*) **~n-fahren** ⟨mot m. m.⟩ *slow-moving congested traffic* **~marsch** m ⟨mil⟩ *march in files* **~steller** m ⟨typewr⟩ *tabulator* **≗weise** adv ⟨mil⟩ *in c.s, in files*

Koloph·onium n ~s/ *rosin*; mit ~ einreiben vt [h] *to rosin* | ~kasten [m] ⟨theat⟩ *resin box*

Koloqu·inte f ~/~n ⟨bot⟩ *bitter-apple*

Kolor·ado n (Staat der U.S.A.) *Colorado* **~kette** f *Front Range* **Kolor·adoplateau** n *Colorado Desert*

Kolorat·ur f ~/~en ⟨mus⟩ *coloratura, grace*(*-note*), *trill* | ~sängerin [f] *florid singer* **Kolori- ~m·eter** n *absorptiometer* **~metrie** f *colorimetric analysis* **kolor·ieren** vt [h] *to colo*(*u*)*r, illuminate* || ⟨mus⟩ *to ornament with florid passages* pl **Kolor·ierung** f ~/ *colouring, coloration, illumination* **Kolor·ist** m ~en/~en **~in** f ~/~nen *colourist* **Kolor·it** n ~(e)s/ ⟨arts⟩ *colouring, coloration, hue*; *colours* pl; farbfrohes ~ *colo*(*u*)*rful pattern*

Kol·oß m –·osses/–·osse *colossus, hulk, behemoth* || ein ~ auf tönernen F. *a c. with feet of clay* **koloss·al 1.** [a] *colossal, immense, huge, tremendous, gorgeous, mighty, enormous*; ⟨fam⟩ *infernal, roaring, corking, devilish, thundering, thumping, ripping* (*fun*) || e–e ~e Dummheit *a gigantic* od *thundering mistake* || *enormous* (*distance*) || ~es Pech *awful bad luck* || *terrible* (*fright*) **2.** [adv] *like blazes* || das hat ihm ~ imponiert .. *made a powerful impression on* .. || ~ liebenswürdig *exceedingly friendly* || es gab ~ viel zu tun *there was a terrible lot to do* || *mighty great pleasure* °**koloss·iv** a ⟨hum⟩ (kolossal + massiv) *ginormous* ⟨sl⟩ **Kol·osserbrief** m *Epistle to the Colossians*

Kolport·age ['tɑːʒə] f ~/~n *hawking* (*of books*, etc) **~artikel** m *hawker's article* **~roman** m *penny-novel*, ⟨sl⟩ *penny-shocker* **-t·eur** [–'tøːə] m ~(e)s/ ~e *hawker, news-* od *street-vendor* **k-t·ieren** vt [h] *to hawk* || ⟨fig⟩ *to spread* (*rumours*)

K·olter[1] m ~s/~ (Steppdecke) *quilt, bedcover*

K·olter[2] n ~s/~ (am Pflug) *coulter*

Kol·umbia, Kol·umbien n *Colombia*; *British Columbia*

Kol·umbus m [npr] *Columbus* || → Ei

Kol·umne f ~/~n ⟨typ⟩ *column*; lebende ~ ⟨typ⟩ *shoulder heading* | ~nbreite [f] *measure*; ~nmaß [n] ⟨typ⟩ *printer's gauge*; ~ntitel [m] *heading* || (laufender) *running title*; ≗nweise [adv] *in columns*

ˣ**Köm** m ~s/ niedd = Kümmelschnaps

K·oma n ~s/~ta ⟨med⟩ *coma* | ≗t·ös [a] *c.tose*

Kombatt·ant m ~en/~en *combatant*

Kombin·at n ~s/~e ⟨SBZ⟩ *combined works* pl **~i·on** [ts] f ~/~en **1.** ⟨philos, chem, math, ftb, chess, etc⟩ *combination* || *a sagacious c.* || *football-players cultivate c.* | *associated employment* | die Presse war auf ~en (Mutmaßungen) angewiesen *the daily press was dependent on conjectures* || dies alles beruht nur auf ~en *this is all based on mere conj.s* **2.** (Unterzeug) *combinations* [pl]: sie trug e–e ~ *she wore c.s* **3.** ([einteiliger] Schutzanzug) ⟨bes Am⟩ *coverall* **~s- ~gabe** f *combining, combinative, constructive power* od *talent, gift of combination* || er hat ~ *he knows to put two and two together* ⟨a. hum⟩ **~dampfbackofen** m *combined steam baking oven* **~gerät** n ⟨el⟩ *c. apparatus*; ⟨wir⟩ *phonograph-radio* **~lehre** f ⟨philos, math⟩ (*theory of*) *c.s* **~schloß** n *puzzle lock* **~tabelle** f *crosstabulation* **kombinat·orisch** a (*clever in*) *combining*, etc; ~e Probleme *combinatorial problems* **kombin·ieren** vt/i [h] *to combine* (*two things*); *to put two and two together*; *to infer, deduce, conclude* || –rt *in combination*; *joint*; –rtes Kabel *combined cable* || –rter Druckstock *combination plate* od *combined line and half-tone block* (⟨Am⟩ *cut*) || (Schulklassen etc) ~ *to throw together* **K·ombistrumpf** m *fully-fashioned stocking with heel knitted on* **K·ombiwagen** m ⟨mot⟩ *beach* od *estate* od *utility car*; *carry-all truck*

Komb·üse f ~/~n ⟨mar⟩ *caboose, cook's room*

Kom·et m ~en/~en *comet* **Kom·eten- ≗artig** a *comet-like*, [adv] *like a c.* **~bahn** f *path of a c.* **~-fernrohr** n, **~sucher** m *c. seeker, c. finder* **~kern** m *nucleus of a c.* **~lehre** f *c.ology* **~maschine** f *c.arium* **~schweif** m *tail of a c.* **~system** n *c.ary system*

Komf·ort [–'fɔːə, –'fɔrt] m ~s/ *comfort, ease* || e–e Wohnung mit allem ~ .. *with all the latest conveniences* || er verzichtete auf allen ~ *he denied himself all comforts* | ≗·abel a *comfortable, cosy* | °≗ion·ös a ⟨sl⟩ *galuptious*

K·omik f ~ *comicality, humour, funniness* || *fun; funny* od *comical things* pl **K·omiker** m ~s/~ *comic actor, comedian* **k·omisch** a *comic(al), humorous, quizzical*; zu ~! *too funny for words*; °gar nicht „komisch" *not really exciting* || ~e Oper, Rolle *comic opera, part* || ~er Kerl, Kauz *comical fellow, queer bird; quiz, original,* ⟨sl⟩ *curiosity* || ~e Figur *droll figure* || ~e Geschichte *curious, strange, quizzical matter* od *story* | [pred] er ist darin sehr ~ *he is very particular, peculiar, odd in these things* || *(don't be so) crotchety*

Komint·ern f ~/ ⟨pol⟩ *Comintern*

Komit·at n ~(e)s/~e **1.** (Geleit) *escort, suite* **2.** (Ungarn: Grafschaft) *county* **Komit·ee** n ~s/~s *committee* || ein ~ einberufen *to summon a c.*

K·omma n ~s/~s & ~ta **1.** ⟨gram⟩ *comma* **2.** ⟨arith⟩ *decimal point*: null ~ drei *point 3* **3.** ⟨mus⟩ (kleinster Tonabstand) *comma* **4.** ⟨ent⟩ *comma (butterfly)* **~bazillus** m *comma bacillus*

Kommand·ant m ~en/~en *commander*; ~ der Übergänge *c. of the crossing sites* || Festungs≈ *fortress c.* || ⟨mar⟩ *captain; c.ding officer (of a cruiser)* || Hafen≈ *harbour captain* | **~·ur** f ~/~en *c.der's*, etc. *headquarters, appointment* | ~bereich [m] *station area* **-d·eur** [døə] ~s/~e (v Bataillon an aufwärts) *c.der; c.g officer*; e–r Division *c.g general*; ~ Logistischer Truppen *Logistical Support Command*; ~ e–s Sicherungsbereichs *C.der, Security Command* N **k-d·ieren** vt/i [h] ⟨mil⟩ *to command, to be in command of* || ⟨fam⟩ *to order a p about* || ⟨mil⟩ *to post,* ⟨Am a.⟩ *to detail* || sie w –rt z *they are told off for, they are temporarily attached to .., appointed to ..* od *for duty as* || er läßt sich nicht ~ *he won't be dictated to* || ~der General *c.ding general; General Officer C.ding*; ~der Admiral *c.der-in-chief naval station* **k-diert** *unassigned* **K-d·ierung** f *temporary duty* auf ~ s *to be on detail*; ~en [pl] ⟨mil, mar⟩ *appointments* **-d·it-** **~anteil** m *limited liability share* **~gesellschaft** f *limited* od *special partnership, sleeping partnership* || ~ auf Aktien *limited stock corporation; company (on shares)* **-dit·är** m ~s/~e = –ditist **k-dit·arisch** a *commanditistic* **K-d·ite** f ~/~n **1.** = –ditgesellschaft **2.** (Zweiggeschäft) *branch(-establishment)* **k-dit·ieren** vt [h] *to invest money in a special partnership; to join a firm as a limited* od *sleeping partner* **K-dit·ist** m ~en/~en *sleeping* (od *limited, special*) *partner* **Komm·ando** n ~s/~s ⟨mil⟩ **1.** (Befehl) *command, order (the c. "Attention"!; the order to fire)* || ~ zurück! ⟨mil⟩ *as you were* || **2.** (Befehlsgewalt) *c.*; einheitliches ~ (über Truppen mehrerer Teilstreitkräfte) *unified c.*; ~ deutscher Streitkräfte (KDS) *German Armed Forces C.*; ~ der Territorialen Verteidigung (KTV) *Territorial Defence, -se C.* || das ~ übernehmen *to assume* (od *take over the*) *c.* (f N. N. *vice N. N.*) || das ~ führen *to (be in) c.* || ⟨mar⟩ das ~ niederlegen (of the admiral) *to strike one's flag* **3.** (Kommandierung) *appointment; detached duty* od *service* **4.** (Behörde) *c., staff* **5.** (Abteilung) *detached unit; detachment, party, detail* || ⟨mil aero⟩ (10–20 Staffeln) *group* || Arbeits≈ *fatigue-party* || *a detail of police* **≈artig** a *c.o type (exercise)* **~brücke** f ⟨mar⟩ *(conning-) -bridge* **~elemente** n [pl] ⟨mar⟩ *transmitter gear* **~gerät** n *automatic engine control*; ⟨artill⟩ *fire director; anti-aircraft computer*; ⟨aero⟩ *predictor* **~gewalt** f *c., control* (über *of*) **~kapsel** f, **~modul** m ⟨a–n⟩ *c. module* **~sache** f: geheime ~ (gKdos) *top secret* **~stab** m *staff of c.* **~stand** m ⟨mar⟩ *conning tower* **~turm** m ⟨aero⟩ *control tower,* ⟨mar⟩ *conning tower* **~wechsel** m ⟨mil mar⟩ *change of c.* **~zeichen** n ⟨mil⟩ *distinguishing flag*

Kommass·ierung f ~/~n [österr] ⟨agr⟩ (Flurbereinigung) *consolidation*

K·ommen n ~s/ *coming, arrival; the coming of spring* || das ~ u Gehen *the come and go (of people)* || *the advent (of Christ)* **k·ommen** vi/(t → E. 2.) [kam/ge~] [s] **A.** ⟨eig⟩ **1. (P)** *to come* ⟨a. sex⟩; bitte ~! ⟨mil-wir⟩ [abs] *over!* || **(an~)** *to arrive* || da kommt er ja! *there he c.s!* || Sie ~ wie gerufen *you (have) c. in the nick of time*; ⟨fam⟩ *well met!* || man kommt *somebody is coming* || der soll nur ~! *just let him c.!* || ~ Sie diesen Weg, bitte! *will you step this way, please* || ~ Sie mit? *will you c. with me?* || ~ Sie denselben Weg? *are you c.g my way?* od *the same way as we?* || wann sind Sie hierher ge~? *when did you c. down here?* || wann ~ wir nach N.? *when do we arrive at N.?* || wie ~ wir nach *N.? how can we get to N.?* || wollen Sie morgen z mir ~? *will you c. to (⟨fam⟩ and) see me tomorrow?* || als er gerade nach N. ge~ war *when he had first c. to N.* od *when he had just arrived at N.* || er kam plötzlich ⟨fam⟩ *he suddenly popped up* || es dauert aber lange, bis sie k–t *she is a long time c.g* || ich k.e **gleich** (hin) *I'll be right down*; ich werde gleich ~ *I'll be round in a minute* || das Kind mußte bald ~ *the child was due very soon* || sie wird bald ~ *she will soon be here,* ⟨fam⟩ *she won't be long* || noch eben zur Zeit ~ *to cut it fine* || komm' nicht in der letzten Minute *don't cut it (too) fine* || ⟨fig⟩ wohin sollte ich ~? *where should I be?* || → zuerst B. **2. (S)** die Jahre (die Erinnerungen) ~ u gehen *the years (reminiscences) c. and go* || der Dampfer, Zug k–t *the steamer, train is approaching* || das Licht k–t v e–r Lampe *the light is from a lamp* || der Tag der Rache k–t *the day of vengeance dawns* || wenn der Frühling k–t *when spring c.s,* ⟨fam⟩ *c. spring* || der Brief k–t u k–t nicht *there is still no letter* || die Stunde ist ge~ *the hour has c.* || ich halte den Augenblick noch nicht für ge~ *I hardly think the right moment has arrived* || wie k–t es (die Ware)? (in welcher Form) *how does it c.?* || woher wohl das Geld k–t? *where may he get the money from?* || in e–r halben Stunde k–t Berlin (im Radio) .. *Berlin will be heard* || er nimmt die Dinge wie sie ~ *he takes things as they c.*; .. anders .. *things are apt to turn out different from expectation* || wenn Sie geradeaus gehen, k–t erst die Kirche .. *straight forward you will c. to the church first* .. || und nun k–t diese Rechnung *and now along c.s this bill* || komme was mag *c. what will; in spite of everything* || k–t Zeit, k–t Rat *in space c.th grace* || die ersten Blüten ~ *the first blossom is c.g out* || das Ende k–t *the end is approaching* || das letzte Stündlein k–t *the last hour draws near* || k–t wieder Krieg? *will there be war again?* || das durfte nicht ~ *that was an unexpected turn* || was k–t, k–t *what will be, will (be)* || wenn es (einmal) s·o weit k–t *when it comes to this* od *to the point* || das sah ich schon lange ~ *I have been expecting that for a long time* || etw ~ **lassen** *to call for a th* | ⟨fig⟩ er wird es wohl nicht so weit ~ l *he will not allow things to go as far as that* **B. (S)** (= **gehören**) die B. ~ in dieses R. *the books belong on this shelf* || das k–t mit auf die R. *that shall go on the bill too* || zwischen zwei Blättern Schreibpapier k–t immer e–e Lage Löschpapier *between each two sheets of letter-paper I should like to find a sheet of blotting-paper* **C. (S)** (= **kosten**) der Schirm k–t (auf) 6 Mark *the umbrella costs 6 marks* || wie hoch *or* teuer k–t das Stück? *what's the price per piece?* || es ~ auf jeden 1 DM *it breaks down to 1 m. a p, it works out at 1 m. a p* **D. (an der Reihe s)** ich k–e vor ihm, nach ihm *it's my turn first* od *before him, after him* || er k–t gleich hinter dem König *he ranges next to the king* **E. [mit Dativ der P] 1. (P)** k–st du mir so? *do you think you can treat me like that?* || k–st du mir so, dann komm' ich dir so! *tit for tat!* || er kam mir grob *he was rude to me* || so darfst du mir nicht ~! *don't try this old game* od *those tricks on me! none of your tricks!* || sie kam mir sehr gelegen *she came very opportunely for me* || mir soll noch e–r ~ und sagen ..! *I'd like to see somebody c. with (that tale)!* || so lasse ich mir nicht ~ *I won't stand that sort of* *thing* || jdm mit e–m Vorschlag ~ *to put a proposition before a p*; komm' mir nur nicht mit unnötigem Kram *don't bother me with trifles* **2.** [vt] ⟨stud⟩ ich komme dir e–n kräftigen Schluck *or* Ganzen [= ganzes Glas Bier] *here's your health*, ⟨fam⟩ *here goes to you*! ⟨fam, vulg⟩ *I looks towards you*! **3. (S)** die S war mir zu plötzlich ge~ *the thing had sprung on me too suddenly* || das k–t mit sehr gelegen, gerade recht, wie gerufen *that suits me to perfection* od *admirably, I just thought of it* || da ~ mir doch Bedenken *I feel scruples about it* || mir kam ein guter Gedanke *I had an inspiration*, .. das Gelüst *I had a sudden hankering after .., I just felt like ..* || die Tränen kamen mir *tears came into my eyes* || ⟨fig⟩ → (in die) Kehle **F. [mit inf] 1.** (mit Absicht) wir w ~ dich ab(zu)-holen *we'll call for you* || er kam es abzuholen *he came to fetch it* **2.** (unbeabsichtigt ~ = geraten) wir kamen auf .. z sprechen *we touched the subject of ..*; man kam auf ihn z spr. *his name came up* || er kam unters Auto z liegen *he fell under the motor--car* || es kam zw m–e Sachen z liegen *it happened to drop between my things* **G. [mit pp]** (an)gelaufen, -gefahren, -geritten ~ *to c. running, driving, riding along* || die Straße heruntergerast ~ *to c. tearing down the road* || e–e Kugel kam geflogen *a bullet came flying* **H. v/imps 1. es** kam ihr der Gedanke *the idea came* od *occurred to her*, es kam mir in den Sinn *it occurred to me, it struck me* || es mußte (so) ~ *it was bound to be, it had to happen, it couldn't have been otherwise* (→ L.), *it was inevitable*; so kam es *so it was*; es mag ~, was da (*or* wie es) will *c. what may, no matter how it goes* || wie's gerade k–t *just as it will turn out* || es k–t ein Gewitter *a thunderstorm is gathering, brewing, threatening* od *is c.g up* || es wird Regen ~ *it is going to rain* || es k–t meist anders als man denkt, ⟨mil, hum⟩ denn erstens k–t es anders und zweitens als man denkt *things generally turn out contrary to expectation* **2.** daß es **so weit** ~ mußte! *that it should have c. to this pass* || es ist so weit ge~, daß .. *matters have come to this pass that ..* || es wird noch **so weit ~, daß ..** *the day will c. when* || es ist **weit** ge~ *things have c. to a pretty pass* || soweit ist's noch nicht ge~ *it's not got to that yet* || **so** k–t es, **daß** .. *hence* od *thus it is that ..; so it c.s to pass that* || **wie** *or* **woher** kam es, daß ..? *how came it that ..*? || wie k–t es, daß ihr noch zweifelt? *how is it possible to be still in doubt*? || und woher k–t es? *and what is the reason of it*?, *why* od *how is that*, ⟨Am fam⟩ *how c.* (*you weren't in*)? || wie kam es, daß ihr euch verfehltet *how came you to miss each other*? **I. ~ lassen**: *to order* (*goods, samples*); laß lieber den Klempner, Arzt ~ *you'd better send for the plumber, doctor* || laß sie nur ~! *Let them c.*! dahin dürfen wir's nicht ~ l *we must not let things go so* (od *thus*) *far* **K. [mit prep] 1. an** e–e Kreuzung, e–n Fluß ~ *to c. to a crossroads, to the banks of a river* || an Ort u Stelle ~ *to arrive at one's destination* || ans Ufer, Ziel ~ *to reach the shore, one's aim* || an(s) Land ~ *to land* || (beim Lesen) an eine Stelle ~ *to c. to a passage* || an jds Stelle ~ *to c. in the place of a p*; *to get a p's post, to succeed to a p's post* || sie war lange nicht mehr an die Luft ge~ *she had not been out-of-doors for a long time* || an den Bettelstab ~ *to be reduced to beggary* | ⟨fig⟩ **an den Tag, ans Licht** ~ *to c.* od *to be brought to light* || wie ~ Sie an diesen Brief? *how did you get hold of* od *c. by this letter*? || wann ~ wir an die Reihe? *when is our turn c.g, when shall we have our turn*? || Sie ~ an die Reihe *it's your turn* || das Gut kam an s–n Neffen *the estate passed into his nephew's hands* || an den Galgen ~ *to* (*live* od *c. to*) *be hanged* || laß es ruhig an dich 'ran ~! *take it* (od *things, life*) *easy*! || er ließ alles viel zu sehr an sich heran~ *he was far too careless, remiss, listless, slow, behindhand in everything*; *he let things drift* || es ist einfach nicht an ihn heran-zu~ *one simply can't get at him* || an–e–a ~ *to c. to blows*; sie waren hart an–e–a ge~ *they were at loggerheads* || er ist an den rechten Mann ge~ *he found* od *met his master* od *his match* || es ist an den rechten Mann ge~ *it has fallen into good hands* **2. auf Grund** ~ ⟨mar⟩ *to ground*; ⟨fig⟩ e–r S auf den G. z ~ suchen *to inquire into the merits of a cause* || auf e–n Berg ~ *to get to* od *to reach the top of a mountain* || auf die Welt ~ *to be born*; *to see the light* (*of this world*) || auf die Füße zu stehen ~ *to light on one's feet*; wieder auf die Beine ~ *to recover one's legs* od *feet* ⟨a. fig⟩ || mühsam auf die Beine ~ *to struggle to one's feet* || wieder auf den Weg ~ *to find one's way again* || auf Festung ~ *to suffer confinement in a fortress* || auf die Schule ~ *to be sent to school* || auf die Hauptstraße ~ *to strike the main road* || wir ~ auf die Straße nach .. *we emerge on the road to* | ⟨**fig**⟩ **auf den Hund** ~ *to go to the dogs* || auf den richtigen Weg ~ *to hit the right road* || er k–t nie auf einen grünen Zweig *he will never make his way* | auf diesen **Einfall** wäre ich nie ge~ *that idea would never have occurred to me* || wie ~ Sie nur auf so 'was? *how do you get hold of such an idea, what may have put such* (*funny*) *ideas into your head*? || wie sind Sie darauf ge~? *how did you find it out*? *how did you happen to think of that*? || ich kam plötzlich auf den Gedanken (etw zu tun) *the idea struck me* (*to do sth*) || wir ~ jetzt auf .. z sprechen *we now c. to ..* od *to talk of, on*; *we now touch the subject of ..* || ich kann nicht auf s–n Namen ~ *I forget* od *can't remember* od *recollect his name* || darauf bin ich nie ge~ *I never thought of that* || auf etw ~ *to catch a th* || ich kann nicht darauf ~ *I cannot call it to my mind* || man k–t mal auf andere Gedanken *your mind has some relaxation, distraction, diversion* || wie ~ Sie auf diese Entdeckung? *what led you to this discovery* || e–r S auf die Spur ~ *to get to the bottom of a th* || e–m auf die Spur ~ *to get upon a p's track* || ich lasse nichts auf ihn ~ *I won't allow him to be put upon, I will hear no ill of him, I see no fault in him* | ihre Rechnung k–t auf 25 Mark *your bill comes* od *runs to 25 marks* || dieser Tee k–t auf 3 Schilling das Pfund *this tea is* od *sells* od *costs* (od *works out at*) *3/- a pound* || es k–t auf dasselbe hinaus *it c.s to the same th* || auf s–e Kosten ~ *to cover one's expenses, to find one's cost repaid*; er wird schon auf s–e K. ~ *he will certainly see that he doesn't lose by it* || es ~ 3 auf jeden *everybody gets three, each p's share amounts to three* || auf 10 schlechte ~ nur 3 gute .. *for ten bad ones there are but three good ones* || es ist mit ihm aufs äußerste ge~ *he has been driven to extremities* || wenn es aufs äußerste k–t *if the worst c.s to the worst* | auf die Nachwelt ~ *to be handed down* od *to c. down to posterity*; es (Ms) ist auf uns ge~ *it has been preserved for us* || nur e–e Beschreibung ist auf uns ge~ *nothing but a description of it remains to us* **3. aus dem Hause** ~ *to stir out* || sie ~ aus Bayern *they c. from Bavaria* || er ist seit .. nicht aus den Kleidern ge~ *for .. he has never been out of his clothes* od *never taken off his clothes* || aus e–r Sitzung ~ *to c. away from a meeting* || sie sind in bestem Einvernehmen aus–e–a ge~ *they parted on the best terms* | diese Worte kamen aus s–m Munde .. *fell from his lips* | **aus der Fassung** ~ *to lose one's self-control* || das k–t mir nicht aus dem Sinn *I can't get it out of my head* od *mind* || es kam mir ganz aus dem Sinn *it has entirely slipped* (*from*) *my memory* || dieser Wunsch kam ihr aus dem Herzen *this was her heartfelt desire* | aus der Mode ~ *to grow* od *get out of fashion* || ⟨mus⟩ aus dem Takt ~ *not to keep time* || das Haus kam aus dem Besitz der Familie *the h. passed out the f.* || ⟨fig⟩ aus dem Regen in die Traufe ~ *to fall out of the frying pan into the fire* **4. außer** sich ~ vor Wut *to lose one's temper* od *self-control with* *rage* || außer Atem ~ *to get out of breath* **5. durch** (e–e Stadt) ~ *to c.* od *pass through* od *via* .. || gut durchs Leben ~ *to get on in life* || durchs Examen ~ *to pass (one's examination)* **6. hinter etw** ~ *to get the hang* od *knack of a th, to discover* od *understand a th, to find out a th* || hinter ein G. ~ *to get behind a secret* || hinter jds Schliche ~ *to find out a p's tricks* od *pranks* || hinter die Wahrheit ~ *to discover the truth* | hinter jdm [dat] ~ *to follow a p* **7. in die Schule** ~ *to be sent to school* || in die Lehre ~ *to be apprenticed* || ~ Sie oft ins Theater? *do you often go to the theatre*? || in den Himmel, die Hölle ~ *to go to heaven, hell* || ins Gefängnis ~ *to be sent to prison* || er war nie in das Haus ge~ *he had never been to that h.* || es kam kein Schlaf in ihre Augen *she did not sleep a wink* || plötzlich kam e–e Unruhe in ihre Augen *alarm flooded her eyes* | **in Fahrt** ~ *to get up* od *gather speed* || die Dinge ~ in Fluß, Bewegung, ins Rollen *things are beginning to move*, .. in Schwung .. *getting into full swing* || in Gang ~ *to be set going* || ins Stocken ~ *to c. to a standstill* | wenn Sie in mein Alter ~ *if you c. to my age* || sie k–t in die Wochen *her confinement is near at hand* | das k–t nicht **in Frage, in Betracht** *that's out of the question* || mir ist (plötzlich) in den Sinn ge~ *it struck me (that ..)* || in die Lage ~ .. zu .. *to have an opportunity of* .. || es ist mit in Anschlag ge~ *it was taken into account* || mit jdm in Konflikt, Kollision ~ *to c. into conflict, collision with a p* || mit jdm in inneren Kontakt, innere Berührung ~ *to c. to close terms with* || mit dem Feinde in Gefechtsberührung ~ *to close with the enemy* || ins Feuer ~ ⟨mil⟩ *to c. under fire* || es ist mir etw in den Weg, in die Quere ge~ *I have met with an obstacle* || in Gefahr ~ *to run into danger* || in Schußweite ~ *to c. within gun-shot* || e–m in den Weg *or* Wurf, in die Quere ~ *to fall in with a p, to run across* od *against a p* || ins Gedränge ~ *to get in among a crowd, to land in a tight place*; ⟨fig⟩ *to get into a pinch* od *scrape* od *into difficulties* pl || in Not, Verlegenheit ~ *to become destitute, embarrassed; to get into trouble* || in den Genuß e–r S ~ *to settle down to the enjoyment of a th* || die Angelegenheit ist in Ordnung ge~ *the matter has been put in order* || wir müssen hierüber ins klare, reine ~ *we must try to see through this matter; we must c. to an understanding about it* || in Wut ~ *to fly into a rage* || in Schweiß ~ *to break out into a perspiration* | **ins** Geleise, Gleichgewicht ~ (S) *to right itself* **8. mit** der (Eisen)bahn, dem Zuge, dem Schiff, dem Auto ~ *to c. by rail(way), train, boat, car* || ich k–e mit e–r Bitte *I have a request* || mit leeren Händen *empty-handed* || **jdm mit Klagen** ~ *to importune a p with complaints* || ~ Sie mir nicht mit Ihrem Unsinn! *none of your nonsense*! **9. nach Hause** ~ *to get home* || ~ Sie gut nach Hause ⟨fam⟩ *take care of yourself*! || wann sind Sie nach B. ge~? *when did you arrive in B.*? || er kam nach D. (wurde dorthin versetzt) *he was transferred to D.* | ⟨fig⟩ gleich nach etw ~ *to be next best thing to* **10. über jdn** ~ *to c.* od *fall upon a p*; ⟨fig⟩ *to happen to a p*; ich will über sie ~ ⟨bib⟩ *I will fall upon them* || über jdm (zu sitzen, stehen) ~ *to be placed above a p* || e–e Wandlung kam über ihn *a change came over his spirit* || wenn solche Zustände über sie ~ *when such moods c. upon her* || *a sense of great loss would descend upon her* || sie fühlte ein heftiges Mitleid über sich ~ *she was conscious of a spasm of pity* || ein stiller Friede kam über mich *a feeling of deep peace came over me* || kein Wort kam über ihre Lippen *not a word passed* od *escaped her lips* || Verzweiflung kam über sie *she was seized with despair* || ~ Sie nicht mehr über m–e Schwelle! *don't cross my threshold again*! || ein großes Unglück ist über ihn ge~ *a heavy piece of misfortune has befallen him* **11. um etw** ~ (= verlieren) *to lose a th, to be deprived of a th*; (= nicht erreichen) *to be disappointed of a th* || ums Leben ~ *to lose one's life* || um sein Hab und Gut ~ *to lose all one's belongings, to be left penniless* || ich bin heute um m–n Schlaf ge~ *I have missed my nap to-day* | **um die Ecke** ~ *to turn the corner* **12. unter** (die) Leute ~ (P) *to mix with other people, to see many people*; (S) *to be made known, to (be) spread abroad* || komm mir nicht wieder unter die Augen! *don't let me see your face again*! || komm mir nicht unter 70 ⟨mot⟩ *don't drop below seventy* [sc *miles an hour*] || das Gut kam unter den Hammer *the estate was put up for auction* || °unter die Räder, den Schlitten ~ *to be a failure* **13. von jdm** ~ *to c. from a p('s house)*; *to approach from (the opposite direction)* || tüchtig vom Flecke ~ *to make headway* || er k–t nicht von der Stelle *he makes no progress* || die Arbeit k–t nicht vom Fleck *the work is at a stand-still, gets on very slowly* || als ich v dort kam *when I came away* || das k–t vom Ungehorsam *that's what c.s of disobedience, that's the result of d.* || von Kräften, Sinnen ~ *to lose strength, consciousness* || seine Krankheit k–t vom vielen Trinken *his illness is attributable to excessive drinking* || meine Glückwünsche ~ von Herzen *my heartfelt congratulations* || von London aufs Land ~ *to come down* || der Wind k–t von Norden *the wind is in the north* || °so was k–t v so was! *there now! that's what was bound to happen! serves you right*!; das k–t davon, wenn man .. *that's what comes of (drinking)* || ich sah es von weitem ~ *I saw it c.g a long way* **14. vor den Richter** ~ *to be brought* od *to appear before a court of law* || kurz vor Toresschluß *at the last moment, in the nick of time* || daß du mir nie wieder vor die Augen k–st *never let me see your face again* **15. zu e-m neuen Hut** ~ *to get* od *come by a new hat*; billig .. *to get sth for nothing*; sie sind zu Geld, zu Vermögen ge~ *they have c. into money, a fortune*; er war durch Zufall zu s–n Erfolgen ge~ *his successes had c. to him by chance*; der Faule wird nie z etw ~ *indolence never leads to success*; er ist z nichts ge~ *he has been a failure in life*; zu e–r S ~ (dazu ~) *to get down to a th* | zu all dem k–t noch .. *on the top of everything else* .. | ich kam nicht **dazu** *I didn't find the time for it* || wie ~ Sie dazu? *how dare you*? || wie k.e ich dazu? *what's it got to do with me* || wie ~ Sie dazu anzunehmen, daß ich .. *what makes you suppose that I* .. || ich weiß nicht, wie ich dazu k.e (zu der Ehre, dem Verdacht) *I'm at a loss to know, how I came to be honoured, suspected in this way* || wie käme ich dazu? *not I*! || wir verstehen, wie der Name dazu ge~ ist .. zu bezeichnen *we understand how the name has c. to denote* .. || er ist dazu ge~, er weiß selbst nicht wie *he hardly knows h.s. how he met with this success* || es ist dazu (= soweit) ge~, daß *it has got to such a pass that* .. | wir ~ jetzt zu den **Räumen,** wo .. *we now gain the rooms where* .. || er ist an e–m S. zur Welt ge~ *he was born on a Sunday* || ich bin mit 20 Jahren zum Militär ge~ *I joined the army at the age of 20* || er kam zur Regierung *he came to reign* [vi] || .. zur Macht .. *into power* | zum **Abendessen** ~ *to c. to dinner* || zum Tee ~ *to drop in for tea* || ich bin noch nicht einmal zum Essen ge~ *I haven't even found time for lunch* || man k–t z Stellen! *you c. to wonderful passages* | das Buch ist mir jetzt zu **Gesicht** ge~ *I have only just seen the book* || zum Vorschein ~ *to appear; to c. to the light of day* || das Gerücht kam uns zu Ohren *the rumour reached our ears* || gleich als es mir zu Ohren kam *when I first heard of it* | ⟨mus⟩ er k–t bis zum hohen C *he can pitch the high C* | ⟨fig⟩ *to arrive at, to proceed to* || **zur Diskussion** ~ *to be open, to c. up for discussion* || zur S ~ *to c. to the point*, ⟨sl⟩ *to get down to brasstacks* || zum Ausdruck, Vorschein ~ *to show* || die Dinge sind oft zur Sprache ge~ *these matters have often been up for discussion* | **jdn zu Worte ~ l** *to give a p permission to speak, to let him speak* || ⟨parl⟩ er kam zu

Worte *he took the floor* ⟨bes Am⟩ ‖ sie ließ ihn nicht einmal zu Worte ~ *she wouldn't as much as give him a hearing* ‖ bei ihm k–t niemand zu W. *with him nobody else can get a word in edgeways* ‖ um zum Ende zu ~ *to make* od *cut a long story short* | **es k-t zum Streit** *a quarrel arises* ‖ es k–t z k–m Konflikt *no conflict is brought about, it c.s to no c.* ‖ wenn es zum Kriege käme *if there were war* ‖ wenn es zum Treffen k–t *when it c.s to an encounter* ‖ es kam zum Kampfe, Blutvergießen *it came to fighting, bloodshed* ‖ es kam zum äußersten *the worst came to the worst* ‖ bis es zur Klage k–t *until legal proceedings are taken* | **er kam zu Fall** ⟨sl⟩ *he came a cropper,* ⟨fig⟩ *he has had a reverse* ‖ .. zu Schaden *he was ruined, he came to grief, he suffered harm*; .. zu Tode *he met his death* | **.. zu Atem** *he recovered his breath*; *let me get my breath first* ‖ .. wieder zur Besinnung *he regained his consciousness, recovered his senses* ‖ sie kam wieder zu sich *she came to* od *round* (od *became herself again*) ‖ er kam zu der Lösung *the solution came to him* ‖ *he came to the conclusion* ‖ zur Ruhe *he came to* (*have time to*) *rest* ‖ wir ~ zu der Überzeugung *we are convinced that* | das Gut kam zur **Versteigerung** *the estate was put up to auction* ‖ wenn es zum Klappen k–t *when it comes to the point* | **mit etw zu Rande,** zu Ende ~ *to succeed in finishing, to accomplish a th* | das Geschäft kam **zustande** *or* zum Abschluß *the transaction was carried out* ‖ **jdm zugute, zustatten** ~ *to profit* od *benefit a p* ‖ das Vermögen s–s Vaters kam ihm sehr zugute .. *proved a godsend* ‖ *his good connections proved a great advantage* ‖ er ließ sich nichts **zuschulden** ~ *he could not be blamed in any way* | sein Leichtsinn wird ihm *or* ihn noch teuer **zu stehen** ~ *some day he will have to pay dearly for his recklessness* **L. [mit a** *or* **adv]** (→ **ab~**) ‖ es ist mir **abhanden** ge~ *I have lost it* ‖ es konnte ja nicht **anders** ~ *it was bound to come* ‖ es wird noch ganz anders ~ *things will get worse still* (→ H.) ‖ → **daher, dahin, daran, davon**; → ~ .. von, **dazwischen, heim~, her~, herab-** etc-~ ‖ **dazu** *or* **hinzu** kam, daß er .. *in addition to that he* .., *it must be added that* .., *what added to the difficulties was that* ..; dazu k–t noch .. *moreover* .. ‖ zum Stolz k–t bei ihm der Geiz dazu *he is miserly as well as proud* ‖ **frei**|~, **los**|~ *to get* (*off*) *free* ‖ jdm **gleich**|-~ *to equal a p, to come up to a p* ‖ °kommste (= kommst du) **heute** nicht, so kommste morgen *I know, you won't be hurried*; *you just dawdle along* ‖ wollen Sie bitte **hierher** ~ *will you step this way, please* ‖ **hierzu** → o. dazu~ ‖ was wird wohl **jetzt** noch ~ *what will be the next th to come?, what next?* ‖ zu **kurz** ~ *to come off badly* (*in*) ‖ komm **mit**! *come along*! ‖ **nahe** ~, **näher** ~ *to draw near, to approach* ‖ jdm sehr nahe-~ ⟨sport⟩ *to challenge a p pretty closely* ‖ wie nahe sie der Natur kam *how nearly she arrived to nature* ‖ jdm zu nahe~ (→ treten) *to wrong a p, to do a p injustice* ‖ **oft** wohin ~ *to frequent* od *haunt a place* ‖ **so** k–t es meistens *that is generally the case* ‖ **(zu) spät** ~ *to be* (*too*) *late,* (*to be behind one's time*) ‖ (gewohnheitsmäßig) spät heim~ *to keep late hours* ‖ spät kommt Ihr, doch Ihr kommt (Schiller, Piccolomini) *you have come late, but you are come*; ⟨prov⟩ *better late than never* ‖ es ist **weit** ge~ *things have come to a pretty pass* ‖ er wird damit nicht weit ~ *he won't get on in this way* ‖ wie weit sind wir in der letzten Stunde ge~? *how far did we get the last time* ‖ nicht weit mit etw ~ *not to get anywhere with* od *doing a th* ‖ **weiter**|~ *to get on, to improve, to make progress* ‖ durch Mut .. *to win one's way by pluck*; damit wirst du .. *that will carry to greater length* ‖ **wie** es auch ~ mag *whatever may happen, come what may* ‖ wer **zuerst** kommt, mahlt zuerst ⟨prov⟩ *first come first served* ‖ mit etw **zurecht**|~ *to accomplish a th, to succeed in* (*finishing*) *a th* ‖ wann k–st du **zurück**? *when shall you come* od *be back?, when will you return?*

k·ommend *coming, approaching* ‖ ~en Dienstag *next Tuesday* ‖ ~e Woche *the coming week, next w.* ‖ ~e Geschlechter, Zeiten *the coming generations, ages* ‖ der ~e Mann *the coming man* ‖ der ~e Volkswagen *the future car for everybody* ‖ für ~e Generationen *for generations to come*

Komm·ende f ~/~n ⟨ec⟩ *prebend*

Komm·ent [kɔ'maŋ] m ~s/~s *regulations* [pl] *for behaviour among German corporate students* **≃mäßig** a *according to the r.s of G. st–ts' corps*; ~er Stoff ⟨Ger stud⟩ *alcoholic beverage, fit* od *good stuff* ‖ ~es Benehmen *proper conduct* (→ vor) ‖ ~er Hieb ⟨fenc⟩ *cut according to fencing r.s* **Komment·ar** m ~(e)s/~e *commentary* ‖ das bedarf k–s ~s *that goes without saying* ‖ ~ überflüssig! *any c. is superfluous* ‖ sich jeden ~s enthalten *to abstain from making any c.* | ⟨comp⟩ *type* **-t·ator** m ~s/–t·oren **1.** (Schreiber, ⟨wir⟩ Sprecher laufender Erläuterungen) *commentator* **2.** (Schr. v Anmerkungen) *annotator* **komment·ieren** vt [h] *to comment on, to annotate*

Komm·ers m ~es/~e ⟨Ger stud⟩ *evening festivity, drinking-bout* **~buch** n *book of songs*

Komm·erz m ~es/ *commerce* **≃i·ell** a *commercial*; *trade* (*profit, loss*) **~i·alrat** ⟨österr⟩, **~ienrat** m ⟨Ger⟩ (Titel) *Councillor of C.*

Kommilit·one m ~n/~n *fellow-student*

Komm·is [–'mi:] m ~/~ [–s] ⟨com⟩ *clerk* ‖ *salesman, shopman* **~stelle** f *clerkship*; ~ Voyageur [m] *commercial traveller* °**Komm·iß** m –isses/ *army, military service, soldier's profession* ‖ ⟨mil sl⟩ *pipe-clay* od *barrack-room life*; ⟨fam⟩ beim ~ *in the army* | [in comp] *commissariat-,* ⟨Am⟩ *government issue* (abbr *G.I.*) **~anzug** m *undress* ‖ (Arbeits-) *fatigue-dress* **~bäcker** m *military baker* **~bluse** f *service* od *undress-blouse* **~brot** n *army bread* **~hengst** m ⟨fig mil sl⟩ = ~stiefel ⟨fig⟩ **≃-mäßig** a *military, commissariat-*; ⟨sl⟩ *pipe-clay* [attr] **~mütze** f *undress* od *service cap* **~stiefel** m pl *army* od *regulation boots* ‖ [sg] ⟨fig mil sl⟩ *pipe clay general, colonel,* etc.; *general terrier* **~vermögen** n *regular portion* **Kommiss·ar, Kommiss·är** m ~(e)s/~e *commissioner, commissary* ‖ ⟨Russ⟩ *commissar* ‖ ⟨mil⟩ *commissariat-officer* ‖ Polizei≃ *police-inspector* **-ssari·at** n ~(e)s/~e ⟨allg⟩ *commissionership* ‖ ⟨mil⟩ *commissariat* **k-ssarisch 1.** [adv] *provisionally*; ⟨com⟩ *by a commissioner* od *deputy* **2.** [a] *by provisional appointment* (*the provisional* Landrat) **Kommissi·on** f ~/~en **1.** *commission, order* **2.** (Ausschuß) *c., committee*; in e–r ~ vertreten s *to be represented on a c.*; e–e ~ einsetzen *to appoint a c.*; *to set up a committee* ‖ in ~ geben, h, nehmen ⟨com⟩ *to sell, have, take goods on c., in consignment* **Kommission·är** m ~(e)s/~e (e–r Behörde) *envoy, c.er* ‖ ⟨com⟩ *agent* **Kommissi·ons- ~agent** m *c. agent* **~artikel** m ⟨com⟩ *article sent on c.* **~bericht** m *report of a c.* od *committee* **~buch** n *order-book* **~bureau** n *agency-office* **~einkauf** m *purchase on c.* **~gebühr** f *c., percentage, factorage* **~geschäft** n **1.** *transaction on c.* **2.** = **~handel** m, **~handlung** f *c. business* **~-verkauf** m *sale on c.* **≃weise** adv *on c.* °**komm·issisch** a ⟨mil⟩ *servicey* → Kommißstiefel **Kommitt·ent** m ~en/~en *employer*; *consignor, consignee* **k-tt·ieren** vt [h] *to commission, commit*

komm·od a *commodious, easy, comfortable* | adv ⟨bes österr⟩ m Sie sich's ~ *make y.s. at home*; ⟨mil⟩ sthehen Sie ~! (*stand*) *at ease*! | **≃e** f ~/~n (*chest of*) *drawers* pl, *dresser* ‖ ⟨Am⟩ *bureau* ‖ (Stollenschrank) *tallboy*; ⟨Am⟩ *highboy,* (auf kl Füßen) *lowboy*

Kommod·ore m ~s/~s ⟨mar; aero⟩ *commodore*

komm·un a *common*; *vulgar, low* **kommun·al** a *communal, municipal* **≃abgaben** f pl *rates* pl ⟨Am⟩ *local tax* **≃anleihe** f *mun. loan,* ⟨Engl⟩ *corporation loan* **≃beamte(r)** m *mun. officer* **≃behörde** f *local authority* **≃fahrzeug** n *public utility vehicle* ≃-

garde f *town militia* **~gericht** n f Mieten *l. rent tribunal* **~politik** f *com. policy* **~schule** f *council* od *parish school* **~steuern** f pl *rates* **~verwaltung** f *L. Government* **~wissenschaft** f *science of local government* **Komm·une** f ~/~n *community, commune*; (*municipal*) *corporation*; Fr *Commune*

Kommunik·ant m ~en/~en *communicant* **-ikati·onskanäle** m pl *channels of communication* **-i·on** f ~/~en *Holy Communion, the Lord's Supper*; an der ~ teilnehmen *to participate in the L.'s S.* || ~skelch [m] *c.-cup, chalice* **-·ismus** m ~/ *communism* **-ist** m ~en/~en *communist* | ~enfresser [m] *McCarthyite*; ~freundlich [a] ⟨Am⟩ *progressive*; ~enhetze [f] ⟨sl⟩ *redbaiting* | **~isch** a *Communist(ic* ⟨dero⟩); ~ m *to communize* || ~e Zersetzung *c.-ist disaffection* **-iz·ieren 1.** vt [h] *to communicate* **2.** vi [h] ⟨ec⟩ *to participate in* od *partake of the Lord's Supper, to receive the sacrament* | ~de Röhren [pl] ⟨phys⟩ *communicating pipes, tubes* pl || ~de Gefäße [pl] *vessels connected by U-tube* **Kommut·ator** m ⟨el⟩ *commutator* | ~motor [m] *series-conduction motor*

Komödi·ant m ~en/~en ⟨cont⟩ *comedian*; *play-actor* ⟨a. fig⟩ || ⟨allg⟩ *actor, performer, player, professional* | **~in** f ~/~nen *player, actress, professional* | **~enhaft** *theatrical* **Kom·ödie** f ~/~n *comedy, play* || Cl·own~, Radau~ *slapstick c.* || in die ~ gehen *to go to the play* || (Verstellung) *make-believe, pretence* || ich habe die ~ durchschaut *I saw through the trick* || das war, gab e–e ~! *that was a regular farce* || ~ der Irrungen (u Wirrungen) *C. of Errors* || die menschliche ~ *Vanity Fair* (Thack.), *Modern Comedy* (Galsw.) || ~ spielen *to act*; ⟨fig⟩ *to sham, dissemble, pretend* **~nhaft** a *theatrical*; ⟨fig⟩ *farcical* **~nhaus** n *playhouse* **~nschreiber** m *c.-writer*; ⟨allg⟩ *dramatist, playwright* **~nzettel** m *play-bill*

Kom- ~pagn·on [ˈkɔmpanjɔŋ] m ~s/~s ⟨com⟩ *partner, associate* || stiller ~ *dormant partner* **~p·akt** a *compact, firm, solid* | ~heit [f] *c.ness, firmness, solidity*; *c. convenience* **~pan·ie** f ~/~n ⟨mil⟩ (= 3 Züge) *company* (= *two platoons*); Fahnen~ *colour c.* || e–e ~ exerzieren l *to exercise* od *drill a c.* || ⟨com⟩ *partnership, company*; die Firma N. & ~ *the firm N. & Co.* | ~bereich [m], ~revier [n] *c. lines* pl; ~chef [m] ⟨mil⟩ *c. commander*; ~exerzieren [n] *c. drill*; ~feldwebel [m] *colour-sergeant*; ~führer [m] *company leader*; ~führung [f] *c. headquarters* pl; ~geschäft [n] ⟨com⟩ *joint business, b. on joint account*; ~weise [adv] *in companies*; ~schreiber [m] *c. clerk*; Angriff in ~stärke [f] *c.-sized attack* **~parat·iv 1.** m ~(e)s/~e ⟨gram⟩ *comparative (degree)* **2.** ~ a *comparative (costs)* **~par·ent** m ~en/~en ⟨jur⟩ *declarant* **~p·arse** m ~n/~n ⟨theat⟩ *super(-numerary), extra* | ~r·ie [f] ⟨fam⟩ *supers, extras* pl

K·ompaß m –asses/–asse *compass*; der ~ ist ruhig .. *is steady*; .. träge .. *hangs*; .. fliegt .. *is wild* || den ~ kompensieren *to adjust the c.* || Hänge~ ⟨mar⟩ *tell-tale c.* || Kreisel~ *gyroscopic c.* || Peil~ *bearing c.* || Steuer~ *steering c.* **~aberration** f *aberration* **~abweichung** f *variation* **~anlage** f *c. system* **~aufhängung** f *c. suspension* **~haus** n *binnacle* **~karte** f *chart* **~kompensierung** f *c. adjustment* **~kurs** m *c. heading* **~linie** f *rhumb line* **~nadel** f *c.-needle* **~rose** f *c.-card* **~strich** m *c. point, rhumb*

Kom- ~pendi·ös a *compendious, succinct* **~p·endium** n ~s/–dien (Auszug) *compendium, abstract* || (Handbuch) *manual* **~pensati·on** f ~/~en *compensation*; ⟨priv l⟩ *set-off (of accounts)*; ⟨crim l⟩ *instantaneous return of an insult etc by like action* | ~sgeschäft [n] ⟨com⟩ *barter*; ~smagnet [m] *c. magnet*; ~smethode [f] *c. method*; ~spendel [n] *c.* od *gridiron pendulum*; ~verfahren [n] ⟨chem⟩ *method of c.* **~pens·ieren** vt [h] *to compensate, counterbalance* || ⟨mar⟩ *to adjust (the compass)* || ⟨com⟩ *make good, to make up for (losses)* || –rt *balanced (aerial, modulation)*; –rte Valuta *compensated rate of exchange* **~pens·ierung** f ~/~en *compensation* **~pet·ent 1.** m ~en/~en *competitor* **2.** ~ a *competent, fit*; *expert (specialist)* || v ~er Seite *from a reliable source, from an expert* od *authority* || ⟨jur⟩ *cognizant* **~pet·enz** f ~/~en *competence, -cy* || strittige ~ *disputed c.ce* || diese Frage gehört zur ~ e–r anderen Behörde *this question is subject to the c.ce of another department* || die ~ besitzen *to be competent (to do)* || ⟨jur⟩ *cognizance* | ~streitigkeiten [f pl] *disputes* pl *about c.ce* **~pilati·on** f ~/~en *compilation* **~pil·ator** m ~s/–·oren *compiler* **~pil·ieren** vt [h] *to compile* **~plem·ent** n ~s/~e ⟨math⟩ *complement* || ⟨gram⟩ *object* | ~werk [n] ⟨comp⟩ *complementer* | ~·är [m] *general partner* | ~·ärfarben [f pl] *complementary colours* pl **~pl·ett** (vollständig) **1.** [a] *complete (copy)* || *entire (breakfast)* || ein ~es Speisezimmer *a dining-room suite* || (P) → dick || ⟨fam⟩ *blithering (fool)* **2.** [adv] du bist ~ verrückt *you're completely mad* **~plett·ieren** vt [h] *to complete* **~pl·ex** m ~es/~e **1.** *total amount*; *whole* **2.** ⟨tech⟩ *aggregate* **3.** *plot of land*; *pile of buildings*: *the brewery is composed in an enormous p. of b.* **4.** ⟨psych⟩ *complex, fixation* **5.** ~bildner [m] ⟨chem⟩ *complexing* od *sequestering agent*; ~bildung [f] *complexing action*; *sequestration*, –b-svermögen [n] *complexing efficiency* **~pl·ex** a **1.** ⟨math⟩ *complex (number)* **2.** *complicated (sentence)* **~pl·ice** m ~n/~n *accomplice (in)*, *(subordinate) partner in crime, confederate* **~plikati·on** [ts] f ~/~en *complication* **~plim·ent** n ~(e)s/~e **1.** (Verbeugung) *bow*, (Knicks) *curtsy* **2.** (Artigkeit) *compliment*, ein fragwürdiges (verbindliches) ~ *a doubtful (courteous) c.* || mein ~! ⟨obs⟩ [österr] *how do you do, sir!* ~, ~! *my congratulations* od *c.s (to you)*; *well done!* || ~e m *to make c.s* || jdm ~e m *to pay c.s to a p* || k–e ~e! *no ceremony!* k–e ~e m *to make very little fuss* od *ceremony*; er macht nicht viel ~e *he is not a man of many words* || leere ~e *flummery* | ~emacher [m] *flatterer, man of compliments*; ~·ieren vt [h] *to compliment, congratulate*; *to flatter* **~pliz·ieren** vt [h] *to complicate, embarrass*; *confound, confuse* **~pliz·iert** a *complicated, intricate, perplexed (matter)*; (P) nicht ~ *uncomplicated* || ⟨fig⟩ *thorny (matter)*; ⟨fam⟩ *(the th was) a can of worms* || ⟨surg⟩ *compound (fracture)* || *complex (disposition, character, situation)* | ~heit [f] ~/ *complexity (of a subject)*; *intricacy* **~pl·ott** n ~(e)s/~e *plot, conspiracy, intrigue* ~e schmieden *to plot*; *conspire (together)*; *intrigue* **~pon·ente** f ~/~n ⟨math⟩ *component* || ⟨phys⟩ Geschwindigkeits~ *c. of velocity* **~pon·ieren** vt [h] *to compose, to set to music* **~pon·ist** m ~en/~en *composer* **~pos·itbau** m *composite building* **~pos·iten** pl ⟨bot⟩ *composite flowers* od *plants* pl; ⟨scient⟩ *compositae* pl L **~positi·on** f ~/~en ⟨arts, mus, tech, met⟩ *composition* || ~ e–r Druckseite *page make-up*, ⟨Am⟩ *page lay-out* | ~slehre [f] ⟨mus⟩ *harmony* **~p·ositum** n ~(s)/–ta & –ten ⟨gram⟩ *compound (word)* **~p·ost** m ~(e)s/ ⟨agr⟩ *compost, mixed manure* | ~·ierung [f] *composting* **~p·ott** n ~(e)s/~e ⟨cul⟩ *preserves, stewed fruit, compote* | ~schüssel [f] *compote-dish*; °~schüsselchen [n] ⟨fig⟩ (Monokel) ⟨fam⟩ *window*; *quiz(zing glass)* **~pr·eß** a ⟨typ⟩ *compact, close, solid* || ~er Satz ⟨typ⟩ *solid* od *close matter* **~pr·esse** f ~/~n *compress, bolster* || kl ~ *pledget* **~pressi·on** f ~/ Motor mit hoher, niedriger ~ *high, low compression motor* | ~saggregat [n] ⟨el⟩ *electro compressor set*; ~shahn [m] *priming cock*; ~spumpe [f] *force-pump*; ~sraum [m] *c. chamber* | ~svolumen [n] *clearance volume*; ~szündung [f] *ignition by compression* **~pr·essor** m ~s/–ess·oren *compressor*; *supercharger* || Hydro~ *c. by fall of water* || Wasserdruck~ *hydraulic c.* | ~motor [m] *s. engine* ⁓**prim·ieren** vt [h] *to compress* (*compressed gas*) **⁓prom·iß** m & n –m·isses/–m·isse **1.** *compromise*; ⟨jur⟩ *agreement to settle legal dispute by arbitration*; ein(en) ⁓ schließen *to* (*make* a) *c.* (mit *with*) **2.** [in comp] *compromise* (*proposal, resolution*) | ⁓los [a] *uncompromising* (*fellow*) || ⁓ kämpfen *to carry on the uncompromising fight* ⁓**promitt·ieren** vt [h] (jdn) *to compromise, expose* (*a p*) || sich ⁓ *to commit o.s., to compromise o.s.* || sich ⁓ mit ⟨fam⟩ *to carry on with*

Komt·eß, Komt·esse f ⁓/⁓(e)n (unverheiratete Tochter e–s Grafen) *countess*

Komt·ur m ⁓(e)s/⁓e *Commander* (*of an order*), ⟨Ger⟩ *knight-c.* **Komtur·ei** f ⁓/⁓en *commandery*

Konch·ylien f pl *shells, shell-fish* [pl konstr]

Kon- **⁓d·ens-** | ⁓milch [f] *condensed milk*, –fabrik [f] *condensery* | ⁓streifen [m] ⟨aero, a–n⟩ *vapo(u)r* od *con(densation) trail*; ⁓topf [m] *steam trap*; ⁓wasser [n] *condensation water*; ⁓-wasserabscheider [m] *water separator*; ⁓wasserrückleitung [f] *condensing water reconductor* **⁓densati·on** f ⁓/ *condensation* || auf ⁓ arbeiten *to work condensing* | ⁓sanlage [f] *condensing plant*; ⁓sapparat [m] *condenser*; ⁓sdampfmaschine [f] *condensing steam engine*; flüssiges ⁓sergebnis *liquid product of condensation*; ⁓skammer [f] ⟨chem⟩ *condensing chamber*; ⁓sröhre [f] ⟨met⟩ *adapter*; ⁓swasser [n] *waste-water* → Kondens- **⁓dens·ator** m ⁓s/–sat·oren ⟨tech⟩ *condenser*; ⟨mot a.⟩ *capacitor* || Berieselungs⁓ *surface evaporative cooler* || Dreh⁓ ⟨wir⟩ *variable condenser* | ⁓abgleich [m] ⟨telph⟩ *balancing by condensers*; ⁓gefäß [n] *condenser tank*; ⁓leiter [f] ⟨telph⟩ *high-pass filter*; ⁓mikrophon [n] *c. transmitter*; ⁓röhre [f] *c. pipe* od *tube* ⁓**densierbar** a *condensable* (*gases, vapo[u]rs*) ⁓**dens·ieren** vt [h] *to condense* || -sierte Milch *condensed* (ungezuckert *evaporated*) *milk* || (Flüssigkeiten) ⁓ *to boil down*; (Text) *to digest* **⁓d·ensor** m ⁓s/–ens·oren ⟨opt⟩ *condenser* | ⁓linse [f] *c. lens* **⁓diti·on** [ts] f ⁓/⁓en (Bedingung) *condition* || (Zustand) *state, condition* || † (Stelle) *situation* ⁓**dition·al** [ts] a *conditional* | K-alis [m] ⁓/ *conditional mood* **⁓satz** m *c. clause* ⁓**dition·ieren** **1.** vi [h] *to be in service* || gut konditioniert (P & S) *well-conditioned* **2.** vt [h] ⟨tech⟩ *to test* (*silk*) **⁓d·itor** m ⁓s/–dit·oren *confectioner, pastrycook* | ⁓farbe [f] *c.y colour* | ⁓form [f] *mold for pastry* | ⁓waren [f pl] *c.y; sweetmeats, sweet* pl **⁓ditor·ei** f ⁓/⁓en *pastry* od *confectioner's shop*; in der ⁓ *at the c.'s* | –(ei)waren [f pl] *confectionery* **⁓dol·enz** f ⁓/⁓en *condolence* | ⁓besuch [m] *visit of c.*; ⁓brief [m], ⁓schreiben [n] *letter of c.* || (Schluß e–s ⁓s: *Believe me in fellowship of sorrow yours* etc.); ⁓telegramm [n] *telegram of c.* ⁓**dol·ieren** vi [h] (jdm) *to condole* (*with a p*)

Kond·om m ⁓s/⁓e ⟨sex engl⟩ *condom*; ⟨fam⟩ *rubber*; ⟨sl⟩ *French letter*

K·ondor m ⁓s/–d·ore ⟨orn⟩ *condor*

Kon- **⁓du·ite** f ⁓/ *conduct, deportment* ***⁓d·ukt** m ⁓s/⁓e *funeral* (*procession*) ***⁓dukteur** [–'tø:ɐ] m ⁓s/⁓e *conductor, guard* **⁓f·ekt** n ⁓(e)s/⁓e *confectionery, confit*, ⟨Am⟩ *candy* || ⁓dose [f] *box of sweets* **⁓fekti·on** f ⁓/⁓en **1.** *dressmaking, manufacture of ready-made articles of dress* || *ready-to-wear production*; *ready-to-wear industry* **2.** (Ware) *confection*; *ready-made* (⟨fam⟩ *reach-me-down*) *clothing*; ⟨fam⟩ *reach-* (⟨Am⟩ *hand-*) *-me-downs* pl ⁓**fektion·ieren** vt [h] –rt *pre-packed* (*chemicals*); *packed* (*developer*) **⁓fektion·är** m ⁓(e)s/⁓e 1. *clothing manufacturer* 2. *dealer in ready-made clothes* **⁓fekti·ons-** ⁓anzug [m] *ready-made suit*, ⟨fam⟩ *reach-me-down*; ⁓geschäft, ⁓haus [n] *ready-to-wear house*, ⟨Am⟩ *clothing store*; ⁓kleidung [f] = ⁓ 2.; ⁓modellschneider [m] *sample maker*; ⁓pelz [m] *r.-m. fur*; ⁓schneider [m] *r.-m. clothing maker*; ⁓ware [f] = ⁓ 2. **⁓fer·enz** f ⁓/⁓en (Jahres⁓) *conference*, ⟨Am⟩ *convention* || (Tagung) *meeting*, ⟨Am⟩ *parley* || e–e ⁓ abhalten *to hold a meeting* | ⁓dolmetscher [m] *conference interpreter*; ⁓-teilnehmer [m] ⟨bes Am⟩ *conferee* || ⁓zimmer [n] *conference-* od *meeting-room*; ⟨school⟩ *staff common room* ⁓**ferieren** vi [h] *to confer, deliberate*, (mit jdm über etw *with a p on s.th*) **⁓fessi·on** f ⁓/⁓en ⟨ec⟩ *confession of faith, creed* || evangelische, katholische ⁓ *Protestant, Roman Catholic faith* od *religion* || ⟨stat⟩ *denomination* ⁓**fession·ell** a *confessional, denominational* **⁓fessi·ons-** ⁓los [a] *creedles*; *undenominational* (*school*); ⁓schule [f] *sectarian* od *denominational* od *voluntary school*; ⁓wechsel [m] *change of creed* **⁓f·etti** n [pl] ⁓[s]/⁓ It *confetti* **⁓firm·and** m ⁓en/⁓en *catechumen, candidate for confirmation, confirmee* | ⁓enunterricht [m] *confirmation classes* pl **⁓firmati·on** f ⁓/⁓en ⟨ec⟩ *confirmation* ⁓**firm·ieren** vt [h] *to confirm* ⁓**fiskati·on** [ts] f ⁓/⁓e *confiscation* ⁓**fisz·ierbar** a *liable to confiscation* ⁓**fisz·ieren** vt [h] *to confiscate, seize*; (Zeitung) *to suppress* **⁓fisz·ierung** f ⁓/⁓en *confiscation* **⁓fit·üren** pl *preserves*; *sweets* pl; *confectionary* | ⁓laden [m] *sweet-shop*, ⟨Am⟩ *candy-store* **⁓fl·ikt** m ⁓(e)s/⁓e *conflict*, (⟨Lit⟩ → *conflict*); ⟨sl⟩ *rumpus* || Verschärfung des ⁓s ⟨theat Lit⟩ *epitasis*; die Interessen stehen (mit–e–a) in ⁓ *the interests are at crosspurposes* || mit dem Gesetz in ⁓ geraten *to come into conflict with the law*, ⟨fam⟩ *to fall foul of the law* || (*of a country*) in feindlichen ⁓ geraten *to be antagonized* || nicht in ⁓ k. mit *to keep on the windy side of* (*the law*) || sich in e–m ⁓ befinden ⟨fam⟩ *to be in hot water* **⁓föderati·on** [ts] f ⁓/⁓en *confederacy* ⁓**föder·iert** a *confederate* || ⟨Am hist⟩ die ⁓en Staaten, die im Bürgerkriege aus der Union austraten *the Confederacy* ⁓**f·orm** a (mit) *conformable* (*to*), *in conformity* (*with*), ⟨math⟩ *conformal* || ⟨com⟩ mit jdm ⁓ gehen *to be in conformity with a p* **⁓formit·ät** f ⁓/ *conformity* **⁓frontati·on** [ts] f ⁓/⁓en *confrontation* ⁓**front·ieren** vt [h] *to confront, to bring .. face to f.* (mit *with a p, a th*) ⁓**f·us** a *confused, in confusion*, ⟨fam⟩ *muddled* (*thinking*), *muddy* (*style*); er wurde ⁓ ⟨fam⟩ *he was getting mixed, his mind became cluttered up with ideas*; *he was perplexed* **⁓fusi·on** f ⁓/⁓e *confusion, muddiness, muddle; perplexity* | ⁓rat [m] *unmethodical p, muddler*, ⟨fam⟩ *muddle-head*

konf·uzisch a *of Confucius, Confucian*

Konf·uzius, Konf·utse m [npr] *Confucius*

Kon- ⁓**geni·al** a *congenial* | ⁓it·ät [f] ⁓/ *congeniality* **⁓gesti·on** f ⁓/⁓en *congestion* **⁓glomer·at** n ⁓(e)s/⁓e *conglomerate, conglomeratic stone* od *rock* || ⟨fig⟩ *aggregation*

K·ongo ['kɔŋgo:] m ⁓s/ **1.** (Land) *Congo* **2.** (Fluß) *the C.* **⁓l·ese** m, **⁓l·esin** f *C.lese*

Kon- **⁓gr·eß** m –·esses/–·esse *congress, convention*; ⟨Am⟩ *the C. of the U.S.* (*Senate and House of Representatives*): *the C. meets* | ⁓abgeordnete [m pl] (eines Staates) *delegation*; ⁓dolmetscher [m] *conference interpreter*; ⁓mitglied [n] *member of a c.*; ⟨Am⟩ *member of C.*, ⟨fig⟩ *gentleman on the hill*; ⁓organisation [f] *c. organisation* ⁓**gru·ent** a *congruent, congruous, equal in all respects* **⁓gru·enz** f ⁓/⁓en *congruity, congruence, perfect equality* ⁓**gru·ieren** vi [h] *to coincide, to be equal in all respects*

K·onia n (türk. Stadt)

Konif·ere f ⁓/⁓n *conifer*(*ous tree*); ⁓nharz [n] *turpentine*; ⁓nöl [n] *conifer oil* → konisch

K·önig m ⁓s/⁓e **1.** *king* || der ⁓ v England *the K. of England* || ⁓ Eduard *K. Edward* || die preußischen ⁓e *the k.s of Prussia* || des ⁓s Rock tragen *to wear the K.'s colours* || der ⁓ und s–e Gemahlin *the K. and his Queen* || jdn z ⁓ ausrufen *to proclaim a p k.* || z ⁓e m *to make .. (a) k.* || Gott erhalte unsern K.! *God save the K.!* || er ist ⁓ seit .. *he has been k. since 1971* || im Namen des ⁓s gegen N. N. *Rex versus N. N.* || die heiligen drei ~e *the* (*three*) (*Eastern*) *k.s* (*of Cologne*), *the three Magi*; das Fest der .. *the Epiphany* **2.** ⟨fig⟩ der ~ aller ~e (Christus) *the K. of K.s* || der Schützen⁓ *the k. of the rifle-shooting* || der Geiger⁓ *the k. of violinists* || der ~ der Wüste, der Tiere *the k. of all animals* **3.** ⟨cards⟩ der Herz~ *the k. of hearts* **4.** (Hütten⁓) ⟨min⟩ *button of metal*, ⟨scient⟩ *regulus* **~-Eduard-VII.-Land** [n] (antarktisch) *King Edward VII Land*; **~-Georg-V.-Land** [n] (antarkt.) *King George V Land* **~gr·ätz** n (böhmische Stadt); Schlacht bei ~ *battle of Sadowa* (1866)

K·önigin f ~/~nen **1.** *queen* || ~mutter *qu. mother* || ~witwe *qu. dowager* **|** ~nensuppe [f] *royal soup* **2.** ⟨chess⟩ sich e–e ~ holen *to queen a pawn* **3.** ⟨bot⟩ ~ der Nacht *qu. of the night*

k·öniglich 1. [a] (Titel) ⁓ *royal*, Seine ⁓e Hoheit *His Royal Highness* || (Insignien) *regal* || (Betragen) *kingly*, *king-like*, *regal* (*port*); ~er Dienst *King's Service* (*to be in the* ..) || ~er Prinz *or* Prinz ~en Blutes *prince of the royal blood* || ~e Personen [pl] *royalty* || ~es Privileg, Besitztum *royalty* || ~es Gewand *King's raiment* || ~gesinnte(r) *royalist* || die ~en [pl] *the Royalists* **2.** [adv] *royally*, sich ~ freuen *or* sich freuen wie ein Schneekönig *to be as pleased as Punch* || wir h uns ~ amüsiert *we enjoyed ourselves immensely*

K·önigreich n ~s/~e *kingdom* (*of* ..), *realm* **|** ⟨fig⟩ nicht für ein ~ *not for the world*

K·önigs- *king-*, *royal* **~adler** m ⟨orn⟩ *golden eagle* **~banner** n *r. banner* **~berg** n ⟨Ger⟩ († Hauptstadt v Ostpreußen) **~blau** n *r. blue* **~burg** f *r. castle* **~fischer** m ⟨orn⟩ *k.fisher* **~freund** m *r.ist* **~geier** m ⟨orn⟩ *k.-vulture* **~gelb** n ⟨paint⟩ *massicot* **~gericht** n ⟨engl hist⟩ *Curia Regis* [L] **~holz** n *k.'s* od *queen's wood* **~kerze** f ⟨bot⟩ (*great*) *mullein*, *high taper*, *Aaron's rod*, *shepherd's club* **~-krone** f *r.* od *k.'s crown* || ⟨bot⟩ *fritillary* **~kuchen** m *fruit-cake* **~mord** m *regicide* **~mörder** m *regicide* **~schlange** f *boa constrictor* **~schloß** n *r. castle* **~schuß** m *best shot* (→ König 2. fig) **~see** m ⟨Ger⟩ (Alpensee bei Berchtesgaden) **~sitz** m *r. residence* **~sohn** m *k.'s son* **~tiger** m *Bengal tiger* **~titel** m *r. title* **~tochter** f *k.'s daughter* ⁓**treu** a *loyal*, *royalistic* **~treue(r)** m *r.ist* [oft auch attr] **~treue** f *loyalty* **~wahl** f *election of a k.* **~wasser** n *aqua regia* **~welle** f ⟨tech⟩ *vertical shaft* **~winter** n ⟨Ger⟩ (Stadt am Rhein) **~würde** f *r. dignity*, *r.ty* **~zapfen** m ⟨tech⟩ *central pivot*, *k. pillar*

K·önigtum n ~(e)s/⁓er [abstr] *royalty*, *kingship* || (Reich) *kingdom*, *realm*

k·onisch a *conic*(*al*), *coniform* || ~e Bohrung *taper hole* || ~es Getriebe ⟨tech⟩ *bevel*(*led*) *gear* || ~es (Zahn-)Rad *bevel wheel*; → Konifere **|** ⁓-schneiden [n] *taper grinding*

Kon- ~jekt·ur f ~/~en *conjecture* || ~politik [f] *conjectural politics* pl **~jugati·on** f ~/~en ⟨gram, zoo, bot⟩ *conjugation* ⁓**jug·ierbar** a *conjugable* ⁓**jug·ieren** vt [h] ⟨gram & scient⟩ *to conjugate* **~junkti·on** [ts] f ~/~en ⟨gram & astr⟩ *conjunction* ⁓**junktion·al, -n·ell** a *conjunctional* **~junkt·iv** [-f] m ~s/~e [və] *subjunctive* (*mood*) **|** ⁓isch [a] *in the* od *as* (*a*) *subjunctive* **|** ~satz [m] *clause in the s. mood*, *s. clause* **~junkt·ur** f ~/~en (*con*)*juncture* (*of circumstances*) || ⟨com⟩ *state*, *turn*, *tide*, *tendency*, *prospects* [pl] *of the market*, *business-outlook*, *market condition*; absteigende, rückläufige ~ *downward movement*, *declining tendency*; *slump* || ⟨com⟩ ansteigende ~ *favourable business juncture*, *upward movement*, *boom*; ⟨Am a.⟩ *swing* **|** ~barometer [n] *industrial b.*; ~bericht [m] *market report*; ~politik [f] *opportunism*, ~ treiben *to trim*; ⟨com⟩ *policy relating to economic trends*; ~politiker, ~ritter [m] *trimmer*, *opportunist*, *time-server*; ~schwankung [f] *economic fluctuation*; ~vorhersage [f] *business forecast*(*ing*); ~zyklus [m] *business cycle*, → *cycle* **~junkturell** a ([adv] ~ bedingt) *due to a general upward trend* ⁓**k·av** a *concave* (*mirror*, *lense*) **~kavit·ät** f ~/ *concavity* **~kl·ave** n ~s/~n *conclave* ⁓**klud·ent** a ⟨jur⟩ (*act*) *permitting conclusion* **~kord·anz** f ~/~en *concordance* (*to Chaucer*) || ⟨geol⟩ ~ der Schichten *conformability of strata* **~kord·at** n ~(e)s/~e *concordate* ⁓**kr·et** a *concrete* (*matter*, ⟨fig⟩ *fact*); *objective*, *representative* (*art*) || in ~em Sinne *in the c.* || ~e Formen [pl] annehmen *to assume c. form* || e–r Idee ~e Form geben *to make* .. *c.*, *to incarnate an idea* ⁓**kretis·ieren** vt [h] *to reify* **~kr·etum** n ~s/–ta ⟨gram⟩ *concrete noun* **~kubin·at** n ~(e)s/~e *concubinage* **~kub·ine** f ~/~n *concubine* **~kurr·ent** m ~en/~en *competitor*, *rival* ⟨Am⟩ *contestant* || ~ in .. *contender for* .. || ⟨sport⟩ ~en [pl] der Weltmeisterschaft *world series* pl **~kurr·enz** f ~/~en (Zusammentreffen) *concurrence*; ⟨jur⟩ *coincidence of several crimes* (od *criminal laws*) || (Mitbewerbung) *competition* (stark *rough*, rücksichtslos *cutthroat*); *rivalry*, *rivalship* || *rival business* od *firm*; Beschränkung etc der freien ~ *restraint of trade* (~verbot [n]) || ⟨sport⟩ *event* || e–a ~ m *to compete with each other* || er fängt an, jdm ~ zu m *he has entered into c.n with a p* || er kauft bei der ~ *he buys in the r. b.* || er ist zur ~ abgewandert, gegangen *he has gone over to the opposition* || e–e ~ ausschreiben *to offer a job for c.n*, *to invite tenders* **|** ⟨fig⟩ e–n Nebenbuhler außer ~setzen *to put a r. out of the running* **|** ⁓fähig [a] *able to compete*, *competitive*; *marketable* (*goods*); ~fähigkeit [f] *ability to meet c.n*; *marketableness*; ~kampf [m] *c.n*, *trade rivalry*; ~klausel [f] *covenant in restraint of trade*; ~lohn [m] *competitive wages*; ~preis [m] *c. price* ⁓**kurr·ieren** vi [h] (mit jdm um) *to rival*, *compete* (*with a p for*) || ~d *rival*; *competitive* (Artikel *lines*); ⟨jur⟩ ~des Verschulden *contributory negligence* **~-k·urs** m –rses/–rse *bankruptcy*, *failure*; ⟨com⟩ *insolvency*; *compulsory winding-up* || ~ ablehnen *to dismiss b.*; ~ abwenden *to avert b.* (*by a composition*) || ~ einstellen *to suspend b. proceedings* || in ~ geraten *to fail*, *to go bankrupt*; (of companies) *to be wound up*; ⟨fam⟩ *to be sold up* || den ~ mangels Masse abweisen *to refuse b. proceedings for lack of assets* od *estate*; ~ anmelden *to declare o.s.* (*a bankrupt* od) *insolvent* || ~ beantragen *to file a petition in b.* || der ~ wird verfügt *debtor is adjudged bankrupt* **Konk·urs- ~delikt** n *act of fraudulent b.* **~erklärung** f ⟨jur⟩ *declaration* od *adjudication of insolvency*, *abjudication*(*-order*); (of companies) *winding-up order* **~eröffnung** f *opening of b. proceedings*; Antrag auf ~ *petition for b.* **~gericht** n ⟨jur⟩ *bankruptcy court* **~masse** f *bankrupt's* od *insolvent estate*, *assets* pl **~ordnung** f *legislation on b.*; *b. act* ⁓**reif** a *insolvent* **~richter** m *referee in b.* **~verfahren** n *proceedings* [pl] *in b.*, ein ~ hinausschieben ⟨Am fam⟩ *to stall* **~verwalter** m *assignee* od *trustee in b.*, *Official Receiver* || Beschluß zur Einsetzung e–s ~s *receiving order*; Vermögenswerte gehen an ~ über *property vests in t.* **~verwaltung** f *receivership*

K·önnen n ~s/ (→ können) *ability*, *faculty*, *power*; *skill*; *efficiency* || ⟨sport a.⟩ *science* || fliegerisches ~ *flying a.* od *s.* || *artistic s.* od *craftsmanship* || alle Welt bewunderte sein ~ *everybody admired his abilities* pl **k·önnen** vt/i [konnte/gekonnt] [h] **1. a.** (etw [**tun**] ~, vermögen, dazu **imstande** s; es ist mir **möglich**) *to be able* (*to do a th*), *to be capable* (*of doing a th*); jeder kann das sehen *it is there for all to see* || ich kann nicht *I cannot*, ⟨Am⟩ *I can not* || nicht ~ *to be unable*, *incapable* **|** .., was sie hätten s ~ (*to remind people of*) *their might-have-beens* **|** (*measures*) *likely to* (*jeopardise*) **|** die Maschine k. ausführen .. *will perform* **|** sie k. nicht **singen** *she cannot sing* || sie k. gut singen *she sings beautifully* || er k. nicht aufstehen *he is not* *able to get up, he cannot get up* || ich k. nicht erkennen *I fail to recognize* || er k. nicht sprechen *speech is beyond him* || **ich habe nicht k** ~ [statt: gekonnt] *I could not (possibly) come* || du k.st das Spaßen nicht l *you will have your joke* || das ~ Sie leicht sagen *it is easy for you to say so* || ich k. mir das Lachen nicht verkneifen *I cannot help laughing* || **der Raum k.** 100 Personen fassen *the room holds* (od *will hold*) *100 persons* || **b. [mit zu ergänzendem inf,** der im Engl. mst stehen muß] etw (tun) ~ *to know how* (etw nicht mehr ~ *to forget*) *to do a th*; ich k. es/ihn nicht **ab** [niedd] *I can't stand it/him*; ich k. auch **anders** *I might change my tone* || ich k. nicht anders *I cannot do otherwise, I cannot help myself* od *it* || ein jeder könnte **das** (tun) *anybody could do that* || ein Mann kennt andere Männer besser als es Frauen ~ *a man knows other men better than a woman can do* || ich k. **es** *I can do it* || *ich* k. nicht **hinein** *I cannot get in* || ich k. nicht dagegen an *I can do nothing to stop it* || uns k. k–r *nobody can touch us* || ich k. nicht mehr *I'm done for* || ich k. nicht mehr mit! *that beats me*! || °es mit jdm gut ~ (= gut mit ihm ausk) *to hit it off, to be in with a p*; ich k. es mit d–m Neffen nicht *your nephew and I don't click* || ich eilte **so** rasch ich nur konnte *I hurried as fast as I could* || ich rannte **was** ich konnte *I tore along with all my might* || ich zog was ich nur konnte *I pulled my hardest, I did my best* || er schrie so laut er konnte *he cried for all he was worth, to the best of his ability, as best he might* || er macht daraus was er nur k. *he makes the best of it* || .. so gut er konnte .. *to the top of his bent* || er war, so gut er konnte, ein guter Fahrer *he was, in his small way, a good driver* || er erkannte die Wahrheit, **soweit** er es konnte .. *according to his light* || ich k. nicht **umhin** zu sagen, .. zu lächeln *I cannot resist saying, I cannot forbear smiling, I cannot but smile* || (erst) ~ vor Lachen *I should smile if I could do that* **2.** vt **(verstehen, beherrschen)** *to understand, to know* || er k. Deutsch, s–e Aufgaben *he knows German, his lessons* || das k. ich auch! *I can do that too* || er k. das *he knows how to do that* || ich k. es auswendig *I know it by heart* || was du k.st, das k. ich auch! *two can play at that game*! || er k. s–e S, sein Geschäft *he knows the ropes* || bei dem Schauspieler ist alles gekonnt *he is a very good* od *able actor, he is able to play any part* **3. (dürfen)** *to be allowed* od *permitted* (*to do* ..) || ich k. *I may* || du k.st hingehen *you may go* (*there*) || der Deckel k. abbleiben *the lid can* od *may be left off* || wir ~ uns Glück wünschen, daß .. *we may congratulate ourselves that* .. || du k.st ausnahmsweise bis 10 Uhr aufbleiben *for once you may stay up until 10 o'clock* || er k. so etwas doch nicht tun! *he dare not do it*! || Sie ~ alles sehen *you are welcome to see everything* **4. (es ist möglich, daß ich ..)** ich k. nicht abk *I cannot* (*get away* od) *be spared* || (es) k. s (*it*) *may be* || es k. nicht s *it cannot be* || das k. man wohl sagen *it may be said* || verdamme ihn nicht, er k. das Geld auch verloren h .. *he may have lost the money* || nicht beigelegt w ~ *to be incapable of settlement* || man k. nie wissen *there's no knowing, you never can tell* || hätte er nur an ihrer Seite stehen ~ *might he but have stood at her side* || ich könnte jetzt .. *I feel like* (*doing*) **5. (für etw ~, dafür ~, schuld sein)** ich k. nicht(s) dafür *I can't help it, it's not my fault, it's no fault of mine* || wer k. dafür? *who can help it* || was ~ wir denn dazu? *what could we have done to prevent it*? *how could we have helped it*? || er k. nichts f s–e Ansichten *he can't help his views* || sie konnte nichts für ihre Stimme, ihren mangelnden Verstand *she could not help her voice .. the lack of her brain* **K·önner** m ~s/~ *very able actor, artist*; *great virtuoso*; *swell* (*at Latin* des Lateins); ⟨Am fam⟩ *whiz*

Kon- ~n·ex m ~es/~e *contact, touch, connection*; ⟨scient⟩ *nexus* [L] | ~i·on [f] ~/~en *c.*, ~en [pl] *influential friends*, ⟨Am pol⟩ *pull* **~niv·enz** f ~/~en *connivance* **~nossem·ent** n ~(e)s/~e ⟨com mar⟩ (Seefrachtbrief) *bill of lading* (abbr *B/L*) **·~rektor** m ~s/–t·oren *vice-principal* (*of a school*), *second master* **~rektor·at** n ~(e)s/~e *vice-principalship, second mastership* **~sekrati·on** [ts] f ~/~en *consecration* **~̂sekr·ieren** vt *to consecrate* **~̂sekut·iv** [i:f] a *consecutive* **~s·ens** m –nses/–nse *consent* **~̂sequ·ent** a *logical, consistent* || ~ s *to be c.* od *stiff in one's back, to act consistently, to act up to one's principles* | adv ⟨a.⟩ *systematically* **~sequ·enz** [–ts] ~/~en **1.** (Folgerung) *consequence* || die ~en ziehen *to take the necessary action*; *to proceed accordingly* **2.** (Folgerichtigkeit) *consistency* || *determination, resolution* **~̂servat·iv** [va'ti:f] a, **~servat·ive(r)** m ~n/~n *conservative, rightist*; *right winger*; er ist ~(er) bis in die Knochen *he is c. to the backbone*, ⟨engl⟩ *he is a true-blue* od *diehard Tory, he is* (*a*) *true-blue* || ~̂er [a] Arbeitervertreter [m] *conservative labourite* **~servati(vis)mus** m *conservatism*, sturer ~ *standpatism*; *hard core* **~serv·ator** [v] m ~s/–at·oren *conservator, keeper* (*of a museum, of manuscripts*, etc.) **~servator·ist** [v] m ~en/~en, ~in ~/~nen [f] *pupil of a conservatoire* Fr (*of music*) **~servat·orium** [v] n ~s/–rien ⟨mus⟩ *academy* od *school of music* || (auf d. Kontinent) *conservatoire* [Fr], ⟨Am⟩ *conservatory* **~s·erve** [v] f ~/~n *conserve, preserve* || ~n [pl] *tinned* (⟨Am⟩ *canned*) *foods* od *goods*; ⟨mil⟩ *p.d provisions* || Fleisch~̂ *p.s of meat, preserved meat* || Gemüse~̂ *tinned* (etc.) *greens* || Obst~̂ *tinned* (etc.) *fruit* || ~ v zus–gekochtem Fleisch u Gemüse ⟨mil engl⟩ *maconochie* | ~nbehälter [m] *food storage container*; ~nbüchse, ~dose [f] (*preserve*) *tin*, ⟨Am⟩ *can*; ~nbüchsenöffner [m] *tin opener*; ~nfabrik [f] *food canning factory, cannery*; ~nfabrikant [m] *canner*, (*food*) *packer*; ~nfabrikation [f] *canning*; ~n(rind)fleisch [n] *bully*; ~nglas [n] *preserving glass, preserve jar* **~̂serv·ieren** [v] vt [h] *to conserve* || (Lebensmittel) *to tin, can, preserve* || (Holz) *to p.* || sich gut ~ (P) *to wear well, to keep up one's good looks, to bear one's age well* | °–rte M. *canned music* **~serv·ierung** [v] f ~/~en (v Häuten) *skin curing* || (v Holz) *timber preserving* || (v Gemälden) *preservation* | ~smittel [n] *preserving preparation, antiseptic, conservation ingredient, preservative*; (f Holz) *wood preserver*; ~ssalz [n] *preserving salt* **~signati·on** f ~/~en *consignment* **~̂sign·ieren** vt [h] ⟨mil⟩ *to confine* || ⟨com⟩ *to consign* **~̂sili·ieren** [i'i:] vt [h] *to rusticate* (*a student*) **~s·ilium** n ~s/–lien *doctors' consultation* | **counsel* **~̂sist·ent** a *consistent, solid, compact* **~sist·enz** f ~/ *consistency, solidity, compactness* **~sistori·alrat** m ⟨Ger⟩ *Counsellor of the Consistory* (title) **~sist·orium** n ~s/–rien *consistory*(*-court*) **~̂skrib·ieren** vt [h] *to enrol, levy* (*soldiers*) **~skripti·on** f ~/–en (⟨Ger⟩ – 1870) (*restricted*) *conscription, levy, enrolment* (*of soldiers*)

Kons·ole f ~/~n (Brett) *bracket* || *pedestal* || *pier-table* || ⟨arch⟩ *console, ancon*(*e*), *corbel*

Kon- ~solidat·ion [ts] f **1.** *consolidation of funds* **2.** *concentration of land-holdings*; ⟨jur⟩ *union of real estate and hypotheca or usufruct in same p* **~̂solid·ieren** vt [h] *to consolidate* || sich ~ *to grow firm* || konsolidierte Staatspapiere = Konsols *consols* (= *consolidated funds*), *gilt-edged shares* **~solid·ierung** f ~ *consolidation* || (v Bergwerken) *amalgamation of mines* **~s·ols** [pl] *consols* pl **~somm·ee** f [kɔ̃sɔ'me:] ~/~s ⟨cul⟩ Fr → Kraftbrühe **~son·ant** m ~en/~en ⟨gram⟩ *consonant* || ~enverbindung [f] *combination of consonants* **~̂son·antisch** a *consonantal* **~son·anz** f ~/~en *consonance, concord, harmony, agreement* **~s·orte** m ~n/~n [mst nur pl] *partner, associate, accomplice* || ~n [pl] *set, gang* || N. N. u ~n *N. N. and Co., and his like, his associates*, etc. **~sorti·al-**

~geschäft [n] *joint business*; ~konto [n], ~rechnung [f] *syndicate account*; ~vertrag [m] *joint agreement* **~s·ortium** [ts] n ~s/–tien *syndicate* (*of bankers*); *pool*; ⟨fam⟩ *set, gang, ring* **≃spi·r·ieren** vi [h] *to conspire, to plot*

Konst·abler m ~s/~ *policeman, constable*

Kon- **≃st·ant** a ⟨math⟩ *constant* (*value*) ⟨a. fig⟩ || ⟨el⟩ *c.* (*current*) || ⟨com⟩ *fixed* (*income, capital*), *standing* (*charges*); *invariable* (*composition*); ⟨comp⟩ *common* (*multiplier*); ⟨ins⟩ *level* (*premium*) | ≃haltung [f] *keeping* od *maintaining c.*; (*electronic*) *stabilization* **~st·ante** f ~/~n ⟨math⟩ *constant* (*quantity*) || ⟨phys⟩ *c.* (*gas-c.*) || ~n [pl] ⟨comp⟩ *constants* **~stantin·opel,** ⟨Turk⟩ Istanbul [n] *Constantinople* **-polit·aner** m, **~in** f *Constantinopolitan* **~st·anz** f ~/ ⟨stat⟩ *constancy, stability* **~stanz** n ⟨Ger⟩ (Stadt am Bodensee) *Constance* **≃stat·ieren** vt [h] *to lay down as a fact, to claim, state*: *I am stating facts* || *to establish* (*a guilt*) || *to notice, observe* || ⟨med⟩ *to diagnose* || (bestätigen) *to bear witness to, to state that* .. **~stellati·on** f ~/~en ⟨astr⟩ *constellation* ⟨a. fig⟩ || *position, state* (*of affairs*); *situation* **≃stern·ieren** vt [h] *to dismay, consternate* || –rt *taken aback*, ⟨fam⟩ *flabbergasted* || vollkommen –rt ⟨fam⟩ *struck all of a heap* **~stipat·ion** [–ts–] f ~/~en *constipation, costiveness* **~stitu·ante** f ~/ ⟨Fr hist⟩ *Constituent Assembly* **≃stitu·ieren** vt [h] *to constitute, to appoint* || ⟨Am pol⟩ *to organize* || **sich** ~ *to form* (*o.s.*); sich [acc] als Ausschuß ~ *to resolve into a committee* sich als Körperschaft ~ *to be incorporated as a company* | ~d [pres p] *constituent* (*assembly*) **~stituti·on** f ~/~en ⟨pol, med⟩ *constitution* || ⟨med a.⟩ *habit* (*of mind and body*) || *a man of strong,*/*corpulent constitution* od *habit* | ~s– *constitutional* (*types*) **~stitutiona·l·ismus** [ts] m ~/ ⟨pol⟩ *constitutionalism* **≃sti·tution·ell** a *constitutional* **≃stru·ierbar** a *constructible* **≃stru·ieren** vt [h] ⟨tech, geom, etc.⟩ *to construct*; *to draw* (*a triangle*) || ⟨gram⟩ *to construe*; falsch ~ ⟨gram⟩ *to misconstrue* || ⟨tech a.⟩ *to develop* || ⟨fig⟩ *to concoct* **~strukt·eur** ['øə] m ~s/~e *engineer, designer, design engineer*; *draughtsman* || ⟨biol⟩ *constructor* (*mutation and natural selection*) **~strukti·on** [ts] f ~/~en *design* || *construction*; *system* || die ~ ist die denkbar einfachste *the c. is of the simplest kind imaginable* | ~saufgabe [f] ⟨geom⟩ (*geometrical*) *construction*; ~sblatt [n] *design sheet*; ~sbüro [n] *technical bureau*; *engineering department*; ~seinzelheiten [f pl] *design features*; ~sfehler [m] *mistake in the drawing, fault* od *defect of construction*; *structural d.*; ~sgedanke [m] *principle of c.*; ~smerkmal [n] *constructional feature*; ~snormen [f pl] *building standards* pl; ~splan [m] *working drawing*; ~sstahl [m] *structural steel*; ~sstück [n] (in zerlegtem Zustand) *piece of c.* (*in dismounted state*); ~szeichner [m] *designer, draughtsman*; ~szeichnung [f] *workshop drawing* **≃strukt·iv** [i:f] a *constructive* **~struktiv·ismus** m [Russ ⟨Lit⟩] (1924) *constructivism* (bes *Selvinski, Tairov*); (⟨a. mod arts⟩)

K·onsul m ~s/~n *consul* || Anerkennung e–s ausländischen ~s *exequator* **Konsul·ar-** [in comp] *consular*; ~gerichtsbarkeit [f] *consular jurisdiction* | **≃isch** a *consular* **Konsul·at** n ~(e)s/~e *consulate, consulship*; v ~ beglaubigt *consular* (*invoice*) | ~sdienst [m] *consular service* od *office*; ~sfaktura [f] *consular invoice*; ~sverweser [m] *acting consul*

Kon- **~sul·ent** m ~en/~en ⟨jur⟩ *counsel, legal adviser* || ⟨allg⟩ *barrister, advocate* **~sultati·on** f ~/~en ⟨med⟩ *consultation* **≃sult·ieren** vt [h] *to consult* **~sum** m ~(e)s/ *co-op*(*erative store*) || ~, Konsum(p)ti·on [f] ~/ ⟨com⟩ *consumption*; übermäßiger ~ ⟨bes Am⟩ *spending* od *buying spree* | ~abgabe [f] *duty on c.n*; ~anstalt [f] *supply stores* pl; ~artikel [m] *article for daily use*; ~genossenschaft [f] = ~verein; ~güter [n pl] *consumer goods*; ~kraft [f] *c.ming power*; ~laden [m] *co-op. store* ~niederlage [f] (*Co-operative*) *Stores* pl; ~steuer [f] *tax on c.n*; ~verein [m] *C.rs' Co-operative Society* || = -niederlage **~sum·ent** m ~en/~en *consumer* **≃sum·ieren** vt [h] *to consume* **≃tagi·ös** [g] a ⟨path⟩ *contagious* **~t·akt** m ~(e)s/~e *contact* || ⟨tech⟩ (*of wheels*) in ~ s *to be in mesh* || ständiger ~ mit dem Computer *real-time processing* | ⟨el⟩ (Schalter) *switch*; ~ herstellen *to make c.*; ~ aufheben *to break c.*; intermittierender ~ *ticker* || ⟨fig⟩ ~ zur Umwelt *way of getting along with people*; ~ halten *to keep in touch* (mit *with*); ~ nehmen *to get in t.* (*with*); den ~ verlieren mit *to lose c.* od *connexion with* | ~abstand [m] ⟨el⟩ *break distance*; ~abzug [m] ⟨phot⟩ *c. print*; ~draht [m] ⟨el rail⟩ *c.-* od *trolley-wire*; ~fläche [f] *area of c.*; ~glühlampe [f] *c. lamp*; ~infektion [f] ⟨path⟩ *contagion*; ~knopf [m] *contact button* od *stud, push button*; ~kopie [f] ⟨rep⟩ *c. copy* od *print* ⟨a. film⟩; ~kopiergerät [n] *c. printer*; ~mittel [n] *c. insecticide*; ~pflege [f] *human relations* (⟨a. com⟩ innerbetrieblich); ~rolle [f] ⟨el rail⟩ (*c.*) *trolley*; ~schelle [f] ⟨el⟩ *c. clip*; ~schnur [f] ⟨el⟩ *flex*(*ible*); ~schuh [m] ⟨el⟩ *collector shoe*; ~schwäche [f] ⟨sex⟩ *frigidness*; ~stöpsel [m] *connecting plug*

kont·ant a *in cash* **≃arbitrage** f *arbitrage in foreign coins* **≃geschäft** n *cash transaction*

kontemplat·iv [–i:f] a *contemplative, meditative*

K·onten- ~bewegung [f] *transaction*, → Konto

K·onter- *counter-* **~admiral** m *rear-admiral* **~bande** f *contraband* (*goods* pl) **~esk·arpe** f ⟨fort⟩ *c.-scarp* **~fei** n *portrait, image, likeness* **~marke** f *c.-mark, pass-ticket, check* **~marsch** m *c.march* **~mine** f *c.-mine* || ⟨com⟩ *bear party, bears* **≃mi·n·ieren** vi [h] *to c.mine* || ⟨com⟩ *to speculate on a fall, be a bear* **~order** f *c.-order* **~revolution** f *c.-revolution* | ~är [m] *c.r.ary* **~tanz** m *square dance, quadrille*

Kontin·ent m ~(e)s/~e *continent* || in ~en denken *to think continentally* | **≃·al** a *continental* | ~abfall [m], ~böschung [f] *c. slope*; ~gletscher [m] *ice cap*; ≃handel [m] *c. trade*; ≃sockel [m] *c. shelf*; ≃sperre [f] (*Napoleon's*) *C. System, blockade of Great Britain*; ~verschiebungstheorie [f] (A. Wegeners † 1930) *c. drift theory*

Konting·ent n ~(e)s/~e *contingent, contribution, quota* (*system*); *share*; ⟨com⟩ *proportion* (*of notes to gold reserves*); ⟨mil⟩ *component* N **≃·ieren** vt [h] *to fix the contingents, to fix a proportion for* .. || ⟨com⟩ *to pool* (*the profits*) || ⟨finance⟩ *to fix a quota for* .. || *to ration* (*food*) || –ierte Waren *quota goods* **~·ierung** f ~/~en *the fixing of a proportion*, etc. (→ vor.)

kontinu·ierlich a *continuous, sustained* **K.-it·ät** f *c.nuity*

K·onto n ~s/–ten & ~s ⟨com⟩ *account*, ⟨fam⟩ *score*; Bank≃ *bank acc.*; Depositen≃ *deposit acc.*; ein ~ h bei *to have an acc. with*; a ~ *on acc.*; ein ~ eröffnen *to open an acc.* (*with a p*); ein ~ ausgleichen *or* saldieren *to balance an acc.*; setzen Sie es auf mein ~ *put it down to my acc.*; auf ~ kaufen *to buy on credit* od ⟨fam⟩ *on tick*; das kommt auf dein ~ ⟨fig⟩ *that lies at your door* **~abschluß** m *settlement of an acc., acc.s to be settled* **~auszug** m *abstract* od *statement of acc.* **~(gegen)buch** (des Bankkunden) n *control-* od *check-book, acc.-, pass-book* **~führung** f *working* od *keeping of an acc.* **~inhaber** m *acc.-holder* **~korrent** n *acc.-current* **~korrentbuch** n *acc.(-)current book* **~stand** m *state* od *condition of an acc.* **~überziehung** f *overdraft*

Kont·or n ~s/~e *office, counting house* || ⟨fig⟩ °ein Schlag ins ~ *a failure, a wash-out* **~arbeit** f *o. work* **~bedarfsartikel** m pl *o. utensils* pl, *o. supplies* pl **~bücher** n pl *account-books* pl **~bursche** n, ~-

diener m *o.-boy* **~einrichtung** f *o. furniture* **~personal** n *staff of an o.* **~stuhl** m *o.-stool, high stool*

Kontor·ist m ~en/~en (*office-*)*clerk* | **~in** f ~/~nen *female* od *lady clerk*

k·ontra L prep *against, contra*; ⟨jur⟩ *versus* | [adv] (*hunt, go, act*) *counter* ‖ (Skat) ⟨cards⟩ ich sage *or* gebe „kontra" *I defy you* (*to win this game*) ‖ jdm Kontra geben *to give a p tit for tat* | das Pro u ≃ *the pros and cons* pl **≃alt** m *contralto* **≃altistin** f (*contr*)*alto* (*singer*) **≃baß** m *contrabass, double-bass* **≃buch** n *customer's book* **~diktat·orisch** a *contradictory* **≃kurve** f *reserved curve* **≃punkt** m *counterpoint* **~punktisch** a *contrapuntal* (*plots*) **~signieren** vt [h] *to countersign*

Kontrah·age [–ʒə] f ~/~n ⟨hist⟩ (*students'*) *challenge for a duel* **Kontrah·ent** m ~en/~en *contractor, contracting party*; ⟨jur⟩ *party to a contract* **kontrah·ieren** vi [h] ⟨stud⟩ ich habe mit ihm kontrahiert *I challenged him* (*to a duel*) | ⟨jur⟩ *to* (*make a*) *contract*

Kontr·akt 1. m ~(e)s/~e *contract, bargain, agreement* ‖ ⟨jur⟩ *c., indenture* ‖ stillschweigender ~ *tacit agreement* ‖ e–n ~ abschließen *to c. a treaty* ‖ ⟨com⟩ ~e abschließen *to c.* ‖ mit jdm e–n ~ abschließen *to make* (od *to enter into*) *a c. with a p* ‖ e–n ~ aufsetzen, brechen *to draft, break a c.* **2.** ≃ a ⟨path⟩ *paralytic, paralysed, lame*; *contracted* (*muscle*) **~arbeit** f *c.-labour* **~bruch** m ⟨jur⟩ *breach of c.* **≃brüchig** [a] ~ w *to break a c.*; *to run out of a c., to jump a c.* **~erfüllung** f *execution of a c.* **~verhältnis** n; zu jdm in (e–m) ~ stehen *to be bound by c. to a p* **≃widrig** a *contrary to c.* **kontr·aktlich, -mäßig 1.** [a] *stipulated, contractual* (*settlement*) ‖ *fixed* (*income, salary*; *wages* pl) **2.** [adv] *by contract*; ~ verpflichtet *indentured* (*labo*(*u*)*r*)

kontr·är a *contrary* ‖ (ungünstig) *unfavourable* ‖ ⟨fam⟩ (widerlich) *loathsome* (*disposition* Geist); *unmanageable* (*child, person*)

Kontr·ast m ~(e)s/~e *contrast*, ⟨fam⟩ *set-off* ‖ die ~e steigern *to tone up contrast* ‖ im ~ stehen zu *to c. with* ‖ als ~ *for c.* | ~arm [a] *flat* (*picture*); ~figur [f] *counterpart* ‖ *point of reference*, → d,; ~losigkeit [f] *lack of c.*; ~mittel [n] ⟨med⟩ *c. medium*; ~pause [f] ⟨rep⟩ *c. dye-line copy*; ≃reich [a] *c.y,* (*picture*) *rich in c.*; ~umfang [m] *c. range* **kontrast·ieren** vi [h] *to* (*form a*) *contrast* (*with*)

Kontraventi·on [ts] f ~/~en *contravention*

Kontributi·on f ~/~en *contribution* ‖ (Steuer, Buße) (*capital*) *levy*

Kontr·oll- *control-* **~abschnitt** m *counterfoil* **~analyse** f *check analysis* **~anlage** f *c.-gear* **~arbeiten** f pl *checks* **~beamte(r)** m *c.ler* **~buch** n *check-, c.-book*; (Bank) *pass-book* **~drucker** m ⟨comp⟩ *monitor printer* **~eingabegerät** n ⟨comp⟩ *c.-input equipment* **~erhebung** f *post-enumeration test*; *quality check* **~gerät** n *check instrument*; ⟨el⟩ *c.ling device* **~gesellschaft** f *holding company* **~karte** f *time card* **~kasse** f *cash-register* **~kommission** f *C. Commission* **~lampe** f *pilot* od *indicator lamp, signal* (⟨comp⟩ *check*) *light* **~lehre** f *master ga*(*u*)*ge* **~liste** f *tally*; ⟨mil⟩ *muster-roll* **~marke** f *union label* ‖ *worker's arrival check, time-keeping-check* **~maßnahmen** f pl *c.ling measures* pl **~muster** n *check sample* **~peilung** f *ch. bearing* **~punkt** m *ch. point* **~rat** *c. commission* (*Allied C. C.*) **~schacht** m (Kanalisation etc) *inspection pit* **~schein** m *counterfoil*, ⟨Am⟩ *check-stub* **~station** f (Raketen≃) *tracking station* **~stelle** f *checkpoint* **~summen** bilden ⟨comp⟩ *to accumulate a hash total* **~system** n *c. system* **~tisch** m ⟨theat⟩ *c. board*, ⟨Am⟩ *switchboard* **~uhr** f *time* (*recording*) *clock*; ⟨tech⟩ *process timer*; ⟨bes Am⟩ *attendance recorder*; die ~ stechen *to clock in* bzw *out* **~untersuchung** f *checkup* ⟨a. med⟩ **~versammlung** f ⟨mil⟩ *muster of reserves* **~zeichen** n *check, tick*; *certification mark, hallmark* **~zettel** m *counterfoil, check*, ⟨Am⟩ *stub* **~ziffer** f *key number* **Kontr·olle** f ~/ *control, surveillance, supervision* (über *of*); *check*(*-up*); *checking* (*of accounts*); *c. experiment*; Fertigungs≃ *supervision of manufacture*; außer ~ geraten *to get out of hand* od *c.* ‖ e–e Stadt unter ~ h *to be in control of a town* ‖ unter jds ~ *under a p's thumb*; (jdn) u. ~ halten *to keep .. on the string, to keep tab on ..* ‖ (unter) staatliche(r) ~ *state control*(*led*) (*railways*) ‖ behördliche ~ *regimentation* ‖ Lager~ *stock c.* ‖ Verkaufs≃ *sales c.* **Kontroll·eur** [–'øə] m *controller* ‖ Bank≃ *bank-examiner*; *auditor* ‖ ⟨el-rail⟩ *time keeper* **kontroll·ieren** vt [h] (→ nachprüfen) *to check* (*up*) | (überwachen, beherrschen) *to control* ‖ jdn ~ *to keep track of*, ⟨Am⟩ *to keep tab on a p* ‖ (Ladung) stückweise ~ *to tally* (*goods*) | vi ⟨mar⟩ *to patrol*

Kontrov·ers- [v] **~prediger** m *controversialist* **~predigt** f *controversial sermon* **~punkt** m *controversial point* **Kontrov·erse** f ~/~n *dispute, controversy*; e–e ~ h mit *to have words with*

Kontum·az f ~/ *contumacy, contempt of court* (*by default of appearance*) ‖ in ~ verurteilen (= *in contumaciam* L) *to fine for contumacy* | ⟨österr vet⟩ *quarantine* **~urteil** n *judgment by default*

Kont·uren f pl *contours, contour-lines, outlines* pl; ⟨telv⟩ *ambit* ‖ ⟨theat⟩ scharfe ~ (e–r Rolle) *a sharply delineated interpretation* ‖ mit ~ versehen *to contour*; abgeschwächte, scharfe ~ *flattened, bold outlines*; ~ auflösen *to soften the outlines* | ~pflügen [n] *contour plowing*; ~sessel [m] ⟨a-n⟩ *c.-seat*

Kontusi·on f ~/~en ⟨path⟩ *contusion*

K·onus m ~/~se *cone* ‖ ⟨tech⟩ *pivot-stand* ‖ Stufen≃ *step cone* **~dorn** m *taper shank* **~kupplung** f *conical coupling* **~lineal** n ⟨mach⟩ *taper turning attachment* **~mühle** f *cone mill*

Kon- ~valesz·ent [v] m ~en/~en *convalescent* **~vekti·on** [ts] f ~/~en ⟨phys, meteor, astr⟩ *convection* | ~s- [in comp] *c.*; ~ofen [m] *convector*, ⟨Am⟩ *space heater*; ~strom [m] *c. current* **~veni·enz-** f ~/~en *convenience* ‖ ~heirat [f] *marriage of c.* **≃ven·ieren** vi [h] (jdm) *to be convenient* (*to a p*), *to suit* (*a p*) **~v·ent** m ~(e)s/~e **1.** *convention, assembly* (*of monks*, ⟨Ger⟩ *of corporate students*) **2.** ⟨hist Fr⟩ *National Convent* **3.** ~wein [m] RC [österr] (*unsweetened*) *altar wine* **~vent·ikel** n ~s/~ ⟨hist Engl⟩ *conventicle* (*of Dissenters*) **~venti·on** f ~/~en *convention, agreement* ‖ streng der ~ folgend *orthodox* ‖ gegen alle ~ verstoßend *unorthodox* (*conduct*) | ~sfuß [m] *monetary standard existing by agreement*; ~sgeld [n] *convention-money*; ~smünze [f] *convention-coin*; ~stheorie [f] *conventional theory of money* **~vention·al-** ~strafe [f] *penalty* (od *fine for late delivery* od *for nonperformance of a contract*); ~wert [m] *conventional value* **≃ventio·ell** a *conventional* **~verg·enz** f *convergence, -cy* **≃verg·ieren** vi [h] *to converge* ‖ ~de Linien *convergent* od *converging lines* **~versati·on** f ~/~en *conversation, talk* **~versati·ons-** ~lexikon [n] *encyclopædia*; ~stil [m] *colloquial style*; ~stück [n] *drawing-room comedy*; ~stunde [f] *lesson in conversation*; ~zimmer [n] ⟨theat⟩ *green-room* **≃vers·ieren** vi [h] *to converse* (mit *with*) **~versi·on** f ~/~en ⟨jur⟩ *confirmation of a legal transaction void of defects of form*; ⟨gram⟩ *zero-derivation*, → d. **~v·erter** m ~s/~ ⟨met⟩ *converter* | ~birne [f] ⟨met⟩ *converter*; ~kipper [m] (P) *converter leverman* **≃vert·ieren** vt [h] *to convert* **~vert·ierung** f ~/~en *conversion* **~vert·it** m ~en/~en *convert* **≃v·ex** a *convex* ‖ ~konkave Linse *convexo-concave lens* | ≃linse [f] *convex* od *converging* od *condensing lens*; ≃spiegel [m] *convex reflector* od *mirror* **~vexit·ät** f ~/ *convexity* **~v·ikt** n ~(e)s/~e *theological seminary* ‖ [bes österr] ⟨school⟩ *students' hostel* ‖ ⟨univ⟩ *free commons* pl, *free board* |

~ler [m] ~s/~ *theological student* (*who eats at commons*) **~v·ivium** n ~s/-vien *banquet* **~voi** ['kɔnvoi] m ~s/~s ⟨mil & mar⟩ *convoy* **~vol·ut** n ~(e)s/~e *bundle, roll, scroll* **~vulsi·on** f ~/~en *convulsion, spasm* **~́vuls·ivisch** [v] a *convulsive, spasmodic* **~́zed·ieren** vt [h] *to concede* **~zentra·ti·on** f ~/~en *concentration*; ~ auf die vorliegende S *c. to the job in hand* | ~sanlage [f] *c. plant*; ~slager [n] *c. camp, camp of detention*; ~sstein [m] *white metal* **~́zentr·ieren** vt [h] *to concentrate* (*one's thoughts*) ‖ (auf [acc]) *to fix* od *centre* (*upon*) ‖ ⟨mil⟩ *to mass* (*troops*) ‖ sich ~ ⟨chem phys⟩ *to concentrate*; ⟨fig⟩ *to focus* (auf *on*), *to bring one's mind to bear on a th* **~́zentr·iert** *concentrated* (*acid*) ‖ ⟨mil⟩ *concentrated* (*fire*); *converging* (*attacks*) ‖ ⟨pharm⟩ in ~er Form *in tabloid form* **~́z·entrisch** a *concentric* (*circles*) ‖ ⟨mil⟩ ~es Feuer *concentric fire* **~z·ept** n ~(e)s/~e *foul* od *rough copy, rough draft* (⟨Am⟩ *draught*), *minute, sketch* ‖ ohne ~ reden *to speak without the book* ‖ ⟨fig⟩ jdn (ganz) aus dem ~ bringen, jdm das ~ verderben *to put a p out* (*of countenance*); *to disconcert, confuse, upset, perplex*, ⟨fam⟩ *to rattle up* ‖ ⟨fig a.⟩ *to put a p off his game* ‖ aus dem ~e k. ⟨fig⟩ *to break down* | ~papier [n] *copy-, draft-paper, scribbling paper* **~z·ern** m ~s/~e ⟨com⟩ *combine, pool* **~́zern·ieren** vt [h] *to unite in a combine* **~z·ert** n ~(e)s/~e *concert* ⟨a. fig⟩ ‖ (Komposition) *c.o* ‖ das Europäische ~ ⟨pol⟩ *the C. of Europe* (→ Schiedsgericht) ‖ Promenaden~́ *prom(enade c.)* ‖ vgl *smoking-c.* ‖ ein ~ geben *to give a c.* ‖ in ein ~ gehen *to go to a c.* **~besucher** m *c.-goer* **~flügel** m *grand piano, c. grand* **~meister** m *leader*, ⟨Am⟩ *c. master* ‖ *conductor* (*of a band*) **~musik** f *musical entertainment* **~qualität** f ⟨rec⟩ *high fidelity* **~saal** m *c.-room, c.-hall*, ⟨Am⟩ *music-hall* **~sänger** m *c.-singer* **~zeichner** m ⟨st exch sl⟩ *stag* **~́zert·ieren** vi [h] *to give concerts* **~zessi·on** f ~/~en **1.** (Zugeständnis) *concession* ‖ jdm ~en m *to concede, grant, admit, allow rights, a privilege, points in game*, etc. *to a p* **2.** (Gebiet mit Ausbeuterecht) *concession*; ⟨min⟩ *licence, -se, grant*; e–e ~ erteilen *to grant a patent, a charter, to give a privilege, franchise* **3.** (Gewerbeberechtigung) *licence* **~́zession·ieren** vt [h] *to license a p, to grant a p a concession* etc. ‖ –rt *chartered* (*bank*); *licensed* (*trades* Gewerbe, *publicans* Gastwirte etc) **~zes·si·ons-** | ~entzug [m] *withdrawal of authorization*, ~erteilung [f] *au. to operate*; ~gebühr [f] *license-fee*; ~geschäft [n] *licensed business*; ~inhaber [m] *concessionary, -aire, patentee* ‖ *licensee* (→ vor.) **~́zess·iv** a *concessive* ‖ ~́satz [m] ⟨gram⟩ *c. clause* **~z·il** n ~(e)s/~e ⟨ec⟩ *synod, council* ‖ ein ~ einberufen *to call a council* **~́zip·ieren** vt [h] **1.** *to conceive, imagine*; *formulate* **2.** *to draw up, to draft*, ⟨fam⟩ *to jot down* **~zip·ierung** f ~/~en *conception* (*of an idea, a poem*) **~́z·is** a *concise, brief, terse* (*style*)

K·oog [o:] m ~s/~e = Kog

Koop- **~er·ator** m ~s/–at·oren ⟨ec⟩ *curate* **~e·rat·ivgenossenschaft** [i:f] f *co-operative association* **~́er·ieren** vi [h] *to co-operate*

Koopt- **~ati·on** f ~/ *co-optation* **~́·ieren** vt [h] *to co-opt, to elect into a body*

Koordi- **~n·aten** f pl ⟨math⟩ *coordinates* pl | ~netz [n] ⟨cart⟩ *coordinate grid system*; ~papier [n] *graph p.*; (Millimeter~́ etc) *coordinate paper*; ~system [n] *frame of reference* **~nati·on** f ~/ *co-ordination* **~́nieren** vt [h] *to co-ordinate* ‖ ⟨a. übtr fig⟩ *to dovetail* **~n·ierung** f ~/~en *co-ordination* | ~sstelle [f] ⟨tact⟩ f das Feuer aller Waffen *fire support c. center* N

Kop·al m ~(e)s/~e *copal* | ~harz [n] *c. resin*; ~lack [m] *c. varnish*

Kop·eke f ~/~n (1/100 Rubel) *copeck*

Kopenh·agen n *Copenhagen*

K·öper m ~s/ (Stoff) *twill*; *cotton tweel* od *serge*, *tweeled* od *twilled cotton* | ~gaze [f] *tweeled gauze*; ~hose [f] *jeans*; ~samt [m] *jean-back* od *Genoa back-velvet*; ~tuch [n] *tweeled woollen cloth* **k·öpern** vt [h] *to twill*; ge–rt *twilled cloth*

kopernik·anisch a *Copernican* ‖ ~es Sonnensystem *planetary system of Copernicus*

K·opf m ~(e)s/~́e **A. 1.** ⟨**eig**⟩ *head* (mst a. v S) ‖ (⟨vulg⟩ → Ballon, Batterie, Birne, Dez, Grützkasten, Krone, Kübel, Molle, Nischel) ‖ (Schädel) *skull* ‖ den ~ betreffend ⟨scient⟩ *cephalic* ‖ ohne ~ ⟨scient⟩ *acephalous* ‖ Rund~́ *bullet-head* ‖ Stifte~́ (Jungenhaarschnitt bei Mädchen) *Eton crop* ‖ Kahl~́ ⟨fam⟩ *bald pate* ‖ ⟨cul⟩ Fisch~́ *jowl* ‖ ~ an ~ *head to head*; ⟨sport⟩ (Rennen) *neck and neck* ‖ ~ oder Adler *or* Wappen! (e–r Münze) *head(s) or tail(s)*! ‖ mein armer ~ *my racking brain* → Kopfschmerzen ‖ sein ~ ist voll davon *his mind is full of these things* ‖ e–n netten ~ voller Haare (*to have*) *a good head of hair*, ⟨fam⟩ (*to be*) *well thatched* **2.** ⟨**übtr**⟩ (= **P**) er setzte e–e Belohnung aus v 1 Pfund auf den ~, wenn Gefangene gemacht würden *he offered a reward of a pound a head for prisoners* ‖ (auf) den *or* je *or* pro ~ *per head, per capita* L, *a head, a piece*; *individual* (*earnings*) ‖ es k *or* (ent)fallen 5 Stück auf den ~ *each gets* od *gives five* ‖ die Menge war einige Tausend ~́e stark *the crowd numbered several thousands* ‖ viel ~́e, viel Sinne (*or* Meinungen) *many men, many minds* **3.** ⟨fig⟩ (= **Leben**) ~ u Kragen riskieren *to risk life and limb*; .. wagen ⟨mil⟩ *to go over the top*; es geht ihm an ~ u Kragen, es gilt s–n ~, darauf steht der ~ *it's a hanging matter, it is death to do it, it is a capital crime*; → B. 6. ‖ und wenn's um den ~ geht! *neck or nothing*! **4.** ⟨fig⟩ (= **Verstand**, Urteilskraft) *understanding, judgment, mind, sense, wits* pl, *mastermind*; ⟨fam⟩ *brains* pl ‖ (Begabung) *genius, brain, parts, talents* pl ‖ ein guter ~ *a clear head, an able thinker* ‖ ein hohler, leerer (Stroh-) ~ *an empty-headed fellow* ‖ unklarer ~ *confused mind* ‖ fähiger ~ *clever fellow, man of parts* ‖ findiger, erfinderischer, heller ~ *inventive, brilliant mind* ‖ der beste ~ im Finanzwesen *the best financial mind*; die besten ~́e des Landes *the best intellects in the country*; ein kluger ~ *an ingenious brain, a man of* (*first-rate*) *wits* ‖ der führende ~ *the brains* (*of the party*); er hat nicht den ~ dazu *he has not the brains*; e–n hellen ~ h *to have one's h. screwed on tight*; ein scharfsinniger ~ *a subtle reasoner*; er hat e–n klaren ~ *he has his head screwed on the right way*; er ist ein objektiver ~ (bes ⟨pol⟩) *he has a detached mind, detached views*, ⟨fam bes Am⟩ *he is very high-brow* od *a highbrow*; ein schlauer ~ *a cunning fellow* | (= **Wille**) s–n eigenen ~ h *to have a head* od *a mind of one's own*: *he will have his own way, he is very stubborn* od *self-willed*; → B. 6. **5.** ⟨fig⟩ (= **oberes Ende** v S) *head* (*of a pin, nail, screw, rivet, beam* etc.) ‖ Molen~́ *mole h.* ‖ (Schriftgießerei) *face*; *head* (*of a letter*) ‖ *stirrup* (*of a boring apparatus*) ‖ ⟨mach⟩ Zylinder~́ *cylinder h.* ‖ ⟨aero⟩ ~ e–s Flugzeugs *nose* ‖ (Bier~́, Schaum) *head* ‖ Brief~́ *letter head, heading of letter-paper* ‖ ~ e–r Zeitung *title* od *heading* ‖ ~ e–s Artikels ⟨Am⟩ *caption* ‖ ~ e–s Berges, Hügels, Kohlenmeilers *top* ‖ ~ e–r Brücke *head* ‖ ⟨bot⟩ *thistle, flower heads* ‖ *head* (*of a bed*) ‖ *crest* (*of a wave*) ‖ Tassen~́ *cup* ‖ Pfeifen~́ *bowl* ‖ Hut~́ *crown*; mit hohem, niedrigem ~ *high-, low-crowned* (*hat*) **6.** ⟨fig⟩ **Kohl**~́ *head of cabbage* ‖ Salat~́ *head of lettuce* **B.** [**mit Verb**] er kann mir nicht den ~ **abbeißen** *or* abreißen *he cannot bite my head off* ‖ e–m den ~ abschlagen *to behead a p, to strike* (⟨fam⟩ *punch, chop*) *a p's head off* ‖ e–n ~ aufsetzen *to insist on having one's own way* ‖ den ~ oben **behalten** *to keep one's h.* (od *pluck*) *up* ‖ mir brummt der ~ v all dem Lärm *this noise has put my h. into a whirl* ‖ hat er s–n ~ nicht wieder **durchgesetzt**? *hasn't he* *got his own way again?*, *to have one's way at all costs* || die ⁓̈e **erhitzten** sich maßlos in der Versammlung *the excitement ran high* .. || mit erhobenem ⁓, e–nen ⁓es *with one's h. uplifted* || s–m ⁓e folgen *to follow one's mind* || s–n eigenen ⁓ **haben** *to have a mind of one's own* || ich habe e–n ganz benommenen ⁓ *I feel quite dazed, stupified* || e–n guten, klaren ⁓ h *to have plenty of brains* || sie hatte wirklich den ⁓ voll *she really had troubles enough* (od *things enough to think about*) || er ließ (vor *or* aus Scham) den ⁓ **hängen** *he hung his h.* (*for shame*), *he moped, desponded, drooped* (*with* ..) || ⟨fig⟩ *he gave up hope*, ⟨fam⟩ *he was down in the dumps* od *mouth* || nur den ⁓ nicht hängen l! ⁓ hoch! *never say die*! *keep smiling*! ⟨sl⟩ *thumbs up*!; es nützt nichts den ⁓ h. z l *gloom doesn't help* || den ⁓ **heben** *to raise one's head* || den ⁓ hinhalten ⟨fam⟩ *to stick one's neck* od *h. out* || den ⁓ hochhalten ⟨sl⟩ *to keep one's pecker up*! || e–m den ⁓ heiß m *to make a p's blood boil*; *to worry a p* || den ⁓ (beleidigt) hochwerfen, hochtragen *to bridle up* || sie holten sich blutige ⁓̈e *they got broken heads* || und sollte es den ⁓ **kosten**! *were I to die for it*! || es kann den ⁓ nicht kosten *he won't bite my h. off* || sich am ⁓ *or* auf dem ⁓ kratzen *to scratch one's head* || jdn e–n ⁓ kürzer m *to behead a p* || **mach** mir doch den ⁓ nicht warm mit .. *don't bother me with* .. || der Schnaps hat dir wohl den ⁓ heiß gemacht! *the spirits seem to have got to your h.* || den ⁓ **neigen** *to bow one's h.* || sie neigte den ⁓ zur Seite *she put her h. on one side* || sie neigte grüßend *or* zum Gruße den ⁓ *she bowed to him* || sie debattierten, bis ihnen die ⁓̈e **rauchten** *they debated till their heads were ready to split* || °ich ochse Geometrie, daß mir der ⁓ raucht *I am sweating away at geometry* || der ⁓ **saust** mir noch von .. *I haven't yet recovered from* .. || den ⁓ **schütteln** *to wag* od *shake one's h.* || finster den ⁓ schütteln *to shake a gloomy h.* || sie schüttelte ablehnend, verwundert den ⁓ *she shook her h. in disapproval, in wonder* || um s–n ⁓ zu **schützen** *to save his neck* || mir schwindelt der ⁓ davon *it makes my h. swim* || s–n ⁓ (= Leben) aufs Spiel **setzen** für .. *to risk one's h. for* ..; den ⁓ zum Pfande setzen *to stake one's h.* (f .. *on* ..) || ich wußte nicht, wo mir der ⁓ stand .. *what to do* (*first*), *which way to turn* || sie **steckten** die ⁓̈e zus *they put their h.s together* || den ⁓ hoch **tragen** *to carry one's h. proudly* || mir tut der ⁓ weh *my h. aches* || sie hat ihm völlig den ⁓ **verdreht** *she has completely turned his h.*, *she vamped him*; *his h. was a little turned by the adulation* || er ist im ⁓ ein wenig verdreht *he has a bee in his bonnet* || den ⁓ verlieren *to lose one's h.* od *wits* (od *presence of mind* od *self-command*); *to go off one's h.*, *to see red*; ⟨vulg & mil⟩ *to do one's nut* || den ⁓ nicht verlieren *to keep one's h.* (od *wits about one*) || ganz *or* total den ⁓ verlieren *to go off the deep-end* || jdm (gehörig) den ⁓ **waschen** (*to reprimand a p*) *to comb a p's hair for him, to tick a p off, to talk to a p like a Dutch uncle, to give a p a rub-down* od *a telling off, to send a p off with a flea in his ear, to haul* od *call a p over the coals*; *to blow a p up* || den ⁓ wiegen *to sway one's h. to and fro* || s–n ⁓ **wetten** *to lay one's h.* || sich den ⁓ **zerbrechen** über *to trouble, cudgel, puzzle, rack, beat, busy one's brains, to bother one's h. about* .., *to quibble over* ..; ⟨sl⟩ *to work one's nut about* .. || sich über etw nicht den ⁓ zerb. *not to trouble one's h. about* || den ⁓ zurückwerfen *or* in den Nacken werfen *to tilt one's chin, to throw* od *toss up one's h.* || er rückte *or* setzte ihm den ⁓ gehörig zurecht *he gave him a severe talking to* (→ ⁓ waschen) **C.** **[mit prep]** er faßte sich **an** den ⁓ *his hand went to his h.* || sich gegenseitig Grobheiten an den ⁓ werfen *to bandy incivilities*; *to throw insults at a p's h.* || sie standen ⁓ an ⁓ *they stood crowded together*, → A. 1. | **auf** den ⁓ fallen *to land on one's h.*; er ist nicht **auf** den ⁓ gefallen *he is no duffer* od *fool* (⟨fam⟩ *no stupid*), *he knows* (*what is what* od *what's o'clock* od) *black from white* od *a th or two*, *he has an eye in his h.* || er hätte längst etw auf den ⁓ bek müssen *he ought to have been called to order long ago* || ⟨mar⟩ ein Feuerschiff auf den ⁓ bek *to hit a lightvessel on the h.* || °jdm auf den ⁓ spucken → ⁓ zurechtsetzen || man sagte ihm die Tat auf den ⁓ zu *he was accused of the deed to his face* || wir l uns nicht auf dem ⁓ herumtrampeln *we will let nobody play the fool with us* || es kostete 50 Pfennig auf den ⁓ *we had to pay -/6 a head* || ich nehme die Verantwortung ganz auf m–n ⁓ *I take all the responsibility on my own shoulders* || e–n Preis auf jds ⁓ setzen *to set a price on a p's h.* || auf s–m ⁓e bestehen *to take h.*, *to insist on one's wishes, to be obstinate* od *strong-headed* || sich auf den ⁓ stellen *to do one's utmost*; und wenn du dich auf den ⁓ stellst *in spite of anything you may do*; ⟨vulg⟩ *I'll see you further first* || sie stellten das Zimmer auf den ⁓ *they turned the room upside-down* || (Flasche etc) auf den ⁓ stellen *to upend, to set on its end, to turn end upwards* || ⟨fig⟩ *to stand* (*a theory*) *on its h.*, *to get hold of the wrong end of the stick* || alles steht hier auf dem ⁓ *everything is at sixes and sevens here*, .. *is topsy-turvy*; .. stellen *to turn* .. *t.-t.*; *to stand* (*the whole town*) *on its ear* || e–e Tatsache auf den ⁓ stellen *to falsify the facts* || ⟨fig⟩ den Nagel auf den ⁓ treffen *to hit the nail on the head, to hit the mark* | **auf den ⁓ zu** fragen *to ask* .. *narrowly* | etw **aus** dem (⟨vulg⟩ nackigen = nackten) ⁓ können *to know a th by heart* od *by rote* || aus dem ⁓e hersagen *to recite from memory, by heart* || du mußt dir den Gedanken aus dem ⁓ schlagen *you must banish that from your thoughts, put that idea out of your h., give it up, get it off your mind* || der Gedanke will mir nicht aus dem ⁓ *I can't get the idea out of my h.* || jdm etw aus dem ⁓e bringen *to put* (⟨fam⟩ *knock*) *a th out of a p's h.* || ich habe mir bald die Augen aus dem ⁓e gesehen *I looked till I was almost blind.* || er verstand es, den ⁓ aus der Schlinge zu ziehen *he understood how to get his h. out of the noose* | sich **bei** den Köpfen kriegen *to come to blows, to fall together by the ears* || jdn beim ⁓e packen *to seize a p by the collar* | ich will mir deine Anregungen **durch** den ⁓ gehen l *I will think over your suggestions* || sich etw durch den ⁓ gehen l *to turn a th over in one's mind* || mir schoß der Gedanke durch den ⁓ *the idea struck me suddenly, flashed through my h.* || sich [dat] e–e Kugel durch den ⁓ jagen *to shoot o.s., to blow out one's brains* | **in** s–m ⁓ hat kein anderer Gedanke Raum *he has thoughts for nothing else* || sich [dat] in den ⁓ setzen, es z tun *to set one's mind on doing it* || etw **im** ⁓ h: (Verstand, ⟨fam⟩ Grips *or* Grütze) *to have plenty of brains*, ⟨fam⟩ *to know a th or two*, ⟨fam⟩ *to know a good th when one sees it*; (Grillen) *he's got a screw loose*, ⟨hum⟩ *he's a h. case* || (große Dinge, ⟨fam⟩ Graupen *or* große Rosinen) *to have high notions, great schemes* || (Heu u Stroh) *to be addle-headed*; (Gedanken) *to be full of thoughts*; andere Dinge im ⁓ h *to have other fish to fry*; was man nicht im ⁓e hat muß man in den Beinen h *a short* od *weak memory makes weary legs* od *makes work for the legs*; was der e–e nicht .., muß der andere in den B. h ⟨m. m.⟩ *it's nice to have a peg to hang things on* || (e–n Rausch) *to have* (*taken* od *had*) *a drop too much*; (Sorgen) *to have cares, troubles and brood over them* || etw noch frisch im ⁓ h *to have sth fresh in memory* || ein Wahn, der in s–m ⁓e spukt *a delusion which haunts him* || es geht mir dauernd im ⁓e herum *it weighs on my mind* || es geht mir (wie) ein Mühlrad im ⁓ herum *my h. is in a perfect whirl* || im ⁓ (aus)rechnen *to compute* od *calculate mentally, to work it out* (⟨fam⟩ *to do it*) *in one's h.* || etw im ⁓ behalten *to remember a th* || es ist mir ständig im ⁓ *it fills my every thought* || sich etw in den ⁓ setzen *to fancy* *sth*; *to take, put* od *get* (*funny* od *absurd notions*) *into one's h.* || setz ihm doch k–e Raupen in den ~ *don't put any silly ideas into his head* || es will mir nicht in den ~ hinein *I can't understand* od *believe, I fail to realize*; *I don't quite see* (daß *that* ..) || sich etw in den ~ gesetzt h *to be possessed of some idea* || was mag ihm nur in den ~ gefahren sein? *whatever can he be thinking of?* || das Blut stieg ihm in den ~ .. *rushed to his h.* || es geht mir im ~e herum *it runs in my h.* || er war durchaus klar im ~ *he had all his wits about him* || klar im ~ *or* mit klarem ~ *clear-headed* | **mit** dem ~ voran *head first* || °mit dem ~ parieren ⟨sport⟩ *to lead with one's chin* ⟨a. fig⟩ || mit dem ~ nicken, wackeln *to nod, wag one's h.* || sie nickte bejahend mit dem ~ *she nodded assent* || den (*or* mit dem) ~ in die Hand gestützt *with one's h. in one's hand* || mit dem ~ rennen gegen *to run* od *beat one's h. against* || ⟨fig⟩ er wollte immer mit dem ~ durch die Wand *he was always wanting to run* od *knock his head against a* (*mill*)*stone* od *brick wall* || mit dem ~e überall durchwollen *to act rashly* || ⟨ftb⟩ (Ball) mit dem ~ stoßen *to head* || jdm mit dem ~ ein Zeichen geben *to nod a h. towards a p* || [prov] das Herz läuft immer mit dem ~ davon *the heart always gets the better of the h.* || er mußte die Verschwörung mit dem ~e bezahlen *the plot cost him his h.* || mit hochroten ≃en *with flushed countenances* | nur **nach** s–m eigenen ~ handeln *to have it all one's own way, to follow nobody's advice but one's own, to follow one's own opinion* || es muß nicht immer nur nach d–m ~ gehen *things must not always be done as you want* || mir steht der ~ nicht danach *I do not feel inclined for it* || es ist ganz nach m–m ~ *it's just as I wished* od *wanted it to be, it suits me to perfection* || Blutandrang nach dem ~ *congestion of the brain* | **über** jds ~ hinweg (*to apply to* ..) *over a p's h.* || sie schlug die Hände über dem ~ zus *she threw up her hands in astonishment, she was taken aback, speechless, beside herself* || das Haus stürzte ihm über dem ~ zus .. *collapsed* od *dropped over his h.* od *came down around his ears* || jdm das Haus überm ~ anstecken *to burn a p's house about his ears* || jdm das Dach über dem ~e nehmen *the war had brought the roof down over her h.* || bis über dem ~ in Schulden *over h. and ears* od *h. over heels in debt* || *up to the eyes in work* || jdm über den ~ wachsen *to outgrow a p*; ⟨fig⟩ *to get beyond a p's control, to get too much for a p*; *she had become more than a match for the old lady* | **um** e–n ~ größer s *to be taller by a h.* || es geht um ~ u Kragen *it's a hanging matter, it's a matter of life and death* || sie band ein Tuch um den ~ *she tied her h. up in* .. | **von** ~ bis Fuß *or* vom ~ bis zu den Füßen *from h. to foot, from top to toe* || nicht von s–m ~ abgehen *not to give way*, ⟨fam⟩ *to stick to one's guns* | jdn **vor** den ~ stoßen *to offend* od *slight a p, to give offence to a p, to disoblige a p*; *to antagonize* (*public opinion*); ⟨fam⟩ *to stand a p on his ears, to rub a p the wrong way* || s–e schroffe Art stieß alle vor den ~ *his rough manners repelled everybody* || wie vor den ~ geschlagen *taken aback* || der Junge hat ein Brett vorm ~ .. *is a blockhead* | jdm **zu** ~e steigen: *the sweetness of the place went to one's h.*; *his h. has been turned by success*; *this wine is heady* od *flies to my h.* || zu ~e steigend *heady* (*liquor*) **~abschlagen** n *beheading, decapitation*; ⟨scient⟩ *decollation* **~ader** f ⟨anat⟩ *cephalic vein* **~anteil** m ⟨com⟩ *share per h.* **~arbeit** f *h.-* od *brain-work, mental work*; ⟨Am fam⟩ *black-coated* od *white-collar occupation* **~arbeiter** m *brain-worker*, ⟨Am fam⟩ *black-coat*(*ed worker*), *white collar* **~arterie** f ⟨anat⟩ *carotid* (*artery*) **~bahnhof** m *rail-h., terminal station, terminus* **~balken** m ⟨carp⟩ *h.-beam* **~band** n, **~binde** f *h.-band, frontlet* **~bau** m *h.-building* **~bedeckung** f *h.-covering, h.-gear*; ohne ~ *hatless* **~beere** f ⟨bot⟩ *ipecacuanha* **~bekleidung** f (e–r Mauer) *top-facing* **~beschwerden** f pl *complaints of the h.* **~besteuerung** f = ~steuer **~bindung** f ⟨el⟩ *top binding* **~blüten** f pl ⟨bot scient⟩ *aggregate flowers* pl **~bohrer** m ⟨surg⟩ *trepan, perforator* **~bolzen** m *set bolt* **~breite** f der Schiene *width of the rail-h.* **~brummen** n *noises in the h.* **~bruststück** n ⟨ent⟩ *cephalothorax* **~decke** f ⟨hors⟩ *mane-sheet* **~drüse** f ⟨anat⟩ *cephalic gland* **~düngung** f ⟨hort⟩ *top-dressing* **~ende** n *h.* (*of a bed*) **≃förmig** a *in the shape of a h.*; ⟨bot⟩ *capitate* **~füßer** m pl ⟨zoo⟩ *cephalopods* pl **~garnitur** f ⟨telph⟩ *h.-and-chest set* **~geschirr** n ⟨hors⟩ *h.-gear* **~geld** n = ~steuer || ⟨crim l⟩ *head money* **~gestell** n ⟨hors⟩ *head stall* **~gicht** f ⟨path⟩ *gout in the h.*, ⟨scient⟩ *cephalagra* **~grind** m *scab on the h., scald, porrigo* **~grippe** f *influenza* **~großaufnahme** f ⟨film⟩ *close-up* **~halter** m *h.-rest*, ⟨surg⟩ *cephalostat* **~hänger** m (Scheinheiliger) *hypocrite*, (Schwermütiger) *mope* **~hänger·ei** f *hypocrisy* || *mopes* pl, *mopishness* **≃hängerisch** a *sanctimonious*, ⟨fam⟩ *saintly* || *mopish, moping* **~haube** f ⟨orn⟩ *crest* **~haut** f *scalp* **≃hoch** a; er steht ~ über .. *he stands h. and shoulders above his contemporaries* **~holz** n *pollard* **~hörer** m ⟨wir⟩ *h.-* od *earphones* pl, *h.-receiver, h.-piece*; (*single*) *earpiece*; (beidseitig) *stethophone* **~jagd** f *h.-hunting* **~keilbein** n ⟨anat⟩ *sphenoid bone* **~kissen** n *pillow* | ~bezug [m] *p.-case* **~kohl** m *h.ed cabbage* **~lage** f (bei der Geburt) *frontal presentation* **~länge** f ⟨racing⟩ *head* **≃lastig** a ⟨aero⟩ *nose-heavy* **~lastigkeit** f *n. heaviness* **~laterne** f ⟨mot, rail⟩ *h.light* **~laus** f *h.-louse* **~leiste** f ⟨typ⟩ *h.-piece* **≃los** a *h.less* || ⟨zoo⟩ *acephalous* || ⟨fig⟩ *giddy, thoughtless, hare-brained, stupid* || ~e Angst *unthinking fear* || ~e Flucht *h.long* od *precipitate flight*, ⟨mil⟩ *stampede* || nicht ~ w *to keep one's wits about one* **~losigkeit** f *h.lessness* || ⟨zoo⟩ *acephalia* || ⟨fig⟩ *giddiness, thoughtlessness, stupidity*; *panic* **~messer** m *cephalometer* **~messung** f *cephalometry* **~naht** f ⟨anat⟩ *suture of the h.* **~nicken** n *nod*(*ding*) **~nikker** m ⟨anat⟩ *annuent muscle* **~nuß** f ⟨fam⟩ *clout* od *blow on the h.* **~prämie** f ⟨ins⟩ *pr. per capita* **~putz** m *headdress* **~rampe** f ⟨rail⟩ *end-loading ramp* **~rechnen** n *mental arithmetic*; ~ schwach! *m. a. weak*! **~rose** f ⟨path⟩ *erysipelas* **~runge** f ⟨rail⟩ *end stanchion* **~rüstung** f ⟨hist hors⟩ *tester* **~salat** m *green salad*, (*cabbage-* od *garden-*)*lettuce* | ~herzen [pl] *hearts of lettuce* **~satz** m ⟨mus⟩ *opening movement* **~scheibe** f ⟨mil⟩ *h.-target* **~scheinwerfer** m ⟨rail⟩ *h.light* **≃scheu** a *shy, skittish, restive* || ⟨fig⟩ (P) *shy, reserved* || ~ m *to alarm, frighten* || ~ w *to take fright*, ⟨hors⟩ *to jib* **~schlag** m ⟨mar⟩ (→ Knoten) *hitch* | ~ader [f] ⟨anat⟩ *cephalic artery* **~schleife** f *topknot* **~schmerz**(en pl) m *h.ache* || ~en h *to have a h.*(*ache*) || jdn v ~en befreien *to take a p's h.ache away* || an ~ leidend, ~ verursachend *h.achy* || heftige ~en *a violent, raving, splitting h.ache*; den ~ vergrößern ⟨fam⟩ *to add another twinge to the h.ache* || ⟨fig⟩ die Furcht es zu tun macht ihm viel ~en *the fear of doing it sits heavy upon him* || mach dir darüber k–e ~en! *no good to let it prey on your mind*! *don't bother your h. about that*! || die Geschäftslage macht ihm viel ~en .. *causes him great anxiety* **~schmuck** m *h.dress, h.gear* **~schraube** f *cap screw* **~schuppen** f pl *dandruff* **~schütteln** n *h.-wagging, shaking of h.s* ⟨cont⟩ (über [acc] *at*) **~schwelle** f ⟨rail⟩ *buffer-beam* **~seite** f ⟨num⟩ *head, obverse*; *face* (*of a stone*) **~sprung** m *h.er, purl* || e–n ~ m *to* (*take a*) *dive, to make* od *take a h.er* (von *off*) **~stand** m; ~ m *to stand on one's h.* || ⟨aero⟩ *to nose over* **~station** f ⟨rail⟩ *terminus, dead-end* **≃|stehen** vi [h] das Bild steht kopf .. *hangs upside down* || er stand kopf vor Staunen *he was struck dumb with astonishment* || es ist reineweg zum ≃! *it strikes me dumb, that beats all*! **~stein** m *cobble* || mit ~en pflastern *to* *c.* | ~pflaster [n] *c.stones* **~steuer** f *poll-tax, capitation fee* **~steuerung** f ⟨aero⟩ *front control* **~stimme** f ⟨mus⟩ *h. voice, falsetto,* ⟨Am⟩ *h. tone* **~stück** n ⟨arch⟩ *h.er*; *inbond brick* ‖ (Zaumzeug) *h.-stall* ‖ (Wagenbau) *h. stock* ‖ ⟨min⟩ (~ e–s Erdbohrers) *stirrup* ‖ ⟨allg⟩ *h.-piece* ‖ ⟨fam⟩ = ~nuß **~sturz** m *vertical dive* ⟨a. aero⟩ **~stütze** f (z Lesen) *h.-rest* **~tuch** n *h.-cloth, h.-scarf, kerchief, wimple* **≈·über** adv *h.-long, h. foremost, h. first, h. over heels* ‖ ≈·über, ≈·unter adv *pell-mell* **≈·unter** adv *h.-down* **~wand** f ⟨rail⟩ *end of a car* **~wäsche** f *shampooing* **~wasser** n *h.* od *hair wash* **~wassersucht** f ⟨path⟩ *water on the brain,* ⟨scient⟩ *hydrocephalus* **~weh** n = ~schmerz **~wunde** f *wound in the h.* **~zahl** f *number of h.s* od *persons* ‖ nach der ~ berechnet *per capita* ‖ nach der ~ abstimmen *to vote by h.* **~zählung** f *capitation* **~zeile** f ⟨typ⟩ *headline,* ⟨Am a.⟩ *banner* **~zerbrechen** n *racking of one's brains, intellectual effort* ‖ jdm ~ m *to puzzle a p*; *to cause a p no little h.ache*; ohne viel ~ *without much pondering* **≈zerbrechend** a *puzzling, brain-trying, severe* **~zeug** n *h.dress* **~ziegel** m *h.-brick* **~zünder** m ⟨mil⟩ *nose-, point-fuze*

K·öpfchen n ~s/~ *small* (od *pretty*) *head* ‖ ~, ~! ⟨fam⟩ *he's got a h.-piece* ‖ ⟨bot⟩ *cluster* **k·öpfen** vt/i [h] **1.** vt *to behead, decapitate* ‖ ich lasse mich ~, wenn .. (*I am*) *blessed if* .. ‖ ⟨ftb⟩ *to head* (*the ball*) ‖ ⟨hort⟩ *to lop, top*; *to poll* (*willows*) ‖ (anköpfen) *to head* (*pins*) **2.** vi [h] (Köpfe bilden) *to put on heart*(*s*) od *head*(*s*) °**K·öpfer** ~s/~ (Kopfsprung) ⟨fam⟩ *ducker* **K·öpfler** m ~s/~ [österr] ⟨swim⟩ = Kopfsprung, ⟨ftb⟩ = Kopfstoß *header* **K·öpfmaschine** f *guillotine*

Kop·ie [österr: ˈko:piə] f ~/~n *copy, duplicate* ‖ ⟨arts⟩ *copy,* ⟨scient⟩ *replica* **Kop·ier-** *copying, printing* **~anstaltarbeiten** f pl *laboratory work* ⟨a. film⟩ **~apparat** m ⟨rep⟩ *printing machine* **~buch** n *letter-, copy*(*ing*)*-book,* ⟨Am⟩ *copy-book* **≈fähig** a ⟨rep⟩ *transparent* (*Pause replica*) **~farbe** f = ~tinte **~film** m *duplicate film* **~gerät** n *c. apparatus*; *reproduction equipment* **~kamera** f *camera printer* **~maschine** f ⟨rep⟩ *coutinuous printer*; optische ~ *optical pr.* **~papier** n *c. paper,* dünnes ~ *flimsy*; ⟨phot⟩ *pr. paper* **~presse** f *letter press, c.-press* **~rahmen** m ⟨phot⟩ *pr. frame* **~stift** m *c.* (*ink*) *pencil* **~tinte** f *c.-ink* **~verfahren** n *c. process* **kop·ieren** vt [h] *to copy, imitate,* ⟨Am fam⟩ *to take* (*a p*) *off* ‖ *to adhere to tradition without being a mere imitator* (ohne zu kopieren) | ⟨phot⟩ *to print* **Kop·ist** m ~en/~en *copyist, copying-clerk*

K·oppe f ~/~n (*dome-shaped*) *top* (*of a moun-*
a ⟨rep⟩ *transparent* (Pause *replica*) **~farbe** f =
tain) (vgl Schnee≈)

K·oppel[1] f ~/~n **I.** (Band) **1.** ⟨allg⟩ *couple, coupling* **2.** (f Hunde) *couple, leash*; v der ~ l *to slip* od *uncouple* (*the hounds*) **3.** (Hürde) *pen* **II.** (Gebundenes) **1.** ⟨hunt⟩ e–e ~ (= 3 Hunde) *a leash of hounds* **2.** (Meute) *pack of hounds* **3.** e–e ~ Pferde (auf dem Markt) *a string* od *set of horses* **4.** *common*; ⟨agr⟩ (eingezäunt) *enclosure* **5.** (Pferde≈) *paddock* **6.** ⟨mus⟩ (Register≈) *joined keyboards, registers, organ-stops* **K·oppel**[2] n ~s/~ ⟨mil⟩ (Leibriemen) (*waist-*)*belt, sword-belt* **K·oppel-** | **~fischerei** f *common* (*right of*) *fishing* **~gerechtigkeit** f, **~recht** n ⟨agr⟩ *right of c.* **~geschäft** n *conditional sale* **~hut** f *c.* (*of*) *pasture, c.* **~knecht** m *teamster* **~jagd** f *c. chase* **~kurs** m ⟨mar⟩ *compound course* **~leine** f, **~riemen** m, **~seil** n ⟨hunt⟩ *leash* (→ Koppel[1] I. 2.) *collar, leash* **~navigation** f *dead reckoning* N | ~srechengerät [n] *d. r. computer* **~schloß** n ⟨mil⟩ *belt buckle* **~stange** f ⟨tech⟩ *drag-bar* **~tisch** m ⟨mar⟩ *plotting board* **~trift** f, **~weide** f *enclosed* od *c. pasture* **~verkauf** m ⟨fam⟩ *tie-in sale* **~verleih** m ⟨film⟩ *block-booking* **~wirtschaft** f ⟨agr⟩ *rotation of crops*

k·oppeln **1.** vt [h] *to couple, leash*; *to string together* (→ Koppel[1]) ‖ ⟨mus⟩ *to join* (*the key-boards, registers, organ-stops*) ‖ ⟨mar⟩ die Kurse ~ *to work the traverses, to keep the dead reckoning* ‖ ⟨agr⟩ *to fence in* (*a field*) ‖ ⟨el, chem⟩ *to connect, couple* ‖ ge–lt ⟨arch⟩ *coupled* (*columns*) **2.** ≈ n ⟨a-n⟩ (e–r Kapsel an die andere) *docking* **K·oppler** m ~s/~ ⟨telph⟩ *coupler* **K·opplung** f ~/~en ⟨allg, el, chem⟩ *coupling*; ⟨mar⟩ *dead reckoning* | ⟨a–n⟩ *docking* | **~s-** ~geschäft [n] *package deal*; ~grad [m] *c. factor*; ~messer [m] *capacity unbalance meter*; ~schwingung [f] *oscillation in coupled circuits*; ~spule [f] *c. coil*; ~verkauf [m] *tie-in sale*; ~wechsler [m] *c. changer*; ~zahl [f] *c. value*

k·oppen vi [h] ⟨hors⟩ *to roar*; *bite the manger*; *be a crib-biter* **K·opper** m ~s/~ *roarer*, etc

K·opra f ~/ *copra*

K·opte m ~n/~n *Copt* **k·optisch** a, das ≈e (⟨(ä)gyptisch⟩) *Coptic*

K·opula f ~/ ⟨log & gram⟩ *copula* **Kopulati·on** [ts] f ~/~en *coupling, marrying*; *marriage-ceremony, nuptial benediction* ‖ ⟨hort⟩ *grafting* **kopul·ieren** vt [h] *to copulate, pair, couple* ‖ (trauen) *to marry* ‖ ⟨hort⟩ *to graft*

k·or 1. & 3. sg ind impf v kiesen

K·orah m, npr ~/ die Rotte ~ ⟨bib⟩ *the company of Korah* ‖ ⟨übtr⟩ *set* od *gang of rogues*

Korak·an f ~/ (Hirse) ⟨bot⟩ *African millet*

Kor·alle f ~/~n *coral* **kor·allen** a *coral, coralline* **Kor·allen-** **≈artig** a *coralline* **~baum** m *coral-tree* **~erz** n ⟨min⟩ *c. ore* **~fang** m *c.-fishing* **≈farbig** *coralline* **~fisch** m *coral fish* **~fischer** m *c.-fisher* **~fischer·ei** f *c.-fishing* **~flechte** f = ~moos **≈förmig** a *c.-shaped* **~halskette** f *c. beads* pl, *c. necklace* **~insel** f *c.-island, atoll* **~kalk** m ⟨geol⟩ *c. lime* **~kraut** n = Scharpelkraut **~moos** n *c.-moss* **~perle** f *c.-bead* **~pilz** m = Ziegenbart **~polyp** m ⟨zoo⟩ *c.-insect,* ⟨scient⟩ pl *coralligena* pl **~riff** n, **~bank** f *c.-reef, c. shelf*; *atoll* **~schnur** f (*string of*) *c.-beads* pl **~schwamm** m ⟨bot⟩ *c. fungus* L **~see** f (*Tasman*) *C. Sea* **~strauch** m *c. plant* **~tier** n = ~polyp

koram·ieren vt [h] ⟨Ger stud⟩ (jdn *coram publico* [L] zur Rede stellen) *to take a p to task*

K·oran m ~(e)s/ *the Koran*

K·orb m ~(e)s/≈e **1.** ⟨eig⟩ *basket*; in Körben *in baskets*; B·agger≈ *dredging bucket*; Ball·on≈ *car, basket, nacelle*; B·eiß≈ *muzzle*; B·ienen≈ *bee-hive, skep*; B·insen~ für Obst *frail*; Brot≈ *bread-b.*; Brut≈ *coop*; Draht≈ *wire b.*; Eß≈ *hamper, provision b.*; Fisch≈ *creel*; Fang≈ ⟨el rail⟩ *guard net,* ⟨Am rail⟩ *cow-catcher*; Flaschen≈ *bottle-hamper*; Förder≈ *drum, cage b.*; Früchte≈ *fruit-b.*; Führer≈ *driver's cab* od *cage* ‖ Geschirr≈; großer ~ *crate*; Kabel≈ *cable b.* ‖ Krankentrage≈ *stretcher*; Lautsprecher≈ ⟨wir⟩ *frame* ‖ Maul≈ *muzzle*; Pack≈ *hamper* ‖ Papier≈ (im Freien) *litter* od *refuse bin, rubbish basket*; (im Zimmer) *waste-*(*paper-*)*b.*; Preß≈ (Kelterei) *press-vat*; Rap·ier≈ *basket hilt*; Reise≈ *travelling b.* ‖ Saug≈ *intake pipe*; Säbel≈ *basket-hilt*; Schanz≈ *gabion*; Sensen≈ *scythe-cradle*; Strand≈ (*roofed*) *wicker-chair* (*for use on the beach*); ⟨theat⟩ *skip,* ⟨Am⟩ *hamper*; Trag≈ (P) *pannier, dosser*; (T) *pannier*; Wäsche≈ *clothes-* od *washing-b.*; Weiden≈ *wicker b.,* ⟨aero⟩ *skep* **2.** ⟨fig⟩ sie gab ihm e–n ~ (wies ihn als Freier ab) *she gave him a denial* od *refusal,* ⟨fam⟩ .. *the definite brush-off,* ⟨sl⟩ .. *the mitten*; *she refused, rejected him,* ⟨vulg⟩ .. *bounced him* ‖ e–n ~ erhalten *to meet with* od *to have a rebuff* ‖ sich e–n ~ holen *to draw a blank,* ⟨sl⟩ *to get the mitten* **3.** **~arbeit** f *b.-making, wickerwork* **~ball**(**spiel** n) m *b.ball* **~binse** f ⟨bot⟩ *frail* **≈blütig** a ⟨scient⟩ *synantherous* **~blütler** m ⟨bot⟩ *composite flower,* pl *compositae* [pl L] **~deckel** m *b. lid* **~degen** m *b.-sword* **~eidechse** f *b. lizard* **~feigen** f pl *figs* pl *in baskets* **~flasche** f *wicker-bottle,* große ~ *demi-*

john, ⟨chem⟩ *carboy* **~flechter** m *b.-maker* **~flechter·ei** f *b.ry* **≗förmig** a *b.-shaped* **~futteral** n *case of osier* **~gefäß** n (des Degens) *b.-hilt* **~geflecht** n *wicker-work* **~gitter** n *b.-grate* **~handel** m *b.-trade* **~henkel** m *b.-handle* **~macher** m *b.maker* **~möbel** n [pl] *b.* od *osier* od *wicker furniture* **~rapier** n, **~schläger** m *b.-hilted rapier* **~schanze** f ⟨mil⟩ *gabionade* **~sessel** m *b.* or *wicker chair* **~trägerin** f *caryatid* **~wagen** m *b.-carriage, b.-phaeton* **~waren** f [pl] *b. ware, b.ry, osier-work* **~weide** f *b.-willow, osier* **≗weise** adv *in b.s* **~wiege** f *wicker cradle* **K·örbchen** n (am B. H.) *cup*

K·ord m ~s/ (Stoff) *cord* | ~samt [m] *corduroy; ribbed velvet*

K·ordel f ~/~n *twine, string, cord, packthread* | ~ader [f] *yarn conductor*

kordi·al a *cordial* **≗it·ät** f ~/~en *c.ity*

Kord·on [–'dɔŋ] m ~s/~s ⟨mil⟩ *cordon, line (of posts)* ‖ e–n ~ um ein Haus ziehen *or* bilden *to draw, post* od *form a c. round a house*

Kordill·eren f pl *Cordilleras* pl

Kordof·an (Landschaft Innerafrikas) *Cordofan*

K·ordova n ⟨span⟩ (Stadt) *Cordova*

Kordu·an m ~(e)s/~e *Spanish leather, cordovan* | ~macher [m] *cordwainer*

k·öre 1. & 3. p sg subj, imperf v kiesen, küren

Kore·aner m ~s/~ *Corean*

Korfi·ot m ~(e)s/~en *Corfiote, man of Corfu*

Korf·u, ⟨a.⟩ **K·orfu** n (Ionische Insel) *Corfu*

Kori·ander m ~s/ (Gewürz) *coriander*

Kor·inth n *Corinth*; **Golf v K.** m *Gulf of C.*

Kor·inthe f ~/~n *dried currant* | ~nkacker [m] → Klugscheißer

Kor·inther m ~s/~; **kor·inthisch** a *Corinthian*; Korintherbrief ⟨bib⟩ *Epistle to the Corinthians*

K·ork m ~(e)s/~e **1.** ⟨bot⟩ (Rinde) *cork* ‖ ⟨scient⟩ *suber* **2.** *float (of an angle)* **3.** = Korken (= Pfropfen) | mit Draht umflochtener ~ *wired cork* ‖ zus-gepreßter ~ *agglomerated c.* **~abfälle** m [pl] *c. chip* **~apparat** m *bottle c.er* **≗artig** a *c.-like, c.y,* ⟨scient⟩ *suberous* **~asbest** m ⟨min⟩ *c.-fossil* **~baum** m, **~eiche** f *c.-tree, c.-oak,* ⟨scient⟩ *suber* **~boje** f ⟨mar⟩ *c. buoy* **~einlegesohle** f *sock of c.* **≗erzeugend** a ⟨scient⟩ *phellogenetic* **~holz** n *c.-wood* **~jacke** f *c. jacket* **~männchen** n *c.-tumbler* **~maschine** f *cask* od *bottle c.ing machine* **~masse** f *c. composition* **~mehl** n *c. dust* od *powder* **~platte** f *c. sheet* od *slab* **~presse** f *c. squeezer* **~rinde** f *suber* **~sauer** a ⟨chem⟩ *suberic* **≗saures Salz** *suberate* **~scheibe** f *c. disk* **~schicht** f ⟨bot⟩ *periderm* **~schneider** m (P) *c.-cutter* ‖ (S) *c.-machine* **~schwimmer** m *(c.) float* **~sohle** f *c. sole* **~stein** m *(agglomerated) c. brick* **~stoff** m *suberin* **~stöpsel, ~pfropf(en)** m *c. stopper* **≗tr·ocken** a *dry as a bone* **~weste** f *c. waistcoat* **~zieher** m *c.-screw* | ~locken [f pl] *c. screws*; ~-Sturzspirale [f] ⟨aero⟩ *spiral dive* **K·orken** m ~s/~ (= Pfropfen, Stopfen, Stöpsel e–r Flasche) *stopper, cork* ‖ der Wein schmeckt nach dem ~ .. *is corked* od *corky* **k·orken** vt [h] *to cork*

K·ormoran m ~s/~e ⟨orn⟩ *cormorant*

°**K·orkser** m ~s/~ *blunderer*

K·orn n ~(e)s/≗er **1.** ⟨allg⟩ (v Pulver, Sand, Samen etc.) *grain* ‖ Samen≗ *grain of seed* ‖ 3 ≗er Sand *three grains of sand* ‖ viele ≗er m e–n Haufen ⟨prov⟩ *many littles make a mickle* (→ ≗chen) **2.** ⟨agr⟩ [koll] (Getreide) *corn, cereals* pl; einzelnes ⟨a.⟩ *kernel* ‖ (⟨engl⟩ Weizen, ⟨Scot⟩ Hafer, ⟨Am⟩ Mais) *corn* ‖ Welsch≗ *maize* ‖ (= Roggen) *rye* ‖ Roggen u Weizen *hard corn* ‖ (Weizen) *wheat* ‖ wie schön das ~ steht! *the c. looks fine, is in good condition* ‖ ~ auf dem Halme *green c.* ‖ brandiges ~ *blasted c.* **3.** (Branntwein) *gin, whisky* ‖ ein ~ *a glass of whisky* (alt *well-matured*) **4.** (am Gewehr) *(fore-)sight,* ⟨Am⟩ *bead*; Kimme u ~ *the s.s*; gestrichen(es) ~ *medium s.*; Voll≗ *full s.*; fein(es) ~ *fine s.* ‖ aufs ~ nehmen *to s.*; *to aim at* .., ⟨mil⟩ *to s.* (*a p*); ⟨fig⟩ (sich dat) e–n aufs ~ nehmen *to mark a p, to have an eye upon*; .. *a design against a p* (⟨a.⟩ jdn auf dem ~ h); sie hat ihn sich aufs ~ genommen ⟨sex⟩ *she set her cap at him* **5.** *standard, alloy, value (of coins)* ‖ v gutem Schrot u ~ *of due weight and alloy* ‖ ⟨fig⟩ v echtem *or* altem Schrot u ~ *of the good old sort, a chip of the old block* **6.** ⟨met⟩ (im Bruch) *grain, crystal* ‖ grobes ~ *coarse g.* ‖ Probe≗ *assay g.* ‖ (kl Stück gediegenen Metalls) *button* **7.** ⟨tech⟩ (an Papier, Leder, Stein, ⟨rep⟩) *grain*; v feinem ~ *finely grained* **8.** (Uhrmacherei) *pivot-hole* **9.** **~ablader** m *wheat shoveler* **~ähre** f *ear of c., head of g.* **~anhäufung** f ⟨phot⟩ *aggregation of g.* **~art** f ⟨min, met⟩ *g.* **≗artig** a ⟨allg⟩ *like a g.,* ⟨scient⟩ *graniform* ‖ ⟨bot⟩ *like c.,* ⟨scient⟩ *frumentaceous* **~aufbau** m *granulometric composition* **~aufkäufer** m *forestaller of c.* **~bau** m *c.-growing,* ⟨Am⟩ *g.-growing; cultivation of cereals* **~beschaffenheit** f ⟨met⟩ *nature of g.* **~bildung** f (des Zuckers) *granulation* **~blei** n *assay lead* **~blume** f ⟨bot⟩ *c.-flower, bluebottle* **≗blumenblau** a ⟨scient⟩ *cyanean, cyaneous* ‖ ⟨fig⟩ *as drunk as a fiddler* od *lord,* ⟨sl⟩ *ripe; tight as a drum* **~boden** m *granary; c. loft* **~börse** f *C.-* (⟨Am⟩ *G.-*) *Exchange* **~brand** m ⟨bot⟩ *smut, blight, rust* **~branntwein** m *c.-brandy, whisky;* ⟨holl⟩ *Hollands* pl **~ernte** f *g. harvest, crop of c.* od *g.* **~fege** f *winnowing-machine* **~feld** n *c.-field* **~fliege** f ⟨ent⟩ *goatfly, c.-fly* → Gicht 2. **≗förmig** a ⟨scient⟩ *granular* **~frucht** f *cereals* pl **~grenze** f ⟨mill⟩ obere ~ *maximum g. size* **~handel** m *c.-trade* ‖ *c.-dealers* pl **~haus** n *granary* ‖ (gutes) **~jahr** n *good g. harvest* **~kaffee** m *c. coffee* **~kammer** f *granary* ⟨a. fig⟩ **~kappe** f ⟨mil⟩ *foresight cover* **~kasten** m *c.-bin* ‖ (Mühlentrichter) *hopper* **~keller** m *silo* **~land** n *c.-* ⟨bes Am⟩ *g.-growing country* **~leder** n *g.ed leather* **~mähmaschine** f *c.-harvester* **~makler** m *c.-factor* **~markt** m *c.-market* **~maß** n *c.measure* **~preis** m *price of c.* **~pulver** n ⟨mil⟩ *granulated (gun-)powder* **~rade** f ⟨bot⟩ *(c.-)cockle* **≗reich** a *abounding in cereals* **~reinigung** f *brushing of c.* | ~smaschine [f] *c.-,* ⟨bes Am⟩ *g.-cleaner; winnowing-mill* **~schrotmaschine** f *c.-bruiser* **~schwinge** f *fan* **~sieb** n *screen, winnowing-sieve* **~sieber** m (P) *screenman* **~sortierer** m (P) *flayman* **~sortierung** f *seed sorting* **~speicher** m *granary* ⟨a. fig⟩, *c. loft* **~sperre** f *embargo on c.* od *g.* **~steuer** f = ~zoll **~trockner** m *g.-dryer* **~verteilung** f ⟨mill⟩ *particle sizing, size distribution* **~waage** f ⟨agr⟩ *g.-scale* ‖ ⟨min⟩ *button-scale* **~wagen** m *c.-waggon* **~walze** f ⟨tech⟩ *toothed roller* **~weih(e f)** m ⟨orn⟩ *hen-harrier* ‖ (Weibchen) *ring-tail* **~wicke** f ⟨bot⟩ *wild vetch* **~wucher** m *profiteering* od *usurious dealing in c.* **~wurm** m *weevil* **~zähler** m *g. counting apparatus, granometer* **~zange** f *large forceps* **~zinn** a ⟨min⟩ *g.-tin* **~zehnte** m *tithe of c.* **~zins** m *c.-rent, -duty* **~zoll** m *c.-tax*

K·örn- [in comp] *granulating* **~büchse** f, **~haus** n (Pulver≗) *gr.-box, gr.-mill* **~platte** f (Leder≗) *graining-plate* **K·örnchen** n ~s/~ *grain, granule* ‖ ⟨fig⟩ *bit; g.n, element, pinch, atom* ‖ ein ~ Wahrheit *a g. of truth* ‖ *an atom of deliberation; a pinch of illustration* ‖ *not an ounce of common sense* ‖ *an ounce of practice is worth a pound of theory* **~bildung** f *granulation* **K·örnen** n ~s/ *granulation* **k·örnen 1.** vt [h] *to corn, grain, granulate (metals)* ‖ *to granulate (powder)* ‖ *to grain, shagreen (leather)* **2.** vi [h] der Weizen körnt *the wheat forms grains* | *the but-roots run to seed* **3.** (sich) ~ v/refl: *sugar granulates* **K·örner-** **≗fressend** a *granivorous* **~frucht** f *corn, grain, cereals* pl **~fritter** m ⟨tech⟩ *granular coherer* **~lack** m *seed-lac* **~leder** n *shagreen* **~mikrophon** n *granular transmitter* **≗tragend** a ⟨bot⟩ *grain-bearing,* ⟨scient⟩ *graniferous* **~zählapparat** m *kernel counting apparatus* **K·örnung** f → Korn 7. & d.

Korn·ett 1. m ~(e)s/~e ⟨mil⟩ *cornet* **2.** n

~(e)s/~e ⟨mus⟩ *cornet (-à-pistons)* **~bläser** m, **Kornett·ist** m *cornet-player*

k·örnig a *granular, granulous* (→ kernig) ‖ [in comp] .. *grained* | **≃keit** f ⟨phot⟩ *graininess*

K·örnung f ~/ *graining (of leather)* ‖ *granulation, granularity (of sugar and metals)*, → Korn, körnen

Korom·andelküste f *Coromandel (coast)*

Kor·ona f ~/–nen **1.** ⟨astr⟩ *corona* **2.** ⟨el⟩ *corona* **3.** ⟨stud⟩ *audience* | ~rthrombose [f] ⟨med⟩ *coronary thrombosis*

K·örper m ~s/~ **1.** *body*; v gesundem ~ *sound in limb and body*, .. u Geist *fit in b. and mind* ‖ ⟨phys, math, chem⟩ *(solid, liquid, gaseous) body* od *substance* ‖ ⟨chem⟩ abgeleiteter ~ *derivate* ‖ ⟨tech⟩ *fixture*: Beleuchtungs≃ *lighting f.*; Porzellan≃ *porcelain f.* ‖ Schiffs≃ *hull* ‖ menschlicher ~ *body*, ⟨cont⟩ *carcass* (→ Figur) ‖ er bebte am ganzen ~ *he shook all over* ‖ sein kl v Fieber geschüttelter ~ *its little frame battling with fever* ‖ der gesetzgebende ~ *the legislature, the legislative assembly* **2.** ⟨fig⟩ der Wein hat (viel) ~ *this is a strong-bodied wine, this is wine of a good body* **~bau** m *structure of the body*; *frame, shape, figure, make*; ⟨fam⟩ *build* ‖ v zartem ~ *delicately shaped* **~beherrschung** f *body-control* **~behinderter** m *physically disabled* od *handicapped p* **~berechnung** f *cubature* **~beschaffenheit** f *constitution* ‖ ⟨med⟩ *condition, physique* **~bildung** f *form* od *shape of the body* ‖ .. schöne ~ *(he had a) fine person* od *appearance* **≃eigen** a: ~e Reize wahrnehmend ⟨eth⟩ *proprioceptive*, → Reize **~erziehung** f *physical education* **~fülle** f *corpulence, stoutness* **~gewicht** n *bodily weight, body-weight* **~größe** f *stature, size* **~haltung** f *carriage, deportment, bearing* **~haushalt** ⟨biol⟩ *metabolism* **~inhalt** m *solid* od *cubical contents, volume* **~kraft** f *physical* od *bodily strength* **~kreislauf** m *systemic circulation* **~kultur** f *physical culture* **~lehre** f ⟨med⟩ *somatology* ‖ ⟨geom⟩ *stereometry, solid geometry* **≃los** a *bodiless, discarnate, without (a) body* ‖ ⟨fig⟩ *incorporeal* od *immaterial state* **~maß** n *stature, size* ‖ ⟨geom⟩ *cubic measure, cubature, measure of capacity*; ~e (e–r Frau) *vital statics* (z. B. 86–53–86 = *34–21–34*) **~masse** f *bulk* **~messung** f ⟨geom⟩ *mensuration of solids* **~pflege** f *personal hygiene, physical culture* | ~instinkt [m] *instinct of comfort*; ~mittel [n] *cosmetic* **~puder** m *talcum powder* **~schwäche** f *bodily weakness* **~stärke** f = ~kraft **~stellung** f *attitude* **~stimmung** f *constitution, temperament* **~strafe** f *corporal punishment* **~strumpf** m *body stocking* **~teil** m *portion* od *part* od *member of the body* **~temperatur** f *body temperature* **~übung** f *gymnastic* od *physical exercise, gymnastics* pl **~umfang** m *waistline* → –maß **~verletzung** f (schwere *grievous*) *bodily harm* od *injury* (mit tödlichem Ausgang *with fatal outcome*; ⟨jur⟩ *manslaughter, murder in the 2nd degree*) **~wärme** f *warmth of a body* ‖ *body* od *physical temperature* **~welt** f *corporeal* od *material world* **~winkel** m ⟨geom⟩ *solid angle* **~wuchs** m → ~bau **~zahl** f *solid number*

k·örperlich **A.** a **1.** ⟨physiol⟩ *bodily (pains), physical (strength, stress, fear, appetite, love)*; ⟨scient⟩ *somatic (cells, death, velocity)*; *constitutional (health)*; ~es Wohlbehagen ⟨a.⟩ *creature comforts*; ~e Beschaffenheit *physique*; ~e Ausbildung *physical training*; ~e Übung (bodily) *exercise* ‖ *corporal (toil, oath, punishment)* ‖ e–n ~en Eid leisten *to take an oath in person* ‖ **2.** (stofflich) *corporeal (being, frame; quantity, property)*; *material (substance, goods)*; *substantial, tangible (things)* ‖ ⟨phys⟩ *corpuscular (theory of light)* ‖ ⟨geom⟩ ~e Festigkeit *solidity*; ~er Inhalt *solid contents* [pl], *volume* **B.** adv **1.** s–e Arbeit reibt ihn ~ auf .. *wears him out*; sie ist ~ leidend *she suffers in body* **2.** ~ u geistig gesund *fit in body and mind* | **3.** ~-seelisch *psychosomatic* (Leiden) **4.** in diesem Bild fehlt **das** ≃**e** *this picture lacks substantiality* | **≃keit** f ~/ *corpor(e)ality, corporeity*; ⟨scient⟩ *somatism* ‖ *substantiality, materiality* ‖ *solidity*, → ~ A. 1. & 2. **K·örperschaft** f ~/~en *corporation*; ~ des öffentlichen Rechts *public corporation*; (juristische P) *body corporate*; öffentliche ~en *public bodies* ‖ ⟨Am⟩ repräsentative ~ (zur Revision der Verfassung) *Convention* ‖ ⟨Am⟩ gr ~ *trust* | **≃lich** a *corporate, collective* **~smitglied** n *corporator, member of a corporation* **~ssteuer** f *corporation profits tax*; ⟨Am⟩ *c. t.*

Korpor·al m ~(e)s/~e ⟨mil, Ger nur noch fam⟩ ⟨mar⟩ *corporal* **~schaft** f *corporalship* ‖ *squad (in barracks)* **~schaftsführer** m *corporal, leader of a squad*

Korporati·on [ts] f ~/~en **1.** = Körperschaft **2.** ⟨Ger stud⟩ *corporation*; ⟨engl⟩ *student's club*, ⟨Am⟩ *fraternity* (→ Corps, Burschenschaft etc) **korporat·iv** [i:f] a *corporate* | adv *(to go) in force (to)* **K·orps** ['ko:ə] n ~ [s]/~ [s] **1.** ⟨mil⟩ *corps* **2.** ⟨Ger univ⟩ (→ Corps, Korporation) **3.** diplomatisches ~ *diplomatic body* **~brud·er, ~bursche** m *member of a C.* **~geist** m *esprit de c.* Fr; ⟨sport⟩ *team spirit*; ⟨pol⟩ *partyspirit*; ⟨allg⟩ *loyalty* **~grenzen** f pl ⟨mil⟩ *c. boundaries* **~kommando** n *c. headquarters* **~manöver** n [mst pl] *manœuvres* pl *of an army c.* **~student** m ⟨Ger⟩ *student belonging to a C.* **~truppen** f pl ⟨mil⟩ *undivisioned units* pl **korpul·ent** a *corpulent, stout, fat, pursy* **Korpul·enz** f ~/ *corpulence, -cy, stoutness*; *fatness*; *obesity* ‖ *(the dignity of an ample) corporation* ‖ °Seine ~ ⟨hum⟩ *his corporation*

K·orpus **1.** °m ~/ ⟨fam⟩ = Körper (→ Corpus) ‖ ~ juris *law-code* ‖ ~ delicti *tangible proof* **2.** f ~/ ⟨typ⟩ *long primer* **~kul·artheorie** f *corpuscular theory (of light)*

K·orreferent m ~en/~en *assistent referee*

korr·ekt a *correct (relations), official (behaviour)* ‖ ⟨ec⟩ *orthodox* ‖ er spricht ein sehr ~es Deutsch *he speaks letter-perfect German* | **≃heit** f ~ *correctness, exactitude*; *purity, chasteness (of style)* **Korrekti·ons-** **~anstalt** f, **~haus** n *house of correction*, ⟨engl⟩ *penitentiary* (für Prostituierte) **Korrekt·iv** [i:f] n ~s/ *corrective* **Korr·ektor** m ~s/ –rekt·oren *proof-reader, press-corrector* **Korrekt·ur** f ~/~en *(proof-)correction* ‖ (Bogen) *proof(-sheet)* ‖ ~ lesen *to read (the) proofs* ‖ letzte ~ *revise, press proof* | Ausführung der notwendigen ~en *working of necessary c.ns* ⟨a. a–n⟩ **~abzug** m *rough print*; *proof(-sheet)* **~bestimmung** f *determination of c.n* **~bogen** m *first proof, proof sheet* **~fahne** f *slip proof* **~lack** m *correctine* **~lesen** n *proof-reading* **~manöver** n ⟨a–n⟩ *c.n manœuvre* **~taste** f ⟨comp, etc⟩ *error key* **~zeichen** n *reader's mark*

Kor- **~rel·at** n ~/~e *correlate, correlative* **~relati·on** [ts] f *correlation* **≃relat·iv** [i:f] a *correlative* **~repet·itor** m ~s/–tit·oren ⟨mus⟩ *opera-singer's rehearser* **≃respektiv** a *dependent* (Verpflichtungen [pl] *agreement*) **~respond·ent** m ~en/~en **1.** *correspondent* Auslands≃ (Zeitung) *foreign c.*, ⟨com⟩ *f. correspondence clerk* **2.** *business friend* **~respond·enz** f ~/~en *correspondence, -cy* ‖ e–e ungeheure ~ unterhalten *to carry on an enormous c.* ‖ s–e ~ erledigen *to write one's letters* ‖ in ~ stehen mit *to correspond with* | ~büro [n] *press-cutting agency*, ⟨Am⟩ *clipping bureau*; ~reeder [m] *ship's husband, managing owner*; ~scheck m *cheque* (⟨Am⟩ *check*) a) *received through the post*, b) *drawn by a bank on itself* **≃respond·ieren** vi [h] **1.** *to correspond* (mit *with*) ‖ mit e–a ~ *to exchange letters* ‖ ~des Mitglied *corresponding member* **2.** mit etw ~ *to correspond to a th*

K·orridor m ~(e)s/~e *corridor, gallery, passage (way* ⟨Am⟩*)* ‖ ⟨pol⟩ (Gebietsstreifen durch fremdes Land) der Polnische ~ *the Polish C.*

Kor- ≂rigierbar a *correctable, -ible* **≂rig·ieren** vt [h] *to correct* || ⟨typ⟩ (Fahnen) *to read the proofs* || (Umbruch) *to revise* || (Text) *to emend* || ⟨astr⟩ *to reduce (observations)* **≂rodierbar** a *corrodible* **≂rod·ieren** vt [h] *to corrode* **Korrosi·on** f ∼/∼en *corrosion*; ∼ verhütend *anticorrosive*; widerstandsfähig gegen ∼ *impervious to corrosion* | ≂sbeständig [a] *c.-proof, c.-resistant; noncorrosive*; ∼sbildner [m] *corroding agent* od *medium* ∼smittel [n] *corroding agent, corrosive* ∼sschutz [m] *anti-corrosion agent*; ∼sschutzverfahren [n] *rust preventing method* **≂ros·iv** [i:f] a *corrosive* **≂rump·ieren** vt [h] *to corrupt, ulcerate* || (bestechen) *to bribe* || ⟨scient⟩ –rte Stellen *spurious passages* pl **≂r·upt** a *corrupt(ed), ulcerated,* ⟨sl⟩ *rotten* **⁓rupti·on** f ∼/ *corruption,* ⟨Am sl⟩ *graft* || politische ∼ *wire-pulling,* ⟨Am⟩ *spoils* pl, *log-rolling, pipe-laying* || Aufdecker v ∼ ⟨Am sl⟩ *muck-raker* | (Bestechung) *bribery*

Kors·ar m ∼(e)s & ∼en/∼en *corsair, pirate, buccaneer*; ∼enschiff *c.r; privateer(ing vessel)*

K·orse m, **K·orsin** f *Corsican* **K·orsika** n *Corsica* **k·orsisch** a *Corsican*

Kors·ett n ∼(e)s/∼e *corset, bodice,* (ein ∼ *a pair of) stays* | ∼macher [m] *stay maker*; ∼-schnur [f] *stay-lace*; ∼stange [f] *busk, bone*

K·orso m ∼s/∼s **1.** (Festung) *corso* **2.** (Straße für Wagenparade) *course, carriage-drive*; in London: *Rotten Row*

Kor·ück m & n [invar] (= **Ko**mmandant, -do des **rück**wärtigen Armeegebiets) *Army Service Command* N

Kor·und m ∼(e)s/∼e ⟨min⟩ *corundum*

Korv·ette f ∼/∼n ⟨mar⟩ *corvette* **⁓nkapitän** m *captain of a corvette* || (Titel) *Commander*

Koryph·äe f ∼/∼n **1.** ⟨Gr⟩ *coryphaeus, leader of the chorus* **2.** ⟨fig⟩ *master-mind, authority*

Kos·ak m ∼en/∼en *Cossack*

Koschen·ille ['iljə] f ∼/ *cochineal* | ∼farbe [f] *carmine of c.* || ∼(schild)laus [f] ⟨ent⟩ *cochineal (insect)*; ∼tinktur [f] *c. tincture*

k·oscher a *kosher, clean, pure (food) according to the Jewish rite* || ⟨fam⟩ die S scheint mir nicht ganz ∼ ⟨sl⟩ *there seems to be sth fishy about it*

K·ose-, ⁓form f, **⁓name** m, **⁓wort** n *pet form, pet name, term of endearment*; ⟨scient⟩ *hypocoristic form,* etc. **k·osen** vi [h] *to make love; to fondle, caress* || *to talk lovingly* (mit *to*) || er koste mit ihr *he spooned with her* || ⟨allg⟩ *to chat, prattle* **k·osig** a *caressing, fondling (p)*; (gemütlich) *cosy; snug (room)*

K·o- ⟨math⟩ **⁓sekante** f ∼/∼n *cosecant* (abbr *cosec* **⁓sinus** m *cosine* (abbr *cos*)

Kosm·etik f ∼/ *cosmetics* | ∼er(in [f]) [m] *beautician* | ∼-Koffer [m], ∼-Tasche [f] *vanity box* od *case* **kosm·etisch** a *cosmetic*; ∼e Aufmachung, Erscheinung *make-up*; ∼er Chirurg *c.* (⟨Am a.⟩ *plastic) surgeon* (⟨Ger⟩ nicht, ⟨Am, engl⟩) staatlich geprüft); ∼e Mittel [n pl] *c.s* pl; ∼er Strumpf etc ⟨med⟩ *surgical stocking, etc*; ∼-pharmazeutische Industrie [f] *c. pharmaceutical industry*; ∼e Wiederherstellung ⟨med⟩ *c. restoration* **k·osmisch** a *cosmic(al)* || ∼er Vorgang *cosmic event* || ∼er Staub *cosmic dust* **Kosmo-** Gr **⁓drom** n ∼(e)s/∼e ⟨Russ a–n⟩ *cosmodrome* **⁓gon·ie** f ∼/∼en [i:ən] *cosmogony* **⁓gr·aph** f m ∼en/∼en *cosmographer* **⁓graph·ie** f ∼/∼n [fi:ən] *cosmography* **≂gr·aphisch** a *cosmographical (instrument)* **≂l·ogisch** a *cosmological (proof for the existence of God)* **⁓n·aut** m ∼en/∼en *cosmo-, astronaut* **⁓n·autik** f ∼/ *cosmo-, astronautics* pl **⁓p·ole** f *cosmopolis* **⁓pol·it** m ∼en/∼en *cosmopolite, cosmopolitan* **≂pol·itisch** a *cosmopolitan* **⁓polit·ismus** m ∼/ *cosmopolitism* **K·osmos** m ∼/ *cosmos, universe*

Koss·at m ∼en/∼en; **Koss·äte** m ∼n/∼n *cottager, cotter, crofter* || ⟨engl⟩ *petty farmer*

K·ost f ∼/ **1.** (Lebensmittel) *food, fare; victuals* pl; leckere ∼ *dainty food*; gute ∼ *good eating and drinking* || magere ∼ *slender fare,* ⟨med⟩ *low diet*; fette, kräftige, nahrhafte ∼ *rich diet*; knappe (magere) ∼ *spare (slender) diet*; reichliche ∼ *full diet*; schwere ∼ ⟨school sl⟩ *stodge* || bürgerliche ∼ *plain food* || fleischlose, vegetarische ∼ *fleshless, vegetarian diet*; auf schmale ∼ gesetzt s *to be on short commons* **2.** (Beköstigung) *board* || freie ∼ *free board* || ∼ u Wohnung *or* Logis *b. and lodging* od *residence* || ∼ u Lohn *b. and wages* || jdm ∼ geben, jdn in ∼ nehmen *to b. a p* || jdm ∼ u Wohnung geben *to b. and lodge a p* || in ∼ geben *to (put out to) b., to b. out* || in ∼ s bei *to b. with* **3.** ⟨**fig**⟩ *the dramatic fare of the period* || schwere ∼ ⟨sl⟩ *stodge* || s–e Schriften sind schwere ∼ *his writing is heavy going* || geistige ∼ *intellectual food* **K·ost-** ([1] → ∼, [2] → ∼en) **≂frei** a *board-free*; jdn ∼ halten *to keep a p in b.* **⁓gänger** m *pensioner, b.er*; ∼ h *to take in b.ers* **⁓geber** m *keeper of a b.-ing-house* **⁓geld** n *allowance for b.* || (der Dienerschaft) *b.-wages* pl; ∼ empfangen *to be on b.-wages* **⁓halter** m *keeper of a b.ing-house* **⁓happen** m, **⁓häppchen** n *dainty bit, titbit* **⁓haus** n *b.ing--house* **⁓schule** f *b.ing-school* **⁓probe** f *relish, sample* || ⟨fig⟩ e–e flüchtige ∼ *a smattering of* [2]**≂spielig** a *expensive, sumptuous; dear, costly* **⁓-spieligkeit** f *e.ness, d.ness, c-liness, s.ness* [1]**⁓verächter** m *fastidious* od *dainty p (as regards food)* || er ist kein ∼verächter *he is not particular* od *fastidious* **k·ostbar 1.** [a] ⟨eig⟩ *costly, expensive, sumptuous, luxurious* || (wertvoll) *priceless, precious, valuable; rich and lustrous (voice)*; ∼es Gut *treasure* || ⟨mus⟩ (of timbre) *rich and lustrous (voice)* | ⟨übtr⟩ ist das nicht ∼! *isn't that priceless, splendid, amusing*! **1.** [adv] *luxuriously, richly (dressed, furnished)* | **≂keit** f ∼/∼en *costliness, e.ness, pr.ness* || [konkr] ∼en [pl] *valuables, jewels* pl; erlesene ∼en *choice and precious things*

Kostar·ika n (in Mittelamerika) *Costa Rica*

k·osten[1] vt [h] (versuchen) *to taste (of a drink); to try (a dish, drink); to (take a) sample, try the qualities (of)* || ⟨fig⟩ *to get the taste of, to experience* || er hat die Freuden des Lebens gekostet *he has enjoyed all the pleasures of life* || sie gab ihm einige Wahrheiten zu ∼ *she gave him a few wholesome truths* || er bekam oft Prügel zu ∼ *he often got a taste of the rod*

k·osten[2] vi(!) [h] *to cost* || ⟨fig⟩ *to take, to require* || die Kleider ∼ mich (*or* mir) sehr viel *the clothes cost me a lot* | was ∼ die Äpfel? (zur Marktfrau:) *what is the price of* .. ⟨fam⟩ *how much (are* od *what are the apples)? how much (does this cost)? what do you charge for this?*; (zur Nachbarin:) *how much* od *what did you pay for .., how much did they charge you for ..*; das Buch wird .. ∼ .. *will sell at 7/6* | was kostet die Welt?! (im Übermut) *what price for the whole town*! || es koste, was es wolle! *whatever it may cost, cost what it may*!; *at whatever cost*! || was es ihn (ihm) selbst auch ∼ sollte, er würde .. *at any cost to h.s. he would do it* || es kostete ihm (ihn) einige Anstrengung z .. *it was with some effort that he ..*; .. sein Leben, s–e Stellung *it cost him his life, his position*; *illness lost him his job*; das hätte ihn sein Geschäft ∼ können *that might have put him out of business* || er ließ es sich viel Geld ∼ *he spent a great deal of money on it*; es sich etw ∼ l *to spare no expenses* | ⟨fig⟩ es wird dir (dich) den Kopf nicht ∼ *it won't cost your life* || es kostete ihn einige A. *it was with some effort that he did it*; es würde ihn viel Überredungsgabe ∼ *it would tax his arts of persuasion* || es kostete mich 5 Stunden *it took me 5 hours* || es wird 3 Stunden ∼ *it will require 3 hours* || sich [dat] etw viel Mühe ∼ l *to take much pains about, to spend much labour on a th*; es sich Geld u Mühe ∼ l *to go to the trouble and expenses*; es wird e–n schweren Kampf ∼ *that will mean a great struggle*

|| es kostet ihn nur ein Wort *it only needs a word of him*

K·osten pl *cost(s* pl), *expense(s* pl), *charges* pl || ⟨jur⟩ *c.s* || die ~ des Baus *the c. of the building* || ·Absatz–, Betr·iebs– (⟨a.⟩ *expenses for running*), S·elbst≃ des Verkaufs, Werbe≃ *distribution, operating, selling, advertising c.(s)*; Gemein≃ *general (manufacturing [and commercial]) e.s*; *factory e.s*; ~ je Stück *unit c.s* || Lager≃ *storage c.s*; Unterhaltungs≃ *c.s of maintenance* || Neben-≃ *petty ch.s, incidental e.s* || große ~ *heavy e.s* || ~, Fracht u Versicherung *c., freight and insurance* (abbr *c. i. f.*) || die Herstellungs≃ verringern *to reduce the c. of manufacture* || die ~ dieser Ausbildung *the c. of ..*; ohne ~ für sich selbst *without c. to h.s.* | die ~ auf jdn abwälzen *to pass the c.s on to a p* | (jdm) ~ **auferlegen** ⟨jur⟩ *to order .. to pay c.s*; ~ festsetzen ⟨jur⟩ *to tax c.* | die ~ **tragen,** bestreiten *bear, defray, pay the c.(s)* || die ~ zurückerstatten *to refund the e.s* || ⟨jur⟩ die ~ festsetzen *to tax the cost* || s–e ~ herausschlagen *to cover one's e.s* || jdm (sich) gr ~ m *to put a p (to go) to great e.* || k–e ~ scheuen *to spare no e.* || nach Abzug der ~ *ch.s deducted* || es lohnt die ~ *it pays* | (es geht) **auf m-e ~** *(this is) at my e.* || das war ein Witz auf m–e ~ ⟨fam⟩ *that was on me*! || es wurde auf s–e ~ gelacht *the laugh was against* (⟨Am⟩ *on) him* || er lebt auf ~ s–s Bruders *he lives* (⟨fam⟩ *sponges) on his brother* || auf ~ e–r S gehen *to take (its) toll in a th*; allzusehr .. g.d *leading to undue impairment of ..* || auf ~ der Gesundheit *at the c. of health* || auf ~ der Qualität *at the e.* od *to the detriment of quality*; *his freedom was bought at the cost of the toil of his slaves* || **auf s-e ~ k** *to make a th pay, to get at one's e.s, to get value for (one's) money, to find one's c.s repaid,* ⟨fam⟩ *to come* od *get home, to pay one's way*; *to get a kick out of a th* | **in die ~** (*or* **zu den ~**) verurteilen *to cast in the c.s* || sich in ~ stürzen *to get o.s. into e.s, to incur great e.* || **mit** *or* **unter** gr ~ *at great e.* **~abbau** m *diminution* od *lessening of cost(s)*, ⟨fam⟩ *the axe* **~anschlag** m *estimate (of c.)*; e–n ~ m *to quote* (f *for*) **~aufstellung** f *c. sheet* **~aufwand** m *expenditure, e.s* pl **~erfassung** f *c. accounting* **~ersparnis** f *saving of e.* **~erstattung** f *compensation, indemnification*; *refund(ment) of c.s* **≃fällig** a = ~pflichtig **≃frei** a *free of c.* od *e.*; ⟨com mst⟩ *clear of all ch.s* **≃los** a & adv *free (of c.* od *of ch.s), for nothing*; ~ u unverbindlich *without charge and obligation* **≃pflichtig** a & adv *with c.s* (abbr *w. c.*); e–n Anspruch ~ abweisen *to dismiss a claim w. c.* **~preis** m *c.-price, first* od *self c.*; unter dem ~ *below c., at a sacrifice* **~punkt** m *(matter of) e.*; den ~ geltend m *to urge the question of e.* **~rechnung** f *bill of c.* od *ch.s*; ⟨bes Am com⟩ *costing* **~sicherheitsleistung** f *security for the c.s* **~überschlag** m, **~v·oranschlag** m *estimate (of c.)* **~vorschuß** m *advance, ch.s* od *e.s advanced*; ⟨jur⟩ *advance of lawyer's fee*

K·oster m ~s/~ *(tea-, wine-) taster* **k·östlich I.** a **1.** *savoury, delicious, luscious, heavenly (fruit)*; *palatable, dainty, delicate (dish)*; *wonderful (dinner)*; *exquisite (food)* **2.** *delectable, pleasant*; *delightful (book), charming (humour)* **3.** (herrlich, famos) *excellent, lovely, priceless, capital*; *grateful (sleep)*; ⟨fam⟩ *(a) divine (little man)*; ⟨sl⟩ *scrummy, scrumptious* || das ist ja einfach ~! *that's delightful*; ⟨fam⟩ *that's capital, ripping*! ⟨iron⟩ *I like that*! || du bist wirklich ~ *you really are the limit*! **4.** * = kostbar **II.** [adv] *delightfully,* etc. || wir h uns ganz ~ amüsiert *we enjoyed it* od *ourselves immensely, we had great fun* | **≃keit** f ~/~en *deliciousness, savouriness, choiceness*

Kost·üm n ~(e)s/~e *costume, dress (Hamlet in modern dress)* || Damen≃ *coat and skirt*; ⟨Am⟩ *tailor-made* || *two-piece c.*; dreiteiliges ~ *ensemble* || Theater≃ *play c.* **~ball** m, **~fest** n *fancy-(dress) ball* od *party* || ⟨hist⟩ ritterliches ~ *carousel* **~-kunde** f *historical study of costumes* **~probe** f ⟨theat⟩ *dress-rehearsal, -parade* **~zeichner** m *dress designer* **~zeichnung** f ⟨theat⟩ *figurine* **köstüm·ieren** vt/refl [h] *to dress (o.s.) up*

K·ot m ~(e)s/ (S) *mud, dirt, sludge, muck, ordure, turd, mire* || (P) *excrement,* ⟨med⟩ *discharge of the bowels,* ⟨scient⟩ *excreta* L, *faeces* pl || (T) *droppings* pl *(of sparrows), dung* || ⟨hunt⟩ *fumets* pl | **mit** ~ bespritzen *to bespatter* || im ~ schleifen l *to bedraggle (one's dress)* || im ~ stekken (bleiben) *to stick in the mud* ⟨a. fig⟩ || ⟨fig⟩ in den ~ ziehen *to drag into the mire* **≃artig** a *faecal(oid)* **~bad** n *dung bath* **~ballen** m *lump of fecal matter* **~brechen** n ⟨path⟩ *stercoraceous vomiting* **~blech** n, **~flügel** m ⟨mot, cycl⟩ *mudguard, dash-board, wing,* ⟨Am⟩ *fender* **~entleerung** f *evacuation* **~fliege** f *dung-fly* **≃fressend** a ⟨zoo⟩ *coprophagous* **~grube** f *dung-hole, sewer* **~jauche** f *sump* **~kratze** f *door scraper* **~lache** f *mud-pool* **~schuhe** m pl *galoshes* pl **~schutzlappen** m ⟨mot⟩ *mud-flap* **~stein** m ⟨geol⟩ *coprolite*; ⟨med⟩ *-lith* **~stoffe** m pl *f(a)eces*; *night soil* **~wetter** n *dirty weather*

K·otangente f ~/~n *cotangent* (abbr *cot*)

Kot·au m ~s/ *ko(w)tow* || ~ m *to ko(w)tow*

K·ote[1] f ~/~n *altitude (of a place)* | ~ntafel [f] *hypsometric(al) tables* pl

K·ote[2] f ~/~n *cot, cottage*

K·öte f ~/~n (der Pferde) *fetlock-joint* | ~ngelenk [n], ~nhaar [n], ~nschopf [m] *fetlock*

K·ötel m ~s/~ *dung* od *dirts* pl *(of dogs, sheep)*

Kotel·ett n ~(e)s/~e & ~s (Hammel- u Schweine≃) *chop,* (Hammel≃ v Bug, Kalbs≃) *cutlet* | ⟨fig⟩ ~en [pl] (Backenbart) *short* od *mutton-chop whiskers* pl; *side-levers,* ⟨Am a.⟩ *s.-burns*

K·öter m ~s/~ **1.** (Hofhund) *(large) watch-dog* **2.** (rasseloser, schäbiger Hund) *cur* ⟨a. fig⟩, *pug*

Koter·ie f ~/~n ⟨mst cont⟩ *clique, set*

Koth·urn m ~(e)s/~e ⟨theat⟩ *buskin, cothurnus* || auf hohem ~ *in a lofty, majestic, tragic* (⟨iron⟩ *pompous) style*

kot·ieren vt [h] *to admit (shares) to the Stock Exchange,* ⟨Am⟩ *to list*

k·otig a *dirty, miry, muddy, mucky* || ⟨med⟩ *faecal(oid), stercoraceous*

K·otillon [–ijɔ̃, –ljɔŋ] m ~s/~s *cotill(ion)*

K·ötner m, **K·otsaß** –assen/–assen *cott(ag)er*

Kotschinch·ina n *Cochin-China*

K·ottische Alpen pl *Cottian Alps*

°**K·otz** m ~es/ so ein ~! *what a bore!, what a disgusting business*! || °~brettchen [n] (Vorhemdchen) *dicky* °**K·otze**[1] f ~/~n *puke, vomit* || ⟨fig⟩ das bringt mir die ~ hoch *that makes me sick* °**k·otzen** (a. kötzeln) vi [h] & sich ~ [h] ⟨vulg⟩ *to retch, vomit, puke*; ⟨sl⟩ *to (shoot* od *sling the) cat* || ⟨aero mot⟩ *to sp(l)utter, chuff,* ⟨Am⟩ *to conk* || jdn zum ≃ bringen ⟨fig⟩ *to make a p puke* od *sick* || es ist zum ≃ (langweilig) *it's awfully slow, it's sickening, it gives me pain in the neck,* ⟨vulg⟩ *it gives me the shits*

K·otze[2] f ~/~n **1.** *coarse cloth* || *coarse woollen blanket* **2.** *coarse great-coat* || *woollen cape* | ~nzeug [n] ⟨weav⟩ *shaggy coverlet*

K·ötzer m ~s/~ ⟨spin⟩ *cop*

Kovari·ante f ~/~n *covariant*

Kraal m [SAfr] → Kral

Kr·abbe f ~/~n ⟨zoo⟩ = Garnele *shrimp* || (Taschenkrebs) *crab*; ~n → *crab* | ⟨arch⟩ *crocket* | ⟨fig⟩ sie ist e–e kl ~ .. *a shrimp* od *dot* || .. e–e muntere ~ *a sweet little th* || ⟨allg fam⟩ *brat, urchin, imp* **Kr·abben- ≃artig** a *crablike,* ⟨scient⟩ *cancriform* **~fang** m *shrimping, shrimp-, crab-catching* **~fleisch** n *crab,* ⟨Am⟩ *crab-meat* **~-spinne** f ⟨zoo⟩ *crab-spider* **~taucher** m ⟨orn⟩ *little auk* **Kr·abbel- ~beutel** m *lucky bag,* ⟨fam⟩ *grab-bag* **~·ei** f ~/~en *crawl(ing), sprawl(ing), wriggling (motion)* | **≃n 1.** vt [h] *to tickle* | v/imps; es krabbelt mir *or* mich in den Beinen *my legs itch*;

I feel a creeping od *tickling, I have a creeping sensation* **2.** vi [s] (klettern) *to climb, scramble* (in *into*) **|** (kriechen) *to crawl, sprawl, grabble, wriggle*

kr·ach! intj *crack*!, *crash*!, *smash*!, *bang*!, *whang*! ‖ **~-bum**! ⟨artill⟩ *whizz-bang*! **Kr·ach** m ~(e)s/~e **1.** ⟨eig⟩ *crack, crash, peal*; e–n ~ tun *to give a crack*; *explosion*; *report* (*of a gun*); ⟨mil sl⟩ *crump* (*of a shell*) ‖ mit lautem ~ *with a whang*; *like a thousand bricks* **2.** ⟨com⟩ *panic, slump, crash, smash*; wir h e–n gr ~ zu erwarten ⟨sl⟩ *we are for the high jump(s)* **| 3.** (Lärm) *row, slam*; ⟨fam⟩ *pother*; (e–n gehörigen) ~ *to make a row, an awful noise*, ⟨fam⟩ *to raise hell*, ⟨sl⟩ *to kick up a row* ‖ mit ~ abhauen [vi] *to bang out* **4.** (Skandal) *dust* **|** (Streit) *row, quarrel*, ⟨sl⟩ *bust-up*; nur mit Ach u ~ *only just, with greatest trouble* ‖ ~ mit– e–a kriegen *to fall out* **~lederne** f (Hose) (*stiff*!) *leather shorts* pl **~mandel** f *shell-a., a. in the shell* **Kr·achen** n ~s/ = Krach *crack(ing)*, etc. ‖ *rattle* (*of musketry*); ⟨mil sl⟩ *crump* (*of a shell*) **kr·achen I.** vi **1.** [h] *to crack, crash*; (Dielen) *creak*; (Rakete) *to rattle*; *to burst with a loud explosion, to fulminate, explode, detonate* ‖ (Donner) *roar, crackle, peal*, (Tür) *to slam*; es –cht im Gebälk ⟨fig⟩ *sth is cracking in the seams* **2.** [s] (krachend einstürzen, zus- *or* entzweibrechen, zus–stoßen etc) *to burst* (od *split, fall*) *asunder, to fall down, collapse with a thundering* od *loud noise*; (Wagen) *to smash* (*into, against*) ‖ ~d z Stehen k *to crash to a stop* **3.** ⟨fig⟩ [s] ⟨com⟩ *to smash, crash, collapse* **II.** vt [h] **1.** *to crack* (*almonds, nuts*) **2.** v/refl ⟨fam⟩ ich habe mich mit ihm gekracht (= verkracht) *I fell out with him* **Kr·acher** m ~s/~ *banger* ‖ ⟨cul⟩ *crackling* **|** (P) °alter ~ *old buffer* od *fog(e)y*, ⟨Am⟩ *backnumber*

kr·ächzen vi/t [h] **1.** (Krähe etc) *to caw, croak* ⟨a. fig⟩ ‖ ⟨fig⟩ (laut atmen) *to wheeze* **|** (äußern) *to rasp, wheeze* ‖ ~d *hoarse, wheezy, rasping* (*voice*) **2.** = ächzen, stöhnen **3.** ≈ n ~s/ *caw(ing)*, etc

°**Kr·ack** n ~(e)s/~e, **Kr·acke** f ~/~n **1.** *jade*, ⟨Am⟩ *plug* **2.** *hovel, bothy* **3.** *young scamp*

Kr·ad n ~(e)s/≈er ⟨mil⟩ (= **Kraftrad**) *motor--cycle* **|** ~melder [m] (*m.-c*) *dispatch rider* ‖ ~-schütze [m] *m.-c. rifler* **Kr·aft** f ~/≈e **1.** *strength, force, power, might*; *vigo(u)r, vitality*; *stamina*; *fortitude, stability* ‖ **ablenkende ~** *deflecting f.* ‖ Angriffspunkt e–r ~ *origin of f.* ‖ Armes≈ *brawn, grip*, ⟨fam⟩ *elbow grease*, ⟨Am sl⟩ *punch* ‖ Aus–e–a–setzung der ≈e *show-down*; **belebende ~** *stimulating f.s* ‖ bindende ~ *bindingness*; **charakterliche ~** ⟨fam⟩ *backbone* ‖ dichterische ~ *poetic f.* od *fire* (in a work); *poetic p.s* (*of a poet*) ‖ durchbiegende ~ *deflecting f.* ‖ Durchschlags≈ ⟨mil⟩ *penetration*; **Einzel**≈ ⟨tech⟩ *single f.*; ⟨el⟩ *power*; ⟨mech⟩ *strength*; ⟨allg phys⟩ *force*; elektromotorische ~ *electromotive f.*; ⟨el⟩ *p., energy*, ~ entfalten *to energize* ‖ ⟨sl⟩ *juice* ‖ finanzielle ~ *money-p., means* **Flieh**≈ *centrifugal f.* ‖ „~ durch Freude" abbr K.d.F. ⟨nazi⟩ "*Strength through Joy*" ‖ **geistige ~** *intellectual, spiritual strength, ability*; *the requisite strength for fulfilling a duty* ‖ (geistige Frische) *vigour* ‖ (Gewalt) *power* ‖ Gesetzes≈ h *to have the f. of law* ‖ die ~ greift in e–m Punkte an *the f. acts on a point* **Hebe**≈ ⟨tech⟩ *lifting p.* ‖ heilende ~ ⟨med⟩ *healing* od *sanitive p.* od *efficacy, virtue* ‖ Heiz≈ *heating effect* **Jugend**≈ (Rüstigkeit) *youthful vigour* ‖ Koerzitiv≈ *coercitive f.* **Körper**≈ *physical st.* ‖ künstlerische ~ ⟨theat⟩ *tragic f.* ‖ lebendige ~ *inertia, vis viva* **Lebens**≈ *nerve*, ⟨fig⟩ *pith* (*of great p.*) ‖ *flush*, ⟨sl⟩ *kick*, ⟨Am sl⟩ *pep*; **magnetische ~** *magnetism, magnetic f.* ‖ magnetomotorische ~ *magnetomotive f.* ‖ (Macht) *p.* ‖ mechanische ~ = Maschinen≈ *mechanical p.s* pl ‖ mit mech. ~ versehen *to p.* ‖ mit eigener ~ ⟨mar⟩ *under her own p.* ‖ ⟨mil⟩ ≈e *f.s* pl; Flieger≈ *air formations* pl ‖ (Nachdruck) *intensity, energy*; **Nähr**≈ (*to boil all*) *the goodness* (*out of meat*); ~ u Saft *succulence*, ⟨sl⟩ *spunk* ‖ Natur≈ *natural f.*; reinigende ~ *purifying f.* ‖ Nutz≈ *effective p.* ‖ ~ e–s **Organs** ⟨med⟩ *tone* (*to lose, recover tone*) ‖ pekuniäre ~ *money-p., means* ‖ Parallelogramm der ≈e *parallelogram of f.s* ‖ **Pferde**≈ *horse-p.* ‖ ⟨phys⟩ *f.* ‖ Rede≈ *p.*, ⟨fam⟩ *punch* (*in a p's remarks*) ‖ resultierende ~ *resultant f.* ‖ Schöpfungs≈ *creative st.* ‖ Schub≈e ⟨tech⟩ *torsional f.s* ‖ schöpferische ~ (P) *genius* ‖ Seiten≈e ⟨tech⟩ *side f.s* ‖ seelische **Spann**≈ *nerve* ‖ (Stärke) *strength* ‖ treibende ~ *moving p.* ‖ *driving f.* ‖ ⟨fig⟩ die tr. ~ s v *to be at the bottom of* ‖ ~ der Überzeugung, **überzeugende ~** *the* (*st. of*) *logic*; *conviction* ‖ (Vermögen) *p.* ‖ mit voller ~ *at full steam* **Wehr**≈ *war-potential* ‖ Widerstands≈ *stamina* pl L [sg konstr] ‖ wirkende, wirksame ~ *dynamic* ‖ ⟨fig⟩ *virtue, efficacy* ‖ ⟨poet, rhet⟩ *potency* (*old passions reincarnated with a new potency*) ‖ *potency* (*of drugs, reasons*) **2. (Gültigkeit)** in ~ treten (of laws) *to become operative, effective*; *to come into operation* ‖ in ~ bleiben *to remain in f.*; in ~ l *to leave in f.* ‖ außer ~ setzen *to declare invalid, to invalidate* **3. (Geschäfts-, Arbeits**≈) (P) erste ~ *a first-rate man*; *he was a p. in his line* ‖ wertvolle ~ der Firma *a valuable servant of the firm* ‖ männliche ~ *male clerk* ‖ Arbeitskräfte *labour, hands, men* ‖ ⟨theat⟩ erste ~ *top-flight performer* ‖ ≈e *available personnel* **4. [mit verb]** alle ≈e **anspannen** *to strain every nerve* od *one's p.s to the utmost, to exert o.s. to the extreme limit of one's p.s*; alle ≈e bestens anwenden, ausnutzen *to make the most of all one's p.* ‖ → aufbieten ‖ geballte ~ *massed p.* ‖ ≈e beanspruchen *to tax the st.* (*seriously*); ihre ≈e w durch .. stark –cht *their st. is rapidly expended during movements* ‖ s–e ≈e entdecken, erkennen *to find o.s.* ‖ die ≈e der Truppe müssen frisch erhalten w *the energy .. must be conserved* ‖ m–e ≈e sind **erschöpft** *my st. is exhausted* ‖ ⟨mil⟩ ≈e vorzeitig festlegen *to tie down forces* ‖ jdm ~ geben *to sustain* od *st.en a p* ‖ er gewann neue ~ in s–m Entschluß *he got a second wind in his resolve* (*to do*) ‖ an ~ gewinnen *the Industrial Revolution slowly gathered f.* ‖ s–e meiste ~ **lagern** in: *he put most of his f. into his characters* ‖ es **nahm** einige ~ **in Anspruch** ⟨fam⟩ *it took some doing* (*to accomplish it*) ‖ Kräfte **sammeln** *to gather st.* ‖ ≈e sparen ⟨mil⟩ *to conserve st.*, spare d–e ≈e *keep your powder dry* ‖ k–e ~ der Welt wird mich überreden *wild horses will not persuade me* (*to do it*) ‖ vereinte ≈e *combined efforts* ‖ s–n Ausführungen bes ~ **verleihen** *to point one's remarks* (durch *by*) ‖ → verlieren ‖ s–e ~ versagte *his st. broke down* od *failed* ‖ s–e ~ versuchen *to try one's wings* ‖ s–e ~ e–r S widmen *to give one's energies to a th* ‖ alle s–e ≈e **zus-nehmen** *to spurt*, ⟨fig⟩ *to buck up* **5. [mit prep] am** Ende s–r ~ s *to be at one's breaking point, to be at the end of one's tether*, nahezu .. *to be about through* ‖ **aus** eigener ~ *of one's own st.*; *by the exercise of one's own faculties, under one's own steam, off one's own bat*; .. emporgek s *to be a self--made man* ‖ (sie schrie) aus allen ≈en .. *at the top of her voice, he ran with all he was worth* od *for all his w.* ‖ **außer** ~ setzen *to cancel, abolish*; *rescind* N (→ 2.) ‖ .. ab heute außer ~ *the decree has been put out of f. from today* ‖ er ist noch **bei** ≈en *he is still in possession of his full st.* ‖ **durch** ~ der Wunder Gottes *by virtue of ..* ‖ **in** ~ treten, → 2. ‖ **jenseits** der Grenze s–r ~ *beyond one's tether* ‖ **mit** aller ~ *with all one's might, with might and main, by main st.*, (*we went at it*) *hammer and tongs* od *tooth and nail, with both hands* ⟨a. fig⟩; *for all one is* (*was*) *worth*; rücksichtslos .. *to go for a th baldheaded*; er schlug ihm mit aller ~ ins G. *he slapped his face as hard as he could* ‖ mit ganzer ~ anrennen gegen *to run full tilt against* ‖ sich mit ganzer ~ f etw einsetzen *to go all-out for a th* ‖ mit starken ≈en angreifen ⟨aero⟩ *to raid in st.* ‖

mit Aufgebot s–r letzten ≈e erreichte er das Ufer *thanks to the exertion of his last ounce of st.* .. ‖ sich e–r S mit ganzer ~ widmen .. *with heart and soul* ‖ **nach** ≈en ausnutzen, benutzen *to make the best of a th* ‖ nach ≈en spielen *to play one's hardest* ‖ das Essen ist **ohne** Saft u ~ *that's a meal without either st. or flavour* ‖ ohne ~ ⟨fig⟩ *ebbed-down* ‖ über jds ≈e *beyond* (od *out of*) *a p's depth*; es ging **über** s–e ≈e *it was beyond him* od *beyond his p.s* od *means* ‖ **von** ≈en k *to lose one's st., to become feeble, to decay* ‖ wieder **zu** ≈en k *to recover* (*one's st.*); *to come to* **kr·aft** prep [gen] *by virtue of; according to* ‖ ~ des Gesetzes *in the name* od *by operation of the Law* ‖ ~ m–s Amtes *by virtue of my office* ‖ *on the st. of his recommendation* **Kr·aft- ~anlage** f ⟨tech⟩ *p.-station* od *plant* **~anstrengung** f *effort, exertion, spurt* ‖ mit **~antrieb** m *p.-driven*; *p.ed* **~artillerie** f *automotive ordnance* **~arm** m ⟨tech⟩ *p.-arm* **~aufwand** m (*expenditure of*) *energy* od *p.* od *f.* **~ausdruck** m *pithy, vigorous, racy, energetic expression, term, phrase*; ⟨fam⟩ *forcible expression*; ⟨sl⟩ *rapper* **~ausdrücke** pl *strong language* **~ausstoß** m → –stoß **~beanspruchung** f *necessary p.* **~bedarf** m *want of p., p. consumption, requisite p., p. required*; geringer ~ *low consumption of p.*; bei geringstem ~ *with a minimum of p. consumption* | ≈smäßig günstig *giving the lowest p. c.* | Maschine f **~betrieb** m *machine for p.-drive* **~brot** n *fortified bread* **~brühe** f ⟨cul⟩ *beef tea, clear soup, emergency soup*; *e. s. stock*; *consommé* Fr **~droschke** f *taxi(-cab)* **~einheit** f ⟨el⟩ *unit* (*of work*) **~entfaltung** f *push* ⟨a. mil⟩, *show-down*; mit größter ~ (*to go*) *all-out* ≈**erfüllt** a *full of st.* od ⟨fam⟩ *go*; *vigorous* **~ersparnis** f *power saving* **~erzeugung** f *generation of p.* **~fahrer** m *motorist,* (*motor*) *driver* | ~brille [f] *motor goggles*; ~hotel [n] *motor court*; ~korps [n] *motorized corps* **~fahr-** ~drehleiter [f] *mobile turn-table*; ~schule [f] *motor-school*; ~sport [m] *motoring*; ~truppe [f] *motors and military transport* (abbr *M.T.*) *service*; ~spritze [f] (Feuerwehr) *motor-engine*; ~wesen [n] *motoring, automobilism*; *automotive industry* (*engineering*); ~zeug [n] *motor vehicle*; ~zeugbau [m] *automotive* (*v. construction* od) *engineering*, ~zeug-Haftpflichtversicherungsschein [m] (internat.) *carte verte*; ~zeugindustrie [f] *aut. industry*, ~zeug-Reparaturwerkstatt [f] *m.-v. repair-shop*, ~zeugverleih [m] *hire-service*, ~zeugwesen [n] *cardom* **~feld** n ⟨el⟩ (*p.-*)*field*; elektrisches ~ *electric f.* **~flußdichte** f *flux density* **~fuhrwerk** n [koll] *motor cars* pl **~fülle** f *fulness of vigour* od *st.*; ⟨fam⟩ *push, go* **~futter** n *concentrated feed* **~gefühl** n *feel(ing) of st.* ≈**geschleppte Artillerie** f *tractor drawn artillery* ≈**gesteuert** a *p.-assisted* **~gewinnung** f *production of p.* ‖ neue ~ ⟨fig⟩ *second wind* **~karren** m *truck* **~korps** n *motorized corps* **~lafette** f *self-propelled mount* **~leistung** f *tour de f.* Fr, *feat*, ⟨sl⟩ *stunt* ‖ ⟨mach⟩ *effective work* **~leitung** f ⟨el⟩ *p. mains* **~linie** f *line of f.* | ≈**los** a *without st.*, etc; (schwach) *feeble, weak, limp*; (P) *effete*; ⟨fig⟩ (*wishy-*)*washy, enervated* (*style*) ‖ ⟨med⟩ *atonic* ‖ (matt) *languid, listless* ‖ (ungültig) *invalid, null and void*; für ~ erklären *to invalidate, cancel, abolish, annul*; ⟨bot⟩ *wilting* **~loserklärung** f *invalidation, abolishment, cancellation, annulment* **~losigkeit** f *lack of strength* od *vigour*; *feebleness*; ⟨med⟩ *atony, debility, asthenia*; ⟨fig⟩ *washiness* (*of style*) **~maschine** f *p.-engine, motor-(-engine)* **~mehl** n *starch, amylum* **~meier** m, **~mensch** m *athlete, a boy all brawn and muscle and no brain*; *live wire*; *he-man*, ⟨Am sl⟩ *tough* **~messer** m *dynamometer* **~messung** f (selbsttätige *automatic*) *load indication* **~mittel** n *efficacious remedy, p.ful means* **~omnibus** m (*motor*)*bus* **~papier** n *kraft* (*paper*) **~post** f *mail-van*; (f P) ⟨Ger⟩ *postal omnibus* **~probe** f *test of st., showdown,* (*artist's*) *feat of st., tour de f.* Fr, ⟨sl⟩ *stunt* **~quelle** f *source of power* od *energy* **~rad** n *motor-(bi)cycle*, ⟨sl⟩ *motor-bike* **~radfahrer** m *motor cyclist* **~radschützenkompanie** f *motorcycle rifler company* ≈**schlüssig** a *stress-free* (System) **~sinn** m *direction of the f.* **~spender** m ⟨tech⟩ *p.-producer* **~sprache** f *pithy* od *strong language*; *bad language* **~spiel** n *dynamics* pl **~sport** m *wrestling, weight lifting, discus*, etc **~station** f *high-p. station* **~stellung** f *p. operating* (*of signals and switches*) **~steuerung** f *boost control* **~stoff** m ⟨mot⟩ *fuel*; *petrol*, ⟨Am⟩ *gasoline*; ⟨sl⟩ *juice* („Sprit"); verbleiter ~ *leaded f.*; ~ mit Zusätzen *doped f.*; mit festem ~ antreiben *to solid-f.* | ~behälter [m] *fuel tank*; ~einspritzung [f] *f. injection*; ~ergiebigkeit [f] *f. mileage*; ~förderung [f] *f. feed*; ~gemisch [n] *f. mixture*; ~-Luft-Gemisch [n] *f.-air mixture*; ~messer [m] *petrol meter*; ~pumpe [f] *f. pump*; ~reiniger [m] *f.-strainer*; ~schnellablaß [m] *f. jettisoning system*; ~sparer [m] *f. economizer*; ~stand [m] *fuel level*; ~- u Rohölindustrie f *fuel industry*; ~uhr [f] *fuel indicator*; ~standanzeiger [m] *f. gauge*; ~verbrauch [m] *f. consumption*; ~verbrauchssatz [m] *rate of f. c.*; ~zuführung [f] *fuel feed*; ~zusatzbehälter [m] (auxiliary) *tank* **~stoß** m ⟨a–n⟩ *surge, burst* (*of p.*) **~strom** m *high p. load* | ~gerät(e pl) *p.ed appliance(s)*; ~kreis [m] *p. circuit*; ~-normverbrauch [m] *normal fuel consumption*; ~stecker [m] *p. plug* **~strömung** f *flux* **~übertragung** f *p. transmission* | ~skabel [n] *electric p. cable* **~- u Schmierstoff** m ⟨aero, mot⟩ *fuel and oil*; ~e [pl] *Petrol, Oil & Lubricants* (*POL*) **~verkehrsamt** n *Transport Office* **~verteilung** f *distribution of energy* ≈**voll** a *full of st.*, ⟨fam⟩ *of push* od *go*; *vigorous, energetic*; *p.ful, sinewy* (*style*) **~wagen** m *autocar,* (*motor-*)*car*, ⟨Am a.⟩ *automobile* ‖ ⟨mil⟩ (Truppen) im ~ verladen, in den ~ einsteigen *to embus* ‖ gel·ändegängiger ~ *cross--country car* ‖ Verkehrs≈ *motor-coach* ‖ Klein≈ (dreirädriger) *cycle-car* ‖ → Sportzweisitzer etc) ‖ Last≈ *motor-lorry* | ~bau [m] *building of motor cars*; ~industrie [f] *motor car industry*; ~kolonne [f] ⟨mil⟩ *mechanical transport column*, ⟨allg⟩ *c. of motor vehicles*; ~lastzug [m] *motor freight car train* **~werk** n *p.* od *generating station*; *central electric st.* **~wort** n *forcible expression* ‖ ~s [pl] *strong language* **~wurz** f = Pestwurz **~zentrale** f ⟨el⟩ (*central*) *p.-station* ≈**zeugtechnisch** a *automotive* (Versorgung) **~zug** m *mechanical transport*; *p. traction* **~zugmaschine** f *tractor*

Kr·äfte- ~bestimmung f ⟨tech⟩ *stress analysis* **~gleichgewicht** n *equilibrium of f.s* **~gruppe** f feindliche ~ *enemy group* **~paar** n *couple of f.s* **~parallelogramm** n *parallelogram of f.s* **~plan** m *stress diagram* **~verbrauch** m *exhaustion of strength*; ⟨mil⟩ *expenditure of combat st.* **~verfall** m ⟨path⟩ *marasmus* **~verhältnisse** n pl *proportion of f.s*; ⟨mil⟩ *relative combat p.* **~verteilung** f ⟨tact⟩ *distribution of f.s*; *tactical grouping* **~zerlegung** f *resolution of f.s* **~zersplitterung** f ⟨tact⟩ *splitting--up* od *dissipation of f.s* **~zustand** m *physical condition* **kr·äftig** a **1.** *strong, brawny, hearty, hardy, rugged, stout*, ⟨Am⟩ *meaty, husky* (*fellow*); *strapping* (*fellow, girl, wench*); *vigorous* (*blow*), ein ~er Junge (Stammhalter) *a healthy boy* ‖ (energisch) *energetic, vigorous* ‖ (mächtig) *powerful, mighty* ‖ (wirksam) *efficacious* ‖ *staunch* (*supporter*) ‖ ⟨cul⟩ *nourishing*; *rich* (*soup*); *potent* (*drink*), *stiff* (Grog); etw ≈es (Schnaps) *sth short*; *square* (*meal*) ‖ ⟨tech⟩ *rigid* (Stahl), *robust* (Lager) ‖ ~er Ausdruck *forcible expression* ‖ ~er Fluch *round oath* ‖ ~e Ausdrucksweise *bold*, ⟨hum⟩ *doughty language* ‖ *rude* (*health*); *sturdy* (*children*); *buxom* (*lass*); *hefty* (*pony*); ⟨phot⟩ *vigorous, hard* (*shadow*) | ich werde einmal ein ~es Wörtlein mit ihm reden *I shall speak to him very energetically*, ⟨fam⟩

I shall haul him over the coals || sich ~ genug fühlen für .. *to feel up to ..* | [adv] ~ gebaut *solidly* od *powerfully built* (*man*) || (*to sing*) *lustily, heartily* || aber ~! *with a vengeance!*, ⟨sl⟩ *with knobs on* **2.** (gültig) *valid* | **~en** vt [h] *to strengthen, to invigorate*, ⟨fig⟩ *to buttress* | **sich** ~ v/refl *to gain strength*; sich durch Ruhe ~ *to rest up*; sich wieder ~ *to recover* (*strength*) | **~er w** *to gain power*, etc | **~̈keit** f **1.** *strength, powerfulness, vigour; energy* **2.** *validity* (*of an objection*), ⟨jur⟩ (*of a marriage*) | **~lich** adv = kräftig adv | **~̈ung** f *strengthening, invigoration* | ~s-mittel [n] *tonic*

Kr·ag- ⟨arch⟩ ~arm [m] *jib arm*; ~stein [m] *stone corbel* od *bracket*; ~stück [n] *ancon, corbel*; ~stütze [f] *bracket support*; ~träger [m] *overhung girder* **kr·agen** vi/t [h] dieser Stein kragt aus *this stone juts out* (*from the wall*) | ich krage den Stein aus *I make the stone jut out* **Kr·agen** m ~s/~ **1.** ⟨eig⟩ *collar* [⟨dim⟩ Kr·ägelchen [n] ~s/~, Pelz- *or* Spitzenkrägelchen f Damen *collaret*(*te*)] || Exerzier~̈ ⟨mar⟩ *blue c.* || Gummi~̈ *india rubber c.* || Hemd~̈ *shirt-c.* || Leinen~̈ *linen* od *white c.* || Mast~̈ ⟨mar⟩ *mast coat* || Matrosen~̈ *sailor collar* || Ministranten~̈ *cape, collar* || Rock~̈ *c.* || Schulter~̈ der katholischen Priester *amice* || Steh~̈ (*stiff*) *stand-up c.*; ⟨ec Engl⟩ *dog-c.* || Stehumlege~̈ (*stiff*) *double c.* || Talar~̈ *tippet* (→ Herrensporthemd) || umgedrehter, hinten schließender ~ *reversed c.* || Umhänge~̈ f Damen *cape*, .. aus Pelz *fur cape, tippet, wrap of fur* | jdn beim ~ packen *to collar a p* **2.** ⟨fig⟩ mit Kopf u ~ *neck and crop*; *to lose neck and crop* || °er packte ihn beim Krips (= Hals) u ~ *he got him by the scruff of his neck* od *by the throat* || es kann ihm Kopf u ~ kosten, es kann ihm an den ~ gehen *it might be a matter of life and death to him, it might cost him his job* od *life* || °da platzte mir der ~ *I flew off the deep end, my tail was out, I flew off the handle* **~bolzen** m (Schmiede) *c.-bolt* **~eidechse** f ⟨zoo⟩ *frill-lizard* **~ente** f *harlequin* **~knopf** m *stud*, ⟨Am⟩ *c. button* **~mantel** m *cloak with cape* **~patte** f *collar patch* **~schoner** m *scarf, muffler* **~spiegel** m ⟨mil⟩ *c. patch* **~stäbchen** n *c. bone*

Kr·ähe f ~/~n ⟨orn⟩ *crow*; Nebel~̈ *hooded c.*; Saat~̈ *rook* || ⟨prov⟩ e–e ~ hackt der andern die Augen nicht aus *dog won't eat dog, there's honour among thieves* || die ~ sagt, daß der Rabe krächze *the pot calls the kettle black* **kr·ähen** vi [h] *to crow* | v/refl; sich heiser ~ *to c. o.s. hoarse* | vt; jdn aus dem Schlafe ~ *to rouse a p by c.ing* | ⟨fig⟩ (*of children*) *to scream* || mit ~der Stimme *with a hoarse voice* || es kräht kein Hahn danach *nobody troubles about it* || du hast zu früh gekräht *you have boasted too soon* **Kr·ähen-** **~̈artig** a ⟨scient⟩ *corvine* **~auge** n (Brechnuß) *nux vomica* **~beere** f ⟨bot⟩ *c.berry* **~̈förmig** a ⟨scient⟩ *corviform* **~fuß** m *c.'s foot* **~füße** m pl **1.** *pot-hooks and hangers* pl **2.** (Runzeln in den Augenwinkeln) *wrinkles* ⟨fam⟩ *c.'s feet* pl **3.** (schlechte Schrift) *scrawl* **~horst** m *c.'s nest, rookery* **~hütte** f = Aufhütte **~nest** n **1.** = ~horst **2.** ⟨fig mar⟩ (Ausguck) *c.'s nest* **~-scharbe** f ⟨orn⟩ *shag* **~vögel** m pl → *crow* **Kr·ähwinkel** n *Gotham* (vgl Kotzebue „Die deutschen Kleinstädter"), ⟨Am⟩ *Podunk* **Krähwinkel·ei** f ~/~en *parochial politics* pl **Kr·ähwinkler** m ~s/~ ⟨fam⟩ *Gothamite, wise man of Gotham, narrow-minded Philistine*

Kr·ain n/npr *Carniola* | **~er** m *Carniolan*

Kr·akau n/npr *Krakow* | ~er(in [f]) m *Krakowian*; → Krakowiak

Kr·ake m ~n/~n; **Kr·aken** m ~s/~ **1.** (Kopffüßer) ⟨zoo⟩ *cuttlefish, octopus* **2.** (Riesen~̈) *kraken*

Krak·eel m ~(e)s/~e *violent quarrel, brawl, tiff, squabble* || (Lärm) *hubbub, noise*, ⟨fam⟩ *row*, ⟨sl⟩ *bobbery* | **~̈en** vi [h] ⟨fam⟩ *to kick up* (od *make*) *a row, to brawl*; ⟨sl⟩ *to* (*tow-*)*row* || *to be boisterous* od *noisy* || *to use abusive language* | **~er** m ~s/~ ⟨fam⟩ *cantankerous* od *quarrelsome fellow, brawler, rowdy; fusser, fuss-box, fuss-pot* | **~̈erisch** a *cantankerous, quarrelsome*

Kr·akel- **~beine** n pl, **~füße** m pl *scrawl* | **~̈n** vi [h] **1.** *to scribble, scrawl* **2.** *to croak* ⟨a. fig⟩ **Krakel·ee** n ~s/~ *crackled glaze* | **~-** *crackle* (*china, glass*)

Krak·owiak m ~s/ (Tanz) *Cracovienne*

Kral m ~s/~e *kraal*

Kr·alle f ~/~n **1.** (Raubtier~̈) *claw* ⟨a. fig⟩ **2.** ⟨orn⟩ *pounce, talon* **3.** ⟨fig⟩ (Hand) *clutch*; ich werde ihm schon die ~n zeigen *I'll show him what's what* **4.** ⟨tech⟩ *claw, clutch* | **~̈n** vi/t [h] *to claw, pounce, clutch* | sich an etw ~ *to hold on to a th* (*by the claws*, etc.), *to cling to a th* **Kr·allen-** ⟨med⟩ *claw* (*foot, hand*) **kr·allig** a *clawed* || scharf~ *with sharp claws*

Kr·am m ~(e)s/~̈e **1.** (**~handel**) *retail* (*trade*) **2.** (**~laden**) *retail-shop, general-store, haberdasher's shop*, ⟨Am⟩ *corner-shop* || *booth, stall, stand*; ⟨vulg⟩ *swag-shop* **3.** ⟨dial⟩ *fair* **4.** (**Ware**) *commodities* pl, *small wares* pl; *grocery, haberdashery, hardware* **5.** (**Plunder**) *stuff, odds and ends, oddments; rubbish, lumber* || der ganze ~ *the whole lot* od *bag of tricks* od *caboodle* ⟨a. fig⟩ **6.** ⟨fig⟩ (**Angelegenheiten**) s–n ~ verstehen ⟨fam⟩ *to know one's onions* || das paßt mir gerade in m–n ~ *or* mir in den ~ *that suits my book* od *purpose* || es paßt mir nicht in m–n ~ ⟨fam⟩ *that won't do at all for me* || jetzt paßt es ihm nicht mehr in den ~ *now the shoe is on the other foot* || er hat den ganzen ~ verdorben .. *the whole business* od *lot* || mach doch k–n ~ *don't* (*make any*) *fuss* **~bude** f → Kram 2. **~laden** m → Kram 2. u 3.

°**Kramb·ambuli** m ~/ (Danziger Kirsch etc) *liquor, spirits, booze* || (Sekt) *sham*

kr·amen vi [h] *to rummage, fumble* (in, unter *in*) || nach etw ~ *to hunt* (*about*) *for a th* || sie hat etw zu ~ *she's busy putting things* (*from one place to the other* od) *in order* **Kr·ämer** m ~s/~ (*rural*) *shopkeeper, retailer, haberdasher; grocer, general dealer*, ⟨Am⟩ *merchant; huckster* | **~in** f ~/~nen *trades woman* **~geist** m *shoppiness* || (P) *huckster* **~gewicht** n *avoirdupois* (*weight*) **~̈haft** a *shoppy, mercenary* **~herrschaft** f *shopocracy* **~innung** f *mercers'* (*grocers'*) *guild* od *company* **~laden** m *retail shop*, (Dorf~̈) *general shop* **~pfund** n *pound avoirdupois* **~seele** f ⟨derog⟩ *merchant* od *any p with low business ethics* **~volk** n *nation of shopkeepers, pettifoggers* pl **~waage** f *common scales* pl **~waren** f pl *chandlery, groceries* pl, *mercery*, → Kram 4. **Krämer·ei** f ~/~en *shopkeeping, retail trading* || (Laden) *retail-shop, general shop* → Kram

Kr·ammetsvogel, Kramts- m ⟨orn⟩ *fieldfare*

Kr·amme, Kr·ampe f ~/~n ⟨carp⟩ *cramp*(*-iron*), ⟨el⟩ *staple* || mit ~n befestigen *to cramp, staple* **Kr·ampf** m ~(e)s~̈e **A.** *cramp* || ⟨med⟩ *spasm, convulsion* || in ~̈e verfallen *to go off into convulsions* || ~̈e h *to have an attack of spasms, to be seized with a cramp* || *he had a crick in his neck* || Mittel gegen ~̈e *antispasmodic*, → Lach~̈ **B.** °⟨fig⟩ **1.** *effort for effect*, ⟨fam⟩ *fuss*; er macht ~ *he fusses* **2.** er geht auf ~ aus *he's out for mischief* **3.** ⟨mil sl⟩ er nahm Urlaub auf ~ *he took leave without permission*, ⟨sl⟩ *he went* AWOL (= *absent without official leave*) **~ader** f *varicose vein*, ⟨scient⟩ *varix* **~̈ad(e)rig** a *varicose* **~aderbruch** m *varicocele* **~anfall** m *convulsive seizure* **~̈artig** a *spasmodic; gusty* (*cough*) **~fisch** m ⟨ich⟩ *cramp-fish* **~husten** m *spasmodic* od *gusty cough* **~̈lösend** a *antispasmodic* **~mittel** n ⟨med⟩ *antispasmodic, a. remedy* **kr·ampfhaft** **1.** [a] *spasmodic, convulsive* || ~ Anstrengungen m *to make strenuous efforts* ⟨sl⟩ *to tie o.s. into knots*; ~es Lachen *convulsive* od *sardonic laugh, hysterical laughing-fit* **2.** [adv] (oft:) *immensely, pain-*

fully, awfully; with immense, strenuous efforts; ~ schluchzen *to shake with sobs;* ~ schlucken *to swallow hard;* (Gesicht) ~ verziehen *to cramp, to work (with emotion);* mit ~ zuckendem Gesicht *with his face twitching;* (Hand) ~ drücken *to clutch*

Kr·ampen m ~s/~ (Spitzhacke) *pick(-ax[e])*

Kr·ampus m ~ses/~e [österr] *St. Nicholas' Devil Servant*

Kran m ~(e)s/~e & ≗e **1.** (Zapfhahn) *tap* **2.** (Hebemaschine) *crane;* mit dem ~ heben *to crane (up), to hoist up with a crane;* Ausleger≗ *jib c.;* Beschickungs≗ *charging c.;* Dr·eh≗ *slewing* od *revolving c.;* f·ahrbarer ~ *travelling c.;* Gr·eifer≗ *c. with crab gear;* Handlauf≗ *travelling c. operated by hand;* H·ellingdr·eh≗ *slipway c.;* K·abel≗ *cableway c.;* Kons·ol≗ *bracket* od *wall c.;* Lauf≗ *travelling c.;* Mont·age≗ *erecting c.;* Pr·atzen≗ *claw c.;* Sch·eren≗ *shear legs c.;* Schw·enk≗ *slewing c.;* Schw·imm≗ *floating c.;* T·urmdr·eh≗ *tower revolving c.;* Verl·ade≗ *handling c.;* Vers·atz≗ *shifting c.;* Wagg·on≗ *derrick wagon c.* **~anlage** f *crane installation* **~arm** m, **~ausleger** m *c. beam* od *jib* **~ausladung** f *outreach of a c.* **~führer** m *c. driver* **~geld** n *cranage* **~gerüst** n *gantry* **~katze** f *crab* **~l·aufkatze** f *c. travelling crab* **~meister** m *crane operator* **~recht** n *cranage* **~schiff** n, Bergungs≗schiff *salvage c. ship* **~ständer** m *c. beam* **~wagen** m ⟨rail⟩ *gantry truck, derrick car*

×**Kr·anewitter** m ~s/ [österr] (Wacholderschnaps) *gin*

kr·ängen vi [h] das Schiff krängt (= neigt sich zur Seite) .. *heels (over), lists, careens* **Kr·ängung** f ~/~en *tilt, heel(ing)* | ~sausgleich [m] *heeling compensation*

Kr·anich m ~(e)s/~e ⟨orn⟩ *crane* (trompetet *trumpets*) ≗**artig** a ⟨scient⟩ *gruiform* **~hals** m *c.'s neck* **~jagd** f *c.-shooting* **~schar** f *flock of c.s* **~schnabel** m ⟨eig⟩ *c.'s bill* ‖ ⟨bot⟩ *stork's-bill, pelargonium* **~vögel** m pl ⟨orn⟩ *gruidae* pl L

Kranio- **~l·og(e)** m *craniologist* **~log·ie** f ~/ (Schädelkunde) *craniology* ≗**l·ogisch** a *craniological* **~metr·ie** f ~/ *craniometry*

kr·ank a **1.** *ill* [= nur pred] a) [pred] er ist ~ *he is ill,* ⟨Am⟩ *sick* ‖ b) [attr] *sick* (**an** Fieber *of a fever*) | der ~e Mann am Bosporus *The Sick Man* (= Türkei) ‖ chronisch ~ *sickly* ‖ (Körperteile mst:) *diseased (heart, mind)* ‖ *bad, sore (tooth)* ‖ *ailing (head) afflicted (mind); stricken (heart);* ~ **an** .. *afflicted with, suffering from (neuralgia)* ‖ (leidend) *in bad* od *ill health,* ⟨fam⟩ *poorly, out of sorts* ‖ ⟨poet⟩ *languid* **2.** [mit verb] ~ w *to fall ill, to be taken ill* ‖ sich ~ fühlen *to feel ill* [nicht: *sick*!] od *indisposed* ‖ ~ darniederliegen *to be confined, to be laid up (with)* ‖ sich ~ stellen *to sham* od *feign illness, to pretend (to be ill),* ⟨mil⟩ *to malinger,* ⟨sl⟩ *to swing the lead* ‖ plötzlich ~ w *to be overtaken by sickness* ‖ sich ~ melden ⟨mil⟩ *to go* od *report sick* ‖ ~ schreiben ⟨mil⟩ *to enter in* od *put on the sick-list* ‖ jdn ~ m ⟨sl⟩ *to give a p the pip* ‖ ⟨fig⟩ ~ m: *that was what ailed India* ‖ ~ schießen ⟨hunt⟩ *to tailor (a hare), to mangle (game) in shooting* ‖ ich habe mich ~ gelacht *I split my sides with laughing* ‖ sich ~ essen *to overeat o.s.* ‖ .. wurde ihr ~ *(her maid) went ill on her* **3.** [mit prep] **an** der Leber ~ s *to be troubled with one's liver* ‖ am Fieber ~ s *to be down* od *laid up with a f.* ‖ an Leib u Seele ~ *diseased in mind and body* ‖ an den Nerven ~ *unstrung* ‖ ⟨fig⟩ ~ am Geldbeutel *short of cash,* ⟨fam⟩ *low in funds, hard up* ‖ **auf** den Tod ~ s *to have a fatal disease* ‖ **nach** jdm *or* etw ~ s *to be yearning for ..* ‖ **vor** Anstrengung ganz ~ s *to be ill with overexertion* | **~meldung** f ⟨mil⟩ *sick report* **Kr·anke** m [ein ~r, der ~] ~n/~n *sick(ly) p, patient* ‖ Lepra≗ *leprous patient* **Kr·änke** f ~/ **1.** ⟨path⟩ = Fallsucht **2.** ⟨fig⟩ °das ist rein um die ~ zu kriegen! *it's enough to drive one mad!* ‖ daß dich die ~! *plague on it!*

kr·änkeln **1.** vi [h] *to be (f)ailing, sickly, suffering, of indifferent health; to sicken;* ⟨fam⟩ *to be poorly* od *out of sorts* ‖ sie begann zu ~ *her health began to decline* od *to give way* **2.** ≗ n *sickliness, poorliness; failing* od *indifferent health* | **~d** a *valitudinarian* **kr·anken** vi [h] (an [dat]) *to be ill* od *afflicted (with), to suffer (from)* ‖ *to be for ever ailing* ‖ ⟨fig⟩ *the business suffers from lack of organisation* ‖ die S –kte daran, daß .. *the difficulty was that ..*

kr·änken **1.** vt [h] (betrüben) *afflict,* (stärker:) *grieve* ‖ (ärgern) *vex, annoy* ‖ (erzürnen) *irritate, anger;* jdn ~ ⟨fam⟩ *to rub a p the wrong way* ‖ (beleidigen) *offend, huff* ‖ (verletzen) *injure; hurt, wound (a p's feelings);* das wird ihn nicht lange ~ *he won't let it hurt him long* ‖ (demütigen) *humble, mortify* ‖ ⟨fig⟩ *to bite* | **~d** *offensive (remark); cutting, galling* (f .. *to a p*) ‖ auf **~de** Art *insultingly,* etc. | **gekränkt** *injured (innocence);* er hat ihn tief *or* sehr ge–kt *he has offended,* etc. *him deeply;* das hat .. *it cut him to the quick;* sich ge–kt fühlen *to feel aggrieved, hurt, mortified, sore (about* über); er ist leicht ge–kt *he is easily offended* od *huffed, he is very touchy;* °sie spielt die ge–kte Leberwurst *she sulks* | [abs] das k–kt *that hurts* | v/imps **es kränkt mich, daß ..** *it annoys, grieves, mortifies me that ..; it is (gall and) wormwood to him* | [mit prep] jdn **an** *or* **in** s–r Ehre ~ *to injure a p's honour;* jdn an *or* in s–n Rechten ~ *to encroach upon* od *to infringe a p's rights;* er fühlte sich **in** s–m Ehrgeiz gekränkt *he felt aggrieved in his ambition; he is wounded in his pride;* jdn **um** etw ~ *to deprive a p of a th,* ⟨sl⟩ *to make a p shell out (money)* ‖ er hat mich um 100 Mark ge–kt *he has lightened me to the extent of a fiver* **2. sich** ~ = sich grämen

Kr·anken- **~anstalt** f *hospital* **~auto** n *ambulance (car)* **~bahre** f *stretcher, litter;* ⟨Ind⟩ *doolie, -ly;* fahrbare ~ *rolling litter* **~baracke** f *barrack hospital* **~behandlung** f *treatment of sick* **~bericht** m *bulletin; case notes* od *record* od *report; hospital-,* ⟨mil⟩ *sick-report* **~besuch** m *call on an invalid,* ⟨med⟩ *(medical) visit, attendance* ‖ ⟨ec⟩ *visitation of the sick* | ~e [pl] *sick visiting;* ~ston [m] *bedside manner* **~bett** n *sick-bed* ‖ ans ~ gefesselt s *to be bedrid(den)* od *confined to one's bed* ‖ vom ~ aufstehen *to have recovered from an illness* **~blatt** n *clinical record* **~buch** n *visiting-book* **~diät** f *invalid (low) diet* **~ernährung** f *sick diet* **~geld** n *sick-allowance, -benefit, -pay* **~geschichte** f *case medical history* **~gut** n ⟨scient med⟩ *patients* pl *(in hospital)* **~haus** n *hospital, infirmary* ‖ jdn in e m ~ unterbringen, ins ~ bringen, überweisen *to hospitalize a p;* er mußte ins ~ *he had to be hospitalized;* im ~ liegen *to be h.d, to lie in hospital* ‖ er starb im ~ *he died in h.* ‖ im ~ wohnender Arzt *interne* ‖ Ausschuß für Sammlungen für Krankenhäuser *begging staff* | ~arzt [m] (dort wohnend) *resident physician;* ~aufnahme, ~einweisung, ~fürsorge [f] *hospitalization;* ~kostenversicherung [f] *hospital (costs insurance* od) *plan* **~kasse** f *sick-fund, health insurance, medical plan;* ~n [pl] ⟨allg⟩ *agencies of the National Health Insurance Plan:* zuständige Pflicht≗ *appropriate agency of .., Local H. I. Commission,* Betriebs≗ *plant* od *company h. i. fund,* Ersatz≗ *substitute h. i. (co-operative) society,* Innungs≗ *guild h. i. fund* | ~narzt [m] *panel doctor;* Liste der ≗e *panel;* Versicherungsschein für die ~ *insurance card;* ~npatient [m] *panel patient;* ~nschein [m] *insurance card; medical card* **~kost** f → –diät; flüssige ~ *slops* pl; ~ bek *to go on slops* **~kraftwagen** m *ambulance* N **~lager** n *sick-bed;* ans ~ Gefesselter *(he is a) shut-in* (wegen *from*) **~liste** f ⟨mil⟩ *sick-list* **~pflege** f *nursing;* freiwillige ~ *voluntary organization in aid of the sick and wounded* | ~artikel [m pl] *hospital requisites;* ~r [m] *sick warder, trained male nurse, ambulance-man, hospital attendant,* ⟨mil⟩

sick berth attendant; ~rin f = -schwester **~revier** n ⟨mil⟩ *dispensary* **~saal** m *ward* **~sammelstelle** f *casualty collecting point* **~schein** m *doctor's certificate*; *medical card* **~schiff** n ⟨mar⟩ *hospital-ship* **~schwester** f (*h.*) *nurse* **~station** f *ward* **~stube** f *sick-room*; (in Anstalten, Kasernen etc) *infirmary* **~stuhl** m *invalid chair*; fahrbarer ~ *bath-chair, motor-chair* **~tasse** f *sickfeeder* **~trage** f = ~-bahre, ⟨mil⟩ *ambulance* **~träger** m ⟨mil⟩ *stretcher bearer, ambulance-man, first-aid man* | ~einheit [f] ⟨mil⟩ *collecting company* **~transport** m *ambulance-service* **~urlaub** m *sick leave* **~verschlag** m ⟨mar⟩ *sick-bay* **~versicherung** f *prepaid medical plan* od *insurance*; *health-* od *sick-insurance*; ⟨soc⟩ *National Health Insurance Plan* | ~sberechtigte(r), (~spflichtige[r]) *p for whom enrolment in the N. H. I. P. is optional* (.. *compulsory*) | ~sschein [m] (*health-*)*insurance card* **~versorgung** [f] f Alte u Arbeitslose ⟨Am⟩ *medicare* **~wagen** m *ambulance* (*car*) **~wärter** m *medical attendant*, (*male*) *nurse*; (im ~haus) *hospital nurse*; ⟨mil⟩ *h. orderly* **~zelt** n *h. tent* **~zimmer** n *sick-room* **~zusatzversicherung** f *supplementary sickness insurance* **Kr·ankfeiern** n *industrial absenteeism* **kr·ankhaft 1.** [a] *morbid, abnormal, diseased* (*appetite, imagination*), *distempered* ⟨a. fig⟩ ‖ ⟨path⟩ *pathological, morbid* (*state of mind, feeling*; ⟨a. fig⟩: *desire, ideas*) ‖ *insane* (*conditions*) ‖ *depraved* (*character, morals*) ‖ *irregular* (*pulse*) ‖ *abnormal* (*imagination, ambition*) **2.** [adv] *psychopathically* (*intense hatred*) ‖ es ist ~ bei ihm, sich (über alles) aufzuregen *he is morbidly inclined to get excited* ‖ *morbidly* (*consciencious, ambitious*) **⁓igkeit** f *morbidity, morbidness, depravity, diseased state* ‖ *abnormality* **Kr·ankheit** f ~/~en *disease, illness, malady* ⟨a. fig⟩; ⟨fig⟩ *ague* ‖ (bes Übelkeit) *sickness*; (chronische ~) (*chronic*) *disease, complaint*; leichtere ~ *ailment, indisposition*; ⟨vet⟩ *distemper* ‖ ⟨bot⟩ *disease* (*in plants*) ‖ ernste, schwere ~ *severe, serious*, bösartige ~ *malignant illness, etc*; langwierige ~ *lingering illness*; schleichende ~ *creeping disease*; akute ~ *acute d.*, ansteckende ~ *contagious d.* ‖ Berufs⁓ *occupational d.* ‖ englische ~ *rickets* pl; ~n [pl] der Schwangerschaft, bei Entbindung u im Wochenbett *diseases connected with pregnancy, delivery, and the puerperism* | sich [dat] e–e ~ **holen** *or* **zuziehen** *to contract a d.* ‖ e–e ~ bek *to catch an illness, to fall* od *to be taken ill* ‖ an e~r ~ leiden, darniederliegen *to suffer from, to be laid up with a d.* ‖ an e–r ~ sterben *to die of a d.* od *of an illness* ‖ von e–r ~ genesen *to recover from a d.* ‖ er hat viele ~en durchgemacht *he has gone through many illnesses* ‖ in N. ist e–e ~ ausgebrochen *an epidemic has broken out at N.* ‖ e–e ~ verursachen *to induce a d.* **Kr·ankheits- ~anfall** m *fit, attack* (*of illness*) **~anlage** f *cachexy*; erbliche ~ *taint* **~bericht** m *doctor's report, bulletin* **~beschreibung** f ⟨scient⟩ *pathography* **~erreger** m ⟨scient⟩ *morbific agent*; *pathogenic, disease, infectious germs* pl; *virus* L **⁓erregend** a *pathogenous* **~erscheinung** f *symptom*; Gruppe v zus–gehörigen ~en *syndrome* **~fall** m *case* (*of illness*); in ⁓en angewandt *applied in illness* **~geschichte** f *history of an illness* **~gift** n *virus* L **⁓halber** adv *owing to* od *on account of* od *through illness* **~herd** m *central seat of a disease, d. focus*; *nidus* L **~keim** m *disease-germ* **~stoff** m *morbid* od *contagious matter, poisonous miasma* **~symptom** n *symptom* ‖ fünf **~tage** m pl *5 days of illness, 5 sick days* **~übertragung** f *contagion, infection* **~urlaub** m *sick-leave* **~verlauf** m *progress of an illness* **~wechsel** m *crisis* **~zeichen** n *symptom* | ~lehre [f] *symptomatology* **~ziffer** f *morbidity* **~zustand** m *state of disease* ‖ (vgl Kranken-) **kr·änklich 1.** [a] *weak in* od *of health, w.ly, sickly, ailing, unhealthy, valetudinarian*; ~ s *to be in ill health*; ~e Menschen *valetudinarians* pl ‖ ~es Kind *peaky child* ‖ ⟨fam⟩ *poorly, shaky, seedy* **2.** [adv] ~ aussehen *to look poorly, peaky, seedy, faintly ill*, etc | **⁓keit** f *sickliness, infirmity, weak state of health, ill h.*, ⟨fam⟩ *seediness, shakiness*, etc. **Kr·änkung** f ~/~en (→ kränken) *vexation, grievance, annoyance, mortification, offence, injury* ‖ kl, schwere ~en [pl] *petty, grievous wrongs* ‖ etw als tiefe ~ empfinden *to be depply hurt, offended by a th*; e–e ~ erfahren *to sustain an injury* ‖ e–e ~ wortlos hinnehmen *to sit down under an injury, to take it lying down* ‖ jdm e–e ~ zufügen *to wrong, offend, mortify, injure a p*

Kranz m ~es/⁓e *wreath, garland* ‖ (um den Kopf) *chaplet*; ~frisur *chaplet coiffure, chaplet of plaited hair* ‖ Advents⁓ *Advent g.* ‖ Ernte⁓ *harvest w.* ‖ Feigen⁓ *string of figs*; (Gebäck) *wreath* ‖ (Gesims) ⟨arch⟩ *cornice* ‖ Jungfern⁓, Braut⁓ *bridal w.*; ⟨fig⟩ *virginity* ‖ Dreh⁓ ⟨artill⟩ *revolving gun mount* ‖ Mai⁓ *may-pole w.* ‖ Myrten⁓ *myrtle w.*, ⟨bot⟩ ~ der Randblüten *corona* ‖ Sieges⁓ *w. of victory* ‖ Schacht⁓ ⟨min⟩ *crib, curb* ‖ Schwung⁓ ⟨tech⟩ *fly wheel* ‖ Spur⁓ *flange* ‖ Zahn⁓ *wheel rim* | e–n ~ **flechten,** winden *to w. a garland* ‖ ⁓e am Ehrenmal niederlegen *to lay w.s on ..* | ⟨poet, fig⟩ *circle* (*of flowering gardens*) ‖ *galaxy* (*of beautiful young ladies*) **~arterie** f ⟨anat⟩ *coronary artery* **~blume** f ⟨bot⟩ *g.-flower* **~brenner** m *annular burner* **~eisen** n (Gießerei) *crown-iron* **~flechterin** f *winder of w.s* **⁓geschmückt** a *wearing a w.* od *chaplet, adorned with g.s* **~gesims** n ⟨arch⟩ *cornice, drip-stone*, ⟨scient⟩ *corona* **~leiste** f ⟨arch⟩ *dripstone, weather-moulding, cornice* **~naht** f ⟨anat⟩ *coronal* **~niederlegung** f *laying of w.s* **~spende** f *floral tribute*; v ~n bitte abzusehen *no flowers by request* **~vene** f ⟨anat⟩ *coronary vein* **Kr·änzchen** n ~s/~ *little g.* od *w.* | ⟨fig⟩ *dancing party* ‖ (*weekly*) *tea--party* ‖ (*ladies'*) *private circle, club*; ⟨Am⟩ *bee*, Spinn⁓ *spinning bee* ‖ *circle* (*of scholars*) **kr·änzen** vt [h] *to g., to w., to crown* (*with w.s*), *to adorn with g.s*

^×^**Kr·anz(e)l** n ~s/~(n) [südd, österr] ([dim] v Kranz) | ~jungfer [f] = Brautjungfer (vgl Jungfernkranz) *bridesmaid*

Kr·äpfel, Kr·apfen m, ×**Kr·äppel** ~s/~ *fritter*

Kr·app m ~(e)s/ ⟨bot & arts⟩ *madder*; **⁓farben** a *m.-coloured* **~farbendruck** m *m. style* **~gelb** n *xanthine* **~karmin** m *m. carmine* **~lack** m *m. lake* **~stoff** m *alizarine*

kr·aß a *crass, gross, crude* ‖ ⟨fam⟩ *awful* ‖ *marked* (*antagonism*); *direct* (*contradiction*); *awful* (*case*); *gross* (*ingratitude*) ‖ ~e Dramatik *realistic drama*; krasser Egoist *grossly selfish p* ‖ *crass* (*stupidity* = *crassitude*) ‖ *thundering* (*lie*) ‖ im krassesten Sinne *in the crass sense of the term* ‖ ⟨iron⟩ *sublime* (*ignorance*) ‖ krasser Fuchs ⟨univ⟩ *freshman* ‖ krasser Anfänger *clumsy beginner* ‖ die Unterschiede sind zu ~ .. *too pronounced*

Kr·ater m ~s/~ *crater* ‖ Mond⁓ *lunar cr.* **~bildung** f ⟨geol⟩ *formation of c.s* **⁓förmig** a *c.--shaped* **~see** m *c. lake*

Kr·atz- ~beere f *bramble-berry* **~bürste** f *scratch-brush, scrubbing-brush, scraper* ‖ ⟨fig fam⟩ *spit-fire, crab, crosspatch* **⁓bürstig** a *cross-grained, crabbed, irritable, peevish, cross* (*as two sticks*), *hedgehoggy*; ~es Wesen *crabbedness, peevishness*, etc. **~distel** f ⟨bot⟩ *fuller's* od *creeping thistle* **~eisen** n ⟨tech⟩ *scraping-iron, scraper* (a. Schuh⁓) **⁓fest** a *mar-resistant* **~fuß** m (*a bow and a*) *scrape*, (*awkward*) *bow* ‖ e–n ~ m *to make* od *scrape a leg* **⁓füßeln** vi [h] *to scrape* (*a leg*) **~kelle** f *notched trowel* **~malerei** f, **~putz** m *graffito* **~spur** f *gall* **Kr·atze** f ~/~n ⟨arts, tech, min⟩ *scraper* ‖ ⟨weav⟩ *card* ‖ Bagger⁓ *rake* ‖ ⟨met⟩ *paddle, rake* **Kr·ätze** f ~/ **1.** ⟨med⟩ *itch, mange*; *scabies*, ⟨scient⟩ *psora* **2.** ⟨met⟩ *dross, sweepings* pl, *parings* pl **kr·atzen** vt/i/refl [h] **I.** vt **1.** ⟨allg⟩ *to scratch, scrape* **2.** ⟨weav⟩ *to card* (*wool*), *to tease* (*cloth*) **3.** [imps] **es kratzt mich** (= juckt mich) überall *I'm itching all over*, .. in der Kehle *I feel irritation* od *a scratching in my throat* **4.** ⟨fig⟩ das Lob hat ihn mächtig ge– *the praise did him no end of good* | etw aufs Papier ~ (schlecht schreiben) *to scribble sth on paper* **II.** vi **1.** (Ohr beleidigend) *to grate, rasp* ‖ auf der Geige ~ ⟨fam⟩ *to rasp* od *scrape on the violin* ‖ die Feder kratzt .. *scratches* **2.** (Schleimhäute reizend) der Wein kratzt .. *has a harsh taste* ‖ der Rauch kratzt im Halse .. *irritates one's throat* **3.** [ell] nicht ~! *don't scratch*! **III.** v/refl **sich** ~ *to scratch* (*o.s.*) ‖ der Hund kratzt sich .. *scratches* ‖ sich am Kopf ~ *to scratch one's head* ‖ bedenklich kratzte er sich hinter dem Ohr *he was full of doubts and scratched his ear* | sich wund ~ *to scratch o.s. sore, to make o.s. sore with scratching* **Kr·atzer** m ~s/~ **1.** ⟨tech⟩ *scraper, scratcher*; *scraping-iron, gall*; ⟨glass⟩ *scratch* **2.** (Schramme) *scrape, mar* **3.** (P) ⟨mus⟩ *scraper* **Kr·ätzer** m ~s/~ **1.** = Kratzer **2.** *bad* od *sourish wine* **3.** *young red wine from the Tyrol* **kr·atzig** a **1.** = kratzend *rasping, grating, reedy, harsh voice* **2.** = kratzbürstig **kr·ätzig** a *itchy, mangy, scabbed*, ⟨scient⟩ *scabious, psorous* **Kr·ätz-** **~milbe** f ⟨ent⟩ *itch-mite* **~salbe** f *salve against the itch*, ⟨scient⟩ *antipsoric*

ˣ**kr·auchen** → kriechen **kr·auen** vt [h] *to stroke* (*the coat of a dog*), *to claw, to scratch softly*

Kr·aul m (Schwimmart) *crawl* | **≃en** *to crawl*

kr·aus a *frizzly, curly* (*hair*) ‖ (Negerhaar) *crips, fuzzy* ‖ *wrinkled* (*forehead*) ‖ *ruffled* (*folds, thoughts*) ‖ ⟨fig⟩ (verwickelt) *abstruse, intricate, complicated* (*matter*); *topsy-turvy* (*world*) ‖ ⟨a.⟩ *vague, dim, faint* ‖ *crude* (*handwriting*) ‖ *tortuous* (*leaf, passage*) | ⟨fig⟩ es wird mir allmählich zu ~ (= bunt) *that goes beyond a joke, you are carrying things too far* (ebenso: [adv] es zu ~ treiben) ‖ ein krauses Gesicht m, die Stirn ~ ziehen *to knit one's brow, to frown, to scowl* **≃bart** m *curled beard* **≃beere** f *cranberry* **≃haar** n *curled* od *curly hair* **~haarig** a *curly-haired, -headed, woolly-haired*, ⟨ethn⟩ *ulotrichous* **≃kohl** m *Savoy cabbage, bore-cole* **≃kopf** m *curly-head*(*ed p*) ‖ (Bohrer) ⟨carp⟩ *countersink* (*bit*) **~lockig** a *curly-headed* **≃machen** n *crisping, ruffling* **≃salat** m *crisped lettuce* **≃tabak** m *shag tobacco* **Kr·ause** f ~/~n (Hals~) *ruff* ⟨a. zoo⟩, (*of dress*) *frill, flounce* ‖ mit e–r ~ verzieren *to frill* | ~minze [f] ⟨bot⟩ *curly-mint* **Kr·äusel-** **~eisen** n *crisping-, curling-iron* **~endivie(n** pl) f *curly endive* **~locken** f pl ⟨cosm⟩ *curly cuts* **~maschine** f (f Tierhaar) *curling machine* **~stoff** m (= Frotté) *ripple-cloth* **~strümpfe** m pl *crimped nylons* **~vorrichtung** f (f Federn) *apparatus for curling* **~werk** n (f Münzen) *milling machine* **kr·äuseln** **1.** vt [h] *to crisp, to curl* ‖ (fälteln) *to frill, gauffer, goffer* ‖ (Münzen) *to mill* **2.** (**sich**) ~ (Wasser) *to ripple, to* (*be*) *ruffle*(*d*) ‖ (Rauch) *to wreathe* ‖ (Stoff) *to pucker, bunch* | ge–lt *in curl*; *frizzed*, ge–ltes Haar *friz* **Kr·äuselung** f *curling*, etc. ‖ (Meer) *ripple, rippling* **kr·ausen** vt [h] *to frill*, etc. → kräuseln 1.

Kr·aut n ~(e)s/≃er *herb, plant* ‖ ≃er [pl] [koll] *herbage* ‖ Medizinal≃er, offizinelle ≃er *medicinal herbs* ‖ Suppen≃er *pot-herbs* ‖ (Krautgemüse) *cabbage* ‖ (rheinisches) Apfel~ *apple jam*, ⟨Am⟩ *apple butter* ‖ [in comp] *wort*; Leber≃ *liver wort* ‖ (Unkraut) *weed* ‖ ⟨fam⟩ (= Tabak) *weed* ‖ Kartoffel–, Rüben≃ *potato-, turnip-tops* pl | ≃er ⟨cul⟩ *fine herbs*; ≃er sammeln *to herborize* ‖ ≃er fressend ⟨zoo⟩ *herbivorous* ‖ ~ einschneiden, einlegen, säuern *to cut, pickle, ferment cabbage* ‖ (v Pflanzen) ins ~ schießen *or* wachsen *to run wild* (od *into foliage*) | ⟨fig⟩ s–e Phantasie ins ~ schießen l *to let one's imagination run riot* ‖ wie ~ u Rüben durch–e–a *higgledy-piggledy* [a, adv], *at sixes and sevens*; ⟨fam⟩ *in a mess* ‖ gegen den Tod ist kein ~ gewachsen *there is no escape from death* ‖ das macht das ~ nicht fett → Kohl **~acker** m *cabbage-field* **≃artig** a *herblike*, ⟨scient⟩ *herbaceous* **~beet** n *c.-bed* **~esel** m ⟨fam⟩ *jackass* **~feld** n *c.-field* **~hacke** f *hoe* **~hobel** m *c.-slicer* **~junker** m ⟨fam⟩ *bumpkin squire*, (*ignorant*) *country squire* **~kopf** m (*head of*) *c.* **~presser** m *c. compressor* **~roulade** f → –wickel **~salat** m *c.-salad*, ⟨Am⟩ *slaw* **~schneidemaschine** f *c. cutter* **~strunk** m *c.-stalk* **~wickel** m ⟨cul⟩ *stuffed c. leaves* **kr·auten** vt [h] ⟨agr hort⟩ *to hoe, weed*

Kr·äuter- **~arznei** f *herb-medicine* **~auszug** m *extract* od *tincture of h.s* **~bad** n ⟨med⟩ *h. lotion* **~bier** n *medicated ale* **~bitter** m → –likör **~boden** m *loft for drying h.s* **~buch** n *h.al* **~butter** f *maitre d'hotel butter* **~frau** f *h.-woman* **≃fressend** a *h.-eating, h.ivorous* **~garten** m *kitchen-garden* **~händler** m *h.alist* **~kammer** f *room for storing h.s* **~käse** m *green cheese* **~kenner** m *h.alist, botanist* **~kenntnis** f *botanical knowledge* **~kissen** n *bag filled with certain h.s, medicated cushion* **~kunde** f *botany* **~kur** f *h.-cure* **~lehre** f *botany* **~likör** m *digestif* Fr **~mann** m *h.-man, gatherer of h.s* **~markt** m *h.-market* **~pflaster** n *cataplasm, h.-poultice* **~presse** f *h. press* **≃reich** a *h.ous, abounding in h.s* **~säckchen** n *sweet-bag* **~saft** m *h.al decoction, juice of h.s* **~salat** m *h.-salad* **~sammeln** n *h.orization* **~sammlung** f *h.arium* **~schnupftabak** m *h.-snuff* **~suppe** f *h.-soup, julienne* Fr **~tabak** m *h.-tobacco* **~tee** m *h.-tea, tea of medicinal h.s, infusion of h.s* **~tonikum** n ⟨cosm⟩ *herbal skin tonic* **~trank** m *decoction of h.s, h.al draught* **~umschlag** m *cataplasm, h.-poultice* **~wein** m *mulled wine, hippocras* **~würstel** n ~s/~(n) [österr] → Kohlroulade **~zucker** m ⟨pharm⟩ *conserve* **Kr·auter(er)** m ~s/~: ⟨mst⟩ alter ~ *old buffer* **kr·autig** a *herblike, herbaceous*

°**Kraw·all** m ~(e)s/~e *rumpus, row, riot, uproar, shindy* ‖ ~ m *to raise hell, to kick up a row* od *shindy* | ~macher [m] *rowdy, rioter, brawler*

Kraw·atte f ~/~n *cravat, tie*; *scarf*; breite ~ → ~nschal | ~nnadel [f] *tie-pin, scarf-pin*; ~nmacher [m] *cravat-maker* ‖ ⟨fig⟩ *stranglehold usurer*; ~nschal [m] *ascot tie*

Kraw·eel- | ~bau [m] *carvel-work*; ~boot [n] (Ggs Klinkerboot) *carvel-built boat*; ≃gebaut [a] *carvel-built*; ~es Fischerboot *nobby*

°**Kraxel·ei** f ~/ *climbing, scrambling* ‖ *mountain-climbing* **kr·axeln** vi [s] *to climb, scramble* (auf *up to*) ‖ *to climb mountains* ‖ mühsam bergauf ~ *to plod* od *plough up hill* **Kr·axler** m ~s/~ (*mountain-*)*climber*

Kr·easleinen n (tierisches) *dowlas, creas*

Kreat·ur f ~/~en *creature* ‖ ⟨fig cont⟩ *creature, satellite, minion, cat's paw, tool* ‖ feile ~ *hireling* ‖ erbärmliche ~ ⟨sl⟩ *squirt* ‖ alle ~ sehnte sich nach Regen *all nature cried out for rain*

Kr·ebs m ~es/~e **1.** ⟨zoo allg⟩ *crab*; weiblicher ~ *hen crab*; Fluß≃ *crayfish*, ⟨Am⟩ *crawfish* | ~e [pl] → *shrimp* **2.** ⟨path⟩ *cancer*; *carcinoma, gangrene*; Haut≃ *cancroid* **3.** ⟨astr⟩ Wendekreis des ~es *Tropic of C.* **4.** ⟨com⟩ *unsold* od *returned book*; ~e [pl] *remainders, returns, dead stock* **≃artig** a **1.** *like a crab, cancriform* **2.** ⟨path⟩ *like cancer, cancerous*; *gangrenous* **~artigkeit** f ⟨path⟩ *cancerousness, gangrenousness* **~augen** n pl *crab's eyes* pl **~bildung** f ⟨path⟩ *canceration* **~butter** f ⟨cul⟩ *crab-cheese, crab's butter* **≃erregend** a *carcinogen*(*et*)*ic* **~erreger** m *carcinogen* **~fang** m *catching of crayfish*, etc **~fänger** m *crayfish catcher* **≃förmig** a ⟨zoo⟩ *cancriform* (→ ≃artig) **~gang** m *sidling* od *crab's walk*; *going backward* (*like a crayfish*); ⟨fig⟩ *retrogradation, decline, decay*; den ~ gehen ⟨fig⟩ *to retrograde, decline*; *to fall off* **~geschwür** n ⟨path⟩ *carcinoma*; *gangrenous* od *cancerous ulcer* **~korb** m = –reuse **~kranke(r)** m *p suffering from cancer* **~nase** f ⟨cul⟩ *shell of crayfish stuffed with paste* **~reuse** f *crayfish bow-net* **≃rot** a (*as*) *red as a lobster* **~schaden** m ⟨path⟩ *cancerous affection*; ⟨fig⟩ *inveterate* od *deep-seated evil, canker*; ⟨a.⟩ *nuisance*

~schale f *crab shell* **~schere** f *claw* od *pincers* pl *of a crayfish* **~suppe** f *crayfish cream-soup*; *bisk, bisque* **~tier** n *crustacean* | ~e [pl] ⟨scient⟩ *crustacea* pl **~zucht** f *crayfish-* od *crab-farming* **kr·ebsen** vi **1.** [h] *to catch crayfish* od *crabs*; ⟨fig⟩ (of oar) *to catch a crab* **2.** [h & s] ⟨fam⟩ *to keep on the move, to drudge* **3.** er geht mit allem ~ *he tries to make use of everything*

Kred·enz f ~/~en | ~tisch [m] *sideboard, buffet* Fr; ⟨ec⟩ *prothesis*; ~teller [m] *salver* ~̈**en** vt [h] *to hand, present* (*a glass of wine*) (urspr.: *after having tasted it*) **Kred·it**[1] m ~(e)s/~e *credit, trust* ‖ (Ruf) *reputation* ‖ Landwirtschafts~̈e *farm loans* pl ‖ langfristiger ~ *long-dated cr.*; laufender ~ *open cr.*; e–n ~ einräumen *to grant cr.*; ~ h *to enjoy cr.*; e–n ~ entziehen *to withdraw a cr.*; e–n ~ kündigen *to call in a cr.* ‖ auf ~ *on cr.*; ⟨fam⟩ *on tick*; auf ~ kaufen [abs] *to run up an account*; ~ geben ⟨fam⟩ *to tick*; jdm e–n ~ geben in Höhe v *to give a p cr. for £ 100*; ~ an .. *cr. to a p* ‖ e–n ~ in Anspruch nehmen *to make use of a cr.* ‖ er hat s–n moralischen ~ erschöpft *he has exhausted his moral cr.* ‖ das muß ihn um allen ~ bringen *that must entirely ruin his cr.* **~aktie** f *cr.-share* **~anstalt** f *cr.-company* → –bank **~aufnahme** f *raising of cr.* **~bank** f *commercial* od *loan bank* **~bedarf** m *demands* pl *for cr.* **~bemessung** f *cr.-fixing* **~beschaffung** f *cr.-supply* **~beschränkung** f *tight-money policy* **~brief** m *letter of cr.* **~dokument** n *cr.-instrument* **~erleichterungen** *cr. facilities* ~̈**fähig** a *reliable, sound* **~genossenschaft** f *cr. union* **~geschäft** n **1.** *cr. business* **2.** *cr.-operation* **~gewährung** f *the granting of cr.s* **~hilfe** f *cr. assistance* **~institut** n *loan institution* **~kündigung** f *notice of withdrawal of a cr.* **~markt** m *cr. market*; die ~̈e stark in Anspruch nehmen *to draw heavily on the cr. m.* **~nehmer** m *borrower* **~rahmen** m *cr. ceiling* **~reisebrief** m *traveller's letter of cr.* **~schädigung** f *defamation that damages a p's cr.* **~schein** m *warant* **~spielraum** *margin available for lending* ‖ auf dem **~weg** *by raising loans* ~̈**-würdig** a [pred] *good cr. risk* | ~keit [f] *cr. worthiness* **Kr·edit**[2] n ~s/~s ⟨com⟩ (Ggs Debet) *credit* **~posten** m *entry on the cr.-side* **~seite** f *cr.-side* **kredit·ieren** vt [h] (jdm etw) *to credit* (*a p with*), *to cr.* (*sth to a p*) | vi [h] *to sell on cr., to give cr.* **Kredit·iv** n ~(e)s/~e *credentials* pl **Kr·editor** m ~s/–t·oren *creditor* **Kr·edo** n ~s/ *creed*

Kr·efeld n ⟨Ger⟩ (Stadt im Rheinland)

°**kr·egel** a (P) *lively, awake*

Kr·eide f ~/~n *chalk* ‖ ⟨tail⟩ *talc, soapstone, tailor's chalk* ‖ ⟨arts⟩ *drawing chalk, crayon* ‖ mit ~ zeichnen, schreiben, bestreichen etc *to chalk, to crayon* | ⟨fig⟩ mit doppelter ~ schreiben *to overcharge* ‖ in die ~ k *or* geraten *to run on tick*; bei jdm .. *to get into a p's debt* ‖ bei jdm mit 100 Mark in der ~ stehen *to owe a p 5 pounds* ‖ tief in der ~ sitzen *to be over head and ears in debt* **Kr·eide-** [in comp] ⟨geol⟩ *cretaceous, chalk-* ~̈**-artig** a *ch.y*, ⟨geol⟩ *cr.* ~̈**blaß**, ~̈**bleich** a (*as*) *white as ch.* od *as a sheet*, (*as*) *pale as a ghost*; ~ aussehen *to look chalky white*; er wurde ~ *his face went deadly pale, ashen*, etc **~bruch** m *ch. quarry* **~erde** f *ch.y soil*; *ch.-earth* **~fels** m *ch.-cliff* **~formation** f ⟨geol⟩ *cr. system* **~grund** m ⟨paint⟩ *gesso-ground* ~̈**haltig** a *ch.y*, ⟨geol⟩ *cr.* **~karton** m *glazed cardboard* **~lager** n *ch.bed* **~mergel** m ⟨geol⟩ *ch.-marl* **~paste** f (~ u Leim) *composition* **~sandstein** m ⟨geol⟩ *upper green sandstone* **~-säure** f ⟨chem⟩ *carbonic acid* **~schiefer** m ⟨geol⟩ *ch.-slate* **~stift** m *ch.(-pencil), crayon* **~strich** m *ch. line* **~system** n ⟨geol⟩ *cr. system* **~vermerk** m *ch. mark* ~̈**weiß** a = ~blaß **~zeichen** n *ch. mark* **~zeichnung** f *crayon(-drawing), ch.-drawing* **kr·eiden** vt [h] *to chalk* **kr·eidig** a *chalky*, ⟨geol⟩ *cretaceous*

kre·ieren vt [h] *to create* ‖ z Peer ~ (ernennen) *to create* (*a p*) *a peer*; *to make, appoint*

Kr·eis m ~es/~e *circle* ‖ großer, größter ~ ⟨math⟩ *great c.* ‖ ⟨astr⟩ ~bahn e–s Planets *orbit* ‖ ⟨geogr⟩ Breiten~̈ *parallel of latitude*; Längen~̈ *meridian* ‖ magnetischer ~ *magnetic circuit* ‖ kl Nebenbild im ~e *inset*, im ~ der König *inset the king* ‖ e–n ~ beschreiben, schlagen, ziehen *to describe* od *draw a c.* ‖ die Quadratur des ~es finden *to square the c.* ‖ im ~e herum *round about, in a round* od *c.* ‖ (P) e–n ~ bilden *to form* (*into*) *a ring* od *c.*; .. um *to form a ring round* (*a p*) ‖ sich im ~e drehen *or* bewegen *to rotate, wheel, revolve, to spin* od *whirl round* od *in a circle*; *to mill* (um *about a p*) ‖ im ~e laufen *or* fliegen *to ring*; Fuchs, der im ~e läuft *ringer* ‖ Störe m–e ~e nicht! *mind my c.s* (Archimedes); ⟨allg⟩ *don't disturb my meditations*! ‖ jds ~e trüben *to queer the pitch for a p* od *a p's pitch* ‖ mir dreht sich alles im ~e (herum) *I feel dizzy, my head swims* od *is swimming* od *goes round* ‖ e–n ~ um jdn schließen, jdn im ~e einschließen *to encircle a p*, ⟨fig⟩ *to hem in a p* ‖ Licht- u Schatten~̈e *pools of light and shadow* | ⟨fig⟩ *set, groups* (*of experts, study g.*); Land~̈, Stadt~̈ ⟨Ger⟩ *district* (vgl ⟨engl⟩ *county*) ‖ (Amtsbezirk) ⟨jur⟩ ⟨Methodisten⟩ ⟨ec Engl⟩ *circuit* ‖ z weißen ~ gehörig *decontrolled* (*town* [*as to rents*]) ‖ ⟨pol⟩ *division, sphere, department, province* ‖ Ideen~̈ *range*, Interessen~̈ *c. of interests* ‖ Wahl~̈, Leser~̈, Abonnenten~̈ *constituency* ‖ ~ des Denkens *sphere of thought* ‖ *field of observation* ‖ in m–m kl ~e (= Arbeits~̈, Wirkungs~̈) *in my own small way* ‖ Freundes~̈ *c. of friends* ‖ geladener ~ *company* ‖ im ~e s–r Familie *in* (*the bosom* od *midst of*) *his family* ‖ (Feier) in kl ~e *in a small c.* ‖ (P) *category*; die gebildeten ~e *the intelligentzia, -tsia*; in gewissen, diplomatischen ~en *in certain, diplomatic quarters*; in allen ~en des Lebens *in every walk of life*; unterrichtete ~e [pl] *informed opinion*; aus gut unterrichteten ~en *on good authority*; die höchsten ~e *the aristocracy, the upper ten* (*thousand*); in weiten ~en *widely* (*admired*); in den besten ~en *in the best society* od *c.s* pl | [in comp] *circle, circular*; *district* **~abschnitt** m ⟨geom⟩ *segment* **~amt** n ⟨Ger⟩ *d. court* od *office* **~amtmann** m ⟨Ger⟩ *d.-bailiff*, ⟨Engl⟩ *first judge of a circuit-court* **~arzt** m *d.-physician, D. Medical Officer of Health* **~ausschnitt** m ⟨geom⟩ *sector* **~ausschuß** m *d. committee* **~bahn** f ⟨astr⟩ *orbit*; ⟨rail⟩ *local* od *branch line*; (Warteschleife) ⟨aero⟩ *orbit* **~beamte(r)** m *d. officer* **~behörde** f *d. board* **~bewegung** f *circuit, c.lar motion* ‖ ⟨astr⟩ *rotation* ‖ *revolution* **~bogen** m *arc*, ⟨arch⟩ *c.lar arch* **~bohrer** m ⟨tech⟩ *borer with c.lar bit* **~diagramm** n *c. diagram* **~direktion** f *d. board* **~direktor** m *director of a d.* **~drehung** f *rotation* **~einteilung** f ⟨geom⟩ *division of a c.* ‖ ⟨pol⟩ *division into d.s* **~ersatzkommission** f ⟨mil⟩ *recruiting commission of a d.* **~evolvente** f *involute of the c.* **~feld** n *roundel* **~fläche** f ⟨geom⟩ *area of the c.* **~förderer** m *c.lar conveyor* **~form** f *c.lar form* ~̈**förmig** a *c.lar* **~förmigkeit** f *c.larity* **~frequenz** f *angular velocity*; ⟨radar⟩ *a. frequency* **~funktion** f *c.lar function* **~-gang** m *revolution* **~gericht** n *d. court*, ⟨vgl engl⟩ *county court* **~geschwindigkeit** f *circulatory velocity* **~hauptmann** m *prefect of a d.* ‖ ⟨vgl engl⟩ *Lord Lieutenant of a county* **~kimme** f *ring sight* **~korn** n ⟨mil⟩ *circular foresight*, ⟨aero fam⟩ *cart-wheel* **~kornvisier** n *annular* od *ring sight*; *speed r. s.* **~lauf** m *circular course, rotation*; ⟨com, tech⟩ *cycle* ‖ ⟨fig⟩ *system circulatory*; *circulation* (*of the blood*), gr kl ~ *major, lesser circulation*; ~ des Kohlenstoffs *organic carbon cycle*; *revolution, periodical return*; *round* (*of affairs*) ‖ (der Jahreszeiten etc) *succession* ‖ (der Pflichten, Veranstaltungen, Freuden) *round*; sich im ~ bewegen *to circulate, to describe a circuit* **~lauf-** (Blut~̈-) *cardiovascular* | ~störung [f] *circulatory trouble* **~leitung** f ⟨nazi, SBZ⟩ *d.* od *party headquarters*

~linie f *circular line*, ⟨geom⟩ *circumference* **~-messer** n ⟨tech⟩ *circular knife* **~messung** f *measurement of the c.*, *cyclometry* **~ordnung** f *d.-regulations* pl **~pendel** n *circular pendulum* **~physikus** m † = ~arzt **~prozeß** m ⟨tech⟩ *cycle of operations* **~richter** m *d.-judge* **⁓rund** a *circular, orbicular*; ~er Querschnitt [m] *c.lar section* **~säge** f (Blatt) *c.lar saw*; (Maschine) *circular saw(ing machine)*; ⟨Am⟩ *buzz-saw*; ⟨fam fig⟩ (Strohhut) *donkey's breakfast* **~schere** f *c.lar trimmer* od *shears* pl **~schule** f *d.-school* **~sekretär** m *d.-prefect's secretary* **~stadt** f ⟨Ger⟩ *d.-town*, ⟨Engl⟩ *county--town*, ⟨Am⟩ *seat* **~stände** m pl (*members* [pl] *of a*) *dietine* **⁓ständig** a ⟨bot⟩ *cyclic(al)* **~strom** m ⟨el⟩ *c.lar current* **~strömung** f *cyclic flow* **~tag** m *dietine, d. council* od *asssembly* **~teilung** f ⟨geom⟩ *cyclotomy*; ~s- *cyclotomic* (*field*) **~umfang** m *periphery, circumference* **~verband** m *d. union* **~-verkehr** m (auf Straßen) *gyratory* od *roundabout traffic*; ⟨mot⟩ *circus*; ⟨wir⟩ *circular radio t.* **~versammlung** f = ~tag **~viereck** n *quadrilateral inscribed in a c.* **~viertel** n *quadrant* **~vierung** f *quadrature of the c.* **~visier** n ⟨mil⟩ *ring sight* **~-wehrersatzamt** n *Recruiting Office* (*Military Subregion*) od *M. S. R. O.* **~wendung** f *pirouette, volt* **~zylinderfläche** f *surface of a c.lar cylinder* **Kreischen** [–sç–] n ~s/~ *small c.*

kreischen [–ʃ–] vi [h] *to scream, squeam* ‖ (stärker) *to shriek* ‖ (vor Angst, Schmerz, bes Vögel) *squawk*; (Kinder) *squall* ‖ (Angst, Schmerz, Zorn; schrill) *screech* (a. Eulenart) ‖ (Kinder vor Schmerz, Angst, Zorn, Freude) *squeal, yell*; ⟨Am a.⟩ *yip* ‖ wie toll ~ *to yell like a fiend* ‖ (Säge) *to grate*; (Türangel) *squeak, creak* ‖ ~d *strident, shrill* (*voice*) | ⟨fig⟩ *loud, gaudy, glaring* (*colour*) | ⁓ n *scream(ing)*, etc. **Kr·eischer** m *screamer, screecher*; *squalling child*, etc

Kr·eisel m ~s/~ (*humming-*)*top*, (*peg*) *top*, *whip(ping)-top* ‖ den ~ treiben, peitschen *to spin* od *whip the top* ‖ (Drehwürfel) *teetotum* ‖ Schiffs-⁓ *gyroscopic stabilizer*; (toy) *gyroscope* **~bewegung** f ⟨tech⟩ *gyration* **~brecher** m *gyratory crusher* **~geradlaufgerät** n (f Torpedos) *torpedo gyro* **⁓gesteuert** a *gyro-controlled* **~kipper** m *rotary tipper* **~kompaß** m *gyro compass*; Drei⁓ *triple g. c.*; ~ für Feuerleitung *g. c. for gunfire control* **~lader** m ⟨aero-mot⟩ *centrifugal supercharger* **~mutter** f ⟨mar⟩ *master compass* **~pumpe** f *centrifugal pump* **~rad** n *turbine* **~radgebläse** n *rotary blower* **~-Schlinger- u Stampfanzeiger** m ⟨mar⟩ *gyroscopic roll and pitch recorder* **~stativ** n ⟨film⟩ *gyro-tripod* **~steuergerät** n ⟨aero⟩ *gyro pilot* **~tochter** f ⟨mar⟩ *repeater compass* **~verdichter** m *centrifugal* (*air*) *compressor* **~verkehr** m ⟨mot⟩ *circus* **~vorrichtung** f *gyroscope* **~wipper** m ⟨tech⟩ *rotary tipper* **~-wirkung** f *gyroscopic* od *gyrostatic effect* **~würfel** m *teetotum* **kr·eiseln** vi [h] *to play at humming-top, to spin the top* | (sich) ~ v/refl [h & s] *to whirl round* ‖ ⟨tech⟩ *to gyrate* **kr·eisen** vi [h] *to turn* (*round*) od *move in a circle, to circle* od *spin* (*round*); *to circulate*; (Planeten) *to revolve, rotate* ‖ *to return periodically* ‖ ⟨orn⟩ *to circle, hover, plane* (über *above*) ‖ ~ l *to pass* (*the bottle*) ‖ die Flasche kreist .. *goes round*; in ~den Bewegungen *using circular strokes* | ⁓ n *circular movement, rotation, revolution* (*of planets*) **Kr·eiser** m ~s/~ (Flurschütz) *keeper*

kr·eißen vi [h] *to* (*be in*) *labour, to travail, to have labour-pains* ‖ ~d ⟨scient⟩ *parturient* | ⁓ n *labour-pains*, ⟨scient⟩ *parturiency, parturition* **Kr·eißerin** f ~/~nen *woman in labour* **Kr·eißsaal** m *delivery room*

Kr·ellschuß m ⟨hunt⟩ *a clean kill*; → weidwund

Kr·em f (⟨vulg⟩ m) ~/~s **1.** ⟨eig, cul, cosm⟩ *cream*; ⟨cul⟩ *custard pudding* ‖ Haut⁓ (*cold-, cleansing-*)*cr.*, *unguent* ‖ Schuh⁓ *polish* ‖ Zahn⁓ *tooth paste* **2.** ⟨übtr⟩ *élite* (*of society, the upper ten* [*thousand*]) **~eis** n *ice-cr.* **~schokolade** f *ch. cr.*

Kremat·orium n ~s/–rien *crematorium* L, ⟨bes Am⟩ *crematory* | ~sauffahrt [f] *cr. drive*

Kr·eml m ~s/ *the Kremlin*

Kr·empe f ~/~n *border, edge, rim*; (*hat-*)*brim* ‖ ohne ~ *brimless* (*hat*); Hut mit schmaler, breiter ~ *narrow-, broad-brimmed hat*; Hut mit teilweise herabgedrückter ~ *slouched hat* ‖ ~ des Kesselbodens *flange of the boiler end* **Kr·empel 1.** m ~s/ *rubbish, lumber*; ⟨sl⟩ *show* ‖ der ganze ~ *the whole caboodle* ‖ was kostet der ganze ~? *How much the whole lot?* ‖ er warf ihm den ~ vor die Füße *he threw up his job at a moment's notice* **2.** f ~/~n ⟨tech⟩ (f Wolle) *card*; (f Tuch) *teasel, teazel, teazle* **~block** m *carding bench* **~kamm** m *card* **~maschine** f *carding machine* **~stube** f *carding-room* **kr·empeln** vt [h] **1.** ⟨tech⟩ *to card* (*wool*) ‖ *to burr, tease, teasel, teazel, teazle* (*cloth*) **2.** er krempelte sein Hemd auf, hoch, zurück (über die Ellbogen) *he rolled his shirt sleeves up* (*above his elbows*) ‖ ich krempele etw um *I turn a th inside out*, ⟨fig⟩ *I knock a th into a cocked hat* **kr·empen** vt [h] *to bend at the edge* ‖ hoch|~, herunter|~ *to cock, slouch* (*the brim of a hat*) **Kr·empziegel** m ~s/~ *pantile*

Kr·emser m ~s/~ *break, sociable, char-a-banc*

Kr·emserweiß n *cremnitz* od *silver white*

Kr·en m ~(e)s/ [sod] → Meerrettich; Knochenmark

Kre·ole m ~n/~n, **-lin** f ~/~nen, **k-lisch** a *Creole*

Kreos·ot n ~(e)s/ *creosote*

×°**kr·epelig** a *peaky* °**K-ling** m *perisher* **krep·ieren** vi [s] (T) *to die, perish* ‖ °(P) ⟨sl⟩ *to kick the bucket, to peg out* ‖ (v Geschossen) *to burst, detonate, explode* ×**Krep·ierl** n ~s/~(n) ⟨sl⟩ *perisher*

Kr·epp m ~s/, **~flor** m *crêpe* Fr | (Trauerflor *black mourning*) *crape* | ~maschine [f] *craping--machine*; ~papier [n] (*toilet*) *crape paper*; ~-seide [f] *crêpe de Chine* Fr; ~serviette [f] *creped serviette*; ~tuch [n] *crape(-cloth)* | **⁓en** vt [h] *to crape*

Kr·esse f ~/~n ⟨bot⟩ *cress, cresses* pl ‖ aufgehen wie ~samen *to spring up like Jack's Bean--stalk*

Kr·eta n *Crete*; aus ~ *Cretan, Cretian* **Kr·eter,** ~s/~; **kr·etisch** a *Cretan*

Kr·ethi und Pl·ethi pl ⟨fig⟩ *Dick, Tom, and Harry*; ⟨cont⟩ *tag-rag* (od *rag-tag*) *and bobtail*

Kret·in [–tɛ̃] m ~s/~s *cretin* Fr, *half-witted p, idiot* | ~bildung [f], ~·ismus [–tiˈnis–] *cretinism*

×**Kr·etscham** m [omd] = Schenke **Kr·etschmer** m = Wirt

kr·euchen vi [h & s] ⟨poet⟩ = kriechen

–(k)reut(h) n [südd] (= Rodung) suff z Bezeichnung v Ortsnamen *e.g.* Bayreuth, Höllriegelskreuth; *cf* Walsrode, Wernigerode; → Rodung, roden

Kr·euz n ~es/~e *cross* **1.** (Formen:) Andr·eas-⁓ *St. Andrew's cr.* ‖ griechisches ~ *Greek cr.* ‖ Haken⁓ *gammadion*; *swastika* ‖ Henkel⁓ *ansated cr.* ‖ Johanniter⁓ *Maltese cr.* ‖ Kleeblatt-⁓ *botonée* Fr ‖ Krücken⁓ ⟨her⟩ *potent*; ~ des Deutschordens *Teutonic cr.* ‖ lateinisches ~ *Latin cr.* ‖ lothringisches ~ *cr. of Lorraine* ‖ Malteser⁓ *Maltese cr.* ‖ päpstliches ~ *papal cr.* ‖ Schräg⁓ ⟨her⟩ *saltier* ‖ Tau⁓ *tau cross* ‖ Wieder⁓ *crosslet* **2.** (Anwendungen:) ⟨anat⟩ (im Rückgrat) (P) *small of the back, loins* pl ‖ das ~ tut mir weh, ich habe Schmerzen im ~ *my back* od *my loins ache* ‖ sich das ~ verrenken, brechen *to strain, break one's back* ‖ ⟨hors⟩ *croup(e), crupper* ‖ (v Rind) *chine* | Anker⁓ *crown, cross* ‖ ⟨astr⟩ ~ des Südens *Southern Cr.* ‖ ⟨cards⟩ *club(s* pl) (= Treff) ‖ Dreh⁓ *windlass* ‖ Ehren⁓ *Cr. of Honour* ‖ Eisernes ~ (Auszeichnung) *Iron Cr.* ‖ Faden⁓ ⟨mil opt⟩ *cr. lines* ‖ Faden⁓visier ⟨mar opt⟩ *cr. wire* *sight* ‖ Fenster≃ *cr.-bar* (*of a window*) ‖ Genfer ~ *Geneva Cr.* ‖ Groß≃ *Grand Cr.* ‖ ⟨her⟩ → 1. ‖ hözernes ~ *wooden cr.*, *cr.piece of wood* ‖ ⟨mus⟩ *sharp, diesis*; mit e–m ~ bezeichnen *to sharp*; ~e u B's *sharps and flats*; durch ein ~ erhöhte Note *sharp* ‖ Rote-~-Medaille *Red Cr. Medal*; Verein v Roten ~ *Red Cr. Society* ‖ ⟨typ⟩ Aufhänge≃ *printer's peel* ‖ (†) *obelisk, dagger* ‖ Warnungs≃ *warning signal* **3.** [mit verb *or* prep] ⟨eig⟩ .. am ~e *Jesus on the cr.*; ans ~ heften, nageln, schlagen *to fasten, fix, nail to the cr., to crucify*; v ~e abnehmen *to take down from the cr.*; das ~ predigen *to preach the cr.*; zu ~e kriechen *to kiss the rod*; *to come to heel*; *to sing small*; *to eat humble pie*, ⟨Am⟩ *to eat crow*; *to eat one's words*, ⟨Am⟩ *to eat dirt*; *to climb down*; *to knuckle under* (vor *to*) ‖ ins *or* über(s) ~ legen, nähen *to lay, sew cr.-ways* od *cr.-wise*; die Arme über(s) ~ falten, verschränken *to cr.* od *fold one's arms* | das ~ schlagen, das Zeichen des ~es m *to make the sign of the cr., to cr. o.s.* (vor jdm *in abhorrence to a p*); ein ~ über jdm m *to trace a blessing for a p*; mit dem ~e segnen *to bless with the cr.* ‖ ein ~ unter eine Schrift m *to put a cr. under a document*; ein ~ vor ein Wort m *to put a cr. against a word*; hinter jdm drei ~e m *to be glad to have got rid of a p* ‖ (als Kreuzfahrer) das ~ nehmen *to take up the cr.* **4.** (in Flüchen:) ~-d·onnerwetter!, ~schweren·ot! *hang* od *damn it all! hell and blazes! damnation!* **5.** ⟨fig⟩ *cr., trouble, affliction, load of mischief*; sein ~ auf sich nehmen *to take up one's cr.*; man hat sein ~ mit ihm *one has no end of trouble with him*; ein schweres ~ z tragen h *to have a hard cr. to bear*, sein ~ geduldig tr. *to bear one's troubles* (od *cr.*) *with patience, patiently*; *to bear one's tribulation*; ⟨prov⟩ jeder hat sein ~ zu tragen *we all have our troubles, every man has his lot* **6.** [adv] **kreuz und quer**, in die Kreuz und Quere *criss-cross, in all directions, all about and about* **~abnahme** f, *deposition* od *descent from the cr.* **~arm** m *transept* **~auffindung** f *Invention of the Cr.*, → ~es- **~aufzug** m ⟨gym⟩ e–n ~ m *to skin a cat* **~band** n *cr.-band* ‖ (Zeitungsschleife) (*postal*) *wrapper* ‖ unter ~ *by book-post* ‖ ⟨carp⟩ *cr.-bar* **~batterie** f ⟨mil⟩ *cr.-battery* **~bau** m ⟨arch⟩ *transept* **~bein** n ⟨anat⟩ *rump-bone, chine-bone*, ⟨scient⟩ *sacrum* **~beitel** m *mortise-chisel* **~berg** m (*Mount*) *Calvary* **~bild** n *crucifix* **~blume** f ⟨bot⟩ *milk-wort* ‖ ⟨arch⟩ *finial* **≃blütig** a *cruciferous* **~blütler** m pl ⟨bot⟩ *cruciferous plants, crucifers*, ⟨scient⟩ *cruciferae* pl L °**~bock** m (Fehler) *howler, boner* **~bogen** m ⟨arch⟩ *groined arch*; *ogive* **~bohrer** m *cr.-mouthed chisel* **~bram-** ⟨mar⟩ ~rahe [f] *miz(z)en-topgallant yard*; ~segel [m] *m.-t. sail*; ~stenge [f] *m.-t. mast* **~brassen** f pl ⟨mar⟩ *m.-top braces* pl **≃br·av** a *honest to the backbone, thoroughly h.*; (bes v Kindern) *as good as gold* **~bruchkerbe** f (e–r Tablette) ⟨pharm⟩ *cross score* **~bund** m *diagonal lashing* **~-d·onnerwetter** n & intj → Kreuz 4. **~dorn** m ⟨bot⟩ *buckthorn* | ~gewächse [pl]; Gattung der ~ *Rhamnaceae* pl L **~drehscheibe** f *two-way turntable* **~eisen** n ⟨arch⟩ *cr. iron* **~fahne** f *banner of the cr.* **~fahrer** m *crusader* | ~heer [n] *army of crusaders* **~fahrt** f *crusade* ‖ ⟨mar⟩ *cruise* **~feld** n ⟨arch⟩ *intersection* **~feuer** n ⟨mil⟩ *cr. fire* ‖ im ~ ⟨fig⟩ *cannon to right of me, c. to left of me* ‖ .. ins ~ nehmen *to take .. between two fires, to expose to a cr.-fire* ⟨a. fig⟩ **≃fid·el** a ⟨fam⟩ *jolly, as merry as a cricket* od *sandboy*; ~ (= gesund) s *to be alive and kicking* od *as fit as a fiddle* **~flügel** m, **~schiff** n ⟨arch⟩ *transept* **≃förmig** a *cr.-shaped*, ⟨scient⟩ *cruciform* **~fragen** f pl *cr.-questioning* **~gang** m ⟨arch⟩ *cloister(s)* ‖ ⟨min⟩ *cr.-cutting* od *-gallery*; *cr. vein* od *lode* **~gasse** f *cr.-street* **~gelenk** n *universal* od *cardan joint* | ~kupplung [f] *universal type coupling* **≃gerändelt** a *cr.wise milled* od *knurled* **~gewebereifen** m ⟨mot⟩ *fabric thread tire* **~gewölbe** n ⟨arch⟩ *groined vault, cr.-vault(ing)* **~gleis** n ⟨rail⟩ *cr.ing track* **~griff** m *four-handed seat* **~gurt** m *cr.-girth, cr.-arch*; ~en [pl] *diagonal ribs* **~hacke** f (*flat*) *pick, pickax(e)*; *mattock* **~haspel** f ⟨tech⟩ *windlass* **~herren** m pl ⟨R. C.⟩ *the Bethlehemites* pl **~hieb** m (Feilen≃) *double cut*; ⟨fenc⟩ *cr.-cut* **~holz** n ⟨mar⟩ *cleat*; ⟨carp⟩ *quarter timber* **~kirche** f *Church of the Holy Cr.* **~klampe** f *belaying cleat* **~knoten** m *double* od *reef* od *sailor's knot* **~kopf** m ⟨tech⟩ *cr.head* (Dampfmaschinenquerhaupt) **~kraut** n ⟨bot⟩ *ragwort, groundsel* **~kröte** f ⟨zoo⟩ *natterjack, rush-toad* **~lafette** f *outrigger gun mount* **≃lahm** a *dead lame*; *broken-backed, lame in the hip* ‖ ⟨hors⟩ *hip-shot* **~lähme** f ⟨vet⟩ *haemoglobinaemia* **~-Leidensweg** m *the Lord's Path of Suffering* **~mars** m ⟨mar⟩ *miz(z)en-top* | ~stange [f] ⟨mar⟩ *m.-t. mast* **~mast** m ⟨mar⟩ *m.-mast* **~meißel** m *cr.-cutting* od *mortise chisel* **~naht** f *cr.(-stiched) seam* **~nimbus** m *cruciferous n.* **~otter** f *common* od *poisonous viper* od *adder* **~peilung** f ⟨mar⟩ *cr.-bearing* ‖ in **~-pflanzung** *staggered* **~pflanzverfahren** n *square-cluster method* **~probe** f (des Blutes) ⟨med⟩ *cr. matching* **~punkt** m = ~ungspunkt **~rahe** f ⟨mar⟩ *miz(z)en-top yard* **~rahmenantenne** f ⟨wir⟩ *cr.-coil aerial* **~rehe** f ⟨vet⟩ = ~lähme **~riemen** m *crupper* **~ritter** m ⟨hist⟩ *crusader*; *crusading knight*; *Knight of the Cr.* **≃saitig** a *over-strung* (*piano*) **~schiff** n ⟨arch⟩ *transept* **~schlag** m ⟨ten⟩ *cr.-drive* | ~hammer [m] *about sledge* **~schlitten** m (Dreherei) *cr.-slide* **~schmerzen** m pl *back-ache*, ⟨med⟩ *lumbago* **~schnabel** m ⟨orn⟩ *cr.-bill*, → d. **≃schnäblig** a *curvirostral* **~schnäbler** m pl ⟨orn scient⟩ *curvirostra* pl L **~schnitt** m ⟨surg⟩ *crucial incision* **~schraffierung** f ⟨arts⟩ *cr.-hatching(s)* **~see** f ⟨mar⟩ *cr.(-running) sea* **~schwerenot** f & intj → Kreuz 4. **~segel** n *miz(z)en-top-sail* **~spinne** f ⟨zoo⟩ *garden-* (od *cr.-*)*spider* **~spreize** f *diagonal stay* **~sprung** m *capriole, caper*; *entrechat* Fr ‖ ⟨hunt⟩ (v Hasen) ≃e m *to double* **~stab** m ⟨tech⟩ *cr.-staff* **≃ständig** a ⟨bot⟩ *cruciate, decussate(d), cruciform* **~stange** f *cr.-guard* **≃steif** a *stiff in the back* od *loins* **~stellung** f *position in form of a cr., decussation* **~stenge** f ⟨mar⟩ *miz(z)en-top mast* **~stich** m (Stickerei) *cr.-stitch* **~stück** n ⟨tech⟩ *cr.*; ⟨rail⟩ *four-way cr.* **~support** m ⟨tech⟩ *cr.-slide rest* **≃tragend** a *cr.-bearing* **~tragung** f *carrying the cr.* ⟨arts a.⟩ *The Procession to Calvary* **~- und Querzüge** m pl *criss-cross* od *cr.-country rambles* pl **~verband** m ⟨med⟩ *cr.-bandage* ‖ ⟨arch⟩ *laying of bricks end-on, headers placed endwise* **~verhör** n ⟨jur⟩ *cr.-examination*; mit jdm ein ~ anstellen, jdn ins ~ nehmen *to cr.-examine a p, to heckle a p*, ⟨Am⟩ *to grill a p* **~verweis** m *cr.-reference*; mit ~en *cr.-indexed* **~visierstab** m *gauging rod* **~weg** m *cr.-way, cr.-road*; *carfax*, ⟨R. C.⟩ *way* od *stations* [pl] *of the Cr.* ‖ am ~ *at a cr.-roads* | ~station [f] ⟨R. C.⟩ *station of the Cr.* od *Calvary* **≃weise** adv *across, cr.-wise*; ~ durchzogen v *criss-crossed with* (*ditches*); (sich) ~ schneiden *to decussate*; ~ gestellt *decussate* **~wicklung** f *cr.-winding*; Spule mit ~ *cr. wound bobbin* **~woche** f *Rogation Week* **~worträtsel** n *cr.-word puzzle*, ⟨fam⟩ *criss-cross* **~wurz** f ⟨bot⟩ = Hauhechel **~zangen** f pl *diagonal ties* **~zeichen** n ⟨typ⟩ (†) *obelisk, dagger* **~zucht-** .. *cr.bred* (*sheep*) **~zug** m *crusade* | ~sidee [f] *crusading spirit*

Kr·euzchen n ~s/~ *crosslet*

kr·euzen I. vt/i & **sich** ~ v/refl [h] **1.** *to cross*; die Arme, Beine ~ *to fold* od *cr. one's arms, to cr. one's legs* ‖ mit jdm die Degen ~ *to cr.* od *measure swords with a p* ⟨a. fig⟩; die Degen ~ sich .. *cross* ‖ ⟨engl⟩ Scheck (mit 2 parallelen Linien) ~ *to cross ..* ‖ die Linien, Straßen ~ sich .. *cut each other, intercross, intersect* ‖ e–e Straße ~ *to cr. a road*; jds Weg ~ *to cr. a p's path*; ⟨fig⟩ jds Pläne ~ *to thwart a p's plans* ‖ die Briefe w sich ~ *the letters will cr.*; unsere Besuche ~ sich .. *overlap* ‖ ⟨phys⟩ sich ~ *to interfere*; verschiedene Interessen ~ sich .. *come into* od *are in conflict* **2.** ⟨rel⟩ sich ~ (u segnen) *to make the sign of the cr., to cr. o.s.* **3.** ⟨mar⟩ ~ *to cruise (about)* ‖ (auf) ~ *to beat up* od *about, to strive, tack* ‖ lange auf der Stelle ~ *to plough the sea* **4.** ⟨zoo, bot⟩ (Vieh) *to cross, hybridize, interbreed*; zur Rassenverbesserung ~ *to grade (up)*; *to produce these flowers two different kinds were cr.ed* ‖ (v Vieh) sich ~ *to interbreed* **II. gekreuzt** pp & a (→ I.) **1.** ⟨bot⟩ *decussate(d), cruciate, cruciform* **2.** ⟨weav⟩ das Weben mit ~er Kette *cr.-weaving*; ~e Knochen *skull and cr.bones* **III. Kreuzen** n (→ I.) *cr.ing, intersection* ‖ *cruising, tacking* ‖ *interbreeding hybridization, hybridism* **Kr·euzer**¹ m ~s/~ ⟨num⟩ [österr] †(= 2 Heller) das ist k–n ~ wert *that's not worth a farthing* **Kr·euzer**² m ~s/~ ⟨mar⟩ *cruiser*; kl schneller ~ *dispatch--boat*; Flak≃ *anti-aircraft cr.*; 10 000-t-≃ *pocket battleship*; leichter *or* kl ~ *light c.*; schnellsegelnder Handels≃ *clipper*; (→ Aviso) **~flotte** f ⟨mar⟩, **~geschwader** n *fleet, squadron of c.s* **Kr·euzes-** (→ Kreuz-) **~aufrichtung** f *Raising of the Cross* **~erfindung** f ⟨ec⟩ (3. Mai) *Invention of the Cr.* **~erhöhung** f (14. September) *Exaltation of the Cr.* **~stamm** m *tree of the cr.*, ⟨hist⟩ *Holy Rood* **~tod** m *death on the cr.* **~zeichen** n *sign of the cr.* **kr·euzigen** vt [h] **1.** ⟨eig⟩ *to crucify* (→ Kreuz 3.) **2.** ⟨fig⟩ sein Fleisch ~ *to mortify one's flesh* **Kr·euzigung** f ~/~en *crucifixion* ‖ ⟨fig⟩ *mortification (of the flesh)* **Kr·euzung** f ~/~en **1.** *cr.ing* ‖ (Straßen≃, → d.) *cr.-roads* pl [sg & pl konstr]; an e–r ~ *at a cr.-roads* ‖ ⟨Am⟩ Ansiedlung an e–r ~ *cr.s-roads* pl ‖ ⟨rail⟩ *intersection*; ~ von Straße u Eisenbahn *level cr.ing*; ⟨min⟩ *intersection* **2.** *cr.ing of breeds, cr.-breeding, interbreeding*, ⟨scient⟩ *hybridation* ‖ (Mischrasse) *cr.-breed*; Kreuzung zw. Negern u Weißen *mulatto, quadroon, octoroon* (1/2, 1/4, 1/8 Neger) ‖ (T) *grade (a grade between the dog and the wolf* **~sader** f ⟨min⟩ *cr.-lode* **~spunkt** m *cr.ing--point* ‖ (v Straße u Eisenbahn *or* v zwei Eisenbahnen) *level-cr.ing* ‖ (Eisenbahnknotenpunkt) *junction* **~sstück** n (Schiene) ⟨rail⟩ *frog*

Kr·ibbel m ~s/ **1.** *itching, tingling sensation*; *pins and needles* **2.** *fretfulness*

kr·ibbelig a *nervy, jumpy, fretful*; ~ s *to be on pins and needles* **Kr·ibbelkopf** m ⟨fam⟩ *excitable, irritable, hot headed p* **kr·ibbeln I.** vi/t [h] **1.** (Käfer) *to crawl, creep*; (Würmer) *to wriggle* ‖ (Ameisen) *to swarm* **2.** (kitzeln) m–e Nase –lt, es –lt mir in der Nase *my nose tickles* ‖ es –lt mir in den Fingern *I have* od *feel pins and needles in my fingers* ⟨a. fig⟩ ‖ ⟨fig⟩ das –lt mich *that vexes me* **II.** ≃ n *crawling*, etc. ‖ *crawling sensation*, ⟨med⟩ *formication*

Kr·ickel m & n ~s/~ *horn of the chamois*

°**Krickel·ei** f ~/~en *scrawl* | *fuss(iness)* °**Kr·ikkel-kr·akel** n ~s/ ⟨fam⟩ *crinkum-crankum* °**kr·ikkeln** vt [h] *to scrawl, scribble*

Kr·ickente f = Kriekente *teal*

Kr·icket n ~s/ ⟨sport⟩ *cricket*, ~ spielen *to play cr., to have a game of cr.* **~spiel** n *game of cr., cr.--match*; internationales ~ *test-match* **~spieler** m *cr.-player, cr.er* (→ Fangpartei, Wicket) **~mannschaft** f *cr.-team*; Oxforder, Cambridger ~ *the Oxford* od *dark, Cambridge* od *light blues*

Kr·iebelkrankheit f ⟨path⟩ *ergotism*

Kr·iech- **~bohne** f ⟨bot⟩ *dwarf-bean* **~erbse** f *d.-pea* **~ente** f ⟨orn⟩ = Kriekente **~graben** m ⟨mil⟩ *shallow communication trench* **~pflanze** f ⟨bot⟩ *creeper, creeping plant* **~rebe** f ⟨Am⟩ *(Japanese) kudzu* **~spur** f ⟨mot⟩ *slow(est) lane* **~stoßschwimmen** n *crawl*; mit ~stoß schw. *to crawl* **~tier** n *reptile* **kr·iechen** vi [h & s] **1.** *to creep*; langsam (Schnecke) *to crawl (along at a snail's pace)*; *to crawl in the dust* ‖ (Wurm) *to crawl, wriggle (into, under)*; wie ein Wurm *to worm one's way*; auf allen Vieren ~ *to crawl on all fours* (⟨a. fig⟩ vor *before a p*) ‖ (P) mühsam vorwärts *or* dahin ~ *to drag o.s. along, to trudge* od *plod along* ‖ ~d ⟨bot⟩ *creeping, trailing*, ⟨scient⟩ *humifuse* ‖ ~des Tier *reptile*; aus dem Ei ~ *to be hatched, to come out (of the egg)*, aus dem Loch ~ *to come* od *creep out of* ..; der Hund ist in s–e Hütte gekrochen .. *has crept into* .. ‖ ins Bett ~ *to turn in between the sheets* ‖ er ist ihr auf den Leim gekrochen *he has allowed himself to be taken in by her* od *to be enticed by her* ‖ vor Angst am liebsten in ein Mauseloch ~ ⟨fam⟩ *to be in a blue funk* ‖ heimlich ~ *to sneak* **2.** ⟨**fig**⟩ (vor jdm) ~ *to cringe, crouch, truckle, kotow, pander (to a p)*; *to grovel (before, to a p)*; *to fawn (on a p)* | **~d** [a] *servile (obsequiousness)*; → Kreuz **Kr·iecher** m ~s/~ (→ vor. 2.) *cringing*, etc. *p*; *cringer, sycophant, toady, time--server, yes man*; ⟨fam⟩ *sneak* **Kriecher·ei** f *cringing*, etc., *servility, toadyism*; ⟨fam⟩ *sneaking*, ⟨Am⟩ *apple polishing* **kriecherisch** *cringing, fawning*, etc., *servile*; ⟨fig⟩ *reptile* [a]; ⟨sl⟩ *slimy* **Kr·iechling** m ~(e)s/~e = Kriekente *teal*

Kr·ieg m ~(e)s/~e *war(fare)* ⟨a. fig⟩ ‖ (Fehde) *feud*, ⟨fig⟩ *contest* ‖ (Streit) *strife, quarrel* ‖ (Feindseligkeiten) *hostilities* | **·Äther**≃ *radio-war* ‖ begrenzter ~ *limited war* Bew·egungs≃ *war of movement, moving war(fare)*; Bl·itz≃ ⟨sl⟩ *blitzkrieg* [Ger], *lightning-war*; B·ürger≃ *civil* od *internal* od *intestine war*; B·usch≃ *bush fighting*; **ch·emischer** ~ (a. G·iftgas≃) *chemical warfare*; Entsch·eidungs≃ *decisive war*; ⟨übtr⟩ *supreme contest*; ⟨fig⟩ *tug of war* (= Tauziehen) ‖ Handels≃ *merchant warfare*; ⟨Arab⟩ der H·eilige ~ (gegen Ungläubige) *the Holy war, jihad, jehad* ⟨a. fig⟩; heißer ~ → Schieß≃; kalter ~ *white* od *cold war*; Kl·ein≃ *guer(r)illa war*; Luft≃ *aerial war*; Nerven≃ *war of nerves*; Schieß≃ *hot* od *shooting war*; See≃ *naval warfare*; **Stellungs**≃ *stationary war--(fare), position war*; totaler ~ *total war, all-out war*; U-Boot≃ *submarine warfare*; ~ der Untätigkeit *war of inertia*; gegenseitiger Vernichtungs-≃ *internecine war*; ~ zu Wasser u zu Lande (u in der Luft) *war on land and water, amphibious (three dimensional) warfare* ‖ der erste **Welt**≃ *the World War I, the first Great War* | der **Deutsch-Französische** ~ *the Franco-German war* ‖ der ~ (von) 1870/71 *the war of* .. ‖ der Dreißigjährige (Hundertjährige) ~ *the Thirty (Hundred) Years' war* ‖ ~ bis aufs Messer, ~ auf Leben u Tod *war to the knife* od *to the bitter end* | ⟨**fig**⟩ der häusliche, eheliche ~ *domestic, matrimonial differences* | ein schwerer, blutiger ~ *a severe, bloody war* ‖ in ~ und Frieden *in peace and war* ‖ im ~e *at war, in time of war* | **das, so ist der** ~! *that's war!*; Bild des ~es *nature, environment of war, war in its outward aspects, the complexion* od *visage of war* ‖ es gibt ~ *that means war* ‖ der ~ ist ausgebrochen *war has broken out* ‖ es ist ~! *there is a war (going on)!*; °..! wir h ~! (eil dich) *there's a war on*; nie wieder ~! kein ~ mehr! *no more war!* | (e–n) ~ **anfangen** *or* beginnen (als Angreifer) *to start* od *begin (a) war, to make war, to begin hostilities*; *Mary went to war with Spain* ‖ ⟨fig⟩ *to unbury the hatchet* ‖ *the object of commanders was to come to handgrips without delay* ‖ der uns aufgezwungene ~ *the war forced upon us* ‖ e–n ~ **entfesseln** ⟨fig⟩ *to let slip the dogs of war* ‖ (e–m Lande) den ~ **erklären** *to declare war (on a country)*; ⟨fig⟩ *to take up the hatchet* ‖ ~ **führen** (mit *or* gegen) (ohne Angreifer zu s) *to wage with, to wage* od *carry on war (with* od *against), to make war (upon)* ‖ in den ~ **gehen** *(of a country) to go to war* ‖ e–n ~ **herbeiführen,** hervorrufen *to make for war*; e–n ~ heraufbeschwören (unbeabsichtigt) *to rush on war* ‖ in e–n ~ hineingezogen w *to be drawn into a war* ‖ ⟨fig⟩ im ~e **leben**: *husband and wife were in a constant state of warfare* ‖ im ~e liegen mit *to war with* ‖ den ~ **mitgemacht** h *to have seen service, to have stood the whole brunt of the war* ‖ zum ~e rüsten *to prepare for war* ‖ im ~e **sein** *to be at war, to be at the front* ‖ am ~e teilnehmend *in the war*

‖ sich in den ∼ stürzen *to rush on war* ‖ zum ∼e **treiben** *to intrigue for war* ‖ mit ∼ **überziehen** *to invade, overrun (a country)* ‖ den ∼ vermeiden *to keep out of the war* ‖ v ∼e verwüstet *war-ravaged, -blasted* ‖ v ∼e zerrissen *war-torn (Spain)* ‖ in den ∼ **ziehen** gegen *to go to war against, to march to battle, to take the field, to go into the war* ‖ *to join up, to go to the front, to go (away) to the war(s)* **≗-fertig** a *ready for war* **≗führend** a *belligerent, engaged in (a) war; at war* ‖ ∼e Macht *belligerent (power)* **≗führung** f *warfare, belligerence, waging of war; strategy, generalship* **≗liebend** a *warlike* **kr·iegen**[1] vi [h] ⟨rhet poet⟩ *to (go to) war, to carry on, make, wage war* (gegen, mit *against*) **kr·iegen**[2] vt [h] **1. (fangen**, fassen) *to catch, get, tag, seize; to catch* (od *lay*) *hold of* ‖ ≗ spielen *to play (at) catch* od *tag* | e–a *or* sich bei den Köpfen ∼ *to fall together by the ears*; ⟨fig⟩ *to get at loggerheads (with)* ‖ sich bei den Haaren ∼ *to pull each other by the hair* ‖ ich will dich schon ∼! *I'll pay you out yet*! **2. (bek)** *to get, obtain; receive (letters)* ‖ *to get (a child, a husband)* ‖ sie h sich ge–gt *they have got each other* ‖ du wirst es (tüchtig) ∼ ⟨fam⟩ *you'll cop it (hot)*; warte, du kriegst gleich ein paar (Schläge) *you'll get a good one* ‖ Hunger ∼ *to get hungry; to catch (a disease)* ‖ was kriegt er dafür? *what does he get for it*? ‖ er wird es mit der P. z tun ∼ *he will have to do with the police* ‖ als wenn er Geld dafür kriegte *like bricks, with a vengeance* ‖ krieg ich was ab? *am I to be in on this*? ‖ jdn auf s–e Seite ∼ *to get a p alongside one* ‖ er ist nicht **klein** z ∼ *he will never give in* ‖ du wirst das Ding doch wohl kl ∼! ⟨hum⟩ *I'm sure you'll be able to break it*! ‖ wir w ihn schon noch kl ∼! *he'll have to eat humble pie yet*! ‖ Wut ∼ *to fly into a wild rage* ‖ (etw) satt ∼ *to be sick of* ‖ es mit der Angst ∼ *to get anxious* **Kr·ieger** m ∼s/∼ *warrior, campaigner, combatant, fighter*; ⟨Am⟩ Guerilla≗ ⟨a.⟩ *bushwhacker* ‖ „alter ∼" "*old campaigner*", *veteran*, ⟨fam⟩ *old sweat*; ⟨hum⟩ (der alles kriegt) *go-getter* | ∼in [f] *female warrior, Amazone* | **∼-bund** m = ∼verein **∼denkmal** n *war memorial* **∼-kaste** f *warrior-caste* ‖ *military c.* **∼leben** n *warrior's* od *m. life* **∼stand** m *m. profession*; [koll] *m. men* pl, *soldiers* pl **∼tod** m *a soldier's death* **∼verband** m *association of m. clubs* **∼verein** m *club of veterans, ex-Servicemen('s club* od *association)* **∼witwe** f *war widow*, ⟨Am⟩ *gold star widow* **kr·iegerisch** a *warlike, bellicose; militant in spirit* ‖ *martial, brave, valiant* ‖ ∼es Wesen [n] *bellicosity*

Kr·iegs- *war, martial, military* **∼adel** m *military nobility* **∼akademie** f *mil. academy, War College, Army Staff College* **∼angelegenheiten** f pl *mil. concern* **∼anleihe** f *war-loan* **∼artikel** m pl *articles of war* **∼atmosphäre** f *war-time atmosphere* **∼ausrüstung** f *armament* **∼ausweitung** f *extension* od *escalation of the theatre of war* **∼baukunst** f *(art of) fortification* **∼baumeister** m *mil. architect* od *engineer* **∼bedarf** m, ∼bedürfnisse [n pl] *requisites of war, mil. stores* pl **∼begeisterung** f *martial enthusiasm* **∼behörde** f *mil. department, War Office* **∼beil** n *axe*; das ∼ begraben (ergreifen) *to bury (take up) the hatchet*; das ∼ schwingen ⟨fig Am⟩ *to wave the bloody shirt* ° **∼bemalung** f *raggery*; in voller ∼ *in full feather* od *fig* **≗bereit** a *ready for war, mobilized* **∼bereischaft** f *readiness for mil. operations, state of mobilization*; in ∼ setzen *to mobilize* **∼bericht** m *war bulletin, communiqué, report* **∼berichter** m *front-line reporter*, ⟨fam⟩ *warco*; L·uftwaffen≗ *air force w. r.* **∼berichter(statter)** m *war correspondent* **≗beschädigt** a *(war) disabled*; ≗e(r) *war disabled ex-Serviceman, invalid, veteran, disabled ex-soldier*; als ∼er entlassen w *to be invalided out of the army* **∼bild** n *pattern of war* **∼blinde(r)** m *war-blinded man*, die ∼n [pl] *the war-blinded* **∼brand** m ⟨fig⟩ *conflagration* | ∼stifter [m] *war mongerer* **∼brauch** m *custom of war* **≗brauchbar** a *fit; useful for mil. purposes* **∼braut** f *war-bride* **∼brücke** f *pontoon-bridge* | ∼ngerät [m] *mil. bridging material, prefabricated b. equipment* **∼budget** n *mil.* (od *army-*) *-budget* **∼dauer** f: auf ∼ *for the duration of the war* **∼denkmünze** f *war-medal* **∼dienst** m ⟨mil⟩ *service*; ∼e tun *to serve in the army* | ∼verweigerer [m] *conscientious objector* **∼drohung** f *threat of war* **∼drommete** f ⟨poet⟩ *war-trumpet* **∼eifer** m *mil. zeal* **∼einquartierung** f *war billeting* **∼einsatz** m; totaler ∼ *total war effort* **∼eintritt** m *entry into the war* **∼entschädigung** f *war indemnity* **∼erfahren** a *skilled* od *experienced in war* **∼erfahrung** f *war experience*; ∼ h *to have seen service* **∼erklärung** f *declaration of war* (an *on, against*) **∼eröffnung** f *opening of hostilities* **∼fach** n *mil. science* **∼fackel** f *torch of war* **∼fahne** f *colours* pl **∼fahrzeug** n ⟨mar⟩ *naval unit* **∼fall** m *casus belli* [L]; im ∼e *in case of war* **∼flagge** f *war* (⟨engl⟩ *white) ensign* **∼-flegel** m ⟨hist⟩ *flail* **∼flotte** f *navy; naval force, fleet (of battleships)* **∼führer** m *war-leader* ‖ die **∼furie** tobt durchs Land *the horrors of war are raging throughout the country* **∼fuß** m, auf ∼ setzen *to put on a war-footing*; Truppen auf ∼ *mobilized troops* ‖ ⟨fig⟩ auf dem ∼ stehen mit *to be at war with, to be at daggers drawn with*, mit der Grammatik .. *to be a duffer at grammar* **∼gebiet** n *war* od *combat area* od *zone* **∼gebrauch** m *usage of war* **∼gefahr** f *danger of war* **∼gefährte** m *companion in arms, fellow-soldier, brother-officer* **∼gefangene(r)** m *prisoner of war* (freilassen *to civilianize*) | ≗ Offiziere [pl] *officer prisoners of war* **∼gefangenenlager** n *P.-o.-W. camp* **∼gefangenschaft** f *captivity*, in ∼ s *to be a P.o.W.* **≗gemäß** a *warlike (equipment)* **∼gerät** n *implements of war, war stores* **∼gericht** [e pl] n (einfaches [Schnell≗] *summary) court*[*s-* pl]*-martial*; oberstes ∼ *general c. (m.)*; jdn vor ein ∼ stellen, über jdn ∼ halten *to c.-m. a p* **≗gerichtlich** adv *by c.-m.* **∼gerichtsrat** m *Judge Advocate* **∼geschichte** f *mil. history* **∼geschrei** n *warcry*, (v Wilden) *war-whoop* **∼geschwader** n *fleet (of men-of-war)* **∼getöse, ∼getümmel** n *din of battle* **≗geübt** a *practised in war* **∼gewinnler** m *(war) profiteer* **∼gewinnsteuer** f *excess profits duty* **∼gliederung** f *battle-array, (table of) wartime organization* **∼glück** n *fortune of war, mil. success* **∼gott** m *god of war, Mars* **∼göttin** f *goddess of war, Bellona* **∼grab** n *war grave* **∼gräber-** ∼dienst [m] *graves registration* N; ∼fürsorge [f] *g. r. (service)*; *War G. Commission*; ∼stätte [f] *soldier cemetery* **∼greuel** n [pl] *war atrocities* pl **∼hafen** m *naval port* **∼handlung** f *act of war*; ∼en [pl] *hostilities* **∼handwerk** n *trade of war* **∼heer** n *army, mil. forces* pl **∼held** m *(war) hero* **∼heldin** f *maiden warrior (Joan of Arc)* **∼heros** m *(war) hero* **∼herr** m *supreme war lord; commander-in-chief (of an army)*; ⟨bib⟩ *lord of hosts* **∼hetze** f *war mongering, war agitation* **∼hetzer** m *warmonger, war agitator, jingo(ist)*, ⟨Am⟩ *war hawk* **≗hetzerisch** a *jingoistic, chauvinistic* **∼hinterbliebene** m [der ∼, ein ∼r] [f ∼]; ∼ pl *surviving dependants of service--men* **∼industrieamt** n *War Industry Board* **∼invalide** m *war invalid* **∼jahr** n *year of war* **∼kabinett** n *war-cabinet* **∼kamerad** m *brother in arms* (→ ∼gefährte) **∼kammer** f ⟨hist⟩ *War-Office* **∼karte** f *war-map, mil. map* **∼kasse** f *war-chest* **∼kassierer** m *paymaster (of the army)* **∼klausel** [f] ⟨ins⟩ *war risk clause* **∼kleidung** f *austerity clothes* pl **∼-knecht** m *trooper, soldier* **∼kollegium** n *War-Office* **∼kommissar** m *mil. commissary* **∼kommissariat** n *mil. commissariat* **∼konterbande** f *contraband of war* **∼kosten** f pl *expenses* od *cost of war, war expenses* **∼kunde** f *mil. science, tactics* pl **≗kundig** a *skilled in war* od *tactics* pl; ein ≗er *a tactician, strategist* **∼kunst** f *art of war, strategy, tactics* pl, *generalship* **∼lage** f *situation*; ⟨mil⟩ *(general, special) idea*; ⟨mil⟩ *war map* **∼lager** n *camp* **∼lärm** m *tumult of war* **∼lasten** f pl *burden of war* **∼läufte** pl *events* pl *of war* **∼lazarett** n *mil. hospital; base* od *general h.* N **~leben** n *mil. life, life in war* **~leistungen** f pl ⟨tech⟩ *war effort* **~leute** pl *soldiers, warriors* **~lied** n *war song* **~list** f *ruse, wile, stratagem of war* **~lust** f *bellicosity* **≈lüstern** a *war greedy, trigger-happy* **~lustig** a *bellicose* **~macht** f (bes zur See) *armament, mil. forces* pl; ⟨pol⟩ *mil. power* **~mann** m *militarist; warrior, soldier* **~-mannschaft** f *troops, forces* pl **~mantel** m *mil. cloak* **~marsch** m *tactical march* **~marine** f ⟨engl⟩ (*Royal*) *Navy*; ⟨Ger⟩ *German navy* **~maschine** f *engine of war* **~material** n *material of war, w. m.*; (incl. Verpflegung) *munition* **~minister** m ⟨Ger⟩ *Minister of War*, ⟨engl⟩ *Secretary of State for War*, ⟨Am⟩ *Secretary of War* **~ministerium** n ⟨Ger⟩ *Ministry of War*, ⟨engl⟩ *War-Office*; ⟨Am⟩ *War Board*, ⟨arch⟩ *Pentagon* **~mode** f *austerity fashion* **≈müde** a *war-weary, -wearied, -worn* **~-munition** f *munitions* [pl] *of war* **~narben** f pl *scars of war*, mit ~ *war-scarred* (*p, country*, etc) **~neurose** f *war fatigue*, (akut) *shell shock* **~not** f *stress* od *calamity of war* **~opferversorgung** f *war victims welfare service* **~partei** f *war-party* **~pfad** m; auf dem ~ s *to be on the warpath* **~pflicht** f *obligation to serve in the army* **≈pflichtig** a *liable to mil. service* **~plan** m *strategic plan*, ≈e [pl] *war plans* **~potential** n *war*(*making*) *potential* **~produktion** f *war production*; Amt für ~ ⟨Am⟩ *Office for Production Management* (*1941*) **~rat** m *war council, council on action*, ⟨engl⟩ *Supreme War Council*; e–n ~ halten *to hold a council of war* **~recht** n *martial law*; ~ verhängen *to proclaim m. l.* (→ ~gericht) **~reserve** f *reserve*(*-force*) **~reserv·ist** m *reserve-man* **~roß** n *charger, war-steed* **~ruf** m *cry of war*; dem ~ folgen *to follow the summons to take up arms* **~ruhm** m *mil. glory* **~rüstung** f *mil. equipment* od *accoutrement*; *armament* **~schäden** m pl *war damage* | ~amt [n] *w. d. commission* **~schauplatz** m *theatre of war* (od *operations*); auf dem afrikanischen ~ *in the African theatre*; ⟨Am⟩ *European Theater* (*of Operations* pl) **~schiff** n *man-of-war, capital ship, war-ship, battle-ship*; ⟨allg⟩ *naval vessel* **~schuld** f *war guilt* | ~lüge [f] *war guilt lie*; *impossible to define the exact share of blame for this vast catastrophe* (Wells); ~verschreibung [f] *warbond* **~schulden** f pl *war debts* **~schule** f *officer candidate school*; vgl. –akademie **~spiel** n *indoor manœuvre* **~sprache** f *mil. language* **~stamm** m *martial tribe* **≈stark** a *fully manned*, [pred] *on a war footing* **~stand** m, **~stärke** f (des Heeres) *manpower*; *war-strength* od *-establishment* | ~- u Ausrüstungsnachweisung [f] *w. e.* **~sterbefälle** m pl *deaths due to operations of war* **~steuer** f *contribution*; *war tax* **~straße** f *mil. road* **~tagebuch** n *war-diary*, ⟨mil⟩ *historic record* **~-tanz** m *war-dance* **~tat** f *warlike deed* **~tauglichkeit** f *fitness for active service* (→ ~brauchbarkeit) **~teilnehmer** m; er war ~ *he has done his bit*; ehemaliger ~ *ex-service-man*, ⟨Am⟩ *veteran* **~-tracht** f (der Wilden) *war-attire* od *-paint* **~trauung** f *war-wedding*, → Fern– **≈tüchtig** a *efficient, fit* **~tüchtigkeit** f *mil. efficiency* od *fitness* **~übung** f *mil. manœuvre* od *exercise* **~unterstützung** f (*war*) *allowance* **~verbrechen** n *war-crime, crime of war* **~verbrecher** m *war criminal* **~verpflegung** f *provisioning of an army* (*in time of war*); *war-rations* pl **~verpflegungsamt** n *commissariat* **~verrohung** f *war-coarsening* **≈versehrt** *a disabled* (*serviceman*, ⟨Am⟩ *war veteran*) **≈verwendungsfähig** a (abbr k.v.) *fit for active service*; *A 1*, ⟨Am⟩ *Class A* || ~ s, ~ geschrieben w *to pass for a. s.* **~volk** n *troops, forces* **~vorbereitungen** f pl *war preparations* **~-vorrat** m mst pl *mil. stores* pl; *initial reserves*; ⟨bes⟩ (*am*)*munition* **~wagen** m ⟨Eg ant⟩ *war* od *charging chariot* **~werft** f ⟨mar⟩ *naval dockyard, arsenal* **~wesen** n *mil. concerns, matters, affairs* pl **~wichtig** a *essential, important military* (*objectives*), *of mil. importance*; Arbeiter in e–m ~en Betrieb *essential worker*; nicht ~ *non-essential*; ~es Ziel *strategic target*; Bombardierung ~er Ziele *st. bombing* **~wirtschaft** f *wartime economy* **~wissenschaft** f *mil.* od *strategic science* | ≈liche Forschung *operations analysis* **~wut** f *warlike fury, rage of war* **~zahlmeister** m *army-paymaster* **~zahlmeister·ei** f *army pay-office* **~zeit** f *time of war*, in ~en *in times of war* **~ziele** n pl *war aims* pl **~zone** f *war zone* **~zucht** f *mil. discipline* **~zug** m *mil. expedition*; *campaign* **~zulage** f *field-allowance, war-bonus* **~zustand** m *state of war* **~zwecke** m pl *purposes of war*

Kr·ikelkrakel n ~s/ = Krickel ..

Kr·im f ⟨geogr⟩ die ~ *the Crimea* **~krieg** m *Crimean war* **~stecher** m † ⟨opt⟩ *field-glasses* pl

°**Kr·imi** m ~s/~s ⟨fam⟩ *deteccer*, → ~nalroman, –film **krimin·al** a (strafrechtlich) *criminal* **Krimin·al- ~abteilung** f *cr.l department*; (in London) *Cr. Office* **~amt, ~gericht** n *cr.l court* **~anklage** f *cr.l charge, presentment* **~beamte(r)** m (*official*) *detective*; *officer of the cr.l department* **~film** m *crime film*, ⟨Am sl⟩ *screamer* **≈gerichtlich** a *cr.l, penal* **~gerichtsbarkeit** f *cr. jurisdiction* **~gerichtsordnung** f *cr.* (*rules of*) *procedure* **~gesetz** n *penal law* **~gesetzbuch** n *penal code* **~klage** f = ~anklage **~komödie** f *comedy thriller* **~polizei** f ⟨Ger⟩ *cr.l police*; *detective force* od *police, cr.l investigation department* **~polizist** m = ~beamter **~prozeß** m *cr. case* **~psychologe** m *psychologist of crime* **~psychologie** f *psychology of crime* **~recht** n *penal law* **~reißer** m *shocker, thriller* **~richter** m *judge in cr.l cases* **~roman** m *crime* od *detective novel*; ~e [pl] ⟨Am fam⟩ *whodunits* **~romanschriftsteller** m *crime novelist* **~sache** f *cr.l case* **~strafkunde** f *penology, criminology* **~stück** n ⟨theat⟩ *crook-drama, gangster-* od *crime-play* **~verfahren** n *cr.l proceeding* **~vergehen** n *indictable offence* **Kriminal·ist** m ~en/~en **1.** *detective*, ⟨sl⟩ *copper*, ⟨Am⟩ *G-man* **2.** (Lehrer) *criminalist, criminal expert* **Kriminalit·ät** f *delinquency, criminality*; Gewohnheits≈ *habitual d.*; Jugend≈ *juvenile d.* **krimin·ell** a *criminal, malfeasant* | ≈**e(r)** m *criminal* | °⟨fam⟩ = Kriminalbeamter

Kr·immer m ~s/ *krimmer*

Kr·impe f ~/ *shrinking, sponging, steaming* (*of cloth*) **kr·impen** vt [h] *to shrink, sponge* (*cloth*) || vi [s] & sich ~ [h] *to shrink* **kr·impfrei** a *thoroughly shrunk, nonshrinking*

°**Krimskrams** m ~/ *trash, rubbish, bits and pieces*; *gadgets* pl, ⟨sl⟩ *junk*; der ganze ~ *the whole caboodle*

Kr·ingel m ~s/~ *curl, curve*; ⟨bak⟩ *cracknel* | ~n *to twist*; z K–n → wälzen

Krinol·ine f ~/~n *crinoline, hoop-petticoat* || ~ngestell n *skeleton of a cr.*; ~nreifen m *spring-hoop*

°**Kr·ipo** f ~/~s = Kriminalpolizei

Kr·ippe f ~/~n *crib, manger* || (Säuglingsheim) *crèche* || *cradle of our Lord*; *Nativity figuriness* || (für Blumen) *flower stand* | ⟨fig⟩ er sitzt an der ~ *he sits at the fountain-head* || sie suchten an die ~ z k *they tried to secure good berths* **Kr·ippen- ~beißer** m = ~setzer **~reiter** m *parasite, sponge* **~-setzen** n ⟨hors⟩ *crib-biting* **~setzer** m *crib-biter, cribber*; *sorry* od *wretched jade* || ⟨fig⟩ *inveterate grumbler* **~spiel** n *Nativity* **~wirtschaft** f ⟨Am pol⟩ *spoils system*

°**Kr·ips** m; jdn beim ~ (u Kragen) packen *to take a p by the collar*

Kr·is m ~ses/~se (malai. Dolch) *kris, creese*

×**Kr·ischan, Kr·ischäning** m [npr] = Christian

×**kr·ischen** vi [h], **Kr·ischer** m → kreischen etc

Kr·ise, Kr·isis f ~/–sen ⟨a. med⟩ *crisis*; geistige, politische, wirtschaftliche ~ *mental, political, economic cr.*; ⟨mil⟩ *critical situation* || bedenkliche, gefährliche ~ *burning cr.* || e–e ~ überwinden *to get over a cr.* || bei dem Kranken tritt die ~ ein *the patient will reach the cr.* || e–e ~ durchm *to* *pass through a cr.*; die ~ überwinden *to turn the corner* | –seneindämmung [f] *cr. management*; –senzeiten [f pl] *times of stress* **kr·iseln** vi [h] ⟨pol⟩ es kriselt *affairs are coming to a cr.*

Krist·all 1. m ~(e)s/~e *crystal* || ~e bilden *to form cr.s, to cr.lize* || ~e scheiden sich aus .. *are precipitated* (*from the solution*) || Lehre v den ~en *cr.lography* **2.** n *cr. goods* [pl] od *ware*; *cut glass* **~-anschuß** m *crop of cr.s* **≗artig** a *cr.line* **~bild** n *image of the cr.* **~bildung** f *cr.lization, formation of cr.s, cr.lizing* **~detektor** m ⟨wir⟩ *cr. detector*; ausbalancierter ~ *balanced cr. detector* | ~apparat [m] ⟨wir⟩ *cr.l set* **~druse** f ⟨min⟩ *cluster of cr.s* **~eis** n *cr.ice* **~fabrik** f *cr.-works* pl [sg konstr] **~fabrikation** f *manufacture of cr.* **~feuchtigkeit** f *cr.line humour* (*of the eye*) **~fläche** f *face of a cr.*; *facet* **~flasche** f *cr. decanter* **~flüssigkeit** f ⟨chem⟩ *liquid of cr.lization* **~form** f ⟨scient⟩ *cr.line form* | ~enbeschreibung [f] *cr.lography* **~gitter** n ⟨phys⟩ *cr. lattice* **~glas** n *cr.* od *flint glass*; englisches ~ *flint cr.* **~glasfabrik** f *cr. glass works* **~goniometer** n *cr. goniometer* **~gravierung** f *cr. engraving* **~habitus** m *cr. shape* **≗hell** a *cr.line, as clear as cr.*; *transparent* **~kante** f *edge of a cr.* **~keim** m *nucleus of cr.lization* **~kiesel** m *cr. pebble* **≗klar** a = ~hell **~kunde, ~(l)ehre** f *cr.lography* **~(l)inse** f *cr. lense* (*of the eye*) **~palast** m *Cr. Palace* **~papier** n *cr. paper* **~schleifen** n *cr. cutting* **~schleifer** m *cutter of cr.* **~seitenfläche** f *lateral plane of a cr.* **~skelett** n *cr. skeleton* **~soda** f *soda cr., cr.lized sodium carbonate* **~spiegelglas** n *cr. glass for mirrors* **~struktur** f *structure of a cr.* **~system** n *cr.*(*line*) *system*; triklines ~ *triclinic system* **~waren** f pl *cr. goods* **~wasser** n *combined water, w. of cr.lization* **krist·allen** a *crystalline, crystal* **krist·allig** a *like crystal* **kristall·in,** krist·allisch a *crystalline* (*schist*); *crystallized* (*iron*) **Kristallisati·on** f ~/~en *crystallization*; ~ des Zukkers *granulation* .. **~sgefäß** n *crystallizer* **~s-wasser** n *water of crystallization*; ohne ~ *anhydrous* **kristallis·ieren** vt/i [h & s] *to crystallize* **Kristallograph·ie** f ~ *crystallography*

Kristi·ania 1. n (⟨mod⟩ = Oslo) *Christiania* (*Norway*) **2.** m ×(⟨a.⟩ Kristl) ~s/~s ⟨ski-ing⟩ *christiania*; ⟨sl⟩ *christie*; e–n ~ reißen *to do a christie*

Krit·erium n ~s/–rien *criterion, touchstone*

Krit·ik f ~/~en *criticism* (an, über *of*), ⟨mil⟩ *critique* || (Buchbesprechung) *review, critique*; ⟨Am fam⟩ *kick* || beißende ~ *knock*; bittere ~ üben *to be bitterly critical* (an *of*) || gute ~en h *to have a good press*; durch heftige ~ verletzen *to scarify*; schlechte ~en h ⟨Am fam⟩ *to get a bad write-up* || niederschmetternde, ungerechte ~ *crushing*; *unfair criticism*; scharfe ~ *diatribe, panning* || e–r ~ unterziehen *to criticize*; *to review* (*a book*); *to pass censure* (scharf tadelnd *stricture*) *upon a p* || ~ hervorrufen *to cause comment* || die ~ wuchs allgemein *the animadversions* (*of the people*) *grew more general* || ⟨fam⟩ **unter** aller ~ *below contempt*; *deplorable, execrable* | ~ = ~er: wie die ~ es tut *as critics do* **≗los** a (& adv) *undiscriminating*(*ly*); *unquestioning*(*ly*); *without critical faculty* **~losigkeit** f *lack of critical faculty* od *of discrimination* **Kritik·aster** m ~s/~ *cristicaster, faultfinder, caviller*, ⟨Am sl⟩ *knocker* || ⟨übtr⟩ *grumbler* **Kr·itiker** m ~s/~ *critic* || *reviewer* (*of books*) || ⟨übtr⟩ *grumbler* **kr·itisch 1.** [a] *critical* [gegen(über) *of*] || (bedenklich) *precarious* || feiner ~er Kopf *fine, judicious, subtle head* od *mind* || ~e Bemerkungen *critical remarks*; *strictures* [pl], *comment* | ~er Augenblick *crisis, critical moment*; ~es Alter *critical age*; ~es Ereignis, ~e Periode *climacteric* || ~e Lage *predicament*; ⟨tech⟩ *liminal* (*temperature*); *bursting, crushing* (*point*); ~e Situation = ~e Lage ⟨fam a.⟩ *pinch* ⟨bes Am⟩; ~er Zeitpunkt *important* (*con*)*juncture* || in ~en Verhältnissen *awkwardly situated* || ~er Tag *crucial* od *eventful day*; ⟨meteor⟩ *critical* od *climacteric day* | [adv] e–r S ~ gegenüberstehen *to be critical of a th* || ~ veranlagt *fault-finding* **kritis·ieren** vt [h] *to criticize* || du hast ewig etw zu ~ *you have always some objections to make* || (besprechen) *to review* || (tadeln) *to censure, trounce*; heftig ~ *to assail, lash, slap, chide, flay, pan*, ⟨fam⟩ *to run down*, ⟨Am sl⟩ *to knock, hammer, kick* || e–a ~ ⟨fam⟩ *to chew one another up* **Krittel·ei** f ~/~en *fault-finding*; *carping criticism*; *cavil* **Kr·itt(e)ler** m ~s/~ *carper, caviller, fault-finder, carping critic* **kr·itt(e)lig** a *censorious*; *captious, fault-finding*; *fastidious* **kr·itteln** vi [h] (an [dat]) *to cavil* (*at*), *to find fault* (*with*)

Kritzel·ei f ~/~en *scrawl*(*ing*), *scribble*; ~en [pl] *scribblings* **kr·itzelig** a *niggling, crabbed, cramped, scrawly* (*handwriting*) **kr·itzeln** vt/i [h] *to scrawl, scribble* (auf *on*) || *to scratch* **Kr·itzler** m ~s/~ *scribbler*

Kro·ate m ~/~n, **-tin** f ~/~nen *Croat* **-tien** [ts] ⟨geogr⟩ *Croatia* **k-tisch** a *Croat*(*ian*)

×**Kr·oatzbeere** f ⟨bot, cul⟩ → Kratzbeere

Kr·ocket n ~s/ *croquet* || ~ spielen *to* (*play*) *croquet* **~hammer** m *mallet* || → Kugel, Reifen **≗t·ieren** vi [h] *to play croquet* **krock·ieren** vt [h] *to roquet*

Krok·ant m ~s/ ⟨cul⟩ *rock* (*almonds*, etc)

Krok·i n ~s/~s (*rough*) *sketch*(*-map*) ⟨a. mil⟩

krok·ieren vt [h] *to* (*rough-*)*sketch*

Krokod·il n ~(e)s/~e *crocodile*; amerikanisches ~ *alligator, cayman*; indisches ⟨a.⟩ *mugger* **~stränen** f [pl] ⟨fig⟩ *c.-tears*; *hypocritical, false tears* **~wächter** m ⟨orn⟩ *c.-bird*

Kr·okus m ~/~ & ~se ⟨bot⟩ *crocus*

Kr·omlech m ~s/~e ⟨praeh⟩ *cromlech*

Kr·on- ~amt n *crown-office* **~anwalt** m *Public Prosecutor*, ⟨engl⟩ erster ~ *Attorney General*, zweiter ~ *Solicitor-General*; ⟨Scot⟩ *Lord Advocate*; ⟨Am⟩ (e–r Stadt) *district* od *circuit attorney* **~beamte(r)** m *crown-officer, officer of the c.* **~bewerber** m *pretender* (*to the c.*) **~bewerbung** f *pretendership* **~einkünfte** f pl *revenue of the c.* **~erbe** m *heir to the c., hereditary prince* **~erbse** f ⟨bot⟩ *c.-pea* **≗förmig** a *c.-shaped* **~gehörn, ~geweih** n *c. of a stag's head, c.ed top* **~glas** n ⟨opt⟩ *c.-glass* **~gut** n *Royal demesne* **~hirsch** m *stag with c.-antlers* **~insignien** pl *insignia of royalty, regalia* pl **~jurist** m *law officer of the C.* **~juwelen** n pl *c.-jewels* pl **~kolonie** f *c.-colony* **~land** n *c.-land, domain* **~lehen** n *fief of the c.* **~lehenhalter** m *tenant* (*in chief* od) *in capite* [L] **~leuchter** m *chandelier* || (mit Glasbehang) *lustre* || (Gas≗) *gaselier* || ⟨el⟩ *electrolier* || (in Kirchen) *jesse* **~-prätendent** m (*royal*) *pretender* **~prinz** m *C. Prince, Prince Royal*; (e–s Kaisers) *Prince Imperial*; ⟨allg⟩ *heir apparent, heir to the throne*; ⟨engl⟩ *Prince of Wales*; ⟨Russ hist⟩ *Czarevitch*, ⟨Fr hist⟩ *Dauphin* **~prinzessin** f *C. Princess*, ⟨engl⟩ *Princess of Wales*; ⟨engl⟩ (älteste Tochter) *Princess Royal* **≗prinzlich** a *belonging to the c.-prince* **~rad** n *c.-wheel* **~rat** m *C. Council* **~räuber** m *usurper* (*of the c.*) **~säge** f *drum-saw* **~schatz** m *c.-treasure* **~-sekretär** m ⟨engl⟩ *Clerk of the C.* **~taube** f *c.-pigeon* **~taler** m = Kronentaler **~werk** n ⟩mil⟩ *c.-work* **~wicke** f ⟨bot⟩ *sickle-wort* **~zeuge** m ⟨jur⟩ *king's evidence* || *approver*; ~ w (of criminals) *to turn king's evidence* (gegen Mitschuldige) **Kr·önchen** n ~s/~ *coronet* || ⟨bot⟩ *coronule* **Kr·one** f ~/~n **1.** *crown* (⟨a. übtr⟩ = Herrscher); ~n rollten v königlichen Häuptern *crowns kept rolling off royal heads* || e–m Könige die ~ aufsetzen *to place the c. on a king's head, to c. a king* || Adels≗, kl ~ *coronet* || päpstliche ~ *tiara* || (Stirnreifen) *diadem*; .. fiel ihm v Haupt ⟨fig⟩ *the d. passed from his brow* | ⟨fig⟩ *acme, perfection*; *flower* od *pink* (*of perfection*); *cope-stone, finishing touch*; die ~ der Schöpfung *the pearl of creation*, die ~ der Frauen *the pearl* od *paragon of womanhood*;

⟨prov⟩ dem Verdienste die ∼! *honour to whom h. is due*! ‖ das setzt der S die ∼ auf *this puts the lid on it, that caps* od *beats all*; *the final touch* (*was put to her disgust by that sight*) **2.** ⟨übtr⟩ **Baum**≃ *top, head*; (v Nadelbaum) *top shoots* pl ‖ Beleuchtungs≃ → Kronleuchter | Blumen≃ (Kranz) (*floral*) *wreath, garland* ‖ Blüten≃ (Dolde) *umbel*; (der einzelnen Blüte) *corol*(*la*) | (e–s Dammes) *summit, top, superior face* ‖ (der Druckerpresse) *cap, hat* | Ernte≃ *harvest c.* | ⟨**num**⟩ *German c., 10 mark gold-piece* = *half a sovereign*; *Danish, Norwegian, Swedish*, etc. *crown* = *1 shilling*; ⟨engl⟩ *a crown* = *5 shillings*, ⟨hum⟩ *cart-wheel*, ⟨sl⟩ *bell* | Geweih≃ des Hirschs *surroyals, crown--antlers*; (= Rehgehörn) *antlers, horns* pl | (Glokken≃) *crown*; Haspel≃ ⟨spin⟩ *swift*; **Huf**≃ *coronet, coronary band* od *cushion*; **Kristall**≃ *lustre*; Lanzen≃ *blunt point of a lance*; Mauer≃ *top, crest, crowning of the wall*; ∼ der Sperrmauer *crown of the dam*; ∼ e–r Schulterwehr *crest*; ∼ am Stechzeug *collar*; ∼ der Taschenuhr *winder*; Wellen≃ *crest*; **Zahn**≃ *crown cap* **3.** °⟨**fig**⟩ (Kopf) *nob, bean*; was ist dir in die ∼ gefahren? *what has come over you*?, *what has befallen you*?; *what have you taken offence at*?; ‖ er ist nicht ganz richtig in der ∼ ⟨fam⟩ *he is not quite right in the upper story* ‖ etw in der ∼ h ⟨fam⟩ a) *to have had a drop too much* b) *to be cross* ‖ das ist ihm in die ∼ gestiegen *that has affected his head* **kr·önen** vt [h] *to crown* ⟨a. fig⟩; *to place the c. on a p's head* ‖ jdn zum Könige ∼ *to c. a p king* ‖ jdn als Kaiser ∼ *to c. a p emperor* ‖ sich zum Kaiser ∼ l *to have o.s. c.ed emperor* ‖ gekrönte Häupter *c.ed heads* ‖ gekrönter Dichter *poet-laureate* | ⟨fig⟩ von Erfolg gekrönt *c.ed with success* ‖ ⟨prov⟩ das Ende krönt das Werk *the end c.s the work* ‖ ⟨tech⟩ gekrönt v *topped by*; ⟨fam⟩ (= vollenden) *to c., finish, top off, cap*; *to put the top-stone on* (*a work*) **Kr·onen-≃artig** a *like a c.*; ⟨scient⟩ *coronary* **∼blatt** n ⟨bot⟩ *petal* **∼bohrer** m *cross-mouthed chisel, crown drill* **∼breite** f (e–s Dammes) *breadth of top* **∼brenner** m ⟨chem⟩ *boiling* od *ring boiler* **∼dach** n *high--pitched roof* **∼fortsatz** m (des Unterkiefers) ⟨anat⟩ *coronoid process* **∼gold** n *eighteen carat gold* **∼höhe** f *crest level* od *elevation* (e–s Deichs) **∼kranich** m ⟨orn⟩ *c.ed crane* **∼mutter** f *castellated* od *horned nut* **∼orden** m (Preußen) *Order of the C.* **∼papier** n *c.-paper* **∼rad** n *face gear*; (e–r Uhr) *canting-wheel* **≃ständig** a ⟨bot⟩ *epipetalous* **∼taube** f ⟨orn⟩ *c.-pigeon* **∼träger** m *c.ed head, sovereign* **∼verschluß** m (Flaschen≃) *crown sealing* **∼welle** (e–r Windmühle) *axle tree*

Kron·ide m ∼n/∼n ⟨myth⟩ *son of Kronos*

Kr·onsbeere f ∼/∼n ⟨bot⟩ *bilberry, cranberry*

Kr·önung f ∼/∼en *crowning, coronation*; ∼ Mariä *Coron. of the Virgin* ‖ ⟨fig⟩ *coping-stone, cope-stone* ‖ die ∼ s: *the fireworks put the last touch on the evening*

Kr·önungs- ∼eid m *coronation oath* **∼feier, ∼feierlichkeit** f *c.-festivities, c.-ceremony, c.-solemnity* **∼mahl** n *c.-banquet* **∼münze** f *coin to commemorate a c.* **∼saal** m *c.-hall* **∼sessel** m *c.-chair, faldstool* **∼tag** m *c. day* **∼werk** n *crowning work* (*of a man*) **∼zug** m *coronation procession*

Kr·opf m ∼(e)s/≃e **1.** ⟨orn⟩ (Vormagen) *crop, craw* **2.** ⟨path⟩ *wen*; *goitre* Fr; ⟨fam⟩ *Derbyshire neck*; ⟨scient⟩ *struma, bronchocele* **3.** ⟨zoo⟩ *swelling* **4.** ⟨bot⟩ *excrescence* **5.** ⟨pap⟩ (∼ e–s Holländers) *breasting backfall* **6.** ⟨arch⟩ runder ∼ *mitre round* **∼achswelle** f ⟨tech⟩ *crank shaft* **≃artig** a ⟨path⟩ *wenny, goitrous*, ⟨scient⟩ *strumous* (*disease*) **∼eisen** n *sling, cran iron, devil's claw* **∼gans** f *pelican* **∼gerinne** n *circular channel* **∼grat** m, **∼kante** f *mitre line* **∼rad** n (e–r Mühle) *breast water wheel* **∼stein** m ⟨arch⟩ *corner stone* **∼taube** f ⟨orn⟩ *cropper, pouter*(*-pigeon*) **kr·öpfen 1.** vt [h] *to cram* (*geese*) ‖ ⟨tech⟩ *to bend at* (*right*) *angles*; ge–fte Aufhängung (e–r Glocke) *cranked suspension* **2.** vi [h] (v Raubvögeln) ⟨hunt⟩ *to gorge* (*o.s.*) ‖ ⟨tech⟩ *to form a knee* **kr·opfig, kr·öpfig** (ˣ⟨a.⟩ kr·opfert) a ⟨path⟩ *goitrous, strumous* ‖ *throaty* (*voice*) ‖ ˣich hab mich kropfert gelacht *I laughed my socks off* **Kr·öpfung** f ∼/∼en **1.** *cramming* (*of geese*) **2.** ⟨tech⟩ *knee*; (e–r Welle) *throw, inside crank* **3.** ⟨arch⟩ *breasting, moulding*

°**Kr·oppzeug** n: kl ∼ *young fry* od *brats* pl

kr·öschen vt [h] ⟨cul⟩ *to crisp, shorten*

Kr·öse f ⟨tech⟩ *notching tool* **∼maschine** f *groove cutting m.* **kr·ösen** vt [h] *to rabbet, groove*

Kr·ösus m [npr] ⟨a. fig⟩ *Croesus, nabob*; er fühlt sich als ∼ *he fancies h.s. a regular C.*

Krot f [–ɔt, ⟨österr⟩ –oːt] ∼/∼(te)n = Kröte ‖ ⟨fig⟩ freche kl ∼ *saucy little girl* od *thing*

Kr·öte f ∼/∼n **1.** *toad* → d., ⟨a.⟩ *paddock, natterjack* **2.** ⟨fig⟩ (P) *ugly wretch*; giftige ∼ *nasty snake*; nette kl ∼ *dear little th* | (Geld) ein paar ∼n ⟨fam⟩ *a bit of money*; *some tin*; nur ein paar ∼n *only a few coppers* **≃nartig** a *toad-like, toadish* **∼neidechse** f *horned t.* **∼ngift** n *t.'s venom* **∼nstein** m *t.-stone*, ⟨geol⟩ *bufonite* **kr·ötig** a ⟨fig⟩ *spiteful*

Kr·oton- ∼öl n ⟨bot, med⟩ *croton-oil* **≃sauer** a *crotonic* **∼säure** f *crotonic acid*

Kr·u f ∼/∼s ⟨mar⟩ *crew*

Kr·ücke f ∼/∼n *crutch* ‖ ⟨brew⟩ *rake, oar* ‖ (Kalkrühr≃) *beater* ‖ ⟨met⟩ *rake* ‖ ⟨pap⟩ *peel* ‖ (Croupier≃) *rake* | an ∼n gehen *to walk on c.es* ⟨a. fig⟩ **Kr·ückenkreuz** n ⟨her⟩ → Kreuz **Kr·ückstock** m *c.ed stick*

Kr·ug m ∼(e)s/≃e **1.** *jug*, ⟨bes Am⟩ *pitcher*; Waschtisch≃ *ewer* ‖ Trink≃ *tankard, toby*; Bier≃ (aus Zinn *pewter-*)*mug*; kl hölzerner ∼ *noggin* ‖ gr brauner irdener ∼ *brown george* | ⟨prov⟩ der ∼ geht so lange z Wasser, bis er bricht *the pitcher which goes too often to the well gets broken at last* | Der Zerbrochene ∼ (Greuze, Kleist) *The Broken Pitcher* **2.** (Schenke) *pot-, ale-house, village-inn* **∼gerechtigkeit** f *publican's license* **≃weise** adv *in jugs*, etc. **∼wirt** m = Krüger **∼wirtschaft** f = Krug 2 ***Kr·üger** m ∼s/∼ *tapster, ale--house keeper, publican* ‖ (*well*), *landlord*, (*he said, you* ..) **Kr·üglein** n ∼s/∼ *small jug* **Kr·uke** f ∼/∼n *stone bottle* od *jar*; Bett≃ *hot water bottle* | ⟨fig⟩ °komische alte ∼ *queer old crank*; ⟨fam⟩ *queer fish, rum fellow*

Kr·ümchen n ∼s/∼ *small crumb* (*of bread*) | ⟨fig⟩ *a wee bit* **Kr·ume** f ∼/∼n *crumb* ‖ (Acker≃) *mould* **Kr·ümel(chen)** n ∼s/∼ = Krümchen **kr·ü-m(e)lig** a *crummy, crumbly, in crumbs* ‖ ∼er Boden *friable soil* **Kr·ümel- ∼kohle** f *small coal* **∼kuchen** m *seed-cake* **∼zucker** m *granulated sugar* **kr·ümeln** vi/t & sich ∼ [h] *to crumble* **kr·umen** vt [h] *to crumble* **kr·umig** a *crumby* (*bread*); *friable* (*soil*)

kr·umm a & adv **1.** ⟨eig⟩ (gebogen) *crooked, bent* ‖ (gekrümmt, geschweift) *curved*, ⟨scient⟩ *sinuous* ‖ (hakenförmig) *hooked*, ⟨scient⟩ *aduncous* ‖ (verdreht) *twisted*, (*a*)*wry* ‖ (bogenförmig) *arched* ‖ (verbogen) *out of shape* ‖ (unregelmäßig) *tortuous, full of twists*; (gewunden) *winding, meandering* | ∼e **Beine** (x–) *crooked legs, knock-kneed legs*; (o–) *bandy-* od *bow-legs*; ∼e B. h *to be crooked-* bzw. *bandy-legged* ‖ e–n ∼en Buckel m *to curve one's back* ‖ ⟨fig⟩ ∼e Finger m *to pilfer, pinch* ‖ ∼e Nase *hook*(*ed*) (seitlich *wry*) *nose* ‖ ⟨fig⟩ e–n ∼en Rücken m *to stoop obsequiously* | jdn ∼ [adv] **anblicken** *to look askance* od *awry at a p* ⟨a. fig⟩; **∼|biegen** *to curve, bend, twist*; **∼|gehen** → gebeugt; es **geht** ∼ mit ihm *th.s are going wrong with him* ‖ sich ∼ **halten** *to stoop* ‖ sich ∼ u schief lachen *to split one's sides with laughing*; **∼liegen** ⟨eig⟩ *to lie in a bent position*; ⟨fig⟩ *to pinch* (*and screw*) ‖ etw ∼ **nehmen** *to take a th ill* od *amiss* od *the wrong way* od *in ill part* ‖ jdn ∼ u lahm **schlagen** *to beat* od *pound a p to a jelly* od *cripple* ‖ etw ∼ [adv] **schlagen** *to hammer crookedly* ‖ **∼ sein** *to be crooked*, etc.; (P) *to stoop*; ∼ u lahm s *to feel cramped* ‖ ~ **sitzen** *to cower, to sit with a crooked back* ‖ ~ **werden** *to bend, curve*; (*of timber*) *to warp*; (P) *to be bowed down* od *bent* (*with age*) **2.** ⟨fig⟩ *crooked, dishonest* ‖ *crooked, tortuous* (*policy*) ‖ *crooked* od *artful* (*ways*) **Kr·umm-~achse** f ⟨tech⟩ *crank* **≃ästig** a *having gnarled* od *crooked branches* **~axt** f *adze* **~bein** n *crook-shanks* pl **≃beinig** a (o-beinig) *bandy*(*-legged*), *bow-legged*; (x-beinig) *crooked-legged, knock-kneed* **≃buck(e)lig** a *crook-backed* **~darm** m ⟨anat⟩ *ileum* L | ~gicht [f] ⟨path⟩ *ileus* **~eisen** n (Küferei) *hollowing knife* **≃flächig** a *with a curved surface* **~hals** m *wry* od *crooked neck*, ⟨path⟩ *torticollis* **≃halsig** a *wry-necked*, ⟨path⟩ *torticollar* **~haue** f (Küferei) *barrel howel*; ⟨carp⟩ *hollow adze* **~holz** n *crook*(*ed*) *timber*; (Schiffsbau) *rising timber, bent wood, knee-, compass-timber* | ~arbeit [f] ⟨min⟩ *long-wall working on small veins*; ~kiefer [f] ⟨bot⟩ *dwarf knee-* od *mountainpine*; ~öl [n] *Hungarian balsam, templin-oil* **~horn** n *crumpled horn* ‖ (Kuh) *crummy* ‖ ⟨mus⟩ *crooked horn*, (*kind of*) *oboe*; (der Orgel) *cromorna* **≃hörnig** a *with twisted horns* **≃linig** a *curvilineal, -linear* **≃näsig** a *hook-nosed* **≃|nehmen** vt → krumm **~säbel** m (Orient) *scimitar* **~schnabel** m ⟨orn⟩ *curlew, crook-bill* **~stab** m *crook* ‖ ⟨ec⟩ *crosier, crozier*; ⟨fig⟩ *episcopal power* **~stehen** n (v Buchstaben) *winding* **~stroh** n *crumpled straw, litter* *crozier*; ⟨fig⟩ *episcopal power* **~|stehen** n (v Buchstaben) *winding* **~stroh** n *crumpled straw, litter* **~werden** n *crooked growth* **~ziegel** m *compass brick* **~zirkel** m *inside callipers, spherical compasses* pl **Kr·umme** m ~n/~n **1.** *hunch-back* **2.** ⟨hunt⟩ *hare* **Kr·ümme** f ~/ **1.** *crookedness, bend*; *curvature*; *circuit*, etc. → krumm **2.** ⟨fig⟩ *crookedness, dishonesty, tortuosity* **kr·ümmen 1.** vt [h] *to crook, curve, bend, twist, crank, buckle* ‖ (den Rücken) *to hog*, (die Schultern) *to hunch* ‖ *to warp* (*wood*) ‖ gekrümmte Fläche ⟨tech⟩ *curved surface, rounded plain* ‖ es soll ihr niemand ein Haar ~ *nobody shall hurt a hair of her head* ‖ dafür werde ich k–n Finger ~ *I shan't lift a finger for that* **2. sich ~** [vrefl] *to grow crooked*, etc.; *to* (*form a*) *bend* od *curve, to crinkle* ‖ (of timber) *to warp, start, wind* ‖ (of rivers) *to wind, meander* ‖ (of worm) *to squirm* ‖ ⟨prov⟩ der getretene Wurm krümmt sich *tread on a worm, and it will turn* ‖ sich ~ u winden *to wriggle, writhe, wince* | ⟨fig⟩ sich (vor jdm) ~ u winden *to cringe and fawn* (*upon a p*), *to stoop* (*before a p*) ‖ sich ~ (vor Verlegenheit, Schmerzen, Lachen) *to squirm* (*with embarrassment*); *to double up, to be doubled up* od *convulsed, to writhe* (*with pain*); *to be convulsed, to split* (*with laughter*) **Krümmer** m ~s/~ ⟨agr⟩ *harrow with colters* **Kr·ümmling** m ~s/~e ⟨arch⟩ *curve-beam of a banister*; *camber-beam* **Kr·ümmung** f ~/~en **1.** (das Krümmen) *crooking, bending*, etc. (→ krümmen); *flexure, crook* (*of an arm*); *with a sweep of his arm* **2.** (Zustand) *crookedness, bend*; *camber* (*of beam, deck, road*); *flexure* (*of a curve*) ‖ ~ des Unterfußes *bend* ‖ *sweep* od *curve* (*in a road*) ‖ ⟨bot⟩ *sinus* ‖ (Windung) *turn, turning, winding, twist*: *full of turns and twists*; ~en [pl] *tortuosities* pl (*of a river*) ‖ *flexion* (*of a limb, joint*) ‖ ⟨path⟩ *contortion*; *curvature* (*of the spine*) **~shalbmesser** m, **~smittelpunkt** m *radius, centre of curvature*

kr·umpen vt [h] *to shrink, sponge, decatize* (*cloth*); → krump(f)frei

kr·umpeln, ≃ vt [h] *to crumple, ruffle, crease*; *to pucker* (*up*) **kr·umpelig** a; ~e Stirn *puckered brow*

Kr·ümper m ~s/~ **1.** *sponger* (*of cloth*) **2.** ⟨mil hist Ger 1808–12⟩ *partially trained reservist* | ~pferd [n] ⟨mil⟩ *supernumerary horse*; ~wagen [m] ⟨mil⟩ *regimental dog-cart*

kr·ump(f)frei a ⟨tail⟩ *pre-shrunk*; *shrink-proof*

Krupp·ade f ~/~n ⟨hors⟩ *croupade*

Kr·uppe f ~/~n ⟨hors⟩ *crupper, croup*(*e*) Fr

Kr·üppel m ~s/~ *cripple*; [pl] *the maimed* ‖ ⟨fig⟩ (schwächliche P) ⟨sl⟩ *crock* ‖ (Mißgestalt) *stunted p* ‖ jdn zum ~ schlagen, schießen *to beat a p black and blue, to cripple a p with a shot* ‖ zum ~ w *to be crippled, maimed* **~grenze** f ⟨bot⟩ *upper crook-timber line* **≃haft, ≃ig** a *crippled, lame, maimed* ‖ v ~er Entwicklung *stunted* (*tree*) **~haftigkeit** f *crippled condition*

Kr·uspel [ˣkruʃpl] m ~s/~(n) ⟨cul⟩ (Knorpel) *gristle* ‖ (Kruste) *crackling* (*of a pie, etc*)

°**kr·usselig** a (kraus) *kinky* (*hair*)

Krustaz·ee [ˈtseːə] f ~/~n ⟨zoo⟩ *crustacean*

Kr·uste f ~/~n *crust* (*of bread*); in der ~ ⟨cul⟩ *en croûte* Fr ‖ *crackling* (*of pork*) ‖ *rind* (*of cheese, bacon*) ‖ (in Portweinflasche) *beeswing* ‖ (im Kessel) *fur* ‖ (Schmutz≃) *caked dirt* (*on shoes*) ‖ (Schorf) *scurf* ‖ ⟨path⟩ (Grind) *scab*, ⟨scient⟩ *porrigo* | e–e ~ bilden, bek, ansetzen *to* (*en*)*crust, to fur* ‖ (sich) mit e–r ~ überziehen *to* (*en*)*crust* **≃nartig** a ⟨scient⟩ *crustaceous* **~nflechte** f ⟨path⟩ *scab* **~ntier** n ⟨zoo⟩ *shell-fish*; *crustacean* **kr·ustig** a *crusty*, ⟨scient⟩ *crustaceous*

Kr·ux f ~/ L *crux*; *sore*; *delicate point* **Kruzi-~f·eren** f pl ⟨bot⟩ *crucifers, cruciferae* pl **~f·ix** n ~es/~e *crucifix* °**~türken**! → Donnerwetter

Kryol·ith m ~(e)s/~e ⟨min⟩ *cryolite*

Kr·yophys·ik f (Physik sehr niedriger Temperaturen) *cryophysics* [sg konstr]

Kr·ypta, -te f ~/–ten ⟨ec arch⟩ *crypt* **Kr·ypto-~g·amen** [pl] ⟨bot⟩ *cryptogams* pl; **≃g·amisch** [a] *cryptogamous*; ~gramm [n] *cryptogram*

Kr·ypton n ~s/ ⟨chem⟩ *krypton*

ks, ks! **kß, kß**! intj *havoc*! ‖ ⟨hum⟩ ich will ja nicht hetzen, aber „kß, kß!" .. *but I cry havoc*

Kuangsi n (südchin. Prov.) *Kwangsi*

Kuangtschouwan n (an Südküste v Kuangtung) *Kwangchow*(*-wan*)

Kuan(g)tung n (chin. Prov.) *Kwan*(*g*)*tung*

K·uba n *Cuba* **Kub·aner** m, **~in** f *Cuban* **kub·anisch** a *of Cuba, Cuban*

K·ubanbrückenkopf m *Kuban bridgehead*

Kubat·ur f ~/~en ⟨math⟩ *cubature*

Kub·ebe f ~/~n, ~npfeffer [m] *cubeb*

K·übel m ~s/~ *tub* (⟨a. hort⟩ für Palmen etc); *bucket*; gr ~ *vat* ‖ ⟨min⟩ *kibble* ‖ Abteuf≃ ⟨min⟩ *sinking bucket* ‖ ⟨fig sl⟩ (Kopf) *pannikin*; (Auto) *rattle-trap* ‖ es gießt wie mit ~n *it's raining cats and dogs* **~tasche** f ⟨mod⟩ *tote* od *bucket bag* **~wagen** m *bin wagon*; ⟨mot⟩ *land-rover*; ⟨mil⟩ *command* (*and reconnaissance*) *car* (abbr *c. and r.*), kl ~ ⟨Am⟩ *jeep*

kub·ieren vt [h] *to* (*raise to the*) *cube* ‖ ≃ n, **Kub·ierung** f *cubation* **Kub·ik-** *cubic* **~dezimeter** n *c. decimetre* **~fuß** m *c. foot* **~inhalt** m *cubage*; *solid contents* pl **~inhaltsberechnung** f *cubature* **~maß** n *c. measure* **~meter** n *c. metre* **~rute** f *c. cord* **~wurzel** f ⟨math⟩ *c. root* (*of 8 = 2*); die ~ ziehen *to extract* od *find the cube-root* (aus 8 *of 8*) **~zahl** f *c. number* od *cube* **~zentimeter** n *milliliter* (*ml*) **~zoll** m *c. inch* **k·ubisch** a ⟨math⟩ *cubic*(*al*) **Kub·ismus** m ~/ *cubism* **K·ubus** m ~/~ & –ben ⟨geom⟩ *cube*

K·üche f ~/~n **1.** *kitchen*; zweite ~ (für Dienstboten) *back-kitchen*; kl ~ *kitchenette* ‖ ⟨mil⟩ *cook-house*; Feld≃ *kitchen car*; (*rolling* od *motor*) *kitchen*; *cooker*; ⟨mar⟩ *cook-room*; *caboose, galley* ‖ Dampf≃ *steam kitchen*; elektrische Klein≃ *portable electric stove* ‖ das Beste was ~ u Keller bieten *the best that cellar and kitchen can offer* ‖ die ~ betreffend *culinary* | des Teufels ~ *hell*, ⟨fam⟩ *blazes*; in des Teufels ~ bringen, k *to get into an awkward, awful* od *a terrible mess, stew, scrape* **2.** (Kochart) bürgerliche, französische, Wiener, feine ~ *plain, French, Vienna, fancy* od *delicate cooking, cookery, cuisine* Fr ‖ die ~ besorgen *to cook, to attend* (⟨fam⟩ *see*) *to the cooking* ‖ e–e gute ~ führen *to keep a good table* ‖ sie versteht die ~ *she understands* od *knows cooking* od *cookery* **3.** (Speise) sie kocht e–e vorzügliche ~ *she makes excellent cooking*; kalte ~ *cold meat, dinner, collation*, etc. || mit kalter ~ vorlieb nehmen *to put up with a cold lunch(eon)*

K·uchen m **1.** *cake, tart* || → Baum≈, Blech≈, Zwetschenkuchen etc **2.** °⟨fam iron⟩ ja ~! *apple-sauce!, fiddle-de-dee!, fiddlesticks!, the devil a bit!, you don't say so!, you may whistle for it!* **~backen** n *making cakes* **~bäcker** m *pastry-cook* **~bäckerei** f *pastry-cook's shop* || = ~backen **~blech** n *griddle, baking-plate* **~form** f *cake-mould* **~rädchen** n *jagging-wheel* **~schaufel** f *cake-server*

K·üchen- ~abfälle m pl *refuse, kitchen-stuff* **~-abwasser** n *scullery water* **~anrichte** f *k. dresser* **~arbeit** f *k.-work* **~bank** f *k.-settle* **~brett** n *chopping-board* **~chef** m ⟨hotel, restaurant⟩ *chef (de cuisine* Fr) **~dienst** m (P&S) ⟨mil⟩ *k. police* (abbr *K.P.*) **~dragoner** m *k.-virago, stout k.-wench* **~-einrichtung** f *k. installation* || *k.-furniture* **~fee** f (*attractive*) *k.-wench* **~gerät** n *k. gadget*; [koll] = **~geschirr** n [koll] *k.-utensils*, ⟨fam⟩ *k.-things* pl, *hollow ware* **~gewächs** n = ~kraut **~herd** m (*k.-*)*range*; *kitchener*; (f Gas) *gas cooker*; ⟨el⟩ *electric stove* od *range* **~junge** m *k.-boy, scullion* **~kombination(smöbel** pl) f *k. unit* **~kräuter** n pl *k.-* od *pot-herbs* pl **~latein** n *apothecary's* (od *monk's, kitchen, garden*) *Latin* **~mädchen** n, ~-magd [f] *k.-* od *scullery-maid* **~meister** m *head--cook, chef* || ⟨fig⟩ bei uns ist Schmalhans ~ *we live in a very poor way, we have to pinch and screw* **~maschine** f *food preparation m.* **~messer** n *k.-* od *case-knife* **~müllwolf** m *garbage grinder* **~personal** n [coll] *persons* pl *employed in a k.* **~schabe** f ⟨ent⟩ *cockroach* **~schelle** f ⟨bot⟩ *pasque(-flower), pulsatilla* L **~schrank** m *cupboard,* (*k.-*)*sideboard*; (Speiseschrank) *larder, pantry* **~stilleben** n ⟨paint⟩ *k.-piece* **~tisch** m *dresser* **~tritt** m *steps* pl **~unteroffizier** m *mess sergeant* **~wesen** n *culinary matters, affairs, concerns* pl **~zettel** m *menu*; (im Restaurant) *bill of fare* **~zeug** n [koll] = ~gerät

×**Kuchel** f ~/~n [südd] = Küche *kitchen*

K·üchlein n ~s/~ *little cake*, → Kuchen || *small kitchen* → Küche

K·üchlein, K·ü(c)ken n ~s/~ *baby chicken; pullet*; Henne mit ~ *hen and chicks* || ⟨fig⟩ (Kind) *chick, pullet* || die ~ [pl] *the brood*

k·ucken vi [h] [nordd] = gucken

K·uckuck m ~(e)s/~e **1.** *cuckoo* (ruft *calls*) **2.** ⟨euph⟩ zum ~! *Oh, hell!, bother!, blame it!, damn it all* || zum ~ mit .. ⟨sl⟩ *blow ..*; ⟨Am⟩ *shoot that hat!* || warum zum ~ ..? *why the hell* od *the dickens*, ⟨Am mil⟩ *the fug* (*have you ..?*) || [eingeschoben] (*they*) *damn well* (*ought to*) || Hol' dich der ~! Geh' zum ~! *bless you! go to hell* od *blazes!* || ich will des ~s s, wenn .. *I'll be hanged if ..* || (das) weiß der ~! *that beats me!* **3.** [intj] ~ rufen *to cry cuckoo* **4.** ⟨Ger hum⟩ *bailiff's seal* (~ statt Adler)

K·uckucks- ~blume f ⟨bot⟩ **1.** *ragged robbin* **2.** *orchid* **~ei** n *cuckoo's egg* || jdm ein ~ ins Nest legen *to lay an egg into another bird's nest* ⟨a. fig⟩ **~lichtnelke** f = –blume 1. **~ruf** m *cuckoo-call* od *-note* **~schaumkraut** n ⟨bot⟩ *c.-flower* **~uhr** f *c.--clock*

°**K·udamm** m ~s/ ⟨fam⟩ f. Kurfürstendamm (Berlin)

°**K·uddelmuddel** m *or* n ~s/~ *mess, muddle*

Kueitschou n (chin. Prov.) *Kweichow*

Kuenlun (Gebirgssystem Innerasiens)

K·ufe[1] f ~/~n (Schlitten≈) *runner*, ⟨Am⟩ *bob* || (Wiegen≈) *rocker* || ⟨aero⟩ *skid* || (Brems≈ für unters Rad) *skid* **~nflugzeug** n *ski-plane*

K·ufe[2] f ~/~n *tub, vat* **K·üfer** m ~s/~ *barrel--maker, cooper* || (Kellermeister) *cellar-man* **~-setzhammer** m *cooper's set-hammer* **Küfer·ei** f ~/~en *cooper's workshop* || *cooper's trade, cooperage*

k·ufisch a *Kufic* (Schrift, Münzen)

K·ugel f ~/~n **1.** ⟨eig⟩ (runde ~) ⟨allg⟩ *ball, globe*; kl ~ *globule* || ⟨geom⟩ *sphere* || ·Aschen≈ *receptacle for ashes*; ⟨bill⟩ *billard-ball*; Blei≈ des Lots *bob*; Brot≈ *pellet*; Erd≈, Himmels≈ *globe, sphere*; F·üll≈n [pl] (*case shot*) *balls* od *bullets, shrapnel bullets*; Gel·enk≈ ⟨anat⟩ *head* (*of a bone*); ⟨her⟩ *ballet, roundel*; *bezant*; Himmels≈ → Erd≈; Hohl≈ *hollow ball*; hölzerne Spiel≈ *bowl*; Kegel≈ (*skittle-*)*ball*; Krocket≈ *ball*; die ~ des Gegners treffen *to roquet*, → krockieren; Lauf≈ *rolling ball*; L·ot≈ *bob*; Marmor≈ *marble*; Papier≈ *pellet* || ~n der Rechenmaschine *beads*; Rinds≈ ⟨cul⟩ *thin flank*; Rosenkranz≈ *bead*; Schuster≈ *shoe-maker's globe*; Schwung≈ ⟨tech⟩ *ball of the governor*; Stahl≈ *steel ball*; Stimm≈ = Wahl≈; Schrapn·ell≈ *shrapnel bullet*; Spiel≈, rote u schwarze Hasard≈ *the red and black ball*; Stoß≈ ⟨gym⟩ *weight, shot*; Sträflings≈ *ball and chain*; Thermometer≈ *bulb*; Wahl≈ *ballot*; jdm e–e schwarze ~ geben *to blackball a p* | ⟨fig⟩ er brachte die ~ ins Rollen *he set the ball rolling* **2.** ⟨mil, hunt⟩ Gewehr≈ *bullet*; *musketball* || Kanonen≈ (*cannon-*)*ball, shell* || *pellet* (*of an airgun*) || ⟨allg⟩ *shot* || ~n u Granaten [pl] *shot and shell* || matte *or* tote ~ *spent ball* od *bullet* || (v ~n) bestrichener Raum *beaten* od *bullet-swept zone, zone swept by fire* || v ~n durchlöchert *riddled with bullets* || jdn auf ~n fordern *to challenge a p* (od *to call a p out*) *with pistols* || ~n wechseln *to exchange shots, to fight a duel with pistols* || die ~n flogen um ihn herum *the bullets were splattering about him* || v e–r ~ getroffen w *to stop a bullet, to stop one*, ⟨sl⟩ *to stop* od *catch a packet* || von e–r ~ getroffen *hit by a bullet* || ⟨prov⟩ e–e jede ~ trifft ja nicht *every bullet has its billet, not every bullet hits home* || sich e–e ~ durch *or* vor den Kopf jagen *to blow out one's brains, to put a bullet through one's head* **K·ugel-** ⟨oft⟩ *spherical* **~abschnitt** m *sph.l segment* **~abweichung** f, ohne ~ ⟨phot⟩ *aplanatic* **≈ähnlich** a *spher(o)ical* **~akazie** f ⟨bot⟩ *American locust-tree* **≈artig** a *sph.l, globular* **~aufsatz** m *knob-like top* **~augen** n pl *beady eyes* **~ausschnitt** m *sph.l sector* **~bahn** f (Spiel) *bowling alley, bowling green* || ⟨tech⟩ *ball race* || (Geschoßbahn) *trajectory* **~bakterien** f pl *cocci, sph.l bacteria* **~baum** m *round-topped tree* **~becher** m (Spiel) *cup-and-ball* **~bildung** f ⟨scient⟩ *conglobation* **~blitz** m *ball-lightning* **~blume** f ⟨bot⟩ *globularia* **~boje** f *ball* od *spherical buoy* **~bolzen** m ⟨tech⟩ *ball pin* **~büchse** f *rifle* **~-distel** f ⟨bot⟩ *globe-thistle, echinops* L **~drehen** n *sph.l turning* **~drehring** m ⟨tech⟩ *ball race* **~-dreieck** n *sph.l triangle* **~fang** m (Spiel) *cup-and--ball* || ⟨mil⟩ (*range-* od *rifle-*)*butt, stop butt* ⟨a. fig⟩ **≈fest** a *ball-, bullet-, shot-proof* **~fisch** m *globe-, swell-fish* **~fläche** f *sph.l surface* **~form** f (Gießform) *bullet-mould* || ⟨geom⟩ *sph.l form* **≈-förmig** a *sph.l, globular* **~fräser** m *cherry*; *sph.l cutter* **~fries** m *bizant, pellet* **~füllung** f *bullets* pl (*of a shrapnel*); ⟨mill⟩ *ball* (od *grinding media*) *charge* **~funktion** f *sph.l harmonics* **~gelenk** n ⟨med⟩ *socket* od *globe joint, whirl-bone* || ⟨tech⟩ *b.-a.-s.(-joint)*; *swivel joint* **~gestalt** f → ~form **~-gewölbe** n ⟨arch⟩ *sph.l vault* **~handgranate** f *sph.l grenade* **~haube** f, **~kalotte** f *sph.l calotte* **~kammer** f ⟨tech⟩ *ball race* **~kocher** m *sph.l bleaching boiler* **~lager** n *b.-(a.-s.-joint) bearing* **~lehre**[1] f ⟨geom⟩ *spherics* **~lehre**[2] f ⟨tech⟩ *ball-gauge, shot--calibre* **~linse** f ⟨opt⟩ *sph.l lens* **~loch** n (Billard) *pocket* **~löffel** m ⟨tech⟩ *bullet-ladle* **~maß** = ~-lehre[2] **~mikrophon** n ⟨wir⟩ *eight-ball* **~mikroskop** n *ball stage microscope* **~mühle** f ⟨tech⟩ (*canon*)-*ball* od *pebble mill* od *crusher* **~mutter** f *ball nut* **~-patrone** f ⟨mil⟩ *ball-cartridge* **~pfanne** f ⟨tech⟩ *ball socket* **~photometer** n *sphere* od *globe photometer* **~regen** m *hail of bullets* od *rifle--shot* **~ring** m ⟨tech⟩ *ball race* **~rinne** f, **~rücklauf** m *ball groove* **≈rund** a (*as*) *round as a ball*

(a. v P = *well-fed*), *globular* **~schaltung** f ⟨tech⟩ *gear lever* **~scharn·ier** n ⟨tech⟩ *ball-and-socket--joint* **~schnitt** m *sph.l section* **~schreiber** m *ball-(point) pen*; ⟨fam⟩ *biro* **~segment** n ⟨geom⟩ *sph.l segment* **~senker** m *cherry*; *sph.l cutter* ≃**sicher** a *bullet-proof*; ⟨mil⟩ *armoured against rifle-fire* **~sonde** f ⟨surg⟩ *bullet-probe* **~spiegel** m *sph.l mirror* **~spiel** n *game of bowls* **~spitzfeder** f *ball-pointed pen* **~spritze** f ⟨hist-mil⟩ *mitrailleuse* Fr **~stoßen** n ⟨gym⟩ *shot put*; *putting the weight* od *shot* **~stoßer** m *shot--putter* **~strahlung** f ⟨ac⟩ *sph.l* od *stereophonic sound* **~streifen** m ⟨geom⟩ *sph.l zone* **~stück** → Blume B. 4. **~tee** m *gunpowder-tea* **~ventil** n *ball valve* **~wahl** f (*election by*) *ballot, balloting* **~wechsel** m *exchange of shots* **~zange** f, **~zieher** m ⟨surg⟩ *ball-extractor, bullet forceps, bullet drawer* **~zapfen** m *ball pivot* **~zone** f ⟨geom⟩ *sph.l zone* **K·ügelchen** n ∼s/∼ *pellet* (*of bread, paper*), *globule, bead*(*let*), *spherule* **k·ugelig** a *globular* **k·ugeln** vi/t [s & h] *to roll* ‖ (Spiel) *to bowl* ‖ (bei Wahlen) *to ballot* | *to roll* (*a ball*) ‖ vrefl **sich ~** [h] *to assume a spherical shape* ‖ ⟨fam⟩ .. vor Lachen *to split one's sides* (*with laughing*) ‖ das ist ja zum ≃! *that's a good'un*!

K·uh f ∼/≃e **1.** *cow* (a. v Wal etc & °⟨fig⟩ = Weib, → Bulle) ‖ junge ∼ *heifer* ‖ unfruchtbare ∼ *freemartin* ‖ ∼, die schwer zu melken ist *hard--yielder* ‖ hornlose ∼ ⟨Am⟩ *mooley* | ⟨fig⟩ dumme ∼! *silly goose* ‖ er stand davor wie die ∼ vorm neuen Tor *he stared at it like a stuck pig* **2.** Blinde ∼ *blind man's buff* **~antilope** f *hart(e)beest*; *pied antelope* **~blatter** f *cow-pox* **~blume** f 1. *dandelion* 2. *hawkbit* 3. *marsh marigold* **~euter** n *cow's udder* **~fladen** m *cow-dung* od *-droppings* pl **~fleisch** n *cow-beef* **~fuß** m *cow's foot*, ⟨mech⟩ (Brecheisen) *crow-bar* **~handel** m ⟨fig⟩ (= Schiebung) *horse-trading*; *job*(*bery*) ‖ *barter* ‖ ⟨pol⟩ *give-and-take* (zw *between*); *shady bargaining*; *log-rolling*; *job*(*bery*) **~haut** f *cow-hide* ‖ ⟨fig⟩ das geht auf k–e ∼ *it's an endless tale* ‖ (unerhört!) *that beats all* **~hirt** m *cowherd*; ⟨Am⟩ *cowboy* **~hornklee** m ⟨bot⟩ *fenugreek* **~käse** m *cow-cheese* **~knecht** m *cowman* **~leder** n *neat's leather* **~lymphe** f *vaccine lymph* **~magd** f *dairymaid* **~milch** f *cow's milk* **~mist** m *cow-dung* **~pocken** f pl *cow--pox* **~pockenimpfung** f *vaccination* **~reigen, ~reihen** m ⟨mus⟩ *cow-brawl* °**~saft** m *milk* ×**~schelle** f ⟨bot⟩ = Küchenschelle °**~schluck** m ⟨sl⟩ (*large*) *swig* od *gulp* **~stall** m *cow-shed, byre*

k·ühl 1. [a] *cool, fresh*; etw ∼ *coolish*; *chilly* ⟨a. fig⟩ ‖ ⟨fig⟩ *cold* (*greeting, answer*), *cool* (*heart, calculator*); *reserved, distant*; ⟨fam⟩ *offish* ‖ ∼e Aufnahme finden *to be taken frostily*; *in a chill manner* ‖ e–e ∼e Blondine *a cold-hearted blond* ‖ ∼ w *to cool down* ‖ es wird ∼er *it is growing cooler* ‖ jdn ∼ behandeln *to give a p the cold shoulder* **2.** [adv] der Wind weht ∼ *there is a cool breeze*; ∼ überlegend *hard-headed* **K·ühl-** ⟨oft⟩ *cooling, refrigerant, -ated, -ating, -ator* [attr] **~anlage** f *c.g plant, r.ating equipment*; ⟨com⟩ *r.g display e.* **~apparat** m *r.ator*; ⟨brew⟩ *cooler* **~bucht** f ⟨tech⟩ *c. chamber* **~flüssigkeit** f ⟨tech⟩ *coolant* **~eimer** m, **~faß** n, **~gefäß** n *c.g-vat, -tub, cooler, r.ator*; ⟨brew⟩ *keelvat* **~halten** n *r.ation* **~haus** n *cold store-(house)* **~hausanlage** f *cold-storage plant* **~mantel** m ⟨mot⟩ *cooling water jacket* **~mittel** n *c.g-agent, remedy, c.g draught*, ⟨scient⟩ *coolant*; *r.ant* **~ofen** m *c.g-furnace, annealing-oven* **~raum** m *r.ating* od *cool chamber, cold room* **~rippe** f ⟨tech⟩ *c.g fin* **~rohr** n *condenser* **~schiff** n *refrigerator ship* **~schlange** f ⟨tech⟩ *c.g coil* **~schrank** m *r.ator*, ⟨fam⟩ *fridge* ∼spirale f ⟨tech⟩ *spiral condenser*; *c.r coil* **~stoffbehälter** m ⟨aero⟩ *glycol tank* **~technik** f *r.ating engineering* **~theke** f *r.ated counter* **~trank** m *c.g drink* ‖ (süßer) ⟨Am⟩ *julep* **~transport** m *r.ated transport* **~truhe** f *r.ating chest* **~vitrine** f *r.ated display case* **~vorrichtung** f *r.ator*; *r.ting plant* **~wagen** m ⟨rail⟩ *r.ator wagon*, ⟨Am⟩ *reefer*; ⟨mot⟩ *r.ator truck* **~wasser** n *c.g water*; ∼ nachfüllen ⟨mot⟩ *to top up the radiator* **K·ühle** f ∼/ *coolness, freshness* ‖ die ∼ der Nacht *the cool hours of the night* ‖ ins ∼ [n] gehen *to go into the fresh air* ‖ ⟨fig⟩ *coldness, reserve* **k·ühlen** vt [h] *to cool* (→ abkühlen) ‖ ⟨übtr⟩ *satisfy* (*thirst*); *assuage* (*pain*) ‖ ⟨fig⟩ s–e Wut ∼, ⟨fam⟩ sein Mütchen an jdm ∼ *to wreak one's anger, to vent one's rage on a p*; ⟨Am⟩ *to get back at a p* **K·ühler** m ∼s/∼ *cooler* (*champagne-c.*) ‖ ⟨mot⟩ *radiator* ‖ S·ekt≃ *ice-pail* | ∼figur [f] ⟨mot⟩ *mascot*; ∼klappe [f] *r. flap*; ∼lamelle [f] ⟨mot⟩ *r. core* **~maske** f *gril(le)* **~schutzhaube** f *r. muff* **K·ühlte** f ∼/ ⟨mar⟩ *fresh* od *stiff breeze* **K·ühlung** f ∼/∼en *cooling* ‖ ⟨tech⟩ *refrigeration*; ⟨mot⟩ *engine-cooling* ‖ Wasser≃ *water-cooling*

K·u(h)le f ∼/∼n [niedd] = Grube, Loch

k·ühn 1. [a] *hardy*; *bold* (*character, deed*); *daring* (*attack, grasp*); *audacious* (*word, step*); *hard* (*rider*); *valiant, dauntless* (*heart, hero*); *adventurous* (*spirit*), *venturesome* (*undertaking*); *rash* (*statement*); *sanguine* (*expectations*) ‖ ich bin so ∼ .. *I take the liberty* .. ‖ ∼ m *to embolden*; ∼ w *to grow bold* **2.** [adv] ∼ geführt *daring* (*attack*) ‖ *vigorously* (*curved lines*) ≃**heit** f ∼/∼en *boldness, audacity*; *daring*; *dauntlessness, venturesomeness*; ⟨übtr⟩ *freedom* (*of conception*) ‖ ∼en [pl] *bold deeds* pl **~lich** adv *boldly, hardily*

°**Kuj·on** m ∼(e)s/∼e *scoundrel, villain* **kujon·ieren** vt [h] *to bully, vex, rag, ill-treat*

K·üken n ∼s/∼ → Kücken

K·ukuruz m ∼(es)/ [österr] *maize*, ⟨Am⟩ *corn*

kul·ant a *accommodating, obliging, polite* ‖ ⟨com⟩ *fair* (*prices*); *easy* (*terms*) **Kul·anz** f ∼/ *obliging ways* pl ‖ ⟨com⟩ *fairness, fair dealing*

K·uli m ∼s/∼s *coolie* ‖ ⟨bes österr, Sw⟩ = Kugelschreiber

kulin·arisch a *culinary*

Kul·isse f ∼/∼n ⟨theat⟩ *wings* pl, *side-scene* ‖ ⟨tech⟩ *slot link* ‖ ⟨st exch⟩ *coulisse* ‖ ⟨fig⟩ das ist nur ∼ .. *mystification* ‖ hinter den ∼n ⟨a. fig⟩ *behind the scenes*; *back-room* (*decisions*); (*by*) *underhand* (*means*) ‖ hinter den ∼n arbeiten *to pull the strings, to work the oracle* (*in one's favour* für sich); h. die ∼n sehen ⟨fig⟩ *to see daylight*; h. den ∼n verschwinden *to back to the side-scenes* **Kul·issen- ~fieber** n ⟨theat⟩ *stage-fright* **~hebel** m ⟨tech⟩ *slotted lever* **~kühler** m ⟨aero-mot⟩ *shutter-radiator* **~maler** m *scene-painter* **~reißer** m ⟨theat & fam⟩ *stage-ranter* **~schieber** m ⟨theat⟩ *scene-shifter* **~steuerung** f ⟨tech⟩ *link motion* **~teil** m (tragbar) *flat* **~wagen** m ⟨theat a-engl⟩ *wing carriage*

°**K·uller** f ∼/∼n *marble* → Klicker °**~augen** n pl *goo-goo eyes*; *saucer(-eye)s*; mit ∼ *pop-eyed*; ∼ m *to give* (*a p*) *the glad eye* **k·ullern** vi/t [s & h] → kollern ‖ °sich kullern *to split* (*one's sides*) *with laughing* °**k·ullerig** a *killingly funny*

K·ulm m ∼(e)s/∼e **1.** *top, peak* **2.** ⟨geol⟩ *culm*

Kulminati·on f ∼/∼en *culmination* **~spunkt** m ⟨astr⟩ *culminating-point* ‖ ⟨fig⟩ *acme* **kulmin·ieren** vi [h] *to culminate* ‖ ∼ in *to centre in*

K·ult m ∼(e)s/∼e (→ Kultus); (Pflege) *cult* (*of arts*) ‖ es wird mit ihm ein richtiger ∼ getrieben *he is the regular object of public worship* **~platz** m *place of worship* **k·ultisch** a *cultic* **Kultiv·ator** m ∼s/–at·oren ⟨agr⟩ *scarifier* ‖ mit e–m ∼ bearbeiten *to scarify* **kultiv·ieren** vt [h] *to cultivate, subdue* (*soil*) ‖ *to grow, tame* (*plants*) ‖ ⟨fig⟩ *to cultivate* (*a p's acquaintance*) **kultiv·iert** a *cultured* (*language*) ‖ *cultivated* (*p*); *civilized* (*nation*); ein sehr ∼er Mann *a man of great culture* **Kult·ur** f ∼/∼en **1.** *cultivation* (*of soil, speech, voice*); *growing* (*of plants*); ⟨for⟩ *young growth* **2.** *culture* (*of oysters, bacteria*, etc.) **3.** (*advanced stage in social development*) *civilization* ‖ (*intellectual development*) *culture* (*a man of the highest c.*); .. v ∼ *civilized* (*states*); „~ des Kindes" *child-centered c.*; → Zivilisation **~annahme** f *acculturation* **~arbeit** f *work of civ.tion* **~ästhet** m *c.d aesthete* **~aufgabe** f *mission of civ.tion* **~austausch** m *c.ral exchange* **~beutel** m *toilet set* od *bag* **~direktor** m ⟨SBZ⟩ *c.ral director* **~drosselung** f *c.ral dim-out* **~einfühlung** f *c.ral empathy* **~erbe** n *c.ral heritage* **≃fähig** a *cultivable, arable* ‖ ⟨fig⟩ *civilizable* **~film** m *documentary, educational, interest, record film* **~fläche** f (tatsächliche) ⟨stat⟩ *cultivated area* **~fortschritt** m *social progress* **~geschichte** f *history of civ.tion, social history* **≃geschichtlich** a *social* **~gruppe** f ⟨SBZ⟩ *amateur players, workshop theatre* **~gut** n *treasures* **~haus** n ⟨SBZ⟩ *clubhouse; civic centre* **~historiker** m *writer on s. h.* **≃historisch** a *socio-historical* **~kammer** f ⟨engl⟩ *the British Council*; ⟨Ger⟩ *Chamber of Culture* **~kampf** m ⟨Ger⟩ *struggle between the State and the Roman Catholic Church, kulturkampf* **~landschaft** f ⟨geog⟩ *c.ral landscape* **~leben** n *the c.ral life* **~lehrfilm** m *instructional film* **~mensch** m *civilized man* **~pflanzen** f pl *cultivated plants* **≃politisch** a *politico-c.ral* **~tasche** f → –beutel **~techniker** m ⟨agr⟩ *drainage engineer* **~träger** m *upholder of civ.tion, c. carrier* **~übertragung** f *acculturation* **~volk** n *civilized nation* **kultur·ell** a *cultural; relating to civilization* ‖ ~e Akklimatisation, Angliederung, ~er Anschluß *acculturation*; ~e Veranstaltungen *cultural activities*

K·ultus m ~/–te *worship, cult, religious rites* pl **~minister** m ⟨Ger⟩ *Minister of Education*; *President of the Board of Education* **~ministerium** n *Ministry of Education*

ˣ**K·ulter** m ~s/~ (Steppdecke) *quilt*

K·umbrisch a ⟨engl⟩ *Cumbrian* (*Mountains*)

K·umm m ~(e)s/~e, **~e** f ~/~n (*wooden*) *trough*; *bowl*; ⟨Am a.⟩ *dinner-pail*

K·ümmel m ~s/ *caraway*(*-seed*) ‖ (Likör) *kümmel* ‖ echter ~ ⟨bot⟩ *cum*(*m*)*in* ‖ °⟨fig fam⟩ e–m den ~ reiben *to call a p over the coals* **~branntwein** m *cum*(*m*)*in-brandy* **~brötchen** n, (**~käse** m) *roll,* (*cheese*) *with caraway-seeds* **~öl** n *cummin-oil* **~spalterei** f *quibbling* **~türke** m ⟨fam⟩ *braggart; philistine, townsman* °**k·ümmeln** vi [h] *to tipple*

K·ummer m ~s/ *grief, affliction, anxiety, sorrow; trouble* ‖ nagender, quälender ~ *harrowing g., agony of sorrow*; .. zehrt an ihr .. *is eating her heart away* ‖ ~ u Not *trials and tribulations* ‖ was hast du denn f ~? *what's your tr.?* ‖ das macht mir wenig ~ *that doesn't tr. me much* ‖ jdm ~ bereiten, m *to grieve a p* ‖ sich ~ m über *to worry* od *fret about* ‖ v ~ gebeugt *careworn*; zu s m ~ *to his distress* od *grief* **K·ümmerer** m ~s/~ **1.** = Kümmerling **2.** ⟨hum⟩ *p who concerns h.s. with other people*; ⟨oft a.⟩ *busybody* **k·ümmerlich 1.** [a] *miserable* (*salary*), *wretched* (*output, remnant*) ‖ (dürftig) *poor, needy; scanty, paltry* (*sum*) **2.** [adv] es geht ihr ~ *she has rather a thin time* ‖ sich ~ durchschlagen *to eke out a scanty livelihood, to live in great destitution* ‖ sie ernährte sich ~ *she barely supported herself* **K·ümmerling** m ~s/~e *miserable creature; undersized animal; stunted plant* **k·ummerlos** a *free from care* od *sorrow; untroubled* **k·ümmern** vi [h & s] ⟨for, hort⟩ *to starve* ‖ die Pflanzen ~ *the plants are stunted* | vt [h] *to grieve, vex, afflict, trouble* ‖ das soll mich nicht ~ *that won't trouble me* ‖ was kümmert's mich? *what is that to me? what do I care?* ‖ (angehen) *to concern, regard* (*that does not concern me*) | **sich ~** [h] **um** *to mind,* (*at*)*tend; to look after; to care about; to concern o.s. with* (*a p*), *to take care of* (*a p*) ‖ ~ Sie sich darum, daß .. *see to it that the work is done* ‖ kümmere dich nicht um Dinge, die dich nichts angehen *mind your own business* ‖ sich nicht ~ um *to be heedless* od *reckless of, to pay no attention to* ‖ *he takes no notice of what people say*; sich um etw gar nicht ~ *not to care a straw about a th*; *he tended to every detail* ‖ er kümmert sich immer um fremde Angelegenheiten *he always has a finger in other people's pie* ‖ wer kümmert sich darum? *who cares?* **K·ümmernis** f ~/–nisse *grief, sorrow, affliction* ‖ –nisse [pl] *woes* ‖ das war e–e gr ~ *that was a great disappointment* **k·ummervoll** a *sorrowful, doleful, rueful, grief-stricken, grievous, afflicted; lugubrious* (*face*); ~er Blick *look of sorrow* | [adv] ~ aussehend *dismal looking*

K·um(me)t n ~(e)s/~e (*horse-*)*collar, hames* pl | ~geschirr [n] *collar-harness*; ~kette [f] *fastening-chain*; ~stöcke [m pl] (*pair of*) *hames*

Kump·an m ~(e)s/~e *companion,* (*good*) *fellow*; ⟨fam⟩ *mate* ‖ lustiger ~ *jolly blade* ‖ e–e Schar fescher junger u älterer ~e in herrlichster Laune *a dashing society of jovial blades old and young* ‖ Zech≃ *boon friend* **K·umpel** m ~s/~ ⟨fam⟩ *chum, pal; fellow-workman,* ⟨bes⟩ *-miner*; ⟨Am fam⟩ *buddy*

K·umpf m ~es/~e **1.** ˣ⟨agr⟩ *whetstone holder* **2.** (⟨a.⟩ ~gefäß n) ⟨archæol⟩ *earthenware bowl*

kumulat·iv [i:f] a *cumulative* **kumul·ieren** vt [h] *to accumulate*

K·umys m ~/~ (alkohol. Stuten-Milchgetränk) *k*(*o*)*umiss, kumys*

k·und a *known, notorious, public* ‖ ~ (w) s *to be*(*come*) *known* ‖ ~ u zu wissen sei hiermit (Formel) *know all men by these presents; we hereby give notice* **k·undbar** a *known, notorious* **k·ündbar** a *subject to notice; s. to being recalled* ‖ (Kapital) *at call* ‖ (Hypothek) *redeemable* **K·unde 1.** f ~/~n (Kenntnis) *knowledge, intelligence, information, notice* ‖ e–m v etw ~ geben *to inform a p of a th* ‖ gebt uns ~, wenn .. *let us know when ..* ‖ schlimme ~ *bad news* ‖ die ~ geht um *the word goes round*; die ~ v etw tragen nach *to carry the tidings of a th to* | (Wissenschaft) *science, lore* [mst in comp ·Erd≃ usw] | ⟨hors⟩ *mark of mouth* ‖ ⟨fig⟩ (P) hat sich die ~n durchgebissen ⟨fam⟩ *is up in the tooth* **2.** m ~n/~n *customer* (*for goods*); ⟨hot⟩ *guest, visitor, c., client; cl.* (*for a service*); *account* (*for advertising*) ‖ eingetragener *registered customer*; regelmäßiger *patron*; ~ s in *to patronize*; voraussichtlicher *prospect* ‖ ~n werben *to tout for c.s*; ~n anlocken *to attract c.s* | ⟨cont; iron⟩ netter ~ *a nice sort of a fellow* ‖ so ein ~! *such a rotter* ‖ ⟨com⟩ (faul) ⟨übtr⟩ *deadbeat; good-for--nothing c.*; (schlau) *a knowing blade, an artful dodger*; (schlimm) *dangerous c.*; (übel) (schwierig) *hard c., nasty piece of work* **k·ünden** vi/t [h] *to announce*; es kündet von .. *it shows* od *proves ..* **K·unden**~beratungsstelle [f] ⟨com⟩ *service department*; ~dienst [m] (*after-sales*) *service*; umfassender ~ *total and continuing s.*; (Lieferwagen) *delivery van,* ⟨Am⟩ *courtesy car*; (Rundschreiben) *circular letter to dealers*; (Scheck) ⟨mot⟩ *s. voucher*; ~gießerei [f] *jobbing foundry*; ~kreis [m] *customers* pl; ~werber [m] *canvasser,* ⟨sl⟩ *tout,* ⟨Am⟩ *solicitor,* ⟨sl⟩ *barker*; ~zahl [f] *connexion,* ⟨fam⟩ *custom* **k·und|geben** vt [h] = ~machen **K·undgebung** f ~/~en *publication, statement, notice; rally, meeting*; ⟨pol⟩ *demonstration* ‖ *manifestation* (*of a Higher Power*); e–e ~ erlassen *to issue a m.* **Künder** m ~s/~ → Dolmetsch ‖ ⟨übtr⟩ *announcer, harbinger* **k·undig** a *knowing, skilful* ‖ (e–r S [gen]) *familiar* od *acquainted* (*with*), *skilled* (*in*), *versed* (*in*), v ~er Seite *from a reliable quarter* ‖ (sachverständig) *expert* ([gen] *at, in*) ‖ **der ≃e** *the expert*; ⟨fam⟩ *one who is in the know*; die ≃en [pl] *the initiated,* ⟨fam⟩ *the knowing ones* pl **k·ündigen** vi/t [h] (jdm) *to give* (*a p*) *warning, to give* (*a p*) *notice* (*to quit*) ‖ zum 1. April ~ *to give notice for April 1st* ‖ e–m mit 3monatiger Frist ~ *to give a p three months' notice* ‖ mir ist ge–gt worden *I am under notice to leave* | (Kapital) *to call in, to recall*; (Hypothek) *to foreclose*; (Vertrag) *to abrogate, denounce* ‖ (Wohnung, Stellung) *to give a p* (*his*) *notice* (*to quit*) ‖ das Abkommen, der Waffenstillstand wurde ge–gt *notice was given to terminate the agreement, armistice* || e–e Freundschaft ~ *to sever a friendship* || den Gehorsam ~ *to refuse obedience* **K·ündigung** f ~/~en *notice, warning*; *n. of termination of employment*; *abrogation, denunciation, foreclosure, recall* || halbjährige ~ *six months' notice* || tägliche ~ *day's notice* || Geld auf tägliche ~ *call-money* || ~ aussprechen, zurückziehen *to give notice, to withdraw a n.* || mit monatlicher, vierteljährlicher ~ *with monthly, quarterly notice* | ~sfrist [f] *period within which notice* od *warning must be given*; ~srecht [n] *right of giving notice*; ~stermin [m] *term of notice* **K·undin** f ~/~nen *lady* od *female customer, client* (→ Kunde 2.) **k·und|machen** vt [h] **k·und|tun** vt [h] *to make known* od *public*; *to give notice of*; *to notify, publish*; *manifest*; *signify* (*wishes, opinions*) **K·undmachung** f ~/~en *publication*; *manifestation, notification*; *proclamation* **K·undschaft** f ~/~en **1.** ⟨com⟩ [koll] *customers* pl, ⟨fam⟩ *custom*; [abstr] *connection, custom, goodwill* || viel ~ h *to have numerous customers* || Gewohnheiten der ~ *buying habits* **2.** (Erkundung) *intelligence* || ~ einholen, ~ einziehen *to collect information* || auf ~ gehen ⟨mil⟩ *to go reconnoitring, to go out scouting* || auf ~ ausschicken ⟨mil⟩ *to send out rec.* || er brachte ~ v Feinde *he brought in information about the enemy* | ≃en vi [h] ⟨mil⟩ *to reconnoitre, scout, feel* | **~er** m ~s/~ *emissary* || ⟨mil⟩ *scout* || *spy* | ~schiff [n] ⟨mar⟩ *scout*

k·ünftig 1. [a] *future* (*life, assistant*), (*generation*) *to come, coming* (*generations*), *prospective* (*partner*) || ~es Jahr *next year* || *next* (*life*) || in ~en Zeiten *in times to come* || s–e ~e Frau *his wife that is to be, his intended* (*wife*) **2.** [adv] = **~hin** *for the future, henceforth* || bitte, dies ~ z unterlassen! *please drop that in future*; → Zukunft

K·unkel f ~/~n *distaff* || [obs] (Weib) *gossip* | ~leh(e)n [n] *petticoat* od *apron-string hold*

Kunlun → Kuenlun

K·unst f ~/≃e *art* || die freien *or* schönen ≃e *the liberal* od *fine arts* || Professor der bildenden ≃e *Art Professor* || ⟨engl⟩ Meister der freien ≃e *master of arts* || angewandte ~ *applied arts* || bildende ~ *decorative art* || ~ u Gewerbe *arts and crafts* || schwarze ~ *black art* || die ~ geht nach Brot *art goes a-begging* || das ist e–e brotlose ~ *there's no money in that*; brotlose ≃e *idle tricks* || was macht die ~? *how is the world with you?* | *craft* (*of metalworking*, etc.), *art* (*of fencing, riding; printing*) | (Geschicklichkeit) *skill, cleverness* || das ist k–e ~! *there's nothing in that, that's nothing!* || er hatte nicht die ~, Menschen zu behandeln *he had not the art of..* || s–e ~ versuchen an *to try one's skill at* || ich bin mit m–r ~ zu Ende *I'm at my wit's end* | ≃e (Kniffe) *practices, tricks* pl; *the dog showed its tricks* **K·unst-** ⟨oft⟩ *artistic, artificial, synthetic* **~akademie** f *academy of arts* **~anlage** f *a.c talent* || ~n [pl] (Lustgarten) *pleasure-grounds* pl, *park* **~arbeit** f *work of art* **~arm** m *a.l arm* **~auge** n (*plastic*) *a.l eye* **~ausdruck** m *technical expression* od *term* **~ausstellung** f *exhibition of works of art*; fahrbare ~ ⟨bes Am⟩ *art-mobile* **~bauten** pl ⟨tech⟩ *constructive works* **~beflissene(r)** m *art-student* **~beilage** a *a.c supplement* **~bein** n (f Oberschenkel-Niederdruck) *suction socket* **~bestrebungen** f pl *a.c efforts* pl **~butter** f *butterine, margarine, imitation* od *a.l butter* **~darm** m *a.l sausage casing* | ~papier [n] *sausage skin paper* **~dichtung** f *learned* od *a.c poetry* **~drechsler** m *toy-man*; *turner in invory* **~druckpapier** n *art paper* od *stock*; *coated paper* || mattes ~ *art matt* || Abzug auf ~ *art pull*, ⟨Am⟩ *glossy print proof* **~dünger** m (*commercial*) *fertilizer*; *a.l manure* **~eis** n *manufactured ice* **~epos** n *literary epic* **~erzeugnis** n *artifact*; *work* od *production of art* **~färber** m *artisan dyer* **~faserplatte** f *wall-board* **~fehler** m ⟨med⟩ *doctor's mistake* **≃fertig** a *skilled* (*in an art*), *skilful*; *craftsmanlike* || ~es Handwerkszeug ⟨archaeol⟩ *artifacts* pl **~fertigkeit** f *workmanship, artistic skill*; *technique, dexterity* **~fleiß** m *industry* **~fliegen** n *aerobatics* pl **~flieger** m *aerobat*(*ic aviator*), *trick-flier, stunt airman* **~flug** m *stunt* od *trick flying, stunt*(*ing*); *acrobatic flight* | ~figur [f] *acr. figure* od *manoeuvre* **~frevel** m *vandalism* **~freund** m *art-lover, lover of the fine arts*; *patron*(*ess* f) *of artists* **≃froh** a *art-loving, fond of art* **~gärtner** m *florist, nursery-gardener, nurseryman* **~gärtner·ei** f *nursery-gardening, horticulture* **~gebaren** n *mode of a.c production* **~gebilde** n *work of art* **~gefühl** n *a.c sense* **~gegenstand** m *art-object, article of virtu* It || ≃e [koll] *virtu* **~gelb** n *silver-stain* **≃gemäß** = –gerecht **~genosse** m *fellow-artist*; ⟨paint⟩ *brother of the brush* **~genossenschaft** f *fellowship of artists* **~genuß** m *a.c treat* **≃gerecht** a *in accordance with the rules of art*, (*a.cally* od *technically*) *correct, workmanlike* (*product*); *dexterous, skilful* (*player*), *workmanlike* **~geschichte** f *history of art* od *of the fine arts* **~geschmack** m *a.c taste*; *virtu* It **~getriebe** n *machinery* **≃geübt** a *skilful* **~gewerbe** n *applied arts, arts and crafts* pl, *industrial arts, a.c handicrafts* pl | ~museum [n] *industrial museum*; ~schule [f] *polytechnic* **~gewerbliche Arbeiten** f pl *applied art work* **~glas** n *a.c glass* **~glied** n *artificial limb* **~graben** m *canal* **~griff** m *trick, artifice, stratagem, dodge, knack*; ⟨med⟩ *manœuvre, manipulation*; schlauer ~ *fetch*; (beim Ringen) *buttock, chip* || er wandte allerlei ~e an *he tried all kinds of dodges* **~haar** n ⟨theat⟩ *crêpe hair* **~handel** m *trade in works of art* **~händler** m *art-dealer, dealer in works of art* **~handlung** f *art dealer's establishment, picture-shop* **~handwerk** n *arts and crafts* pl; *handicraft* **~handwerker** *artificer, craftsman* **~harz** n *s. resin*; *bakelite* | ~preßstoff [m] *synth. plastic material* **~historiker** m *art historian* **~jünger** m *art student* **~kenner** m *connoisseur* **~kniff** *dodge* → ~griff **~kraftsport** m *theatrical* od *circus gymnastics* **~kritik** f *art-criticism* **~kritiker** m *art reviewer* **~laufen** n (Eissport) *figure-skating* **~leder** n *leatherette, imitation leather* | ~pappe [f] *a.l leather board* **~lichtaufnahme** f ⟨phot⟩ *a.l light exposure* **~liebhaber** m *virtuoso, amateur, dilettante* **~liebhaberei** f *virtu* It **~lied** n *art-song* **≃los** a *artless, rude* (*style*) **~losigkeit** f *artlessness* **~maler** m *painter* **≃mäßig** a *a.c, technical* || = ~gerecht **~mittel** n *a.l means* **~pause** f ⟨rhet, iron⟩ *pause*: *very good orators, when they are out, they will spit* (m e–e ~) (Shak) **~prosa** f *rhythmic prose* **≃reich** a *a.c, ingenious* **~reise** f (*artist's*) *professional tour* **~reiter** m *trick-rider, equestrian*; ~in [f] *equestrienne* **~reiter·ei** f *trick-riding, equestrianism* **~richter** m (*art*) *critic* **≃richterlich** a *critical* **≃richtern** vi [h] *to criticize* **~richtung** f *a.c school* **~sammlung** f *collection of works of art, art collection* **~schaffen** n *artistry, artistic creation* **~schätze** m pl *art treasures* pl **~schlosser** m *art-metal-worker* **~schnitzer** m *toy-man* **~schreiner** m = ~tischler **~schule** f *school of arts* (→ –richtung) **~schütze** m *trick shot* **~schweißen** n *trick welding* **~schwimmen** n *water ballet* **~seide** f *synthetic* (od *near-*)*silk*; *acetate*; *rayon* Fr **~sinn** m *a.c taste, artistry, virtuosity* **≃sinnig** a *a.c* **~speisefett** n *shortening* **~sprache** d (Esperanto) *a.l* od *constructed language* **~springen** n *diving* **~stätte** f *home of art* **~sticker·ei** f *fine-art needlework* **~stoff** m *plastic* | ~formstück [n] *pl. moulding*; ~schichtplatte [f] *laminated pl.* **~stopfen** n, **~stopfer·ei** f *fine-drawing* **~straße** f *turnpike road, highroad* **~stück** n *trick*, (*clever*) *feat, sleight-of-hand*, ⟨sl⟩ *stunt* || ≃e m *to do* (*parlour-*)*tricks* od *-stunts* || das ist kein ~! *there is nothing clever in that!* || ~! ⟨iron⟩ *it's as easy as ABC!* **~tätigkeit** f *artifice* **~tischler** m *cabinet-maker* **~trieb** m *a.c* od *mechanical instinct*

~turnen n *acrobatic exercises* **~verein** m *art-union* **~verlag** m *fine art publishers* pl **~verstand** m *a.c insight* **~verständige(r)** m *expert, adept* **≃voll** a → –reich; ~ angelegt *elaborate, a.c, ingenious*; ~e Anlage [f] *ingenuity* **~werk** n *work of art*; abstrakte ~e *abstractions* pl | ~stätte [f] *workshop for arts and crafts* **~welt** f *world of art* **~wert** m *virtu* It **≃widrig** a *contrary to the rules of art, inartistic* **~wissenschaft** f *science of art, æsthetics* pl **~wolle** f *shoddy, a.l wool*; ~ aus Tuchlumpen *mungo* **~wort** n *technical term* **~zweig** m *branch of art* **Künstel·ei** f ~/~en *artificial work* ‖ *artificiality* ‖ (im Stil) *mannerism* ‖ (Geziertheit) *affectation, affected ways* **k·ünsteln** vi [h] *to subtilize* ‖ ~ an *to bestow great pains on a th* | vt *to over-refine* ‖ er künstelte es aus *he puzzled it out* | **gekünstelt** (*over-*)*refined* (*language*) ‖ *fictitious* (*character*) ‖ *stilted* (*style*) ‖ *forced, affected* (*gaiety*) **K·ünstler** m ~s/~ (~in f) *artist* (bes ⟨paint⟩); ⟨mus & theat⟩ *performer*; Geigen≃ *p. on the violin* ‖ ⟨com⟩ *commercial a.* od *designer*; Werbe≃ *advertising a.*; *poster a.* ‖ ausübender ~ *practitioner* ‖ (Artist, Koch≃, Haar≃ etc) *artiste* **~arbeit** f *art work* **~druck** m *a.'s proof* **~leben** n *a.c life* **~name** m *pen-name*, ⟨theat⟩ *stage-n.* **~ruhm** m *a.'s fame* **~schrift** f ⟨typ⟩ *fancy type* **~verein** m *a.'s society* **~volk** n ⟨theat⟩ *show folk* **~werkstatt** f *studio* **~zimmer** n *green-room* **k·ünstlerisch 1.** [a] *artistic*; *artist-like* ‖ ~es Können *artistry*; ~er Leiter *art director* **2.** [adv] *artistically* ‖ ~ wertvoll ⟨film⟩ *a. meritorious* **K·ünstlerschaft** f **1.** [koll] *body of artists* **2.** = **K·ünstlertum** n **1.** *artistry, craftsmanship* **2.** [koll] *the artists, the artistic world* **k·ünstlich 1.** [a] (kunstvoll) *elaborate, artistic* ‖ (sinnreich) *ingenious* | (nachgemacht) *artificial* (*flower, limb, eye, breathing*), *man-made* (*flower, moon*) ‖ *false* (*hair, teeth*) ‖ ~es Gebiß *denture, false set of teeth* ‖ ~e Diamanten *imitation diamonds* ‖ ~es Bein *joint-leg* ‖ *synthetic* (*indigo*) **2.** [adv] ~ erzeugt *forced* (*draught*); *over* .. (*oversimplify*) | **≃keit** f /~ *artificiality* ‖ *elaborateness*

k·unterbunt 1. [a] *parti-coloured* | *confused, pell-mell* **2.** [adv] (wirr) *in a heap* (*of confusion*), *topsy-turvy, higgledy-piggledy*

K·üpe f ~/~n *tub, coop* ‖ (Färber≃) *copper, vat* | ~nfärbung [f] *vat-dyeing*; ~nrahmen [m] *dipping-frame* **K·üper** m ~s/~ *cooper* **~lohn** m *cooperage*

Kup·ee n ~s/~s **1.** ⟨rail⟩ † & ⟨österr⟩ *compartment* **2.** ⟨mot⟩ *coupé*

K·upfer n ~s/ *copper* ‖ (Geld) *c. money, c.s* pl ‖ schwefelsaures ~ *cupric sulphate* ‖ (Kupferstich) *c.plate* (*print*): *a book with many c. illustrations* **≃artig** a *c.y, c.ish* **~asche** f *c.-ashes* pl **~ätzung** f *etching on c.* **~ausschlag** m ⟨path⟩ *red pimples* pl **~bergwerk** n *c.-mine* **~blatt** n *c.-plate* **~blau** n *blue-ashes* pl **~blech** n *sheet-c.* **~blüte** ⟨min⟩ *c.-bloom* **≃braun** a *c.y, c.-coloured, brazen* **~draht** m *c. wire* **~druck** m *c.-plate* (*-print*[*ing*]) ‖ [konkr] ⟨Am a.⟩ *rotogravure* **~druckpapier** n *plate-paper*; *c. printing paper* **~erz** n *c.-ore* **≃farben** a = ≃braun **~gang** m ⟨min⟩ *c.-lode* **~gelb** n *coarse c.* **~geld** n *c. coin* od *money, c.s* pl **~geschirr** n *c. utensils*, ⟨fam⟩ *c.s* pl **~gesicht** n *c.-coloured face, carbuncled face* **~glanz** m ⟨minr⟩ *c.-glance* **~glucke** f ⟨ent⟩ *lappet moth* **~grün** n ⟨minr⟩ *mountain-green* **≃haltig** a *c.y, containing c.*; ⟨scient⟩ *cupreous, cupriferous* **~hammer** m *c.-mill, c.-works* **~haut** f *c.-sheathing* (*of a ship*) **~hütte** f *c.-works* [sg konstr] | ~narbeiter [m] *c.-smelter* **~kalk** m *c. calx* | ~brühe [f] *Bordeaux mixture* **~kies** m ⟨minr⟩ *yellow c.-ore* **~könig** m ⟨minr⟩ *regulus of c.* **~lichtdruck** m *photogravure* **~litze** f *c. strand* **~münze** f *c. coin* **~nase** f ⟨fig⟩ *c.-nose, grog-blossom* (Hardy) **~platte** f *c.plate* **≃plattiert** a *c.clad* **~pol** m ⟨el⟩ *negative pole* **~rost** m *verdigris* **≃rot** = ≃braun **~sammlung** f *c.plate collection* **~schlacke** f *c.-slag* **~schmied** m *c.-smith, brazier* **~spat** m ⟨minr⟩ *malachite* **~stechen** n *engraving on c.* **~stecher** m *engraver* (*on c.*), *c.plate-engraver* **~stecherkunst** f *c.-engraving* **~stich** m *c.plate, engraving, print* | ~händler [m] *print-dealer*; ~kabinett [n] *department of prints* **~vergiftung** f *c.-poisoning* **~vitriol** m &n *blue* od *c.-vitriol* **~wasser** n *c.as* **~werk** n **1.** *book containing prints* **2.** = Kupferhammer **k·upferig** a *coppery* **k·upfern** a *copper, of c.*

kup·ieren vt [h] **1.** (Pferd, Hund) *to dock, round* **2.** *to cut* (*the cards*) **3.** ⟨mil⟩ kupiertes Gelände *broken* od *intersected ground* **4.** *to adulterate* (*wine*)
Kup·on m ~s/~s = Coupon (Fr) *coupon, check*; *counterfoil* | ~bogen [m] *coupon sheet*

K·uppe f ~/~n *knob, knoll*; *top, summit* ‖ (Nagel≃) *head*; *finger-, screw-end* → Koppe **K·uppel** f ~/~n *cupola, dome* **~bau** m *domed building*; ⟨Ind arch⟩ *stupa* **~dach** n *dome-shaped roof* **≃förmig** a *domic*(*al*) **~gewölbe** n *dome-shaped vault, cupola*

Kuppel·ei f ~/~en *match-making* ‖ ⟨dero⟩ *procuring*; ⟨jur⟩ (schwere *aggravated*) *procuration* **k·uppeln** vt (mst koppeln) & vi [h] *to connect, to throw into gear*; ge–lt mit ⟨tech⟩ *locked with*; ⟨wir⟩ *to couple*; ⟨fam⟩ (= Ehe vermitteln) *to make a match, to play the go-between* | ⟨dero⟩ *to procure* **K·uppel- ~pelz** m ⟨fam⟩ *reward for bringing about a match* **~stange** f ⟨rail⟩ *drag bar* **K·upp(e)lung** f ~/~en ⟨tech, wir, rail⟩ *coupling* ‖ ⟨mot⟩ *clutch* ([aus-] einrücken *to* [*dis*]*engage*; selbsteinrückend *self-actuating*) | ~sbelag [m] *clutch facing*; ~shebel [m] *coupling lever*; ~sklaue [f] *clutch dog*; ~smanöver [n] ⟨a-n⟩ *docking manœuvre* **K·uppler** m ~s/~ ⟨rail⟩ *shunter*; ⟨sex⟩ *match-maker, go-between, pander* ‖ ⟨dero⟩ *procurer* (f *procuress*); *bawd* | **≃isch** a *match-making*, ⟨dero⟩ *procuring*

K·ur[1] **(K·ür)** f ~/~en (Wahl) *election* **~fürst** m *elector* (f *electress*) **~fürstentum** n *e.ate* **≃fürstlich** a *e.al* **~pfalz** f *the Palatinate* **≃pfälzisch** a *Palatine* **~prinz** m *e.al prince* (f *e. princess*) **~würde** f *e.al dignity, e.ate*

Kur[2] f [invar] (Fr cour) er macht *or* schneidet ihr die ~ *he courts, wooes her*; *makes love to her*; *pays her attentions* **~machen** n, **~macherei** f *courting*; *love-making*

Kur[3] f ~/~en (Heilung) *cure* ‖ e–e ~ m *to do a cure*; e–e ~ gebrauchen *to go through a course of* (*medical*) *treatment, to take the waters* od *the baths* ‖ die ~ in N. hat angeschlagen *the treatment at N. has proved successful* | ⟨fig⟩ wir w ihn einmal in die ~ nehmen *we will call him to account* **~anstalt** f *sanatorium* **~arzt** m *physician of a watering-place* **~gast** m *patient, visitor at a w.-p.* **~gelegenheit** f *pumproom faculties* pl **~haus** n *pump-room, spa hotel, assembly-rooms* pl **~kosten** pl *expenses of a cure* **~liste** f *list of visitors* **~ort** m *w.-p., spa, health resort* **~pfuscher** m *quack* | ~ei [f] *quackery* **~saal** m *assembly-room* **~schmied** m *farrier* **~stadt** f *resort city* **~taxe** f *visitor's tax*

K·ür f ~/~en *free figures* ⟨a. skating⟩, *extempore* L (→ küren) | ~übung [f], ~turnen [n] *ad libitum* od *free exercise gymnastics* pl; *free figures*

Kur·a m (Fluß in Georgien) *Kur*(*a*)

Kur·ant m ~(e)s/ *currency* **kur·ant** a *current*

K·üraß m –asses/–asse *cuirass* **Küras·sier** m ~(e)s/~e *cuirassier*

Kurat·el f ~/~en *trusteeship, guardianship* ‖ ⟨jur⟩ unter ~ stehen *to be in ward* od *under t.*; unter ~ stellen *to put under t.* **Kur·ator** m ~s/–at·oren ⟨jur⟩ *trustee, guardian*; (Museums≃; ⟨univ⟩) *curator* **Kurat·orium** n ~s/–rien ⟨jur⟩ *board* (*of trustees*); ⟨univ⟩ *c.'s office*

Kurb·ayern n ⟨Ger hist⟩ *Electorate of Bavaria*

K·urbel f ~/~n *crank, winch*(*-handle*) ‖ An·ruf≃ *call crank* ‖ Br·ems≃ *brake handle* ‖ H·and-

≃ *hand-drive* ≃**achse** f *cr.-axle* ~**antrieb** m ⟨mot⟩ *connecting rod assembly* ~**arm** m *cr.-lever, cr.--arm* ~**bewegung** f ⟨tech⟩ *cr.-motion* ~**dynamo** n *hand-operated dynamo* ~**fenster** n *lowering window* ~**gehäuse** n *cr.-case* ~**lager** n *cr.-bearings* pl ~-**presse** f *lever press* ~**stange** f ⟨tech⟩ *connecting-rod* ~**trieb** m *cr. gear* ~**wanne** f ⟨mot⟩ *sump* ~**welle** f *eccentric shaft, cr.shaft* ~**zapfen** m *cr.-pin* **k·urbeln** vi [h] *to turn the crank* ‖ (Film) *to wind*, ⟨Am⟩ *to shoot* **Kurb·ette** f ~/~n ⟨hors⟩ *curvet* **kurbett·ieren** vi [h] ⟨hors⟩ *to curvet*

K·ürbis m –isses/–isse *gourd, pumpkin* ~**flasche** f *gourd-bottle* ≃**förmig** a *gourd-shaped* ~**gewächse** pl *cucurbitaceous plants* pl ~**kern** m *seed of a g.*

Kurbr·andenburg n ⟨Ger hist⟩ *Electorate of Brandenburg*

K·urde m, **K·urdin** f *Kurd* **k·urdisch** a *Kurdish* **K·urdistan, Kurdist·an** n (Landschaft am oberen Tigris) *Kurdistan* **kurdist·anisch** a → kurdisch

k·üren vt [kürte & kor/gekürt & gekoren] [h] *to choose, elect*

Kurh·essen n ⟨Ger⟩ → Hessen-Kassel

Kuri·alstil m *law-style, legal style*

K·urie f ~/~n **1.** ⟨Roman ant⟩ *curia* **2.** ⟨Ger⟩ *electorate* **3.** (Vatikan) *Papal Court, Curia*

Kur·ier m ~(e)s/~e *special messenger, courier, express* ‖ ~ reiten *to ride post* ~**stiefel** m pl *jack-boots* pl

kur·ieren vt [h] *to cure* ⟨a. fig⟩ ‖ gründlich ~ *to effect a cure* ‖ ⟨fig⟩ er ist von s–n Vorurteilen –rt *he is cured of ..* ‖ wieder ganz –rt *quite restored* ‖ zu Tode –rt *killed by doctoring*

Kur·ilen pl (sowjetische Inseln) *Kuriles*

Kur·ilisch a *Kuril*; ~er Graben ⟨mar⟩ *Kuril Trench*; ~e Schwelle ⟨mar⟩ *Kuril Ridge*

kuri·os a *curious, singular, queer, odd* ‖ ~er Kerl *or* Kauz ⟨fam⟩ *queer* od *rum fellow* ≃**it·ät** f ~/~en *curiosity* ‖ (Sammlungsstück) *curio(sity)* | ~enhändler [m] *dealer in curiosities* **Kuri·osum** n ~s/–sa L *curious fact* ‖ *curiosity*

K·urisches Haff n (vor Memel-Mündung) ⟨a.⟩ *Kurishes Haff* **K·urische Nehrung** f *Kurishe Nehrung*, → Nehrung

K·urland n *Courland* **K·urländer** m, ~**in** f *Courlander, inhabitant of Courland* **k·urländisch** a *(of) Courland*

k·urren vi [h] **1.** (Fischerei) *to trawl* **2.** = knurren; (Magen) *to rumble*

Kurr·ende f ~/ *itinerant choir* | *circular letter (singing in the streets)*

Kurr·entschrift f *running hand* | *italics* pl

k·urrig a **1.** *quarrelsome* **2.** *strange*

K·urs m ~es/~e **1.** ⟨com⟩ (Umlauf) *currency, circulation* ‖ (Kurswert) *(rate of) exchange quotation* ‖ zum gegenwärtigen ~ *at the present ex.* ‖ im ~ stehen *to be current, quoted (at)* ‖ in ~ setzen *to circulate* ‖ im ~ zu *or* zum ~ von *at the rate* od *ex. of* ‖ die Kurse ziehen an, bröckeln ab *qu.s are hardening, easing* ‖ im ~ steigen *to rise, to go up* ‖ die Kurse sind gefallen *the prices have gone down* ‖ ohne ~ *without (official) qu.* ‖ außer ~ setzen *to call in, to demonetise, to withdraw from cir.* ‖ ⟨übtr⟩ Ehrlichkeit stand nicht hoch im ~ *honesty was at a discount* ‖ er steht bei ihm hoch im ~ *he is in high favour with him*; sein Ansehen steigt im ~ *his stock is rising* **2.** (Lehrgang) *course*; ⟨Am⟩ *institute* **3.** ⟨mar & fig⟩ *course*; *heading* ‖ ⟨fig⟩ *(collision) c.* ‖ (miß-), rechtweisender ~ *(magnetic), true c.* ‖ zurückgelegter östlicher ~ *easting* ‖ ~ geradeaus! *straight ahead!* ‖ ⟨fig⟩ der neue ~ ⟨pol⟩ *the new c.* od *drift* ‖ ~ absetzen *to lay (off) the c.* ‖ ~ ändern auf *to alter c. to* ‖ den ~ ändern *to haul (the wind)*, ⟨fig⟩ *to change one's tack* ‖ den ~ (beibe)halten *to keep the c.*; (auf) ~ halten *to steady, to hold heading* ‖ e–n neuen ~ einschlagen ⟨fig⟩ *to take a new tack* ‖ nördlichen ~ fahren *to bear north* ‖ ~ h auf *to make* od *steer for* ‖ nicht geraden ~ halten *to yaw* ‖ den ~ innehalten *to hold on one's c.* ‖ die Schiffe liefen mit ~ West ab *the ships steamed off towards the west* ‖ den ~ nachprüfen *to check the c.* ‖ ~ nehmen *to head (auf for)* ‖ ~ nehmen *or* setzen auf *to shape a c. for, to set the c. for* ‖ den ~ nach dem offenen Meer nehmen *to head out to sea* ‖ die Flugzeuge ziehen ihren ~ gegen .. *fly their c. on a cruise against* ~-**abschlag** m *drop in prices* ~**abweichung** f (Rakete) *yawing* ~**änderung** f *change in c.* ~**anstieg** m ⟨st exch⟩ *advance in price* ≃**anziehend** a ⟨com⟩ *rising* ~**bericht** m ⟨com⟩ *market report, st.-ex.-r.* ~**bestimmung** f *course determination* ⟨a. a–n⟩ ~**blatt** n = ~bericht ~**buch** n *railway-guide, time-table*; ⟨engl⟩ *Bradshaw*, ⟨Am⟩ *schedule* ≃**fähig** a *lawful (money, currency)* ~**flugzeug** n *airliner* ~**gewinne** m pl *market profit* ~**korrekturmanöver** n ⟨a–n⟩ (z Eliminierung v Brennschlußfehlern *midcourse) correction manœuvre* ~**kreisel** m *directional gyro* ~**kreuzung** f *crossing of c.s* ~**linie** f ⟨aero⟩ *on-c.*; ~ am Kompaß ⟨mar⟩ *lubber's line* ~**notierung** f *(market-)qu.* ~**rechengerät** n ⟨aero⟩ *(time/distance/speed) computer* N ~**schiff** n *liner* ~**schreiber** m ⟨mar⟩ *c. recorder* ~**schwankung** f ⟨com⟩ *fluctuation in the rate of ex.* ~**stand** m ⟨com⟩ *rate of ex.* ~**steuerung** f ⟨aero⟩ *automatic* od *robot* od *gyro pilot* ~**sturz** m ⟨com⟩ *sudden fall of prices* od *in the rate of ex.*, ⟨sl⟩ *slump* ~**teilnehmer** m = Kursant ~**treiber·ei** f ⟨com⟩ *market-rigging* ~-**verlust** m *loss in (the) ex.* ~**versetzung** f *heading displacement* ~**wagen** m ⟨rail⟩ *through-coach* ~-**wechsel** m *alternation of c.*; ⟨pol⟩ 100%iger ~ *turnabout* ~**weiser** m ⟨aero⟩ *direction indicator* ~**wert** m *market value* ~**zeichen** n ⟨aero⟩ *on-c. signal* ~**zettel** m = ~bericht ~**zuschlag** m *contango, carrying-over rate* **Kurs·ant** m ~en/~en ⟨SBZ⟩ *student, trainee*

K·ürschner m ~s/~ *furrier, skinner* ~**geselle** m *journeyman furrier* ~**handwerk** n *furrier's trade* ~**innung** f *corporation of furriers* ~**ware** f *furs and skins* pl **Kürschner·ei** f ~/~en *furrier's trade* ‖ (Werkstatt) *f.s shop*

kurs·ieren vi [h] *to be current* ‖ (Geld) *to circulate* ‖ (Gerücht) *to be afloat, to fly about* ‖ Anekdoten ~ über ihn *there are anecdotes about him* **kurs·iv** adv; ~ gedruckt *in italics* pl ≃**schrift** f *running hand*; ⟨typ⟩ *italics* pl **kurs·orisch** a; ~e Lektüre *cursory reading* **K·ursus** m ~/–se *course* ‖ e–n ~ in .. [dat] durchmachen *to go through a course of ..*

Kurt·ine f ~/~n ⟨fort⟩ *curtain* | ⟨theat⟩ (Zwischenvorhang) *drop-scene*

Kurtis·ane f ~/~n *courtesan*

Kurvat·ur f ~/~en *crook* **K·urve** f ~/~n [w] *curve, bend*; (steil)abfallende ~ *(dipping) downward-sloping c.* ‖ ~n zeichnen, beschreiben *to draw, describe c.s* ‖ scharfe ~ *hairpin bend*; e–e ~ ausfahren *to round a c.*; in der ~ liegen *to negotiate a c.* od *b.*; **aus** der ~ fliegen *to fly off the c.*; e–e ~ schneiden *to cut a b.*; **in** die ~ gehen *to enter a c.* ‖ in ~n davonfliegen *to swerve off*; ⟨racing⟩ in der innersten ~ liegen *to have the pole*; (Straßen≃) e–e ~ (zu knapp) nehmen *to take a corner (to short)*; zu scharf in die ~ gehen *to overbank*; ⟨fig⟩ °du hast die ~ raus *you've got the hang of it* **k·urven** vi [h] *to curve, circle* **K·urven-**~auswertung [f] *plotting of c.s*; ~bild [n] *graph*; ~kampf [m] ⟨aero⟩ *turning combat*, ⟨sl⟩ *dog--fight*; ~lage [f] ⟨mot⟩ *cornering characteristics*; ~lineal [n] *French c.s*; ≃reich [a] *winding (road)*; *curvaceous (lady)*; ~e Strecke [f] ⟨mot⟩ *bends for 2 miles*; ~überhang [m] ⟨rail⟩ *superelevation*; ~verlauf [m] ⟨geom stat⟩ *run of a c.*; ~zeichengerät [n] ⟨comp⟩ (programmgesteuert) *plotter*

k·urz 1. [a] (räumlich, zeitlich) *short (arm, hair, sleeves, pipe, grass, steps; time, memory, way, syllable, grace-note, notice)* ‖ (zeitlich) *brief* ‖ (bündig) *brief, concise*; ~ u treffend *laconic, pithy* ‖ ⟨dero⟩ *abrupt, curt* ‖ ~ u dick *stubby, dumpy,* *podgy* || ~ u stämmig *stumpy, squat* || ~ u untersetzt *stocky, thickset* || ~e, heftige Anstrengung, ~es Aufflammen ⟨fig⟩ *spurt* || er hat e–n ~en Atem *he is sh.-winded* || ~er Augenblick *snatch(es* pl) (*of sunshine*); ~er Besuch *flying visit*; ~e Charakterskizze *thumbnail character portrait*; ~er Flug ⟨aero sl⟩ *flip* || ~e Hosen *sh.s*; *brief* (*linen cloth* ⟨Eg⟩) || mit etw ~en Prozeß m *to make sh. work of a th* || ⟨mar⟩ *chopping* (*sea*) || ~e Übersicht *summary review* || ~e Waren [pl] *small ware*; *metal ware* od *goods* pl || in ~en Worten *in a few words* || ~e Wechsel [pl] ⟨com⟩ *sh. papers, sh.s* || **auf** ~e Sicht ⟨com⟩ *at sight* **2.** [adv] *sh.ly*; zu ~k (bei Landung) ⟨aero⟩ *to undershoot* || (kurzum) *in sh., briefly* || **binnen** ~em *before long, within a sh. time* || **bis vor** ~em *until very recently* || **in ~em** *sh.ly* || nach ~em *a sh. time after* || **(erst) seit ~em** *just lately, (but) for some little time* || **über** ~ oder lang *sooner or later, sh.ly, before long, one of these days* || **~ und bündig** *trite(ly), terse(ly), concise(ly)* || ~ **und gedrängt** *succinct(ly)* || ~ **und gut** *to make a long story short*; *in sh., the long and the sh. of it is* || **~ und klar** geschrieben *succinctly and clearly written* || **~ und treffend** *laconically, to the point* || **vor ~em** *recently, a sh. time ago, a little while since, the other day* || erst vor ~em *but a short time since* || bis vor ~em *up to the other day* || es war **~ vor** 1 Uhr *it was not far off one o'clock* || ~ vor der Stadt *sh. of the town* || **~ vorher** *sh.ly before* **3. ~ abbrechen** *to break off suddenly* || e–n **~ abfertigen** *to cut a p sh.* || e–e S **~ abmachen** *or* **abtun** *to dispatch a th quickly* || ~ abschlagen *to refuse flatly* || in **~ abgeschnittenen** Worten *in clipped words* || jdn ~ abweisen *to be sh. with a p*; **~ andeuten** *to give a brief indication of*; **~ angebunden** *abrupt*; *standoffish*; ~ a. s mit .. *to be short with a p*; jdn ~ vorher **benachrichtigen** *to give a p sh. notice* || **~ charakterisieren** *to characterize briefly* || **~ erwidern** *to give a terse* od *abrupt reply* || **faß** dich ~! *be brief! cut it sh.!, come to the point!* || e–n **~ halten** *to keep a p sh. of money* || (ein Pferd) ~ halten *to tighten the reins* || die S **ist ~** folgende *the long and the sh. of it is* || **zu ~ k** *to be neglected, to come off badly* || *to come up a loser* (bei *in*) || um es ~ zu **m** *to cut the matter sh., to put it briefly* || er machte es ~ *he was quick in doing it* || **~ gesagt** *in a word, briefly put* || ~ und klein **schlagen** *to knock to pieces*: *I'll break every stick in this house* || **~ schließen** ⟨el⟩ *to short-circuit* || (Haare) **~ schneiden** *to bob*; sich die Haare ~ schneiden l *to have one's hair cropped* || ihr Haar ist ~ geschnitten *her hair has been cut sh.* || (Mähne) ~ schneiden *to hog* || **~ geschnitten, ~ geschoren** (Haar) *close-cropped* || **~ skizzieren** *to thumb-nail* || sie **trägt** das Haar ~ *she wears her hair sh.* || um es **~ zus-zufassen** *to give it you in a nutshell* **4.** ein ≃er, etw ≃es *a short drink* **5.** [compr] **k·ürzer**: ~ m ⟨tail⟩ *to chop off*; er wurde (um) e–n Kopf ~ gemacht *he was beheaded, his head was cut off* || die Tage w ~ *the days are shortening* (od *drawing* od *closing in*); sich ~ fassen als .. *to write at less length than ..* || (dabei) den ~en ziehen *to get the worst of it, to be worsted,* ⟨fam⟩ *to come off second-best, to feel the draught*; im Kampf .. *to be left behind in the struggle* ⟨fig⟩; wer den ~en zieht, bezahlt! *off man pays!*; die Armen ziehen den ~en *the dice are loaded against the poor* **6.** [sup] **k·ürzest**: am ~en *shortest* || auf das ~e *in the shortest way* **K·urz- ~arbeit** f *undertime work* **~arbeiter** m *half-time* od *part-time worker*, ⟨fam⟩ *part-timer* **≃armig** a *sh.-armed* **≃atmig** a *scant of breath, pursy, asthmatic, sh.-winded* || ⟨vet⟩ *broken-winded* **~atmigkeit** f *sh.-ness of breath, pursiness* **~befehl** m *fragment order* N **≃beinig** a *sh.-legged* **~biographie** f *profile* **~brüchigkeit** f ⟨met⟩ *shortness, brittleness* **≃dauernd** a *transient, passing* **~fassung** f ⟨wir⟩ (*news*) *summary* **~film** m *sh., featurette* **~flügler** m ⟨ent⟩ *rove beetle* **~form** f *curtailed* od *abbreviated form* **~frage** f ⟨quiz⟩ *quicky* **≃fristig** a *short* (*loan*); *sh.-term* (*debt, forecast*); bei ~er Ansage *or* Anmeldung *at a moment* (*or two*)*'s notice* **≃gefaßt** a *synoptic(al)* **~geschichte** f ⟨Lit⟩ *sketch*; *sh. story* **≃halsig** a *sh.-necked* **~hemdchen** n ⟨mod com⟩ *camisette* **≃köpfig** a *brachycephalic* **~lage** f ⟨artill⟩ *short-fall* **≃lebig** a *sh.-lived, ephemeral* **~nachrichten** f pl *newslets* **~schießer** m pl ⟨eig artill⟩ *drop-sh.s* **~schluß** m ⟨el⟩ *sh. circuit*; ~ verursachen *to sh.-circuit* [vi] | ~handlung [f] ⟨psych⟩ *impulsive act*; ~läufer [m] ⟨tech⟩ *squirrel-cage rotor*; ~l.motor [m] *sq.-c. motor* **~schrift** f *sh.hand(-writing), stenography* **~schriftler** m *sh.-writer* **~schuß** m *shot falling sh., sh. shot*; ≃e pl ⟨artill⟩ *dropping-shorts* **~schwanz-** *sh.-tailed* **~schwert** n *scramasax* **≃sichtig** a ⟨eig⟩ *sh.-* od *near-sighted*; ⟨fig⟩ *narrow-minded, sh.-sighted, purblind* | ≃keit [f] *sh.-s.ness, myopia*; ⟨fig⟩ *sh.-s.ness, narrow-mindedness* **~spruch** [m] mit unverschlüsselter Anschrift ⟨mil⟩ *abbreviated plaindress* **~start** m ⟨aero⟩ *short takeoff (and landing)* **≃stielig** a *sh.-handled*; ⟨bot⟩ *sh.-stalked*, ⟨scient⟩ *subsessible* **~strecken-** *short range* [attr] | ~flug [m] ⟨fam⟩ *hop*; ~lauf [m] *sprinting*; ~läufer [m] *sprinter* **≃treten** vi [h] ⟨fig⟩ *to soft-pedal* ⟨sl⟩ **≃·um** adv *in sh.* **~waren** f [pl] (Eisen-) *hardware* || (Posamenten) *small* od *petty ware(s* pl), *haberdashery*, ⟨Am⟩ *notions* pl | ~händler [m] *dealer in hardware, haberdasher*; ~handlung [f] *thread-and-needle shop* **~weil** f *pastime, play, amusement, sport, jest, joke*; ~ treiben *to make merry, to disport o.s.*; allerlei ~ treiben *to have all kinds of amusement* **≃weilig** a *diverting, amusing, funny* **~welle** f ⟨wir⟩ *high frequency*; *sh. wave* | ~nsender [m] *sh.-w. transmitter* **~wort** n *acronym* **≃wollig** a *sh.-napped* **~zeit-** ~beschäftigung [f] *part-time employment*; ~messung [f] *microchronometry* **K·ürze** f ~/~n (Raum & Zeit) *sh.-ness* || (Bündigkeit) *brevity* || *sh. syllable* || (Barschheit) *curtness* || wir w in ~ bei euch s *we shall soon be with you* || in aller ~ *briefly, succinctly, in a nutshell* || das ist in ~ die ganze Geschichte *that's the long and short of it* || der ~ halber *for sh.* || in der ~ liegt die Würze *brevity is the soul of wit* (Shak) **K·ürzel** n ~s/~ *logogram*; (Wort) *grammalogue* **k·ürzen** vt [h] *to shorten* (*skirt, essay*) || ⟨math⟩ *to simplify, reduce* (*fraction*) || *to curtail*; *to cut down*, ⟨Am⟩ *to slash, dock* (*wages*) **k·ürzer, k·ürzest** → kurz **k·urzerhand** adv *abruptly*; *offhand, without hesitation*; ~ erfunden (*tale*) *just invented*; *on the spot*; *briefly* **k·ürzlich** adv *lately, newly, recently, latterly*; erst ~ *quite recently* **k·urz·um** adv *in short* **K·ürzung** f ~/~en *abbreviation, abridgment* || ⟨math⟩ *reducing* || ⟨theat⟩ *cutting down*; *cut* **k·urzw·eg** adv *briefly*; *abruptly, curtly*

kusch!, ~ dich! [intj] (*lie*) *down!* **k·uschen** vi [h] *to crouch, to lie down* || ⟨fig⟩ er muß (sich) ~ *he must keep quiet* od *do as he is told*

Kus·ine f ~/~n (*woman* od *girl*) *cousin*

K·uskus m ~/~ ⟨cul⟩ (Art Grütze) *couscous*

K·uß m Kusses/Küsse, ⟨dim⟩ Küßchen [n] *kiss*; ⟨fam⟩ *buss* || Küsse tauschen *to exchange k.es* || e–m e–n ~ zuwerfen *to blow a p k.* || flüchtiger ~ ⟨sl⟩ *peck* || schallender ~ *smacker* || heiße Küsse *ardent, passionate kisses* || e–m e–n Gute-Nacht ≃ geben *to k. a. p. good night* **≃fest** a *kiss-proof* (*lip-stick*) **~täfelchen** n *osculatory*

küß' die Hand! ⟨oft⟩ [ksˈtɛənt] österr **1.** *How do you do, madam!* **2.** *No, thank you!*

K·üssen n ~s/ *kissing* || zum ~ schön *charmingly sweet*

k·üssen vt [h] *to kiss* ⟨a. fig⟩ = leise berühren, ([Ball] *to snick*) || sie ~ sich *they k. each other* || ⟨fig⟩ die Erde ~ (hinfallen) *to embrace the earth* || e–n auf die Wange ~ *to k. a p's cheek* || e–n aus dem Schlafe ~ *to rouse a p with k.ing* || e–n zum

Abschied ~ *to k. a p good-bye* **Küsser·ei** f ~/ ⟨fam⟩ *billing and cooing* **K·ußhand** f; jdm e–e ~ zuwerfen *to kiss one's hand to a p, to blow* od *to throw a kiss to a p* || das nehme ich mit ~ *I'll accept that with (the greatest) pleasure* **k·ußlich, k·üßlich** a *made for kissing, kissable*

K·usseln f [pl] ⟨mst mil⟩ *shrubbery*

K·üste f ~/~n *(sea)coast, shore* || (Strand) *beach* || unreine ~ *foul c.* || an der ~ *by the sh.-side* || an der ~ stationiert *sh.-based (aircraft)* || an der ~ entlangfahren *to proceed* od *sail along the c.* || sich unter der ~ halten *to hug the c.* || die ~ sichten *to raise the c.* **K·üsten- ~abschnitt** m *c.al frontier* **~artillerie** f *c. artillery* **~batterie** *c.al battery* **~befestigung** f *c.al fortification*, ~en *c.al defences* **~beschuß** m (v See aus) *ship-to-shore attack* **~bewohner** m *inhabitant of the c.*; ⟨fam⟩ *seasider* **~dampfer** m *c.ing steamer* **~dünen** pl *links* pl **~ebene** *c.al plain* **~fahrer** m *c.er* (a. P), *c.ing vessel* **~fahrt** f *c.ing* **~feuer** n *c.al light* **~fischerei** f *c.al* od *inshore fishery* **~gebiet** n *littoral*; *c.al district* od *area*; ⟨Am⟩ *tide-water* **~gegend** f *sh.-side* **~geleitboot** n *c. escort* **~geschwader** n *home squadron* **~gewässer** n [pl] *c.al waters* pl **~handel** m *c.ing trade, c.wise traffic* **~land** n, **~strich** m *littoral, maritime country*; *stretch of c.* **~licht** n *c.al light* **~panzer** m *c.al defence vessel* **~provinz** f *maritime province* **~schiffahrt** f *cabotage*; *c.wise shipping* **~schutz** m *c.guards* pl | ~dienst [m] *offshore patrol*; ~flugzeug [n] *c.al defence aeroplane*; ~kommando [n] *c.al command* **~sicherung** f *c.al security* **~stadt** f *sea-side town* **~straße** f *c.al road* **~streifen** m *c.al strip* **~strich** m = –land **~telegraph** m *c.al signal mast* **~verkehr** m ⟨mar⟩ *c.wise traffic* **~vermessung** f *survey of the c.* **~verteidigung** f *c. defence* | ~sbereich [m] *defensive c.al area* **~wachboot** n *seaward patrol craft* **~wache, ~wacht** f *c.-guard* **~wachschiff** n *c.-guard vessel* **~wasser** n *tide-water*

K·üster m ~s/~ *sexton, verger* **Küster·ei** f ~/~en *s.'s house* od *office* **K·ustos** m ~/Kust·oden *custodian, keeper, curator* || ⟨typ⟩ *catch-word*

Küstr·in ⟨†Ger⟩ (Stadt an der Oder)

K·utsch- ~bock m *(coach-)box, driving-seat* | ~decke [f] *hammer-cloth* **~kasten** m *well* od *boot of a coach* **~pferd** n *coach-* od *carriage-horse* **~wagen** m → folg & Wagen **K·utsche** f ~/~n (→ Wagen) *coach, carriage, trap* || Bahnhofs≗ *(station-)fly* || ⟨Am⟩ (2 Räder, 1 Pferd) *buggy, sulky, rig* || sechsspännige ~ *coach-and-six, mail-coach* || ~ u (2) Pferde halten *to keep a carriage and pair* || in e–r ~ fahren *to ride in a coach* **K·utschen- ~bauer** m *coach-builder* **~bock** = Kutsch– **~gestell** n *c.-frame* **~himmel** m *c.-top, roof of a c.* **~leder** n *apron* **~schlag** m *carriage-door* **~tritt** m *foot-board, steps* pl **K·utscher** m ~s/~ *coachman, driver* || das kann mein *or* Lehmanns ~ auch *anybody can do that* **~bock** m, **~sitz** m = Kutsch– **~handschuh** m *driving-glove* **kutsch·ieren** vi [h & s] *to drive ([in] a coach)* || [s] *to ride in a coach* || er –rt ausgezeichnet *he is an excellent whip*

Kutsch Behar n (Vorderind. Bezirk) *Cooch Behar*

K·utte f ~/~n *cowl* || die ~ anlegen ⟨fig⟩ *to don the monk's garb* || jdn in die ~ stecken *to make a monk of a p*

K·uttel- ~fisch m *sepia, cuttle-fish* **~flecke** m [pl] *tripe, chitterlings* pl **~hof** m *shambles* pl **~markt** m *tripe-market* **K·utteln** f pl ⟨cul⟩ *chitterlings* pl, *fry*, (bes Rind) *tripe*

K·utter m ~s/~ ⟨mar⟩ *cutter* || Wal≗ *whaler*

Kuv·ert n [kuw'e:ə] ~(e)s/~e ['ertə] *envelope, wrapper* || unter ~ *under cover* | (Gedeck) *cover* **≗·ieren** vt [h] *to wrap, to (put in an) envelope* **Kuvert·üre** f ~/~n ⟨cul⟩ *couverture*

K·ux m ~es/~e ⟨min⟩ *cost-book mining(-)-share* | ~inhaber [m] *c.-b. shareholder*; ~schicht [f] ⟨min⟩ *day's shift*

Kwangtung (Prov. Chinas)

Kybern·etik f ~/~en *cybernetics* [sg konstr]

K·yffhäuser [ki-] ⟨Ger⟩ (Berg) *Kyffhauser* **~sage** f *K. Saga* (v Kaiser Barbarossa † 1190)

Kykl·aden f pl → Zykladen

k·ymrisch a *Cymric*

Kyren·aika n (Land in Nordafrika) *Cyrenaica*

K·yrie|el·eis(on)! Gr *Lord, have mercy upon us! kyrieeleison!*

kyr·illisch a *Cyrillic* (Schrift)

L

L, l [el] n ~/~ *L, l* || l³ (= l hoch³) → Leitung L-Zug [m] = Luxuszug

la intj **1.** ⟨mus⟩ *lalalala*; (Kehrreim) *falderal* **2.** nur so lala (= mäßig) *nothing to boast of, pretty middling* || (es geht in allem nur) so lala *(that's all) so-and-so*; ⟨Am⟩ *so so*; *all-right, I guess*

L·ab n ~(e)s/ *rennet* **~drüse** f *pepsine gland* **~kraut** n ⟨bot⟩ (gelbes) ~ *(Our Lady's) bedstraw* **~magen** m *rennet-stomach, -bag*

°**L·aban** m ~s/~e ⟨fig⟩ → Lulatsch

L·abbe f ~/~n ⟨sl⟩ *hanging lip* **l·abber** a: ~e Kühlte ⟨mar⟩ *light breeze, calm* °**l·abberig** a *wishy-washy, sloppy*; ~es Gesöff ⟨sl⟩ *lap* **l·abbern** vi/t [h] *to lap* || (schwatzen) ⟨vulg⟩ *to twaddle, babble* || (küssen) *to slobber* || ⟨mar⟩ (Segel) *to flap about*

L·abe f ~/ = Labsal **~becher** m *refreshing cup* **~flasche** f ⟨mil⟩ *(water-)flask*; *bottle of cordial* **~trunk** m *r. drink* **l·aben** vt [h] *to refresh, cheer* || **sich ~ an** *to refresh, regale, comfort o.s. with*

L·aberdan m ~s/ ⟨ich⟩ *salt* od *cured cod*

labi·al a *labial* **≗laut** m, **Labiale** f ~/~n *labial*

lab·il a *unstable (equilibrium)* || *unstable, weak (character, health)*; seelisch ~ *psychologically unstable*; labile || *fluid (situation)* || ⟨scient⟩ *labile* | **≗it·ät** f *disequilibrium, lability* ⟨a. fig⟩; *instability*; ⟨fig⟩ *unsteadiness*

°**Lab·or** n ~s/~e ⟨fam⟩ *lab* **~·ant(in** f ~/~nen) m ~en/~en *lab assistant* od *technician* **~at·orium** n ~s/–rien *laboratory*, ⟨fam⟩ *lab*, → Labor **≗·ieren** vi [h] *to labour, to do laboratory-work* || (an [dat]) *to suffer (from), to be afflicted (with)*

Labrad·or n *Labrador* **~strom** n (kalte Meeresströmung) *Labrador Stream*

L·absal n ~(e)s/~e, **L·abung** f ~/~en *refreshment, restorative, cordial*; ⟨fam⟩ *pick-me-up* || ⟨fig⟩ *treat, comfort, cordial*

L·abskaus n ~/ ⟨mar⟩ = Eintopfgericht

Labyr·inth n ~(e)s/~e ⟨myth, anat, fig⟩ *labyrinth*; ⟨hort, fig⟩ *maze* || **≗isch** a *l.ine, mazy*

L·ach- (→ Lache ²⁻³) **~anfall** m *fit of laughter* **~baum** m *notched tree, boundary-tree* **~falte** f *laughter-line* **~film** m ⟨fam⟩ *laughy* **~gas** n *laughing-gas, nitrous oxide* **≗haft** a *ridiculous* **~krampf** m ⟨med⟩ *convulsive fit of (hysterical) l.r*; ≗e bek *to go into convulsions of l.r*; .. verursachen *to throw into ..* **~lust** f *inclination to laugh*; *risibility* **≗lustig** a *fond of l.ing*; *risible* **~möwe** f ⟨orn⟩ *l.ing-gull* **~muskel** m ⟨anat⟩ *risorial* od *risible muscle* **~salve** f *peal of l.r* | ~nprovokateur [m] ⟨theat, etc⟩ ⟨Am sl⟩ *stooge* **~sturm** m *tempest of l.r* **~taube** f *l.ing-dove*

L·ache¹ f ~/~n *pool, puddle (of blood, oil)*

L·ache² *notch made in a tree, boundary mark*

Lache³ f ~/~n *laugh(ter)* ‖ e–e gellende ~ anschlagen *to burst into a roar of l.ter* ‖ sie hat e–e komische ~ *she has a funny way of l.ing*; in e–e ~ ausbrechen *to fall a-l.ing* **L·ächeln** n ~s/ *smile* (schwach *faint*, müde *faint*) ‖ (geziert) *smirk* ‖ (höhnisch) *sneer* ‖ e–n mit e–m ~ hereinbitten *to smile a p in* ‖ sie dankte ihm für den Empfang mit e–m ~ *she smiled acknowledgement of his welcome* ‖ geziertes ~ *simper*; ein häßliches, sardonisches ~ aufsetzen *to smile* od *give a hideous, sardonic smile* ‖ es mit e–m ~ abtun ⟨fam⟩ *to laugh it off* ‖ mit e–m unterdrückten ~ *tongue in cheek* ‖ mit Gewalt ein ~ zustandebringen *to force a smile to one's lips* **l·ächeln** vi/t [h] *to smile* (über *at*), *to give a smile* ‖ (geziert) ~ *to smirk, simper* ‖ (höhnisch) ~ *to sneer* (über *at*) ‖ heimlich ~d *tongue in cheek* ‖ kaum ~ *to smile faintly* ‖ kühl u höflich ~ *to smile with cool politeness* ‖ ihm lächelt kein Glück *fortune does not smile on him* ‖ mitleidig über jdn ~ *to think a p small beer* ‖ vor sich hin ~ *to smile to o.s.* ‖ er lächelte über das ganze Gesicht *his face was all smiles*, ⟨fam⟩ *he smiled from ear to ear* ‖ mit ~der Verbeugung *with a smile and a bow* ‖ strahlend hinter e–m her- ~ *to beam after a p* ‖ die Sonne lächelte u strahlte *the sun smiled his broadest* ‖ e–n ~d hereinbitten *to smile a p in* ‖ höflich ~ *to smile a polite smile* ‖ zu e–m hinüber|~ *to smile across at a p* ‖ zustimmend ~ *to smile one's agreement* ‖ ohne zu ~ *unsmiling*; nicht ~ *to be unsmiling* | ihr Auge lächelt Freude *her face beams with joy* ‖ → grinsen lachen, feixen **L·achen** n ~s/ *laugh, laughter, laughing* ‖ fröhliches ~ *light laugh*; höhnisches ~ *fleer* ‖ lautes, schallendes ~ *roars* [pl] *of l.ter, horse-l.* ‖ gut ~ h *to think o.s. lucky*; das ist nicht zum ~ *it's no joke*; e–n z ~ bringen, reizen *to make a p l.*; sich vor ~ biegen *to howl with l.er*; vor ~ fast platzen (→ vergehen) *to split one's sides*; *to l. fit to burst*; ihr ~ *their l.ing voices* ‖ wir kamen nicht aus dem ~ heraus *there was no end to our l.ter* ‖ die S ist z ~ *that is a l.ing-matter, that's ridiculous* ‖ erst können vor ~! *fancy*! z ~ komisch ⟨Am⟩ *funny as a crutch* ‖ er konnte sich des ~s nicht erwehren *he could not help l.ing* ‖ die Gags reizten z ~ ⟨theat⟩ *the gags drew a laugh* ‖ sich das ~ verbeißen *to suppress one's l.ter, to choke back a smile* ‖ ⟨prov⟩ am vielen ~ erkennt man den Narren *the loud l. bespeaks a vacant head, empty vessels make the most noise* **l·achen 1.** vi [h] *to laugh* (über [acc] *at*) ‖ bitter ~ *to give a bitter l.* ‖ höhnisch ~ *to snigger, sneer, fleer* ‖ aus vollem Halse ~ *to roar with l.ter, to burst out l.ing* ‖ übers ganze Gesicht ~ *to smile from ear to ear* ‖ laut ~ *to l. out loud; to guffaw, chortle* ‖ unbeherrscht ~: *she had a l. like a trooper* ‖ hohl ~ *to l. a hollow l.* ‖ brüllend *to yell*; strahlend *beam*; vergnügt *chuckle* ‖ gezwungen ~ *to l. wanly, to give a forced l.*, ⟨fam⟩ *to l. on the wrong side of the mouth* ‖ in sich hinein ~ *to l. inwardly*; verschmitzt ~d *the eyes twinkling with l.ter* | **(S)** *to smile*: *all nature smiled* od *looked smiling* | e–m ins Gesicht ~ *to l. in a p's face* ‖ das wäre (ja) gelacht, (wenn) *it would be ridiculous* (*if*); *is there any doubt? that's* (*a*) *child's play* ‖ du hast schön *or* gut ~ *it's all right for you*; wer lacht da –! *who laughs now*!; daß ich nicht lache! *don't make me l.*! *that's enough to make one l.*; da ~ ja die (ältesten Suppen-)Hühner *that's enough to make a cat* od *monkey l.* ‖ da ist nichts **zu** ~ *there is nothing to l. at*; er hat nichts zu ~ *it's no joke for him*, ⟨fam⟩ *it's no giggle*; du hattest (auch) nichts zu ~ ⟨sl⟩ *you had no blooming picnic* ‖ das Herz lachte mir im Leibe *it did my heart good* ‖ ⟨prov⟩ wer zuletzt lacht, lacht am besten *he l.s best who l.s last* **2.** vt [h] wir lachten Tränen *we l.ed till we cried* **3. vrefl** ⟨fam⟩ **sich** bucklig, krank, schief, tot ~, (sich [dat] e–n Ast ~) *to l. enough to split, to split* (*one's sides*) *with l.ing, to l. fit to burst, to l. one's head off*; wir lachten uns krumm u schief *we almost died with l.ing* ‖ sich [dat] ins Fäustchen ~ *to l. in one's sleeve* **l·achend** a *laughing* ‖ *joyful* (*heirs*); der ~e Dritte *the "tertius gaudens"* ‖ ⟨fig⟩ *bright* (*sunshine*) ‖ der ~e Mai *the smiling month of May* ‖ ~e Gefilde *smiling fields* ‖ das ~e Leben *the joyous life* ‖ er ist der ~e Dritte *he is the third man and has the l. on his side* **L·acher** m ~s/~ *laugher*; die ~ auf s–r Seite h *to have the laugh on one's side* ‖ die ~ waren auf der anderen Seite *the laugh was against* (⟨Am⟩ *on*) *me, him*, etc. **l·ächerlich** a **1.** (Lachen erregend) *ridiculous, laughable* ‖ *comical, droll, ludicrous*; *funny*; *grotesque* ‖ es ist ~, daß e–r tut *it is absurd for a p to do* ‖ ~! *bosh*! ‖ Zahlen – ~! *figures, indeed*! | [adv] ~ gering *derisive, derisory* (*amount*) ‖ *absurdly, preposterously* (*narrow*) | e–n ~ **machen** *to make fun* od *game of a p, to ridicule a p, to hold a p up to ridicule*; ⟨Am⟩ *to guy a p* ‖ **sich** ~ m *to make an ass* od *exhibition* od *a fool of o.s.* **2.** ⟨fam⟩ (vergnügt) ihm war nicht ~ zu Mute *he did not feel inclined to smile* od *in a laughing mood* **3. das** ~̊**e** *the ridiculous*; das ~ste daran war .. *the most ridiculous part of it was ..* ‖ ins ~e ziehen *to make fun of, to* (*turn into*) *ridicule* ‖ man muß nicht alles ins ~e ziehen *one must not try to make everything seem ridiculous* | ~̊**keit** f ~/~en **1.** (Zustand) [ohne pl] *ridiculousness* ‖ jdn der ~ preisgeben *to expose a p to ridicule*; e–r S den Anstrich v ~ geben *to make a th faintly absurd* **2.** (Gegenstand) [mit pl] *trifle*, (*a mere*) *farce* ‖ solche ~en kümmern mich nicht *I don't trouble about such trivial matters* **l·ächern 1.** v/impers [h]: mich lächert *or* es lächert mich *I feel inclined to laugh* **2.** vt: die S lächert mich *it makes me laugh* **L·ächler** m ~s/~; **~in** f ~/~nen *smiling one*

l·achig a *full of puddles* (→ Lache¹)

Lachs m ~es/~e *salmon*; ⟨Swed, Norw⟩ *lax*; vorm Ablaichen *rawner, baggot* ‖ junger ~ *par(r)* ‖ (vor [nach] erster Rückkehr nach [aus] dem Meere) *smolt* [*grilse*] **~angel** f *s.-tackle* **~fang** m, **~fischerei** f *s.-catching* **~fische** m [pl] Sippe der ~ *Salmonidae* [L pl] ~̊**farben,** ~̊**farbig,** ~̊**rot** a *s.(pink)* **~forelle** f *finnock, schoder*; *grey* od *s.-trout* **~haken** m (am Unterkiefer) *neb* **~kopf** m *head of a s., jowl* **~schinken** m *lax ham*

ˣ**L·achter** f ~/~n; n ~s/~ (= 2 m) *fathom* **~baum** m *boundary-tree*

L·ack m ~(e)s/~e *varnish* (*oil*), *lacquer* (*nitrocellulose* od *solvent type*) ‖ ⟨fig⟩ der ~ der Bildung *the veneer* (Fournier) *of culture* ‖ fertig ist der ~! *that's done*!, *that's that*! °**~affe** m *fob, dandy* **~arbeit(en)** f (pl) *Japan-work, lacquered work* **~arbeiter** m *varnisher* **~entferner** m ⟨cosm⟩ *l. removing shampoo* **~farbe** f *varnish paint, enamel paint* **~harz** n *gum-lac* **~holz** n *dwarf mountain-pine* **~leder** n *patent leather* **~mantel** m (Damenmode) *oilskin coat* **~schuhe** m pl *p. l. shoes*, ⟨Am fam⟩ *p. l.s* **~stiefel** m *p. l. boot, dress-boot* **~waren** f pl *japanned* od *lacquered goods* pl **lack·ieren** vt [h] **1.** *to lacquer, varnish, japan* **2.** ⟨fig⟩ °e–n ~ (⟨hum a.⟩ lackmeiern) ⟨fam⟩ *to do a p in the eye* ‖ ich war der Lackierte *I was the loser* od *pigeon* **Lack·ierer** m ~s/~ *varnisher, lacquerer* **Lack·ierung** f ~/~en *enamel finish*

°**L·ackel** m ~s/~ *churl, boor*

L·ackmus m, n ~/ ⟨chem⟩ *litmus* **~kraut** n ⟨bot⟩ *turnsole* **~papier** n *litmus-paper*

L·acknau n → Lakhnau

L·ade f ~/~n *box, case, chest* ‖ (für Wäsche etc) *press* ‖ (Schub~̊) *drawer* ‖ Bundes~̊ *Ark of the Convention* ‖ ⟨weav⟩ *batten, lathe* ‖ ⟨fig⟩ sie sieht aus wie gerade aus der ~ genommen *she looks as if she had just come out of the band-box* **~bahn** f *loading chute* **~baum** m ⟨mar⟩ *derrick* **~behandlungsgebühr** f ⟨rail⟩ *handling charges* pl **~brief, ~schein** m ⟨com⟩ *bill of lading* **~bühne** f, **~plattform** f ⟨tech, rail⟩ *loading platform* **~druck**

m *boost* | ∼regler [m] ⟨mot⟩ *manifold pressure control*; ∼messer [m] *b. p. ga(u)ge* **∼fähigkeit** f ⟨mar⟩ *tonnage, loading capacity* **∼geld** n *loading-charges* pl **∼geschirr** n ⟨mar⟩ *loading tackle* od *gear* **∼geschwindigkeit** f ⟨mil⟩ *speed of loading* **∼gewicht** n *weight loaded* **∼hemmung** f (*gun*) *jam, stoppage* **∼hub** m *intake stroke* **∼kanonier** m *charger* **∼lehre** f ⟨rail⟩ *gauge of goods-vans* **∼linie** f ⟨mar⟩ *load-line* **∼liste** f *loading bill* **∼loch** n ⟨artill⟩ *breech-block hole* **∼luft** ⟨aero-mot⟩ *boost air* | ∼kühler [m] ⟨mot⟩ *compressor intercooler* **∼marke** f ⟨mar engl⟩ *Plimsoll line* **∼maß** n *loading ga(u)ge* **∼pforte** f ⟨mar⟩ *port* **∼pfropf** m *wad* **∼plan** m ⟨mar⟩ *stowage plan* od *table* **∼platz** m *loading-place*; ⟨mar⟩ *wharf* **∼rampe** f ⟨rail⟩ *loading ramp*, ⟨Am⟩ *l. platform* **∼raum** m ⟨mar⟩ (*ship's*) *hold*; ⟨mil⟩ *chamber*; ⟨aero⟩ *stowage compartment* ‖ *cargo capacity* **∼rost, ∼schlitten** m *pallet* **∼schein** m *inland waterway bill of lading* **∼stock** m *ramrod*; ⟨artill⟩ *loading-pug* **∼streifen** m ⟨mil⟩ *charger*, (*cartridge-*)*clip* **∼stromstoß** m ⟨el⟩ *charging current impulse* **∼übersetzung** f *blower ratio* **∼verzug** m ⟨artill⟩ *dead time* **∼vorrichtung** f ⟨artill⟩ *breech mechanism* **L·aden** m ∼s/∼ & ≃ *shop* ⟨a. fig⟩, ⟨Am⟩ *store* ‖ (Fenster≃) *shutter* | e–n ∼ eröffnen *to start a shop* ‖ den ∼ öffnen *to take down the shutters* ‖ °⟨**fig**⟩ *shop*; der ganze ∼ ⟨sl⟩ *the whole show*, ⟨Am sl⟩ *the whole shebang*; müder ∼ *dead-tired routines* pl; °den ∼ schmeißen *to deliver the goods* ‖ er kann s–n ∼ zumachen *he is done for* ‖ °der ∼ klappt *the matter is in order* ‖ ⟨aero sl⟩ °den ∼ vollrotzen (Flugzeug beschießen) *to paste away at*, ⟨Am⟩ *to loose off* **l·aden vt/i I. vt** [lud/ge∼] [h] **1.** **(Last)** ⟨mar⟩ *to lade* ‖ (als Fracht) *to freight* ‖ (Güter) *to load* (auf e–n Wagen *on to a lorry*); (Flugzeug) mit Bomben ∼ *to bomb up* ‖ aus (e–m Wagen) ∼ *to unload* (*a cart*) ‖ zuviel ge∼ h *to be overloaded* ‖ (Gewehr etc) *to load* ⟨a. el⟩, *to charge*; (Batterie) ⟨el⟩ *to charge up*; (Draht) *to electrify* | ⟨fig⟩ die Atmosphäre war ge∼ *the a. was surcharged* ‖ die A. war mit Mißtrauen ge∼ .. *was charged with mistrust* ‖ (P) mit Energie ge∼ *full of energy* | der Fuhrmann hat Holz ge∼ *the carter has loaded up timber* ‖ der Kahn hat Weizen ge∼ *the barge is loaded with wheat* | e–e Schuld **auf** sich ∼ *to burden o.s. with guilt* ‖ ich möchte nicht d–n Zorn auf mich ∼ *I don't want to incur your wrath* ‖ e–e gr Verantwortung auf sich ∼ *to undertake a great responsibility* | ⟨fig⟩ er hat schwer ge∼ *he is half-seas-over* od *well lubricated, he has had quite enough* | er ist schwer **auf** dich ge∼ *he is highly incensed against* od *with you* **2. (P) (einladen)** *to invite, ask* ‖ **(vorladen)** *to summon, cite* ‖ vor ge∼en Gästen *before invited guests* ‖ er ist als Zeuge ge∼ *he has been called as witness* ‖ e–n zu Tische ∼ *to ask a p to dinner* ‖ e–n vor Gericht ∼ *to serve a summons on a p* **II. vi** (*of ship*) *she takes her loads* **III.** ≃ n *loading* (*of the camera*, etc) **L·aden- ∼aufseher** m *floor-* od *shop-walker* **∼besitzer** m *shop-*(⟨Am⟩ *store-*)*keeper* **∼bursche** m *shop-boy* **∼dieb** m *shop-thief*, ⟨fam⟩ *shop-lifter*, ⟨sl⟩ *snatch, grabman* **∼diener** m *shopman, shop-assistant* **∼fenster** n *shop-window* **∼gaumer** m ∼s/∼ Sw = **∼hüter** m ⟨fig⟩ *drug in the market, dead stock*; *deadwood*; ⟨Am sl⟩ *sticker, plug*; ⟨com⟩ ∼ [pl] *dead stock* **∼inhaber** m *shopkeeper*, ⟨Am⟩ *storekeeper* **∼kasse** f *till* **∼mädchen** n *shopgirl* **∼miete** f *shop-hire, shop-rent* **∼preis** m *retail-price, selling-price* ‖ (Buchhandel) *publishing price* °**∼schickse** f = –mädchen, ⟨fam⟩ *shoppy* **∼schild** n *sign, facia* **∼schluß** m *shutting up shop*; *shop closing hour(s)*; Vorschrift über ∼ *shop hours rule*; nach ∼ *after hours*; früher ∼ *early closing* **∼schwengel** m ⟨fam cont⟩ *counter-jumper* **∼tisch** m *counter*; über den (unter dem) ∼ verkaufen *to sell across* (*under*) *the c.*; Auslage auf dem ∼ *c. display* **∼tür** f *shop-door* **∼verkäufer** m *sales clerk* **L·ader** m ∼s/∼ *loader* ⟨a. artill⟩, *charger*; ⟨mot⟩ *supercharger, compressor*; ⟨aero mot⟩ *blower* **∼getriebe** n *bl. drive* **∼lohn** m *loading* od *lading charges* pl **∼motor** m *bl.-fed engine* **L·adung** f ∼/∼en **1.** *loading, lading* ‖ (Güter) *freight*, (v best Gewicht) *load* (*of hay*) ‖ ⟨mar⟩ *cargo, shipment* ‖ die ∼ löschen *to discharge the cargo* ‖ ∼ einnehmen *to load*, ⟨mar⟩ *to take in cargo* **2.** (e–s Gewehrs etc & ⟨el⟩) *charge* ‖ **volle ∼** *full load*, etc. ‖ (Geschütz) *full charge* ‖ ⟨fam fig⟩ er hat s–e volle ∼ (Bier) *he is top-heavy, he's well lubricated* ‖ **geballte ∼** ⟨mil⟩ *concentric charge*; gestreckte ∼ *distributed charge*, ⟨at⟩ *elongated ch.*; verdichtete ∼ *compressed ch.* **3. (P) (Vor≃)** *summons* ‖ e–e gerichtliche ∼ erhalten *to be served with a summons* (vor *to*) | **(P) (Ein≃)** *invitation* **L·adungs- ∼aufseher** m *super-cargo* **∼platz** m = Ladeplatz **∼raum** m *powder* od *cartridge chamber* **∼versicherung** f *cargo insurance*

läd·ieren vt [h] (beschädigen) *to injure, damage* ‖ (verletzen) *to hurt*

Laf·ette f ∼/∼n (*gun-*)*carriage, mount*(*ing*) ‖ Gelenk≃ *pivot carriage* ‖ auf die ∼ heben *to mount* ‖ von der ∼ heben *to dismount* **Laf·etten- ∼drehkranz** m *base ring* **∼holm** m *outrigger* **∼kasten** m *trail-box* **∼rahmen** m *carriage chassis* **∼schwanz** m *trail* **∼sitz** m *carriage seat* **∼sporn** m *trail spade* **∼wand** f *bracket, carriage side* **Lafett·ierung** f *mounting*

L·affe m ∼n/∼n *fop, pup(py), popinjay, squirt*

L·affe f ∼/∼n (Schöpfteil des Löffels) *bowl*

l·ag 1. & 3. sg pret v liegen **L·age** f ∼/∼n **1.** *situation, location*; *position* (l sich in 3 verschiedene ∼n bringen ⟨tech⟩ *can be adjusted to 3 different p.s*) ‖ (e–s Hauses) *site* ‖ *the lie* (*of the land, of the upper floor*); ∼ nach Süden *southern aspect* ‖ (Zustand) *state, condition* ‖ (Haltung) *attitude* ‖ ⟨fenc⟩ *guard* ‖ ∼ der Dinge *state* (*of affairs*) *status, situation, condition, circumstance, predicament, how ths stand* ‖ **bei** *or* **in** drängender, dringender ∼ *in critical, urgent situations, if the situation is critical*; in gespannter ∼ *during a dense s.* ‖ die ∼ der Dinge **erfordert** es *the* (*present*) *state of affairs ..* ‖ der Krieg schuf e–e neue ∼ *the war has put a new face on ths* | versetze dich **in m-e ∼** *put* od *imagine y.s. in my position* ‖ (nicht) **in der ∼ s, zu ..** *not to be in a position to*; ich bin nicht in der ∼, zu .. *I am not able* od *prepared to .., I don't see my way to* (*doing*) ‖ **nach der ∼** der Dinge *in view of the conditions, in the nature of ths* | (*the present*) *status* (*of art*) | die **allgemeine ∼** *the outlook* (*of trade*; *in Europe*) ‖ **(P)** in **bedrängter** ∼ s *to be in distress, to be hard set* od *up*; bequeme ∼ (e–s Kranken) *comfortable position*; in e–r **furchtbaren** ∼ s *to be in an awful plight*; **gefährliche,** mißliche, dumme, fatale ∼ *predicament* | **(S)** geneigte ∼ *cant* ‖ es herrscht e–e gespannte ∼ *the conditions are somewhat strained* ‖ gesunde ∼ (Stadt) *healthy position* | **(P)** in der gleichen ∼ wie *in the same boat with*; in der glücklichen ∼ s *to be fortunate enough*; in e–r weniger glücklichen ∼ s *to be less fortunately placed* | (Weinberg) in **guter** ∼ *favourably situated* ‖ ⟨mot⟩ → Straßen≃; in guter (finanzieller) ∼ *doing well*; ⟨fam⟩ *sitting pretty* ‖ **heikle** ∼ *tight corner* ‖ in hilfloser ∼ *on the ropes* ⟨fig⟩ ‖ geschützte ∼ *lee* ‖ **kritische** ∼ *pass* (*ths have come to a* [*strange*] *pass*) ‖ in **mißlicher** ∼ *in a trying situation, under trying conditions* pl | **(P)** in e–e mißliche ∼ geraten *to get into a scrape*; ich bin in der **peinlichen** ∼ *I feel under the painful necessity* (*of ..*) | **(P)** etw in die **rechte** *or* richtige ∼ bringen *to put sth in proper order* od *in its right position*; ⟨mar⟩ *to ship* (*rudder*) ‖ in richtiger ∼ halten *to keep in place*; **schiefe** ∼ (Schiff) *sheer* | (P) ⟨fig⟩ e–n in e–e schiefe ∼ bringen *to land* od *put a p in an awkward* od *a false position*; schlechte *or* schlimme ∼ (*evil*) *plight* ‖ in e–r schlimmen ∼ s *to be in a tight fix* od *in a bad way*;

geldlich .. *to be on one's beam-ends* ‖ jdn in die ~ versetzen z tun *to enable a p to do* ‖ in der schwierigen ~ s, tun zu müssen *to be in the difficult position of doing* | **sonnige** ~ (Haus) *sunny situation* | die **tatsächliche** ~ kennen ⟨fam⟩ *to know the score* | in e–r **üblen** ~ s *to be in a fix, to be down on one's luck* ‖ in e–r **unangenehmen** ~ s *to be awkwardly circumstanced* ‖ ich bin in e–r **verflixten** *or* verteufelten ~ *I am between the devil and the deep sea* | jdm gegenüber in vorteilhafter ~ s *to have the wind of a p* **2.** ⟨mus⟩ (Geige etc) die dritte ~ *the third position*; in e–e höhere ~ gehen *to shift to a higher position* **3.** *coat*(*ing*) (*of colours*) **4.** ⟨geol⟩ *layer, bed*; ⟨scient⟩ *stratum* [pl *strata*] **5.** (Satz, Gruppe) *set*; (Papier) *gathering*; drei ~n Pappe *three thicknesses of cardboard* ‖ e–e ~ Bier ausgeben *to stand a round of beer*, e–e ~ v Wirt *one on the house* ‖ (Kabel) *tier* (*in ~s*) ‖ *cake* (*of tobacco*) ‖ *skein* (*of wool*, etc.) ‖ ⟨artill⟩ (Lagenfeuer) *volley, group, tier* ‖ e–e ~ feuern *or* abgeben *to fire a volley*, ⟨mar⟩ *to fire a broadside* **~bericht** m, **~meldung** f ⟨mil⟩ *situation report* N **~beurteilung** f *evaluation* od *estimation of situation* **~empfindlichkeit** f *sensitiveness to position* **~entwicklung(en)** f begegnen *to react to developments in the situation*; den ~ anpassen *to adapt to the changing s.s* **~plan** m *general* od *ground plan*; *plan view, site plan* **~zimmer** n ⟨mil⟩ *war room* **L·agen~feuer** n *tiers* [pl] *of fire* **~karte** f ⟨mil⟩ (gr *general*) *situation map* **~plan** m *plan of site* **~tisch** m ⟨mil⟩ *operation board* ‖ e–e **~veränderung** erfahren *to have one's position changed* **≈weise** adv *in beds* etc. → Lage 4. ‖ ⟨artill⟩ (*firing*) *in groups*

L·ager n ~s/~ **1.** (Bett) *bed, couch* ‖ (Bahre) *stretcher* ‖ (Nacht≈) *night's lodging*; (Pritsche) *board-* od *plank-bed* ‖ ein bescheidenes ~ *a shake-down*; (sich) ein ~ bereiten *to shake down* ‖ e–m ein (Not-)Lager einrichten *to rig a p up a shake-down*, ⟨Am⟩ *makeshift bed, an improvised couch* ‖ nach langem Kranken≈ *after a long illness* ‖ e–e Krankheit warf ihn auf das ~ *sickness confined him to his bed* **2.** ⟨mil & fig⟩ *camp, encampment* ‖ (Depot) *depot* N (*ammunition d.* od *dump*) ‖ Arbeits≈ *labour camp*; (Ausbildungs≈) *training centre*; Baracken≈ *hut camp* | ein ~ aufschlagen (abbrechen) *to pitch* (*strike* od *raise*) (*a*) *camp* ‖ **im** ~ *in unit lines*; **in** e–m ~ unterbringen *to camp* (*troops*) ‖ internationales Pfadfinder≈ *World Rover Moot* ‖ Feinde **im eigenen** ~ *foes in one's own household* ‖ ⟨pol⟩ sich in mehrere ~ spalten *to split up into several parties* ‖ er steht in unserem ~ *he is on our side* **3.** ⟨hunt⟩ (v Wild) *lair*, (Fuchs≈) *kennel* **4.** ⟨geol, min⟩ *bed, deposit* **5.** ⟨com⟩ *warehouse, storehouse* ‖ (Vorrat) *store, stock, assortment, supply* ‖ das ~ aufnehmen **(räumen)** *to take* (*clear*) *stock*(*s*) ‖ ab ~ *free our warehouse* ‖ auf ~ *on hand*, solange auf ~ *while in stock*; normalerweise auf ~ gehalten (*goods*) *carried in one's normal stock* ‖ aufs ~ bringen *to store* ‖ auf ~ h *to keep in stock*, ⟨fig⟩ *to have on hand, to have a stock-in-trade* (*of catchwords*, etc) ‖ ein gut assortiertes ~ h *to be well stocked* ‖ nicht mehr auf ~ h *to be out of* ‖ geheimes ~ (v Waffen, Lebensmitteln) *cache* Fr ‖ Faß≈ (Unterlage) *cask support, gantry* ‖ ein gutes ~ v Weinen h *to have a good cellar* (*of wine*) ‖ (Wein) auf ~ *on tap* ⟨a. fig⟩ **6.** ⟨tech⟩ *bearing*[*s* pl]; ein ~ ausrichten *to true a b.*; das ~ läuft aus *th b. runs down* ‖ Drehzapfen≈ (Eisenbau) *centre plate* ‖ Druck≈ *thrust b.* ‖ Feder≈ ⟨mot⟩ *spring b.* ‖ Gleit≈ *slide b.* ‖ Hals≈ *collar b.* ‖ ~ der Hauptwelle *bed of the main shaft* ‖ staubdicht geschlossenes Kugel≈ *dust-proof enclosed ball b.* ‖ Kupplungs≈ *radial clutch b.* ‖ Vorgelege≈ *countershaft b.* ‖ ~ e–r stehenden Welle *step b.* **~aufnahme** f *stock-taking* **~aufseher** m *warehouse-keeper* od *-man, storekeeper* **~bedingungen** f pl *storing conditions* **~bestand** m *stock, inventory* | ~skontrolle [f] (mit Berichterstattung) ⟨comp⟩ *st. control* (*statement*), tägliche *daily record of the st. position* **~bewegung** f *st. movement* ⟨a. comp⟩ **~bier** n *lager*(*-beer*) **~bock** m *bearing support* **~buch** n *store-book* **~buchse** f *b. bush* **~diener** m *w.h.-clerk* **~dienst** m ⟨mil⟩ *camp-duty* **~empfangsschein** m *w.h. receipt* **~fähigkeit** f *shelf life*; *keeping quality* **~faß** n *storage cask*, ⟨brew⟩ *stock tub* **~fieber** n *camp-fever* **~frist** f *period of retention* **~fugen** f pl *groovings, furrows* **~gang** m ⟨geol⟩ *sill* **~geld** n, **~gebühren** f pl ⟨com⟩ *storage, w.h.-rent*, ⟨rail⟩ *st. charges*; ⟨mar & rail⟩ bei verzögerter Entladung *demurrage* **~größe** f ⟨com⟩ *stock-size* **~halter** m *store-clerk, store-keeper* **~haltung** f *stock-keeping* **~haus** n *w.h., store*(*house*) | ~schein [m] ⟨com⟩ (*dock-*)*warrant* **~hof** m *dock*(*yard*) **~keller** m *storage cellar* **~koller** m ⟨mil, etc⟩ *barbed wire blues* **~kontrolle** f *stock control* **~kosten** [pl] *storage costs* pl **~krankheit** f *camp-sickness* **~meister** m *storeman* **~metall** n *white, anti-friction, bearing, babbitt metal* | ~schale [f] *babbitt bushing* **~miete** f *housing, storage* **~obst** n *fruit kept over winter* **~platz** m *camping site*; *storage yard*; *depot*; (im Freien) *dump*; = ~stätte **~raum** m [abstr] *storage space*; [konkr] ≈e [pl] *st. premises* **~reibungskraft** f ⟨rec⟩ (*tone-arm*) *bearing friction* **~schale** f *half b.g* ⟨mot⟩ ~ anfertigen *to* (*re*)*metal a bearing* **~schein** m *warrant*, ⟨Am⟩ *w.h. receipt* **~seuche** f *infectuous camp-disorder* **~stätte** f, **~stelle** f *resting-place* ‖ (Bett) *couch, bed* ‖ ⟨geol⟩ *deposit bed* **~verwalter** m *storekeeper* **~vorrat** m *stock* **~wache** f *camp-watch* **~zeit** f *storing time* **Lager·ist** m ~en/~en *w.h.-clerk* **l·agern** vt [h] *to lay down* ‖ (Waren) *to store, to w.h.* ‖ (Truppen) *to encamp* | vi [h] & sich ~ *to lie down* (od [of corn] *flat*); *to rest*; im Freien ~ *to camp out* ‖ ⟨mil⟩ *to* (*be*) *encamp*(*ed*) ‖ sie hatten sich im Gras ge–rt *they had chosen a resting-place* .. ‖ Wolken lagerten auf den Bergen *clouds had settled on the hills* od *brooded over* .. ‖ ⟨com⟩ *to be stored* od *in stock* ‖ gut ge–rt *well seasoned* (*wine*) ‖ die Waren ~ noch bei uns .. *are still on our hands* **L·agerung** f ~/~en ⟨com⟩ *storage, warehousing* ‖ ⟨mil⟩ *encampment* ‖ ⟨geol⟩ *stratification* | ~seigenschaften [f pl] *keeping properties*; ~sstörung [f] ⟨geol⟩ *dislocation*; ~szeit [f] (bei radioaktiver Altersbestimmung) *deposition date*

L·ago Maggi·ore [maˈdʒɔːrə] m ⟨It⟩ (See)

Lag·une f ~/~n *lagoon* | ~ngebiet [n] *the L. area*; ~neninseln [f pl] (im Süd-Pazifik) *Ellice Islands* pl; ~nstadt [f] *City of L.s*

lahm a *lame* (*leg*) ‖ *crippled* (*arm*) ‖ ⟨path⟩ *paralysed* ‖ (hinkend) *limping, halting* ‖ e–n ~ schlagen *to lame a p* | ⟨fig⟩ *weak*(*-kneed*), *wretched, poor* ‖ *dull* (*business*) ‖ *lame* (*excuse*) ‖ *game, rickety* (*chair*) ‖ *slow*, ⟨Am⟩ *dateless* (*girl*) **l·ahmen** vi [h] *to be lame* od *crippled* ‖ (lahmgehen) *to limp, halt* ‖ (Pferd) *to go lame* (auf e–m Bein *on one leg*) **l·ähmen** vt [h] ⟨a. fig⟩ *to lame, paralyse* ‖ ⟨fig⟩ *cripple* ‖ gelähmt *paralysed* (vor *with*), ⟨fig com⟩ *dull, benumbed, languishing, flagging* (*business*); ⟨mil⟩ *to cripple*, ⟨tact⟩ *immobilize* ‖ ⟨fig⟩ lähmend *paralysing* (*dismay, care*), *enervating* (*heat*) **L·ahmheit** f ~/ *lameness*, ⟨path⟩ *paralysed state* ⟨a. fig⟩ **l·ahm|legen** vt [h] ⟨fig⟩ (Verkehr) *to obstruct* ‖ (Handel) *to paralyse* ‖ (Entwicklung) *to cripple, amputate* ‖ e–n vollkommen ~ *to whip-saw a p* **L·ahmlegung** f ⟨tact⟩ *neutralization*; **L·ähmung** f ~/~en ⟨a. fig⟩ *paralysation, laming*; ⟨mil⟩ ~en [pl] *p.* od *denial measures, neutralization* (*of facilities*) ‖ (Gelähmtheit) *paralysis* ‖ einseitige ~ *hemiplegia*; beiderseitige Bein≈ *paraplegia*; unvollständige ~ *paresis*

L·ahn f ~/~en [bay-österr] = Lawine, → d.

L·ahn m ~es/~e *flattened wire*; *tinsel*

Lah·ore n (Stadt in West-Pakistan)

L·aib m ~(e)s/~e (Brot) *loaf* ‖ ~ (Käse) *whole*

L·aibung f ~/~en ⟨arch⟩ *reveal*

L·aich m ∼(e)s/ *spawn* ‖ Austern∼̈ *spat* ‖ ∼e, ∼zeit [f] *sp.ing-time* | ∼grube [f] (*salmon & trout*) *redd*; ∼kraut [n] *pond-weed* **l·aichen** vi [h] *to spawn* ‖ (Auster) *to spat* ‖ Fisch nach dem ∼̈ *spent fish*

L·aie m ∼n/∼n ⟨a. fig⟩ *layman* ‖ ⟨fig⟩ *uninitiated p, novice, amateur, dilettante* ‖ die ∼n *the laity* ‖ ein blutiger ∼ *a greenhorn* **L·aien- ∼behandlung** f *medical treatment by laymen* **∼bruder** m *lay brother* **∼̈haft** a *like a layman, lay* (*reader*) ‖ *unprofessional* **∼helfer** m *lay-helper*; ⟨aero⟩ *civilian assistent* ‖ *first-aid* (*lay*)*man* **∼helferin** f *f.-a. laywoman, female lay-helper*, (Luftschutz) *shelter nurse* **∼priester** m *lay priest* **∼richter** m *lay judge* **∼schwester** f *lay sister* **∼stand** m *laity* **∼tum** n *laymanship*

Lak·ai m ∼en & ∼s/∼en *lackey, footman* ‖ ⟨mst dero⟩ ⟨a.⟩ ∼enseele [f] *flunkey, cringer* | ∼̈enhaft [a] *fl.-like, cringing* ‖ adv *like a fl.*

L·ake f ∼/∼n (Salz∼̈) *brine, pickle*

L·aken n ∼s/∼ (Bett∼̈) *sheet* ‖ (Toten∼̈) *pall, shroud*

L·akhnau n (Vorderind. Bezirk) *Lucknow*

Lakkad·iven pl (Inselgruppe im Arab. Meer) *Laccadive Islands* pl

†**Lak·onien** n ⟨Gr⟩ (Landschaft) *Laconia* †**Lak·onier** m, **∼in** f *Laconian, Lacedæmonian* †**lak·onisch** a *Laconian* **lak·onisch** a *laconic* (*brevity, answer*)

Lakr·itze f ∼/∼n *liquorice, licorice* ‖ ∼nholz [n] *stick-liquorice* ‖ ∼nsaft [m] *l.-juice* ‖ ∼nstengel [m] *l.-cake* ‖ ∼nwasser [n] *l.-water*

Lakt·ose f ∼/ *lactose* (*milk-sugar*)

l·ala → la **l·allen** vt/i [h] (Kind) *to babble, stutter* ‖ (Betrunkener) *to speak thick* | *to stammer* (*a prayer*), *to hum* (*a tune*) ‖ *to lull* (.. *to sleep*)

L·ama m ∼s/∼s ⟨Tibet. rel⟩ *lama*

L·ama n ∼s/∼s ⟨zoo⟩ *llama* ‖ ∼garn [n] *ll.*(-(-*yarn*); ∼wolle [f] *ll. hair*

Lam·arck: Anhänger ∼s *Lamarckian*

L·ambertsnuß f ⟨bot⟩ *filbert*

L·ambrequin [ˈlambəkɛ̃] m ∼s/∼s ⟨decor⟩ *pelmet*

Lambr·is [–i] m ∼/∼ *panelling*

Lam·é m ∼s/ (metalldurchwirkter Stoff) *lamé*

Lam·elle f *lamella*, ⟨el⟩ *lamina* [pl *–ae*] ‖ Kollektor∼̈ *commutator bar* ‖ (Pilz∼̈) *gill* | ∼nkühler [m] ⟨mot⟩ *ribbed radiator*; ∼nkupplung *multiple disc clutch*; ∼nmagnet [m] *lamellar magnet*

Lamentati·on [ts] f ∼/∼en *lamentation* **l-t·ieren** vi [h] *to lament* (um *for*; über [acc] *over*), *to wail* (*over*) **Lam·ento** n ∼s/∼s *lamentation* ‖ er machte ein gr ∼ über .. *he raised great lamentations about* ..

Lam·etta f, (n) ∼(s)/ *lametta* ‖ ⟨fig mil fam⟩ (Orden) *gongs* pl, (Ordenschnallen) *fruit salad*

lamin·ar a *laminar* | laminieren vt [h] *to laminate* ‖ in 3 Schichten ∼ *to sandwich*

L·amm n ∼(e)s/∼̈er *lamb* ‖ kl ∼ *l.kin* ‖ ⟨ec⟩ ∼ Gottes *the Holy L.* **∼̈artig** a *l.like* **∼braten** m *roast l.* **∼fell** n *l.skin* **∼fleisch** n *l.* **∼̈fromm** a (*as*) *gentle* od *meek as a l.* **L·ämmchen** n ∼s/∼, **L·ämmlein** n ∼s/∼ *l.kin* ‖ (→ Lamm) ‖ [pl a.] Lämmerchen **l·ammen** vi [h] *to cast l.s*; *to ewe, l.* **L·ämmer-∼geier** m ⟨orn⟩ *griffin-* od *barbed vulture*; *lammergeyer* [Ger] °**∼hüpfen** n ⟨fig⟩ → Knospenball **∼stall** m *stall* od *pen for l.s* **∼weide** f *pasture for l.s* **∼wölkchen** n pl *lambs, flocks*; mit ∼ bedeckt *fleeced*; **∼wolke** f *cirro-cumulus* **∼wolle** f *l.'s-wool* **∼zeit** f *ewing-time*

L·ampe m: Meister ∼(rt) *Puss* (*hare*)

L·ämpchen n *small lamp* ‖ *Chinese lantern* ‖ farbiges Glas∼̈ *glass fairy-lamp* **L·ampe** f ∼/∼n **1.** *lamp* (mattiert *frosted*) ‖ ⟨ec⟩ ewige ∼ *everburning l.* ‖ e–e ∼ anzünden (putzen) *to light* (*trim*) *a l.* ‖ das Buch riecht nach der ∼ (gelehrt) *the book smells of the midnight oil* ‖ ⟨fig⟩ °e–n auf die ∼ gießen ⟨fam⟩ *to wet one's whistle* **2.** ⟨theat⟩ gefärbte ∼ *colour-dipped lamp*, ⟨Am⟩ *d. l.*; die ∼n [pl] (Rampenlichter) *the foot-lights* pl ‖ ein Stück vor die ∼n bringen *to stage* .. **3.** Steh–, Nachttisch–, Löt–, ⟨min⟩ Wetter∼̈ *standard, bedside, soldering, Davy-lamp* **L·ampen- ∼anzünder** m *lamp-lighter* **∼docht** m (*l.-*)*wick* **∼fassung** f *l.holder* **∼fieber** n *stage fright* **∼fuß** m *l.-stand* **∼glas** n *l.-glass*, (*l.-*)*chimney, funnel* **∼glocke** f (*l.-*) *-shade* **∼licht** n *l.light* **∼putzer** m *l.lighter* **∼ruß** m *l.-black* **∼schalter** m *l. switch* ⟨a. mot⟩ **∼schirm, ∼schleier** m *l.-shade* **∼schwarz** n ⟨paint⟩ *l.-black* **∼stock** m *sconce* **∼strahler** m ⟨mot⟩ *l. switch* **∼teller** m *l.-mat* **∼wärter** m ⟨min⟩ *davy-man* **∼zylinder** m = –glas

Lampi·on [–piˈɔŋ, –piɔ̃:] m & n ∼s/∼s *lampion, Chinese* od *paper lantern*

Lampr·ete f ∼/∼n ⟨ich⟩ *lamprey*

lanc·ieren [laŋˈsi:rən] *vt* [h] *to launch* (*torpedo*) ‖ *to bring into fashion*; (Buch etc) *to push* ‖ jdn ∼ *to give a p a start, to carve out a career for a p, to pitchfork a p* (in *into*) (in e–e Stellung) ‖ lanc·iert: *now that you are lanced in the world*

L·and n ∼(e)s/∼̈er **1.** (Ggs: Wasser) *land* ‖ festes ∼ *dry l., continent* ‖ ∼! ⟨mar⟩ *l. ho*! ‖ das Innere des ∼es *the upcountry* ‖ im Innern des ∼es gelegen *upcountry* (*lake*) **2.** (Ggs: Stadt) [ohne pl] *country* ‖ (als Schauplatz a. plattes ∼) *countryside*: *the English c., inhabitants of the c.* **3.** (Boden, Ackerland) *ground, soil, land* ‖ (un)fruchtbares ∼ (*in*)*fertile*, (*un*)*fruitful soil* ‖ brachliegendes ∼ *fallow* (*l.*); *wasteland* ‖ flaches *or* plattes ∼ *flat* od *open country, level ground* ‖ ein Stück ∼ *a piece of l.*; ⟨Am⟩ *homestead*, .. ∼ erwerben *to h.* **4.** (Gebiet) *territory*, [pl] ∼e *regions*; in deutschen ∼en *in German countries* ‖ (Staatsgebiet) *land, country*; ⟨Ger⟩ ∼̈er [pl] (*member*) *states* ‖ das ∼ m–r Väter *the l. of my fathers* ‖ das Deutsche Reich umfaßte verschiedene Länder .. *various states* ‖ er wurde des ∼es verwiesen *he was banished from the country* ‖ woher des ∼es? *where do you hail* od *come from*? ‖ das ist des ∼es nicht der Brauch *that is not the custom with us* | ⟨bib⟩ das **Gelobte,** Verheißene ∼ *the Promised L.*; ∼ der Verheißung, ∼ der unbegrenzten Möglichkeiten ⟨a.⟩ *L. of Promise* ‖ das Heilige ∼ (*the*) *Holy L.* ‖ Gottes ∼, ∼ v Gottes Gnaden (= Amerika) *God's Own Country* ‖ ackerbautreibendes ∼ *agrarian c.* ‖ ⟨übtr⟩ (= Bewohner) das ganze ∼ *the whole c.* ‖ ⟨fig⟩ das ∼ (Reich) der Phantasie *the realm of imagination* ‖ das ∼ der Träume *the l. of dreams* **5. ∼ anlaufen,** erreichen *to make the l.* ‖ **∼ ansteuern** *to make for the shore* ‖ das ∼ **bebauen** *to cultivate the soil* ‖ ∼ **entdecken** ⟨mar⟩ *to descry l.* ‖ das ∼ zu Gesicht bek *to sight the l.* ‖ ∼ u Leute **kennen** lernen *to see the world* ‖ *to get acquainted with l. and people* ‖ ⟨fig⟩ endlich ∼ **sehen** *to see light at last* ‖ ∼ **sichten** *to make land* **6. am** ∼e *ashore* ‖ **an** ∼ gehen *to l., disembark*; ⟨mar⟩ *to go ashore*; in Schwärmen .. *to swarm ashore* (→ anlanden) ‖ das An∼̈gehen *the shore-going*, an ∼ gehend *sh.-going* ‖ **ans** ∼ bringen *to bring to sh., to put on l.* ‖ ans ∼ steigen *to l., disembark*; ⟨mar⟩ *to go ashore* ‖ **auf** dem ∼e *in the c.*; ⟨mar⟩ *on sh.* ‖ aufs ∼ ziehen *to remove to the c.* ‖ aufs ∼ gehen *to go into the c.* ‖ **aus** aller Herren ∼̈ern *from all quarters of the globe, from all over the world* ‖ **außer** ∼es gehen *to leave the c.* ‖ außer ∼es s *to be in foreign parts, to be abroad* ‖ **für** das ganze ∼ *national* ‖ **im** eigenen ∼e hergestellt (erzeugt etc) *home-made* (*-grown, -bred*), ⟨Am⟩ *domestic*; sich im ∼e verproviantieren *to live off the l.*; im ganzen ∼ *nationally* ‖ viele Jahre gingen seither **ins** ∼ *many a day has passed* od *many a year has come and gone since then* ‖ **über** ∼ reisen *or* gehen *to travel across c.*; ü. das ganze ∼ (*all*) *across the c.*; ü. ∼ u Meer *by l. and sea* ‖ Propaganda ü. das ganze ∼ *c.-wide pr.* ‖ **unter** ∼ ⟨mar⟩ *in sh.*, u. ∼ bleiben *to keep to the sh.* ‖ **vom**

~e s *to be a c.(wo)man* ‖ v ~e eingeschlossen *l.-locked (harbour)* ‖ v ~e *countrified* ‖ v ~e wegziehen *to abandon the country-side* ‖ v ~e stoßen *to put to sea* ‖ die Unschuld v ~e *an innocent c.-girl* ‖ Gottes Wort v ~e (⟨hum⟩: Dorfgeistlicher) *a c.-parson* ‖ **von** ~ abhalten ⟨mar⟩ *to keep off from the sh.* ‖ **zu** Wasser u zu ~e *by water and by l.* (reisen) ‖ zu ~e, zu Wasser u in der Luft *on l., at sea, and in the air*; *triphibian (strategy)* ‖ e–e Verteidigung zu Wasser u zu ~e *an amphibious defence* ‖ hierzu⁓e *in these parts, in this c.* ‖ bei uns zu⁓e *with us* **~adel** m *(landed) gentry, provincial nobility*; ⟨Ger⟩ kl ~ *backwoods nobility* **~arbeit** f *rural* od *rustic employment* **~arbeiter** m *agricultural labourer, farm hand*; ⟨Am⟩ *laborer, ranchman* | ~in [f] ⟨Am⟩ *farmerette* **~armee** f *land-force*[s pl] **~arzt** m *country doctor* od *physician* **~aufenthalt** m *stay in the c.* ‖ e–n solchen Pfarrer finden Sie ⁓**·auf,** ⁓**·ab** [adv] nicht wieder *you can go all over the c. without finding another parson like him* ⁓**·aus,** ⁓**·ein** adv *from c. to c.* **~bau** m *agriculture* **~bauer** m *husbandman; farmer* **~besitz** m *l.ed property*, ⟨jur⟩ *real estate* **~besitzer** m *l.ed man* od *proprietor*; die ~ [pl] (~klasse [f]) *l.ed gentry (l.ed class)* **~bestellungsurlaub** m *agricultural leave* **~bevölkerung** f *c. people, rural population the c.side* **~bewohner** m *p living in the c.*; *c.-man* **~bote, ~briefträger** m *rural postman* **~brot** n *brown bread* **~buch** n *register of l.* **~bund** m ⟨pol⟩ *c. party* **~dienst** m ⟨mar⟩ *service on sh.*; ⟨Ger⟩ *service in the c.* **~drost** m *high-bailiff* **~edelmann** m *(c.-)squire* **~eigentümer** m *l.ed proprietor, l.owner* ⁓**·einwärts** adv *up-c.*; 200 m ~ *200 m inland*; Wanderung ~ *migration inland* **~enge** f *isthmus, neck of l.* **~farbe** f *countrified complexion* ⁓**fern** a ⟨mar⟩ *far from l.* ⁓**fest** a (geworden) ⟨geog⟩ *land-tied (island)* **~flecken** m *c. hamlet* **~flucht** f *flight from the l., rural exodus, drift to the towns* ⁓**flüchtig** a *fugitive* **~flugzeug** n ⟨aero⟩ *l.-plane* **~formenkunde** f *geomorphology* **~fracht** f *l.-freight* **~frau** f *c.woman* **~fräulein** n *c.-miss* **~fremde(r)** m *alien, stranger* **~friede(n)** m *national* od *public peace, the (king's) peace*; ⟨Ger⟩ *L. Peace* **~friedensbruch** m *breach of the (king's) peace* **~fuhre** f *carriage by l.* **~gebiet** n *rural area* **~gegend** f *c. side*, die ~en [pl] *the ~s pl* **~geistliche(r)** m *c. clergyman, village parson* **~gemeinde** f *rural community; village; parish* **~gendarm** m *c. constable* **~gericht** n *provincial court; c. court* **~gewinn** m durch Rückgang des Wasserspiegels *dereliction* **~gewinnung** f (v Meer) *l. reclamation* **~graf** m *l.grave* (f *l.gravine*) ⁓**gräflich** a *l.gravial* **~grafschaft** f *l.graviate* **~gut** n *l.ed property, estate, countryseat* **~handel** m *trade by l.* **~haus** n *c.-house, cottage*; ⟨Am a.⟩ *farm* **~heer** n *l. force(s pl)* **~hunger** m *l. hunger, greediness for l.* **~innere** n *the upcountry, inland, interior* **~jahr** n ⟨Ger⟩ *year's rural service, "c.-year"* **~junker** m *(c.-)squire* **~karte** f *map* **~kind** n *c.-bred p* **~klima** n *l.-controlled* od *continental climate* **~kreis** m ⟨Ger⟩ *(rural) district* **~krieg** m *l.-warfare, war on l., territorial campaign* ⁓**kundig** a *notorious* **~kutsche** f *stage-coach* **~läufer** m *vagabond, vagrant* ⁓**läufig** a *common, customary, conventional, current, general, orthodox, accepted (view)* **~leben** n *c. life; the c.side*; das ~ schildernd *bucolic, pastoral (poem)* **~leute** pl *c. people* pl, *peasantry* **~luft** f *c. air* **~macht** f *l.-force(s pl), the army* **~mädchen** n *c.-girl* **~makler** m ⟨Am⟩ *realtor* **~mann** m *rustic, peasant, c.man* (vgl Landsmann) **~marke** f ⟨mar⟩ *l.mark* **~markt** m *c. market* **~maschinenbau** m *agricultural machine industry* **~messer** m *surveyor* **~meßkunst** f *(art of) surveying* **~miliz** f *militia*, (zu Pferde) *yeomanry* **~nahme** f *settlement in a c.; colonization of a c.; the taking possession of a c.; occupancy, occupation* **~nehmer** m *settler* **~oberfläche** f *l.* od *continental surface* **~pächter** m *sharecropper* **~partie** f *rural excursion, outing, excursion in(to) the c., picnic* **~parzelle** f *plot of l.* **~pfarre** f *c. parsonage* **~pfarrer** m *c. parson* **~pfleger** m *governor of a province* **~plage** f *epidemic* ‖ ⟨fig⟩ *national* od *public calamity* ‖ e–e wahre ~ *a public nuisance* **~polizei** f *rural police* **~pomeranze** f ⟨fam⟩ *c.-miss*; ⟨Am sl⟩ *girl rube* ‖ *she looked like a bouncing c.-wench* **~post** f 1. *rural post*, 2. *stage-coach* **~postzustellung** f ⟨Am⟩ *rural free delivery* **~prediger** m = ~pfarrer **~rat** m *country warden, landrat* **~ratte** f ⟨mar fam⟩ *l.lubber* **~raum** m *region* **~recht** n *common law* **~regen** m *steady (down)pour, general rain* **~reise** f *journey, overland journey, journey by l.* **~richter** m *judge of a provincial court, c.-court judge* **~route** f *overland route* **~rücken** m *ridge of l.* od *hills* **~saß** m *tenant, freeholder* **~schaft** etc → d. **~scheide** f *boundary* **~schule** f *c.* od *village school* **~schulheim** n *c. hostel provoding for open-air instruction* **~schutz** m ⟨mar⟩ unter ~ gehen *to run for port* od *cover* **~-See-Beförderungsmittel** n *surface transport*; auf dem ~-Seewege *by s. tr.* **~seuche** f *epidemic* **~sichtung** f ⟨naut⟩ *l.fall* **~sitz** m *c. seat* **~spitze** f *head of l., cape, naze, promontory* **~stadt** f *c. town* **~stände** ⟨hist⟩ m pl *states* [pl] *of the c.* od *province* **~steuer** f *l.-tax* **~straße** f (1. Ordnung) *highway, highroad*; an der ~ *by the roadside*; auf der ~ *on the road*; erhöhte ~ *causeway* | ~n-philosoph [m] ⟨Am⟩ *hobo* **~streicher** m *vagabond, prowler, tramp*; ⟨vulg⟩ *gook, bum*; ⟨Am sl⟩ *hobo* [pl *~es*], sich als ~ durchschlagen *to hobo it* | ~tum [n] *vagabondage, vagrancy* **~strich** m *stretch tract of l., region, district; clime, zone* **~sturm** m *general levy, last reserve*; [Ger] *landsturm* | ~mann [m] *home guard* **~stützpunkt** m; Flugzeug mit ~ *sh.* (od *l.*)*-based aircraft* **~tag** m *diet*; ⟨Ger hist⟩ *the Representative Assembly* ‖ e–n ~ ausschreiben *to convene the states* **~transport** m *l.-carriage, l.-conveyance* **~truppen** pl *l. forces* **~urlaub** m ⟨mar⟩ *sh. leave*; allg ~ *free gangway* | ~skluft [f] *go-ashores* pl **~verbindung** f *overland communication* **~vermessung** f *l.-surveying* **~vogt** m *governor, high bailiff* **~vogtei** f *bailiwick* **~volk** n *c. people* pl; *c.folk, peasantry* ⁓**wärts** adv *l.ward, towards the l.* **~w·asserflugzeug** n *sea and l. aircraft, amphibian* **~weg** m 1. *overland route*, 2. *(secondary) c.-road* ‖ auf dem ~ *overland* **~wehr** f ⟨engl⟩ *territorial army, territorials* pl ‖ *militia*; berittene ~ *yeomanry* **~wein** m *local wine* **~welle** f *swell* **~wind** m *offshore wind* **~wirt** m *farmer, husbandman, agriculturist* ‖ vornehmer ~ *gentleman-farmer* ‖ Bund der ~e *agricultural association*, ⟨Am⟩ *grange* **~wirtin** f *farmer's wife* **~wirtschaft** f *agriculture, farming, husbandry* | ~lich [a] *agricultural, farming*; ~e Aktienbank [f] *joint-stock l.-bank*; ~e Verschuldung [f] *rural indebtedness*; ~sausstellung [f] *agricultural fair*; ~sschule [f] *academy for agriculture* **~wirtswetter** n *growing w.* **~wohnung** f *c.-house* **~zunge** f *neck* od *spit (of land)* **L·andauer** m ~s/~ (Wagen) *landau* **L·ändchen** n ~s/~ *small country* ‖ *petty state* **L·ände** f ⟨mar⟩ *landing-place*

L·ande- (→ Landungs-) **~bahn** f ⟨aero⟩ *(landing) runway* N, *l. strip* | ~befeuerung [f] *r. lighting*; ~flutlicht [n] *apron floodlight*; ~feuer [n] *contact* od *r. light*; ~-Hauptbake [f] *r. localizer* **~deck** n ⟨aero⟩ *l.* od *flight deck* **~einrichtung** f *l. facility* **~fläche** f ⟨aero⟩ *alighting area* **~genehmigung** f *l. clearance* **~geschwindigkeit** f *l.-speed* **~hilfe** f *aid to l.* **~hilfsmittel** pl *l. aids* **~klappe** f ⟨aero⟩ *l. flap*; ~n aus-(ein)fahren! *flaps down (up)!* | ~nbetätigung [f] *flap control* **~kopf** m ⟨mil⟩ *beachhead* N **~kreuz** n ⟨aero⟩ *l. cross* od *T, ground strip* **~kufe** f ⟨aero⟩ *runner* **~kurssender** m *r. localizer* **~licht** n ⟨aero⟩ *l. search light* ‖ *aerodrome beacon* **~meldung** f *arrival message* **~möglichkeit** f *l. facility* **~platz** m ⟨mar⟩ *quay, wharf, pier*; ⟨aero⟩ *l. ground; runway, aerodrome*; ⟨mil⟩ *l. field* N **~punkt** m (vorgesehener [Mond⁓])

⟨a–n⟩ *footprint* **~stelle** f (Fluß-) ⟨Am⟩ *levee*; (schwimmende) *l. stage* **~stoß** m *l. impact* **~strahl** m *l. beam* **~strecke** f *l. run* od *distance* **~streifen** m ⟨aero⟩ *air strip*; beleuchtet *flare path* **~stütze** f ⟨a-n⟩ *shock-absorber* od *l. leg* **~trupp** m *l. team* N **~zeichen** n *l. mark* **l·anden,** Sw ≗ vi/t [s/h] *to land, to disembark* ([vt] *troops*) ‖ ⟨mar⟩ *to touch* (*at*), *to beach* ‖ ⟨aero⟩ *to make a l.ding, to touch down* ⟨Am a.⟩ *to come d.*; auf dem Wasser ~ *to alight on the water*; aus der Luft ge–dete Truppen *airborne elements* | ⟨fig⟩ *to l.* (*in a ditch, on one's feet*), *to end up* (*in a police court*); *to find one's way* (*to* ..); ⟨übtr⟩ *to end* od *wind up* (bei [abstr] *in*) ‖ *to reach one's destination* ‖ man kann nicht wissen, wo die beiden heute nacht noch ~ w ⟨Am⟩ *no knowing where they'll barge off to later* ‖ °bei ihr kannst du nicht ~ *you won't get any change out of her* | ⟨sport⟩ [vt] *to l.* (*an upper-cut*); *to secure* (*a win*); °e–m e–e ~ *to l. a p a blow, to get home* | **beim** ≗ *on l.ing* **L·änder-** **~beschreibung** f *chorography* **~gier** f *thirst for new territory, land-hunger* **~kammer** f ⟨Ger⟩ *Laender Chamber* **~kunde** f *geography, knowledge of countries* **~namen** m pl *names of the countries* **~rat** m ⟨Ger⟩ *State Co-ordinating Agency* **~raub** m *land grabbing* **~regierungen** f pl *regional governments*, ⟨Ger⟩ *land* od *state governments* **~teilung** f *distribution of provinces* **~verfassungen** f pl *land* od *state constitutions* **Länder·ei(en)** f (pl) *landed property*; *estates, lands* pl

L·andes- **~adel** m *nobility of the country* **~angehörige(r)** m *citizen, subject* **~angehörigkeit** f *citizenship, nationality* **~anleihe** f *domestic loan* **~art** f *manner* od *custom of the c.* **~aufnahme** f *geodetic survey* N **~bank** f *national bank* **~beschreibung** f *topography* **~erzeugnis** n *home produce* **~farben** f pl *national colours* pl **~fürst**, **~herr** m *reigning prince*; *sovereign, monarch* ([f] *r. princess*, etc) ≗**fürstlich** a *relating to the s., crown-* **~gebrauch** m = ~art **~gesetz** n *state-law*; ⟨Ger⟩ *individual st.-law* **~grenze** f *frontier, boundary* **~hauptmann** m ([österr] = Chef der Regierung e–s Bundeslandes) *governor* **~herr** m = ~fürst **~herrschaft** f *s.ty, supremacy* **~innere** n *upcountry* **~kind** n *native* (*of the c.*) **~kirche** f *national* od *regional* (⟨engl⟩: *established*) *church* (vgl Landkirche) **~mutter** f *s. lady*, ⟨Ger⟩ *wife of a* (*former*) *reigning prince* **~obrigkeit** f *supreme authority, government, authorities* pl **~produkt** n = ~erzeugnis **~recht** n ⟨Ger⟩ *state law* **~regierung** f *government* (*of the* [*a*] *c.*) **~schuld** f *national debt* **~sprache** f *vernacular* od *native language, l. of a c.* ‖ (Volkssprache i. Ggs z. Latein) *vulgar tongue* **~tracht** f *national costume, c. dress* **~trauer** f (anlegen) (*to go into*) *public mourning* ≗**üblich** a *usual in the c., national, customary, as used locally* ‖ es ist ~ *it is general practice* ‖ dieser Brauch ist ~ *this is a national custom* **~vater** m *prince, sovereign, father of the people* **~vermessung** f *ordnance-survey* **~verrat** m (*high*) *treason* **~verräter** m *traitor to his c.* **~verteidigung** f *national* od *home defence* **~verweisung** f *banishment, exile* **~verwiesene** m [der ~, ein ~r] *exile* **~währung** f *national currency* **~wohl** n *well-being* od *interest of a c.* **~zeit** f *zone time* **~zeitung** f *official gazette* **L·ändler** m ~s/~ *slow waltz* **l·ändlich** a *rural* (*district, stillness*); *rural, rustic, country-like* (*simplicity*); *bucolic, pastoral, Arcadian*; *provincial* ‖ ~es Leben *c.-life* ‖ *village, villatic* (*fowl*) ‖ ~e Einfachheit *rusticity* ‖ ⟨prov⟩ ~, sittlich *when at Rome, do as the Romans do* ≗**keit** f ~/ *rural character* (*of a scenery*) ‖ *rusticity*

L·ands- **~berg** n ⟨Ger⟩ Stadt **1.** am Lech **2.** † an der Warthe **~knecht** m ⟨hist⟩ *lansquenet, mercenary*; fluchen wie ein ~ *to swear like a trooper* **~leute** pl *a p's people*; *fellow-countrymen* pl ‖ s–e schottischen ~ *his brother Scots* **~mann** m *compatriot,* (*fellow-*)*countryman* (→ vor) ‖ was für ein ~ sind Sie? *what is your native country?* **~männin** f (*fellow-*)*country-woman* **~mannschaft** f *compatriots* pl ‖ ⟨Ger univ⟩ *association of* (urspr. *compatriot*) *students* **L·andschaft** f ~/~en *countryside, landscape, scenery* ‖ ⟨paint⟩ *landscape* ‖ (Provinz) *district, region, territory, province*; N. u die umliegende ~ *N. and the country round* ‖ *rural outskirts* od *surroundings* ‖ (Landstände) *representative chamber of a country* **~sfilm** m *scenic, sceneric*(*al*) **~sgärtnerei** f *landscape-gardening* **~smaler** m, **L·andschafter** m ~s/~ *l.r, l.-painter* **~sschutz** m *preservation of rural amenities* **l·andschaftlich** a *provincial* ‖ die ~e Schönheit *the beauty of the scenery* ‖ die ~e Beschaffenheit *the topography* (*of a district*) ‖ ~er Ausdruck *provincialism* | das ≗e *the region* °**L·andser** m ~s/~ ⟨Ger⟩ *landser*; ⟨engl⟩ *private* (*soldier*); ⟨fam⟩ *Tommy*, ⟨Am⟩ *G.I.* (abbr f *government issue*)

L·andung f ~/~en *landing, debarkation*; *arrival* ‖ ⟨aero⟩ *l., alighting, descent*, ⟨a.⟩ *touch-down* (*on the moon*); außerhalb e–s Flugplatzes *off-field l.*; ~ ohne Gas *l. with engine cut off*; vom Boden aus geleitet → GKL-; bei ~ zu weit k *to overshoot* ‖ Außen≗ *off-field l.*; Bauch≗ *belly l.*; Blind≗, (Bums≗) *blind* (*rough*) *l.*; Bruch≗ *crash-l.* ‖ Deck≗ ⟨aero mar⟩ *deck landing* ‖ Dreipunkt≗, (Durchsack≗) *three-point* (*pancake*) *l.*; glatte ~ *safe* od *good l.*; Not≗ (Rückenwind≗) *forced* (*down-wind*) *l.*; weiche ~ *soft l.*, dazu: *to soft-land*; Ziel≗ *precision l.* | glatte ~ m *to make a good l.*; ⟨Am sl⟩ *to drop her down like a gentleman* | ⟨a–n⟩ ~ (der Kapsel im Wasser) *splashdown* ‖ zur ~ bringen *to ground*; die ~ einleiten *to prepare for the l.* **L·andungs-** (→ Lande-) **~abteilung** f ⟨mar⟩ *landing party* **~bake** f ⟨aero⟩ *approach beacon* **~boot** n ⟨mil⟩ *landing craft* od (kl) *barge* (*L. C.*) **~brief** m ⟨com⟩ *pratique* **~brücke** f ⟨mar⟩ (*l.-*)*stage, pier, jetty* **~damm** m *pier* **~fahrzeug** n ⟨mil⟩ *l. craft* **~geschwindigkeit** f *l. speed* **~kosten** pl *l.-charges* pl **~platz** m ⟨mar⟩ *l.-place* **~schein** m *l.-certificate* **~schiff** n *l. ship* N, *attack transport* **~steg** m *gang-plank* **~stelle** f ⟨tact⟩ *l. point* **~truppen** f pl *l. troops* pl **~übung** f *amphibious* od *disembarking exercise* **~unternehmen** n ⟨mil⟩ *sea-borne invasion* **~versuch** m *l. attempt* **~welle** f *boat wave* **~zeichen** n *l. mark*

l·ang I. a **1. räumlich**: *long* ‖ (v P a.) *tall* ‖ (v Haar a.) *ample* ‖ etw ~ geraten *l.ish* ‖ er fiel (die Länge) ~ hin auf *he came down full length upon* ‖ ~ u dünn *lathy* (*girl*) ‖ er ist e–e ~e Latte *he is as l. as a hop-pole* ‖ Rock mit ~en Schößen *l.-skirted coat*; mit ~em Griff *l.-handled* ‖ zehn Meter ~ *ten metres l.* od *in length* ‖ e–n Finger ~ (*of*) *the length of a finger* ‖ ein e–e Viertelmeile langer u halb so breiter Raum *a space of a quarter of a mile in length and half as broad* ‖ sie sind gleich ~ *they are equally l.* od *of equal length, they have the same length* ‖ zehn *m* lang u fünf *m* breit *ten metres by five* ‖ es ist so ~ wie breit ⟨a. fig⟩ *it is as broad as it is l.* ‖ ein endlos langer Vortrag *an endless lecture* ‖ länger w *or* m *to lengthen* ‖ sein Gesicht wurde länger *his countenance fell* ‖ länger m ⟨fig⟩ *to extend, prolong* | ⟨fig⟩ → **Bank** ‖ Neuigkeiten h ~e Beine *news travel fast* ‖ °~e **Brühe** ⟨cul fam⟩ *slops* pl ‖ ~e **Finger** m *to be light-fingered* ‖ ein ~es (enttäuschtes) **Gesicht** m *to pull a l. face* ‖ e–n ~en **Hals** m *to crane* (*one's neck*) *forward* ‖ etw v ~er **Hand** vorbereiten *to make preparations well in advance* ‖ er hat e–e ~e **Leitung** (→ lausig) *he is a slow coach*, ⟨Am a.⟩ *slow poke* od *just like an Englishman* ‖ e–m e–e ~e **Nase** m *to bamboozle a p*; ⟨Am⟩ *to l. one's nose to a p* ‖ mit ~er N. abziehen *to be down in the mouth* → Nase ‖ der ~en **Rede** kurzer Sinn ist der .. *to cut a l. story short* ‖ ~e **Zähne** m *to be disgusted with one's food* **2. zeitlich**: ein ~er Winter *a l. winter*; zehn ~e Stunden *ten wearisome hours*; e–e drei Tage ~e Reise *a three days' journey* ‖ ⟨com⟩ auf ~e Sicht *at l. sight* ‖ ein ~es Krankenlager *a l.* (od *protracted*) *illness*; ⟨med⟩ *chronic* (*exposure*) || ~e Zeit hindurch, auf ~e Z. *for a l. time* || nach ~en Jahren *after many years* || die Zeit nicht (zu) ~ w l *not to let the hours drag*; vor nicht ~er Z. *not so l. ago* || den lieben ~en Tag *the whole* od *livelong day* || die ≈ste Z. s–s Lebens *the greater part of his life* || vor ~er Z. festgesetzt, ergangen *l.-standing* (*engagement, invitation*) || du bist die ≈ste Z. hier gewesen *you will not be here much l.er* || für ≈ere Zeit *for a prolonged period* od *stay*, etc., *for some time* || über kurz oder ~ *sooner or later* || in nicht allzu ~er Zeit *before l.* || er braucht e–e ~e Zeit z Kommen *he is l.* (*in*) *coming* || mir wird die Zeit ~ *time hangs heavy on my hands, I don't know how to beguile the time, I find it very slow* **II.** **≈e(s)** n etw ~s, ein ~r *a long drink*; [mst klein geschr.] seit ~em *this l. time, for a l. while* (*past*), *for years and y.*; ⟨Am⟩ *in many a long day*; *in y. and y.* || er erzählte uns ein ~es u breites über *he made a song of*; *he span us a l. yarn about* || (Thema) des ~en u breiten behandeln *to dwell upon* (*a th.*) || sich etw des ~en u br. überlegen *to consider a question in all its aspects* || sich des ≈eren über etw auslassen *to enlarge upon a th* **III. adv 1. räumlich**: ⟨vulg⟩ die Straße ~ (entlang) *along the street*; viele Meilen ~ (weit) *extending for many miles*; sich ~ hinziehend *l. straggling* (*village*); sich ~ legen *to stretch out* **2. zeitlich**: [mst ~e] ~e schlafen *to sleep late*; (fünf) Tage, Jahre ~ *for* (*five*) *days, years* | ~e dauern, währen *to last a l. time* || es dauerte nicht ~e *it didn't last l.*; da kannst du ~e warten *you can wait a l. time* || bleib nicht zu ~ *don't stay too l.*; sehr ~e *ever so l.*; so ~ ich mich erinnern kann *ever since I can remember*; nicht ~e u er kam *it was not l. before he came*; ~e **her** ⟨Am fam⟩ *way back*; ~, ~ ist's her *l., l. ago*; ewig ~e *ever so l.*; es ist nicht so ~e her, (daß) *it is not so l. ago* (*someone broke it open*), *it is not so l. since* ..; viele Jahre ~ *for many years together* || es ist schon (noch nicht) ~e her, seit .. *it is a l. time since* .. (*it is not l. since*); das ist schon ~e her *that was a l. time ago*; ~e bevor er mir's sagte *l. before he told me*; die ~e vergangene Zeit *the l.-ago time*; er macht aber ~e! *he takes his time about it*!; er dachte nicht erst ~e nach *he did not pause to consider*; ⟨fam⟩ er wird's nicht mehr ~e m (bald sterben) *he won't last much l.er*; sie hat diese Gew. schon von ~e her *this has been her habit for years*; noch ~e nicht *far from* .., *not for some time yet*; so ~e bis *until, till*; noch auf ~e hinaus *for a l. time yet to come*; wie ~e noch? *how l. still*? || ich kenne sie schon viele J.e ~ *I have known her these many years* || wie ~e warten Sie schon? *how l. have you been waiting*?; nur e–e S. ~ las er deutlich *he only read one page clearly*; ~ ersehnte Hilfe *l.-desired relief*; ~ anhaltender Beifall, Regen *prolonged applause, continuous rain*; ~e erwartet *long looked for* | ⟨übtr⟩ das ist noch ~e nicht genug *that's nothing like enough*; es ist noch ~e nicht fertig *it isn't nearly ready* (*yet*); das ist für ihn ~e genug *that's plenty and enough for him*; es ist ~e nicht so billig wie *it is nothing* od *not anything like as cheap as*; ~e nicht gut genug *not half good enough*; ~e noch nicht erreicht *not yet, by a l. way, reached* **3.** [compr] **länger,** *prolonged* (*period*); [sup] **längst**: je l.r, je lieber, *the l.er the better*; ich kann's nicht l.r mit ansehen *I can't stand it any l.er*; ich hab' das schon l.r bemerkt (seit einiger Zeit) *I have noticed that l. ago* od *for some time* (*past*); ~ bleiben als erwünscht *to be overstaying one's welcome*; wir können nicht l.r leben *we cannot continue to live*; das wird am l.sten gedauert haben *that won't last much l.er*; das weiß ich l.st (= seit langem) *I have known that* (*for a l. while* od) *all along*; l.st vergangene Zeiten *times l. past*; *far-off ages*; l.st fällig *overdue*; du solltest l.st .. *you should be in your bed hours ago* | ⟨übtr⟩ l.st = bei weitem: du bist l.st nicht so groß wie ich *you are not nearly as tall as I am*; das ist noch l.st nicht die Hälfte *that's nothing like half*; sie war l.st nicht mehr jung *she was far from young* | **längstens** *at* (*the*) *longest, at the farthest*; (spätestens) *at the latest* || (höchstens) *at the most* **l·ang-~ährig** a *l.-eared* **~ärmelig** a *l.-sleeved* (*shirt*) **~-armig** a *l.-armed* **~atmig** a ⟨a. fig⟩ *l.-winded* (*story*); *verbose* (*statement*); ⟨fig⟩ *wordy* **≈atmigkeit** f ⟨a. fig⟩ *l.-w.ness* **≈basisgerät** n ⟨artill⟩ *two--station range finder* **≈baum** m (e–s Wagens) *pole, perch* **≈bein** n (l.-)legs [sg konstr] **~beinig** a *leggy, l.-legged*; ~e Mücke, Schnake *daddy-l.-legs* **~faserig** a *l.-stapled* (*cotton*) **≈finger** m *pickpocket, pilferer* **~fingerig** a *light-fingered* **~flammige Kohle** *cannel coal* **≈format** n ⟨typ⟩ *oblong size* **~-fristig** a *l.-range* (*proposals*), *l.-term* (*credit*); *fixed* (*investments*) || *l.-sighted* (*weather forecast*), ⟨com⟩ *l.-dated, l. time-*(*draft*) **~gestreckt** a *elongated*; *linear* **~gestreift** a *vertically striped* **~-gewachsen** a (P) *of tall stature* **~gliedrig** a *l.-limbed* || *l.-link* (*chain*) **~haarig** a *l.-haired, shaggy*; °~e Rasse (⟨fig⟩: Weib) ⟨sl⟩ *hair, the skirt*, ⟨Am⟩ *twist* **~händig** a *l.-handed* **~haus** n = –schiff **~-holz** n ⟨for⟩ *l. wood* || ⟨arch⟩ *l. beam*; *grain timber* | ~wagen [m] *t. wag*(*g*)*on* **~hübig** a *l.-stroke* (*engine*); *l.-throw* (*crank*) **~jährig** a *of l.* (od *many years'*) *standing*; *l.-time* (*friend*) **~lebig** a *l.-lived*; *durable* (*goods*) **~lebigst** a *l.est-lived* **≈-lebigkeit** f *l.evity* **~loch** n ⟨tech⟩ *slotted hole* | ~-hobel [m] *dado planer* **≈mut** f *patience, forbearance* **~mütig** a *forbearing, patient, l.-suffering* || adv *with patience* od *forbearance* **≈mütigkeit** f = Langmut **~nasig** a *l.-nosed* **≈ohr** n & m ⟨fam⟩ *l.-ear*(*s*), *jackass*; ein Esel schilt den andern ~ *it's like the pot calling the kettle black* **~ohrig** a *l.-eared* **~rolle** f ⟨Jap paint⟩ 1. (vertikal) *kakemono* 2. (horizontal) *makimono* **~rund** a *oval* **≈schädel** m *dolichocephal* **~schädelig** a *d.ic* **≈schäfter** pl *top-* od *high boots* pl, *Wellingtons* pl **≈schiff** n (e–r Kirche) *nave* **≈schläfer** m *slug-a-bed, lie-a--bed*; ⟨Am sl⟩ *bedbug* **~schößig** a *l.-skirted* **≈schwelle** f ⟨rail⟩ *l.itudinal sleeper* **≈seite** f *l. pane* (*of a roof*) **~sichtig** a ⟨com⟩ *l.-sighted, drawn at l. sight* **≈spiel-** ~band [n] ⟨wir⟩ *recording tape* || ~platte [f] *l.-playing* od *microgroove record*, ⟨fam⟩ *l.player*; ~n [pl] ⟨a.⟩ *extended play* (*EP*) **~stielig** a *l.-handled, with a l. stalk, stalky* || ⟨fig⟩ = –weilig **≈strecken-** *l. range* (*bomber, plane*), *l. distance* (*flight, race runner*) || ⟨mot⟩ *grand tourisme* (*car*) **≈tau** n *l. rope* **≈weile** f *weariness, boredom, tediousness*; *ennui* Fr → Langeweile **~weilen** vt [h] *to tire, bore*; ⟨Am⟩ *to make tired* || ge–lt ⟨a.⟩ *dull* || das Stück l.lt *the play drags* || sich ~ *to feel bored* od *dull, to find time hang heavy on one's hands* **≈weiler** m ⟨fam⟩ *bore, yawner-at, slowpoke* **~weilig** a *tedious*; *dull* ⟨a. cul⟩ *tiresome*; (P) *slow, stodgy, stuffy*; *beastly* || ~ m *to stale*; ~ w (*of play*) *to drag* || es ist zum Sterben ~ *it bores me stiff* || höchst ~ (*of play*) *as dull as ditch-water*; (*of book*) *as dry as dust* || die Zeit ~ finden *to find time hang heavily* || ~e P ⟨fam⟩ *stick, bore*; es ~ finden *to be bored by it* **≈weiligkeit** f *tediousness, heaviness* **≈wellen-** *l. wave* od *low frequency* (*station*) **~wellig** a ⟨phys⟩ *of l. w. length* **~wierig** a *of l. duration, wearisome, protracted, long, lengthy*; ⟨a.⟩ *slow* (*journey*), *unending, interminable*; ⟨med⟩ *chronic* **≈wierigkeit** f *wearisomeness, tediousness, lengthiness* **≈-zeile** f ⟨pros⟩ *l. line* **≈zeitzünder** m: Bombe mit ~ *large time bomb* **l·ange** adv = lang **L·änge** f ~/~n **1. räumlich**: *length*, ⟨film⟩ *footage* || (Größe) *tallness, size* || ⟨astr, geogr⟩ geographische ~ (*Greenwich*) *longitude*; Berlin liegt unter 13° östlicher ~ *B. lies at 13 degrees east*(*ern*) *l.de* (abbr *E.L.*); es hat *or* mißt 100 *m* in der ~ *it measures* od *is 100 metres long* od *in length* || (Maß) e–e ~ .. genügt *a l. of a gas-pipe will do*; ⟨sport⟩ das

Boot, Pferd führte, siegte mit zwei ~n .. *led, won by two l.s* || sind alle v derselben ~? *are all of them the same l.?* || das Land in der ~ u Breite durchreisen *to travel through the l. and breadth of the c.* || das Haus stand in s–r ganzen ~ in Flammen *the whole l. of the h. was in fl.*; sich der ganzen ~ nach erstrecken (S) *to lie along ..*; der ~ nach aufgeschlitzt .. *hogs split open l.wise* od *the l. of their bodies* || der ~ nach *or* lang hinfallen *to fall down (at) full l.* od *at one's l.*, ⟨a.⟩ *to measure one's l.*; sich der ~ lang hinlegen *to sprawl one's l.*; der ~ lang liegen *to be sprawling full l.* || sich in die ~ ziehen (*of a road*) *to l.en out* || ⟨mil⟩ der ~ nach beschießen *to enfilade* **2. zeitlich**: *length* || (Dauer) *duration* (*of a visit*) || ⟨pros⟩ ~ e–r Silbe *l.* od *quantity of a syllable* || ~ (lange Silbe) *long s.* || auf die ~ (der Zeit) *in the long run* || auf die ~ ertrag ich das nicht *I can't stand that for any l. of time* || ⟨theat⟩ das Stück hat s–e ~n .. *has its dragging passages* || in die ~ **ziehen** *to draw out, protract* (*debate*), *spin out* (*story*) || **sich** in die ~ z. *to grow* od *last long*; ⟨med⟩ *to linger* (*l.ing disease*); (S) *to take a long time, to hang fire*; (Krieg) *to drag on*; *to drawl* (*a word*) *out*; die Verhandlungen z. sich in die ~ .. *are of a protracted nature* **l·ange-~·anhaltend** a *long-standing* (*illness*) **~d·auernd** a *long-drawn* (*struggle*) **l·ängelang** adv (*at*) *full length* || sich ~ hinlegen *to lie down full l.*; *to go down sprawling* **l·angen** vt/i [h] *to seize, grasp* || (e–m etw) ~ *to reach, hand, give a p sth* || ⟨fam⟩ ich langte ihm e–e (Ohrfeige) *I boxed his ears, I fetched* od *landed* (od *passed, fetched*) *him one* (od *a blow*; *a clout* [Kopfnuß]) || ich werde ihn mir noch ~! *I'll get hold of him yet!* || (etw) **aus** der Tasche ~ *to take .. out of ..* | vi [h] **nach** etw ~ *to stretch out one's hand to reach for a th* || er mußte **in** die Tasche ~ *he had to bleed* (= *pay*) || ~ **in, unter** *to reach in, under* | (genügen) *to suffice, to be enough* od *sufficient* || das wird weit ~ *that will go far* || ich lange damit e–n Monat (komme aus) *I keep myself a month on it*, ⟨fam⟩ *I make it do a month* **l·ängen** vt [h] ⟨tech⟩ *to extend* **L·ängen-~ausdehnung** f ⟨phys⟩ *linear dimension* od *expansion* **~durchschnitt** m *longitudinal section* **~-einheit** f *unit of l.th* **~fehler** m *error in range* **~grad** m ⟨geog⟩ *degree of longitude*; *meridian* **~kreis** m ⟨geog⟩ *circle of l.de* **~maß** n *long* od *linear measure* || (Gerät) *instrument for measuring l.ths* **~maßstab** m *scale of l.th* **~messung** f *measurement of l.ths, linear measurement* **~schwingung** f *l.dinal oscillation* **~streubereich** m ⟨artill⟩ *depth* **~stück** n ⟨arch⟩ *string-piece*

Lang·ette f ~/~n *scallop* || ~nstich [m] *buttonhole stitch* || mit ~n besticken, **l-tt·ieren** vt *to scallop*

Langew·eile = Langweile || aus Langerweile *out of boredom*

l·änglich a *oblong, longish* || ~ u rund *oval*

Langob·arde m, **Langob·ardin** f *Longobard, Lombard* **langob·ardisch** a *Longobardian, Longobard*

l·ängs prep [mit gen] *along, alongside of* || ~ der Küste *along shore* || ~ der Küste fahren *to hug the coast* **L·ängs-~bestreichung** f ⟨mil⟩ *enfilade* **~druck** m *thrust load* **~einschnitt** m *longitudinal incision* **≃elastisch** a ⟨tex⟩ (Stoff) *elastomerised in warp* **~feld** n (im Geschützrohr) *chase* **~feuer** n ⟨mil⟩ *enfilade* **~naht** f ⟨tech⟩ *longitudinal joint* **~neigungsmesser** m ⟨aero⟩ *pitch indicator* **~richtung** f *l. direction* **~riß** m *split* **≃schiff** n adv *for-and-aft* **~schnitt** m *l. section* | ~tafel; ~ziffer [f] ⟨demog⟩ *generation table*; *g. rate* **~-schwelle** f ⟨rail⟩ *string-piece* **≃seits** adv (gehen) (*to go*) *alongside* **~streifen** m [pl] ⟨tex⟩ *longitudinal stripes* **~teilung** f *linear pitch* **~träger** m ⟨arch⟩ *main girder* **~verstrebung** f *l. stays* pl

l·angsam a & adv **1.** *slow* ⟨a. artill⟩ (*fire*); (*speed*); ⟨aero⟩ *lazy* (*8*); ~ wie e–e Schnecke *snail-like* || ~, ~! *steady, steady!* || (säumig) *tardy*, ⟨fam⟩ *dawdling* || ~ s *to dawdle* || (bedächtig) *leisurely, deliberate* || (schwerfällig) *dull, heavy* || (→ allmählich) *gradually, by degrees*, etc || (bequem) *easy-going*, ⟨com⟩ *slack* (*sale*) || *unhurried* (*steps*) || *lingering* (*death*) || so ~ wie möglich *dead slow* || ~ v Begriff *dull of comprehension* || ~ aber sicher!, immer ~ voran! *slow but sure!* || wer ~ **geht**, kommt auch ans Ziel *fair and softly goes far, slow and steady does it* od *wins the race* || ⟨mil⟩ ~er Schritt *goose-step* || ~e Fahrt *slow speed*; ~ fahren! *slow!*; *drive slowly* **2.** ~ **abgehen** ⟨com⟩ *to go off slowly* || arbeitend *sluggish* (*liver*) || auffassen *to be dull of comprehension*, ⟨fam⟩ *to be a slow-coach* || ⟨film, wir⟩ ~ auftauchen l *to fade in* || sich nur ~ **durchsetzen**: *the plough made but a slow conquest of Britain* || ~er **fahren** ⟨mot⟩ *to slow down* || ~er fahren l ⟨mar⟩ *to ease* (*her*) || ~ fließend *sluggish* (*river*) || ~ **gehen** *to walk slowly* od *gently*: *he inched into the room* || ~er gehen *to slacken one's pace* || die Uhr geht zu ~ *the clock loses* || ~ **m** ⟨sl⟩ *to go slow* || ~er **m** *to slacken* || ~ sprechen ⟨a.⟩ *to be slow of speech* || etw ~ **tun** *to be slow about a th* || die Wochen vergingen ~ .. *slagged* || ⟨film, wir⟩ ~ verschwinden l *to fade out* **≃ausschalter** m ⟨el⟩ *slow-break switch* **~läufer** m ⟨mach⟩ *slow runner*; ⟨mill⟩ *slow-speed grinder* **~streik** m ⟨post⟩ *working to rule* **L.erwerden** n *slackening* **L.keit** f ~/ (→ langsam) *slowness, deliberation, tardiness, dawdling, dullness, heaviness, slackness*

l·ängst(ens) adv → lang III., 3.

Langued·oc [lɑ̃g'dɔk] n ⟨Fr⟩ (Südfrankreich)

Lang·uste f ~/~n *spiny lobster*

Lanol·in [i:n] n ~s/ ⟨chem⟩ *lanolin, wool-fat*

Lantschou n (Stadt in China) *Lanchow*

L·anze f ~/~n **1.** *spear*, ⟨mil, tech⟩ *lance* (a. Bewaffneter) || mit eingelegter ~ *with couched l.* || mit e–r ~ angreifen *to l.* || e–e ~ brechen f ⟨fig⟩ *to break a l. for, to take up the cudgels for*, ⟨a.⟩ *to weight the scales in favour of*, ⟨Am a.⟩ *to bat for a p* || e–e ~ brechen mit ⟨fig⟩ *to enter the lists with, to cross swords with* **2.** °⟨sex⟩ *weapon*; °e–e ~ brechen mit *to break a l. with ..* **L·anzen-~brechen** n ⟨hist⟩ *joust*(*ing*), *tilting, tournament* **~fähnlein** n *l.-pennon* **≃förmig** a *sp.-shaped* **~reiter** m ⟨mil⟩ *l.r* **~rennen, ~spiel, ~stechen** n = ~brechen **~revers** m ⟨tail⟩ *peak lapel* **~stecher** m → Phantom **~stoß** m *thrust with a l.* **~träger** m *sp.man, l.-bearer* **Lanz·ett-~besteck** n ⟨surg⟩ *case with lancets* **≃blätt(e)rig** a ⟨bot⟩ *lanceolate* **~fisch** m ⟨zoo⟩ *lancelet* **≃förmig, ≃lich** a *spear-shaped* **Lanz·ette** f ~/~n ⟨surg⟩ *lancet*

L·aos n (Staat in Hinter-Indien)

Lapid·arstil m *lapidary style*

La Plata 1. [m] Rio de L. P. **2.** [n] (Stadt)

La-Plata-Staaten m pl *La Plata states*

Lapp·alie f ~/~n *trifle, bauble, fiddle-faddle, paltry matter, small concern* **L·äppchen** n ~s/~ (→ Lappen) ⟨bot, anat⟩ *lobule* **L·appen** m ~s/~ *flap*, (Wisch≃) (*piece of*) *cloth*, (Lumpen) *rag*, (Flicken) *patch* || (Staub≃) *duster* || ⟨anat & bot⟩ *lobe* || fleischiger ~ (*of fowl*) *wattle, gills* || Fuß≃ *foot-rag* || ⟨hunt⟩ ~ [pl] *toils* pl; ⟨fig fam⟩ e–m durch die ~ gehen *to bolt from a p, to give a p the slip* **~bildung** f ⟨scient⟩ *lobation* **~jagd** f *hunting with toils* **Läpper·ei** f ~/~en = Lapp·alie **l·äppern** vt/i [h] **1.** *to sip, lap*; es läppert mich nach Schokolade *I just feel like chocolates* **2.** sich zus~: es läppert sich zus *it runs up* od *accumulates* (*by degrees*) **L·äpperschulden** f pl ⟨fam⟩ *petty debts* pl **l·appig** a (aus Lappen bestehend) *ragged* || (mit Flicken besetzt) *patched* || ⟨anat, bot⟩ *lob*(*ulat*)*ed* || (schlaff) *flabby*, (*wishy-*)*washy* || (dünn) *sloppy*, ⟨Am⟩ *pussyfoot* (*tea*) || *languid* (*movement*)

L·appe m, **L·appin** f, **L·appland** n *Lapland* **L·appländer** m, **~in** f *Lapp, Laplander* **l·appländisch** *Lapp, Lappish, Laplandish, Lapponian*

l·äppisch a (→ Laffe) *silly, apish, foolish* || (unbedeutend) *fiddling* || *senseless, insipid* || *childish* || ~es Zeug *rubbish, stuff and nonsense* || (weichlich) *coddled*; ~er Mensch ⟨fam⟩ *milksop*

L·appschweißen n ⟨tech⟩ *lap welding*

L·apsus m ~/~ *slip of the tongue* bzw *pen*

Laramie-Kette f *Laramie Range* (U.S.A.)

L·ärche f ~/~n ⟨bot⟩ *larch*; amerikanische ~ *tamarack* || ~nschwamm [m] *agaric*

L·aren m pl ⟨L ant⟩ *lares* L, *household gods* pl

°**larif·ari**! intj *stuff and nonsense*! *rubbish*!

L·ärm m ~(e)s/; L·ärmen [n] ~s/ *noise, din* || ⟨fam⟩ *hubbub*; (stärker:) *racket*; (Aufruhr) *row, tow-row, turmoil*; (Geschrei) *clamour* (a. in der Presse) || ⟨sl⟩ *hullaballoo* || ein Höllen~ *a regular bedlam* || blinder ~ *false alarm* || ~ blasen, ~ schlagen *to sound* (od *beat, give*) *an alarm* || blinden ~ schlagen ⟨a.⟩ *to cry wolf* || ~ m *to make a n., to tow-row*; viel ~ m *to make a great n.* od *to-do* (um *about*); ⟨fam⟩ *to kick up a great row* || wozu all der ~? *what is all this n. about*? || ⟨prov⟩ viel ~ um nichts *much ado about nothing* **~apparat** m *alarum* **~bekämpfung** f *sound-level* od *n. control* **~belästigung, ~plage** f, **~unfug** m *n. nuisance* **~frei** a ⟨mach⟩ *silent* (*operation*) **~glocke** f *alarmbell* **~macher** m *alarmist* ⟨a. fig⟩ || *noisy person* **~spiegel** m *n. level* **~zeichen** n *alarm-signal*

l·ärmen **1.** vi [h] (→ poltern, toben, wüten) *to make a noise*, ⟨fam⟩ *to kick up a row, to tow-row* || (streitend) *to brawl* || (schreiend) *to clamour, shout* || (schimpfend) *to bluster* **2.** vt [h] jdn wach ~ *to waken a p with noise* **l·ärmend** a [pres part] *noisy, rampageous* (*play*); *garish* (*cinema*); (unbeherrscht) *obstreperous* || (lustig ~) *riotous* || *blustering, blustery*; *turbulent, tumultuous, raging, storming, wild, rampant, fiery, heated*; ~ laut *boisterous* || die ~e Menge *the mob*

larmoy·ant [larmwaj'ant] a *snivelling* (*character*) || *pathetic* (*play*)

L·ärvchen n ~s/~ → **L·arve** f ~/~n *mask* || (Gesicht) *face*, ⟨fam⟩ *phiz* || ein niedliches Lärvchen *a pretty little face* od *girl* || (Gespenst) *larva, monster*, ⟨fam⟩ *bogy* || ⟨ent⟩ *grub, nymph, larva* || jdm die ~ vom Gesicht reißen *to unmask* od *expose a p, to tear the mask off a p's face*

l·as 1. & 3. sg pret (**l·äse** subj) v lesen

l·asch a *flabby, limp, lax* | ~**heit** f ~/ *laxity*

L·asche f ~/~n ⟨tail⟩ (Keil) *gore, gusset* || (Taschenklappe) *flap* || (Schuh~) *flap, tongue* || ⟨tech⟩ *tongue, fish* || ⟨rail⟩ *fish*(*-plate*); mit ~n verbinden *to fish* || ⟨arch⟩ *strip* || ⟨carp⟩ *groove* || (*filmpack*) *paper leader* **l·aschen** vt [h] *to put in a gore* || *to furnish with flaps*, etc.; ⟨mar⟩ *to sling* || ⟨carp⟩ *to join by means of grooves*

L·aser m ~s/ ⟨phys⟩ *laser*, → Lichtverstärkung

las·ieren vt [h] ⟨paint⟩ *to glaze*; → Lasur

l·aß a *weary*; *indolent* | ~**heit** f *w.iness, i.nce*

laß! imp v lassen **L·aßbecken** n ~s/~ ⟨surg⟩ *bleeding-basin* **l·assen I.** vt/(i → I. 4. von) [ließ/gelassen] [h] **(fortlassen, verlieren) 1.** sein Leben ~ *to lose one's life*; er ließ sein L. für .. *he gave* od *sacrificed his life for* .. || *to shed* (*blood*); er mußte Blut ~ *he had to bleed* od *to be bled*; e–m Blut ~ *to bleed a p* || er ließ Haare (erlitt Verluste) *he was fleeced* || er ließ viel Geld in der Kneipe *he spent a lot of money in drink*; .. beim .. *at his tailor's* || (sein) Wasser (Urin) ~ *to pass one's water* | **(hinterlassen)** *to leave*; e–m etw ~ *to bequeath a p a th* || (bei Tisch) ~ wir den Gästen auch noch etw **(übrig)**! *family hold off*! || **(unterbringen)** *to place*; *to park the children with their aunt* || er weiß sich vor Freude nicht zu ~ *he is beside h.s. with joy* || wo ~ Sie das alles? *where do you put it all*? **2. (unterlassen)** *to desist, abstain* (*from*) || laß das Weinen (usw)! *stop crying, give up* (*mourning*), *stop* (*that noise*) || °tu was du nicht ~ kannst *do it if you think you must*; sie wußte nicht, was sie tun oder ~ sollte .. *or leave undone*; *whatever he does or doesn't do*; tun u ~ können .. *to be free* od *welcome to do* (*as one pleases*) || Sie ließen besser das Rauchen *you had better abstain from smoking* od *avoid s.* || ich kann es nicht ~ *I can't help* ([*doing*] *it*); *he can't leave it alone* || du kannst das Spaßen nicht ~ *you will have your joke* || ~ Sie das °(unterwegs) *don't*!, *leave that alone*!, ⟨fam⟩ *drop that*!; *stop it*! ⟨Am⟩ *cut it out*!, *lay off*! || (wenn Sie mir es nicht billiger ~), laß ich's (*if you don't let me have it at a lower price*) *I will do without it* **3. (in e-m Zustand belassen)** die Dinge beim alten ~ *to leave ths as they are* || *to leave* (*open, shut, undone*), *to leave off* || laß mich in Frieden *or* zufrieden! *let me alone*! || etw auf sich beruhen ~ *to leave a th as it is* || laß mich aus dem Spiele *don't draw me into the affair* || ungesagt ~ *to leave undiscussed* || e–n unbestraft ~ *to let a p go free* || unbeschrieben ~ *to leave blank* || es dabei bewenden ~ *to leave it at that* || laß (es) gut s! *never mind*! || stehen ~: *I've left my stick in the bus* | **e-m etw** ~ *to leave a th in a p's hands* || laß es ihm *let him keep it* || das muß man ihm ~ *one must give him credit for that*; das muß man Ihnen ~! *I'll say that for you*! || das muß man ihm ~, er ist offen *you must admit he is frank* || ich will Ihnen die Wahl ~ *you shall have the choice* || ~ Sie es mir billiger (→ I. 2. [Ende]) || ~ Sie uns freie Hand *give us a free hand* || ~ Sie sich Zeit *take your time* || ich will dir genug Zeit ~ *I will allow you enough time* || sich [dat] etw f zuletzt ~ *to reserve a th to the last* **4. [mit prep]** kein gutes Haar **an** e–m ~ *to have not a single word to say in a p's favour* || sich **auf** die Knie fallen ~ *to go down on one's knees*, sich aufs Knie fallen ~ *to bow the knee* (vor *to*) || nicht **aus** den Augen ~ *to keep an eye on* || aus dem Hause ~ *to let out of the h.* || nicht aus den Händen ~ *not to let slip* (*from one's hands*) || laß mich aus dem Spiele *don't draw me into the matter* || **außer** acht ~ *to take no notice of* || ~ wir's **beim** alten *let's leave ths as they are* || ~ wir das lieber **beiseite** *we had better pass that over*; ~ wir allen Spaß b. *all joking apart*! || etw **hinter** sich ~ *to leave a th behind one*; das läßt alles weit h. sich *that is better* od *worse than anything we've ever heard of before*; (Verfolger) weit h. sich ~ *to fling* (..) *off* || e–n **im** Stich ~ *to leave a p in the lurch* || im unklaren ~ *to leave in the dark* (über *about*) || e–n im Amt ~ *to continue a p in office, to keep him in one's employ* || ~ Sie mich (damit) in Ruhe! *leave me alone*! (*nothing of that* [*any more*])! || ich kann ihn nicht **von** mir ~ *I can't part with him* || Bier vom Faß ~ *to draw beer from the cask* | **[vi]** sie kann nicht v ihm ~ *she cannot leave him* od *live without him* || .. *give up gambling*! *he still retains* od *can't help retaining* (kann nicht ~) *his passion for gambling* || sie ließen nicht v–e–a *they stuck to one another* || ich kann nicht v m–r Meinung ~ *I cannot change my opinion* | e–n **vor** sich ~ *to admit a p to one's presence* || er läßt niemand **zu** sich *he won't see* od *receive anybody* || etw zum Pfand ~ *to pawn* od *pledge a th* || e–n zur Ader ~ *to bleed a p* **II.** v/aux [h] **(zulassen, veranlassen) 1. (zulassen, erlauben)** *to allow, let, permit* || **(dulden)** *to suffer a th* (*to be done*) | (→ a. 3.) er läßt sich nichts abgehen *he doesn't stint h.s. in anything* || ich lasse mich nicht (anführen etc) *I am not to be* (*swindled*, etc) || ich lasse es darauf ankommen *I'll take my chance* (*of that*) || er läßt sich nicht befehlen *he won't be ordered* (*stand ordering*) *about* || laß es dabei (bewenden) *leave it at that* || sich gerne bewundern ~ *to like admiration* (od *to be admired*) || das Licht brennen ~ *to leave the light burning* || ein Gesetz durchgehen ~ *to pass a bill* || E. durchgehen ~ *to allow electricity to pass through* || laß dir das nicht einfallen *you must not think of such a th* || (das Kleid) läßt sie größer erscheinen .. *makes her look taller* || fallen ~ *to drop* (⟨a. fig⟩ *a bill*, *subject*) || laß dir ein Glas Bier geben! *have a gl. of b.*! || das ~ wir uns gefallen! *that's not half bad*, ⟨fam⟩ *that's sth like* || das lasse ich mir nicht gefallen *I won't stand that*! || die Dinge einfach **gehen** ~ *just let ths go* || sich g. ~ *to be careless of one's p*; *to relax*; laß es dir gut g. ⟨fam⟩ *fare-thee--well* || Gott lasse es geschehen, daß *God grant that* .. || sie wollte sich v niemand helfen ~ *she would allow no one to help her, she would not let anyone help her* || hören ~ *to sound* (*a note*) || etw zur Ruhe **k** ~ *to allow a th to come to rest* || sein Licht leuchten ~ *to let one's light shine before men* || sich nicht in (e–n Hinterhalt) locken ~ *to avoid being drawn into* .. || ~ Sie mich nur **m**! *leave that to me*!; .. ihn *give him his head* || sich gerne Komplimente **m** ~ *to like to receive* od *hear c.s* || sich nichts merken ~ *not to betray one's feelings* od *o.s.*; laß dir nichts m. *don't give y.s. away*; *don't betray y.s. don't show it*; *pretend like you know nothing* || °etw mitgehen ~ ⟨euph⟩ *to borrow a th* (bei *from*) || er ließ sich nicht raten *he would not be advised* || mit sich reden ~ *to listen to reason* || ich mag es mir nicht v ihm sagen ~ *I don't care to have him say it to me* || laß dir das ein- f allemal gesagt s *let me tell you once* (*and*) *for all* || er läßt ihn frei schalten u walten *he lets him do just as he likes* || schlafen ~: *the wind would not suffer* od *allow me to sleep* || sehen ~ *to show* || sich (nicht) sehen ~ *to present o.s.* (*to keep out of sight*); .. nirgends .. *she doesn't go anywhere*; laß dich nicht sehen! *keep out of sight, don't show your face*! || das kann sich sehen ~ *that's not half bad* || laß das sein! *stop that*! || laß (es) gut sein! *never mind*! || den Mut nicht sinken ~ *to keep up one's courage* || °etw springen ~ (Zeche m) *to run up a big score* || das hatte ich mir nie träumen ~ *I should never have thought* od *dreamt of it* || sich nicht **über**setzen ~: *the idiom is not capable of translation* || **un**beschrieben ~ *to leave blank* || das läßt **v**ermuten, daß *that causes a suspicion that* || Milde **w**alten ~ *to show mercy* || warten ~ *to keep waiting* || laß das Wasser kühl **w** *leave the water to cool, let it cool* || es laut w ~ *to let it become known* || er wollte ihn nicht Maler w ~ *he refused to have him become a painter* || sich etw sauer w ~ *to take much pains with a th* || jdn etw wissen ~ *to give notice of a th to a p* || er ließ sichs dort wohlsein *he made h.s. quite comfortable there* | **[imp]** laß sehen! usw. *let me see*!, *let me hear from you*!, *let me know the result* || laßt uns spazieren **gehen** *let us take a walk* || **(sich vorstellen)** laß ihn nur erst selbst verheiratet s *just imagine him a family-man h.s.* (→ o.) **2. (veranlassen, e-n zu etw nötigen)** *to make, cause*, (befehlen) *order* (*to be done*); *to have* (*done*); e–n etw tun ~ *to get a p to do* || *to arrange for a beam of light to strike the bottom* || das Haus, das sie hatte **b**auen ~ *the house she had had built* || **d**rucken ~ *to have printed* || **f**liegen ~ *to let fly* (*bird*); *to fly* (*kite*) || ich lasse ihn **gr**üßen *I wish to be kindly remembered to him* || **h**olen ~ *to send for* (*a letter, the doctor*) || v sich hören ~ *to send news* || der König ließ ihn **k** *the king ordered him to be brought before him* || laß sie sofort heraufk *have them up at once* || er ließ ihn (v der Universität) nach Hause k *he had him down* || **l**egen ~: *he caused it to be placed on the table* || auswendig lernen ~: *she made them learn it by heart* || laufen ~ *to run* (*a canteen, an engine*) || .. unter der Erde laufen zu ~: *it is convenient to have the wires running under ground* || sich malen, **p**hotographieren ~ *to have one's portrait painted, photograph taken* || er ließ e–e Tasche **m** *he had a satchel made* || er läßt sich [dat] e–n Anzug m *he is having a suit made* || **r**ufen ~ *to send for* || er ließ ihm sagen, daß *he had him told that, he sent him word that* || ich habe mir sagen ~ *I have heard, I have been told* || laß ihn an mich schreiben *get him to write to me* || springen ~: *he made the dog jump*; *he jumped her up and kissed her*; alle Minen springen ~ *to leave no stone unturned* | (schildern) *poets let* od *make their heroes do, represent them as doing* || ich lasse ihm gute Reise wünschen *will you wish him from me a safe journey* **3. vrefl (P & S) a.** (S) sich abspülen ~ *to rinse off* **das läßt sich aushalten** *that is quite endurable* || es l. sich nicht **b**eschreiben *it defies description* || es l. sich biegen *it will stand bending* || das l. sich **d**enken *I should* (*just*) *think so*; wie sich d. l. *as may be imagined* || .. l. sich **e**ssen *that is sth like a cake*! .. l. sich kaum essen .. *is hardly eatable* || das l. sich **h**ören! *that is plausible, that sounds well*, ⟨fam⟩ *that is sth like*! || es l. sich nicht mit ihr leben *there is no living with her* || es l. sich nicht leugnen *there's no denying that* || das l. sich **m** *that can be done* || es l. sich nicht **l**eugnen, daß *there is no denying* (*the fact*) *that* || .. **r**auchen *this cigar is worth smoking* || darüber l. sich reden *that admits of further discussion* || das l. sich leichter **s**agen als tun *that's more easily said than done* || hier l. es sich gut sitzen *it's very pleasant sitting here* || sich **t**ragen ~: *the load is not too heavy to carry* || das wird sich nicht umgehen, vermeiden ~ *that cannot be avoided* || sich trinken ~: *this wine is very drinkable* || sich gut **v**erarbeiten ~: *this material can be easily worked up* || das l. vermuten, daß *that suggests that* || es l. sich nicht mit ihm **zus** leben *there is no living with him* **b.** (P) (→ a. II. 1., 2.) **er läßt sich nicht abschrecken** *he doesn't allow h.s. to be disheartened* || .. abweisen *he takes no denial* od *refusal* || laß dich's nicht anfechten *never mind* || laß dich **be**lehren! *be advised*! || laß dich nicht **e**rwischen *don't let y.s. be caught* || er l. sich **g**ehen *he is careless of his p* || er l. sich's etw **k**osten *he spends a lot of money on it* || er l. sich nicht lange **n**ötigen *he doesn't wait to be invited twice, he requires very little pressing* || sie l. sich nirgends **s**ehen *she doesn't go anywhere* || sich **t**ragen ~ (P) *to be carried* || er l. sich's nicht **v**erdrießen *he spares no trouble* || er l. sich verleugnen *he won't see anybody* **III.** v/imps * **(aussehen)** das läßt schön *that is beautiful* || (e–m gut anstehen) *to befit, become* (*a p*) || das Kleid läßt (= steht) ihr gut .. *suits her well* **IV.** ≗ n ~s/ unser Tun u ≗ *our commissions and omissions* pl **l·ässest** = läßt 2. sg ind pres v lassen

l·ässig a (faul) *lazy, indolent, idle* || (schlaff) *sluggish, lackadaisical* || *languid* (*pose*) || (sorglos) *careless* || (nachlässig) *negligent, shiftless, remiss* | ≗**keit** f ~/ *laziness, indolence, idleness*; *sluggishness*; *carelessness*; *negligence* **l·äßlich** a ⟨allg⟩ *pardonable, excusable*; ⟨ec⟩ *venial* (*sin*) | ≗**keit** f ~/ *veniality* | ~en [pl] *venial sins* od *faults*

L·asso m & n ~s/~s *lasso*; [dazu:] *to lasso*

last, not least *last but not least*

Last f ~/~en **1.** ⟨eig⟩ *load, weight*, ⟨Am⟩ (e–s Wagens) *haul*; (Bürde) *burden, burthen* || (*she wore a*) *power* (*of rings*) | ⟨fig⟩ *burden, charge, encumbrance*; *w.* (*of evidence*); *nuisance, bother, trouble* || (Plage) *trial* || (kostspielige ~) ⟨a.⟩ *white elephant* || *onslaught* (*of years*) || drückende ~ *dead w.* || *brunt* (*of a battle*) **2.** ⟨mar⟩ *cargo, freight*; (Tragfähigkeit) *tonnage* **3.** ⟨com⟩ *charge* (auf .. *on property*) || (Hypotheken-, Schulden≗) *encumbrance* || zu ~en jds *to the debit of a p*; zu ~en des Käufers *to be paid by the buyer* || (Abgaben) *taxes, fiscal, social burdens* pl **4.** e–m e–e ~ **abnehmen** *to take a b. off a p's shoulders* || e–m ~en aufbürden *to heap b.s on a p* || der Tisch **bog** sich unter der ~ der Speisen .. *groaned with food* || ⟨com⟩ e–m etw zur ~ **bringen** *to debit a p's account for* .. || wir buchen es zu Ihren ~en *we d. it to your account* || es **fällt** mir e–e ~ v Herzen *a load falls from my h.* || e–m zur ~ fallen *to be a b. to a p, to be a nuisance*; *to be thrown upon a p's resources*; *to be a charge upon a p* || e–m mit etw ..:

⟨fam⟩ *I won't inflict the family on you* ‖ e–e ~ auf sich **laden** *to impose a b. on o.s.* ‖ e–m etw zur ~ legen *to charge* od *reproach a p with a th, to lay a th to a p's charge* od *at a p's door*; es wird ihm zur ~ gelegt *it lies at his door* ‖ Sie **nehmen** mir e–e ~ v der Seele *you are lifting a load from my spirit* ‖ auf dem Hause **ruhen** erhebliche ~en *the h. is heavily encumbered* ‖ e–e ~ **schleppen,** tragen *to drag, carry a load* ‖ er ist mir e–e schwere ~ *he is a great drag on me* ‖ ⟨com⟩ e–m (e–e Summe) [Waren] zur ~ schreiben *to debit .. to a p, to charge [goods] to a p's account* ‖ sich selbst zur ~ **w** *to get a nuisance* od *b. to o.s.* ‖ die Zeit wird mir zur ~ *time hangs somewhat heavily on my hands* **~auto** n = ~kraftwagen **~dampfer** m *cargo-steamer* **~esel** m *sumpter-mule* **~fracht** f ⟨mar⟩ *freight per ton* **~fuhre** f *goods-van* **~fuhrunternehmer** m *haulier* **~gebühr** f, **~geld** n *tonnage* **~kahn** m *barge, lighter* **~kraftwagen** m (abbr Lkw [elka've:]) *(motor-)lorry, van, camion*; ⟨Am⟩ *(auto-)truck*; ~ mit Anhänger [m] *lorry-, truck-trailer*; durch ~ gezogen *truck drawn*; mit ~ befördert *lorry-borne (troops)* | ~fahrer [m] *lorry-driver*; ~kolonne [f] *truck column*; ~-Verladestelle [f] (P & S) *entrucking point* N **~magnet** m *lifting m.* **~pferd** n *pack-horse* **~schiff** n *tramp-boat*, ⟨mar a.⟩ *hulk* **~schrift** f ⟨com⟩ *debit* | ~beleg [m] *d. voucher* **~tier** n *beast of burden, pack-animal*; wie ein ~ arbeiten *to work like a horse* **~träger** m *porter* **~transport** m *drayage* **~übertragung** f *loading transmission* **~vieh** n *beasts* [pl] *of burden* **~wagen** m *van, wag(g)on*; ⟨mot⟩ *lorry*, ⟨Am⟩ *truck* **~zug** m ⟨mot⟩ *lorry and trailer, tractor-trailer train* **l·astbar** a *capable of being loaded* od *of bearing a burden* **l·asten** vi [h] *to be heavy* ‖ *to weigh, press* (auf *upon*) ⟨a. fig⟩: *the matter weighed* od *was dwelling upon his conscience* od *mind*; *there were too many ths on her mind*; *the whole responsibility lay* od *rested on his shoulders*; *it was a heavy burden to him* ‖ auf dem Hause ~ erhebliche Schulden *the house is heavily encumbered with mortgages* **L·asten- ~aufzug** m *goods* (⟨Am⟩ *service*) *lift* od *elevator* **~ausgleich** m ⟨Ger⟩ *equalization of burdens* **~fallschirm** m *cargo-parachute* **~flugzeug** n *goods airplane* **~̂frei** a *free from taxes* ‖ *unencumbered* (*estate*); *we bought the house free from all debts* **~roller** m (3-rädrig) *tricar* **~segler** m ⟨aero⟩ *transport glider* °**L·aster** m ~s/~ = Lastauto, -wagen

L·aster n ~s/~ **1.** ⟨eig⟩ *vice*; ⟨allg⟩ *depravity, viciousness* ‖ kein ~ h *to have no vices*; dem ~ frönen *to indulge in vice*; sich e–m ~ hingeben *to pursue a profligate life*; dem ~ nachgehen *to gloat on vice* ‖ Haus des ~s *disorderly house* **2.** ⟨übtr⟩ *infamous fellow*; (Weib) ⟨fam⟩ *bad wench* ‖ ⟨hum fam⟩ langes ~ *six feet of wickedness*; so ein langes ~ *such a tall piece of w.* **~höhle** f *den of vice* **~leben** n *vicious life* **~pfuhl** m *sink of iniquity* **~stätte** f *pandemonium* L **~tat** f *villainous* od *heinous action* **~̂voll** a *vicious, depraved* **L·ästerer** m ~s/~ *calumniator, defamer, slanderer, scandal-monger, backbiter* ‖ (Gottes~̂) *blasphemer* **L·äster- ~allee** f ⟨hum⟩ *lane of mockers* **~chronik** f *scandal, gossip* **~geschichte** f *scandalous story* **~maul** n *black mouth*; *slanderer, scandal-monger, backbiter* **~rede** f *slanderous* od *defamatory language* **~schrift** f *libel, lampoon* **~schule** f *school for scandal* **~sucht** f *calumnious disposition* **~̂süchtig** a *slanderous* **~wort** n *slander*; ⟨ec⟩ *blasphemy* **~zunge** f *black mouth* ‖ = ~maul **l·asterhaft** a *vicious, profligate, dissolute* (*life, fellow*) ‖ *lascivious, depraved, abandoned* (*woman*) ‖ ⟨allg⟩ *wicked, corrupt* **~̂igkeit** f ~/ *viciousness, profligacy, dissoluteness*; *lasciviousness, depravity*; *wickedness, corruptness* **l·ästerlich** a **1.** *slanderous, abusive*; *calumnious* ‖ (gottes~) *blasphemous* **2.** (schändlich) *scandalous, disgraceful* **l·ästern** vt [h] *to slander, defame* ‖ *backbite* ‖ *abuse, malign*: *the much maligned Chamber* ‖ (Gott) ⟨a.⟩ vi [h] *to blaspheme* ‖ ~d *blasphemous* **L·ästerung** f ~/~en *calumny, calumniation, abuse, slander* ‖ ⟨ec⟩ *blasphemy*

-l·astig a [nur in comp] zw·ei~ *carrying two loads* ‖ ·achter–, k·opf~ ⟨mar⟩ *down by the stern, head* **L.keit** f ~/ ⟨mar⟩ *capacity, tonnage* | ~sregelung [f] ⟨mar etc⟩ *trimming* **l·ästig** a *burdensome, cumbersome* ⟨a. fig⟩; (ärgerlich) *bothersome, irksome* (*duties*); *annoying* (für *to*); (beschwerlich) *troublesome, tiresome* (*fellow, illness, duty*); *fashious* ‖ (anspruchsvoll) *importunate* (*p*); *exacting* (*invalid*); *undesirable* (*alien*) ‖ ~er (kostspieliger) Besitz *a white elephant* ‖ (unbequem) *incommodious* | e–m ~ fallen *or* w *to be a bore, to become a burden* od *trouble to a p*; sich ~ m *to make a nuisance of o.s.* ‖ *to incommode, bore, oppress, importune, molest* vt ‖ [abs] ~ s *to be a nuisance* (flies) od *a burden* (overcoat on warm days) | **~̂keit** f ~/ *b.ness* ‖ *i.ness t.ness*; *bore*; *inconvenience*; *weariness*

L·astexhose ® f *stretcher trousers, stretch pants*

L·asting [ɑ:] m ~s/ (Kammgarnstoff) *prunella*

Las·ur f ~/~en *colouring blue* ‖ (Anstrich) *azure coating* **~blau** n *ultramarine* | **~̂** a *azure* **~farbe** f = ~blau ‖ ⟨allg⟩ *transparent colour* | ~̂n [a] = ~̂blau **~grün** n *bice* **~stein** m = **Lasur·it** m ~(e)s/~e *lapis-lazuli*

lasz·iv [–f] a *lascivious* | **~̂it·ät** f ~/ *l.ness*

Lät·are; Sonntag ~ *Mid-Lent-Sunday*

L·ate ⟨sl⟩ = **Lat·ein** n ~s/ *Latin* ‖ mit s–m ~ zu Ende s ⟨fig⟩ *to be at one's wits' end*, ⟨fam⟩ *to be nonplussed* od *at a nonplus*; da bin ich mit m–m ~ z Ende ⟨Am fam⟩ *you've got me there* **~am·erika** n *Latin America* | ~ner [m] *L.-A.n*, ⟨sl⟩ *greaser* **~schule** f *grammar school* **Lat·einer** m ~s/~ *Latinist* **lat·einisch** a *Latin* (*tongue, characters* pl) ‖ ⟨typ⟩ (Antiqua) *Roman*; (Kursiv) *italics* pl ‖ → Kreuz ‖ ~es Segel *lateen* ‖ ~e Volkssprache *low Latin*

La-Tène-Zeit f ⟨praeh⟩ *late Celtic period*

lat·ent a *latent, potential* ‖ ~e Kraft *potential(ity)* **Lat·enz** f ~/ *latency* **~zeit** f ⟨med⟩ *l. period*

Lat·erna m·agica f ~/ *magic lantern* **Lat·erne** f ~/~e *lantern* ⟨a. arch⟩; *lamp*; ⟨a.⟩ *light* | Bl·end~̂ *dark lantern*; H·of~̂ *yard l.p*; K·opf~̂ ⟨mot, rail⟩ *headlight*; Öl~̂ *oil l.p*; Pap·ier~̂ *Chinese l.n*; Positi·ons~̂ ⟨mar⟩ *position l.p*; Schl·uß~̂ *tail l.p*; St·allaterne *stable l.n*; Str·aßen~̂ *street l.p*; St·urm~̂ *storm* od *hurricane l.p* od *l.n*; T·aschen~̂ *electric torch*, ⟨Am⟩ *flashlight* | e–e ~ anzünden *or* anstecken, auslöschen *to light, put out a l.* ‖ °jetzt geht mir e–e ~ auf *now I get it, it dawns upon me* ‖ etw am Tage mit der ~ suchen *to burn a l.p in broad daylight* **Lat·ernen- ~anstecker, ~anzünder** m *l.plighter* **~arm** m *l.n-crank* **~eisen** n ⟨mar⟩ *l.n-braces* pl **~fisch** m ⟨ich⟩ *l.n-fish* **~halter** m ⟨cycl⟩ *l.p-bracket* **~pfahl** m *l.npost*; ein Wink mit dem ~ ⟨fig⟩ *a broad hint* **~träger** m *l.n-bearer* ‖ ⟨ent⟩ *l.n-fly*

L·atex m ~/ (Kautschukmilch) *latex*

Latif·undien n pl *large estates, latifundia* pl

†**Lat·iner** m, **~in** f *Latin, inhabitant of ancient Latium*; ~ [pl] *Latins, Latini* L pl †**lat·inisch** a *Latin* **latinis·ieren** vt [h] *to latinize* **L-·ismus** m ~/–men *Latinism* **L-·ist** m ~en/~en *Latinist* **L-it·ät** f *Latinity* †**L·atium** n *Latium*

Latr·ine f ~/~n *latrine* ‖ behelfsmäßige ~ *pole-seat* | ~ngerücht [n] ⟨mil⟩ *cook official*; ⟨sl⟩ *scuttlebutt*; *latrine-* od ⟨Am⟩ *jungle-wireless*, ⟨aero sl⟩ *phon(e)y gen*; ~graben [m] *straddle trench*

°**L·atsch** m ~es/~e; **L·atsche** m ~n/~n (schlapper Mensch) *lackadaisical fellow* **L·atsche** f ~/~n **1.** ⟨bot⟩ *mountain pine* **2.** ⟨vulg⟩ (*down-at-heel*) *slipper* **l·atschen** vi [s] *to shuffle, slouch* (*along*), *to foot-slog* **l·atschig** a *shuffling, slouching*, *jogging* ‖ ⟨fig⟩ *slovenly* ‖ (schlapp) *lackadaisical (fellow)* ‖ sich ~ lehnen gegen *to lounge against*

L·atte f ~/~n **1.** *lath* ⟨a. sport⟩, *batten*; mit ~n versehen *to batten* ‖ e–m durch die ~n (statt: Lappen) gehen *to slip through a p's fingers* ‖ *rung (of a blind)* ‖ ⟨ftb⟩ *cross-bar*; ⟨aero sl⟩ *prop(eller)* **2.** ⟨fig⟩ (P) lange ~ *hop-pole, maypole* **3.** *a heavy score to pay* **4.** °⟨vulg sex⟩ *long Tom* **l·atten** vt [h] *to lath* **L·atten-** **~gestell** n *lathwork* **~gitter** n *lattice-work* **~holz** n *lath-wood* **~kiste** f *crate* **~rost** m *board-walk* **~verschlag** m **1.** *latticed partition* **2.** (–kiste) *wooden packing boards* pl **~werk** n *lath--work, lattice(-work)* **~zaun** m *paling, lath-fence, stockade*; mit e–m ~ umgeben *to stockade* **~ziegel** m *lath-brick*

L·attich m ~(e)s/~e *lettuce* | ~salat [m] *garden l.*

°**Lat·üchte** f ~/~n ⟨hum⟩ (→ Laterne + Leuchte)

Latw·erge f ~/~n *electuary (confection)*

L·atz m ~es/≈e (Hosen≈) *fly* ‖ (Kinderlätzchen, Schürzen≈) *bib* ‖ (Schürze) *pinafore* | ~hös|chen [n] ⟨tail⟩ *bib slacks* ‖ ~hose [f] ⟨tail⟩ *bib and brace overall*

l·au a *lukewarm (water)*; *tepid (tea)* ‖ *warm (evening)*; *genial (wind)* ‖ ⟨fig⟩ *indifferent, half--hearted (devoutness, attempt), tepid (assent), l.w. (zeal, sympathy, friendship)* ‖ *casual (friend)* | **ein ≈er** *a half-and-halfer* **≈heit** f ~/ *tepidity* ‖ ⟨fig⟩ *half-heartedness* **~warm** a = lau

L·aub n ~(e)s/ (mst) *leaves* pl; *foliage, leafage* ‖ sich mit ~ bedecken (Baum) *to put on leaves*; ~ verlieren *to shed leaves* ‖ mit ~ bedeckt *frondose* **~baum** m *broadleaf* od *deciduous tree* **≈bekränzt** a *wreathed in foliage* **~dach** n *leafy roof* **~fall** m *fall (of the leaves)* **~frosch** m *tree-frog* **~gehänge** n *festoon* **~gewinde** n *garland* **~holz** n *leaf-wood, deciduous trees* pl **~hütte** f ⟨bib⟩ *tabernacle* | ~nfest [n] *Feast of (the) T.s* **≈reich** a *leafy* **~säge** f *fret-* od *scroll-saw* | ~arbeit [f] *fretwork* **~soffitte** f ⟨theat⟩ *foliage border* **~streu** f *litter of leaves* **≈tragend** a *leafy*; ⟨scient⟩ *frondiferous, frondescent* **~verzierungen** f pl ⟨arts⟩ *leaf-work* **~wald** m *hardwood forest*; *deciduous* od *leafy wood* **~werk** n *foliage* ‖ ⟨arch⟩ *leaf-work*; ⟨arts⟩ *scroll of tendrils* **L·aube** f ~/~n *arbour, bower* ‖ *summerhouse* ‖ ⟨arch⟩ *loggia, arcade*; ⟨theat⟩ = Loge ‖ ~n [pl] *arcade of shops* ‖ ⟨fig⟩ fertig ist die ~ *so that's that, that's finished anyway* **~ngang** m *covered walk, arcade*; *pergola* **~nkolonie** f *allotment, garden district* **~pieper** m ⟨hum⟩ = Schrebergärtner **~vogel** m ⟨orn⟩ *bower-bird* **l·aubig** a *leafy, leaved*

L·auch m ~(e)s/~e ⟨bot⟩ *leek* **~farbe** f *l.--colour* **≈grün** a *l.-green, prasine, porraceous*

L·auer f ~/ *lurking-place, ambush* ‖ sich auf die ~ legen *to lay an ambush (for a p)* ‖ auf der ~ s *or* liegen *to lie in ambush* od *in wait, to be on the lookout (for a p)* | ~stellung [f] ⟨mil⟩ *waiting position* **l·auern** vi [h] (auf [acc]) *to (be on the) lurk, to lie in wait (for), to watch (for)* ‖ ⟨fam⟩ (warten) *to wait (for a p, an opportunity)*; auf die Erbschaft ~ *to wait for dead men's shoes* ‖ **~d** *expectant (silence)*; (hinterhältig) *searching, cunning (look)*; *creeping (danger)*

L·auf m ~(e)s/≈e **1.** ⟨eig⟩ *run(ning)* ⟨a. sport & mach⟩; *spin* ‖ (Wett≈) *race*, ⟨sport a.⟩ *heat* ‖ ⟨astr⟩ *course, movement* ‖ (des Wassers) *current, drift* ‖ *course (of a river)* ‖ in vollem ~e *at full* od *top speed, in full career*; ⟨hors⟩ *at full gallop* ‖ ⟨crick⟩ *run*; 100 (u mehr) ≈e m *to reach three figures*; 6 Bälle ohne ≈e *maiden over* ‖ schiefer ~ (e–r Kugel) *bias* ‖ ⟨mach⟩ *running* ‖ ⟨fig a.⟩ *sweep (of civilisation)* **2.** (Bahn) *track* ⟨a. sport⟩; ⟨allg⟩ *path* ⟨a. fig⟩: *the p. of civilisation* ‖ ⟨astr a.⟩ *orbit* ‖ *circulation (of the blood)* ‖ ⟨mar⟩ *course*; s–n ~ richten nach *to shape one's course for* **3.** ⟨mus⟩ *run, cadence*; perlender Koloratur *roulade*; schneller ~ *hurry* **4.** ⟨hunt⟩ *(4 footed game & dog) foot, leg* **5.** (e–s Gewehrs etc) *barrel* ‖ gezogener, glatter ~ *twisted, smooth barrel* ‖ (e–r Kanone) *bore* ‖ Gewehr mit e–m ~ *single-barrelled gun* ‖ ⟨hunt⟩ vor den ~ k *to come within shooting range* **6.** ⟨übtr⟩ (Verlauf) im ~e der Zeit, des Jahres, des Gesprächs *in (the) course* od *process of time, of the year, of the conversation*; *with the passage of years*; *(was altered) over the years* ‖ im ~e e–s Jahrhunderts *in a century's time* ‖ im ~e v 2 Jahren seit .. *within two years of (her ascension)* **7.** **s-n ~ h** *or* **nehmen** *to go on its course*; *fate takes its c.*; *the charge will have to go forward* ‖ der Gerechtigkeit ihren ~ l *to let justice take its c.* ‖ den Dingen ihren ~ l *to let ths slide*; *let ths follow their own course* ‖ [dat] freien ~ l ⟨a. fig⟩ *to give (a horse, a p) rein*; *to give a loose (to one's passion)*; *to give vent (to a th)* ‖ s–n Gedanken freien ~ l *to give full play to one's thoughts*; den Dingen .. *to give full scope to ths*; s–n Gefühlen .. *(to allow o.s.) to give way to ..*; dem Schmerz .. *to let the pain ride* ‖ ⟨prov⟩ das ist der ~ der Welt *that's the way of the world, such is life* **~achse** f ⟨rail⟩ *dead axle* **~bahn** f ⟨sport⟩ *track* ‖ ⟨hors⟩ *course* ‖ ⟨tech⟩ (e–s Lagers) *race* | ⟨fig⟩ *career*; *walk of life*; e–e ~ einschlagen *to enter upon a career* **~band** n ⟨tech⟩ *conveyor* **~bank** f = ~stuhl **~brett** n ⟨mot⟩ *running-board* **~brücke** f ⟨mil⟩ *light bridge*; ⟨mar, arch⟩ *gangway* **~buchse** f ⟨tech⟩ *liner* **~bursche** m *office-, errand-boy, messenger-boy, roundsman*; ⟨hot⟩ *page(-boy)*; (Druckerei≈) *printer's devil* **~feuer** n ⟨for⟩ *surface fire*; ⟨mil⟩ *running-fire* ‖ *train of (gun-)powder* ‖ sich wie ein ~ verbreiten *to spread like wildfire* **~fläche** f ⟨mot, rail⟩ (of tyre, wheel, rail) *tread*; ~ erneuern ⟨mot⟩ *to recap* **~gang** m *walking way* ‖ ⟨arch⟩ *gallery* ‖ ⟨aero⟩ *walkway* ‖ *gallery* ⟨a. a-n⟩ **~gärtchen** n *playing pen* **~geschwindigkeit** f ⟨tech⟩ *operating* od *running speed* **~gewicht** n *sliding weight, rider* | ~swaage [f] *steelyard* **~graben** m ⟨mil⟩ *(communication) trench*; *approach, sap* **~huhn** n ⟨orn⟩ *rail* **~junge** m = ~bursche **~käfer** m *ground beetle* **~karte** f ⟨tech⟩ *process card* **~katze** f ⟨tech⟩ *travelling crab, trolley*; ⟨film⟩ *cat--walk* **~kleid** n *walking* od *street dress* **~kran** m *travelling crane* **~kunde** m ⟨com⟩ *chance customer* **~mantel** m *barrel-casing* **~masche** f (im Strumpf etc) *ladder*, ⟨Am⟩ *run* **~mündung** f *muzzle, mouth (of the cannon)* **~paß** m *dismissal*, ⟨fam⟩ *sack* ‖ jdm den ~ geben *to dismiss a p*; ⟨fam⟩ *to give a p marching orders* od *the sack*, ⟨Am sl⟩ *the gate* od *slip* ‖ sie gab ihm den ~ *she jilted him, gave him the mitten* od *push* **~planke** f ⟨mar⟩ *gang-board, -way* **~rad** n ⟨aero⟩ *landing-wheel, skid* **~rädchen** n *caster* **~richtung** f *machine direction* **~riemen** m ⟨mach⟩ *driving belt* **~rolle** f ⟨el⟩ *trolley*; ⟨theat⟩ *bobbin*, ⟨Am⟩ *spool* **~salve** f *salvo* **~schiene** f *rail* **~schrift** f ⟨el⟩ *light writing, travelling letter signs*; *speed advertising*; *running message display* **~schritt** m ⟨sport⟩ *double time*; *double(-quick) step*; im ~ *at the run, at the double* ‖ im ~, marsch-marsch! ⟨mil⟩ *double-quick, march!* **~sitz** m ⟨tech⟩ *running fit* **~sohle** f *outsole* **~spur** f *trail, wake, track (of a torpedo)* **~stall** m *pen* **~steg** m *light* od *foot bridge* ‖ ⟨aero⟩ *keel* **~stuhl** m, **~wagen** m (für Kinder) *baby-walker, go-cart* **~vogel** m *runner* **~weg** m ⟨arch⟩ *aisle* **~wettkämpfe** m pl *track events* **~werk** n *mechanism*; *running gear*; ⟨mot⟩ *rolling gear* **~zeit** f ⟨rec⟩ *playback time* ‖ ⟨theat⟩ *running time*; ⟨film⟩ *screen time*; *showing, performance* ‖ ⟨tech⟩ *running time*; *hours of operation* ‖ ⟨zoo⟩ *rut(-time)*; die ~ h *to be on heat* ‖ ⟨com⟩ *currency* ‖ ⟨contract⟩ *duration* | ~spektrograph [m] *velocitron* **~zettel** m *circular (letter)*; *tracer*; *transmittal slip, control tag*, ⟨bes mil⟩ *clearance chit* **l·aufen** **I.** vi/t [s] & **sich** .. v/refl [h] **1.** **(gehen** *to walk* ‖ wir sind ge~ (*not* gefahren) *we came here* od *went there on foot* || *you can walk one way, an hour, 5 kilometres* || ⟨fam⟩ er mußte immerzu ~ *he was constantly running to the W.C.* | (S) *engines run, wheels turn* **2.** (**Ggs gehen**) *to run* (⟨a. rail⟩ v Zügen) || schnell ~ *to run swiftly; to tear; to rush, career; to scamper* ([like] *playing child, frightened animal*) || (geradeaus, schnell u leicht ~) *to scud, skim along* || ⟨fam⟩ wie ein Wiesel *or* Besenbinder *or* ⟨hum⟩ geölter Blitz ~ .. *like mad, as quick as lightning* || um die Wette ~ *to race (for a wager)*; mit e–m .. *to race a p* || in gr Schritten *or* Flüchten ~ *to lope* || ⟨sport⟩ über kz Strecken ~ *to sprint* || ge~ k *to come at the* od *a run* || schneller ~ als *to outrun (a p)* | ⟨mar⟩ **10 Knoten** die Stunde ~ *to do* od *make 10 knots an hour* || ⟨mot⟩ *what will the car do to the gallon*? **Trab** ~ *to trot*; Galopp ~ *to gallop* || **s-s Weges** ~ *to go*, etc. *one's way* | (P) e–n **Gang** ~ *to go on an errand*; **Gefahr** ~ *to run into danger, to run a great risk*; → Schlittschuh, Ski, Spießruten; **Sturm** ~ *to storm, charge* **3.** (**auslaufen**) [abs] das Faß läuft *the barrel leaks* od *runs* || das Bier läuft (flott) *the beer is drawn quickly* **4. sich** ~ v/refl; sich außer Atem ~ *to run o.s. out of breath* || sich müde ~ *to tire o.s. with running* || sich [dat] die Schuhsohlen entzwei ~ *to wear out one's shoes*; sich die Füße wund ~ *to run one's feet sore* || sich [acc] zu Tode ~ *to kill o.s. with r.g* | v/imps **es läuft sich** hier schlecht *it is bad w.ing, r.g, skating here* **5.** [mit adv *or* prep] **auf** Bälle ~ *to run to balls* || ⟨mar⟩ auf Grund ~ *to run aground* || auf e–e Mine ~ *to hit a m.* || auf den Sand ~ (of a boat) *to shelve on to the sand*; auf den Strand ~ *to be stranded* || auf den Straßen (umher) ~ *to run the streets* || der Faden läuft auf die Spule *the thread is wound up on the spool* || das Schiff läuft **aus** (dem Hafen) *the ship leaves the harbour* || sie lief aus dem Dienst *she ran away from her service* || mit dem Kopf **gegen** die Wand ~ *to run one's head against the wall* ⟨a. fig⟩ || **hin und her** ~ *to run to and fro*; immer hin u her ~ *to be always r.g about* || **hinter** e–m her|~ *to run after a p* ⟨a. fig⟩ || e–m **in** die Arme ~ *to run* od *butt into a p* || es läuft ins Geld *it is expensive* || in den Hafen ~ *to run into harbour*; ins Verderben ~ *to rush into destruction*; jdm in die Arme ~, jdm in den Weg ~ *to come* od *run across a p*; ins Zimmer *into the room* || die Feder (das Seil) läuft **über** das Papier (die Rolle) .. *runs over* .. || er lief Hals über Kopf davon *he rushed headlong away* || **um** die Sonne ~ *to revolve* od *move round the sun* || ums Haus ~ *to run round the h.* || um die Wette ~ → I. 2. || der Faden läuft **von** der Spule .. *runs from* || das Schiff lief vom Stapel .. *was launched* || **vor** e–m (davon)|~ *to flee from a p* **II.** [**nur vi**] **1.** (**rinnen, fließen, aus**|~) *to trickle down; to flow, leak* || *the blood circulates* (in *or* durch *in*) || *the tap drips* || *the barrel runs* od *leaks* || *the candle gutters* || *the el. current flows* || Tränen liefen ihr über die Wangen *tears trickled* od *rolled down her cheeks* || mir läuft die Nase *my nose is r.g* || er arbeitete, daß ihm der Schweiß lief .. *that he was sweating* | ⟨fig⟩ es lief mir eiskalt (*or* ein Schauer) über den Rükken *I felt a shudder all over me*, es lief mir dabei .. *it gave me the creeps, it made my flesh creep* || ein Gemurmel lief durch die Reihen *muttered words passed down the ranks* || ein Zittern lief durch ihren Körper *she trembled in every limb* || ⟨com⟩ die Schatzanweisungen ~ über M 100.– etc *the bonds are denominations of M 100.–*, etc **2.** (**verlaufen, enden**) *to run, extend; end* || das Gebirge läuft v Norden nach Süden *the range of hills runs from n. to s.* || der Weg läuft durch Kornfelder .. *runs through* .. || zus|~ *to come together, to run into one* .. || parallel ~ mit *to run parallel with* || es läuft ziemlich auf (ein u) dasselbe hinaus *it comes to much the same th* || es läuft das Gerücht, daß .. *there is a rumour about* od *afloat that* **3.** (**zeitlich**) wie lange läuft der Vertrag, Wechsel? *how long has the contract, draft still to run?, when does the draft fall due?* || (**vergehen**) *time goes by, passes, elapses* || ([aus]~) *the matter may turn out any way* (so oder so) || (im Gange s) die Sache läuft *the matter takes its course* || ⟨theat⟩ das Stück läuft schon 8 Wochen *the play has had a run of 8 weeks* **4.** ~ **lassen**: laß ihn ~ (entwischen)! *let him go*! (s–r Wege gehn) *let him off* od *rip; turn him off, give him the sack*! || laß die Dinge ~ *let ths slide* od *rip* || (Segel) ~ l *to dowse* || Wasser ~ l *to run water* || sein Pferd ~ l a) *to urge one's horse* b) *to let it go as it likes* c) *to enter it for a race* || (Schiff) v Stapel ~ l *to launch*, auf den Strand ~ l *to strand* **III.** ~ n ~s/ → Lauf *course, rush; running scampering*; schweres ~ ⟨mot⟩ *labouring* || zum ~ bringen *to set going* **l·aufend** a *running (interest)* || *current (account, price, expenses* [pl], *number)* || ~e Arbeiten *routine work; what jobs there are* || ⟨ins⟩ *open, floating (policy)*; *(insurance) in force* || ~e Nummern [pl] *consecutive numbers; serial (numbering)*; ⟨comp⟩ Karte mit ~er N. *serial numbered card* || *regular (payments)* || 25 ~e Meter *25 metres in length* || es kostet 40 Pf. der ~e Meter .. *a metre, per metre run* || ⟨com⟩ ~en Monats *instant* (mst abbr *inst.*) || das ~e Jahr *the present* od *current year* || *day-to-day (matters)*; *routine* (Wartung); ~e Geschäfte *daily* od *pending business* || *standing (patrols)* || ⟨tech⟩ *serial* || ~es Band *conveyor, endless* od *moving band*; °am ~en B. = ununterbrochen; am ~en B. arbeiten *to work on the continuous transfer system, .. on the tape* || ~es Gefecht ⟨mar⟩ *running fight* || ~er Wechsel ⟨com⟩ *running bill* || etw ~ ergänzen *to keep up-to-date (by running addenda)* || jdn **auf** dem ~en halten (über ..) ⟨fig⟩ *to keep a p posted* od *informed (of current events)* || **auf** dem ~en bleiben über *to keep in touch with, to be well up, to keep posted* (mit *in*); auf dem ~en s ⟨fam⟩ *to be in the swim* | adv ~ numerieren *to number serially* **-läufer** m (Wagner~) *W. addict* od *fan* **L·äufer** m ~s/~ *runner*, ⟨sport a.⟩ *cinder-man*; ⟨orn⟩ → *sandpiper* || (Diener) *(running-) footman*; ⟨mar⟩ *messenger*, ⟨fam⟩ *peggy*; ⟨mil⟩ *orderly* || ⟨ftb⟩ *half-back* [pl *h.b.s*, ⟨fam⟩ *halves*], Mittel~ *centre half-back* || sie ist eine gute ~in *she is a good runner* od *walker* | ⟨chess⟩ *bishop* || ⟨mus⟩ *run, running passages* pl || ⟨arch⟩ (Stein) *stretcher, runner* || ⟨mech⟩ *slider* || ⟨el⟩ *armature, rotor*; ⟨turbo⟩ *driven torus; compressor* || (Mühlstein) *runner*; ⟨mill⟩ *muller* || ⟨spin⟩ *traveller* || (Farbenreiber) *muller*, ⟨typ⟩ *brayer* || ⟨hort⟩ *runner, tendril* || (Teppich) *strip of carpeting, (carpet-)runner* || (Treppen~) *stair-carpet* || (Tisch~) *(table-)runner* **~gewicht** n *sliding weight* **~mühle** f *vertical mill* **~schicht** f ⟨arch⟩ *course of stretchers* **~schwein** n *shoat* **~stange** f (Treppen~) *stair-* od *carpet-rod* **~verband** m ⟨arch⟩ *longitudinal laying of bricks* **Laufer·ei** f ~/~en *running about* || viel ~ verursachen *to cause a lot of trouble*; jdm .. *to keep a p on the move* **l·äufig, l·äufisch** a (T) ⟨allg⟩ *hot*, ⟨hunt⟩ *ruttish*, (Hündin) *on heat*

L·auge f ~/~n *lye, buck* || *alkaline* od *caustic solution* || schwache, starke ~ *weak, strong wash* || ⟨fig⟩ ~ des Spottes *biting sarcasm* **l·augen** vt [h] *to buck, to soak in lye, to lye; to lixiviate* **~artig** a *alkaline* **~asche** f *alk. ashes* pl **~brezel** f *pretzel* **~bütte** f *lye-vat* **~verätzung** f *lye burn* **~wasser** n *lye* **Lauger·ei** f ~/~en ⟨tech⟩ *leaching plant*

L·auheit, L·auigkeit f ~/ *tepidity, luke-warmness* || ⟨fig⟩ *half-heartedness, indifference*

L·aune f ~/~n *humour, temper* || *(bad) t.*; *(gloomy) h.*; *(merry) mood*; heitere ~ *high spirits* pl; rosige ~ *a cheerful t.*; schlechte ~ *ill-h.*, ⟨fam⟩ *tantrums* pl; schlechter ~ ⟨fam⟩ *liverish*; üble ~ *peeve* || in ~ s für *to be in the h.r for* || *changeableness (of the weather)* || *uncertainty (of luck)* | (Einfall, Grille) *freak, whim, caprice, fancy*

|| *the vagaries* od *hazards* (*of the weather*) | sie hat ihre ~ *she is cross* || sie hat ihre ~n *she is very whimsical* || wie es ihre ~ ergab *as her whim was* || je nach ihrer ~ .. (*administered or not*) *at her caprice* || übler ~ *ruffled* || übler ~ s ⟨sl⟩ *to have the hump* || die ~ verlieren *to be put out of h.r* || °das gibt/schafft ~ *that gives* (od *will give*) *us fun* || jdn bei guter ~ erhalten *to h.r a p, to keep a p in good spirits* || nicht bei ~ s *to be out of h.r, to be the wrong side out* || bei guter ~ s *to be in good spirits*, od ⟨fam⟩ *in high feather* || sich bei (guter) ~ erhalten *to keep one's spirits up* || besonders guter ~ s *to be in high* od *quite special spirits* || wenn ihn die ~ anwandelt *when the fit takes him, if he feels like it* **l·aunenhaft** a *capricious, whimsical, erratic, fitful, fancyful* || *fickle* (*fellow*) || *uncertain*; *changeable* (*weather*) | ≃**igkeit** f *c.ness, wh.ity* **l·aunig** a (nur positiv wertend, → fol) *humorous* || *droll, comical* || *entertaining* | ≃**keit** *h.ness* || *d.ness*, etc. **l·aunisch** a ⟨nur derog⟩ **1.** *out of humour, peevish, sulky, cross, ill-h.ed* **2.** *capricious, whimsical, splenetic* || ein ~er Mensch *a man of moods*; (ungleichmäßig) *fitful, spasmodic* || ~ wie der April *as changeable as the weather*; *wayward* (*fortune*)

L·aurer m ~s/~ *spy, lurker*, → lauern

L·aus f ~/≃e *louse* [pl *lice*]; ⟨fam⟩ *crawler* || mit Läusen behaftet *lousy* | ⟨fig⟩ ihm ist e–e ~ über die Leber gekrochen *he is ruffled* || e–m ≃e in den Pelz setzen *to cause a p vexation* °**~bub(e)** m *saucy stripling, bumptious fellow*; *young scamp*; ⟨hum⟩ *rogue, rascal* | ~nstreich [m] *prank*, ⟨bes Am⟩ *shenanigan*

Laus·anne [lo'zan] n ⟨Swiss⟩ (Stadt)

L·ausch- ~dienst m ⟨telph⟩ *wire intercept service* **~zange** f *w.-tapping clamp* **L·ausche** f ~/~n; auf der ~ s *to be watching, listening, eavesdropping*; *lurking* **l·auschen** vi [h] *to listen, eavesdrop* || niemand kann ~ *nobody can overhear* || e–m gespannt ~ *to hang on a p's lips* || ~d warten auf *to listen for*; (lauern) *to lie in wait for* **L·auscher** m ~s/~ **1.** *listener, eavesdropper* || ⟨prov⟩ der ~ an der Wand hört s–e eigne Schand' *listeners seldom hear good of themselves* **2.** ⟨hunt⟩ (v Wild) *ear* **l·auschig** a *snug, cosy* (*corner*) || *peaceful and pleasant* (*place*) || *secret* od *hidden* (*path*)

L·ause- °**~geld** n ⟨vulg⟩ *beggarly sum, pittance* °**~junge,** °**~kerl** m ⟨fig⟩ *blackguard, lout*; ⟨hum⟩ *rascal, rogue* (→ Lausbub) **~kamm** m *small-tooth comb*, ⟨fam⟩ *louse-trap* °**~nest** n ⟨fig⟩ *dirty hole* **~pulver** n, **~salbe** f *powder, ointment against lice* **l·ausen** vt [h] *to louse* || ⟨vulg⟩ *to fleece* (*a p*) || °ich dachte mich laust der Affe *I was staggered*, ⟨fam⟩ *flabbergasted* od *thunderstruck, I thought I had grown mad* **Lauser·ei** f ~/~en ⟨vulg⟩ *stinginess* || (Kleinigkeit) *trifle, flea-bite* **l·ausig** a *lousy* ⟨a. °fig⟩ | °⟨fig⟩ *rotten*, ⟨Am sl⟩ *bum* || *stingy* (*p*) || *paltry* (*sum*) | adv *beastly* (*cold*); ⟨fam sl⟩ *precious* (*dear*) || *bloody* (*boring*) || ⟨fam⟩ er hat eine ~ lange Leitung, ⟨hum⟩ bei ihm L hoch drei (l^3) (→ lang I. 1. ⟨fig⟩) *he is beastly slow-witted*; ~ l. L.! *slowcoach*!

L·ausitz f *Lusatia* || **~er** m & a *Lusatian*

L·aut m ~(e)s/~e *sound*, ⟨mus⟩ *tone* || e–n (k–n) ~ v sich geben *to utter a sound* (*not to breathe* [*a word*]) || k–n ~ mehr! *not another word*! || ⟨hunt⟩ ~ geben *to give tongue, to bark* **l·aut 1.** a *loud* || (lärmend) *clamorous, noisy* (*street*), *boisterous* (*fellow*), *loud-voiced* (*husbands*), *rampageous* (*play*) || (tönend) *resonant, sonorous* (*voice*), *vocal* (*stillness*) || widerlich ~ *blatant* || durch ~e Stimme gekennzeichnet *or* auffallend *loud-voiced* || ~es Durch–e–a–reden *splutter* | (hörbar) *audible* || (deutlich) *distinct, clear* (*voice*) || (öffentlich) *public, before everybody* | ⟨fig⟩ *strident* (Kritik); (grell) *showy, crude*; *large*; ~ w *to become audible, to grow loud*; ⟨fig⟩ *to become public*; *it was noised abroad that*; ~ w l *to betray, express* (*feelings*); *to divulge*; in ~e Meinungsverschiedenheiten geraten über *to have high words upon* **2. adv** *loudly*, ⟨mst⟩ *aloud* || ⟨mus⟩ *forte*, sehr ~ *fortissimo* It || (*to call, yearn, talk, complain*) *loudly*; (*he said*) *aloud* od *clearly*; ~ antworten *to answer up*; etw ~ heraussagen *to say a th out loud*; ~ auflachen *to laugh outright*; ~ rufen *to bay out*; er schrie so ~ (wie) er nur konnte *he was yelling his loudest* od *at the top of his voice*; ~ bemerken *or* v sich geben *to boom*; ~ z·ufallen *to bang shut* | **~er** sprechen *to speak up, to elevate the voice*; sprich ~er! *or* ~er sprechen! *speak up*!, ⟨Am⟩ *louder*! **3. prep** [mit gen & dat: ~ Bericht] *according to, in pursuance of* (*the law*); ~ des Vertrages *under the treaty*; ~ (kraft) des Befehls *by order* || ⟨com⟩ *as per* (*receipt*, etc.) || ~ Bericht, Vorschrift *in conformity with the report, regulations* || ~ Vollmacht *by virtue of power of attorney*

L·aut- ~angleichung f ⟨phon & gram⟩ *assimilation* (*of sounds*) **~bezeichnung** f *soundnotation* **~-bildung** f *phonation* **~gesetz** n *phonetic law* **~lehre** f *phonetics* pl || *phonology* ≃**malend** a *onomatopoe*(*t*)*ic* **~malerei** f *onomatopoeia* ≃**nachahmend** a *imitative* (→ vor) **~schrift** f *phonetic spelling* od *writing* **~schwund** m *fading* **~sprechanlage** f *public address system* **~sprecher** m ⟨wir⟩ *loud speaker*; *megaphone*, ⟨fam⟩ *meg*(*ger*), (tief) *woofer*, (hell) *tweeter* || ⟨rec⟩ *speaker* || am ~ sitzen *to be tuned in*; durch ~ übertragen *to relay* | ~wagen [m] *l.-sp. van*, ⟨bes Am⟩ *sound truck* **~stärke** f ⟨ac⟩ *loudness level*; (objektiv) *volume* (~regler *-regulator*); ⟨allg⟩ *audibility*; *intensity of sound* | ~regelung [f] ⟨wir⟩ *volume control*; ~schwankungen [f pl] *fluctuations* pl *of sound* **~system** n *phonetic system* **~tafel** f *sound-chart* **~verschiebung** f *consonant-shift*(*ing*), *Grimm's law* **~verstärker** m (*sound-*)*intensifier* od *amplifier* **~zeichen** n *phonetic symbol* || ⟨wir⟩ *station signal*; ~ synchronisieren ⟨aero⟩ *to pip in* **l·autbar** a *known, public, notorious* || es ist ~ geworden *it has got abroad*

L·äutewerk n → dort **L·aute** f ~/~n [urspr *Arab*] *lute*; Lieder zur ~ *songs accompanied by the l.* || die ~ spielen *or* schlagen *to play the l.* || etw auf der ~ spielen .. *on the l.* | ~nmacher [m] *l.-maker*; ~nschläger, ~spieler [m] *l.-player* **l·auten** vi [h] *to sound*, ⟨a. fig⟩: *that sounds plausible, strange* || (des Inhalts s) *to run, read*: wie lautet ..? *how does the passage read*? *what does the letter say*? *what were his words*?; es –tet so *it runs thus, what are the words of the first commandment*? || ⟨jur⟩ das Urteil –tet auf Tod *the sentence is death* || es –tet günstig *it is favourable* || auf den Inhaber ~d *not transferable* (*bonds*), ⟨com⟩ *payable to bearer* **L·äuten** n ~s/ *peal, knell* || (langsam gleichmäßig) *toll* || beim ~ der Glocken *to the pealing of the bells* od *toll of the bell* **l·äuten** vi/t [h] *to ring* (*the bells*), *to peal* || es –tet *I hear a bell, the bell is ringing* || Sie h ge–tet? *You rang*? || es –tet *there's the bell*; es hat ge–tet *the bell has gone* || es –tet Angelus *it is ringing for the angelus* | die Glocken ~ *the bells are ringing* || mit allen Glocken ~ *to set all the bells going* || es –tet zum zweitenmal (zur Kirche) *the second bells are ringing* | man –tete ihn zu Grabe *his death-knell was* (*being*) *tolled* | ⟨telph⟩ *to trill, jangle*: *the telephone bell rang*

l·auter a **1.** *clear, pure*; *unalloyed, unmixed* || (echt) *genuine* (*intentions*) || *sterling* od *pure* (*gold*) || (ehrlich) *true, candid*; *sincere*; *single-hearted, -minded* || aus ~er Quelle ⟨fig⟩ *from a reliable quarter* || ~e Gesinnung *flawless character* || die ~e Wahrheit *the very, unvarnished, plain*, ⟨fam⟩ *blessed truth* **2.** [inv] (nichts als) *mere*; *nothing but* || ~ Lügen *a pack of lies* || *stark* (*nonsense*) || *so many* (*rascals*) || *so much* (*waste of time*) || aus ~ Neid *out of sheer envy* || sie besteht aus ~ Widersprüchen *she is all inconsistency* || es gibt nicht ~ Engel wie du *the world is not all made up of angels* *like you* || du siehst den Wald vor ∼ Bäumen nicht *you cannot see the wood for trees* **L·äuter-∼bottich** [m] ⟨brew⟩ *lauter tub*; ∼vorrichtung [f] *straining apparatus* **L·äuterer** m ∼s/∼ *cleanser, purifier* || *refiner* **L·auterkeit** f ∼/ *clearness, pureness* || *purity* (*of character*); *integrity* || *single--mindedness, sincerity, candour* **l·äutern** vt [h] (Branntwein) *to clear* || (aufbereiten) *to clear* || (Glas, Metalle, Zucker) *to refine* || (Flüssigkeiten) *to clarify, purify* (⟨a fig⟩ *from sin*); (destillieren) ⟨chem⟩ *rectify* || ⟨tech⟩ *to cleanse, purge* || ⟨fig⟩ (Menschen) *to chasten, ennoble* **L·äuterung** f ∼/∼en *clearing, refining, clarification* || *purification, refinement* || *rectification* || (*the*) *purging* (*of the soul*) | ∼sbecken [n] *clarifying tank*; ∼skessel [m] (Salpeter) *refining boiler*; (Schwefel) *melting pot*; ⟨allg⟩ *clarifier*

L·äutewerk n ∼s/∼e *ringing-apparatus* || ⟨rail⟩ halt, wenn das ∼ ertönt! *stop when the bell is ringing* **L·autheit** f ∼/ (→ laut) *loudness, distinctness* **laut·ieren** vi/t [h] *to read phonetically* **Laut·iermethode** f *phonetic method* **l·autlich** a & adv *of sound* || *phonetic* **l·autlos** a *silent, mute* || *hushed, breathless, deep* (*silence*)

L·autung f ∼/∼en *articulation*

L·ava f ∼/-ven *lava*; ⟨tech⟩ *volcanic dust* | ∼glas [n] ⟨min⟩ *obsidian*; ∼schlacke [f] *l. slag*; ∼strom [m] *stream of l.*

Lav·abel m ∼s/∼ *washable fabric* || *washable* [s]

Lav·endel m ∼s/ ⟨bot⟩ *lavender* | ∼blüte [f] *l.-flowers* pl; ∼gras [n] *sweet vernal grass*; ∼-kopie [f] ⟨film⟩ *l.*; ∼öl [n] *spike oil*; ∼parfüm, ∼wasser [n] *l.-water*

lav·ieren 1. vi [h & s] ⟨mar⟩ *to veer, tack* (*about*) || ⟨fig⟩ *to shift, to steer a middle course* || gegen den Wind ∼ *to ply* || ∼ nach *to be on* (*the port tack*) **2.** ⟨paint⟩ *to wash* | L–rung [f] *wash*

Law·ine f ∼/∼n *avalanche* || e–e ∼ geht nieder *or* zu Tal .. *falls* | ∼nsturz [m] *snow-slip*

l·ax a *lax, loose* || (Moral) *easy* || (Sitten) *licentious* | **≗heit** f ∼/∼en *laxity, laxness*

lax·ieren vi [h] *to take an aperient* || ∼ vt *to purge* || **∼d** *aperient, laxative* **Lax·iermittel** n ⟨med⟩ *laxative, purge*

Lazar·ett n ∼(e)s/∼e *infirmary,* (*military*) *hospital* || → Feld≗ *casualty clearing station* **∼behandlung** f *h. treatment* **∼einweisung** f *h.ization* **∼fieber** n *h.-fever* **∼gehilfe** m *dresser* **∼kleidung** f *h. blue* **∼raum** m ⟨mar⟩ *cockpit* **∼schiff** n *h.-ship* **∼zug** m ⟨rail⟩ *h.-train, ambulance train*

†**Lazed·amon** n *Lacedæmon, Laconia* †**Lazedäm·onier** m, **∼in** f, **lazedäm·onisch** a *Lacedæmonian, Laconian*

L·eb- ∼kuchen m *ginger-bread*; dazu: *g.-b. baker*; → Laib

l·eb- ∼los a *lifeless, inanimate*; *inert*; *limp*; *dull, flat* **≗losigkeit** f *lifelessness* || ⟨fig⟩ *impassiveness, coldness* || ⟨com⟩ *stagnation, dullness* **≗t·age** m pl *days* pl *of life* || m–e ∼ (*in*) *all my life*; mein ∼ nicht *never* (*before*) **≗zeiten** f pl; bei s–n ∼ *in* od *during his lifetime* **L·ebe- ∼dame** f *society lady* **∼h·och** n *cheer*(*ing*) || ∼! *cheers*!; ein ∼ auf e–n ausbringen *to give three cheers for a p* **∼lang** n; mein ∼ *all my life*; *during my life time* **∼mann** m *man about town, man of the world*; *worldling*; ⟨a.⟩ *free-liver*; *bon-vivant* Fr || ⟨dero⟩ *rake* || ⟨sl⟩ *buck, dandy, swell, masher* || flotter ∼ ⟨Am⟩ *high-roller*; alter ∼ ⟨Am⟩ *sugar daddy* **∼welt** f *fashionable world, society people* pl **∼wesen** n *animal*; *living creature*; pl ⟨a.⟩ *living organisms*; kleinste ∼ [pl] ⟨scient⟩ *animalcules* pl **∼wohl** n *farewell, adieu*; ∼ sagen *to bid farewell*

L·eben n ∼s/∼ **1. Bedeutungen:** *life* || (Bestehen) *existence* || (Welt) *things* (*in general*) || (∼[sführung]) *living* (*wisdom about living*) || (Einzelleben) *life*; *years* (*the story of all his years*; (*he had told more lies in*) *his time* || (Lebewesen) *living creature*; (*many a*) *young life* (*was ended*) || (Fleisch) *quick* (*he cut h.s. to the quick*) || (Leben[sbeschreibung]) *biography, life* || (Wirklichkeit) *reality, existence* || (Treiben) *animation, movement*; *commotion,* ⟨fam⟩ *to-do*; *stir, bustle* (*on the stage*) || (Munterkeit) *liveliness, cheerfulness, animation*; voll(er) ∼ *all alive*; es ist kein ∼ in ihm *there is no life* od ⟨fam⟩ *go in him*; plötzlich war ∼ in ihn gek *he had suddenly come to l.*; (∼[skraft]) *vitality, vital power*; *mettle, ardour, vigour*; *high* od *great spirits* pl || (∼[sweise] *manner of*) *life*; (*to lead a simple life*) **2.** den **Ernst** des ∼s kennen lernen *to feel the seriousness of l.*, das ∼ ernst nehmen *to be serious about l.* || Morgen usw des ∼s, Frühling usw des ∼s *spring* etc. *of life* || noch leuchtet mir die Sonne m–s ∼s *the sunshine of my life is still about me* || es ist kein Funken *or* Hauch v ∼ mehr in ihm *he does not show the slightest sign of life any more* | **bürgerliches** ∼ *l. in the middle classes*; elendes ∼ *sorry l.*; geistiges ∼ *intellectual l.*; ein Ausdruck des gemeinen ∼s *an every-day expr.*; geregeltes ∼ *disciplined l.*; geselliges ∼ *social l.*; gesellschaftliches ∼ *l. in the world of society*; das **irdische** ∼ *l. on earth*; kaufmännisches ∼ *business l.*; das künftige ∼ *future* od *heavenly l., l. to come, afterlife*; liederliches ∼ *loose-living*; das praktische *or* wirkliche ∼ *the realities of l.*; das Soldaten≗ *military l.*; sorgenvolles ∼ *l. full of cares and auxieties*; zurückgezogenes ∼ *l. of retirement* || die (aller)größte Überraschung ihres ∼s *the surprise of her life* ([pl] *of their lives*) **3. am** ∼ bleiben *to remain alive, to escape, survive* || der einzige, der am ∼ blieb *the only survivor*; nur noch mit e–m Faden am ∼ hängen *to hang on to mortality by a thread* || e–n am ∼ l *to spare a p's l.* || noch am ∼ s *to be spared,* ⟨sl⟩ *to be alive and kicking* || es ging ihm ans ∼ *his l. was in peril* || am ∼ strafen *to punish with death* || ein Kampf **auf** Tod u ∼ *a life-and-death struggle, a fight to the death, a mortal combat*; e–n K. auf T. u ∼ führen mit *to fight for l. or death with* || auf ∼ u Tod *come life, come death* || **aus** dem ∼ gehen *or* scheiden *to depart this l.* || aus dem ∼ gegriffen *taken from actual l.* || **bei** Leib u ∼ *under penalty of death* || **durch** → hindurch || gut durchs ∼ k *to get on very well* || sich allein durchs ∼ schlagen *to fend for o.s.* || ich möchte **für** mein ∼ gern *I would give anything to .., I like it above all ths ..*; er spielt Kricket f. s. ∼ gern *he is passionately fond of c.,* ⟨sl⟩ *he is hot on c.* || ein Bund fürs ∼ *a life-long union*; ich darf es f. mein ∼ nicht sagen *I dare not for the l. of me say it* || sein ganzes ∼ **hindurch** *all his days* od *l., the whole of his l.* || **im** gemeinen ∼ *ordinarily*; im öffentlichen ∼ stehen *to stand in public l.*; so geht es immer im ∼ *that's the way of the world*; nie im ∼! *not on your l.*!; lachen wie nie im ∼ *to get the laugh of one's l.*; mitten im ∼ (*or* im Strudel des ∼s) stehen *to be at the hub of ths* || **in** diesem u jenem ∼ *in this l. and in the l. to come* || das erste Mal im ∼ *for the first time in my l.* || e–n **ins** ∼ einführen *to introduce a p to l.* || ins ∼ eintreten *to make one's appearance in l.* || ins ∼ rufen *to bring forth*; *to generate, produce, evoke, spawn*; *to call into being, to originate, to set on foot*; *to bring into existence, to start*; *to organize, conceive* (*institution*); ⟨com⟩ *to float*; (neue Zeit) *to inaugurate*; (Zeitung) *to launch*; → schaffen || ins ∼ schneiden *to cut to the quick* || ins ∼ treten *to come into existence* od *being* || ein ∼ **lang** *for a l.-time*; ihr ∼ lang *her l. long* || **mit** dem [nackten] ∼ davonk *to escape* (*with one's* [*bare*] *l.*) || mit Leib u ∼ *with body and soul* || er bezahlte es mit s–m ∼ *he sacrificed his l. for it* || e–m **nach** dem ∼ trachten *to seek* od *attempt a p's l., to compass a p's death* || nach dem ∼ zeichnen *to draw to the l., to draw from nature* od *l.*; dem ∼ abgelauscht *taken from l.* || **um** ∼s u Sterbens willen *to make quite sure* || um sein ∼ bitten *to pray for one's l.* ||

sie fürchten um ihr ~ *they are frightened of their skins* || **ums** ~ *for dear l.* (laufen) || e–n ums ~ bringen *to put a p to death, to kill* od *murder a p*; sich .. *to commit suicide* || ums ~ k *to perish, to lose one's l., to be killed* || **zeit** m–s ~s *all my l.-time* || genug **zum** ~ verdienen *to get a sufficient living* || zu neuem ~ erwecken *to galvanize (a business) into new l.* **4.** ein anders, neues ~ **anfangen** *to turn over a new leaf* || sein ~ **aushauchen** *to breathe one's last* || er **brachte** neues ~ in die S *he infused new l. into the affair* || e–r S wieder ~ **einflößen** *to bring a th back to l.* || sein ~ einsetzen *to stake one's l.* || das ~ erlischt *l. passes by* || das ~ **fließt** schnell dahin *time flies* || sich des ~s freuen *to take pleasure in l., to enjoy one's l.* || ein unruhiges ~ führen *to lead* od *live a troubled l.* || ein (zu) flottes ~ führen ⟨sl⟩ *to go the pace (too hard)* || sie **gab** *or* schenkte e–m Knaben das ~ *she gave birth to a boy* || e–r S ~ geben *to blow a th to l.* || sie h ihr ~ gegeben *or* gelassen *they have laid down* od *given their lives* || .. gibt s–m ~ Inhalt .. *gives him sth to live for* || sein ~ geht zu Ende *his sands are running out* || das ~ genießen *to enjoy l.*; er hatte das ~ nicht wenig genossen *he had sown no few wild oats* || der ganze Platz gewann ~ .. *came to life* || das Gemälde **hat** ~ .. *is endowed with l.* || sein ~ für e–n hingeben *to sacrifice one's l. for a p* || °da **kam** ~ in die Bude *ths became lively* || sein ~ **l** (für e–e S: → .. hingeben) → .. aushauchen || sich das ~ leicht **m** *to lead an easy l.* || e–m das ~ sauer m *to make it hot for a p* || jdm das ~ z Qual m *to lead a p a dog's l.* || e–m (sich) das ~ **nehmen** *or* rauben *to take a p's (one's own) l.; to kill a p (o.s.); to make away with a p (o.s.)* || er **schenkte** ihm das ~ *he spared his l.* (→ sie gab ..) || sein ~ aufs Spiel setzen *to risk one's l.* || sein ~ in die Schanze schlagen *to fling away one's l.* || ≗**spendend** a *l.-giving* ≗**sprudelnd** a *full of vitality* ⟨fam⟩ *of beans* || sein ~ teuer **verkaufen** *to sell one's l. dearly* || die Tage s–s ~s sind gezählt *his days are numbered* **l·eben I.** vi [h] **1.** ⟨**eig**⟩ *to live, to be alive, to have life* || lebt er noch? *is he still alive?* || das Kind hatte gelebt *the child came living into the world* || so wahr ich lebe! *(as sure) as I'm alive! as I live!* || er wird nicht lange ~ *his days are numbered* || solange N. lebt, kann .. *in N.'s life-time there can ..* || sie kennen ihn schon solange sie leben *they've known him all their lives* || er lebt eben noch *he's just alive* || ich kann nicht ewig ~ *I can't last for ever* || ~ **bleiben** *to stay alive* || wenn ich ~ bleibe *if I am spared* || °(wie geht's?) man lebt! *so-so, just fair; we do see life* || in der Wirklichkeit ~ *to be concerned with reality* || er lebt nur der (*or* f die) Wissenschaft *he lives a life wholly devoted to researchwork* od *science* || noch einmal ~ *to have one's time over again* **2.** (**existieren**) *to exist* || so wahr Gott lebt *by the living God! as sure as there's a God in heaven* || *Christ lives in us* || in mir lebt die Hoffnung *I live in hopes (of* od *that)* **3.** (**sich nähren**) *to live, feed, subsist* (v *on*) (v e–m Beruf *by*) || *to live (on one's income)* || (schmarotzend) *to pray upon* || zu ~ h *to have a competency, to have enough to live on* || davon kann ich kaum ~ *I can barely exist on that* || wovon lebt er eigentlich? *how does he manage to live?* || sie ~ gut ⟨vulg⟩ bon [bɔŋ] *the live well* || kümmerlich ~ *to lead a precarious existence, to live miserably* || üppig ~ *to live high* || er lebt v s–r Hände Arbeit *he lives by the sweat of his brow,* .. v der Hand in den Mund .. *from hand to mouth,* von der Luft *on air,* v Spiele *by gambling* **4.** (**wohnen**) er lebt in Berlin *he lives* od *resides in B.,* in Marburg *at M.* || im Auslande ~ *to stay* od *reside abroad* || wie lange ~ Sie schon in England? *how long have you been living ..?* **5.** (**sich führen**) er weiß zu ~ *he is well-bred, he has good manners; he knows how to make life easy* || gesellig, zurückgezogen ~ *to live sociably, to live a retired life* || auf gr Fuße, flott, in Saus u Braus ~ *to lead a gay life, to live in a grand style, in a whirl of pleasure* || wie Gott in Frankreich, wie im Himmel, herrlich u in Freuden ~ *to lead a heavenly life* || in den Tag hinein ~ *to live without a thought for the morrow* || wie Hund u Katze ~ *to lead a cat's and dog's life* || sie ~ mit–e–a auf gespanntem Fuße *their relations are somewhat strained* || lebe **wohl**! *farewell! good-bye!* || mit ihm ist gut ~ (ausk) *he is a good fellow to live with* || **nach** e–m Grundsatz ~ *to live up to a principle* || nach demselben Vorbild ~ *to follow the same pattern* || **in** dürftigen Verhältnissen ~ *to live in a small way* || **in** der Vergangenheit ~ *to live in the past,* in s–r Kunst ~ .. *in one's art* || bescheidener ~ *to draw in one's horns* || für sich ~ *to live to o.s.* || die Pferde ~ dort **wild** .. *run wild there* **6. für etw** ~, e–r S [dat] ~: *he lives solely for his health, his ideas; she only lives for her children* **7.** (**fortdauern**) sein Gedächtnis lebt in unsern Herzen weiter .. *is still fresh in our hearts* || sein Name lebt .. *still lives* || er lebt in s–m Sohne weiter *he lives again in ..* || Sprichwörter, die in aller Munde ~ *proverbs which everybody knows* || es lebt weiter *it perpetuates itself* || ⟨fig⟩ (of words) *to be in living use* **8.** (**lebendig wirken**) es lebt alles an ihm *he is all life* od *very much alive* || die Statue lebt förmlich .. *seems actually alive* od *to breathe* **9. e-n hoch ~ l** *to cheer a p*; (bei Tisch) *to drink a p's health* || es leben die Damen *I give you the ladies!* || es ~ die Frauen! *here's to the women* || es lebe die Freiheit! *hurra for freedom!* || N. lebe hoch! *three cheers for N.,* (offizieller) *here is to the health of N.!* || es lebe der König! *long live the k.!,* ~ Sie **wohl**! → I. 5.; ⟨fam⟩ *be good!,* ⟨Am⟩ *take care of y.s.!* **10. Wendungen**: in ihm ~, weben u sind wir *in him we live and move and have our being* || was auf Erden lebt u webt *all that is alive and astir on this earth* || man lebt nur einmal in der Welt *Christmas comes but once a year* || ⟨prov⟩ solange man lebt, solange man lernt *we live and learn* || das ist er, wie er leibt u lebt *it is his very self* || er ist sein Vater, wie er leibt u lebt *he is the very image* (⟨vulg⟩ *spit*) *of his father* || nicht ~ u nicht sterben können *to have hardly enough to keep body and soul together* || so etw lebt nicht! *well, I never!* || ~ u ~ l, °laß sie ~ (sc Läuse), was sie fressen zahl ich! *live and let live; (there must be) give and take* **II. vt** [h] **1.** sein Leben noch einmal ~ *to live one's life over again* || e–n Gedanken ~ *to be moved by an idea* **2.** v/imps/refl **hier lebt sich's** angenehm *it is pleasant living here* **l·ebend 1.** pres p & a *living, alive* || ~e Bilder *tableaux vivants* Fr, *(living pictures)* || ein noch ~er Zeuge *a still-living witness* || kein ~es Wesen *not a living soul* || *quick set (hedges); natural (flowers); modern (languages)* || das ~e Inventar *the live-stock* || *walking (dictionary)* (P) || wild ~e Menschen *savages* || ein hier ~er Dichter *a poet living here* || lange ~ *long-lived* || ~ gebären *to be viviparous* || z Bekämpfung ~er Ziele *anti-personnel* [attr] **2.** ≗**e(r)** m, ≗**e** f *living p* || ~e wie Tote *living and dead alike*; ⟨bib⟩ *the quick and the dead* || die einzigen noch ~en *the only survivors* pl ≗**geborenes** n, ≗**geburt** f *live birth* ≗**gewicht** n *live weight* **leb·endig** a & adv **1.** (**lebend**) *living* || k–e ~e Seele *not a l. soul* || ~e Junge gebären *to bring forth young alive* || sie hatte 9 ~e Junge (, eins war tot) *she had 9 puppies alive* od *l.* (, ..) || mehr tot als ~ *more dead than alive* || ~ *or* bei ~em Leibe verbrannt [pp] *burnt alive* || wieder ~ w *to come to life again* || wieder ~ m *to revive, to bring back to life* || ~ machend *vivifying* (a. fig) || ~ machende Gnade *quickening grace* | ⟨übtr⟩ *l. (force* ⟨a. tech⟩, *faith)* || *live (coals* od *coal)* || *the l. word of God* || *by the l. God!* || *lively (interest), vivid (description), animated, spirited (conversation); alive (happiness); telling, striking (picture); l. (unity)* || die ~e Art, .. *the verve with which he reproduced the gestures* || *to be in l. touch with* || *all his charac-*

ters are alive || etw ~ erhalten *to keep (a name) alive* || ~ m *to vivify* || ein Stück ~ m *to make a play live* || ~ w *to spring to life*; (of feelings) *to come alive* (→ lebend) | ⟨fig⟩ (bewegt) *the streets are full of life and bustle* || es wird ~ auf den Straßen *the people are astir in the streets* **2.** (**lebhaft**) *active (mind)*; *lively (imagination)*; *intense (emotion)* || *vivid (light, colour)* || (P) *energetic*; *keenly sensitive*; *brilliant (talent)*; ein sehr ~es Kind *a child full of vitality* od *life* || *full of vigour* **Leb·endiggeb·ären** n ~s/ *viviparity, viviparousness* | **≃d** a *bringing forth young alive*, ⟨scient⟩ *viviparous* **Leb·endigkeit** f ~/ *aliveness*; ⟨fig⟩ *vivacity, liveliness, vitality* (→ lebendig, Lebhaftigkeit) **L·ebens-** *vital*; *life-, of l.*; *living* **~abend** m *declining years*; *late y.s of l.*; *evening, decline, autumn, sunset of l.*; ein schöner ~ *a beautiful old age* **~abriß** m *biographical notes* pl **~abschnitt** m *age period, part of l.* **~ader** f *v. artery* **~alter** n *age* **~angst** f *biophobia* **~anschauung** f *conception, view, philosophy of l., outlook on l.* **~art** f *way of l.g* || (Benehmen) *behaviour, manners* pl; *savoir vivre* Fr || gute *or* feine ~ *good breeding* od *manners* pl; er hat k–e ~ *he is wanting in g. br.* **~aufgabe** f; m–e ~ *the task of my l., my l.-task* **~balsam** m ⟨med⟩ *restorative*; ⟨poet⟩ *balm of l.* **~baum** m ⟨bib⟩ *tree of l.* || ⟨bot⟩ *arbor vitae* **~bedingungen** f pl *conditions* pl *(of l.), standards of l., essential conditions* **~bedürfnisse** n pl *necessaries* pl *of l.* **~bejahung** f *affirmation* od *acceptance of l.* **~beruf** m *vocation* **~beschreibung** f *biography, l.* **~bild** n *biographical sketch* **~blut** n *l.-blood* **~blüte** f *prime* od *bloom of l.* **~dauer** f *duration of l.* || auf ~ *for l.* || lange ~ *longevity* | ⟨tech⟩ *l.time*; *accuracy l.* || kz *short-l. (item)* **~element** n: *it was the breath of his nostrils* **~elixier** n ⟨cosm⟩ *elixir of l.*; (Schnaps) *aqua vitae* L, *corpse-reviver, pick-me-up* **~ende** n; bis an mein ~ *to the end of my days* **~erfahrung** f *practical experience* **~erwartung** f *l.* ⟨bes ins⟩ *expectancy, expectation of l.* **~faden** m *thread of l., fatal thr.* **≃fähig** a *capable of l.g*, ⟨a. fig:⟩ *possessing vitality*, ⟨med⟩ *viable*; nicht ~ *non-v.* **~fähigkeit** f ⟨med⟩ *viability*, ⟨fig⟩ *vitality* **~feuer** n *energy, vital powers* pl **~flamme** f *v. spark* **~form** f *l. pattern* **~frage** f *matter of l. and death, v. question* **~freude** f *zest*; *joy in l.g, delight in l., joie de vivre* Fr; Überschäumen der ~ *the surge of joy of l.g* **~frist** f *lease of l.* **~führer** m *guide to l.g* **~führung** f *way of l.*; *line of conduct*; strenge ~ *severe regimen*; sittliche ~ *morality* || der letzte **~funken** *l.'s last embers* pl **~gebiet** n *walk of l.* (*in different, all ~s of l.*) **~gefahr** f *danger of l.*; ~! *d.!*; in ~ schweben *to go in fear of one's l.*; k–r ist in ~ *none are in danger (of their lives)*; mit eigener ~ *at the risk of one's (own) l.* **≃gefährlich** a *perilous, mortal*; *l.--threatening* | adv *dangerously (ill)* **~gefährte** m, **~gefährtin** f *partner for l. (the p. of my days)* **~gefühl** n *vitality, vital consciousness* **~geister** m pl *vital, l.g, animal spirits* pl **~gemeinschaft** f *partnership*; ⟨biol⟩ *association, community* **~genuß** m *enjoyment of l., comfort* **~geschichte** f *l.--history* **~gestaltung** f *forming* od *shaping of l.* **~gewohnheiten** f pl *l.g habits* **≃groß** a *as large as l., l.-size(d)* **~größe** f *full size, l.-size* || in ~ *full length, l.-size*; *he turned up again as large as l.* || → Porträt **~haltung** f *mode of l., mental attitude* || *standard of living*, ⟨med⟩ *regimen* | ~sindex [m] *consumer price index (CPI)*; ~skosten [pl] *cost of l.g*, ~index [m] *c. of l.g i.* | ~skosten [pl] *l.g expenses* **~hunger** m *zest for l.* **~inhalt** m: jds einziger ~ *the only concern of a p's l.* **~jahr** n: ins 40. ~ treten *to be rising forty* **~kampf** m *struggle for existence* **≃klug** a *worldly wise* | ~heit [f] *w. wisdom* **~kraft** f *l.g strength, v. power, v.ity, vigo(u)r* || mit ~ erfüllen *to vitalize* **≃kräftig** a *vigorous (child)*; *sound, healthy (undertaking)* **~künstler** m *master of the art of l.g, l.manship* **~lage** f *station* od *walk of l.* || jeder ~ gewachsen *equal to every emergency*; ~n [pl] *circumstances* **≃lang** [adv] *during l., for l.* || [a] *l.long* **~länge** f *length of l.* **≃länglich** [a] *l.long, for l.* || ~e Rente *for l. annuity* || ~e Zuchthausstrafe *penal servitude for l., l.-imprisonment*; ~ h *to serve l.* || [adv] *during l., (he is king) for l.* | **≃er** [m] *convict under a l. sentence*, ⟨sl⟩ *l.r* **~lauf** m *course of l.* || (Bericht) *particulars about one's l., curriculum vitae* **~licht** n (*lamp of*) *l.* || jdm das ~ ausblasen *to take a p's l.*; ⟨fam⟩ *to do for a p* **~linie** f (der Hand) *v.* od *l. line* ⟨a. fig⟩ **~luft** f *v. air* **~lust** f *love of l.* **≃lustig** a *pleasure-loving, gay, jovial, merry, full of animal spirits* **~mark** n *v. strength* **~mittel** n pl *food(stuffs* [pl]); ein ~ *an article of food*; mit ~n versehen *to victual*; ~ einkaufen *to market* | ~amt [n] *food office*; ~chemiker [m] *food chemist*; ~farbstoff [m] *edible dye*; ~gefriertrocknen [n] *freeze-drying* ~geschäft [n] *g.'s shop*, ⟨Am⟩ *g.'s store*; ~händler [m] *grocer*; ~industrie [f] *food manufacturing*; Waren der ~ *prepared foodstuffs*; ~karte [f] *food-* od *ration-card*, ~kartenabschnitt [m] *f.r. ticket, point*, ~kartenstelle [f] *food office*; ~knappheit [f] *f. shortage*; ~konserven [f pl] *canned food*; ~mangel [m] *lack of food*; ~packungen [f pl] *food wrappers*; ~preise [m pl] *prices of foodstuff*; ~überwachung [f] *food control*; ~versorgung [f], ~vorrat [m], ~zufuhr [f] *food-supply* **~möglichkeit** f *possibility to exist, capacity to survive* **≃müde** a *weary of l.* **~mut** m *courage to face life* **≃nahe** a *close to l., practical, representing the realities of l.* **~nähe** f *closeness to l.* **~notdurft** f *necessaries* pl *of l.* **~notwendig** a *v.* (für *to*); ~e Güter [n pl] *necessities of l.* | **≃keit** [f] *v. necessity (the very breath of one's nostrils)* **~periode** f; frühe ~ *early years (of a p)* **~philosophie** f *philosophy of l.g* **~prozeß** m *v. functions* pl **~raum** m *do.*; *l. space* || *sphere of existence* | ~forschung [f] *ecology* **~rechte** n pl *v. rights* pl **~regel** f *rule of l., maxim* **~retter** m *l.-saver* **~rettungsapparat** m *l.-saving apparatus* || (Gürtel) *l.--belt* || (Feuerwehr) *fire-escape* **~saft** m *l.-sap* **≃satt** a *weary* od *tired of l.* **≃schwach** a *immature* (Kind) **~standard** m *standard of l.* **~stellung** f *walk of l.* **~strafe** f *capital punishment* **≃treu** a *true to l.* **~treue** f *truth to l.* **~trieb** m *v. instinct, v.ity, animalism* **≃überdrüssig** a = **≃**müde **≃unfähig** a *incapable of survival* **~unterhalt** m (auskömmlich *fair*) *l.*; bewilligter ~ *l. allowance*; *livelihood, maintenance, sustenance, subsistence*; ⟨fam⟩ *bread and butter* || (jdm) ~ gewähren *to support*; sie hat nicht das Nötigste für ihren ~ *she lacks the very necessities of l.* | ~sindex [m] *index--number of cost of l.g* **~verhältnisse** n pl *living conditions* pl **~verlängerung** f *extended l. span*; *increased longevity* **~verlust** m *loss of l.* **~verneinung** f *negation of l.* **~versicherung** f *l.-assurance* od *-insurance* || abgekürzte ~ *endowment assurance* **≃voll** a *full of l.* **≃wahr** a *l.-like, realistic* **~wandel** m (*course of*) *l., conduct (of l.)* || sein schlechter ~ *his evil l.g, disreputable l.* || e–n makellosen (lockeren) ~ führen *to lead a stainless (dissolute) l.* **~wasser** n, **~wecker** m → ~elixier **~weg** m *walk* od *course of l.*; *passage throught l., path through l.* **~weise** f *mode* od *way of l., manner of l.g, line of conduct, habits* pl || sitzende ~ *sedentary l.* || ⟨med⟩ *regimen* (salzlos *salt-free*); einfache, strenge ~ *austerity* **~weisheit** f *practical wisdom* od *philosophy, w. of l.* **~werk** n *l.-work* **≃wichtig** a *v., integral, of v. importance* || ~e Betriebe *key-industries* **~wille** m *the will to live* **~zeichen** n *sign of l.* || wir h noch immer kein ~ v ihm *we still have had no news of him* **~zeit** f *l.time* || auf *or* für ~ *for (the rest of one's) l.* || bei ~ *in his l.time, when (still) alive*; erste ~ *neo-natal period* **~ziel** n *aim* od *goal of l.* **~zuversicht** f neue ~ *a new lease of* (⟨Am⟩ *on*) *l.* **~zweck** m *purpose* od *aim of l.*

L·eber f ∼/∼n *liver* (gebacken *fried*) ‖ Lehre v der ∼ *hepatology* ‖ er hat's an der ∼ *he's l.ish* ‖ °frei v der ∼ weg reden *to speak up* od *frankly, to speak one's mind* (*freely* od *without mincing matters*); ⟨fam⟩ *to cut loose*; °es muß mir v der ∼ herunter *I must get it off my mind* od *chest*; es frei v der ∼ sagen *to make a clean breast of it*; °was ist denn dir über die ∼ gelaufen? ⟨m. m.⟩ *who has stolen his cookie? what's eating him?*

L·eber- *liver*, ⟨med⟩ *hepatic* (*duct, colic*), *hepato-*(*cirrhosis*) **∼blümchen** n ⟨bot⟩ *l.leaf, hepatica* **≃braun** a *l.-coloured* **∼egel** m ⟨zoo⟩ *l.-fluke* **∼entzündung** f *hepatitis* **∼farbe** f *l.-colour* **≃farben**, **≃farbig** a *l.-coloured* **∼fleck** m *mole, freckle* **∼krankheit** f *l.-complaint* **∼kraut** n ⟨bot⟩ *l.wort* **≃leidend** a *l.ish* **∼pastete** f ⟨cul⟩ *l. loaf* **∼raute** f ⟨bot⟩ *moon wort* **∼reim** m *foolish* od *pointless rhyme* **∼stein** m ⟨geol⟩ *hepatite* **∼tran** m *cod-l. oil* **∼wurst** f ⟨Ger⟩ *l.-pudding* od *-sausage*; ⟨Am, Austr⟩ *l.wurst* ‖ er spielt die gekränkte ∼ *he is huffed and shows it*, ⟨Am⟩ *he has a chip on his shoulder*

l·ebhaft [a] *lively, vivacious, quick, animated* ‖ *buoyant* (*spirits*) ‖ *bright* (*eye, child*) *impulsive* (*man*); *quick* (*movement*); *sprightly* (*air* Melodie) ‖ *high, bright, gay, lively, eager* (*colour*); *mobile* (*face*); *ruddy* (*complexion*); *cheery* (*pace*); *active* (*mind*); *brisk* (*activity*); *keen* (*interest*); *vigorous* (*applause*); *vivid* (*description, recollection*); *spicy* (*horse*); *humming* (*trade*); *l.* (*fighting* Kämpfe); *heated* (*discussion*); *busy* (*street*) ‖ ⟨com⟩ *strong* (*demand* Nachfrage, *for* nach); ⟨com, exch⟩ *brisk* ‖ ∼ w *to become heated* od *animated* | [adv] *in a l. manner, with animation* ‖ (*to talk*) *brightly*; (*to write*) *incisively*; (*to regret*) *sincerely, deeply, exceedingly* ‖ jdn ∼ vor sich sehen *to have a l. picture of a p*; ich kann mir ∼ vorstellen, daß *I can readily imagine that* ‖ etw ∼ fühlen *to be alive to a th* ‖ ∼! *look alive!* **≃igkeit** f ∼/ *liveliness, vivacity, quickness, briskness* ‖ *buoyancy* ‖ (Angeregtheit) *animation* ‖ (Leben) *stir, bustle* ‖ (Munterkeit) *sprightliness, cheerfulness*

Lech m (Nebenfluß der Donau) *Lech* **L·echfeld** n ⟨hist⟩ *region between the Lech and the Wertach* **Lechtal** n *valley of the Lech, Lech-valley* **L·echtaler Alpen** pl *Lechtal Alps* pl

l·echzen vi [h] *to be parched with thirst* ‖ ⟨bot⟩ *to languish* ‖ ⟨fig⟩ (nach) *to long, languish, pant, yearn* (*for*); *to hanker* (*after* [*gold*]) ‖ nach Blut ∼ *to thirst for blood* ‖ *he is dying for a drink of water*

leck a *leaky, leaking* ‖ ∼ s *to make water, to be leaky, to leak* ‖ ∼ w *to become leaky*, ⟨mar⟩ *to spring a leak* **L·eck** n ∼(e)s/∼e *leak* ‖ ein ∼ bek, dichten *to spring* (*stop*) *a l.* **∼gruppe** f ⟨mar⟩ *wreckage party* **∼segel** ausbringen *to place a collision mat* **∼sicherung** f ⟨mar⟩ *damage control* **Leck·age** [–ʒə] f ∼/∼n ⟨com⟩ *leakage* **≃dicht**, **≃fest** a *leak-proof, tight* **l·ecken**[1] vi **1.** [h] (undicht s) *to leak*, ⟨mar⟩ *to have* (*sprung*) *a leak* **2.** [s] (rinnen) *to leak* od *ooze out* ‖ (tröpfeln) *to trickle* od *drip out* ‖ *the candle drips* **3.** ≃ n *leak*(*age*)

L·ecke f ∼/∼n *salt-lick* (a. Leckstein) **l·ecken**[2] vt/i [h] *to lick* (a. sich *o.s.*) ‖ *to lap*; auf∼ *to lap up* ‖ *lambent* (*flame*) ‖ die Flammen ∼ am Dach .. *leap up to the roof* ‖ er leckte ihr die Hand (of dog) *he licked her hand* ‖ er leckte sich den Mund *he licked his chops* ‖ Blut ∼ (of beasts) *to taste blood* ⟨a. fig⟩, e–n Hund Blut ∼ l *to blood a hound* ‖ am Bleistift ∼ *to lick one's pencil* ‖ das Wild leckt gern Salz *the game is fond of a salt-lick* | den Teller **rein∼** *to lick one's plate clean* | (küssen) sie ∼ sich (ab) ⟨fam⟩ *they slobber over each other* (*with kisses*) | (sauber ausarbeiten) .. zu geleckt *the picture is too carefully finished* ‖ ein geleccktes Herrchen *a young fop* ‖ er sieht aus wie geleckt *he looks as if he had just come out of a band-box* | ⟨fig⟩ sich [dat] die Lippen, alle zehn Finger nach etw ∼ *to be greedy after a th* ‖ j–s Speichel ∼ *to lick the dust before a p's feet* ‖ vorne ∼ u hinten kratzen *to smile to a p's face and to stab him in the back* **l·ecken**[3] [† nur]: wider den Stachel ∼ *to kick against the pricks*

l·ecker a **1.** *nice, delicate, savoury, dainty* (*dish*); ∼es Mahl *regale* ‖ ⟨allg⟩ *delicious* ‖ *sweet, hugsome* (*girl*); ⟨hum⟩ *goluptious* **2.** (genäschig) *greedy, lickerish* **3.** (wählerisch) *finical, fastidious* **L·ecker** m ∼s/∼ → Feinschmecker ‖ ⟨hunt⟩ (Haarwild) *tongue* **∼bissen** m *dainty* (*bit*), *delicacy, titbit, regale* ‖ ⟨fig⟩ *treat, plum* (*the* ∼*s of the repertory*) ‖ °(Frau) *tart, dish* **∼maul** n, **∼zahn** m *dainty feeder, dainty p* ‖ ein ∼ s *to have a sweet tooth* **Lecker·ei** f ∼/∼en **1.** [abstr] *greediness, daintiness* **2.** [konkr] *dainty* (*bit*), *delicacy* (→ Leckerbissen) **3.** (Küssen) *slobbering* **l·eckerhaft** a *greedy, dainty, lickerish* **≃igkeit** f ∼/ *greediness, daintiness, fastidiousness* **l·eckern** vt/i [h] *to relish* | (nach) *to long* (*for*); ⟨fam⟩ *to be sweet* (*on*)

L·eder n ∼s/∼ *leather, skin* (⟨a. fig⟩: Haut); ⟨ftb⟩ (Ball) *pigskin, leather* ‖ in ∼ gebunden *calf-bound* ‖ abgenarbtes ∼ *smooth l.*; alaungares ∼ *alumed l.*; ⟨bookb⟩ in biegsamem ∼ *in yapp*; dänisches ∼ *Danish skin* ‖ englisches ∼ ⟨weav⟩ *sateen, moleskin*; Fensterputz≃ *window l.*; gegerbtes ∼ *tanned skin*; gelbe Farbe gegerbten ∼s *tan*; G·ems≃ *chamois*; genarbtes ∼ *grained l.*; H·aifisch≃ *chagrin*; J·uchten≃ *Russian l.*; N·anking≃ *chamois*; R·ind≃ *neat's l.*; Saffian≃ *morocco*; sämisches (Putz-, Wasch≃) ∼ *chamois*; weißgares ∼ *tanned* od *tawed l.* | zäh wie ∼ (*as*) *tough as l.* ‖ jdm das ∼ gerben *or* versohlen *to thrash a p*; *to tan a p*(*'s hide*); .. was das ∼ hält .. *as hard as one can* ‖ ans ∼ gehen ⟨fam⟩ *to go it strong*; ran ans ∼ ⟨vulg⟩ *lump into it* ‖ v ∼ ziehen *to draw* od *unsheathe one's sword*, ⟨fig⟩ *to let* od *blow off steam* (*to* [*give*] *vent* [*to*] *one's feelings*), *to say one's say*, tüchtig .. *to come* od *go it strong*, jdm gegenüber .. *to give a p a piece of one's mind* **∼abfälle** m pl *l. cuttings* pl **∼apfel** m ⟨bot⟩ *l.-coat* **∼appretur** f → –paste **∼arbeiter** m *workman in l., currier* **≃artig** a *l.y, coriaceous* **∼band** m (Buch) *calf-binding* ‖ (Riemen) (*l.*) *strap* **∼bereiter** m *l.-dresser, currier* **∼bereitung** f *l. dressing* **≃braun**, **≃farben**, **≃gelb** a *tawny, tan, buff* **∼ecken** f pl ⟨bookb⟩ *l. tags* pl; mit ∼n versehen *l.-tipped* **∼fett** n *dubbing* **∼gamaschen** f pl *l.s* pl, *leggings* pl **∼handel** m *l. trade* **∼händler** m *dealer in l.* **∼handschuh** m *l.-glove* **∼haut** f ⟨anat⟩ *corium, cutis* **∼hosen** f pl *l.s* [pl], *l. breeches* pl **∼hülsenbaum** m *honey locust* **∼imitation** f *l.oid* **∼koffer** m *l. trunk* **∼koller** m ⟨mil⟩ *buff-coat* **∼lack** m *pouch-varnish* **∼narbe** f *l.-grain* **∼papier** n *l.ette* **∼paste** f *clobber* **∼riemen** m *l. strap*; (für Rasiermesser) *strop* **∼rücken** m ⟨bookb⟩ *l.-back*; mit e–m ∼ versehen *l.-backed* **∼sitz** m *l. bottom* **∼streifen** m *thong* **∼strumpf** (*Cooper's*) *L.-stocking* **∼tuch** n *American l.* **∼überzug** m *l. case*; mit ∼ *covered* od *cased in l.* **∼- und Sattlergeschäft** n *l.-and-harness shop* **∼waren** f pl *l. goods* **≃weich** a (*as*) *soft as l.*; ∼ schlagen ⟨fig⟩ *to beat to a jelly* **∼zeug** n ⟨mil⟩ *l.s* pl, *straps and belts*; *l. straps* pl **∼zucker** m *marsh mallow* (*paste*) **∼zurichter** m *l.-dresser, currier* **L·ederer** m ∼s/∼ [südd] = Gerber, →–zurichter **l·edern** vt [h] *to l., to furnish with l.* ‖ (Fenster) *to clean with wash-l.*; ⟨fam⟩ (prügeln) *to thrash, hide* **l·edern** a *l.n*, (*of*) *l., coriaceous* ‖ ⟨fig⟩ *tough* (*meat*); *dry* (*lecture*); *dull* (*book*); *heavy* (*play, p*); *wooden* (*expression*) ‖ ⟨sl⟩ *chippy*; ein ∼er Kerl *a Dryasdust, a bore*

l·edig I. [a] **1.** (unverheiratet) *single, unmarried*; ⟨demog⟩ nicht ∼e P *ever-married p*; Abgangsordnung [f] der ≃en *net nuptiality table* ‖ (der) ∼e *bachelor*; (die) ∼e *spinster* ‖ ∼ s *to be single*, ⟨hum⟩ *to live in s. blessedness* ‖ ∼ bleiben *to stay* od *remain s.* od *a bachelor* (*spinster*) ‖ ∼er Stand *s. state*; *celibacy* ‖ ein ∼es Kind *an illegitimate* *child* || ~e Mutter (Tochter) *unmarried m., d.* **2.** (entbunden) e–r S [gen] *or* von etw ~ s *to be exempt* od *free of a th* || dieser Sorge war er ~ *he was rid of* od *freed from this anxiety* **3.** (unbehindert) los u ~ s *to be absolutely free, to have no ties*; aller Fesseln ~ s ⟨fig⟩ *to have cast off all one's chains* || e–n los u ~ l *to release a p* || sich v etw los u ~ m *to free o.s. from a th* || e–n los u ~ sprechen *to absolve a p entirely* **4.** (unbesetzt) *unoccupied* (*seat*) || ⟨hors⟩ *without riders* || *vacant* (*office*); ~ Stelle *vacancy* **II.** **~, ~lich** [adv] *exclusively, merely, solely, purely, only* || *he is devoted entirely to money-making*

L·edischiff n Sw = Lastschiff

L·ee f ~/ ⟨mar⟩ *lee(-side)* (Ggs Luv) || in ~ fallen *to come by the lee* || nach ~ treiben *to drift lee-ward* || ~ m *to give a lee* **~bord** n *larboard*, ⟨mst⟩ *port* **~brassen** f pl *lee-braces* pl **≏gierig** a *carrying lee helm* **~küste** f *lee shore* **~segel** n *studding-sail* **≏wärts** adv *leeward* **~weg** m *leeway*

l·eer 1. [a] *empty*; *unfurnished* (*flat*) || (bar) *void* || (bedeutungslos) *void, vain* || (wertlos) *hollow, futile* || (unbesetzt), *unoccupied, vacant* (*room, place*), *free* (*chair*) || ~e Fässer etc [pl] *empties* pl || (ausdruckslos) *vacant, blank* (*mind*); *vacuous* (*stare*); *vapid* (*conversation, compliments*) || ~es Papier [n] *blank* || *lame* (*excuse*); *idle* (*gossip, statement*); *vain* (*threats, hopes, promises*) || ~ ausgehen *to be left out in the cold*; sich ~ (hungrig) fühlen *to feel hollow* || vor ~en Bänken spielen ⟨theat⟩ *to play before a thin audience* || ~es Geschwätz *wind, bunk(um)*, ⟨sl⟩ *hot air*, ⟨Am sl⟩ *punk* || mit ~en Händen *empty-handed* || ⟨tech⟩ ~laufen *to race, to run light*, ⟨fig⟩ *to run idle*; (Staubecken) ~laufen l *to run dry* || das Nest ist ~ ⟨mst⟩ *the birds are flown* || ~es Stroh dreschen *to thresh empty straw* || ~er Schein *mere pretence* || ~e Stelle *vacancy* || die Straße ist ~ .. *deserted* || *bare* (*wall*) || die Wohnung steht ~ [adv] .. *is to let* || ~ l *to leave* (*a line*) *blank* || wüst u ~ *without form and void* ⟨bib⟩ **2. das ≏e** *vacancy* (*to gaze into v.* od *space*) || ⟨phys⟩ *vacuum* || ⟨allg⟩ *vacant space* || *void* (*the v. created by his absence*) || ins ≏e arbeiten *to waste o.s. on emptiness* **L·eer-** (→ a. Lehr-) **~aufmachung** f (Schaupackung) *dummy* **~aufnahme** f ⟨phot⟩ *blank exposure*, ⟨film⟩ *b. e.s* **~darm** m ⟨anat⟩ *jejunum* L **~faß** n *emptying-vat* **~gewicht** n *weight empty, unladen w., dead-w.* ⟨a. aero⟩; *tare* **~gut** n *empties* pl (*barrels, casks*) **~lauf** m ⟨mot⟩ *idling*; ⟨tech⟩ *dead* od *lost motion*; *dead travel, idle running* || (Wasserbau) *waste-pit*; ⟨fig⟩ *wastage, loss by waste* | ~handlung [f] ⟨eth⟩ *vacuum activity*; ~prüfung [f] ⟨mot⟩ *dry running*; ~scheibe [f] *loose pulley*; ~strom [m] ⟨el⟩ *no-load current* **~lokomotive** f ⟨rail⟩ *pilot engine* **~spalte** f ⟨comp⟩ *blank column* | ~nkontrolle [f] *b. c. detection device* **~stehen** n *untenanted state* **≏stehend** a *empty, unoccupied, vacant* (*flat, room, bed*) **~takt** m *idle stroke* **~taste** f ⟨typewr⟩ *space bar* **~versuch** m ⟨pharm⟩ *blank experiment* od *test* **~weg** m *dead travel*

L·eere f ~/ *emptiness, void(ness)*; (*empty*) *space* || (leerer Raum) *vacuum* || *lameness, idleness, nothingness, vainness* || *the void created by his absence* || *vapidity* (*of a p*) || ⟨biol⟩ *inanition* || geistige ~ *vacancy* || *vacuity* (*of expression*) || ⟨theat⟩ gähnende ~! *an exceedingly thin house*!; ins ~ starrend (of eyes) *fixed on space* **l·eeren 1.** vi [h] *to empty, void, clear, evacuate*; *clear* (*dish*) || (Glas) bis auf den Grund ~ *to drain* || *to pump a well dry* || Briefkästen ~ *to collect letters* || **sich** ~ *to* (*become*) *empty* || (of room) *to be thinning* **2.** ≏ [n] *emptying*, etc. || *clearance* (*of a letter-box*), *collection* (*of letters*) || *evacuation* (*of a country*) **L·eerheit** f ~/ **1.** = Leere [f] **2. ~en** pl *trivialities, inanities* **L·eerung** f ~/~en = Leeren 2.

L·efze f ~/~n *lip* || *flew* (*of bloodhound*)

L·eg(e)- ~angel f *trimmer, night-line* **~henne** f *laying hen*; (*good*) *layer* **~föhre** f → Latsche **~horn** n *leghorn* (*fowl*) = Livorno **~röhre** f ⟨ent⟩ *ovipositor* **~zeit** f ⟨orn⟩ *laying-season*

leg·al a *legal, lawful* **~is·ieren** vt [h] *to legalize, to authenticate* **≏is·ierung** f ~/ *legalization* **≏it·ät** f ~/ *legality* **leg·aliter** adv [L] *legally*

Leg·at 1. m ~en/~en (Abgesandter) *legate* **2.** n ~(e)s/~e (Vermächtnis) *legacy*, (of real estate) *devise*, (of chattels) *bequest* **~·ar** m ~(e)s/~e *legatee, legatary* **~i·on** [ts] f ~/~en *legation, embassy* | ~srat [m] ⟨Ger⟩; ~ssekretär [m] *councillor, secretary to an embassy*

L·egel n ~s/~ ⟨mar⟩ die ~ [pl] *the cringles* pl

l·egen vt [h] **1.** *to lay, put, place* (*a book on a table*) | [refl] **sich** ~ *to lie down* || (krank) *to take to one's bed* || sich (schlafen) ~ *to lie down* (*to sleep*), *to go to bed* || ⟨agr⟩ (v Getreide) sich ~ *to be beaten* od *weighed down* || (v Wind etc) *to calm* od *settle down, die away, abate, fall*; (Sturm) *to blow over* || er hat sich gelegt (ist krank) *he has taken to his bed* || sein Erstaunen legte sich .. *abated* || die Erregung, Furcht, der Schmerz legte sich .. *subsided*; *his rage went dead*; der Lärm legte sich *the hubbub quiet(en)ed down* || *the first excitement had blown over* **2.** [**mit best Objekt**] *to sow* (*beans, peas*) || *to lay down* (*floors, a floor, a pavement, a drainage system*) || *to lay* (*eggs*); [ell] die Hühner ~ fleißig .. *are good layers*; frisch gelegte Eier *new-laid eggs* || das Fundament, den Grund(stein) zu (etw) ~ *to lay the foundation* (*-stone*) *to* || ⟨fig⟩ e–m das Handwerk ~ *to stop a p's proceedings* || *to lay* (*cables*) || (die) Karten ~ *to lay the cards* || *to plant* (*potatoes*) || (Leitung) ⟨el⟩ *to run* || *to lay* (*mines*) || *to lay down* (*pipes, a carpet*) || Schlingen ~ *to set traps* || Senkreiser ~ *to put layers into the ground* || Wäsche ~ *to lay the linen* **3.** [**mit prep** *or* **adv**] ad acta ~ *to shelve* (⟨a. fig⟩: *plan*) | an etw ge~ s → liegen || **an-e-a-|~** *to join* || ans Feuer ~ *to put to* od *near the fire* || die Axt an den Baum ~ *to lay the axe on the tree* || Hand an etw ~ *to turn one's hand to a th* || Hand an sich ~ *to take one's own life* || (die) Hand an e–n ~ *to lay hands upon a p* || die letzte Hand an etw ~ *to put the finishing touches to a th* || *to set fire to a h.* || e–m etw ans Herz ~ *to recommend a th warmly to a p* || *to put the dog on the chain* || an den unrechten Platz ~ *to mislay* || etw wieder an s–n Platz ~ *to put a th back to its place* || sie legte den Kopf an s–e Schulter *she rested her head against his sh.* || an den Tag ~ *to display, evince, show* | **sich ~ auf** *to lie* (*down*) (*on the sofa*), *to lower o.s. to* (*the ground*); ⟨fig⟩ *to apply* od *devote o.s. to, to occupy o.s. with, to go in for, to take up* (*fishing*); *fishing has become his hobby*; (S) sich fest ~ auf *to fit down on* || s–n **Arm** ~ auf *to rest one's arm upon* || *to place restrictions on* (*the use*) || *to lie down on the bed* || sich aufs **Bitten** ~ *to take recourse to entreaties* || der Rauch legte sich mir auf die Brust .. *settled on my ..* || auf–e–a–|~ *to lay one on the top of the other, to pile up* || *he rested the rifle upon the saddle* || (etw) auf ein Gestell ~ *to rack* || **Gewicht** ~ auf *to attach importance to* || *he rested his hands upon my shoulders* || .. aufs **Herz** *she put her hand to her heart* || *she superposed her hands on his* || sich auf die faule Haut, aufs Ohr ~ ⟨fig⟩ *to take things easily, to lead an idle life* || Geld auf die hohe **Kante** ~ *to put by money* || sich auf die Lauer ~ *to lie in ambush* || **N**achdruck ~ auf *to lay special emphasis on* || *to apply a plaster to* (*the chest*), *to put a pl. on* (*a wound*) || das legte sich mir schwer auf die **S**eele *that lay heavily on my heart* || ⟨mot⟩ der Wagen legte sich auf die linke Seite *the car lurched to the left* || sich auf die Seite ~ *to roll od turn over on one's side*, (of ship) *to heel*; (Schiff) auf die S. ~ *to heel* || etw **wieder** auf den **T**isch, in die Schublade ~ *to return* od *restore a th to* .., .. || Geld auf **Z**insen ~

to invest capital || hohen Zoll auf etw ~ *to place a heavy duty on a th* || e–m die Worte auf die Zunge ~ *to put .. into a p's mouth* | **aus** der Hand ~ *to put* od *lay aside* || aus–e–a| ~ *to unfold* || **beiseite**| ~ *to put aside* od *by*; *to store up*; (aufgeben) *to discard* || etw **bereit**|~ *to keep a th ready* | **durch-e-a**|~ *to jumble up* || ⟨mar⟩ sich **fest**|~ *to berth, moor* | e–n **hinter** Schloß u Riegel ~ *to put a p under lock and key* || etw hinter sich ~ (sparen) *to put sth by* | **in** etw ~ *to deposit* od *lay down in* || in **A**sche ~ *to incinerate, to turn* od *reduce to (dust and) ashes* || sich ins **B**ett ~ *to go to bed, to lie down in bed*; sich mit e–m ins Bett ~ *to go (in)to bed with a p* || in Falten ~ *to gather up, to fold*; das Gesicht .. *to frown* || in Fesseln ~ *to put a p in(to) chains* od *irons* || e–n ins **G**rab ~ *to inter a p* || das Kinn in die **H**ände gelegt ⟨fig⟩ *her chin cupped in her hands* || in jds Hände ~ *to put .. in a p's hands* ⟨a. fig⟩; *the administration is rested in the Secretary of State* || e–m Einquartierung ins Haus ~ *to billet soldiers on a p* || in den **K**orb ~ *to throw into the b.* || sich ins Mittel ~ *to interpose, intervene, interfere, to step in* || in d. Mund → auf d. Zunge ~ || Eier ins Nest ~ *to lay eggs in the nest* || sich ins **R**uder ~ *to row with all one's strength*, ⟨fig⟩ *to act with might and main* || die Hände in den Schoß ~ *to sit doing nothing* || Besatzung in e–e Stadt ~ *to garrison a town* || s–n Einfluß in die Waagschale ~ *to throw one's influence into the scales* || e–r S gr Hindernisse in den **W**eg ~ *to put* od *interpose great obstacles in the way of (commercial intercourse)* || sich ins Zeug ~ *to pull one's weight, to put one's shoulder to the wheel* | etw **lahm** *to paralyse a th* | sich längsseits e–s Schiffes ~ ⟨mar⟩ *to go alongside of a ship* | der Reihe **nach** ~ *to arrange in regular* od *proper order* || e–m etw **nahe** ~ ⟨fig⟩ *to suggest a th to a p* | **schief** ~ *to lay askew* | **trocken** ~ *to drain, to dry up* | **über**-–e–a| ~ *to put on top of each other* | ein Knie über das andere ~ *to cross one k. over the other* || e–e Decke über den Tisch ~ *to spread .. over ..* || *a haze settled down over the country* || *calm had come upon the town* || *darkness, silence closed over the garden* | ~ **um** *he put his arm round her*; fest um .. *his arm tightened about her, his fingers closed upon her hand* || *to pass a rope round a tree* || *he wrapped a shawl round her shoulders*; .. fest .. *to hitch about ..*; .. sorgfältig .. *to drape* od *arrange round ..* || *to clasp a bracelet round one's wrist* | **unter** Siegel ~ *to seal up* | **von** sich ~ *to lay aside*; (Kleid, Schmuck) *to take off* || sich **vor** Anker ~ *to cast anchor* || ein Schloß vor die Tür ~ *to put a padlock to the d.* || ⟨mil⟩ sich vor e–e Stadt ~ *to besiege a town* | **zu**–e–a| ~ *to join* || sich zu Bett ~ *to go to bed*; .. krank .. *to take to one's bed* || e–m etw zur Last ~ *to charge a p with a th* || sich zur Ruhe ~ *to lie down* || zum übrigen ~ *to add to the rest* || *she put the key with her gloves* | ein Lehrbuch **zugrunde**|~ *to work on the basis of a text-book* | **zurecht**|~ *to arrange, drape* | ⟨fig⟩ sich da**zwischen**|~ *to intervene between* (→ ins Mittel ~)

legend·arisch, leg·endenhaft a *legendary* **Leg·ende** f ~/~n *legend (Golden L.)*, ⟨a. cart⟩ || ⟨typ⟩ *key*; (Bild≗) *underline* **~nbuch** n, **~nsammlung** f, **~nschreiber** m *legendary*

leg·er [leʒeːə] a Fr *easy, unforced, unaffected, casual*

L·e(e)gerwall m ~s/ *lee-shore*

Leg·ierung f ~/~en *alloy(ing)* (~ auf A.basis *aluminium-base alloy*) **leg·ieren**[1] vt [h] ⟨jur⟩ *to bequeath, leave as a legacy* **leg·ieren**[2] vt [h] ⟨met⟩ *to alloy* || ⟨cul⟩ *thicken, bind*; –rt *thick (soup, etc)*

Legi·on f ~/~en *legion* || ihre Zahl ist ~ *their number is l.* | **~·är** m ~s/~e *legionary*

legit·im a *legitimate, lawful* **Legitimati·on** [ts] f ~/~en *legitimation* || (Ausweis) *proof of identity* | ~spapier [n] *paper of identification* **legitim·ieren** vt [h] *to legitimate, identify* || sich ~ [h] *to prove one's identity* **L-it·ät** f ~/~en *legitimacy*

Legu·an m ~s/~e ⟨zoo⟩ *iguana*

L·eh(e)n n ~s/~ *fief, fee, feud(al tenure)*; auf Leibeserben beschränktes ~ *estate in fee tail* || e–m etw zu ~ geben *to enfeoff* od *invest a p with ..* || zu ~ tragen *to hold in fee* **~bauer** m *peasant holding a feudal tenure* **~besitz** m *f. t.* **~brief** m *bill of feoffment* **~buch** n *register of f. t.s* **~dienst** m *f. service* **~erbe** m *f. heir* **~gut** n *feud, fee, estate in fee* || (freies) *freehold* **~(s)herr** m *(f.) lord, liege(-lord)* **~(s)hof** m *farm held by a f. t.* **~recht** n *f. law* | ≗lich [a] *under f. l.* **~(s)wesen** n *f.ism* **~-wort** n ⟨gram⟩ *loan-word, borrowed word* **L·eh(e)ns-** **~eid** m *oath of allegiance* **~fall** m *vacancy of a f. t.* **~folge** f *succession to a fief* **~herrlichkeit, ~herrschaft** f *quality* od *domination of a f. lord* **~leute** pl → **~mann** m *f. tenant, vassal* **~pflicht** f *fealty, feudal duty* **~träger** m *feoffee, feudal tenant* **~treue** f *f. faith* **~verfassung** f *f. system*

L·ehm m ~(e)s/~e *loam, clay* **~boden** m *l.y soil, c.ey ground* **~fußboden** m *earthen floor* **~grube** f *l.-pit, c.-pit* **~grund** m *l.y bottom* **~hütte** f *mud-cottage* **~kübel** m *hod* **~wand** f *mud-wall* **~wüste** f *l.y desert* **l·ehmig** a *clayey, loamy*

Lehn- **~bank** f *bench with a back (to it)* **~sessel, ~stuhl** m *armchair, easy chair* **L·ehne** f ~/~n **1.** *support, prop* || (Rück≗) *back* || (Arm≗) *arm-rest* || Stuhl mit hoher ~ *high-backed chair* **2.** (Abhang) *slope* **3.** ⟨pap⟩ *gallows* pl **l·ehnen** vi/t [h] *to lean* || das Brett lehnt an der Wand .. *leans against the w.* | er lehnte das Brett an die Wand *he leant .. against the w.* || etw gegen e–e Stütze ~ *to prop up a th against a support* || sie lehnte den Kopf an s–e Brust *she rested her h. against his br.* | **sich ~** **(an** [acc]) *to lean (against)* || (sich) ~ auf *to rest (o.s.) on* || sich aus dem Fenster ~ *to lean from* (od *out of*) *the window*

L·ehr- (→ a. leer) **~amt** n *teacher's profession, t.ship*; ⟨univ⟩ *professorship* || das ~ antreten *to enter upon a mastership*; sein ~ aufgeben *to resign one's position as teacher* **~amtsprüfung** f *t.'s examination* **~amtszeugnis** n *t.'s diploma* **~anstalt** f *academy, school*, höhere ~ *secondary school* **~apparat** m ⟨rec, phot, telv⟩ *teaching machine* **~art** f *method of t.g* **~auftrag** m *t.g assignment*; *(invitation to lecture* [für *on*]) **~bataillon** n *training b.* **~begierde** f *desire to teach* **~beruf** m *t.'s calling, scholastic profession* **~brief** m *(apprentice's) indenture(s* pl), *certificate of apprenticeship* **~bube** m *apprentice* **~buch** n *manual, textbook, compendium*; ~ f Selbstunterricht *know-how book* **~bursche** m *apprentice* **~dichtung** f *didactic poetry* **~erfahrung** f *t.g experience* **~fach** n *(profession of) teaching* || *subject (of study)*; *how many subjects do you take?* **~film** m *instructional film*; *educational film* **~flugzeug** n (Modell) ⟨aero-sl⟩ *penguin* **~freiheit** f *freedom of t.g* **~gabe** f *talent for t.g* **~gang** m *class, course*; ⟨mil⟩ *training course* | ~steilnehmer *trainee* **~gebäude** n ⟨fig⟩ *system (of philosophy* od *t.g etc.)* **~gedicht** n *didactic poem* **~gegenstand** m *subject of instruction* **~geld** n *tuition for apprenticeship* || ~ geben *or* zahlen ⟨fig⟩ *to pay dearly for experience* **~herr** m *master, employer*, ⟨sl⟩ *boss* **~hilfsmittel** n pl *t.g aids* **~jahre** n pl *(years of) a.ship*; s–e ~ durchmachen *to serve one's articles* **~junge** m = Lehrling **~kanzel** f [österr] = –stuhl **~kontrakt** m *indenture(s* pl) *of a.ship* **~körper** m *t.g staff*; ⟨univ⟩ *professiorate*, ⟨Am⟩ *faculty* **~kraft** f *t.*; *faculty member* **~mädchen** n *girl-apprentice* ≗**mäßig** a *doctrinal, dogmatic* **~meinung** f *dogma, doctrine* **~meister** m *t., instructor*; *tutor*; *professor* || (beim Handwerk) *master* **~meisterin** f *mistress* **~methode** f = ~art **~mittel** n pl *instructional* od *teaching aids, means* pl *of instruction, instruction media*; akustische ~ (Tonträger) *sound media* **~plan** m *plan of instruction, syllabus, (school) curriculum*; *curricular planning*, außerhalb des ~s *extracurricular*; (Stunden-) *time-table, routine,* ⟨Am⟩ *schedule* ~̽**reich** a *instructive* **~saal** m *lecture-, class-room*; *auditory* **~satz** m *proposition, tenet, dogma, rule* ‖ ⟨math, log⟩ *proposition*; *theorem* **~schwester** f *student nurse* **~spruch** m *sentence, maxim, aphorism* **~stand** m *scholastic* od *t.g profession* **~stätte** f *institution of learning*; *t.g centre*; *seat of t.g* **~stelle** f *office of a t.*; *apprenticeship* **~stube** f *lecture-room, school-room* **~stuhl** m (*professor's*) *chair, pr.ship* **~stunde** f *lesson, lecture* **~tafel** f *graphic tr.g aid* **~ton** m *dogmatical manner* **~verfahren** n *method* **~vertrag** m = ~brief **~weise** = ~art **~weisheit** f *scholastic wisdom* **~werkstätte** f ⟨ind⟩ *industrial tr.g division* **~zeit** f = ~jahre ‖ (*of an author*) *novitiate* **~zimmer** n *schoolroom* **~zwang** m *compulsory instruction* od *t.g* **L·ehre** f ~/~n **1.** (theoretische) *doctrine, theory* ‖ ⟨ec⟩ *tenets* [pl], *doctrinal t.g*; ~ verbreiten *to disseminate the t.g of the gospel* ‖ die ~ v Schall *the theory of sound* ‖ (praktische) *advice, rule, precept* ‖ (moralische) *lesson*; e–m e–e ~ geben *to read a p a l.*; durch die ~ gewitzigt *wiser for the l.*; e–e ~ ziehen aus *to take warning from*; e–e hohe sittliche ~ vermitteln *to teach a high moral l.* ‖ laß dir das e–e ~ s! *let that be a w. to you!*; *take that for a l.* ‖ (Nutzanwendung) *application* ‖ (e–r Fabel etc) *moral* ‖ (das Lehren) *tuition*: in s–r ~ *under his t.* ‖ (Unterricht) *system of instruction*; in guter ~ s *to be at a good school* od (beim Handwerk) *apprenticeship*; (bei e–m) in der ~ s *to be serving one's a.ship* (*to serve as a. with a p*); zu jdm in die ~ k *to be a. to a p*; in die ~ nehmen *to take as a.*; in die ~ geben *or* tun *to bind a., to a., to article* (bei, zu *to*) ‖ ⟨übtr⟩ jdm e–e ~ geben *to teach a p a lesson*; du kannst bei ihm noch in die ~ gehen *you can learn a lot from him* ‖ ~ ziehen aus: *from the errors of others a wise man corrects his own* **2.** ⟨tech⟩ *gauge* ‖ (Muster) *pattern* ‖ ⟨arch⟩ *centering* ‖ ⟨carp⟩ *pattern* ‖ (Kaliber) *calibre, size* ‖ ⟨min⟩ (*jointing*) *rule* ‖ ⟨sculp⟩ *model* ‖ ⟨typ⟩ *type gauge* ‖ (Guß) *loam board* ‖ (Meßstock) *staff* ‖ (Töpferei) *templet* **l·ehren 1.** vt [h] *to teach* ‖ (belehren) *to inform, instruct* ‖ e–n (falsch: e–m) etw ~ *to t. a p sth, to put a p up to sth* ‖ e–n schreiben ~ *to t. a p writing* od (*how*) *to write* ‖ (dartun) *to show*: die Zeit wird's ~ *time will sh.* ‖ (öffentlich) ⟨univ⟩ *to profess* ‖ *the M. School preached the doctrine of* .. **2.** ~̽ n ~s/ *t.ing, giving lessons* **L·ehrer** m ~s/~, **~in** f ~/~nen *teacher* (⟨a. fig, iron⟩: danke, Herr ~! *thank you, t.!*), *master, instructor* ‖ ⟨Am⟩ (Titel f jede Art) *professor* ‖ ~ der Mathematik *mathematical t., t. of mathematics* ‖ (v Beruf) *preceptor, professor* ‖ (Privat~) (*private*) *tutor* ‖ (Klassen~̽) *formmaster* ‖ (Turn~̽) *instructor* ‖ ⟨univ⟩ *professor, lecturer* (f [*lady* od *female*] *t., governess,* ⟨Am fam⟩ *schoolma'am*) **~bildungsanstalt** f = ~seminar **~kollegium** n *staff* (*of t.s*), *magistral staff* **~konferenz** f *meeting of the* (*teaching*) *staff* **~(innen)seminar** n *training-college* (*for teachers*) **~stand** m *scholastic profession* **~stelle** f *mastership* **L·ehrerschaft** f ~/~en [koll] *body of teachers* **l·ehrhaft** a *instructive* (*lesson*), *didactic* (*poem*) **L·ehrling** m ~(e)s/~e *apprentice* ‖ ⟨fig⟩ *disciple, novice, tyro*; ⟨allg⟩ *beginner* ‖ als ~ ein Handwerk lernen *to be apprenticed to a trade* ‖ ⟨Am a.⟩ *cub*: als ~ dienender Pilot *cub pilot* ‖ Sattler~̽ *apprentice saddler* **~sverhältnis** n *a.ship*

L·ei f ~/~en (Fels) vgl. Lore~̽, Erpeler Lei

.. lei suff [zur Bildung v a wie] aller~ (*of*) *all sorts*, 20er~ *20 different ths, of 20 d. kinds*

Leib m ~(e)s/~er **1. Bedeutungen**: (Körper) *body* ‖ (Unterleib) *belly* ‖ (Mutter~̽) *womb,* ⟨scient⟩ *matrix*; → Eingeweide ‖ (Rumpf) (*of horses, cows*) *barrel* ‖ toter ~ *corpse, dead body*; (T) *carcass* ‖ ⟨rel⟩ unser irdischer ~ *our mortal clay* ‖ → Leben **2. [mit verbs] offenen ~ h** *to have easy motions*; verstopften ~ h *to be constipated* ‖ s–n ~ pflegen, s–m ~e etw zugute tun *to pamper o.s.* ‖ gesegneten ~es s *to be with child* ‖ sie sind ein ~ u e–e Seele *they are in perfect union* ‖ °sich den ~ vollschlagen ⟨fam⟩ *to fill one's belly* ‖ ~ und Leben wagen *to risk one's life* ‖ ~ u Seele zus–halten *to keep* (*the*) *body and soul together* **3. [mit prep]** alles was man **am** ~e hat *every stitch*; *all one stands up in* ‖ sich etw am eigenen ~e abdarben, absparen *to stint o.s. of a th*; .. erfahren *to experience .. personally*; er erlebte .. am eigenen ~e *he lived to be blackmailed h.s.* ‖ am ganzen ~e vor Furcht zittern *to tremble all over with fear* ‖ am ganzen ~e zitternd *all of a tremble* ‖ am ~e strafen *to inflict corporal punishment upon* ‖ es ging ihm an ~ u Leben *his life was at stake* ‖ sich alles an den ~ hängen *to put all one's money on one's back* ‖ k–n Rock **auf** dem ~e h *to have no coat to one's back* ‖ (*to conceal a th*) *upon one's person* ‖ nur mit dem, was er auf dem ~e hatte *with the clothes he was wearing and no more* ‖ die Rolle war ihm (wie) auf den ~ geschrieben *the part suited him to a T* ‖ e–m auf den ~ rücken *to attack a p,* ⟨fig⟩ *to press a p hard* ‖ sich die Lunge **aus** dem ~e reden *to talk o.s. to death* ‖ **bei** ~e (beileibe) nicht! *on no account!, not for the life of me* ‖ bei lebendigem ~e *alive* ‖ gut bei ~e s *to be stout* od *corpulent* ‖ k–e Ehre **im** ~e h *to have no sense of hono(u)r to be devoid of all honourable feeling*; kein Herz .. *to have no h.* ‖ ich habe heute noch nichts im ~e *I have eaten nothing the whole day* ‖ kein Herz im ~e h *to be heartless* ‖ Grimmen im ~e h *to have a stomach-ache* ‖ das Herz lacht mir im ~e *my h. leaps for joy,* ⟨fam⟩ *it does my h. good* ‖ er hat den Teufel im ~e *he is a wicked* od *wily fellow* ‖ das Herz drehte sich mir im ~e herum bei .. *I was disgusted at* (*the sight*) ‖ °sich die Beine in den ~ stehen *to get tired standing* (*for hours*) ‖ °sich das Essen in den ~ jagen *to bolt one's meal* ‖ e–m ein Messer in den ~ stoßen *to drive a knife into a p* ‖ **mit** ~ u Seele für e–e *or* bei e–r S s *to be heart and soul with* (od *in, for*) *a th* ‖ er ist mit ~ u S. bei der Arbeit *he puts his h. in his work* ‖ er hat sich ihm mit ~ u Seele verschrieben *he has given h.s. over to him b. and s.* ‖ e–n **um** den ~ fassen *to put one's arm round a p's waist* ‖ sein Pferd wurde ihm **unter** dem ~e erschossen *his h. was shot under him* ‖ e–m nicht **vom** ~e gehen *to dangle after a p, to hang on to a p* ‖ sich [dat] jdn (drei Schritt) v ~e halten *to keep a p at a distance* (*at arm's length*); .. so weit wie möglich .. *to get a p at as great a distance from o.s. as one can* ‖ bleib' mir v ~e!, drei Schritt v ~e! *stand* od *keep off! clear off!* ‖ bleib' mir damit v ~e! *don't trouble me with that* (→ Hals C. 2.) ‖ e–m **zu** ~e gehen *to assault a p* ‖ e–m zu ~e wollen *to have a design upon a p* ‖ e–r S zu ~e gehen *to pursue*; *tackle sth, to cope* od *grapple with a th* ⟨Am fam⟩ *to wade into* .. ‖ e–r Kr. wirksam zu ~e gehn *to wage effective war upon a disease* ‖ geh der Schwierigkeit nur energisch zu ~e! *grasp the nettle!* **~arzt** m *personal physician* ([+ gen] *to a p*) **~binde** f *waistband, flannel belt*; ⟨surg⟩ *abdominal belt*; ⟨mil⟩ → Schärpe **~bursch** m ⟨Ger⟩ *student who is in comradeship especially attached to a student junior to him called* "Leibfuchs" **~diener** m *body servant* (bei *with*), *personal attendant* ~̽**eigen** a *in bondage*; ~ m *to enthral* **~eigene(r)** *bondsman, serf* (f *bondswoman*) **~eigenschaft** f *bondage, serfdom*; *chattel slavery* **~essen** n → ~gericht **~farbe** f ⟨fig⟩ *favourite colo(u)r* **~fuchs** m → ~bursch **~garde** f *body-guard,* ⟨engl⟩ *Life-Guards* pl **~gardist** m *Life-Guardsman,* ⟨engl⟩ *Yeoman of the Guard* **~gedinge** n *pension, life-annuity*; (Wittum) *jointure* **~gericht** n ⟨cul⟩ *favourite dish* **~gürtel** m *waist-belt* **~gut** n *estate for life* **~jäger** m **1.** *huntsman in ordinary* **2.** = ~diener **~koch** m *cook to a royal* od *high person-*

age **~kompagnie** f *colonel's company* **~kutscher** m *state coachman* **~lied** n *favourite song* **~medikus** m = ~arzt **~pacht** f *tenure for life* **~page** m *page of the presence* od *in ordinary* **~pferd** n *favourite horse* **~regiment** n *Sovereign's Own (regiment)* **~rente** f *life-annuity* **~riemen** m ⟨allg⟩ *waist-belt*; ⟨mil⟩ *garrison b.*; ⟨hist⟩ *sword b., crossb.* ‖ sich den ~ enger schnallen *to tighten one's belt* **~rock** m ⟨hist⟩ *dress-coat* ‖ ⟨ec R. C.⟩ *soutane* ‖ ⟨mil⟩ → Dolman **~schmerzen** m pl, **~schneiden** n *stomach-ache, colic, bellyache, gripes* pl, ⟨med⟩ *abdominal discomfort* od *pains* pl **~speise** f ⟨hum⟩ L.- und Magenspeise [f] *favourite dish* **~spruch** m (Lieblingsausdruck) *motto, device* **~standarte** f ⟨nazi⟩ *SS Life-Guards* pl **~stück** n *favourite air* **~wache** f ⟨allg⟩ *body-guard*; ⟨engl⟩ Kgl. ~ *the Honourable Corps of Gentlemen-at-Arms, the Queen's B.-G. of the Yeomen of the G.*; ⟨hist⟩ (Rom) *praetorian g.* **~wäsche** f *body-linen, underwear*; (Frauen≈) ⟨fam⟩ *undies* pl; ein Stück ~ *an undergarment* **~weh** n = ~schmerz **L·eibchen** n ~s/~ (am Frauenkleide) *bodice* ‖ (Korsett) *stays* pl **l·eiben** vi [h] ~ u leben → leben: da ist er wie er leibt und lebt ⟨fam⟩ *that's him all over* **L·eibes-** **~beschaffenheit** f *constitution (of body)*; (Erscheinung) *physique* **~beschwerden** f pl *infirmity* **~bewegung** f *bodily exercise* ‖ sich [dat] ~ m *to take exercise* **~erbe** m *natural heir*; *offspring* | ~n [pl] *issue (without ~)* **~erziehung** f *physical training* **~fehler** m *defect* od *blemish of the body* **~frucht** f *embryo, fœtus, fetus* ‖ Tötung der ~ *prolicide* **~gefahr** f *danger of life* **~gestalt** f *shape of the body*; *figure* **~größe** f *stature* **~kraft** f *bodily strength* ‖ aus ≈en *with all one's might, with might and main*; ⟨fam⟩ *for dear life*; *for all one is worth*; .. schreien *to shout at the top of one's voice* **~mitte** f *waist* **~nahrung** f *food*; ~ u Notdurft *food and clothing* **~öffnung** f *openness of the bowels* **~pflege** f *bodily hygiene* **~schwäche** f *corporal infirmity* **~strafe** f *corporal punishment* **~übungen** f pl *bodily exercises* pl, *physical training* (abbr *P. T.*); ⟨fam⟩ *ph. jerks*; (Turnen) *gymnastics* **~umfang** m *corpulence* **~verstopfung** f *constipation* **~visitation** [–tsion) f ⟨Kriminalpolizei⟩ *search* **l·eibhaft, leibh·aftig 1.** [a] *bodily, living, corporeal, in p* ‖ (wirklich) *real, true* ‖ er ist es ~ *it is h.s.* ‖ er ist der ~e .. *he is the very ..* ‖ der ~e Teufel *the devil incarnate* ‖ die ~e Geduld ⟨hum⟩ *patience on legs* ‖ der ~ige Vater *a chip of the old block* **2.** [adv] *in one's own p, bodily, p.ally*; (*to see a p*) *in the flesh* od *as large as life* .. **leibig** suff [zur Bildung v a wie] fett~ *fat-bodied* **l·eiblich** a *corporal (beauty)*; *bodily (needs)* [a. adv] ‖ *physical* → Wohl ‖ (materiell) *corporeal* ‖ (irdisch) *worldly, earthly* ‖ (leibhaftig) → dort ‖ ~er Bruder *own* od *full brother (to a p)* ‖ ~er Vetter *cousin-german* ‖ ihr ~er Sohn *her own son*; *her flesh and blood* ‖ m–e ~en Augen *my own eyes* **L·eibung** f ~/~en ⟨arch⟩ *intrados, soffit, jamb, body embrasure* | ~sbogen [m] *back arch*

Leich m ~(e)s/~e ⟨hist mus⟩ *lay*

L·eich- **~dorn** m *corn* ‖ ~operateur, ~schneider [m] *corn-cutter, chiropodist* **~huhn** n *lich-owl* **L·eiche** f ~/~n **1.** *dead body* (nur über m–e ~ *over my d. b.*); *corpse*; ⟨cont⟩ *carcass*; ⟨sl⟩ *stiff* (*'un*) ‖ er geht über ~en *he sticks at nothing* ‖ wandelnde ~ *living skeleton* ‖ die ~ wurde aufgebahrt *the body was laid out in state* ‖ e–n zur ~ m ⟨fam⟩ *to do for a p* **2.** (Begängnis) *funeral* ‖ zu e–r ~ gehen *to attend a f.* **3.** ⟨typ⟩ *omission, word* od *sentence left out* **4.** °(leere Flasche) ⟨fam⟩ *dead marine* od *soldier* **L·eichen-** **~acker** m = Gottesacker **~alkaloide** n pl *cadaveric alkaloids* pl **≈artig** a *cadaverous* **~ausgrabung** f *exhumation* **~bahre** f *bier* **~begängnis** n *funeral, burial* **~begleitung** f *f. train* **~beschauer** m *coroner* **~besichtigung** f = ~schau **~besorger, ~bestatter** m *undertaker*; ⟨Am⟩ *f. director*; *mortician* **~bitter** m *undertaker's man* | ~miene [f] *woe-begone face* **≈blaß** a *livid*; *pale as death, deadly pale*; (*face*) *as white as a sheet* **~blässe** f *deathlike pallor* **~feier** f *funeral, obsequies* pl **~fett** n ⟨anat⟩ *adipocere* **~finger** m **1.** ⟨bot⟩ = Stinkmorchel **2.** *cheese shaped like a finger* **~fledderer** m *plunderer of corpses* **~frau** f *layer-out* **~gebühr** f *burial-fee* **~gepränge** n *funeral rites* pl **~geruch** m *cadaverous smell* **~gerüst** n *catafalque* **~gesang** m *dirge* **~gewölbe** n, **~gruft** f *f. vault, catacomb* **~gift** n *ptomaine*; *pt. poison* **~halle** f, **~haus** n **1.** ⟨ec⟩ *mortuary*, ⟨fam⟩ *dead-house* **2.** (öffentlich) *morgue* **~hemd** n *shroud* **~huhn** n *lich-owl* **~kammer** f *death-chamber*; ⟨anat⟩ *dissecting-room* **~musik** f *f. music* **~öffnung** f *post-mortem examination*; ⟨med⟩ *autopsy* **~predigt, ~rede** f *f. sermon* od *oration* **~räuber** m *body snatcher/stripper* **~schändung** f *desecration* od *abuse of a dead body* **~schau** f *inquest (on a d. b.)* | ~schein [m] ⟨med⟩ *certificate of death* **~schmaus** m *f. repast* **~starre** f *rigor mortis* L **~stein** m *tombstone* **~träger** m *bearer* **~tuch** n *pall, shroud*; ⟨fig⟩ *shroud (of snow)* **~verbrennung** f *cremation* | ~sofen [m] *cremator* **~wache** f *death-watch* **~wagen** m *hearse* **~zug** m *funeral procession, cortège* [Fr] **l·eichenhaft** a *cadaverous* **L·eichnam** m ~(e)s/~e *(dead) body, corpse* ‖ lebender ~ *dead man alive*; ⟨path⟩ *walking skeleton* ‖ Veränderungen am ~ *cadaveric changes* ‖ °⟨hum⟩ mein sterblicher ~ *my apple-cart* ‖ s–n ~ pflegen ⟨fam⟩ *to look well after number one*

l·eicht I. [a] **1.** ⟨eig⟩ *light (burden*; ⟨übtr⟩ *fetters, music, wine, food, soil, troops, cart)* ‖ ⟨com⟩ zu ~ *under weight*; *worn, too light (coin)* | ⟨fig⟩ leichten Fußes *nimbly, at a light-footed pace* ‖ *easy (gait)* ‖ e–e ~e Hand h *to have a light touch* ‖ *thin* od *light (clothing)* ‖ *wan smile* ‖ *mild (tobacco)* ‖ *trivial (expenses)* ‖ e–n ~en Schlaf h *to sleep lightly* ‖ *weak (wine)* | ~er m, ~er w *to lighten* ‖ ⟨occultism⟩ ~er w *to levitate* ‖ sich den Kopf ~ m *to clear one's brain* ‖ sich ~ m *to relieve o.s.* od *one's bowels* **2. (leichtfertig)** *swift, fast, frivolous, (dead) easy, light-minded (girl)*; ~es Mädchen ⟨vulg⟩ *gay* od *merry bit, push-over*; das Mädel hat e–n ~en Sinn .. *is rather fast* ‖ ~er Bruder *gay customer* ‖ ~en Sinnes *easy-going* **3. (unbedeutend)** *slight (doubt, troubles, illness)* ‖ *gentle (reproof)* ‖ ~es Fieber h *to be a little feverish*; *minor (wound)* **4.** ⟨fig⟩ (geringe **Mühe** bereitend) (Ggs hart) *sitting (target* Beute); *easy (task)* ‖ *soft*, ⟨sl⟩ *cushy (job)*; *slight (exertion)*; *smooth (working)*; *fractional (raising of a finger), facile (tears)* ‖ *light (style)* ‖ ⟨sl⟩ *potty (questions)* ‖ leicht zu lernen *easy (language)* ‖ e–e ~e S ⟨fam⟩ *a snip* ‖ k–e ~e S ⟨fam⟩ *no picnic* ‖ °das macht mich um 100 M-chen (⟨vulg⟩ Eier) ~er *that puts me out of 5 quid* | [mit nouns] ⟨com⟩ ~en **Absatz** finden *to meet with ready sale* ‖ → Achsel ‖ ~en Kaufes davonk *to get off cheaply* ‖ mit ~er Mühe *with little trouble* ‖ er nahm es v der ~en Seite *he looked at it from the bright side* ‖ mit e–m ~es Spiel h *to beat, manage, persuade a p easily* ‖ ~er Treffer ⟨sl⟩ *sitter* | [mit verbs] **es ist** ~ mit ihm auszuk *he is easy to get on with* ‖ er macht sich's ~ ⟨fam⟩ *he takes it easy* ‖ ~er gesagt als getan *more easily said than done* ‖ es ist (mir) ein ~es *it is a trifling matter (to me)*, ⟨Am sl⟩ *it's a cinch* ‖ es wäre ein ~es gewesen *it would have been easy enough* ‖ er ist nicht ~ zu verstehen *he is not easy to understand* ‖ es wird ihm alles ~ *he shows great ease in everything* **II. [adv]** leicht annähen *to sew on lightly* ‖ *to breathe gently* ‖ *lightly built* ‖ etw ~ bek können *to have ready access to a th* ‖ sich ~ bewegen (P) *to move easily*; (S) *to move slightly* (wenig) ‖ ~ entzündlich *highly inflammable* ‖ ~ erhitzen *to heat gently* ‖ sich ~ erkälten *to be liable to colds* ‖ es fällt ihm ~ *it is easy for him to do*; es wird ihm nicht ~ fallen *it is going to be a little difficult for him (to ..)* ‖ ~ gehend *easy-rol-*

ling (*drawer*) ‖ das wird nicht so ~ wieder geschehen *that is not likely to happen again* ‖ ~ gewinnen *to win hands down* ‖ er hat es (nicht) ~ *he has an* (*no*) *easy time of it*, (⟨Am⟩ *he is hard put to it*) ‖ ~ z glauben *easy of belief* ‖ °sie ist nicht ~ z h *she's no push-over* ‖ ~ irreführend *apt to be misleading* ‖ ~ laufen: *the engine runs sweetly* ‖ ~ lesbar *easy to read* ‖ ~ z lösen *easy of solution* ‖ etw ~ nehmen *to make light, to think lightly of a th*; *to trifle with a th* ‖ du wirst das nicht so ~ schlagen ⟨sl⟩ *you will not beat that in a hurry* ‖ es konnte ~ s, daß *it could well be that* ‖ sie ist ~ gekränkt *she soon takes offence* ‖ ~ tanzen *to dance lightly* ‖ → traben ‖ etw ~ tun: *you could have done it with a feather* ‖ (nicht) ~ übelnehmen *to be* (*slow*) *quick to take offence* ‖ ~ verdaulich *light of digestion* ‖ ~ verdient *easy* (*money*) ‖ ~ vergessen *to be apt to forget* ‖ sich [dat] etw zu ~ vorstellen *it is not as easy* (*a matter*) *as one thinks*; sich ~ vorstellen können: *you may easily imagine* ‖ er wird ~ böse *he is easily roused* ‖ e–m ~er w als: *this life sits lighter on them than upon you* ‖ ~ zugänglich (P) *easy of access*; ⟨mach⟩ *readily accessible* **L·eicht- ~athletik** f (*light*) *athletics* sg & pl; '*track-and-field*' **≗bedeckt** a *lightly covered* **~benzin** n *light petrol, high grade p., etc* **≗beschwingt** a *light-winged*; ⟨fig⟩ *springy* (*steps*) **≗bewaffnet** a *light-armed* **≗blütig** a *sanguine, cheerful, buoyant* | ~keit [f] *s.ness* **≗faßlich** a *lucid*; *easy to understand* **≗fertig** a *light*(*-headed*), *frivolous, volatile*; (im Reden) *flippant*; (lose) *loose, giddy*; ~es Frauenzimmer *fast woman*; (gewissenlos, unbeständig) *fickle*; (mutwillig) *wanton* (*stealing*); (unbedacht) *feckless*, → fahrlässig; (gewissenlos) *irresponsible*; (unbedacht) *thoughtless* | adv *with levity*; etw ≗ behandeln *to make light of a th*; ~ spielen *to play fast and loose*; ~ umgehen mit *to play with* (*fire*); sich ~ benehmen ⟨a.⟩ *to play the giddy goat* | ~keit [f] *levity, frivolity, volatility, looseness, flippancy* **≗flüchtig** a *highly volatile* **≗flüssig** a *easily fusible* **~fuß** m ⟨fig⟩ *madcap, giddy-head, gay young spark* **≗füßig** a *nimble, light-footed* ‖ ⟨fig⟩ = ≗fertig **≗geschürzt** a *with one's clothes tucked-up* **~gewicht** n ⟨box⟩ (bis 122 Pfd) *light-weight* (⟨engl⟩ bis *135 lbs*) **≗gläubig** a *credulous*; ⟨fam⟩ *gullible*, ein ~er Mensch *an easy mark*, ⟨Am sl⟩ *a sucker* | ~keit [f] *credulity*, ⟨fam⟩ *gullibility* **≗hin** adv *lightly*, ⟨fig⟩ *off-handedly*; (*to answer*) *casually*; so ~ *in an* od *this off hand way, flippantly, airily*; ~ abtun *to shrug off* **~industrie** f *light engineering i.* **~kraftrad** n *l. motor cycle* **~kranke(r)** m *ambulatory case* **≗lebig** a *easy-going, gay, fast, flippant*, ⟨a.⟩ *Bohemian* .. **~matrose** m *ordinary seaman* **~metall**-Legierung f *light metal alloy*; ~karosserie *l. m. body* **~motorrad** n *light motor bicycle* **~schwergewicht** n ⟨box⟩ (bis 159 Pfd.) *light-heavy weight, cruiser-weight* (⟨engl⟩ bis *175 lbs*) **~sinn** m *levity, carelessness, frivolity* ‖ es ist ein gr ~ v dir *it is frightfully careless of you* (*to do*) **≗sinnig** a *light, frivolous, careless, feckless, harum-scarum, flighty, fast, giddy, light-minded*; (liederlich) *dissipated, debauched, profligate, licentious* | ~erweise [adv] *thoughtlessly, light-heartedly* **~verbrecher** m *star-prisoner* **≗verderblich(e Waren** f pl) [a] *perishable*(*s* pl) **≗verständlich** adv *in simple language* **≗verwundet** a *slightly wounded*; ein **≗er** m ⟨mil⟩ *a walking case* (Ggs *transport case*) **L·eichter**(- ~fahrzeug [n]) m ⟨mar⟩ *lighter, tender, scow, barge*; ~lohn [m] *lighterage* **l·eichtern** vt/i [h] ⟨mar⟩ (ein Schiff) ~ *to lighter* (*cargo*) | das Schiff leichtert .. *lightens* **L·eichtigkeit** f ~/ ⟨eig⟩ *lightness* → leicht I. 1. ‖ ⟨übtr⟩ *nimbleness, agility*; (muntere ~) *jauntiness* ‖ ⟨fig⟩ *effortlessness*, (→ leicht I. 4.) *ease, easiness, facility* ‖ ⟨mech⟩ *sweetness* (*in running*) ‖ → Kinderspiel ‖ mit ~ gewinnen *to win hands down* ‖ e–e ~ ⟨sl⟩ *a sitter* ‖ ⟨sport⟩ *it was a walk-over* ‖ ⟨Am sl⟩ *it's a cinch* ‖ k–e ~ ⟨fam⟩ *no picnic* ‖ ich hätte es mit ~ tun können *I could have done it with a feather* **l·eichtlich** adv *easily* → leicht II.

L·eid n ~(e)s/* ~en **1.** *harm, injury* ‖ (Unrecht) *wrong* ‖ sich [dat] ein ~(s) antun *to lay hands upon o.s.*; *to do o.s. a mischief* ‖ er hatte nie e–m Menschen etw zu≗e getan *he had never done mortal a wrong*; er tut k–r Fliege etw zu≗e *he can't harm* od *hurt a fly*; .. als könne er .. *he looks as if butter would not melt in his mouth* ‖ dir soll kein ~ geschehen *you shall suffer no harm* ‖ e–m ein ~ antun *to do a p an injury, to inflict wrong on a p* **2.** *affliction, sorrow, woe, grief* ‖ *pain* ‖ *calamity, misfortune* ‖ jds ~ lindern *or* heilen *to cure a p's woe* ‖ e–m sein ~ klagen *to complain to a p about one's wrongs, to tell a p one's plaintive story* ‖ ~ tragen *to be in mourning*; .. um e–n Toten *to mourn for a p* ‖ sie hielten in Lieb' u ~ zus *they held together for better and worse* ‖ ~en u Freuden *griefs and pleasures*; in Freud' u ~ *in joy and sorrow, in good and evil days* ‖ vor ~ vergehn *to pine away for grief* ‖ über e–e Sünde Reue u ~ empfinden *to have regrets for a sin* ‖ Freude u ~ *the joy and the anguish* (*of life*) **l·eid** a; es ist *or* tut mir furchtbar ~ *I am awfully sorry, I regret* (daß *that*) (sagen zu müssen *to say*); *I'm afraid* (*I can't give you the address*); *I'm afraid* (*I don't know*) ‖ das tut mit ~ *it grieves me*; *I'm afraid I can't help it* ‖ es tut mir ~ für dich, du tust mir ~ *I am sorry for you*; *I pity you* ‖ e–m etw ~ m *to make a p regret a th* ‖ sind ihm s–e Zusagen wieder ~ geworden? *does he regret his promises*? ‖ es wird dir schon noch ~ w! *you will be sorry for it yet*! | **sich** [dat] (selbst) ~ tun *to be sorry for o.s.* **L·eid- ≗tragend** a *in mourning* **~tragende(r)** m *mourner*, die ~en *the bereaved relatives* ‖ ⟨fam übtr⟩ (*I am*) *the victim* **~wesen** n; zu m–m ~ muß ich .. *to my* (*great*) *regret* od *sorrow, distress, dismay I must* .., *much to my s.*; *I regret having to* .. **L·eideform** f ~/~en ⟨gram⟩ *passive* (*voice*) **L·eiden** n ~s/~ *suffering*; gr ~ *agony* ‖ ⟨fig⟩ (Elend) *affliction, misfortune* ‖ W.s ~ *The Sorrows of Werther* ‖ ⟨med⟩ *complaint*; ein unbedeutendes ~ *a minor ailment* ‖ *an acute, chronic illness* ‖ (Christi) *passion* ‖ er sieht aus wie das ~ Christi (⟨mil⟩ °zu Pferde) *he looks a picture of misery* **l·eiden** vt/i irr [h] **1.** *to suffer* (an [dat] *from*) ‖ er leidet an der Leber *his liver is out of order*; an Leberschwellung *he is running to liver*; an k–r Krankheit ~ ⟨off⟩ *to be free of disease*; .. an den Nerven *his nerves are upset*; .. an Ohnmachten *his is subject to fainting fits* ‖ woran leidet er? *what does he ail from*? ‖ ~ unter *to smart from* (*wounds*) ‖ z ~ h unter *to labour under*; z ~ h v jdm *to suffer at a p's hands* ‖ durch Tragen gelitten h *to be the worse for wear* ‖ nicht (not) ~ l *not to impair*; nicht ~ dürfen unter *not to be sacrificed to* (*brevity*) **2.** **(aushalten)** *to bear, undergo*; *to endure* (*thirst, hunger*), *to suffer* (*great damage, shipwreck, punishment, a great loss*) **3.** **(zulassen)** *to tolerate, permit, allow* ‖ die S leidet k–n Aufschub .. *admits of no delay* ‖ das leid' ich nicht *I won't have that* ‖ zweifache Auffassung ~ *to be open to two interpretations* ‖ er litt ihn nicht im Zimmer *he would not have him in the room* **4.** ~ **mögen** *to like* ‖ ich mag ihn nicht ~ *I cannot endure, stand*, ⟨fam⟩ *abide*, ⟨sl⟩ *stick him*; *I don't like him*; ⟨sl⟩ *I have it in for him, I got my knife into him, I cannot away with him*; ⟨Am⟩ *I have a down on him* ‖ er ist überall wohl gelitten *he is a favourite with everybody*; ich bin bei ihm w. g. *I'm in his good books* **l·eidend** a *suffering* ‖ (kränklich) *sickly, ailing* ‖ an e–r tödlichen Kr. ~ *stricken with mortal illness* ‖ ~ s *to be failing in health, to be in ill h.* ‖ ~ an *afflicted with* ‖ er ist schon lange ~ *he has been a sufferer for a long time* ‖ ⟨gram⟩ *passive* **L·eidende** m [der ~/ein ~r] ~n/~n *sufferer* ‖ *patient, sick p., invalid* **L·eidener** → Leydener **L·eidens- ~becher** m =

∼kelch **∼gefährte, ∼genosse** m *fellow sufferer, companion in adversity*; ∼n s *to be in the same boat* **∼geschichte** f *history of a p's sufferings* ‖ ⟨rel⟩ *Christ's Passion* **∼kelch** m ⟨fig⟩ *cup of bitterness* **∼probe** f *trial* **∼station** f ⟨rel⟩ *Station of the Cross* **∼stätte** f *place of suffering*; ⟨rel & fig⟩ *Golgatha* **∼weg** m; Christi ∼ *Jesus' bitter path to the cross*; ein einziger ∼ .. *an unbroken life of suffering* **∼werkzeuge** n pl (Christi) *Instruments of the Passion* **∼woche** f *Passion* od *Holy Week* **∼zeit** f *years of tribulation* **L·eidenschaft** f *passion, emotion* ‖ edle ∼ ⟨a.⟩ *sacred fire* ‖ wilde ∼ *towering fury* od *rage* ‖ die Wellen der ∼en gingen hoch *p.s ran high* ‖ e–n in s–n ∼en bestärken *to pander to a p's p.s*; die ∼ in jdm schüren *to stir the fire of a p's passion* ‖ s–n ∼en frönen *to give way to one's p.s* ‖ die ersten Wogen der ∼ *the first transports* ‖ ∼en [pl] *likings* pl ‖ Spiel≗ *p.* od *zest for gambling* ‖ Reisen ist s–e ganze ∼ *travelling is a downright p. with him* ‖ mit aller ∼ *with all one's heart* **l·eidenschaftlich** a *p.ate* (*character, mood*) ‖ *rapturous* (*joy*) ‖ *ardent* (*love*) ‖ *vehement* (*gesture*) ‖ *burning, ardent* (*desire, longing*) ‖ *enthusiastic* (*admirer*) ‖ *hot* (*workman*) ‖ *impassioned* (*address*) ‖ *violent* (*hate, language*) ‖ ein ∼er Mensch *an impetuous spirit* ‖ er ist ein ∼er Ruderer *he goes in for rowing in a big way* | er liest ∼ [adv] gern *he is p.ately fond of reading, reading is a p. with him* **≗keit** f *p.ateness, ardour, vehemence* ‖ *pathos* ‖ *impetuous spirit* **L·eidenschafts- ∼ausbruch** m *heat* **≗los** a *dispassionate, unemotional* (*manner*) ‖ (unempfindlich) *callous, hard-hearted* ‖ (sachlich) *matter-of-fact, cool*(*-blooded*) **∼losigkeit** f ∼/ (→ vor) *d.ness* ‖ *c.ness, cool-b.ness, m.-of-f.ness*

l·eider ∼! intj *alas*! *sad to say*; *to my* (etc) *sorrow*; ∼ Gottes! *worse luck*! ‖ adv *unfortunately* ‖ sie ist ∼ krank *I am sorry* (*we grieve*) *to say, she is ill* ‖ wir h euch ∼ nicht angetroffen *we are sorry that* .. ‖ ich muß Ihnen ∼ mitteilen, daß .. *I regret to inform you that* .. ‖ ∼ nicht viel *not much, I'm afraid*; (*I don't know*), *I'm sure* ‖ wir k ∼ nicht .. *we regret our inability to c.* ‖ es ist ∼ wahr *it is unfortunately true* **l·eidig** a *tiresome, troublesome, disagreeable* ‖ (verdrießlich) *vexatious* (*accident*) ‖ *unfortunate* (*circumstances*) ‖ (schlimm) *fatal, dismal* ‖ das ∼e Geld! *cursed Mammon*!; .. Trost *a poor consolation* **l·eidlich** a *tolerable* ‖ ganz ∼ *well enough, not so bad* ‖ (mittelmäßig) *moderate, passable, indifferent* | ⟨fam⟩ [a. adv] *middling* | [adv] *passably*; *tolerably, reasonably*; *his condition is fairly satisfactory* ‖ es geht so ∼ *I am managing* od *getting on fairly well* od *tolerably*; *it is so-so* od *pretty middling* od *after a fashion* ‖ er wird s–e S ∼ m *he'll pass muster all right* ‖ er ist noch so ∼ davongek *he got off pretty cheaply* **≗keit** f ∼/ *t.ness, mediocrity*

L·eier f ∼/∼n *lyre* ‖ ⟨astr⟩ *Lyra* ‖ ⟨fig⟩ *hackneyed tune* ‖ die alte ∼ *the* (*same*) *old song* od *tune* ‖ immer dieselbe ∼ anstimmen *to be for ever harping on the same string* **∼antilope** f → Kuh .. **≗förmig** a *lyre-shaped* **∼gang** m; der alte ∼ *the old jog-trot* **∼kasten** m *barrel-organ, hurdy-gurdy* **∼(kasten)mann** m *organ-grinder* **∼schwanz** m ⟨orn⟩ *lyre-bird* **Leier·ei** f ∼/ → Geleier, Leier ⟨fig⟩ **l·eiern** vi [h] *to play on the hand organ* ‖ *to grind a barrel-organ* od *tune* ‖ ⟨fig⟩ *to drawl, drone* ‖ e–m die Ohren voll| ∼ *to din one's tale into a p's ears* ‖ ⟨allg⟩ (kurbeln) *to turn a crank* | ⟨fig⟩ *to muddle* od *potter about* ‖ °e–m etw aus dem Kreuze ∼ *to make a p come down with a th*

L·eih- ∼amt n *pawnbroker's office* **∼bibliothek** f *circulating library*, ⟨Am⟩ *rental l.* ‖ (öffentliche) *lending l.* **∼gabe** f ⟨arts⟩ *loan* **∼gebühr** f *lending fee* **∼haus** n *pawnbroker's shop*; ins ∼ tragen *to put into pawn*, ⟨fam⟩ *to put up the spout* **∼- und P·achtgesetz** ⟨Am⟩ *Lend-Lease Act* (11.3.1941) **∼(ver)packung** f *returnable packaging* **∼wagen** m ⟨mot⟩ *car hired out* (*gratis*) **l·eihen** vt [lieh/geliehen] [h] **1.** (jdm) *to lend* (*a p*); ⟨Am a.⟩ *to loan* ‖ *to advance* (*a p money*), *to accomodate* (*a p with m.*) ‖ (Gemälde) *to loan* **2.** (v jdm entlehnen) *to borrow* (*of* od *from a p*) ‖ (mieten) *to hire* (*a horse from a p*) ‖ ich habe es mir ∼ l (*or* geliehen) *I had it lent me*, (gemietet) *I took it on hire* ‖ ⟨fig⟩ e–m sein Ohr ∼ *to lend an ear to a p* **L·eiher** m ∼s/∼ **1.** *lender* **2.** *borrower* **l·eihweise** adv *on loan* ‖ (mietweise) *on hire* ‖ kann ich .. ∼ h? *may I have the loan of* ..? etw ∼ erhalten *to have a th on loan* (v e–m *from a p*)

Leik n ⟨mar⟩ = Liek **L·eilach** n = Leinlaken

L·eim m ∼(e)s/∼e *glue* ‖ (zum Steifen etc) *size* ‖ ⟨pap⟩ *animal sizing, size* ‖ (Vogelfang≗) (*bird-*)*lime* ‖ ⟨chem⟩ *lute* ‖ ⟨fig fam⟩ das ist ein elender ∼ .. *a wretched take-in*; auf den ∼ gehen *to fall into the trap, to rise to bait, to swallow b.*; e–m .. *to be taken in by a p*, ⟨Am⟩ *to fall for a p's line*; ich bin nicht auf den ∼ gegangen *the trap is down*! *the trick to do me has failed* ‖ **aus** dem ∼ ⟨fig⟩ *off the hinges*, ⟨bes Am fam⟩ *out of kilter*; ⟨fam⟩ **aus** dem ∼ gehen *to get out of joint*; ganz .. *to fall to pieces* (⟨a. übtr⟩ v Freundschaft) **≗artig** a *glue-like*, ⟨scient⟩ *glutinous* **∼druck** m ⟨typ⟩ *size printing* **∼farbe** f *limewater-colour* ‖ ⟨arts⟩ *distemper* **∼fuge** f *glue-joint* **∼grund** m *glue-priming* **∼knecht** m (S) *g. press* **∼kraut** n ⟨bot⟩ *catchfly, fly-bane* **∼ring** m ⟨hort⟩ *greaseband* **∼rute** f *lime-twig* **∼sieder** m *glue-boiler* ‖ ⟨fig fam⟩ *slow--coach* **∼stoff** m ⟨chem⟩ *gluten* **∼tiegel, ∼topf** m *glue-pan, -pot* **∼wasser** n *glue-water* **∼zwinge** f (Werkzeug) *screw-clamp* **l·eimen** vt [h] *to glue* ‖ (Papier) *to size* ‖ ⟨bookb⟩ *to glue up*; geleimtes Buch *paperback*; sich [acc] ∼ l ⟨fig⟩: *ths can be patched up* ‖ ⟨hunt⟩ (e–n Vogel) *to lime* ‖ °jdn ∼ ⟨fam⟩ *to take a p in* ‖ der Geleimte *the dupe* **l·eimig** a *gluey, viscous*

.. lein n ∼s/∼ [dim suff] (Lämmlein *lambkin*; *ringlet*, Dörflein *hamlet*) (→ .. chen)

L·ein m ∼(e)s/∼e (∼samen) *linseed* ‖ (Flachs) *flax* **∼bau** m *cultivation of f.* **∼dotter** m ⟨bot⟩ *gold of pleasure* **∼kraut** n ⟨bot⟩ *wild flax* **∼kuchen** m *oil-cake* **∼laken** n = –tuch **∼ölfirnis** m *boiled linseed-oil* **∼pfad** m *tow*(*ing*)*-path* → Leine **∼saat** f, **∼samen** m *linseed* **∼tuch** n *linen cloth* od *sheet* **∼wand** f → d. **∼weber** m *linen-weaver* **∼zeug** n *linen* **L·eine** f ∼/∼n *line, cord* ‖ Fang≗ *harpoon-line* ‖ Hunde≗ (*dog-*)*lead, leash* ‖ Wäsche≗ (*clothes-*)*line* ‖ Zug≗ *towing rope* ‖ sie nahm den Hund an die (ließ ihn v der) ∼ *she put him on* (*let him off*) *his lead, slipped him* ‖ durch e–e ∼ (ab)sperren *to cord off* ‖ ⟨fig fam⟩ ∼ ziehen *to clear out* **L·einen** n ∼s/∼ (⟨theat⟩ *opaque*) *linen* ‖ grobes ∼ *drabbet* ‖ feines weißes ∼ *cambric* ‖ Steif≗ *buckram* ‖ Gerstenkorn≗ *huckaback* **l·einen** a (*made of*) *linen* **L·einen- ∼band 1.** n *tape* **2.** m ⟨bookb⟩ *cloth binding* **∼damast** m *l.-damask* **∼garn** n *l. yarn* **∼gewebe** n *l. woof* **∼kittel** m *smockfrock* **∼papier** n *l. paper* **∼tuch** n *l. cloth* **∼waren** f pl, **∼zeug** n *l.* (*goods* pl) **∼zwirn** m *l. tread* **L·einwand** f ∼/ *linen, cloth*; grobe ∼ *burlap* ‖ ⟨paint⟩ *canvas* ‖ ungebleichte ∼ (*brown*) *holland, unbleached l.* ‖ Zupf≗ *lint* ‖ auf die ∼ werfen ⟨film⟩ *to screen*; *to project on to a sc.* ‖ in ∼ gebunden *bound in cloth* **∼band** m *c. binding* ‖ *volume bound in c.* **∼bleiche** f *bleaching* ‖ (Platz) *bl.-ground* **∼handel** m *l.-trade* **∼händler** m *l.--draper* **∼kittel** = Leinenkittel

L·eipzig n ⟨Ger⟩ (Stadt in Sachsen) | ∼er Allerlei [n] n ∼s/ ⟨cul⟩ *mixed vegetables*; ∼er Mustermesse [f] *Leipzig Fair*; ∼er Titeldruck [m] = Katalogkarten (internat. 7,5 × 12,5 cm)

l·eis(e) 1. [a] *low* (*voice*) ‖ *faint, slight* (*noise*) ‖ *light* (*step*) | ⟨übtr⟩ (sachte) *soft* ‖ (sanft) *gentle* (*rain, breath*) ‖ (zart) *delicate, faint* ‖ *slight* (*hint, suspicion*) ‖ *faint* (*doubt*) ‖ bei der ∼sten Frage *at the shadow of a question* ‖ ich habe e–e ∼ Ahnung, daß sie k *I have an inkling of their coming*

|| nicht die ~ste Aussicht *not a dog's chance* (auf *of*); nicht die ~ste Ahnung *not the faintest idea* od *vaguest notion*; jede ~ste *any faint* (*discrimination*) || ein ~s Gehör h *to be sharp of hearing* || e–n ~en Schlaf h *to sleep lightly, to be a light sleeper* **2.** [adv] (*to speak*) *low* od *under one's breath* od *in a low voice* || (*to knock*) *softly, gently* || ⟨theat⟩ *aside* || er hört sehr ~ *he has a quick ear* || ~ auftreten *to tread softly* || (*to touch*) *lightly* || ⟨fig⟩ ~ treten *to slime, sneak*; *to sing small, to draw in one's horns* °**L·eisetreter** m ~s/~ ⟨fig⟩ *spy, slink, pussyfoot, sneak, hypocrite* || ⟨Am⟩ *pussyfoot*(*er*) || er ist ein ~ *he is a bit of a sneak* | **~·ei** f *sneaking* | **≗isch** a *pussyfooting, flannel--mouthed*

l·eistbar a *feasible, practicable*

L·eistchen n ~s/~ ⟨arch⟩ *bandelet* **L·eiste**[1] f ~/~n *ledge, border* || ⟨arch⟩ *fillet* ⟨a. theat⟩; *reglet* || Dach≗ *cornice* || Fuß≗, Wand≗ *skirt--board* || ⟨tech⟩ *border, ledge*; *strip*; *batten* || (Tuch) *selvage, list, ledge*

L·eiste[2] f ⟨anat⟩ *groin* || ~n- *inguinal*

L·eisten m ~s/~ ⟨tech⟩ *last, form, model* || (zur Erhaltung der Form) *shoe-, boot-tree* || über den ~ schlagen *to put upon the block* od *last*; *to tree* || alles über einen ~ schlagen ⟨fig⟩ *to treat all ths alike, to tar everything with the same brush* || ⟨prov⟩ Schuster, bleib bei d–m ~! *every jack to his trade*!

l·eisten vt [h] (→ Leistung) *to do* (*one's duty*) || (verrichten) *to perform* (*a piece of work*) || (erfüllen) *to fulfil, accomplish* || (ausführen) *to carry out* || (verwirklichen) *to effect, realize* || etw ~ *to achieve, accomplish*, ⟨Am fam⟩ *to toe the mark* | **mehr** ~ als *to prevail over* || er leistet **viel** *he is a wizard*; im Malen h sie nie viel ge–tet *they have never been clever at painting*; er –tet soviel wie zwei andere Arbeiter *he does the work of two other workmen*; **wenig** ~ *to do little* | **Abbitte** ~ *to apologize*; Anzahlung ~ *to make a deposit*; er wird nichts Außergewöhnliches ~ *he won't set the Thames on fire*; e–n **Beitrag** ~ z .. *to make a contribution to* ..; **Bürgschaft** ~ *to give security*; .. für jdn *to go bail for a p* || Buße ~ *to do penitence* || (e–m) e–n **Dienst** ~ *to render a service* (*to*); D.e ~: *to do most important service for* ..; Namen ~ uns hier gute D.e *names here stand us in good stead* || e–n **Eid** ~ *to take an oath* || Ersatz ~ *to make restitution* || e–r Einladung Folge ~ *to accept an invitation* || **Gehorsam** ~ *to yield obedience* || Genugtuung ~ *to give satisfaction* || → Gesellschaft, Gewähr || Großes ~ *to achieve great ths* || **Hilfe** ~, hilfreiche Hand ~ *to give assistance, to lend a* (*helping*) *hand* || Hervorragendes ~ in *to excel in* || das Höchste z ~ suchen *to aspire to a high level of excellence* || Huldigung ~ *to do* od *render homage* || er hat sein möglichstes ge–tet *he has done his best* || **nichts** ~ *to be inefficient*; er leistet nichts außer in *he is no good except in* || er wird nie etw **Ordentliches** ~ *he will never do much* || e–n **Schwur** ~ *to swear an oath* || Sicherheit ~ *to give security* || etw **Tüchtiges** ~ in *to do well in, to show proficiency in, to make a mark on a th* || sie ~ Übermenschliches *their efforts are almost superhuman*; → **Verzicht** || Vorschuß ~ auf *to advance money on* || Vorzügliches ~ *to achieve excellent results, to do excellently well* || e–m **Widerstand** ~ *to offer* od *make resistance* od *opposition to a p*; nur kurz W. ~ *to put up but a short resistance* | **sich etw** ~ *to treat* (⟨Am sl⟩ *blow*) *o.s. to a th* || sich etw ~ können *to be in a position to do a th*; ich kann *or* darf mir es (nicht) ~ *I can*(*not* od *ill*) *afford it* (z tun *to do*); (aus freien Stücken) *to volunteer* (*a remark*) || er –tete sich die freche Antwort, daß .. *he had the cheek to answer that* .. || °da hat er sich [dat] etw Nettes ge–tet! ⟨vulg⟩ *he has been and gone and done it*!; sich e–n Witz an/mit jdm ~ ⟨fam⟩ *to come a joke on a p*

L·eisten- ~beule f [Leiste[2]] ⟨path⟩ *bubo* **~bruch** m ⟨path⟩ (*inguinal*) *hernia, rupture in the groin* **~drüse** f *i. gland* **~gegend** f *groin*, ⟨scient⟩ *i. region* **~hobel** m [Leiste[1]] *fillet-* od *ogee-plane* **~holz** n [Leisten] *wood for lasts* **~schneider** m *last-cutter* **~werk** n [Leiste[1]] *mouldings pl*

L·eistung f ~/~en **1.** (das Leisten) *performance, accomplishment, execution, proficiency, efficiency* || ⟨mech⟩ *power, capacity* || ⟨mot⟩ *horsepower rating* || ~ ist die in der Zeiteinheit getane Arbeit *power is the rate at which work is done, and implies time measurement*; ~ erfolgt *p. is acting* || *taking* (*of an oath*) **2.** (das Geleistete) ⟨phys, mach⟩ *result, effect*; (P) *feat* || bedeutende ~ ⟨tech⟩ *engineering feat* || (e–r Fabrik *or* Maschine) *production, output* (höhere ~ bei geringerer Mühe *higher o. at less effort*); *performance* (die besten ~en erzielen *to achieve maximum p.*); *ratings* pl || ⟨ins⟩ *benefit* || *service*(*s*) *rendered* || (*excellent*) *workmanship* od *piece of work* || ⟨el⟩ *wattage* || ⟨arts⟩ *workmanlike* od *artistic performance* || ⟨sport sl⟩ *stunt, performance* (*of a team*) (sinkt ab *deteriorates*) || ⟨com⟩ *disbursement* || ⟨tech⟩ die ~ steigern *to tune up* || s–e guten ~en im Latein *his skill at L., his proficiency* od *attainments in L.*; jds ~en beeinträchtigen *to cramp a p's style* || das war e–e ~! *that was a great th to do* od *a fine effort*! || die Truppen h erstaunliche ~en vollbracht .. *did astonishingly good work*; ihre ~en *their triumphs*; an ~en gewöhnt *conditioned to achievement*; e–e geniale ~ *a stroke of genius* || k–e geringe ~ *no small feat* || Glanz≗ ⟨sl⟩ *stunt*; höchste Glanz≗ *acme* || Kraft≗ *tour de force* Fr ⟨a. übtr⟩ **3.** ⟨**tech**⟩ a) (Kraft≗) *power* | b) (ausgebrachte Menge) (*work*) *output, production* | c) (Menge durch Zeit) *rate of output, production rate* | d) (Kapazität = mögliche Menge durch Zeit) (*work*) *capacity* **L·eistungs- ~aufnahme** f ⟨el⟩ *input*; ⟨tech⟩ *power consumption* **~ausschluß** m ⟨ins⟩ *exclusion of benefits* **~beschreibung** f ⟨mach⟩ *specifications* **~blatt** n *record sheet* **~empfänger** m *p to whom the services are supplied* **≗fähig** a (P) *efficient* || ⟨mach⟩ *powerful*; (Fabrik etc) *productive* || ⟨com⟩ *solid, solvent*; ~er s als *to outperform* | ~keit [f] *efficiency*; *capacity, productivity, productive power*; ⟨tech, phys⟩ *power*; gr ~ ⟨mach⟩ *high output capacity*; ⟨com⟩ *solvency*; ⟨mil⟩ *effectiveness* **~gewicht** n *weight per HP* **~höhe** f *pitch* od *level of proficiency* **~klage** f ⟨jur⟩ *action for specific performance* **~kurve** f ⟨tech⟩ *power curve, performance graph* **~lohn** m (bei Akkordarbeit) *payment by results*; progressiver ~ *accelerating incentive* **~merkmale** n pl *characteristics* **~niveau** n *competency* (*in teaching*, etc) **~ort** m *place of performance* **~prüfung** f *efficiency test* **~reaktor** m *power reactor* **~religion** f *r. according to which one tries to be saved by one's own efforts*; ⟨übtr⟩ der ~ nachhängen *to make a god of efficiency* **~schau** f (z. B. *industrial*) *trade-fair* **~segelflugzeug** n *p.-type glider* **~spitze** f ⟨com⟩ *ceiling* **~sport** m *competitive sports* pl **~verlust** m *waste power, lost effect* **~vermögen** n *capacity* **~verzug** m *delay of obligation*

L·eit- ~artikel m (e–r Zeitung) *editorial*; ⟨fam⟩ *leader, lead-off* **~bake** f ⟨mar⟩ *leading beacon* **~band** n → Gängelband **~batterie** f ⟨artill⟩ *lead* od *central b.* **~bild** n = Ideal *image* **~blech** n (f Kraftstoff) *baffle* ⟨a. aero⟩ **~block** m ⟨mar⟩ *leading-block* (*for a rope*) **~bomber** m *master--bomber* **~faden** m ⟨fig⟩ *clue, guide*; (Buch) *manual, textbook, introduction, gradus* (der Botanik *to botany*) **~fähigkeit** f ⟨el⟩ *conductivity* **~feuer** n *leading light* **~flugzeug** n *pathfinder* N **~gedanke** m *principle*; *leading idea* **~hammel** m *bell-wether* ⟨a. fig⟩ **~karte** f ⟨comp⟩ *master card* **~linie** f *white line* (*for pedestrians*); ⟨mot⟩ (un)-

unterbrochene ~ (*solid*) *broken line*; er reitet auf der ~ *he takes his half out of the middle* **~motiv** n ⟨mus⟩ *leading motif, leitmotiv* **~offizier** m ⟨aero⟩ *controller* **~planke** f ⟨mot⟩ *safety fence* **~riemen** m *leash*; ⟨hors⟩ *driving rein* **~rolle** f ⟨tech⟩ *guide--pulley* **~satz** m *guiding principle* **~scheinwerfer** m *master s.* **~schiene** f ⟨rail⟩ *guard-rail, switch* **~seil** n *guide-rope*; ⟨hunt⟩ *leash* **~sprache** f (bei Übersetzung) *source language* **~stand** ⟨mar, mil⟩ *control station* **~stange** ⟨tech⟩ *conducting rod* **~-stern** m ⟨astr⟩ *polar star*, ⟨fig⟩ *lodestar, leading star* **~strahl** m ⟨aero⟩ *radio beam* | ~anflug [m] *beam approach*; ~anlage [f] *r. directive device* **~tier** n ⟨hunt⟩ *leader* **~weg** m ⟨post⟩ *route, via* **~werk** n ⟨aero⟩ *controls* pl, *empennage*; *tail-fin* (*of a bomb*) **~zügel** m *leading rein*, → leiten

L·eite f ~/~n (Abhang) *declivity, slope*

l·eiten vt [h] **1.** *to lead, guide* || *conduct* (*negotiations, a concert*, ⟨a. phys⟩) || (*the wires*) *transmit* (*the current*); ⟨comp⟩ *to transfer*; z Speicher *to store*; ⟨aero⟩ *to vector* || ⟨traffic⟩ *to route* (*all cars were r.d via M.*) || (e–n auf den rechten Weg) *to direct*; ⟨fig⟩ *to put in the right way*; *if reason had swayed our policy* || e–n ~ ⟨fam⟩ *to run a p* || auf die Spur ~ *to point to the track* || (Stoff) *to pass* (über *over* [*platinum*]) || (Gas durch Röhren) *to convey* || e–n Fluß in ein anderes Bett ~ *to divert .. into ..* || ein Gesuch an .. (weiter) ~ *to pass on .. to ..* || (Abwässer) *to drain* (*sewage*) (in *into*) | **sich** ~ l v .. *to govern one's action by ..*; sich v dem Gedanken ~ l an *to be affected by the thought of*; sich ganz v jdm ~ l *to be quite in a p's hands*; sich schwer ~ l *to be difficult to manage*; sich v den Umständen ~ l *to be ruled by circumstances* || sich v nichts ~ l können *to have nothing to go by* **2.** (**beaufsichtigen, verwalten**) *to direct, manage, conduct, control* || *to have control of* (*a department*); ⟨Am⟩ *to preside over* || (Gottesdienst) *to conduct* || (Inszenierung) ⟨theat⟩ *to be in charge of* (*the production*) || *to be at the head of* (*a school*) || (Versammlung) *to preside over* (*a meeting*) || *to run* (*a canteen, house*) || *to have* (*an investigation*) *in charge*; ⟨Am⟩ *the inquest was presided over by N.* || *to rule* (*the state*) **leitend** a *leading* (*idea*), *conducting* ⟨a. phys⟩ || ⟨el⟩ nicht ~ *non-conducting* || *guiding* (*hand*) || *key* (*member*) || die ~en Kreise *the governing classes* || ~e Stellen [pl] ⟨com, ind⟩ *executive positions* || ~er Zug *dominant note* **L·eiter**[1] m ~s/~ **1.** *leader* (expedition), *guide* (education) || *conductor* ⟨a. mus⟩ (f *conductress*) || technischer ~ *chief engineer* || (e–s Geschäfts) *manager*(*ess* f); ⟨com Am a.⟩ *president*; ⟨sl⟩ *boss* || verantwortlicher ~ *executor* || *chief engineer* || ⟨tech, mil⟩ *director* (*of manœuvres*, der Personalabteilung *of personel services* pl) || ⟨wir⟩ *program supervisor*; *supervising engineer* || (e–r Schule) *head master* (f *head mistress*) || ⟨mil⟩ ~ der Fla *antiaircraft defence commander* N; ~ der Generalstabsabteilung *Assistant Chief of Staff* N, → G 1–4 | Abteilungs~̣ *head of the department* || Partei~̣ *manager*, ⟨dero⟩ *wire-puller*, ⟨Am⟩ *boss* || Propaganda~̣ *press agent* || Spiel~̣ ⟨theat⟩ *stage-manager* || Verkaufs~̣ *sales manager* || Versammlungs~̣ *chairman*; ⟨engl parl⟩ *leader of the House* || Wahl~̣ *voting steward* **2.** ⟨phys⟩ *conductor*

L·eiter[2] f ~/~n *ladder* || Feuer~̣ (mechanische ~) (*telescopic*) *fire-l., f.-escape* (*l.s were telescoped* wurden in–e–a geschoben); (drehbare ~) *turntable l.* || Folter~̣ *rack l.* || Hühner~̣ *hen-l.* || schwedische ~ (Sprossenwand) ⟨gym⟩ *wall-bars* || Steh~̣ *step-l.*, (*pair of*) *steps* pl || Strick~̣ *rope-l.* | e–e ~ an–, aufstellen *to put up a l.* || mit ~n ersteigen *to mount with l.s*, ⟨mil⟩ *to scale* || v e–r ~ fallen *to fall off a l.* | ⟨fig⟩ die soziale ~ immer tiefer hinabsteigen *to sink lower and l. in the social scale* **~baum** m *l.-beam* **~ersteigung** f *mounting of* od *with l.s*, ⟨mil⟩ *scaling* **~-fahrzeug** n *mobile turn-table* **~̣förmig** a *l.-shaped* **~gerüst** n *mason's scaffold* **~haken** m *roof hook* **~sprosse** f *rung* (*of a l.*), *l.-step* **~übungen** f pl *l. work* **~wagen** m *rack-, l.-wag(g)on*, ⟨mst⟩ *open van*, ⟨a.⟩ *break*

L·eitung f ~/~en (→ l·eiten) **1.** (das Leiten) *leading, management, leadership, guidance, direction*; ~ des Auges *visual guidance* || oberste ~ *headship* || *board* (*German Coal Mining B.*) || unter jds ~ arbeiten *to work* od *labo(u)r under a p* || ⟨mil⟩ *control* || *running*, ⟨Am⟩ *operation* (*of schools*) || die ~ in die Hand nehmen *to undertake the management* || unter s–r ~ *under his control, direction, tutelage*, ⟨mus⟩ *conduction*; *Mr. N. conducting* **2.** ⟨phys⟩ (Vorgang) *conduction, convection* **3.** ⟨tech, mach⟩ *guiding-bar, transmission* || (Verbindungsstück etc) *connexion* || Licht~̣ *lighting connexion* || ⟨el⟩ *lead* || ⟨telph⟩ *line, wire*; e–e ~ belegen *to seize a l.*; die ~ ist besetzt *the line is busy*; Haupt~̣ *main*; oberirdische ~ *overhead line*; el. ~ in e–m Zimmer anlegen *to wire a room for electricity* || (Rohr~̣) *conduit* (*-pipe*), *plumbing, pipe-line, pipes* pl || ⟨fig⟩ °er hat e–e lange ~ → lang, lausig **L·eitungs- ~bündel** n ⟨el⟩ *bunched circuit* **~draht** m *conducting-wire, telegraph wire* **~fähigkeit** f ⟨el⟩ *conductivity* **~führung** f *wiring* **~mast** m *telephone pole* || *tower for aerial lines* **~netz** n ⟨el⟩ *supply network*; ⟨tech⟩ *distribution, water system* **~prüfer** m ⟨el⟩ *fault-finder* **~rohr** n *conduit-pipe, delivery-tube* || (für Gas, Wasser) *main* **~schnur** f *cord* **~störung** f *line fault* **~system** n *wiring* **~- u Schiedsrichterdienste** m pl *control and umpire service* sg **~vermögen** n ⟨tech⟩ *conductibility, conducting power* **~wasser** n *company's water, main* od *tap water* **~widerstand** m ⟨el⟩ *resistivity*

L·eitzordner ® m *arch file*

Lekti·on f ~/~en *lesson* || ⟨fig⟩ *lecture*; jdm e–e ~ geben ⟨fig⟩ *to lecture a p* **L·ektor** m ~s/Lekt·oren *lecturer*; (Verlags~̣) *reader* || ~stelle [f] *post of a l.* **Lekt·üre** f ~/~n *reading*; (*a lot of*) *r. matter* || (Bücher) *books* pl || in m–r ~ *in the course of my r.* || m–e ~ *my r.s* pl

L·emberg n (Stadt der UdSSR)

L·emma n ~s/~ta ⟨a. lexicography⟩ *lemma*

L·emming m ~(e)s/~e ⟨zoo⟩ *lemming*

L·emnos n (Insel im Ägäischen Meer)

Lem·ure m ~n/~n **1.** ⟨myth⟩ ~en [pl] *lemures*, ⟨allg⟩ *ghosts* **2.** ⟨zoo⟩ *maki*

L·ena f (sibir. Fluß)

L·ende f ~/~n *loin*[*s* pl] || (Hüfte) *haunch, hip* || (Schenkel) *thigh* **L·enden- ~braten** m *roast loin*; (vom Rind) *joint, sirloin* **~gegend** f *lumbar region* **~kleid** n (der Malaien) *sarong* **~knochen** m *hip--bone* **~lahm** a *hip-shot*; ⟨fig⟩ *weak-kneed* **~-schmerz** m *lumbago* **~schurz** m *breechclouts* pl **~stück** n *loin, sirloin, fillet steak*; ⟨Am⟩ *tenderloin* **~tuch** n *loin-cloth* **~weh** n *lumbago*

L·eningrad n ⟨Russ⟩ (Stadt) *Leningrad*

L·enk- ~achse f ⟨tech⟩ *steering axle* ⟨a. mot⟩ || ⟨rail⟩ *leading bogie* **~arm** m ⟨mot⟩ *st.g arm* **~beil** n *hatchet* **~gehäuse** n *st.g box* **~hebel** m ⟨mot⟩ *st.g knuckle* **~kabel** n ⟨aero⟩ *check cable* **~körper** m *guided missile* **~rad** n ⟨mot⟩ *st.g* od *castor wheel* | ~schaltung [f] *st.g-column control* **~riemen** m, **~seil** n *reins* pl **~rolle** f *guide pulley* **~säule** f *st.g column* **~schloß** n (→ Schloß 1.) *steering* (*column*) *lock* **~schnecke** f ⟨tech⟩ *st.g worm* **~-segment** n ⟨mot⟩ *st.g quadrant* **~spindel** f *st.g wheel spindle* **~stange** f ⟨tech⟩ *st.g tie rod*; ⟨cycl⟩ *handle-bars* pl **~system** n : elektronisches ⟨a–n⟩ ~ *e.c guidance s.* **~vorrichtung** f ⟨mot⟩ *st.g gear* **~-waffe** f *guided* od *homing missile*; mit ca. 8000 km Reichweite *intercontinental ballistic m.* (*ICBM*) **l·enkbar** a *guidable, manageable, tractable, governable, manœuvrable* || ⟨tech⟩ *dirigible* || ~es Luftschiff *dirigible* (*airship*), *steerable* od *navigable balloon* | **~̣keit** f *tractability, m.ness* || *dirigibility*

l·enken vt [h] *to direct, guide* || (wenden) *to turn, bend*; er lenkte s–e Schritte heimwärts *he made his way homewards* || (ein Pferd) *to govern*; *to ride* (auf *to*); er weiß ein Pferd zu ~ *he knows how to manage a h.* || (ein Fahrzeug) *to drive*, ⟨mar⟩ *to steer, navigate*, (als Lotse) *to pilot* ⟨a. aero⟩; (Rakete) *to aim* | ⟨fig⟩ *to direct* (*a battle*); *to rule, manage*; *to sway* (*opinion*); richtunggebend ~ *to channel* || *to conduct* (*policy*); (heimlich) ⟨pol⟩ *to wirepull*; *to dispose* (*men's feelings to one's wish*) || s–e Gedanken rückwärts ~ *to throw one's mind back* || (Aufmerksamkeit ~ auf [acc]) *to call* (*to*), *to turn* (*upon*); .. auf sich ~ *to catch* (*a p's attention*), *to attract* (*people's a.*) || es war schwer, ihn zu ~ *he was difficult to direct* || sich ~ l *to be manageable* || etw in neue Bahnen ~ *to give a new direction to a th* **L·enker** m ~s/~ **1.** *ruler, governor* || *driver* (*of a car*); als ~ des Wagens *in charge of the car* || ~ der Rosse *charioteer* || ⟨rel⟩ der ~ des Weltalls *the Lord of the Universe* **2.** ⟨mach⟩ *guiding-rod* **3.** ~konstruktion [f], ~system [n] ⟨mot⟩ *wheel control linkage* **l·enksam** a *manageable, tractable, pliable* (→ fügsam, gefügig) | ≃**keit** f ~/ *m.ness, tr.ness, pl.ness, docility* **L·enkung** f ~/~en *guidance* || *governing, ruling* || ⟨pol⟩ *leadership* || *management* (*of affairs*) || (e–s Fahrzeugs) *driving, steering, piloting* | ~sanschlag [m] *st.g stop*; ~ausschuß [m] *st.g committee*; ~sgenauigkeit [f] *steering precision* od *accuracy* ⟨a. a–n⟩

L·enz[1] m ~es/~e ⟨poet⟩ *spring* || ⟨fig⟩ *prime* (*of life*) | ~monat [m] *spring-month, March* || sie zählte erst 20 ~e *she was but 20* (*years of age*) | **~en** vi [h] es lenzt *spring is near*

L·enz-[2] **~einrichtung** f ⟨mar⟩ *pumping arrangement* **~ejektor** m *bilge-ejector* **~pumpe** f *b. pump* ≃**pumpen** vi [h] *to free the ship* **l·enzen** vi [h] ⟨mar⟩ **1.** (vor Topp und Takel) ~ *to scud* (*under bare poles*) **2.** *to free the ship*

leon·inisch a *Leonine* (*verse*)

Leop·ard m ~en/~en ⟨zoo & her⟩ *leopard* **~enfell** n *leopard's skin* **~enweibchen** n *leopardess*

L·epra f ~/ *leprosy* ≃**krank** a *leprous* **Lepr·osenhaus** n *lepers' hospital*

L·erche f ~/~n ⟨orn⟩ *lark, skylark* || Wiesen-, Heide≃ *woodlark* | ⟨fig⟩ °e–e ~ schießen ⟨sl⟩ *to come a cropper* | ~n [pl] → *lark* **L·erchen- ~fang** m *catching of larks* **~garn** n *net for c. l.* **~gesang** m *singing of l.* **~herd** m *decoy for l.* **~strich** m *flight* od *passage of l.* || (Fang) *c. of l.*

L·ern- ~begierde f *desire of learning, studiousness* ≃**begierig** a *desirous of l. studious* **~eifer** m *eagerness to learn* **~schwester** f *cadet nurse*; *probitioner* **~vermögen** n (*innate*) *disposition to learn* **~zeit** f *time of l.* || *apprenticeship* **l·ernen** vt/i [h] **1.** *to learn, to study* || ⟨vulg⟩ [statt lehren!] ⟨vulg⟩ *to l.* (*I'll l. you*) [statt] *to teach* || v e–m ~ *to l. from a p*; aus .. *from books*, durch .. *from experience* || über .. (*of life*); bei wem lernt ihr Englisch? *who is your master in E.*? | **Französisch** ~ *to l. French*; .. schnell ~ *to be quick at* .. || lesen ~ *to l. to read* || kochen ~ *to l. cooking* || Geige spielen ~ *to l. the violin* || jdn kennen|~ *to meet a p*; (näher) *to make a p's acquaintance* || den er sehr bewundern gelernt hatte *whom he had come greatly to admire* || etw (langsam) lieben ~ *to get to like a th* | auf Bäcker ~ *to learn to be a b.*; *to train for a masseuse* | **auswendig** ~ *to l. by heart, to con*; ⟨theat⟩ *to study* (*one's part*) || gelegentlich ~ *to pick up* || gründlich ~ *to acquire* (*English*) *thoroughly* || ⟨theat⟩ s–e Rollen schnell, langsam ~ *to be a quick, slow study* || selbständig ~ *to teach o.s.* (*Italian*) || er lernt gut *he is an apt scholar* | ⟨prov⟩ lerne was, so kannst du was *l., and you will know* || man –nt, solang man lebt *one lives and learns* || es will alles gelernt s *everything has to be l.t* | die Verse ~ sich leicht .. *are easily l.t* **2.** (**zunftmäßig**) er lernt Konditor *he is apprenticed to a confectioner* || er lernt noch *he still serves his apprenticeship* (bei *with*) || er ist ein gelernter Bäcker *he is a baker by trade* **3.** **das** ≃ *l.ing* || das ~ fällt ihm schwer *he is slow in l.ing*

L·esart f ~/~en *reading, version* || ~en [pl] *variants* pl || e–e andere ~ *a various r., a variant* **l·esbar** a **1.** *legible* (⟨a. comp⟩ gut ~) **2.** (unterhaltend) *readable, worth reading* | ≃**keit** f *readability, readableness* **L·ese** f ~/~n *gathering* || (Wein≃) *vintage* || (Ähren≃) *gleaning* || → Blüten≃; → lesen I., 2. **L·ese- ~abend** m *evening g.g for reading* **~brettchen** n ⟨weav⟩ *hole-board* **~brille** f *r.g-glasses* pl **~buch** n *r.r, manual* **~drama** n *book-, closet--drama* **~fibel** f *first r.r, primer* **~früchte** f pl *gleanings* (*from books*); *collectanea* **~gerät** n ⟨comp⟩ *reading device* | Mikrofilm≃ ⟨rep⟩ *microfilm reader* **~gesellschaft** f *literary society* **~gewohnheiten** f pl *r.g habits* **~halle** f, **~kabinett** n (*public*) *r.g-room* **~kränzchen** n **1.** *r.g-club* **2.** → ~abend **~kreis** m *circle of r.rs* || (Verein) *r.g--society* **~lampe** f *r.g lamp* **~lupe** f (*microfilm*) *r.g--glass* ≃**lustig** a *fond of r.g* **~probe** f ⟨theat⟩ *r.g rehearsal* **~publikum** n *r.g public* **~pult** n *r.g-desk* °**~ratte, ~ratz(e)** ⟨fam⟩ *bookworm* **~saal** m *r.g--room* **~/Stanzeinheit** f ⟨comp⟩ *Input/output unit* **~stoff** m *r.g* (*matter*) **~stunde** f *r.g-hour* **~sucht** f = ~wut ≃**süchtig** a *madly fond of r.g* **~tisch** m (Klaube-) ⟨tech⟩ *picker table* **~übung** f *r.g exercise* **~unterricht** m *instruction in r.g* **~verein** m = ~zirkel **~welt** f *r.g public* **~wut** f *r.g mania* **~zeichen** n *bookmark*(*er*); e–n Finger als ~ benutzen *to close a book upon a finger* **~zeit** f *r.g--time* || (Wein≃) *vintage* **~zimmer** n = ~halle **~zirkel** m *r.g-club* **L·esen** n ~s/ *reading* || mit ~ beschäftigt (*engaged in*) *r.* || (Universität) *lecturing* | *gathering* || *vintage* → Lese **l·esen I.** vt/i [las/ge~] [h] **1.** (auflesen) *to gather, to pick up* || (Ähren) *to glean* || (Trauben) *to pick* || (Erbsen) *to pick* od *clean* **2.** (Schrift) *to read* || genau ~ *to study* (*a book*) || ~, schreiben, rechnen lernen ⟨fam⟩ *to learn the 3 R's* (*r.g*, [*w*]*riting*, [*a*]*rithmetic*) || ich kann es kaum ~ ⟨a.⟩ *I almost can't make it out* || nicht zu ~ *illegible* || man kann es ~ (muß aber nicht) *it is r.able* || etw laut ~ *to r. a th out* || mit verteilten Rollen ~ .. *with assigned parts* || sehr viel ~ *to r. a great deal* || vielgelesen *much r.* [red] (*novel, author*) | ⟨typ⟩ e–e Korrektur ~ *to r. a proof* || die Messe ~ *to say mass* | ich habe nur 3 Tage **an** dem Buch ge~ *it took me but three days to r. the book* || ~ **in** .. *to r. in* (*the stars, her eyes*); in jds Zügen ~ *to peruse a p's face*; .. z ~ s: *her thoughts showed in her face*; mit jdm zus aus/in e–m Buch ~ *to look on with another p* || zwischen den Zeilen ~ *to r. between the lines* **3.** ⟨univ⟩ *to deliver lectures* || er liest (über) m. G. *he lectures on modern history* **4.** [v/refl] **sich** halb blind (in den Schlaf) ~ *to r. o.s. half-blind* (*to sleep*) || das Buch liest sich gut, läßt **sich** nicht ~ *the book r.s well, is unreadable* **5.** ⟨fig fam⟩ e–m die Episteln, die Leviten, den Text ~ ⟨fam⟩ *to lecture* od *rebuke a p*, ⟨Am⟩ *to tell a p where to get off* **II.** ≃ n: ~- u Schreibenkönnen [n] *literacy* **~swert** a *rewarding*; *worth r.ing*; *readable*; nicht ~ *unreadable, hopelessly dull* || ~ s *to repay r.g* **L·eser** m ~s/~ **1.** *gatherer, gleaner, vintager, picker* (→ lesen 1.) **2.** (v Schrift) *reader* || der (geneigte) ~ *the gentle r.* || die (geneigte) ~in *the fair r.* || ein eifriger ~ *a hard r.* **~analyse** f *r. ship analysis* **~kreis** m *circulation, constituency* || der Dichter hat e–n weiten ~ .. *is widely r.* [red] || Zuschrift aus dem ~ *letter to the editor* **Leser·ei** f ~/~en *incessant reading* **l·eserlich, l·eslich** a *legible* || gut ~ *easy to read* | ≃**keit** f *legibility* **L·eserschaft** f ~/~en *the readers* pl **L·esung** f ~/~en **1.** ⟨parl⟩ *reading* (*of a bill*) || .. kam zur dritten ~ *the bill was read for the third time* || die erste ~ *the first reading* **2.** (Lesart) abweichende ~ *variant*

l·esbisch a *lesbian* (*love*); *of Lesbos*

Let n ~s/~s ⟨ten⟩ *let, net*

let·al a (tödlich) *lethal* | ≗it·ätsziffer [f] ⟨stat⟩ *case fatality rate*

Letharg·ie [i:] f ~/~n [ˈi:ən] *lethargy*

L·ethe f ⟨myth⟩ ~ trinken *to drink of the river Lethe*

L·ette m ~n/~n, **L·ettin** f ~/~nen *Lett* **let·tisch** a *Lettic, -ish*; **das** ≗**e** *Lett(ish)* **L·ettland** n *Latvia*

L·etten m ~s/~ (*potter's* od *red*) *clay* ≗**artig** a *c.ey* **~boden** m *c.ey soil* **~kluft** f ⟨min⟩ *weigh--board* **l·ettig** a *clayey*

L·etter f ~/~n (Buchstabe) *letter, character, type* ‖ der Tag wird in den Annalen mit roten ~n verzeichnet w *in the annals the day will go down as a red letter day* **L·ettern** pl *lettering* **~art** f *typeface* **~druck** m *printing* **~gießmaschine** f *type-founding machine* **~gut** n *type-metal* **~holz** n *tiger-wood* **~messer** m *typometer* **~metall** n = ~gut

L·ettner m ~s/~ ⟨ec⟩ *lectern, reading-desk* ‖ ⟨ec arch⟩ *rood-screen, -loft; choir-screen, jube*

letz a [obd] = verkehrt

L·etzi f ~/~nen Sw = Grenzschutz(wehr)

l·etzen vt [h] **1.** *to regale, comfort, cheer* | **sich** ~ an [dat] *to relish, to enjoy* **2.** sich mit s–n Freunden ~ *to give a farewell dinner*

letzt I. [a] **1.** *last, ultimate* ‖ (am Ende) *final* (⟨mill⟩ Sieb); *extreme* (*unction*) → u.; ⟨med⟩ *terminal* (*illness*) ‖ (höchst) *top* (*step*) ‖ (niedrigst) *lowest* (*level*), ⟨fam⟩ *bottom* (*part*) ‖ (neuest): *his latest novel* | bis zum ~en **A**temzug *to one's last breath* ‖ die Letzten **D**inge *the end of all ths* ‖ e–m die ~e **E**hre erweisen *to show a p the last honours, to pay a p the last tribute of respect* ‖ das ~e Ende *the fag-end* (*of a cigar*); *the heel* (*of a loaf*) ‖ ~en Endes *in the long run, in the last analysis*; ich bin ~en Endes (im Grunde) froh darüber *I am at the bottom of my heart glad of it* ‖ ⟨sport⟩ bis zur ~en Entscheidung *to the finish* ‖ ~es **G**eleit geben (→ ~e Ehre) *to attend a p's funeral* ‖ ~es Gericht *Day of judgement* ‖ ~e **H**and → legen an ‖ bis zum ~en Heller *to the last penny* ‖ die ~en **J**ahre *of recent years*; ~es Jahr *last y.*, ⟨a.⟩ *yesteryear* ‖ das war das ~e **M**al, daß ich ihn sah *that was the last time I saw him, that was the last I saw of him* ‖ bis auf den ~en Mann (*to fight*) *to the last man*; (*they were all present*) *to a man* ‖ ~es Mittel *extreme measures* pl ‖ .. im ~en Moment .. *with only seconds to spare* ‖ ~en Monats ⟨com⟩ *ultimo* (abbr *ult.*) ‖ ~e **N**euheit *latest news* ‖ ⟨ec R. C.⟩ ~e **Ö**lung *extreme unction* ‖ den ~en **P**fennig los w *to get rid of every penny/cent one has* ‖ ~es Rennen, Spiel etc *nightcap* ‖ bis auf die ~e **S**pur vertilgen *to destroy root and branch* ‖ an ~er Stelle *lastly* ‖ sein ~es Stündlein hat geschlagen *his last hour has come* ‖ ~er **V**ersuch *last attempt, supreme effort* ‖ sein ~er **W**ille *his last wishes* pl, ⟨jur⟩ *his last will and testament* ‖ das ~e Wort ⟨fig⟩ *ultimatum*; das ~e Wort h *to have the last word*; s–e ~en (Sterbe)Worte *his dying words* ‖ in der ~en **Z**eit; → III. 2. ‖ in den ~en Zügen liegen *to be breathing one's last* **2.** [im compr] **der, die, das, ~ere**; **~er, ~e, ~es** *the latter* ‖ im ~eren Falle *in the latter case* **II. ~e(r)** m, **~e** f, **~e[s]** n **1. der (die) ~e** *the last* (*one*) ‖ er wäre der ~e, der wünschte *he would be the l. to desire* ‖ er ist der ~e, den ich wählte *he is the l.* (*p*) (*that*) *I should choose*; der ~, der erfunden hätte *the last man to invent* ‖ sie war die ~e, an die ich denken konnte *she was my l. guess* ‖ der ~e (des Monats) *the l.* (*day of the month*) ‖ er ist der ~ in der Klasse (Schule) *he is at the bottom of his class* (⟨sl⟩ *he is ultimus omnium, he is lag*) ‖ der ~e s–s Geschlechts, Namens *the l. of his race, name* ‖ °e–m den Letzten geben *to tag a p* ‖ ⟨prov⟩ den ~en beißen die Hunde *the devil take the hindmost* **2. das** ≗**e** *the l. th* ‖ das wäre mein ≗es (Tod) *that would be the end of me* ‖ der Vorwurf unreif zu s ist ungefähr das Letzte, was man zugibt *whatever charge one will admit it is not the charge of being immature* ‖ aus e–r S das ~e herausholen ⟨sl⟩ *to knock hell out of a th* ‖ **bis zum** ≗en (Äußersten) *to the l. extremity, to the bitter end* ‖ sein ~es hergeben *to exert o.s. to the extreme limit of one's powers*; er gäbe sein ≗es hin *he would give his l. penny, his very life, sacrifice everything* ‖ **bis ins** ~e *down to the last detail*; **zum** ≗en greifen *to take extreme measures, to cling to the l. straw* **III.** [adv] **1.** *finally, in the end* ‖ der ~ Genannte *the l. named* ‖ der ~ Kommende *the l. comer* **2. ~, ~ens, ~hin, ~lich** (in der ~en Zeit) *recently, latterly, lately, of late, the other day* **3. ~ens** (in Aufzählungen) ⟨a.⟩ *l.ly, in the l. place* ‖ am ~en, zum ~en *finally, at l., in the end* ‖ (auf Auktionen) zum – ~en! *for the l. time!* es ist bei ihm Matthäi am ~en ⟨fam⟩ *he is on his l. legs* **IV. Letzt** f ~ [= die Letzte] auf die ~ *in the end* ‖ zu guter ~ *in the end*; *at late* od *long l.*; *l. but not least*; *as my l.*; *to finish up with* ‖ bis zu guter ~ *to the very l. moment* **L·etzt- ~bietende(r** m) f *l. and highest bidder* ≗**erwähnt** a *l.-mentioned* ≗**jährig** a *l. year's* (*play*) **~lebende(r** m) f *l. survivor* ≗**willig** [adv] *by will* ‖ [a] ⟨jur⟩ *testamentary* (*disposition*) = ~e Verfügung *will* **l·etztens, l·etzthin, l·etztlich** adv ⟨a.⟩ *ultimately*; → letzt III. 2. **l·etzterer** compr v letzter → letzt I. 2.

Leu m ~en/~en ⟨poet⟩ *lion* ‖ „verderblich ist's den ~ zu wecken" *let sleeping dogs lie*

L·eucht- [in comp] *luminous* (*body, paint, sight*); *illuminating* (*power*); *signalling* →-rakete **~bake** f ⟨mar⟩ *light beacon* **~bild** n *transparency* **~boje** f *light buoy* od *float* **~bombe** f *flash-bomb, flare* (*bomb*), ⟨Am⟩ *light bomb* **~brunnen** m *illuminated fountain* **~dichte** f ⟨el⟩ *brightness*; ⟨phys⟩ *H*(*elios*), *L*(*uminence*) **~elektron** n *photo-e.* **~-draht, ~faden** m ⟨bes el⟩ *luminous filament* **~fakkel** f *flare, torch* **~fallschirm(rakete** f) m *parachute flare* **~farbe** f *luminous paint* **~feuer** n ⟨mar⟩ *beacon* (*light*), *signal fire*, (*coast*) *light* **~feuerverzeichnis** n *Light List* **~fleck** m ⟨radar⟩ *blip* **~gas** n (*lighting-*)*gas, coal* od *natural gas*; *commercial* (⟨Am⟩ *city*) *gas* **~geschoß** n *star shell* **~granate** f *candle-bomb* **~käfer** m *glow-worm* **~kegel** m *cone of light* **~kompaß** m *luminous c.* **~körper** m *illuminant* **~kraft** f *illuminating power*; ⟨paint⟩ *brilliancy, -ce*; *brightness*; ⟨phot⟩ *saturation*; *luminosity* **~kugel** f *fire-ball, signal rocket, flare*; ⟨mil⟩ *tracer* (*bullet*), ⟨aero⟩ *flare* **~masse** f *phosphorescent compound* **~mine** f *trip flare* **~mittel** n *illuminant* **~patrone** f *Very light, tracer cartridge* **~pedal** n *luminous p.* **~pilz** m *phosphorescent agaric* **~pistole** f *Very* od *signal*(*ling*) *pistol* **~rahmensucher** m ⟨phot⟩ *bright-frame viewfinder* **~rakete** f *light-rocket*, ⟨aero⟩ *flare*; *parachute light* **~rohrbeleuchtung** f *strip lighting* **~röhre** f ⟨el⟩ *fluorescent* (od *vacuum tube*) *lamp* **~satz** m *flare composition* **~schicht** f *fluorescent coating* **~schiff** n *lightship*; *floating light* **~schirm** m *fluorescent screen* **~schrift** f *moving news panel* **~skala** f *luminous dial* **~spur** f *tracer streak* | ~brandgeschoß [n] *incendiary tracer* N; ~geschoß [n] *tracer* (*bullet* od *shell*); ~munition [f] *tracer ammunition* **~stab** m *electric torch* **~stärke** = ~kraft **~stoff** m *luminous matter* **~tiere** n pl ⟨ent⟩ *phosphorescent animals* pl **~tonne** f = ~boje **~turm** m *light--house*; ⟨aero⟩ *air-way light-house* **~wand** f *luminous panel* **~wirkung** f *luminous effect* **~zeichen** n *signal* od *Very light* **~ziffer(blatt** n) f *luminous figure* (*l. dial*) **L·euchte** f ~/~n *light, lamp, lantern* ‖ ⟨fig⟩ *star, shining light*; *luminary* (*in science*); *wizard* ‖ ⟨sport sl⟩ *big knob* **L·euchten** n ~s/ *lighting* ‖ *shining, blaze* ‖ (Blitzen) *lightning* ‖ (Meeres≗) *phosphorescence* ‖ ⟨phys⟩ *coruscation*; (faulen Holzes) *fox fire* **l·euchten** vi [h] **1.** (Licht geben) *to light* ‖ (of stars) *to shine, to emit light* ‖ (strahlen) *to beam, radiate* ‖ (blinken) *to glitter, gleam* ‖ (hell w) *to light up* ‖ (funkeln) *to sparkle* ‖ *to blaze with light* ‖ (of eyes) *to shine*; (of light a.) *to wink*; (of flowers a.) *to blaze*; (vom Meere) *to phosphoresce* | die Blitze ~, es leuchtet *it lightens* **2.** ⟨fig⟩ sein Licht ~ l *to let one's light shine* || das leuchtet in die Augen (ist augenscheinlich) *that is obvious* od *evident* **3. e-m** ~ *to light a p* (*with a candle*, etc., [*on*] *his way*), *to hold the light for a p* || e–m heim *or* nach Hause ~ *to see a p home with a lantern*; ⟨fig⟩ → heimleuchten || er leuchtete mir ins Gesicht *he threw the light on my face* **4. leuchte in** die Ecke *light up the corner* **l·euchtend** a *shining, bright, resplendent* || *radiant, lustrous*; *beaming*; *gleaming, glowing, glaring*; *dazzling, glistening, glittering, shimmering* || *luminous* (*dial*, etc.) || ⟨her⟩ *beautiful, glancing* (*arms*) || *brilliant, vivid* (*colour*) || ⟨fig⟩ *brilliant, shining* (*example, model*) **L·euchter** m ~s/~ *candle stick* || (Kron≃) *chandelier, lustre* || (Wand≃, Klavier≃) *sconce* **~arm** m *sconce, bracket* (*of a chandelier*) **~gehänge** n *lustres* pl **~tisch** m *candle-stand* **~tülle** f *socket*

L·eugnen n ~s/ *denial, negation* || *disavowal* || (Widerrufen) *retrac(ta)tion* **l·eugnen** vt/i [h] *to deny, disown* || ⟨jur⟩ er leugnet *he denies the charge* || *to deny* (*the existence of God*) || (bestreiten) *to contest* || *to gainsay* (*a fact*) || (widerrufen) *to recant, retract* || (in Abrede stellen) *to disavow*; sie ~, daß er es tat *they deny his having done it*; er leugnet es rundweg (*or* steif und fest) *he flatly denies it*; es frech ~ *to brazen it out*; es ist nicht z ~, daß *there is no denying that, it cannot be denied, it is undeniable that* **L·eugner** m ~s/~ *denier* | **≃isch** a *disowning*, ⟨jur⟩ *traversing* **L·eugnung** f *denial* (⟨a.⟩ un(ter)bewußt ⟨psych⟩)

Leuk- Gr **~äm·ie** f ~/ Gr *leukaemia* **~o-pl·ast**® n ~(e)s/ *adhesive plaster* (⟨Am⟩ *tape*); °*elastoplast*® | ~bomber [m] ⟨mot⟩ *rattletrap* **~orrh·öa** f ~/ ⟨med⟩ *leucorrhœa*; *the whites* pl **~otom·ie** f ~/ *leucotomy, lobotomy*

L·eumund m ~(e)s/ *renown, reputation* || guter ~ *good reputation* || böser ~ *ill fame* || in bösen ~ bringen *to defame, to bring into disrepute* **~ser-forschung** f *inquiry into a p's character* **~szeugnis** n *certificate of good conduct*; ⟨com etc⟩ *character*

L·eut- ~priester m *secular priest* **≃selig** a *affable, cordial, condescending* || *pleasant* (*superior*) || *courteous* (*manners*) | (P) *homy*; *affable*; *condescending*; ⟨Am⟩ *folksy* | ~keit [f] *affability, condescension, cordiality* **L·eutchen** pl [dim v Leute] *little people*; die guten ~ *the good folk* pl || liebe ~! *my good people*! **L·eute** pl **1.** *persons* pl, *people* pl, *men* pl, *folk(s)* pl || es sind ~ bei ihm *he has visitors* || m–e ~ (Angehörigen) *my people* || unsere ~ (Partei) *our own people* od *set* || (Dienerschaft) *domestics, servants* pl || (Arbeiter) *hands* pl || allerlei ~ *all sorts of men* || feine ~ ⟨sl⟩ *nobs* || kl ~ *little people* || junge, alte ~ .. *folk* || s–e ~ kennen *to know one's customers* od *whom one is dealing with* || Land u Leute *the country and its inhabitants* || die reichen wie die armen ~ *both the rich and the poor people* pl || es gab ~, die sagten *there were those who said* || das sind die rechten ~ *those are the right sort* || die gebildeten ~ *the gentry* pl || wir sind geschiedene ~! *I have finished with you*! **2.** ⟨fam⟩ liebe ~! *my dear friends*! || die ~ *the boys*, ⟨Am⟩ *guys* || ⟨mil⟩ ~! *lads*! || ⟨cont⟩ *gentry* (*light-fingered g.* langfingrige ~); sonderbare ~ *strange folk* || ⟨iron⟩ das sind mir nette ~! *they are a fine set of fellows* **3.** [koll] *the world* [sg] || die ~ sagen *people say, it is said* || was w die ~ sagen! *what will the world* (⟨fam⟩ *Mrs. Grundy*) *say*? | **unter** die ~ gehen *to go into society*; (in die Welt hinaus) *to go abroad* || nicht unter die ~ gehen *to shun society, to see nobody* || er ist unter ~n gewesen *he has seen the world* || → Geld, Gerede || (Gerücht) unter die ~ bringen *to spread abroad* || (S) unter die ~ k *to become known, to transpire*; (P) *to be seen abroad* **4.** (Erwachsene) aus Kindern w ~ *boys will be men* **~betrüger** m *common cheat* **~placker, ~scherer** m = –schinder **≃scheu** a *shy, retired*; *shunning company* **~schinder** m *oppressor, sweater*, (*slave-*)*driver*; ⟨mil⟩ *martinet* **~schinderei** f *oppression, sweating*

L·eutnant m ~s/~e *second lieutenant*; ⟨fam Am⟩ *looey* || ~ zur See *sub-l.*, ⟨Am⟩ *ensign* || Herr ~! *sir*! || ⟨fig⟩ ein ~ bezahlt s–e Schulden! *it's a Quaker-meeting*! **~sschulterstück** n *l.'s shoulder-knot* **~sstelle** f *l.'s commission*

Leuz·it m ~s/ ⟨min⟩ *leucite, white garnet*

Lev·ante [v] f *Levant, East, Orient* **lev·antisch,** levant·inisch [a] *Levantine*

Lev·it [v] m ~en/~en *Levite* || → lesen

Levk·oje f ~/~n ⟨bot⟩ *gilly-flower*

Lewis·it n ~s/ ⟨mil⟩ (Gelbkreuzgas) *lewisite*

Lex·em n ~(e)s/~e (*meaningful speechform that is an item of the vocabulary of a language*; → Litotes) *lexeme* **lexi- ~kalisch** a *lexical* **≃ko-gr·aph** m ~en/~en *lexicographer* **≃kographie** f *lexicography* **≃kogr·aphisch** a *lexicographic(al)* ·**≃kon** n ~s/–ken, –ka *dictionary, lexicon*; *encyclopaedia*; ⟨geog⟩ *gazeteer*

L·eyden, L·eiden [-ai-] n (Stadt in den Niederlanden) *Leyden* | **~er** a (*of*) *L.* || ~ Flasche [f] ⟨el⟩ *L. jar*

Lh·asa n (Hauptstadt v Tibet) *Lhasa, Lassa*

L'hombre = Lomber ⟨cards⟩ *ombre*

Liais·on [liɛ'zɔ̃:] f ~/~s Fr *liaison*

Li·ane f ~/~n ⟨bot⟩ *liana*; ⟨fam⟩ *supple-jack*

L·ias f ~/ ⟨geol⟩ *Lias*; ~formation [f] *L.sic f.*

L·ibanon ~s/ **1.** m (*Mount*) *Lebanon* **2.** n (Land) *Lebanon*

Lib·ell n ~(e)s/~e *libel* **~·ist** m ~en/~en *libeller* **libell·ieren** vt [h] ⟨jur⟩ *to libel*

Lib·elle f ~/~n ⟨ent⟩ *dragon-fly* || ⟨tech⟩ (Röhren≃) *level tube* || ⟨artill⟩ *spirit bubble* : die ~ einspielen l *to centre the b.*

liber·al a *liberal*; ⟨pol⟩ *Liberal* || die ≃en *the L.s*; links~ *radical* | **≃isierung** f *l.ization* (*of trade = trade l.*) | **≃it·ät** f *generosity, liberality* **Liber-t·iner** m ~s/~ *libertine*

Lib·eria, Lib·erien n *Liberia*; Bewohner(in) v ~ *Liberian*

Libr·etto n ~s/~s & –tti *libretto, book*; *words* pl

L·ibyen [-by-] n *Libya* **L·ibyer** m, **~in** f, **l·ibysch** a *Libyan* | ≃e Wüste f *Libyan Desert*

.. lich lebendes *suff* als *dim* v *adj*: schwarz/≃lich

L·icht n ~(e)s/~e (= Kerzen) & ~er (= Flammen, ⟨arts, hunt⟩) **A. Bedeutungen**: **1. (Schein)** *light* ⟨a. fig⟩ || auf-/-aus-/durchfallendes ~ *incident/emergent/transmitted l.* || helles, strahlendes ~ *bright, radiant l.* || schwaches, gedämpftes ~ *faint, dimmed l.* ⟨a.⟩ *faint glare*; grelles ~ *hard l.*; *glare* || dämmerndes ~ *a half l.* || indirektes ~ ⟨paint⟩ *false l.* || wechselndes ~ ⟨fig⟩ *a cross-l.s* (*of modern philosophy*) || ⟨fig⟩ bezeichnendes ~ (werfen auf) (*to throw a*) *striking l.* (*on*) || (Helle) *brightness, lustre* || ~ des Tages *day-l.* || es ist ~ im Zimmer *there is* (*a*) *l.* od *there are l.s* .. || ~ des Mondes, e–r Kerze *moon-l., candle-l.* || ⟨paint⟩ **~er** pl (*high*) *l.s* (u Schatten *and shadows*) || ~er e–s Edelsteins *lustre, fire* sg | ⟨bib⟩ es werde ~ *let there be l.* || ~ aufblitzen l *to flash l.* || helles ~ werfen auf *to shed* od *let a striking l. on* || grünes ~ ⟨fig⟩ (Erlaubnis) *green l.* **2. (Klarheit)** *the l. of truth* || *clearness of intellect* || ~ bringen in ⟨fig⟩ *to elucidate a th* || ~ verbreiten über *to diffuse l. over* **3. (Leuchte)** das Ewige ~ *the ever-burning* od *sanctuary l.* || ⟨mar⟩ (Leuchtfeuer) *beacon, l.*; mit allen ~ern fahrend (*ship*) *with all navigation l.s* || ein tropfendes ~ *a dripping candle*; gezogenes ~, Talg≃ *dip-* od *tallow candle* || ~e ziehen *to dip c.s* || ein ~ gebrauchen ⟨sl⟩ *to use a glim* || Glanz der ~e *resplendence of the c.s* || Weihnachtsbaum≃e *Christmas-tree c.s* || das ~ anzünden (auslöschen), ⟨el⟩ an-, (aus-) knipsen *to light* (*put out*) *the candle*, ⟨el⟩ *to switch* od *turn on* (*off*) *the l.* || die ~e des Weihnachtsbaums anstecken *or* anzünden *to light the c.s on the Ch.-t.* || ~ aus! ⟨sl⟩ *douse the glim* || die ~er gingen an *the l.s came on* | (Gestirn) *luminary* || das neue ~ *the new moon* **4.** (**Beleuchtung**) *illumination* || elektrisches ~ *electric l.* || bengalisches ~ *Bengal l.s* pl || in halbem ~ *in a dim* od *subdued l.* **5.** ⟨hunt⟩ ~er (des Wildes) *l.s, eyes* pl **B. Wendungen**: ⟨mst fig⟩ e–m ein ~ **aufstecken** über etw *to open a p's eyes to the real facts of a th* || ~ in e–e S bringen *to clear a matter up, to throw l. upon a th* || das ~ der Welt erblicken *to come into the world, to see the l.* || es **geht** mir ein ~ auf *I begin to see day-l.*; plötzlich .. *a sudden l. dawns upon me* || er **ist** (k)ein großes ~ .. *a shining* (*no great*) *l.* || wo viel ~ ist, ist viel Schatten *strong l. casts deep shadows* || e–m ~ u Luft s *to be meat and drink to a p* || sein ~ leuchten l *to show o.s. to advantage*; ⟨fam⟩ *to put it on* || das ~ **scheuen** *to avoid the l. of day* || sein ~ (nicht) unter den Scheffel stellen (*not*) *to put one's l. under a bushel* || ein ungünstiges ~ werfen auf e–n, etw *to put a p, a th in an unfavourable l.* || ganz neues ~ werfen auf *to shed a wholly new l. on* || ein schlechtes ~ werfen auf *to reflect upon* | **ans** ~ bringen *to bring to l., to disclose, to turn up*; (Wahrheit) *to elicit*; (öffentlich) *to make known* || ans ~ k *to come to l.* || ans ~ der Öffentlichkeit ziehen *to drag into the l. of day* | geh mir **aus** dem ~e! *stand* od *get out of my l.* | **bei** ~e (arbeiten) .. *by lamp-light* || bei gedämpftem ~e *in subdued l.* || bei ~e besehen ⟨fig⟩ *to examine narrowly* od *closely* || bei ~e betrachtet *taking a general view of the case* || gegen das ~ halten *to hold up to the l.* | **hinter**: e–n hinters ~ führen *to trick, double-deal, humbug*, ⟨sl⟩ *dope a p* | **im** ~e e–r Kerze prüfen *to examine by the l. of a c.* || im ~ s–r Erfahrung gesehen *measured by the standard of ..* || im ~e der Öffentlichkeit *in the limelight of publicity* || etw im wahren ~e betrachten *to take a wide view of a th* || sich im wahren ~e zeigen *to show one's colours, to come out in one's true c.s* || e–m, sich im ~e stehen *to stand* od *be in a p's, one's own l.* od *way* ⟨a. fig⟩ || im besten ~e zeigen *to show up to the best advantage* | etw **in** anderem ~e erscheinen l *to put a different complexion on a th* || in ein falsches ~ stellen *or* rükken *to colour* || sich bei jdm in ein gutes ~ setzen wollen *to curry favour with a p* || jdn ins beste ~ stellen *to parade a p*; jdn ins rechte ~ setzen *to make a p look good, to show a p in the right l.*; die Tatsachen ins richtige *or* in helles ~ setzen *to bring on the facts in full relief, to throw the limelight on them* || alles in rosigem ~e sehen *to look only on the bright side of ths, to take a br. view of everything*; jdm in vorteilhaftem ~ erscheinen, sich bei jdm in v.s ~ stellen *to appear to advantage in a p's eyes* | **mit** ~ überschwemmen *to floodlight* | **zwischen** ~ u Dunkel *between two l.s, in the twilight* **licht** a **1.** *light*, (glänzend) *bright, shining* || (v Farben) *l.(-coloured)*; ~es Ocker *pale ochre* || bei ~em Tage *in broad daylight* || ein heller, ~er Morgen war angebrochen, es war bereits heller, ~er Tag *the morning had risen stark and clear* || es wird ~er *it is brightening up* || ⟨fig path⟩ ~er Augenblick *lucid interval, sane moment* **2.** (**durchsichtig**) ~e Maschen *open meshes* || ~e Stelle (im Walde) *glade, clearing*, (am Wolkenhimmel) *break in the clouds* || ⟨mil⟩ ~e Reihen *thin ranks, narrow lines* || ~ m *to clear* (*a wood*), *to thin* (*the ranks*) || ⟨tech⟩ ~e Weite, Höhe *clear width, hight; inside width; free headroom, overhead clearance* || ⟨typ⟩ ~e Schrift *contour face* || ~ w (of ranks) *to thin*; (of hair) *to get thin* || ~e Fassung *clear setting*, ~gefaßt *set transparently, set a jour* Fr **3.** ⟨tech⟩ **das** ~e *clear space* || im ~en (gemessen) *in the clear* **L·icht-** *l.(ight), l.(uminou)s, l.(umini)ferous* **~abschluß** m *exclusion of l.* **~arbeit** f *working* (od *work done*) *by lamp-l.* **~arm** a *wanting in l.* **~äther** m *luminiferous ether* **~auge** n ⟨hors-vet⟩ *wall-eye* **~ausbeute** f ⟨phys⟩ *l. efficiency* (*in lumens per watt*) **~ausfall** m *l. leakage* **~bad** n *solar bath, insolation* **~bandbeleuchtung** f *strip l.ing* **~behandlung** f ⟨med⟩ *treatment with l.* **~beugung** f ⟨phys⟩ *refraction* **~bild** n *photo(graph)* | ~auswertung [f] *photogrammetry*; ~erkundung [f] ⟨aero, mil⟩ *photographic reconnaissance flight* **~bilder** n pl (für e–n Vortrag) (*lantern-*)*-slides* | ~vortrag [m] *lantern(-slide) lecture*; (Reisebericht) ⟨Am⟩ *travelogue* **~bildlich** a *photographic* **~bildner(in** f) m *ph.pher* **~bildner·ei** f *ph.phy* **~blau** a *l.-blue* **~blick** m *beam, glimpse, glint of l.* || ⟨fig⟩ *bright spot*; *a sight for sore eyes* **~blond** a *fair* **~bogen** m ⟨el⟩ *arc* | ~ofen [m] *electric arc furnace*; ~schweißung [f] *arc welding*; ~zündung [f] *arc ignition* **~braun** a *l.-brown* **~brechung** f *refraction of l.* **~dämpfer** m *extinguisher* **~dämpfung** f *subdueing* od *dimming of l.*, **~druck** m *photographic printing, ph.typy* || (Bild) *ph.type* | ~papier [n] *ph.copying paper* **~durchflutet** a *flooded with l.*; ⟨tech⟩ *flood-lighted* **~durchlässig** a *transparent* | ~keit [f] *l. transmission* **~echt** a *fadeless* (*material*), *fast to light* **~effekt** m ⟨arts⟩ *luminous* od *lighting effect*; ⟨theat⟩ *optical e., trick of l.* **~empfindlich** a ⟨phot⟩ *sensitive* || ~ m *to sensitize* || ~machen [n] *sensitization* | ~keit [f] *sensitivity*, ⟨phot m. m.⟩ *speed* | ~smesser [m] *sensitometer* **~empfindung** f *sensation caused by light* **~energie** f ⟨phys⟩ *luminous e.* **~erscheinung** f *l.s appearance* **~farbendruck** m *heliograph* **~feind** m ⟨fig⟩ *obscurant(ist)* **~fleck** m *spot of light, light-spot*; → –hof(bildung) **~fluter** m *floodlight lamp* **~form** f *candle-mould* **~fuchs** m *light chestnut(-horse)* **~führungsgrenze** f ⟨mil mot⟩ *no-vehicle-l. line* **~gaden** m ⟨ec arch⟩ *clerestory* **~gebend** a *l.ferous* **~gelb** a *l.-yellow* **~geschmack** m ⟨brew⟩ *sun flavour* **~geschwindigkeit** f *speed of l.*; mit ~ *at the s. of l.* **~gestalt** f ⟨poet⟩ *l.s* od *radiant form* **~gießer** m *chandler* **~glanz** m *brightness* **~grau** a *pale-grey* **~hell** a *brilliant* **~helle** f *radiance* **~hof** m 1. ⟨arch⟩ *well of a court, inner c., glass-roofed c.* 2. ⟨phot⟩ *halation* 3. ⟨astr⟩ *halo, corona* | ~frei [a] *non-halation*; ~ m ⟨phot⟩ *to back up*; ~bildung [f] *halation*; ~schutz [m] ⟨phot⟩ *anti-halo coating* od *backing* **~höhung** f ⟨paint⟩ *high l.* **~hütchen** n *extinguisher* **~impuls** m ⟨opt⟩ *l. pulse* **~jahr** n *l.-year* **~kabel** n *electric-l. cable* **~kanone** f →–verstärkung **~kegel** m ⟨astr⟩ *cone of rays*; breiter ~ *wide-angle beam* **~knecht** m ⟨tech⟩ *save-all* **~kontrast** m *subject c.* **~kräftig** a *l.s* **~kupferdruck** m *heliogravure* **~lehre** f ⟨phys⟩ *photology, optics* **~leistung** f *l. output* od *yield* **~leitung** f *l.ing mains* pl; *branch circuit*; ⟨wir⟩ sich an die ~ anschließen l *to operate on the mains* **~magnetzünder** m *mag-dynamo* **~manschetten** f pl *cut paper* od *glass ornaments* pl *for candlesticks* **~maschine** f ⟨mot⟩ *dynamo* **~masse** f *mass of l.* **~meer** n *ocean of l.*; *one blaze* **~meß** f *Candlemas* **~meß**(verfahren) n *flash ranging* N | ~batterie [f] *f. spotting b.* **~messer** m (Instrument) *photometer* **~meßtrupp** m *flash-ranging section* **~motte** f *candlemoth* **~mühle** f ⟨phys⟩ *radiometer* **~nelke** f ⟨bot⟩ *campion* **~paus-** ~film [m] ⟨rep⟩ *diazo f.*; ~papier [n] *diazotype materials* pl; ~verfahren [n] *d.t. printing* **~pause** f *d. print*; *phototype*; *heliographic pr.*; *photostat*; *blueprint* **~polarisation** f ⟨phys⟩ *l.s polarization* **~punkt** m *bright* od *l.s point* || ⟨fig⟩ *ray of hope* || ⟨arts⟩ *high l.* **~putze** f, **~(putz)schere** f (e–e *a pair of*) *snuffers* pl **~rakete** f *flare* **~quantum** n ⟨phys⟩ *photon* **~quelle** f *l. emitter*, starke ~ *high-power l. source* **~raumprofil** n *obstruction ga(u)ge limit* **~reklame** f [konkr] *sky-sign* od *electric sign*; [abst] *l.s advertising* **~rot** a *bright-red* **~rufanlage** f *l.s signalling installation* **~säule** f ⟨theat⟩ *l.ing tower*; → Friedhofs– **~schacht** m *well* **~schein** m *lustre* || *gleam* od *ray of l.* || heller ~ *pool* (od *bright glare*) *of l.* **~schere** f = ~putze **~scheu 1.** f *dread of l.* **2.** ~ a *shunning the l.* || ⟨fig⟩ *shady*; *obscurantist* [attr] || ~es Gesindel *the underworld that shuns the l.* **~schirm** m *screen*, (*lamp-*)*shade* **~schleuse** f *l. trap*; *l.-locked passage* **~schnitt** m ⟨film⟩ *cutting* **~schnuppe** f *candlesnuff* **~schutzmittel** n *antifading agent* **~schwach** a ⟨phot⟩ *giving off feeble l.*, *dull*; *low-speed* (Objektiv) **~seite** f ⟨fig⟩ *bright*, *favourable*, *sunny side* (*of ths*) **~setzmaschine** f ⟨typ⟩ *photo-composing machine* **~sicher** a *l.-proof* **~signal** n ⟨mot⟩ *stop-l.*; ⟨rail⟩ *l. unit* **~sparer** m *save-all* **~sphäre** f *l.s sphere* **~spiele** n pl *movies* pl, *cinema* **~spiel-** ~bühne [f], ~theater [n] *cinematographic* od (*motion-*, *moving-*)*picture theatre* (od *house*) **~sprech-** ~gerät [n] *optophone*; ~verkehr [m] *o. traffic*; ~en vi/t [h] *to optophone* **~stark** a *high-power* (*lens*) **~stärke** f *l.s intensity*; *focus number* | ~messer [m] *photometer* **~stoff** m *l.s matter* **~strahl** m (kl) *ray*, (gr, kl) *beam thread of l.* | ~lenmesser [m] ⟨phys⟩ *actinometer* **~strom** m *luminous flux* **~stumpf** m *candle-end* **~therapie** f ⟨med⟩ *phototherapeutics* **~ton** m *optical sound* | ~wert [m] ⟨film⟩ *printer factor*; *density* **~umstrahlt** a *radiant* **~undurchlässig** a *opaque* **~verhältnisse** n pl ⟨phot⟩ *taking conditions* **~versatz** m ⟨theat-el⟩ *groundrow* **~verstärkung** f *l. amplification by stimulated emission of radiation* (*Laser*) **~voll** a *l.s*, *bright*, ⟨fig a.⟩ *lucid*, *clear* **~wanne** f *multibulb flood-l.* **~weite** f ⟨arch⟩ *open space*; ⟨tech⟩ *clear width* **~welle** f *wave of l.* **~wert** m ⟨phot⟩ *exposure value* | ~skala [f] *l.-v. scale* (LVS) **~wesen** n *celestial being* **~wirkung** f *l.s effect* **~zeichen** n *flash*(*-signal*) **~zeiger** m *l. beam pointer* **~zeitung** f *l.-writing motogram*, *travelling news sign* **~ziehen** n *dipping* od *making of* (*tallow-*)*candle* **~zieher** m *candle-maker*, *chandler* **L·ichte** n ~n/: im ~n ⟨arch⟩ *with the clear*, → lichte Höhe **l·ichten** vt [h] (Wald) *to clear* || (Reihen, Haar; a. sich ~) *to thin* (*out*) || sich ~ ⟨a.⟩ *to grow* od *get thin*(*ner*) || die Zuschauer h sich gelichtet *the audience has thinned out*

l·ichten vt [h] ⟨mar⟩ *to weigh* (*anchor*) || *to lighten* (*a ship*) **L·ichter** m (→ Leichter) **~geld** n *lighterage*

L·ichter n pl v Licht **~chen** n pl v Lichtchen **~führungsgrenze** f ⟨mil mot⟩ *l. line* **~glanz** m *bright illumination of candles* **~meer** n *blaze* od *sea of lights* **~rechen** m ⟨R C⟩ *triangular candlestick* **l·ichterloh** adv *blazing*, *in full blaze*; *all aflame* od *ablaze* || er brennt ~ (vor Liebe) *he is madly in love* **l·ichtlos** a *dark* **L·ichtung** f ~/~en *clearing* || ⟨mil⟩ *thinning* || ⟨for⟩ *clearing*, *opening*; *open space*; *glade*

L·id n ~(e)s/~er *eye-lid* | ~schattenstift [m] ⟨cosm⟩ *eye shadow stick*; ~spalte [f] *palpebral fissure*

l·idern vt [h] ⟨tech⟩ *to pack*, *leather* (→ Leder) **L·iderung** f ~/~en ⟨tech⟩ *packing*, *leathering* | ~sdeckel [m] *packing-washer*

L·ido m ~s/~s *barrier beach*, *offshore bar*, *lido* It | ~hemd [n] *short sleeved leisure shirt with breast pocket*

l·ieb I. [a] **1. [attr] (P)** *dear*, *beloved* || *esteemed* || der ~e Gott *the Lord*, *the Almighty* || ~er Gott! *good God*! *good Lord*! || Unsere ~e Frau *our* (*Blessed*) *Lady* || *dear* (*father*, *friends*!) || *a good fellow* || so ein ~es Ding *such a little darling* || ~er Herr N.! *Dear Mr. N.*; ~er N.! *my dear N.* || ~er Junge! *old man*! *old th*! || sich ~ Kind m bei ⟨fig⟩ *to ingratiate o.s. with*, *to endear o.s. to*, *to curry favour with* || (bei jdm) ~(es) Kind s ⟨fig⟩ *to be a favourite* (*with a p*) | **(S)** m–e ~ste Beschäftigung *my favourite occupation*, *the oc. I like best of all* || das ~e Brot *the daily bread* || um des ~en Friedens willen *for peace and quietness' sake* || das ~e Geld *the Golden Calf* || ~er Himmel! *good heavens*! ⟨fam⟩ *good gracious*! || das weiß der ~e H.! *Heaven only knows*! || er hat kaum das ~e Leben *he has just enough to live upon*, *he is a bare existence* || ⟨emph⟩ sie h ihre ~e Not mit ihm *they have a nice trouble with him*; den ~en langen Tag *all day long*, *the livelong day* || ⟨iron⟩ nun hat die ~e Seele Ruh'! *now you are happy*, *arn't you*? || die ~e Zeit! *goodness* od *dear me*! **2. [pred]** *amiable*, *charming* || *pleasant*, *agreable* || seien (*not* sind!) Sie so ~, mir z helfen *or* u helfen Sie mir *be kind* od *an angel and help me* || sei (so) ~ *or* du bist auch ~! *there's a dear* (*child*) od *darling*! || das Kind ist wirklich ~ *it is a sweet child* || es ist mir ~, daß .. *I'm glad* (*that*) (*you have come*); *I am pleased* (*to hear* od *see*) *that* .. || er ist mir ~ u wert *he is very dear to me*, *I love and esteem him* || es ist mir gar nicht ~ z sehen *I am anything but pleased*, *I'm sorry* (*to find*) *that* || wenn dir dein Leben ~ ist *if* od *as you value your life* (*don't*) || sich etw ~ s l, mit etw für~|nehmen *to make shift with a th* || sie hatte ihn ~ gewonnen *she had become fond of him* || jdn, etw ~ gewinnen *to take* (*kindly*) *to a p*, *a th*; sie ist uns ~ geworden *we have become attached to her* || (of qualities) (jdn) lieb m *to endear* (jdm *to a p*) **3. lieber** [compr zu lieb & gern] *dearer*; *more pleasant*, etc. || **adv** *more willingly*; *sooner* (*today than tomorrow*); *rather*, *better* || ich möchte ~ nicht *I had* od *I'd rather not* || *to obey God rather than man* || laß es ~! *you had better leave it* || ~, als daß .. *in preference to* (*going*) || ~ h, mögen, sehen, wollen *to like better*, *to prefer* || ich hätte ~ nicht k sollen *it would have been better to stay away*; ich wäre ~ zu Hause geblieben *I did rather want to stay at home*; ich wüßte nicht, was ich ~ täte *I don't know what I would sooner do* || wir sollten ~ [Litotes] *it would be as well* .. || ~ tot als Sklave! *rather death than slavery* || ~ tot! *I shall die first*! || .. desto ~ ist es ihm .. *the better he likes it* **4. liebst** [sup zu lieb & gern] *my best friend*; *my favourite dish* || **am ~en** dies *preferably this one* || das h wir am ~en *we like that best* (*of all*) || ich möchte am ~en .. *I feel inclined to* (*flog him*) **II.** [subst] **1. Liebe(r** m) f: mein ~r! (f: m–e ~!) ⟨fam⟩ *dear fellow*, *old th* od *man* (*dear woman* od *lady*!, *old girl*!) || ⟨oft iron⟩: (*my*) *precious* (*you mustn't be so morbid*, *pr.*!); (Frau zum Mann) ⟨a.⟩ *boy*!; m–e ~n [pl] *my dear ones* od *dear friends*!, ⟨fam⟩ *my dears*! pl **2. Lieb(chen)** n (Geliebte): ~! *love*, *darling*, *dear girl*, *beloved*! **3. Liebe(s)** n [das ~, etw ~s] *pleasant thing*[*s* pl] || viel ~es! *much love*! e–m viel ~s antun *to be very kind to a p*, *to show a p great affection* **4. der, die Liebste** *his*, *her beloved* (*one*), *best girl*, *sweetheart*, (m ⟨a.⟩ *lover*, f ⟨a.⟩ *love*) || ~(r)! *darling*! **5. das Liebste** *the most precious th one possesses*, *the th one cherishes most* || das wäre mir das ~ *I should like that best* (*of all*) **L·ieb- ~äugel·ei** f *amorous glances* pl; ⟨fam⟩ *ogle*, *ogling* **~äugeln** vi [h] mit jdm *or* etw ⟨fam⟩ *to ogle* (*a p*, *a th*); ⟨Am⟩ *to neck* || ⟨iron⟩ *to make sheep's eyes* (*at a p*) || *to toy* (*with an idea*) || ⟨fig⟩ *to flirt* (*with the socialists*) **~diener** m = Liebe- **~frauen-** ~kirche [f] *St. Mary's* (*Church*); ~milch [f] *Rhenish wine grown near Worms* **~|gewinnen** vt [h] *to take* (*a fancy*, ⟨Am⟩ *a shine*) *to*, *to become*, *get*, *grow*, *attached to* od *fond of*, *to come to like a p* **~|haben** vt [h] *to love*, (schwächer) *to like*, *to be fond of* || hab mich lieb *be kind to me*, *love me* **~haber** m *lover*, *admirer* || (Kunst~) *amateur*, *dilettante* || (*bird-*, etc.) *fancier* || *connoisseur* (*of pictures*) || ~ des Rennsports *racing man*, *turfite* || leidenschaftlicher ~ ⟨sl⟩ (*film-*, etc.) *fan* od *fiend*; ein l. ~ s v *to be passionately fond of* || ⟨theat⟩ Erster ~ *leading gentleman* (f *lady*), *the romantic lead* | ~·ei [f] (für) *partiality*, *fancy* (*for*, *to*), *fondness* (*of*) || (Gegenstand) *favourite pursuit*, *hobby* || *gardening is an indulgence of mine* || übertriebene ~ *extravagance* || aus ~ *as an amateur*, *for amusement's sake* | ~einband

[m] *amateur* od *collector's binding*; ~preis [m] *fancy price*; ~rolle [f] *lover's part*; ~theater [n], ~vorstellung[en pl] [f] *private* (od *amateur*) *theatricals* pl ≃**k·osen** vt [h] *to caress, fondle, cuddle* | ~d [adv] *caressingly* **~k·osung** f *fondling, caress(es* pl) ≃**los** a *unkind; unloving, unlovable; unfeeling, uncharitable, unsympathetic* **~losigkeit** f *unkindness, uncharitableness* ≃**reich** a *full of kindness; kind, amiable; affable, benevolent* **~reiz** m *charm, grace(fulness), attractiveness*; ⟨fam⟩ *sweetness* ≃**reizend** a *lovable; charming, attractive; graceful*; ⟨fam⟩ *sweet* **~stöckel** m & n ⟨bot⟩ *lovage, leviticum* ≃**wert** a *beloved and esteemed* **L·iebchen** n ~s/~ *sweetheart, love* **L·iebden** [obs] Euer ~ (Ew. ~!) *Cousin*! (*title*) **L·iebe** f ~ **1.** ⟨eig⟩ *love* (zu *of, for, to*[*wards*]) ‖ e–e alte (= frühere) ~ *an old flame* ‖ (*filial*) *affection* ‖ (*Christian*) *charity* ‖ berechnende ~, (die durch den Magen geht) *cupboard-l.*; abgöttische ~ *idolatry*; unglückliche ~ *disastrous l.*; verschmähte ~ *disdained l.* | das ist die ~! [statt engl mst] *c'est l'amour*! **zu:** *l. for one's neighbour*; *l. of one's country* ‖ **aus** ~ **(zu)** *for love* (*of*) ‖ aus ~ zum Kampf *for the l. of fighting* ‖ gegen ~ gefeit *heartwhole* ‖ aus ~ heiraten *to marry for l.* ‖ Heirat aus ~ *l.-match* ‖ **heiße** ~ *passion* ‖ vernarrte ~ *infatuation* (zu *for*) ‖ der jungen ~ erster Traum *l.'s young dream* ‖ was macht die ~? *how have your* (*young*) *l.s prospered*? ‖ e–e unglückliche ~ *an unfortunate l.-affair* ‖ unerwiderte ~ *unrequited l.* od *attachment* | kalte Hände, warme ~ *a cold hand, a warm heart* ‖ die ~ ist blind *l. is blind* ‖ ~ entflammen *to excite l.*; sich [dat] jds ~ erwerben durch *to get endeared to a p by* ‖ mit ~ erreicht man meist mehr als mit Gewalt *a little kindness goes a long way* ‖ alte ~ rostet nicht *old l. lies deep* **2.** (**Gefälligkeit**) tun Sie mir die ~ *do me the favour* ‖ e–e ~ ist der anderen wert *one good turn deserves another* **~diener** m *time-server, toady, pickthank* | ~ei [f] *time-serving, cringe, cringing*; ≃isch [a] *t.-s., fawning, cringing*; ≃n [vi h] *to cringe, truckle, toady*; jdm ~ *to play up to a p* ≃**glühend** a *glowing with l.* ≃**krank** a *l.-sick* ≃**leer** a *devoid of* od *lacking in l.* ≃**voll** a *loving, fond, affectionate, devoted; caressive* (*look*) ‖ ~e Fürsorge *loving care* **Liebel·ei** f ~/~en *amour,* (*l.-*)*intrigue, flirtation, l.-affair* ‖ *dalliance* **l·iebeln** vi [h] *to flirt, spoon; to make l.* ‖ *to dally* (mit *with*) **L·ieben** n ~s/ *l.-making* ‖ → Liebe

l·ieben vt [h] *to love* (a. vi [h]) ‖ sie ~ sich *or* e–a *they l. each other* od *one another* ‖ er sehnte sich danach jdn ~ zu lernen *he began to wish to make l. to someone, .. to have someone to l.* ‖ v ganzem Herzen *with all one's h.*; innig ~ *to adore* ‖ (gern h) *to like, to be fond of* ‖ (Zuneigung h) *to be attached to, to cherish* ‖ närrisch ~ *to dote on* ‖ unglücklich ~ [vi] *to be crossed in l.* | ⟨übtr⟩ *to go in for* (*small hats*) ‖ *violets like the shade* ‖ *artists in whom he delighted* ‖ *the school he so greatly fancied* ‖ *such scenes he fancied* ‖ es ~, etw zu tun *to delight in doing, to be fond of doing* **geliebt** [a] *beloved*; geliebte J.! *dearest Jenny* **l·iebend** a *loving; heartfelt* (Verehrung) ‖ die ≃en *the two lovers* ‖ Briefschluß: Dein Dich ~er (Bruder) N. *affectionately Yours* (*Your affectionate brother*) *N.* **L·iebens-** ≃**wert** a *lovable,* (*temperament*) ⟨Am⟩ *lovely* | (S) *delightful* ≃**würdig** a *amiable, lovable, lik(e)able; kind, genial, pleasant, nice; warm-hearted* ‖ das ist sehr ~ v Ihnen *that is very kind of you* | ~erweise [adv] *amiably, kindly*; ~keit [f] *amiability, kindness* ‖ Sie besaßen die ~, es zu tun *You were kind enough to do it*; ~en [pl] ⟨iron⟩ *scoffing remarks* **l·ieber** a → lieb I. 3. **L·iebes- ~abenteuer** n *love-adventure* ‖ auf ~ ausgehen *to go in search of gallant adventures* ‖ ein Mann v ~n *a man of gallantry* **~affairen** f pl *affairs of the heart* **~angelegenheit** f (*l.-*)*affair* **~antrag** m *l.-suit* **~apfel** m *l.-apple* **~band** n *tie of l.* **~becher** m *loving-cup* **~bedürfnis** n *desire for l.* **~beteuerung** f *protestation of l.* **~bezeigung** f *l.-making* **~blick** m *amorous* od *adoring glance* **~brief** m *l.-letter* **~briefchen** n *billet-doux* Fr **~dichter** m *erotic poet* **~dienst** m *good turn, favour, kindness, kind office* ‖ jdm e–n ~ erweisen *to do a p a good turn* **~erklärung** f *declaration of l.* **~feuer** n *ardent l.* **~fieber** n *l.-fit* **~flamme** f *flame of l.* **~gaben** f pl *pittance* sg; ⟨mil⟩ *comforts* pl **~gedanke** m *l.-thought* **~gedicht** n *amatory poem* **~genuß** m *enjoyment of l.* **~geschichte** f **1.** *l.-story, l.-tale* **2.** = ~angelegenheit **~geständnis** n *confession of l.* **~glück** n *l.rs' happiness* **~glut** f *flame* od *fervour of l.* **~gott** m *god of L.* (*Cupid*) **~göttin** f *goddess of L.* (*Venus*) **~handel** m *amour, intrigue,* (*l.-*)*affair* **~heirat** f *l.-match* **~klage** f *amorous complaint* °**~knochen** m ⟨sex vulg⟩ *jiggling-bone* | ⟨bak⟩ *éclair* Fr **~knoten** m *true l.r's knot* ≃**krank** a *l.-sick* **~kummer** m *l.r's grief* **~kuß** m *kiss of l.* **~lied** n *l.-song* **~lyrik** f *amatory lyrics* pl **~mahl** n *l.-feast* ‖ ⟨mil⟩ *regimental dinner* **~mangelschaden** m *infantile damage caused by lack of affection*; → *juvenile* **~müh'** f: das ist vergebliche ~ *that means L.'s labour's lost* **~paar** n *couple* od *pair of l.rs* **~pfand** n *l.-token* ‖ (Kind) *pledge of l.* **~pflicht** f *charitable duty* **~qualen** f pl *pangs of l.* **~rausch** m *transport of l.* **~roman** m *l.-story* **~sache** f *l.-affair* **~schwur** m *l.r's oath* **~spiel** n = Liebelei ≃**toll** a *mad with l.* **~trank** m *l.-potion* **~verhältnis** n (*l.-*)*affair, intrigue* **~wahnsinn** m *l.'s frenzy* **~werbung** f *courting, courtship* **~werk** n *work of charity, charitable office* **~wonne** f *pleasure of l.* **~wut** f *l.-passion, -fit* **-zauber** m *l.-spell* **~zeichen** n *l.-token* **l·ieblich 1.** [a] ⟨allg⟩ *pleasing* ‖ *lovely, adorable*; ⟨fam⟩ *sweet* (*girl*) ‖ *charming* (*view*) ‖ *delightful* (*place*) ‖ *delicious* (*smell, taste*) ‖ *caressive* (*voice*) ‖ ⟨iron⟩ das ist ja ~! *that's a fine mess*! **2.** [adv] ~ duftend *sweet-scented* ‖ ~ klingend *melodious* ‖ ~ süß *benignly sweet* ‖ (*to smell*) *sweet, nice* ‖ (*to stir the leaves*) *pleasantly* | ≃**keit** f ~ *loveliness, amiability, charm, gracefulness* ‖ *delightfulness, deliciousness* ‖ (P, Ort) *amenity* ‖ *sweetness* ‖ *melodiousness* **L·iebling** m ~(e)s/~e *darling, pet*; (lamb) *cosset* ‖ (*come on*), *lass* ‖ ⟨fam⟩ *honey* ‖ ⟨dero⟩ *minion* ‖ (Günstling) *favourite*; ⟨school⟩ (Vorzug) *nevvy* ‖ ⟨sex⟩: ~ der Frauen *fair-haired boy*; *a devil with the women* **L·ieblings-** [in comp mst] *favourite* (*book, daughter, dish, poet, occupation*) ‖ *pet* (*dog*) ‖ *greatest* (*wish*) **L·iebschaft** f (*love-*)*affair, intrigue, amour* ‖ (oberflächliche) *flirtation* ‖ e–e ~ h mit *to have* (od *carry on*) *an affair with*; .. anfangen mit *to take up with* **L·iebste(r)** m, **L·iebste** f ~n/~n → lieb II. 4.

L·ied n ~(e)s/~er *song* (→ Gedicht) ‖ (Weise) *air, tune, lilt, melody* ‖ kz ~ *lay* ‖ (Solo≃ zur Laute) *air*, ⟨hist⟩ *ayre* (→ Madrigal) ‖ (Volks≃) *ballad* ‖ (Jubel≃) *carol* ‖ (mehrstimmiges) *glee* ‖ (geistliches) *hymn*; (der Neger) ⟨Am⟩ *spiritual* ‖ ⟨mus⟩ ~er pl *lieder* ‖ ⟨Lit⟩ *Lay* (*of the Nibelungen*) | e–m ein ~ zum besten geben *to favour a p with a s.* ‖ ein ~ anstimmen *to strike up* od *intone a s.* ‖ sing uns ein ~ *give us a s.*! ‖ wie es im ~ heißt *as the ballad puts it* | ⟨fig⟩ das alte ~ *the old story* ‖ das Ende v ~e *the end of the matter* ‖ davon kann ich ein ~(chen) singen *I can tell you a tale about that* **L·iedchen** n ~s/~ *ditty* **L·ieder- ~abend** m *lieder-evening; singing; song recital* ≃**artig** a *s.-like*; ⟨mus⟩ *cantabile* **~buch** n *s.-book* ‖ ⟨ec⟩ *h.-book* **~dichter** m *lyrical poet, s.-writer* **~dichtung** f *lyrical poetry, s.-writing* **~hort** m *s.-book, treasury of s.s* **~komponist** m *composer of s.s* **~kranz** m, **~tafel** f *choral society* ≃**reich** a *rich in s.s* **~sänger** m *ballad-singer* **~spiel** n *musical play* **~texte** m pl ⟨fam⟩ *lyrics* **~zyklus** m *cycle of romances*

°**L·iederjahn, L·iedrian** m ~s/~e *loose* od *fast fellow, rake, sloven* **l·iederlich** [a] **1.** (unordentlich) *careless, slovenly* ‖ *sloven* (*clothing*) ‖ *slipshod,* *disorderly* (*fellow*) || *unkempt* (*appearance*) || *floppy, negligent* (*style*) || *topsy-turvy* (*room*) || *sloppy* (*work*) | [adv] ~ arbeiten ⟨fam⟩ *to scamp one's job* **2.** (ausschweifend) *loose, dissipated, wanton* || (lasterhaft) *dissolute, debauched, disreputable* || ~er Kerl *loose fish*; *rake, profligate fellow, bad lot* || Bruder *or* Hans ≗ *Jack Rake, Lovelace, Mr. Scapegrace* || ~es Frauenzimmer *loose, gay, fast woman*; ⟨sl⟩ *bad 'un* || ~es Leben *profligacy*; ein .. führen *to lead a loose, fast, profligate life* | **≗keit** f ~/~en *carelessness, slovenliness, negligence* | *looseness, profligacy, debauchery, dissoluteness*

l·ief 1. & 3. sg pret v laufen

L·iefer- **~auftrag** m *order of delivery* **~bote** m *d.y-man* **~fähigkeit** f ⟨m. m.⟩ *available output* **~-frist,** **~zeit** f *term of d.y*; Verlängerung [f] der ~ ⟨contr⟩ *extension of time of d.y* **~menge** f *quantity d.ed* **~schein** m *bill of d.y, d.y* od *supply note, docket* **~termin** m (vertraglich) ⟨com⟩ *contract date* **~wagen** m *d.y-van* ⟨Am⟩ *d.y truck*; (Milch-, Brot≗) ⟨engl⟩ *panel truck* | ~dieb [m] ⟨sl⟩ *van-dragger* **Liefer·ant** m ~en/~en *supplier, purveyor* || (ins Haus) *roundsman*; ⟨mil⟩ *contractor* || (v Kleidung) (⟨mar⟩ *naval*) *outfitter* || (v Lebensmitteln) *caterer, provider* || (v Möbeln) *furnisher* **l·ieferbar** a *d.able, to be d.ed* (an *to*) || sofort ~e Waren *spot goods,* ⟨fam⟩ *spots* pl; in kurzer Zeit ~ *available on short d.y*; noch ~ *still on sale*; (Buch) *still in print*; nur beschränkt ~ s *to be in short* od *limited supply* **l·iefern** vt [h] e–m etw ~ *to deliver a th to a p* || (beschaffen) *to furnish, provide, supply a p with a th*; *to purvey a th for* (*the army*), *to furnish* (*evidence, proofs*), *to yield* (*informations*) || (auf Bestellung) *to supply a th* (*to order*) || (Lebensmittel) *to cater* .. (*for a feast*) || (Schauspieler etc) *to supply a p with* (*actors*) || in Heften ~ *to issue* od *publish in numbers* || (Ertrag, Ernte) *to yield* || e–e Schlacht ~ *to give battle* (e–m *to* ..) || ⟨fig⟩ jdn ~ *to ruin a p* || er ist ge–rt ⟨fam⟩ *he is done for, it's all over with him* || sich in jds H. ~ *to put o.s. in a p's hands* **L·ieferung** f ~/~en (Tätigkeit & Gegenstand) *delivery, supply* (an *to*) || *providing, furnishing* || *yielding* || ⟨mil⟩ ~ m für *or* an *to make issues to the army* || (e–s Werkes) *part, instalment, number* || zahlbar bei ~ *payable* od *cash* (⟨Am⟩ *collect*) *on delivery* (abbr *C.O.D.*) **L·ieferungs-** **~angebot** n ⟨com⟩ *tender* ⟨Am a.⟩ *bid* od *proposal* (auf *for*) **~bedingungen** f pl *terms* [pl] *of d.* **~geschäft** n *indent-business* || (auf Zeit) *time-bargain* **~preis** m *contracted price* **~schein** m = Lieferschein **~tag** m *day of* (od *fixed for*) *d.* **~vertrag** m *contract for d.* **≗weise** adv *in parts* od *instalments* **~werk** n *serial* **~zeit** f = Lieferfrist

L·iege f ~/~n → Kautsch || ⟨a.⟩ *ottoman* ⟨rail⟩ *shelf, sleeperette* ⟨a. aero⟩; ⟨bes Am⟩ *couchette* **~geld** n ⟨mar⟩ *demurrage* **~kur** f (*bed*) *rest cure,* ⟨med⟩ *clinotherapy* **~platz** m ⟨mar⟩ *berth,* ⟨Am⟩ *slip* **~sitz** m ⟨mot, rail, a–n, etc⟩ *reclining seat* **~stuhl** m *deck-chair* **~stütz** m ⟨gym⟩ *push-up* (*to do a few p.-ups*) | ~übungen [f pl] ⟨gym⟩ *press-ups* **~zeit** f ⟨mar⟩ *lay-days* pl

l·iegen I. vi [lag/gelegen] [h] **1.** *to lie* (*on the table, floor,* etc) || sich befinden *to be* (*placed*), (⟨geogr⟩ *situated, located*) || da liegt es *there it is* (od *lies*) || *a city lies* od *stands on a river* (an), *is set upon a hill* (auf), *lies* (*to the*) *west of* .. (westlich v ..) || *a ship is berthed* od *moored* (liegt festgemacht) || hier liegt .. *here lies the body of* .. || ⟨fig⟩ wie die Dinge ~ (S –gt) *in the nature of things*; da liegt der Hund begraben, der Knoten *there's the rub* || ⟨mot⟩ s. u. gut liegen | (gebreitet s) es liegt e–e Decke auf dem T. .. *is spread over the table* || Stille lag über dem Dorf *stillness brooded over* .. || um den Balken liegt ein Ring *a ring is laid round the* .. | [mit dat] (passen) **es liegt mir** (nicht) *walking is*(*n't much* od *nothing*) [*in*] *my line*; *it does* (*not*) *suit me*; *I* (*don't*) *like it*; *it is* (*not*) *in him to do that*; *that does* (*not*) *appeal to her* || es kam ihm gelegen *it came opportunely for him* | [abs *or* ell] (T) *to couch* || er liegt *he lies in bed* || es liegt (zwei Fuß hoher) Schnee *there is a coat of snow* (*the snow is* od *lies two feet deep*) || ⟨fig⟩ (stocken) *to be at a standstill, to languish* || zu gelegener Zeit *at a suitable moment* **2.** [mit adv *or* adv Bestimmung] **ausgestreckt** ~ *to lie* (*at*) *full length*; **behaglich** ~ *to nestle*; bereit ~ *to be ready* (*at hand*); der Stoff liegt e–n *m* breit .. *is one metre wide*; **dicht** ~ auf *or* an *to huddle on*; dick *or* dünn ~ auf: *thick dust films the piano* || **es lag mir fern** .. zu .. *it was not in my intention* od *I had no wish to offend you*; *far be it from me* (*to do*); **nichts** liegt uns ferner, als .. *there is nothing further from our minds than* ..; fest ~ ⟨hunt⟩ (*snipe*) *lie well*; **geeignet** ~ für: *the place is favourably situated for* || das Auto liegt **gut** auf der Straße *the car has a favourable position* (⟨Am⟩ *location*) *of the centre of gravity*; *the car is well hung, has a favourable clearance over the road*; → Straßenlage || der Schnee auf der Straße lag **hoch** *the snow was deep in the st.* || hoch, niedrig ~ (of prices) *to rule* (*high, low*) || er liegt **krank** *he is laid up with an illness,* → ~d || das Wasser lag **schwarz** um ihn her *the w. was bl. all round about him* || **schwer** ~ auf *to weigh heavy upon* (*loneliness weighed down her heart*) || die S liegt so: .. *the matter can be summed up as follows*; **voll** ~ v *or* voller .. ~ *to be covered with* (*stones*), *to be littered up with* (*books*); **weich** ~ *to have a soft bed* || **[nach neg]** so weit *or* was an ihm läge *if he could help it* || wie die Dinge ~ *as matters stand*; er sah, wie die D. lagen *he saw how the land lay* || es liegt weit **zurück** *it goes back a long way* || zurückgelehnt ~: *she had been reclining on a settee* **3.** ~ **bleiben** [s] *to remain* od *continue lying* od *in bed, to keep one's bed*; (*snow*) *sticks*; (unterwegs) *to break down*; ⟨rail⟩ *to be held up*; (Arbeit) *to be discontinued, to stand over*; *to be brought to a standstill, to come to a dead stop*; (Briefe) *not to be sent off*; (Waren) *to remain on hand*; ⟨parl⟩ (verschoben w) *to lie on the table* || ⟨mot⟩ (of car) *to strand, to get stranded*; (*vehicles which have*) *to drop out of the column*; ~geblieben *broken-down* || (of attack) *to hang fire, to cease, abate* | Geld auf der Bank ~ **haben** *to have money at the b.* (*on deposit*) || (Wein) *to have* .. *in the cellar* | (beim Fall) zu ~ **k** auf *to land on* | ~ **l** *to let lie, to abandon, to leave* od *let alone* || *to leave* (*a th*) *lying about*; *I left my umbrella* (*behind*) *somewhere* || rechts ~ l *to leave* (*a th*) *on one's right* || ⟨fig⟩ (Ort) links ~ l *to leave* .. *unvisited*; (P) *to ignore, disregard, cut a p* || e–n für tot ~ l *to leave a p for dead* **4. am** Boden ~ ⟨a.⟩ *to be down* || *to lie on a p's breast* || an–e–a ~ *to join* od *touch each other* || an der Erde ~ *to lie on the ground* || am Fieber krank ~ *to be down* od *laid low with a f.* || mir liegt etw am H. *I have a th very much at heart, it is nearest to my h.* || *the pub lies on the way* || ⟨mar⟩ hart am W. ~ *to sail close to the wind* | **es liegt d·aran, daß** *the reason is that* | es liegt an ihm *it rests with him,* .. nicht an **mir** *it is not my fault* || die Schuld liegt an ihm *the fault lies with him, he is to blame* || mir liegt viel **daran,** es ist mir sehr daran gelegen *I care very much* (zu tun *to do*; ob *whether*); *I am anxious* (*for it*; *to do*); *it is of great moment* od *consequence to me*; *I am greatly* (*little*) *interested* (*in it*) od *concerned* (*about it*) || mir liegt nichts (°ein Dreck *or* Quark) daran *it doesn't matter* (*to me*) (*at all* od ⟨fam⟩ *a bit*), ⟨fam⟩ *I don't care a fig* || was liegt mir dran? *what is that to me*? || soviel *or* was **an** mir liegt *as far as it lies in my power* || **auf**: → Bärenhaut, flach || auf Flaschen ~ *to be in bottles* || e–m auf dem Halse ~ *to be always at a p's elbows, to bore* od *pester a p* || es liegt auf der Hand *it is obvious* || auf e–m Haufen ~ *to lie in a heap, to be piled up* || es liegt mir auf dem Herzen *or* Gewissen *it lies heavily on my conscience* || → Knie, Lauer || der Ton liegt auf der ersten Silbe .. *is on* .. || e–m auf der Tasche ~ *to live at a p's expense* || er lag auf den Tod (krank) *he was not expected to live* || das Geld liegt auf der Straße *m. can be picked up in the st.* || → Weg || das Wort lag mir auf der Zunge *I had the w. at the tip of my t.* || **aus** [dat]: *to lean out of the window* || das liegt **außer** m–m Bereich (m–n Berechnungen) *that lies, is (goes) beyond my province (calculations)* || sie ~ **bei** den anderen *they are with the others* || der Durchschnitt liegt bei nur e–m Morgen *the average is as low as one acre* || ~ bei → Entscheidung || alles liegt **durch**–e–a *everything is topsy-turvy* || **gegen** Süden ~ (Land) *to lie to* (Haus: *to face*) *the south* | es lag nicht **in** s–r **A**bsicht *it was not his intention* (zu tun *to do*) || im Anschlag ~ *to aim a gun* || .. im **B**ereich des Möglichen *that is not within the range of p.y* || im Bette ~ *to be* od *lie in bed*; (krank) *to keep to one's bed, to be down* od *laid up* (an, mit *with*) || das liegt im Blut (*or* in der **F**amilie) *that runs* od *is inherent in the bl.* (od *f.*) || ⟨mil⟩ im Felde ~ *to be (encamped) on the line* od *in the field* || es liegt mir schwer wie Blei in den **G**liedern *I feel as heavy as lead* || → Grün || .. liegt in den **H**änden des .. *the responsibility is vested in the Minister*; *it rests with him*; *happiness rests in spiritual ths* || sich in den Haaren ~ *to be at loggerheads* || → Hinterhalt, **M**agen || die Wahrheit liegt in der Mitte .. *lies half-way* || das liegt im Menschen *it is part of human nature* || es liegt nicht in s–r Natur *it is not in him* || e–m mit (etw) in den **O**hren ~ *to be (for ever) bothering a p with* || °da liegt der Hase im **P**feffer *there's the rub* || → Quartier, Scheidung, Schützengraben, Schlaf, Streit || im Sterben ~ *to be* od *lie dying* || ständig in den **W**irtshäusern ~ *to hang about pubs* || in den letzten **Z**ügen ~ *to lie at death's door* | **mit** dem Bauch **auf** der Erde ~ *to lie pronely on the ground* od *on one's stomach* || **mit** dem Gesicht **gegen** die Wand ~ *to lie with one's face to the wall* || das Haus liegt **mit** der Front **nach** dem Fluß .. *faces the river*; **nach** Süden *faces the south*; *its façade opens on N.-Square* || *the room overlooks* (od *looks onto*) *the garden* || .. ~ der Reihe nach *the sheets are arranged in perfect order* || **über** etw ~ *to overhang a th* || ⟨fig⟩ immer über s–n Büchern ~ *to plod at one's books* || *a mist hung over the country* || *melancholy was upon the suburb* || ~ **um** *to cluster round* || **unter** der Erde ~ *to rest in one's grave, to be bedded beneath the sods*; ⟨mil sl⟩ *to be kicking up the daisies* || unter der Oberfläche v etw ~ *to underlie a th* || ~ **vor**: *there is a garden in front of the house* || ⟨mar⟩ vor Anker ~ *to be, ride, lie at anchor* || es liegt klar vor Augen *or* zu Tage, daß *it is perfectly clear that* || (zeitlich) lange ~ vor *to have been long anterior in date to* || ⟨fig & sport⟩ vor jdm ~ *to lie ahead of a p* || ⟨mil⟩ vor e–r Stadt ~ *to lay siege to a town* || **zu** Bette ~ *to keep (to) one's bed* || jdm zu *or* zu jds Füßen ~ *to lie at a p's feet* || → zugrunde ~ || (of events) ~ **zwischen** *to intervene between* **II. sich** ~ [v/refl]: ⟨a.⟩ sich [acc] (*or* sich [dat] den Rücken) wund ~ *to become bedsore* **III.** ≗ [n] *lying, prostration* || ich bin das ~ *or* des ~s müde *I am tired of lying* od *of my bed* **l·iegend I.** [a] *lying (down)*; (krank) ⟨mil⟩ *litter* [attr] || (örtlich) *situated* || (ruhend) *reclining, recumbent* || (hingestreckt) *reclining, reposing prostrate* || (auf dem Bauche) *prone* || (auf dem Rücken) *supine* || unter Feuer etc ~ *stricken (area)* || ⟨her⟩ *couchant* || (waagerecht) *horizontal* || ⟨P & geol⟩ *recumbent* || ⟨bot⟩ *procumbent* || ~e Güter *or* Gründe [pl] *real od landed estates* pl od *property, immovables* pl **2.** das ≗**e** n ⟨min⟩ *the foot-wall*, ⟨geol⟩ *lower bed, underlying stratum* **L·iegenschaft** f ~/ (mst) ~en = liegende Güter, ⟨off⟩ *accomodations*

l·ieh 1. & 3. sg pret v leihen

L·iek n ~(e)s/ ~en ⟨mar⟩ *bolt-rope, leech* | ~garn [n] *roping twine*

l·ies imp v lesen (abbr l.)

Lieschen Müller ⟨fig⟩ *Mrs Jones*

L·iesch(gras) n ⟨bot⟩ *timothy(-grass)*

L·iese f ~/ ~n **1.** *Lisa* || dumme ~ *silly goose* **2.** ⟨min⟩ *narrow fissure* **3.** ~**n** f pl *inside fat of pork*

l·iest 2. u 3. sg prs v lesen

l·ieß 1. u 3. sg pret v lassen

Lift m ~(e)s/ ~e *lift* ⟨a. rec⟩

L·iga f ~/–gen *league* (*Arab L.*) ~**m·ent** n ~(e)s/ ~e *ligament* ~**t·ur** f ~/ ~en ⟨mus, typ, surg⟩ *ligature* **Lig·ist** m ~en/ ~en, ~**in** ~/ ~nen *leaguer* | ≗**isch** a *of the league*

Lign·in n ~(e)s/ ~e *lignin(e)*

Lign·it m ~(e)s/ ~e ⟨min⟩ *lignite*

†**Lig·urer, Lig·urier** pl ⟨It⟩ *Ligurians* †**Lig·urien** n *Liguria* **lig·urisch** a *Ligurian* (*Alps* pl) **Lig·urische Meer,** das ⟨ehem.⟩ *the Ligurian Sea*, ⟨jetzt⟩ *the Gulf of Genoa*

Lig·uster m ~s/ ⟨bot⟩ *privet* | ~hecke [f] *p.-hedge* || ~schwärmer [m] ⟨ent⟩ *p.-hawk(moth)*

li·ieren: sich ~ [h] (mit) *to ally (with)* || ⟨com⟩ *to become a partner* od *associate (of)* **Li·ierung** f *(forming an) alliance*

Lik·ör m ~(e)s/ ~e *liqueur, cordial* | ~bohne [f] *chocolate liqueur*; ~fabrik [f] *l.-distillery*

Likt·orenbündel n pl *fasces* [pl L]

L·ila n ~s/ *lilac(-colour)* | ≗ *lilac(-coloured)*

L·ilie f ~/ ~n ⟨bot⟩ *lily*, → d. || ⟨her⟩ *fleur-de-luce* **L·ilien-** ~**arm** m ⟨poet⟩ *lily-white arm* ≗**artig** a ⟨bot⟩ *liliaceous* ≗**weiß** a *lily-white, (as) white as a l.* ~**zwiebel** f *bulb of a lily*

L·iliput- *midget* [attr] ~**·aner** m ~s/ ~ *Lilliputian*

L·ille n (seit 1667 franz. Stadt)

L·ima (Hauptstadt v Peru)

Lim·an m ~s/~e ⟨Turkey⟩ *lagoon, estuary almost completely separated from the sea*

L·imba n ~s/ (Furnierholz) *limba, afara, ofram*

L·imburg n **1.** niederländ.-belg. Provinz || ~er (Käse) m *Limburger (cheese)* **2.** ⟨Ger⟩ (Stadt an der Lahn)

L·imit n ~s/ ~s L·imitum [n] ~s/–ta *limit* || ein ~ stellen *to fix a l.* ≗**·ieren** vt [h] *to l.*

Lim·oges [–o:ʒ] n ⟨Fr⟩ (Stadt) → Email

Limon·ade f ~/ ~n *carbonated soft drink (made of fruit-juice)* **Lim·one** f ~/ ~n *lime (fruit)*

Limous·ine f ~/ ~n *berlin(e)(-coach)* || ⟨mot⟩ *saloon(-car), limousine*, ⟨Am⟩ *sedan*

L·inde f ~/ ~n ⟨bot⟩ *lime(-tree), linden*, → d. | ~nallee [f] *lime-tree walk* od *avenue*; ~nschwärmer [m] ⟨ent⟩ *lime-hawk(moth)*

l·ind a *soft, gentle* **L·inderer** m ~s/ ~ *soother, comforter* **l·indern** vt [h] *to soften*; *mitigate (evils)*; *assuage (pains), alleviate (want)*; *soothe (pains)*; *allay (troubles), relieve (poverty)* | **sich** ~ (of spasms) *to abate* | ~der Balsam *lenitive ointment* **L·inderung** f ~/ ~en *softening, mitigation, alleviation* || *relief* || *abatement* || ⟨path⟩ *palliation* ~**s-mittel** n ⟨med⟩ *lenitive, palliative, anodyne* **L·indheit** f ~/ *mildness, lenity*

L·indwurm m *dragon*

Line·al n ~(e)s/ ~e *ruler*; *straightedge*; *rule* (mit Metalleinlage *with strengthened edge[s]*) || .. als hätte er ein ~ verschluckt (*he looks*) *as if he had swallowed a poker* || (zum Messen) *rule* || Vis·ier≗ *alidade* || → Nonius || ⟨typ⟩ *guide* **Line·am·ent** n ~(e)s/ ~e *lineament, feature* **line·ar** *linear* | ≗beschleuniger [m] ⟨at⟩ *l. accelerator*; ≗maßstab [m] *l. scale*; ≗perspektive [f] *l. p.* ≗**is·ierung** f ⟨phot⟩ *correction of nonlinear distortions*

.. ling m [dim suff] z. B. in: Dichterling

L·inga(m) n ~s/ ~e ⟨Ind myth⟩ (Phallus) *lingam*

Linge f ~/ [lɛ̃ʒ] Sw = Wäsche ~**er·ie** f ~/ ~n = W.kammer

.. lings [adv suff] z. B. in: blindlings *blindly*

Lingu·allaut m ⟨gram⟩ *lingual* **Lingu·ist** [–gw–] ∼en/∼en *linguist* | **∼ik** f *linguistics* pl

L·inie f ∼/∼n **1.** *line* ⟨a. fig, rail, mil⟩ ‖ Abstammungs≃ *lineage, descent* ‖ Äquator≃ *line* ‖ Ausgangs≃ *base* ‖ ausgezogene ∼ *solid l.* ‖ fließende ∼ *sweep* (*of drapery*) ‖ gestrichelte ∼ *broken l.* ‖ Grenz≃ *limit* ‖ ⟨rail⟩ Haupt≃ *trunk line* ‖ ⟨fenc⟩ Mensur≃ *l. of distance* ‖ ⟨mot⟩ → Leit≃ ‖ ohne ∼n *unlined* ‖ Schiffahrt≃ *route* (*on this r.*) ‖ schlanke ∼ *slim figure*; neue ∼ ⟨tail⟩ *new look* ‖ Schützen≃ *skirmishing l.* ‖ Setz≃ *composing rule* ‖ Start≃ *starting-l.* ‖ Tast≃ (Fingerabdruck) *tactile l.* ‖ ⟨traffic⟩ *line, route* ‖ Wasser≃ *water level* ‖ weibliche ∼ *distaff-side* (*on the* ..) ‖ Widerstands≃ *line of resistance* **2.** ⟨mil⟩ ∼ zu 1 Glied *line*, Kompanie in ∼ *c.y drawn up in l.* ‖ (Linientruppen) (*to serve in the*) *line* **3. auf** der ganzen ∼ ⟨mil⟩ (*progress*) *all along the l.*; *sweeping* (*victory*); ⟨fig⟩ *all the way along*, ⟨Am⟩ *right along*; (*to make peace*) *all round* ‖ ⟨fig⟩ sich auf gleiche ∼ mit e–m stellen *to put o.s. on the same footing with a p* ‖ auf der mittleren ∼ liegen *to lie midway* ‖ auf gleicher ∼ mit ⟨fig⟩ *on a level with* ‖ **in** erster ∼ *mainly*; *first and foremost* ‖ ⟨mil⟩ in vorderster ∼ *in the front line* ‖ in e–r ∼ stehen, liegen *to be in line* ‖ in e–r ∼ aufstellen *to draw up in* (*a*) *l.*, *to aline* ‖ in gerader ∼ abstammend *lineally descended*; .. Abstammende(r) *direct descendant* ‖ der Künstler kommt erst in zweiter ∼ in ihm *the artist is only secondary in him* ‖ **zur** ∼ einschwenken (l) ⟨mil⟩ *to wheel into l.* **4.** ∼ **halten** *to keep in* od *to the l.* ‖ ⟨typ⟩ *to line*; ⟨pol⟩ e–e mittlere ∼ einhalten *to keep a middle course*; e–e klare ∼ verfolgen *not to lose track*; s–e Pläne **wahren** die große ∼ .. *are always on a grand scale* **L·inien-** *line* **∼blatt** n (*sheet with*) *ink-l.s* pl **∼dienst** m ⟨aero, rail, etc⟩ *scheduled service* **∼flugzeug** n *airliner* **∼frachter** m ⟨mar⟩ *cargo liner* **∼führung** f *tracing*; *contour l.s* pl; *l.ation* ‖ ebenmäßige ∼ *harmony of l.s* ‖ ⟨traffic⟩ *route, routing* **∼manier** f ⟨arts⟩ *l.-engraving* **∼netz** n ⟨el⟩ *grid*; ⟨rail⟩ *network* **∼papier** n *ruled paper* **∼regiment** n *regiment of the l.* **∼richter** m ⟨sport⟩ *l.sman* **∼schiff** n *l.r*, (*l.-of-*) *-battleship* **∼soldat** m *regular*, *l.sman* **∼system** n ⟨mus⟩ *diatonic scale* **≃treu** a *true to the party-l.*; *Communist*-etc-*l.* [attr]; ⟨pol⟩ *regular* (*ticket* Parteiliste, *party member*); ∼ s *to follow the party-l.*, *to toe the l.* **∼treue** f *loyalty to the p.-l.* **∼truppen** f pl (*troops of*) *the l.*, *regulars* pl **∼umschalter** m ⟨el⟩ *commutator* **lin(i)·ieren** vt [h] *to rule, line* **L-rung** f ⟨phot⟩ *cross-ruling* (*of the focussing screen*) **Lin(i)·ier- ∼brett** n *ruling-board* **∼feder** f *r.g-pen* **∼maschine** f *r.g-machine*

l·ink a (Ggs: recht) *left, l.-handed*; *l.-hand* (*edge*) ‖ ⟨her⟩ *sinister* ‖ ⟨mot⟩ *near* (*front wheel*) ‖ ∼e Seite *l.*(*-hand*) *side*, *l.* (*hand*); ⟨com⟩ *debtor's* (od *debit-*)*s.*; (des Schiffes) *port*; (v Stoffen) *under* od *wrong s.*; (Kehrseite) *reverse*; ⟨hors⟩ (des Pferdes) *near s.* ‖ ⟨hors⟩ ∼e Hand, ∼er Fuß (des Reiters) ⟨a.⟩ *bridle-hand, stirrup-foot* ‖ ⟨sport⟩ mit der ∼en Hand schlagend *l.-handed*, ⟨Am hum a.⟩ *southpaw* ‖ sich zur ∼en Hand trauen l *to marry with the l. hand, to contract a morganatic marriage* ‖ ∼s s *to be l.-handed* ‖ mit dem ∼en Fuß zuerst aufgestanden s *to have got out of bed the wrong way* ‖ mein ∼er Nachbar (im Glied) *my l.-hand man* **L·inke** f *the l.* (*hand* od *side*) ‖ ⟨parl⟩ *the L.* ‖ zu jds ∼n *on* od *at a p's l.* (*side*) ‖ ⟨parl⟩ Anhänger der ∼n *l.ist* **L·inke** m [der ∼, ein ∼r] ⟨box⟩ *left*(*-hander*) **l·inkerhand, -seits** adv *on the left* (*hand* od *side*) **l·inkisch** a ⟨mst fig⟩ *awkward, clumsy, gawky, ungainly*; ⟨fam⟩ *fumbling, thumby* ‖ ∼er Bursche *hobbledehoy* ‖ ∼es Wesen *awkwardness, clumsiness*, → links

Linkr·ustapapier n ∼s/∼e *linen croster*

l·inks adv *to* od *on the left*; *on the l.* od *wrong* od *reverse side* (→ link ⟨fig⟩, → liegen I. 3.) ‖ ⟨traffic⟩ (rechtsfahrend) *offside* ‖ weder ∼ noch rechts sehen *to look neither right nor l.* ‖ ∼ stricken *to purl* ‖ ⟨bot⟩ ∼ windend *sinistrorse* ‖ ⟨crick⟩ ∼ ab *long-on* ‖ nach ∼ *to the l.*, *l.wards* ‖ ∼ (= verkehrt) anziehen *to put* (*a stocking*) *on inside out* ‖ ∼ [a] s *to be l.handed* ‖ ∼ [adv] s ⟨fig⟩ *to be on the wrong track* ‖ ⟨parl⟩ ∼ stehen *to be a l.ist*; weit ∼ stehen *to be very far to the L.* ‖ das Bild ∼ unten .. *at the lower l.* ‖ ⟨mil⟩ ∼ um! *l.* (*about*) *turn*! *l.* (⟨fam⟩ *hep*) *face*!; ∼ schwenkt marsch! *l. wheel*!; (im Marsch) ∼ um! *by the l. flank, march*! ‖ ⟨theat⟩ (P & S) *stage l.*; *prompt side* ‖ ⟨ftb⟩ ∼ außen *outside-l.* ‖ ∼ gehen *to keep to the l.*; ∼ fahren! *drive on the l.* ‖ ⟨typ⟩ ∼ oben *at the top l.*; v ∼ o. *from upper l.*; v ∼ nach rechts *l. to right* ‖ ⟨knit⟩ 2 ∼, 2 r. *2 purl, 2 plain* **L·inks- ∼abweichung** f *levogyration* **∼·außen** m ⟨ftb⟩ *outside l.* **∼drall** m *l.hand twist* **≃drehend** a *l.-handed* (*propeller*) **∼drehung** f *anticlockwise rotation*; ⟨scient⟩ *sinistration*; ⟨opt⟩ *levogyration* **≃gängig** a *l.-handed* (*screw*) **≃gewunden** a *sinistrorse* **∼händer** m *l.-hander*, ⟨Am, hum a.⟩ *lefty, southpaw* **≃her, ≃hin** adv *from, to the l.* **≃herum** adv *over the l.* (*shoulder*); sich ∼ drehen *to turn counter-clockwise* **∼kurve** f *l.-hand turn* od *bend* **∼lauf** m → –drehung **∼lenkung** f *l.-h. drive* **∼liberale(r)** m *Radical* **≃rheinisch** a *on the l. side of the Rhine* **≃seitig** a *l.-sided* **∼stricken** n *purl* **≃um** → links **∼verkehr** m *l. traffic* **L·inkser** m ∼s/∼ = Linkshänder

L·innen n = Leinen; ≃ a = leinen **Lin·oleum** n ∼s/, ∼teppich [m] *linoleum*; mit ∼ ausgelegt *linoleum floored* ‖ ∼schnitt [m] ⟨arts⟩ *linocut*; ∼stock [m] *l.block* **Linotype**-Setzmaschine f *l.type*

L·inse f ∼/∼n **1.** ⟨bot⟩ *lentil* **2.** ⟨opt⟩ *lens* ‖ ∼ des Auges *crystalline lens* ‖ ⟨phot⟩ nicht verzerrende ∼ *aplanat*(*ic lens*) **L·insen- ≃artig** a, **≃förmig** a *lens-shaped*; ⟨scient⟩ *lentiform, lenticular* **∼folge** f *optical combination* **∼gericht** n *dish* (⟨bib⟩ *pottage*) *of lentils* **∼glas** n ⟨opt⟩ *lens* **∼mehl** n *meal of lentils* **∼prüfer** m (S) *focimeter* **∼scheinwerfer** m ⟨theat⟩ *lime-light* **∼suppe** f *lentil-soup* **∼trübung** f *clouding of lens* **∼wicke** f ⟨bot⟩ *lentil vetch* **∼zussetzung** f *lens assembly*

ˣ**l·insen** vi [h] → lunzen

Linz n (oberösterr. Stadt) | ∼ertorte [f] *jam tart with criss-cross pastry*

Lip·arische Inseln pl *Lipari Islands*

L·ippe ⟨Ger⟩ ([f] Fluß & [n] †Land)

L·ippe f ∼/∼n *lip* ‖ aufgesprungene *cracked*, aufgeworfene *pouting*, geschwungene *curved*, zusgekniffene *pursed-up* (*lips*); wulstige ∼n ⟨fam⟩ *blubber-lips* ‖ die ∼n aufwerfen *to purse up* .., schürzen *to curl one's lips* ‖ die ∼n hängen l *to mope* ‖ .. öffnen *to part* .. ‖ ein Lächeln kräuselte ihre ∼n *her face was wreathed in smiles* ‖ .. verziehen .. *his lips broke into a broad smile* ‖ °er riskiert e–e ∼ *he is lippy, impudent* ‖ °riskier k–e solche ∼! *not so much lip*! ‖ .. ∼n zus–kneifen *to pinch, fold, tighten* ..; s–e ∼n zuckten *his mouth twitched*; .. wurden ganz schmal *his lips became a line* | **an** jds ∼ hängen *to hang upon a p's words* ‖ **auf** jedermanns ∼n s *to be on everybody's lips* ‖ er legte e–n Finger auf die ∼n *he laid a f. to his lip* ‖ sich auf die ∼n beißen *to bite one's lips* ‖ das Wort schwebte mir auf den ∼n *I had the w. on the tip of my tongue* ‖ **über** die ∼n bringen *to utter* ‖ das soll nicht über m–e ∼n k *it shall not pass my lips, I'll keep it a dead secret* ‖ **von** den ∼n lesen *to lip-read* ‖ **zwischen** Lipp' und Kelchesrand schwebt der finstern Mächte Hand *there's many a slip 'twixt the cup and the lip* **L·ippen- ∼andacht** f *lip-service* **∼bär** m ⟨zoo⟩ *Indian bear* **∼bekenntnis** n (*mere*) *words* pl **∼blüte** f, **∼blütler** m *labiate*([*d*] *flower*) **≃blütig** a *labiatifloral* **≃förmig** a *lip-shaped*; ⟨bot⟩ *labiate*(*d*) **∼füßer** m ⟨zoo⟩ *chilopod*

~kerbe f *lip furrow* **~laut** m ⟨phon⟩ *labial* (*sound*) **~pflock** m (als Schmuck) *labret* **~pomade** f *lipsalve* **~stift** m *lipstick* **l·ippig** a **1.** *lipped*, ⟨bot & zoo⟩ *labiate*(*d*) **2.** [in comp] **..lippig**: schmal~ *with thin lips*

L·iquida f ~/~ä, -den ⟨phon⟩ *liquid consonant* **~ti·on** f ~/~en ⟨jur⟩ *liquidation* ‖ ⟨com⟩ *settlement*; *winding-up* ‖ *doctor's* od *lawyer's bill* **~s-büro** n *Stock-exchange clearing-house* **liquid·ieren** vt/i [h] ⟨com⟩ *to liquidate* ‖ *to clear* od *settle* (*accounts*), *to wind up* (*a firm*) ‖ (Geldbetrag) *to charge* ‖ *to settle* (*a conflict*) ‖ ⟨nazi⟩ (P) *to "l."*, *to polish* (⟨Am⟩ *bump*) *off* **Liquidit·ät** f ~/ *liquidity*; *solvency*

l·iruml·arum! *fiddlesticks*!

Lis·ene f ~/~n ⟨arch⟩ *pilaster-strip*

Lisi·ere f ~/~n Fr = Saum, Kante; Rand

l·ismen vi/t [h] Sw = stricken **L·ismer** m ~s/~ Sw Strickweste

L·ispellaut m *lisped sound* **L·ispeln** n ~s/ *lisp*(*ing*); *whisper*(*ing*); *murmur*(*ing*) ‖ ⟨scient⟩ *susurration* | ≗ vi/t [h] *to lisp* ‖ (flüstern) *to whisper* ⟨a. fig⟩ (v Wind) ‖ (v Wasser) *to ripple*, *murmur* **L·ispler** m ~s/~ (f ~in) *lisper*

L·issabon n (Hauptstadt u Hafen Portugals) *Lisbon*, [port] *Lisboa*

L·ist f ~/~en *cunning*, *craft*(*iness*); ⟨fam⟩ *depth* ‖ (Kunstgriff) *trick*, *stratagem*, *ruse*, *artifice* ‖ ~ anwenden *to use* od *employ c.* od *trickery* ‖ e–e ~ anwenden *to resort to a ruse*, *to employ underhand work* ‖ frei v ~ *guileless*, *ingenuous* ‖ mit ~ u Tücke zustandebringen *to wangle* (*an agreement*), .. versuchen *to wangle* (*to do*) ‖ ~ gegen ~ *diamond cuts diamond* ≗**enreich** a *resourceful*; *full of c.*, *cr.*, *deceipt*

L·iste f ~/~n *list* ‖ (beschreibende) *catalogue*; ~ v Einheitsbezeichnungen v Gegenständen *standard* (*equipment*) *nomenclature list* N ‖ namentliche ~ *collective schedule* ‖ (Wahl≗) *ticket* (*I'm voting the t. one*) ‖ (~ v Wahlkandidaten) ⟨Am⟩ *slate* ‖ (Toten–, Steuer≗) *roll* ‖ (Preis≗) *rate-card* ‖ (amtliche ~) *register* ‖ (~ der Geschworenen, Kassenärzte) *panel* ‖ (Mitglieder≗) *roll* (z. B. des *H.L.*) ‖ e–e ~ führen *to keep a l.*, etc. ‖ in e–e ~ eintragen *to l.*, *enrol*, *register*, *schedule*, *catalogue*, *empanel* ‖ auf die schwarze ~ k *to be put on the black l.*, *to be blackl.ed* ‖ jdn aus e–r ~ streichen *to strike a p off a l.*, *to erase his name from a l.*, etc **~nverbindung** f ⟨pol⟩ *block*

li·stig a *cunning*, *subtle*, *sly*; *crafty* (*eyes*) ‖ er ist ein ~er Fuchs *he is a tricky fellow*, *a deep one*, *a sly fox* | ≗**keit** f ~/ *craftiness*; *slyness*, *artfulness*

Litan·ei f ~/~en ⟨ec⟩ *litany* ‖ ⟨fig⟩ *longwinded story*, *rigmarole*

L·itauen n ~s/ (Land) *Lithuania*

L·iter n (& m) ~s/~ *litre*, ⟨Am⟩ *liter*; ≗weise [adv a] *by the l.*

Liter·arhistoriker m *historian of literature* **liter·arisch** a *literary* ‖ ~er Diebstahl *plagiarism*; die ~e Welt *the republic* od *world of letters*; ~er Wert ⟨a.⟩ *readability* **Liter·at** m ~en/~en *literary man*; *man of letters*, *writer* ‖ die ~en [pl] *the literati* It, *the penmen* pl **Literat·ur** f ~/~en *l.ture*, *learning*, *letters* pl ‖ wissenschaftliche ~ *scientific writing* ‖ die einschlägige ~ *the bibliography* ‖ schöngeistige ~ *belles lettres*; (*pure*) *literature* ‖ der ~ angehören *to be of l.ry value* **~angabe** f *b.phy* **~beilage** f *l.ry supplement* (z. B. der Times) **~blatt** n *l.ry review* **~geschichte** f *history of l.ture*, *l.ry history* **~hinweis** m, **~nachweis** m *reference* **~sprache** f *written language* **~verein** m *l.ry society* **~verzeichnis** n *b.phy* **~wissenschaftler** m = Literarhistoriker; vergleichender ~ *comparativist* **~zeitung** f *l.ry paper*, *critical review*

Lit·ewka f ~/–ken *litevka* ‖ *undress jacket*

L·itfaßsäule f ~/~n ⟨Ger⟩ *advertising pillar*

L·ithiumsalz n *lithia salt*

Lithogr·aph m ~en/~en *lithographer* **Litho-graph·ie** f ~/~n *l.phy* ‖ (Bild) *l.ph* | ≗**ren** vt [h] *to l.ph* **L.ph·ierpapier** n *l.phic paper* | **l.gr·aphisch** a *l.phic* ‖ ~e Anstalt [f] *l.phic establishment*

Lit·otes f ~/~en ⟨gram⟩ *litotes*, ⟨bes engl⟩ *understatement* (z. B. *rather*, *fairly*, *somewhat*, *in a way*, *to a certain extent*; *it is not altogether unknown to me* (ich weiß sehr wohl); *not bad* (sehr gut); *with some trouble* (mit viel Mühe)

l·itt 1. & 3. sg pret v leiden

Liturg·ie f ~/~n [–i:ən] *liturgy* **lit·urgisch** a *liturgical*

L·itze f ~/~n *lace*, *cord*, *string*, *braid* ‖ ⟨el⟩ *cord*, *strand*, *flex*(*ible*) ‖ ⟨mil⟩ *galloon*, (*patch of*) *braid*; ~n [pl] *braiding* ‖ ⟨weav⟩ *heddle* **~nbesatz** m *braiding* **~ndraht** m ⟨el⟩ *standard wire* **~nöhr** n ⟨weav⟩ *heddle-eye* **~nschnur** f *cord* **~n-zwirn** m ⟨tech⟩ *heddle-thread*

L·iverpool ['livəpu:l] n ⟨engl⟩ **~kette** f (in Neu-Süd-Wales, Australien) *L. Range*

L·ivingstone [-stən] (Stadt in Rhodesien)

L·ivland [-i:f-] n (im Baltikum) *Livonia* ≗**er** m ~in [f] **l.**≗**isch** a *Livonian*

Liv·orno [-v-] n ⟨It⟩ (Stadt u Prov.) *Leghorn*, *Livorno* **liv·ornisch** a *Leghorn*, *Livornese*

Livr·ee [–e:] f ~/~n [–e:ən] **1.** *livery* **2.** [koll] s–e ~ *his l.-servants* pl **~bediente(r)** m *l.-servant*; *flunkey* ⟨mst cont⟩ ‖ junger ~ (*boy in*) *buttons* **~borte**, **~tresse** f *galloon*

Lizenti·at m ~en/~en ⟨Ger ec; engl med⟩ *licentiate* **Liz·enz** f ~/~en *licence* ‖ e–m e–e ~ erteilen *to license a p* **~gebühren** f pl *licensing fees*; *royalties* pl *for the use of patents* **~inhaber**, **~träger** m *licensee*, *permittee*

Ll·oydvorschriften f pl *Lloyd's regulations* pl

.. ln [inf], **-le** (1. P), **-lt** (3. P) *verb-dim-suff*: husten/hüsteln, lachen/lächeln

L·ob n ~(e)s/ *praise* ‖ (Empfehlung) *commendation* ‖ (Ruhm) *fame* ‖ (Lobrede) *eulogy* ‖ gottlob!, Gott sei ~ u Dank *thank heaven*! ‖ des ~es voll *loud in one's pr.s*, *having nothing but pr.* ‖ mageres, spärliches, übertriebenes ~ *cold*, *faint*, *fulsome pr.* | jdm ein gutes (schlechtes) ~ erteilen, spenden, zollen *to bestow great* (*poor*) *pr. upon a p*; ~ u Tadel austeilen *to hand out p. and blame*; durch lauwarmes ~ herunterreißen *to damn with faint pr.*; sein eigenes ~ singen *to blow one's own horn*; jdm ~ spenden *to accord pr. to a p*; jdn mit ~ überschütten *to lavish pr. on a p* ‖ ⟨school⟩ ein ~einschreiben *to enter a good mark* | **über** alles ~ erhaben *beyond* (od *above all*) *pr.* ‖ **zu** s–m ~e *in his pr.* ‖ es gereicht ihm sehr zum ~e *it is a feather in his cap*; .., daß .. *it does him great credit that* .. **~begierde** f *desire of pr.* ≗**begierig** a *desirous* od *greedy of pr.* **~gedicht** n *laudatory lines* pl od *poem*, *panegyric* ‖ ~ auf jdn *poem in pr. of a p* **~-gesang** m *hymn*, *song of pr.* **~hudel·ei** f *nauseous adulation*, *coarse* od *base flattery* ≗**hudeln** vi/t [h] *to cry up* | (etw) *to magnify*, (e–m) *to give a p fulsome pr.*, ⟨fam⟩ *to grease to a p* **~hudler** m *mean flatterer*, *adulator*, *sycophant* ≗**hungrig** a *eager for pr.* **~lied** n *hymn* ≗**preisen** vt [h] *to pr.*, *eulogize*, *extol*, *glorify* **~preiser** m *pr.r*, *extoller*, *eulogist* **~preisung** f *pr.*, *glorification* ‖ ⟨ec⟩ *doxology* ‖ ⟨com⟩ überschwengliches ~ *blurb* **~psalm** m *hymn* ‖ ⟨fig⟩ *high c.ation* **~rede** f *eulogy*, *panegyric*, *encomium* (auf *on*) ‖ auf e–n Toten *eulogium* **~redner** m *panegyrist*, *encomiast* ≗**singen** vi [h]; jdm ~ *to extol a p*, *to sing a p's pr.s* **~spruch** m *encomium*, *eulogy* **l·oben** vt [h] *to praise* ‖ (empfehlen) *to commend* (für, um, wegen *for*) ‖ (rühmen) *to eulogize*, *extol*, *glorify* ‖ übermäßig (⟨fam⟩ über den grünen Klee) ~ *to laud up to the skies*, ⟨fam⟩ *to crack up*; ⟨Am sl⟩ *to boost*; ⟨com⟩ *to puff* ‖ ~d sprechen über *to applaud*; *to speak highly of* ‖ .. nicht genug ~ *I cannot speak too highly of him* ‖ es läßt sich ~ *it is pr.worthy* (an e–m *in a p*) | da lobe ich **mir** ..! *give me* (*the old good times*!), *commend me* (*to E. above* *all cities!*), *he is* (*the man*) *for me!* | 〈prov〉 gute Ware lobt sich selbst *good wine needs no bush* **⁓swert, ⁓swürdig** a *pr.worthy, worth praising* || *laudable* **l·obesam** a [obs mst nachgestellt] *worthy, noble, worshipful* **L·obes- ⁓ausdruck** m *eulogism* **⁓erhebung** f (*high*) *praise, extolling, high c.ation, encomium* || sich in ~en ergehen über jdn *to pr.* od *extol a p to the skies* **⁓wort** n *laudation* **l·öblich** a *laudable, c.able, meritorious* || (Titel) *worshipful* | **~̈keit** f ~/ *laudableness, meritoriousness*

L·obby f ~/~s & –bies (Wandelhalle) *lobby* | ~·ist [m] ~en/~en *lobbyist* (Agent zur Beeinflussung der Abgeordneten)

lobul·är a 〈med〉 *lobular*

L·och n ~(e)s/~̈er **1.** *hole* 〈a. fig〉; 〈bill〉 *pocket*; 〈golf〉 *hole* (a. gesamte Zielbahn) || blindes ~ 〈tech〉 *dead h.* || Bohr~̈ *bore-* od *drill-h.* || °(Gefängnis) 〈sl〉 *jug, quod, chok*(*e*)*y*, 〈Am sl〉 *bullpen*, (im ~ *in jug*) || Guck~̈ *spy-* od *peep-h.* || (Höhlung) *hollow, cavity* || 〈hunt〉 → Bau .. || (Mauerlücke) *breach* || 〈met〉 (Gieß~̈) *sprue* || 〈mot〉 (im Reifen) *puncture* || (e–s Mühlsteins) *eye* || 〈mus〉 (e–s Blasinstruments) *finger-h., stop* || Niet~̈ *rivet h.* || (Öffnung) *opening* || (Riß) *tear* (*in a carpet*) || Schlag~̈ (auf der Straße) *pot-h.* || (im Schuh) *leak* || (Schuttloch; °kl Ort 〈sl〉) *dump* || °〈sex〉 *blind alley, h., hatchway* | Spund~̈ *bung-h.* || Stemm~̈ *mortise h.* || tiefes ~ 〈a.〉 *crater* || (Wohnloch, Hütte) *dirty h., den, kennel, hovel*, 〈Am〉 *hang-out* (→ Bude) | ein ~ ausfüllen *to stop a gap* || ein ~ bek (sock) *to spring a leak*; es hat ~̈er bek *it has all gone into h.s, has got h.s* || sich ein ~ in den Kopf fallen *to fall and break one's head* || ~̈er h *to be in h.s* || (in etw) ein ~ m *to make, pierce a h.* || °ins ~ spazieren 〈fam〉 *to be cooped up, to go to jug* (*prison*); °ins ~ stecken 〈fam〉 *to put into quod* || 〈golf〉 ins ~ spielen *to h.* || 〈bill〉 ins ~ stoßen *to pocket* || °das ~ versohlen *to spank* (*a child*) || **2.** 〈fig〉 ein ~ aufreißen, um ein anderes zuzustopfen *to rob Peter to pay Paul* || °e–m ein ~ in den **B**auch fragen 〈fam〉 *to pump a p dry*; sich ein ~ in den B. lachen *to laugh enough to split one's sides*; °jdm ein ~ in den B. reden *to talk the hind leg off a donkey* || das hat ein böses ~ in m–n Beutel gerissen *that has made a big h. in my pocket*; sich ein ~ in den K. stoßen *to cut one's head open* (an *against*) || ein ~ in die **L**uft gucken *to stare vacantly*; er starrte ~̈er in die L. *his mind went blah*; ein ~ in die L. schlagen *or* schießen *to make a bad miss* || aus e–m andern ~e **p**feifen *to change one's tone*; °aus dem letzten ~e pfeifen *to be on one's last legs* od 〈sl〉 *pegs* || er säuft wie ein ~ *he can drink* od *drinks like a lord* od *fish* || e–n anderen vor's ~ **sch**ieben *to let somebody else bear the brunt* **⁓band** n *punch*(*ed*) od *perforated tape*, → –streifen **⁓bandlesegerät** n *tape reader* **⁓beitel** m *mortise chisel* **~̈bereit** a 〈comp〉 (*result*) *ready for transfer* **⁓bohrer** m *auger* **⁓dorn** m, **⁓eisen** n *punch* **⁓feile** f *entering file* **⁓feld** n 〈comp〉 *card field* **⁓fraß** m 〈tech〉 *pitting* **⁓hammer** m *drift* **⁓kamera** f *pinhole c.* **⁓karte** f *punch*(*ed*) *c.*; 6000/80stellige ~n je Stunde *a speed of 100 c.s per minute, using 80-column c.s* | ~nabteilung [f] *tabulating center*; ~nanlage [f] *punched c. machine installation*; ~nausgabe [f] *punch c. output*; ~n-datenverarbeitung [f] *p.ed c. data processing* ~n/Stunde [f] 〈m. m.〉 *p. c.s a minute* **⁓kathode** f *pierced c.* **⁓lehre** f *h. gauge* **⁓maschine** f *punch*(*ing* od *mortise machine*) **⁓meißel** m = ~beitel **⁓position** f 〈comp〉 *p.ing position* **⁓prüfer** *m* 〈comp〉 *verifier* **⁓reihe** f *row of h.s* **⁓säge** f *fret-saw* **⁓-schriftübersetzer** m 〈comp〉 *interpreter* **⁓stahlplattenbelag** m *pierced steel planking* N **⁓stanze** f *punching machine* **⁓stein** m 〈arch〉 *perforated brick* **⁓stengel** m 〈comp〉 *p.ing knife* **⁓streifen** m *p.*(*ed*) *tape*; ~ benutzen *to p. paper t.* | ~betrieb [m] 〈telg〉 *t. relay*; ~leser [m] 〈comp〉 *p.-t. reader*; ~sender [m] *tape transmitter* **⁓taste** f *p. key* **⁓taster** m *inside calipers* pl **⁓visier** n *peep-sight* **⁓weite** f *aperture* **⁓zange** f *punch pliers* pl **L·öchelchen, L·öchlein** n *little* od *small h.* **l·öcheln** vt [h] *to make small h.s in, to perforate*, → **l·ochen** vt [h] *to make a hole in* || (Fahrkarten etc) *to punch* | ~̈ n 〈comp〉 *p.ing*; ~ eingeschaltet "*p. on*"; ~ der Ergebnisse 〈m. m.〉 *p. results* **L·ocher** m *punch*(*er*) || (für Papiere) *file-punch, perforator* **l·öcherig** a *full of h.s* || 〈met〉 *honeycombed, porous* **L·ochung** f ~/~en *perforation*, → Lochen | ~sablauf [m] 〈comp〉 *punching operations* pl

l·ock- ⁓artikel m 〈com〉 *window attraction* **⁓bieter** m (Auktion) *mock-bidder*, 〈sl〉 *punter* **⁓ente** f *decoy-duck* **⁓flugzeug** n *d. aircraft* **⁓mittel** n, **⁓speise** f *inducement, lure, bait*; 〈com sl〉 *gimmick* **⁓pfeife** f *bird-call* **⁓ruf** m 〈orn〉 *call*(*-note*) **⁓speise** f 〈a. fig〉 *sugarplums* pl **⁓spitzel** m *catch, agent provocateur* Fr **⁓vogel** m *decoy*(*-bird*) || 〈fig〉 *bait, lure* **l·ocken I.** vt [h] *to decoy, bait, allure* || *the hen calls its chickens* || ins Garn *or* Netz ~ *to tempt into a trap* 〈a. fig〉 | 〈fig〉 *to attract, entice* || das kann mich nicht ~ (reizen) *that won't tempt me* || e–m das Geld aus der Tasche ~ *to fleece a p* || sich in e–n Hinterhalt ~ l *to be drawn into an ambush* **II.** ~̈ n 〈mil〉 *tattoo, call* **L·ockung** f ~/~en *allurement, enticement* || *temptation* || (S) *enticement, bait* || 〈fig〉 e–r ~ folgen *to jump at a bait* || e–r ~ erliegen *to fall to a temptation*

L·ocke f ~/~n *lock of hair*; *curl, ringlet*; lose ~n *wanton curls* || (Stirn~̈) *quiff* || e–m ~n brennen *to frizzle a p's hair* **l·ocken** vt [h] & **sich** ~ v/refl *to curl* || gelocktes Haar *curly hair* **L·ocken- ⁓haar** n *curly hair* **⁓kopf** m *c. head*; *c.-headed p* **⁓papier** n *curl-paper* **⁓perücke** f *full-bottomed wig* **⁓wickel** m *curler* **l·ockig** a *curled, curly* | [pred] *in curls*

l·ocker a **1.** *loose, slack* || (P) *relaxed*; [pred] *at ease*; *fluffy* (*hair*) || *light, loose* (*soil*); ~es Gewebe *loosely woven material*; *loose* (Gliederung *division*) || (nachgebend) *giving way* || (wacklig) *tumbledown, shaky* || *spongy* (*bread*) || *threadbare* (*connexion*) || ~ m *to make loose* (→ lockern) || (Tau) ~ l *to pay out* || die Zügel ~ l *to keep a slack hand on the reins* 〈a. fig〉 || ~w *to work loose*; *to* (*be*)*come loose* (a. v Zähnen) || 〈fig〉 nicht ~ l *to insist*; er läßt nicht ~ *he won't give in, sticks to his guns, stands firm* **2.** (P) (ausschweifend) *dissolute* (*habits*), *fast* (*p*) || *lax* (*morals*) || ~ [adv] leben, ein ~es L. führen *to lead a loose*, (*gay and easy*), *disorderly life* || ~er Vogel *or* Zeisig 〈fam〉 *loose fish, sad dog* | **~̈heit** f ~/ *looseness, slackness* || *sponginess* | *dissoluteness, laxity* **l·ockern** vt [h] **1.** *to loosen, slacken*; *to dislodge* (*a stone*) || *to start* (*a nail*) || (Seil) *to pay out* (*a foot at a time*) || *to break up, hoe, scarify* (*the soil*) || 〈fig〉 *to relax* (*the control*) **2. sich** ~ v/refl *to loosen, to* (*be*)*come* od *work loose* || (of nail) *to start* || (plötzlich) (of rope) *to surge* | 〈fig〉 *to relax* **L·ockerung** f ~/~en *relaxation*; *slackening* (*of tension*) || (~ der Einschränkungen) *derestriction* | ~sübung [f] 〈gym〉 *limbering-up exercise*

°**L·ocus** m ~/–sse *W.C.* || auf den ~ gehn *to go to the privy* | ~papier [n] 〈sl〉 *bumf*(*odder*)

Lodder·ei f = Lotterei **l·odderig** a = lotterig

L·oden m ~s/~ *coarse woollen cloth, frieze, shag* || die ~ [pl] 〈fam〉 *clothes* pl, *hair*

l·odern vi [h] *to blaze, flare, flame* || 〈fig〉 (of face) *to glow*; *to burn* (*with love*) || **⁓d** 〈fig〉 *flaming* (*patriotism*); *burning* (*enthusiasm*)

Lodz n [lctʃ] (poln. Prov. & Stadt)

L·öffel m ~s/~ *spoon* || (gr) *ladle* || 〈hunt〉 *ear* (*of a hare*, 〈fam〉 *of a p*) | 〈fig〉 er tut so, als hätte er die Weisheit mit ~n gegessen *he makes a great pretence of wisdom* || mit e–m silbernen ~ geboren s *to be born with a silver spoon in one's mouth* || sperr d–e ~ auf! *keep your ears open* || schreib dirs hinter die ~! *mark my words!* || du kriegst noch e–n hinter die ~ *you'll get your ears boxed yet* || °jdn übern ~ barbieren ⟨fam⟩ *to do a p in the eye; to sell a p a bill of goods*; über die ~ barbiert w ⟨Am⟩ *to get taken for a ride* **~bagger** m *shovel excavator, steam navvy*; ⟨Am⟩ *st. sh.* **~biskuit** n ⟨m. m.⟩ *lady-finger* **~blech** n, **~brett** n *sp.-rack* **~bohrer** m *shell auger, whimble* **~ente** f ⟨orn⟩ *shoveller* **~gans** f ⟨orn⟩ *sp.-bill* **~korb** m *knife-tray* **~kraut** n ⟨bot⟩ *sp.-wort* **~stiel** m *sp.-handle* **~voll** m *sp.ful*; zwei ~ *two sp.fuls* **≈weise** adv *by sp.fuls od l.fuls* **l·öffeln** vt [h] *to eat with a sp.* || *to l.* od *sp. out* | ⟨fig⟩ *to grasp (understand)* | °⟨stud⟩ **sich** ~ *to return a p's (drinking) pledge* **Löffler** m ⟨orn⟩ *spoonbill*

Lof·oten pl (norw. Inselgruppe) *L.e Islands*

l·og 1. & 3. sg pret v lügen

L·og n ~(e)s/~e ⟨mar⟩ *log*; das ~ auswerfen *to (stream the) log* | ~buch [n] *log(-book)*; ins ~ eintragen *to enter in the log*; ~leine [f] *log-line*; ~rolle [f] *log-reel*; ~scheit [n] *log-ship*

Logar·ithmus m ~/–men *logarithm*; dekadischer ~ *common l.* | –mentafel [f] *table of l.s* **l.misch** a *-mic*

L·oge ['lo:ʒə] f ~/~n ⟨theat⟩ *box*; (im 1. Rang) *dress-box*; reservierte ~ *private box* || (⟨arch⟩ & Freimaurer≈) *lodge* || in ~n abteilen *to box off* **L·ogen- ~bruder** m *freemason* **~gang** m ⟨theat⟩ *lobby* **~meister** m *master of a lodge* **~schließer, ~wärter** m *box-keeper*

l·oggen vi [h] ⟨mar⟩ *to (stream the) log*

L·ogger m ~s/~ *lugger* | ~segel [n] *lug-sail*

log·ieren [lo'ʒi:rən] vi [h] *to stay, lodge*, ⟨Am⟩ *to room* (in *at*, bei *with*) | vt [h] (jdn) *to lodge, accommodate, to put up* **Log·ier- ~besuch** m ~(e)s/~e *staying guest(s* pl) **~haus** n *lodging-house*; (billiges) ⟨sl⟩ *doss*; ⟨Am⟩ *rooming-house* **~zimmer** n *spare room* **Logis** [lo'ʒi:] n ~/~ *lodgings apartments* pl | ~geld [n] *l.g m.*

L·ogik f ~/ *logic*; weibliche ~ *woman's reasoning* | **~er** m ~s/~ *logician* **l·ogisch 1.** [a] *logical* || ~er Zus–hang *connectedness, coherence* **2.** [adv] ~ denken *to think connectedly, straight* || ~ denken können *to have a consecutive mind*; ~ durchdenken *to reason out* **~erw·eise** adv *logically* **Log·istik** f ~/ *logistics* [sg konstr] (Produktion, Beschaffung, Lagerung, Transport, Nachschub, Wartung, Personalverwaltung) N

l·oh[1] a & adv = lichter~ | ≈feuer [n] *blazing fire* **L·ohe**[1] f ~/~n *flame, blaze*; wabernde ~ *bl.g f.* **l·ohen**[1] *to be ablaze* od *in flames*

L·oh-[2] **~bad** n *tan-bath* **≈braun** a *tawny* **~beize, ~brühe** f *ooze* **~farbe** f *t.-colour* **≈farben** a *t.-coloured, tawny* **~faß** n *t.-vat* **≈gar** a *prepared with t., t.ned* **~gerber** m *t.ner* **~gerberei** f *t.nery, tanyard* **~grube** f *t.-pit* **~kuchen** m *t.-turf, t.-ball* **~rinde** f *t.-bark* **~mühle** f *t.(ning)-mill* **L·ohe**[2] f ~/~n *(tanning-)bark*; *tan* **l·ohen**[2] vt [h] *to (steep in* od *to treat with) tan*

L·ohn m ~(e)s/≈e **1.** (ohne pl) (Entgelt) *return, compensation* || (Belohnung) *recompense*; *reward (of valour, labour; treason)* || s–n (wohl)verdienten ~ empfangen *to get one's due* || e–m s–n ~ abstatten, erstatten, geben *to give a p his deserts* pl || schlimmen ~ empfangen *to be ill rewarded (for one's trouble)* || ⟨prov⟩ → Undank || zum ~ f *in return for, as a reward for* **2.** [mit pl] (Arbeits≈) *wages* pl, *hire, gain* || (Gehalt) *salary*; ≈e u Gehälter *accrued payrolls* || (Gebühr) *fee* || (Zahlung) *pay(ment)* || (Vergütung) *remuneration* || ausreichender ~ *a living wage*; ausgezahlter ~ *take-home pay* || in jds ~ stehen *to be in a p's pay* od *service* || e–n um ~ u Brot bringen *to deprive a p of his livelihood* || ⟨prov⟩ jede Arbeit ist ihres ~es wert *a good day's w.s for a good day's work* || höhere ≈e! ⟨Am fam⟩ *higher brackets!* **~abbau** m *wage-deflation, wage cut* **~abrechnung** f *payroll accounting* **~arbeit** f *paid labour; job-work* (z. B. *job-printing*) || literarische ~ *pot-boiler* **~arbeiter** m *journeyman, paid workman*; ⟨Am⟩ *hired man*; ~in [f] *workwoman, charwoman*, ⟨Am⟩ *hired woman* **~ausgleich** m *levelling of wages* **~auszahlung** f *payment of w.s* **~buch** n *w.s-book* **~büro** n *pay office* **~diener** m *odd man, sham butler, valet* **~drückerei** f *sweating* **~empfänger** m *w.-earner* **~erhöhung** f *advance of w.s* **~fuhre** f *(ride in a) hackney-carriage* **~gefälle** n *differential tariff* **~-gelder** n pl *w. money* **~herr** m *employer* **~kellner** m *odd waiter, daywaiter* **~kosten** pl *labo(u)r costs* **~kürzung** f *cut in wages, w.s cut* **~kutsche** f *hackney-coach, hired coach* **~kutscher** m *h.-c.man* **~liste** f *payroll* **~niveau** n, **~spiegel** m *level of w.s* **~pfändung** f *garnishment of w.s* **~satz** m *rate of pay* **~schreiber** m *hackwriter* || (für Zeitungen) *penny-a-liner* **~steuer** f *tax on w.s* od *salary* **~stop** m *w. freeze*; ~ durchführen *to freeze w.s* **~streifen** m ⟨comp⟩ *payroll* **~streit** m *w.-squabble* **~tag** m *pay-day* **~tarif** m *scale of w.s* **~tüte** f *p. envelope, p. packet* **~- u Gehaltsabrechnung** f *compute payroll* **~- u Preisschraube** f *inflationary spiral* **~veredelung** f *transformation under sub-contract*; ⟨cust⟩ *customable goods which have been cleared for the purpose of processing against payment* **~zettel** m *w.s-* od *p.-sheet, p.-slip*; ⟨Am⟩ *p.roll* **l·ohnen** vt/i [h] **1.** e–m etw ~ *to reward, recompense a p for a th, to repay a p* (mit *with*) || Gott lohn's! *God bless you (for it)!* **2.** e–n ~ *to pay a p* **3.** (mit acc *or* gen der S) alle Mühe ~ *to repay all the pains* || was lohnt es? *what does it bring in?* || es lohnte die [acc] *or* der [gen] Mühe nicht *it was not worth while, the game was not worth the candle* || es lohnt die Ausgabe nicht *it does not pay* **4.** [abs mst refl] **es lohnt (sich)** nicht *it doesn't pay* od *answer*, .. für mich *it is not worth my while*; .. kaum *there is not much in it*; .. nicht im geringsten, es z tun *there is no use whatever in (it's no use) doing it*; .. nicht z erwähnen *it is not worth mentioning*; l. sich's hinzugehen? *does it pay to go?* es l.! *it pays! it's worth it* || die Arbeit l. (sich) *it is a good paying job*; das U. l. sich *it is a p.g, remunerative, profitable enterprise* || es lohnt die Mühe *it is worth the bother* **l·ohnend** a [pres p] *remunerative, paying*; ⟨Am⟩ *worth-while (excursion)* || etw ~ gestalten *to put .. on a paying basis*; sich als ~ erweisen *to prove rewarding*

l·öhnen vt [h] *to pay wages to* || ⟨mil⟩ *to pay (soldiers)* **L·öhnung** f ~/~en *payment* || (Geld) *(soldiers') pay* | ~sappell [m] *pay parade* || ~stag [m] *pay-day*

Loire f [lwar(ə)] ⟨Fr⟩ (Fluß)

°**Lok** f ~/~s = Lokomotive | ~führer [m] *engineer* N; ~heizer [m] ⟨fam⟩ *footplateman*

Lok·al n ~(e)s/~e *locality, place* || (Laden) *room, shop* || (Räume) *premises* pl, *office* || (Gastwirtschaft) *restaurant, inn, ale-house, public house*, ⟨fam⟩ *pub, tavern* || ⟨Am sl⟩ *joint*, verrufenes ~ *dive* || (Tanz~) *dancing-rooms* pl **lok·al** a *local* || ⟨med⟩ *topical (pains)* | ≈e(s) n *local news* **Lok·al- ~bahn** f *local railway, bay-line* **~behörden** f pl *l. authorities* pl **~blatt** n *l. paper* **~farbe** f ⟨arts⟩ *l. colouring* **~größen** f pl (P) *l. celebrities* **~kenntnis** f *l. knowledge* **~kolorit** n ⟨Lit⟩ *l. colour* **~miete** f *office-rent* **~nachrichten** f pl *l. news* pl **~patriotismus** m *parochialism* **~termin** m ⟨jur⟩ *hearing* od *investigation on the spot; summons in situ; reconstruction of the crime* od *accident at the scene of the crime*, etc **~verhältnisse** n pl *l. concerns* pl **~-verkehr** m *l. traffic* **~zug** m ⟨rail⟩ *l. train* **lokalis·ierbar** a *locatable* **lokalis·ieren** vt [h] *to localize, locate* **Lokalit·ät** = Lokal

L·oko .. *spot-(business, goods)* **~mob·ile** f ~/~n *locomobile, portable steam engine* || (Straßenwalze) *steam-roller* **~mot·iv ..** ⟨rail⟩ ~führer [m] *train (od engine-)driver*, ⟨Am⟩ *engineer*; ~führerstand [m] *cab*; ~kilometer [m] *unit k.*; ~leerfahrt [f] *light running*; ~pfeife [f] *steam-whistle*;

∼schuppen [m] *engine-house* **Lokomot·ive** f ∼/∼n ⟨rail⟩ *engine*; Versuchs≂ *pilot-e.* || kl Rangier≂ *pony-e.*

°**L·okus** m ∼/–usse → Locus

L·olch m ∼(e)s/∼e ⟨bot⟩ *rye-grass, darnel*

°**L·ollo** f ∼/∼s *sweater girl*; *A-bomb* | m ∼s/∼s *ample bosom*; *tight-fitting girl's pullover*

Lomb·ard m & n ∼(e)s/∼e *deposit-bank, loan--bank* | ∼geschäft [n] *deposit-business*; ∼kredit [m] *collateral loan*; ∼nuß [f] *Barcelona nut* **Lomb·arde** m, –din [f], l–disch [a] *Lombard*; L–d·ei [f] *Lombardy*; → Langobarde

l·ombern vi [h] ⟨cards⟩ *to play at ombre*

L·ompenzucker m *lump-sugar*

L·ondon n ∼s/: e–e Woche in ∼ s *to be up in L. for a week* | **∼er 1.** m *Londoner*, ⟨fam⟩ *cockney* **2.** a *London* (*L. people, season*); ∼ Bahnsteig *up--platform*; ∼ Gleis *up-line*

L·onge ['lɔŋʒə] f ∼/∼n ⟨hors⟩ *lunge*, ⟨Am⟩ *longe* **Long·ier-** [in comp] *lungeing* (∼zügel *l. rein*) **long·ieren** vt [h] (Pferd) *to lunge*/*longe*

Long Island [lɔŋ'ailənd] n (Insel am Ausfluß des Hudson, gegenüber New York)

L·ooping [u:] m & n ∼s/∼s (vorwärts *outside*) *looping* (⟨aero⟩ senkrechter Kreis)

L·orchel f ∼/∼n ⟨bot⟩ (Pilz) *edible turban-top*

L·ordschaft f ∼/∼en: s–e ∼ *his lordship*

L·orbaß m –asses/–asse [ond] = Lümmel, Taugenichts

L·orbeer m ∼s/∼en ⟨bot⟩ *laurel*, → d.; *bay* || ⟨fig⟩ ∼en ernten *to wind* od *gain l.s* pl || auf s–n ∼en ausruhen ⟨fig⟩ *to rest on one's oars* od *l.s* **∼baum** m *sweet bay* ≂**bekränzt** a *l.-crowned* || ∼er Dichter *poet laureate* **∼blatt** n *bay-leaf* **∼kranz** m *wreath of l.* **∼kraut** n ⟨bot⟩ *spurge-l.* **∼öl** n *bay-oil* **∼rose** f ⟨bot⟩ *oleander* **∼spiritus** m *bay--rum* **L·orbeere** f ∼/∼n (Frucht) *l.-berry, bay--berry*

L·ore f ∼/∼n *lorry, truck*

L·ore f [npr] am Tore *Sally in our Alley*

Lorel·ei ⟨Ger⟩ (∼felsen am Rhein)

L·orenzstrom m → Sankt-Lorenz-Strom

Lor·et(t)o n ⟨It⟩ (Wallfahrtsort) *Loretto*

Lorgn·ette f [lɔrn'jɛtə] f ∼/∼n *lorgnette, eye--glasses* pl (e–e ∼ *a pair of* ..) **lorgnett·ieren** vt [h] *to observe through a l.* **Lorgn·on** [lɔrn'jɔŋ, lɔrn'jɔ̃:] n ∼s/∼s **1.** *monocle, eye-glass* **2.** = Lorgnette

L·ori m ∼s/∼s **1.** ⟨zoo⟩ *loris* **2.** ⟨orn⟩ *lory*, → d.

L·os n ∼es/∼e **1.** *lot* || durchs ∼ entscheiden *to decide by lot* || die ∼e sind gefallen *the die is cast*, ⟨fam⟩ *we are in for it* || das ∼ werfen *or* ziehen *to cast* od *draw lots* (über *for*) **2.** (Lotterie≂) (*lottery-*)*ticket* || das gr ∼ *the great* od *first prize* (fiel auf *went to*) || das gr ∼ ziehen *to draw the winner*; ⟨fig⟩ *to strike oil* || ich warte, bis ich das gr ∼ ziehe *I'll wait till my ship comes home* **3.** (Anteil) *lot, portion, share* || (Stück Land) *allotment*, ⟨Am⟩ *lot* **4.** ⟨min⟩ *heap of ore* **5.** ⟨fig⟩ (Schicksal) *fate, destiny* || *a bitter fate, an easy lot, a hard destiny*; *hard lines* pl || .. unser aller ∼ *it's all in a lifetime* || sein ∼ ist nicht zu beneiden *his position is not an enviable one* || das gleiche ∼ erfahren *to fare alike* || sie hatten das gleiche ∼ *they shared the same fate* || das ∼ mit (jdm) teilen *to throw in one's lot with*, ⟨Am⟩ *to throw in with* || sein ∼ tragen *to bear one's destiny*; → losen

l·os[1] [nur pred] a [attr a → lose] **1.** [ohne Objekt]: *the rope is loose, slack, off, detached* || (T) *loose* || *the prisoner is free* || *the dog is off his chain* (v der Kette ∼) od *unchained* || ⟨fig⟩ bei ihm ist e–e Schraube ∼ *he has a screw loose, he has a bat in his belfrey* **2.** [ell imp] ∼! (**angefangen**!) *go*! *go on*! ⟨Am fam⟩ *go to it*! || auf „∼" geht's ∼ *on the word "go" we* (*you*) *start* || wann geht's ∼? ⟨Am⟩ *when does it come off*? || nun aber ∼! *hurry up, now*! *look alive*! *quick march*! || lauf ∼! *run along*! ⟨fam⟩ *fire away*! || drauf ∼! *at it*! *now for it*! *go it*! || geh' ∼! *get away with you* || laß ∼! *let go*! || nun also ∼! *come along, now*! || ∼, komm! *here, come*! || (to o.s.) also ∼ denn *so* od *well, here goes*! **3.** ⟨fig⟩ (**im Gange**) °ist (irgend et)was ∼? *is sth wrong*?, (*is*) *anything up* od *wrong*? || was ist ∼ (mit ihm)? *what is up* (*with him*)?; *what is it, Henry*? *what's the matter*? || *what's gone wrong with this door*? || was ist hier ∼? *what's going on here*? || was ist denn (nur *or* bloß) ∼? ⟨fam⟩ *what's the row*? || was ist denn (bloß nun schon wieder) ∼? *what is it now*?, *what's doing*?, *what's cooking*?, *what's the trouble, now*? || was ist denn (nun) eigentlich ∼? *what exactly is the matter*?, *what's the* (*big*) *idea*? | (Unterhaltendes) °hier ist was (nichts) ∼! *there is sth* (*nothing*) *doing here* || hier ist immer was ∼ *there is always sth* (*going*) *on here*; *there is sth special on* (*foot*) | da war der Teufel ∼ *there was a deuce of a row* || es ist etw ∼ mit ihm *there is sth amiss* (od *the matter*) *with him*; es ist etw mit s–n Nieren ∼ *he has sth the matter with* .. || mit dem Jungen ist immer was ∼! *bless the boy*! || es ist nicht viel ∼ damit *it is very small beer* || (ich habe nur eins) u damit ist auch nicht viel ∼ .. *and that's not very gaudy* || mit ihm ist nicht viel ∼ ⟨fam⟩ *he is not up to much* || °da ist nicht viel ∼ mit *it is no great ths* od *shakes* | *I'll just see what is up* || *he went out to see what was toward* || sehen, ob wirklich etw ∼ ist .. *if anything is really the matter* || *before he knew where he was* (was ∼ war) || ⟨fam⟩ *what really is the dickens with us is* .. | °da wird allerhand ∼ s ⟨sl⟩ *there'll be dirty work* || *sth was astir in the cottage* | °**etw** (wenig) **∼ h** *to know sth* (*very little*) || darin hat er etw ∼ *he is rather good at that* **4. eine**[**r** gen] [acc] **S** *or* **v e-r S ∼ s** *to be rid* od *quit of a th* || m–e Uhr bin ich ∼ *I've lost* (od *I'm done out of*) .. || etw ∼ s (w) *to be* (*get*) *rid of a th* || ich kann die Ware nicht ∼ w *I cannot sell* ..; *to shake off* (*a cold*, etc); den Gedanken an etw ∼ w *to get a th off one's mind*; jdn ∼ w *to see the back of a p*; e–e Tochter ∼ w *to get a d. off one's hands* || ∼ v Rom! *away from* .. || e–n ∼ w *to get rid of a p* || den sind wir ∼! *a good riddance*!; den wären wir lieber wieder ∼ *he is a good riddance*

los[2] adv, **los**|.. pref [betont trennbar vor Verben] **1.** (Loslösung v) z. B. ∼|machen *to undo*, ∼|haken *to unhook* **2.** (sich entfernen) v etw ∼|stürzen v, aus .. *to dash from* (od *out of*) **3.** (Ziel) auf jdn ∼gelaufen k *to come running to a p* **4.** (Beginn e–r Handlung) er schimpfte los *he started a terrific row* || er schoß ∼ *he delivered his fire* .. **los**[3] suff (Mangel) **1.** harm∼ *harmless* **2.** erwerbs∼ *unemployed* **3.** furcht∼ *without fear* **4.** hoffnungs∼ *past hope, hopeless* **5.** leidenschafts∼ *dispassionate* **l·os- ∼|arbeiten** vt [h] *to loosen, to work off, to disengage* | [vi] darauf ∼ *to work away* (auf [acc] *at*) | [vrefl] sich ∼ *to disengage* od *extricate o.s., to get loose* °∼|**ballern** vi/t [h] *to pop off* **∼|bek** vt [h] **1.** *to disengage* **2.** ⟨fam⟩ (*to begin to understand*), ⟨fam⟩ *to get the hang* od *knack of* **∼|binden** vt [h] *to unbind, to untie*, ⟨mar⟩ *to unfurl* (*a sail*) **∼|bitten** vt [h] *to beg for a p's release, to beg a p off* **∼|brechen** vt [h] *to break off* || vi [s] *to burst* (*out*), *to break* (*out, loose, forth*) **∼|brennen** vt [h] *to fire, discharge* **∼|bröckeln** vt/i [h/s] *to crumble off* **∼|donnern** vi [h] *to thunder away* || ⟨fig⟩ *to burst forth, to fulminate* (*against*) **∼|drehen** vt [h] *to unwring, unscrew* **∼|dreschen** vi [h] *to thrash* (*freely*) (auf *at*) ⟨a. fig⟩ **∼|drücken** vi [h] *to push off* || *to discharge*; *to fire* (*off*) **∼|eisen** vt [h] *to clear of ice* || ⟨fig⟩ *to disentangle* || (Geld) *to screw* .. *out* (*of a p*) **∼|fahren** vi [s] *to rush* (auf *upon*) || fahr ∼! ⟨sl⟩ *buzz off* || ⟨fig⟩ *to leap out* (auf *at*) || ⟨mar⟩ *to make straight for* (*land*) || ⟨fig⟩ *to burst forth*; auf jdn ∼ ⟨fig⟩ *to go on at a p* **∼|feuern** vt [h] *to fire* (*a shot*) || *to discharge* (*a gun*) | vi [h] *to fire* (*at a p*), *to deliver one's fire* **∼|geben** vt [h] *to set free, to release* ≂**gebung** f ∼/ *setting free, emancipation* **∼|gehen** vi [s] *to come* *off* ‖ *to pop* ‖ (sich lockern) *to work*, (*be*)*come*, *get loose* ‖ (Knoten) *to slip* ‖ (Gewehr, Schuß) *to go off*; leicht ~ (Gewehr) *to have a light action* ‖ (losbrechen) *to break out* ‖ (anfangen) *to begin* ‖ geh mir nur los mit d–n Kniffen! *none of your tricks*! ‖ geh los und tu es *trot along and do it* ‖ auf jdn (etw) ~ *to fly* (*out*) *at a p*, *to attack a p*, *to go* od *make for a p*; .. gerade .. *to go right up to a p*; *to head for*, *to go at a th*; mutig .. *to breast a th* ‖ *to march against* (*the enemy*) ‖ *they let out at one another* ‖ gerade darauf ~ *to go straight to the point*, *to make no bones of the matter* ‖ wann geht's ~? ⟨fam⟩ *when is it to come off*? ‖ jetzt geht's ~! *now for it* ‖ dann ging's erst richtig ~ *then came the fun*, *row*, etc ‖ nicht ~ (Gewehr) *to miss fire* ‖ das Gewehr geht schwer ~ *the gun hangs fire* ≃**gelöstsein** n *detachment* (*from*) **~gerissen** a *scattered* (*from their homes*); v der Welt ~ s *to be out of ths* °**~|gondeln** vi [s] *to push off* **~|gürten** vt [h] *to ungird* **~|haben** → los[1] 3. (Ende) **~|haken** vt [h] *to unhook* **~|hauen** vt [h] *to strike off* | vi ⟨fam⟩ auf e–n ~ *to batter a p about* **~|helfen** vi [h] (jdm) *to assist a p to get loose* od (*in getting*) *free* ≃**kauf** m *buying off* ‖ *ransoming*, *redemption* (*of prisoners*) **~|kaufen** vt [h] *to redeem*, *ransom*; *to buy off* (a. v Militärdienst) ‖ sich ~ v *to buy o.s. out of* (*an obligation*) **~|ketten** vt [h] *to unchain* **~|knallen** vt [h] *to discharge*; *to fire off* | vi [s] *to explode*, *to go off with a bang*, *to bang off* **~|knüpfen** vt *to untie* **~|k** vi irr [s] *to come off*, *to get loose* od *free*; *to be set free* ‖ auf e–n ~ *to advance upon*, *to come for a p* ‖ ⟨aero⟩ v Boden ~ *to get off* (das ≃ *the get*[*ting*]-*off*) ‖ v jdm ~ *to get rid of a p*; *to get off* (*a contract*) ‖ *to get away* (v *from one's job*); ~ v *to shake off* (*a th*, *a p*) **~|koppeln** vt *to unleash*, *uncouple* **~|kriegen** vt [h] (etw) (v) *to get* (*a th*) *loose* (*from*) ‖ ⟨fig⟩ 1. *to disengage*, *to free* 2. = ~bek ⟨fig⟩ **~|kuppeln** vt [h] ⟨mach⟩ *to disengage*; ⟨rail⟩ *to uncouple* **~|lachen,** laut ~ vi [h] *to guffaw* **~|l** vt [h] *to* (*let*) *loose*, *to let go* od *off*, *to leave* (od *loose*, *miss*, *one's*) *hold of* (od *on the handle*) ‖ nicht ~! *hold fast*! ‖ laß mich los! *unhand me*! ‖ *he let go* (*of*) *the handle* ‖ (freigeben) *to set at liberty*, *set free*; jdn ~ auf *to turn loose on*; *to pour* (*one's energy*) *upon* ..; *throw off* (*a dog*) ‖ *to vomit*, *launch* (*a lampoon*) ‖ *to fire off* (*a joke*, *a string of questions* [auf *at*]) **~|leben** vi [h] ⟨fam⟩ drauf ~ *to live a fast life*, *to l. thoughtlessly* **~|legen** vi [h] ⟨fig⟩ *to begin*, *set about* (*doing*) ‖ *to blaze away* ‖ (sprechen) ⟨fam⟩ *to lay it on*; .. gegen .. *to sail into* ..; (wieder) ~ *to be off* (*again*) (*there he goes again*) ‖ tüchtig ~ *to let off steam* ‖ (gegen jdn) *to inveigh* (*against a p*), *to denounce* (*a p*) **~|lösen** vt [h] *to detach* | sich ~ *to come off* ‖ (Haut) *to peel off* ‖ ⟨fig⟩ *to sever o.s.* (v *from*); ⟨mil⟩ *to break contact* (v *with*) ≃**lösung** f *detachment* **~|m** vt [h] *to free*, *deliver* (v *from*) ‖ *to loosen*, *undo*, *untie*, *unfasten* ‖ *to slip* (*a catch*) | sich ~ *to disengage* (*o.s.*) (v *from*); *to break away* (*from*) ‖ *to disentangle o.s.* **~|marschieren** vi [s] *to march straight* (auf *towards*) **~|pflöcken** vt [h] *to unpeg* **~|platzen** vi [s] *to burst forth*, *to explode*, *to break out* ‖ ⟨fig⟩ *to blurt out* (mit etw [*with*] *a th*) **~|reden** vi [h] drauf ~ *to talk on and on* **~|reißen** vt irr [h] *to break loose* ‖ *to dislodge* (*a stone*) ‖ *to pull a p off a p* ‖ *uprooted from* (v) *their homes* ‖ *he wrenched her loose* (v sich) ‖ **sich** ~ *to disengage o.s.* (*by force*), *to bear o.s. away*, *to break away*; *to tear o.s. free* (*from*) ‖ (*of dogs*) *to get loose* ‖ ⟨mar⟩ *to break adrift*; .. v Anker *to part anchor* **~|rennen** vi [s] *to race towards* (auf) **~|sagen, sich** [h] (v etw) *to renounce* (*a th*), *to cut o.s. loose*, *to dissociate o.s.*, *to make a clean break* (*from a th*), *to give up* (*a th*); *to disown* (*a p*) ‖ *to cry off from* (*a treaty*) ‖ ⟨pol⟩ *to bolt the ticket*; *Iceland has cast its ties with Denmark* **~|sausen** vi [s] *to shoot away* °**~|schieben** vt/i [h & s] *to push off* [vt/i] **~|schießen** vt/i [h] *to discharge* (*a gun*), *to fire* (*off*) ‖ ⟨fig⟩ [abs] ⟨fam⟩ *to fire away*, *to give a piece of one's mind* | vi [s] auf e–n ~ *to rush at a p* ‖ ⟨fig⟩ schieß ~! *go ahead*! ⟨Am sl⟩ *shoot*! **~|schlagen** vt/i [h] *to beat loose*, *knock off* ‖ (*it gave him a chance*) *to strike* vi ‖ *to deliver one's blow* ‖ *to let fly* (*with one's fists*) ‖ (verkaufen) *to dispose of*, *to clear off* (*goods*); (spottbillig) *to sell off dirtcheap* od *for a mere song* | vi [h] ⟨mil⟩ *to take the field*, *to commence hostilities*, *to open the attack* ‖ auf jdn ~ *to attack a p* **~|schnallen** vt [h] *to unstrap*, *unbuckle* **~|schneiden** vt [h] *to cut off* **~|schrauben** vt [h] *to unscrew* **~|s** vt [s] → los[1] 4. **~|sprechen** vt [h] *to absolve* ‖ (frei|m) *to free* ‖ e–n Lehrling ~ *to declare an a. free* ‖ (v etw) *to acquit* (*of a th*) | vi drauf ~ *to talk at random* ≃**sprechung** f ~/ *absolution*, *acquittal* **~|sprengen** vt/i [h & s] *to burst off* | auf e–n ~ *to gallop towards a p* **~|springen** vi [s] *to jump off* ‖ (S) *to burst off* ‖ (auf [acc]) *to rush upon*, *to fly* od *jump at* **~|steuern** vi [s] (auf [acc]) *to head* od *make* (*for*) **~|stürmen** vi [s & h] (auf [acc]) *to rush* (*at*); ⟨Am⟩ *to break* (*for*) **~|stürzen** vi [s] (auf [acc]) *to dash*, *run*, *rush* (*at*) **~|trennen** vt [h] *to unstitch*, *unsew* ‖ ⟨fig⟩ *to sever*, *separate* ≃**trennung** f *separation* **~|w** vt [s] → los[1] 4. **~|werfen** vt [h] *to cast off*; → abstoßen **~|wettern** vi [h] *to be in full cry* (gegen *against*) **~|wickeln** vt [h] *to uncurl*, *disentangle*, *unwind*, *untwist*, *unravel*; (Paket) *to undo*, *unwrap* **~|ziehen** vi [s] *to set out*, *to march away* ‖ gegen *or* über jdn ~ *to inveigh*, *declaim against a p*, ⟨fam⟩ *to run a p down*; wütend .. *to get off on a harangue against a p*

Los ·Angeles [loːsˈanʒələs] n (Stadt) (U.S.A.)

l·ösbar a *soluble* (*problem*; *in fluids*) ‖ *solvable* (*knot*; *problem* ⟨a. math⟩); (→ lösen)

L·ösch- (→ löschen) *ex*(*tinguish*), *q*(*uench*) [1]**~anlage** f (f Kalk) *lime slaking plant* ≃**bar** a *extinguishable*; (Durst) *quenchable* **~blatt** n *blotting-paper* **~eimer** m, **~faß** n 1. *fire-bucket* 2. ⟨tech⟩ *q.ing-tub* **~funke** m ⟨el⟩ *q.ed spark* [2]**~geld** n ⟨mar⟩ *wharfage* [1]**~gerät** n *utensils* pl *for ex.ing* od *q.ing fire* [2]**~hafen** m ⟨mar⟩ *port of discharge* [1]**~horn** n, **~hütchen** n *ex.er* **~kohle** f *q.ed charcoal* **~kommando** n *fire-squad* **~kopf** m ⟨rec⟩ *erasing head* **~kurbel** f ⟨comp⟩ *effacer* **~mannschaft** f *f.men* pl, *f.-brigade* **~mittel** n *f.-ex.er* **~papier** n = ~blatt [2]**~platz** m *pier*, *wharf*, *port of discharge* [1]**~rolle** f *desk blotter* [1]**~trupp** m ⟨mil⟩ *f.-party* **~turm** m (Koks≃) *q.ching t.* **~vorrichtung** f 1. = ~gerät 2. [2]⟨mar⟩ *discharging device* [1]**~wasser** n (Schmiede) *q.ing water* **~wiege** f = –roller [2]**~zeit** f ⟨mar, com⟩ *running days for discharging* **L·ösche** f ~/ ⟨tech⟩ *cinder*, *coal dust*, *breeze* **~beton** m *cinder concrete* **l·öschen**[1] vt [h] **1.** *to put out* (*a light*, *a fire*) ‖ *to extinguish* ‖ *to quench* (*flames*, *coke*, *thirst*) ‖ *to slake* (*lime*, *one's thirst* [*for vengeance*]) ‖ °s–n Brand ~ *to cool one's coppers* **2.** (tilgen) *to cancel* (*an item*) ‖ *to efface*; *to blot out* ‖ ⟨rec comp⟩ *to erase* (*without recording* [Neuaufnahme]) (dazu: *erasure*) ‖ ⟨jur⟩ ~ *to pay off* (*a mortgage*) ‖ *to cancel* (*outstanding debts*) ‖ *to liquidate* (*a firm*); *to cancel* (*trade names*) ‖ *to close* (*an account*) | (ablöschen) *to blot* (*ink*) **l·öschen**[2] vt [h] ⟨mar⟩ (ausladen) *to unload* (*cargo*), *empty*; *lighten*, *discharge* (*a ship*) ‖ *to land*, *unship* (*goods*) ‖ ~ u laden (of ship) *to turn round* **L·öscher** m ~s/~ (→ löschen[1] u [2]) **1.** (f Flamme) *ex.er* **2.** (f Geschriebenes) *blotter* **3.** ⟨mar⟩ *unloader*, *discharger* **L·öschung** f ~/~en (→ löschen[1] u [2]) *ex.ing*, *effacement* ‖ ⟨comp⟩ automatische ~ bei unrichtigen Salden (Albus) *automatic rejection of incorrect balances* (*Arib*) | (v Schiffen) *discharging*, *unloading* ‖ (v Waren) *landing*, *unshipping* **~shafen** m *d.ing port*

L·ose n ~n/~n ⟨mar⟩ *slack* (*of a rope*) ‖ ~ durchholen *to haul in the sl.* ‖ ~ geben *to pay out* ‖ ~ h *to be sl.* **l·ose** [a] **1.** = locker 1. **2.** (beweglich) *movable* ‖ (zus–hanglos) *incoherent* ‖ ~s Geld (*small*) *change*, ⟨com⟩ *bulk* (*item*), *loose* (*goods*) || *unwound* (Trumm) || *straggling* (*group*) || ~ w *to come untied* bzw *unglued* | [adv] ~gepackt *loosely packed*; ~ hängend *loose* **3.** ⟨fig⟩ *free and easy*, *loose* (*life*) || *fickle, volatile* (*character*) || (liederlich) *dissolute, dissipated, fast* (*man* bzw *woman*) || *wanton, gay* (*girl*), *naughty* (*trick*) || ~es Geschwätz *loose talk* || ein ~s Maul *or* Mundwerk h *to have a loose, malicious, bad tongue* || ~r Vogel ⟨fig⟩ *rogue, wag*; *sad dog* | du Loser! *you waggish rogue*! **~blatt-** *loose-leaf* [attr] **L·öse- ~geld** n *ransom* **~mittel** n *solvent*; (im Lack) *vehicle* ⟨med⟩ *expectorant* **l·ösen** vt/refl [h] **I.** ⟨eig⟩ **1.** *to loosen, unknot, unbind* || *to untie* (*a knot*) || *to undo* (*a tie*) || *to release* (*a brake*); *to break* (*a seal*) || *to unwind* (*a scarf from one's neck*) || (in Teile) *to undo, to take to pieces* || (abtrennen) *to detach* (*a bone*) || **2.** (locker m) e–m die Z. ~ ⟨fig⟩ *to loosen* od *unlock a p's tongue*; schleim~d *phlegm-loosening* (*medicine*); *sleep relaxes the limbs*; *to break up* (*the strain*) **3.** ⟨fig⟩ (Bande) ~ *to untie, unknot*; *to sever* (*a tie*) || den Knoten (e–s Dramas) ~ *to unravel the plot* || *to free* (aus *from*) **4. sich** ~ (vgl 1) *to get loose, to come undone* od *untied* || (of nails) *to start* || (of boards) *to come away* || (of paper) *to come loose, to fall away* || (of feelings) *to break loose* (*in a p*) || sich v jdm ~ *to separate from, to break with a p* || ⟨mil⟩ sich v Feinde ~ *to disengage from* .. **5.** (befreien) *to free, deliver* || jdn ~ aus/v *to release a p from his bonds, obligations* || (lossprechen) *to absolve* || (mittels Lösegeld) *to ransom, redeem* **6.** (einlösen) *to redeem* (*a pledge, a promise*) **7.** e–e Eintrittskarte ~ (im Vorverkauf) *to book a seat*; (⟨theat⟩ an der Kasse & ⟨rail⟩ Fahrkarte) *to take* od *buy a ticket* **8.** (aufheben) Bann ~ *to withdraw* .. || Ehe *to dissolve* .. || *to cancel* (*an obligation*) || *to set aside* (*a contract*) || *to discontinue, to break off* (*a connexion, an engagement*) **9.** (Aufgabe etc) *to solve* (*problems, questions, riddles*); *to perform* (*a task*); *to surmount* (*a difficulty*); *to clear up* (*contradictions, some confusion, a doubt*) || ⟨pol⟩ *to deal with* (*special problems*); z ~ suchen *to tackle* (*a problem*); das löst mein Problem nicht *that won't meet my case*; die Frage mit Gewalt ~ *to force the issue* **10.** *to discharge, fire* (*a gun*) **11.** (schmelzen) (sich) ~ *to dissolve, melt* || sich leicht ~ l *to be easily d.d* **12.** ⟨com⟩ (Geld) *to get* od *make m.* (*out of a th*) || sie h nur wenig gelöst *their returns* od *takings* pl *have been poor*; → Losung[2] **l·öslich** a *dissolvable*; sofort ~ *instant* (*coffee*); in Wasser ~ *water-soluble* || ⟨chem⟩ *soluble* | ≗keit f *dissolvability* || ⟨chem⟩ *solubility*

l·osen 1. vi [h] *to draw lots* od *cuts* || *to cast* od *draw lots*; *to draw straws* || (würfeln) *to raffle* || ⟨ten⟩ *to toss*; ~! *rough or smooth*! || (mit Münze) *to toss* (*up*); ~ wir! *heads or tails*! || mit jdm ~ *to toss a p* (um *for*) || ⟨mil⟩ sich fest (frei) ~ *to draw a bad* (*good*) *number* **2.** ≗ n; beim ≗ gewinnen *to win the toss*

L·öß m Lösses/Lösse ⟨geol⟩ *loess*

L·ost m ~(e)s/ = Gelbkreuz(gas)

L·osung[1] f ~/~en, **~swort** n ⟨bib⟩ *text, lesson*; ⟨mil⟩ *password, watchword*; ~! *friend or foe*! || ⟨übtr⟩ *signal*; *cry* (*of the day*) || (Geschrei) *battle-cry, slogan* ⟨a. fig⟩; e–e ~ prägen *to put forward a sl.* || das ist m–e ~ *that's my ticket* || das ist die ~ *that's the th*

L·osung[2] f ~/~en ⟨com⟩ *returns, takings* pl

L·osung[3] f ~/~en ⟨hunt⟩ (des Wildes) *fumets, droppings* pl || ~ des Fuchses *billet*, → lösen

L·ösung f ~/~en *loosening* || (e–s Rätsels & math etc) *solution*; *answer* || s–e ~ finden *to be solved* || ⟨theat⟩ (~ des Knotens) *unravelling*; *dénouement*; unerwartete ⟨oft⟩ *deus ex machina* || (of guns) *firing off* || ⟨chem⟩ *solution*; arme *or* schwache ~ *dilute* od *weak solution* | ⟨fig⟩ *key* (zu *to*) | **sich** [acc] an die ~ des Problems m *to set one's wit to* .. | **~s-** ~geschwindigkeit [f], ~zeit [f] *dissolution speed*; *d. time*; ~mittel [n] *solvent*

L·ot n ~(e)s/~e **1.** ⟨arch⟩ *plumb-rule* **2.** ⟨mar⟩ (Senkblei) *lead, plummet* || ⟨el⟩ *sounder* || Echo≗ *echosounder* || Hand≗ *lead and leadline* || Tief≗ *deap-sea lead* || ⟨mar⟩ das ~ besetzen *to man the lead* || das ~ werfen *to take soundings* **3.** (Gewicht) *half an ounce* || Neu≗ *ten grammes* || Freunde in der Not gehn hundert auf ein ~ *friends in need are scare indeed* **4.** (Löte) *solder* **5.** ⟨math⟩ *perpendicular* (*line*) || ein ~ errichten (fällen) *to raise* (*drop*) *a perpendicular* (*on a line*) | ⟨fig⟩ im ~e s *to be in good order* || etw ins ~ bringen *to put ths right* || aus dem ~e bringen *to disturb* || nicht im ~e s *to be out of plumb* || nicht ganz im ~e s *not to be up to the mark* **~achse** f *vertical axis* **~gast** m ⟨mar⟩ *leadsman*; ≗e ans Lot! *l.men in the chains*! **~leine** f *fathom-, lead-, sounding-line* **~maschine** f ⟨mar⟩ *s.g machine* **≗recht** [a] *plumb, perpendicular* | [adv] *by the pl.-line* **~rohr** n ⟨mar⟩ *s.g tube* **~waage** f *pl.-level* **~wurf** m *cast of the lead*

L·öt- ~apparat m (f Hartlot) *brazing outfit* **~blei** n *lead solder* **~flamme** f *blowpipe flame* **~flußmittel** n *s. flux* **~kolben** m *soldering-bit, s.-iron* **~lampe** f *s.-lamp*, → Schweißbrenner **~rohr** n *s.-pipe, blowpipe* **~stelle** f *s. point* **~wasser** n *s.-water* **~zinn** n *tin* od *soft solder* **l·ötbar** a *solderable* **L·öte** f ~/ *solder*(*ing*) **l·oten** vi [h] **1.** ⟨arch⟩ *to plumb, to set to the pl.-line* **2.** ⟨mar⟩ *to take soundings, to* (*heave the*) *lead, to sound, to pl.* (→ Lotgast) noch (nicht mehr) ~ können *to be in* (*to lose* od *to be out of*) *soundings* **l·öten** vt [h] weich ~ *to solder* (an *to*) || hart ~ *to braze* **l·ötig** a *weighing half an ounce* (*or* [Neulot] *ten grammes*) || (v edlen Metallen) *pure* || *of due alloy* | ≗keit f *fineness*

L·othringen n *Lorraine* ⟨Fr⟩, †*Loth*(*a*)*ringia* **L·othringer** m, **~in** f *Lorrainer, Lotharingian* **l·othringisch** a *Loth*(*a*)*ringian, Lorrainese*

L·otos, L·otus m ~/~; ~blume [f] ⟨bot⟩ *lotus-flower* **~pflaume** f ⟨bot⟩ *date plum*

L·otse m ~n/~n *pilot* **l·otsen** vt [h] *to pilot* || ⟨fig⟩ *to drag* (*a p*) *along*; *to nurse* (in *into*), *to steer* .. *around* (*to*) **L·otsen- ~amt** n *P. Office* **~barke** f, **~boot** n *p.-cutter* **~fahrzeug** n *p.-vessel* **~fisch** m *p. fish* **~freiheit** f *free p.age* **~gebühr** f, **~geld** n *p.age* **~kunst** f *p.age* **~station** f = ~amt **~zwang** m *compulsory p.age*

L·otter- ~bett n *lazy-bed* **~bube** m *young rascal, bad egg* od *lot, vagabond* **~leben** n *dissolute life, life of dissipation* || ein ~ führen *to lead a disorderly life* **~wirtschaft** f *slovenly household* **Lotter·ei** f ~/~en 1. *slipshod*(*i*)*ness* 2. *laziness* 3. *dissipation* **l·otterig** a **1.** *slovenly, slipshod, sluttish* **2.** *dissolute, dissipated, fast*(*-looking*), *rakish, raffish*

Lotter·ie f ~/~n *lottery* || (in e–r) ~ spielen *to take l. tickets* **~einnahme** f *l.-office* **~einnehmer** m *l.-office keeper* **~gewinn** m *prize* **~kollekte** f = ~einnahme **~kollekteur** m = ~einnehmer **~los** n (*l.*) *ticket* **~plan** m *scheme of a l.* **~spiel** n (*playing in a*) *l.* **~vorstellung** f (Eintrittskarte = Los) ⟨bes film⟩ *bank night* **L·otto** n ~s/~s *lotto* || ~ spielen *to play at l.*

L·otung f ~/~en ⟨mar⟩ *sounding, plumbing*

L·ötung f ~/~en *soldering* | **L·otus-** → Lotos–

L·otus m ~/~ (Hornklee) *sweet clover*

Louisiade-Archipel m *Louisiade Islands*

Louisi·ana n (Staat der U.S.A.)

Louisville [lui'vil] n (Stadt) (*Ky. U.S.A.*)

L·öwe m ~n/~n ⟨a. fig⟩ *lion* (f *lioness* L·öwin) ⟨a. fig⟩ || ⟨astr⟩ *Leo* || im „Löwen" *at the Lion* (*Hotel*) || der ~ des Tages ⟨fig⟩ *the hero* .. **L·öwen-** ⟨bot⟩ → *Lion's* **~anteil** m ⟨fig⟩ *lion's share* **≗artig** a *l.-like*, (⟨scient⟩ *leonine*) **~bändiger** m *lion-tamer* **~fuß** m ⟨bot⟩ *lion's-foot* **~grimm** m *leonine fury* **~grube** f *l.'s den* **~haut** f *l.'s skin* **~herz** n ⟨fig⟩ *l.-heart* (*Richard L.-h.*) **~jagd** f *l.*

hunting **~junge(s)** n *l.'s cub, puppy, whelp* **~klaue** f *l.'s claw* **~maul** n ⟨bot⟩ *snapdragon* **~mut** m *l.-like courage* **~orden** m *Order of the L.* **~stärke** f *l.-like force* **~tatze** f *l.'s paw* **~wärter** m *l.-keeper* **~zahn** m ⟨bot⟩ *dandelion, taraxacum*

L·öwen n (belg. Stadt) *Louvain* [Fr]

loy·al a *loyal, staunch* **Loyalit·ät** f ~/ *loyalty*

Loyalit·ätsinseln [lwaja-] f pl (im Stillen Ozean) *Loyalty Islands*

Lübeck n ⟨Ger⟩ (Stadt) *Lubeck* **L·übecker** m, **~in** f *inhabitant of L.* **l·üb(i)sch** a (*of*) *Lubeck*

L·uch f ~/~̈e (Sumpfwiese) *bog, marsh*

L·uchs m ~es/~e **1.** ⟨zoo⟩ *lynx*, ⟨Am⟩ *catamount* || aufpassen wie ein ~ *to watch like a hawk* **2.** ⟨fig⟩ (*sly old*) *fox* **~auge** n ⟨a. fig⟩ *l.-eye* **~̈äugig** a *l.-eyed, lynsean* **~katze** f *wildcat* **l·uchsen** vi/t [h] *to keep a sharp eye on* (nach) || *to lie in ambush* | e–m etw (ab)~ ⟨sl⟩ *to sneak* od *filch a th from a p*

L·ücke f ~/~n *gap* || mit vielen ~n *gappy* || (offene Stelle) *blank* || (Auslassung) *omission* || (im Text) *lacuna, hiatus* || (Riß, Bruch) *breach* || (Mangel) *deficiency* (in *in*) || e–e ~ ausfüllen *to fill up* od *to stop a gap*; die ~n ausf. *to fill in the missing pieces* || ⟨fig⟩ e–e empfindliche ~ ausfüllen *to supply* od *satisfy a long-felt want, to fill an aching void* od *a crying need* || ⟨school⟩ ~n ausfüllen ⟨Am⟩ *to work off conditions* || e–e ~ reißen ⟨Am⟩ *to make a dent* (*in a sum*); ⟨mil⟩ *to open a breach* (*in the enemy's ranks*); auf ~ setzen *to stagger* **L·ücken-** **~büßer** m *stop-gap, makeweight* || ⟨liter⟩ *padding, expletive* || (Behelf) *makeshift* || (P) *man of straw* **~̈haft** a *having gaps, gappy*; ⟨fig⟩ *fragmentary, imperfect, defective, incomplete* **~haftigkeit** f *imperfection, defectiveness, incompleteness* **~̈los** a *without a break* od *gap, uninterrupted; complete, full*; ⟨übtr⟩ *watertight* ⟨fig⟩ **~zahn** m ⟨anat⟩ *premolar*

l·ud [1. & 3. sg pret] v laden

L·uder n ~s/~ (Aas) *carrion* || (Köder) *lure* || ⟨vulg⟩ *beast, cad, damned wretch*, ⟨sl⟩ *sod* || dummes ~ *ass, fat-head* || armes ~ *pitiable object* || °falsches ~ ⟨derog⟩ *cad*; ⟨Am sl⟩ *double-crosser*; (Weib) *baggage, trollop* || °unter allem ~ *abominable, below criticism* **~hütte** f ⟨hunt⟩ *rook-shooting hut* **~leben** n *life of low debauchery* °**~̈mäßig** adv ⟨fam⟩ *devilishly* **l·udern** vt/i ⟨h⟩ (ködern) *to lure, to bait* | ⟨vulg⟩ *to lead a life of l. d.*

L·ues f ~/ *lues, syphilis*

L·uffa f ~/~s ⟨bot⟩ *luffa, loofah* [a. attr]

L·uft f ~/~̈e **A.** Bedeutungen **1.** *air* || frische, rauhe ~ *fresh, raw air* || stickige ~ *fug*, ⟨fam⟩ *frowst* **2.** (Luftzug) *breeze, draught of air* || bewegte, frische ~ *fresh breeze*; leicht bewegte ~ *gentle br.* **3.** (Atem) *breath* **4.** (im Freien) (*the open*) *air, outdoors* **5.** °⟨fig⟩ heiße ~ (u Steine)! *hot air! gas! froth!* ⟨vulg⟩ *piss and wind!* → B. 2. **6.** ⟨tech⟩ (Lager) *clearance, slackness* **B. 1.** die ~ **anhalten** *to hold one's breath* || ⟨fam⟩ halt die ~ an! *spare your breath to cool your porridge with* || jdn wie ~ behandeln *to cut a p* (*dead*) || wieder ~ **bek** *to breathe again*, ⟨fig⟩ *to get breathing room* || °erschüttere die ~ nicht so! ⟨fam⟩ *draw it mild!* || k–e ~ **h** *to be short* (od *out*) *of breath*; *the cigar doesn't draw* || ⟨fig⟩ etw ~ h *to breathe again, to have time on one's hands* || die Reifen h nicht genug ~ ⟨mot, cycl⟩ *the tyres are underinflated*; aus e–m Reifen die ~ ablassen *to deflate a tyre* || °~ in ein Glas **l** ⟨fam⟩ *to take the inside out of a g.* (*to drink*) || (e–m) ~ **m** *to unburden, ease, relieve* || sich ~ m *to find vent, to burst out* (*in dry jokes*) || s–n Gefühlen, s–m Herzen ~ m *to relieve* (od *give vent to*) *one's feelings* (gegenüber jdm *on a p*); (*he unburthened h.s. of his indignation to the major*); *to work off* .. (in *in*), *to unbosom o.s.*; ⟨fam⟩ *to blow off one's steam* || sich ~ **schaffen** *to win breathing room* || ~ (Ordnung) schaffen in *to clear sth up* || ⟨fam⟩ frische ~ schnappen (*to get out*) *to have a breath of air*; ⟨Am⟩ *to have a blowout* || (frische) ~ schöpfen *to draw breath, to take the air, to breathe fresh air*; *to air* (*o.s.*); wieder .. *to breathe again, to recover one's breath* || es **weht** kein Lüftchen *there is not a breeze stirring*; wenn nur ein ~̈chen weht fällt er um *a puff of air will knock him over* || ⟨fig⟩ ein neues ~̈chen weht ⟨fig⟩ *new winds are blowing*; es weht ein anderes ~̈chen *there is a different atmosphere* || die ~ zerreißen: *the gun crash tore the air* **2.** ⟨fig⟩ die ~ **ist rein** *the coast is clear*; warten bis die ~ rein ist *to wait for a clean field* || °⟨fig⟩ es (dort) ist **dicke** ~! *there's trouble brewing*; ⟨mil⟩ *it's blue hell, it's a warm corner* || er ist ~ für mich *he is nothing to me*, → A. 5. **C. an** die ~ bringen *to air*, .. gehen *to take an airing, to go out* || an *or* in der (freien) ~ s *to be in the* (*open*) *air* || ⟨fam⟩ e–n an die ~ setzen *to turn* od *put a p out of doors*, ⟨com⟩ *to give a p his walking papers*; ⟨Am sl⟩ *to give a p the air* || Ansicht **aus** der ~ *view from the air* || ⟨fig⟩ (völlig) aus der ~ gegriffen *pure invention!*; .. s ⟨fam⟩ *to have no leg to stand on* || (über e–m) **in** der ~ *overhead* || ⟨aero⟩ (Gegend) in der ~ beherrschen *to dominate .. aerially* || in die ~ fliegen (*of birds*) *to take wing* od *to the air*; ⟨fig⟩ (S) *to be blown up, to explode, to go* od *blow up* (⟨fam a.⟩ in die ~ gehen) || (P) ⟨fig⟩ °in die ~ gehen ⟨sl⟩ *to hit the ceiling* od *roof* || in die ~ greifen *to grasp at nothing* || es hängt *or* schwebt in der ~ 1. = ist aus der ~ gegriffen 2. .. noch .. *it is undecided yet* || ⟨aero⟩ in der ~ herumfliegen *to navigate* od *travel the air*; in der ~ bleiben *to stay aloft* || etw liegt in der ~ *sth is coming*, .. *is in the air* (od *wind, offing*) || (Bombe) in die ~ sprengen *to blow up*; (etw) .. *to blow .. to bits* || (Ball) hoch in die ~ treiben *to sky* || ⟨fig⟩ in ~ zerfließen *or* zergehen *to vanish into air* || **mit** ~ gefüllt *pneumatic* || mitten in der ~ *in mid-air* || **nach** ~ ringen *or* schnappen *to gasp for breath* || **von** ~ leben: (*one cannot*) *live on air* **~abk** n *air convention* od *pact* **~abscheider** m (Entlüfter) *air separator* **~abschluß** m [abstr] *exclusion of air*; [konkr] *air* od *hermetic seal*; unter ~ *airtight* **~abwehr** f *anti-aircraft* (*defence*), *air defence* | ~geschütz [n] *a.-a. gun*, ⟨sl⟩ *archie*; ~stelle [f] *a. d. department* **~abzug** m *air exhaust* **~akrobat** m (Zirkus) *aerialist* **~akrobatik** f *air stunting* **~alarm** m *alert*; *air-raid alarm* od *warning* **~angriff** m *air-raid* (bei e–m ~ *in an* ..); ~ mit Brandbomben *fire blitz*; Maßnahmen gegen ~e *a.-r. precautions* (*A.R.P.*) **~ansicht** f *aerial view* **~antenne** f *overhead aerial* **~armada** f *air armada*, ⟨Am⟩ *airmada* **~̈artig** a *aeriform, gaseous* **~aufbereitung** f ⟨arch⟩ *air conditioning* **~aufklärung** f ⟨mil⟩ *air scouting, aerial reconnaissance*; strategische ~ *distant air rec.* **~aufnahme** f *a.l photograph* od *survey*; *bird's eye photo, a.l view*; ⟨surv⟩ *a.l.mosaic* **~aufrüstung** f *a.l rearmament* **~auslaßventil** n *outlet-* od *escape valve* **~bad** n *air-bath*; Anzug f ~ *sun-bathing costume* **~ballon** m (f Kinder) *toy-balloon*, ⟨aero⟩ *balloon* **~beförderungsunternehmen** n *airline* **~behälter** m 1. ⟨orn⟩ *air-sac* 2. ⟨tech⟩ *air bottle*, etc. **~beobachter** m ⟨aero⟩ *spotter* **~beobachtung** f *overhead observation* **~̈bereift** a *pneumatic tyred* **~beschuß** m *fire from aircraft* **~bild** n *vision*; ⟨aero⟩ *a.l view*; *air-photo*, ⟨Am⟩ *airscope* | ~aufklärung [f] *photographic reconnaissance*; ~auswertung [f] *photographic interpretation*; ~reihe [f] *ph.c strip*; ~flug [m] ⟨fam⟩ *smile-please run*; ~gerät [n] *a.l camera*; ~karte [f] *aerophotographic map, photomap* **~blase** f *bead*; ⟨ich⟩ *air-bladder*, ⟨fig⟩ *bubble*, ⟨tech⟩ *air-lock*, ⟨pap⟩ *air bell* **~bombe** f *flying b.* **~bremse** f *air brake* ⟨a. a-n⟩ **~brennstoffgemisch** n *fuel-air mixture* **~brücke** f *air lift*; über die ~ befördern *to a.-l.* **~deckung** f ⟨aero⟩ *air cover* **~̈dicht** a *air-tight*; *sealed* (*cabin*) || adv *hermetically* (*closed*) **~dichte** f *air density* **~dienst** m *Air Mail Service* **~drahtumschalter** m *a.l change* **~druck** m ⟨phys⟩ *atmospheric pressure*; allg. ~anstieg [m] ⟨meteor⟩ *surge* ‖ (bei Explosion) *blast* | ~bremse [f] *atmospheric* (⟨Am⟩ *air*) *brake*; ~gradient [m] ⟨meteor⟩ *pr. gradiant*; ~-messer [m] ⟨phys⟩ *barometer*; ⟨mach⟩ *air pressure gauge*; ~verminderung [f] *decompression*; ~wirkung [f] *blast effect* **~düse** f *air-nozzle*; ⟨aero⟩ *fresh air inlet valve* **~einlaß** m *air intake* **~-elektrizität** f *atmospheric el.* | ~smesser [m] *electroscope* **~erscheinung** f *atmospheric phenomenon* | ~slehre [f] *meteorology* **~fahrer** m *aeronaut, balloonist* **~fahrt** f *aeronautics* pl, *a.l navigation, balloon ascent, a.l voyage* | ~attaché [m] *air-attaché*; ~behörde [f] *aeronautical authority*; ~gesellschaft [f] *airways company*; ~industrie [f] *aircraft ind.*; ~linie [f] *air-line*; ~medizin [f] *aeromedicine*; ~minister [m] *Air Minister, Secretary of the Air Force*; ~ministerium [n] *Air Ministry*; ~politik [f] *air policy*; ~wege *airlanes* pl **~fahrzeug** n & ~e [pl] *airplane(s), aircraft* (*300* ~); (Ballon) *aerostat*; *lighter-than-air aircraft* | ~ausrüstung [f] *a.c. equipment*; ~kennzeichen [n] *a.c. identification*; ~prüfer *licensed a.c. engineer* **~fanatiker** m *fresh-air fiend* **~fänger** m ⟨mot⟩ *air-scoop* **~farbe** f *sky-colour* **~feder** f *air spring* od *suspension* | ~kissen [n] *a. s. cushion* **~federung** f ⟨mot⟩ *a. s.* **~feuchtigkeit** f *atmospheric humidity* | ~smesser [m] *hygrometer* **~filter** m *air cleaner* **~-flasche** f ⟨tech⟩ *compressed-air cylinder* **~flotte** f *air-fleet*; ⟨engl⟩ *Royal Air Force* (*R.A.F.*) | ~n-stützpunkt [m] *air base* **≗förmig** a *gaseous, aeriform* **~fracht** f *airfreight*; als ~ verladen *to a.f.* | ~dienst [m] *air delivery service* **~frachter** m *air freighter* **~frühwarnung** f *air early warning* **~gang** m ⟨zoo & bot⟩ *a.l duct* **~gebilde** n *a.l. form* **≗gefährdet** a *vulnerable to air attacks* **~geist** m *sylph* **≗gekühlt** a *air-cooled* **~gemisch** n *air mixture* **~-geschwindigkeit** f *air-speed* **~gewehr** n *air-gun* **~-hafen** m *aerodrome, air-port* **~hammer** m *pneumatic h.* **~härtestahl** m *air hardening steel* **~hauch** m *breath of air* **~hebel** m *air lever* **~heizung** f *hot-air heating* | ~sapparat [m] *calorifier, hot-air heating-apparatus* **~herrschaft** f *air supremacy* od *mastery*; *control of the air* **~hiebe** [m pl] schlagen *to beat the air* **~hoheit** f *sovereignty of the air* **~-horchdienst** m *air-defence listening service* **~hülle** f *atmosphere* **~Infanterie** f *air(borne) inf.* **~isolierschicht** f *insulating air cushion* **~kabel** n ⟨el⟩ *a.l* od *overhead cable* **~kammer** f *air-chamber* **~kampf** m *air* od *a.l combat, airfighting, battle in the skies,* ⟨sl⟩ *scrap, dog-fight* | ~flugkörper [m] *air-to-air missile* N **~karte** f *airway* od *a.l map* **~kessel** m *air vessel* **~kissen** n *air-cushion* | ~boot [n] *hovercraft*; ~bus [m] *hoverbus*; ~fahrzeug [n] *a.-c. vehicle* (*ACV*), im ~ fahren *to hover* **~klappe** f *air-valve, ventilator*; *ventilation damper*, ⟨mot⟩ (Seitenfensterchen) *ventipane*, ⟨tech⟩ *air-control*, ⟨aero⟩ *air flap* **~kolben** m *pneumatic piston* **~kondensator** m *air condenser* **~körper** m *a.l body* **~korridor** m *air lane* od *corridor* **~krankheit** f *airsickness* **~kreis** m *atmosphere* **~kreuzer** m *air cruiser* **~krieg** m *a.l warfare*), *war in the air* | ~srecht [n] *air war right*; ~sleitung [f] *air-staff* **~kühlung** f *air cooling* **~-kunde** f *aerology* **~kurort** m (*climatic*) *health resort* **~kursbuch** n *air timetable* **~lage** f ⟨meteor⟩ *air stratum*, ⟨tact⟩ *a. situation* **~lande-** ~angriff in Zus–arbeit mit mot. Truppen ⟨tact⟩ *vertical envelopment*; ~brigade [f] *a. landing br.*; ~brükkenkopf [m] *airhead*; ~raum [m] *drop zone* N; ~transport [m] *a.l troop transport*; ~truppen [f pl] *airborne troops, parachute* (⟨fam⟩ *para-*) *-troops*; ~unternehmen [n] *airborne operation* **~-landung** f *airborne landing* **≗leer** a *airless, void of air*; ~er Raum *vacuum*; ~ m *to evacuate air from* **~leere** f *void, vacuum* **~leitung** f ⟨el⟩ *overhead line* od *wire* ‖ ⟨tech⟩ *air piping* **~linie** f *bee-line*, ⟨Am⟩ *air-line*; 3000 km in ~ *3000 straight-line km.* ‖ ⟨aero⟩ *airway* ‖ (in der) ~ *as the crow flies*; *by the string rather than the bow* | ~nentfernung [f] *st.-l. distance* **~loch** n *airhole, vent*; ⟨aero⟩ (*air*)-*pocket* **~-Luft-Rakete** f ⟨aero⟩ *air-to-air missile* **~macht** f *air-power* **~mangel** m *want of air* **~-marschall** m *Air Marshal* **~masse** f ⟨meteor⟩ *air mass* **~mast** m (U-Boot) *breathing mast* **~matratze** f *air mattress* **~meer** n *atmosphere* **~melde-** ~-dienst [m] *aircraft reporting service*; ~quadrat [n] *a.l reference square* **~messer** m *aerometer* **~-meß-** ~bild [n] *survey photograph* **~mine** f *parachute* od *a.l mine* | ~nabwurf [m] *mining from the air* **~mischgehäuse** n *air mixing chamber* **~mischung** f *air mixture* **~nachrichten-** ~helferin [f] *Wraf*; ~truppe [f] *air intelligence division* **~not-netz** n *search and rescue* (*net*) N **~ortung** f *a.l navigation* **~parade** f ⟨aero⟩ *fly-past*, ⟨Am⟩ *flyby* **~perspektive** f *a.l perspective* **~pflanze** f *aerophyte* **~photobrief** m *airgraph*, ⟨Am⟩ *V-mail* **~photographie** f *a.l photography* **~pistole** f *air-pistol* **~planquadrat** n *a.l reference square* **~polster** n *air cushion* **~post** f, (durch) ~! (*by*) *airmail*! durch ~ schicken *to airmail*; ~- u Eilbotenzustellung [f] *airexpress* | ~aufnahme [f] (im Fluge) *airmail pickup*; ~brief [m] *air letter*; ~leichtbrief [m] *aerogram(me)*; ~papier [n] *airmail stationery*; ~verkehr [m] *air mails* **~presser** m *air compressor* **~prospekt** m ⟨theat⟩ *sky-cloth*, ⟨Am⟩ *sky drop* **~pumpe** f *air-pump*, ⟨mot & cycl⟩ *pump*; mechanische ~ *power pump* **~rakete** f ⟨Am⟩ *anti-tank aircraft rocket* N **~rat** m ⟨engl⟩ *Air Council* **~raum** m *atmosphere, a.l region, sky, skies* pl; *air space* (*to violate foreign a. sp*); Beherrschung des ~s *control of the air* | ~beobachter [m] *air observer*; ~-beobachtung [f] *look-out*; ~späher [m] *air guard* **~reich** n *kingdom of the air* **~reifen** m (*pneumatic*) *tyre* **~reiniger** m *air freshener*; gr ~ *precipitron* **~reinigung** f *ventilation* **~reise** f *a.l voyage, air travel* | ~dienst [m] *air-passenger service* **~re-klame** f *sky advertising* **~riese** m ⟨aero⟩ *sky giant* **~röhre** f *air-tube* ‖ ⟨anat⟩ *windpipe, trachea* | ~n-deckel [m] ⟨anat⟩ *epiglottis*; ~nentzündung [f] ⟨med⟩ *quinsy*; ~nkatarrh [m] *bronchitis*; ~n-schnitt [m] *tracheotomy*; ~nschwindsucht [f] ⟨path⟩ *tracheal phthisis* **~route** f *airway, skyway* **~rüstung** f *air armament* **~sack** m ⟨aero⟩ *ballonet* Fr **~sauger** m *vacuum fan, air exhauster* **~säule** f *column of air* **~schacht** m *ventilating shaft* **~schaukel** f *swing-boat* **~scheibe** f ⟨aero mil⟩ *air target* **≗scheu** a *afraid of the air* **~schicht** f *air layer* **~-schiff** n *air-ship*, ⟨Am⟩ *zep*; Lenk≗ *dirigible*; kl. unstarres ~ *blimp*; halbstarres ~ *semi-rigid airship*; ~halle [f] *hangar* **~schiffahrt** f *air* od *a.l navigation, aeronautics* **~schiffer** m *airman, aeronaut* | ~abteilung [f] ⟨mil⟩ *aeronautic department* **~schirm** m ⟨tact⟩ *air-umbrella* **~schlacht** f *air battle* (um England *of Britain*) **~schlange** f *paper streamer* **~schieppscheibe** f *target banner* **~schleuse** f ⟨tech⟩ *air lock* **~schlösser** n pl *castles in Spain*; ~ bauen ⟨fig⟩ *to build castles in the air* **~schraube** f ⟨aero⟩ *air-screw, propeller*, ⟨fam⟩ *prop* | ~ndrehzahl [f] *pr. RPM*; ~nsteigung [f] *pr. pitch*, kl ~ *low pitch*; ~nstrahl [m] *slip stream*; ~nverstellung [f] *change of pitch* **~schutz** m *air-raid protection* (*ARP*), *aerial defence* | ~bund [m] *air defence league*, ⟨engl⟩ *Civil Air Guard*; ~helfer [m] *civil defence worker*; ~keller [m] *bomb proof refuge, air-raid* od *ARP-shelter*; in den ~ gehen *to take shelter*; ~pumpe [f] *stirrup pump*; ~raum [m] (*air-raid*) *shelter*; ~vorkehrungen [f pl] *a.-r. precautions* pl (*ARP*); ~warnzentrale [f] *a.-r. control centre*; ~wart [m] *air-raid warden* **≗segeln** vi ⟨aero⟩ *to soar* **~sieg** m *victory in the air*; den 100. ~ erringen *to bring the total of one's victories to 100* **~soffitte** f ⟨theat⟩ *sky border* **~späher** m *air guard* **~sperre** f *air barrage*

~sperrgebiet n (Fla) *inner artillery zone* N **~spiegelung** f *mirage, fata morgana* **~sport** m *sport flying* **~sportler** m *amateur flier* od *pilot* **~sprengpunkt** m *high burst* **~springer** m *caperer, vaulter* **~sprünge** [m pl] m *to cut capers, to throw somersaults*; *to caper, gambol* **~störungen** f pl *atmospheric disturbances* **~stoß** m *gust of air*, ⟨artill⟩ *blast concussion* **~straßenkreuz** n *a.l crossroads* [sg konstr] **~strecke** f ⟨aero⟩ *airway* **~streitkräfte** f pl *Air Force* **~strom** m *current of air*; ⟨phys⟩ *air stream* **~strömung** f *movement of a mass of air*; horizontale ~ *advection* | ~smesser [m] *anemometer* **~strudel** m ⟨aero⟩ *wash* **~stützpunkt** m *air base* N **~taktik** f *a.l tactics* pl **~tätigkeit** f *a.l activity* **~tauglichkeit** f = –tüchtigkeit **~taxi** n *taxiplane, helibus* **~ton** m ⟨arts⟩ *air-tone, air* **~torpedo** n *a.l torpedo*, ⟨sl⟩ *flying pig* **~transport** m *air conveyance* | ~versicherung [f] *aviation insurance* **≗trocken** a *air-dry* **~tüchtigkeit** f *air-worthiness* **~überlegenheit** f *air supremacy*, bei feindl. ~ *where the enemy has air superiority* **~überwachung** f *air surveillance* **~ventil** n *air inlet* **~veränderung** f = ~wechsel **~verdichter** m *air-compressor* **≗verdünnt** a *rarefied* (Raum *air space*) **~vergütung** f ⟨arch⟩ *air conditioning* **~verkehr** m *air traffic* od *transports* pl | ~snetz [n] *air line network*; ~slinie [f] *air-line* od *service*; ~splan [m] *flying schedule*; ~svorschriften [f pl] *air-traffic rules* pl **~verlegung** f ⟨tact⟩ *air move* **~versorgung** f ⟨aero⟩ *air-to-air-supply* **~verteidigung** f (bodenständig *static*) *air defence* (*system*) **~verunreinigung** f *atmospheric pollution* **~waage** f *aerometer* **~waffe** f ⟨aero⟩ *air-arm, air corps, Air Force*, ⟨engl⟩ *Royal Air Force* | ~nattaché [m] *air attaché* N; ~nbauabteilung [f] *aviation engineer division*; ~nhandbuch [n] *aeronautical information publications* pl; ~n-Kommando [n] f Forschung u Entwicklung *Air Research and Development Command* N; ~n-Nachrichtenzentrale [f] *Air Information Center* N; ~npolizei [f] *air police* **~wechsel** m *ventilation* (*in a room*), ⟨med⟩ *change* (*of air*) **~weg** m ⟨anat⟩ obere ~e [pl] *upper respiratory tract*; Krankheiten der ob. ~e *u. r. t. diseases* || ⟨aero⟩ *air-route, air-line* || auf dem ~e *by air* || auf dem ~e befördert *airshipped* || *airborne* (*troops*) **~werbung** f *sky advertising, skywriting* **~wettfahrt** f *a.l race* **~widerstand** m *air resistance*; ⟨aero⟩ *drag* **~wirbel** m *wake*; *whirl, vortex* **~zelle** f *air-cell* **~zeug-** [in comp] *aircraft* (*-carrier* -träger, *works* -werke) **~ziegel** m *air-(dried) brick* **~ziel** n *a.l objective* | ~- ⟨Fla⟩ *ground-to-air* [attr] (*firing*); ~beschuß [m] *anti-aircraft fire* **~zufuhr** f *ventilation*; *supply of fresh air* **~zuführung** f ⟨mot⟩ *main air bleed* | ~sschlauch [m] *airpipe* **~zug** m *current of air, draught, breeze* || ⟨fig⟩ ein neuer ~ *a new spirit* **~zustelldienst** m *air delivery service* **~zutritt** m *free access of air* **~zwischenraum** m *air gap* **L·üftchen** n ~s/~ → Luft A. 2. u. B. es weht .. **l·üften** vt/refl [h] **1.** *to* (*expose to the*) *air* (*beds, clothing*) || *to aerate* (*the soil*) || *to prune* od *lop* (*a tree*) **2.** *to ventilate* (*a room*) **3.** *to lift* od *raise* (*one's hat, a curtain*), *to take off* (*one's hat*) || *to release* (*a brake*) | ⟨fig⟩ *to reveal* od *unveil* (*a secret*), *to drop* (*the mask*) **4. sich** ~ *to go into* (od *to take*) *the air* || ⟨fig⟩ = (s–n Gefühlen) Luft m **L·üfter** m ~s/~ ⟨tech⟩ *fan*; *air blower*; *ventilator* || (Saug≗) *exhauster* | ~kopf [m] (*ventilation*) *cowl* **l·uftig** a *airy* (*substance*) || *aerial* (*being*) || *breezy* (*height*) || *exposed to the air* || (gasartig) *gaseous* | *light, loose, thin* (*garment*) || ⟨fig⟩ *flighty, giddy* (*p*) || ein ~er Bruder = Luftikus | **≗keit** f ~/ *airiness* || *thinness* || ⟨fig⟩ *flightiness, giddiness* °**L·uftikus** m ~/ ⟨fam⟩ *gas-bag, windbag* **L·üftung** f ~/~en *airing* || *ventilation* || (Hebung) *lifting* **~sanlage** f *v.tion plant* **~sgerät** n *aerating apparatus* **~srohr** n *v.ting pipe* **~sschacht** m *vent(ilation shaft)* **~sschleuse** f *ventilation baffle*

L·ug m ~(e)s/ *lie* || ~ u Trug *lies and frauds* pl, *pack of lies, fraud and falsehood* || *falsehood and deceit* || er ist voller ~ u Trug *he is a liar and a cheat*, → lügen

Lug·aner See m ⟨It⟩ *Lake* (*of*) *Lugano*

L·ug- ~·aus m ~/~ *lookout*, ⟨mar⟩ *watch* **~insland** m ~/~ *watch-tower* **~loch** n [bes österr] → Guckloch; → lugen

L·üge f ~/~n *lie*, (grobe *gross*) *falsehood* || ⟨fam⟩ *story, fib*, ⟨bib⟩ *lease* || dreiste, unverfrorene ~ *cool, most brazen lie*, ⟨fam⟩ *tall story* || e–e faustdicke *or* glatte ~ *a whacking big lie*; ⟨sl⟩ *a corker, plumper, nailer* || kl *or* fromme ~ *white lie* || (es sind) lauter ~n *it's all a lie, it's a pack of lies* || über jdn ~n verbreiten *to tell lies of a p* || jdn e–r ~ zeihen *or* bezichtigen *to accuse a p of telling lies* || jdn ~n strafen *to give a p the lie* (*direct*), ⟨Am⟩ *to belie a p* || etw ~n strafen *to give the lie to* (*slanders*) || jdm e–e ~ aufbinden *to sell a p a packet* || ⟨prov⟩ ~n h kurze Beine *lies have short legs* od *wings* || → zurückweisen, derb 2

l·ugen vi [h] (nach etw) *to look out, to look* (*for a th*) || *to peep* od *peer* (*round the corner*); → Lug-

l·ügen vi [log/gelogen] [h] **1.** *to* (*tell a*) *lie, to tell lies* od *a falsehood* od ⟨fam⟩ *stories* || etw ~ *to invent a th* || (vorgeben) *to pretend* || (flunkern) *to tell a fib* | er lügt wie gedruckt *he lies like truth, like a book* || .. das Blaue v Himmel .. *like a trooper*, .. *in his throat* || du lügst! *you are a liar* || nein, d·u lügst! *it's you that's the liar* || ich müßte ~, wenn *I should be telling a lie if* || er lügt, wenn er nur den Mund aufmacht *he can't open his mouth without telling a lie* || wer lügt, der stiehlt *show me a liar, and I'll show you a thief* **2.** vt *to invent* **3.** ⟨fam⟩ e–m die Ohren (°die Hucke) voll ~ *to cram a p with lies* **4.** ≗ n *lying, telling lies* || ⟨fam⟩ *fibbing, story-telling* || → Verlogenheit **L·ügen-** °**~beutel** m *fibber*; *habitual* od *incorrigible liar* **~detektor** m *lie detector* **~feldzug** m *lie campaign* **~fürst, ~geist** m *Father of Lies, Satan* **~geschichte** f *cock-and-bull story*; *fable* **~gewebe** n *net of lies* od *falsehoods*, ⟨Am⟩ *a lie out of whole cloth* **~märchen** n *stretcher* **~maul** n *impudent liar* **~propaganda** f *political lie pr.* **~prophet** m *false* od *lying pr.* **~schmied** m *inventor of shameless lies* **l·ügenhaft** a (P) *lying, false, deceitful, mendacious* || (S) *untruthful, invented* **≗igkeit** f ~/ *mendacity, falsehood, deceitfulness* **L·ügner** m ~s/~ *liar*, ⟨fam⟩ *story-teller* || gemeiner ~ *dirty liar* || sich v jdm ~ heißen l *to take the lie from a p*; jdn als ~ hinstellen *to make a p out a l.*; jdn z ~ m *to prove a p a liar, to expose his lies* **l·ügnerisch** a *lying* (*tongue, speech*) || *mendacious* (*character*) || in ~er Weise *lyingly*

L·uke f ~/~n **1.** *dormer-window* **2.** ⟨mar⟩ (⟨mil-mar⟩ a. Luk [n]) *hatchway* ⟨a. a-n⟩; die ~n schließen *to close down the hatches* || (Lade≗) *cargo hatch* | ~ndeckel [m] ⟨mar⟩ *cover of a hatchway*

lukrat·iv a *lucrative*, → einträglich

L·uksor n (ägypt. Dorf) *Luxor*

luk·ullisch a ⟨cul⟩ *luxurious, sumptuous*

°**L·ulatsch** m ~es/~e *long stripe, long legs* [sg]

l·ullen vt/i [h] *to lull* || in Schlaf ~ *to lull to sleep*

lumb·al a (= Lenden-) *lumbar*

L·umen n ~s/ (Einheit des Lichtstroms) *lumen* || ⟨fig⟩ (P) *luminary, light*

°**L·umig** m ~s/~e *lout* → Lümmel

Luminesz·enz f ~/ *luminescence* (*e.g. of fire-flies*)

L·umme f ~/~n ⟨orn⟩ *guillemot*, → d.

L·ümmel m ~s/~ *rough, lubber, bumpkin, hog, lout*; ⟨Am sl⟩ *hick, hoodlum* | ⟨übtr⟩ ein gr, starker ~ *a long-limbed fellow* **Lümmel·ei** f ~/~en *lubberly behaviour, unmannerliness, insolent act* od *remark* **l·ümmelhaft** a *lubberly, loutish, boobyish* **≗igkeit** = Lümmelei **l·ümmeln** vrefl; sich ~ *to sprawl, loll* (*in a chair*)

L·ump m ~(e)s & ~en/~e(n) (zerlumpt) *ragamuffin* ‖ (jämmerlich) *wretch, scamp* ‖ (Schuft) *knave, blackguard, rotter, scoundrel* ‖ ⟨Am sl⟩ *scalawag* ‖ dieser ~ v e–m Kerl *that rag of a fellow* ‖ dieser ~ v e–m I. *that ragamuffin Italian* **~(fisch)** m ⟨ich⟩ *lump-fish* **L·umpen** m ~s/~ *rag, tatter* ‖ (Wischtuch) *clout* ‖ die ~ [pl] *rags and tatters* ‖ alte ~ [pl] *duds* pl ‖ ⟨fig⟩ jdn aus den ~ schütteln *to haul* od *call a p over the coals*; ⟨bes mil sl⟩ *to shake down* **l·umpen** vi [h] ⟨fam⟩ *to lead a life of dissipation* ‖ sich nicht ~ l *to come down* (od *to do ths*) *handsomely* ‖ er will sich nicht ~ l *he won't be called shabby*; er ließ sich nicht ~ *money was no object* **L·umpen- ~baron** m ⟨vulg⟩ *trumpery baron* **~beutel** m *rag-bag* **~brei** m ⟨pap⟩ *pulp* **~ding** n *paltry th* ‖ ⟨fam⟩ (Kind) *little scrub* **~geld** n ⟨fam⟩ *paltry sum, trifling expense* ‖ für ein ~ *dog-, dirt-cheap* **~gesindel** n *rabble, riffraff* **~handel** m *rag-trade* **~händler** m *rag-merchant, dealer in rags* **~hund, ~kerl** m ⟨vulg⟩ *ragamuffin, rascal* **~kram** m *trash, rubbish* **~leben** n *loose life* **~mann** m *rag-picker, ragman* **~pack** n = ~gesindel **~papier** n *paper made of rags* **~sack** m *rag-bag* **~sammler** m *ragman, rag-picker* ‖ °⟨fig⟩ (*last train, tram*) *Flying Fornicator*, ⟨Am fam⟩ *owl-car* **~volk** n = ~gesindel **~wolle** f *shoddy* **~zucker** m *lump-sugar* **Lumper·ei** f ~/~en *shabby trick* ‖ (Kleinigkeit) *trifle, mere flea-bite, nothing to speak of* **l·umpig** a *ragged, in rags* ‖ *poky* (*dress*) ‖ ⟨fig⟩ *shabby, mean, paltry* ‖ (trivial) *measly* ‖ *beggarly* (*fiver*) ‖ ~e Pfennige *paltry* od *beggarly pence*; *two hundred miserable dollars* ‖ ~e vier Jahre *a paltry four years* | ≗keit f *raggedness, paltriness* ‖ [konkr] die ~ v ein paar Mark *the paltry sum of* ..

lun·arisch a *lunar* (*month, nodes, rainbow*)

L·üneburg n ⟨Ger⟩ (Stadt) *Luneburg* **L·üneburger** m, **~in** f *inhabitant of Luneburg* **L·üneburger Heide** f *Luneburg Heath*

Lün·ette f ~/~n ⟨arch⟩ *tympanum*; ⟨fort⟩ *lunette*

L·unge f ~/~n *lung*; *lungs* pl (e–e ~ *a pair of l.s*) ‖ ~n [pl] (T) *lights* pl | ⟨fig⟩ e–e gute *or* starke ~ h *to have good l.s* ‖ es auf der ~ h *to be troubled with one's l.s, to be chesty* ‖ schone d–e ~ *save your breath* ‖ sich [dat] die ~ aus dem Halse schreien *to scream one's l.s out, to scr. o.s. into fits* od *one's head off* ‖ auf ~ rauchen *to inhale* ‖ aus voller ~ *one's loudest* **L·ungen- ~ader** f ⟨anat⟩ *pulmonary artery* **~balsam** m *balsam for the l.s* **~bläschen** n ⟨anat⟩ *air-cell of the l.s* **~blutung** f *bleeding of the l.s* **~drüse** f *bronchial gland* **~entzündung** f *pneumonia* L **~fäule** f ⟨path⟩ *p.y consumption, phthisis*; ⟨vet⟩ *dry-rot* **~fieber** n ⟨path⟩ *p.y fever* **~flechte** f ⟨bot⟩ *tree-lichen* **~flügel** m *lobe of the l.s* **~geschwür** n ⟨path⟩ *ulcer* od *abscess in the l.s* **~haschee** n ⟨cul⟩ *hashed calf's lights* pl **≗krank** a, **~kranke(r)** m *consumptive* **~krankheit** f *p.y disease* **~kraut** n ⟨bot⟩ *l.wort* **~kreislauf** m *lesser circulation* **~lappen** m = ~flügel **~leiden** n = ~krankheit **~mus** n ⟨cul⟩ = ~haschee **~öd·em** n ⟨path⟩ *œdema of the l.s* **~öffner** m ⟨gym⟩ *pipe-opener* **~probe** f *experiment on the l.s* **~schützer** m 1. *respirator* 2. *l. protector* **~schwind-** ~sucht [f] *p.y consumption* od *disease, phthisis* | ≗süchtig [a] *consumptive, phthisical* **~spezialist** m *doctor who specializes in chest* (*diseases*) **~tuberkulose** f ⟨path⟩ *tuberculosis* (*of the lungs*); = –fäule

L·ungerer m ~s/~ *idler, loafer* **L·ungerleben** n *idle* od *lazy life* **l·ungern** vi [h & s] **1.** *to idle* od *loiter* (*about*) ‖ *to lead a lazy* od *vagabond life* **2.** [h] nach e–m *or* etw ~ *to long after* ..

L·unker m ~s/~ (als Schwindungserscheinung) *shrinkhole, shrinkage void*; (als Gaseinschluß) *blow-hole*; (im Gußblock) *pipe* ‖ ≗freier Guß *flawless casting*

L·ünse f ~/~n *linch-pin*; → Nabennagel

L·unte f ~/~n **1.** (*slow-*)*match* ‖ ~ riechen ⟨fig⟩ *to smell a rat, to scent danger* **2.** ⟨hunt⟩ *brush* (*fox's* od *wolf's tail*) **3.** ⟨tex⟩ (Faserstoffhalbzeug) *rove* **L·unten- ~gewehr** n *match-lock* **~kästchen** n *slow-match case* **~schloß** n *match-lock* **~spitze** f (Fuchs≗) *tag* **~stock** n *linstock*

l·unzen vi [h] *to peep, to look furtively*

L·upe f ~/~n *pocket-lens, magnifier, magnifying-glass*; starke ~ *high-power magnifier* ‖ durch die ~ besehen, unter die ~ nehmen ⟨fig⟩ *to scrutinize narrowly, examine closely, take a hard look at*, ⟨Am⟩ *to make a check-up of* (*a th*)

l·upfen, ≗ vt [h] *to lift gently* od *slightly*

Lup·ine f ~/~n ⟨bot⟩ *lupin*(*e*)

L·uppe f ~/~n *hollow billet* (*for tubes*) | ~neisen [n] *puddled iron*; ~nfeuer [n] *bloomery*

Lurch m ~(e)s/~e ⟨zoo⟩ *amphibian, batra chian*

†**Lusit·anien** n (röm. Prov. im alten Spanien, jetzt etwa Portugal) *Lusitania* **Lusit·anier** m, **~in** f, **lusit·anisch** a *Lusitanian*

Lust f ~/≗e [pl nur bei 2.] **1.** (Neigung, Verlangen) *inclination, mind, disposition, liking*; *wish, desire*; ~ u Liebe zu .. *zest for* ‖ s–e ~ (voll u ganz) **befriedigen** *or* büßen *to satisfy one's desire* (*to the top of one's bent*) ‖ ich bekam gr ~ zu *I felt highly inclined, I was seized with a desire to do* ‖ ich **fühle** gr ~ dich zu verprügeln *my fingers itch to beat you* ‖ ich **habe** k–e ~ **auf** .. (*meat*) *doesn't tempt me* ‖ ~ **h zu** *to have a liking for* od *a mind to* (*do*), *to feel inclined to* (*do*), ~ dazu h *to feel like it*; ganz wie Sie ~ h *just as you like, do as you please* ‖ fast (*or* nicht übel) ~ h *to have half a mind* ‖ wenig ~ h *to be unwilling* (*to do*) ‖ [mst neg *or* interr] *do you* (*I don't*) *care to do* ‖ e–m ~ **m** (zu) *to give a p a desire* (*for*), *to inspire a p with pleasure* (*in*) ‖ mir ist die ~ dazu **vergangen,** ich habe die ~ dazu verloren *I have lost all liking for it* ‖ ich verspürte ein ≗chen dazu *I had rather a fancy for it, I felt like* (*watching her*) ‖ es **wandelte** mich die ~ an = ich bekam ~ ⟨a.⟩ *the fancy took me* (*to write*) | **mit** ~ u Liebe, **nach** Herzenslust *with a will, with heart and soul* ‖ mit ~ u Liebe bei e–r S s *to put one's whole heart into a matter* **2.** [mit pl] (Sinnen≗) *the lusts* (*of the flesh*) ‖ *evil, carnal, worldly, sinful desire* od *appetite* ‖ (Wollust) *titillation* ‖ s–e ~ befriedigen *to satisfy one's passion* ‖ s–n ≗en frönen *to gratify one's evil passions* **3.** (Freude) *pleasure, delight*; *joy, enjoyment* ‖ (Fröhlichkeit) *mirth* ‖ (Genuß) *enj.t* ‖ (s–e) ~ an etw finden *or* h *to take* (*a*) *pl.* od *d. in a th* ‖ es gereicht ihm zur ~, es gewährt ihm ~ *it gives him pl.* ‖ da kann e–m die ~ daran vergehen *it makes one lose one's liking for it* ‖ es ist e–e wahre ~ zu sehen, wie .. *it is quite d.ful to see how* .. ‖ er tat es, daß es e–e ~ war .. *like a brick, with a vengeance* ‖ → Leid **~anlagen** f pl *pl.-grounds* pl **≗betont** a *pleasurable* **~dirne** f *prostitute* **~empfindung** f *pleasant sensation* **≗erregend** a *appetizing* **~fahrt** f *pl.-trip, excursion*, ⟨Am mot⟩ *joy-ride* **~garten** m *pl.-grounds* pl **~gefühl** n *feeling of pl.* **~greis** m ⟨bes Am sl⟩ *sugar daddy* **~haus** n *summer-* od *pl.-house* **~häuschen** n *box in the country*; (Laube) *arbour* °**~knochen,** °**~knüppel** m ⟨sex & aero⟩ *joystick* **~lager** n *holiday-camp*; ⟨hist⟩ *pl.--camp* °**~molch** m *lecher* **~mord** m *rape and murder*; *murder associated with sex* **~partie** f *pl.--party* **~reise** f *pl.-trip* **~reisende(r)** m *traveller for pl.* **~schiff** n *pl.-boat* **~schloß** n *pleasance, pl.-seat* **~seuche** f ⟨path⟩ *veneral disease, syphilis* **~sitz** m = ~schloß **~spiel** n *comedy* | ≗artig [a] *comic*; ~dichter [m] *writer of comedies*; ~gattung [f] *kind of comedy* **~wald** m *park, grove* | ≗chen [n] *shrubbery* **≗wandeln** vi [s] *to take a walk, to stroll about, to promenade* **~wandler** m *stroller* **L·ustbarkeit** f ~/~en *amusement, diversion, pleasure, sport, entertainment, festivity*; ⟨fam⟩ *jollification, merry-making* ‖ e–e ~ veranstalten *to arrange a j.* ‖ ~en [pl] *gaieties* pl **~ssteuer** f *entertainment tax* **l·üsten** vi/imps [h] = gelüsten

L·üster m ~s/~ **1.** (Stoff, Glanz) *lustre* **2.** (Leuchter) *chandelier* | ~dekor [n] *lustrous glaze*; ~klemme [f] ⟨rec-el⟩ *Hirschmann-type connector*

l·üstern a (→ Lust) (nach) *longing* (*for*), *greedy* (*of, for*), *desirous* (*of*) | (sinnlich) *lascivious* (*eyes*), *lewd* (*pictures, jokes*) || *lecherous, wanton, prurient* (*p*) || *voluptuous, lustful* (*glance*) || *slippery, spicy* (*tale*) || ~ s (nach etw *or*) es zu tun *to have a violent desire* (*for a th* od) *to do it* || mit ~en Augen ansehen *to cast longing eyes* od *lustful glances at* | ≈**heit** f ~/~en *longing, greediness* || *lust, lasciviousness, concupiscence* || *lewdness, lubricity, lititiousness, prurience, -cy* **l·ustig** [a] **1.** *gay, merry, cheerful* || (unterhaltend) *amusing, funny* || (drollig) *droll, comical* | ~er Abend *jolly evening, spree*, ⟨Am sl⟩ *bat* || ~er Bruder *j. fellow* || Bruder ≈ *Merry Andrew* || ~er Bursche *j. blade* || e–e ~e Gesellschaft *a merry party* || ~e Leute *amusing people* || ⟨theat⟩ ~e P *comical character*; (derb) *low comedian* || *sprightly* (*air*) || *rollicking* (*song, pantomime*) || ~er Scherz *fine fun*, ⟨fam⟩ *lark* || ~er Streich *merry trick*, ⟨fam⟩ *jolly lark* || ~ s *to make merry* || sich [dat] e–n ~en Tag m *to make a j. day of it* || *j., skittish* (*widow*) | [adv] da ging's ~ her *there was plenty of fun going on* || nun aber ~ (= flink) an die Arbeit! *now, wire in!, now, to your work!*, ⟨fam⟩ *buck up!* || das kann ja ~ w! *that may turn out a pretty mess!* **2.** (lächerlich) sich ~ m über jdn *to make fun, sport, game of a p, to banter a p, to poke fun at a p*; ⟨Am a.⟩ *to have a good laugh at a p*; man machte sich in .. über ihn ~ *he was quite a joke in our company*; .. über etw *to mock* (od *poke fun*) *at a th* || alles macht sich über ihn ~ *he is the laughing-stock of everybody* **3.** .. ~ [in comp z. B.] arbeits~ *fond of work, taking pleasure in one's work*; kauf~ *prospective* (*customer*) | ≈**keit** f *cheerfulness, mirth, jollity, gaiety*; ausgelassene ~ *unrestrained mirth* || *merriment* || *amusement, fun* || *drollness, comicality* | ≈**macher** m ~s/~ *jester, buffoon, Merry Andrew* || → Spaßmacher **L·üstling** m *sensualist, debauchee, libertine, voluptuary* **l·ustlos** a *listless* || ⟨com⟩ *dull, stagnant, lifeless, slack* || *dull* (*market*) || *lifeless* (*change*) || die Börse schloß ~ .. *closed in a dull tone* | ≈**igkeit** f *listlessness* || *dullness*

L·ustrum n ~s/–ren & –ra (5 Jahre) *lustrum*

Luther·aner m ~s/~, **l·utherisch** a *Lutheran*

L·uthertum n ~(e)s/ *Lutheranism*

L·utsch- ~**beutel,** ~**er** m ~s/~ *sucking-bag, comforter*, ⟨Am⟩ *pacifier* ~**bonbon** n *sucker, rock* ~**stange** f *lollipop* **l·utschen** vi [h] *to suck* || am Daumen ~ *to suck one's thumb*

l·ütt a [niedd] = klein | ≈e [m] ~n/~n = Schnaps | ≈e [n] der, die, das ≈e (Kind) *the little one*

L·utte f ~/~n ⟨mil⟩ *drain* || ⟨min⟩ *air conduit*

L·utter m ~s/~ ⟨distil⟩ *singlings* pl

L·üttich n (belgische Stadt) *Liège* [Fr]

L·uv f ~/ ⟨mar⟩ *luff, weather side* || (Feuer≈) (im Gefecht) *engaged side* || ~ halten *to keep the wind* ~**baum** m *outrigger* ≈**gierig** a *weatherly* ~**seite** f = ~ | ~**wall** m *weather-shore* ≈**wärts** adv *in the wind's eye*; *to windward* || ~ v e–m Schiff fahren *to weather a ship* || etw ~ anfahren *to weather a th* ~**winkel** m *wind correction angle*, ⟨aero⟩ *crab a.*

L·uxemburg n **1.** (Land & Stadt) *Luxemburg* **2.** (belg. Prov.) *Luxembourg* **L·uxemburger** m, ~**in** f *inhabitant of Luxemburg* (bzw *Luxembourg*) **l·uxemburgisch** a *Luxemb*(*o*)*urg*

Lux n ~/~ (Einheit der Beleuchtungsstärke) *lux* ~**wert** m *lux value*, → *Lux*

luxuri·ös a *luxurious* (*life*), *sumptuous* (*furniture*)

L·uxus m ~/ *luxury, sumptuousness* || kein ~ ⟨sl⟩ *no swank*; ⟨Am oft⟩ (Neureich≈) *razzle-dazzle* ~**artikel** m *fancy-article, novelty, luxury* ~**ausführung** f *de luxe model* ~**ausgabe** f *fine edition, e. de luxe* Fr ~**einband** m *rich binding* ~**gesetz** n *sumptuary-law* ~**güter** n pl *luxury goods* ~**kajüte** f *stateroom* ~**papier** n *fancy-paper* ~**steuer** f *luxury tax* ~**verwahrlosung** f *juvenile demoralization* (*caused by too high a standard of life*) ~**wagen** m ⟨mot⟩ *l.y car*; *saloon*(*-car*) ~**zug** m *saloon-train*

Luzern n (schweiz. Stadt u Kanton) *Lucerne*

Luz·erne f ~/ ⟨bot⟩ *lucern*(*e*), *purple medic*

Luz·erner m, ~**in** f *inhabitant of Lucerne*

†**L·ydien** n (Landschaft in Kleinasien) *Lydia*

L·ydier m, ~**in** f, **l·ydisch** a *Lydian*

Lykop·odiumtopf m ⟨theat⟩ *lycopodium pot*

L·ymph- ~**bereitung** f *lymphopoiesis* ~**drüse** f *lymphatic gland* ~**gefäß** n ⟨anat⟩ *lymphatic vessel, lymph-duct* **lymph·atisch** a *lymphatic* **L·ymphe** f ~/~n *lymph* || ⟨med⟩ *vaccine* (*matter*)

l·ynchen vt [h] *to lynch* **L·ynchjustiz** f *lynch law*

Lyon [li'ɔ̃:] n ⟨Fr⟩ (Stadt) *Lyons* || ~**·eser,** ~**er(in f)** m *inhabitant of L.*

L·yra f ~/–ren *lyre* || ⟨astr⟩ *Lyra* **L·yrik** f ~/~en *lyric poetry* || *lyrics* pl | ~**er** ~s/~ *lyric poet* **l·yrisch** a *lyric* (*poems, poets, poetry, drama, muse*) | *lyrical* (*emotion, praise, sorrow, tenor, humo*(*u*)*r*)

L·ysa G·ora f [sg] ⟨poln⟩ (Gebirge) *Lysogóry* [pl]

Lys·ol® n ~(e)s/ ⟨chem⟩ *lysole*

Lyz·eum n ~s/–zeen *lyceum, grammarschool*

M

M, m n ~/~ *M, m* || DM = Deutsche Mark || es kostet 2 M [°sprich: em] *it costs two marks*

Mä·ander m (Fluß in Kleinasien) *Meander*

Mä·ander m ~s/~ (*Greek*) *fret* | ~streifen [m] *fretwork* **mä·andrisch** a *meandrian, meandering, winding*

M·aar n ~(e)s/~e *dell*; *maar* || (*volcanic*) *lake*

Maas f (link. Nebenfluß des Rheins) *Meuse*

Maastr·icht n ⟨holl⟩ (Stadt) *Maestricht*

M·aat m ~(e)s/~e ⟨mar⟩ 1. *mate*, ⟨fam⟩ *pal* 2. (*ship's*) *mate*; ⟨allg⟩ *petty officer* || ~e u Matrosen *the lower deck* ~**schaft** f 1. (*ship's*) *crew* 2. (*trading*) *company* 3. *comradeship*

M·acchie [-kiə] f ~/~n It *macchia*, Fr *maquis*

Maced·onien n → Mazedonien, Makedonien

Mach·andel m ~s/~ (Wacholder) [niedd] *juniper*(*-tree*)

M·ach- ~**art** f *make* (*in style* & *m.*) || *workmanship* (*elaborate w.*) ~**werk** n *product, concoction, bungling work, patch work*; ⟨fam⟩ *put-up job* || elendes ~ *clumsy* od *poor piece of work* || (literarisches) *pot-boiler* **M·ache** f ~/ **1.** *make, style, workmanship* || ⟨fam⟩ *put-up job*; die S ist in der ~ ⟨fam⟩ *the matter is on the move* **2.** (Täuschung) *humbug, make-up, sham* || *pomposity* | das ist nur ~ *that is all eye-wash* || bewußte ~ *intentional dodgery* || ⟨fam⟩ etw in der ~ h *to have sth in hand, to be having it made* || ⟨fig⟩ **a.** e–n in der ~ h *to be licking a p into shape* **b.** *to belabour a p* || das Stück zeigt e–e geschickte ~ *the play is written in a clever style* || sich auf die ~ verstehen *to know the tricks of the trade*; ⟨fam⟩ *he knows a th or two*; ⟨prov⟩ wie die ~, so die S *as the bake so the cake*

m·achen I. vt [h] **1.** (**anfertigen,** herstellen) **a.** *to make* (*boots*) || ~ l *to have* (*order, get*) *made* || *where do you get your clothes made*? || (Schnittmuster) *to cut out* (*a pattern*) **b.** *to make up* (*a medicine*) ‖ *to prepare* (*a meal*) ‖ *to make* (*butter, tea, sausages*) **c.** *to take* (*a copy*) ‖ *to prepare* (*one's homework*) ‖ Feuer ~ *to make a fire* ‖ das macht Appetit (..) *that gives you an appetite* (*sleepless nights*) **2.** (**herrichten**) *to make beds* ‖ *to tidy* (*a room*) ‖ sich das Haar ~ *to do one's hair* ‖ ⟨fam⟩ *to fix* (*a bed, the fire, one's hair*); sich die Zähne ~ l *to have one's teeth looked after* **3.** (**tun**) *to do* ‖ ich mach's *well, here goes*!, *I'll do it*! ‖ er macht es gerade *he is just about it*; es ~ *to manage* (*it*); *to turn the trick*; was h Sie heute ge–cht? *what have you done with y.s. today*? ‖ mach, was du willst *do as you please*; *take it or leave it* ‖ so etw macht man nicht *it isn't done* ‖ nicht wissen, was man (zuerst) ~ soll *not to know which way to turn* ‖ man kann nichts dagegen ~ *you can't help it*; °⟨hum⟩ kann man dagegen nichts ~? *do you* (⟨vulg⟩ *yer*) *feel like that*? ‖ ° ~ wir! *let's* ‖ °es ihr ~ ⟨sex vulg⟩ *to do a woman's job for her* **4.** (**bewirken**) *to effect* ‖ (verursachen) *to cause*; *his conduct occasions* od *causes me great anxiety* ‖ (schaffen) *to create* ‖ (erzeugen) *to produce, fabricate, manufacture* ‖ (gestalten, bilden) *to form, shape, fashion* (aus *from, out of*; zu *into*) ‖ ⟨theat⟩ wer macht (spielt) den Hamlet? *who performs the part of H.*? ‖ (errichten) *to erect, construct* ‖ (erheben zu) *to raise into* ‖ (ergeben) 2 + 2 macht 4 *two and two are* (*make, is*) *four* ‖ (verwandeln) ⟨arith⟩ Pfge zu M ~ *to reduce pfennigs to marks* ‖ (gehen, zurücklegen) *to go* (*a way*) ‖ denselben Weg zweimal ~ *to cover the same ground twice* ‖ (ausmachen) 20 Schilling(e) ~ ein Pfund *twenty shillings make* (od *go to*) *a pound* **5.** [**mit best. Objekt**] (mst *to make*) → **A-a** ‖ e–n Abstecher ~ nach *to take a trip to* ‖ e–m Angst ~ *to alarm a p* ‖ Anspruch ~ auf etw *to lay claim to a th* ‖ Anstalten ~ *to take measures* ‖ e–m Mädchen e–n Antrag ~ *to propose to a girl* ‖ gute Arbeit ~ *to do good work* ‖ kein Aufhebens ~ v etw *to make no fuss about a th* ‖ du wirst Augen ~ *you will be amazed* ‖ s–e Aussage ~ *to give one's evidence* ‖ gute Aussichten ~ *to offer good prospects* ‖ ⟨bill⟩ e–n **Ball** ~ *to score* od *pocket a ball* ‖ sich e–n Begriff ~ v *to get some idea of* ‖ e–e Bemerkung ~ *to pass a comment, to observe*; *to make a remark* ‖ sich [dat] Bewegung ~ *to stretch one's legs*; sich viel B. ~ *to take a great deal of exercise* ‖ e–n Bogen ~ *to go a roundabout way* ‖ ⟨fam⟩ den *or* s–n **Doktor** ~ *to take a doctor's degree* ‖ Dummheiten ~ *to play the fool* ‖ ⟨fam⟩ den Dummen ~ *to be the pigeon* ‖ e–m Durst ~ *to make a p thirsty* ‖ e–m **Ehre** ~ *to be a credit to a p* ‖ Einwände ~ *to raise objections* ‖ Ernst ~ *to take serious measures* ‖ → **Federlesen,** Feierabend, Finger, Fiasko ‖ e–e traurige Figur ~ *to cut a sorry figure* ‖ *to give* (*a p pleasure, joy, work, an impression*) ‖ → **Garaus,** Gebrauch ‖ sich [dat] Gedanken ~ über *to be disquieted about* ‖ ein Geschäft ~ *to conclude a transaction* ‖ Geschäfte ~ *to do business* ‖ → Geschichte, Geschrei ‖ ein Gesicht ~ *to pull a long face* ‖ **Haar** → ~ 2, Halt ‖ den Handlanger ~ *to act as handy man* ‖ ein gr Haus ~ *to keep an open house* ‖ Hochzeit ~ *to get married* ‖ Holz (kl) ~ *to chop wood* ‖ sich [dat] **Illusion** ~ über *to have illusions as regards* ‖ ein **Komma** ~ *to put a comma* ‖ → Kasse, Karriere ‖ jdm sein Kompliment ~ *to congratulate a p*; K.e ~ *to pay compliments* ‖ **Licht** ~ *to strike a light, to light the candle, etc.*, ⟨el⟩ *to switch on the light* ‖ → Luftsprung ‖ den wilden **Mann** ~ *to rave like a madman* ‖ Männchen ~ (Hund) *to sit up* ‖ Musik ~ *to play* (*the piano, etc.*) ‖ e–m Mut ~ *to encourage a p* ‖ sich [dat] e–n **Namen** ~ *to make a name for o.s.* ‖ e–m viel Not ~ *to give a p a good deal of trouble* ‖ **Ord**nung ~ *to tidy up* ‖ e–e **Partie** ~ *to play a game*; e–e gute P. ~ *to make a good match* ‖ → Pleite ‖ ⟨fig⟩ e–n Punkt ~ *to* (*come to a full*) *stop* ‖ **Quartier** ~ *to prepare quarters* ‖ **Radau** ~ *to kick up a row* ‖ bunte Reihe ~ *to arrange ladies and gentlemen in couples* ‖ das Rennen ~ *to win the race* ‖ mach k–e **Sachen** *don't raise any difficulties*; *do people really do this sort of things*? ‖ jdm **Schande** ~ *to bring shame upon a p* ‖ ein Schläfchen ~ *to take a nap* ‖ ⟨fig⟩ s–n Schnitt ~ *to feather one's nest* ‖ Schulden ~ *to run into debt* ‖ e–e Schwenkung ~ ⟨mil⟩ *to wheel round* ‖ e–n Seitensprung ~ *to have an escapade* ‖ e–m **Sorgen** ~ *to give a p anxiety*; sich S. ~ *to experience anxiety* ‖ er machte sich k–e S. um Ausgaben *he cared nothing for expense* ‖ das macht **Spaß** *that is fun* ‖ Späße ~ *to crack jokes* ‖ → Sprung, Staat ‖ dumme **Streiche** ~ *to indulge in mad freaks* ‖ e–n Stich ~ ⟨cards⟩ *to take a trick* ‖ sich e–n guten **Tag** ~ *to have a good day* ‖ → Testament ‖ reinen Tisch ~ *to clear ths up* ‖ ⟨sport⟩ ein Tor ~ *to score a goal* ‖ → **Umweg** ‖ e–m **Verdruß** ~ *to cause a p grief* ‖ sich ein Vergnügen ~ aus *to take pleasure in* ‖ sich [dat] ein Vermögen ~ *to make one's fortune* ‖ jdm Vorschläge ~ *to make a p suggestions* ‖ e–m Vorstellungen (→ o. Begriff ~), Vorwürfe ~ *to remonstrate with a p, to reproach a p* ‖ ⟨parl⟩ die **Wahlen** ~ *to influence the election* ‖ viel Wesens ~ um *to make a fuss about* ‖ mach k–e Witze! *don't try to be funny*! ‖ viele Worte ~ *to talk too much* **6.** [**pron. Objekt**] **das** macht man so *that's how it's done* ‖ das macht man anders *you must manage* od *do that differently* ‖ .. *but we cannot do this with air* (mit) ‖ °das können andere ~ *let George do it* ‖ ich mach **es** (vgl. I. 3. u 11.) ‖ ⟨com⟩ unter dem macht er's nicht *he won't do it for less* ‖ wir w es schon ~ *we'll be all right* ‖ es e–m wie dem anderen ~ *to treat all alike* ‖ (es) wird gemacht! *right-ho*!, *righto*! ‖ er macht es nicht mehr lange *he won't live long* ‖ **was** macht(e) das?, was kann das ~? *what of it* od *that*?, *what does* (*did*) *it matter*?; *that cuts no ice*! ‖ was ~ Sie? *what are you doing* (od *up to*)?; (gesundheitlich) *how are you*?, *how do you do*? ‖ was macht die Kunst?, was ~ Sie Schönes? ⟨fam⟩ *how is the world with you*? ‖ was soll ich nur ~? *what am I going to do about it*?; was ~ wir bloß? *what are we to do*? ‖ was ist z ~? *what is to be done*? ‖ *what did you do with the key*? (mit) ‖ *what am I to make of it* (*him, all these ths*) (aus der S, ihm, allem) ‖ was du dir schon daraus machst! *for all you care*! ‖ was macht es (die Rechnung)? *what does it* (.. zusammen .. *the sum total*) *amount to*?, ⟨fam⟩ *how much* (*is it*)? **7.** (das *or* es) macht **nichts** [Objekt]! *that doesn't matter*!, *never mind* (*that*)!, *that's of no consequence, that's quite all right* ‖ es machte nichts, daß .. *it made no difference that* **8.** [**Subjekt**] was macht **das** schon? *what's the odds*? **das** macht (⟨hum⟩ fast) gar nichts ⟨fam⟩ *no odds*!; *thank you for nothing*; **nichts zu** ~! *no go*!, *nothing doing*!, *no fear*! (→ a. 9.) ‖ (da ist dann) nichts zu ~, da kann man nichts ~ (*there is*) *nothing doing* (*then*)!, *there is no help for it then*!, *it can't be helped*! ⟨fam⟩ *there is nothing for it*! (vgl ~ bei) **9.** [**mit prep**] **an**: *much had been done to the room since then* ‖ sich **an** e–e Aufgabe ~ *to set one's hand to a task*, .. **daran** .. *to it*; *to settle down to it*; mach dich daran! *get with it*! ‖ **auf:** *put the lid on the pot*! ‖ **aus** jdm etw ~ *to build a p up* ‖ *she took* od *got the stains out of it* ‖ sich [dat] aus e–r S etw (nichts) ~ *to lay* (*no*) *weight upon a th* (*not to mind a th*, ⟨fam⟩ *not to care a pin* od *a fig* [od *a brass farthing*] *for*) ‖ *he did not care the least about her* ‖ sich viel (wenig) aus etw (jdm) ~ *to care much* (*little*) *for a th* (*a p*) ‖ ich mache mir nichts **daraus** *I don't care a pin* (etc.) ‖ mach dir nichts draus! *keep smiling*!; ⟨fam⟩ *skip it*!, *take it easy*!, ⟨Am⟩ *grin and bear it*! ‖ etw (viel) aus e–r S ~ *to make sth* (*much*) *out of an affair* ‖ er macht sich [dat] durchaus nichts aus .. *he cares nothing for books*; er macht sich nichts daraus *it* (*music*) *does not appeal to him*; sie ~ sich nichts daraus 100 Pfd. zu bezahlen *they think nothing of paying £ 100*; sich kein Gewissen daraus ~ *to have no scruples about* (zu tun *doing*) ‖ er ist nicht, was die Leute aus ihm ~ *he is not the man one imagines him to be* ‖ aus etw kein Geheimnis ~ *to make no secret of a th* ‖ *of the servant girls she made nurses* ‖ *what could we do with our lives* ‖ *what circumstances had done to him* ‖ *it made a different woman of her* ‖ aus e–m Pf. zwei ~ *to turn one penny into two* ‖ *she made our island into a great country* (vgl ~zu) ‖ **bei** mir ist nichts zu ~! *no use trying it on with me*! (vgl 8.) ‖ bei der S ist nicht viel zu ~ *there is not much to be gained by it* ‖ [ell] **in** die Hosen ~ *to have an accident in one's trousers* ‖ es war **mit** ihr nichts zu ~ *there was nothing to be done with her* ‖ was mußt du mit Wasser ~, um .. *what do you have to do to water to turn it into vapour* ‖ ⟨com⟩ wir ~ damit 10% *we are making ten per cent. out of it* ‖ jdn **zum** Doktor ~ *to confer a doctor's degree upon a p* ‖ e–n zu s–m Freunde ~ *to make friends with a p, to make a friend of a p* ‖ e–n z Gef. ~ *to take a p prisoner* ‖ etw zu G. ~ *to turn a th into money* ‖ e–n z G. ~ *to make* (*choose, elect, appoint*) *a p general* ‖ e–n z Gespött ~ *to ridicule a p* ‖ sich zur Aufgabe, zum Prinzip ~ zu tun *to make a point of doing* ‖ er machte die Nacht z Tage *he turned his nights into days* (vgl ~ aus) ‖ er machte es nur z Spaß *he .. in* (⟨Am⟩ *for*) *fun* ‖ zu eigen, zunutze ~ → I. 10. b. **10. [mit Adjektiv als Objekt]** ⟨mst⟩ *to make*, [bei Zustandswandel a.] *to render* **a. (P)** e–m **angst** u bange ~ *to instil the fear of God into a p, to frighten a p to death* ‖ e–n arm ~ *to m. a p poor, to impoverish a p* ‖ e–n aufmerksam ~ auf *to draw a p's attention to* ‖ böse *to m. a p angry*; **dumm** *to m. a fool of a p* ‖ geneigt *to m. a p feel well-disposed* ‖ gesund *to cure a p* ‖ glücklich *to m. a p happy* ‖ wieder jung *to m. a p feel young again* ‖ → kirre, mundtot ‖ namhaft *to mention a p by name* ‖ nervös *to get a p nervous* ‖ °e–n schlecht ~ ⟨fam⟩ *to run a p down* ‖ **stutzig** *to puzzle a p* ‖ verrückt *to send a p crazy* ‖ zugänglich *to render a p accessible* **b. (S)** e–m etw begreiflich ~ *to m. a p realize a th* ‖ deutlich *to m. quite clear* ‖ glaubwürdiger *to render more plausible* ‖ **klar** .. *to get a th across* ‖ leer *to empty* ‖ es (un)möglich ~ *to render* od *make it* (*im*)*possible* ‖ e–m etw mundgerecht ~ *to suit a th to a p's taste* ‖ rückgängig ~ *to cancel* (*an obligation*) ‖ sich etw schwer ~ *to do a th the hard way* ‖ sich etw zu eigen ~ *to appropriate a th*; *to acquire* (*knowledge*); e–m .. *to dedicate .. to a p* ‖ sich etw **zunutze** ~ *to turn a th to* (*good*) *account* **11. [mit Adverb]** er macht's nun mal nicht **anders** *that's his way of doing ths* ‖ es kann nicht anders gemacht w *it cannot be done any other way* ‖ es zu arg ~ ⟨fam⟩ *to come it too strong* ‖ es sich bequem ~ *to make o.s. comfortable* od *at home* ‖ **mach's** gut! (beim Abschied) *cheerio*! ⟨Am⟩ *take care of yourself* ‖ er macht's so gut er's kann *he is doing his best* ‖ mach's kurz! *cut it short* ‖ niemand kann es ihm recht ~ *nobody can satisfy him* ‖ ihm ist nichts recht zu ~ *for him you can do nothing right* ‖ man kann's nicht allen recht ~ *you cannot please everybody* ‖ wir wollen das lieber schriftlich ~ *it will be better to give* od *have that in writing* ‖ er hat mir's schon öfter so gemacht *he has often treated me like that* ‖ wie man's macht, ist's falsch *no matter what we do, it turns out wrong* **12. a. [mit acc & inf]** er hat sie glauben ~ *or* gemacht, daß .. *he made her think, he imposed on her that* .. ‖ er macht alle von sich reden *he sets all the world talking*; [ell] macht v s. r. *he makes people talk about him* ‖ **b.** etw **geltend** ~ *to make a th valid* ‖ ⟨jur⟩ *to plead* (*prescription* Verjährung) ‖ vgl II. 5. **II. sich ~ vrefl 1. (P)** er macht sich *he is getting on now*; .. geltend *he asserts h.s.*; *he* (a. *it*) *makes his* (*its*) *influence felt*; .. gut *he does well* (im Sport, Beruf); *he acquits h.s. well* ‖ er wird sich ganz gut ~ *he'll pass muster all right* ‖ er macht sich wieder (gesundheitlich) *he is all right again*; *he is mending, improving, getting better* **2. (S)** (geschehen) sich ~ (daß) *to happen, to come about* (*that*) ‖ (fortschreiten) *to advance, progress, get on* ‖ (wie geht's? –) ⟨fam⟩ es macht sich! (..) *pretty well*!, ⟨fam⟩ *pretty middling*! ‖ **es** macht sich *it will do* od *the th will go*; *it's in a fair way*; *it's picking up* ⟨a. st exch⟩ **es** macht sich wieder ‖ es wird sich schon (noch) alles ~ *all will come right* (*in the end*) ‖ **es** wird sich schon noch ~ 1 *I* (*we* etc) *shall be able to do it* (*somehow or other*) (*after all*) ‖ es wird sich schwer ~ 1 *I don't see how I can do it*; *I'm afraid I can't* (*do it*) ‖ **es** wird sich (alles) schon noch von selbst wieder ~ *all will come round again in time* ‖ es läßt sich nichts daran ~ *it can't be altered* **3. (erscheinen)** das macht sich gut *that seems, sounds, looks well enough* ‖ (kleiden) *that is very becoming, looks very well* **4. [mit prep] sich an etw** ~ *to set about, to begin*; .. mit Eifer *to attack .. with zeal, to put one's heart and soul into* .. ‖ sich an jdn heran| ~ *to approach, accost*, ⟨fam⟩ *tackle a p* ‖ sich eifrig an etw ~ *to buckle to a th* ‖ sich daran ~ zu tun *to set out* od *about to do* od *doing*; *to take to doing* ‖ sich **auf** den Weg (⟨fam⟩ die Beine) ~ *to set out* od *off, to depart, to get on one's way, to be getting along* ‖ sich **aus** dem Staube ~ *to decamp, bolt*, ⟨fam⟩ *to make off* ‖ sich **hinter** die Arbeit ~ *to set to work* ‖ sich **über** (e–n, etw) her| ~ *to rush* od *fall upon* ‖ sich ~ **zu** *to constitute o.s.* (*her companion*), *to make o.s.* (*master of* ..) ‖ sich zum Herrn e–s Landes ~ *to conquer a country* **5. [mit Adjektiv mst]** *to make* ‖ sich angenehm ~ *to m. o.s. agreeable* ‖ °sich dünn ~ *to clear out* ‖ sich gefürchtet ~ *to m. o.s. feared* od *an object of fear* ‖ sich schmuck, schön ~ *to smarten o.s. up* ‖ sich selten (rar) ~ *to m. o.s. scarce* ‖ sich verbindlich ~ zu tun *to engage* (od *to pledge o.s.*) *to do* ‖ sich um etw, e–n verdient ~ *to deserve well of a th, a p* ‖ sich verständlich ~ *to m. o.s. understood* ‖ °sich voll (schmutzig) ~ *to dirty o.s.* ‖ sich wichtig ~ *to put on an air of importance* **III. vi** [h] *to do, manage, see* **1.** wie macht der Hund? *what does the dog say* od *do*? (wauwau) ‖ der Hund macht schön .. *sits* od *stands on its hindlegs and begs* ‖ er machte „brr!" (z Pferde) "*whoa*", *he said* ‖ (Bewegung) er machte so *he went like this* od *so* ‖ linksum ~ *to wheel left about* ‖ sie ~ lange *they are a long time coming* **2.** ~ Sie doch (schnell)! *be quick, go on*, (*make haste*), *hurry up, look sharp*, ⟨fam⟩ *knock up*; ⟨Am sl⟩ *step lively, step on it* | ~, **daß** man fortkommt *to be off, to get out, to make off* od *away*; imp *get thee gone*!, *go your way, you cad*!, *away with you*!, *be off*! ‖ *see that you get there in time* **3.** e–n ~ 1 *to let a p do as he pleases* ‖ laß mich nur ~! *don't worry, I'll see to it*! **4.** ⟨com⟩ **in** Tee etc ~ *to deal in tea* ‖ in Tee wird wenig gemacht *there is little dealing in tea* ‖ ⟨fam⟩ in D. ~ *to work* (⟨fam⟩ *to dabble*) *in democracy* ‖ in Politik ~ *to busy o.s. with politics* **IV. gemacht** → I.–III. ‖ **1.** ~! *agreed*! ⟨sl⟩ *right oh*! ⟨Am sl⟩ *O.K.*!, *okay*! **2.** er ist ein gemachter Mann *he has reached the top of the tree*, ⟨fam⟩ *he is a made man* | v Menschen gemacht *man-made* (*system*) **3.** *artificial* (*flowers*), *feigned* (*indignation*) **4.** .. wie für Sie gemacht .. *fits you to a T* od *like a glove*

M·achenschaft f ~/~en *intrigue, machination*; ⟨sl⟩ *wangle*; ⟨Am sl⟩ *frame-up* ‖ durch ~ erreichen *to wangle* ‖ durch die ~ jds *through the practice of a p* ‖ dunkle ~en *evil machinations* ‖ unsaubere *dishonest, fraudulent, underhand m.s*

M·acher m ~s/~ **1.** *maker, producer* **2.** ⟨parl⟩ *wire-puller* **3.** ⟨fam⟩ *manager*; ⟨sl⟩ *big pot* **~lohn** m *cost of* (od *charge for*) *making, manufacturing-price*

Macher·ei f ~/~en *making*

|| *inferior make* || *blundering, bungling* || ⟨pol⟩ *wire-pulling*

Machiavell·ismus m ⟨pol⟩ *Machiavelli(an)ism*

Machinati·on f ~/~en *artifice, machination, intrigue, deep plot*

M·achsche Z·ahl *Mach number*, ~r Stamm *M. stem*

M·acht f ~/≃e [pl nur B.] **A. [abstr] 1.** *power* (über *over, of*) || (Herrschaft) *command, control* (*of*); *dominion* (*over*); *grip* (*on*); ⟨pol⟩ *authoritarian power* || (innere) *hold* (*of*, ⟨fig⟩ *on*); *sway* (*over*) || (gesetzmäßige) *authority* || (geistige) *ascendency* || e–e höhere ~ *an Act of God*, (vgl höhere Gewalt) || (mögliche) *potentiality* **2.** (Kraft) *force, strength*; (körperlich & geistig) *might, power* | geringe, gr ~ *limited, great power* || *power* (*of sin, seduction*) || *might* (*of corruption*) || (geheime) *influence* || ⟨fig⟩ *key* (*to*) || (vollkommene) *strangle-hold* (*on*); *convention has no hold on him* (über ihn) || *power over life and death* || *the might of British arms*; *the whole might of the Empire*; *the military might of a country* || *the force of habit* || ⟨fig⟩ *the irresistible potency* (*of her personality*) **B. [konkr] 1.** (Nation) *power* || e–e bedeutende ~ *a great p.* || ⟨fig⟩ *the heavenly p.s, the p.s of darkness*; *evil p.s* || ⟨pol⟩ *the Concert of the Great P.s* || Groß≃ *major p.* || die Achsen≃e [pl] *the Axis p.s* pl || *the British p.* || e–e fremde ~ *an alien p.* || *the Habsburg p.*; *the imperial p.* || Gleichgewicht der pol. ≃e (auf dem Kontinent) *Balance of P.* || Neun-≃e-Abkommen *Nine-P. Treaty* || Drei≃epakt *Tripartite Pact* **2.** (Heer) *military force(s* pl), *troops* pl || bewaffnete ~ *armed force* **C. 1.** s–e ganze ~ **aufbieten** *to exert all one's power* || ⟨pol⟩ s–e ~ aufzwingen *to impose its/her p. and flag* || die ~ **bek,** erreichen *to reach p.* || s–e ~ behalten über *to maintain one's hold over* || → Erweiterung || die ~ ergreifen, übernehmen *to ascend to p., to assume p.*; *to usurp the reins of government* || e–m ~ u Gewalt **geben** zu tun *to authorize a p to do* || ~ über (e–n) gewinnen, erringen *to gain p. over* || die ~ über etw in Händen **h** *to hold .. in one's p., to have mastery of* od *full p. over* || zu etw Fug u ~ h *to have full authority to do ..* || es **stärkte** die ~ der M. *it strengthened the hands of the monarchy* || die ~ **verlieren** *to go out of p.*, wieder übernehmen *to return to p.* | ⟨prov⟩ ~ geht vor Recht *might is right* **2. an** der ~ s, bleiben *to be, remain in p.* || schon lange an der ~ s ⟨engl parl⟩ *to have had a long innings* || (Kräfte) an die ~ bringen *to bring into the ascendent* || an die ~ gelangen *to ascend to p.* || **auf** dem Gipfel der ~ stehen *to have reached the zenith of one's p.* || **aus** eigener ~ *on one's own responsibility* || **durch**: *by the p. of his wealth* || sich **in** der ~ behaupten *to maintain one's p.* || jdn, etw ganz in s–r ~ h *to hold a p, a th in the hollow of one's hand*; sich in der ~ h *to keep o.s. under control* || es steht (nicht) in m–r ~ *it lies in my p.* (*it is outside of my control*) || er hat es ganz in s–r ~ ⟨fig⟩ *he has the ball at his feet* || **mit** aller ~ *with all one's might, with might and main, by main force*, (*he backed the Forum*) *for all it's worth*, (*we went at it*) *hammer and tongs* od *tooth and nail* || (*he hurled it*) *with all his strength* od *with a vengeance*, (*to strive*) *to the top of one's bent* (*after beauty*); *to go all out for a th* || **über** s–e ~ *beyond one's strength* || **von** der ~ fernhalten *to keep from power* || **zur** ~ k *to come* od *rise to p.*; wieder .. *to make one's come-back* || *the Conservatives came into office* **~befugnis** f *authority, competence*; e–m –sse übertragen *to delegate powers to a p* **~bereich** m *sphere of influence*; den ~ e–s Staates erweitern *to aggrandize a state* **~entfaltung** f *expansion of power*; größte ~ (*reached his*) *high-water mark* **~ergreifung** f *seizure of p., assumption of supreme authority* **~fülle** f *plenitude of p.* **≃gebietend** a *predominant* **~gebot** n *authoritative order* **~gefühl** n *sense of p.* **~gier** f *lust of p.*; *thirst for* (*pursuit of*) *p.* **~haber** m *potentate, ruler, lord*; *wielder of p.*; kl ~ *boss* ⟨a. pol⟩ **≃haberisch** a *dictatorial, despotic* **~handlung** f *despotic act* **~kampf** m *struggle for p.* || ⟨pol⟩ (bes ⟨a.⟩ interkontinental) *power-game* **≃liebend** a *p.-loving* **≃los** a *p.less* (gegen *against*), *impotent*, ⟨fig⟩ *numb*; ~ s ⟨a.⟩ *to be lost* (*before a p's intrigues*) || da ist man ~ *there you are* **~losigkeit** f *impotence, weakness* **~organisation** f ⟨pol⟩ *p. concentration* **~politik** f *p.-politics* **≃politisch** adv *by force* **~probe** f *trial of strength* **~sphäre** f *orbit* **~spruch** m *authoritative dictum* od *decision, fiat*; e–n ~ tun *to give a peremptory order* **~staat** m *totalitarian state* **~stellung** f *ascendency*; *p.ful position* **~streben** n *striving for p.* **≃trunken** a *p.-happy* **~übernahme** f *assumption of p.* **~verhältnis** n *balance of p.* **~vermehrung** f *aggrandizement* **≃voll** a *p.ful* (*personality, offensive*), *impressive* (*manifestation*) **~vollkommenheit** f *absolute p.*; aus eigener ~ *on one's own authority* **~wille** m *will to p.* **~wort** n *absolute command*; ein ~ sprechen *to speak a decisive word*; *to interpose one's authority*; durch ein ~ entscheiden *to pronounce a decisive judgement* (*as to*) **~zentrum** n ~s/–zentren *centre of p.* **~zusammenballung** f *concentration of p.* **m·ächtig A. I.** [a] **1.** *mighty* (*arches*); *powerful, strong* (*ruler, chap, voice, movement*); *hefty* (*fellow*); *great* (*nation*); ⟨rhet⟩ *potent* (*reasons*) **2.** (bedeutend) *considerable, formidable, immense, huge*; *massive* || *big* (*beard*), *good* (*luck*) || ⟨min⟩ *thick, wide, rich* **II. [adv]** *considerably, very, mighty* (*cold*) || ~ viel *a lot*, ⟨vulg⟩ *a mighty lot* || (*to press*) *hard* || (*to annoy*) *a lot* || (*to work*) *like a horse, with a vengeance* **B. [mit gen]** e–r P *or* S ~ s *to be master, lord of, over ..*; *to have mastery, authority over ..* || *.. command* (*of eloquence, of a language*); *.. the use* (*of only one hand*) || *he was hardly master of his senses* || s–r selbst nicht ~ s *to be out of one's senses* **III.** die **Mächtigen** pl dieser Welt *the powerful* od *mighty of this world* **M·ächtigkeit** f ~/ (→ vor.) ⟨math⟩ *power, potency* || ⟨min⟩ *thickness, width, richness* (*of a lode*) || ⟨allg⟩ *hugeness*

M·acker ~s/~ *pal, mate*; ⟨teens⟩ *hepcat*

m·acklich a *handy* (*boat*)

Madag·askar n (ostafrik. Insel) *Madagascar*; → Madegasse

M·ädchen n ~s/~ **1.** *girl* || ⟨poet⟩ *maid(en)*, *lass* || kl ~ *chit* || junges ~ *young lady*, ⟨fam⟩ *damsel*; ⟨stat⟩ *young woman* od *person*; ⟨fam⟩ *wench* || ⟨Am sl⟩ *squab* || anständiges ~ *decent, respectable girl*, ⟨mil fam⟩ *square bit* || gefallenes ~ *fallen girl* || spätes ~ *spinster, old maid* || modernes ~ *girl of the period* || unberührtes ~ *virgin* || ⟨nazi⟩ Bund Deutscher ~ (B.D.M.) *The Girl's Association of Germany* | sein ~ *his sweetheart, his best girl* || °~! (Ehefrau) *old girl!* || mit e–m ~ ausgehen ⟨fam⟩ *to trot out a judy*; er hat ein ~ geschwängert *he got a g. in trouble* **2.** (Dienst≃) *maid* || ~ für alles *maid-of-all--work* ⟨a. fig⟩, *general* (*servant*); ⟨sl⟩ *skivvy, slavey* **~anstalt** f *ladies' school* **~erziehung** f *female education* **~gymnasium** n *girl's college* **~handel** m *white slave trade, whiteslavery*; *pimping* (*trade*) **~händler** m *pimp, bawd, whiteslaver* **~heim** n, **~hort** m *home for young girls* **~jäger** m *fop lady-killer, masher* **~kammer** f *servant's bedroom* **~name** m *girl's name*; (e–r Frau) *maiden-name* **~pensionat** n *young ladies' boarding-school* **~raub** m *rape* **~räuber** m *ravisher* **~rolle** f ⟨theat⟩ *girl's part* **~schule** f *girls' school* **~stand** m *girlhood* **~stimmen** f pl *girls' voices* pl **~tratsch** m *girls'* (⟨Am sl⟩ *gals'*) *chatter* od *gossip* **~turnen** n *callisthenics* [sg] **~verbindung** f ⟨Am univ⟩ *sorority* **~zimmer** n *maid's room* **m·ädchenhaft** a *girlish, maidenly* || ⟨fig⟩ *modest, bashful* || etw ≃es zur Schau tragen *to cultivate girlish manners* | **≃igkeit** f *girlishness*; ⟨fig⟩ *bashfulness* **M·adel,** ≃ n ~s/~ *girl, girlie*; ⟨fam⟩ *filly*, ⟨vulg⟩ *gal* || ⟨Am sl⟩ *frail* || ein reizendes, liebes ~ *a perfect duck* ‖ hübsches ~ *flyer* ‖ ⟨sex vulg⟩ *bird, bit*

M·ade f ~/~n *maggot, (cheese-)mite* ‖ (Fliegen~̈) *gentle* ‖ ich sitze hier wie die ~ im Speck *I'm as snug as a bug in a rug* **m·adig** a *maggoty* ⟨*cheese*⟩, *full of mites* ‖ *worm-eaten* (*fruit*) | ⟨fig⟩ *paltry* (*fellow*) ‖ e–n ~ m *to speak ill of a p, to run down a p*

Madeg·asse m ~n/~n, **-ssin** f ~/~nen (Bewohner von Madagaskar) **m-ssisch** a *Malagasy*

Mad·eira [maˈdeːra] n (portug. Atlantikinsel)

Madj·ar m → Magy·ar

Mad·onna f ~/–nnen *the Madonna, the Holy Virgin*; ⟨paint⟩ ~ in der Felsengrotte *V. of the Rocks*, Stillende ~ *V. Suckling the Child* **Mad·onnen-** **~bild** n *image of the V.* **~̈haft** a *M.-like* **~scheitel** m (*woman's*) *middle-parting* **~verehrung** f *M.-worship*

M·adras n (vorderind. Staat & Stadt) *Madras*

Madr·id n ⟨Span⟩ (Hauptstadt) **Madr·ider** m, **~in** f *Madrilenian*

Madrig·al n ~s/~e *madrigal*

Mad·ura n **1.** (Sunda-Insel) **2.** (Stadt der vorderind. Prov. Madras)

m·ag [1. & 3. sg pres] v mögen; ~ s! *may be*!

Magalhães- [magalˈjɑːẽŋs] od **Magell·anland** n *Magellan's Land* **Magalhães-** od **Magell·anstraße** f *Strait of Magellan*

Magaz·in n ~(e)s/~e *warehouse, storehouse* ‖ im ~ aufbewahren *to store, w.h.* ‖ ⟨mil⟩ *stores* pl, *depot*; (am Gewehr) *magazine* ‖ ⟨theat⟩ *scene dock* ‖ ⟨comp⟩ *feed* | (Zeitschrift) *m., review* **~aufseher** m *storeman* **~gewehr** n *repeating rifle* **~schönheit** f *pin-up girl* **~sendung** f ⟨telv⟩ z. B. *Report, Panorama* **~streifen** m (am MG) *container* **~verpflegung** f ⟨mil⟩ *provisioning from depots* **~verwalter** m *storekeeper* **~verwaltung** f *administration of stores* **~̈·ieren** vt [h] *to w.h., to store*

M·agd f ~/~̈e (*maid-*)*servant*, (*serving-*)*maid* ‖ Hausfrau u ~ *mistress and maid* ‖ ⟨poet⟩ *maiden* ‖ ⟨fig⟩ *handmaid* (*of theology, of the Lord*) | **~̈lein** n ~s/~ *little maid, girl* ‖ ⟨poet⟩ *maiden* ‖ ⟨urspr. Sc⟩ *lassie*

Magdal·enenstrom m (in Kolumbien) *the Magdalena*

M·agdeburg n ⟨Ger⟩ (Stadt an der Elbe)

M·agen m ~s/~̈ *stomach*, ⟨fam⟩ *tummy*; *inside, little Mary*, ⟨sl⟩ *craw* ‖ ⟨zoo⟩ *maw*; ⟨orn⟩ *gizzard* ‖ auf den leeren ~ *on an empty st.* ‖ (of anger) sich auf den ~ legen *to affect the st.* ‖ empfindlicher ~ *queasy* od *weak st.* ‖ e–n guten ~ h *to have a good digestion* ‖ (of food) schwer im ~ liegen *to sit heavy on the st.* ‖ ⟨fam⟩ *it sticks in my gizzard* ‖ er hat mit dem ~ zu tun *he has got a st.* ‖ sich [dat] den ~ anstopfen mit *to fill one's belly with*; .. verderben *to upset one's st.* ‖ e–n verdorbenen ~ h *to suffer from indigestion*(*s* pl) ‖ ⟨fig⟩ es dreht sich e–m der ~ um *one feels sick in one's st.* ‖ er (es) liegt mir im (fällt mir auf den) ~ ⟨fam⟩ *I am sick of him* (*it*) ‖ ich habe ihn im ~ *I cannot stand him* **~beschwerden** f pl *indigestion* **~bitter** m (*cordial*) *bitter*(*s* pl) **~brei** m *chyme* **~brennen** n *heart-burn*; (*water*) *brash*, ⟨med⟩ *pyrosis* **~-Darm-Kanal** m *gastro-intestinal tract* **~drücken** n *pain in* od *pressure on the st.* **~elixier** n *st.-elixir* **~erweiterung** f *dilatation of the st.* **~essenz** f *cordial drops* pl **~fieber** n *gastric fever* **~gegend** f *epig.c region* **~geschwür** n *g.c ulcer* **~grippe** f *g.c influenza* **~grube** f *pit of the st.*; ⟨box⟩ *wind* **~katarrh** m *cold in the st.* **~knurren** n ⟨fam⟩ *collywobbles* pl **~krampf** m *st.-spasms* pl ‖ *cardialgy* **~̈krank, ~̈leidend** a *dyspeptic* **~krankheit** f, **~leiden** n *st.-complaint* **~krebs** m *cancer in the st.* **~mittel** n *st.ic* **~mund** m ⟨anat⟩ *orifice of the st.* **~pflaster** n *st.-plaster* ‖ ⟨fig fam⟩ *square meal* **~saft** m *g.c juice* **~säure** f *acidity, g.c acid* **~schmerzen** m pl *st.-ache* **~schnitt** m ⟨surg⟩ *gastrotomy* **~schwäche** f *dyspepsia* **~spülung** f *g.c lavage* **~̈stärkend** a *st.ic, tonic* **~stärkung** f *st.ic* **~tropfen** m pl *cordial drops* pl, *digestive tonic* **~verstimmung** f ⟨med⟩ *disordered st.* **~wand** f ⟨anat⟩ *coat of the st.* **~weh** n *st.-ache* **~wein** m *st.ic wine*

m·ager I. [a] *lean, fatless* (*meat*), *thin* (*p*) ‖ *slender* ‖ *scraggy*; ⟨Am a.⟩ *scrawny* ‖ (hager) *ill-conditioned, emaciated* ‖ (Kost) *jejune, meagre* ⟨a. fig⟩, *slender, frugal* (*diet*) | ⟨fig⟩ *barren* (*soil*) ‖ *poor* (*crop, lime, result*) ‖ *meagre* (*outcome, concrete*) ‖ *small* (*profit*) ‖ ⟨min⟩ *attle, mute* ‖ *non-* od *semi-bituminous* (*coal*) ‖ ⟨typ⟩ *lean-faced* (*type*), *prosy, dry* (*book*) | die sieben ~en J. *the seven lean years* od *y. of famine* ‖ ~e P *scrag* ‖ ~ w *to thin down*; (v Vieh) *to fall away* **II. das ~̈e** n ⟨cul⟩ *the lean* | **~̈keit** f ~/ *leanness, meagreness* ‖ *thinness, slenderness* ‖ etc. ‖ *prosiness* **~̈käse** m *lean cheese* **~̈milch** f *skim*(*med*) *milk* | ~pulver [n] *powdered skim m.* **~sucht** f *leanness*

Mag·ie f ~/ *magic* (*art*) ‖ *the black art* **M·agier** m ~s/~ *m.ian* **m·agisch** a ⟨fig⟩ *m.* (*square*); *m.al* (*illuminations*) ‖ ⟨fig⟩ *irresistible* (*power*)

Mag·ister m ~s/~; ~ der freien Künste (Artium) *Master of Arts* (*M.A.*) ‖ (Schulmeister) (*school*)*master* **Magistr·at** m ~(e)s/~e *municipal board, B. of Control* ‖ *municipal* (od *town*) *council*

Magistr·ats- **~beamte(r)** m *municipal officer* **~mitglied** n, **~p** f *magistrate, town-councillor* **~sitzung** f *meeting of the t. council* **~würde** f *magistracy*

M·agma n ~s/–men *magma*

Magn·at m ~en/~en *magnate, grandee*; ⟨Am fam⟩ *tycoon*; ⟨sl⟩ *czar* (z. B. *cinemaczar*)

Magn·esia f ~/; gebrannte ~ *burnt magnesia*

Magn·esium n ~s/ *magnesium*

Magn·et m ~(e)s/e *magnet* ‖ ⟨min⟩ *loadstone* **~anker** m *armature* **~apparat** m *m.o* **~band** n *magnetic tape* | ~schreiber [m] *m.ic* od *tape recorder*; verschiedene ~systeme [pl] *range of m.ic t. systems*; ~test [m] *m.ic t. testing* **~eisenstein** m → Magnetit **~feld** n *m.ic field* **~kies** m ⟨min⟩ *m.ic pyrites* **~kupplung** f *m.ic clutch* **~mine** f *m.ic mine* **~nadel** f; Ausschlag der ~ *deflection of the m.ic* od *compass needle* **~schalter** m ⟨mot⟩ *ignition switch* **~schenkel** m ⟨el⟩ *pole piece* **~spule** f ⟨el⟩ *m.ic coil* **~stäbchen** n *m.ic bar* **~stein** m *loadstone* **~ton-** ~film [m] *m.ic film*; ~kamera [f] *sound c.*; ~läufer [m] ⟨rec⟩ *soundhead* **~trommel** f ⟨comp⟩ *m.ic drum store* **~zünder** m *m.o* **~zündung** f *m.o-ignition* **magn·etisch** a *m.ic* (*force, storm*; *trance*); ~e Pole der Erde *terrestrial m.ic poles*; ~e Wasserkrafterzeugung *magneto-hydrodynamics* ‖ ~ Nord *compass north* ‖ ~ m *to m.ize*

Magnetis·eur [magnetiˈzøːə] m ~(e)s/~e *m.izer, mesmerist* **magnetis·ierbar** a *m.izable* **Magnetis·ieren** n ~s/ *m.ization* ‖ *mesmerization, hypnotization* **magnetis·ieren** vt [h] *to m.ize* (*iron*, etc) ‖ *to mesmerize, hypnotize* (*a p*) **Magnetis·ierung** f *m.ization*, etc | ~sstärke [f] ⟨phys⟩ *m.ic field strength, m.ic force* **Magnet·ismus** m ~/ *m.ism* (remanent *residual*) ‖ = Mesmerismus ‖ Lehre (f) vom ~ *m.ics* **Magnet·it** m ~(e)s/~e *magnetite* | ~trübe [f] *m. densemedium* **magn·eto-** **~elektrisch** a *m.o-electrical* **~̈induktion** f *m.ic induction* **~̈phon**® n (*m.ic*) *tape recorder* | ~band [n] *recording tape, t. recorder*

Magnifiz·enz f ~/~en ⟨Ger univ⟩ (Rektortitel) Eure, seine ~ *Your, His magnificence*

Magn·olie f ~/~n ⟨bot⟩ *magnolia*; → *bay*

magst [2. sg ind. pres] v mögen

Magy·ar(e) m, **Magy·arin** f *Magyar* **magy·arisch** a *Magyar, Hungarian*

mäh intj (der Schafe) *bah*!

Mahag·oni n ~s/ *mahogany* (*wood*)

Mahar·adscha m ~s/~s *maharajah*

M·ahd f ~/~en (das Mähen) *mowing* ‖ (Schwaden) *swath* ‖ (Ernte) *haycrop* ‖ *day's work of a* *mower* || Sw [n] *Alpine meadow* **M·äh- ~binder** m *reaper-and-binder* **~drescher** m ⟨agr Am⟩ *combine (-harvester)* **~maschine** f *mower, reaper, harvester*; ⟨hort⟩ *lawn-mower* | ~nführer [m] *reaping machine driver* **M·ähen** n ~s/ *mowing* **m·ähen** vt/i [h] *to cut, crop (grass), to reap (corn)* **M·äher** m ~s/~ *mower* || *harvester, haymaker*

M·ahl[1] n ~(e)s/~e & M·ähler *meal, repast* || (festliches ~) *banquet* (→ ~zeit) **~schatz** m *dowry, portion* **~stätte** f *meeting place* || *place of execution* **~zeit** f *meal, repast* || anständige ~ *square meal* || ~ halten, einnehmen *to have, eat, take a meal* || gemeinsame ~ ⟨engl univ⟩ *(he ate his) commons (= dined in hall)*; nach der ~ *after hall*; ⟨mil⟩ *after mess* || kalte Abend≈ ⟨engl⟩ *(meat-)tea (she ate an excellent tea)* || ⟨rail⟩ *service (book for the first s.)* || sie trafen sich bei Tisch zu e–r ~ *they met at table over a meal* || ~en [pl] *meals*, ⟨Am sl⟩ *eats* pl || (gesegnete) ~! (Engl & Am ungebräuchlich [etwa: *I hope you will enjoy* bzw *have enjoyed your dinner*]) || ⟨vulg⟩ (als Gruß) etwa: *hallo, chaps!* || ⟨fig iron⟩ prost ~! *no idea of it!, I'll see you further first* || Bett? Prost ~! *Bed, indeed!* || da h wir die Proste ~ *here we are (in a nice mess)!*

m·ahlen vt/i [h] *to grind* || grob ~ *to crush, bruise* || fein ~ *to pulverize* || ⟨mot⟩ *(the wheels) skid (in the sand)* || ⟨pap⟩ *to beat*: rösch ge~ *free beaten*, schmierig ge~ *wet-beaten* || ⟨mill⟩ (Halbzeug) *to break* **M·ahl**[2]- **~aggregat** n *grinder* **~anlage** f *grinding plant* **~bahn** f ⟨mill⟩ *g.ing zone* od *track* **~fläche** f ⟨tech⟩ *rubbing-surface* **~gang** m *set of mill-stones* **~gast** m *miller's customer* **~geld** n *miller's fee* **~gerinne** n *mill-trench* **~gut** n *grist*; ⟨tech mill⟩ *raw material; material under treatment; finished product* | ~eintragung [f] *feed(ing)*; ~eintritt [m] *raw feed entrance*; ~stück [n] *feed piece* **~holländer** m ⟨pap⟩ *beater* **~knecht** m *miller's man* **~korn** n *corn to be ground* **~körper** m *g.ing rollers* | ~füllung [f] *g.ing media* pl **~kranz** m *g.ing ring* **~mühle** f *(flour- od corn-) -mill*, ⟨Am⟩ *(grist-)mill* || ⟨min⟩ *crushing drum* **~platte** f *g.ing track* **~recht** n *right to mill* || **~sand** m ⟨geog⟩ *quicksand* **~schüssel** f ⟨mill⟩ *g.ing table* **~stein** m *millstone* **~steuer** f *duty on ground corn* od *on g.ing* **~strom** m → Malstrom: *maelstrom* **~trommel** f *g.ing drum* **~werkzeuge** pl *disintegrating* od *g.ing elements* **~zahn** m *molar, grinder* **m·ahlbar** a *millable (wheat)*

m·ählich a = allmählich; gemach, ≈lich

M·ahn- ~brief m, **~schreiben** n *hortatory letter* || (e–s Gläubigers) *dunning-letter, request of payment* **~glocke** f *warning bell* **~mal** n *monument, memorial* **~ruf** m *warning cry* **~schreiben** n *hastener* **~verfahren** n *hortative process* **~wort** n *(word of) exhortation* **~zettel** m *reminder* **m·ahnbar** a *claimable (as a debt), demandable* **m·ahnen** vt [h] *to remind, warn, admonish* || e–n an etw ~ *to remind a p of a th, to recall a th to a p's mind* || ~d *admonitory (finger)* || e–n zu etw ~ *to exhort a p to do a th* || e–n brieflich ~ *to write a monitory letter to a p* || (e–n wegen e–r Schuld ~) *to demand payment of, to dun, to press a p for payment* || (brieflich) *to claim one's debts from a p* | [abs] ⟨anti-aero⟩ *to sound a* od *the warning*; die Dämmerung mahnt zur Eile *the dusk makes us realise the necessity for haste* **M·ahner** m ~s/~ *admonisher, monitor* || (Gläubiger) *creditor, dun(ner)* || (Gewissen) *conscience* **M·ahnung** f ~/~en *reminder, exhortation, admonition, warning*; ~ z Vorsicht *cautionary note* || (um e–e Schuld) *summons to pay, demand of payment, dunning*

M·ähne f ~/~n ⟨zoo⟩ *mane* || (P) *head of hair, long hair* **~nschaf** n *maned sheep*

Mah·onie f ~/~n ⟨bot⟩ *mahonia* → d.

M·ahr m ~(e)s/~e *nightmare*

Mahr·atte, Mar·athe m, **Mahr·attin, Mar·athin** f (Angehörige[r] e–s Hinduvolks) *Mahratta*

M·ähre f ~/~n (Stute) *mare* || ⟨dero⟩ *jade*

M·ähre m, **M·ährin** f *Moravian* **M·ähren** n *Moravia* **m·ährisch** a *Moravian*; ≈ **Schönberg** n *Sumperk* **M·ährisches Ges·enke** n *M. Mountains* pl, *M. Chain*

×**m·ähren** vi [h] *to dawdle*

M·ai m [~ & ~(e)s, ⟨poet⟩ ~en/] *May* || im ~ *in M.* || im Wonnemonat ~ *in the blissful month of M.* || der 1. ~ *the first of M.* || des Lebens ~ *the prime of life* **~baum** m *May-pole* **~blume** f = ·~-glöckchen **~bowle** f = ~trank **~feier** f *May-day* **~fest** n ⟨a.⟩ *beltane* **~glöckchen** n ⟨bot⟩ *lily of the valley* **~grün** n *first verdure* || (Farbe) *celadon* **~käfer** m ⟨ent⟩ *cockchafer*, ⟨bes Am⟩ *may bug* || °⟨fig⟩ er denkt über die Unsterblichkeit der ~ nach *he thinks about breakfast* °≈**käfern** vi [h] *to think over a speech, to chew the cud* **~kätzchen** n ⟨bot⟩ *catkin* **~königin** f *Queen of (the) May* **~lüftchen,** ≈**lüfterl** n *vernal breeze* **~trank** m ⟨Ger⟩ *May-wine, wine flavoured with woodruff*

M·aid f ~/~en *maid, maiden*, → Magd

M·aie f ~/~n ⟨bot⟩ *birch* || *green bough* **M·aien-** → Mai- **~blüte** f *flowering-season* || ⟨fig⟩ in s–r Sünden ~ *in the flush prime of his sins* || in der ~ des I. *when Imperialism was flourishing*

M·ailand n ⟨It⟩ (Stadt) *Milan* **M·ailänder** m, **~in** f, **m·ailändisch** a *Milanese*

Main, der ⟨Ger⟩ (Fluß) *the Main*

Maine [mein] n (Staat der U.S.A.)

Mainz n ⟨Ger⟩ (Stadt am Rhein) *Mayence*

M·ais m [~ & M·aises/] *maize*, ⟨Am⟩ *(Indian) corn*; grüner ~ *niblets* pl **~brei** m ⟨Am⟩ *hominy* **~brot** n ⟨Am⟩ *pone* **~flocke** f *corn flake* **~grieß** m (grober) *samp* **~kolben** m ⟨Am⟩ *corn-cob* **~kuchen** m *hoecake* **~mehl** n ⟨Am⟩ *Indian meal* **~whisky** m *corn*, ⟨sl⟩ *c.mule*

M·aischbottich m *mash(ing)-tub*; ⟨brew⟩ *keeve* **M·aische** f ~/~n *mash* **m·aischen** vt [h] *to mash*

M·aisur n (Vorderind. Bezirk) *Mysore*

Maitr·esse [mɛːˈtresə] f = Mätresse

Maj·estas f (Mariae) ⟨arts⟩ *Majesty* **Majest·ät** f ~/~en *majesty* ⟨a. fig⟩ || Eure ~ *Your M.* | ≈**isch** a *majestic* || ⟨fig⟩ *grand, imposing, awe-inspiring* || der Berg lag ~ vor mir .. *lay before me in all its m.y* | adv *m.ically*; ~ hineinsegeln, ~ hereink ⟨fig fam⟩ *to sail in* **Majest·äts- ~beleidigung** f *lese-majesty* **~brief** m *charter* **~plural** m "*We*" *used by sovereigns* **~recht** n *sovereign's prerogative* **~verbrechen** n *high treason* **~verbrecher** m *offender against the sovereign*

Maj·olika f ~/–ken *majolica* **~fabrik** f *pottery*

Majon·äse f → Mayonnaise

Major·an m ~s/ ⟨bot⟩ *marjoram*; wilder ~ *origan*

Maj·or m ~s/~e ⟨mil⟩ *major* || Herr ~! *Major!* | **~in** f ~in/~innen *major's wife* **~secke** f *critical period in an officer's career* **~srang** m *majorship* **Major·at** n ~(e)s/~e *(right of) primogeniture* || (Gut) *entail* **~sherr** m *owner of entailed property* **Majord·omus** m ~/~ ⟨hist⟩ *mayor* od *steward (of the palace)* || ⟨fam⟩ *major-domo* **major·enn** [pred a] *of (full) age, major (you are m.)* || ~ w *to come to one's majority, to come of age* ≈**it·ät** f ~/ *majority, full age* **majoris·ieren** vt [h] *to beat by a majority of votes* **Majorit·ät** f ~/~en *majority* || absolute ~ *absolute m.*; ⟨Am⟩ *m.* **~sbeschluß** m *resolution carried by a m.* **Maj·uskel** f ~/~n ⟨typ⟩ *capital (letter)*

Maj·orca, Maj·orka, Mall·orca n (span. Insel im Mittelmeer) *Majorca*

Makad·am- ~pflaster n *macadam pavement* **~straße** f *m.ized road* ≈**isieren** vt [h] *to m.ize*

Maked·onien n → Mazedonien

M·akel m ~s/~ *spot, stain* || *blot* ⟨a. fig⟩ *(on a p's character)* || ⟨fig⟩ *blemish, flaw, defect, stigma* || *odium (to bear the o. of ..)*; (Beschuldigung) *imputation* || ohne ~ *immaculate, without blame* || mit e–m ~ behaftet *afflicted with a blemish*;

tainted **Mäkel·ei** f ~/~en *fault-finding, carping* || *c.g criticism* || (im Essen) *fastidiousness* **m·äkelig** a *f.-f.g*, ⟨fam⟩ *fussy*; (im Essen) *fastidious* **m·akellos** a *spotless, stainless, flawless, undefiled*; *virgin*; *unblemished*; *perfect* || *immaculate* ⟨a. theol⟩ | adv ~ weiß *virgin white* | **≗igkeit** f ~/ *flawlessness, spotlessness, immaculateness* **m·äkeln** vi [h] (an [dat]) *to find fault* (*with*), *to pick* (*at* [*a p, one's food*]) || (über [acc]) *to cavil* (*at, about*) || mäkele nicht! *don't be finding fault* (*with everything*)! **M·äkler** m ~s/~ *fault-finder, caviller*

m·akeln vi [h] *to act as broker* **M·akler** m ~s/~ ⟨com⟩ *agent, factor*, ⟨Am⟩ *solicitor* || (Börsen≗) (*inside-*)*broker* || (Güter≗) *land jobber* **Makler·ei** f ~/~en ⟨com⟩ *commission business* || *agent's* od *broker's dealings* **M·akler-** **~gebühr** f *brokerage* **~geschäft** n *broker's business* **~lohn** m, **~provision** f *brokerage* **~stand** n [konkr] *pit*

M·aki m ~s/~s ⟨zoo⟩ *maki* → Lemure, Halbaffe

Makkab·äer m pl ⟨bib⟩ *Maccabees*

Makkar·oni pl *macaroni* pl

Makr·ele f ~/~n ⟨ich⟩ *mackerel* (*shoals of m.*) **~nfang** m *m.-catching* **~nfänger** m *m.-boat*

Makrok·osmos m ~/ *macrocosm*

m·akromolekul·ar a *macromolecular*

Makr·one f ~/~n (Gebäck) *macaroon*

Makulat·ur f ~/~en *waste-paper*; ⟨print⟩ *spoilage* || ⟨fig⟩ *worthless book* || reden Sie k–e ~! *don't talk rubbish*! **~bogen** m *waste* od *spoilt sheet* **~papier** n *waste paper*

M·al 1. n ~(e)s/~e *time* || ein anderes ~, ein ander≗ *another time, some other time* || dieses ~, dies≗ *this time* od *bout, this once* || drei≗ *thrice, three times*, drei≗ so alt wie er *three times his age*; drei≗ vier ist zwölf *three times four are twelve* || drei- bis vier≗ *three or four times* || ein- bis zwei≗ *once or twice* || da war das eine ~, als *there was the occasion on which* || dieses eine ~ *this once* || einige ~e *once or twice, sometimes* || das einzige ~ *the only time* || ein einziges ~ *a single time* || etliche ~e *several times* || das erste (u das letzte) ~, ein erstes ~ *the first* (*and the last*) *time* (→ erste C., jedes≗, kein≗) || manches (liebe) ~ *sometimes, many* (*and many*) *a time* || mehrere ~e *several times* || nächstes *or* das nächste ~ *next time* || ein paar ~e *a few times* || unzählige ~e *countless times, times without number* || die vielen ~e *the number of times* || voriges ~ *last time* | **beim** ersten ~e (*at*) *the first time*, ⟨fam⟩ *at the* od *one's first go*(*-off*) || beim letzten ~e *on the last occasion* || **für** das *or* dies e–e ~ *this time, for once, for the nonce* || ein für alle≗ *for good, once* (*and*) *for all*; ⟨Am a.⟩ *first, last, and all the time*; .. aus s *to be gone and done with* || **mit** e–m ~e *all at once, all of a sudden*; *with a leap, at one go* || **noch** einmal *once more* || ein **über** das andere ~ *over and over again* || ein **ums** andere ~ *alternately, by turns* || **zum** andern ~e *a* (od *for the*) *second time* || zum letzten≗ *for the last time* || zum soundsovielten ~e *time* (od *again*) *and again* || zu tausend ~en *many thousand times* || zu verschiedenen ~en *at various times* || zu wiederholten ~en *repeatedly, time after time, time* (od *again*) *and again* || e–n zum letzten ~e ansehen *to look one's last at a p* || zum wievielten ~e? *how often*? || zum zweiten ~e *the second time* **2.** n [~(e)s/~e & ≗er] *spot, stain*; (Wundmal[e]) *stigma*[*ta*] || (am menschlichen Körper) (*birth-*)*mark, mole*; ⟨med⟩ *naevus* || ein blaues ~ *a bruise* || (Zeichen) *mark, sign, token* || (Grenz~) *boundary* || ⟨sport allg⟩ *post, base* || (Ziel) *goal* || (Ablauf~) *start*(*ing-point*) **~linie** f ⟨crick⟩ *bowling-* (Schock-), bzw *popping-line* (Schlag-) **~stein** m *landmark*

mal[1] (= einmal) (im Märchen) es war (ein)~ *once* (*upon a time*) *there was* | ⟨**fam**⟩ *just* (*come here*!); sieh (**doch**) ~ *look at that*; sieh ~ e–r an! *well I never*!, laß ~ sehen *let me* (*just*) *have a look*!; wenn du ~ vorbeikommst, .. *if you should come past* .. | **noch**~ *once more* || du könntest ~ zu ihm gehn *you might take an opportunity to call on him* || das ist ~ 'ne Familie! *that is a family, that is*! || es ist **nun** ~ nicht anders, das ist nun ~ so *it can't be helped, such is life* || aber es ist nun ~ so *but there it is* || so sind wir nun ~ *that is how we are* || er ist nun ~ so *he is like that* || da die Dinge nun ~ so liegen *things being what they are* | wenn das ~ (= **nur**) gut geht! *let's hope it will turn out all right* | es ist **nicht** ~ wahr *it isn't even true* || **sag**' ~! *I say*!, *just tell me*! || geh' ~ hin *just go there* || *now and then* (*let us hear from you n. & th.* || schreib' ~! *write sometime* | **.. mal** [suff] ein~ *once*, zwei~ *twice*, drei~ *three times, thrice* | **.. malig** [suff] .. *fold* (*a threefold warning*) ein~ *unique* (*opportunity*)

m·al[2] adv **1.** ⟨math⟩ (→ Mal) [schreib × *or* ·] 3 × 3 ist *or* macht 9 *3 times 3 are/make* ⟨Am⟩ *equals 9*; 2 · 2 = 4 *twice 2 are/make* ⟨Am⟩ *equals 4*; ein~ ist kein~ ⟨prov⟩ *once does not count*

m·al- **~nehmen** vt [h] *to multiply* (*m. 6 by 4 and the product is 24* od *6 m-ied by 4 is 24*) | ≗ n *multiplying, multiplication* **≗zeichen** n *multiplication mark* od *sign*

M·al- (→ malen) **~gerüst** n ⟨bes theat⟩ *paint-frame* **~grund** m (→ Bild–) *support* | (Grundierung) *groun*(*ding*) **~kasten** m *colour-box* **~kunst** f *art of painting* || die ~ *the brush* **~stock** m ⟨arts⟩ *maulstick* **~utensilien** pl *painting material*

M·alabar n (vorderind. Bezirk) *Malabar*

Malach·it m ~s/~e ⟨min⟩ *malachite*

M·alaga m ~s/~s (Wein) *Malaga*

Mal·aie m, **Mal·aiin** f *Malay* (*man*, f *woman*), *Malayan* **mal·aiisch** a *Malay*(*an*); ≗e H·albinsel [f] → Malakka; ≗er Archip·el [m] *Malaysia*

Mal·ak(k)a, Halbinsel (in Hinterindien) *Malacca* (*peninsula*); Straße v ~ *Strait of M.*

Mal·aria f ~/ ⟨med⟩ *malaria*

M·älarsee m (in Schweden) *Lake Maelar*

Mal·aysia n *Malaysia*

Mal(e)d·iven f pl *Maldive Islands, Maldives*

Malef·iz- **~junge, ~kerl** m ⟨fam⟩ *rascal, scamp*

m·alen vt [h] *to paint* (a. vi [h]), ⟨fam⟩ *to do* || er malt *he is a p.er* || sie malt etw *she does a little p.ing* || → streichen || in leicht getöntem Weiß gemalt *p.ed a faded white* || sie ist zum ≗ schön *she is a perfect picture* || es ist zum ≗ *it is worth painting* || ⟨fig⟩ *to represent, delineate*; *to portray* | **an** e–m Bilde ~ *to be p.ing a picture* || **auf** Glas ~ *to p. on glass* || **in** Email ~ *to anneal, to enamel* || in Öl ~ *to p. in oils* || **nach** e–m Muster .. *from a model*; nach dem Leben, der Natur *from life, from nature* || **sich ~ l** *to have one's picture taken, to sit for one's portrait* | ⟨übtr⟩ die Buchstaben ~ *to take pains with one's writing* || auf s–m Antlitz malte sich Entsetzen *an expression of horror came into his face* || der Sonnenuntergang malt sich im Wasser *the sunset is reflected in the water* || mit gemalten Wangen *with rouge on her cheeks* | **Redensarten**: mal' den Teufel nicht an die Wand! *talk of the devil and* (*he will appear*) || mal dir 'was! *you may go and whistle for it*!, *catch me doing it*! *not I*! || ich werde ihm was ~ *I'll give him a bit of my mind* **M·aler** m ~s/~ *painter* (f *paintress, lady-p.er*); ~ der Bewegung *action p.er* || (= Künstler) *artist* (f *lady artist*) || (gewerblich) *house-p.er* (*by trade*) **~akademie** f (*p.ing-*)*academy, academy of p.ing* **~arbeiten** f pl *decorations* pl, *p.ing* **~atelier** n (*artist's*) *studio* **~beruf** m *pictorial calling* **~esel** m *easel* **~farbe** f *p.er's colour* **~gold** n *p.er's gold, ormolu* **~instinkt** m *p.er sense* **~leinwand** f *canvas* **~muschel** f ⟨zoo⟩ *p.er's gaper* **~pinsel** m *p.er's brush* **~schule** f 1. *academy of p.ing* 2. *Dutch*, etc. *school of p.ers* **~silber** n *silver powder* **~staffelei** f *easel* **~stock** m *maulstick* **~stuhl** m *sketching-stool* **Maler·ei** f ~/~en (Kunst) (*art of*) *p.ing* || (Gemälde) *picture, p.ing* || ~ grau in grau *grisaille* || (auf e–r Vase) *p.ing* **m·alerisch** a *picturesque*, *romantic; scenic* | adv *romantically (situated)*; ~e Schönheit *p.ness* || das ≈e *the p.*

Malh·eur [ma'løə] n [~s/~s & ~e] *misfortune, mishap* || es ist ihm ein kl ~ passiert *he has had a little mishap* **malizi·ös** a *malicious, spiteful*

M·all n ~(e)s/~e ⟨mar⟩ *mould, model*

Mall·orka, -ca → Majorca

M·almö (schwed. Stadt)

°**mal·ochen** vi [h] ⟨sl⟩ (in jail) *to do time*

M·alstrom m ~s/~e *maelstrom, whirlpool*

M·alta n (Mittelmeerinsel) **Malt·eser** m, **~in** f (Bewohner Maltas) *Maltese*

M·alter m & n ~s/~ (Holzmaß etwa:) *cord* || (Getreidemaß) *12 bushels* pl

Malt·eser- ~kreuz n *Maltese cross* **~orden** m *order of Malta* **~ritter** m *Maltese Knight*

malträt·ieren vt [h] *to ill-treat*

Malvas·ier m ~s/ (Wein) *malmsey*

M·alve f ~/~n ⟨bot⟩ *mallow* **≈nartig** a *malvaceous* **≈nfarben** a *mauve*

M·alz n ~es/ *malt* || ⟨fig⟩ an ihm ist Hopfen u ~ verloren *it's all thrown away on him, he's a hopeless case* **~bereitung** f *m.ing* **~bier** n *m.-beer, ale* **~boden** m *m.-loft* **~bonbon** n *cough-lozenge* **~darre** f *m.-kiln* **~extrakt** m *extract of m.* **~keime** m pl ⟨brew⟩ *m. sprouts* **~steuer** f *m.-tax, m.-shot* **~tenne** f *m.-floor* **~trank** m *m.-drink* **~zucker** m ⟨chem⟩ *m.ose* **m·älzen** vt/i [h] *to malt* **M·älzer** m ~s/~ *maltman, maltster* **Mälzer·ei** f ~/~en 1. *malting* 2. *malt-house*

Mam·a f ~/~s *mamma* || ⟨fam⟩ Mammi *ma, mum(s), mummy*; ⟨Am⟩ *mom*

Mamel·ucken m pl (oriental. Leibwache) *Mamelukes* pl

M·ammon m ~s/ *mammon, pelf* || dem ~ dienen *to worship M.* || Liebe zum ~ *love of gold* || der schnöde ~ *filthy lucre* **~sdiener** m *worldling, m.ist* **~sdienst** m *m.-worship*

M·ammut n [~(e)s/~s & ~e] ⟨hist-zoo⟩ *mammoth* **~baum** m *m. tree*, ⟨bot⟩ *sequoia* **~sendung** f ⟨telv⟩ *telethon* (vgl *Marathon*) **~vergrößerung** f *giant enlargement* **~zahn** m *m. tusk*

m·ampfen vt/i [h] *to munch (like a cow)*

Mams·ell f ~/~en & ~s *shop-girl, miss* || ⟨fam⟩ *damsel* || (Wirtschafterin) *housekeeper* || kalte ~ *waitress who distributes cold dishes only*

m·an 1. [indef pron] [dat e–m; acc e–n] *one, people, men, we, you, they*; ⟨fam⟩ *a fellow (can't a f. ask?)* | ~ klopft *somebody is knocking* || wenn e–m nicht wohl ist, bleibt ~ „ *if one does not feel well one had better stay at home* || der Eindruck, den ~ hatte, war *one's impression was* | *you (never know what may happen to you)* || *you (never had a moment's peace)* || *this woman, you felt* (fühlte ~), *would* .. | und da sagt ~ *and they* od *people say*; ~ staunt *people wonder* || ~ saß .. *they, we were seated about the table* || ~ sagte mir .. *they told me; I had been told* .. | ~ stellte e–e Besserung fest *a recovery was reported* || diese sieht ~ nicht oft *these are not often seen* || ~ muß es tun *one must do it, it must be done* || ~ kann nie wissen *one never can tell, there is no telling (whether)* || *you know all there is to know about* .. (was ~ wissen muß über) || ~ hört dich .. *you'll be heard in the street* || ~ reist jetzt schneller *travelling is quicker nowadays* || wenn ~ ihn hört .. *to hear him (one would think)* | ~ nehme *take* (!) || ~ verbinde *join* (!) **2.** adv ⟨fam⟩ (Füllwort) (= nur) || ~ sachte! *come, come! draw it mild!* || er soll's ~ versuchen *let him try* || na, denn ~ los! *come along, then!* ~ zu! *get going!* || sei ~ nicht böse! *don't be angry!* || es kostet ~ 3/– *it costs only 3/–* || → begraben | [intensitiv] wer war das ~ nur? *whoever was that?* || ich möchte ~ (bloß) wissen *I wonder* (ob *if*) || wenn ich ~ nur wüßte *if only I knew* || komm' ~ mit! *do come with me* || ~ nur nicht bange! *never fear!* (vgl mal[1] = nur)

Män·ade f ~/~n ⟨Gr myth⟩ *mænad*; → Man·ie

°**m·anagen** ['mɛnɛdʒən] vt [h] -gte/ge-gt [-tʃt] ⟨sl⟩ *to pull (it) off; to wangle* **M·anager- ~geist** m *managerialism*; v ~ durchdrungen *m.ialized* **~krankheit** f *m.ial* od *stress disease* **~tum** n *managership; m.ial attitude*, ⟨fam⟩ *bossiness*

m·anch; **~er, ~e, ~es** [indef pron] *many a (man, etc.)* || ~e arme Leute *many poor people* || ~es Mal *many a time* || ~ e–r, ~ e–e *many a one* || ~ anderer *many another* || er ist schon ~es Jahr hier *he has been here some* od *many years, many a year* || in ~em hatte er recht *he was right in many things* | [intensiv] so *or* gar ~er *a good many people* || so *or* gar ~es *so many ths, a great deal, so much, plenty* **2. ~e** pl (= einige) ~e Leute *some* od *several people* || ~e [gen] *some of the prisoners* **~erlei 1.** [a] *several (people), various (ths)*, auf ~ Art *in sundry ways* **2.** ~ [n] *all* od *several sorts of ths* **~erorts** adv *in many a place* **~mal** adv *sometimes*

Manche 1. (Canal de la M.) **2.** (franz. Departement)

Manch·ester m ~s/ (Stoff) *velveteen, corduroy* **~tum** n ~s/ *Cobdenism (Free Trade!)*

M·andalai n (Hptst. Oberbirmas) *Mandalay*

Mand·ant m ~en/~en ⟨jur⟩ *client, mandator* || ⟨com⟩ *committer, consignor* **Mand·at** n ~(e)s/~e ⟨com⟩ (Auftrag) *order* || ⟨pol⟩ *mandate* || (Vollmacht) *warrant* || ⟨jur⟩ *authorization, brief* || (e–r Behörde) *writ* || sein ~ niederlegen *to resign one's seat* **Mandat·ar** m ~(e)s/~e *mandatory, authorized agent* || (Vertreter) *representative* **~macht** f ⟨pol⟩ *Mandatory Power* **Mand·ats-** [in comp] *mandated (colonies)*

Mandar·in m [~s & ~en/~e(n)] *mandarin* | **~e** f ⟨bot⟩ *tangerine; mandarin* **~enamt** n *m.ate* **~enherrschaft** f *m.ism* **~ente** f ⟨orn⟩ *mandarin*

M·andel[1] f ~/~ (Zahl) **1.** *(a sitting of) fifteen* || 2 ~ Eier *thirty eggs* **2.** ⟨agr⟩ (= 15) *shock* **m·andeln** vt [h] 1. (Eier) *to arrange in sittings of 15* 2. ⟨agr⟩ *to shock (corn), to put into shocks* **m·andelweise** adv *in sets of 15*; etc

M·andel[2] f ~/~n ⟨bot⟩ *almond* (schälen *to skin*); gebrannte ~ *praline* || ⟨anat⟩ *tonsil* || die ~n herausnehmen *to cut, remove, excise the tonsils* || geschwollene ~n *enlarged* od *inflamed tonsils* **~baum** m *a.-tree* **~entzundung** f ⟨path⟩ *mumps* pl; ⟨scient⟩ *tonsillitis* || eitrige ~ *quinsy* **≈förmig** a *a.-shaped, amygdaloid* **~karamel** n *hard-bake* **~kern** m *almond* **~kleie** f *a.-powder* **~krähe** f ⟨orn⟩ *roller* **~milch** f *emulsion of a.s* **~nuß** f *white filbert* **~öl** n *a.-oil* **~pudding** m, **~speise** f *blancmange* **~seife** f *a.-soap*

M·andl n ~s/~(n) [österr, bay] („Männlein") *stones heaped up to form a "monument"* || *scare--crow*

Mandol·ine f ~/~n *mandolin*

M·andorla f ~/–len ⟨arts⟩ *almond(shaped glory)*

Mandr·ill m ~(e)s/~e *mandrill*

M·andschu, Mandsch·uren pl (Zweig der Tungusen) *Manchus* **Mandsch·ukuo** *Manchoukuo* **Mandschur·ei**, die [f] *Manchuria*

Man·ege [ma'ne:ʒə] f ~/~n *ring, arena*

M·anen pl ⟨Roman rel⟩ *Manes* pl

°**m·ang** prep *among* || *(in)between*

M·ang- ~futter n *mixed grain* **~korn** n *meslin*

Mang·an n ~(e)s/ ⟨chem⟩ *manganese* **~blende** f *alabandin(e)* **~eisen** n *m.ese iron* **~erz** n *m. ore* **≈haltig** a *m.iferous* **≈saures Salz** n (heute: Mangan·at) ⟨chem⟩ *m.ate*

M·ange f ~/~n (gr Korb) *hamper*

M·ange(l)[1] f ~/~n *mangle* || (f Tuch) *calender* | **≈n** vt [h] *to c.*; (Wäsche) *to m.* **~brett** n *mangling board* **~maschine** f *m.ling machine*

M·angel[2] m ~s/≈ (an) *lack (of courage, sleep, comprehension, manners)*; *deficiency (of revenue)* || *want (of affection)* || (Fehlbetrag) *deficit* ||

shortage (*of food, houses*) || ([verborgener] Fehler) (*hidden*) *defect*; *blemish, shortcoming* || die ⁓ des Buches *the faults in the book* || ⁓ aufweisen *to be defective* || ⁓ beseitigen *to make good the d.s*; ⁓ feststellen *to discover deficiencies*; ~ der Gegenleistung ⟨com⟩ *failure of consideration* | ~ an Selbsterkenntnis *ignorance of one's own heart*; der gr ~ an .. *the gross absence of* ..; (Not) *indigence* || ~ an Zucht *indiscipline*; ~ an Geld *impecuniosity* || ~ an Lebensmitteln *shortness of provisions* || vollkommener ~ an Wasser *water-famine* || ~ leiden *to be in distress, to live in poverty, to be destitute*; *to be* od *go in want of* (an) || großen ~ leiden *to be in utter destitution* || **aus** ~ an, mangels *for* od *from want of*; aus ~ an Beweisen *in default of evidence*, .. an Inf. *in the absence of further information* || ~ **h** an *to be short of* || sie h ~ an Arbeitskräften *they are short-handed* || e–m dringenden ~ abhelfen *to supply a much-felt want* **⁓anzeige** f *notice of defects* **~beruf** m *occupation with a great number of vacancies*; ⟨a.⟩ *shortage of labo(u)r, critical occ.* **~erkrankung** f = –krankheit **~ernährung** f *malnutrition* **⁓frei** *faultless*; *free from defect* **~krankheit** f *avitaminosis*; *deficiency disease* **~lage** f *shortage* | ohne **⁓gewähr** f *with all faults* **~material** n *d.y* od *critical materials* pl **⁓rüge** f *disapproval* **~ware** f *deficiency-* od *shortage-goods* pl **m·angelhaft** a *defective* ⟨a. gram⟩, *deficient* || *imperfect* || ~e Drüsenfunktion ⟨med⟩ *glandular deficiency* | adv *not properly* (*done*) | **⁓igkeit** f ~/ *defectiveness* ⟨a. gram⟩; *imperfection* **m·angeln** vi [h] (an [dat]) *to be wanting, lacking, deficient* (*in*) || *to be in want* (*of*) || *to want, fail, lack* | **es** –lt ihm an Mut *he lacks courage* || es ~lt uns an Lebensmitteln *we are in want of* od *short of victuals* || es –lt ihm an Bildung *his manners are faulty* | es –lt an allem *there is a shortage in everything* || es –lte an W. *water failed* od *was lacking* | an mir soll es nicht ~ *I will do my part* od *my best, I shall spare no pains* || er läßt es sich an nichts ~ *he does not deny h.s. anything* | ~d [+ subst] = Mangel an; wegen ~der Zeit *for lack of time* **m·angels** prep [gen] *in default of* || ~ Masse ⟨com⟩ *on the grounds of insufficiency of assets*

M·ango- ~baum [m] *mango* (*-tree*), ~frucht, ~pflaume [f] *mango* [pl *-oes*]

M·angold m ~s/ (*white*) *beet*; *chard*; *mangel*

M·angostane f ~/~n ⟨bot & cul⟩ *mangosteen*

Mangr·ove f ⟨bot⟩ *mangrove* || *m. woods*

Mang·uste f ~/~n ⟨zoo⟩ *mongoose*; *ichneumon*

Manich·äer m ~s/~ *Manichee* || ⟨fig fam⟩ *dun*

Man·ie f ~/~n *madness, mania*; *cacoethes* (*for writing*) || es ist bei ihm zur ~ geworden *it has become a mania with him*; → Mänade

Man·ier f ~/~en *manner, fashion, mode*; ⟨arts⟩ *handling* || *habit* | ~en [pl] (*to have good, bad*) *manners* pl; *address*; eine P mit guten ~en *a well-mannered p* || komische ~en *funny ways* || mit guter ~ *with a good grace* || ⟨arts⟩ gesuchte ~ *affected manner* od *style* || das ist nur ~ *it is all affectation* | (Weise) in solcher ~ *in such a way* || das ist k–e ~! *that is not the way to do it* (od *to behave*)! || e–n auf gute ~ los|w .. *in a decent way* || auf gute ~ davon|k *to have a lucky escape* **manie·r·iert** a *affected* || ⟨arts⟩ *mannered*; *stilted* (*style*) | **⁓heit** f *affectedness, affectation*; *trick* || ⟨arts⟩ *mannerism* **Manier·ist** m ~en/~en *–ist* **man·ier·lich** [a] *mannerly, civil, polite* || *wellbehaved, -bred, -mannered* | [adv] sich ~ betragen *to behave o.s.* | **⁓keit** f *mannerliness, civility, politeness*

Manif·est n ~(e)s/~e (*public*) *statement* **~a·ti·on** [ts] *demonstration, manifestation* **⁓·ieren** vt [h] 1. *to manifest*; *display* 2. *to swear a declaration*

Manik·üre f ~/~n *manicure* **manik·üren** vt *to m.*

Man·ila n (Hauptstadt der Philippinen) *Manil(l)a* || **~-** *Manila* (*cigar, hemp*)

Mani·ok m ~s/~e ⟨bot, cul⟩ *cassava*

Man·ipel 1. m ~s/~ ⟨mil hist⟩ *maniple* 2. f ~/~n ⟨R. C.⟩ *maniple* **M-pulati·on** f ~/~en *manipulation* **m-pulieren** vt [h] *to manipulate, handle* || (Währung) *to manage*

M·anipur n (Bezirk in Assam) *Manipore*

m·anisch *a manic* (*depressive insanity*)

Manit·oba n (kanad. Prov.)

M·anko n ~s/~s ⟨com⟩ *defect, shortage, short measure* od *weight* || (Fehlbetrag) *deficiency* || *deficit* (*of cash*) **~geld** n (f Kassierer) *risk money*

Mann m [~es/⁓er; ⟨poet⟩ pl ~en] [pl a. ~] → A. 5. **A. Bedeutungen 1.** *man* || ⁓er [pl] *men, men-folk* pl, *manhood* (*the whole m. of the country*) || ⟨fam⟩ *bloke* || (Anrede) *man* (*hurry up man!*); ⟨Am sl⟩ *bo* || lieber ~! ⟨vulg⟩ *my bloater* || ~ Gottes! *man alive!*; das ist unser ~! ⟨fam⟩ *he's our measure* **2.** (Ehemann) *husband*, ⟨vulg⟩ *man*; mein ~ *my h.* || ~ u Frau *man* od *h. and wife*; Ihr lieber ~ *your good h.*; mein ~ u Ihr Gatte *my h. and yours* **3.** [koll] der gemeine, etc. ~ → B. 1. **4.** ⟨cards etc⟩ *partner* || den vierten ~ m *to take the fourth hand* **5.** ⟨mil⟩ 10 ~ *ten men* || drei ~ hoch *three men deep* || ~ u Roß *man and horse, horse and rider* || 1000 ~ *1000 troops* N, .. z Fuß *1000 foot* || gut (schlecht) der ~!, wie heißt der ~? *take his name, sergeant-major!* ⟨a. fig⟩ | ⟨mar⟩ alle ~ *all hands* **6.** (Lehnsmann) [pl ~en] *follower, retainer, vassal* || ⟨mil⟩ *warrior*; ⟨engl⟩ *fighting* od *merry man* **B. 1. [mit Adj.]** **alter** ~ *old, aged man, man advanced in years* || ⟨fam⟩ *old boy*; ⟨min fig⟩ *gob*; a. ~ ist doch kein D-Zug! ⟨m. m.⟩ *my name is Simpson not Samson, I'm not as young as I was* || feiner ~ *gentleman* || den feinen ~ spielen *to do the swell* || er ist ein ganzer ~ *he is the right sort* (*of man*), *quite a man*, ⟨fam⟩ *a fine fellow* || gebildeter ~ *man of culture* || der gegebene *or* geeignete ~ f etw s *to fill the bill* || der gemeine ~ [koll] *the common people* pl || der gewöhnliche ~ *the man in the street* || ein **gr** ~ (geistig) *a great man* || der biedere, gute ~ ⟨hum⟩ *the worthy man* || hervorragender ~ *prominent man* || junger ~ *young man*; ⟨com⟩ mein junger ~ *my clerk* od *man* || der **kl** ~ [koll] *small people* pl, (*a small man's paradise*) || der rechte ~ *the right sort* (*of man*) || richtiger, kräftiger ~ *he-man* || schöner ~ *handsome man* || der schwarze ~ *the* (*black*) *bogy*(*-man*) || °den **st**arken ~ markieren *to play the strong man* || starker ~ ⟨Am⟩ *he-man* || verheirateter ~ *family man* || ein vielseitiger ~ *an all-round man* **2. [mit Verb]** wie ein ~ **aufstehen**: *the nation rose as one man* || als ~ auftreten *to play the man* || e–n ~ bek *to get married* || der ~ muß noch geboren w .. *is not born yet* (*who*) sich als ~ bewähren *to prove a true man* od *o.s. a man* || dieser Beruf ernährt s–n ~ *this vocation is a lucrative one* || s–n ~ finden *to find* od *meet one's match* || e–n ~ h *to have a husband* || als *or* wie ~ u Frau leben *to live in concubinage* || e–n ~ nehmen *to marry* || ~s genug s zu tun *to be able to do* od *equal to doing* (*he is man enough for that*) || er ist mein ~ *he is my man* || s–n ~ stehen *to hold one's own, to stand one's ground, to keep one's end up*; ⟨fam⟩ *to come up to* (*the*) *scratch*; *to face the music* (*like a man*) || s–n ~ stellen *to stand one's ground*; *to contribute one's share* || sich als ~ zeigen *to show o.s. a man* **3. [mit prep]** s–e Ware **an** den ~ bringen *to get rid of* od *to dispose of one's goods*; (Kenntnisse ..) *to display*; *to show off*; (Mädchen ..) *to find a husband for* .. (⟨fam⟩ *he got her off*), .. nicht .. z bringen *unmarriageable*; ⟨com⟩ .. wollen *to try to sell a th* || ~ **an** ~ gedrängt *crowded together* || wenn Not am ~ ist *if help is needed, if the worst comes to the worst, in case of emergency* || an den unrechten ~ k ⟨fam⟩ *to come to the wrong shop, to get into the wrong box* || 3 Sch. **auf** den ~ *3 s a head* || (Hund) auf den ~ dressiert *trained to take a man* || bis auf den letzten ~ *to the last* (od *to a*) *man* || **durch** e–n dritten ~ (gehend) *done by attorney* ‖ ~ **für** ~ *man by man* ‖ für einen ~ stehen *to stand up for each other* ‖ „(Für) Männer" "*(For) Gentlemen*" ‖ ~ **gegen** ~ kämpfen *to fight man against man* od *hand to hand* ‖ **mit** ~ u Maus untergehen ⟨mar⟩ *to sink with all hands* ‖ bis **zum** letzten ~ *to the last man* ‖ zum ~ heranwachsen *to grow up to be a man* | er ist der ~ **an** der Spitze *he is the manager* ‖ ein ~ **aus** dem Volke *a man of the people* ‖ der ~ aus dem Volke *the man in* ⟨Am *on*⟩ *the street* ‖ ein ~ **für** alles *a (general) handy man* ‖ der ~ **im** Monde *the man in the moon* ‖ sie ist der ~ im Hause ⟨fam⟩ *she wears the trousers* ‖ ~ **über** Bord *man overboard* ‖ ein ~ **von** Bedeutung etc *a man of importance, character, courage* ‖ .. v Talent, Takt *a talented, tactful man* ‖ ~ v der Straße *man in* ⟨Am *on*⟩ *the street* ‖ ~ v Wort *a reliable man* ‖ er ist nicht der ~ **dazu** *he is not the man to do it* **4.** **[mit Subst]** der ~ des Tages *the man of the day* ‖ ein ~ der Tat *an energetic man* ‖ ein ~ des Todes *a lost man,* ⟨Am fam⟩ *goner* **C. Wendungen**: ein ~ ein Wort! *an honest man's word's as good as his bond!, honour bright!* ‖ *I rely on you!* **~loch** n ⟨mach⟩ *man-hole*; ⟨mil⟩ *man-hole* **⩪toll** = ~stoll **~weib** n *virago* **m·annbar** a *marriageable* ‖ ~ w *to reach (wo)manhood* | **⩪keit** f *(wo)manhood* ‖ (v Jüngling a.) *puberty* ‖ (v Mädchen a.) *marriageable age* **⩪werden** n *pubescence* **M·ännchen** n ~s/~ **1.** *manikin, little man* ‖ ein altes ~ *an old little man* **2.** (Anrede) liebes ~ *dear old man* **3.** (T) *male* ‖ (Elefant, Rind, Wal) *bull* ‖ (Hase) *buck (buck-rabbit)*; ⟨orn⟩ *cock(-bird)* ‖ Sperlings⩪ *cock-sparrow* [pl *c.-s.s*] ‖ ~ u Weibchen *male and female, he and she* **4.** (v Hund u Hasen) ~ m *to sit up* ‖ °nicht mehr wissen, ob man ~ oder Weibchen ist → durchgedreht s °**M·änne** (⟨fam⟩ Anrede f Mann) ⟨vulg⟩ *hubbykins!*; mein ~ *my hubby* **M·änner** [pl v Mann] ‖ „~" *Gentlemen* ‖ zu den „~n" gehen *to do the gentleman* **M·ännerchen** n pl [dim v Männer pl] *manikins, little men* **M·annequin** m ~s/~s *mannequin* Fr **M·änner- ~abend** m *bull session* | nach **~art** [f] *in a mannish way* **~chor** m *choir of male voices* ‖ ⟨theat⟩ *chorus of men* **~gesangverein** m *men's singing-club* **~kindbett** n *couvade* Fr, *man-childbed* **⩪mordend** a *homicidal* **⩪scheu** a *afraid of men* **⩪süchtig** a *mad after men* **~treu** f ⟨bot⟩ *creeping forget-me-not* **~volk** n *men* pl **M·annes- ~alter** n *man's age* od *estate, manhood; adulthood* ‖ im besten ~ *in the prime of life* **~art** f *man's ways* pl **~kraft** f *manly vigour, virility* **~mut** m *manhood, manly courage* **~sinn** m *manly feeling* **~stamm** m *male line* **~stolz** m *manly pride* **M·annestum** n ~s/ 1. *manly discipline* 2. *manliness* **~-wort** n *man's word* **~würde** f *dignity of man* ‖ → Manns- **m·annhaft** a *manly, stout, valiant, spirited* ‖ ~ auftreten *to play the man* ‖ er tritt ~ dafür ein *he resolutely stands up for it* | **⩪igkeit** f *manfulness, manliness, stoutness, spirit* **M·annheit** f ~/ **1.** *masculinity* **2.** *virility* **3.** *manliness* **M·ännin** f ~/~nen (Mannweib) *virago* **m·ännlich** a *male (child, heir, animal, plant)* ‖ ⟨gram⟩ *masculine (gender)* ‖ ~er Bekehrter *man convert* ‖ ~es Personal *man-power* ‖ das ~e Glied *male membrum, penis*; ~es Geschlechtshormon *androgen*, ~e Eigenschaften hervorrufend *androgenic*; ~e Generation *paternal g.* | ⟨fig⟩ *manly (attitude)* ‖ *virile (face)* ‖ ~e Kleidung *man's clothing* ‖ *male (rhyme, thread* [Gewinde], *tank* ⟨mil⟩) | **⩪keit** f ~/ *masculinity, manhood, maleness, virility* **M·anns-** °**~bild** n *man, male p.*; Mittagessen der ~er ⟨sl⟩ *buck* [nur attr] *lunch* **⩪dick** a *of the thickness of a man* **~gestalt** f *male figure, shape of a man* **~hand** f *man's hand(writing)* **~hemd** n *shirt* **⩪hoch** [a & adv] *of a man's height, man-tall* **~länge** f *man's length, man's size* ‖ ⟨fam⟩ **~leute** pl *men* pl, *male folk* **~person** f *male p, man* **~pflicht** f 1. *marital duty* 2. *duty of a man* **~stamm** m *male line* **~sucht** f *nymphomania* **⩪tief** a *fathom deep* **⩪toll** a *man-mad, mad after men*; ⟨scient⟩ *nymphomaniac*; ⟨vulg⟩ *cock-smitten* **~tollheit** f = ~sucht °**volk** n *men* pl **~zucht** f *discipline*; ohne ~ *undisciplined* **M·annschaft** f ~/~en **1.** *(body of) men* pl ‖ (Arbeiter) *gang of men* **2.** ⟨mil⟩ *squad (of men), hands troops* pl ‖ alte ~ *veterans* pl ‖ junge ~ *young recruits* pl ‖ die ~en *the ranks, the rank and file*; ⟨Am⟩ *the enlisted men* N; ohne ~en (z. B. Panzer) *without troops* **3.** ⟨mar⟩ *crew, company*; ⟨mil-mar⟩ *forecastle* (Ggs *quarter-deck)* ‖ die ganze ~ *all hands* pl ‖ Geschütz⩪ *gun crew* **4.** ⟨aero⟩ *crew*, Boden⩪ *ground-crew* **5.** ⟨sport⟩ *team,* ⟨Am a.⟩ *squad*: in e-r ~ spielen *to play in* (⟨Am⟩ *on*) *a team* ‖ Ersatz⩪ ⟨Am⟩ *scrub* **M·annschafts- ~anwerbung** f ⟨mil & mar⟩ *enrolment of men* **~deck** n ⟨mar⟩ *mess-deck* **~dienstgrad** m (P) *private* **~ersatz** m *replacement* N **~führer** m ⟨sport⟩ *captain, skipper* **~geist** m *team-spirit* **~quartiere** n pl *other ranks' billets* **~raum** m ⟨mar⟩ *crew's space, mess quarters forward* **~stammrolle** f ⟨mil⟩ *muster-roll* | aus dem **~stand** z Offizier befördert w *to rise from the ranks*; a. d. ~ hervorgegangener O. *ranker* **~stube** f ⟨mil⟩ *troop-room* **~wagen** m ⟨mil⟩ *troop-carrier* **~wertung** f *team-classification*

M·anna n ~s/ ; f ~/ *manna* | ~esche [f] *m.-ash*; ⩪gebend [a] *manniferous*; ~gras [n] *m.-grass*; ~grütze [f] *m.-croats* pl; ~lese [f] *gathering of m.*

m·annigfach, m·annigfaltig a *manifold, various, diverse, multifarious, multiplex, chequered, variegated* **M·annigfaltigkeit** f ~/ *manifoldness, variety, diversity, multiplicity*; *diversification* **m·ännig-lich** [pron] *each and every one, all and sundry*

Manom·eter n & m ~s/~ *manometer, ga(u)ge* ‖ °⟨hum⟩ ~! *man alive!* **~druck** m ⟨Am⟩ *gage pressure* **~stand** m *reading of pr. g.*

Man·över n ~s/~ ⟨mar⟩ *naval manœuvre* od *evolution* ‖ Flotten⩪ [pl] *naval m.s* ‖ Landungs⩪ *landing m.* ‖ ⟨mil⟩ *m.s* pl ‖ ins ~ ziehen *to go the m.s* | *field training*; *exercise* N ‖ ⟨fig⟩ *stratagem, trick*; ⟨pol⟩ *politics* ‖ allerlei ~ m *to play all sorts of dodges* **~anzug** m *field-dress* **~gelände** n *m.* od *exercise area* **~-Salutkartusche** f *blank cartridge* **manövr·ieren** vi/t [h] *to m.* ‖ ⟨mar⟩ *to practise (tactical evolutions)* | ⟨fig⟩ (e–n) *to engineer, shepherd* ‖ *to conjure (from .. into ..)* **manövr·ier- ~fähig** a *manœuvrable, manageable* **⩪eigenschaften** f pl *manœuvring capabilities* **⩪vorrichtung** f ⟨tech⟩ *control mechanism*

Mans·arde f ~/~n *garret, attic* **~ndach** n *curb-roof* **~nfenster** n *dormer-window* **~nwohnung** f *lodgings in a garret* **~nzimmer** n *garret-room*

°**M·ansch** m ~(e)s/~e, **~e** f ~/~n *hodge-podge*; ⟨fam⟩ *mess* | **⩪en** vt/i [h] *to mix* ‖ *to puddle, splash,* ⟨fam⟩ *to mess about* (in *in*, mit *with*) | **~er** m ~s/~ *dabbler, puddler* | **~er·ei** f ~/~en *puddling, dabbling* ‖ *hodge-podge, mess* | **⩪ig** a *sloppy (road)*

Mansch·ette f ~/~n *cuff* ‖ (falsche) *wristband* ‖ (altmodische mit Spitzen) *ruffle* ‖ ~n h vor [dat] *to stand in awe of,* ⟨sl⟩ *to funk* (vt/i) ‖ e–m ~n m *to keep a p in awe, to make a p funk* | ~nhemd [n] *ruffled shirt*; ~nknopf [m] *stud* ‖ (doppelter) *(sleeve-)links, cufflinks* pl

M·antel m ~s/⩪ **1. Bedeutungen**: *cloak, (over-)coat* ‖ beidseitig z tragender ~ *reversible* ‖ (f Frauen) *mantle* ‖ (kurzer) *short cape* | → Abend⩪ f Damen *wrap* ‖ Aktien⩪ *bearer-certificate of shares, share warrant* ‖ → Bade⩪ *bath-gown, bathing wrap* ‖ Blei⩪ (f Kabel) *lead sheath* ‖ Chor⩪ (Pluviale) ⟨R. C.⟩ *cope* ‖ Form⩪ ⟨found⟩ *coat (of a mould)* ‖ Frisier⩪ *dressing jacket* ‖ ⟨geom⟩ *surface* ‖ Geschoß⩪ *coating, jacket* ‖ Gießerei⩪ *cope* ‖ Gummi⩪ *caoutchouc cloak* ‖ Hochofen⩪ *shell* ‖ Hülsen⩪ *(wall of a) cartridge case* ‖ Kamin⩪ *mantel* ‖ Kessel⩪ *boiler jacket* ‖ Kreissägen⩪ *casing* ‖ Krönungs⩪ *coronation robe* ‖

Lauf≗ (Gewehr) *barrel casing, jacket* || Luftreifen≗ *cover* || Kegel-, Pyramiden-, Zylinder≗ *convex surface* || ⟨mil⟩ gerollter ∼ *cloak slung over the shoulder* || ⟨mot⟩ (*outer*) *cover*; der ∼ ist aus der Felge gesprungen *the c. has sprung out of the rim*; ∼ auswechseln (auflegen) *to change the* (*fit on a*) *c.* || Ofen≗ *lining* || Regen≗ *mackintosh,* ⟨fam⟩ *mac*(*k*) || Rohr≗ *jacket* || Schützengraben≗ *trench-coat* || Schlauch≗ *cover* || ⟨tech⟩ *jacket, case, casing, shell* || Wappen≗ *mantling, drapery* || Wetter≗ *waterproof coat* || Winter≗ *greatcoat* || ⟨zoo⟩ (der Weichtiere) *mantle* || Zylinder≗ *cylinder jacket* **2.** den ∼ **anziehen** *or* umhängen (ausziehen *or* ablegen) *to put on* (*take off*) *one's cloak* | ⟨fig⟩ mit dem ∼ der Liebe zudecken *to cover with the cloak of charity* || den ∼ auf beiden Schultern tragen *to hold with both parties* || den ∼ nach dem Winde hängen *to turn one's coat*; *to be a time-server, to temporize* **∼-Aufhängestange** f *coat rail* | wir haben e–n **∼defekt** *there is a d. in the o. c.* **∼elektrode** f *sheathed e.* **∼gesetz** n *covering law* **∼geschoß** n *jacketed bullet* **∼kragen** m 1. *coat-collar*, sein ∼ *the collar of his coat* 2. *cape* **∼linie** f (am Zylinder) *generating line* **∼pavian** m *sacred baboon* **∼riemen** m ⟨mil⟩ *cloak-strap* **∼rohr** n *jacket* **∼rolle** f ⟨mil⟩ *rolled greatcoat* **∼sack** m *portmanteau,* ⟨mil⟩ *valise* **∼soffitte** f ⟨theat⟩ *drapery border* **∼takel** n ⟨mar⟩ *runner-purchase* **∼tasche** f *coat pocket* **∼tier** n ⟨zoo⟩ *tunicate* **∼träger** m ⟨fig⟩ *time-server,* ⟨pol⟩ *opportunist* **∼tuch** n, **∼zeug** n *mantling* **∼vertrag** m *covering agreement* **Mäntelchen** n ∼s/∼ *short cloak, mantlet, cape* | sein ∼ nach dem Wind hängen ⟨fig⟩ *to trim one's sails to every w., to blow hot and cold* | e–r S ein ∼ umhängen *to palliate* od *colour a th* || sich ein soziales ∼ umhängen *to affect social feelings* **Mant·ille** [–iljə] f ∼/∼n *mantilla* (Sp)

Mant·isse f ∼/∼n ⟨logar⟩ *mantissa*

Man(t)sch etc → Mansch etc

M·antua n ⟨It⟩ (Stadt & Provinz) *Mantua*

Manu- **∼·al** n ∼s/∼e 1. ⟨mus⟩ *key-board* 2. *notebook* | ∼akten [f pl] ⟨jur⟩ *manuals* pl **∼fakt·ur** f ∼/∼en (Fabrik) (*manu*)*factory* || (Erzeugnis) *manufacture* || (Herstellung) *manufacturing* | ∼arbeiter [m] *factory-hand*; ∼erzeugnisse [n pl], ∼waren [f pl] *manufacture*(*d goods* pl); kl ∼ *manufactured articles* || ⟨Am⟩ *dry goods* pl **∼fakt·ur·ist** m ∼en/∼en *manufacturer* **∼skr·ipt** n ∼(e)s/∼e **1.** *manuscript* (abbr *MS.*, pl *MSS.*) **2.** ⟨typ⟩ *copy, matter* | als ∼ gedruckt *privately printed*; ⟨theat⟩ *right of acting reserved* || ∼ berechnen *to cast up copy*

†**Mä·otischer See** m → Asowsches Meer

M·appe f ∼/∼n (unter dem Arm zu tragen) *portfolio* (⟨a. arts⟩ *lithograph p.*) || (Schul≗ [f e–e Schulter]) *satchel,* [f den Rücken] *school-bag* || (Schreib≗) *writing-* od *blotting-case* || alphabetische Brief≗ *alphabetical file* || Akten≗ *brief-case* **Mapp·ierung** f ∼/∼en *topographic*(*al*) *survey*

M·arabu m ∼s/∼s ⟨orn⟩ *marabou*

Mar·al m ∼s/∼e (Hirsch des Kaukasus) *maral*

Mar·amba n (in Zambia) (†→Livingstone)

Mar·äne f ∼/∼n ⟨ich⟩ *whitefish*

Mar·athen pl → Mahratten

M·arathonlauf m *marathon* (*race*[*r* –≗er])

M·arbel, M·ärbel m ∼s/∼ *marble*

Marburg-Lahn n ⟨Ger⟩ (älteste protestantische Universität, seit 1527)

M·arder m ∼s/∼ ⟨zoo⟩ *marten*

Mär(e) f ∼/∼en (*old* od *fairy-*)*tale* || ⟨fig⟩ *news, report, tidings* pl **∼chen** n ∼s/∼ *fairy-tale* || *legendary fiction* || ⟨fig⟩ *myth* (*spread by publicists*) || (Gerücht) *rumour* || (Lüge) *fib, cock-and-bull story* || ∼ aus Tausendundeiner Nacht *Arabian Nights tale* || es war wie aus e–m ∼ *it was out of a story-book* | ∼buch [n] *book of fairy tales*; ∼erzähler [m] *story-teller*; ∼kunde [f] *storiology*; ∼schatz [m] *folk-lore*; *collection of fairy-tales*; ∼spiel [n] *fairy play*; ∼welt [f] *world of romance* **m·ärchenhaft** a *fabulous, legendary* || ⟨fig⟩ *fairy-like* (*landscape*) || *fantastic* (*stage-scene*) *magical* (*velocity*) | adv *fabulously* (*rich*) | **≗igkeit** f ∼/ *fabulousness* || ⟨fig⟩ *fictiousness*

Mar·emme f ∼/∼n *maremma* It

Margar·etenblume, Marger·ite [f] ⟨bot⟩ *marguerite,* ⟨Am⟩ *daisy*; Strauch≗ *Paris Daisy*

M·arge [–ʒə] f ∼/∼n ⟨com⟩ *margin*

Margar·ine f ∼/ (⟨Am⟩ *oleo*)*margarine,* ⟨mst⟩ *margerine* | Margarin(e)säure [f] *margaric acid*

Margin·alien pl *marginal notes* pl

Mar·ia f [∼s *or* –riä/–rien] *Mary* || die Jungfrau ∼ ⟨ec⟩ *the Virgin Mary* || Ave ∼! *Hail Mary* || ⟨paint⟩ M-ä Geburt, Verlobung, Tod *Birth, Marriage, Death of the V.*; ∼ im Rosenhag *Madonna in the Rose Arbo*(*u*)*r* || Mariä Heimsuchung [f] ⟨ec⟩ (*Feast of the*) *Visitation* || Mariä Verkündigung [f] ⟨ec⟩ *Annunciation*

Mari·age [–ʒə] f ∼/∼n ⟨cards⟩ *marriage*

Mari·anen f pl (Mikronesien) *Mariana-Islands*

Mar·ien- **∼anbetung** f ⟨ec⟩ *Mariolatry* **∼bad** n ⟨cul, chem⟩ *water-bath* **∼balsam** m *poon-oil* **∼bild** n *image of the Virgin Mary* **∼blume** f *ox-eye* (*daisy*), *marguerite* **∼blümchen** *daisy* **∼dienst** m *worship of the Virgin Mary* **∼distel** f *lady's-thistle* **∼fäden** m pl *gossamer* **∼fest** n *Lady-Day* **∼flachs** m *toad-flax* **∼garn** n *gossamer* **∼glas** n ⟨min⟩ *mica, selenite* **∼glöckchen** n ⟨bot⟩ *Coventry-bell* **∼käfer** m ⟨ent⟩ *lady-bird,* ⟨Am⟩ *-bug* **∼kirche** f *St. Mary's church* **∼kult(us)** m *worship of M. the V.*; *Mariolatry* **∼tag** m *Lady-Day, Annunciation-Day*

Marihu·ana n ∼s/ *marihuana, -iju-* | ∼-Zigarette [f] ⟨sl⟩ *reefer, drag, joint*

Mar·ille f ∼/∼n [österr] (*small*) *apricot*

Mar·ine f ∼/∼n *Marine*(*s* pl); Handels≗ *merchant m.* || Kriegs≗ *navy*; ⟨engl⟩ *Royal N.,* ⟨Am⟩ *United States N.* || er ist bei der ∼ *he is in the M.s* || bei der ∼ dienen *to serve in the n.* || zur ∼ gehen *to join* od *enter the n.* || reitende Gebirgs≗ ⟨hum⟩ *horse marines* pl **∼akademie** f *Naval College* **∼amt** n *n.l board*; ⟨engl⟩ *the Admiralty,* ⟨Am⟩ *N. Department* **∼arsenal** n *n.l repair base*; *n.-yard* **∼artillerie** f *n.l, artillery* **∼arzt** m = ∼sanitätsoffizier **∼attaché** m *n.l attaché* **∼blau** a & n *m. blue* **∼einheiten** f pl *n.l ratings* pl **∼etat** m *n.l estimates* pl **∼flieger** m *n.l pilot* od *flier* **∼flugwesen** n *n.l aviation* **∼flugzeug** n *n.l airplane*; *seaplane* **∼gericht** n *n.l court* **∼haushalt** m = ∼etat **∼infanterie** f *M. Corps* N; ⟨hist⟩ (*Red*) *M.s* pl **∼ingenieur(offizier)** m *engineer officer* (*N.*) **∼konstrukteur** m *n.l designer* **∼leitung** f (⟨Ger hist⟩ Oberkommando der Kriegsmarine), → ∼amt; nautische Abteilung *Hydrographic Office* **∼landetruppen** f pl *Marine Corps* **∼landungstrupp** m *n.l landing party* **∼luftwaffe** f ⟨engl⟩ *Fleet Air Arm* **∼maler** m *sea*(*scape*)*-painter* **∼mannschaften** f pl *n.l ratings* pl **∼minister** (nicht deutsch) m *minister of n.l affairs*; ⟨engl⟩ *First Lord of the Admiralty* || (*U.S.A.*) *Secretary of the N.* **∼ministerium** n (nicht deutsch) *n.l department, n. board, Ministry of N.l Affairs* || ⟨engl⟩ *Admiralty* || (*U.S.A.*) *Department of the N.* **∼offizier** m *n.l officer* **∼rangliste** f *N. List* **∼sanitätsoffizier** m *medical officer* (*R.N.*) **∼schule** f *N.l College* **∼stammdienststelle** f *n.l personnel office* **∼station** f *n.l station* **∼soldaten** m pl, **∼truppen** f pl *m.s* pl **∼stück** ⟨paint⟩ *seapiece, seascape* **∼verwaltungsoffizier** m *accounting officer* (*N.*) **∼waffenamt** n *n.l ordnance office* **∼werft** f *n.-yard* **∼wesen** n *n.l affairs* pl **∼zahlmeister** m = ∼verwaltungsoffizier **marin·ieren** vt [h] *to pickle, souse, marinade* || –rter Hering *soused herring* **marit·im** a *maritime*

Marion·ette f ∼/∼n *marionette, puppet* **∼nregierung** f *p. government* **∼nspiel** n *p.-play* **∼nspieler** m *p.-man* **∼ntheater** n *p.-show*; ⟨engl⟩ *Punch and Judy* (*show*)

Mar·itza f (Fluß der Balkanhalbinsel) *Maritsa*

M·ark[1] n ∼(e)s/ *marrow* ‖ (v Früchten) *pulp* ‖ (im Holz) *pith* | ⟨fig⟩ *the very marrow* od *pith* ‖ (Kraft) *mettle, backbone* ‖ bis ins ∼ dringen ⟨fig⟩ *to cut* od *touch to the quick* ‖ e–m durch ∼ u Bein gehen *to pierce a p to the bone*; es ging mir durch ∼ u B. (⟨hum⟩ u Pfennig) (*the shriek*) *made my blood run cold*; *my blood curdled* (*with terror*); *it cut me to the quick* ‖ bis ins ∼ (*French*) *to the core*, (*rotten*) *at the core* ‖ bis aufs ∼ quälen *to torment to death* ‖ e–m das ∼ aus den Knochen saugen *to suck a p's blood*; bis ins ∼ getroffen *chilled to the marrow* **≗durchdringend** a *piercing* (*cry*) **~kürbis** m *marrow squash*

Mark[2] f ∼/∼en **1.** *boundary, border*(*-land*) ⟨hist⟩ *marches* pl (*the Welsh M.*) ‖ die ∼ (Brandenburg) *the March of B.* **2.** ⟨ftb⟩ *touch* **3.** (Dorfflur) *common*; *village bounds*

Mark[3] f ∼/∼ **1.** (Gewicht f edle Metalle ½ Pfund) *mark, six ounces* **2.** (= 100 Pfennig(e) abbr *M*) *mark* 50 ∼ *fifty marks* pl

M·ark-[2] **~graf** m *margrave* **~gräfin** f *margravine* **≗gräflich** a *relating to a margrave* od *to a margraviate* **~grafschaft** f, **~grafentum** n *margraviate* [1]**≗haltig** a ⟨anat⟩ *medullary* **~klößchen** n pl ⟨cul⟩ *marrow-balls* pl **~knochen** m *marrow-bone* [2]**~linie** f ⟨ftb⟩ *touch-line* [1]**≗los** a *marrowless* ‖ ⟨fig⟩ *pithless* [2]**~ordnung** f *rules respecting boundaries* **~scheide** f *boundary* **~scheide-** ∼kunst [f], ∼wesen [n] *surveying* **~scheider** m *surveyor* ‖ *mine-s.r* **~stein** m *landmark* ⟨a. fig⟩, *boundary-stone* ‖ ⟨fig⟩ *mile-stone, epoch-making event* ‖ dies bedeutete e–n ∼ *this marked an epoch* (*in*) [3]**~stück** n *mark-piece* [1]**~substanz** f *medullary substance* **≗voll** a *pithy*

Mark Br·andenburg f → Brandenburg

mark·ant a *striking* (*features, style*), *prominent* (*personality, point*) ‖ *marked* (*divergence*) ‖ *well-cut* (*features*) ‖ e–e ∼e Persönlichkeit *a man of mark* **M·arke** f ∼/∼n *mark, token* ‖ ⟨mar⟩ Lade≗ *load-mark*, Tiefgangs≗ *draught mark* ‖ *label* ‖ ⟨com⟩ (Schutz≗) *trade-mark*; (→ Lebensmittel-) ∼en abgeben *to spend coupons* ‖ (Sorte) *brand, quality, make, type, shape, growth, style* ‖ (Eß-, Eintritts-≗) *ticket* ‖ (Steuer≗) *revenue stamp* ‖ (Brief≗) (*postage-*)*stamp* ‖ (Lebensmittel≗) *coupon*; Fleisch≗ *meat-c.* ‖ (Spiel≗) *counter, chip* ‖ (Garderobe≗) *check* | ⟨fig⟩ °(P) *a rum cuss*; e–e üble ∼ ⟨sl⟩ *a tough proposition* **m·arken** vt [h] *to mark* ‖ *to settle a boundary* **M·arken-** (→ Lebensmittel-) **~abschnitt** m *point* (*cereals are on p.s*) **~album** n *album for postage stamps* **~artikel** m pl *branded* od *patent* (od *propriet*[*ar*]*y*) *articles* od *goods*; *brands*; *brand-name goods*; führende ∼ [pl] *b. leaders* **~fälschung** f *infringement of trade-marks* **≗frei** a *unrationed* (*goods*); [pred] *off the ration* **~heft** n (Brief≗chen) ⟨post off⟩ *stamp book* **~milch** f *accredited m.* **~name** m *trade* od *b. name* **≗pflichtig** a *coupon* (*goods*) **~sammler** m *stamp collector* **~sammlung** f *stamp-collection* **~schutz** m *protection of trade-marks*

M·ärker m, **~in** f *inhabitant* (od *native*) *of the March of* → *Brandenburg*; *Brandenburger*

Mark·esasinseln (Polynesien) *Marquesas Islands*

Market·ender m ∼s/∼ (f **~in**) *sutler, canteen-(wo)man* **~bude** f *canteen* **~wagen** m *sutler's van* | ∼dienste [m pl] *exchange service* N → **Marketender·ei** f ∼/∼en **1.** *sutler's trade* **2.** *stores* pl; ⟨Am⟩ *Post Exchange* (abbr *P.X.*) **market·endern** vi [h] *to be a sutler*

Marketer·ie f ∼/∼en *marquetry*

mark·ieren vt [h] **1.** (kennzeichnen) *to mark* (*goods*) ‖ *to mark out* (*a road*) ‖ *to blaze* (*trees*) ‖ *to earmark* (*cattle*) ‖ m–rt *tagged* (*atom*) ‖ ⟨bill⟩ *to mark* ‖ ⟨phot⟩ scharf ∼ *to define sharply* **2.** (hervorheben) *to emphasize, accentuate* ‖ ⟨theat⟩ *to show off* ‖ (*well-marked* [*features*]) **3.** (andeuten) ⟨mil⟩ *to mark, indicate* (*the enemy*) ‖ markierter Feind *skeleton enemy* ‖ ⟨theat⟩ *to indicate* (*one's rôle*) **4.** °(vortäuschen) er markiert Blindheit, den Harmlosen *he pretends to be blind, harmless* **Mark·ierung** f ∼/∼en *marking*; ⟨mus⟩ *phrase mark* | ∼sbake [f] ⟨aero⟩ *marker light*; ∼sbombe [f] *marker b.*; ∼sfeuer [n] *m.er beacon*; ∼svorrichtung [f] *m.g device*

m·arkig a *marrow-like, marrowy* | ⟨fig⟩ *pithy* (*speech*), *strong* (*word*), *vigorous* (*handshake*), *racy* (*expression*); → Mark[1]

Mark·ise f ∼/∼n (*sun-*)*blind* ‖ (*window*) *awning*

†**Markom·annen** pl (german. Volksstamm) *Marcomanni* [L] pl

Mark·ör m ∼s/∼e †(Billard≗) *scorer, marker*

M·arkt m ∼(e)s/≗e *market* **1.** *America is the best m. for* ..; empfindlicher ∼ *sensitive m.* ‖ e–n neuen ∼ erobern *to win a new m.*; den ∼ überschwemmen *to glut th m.*; sich durch s–e Preise aus dem ∼ ausschalten *to price o.s. out of the m.* **2.** auf den ∼ bringen *or* werfen *to* (*bring* [*in*]*to* od *to throw* od *put on the*) *m.*, ⟨Am a.⟩ *to put .. out*; ⟨exch⟩ (Papiere ..) *to unload*; e–e Anleihe .. *to issue a loan* ‖ (*of estates*) auf den ∼ k *to come into the m., to be in the m.* ‖ wieder dem freien ∼ übergeben *to unfreeze* (*prices, wages*); Gemeinsamer ∼ *Common M.*; grauer, schwarzer ∼ *grey, black m.*; guter ∼ *seller's m.*; e–n guten ∼ finden *to meet with a ready m.* od *sale* ‖ organisierter ∼ *organized m.ing* **3.** (∼tag) wir h zweimal ∼ *we have m.-day twice a week* ‖ Samstag wird ∼ abgehalten *S. is our m.-day*; den ∼ abzapfen *to tap the m.* (nach *for*) ‖ zum ∼e fahren, (Vieh) zu ∼e treiben *to drive* [vi/t] *to m.* ‖ zu ∼e *or* auf den ∼ gehen *to go m.ing* ‖ den ∼ beschicken (besuchen) *to send goods* (*to go*) *to m.* ‖ den ∼ untersuchen *to comb the m.* (*for*) ‖ ⟨fig⟩ s–e Haut (nicht) zu ∼e tragen *to risk one's life* (*to save one's bacon*) **4.** Jahr≗ *fair*; Märkte beziehen *to frequent fairs* **5.** *m.*(*-town*), *emporium* **6.** *bargain, business, sale, trade* ‖ der Baumwoll≗ ist ruhig *cotton is a quiet m.* ‖ den ∼ drücken *to bring down prices* **7.** *m.-square* od *-place* ‖ am ∼e wohnen *to live on the m.-sq.* ‖ auf dem ∼e *in the m.-sq.* **~abgabe** f *m.-due* **~absatz** m (*m.-*)*sale* **~amt** n *m.-board* **~analyse** f *m. investigation* **~beherrschung** f *control of the m.* **~bericht** m *m.-report* **~bude** f *booth, stall* **~einführung** f *commercialization* (*of a product*) **~einkäufe** m pl *m.ing* | (nicht) **≗fähig** a (*un*)*m.able*, (*un*)*saleable*; ∼e Mengen *commercial quantities* **~fähigkeit** f *m.ability* **~flecken** m *borough, m.-town* **~forschung** f *m. research* **~freiheit** f *m.-privilege* **~gang** m 1. *going to m., m.ing* 2. *m.-rate* **≗gängig** a *m.able, current*; überall ∼ *fungible* (*article*); ∼e Preise [m pl] *usual m.-prices* pl **~gebühren** pl *m.-dues* **~geld** n *money taken at a fair* ‖ (im Haushalt) *m.-penny* ‖ (Standgeld) *stallage* **~genossenschaft** f *m.ing society* **~gerechtigkeit** f = ∼freiheit **~gut** n *m.-wares* pl **~halle** f *covered m.* **~helfer** m ⟨com⟩ *porter* **~korb** m *m.-basket* **~lage** f *mood of the m.* (angespannt *tight*) **~leute** pl *keepers of stalls, m.-folk* **~meister** m *m.-inspector* **~ordnung** f *m.-regulations* **~platz** m *m.-place* **~preis** m *m.*(*-price*), *to-day's rate* **~recht** n 1. = ∼ordnung 2. = ∼freiheit 3. = ∼zoll **~sachverständiger** m *m.ing expert* **~schreier** m *cheap-jack, quack, charlatan* **~schreier·ei** f *quackery, puffing, charlatanism*; ⟨Am sl⟩ *ballyhoo* **≗schreierisch** a *quackish, charlatan* ‖ (laut) *blatant, showy, ostentatious*; ∼e Anzeige *puff*(*ing*); in ∼er Weise *in showmen's language* **~stand** m = ∼bude | ∼geld [n] *stallage* **~tag** m *m.-day* **~tasche** f *m.ing bag* **~tendenz** f *trend in the m.* **~untersuchung** f = –analyse **~verkehr** m *business done at the m.* od *on 'Change*; *m.*(*-business*) ‖ *traffic in the m.* ‖ offener ∼ *open m.* **~vogt** m = ∼meister **~weib** n *m.-woman* | freie **~wirtschaft** f *free m.* od *economy* od *enterprise*; soziale ∼ *socially-orientated m. ec.*, ⟨Ger⟩ *Erhard system* (*of free competition with special regard to its social aspect*) **~zettel**

m *list of m.-quotations* **~zoll** m *m.-duty* **m·arkten** vi [h] *to haggle* (um, über *about*), *to bargain* (*for*)

M·arkung f ~/~en = Mark² 1. u 3.

M·arkuskirche f *St. Mark's church*

m·arlen vt [h] ⟨mar⟩ *to marl(ine)* (*ropes*)

M·arl- ~leine [f] (a. Marling f) ⟨mar⟩ *marline*; ~spieker [m] ⟨mar⟩ *marline spike*

M·armarameer n *Sea of Marmora*

Marmel·ade f ~/~n *jam*, ⟨fam⟩ *squish* ‖ (v Apfelsinen, ⟨Am⟩ allg) *marmalade* | ~ndose [f] (*jam-*)*jar, jam-pot*

M·armel m ~s/~, ~kugel [f] *marble* **~spiel** n ⟨fam⟩ *bonce* **~stein** m ⟨poet⟩ = **M·armor** m ~s/~e *marble* ‖ Gips~̈, künstlicher ~ *artificial m., impastation* ‖ Zwiebel~̈ *cipolin* **~ader** f *vein in the m.* **~arbeit** f *m. working* **~bild(werk)** n *m.* (*statue*) **~bildhauen** n *m. carving* **~bruch** m *m.-quarry* **~busen** m ⟨poet⟩ *m. breast, snowy bosom* **~imitation** f *impastation* **~kuchen** m *mocha layer cake* **~mühle** f *m.-mill* **~palast** m *m.-palace* **~platte** f *m. plate, slab of m.* **~säule** f *m. column* **~schleifer** m *m.-cutter, m.-polisher* **~schleifer·ei** f *m.-works* pl **~schnitt** m ⟨bookb⟩ *m.d edges* pl **~stein** m *m.* **~tisch** m *m.-topped table* **~treppe** f *m. stairs* pl **marmor·ieren** vt [h] *to m., vein, grain* ‖ –rt *sprinkled* ‖ mit –rtem Schnitt ⟨bookb⟩ *m.-edged* **Marmor·ierung** f *marbleization, marbling* **m·armorn** a (*made of*) *m.*

M·arne f ⟨Fr⟩ (Nebenfluß der Seine)

mar·od(e) a *knocked up, tired* (⟨fam⟩ *fagged*) *out* ‖ (krank) **Marod·eur** [–'dø:r] m ~s/~e *marauder* **marod·ieren** vi [h] *to go marauding, to pillage*

Marokk·aner m, **~in** f *inhabitant of Morocco, Moroccan* **marokk·anisch** a *Moroccan*, (*of*) *Morocco* **Mar·okko** n *Morocco*

Mar·one f ~/~n *sweet* od *edible chestnut* ‖ glasierte ~ *candied ch.*; (→ Kastanie) **~npilz, ~nröhrling** m *chestnut bolete*

Maroquin [–'kɛ̃] m ~s/~s *Morocco-leather, morocco* ~̈**·ieren** [–kin'i:rən] vt [h] *to morocco*

Mar·otte f ~/~n *caprice, whim, piece of folly* ‖ (Steckenpferd) *fad, hobby*

Marqu·esasinseln → Mark·esasinseln

Marqu·eur = Markör

Marquis [mar'ki:] m ~/~ *marquess, marquis* **~·at** n ~(e)s/~e *marquisate* | **~e** f ~/~n ⟨engl⟩ *marchioness*, ⟨a-engl⟩ *marquise*

M·ars¹ m ~/ ⟨astr⟩ *Mars* ‖ auf dem ~ *on M.* | ~bewohner [m] *Martian*

M·ars² m & f ~/~en ⟨mar⟩ *top* ‖ der gr ~ *main-top* ‖ Fock~̈ *fore-top* ‖ Gefechts~̈ *fighting top* **~brassen** f pl *top-braces* pl **~laterne** f *top-lantern* **~segel** n *topsail* **~stange** f *topmast*

M·arsch¹ **1.** m ~es/~̈e *march(ing)*; ⟨mil⟩ *road movement* ‖ ⟨mus⟩ *m.* ‖ flotter ~ *brisk m.* ‖ in verdeckten, eiligen ~̈en *in* od *by stolen, forced m.es* | **auf** dem ~ *on the move*; *en route* N; sich **auf** den ~ begeben *or* m, sich in ~ setzen *to set* od *m. out* ‖ e–n ~ m *to march* ‖ Truppen auf den *or* in ~ setzen *to m. troops* ‖ durch ~̈e übermüden *to overmarch* ‖ dem Feind e–n ~ abgewinnen *to steal a m. upon ..* ‖ den ~ schließen *to bring up the rear* ‖ wieder auf dem ~ s *to be on the move* od *m. again* | e–n ~ aufspielen *to blaze into a m., to strike up* od *play a m.* ‖ ⟨fig⟩ e–m den ~ blasen, m, schlagen *to give a p his m.ing orders, to send a p about his business*; *to haul a p over the coals* | ⟨fig⟩ die Elektrifizierung ist auf dem ~e .. *is progressing* **2.** marsch! [intj] *m.! go on!* ⟨fam⟩ *be off! hop it! get out!* ‖ ⟨mil⟩ vorwärts ~! *forward, m.!* ‖ ~, ~! *double* (*the pace*)! *double march!* **~abstand** m *distance, gap* (od *time interval*) *between serials* (od *units*) **~anmeldung** f *r. m.t bid* **~anzug** m *m.ing-kit* **~bataillon** n *battalion on the m.* **~befehl** m *m.ing order*(*s* pl); *movement* od *march order* N; (Schein) *official travel order*, ⟨Am⟩ *order of m.t*; ~ erhalten *to get the route* [raut] (nach *for*); ~ h *to be under m.ing-orders* ~̈**bereit** a *ready to m.* **~breite** f *front of m. column* **~dauer** f = –zeit **~erleichterung** f *relaxation of uniform regulations*; ~! *at ease march!* ~̈**fähig** a *fit for m.ing*; *walking* (Verwundeter) **~folge** f *order of m.* **~gliederung** f *m. formation* **~gruppe** f *m. serial* od *group* **~halfter** m ⟨hors⟩ *headstall with head rope* **~geschwindigkeit** f (*m.ing*) *pace, rate of m.ing* **~kolonne** f *troops on the m., m. column, c. of route, m.ing c.*; gesicherte ~ *governed c.* ~̈**krank** a *footsore*; ~e [pl] *m. casualties* **~kredit** m ⟨mil⟩ (*r.*) *m. credit, m. authorization* **~lager** n *bivouac* **~längen** f pl *road spaces* **~leistung** f *m.ing performance*; *m. distance* od *capacity* **~linie** f *line of m.* **~lied** n *m.ing song* **~mäßig** a & adv *in m.ing-style* **~ordnung** f *route order* **~richtung** f *direction of a m.* **~route** f *route, line of m.* **~sicherung** f *security on the m.* **~skizze** f *strip map* **~strecke** f = –route **~tag** m *m.ing day, day of departure* **~tempo** n *rate of m.ing* ‖ ⟨mil⟩ *quick time*; Marschieren [n] im ~ *quick m.*; Schritt im ~ *quick step* **~tiefe** f *length* od *depth of m.ing column* **~turbine** f *ahead t.* **~überwachung** f *m.t control* N **~verpflegung** f *supply for* od *on the m., m.ing ration, haversack r.* **~weg** m *route* **~ziel** n *destination* N; Linie der gleichzeitig zu erreichenden ~e *phase line*

M·arsch² f ~/~en (Ggs Geest) *marsh*(*y land*), (*fen-*)*marsh* ‖ (am Meer) (*salt-*)*marsh* **~boden** m *m.y soil* **~fieber** n *m.-fever* **~land** n *m.*(*y*) *land, fen-l.* **~länder** m *inhabitant of a m. country*, → marschig

M·arschall m ~s/~̈e *marshal* ‖ die Frau ~(in) *the Marshal's lady* **~amt** n *marshal's office* **M·arschallinseln** f (in Mikronesien) *Marshall Islands* pl **~stab** m *m.'s baton* **~würde** f *marshalship*

marsch·ieren vi [s & h] *to march* ‖ in (e–r) Reihe ~ (l) *to file* [vi/t] (*troops*) ‖ nach Norden ~ *to proceed northwards* ‖ auf e–e Stadt (zu *or* los) ~ *to march on a town* ‖ Truppen an sich vorbei~ l (= Parade abnehmen) *to take the salute of the troops* ‖ in aufgelösten Reihen ~ *to march in a straggle* ‖ sie ~ nach der Musik *they step out to it* ([band] *bravely*) | ⟨fig⟩ *to stride* (*Walter strode in front*) ‖ *to troop* (*they trooped into the room*) ‖ ⟨fam⟩ du kannst ~! (*you may*) *be off!* ‖ ⟨cul⟩ ~ l *to start, to put .. on* **Marsch·ierer** m; alter ~ *old sweat*

m·arschig a *marshy, boggy*, → Marsch²

Mars·eille [-sej] n ⟨Fr⟩ *Marseilles*

†**M·arser** pl (Volk in Mittelitalien) *Marsi* [L] pl

M·arshall-Plan m *European Recovery Program* ⟨Am⟩ (ERP)

M·arstall m ~(e)s/~̈e *stud*; *mews, stable*(*s* pl)

M·arter f ~/~n **1.** *torment, torture* ‖ *pang, agony* ⟨a. fig⟩ ‖ unter ~n sterben *to die in agony* ‖ *martyrdom* **2.** = Folter **~bank** f *rack* **~gerät** n *instrument*(*s* pl) *of torture* **~holz** n ⟨ec⟩ *Christ's cross* **~kammer** f *torture-room* **~pfahl** m *stake* (*of torture*); ⟨arts⟩ Christus am ~ *Scourging of Ch.* **~tod** m *martyr's death, d. by torture* ~̈**voll** a *excruciating, torturing* **~werkzeug** n = ~gerät **~woche** f *Passion-week* **M·arterer** m ~s/~ *torturer, tormenter* **M·arterl** n ~s/~ *memorial tablet* od *cross* (*at place of accident* od *murder*) **m·artern** vt/refl [h] *to torture* (*o.s.*), *torment* (*o.s.*), *excruciate* (*o.s.*), *to* (*put to the*) *rack* ‖ *to harrow* gemartert *martyred* (*saint*) ‖ zu Tode ~ *to torment to death* | ⟨fig⟩ *to rack* (*one's brain*)

marti·alisch [–tsi–] a *martial, warlike*

M·artin(s)- **~fest** n *Martinmas* **~gans** f *Martinmas-goose* **~stahl** m *open-hearth steel* **~tag** m *St. Martin's day, Martinmas*

Martin·ique [-ik] n ⟨Fr⟩ (e–e der kl. Antillen)

M·ärtyrer m ~s/~ (f **~in**) *martyr* ‖ e–n z ~ m *to make a martyr of a p* ‖ ⟨fig⟩ z ~ w *to become a victim* **~geschichte** f *martyrology* **~krone** f *crown of martyrdom* **~tod** m *martyr's death* ‖ den ~

sterben *to suffer martyrdom* **~tum, Mart·yrium** n *martyrdom*

Mar·unke f ~/~n (Pflaume) *red egg-plum*

Marx·ismus m ~/ *Marxism* **marx·istisch** a *Marxist, Marxian*

M·aryland n (Staat der U.S.A.)

M·ärz m [~en & ~(es)/~e] *March* **~becher** m ⟨bot⟩ *large snow-drop* **~bier** n *March ale* **~blümchen** n ⟨bot⟩ *yellow trefoil* **~ente** f *mallard* **~feld** n ⟨hist⟩ *champ de Mars* Fr **~hase** m *March hare* **~schnee** m *snow in March* **~veilchen** n *sweet violet*

Marzip·an m ~(e)s/~e *marzipan*, † *marchpane*

M·asche f ~/~n *mesh* ⟨a. fig [*of the law*]⟩, (in knitting) *stitch* (*of mail*) ‖ e–e ~ aufheben *or* aufnehmen (fallen l) *to pick up* (*drop*) *a stitch* ‖ °⟨fig⟩ das ist die ~! *that's the correct card*! *the gadget*! *the idea*! ⟨sl⟩ *posh*! [mst] *that's it*!, *that's all the kick* od *go*! | **~n** pl *net*(*work*) **~ndraht** m *netting wire, screen-wire* **≈nfest** a *ladder-proof, non-slip*, ⟨Am⟩ *non-run* (*hosiery*) **~ngrund** m *meshed work* **~nnetz** n *mesh network* **~nsieb** n *mesh-screen* **~nweite** f *mesh size* **~nwerk** n *network* **m·aschig** a *meshy, netted*

Masch·in- [in comp] österr → ~en-

M·aschine f ~/~n **1.** *machine* ‖ ⟨rail etc⟩ *engine* ‖ ⟨aero⟩ *m.*, ⟨fam⟩ *job* ‖ *machinery*; *apparatus* ‖ ⟨cycl⟩ *m.*; e–e erstklassige ~ *a thorough-bred* ‖ menschliche ~ *robot* ‖ (~nwerk) *m.ry*; das Zeitalter der ~ *the age of m.ry* | Dampf≈ *steam-e.* ‖ dampfhydraulisch betriebene ~ *steam-hydraulic m.* ‖ dreizylindrige ~ *triple-cylinder e.* ‖ dynamoelektrische ~ *dynamo-electric m.* ‖ einzylindrige ~ *single-cylinder e.* ‖ hydraulisch betriebene ~ *hydraulically operated m.* ‖ Kraft≈ *power unit* ‖ Näh≈ *sewing m.* ‖ Papierherstellungs≈ *m. for the manufacture of p.* ‖ ~ v 80 Pferdestärken *80 horse-power e.* ‖ mit Riemen angetriebene ~ *belted m.* ‖ Schreib≈ *typewriter* ‖ Schiffs≈ *e.* ‖ ~ f Sonderzwecke *single-purpose m.* ‖ universell brauchbare ~ *allround m.* ‖ unmittelbar angetriebene ~ *directly operated m.* ‖ Zug≈ (*motor-*)*tractor* | die ~ ist betriebsunfähig *the e.* (*m.*) *has broken down* ‖ e–e ~ anlassen, in Gang *or* Betrieb setzen *to start a m., to set her going* ‖ abstellen *to stop* ‖ aufstellen *to adjust* ‖ neue ~n aufstellen *to lay down new m.ry* ‖ die ~ ist im Gange (in Betrieb) .. *is in motion* (*service*), läuft *is running* ‖ mit *or* auf der ~ bearbeiten, herstellen *to m.* ‖ mit der ~ gemacht *m.-made* ‖ auf der ~ geschrieben *typed* od *type-written* ‖ Übernahme der Arbeiten auf die ~ ⟨comp⟩ *implementation* **2.** ⟨fig⟩ die ~ des Staates *the state-m.ry* ‖ *they were m.s in the hands of their superiors* ‖ wie e–e ~ arbeiten *to do one's work mechanically* | °ist das aber 'ne ~! (dicke Frau) *isn't she a whacker*! **maschin·ell** a: ~e Holzverarbeitung *wood machining* | adv ~ bearbeiten *to machine, work on a m. tool* **Masch·inen- ~antrieb** m, mit ~ *power-driven* **~arbeit** f *m.-work* ‖ *mechanical labour* **~arbeiter** m *machinist*, ⟨Am a.⟩ *shopman* **~bau** m *e.-building*; *mechanical engineering* | ~er [m] (*mechanical*) *engineer*; *millwright* | ~kunst [f] *engineering*; ~schule [f] *engineering-school*; ~werkstatt [f] *m.-shop* **~belastung** f *m. loading* **~bearbeitung** f *machining* **~betrieb** m *m.ry* **~buchhalter** m *bookkeeping-m. operator* **~bütten** n ⟨pap⟩ *mould-made paper* **~code** m ⟨comp⟩ *machine code* **~druck** m *m.-impression* **~element** n → –teil [n] **~fabrik** f *m.-works, engineering works* [sg konstr] **~flak** f ⟨mil⟩ *automatic anti-aircraft gun* **~führer** m ⟨rail etc⟩ *e.-driver*; ⟨tech⟩ *plant operator* **~fundament** n *e.-seating* **~garn** n *twist, m.-spun yarn* **~gewehr** n, leichtes (schweres) ~ *light* (*heavy*) *m.-gun*; mit dem ~ beschießen *to m.-gun*; gekoppeltes ~ *coupled m.-g.* | ~aufsatz [m] *sight-bar*; ~feuer [n] *m.-g. fire*, mit ~ belegen, beschießen *to m.-g.*; ~gurt [m] *cartridge belt*; ~kampfwagen [m] *female tank*; ~kanzel [f] ⟨aero⟩ *gunner's cockpit*; ~kompanie [f] *m.-g. company*; ~nest *m.-g. nest*; ~schütze [m] *m. gunner*; ~stand [m] ⟨aero⟩ *gunner's station* **≈glatt** a ⟨pap⟩ *m.-finished* **~gondel** f ⟨aero⟩ *power gondola, e. nacelle* **~halle** f, **~haus** n *e.-house, e.-room, e.-shop, e.-shed*; ⟨el⟩ *powerhouse* **~ingenieur.** m *mechanical engineer* **~kanone** f *automatic gun* **~kraft** f *e.-power* **~kunde, ~lehre** f *engineering, mechanics* **~leistung** f *e. power* **≈mäßig** a *like a m., mechanical* ‖ ⟨fig⟩ *automatic, instinctive* **~meister** m (*master-*)*machinist*; ⟨rail⟩ *traffic-manager, manager of the rolling stock*; ⟨typ⟩ *conductor*; ⟨theat⟩ *scene-shifter, stage-mechanician* **~näherei** f *m. stitch* **~name** m (symbolischer ~) ⟨comp⟩ *mnemonic name* **~papier** n *m.-made paper*, Rolle ~ *web, endless paper* **~park** m *m.ry* **~personal** n *e.-room staff*, ⟨mar⟩ *e.-r. complement* **~pflege** f *equipment maintenance* **~pflug** m *steamplough* **~pistole** f (*automatic*) *sub-m.-gun, m.-pistol* **~programm** n ⟨comp⟩ *object program* **~putzer** m ⟨rail⟩ *cleaner* **~raum** m *e.-room* ⟨a. mar⟩ **~riemen** m *e. belt* **~satz** m ⟨typ⟩ *m. composition* **~schaden** m *e. trouble* **~schlosser** m (*metal*) *fitter* **~schreiber(in** f) m (*female* od *lady*) *typist* **~schrift** f *type-script, type-written characters* pl, *typewriting*; in ~ *type-written*, 10 Bogen ~ *ten sheets of type-written paper* **~schweißen** n *machine welding* **~setzer** m ⟨typ⟩ *m.-operator* **~sprache** f ⟨comp⟩ *computer language* **~tagebuch** n *e.-room register* **~teil** n (Bauteil) (*machine*) *part, part of a m.* **~teil** m, verschiebbarer ~ *rider* **~waffe** f *automatic weapon* **~webstuhl** m *power-loom* **~wechsel** m ⟨rail⟩ *change of e.s* **~wesen** n *engineering* **~zeichnung** f *engineering drawing* **~zeitalter** n *m. age* **~zentrale** f *central power-plant* **Maschiner·ie** f ~/~n *machinery, plant* **Maschin·ist** m ~en/~en *machinist, operator* ‖ ⟨rail⟩ *engine-driver* ‖ ⟨theat⟩ *scene-shifter, stage mechanician*

MASER (Maser) m *Maser* (*maser*) = *microwave amplification by stimulated emission of radiation*

M·aser f ~/~n *spot, mark, speck*; (im Holz) *vein, streak, grain* **~fleck** m = ~ | **~n** [pl] ⟨med⟩ *measles* pl; die ~n h *to have* (od *suffer from*) *the m.* **m·aserig** a *veined* (*wood*); *streaked, speckled, streaky* **m·asern 1.** [vt] [h] *to vein, grain, spot* **2.** [a] *veined* (*wood*) **M·aserung** f (Holz≈) *veining, grain*

Maskar·enen, Maskar·enische Inseln f pl (Réunion, Mauritius, Rodriguez im Ind. Ozean) *Mascarenes, Mascarene Isles* pl

M·aske f ~/~n *mask* ⟨a. fig⟩ ‖ ⟨fenc⟩ *visor* ‖ ⟨phot⟩ (*slide*) *mask* ‖ ⟨mil⟩ *screen* ‖ (P) *masker*(*ader*), *figure* ‖ ~ anlegen, tragen, ablegen *to put a m. on, to wear a m., to take off one's m.* od *to unmask* ‖ ohne ~ *unm.ed* ⟨a. fig⟩ | ⟨fig⟩ sein Gesicht erstarrte zu e–r ~ *his features set in a m.*; e–m die ~ v Gesicht reißen *to unm. a p* ‖ die ~ fallen l *to drop* od *abandon all pretence, to show one's true face* od *one's colours* ‖ unter der ~ der F. *behind* od *under the m.* od *under the pretence of friendship* ‖ .. ist nur ~ *his amiability is nothing but sham* | °so 'ne ~! (P) *what a guy*! **M·asken- ~anzug** m *fancy-dress* **~ball** m; auf e–m ~ *at a f.-(d.) ball, masked ball* **~fest** n ~ball **~freiheit** f *freedom of a masquerade* od *during a carnival* **~kleid** n, **~kostüm** n *f.-d.* **~scherz** m *mummery* **~tanz** m *masque* **~verleiher** m *costumier* **~zug** m *masquerading procession* **Masker·ade** f ~/~n *masquerade, f.-d. ball*; (*game of*) *disguise* **mask·ieren** vt [h] (Gesicht) *to mask* ⟨a. mil & fig⟩ ‖ ⟨mil⟩ *to camouflage* | **sich** ~ *to masquerade, to put on a mask* ‖ (verkleiden) *to disguise o.s.* ‖ (zum Ball) *she dressed h.s. up as a shepherdess* | ⟨übtr⟩ *the central heating was concealed by a fireplace* **Mask·ierung** f ~/~en *masking* ⟨a. mil & fig⟩, *masquerade* ‖ ⟨mil⟩ *camouflage, screening*

Mask·otte f ~/~n *mascot*

Maskul·inum n ~s/–na ⟨gram⟩ *masculine noun*

Mas·owien n (poln. Landschaft) *Masovia*
m·aß, (m·äße) 1. & 3. sg pret (subj) v messen
M·aß A. 1. n ~es/~e *measure* ‖ (Ausdehnung) *dimension, extent* ‖ (Größe) *size* ‖ ⟨tail, etc.⟩ (*a p's*) *measurements* pl ‖ ⟨mus⟩ *time* ‖ (Mäßigung) *moderation, propriety* ‖ (Verhältnis) *proportion* **2.** (Eich-, Normal≃) *gauge* ‖ deutsches, engl. ~ .. *standard unit* **3.** f ~/~ *tankard* (*1.76 pt*); zwei ~ *two pots* od *quarts* (*of beer*) **B. geringes** ~ *modicum* (*of knowledge*) ‖ gerütteltes ~ = volles ~ ‖ ein gewisses ~ v Erfolg *a measure of success* ‖ e–m ein **hohes** ~ v Vertrauen entgegenbringen *to have full confidence in a p* ‖ höchstes ~ *maximum* ‖ etw in **natürlichem** ~e nachbilden *to take a lifesize copy of a th* ‖ unumgänglich notwendiges ~ *unavoidable minimum* ‖ etw in **vergrößertem** (verkleinertem) ~e zeichnen .. *on an enlarged* (*reduced*) *scale* ‖ ein **volles** ~ *full measure*; *a generous portion* (*of*) ‖ ⟨fig⟩ das ~ ist voll! *I've had enough of it!, the cup is full to the brim!* ‖ er hat sein volles ~ *he has his full measure* od *his fill* **zweierlei** ~ *two standards* **C.** sich in demselben ~e **entwickeln** wie: *the development kept pace with* .. ~ **halten** *to keep within bounds, to observe moderation, to be moderate,* .. im Essen *to be a moderate eater* ‖ weder ~ noch Ziel halten *to go to extremes*; wissen ~ z h. *to know when/where to draw the line* ‖ e–m (das) ~ **nehmen** für *or* zu *to measure a p for* (*a suit*), *to take a p's measurements for* ‖ das ~ **überschreiten** *to exced all bounds* (*of moderation*) ‖ das ~ e–r S **vollmachen** *to put the lid on a th* **D.** er hielt die Kritik **auf** dem rechten ~ *he kept criticism within its proper bounds* ‖ die Zahl auf ein vernünftiges ~ beschränken *to reduce the number to reasonable proportions* ‖ **in** dem ~e, daß *to such a degree as to* ‖ in dem ~e wie *in the same measure as, at the rate which, as much* od *intensely as, according as* ‖ in diesem ~e *at this rate* ‖ in erstaunlichem ~e *in an astonishing way* ‖ in bedrohlichem ~e *at a fearful rate* ‖ in geringem (hohem) ~e *on a small* (*large*) *scale* ‖ in gleichem ~e *at a corresponding rate* ‖ in hohem ~e *in a high degree, to a large* od *great extent*; *highly, richly, amply, eminently*; *vitally*; ⟨fam⟩ *to a degree* ‖ in höchstem ~e *to the utmost limit* ‖ er genoß mein Vertrauen in reichem (vollem) ~e *I had great* (*full*) *confidence in him* ‖ in so reichem ~e *in such abundant measure* ‖ in noch stärkerem ~e *at a still greater rate* ‖ in verstärktem ~e *additionally* ‖ in vollem ~e *to the full*; *fully, largely, abundantly* ‖ in zunehmendem ~e *increasingly* ‖ **mit** ~(en pl) *in moderation* ‖ mit ~ u Ziel *in reason* ‖ alles mit ~ u Ziel! *there's a limit to everything* ‖ man kann nicht alle mit gleichem ~e messen *one can't judge everybody by the same standard* ‖ **nach** ~ *to order* ‖ ⟨tail⟩ *made to measure,* ⟨Am⟩ *custom-made* ‖ nach ~ angefertigter Anzug *bespoke suit,* ⟨Am⟩ *custom-suit* ‖ nach ~ kaufen *to buy to measure*; nach ~ u Gewicht *according to m. and weight* ‖ ohne ~ *without moderation* od *restriction* ‖ ohne ~ u Ziel *immoderately, without limits* ‖ **über** die *or* alle ~en *beyond m., b. all bounds, excessively, immeasurably, outrageously, exceedingly* ‖ *no end* (*grateful*) ‖ *an atrociously bad lunch* ‖ *supremely, deliriously,* ⟨Am⟩ *tremblingly* (*happy*) ‖ *helplessly* (*unprotected*); (*exasperated*) *beyond all endurance* ‖ *acutely* (*jealous*) ‖ ⟨sl⟩ *horribly* ‖ über die ~en groß *or* gewaltig *overwhelming* (*power*) ‖ über alle ~en loben *to praise to the skies*; über jedes vernünftige ~ *beyond reason*; etw über die ~en vergrößern *to enlarge a th out of all proportion* ‖ s–e Anschuldigungen gingen über das übliche ~ hinaus .. *exceeded the usual bounds* **~abteilung** f *bespoke* (Am *custom*) *department* **~abweichung** f (zulässige ~) ⟨tech⟩ *allowance* **~analyse** f ⟨chem⟩ *titration, volumetric analysis*; e–e ~ an e–r Lösung ausführen *to titrate a solution* **~anfertigung** f *custom-order* **~anzug** m *made-to-measure suit* **~arbeit** f *a th made to measure*; *bespoke work* **~bestimmung** f *measurement* **~einheit** f *unit of measure* **~fehler** m *faulty dimension* **~gabe** f *measure, proportion* ‖ (jedoch) mit der ~, daß *on the condition that*; *with the provision* od *proviso that* ‖ nach ~ der folgenden Bestimmungen ⟨contr⟩ *subject as hereinafter set out* ‖ nach ~ des Preises *according* (od *in proportion*) *to the price* ‖ nach ~ der Regierung *as directed by the G.* **≃gebend** a *standard* ‖ *decisive* (f *for*) ‖ *authentic* (*text*); *dispositive* (*clause*); *proper* (*authority*) ‖ *overriding* (*necessity, factor, requirements*) ‖ ~ f die S ist *essential is* ‖ v ~er Seite *from authoritative quarters*; an ~en Stellen *in a. qu.*; ~e Kreise *influential circles* pl ‖ ~ s *to be a governing consideration*; ~ s f ⟨a.⟩ *to govern*; f (die Größe) ist ~ (*the size*) *shall be determined by* .. ‖ er (das) ist nicht ~ für *he* (*that*) *is no criterion for* ‖ der lateinische Text ist ~ .. *prevails* ‖ ~ ist .. *what finally matters is* .. **≃geblich 1.** [adv] *considerably* (*interested, concerned*); ~ beeinflussen *to exert a telling influence on* **2.** [a] *consequential* ‖ etw als ~ ansehen *to regard a th as a determining factor*; diese Daten sind nur annähernd ~ *the data constitute only an approximate guide* **≃gerecht** a *in correct scale* **~geschäft** n *bespoke business* od *trade* **≃|halten** vi [h] → Maß **~halten** n *moderation, restriction* **≃haltend** a ⟨phot⟩ *nondeforming* (*film*) **~haltigkeit** f ⟨phys⟩ *dimensional stability*; ⟨rep⟩ *stability*; *absolutely constant dimensions* **~holder** m ⟨bot⟩ *field-maple* **~kanne** f *quart, tankard* **~kolben** m *volumetric flask* **~krug** m *quart-jug,* ⟨Am⟩ *stein* **~lieb** n, gr ~ *ox-eye daisy* **~liebchen** n *daisy* **≃los** [a] *immoderate, measureless* ‖ ⟨fig⟩ *extravagant, reckless* ‖ [adv] *beyond all bounds, without any sense of proportion, incredibly, recklessly, exceedingly* **~losigkeit** f *intemperance, -rateness*; *want of moderation* ‖ ⟨fig⟩ *extravagance* **~nahme** f *arrangement, action, move* ‖ erste ~n *emergency measures*; Gesamtheit der ~n *group of actions* ‖ als vorübergehende ~ *as a temporary measure* ‖ dem müssen die eigenen ~n Rechnung tragen *this factor must be recognized and provided for* ‖ ~n treffen *or* ergreifen *to take m.s* od *steps* ‖ die äußersten ~n ergreifen *to go* od *proceed to extremities* **~prüfer** m *measure tester* **~regel** f *measure*; ~n ergreifen, nehmen, treffen *to take m.s*; .. gegen (= e–n maßregeln) *to censure, reprimand, discipline a p, to inflict disciplinary punishment on a p* **~röhre** f *burette* **~schneider** m *bespoke* (⟨Am⟩ *custom-*) *tailor* **~schuhe** m pl *custom-made shoes* **Maßstab** m *measuring rod* ‖ *yardstick* ⟨a. fig⟩; *measure*; *ratio of dimensions* ‖ (Strichmaßstab) *line standard* ‖ (Karten≃) *scale*; Karte gr ~es *large-sc. map*; im ~ v *drawn to a sc. of one inch to 60 miles* (*a one-inch-to-60-miles map*); im selben ~ *drawn to the same sc.* ‖ vergrößerter (verkleinerter) ~ *enlarged* (*reduced*) *scale* ‖ das ist kein ~ *you can't go by that* ‖ in kl ~ *small-scale* (*settlement*) ‖ in e–m kl (gr., großartigen) ~e *on a small* (*large, gigantic*) *scale* ‖ ⟨fig⟩ *standard* (*by German st.s* nach ..) ‖ e–n ~ festsetzen *to set up a st.* ‖ wenn *or* sobald man .. als ~ nimmt *in terms of* (*economics*); mit den ≃en .. gemessen, interpretiert *in terms of* (*western experience*) ‖ sich nach e–m ~ richten *to go by a st.* ‖ e–n ~ an etw legen *to apply a st. to a th* ‖ sie h jeden ~ verloren *they are without any sense of proportion, they have lost all s. of pr.* | ≃gerecht, ≃getreu [a] (*according*) *to scale*, nicht ~ *out of sc.* **Maß- ~stock** m ⟨tech⟩ *rule* **~verhältnisse** n *proportions* pl **≃voll** a *moderate, temperate, measured* ‖ *discreet* (*behaviour*) ‖ *lenient* (*criticism*) ‖ alles, was sich in ~en Grenzen bewegt *anything in reason* ‖ ~ leben *to live a life of moderation* **≃weise** adv *in quarts* **~werk** n *tracery, lights* pl **~zahl** f ⟨stat⟩ *statistic*; Prüf≃ *test st.*, Zuordnungs≃

classification st. **~zeichnung** f *dimensioned drawing*

Massach·usetts [-tʃ-] n (Staat der U.S.A.)

Mass·age [-ʒə] f ~/~en *massage*; → Masseur **massakr·ieren** vt [h] *to massacre, slaughter*

M·asse f ~/~n **1.** **(S)** *substance, mass* || ⟨cul⟩ *mixture, filling* || breiige ~ *pulp* || dicke, feste ~ *blubber* || ⟨found⟩ *charge of metal* || gestampfte ~ *rammed stuff* || ~ homogener Teile *aggregate* || kl runde ~ *blob* || knetbare ~ *magma* L (bes ⟨geol⟩ des Erdinnern) || körperliche ~ *substance* || *plastic (substance)* || rollige ~n ⟨min⟩ *unfixed masses* || teigige ~ *dough(y mass), paste* || (Töpfer-~) *paste* || weiche ~ *soft substance* || wirre ~ *welter (of stone)* || zähe ~ *tough substance* || zusammenhängende ~ *block* **2.** (Menge) *quantity, volume* || (Haupt~) *bulk* || **in** ~(n) *in large quantities* || e–e ~ Geld *a lot of money* || sie h alles in ~n .. *in abundance* || in ~n herstellen *to mass-produce* **3.** **(P)** *multitude* || die ~ des Volkes *the mass* [pl konstr] *of the population* || arbeitende ~n *toiling masses* || die breite *or* gr ~ *the masses, the vast numbers, the common herd* od *people* || (Menschen~n) *masses of people* pl || die ~ der Junker *the rank and file of squires* || sie kamen in ~n .. *in crowds* **4.** ⟨com⟩ Vermögens- (Konkurs-) ~ *(bankrupt's) estate; fund(s)* || → mangels ~ wurde das Konkursverfahren eingestellt *the bankruptcy proceedings were stopped for lack of assets* | (Umsatz) die ~ muß es bringen *the number of buyers must ensure a good turnover* **~kabel** n ⟨el mot⟩ *earthing lead*

M·assel[1] f ~/~n ⟨met⟩ *pig*

°**M·assel**[2] m ~s/ [hebr] ⟨vulg⟩ (Glück) *luck*

m·aßen †* [conj] (= weil) *inasmuch as* .. **maßen** [adv-suff] ·anerkannter~ *admittedly, as generally acknowledged* || bek·annter~ *notoriously* || der~ *in such a degree* || → einiger~, folgender~ || erklärter~ *declaredly* || gebührender~ *duly* || solcher~ *in such a degree* od *manner, so much so* (daß *that*) || unverdienter~ *undeservedly* || versprochener~ *as promised*

M·assen- °**~abfütterung** f *feeding of large numbers* **~absatz** m *wholesale* **~absprung** m ⟨aero⟩ *mass-jump* **~abwurf** m (Bomben) *salvo* **~angriff** m *m.-attack* **~angst** f = **~flucht** **~anschluß** m ⟨el mot⟩ *earth connection* **~anziehung** f *gravitation* **~armut** f *pauperism* **~artikel** m *wholesale ware, m. production article* **~aufgebot** n *general levy* **~austritt** m *m. exodus* °**~bach** adv ⟨hum⟩ = –weise **~bedarf** m *volume demand* **~bildung** f ⟨mil⟩ *m.ing (of troops)* **~demonstration** f *m. demonstration* **~elektrode** f *ground e.* **~erhebungen** f pl *m. risings* **~feuer** n ⟨mil⟩ *g.l volley* **~flucht** f *stampede* **~gebirge** n *mountain m.(if)* **~grab** n *g.l tomb, common grave* **~gräber** n pl ⟨hist⟩ *barrows* pl, *tumuli* L pl **~gutfrachter** m *bulk good freighter* **~herstellung** f *m.-production, quantity* (od *large-scale*) *manufacturing* od *production* **~kommunikationsmittel** n pl *mass c.tion means* **~mensch** m *m. man, collective man* **~mord** m *(g.l) massacre, holocaust; wholesale murder; butchery, slaughter* **~nahverkehr** m *m. transit* **~opfer** n ⟨fig⟩ *hecatomb* **~orchester** n *m.ed bands* pl **~produktion** = ~herstellung **~prophylaxe** f *collective pr.* **~psychose** f *m. psychosis* **~quartier** n *doss-house* **~schaden** m ⟨ins⟩ *heavy loss* od *damage* **~schlachtung** f *massacre*, ⟨fig⟩ *hecatomb* || → ~mord **~speiselokal** n *m. catering establishment* **~sturz** m ⟨racing, etc⟩ *pile-up* **~szene** f *crowd-scene* **~verbrauch** m *bulk consumption* **~verkauf** m *heavy sales* pl **~vernichtungswaffe** f *mass destruction weapon* **~versammlung** f *m. meeting* **~verwalter** m ⟨jur⟩ *assignee* **~wanderung** f *m. movement; rush* **~weise** adv *in shoals, in large quantities* **m·assenhaft** a *abundant, numerous; wholesale* [attr]; *plenty of* ..; *loads of (time)*; ⟨com⟩ *volume (demand)* || adv *in crowds* od *shoals* || ~ enthalten *to be full of* || ~es Auftreten v .. *swarms* od *myriads of (gnats)* **~igkeit** f ~/ *abundance*

Mass·eur [–ˈsøə] m ~s/~e [–ørə] *masseur* **-·euse** [–ˈsø:zə] f ~/~n *masseuse* **mass·ieren** vt [h] *to massage, knead*; (nach dem Bade) **to shampoo* || auf schlanke Linie ~: *my masseuse is taking me off three times a week*

mass·ieren vt [h] ⟨mil⟩ *to mass (troops)* || massierte Erdziele ⟨mil⟩ *compact ground targets* pl **Mass·ierung** f ⟨mil⟩ *concentration* **m·assig** [a] *bulky, solid, massy, ponderous, voluminous; colossal (statue), stout (p); thick (tree)* | [adv] °er hat ~ viel Geld *he has a huge lot of m.*

m·äßig a *moderate (heat, cold, claims)* || (enthaltsam) *frugal* || (im Trinken) *sober, temperate* || *conservative (estimate)* || *moderate* od *reasonable (prices)* || *sober (conduct)* | ⟨mus⟩ *andante* | (mittel~) *middling* || *mediocre (worker)* || *indifferent (health, player)* || ein sehr ~er Ersatz *an apology* (f *for*) || ~! *bad show!* .. **mäßig** [in comp] **1.** *measuring* .. **2.** kavalier~ *cavalierly* || helden~ *like a hero*; → Maß

m·äßigen vt/refl [h] (sich) ~ *to moderate (o.s.)* || (lindern) *to mitigate, temper, assuage; to soften (down); to tone down (one's speech)* || ~ Sie Ihren Zorn *or* sich *curb* od *keep your temper!, compose* od *restrain y.s.* || ~ Sie sich im Essen *control your appetite!, be moderate in eating* || ge–gt *temperate (zone), moderate (Republicans)* || *to keep within bounds* || (verringern) *to lessen* || (langsamer m) *to slacken* **M·äßigkeit** f ~/ *moderation* || *temperance, frugality, sobriety* || *reasonableness (of prices)* | (Mittel~) *mediocrity* **M·äßigkeits- ~apostel** m *apostle of temperance* **~verein** m *t. society, Band of Hope* **~vereinler** m *teetotaller, blue-ribbonite* **M·äßigung** f ~/ *moderation* || *mitigation*

mass·iv **1.** [a] *massive (statue, silver chain; retaliation)* || *solid, pure (gold)* || *squat* (od *well built*) *(house)* | ⟨fig fam⟩ er wurde ~ *he cut up rough* **2.** ~ [n] ⟨geol⟩ *block massif*

M·ast[1] m ~es/~e(n) ⟨mar⟩ *mast* || ⟨aero⟩ Anker~ *pylon; mooring m.* || ⟨mar⟩ Besan~ *mizzen m.* || Behelfs~ *jury-m.* || Fock~ *fore-m.* || Groß~ *main m.* || Telegraphen~ *telegraph-pole* | e–n ~ abtakeln *to unrig a m.* || .. einsetzen *to step a m.* || den ~ aufrichten, kappen (umlegen) *to hoist, cut (take down) the m.* || mit ~en versehen *to m.* || *(of ships)* den ~ einbüßen *to be dismasted* || den ~ zutakeln *to rig the m.* || die Segel auf den ~ brassen *to back the sails* **~backe** f *m.-cheek* **~band** n *m.-hoop* **~baum** m *mast* **~fesselgeschirr** n ⟨aero⟩ *m.-mooring gear* **~gast** m *m.man* **~korb** m *top, m.-head, crow's nest* **~los** a *m.less dism.ed* **~montage** f *pole mounting* **~schalter** m ⟨el⟩ *pole switch* **~spur** f *m.-step* **~stenge** f *main-topmast* **~verankerung** f ⟨aero⟩ *m.-mooring* **~wache** f *look-out* **~werk** n *masts* pl **m·asten** vt [h] *to m. (a ship)* .. **mastig** a suff ⟨mar⟩ drei~ *three-m.ed*

M·ast[2] f *food, mast* || *fattening (pigs,* etc.) || Schweine zur ~ halten *to fatten pigs* || Gänse zur ~ füttern *to stuff geese* || in die ~ tun *to set to fatten* **~darm** m ⟨anat⟩ *straight gut*, ⟨scient⟩ *rectum* | ~entzündung [f] *rectitis*; ~spiegel [m] *rectoscope* **~futter** n *fattening-pasture* **~hähnchen, ~huhn** n *(fattened) roasting* od *battery chicken* **~kur** f ⟨med⟩ *su(pe)ralimentation*; e–e ~ nötig h *to need feeding up* **~nutzung** f *pannage* **~schlachtvieh** n *fatstock* **~schwein** n *fattened pig; porker* || ⟨fig⟩ *fat sow* **~stall** m *fattening-stall* **~vieh** n *cattle to be fattened* || *f.ed cattle* **m·ästen** vt [h] *to feed, to fatten; to cram, stuff, noodle (geese)* || sich ~ [h] *to fill one's fat belly; to grow fat, to batten (an on)*; ⟨fam⟩ *to grease the gills* || gemästet *stall-fed*, ⟨fig fam⟩ *well-fed* || ⟨bib⟩ das gemästete Kalb schlachten *to kill the fatted calf* **Mastung,** ~ f ~/ *feeding, fattening*; (Schaf) *flushing* || (v Vögeln) *cramming*

M·astix m ~(es)/ *mastic, mastic-tree*

Mas·uren pl **1.** (poln. Volksstamm in den Landsch. Masovien) *Masurians* pl **2.** †(der südl. Teil v Ostpreußen)

Mas·urka f ~/~s (Tanz) *mazurka*

Matad·or m ~s/~e *matador* | ⟨fig⟩ *big gun*; (Haupt≁) *top sawyer* || *crack player* || ⟨mil⟩ *king* ⟨a. fam⟩ || ⟨cards⟩ *master card*

Match- ~beutel, ~sack [m] *duffle* (od *carry-all*) *bag*

M·ater f ~/~n ⟨typ⟩ *matrix*, ⟨fam⟩ *mat*

Materi·al n ~s/~ien **1.** *material* || ⟨rail⟩ *rolling-stock* || Menschen u ~ verlieren *to lose man-power and m.s* || aus schlechtem ~ herstellen *to fake* || stimmliches ~ *vocal m.* | (P) brauchbares ~ *useful men* || prächtiges ~ s *to be first rate* **2.** **~ien** [-iən] pl *groceries, drugs* || (Roh≁ien) pl *raw m.* **~beanspruchung** f *m. stress* **~beute** f *booty in m.* **~einlauftrichter** m *raw feed input hopper* **~eintrag** m ⟨mill, etc⟩ *feed of m.* **~erhaltung** f *maintenance* **~ermüdungsmesser** m *fatigue meter* **~lager** n *stock of m.s*; *stockpile* **~plan** m *m. schedule* **~schaden** m *m. damage* | durch **~überlegenheit** besiegen, schlagen ⟨mil⟩ *to outmachine* **~verwalter** m *supply clerk* **~waren** f pl *groceries, colonial products* pl || (Drogen) *drugs* pl | ~händler [m] *grocer, druggist*; ~handlung [f] *grocery, grocer's shop* **Material·ismus** m ~/ *materialism* **material·istisch** a *materialistic* **Mat·erie** f ~/~n *matter, stuff* || *a question not of form but of substance* || *to oppose mind to matter* || *the power of mind over matter* | ⟨med⟩ *matter, pus* | ⟨philos⟩ *hyle* **materi·ell** [a] *material* (*reason, position*) || ~er Aufwand *expenditure of m.*; die ~en Annehmlichkeiten des Lebens *the creature comforts* || in ~er Hinsicht *m.ly* || ~es Recht *substantive law* || ~e Sorgen *material cares* | [adv] ~ denkend *m., of a worldly mind* || nicht ~ gesinnt *unworldly* || sich ~ gut stehen *to be well-off* || ~ unabhängig *of independent means*

Mathemat·ik f ~/ *mathematics* [pl, mst sg konstr]; ⟨fam⟩ Mathe(se) *matha* **~lehrer** m *mathematical master* **Mathem·atiker** m ~s/~ *mathematician* **mathem·atisch** a *m.cal* || ~er Satz *m.cal proposition* || ~e Gesetze *laws of m.cs* || ~e Geographie *astronomical geography* || mit ~er Sicherheit, Pünktlichkeit *with m.cal certainty, exactness*

Matin·ee [′ne:] f ~/~n [–′ne:ən] *morning performance, matinée* || (Frauenmorgenrock) *peignoir, wrapper*

M·atjeshering m *white herring*; *matie, matje*

Matr·atze f ~/~n *mattress* || (Sprungfeder≁) *spring-m.* || Woll≁ *flock bed* || ⟨a–n⟩ *couch* || °an der ~ horchen (gehen) ⟨fam⟩ *to go between the sheets*

Mätr·esse f ~/~n (*kept*) *mistress* || *paramour, concubine* || ⟨Gr ant⟩ *courtesan, -zan* || sich e–e ~ halten *to keep a m.* || sie h ~n *they have m.es* | –ssenwirtschaft [f] *reign of m.es*

Matriarch·at n ~(e)s/~e *matriarchy*

Matr·ik [österr], **Matr·ikel** f ~/~n ⟨univ⟩ *register, roll*; ⟨scient⟩ *matricula* || in die ~ eintragen *to register, to matriculate* **M·atrix** f ~/ Matr·izen ⟨math⟩ *matrix* **Matr·ize** f ~/~n *matrix* || (f Schreibmaschine) *stencil* || (Stempel) *die* || (Galvanoplastik, Stereotypie) *mould* | ⟨typewr⟩ ~nfarbe [f] *stencil ink*; ⟨comp⟩ ~-karte [f] *master balance card, descriptive c.*; ~n-papier [n] *stereo-flong*; *stencil paper*; ~rechnung [f] *matrix calculus* **Matr·one** f ~/~n *matron* ≁**nhaft** a *matronly*

Matr·ose m ~n/~n *sailor, seaman* || ⟨fam⟩ (*jack-*)*tar*; ⟨sl⟩ *jolly*; ⟨Am sl⟩ brit. ~ *lime-juicer* || ⟨mil mar⟩ *blue-jacket* || gemeiner ~ *deck hand*; als gewöhnlicher ~ *before the mast* || erfahrener ~ *able seaman* || ~ auf Landurlaub *liberty man* **Matr·osen-** **~anzug** m *sailor-suit* **~art** f *s.-fashion*; auf ~ *s.-like* **~hut** m *s.-hat* **~jacke** f *s.-jacket, pea-j.*, ⟨fam⟩ *monkey-j.* **~kleider** n pl ⟨fam⟩ *slops* pl **~kragen** m *s.-collar* **~lied** n *mariner's song, sea-shanty* **~makler** m *crimp* **~mütze** f *s.* (*dress*) *cap* **~schenke** f *s.'s pub* **~schneider** m *slop-maker* **~stoff** m (f Kinder) *galatea* **~werber** m = ~makler

M·atsch[1] m ~es/ (Brei) *pulp, squash* || (v Obst etc) z ~ w *to be squashed up* || (Schlamm) *mud, slush* || (Pfütze) *puddle* °**~auge** n *black eye* **m·atschen** vt [h] *to squash, mash* **m·atschig** a *mashy*, ⟨fam⟩ *squashy, messy* || (schlammig) *muddy, slushy, sludgy* **Matsch- u Schnee-Reifen** m *mud and snow tire*

M·atsch[2] m ~es/ (Spiel) *capot, loo* || ~ m *to capot, to make all the tricks* || ~ w *to be capotted, to lose all the tricks* **m·atschen** vt [h] (Spiel) *to capot*

M·att n ~/ (Schach) *mate* | ≁ a (schach≁ *check and*) *mate* ⟨a. fig⟩; jdn ~ setzen *to checkmate a p*

m·att a **1.** (P) *tired, exhausted, worn* (⟨fam⟩ *fagged*) *out* || (schwach) *feeble* || *faint, languid* || ~ s *to feel faint* (vor .. *with thirst, pain*) | ⟨hunt⟩ ~ hetzen *to bring* (*a stag*) *down* **2.** (S) *weak, limp* || (Augen) *dim*; mit ~en Augen *pale-* od *dim-eyed* || (im Ausdruck) *bald, lame* || (Bewegung) *limp* || (Bier) *flat* || (Blau) *dull, dead* || (Börse) ⟨com⟩ *dull, lifeless, stagnant* (*market*) || (Dichtung) *weak* || (Echo) *feeble* || (Entschuldigung) *lame* || (Farben) *subdued* || (Geschäft[sgang]) *dull* (*business*) || (Glas) *opaque, frosted* || (Gold) *dull, dead* || (Kugel) ⟨mil⟩ *spent* (*ball*) || *faint* (*smile*) || (Licht) *subdued* || (Papier) *mat, unglazed* || (Puls) *weak* || (Stil) *meagre, flabby, jejune, bald, monotonous* || (Stimme) *faint, feeble* || (Wetter) *oppressive* (*air*) || (Witz) *stale, poor* || (Worte) *feeble* | ~ [adv] ätzen *to mat, frost* (*glass*) || ~ satiniert *friction glazed* (*paper*) || ~ w (of efforts) *to wear thin* || ⟨fig⟩ ~ wirken *to fall flat* **~äugig** a *dim-* od *pale-eyed* **~blau** a *of a dull blue* ≁**druck** m ⟨typ⟩ *mat impression* ≁**farbe** f (Vergoldung) *deadening matter* **~geworden** a ⟨paint⟩ (of colours) *drunk in* [adv] ≁**gold** n *dead gold* **~golden** a *pale gold* (*hair*) **~grün** a *pale-green* **~herzig** a *poor-spirited, half-* od *faint-hearted* | ≁keit [f] *f.-* od *h.-h.-ness, poor-spiritedness* ≁**kolbenlampe** f *frosted lamp* ≁**scheibe** f ⟨phot⟩ *ground* [pp] *glass, focussing screen* || °~ bek (ohnmächtig w) *to go black*, ⟨sl⟩ *to black-out* || °bei mir ~! *I'm not quite myself* | ~nsucher [m] *reflex viewfinder* **~schwarz** a *dull black* **~vergoldet** a *dead-gilt* **~weiß** a *dull white* **M·attheit** f *tiredness, exhaustion* || *languidness, lassitude* || *faintness, feebleness* || ⟨com⟩ *dullness, lifelessness*; *stagnancy* (*of the market*) || *dimness* (*of glass*), *dullness* (*of gold*) **matt·ieren** vt [h] (= matt schleifen) *to mat, deaden* (*gold*) || *to tarnish* (*metal*) || *to frost* (*glass*) **M·attigkeit** f ~/ *faintness, weakness* || *exhaustion* || *languor*

M·atte[1] f ~/~n (*Alpine*) *meadow* || ⟨poet⟩ *mead*; die grünen ~n *the green fields* pl

M·atte[2] f ~/~n *mat* || chinesische ~ *China m.* || englische ~ *wrought m.* || K·okos≁ *cocoanut m.* || Str·oh≁ *straw m.* || Tür≁ *door-m.* **M·atten-** **~binse** f *m.-weed* **~damm** m *m. dike* **~flechter** m *m.-maker* **~geflecht, ~stoff, ~zeug** n *m.ting*

Matth·äus m *Matthew* || ~-Evangelium [n] *Gospel according to St. M.* || ⟨fam⟩ mit ihm ist's Matthäi am letzten *it's all over with him*; bei mir ist .. (mit dem Gelde) *I am at the end of my tether*

M·attra n (vorderind. Bezirk) *Muttra*

Mat·ur(a) f ~/ = Reifeprüfung

Maturit·äts- **~examen** n ⟨Ger⟩ *final* od *leaving examination* (*at a secondary school*) || das ~ m *to pass one's f.l ex.* **~zeugnis** n *leaving certificate, c. of maturity*

M·atz m ~(e)s/≁e 1. *simpleton, noodle, nincompoop* (→ Hemden≁) 2. (Vogel) *dicky-bird, starling* (= Piepmatz) **M·ätzchen** n ~s/~ **1.** [dim] **2.** ⟨fam⟩ *trick, antic*; ⟨Am sl⟩ *gimmick*;

⟨hors⟩ *gambade* ⟨a. fig⟩ || ~ m *to play the fool, to play tricks*

M·atze f ~/~n, **M·atzen** m ~s/~ ⟨Hebr⟩ *Passover* od *unleavened bread*

°**mau** a **1.** ⟨sl⟩ *dicky* (*business*) || das ist ~ *it's pretty middling* **2.** mir ist ~ [adv] (ich bin unwohl) *I feel faint* (→ matt, Mattscheibe)

M·auer f ~/~n *wall* || ausgebauchte ~ *battering* od *shrinking w.* || Außen~̈ *outer w.* || blinde ~ *dead* od *blind w.* || Brand~̈ *fire w.* || einhalb Stein starke ~ *wall half a brick thick* || fensterlose ~ = blinde ~ || fluchtlose ~ *slovenly-built w.* || gezinnelte ~ *embattled w.* || Giebel~̈ *gable w.* || Grund~̈ *foundation w.* || Haustein~̈ *w. of free-stone* || „hölzerne ~n" (Schiffe) *wood w.s* || Kai~̈ *quay* (*w.*), *embankment, pier* || stehengebliebene ~n → -reste || Stirn~̈ *face w.* || Stütz~̈ *supporting* od *retaining w.* || trockene ~ *dry w.* || Wolken~̈ *curtain of clouds* || Ziegel~̈ *brick-w.* || Zwischen~̈ *partition w.* | außerhalb (innerhalb) der ~n *extramural* (*intramural*) || in Marburgs ~n *within the walls of M.* || die ~ senkt *or* setzt sich .. *sinks in* od *settles* || mit e–r ~ umgeben *to w.* (*in*) || mit weißen ~n *white-walled* | ⟨fig⟩ fest wie e–e ~ (*as*) *firm as a rock* || ⟨fig⟩ ~n zw Klassen *class-barriers* **~abdeckung** f *coping* **~absatz** m *offset* **~anker** m *w. clamp* **~anschlag** m *poster* **~-arbeit** f *masonry* **~assel** f *woodlouse* **~auskleidung** f *brickwork lining* **~band** n ⟨arch⟩ *string-course* **~bettung** f *bed of masonry* **~blende** f *niche of a w.* **~blümchen** n ⟨bot & fig⟩ *w.-flower* **~brecher** m *battering-ram* **~brüstung** f *cornice* **~damm** m ⟨min⟩ *dam of brickwork* **~ecke** f *quoin* **~eidechse** f ⟨zoo⟩ *w.-lizard* **~eppich** m ⟨bot⟩ *ivy* **~feld** n *pane of a w.* **~fläche, ~flucht** f *plain of a w.* **~fuchs** m ⟨ent⟩ *w. butterfly* **~fuß** m *bottom of a w.* **~gecko** m ⟨zoo⟩ *w.-gecko* **~hut** m, **~kappe** f *coping* **~kalk** m *mortar* **~kelle** f *trowel* **~konsole** f *w. bracket* **~krone** f *mural crown*; (Sperr~̈) *dam crest* **~-krönung** f *coping* **~meister** m *master mason* **~pfeffer** m ⟨bot⟩ *stone-crop*; scharfer ~ *w.-pepper* **~pfeiler** m *buttress* **~polier** m *bricklayer's foreman* **~rand** m (innerer) *parapet* **~raute** f ⟨bot⟩ *w.-rue* **~reste** m pl *remains* od *remnants of w.s* **~salpeter** m *w.-saltpetre* **~salz** n *w.-salt* **~sand** m *sand used by bricklayers* **~schlitz** m *loophole* **~-**schwalbe f ⟨orn⟩ *black martin, martlet, swift* **~-sockel** m *plinth w.* **~spalte** f *crevice, crack, chink of a w.* **~specht** m ⟨orn⟩ *spider-catcher* **~stein** m *brick* **~strecke** f *pane of a w.* **~verband** m *bond*; (Läufer) *stretcher*; (Binder) *header* **~verkleidung** f *lining of a w.*; ⟨fort⟩ *revetment* **~vertiefung** f *recess* **~werk** n *masonry, brickwork* **~zacke** f ⟨arch⟩ *cop* ⟨fort⟩ *merlon* **~ziegel** = ~stein **~zinne** f ⟨fort⟩ *battlement* **m·auern 1.** vt/i [h] *build* (*in stone* od *in brick*) | *to lay bricks* **2.** vi [h] ⟨übtr ftb⟩ *to stone-wall* || ⟨cards⟩; *to play for safety* → Maurer

M·auke f ~/ **1.** ⟨vet⟩ *malanders* pl **2.** *hidingplace* °**~pantoffel** m pl *spats* ⟨a. fig aero⟩

M·aul[1] n ~(e)s/~̈er **A.** ⟨zoo⟩ *mouth, muzzle* | °(P) ⟨fam⟩ *jaw, chops* pl || °ein gottloses, grobes, loses, ungewaschenes ⟨fig⟩ ~ *a wanton, rough, loose, cheeky tongue*; ein schändliches ~ *a foul mouth* | ⟨übtr⟩ °die bösen ~̈er *the scandal-mongers* || °alle ~̈er sind voll davon *everybody's tongue is wagging about it*; hungrige ~̈er ⟨sl⟩ *peckers* **B.** °**Wendungen**: sich etw am ~ absparen *to stint o.s. of a th* || das ~ (nicht) aufmachen *or* auftun *to open one's lips* (*not to say bo to a goose*) || das ~ aufreißen *to brag* || das ~ aufsperren *to stand gaping*; ⟨fig⟩ *to gasp* || ~ u Nase aufsperren *to be flabbergasted* || das ~ brauchen *to use one's tongue* || er hat 10 ~̈er zu ernähren *he has to maintain a family of ten persons* || e–m übers ~ fahren 1. *to snap a p up, to cut a p short* 2. *to give a p the lie* || nicht aufs ~ gefallen s *to have the gift of the gab, to have a ready answer* od *tongue* || e–m ums ~ gehen *to flatter a p to his face* || das gr ~ h *to talk big, to brag*; *to talk everybody down* || das ~ halten ⟨sl⟩ *to shut one's trap, to shut up, to cut the cackle, to stop one's gab*; halt's ~! *shut up!*, *hold your jaw* od *row! dry up! ring off!* ⟨Am sl⟩ *can it!* || das ~ hängen l *to pull a long face, to pout, to be down in the mouth* || in der Leute ~̈er k *to become the talk of the town* || ein (schiefes) ~ m *to make a wry face* || ein süßes ~ m *to sham friendliness* || kein Blatt vors ~ nehmen *to call a spade a sp.* || das ~ voll nehmen *to brag* || e–m nach dem ~e reden *to chime in with a p* || e–m die Antwort ins ~ schmieren *to put the right words into a p's mouth* || e–m Brei, Honig, Pappe ums ~ schmieren *to buoy a p up with vain hopes* || das ~ nach etw spitzen *to be keen on sth* || e–m das ~ stopfen *to stop a p's talk* || das ~ steht ihr k–n Augenblick still *she talks nineteen to the dozen* || e–m das ~ verbieten *to tell a p to hold his tongue* || sich das ~ verbrennen *to put one's foot in it* || e–m das ~ wäßrig m *to make a p's mouth water* || ich durfte mir nur das ~ wischen (bekam nichts) *I could only wipe my mouth* | ⟨prov⟩ dem fliegen die gebratenen Tauben ins ~ *he is living in the land of milk and honey* **~affe** m *booby, jackanapes* [sg]; ~n feilhalten *to stand gaping* **~drescher** m *chatterbox* ~̈**faul** a ⟨fam⟩ *averse to speaking, too lazy to speak* **~fäule** f ⟨vet⟩ *flaps* pl **~fertigkeit** f *loquacity* **~freund** m *lip-friend, flatterer* **~hänger** m *pouter*; *sulky person* **~hängerei** f *sulks* pl, *sulking, moping* **~held** m *braggart*; ⟨Am a.⟩ *mouth-artist*, ⟨sl⟩ *windjammer* **~heldentum** n *bragging* **~klemme** f *lock-jaw* **~korb** m *muzzle* || (e–m Hund) den ~ anlegen *to muzzle* || ohne ~ *unmuzzled* **~schelle** f *box on the ear*, ⟨fam⟩ *muzzler* || jdm e–e ~ geben *to slap a p's face* **~sperre** f = ~klemme **~spitzen** n; da hilft kein ~, es muß gepfiffen w [etwa:] *in for a penny, in for a pound* **~tasche** f = 1. ~schelle 2. ~held 3. ~hänger **~trommel** f *Jew's harp* **~- u Klauenseuche** f ⟨vet⟩ *murrain, foot-and-mouth disease* **~werk** n ⟨fam⟩ (*gift of the*) *gab* **M·äulchen** n ~s/~ *little mouth* || ⟨fam⟩ *kiss* || ein ~ m *to purse up one's lips* **m·aulen** vi [h] ⟨fam⟩ *to pout, to be sulky, to pull a long face* || *to grumble*, ⟨sl⟩ *grouse*

Maul[2]**-** ~beerbaum [m] *mulberry*(*-tree*); ~-b.feige [f] *sycamore*, ~beere [f] *m.*

Maul[3]**-** **~esel** m (Bastard v Pferdehengst u Eselin, *a stallion is the sire and a donkey is the dam* [vgl –tier]) ⟨eig⟩ *hinny*; ⟨mst⟩ *mule* || ⟨fig⟩ → Mulus || wie ein ~ *mulish* | ~treiber [m] *mule-driver, muleteer* **~tier** n (Bastard v Eselhengst u Pferdestute [vgl –esel]) *mule*; auf ~en beritten *m.-mounted* (*infantry*) | ~treiber [m] *muleteer*

Maul[4]**-** **~wurf** m ⟨zoo⟩ *mole* | ~sfalle [f] *m.-trap*; ~sfell [n] *m.skin*; ~sgrille [f] ⟨zoo⟩ *m.-cricket*; ~shaufen, ~shügel [m] *m.-hill*

°**M·äuler** pl v Maultier & Maul

M·aure m (–rin [f]) *Moor*(*ess f*); spanischer ~ *Spanish Moor, Morisco* | ~nkappe [f] *morion*; → Birnhelm; → Mauretanien

M·aurer m ~s/~ *mason, bricklayer* (→ Mauer) **~arbeit** f *b.-l.ing, b.work* **~gesell(e)** m *journeyman m.* **~handwerk** n *m.ry* **~kelle** f (*m.'s*) *trowel* **~-meister** m *master-m.* **~pinsel** m *whitewash-brush* **~polier** m *b.l.r's foreman*

Mauret·anien n (in NW-Afrika) *Maure–, Mauritania*

maurisch (Stil, Bau) *Moorish*

Maur·itius n [-ts-] (Insel im Ind. Ozean)

M·aus f ~/~̈e → *shrew, vole, mouse* **A. 1.** ⟨eig⟩ *mouse* [pl *mice*] || ⟨fig⟩ Asphalt~̈ *or* weiße ~ = Verkehrspolizist ⟨sl⟩ *cop*(*per*), *speed-cop* **2.** (Anrede) = Mäuschen **3.** ⟨anat⟩ (*thick part of the thumb*) *thenar* **B.** die ~ knabbert, pfeift (*or* piept), raschelt .. *nibbles, squeaks, rustles* || wie e–e ~ *m.-like* **C.** ⟨fig⟩ wie die ~ in der Speckseite leben *to live like fighting-cocks* || das ist den ~̈en gepfiffen *that's waste of time* || mit e–m spielen wie die Katz' mit der ~ *to play cat and m. with a p* ‖ da beißt k–e ~ den Faden ab *it can't be helped!, that's final!, and there it stands!, there you are!* ‖ (weiße) ~e sehen (im Delirium) *to see snakes* ‖ das trägt die ~ auf dem Schwanze fort *a m. could run away with that* **D.** ⟨prov⟩ mit Speck fängt man ~e *good bait catches fine fish* ‖ wenn die Katze nicht zu Hause ist, tanzen die ~e *when the cat's away the mice will play* **~farbe** f *m.-colour* **~farben** a *m.-c.ed*

Mauschel·ei f *Yiddish speech* od *haggling* **m·auscheln 1.** vt/i [h] *to mouth Yiddish* **2.** ⟨fig⟩ ~ n ⟨cards⟩ *game of hazard*

M·äus|chen n ~s/~ (→ Maus A. 1., → Maus A. 2.) *little mouse* ‖ da möcht' ich ein ~ s *I should like to be a clandestine listener* | ⟨fig⟩ mein ~! ⟨fam⟩ *my duck(ie)!, love!, pet!* | °*prostitute; lady of easy virtue;* ⟨fam⟩ *loose fish* | sich ans ~ stoßen *to knock against one's funny-bone* **~still** a *stone-, stock-still, as still as a mouse, mousy* ‖ es war ~ *one might have heard a pin drop* ‖ (P) ~ s *to keep absolutely quiet* **M·ause-** (→ a. Maus-, Mäuse-) **~falle** f *m.-trap* **~katze** f *(good) m.r* **~kätzchen** n ⟨fam⟩ mein ~! *my little pet* **~loch** n *m.-hole* ‖ ⟨fig⟩ ins ~ kriechen ⟨fam⟩ *to be shivering in one's shoes* **~tot** a *stark dead, as dead as mutton* (od *as a duck*) ‖ er ist ~ *he is dead and gone* **~zahn** m ⟨fig⟩ *little tooth*

M·äuse- ~bussard m ⟨orn⟩ *common buzzard* **~dorn** m ⟨bot⟩ *butcher's broom* **~dreck** m *mice-dirt* **~falke** m ⟨orn⟩ *mouse-hawk* **~fang** m *catching mice* ‖ (v Katzen) *mousing* **~fänger** m *mouser* **~fraß** m *damage done by mice* **~gerste** f ⟨bot⟩ *waybent (barley-grass)* **~gift** n *ratsbane* **~katze** f *(good) mouser* | sein Getue etc ist z **~melken** .. *will send me crackers* **~not** f *plague of mice* **m·ausen 1.** vi [h] *to mouse, to catch mice* ‖ die Katze läßt das ~ nicht *cats will catch mice, what's bred in the bone comes out in the flesh* | ⟨fig⟩ *to sneak about; to prig* **2.** °vt/i [h] ⟨fam⟩ *to pilfer, filch* ‖ ⟨sl⟩ *to hook, swipe, snaffle, lift, sneak, bone, pinch* °**M·auser** m ~s/~ *pilferer* | **~ei** f ~/~en *pilfering*, etc **m·auserig** a Sw = verdrießlich °**m·ausig** a: **sich ~ m** *to give o.s. airs, to put on airs* ‖ *to take liberties*

M·auser f ~/ *moult(ing[-season])*; in der ~ s *to be moulting* **m·ausern** (a. sich ~) [h] *to moult; to shed feathers* ‖ ⟨fig⟩ (P) sich ~ *to start a new life* ‖ *to change one's coat* ⟨fig⟩ od *opinion*

Mausol·eum n ~s/–l·een [–e:ən] *mausoleum*

M·aut f ~/~en *duty, toll, custom(s pl), excise* ‖ (Zollhaus) *c.-house* **~amt** n *c.-h.* **~beamte(r)** m *c.-h. officer* **~einnehmer** m *receiver of c.s* **~frei** a *toll-free, duty-free* **~straße** f *turnpike* **M·autner** = Mauteinnehmer

Maxi- (Ggs Mini-) ⟨mod⟩ ~mantel [m] *maxicoat*

maxim·al adv *(up to) a maximum of* .. **Maxim·al- ~arbeitstag** m *maximum of working-hours* **~automat** m ⟨el⟩ *m. automatic device* **~betrag** m *highest amount* **~bevölkerung** f ⟨demog⟩ *m. population* **~gefälle** n ⟨rail⟩ *greatest gradient* **~geschwindigkeit** f *greatest speed* **~überdruck** m *peak overpressure* **Max·ime** f ~/~n *maxim* **M·aximum** n ~s/–ma *maximum; (curve) peak* | ~-(u Minimum-)Thermometer [n] *(self-registering)* bzw *m. th.*

M·aya [-j-] pl (Indianerstamm) *Maya*

Mayonn·aise f ~/~n [–'e:zə] ⟨cul⟩ *mayonnaise*

Mazed·onien n *Macedonia* **Mazed·onier** m, **~in** f, mazedonisch [a] *Macedonian*

Mäz·en m ~(e)s/~e *Maecenas, patron (of arts and letters), protector* **~·atentum** n *patronage*

Maz·urka f ~/~s (Tanz) → Masurka

Mech·anik f ~/~en (Lehre) *mechanics* pl ‖ Fern~ *telemechanics* | (Triebwerk) *mechanism; mechanical device* od *contrivance* **Mech·aniker** m ~s/~ *mechanic(ian), engine builder;* ⟨wir⟩ *operator, m.c;* Maschinen~ *m.c workman* ‖ ⟨aero hum⟩ *plumber* | ~drehbank [f] *brass-finisher's lethe* **mech·anisch** [a] *m.cal (method, drive, loom, philosophy)* ‖ ~es Wärmeäquivalent *equivalent of heat in units of work* ‖ ⟨tech⟩ ~e Kraft *or* Leistung *power* | [adv] *m.cally (driven)* ‖ *(to learn) by rote* ‖ *(to recite) in a humdrum way* **mechanis·ieren** vt *to mechanize* (⟨mil⟩ *m.d forces*) **Mechanis·ierung** f ~/ *mechanization (of labour, of the art of warfare, of conduct in life)* **Mechan·ismus** m ~/–men *mechanism* ‖ (Uhrwerk a.) *works* pl **mechan·istisch** a *mechanistic*

M·echeln n (belg. Stadt) *Mechlin; Malines* Fr

m·eckern vi [h] *to bleat;* (Bekassine) *to scrape* ‖ (P) *to speak in* od *with a thin and tremulous voice* ‖ °⟨fig⟩ (mäkeln) *to grouse, carp;* ⟨Am sl⟩ *to kick, knock, holler, natter* ‖ er hat immer etw z ~ *he has always sth to grumble about* **M·eckerer** m ~s/~ ⟨fig⟩ *grumbler;* ⟨sl⟩ *bellyacher, chiseller,* ⟨Am⟩ *knocker*

M·ecki m ~/~(s) (Igel-Scherzgestalt) *urchin* **~schnitt** m ⟨cosm⟩ *butch*

M·ecklenburg n ⟨Ger⟩ (~-Schwerin, ~-Strelitz) **~er(in** f**)** m *inhabitant of M.* | ~ Bucht [f] *M. Bay* **m–gisch** a *(of) M.*

Med·aille [me'daljə] f ~/~n *medal* ‖ e–e ~ schlagen, scheiden *to stamp, cut a m.* ‖ ⟨fig⟩ die Kehrseite der ~ *the dark side of the question* ‖ Inhaber e–r goldenen ~ *gold medallist* **~nsammler** m *medallist* **~nstecher** m *engraver of medals* **Medailleur** [medal'jøə] m ~s/~e *medallist, medal-coiner* **Medaillon** [medal'jɔŋ, meda'jɔ̃:] n ~s/~s ⟨arch, arts⟩ *medallion* ‖ (Kapsel als Schmuck) *locket*

†**M·eder** pl (Volk im heutigen Persien) *Medes*

M·edia f ~/–iae *or* –ien *voiced-stopped consonant* (b, d, g) **medi·al** a *voiced-stopped* **medi·an** a ⟨ent⟩ *median (vein)* **~alter** n ⟨demog⟩ *m. age* **~folio** n *demi-folio* **~größe** f *median size* **~papier** n *medium (paper)* (⟨engl typ⟩ *18 × 28 inches*)

Medi·ante f ~/~n ⟨mus⟩ *mediant* **mediatis·ieren** vt [h] ⟨hist, pol⟩ *to mediatize*

mediäv·al [v] a *medieval* | ~ f ⟨typ⟩ *old style*

Medikam·ent n ~(e)s/~e *remedy, medicine* **~·ös** a *drug (treatment); physicky (smell)* **Medik·aster** m ~s/~ *quack* **M·edikus** m ~/Medizi *physician, practitioner*

Med·ina n (arab. Stadt) *Medina*

Meditati·on f ~/~en *meditation* **medit·ieren** vi [h] *to meditate, ponder*

M·edium n ~s/–dien ⟨psych, chem⟩ *medium* ‖ (Flaschenmaß 0,61) *m.; imperial pint (1.05 pt)*

Mediz·in f ~/~en **1.** *(science of) medicine;* innere ~ (Fach) *chemical m.* ‖ ~ studieren *to study m., to walk the hospitals* ‖ Doktor der ~ *doctor of m.* (abbr. *M.D.*) ‖ Schul~ *scientific m.* ‖ gerichtliche ~ *medical jurisprudence* **2.** (Arznei) (einnehmen *to take*) *m.,* ⟨fam⟩ *physic* (gegen Gicht *for gout*) ‖ ~ verschreiben *to give the prescription* **~flasche** f *m.-bottle;* kl *vial* **~glas** n *phial* **~karren, ~wagen** m *medicinal canteen* **~mann** m *medicine-man;* °⟨sl⟩ *medico* **Medizin·al- ~beamte(r)** m *medical officer* **~gewicht** n *troy weight* **~kollegium** n *Board of Health* **~kräuter** n pl *medicinal herbs* **~rat** m *medical councillor* (German title) **~verordnungen** f pl *sanitary regulations* **~ware** f *medicinal drugs* pl **~wein** m *medicated wine* **~wesen** n *medical practice* od *system* **Mediz·iner** m ~s/~ *physician, medical man* ‖ (Student) *m.l student* ‖ er ist ~ *he is a* .. **mediz·inisch** a (arzneilich) *medicinal (herbs)* ‖ (ärztlich) *medical (man);* ~e Altersversorgung ⟨Am⟩ *medicare;* ~e Verpflanzung (skin, limbs, organs) *medical transplantation* ‖ → Fakultät ‖ v ~en Standpunkt *medically* | ~-soziologisch [a] *socio-medical*

Med·use f ~/~n ⟨zoo⟩ *medusa* | **~nhaft** a *gorgonian* ‖ ⟨zoo⟩ *medusan* | adv *like Medusa*

M·eer n ~(e)s/~e (→ See) **1.** sea ‖ Welt~

ocean ‖ das ~ ⟨poet⟩ *the blue*, ⟨sl⟩ *the briny* ‖ bewegt, glatt, still, stürmisch *rough* od *choppy, smooth, peaceful, stormy* ‖ das offene ~ *the high seas* pl, *the main, offing* ‖ das tiefe ~ *the deep* (*sea*) ‖ das weite ~! *the main* ‖ v ~e bespült *washed by the sea* | Adriatisches ~ *Adriatic Sea*; Japanisches ~ *S. of Japan* ‖ Mittelländisches ~ *Mediterranean* ‖ Rotes, Schwarzes, Totes ~ *Red, Black, Dead Sea* | **am** ~ *on the seashore, at the seaside*; .. befindlich *maritime* ‖ Schloß am ~ .. *on the s.* ‖ **auf** dem ~ (*out*) *at s.*; ⟨poet⟩ *on the main* ‖ auf dem ~ fahren *to sail on the s.* (*I have never been ill on the s.*) ‖ die Sonne steigt **aus** dem ~ .. *rises from* .., versinkt **im** *or* ins ~ *goes down in* .. ‖ ein Tropfen im ~e *a drop in the ocean* ‖ **jenseits** des ~es (befindlich) *over-sea, transmarine* ‖ **nach** dem ~e zu (*to advance*) *seaward* ‖ 200 m **über** dem ~e .. *above the s.* ‖ übers ~ *over s.*; .. wandern *to travel across the seas*; .. gehen *to go over-seas* ‖ **unter** dem ~e *submarine* ‖ der einzige Weg **zum** ~e *the only water-way out* **2.** ⟨**fig**⟩ in e–m ~ v Arbeit versinken *to be over head and heels in work* ‖ *a blaze* (*of flowers, colours*) ‖ das ~ der Leidenschaften *the depths of passion* ‖ *a flood* (*of light*) ‖ *the waste* (*of air*) ‖ ein wogendes ~ v M. *a seething mass of people* ‖ das Steinerne ~ *the rocky heights* ‖ ein ~ v Trümmern *a wilderness of ruins* ‖ *the ocean* (*of time*) **~aal** m ⟨ich⟩ *conger(-eel)* **~anwohner** m *inhabitant of a seaside district* od *town* **~äsche** f ⟨ich⟩ (*grey*) *mullet* **~assel** f *sea-slater* **~barbe** f ⟨ich⟩ *surmullet* **~beherrscherin** f *queen of the seas, ruler of the waves* **~beschreibung** f *oceanography* **≃bespült** a *sea-bathed* **~bewohner** m *inhabitant of the sea* **~brassen** m ⟨ich⟩ *sea-bream* **~busen** m *bay, gulf* ‖ Bottnischer, Finnischer, Rigaischer ~ *Gulf of Bothnia, Finland, Riga* **~deich** m *sea-wall* **~drache** m *sea--dragon, horned ray* **~enge** f *strait*(*s* pl), *sound, narrows* pl, *channel* **~engel** m ⟨ich⟩ *angel-fish* **~fahrt** f *sea-trip* ‖ (Überfahrt) *passage* ‖ (längere Reise) (*sea-*)*voyage* **~farbe** f, **≃farben** a *sea-green* **~fenchel** m ⟨bot⟩ *sea-fennel* **~forelle** f *finnock, schoder* **~frau** f *mermaid* **~gans** f *barnacle-goose* **~gegend** f *maritime region* **~gewächs** n *sea-plant* **~gott** m *sea-god*, ⟨myth⟩ *Neptune* **~greis** m ⟨fig⟩ *old fogey with oldfashioned views* **≃grün** a *sea--green* **~grünstein** m *beryl* **~grundel** f ⟨ich⟩ *sea--gudgeon, rockfish* **~hecht** ⟨ich⟩ m *hake* **~handel** m *maritime trade* **~herrschaft** f *supremacy at sea* **~jungfrau** f *mermaid* **~katze** f ⟨zoo⟩ *Guenon monkey* **~leuchten** n *phosphorescence* (*of the sea*) **~linsen** f pl *duckweed, fen-lentils* pl **~luft** f *sea--breeze* **~mädchen** n *mermaid* **~muschel** f *sea-shell* **~nessel** f *sea-anemone, nettle-fish* **~nymphe** f *sea--maid, Nereid, mermaid* **~ohr** n (Schnecke) *ormer* **~rettich** m *horse-radish* **~salz** n *sea-salt* **~schaum** m ⟨fig⟩ *meerschaum* | ~pfeife [f] *m.* (*pipe*); ~spitze [f] *m. cigar-holder* **~schnecke** f *sea-snail* **~schwalbe** f ⟨orn⟩ *sea-swallow, tern* **~schwamm** m *sponge* **~schwein** n ⟨zoo⟩ *sea-hog, porpoise* **~schweinchen** n ⟨zoo⟩ *guinea-pig* **~senf** m ⟨bot⟩ *sea-mustard, sea-rocket* **~strudel** m *whirl-pool* **≃umschlungen** a ⟨poet⟩ *sea-encircled, sea-girt* **~ungeheuer** n *sea-monster* **≃wärts** adv *seawards* **~wasser** n *sea-water, brine* | ~aquarium [n] *sea-quarium, oceanarium*; ~stein [m] ⟨minr⟩ *beryl* **~weib** n *mermaid* **~wunder** n *sea-monster* **~zwiebel** f ⟨bot⟩ *sea-leek, squill* **M·eeres- ~arm** m *arm of the sea*; *inlet*; *firth* (*of Scotland*), *fjord* (*of Norway*) **~boden** m *bed* od *bottom of the ocean*; flacher, kontinentaler ~ *continental shelf* **~brandung** f *breakers* pl, *surf* **~fauna** f *marine animals* **~fläche** f *surface of the sea* **~flut** f *waves of the sea* ‖ *high-water* **~früchte** f pl ⟨cul⟩ *seafood* **~grotte** f *ocean cavern* **~grund** m *sea-bed, bottom of the sea* ‖ ⟨fam⟩ *Davy Jones's locker* **~güter** n pl *resources of the sea* **~höhe** f (in *at*) *sea-level* N **~kunde** f *oceanography* **~küste** f *sea-cost, seaboard* **~schaum** m *sea-foam, froth* **~schlund** m *deeps* [pl] *of the sea* **~spiegel** m *sea-level*, über dem ~ *above the s.-l.* N **~stille** f *calm* (*at sea*), völlige ~ *dead calm* **~strand** m *sea-shore, beach* **~strömung** f *ocean-current*; ⟨mar⟩ *drift* **~tiere** n pl *oceanic animals* **~ufer** n *sea-shore* **~woge** f *billow*

mef·itisch a *mephitic*(*al*)

Mega- [Gr groß] **~hertz** n (= 10^6 Hertz) *megahertz* (*1000000 cycles per second*) N **≃l·ithisch** a *megalithic* **~l·ithkultur** f *m. age* **~ohm** n ⟨el⟩ *megohm* (= *1000000 ohms*) **~ph·on** n ~s/~e *megaphone* **~tonne** f (1 Mio t)

Meg·äre f ~/~n ⟨fig⟩ *shrew, virago, vixen, fury*

M·ehl n ~(e)s/ (grobes) *meal*; *middlings* (Vollkorn) ‖ (feines) *flour*, feinstes ~ *superfine fl.* ‖ (Staub) *dust, powder* ‖ ⟨bot⟩ *farina* ‖ Gersten≃ *barley m.* ‖ Kartoffel≃ *potato fl.* ‖ Knochen≃ *bone m.* ‖ Kork≃ *cork p.* ‖ Roggen≃ *rye fl.* od *m.* ‖ aus ~ bestehend *farinaceous* ‖ zu ~ mahlen *to fl.* ‖ mit ~ bestreuen *to fl.* (*over*) **~abkühler** m *hopper boy* **≃arm** a *yielding little fl.* **≃artig** a *farinaceous* **~baum** m, **~bank** f *m.l-bench* **~beerbaum** m ⟨bot⟩ *whitebeam*; *Sorbus* od *Pyrus aria* **~beere** f *haw* **~beutel** m *fl.-bag* ‖ (Müllerei) *bolter* **~birne** f *m.y pear* **~brei** m (*m.-*)*pap* **~faß** n *m.-tub*; (kl) *fl.-box* **~früchte** f pl *cereals* pl **≃haltig** a *farinaceous* **~händler** m *corn-chandler* **~käfer** m *m.-beetle* **~kasten** m *m.-box* **~kleister** m *paste* **~kloß** m *dumpling*, ⟨Am⟩ *doughboy* **~kraut** n ⟨bot⟩ *meadow-sweet* **~primel** f *bird's eye primrose* **≃reich** a *fl.y* **~sack** m *fl.-bag* od *-sack* ‖ ⟨fig⟩ (P) *dumpy* **~schwitze** f ⟨cul⟩ *roux*; *fl. roasted in fat* **~sichter** m *fl. sifter* **~siebanlage** f *fl. sifting plant* **~speise** f *farinaceous food*, ~n pl *f. dishes*; *pudding, pastry*; *sweets* pl; (z Frühstück) *cereals* **~staub** m *fl.-dust* **~suppe** f *water-gruel* **~tau** m *mildew, blight*; dazu: *mildewy, blighted* **~teig** m *paste, dough* **~trichter** m *chute* **~wurm** m *m.--worm*; *miller* **~zucker** m *powdered sugar* **m·ehlig** a *mealy, floury, farinaceous* ‖ *floury* (*potato*) ‖ *sleepy, juiceless* (*fruit*)

m·ehr [compr v viel & sehr] **I.** [adv] **A. 1. [mit Subst]** ~ Feinde **als** Freunde *more .. than ..* ‖ er hat ~ Geld als du (denkst) .. *more m. than you* (*imagine*) ‖ mit ~ Hoffnung *with better hopes* ‖ etw mit ~ Recht behaupten *to say sth with greater truth* ‖ du hast ~ Glück gehabt als andere *you have prospered beyond other people* | [qual] er ist ~ Gelehrter als Künstler *he is more* (*of*) *a scholar than* (*of an*) *artist* | *increased* (*destruction*) **2. [mit Verb]** [quant] [abs] bald ~ *more to come* ‖ man soll nicht ~ versprechen als man halten kann .. *more than* .. ‖ es kostet ~ *it costs more* ‖ ich habe ~ zu tun als dir zuzuhören *I have sth better to do than to* .. ‖ ich will nicht ~ (als das) *that's all I want* ‖ ich habe (drei) ~ als du *I've got* (*three*) *more than you* ‖ ~ v etw h *to get more out of a th* (wenn *or* indem man tut *by doing*) | [qual] (→ besser, eher) du mußt ~ achtgeben *you must take greater care* ‖ er wird ~ verehrt als sie *he is held in higher esteem than she* ‖ ~ zusagend (statt: zusagender) *more congenial* (*occupation*) ‖ e–n ~ begünstigen ⟨oft⟩ *to do more to favour a p* **3. [mit Zahlwort]** 4 oder ~ *a minimum of four*; 3 Monate u (*or* wenn nicht) ~ *3 months and better*; ~ **als** (= über) 10 Mark *more than* ‖ ~ als 100 (Jahre), ein Dutzend *upwards of one hundred* (*years*), *a dozen* ‖ sie ist ~ als 30 Jahre alt *she is on the wrong* od *shady side of thirty* ‖ ~ als 9 Uhr *past nine* ‖ er hat sich um ~ als das Doppelte verrechnet *he was more than doubly out of his calculations* | ~ als **genug** *more than enough, more and to spare* ‖ es gibt **deren** ~ als genug *there are too many of them* (*already*) ‖ das ist ~ als **zuviel** *that is far too much* **4. [mit Adj]** ~ gr als kl *rather big than small* ‖ ~ lang als breit *the length greater than the width* ‖ ~ tot als lebendig *more dead than alive* | das ist ~ als schlimm *that is worse than all* ‖ das ist ~ als frech *that puts the lid on* | das ~ als magere Ergebnis *the more than meagre results* | ~ liebenswürdig = liebenswürdiger || ein ~ heiterer Tag = ein heiterer Tag **5.** **[mit prep]** ~ **aus** Langeweile als aus Vorsatz *more from boredom than from design* || ~ **nach** m–m Geschmack *nearer to my taste* | das schmeckt **nach** ~ *that tastes of more* (⟨fam⟩ *tastes morish*) **B.** **(weiter, sonst)** was willst du ~? *what else do you expect* od *want*? || was gibt's ~? *what else is there*? **C.** **[mit Negation]** [in Antworten] nicht ~ *no more* || nie ~ *never again* || niemand ~ *nobody else* || nichts ~ *nothing more, just that* || nicht ~ als *just* (*a minute*) || kein Wort ~! *not another word*! | ich **bin** kein Kind ~ *I am no child any longer* || er **ist** nicht ~ *he has passed away* || er ist nicht ~ hier *he is no longer here* || du bist nicht ~ als ich *you are no*(*thing*) *better than I am* || das ist nicht ~ als d–e Pflicht *that is nothing more than your duty* || das ist nicht ~ als recht u billig *that's only fair* || das ist kein Spaß ~ *this is beyond a joke* | es **besteht** k–e Hoffnung ~ *there is no longer any hope* || es bleibt nichts anderes ~ übrig *there is nothing else left* || es **dauert** nicht ~ lange *it won't last much longer* || ich kann nicht ~! ⟨fam⟩ *I'm done* (*for*)! || nicht ~ arbeiten **können** *to be past one's work* || er lebt nicht ~ *he is no longer alive* || es gab nichts, das sie ~ liebte *there was nothing she liked better* (*than to write*) || ~ kann man nicht verlangen *that's all one can expect* || sie **wußte** sich nicht ~ zu helfen *she did not know what else to do* **D.** **~ als** → I. A. 1.; es ist ~ als wahrscheinlich *there is more than an even chance* || u **andere** ~ (abbr u.a.m.) *and some others* || u anderes ~ *and what not*! || u **dergleichen** ~ (abbr u. dgl. m.) *and the* (od *such*) *like* || ~ **denn je** *more than ever* || **immer** (noch) ~ (*still*) *more and more* || **je** ~ er hat, je (*or* desto) ~ er will *the more he has the more he wants* || ~ **u** ~ anwachsend *ever increasing* (*outpout*) || **noch** ~ *still more* || was noch ~? *what else*? || die anderen h noch ~ .. *have even more* || .., ja sie waren es noch ~ (*the Tories were as intolerable as ever*) *indeed they were more so* || *we have yet more* (noch ~) *plays from his pen* || er hatte **nur** ~ den Gedanken *he had only the one idea now* || **um so** ~! *so much the more*! || um so ~ als *particularly as, all the more as, the more so as* || **viel** ~ *much more*, ⟨fam⟩ *a lot more* || ~ **oder weniger** *more or less, in a way, to a certain extent*; ~ o. w. dasselbe *pretty much the same th*; vielleicht einige 100 ~ o. w. *give or take a few hundred* || nicht ~, nicht weniger *no more and no less* **II.** **Mehr** n ~/ *majority* (*of two votes*) || ⟨com⟩ *over* || (Überschuß) *surplus* || (Zuwachs) *increase* **~achsantrieb** m *multi-axle drive* **~achser** m *m.-a. vehicle* **~arbeit** f *added* od *extra work* **≃armig** a *with several arms* (→ Leuchter) **≃atomig** a *polyatomic* **~aufwand** m, **~ausgabe** f *additional expenditure* **≃bändig** a *in several volumes* **~bedarf** m *excess demand*; *additional r.ts* **~belastung** f *surplus load*; *overload* **~bereichs-** ⟨mot⟩ *multigrade* (Öl) **~bestand** m *excess stock* **~betrag** m ⟨com⟩ *excess, surplus* **~bieter** m *higher bidder* **~decker** m *multiplane* **≃deutig** a *ambiguous* | ~keit [f] *ambiguity* **~ehe** f *polygamy* **~einnahme** f *surplus* od *increase of receipts* **~ertrag** m *surplus* **≃fach,** **≃fältig** [a] *manifold, repeated* || *multiplex* || *multiple* (*expansion engine*) | adv *repeatedly* | das ~e *the multiple* | M–belichtungs- *multiple-exposure* (*shutter*); M–betrieb [m] ⟨telv⟩ *multiplex operation*; M–bild [n] ⟨telv⟩ *multiple image*; M–blitz [m] ⟨phot⟩ *multiflash*; M–druck [m] *cascade printing*; M–leitung [f] ⟨telv⟩ *multiple line*; M–röhrenempfänger ⟨wir⟩ *receiver for multiple tubes*; –schnur [f] *multiple cord*; ~täter [m] *old lag*; –telegraphie [f] *multiplex telegraphy*; ~werfer [m] *multiple launcher* **~familienhaus** n *multiple f. dwelling* **~f·arbendruck** m *colour-* (⟨Am⟩ *color-*) *-print*(*ing*) **≃farbig** a *polychromatic* | ≃keit [f] *polychromy* **~forderung** f *increased demand* **~förderung** f *incr. delivery* **~frontenkrieg** m *war on several fronts* **~gängig** a *multiple*(*x*) (Gewinde *thread*); ~e Schraube *m. th. screw* **~gebot** n *higher bid*; *advance* (über *on*); *outbidding* **~gewicht** n ⟨rail⟩ *excess weight* **~gewinnsteuer** f *excess profits tax* **~gitter-** f ⟨wir⟩ *multigrid* (*valve*, ⟨Am⟩ *tube*) **≃gleisig** a *with several tracks* **≃jährig** a *several years old*; *of s. y.s* **~kanal-** *multichannel* (*TV*) **≃kantig** a *many-sided* **≃kernig** a ⟨at⟩ *polynuclear* **~kosten** pl *additional* od *extra expenses* od *charges* **~lader** m ⟨mil⟩ *magazine-rifle, repeater* **≃läufiges** Flugabwehr-M.G. *multiple pom-pom* **~leiterkabel** n ⟨el⟩ *multicore* (⟨Am⟩ *multiconductor*) *cable* **≃malig** a *repeated, reiterated* **≃mals** adv *several times, more than once* **≃motorig** a *multi-engine*(*d*) (*plane*) **~phasenstrom** m ⟨el⟩ *polyphase current* | zu geringem **~preis** *at slight additional charge* **~röhren-** ⟨wir⟩ *multi-valve* (*receiver*) **~schicht-** *multi-shift* (*work*) **≃schichtig** a *multilayered* **≃seitig** a *with several sides*; ⟨übtr⟩ *multilateral* (*agreement*), ⟨fig⟩ *multifarious* **≃silbig** a *polysyllabic* **~sitzer** m ⟨aero⟩ *multiseater* **≃sprachig** a *polyglot* | ≃keit [f] *plurilingualism* **~stellig** a (*number*) *of several places* **≃stimmig** a *concerted*; ~er Gesang, ~es Lied *part-singing, -song* **~stufe** f ⟨gram⟩ *comparative* **≃stufig** a *multistage* || ⟨a–n⟩ *multiple-stage* (*rocket*) **≃stündig** a *lasting for hours* **≃tägig** a *of several days' duration* **~verbrauch** m *additional consumption* **≃teilig** a *complex, sectionalized*; *consisting of several parts* **≃völkisch** a *multinational* (*state*) **~wert** m *overvalue*; *surplus v.*; *increment v.* | ~steuer [f] *increased value tax, Value-Added Tax* **≃wertig** a ⟨chem⟩ *polyvalent* || *multiple-valued* (*logic*) **≃wöchig** a *of several weeks* **~zahl** f ⟨gram⟩ *plural* (*number*) || (Mehrheit) *majority*; die überwiegende ~ *the vast m., the bulk*; in der ~ der Fälle *in the m. of cases* **~zahlung** f *extra-pay* **~zweck-** *general purpose* [attr]; *utility* [attr] N; *multipurpose* (*aircraft, arm*) **m·ehren** vt [h] *to multiply, augment* || *to raise, increase* || sich ~ *to proliferate*; *to increase in number*, ⟨a.⟩ *to rise* || die Anfragen ~ sich *the number of enquiries is increasing* **M·ehrer** m ~s/~ *enlarger, augmenter, increaser* **m·ehrere** pron pl *several* (*people, times*) || ~ v uns *some of us* || *divers* (*methods, kinds*) (verschiedene) *different* || ⟨sl⟩ *umpteen* **M·ehrheit** f ~/~en *majority*, ⟨Am⟩ *plurality*; absolute, einfache ~ *absolute, simple m.*; arbeitsfähige ~ ⟨pol⟩ *working m.*; totale ~ *overall m.*; überwältigende ~ *overwhelming odds* pl; mit 3 Stimmen ~ *by a m. of three*; vorgeschriebene ~ *qualified m.* (etwa: $^2/_3$, $^3/_4$); ⟨gram⟩ *plural* (*number*) || mit knapper ~ *by a narrow m.* **~sbeschluß** m *resolution by a m.*; durch ~ *by a m. of votes*, ⟨Am⟩ *by a plurality* **~spartei** f *m. party* **~swahl** f *m. election* **Mehrlingsgeburt** f *multiple birth* od *delivery* ˣ**mehrschdend·eels** adv = meistenteils, ˣ**m·ehrschdens** adv = meistens **M·ehrung** f ~/~en *multiplication, augmentation, increase, rise, growth* || zur ~ e–r S beitragen *to add to a th*

m·eiden **1.** vt [mied/gemieden] [h] *to avoid, eschew, shun* (*I shunned him like the plague*); *not to* (*to refuse to*) *come close to* || *to steer* od *keep clear of* || *to give a wide berth to* || ⟨fam⟩ *to fight shy of* || Gesellschaft ~ *to keep o.s. to o.s.* || geloben jdn zu ~ *to forswear a p's company* || Glück u Schlaf ~ mich *luck and sleep shun me* || die Sünde ~ *to eschew evil, to shrink from evil* **2.** ≃ n *avoidance*; *shunning*, etc.

M·eidinger m ~s/~ ⟨m. m.⟩ (Kalauer) *chestnut*

M·eier m ~s/~ (Pächter) (*tenant-*)*farmer* || (Gutsverwalter) *steward* || ⟨Ger hist⟩ (Haus≃) *majordomo* || ⟨fig⟩ *daddy-long-legs* **~gut** n, **~hof** m *farm, homestead* **~zins** m *farm-rent* **M·eier, M·üller u Sch·ulze** npr *Brown, Jones and Robinson*

Meier·ei f ~/~en *dairy-farm* || *dairy(-house)* | ~erzeugnisse [n pl] *d.-f. products* pl °**m·eiern** vt [h] *to take a p in, to do a p (in the eye)* || der Gemeierte *the jay*

M·eile f ~/~n *mile* (⟨Ger⟩ 7500 m; ⟨engl⟩ *1760 yards, 1609 m*) || französische ~ *league* (4450 m) || geographische ~ *geographical mile* (⟨Ger⟩ 7420 m) || ⟨mar⟩ See≈ (abbr sm, 1852 m) *nautical mile* || 12 sm laufen *to do 12 knots* **M·eilen- ≈breit** a *several miles broad* **~fahrt** f *speed trial over the measured mile* **~geld** n *mileage* **~länge** f *a mile's length* **~maß** n *mile-measure* **~stein** m *milestone* **~stiefel** m pl *seven-leagued boots* pl **≈weit** a *(extending) for miles around* || ~e Felder *miles and miles of fields* | adv (he *walked) mile upon mile*; *I ran for miles* || ⟨fig⟩ ~ entfernt bleiben v etw *to miss a th by a m., to be very far from it* **~zahl** f *mileage* **~zeiger** m *milestone*

M·eiler m ~s/~ *charcoal-kiln, pile*; ⟨at⟩ → Kernreaktor **~decke** f *turf covering of a pile* **~kohle** f *charcoal*

m·ein 1. [gen v ich †] ⟨poet⟩ = meiner: gedenke ~ *remember me* **2.** (mir gehörig) das Haus ist ~ .. *is mine, belongs to me* || du bist ~ *you are mine* || alles, was ~ ist, ist auch dein *what is mine also belongs to you* || ~ u dein unterscheiden *to distinguish meum and tuum* od *mine and thine* **3. mein(e** f), m, n [pron poss] [⟨poet⟩ oft *invar* nachgestellt] *my (house)* || s–e Sachen und (die) ~e(n) *his things and mine* || ~er Ansicht nach *or* ~es Erachtens *in my opinion* || ~es Wissens *as far as I know* || ~e Herren! *gentlemen!* || ~ Zug *my train* || dieser ~ Sohn *this son of mine* | ach du ~e Güte!, ach du ~ [Gott]! *good(ness) gracious!* ⟨fam⟩ *oh, my!* **4.** das Meine *my property* || ich habe das ~ getan *I've done my bit* od *best* || die ~n *my relations, people, family*

M·eineid m ~(e)s/~e *(false oath) perjury* || e–n ~ schwören *or* leisten = ≈ig w | **≈ig** a *perjured* || ~ig w *to swear falsely; to forswear* od *perjure o.s.*; ⟨jur⟩ *to commit perjury* | **~ige** m [der ~, ein ~r] *perjurer*

m·einen vi/t [h] → Meinung **A. 1.** (denken, glauben, wähnen) *to think, imagine, fancy, believe* || (behaupten) *to assert* || (der Ansicht s) *to be of opinion, to find, suppose* **2.** (beabsichtigen, im Sinne h) *to mean, intend, purpose* || *to have in view, to aim at* || (sagen wollen) *to mean* (mit *by*) **3.** ⟨poet⟩ (minnen, lieben) *to love* **B. 1.** ~ Sie? *do you think so?* || nein, meinte er, .. *no, said he,* .. || ich meine, **daß** er recht hat *I think he is right* || ich meinte **dich** im Recht *I thought you were in the right* || meinst du s–r Rache **zu** entgehen? *do you imagine that you can escape his r.?* || er meinte gar nicht zu fliehen *he did not intend to escape at all* || **damit** bist du gemeint *that's meant for you* **2. das** möchte *or* sollte ich doch ~ *I should think* od *say so* || das will ich (aber) ~! *I should (just) think so!, to be sure!* || das will ich wohl ~ *I quite believe so* | **man** sollte ~, er sei verrückt *one would think he had gone mad* | **es böse** mit e–m ~ *to mean no good to a p* || es nicht böse ~ *to mean no harm* || es war nicht böse gemeint *it was meant for the best* || es **ehrlich** *or* **gut** ~ *to have honourable intentions, to mean well* || es **ernst** ~ *to be in earnest* || ~ Sie das ernstlich? *do you really mean it? I mean it!* || es mit e–m **gut** ~ *to wish* od *mean a p well* || wir ~ es nur gut mit dir *we have only your welfare at heart* || die Sonne meint es gut .. *is very hot* | **so** war das nicht gemeint *that was not my intention, it wasn't meant, I didn't mean that* || ich meinte nur so *it just strikes me* | verstehen Sie, **was** ich meine? *do you see my point?* ⟨fam⟩ *do you get me* | **was** ~ Sie damit? *what do you mean by that* || was ~ Sie dazu? *what do you think of it?, what is your opinion about it* || was ~ Sie zu .. *what* od *how about (oysters)?* | **wenn** Sie ~ *if you say so, sir* || wenn Sie es so ~ *if you look at it in that way* || nun, wenn Sie ~ *well, if you think so* || wenn Sie es wirklich so ~ *if that is really what you mean* || .. u ich meinte es wirklich .. *and I meant it* | **wie** ~ Sie? *I beg your pardon!* | sie ~ **wunder** wer sie sind ⟨fam⟩ *they fancy themselves* || sie ~ wunder, was sie getan h *they think they have been doing great things*

m·einer → mein || ⟨sport⟩ ~! ⟨sl⟩ *bags I!* **m·einerseits** adv *as for* od *to me* od *m.s., as far as I am concerned* || *on* od *for my part* || ich ~ *I personally; I for one* || ~! *it was a pleasure to me! the pl. was entirely mine!* **m·eines- ~gleichen** pron *my equals* pl || *people like me, the like(s) of me* | **~teils** adv *for my part* **m·einet- ~halben, ~wegen, um ~willen** adv *on* od *in my account, for my sake* od *part, on my behalf* || *as far as I am concerned* || ~ kannst du denken, was du willst *you are welcome to your own opinion* || *we may as well have a look at it* | (ja,) ~ (..)! *I don't mind* od *care! I don't care if I do! for all* od *aught I care (..)!* || *all right then!* ⟨Am⟩ *okay!* **m·einige** (der, die, das ~) [pron poss] *mine* || die ~n [pl] *my family, my people* pl

M·einung f ~/~en → meinen **A.** (Ansicht) *opinion, notion, view* (über *of*) || (Glaube) *belief* || (Überzeugung) *conviction* || (Absicht) *intention* || (Gesinnung) *mind, sentiment* || (Bedeutung) *meaning, significance* **B.** falsche, irrige ~ *wrong opinion, misconception* || maßgebliche ~ *opinion of official quarters*; geringe ~ *poor o.* (v *of*); e–e hohe ~ v sich h *to think a lot of o.s., to be taken up with o.s.* || die öffentliche ~ *(the) public o.* od *mind* || übereinstimmende ~ *consensus of o.* || die verschiedensten ~en *all shades of o.* || vorgefaßte ~en *prejudice, preconceived ideas* pl **C. nach** m–r ~, m–r ~ nach *in my o., to my mind* od *thinking, as I see* od *take it*; .., *I take it,* .. || nach m–r ~ ist .. *my judgment is that* ..; m–r ~ nach wird .. *he will cheat you if you ask me*; nach m–r ehrlichen ~ *in my candid judgement*; s–r ~ nach *according to him*; nach herrschender ~ *by the weight of authority*; nach der ~ einiger Kritiker *by some reviewers' opinions* **D.** s–e ~ über etw abgeben *to pass o. on a th* || s–e ~ **ändern** *to change one's mind*; .. ständig .. *to chop and change* || sich der ~ anderer anschließen *to join issue* || s–e ~ offen aussprechen *to speak one's mind* || e–m e–e bessere ~ **b**eibringen v *to make a p think better of* || auf s–r ~ **b**estehen *to stick to one's o.*; .. nachdrücklich .. *to press one's point* || sich e–e ~ **b**ilden *to form an o., to take a view* || jds ~ **e**rfahren *to have a p's o.* || e–n um s–e ~ über jdn **f**ragen *to ask a p's o. of a p*; (Bevölkerung) nach der ~ fragen *to opinion-poll* || was **g**eht mich die ~ der Leute an *what do I care about Mrs Grundy* od *about what people think* | e–e ~ **haben** *to have an o.*; s–e eigene ~ h *to do one's own thinking* || °er hat dafür k–e ~ *he does not think much of it* || k–e feste ~ h *not have settled o.s.* || über jdn e–e falsche ~ h *to wrong a p* || e–e gute, schlechte ~ h v *to think well, badly* od *ill of* || e–e zu gute ~ v sich (selbst) h *to have too good an o. of o.s., to be conceited* | es **h**errscht nur e–e ~ darüber *there is a general consensus of o. about it* || wenn du m–e ~ **h**ören willst .. *if you ask me (I think ..)* || s–e ~ **k**undgeben *to declare o.s.* || zu e–r ~ **n**eigen *to incline to an o.* | s–e ~ **sagen** *to say one's say*; jdm .. *to let a p know one's mind*; offen u frei .. *to speak out* || e–m gehörig *or* gründlich die ~ s. *to give a p a bit* od *piece of one's mind, to tell a p some home-truths*; s–e ~ s. dürfen *to have one's say* | der ~ **sein,** daß *to be of (the) opinion, to hold that* || ich bin leider anderer ~ *I beg to differ* || durchaus der ~ s, der festen ~ s *to feel strongly (that)* || mit e–m in allem derselben ~ s *to be wholly with a p in thinking* || e–r(lei) ~ s *to agree* (mit *with*); wir sind e–r ~ *we are of the same o.* || ein u derselben ~ s *to be at one* (über *on*) || (es war) ganz m–e ~

I thought as much m.s.; "*that's what I think*", *he said*; ich bin ganz Ihrer ∼ *I quite agree* (*with you*) ‖ geteilter ∼ s *to be devided* (über *on*); *to be in two minds* (über *as to, about*), man konnte nicht .. *there could be no two minds* | zu s–r ∼ **stehen** *to have the courage of one's o.* ‖ jds ∼ teilen *to share a p's o., to agree with a p's o.* ‖ e–e ∼ verfechten, vertreten *to defend, advocate an o.*; *to preach one's theme* ‖ die ∼ wandte sich gegen .. *the tide of o. turned against* .. **M·einungs- ∼äußerung** f *expression of opinion* **∼austausch** m *exchange of views* (über *on*) **∼befragung, ∼forschung** f (*public*) *opinion research* ⟨Am⟩ *poll*(*s*) od *survey* **∼befragte(r)** m *pollee* **∼forscher** m *expert on* od *investigator of p.c o.* ⟨Am⟩ *pollster* **∼freiheit** f *freedom of thought and speech* **∼pflege** *public relations* **∼umfrage** f *p.c o. poll* **∼verschiedenheit** f *divergence* od *disparity of views*; *dissent, disagreement, controversy* (über *about*) | völliger ∼wechsel m *about-face*

M·eise f ∼/∼n ⟨orn⟩ *titmouse* [pl *titmice*] → *tit*

M·eißel m ∼s/∼ *chisel*; (Schneidstahl) *single-point* (*cutting*) *tool* ‖ ∼bohrer [m] (*flat*) *jumper* | **≗n** vt [h] *to chisel, carve, sculpture* ‖ wie gemeißelt *sculpturesque* ‖ *a chiselled face*

M·eißen n ⟨Ger⟩ (Stadt) *Meissen, Misnia* | Meißner [a] ∼ Porzellan *Dresden China*

M·eißner m ⟨Ger⟩ (Gebirge)

m·eist 1. [a] *most* ‖ die ∼en Häuser *most of the h.s* ‖ die ∼en M. *most* (od *the majority of*) *people* ‖ in den ∼en Fällen *in most cases, more often than not, as a general rule, for the most part* ‖ bei den ∼en Leuten *with the general of people* | [**abstr**] die ∼e Freude *the greatest joy* ‖ die ∼e Zeit (*for*) *most of the* od *one's time* ‖ die ∼e Zeit des Jahres *during the greater part of the year* | **die ∼en** pl *most people, the greater part, number, the majority* (*of people*) ; .. als die ∼en anderen *they run faster than almost any other* ‖ die ∼en v uns *most of us* | **das meiste** *the greater* od *best part, the bulk* (*of it, of their income*) **2.** [adv] (meistens) *mostly, generally, usually, as a rule* ‖ am ∼en *most* ‖ am ∼en bekannt *best known* ‖ wer am ∼en bietet, bekommt es *it goes to the highest bidder* **∼begünstigt** a *most favoured* **≗begünstigung** f (im Zoll) *preference* | ∼sklausel [f] (im GATT) *most favoured nation clause* **≗betrag** m *highest amount* **∼bietend** a *bidding highest*; ∼ [adv] verkaufen *to put up for sale* **≗bietende(r)** m *highest bidder* **≗gebot** n *best offer, highest bid* **∼gekauft** a: ∼es Buch etc *bestseller* **∼stufe** f ⟨gram⟩ *superlative* **m·eistens** adv *mostly, generally, usually*; *as often as not, more often than not* **m·eistenteils** adv *for the most part*

M·eister m (∼in f) ∼s/∼ *master* ‖ (e–s Handwerks) *master*(*-workman*) ‖ ⟨sl⟩ *boss*, (Anrede:) *gov*(*ernor*) ‖ (Frau) ∼in *master's wife* ‖ Bäcker≗ *m. baker* ‖ ∼ v der Elle *snip* ‖ ⟨übtr⟩ *doyen* (*of British Geology*) ‖ ⟨sport⟩ *champion* (f *ch.ess*); ∼ des Fußballs *ch.* od *first-class football player* ‖ ∼ im Hochsprung *high jump ch.* | ⟨fig⟩ wahrer ∼ *past-master* (in *in*), *swell* (*at Latin, tennis*) ‖ ⟨fig⟩ ∼ Petz *Bruin*; ∼ Pfriem *cobbler*; Christus unser ∼ *Christ, our Lord*; ∼ der Malerei *m.-painter*; ∼ v Stuhl *m. of the Lodge*, (Anrede:) *worshipful m.* | ∼ w *to become a m. of a company*; ⟨fig⟩ (e–s Dinges) *to m.* (*a th*) ‖ wir sind nicht ∼ des Zufalls *we have no control over chance* ‖ s–n ∼ finden (in, an), *to meet with one's match* (*in*) | ⟨prov⟩ es ist noch kein ∼ v Himmel gefallen *no man is born a m.* **∼arbeit** f *m.-work* **∼bauer** m ⟨SBZ⟩ *m. farmer* **∼flieger** m ⟨aero⟩ *ace* **∼gesang** m ⟨Ger⟩ *song of a m.-singer* **∼hand** f *m.-hand* **∼marke** f, **∼stempel** m *maker's mark* **∼recht** n *freedom of a company* **∼sang** = ∼gesang **∼sänger**, **∼singer** m *m.-singer* **∼schuß** m *capital* od *best shot* **∼schütze** m *marksman, dead shot*, ⟨fam⟩ *crackshot* **∼singer** m = ∼sänger **∼spiel** n *m.ly play*(*ing*) od *performance* **∼spieler** m *brilliant* od *crack player* od *professional* **∼stück, ∼werk** n *m.piece*; ⟨Lit⟩ *classic* **∼würde** f *m.ship* **m·eister- ∼haft, ∼lich** a *masterly* (*skill*) | adv *brilliantly, in a m.ly manner, to perfection* **∼los** a Sw = eigenwillig, unbeherrscht **m·eistern** vt [h] **A.** (beherrschen) *to master* (*a problem, one's tongue*), *to govern* ‖ (unterwerfen) *to subdue* ‖ (übertreffen) *to surpass, outdo*; *to get the better of* ‖ (mäkeln) *to censure, to cavil* (*at*) **B.** *he could not curb his impatience* ‖ *he strove to get a grip on life* (das L. z ∼) ‖ *to come through all right with* ..; *she carried off the situation with a lift of the eyebrow* **M·eisterschaft** f ∼/ **1.** [abstr] *proficiency, m.ship, m.ly skill* (*his kill is undeniable*) ‖ ⟨sport⟩ *championship, title*; sich um die ∼ bewerben *to compete for the ch.*; die ∼ austragen *to decide the ch.* **2.** [konkr koll] *guild, company* **∼srennen, ∼streffen** n *ch.-meeting*; **∼sspiel** n *ch. match*; **∼sturnen** n *ch.-meeting*

M·ekka n (arab. Stadt) *Mecca*

M·ekong m (Strom in Hinterindien)

Melanchol·ie f *melancholy, spleen* **M-·oliker** m ∼s/∼ *hypochondriac, m.liac* **m.-·olisch** a *m.ly, h.cal*; (*to look*) *blue*

Melan·ese m, **-sin** f = Melanesier **Melan·esien** n *Melanesia* **-sier(in)**, **≗sisch** a *Melanesian*

Melange [me'laŋʒə, me'lɑ̃:ʒ] f ∼/∼n *mixture* ‖ ⟨bes österr⟩ → Milchkaffee

Mel·asse f ∼/∼n *molasses* pl [sg konstr], *treacle*

M·elbourne ['melbɔ:n]; ⟨engl⟩ ['melbən]

M·elchter f ∼/∼n Sw *wooden milk-can*

M·elde f ∼/∼n ⟨bot & Ger mil cul⟩ *orach*

M·elde- ∼abwurf m ⟨aero⟩ *message dropping* **∼amt** n ⟨Ger⟩ *office for registration* **∼apparat** m ⟨aero⟩ (*anti-aircraft*) *predictor* **∼blatt** n ⟨mil⟩ *message form* **∼bogen** m *questionary* **∼boot** n *aviso, advice-boat* **∼dienst** m ⟨mil⟩ *message* od *dispatch-carrying duty* ‖ *intelligence service*; ⟨aero⟩ *detector-service* **∼dosis** f *reportable radiation dosage* **∼fahrer** m ⟨mil⟩ *dispatch-rider* N **∼gänger** m *runner* **∼hund** m *messenger dog* **∼lämpchen** n ⟨el⟩ *lamp repeater* **∼liste** f ⟨sport⟩ *list of entries*; *entry* **∼pflicht** f *obligation to report o.s.*; *obligatory reporting* **≗pflichtig** a *reportable notifiable* (*disease*); *subject to registration* **∼reiter** m ⟨mil⟩ *dispatch-rider* **∼sammelstelle** f ⟨mil⟩ *pick up* **∼schiff** n = ∼boot **∼schein, ∼zettel** m ⟨Ger⟩ *entry-* od *registration-form* ⟨a. hot⟩ **∼stelle** f (f Feuer) *fire-alarm, fire-station* **∼tasche** f *message bag* **∼weg** m [abstr] *path* (*to be*) *travelled by reports* **∼wesen** n *registration service* ‖ *intelligence service* **m·elden I.** vt/i [h] **1.** (ankündigen) *to announce, notify* ‖ jdm etw (schriftlich) ∼ *to inform a p of a th* (*in writing*); amtlich, (dienstlich), [telegraphisch] *to notify*, (*report*), [wire] *a th to a p*, ⟨mil a.⟩ *to advise* ‖ den Empfang e–r S ∼ *to acknowledge* (*the*) *receipt of a th* ‖ e–m ∼ l *to send a p word* ‖ e–n ∼ *to announce a p*; wen darf ich ∼? *what name, please*? ‖ ⟨bes mil⟩ ich werde Sie ∼ *I shall report you* ‖ ⟨rail⟩ (Zug) *to signal* ‖ der Heeresbericht meldet .. *announces* ‖ die Zeitungen ∼ .. *publish reports of* ‖ ⟨sport⟩ *to nominate*; ge–det s *to have been entered* **2.** (sagen, erwähnen) *to tell, mention*; *to make mention of* ‖ wie oben ge–det *as stated above* ‖ °du hast nichts zu ∼ *you have nothing to say* (*in this matter*) ‖ mit Respekt zu ∼ *with all due respect to you* **3.** ⟨cards⟩ *to call* (*tricks, a solo*) ‖ Sie h z ∼ *it is your turn to say* **II. sich** (zur Stelle) ∼ [vrefl] ⟨bes mil⟩ *to report o.s.* (bei *to*) (zum Dienst *for duty* od *service*; Leutnant N. –det sich als O.v.D. *Sir, I report as new officer of the day*; v Urlaub zurück *back from leave*) ‖ sich polizeilich ∼ *to register one's address* (*with the police authorities*) ‖ sich beim Fundbüro ∼ *to report sth lost in the Lost-property Office* ‖ sich ∼ ⟨wir⟩ *to sign on* [adv]; wir ∼ uns um 5° wieder *we are on the air again at 5*; es –dete sich niemand ⟨telph⟩ *the t. was not answered*; sich krank ~ ⟨bes mil⟩ *to report (o.s.) ill, to go sick* ‖ ⟨com⟩ (v Gläubigern) *to come forward* ‖ ⟨sport⟩ *to enter (for)* ‖ das Kind meldet sich (zum Stillen) .. *makes itself heard* ‖ sich ~ l *to send in one's name* ‖ bitte, ~ Sie mich dem Herrn Direktor *please tell the d. that I am here* od *that I should like to see him* | ⟨fig⟩ der Hunger, Magen meldet sich *hunger makes itself felt* ‖ der Winter meldet sich *winter is setting in* ‖ das Alter meldet sich bei ihm *age is telling on him* | sich ~ **zu** *or* **für** *to put up* od *apply for (an appointment)* ‖ *to enter (one's name) for (an examination)* ‖ sich zum Wort ~ *to try to catch the chairman's*, etc. *eye* **meldend**: der ⩯e *the originator of a report* **M·elder** m ~s/~ *dispatch-rider, runner* **M·eldung** f ~/~en *announcement, notification, advice, notice, information* ‖ *mention* ‖ ⟨mil⟩ *report*; (Termin⩯) *return*; ~ nach dem Einsatz *debrief(ing)* N; ~ **über** gelagerte Bestände *stock storage report* N; .. feindliches Feuer ⟨artill⟩ auf eigene Truppen *shelling r.*; .. Gefechtsverluste *casualty r.* N ‖ ⟨sport⟩ *entry* | Abend⩯ *night-r.* ‖ Flieger⩯ *air-r.* ‖ Geheim⩯ *secret message* ‖ Sensations⩯ ⟨Am sl⟩ *scoop, beat* | ~ abwerfen *to drop a message* ‖ ⟨sport⟩ s–e ~ zurückziehen *to scratch* | nach bisher vorliegenden ~en ⟨mil⟩ *according to reports so far to hand*

mel·ieren vt [h] *to mix, mingle* ‖ grau meliert *mixed with gray* ‖ er hat gr. m.tes Haar *his hair is flecked with grey* ‖ braunmeliert *whitey-brown* ‖ ⟨com⟩ meliertes Tuch *pepper and salt*

Meliorati·on f ~/ *(a)melioration, soil improvement* | ~smittel [n] *soil conditioner* **melior·ieren** vt [h] *to ameliorate*

Mel·isse f ~/~n ⟨bot⟩ *balm(-mint)*

m·elk a *milch, giving milk* ‖ (trächtig) *with young* **M·elk- ~eimer** m, **~faß** n, **~kübel** m *milking-tub, milk-pail* **~kuh** f *milch cow* **~maschine** f *milking m.* **~schemel** m *milking-stool* **~zeit** f *m.g--time* **m·elken 1.** vt [molk/gemolken] [h] *to milk* ‖ ⟨fig⟩ *to fleece (a p)* ‖ frisch gemolkene Milch *milk fresh from the cow* ‖ sich ~ l *to milk* **2.** vi [h] *to give milk* ‖ ⟨fig⟩ die ~de Kuh *the goose that lays the golden eggs* **M·elker** m ~s/~ *milker* | **~in** f *milker, milk-maid* **Melker·ei** f ~/~en 1. *milking* 2. *cow house, dairy(-farm)*

Melod·ie f ~/~n [i:ən] *melody, tune, air, strain* ‖ wie geht die ~? *how does the tune run?* ‖ nach der ~ von *to the tune of* | ⩯nreich [a] *tuneful* **⩯nselig** a *melodious* **Mel·odik** f ~/ *melodics* pl **melodi·ös, mel·odisch** a *melodious, tuneful, tuny* ‖ *musical* **Melodr·ama** n ~s/–men *melodrama* **melodram·atisch** a *melodramatic*

Mel·one f ~/~n *melon* ‖ °⟨fig⟩ *hard-hat, bowler(-hat), billy-cock, pot* **~nkürbis** m *squash, gourd*

M·eltau m ~(e)s/ *honey-like excrement of leaf-lice*

M·elvillebai (an der Westküste Grönlands) *Melville Bay* **M·elvillehalbinsel** f *M. Peninsula*

Membr·ane f ~/~n ⟨anat⟩ *membrane* ‖ ⟨telph⟩ *diaphragm*

M·emel 1. f (Fluß) *Niemen* **2.** n ⟨†Ger⟩ (Stadt) *Memel* **~gebiet** n *M. District*

M·emme f ~/~n *dastard, coward, poltroon*, ⟨Am sl⟩ *sissy* | **⩯nhaft** a *cowardly*

Memoire [me'mwa:r] n ~s/~s *memoir* | ~nschreiber [m] *memoirist, author of memoirs* **Memor·andum** n *memorandum (diplomatic note)* **Memori·albuch** n ⟨com⟩ *waste-book, memorandum--book* **memor·ieren** vt [h] *to get* od *learn by heart, to commit to memory* ‖ s–e Rolle ~ *to learn one's part* ‖ gut memoriert h *to know thoroughly*

Men·age [me'na:ʒə] f ~/~n *plate-basket*; *set of dishes*, ⟨Am⟩ *dinner-pail* ‖ (f Essig u Öl) *casters* pl, *cruet-stand*; *condiments set* | ⟨bes österr mil⟩ *provisioning* („Erst kommt die ~ ['menaʒ] u F·urage u dann die Blamage") **Menager·ie** [menaʒə'ri:] f ~/~n *menagerie* **menag·ieren** [mena'ʒi:rən] **1.** vt *to manage* ‖ (sparen) *to economize* **2. sich** ~ *to moderate o.s.*

M·enaikanal m (zw Carnavonshire u der Insel Anglesey, Wales) *Menai Strait(s)*

m·endeln vi [h] *to mendelize*; M–lsche Regeln, Gesetze *Mendelism, Mendel's laws*; M–lsche Vererbung *Mendelian inheritance*

M·eng- ~futter n *mash* **~korn** n *wheat and rye mixed* **m·engbar** a *capable of being mixed* **m·engen** vt [h] *to mix, to mingle* ‖ (Tee etc) *to blend* ‖ → mischen ‖ ⟨fig⟩ (im Reden) eins ins andre ~ *to mix ths up* | sich unter die Leute ~ *to mingle with the crowd* ‖ sich in e–e S ~ *to meddle with, to interfere in a th* ‖ er mengt sich in alles *he puts* od *pokes his nose in everywhere, he has an oar in everyman's boat, he is a meddler* **Menger·ei, M·engung** f ~/~en *mingling, mixing, blending* ‖ *mixture, blend* **M·engsel** n ~s/~ *mixture, medley, hodge-podge*

M·enge f ~/~n (→ Haufe, Masse, Un⩯) **1.** *quantity* ‖ ⟨math⟩ *set, aggregate* ‖ (Fülle) *plenty* ‖ jede beliebige ~ *any amount* ‖ effektive ~ ⟨comp⟩ *quantity good* ‖ erlaubte ~ *allowance* ‖ e–e ganze ~ ⟨fam⟩ *a good few* ‖ gr ~ *great* od *large number (of people), quantity (of fruit)* ‖ schöne ~ *fine* od *pretty lot* od *crop* | e–e ~ Bücher etc, Bücher etc die ~ *or* in ~ *a great many books*; *a fleet of cars*; *a mass of details*; *a host of difficulties* ‖ *a pack of fools, lies, nonsense* ‖ *scores of friends* ‖ *fruit in abundance* ‖ *large volumes of information* ‖ *a shower, a fine crop of letters* ‖ *plenty of meat, money* ‖ ⟨fam⟩ *lots* od *a mint of money* ‖ *a host* od *scores of names* ‖ *a crowd* od ⟨sl⟩ *power, sight of people*; *a great many people, shoals*, (⟨Am⟩ *rafts*), *myriads of p.* ‖ *a peck, sea, world of trouble* ‖ *a world* od *a large body of water* | e–e gr ~ v Literatur *an ocean of l.* | **in** gr, ⟨fam⟩ schweren, °rauhen ~en *abundantly, in (great) abundance, in bulk*; *(in) galore (quarrels galore)*, (P & T) *in crowds* ‖ *(to be found) freely* ‖ in gr ~en auftreten *to come in a flood, to shoal* | die ~ muß es bringen *numbers must do it*; → Masse ‖ **es gibt** e–e ~ G., daß .. *r.s are rampant that ..* ‖ es gab e–e ~ zu tun *there was plenty to do*; in ~n herstellen ⟨a.⟩ *to produce on the line* **2.** [abs] die ~ (das Volk) *the multitude, crowd, million*; *the masses* pl, *hoi polloi* (Gr); das Interesse der ~ *the popular i.* | sich **aus** der ~ herausheben *to rise out of the ruck* ‖ (er, es) fällt **in** der ~ nicht auf *may pass in a crowd* **~nlehre** f ⟨math⟩ *theory of sets, theory of aggregates* **⩯mäßig** a *quantitative* **~nrabatt** m *quantity discount*

M·engsel → o. Meng-

M·enhir m ~s/~e ⟨praeh⟩ *menhir*

Men·iskus m ~/–ken ⟨anat⟩ *meniscus*

°**Menk·enke** f, ~ m *to be formal* ‖ mach k–e ~! *don't fuss!*; *none of your tricks!*

M·ennig m ~(e)s/ **~e** f ~/ *minium, red lead*

M·enopause f ⟨biol⟩ *climacteric, menopause*

Men·orca, Min·orka n ⟨Span⟩ *Minorca*

M·ensa f ~/–sen ⟨univ⟩ *hall*, ⟨Am⟩ *commons*

M·ensch 1. [m] ~en/~en *man, human being, p* ‖ *a young, handsome, brave, noble man* ‖ *a stupid, smart, clever, mean, cowardly p* ‖ ein solcher ~ *such a one as he* ‖ ėr ist die Seele v e–m ~en *he is a capital fellow* ‖ der griechische (innere) ~ *the Greek (inner) man* ‖ ~en 2. Klasse *second raters* ‖ der ~ im Betrieb *the human factor in business* ‖ Beziehungen v ~ zu ~ *interhuman relationship* | ~! *old man! my dear fellow!* ‖ aber ~! *man alive!* ~ ärgere dich nicht! (Spiel) *ludo* | [pl] die ~en *men* pl, *mankind, humanity, people, the world* | welcher ~? *who?* ‖ jeder ~ *everybody, all the world*; ⟨emph⟩ *every living soul* ‖ kein ~ *nobody* | ~ geworden *incarnate* ‖ ~ w *to be made flesh* ‖ z gesitteten ~en m *to humanize* ‖ unter die ~en k *to go into society* ‖ viele ~en k ums Leben *many* (*people*) *lose their lives* ‖ der ~ denkt, Gott lenkt *man proposes, God disposes*; des ~en Sohn *the Son of Man* (*Christ*) ‖ e–n neuen ~en anziehen *to moult*; *to become a new man* ‖ er ist auch nur ein ~ *he is only human* ‖ mein ganzer ~ war ergriffen *I was moved to the heart* **2.** [n] ~es/~er ⟨vulg⟩ *wench, hussy*, ⟨fam⟩ *baggage* ‖ derbes ~ *whacker, strapper* ‖ (Dirne) *strumpet* **M·enschen-** mst *h.* (*human*) bzw *h.e* (*humane*) **~affe** m *man-ape, anthropoid ape* **≃ähnlich** a (v Affen) *a.pomorphous, a.poid* | ≃keit [f] *resemblance to a man* **~alter** n *generation, age* **~antlitz** n *h. face* **~art** f: das ist ~ *that's the way of the world, such is h. nature* **~begegnung** f *human relations* pl **~beglücker** m ⟨dero⟩ *do-gooder* **~blut** n *h. blood* **~dasein** n *h. existence* **~dieb** m *kidnapper* **~familie** f *h. race* **~feind** m *misanthrope, m.pist* **≃feindlich** a *m.-pic*(*al*) **~fleisch** n *man's flesh, h. flesh* **≃fressend** a *man-eating* **~fresser** m *man-eater, cannibal*; (im Märchen) *ogre*; ~in [f] *ogress* **~fresserei** f *cannibalism* **~freund** m *philanthropist* **≃freundlich** a *h.e, kind, ph.pic* **~freundlichkeit** f *h.eness, h.ity, ph.py* ‖ *geniality, affability* ‖ *benevolence* **~furcht** f *fear of man* **~gattung** f *h. species* **~gebeine** n pl *h. bones* pl **~gebot** n *h. law* **~gedenken** n *memory of man* ‖ seit ~ *time out of mind, within* (vor *beyond*) *living memory* od *the memory of man, from time immemorial* **~gefühl** n *h.e feeling* **~geschlecht** n *mankind* **~gestalt** f *h. shape* od *form* **~gewühl** n *crowd of men* **~glück** n *h. happiness* **~haar** n *h. hair* **~handel** m *man-, slave-trade* **~haß** m *misanthropy* **~hasser** m *m.pe* **~heil** n *salvation of mankind* **~herz** n *h. heart* **~hilfe** f *h. assistance* **~jagd** f *man-hunt* **~kenner** m *judge of men* od *h. character*; er ist ein ~ *he knows h. nature* **~kenntnis** f *knowledge of mankind* od *of h. nature* **~kind** n *h. being*; so ein armes ~ *such a poor fellow, the poor dear* **~knochen** m *h. bone* **~kunde** f = ~lehre **~leben** n *h. life*; ~ [pl] fordern *to claim lives* **≃leer** a *deserted* **~lehre** f *anthropology* **~liebe** f *love of humanity, philanthropy* **~material** n ⟨mil⟩ *man-power* **~menge** f *crowd* **≃möglich** a *h.ly possible, within h. power*; nicht ~ *impossible*; alles was ~ ist *all that is in any way possible* **~mord** m *homicide*; (böswilliger) *murder* **~natur** f *h. nature* **~opfer** n *h. sacrifice* | das 1. **~paar** *our first parents* **~pflicht** f *duty of a h. being* **~potential** n *manpower* **~raub** m *kidnapping* **~räuber** m *k.per* **~recht** n *law of man*; ~e [pl] *rights of m., h. rights* **≃reich** a *populous* **~satzung** f *h. institution* **~scheu** f *shyness, unsociableness* **≃scheu** a *shy, unsociable* **~schinder** m *oppressor, slave-driver, extortioner* **~schlag** m *race of men*; ein anderer ~ *a different kind of people* **~seele** f *h. soul*; k–e ~ *not a living soul*; jede ~ *every man Jack* **~sinn** m = ~verstand **~skind** ⟨fam⟩ *man alive*!; ~er! *fellows*! *chaps*! **~sohn** m (*the*) *Son of Man* **~stimme** f *h. voice* **~typ** m; frühe ~en *hominids* pl **~typus** m *type of h.ity* **~verächter** m *cynic* **~verstand** m *h. understanding* ‖ gesunder ~ *common sense*, ⟨Am a.⟩ *horse s.* **~weisheit** f *h. wisdom* **~welt** f *h. world, mankind* **~werk** n *work of man* **~witz** m *h. understanding* **~wohl** n *h. weal* **~würde** f *dignity of m.* od *h. dignity* **≃würdig** a *decent* **M·enschentum** n ~s/ 1. *human race* 2. = Menschlichkeit **M·enschheit** f ~/ 1. *man*(*kind*), *humanity, human race*; *for the welfare of man* 2. *h. form* od *nature* 3. = Menschenmenge | ~s- → Menschen- **M·enschlein** n *mannikin, little bit of a man* **m·enschlich** a 1. *human* (*life*) 2. (fühlend) *humane* 3. *decent, tolerable* | ~e Bedürfnisse *man's needs* ‖ ~es Empfinden *h.ity* ‖ nach ~em Ermessen *h.ly speaking* ‖ *humane* (Pflicht); nach ~er Voraussicht *as far as we can foresee* ‖ ~e Vorstellungen *man's ideas, notions* ‖ sollte mir etw ≃es zustoßen *in case anything should happen to me* ‖ ihm ist etw ≃es passiert *he has made a mistake*; *he has died* ‖ er fühlte ein ~es Rühren *h. compassion stirred his breast*, ⟨hum⟩ *he felt hungry* | Irren ist ~ *to err is human* | **≃keit** f ~/ 1. *humanity, human nature* 2. *humaneness, humanity* ‖ ~ im Betrieb *human relations* pl; aus Gründen der ~ *for humanitarian reasons* **M·enschwerdung** f ~/ *incarnation* | (der Affen) "*development of apes into men*"

Menstruati·on [ts] f ~/~en *menstruation*

Mens·ur f ~/~en *measure*, → Meßglas ‖ ⟨mus⟩ *diapason* ‖ ⟨fenc⟩ *proper distance*; (Tätigkeit) *students' fencing* ‖ (Ort) *ground measured for a duel, fencing, duelling-ground* ‖ auf (die) ~ gehn *to go fencing*

Mentalit·ät f ~/ *mentality* **Ment·alreservation** f *mental reservation, reservatio mentalis* L

Menth·ol n ~s/ *menthol*

M·entor m ~s/–t·oren *mentor, tutor* (jds *to a p*)

Men·ü n ~s/~s *bill of fare*; *menu* | *table d'hôte dinner* | ~karte [f] *menu* (*card*)

Menu·ett n ~(e)s/~e *minuet*

meph·itisch = mefitisch

mephistoph·elisch a *Mephistophelian, Mephistolean*

Mer·an n ⟨It⟩ (Stadt) *Meran*(*o*)

Merc·atorprojection f ~/~en *Mercator projection*

M·ergel m ~s/ ⟨geol⟩ *marl* **~ablagerung** f *bed of m.* **≃artig** a *m.y* **~düngung** f ⟨agr⟩ *m.ing* **~erde** f *earthy m.* **~grube** f *m.-pit* **~kalk** m *m.y limestone* **~schiefer** m *slaty m.* **~ton** m *argillaceous m.* **m·ergelig** a *m.ly* **m·ergeln** vt [h] ⟨agr⟩ *to m.*

Meridi·an m ~s/~e *meridian* ‖ durch den ~ gehen *to culminate* ‖ ~höhe *m. height* **m.n·al** a *meridional* **≃kreisel** m ⟨aero⟩ *meridian gyro*

Mer·inge f ~/~n (*cream-*)*meringue* Fr **~masse** f *m. mixture*

Mer·ino m ~s/~s *merino* (a. –schaf, –wolle)

Mer·iten pl: er hat s–e ~ *he has his merits*

M·erk m ~(e)s/ ⟨bot⟩ (*Sium*) *skirret*

merkant·il a *commercial, mercantile* (*system*)

M·erk- **~blatt** n *data sheet*; *memorandum* ‖ (*instructional*) *leaflet, pamphlet*; *directives* pl **~buch** n *note-book* **~mal** n *mark, token, characteristic*; (*significant, prominent, characteristic, distinctive*) *feature, sign, attribute*; ⟨comp⟩ *label*; artgemäßes ~ ⟨demog⟩ *quality* ‖ besonderes, unterscheidendes ~ *special peculiarity, speciality* ‖ ⟨biol⟩ *character* **~spruch** m *popular saying* **~welt** f ⟨eth⟩ *perceptual world* **~wort** n ⟨theat⟩ *cue* ‖ ⟨typ⟩ *direction-word* **≃würdig** a *noteworthy* (*event*), *remarkable* (*occurrence, district*) ‖ (seltsam) *curious* (*fellow*), *strange* (*story*) ‖ *marvellous* (*composure*) ‖ äußerst ~ *curiously enough* ‖ das ist ~ *that is extraordinary* | sie hat e–e ~ [adv] hohe Meinung v sich *she thinks an awful lot of h.s.* | ≃erweise [adv] *curiously, oddly* ‖ *strange to say* (*he did it*) | ~keit [f] *remarkableness, curiousness, curiosity*; ~en [pl] *remarkable ths, sights* pl (*of a town*) **~zeichen** n *mark* ‖ mit e–m ~ versehen *to mark* (*with*) **m·erkbar** a *perceptible, noticeable* ‖ e–e ~e Besserung *a marked improvement* **m·erken I.** vi [h] **1.** †(aufpassen) *to listen* **2.** der Junge merkt gut .. *has a good memory* **3. auf** etw ~ *to take heed of, to pay attention to, to attend to, to mind a th* **II.** vt [h] **1.** ⟨dial⟩ (bezeichnen) *to mark* ‖ (aufschreiben) *to note* (*down*) **2.** (verstehen) *to understand, realize* ‖ (wahrnehmen) *to notice, feel, perceive* ‖ sie h es sofort ge–kt *they knew at once what was up* ‖ ich –kte s–e Absicht *I recognized* .. ‖ sie h nichts ge–kt *they didn't notice anything* ‖ ich –kte etw *I smelled a rat* ‖ ich –kte es k *I felt it coming* | jdn ~ l, daß *to let a p see that*; h Sie ge–kt, daß ..? *are you aware that* ..? ‖ man –kte es **an** ihrer Aufregung, daß .. *her excitement showed you that* .. ‖ du –kst auch alles *you are of too noticing a nature* **3. sich** [dat] etw ~ (einprägen) *to retain, note, remember a th* ‖ *to make* (*a mental*) *note of, to take good note of* ‖

merk dir's! (..) *bear it in mind! keep it! now mark* (..)! || ich werde mir's ~ *I shall not forget it, I'll bear it in mind* || ~ Sie sich, was ich sage! *mark my word! remember what I say* || leicht (schwer) z ~ *easily remembered* (*hard to remember*) || ~ Sie wohl! wohlgemerkt! *mind you! mark me!* **4.** etw ~ l (verraten) *to show, betray*, ⟨fam⟩ *to let out a th* || nicht ~ l *to dissemble, to keep snug* | **sich nichts ~ l** *not to betray anything, to make no sign, to seem to know nothing* (*of a th*), *not to give o.s. away* || *he let nothing* (*of this*) *be seen* | ich werde es **ihn** ~ l *I'll let him know what's what*

M·erker m ~s/~ **1.** *scorer, marker* || ⟨arts hist⟩ *critic* **2.** °du bist ein richtiger ~ *you do notice everything*; *you are of too noticing a nature* || du hast den richtigen ~ *you are quick in observing*

m·erklich a *noticeable, perceptible* || *visible* || *obvious, evident* || *sharp* (*contrast*) || *marked* (*difference*) || kaum ~ *very little* | adv *visibly* (*not v. larger*) || *considerably, appreciably* || *perceptibly* (*improved*) || (*to differ*) *perceptibly* °**M·erks** m *brains* pl, ⟨fam⟩ *gumption, nous*

Merk·ur m ~s/ ⟨alchemy⟩ m & n *mercury* || ⟨astr⟩ *Mercury* **Merkuri·al-** [in comp], ≃**isch** a *mercurial* (*ointment*) **~mittel** n *mercurial*

M·erle f ~/~n ⟨orn⟩ *blackbird*

°**m·erschten,** die ~ ⟨dial⟩ = die meisten

M·erz- **~schafe** n pl *cast-off sheep* **~vieh** n *rejected cattle, culls* pl

merzeris·ieren vt *to mercerize*

Mes·abigebirge n *Mesabi Range* (*Minn.*)

Mesalliance [–'ã:s] f ~/~n *misalliance*

mesch·ant a = boshaft, bösartig ⟨a. med⟩

°**mesch·ugge** a [Hebr] ⟨sl⟩ *loony*, ⟨Am⟩ *meshug*(*g*)*a*(*h*)

mesmeris·ieren vt [h] *to mesmerize* **Mesmer·ismus** m ~/ *mesmerism*

M·esner m ~s/~ *sexton* || ⟨R. C.⟩ *sacrist*(*an*)

Mesopot·amien n *Mesopotamia* **Mesopot·amier** m, **~in** f, **mesopot·amisch** a *Mesopotamian*

m·esoz·oisch a ⟨geol⟩ *mesozoic* **M·esoz·oikum** n *Mesozoic*

M·eß- (→ Messe, messen) [3]**~achsen** der Kreisel ⟨a–n⟩ *gauge axes of gyros* [1]**~amt** n ⟨ec⟩ (*service of the*) *mass* || [2]⟨com⟩ *office of* (*Leipzig*) *fair* [3]**~band** n (*rule* od *measuring-*)*tape* **~becher** m [3]= –glas; [1]⟨ec⟩ *beaker* [3]**~bereich** m *effective range* **~bild-** ~kamera [f] *photogrammetric c.*; ~verfahren [n] *photogrammetry* **~brief** m ⟨mar com⟩ *bill of tonnage* [1]**~buch** n ⟨ec⟩ *missal, mass-book* [2]**~bude** f *booth, stall* (*at a fair*) [1]**~diener** m (= Mesner) *acolyte* [3]**~entfernung** f *subject distance* **~fahne** f *surveyor's flag* **~fehler** m *error in measurement* [3]**~flug** m *test flight* [2]**~freiheit** f *privilege of holding a fair* **~fremde** m pl *merchants attending a fair* [1]**~gerät** n ⟨ec⟩ *mass-requisites* || [3]*range-finder*, ⟨mech⟩ *measuring instrument* [2]**~geschenk** n *fairing* [1]**~gewand** n ⟨ec⟩ *chasuble, vestment* [3]**~glas** n *graduated measure* [1]**~glocke** f *mass-bell* [3]**~größe** f ⟨comp⟩ *measurable variable*; *mesurand* [2]**~gut** n *goods* [pl] *sent to a fair* **~helfer** m *packer, porter* (*at a fair*) [1]**~hemd** n ⟨ec⟩ *alb* **~kännchen** n *altar cruet* **~kelch** m *chalice* [3]**~kette** f *surveyor's chain* [1]**~knabe** m ⟨ec⟩ *little server* [3]**~kunde** f *surveying* **~kunst** f *geometry* **~latte** f *surveyor's staff*, ⟨Am⟩ *rod* **~okular** n *measuring eyepiece* [1]**~opfer** n ⟨ec⟩ (*sacrifice of the*) *mass* **~priester** m *mass-priest* **~pult** n *mass-book desk* [3]**~rute** f *surveyor's rod* od *perch* **~schnur** f *measuring cord* **~schraube** f *micrometer caliper* **~stab** m ⟨mot⟩ (f Öl) *dip stick* **~stange** f = ~rute [2]**~stadt** f = Messestadt [3]**~strecke** f ⟨mot, aero⟩ *speed course* **~sucher** m ⟨phot⟩ *range finder* **~tafel** f *test board* **~technik** f *technique of measurement*; *measuring* **~tisch** m *chart-, plane-* od *surveyor's table, surveying-board* (dazu: *to plane-table*) | ~aufnahme [f] *plane-table sketch*; ~blatt [n] (1 : 25000) ⟨mil⟩ *ordnance* (*survey*) *map* **~trupp** m *survey section*; ⟨mil⟩ *ranging squad* [1]**~tuch** n ⟨ec⟩ *communion-cloth* [3]**~uhr** f *dial ga*(*u*)*ge* (*indicator*) | ~anzeige [f] *meter reading* [3]**~vorgang** m *measurement*; *measuring proceedings* pl [2]**~ware** f = ~gut [1]**~wein** m *sacramental wine* [3]**~wert** m *measured value* || ⟨aero⟩ *datum* (erflogen *obtained during flight*) || Eingabe v ~en u Kommandos ⟨a–n–comp⟩ *input of index numbers and orders* ~übertragung [f] *data transmission* **~wesen** n *measurements* pl [2]**~woche** f *fair-week*

m·eßbar a *measurable* ≃**keit** f ~/ *measurability*

M·esse f ~/~n [1]⟨ec⟩ *mass* || hohe (stille) ~ *high* (*low*) *mass* || [2](Markt) *fair*, die Leipziger ~ *the Leipzig Fair* | e–e ~ abhalten *to hold a fair* | die ~ beschicken *to send goods to the f.* || die ~ besuchen *to attend the f.*; sich z ~ anmelden *to register for a f.*; auf e–r ~ ausstellen *to display goods at a f.* | [1]~ lesen ⟨ec⟩ *to say mass* || in die *or* zur ~ gehen *to go to mass* | [2]**~besucher** m *fair goer*; *visitor to a f.* **~onkel** m ⟨etwa⟩ *sugar daddy* **~ordnung** f *fair regulations* pl **~stadt** f *fair-town* **~stand** m *fair stand*

M·esse f ~/~n ⟨mar⟩ (*officers'*) *mess* || Kadetten≃ *gun-room* || *ward-room* **~jackett** n *mess jacket* **~weste** f (*white*) *evening waistcoat*

m·essen I. vt [h] **1.** *to measure* (*width, size, speed*) || Band nach dem Meter (, ..) ~ *to m. ribbon by the metre* (*milk by the litre*) || zwei Dinge mit– *or* an–e–a ~ .. *against each other* || mit dem Metermaß, e–r Schnur ~ *to meter, to cord* || (Ausmaß feststellen, eichen) *to gauge* (*rainfall, heat, wind*; *casks, wire*, etc.) || jds T. ~ *to take a p's temperature* || (Land) *to survey* || (Winkel) *to determinate* | ⟨übtr⟩ (**betrachten**) *to take in* || (beurteilen) mit zweierlei Maß ~ *to judge by two different standards* || ge~ an s–n Fähigkeiten ist er .. *considering his abilities ..* || an kontinentalen Maßstäben ge~ *put to the test of ..* || (mustern) *to measure* (*a p with looks*); .. verächtlich *to look a p down* | ⟨fig⟩ er kann das G. mit Scheffeln ~ *he is rolling in money* || ge~e Haltung *dignified demeanour* || mit ge~en Schritten *with measured steps* **2. sich mit e-m** ~ *to match a p, to measure o.s. with* od *against a p* (an in) || *to cope with, to spar at* od *with* || .. im Laufen *to run against a p, to race a p* || ich kann mich ~ mit *I can hold my own with* od *cope with* | ⟨fig⟩ *to measure swords, to try conclusions* || sich nicht ~ können mit *to be no match for*; sich nicht mit etw ~ können *not to be up to the standard of a th*; s–e Kräfte *or* sich an etw Größerem ~ *to try one's hand at sth bigger* | **ge~ an,** wenn wir .. ~ an *in terms of* (*trade, other currencies*) **II.** vi *to contain* (*a foot c.s 12 inches*) || ich messe 1,80 m *I am 1.80 metres high*; er mißt .. ohne Schuhe *he is 6 feet tall in his stocking feet*

M·esser[1] m ~s/~ **1.** (P) *measurer* **2.** (Gerät) *ga*(*u*)*ge, measuring instrument* | [in comp] mst *-meter* || Dr·uck≃ *pressure gauge* || Entf·ernungs≃ *range-finder* || Geschw·indigkeits≃ *speedometer*, ⟨mar⟩ *speed indicator* || Sp·annungs≃ ⟨el⟩ *voltmeter* || Umdr·ehungs≃ *revolution indicator* || Wasserstands≃ *water gauge* || Wellen≃ ⟨wir⟩ *wavemeter* || Wind≃ *wind gauge* || Zeilen≃ *line measure*

M·esser[2] n ~s/~ *knife* || ~ u Gabeln [pl] *cutlery* | B·aum≃ *pruning-k.* || D·olch≃ *whinger* || elektrisches ~ *radio k.* || feststehendes ~ *fixed k.* || F·isch≃ *fish-k.* || gr ~ *snickersnee* || H·ack≃ (*meat*) *cleaver, chopper* || H·obel≃ *cutter* || Kl·app≃ *jack-k.*, ⟨med⟩ *bistoury* || Krebs≃ *crayfish k.* || Obst≃ *fruit k.* || Okulier≃ *budding-k.* || Ras·ier≃ *razor* || R·eb≃ *billhook* || Sch·ab≃ *burin* || Sp·argel≃ *cutter* || St·anz≃ *punching tool* || T·aschen≃ *pocket-k.* || W·iege≃ *cradle* || zweiklingiges ~ *double-bladed k.* | **bis** aufs ~ *to the k.*; *tooth and nail* || ein ~ abziehen *to hone a k.* || e–n jdm ans ~ liefern *to give a p up to a p* || ⟨fig⟩

e–m das ~ an die Kehle setzen *to hold a k. to a p's throat* || das ~ saß ihm an der Kehle *he felt the k. at his th.* || (e–n) **mit** dem ~ stechen, (etw) mit d. ~ (aus)schneiden *to k.* || ⟨fig⟩ er führt das lange ~ *he brags* || e–m ein ~ in den Leib **jagen,** stechen *to run a k. into* od *through a p* || auf (des) ~s **Schneide** stehen *to be* od *balance on the razor's* (od *k.-)edge*; auf (des) ~s Schneide stehend *snickersneed (condition)* | **~bänkchen** n *k.-rest* **~besteck** n *k.-case* **~egge** f *scarifier* **~flug** m ⟨aero⟩ *vertical bank* **~gras** n ⟨bot⟩ *k.-grass* **~griff** m, **~heft** n *k.-handle* **~händler** m *cutler* **~held** m *hooligan, cut-throat,* ⟨sl⟩ *knifer* **~klinge** f *k.-blade* **~kontakt** m ⟨tech⟩ *k.-blade c.* **~korb** m *k.-tray* **~putzbrett** n *k.-board* **~rücken** m *back of a k.* **~schalter** m ⟨tech⟩ *k.-switch*; ⟨wir⟩ → Erdung **~schärfer** m *k.-sharpener* **~schmied** m *cutler* **~schmiede** f *cutler's workshop* **~schneide** f *k.-edge* **~spitze** f *point of a knife* **~stecher** m = –held **~stich** m *k.-thrust* **~tuch** n *k. towel* **~waffe** f *snickersnee* **~walze** f *cylinder cutter* **~waren** f pl *cutlery,* .. aus Solingen *S. goods* **~wunde** f *k. wound*

messi·anisch a *Messianic* **Mess·ias** m *Messiah*

Mess·ina n ⟨It⟩ *Messina*; Bewohner(in) v ~ *Messinese*; Straße v ~ *Strait(s) of Messina*

M·essing n ~s/ *brass* | ~beschläge [m pl] *b. (mounting)*; mit ~ beschlagen *b.-bound (trunk)* **~blech** n *sheet-b.* **~draht** m *b. wire* **~geschirr** n *b. untensils* pl, *b.es* pl **~gießer** m *b.-founder* **~hammer** m, **~hütte** f *b.-forge* **~platte** f, **~schild** n *b. plate* **~schmied** m *brazier* **~ware** f *brazier's ware* **m·essingen** a *(made of) brass, brazen*

M·essung f ~/~en *measurement* || ⟨math⟩ *mensuration* || (Entfernungs~̂) *range finding* || e–e ~ m *to take a measurement,* ⟨surv⟩ .. *bearings*

Mest·ize m ~n/~n *mestizo*

M·et m ~(e)s/ *mead*

Met·all n ~(e)s/~e *metal* [–*ll*–] || (Messing) *brass* || (un)edle ~e *precious (base) metals* pl || Schlagen der ~e zu Blättern *foliation* || ~ angreifen *to attack m.* || ⟨fig⟩ sie hat ~ in der Stimme *her voice has a metallic ring* od *timbre,* .. wenig, viel .. *has poor, rich timbre* **Met·all-** **~ader** f *m.lic vein* od *lode* **~̂angreifend** a *corrosive to m.s* **~arbeiter** m *m.-man, m.list, worker in m.(s)* **~̂artig** a *m.lic* **~bearbeitung(smaschine)** f *m. working (machine)* **~bedachung** f *m. covering* **~blatt** n *m.lic foil,* ⟨weav⟩ *m.lic reed* **~blechstanzen** n *sheet m. punching* **~draht** m *m.lic wire* **~fadenlampe** f *m.lic filament lamp* **~färbung** f *m. colouring* **~flugzeug** (Ganz~̂) n *(all-)m. aeroplane* **~futter** n *bush* **~gehalt** m ⟨min⟩ *yield of ores* **~geld** n *specie* **~gemisch** n *mixture of m.s, alloy* **~glanz** m *m.lic lustre* **~gold** n *Dutch gold* **~guß** m *m. cast(ing)* **~̂haltig** a *m.line, m.liferous* **~haut** f ⟨aero⟩ *m. envelope* **~komposition** f *m.lic compound* **~könig** m ⟨chem⟩ *regulus (of m.)* **~kunde** f *m.lurgy* **~niederschlag** m *deposit m.* **~oxid** n ⟨chem⟩ *m.lic oxide* **~probe** f *assay* **~ring** m ⟨tech⟩ *thimble* || ⟨allg⟩ *ferrule* **~säge** f *hacksaw* **~scheidung** f ⟨el⟩ *electrolytic parting* | mit e–r **~schicht** überziehen ⟨el⟩ *to galvanize* **~schild** n *m. sign* **~spiegel** m *m.lic mirror* **~spritzverfahren** n *m. spraying* **~̂verarbeitend** a *metal-processing (plant)* **~versetzung** f *alloy* **~vorrat** m (der Bank) *stock of bullion* od *specie* **~waren** f pl *hardware* **met·allen** a *metal (tray)* || *metallic (gleam)* **met·allisch** a *m.lic (material, voice, appearance)* || *m.line (water)* **metallis·ieren** vt [h] *to m.lize (paper, wood), to impregnate with metal* **Metall·urg** m ~en/~en *m.lurgist* | **-urg·ie** f *m.lurgy* **metall·urgisch** *m.lurgic(al)* || ⟨exch⟩ *mining (shares* pl)

Met·a- **~̂m·orph** a ⟨geol⟩ *metamorphic (changes)* | ~̂·ose [f] ~/~n *m.phosis* | ~os·ieren vt [h] *to m.phose, transform* **~pher** f ~/~n *metaphor* (sinnentleert *dead*; *e. g.: the head of the firm*) **~̂ph·orisch** a *m.ical (expression)* || *figurative (sense)* **~phys·ik** f ~/ *metaphysics* pl [oft sg konstr] **~ph·ysiker** m ~s/~ *m.ian* **metaph·ysisch** *a m.ical* **~sprache** f *meta-language* **~st·ase** f ~/~n ⟨path⟩ *metastasis* **~th·ese** f ~/~n ⟨gram⟩ *metathesis* **~z·entrum** n ~s/–tren ⟨mar⟩ *metacentre*

Metempsych·ose f ~/~n *metempsychosis*

Mete·or m ~s/~e *meteor* | ~̂artig, ~̂isch [a] *m.ic*; ~eisen [n] *m.ic iron*; **~ol·oge** m ~en/~en *m.ologist,* ⟨Am⟩ *weather scientist,* ⟨fam⟩ *weatherman* **~olog·ie** f ~/ *m.ology* **~̂ol·ogisch** a *m.ological (station)*

M·eter n ~s/~ *metre,* ⟨Am⟩ *meter* || → drei || nach dem ~ *by the m.* .. **meter** n [in comp:] *barometer, manometer* || [m] *hexameter* **~kerze** f ⟨el⟩ *m.-candle* **~kilogramm** n *kilogrammetre* **~̂lang** a *a m. long* **~maß** n *metre rule* || *metric measure* **~ware** f *piece goods* **~̂weise** adv *by the m.*

Meth·an n ~s/ *methane* **~·ol** n ~(e)s/ *methanol*

Meth·ode f ~/~n *method* || (Art u Weise) *way, manner, line*; *approach (to a problem)* || .. anwenden *to employ* ..; falsche ~n .. ⟨a.⟩ *to go on wrong lines* || es hat ~ *there is m. in it (Hamlet II, 2)* || er hat so s–e ~ *that is his usual m.* || nach e–r ~ arbeiten .. *on a system* || *he has brought system into the undertaking* || jeder nach s–r ~ .. *to his own m.* || *it was his plan to read a piece slowly* **~nlehre** f, **Meth·odik** f ~/ *m.ology* **Meth·odiker** m ~s/~ *m.izer* **meth·odisch** a *m.ical* || ~e Behandlung *m.ization*

Method·ist m ~en/~en *methodist* **~enprediger** m *Methodist preacher* | **~̂isch** a *methodistical* **–dolog·ie** f *methodology*

Meth·yl n ~s/ *methyl* **~alkohol** m *methanol* **~äther** m *m.ic ether* **~·en(blau)** n ~s/ *m.ene(-blue)*

Metier [meˈtjeː] n ~s/~s *profession, business, trade, calling*

Metonym·ie f ~/~n [–iːən] *metonymy* (Neptun = Meer, „Leder" = Fußball; Bonn = Regierung) **meton·ymisch** a *metonymical*

M·etrik f ~/ *prosody, metrics* pl [a. sg konstr] | **~er** m ~s/ *metrist* **m·etrisch** a *metrical*; ~es System *metric system* **Metron·om** n ~s/~e *metronome* **M·etrum** n ~s/–ren & –ra *metre*

Metrop·ole f ~/~n („Mutterstadt") *metropolis*

M·ett n ~(e)s/ [niedd] *fatless minced pork*

M·ette f ~/~n ⟨ec⟩ *mat(t)ins* pl

Metteur m ~s/~e *maker-up*; *make-up hand*

M·ettwurst f *Bologna* od *German sausage*

Metz n [†Ger], ⟨Fr⟩ (Stadt in Lothringen)

M·etze f ~/~n **1.** *measure for corn, peck* **2.** ⟨vulg⟩ (Dirne) *strumpet, harlot, whore*

M·etzel- **~bank** f *shambles* pl **~suppe** f *pudding-broth* **Metzel·ei** f ~/~en *slaughter, butchery*; *massacre* **m·etzeln** vt [h] *to massacre, butcher, slaughter* **M·etzge** f ~/~n [sd] = Schlachtbank, Metzgerei **m·etzgen** vt [h] *to butcher* **M·etzger** m ~s/~ *butcher* **~beil** n *b.'s cleaver* **~hund** m *b.'s dog* **~knecht** m *b.'s man* **Metzger·ei** f ~/~en *b.'s business, shop, trade* || *butchering*

Meublem·ent [–œ–mɑ̃ː, –maŋ] n ~s/~s *furniture*

M·euchel- **~mörder** m *foul assassin* || gedungener ~ *hired a., bravo* It **~mord** m *foul a.ation* **~̂mörderisch** a *a.-like* **m·eucheln** vt [h] *to a.ate* **m·euchlerisch** a *treacherous, insidious* **m·euchlings** adv *i.ly, t.ly*

M·eute f ~/~n ⟨hunt⟩ *pack (of hounds), the hounds* || ⟨übtr⟩ *the numbers (of pursuers)*

Meuter·ei f ~/~en ⟨allg⟩ *sedition* || ⟨mil, mar⟩ *mutiny* **M·euterer** m ~s/~ *mutineer* **m·euterisch** a *mutinous, seditious* **m·eutern** vi [h] *to mutiny, mutineer* || ~d *mutinous*

Mexik·aner m, **~in** f *Mexican* **mexik·anisch** a *Mexican, of Mexico*; ⟨Am fam⟩ *greaser*

Mexik·anische Meerbusen, der *the Gulf of Mexico* **M·exiko** n *Mexico*

MG-Stand m → Maschinengewehr~́
Mi·ami n (Stadt) (*Fla., U.S.A.*)
Mi·asma n ~s/–men *miasma* **m-·atisch** a *m.tic*
mi·au! *mew!* | **~en** vi [h] *to mew, to caterwaul*
m·ich pron [acc (nom: ich)] *me* || ~ selbst *myself* || ich kenne ~ .. *m.s.* || ich setze ~ *I sit down* || → freuen, fürchten || ich ziehe ~ an *I am dressing* | ⟨fam oft⟩ *us* (*let's have it*)
Micha·eli(s) *Michaelmas* || zu ~ *at M.* **~fest** n *M., M.-day* **~messe** f *M.-fair* **~tag** m = ~fest
M·ichel m npr *Michael, Mick, Mike* || ⟨fig⟩ *clumsy* od *stupid fellow* || deutscher ~ ⟨fig⟩ *plain honest German, Fritz* || grober ~ *boor*
M·ichigan n [–ʃ–] (Staat der U.S.A.) *Michigan, the Lake State* **~-See** m *Lake Michigan*
Michoac·án [–tʃ–] (Staat in Mexiko)
°**mick(e)rig** a 1. *sickly, peaky* 2. *stingy*
M·idi- (knieumspielend) *midi* → Maxi-
mied(e) 1. & 3. sg indic (subj) pret v meiden
M·ieder n ~s/~ *bodice* || ⟨hist⟩ *stomacher*
°**M·ief** m ~(e)s/ *fug, fust,* ⟨mil sl⟩ *niff* | **~́ig** a *stuffy*
M·iene f ~/~n *mien, air, countenance* || (Gesichtszug) *feature* || ~ m etw z tun *to seem to be on the point of doing, to look as if one were about to do, to offer to do a th* || bekümmerte ~ *worried face* || e–e ernste ~ bewahren *to keep one's c.* || böse *or* finstere ~ *black looks* pl, e–e .. m *to look black* (e–m *at a p*) || e–e kecke ~ aufsetzen *to put on a bold front* || mit guter ~ *with a good grace*; gute ~ z bösen Spiel m *to make the best of it* od *of a bad bargain* od *job, to come up smiling, to grin and bear it* || e–e eiserne ~ annehmen *to set one's face like iron* || mit gleichgültiger ~ *with an impassive face* || offene, verschlossene ~ *open, reserved air* || e–e saure ~ m *to put on a sour c.* || e–e strenge ~ aufsetzen *to take on a severe look* || ohne e–e ~ zu verziehen *without turning a hair* od *moving a muscle* od *wincing* || e–e unschuldsvolle ~ vortäuschen *to assume an air of innocence* **M·ienen-~spiel** n *mimicry, pantomime* || ⟨theat a.⟩ *business* **~sprache** f *play of the features, pantomime*
M·iere f ~/ ⟨bot⟩ *chickweed*
°**m·ies** a *beastly, breamy*; e–e ~e S *a rotten affair* || *poor, paltry* (*shop*) || das sieht ~ aus *that looks bad* °**~́epeter** m *creep* °**~epetrig** a *paltry, poor* || *drizzerable* (*weather*) || (P) [pred] *off colo(u)rs* °**~́macher** m *pessimist, croaker, defeatist*; ⟨fam⟩ *wet blanket* || ⟨Am sl⟩ *knocker* °**~́macherei** f *defeatism*
M·iesmuschel f ~/~n *edible (sea-)mussel*
M·iet- **~ausfall** m *loss of rent* **~auto** n *taxi-cab* **~droschke** f *cab, fly* || ⟨engl⟩ *hansom (cab)* **~einigungsamt** n ⟨m. m.⟩ *Rent Tribunal* **~ertrag** m *rental* **~forderungen** f pl *rent receivables* ⟨a. bal⟩ **~́frei** a *rentfree* **~fuhre** f *hired carriage* **~geld** n *hire, earnest(-money)* **~haus** n *apartment-house*; *block of flats*; ~ ohne Fahrstuhl ⟨bes Am⟩ *walkup* **~herr** m *landlord* || *lodger* **~kontrakt** m *agreement, lease, tenure* **~kutsche** f *hackney--coach, job-carriage,* ⟨Am⟩ *hack* **~kutscher** m *h.-c.man* **~lakai** m *hired servant* **~leute** pl *lodgers, tenants* pl **~pferd** n *hired horse, job-h.* **~schreiber** m *hack*; (Memoiren~́) *ghost writer* **~schutz** m *rent control* **~skaserne** f *tenement-* od *apartment--house, block of flats,* ⟨bes Am⟩ *flat-house*; ⟨sl⟩ *rookery* **~smann** m *lodger, tenant* **~(s)recht** n *tenant-right* **~soldat** m *mercenary* **~stall** m *livery--stable* **~truppen** f pl ⟨mil⟩ *mercenary* od *hired troops* pl **~vertrag** m = ~kontrakt **~wagen** m = ~kutsche; ⟨mot⟩ *hire car* **~́weise** adv *on hire* **~-wohnung** f *lodgings* pl, *flat, tenement,* ⟨Am⟩ *apartment*; ⟨demog⟩ neue ~ *new letting*; teure ~ *high--rental a.t* **~zeit** f *term of lease* od *hire* **~zins** m *rent* **~zinssteuer** f ⟨Ger⟩ *rental tax* **m·ietbar** a *rentable, tenantable* **M·iete** f ~/~n **1.** ⟨agr⟩ (Heu~́) *rick,* (Getreide~́) *stack, shock* || (Kartoffel~́, Rüben~́) *pit* || .. anlegen *to lay down* .. **2.** *rent, hire* || f ein Zimmer *lodging money* || zur ~ wohnen *to live in l.s* od *as a lodger* || zur ~ geben *to let (out)* || e–n in ~ nehmen *to hire a p* || die ~ kündigen *to give notice* **m·ieten** vt [h] **1.** *to rent (a house)* || *to engage (a room, l.s)* (bei *with*) || monatlich *by the month* || (Diener) *to engage* || (Droschke) *to take* || (Pferd) *to job* od *hire* || (Schiff) *to charter* **2.** ⟨agr⟩ *to stack (hay)* || *to store (potatoes)*
M·ieter m ~s/~ *tenant, lodger*; → Pächter || ⟨jur⟩ *lessee* **~schutz** m ⟨Ger⟩ *rent control, c.led r.s* | ~gesetz [n] *Rent Restriction Act*; ~verein [m] *tenants' association* **M·ieterschaft** f *tenantry*
M·ietling m ~(e)s/~e *hireling, mercenary*; *tool*
M·ietung f ~/~en *hiring*
M·iez(e) f ~/~en (a. ~ekatze) ⟨fam⟩ *puss, pussy(-cat), mogger, moggy* || ⟨sex vulg⟩ *cat*
Mignon ['miɲõ], ~sockel [m] ⟨theat⟩ *small Edison screw,* ⟨Am⟩ *screw base*
Migr·äne f ~/~n ⟨med⟩ *nervous* od *sick headache, migraine* Fr
M·iko m ~s/~s ⟨hum⟩ → Abkürzungen
Mikrat n ~(e)s/~e ⟨rep⟩ *miniature*
Mikr·obe f *microbe* **mikr·obisch** a *m.bial, m.bic*
M·ikro- **~archiv** n ⟨rep⟩ *archives* pl *for microcopies* **~bar** n *milli-dyne per sq. cm.* **~film** m *microfilm* | ~durchlaufgerät [n] *m.f. flow camera*; ~entwicklungsgerät [n] *m.f. processor*; ~kopie [f] *bibliofilm*; ~streifen [m] ⟨rep⟩ *microstrip* **~-gefüge** n *microstructure* **~karte** f ⟨rep⟩ *Microcard®* **~k·osmos** m ~/ *m.cosm* **~küvette** f ⟨Kalorimetrie⟩ *microcell* **~m·eter** n (10^{-6} m) *micron,* → Meßschraube **~n·esien** n *Micronesia* **~n·esier** m *Micronesian* **~organismus** m *m.-organism* **~phon** n ~s/~e *m.phone* **~photographie** f *microphotography* **~rollfilm** m *roll microfilm* **~sekunde** f *micro-second* **~skop** n ~s/~e *m.scope* | ~-Filmaufnahme [f] *cine-photomicrography* **~́sk·opisch** a *m.scopic(al)* **~zephale** m ~n/~n *microcephalous p*
Mil·an m ~s/~e ⟨orn⟩ *kite*
M·ilbe f ~/~n ⟨ent⟩ *mite, tick* **m·ilbig** a *mity*
M·ilch f ~/ *milk* || ⟨ich⟩ *milt, soft roe* || fette ~ *rich m.* || dicke ~ *curds and whey* || geronnene, saure ~ *sour, curdly m.* || die ~ ist geronnen .. *has curdled* od *turned sour* || kondensierte ~ *Swiss m.*; Mager~́ *skim(med) m.*; Trocken~́ *dried m.*; Voll~́ *whole m.* || k–e ~ mehr geben *to run dry*; ~ taufen *to simpson*; ge–fte ~ *simpson* || ~ aus Trocken~́ *reconstituted m.* | ⟨fig⟩ ein Antlitz wie ~ u Blut *a face all like milk* od *lilies and roses* || die ~ der frommen Denkungsart (Schiller) *the m. of human kindness* (Shak) **~ader** f ⟨anat⟩ *lacteous vein* **~́artig** a *l., m.y* **~bar** f *m. bar* **~bart** m *downy beard,* ⟨fig⟩ *young shaver, greenhorn, m.sop* **~́bärtig** a ⟨fig⟩ *green* **~brei** m *bread and m., m.-porridge* od *-pap* **~brötchen** n (*French*) *m. roll* **~bruder** m *foster-brother* **~drüse** f ⟨anat⟩ *lactiferous gland* **~eimer** m *m.-pail* **~fieber** n *m.-fever* **~frau** f *dairy-woman* **~́gebend** a ⟨scient⟩ *lactiferous*; reichlich ~ *uberous* **~gefäß** n ⟨anat⟩ *lacteal vessel* **~gesicht** n *angel face*; ⟨dero⟩ *whey-face* **~glas** n *porcelain glass*; → Mattglas **~haar** n *down* **~halle** f *m.-bar* **~́haltig** a *lactiferous* **~kalb** n *sucking calf* **~kaffee** m *white coffee, café au lait* Fr **~kammer** f *dairy* **~kännchen** n *m.--jug* od *-pot* **~kanne** f; gr ~ *m.-can*; (z Buttern) *churn* **~kost** f *m. diet* **~kuh** f *m.-cow, milcher* **~kur** f *m.-diet, -cure* **~mädchen** n *m.maid* **~mädchen-rechnung** f *account made up on false premises* || das ist e–e ~; nur k–e ~! *don't count your chickens before they are hatched!* **~magd** f *dairy-maid* **~-mangel** m ⟨med⟩ *agalactia* **~mann** m *m.man, dairyman* **~messer** m *galactometer, lactoscope* **~mixgetränk** n *m. shake* **~napf** m *m.-cup, m.--bowl* **~pan(t)scher** m *adulterator of m.* **~probe** f *m. sample* **~prüfer** m *m. tester* **~pulver** n *m. powder, p.ed m.* **~pumpe** f ⟨med⟩ *breast-glass* **~-rahm** m *cream* **~reis** m *rice-m.,* ⟨Am⟩ *m.-rice* **~-**

saft m *m.y juice*; ⟨scient⟩ *chyle*; ⟨bot⟩ *latex* **~säure** f ⟨chem⟩ *lactic acid* **~schokolade** f *m. chocolate* **~schwester** f *foster-sister* **~speise** f *m.-food* **~spindel** f *lactometer* **~stern** m Pyrenäen-~ ⟨bot⟩ *Spiked Star of Bethlehem* **~strahl** m *m.-jet* **~straße** f ⟨astr⟩ *M.y Way*, ⟨scient⟩ *galaxy* **~suppe** f *m.-soup*; ⟨fig meteor⟩ *soup* **~topf** m *m.-pot* **~treibend** a *lactiferous* (Futter) **~viehhaltung** f *dairy husbandry* **~wagen** m *m. float* | ~pferd [n] *m.(-waggon) horse* **~weiß** a *m.-white* **~wirtschaft** f *dairy(-farm)*; eigene ~ *own dairy produce* || ⟨fig sex⟩ *dairies, m.y way* **~zahn** m *m.-tooth* **~zentrifuge** f *separator* **~zucker** m *sugar of m., lactose* **~zuckersäure** f ⟨chem⟩ *saccholactic acid* **m·ilchen 1.** vi [h] *to yield* od *give milk* || ~d *(cow) in milk*, ⟨übtr bot⟩ *lactescent* **2.** a *milch (cow)* || ⟨ich⟩ *milt (herring)* **m·ilchig** a *milky* **M·ilch(n)er** m ~s/~ ⟨ich⟩ *milt(er)*, (Fisch) *soft-roe(d) fish*

m·ild a (Wetter, Strafe, Tabak, Bier, Seife etc) *mild* || (Wetter) *soft, temperate, genial*; ~er w *to soften* || (Winter) ⟨a.⟩ *open* || (Wind, Luft, Regen, Worte) *soft*; *assuasive (air)* || (Hauch, Hitze, Tadel, Tag, Medizin) *gentle* || (Licht) *subdued* || (Sitten) *benevolent* || (Strafe) *slight* || (Tadel) *light* || (Spende) *charitable* || (Fleischstück, Herz) *tender* || (Wein, Frucht) *mellow* | (freigebig) *liberal* || s–e ~e Hand auftun *to give with an open hand* (→ Gabe) || (nachsichtig) *lenient, indulgent* | adv *blandly* || *(to act) kindly* || ~ gesagt *to put it mildly*; ~ gestimmt s *to feel (almost) mellow* || ⟨med⟩ *of a mild description* || ~ urteilen *to criticize mildly*; ⟨jur⟩ *to give a lenient sentence, to judge l.ly* **~gesinnt** a *of gentle disposition* **~herzig** a *tender-hearted* || *charitable* **~herzigkeit** f *kind-heartedness* || *charitableness* **~tätig** a *charitable, munificent* || *benevolent* **~tätigkeit** f *ch.ness, liberality, munificence, charity* **M·ilde** f ~/ *mildness, softness* || *gentleness, tenderness*, etc. (mild); *charity* || *(fatherly) indulgence* || *(ill-placed) leniency* || ~ walten l *to practise benevolence* || *(to appeal to the) mercy* od *clemency (of a p)* || er versuchte es mit ~ *he tried it by g.ness* **m·ildern** vt [h] *to soften, mitigate* || *assuage (p, feelings, pain; desire)* || *to relax (discipline, a rule)* || (Schmerz etc) *to soothe, alleviate* || (Ausdruck) *to qualify* || (Strafe) *to mitigate* || (Besorgnis) *to allay* || (Spannung etc) *to reduce* || (Herbheit) *to sweeten* || ⟨chem⟩ *to correct* || sich ~ *to grow milder* (a. Wetter) || ~de Umstände ⟨jur⟩ *extenuating circumstances*, .. zubilligen *to make allowances for ..* || *(the severity of the etiquette was allowed) to lapse* (.. wurde gemildert) **M·ilderung** f ~/~en *mitigation, moderation, alleviation* || *soothing* || *relaxation* || *qualification* || *correction* | zur ~ v *in extenuation of* **~sausdruck** m *euphemism* **~sgrund** m ⟨jur⟩ *extenuating cause* od *reason*, ⟨a.⟩ *excuse* **~smittel** n ⟨med⟩ *lenitive*

†**Mil·et** n (Stadt in Kleinasien) *Miletus*

Mili·eu, Milj·ö n ~s/~s *milieu* Fr || *(atmo)-sphere*; ⟨Lit⟩ *scene, background* || *environment, (social) surroundings* pl **~drama** n *m.-drama* **~färbung** f *local colour* **~gestört** a *maladjusted*

Milit·är 1. n ~s/ *military, army, soldiery* || z ~ gehen *to join the a.* || beim ~ s *to be in the a.* **2.** m ~s/~s *soldier, military man, officer* **~abk** n *M. Concordate* N **~ähnlich** a *param.* (*force* Verband) **~akademie** f *m. academy* **~anwärter** m *soldier entitled to a civil appointment* **~arzt** m *a. surgeon* **~attaché** m *m. attaché* **~ausschuß** m *M. Committee* N **~beamte(r)** m *commissary, m. official* **~behörden** f pl *m. authorities* pl **~bereich** m *district command* **~bevollmächtigte(r)** m *plenipotentiary officer* **~dienst** m *m. service*; aktiver ~ *active s.* | ~pflicht [f] *compulsory (m.) service*; ~pflichtig [a] *bound to serve in the a.*; ~tauglich [a] *fit for m. s.*; ~zeit [f] *national s. period* **~diktatur** f *m. dictatorship, sword-law* **~etat** m *a. budget* **~fahrschein** m *travelling warrant* **~flugzeug** n *service machine* **~frei** a (~ h *or* s *to be) off duty* **~fromm** (Pferd) *trained to stand fire* **~geld** n *Armed Forces Special Vouchers* pl **~gericht** n *m. court* | ~shof [m] *m. tribunal* **~gesetzbuch** n (⟨Ger⟩ bis 1945) *Code of M. Law* **~gewalt** f *sword law, the sword* od *the sabre* **~herrschaft** f *militarism* **~intendant** m *commissary general* **~intendantur** f *commissariat* **~justiz** f *m. law*; Chef der ~ *Judge Advocate General* **~kabinett** n königliches ~ *the king's m. advisers* **~kapelle** f *m. band* **~macht** f *m. power* **~maß** n *m. standard* **~medizinalwesen** n *a. medical service* **~musik** f *m. band, martial music* **~musiker** m *m. bandsman* **~mütze** f *forage-cap* **~person** f *member of the armed forces* **~pflicht** f *compulsory m. service*; s–r ~ genügen *to serve one's time* **~pflichtig** a *liable to m. service* **~polizeitruppe** f *Corps of M. Police* **~recht** n *m. law* **~regierung** f *m. government* **~schriftsteller** m *writer on m. affairs* **~seelsorge** f *religious welfare* **~seelsorger** m *army chaplain* **~stand** m *profession of arms* (→ Militär) **~stiefel** m ⟨fig⟩ *regulation boot* **~strafgesetzbuch** n *m. penal code*; *Uniform Code of M. Justice* N **~straßengrundnetz** n *Basic M. Road Network* N **~tuch** n *a. cloth* **~vertreterausschuß** m *M. Representatives Committee* N **~verwaltung** f *m. administration, m. department*; ⟨engl⟩ *A. Board* **~vorlage** f *a. bill* **~wesen** n *m. affairs* pl **~wirtschaft** f *militarism* **~wissenschaft** f *m. science* **~zeit** f *(his) soldiering days* pl, *time* od *period of service* **Milit·aria** pl ~/ *(book on) military affairs* pl **milit·ärisch** a *military (training)* || *soldierly (bearing)* || *martial, soldierlike (appearance)* || ~e Landesverteidigung *national mil. defence, -se* N; ~er Straßenverkehr *mil. road traffic* **Militar·ismus** m ~/ *militarism* **Mil·iz** f ~/~en *militia* || (berittene) ⟨engl⟩ *yeomanry* **~soldat** m *militiaman*

Millefi·origlas n *Murrhine glass* **M·illi- ~ard·är** m ~s/~e *multi-millionaire* **~·arde** f ~/~n (= 1000 Mio) *a thousand millions, milliard*; ⟨Am⟩ *billion*; 1 M–dstel Meter (μμ) *bicron* **~gramm** n (abbr mg) *milligram(me)* **~meter** n (abbr mm) *millimetre* | ~papier [n] *graph* od *squared paper*; ~teilung [f] *metric pitch* **~mikron** n *millimicron* (mμ) **~·on** f ~/~en *million* || ~en u aber ~en *m.s upon m.s, tens of m.s (of ..)* || es geht in die ~en *it runs into (the) m.s* || zu ~en *by the m.* || 20 ~en Menschen *twenty m.(s of) people* || tausend ~en *a milliard* ⟨Fr & Am⟩ || 1 ~ ~en *a billion* || ~en ~en [pl] *million million* [sg] *(stars)* **~enfach** adv *a m. times* **~onär** m ~s/~e *millionaire* **~·onste** a *millionth* **~·onstel** n *millionth* || ⟨el⟩ ~ Ampere [n] *microampere*

Milwaukee [mil'wɔ:ki:] n (Stadt) (*Wisc.*) USA

M·ilz f ~/~en ⟨anat⟩ *milt, spleen* **~ader** f ⟨anat⟩ *splenic vein* **~beschwerden** f pl ⟨med⟩ *spleen* **~brand(ig** a) m ⟨vet path⟩ *(suffering from) anthrax* L **~entzündung** f *splenitis* **~farn** m ⟨bot⟩ *spleen wort* **~krank** a = ~süchtig **~krankheit, ~sucht** f *hypochondriasis, spleen* **~süchtig** a *splenetic, h.driacal* **~stechen** n ⟨path⟩ *stitches* pl *in the side*

M·ime m ~n/~n *mime, mimic* **M·imik** f ~/ *mimicry, mimic art* | **~er** m ~s/~ *mimic* | **~ry** f *m.ry*; ⟨biol a.⟩ *mimesis* **m·imisch** a *mimic(al)*

Mim·ose f ~/~n ⟨bot⟩ *mimosa* || er ist die reinste ~ *or* v ~nhafter [a] Empfindlichkeit *he is as sensitive as a m.* || sie zog sich ~nhaft [adv] zurück *she retired at once into her shell*

Minar·ett n ~(e)s/~e *minaret*

M·inas Geraes [ʒ–] (Staat in Brasilien)

Mindan·ao, Mind·oro n (Philippineninseln)

m·inder a *less(er)* || (kleiner) *smaller* || (geringer) *minor, inferior* | adv *less* || nicht ~ *quite as much*; *likewise* || nicht mehr u nicht ~ *neither more nor less* || mit mehr oder ~ gr Sorgfalt *more or less carefully* **M·inder- ~ausgabe** f *less expense* **~begabt** a *not gifted, unintellectual* **~begünstigt,** ~-

bemittelt a *underprivileged* ([*the*] *poorer* [*classes*], *those in the lower income brackets*) ⁓**belastet** a ⟨jur⟩ *less incriminated* ‖ ein ⁓er *a probationer* **~betrag** m *deficit, shortage* ⁓**durchblutet** a *lacking regular blood supply* **~einnahme** f *decrease of receipts* **~ertrag** m *short proceeds* pl ⁓**gebildet** a *poorly educated* (*p*) **~gewicht** n *deficiency in weight* ⁓**jährig** a *under age*; *minor* | M–keit [f] *minority*; *non-age* **~wert** m ⟨ins⟩ *decrease in value* ⁓**wertig** a *sub-standard* (Ware); *trashy, rubbishy*; *of inferior value* od *quality* ‖ *inferior* (*quality*); [pred] *no class*; *C 3* | M–keit [f] *trashiness, inferiority*; geistige ~ *mental retardation*; M–keitsgefühl [n] *inferiority complex* **~zahl** f *smaller number, minority* (*to be in the m.*) **M·inderheit** f ~/~en *minority* ⟨a. pol⟩ ‖ sich in der ~ fühlen *to feel outnumbered* | ~engruppe [f] *m. group* **m·indern** vt [h] *to diminish, lessen* ‖ (herabsetzen) *to reduce, abate*; *slacken* (*speed*) ‖ ⟨mar⟩ *shorten* (*sail*) | **sich** ~ *to grow less, decrease*; *to fall off* **M·inderung** f ~/~en *diminu*(*a*)*tion, decrease* ‖ *reduction, abatement*; Dämpfungs⁓ *de-attenuation* **M·indest-** **~abstand** m (v Erdboden) ⟨el⟩ *minimum clearance* (*to ground*) **~arbeitslohn** m → –lohn **~auflage** f *m. circulation* **~betrag** m *m.* **~bietende(r)** m *lowest bidder* **~flug-** ~geschwindigkeit [f] *m. flying speed*; ~höhe [f] *m. flight altitude* **~fordernde(r)** m *p charging* od *asking the l.st price* **~gebot** n *l.st bid* **~gebühr** f ⟨rail⟩ *m.m* od *l.st charge* (*for goods*, etc) **~gehalt** m *l.st percentage* ‖ ~ [n] (*or* **~lohn** m) *m. pay* (od *wages* pl); *floor* **~leistung** f *m. rate* **~maß** n (*irreducible*) *m.* (an *of*); auf ein ~ verringern *to minimize* **~preis** m *m. price* **~wert** m *m.* od *lowest value* **m·indeste** a *least, smallest, lowest* ‖ nicht die ~e Aussicht *not the slightest* (⟨fam⟩ *not a ghost of a*) *chance* ‖ nicht das ~ *absolutely nothing*; ⟨fam⟩ *not the least bit* ‖ nicht das ~ verstehen v *not to have the slightest idea of* ‖ ich weiß nicht das ~ v .. *I know nothing whatever of* .. ‖ nicht im ~n *not in the least, not at all* (vgl gering III. C. 2. b.) ‖ zum (aller)~ *at the* (*very*) *least* ‖ wir trauen ihm nicht im ~ .. *not* .. *as far as we can see him* **m·indestens** adv *at least* ‖ vor ~ 20 Jahren *the best part of 20 y.s ago* ‖ .. ~ 65 Jahre *he must be 65 now if a day* ‖ ~ 50 G. wert *worth 50 guineas if w. anything* od *a penny* od *a crown* ‖ ⟨iron⟩! (Antwort) *Like to see m.s. doing it*!

M·ine f ~/~n **1.** ⟨min & mil⟩ *mine* ‖ ⟨mar, mil⟩ ~n legen *to lay m.s* ‖ auf e–e ~ laufen *to strike a m.* ‖ e–e ~ abschießen *to sink a m.* (*by gunfire*) ‖ ~n räumen *to sweep m.s.* ‖ e–e ~ springen l *to spring a m.* ‖ alle ~n springen l ⟨fig⟩ *to make every effort, to leave no stone unturned* **2.** (Bleistift⁓) *lead* **3.** ⟨hist Gr⟩ (Gewicht & Münze) *mina* **M·inen-** **~aktie** f ⟨com⟩ *mining-share* **~arbeit** f *m.g* **~arbeiter** m *miner* **~auge** n *entrance to a mine* **~bau** m *m.g operations* pl **~bombe** f *high explosive bomb* **~bomber** m ⟨mil, a. fig⟩ *block-buster* **~falle** f *booby trap* **~feld** n ⟨mil, mar⟩ *m.-field* **~gang** m ⟨min⟩ *gallery* **~gebiet** n *m.d zone* **~gerät** n *m.r's tools* pl **~gräber** m ⟨mil⟩ *sapper* **~gründe** m pl *m.g plots* pl **~hals** m *outlet to a gallery* **~krieg** m *subterranean* (⟨mar⟩ *m.*) *warfare* **~kreuzer** m *m.-laying cruiser* **~leger** m ⟨mil⟩ *m. layer*; ⟨mar⟩ (Schiff) *M. Planter* N **~räum-** ~gerät [n] *sweep*; v ~ nicht unschädlich z m *unsweepable*; ~panzer [m] *flail tank* **~sperre** f *m. barrier* **~sperrkrieg** m *m. warfare* **~sucher** m (⟨mil⟩ P) (⟨mar⟩ Boot) *m.sweeper* **~trichter** m *crater* od *funnel of a m.* **~werfer** m ⟨mil⟩ *trench-mortar, m.-thrower*; ⟨sl⟩ *Minnie* **~zünder** m *detonator* **~zündung** f *firing of m.* **Miner·al** n ~s/~e & ~ien *mineral* **~quelle** f *m. spring* **~reich** n *m. kingdom*; ⁓ [a] *m.-laden*; *rich in m.ls* **~reichtum** m *abundance of m.ls* **~wasser** n *m.l* od *aerated* od *soda water*; ⟨bes med⟩ *tonic* (*water*) **Miner·alien-** **~kabinett** n, **~sammlung** f *collection of m.ls* **~kunde** f *m.logy* **miner·alisch** a *m.l* **Mineral·og(e)** m ~en/~en *m.logist* **Mineralog·ie** f ~/ *m.logy* **mineral·ogisch** a *m.logical* **Min·ette** f ~/~n ⟨min⟩ *minette*

Mingr·elien n (Landsch. in Georgien) *Mingrelia* **Mingr·elier** m, **mingr·elisch** a *Mingrelian*

M·ini- (*minibus, -cam*(*era*), *-car*) | ~fußball [m] *miniature football*, ⟨fam⟩ *baby-foot*; ~golf [n] *m.e golf*; ~mädchen [n] = leichtes Mädchen; ~rock [m] (im) ~ *miniskirt*(*ed*)

Mini·ator m ~s/–·oren *limner* **Miniat·ur** f ~/~en *miniature* **~ausgabe** f *m. edition* ⟨a. fig⟩ **~flügel** m ⟨mus⟩ *baby grand* **~gemälde** n *m.* **~-handschrift** f *illuminated manuscript* **~maler** m *m.-painter* **~maler·ei** f *m.-painting* **~is·ierung** f *miniaturisation*

Min·ier- **~arbeit** f ⟨fig⟩ *intriguing* **~kunst** f *art of mining* ‖ ⟨mil⟩ *underground engineering* **~rahmen** m *gallery frame* **min·ieren** vt [h] *to* (*under*)*mine, to sap* **Min·ierer** m ~s/~ *miner, sapper*

minim·al a *infinitesimal*; ⟨fig⟩ *insignificant* ‖ *extremely low* (Verbrauch); ~e Verluste *a minimum of losses* ‖ ~er Preis *m. price* ⁓**betrag** m *m.*; *lowest amount* ⁓**thermometer** n (usw) *m. thermometer* (*m. weight, price, rate*, etc) **Minim·ierung** f ~/ *minimization* **M·inimum** n ~s/–ma *m.*; ~ an Gewinn *m. profit margin*

Min·ister m ~s/~ *minister* ‖ ⟨engl⟩ *Secretary of State* (*for Dominion affairs*, etc.) ‖ ~ des Äußeren *or* Auswärtigen *Minister of Foreign Affairs*, ⟨engl⟩ *Foreign Secretary* ‖ ~ des Inneren ⟨engl⟩ *Home Secretary* ‖ → Finanz- usw ⁓ ‖ ~ für die Kolonien ⟨engl⟩ *Colonial Secretary* ‖ ~ ohne Geschäftsbereich *m. without portfolio* **~bank** f *m.ial bench, Treasury b., front b.* **~konferenz** f *conference of m.s* **~krise** f *m.ial crisis* **~präsident** m *Prime M.*; ⟨a-engl⟩ *M. President* [pl *M.s P.*] **~rat** m *Cabinet Council*, oberster ~ (f. d. Krieg) *war-cabinet* **~stelle** f *m.ial office* **~wechsel** m *change of the ministry* **Ministeri·al** **~beamte(r)** m *official of a m.ial department* **~direktor** m *M.ial Director* **~erlaß** m *m.ial order*; ⟨engl⟩ *order of the Privy Council* **~gebäude** n *government offices* **~rat** m ⟨Ger⟩ *counsellor of a m.ial department* **ministeri·ell** a *m.ial* **Minist·erium** n ~s/–rien *ministry* (*of Health*, etc) ‖ [koll] ⟨engl⟩ *Cabinet Ministers* ‖ ⟨Am⟩ *Department* (*of Defense* N, *Justice, War*, etc.) ‖ ~ des Innern ⟨engl⟩ *Home Office* ‖ ~ des Äußeren ⟨engl⟩ *Foreign Office* **Ministr·ant** m ~en/~en ⟨R. C.⟩ *altar boy* **ministr·ieren** vi [h] ⟨R. C.⟩ *to officiate, minister*

M·inna npr; °Grüne ~ (*prisoners'*) *Black Maria*; ⟨Am sl⟩ *paddy wagon*

M·inne f ~/ ⟨poet⟩ *love* ‖ *wooing* **~glück** n *joy of l.* **~hof** m *court of l.* **~lied** n *l.-song* **~sang** m *minnesong*; ~s Frühling *the minne-singer's l.-songs* **~sänger** m ⟨Ger⟩ *minnesinger* (*minstrel*) **~sold** m *l.r's reward* **~werben** n *l.r's wooing* **m·innen** vt [h] ⟨poet⟩ *to l., court* **m·innig(lich)** a *lovely, charming* ‖ *lovable, love-inspiring* ‖ *loving*

Minne·apolis n (Stadt) (*Minn. U.S.A.*)

Minnes·ota n (Staat der U.S.A.)

Min·oisch a *Minoan* (*Age, Epoch*)

Min·orca n → Menorca

minor·enn a *under age, minor* ⁓**it·ät** f ~/ *m.ity* **Minor·it** m ~en/~en *M.ite, Franciscan brother* **Minorit·ät** f ~/~en *minority* **Minu·end** m ~en/~en ⟨math⟩ *minuend* **m·inus** adv *minus* (10—2) (*ten minus two*) ‖ °(etw) ~ m *to lose*; (durch Dieb) *to be eased of* .. **M·inus** n ~/ *deficit* | ~blau [n] etc ⟨phot⟩ *minus blue*, etc; ~pol [m] ⟨el⟩ *negative pole* od *terminal*; ~zeichen [n] (—) ⟨math⟩ *negative* od *minus sign* (—) **Min·uskel** f ⟨typ⟩ *minuscule, small letter* **Min·ute** f ~/~n (Zeit- & Winkel⁓) *minute* ‖ jdn e–e ~ (unterbrechen) .. *for a m.* (od *moment*) ‖ es wird k–e ~ dauern *it won't be a m.* ‖ laß es 5 ~n kochen .. *for 5 m.s*;

knapp 5 ~n *a short 5 m.s* ‖ Geschütz, das in Abständen v e–r ~ feuert *m.-gun* | **auf** die ~ *to the (very) m.; punctual to the moment* ‖ auf die ~ bestimmen *to fix (a time) to a m.* ‖ **in (nach)** e–r ~ *in (after) a m.* ‖ in der nächsten ~ *in another m.* ‖ (in) jede(r) ~ zus–brechen *to collapse any m.* ‖ (..) in der letzten ~ *last-m. (change)* ‖ komm' nicht in der letzten ~ *don't cut it too fine* ‖ **von** ~ zu ~ *momently* ‖ bis **zu** dieser ~ *to this m.* **Min·uten-** ≃**lang** a *lasting a minute* od *several m.s* | adv *for (several) m.s* ~**photographie** f *while-you-wait ph.* ~**uhr** f *m.-watch* ≃**weise** adv [& a] *every m., by m.s* ~**werk** n *m.-works* pl ~**zeiger** m *m.-hand* **minuzi·ös** a *minute* [–'ju:t] (*work, inquiry, inquirer*); *painstaking, careful (investigation)*

Minsk n ⟨Russ⟩ (Stadt)

M·inze f ~/~n ⟨bot⟩ *mint*

M·io ⟨bank⟩ = Million(en) → Abkürzungen

Mioz·än n ~s/ ⟨geol⟩ (untere Jungtertiärstufe) *miocene*; → –zän

m·ir pron [dat v ich] (*to*) *me* ‖ er gab es ~ *or* ~'s *he gave it (to) me* ‖ ⟨vulg⟩ *us (give us a bit more)* ‖ das brauchst du ~ nicht zu sagen *you needn't tell me that* ‖ ich schnitt ~ in den Finger *I cut my f.* | ~ **ist('s)** kalt *I feel cold* ‖ ~ **wird** ganz elend *I am feeling very poorly* | jetzt ist's **an** ~ *it's my turn now* ‖ ein F. **von** ~ *a friend of mine* ‖ ein Buch v ~ .. *written by* (od *belonging to*) *me* | ⟨prov⟩ **heute** ~ morgen dir *everyone in his turn* ‖ ~ **kann** k–r! *nobody can do me!*, ⟨Am⟩ *no flies on me!* ‖ °~ können sie alle! *you are all welcome to your own tastes* ‖ [dativus ethicus] (unübersetzt!) **laß** ~ das ja bleiben! *Don't! Leave that alone!* ‖ ~ **nichts,** dir nichts [adv] *willy-nilly, without ceremony, w.t more ado*; ⟨fam⟩ *(quite) coolly* ‖ ~ u mich **verwechseln** *to be uneducated* (vgl *to drop one's hs*) ‖ **von** ~ aus! (⟨fam & dial⟩ wegen ~!) *I don't mind!* ‖ *for my sake!* **wie** du ~ so ich dir! *(that was) tit for tat! scratch me and I'll scratch you*

Mirab·elle f ~/~n *mirabelle-plum, yellow plum*

Mir·akel n ~s/~ *miracle* ~**spiel** n *m.-drama*

Mirs·apur n (vorderind. Bezirk) *Mirzapur*

Misanthr·op m ~en/~en *misanthropist* | **-op·ie** f ~/ *misanthropy* | ≃**isch** a *m.pic(al)*, → Miso-

M·isch- [in comp] mst *mixed* ~**apparat** m *mixer* ~**art** f *cross-breed* ~**becher** m *shaker* ~**bestand** m *m. crop*, ⟨for⟩ *m. wood* ~**bildung** f *hybridity* ~**blende** f ⟨wir⟩ *fader* ~**bottich** m *blending vat* ~**decke** f (Straßen≃) *pre-mix carpet* ~**düngemittel** n *compound fertilizer* ~**dünger** m ⟨agr⟩ *compost* ~**ehe** f *m.-religion marriage*; e–e ~ eingehen *to marry across religious lines* ~**farbe** f *m.* (od *secondary*) *colour* ~**form** f ⟨gram⟩ *hybrid* ~**futter** n *m. provender* ~**gas** n *semi-water gas* ~**gefäß** n *mixing vessel*, etc. ~**gericht** n *ragout* ~**getränk** n *mixture*, ⟨Am⟩ *soda* ~**heirat** f = ~ehe ~**korn** n *wheat and rye m.* ~**krug** m *mixer* ~**kultur** f ⟨bact⟩ *anaculture* ~**masch** m *hotchpotch, medley; farrago; olio*; ⟨fam⟩ *junket, mix(-up)* ~**metall** n *alloy* ~**probe** f *average sample* ~**pult** n ⟨film⟩ *mixing console*; ⟨wir⟩ *m.g table, mixer unit* ~**rasse** f = ~art ~**schnecke** f ⟨tech⟩ *m.g screw* ~**sprache** f *hybrid language* ~**trank** = ~getränk ~**trommel** f *pug-mill* ~**volk** n *m. race* ~**wald** m *m. forest* ~**wort** n *acronym* → d. ~**wuchs** m *m. growth* **m·ischbar** a *miscible, mixable* | ≃keit f *mixability* **m·ischen** vt [h] **1.** *to mix, mingle* ‖ (Arznei) *to make up*; *to shake (a cocktail)* ‖ (Bestandteile) *to incorporate* ‖ (Metall) *to alloy* ‖ ⟨comp⟩ *to merge* (≃ [n] *merging process*) ‖ ⟨chem⟩ *to combine* ‖ ~ mit *to mix with* ‖ Wasser in *or* unter den Wein ~ *to adulterate wine with water* ‖ ~ unter *to jumble up with* ‖ eins ins andere ~ *to jumble th.s up* ‖ .. das aus .. gemischt war *a feeling in which curiosity and pity played their parts* | **gemischt** a *mixed (feelings, number, school, diet, spirits)* ‖ g.e Gesellschaft *omnium gatherum* ‖ *miscellaneous (committee)* ‖ *adulterated (wine, etc.)* ‖ ⟨cul⟩ *assorted* | [adv] auf dem Fest ging es recht gemischt zu *the entertainment was of a rather mixed character* **2.** *to shuffle*, (betrügerisch) ⟨fam⟩ *to doctor (the cards)* ‖ wer mischt? ⟨fam⟩ *whose deal is it?* **3. sich** ~ *to commingle, to be mingled* ‖ Öl u Wasser ~ sich nicht *oil will not mix with water* ‖ sich in fremde Dinge ~ *to meddle with* od *interfere in other people's affairs* od *business* ‖ sich ins Gespräch ~ *to join in a c.* ‖ sich unter das Volk ~ *to mix with the crowd* **M·ischer** m ~s/~ ⟨comp⟩ *collator* **M·ischling** m ~s/~e *hybrid, mongrel* ‖ (Rassen-≃) *half-breed* od *-caste* ‖ ~s- [in comp] *half-caste* .. °**Mischp·oche, -·oke** f ~/~n ⟨Hebr⟩ *family*; ⟨fam⟩ *lot, set* **M·ischung** f ~/~en [abstr] *mingling* ‖ [konkr] *mixture* ‖ (Met·all≃) *alloy* ‖ Tabak≃ *blend* ‖ ⟨chem⟩ *composition, combination*; ⟨fig a.⟩ *concoction* ~**sgewicht** n ⟨chem⟩ *combining weight* ~**sverhältnis** n *proportion of mixture, mixing rate; mixture ratio* od *strength* ~**sverwandtschaft** f *chemical affinity*

miser·abel [a] *miserable (handwriting), wretched (fellow, humour), rotten (play)*, ⟨fam⟩ *villainous (hotel), filthy (coffee)*; ~! ⟨mil⟩ *breamy*; ⟨Am⟩ *punk, crummy* ‖ [pred] *not good enough* | [adv] mit ist ~ zumute *I am in a wretched humour* **Mis·ere** f ~/~n *misery, w.dness* ‖ *the miseries* pl (*of life*) **Miserik·ordie** f ~/~n ⟨ec arts⟩ *misericord* **Miser·ere** n ~(s)/~ ⟨ec & path⟩ *miserere*

Misog·yn m ~(e)s/~e *misogynist*

M·ispel f ~/~n ⟨bot⟩ *medlar* ‖ *m.(-tree)*

m·iß imp **mißt** 3. sg pr v messen

M·iß- pref [untrennbar; wenn getrennt ⟨hum⟩] *amiss, dis-, mis-* ‖ *bad, false, wrong* [pp mst ohne –ge–, also: mißdeutet (*mißgedeutet)] ≃**·achten** vt [h] *to slight, despise* ‖ (vernachlässigen) *to disregard, neglect* ‖ (Gesetz) a *to set at naught* ~**·achtung** f *disdain, contempt; disregard* (v, gegenüber *of, for*); feindselige ~ *contempt and hostility*; allgemeiner ~ ausgesetzt *exposed to public contempt* ‖ sich die ~ jds zuziehen *to draw down on o.s. the disdain of a p* ‖ voller ~ *disrespectful (to)* ≃**·arten** vi [s] [pp mißgeartet] *to degenerate* ~**behagen** n *displeasure, discomfort, uneasiness; dislike, distaste; discomposure; uncomfortable feeling; discontent* ‖ (ein) lebhaftes ~ empfinden *to feel extremely uncomfortable* ≃**behagen** vi [h] (jdm) *to displease (a p)* ‖ es –behagt mir *I am ill at ease about it* ≃**behaglich** a *unpleasant, disagreeable*; sich ~ fühlen *to feel uncomfortable* ~**belieben** n *displeasure* ≃**b·ilden** vt [h] [pp ~gebildet] *to misshape* (→ entstellen) ~**bildung** f *malformation, deformity* ≃**b·illigen** vt [h] (etw) *to deprecate, discountenance; veto; to disapprove (of), to object (to)*; .. entschieden .. *to set one's face against a th*; .. öffentlich .. *to cry out against* od *on a th* | ~d [pres p & a (adv)] *disapproving(ly)* ~**billigung** f *disapproval, disapprobation, reprobation* (über *of*); mit ~ betrachten *to take a dim* od *poor view of* ~**brauch** m *abuse* (grob *crying*) (*of powers* Befugnisse) ‖ (falsche Anwendung) *misuse*; ~ treiben mit *to misuse; to misuse (one's authority)* ‖ e–n ~ abstellen *to remedy an abuse* | ~sicher [a] *foolproof* ≃**br·auchen** vt [h] *to abuse* ‖ (Gewalt) *to misuse* ‖ *to make wrong use of (one's rights)* ‖ *to take advantage of ..; to encroach, impose, presume upon (a p's good-nature)* ‖ ⟨bib⟩ *to take (the name of the Lord) in vain* ‖ → vergewaltigen ≃**bräuchlich** a *improper, abusive*; ~e Verwendung *diversion* | etw ~ verwenden f *to divert a th to* ≃**d·euten** vt [h] *to misinterpret* ‖ ⟨fig⟩ *to misconstrue, misrepresent, to take amiss* ~**deutung** f *misinterpretation* ‖ *misconstruction, misrepresentation* ~**erfolg** m *failure*, ⟨sl⟩ *wash-out*; gr ~ ⟨sl⟩ *frost; flop (of a book)*; (im Examen) *plough*; ~ h ⟨sl⟩ *to come a cropper*; zu ~ führen *to invite failure*; er wird mit ~ enden *he plays a losing game* ~**ernte** f *bad harvest*; ~n [pl] *crop failures* ~**f·allen** n *displeasure,* *dislike; disapproval* (an *of*) ‖ ~ erregen *to be disapproved of*, ⟨theat⟩ *not to be well received*; jds .. *to displease a p*; *to incur a p's displeasure* ‖ sein ~ (unmißverständlich) ausdrücken *to express one's (unqualified) disapproval* ≗**f·allen** vi irr [h] (jdm) *to displease* (*a p*) ‖ mir –f·ällt die S aufs höchste *I am not in the least pleased with it*; er/es –fällt mir *I regard him/it with displeasure* ≗**fällig** a *displeasing, disagreeable, unpleasant* ‖ (anstößig) *shocking* ‖ (mißbilligend) *disparaging* | [adv] sich ~ über etw äußern *to find fault with a th* ~**fälligkeit** f *disparagement* ~**farbe** f *disagreeable colour* ≗**farbig** a *discoloured* ≗**förmig** a *misshapen* ≗**gebären** vi [irr] [h] ⟨med⟩ *to miscarry* ~**geburt** f ⟨med⟩ *miscarriage, abortion* ‖ (Kind) *monster* ‖ ⟨fig⟩ *monstrosity, abortion*, (P) *misfit, freak* ≗**gelaunt** a *illhumoured* ~**geschick** n *misfortune, bad luck*; *adverse fortune*; *adversity* ‖ (Unfall) *misadventure, mishap, disaster* ~**gestalt** f *deformity* ‖ (Wesen) *deformed being, monster* ≗**gestalt(et)** a *misshapen, deformed* ~**gestaltung** f *deformity* ≗**gestimmt** a *moody, out of sorts* ~**gewächs** n *monstrous growth* ≗**gl·ücken** vi [s] *to miscarry, to fail, to fall flat* ‖ es ist mir –ckt *I have not succeeded* | ≗ [n] *failure, ill success* ≗**gl·ückt** a *abortive* (*attack*) ≗**g·önnen** vt [h] (jdm etw) *to envy, grudge* (*a p a th*) ~**griff** m *mistake, blunder* ‖ (Stil) *infelicity, lapse* ‖ e–n ~ m *to get the boot on the wrong foot* ~**gunst** f *envy, grudge, jealousy* ‖ *ill-will, malevolence* | ⟨fig⟩ (P) „~" *dog in the manger* ≗**günstig** a *envious, grudging, jealous* ‖ *uncomplimentary* (*rumour*) ≗**h·andeln** vt [h] *to ill-treat, -use*; *brutalize, manhandle, mishandle*, ⟨Am⟩ *to rough-house* (*prisoners*) ‖ *to maltreat* (*a violin*) | vi [h] *to act wrongly* ~**h·andlung** f *ill-usage, ill-treatment* ‖ ⟨jur⟩ tätliche ~ *assault and battery* ~**heirat** f *ill-advised marriage, ill-assorted match, misalliance* ≗**hellig** a *dissentient, discordant* | M–keit [f] *friction, unpleasantness, discord, dissension* ‖ ~en [pl] *unpleasantness* (*between*); ~en beilegen *to settle misunderstandings* ~**klang** m *jarring note*; *dissonance*; *disharmony* ⟨a. fig⟩ → Streit ≗**klingend** a *discordant* ~**kredit** m *discredit, disrepute* ‖ in ~ bringen *to discredit* (bei *with*); *to get* (*a p*) *in wrong*; sich .. *to bring discredit on o.s.* ‖ in ~ k *to become discredited* ‖ im ~ stehen (S) *to be at a discount* ≗**launisch** a *ill-humoured* ~**laut** m *dissonance, discord* ≗**l·eiten** vt [h] *to misguide, mislead*; *lead astray*; *to seduce* ≗**liebig** [a] *obnoxious, objectionable, odious, not in favour* ‖ ~ w *to become unpopular* (bei *among, with*) | [adv] ~ aufnehmen *to take amiss* | M–keit [f] *unpopularity* ≗**l·ingen** vi [s] *to miscarry, fail*; *turn out ill*; *prove a failure*; *go wrong* ‖ es –l·ang ihm ganz *he met with total failure* ~**l·ingen** n *failure* (→ ~glücken) ~**l·ungen** a *abortive, vain, ineffectual* (*attempt*); e–e (ganz) ~e S *a* (*dead*) *frost* od *failure* ~**mut** m *displeasure, ill-humour, discontent*; ⟨fam⟩ *tiff* ‖ ⟨psych⟩ *dejection, the blues* pl ≗**mutig** a *ill-humoured, sullen, cross, discontented* ‖ *dejected* ~**pickel** m ⟨min⟩ *arsenopyrite* ≗**r·aten** vi [irr] [s] = –l·ingen ‖ ~e Kinder *ill-bred children* ~**stand** m (Übelstand) *grievance, nuisance* ‖ schreiende ≗e abschaffen *to remedy crying abuses* ‖ (Fehler) *defect* ‖ (Mißlichkeit) *unsuitableness, impropriety, inconvenience* ≗**stimmen** vt [h] *to put out of tune* (⟨fig⟩ .. *temper*) | vi [h] *to be discordant* ~**stimmung** f *discord(ance), difference, dissension* ‖ (Mißmut) *ill-humour*; es kam k-e auf *no ill-feeling arose*; ohne jede ~ *without any discordant note* ~**ton** m *discordant tone* ⟨a. fig⟩, *jar*; ⟨fig⟩ *discord, dissonance*; *sour chord* ‖ e–n ~ verursachen *to jar* ≗**tönen** vi [h] *to sound wrong, to jar, to be dissonant* od *out of tune* ≗**tönig** a *dissonant, jarring, grating* ~**trauen** n *distrust* (wecken *to sow*; gegen *in, of*), *suspicion* (*of*) ‖ (gegen sich selbst) *diffidence*; ~ erregen *to awaken suspicion*; jedes ~ beseitigen *to disperse any lack of confidence*; ~ hegen *to be suspicious* (gegen *of*); etw mit gr ~ betrachten *to view a th with a highly suspicious eye* | ~santrag [m], ~svotum [n] *motion* bzw *vote of censure* (od *of no-confidence*); mit ~ betrachten *to take a dim* od *poor view of* ≗**trauisch** a *distrustful* (gegen *of*) ‖ *diffident* (betr *about*) ‖ *suspicious* (*of*); *leery* | adv *mistrustfully*; ~ ansehen *to look askance at* ~**vergnügen** n *dissatisfaction, displeasure, discontent* ≗**vergnügt** a *d.fied, d.sed, d.ted*; *repining* ‖ ⟨pol, mil⟩ *malcontent* | ~e(r) [m] *malcontent, grumbler* ~**verhalten** n *misconduct, misbehaviour* ~**verhältnis** n *disproportion, imbalance, incongruity*; bei e–m sehr starken ~ der Stimmen *by a lopsided margin* ≗**verständlich** a *erroneous* ‖ ~e Auffassung *misconception* | adv *by mistake* ~**verständnis** n [a. –nisse pl] *misunderstanding, misapprehension, misconception, mistake* ‖ (leichter Streit) *dissension* ‖ ⟨fam⟩ *breeze, tiff* ‖ um ein ~ z verhüten *that there may be no mistake*, etc. ≗**verstehen** vt [irr] [h] *to misunderstand*; *mistake, misconstrue* (*a p's intentions*); *to get .. wrong* ‖ die S ganz ~ ⟨fam⟩ *to get hold of the wrong end of the stick* ‖ e–a ~ *to be at cross-purposes*; nicht –zuverstehend *unmistakable* ~**wachs** m *failure of crops, bad harvest* ≗**weisend** a ⟨mar⟩ *magnetic* (*bearing, course track, north*) ~**weisung** f *variation*; Orts≗ *true declination* od *bearing* ~**wirtschaft** f *maladministration, mismanagement, deficit economy* ~**zustände** m pl *abuses* pl (*of a system*), *calamity*

m·issen vt [h] *to miss, want*; *do without* ‖ e–n leicht (schwer) ~ können *to spare a p easily* (*to miss a p badly*) ‖ e–n ungern ~ (verlieren) *to grieve to lose a p* **M·issetat** f *misdeed*; *crime*; *wrongdoing*; *evil action*; (vollbringen *to commit*); ~en [pl] *evil doings* pl **Misset·äter** m *malefactor, wrongdoer, evildoer, criminal, malignant* ‖ ⟨jur⟩ *felon, offender, delinquent*

Missi·on f ~/~en ⟨ec & pol⟩ *mission* ‖ innere ~ *home* (⟨Am⟩ *domestic*) *m.*; äußere ~ *foreign m.*; ~ treiben *to do m.ary work* **-on·ar, -on·är** m ~s/~e *m.ary* ≗**·arisch** a *m.ary* (*work*) ~**sanstalt** f *m.(-house)* ~**sgesellschaft** f *m.ary society* ~**stätigkeit** f *m.ary labours* (*of the Church*)

m·ißlich a *awkward* (*affair, position, problem, situation, turn*), *inconvenient* (*appointment*) ‖ (gefährlich) *dangerous, hazardous* ‖ (bedenklich) *critical* (*conditions*) ‖ *delicate* (*question*) ‖ (schwierig) *difficult, trying, precarious* (*conditions*) | [adv] .. steht ~ *is in a critical position*, .. *has reached a c. point* | es ist etw ≗**es** um .. *there are doubtful* od *uncertain points in* .. | ≗**keit** f ~/ *a.dness, in.ience* ‖ *danger, difficulty* ‖ *pr.ness*

Missol·unghi [–ŋgi] n ⟨Gr⟩ (Stadt) *Missolonghi, Mesolóngion*

Miss·ouri [–u:] **1.** m (amerik. Fluß) **2.** n (Staat der U.S.A.); Bewohner(in) v ~ *Missourian*

M·ist m ~es/ **1.** ⟨mar⟩ *mist, fog* **2.** *dung, manure* ‖ (Schmutz) *dirt*; ⟨fam⟩ *muck* ‖ (Tier≗) *droppings* pl ‖ ⟨fig fam⟩ *rubbish, muck, rot, stuff*; ⟨sl⟩ *tripe, bilge*; ⟨Am⟩ *blah, crap*; reiner ~! *tommy* od *absolute rot*!, *sheer muck*! ‖ °verfluchter ~! ⟨vulg⟩ *mess*! ‖ rede k–n ~! *don't talk through your hat*, ⟨Am sl⟩ *can that stuff* ‖ was für ein ~! *what rubbish*! ‖ der übliche ~ *the usual junk*; alten ~ aufrühren *to rake up the muck of the past* ~**bauer** m ⟨fig⟩ *clodhopper* ~**beet** n *hotbed* | ~fenster [n] *garden-* od *forcing-frame* °~**ding** n ⟨sl⟩ *lemon* °~**fink** m ⟨fig⟩ *pig, mud-lark* ~**fuhre** f *load of m.* ‖ *d.-cart* ~**gabel** f *d.-* od *pitch-fork* ~**grube** f *d.-hole* od *-pit* ~**haken** m *d.-hook* ~**haufen** m *d.hill*, ⟨fig fam⟩ *muck-heap* ~**hof** m *stableyard* ~**jauche** f *liquid m.* ~**käfer** m *d.-beetle* ~**karren** m, ~**karre** f *d.-barrow, d.-cart* ~**lache** f *puddle* ~**stock** m Sw = –haufen ~**streuer** m *manure spreader* ~**wagen** m *d.-wag(g)on* **m·isten** vt [h] *to dung, manure* (*fields*) ‖ *to clean* (*stables*) | vi [h] (T) *to dung* **m·istig** a **1.** ⟨mar⟩ *misty, foggy* ‖ ⟨fig⟩ *stuffy* **2.** °⟨fig fam⟩

mucky || e–e ~e Angelegenheit *a pretty kettle of fish*

M·istel f ~/~n ⟨bot⟩ *mistletoe* **~drossel** f *mistle* od *missel thrush* (sic!) **~zweig** m *mistletoe bough*

m·it I. adv [& trennbares pref v verbs = *co-*, (*along* od *in common*) *with, simultaneously*, etc] *also, as well, likewise, too* | ~ der beste *one of the best* || ihr ~ der liebste *of those she likes most* od *best* | → anfassen etc || das **gehört** ~ dazu *that is part* (*and parcel*) *of it, that belongs to it too* || da **kann** ich nicht ~ (geistig) *I can't keep up, that's beyond my comprehension*; *that beats me* || (geldlich) *I can't go the pace* || da kann er gar nicht ~ *he's completely out of the running, he can't hold his own* || **komm** ~! *come on* od *too*!, *come along with me* (*us*)! || komm doch mal ~ bei mir vorbei! *look me up too when you have time* || ~ dabei **sein** *to be there too, to be* (*one*) *of the party* (a. ~ v der Partie s); *to make one of a number, to be concerned in a matter* || da war .. ~ im Spiel (*treason*) *played a part in it* || ~ **wollen**: *children like to be in it* **II.** prep [dat] **A.** *with* || ~e–a *with each other*; *together* || alle ~e–a *all together, all at the same time* || zus ~ *along with* | (Begleitung) *in the company of* | (versehen ~) suff *-ed*: *blue-eyed, low-windowed* | *and*: *a carriage and four* (~ 4 Pferden) || *a blue coat and brass buttons* | (habend, haltend etc) *a girl in rosy cheeks* || ~ dem Hute in der Hand (*Mr. N.*,) *hat in hand*(, *said* ..); (so:) *beak down*, etc || .. begrüßte mit strahlendem Gesicht *Miss N., her face beaming, welcomed* | (voll v) *a basket* (*full*) *of pears, a pot of jam* | ~ **sich** bringen *to impose* (*heavy burdens*) | [instrumental:] *by this expression, by bus* || der Faden, ~ dem sie .. hatte .. *with which she had sewn* od .. *she had sewn with* | [temporal] *at, in, from, on* → **B.** [mit subst, oft [abstr] mit adv-Bedeutung] ~ **Absicht** *with* (*full*) *intention, intentionally*; (so:) *with caution, deliliberation*; *cautiously, enthusiastically, deliberately, regretfully, rightfully, zealously*; ~ dem **Abend** *in the e.* || ~ den **Augen** zwinkern *to wink one's eyes*; ~ der **Bahn** *by rail*; ~ **Blei**(stift) *in pencil*; ~ goldenen Buchstaben *in golden characters*; ~ dem **Finger** auf etw zeigen *to point one's f. at a th*; ~ dem **Fuß** stampfen *to stamp one's f.*; ~ barem **Gelde** *for ready m.*; ~ der ersten Gelegenheit *by* od *at the first opportunity*; ~ offener Gewalt *by main force*; ~ allen Glocken läuten *to ring all the bells*; ~ dem Glockenschlage *as the clock struck, on the stroke of* (*twelve*); **Hut** → II. A.; ~ 20 **Jahren** *at* (*the age of*) *20*; ~ **Lebensgefahr** *at the risk of one's life*; ~ e–m **Male** *all at once, suddenly, all of a sudden*; ~ Muße *at leisure*; ~ **Namen** *called, .. by name, by the name of ..*; ~ der **Post** *by p.*; ~ Protest *under pr.*; ~ e–m **Schlage** *at a blow*; ~ lauter **St.** *in a loud voice*; ~ 16 gegen 2 St.n *by 16 votes to 2*; ~ dem heutigen **Tage** *from to-day* (*forth*); ~ Tagesanbruch *at day-break*; ~ **Verlust** *at a loss*; ~ Volldampf *at full steam* od *speed*; mit anderen Worten *in other words*; ~ e–m Worte *in a w.*; ~ diesen Worten [zeitlich] *with these words*; ~ der **Zeit** *by and by, in* (*the course of*) *time* **C.** [mit Adjektiv] sparsam, zufrieden ~ *sparing, satisfied with* **D.** [mit Verb] (als pref oft: *to play one's part in* [*building, forming a th*]) **anfangen** ~ *to begin with*; **bedecken** ~ *to cover with*; sich ~ etw **beeilen** *to make haste with a th*; ~ 3 Mark **berechnet** w *to be charged at 3 s*; ~ e–m **fühlen** *to feel for* od *sympathize with a p*; er **geht** ~ ihr *he is her lover*; .. auf u ab *he walks her up and down*; wie geht es ~ ..? *how is* (*he* od *it*)?; ~ diesen Dingen geht es wie ~ .. *it is with those ths as with* .. || ~ etw **geizen** *to be niggardly of a th*; → kämpfen; ~ der Peitsche **knallen** *to crack one's whip*; ~ e–m **reden** *to speak to a p*; er **schlug** ihn mit 3 u 2 ⟨golf⟩ *he defeated him 3 and 2*; ~ e–m gleichen Alters **sein** *to be of the same age as a p*; was ist ~ ihm? *what is the matter with him*?, *what has happened to him*?; wie weit **ist** er ~ s–r Arbeit? *how far has he advanced with his work*?; es ist ~ s–n Kenntnissen nicht weit her *his knowledge is very limited*; ~ den Worten **spielen** *to play on words*; **Böses** ~ Gutem **vergelten** *to return good for evil* || was hat sie ~ ihm **vor**? *what plans has she regarding him*?

M·it- [pref vor subst] mst *co*(-) .., *col* .., *com* .., *con* ..; *brother* ..; *fellow-* ..; *joint* ..; *part-* .. || *common* || *simultaneous* **m·it-** pref [immer trennbar] vor den meisten verbs: *co*(-) .., *col* .., *com* .., *con* .. || *jointly, simultaneously, at the same time* || *in common* (*with*), (*along*) *with* || [oder durch verbs:] *to aid* od *assist in* || *to join, participate, share, take part in* **M·it-** ≃**anhören** vt [h] (zufällig) *to overhear* **~anspruch** m *competition* **~arbeit** f *co-operation, collaboration* (*with*) ≃|**arbeiten** vi [h] *to collaborate, co-operate* (bei, an *in*) || tüchtig ~ *to pull one's weight* (*to do*) || (Werk, Zeitung) *to contribute* (an *to*), *to be on the staff* (*of*) **~arbeiter** m *assistant, fellow-, co-worker* || *assistant, coadjutor* || N. u s–e ~ [pl] *N. and his associates* || freier ~ *guest designer*, etc | ⟨Am⟩ *coworker* || (Zeitung) *contributor, correspondent, columnist*; freier ~ (e–r Zeitung) *outside contributor* || pl (e–s Werkes etc) *staff* (*to*) | ~beziehungen [f pl] *human relations*; ~gruppe [f] *staff*; ~schaft [f] *personnel* || (Zeitung) *correspondents' position* **~bedeutung** f *connotation* ≃|**begreifen** vt [h] *to include* **~beklagte(r)** m ⟨jur⟩ *co-defendant* ≃|**bek** vt [→ k] [h] *to get .. for one's portion* || (mit anderen) *to receive together with others* || *to r. when leaving* || (als Mitgift) *to get as dowry* || °das hab' ich nicht ganz ~ ⟨fam⟩ *I didn't quite catch* od *get* (*understand*) *it* || hast du das ~? *do you get me*? **~belehnung** f *co-investiture* **~besitz** m ⟨jur⟩ *j. possession* od *ownership* **~besitzer** m *j. proprietor* od *owner, copartner* **~bestimmung** f *co-determination* | ~srecht [n] (*right of*) *co-det.*; *co-rule*; ⟨pol⟩ *r. of co-decision* ≃**beteiligt** a *partaking* (*in*) || ich war nicht ~ *I had no part* od *share in it* **~beteiligte(r)** m ⟨com⟩ *partner* || ⟨jur⟩ *interested party*; *accomplice* (*in a crime*) **~bewerb** m *competition* ≃|**bewerben**: sich ~ [irr] [h] (um) *to compete* (*for*) **~bewerber** m *competitor, rival* **~bewerbung** f = –bewerb **~bewohner** m (e–s Hauses) *f.-lodger*; *inmate* ≃|**bezahlen** vi/t [h] *to pay one's share, to pay for someone else as well* ≃|**bezeichnen** vt [h] *to connote* ≃|**bieten** vi [irr] [h] *to bid together* ≃|**bringen** vt [irr] [h] *to bring* od *carry along* (*with*) || *to bring as dowry* || (v der Reise) *to bring a present*: *what have you brought me*? || (an Fähigkeit) *to bring* (f etw *to a th*), *to be qualified* (*for*) || *bring your book, friend* (*along with you*) || *he brought a stick with him* || *documents must be brought* **~bruder** m *f., comrade, colleague* || ≃ pl ⟨ec⟩ *brethren* | ≃schaft [f] *f.ship, brotherhood* **~bürge** m *j.-bail, j.-security*; *cosponsor* **~bürger** m *f.-citizen* | ~schaft [f] [abstr] *f.-c.ship*; [konkr.koll] *f.-c.s* pl **~christ** m *f.-Christian* ≃|**dürfen** vi [irr] [h] *to be permitted to go along* (*with a p*) || ⟨fam⟩ darf ich mit? *may I come too*? **~eigentum** n *j.-property*; ~ nach Bruchteilen *tenancy in common*; ~ an ererbten Grundstücken ⟨jur⟩ *parcenary* **~eigentümer** m *co-proprietor, j.-owner* ≃**ein·ander** adv *together, j.ly* || alle ~ *one and all, all and sundry* || ~ in Verbindung stehen *to intercommunicate* ≃|**einbegreifen** vt [irr] [h] *to connote, include* || alles .. –griffen *everything included, including e.g* ≃|**empfinden** vt [irr] [h] *to feel* (*with, for*), *to sympathize* (*with*) **~empfindung** f *sympathy* ≃|**enthalten** vt [h] *to imply, implicate* ≃|**entscheiden** vt [h] *to have some say* (über *in*) | ~d *co-decisive* (*significance*) [*along with other factors*] **~erbe** m *coheir, j. heir* ≃|**erben** vt [h] *to partake of an inheritance, to come into one's share* **~erbschaft** f ⟨jur⟩ *co-i.e* **~erkrankung** f ⟨med⟩

involvement (*of an organ*) ~|**essen** vt/i [h] (mit) *to eat, dine* (*with a p*), *to partake of a p's dinner*, etc || alles ~ *to eat up everything* **~esser** m (in der Haut) *comedo, blackhead* ~|**fahren** vi [s] *to ride, drive, go, travel* (*with a p*) || mit jdm ~ *to depart with a p* || ⟨rail⟩ *to be on the train* || ⟨mot⟩ willst du ~? *will you come for a ride*? || jdn ~ l *to give a p a lift* od *ride* **~fahrerzentrale** f ⟨Am⟩ *carpool* ~|**fangen** vt [h] *to catch with others* || –ge–, –gehangen *caught together, hanged t.r* ~|**fechten** vi [h] *to join in a fight* ~|**folgen** vi [s] *to follow with others* ~|**formen** vt [h] *to play one's part in shaping* od *achieving a th* **~freude** f *c. joy, sympathy* **sich** ~|**freuen** vrefl *to rejoice with others* ~|**fühlen** vt/i [h] *to sympathize* || ~d *feeling* (*heart*) || ~des Verständnis ⟨arts⟩ *rich sympathy* (f *with*) ~|**führen** vt [h] *to carry along* (*with one*), *to have with one*; ge–rt w *to be tided* **~gabe** f = ~gift **~gäste** m pl *brother guests* pl ~|**geben** vt [h] *to give along* (*with a th*) || *a constable was detached to pilot him* || *a guide was sent* (*along*) *with him* || (Mitgift) *to give as a marriage-portion* od *dowry* || (Proviant) *to provision a p* **~gebrauch** m *j. use* **~gefangene(r)** m *f.-prisoner* **~gefühl** n *sympathy, f.-feeling* (mit *for*) || e–m sein ~ aussprechen *to express s.y with a p* (*in a loss*) || (Brief) in ~ mit .. *in f.ship of sorrow* (*yours* ..); jdm ~ entgegenbringen *to sympathize with a p*; bei herzlosen Menschen kann man kein ~ erwecken *we cannot get blood out of a stone* ~|**gehen** vt (mit jdm) [s] *to go along with* od *to accompany a p* || *to take part* (*in a game*) || gehst du ~? *are you coming with me*? || *to keep pace* (*with the times*) || ⟨cards⟩ *to come in* || die Zuhörer gingen ~ *the audience was carried away* || → –fangen || das geht so (mit) *that will do at a pinch* || °~ l *or* heißen ⟨fam⟩ *to pilfer, pocket*; ⟨fam⟩ *to go off with a th* ~|**genießen** vt/i irr [h] *to enjoy with a p* ~**genommen** pp & a ⟨fig⟩ *worried* od *ravaged* (v, durch *by, with*), *unstrung* (*from*) || arg ~ (s *to be*) *the worse for wear, battered* (*hat*) || (P) *shaken to have been in the wars*; .. w ⟨sl⟩ *to get it in the neck*; → ~nehmen **~genuß** m *participation* ~**gerechnet** pp; X ~ *counting X* **~geschöpf** n *f.-creature* **~gesell(e)** m *f.-journeyman, companion* **~gift** f *dowry, portion* || mit e–r ~ ausstatten *to dower* | ~jäger [m] *fortune-hunter* **~glied** n *member*, altes ~ *old-timer*; ⟨univ etc⟩ *f.*, ⟨parl⟩ *m.* || e–n als ~ eintragen *to enrol a p* (*in a society*) || ~ e–s A.es s *to sit on a committee* || eingetragenes ~ s *to be on the books* || ordentliches ~ *full m.* || zahlendes ~ *auxiliary* od *contributing m.* || ~ w *to join* (*a club*) | ~erzahl [f] *m.ship, enrolled strength* (*of a party*); ~sbeitrag [m] *m.ship fee*; ~skarte [f] (*m.'s*) *ticket*; ~schaft [f] *m.ship* (*in a club*) || *f.-ship* ~|**h** vt *to have* (*taken*) *with one* ~|**halten** vi [h] *to be one of the party* || ich halte mit *I'll join you* || wacker ~ *to hold one's own*; ~ mit *to match, equal* || vt (Zeitung) *to take .. in together* ~|**helfen** vi [h] → helfen II. || *to lend a helping hand* || bei etw ~: *she had helped with the cakes* || an e–m Gedicht ~ *to help to write* .. **~helfer** m *aider, helper, assistant, helpmate* || ⟨jur⟩ *accomplice* **~herausgeber** m *coeditor* (f *coeditress*) **~herrschaft** f *j. rule, co-regency* **~herrscher** m *co-regent* **~hilfe** f *assistance, aid, help, co-operation* || (durch das Gewährenlassen) unter, durch ..: *with the connivance of* ~**h·in** conj *consequently, therefore* || *so, then, thus* ~|**hören** vi/t *to listen in* (*and hear*) || (unberchtigt) *to tap*; *intercept* ⟨mil wir⟩ (~ [n] *monitoring*) || ⟨wir⟩ *to tune in* **~hör**-~regler [m] ⟨rec⟩ *monitoring control*; ~taste [f] *listening key* **~inhaber** m *copartner* **~interessent** m *partaker, sharer* ~|**kämpfen** vi [h] *to take part* od *to join in a combat, to see action* (bei *at*) **~kämpfer** m *comrade-in-arms, f.-combatant* ~**klagen** vi [h] ⟨jur⟩ *to join as defendant* **~kläger** m *j.* od *co-plaintiff* ~|**k** vi [s] (→ mit I.) *to come along* (*with a p*) || komm ~! *come on*!; .. zu ihm hinüber *come on over to him*! || k Sie mit? *are you coming my way*? || .. *wouldn't you care to come*? || (Schule) *to keep up, follow* || mit jdm ~ *to keep up with a p* ~|**können** vi [h] → mit I. **~kontrahent** m *j.-contractor* ~|**koppeln** vi [h] ⟨mar⟩ *to keep the dead reckoning* ~|**kriegen** vt [h] ⟨fam⟩ = ~bek ~**lachen** vi [h] *to laugh with the others, to join in the laugh* **~laufachse** f ⟨rec⟩ *rotating record spindle* **~läufer** m ⟨sport sl⟩ *passenger*; ⟨pol⟩ *nominal member*; *follower*; *trimmer*; *fellow-traveller* **~laut(er)** m ⟨gram⟩ *consonant* **~lebende(r)** m *co-eval* **~leid(en)** n *compassion, commiseration*; *sympathy*; *pity* || aus bloßem ~ *merely out of p.* || mit jdm ~ h *to p. a p, to take* od *have c.* od *p. on a p*, ⟨fam⟩ *to feel for a p*; .. mit jds Notlage *to be pitiful to a p's distress* || kein ~ h *to have no p.* od *bowels*; ~erregend *pitiful, piteous, pathetic*; voller ~ *c.ate* **~leidenschaft** f *sympathy* || in ~ ziehen *to affect, involve* (*an organ, a p, a th*) ~**leidenswert** a *pitiable, piteous, deserving pity* ~**leidig** a *pitiful* || *compassionate* (*to*) || *charitable* (*hearts*) || ⟨fig⟩ *indulgent* (*smiles*) | adv *pitifully, with pity* || ~ tun *to simulate p.*; ~ über jdn lächeln *to think a p small beer* ~**leidlos** a *pitiless, uncharitable, unfeeling* **~leidsbezeigung** f *condolence* ~**leidvoll** a *full of pity, compassionate* ~|**lesen** vt [h] (Zeitung etc) *to take in together* ~|**locken** vt [h] *to entice to go* od *come along* (*with a p*) ~|**m** vi/t [h] *to follow the rule* od *crowd, to swim with the stream*; *to do as others do, to be in it, to join in* (etw *in a th*), (den Tanz *to join the dance* ⟨a. fig⟩) || helfend ~ *to chip in* || da mach ich nicht mit *catch me* (*doing that*), .. nicht mehr mit *I draw the line at that*, ⟨Am sl⟩ *this is where I get off* || alles ~ *to be game for anything*; (erleben) *to go through, to see* || etw ~ *to take part in a th, to go to* (*a ceremony*), *to see* (*parties*) || die Mode ~ *to go* (od *take up*) *with* od *to follow the fashion* || ⟨cards⟩ *to take a hand* (*at whist*), (Poker) *to come in* || wollen Sie (den Ausflug) ~ *will you join us* (*in the exc.*), *will you make one of the party*? || (wie geht's?) – °Man macht so mit! .. *so-so, just fair*; *we do see life* || viel ~ *to keep company* || etw bis zu Ende ~ *to see a th out, to sit through* (*a meeting*) || –gemacht h ⟨mil⟩ *to have seen service* (od *action* [at]), *to have been in* od *through two wars* || °sie macht (alles) mit *she's a good sport* ⟨a. sex⟩ || ~ wollen ⟨teens⟩ *to sweat* **~mensch** m *f.-man, -creature, -being* ~**menschlich** a: ~e Beziehungen *human relations* ~|**mögen**, ~|**müssen** vi [h] *to feel inclined, to be obliged to join the others* ~|**nehmen** vt [h] *to take out* od (*along*), *to carry away with one* || nimm mich ~! *let me come*!, ⟨mot⟩ *give me a lift*! || sich ~ l ⟨sl⟩ *to hitch-hike* || (auf der Reise e–n Ort „~") *to call at* (*a place*), *to visit* (*sights*); ⟨mot rail⟩ (jdn) ~ *to pick up* || ⟨fig⟩ etw ~ *to avail o.s. of a th* || ich nehme alles mit *all's fish that comes to my net* || das kann man gerne ~ ⟨fam⟩ *it's not to be sneezed at* || *to make a profit by the way* | (schwächen) *to exhaust, weaken*; *to wear* (*out*) || (arg zurichten) *to punish a p* (→ angreifen, Anspruch B. 2.) *to handle roughly, to punish, to treat harshly, to take toll of* (*a p*), *to hit hard, to cut up badly* || *he was affected by it*; *it told* od *wore on him terribly*; *he seemed very much pulled down* od *rather knocked about*; *he looked as if he had been in the wars* || (Stunde etc ~) *to partake of a lesson* || *to join a class* | zum ~ (*cakes*) *to go* **~nehmer** m ⟨tech⟩ (Stift) *driving plate pin*; (am MG) ⟨mil⟩ *cam* ~**n·ichten** adv *by no means, in no way, not at all* **~pächter** m *j. tenant* **~pate** m *co-sponsor* ~|**rechnen** vt/i [h] *to include in the account* od *in the reckoning* || ⟨fig⟩ *to i.* || –ge–et *i.ding* (*the costs*) || nicht ~ *to leave out of account, to discount* || nicht –ge–et *not counting* (*the two*) | vi [h] (zählen) *to count* || er rechnet nicht mit *he is of no account* ~|**reden** vi [h] *to join in a conversation*, etc || (gelegentlich) *to put in a word or two* | vt [h]; ein

Wörtlein ~ *to have one's little say*, .. (nichts) –zu–h *to have a voice (nothing to say) in the matter*; *(it's no concern of yours!)* **~reeder** m *j.-owner of a ship* **~reederei** f *j. ownership* **~regent** m *coregent* **~regentschaft** f *coregency* ≗|**reisen** vi [s] *to travel along (with a p)* **~reisender** m *f.-passenger* od *-traveller* ≗|**reißen** *to carry along* (⟨a. fig⟩ *by a speech)* ‖ er riß alles mit ⟨theat⟩ *he swept the audience off their feet* ≗**reißend** a *enthusiastic*; *motivating (influence)* **~sammen** → zus–, gemeinsam ≗**s·amt** prep [dat] *as well as, together with* ‖ s–n Freund ~ dem Stuhl .. *his fr., chair and all*, .. ≗**schreiben** vt [h] *to take a record of (a speech)* **~schuld** f *complicity, accessoriness* ‖ ~ h an *to be implicated in* ≗**schuldig** a *accessory* (an *in*) ‖ er machte sich ~ an *he made h.s. an accessory to* **~schuldige(r)** m *accomplice, accessory*; *confederate* (vgl Dritte) ‖ sich als ~n bekennen *to admit complicity* **~schuldner** m *j. debtor* **~schüler** m *school-f., f.-pupil*; *book-mate* **~**|**schwingen** n ⟨wir, el⟩ *resonance* ≗|**sein** vi [mst ell:] er war mit *he went, rode, sailed, etc. with the others, he joined the party* ≗|**singen** vt/i *to join in (singing) (the chorus* Kehrreim) ≗|**sollen** vi [h] [ell] *to be supposed to go with a p* ≗|**spielen** vt/i [h] *to play (with a p), to join in play* ‖ ⟨theat⟩ *to appear*, ⟨übtr⟩ (S, P) *to play a* (od *one's*) *part (in a th)* ‖ nicht mehr ~ *to give up playing*, ⟨cards⟩ *to throw up the cards*, ⟨fig⟩ *to resign, withdraw* ‖ ⟨übtr⟩ die Geldfrage spielt mit .. *enters into consideration* ‖ nicht ~ ⟨cards⟩ *to cut out* | jdm übel ~ ⟨fig⟩ *to do a p a bad turn, to use a p ill, to play havoc (among), to play the prank (on)* ‖ (P) *to do the dirty on a p*, ⟨bes Am⟩ *to give a p a raw* od *rough deal* ‖ es hat uns übel –ge–lt ⟨sl⟩ *it did us dirty* **~spieler** m (Kind) *playf.* ‖ (derselben Partei) *partner* ‖ ⟨theat⟩ *supporting player* **~spracherecht** n *right to say one's opinion* ≗|**sprechen** vi/t [h] = ≗reden; ein Wort ~ *to put in a word* ‖ (Gebet, in e–r D.) *to join in a prayer, discussion* ‖ ⟨übtr⟩ (S) *to play a part (in a th)* **~streiter** m *comrade-in-arms* **~täter** m *accomplice, accessory*; ⟨a.⟩ *co-principle*; ⟨civ l⟩ *j. tortfeasor* | ~schaft [f] *accomplicity* ≗**teilbar** a *communicable* ‖ ⟨med⟩ → ansteckend ≗|**teilen I.** vt [h] jdm (etw) **1.** †⟨bib⟩ *to let a p partake (of a th)* **2.** *to let a p know (where, etc)*; *let me know your decision*; *to make known (to a p)*; *to communicate (to a p)*; sofort *to flash*; (vertraulich) *to impart, confide* ‖ jdm etw ~ *to inform* (⟨com⟩ *advise*) *a p of a th*, (Ansicht) *to give a p one's opinion* ‖ *to my regret I must inform you that* .. ‖ ich erlaube mir, Ihnen –zu–, daß *I beg to inform you that* ‖ *ths have forced me to say that* .. **3.** (ausrichten) kann ich etw ~? *can I take a message*? **4.** (amtlich) *to notify a p of a th* **5.** (eröffnen) *to break a th* (die Nachricht *the news*) *to a p* **II. sich** jdm *or* e–r S ~ **1.** *her spirit infected him* (od *communicated itself to him*) ‖ *the heat spreads over the surroundings*; *her alarm affected him, he was aff. by her al.*; *the motion passed on to* .. **2.** *to open one's heart to a p* ≗**teilsam** a *communicative* (→ aufgeschlossen) ‖ *expansive, effusive, outgoing*; ~ w gegenüber *to unbend toward* ‖ nicht ~ *ineffusive*, etc ‖ (schwatzhaft) *talkative* | ≗keit [f] *communicativeness* **~teilung** f *communication*; *information* ‖ *intimation* ‖ ⟨com⟩ *advice* ‖ (amtliche) *notification*; vertrauliche ~ *confidence* ‖ ~ m *to make* .. ‖ *to advise (all concerned)* N ‖ e–e ~ übermitteln *to send a message* ‖ wir bitten um ~ über *please inform us about*; *kindly let us know* (od *have some information) about* od *whether* ‖ e–e ~ *a piece of knowledge* ‖ telephonische ~ *telephone message* | ~sblatt [n] *bulletin* N ≗|**tönen** vi [h] *to sound simultaneously* ≗|**tragen** vt [h] *to carry*, etc *j.ly* ‖ (Verluste) *to share* ‖ –ge– w *to ride on the back* (v .. *of other products*) ≗|**trinken** vt/i [h] *to drink (with)*; bei .. *to drink part of a p's* ≗**·unter** adv *(every) now and then, occasionally, sometimes* ≗|**unterschr·eiben** vt/i [h], ≗|**unterz·eichnen** vt/i [h] *to sign also, to countersign* **~unterschrift** f *j. signature* **~unterz·eichner, ~unterz·eichnete(r)** m *co-signatory, co-sponsor* **~urheber** m *j. author* **~ursache** f *concurring (additional, secondary) cause* ≗**verantwortlich** a *sharing the responsibility (with)* **~verbrecher** m *accomplice* **~vergangenheit** f → Imperfekt (z. B. er sang, als ich ..) **~verschulden** n *contributory negligence* **~verschworene(r)** m *co-, f.-conspirator* **~verwaltung** f *coadministration* **~vormund** m *j.-guardian* **~vormundschaft** f *co-guardianship* **~welt** f *the present generation* od *age, the age* od *time we live in*; *our*, etc. *contemporaries* pl ≗|**wirken** vi [h] (an, bei [dat]) *to co-operate (in)*; helfend ~ *to chip in* ‖ ⟨theat⟩ *to take part (in a play)*; *to be in the cast* ‖ *to assist (in clearing up a matter), to contribute (to a newspaper*, etc.) ‖ ohne sein ≗ *without his assistance* ‖ ~er Umstand *assisting factor, coefficient* **~wirkung** f *cooperation*, etc. **~wissen** n *j.-knowledge, privity* ‖ ohne mein ~ *unknown to me, without my knowledge* (od *cognizance*) ‖ mit jds ~ *with the connivance of a p* ‖ *with his privity* ≗|**wissen** vt [h] um etw ~ *to know (to be privy) of a th* | ~schaft [f] = –wissen [n] **~wisser** m *party, accessary* ‖ er hatte k–n ~ *he let nobody into the secret* (bei *of*) | ~schaft [f] ⟨jur⟩ *guilty knowledge* ≗|**wollen** vi [h] = ≗gehen etc wollen ≗|**zahlen** vt [h] *to pay one's share* ≗|**zählen** vt [h] = –rechnen *to count in (those absent)* ‖ (etw) nicht ~ *to discount* | vi *to count also* ‖ *please also keep count* ≗|**zechen** vi [h] *to keep (a p) company in a drinking-bout* **~zeuge** m *f.-witness* ≗|**ziehen** vt [h] *to pull with (others)* ‖ *to drag a th along with one* | vi [s] *to travel*, etc. *with (others)* **~zweck** m *additional purpose*

M·itra f ~/–ren *mitre*, ⟨Am⟩ *miter* **~bänder** n pl *wimples*

M·ittag m *midday, noon(tide)* ‖ (→ mittags) ‖ heute ~ *at noon to-day* ‖ S. ~ *Sunday noon* ‖ es ist ~ *it is twelve o'clock* ‖ ⟨fig⟩ *the meridian (of life)* (.. hinter sich h *to have crossed* ..) ‖ ⟨geog⟩ (Süd) *south* ‖ gegen ~ *towards noon*; *southerly* | zu ~ essen *to lunch* ‖ zu ~ bleiben *to stay to lunch* (od *early dinner*) ‖ ~ m *to halt for midday rest* **~essen** n *lunch(eon), early dinner* **m·ittägig, m·ittäglich** a *midday, noontide (event), happening at noon* ‖ ⟨geog⟩ *southern*, ⟨scient⟩ *meridian, meridional* **m·ittags** adv *at noon* **M·ittags- ~ausgabe** f *noon edition* **~besteck** n ⟨mar⟩ *n. position* **~blume** f *mesembrianthemum*; *fig-marigold* **~frühstück** n *brunch* (= *breakfast* + *lunch*) **~gast** m *luncheon-* od *dinner-guest* **~gegend** f *southern region, meridional country* **~gesellschaft** f *company to lunch* od *(early) dinner* **~glocke** f *n.-* od *dinner-bell* **~glut, ~hitze** f *n.day heat* **~höhe** f *meridian* ‖ (der Sonne) *altitude* **~kreis** m, **~linie** f *meridian* **~luft** f *n.day air, southern breeze* **~mahlzeit** f = Mittagessen; leichte ~ *(farmer's) nooning* **~pause** f *lunch-hour*; *recess* **~ruhe** f, **~schläfchen** n *after-dinner* od *afternoon nap, doze, siesta* (halten *or* m *to take one's* ..) **~seite** f *South side* **~sonne** f *n.tide sun* **~sonnenstand, ~stand** m *station of the sun at n.* **~stunde** f *n.tide, n.* ‖ (Eßstunde) *lunch-* od *dinner-hour* **~tisch** m *lunch, dinner* ‖ fester ~ *ordinary* ‖ gut bürgerlicher ~ *good plain dinner* **~zeit** f *n.(tide)* ‖ (Eßzeit) *lunch-* od *(early) dinner-time* ‖ um die ~ *towards n.* ‖ während der ~ *during the n. hour* **M·itte** f ~/~n **A.** *middle, midst* ‖ (Mittelpunkt) *centre*, ⟨fig a.⟩ *navel* ‖ (Mittelweg) *mean* ‖ ⟨parl⟩ *the m.e party*; Mann der ~ *centrist* ‖ ⟨ftb⟩ ~! *centre*! | genaue ~ *exact m.e* ‖ goldene (rechte) ~ *golden (happy) mean* ‖ die gute ~ treffen *to hit the happy medium* ‖ ungefähre ~ *approximate centre* | *body (of the church)* ‖ ~ der Scheibe *bull's eye* ‖ ~ des Sommers (Winters) *midsummer (midwinter)* | ~ Mai *in mid-May*; gegen .. *about the m.e of May* ‖ er ist ~ Vierzig(er) (*or* der Vierziger) *he is halfway* *between forty and fifty*, .. *in his m.e forties* | Reich der ∼ (China) *Central Kingdom* **B. auf** der ∼ des Marsches *in the mid-march* ‖ **aus** unserer ∼ *from among us, from our midst, of our company* ‖ ⟨fam⟩ ab **d·urch** die ∼ ⟨urspr. theat⟩ *clear out*! ‖ **in** der ∼ *in the m.e* (*of the road*); ⟨paint⟩ *in the m.e distance*; ⟨fam⟩ *medially* ‖ in unserer ∼ *in our midst, among us* ‖ (wir nahmen ihn) in unsere ∼ (*we took him*) *in the midst of us*; ⟨mil⟩ (..) *between two fires* ‖ in der ∼ des 19. Jh. *in the mid 19th c.* ‖ das Haus liegt in der ∼ der Straße .. *is half-way down* .. ‖ in der ∼ durchreißen (.. schneiden) *to tear* (*cut*) *across* ‖ **zur** ∼ ⟨theat⟩ *on-stage* **m·ittel** a (∼mäßig) *middling* ‖ unter ∼ *below the average*; vgl mittler(e) **M·ittel** n ∼s/∼ (Mitte) **A.** *middle, midst* ‖ (Durchschnitt) *average* (im ∼ *on the a.*); ⟨stat⟩ gewogenes ∼ *weighted a.* od *mean*; die Temperatur betrug im ∼ *the a. temperature amounted to* | (Hilfs≗) *means* pl [sg konstr], *resources* pl ‖ ∼ der Berichterstattung *information media* L pl ‖ (Ausweg) *expedient, way* | jedes brauchbare ∼ *any means to the end*; ein gewaltsames ∼ *strong measures*; letztes ∼ *resort* (zu *to*), *last measure*; sicheres ∼ *reliable method* ‖ ein ∼ z Zweck *a means to an end*; *the means to attain one's purpose* (→ Zweck) | (Heil≗) *remedy*; (wirkendes) *agent*; (*alleviatory*) *medicine*; ∼ gegen Fieber *antipyretic drug* | ⟨math⟩ (*arithmetical, geometrical, harmonic*) *mean* ‖ ⟨tech⟩ *equipment* ‖ ⟨phys⟩ *medium* ‖ ⟨chem⟩ ∼ [pl] *reagents* pl | ∼ [pl] (Geld) *means* pl, *funds* pl, *substance, money* ‖ (Vermögen) *fortune* ‖ **mit** geringen ∼n (*a man*) *of few possessions*; ohne ∼ *stranded* ‖ mit allen ∼n versuchen *to make every effort*; ⟨mil⟩ *to push the attack to a successful conclusion with ev. e. at one's command* **B.** alle erdenklichen ∼ **an**wenden *to use* od *try every possible means*; .. *any m.s* (*to the end*); neue .. *to change one's method* ‖ mit den schärfsten ∼n **be**kämpfen *to oppose* .. *with the strongest measures* ‖ die ∼ besitzen zu tun *to be in a position to do* ‖ die ∼ bewilligen *to grant the money* (*for*) ‖ m–e ∼ erlauben es mir nicht *I can't afford it* ‖ ∼ u Wege **finden** *to find ways and means* (*some means has to be found* [*of doing, to do*]); .. für etw *to manage a th* ‖ als ∼ z Zweck **ge**brauchen *to use as a means to an end* ‖ kein ∼ mehr **h** *to be at one's wit's end* ‖ ins ∼ **treten, sich** ins ∼ legen *to step* od *weigh in*, ⟨Am sl⟩ *to horn in* ‖ *to interpose*; *to mediate, interfere, intercede, intervene* (*between*, für jdn *on a p's behalf, in a matter*) ‖ kein ∼ **un**versucht l *to leave no measures untried, to leave no stone unturned*; ⟨a.⟩ *to explore every avenue* **∼abschnitt** m ⟨mil⟩ *central sector* **∼alter** n *M.e Ages* pl; das frühe *or* finstere ∼ *the Dark Ages* **≗alterlich** a *mediæval*; ⟨fig⟩ *oldfashioned* (*ideas*) **∼amerika** (–asien etc) n *Central A.* **∼arrest** m ⟨mil⟩ *solitary confinement* **∼artillerie** f ⟨mar⟩ *medium-calibre guns*; (bei gr Schiffen) *secondary armament* **∼begriff** m *medium*; *m.e term* **∼blech** n [qual] *jobbing sheet* **∼deck** n ⟨mar⟩ *m.e decks* pl, *steerage* **∼decker** m ⟨aero⟩ *midwing* (*mono*)*plane* **∼deutschland** *C. G.* **∼ding** n *sth intermediate* (*between two ths*); ⟨fig⟩ *there is no half-way house* **∼druck** m *medium pressure* | ∼schieber [m] *i.e slide-valve* **∼england** n *the Midlands* pl **∼ernte** f *average harvest* **≗europäische Zeit** f *C.l E. time* **∼farbe** f *m.e colour, mezzotint* **≗fein** a ⟨com⟩ *fine-middling, good medium* **∼feld** n *centre-field* **∼-finger** m *m.e-finger* ⟨a. °fig sex⟩ **∼form** f ⟨gram⟩ *participle* **∼frequenz** f ⟨wir⟩ *medium fr.* (*MF*) **∼-fuß(knochen)** m ⟨anat⟩ *metatarsus* **∼gang** m *c.l passage*; ⟨ec⟩ *m.e aisle*, → Gang **∼gattung** f *i.e kind* **∼gebäude** n *c.l building* **∼gebirge** n *uplands* pl, *hill country* | *c.l chain of mountains* **∼gewicht** n ⟨box⟩ *m.e-weight* (bis 145 Pfd, ⟨engl⟩ *160 lbs*) **∼glied** n *m.e joint*, ⟨math⟩ *m.e term* **≗groß** *medium-sized, of m.m size*; nicht über ∼ *of no more than average height* **∼grund** m ⟨paint⟩ *m.e distance, c.e-ground* **≗gut** a ⟨com⟩ *middling, of second quality, s.-rate* **∼hand** f ⟨anat⟩ *metacarpus*; ⟨cards⟩ *s. hand* **∼hart** a *medium hard* **≗hoch-deutsch** a *M.e High G.* **∼klasse** f ⟨sociol⟩ *m.e classes* pl ‖ Auto der ∼ *compact car* **∼kraft** f ⟨tech⟩ *resultant* **≗ländisch** a *inland* ‖ das ∼e Meer [n] *the Mediterranean* **∼latein** n *Low Latin* **∼linie** f ⟨geogr⟩ *equator*; ⟨phys⟩ *neutral zone*; ⟨geom⟩ *bisector*; ⟨ftb⟩ *c.e line*; ⟨ten⟩ *half-court line*; ⟨theat⟩ *centre mark*, ⟨Am⟩ *center l.*; ⟨mil⟩ *center l.* N **∼loge** f ⟨theat⟩ *balcony-box* **≗los** a *penniless*; ⟨off⟩ *without means of support*; *destitute*; ∼e P *medically indigent p* ‖ er stand ∼ da *he was left penniless* **∼losigkeit** f *poverty, destitution* **∼mächte** f pl ⟨pol⟩ *C.l Powers* pl **∼mann** m ⟨com⟩ *m.eman* **∼maß** n *average* **≗mäßig** a *mediocre, middling* (*achievements*); *moderate* (*ability*); *indifferent* (*dramatist, meal*); ⟨com⟩ *fair, m.m* (*quality*) ‖ adv *indifferently* **∼mäßigkeit** f *mediocrity* **∼mast** m ⟨mar⟩ *mainmast* **∼meer** n *Mediterranean* | ∼raum [m] *M. area* **∼ohrent-zündung** f *otitis media* **∼partei** f ⟨parl⟩ *moderate* od *c.l party* (→ Zentrum) **∼pfeiler, ∼pfosten** m *upright post* **∼pferd** n *centre horse* °**≗prächtig** a *not bad* **∼preis** m *average price, m.m-price*; sich auf den ∼ einigen *to split the difference* **∼punkt** m *centre*; ⟨fig⟩ *heart* (*of a town*), *focus, hub* (*of the universe*), *c.l point* (*of society*); *she was the life of the party*; im ∼ e–r S stehen *to be at the core of a th*; im ∼ s–r Überlegungen steht .. *a prime consideration is* ..; den ∼ der Unterhaltung bilden *to hold the stage*; im ∼ des Interesses stehen *to take the limelight* **∼rippenstück** n ⟨cul⟩ *entrecote* Fr **∼schiff** n ⟨arch⟩ *nave* **∼schlag** m, **∼sorte** f *middling, m.e sort* ‖ ⟨com⟩ *m.gs* pl **∼schule** f *continuations school, lower grade secondary school* **∼spannung** f ⟨el⟩ *medium voltage* (*250–650 V*) **∼sprosse** f (am Geweih) *royal, terz* **∼staaten** m pl *states of secondary importance* **∼stadt** f *m.e-sized town* **∼stand** m *m.e classes* pl | ∼s– *m.e class* (*manners*) **∼statur** f *middling size* | e–e **∼stellung** einnehmen *to take an intermediate position* ⟨a. fig⟩ **∼straße** f *m.e road* ‖ ⟨fig⟩ *m.e course, mean, m.m*; goldene ∼ *golden mean* **∼streckenlauf** m *half-long distance race* **∼streckler** m ⟨sport⟩ *m.e distance runner* **∼streifen** m ⟨mot⟩ (grüner) *c.l reservation*, ⟨Am⟩ *median* **∼stromschlene** f ⟨el⟩ *centre conductor rail*, ⟨Am⟩ *center contact rail* **∼stück** n *centre-piece*; ⟨cul⟩ *m.e cut*; °⟨f sex⟩ *masterpiece*; *Midlands* **∼stufe** f *intermediate degree*; ⟨school⟩ *i. class*; *secondary education* **∼-stürmer** m ⟨ftb⟩ *centre-forward* **∼tarif** m ⟨com⟩ *equated rate* **∼ton** m ⟨arts⟩ *half tint*; ⟨mus⟩ *mediant* **∼tormann** m ⟨crick⟩ (rechts) *mid-off*, (links) *mid-on* **∼treffen** n *centre* (*of an army*) **∼-wasser** n *half tide* | ∼stand [m] (MW) *mean water level* **∼weg** m *m.e course* (einschlagen *to adopt*) (→ ∼straße) **∼welle** f ⟨wir⟩ *medium frequence* od *wavelength* | ∼nfunk [m] *standard broadcast* **∼-wert** m *average* od *mean value* **∼wort** n ⟨gram⟩ *participle* **∼zimmer** n *centre-room* **∼zustand** m *intermediate state* od *condition, neutrality* **m·it-telbar** a *mediate*; *indirect* (*consequence, possession*) **M·ittelchen** n ⟨med⟩ *slight remedy* ‖ ⟨fig⟩ *trick*: mit allerlei ∼ suchte er .. zu tun *he tried all sorts of tricks to do* .. **mittels**(t) prep [gen] *by means of, with the assistance of* **M·ittels- ∼mann** m, **∼person** f *agent, middleman, mediator* ‖ ⟨fam⟩ *go-between* **m·ittelste(r)** a *middlemost, central* **m·itten** [adv], ∼ in (an, auf, unter) *in the midst* od *middle* (*of*), *amidst*; *mid* ‖ ∼ **am** Tage *in broad daylight*; ∼ **auf** der Straße *in the open street* ‖ ∼ auf dem Wege *well on the way*; ∼ **aus** *from amidst*; (.. e–r Menge) *from among*; ∼ aus der Versammlung *from the midst of the assembly*; | **darin** *or* darunter *or* inne (*right*) *in the* (*very*) *centre* od *midst* (*of it, of them*); ∼ **durch** die Stadt *right through* (*the*) *town* ∼ **durch**|hauen *to cut across*; ∼ **entzwei** (*broken*) *right in two*; ~ **(hin)durch** (*right*) *across, through the midst*; ~ **hinein** *in medias res* L, *into the heart* (od *very middle*) *of ths*; ~ **im** Schreiben *in the middle of writing*; ~ im Winter *in the dead* od *depth of w.*; ~ **in** der Arbeit sterben .. *in harness*; ~ in e–r Krise *in the thick of a cr.* || ~ in die *or* der Luft *in mid-air*; ~ in der Nacht *in the dead of night, at midnight*; ~ in der Unterredung (über) *well away* (*on a subject*); ~ **ins** Herz *right into the heart* || ~ ins 19. Jh. *well into the 19th c.*; → zwischen **M·itter-** **~nacht** f *midnight* || es schlägt ~ *it is striking the hour of m.* || (Nord) *north* || um ~ *at m.* || Schlaf vor ~ *beauty-sleep* **≗nächtig, ≗nächtlich** a *m.* (*silence*), *nocturnal* || zu ~er Stunde *at the hour of m.* || (nördlich) *northern* **≗-nachts** adv *at m.* **~nachtsonne** f *m. sun* **~nachtzeit** f *m.* **M·itt-** **~fasten** pl *Mid-Lent* **≗schiffs** adv (*a-*)*midships* **~sommer** m *midsummer* **≗wegs** adv *midway* .. **m·ittig** [suff] *centrally* **M·ittigkeit** f ⟨tech⟩ *concentricity, co-axiality* **M·ittler** m ~s/~ *agent, mediator* (f *mediatress*) || ⟨com⟩ *middleman* | ~amt [n] *mediatorship* **m·ittlere(r, -s)** a *middle, central* (*sector*) || der ≗ Osten *the M. East* || (durchschnittlich) *average* (*size, harvest*) || *mean* (*pressure* [*quantity of*], *precipitation*) || (mittelmäßig) *medium* (*estate, speed, temperature*) || ⟨stat, demog⟩ *standard* [attr] || ⟨phot⟩ ~s Grau *m.m grey* || ⟨math⟩ *mean* (*proportional*) || (Staat etc) ~r Größe *m.m-rank* [attr] || in ~n Jahren *m.e-aged* || in den ~n Fünfzigern *in the m.e fifties* || v ~r Größe *m.m-sized* || → Mittelartillerie **m·ittlerweile** adv *meanwhile, in the meantime, by the time, all the while* || *by now, by then* **M·ittwoch** m ~(e)s/~e *Wednesday*; [→ Montag]

M·ix m ~es/~e *mixer* | ~becher [m] *shaker*; ~glas [n] *mixing glass*; ~pickles [pl] *mixed pickles* **Mixt·ur** f ~/~en *mixture* || ⟨pharm⟩ *draught*

Mnem·onik f ~/~ *mnemonics* pl **mnem·onisch** a *mnemonic* **Mnemot·echnik** f ~/ *mnemotechnics*

M·ob m ~s/ *mob, crowd, throng*

M·ob- (→ ~il[machung]) ~kalender [m] *mobilization plan*; ≗mäßig [a] *according to war establishment*; ~verbände [m pl] *m. units*

M·öbel n ~s/ *piece of furniture* || ~ [pl] *f.* | (⟨fig⟩ altes ~ (P) *institution*; *fixture*) || unnützes ~ *good-for-nothing sort of p* **~händler** m *f.-dealer* **~kattun** m *chintz* **~lager** n *f.-warehouse* **~politur** f *f.-polish* **~spediteur** m *f.-remover*, ⟨Am⟩ *movingman* **~speicher** m *pantechnicon, warehouse* **~stil** m *f.-style* **~stück** n *piece of f.*; *fitment*; ⟨Am sl⟩ *stick* **~tischler** m *cabinet-maker* **~transport** m *f.-removing*; ~ ausführen *to remove f.* | ~geschäft [n] *f.-removers* **~überzug** m *cover* **~wagen** m *moving* od *f.-van*; *pantechnicon*; ⟨Am⟩ *moving van* || ⟨aero fam⟩ (2- u mehrmot.) *bus, taxi, sky wagon*

mob·il a (beweglich) *movable* | (flink) *active, quick* || gesund u ~ *hale and hearty* | ⟨mil⟩ *mobile* (*unit*) || ~e Löhnung *war pay* || ~|m = mobilisieren || ⟨fig⟩ etw ~ m *to embattle* od *mobilize a th* (f *for*, gegen *against*) **M·obile** n ~s/~s ⟨"arts"⟩ *mobile* **Mobili·ar** n ~(e)s/~e *movables* pl, *household goods* pl, *furniture* **~erbe** m ⟨jur⟩ *heir to the personal property* od *estate* **~hypothek** f ⟨engl⟩ *chattel mortgage* **~versicherung** f *insurance of contents* **~vermögen** n, **Mobilien** pl ⟨jur⟩ *p.l p.y* od *e.* **mobilis·ieren** vt/i [h] ⟨mil⟩ *to mobilize* **Mobilit·ät** f ~/ ⟨geog⟩ *spatial mobility* | ~sziffer [f] ⟨demog⟩ *migration rate* **Mob·ilmachung** (**Mobilis·ierung**) f ~/~en ⟨mil⟩ *mobilization* | ~sbefehl [m] *m. order*; ~sgeld [n] *field-allowance*; ~skalender [m] *m. plan*; ~smaßnahmen [f pl] *m. measures*; ~splan [m] *plan of m.*; 1. ~stag [m] *M-day*; ~svorschrift [f] *M. Regulation* N; ~zulage [f] = ~geld || → Mob- **möbl·ieren** vt [h] *to furnish, to fit up* (*rooms*) || neu ~ *to refurnish* || ⟨fam⟩ **möbl·iert** wohnen *to live in lodgings* || ~er Herr *lodger* **Möbl·ierung** f ~/~en *furnishing*

m·ochte, (≗) 1., 3. sg pret (conj) v mögen **M·öchtegerne** m ~/ *would-be* | ~-Großmacht [f] *w.-be big power*

mod·al a *modal* | ≗satz [m] *adverb*(*ial*) *clause* **Modalit·ät** f ~/~en *modality*

M·odder m ~s/ *mud* | ~grund [m] *muddy* od *slicky ground*; ~prahm [m] *ballast lighter, drag boat* **m·oddern** vt [h] *to stir up the ground*

M·ode f ~/~n **A.** *fashion*; *vogue*; die letzte ~ *the last cry* || (Brauch) *custom, use* **B. aus** der ~ k (.. gek) *to grow* od *go out of f.* (*outmoded* [*hat*]) || **in** (der) ~ *f.able, in f., in general wear*; (P) *f.able* (*artist, writer*, etc); ⟨fam⟩ *all* od *quite the go* od *rage, in vogue*; in (die) ~ bringen *to bring into v.*; in (die) ~ k, ~ w *to come into f.*; in (der) ~ s ⟨a.⟩ *to be in the movement, to flourish*; **mit** der ~ gehen *to go with the f.s*; **nach** der neuesten ~ *according to the latest f.* od *craze* || sich nach der (neusten) ~ kleiden *or* tragen *to follow the f., to dress after the latest f., to be dressy* **C.** die **~angeben** *to set the f.* || (in) ~ **bleiben** *to continue in f.* || e–e neue ~ **kam auf** .. *crept in* || die ~ (alle ~n) **mit**|m *to follow the f.* (*every f.able fad*), *to be in the f.* || (in) ~ **s** *to be the f.* od *taste* || ganz die ~ *or* die gr ~ s *to be all the rage* || es wurde allgemein ~ ⟨Am fam⟩ *the fad took hold of the nation* **D.** ⟨fig⟩ das wäre die neueste ~! *that would be a nice sort of game!, there's nothing doing!* **~artikel** m *fancy-article* || ~ [pl] *novelties* pl **~ausdruck** m *fashionable expression, vogue-word* **~ausstellung** f *fashion show* **~bild** n *f.-plate* **~buch** n *best-seller* **~dame** f *lady of f.* **~dichter** m *poet of the day* **~farbe** f *f.able colour* **~fex** m = ~narr **~händler** m *milliner* **~herr** m *f.able gentleman* **~herrchen** = ~narr **~journal** n = ~zeitung **~krankheit** f *f.able complaint*; ⟨fig⟩ *folly in f.* **~kupfer** n = -bild **~laune** f *vagary of f.* **~n|-** ~geschäft, ~haus [n] *fashion house*; *millinery*; ~schau [f] *dress* od *f.-parade* **~narr** m *slave of f., dandy, johnny, fop, swell*; ⟨fam⟩ *masher*; ⟨sl⟩ *high-stepper* **~närrin, ~puppe** f *fine* od *f. doll* **~sache** f *passing fancy*; *fad* **~schau** f *dress* od *f. show*; *mannequin parade*, (intim) *floor-show* **~schmuck** m *costume jewellery* **~schöpfer** m *fashion creator, fashion designer* **~-schöpfung** f (*latest*) *f. creation* **~schriftsteller** m *f.able author* **~stoff** m *fancy-stuff* od *cloth* **~sucht** f *mania for new f.s* **~torheit** f (*f.able*) *craze* **~ware** f *millinery, fancy-goods* pl **~welt** f *f.able world* **~-wort** n = ~ausdruck **~zeichner** m *f. designer* **~-zeitung** f *ladies'* od *f.-paper, magazine of f.s* **M·odel** m ~s/~(n) ⟨arch⟩ *module* || *pattern* || (*cotton-printing*) *block* || ⟨bak⟩ *matrix, mo*(*u*)*ld* **Mod·ell** n ~(e)s/~e ⟨arts⟩ *model, sitter* || ⟨tech⟩ *pattern*; *model*; verkleinertes ~ *mock-up* || (Muster) *pattern*; ⟨mil⟩ *trial model* || (*anatomical*) *cast* || jdm ~ stehen *to serve* od *pose as* (*a*) *m.l for a p* || ⟨fig⟩ (zu) *to be the prototype* (*of*) **~fall** m *test case* **~-puppe** f *lay-figure* **~sammlung** f *collection of m.ls* **~sand** m ⟨met⟩ *facing sand* **~schreiner, ~schlosser** m *pattern-maker* **~skizze** f *academy figure* **~steher** m (*painter's*) *m.l* **~versuch** m *small scale test* **~zeichnen** n *m.l-drawing* **~zeichnung** f *academy figure* **modell·ieren** vt [h] *to model, mould* (nach *on*) || *to fashion, shape* **Modell·ierer** m ~s/~ *modeller, pattern-maker, moulder* **Modell·ierholz** n *boasting tool* **m·odeln** **1.** = modellieren **2.** (Sätze etc) *to polish* **3.** ⟨weav⟩ *to figure* **4.** (ändern) *to change*

M·odena n (Stadt in N.-Italien)

M·oder m ~s/ (Fäulnis) *mould, mustiness* || (Schlamm) *mud* || *musty air* **~duft, ~geruch** m *musty smell* **~erde** f *mould* **~fleck** m *mildew* **~luft** f = ~ **m·oderig** a *mouldy, musty, frowzy* || *decaying* || ~ w *to go mouldy* **m·odern I.** vi [h] (Holz) *to rot* || (im Grabe) *to moulder, putrefy, decay* **II.** ≗ n *mouldering*, etc || *putrefaction, decay*

mod·ern I. a (neuzeitlich) *modern, advanced*;

(*appliances*) *of our time* ‖ (modisch) *fashionable, stylish, trendy*; ~st *down to date*; aufs ~ste gekleidet *attired in the highest style of fashion* ‖ (fortschrittlich) *go-ahead, progressive, up-to-date, modern* (*views*); (P) *sophisticated*; (ganz ~) *up--dating, exclusive* (*patterns*) ‖ *latter-day* (*saints*) | ⟨dero⟩ *new-fangled* **II. die ≃en** *the modern world*; *the modernists* pl | **≃e** f ~/ *modernity*; *modern times* od *representatives* pl **~is·ieren** vt [h] *to modernize*; *to stream-line* (*production methods*) **≃is·ierung** f (e–r Fabrik) *redeployment* **≃it·ät** f ~/ *modernness*

Modifikati·on [ts] f ~/~en *modification* **modifiz·ieren** vt [h] *to modify* ‖ ⟨gram a.⟩ *to qualify*

m·odisch a *fashionable, modish, stylish*; [pred] *all the kick* ‖ **≃e** n ~n/ *modishness* **Mod·istin** f ~/~nen *milliner, modiste*

M·odul m ~s/ ⟨allg tech⟩ *module*; ⟨math⟩ *modulus* L **~ati·on** [ts] f ~/~en *modulation, intonation* | ~sfähigkeit [f] *adaptability* (*of voice*); ~sgrad [m] *percentage* od *depth of m.* **modul·ieren** vt [h] *to modulate* **M·odus** m ~/M·odi *mode, manner, fashion*; *rule* ‖ ⟨gram⟩ *mood* ‖ e–n ~ finden z tun *to find means for* od *a way of doing*

Mofa n → Motorfahrrad

Mof·ette f ~/~n ⟨geol⟩ *mofette* (*vent of gaseous exhalation*)

°**Mogel·ei** f ~/~en *cheating, trickery* **m·ogeln** vi [h] ⟨fam⟩ *to cheat, trick*; ⟨sl⟩ *to wangle, gyp* **M·ogler** m ~s/~ *cheat*; *card-sharper*

m·ögen [mochte/gemocht] [h] **I.** vt (gern ~) *to like*; ich mag es gern, vertrag's aber nicht ⟨cul⟩ *I l. it but it doesn't l. me* ‖ sie ~ sich *they are fond of each other* ‖ Kinder ~ ihn *children take to him* | **nicht** ~ *to dislike*; *to object to* (*a th*); *I don't fancy* (*being ordered about*) ‖ ich mag sie nicht (**leiden**) *I don't like her*; (stärker) *I can't bear her* ‖ sie ~ es nicht *they don't care for it* | **lieber** ~ *to like better, to prefer* ‖ ich möchte (viel) lieber Fisch *I'd* (*much*) *rather have fish* **II.** v/aux **1.** (**Erlaubnis**) sie ~ es (meinetwegen) tun *let them* (od *they may*) *do it* (*if they like*) ‖ es mag geschehen *very well, let's have it, I don't care* ‖ er mag nur reden *let him talk as much as he likes* ‖ wenn .., mag er es h *if .., let him* (od *he may*) *have it* ‖ hier mag erwähnt s, daß .. *let me say here that* .. **2.** (**Wunsch**) (gern ~) *to desire, wish, like, to have a mind* (*to do*) ‖ (wollen) *to be willing* ‖ ich (er) möchte wohl *or* gern(, wenn ich (er) nur könnte) *I should* (*he would*) *like to* (*if I* (*he*) *could*) ‖ ich möchte gerne mit Ihnen sprechen *I should like* (od *allow me*) *to speak to you*; .. wissen, ob .. .. *to know whether* | möchten Sie sich nicht setzen? *would you care to sit down*? | ich möchte, **daß** er käme *I wish he would come* ‖ ich möchte nicht, daß er es erführe *I don't want him to hear about it* ‖ ich möchte, daß du ihm schreibst *I want* od *would like you to write to him*, ⟨Am a.⟩ *I want you should write to him* ‖ ich wünsch(t)e, daß er k möge (möchte) *I wish*(*ed*) *him to come*, [*that*] *he may* (*might, would*) *come* | ich ließ ihm ausrichten, er möchte zu mir k *I sent him word to call on me* | möge, möchte er Erfolg h! *may he succeed*! ‖ möchte es doch geschehen! *how I wish it would happen*! | ⟨iron⟩ das möchte ich denn doch mal sehen! *well, I should like to see* (*him do*) *that*! ‖ möge es ihm wohl bek! *much good may it do him*! | [inf + inf statt pp] ich habe es ihm nicht sagen mögen *I should not have liked to tell him*; .. tun ~ *I did not care* od *like to do it* ‖ ich habe nie bleiben ~ *I never cared for staying* | [**irrealis**] ich möchte am liebsten davonlaufen *I feel half inclined to run away*; man möchte rasend w *it's enough to drive one mad*; ich möchte tot u begraben s! *I wish I were dead*!; (ich) möcht's bezweifeln *I doubt it, I have my doubts*; ich möchte den sehen, der es wagt *I defy anyone to dare it* ‖ ich möchte heulen, wenn .. *I feel like crying when* ..; das Herz möchte mir zerspringen *my h. is ready to break* **3.** (**Ablehnung**) ich mag **nicht** *I will not, I don't like it, I don't care about it, I don't want to* (nach Hause gehn *go home*) ‖ *I hate doing* (od *to do*) *it* ‖ *I don't feel like going* **4.** (**Möglichkeit**) Sie ~ recht h *you may be right* ‖ das mag wohl s *that is very likely*, ⟨fam⟩ *that's as may be* ‖ er mag krank s *he may* (*possibly*) *be ill* ‖ sie mochte 20 (Jahre alt) s *she might* od *would be 20* ‖ es mögen, mochten etwa 20 Leute da gewesen s *about 20 people might have been there* ‖ es mochte wohl schon 9 Uhr s, als er .. *it was perhaps as late as 9 o'clock when he* .. ‖ es mag (mochte) später gewesen s *it may* (*might*) *have been later* ‖ er mochte lächeln *he might smile* ‖ der Geier, Henker, Teufel mag wissen, wo .. *the d– only knows* .. | (**mildernd**: [pret subj]) das möchte schwer zu beweisen s (*I fear* od *I am afraid*) *it will be difficult to prove that* ‖ Sie möchten sich wohl irren *I am afraid you are mistaken* ‖ es möchte wohl besser s, wenn .. *it would doubtless be better if* .. ‖ daraus möchte kaum etw w *very likely nothing will come of it* | (**fragend**) wer mag ihm das gesagt h? *who can* od *may have told him that*? ‖ .. mochte .. *how old would he be*? ‖ wie mag es ihm gehn? *how may he be*? ‖ was mag das s? *what can that be*? **5.** (**Einräumung**) ~ sie **auch** reich s .. *though they be rich* .. ‖ wie dem *or* das a. s mag *be that as it may* od *might* ‖ wo er a. s mag *wherever he may be* ‖ was er a. tun mochte .. *do what he would*, (*he could not* ..) ‖ was ich a. immer tun mag *whatever I may do* | es mag (wohl) s, **daß** .. *it may be true that* .. ‖ ~ sie **noch so** reich s *let them* (od *may they*) *be ever so rich* ‖ er mochte arm s **oder** reich *whether* (*he was*) *poor or rich* ‖ mochte es so o. so heißen *be it called so or so* ‖ er mag wollen o. nicht *no matter whether he wants to or not* ‖ .. **und wie** sie alle heißen mochten *whatever their names were* ‖ sie mag tun, **was** sie will *no matter what she does* ‖ du magst sagen, was du willst *whatever you may say*; *you may say what you like* ‖ es mag kosten, was es will *or* wolle *it may cost what it will* ‖ es mag daraus w, was da wolle *whatever may come of it* ‖ mag *or* möge da k, **wer** will, .. *no matter who comes* .. **6.** (**Befehl**) das ~ Sie Ihrer Waschfrau erzählen! (*you may*) *tell that to the* (*horse-*) *marines*! ‖ niemand möge glauben, daß .. *let no one think that* ..! ‖ ~ sie sich darüber beschweren! *let them complain of it*! ‖ sie ~ sich (davor) hüten, noch einmal so zu handeln! *they should be careful how they act like that again* ‖ sie ~ sich in acht nehmen *let them beware* (od *look out*)!, *they should be on their guard* ‖ sag ihm, er möge, möchte heim k *tell him to come home* ‖ mag es tun, wer kann! *let anybody do it who can*! **m·öglich I.** [a] **A.** *possible* ‖ (ausführbar) *practicable, feasible* ‖ (ungewiß) *contingent* ‖ (etwaig) *eventual*; *potential* (*readers*) **B. 1. alle** ~en .. *diverse* .., .. *of all kinds* ‖ durchaus ~e Aussicht (*to have a*) *sporting chance* ‖ alle ~n Fälle (**jede** ~e Hilfe) *all possible emergencies* (.. *assistance*) ‖ aller Trost, der ihr (zu spenden) ~ war *such consolation as she might* .. ‖ auf alle *or* jede nur ~e Weise *in all possible* od *feasible ways, in any and every way*; *by* (*any and*) *all means* **2. alles** ~e *all that is* (*was*) *p.*; .. aufbieten (versuchen) *to do everything in one's power, to do one's utmost*; *to try e.g p.* od *imaginable* ‖ er tat alles ~e *he went out of his way* (*to be nice*) ‖ alles ~e versprechen *to make all kinds of promises* **3. nicht** ~ *impossible* ‖ [intj] nicht ~! *no*! *you don't say so*! *did you now*?; *really*?; *oh, indeed*!, (*He always does*) – *Does he, now*? ‖ ist's ~! *fancy*! **4.** es ist ~, **daß** er kommt *he may possibly come* **5.** das einzige **mir** ~e Mittel .. *in my power* ‖ es war mir nicht ~ *I was unable to do it, it was beyond my power, ability, it was impossible for me* (*to find*) ‖ ich hoffe, daß es Ihnen ~ s wird *I trust you will see your way* (*to do it*) **C.** es ist **durchaus, leicht** ~ *it may quite well be*,

⟨fam⟩ *it is on the cards* (*that*), *it will be all right* (*to see her*); das ist **eher** ~ *that is more likely*; was **irgend Menschen** ~ war *whatever was within human possibility*; das ist leicht, wohl ~ *that may well be p.* **D.** [mit verbs] etw ~ **finden** *to find sth p.* ‖ es kaum f ~ **halten** *to scarcely believe one's ears* ‖ ich halte es sogar f ~ (daß ..) *for all I know* (*it may have been* ..) ‖ ~ **m** *to make p.*, *to render feasible* ‖ es ~ m *to see one's way* (*to do*) ‖ es e–m ~ m *to make it p. for a p* (*to do*) ‖ wie soll man es ~ m? *how is it to be done?* ‖ (es ist) kein Z. mehr ~ *no possibility of doubt* **II.** **[adv]** **1.** **so .. wie** (nur irgend) ~ *as quickly as might be*, *as quick as quick can be* ‖ *be as quick as ever you can* ‖ *he is as unhappy as he can be* ‖ *they were polite as polite would be* ‖ *he is as decent as they come* ‖ *he is as poor as they make him* ‖ so gut es dir ~ ist *to the utmost of your power* **2.** **sobald** wie ~, **~st** bald, bald~st *as soon as* (*ever*) *p.*; *any time* ‖ sobald es mir (Ihnen) ~ ist *as soon as I can make it p.* (*at your earliest convenience*) **3.** **wo** (wenn) ~ *if p.*, *if anything* **III.** **sup** **[a & adv]** **1.** [adv] **~st** *if possible*, **~st** genau (viel) *as clearly* (*much*) *as p.*; ~st viele *the largest possible number of*; ~st dicker Draht *wire as thick as p.* ‖ ~st kl *minimum* (*loss*) ‖ *a list of as many ths as you can*; ~ bis zum .. ⟨a.⟩ *preferably by May 1st*; ~st nie *never if I can help it* | **auf** ~st ö. Art *in as economic a way as p.* ‖ **in** ~st kurzer Zeit *in the shortest p. time* ‖ in ~st wenigen Worten *in the fewest p. words* od *words p.* ‖ mit ~ster (~st gr) Eile *with all p. speed* **2.** **best~** adv (falsch: -st) *in the best p. way* | größt~e (kleinst~e) Abstände *greatest* (*smallest*) *p. distances* **IV.** s **das** ≃e: im Bereich des ~en *within the realm of possibilities* ‖ **sein** **~stes tun** *to do one's utmost* (.. *level* od *very best*), ⟨sl⟩ *damnedest*; *to be on one's mettle*, *to strain every nerve*; *to put one's shoulder to the wheel* ‖ sein ~stes getan h *to have shot one's bolt* **m·öglichenf·alls** adv *if* (*it be*) *possible*, etc **m·öglicherw·eise** adv *possibly*; *by any possibility* ‖ ~ fragen sie ihn *it is possible that they ask him* **M·öglichkeit** f ~/~en *possibility*, *opportunity* ‖ (Tunlichkeit) *practicability*, *feasibility* ‖ (möglicher Fall) *eventuality*; *contingency* (*of abdication*, *of his marriage*) ‖ *approach* (zu *to*) ‖ ⟨scient⟩ *potentiality*; ~ e–e Ware abzusetzen *a product's performance* ‖ entfernte ~ ⟨fam⟩ *long shot*; reichliche ~ zu *plenty* (*enough*) *rope to* | **~en** pl ⟨a.⟩ *ways and means* pl; ~(en) ⟨comp⟩ *feasibility* ‖ ~en des eigenen Handelns *courses of action*; ~en (der Versorgung) *the* (*logistical*) *capabilities and limitations* | ist es die ~! *well, I never!*, *you don't say so!* | **alle** ~en *all possible combinations* ‖ **besondere** ~ *privilege* ‖ dann bleibt die **einzige** ~ *then the only alternative would be* (*to do*) ‖ nicht die **entfernteste** ~ *not the remotest chance* ‖ ich sehe zunächst k–e ~ zuzustimmen *I don't see my way clear yet to say okay* ‖ wenn e–m nur die **leiseste** ~ gegeben wäre *given the ghost of a ch.* ‖ jene **letzte** ~ *that odd ch.* ‖ als letzte ~ *as a last resource*, *in the last resort*; nach der (aller)letzten ~ greifen *to grasp at straws* ‖ **unbegrenzte** ~en *unlimited poss.ies* | ~en nicht **ausnutzen** *to ignore poss.ies* ‖ e–m die ~ **bieten** *to give a p a chance* (zu *to*) ‖ es **besteht, gibt** die ~ *there is a ch.* (z tun *of doing*); hierbei besteht die ~ zu rekonstruieren *allowing the reconstruction should necessity arise* ‖ die ~ ist **gegeben** *it is just possible* ‖ ich **finde, habe, sehe** k–e ~ *I see, have no way*, *I cannot see any ch.* (*of doing*) ‖ *I don't see my way to do it*; die ~ h *to have a ch.* od *opp.*; *to stand a ch.*; *to run a good ch.* ‖ e–m die ~ **verschaffen** *to put a p in the way* (*of doing*) ‖ die letzte ~ **versuchen** *to try every possible means* | ⟨scient⟩ **in** der ~ *potentially* ‖ **nach** ~ *as far* (*much*) *as possible*, *in the best way p.*, *as much as one can* ‖ **von** s–n ~en guten Gebrauch m ⟨fam⟩ *to play one's cards well*

Moh·air, Moh·är m ~s/~e *mohair*

Mohi·kaner m ~s/~ *Mohican* ‖ ⟨fig⟩ der letzte ~ (Hunderter) *the last rose of summer* (*5 £-note*)

°**M·öhlfritze** m *soggy type* → Langweiler

M·ohn m ~(e)s/~e ⟨bot⟩ *poppy* **≃artig** a *papaverous* **~kapsel** f, **~kopf** m *poppy-head*

M·ohr **1.** m ~en/~en *Moor*, *negro*, *blackamoor* (f *negress*) ‖ ⟨fig⟩ e–n ~en weiß waschen wollen *to try to wash an Ethiopian white* **2.** m ~s/~e (Moiré) *watered silk* **M·ohren-** **~fürst** m *Moorish prince* **~gesicht** n *blackamoor's face* **~hirse** f *Caffre-corn*; *sorghum*, *-gho* **~kopf** m *Moor's head* **~land** n *Ethiopia* **~sklave** m *negro slave* **~tanz** m *morris-dance* **~tänzer** m *morris-dancer* **~wäsche** f ⟨fig⟩ *vindication* **m·ohrisch** a *Moorish*

M·öhre f ~/~n, **M·ohrrübe** f *carrot*

Moiré [mwa're:] m & n ~s/~s *moire*, *watered silk*, *tabby* | ~kleid [n] *tabby* (*gown*) **moir·ieren** vt [h] *to water*, *wave*, *tabby* **moir·iert** a *moiré* ‖ moirierter Stoff [m] *tabby*, *clouded stuff*, *moire*

Mok·adeteppich m ⟨engl⟩ *Wilton carpet*

mok·ant a *sneering*, *mocking* **mok·ieren,** sich ~ [h] (über [acc]) *to sneer* (*at*)

Mokass·in m ~s/~e (Indianerschuh), **~**(**schlange**) f ⟨zoo⟩ *moccasin*

M·okka **1.** n (arab. Hafenstadt) *Mocha* **2.** m ~(s)/~s *Mocha coffee*, *mocha*

M·ol n ~s/~s (Gramm-Molekül) *mol*(*e*); *gram molecule* | **≃·ar** a *molecular* (*volume*); *molar* (*concentration*)

Mol·ar m ~s/~e *molar*, *m. tooth*

Mol·asse f ~/~n ⟨geol⟩ *molasse* Fr

M·olch m ~(e)s/~e *newt*; ⟨fig⟩ *old lecher*

M·oldau f **1.** (Landschaft in Rumänien) *Moldavia* **2.** (Fluß) *Moldau* (in Böhmen)

M·ole f ~/~n *mole*, *pier*, *jetty*; *breakwater* | ~nkopf [m] *p.-head*

Molek·ül n ~s/~e *molecule* **Molekul·ar-** *mol*(*ecul*)*ar* (*biology*, *forces*, *heat*, *motion*, *physics*, *theory*, *weight*) **Molekul·ator** m ~s/~en ⟨mill⟩ *moleculator*, *-ku-*

***m·olk** 1. & 3. sg pret v melken **M·olken** f pl *whey*; heiße ~ mit Schuß *posset* **~käse** m *green cheese* **~kur** f *whey-cure* **~säure** f *acid of milk* **~trank** m *posset* **~wirtschaft** f *dairy* **Molker·ei** f ~/~en *dairy*(*-farm*[*ing*]); *creamery*; *milk plant* **~genossenschaft** f *dairy-farmers' association* **~wirtschaft** f *dairy industry* **m·olkig** a *wheyish*, *wheyey*

M·oll n ⟨mus⟩ *minor* (*key*) **~akkord** m *m. chord* **~tonart** f = ~ ‖ **~tonleiter** f *m. scale*

°**M·olle** f ~/~n **1.** = Mulde; *large* (Berlin) *beer-glass* ‖ mit ~n gießen *to rain cats and dogs* **2.** (Kopf) *pannikin* **M·öller** m ~s/~ ⟨met⟩ *burden*

m·olle(r)t [österr] (P), **m·ollig** a ⟨fam⟩ **1.** *soft* ‖ *plump and pleasant*, ⟨sl⟩ *crummy* (*little woman*); *plump and wellrounded* (*legs of a child*) **2.** *comfortable*, *snug* ‖ hier ist's hübsch ~ *it's nice and cosy here*

Moll·uske f ~/~n *mollusc*, *mollusk*

M·oloch m ~s/~e *Moloch*, *Juggernaut*

M·olotowcocktail m *Molotov cocktail*

M·olton m ~s/~s (Stoff) *baize*; *quilting*

Mol·ukken pl → Gewürzinseln

Molybd·än n ~(e)s/ ⟨chem⟩ *molybdenum*

Mom·ent ~(e)s/~e **I.** m *moment* → Augenblick ‖ ~ mal! *wait a bit!* °*half a mo*; jeden ~ *every little while*; im letzten ~ *in the nick of time*; *in the 11th hour*; *at the crucial*, *psychological*, *decisive moment*; im ~ der Dämmerung *at the crack of dawn* **II.** n ⟨tech⟩ *momentum* | (Antrieb) *impulse*, ⟨psych⟩ *impetus* ‖ ausschlaggebendes ~ *important point*, *decisive reason* ‖ ein entrinnbares ~ *an element of escape* ‖ ⟨theat⟩ erregendes ~ *inciting moment*, *initial impulse* | (Beweggrund) *motive* ‖ hauptsächliches ~ *main point* od *factor* ‖ retardierendes ~ *moment of last suspense*, → psychologisch ‖ wesentliches ~ *element* **~aufnahme** f ⟨phot⟩ *snapshot*, *instantaneous photo-*

graph; sehr kurze ~ *high-speed exposure* || e–e ~ m *to snapshot* (v e–m *a p*) **~kupplung** f ⟨mot⟩ *instantaneous clutch* **~stoß** m ⟨mech⟩ *momentum kick* **~verschluß** m *i. shutter* **moment·an** a *momentary, instantaneous* | ~ adv *instantly*; *right now, for the present*

M·onaco n (Fürstentum an der Riviera)

Mon·ade f ~/~n *monad* || ~nlehre [f] *m.ism*

Mon·arch m ~en/~en *monarch* (f *female sovereign*; *queen*) | **~·ie** f *monarchy* | **≈isch** a *monarchic(al)* | **~·ist** m *monarchist*

M·onat m ~(e)s/~e *month* || der ~ Mai *the m. of May* || am 15. dieses (*or* des laufenden) ~s *on the 15th of this m.*, ⟨com⟩ *on the 15th instant* || in 6 ~en (*with*)*in 6 m.s*, *this day 6 m.s* || vor anderthalb ~en *six weeks ago* || 500 Mark im ~ *500 marks per m.* od *m.ly* || ein 6 ~e altes Kind *a six--m.s-old baby* || die Frau ist im vierten ~ .. *is in the .., is four months gone with child* || er hat zwei ~e (Gefängnis) bek *he got a sentence of two m.s* | [in comp mst] *m., m.ly* **≈elang** a & adv *lasting for m.s* **~sabrechnung** f *m. end total* **~sabschluß** m ⟨com⟩ *m.ly balance* **~saufstellung** f, **~sbericht** m *m.ly report* od *statement* **~sbinde** f *sanitary towel* **~sbuch** n *m.ly book*; *ledger* **~sblutung** f, **~sfluß** m ⟨med⟩ *menses* pl, *m.ly courses* pl, *menstruation* **~sfrist** f *term* od *space of a m.* || binnen ~ *within a m.* **~sgeld** n *m.ly wages* pl, *m.ly allowance* od *pay* **~skarte** f *m.ly season-ticket* **~srate** f *m.ly instalment, sum falling due every m.* | erste **~sregel** f *menarche* **~srose** f *m.ly rose* **~sschrift** f *m.ly* (*journal* od *magazine*); ~en [pl] *m.lies* || Halb≈ *fortnightly review* || Drei≈ *quarterly* **~stag** m *day of the m., date* **~stampon** n *tampax*; *sanitary tampon* **~suhr** f *clock which goes for a m.* **~s-swechsel** m (*student's*) *m.ly allowance* **≈sweise** adv *by the m., m.ly* **~szyklus** m ⟨biol⟩ *menstrual cycle* .. **m·onatig** a drei~ etc *three-m.s'* (*tour, calf*); (*a child*) *of 3 m.s* **m·onatlich** **1.** a *monthly* (*number, instalments*) | adv *every* (od *by the*) *month* **2.** drei~ *quarterly* **3.** **das ≈e** = Monatsfluß

M·önch m ~(e)s/~e **1.** *monk, friar* **2.** *ridge* od *hip tile* **3.** ⟨typ⟩ *monk* **4.** ⟨arch⟩ (e–r Wendeltreppe) *spindle* || (e–s Fensters) *mullion* | **≈isch** a *monkish, monastic* **M·önchs- ~bogen** m ⟨typ⟩ *friar, blank sheet* **~geist** m *monastic spirit* **~grasmücke** f ⟨orn⟩ *blackcap* **~kappe** f *monk's hood, cowl* **~-kloster** n *monastery* **~kolben** m ⟨tech⟩ *plunger* **~-kutte** f *frock* **~leben** n *m.c life* **~orden** m *religious* od *m.c order* **~schrift** f ⟨typ⟩ *black-letter* **~wesen** n *m.cism* **~zelle** f *monk's cell* **M·önchtum** n ~(e)s/ *monachism, monkhood*

M·ond m ~(e)s/~e *moon* (a. ⟨poet⟩ = Monat) || ~e *satellites* (*of Jupiter*) || halber ~ *crescent* || voller ~ *full m.* || zunehmender (abnehmender) ~ *increase* (*wane*) *of the m.* || der ~ nimmt zu (ab) [scheint] *the m. is waxing* (*waning*) [*shining*] || Rückseite [f] des ~es *far side of the moon* || Schuß [m] nach dem ~e ⟨a–n⟩ *moon shot* || der ~ schien *there was a m.*; .. hell *the m. shone with a clear lustre* || v ~e beschienen *m.lit* || der ~ schwebt .. *rides* (*between the trees*) || der Mann im ~e *the man in the m.* || den ~ betreffend ⟨scient⟩ *lunar* || unter dem ~e ⟨scient⟩ *sublunary* | ⟨fig⟩ hinter dem ~e *behind the times* || auf dem ~e leben *to be up in the air, to be m.struck* || m–e Uhr geht nach dem ~e ⟨sl⟩ *my watch is all to hell, goes on shirt-buttons* | ⟨übtr fort⟩ Halber ~ *ravelin* | ⟨fig⟩ → Glatze **~aufgang** m *m.rise* **~bahn** f *m.'s orbit* **~beben** n *moonquake* **≈beglänzt, ≈beschienen** a *m.lit* (*hall*) **~beschreibung** f *selenography* **~bewohner** m *lunarian* **~fähre** f *lunar module* (*LM*) **~fahrer** m *lunarnaut* **≈fernster Punkt** ⟨a–n⟩ *apolune* **~finsternis** f *eclipse of the m., lunar eclipse* **~flecken** m *spot on the m., macula* **≈förmig** a *m.-shaped* || ⟨bot⟩ *lunulate* **~forscher** m *selenologist* **~gebirge** n ⟨astr⟩ *Lunar Mountains* **~gesicht** n *m.-face* **≈hell** a *m.lit* **~jahr** n *lunar year* **~kalb** n *m.calf*; ⟨med⟩ *false conception* **~-Landefahrzeug** n *Lunar Excursion Module* (*LEM*) **~-Landegerät** n *moon landing gear* **~-Landeunternehmen** n *moon landing enterprise* **~landschaft** f *m.lit landscape* || ⟨a–n⟩ *moonscape* **~landung** f *touch-down on the m.* **~licht** n *m.light* **~meer** n *lunar sea* **≈nächster Punkt** ⟨a–n⟩ *perilune* **~nacht** f *m.lit night* **~-oberfläche** f *luna surface, surface of the moon* **~rakete** f (*circum*)*lunar rocket* **~rückseite** f *far side of the m.* **~scheibe** f *disk of the m.* **~schein** m *m.shine, m.light* || ⟨fam⟩ *bald-headedness* || er hat e–n mächtigen ~ *he is* (*as*) *bald as a badger* || es war (kein) ~ *there was a m.* (*no m.*) || bei ~ *in the m.light* || er kann mir im ~ begegnen *he can go and be hanged*; ⟨Am⟩ .. *go jump in the lake* **~sichel** f *crescent* **~sonde** f (Rakete) ⟨Am⟩ *Ranger, Surveyor*; *Lunar orbiter*; ⟨Russ⟩ *Lunik* **~stein** m ⟨min⟩ *m.stone* **~sucht** f ⟨med⟩ *m.--madness, somnambulism* **≈süchtig** a *m.struck* **~uhr** f *lunar dial* **~umkreisungskapsel** f ⟨a–n⟩ *Lunar Orbiter* **~umlaufbahn** f ⟨a–n⟩ *circular path around the m.* **~viertel** n *quarter* (*of the m.*) || **~-wechsel** m *change of the m.* || es ist ~ *the m. changes*

Mondam·in ® n ~s/~e ⟨Am⟩ *corn-flour*

mond·än a *smart, fashionable*; *super-elegant*

°**Mon·eten** pl ⟨fam⟩ (Geld) *chink, tin, L.S.D.* (f *£ s d*) || ⟨sl⟩ *dough*; *dibs* pl, ⟨Am sl⟩, *spondulicks, shekels* pl || Haufen ~ *big dough*

Mong·ole m, **Mong·olin** f *Mongol*(*ian*), *Mogul*

Mongol·ei f *Mongolia* **mong·olisch** a *Mongol, Mongolian, Mongolic, Mogul*

Mon·ier- ~bau m *Monier's building* **~eisen** n *reinforcement iron* **~gewölbe** n *M.'s arch* od *vault* **~platte** f *M. slab*

mon·ieren vt [h] *to censure, criticize* **M·onitum** n ~s/–ta *admonition* || (Verweis) *censure*

Mono- ~gam·ie f ~/ *monogamy* **≈g·amisch** a *monogamous* **~gr·amm** n ~(e)s/~e *monogram* **~graph·ie** f ~/~n *monograph, treatise* **·~kel** n ~s/~ *monocle,* (*single*) *eyeglass* || einklemmen: *he screwed in his m.* | ~linse [f] *monocular lens, watchmaker's eyeglass* **~k·ini** m = Bikini ohne (Oberteil) **~l·ith** m ~s/~e ⟨praeh⟩ *standing stone*; *monolith* **~l·og** m ~(e)s/~e *monologue, soliloquy* **≈logis·ieren** vi [h] *to soliloquize* **~-man·ie** f ~/~n *monomania* **~photo-Filmsatz** m *mono-photo type-setting* **~p·ol** n ~(e)s/~e *monopoly* (auf *of*, ⟨Am⟩ *on*) | ~abgaben [f pl] *m. taxes*; ~artikel [m] *proprietary article* **≈polis·ieren** vt [h] *to monopolize* || **-is·ierung** f ~/~en *monopolization* || **-·ist** m ~en/~en *monopolist* **~the·ismus** m ~/ *monotheism* **≈t·on** a *in the same key*; *monotonous*; *humdrum* || *grey*; *drab* (*colours*) **~ton·ie** f ~/~n *monotony*

M·onstr- ~·anz f ~/~en ⟨ec⟩ *monstrance, pyx* **~·ös** a *monstrous* **~osit·ät** f ~/~en *monstrosity, enormity* **·~um** n ~s/–ra *monster*

Mons·un m ~(e)s/~e (½jährig. Wind) *monsoon*; in e–n ~ geraten *to strike a m.*

M·ontag m ~(e)s/~e *Monday* || blauer ~ *holiday* od *idle Monday* || am ~ *on M.*, ⟨Am⟩ *M.* || (des) ~s *every M., on M.s* || ~ abend *M. evening* **~spost** f *M.'s mail* **~szeitung** f *M. journal*

Mont·age f ~/~n = Montierung || ⟨film⟩ *sequence*; *editing* || ⟨tech⟩ *assembly* | fahrbares ~gestell [n] *dolly*; ~halle [f] *fitting shop, ass. hall*, ⟨aero⟩ *ass. hangar*; ~haus [n] *pre-fab*; ~straße [f] *ass.-line*; ~teile [pl] *assemblies*; ~-zubehör [n] *hardware*; **Mont·ana** f (nordwestlicher Staat der U.S.A.) **Mont·an- ~aktien** f pl *mining-shares* pl **~industrie** f *mining industry* **~-union** f *European Coal and Steel Community* **~-wachs** n *montan wax* **Mont·eur** [mɔn'tøːr] m ~s/~e *mounter, fitter* || ⟨aero⟩ → Bordwart; Leitwerk≈ *rigger* | ~anzug [m] *combination, overall*; ~hebel [m] ⟨mot⟩ *tire lever* **Mont·iereisen** n ⟨mot⟩ *tire lever* **mont·ieren** vt [h] ⟨tech⟩ *to assemble*; *fasten*; *to fit* (*up*), *to fix* (*a tire*)

|| *to erect (an engine)* || ⟨aero⟩ *to rig* || (Geschütze) *to mount* **Mont·ierung** f ~/~en **1.** ⟨tech⟩ *assembly; fitting (up); erection, adjusting* || *mounting* || ⟨aero⟩ *rigging* || ⟨arts⟩ *mount* **2.** ⟨mil⟩ (a. **Mont·ur** f) *regimentals* pl, *uniform* || *equipment* || (der Dienerschaft) *livery*

Montbl·anc [mɔ̃'blɑ̃] m *Mont Blanc*

Mont Cen·is [–i] m (Alpenberg)

Montenegr·iner m, **~in, montenegr·inisch** a *Montenegrine* **Monten·egro** n (südslaw. Bundesstaat)

M·onte R·osa m (Alpenberg)

Montevid·eo n (Hauptstadt v Uruguay)

Montre·al n (Stadt in Kanada)

Monum·ent n ~(e)s/~e *monument* **monument·al** a *monumental (work, structure,* etc.)

M·oor n ~(e)s/~e *fen, bog, swamp* || (Heideland) *wold, moor* **~bad** n *m.bath, peatbath* **~boden** m *marshy* od *fenny soil* **~bruch** [–u:–] m & n *moss-hag* **~erde** f *bog-earth, moor-earth* **~grund** m *moorland* **~hahn** m ⟨orn⟩ *gorcock* **~huhn** n ⟨orn⟩ *moor-fowl; grouse* **~land** n *moor(land), marshy district* **~loch** n *boghole* **~schneehuhn** n *willow grouse* **~schnepfe** f ⟨orn⟩ *jack snipe* **~see** m *boglake* **~wasser** n *marshy* od *muddy water* **m·oorig** a *marshy, boggy* || *moory*

M·oos n ~es/~e *moss* || (irisches) *carrageen* || Island*⌅* *Iceland m.* || Torf*⌅*, Sumpf*⌅* *sphagnum* | °⟨fig⟩ (Geld) *brass, dust;* ⟨Am⟩ *oof, kale* **~achat** m ⟨minr⟩ *m.-agate* **~beere** f *cranberry; fenberry* **⌅bewachsen** a *m.-grown, m.y* **~kapsel** f *pyxidium* **~kunde** f *muscology* **~rose** f *m.-rose* **~tierchen** n pl *polyzoa* pl **m·oosig** a *m.y, m.-grown*

M·oped n ~s/~s *motor-assisted bicycle,* ⟨fam⟩ *auto-bike*

M·ops m ~es/⌅e *pug(-dog)* | ⟨fig⟩ *blockhead* || *grumbler* | ~gesicht [n] *pug-face* °**m·opsen I.** vt [h] *to pilfer* || das wird ihn ~ *that will upset him* **II. sich** ~ *to feel dull, to be bored to death* **m·opsig** a *like a pug, pug-nosed*

M·ora f ~/–ren Gr ⟨pros⟩ *mora,* → d.

Moradab·ad n (vorderind. Bezirk)

Mor·al f ~/ *morals* pl || doppelte ~ *double-faced m.s* || (Sittlichkeit) *m.ity* || ⟨mil⟩ *m.e* || (e–r Fabel) *m.* (v der Geschicht' *of the matter*) | ⌅analoges Verhalten ⟨eth⟩ *behavioural analogies to morality;* ~predigt [f] *(m.) lecture* || ⟨sl⟩ *pep talk* | ⟨fig⟩ e–m e–e ~ halten *to read a p a homily* °**Moral·in** n ~s/ ⟨nazi⟩ *hypocrisy* || **⌅sauer** a *hypocritical* **mor·alisch** a *moral* || ~e Betrachtungen anstellen *to m.ize;* ~e Entgleisungen *abominable ethics;* ~er Grundsatz *moral;* ~e Wirkung *moral* od *demoralizing effect;* ⟨mil⟩ *effect on morale* || **⌅e(r)** m [ell] e–n **⌅en** bek, h *to feel m. twinges* **moralis·ieren** vi [h] *to m.ize* **Moral·ist** m ~en/~en *m.ist* **Moralit·ät** f ~/ *m.ity* || ⟨theat⟩ ~en [pl] *m.ities*

Mor·äne f ~/~n ⟨geol⟩ *moraine* || End-, Grund-, Innen-, Mittel-, Ober-, Seiten-, Stirn⌅ *terminal, ground, englacial, medial, upper, lateral, frontal m.* **~-nschutt** m *till*

Mor·ast m ~es/~e & ⌅e *morass, bog, fen, marsh, swamp, slough* || (Schmutz) *mud, mire* || im ~e stecken bleiben *to stick in the mud* ⟨a. fig⟩ || ⟨fig⟩ im ~e waten *to wallow in the mire* **~loch** n *slough, puddle* **mor·astig** a *boggy, marshy* || (schmutzig) *muddy, miry*

Morat·orium n ~s/–rien ⟨pol⟩ *moratorium* || ⟨jur⟩ *(letter of) respite*

morb·id(e) a *morbid (mind, ideas), sick; given to m. feelings; sick (jokes)* **Morbidit·ät** f ~/ *m.ity;* Maßzahlen der ~ ⟨demog⟩ *m.ity rates*

M·orchel f ~/~n ⟨bot⟩ *morel (edible fungus)*

M·ord m ~(e)s/~e (vorsätzlich) *murder, assassination* ([vor 1943] vorbedachte Tötung e–s Menschen) ⟨m. m.⟩ *murder in the 1st degree;* ([seit 1943] e–e Art qualifizierter Totschlag [§ 211f. StGB]) → Totschlag || e–n ~ begehen *to commit m.* || ~ u Brand schreien *to yell tremendously* || ~ brüten *to meditate m.* || e–n z ~ anstiften *to instigate a p to commit m.* | ⟨fig⟩ es wird ~ u Totschlag geben *it will end in bloodshed (and death)* || ~ u Totschlag! *blood and thunder* || das ist ja (der reinste) ~! *that's an awful business (that is nothing better than m.)* **~anfall** m *m.ous assault* **~anschlag** m *m.ous plot* **~brenner** m *incendiary, bloody villain,* ⟨Am⟩ *bad man* **~brenner·ei** f *incendiarism* **⌅brennerisch** a *incendiary* **~bube** m *m.er, assassin* **~elem·ent**! intj *blood and thunder* **~geschichte** f *tale of m.* **~geschrei** n *cry of m.* (→ –sgeschrei) **~gesell(e)** m *cutthroat* (vgl ~bube) **~gewehr** n *m.ous weapon* **~gier** f *bloodthirstiness* **⌅gierig** a = ~lustig **~lust** f *m.ous lust, thirst for blood; homicidal insanity* **⌅lustig** a *bloodthirsty, sanguinary* **~nacht** f *night of (a) m.* **~stahl** m *m.ous sword* od *dagger* **~sucht** f = ~lust **~tat** f *m.(ous deed)* **~versuch** m *m.ous attempt* || e–n ~ auf jdm m *to make an attempt upon a p's life* **~waffe** f = ~gewehr **~wanze** f ⟨ent⟩ *assassin-bug* **~wespe** f ⟨ent⟩ = Grabwespe **~wut** f *m.ous rage* **m·orden** vt/i [h] *to murder* | ⌅ n ~s/ *murdering* || ein fürchterliches ~ *terrible butchery* **M·örder** m ~s/~ *murderer* (f *murderess*); *assassin* (a. ⟨fig⟩ z. B. Bazillus) || ⟨zoo⟩ = Schwertwal) || gedungener ~ *bravo, hired m.* || ⟨fig⟩ *destroyer* **~grube** f *den of cutthroats* || aus s–m Herzen k–e ~ m *to be very outspoken* **m·örderisch** a *murderous, slaughterous* || *sanguinary (battle)* || (Klima etc) *deadly* | ⟨fig⟩ *cutthroat (prices);* ~es Tempo *killing pace;* ~e Wut *k.g rage; dreadful, terrible* | adv ⟨fam⟩ *excessively, confoundedly* || ~ fluchen *to swear like a trooper* **m·örderlich** a *murderous, violent* || ⟨fam⟩ *confounded, terrible, cruel* || ⟨sl⟩ *enormous, fearful* || e–n ~ verhauen *to beat a p within an inch of his life* **m·ordio;** ~ schreien *to cry murder* °**M·ords-** *wizard* [attr]; ⟨Am sl⟩ *big-time* [attr] (blühend) *booming* || *hell of a (mess)* || *the father of a (hiding)* **~·angeber** m *heavy swell* **~·angst** f *mortal fear* **~arbeit** f ⟨fam⟩ *man-sized job* **~b·ammel** m ⟨sl⟩ *blue fear* od ⟨sl⟩ *funk* || e–n ~ h *to be in a b. f.* (vor *about*) **~d·ampf** = ~bammel **~d·ing** n ⟨sl⟩ *smatterer, scorcher, whopper, smasher, screamer;* ⟨Am⟩ *whaler* **~durch-e-a** n *devil of a mess* **~·eile** f *mortal hurry* **⌅eingebildet** a *up on o.s.* ⟨sl⟩ **~erfolg** m *smashing success* **~g·audi(um)** n *loud rejoicing* **~gesch·ichte** f *tall* od *cock-and-bull story* **~geschr·ei** n *loud shouting* || ein ~ erheben *to raise a terrible outcry* **~glück** n *powerful good luck* **⌅groß** a *walloping great; whacking* **~k·atzenjammer** m *a hang-over that will make history* **~k·erl** m *devil of a fellow; great lad;* ⟨fam⟩ *topper, trump, stunner, crackerjack;* ⟨Am fam⟩ *jim-dandy* || ⟨sl⟩ *whacker* **~könner** m ⟨univ sl⟩ *shark* **~lärm** m; e–n ~ m ⟨Am sl⟩ *to raise the roof* **~lüge** f *corker, cracker, twister* **⌅m·äßig** a *awful, enormous, man-sized (work)* | adv *awfully, enormously, cruelly, murderously (hard work)* **~propag·anda** f ⟨Am fam⟩ *ballyhoo* **~r·ausch** m; e–n ~ h *to be far from sober, to be dead drunk* **~sch·iß** m: e–n ~ h *to be in a blue funk* (vor *about*) **~schnupfen** m *streaming cold* **~schreck** m ⟨fam⟩ *turn* **~schwein** n *bread buttered on both sides* **~skand·al** m *a jolly old row* **~sp·aß** m *some fun* **~spekt·akel** m *pandemonium, terrific row, dreadful noise,* ⟨fam⟩ *hullabaloo* **~t·empo** n; im ~ *at a rattling* od *terrific pace* od *speed* **~·ulk** m *flare-up; side-splitter* °**⌅trum** a [österr] = –mäßig **~viel** [a] halten v *to think no small beer of* **~zigarre** f ⟨fig mil fam⟩ (strenger Verweis) *rocket*

Mor·ea n ⟨Gr⟩ (Halbinsel); auf ~ *in the Morea*

Mor·elle f ~/~n ⟨bot⟩ *morello (cherry)*

M·ores; jdn ~ lehren *to teach a p manners*

morgan·atisch a ⟨jur⟩ *morganatic, left-handed*

M·orgen I. m ~s/~ **A. 1.** *morning* (⟨poet & fig⟩ *morn*) || ⟨fig⟩ *dawn* **2.** (Osten) *east;* gegen ~ *towards the e.* **3.** (Land, 25,53 Ar) *acre, rod* || 20 ~

Land *20 acres of land* **B.** anbrechender ~ *dawn, day-break, dawn of day* || heiterer ~ *bright morning* || taufrischer ~ *m. bathed in* (od *fresh with*) *dew* **C.** guten ~! ⟨fam⟩ ('n) ~! (*good*) *m.*! || e–n schönen guten ~! ⟨Ir⟩ *the top of the m.* (*to you*) || e–m e–n guten ~ wünschen *to bid a p a good m.* **D.** alle *or* jeden ~ *every m.* || **des** ~s *in the m.* || des ~s früh *early in the m.* || diesen ~ *this m.* || e–s schönen ~s *one* od *some fine m.* || heute, (am) Dienstag ~ *this, Tuesday m.* || (vor)gestern ~ *yesterday m.* (*the m. of the day before y.*) | **(am)** nächsten ~ *the next* od *following m.* || am (frühen) *or* (früh) am ~ (*early*) *in the m.* || am ~ des 5. Mai *on the m. of May 5th* || an e–m schönen ~ *on a b. m.* || **gegen** ~ *towards* (*the*) *m.* || bis **in** den hellen ~ hinein *right through to the bright m.* || **mit** anbrechendem ~ *at break of day* || **vom** ~ bis zum Abend *from m. till evening* **E.** der ~ **dämmert,** bricht an *the m. dawns* || den ~ erwarten *to look forward to day-break* || es **ist** schon (heller) ~ *it is* (*broad*) *daylight* || den ~ verschlafen *to sleep away the m.* || die Nacht weicht dem ~ *the n. retires before the day* || es **wird** ~ *the day is breaking, day-break is near* **F.** ⟨fig⟩ *the morn of life, of freedom* || sie sieht aus wie der taufrische ~ *she looks as fresh as a daisy* **II. m·orgen** adv *to-morrow* || ~ abend, früh, mittag *to-morrow evening, morning, noon* || morgen über (in) 8, 14 Tage(n) *to-morrow week, fortnight* || ⟨fig⟩ der Stil v ~ *the style of the future* | ~ verreisen wir *to-m. we are going away* || komm ~ wieder *come again to-m.* || jdn auf ~ vertrösten *to hold out a p's hopes for the next day* || ⟨iron⟩ ~! = Kuchen! || ~ ist auch ein Tag *that's enough for one day* || „~, ~, nur nicht heute" sagen alle faulen Leute *there is no time than the present* **III. das Morgen** *the coming day*; *the morrow* ⟨a. bib⟩; *the future* **~andacht** f *morning-prayers* **~anzug** m *m.-dress, undress* **~ausgabe** f (Zeitung) *m.-edition* **~besuch** m *m. call* **~blatt** n *m. paper* **~dämmerung** f *day-break, dawn, m. twilight*; in der ~ *in the early twilight* || ⟨fig⟩ *dim beginning* **~gabe** f *dowry* | *bridegroom's gift to his bride the m. after their marriage* **~gebet** n *m. prayer* **~gesang** m *m. song* **~glocke** f *m.-bell* **~grauen** n; beim ~ *at the break of day* **~gymnastik** f *setting-up exercises* pl (m *to take* ..) **~haube** f *boudoir-cap* **~himmel** m *eastern sky* **~kleid** n *morning-gown* **~land** n *the East, Orient*; die 3 Weisen aus dem ~e *the three Magi* **~länder** m *Oriental* **≈ländisch** a *oriental, eastern* **~licht** n *m.-light* **~lied** n *m. hymn* **~luft** f *m. air, m. breeze* **~nebel** m *early haze* **~post** f *first mail* **~punkt** m *due east* **~rock** m *dressing-gown*; ⟨Am⟩ *bathrobe* **~rot** n, **~röte** f *aurora, rosy dawn* || ⟨fig⟩ *dawn, prime* **~schlaf** m *m.-sleep* **≈schön** a *beautiful as the early day* **~segen** m *m. prayers* pl **~seite** f *east*(*ern*) *side* **~sonne** f *m.-sun* **~spaziergang** m *m.-walk* **~ständchen** n *m. music* **~stern** m *m. star, day-star* || (Waffe) *spiked club*; *flail* **~strahl** m *ray of the m.-sun* **~stunde** f *m. hour* || in früher ~ *in the early m.* || in den frühen ~n *in the small hours* (*of May 5th*) || ~ hat Gold im Munde (*the*) *early bird catches the worm* **~tau** m *dew* **~traum** m *m. dream* **~trunk** m *m. draught* **~veranstaltung** f *morning performance* **~wache** f *watch* **≈wärts** adv *eastward* **~wind** m *m. breeze* | *east wind* **~zeit** f *m.-hours* pl **~zeitung** f = ~blatt **m·orgend** a *of to-morrow* || der ~e Tag *to-m.* **m·orgenlich** a *matutinal* **m·orgens** adv *in the morning* | *every m.* || ~ früh *early in the m.* || um 1 Uhr ~ *at one in the m.* || v ~ bis abends *from m. till night* **m·orgig** a *of to-morrow, to-m.'s* || der ~e Tag *to-m.*

Mor·iske m (= Maure) *Moor* | ~ntanz [m] *morris dance*

Morm·one m ~n/~n *Latter-Day Saint, Mormon*

mor·os a *morose* **≈it·ät** f ~/ *m.ness*

Morphin·ist m ~en/~en *morphia-eater* od *-addict* **M·orphium** n ~(s)/ *morphia, morphine* | ~spritze [f] *m. injection*; ~sucht [f] *m. habit*

Morpholog·ie f ~/ *morphology*

m·orsch a *rotten* (*timber*) || *dilapidated, shaky* (*edifice*) || ⟨pol⟩ *decayed* (*state*) || *pulpy* (*apple*) || (brüchig) *brittle* || *carious* (*tooth*) | ⟨fig⟩ *mouldy, stale, old-fashioned* | ~ w *to rot, decay* | **≈heit** f ~/ *brittleness* || *rottenness* ⟨a. fig⟩

M·orse- ~alphabet n *Morse code* **~apparat** m *M. telegraph* **~taste** f *M. key* **~zeichen** n pl *M.* od *dot-and-dash signals* od *symbols*

M·örser m ~s/~ ⟨a. mil⟩ *mortar*; ⟨artill⟩ *heavy howitzer* **~batterie** f *m.-battery* **~keule** f *pestle* **~lafette** f *m.-carriage*

Mortalit·ät f ~/ *mortality*

M·örtel m ~s/~ *mortar* || ~ anmachen *to mix up m.* || mit ~ bewerfen *to rough-cast* **~kelle** f *trowel* **~maschine** f *mixer* **~trog** m *hod*

Mosa·ik f ~/~en *or* n ~s/~e *mosaic*(*-work*) || in ~ gearbeitet *tessellated* **~arbeit** f *inlaid work* **≈förmig** *tessellated,* ~ zus–setzen *to tessellate* **~fußboden** m *tessellated pavement*

mos·aisch a *Mosaic* (*Law, in Pentateuch*)

Mosamb·ik n (in Ost-Afrika) *Mozambique*

Mosch·ee f ~/~n *mosque* [–sk] | ~kanzel [f] *mimbar*; ~turm [m] *minaret*

M·oschus m ~/ *musk* **~beutel** m *m.-bag* **~blume** f *sweet sultan* **~bock** m ⟨ent⟩ *m.-beetle* **~drüse** f *m.-gland* **~geruch** m *scent of m.* **~kraut** n ⟨bot⟩ *moschatel* **~ratte** f *musk-rat* **~rose** f *m.-rose* **~tier** n *m.-deer* **~ziege** f *m.-goat*

°**M·öse** f ⟨sex vulg⟩ *fanny, cat* → Döschen

M·osel 1. f (Rhein-Nebenfluß) **2.** m ~s/ *Moselle* || e–e Fl. ~ a *bottle of M.*

M·oses m *Moses* || ~ u die Propheten h ⟨fam⟩ *to have the wherewithal* od *tin* || die 5 Bücher Mosis *or* Mose [gen] *the Pentateuch* || ⟨arts⟩ ~ schlägt Wasser aus dem Felsen *M. Striking the Rock*

M·oskau n *Moscow* **M·oskauer** m, **~in** f *Muscovite* **m·oskauisch** a *Muscovite*

Mosk·ito m ~s/~s *mosquito* **~stich** m *m.-bite*

Moskov·iter(in f) m, **M·oskauer(in)** *Muscovite*

Moskw·a f ⟨Russ⟩ (Fluß) *Moskva*

M·oslem m ~s/~s *moslem, muslim*; ⟨a.⟩ *Moslem, Mussulman* [pl *M.s*]

M·ost m ~es/~e *must, stum,* (*new wine*) || Apfel≈ *cider* || Birn≈ *perry* || wissen wo Barthel den ~ holt ⟨fam⟩ *to know the ropes* **~kelter** f *wine-* (*cider-*)*press* **m·osten** vt/i [h] *to press the grapes*, etc

M·ostrich m ~(e)s/~e *mustard*; ⟨mst⟩ Senf

Mos·ul n (Land & Stadt in Mesopotamien)

Mot·el n ~s/~s *motel*, ⟨Am a.⟩ *motor court*; (im Stadtinneren) *motor inn*

Mot·ette f ~/~n ⟨ec mus⟩ *motet*

Mot·iv n ~(e)s/~e *motive* || ⟨arts & tail⟩ *motif* Fr, ⟨mus⟩ *theme*, ⟨paint & phot⟩ *subject*; ~ in schneller Bewegung *high-speed action s.*; das ~ vom Hintergrund abheben *to make the s. stand out from* .. | ~sucher [m] ⟨phot⟩ *s. finder* | edle ~e *noble impulses* od *promptings* || durch persönliche ~e bestimmt *personally motivated* **motiv·ieren** vt [h] *to state the motive of, to justify, to account for* || (begründen) *to bring forward arguments in support* (*of a resolution*) **Motiv·ierung** f, mit der ~, daß .. *on the plea that* .. **M·otor** [⟨vulg⟩ Mot·or] m ~s/Mot·oren *motor* ⟨a. fig⟩, *engine* | Diesel≈ *Diesel engine* || ~ mit mehreren Drehzahlstufen *multiple speed* (⟨Am⟩ *multispeed*) *m.* || Explosions≈ *internal explosion e.* || Flugzeug≈ *aero-m.* || geschlossener ~ *protected m.* || Mehrzylinder≈ *multicylinder m.* || Reihen≈ *engine with cylinders in line* || Stern≈ *radial e.* | den ~ ab-, anstellen *to stop, start the m.* || laufender ~ *revving engine* || nachsehen *to check over* || der ~ springt an .. *picks up* || mit vollaufendem ~ *with full throttle*, ⟨Am⟩ *opened up*; den ~ auf Touren bringen *to rev up*, .. langsamer laufen l *to rev down* **∼anlasser** m *engine-starter* **∼antrieb** m *e. drive*; mit ∼ *m.-* od *power-driven* (*vehicle*) **∼boot** n *m.-boat* **∼defekt** m *e.-trouble* **∼droschke** f *m. cab* **∼fahrrad** n *motor-assisted bicycle*; → Moped **∼flugzeug** n *power plane* **∼harke** f *rake dozer* **∼haube** f *e.-bonnet*, ⟨aero⟩ *e. cowl* **∼leistung** f *rating of an e.* **∼locher** m ⟨comp⟩ *automatic key punch* **∼lochprüfer** m *aut. verifier* **∼mäher** m *m.-scythe* **∼(omni)bus** m *m.* (*omni*)*bus* **∼panne** f *e.-trouble* **∼pflug** m *tractor-plough* **∼rad** n *m.-*(*bi*)*cycle* ‖ ∼ fahren *to ride a m.-c.* **∼radbrille** f *m.-cycling goggles* **∼radfahrer** m *motor cyclist* **∼radhaube** f *m.-cyclist's helmet* **∼radhindernisrennen** n *scramble* **∼raum** m *e. compartment* **∼regler** m ⟨aero⟩ *e. governor* **∼rennboot** n *racing m.-b.* **∼rettungsboot** n *m. life-b.* **∼roller** m *m. scooter* **∼säge** f *power saw* **∼schalter** m *switch for the m.* **∼schlepper** m *m.-tractor* **∼schlitten** m *snowmobile* **∼spritze** f *fire-e.* **∼staffel** f ⟨bes mil⟩ *m.*(*-caval*)*cade* **∼störung** f *e. failure* od *trouble* **∼taste** f ⟨comp⟩ *m. bar* **∼unfall** m *m. accident* **∼wagen** m *m.-car* ‖ im ∼ fahren *to* (*go in a*) *m.* **∼wechsel** m *e. replacement* **∼wesen** n *motoring* **∼winde** f *m. winch* **∼zylinder** m *cylinder of the e.* **M·otoren- ∼anlage** f *power-plant* **∼gondel** f ⟨aero⟩ *p.-gondola*, ⟨Am⟩ *p. car* **∼haus** n *p.-house* **∼lärm** m ⟨bes aero⟩ *power roar* **∼raum** m *engine-room* **∼schaden** m *e. failure* .. **mot·orig** a, dr·ei∼ *triple-engined* **mot·orisch** a *motorial, kinetic* ‖ ⟨anat⟩ *motor*(*y*) ‖ ∼e Kräfte *motor power* **motoris·ieren** vt [h] *to motorize* (*m.ed units*); –rte Truppe *mechanized force* **Motoris·ierung** f ∼/∼en ⟨mil⟩ *mechanization*

M·otte f ∼/∼n *moth* ‖ B·aum∼̈ → Glucke ‖ Gespinst∼̈ *ermine m.* ‖ etc → *moth* ‖ Kleider∼̈ (*clothes-*)*m.* | voll ∼n *full of moth* ‖ v ∼n zerfressen *m.-eaten* | ⟨fig⟩ ∼n *funny ideas* ‖ du kriegst die ∼n! *my eye! what* od *why the dickens!* ‖ das ist um die ∼n zu kriegen *it's enough to give one the hump!* | kesse ∼ (Mädchen) ⟨sl⟩ *hot number* **∼̈necht** a *moth resistant* (*carpet, cloth, fabric*) **∼nfraß** m *m. damage* **∼nkraut** n ⟨bot⟩ → Hahnensporn **∼nkugel** f *m.-ball* **∼nsack** m (f Kleider) *garment* od *wardrobe* od *foldable plastic bag* **∼npulver** n *moth-repellent*

M·otto n ∼(s)/∼s *motto, device* ‖ *epigraph*

Mount ·Everest m (Himalayagipfel)

mouss·ieren [mus–] vi [h] *to effervesce, sparkle, bubble* ‖ ∼d *sparkling* (*wine*) ‖ *effervescent* (*spring*)

M·öwe f ∼/∼n ⟨orn⟩ → (*sea-*)*gull* od *-mew*, → *skua*

M·ozartisch a *Mozartian* (*divertimento*)

Moz·ette f ∼/–en ⟨R C⟩ (Cape mit Kapuze) *mozetta*

M·uck m ∼s/∼e, **M·ucks** m –ses/–se *faint noise* ‖ k–n ∼ tun *not to utter a sound* ‖ °k–n ∼ h *to have no spunk* ‖ k–n ∼ mehr! *not another word!*

M·ucke f ∼/∼n *whim, caprice* (vgl folg. [Ende]) ‖ pl *pranks* pl ‖ (S) s–e ∼n h *to be a bit tricky* ‖ (T) *to be vicious* ‖ e–m die ∼n vertreiben *to cure a p of his whims* (*an animal of its caprices*)

M·ücke f ∼/∼n → *gnat, midge* ‖ ⟨dial⟩ → *fly* ‖ Fieber∼̈ *anopheles* L ‖ ∼n seihen *to strain at a gnat* ‖ ∼n fangen ⟨fig⟩ *to stand gaping* ‖ e–e ∼ am Spieß braten *to break a fly on a wheel* ‖ aus e–r ∼ e–n Elefanten m *to make a mountain out of a molehill* ‖ mit Geduld u Spucke fängt man e–e Mucke *patience and a snare catch many a hare* **∼nfang** m ⟨bot⟩ *fly-bane, catch-fly* **∼nfänger** m *fussy p* ‖ *idler* **∼nfängerei** f *fussiness* **∼̈ngroß** a *midget-size* **∼nfett** n *mare's nest* ‖ e–n nach ∼ schicken *to send a p on a fool's errand* **∼nflor** m *mosquito-net* **∼npulver** n *insect-powder* **∼nschwarm** m *host of gnats* **∼nseiher** m *fussy p* **∼nstich** m *gnat-bite* **∼nwedel** m *fly-flap*

°**M·uckefuck** m ∼s/∼e → Malzkaffee, Kaffee-Ersatz

°**M·ucke-picke** f ∼/∼n ⟨mot⟩ *pip-squeak*

m·ucken vi [h] **1.** *to grumble* ‖ *to sulk* **2.** *to utter a faint sound* **3.** = mucksen **4.** *to be silent* od *glum* **5.** *to be whimsical* | m–e Zähne ∼ *my teeth are grumbling* od *aching* ‖ nicht gemuckt! *not another word!, don't argue!* ‖ die S muckt .. *is hanging fire* **M·ucker** m ∼s/∼ **1.** *bigot, hypocrite*, → Duckmäuser **2.** *grumbler*; *sulky p* **Mucker·ei** f ∼/, **M·uckertum** n ∼s/ *bigotry, cant, hypocrisy* ‖ *grundyism* **m·uckerhaft** a *canting, hypocritical* **m·uckern** vi [h] **1.** *to play the hypocrite* **2.** = mucken **m·uck(i)sch** a *sulky, sullen, peevish*

M·ucks m → Muck **∼̈(mäuschen)still** a *as quiet as a mouse* **m·ucksen** vt [h] & sich ∼ [h] *to move, stir* ‖ er darf nicht ∼ *he dare not say a word* ‖ nicht gemuckst! *don't stir!*, ⟨Am fam⟩ *stay pat!*

m·üde a **1.** *tired* (*p, eyes, legs*); ⟨child's⟩ müdi *tyoh* ‖ *weary* (*features, steps*) ‖ *sleepful, drowsy* ‖ *jaded* (*appearance*) ‖ [mst pred] *spent* | ∼ heimk *to come home tired out* ‖ ∼ umherschleichen *to creep about wearily* | ∼ u abgekämpft *weak and weary* ‖ ∼ u matt *tired and worn out*; (erschöpft) *fatigued* ‖ ∼ v der Arbeit *fagged out* od ⟨fam⟩ *knocked up by hard work* ‖ zum Umfallen ∼ *ready* od *fit to drop, bone-tired, dead-beat* | ∼ m *to tire* (*out*), *to weary* ‖ ein Pferd ∼ reiten *to ride a h. till tired-out* ‖ sich ∼ laufen *to walk o.s. into exhaustion* ‖ sich ∼ reden *to tire o.s. with talking* ‖ ∼ w *to be getting tired* ‖ ∼ w z tun *to wear o.s. out doing, to become tired of doing* | ⟨übtr⟩ °∼r Laden *dead-t. routines* **2.** (überdrüssig) [mit acc or gen] ich bin es ∼ *I'm sick of it* (.. z hören .. *of hearing*), *I've had enough of it* ‖ jds ∼ w *to weary of a p* ‖ des Lebens ∼ s *to be weary of life* **M·üdigkeit** f ∼/ *weariness, fatigue*; *languor*; (vornehm) *lassitude* ‖ vor ∼ umsinken *to drop down from* (*sheer*) *exhaustion*, ⟨fam⟩ *to be done up* ‖ k–e ∼ vorschützen! *don't plead weariness as an excuse!*

°**M·udelfritze** m ∼n(s)/∼n *soggy type* **m·udeln** vi [h] *to dawdle*

M·uff m ∼(e)s/∼̈e **1.** (Händewärmer) *muff* °⟨a. fig sex vulg⟩ **2.** (Schimmel) *mould*(*iness*), *mildew* **3.** ⟨vulg⟩ (Mief) *fug* ‖ *mouldy smell* **4.** *deep bark* **5.** *growling dog* **6.** *pouter, moper*; *sulky p* **M·üffchen** n *cuff, mitten* **M·uffe** f ∼/∼n ⟨tech⟩ (Verbindungshülse) (*pipe-*)*coupling*; (Rohrende) *socket, bell* | ∼nkupplung [f] ⟨mach⟩ *socket-joint*; ∼nverbindung [f] *sleeve-j.*

M·uffel[1] m ∼s/∼ **1.** *snout, muzzle* | ⟨fig⟩ *potato-trap* **2.** ⟨arch⟩ *lion's*, etc *face* (*as spout*) **3.** (P) *growler, mumbler* **∼gesicht** n *pudding-face* **∼tier** n = Mufflon **m·uffelig** a *sullen, sulky* ‖ *blubber-faced* ‖ *cross, vexed*

M·uffel[2] f ∼/∼n ⟨chem, tech⟩ *muffle* **∼farben** f pl *muffle-colours* pl **∼ofen** m *muffle-kiln*

m·uffeln vt/i [h] **1.** *to mumble* **2.** *to munch* **3.** *to sulk, mope*

m·uffen vi [h] *to be sulky* ‖ *to grumble, mutter*

m·üffen vi [h] ⟨fam⟩ *to smell musty* od *fusty* **m·uffig, m·üffig** a **1.** *grumbling* **2.** *glum, sulky* **3.** (Geruch) *musty, frowsty, frowzy*; *fuggy* (*air*); *faint* (*meat*) | ∼e Luft *fug, frowst* ‖ ∼er Geruch *muggy smell*; *reek* ‖ es riecht ∼ *there is a fusty smell* ‖ in der ∼en Stube hocken *to fug*

M·ufflon m ∼s/∼s ⟨zoo⟩ *mouf*(*f*)*lon*

m·ugelig a (of gems) *en cabochon* Fr

m·uh! intj (of cows) *moo!*; → muhen

M·ühe f ∼/∼n *trouble, pains* pl ‖ (Arbeit) *labour, toil* | die ∼n des Lebens (Tages) *the tr.s of life* (*the daily tr.s*) | große, viel ∼ *great p.s, much tr.* ‖ leichte ∼ *little tr.* ‖ schwere ∼ *great exertion* ‖ unbeschreibliche, vergebliche ∼ *indescribable, useless efforts* pl ‖ verlorene ∼ *waste of time, tr. for nothing*; ⟨fam⟩ *beating the air* | **mit** ∼ *with difficulty*; mit gr ∼, mit ∼ u Not *by dint of great exertion*, .. s–n Weg m *to creak one's way through*; er brachte die W. nur mit ∼ heraus *he could hardly get the words out*; er konnte sein Geld nur mit ~ retten *he was hard put to it to save his m.* || **ohne** jegliche ~ *effortlessly, without* (*the slightest*) *tr.* od *effort*, ⟨urspr sport⟩ *hands down*; ohne ~ kein Lohn *no pains no gains* | es ist (schon) der ~ [gen] **wert** *it is worth* (*one's*) *while*, od *the tr.* (*to do, doing*), ⟨fam⟩ *it's w. it* | ~ **anwenden** (zu tun) *to bestow infinite p.s on drawing* || **danken**: *thank you for your tr.* || **sich** [dat] (alle erdenkliche) ~ **geben** *or* **m** *to make an effort* (*to do*), *to take p.s* (mit *with*) od *much tr.* (*about*), *to tr. o.s.*; *to try and try*; *to strive* (*to do a th*), *to do one's level best*; ⟨Am fam⟩ *to put one's mind to it*; (*to put o.s. out*) || sich die ~ geben *or* m *to* [*go to the*] *tr.* (*to do*); sich (k–e) ~ geben etw z tun (*not*) *to bother to do a th*; geben Sie sich k–e ~ *you can spare y.s. the tr.*, *you are wasting your time* || sich besondere ~ geben *or* m *to go out of one's way* (*to do*) (f, um *for*) || ~ **h** *to have difficulties* od *some tr.* (mit *with*, zu tun *in doing*), *to have a hard time* (*doing*) || viel ~ **kosten** *to be an awful* od *a horrible sweat*; jdn ~ kosten *to put a p to tr.* || e–e Arbeit kostet, macht, verursacht gr ~ *a job costs, makes, causes a lot of tr.*; die ~ u die Kosten h *to be at the pains and charges* || es **lohnt** die ~ nicht *it is not worth while* || e–m ~ **m** *to give a p tr.*, *to put a p to great tr.* || es macht mir viel ~, es zu tun *I find it a great tr. to do it* || es macht ihm k–e ~ *it isn't any tr. to him* || sich die ~ m *to tr. o.s.*, *to bother* (zu tun *to do*) || *it's very good of you to have b.ed* || *if it is not too much tr.* .. || sich gr ~ m *to go to much tr.* (*to do*) || sich bes ~ m *to put o.s. out of the way* (wegen *for*, z tun *to do*) || sie m sich nicht (einmal *or* erst) die ~ *they don't tr.* (*to write*) || m Sie sich k–e ~ *don't bother* (*y.s.*) (damit *about it*); *don't put y.s. out* (meinetwegen *on my account*) || sich die ~ **nehmen** *to take the tr.* (z tun *to do*) || k–e ~ **scheuen** *or* sparen, sich jeder ~ **unterziehen,** sich k–e ~ **verdrießen l** *to grudge* od *spare no p.s*, etc., *not to mind any tr.*; *to go out of one's way* || **verursachen**: *he gave no tr.* || e–m: *to put a p to tr.* || das v–chte gerade die ~ *that was half the tr.*

M·ühe- **≃los** a *without trouble, effortless, easy*; *facile* **~losigkeit** f *easiness* **≃sparend** a *labour-saving* **≃voll** a *troublesome, hard, difficult* **~waltung** f *trouble, efforts* pl, *care* **m·ühen,** sich ~ [h] *to exert o.s., to toil, to trouble o.s.* (→ bemühen)

m·uhen vi [h] (of cow) *to moo, low*; → muh!

M·ühl- **~bach** m *mill-brook* **~beutel** m *bolter* **~bursche** m *miller's man* **~damm** m *mill-dam* **~gang** m *mill-stones* pl **~gerinne** n, **~graben** m *mill-race*, ⟨Am⟩ *raceway* **~knappe** m *miller's man* **~lauf** m *drum* **~rad** n *mill-wheel* || es geht mir wie ein ~ im Kopf herum *my head is perfectly dizzy* **~stein** m *millstone* (*runner*); *grindstone* **~teich** m *mill-pond* **~trichter** m *mill-hopper* **~wasser** n *mill-race* **~wehr** n *mill-dam* **~werk** n *mill*(*-work*) **M·ühle** f ~/~n *mill*; Grob-/Fein-/Feinst≃ *crusher/grinder/pulverizer* || ⟨tech-mill⟩ Doppelhart≃ *double hard ball m.*; Dreiwalzen≃ *ring mill*; Hammer≃ *h. m.*; Hart≃, Kugel(fall)≃ *ball m.*, Luftstrom≃ *air-swept m.*; Mehrkammer≃ *multi-chamber m.*; Müll≃ *garbage grinder*; Schlag≃ *impact m.*; Schlagzeug≃ *cross beater m.*; Schrot-, Quetsch≃ *bruiser*; Siebkugel≃ *screen ball m.*; Strahl≃ *jet mill*; Walzenschüssel≃ *roller m.* | (Brettspiel) *nine men's morris* || ⟨gym⟩ *grinder* || ⟨aero hum⟩ *crate, bus, kite* || °⟨f sex⟩ *mill* | das ist Wasser auf s–e ~ ⟨fig⟩ *that is grist to his mill, that is nuts to him* **M·ühlen-** **~bau** m *m.-building* **~bauer** m *m.-wright* **~einlauf** m *m. inlet* **~flügel** m *sail of a windmill* **~rohr** n *grinding shell* **~sockel** m *m. plinth* **~staub** m *m.-dust* **~teich** m *m.-pond*

M·uhme f ~/~n [obs] *aunt* ([dim] *aunty*) || → Cousine, Nichte || (Kinder≃) *nurse*

M·ühlsal n ~(e)s/~e; f ~/~e *hardship* (*great h.s*), *toil, trouble* || (Elend) *misery* **m·ühsam** a *wearisome, toilsome, troublesome, laborious, painstaking* || *hard* (*life*) || *laboured* (*breathing*); *uphill* (*work*) | adv *with an effort, with difficulty* || ~ erarbeitetes Wissen *hard-won kn.*; sich ~ ernähren *to struggle for a living*; ~ verdient *hard-earned* (*money*); (*to earn a th*) *the hard way*; sich [acc] ~ wieder aufrichten *to struggle to one's feet*; sich ~ fortschleppen auf .. *to trudge down a road* | **≃keit** f ~/ *troublesomeness, laboriousness* **m·ühselig** a *painful, toilsome, laborious*; *arduous* (*duty*) | (elend) *miserable, wretched* (*life*), *thorny* (*path*) | **≃keit** f ~/ *p.ness, t.ness, l.ness* | *misery, w.ness* | (etw Mühseliges) *toil, hardship, uphill work*; *fatigues* pl

°**M·ui** f ~/~s ⟨fam⟩ (→ Mutti) *mums, mummy*

M·ukden n († Hauptstadt der Mandschurei)

Mul·atte m ~n/~n *mulatto* (f [*female*] *mulatto*)

M·ulde f ~/~n *tray, trough* || Back≃ *hutch* || ⟨fig⟩ es groß wie mit ~n *it was raining cats and dogs* || (Eisenmassel) *iron pig*; e–e ~ Blei *a pig of lead* || ⟨min⟩ *hole, cavity* || ⟨geol⟩ *syncline* (*of strata*); ⟨mar geog⟩ *basin*: Westafrikan. ~ *South Eastern Atlantic B.*; Kap≃ (S.-Afrika) *Cape B.* || (Tal) *depression, valley, coomb, basin, hollow, trough* **M·ulden-** **~blei** n *pig-lead* **≃förmig** a *trough-shaped*, ⟨geol⟩ *synclinal* (*fold*) **~kipper** m *tip-up truck*, ⟨bes Am⟩ *V-dump car*

M·ülhausen n ⟨Ger⟩ (Stadt im Elsaß) *Mulhouse* [Fr]

M·ull m ~(e)s/ *thin* od *Indian muslin, mull* | ~bausch [m] *tampon*; ~gaze [f], ~pfropfen [m] *tent*; (Wunde) durch ~ offen halten *to tent*; ~kleid [n] *muslin dress*

M·üll m ~(e)s/ *dust*; *rubbish, refuse, garbage* **~abfuhr** f *carting of dust*; *refuse disposal* od *collection* **~abladeplatz** m *dump*(*ing place*), *waste area* **~eimer** m *dust-bin, ash-can*, ⟨Am⟩ *garbage pail* od *can* **~grube** f *dust-hole* **~haufen** m *scrap-heap* **~kasten** m (*domestic*) *dust-bin*; *refuse* od *garbage container* **~kübel** m → -eimer **~kutscher** m *dustman* **~schacht** m *refuse* (⟨Am⟩ *garbage*) *chute* **~schaufel** f *dustpan* **~schlucker** m *waste-disposer*, ⟨Am⟩ *garbage chute* **~verbrennung** f *refuse incineration* | ~sofen [m] *destructor* **~wagen** m *dust-cart*; *garbage lorry* **~werker** m *dustman* **~wolf** m *garbage grinder*

M·üller m ~s/~ *miller* (f **~in** *m.'s wife* auf, nach ~inart [f] ⟨cul⟩ *meunière* [*style*]); ~bursche [m] *m.'s man* od *boy*; ~esel [m] *m.'s ass*; ~geselle, ~knappe, ~knecht [m] *m.'s man*

°**m·üllern** vi [h] ⟨gym⟩ *to do one's daily dozen*

M·ulm m ~(e)s/ *dust* || *rotten wood* || *mouldiness, rot*(*tenness*) **m·ulmig** a *dusty, mouldy, rotten* || *fuggy, sticky* (*air*) || *worm-eaten* (*wood*) || *decayed* (*stone*) || ⟨fig fam⟩ *rotten* (*affair, weather*), *snickersneed* (*condition*) || [pred a.] *in a mess* || ⟨mil⟩ heute wird's ~ *it's going to be a heavy day*

M·ultebeere f ⟨bot⟩ *cloudberry*

m·ultilater·al a *multilateral*

mult·iple Skler·ose f ~n/~n *multiple sclerosis*

Multiplik·and m ~en/~en ⟨math⟩ *multiplicand* | ~/Dividend/Quotient-Register [n] ⟨comp⟩ *m./d./q.* (*MC/DD*) *register* | **-kati·on** f ~/~en *m.cation* | **-k·ator** m ~s/–at·oren *m.cator*; ⟨phot⟩ *filter factor* **multipliz·ieren** vt [h] *to multiply*; 6 mit 3 ~ *to m. 6 by 3* || mit sich selbst ~ *to square*

Multivitam·intablette f *compound vitamin tablet*

M·ulus m ~/–li (Maulesel) ⟨fig⟩ *freshman* (*before going to the university*)

M·umie f ~/~n *mummy* ⟨a. fig⟩ | ≃nhaft, mumifiziert [a] *mummified*

°**M·umm** m ~/ **1.** *inclination* (*to tackle a job*) **2.** *pluck, ginger*, ⟨fam⟩ *zip*; ⟨sl⟩ *guts* pl, ⟨Am⟩ *pep, tuck* || mit ~ *full of beans* || k–n ~ in den Knochen h *to have no guts*; (*there's no go in him*)

M·umme[1] f ~/ (*strong*) *Brunswick beer*

M·umme[2] f ~/~n *mask* || *masked p*

M·ummel f ~/~n ⟨bot⟩ *water-lily*

M·ummelgreis m ⟨sl⟩ *geeser, geezer*

m·ummeln vi [h] *to mutter, mumble (to o.s.)*
m·umme(l)n vt [h] *to muffle up*
m·ümmeln vt [h] *to munch*
Mummer·ei f, **M·ummenschanz** m *masquerade*
M·umpitz m ~es/~e; ~! *bosh! stuff (and nonsense)!, rubbish! flim-flam! humbug!* ⟨Am sl⟩ *shenanigan!* || mach k–n ~ *don't play the fool!*
M·umps m –ses/ ⟨med⟩ *mumps; parotitis*
M·ünchen n (Hauptstadt v Bayern) *Munich*
M·ünchener m, **~in** f *inhabitant of Munich*
M·ünchhauseni·ade f ~/~n *cock-and-bull story*
M·und m ~(e)s/~e & ~̈er **A.** *mouth* || *lips* pl || ⟨zoo⟩ *stoma* | ⟨fig⟩ *head (of a shaft)* || *the (metal) m. (of a bell)* **B. beredter** ~ *fluency of speech*; lügnerischer ~ *lying tongue*; rosiger ~ *rosy lips* pl; sinnlicher ~ *sensuous m.*; je voller der ~, desto deutlicher die Aussprache ⟨hum⟩ *the fuller the m. the better the pronunciation* | e–n ~ voll *a m.ful* **C.** sich den ~ **abwischen** *to wipe one's m.* (an, mit *on*) || nur den ~ auf–zumachen brauchen um zu erlangen, was man will *to have one's own way for the asking* || den ~ **aufreißen** *to brag*; vor Staunen (a. aufsperren) *to gape* || ~ u Nase **aufsperren** *to stand staring and gaping* || den ~ **auftun** *to open one's m.*; .. nicht .. können *to be close-mouthed: he cannot say bo to a goose* || sie ist nicht auf den ~ **gefallen** *she knows all the answers*; .., °aber zugänglich *she's free of her lips, free of her hips* || ihr ~ **geht** den ganzen Tag *her jaws are going all day* || e–n gr ~ **h** ⟨fig⟩ *to brag*; e–n losen ~ h *to be slack-jawed; to answer back*; den ~ auf dem rechten Fleck h *to have the gift of the gab* || **halt** den ~! *hold your tongue; shut your m.; shut up!*; halt d–n ungewaschenen ~! *wash out your m.!*; den ~ halten *to hold one's tongue* (⟨fam⟩ *noise, jaw*); ⟨fam⟩ *to dry up*; .. über *to keep one's m. shut about* || reinen ~ halten *to keep counsel* od *a secret* || jdm den ~ **öffnen** *to persuade a p to speak* || den ~ **spitzen** *to screw up one's lips* || jdm den ~ **stopfen** *to stop a p's tongue, to shut a p up* || e–m den ~ **verbieten** *to forbid a p to speak*, ⟨fam⟩ *to muzzle a p* || sich den ~ **verbrennen** ⟨fig fam⟩ *to put one's foot in (it)* || du hast wohl den ~ **verloren** *you seem to have come without your tongue* || den ~ **verziehen** *to pucker up one's m.* || den ~ **vollnehmen** *to talk big, to m., boast, brag, swagger* || sich den ~ **vollstopfen** *to gorge o.s.* || der ~ **wässert** e–m danach, es wird e–m der ~ wässerig danach, es macht e–m den ~ wässerig *it makes one's m. water* || sich den ~ **wischen** *to wipe one's m.* ⟨a. fig⟩ || er preßte den ~ zus *his m. hardened* **D. an** den ~ führen *to put to one's m.* || an jds ~e hängen *to hang on a p's lips* || sich etw am ~e absparen *to stint o.s. of a th.* | (nicht) **auf** den ~ gefallen s *to love one's tongue (to have a ready t., to know all the answers)* || jdm eins auf den ~ geben *to hit a man in the m.* || auf den ~ küssen .. *on ..* || wie auf den ~ geschlagen *dumbfounded* | es **aus** s–m ~e h *to have it from his m.* || Sie nehmen mir die Worte aus dem ~e! *you are taking the very words out of my m.!, that's what I was going to say*; aus berufenem ~e *from an authoritative source*; ⟨fam⟩ *straight from the horse's m.* || aus dem ~e riechen *to have a bad breath* | das Wasser lief ihm **im** ~e zus *his m. watered* || mir blieb der Bissen (das Wort) im ~e stecken *I nearly choked [for fear] (the words stuck in my throat)* || e–m das Wort im ~e umdrehen *to twist the words in a p's m.* || (den Namen Gottes) unnütz im ~e führen *to take in vain*; ein Wort viel im ~e f. *to make frequent use of a w.* | **in** aller ~e s *to be on everyone's lips* od *the talk of the town*; (*the artist's name is in everybody's m.*) || in den ~ legen *to suggest*; (*to put words in a p's m.*) || e–m die Bissen in den ~ zählen *to grudge a p every morsel* || e–m etw in den ~ schmieren *to make sth quite clear to a p* || ich mag das Wort nicht in den ~ nehmen .. *to utter ..* | **mit** offenem ~e *open-m.ed, gaping* || mit vollem ~ reden *to speak with* (od *between*) *m.fuls* || nur mit halbem ~e lachen *to laugh on one side of the m.* || sie ist immer mit dem ~e vorweg *she has a forward tongue* | e–m [den Leuten] **nach** dem ~e reden *to chime in with (to flatter) a p, to fawn on a p [to be a mealy-m.ed p]* | e–m **über** den ~ fahren *to pick a p up*; ⟨sl⟩ *to jump down a p's throat* | e–m Honig **um** den ~ schmieren *to butter a p up* | **von** ~ zu ~e gehen *to pass from m. to m., to be the talk of the town, to be in everybody's m.* | Schaum **vor** dem ~e h *to foam at the m.* || kein Blatt vor den ~ nehmen *not to mince matters* || ein Brett vor dem ~ h *to be tongue-tied* || e–m das Brot vor dem ~e wegnehmen .. *out of ..* **M·und-~art** f *dialect* || *provincialism* || irische ~ *brogue* **~artenforscher** m *dialectician* **-forschung** f *dialectology* **~̈artlich** a *dialectal* || *provincial* **~bedarf** m *victuals* pl, *provisions* pl **~entzündung** f ⟨path⟩ *stomatitis* **~̈faul** a = maulfaul **~fäule** ⟨path⟩ *thrush*, ⟨scient⟩ *stomatitis* **~fertigkeit** f *readiness of one's tongue*; ⟨fam⟩ *gift of the gab* **~̈gerecht** a *palatable*; e–m (etw) ~ m *to adapt to a p's fancy* od *taste* **~geruch** m ⟨med⟩ *halitosis* **~geschwür** n ⟨path⟩ *ulcer in the m.* **~harmonika** f *m.-organ, harmonica* **~höhle** f *oral cavity* **~klemme** f = ~sperre **~koch** m *prince's cook* **~loch** n *orifice* || ⟨tech⟩ *blow-* od *fuse-hole* || (Schacht) *mouth* || (e–r Flöte) *blowing-hole* **~pflege** f *care of the m.* **~pfropfen** m ⟨mar artill⟩ (*muzzle*) *tampion* **~portion** f *ration* **~raub** m (*minor*) *theft of food*, etc *for immediate consumption* **~̈recht** = ~gerecht **~scheibe** f (e–r Gasmaske) *m. opening* **~schenk** m *cup-bearer* **~schwamm** m ⟨path⟩ *thrush* **~sperre** f ⟨path⟩ *lock-jaw* **~spiegel** m ⟨med⟩ *stomatoscope* **~stellung** f ⟨phon⟩ *position of the m.* (od *its parts*) **~stück** n (⟨mus⟩ & an Gasmaske) *m.piece* (⟨a.⟩ P Wortführer); (der Zigarette) *tip*; ⟨hors⟩ *bit*; (am Blasebalg) *nozzle*; ⟨artill⟩ *muzzle*; ⟨fig vulg⟩ = ~werk **~̈tot** a *not allowed to speak*; ⟨jur⟩ *dead in law* || ~ m *to (reduce to) silence*; ⟨fig⟩ *to muzzle, gag*, ⟨school⟩ *to floor* **~tuch** n *napkin* **~̈voll** m *m.ful; sup* **~vorrat** m = ~bedarf **~wasser** n *m.-wash; gargle* | ~schale [f] *finger-bowl* **~werk** n ⟨vulg⟩ *potato-trap; glib* od *voluble* od *loose tongue; her t. runs continually* || ein gutes *or* loses ~ h *to have the gift of the gab* od *one's tongue well oiled; to have a tongue* **~winkel** m *corner of the m.*; e–n ~ verziehen *to smile at one side of the m.*

M·ündel m & n ~s/~ *ward, pupil* **~geld** n *ward m.* **~gut** n *property of a ward* **~̈sicher** a; ~e Papiere *gilt-edged* (od *trustee*) *securities* (od *stock*) **~stand** m *pupilage* **m·ündig** a *of age* || ~ w *to come of age* || für ~ erklären *to declare of age* | **~̈keit** f ~/ *majority, full age* || (das ~̈werden) *coming of age*; → Muntbruch

m·unden vi imps [h]; es mundet mir *I like* od *relish it* || es mundet köstlich *it has a delicious taste, it tastes excellent* **m·ünden** vi [h] (in [acc]) (Fluß) *to fall, flow (into)* || (Straße) *to run (into)* || (Kanal) *to end (in)* | ~d in *affluent of (a river), discharging itself into (the ocean)* **m·ündlich** a *verbal (agreement, order, threats); viva voce, oral (examination); vocal [and written] (demonstration); personal* (Auskunft) || *nuncupative* (Testament) || ~e Vernehmung ⟨jur⟩ *parole evidence* | adv *by word of mouth, orally, verbally* || (Brief) alles andere ~! *all other news when we meet* **M·ündung** f ~/~en (e–s Flusses) *mouth* (an der ~ *at the m.*) || (weite) *estuary, firth* || (Nebenfluß~̈) *junction with main stream* || (Gefäß-, Rohr~̈) *orifice, opening* || (Gewehr~̈) *spout* || (Geschütz~̈) *muzzle* **~sarm** m *distributary* **~sbremse** f *muzzle-brake* **~sdeckel** m *m.-cap* **~senergie** f *m.-energy* **~sfeuer** n *flash* | ~bereich [m] *blast area*; ~vorsatz [m] *flash-hider* **~sgebiet** n *delta* **~sgeschwindigkeit** f *m. velocity* **~sknall** m *puff* **~spropfen** m ⟨artill⟩ *tampion* **~strichter** m ⟨geog⟩

estuary **~süberzug** m, **~sverschluß** m = ~sdeckel **~sweite** f ⟨artill⟩ *bore*

M·ungo m ~s/~s ⟨zoo⟩ *mongoose*

Munifiz·enz f ~/~en *munificence*

Muniti·on f ~/~en *ammunition*, (⟨fam⟩ Muni- [in comp] *ammo*), ⟨sl⟩ *confetti* ‖ ~ gurten *to fill am. belt* | **~s- ~arbeiter(in** f) m *munition-worker* **~ausgabe** f *issue of am.* **~ausstattung** f *allowance of am.* **~bestand** m *am. to hand* **~ersatz** m *replenishment of am.* **~fabrik** f *am.-factory*; in die ~ gehen *to go into munitions* **~kammer** f *magazine* **~karren** m *tumbrel* **~kasten** m *caisson* **~kolonne** f *am.(supply)column* **~lager** n *am.-dump* od *depot* | ~bereich [m] *explosives area* **~kanoniere, ~-männer** m pl *am. passers* pl; *supply party* **~räumtrupp** m *explosive ordnance disposal unit* **~schütze** m *am. handler* **~nachschub** m, **~versorgung** f *am. supply* **~wagen** m *tumbril, caisson* **~zuführung** f *feed chute*

m·unkeln vi/t [h] *to whisper about* ‖ man munkelt *there is a rumour (abroad), there are whispers afloat (that)* ‖ wir h davon ~ gehört *or* hören *we have heard it rumoured* | ⟨prov⟩ im Dunkeln ist gut ~ *night is the friend of lovers*

M·ünster n (& m) ~s/~ *minster, cathedral*

M·ünster n ⟨Ger⟩ (Stadt) *Munster* **M·ünsterland** n *country of M.* **m·ünsterisch** a *of M.*

M·untbruch m ~(e)s/~̈e ⟨jur⟩ *child-stealing*; → Mündel

m·unter [a] *awake, watchful; jaunty, quick, spritited* ‖ ⟨fig⟩ (lebhaft) *lively (child); active, sprightly, nimble* ‖ *bright (complexion, colours)* ‖ (rüstig) *vigorous* ‖ *(at a) cheery (pace)* ‖ (heiter) *gay* ‖ (fröhlich) *merry*, (unstet) *mobile (eyes)* | ~! *cheer up!, look alive!* | gesund u ~ *hale and hearty* ‖ du bist wohl nicht ganz ~? *are you mad* (⟨Am⟩ *crazy*)? ‖ wie ein Eichhörnchen (*or* wie ein Fisch im Wasser) *(as) merry as a grig*; (gesund) *(as) fit as a fiddle*; .. Schwalbe *she was as gay as a lark* ‖ schon ~ s *to be astir* (od *up and doing*) ‖ e–n ~ m *to wake a p* | [adv] *briskly, joyously, lustily*; *(to jump) for joy* | **~̈keit** f ~/ *liveliness, vivacity, alacrity, sprightliness, briskness* ‖ *gaiety, mirth* ‖ *vigour*, etc. → vor.

M·ünz- ~abdruck m *impression of a coin* **~amt** n, **~anstalt** f *mint, bullion-office* **~arbeiter** m *m.-man* **~automat** m *coin-operated machine* (⟨a.⟩ Straßen-) **~beamter** m *official of a m.* **~beschikkung** f *alloyage* **~beschneider** m *c.-clipper* **~einheit** f *uniform c.age; monetary unity, unit* od *standard of currency* **~einwurf** m *c. slot* **~fälscher** m *(false) c.er* **~fälschung** f *(false) c.ing* **~fernsehen** n *pay-as--you-view TV* **~fernsprecher** m *call-box, c.-box*; ⟨Am⟩ *pay-phone* **~freiheit** f *privilege of c.ing* **~-fuß** m *(monetary) standard* **~-Gaszähler** m *prepayment gas meter* **~gebühr** f, **~gefälle** n *m.age* **~gehalt** m *standard of alloy* **~gepräge** n *m.-stamp* **~-gesetz** n *c.age act* **~herr** m *master of the m.* **~inschrift** f *superscription* **~just·ierer** m *m.-assayer* **~kabinett** n = ~sammlung **~kenner, ~kundiger** m *numismatist* **~kunde** f *numismatics* pl **~meister** m *m.-master, officer of the m.* **~prägung** f *c.age* **~presse** f *c.ingpress* **~probe** f *assay (of a c.)* **~rand** m *edge* od *rim of a c.*; *milled edge* **~recht** n *right of c.age* **~sammlung** f *collection of c.s* **~schlag** m *c.age* **~silber** n *standard silver* **~sorte** f *species* [a. pl] *of c.* **~stecher** m *die-sinker* **~stempel** m *die* **~-system** n *monetary system* **~umlauf** m *monetary circulation* **~verbrechen** n *false c.ing* **~verschlechterung** f *debasement of c.(age)* **~währung** f *standard* **~ward·ein** m *assay-master* **~wesen** n *c.age, monetary system* **~wissenschaft** f *numismatics* pl **~zähler** m *slot-meter* **~zeichen** n *c.er's mark* **~zusatz** m *alloy* **M·ünze** f ~/~n (Münzanstalt) *mint* ‖ (Geld) *coin, money* ‖ (Denk~̈) *medal* | (kl ~) *change* ‖ klingende, bare ~ *hard, ready cash* ‖ abgegriffene, falsche ~ *worn, base coin* ‖ ~n schlagen *to coin, to mint coins* ‖ ~n beschneiden *to clip coins*; ⟨**fig**⟩ (e–m) mit *or* in gleicher ~ (heim)zahlen *to retaliate in kind (to pay a p back in his* [*own*] *coin); to give as good as you get*; ⟨fam⟩ *to give a p a pig of his own sow* ‖ (alles) für bare ~ nehmen *to believe implicitly, to take (a report) at its face value (to swallow hook, line, and sinker)* ‖ in klingende ~ umsetzen *to get a quid pro quo* **m·ünzen** vt [h] *to mint, coin* ‖ gemünztes Gold *specie* | ⟨fig⟩ das ist auf dich gemünzt *that is meant for you* **M·ünzer** m ~s/~ *minter, coiner*

Mur·äne f ~/~n ⟨ich⟩ *murӕna*

m·ürbe a (reif) *mellow* ‖ (Fleisch) *tender, soft*; ~ m *to hang* ‖ (durch) *well done* ‖ (Gebäck) *crisp, short* ‖ (brüchig) *brittle* | ⟨fig⟩ (P) *worn*; jdn ~ m *to wear a p down, to curb* od *humble a p* ‖ ~ w *to grow weary*; (nachgeben) *to give in* ‖ ~ gemacht *broken* **M·ürbe- ~braten** m *roast rump(--steak)* **~kuchen** m *short cake*; *short pastry* **~-macher** m (Gewürz) *tenderizer* **~teig** m *short paste* **~teiggebäck** n ⟨Am⟩ *angel cake* **M·ürbigkeit** f ~/ *mellowness* ‖ *tenderness* ‖ *softness* ‖ *crispness* ‖ *brittleness* ‖ *shortness*

M·urcia [–θia] n ⟨Span⟩ (Provinz)

M·ure f ~/~n, **M·urgang** m ~es/ ⟨geol⟩ *landslip, débâcle* Fr ‖ *rock stream, torrential wash*

°**M·urks** m –ses/ *bungle; bungling* °**m·urksen** vi/t [h] *to bungle* | vt *to murder*

M·urmanküste f (Nordküste der Halbinsel Kola) *Murman Coast* **M·urmansk** ⟨Russ⟩ (Provinz & Gebietshauptstadt) ⟨a.⟩ *M. (Region)*

M·urmel m ~s/~n *marble* **~spiel** n *game at m.s*

m·urmeln vt/i [h] *to murmur, mutter* ‖ sie ~ zustimmend *they murmur their assent* ‖ vor sich hin ~ *to .. to o.s.* ‖ (Bach) *to babble, purl* ‖ undeutlich ~ *to burble* | **das** ~̈ ⟨a.⟩ *susurration*

M·urmeltier n *marmot*, ⟨Am⟩ *groundhog* ‖ wie ein ~ schlafen *to sleep like a top* od *dormouse*

M·urr m ~(e)s/ **1.** (Kater) *Grimalkin* **2.** = Mumm 2. ‖ **~kopf** m *grumbler* **~̈köpfig** a *morose, grumbling, surly, peevish* **m·urren 1.** vi [h] *to growl, murmur; to grumble* (über *about*); ⟨Am a.⟩ *to grouch* ‖ ohne zu ~ *unmurmuringly, without a murmur*; *(to take one's fate) unquestioning* **2.** ~̈ n *murmurs* pl, *groans* pl, *grumbling* **m·ürrisch** a *peevish, peeved; crusty, gruff; curt, short; blunt; glum; morose, surly, sullen, sulky; sore; bad--tempered, ill-humoured; irascible; cross; petulant; churlish; querulous* ‖ (brummig) *grumbling, grouchy*; ⟨fam⟩ *grumpish, –py; cantankerous* ‖ ~er Mensch *grumbler*, ⟨fam⟩ *crosspatch* ‖ ~es Wesen *moroseness, sullenness*, etc | adv ~ dreinschauend *sullen-eyed*

M·urray ['mʌri] m ⟨Aust⟩ (Fluß)

M·us n ~es/~e *mash, pap* ‖ *stewed fruit; jam* ‖ (Apfelsine) *marmalade* ‖ zu ~ m *to mash* | ⟨fig⟩ °e–n zu ~ schlagen *to beat a p to a jelly* °**~spritze** f (Schirm) *brolly*, ⟨Am⟩ *bumber-shoot*

Musag·et m ~en/ ⟨myth⟩ *(Apollo) Musagetes*

M·uschel f ~/~n ⟨zoo⟩ (Tier) *shell-fish*, (zweischalige) *mussel* ‖ eßbare Meeres~̈ *clam* ‖ (Schale) *shell* ‖ ⟨anat⟩ *conch* ‖ ⟨telph⟩ *ear-piece* **~abfallhaufen** m ⟨praeh⟩ *shell heap* **~̈förmig** a *mussel--shaped, conchoidal, conchiform* **~gehäuse** n = ~schale **~geld** n *cowry* **~gericht** n *sea-food* **~gold** n *painter's gold, ormolu* **~hut** m *cockle-hat* **~-kalk** m *muschelkalk* **~kenner** m *conchologist* **~kunde** f *conchology* **~sand** m *powdered shell* **~-schale** f *mussel-shell*; ⟨cul⟩ *coquille* **~silber** n *shell-silver* **~tier** n *shell-fish* **~werk** n *shell-work, grotto* **m·uschelig** a **1.** *shelly* ‖ ⟨minr⟩ *conchoidal (fracture)* **2.** *snug* **3.** *tricky*

M·uschik m ~s/~s (russ. Bauer) *moujik, muzhik*

°**Muschk·ote** m ~n/~n (Musketier) *private (soldier)*; ⟨Am⟩ *G. I.* (abbr für *government issue*)

M·uselman m ~en/~en, **-mann** m; **m-m·anisch, m-männisch** a *Mussulman, Moslem* [a. f]

M·use f ~/~n ⟨myth⟩ *Muse*; leichte, 10. ~

⟨m. m.⟩ *light verse* (z. B. *Aristophanes, Sh.'s songs Limericks*, etc) **muse·al** a *like a museum* **M·usen-~almanach** m *poetical annual* **~berg** m *Mount Parnassus* **~quell** m *well of the Muses, Pierian fount* **~roß** n *Pegasus* **~sitz** m ⟨fig⟩ *university* **~-sohn** m *poet; student* **Mus·eum** n ~s/–een [eːən] *museum* | ~skunde [f] *museography*; ~sstück [n] *piece worthy to go into a m.* **Mus·ik** f ~/ *music* (alt *early*) ‖ (Musikanten) *band of m.ians* pl ‖ ~ m *to make m.* ‖ in ~ setzen *to set (to m.)*; *to write the m. of* ‖ die ~ zu e–r Oper, etc schreiben *to write the score to an opera, to a text* | ⟨fig fam⟩ ohne ~ abziehen *to steal away* ‖ da liegt ~(e) drin *there is sth to that, that's the th!* **~akademie** f *m.al academy* **~aufführung** f *m.al performance; concert* **~automat** m *coin-operated gramophone*, ⟨bes Am⟩ *juke box* **~begleitung** f *accompaniment* **~direktor** m *chief conductor* **~dirigent** m *conductor* **~dose** f *m. box* **~drama** n *opera* **~fest** n *m. festival* **~folge** f *program* **~instrument** n *m.al instrument* **~kenner** m *m. expert* **~korps** n ⟨mil⟩ *band* **~lehrer** m *m.-master* **≃liebend** a *fond of m.* **~liebhaber** m *music-lover* **~meister** m ⟨mil⟩ *bandmaster* **~pavillon** m *band shell* **~podium** n *bandstand* **~probe** f *rehearsal* **~reiten** n *riding to m.* **~saal** m *concert hall* **~schrank** = ~truhe **~-schule** f *conservatory* **~stück** n *composition, piece of m.* **~stunde** f *m.-lesson* **≃treibend** a *cultivating m.* **~truhe** f ⟨wir⟩ *radio-phonograph console model*; mit Plattenwechsler *auto-r.* ‖ *radio-record combination* **~- u Sprachaufnahmen** pl ⟨rec⟩ *recording of music and sound* **~unterricht** m *m. lesson(s)* **~verein** m *m.al society* **~verleger** m *m.--publisher* **≃verständig** a *appreciative of m.*; er ist ~ *he appreciates m.* **~verständiger** = ~kenner **~verständnis** n *m.al appreciation* **~wissenschaft** f *musicology* | ~ler *m.gist* **~zeichen** pl *m.al symbols* **Musik·alien** pl (*printed*) *music* | ~händler [m] *owner of m. store*; ~handlung [f] *m.-shop* **musik·alisch** a *m.al* (*evening, family, inclination, feeling*) ‖ ~e Stühle (Spiel) *m. chairs* ‖ ~er Teil (e–r Operette) *score*, (e–s Abends) *program* ‖ ~e Veranlagung *m.al talent* od *inclination* ‖ ~e Veranstaltung, ~er Vortrag *m. performance, musicale, recital* ‖ ~ s *to be m.al* **Musikalit·ät** f ~/ *m.ality musicianship* **M·usik·ant** m ~en/~en (*itinerant*) *musician* ‖ *indifferent player* ‖ böhmische ~en [pl] *German band* | °⟨fig⟩ ~en *ready cash* **~enknochen** m *funny-bone* **~entum** n *musicianship* **M·usiker** m ~s/~; **M·usikus** m ~/Musizi *musician* ‖ ausübender ~ *performing artist* od *musician* **m·usisch** a *art-loving* ‖ ~e Erziehung *instruction in arts and music* **musiz·ieren** vi [h] *to practise* od *have* od *make music* ‖ viel ~ *to play a good deal on the piano*, etc. ‖ es wurde musiziert *we had* od *there was (some) music* ‖ wenn musiziert wird *at music* | gesellschaftliches ≃ *music played at social gatherings*

Mus·iv-~arbeit f *mosaic (work)* **~gold** n *mosaic--gold* **mus·ivisch** a *mosaic*

°**Musj·e** m ~s/~s (= monsieur Fr) *sir*, ⟨archaic⟩ *sirrah*, ⟨Am⟩ *sir(r)ee*

Musk·at m ~(e)s/~e; **~e** f ~/~n = **~nuß** f *nutmeg* | ~baum [m] *n.-tree*; ~blüte [f] *mace* **~·eller** m ~s/~ (Wein) *muscatel* | ~apfel [m] *musk-apple*; ~birne [f] *musk-pear*; ~traube [f] *muscadine (grape)*; ~wein [m] *muscatel*

M·uskel m ~s/~n ⟨anat⟩ *muscle* ‖ ⟨übtr⟩ ~n [pl] (Kraft) *brawn* **~anstrengung** f *muscular exertion* **~band** n ⟨anat⟩ *m.r ligament* **~bewegung** f *m.r movement* **~faser** f *m.r fibre* **~haut** f *m.r membrane* **~kater** m *pain after m.r exertion*; ⟨Am fam⟩ *Charley horse* **~kraft** f *m.r power* od *strength*; *m.rity* **~lehre** f *myology* **~mann** m ⟨arts⟩ *skinless figure* °**~protz** m *m.-man*, ⟨fam⟩ *beefcake* **~-rheumatismus, ~schmerz** m *pains in the m.s*, ⟨scient⟩ *myalgia* **~schwund** m *m.r dystrophy* **≃-stark** a *muscular* **~stärke** f *m.r strength, m.rity* **~strecker** m *expander* **~zerrung** f *sprained muscle*; sich e–e ~ zuziehen *to sprain a muscle* **m·usk(e)lig** a *muscular* **Muskulat·ur** f ~/~en *musculature; muscular system* **muskul·ös** a *muscular, brawny*

Musk·ete f ~/~n *musket* **Musk·eten-~feuer** n *volley of m.ry* **~kugel** f *m.-ball* **~salve** f *volley of m.ry* **~schuß** m *m.-shot* **Musket·ier** m ~(e)s~e *musketeer* **Musk·ote** m → Muschkote

M·üsli n ~s/ ⟨cul⟩ *raw cereals and fruit with milk*

M·uße f ~/ *leisure, ease* ‖ ~ h *to be at l.* ‖ mit ~ *at one's l., in a l.ly way* ‖ Zeit u ~ h, finden *to have, find time and l.* (für *for*) **~stunde** f *an unoccupied hour* **~zeit** f ⟨fam⟩ *off-time* **m·üßig** → d.

Mussel·in m ~(e)s/~e *muslin* | **≃en** a *muslin*

m·uß [1. & 3. pres] v müssen **M·uß** n ~/ (*hard*) *necessity; must* ⟨a.⟩ [attr]; *an absolute m.*, → müssen 9. ‖ es ist ein ~ *it is a n.* ‖ es ist kein ~ *there is no real need for it, it is optional* | ⟨prov⟩ ~ ist e–e harte Nuß *necessity is a hard master* **~heirat** f *shotgun marriage* **~preuße** m *Pr. against his own wishes* **m·üssen** vi [muß/mußte/gemußt] [h] **A. 1.** [vor anderem inf steht ~ = gemußt: B. 8., C. 4., D. 3.] **2.** *must* [fast nur im indic pres: → B. 9. & C.] **B. 1. (Naturnotwendigkeit)** alle M. ~ sterben *all men must die* ‖ ich, er muß *I, he must* ‖ der Hund muß sich auch immer kratzen *that dog will scratch h.s.* **2. (Logik)** *what is not right must be wrong* ‖ *yes, that must be so* ‖ *he must be very clever* ‖ *the fugitives must have suffered severely* (vgl 12.) **3. (Zwang)** *to be forced*, (nur v P) *compelled (to do)* ‖ wir ~ gehen *we must (needs) be going* (od *be off*) ‖ ich muß lachen *I cannot help laughing* (wenn *if*) ‖ die Briefe ~ geschrieben w .. *require to be written* ‖ es mußte mich einfach interessieren *I could not help being interested*; .. muß zurückgegeben w .. *will be returned* **4. (Verabredung)** *he is due to speak tonight* ‖ *the train is due at 7.30* (muß k) **5. (Verpflichtung)** (vgl 9.) *to be bound (to do)* ‖ das mußt du selbst beurteilen *that's for you to judge* ‖ er muß abgehen *he is due to retire* ‖ *he acts as he should* (muß) **6. (Wunsch)** du mußt mitk *do come (with us)!* ‖ die Wahrheit muß an den Tag! *I wish the truth may come out* ‖ ich muß mit ihr sprechen *I must* (od *want to*) *speak to her* **7. (Befehl)** *you must obey* **8. (Sollen)** *to have got to* ‖ Sie ~ wissen *you ought to know* ‖ er hätte mehr arbeiten ~ *he ought to have worked harder* ‖ ein Ehemann, wie er s muß *a model* od *pattern husband* **9. (umständehalber)** (vgl 5.) *to must* (→ A. 2.), *to have to, to be obliged to, to be bound by duty*, etc. ‖ *he acted as he had to* ‖ .. muß berücksichtigt w .. *is a consideration*; .. man h *they are absolute musts*; du mußt die Augen offen halten *you want to keep your eyes open*; das hatte er ja nur sagen ~ *he should have said it* ‖ ⟨fam⟩ *sth has (got) to be done* (muß geschehen) ‖ ich mußte telephonieren *I had occasion to telephone* ‖ .. mußte sie nun tragen *that burden was now for her to bear* ‖ du wirst es tun ~ *you will have to do it* ‖ was er wissen muß *what he needs to know* **10. [ell]** sein letzter Taler mußte **dran** .. *had to be sacrificed* ‖ ich muß **fort** *or* weg *I must go* (vgl 3) ‖ °er muß **ins** Loch *he must go to prison* ‖ wir ~ **nach** Hause (zu ihm) *we must go home (go to him)* ‖ die Briefe ~ **zur** Post .. *must go to the post, must be posted* **11. (unzweifelhaft)** sie ~ **doch wohl** bald k *they are bound to come soon, they must soon be here* ‖ es muß (wohl) wahr s *it must be true, it is undoubtedly true* ‖ er muß doch dankbar s *he cannot but be grateful* ‖ du mußt doch zugeben .. *you must admit* .. **12. (vermutlich)** (vgl 2.) es muß **wohl** schon Zeit s *it must be time by now* ‖ er muß wohl krank s *very likely* (od *I suppose*) *he is ill* ‖ er muß es noch nicht wissen, sonst .. *he cannot know it yet, or he would* .. **13. nicht** ~ *not to be supposed (to do)*; du mußt es nicht tun, wenn du nicht willst *you need not do it,* *if you do not like it* | Sie ~ sich nichts v ihm befehlen l *don't let him order you about* | [abs] ich muß (= darf) nicht vergessen *I must not forget* **14. (Frage) warum** mußten Sie das sagen *what made you say that* || **wer** muß **nicht** denken an ..? *who can help thinking of* ..? | [obs] wer muß (= mag) es ihm gesagt h? (jd muß, aber wer?) *who may, can, could have told him* | muß das wirklich getan w? *must that needs be done*? || mußtest du auch gerade heute k? *pity that you had to come today* || ⟨iron⟩ muß das s? *do you* (⟨vulg⟩ *yer*) *feel like that*? **15. wenn** es s muß *if it can't be helped* **C. [pret] mußte 1.** *had to, was forced* od *obliged to* (od *compelled to* nur v P) **2.** [in abhängiger Rede] *must* **3.** er m. abreisen (die Schule früh verlassen) *he had to leave* (*school at an early age*) || es m. (nun) einmal so sein [.. sich gerade so fügen, daß ..] *it had to be so, chance* od *fate would have it so* [*have it that* ..] **4.** sie **h es tun** ~ (vgl A. 1.) *they have been obliged to do it* **D. müßte 1.** (Vermutung) welches Vergnügen m. es s *what pleasure it would be* **2.** (moralische Verpflichtung) wir m.n (= sollten eigentlich) .. *we ought to love our neighbours* || *you ought to know better* || *you should sink into the ground for shame* **3.** (umständehalber) er hätte es (eigentlich) wissen ~ *he ought to have known it* || es m. spätestens morgen geschehen *it ought to be done by to-morrow* || der Zug m. längst da s *the train is over-due* **4.** das ist **als** m. es so s *that seems as if it could not be otherwise* **5.** ich m. mich sehr irren, **wenn** *I should be very much mistaken, if* **6.** er kommt sicher, er m. **denn** krank s *he is sure to come, unless he is ill* || das werde ich nie glauben, er m. es mir denn selbst sagen .. *unless I have it from his own lips*

m·üßig [a] **1.** *idle* (*hand*); *vacant* (*hour*); *lazy* (*life*) || *idling* (*loafers*) || (zeitweise) *disengaged* || *unemployed* (*time*) || nicht ~ s ⟨fig⟩ *not to let the grass grow under one's feet* | [adv] ~ gehen *to be idle, to saunter* || ~ dabeistehen *to stand idly by* (u warten *waiting*) || ⟨com⟩ (v Geld) ~ liegen *to lie idle* **2.** (zwecklos) *vain, fruitless, futile, useless* (*talk*); *idle* (*thoughts*); *frivolous* (*question*) ≈**gang** m *idleness, laziness*; sich dem ~ hingeben *to eat the bread of i.* || ⟨prov⟩ ~ ist aller Laster Anfang *Idleness is the root of all evil* ≈**gänger** m *idler, loafer* || ⟨fam⟩ (Faulpelz) *lazy-bones* | ≈**risch** [a] *idling, lazy* ≈**keit** f *idleness*; → Muße

M·ustang m ~s/~s ⟨Am⟩ *mustang* (*wild horse*)

M·uster n ~s/~ *model*; *test piece* || (Probe) *sample* || (Vorlage) *pattern, design* || (Richtschnur) *standard* || ⟨fig⟩ *example* (*of true friendship*) || das ewige ~ *the ideal* || ~ ohne Wert *by s.-post* | die neuesten ~ *the latest p.s* | **nach** dem ~ v *on the line of* || nach englischem (sozialistischem) ~ *after the E. p.* (*on a socialist p.*) || nach e–m ~ arbeiten *to work from a p.* || nach ~ *according to pattern* || *to organize on the m. of* (nach dem ~ v) || 3 Flugzeuge **vom** ~ Beaufighter *three B.s* | ~ zus–stellen *to make a collection of s.s* || *to embroider a p.* | *she is a m.* (das ~ e–r) *of a good house-wife, the pink of politeness, a pattern of domestic virtues* || das ~ v e–m Schüler *a m.-scholar* | **als** ~ hinstellen *to hold up as a m.* || sich ein ~ nehmen **an** *to m. o.s. on*; .. e–n **zum** .. *to follow a p's example, to p. o.s. after a p*; ⟨fig⟩ *to take a leaf out of a p's book* **~abzug** m *film copy* **~bedingungen** f pl ⟨ins⟩ *standard* od *uniform policy conditions* **~beispiel** n *model, ex.*; *test case*; ein ~ geben *to set a p.* (für *of*) **~betrieb** m *pilot* od *m. plant, farm*, etc **~bezeichnung** f *type-designation* **~bild** n (*proto*)*type, paragon, ideal* **~buch** n *book of p.s* **~gatte** m *p. husband* ≈**gültig** a *st., classical, ideal* (*order*) || *exemplary, model* (→ ~haft) | ~keit [f] *ex.riness* **~gut** n *m. farm* **~karte** f ⟨com⟩ *p.-* od *show-card* **~kasten** m ⟨com⟩ *box of s.s* **~klammer** f *paper-fastener* **~knabe** m *m.* od *show boy*, ⟨dero⟩ *swot, prig* | Ihre ganze **~kollektion** *a full range of your s.s* **~lager** n *stock of s.s, s. stock, showroom* **~leistung** f *record* **~messe** f *s. fair* **~modell** n *master p.* **~presse** f *tuck press* **~probe** f *pattern* **~reisende(r)** m *commercial traveller* **~rolle** f ⟨mil⟩ *muster-roll* **~sammlung** f ⟨com⟩ *collection of s.s* || ⟨Lit⟩ *anthology* **~schneider** m *p.-maker* **~schriftsteller** m *classical* od *st. author* **~schule** f *m. school* **~schüler** m *show boy*; ⟨sl⟩ *swot* **~schutz** m 1. Gebrauchs≈ *registration* (*and protection*) *of designs* 2. Geschmacks≈ *copyright in d.s* | ~gesetz [n] ⟨m. m.⟩ *Designs Act*, → Gebrauchs≈ **~stück** n (*good*) *specimen, exhibit*; *pattern*; ⟨arts⟩ *study* **~tabellierungen** f pl ⟨comp⟩ *s. tabulations* **~werk** n *st. work* **~wirtschaft** f *m. farm* **~wort** n ⟨gram⟩ *paradigm* **~zeichner** m *p.-drawer, d.er* **~zeichnung** f *p., d.* **~zimmer** n *show-room* **~zulassung** f *type-approval* **m·usterhaft** a *exemplary, model* (*behaviour*) || *perfect, ideal* (*order*) || ~e Haltung ⟨mil⟩ *excellent behaviour* || *excellent* (*workman*) | adv *wonderfully well* || ~artig (Kind) *good as gold* | ≈**igkeit** f ~/ *exemplariness* **-musterig** a gr·oß-, kl·ein~ *with large, small designs* **m·ustern** vt [h] **1.** *to examine, view*; *to* (*pass in*) *review* || *to eye*: .. v Kopf zu Fuß *he eyed him from head to foot, he looked him up and down* || .. sich, e–a *they measured each other with their eyes*; sich (selbst) [jdn] ~ *to look o.s.* [*a p*] *over* **2.** ⟨mil & mar⟩ *to review* od *inspect* (*troops*); *to muster* (*recruits*) **3.** ⟨tech⟩ *to* (*apply a*) *pattern* (*to*) (*a wall*) || (Stoffe) *to figure* | **gemustert** *figured* (*ribbons, wall-paper*) || –ter Stoff *fancy-material* **M·usterung** f ~/~en *examination, inspection, scrutiny* || *review* || ⟨com⟩ *pattern, design* (*of textiles*, etc) | ⟨mil⟩ *muster-parade, inspections* pl || *muster*(*ing*) || e–e ~ halten *to hold a review, to review troops* **~sgeschäft** n ⟨mil⟩ *mustering, recruiting* **~skommission** f ⟨mil⟩ *board of ex.*(*s*)

M·ut m ~(e)s/ **1. A.** *courage* || (Herzhaftigkeit) *heart, spirit, mettle* || (Kühnheit) *hardihood, boldness* || ⟨moral philos⟩ *fortitude* || ⟨mil⟩ *bravery, valour, valiance, fight* (*no f. was left in them*) || ⟨fam⟩ *kick, pluck* || ⟨sl⟩ *guts* pl, *ginger, grit* || ⟨Scot sl⟩ *spunk* (*to have the sp. to do*) || ⟨Am sl⟩ *sand* **B.** angetrunkener ~ *Dutch courage, pot-valour*; mit a.m ~ *well-fortified* || eherner, fester, frecher, kecker ~ *iron, unswerving, wanton, audacious c.* || moralischer ~ *moral c.* || sinkender ~ *sagging spirits* || unerschrockener ~ *undaunted c.* || trauriger ~ *deplorable hardihood* (*to betray*) || zager ~ *faint-hearted c.* **C.** [als Subjekt] sein ~ steigt *his boldness grows* || sein ~ ging ihm aus; schwand, verließ ihn *his c.* od *nerve failed* od *deserted him*; *his heart failed him* od *sank*; ~ gehört nun mal dazu *it simply takes grit* **D.** [als Objekt] s–n ~ aufs höchste anspannen *to screw one's c. up to the sticking point*; ~ **bek** *to win c.*; wieder .. ⟨sl⟩ *to get one's pecker up* || ~ beweisen *to show c.* || ~ erfordern: *it takes c.* || ~ fassen *to take* od *gather c.* od *heart* || fasse ~! *take your c. in both hands*!, *pluck up*! || frischen ~ fassen *to screw up one's c., to nerve o.s.* || es gibt mir neuen ~ *it gives me new heart* || ~ **h** *to possess c.* || sie h k–n ~ *their hearts fail them* || den ~ dazu h *to have the nerve* (od ⟨fam⟩ *grit*) (*to do*), ⟨sl⟩ *to have got the guts* || sich ~ **m** *to get one's c. up* || den ~ (nicht) sinken l *to lose c.* (*to keep up one's c.*, ⟨sl⟩ *to keep one's pecker up*, ⟨bes sport⟩ *to come up smiling* || den ~ verlieren *to lose c.* od *one's nerve*; nur nicht den ~ v.! *never say die*! || (all) s–n ~ zus–nehmen *to summon one's c.* (*to take one's c. in both hands*) **E. jdm** ~ einflößen *or* m *to give a p c., to put c. into a p* || jdm den ~ (be)nehmen *to discourage* od *unnerve a p*; .. allen .. *to deprive a p of all c.* || jds ~ stärken *to brace a p's c.* || in jdm den ~ wecken *to inspire a p with c.* || jdm ~ zusprechen *to cheer a p up* **F.** [intj] (nur) Mut! *cheer up*! *pluck up* (*your c.*) || nur den ~ nicht verlieren! *don't lose heart*!, *never say die*! **2. A.** ⟨**psych**⟩ *mood, frame of* *mind* **B.** frischen, frohen, guten *or* gutes ~(e)s s *to be of good cheer* od *heart* ‖ getrosten ~(e)s s *to be confident* | etw heiteren ~(e)s tun .. *cheerfully* **C. zu ~e** *or* **zumute**: wie ist dir z.? *how do you feel?* ‖ du weißt nicht, wie mir z. war *you little know what I felt* od *suffered* | mir ist nicht lächerlich z. *I'm not in a laughing humour* ‖ .. schlecht z. *I feel ill at ease* ‖ .. sonderbar z. *I feel queer* ‖ .. übel z. *I am sick at heart* ‖ .. nicht wohl z. *I do not feel well*, .. dabei .. *it makes me feel uncomfortable* **≗beseelt, ≗erfüllt** a *high-spirited, full of c.* **≗los** a *disc.d, dejected; despondent, deflated; languid, afraid* (*to do*) ‖ ~ m *to dishearten, discourage* **~losigkeit** f *disc.ment, dejectedness, dejection, despondency* **≗maßen** vt [h] *to surmise, suppose, presume, conjecture, guess* **≗maßlich** a *hypothetical, conjectural; probable, presumable; supposed, putative* (*father*) ‖ ~er Erbe *heir presumptive* | adv *to all appearance* **~maßung** f *conjecture* (über *about*), *surmise, supposition, guess*(*work*) ‖ ~en anstellen *to form conjectures, to conjecture* **≗maßungsweise** adv *as a guess* **≗voll** a *high-spirited, courageous*, ⟨fam⟩ *plucky* **~wille** m *frolicsomeness, playfulness, sportiveness*; (Schelmerei) *waggery, mischievousness*; (Schelmenstreich) *mischief, pranks* pl | ⟨dero⟩ *wantonness*; ⟨bib⟩ *temerity*; (Bosheit) *malice* | s–n ~n an jdm auslassen *to let off one's high spirits on a p* ‖ ~n treiben *to play tricks* (mit *on*) ‖ aus reinem ~n *from love of mischief* **≗willig** a (ausgelassen) *frolicsome, playful, sportive* ‖ (absichtlich) *deliberate, voluntary* ‖ ~e Beschädigung e–r S *wilful damage on a th* ‖ (Streiche machend) *mischievous* ‖ ⟨dero⟩ (frevlerisch) *wanton, malicious* ‖ *fraudulent* (*bankruptcy*) ‖ (unnötig) *gratuitous* (*lie*) | adv (*to torment animals*) *wilfully* ‖ (*to behave*) *wantonly* ‖ ~ ins Verderben rennen *to rush headlong into destruction* | ~keit [f] *mischievous disposition* | ⟨dero⟩ *wantonness* | *gratuitousness* **M·ütchen** n ~s/; sein ~ an jdm kühlen ⟨fig⟩ *to wreak one's anger upon a p, to vent one's spleen on a p*; ⟨Am⟩ *to take it out on a p* **m·uten 1.** vt/i [h] *to apply for a mining-concession* → Mutung **2.** vi [s] [nur pp gemut(et):] wohl gem. s *to be cheerful* **m·utig** a *courageous, mettlesome* ‖ *bold* (*hero, heart, attack*) ‖ *brave* (*deed*) ‖ ⟨fam⟩ *gritty* ‖ *game* (*dog*) ‖ ~e Tat *adventure* | ⟨prov⟩ dem ≗en gehört die Welt *go in and win* | adv *courageously* ‖ ~ sterben *to die game* ‖ nur ~ weiter! *more power to your elbow!* | **≗keit** f ~/ *mettlesomeness, mettle*

M·uta f ~/–tae ⟨gram⟩ *mute* (*consonant*)

mutag·en a ⟨biol⟩ *mutagenic* **Mut·ant** m ~(e)s/ ~e (P im Stimmwechsel ~en/~en), **Mutante** f ~/~n ⟨biol⟩ *mutant* **Mutation** f ~/~en ⟨biol⟩ *mutation, sport* | ~sstämme [pl] ⟨biol, bact⟩ *mutant strains* **mut·ieren** vi [h] ⟨biol⟩ *to mutate, sport*; (voice) *to break* | ≗ n *mutation*

M·utter 1. f ~(s Hut)/≗ *mother* (⟨a. fig⟩ *m. earth*) ‖ ⟨sl⟩ *mater* L ‖ (Ehefrau) ⟨fam⟩ *ma* ‖ (alte Frau) *matron, old woman, dame* ‖ (T) *dam* ‖ die ~ Gottes *the Holy Virgin, the Madonna*; ~ des Erbarmens *V. of Mercy* ‖ **bei** ~ Grün übernachten *to sleep with Mrs. Green* od *under a tree* ‖ wie bei ~(n) *as comfortable as at home, like m. makes it* | **zur** ~ m *to get with child, to make* (*a girl*) *a m.* ‖ m–r ~ [gen] Sohn *this child* | werdende ~ *expectant m.* ‖ wie e–e ~ *m.ly* ‖ sie war ganz ~ *she was all maternal* **2.** ⟨anat⟩ = Gebär≗ **3.** ⟨tech⟩ f ~/~n (Schrauben≗) *nut* ‖ Flügel≗ *butterfly nut* ‖ Gegen≗ *lock nut* ‖ Kapsel≗ *capped nut* ‖ Kolben≗ *piston rod nut* **~auge** n *m.'s eye* **≗beratung** f abhalten *to hold antenatal clinic* **~beschwerden** f pl *uterine complaint* **~boden** m *top* od *surface soil*, ⟨anat & fig⟩ *matrix* **~bruder** m *m.'s brother, maternal uncle* **~brust** f *m.'s breast* **~erde** f *garden-mould*; ⟨fig⟩ *native soil* **~fieber** n *puerperal fever* **~flecken** m = ~mal **~flugzeug** n (das Roboter-Drohnen lenkt) ⟨aero fam⟩ *queen* **~freuden** f pl *m.l joy* ‖ ~ [dat] entgegensehen *to be with child* **≗fürsorge** f *maternity service* **~gestein** n *bedrock* **~g·ottesbild** n *image of the* (*Blessed* od *Holy*) *Virgin* **~halter** m (Gebär≗) *pessary* **~herrschaft** f *matriarchy* **~herz** n *m.l* od *m.'s heart* **~hilfe** f *M.'s Aid Society* **~instinkt** m *m. instinct* **~kind** n *pet* od *spoilt child* | ~-Kind-Beziehung [f] *parenthood* **~kirche** f *m.-church* **~kompaß** m *master compass* **~korn** n *ergot* **~kraut** n ⟨bot⟩ *fever-few* **~kuchen** m ⟨anat⟩ *placenta* L **~lamm** n *ewe-lamb* **~land** n (e–r Kolonie) *m.-country* **~lauge** f *m.-liquor*; ⟨Saline⟩ *bittern* **~leib** m *womb*, ⟨scient⟩ *uterus* ‖ vom ~e an *from one's birth* **~liebe** f *m.l* od *m.ly love* **≗los** a *m.less* **~mal** n *mole, birth-mark* **~milch** f *m.'s milk* ‖ mit der ~ einsaugen *to be born and bred to ..; to cut one's teeth on* (*a th*) **~mord** m, **~mörder** m *matricide* **≗mörderisch** a *matricidal* **~pause** f (*reproducible*) *master copy* od *print* **~pferd** n *mare* **~pflanze** f *parent plant* **~pflicht** f *m.l duty* **~rohr** n ⟨artill⟩ *outer* od *B-tube* **~schaf** n *ewe* **~schiff** n *m. ship*; (f Versorgung) *tender* ‖ ⟨aero a.⟩ *aircraft tender* **~schlüssel** m *spanner, screw-wrench* **~schoß** m *m.'s lap* ‖ ⟨fig⟩ *tender care* **~schraube** f *bolt with head and nut* ‖ *nut; female screw* **~schutz** m *protection of motherhood* **~schwein** n *sow* **~schwester** f *m.'s sister, m.l aunt* **~seele** f; k–e ~ *not a* (*living*) *soul* **≗seelenall·ein** a *quite alone* **~söhnchen** n *m.'s darling* ‖ ⟨dero⟩ *milksop, spoilt child*, ⟨fam⟩ *molly*(*-coddle*) **~sprache** f *m.-tongue, native language, vernacular* **~stadt** f *native town* ‖ (e–r Kolonie) *m.-city* **~stand** m *m.hood* **~stelle** f *place of a m.* ‖ ~ vertreten (an [dat], bei) *to be a second m.* (*to*) **≗sterblichkeit** f *puerperal* od *maternal mortality* **~tag** m *Mothers' Day* **~teil** n *m.l portion* **~tier** n *dam* **~trompete** f ⟨anat⟩ *oviduct* **~witz** m *m.-wit, commonsense, gumption* **~wurz** f ⟨bot⟩ *mountain arnica* **M·uttchen** n ~s/~ ⟨fam⟩ *mummy* **M·ütterchen, M·ütterlein** n ~s/~ *beloved m., dear little m.* ‖ ⟨fig⟩ *good old woman, granny* **m·ütterlich** a *mother*(*ly*), *maternal* ‖ ~ verwandt *related on the m.'s side* ‖ e–e Tante **~erseits** [adv] *a m.l aunt* ‖ s–e Familie ~ *his m.'s family* **M·utterschaft** f ~/ *motherhood, maternity; parenthood* **M·utti** f ~(~s Hut)/~s ⟨fam⟩ *mammy, mum*; ⟨Am⟩ *mom*

M·utung f ~/~en ⟨min⟩ *claim* → muten

°**Mutz** f ~/~en (Tabakpfeife) *nose-warmer*

M·ütze f ~/~n *cap* | B·ade≗ *bathing cap* ‖ → Baskenmütze ‖ Damen≗ bonnet ‖ ⟨mil⟩ *hat*; ⟨mil⟩ → a. Feldmütze ‖ Kaffee≗ *cosy* ‖ (Kugelabschnitt) *spherical cap* ‖ Ohrenschutz≗ *comforter cap* ‖ P·elz≗ ⟨mil⟩ *busby* ‖ Sch·irm≗ *peaked cap* ‖ Sch·otten≗ *bonnet, tam o'shanter* ‖ Sch·ul≗ ⟨Ger⟩ *school-cap*, ⟨engl⟩ (*square*) *college-cap*, ⟨fam⟩ *mortarboard* ‖ Sp·ort≗ *tweed cap* ‖ Zipfel≗ *jelly-bag cap* | die ~ abnehmen vor *to take off one's cap to ..* **M·ützen- ~aufschlag** m *turned-up part* **~band** n *cap* od *bonnet ribbon* **~deckel** m *flat crown* **~macher** m *capmaker* **~rand** m *edge, rim* **~schirm** m *peak* **~stoß** m *edging*

†**Myk·ene** n ⟨Gr⟩ (Stadt) *Mycenæ* **myk·enisch** a *Mycenæan*

M·yon n ~s/ ⟨phys⟩ *muon*

Myri·ade f ~/~n *myriad* ‖ ~n Sterne *m. s of stars*

M·yrrhe f ~/~n ⟨bot⟩ *myrrh* **~öl** n *oil of myrrh*

M·yrte f ~/~n ⟨bot⟩ *myrtle* (→ Eukalyptus) ‖ die jungfräuliche ~ der Braut *the virginal m.-wreath* **~nzweig** m *myrtle-branch*

†**M·ysien** n (kleinasiat. Landschaft) *Mysia*

mysteri·ös a *mysterious* (*event, darkness*) ‖ das Mysteriöse *m.ness* **Myst·erium** n ~s/–rien *mystery* ‖ ⟨theat⟩ *miracle-play* **Mystifikati·on** [ts] f ~/~en *mystification* **mystifiz·ieren** vt [h] *to mystify* **M·ystik** f ~/ *mysticism* ‖ ~er [m] ~s/~ *mystic* **m·ystisch** a *mystic* (*writer*) ‖ *mystical* (*doctrine, intercourse, p, darkness, affair*); die ~e

Atmosphäre *or* das ~e *mystique* **Mystiz·ismus** m ~/ *mysticism*

M·ythe f ~/~n *fable, myth* || die nordischen ~n *the Norse m.s* **~nbildung** f *formation of m.s* **~nforschung** f *m.ology* **m·ythenhaft, m·ythisch** a *m.ic* || ⟨fig⟩ *m.ical* || ~e Gestalt *m.(ical shape)* || ins ~e wachsen *to become a m.* **Mythol·og** m ~en/~en *m.ologist* **-log·ie** f ~/~n *mythology* **m-l·ogisch** a *mythologic(al)* **M·ythos, -thus** m ~/-then *myth* || mit e–m ~ aufräumen *to explode a m.*; → Mythe, Fabel

Myz·el n ~s/~e ⟨bot⟩ *mycelium*

N

N, n [n] ~/~ *N, n* || 3^n 3^n; → hoch

n·a intj (auffordernd) *well! now! then!* || (zustimmend) ~ **also!** *there you are!* || ~ **eben!** *even so* || (fragend) ~? *well?* || (zögernd) *well then (I'll proceed)* || (beschwichtigend) ~, ~! *come, come!, there, there!* || ~ **n·u!** ~ ·aber! *well, I never!, I say! what next!* || ⟨iron⟩ ~ das wäre! *nonsense!*; ~, ~! (ungläubig) *well, well!, gently!* || (erstaunt) ~, **so was!** *there now!* || ~ **(und) ob!** *rather! most certainly!, shouldn't I, now?* || ~, **warte!** *just wait!*

N·abe f ~/~n *hub, nave* || ⟨cycl⟩ *cycle hub*, Freilauf~ *freewheel hub* || ⟨mar⟩ (der Schraube), ⟨aero⟩ (des Propellers) *boss* || ⟨tech mill⟩ *boss (of drum)* **N·abel** m ~s/~ ⟨anat⟩ *navel* || ⟨geom & ant⟩ *umbilicus (of a spiral, a sea)* || ⟨her⟩ *nombril* || ⟨bot⟩ (Samen~) *eye*, ⟨scient⟩ *hilum* **~binde** f *umbilical band* **~bruch** m *u.l rupture*, ⟨scient⟩ *omphalocele* **~förmig** a *n.shaped, u.l* **~frei** a ⟨bes Am⟩ *peek-a-boo (dress)*; → taillen– **~kraut** n ⟨bot⟩ *n.-wort*, gemeines ~ *penny-wort* **~schnitt** m ⟨med⟩ *omphalotomy* **~schnur** f *n.-string* **~schwein** n ⟨zoo⟩ *tajacu, peccary* **~stück** → N. ⟨anat⟩ **n·abeln** vt [h] (Kind) ~ *to dress a (child's) n.* **n·aben** vt [h] *to furnish with a nave* **N·aben-~bolzenschraube** f ⟨aero⟩ *airscrew boss bolt* **~bremse** f *hub brake* **~buchse** f *n.-box* **~drechsler** m *n. turner* **~ring** m *axle-hoop* **~scheibe** f *n. disc*

N·abob m ~s/~s ⟨Ind⟩ *nawab*, ⟨Moham & AInd⟩ *nabob*

nach I. prep [dat] [oft nachgesetzt [adv] *or* trennbar [pref]] **A. 1. (Zeit)** *after* || ~ Ablauf der Frist *at the expiration of the appointed time* || ~ getaner Arbeit *after (when) the work was (is) done* || im Jahre .. ~ Chr. (G.) *in the year .. of our Lord* | ~ Eingang Ihres Briefes *(up)on receipt ..* || ~ dem Essen, der Tafel, ~ Tisch *after the meal, after lunch, dinner* || ~ 30 Jahren *30 years later*; noch ~ Jahrhunderten *even in centuries to come* || ~ der Kirche *after church, after divine service* || ~ etwa 20 Minuten *in about 20 minutes' time*; ~ genau 20 M. *just 20 m.s later*; 5 M. ~ 3 (Uhr) *5 m.s past* (⟨Am⟩ *after*) *3* || ⟨com⟩ ~ Sicht *at sight* || ~ e–r Weile *after a time* || ~ einiger Zeit ⟨a.⟩ *by-and-by* || ~ langer Zeit *a long time later* | *(on the morning) succeeding (the festival)* || ~ e–r Lobrede .. *after praising (the progress he said)* | **(gleich)** ~ s–m Eintritt, s–r Rückkehr *on his entrance* || **unmittelbar** ~ *(the conditions) immediately following (the war)*; .. *following sharply upon* || *upon* [nicht *after*] *his accession it became known* **2. (Reihenfolge)** *after, behind* || e–r ~ dem anderen *one after another, one by one* || e–n .. ~ dem anderen: *he wrote letter after l.*; *day after d.*; *cigar after c.* || ~e–a *successively*; gleich ~e–a *in quick succession* | ~ Ihnen! *after you!* || **gleich** ~ dem D. *next to the director (he was ..)* || er war der tüchtigste ~ dem K. *he was .. if we except the king* | ⟨gram⟩ **stehen** ~ *to follow (the noun)* || ~ **sich ziehen** *to bring on, to cause, to be followed by* || **unmittelbar** folgen ~ *to follow on the heels of* **B. 1. (Ziel, Richtung)** *to(wards), for* || ~ Abend (zu) *westward*; ~ links *to the left*; ~ Norden *to(wards) the Noth*; *(on the way) North* || ~ oben *upwards, on high*; ~ unten *downwards* || ~ rechts (zu) *toward the right* || ~ vorn *ahead* | **bestimmt** ~ .. *bound for (France)*; ~ der Heimat b. *homeward--bound*; ~ England b.te Post *mail for E.* | Flucht ~ Ägypten .. *into ..* | ~ jeder Richtung *in every direction* || ~ der Straße *facing the street* | → bis I. A. || ~ dort (hier) = dorthin (hierher) **2. [mit Verb]** sich ~ London **aufmachen**, ~ L. aufbrechen *or* abreisen *to go to, start* (od *set out*) *for L.* || *the Gulf Stream brings them about our shores* || ~ **B.** hinein .. *to bring into Berlin* || ~ Hause **ge**hen *to go home*; ~ der **S**tadt .. *to go to town* || das Fenster geht ~ der Str. .. *looks into the street* || ~ England **reisen** *to go to E.*; er ist nach E. gereist *he has left for E.* || ~ dem Arzte **schi**cken *to send for the doctor* || ~ e–m schießen *to shoot at a p* || ~ Java **segeln** *to sail for J.* || ~ der Uhr sehen *to look at one's watch* || *he stretched his legs to the fire* || sich ~ etw **umsehen** *to look about for a th* || er **warf** e–n Stein ~ dem Hunde *he threw a stone at the dog* **C.** (= **um**) *about, for* || ~ etw fragen *to inquire* od *ask about a th* || ~ Wasser gehen *to fetch (go for) water* || ~ Brot schreien *to cry for bread* || der Fisch schreit ~ Wein *the enjoyment of fish calls for wine* **D. 1. (Art, Vorbild, Maß, Richtschnur)** *from, according to, in conformity, accordance with, after the manner of, on the authority of, agreeably to*; ein Stich ~ Raffael .. *after R.* || *a comedy from the Italian* | ~ dem **A**bc *alphabetically* || → Anschein || ~ m–r Ansicht *or* Meinung *according to my view, in my opinion* || ~ s–r Aussage *from his account* || ~ den **B**edingungen .. *under the terms (of the bequest)* || ganz ~ Belieben *just as you please* od *like* || *the books I was brought up on* || ~ der geltenden **D**efinition *under the existing d.* || ~ deutschem **G**elde *in G. m.* || ~ franz. Geschmack *in the French fashion, style, taste*; *this was a girl after his desire* || ~ dem Gesetz v 1962 *under the law of ..* || ~ dem Gewicht *by the weight* || ~ dem innersten Grunde (verstehen) .. *to the bottom* || ~ **H**erzenswunsch *to one's heart's desire* || ~ dem **M**eter *by the meter* || ~ jds Musik tanzen .. *to a p's music* || dem **N**amen ~ *by name* || ⟨fam⟩ immer der Nase ~ *straight ahead* || ~ der Natur (gezeichnet etc) *from nature* || ~ Noten (spielen) .. *from music*; ⟨fig⟩ (können) *to perfection* || der **R**egel ~ *according to the rules, as a rule, generally* || ~ der Reihe *in turn, by turns* || je ~ den **U**mständen *according to circumstances* || ~ **V**erdienst *according to deserts* || ~ franz. **W**ährung *according to French currency* || der Wirklichkeit ~ *in reality* || ~ s–r Weise *in his (usual) way* || ~ bestem Wissen *to the best of one's knowledge* **2.** (**[zu urteilen]** ~) *by* od *from (what I have heard)* || allem Anschein ~ *from all appearances* || *considering* (od *in view of*) *his education* || *by the expression of the man's face* || *to judge from his clothes* || *it is 1 by my watch* **3. [mit Verb]** wenn es ~ mir ginge *if my wishes were to be carried out* || wenn es ~ ihm ginge *if one may believe him,* .. ~ s–m Kopfe ginge *if he had his way* || ~ Diät leben *to keep one's diet* || ~ Diktat schreiben .. *from dictation* || es riecht, schmeckt ~ Fisch *it smells, tastes of fish* || ⟨fam⟩ das schmeckt ~ mehr *that gives me an appetite for more* **II. adv** → I. **1.** [oft ell] mir ~! *follow me!* ||

auf und ihm ∼! *up and after him!* || wir wollen ihm ∼! *we will go* od *run after him* **2.** [adv & trennbares pref] *after, behind* || hinten ∼ *afterwards, behind* **3. nach u nach** *by degrees, by little and little, little by little, by and by, bit by bit, gradually*; → langsam || *by now, by this time* (*you ought to know it*) || **nach wie vor** *now as ever* od *before, as usual; still*; n. w. v. tun *to continue to do* **N·ach-, n·ach-** pref [in comp] **I.** [nouns] (mst nachträgliches Tun) *subsequent* (*payment*), *additional, supplementary* (*order*); *aftermath, aftertaste* **II.** [adjectives] *secondary*, (mst zeitlich) ∼christlich *post-Christian* **III.** [verbs] [trennbares pref] **1.** (Wiederholung) ∼|bestellen *to repeat an order, to order some more* (*of a dish*); ∼|buchstabieren *to spell over again*; ∼|gären *to ferment again*; ∼|-bohren, ∼|reißen *to bore, tear wider* **2.** (Nachahmung) ∼|arbeiten *to work after* od *from*; e–m ∼|buchstabieren *to spell after a p* **3.** (zeitliche Reihenfolge) sich ∼|bilden *to complete one's education*; ∼|bewilligen *to grant subsequently* od *additionally*; ∼|beten *to resound*; ∼|dröhnen *to rumble after* **4.** (Verfolgen) e–m ∼|bellen *to bark after a p*; e–m ∼|blicken *to follow a p with one's eyes*; e–m ∼|schreien (∼|drohen) *to pursue a p with invectives* (*threats*) **N·ach-** ≃|**achten** vi [h] [dat] *to observe* (*a rule*) **∼achtung** f *observance* || zu Ihrer ∼! *for your guidance* ≃|**äffen** vt/i [h] [dat] *to ape, imitate, copy*; ∼d *mimicking*; die Vornehmen ∼d *snobbish* **∼äffer** m *mimic, aper, servile imitator*; ⟨fam⟩ *copycat* **∼äffer·ei** f *mimicry, aping* **∼äffung** f *aping, servile imitation* ≃|**ahmen** vt/i [h] [dat] *to imitate* (in *in*), *to copy* || e–n ∼ *to mimic, imitate a p*; (lächerlich) *to mock a p*; (gewinnsüchtig etc) *to take one's colours from a p, to steal a p's thunder* || (verfälschen) *to counterfeit, adulterate* (→ ≃|m) ≃**ahmenswert** a *exemplary, worth imitating, worthy of imitation* **∼ahmer** m = ∼äffer; *echo* **∼ahmer·ei** f *slavish imitation; plagiarism* **∼ahmung** f *i.n, counterfeit*; (Gegenstand) *copy, replica*, ⟨fig⟩ *false coin* || ∼ verboten *copying forbidden* || ∼ finden *to be copied, imitated* | *imitation, copy(ing); emulation; simulation; mimicry*; ⟨bes paint⟩ [konkr] *pastiche* Fr; vor ∼en wird gewarnt *beware of substitutes* **∼ahmungs-** ∼gabe [f] *imitative faculty*; ∼trieb [m] *i.ve instinct*; ∼sucht [f] *mania for i.n* **∼apostolisch** a *post-apostolic* **∼arbeit** f *extra work* || *last finish* ≃|**arbeiten** vt [h] *to copy* (e–m *a p*), e–m Muster ∼ *to work from a pattern*; ein M. ∼ *to copy a p.* || das Versäumte ∼ *to make up for lost time* || ⟨school⟩ müssen *to be kept in* || (verbessern) *to touch up, retouch* || sich nur mühsam (jdm) ∼ *to follow* (*a p*) *with great difficulty* ≃|**arten** vi [s] [dat] *to take after, to resemble* **∼aufnahme** f ⟨film⟩ *retake* ≃|**beben** vi [h] *to resound* | ≃ n *last shocks of an earthquake* ≃**bedacht** a *considered after the occurrence, remembered too late* **∼behandlung** f *subsequent treatment; after care* ≃ **belichten** vt [h] ⟨phot⟩ *to burn in, to overprint* **∼belichtung** f *post-exposure* **∼beobachtung** f ⟨a.⟩ *follow-up* ≃**berechnen** vt [h] *to make a supplementary charge for ..* ≃|**bessern** vt [h] *to mend, improve* || *to touch up, retouch*; ⟨for⟩ *to replant* ≃|**bestellen** vt [h] (etw) *to repeat* od *renew an order* (*for*) || *to order another helping* (od *some more*) (*of a dish*) **∼bestellung** f *additional* od *repeat-order*; (im Lokal) *seconds* ≃|**beten** vt/i [h] ⟨fig⟩ *to repeat mechanically*, (e–m) *to echo* (*a p*) **∼beter** m (*thoughtless*) *repeater, echo*, ⟨fam⟩ *parrot* **∼beter·ei** f *thoughtless repetition, echoing* ≃|**bezahlen** vt/i [h] *to pay afterwards, pay the rest* (*of*) **∼bezahlung** f *subsequent* od *additional payment* **∼bild** n *copy, replica* || ⟨opt⟩ *ocular spectrum*; ⟨physiol⟩ *after-image, persistence of vision* ≃|-**bilden** vt [h] *to copy, imitate, duplicate* **∼bildung** f *copying* || (Kopie) *copy, imitation, reproduction* || (betrügerische) *forgery* || (genaue) *facsimile* ≃|-**blättern** vt/i [h] *to look up, search for* (*a passage*) ≃|**bleiben** vi [s] *to remain, lag, linger, stay behind to be left* || ⟨fam⟩ es ist ∼geblieben *it was not done* || ⟨school⟩ *to be kept in* ≃|**blicken** vi [h] (jdm) *to look after* (*a p*), *to follow* (*a p*) *with one's eyes* **∼-blüte** f *second bloom* || ⟨fig⟩ *aftermath* ≃|**bohren** vt/i [h] *to bore again* || *to enlarge* (*a hole*) **∼brennen** n (Turbinenluftstrahlwerk & Rakete) *after-burning*; ⟨mil⟩ *hangfire* ≃|**bringen** vt [h] *to carry after* od *later*; *to bring on* || *to push on* (*a pupil*) ≃|**buchstabieren** vt [h] *to spell over again* || (jdm) *to spell after a p* **∼bürge** m, **∼bürgschaft** f *collateral security* ≃**christlich** a *post-Christian* ≃|**datieren** vt [h] *to postdate* ≃|**denken** vi [h] *to think, reflect, meditate, muse, ponder, ruminate, deliberate* || tief ∼ *to cogitate* (über *on*), angestrengt ∼d *hardthinking* || e–m ∼ *to follow a p's thoughts* || denk mal n.! *think it over!* || ∼d (*she stood*) *considering* | **über** e–e S ∼ *to ponder* od *brood over* od *to meditate, speculate on a th* || über sich ∼ *to consider o.s.* || nun er darüber n.dachte *now that he came to think of it* | ≃ [n] *reflection* || *cogitation, speculation, musing* || eigenes ∼ *own meditation* || beschauliches ∼ *contemplation* || über sich *self-consideration* || (*a matter of*) *reasoning* || (*after long*) *thought* || in ≃ dastehen *to stand in thoughtful mood* || bei weiterem ≃ *on second thoughts, on reflection* || in tiefes ∼ versunken *in deep thought* ≃**denklich** a *pondering, reflecting, reflective, speculative, museful, pensive, wistful* || *thinking* (*mind*), *thoughtful* (*air*), *contemplative* (*p*), *meditative* (*tone, p*) || e–e ∼e S *a serious affair* od *business* || ∼ machend *thought-provoking* (*book*), ∼ stimmen *to give pause .., to set* (*a p*) *thinking* || ∼ w *to turn thoughtful* || e–n ∼ m *to stagger a p, to set a p thinking* | adv *pensively*, etc; *in deep thought, thoughtfully*; ⟨fam⟩ *in a brown study* | ≃keit [f] *p.ness, th.ness, m.ness, w.ness* ≃|**dichten** vt [h] *to imitate* (*a poet's work* od *style*) | ⟨tech⟩ vt/i [h] *to tighten* | *to become tight, to tighten* **∼dichtung** f *paraphrase* ≃|**drängen** vi/t [h] *to press* od *crowd after* || ⟨mil⟩ *to pursue closely*; mit aller Kraft ∼ *to exert all possible pressure on the enemy* || sich ∼ *to force one's way in* | ≃ [n] ⟨tact⟩ *direct pressure* od *pursuit*; durch scharfes ≃ *by exerting heavy pressure* ≃|**dringen** vi [s] *to follow* od *press after* || e–m ∼ *to pursue a p* ≃|**drohen** vi [h] e–m ∼ *to pursue a p with threats* ≃|**dröhnen** vt [h] *to rumble after* **∼druck** m ⟨typ⟩ *reprint, reproduction* || (unerlaubter) *piracy*; *pirated edition* || ∼ verboten! *all rights reserved!* | ⟨emph⟩ *stress, emphasis* || (e–n) ∼ legen auf [an] *to lay stress upon*; *to emphasize* (*a word*); bes ∼ l. auf *to dwell particularly on* (*a th*) || e–r S ∼ verleihen *to give* od *lend point to a th, to emphasize* od *urge, energize a th* || mit ∼ *emphatically, energetically, vigorously* || mit ∼ aufrecht erhalten *to press* (*the charge against a p*); (*to speak*) *with assurance* ≃|**drucken** vt [h] *to reprint* || (unerlaubt) *to pirate* **∼drucker** m *piratical publisher* ≃**drücklich, ≃drucksvoll** a *firm, energetic, emphatic, expressive, poignant*; *vigorous* (*measures*) | adv *emphatically*, etc || (*to ask*) *pointedly*; ∼ betonen or hervorheben *to emphasize*; *to urge* (*a point*) || jdm etw ∼ z Bewußtsein bringen *to emphasize a th to a p, to bring a th home to a p* || ∼ Einspruch erheben *to put one's foot down* ≃|**dunkeln** vi [h] ⟨arts⟩ *to grow darker, to deepen* ≃|**eichen** vt [h] *to recalibrate* **∼eiferer** m *emulator* ≃|**eifern** vi [h] (jdm) *to emulate* (*a p*), *to vie* od *compete with a p* **∼eiferung** f *emulation* **∼eile** f ⟨mar⟩ *hot pursuit* ≃|**eilen** vi [s] *to hasten* od *run after* ≃**ein·ander** adv *successively, in succession, progressively, piecemeal; one by one, one after another* od *the other* || (*to do*) *in turns, alternately* || (*she had*) *in turn* (*been the wife of .., of ...*) || ∼ gehen, ziehen *to file* (*out of the house*) ≃|**empfinden** vt [h] (jdm) *to feel with* (*a p*), *to enter into* (*a p's*) *feelings* || e–e

Dichtung ~ *to have feeling for* .. | ≃ [n] *feeling, sympathy* **~erbe** m *second heir, after-heir* **~erbfolge** f *revisionary succession* **~erbschaft** f *remainder* **~ernte** f *aftermath, -crop* **≃|ernten** vi [h] *to glean* **≃|erzählen** vt [h] *to repeat* ‖ dem Englischen nacherzählt *adapted from the English* ‖ (Gerüchte) *to retail* ‖ e–m etw ~ *to repeat slanderous tales about a p*; –erzählt w *to be circulated* **~erzählung** f *recountal* **≃|exerzieren** vi [h] *to do extra drill* ‖ ⟨fig⟩ *to do an extra task* **~fahr** m *descendant* ‖ ~en [pl] *posterity* **≃|fahren** vi [h] *to follow* (*in a carriage* od *boat*); jdm ~ *to go after a p* **≃|färben** vt [h] *to colour* od *dye a second time* **~faßbrief** m ⟨com⟩ *follow-up* **~faßwerbung** f ⟨com⟩ *follow-up advertising* **~feier** f *subsequent celebration, extra fête* **≃|feilen** vt [h] ⟨fig⟩ *to retouch* **≃|feuern** vi [h] *to keep up the fire* ‖ vt/i e–m ~ *to fire at a p* **~flammer** m *hangfire* **~folge** f (im Amt) *succession* ‖ (Reihenfolge) *sequence* ‖ ⟨fig⟩ *imitation* (*of Christ*) ‖ jds ~ antreten ⟨a.⟩ *to step into a p's shoes* | ~gesellschaft [f] *successor company*; die ~staaten *the Succession States* **≃|folgen** vi [s] [dat] *to follow* ‖ *to succeed* (*a p in his office*) ‖ ⟨fig⟩ *to imitate, to tread in the footsteps* (*of Jesus*) ‖ auf den Fersen ~ *to be at a p's heels* **≃folgend** a *following* ‖ (S) *subsequent* ‖ ⟨mil⟩ *pursuing* (*infantry*); *trailing* (*units, elements*) **~folger** m *follower* ‖ *successor* (*to a p*) ‖ ⟨fig⟩ *imitator, disciple* ‖ als ~ v *in succession to* **~forderung** f *afterclaim* ‖ *extra charge* **~f·ormschleifen** n ⟨tech⟩ [abstr] *profile copy grinding* **~|forschen** vi [h] *to inquire* (wo *where*) ‖ [dat] *to investigate*; *to give attention to*; *to search* (*after*), *to inquire* od *spy* (*into*) ‖ ~ über *to speculate as to* **~forschung** f *investigation, search, inquiry, examination* ‖ (gelehrte) *research* ‖ ~en anstellen (nach) *to make inquiries* (*about after*) | ~sabteilung [f] *tracing department* **~frage** f **1.** = ~forschung ‖ ~ halten (nach) *to make inquiry* (*for, into, after*), *to inquire* (*after*) ‖ danke für (die) gütige ~! *thanks for* (*your*) *kind inquiries*! **2.** ⟨com⟩ *demand, call, market* (nach *for*) ‖ (Bedarf) *need* (*for*) gute ~ *seller's market*; starke ~ *boom*; *great* od *bad run* (*on*), *rush* (*for*) ‖ lebhafte (schwache) ~ *brisk* (*slack*) *demand* (*for*) ‖ ~ auf dem Arbeitsmarkt *requests for employment*; es war große (wenig) ~ nach Eisen *iron was greatly* (*little*) *in demand* ‖ in beständiger ~ *in steady demand* ‖ Angebot u ~ *supply and demand* **≃|fragen** vi [h] (nach) *to inquire* od *ask* (*after*) ‖ ich werde ~ *I'll inquire* ‖ er fragt nichts danach *he cares nothing about it* **~frist** f (*additional*) *respite, prolongation of time*; ⟨bes ins⟩ *days of grace* **~frost** m *late frost* **~frühling** m *second spring* **≃|fühlen** vt [h], jdm etw ~ *to understand, to enter into* od *to appreciate a p's feelings about a th* ‖ es jdm ~ (können) *to feel* od *sympathize with a p*; *to know a p's feelings*; das kann ich Ihnen ~ *don't I know that feeling* **≃führen** vt [h] ⟨mil⟩ *to move .. forward* | ≃ [n] *displacement* (*in longer moves*) **≃|füllen** vt [h] *to fill up, to replenish* ‖ (Lager) *to assort*; ⟨mot⟩ f. Sie 5 l Öl nach *put in 5 litres of oil* das Kühlwasser ~ *to top up the radiator* | ≃ [n] ⟨mot⟩ *topping up* | im **~gang** zu (Brief) *pursuant .., further to* .. **≃|geben** vt [h] *to give later*; *to make up for* ‖ *to add* ‖ *to knuckle under*; jdm nichts ~ *to be a p's equal, to be equal to a p, to yield to a p in nothing* ‖ vi [h] (Spannung) *to relax, slacken*; *to give way* ‖ (weichen) *to yield*; *the ground y.ed under him*; *the rope came away* ‖ (*he tried the handle*;) *it gave* ‖ (Geröll) *to slip*; (Zweig, Stoff) *to give* ‖ ⟨com⟩ (Kurse): *the exchange has declined*; (of prices) *to ease off, to soften*; *to climb down* | (sich umstimmen l) *to relent, to come round, to surrender* ‖ etw ~ *to soften a little, to thaw* ‖ jdm ~ *to give way* od *in to a p, to yield to a p* ‖ *to comply with a p's wishes* ‖ (nachsichtig) *to indulge* od *humour* (*a child*) ‖ (einsichtig) *to accede, defer to* (*a p's judgement*) ‖ nur nicht ~! *never say die*! **≃gebend** a *complying, indulgent* ‖ nicht ~ *unshrinking* **≃geboren** a (nach Vaters Tode) *posthumous* ‖ (jünger) *junior, younger*; ~er Sommer *Indian s.* **~gebühr** f *postage-due, excess postage* **~geburt** f *after-birth, placenta* **~gedanke** m *after-thought* **≃gedunkelt** a (Bild) *darkened* **~gefühl** n *after-feeling* **≃gehen** vi [s] [dat] ~ *to investigate a th, to follow* (*a th*) *up*, → –forschen; *to indulge* (*in a th*) ‖ *to seek* (*pleasure*), *to look into* (*a question*) ‖ *to entertain* (*a suggestion*) ‖ dem Geschäft hat alles andere –zu– *business first* | s–n Geschäften (s–r Praxis) ~ *to attend to one's business* (*practice*), *to get* od *go about one's affairs* ‖ (e–r S, e–m Beruf) *to pursue*; *to follow* (*a trade*) (jdm) *to go after, to follow* (*a p*); auf Schritt u Tritt *to follow at a p's heels* | (v Uhren) *to be* (*3 minutes*) *slow* (gegen *to be slower than*) ‖ täglich 5 Min. ~ *to lose .. a day* **≃gelassen** a (v literarischen Werken) *posthumous* **≃gemacht** a *imitated, counterfeit, sham, false*; ⟨sl⟩ *fake* (*necklace*) ‖ ~e Ware *imitation goods* ‖ (künstlich) *artificial* **≃geordnet** a *lower* (*authority*); [dat] *subordinate to* **≃gerade** adv *by this time, by now* (→ n. u n.) **~gesang** m *epode* **~geschmack** m (*after-*)*taste* **~geschwader** n *rear of a fleet* **≃gestalten** vt [h] *to reproduce* **≃gesteuert** a (*bomb*, etc) *with trajectory correction* **≃gewiesenermaßen** adv *as has been shown* od *proved* **≃giebig** a *acquiescent, yielding, compliant*; *complaisant, facile* ‖ (nachsichtig) *forbearing, indulgent* ‖ ~ w *to relent* (gegen *towards*) | ⟨tech⟩ *flexible*; *soft* (*shoulder of a road*; *spot* ⟨a. fig⟩) | ≃keit [f] *yieldingness, compliance, complaisance* ‖ *indulgence* | *flexibility* **≃|graben** vi [h] [dat] *to dig* (*for*), *to excavate* **~grabung** f *excavation* **~grübeln** n *speculation, musing* ‖ *meditation* ‖ *deep thinking*, ⟨fam⟩ *brown study* ‖ ≃ vi [h] *to speculate, muse* ([dat] *or* über [acc] *on*), *to ponder, brood* (*over*) **≃|gucken** vi [h] e–m ~ *to follow a p with one's eyes* **~guß** m ⟨tech⟩ *second cast* ‖ (Tee) *second brew, washy tea* **~hall** m *echo, reverberation* **≃|hallen** vi [h] *to echo, resound* **≃|halten** vt/i [h] *to celebrate later* ‖ *to make up for* (*a lesson missed*) | *to last, to hold out a long time* **≃haltig** a *lasting, enduring, persistent* (*effect*) ‖ ⟨mil⟩ *lasting* (*resistance*) | [adv] ‖ *for an extended period*; *effectively*; jdn ~ beeinflussen .. *greatly* | ~keit [f] *lastingness* ‖ *persistence* **≃|hangen, ≃|hängen** vi [h] [dat] *to follow*; *to be given* od *addicted to*; *to indulge in* ‖ *to give way to* (*melancholy*) ‖ s–n Gedanken ~ *to muse, to give rein* od *free play to one's fancy* od *thoughts* ‖ e–m Plan ~ *to give o.s. up to a plan* **≃|hauen** vi [h] ⟨fenc⟩ *to parry and thrust* ‖ ⟨mil⟩ *to pursue* **~h·ausegehen** n *going home* ‖ beim ~ *on one's way home* **≃|heizen** vi [h] *to replenish* od *keep up the fire* **≃|helfen** vi [h] [dat] *to assist* (*a pupil*) ‖ *to jog* (*a p's memory*) ‖ e–m ~ *to help a p* (*on*), ⟨fam⟩ *to give a p a lift* ‖ e–r S ~ *to push a th on*; ⟨arts⟩ *to retouch* **~helfer** m *helper* **≃her** adv *afterwards, later, subsequently* ‖ bis ~! *so long*! *see you later*! ‖ vorher u ~ *before and since* **≃h·erig** a *subsequent* **~hieb** m ⟨fenc⟩ *remise* (e–n ~ m *to make r.*) ‖ *cut after parrying* ‖ ⟨mil⟩ *immediate pursuit* **~hilfe** f *help, assistance* | ~kurs [m] *supplementary course*; ~stunden [f pl] *repetitional* od *private lessons, coaching* **≃|hinken** vi [s] [dat] *to halt* od *hobble after* od *behind* ‖ ⟨fig⟩ ~gehinkt k *to lag behind, to be late* ‖ ⟨fig⟩ *to imitate clumsily* **~holbedarf** m ⟨com m. m.⟩ *pent-up* od *postponed demand* **≃|holen** vt [h] *to make good*; *to make up for* (vgl n.halten) ‖ Versäumtes ~ ⟨fig⟩ *to recover, to make up leeway* ‖ Schlaf ~ *to catch up on sleep* **~hut** f ⟨mil⟩ *rear*(*-guard*); ⟨a.⟩ *trail party* ‖ die ~ bilden *to bring up the rear* **≃|jagen** vi [s] [dat] *to chase, pursue*; *to hunt after* ⟨a. fig⟩ | vt [h] e–m e–e Kugel (e–n Eilbrief) ~ *to fire a shot* (*to send an express-letter*) *after a p* **≃|kauen** vt [h] *to* *chew again* || ⟨fig⟩ e–m etw ~ *to repeat mechanically another p's views and words* **~klang** m *lingering tone* || ⟨phys⟩ *resonance* || ⟨fig⟩ *after-effect* || ~e [pl] ⟨fig⟩ *reminiscences* pl ~|**klappen** vi [h] ⟨mus⟩ *to drag* ~|**klingen** vi [h] *to linger in the ear, to re-echo* **~kommando** n *rear party* od *element* **~komme** m *descendant* || ~n [pl] *descendants* pl, *progeny, offspring* (*their seven o.*); *generation* (neue *of children*) || ohne ~n *without issue,* ⟨jur⟩ *obiit* (er starb) *sine prole* (*ob. s. p.*) ~|**k** vi [s] [dat] *to come after, to follow* || *to join* (*I'll join you in 10 minutes*) || ⟨fig⟩ *to come up* od *fall in with, to comply with* (*a p's wishes*) || e–r Aufforderung etc ~ *to answer a call, etc* || e–r Bitte ~ *to accede to a request* (*that .. should,* od *to do*) || ~ *to keep* (*one's promise*) || *to follow* (*directions*) || *to obey* (*orders*) || *to do* od *discharge* (*one's duty*) || *to come up to, to meet* od *fulfil* (*one's engagements*); *to fill* (*the needs*); er ist .. nicht –gek *he has failed to meet his engagements* || Ihrer Bitte ~d *in compliance with your request* || nicht ~ können *not to be able to follow*; er ging so schnell, daß ich kaum ~ konnte ⟨a.⟩ *he walked my legs off* | e–m (mit e–m kräftigen Schluck) ~ *to respond to a p's pledge, to pledge a p's toast* **~k-schaft** f = N.-kommen [pl]; ⟨demog⟩ endgültige (tatsächliche, vorläufige) ~ *completed* (*cumulative, incomplete*) *fertility,* **~kömmling** m = N.komme ~|**können** vi [h] [ell] = ~k können **~kost** f *dessert* **~kriegs-** [in comp] *post-war* (*phase*) **~kur** f *after-treatment, rest after a treatment* ~|**lallen** vt [h] *to repeat stammering* **~laß** m *slackening, relaxation* || ohne ~ (arbeiten) .. *without intermission, incessantly* || (Strafe) *remission* (a. *of taxes*) || ⟨com⟩ *rebate, abatement, deduction, reduction* (.. gewähren *to allow* ..) || unter ~ von 3% *allowing a discount* od *reduction of 3%* || (Hinterlassenschaft) *assets* pl, *estate* || literarischer ~ *literary remains* od *bequest* | ~gericht [n] *Probate Court*; ~pfleger, ~verwalter [m] *administrator*; ~staffel [f] *scale of discounts, sliding scale*; ~steuer [f] *estate duty*; *transfer tax*; ~verzeichnis [n] *estate inventory* ~|**lassen 1.** vt [h] *to leave behind* || (hinterlassen) *to bequeath* || (lösen) *to loosen* (*a screw*) || *to relax, slacken, loosen* (*a rope*) || *to slacken* (*the reins*) || nicht ~! *keep the ball rolling*!; er ließ nach *he eased up* || (mildern) *to mitigate* || (unterlassen) *to discontinue*; *to leave off* (*smoking*) | Laß **das** nach! *Do stop*!, *Have done*! | **etw** am, im, vom Preise ~ *to make a reduction* || etw von e–r Forderung (Strafe) ~ *to abate one's demands*; *to remit part of a claim* (*punishment*) || ⟨com⟩ beiderseits etw ~ *to split the difference* || k–n Pfennig ~ *not to knock off a single halfpenny* | **-ge-** *bereaved* (*widow*) || *posthumous* (*works*) **2.** vi [h] *to abate* (⟨a.⟩ v Angst, Schmerz; ⟨a.⟩) *to ease off, to lessen*; nicht ~ ⟨fam⟩ *to hang on*; (aufhören) *to cease* || (milder w) *to relent, soften* || (Spannkraft verlieren) *to slacken, relax, flag*; *to slack off* || (sich vermindern) *to diminish* | *the cold abated* || *the heat cooled down* || *the rain, storm abated, subsided* || *the wind calmed down, fell, waned, abated* | *to decline, to ooze out*; *life ebbed away* || *his interest, ardour slackened, subsided, flagged* || *the spirit of imitation flagged* || *her health gave way* || *her sobs died down* || *his strength, resistance gave out, weakened, ebbed* || ⟨com⟩ *the demand grew less brisk*; *sales fell off* | ⟨school⟩ [ell] er hat –ge– *his work has deteriorated* || gänzlich .. ⟨mil⟩ *the fire died down* | **nicht** ~! *don't get slack*! || nicht ~ bis .. ⟨Am⟩ *not to let up until ..* || nicht ~d *unremitting* | **an** *or* **im** Eifer ~ *to slack*; **in** s–n Bemühungen ~ *to relax one's efforts* (*to do*); *to abate in, to grow weary in one's efforts* || in den Leistungen ~ ⟨a.⟩ *to run to seed*; ⟨school⟩ *to fall behind in one's studies* || im Fleiß ~ *to become less diligent, to relax* od *flag in one's zeal* || **in** *or* **mit** der Verfolgung ~ *to slacken in the pursuit* || laß nie nach mit Beten *never grow slack of prayers* || ~ **von** *to desist, abstain from* **II. N·achlassen** n [gen] *abatement, reduction* || *relaxation* (*of* od *in discipline*); *flagging* || *diminution* || *subsidence, cessation* || → –laß, –lassung ~|**lässig** a *remiss* (v mir *of me*) || *dilatory, slack* (*in doing*) || *negligent, careless, indolent* || ⟨Am⟩ *derelict* (in *in, in doing*) || *slovenly, sloppy* (*speech*); *slipshod* (*style*); *slapdash* (*work*); *dowdy* (*dress*) || ~ in bezug auf *casual about* | [adv] etw ~ behandeln ⟨a.⟩ *to treat like a stepchild*; an etw ~ herangehen *to make a bits-and-pieces approach at a th* | ~keit [f] *negligence* (strafbar *actionable*); *carelessness*; *remissness*; *indolence* **~lassung** f *remission* || *bequest* (→ –laß, –lassen II.) **~lauf** m ⟨rep, rec⟩ *trailer*; (of engine) *after-running*; (heating system) *purge system*; (wheel) *castor* ⟨a. aero⟩; (*in destillation*) *tails*; *last running* ~|**laufen** vi [s] [dat] *to run* od ⟨fam⟩ *tag after* ⟨a. fig⟩ || *to hang about after* || *to dangle after* (*girls*) **~läufer** m ⟨bill⟩ *fellow* ~|**leben** vi [h] (e–m Grundsatze etc) *to live up to, to observe* || *to live in accordance with* (*a p's advice*) ~|**legen** vt/i *to add to* || *to put on more coal,* etc (*to the fire*) **~lese** f [abstr] *gleaning* || ~ halten *to glean* | [konkr] *gleanings* pl || ⟨fig⟩ *second selection*; ⟨lit⟩ *supplement* ~|**lesen** vt [h] ⟨agr⟩ *to glean* | *to read again* || *to read* (*a passage previously missed*) || *to look up* (*a passage*) | beim ~ *on reading again* || lies nach! *mind your book*! **~leser** m *gleaner* ~|**liefern** vt [h] *to supply* od *deliver subsequently* **~lieferung** f *subsequent delivery, completion* ~|**lösen** vt/i [h] ⟨rail⟩ *to take a supplementary ticket* **~löseschalter** m *excess-fare office* ~|**m** vt [h] (jdm etw) *to imitate* (*a p, a th*) || das soll mir mal e–r ~! *I defy anybody to do that* od *to do it like me* || mach es mir n.! *do as I do*! | (betrügerisch) *to counterfeit, forge*; ⟨sl⟩ *to fake* || –ge–cht *imitated, artificial, imitation* (*flowers*) | (parodieren) *to mimic*; ⟨Am⟩ *to take* (*a p*) *off* **~macher** m *imitator* || *forger* **~macher·ei** f *imitation* || *forgery* **~mahd** f *aftermath* ~|**malen** vt [h] *to copy* **~mast** f *aftermast* ~|**messen** vt [h] *to verify, to measure again* || *to resurvey* | ~ [n] *resurvey* **~mittag** m *afternoon*; später ~ ⟨Am⟩ *evening* || spät am ~ *late in the a.* || heute ~ *this a.* ~**mittägig** a *afternoon* ~**mittags** adv *in the afternoon(s)* || ⟨bes rail⟩ *p. m.* (= *post meridiem*) || spät ~ ⟨a.⟩ *late of an afternoon* | ~aufführung [f] *matinee*; ~kleid [n] *tea-gown*; ~ruhe [f], ~schläfchen [n] *afternoon* od *post-prandial nap*; *forty winks* pl; ~sitzung [f] *afternoon session* || ~sonne [f] *westering sun* || ~vorstellung [f] *matinée* **~nahme** f *cash* (⟨Am⟩ *collect*) *on delivery* (abbr *C.O.D.*) || e–e ~ einlösen *to meet a cash delivery* || unter ~ (*per*) *C.O.D., to be paid for on delivery* (*P.O.D.*) || ⟨com⟩ unter ~ der Fracht, der Spesen *charges forward* | ~gebühr [f] *collection-fee*; ~karte [f] *reimbursement-card*; ~sendung [f] *C.O.D. parcel* **~name** m *surname, byname* ~|**nehmen** ⟨com⟩ *to charge forward*; *to reimburse o.s. for*; ⟨post⟩ *to collect* **~nennung** f ⟨racing, etc⟩ *late entry* ~|**ordnen** vt *to rearrange* || *to class next, after* || –ge–net (Stellen) *lower* (*offices, authorities*) ~|**pfeifen** vt/i [h] *to whistle by ear* || [dat] *to whistle after* || m–m Gelde kann ich ~ *I may whistle for my m.* ~|**plappern** vt [h] *to repeat, echo* **~porto** n *additional charge, surcharge* | ~marke [f] *extra-postage stamp*; ⟨Am⟩ *p.-due st.* ~**prüfbar** a *verifiable* ~|**prüfen** vt [h] *to make sure* || etw (auf s–e Richtigkeit) ~ *to verify a th* || ⟨Am⟩ *to check up*; *to recheck* || (Entscheidung) *to reconsider* **~prüfung** f *verification* || ⟨school⟩ *second examination* || (Wahl~) ⟨pol⟩ *recount* || ~skommission [f] *Board of Review* ~|**rechnen** vt [h] *to examine* || *to check* (*an account*) || *to reckon over again*; ich habe nicht –ge–net *I have lost account* **~rechnung** f *examination, checking* **~rede** f *epilogue* || üble ~ *ill* od *evil report, slander* || jdn in üble ~ bringen *to* *slander a p, to injure a p's reputation* || üble ~ verbreiten *to spread vile gossip* ≃|**reden** vt [h] (jdm) *to repeat a p's words* || jdm Übles ~ *to asperse, slander, backbite a p; to speak ill behind a p's back* || jdm Gutes ~ *to speak well of a p* ≃|**regeln** vt [h] *to readjust* ≃|**reichen** vt [h] *to submit .. later*; → -gang ≃|**reifen** vi [s] *to ripen later* ≃|**rennen** vi [s] (jdm) *to make after (a p)* || → Nachricht **⁓richter** m *executioner* ≃|**rücken** vi [s] (jdm) *to move* od ⟨mil⟩ *march after (a p)* || (im Rang) *to move up, to be promoted* | vt [h] *to advance* **⁓ruf** m *obituary; obituary notice* od *poem* | (Zeitung) ~abteilung [f] *morgue* ≃|**rufen** vt [h] [dat] ⟨fig⟩ *to speak (words of sympathy at a p's grace)* **⁓ruhm** m *posthumous fame, renown after death* ≃|**rühmen** vt [h]; jdm etw ~ *to speak well of a p in his absence* || ⟨fig⟩ *to say sth to a p's credit* od *in praise of a p* ≃|**sagen** vt [h] (jdm etw) → nachreden, anhängen || es wird ihm Stolz -ge-gt *he has a reputation for pride* || sich ~ l: *you must not let people say such ths about you* || °mir kann k-r nichts ~! ⟨Am vulg⟩ *they've got nothing on me* **⁓satz** m *conclusion, minor* || ⟨gram⟩ *concluding sentence* ≃|**schaffen** vt ⟨arts⟩ *to copy* || (anschaffen) *to renew* ≃|**schallen** vi [h] *to resound, to echo* ≃|**schauen** vi [h] → -sehen, schau mal nach, ob .. *look and see if ..* ≃|**schicken** vt [h] = ~senden ≃|**schießen** vi [s] [dat] ⟨fig⟩ *to rush after a p* | vt [h] ⟨fig⟩ (Geld etc): *to add what is wanting, to make an additional payment* ≃|**schimpfen** vi [h] (jdm) *to hoot (a p)* **⁓schlag** m ⟨mus⟩ *grace-note (after a trill,* etc); ⟨cul⟩ *second helping* **⁓schlagebuch** n *book of reference, r. b.* ≃|**schlagen** vt [h] (ein Buch) *to consult, to refer to* || (ein Wort etc) *to look up* || [vi] e-m ~ ⟨fig⟩ *to take after a p* ≃|**schleifen** vt/i [h] *to trail .. after one*; es schleift nach (*dress*, etc) *it trails, drags*; ⟨fam⟩ *to drag up (child)* || ⟨tech⟩ (Messer) *to stone; to true (tool, wheel,* etc) | ≃ [n] *truing* ≃|**schleppen** vt [h]; e-m ~ *to carry after a p* || *he drags one leg after him* **⁓schlüssel** m *master-key* || (Dietrich) *false key; picklock* ≃|**schmecken** vi [h] *to leave a taste behind* ≃|**schöpfen** vt [h] ⟨mus⟩ *to intuitively re-create* ≃**schöpferisch** a *capable of re-creating intuitively* ≃|**schreiben** vt [h] *to copy; to write* od *to take down* || *to write from dictation* || [dat] *to imitate (a p's) writing* || *to plagiarize* **⁓schrift** f (*writing from a) dictation* || *transcript (of a speech)* || (in Briefen) *postscript* (abbr *P.S.*) **⁓schub** m ⟨bowling⟩ *next throw* || ⟨mil⟩ *reinforcements* pl; *supply*; ~ erfolgt .. *s. action will be taken* N | ~artikel [m] → -gut | ~basis [f] *supply base*; ~gut [n] *s. item*; ~kolonne [f] *s. column*; ~n [pl] *s. train* || ~stab m *administrative command* N; ~straße [f] *route* od *line of communication*; ~truppen [f pl] *servicing troops* ~- u Verpflegungswesen n *s. and victualling*; ~wesen [n] *logistics* [sg konstr]; ~zug [m] *s. train* ≃|**schüren** vt [h] *to add fuel to* **⁓schuß** m (von Geld etc) *subsequent* od *fresh* od *additional payment* ≃|**schütten** vt [h] *to add to* || Kohlen ~ *to make up the fire* ≃|**schwatzen** vt [h] *to repeat (gossip)* ≃|**sehen** vt/i [h] (e-m) *to look after (a p)*; (etw) *to look after (a th), to look into (one's bag); to examine, inspect, revise* || *to overhaul*, ⟨Am⟩ *to check (a machine)* || ⟨school⟩ *to correct (the books)* || (Schriftstück) *to look over* || (nachschlagen) (in e-m Buch) *to look up*; (Buch) *to consult; to refer to* || er sah dem Wagen n. *his eyes followed the car* || sie sieht n., daß es geschieht *she sees (to it* od*) that it is done* || [abs] *to go and look* || ~, wer .., wo .., ob .. *to (go* od *look and) see who .., where .., whether* od *if ..*; (⟨a.⟩ *make sure you've got a hanky)* | ⟨fig⟩ (jdm etw) *to indulge (a p in a th)* | **das** N.- h *to be the loser, to be the worse for it, to whistle for one's money* || *to be left out in the cold* || mir blieb das N. *I was too late in the field* ≃|**sein** vi *to lag behind* || [ell] er ist n. *he has made up for the time lost*, .. ihm .. *he has reached him, he is after him* ≃|**senden** vt [h] *to send after* || (Brief) *to redirect* || *please forward!* ≃|**setzen** vt [h] *to set, put, place after* || (im Spiel) *to increase one's stake* || ⟨fig⟩ (hintansetzen) *to think less of, to set less value upon, to consider inferior* (od *of less value than*) | vi [s] (jdm) *to run*, etc *after a p, to chase, pursue* **⁓setzung** f *hot pursuit* || (Geringschätzung) *disregard* **⁓sicht** f *forbearance, indulgence; tolerance* || (Ggs Vor-) ⟨hum⟩ *hind-sight* || (Milde) *leniency, clemency* || (Geduld) *patience* (mit *with*) || ⟨com⟩ *respite* || ~ h mit *to be indulgent towards, to excuse, to be patient with; to make allowance for* || e-n um ~ bitten *to ask a p's indulgence* || gegenseitige ~ üben *to bear and forbear* || ⟨prov⟩ Vorsicht ist besser als ~ *prevention is better than cure* ≃**sichtig** a *indulgent, lenient* (gegen, mit *to*), *gentle (with), considerate, forbearing; soft (education)*; ~ s *to stretch a point*, .. gegen *to indulge (a th, a p)* || allzu ~ *fond (mother)* | ~keit [f] *indulgence, forbearance; charitableness* **⁓sichts-**~tage [m pl] ⟨com⟩ *days of grace*; ≃los [a] *stern, unrelenting*; ≃voll [a] *very indulgent* **⁓silbe** f ⟨gram⟩ *suffix* ≃|**sinnen** vi [h] ([dat] *or* über [acc]) *to deliberate, muse, meditate, reflect, ruminate (on)* | ≃ [n] *reflection, meditation* || in tiefes ≃ versunken *in a brown study* ≃|**sitzen** vi [h]; ~ (müssen) ⟨school⟩ *to be kept in* || (Schüler) ~ l *to keep in, to detain* | ≃ [n] *detention* **⁓sommer** m *after-, late, Martin's, Indian summer* ≃|**spähen** vi [h] (jdm) *to watch (a p) closely, to spy after* || *to dive* od *pry into (secrets)* **⁓spann** m ⟨film etc⟩ *final title strip* | ~vorrichtung [f] *tensioning equipment* ≃|**spannen** *to adjust* **⁓spiel** n ⟨theat⟩ *afterpiece* || ⟨mus⟩ *postlude* || ⟨ec⟩ *concluding voluntary* || ⟨fig⟩ *after-clap, subsequent result; sequel (of* od *to)* || übles ~ *bad consequences* pl ≃|**spielen** vt/i [h] ⟨fig⟩ *to imitate* || ⟨cards⟩ *to return (a suit* od *lead)* || e-e andere Farbe *to lead another suit* **⁓spitze** f ⟨mil⟩ *rear(guard) point* ≃|**spotten** vi [h] [dat] *to mock, mimic; to take off* ≃|**sprechen** vt [h] (jdm etw) *to repeat a p's words, to echo a p* ≃|**spüren** vi [h] [dat] *to trace, track* || ⟨fig⟩ *investigate* || (spionieren) jdm ~ *to spy on a p* || e-r S ~ *to spy* od *look into a th* || *to explore a th* || e-m ~ l *to dog a p('s footsteps)* || ⟨hunt⟩ *to scent* || ~d *inquisitional* | vt *to feel the after-effects of* **⁓spürung** f *tracing, tracking* || ⟨fig⟩ *investigation, search* ≃|**stehen** vi [h] *to follow* || ⟨gram⟩ *to be placed after* || (jdm) *to be inferior* od *second (in importance) to; to come after (one's pretty sister)* || *to yield to* (in *in*) || e r S ~ *to be subordinate to; to fall* od *come short of a th* || °k-m in nichts ~ *to ask no odds from any one; not to play second fiddle to* || k-m ~d *yielding* od *second to none* || jdm nicht viel ~ *to make a good second to a p* || ~d [a & adv] *following (passage), subjoined (list); (goods) specified below* || ~d aufgeführte Namen *names listed below* od *hereinafter set forth* || im ≃den teile ich mit, daß *herewith I beg to inform you that* ≃|**steigen** vi [s] [dat] ⟨fig⟩ *to follow* || man steigt nach! *always follow a pretty girl!* ≃**stellbar** a *adjustable* ≃|**stellen** vt [h] *to place behind* od *after* || (Uhr) *to put back* || (Schraube) *to adjust* | vi (jdm) *to be on the track of; to lay snares for, to lie in wait for (a p)*, ⟨fam⟩ *to be after (a girl)* **⁓stellung** f (Verfolgung) *persecution* || (Fallstrick etc) *snare, ambush* **⁓steuer** f *additional tax* ≃|**stöbern** vi [h] [dat] *to rummage (in; for, after)* **⁓stoß** m *after-thrust, -kick*; ⟨fenc⟩ *counterthrust*; ⟨ad⟩ *follow-up* ≃|**stoßen** vi [h] ⟨fenc⟩ *to parry and thrust* || ⟨mil⟩ *to follow up, to pursue*; unablässig ~ *to relentlessly push after the withdrawing enemy* ≃|**streben** vi [h] [dat] *to strive (after)* || jdm ~ *to emulate a p* **⁓strom** m (Sog) ⟨aero⟩ *wake* ≃|**strömen,** ≃|**stürmen,** ≃|**stürzen** vi [s] [dat] *to rush, jump, crowd,* etc. *after* ≃|**suchen** vt/i [h] *to search (after* od *for), to seek (after)* | (um) *to apply (for)* **⁓suchung** f *search, inquiry* || *suit, petition* **⁓synchronisation** f *post-scoring* od *-synchr.* ~|**tanken** vi/t *to refuel* | ~ [n] in der Luft *flight refuelling* **~tat** f *secondary action* (straflos *non-punishable*) **~teil** m *disadvantage; drawback* (*to*), *shortcoming* (*in*); *bane* (Ggs *boon*) || *the penalty* (*of greatness*) || ⟨a.⟩ *objection* (*to*) || (Schaden) *loss, prejudice, damage, detriment* || ⟨fig⟩ *flaw* (*in*) || ohne ~ f s–e Ehre *without detriment to his honour* || im ~ *disa.d*, ⟨com⟩ (*to be*) *at a competitive disa.* || zum ~ [gen] *to the prejudice of* || zu m–m ~ *to my loss, unfavourably* || sich zu s–m ~ entwickeln (P) ⟨hum⟩ *to wear thin* || den ~ h z s *to labour under the disa. of being* || im ~ s *to be at a disa.* || zum ~ v *at the expense of*; z ~ gereichen *to be detrimental*; z ~ des Urhebers aus-, fehlschlagen ⟨fam⟩ *to backfire* || jdn in den ~ setzen *to handicap a p* || mehr ~e als Vorteile aus e–r S h *to get more kicks than ha'pence out of a th* || mit ~ verkaufen *to sell at a loss* ~**teilig** a *disa.ous, prejudicial, prejudicious, detrimental, injurious, harmful* ([dat] *to*) || ~ s f *to be a disadvantage for* || über ihn ist nichts ~es bekannt *nothing is known against him* | adv; ~ beeinflussen *to affect prejudicially*; die Gesundheit ~ b. *to be detrimental to one's health* || ~ behandeln *to discriminate against* | ~keit [f] *disadvantageousness, injuriousness* **~therapie** f *follow-up treatment* **~tisch** m ⟨engl⟩ (Obst) *dessert*; (Pudding etc) *sweets* pl || ⟨Am⟩ (beides) *dessert* || als *or* zum ~ *for dessert* ~|**tönen** vi [h] *to resound* || (v Noten ⟨a.⟩) *to linger* **~trab** m ⟨mil⟩ *rear(-guard)*; ⟨fig⟩ im ~ s *to be behind the times* ~|**trachten** vi [h] [dat] → –streben, –stellen **~trag** m *addition, supplement* || (Brief~) *postscript* || (Testament~) *codicil* || als ~ *supplementary* || e–n ~ bilden zu *to be supplementary to* | ~sband [m] *supplement(ary volume)*; ~szahlung [f] *payment of arrears* **~träge** pl *addenda* pl ~**~tragen** vt [h] *to carry* od *bear after* || (hinzufügen) *to add, append, supply* || *to book* (*an omitted item*) || (jdm etw) *to bear* (*a p*) *a grudge, to be resentful* (*of a th*), *to resent* (*a th*) || nichts ~ *to bear no malice, to harbo(u)r no ill--feeling*; hoffentlich trägst du mir nichts n. *no ill--will, I hope*; ich trage es dir nicht nach *no hard feelings! let bygones be bygones* || er ist nicht ~d *he doesn't bear any enmity* || ~d, **~trägerisch** a *unforgiving, vindictive, resentful, spiteful* ~**träglich** a (später) *subsequent; deferred* || (ergänzend) *supplementary, additional* || ~er Gedanke *afterthought* (so: *aftergrowth*, etc) || ~ [adv] *by way of addition; further, subsequently; after the event* || (zeitlich) *later* || ~ wirkende Kraft *after-power* od *-effect* **~trags-** *supplementary* (→ –trag) ~|**trauern** vi [h] → trauern || *it's no use crying over spilt milk* (e–r verpaßten Gelegenheit [dat]) ~|**treten** vi [s] (jdm) *to step after* (*a p*), *to follow* (*a p*) *closely* **~treter** m (*blind* od *servile*) *follower* || ⟨fig⟩ *imitator* **~trieb** m ⟨agr⟩ *after-shoot* ~|**tropfen** vi [h/s] *to dribble* **~trupp** m ⟨mil⟩ *rear-guard support* ~|**tun** vt [h] *to add* (in, zu *to*) || jdm etw ~ *to imitate a p* || es jdm ~ wollen (nicht ~ können) *to emulate* (*not to come up to*) *a p* **~überträger** m ⟨telph⟩ *output transformer* **~untersuchung** f *re--examination*; ⟨tech⟩ *maintenance check*; ⟨med⟩ *check-up* **~urlaub** m *extended vacation* od ⟨mil⟩ *leave* **~verbrenner** m ⟨aero⟩ (*jet*) *afterburner* **~vermächtnis** n *reversionary legacy* ~|**versichern** vt [h] *to reinsure; to insure for a larger amount* **~versicherung** f *re-, additional insurance* **~|vollziehen** vt [h] *to fulfil, perform, sign, ratify later* ~|**wachsen** vi [s] *to grow afterwards* od *later* od *again* || (*new generations*) *grow up* || die Haare wachsen ihm nach *he is having new hair* ~|**wägen** vt [h] = ~wiegen **~wahl** f *final choice* || ⟨pol⟩ *by-election* **~weh** n *after-pain* **~wehen** pl *after-throes, after--pains* pl || ⟨fig⟩ *unpleasant* od *painful consequences* pl ~|**weinen** vt/i [h] e–m (Tränen) ~ *to bewail a p's death, to mourn the loss of a p*; e–r S ~ *to regret a th, to lament for a th* **~weis** m *proof* || *certificate, voucher* || (Arbeits-) *Labour Exchange* || ~ der Richtigkeit *verification*; es fehlt uns der ~, daß *we are without evidence that*; den ~ liefern, führen, erbringen *to prove; to adduce evidence*; .. f (als) *to qualify for* (*as*) || er erbrachte den unwiderleglichen ~ *he furnished irrefutable proof* (daß *that*) || ⟨mil⟩ (Stärke~ etc) *table of organization* | ~buch [n] ⟨mil⟩ *army book*; ~führung [f] *documentation* (über *of*); ~pflichtig [a] *accountable* (*document*) ~**weisbar,** ~**weislich** a *provable, demonstrable, traceable* **~weisbureau** n *intelligence-office* ~|**weisen** vt [h] *to point out* || *to refer to* || *to show, demonstrate* (*a mistake*) || (beweisen) *to prove, establish* || *to identify* || *to authenticate* (*one's birth*) || –zu– suchen *to argue that* || ~, daß jd unrecht hat *to prove a p wrong* || jdm etw (Gewünschtes) ~ *to inform a p about a th*; (Arbeit) *to get work for a p*; (Verbrechen) *to convict a p of a crime*; *to make good* (*one's claim*) **~weiser** m *index* || *book of reference* || (f Adressen) *directory* **~weisung** f *intelligence, information* || (Verweisung) *reference* || (Beweis) *proof* || (Buch, Liste) *tables* (*of equipment*); Stärke- u Ausrüstungs~ (*STAN*) *table of organization and equ.*; Bestands~ ⟨bes mil⟩ *return, report*; ⟨tax⟩ *summary* (*of expenses*, etc) **~welt** f *posterity; futurity* || für die ~ *for p.* || der ~ überliefern *to hand down to p.* ~|**werfen** vt [h] [dat] *to throw a th after a p* ⟨fig⟩ jdm ein Examen ~ *to pass a p without difficulty*; ein Ex. –geworfen bek *to pass an exam without diff.* ~|**wiegen** vt [h] *to weigh* (*over*) *again* **~winter** m *late* od *second winter* ~|**wirken** vi [h] *to be felt afterwards, to have an after-effect, to operate afterwards* || ~d *lingering* (*taste*) **~wirkung** f *after-effect, after-math* (*of war*) || *consequences* pl || *persistence* (e–s Eindrucks) ~|**wollen** vi [h] [ell]; ich will ihm nach *I'll go after him* **~wort** n *epilogue* **~wuchs** m *after-growth* || *young shoot* od *wood* || ⟨sport⟩ *colts* pl || Kälber~ *calf crop* || ⟨fig⟩ *vintage* || ⟨fig⟩ *coming* od *rising generation* || ~ heranbilden *to educate successors* | ~star [m] ⟨film⟩ *starlet* ~|**zahlen** vt/i *to pay later* od *extra* od *in addition* || ⟨theat, rail⟩ *to pay the difference* ~|**zählen** vt [h] *to count* (*up* [od *over again*]) || (Waren) *to tally* **~zahlung** f *additional* od *supplementary payment, payment of arrears, extrapayment; back-pay*; ⟨rail⟩ *excess fare* **~zählung** f *second counting* ~|**zeichnen** vt [h] ⟨arts⟩ *to draw* (*from*) || [a. vi] *to copy* || ⟨com⟩ *to subscribe for more* (*shares*) **~zeichnung** f *drawing after, copy(ing)* || ⟨com⟩ *subsequent subscription* **~zeit** f die ~ *the afterwards* ~|**ziehen** vt [h] *to draw after*, ⟨mar⟩ *to tow* || (Strich etc) *to trace* || (Augenbrauen) *to pencil* || *to tighten up* (*screws*) || *to drag* (*one foot*) || (mit sich bringen) *to involve* | vi [s] [dat] *to march after, to follow* **~zins** m *quit-rent* ~|**zotteln** vi [s] ⟨fam⟩ (jdm) *to trot after* **~zucht** f (Geflügel) (*last*) *brood* || (Bienen) *last swarm* || ⟨agr⟩ *planting*; ⟨bes for⟩ *regeneration* **~zug** m *marching after* || ⟨mil⟩ *rear(-guard)* || ⟨chess⟩ *next move* | ~sgläubiger [m] ⟨jur⟩ *deferred creditor* **~zügler** m ⟨mil⟩ *straggler; camp-follower* || (Kind) *belated birth*; → Versprengter **~zündung** f → –brennen, ⟨mot⟩ *late* od *retarded ignition*

N·achbar m ~s & ~n/~n *neighbour* (⟨a. fig⟩ *our western n.s* [*France*]) || nächster ~ (Haus- u Zimmer~) *next-door n.* || (im selben Haushalt etc) *fellow-lodger* | ~- *adjacent* (⟨telv⟩ *channel*, ⟨mil⟩ *unit*) **~arten** f pl ⟨biol⟩ *closely related species* pl **~gemeinschaft** f *n.hood unit* **~dorf** n *n.ing village* **~eigentümer** m *adjoining owner* **~haus** n *adjoining house*; .. im ~ (*they live*) *next door* **~land** n, **~staat** m etc *n.ing country, state*, etc **n·achbarlich** a *neighbour* (*policy*) || *n.ly* (*intercourse* Beziehungen pl) || *n.'s* (*house*) || *n.ing* (*garden*) | [adv] ~ verkehren *to be on n.ly terms* (mit *with*) **N·achbars- ~frau** f *neighbour; lady next door* **~leute** pl *n.s* **N·achbarschaft** f ~/ *n.hood* (a.

= alle Nachbarn) || (Nähe) *vicinity, proximity* || in der ~ *adjoining* || in nächster ~ *in close vicinity* || sie ist e–e gefährliche ~ .. *a dangerous n.* (f *for*) || gute ~ halten *to have friendly intercourse with one's n.s* || die Schulen der ~ ⟨Am⟩ *the n.hood schools* | [koll] *n.s* pl

nachd·em I. [adv] *afterwards, after that* **II.** [conj] **1.** (zeitlich) *after, when*: *after the war had been lost, when the war was lost* || gleich ~ er .. *when first he came here* || ~ C. ermordet war, mußte B. fliehen *C. having been murdered B. had to fly* || [bei gleichem Subjekt]: *after looking* (od *having looked*) *at it they went home* || ~ er A. gewesen war, wurde er .. *from being an Anglican he became* ..; *once* (*he had read it* ..) **2.** ⟨dial⟩ [kausal] *because* **3. je** ~ .. *according as* (*he was young or old*) || je ~ es kommt *just as it may happen* || je ~ (wie) er sich benimmt *according to his conduct* | [ell] je ~ *as the case may be*; *according to the subject* od *circumstances* || ⟨fam⟩ [ell] *it* (*all*) *depends*

N·achen m ~s/~ *boat, skiff* || (flacher) *punt* | ~führer [m] *boatman, punter*

nachh·er adv *afterwards, after that* || (darauf) *then* || bald ~ *presently*; *soon after* || vorher u ~ *before and since* || (*a dessert*) *to follow* **nachh·erig, n·achmalig** a *subsequent, later*; *posterior*; *following* || *future* **n·achmals** adv *afterwards, subsequently* || *since* (*then*)

N·achricht f ~/~en (Neuigkeit) *news* (über *of a p*) || *the news is* .. || e–e s–r ~en war .. *one piece of his news was* .. || *two pieces of good news* || (Bericht) *account, report* || (schriftliche etc) *communication* (an *to*) ⟨a. mil⟩; ⟨mil⟩ *report* || (Auskunft) (*piece of*) *information* || (kurzer Bericht) *notice* || (Kunde [f]) ~en [pl] *intelligence*; Neueste ~en aus aller Welt ⟨Am⟩ *Newsfronts of the World* || letzte ~en *stop-press* || verspätete ~ *belated post* || vermischte (Zeitungs)~en *miscellanies* pl || ⟨com⟩ *advice* || ~en für Seefahrer (N.f.S.) *notices to Mariners* || zur ~ *for your guidance* od *information* || ~ bek v *to receive news* od *intelligence, to hear from a p* || ~ einholen *to make inquiries* (über *about*) || ⟨mil⟩ ~en einziehen *to gather* od *gain intelligence* || ich erfuhr ~en über ihn *I learned his news* || ~ geben ⟨a.⟩ *to write* || jdm ~ geben *to give a p information, advice, notice* (über *about*) (*till when am I to give notice*?); (amtlich) *to notify a th to a p*; *to send a p word, to let a p know, to advise a p* || geben Sie mir von Zeit zu Z. ~! *keep me advised*! || ~ v sich geben *to send news of o.s.* || ~en gewinnen *to acquire inf.* || ~ h *to have news*; ich habe k–e ~ v ihr *I have not heard from her* || e–e ~ geht *or* trifft ein, kommt an *news comes to hand* || als die ~ kam ⟨bes Am⟩ *when the news broke* || die ~ melden *to break the news* || e–e ~ verbreiten *to circulate a report* **N·achrichten- ~abteilung** f ⟨mil⟩ **i**(*ntelligence*) *department*, ⟨mar⟩ *naval i. division*, ⟨pol⟩ *News Department* **~agentur** f, **~büro** n *news agency*; (e–r Zeitung) *news-room* **~ansager** m ⟨wir, telv⟩ *newscaster* **~beschaffung** f *collection* od *procurement of inf.* **~dienst** m ⟨wir⟩ *news service*; ⟨mil⟩ *i.* (*s.*), (geheim *Counter*) *I. S.* (*I.S.*) od *Corps*; ⟨wir⟩ *last news*; ⟨mil fam⟩ *Q department*; (Geheim) *I. Department* **~gerät** n *signalling apparatus* **~gewinnung** f *production of i.* **~kompanie** f *signal c.* **~material** n ⟨mil⟩ (Feind-) *inf.*; (ausgewertet) *i.* [koll] **~mittel** n *means of intercommunication, comm. facilities* **~netz** n *i. net*; *communication network* **~offizier** m *i. officer* **~sammelstelle** = ~zentrale **~satellit** m *comm.s satellite* **~schlager** m ⟨Am⟩ *beat* **~sender** m ⟨wir⟩ *newscaster* **~sendung** f ⟨wir⟩ *news cast* **~sperre** f *news ban* od *black-out* **~sprecher** m ⟨wir⟩ *newscaster, newsreader* **~stelle** f *information centre*; ⟨mil⟩ *i. office* **~technik** f (als Fachgebiet) *comm. engineering*; (Mittel) *means of communication* **~träger** m *news medium*, pl *-ia* **~truppen** f pl *signal corps*; ⟨engl⟩ *Royal Corps of Signals* (*R.C.S.*) **~übermittlung** f *transmission of i.*; (drahtlos) *radio signalling* **~verarbeitung** (u –übertragung) f *inf. handling*; ⟨comp⟩ *processing of inf.* || **~verbindung** f *i. contact*; *intercomm.* | ~swesen [n], **~verkehr** m *comm.s* **~werfer** m *message projector* **~wesen** n *i. service*; *communication*(*s*) **~zentrale** f *i. centre* **n·achrichtlich** adv *by way of notice* od *information*; *for inf.*; ~ an: *inf. addressee*: .. *serving as advice*

n·ächst prep *next to, next after* || [a] *next-door* (*neighbour*) || adv *next* **~b·este** a *second-best, next in quality* **~d·em** adv *next to that, thereupon, besides* **~f·olgend** a *next* **~liegend** a *nearest* (*at hand*) **~vorh·ergehend** a *immediately preceding* || der **~w·ichtigste** nach Sh. *the most important next to Sh.* **~w·ohnend** a *next-door* (*neighbour*)

n·ächste I. a (→ nahe) **1.** (räumlich) *nearest* (*warehouse*) || *next-door* (*neighbour*) || .. im ~n Hause (*he lives*) *next door* || (Weg) *nearest* od *shortest* (*way, cut*) || der ~ beste *the first that comes*; *any* **2.** (Beziehungen) *closest* od *most intimate* (*relations, friends*) || *immediate* (*heir*) || *nearest* (*relatives*) **3.** (Zeit, Reihenfolge) *next* || im ~n Augenblick *in another moment, a m. afterwards, the next m.* || bei ~r Gelegenheit *at the first opportunity* || in den ~n 20 Jahren von jetzt ab *within* (*the next*) *20 years from now* || das ~ Mal *the next time* || ~e Michaeli .. (*he was 63*) *come Michaelmas* || ⟨com⟩ ~n Monats *proximo* (abbr *prox*) || mit ~r Post *by return of post* || (in Erzählungen [nicht v der Gegenwart aus]) den ~n Tag, am ~n Tage *the next* od *following day* || ~r Tage *as soon as possible* || (in) ~r Zeit *before long, very soon* | ⟨prov⟩ jeder ist sich selbst der ~ *near is my shirt, but nearer my skin*; *charity begins at home* **II.** adv **1. am ~n** *nearest, next* || was (e–r Frage, S) am ~n kommt *the nearest approach to* .. || die, die ihm am ~n waren *those who were nearest to him* || er kommt ihm am ~n *he comes next to him* (an *in*) || Mars wird der Erde am ~n s .. *will be at its nearest to* .. || er steht ihr am ~n *he is nearest to her heart* **2. fürs** ~ *for the present* **N·ächste(r)** m ~n/~n *fellow-creature* od *-man*, ⟨bib⟩ *neighbour* (→ nächste I. 3. prov) **N·ächstenliebe** f ~/ *charity, altruism* **n·ächstens** adv (*very*) *soon, shortly*; *presently*; *one of these days*; *next time*

N·acht f ~/⸚e **A.** *night* ⟨a. fig⟩ || ⟨fig a.⟩ *darkness* | ⸚s *or* des ~s [irr gen] = bei ~ || heute, morgen, gestern ⸚ *to-night, to-morrow n., last n.* || es hat diese ~ geregnet .. *during the n.* || gute ~! *good n.*! ⟨iron⟩ gute ~, lieber Herrgott! (es ist alles aus) *good night*! || die Heilige ~ *Christmas Eve*; „Stille ~, Heilige ~" "*Silent N., Holy N.*"; durchzechte ~ *white n.* **B.** die **ganze** (lange) ~ (hindurch) *all n.* (*long*) || ganze ⸚e **lang** *whole nights together* || (drei) ⸚e lang (hinter–e–a) *for several n.s* (*at a time*) || e–e ~ **ohne** Alarm *a n. off* **C. bei** ~, **in** der ~ *at* od *by n., in* od *during the n.*; spät in der ~ ⟨a.⟩ *last th* [abs] || bei dunkler ~ *in the darkness of n.* || bei ~ u Nebel ausziehen, davongehen *to escape under cover of the n.*, °*to shoot the moon* || ~ **für** ~ *n. after n.* || **in** (→ a. bei ~, zur ~) || in e–r dunklen ~ *on a dark n.* || in tiefer ~, in der Stille der ~ *at dead of n.* || in e–r Winter⸚ *on a winter n.* || in der ~ zum 25. Juli *during the n. following July 24th* || (bis) tief *or* spät in die ~ (hinein) [arbeiten] *till late in the* od *at n.* [*to burn the midnight oil*] || **mit** Anbruch *or* Eintritt der ~, mit einbrechender ~ *at n.fall* || **mitten** in der ~ *in the middle of the n.* || **über** ~ *in one n. over-n.*; *during the n., at n.*; *the whole n.*, ⟨fig⟩ *unexpectedly* || über ~ bleiben *to stay the n.* (*in, at*) || **zu** ~ essen *to sup* || zur späten ~, spät in der ~ *late at n.* || zw e–r ~ u der anderen *between n. and n.* **D.** °e–e **durchbummelte** ~ *a n. on the tiles* || sich die ~ um die Ohren schlagen, die ganze ~

durchm *to make a n. of it* || die ~ zum Tage m *to turn n. into day* || es ist ~ *it is n. time* || u ist die ~ auch noch so schwer, es muß doch Morgen w *every cloud has its silver lining* || v der ~ überrascht w *to be benighted* || die ~ bricht herein, sinkt nieder, zieht herauf (*the*) *n. is setting* od *gathering in* || es wird ~ *n. is setting in* od *coming on*; *it is growing* (⟨fam⟩ *getting*) *dark* || ⟨fig⟩ es wird ~ vor m–n Augen *my eyes are darkening* || (jdm) gute ~ wünschen *to bid* (*a p*) *good n.* **E.** häßlich **wie** die ~ *ugly as sin* || schwarz wie die ~ (*as*) *black as coal* || ⟨prov⟩ bei ~ sind alle Katzen grau *when candles are out, all cats are grey* **~affe** m ⟨zoo⟩ = Lori **~anbruch** m *nightfall* **~angriff** m *night-attack* **~angst** f *n. terrors* pl **~anzug** m *n.-dress* **~arbeit** f *n.-work*; (Studium) *lucubration*; ⟨Am a.⟩ *moonlighting* **~arbeiter** m ⟨a.⟩ *sundowner* **~ausgabe** f (Zeitung) *final*; *extra special* **~becken** n *commode* **~besuch** m *n.-call* (*of a doctor*) **~blindheit** f ⟨path⟩ *n.-blindness*, ⟨scient⟩ *nyctalopia* **~bogen** m ⟨astr⟩ *nocturnal arc* **~bomber** m *n.-bomber* **~bummler** m *fly-by-night* **~dienst** m *n.-service* od *-duty* **~essen** n *supper* **~eule** f *n.-* od *screech-owl*, ⟨fig⟩ *fright* **~falter** m ⟨ent⟩ (*hawk-*)*moth* || ⟨fig⟩ (P) *n. owl* **~fernglas** n ⟨Am fam⟩ *snooperscope* **~flug** m *n. flying* **~frost** m *n.-frost* **~gebet** n *evening-prayer* **~gefecht** n *n.-action* **~geist** m, **~gespenst** n *ghost, spectre* **~geschirr** n *chamber*(*-pot*) || ⟨fam⟩ *pot* (kindlich *pon*) **~gleiche** f *equinox* **~glocke** f *n.-bell* **~haube** f *n.-cap* **~hemd** n *n.-shirt*; (f Frauen & Kinder) *n.-gown* od *-dress* **~herberge** f *n.'s lodging*; *lodging-house* **~hyazinthe** f ⟨bot⟩ *tuberose* **~imbiß** m *supper* **~jacke** f *n.-jacket* **~jagd** f ⟨aero⟩ *n. interception*; helle ~ *illuminated n.-fighting* **~jäger** m ⟨aero⟩ *n.-fighter*, ⟨fam⟩ *cricket* **~käfer** m *n. flying beetle* **~kerze** f ⟨bot⟩ *evening primrose* **~kleid** n *n.-dress*, *n.-gown*, *deshabille* **~klub** m *night club* **~lager** n *n.'s lodging*; ⟨fam⟩ *shakedown* (*to give a p a sh.*) || (Unterkunft) *accommodation* od *quarters* pl *for the n.* || ⟨mil⟩ *bivouac* **~leuchter** m *bedroom candlestick* **~licht** n *n.-light* **~lokal** n *n.-club*, *dancing-room*(*s* pl); (teures) ⟨Am fam⟩ *swank spot* **~luft** f *n.-air* **~mahl** n *supper* **≃mahlen** vi [h] [österr] *to have s.* **~mahr** m *n.-mare* **~marsch** m *n.-march* | ~beleuchtung [f] *convoy light* **~mette** f ⟨ec⟩ *matins* pl **~musik** f *serenade* **~mütze** f *n.-cap* || ⟨fig fam⟩ *dullard* **~pfauenauge** n *emperor-moth* **~portier** m *n.-porter* **~posten** m ⟨mil⟩ *n.-guard* °**~pott** m *jordan*, ⟨vulg⟩ *po* **~quartier** n = ~lager || jdm ~ geben ⟨fig⟩ *to accommodate a p for the n.* **~rabe, ~reiher** m ⟨orn⟩ *n.-heron* **~reise** f *journey by n.*, *overnight journey* **~rock** m *dressing-gown* **~ruhe** f *n.'s rest* **~runde** f *patrol* **~schaltergebühr** f ⟨post⟩ *late fee* **~schatten** m ⟨bot⟩ (*deadly* od *black*) *n.-shade* | ~gewächse [n pl] ⟨bot⟩ *solanaceæ*, → *vine* **~schicht** f *n.-shift* || in ~ arbeiten *to work on n.-sh.* | zu **≃schlafender** Zeit *at this unearthly hour* (*in the middle of the n.*) **~schmetterling** m = ~falter **~schwalbe** f = Ziegenmelker **~schwärmen** n, **~schwärmerei** f *n.-revelling* **~schwärmer** m = ~falter || ⟨fig⟩ *n.-bird*, ⟨Am⟩ *n. crawler* **~schwester** f *n.-nurse* **~seh-** ~gerät [n] *evaporograph*; ~vermögen [n] = **~sicht** f *vision by n.*, *n. v.* **~ständchen** n = ~musik **~stille** f *silence of the n.* **~stück** n ⟨arts⟩ *n.-piece* **~stuhl** m *close-* od *n.-stool*, (*n.-*)*commode* **~stunde** f *hour of the n.*, *n.-hour* **~tarif** m *n. rate* | jdm etw in e–m **~telegramm** [n] mitteilen etc *to cable a p a th in a night-letter* **~tisch** m *n.-* od *bed*(*side*)*-table* **~topf** = ~geschirr **~trunk** m ⟨fam⟩ *n.-cap* **~übung** f ⟨mil⟩ *n.-training*; *n.-manœuvre* **~urlaub** m ⟨mil⟩ *late pass* **~viole** f ⟨bot⟩ *dame's violet* od *wort* **~visier** n ⟨mil⟩ *n.-sight* **~vogel** m *n.-bird* **~wache** f *vigil*, *n.-watch* ⟨a. paint⟩ || *n.-nurse* || ⟨mil⟩ *n.-guard* **~wächter** m *watchman* | ⟨fig fam⟩ *dullard*, ⟨Am sl⟩ *dub* || ⟨vulg⟩ *turd* **~wandeln** n *sleep-walking*, *somnambulism* | ≃ vi [s] *to walk in one's sleep* **~wandler** m *sleep-walker*, *somnambulist* **~wärter** m *n.-nurse* **~wäsche** f *n.-things* **~zeit** f *n.-time* (zur ~ *at n.-t.*) **~zeug** n *n.-dress* od *-ths* pl **~zug** m ⟨rail⟩ *n.-train* **n·ächtelang** adv → Nacht B. **n·achten** vi imps [h] *to grow night* od *dark* **n·ächtens** adv ⟨poet⟩ = nachts (→ Nacht A.) **n·ächtig** a *dark*, *gloomy* **N·achtigall** f ~/~en *nightingale* | ~enschlag [m] *warbling of the n.* **n·ächtigen** vi [h] *to pass the night* **n·ächtlich** a *nightly*, *nocturnal*; *night* (*attack*); *darksome*, *gloomy* (*sky*); *overnight* (*assault*) || auf dem ~en Bummel s ⟨sl⟩ *to be on the tiles* | adv *n.ly*, *every n.* | ~erw·eile [adv] *in the* od *at n.-time* **n·achts** adv → Nacht A.

°**Nackedei** m ~s/~ *naked child*; süßer Backfisch≃ ⟨hum⟩ *beguiling teenage bobby soxer sans sox* (ohne Rollsocken)

N·acken m ~s/~ (*scruff* od *nape of the*) *neck* || e–n beim ~ packen *to catch a p by the neck* || e–n Schelm im ~ h *to have a roguish disposition* || den Kopf in den ~ werfen *to throw back one's head* | ⟨fig⟩ jdm immer auf dem ~ s *to be forever at a p's heels* || störrischer ~ *obstinate n.* || den ~ beugen *to submit* || .. saßen ihm im ~ *the pursuers hung on his heels* **~feder** f (Hahn≃) *hackle* **~haar** n *back-hair* **~hebel** m ⟨wrestling⟩ *double Nelson* **~schirm** m ⟨hist⟩ *nape-guard* **~schlag** m *blow from behind* || ⟨fig⟩ *drawback*; (jdm) ≃e versetzen *to rabbit-punch*; e–n ~ erhalten *to get it in the neck* ⟨a. fig⟩ **~stück** n ⟨cul⟩ *scrag-end* **-nackig, -≃** a *-necked* (*long-*, *stiff-n.*)

n·ackt (a. nackend, ⟨fam⟩ nackig) *naked*; ⟨bes arts⟩ *nude* || (ohne Federn) *callow* || *bare* (*arms, feet*); *naked* (*limbs*) | ⟨fig⟩ *bare* (*life, trees, ground*) || *naked* (*eyes*) || *abject* (*poverty*) || *blunt* (*fact*) || *plain* od *blunt* (*truth*) || ~e Gewalt der Umstände *brute circumstances*; in ~em Zustand *in the nude* | (sich) ~ ausziehen *to strip* || ~ schwimmen *to swim in the nude* | ⟨tech⟩ *unlagged* (Rohr etc), *stripped* (Chassis) **N·ackt- ~beinchen** n ⟨fig Am⟩ *bobby soxer* (Mädel mit Rollsocken) °**~frosch** m *naked child* **~kultur** f *nudism* **~samige** f ⟨bot⟩ *gymnosperm* **~schnecken** f pl ⟨zoo scient⟩ *limacidae* **~studie** f ⟨phot⟩ *nude figure study* | als **~tänzerin** auftreten *to do strip-tease dances* **N·acktheit** f ~/~en *nakedness, nudity* || *callowness* || ⟨fig⟩ *bareness* (*of the soil*); *bareness* (*of a landscape*)

N·adel f ~/~n **A.** *needle* ⟨a. minr⟩; ⟨bot⟩ *needle*(*-leaf*) **B.** ·Ansteck≃ *pin*; ·Ätz≃ *style*; B·usen≃ *breast-pin*; ·Eis≃ *ice-needle*; Grammoph·on- etc -≃ *style*; H·aar≃ *hair-pin*; H·äkel≃ *crotched-hook*; Ins·ekten≃ *setting pin*; K·upferstech≃ *dry-point*; Magn·et≃ *magnetic needle*; N·äh≃ *needle*; N·etz≃ *netting n.*; Rad·ier≃ *style*; R·eiß≃ *mark scraper*; Schl·ips≃ *scarf-pin*; S·icherheits≃ *safety pin*; St·eck≃ *pin*; St·opf≃ *darning-n.*; Str·ick≃ *knitting-n.*; Vorst·eck≃ (*bar*) *pin*; Z·ünd≃ ⟨mil⟩ *needle* **C.** e–e ~ einfädeln *to thread a n.* || mit ~n ab-, feststecken *to pin*; die Steck≃n herausnehmen aus *to unpin* || ⟨surg⟩ ~n legen *to put stitches in* || sich auf die ~ verstehen *to be clever at n.-work* | ⟨fig⟩ mit der heißen ~ genäht ⟨fam⟩ *just blown together* || wie auf ~n sitzen *to be on thorns* od *tenter-hooks* || nach e–r ~ im Heuwagen suchen *to look for a n. in a bottle of hay* od *in a haystack* **~abweichung** f *magnetic declination* **~arbeit** f *needlework* **~ausschlag** m *variation of the* (*magnetic*) *n.* **~baum** m ⟨bot⟩ *conifer*, ⟨for⟩ *evergreen tree* **~brief** m *paper of pins* **~buch** n *n.-book* **~büchse** f *n.-* od *p.-case* **~draht** m ⟨tech⟩ *n.-*(bzw *p.-*)*wire* **~fabrik** f *n.-factory* **≃förmig** a *n.-shaped*; *acicular* || ⟨bot⟩ *aculeate* **~geld** n *pin-money* **~holz** n ⟨for⟩ *soft-wood* | ~baum [m] *conifer*(*ous tree*); ~zellstoff [m] *c.s wood* od *softwood pulp* **~hölzer** n pl *conifers* pl, *pines and firs* pl **~kissen** n *pincushion* **~kluppe** f (f Kupferstich) (*dry-*)*point* **~kopf** m *p.'s* (od *p.-*)*head* **~öhr** n *eye of a needle* **~palme** f ⟨bot⟩

raffia **~sonde** f ⟨surg⟩ *n.-bearer* **~spitze** f *point of a n.* **~stich** m *p.-hole, prick, stitch* ‖ (Verwundung) *p.-prick* ⟨a. fig⟩ ‖ jdm e–n ~ versetzen *to pin-prick a p* **~ventil** n *n. valve* **~verfahren** n *compass method* **~wald** m *fir-, pine-*, ⟨scient⟩ *conifer(ous) wood* **n·adeln 1.** [vt] [h] *to pin* ‖ *to sew (boots, gloves)* **2.** [vi] der Baum nadelt .. *sheds its needles* **N·adler** m ~s/~ *needle-* od *pin-maker* **~ware** f *pins and needles* pl

Nad·ir m ~s/ *nadir* (Ggs Zen·it *zenith*)

Nagas·aki n (japan. Stadt)

N·agel m ~s/≗ **1.** ⟨tech⟩ *nail* (vgl Bolzen, Kloben, Krampe, Stift) **A.** ·Achs≗ → Lünse ‖ geschnittener ~ *cut n.* ‖ gr ~ *spike* ‖ H·aken≗ *tenter-hook* ‖ H·olz≗ *peg*; *nog*; *dowel*; ⟨mar⟩ *treenail, trennel* ‖ H·uf≗ *horse-nail* ‖ kl ~ *(tin-) -tack*; .. ohne Kopf *sprig*; .. ohne K. f. Schuhe *sparable* ‖ langer ~ mit kl Kopf *brad* ‖ Reiß≗ *drawing-pin* ‖ Schmiede≗ *forged n.* ‖ schmiede-eiserner ~ *wrought n.* ‖ Schuh≗ *shoe-n.* ‖ Sohlen-≗ f. ~schuhe *hobnail* ‖ Stift≗ *pin* ‖ ~ mit Widerhaken *barbed n.* ‖ Zier≗ *upholsterer's n.* **B.** etw an e–n ~ **aufhängen** *to hang sth up on a n.* ‖ Schuhe mit ≗n beschlagen *to stud boots with n.s* ‖ e–n ~ einschlagen in .. *to drive a n. into ..* ‖ der ~ zieht .. *takes* ǀ ⟨fig⟩ an den ~ hängen *to shelve (to give up)*; die S .. *to throw up the cards* ‖ den ~ auf den Kopf treffen *to hit it* od *the mark*; *to hit the (right) n. on the head*; ⟨fig a.⟩ *to hit the bull's eye* ‖ e–n ~ im Kopf h *to have a bee in one's bonnet* ‖ ein ~ zu m–m Sarge *a n. in my coffin* **2.** ⟨**anat**⟩ ≗ [pl] *nails* pl ‖ abgekaute, gepflegte ~ *bitten, well-kept n.s* ‖ an den ~n kauen, sich die ~ schneiden (putzen) *to bite, cut* (⟨fam⟩ *do*) *one's n.s* ǀ ⟨fig⟩ k–n ~ breit *not an inch* ‖ (die Arbeit) es brennt mir auf den ~n *I am hard driven (with my work)* ‖ °⟨fig⟩ sich etw untern ~ reißen *to clean up sth.*, ⟨mil⟩ *to swipe ..* **3.** °⟨fig⟩ sich e–n ~ ins Kreuz schlagen ⟨sl⟩ *to put one's foot into one's mouth* **~auszieher** m ⟨tech⟩ *nail-drawer* **~bank** f ⟨mar⟩ *cross-piece* **~blüte** f *n.-spot* **~bohrer** m *gimlet* **~bürste** f *n.--brush* **~eisen** n *n.-rod* ‖ *heading-tool* ‖ *n.-mould* **~feile** f *n.-file* od *-trimmer* ≗**fest** a *fastened with nails, nailed* ‖ ⟨jur⟩ *immovable* **~fluh** f ⟨geol⟩ *nagelfluh* **~geschwür** n *whitlow* **~glätter** m *n.-pad* **~hautentferner** m *cuticle remover* **~kopf** m, **~kuppe** f *head of a n.* **~lack** m *nail polish, nail enamel*, roter ~ *sang-de-bœuf*; ~entferner [m] *n. e. remover* **~mal** n *n.-mark* ≗**neu** a *hard as nails, bran(d)-new, spick and span* **~pflege** f *manicure* **~polierer** m *buffer* **~probe** f; die ~ m *to leave no heel-taps, to thumb one's glass* **~schmied** m *n.-maker* od *-smith* **~schmiede** f *n.--forge* **~schuhe** m pl *spiked* od *nailed* od *studded boots* od *shoes* **~tritt** m ⟨hors⟩ *picked-up nail* **~verbindung** f *nailed joint* **~weißstift** m *manicure white pencil* **~wurzel** f *root of a n.* **~zange** f *nippers* pl **~zieher** m *claw-wrench* **N·ägelein** n ~s/~ ⟨obs & poet bot⟩ *clove* **n·ageln** vt [h] *to nail, spike* ‖ die Genagelten [pl] (= Schuhe) *the nailed boots* **N·agler** m ~s/~ *nailer, nail-smith*

n·agen vt/i [h] (an [dat]) *to gnaw (a piece of bread) (on one's lips), to nibble (at)* ‖ *to pick (a bone)* ‖ nichts z ~ noch z beißen *neither bite nor sup* ‖ *the surf wears away the shore* ǀ ⟨fig⟩ es nagte an mir *it rankled in my mind, it preyed upon my mind, it nagged at my heart (when)* ‖ der Kummer nagt ihm am Herzen *his heart is consumed with grief* ǀ ~d *gnawing* ⟨a. fig⟩ ‖ *ravenous (hunger)* ‖ *cankering (remorse)* ‖ *poignant (grief)* ‖ *troublesome (doubts)* ‖ *(slights) that rankle in the breast* ‖ *carking (care wears her down)*; *corrosive (fear*, etc) **N·ager** m ~s/~; **N·agetier** n *rodent, gnawer*

N·agoja n (japan. Stadt) *Nagoya*

N·agpur n (vorderind. Bezirk)

N·ah- ~angriff m *close range attack* **~aufklärer** m *tactical reconnaissance aircraft* **~aufklärung** f ⟨mil⟩ *close patrol, short range reconnaissance* **~aufnahme** f ⟨film⟩ *close-up* ǀ ~vorsatzlinse [f] *c.-up lens* **~bereich-**Navigationsverfahren n *short range navigation* N (*SHORAN*) **~kampf** m *close(--range) action* od *fight, hand-to-h. fighting, fight at close quarters* ‖ ⟨box⟩ *infighting, clinch* ǀ ~artillerie [f] *close-support artillery*; *forward guns*; ~mittel [n] *short-range weapon*, ~ [pl] *cl.-r. arms*; ~wagen [m] *cl.-r. tank* **~ost** m: in ~ *in the Middle East* ǀ ~- *M.E. (war)* **~selektion** f ⟨telv⟩ *adjacent channel selectivity* **~transport** m *sh.--distance tr.* **~treffer** m *near hit* ⟨a. fig⟩ **~unterstützung** f *close support* N **~verkehr** m *short--distance* od *local traffic*; ⟨rail⟩ *junction traffic* ǀ Flugsicherung im ~sbereich *terminal air traffic control* **~ziel** n *immediate objective* od *target*; → nah(e)

N·äh- ~arbeit f *needlework, sewing* **~garn** n *s.-cotton* **~kästchen** n *(lady's) work-box* **~kissen** n *s.-cushion* **~kloben** m ⟨tech⟩ *s.-block* **~korb** m *s.* od *w.-basket* **~kränzchen** n *ladies' w.ing party* (⟨Am⟩ *bee*) **~mädchen** n = Näherin **~maschine** f *s.-machine* **~nadel** f *(s.-)needle* **~rahmen** m *frame for needlework, s.-frame* **~ring** m *tailor's thimble, s.-ring* **~schule** f *s.-school* **~seide** f *s.-silk* **~stube** f *s.-room* **~täschchen** n *needle-case*; *house-wife* ['hʌzif] **~tisch** m *lady's work table* **~zeug** n *s. implements* pl **~zwirn** m *s.-thread* **n·ähen** vt [h] *to sew, stitch* (an *to*) ‖ ⟨med⟩ *to stitch (a cut)*; *to suture (up)* ‖ mit gr Stichen ~ *to baste*, überwendlich ~ *to whip, oversew* ‖ genäht *welted (shoes)*; mit der Hand g. *sewed by h.* ‖ sich [dat] die Finger wund ~ *to sew the flesh off one's bones* **Näher·ei** f ~/~en *sewing* ‖ *needlework* **N·äherin** f ~/~nen *needlewoman, seamstress*; → Naht

n·ah(e) a & adv [compr: näher *nearer*; sup → nächst] **A.** *near (presence)* ‖ ⟨obs, poet, dial⟩ *nigh* ‖ *close (friend[ship])* ‖ *neighbouring (town)* ‖ *near (relation)* ‖ ⟨Am a.⟩ *nearby (house, future)* ‖ ganz ~ [adv] *within a stone's throw* ‖ (bevorstehend) *impending (arrival, danger)*; *imminent (danger)* ‖ der ~e Tod *the approach of death* ‖ der Sommer ist ~ .. *is drawing near* **B. nähere** Umgebung etc *near surrounding, relations* (Verwandte); *fuller (information)*; *stricter (inquiries)*; *more valid (claims, rights)*; *more intimate (relations* Beziehungen); jds nähere Bekanntschaft m *to become more intimately acquainted with a p* ‖ → näher **C.** ~ bekannt *intimately acquainted* ‖ ~ verwandt *near akin, closely related* (mit *to*), *near a p in blood*; *(they are) near relatives* ǀ in ~er Aussicht *near at hand* ǀ er war e–r Ohnmacht (der Verzweiflung) ~ *he nearly fainted (was almost desperate)* ‖ das Weinen war mir ~ *I was near crying, I felt inclined to cry* **D.** ~ **am** Fenster etc *by the window*; *near* od *close to (the lamp)* ‖ ~ an (die) 80 (Jahre) *close (up)on eighty* ‖ es waren ~ an die tausend *there were nearly a thousand of them* ‖ ⟨ftb⟩ ~ am Ball s *to be on the ball* ‖ ⟨fig⟩ ~ am Bankrott *within measurable distance of b.* ǀ ~ **an-e-a** *close together, close to one another*; *contiguous* ǀ ~ bei *close to (the house)*; *handy to (the door)*; *close to him was a window* ǀ ~ **daran** s zu tun *to be near* (od *on the point* od *verge of*) *doing* ‖ *to be about to do* ‖ *I very nearly did it* ‖ Betrug oder ~ daran *fraud or near neighbour to it* ‖ es war ~ daran, daß *it was touch and go that I was swept*; *it nearly happened that* ǀ **(von)** nah u fern *(from) far and near* ‖ **von nahem** betrachten *to examine at close quarters* **E.** es **berührte** ihn ~ *it came home to him* ‖ ~ **bevorstehen** → A. ‖ ~ an etw **grenzen** *to border on (be adjacent to) a th* ‖ → ~k, ~legen, ~liegen ‖ ~ **k** (treten etc) *to come (step*, etc) *near* ‖ e–m zu ~ k = .. treten ‖ komm' mir nicht zu ~! *stand off!, keep away!* ‖ e–r S ~ **sein**: *he was verging on the age of ..*; *he was near his end* od *death* ‖ e–m zu ~ **treten** *to hurt a p('s feelings), to offend a p*; ohne Ihnen (Herrn N.) zu ~ treten zu wollen *no* od *without disparagement to you (to Mr. N.)*; *pace* *tua* L (*pace Mr. N.*) ‖ (e–r S) zu ∼ treten *to question* (*encroach upon*) (*a p's authority*), *to violate* (*truth*) **n·ahe- ∼bei** adv *near* od *hard* od *close by* **∼|bringen** (e–m etw) *to make a p familiar with a th*; *to drive* (*a truth*) *home to a p* **∼|gehen** ⟨fig⟩ [dat] *to go to one's heart*; es geht ihm n. *it touches him*; es (etw) geht mir nahe *it affects* od *grieves me to the heart* (*I am much grieved at a th*) ‖ sich etw (zu) ∼ l *to take a th* (*too much*) *to heart* **∼hin** adv = ∼zu **∼|k** [dat] *to approach*; *to come near to*; *to get at* (*the truth*) ‖ *nobody could get near him* ‖ (S) *to run close second to*; *a shyness approximating to cowardice* ‖ ⟨fig⟩ jdm ∼ *to run a p close* **∼|legen** (e–m etw) *to intimate, prompt, suggest* (*a th to a p*), *to encourage a p* (*to take interest in a th*); .. dringend .. *to urge a th on a p*; das legt den Gedanken ∼, daß .. *that suggests that* .. **∼|liegen**: *the forest is quite near* od *is close by*; .. *is close to* (od *borders upon*) *the town* ‖ ⟨fig⟩ *to be obvious*; es liegt n. zu tun *one easily does*; *there is a suggestion* (daß *that*) | ∼d [a] *obvious* **∼|stehen** vi [h] [dat] *to be intimately connected with* **∼|treten** vi [s] [dat] *to come into close contact with*; jdm nicht zu ∼ wollen *to mean no offence to a p* | **∼zu** adv *almost, nearly*; *practically* (*impossible*); *best part of* (*a week*); *wellnigh* (*hopeless*) **N·ähe** f ∼/∼n *nearness, proximity* ‖ (örtlich a.:) *vicinity, neighbourhood,* (zeitlich a.:) *imminence* | **in** der ∼ (*other houses*) *thereabouts*; (*there was no one*) *about*; (*a wolf was*) *by* ‖ in nächster *or* unmittelbarer ∼ *near at hand, close by, at close quarters*; *in close proximity*; aus .. schießen *to fire at close quarters* ‖ ganz *or* hier in der ∼ ⟨a.⟩ *within call, next door* ‖ in der ∼ der Stadt *near the town*; sich in der ∼ aufhalten *to stay around*; .. e–r S .. *to hang round about a th*; .. e–r P .. *to be at a p's elbow* ‖ in der ∼ betrachten *to look closely at, to examine closely* ‖ in jds ∼ k *to come near a p* **n·ahen** vi [s] & sich ∼ [h] *to draw near, to approach* ‖ [dat]) *nobody could get near him* **n·äher** [compr v → nahe] *my h. is nearer* (an) *the shore than his* ‖ treten Sie ∼! *this way, please!* | ∼e Bedingungen, Bestimmungen *qualifications*; bei ∼er Betrachtung *on further consideration* ‖ ⟨gram⟩ ∼es Objekt *direct object* ‖ ∼e Umstände = Näheres | [adv] sich ∼ mit etw beschäftigen *to give a th greater attention* ‖ etw jds Verständnis [dat] ∼ bringen *to bring a th more within a p's comprehension* ‖ auf etw ∼ eingehen *to go into a matter more closely* ‖ je ∼ sie dem Hause k *the nearer they approach the h.* ‖ (immer) ∼ k *to close in* (*and in*) ‖ dem Ziele ∼ k *to advance towards the goal* ‖ e–r S ∼ k *to get to the bottom of a th* ‖ e–r S ∼ rücken *to app. a th* | ∼ bestimmen *or* bezeichnen *to qualify* ‖ ⟨übtr⟩ e–m etw ∼ bringen: *that drives the conviction further home* **N·ähere(s)** n ∼n/ *details* pl ‖ wenn Sie ∼s wissen wollen *if you want d.* ‖ ∼s erfahren *to learn* (*further*) *particulars* ‖ sich des ∼n entsinnen *to remember all the circumstances* | das ∼ aus–e–a–setzen *to explain fully* **n·ähern** vt [h] *to bring* (*closer together* od) *near* | **sich** (jdm) ∼ [h] *to draw near, to approach* (*a p*) ‖ *to strike up an acquaintance with* (*a lady*) ‖ sich jdm, e–r S ∼ *to close in upon, to draw to*(*wards*) *a p, a th* ‖ *nobody could get near him* ‖ *to near* (*the port*) ‖ *to lapse towards* (*a type*) ‖ *to be nearing* (*the thirties*) ‖ *to be verging towards* (*a quarrel*) ‖ sich wieder ∼ (S) *to reconverge* **N·äherung** f ∼/∼en *drawing near, approach* | **∼sverfahren** n *rational approximations* pl (*e. g. for the elementary functions*) **≗sweise** adv *by approximation*; **∼swert** m ⟨math⟩ *approximate value* **∼zünder** m *proximity fuse*

Näher·ei, Näherin → o. (nach:) nähen & Naht

nahm (**nähme**) 1. & 3. sg (subj) v nehmen

N·ähr- ∼boden m *fertile* od *fostering soil* ‖ ⟨bact⟩ (*culture-*)*medium* ‖ ⟨fig⟩ *matrix, substratum, breeding-ground* **∼creme** f ⟨cosm⟩ *skinfood* **∼gehalt** m *sustenance* **∼geld** n *alimony* **∼hefe** f ⟨cul⟩ *nutritional yeast* **∼kraft** f *nutritive power* **∼mittel** n [mst pl] (*prepared*) *food-stuffs*; *nutriment, nutritive*; *cereals* pl **∼mutter** f *foster-mother*; ⟨univ⟩ *alma mater* L **∼präparat** n *patent food* **∼salze** n pl *nutritive salts* **∼stand** m *peasantry* ‖ *working* od *labouring class* **∼stoff** m *nutritious matter, nutritive* (*material*), *aliment*; *foodstuff* **∼wert** m *nutritive* od *caloric value* od *quality* | ≗arm [a] *oligotrophic*; ≗reich [a] *eutrophic*; ohne ∼ *jejune, innutritious* **n·ähren 1.** vi [h] *to be nourishing* **2.** vt [h] *to nourish* ‖ *to suckle* (*a baby*) | ⟨übtr⟩ *to feed* (*a fire*); (Angriff) *to sustain* | ⟨fig⟩ *to foster*; *pamper* (*feelings*); *to entertain* (*suspicion, resentment*); *to nurse* (*a wish*) ‖ **sich** ∼ (v) *to feed* od *to live* (*on*) ‖ ⟨fig⟩ *to gain a livelihood, to earn one's living* ‖ sich kümmerlich ∼ *to earn a scanty living* **n·ahrhaft** a *nutritious, nourishing, nutritive* ‖ *substantial* (*meal, fare*) ‖ *rich* (*diet*) ‖ *strengthening* (*food*) | ⟨übtr⟩ *productive* (*soil*) | **≗igkeit** f ∼/ *n.sness* ‖ *s.ity* ‖ *richness* ‖ etc **N·ahrung** f ∼/ *food, nourishment, nutriment, nutrition* ‖ *diet* ‖ *comestibles* pl ‖ (Unterhalt) *livelihood, sustenance, support, living* | ⟨fig⟩ (*the daily*) *fare*; *reinforcement* | **zur** ∼ gehörig *nutritional* | geistige ∼ *mental food* od *nutriment* ‖ gesunde ∼ *healthy diet* ‖ kärgliche ∼ *scanty sustenance* ‖ pflanzliche ∼ *vegetable food* ‖ reichliche (schlechte) ∼ *good* (*poor*) *nourishment* | e–m ∼ u Kleidung **geben** *to find a p in board and clothing* ‖ dem Vieh Gras als ∼ geben *to feed cattle on grass* ‖ .. ∼ an K. u Seele *he gave her food of both the body and the soul* ‖ ⟨fig⟩ [dat] ∼ geben *to strengthen* (*a suspicion*), *to* (*be fresh fuel* od) *add f. to* (*the flames of a passion*) ‖ s–r ∼ nachgehen *to attend to one's business* ‖ ∼ zu sich **nehmen** *to take food* od *nourishment* ‖ jdn in ∼ **setzen** *to employ a p* ‖ ∼ **ziehen** aus *to draw nourishment from* **N·ahrungs- ∼aufnahme** f *reception of food*; *ingestion* **∼bedürfnis** n *want of food* **∼brei** m *chyme* **∼flüssigkeit** f *chyle* **∼kanal** m *alimentary canal* **≗los** a *without food* (⟨übtr⟩ *resources*); *hard* (*times*) **∼losigkeit** f *lack of food*, etc ‖ *unproductiveness* (*of the soil*) ‖ *hardness* (*of times*) **∼mangel** m *lack, want* od *scantity of food* (*provisions, nourishment*); *innutrition* **∼mittel** n *article of food* ‖ [pl] *provisions, victuals* pl; *food-stuffs* pl; hochwertige ∼ [pl] *food of high nutritive value* | ∼fälschung [f] *adulteration of food*; ∼gewerbe [n] *food trades* pl; ∼industrie [f] *provision-industry*; ∼knappheit [f] *food shortage*; ∼lehre [f] ⟨physiol⟩ *sitology*; ∼steuer *duty on provisions*; ∼zufuhr *food-supply* **∼pflanze** f *food-plant* **∼saft** m *chyle* **∼sorgen** f pl *struggle for bread, cares of subsistence* od *life*; ∼ h *have difficulty in making both ends meet, to be hard up* **∼stoff** m *nutritious matter, nutriment* ‖ ∼e [pl] *food-stuff* | auf **∼suche** [f] *in search for food* **∼verordnung** f → –vorschrift **∼verweigerung** f ⟨path⟩ *sitophobia* **∼vorschrift** f *regimen, diet* **∼zufuhr** f *taking nourishment*

N·aht f ∼/≗e *seam* ‖ ⟨anat, surg, bot⟩ *suture*, ⟨tech⟩ *seam*; ⟨mar⟩ *seam* (*of planks*) ‖ doppelte ∼ ⟨mar⟩ *flat seam* ‖ falsche ∼ *mock s.* ‖ Löt≗ *soldered s.* ‖ (Schweiß≗) *weld*(*ing*) *s.* ‖ überwendliche ∼ *overcast* | ≗e anlegen *to put in stitches* ⟨a. med⟩; e–e ∼ auftrennen *to rip open a seam* ‖ die ∼ ist geplatzt .. *has burst* | ⟨fig fam⟩ *a lot of* (*cherries*, etc) ‖ e–m auf die ∼ fühlen *to test a p* **∼los** a ⟨tech⟩ *jointless, seamless* (Rohr) **∼schweißung** f *seam welding* **∼stelle** f ⟨tact⟩ *boundary position* **Nähter·ei** f = Näherei **N·ähterin** = Näherin

na·iv [–f] a *naïve* (od *folk* [*artist*]); *artless, guileless, ingenuous* ‖ *simple-minded* (*girl*) ‖ *objective* (*poetry*) | den ≗en [–v–] spielen *to play the unsophisticated* ‖ die ≗e spielen ⟨theat⟩ *to play naïve parts* **Naivit·ät** [–v–] f ∼/∼en *naiveté,* *artlessness, guilelessness, ingenuousness; objectivity*

Naj·ade f ~/~n ⟨myth & zoo⟩ *naiad*

N·ame(n) m ~ns/~n **A.** *name*; ein angenommener ~ *an alias* ‖ Deck≃ *code n.* ‖ erfundener ~ *fancy n.* ‖ Gattungs≃ *generic n.* ‖ irrtümlicher ~ *misappellation, misnomer* | (Benennung *appellation* ‖ (Ruf) (guter *good*) *renown, reputation*; *good name in men and women* (Shak) **B.** e–e Insel des ~s N. .. *of the n. of N.* ‖ der ~ e–s Wissenschaftlers *the n. of scientist* ‖ der 5. B. des ~ns *the 5th baronet to bear the n.* ‖ H., s–s ~ns der Vierte *Henry the fourth of his n.* ‖ der ~ f die Beere *the n. of the berry* ‖ die einzelnen ~n *the personnel* (*of a commission*) ‖ wie ist Ihr ~? *what is your name*? wie war noch Ihr (⟨vulg⟩ werter) ~? *I haven't the advantage of your n.* **C.** e–n ~n **angeben** (nennen) *to give a n.* ‖ was bedeutet schon ein ~? *what's in a name*? (Shak) ‖ s–n ~n **beflecken** *to stain one's reputation* ‖ → beilegen ‖ kaum dem ~n nach bekannt s: (*distress*) *almost wants a n.*; s–n ~n darunterschreiben *to sign* (*one's n., a document*) ‖ e–n ~n führen *to be named* ‖ **hat** das Kind schon e–n ~n? *has the ch. already been christened*? ‖ die S muß doch e–n ~n h .. *must have a n. of some sort* ‖ e–n guten ~n h *to be of good report* ‖ ihr ~ hat k–n guten Klang *her n. is not in good repute* ‖ dem Kind (durch Heirat) e–n ehrlichen ~n geben ⟨fam⟩ *to parson* [vi]; s–n ~n **hergeben** f *to lend one's n. to* ‖ sich e–n ~ **m** *to win a high reputation, to make one's mark, to make a n. for o.s.*; ⟨Am⟩ *to go on record* | e–n beim *or* mit ~n **nennen** .. *by n.*; k–n ~n n. *to name no names*; ⟨parl⟩ ~n n.! *name*!; er wollte s–n ~n nicht n. *he would not give his n.*; die Dinge beim richtigen ~n n. *to call ths by their proper n.s, .. a spade a spade* | ~n verlesen *to call the roll* ‖ s–n ~n wahren *to maintain one's prestige* **D. auf** den ~n lautend *bearing the* (*one's*) *n., not negotiable*; ⟨com⟩ *payable to order* ‖ ein Fleck auf jds ~n *a blot on a p's escutcheon* ‖ auf jds ~n (ausstellen) *in the n. of a p* ‖ er hört auf den ~n N. *he answers to the n. of N.* | **im** ~n jds *or* v jdm *on behalf of a p* ‖ im ~n des Gesetzes *in the n. of the law* ‖ in s–m ~n *in his n.* ‖ im ~n Gottes! *in God's n.*! ‖ °in Gottes ~n! *for God's sake* (*have it*)! ‖ °in des Teufels ~n! *hang it all*!, (*go and be*) *damned*! | **mit** dem ~n N. *by* od *of the n. of N.* ‖ mit ~n erwähnt *mentioned by their n.s* | dem ~n **nach** *nominally*; *nominal* (*fine*) ‖ (*only king*) *in name* ‖ (*to know a p*) *by n.* | ohne ~n *no n.* (*tobacco, orchestra*, etc) | **unter** e–m ~n auftreten, bekannt s *to go by* od *under a n.* ‖ unter dem (falschen) ~n N. reisen *to be masquerading under the n. of N.* ‖ ⟨fig⟩ u. d. ~n [gen] *under the pretext* (*of charity*) | **v** ~n u Klang *of international reputation* **N·amen-** **~brett** n *name board* **~buch** n *register of proper n.s* **≃gebend** a *eponymous* (*hero*) **~gebung** f *n.-giving, naming*; *christening*; ⟨scient⟩ *nomenclature* **~liste** f *roll*, ⟨pol⟩ *poll* **≃los** a *n.less, anonymous* ‖ (unsäglich) *boundless, indescribable, unspeakable* (*pain*), *unutterable, inexpressible* (*misery*) **~losigkeit** f *n.lessness*, etc. **~papier** n *stock payable to order* **~register, ~verzeichnis** n *list of n.s* od *authors*; *n. index* **~schild** n *n.-plate*; (am Haus) *n.-board* **~verlesung** f *call-over* **~verwechs(e)lung** f *mistake in n.* **~vorspann** m ⟨film⟩ *credit titles*; *credits* **~zeichen** n pl (f Wäsche) *name taps* pl **n·amens 1.** *named* **2.** prep [gen] *in the name of* ‖ *on behalf of* (*the secretary*) **N·amens-** **~aktie** f *registered share* **~aufruf** m *roll-call* **~bruder** m *namesake* **~fest** n, **~tag** m ⟨R. C.⟩ *n.-day* **~nennung** f; ohne ~ *anonymously* **~unterschrift** f *signature* **~vetter** m *n.sake* **~zug** m *signature*; eigenhändig mit ~ versehen *to autograph* **n·amentlich** adv *by name, namely* ‖ ~ anführen *to mention individually* od *by name* | (insbesondere) *particularly, especially, in particular* | [a] ⟨parl⟩ ~e Abstimmung f *name-poll* **n·amhaft** a *distinguished, renowned*; *noted* (*orchestras*) ‖ (beträchtlich) *considerable* (*difference*); *large* (*sum*) ‖ ~ m *to name, specify* **n·ämlich** adv **1.** *namely, to wit, that is* (*to say*) (abbr *i.e.* od *viz*) **2.** (begründend) *because*; *you know* od *see* **n·ämliche** (der, die, das) a *the same*; *the very* (*man*) **Nämlichkeitsbescheinigung** f (Zollwesen) → Identitätsnachweis

Nam·ur [–yr] n (belg. Stadt & Prov.)

N·ancy ['nɑ̃si] n ⟨Fr⟩ (Stadt)

N·anga P·arbat (ein Himalayagipfel)

N·änie ['nɛːniə] f ~/~n [Gr] *nenia, dirge*

N·anking n **1.** (chin. Stadt) *Nankin* **2.** ~s/~e & ~s ⟨com⟩ *nankeen* | ~leder [n] *chamois* **≃en** a *nankeen*

Nanschan n (Gebirge in China) *Nan Shan*

Nantes [nɑ̃t] n ⟨Fr⟩ (Stadt an der Loire)

°**nan·u** intj *now*! *I say*!, ⟨Am⟩ *gee* → na

N·apf m ~(e)s/≃e *bowl, basin, cup* ‖ Eß≃ *porringer* ‖ Farben≃ *saucer* **~kuchen** m *pound-cake, savarin, baba*

N·aphtha n ~s/~s *n.a* | **~l·in** n ~s/ *naphthalene*

Nap·oleon(d·or) m ~s/~e ⟨Fr⟩ *napoleon* (*20 francs*)

N·appaleder n *nappa*

N·arbe f ~/~n *scar* ‖ ⟨surg⟩ *cicatrice*; ⟨med⟩ *pit* (*of the small-pox*) (→ vernarben); (des Leders) *grain* ‖ ⟨bot⟩ *stigma* ‖ ⟨agr⟩ *top-soil* ‖ e–e ~ hinterlassen *to leave a scar* **n·arben** vt [h] (Leder) *to grain, pommel, shagreen* ‖ ⟨agr⟩ *to take off the top-soil* | **sich** ~ *to scar*; ⟨surg⟩ *to cicatrize* **N·arben-** **≃bedeckt** a *scarred* (*face*) **~bildung** f *formation of a scar* ‖ ⟨surg⟩ *cicatrization*; ⟨at⟩ *keloid* **~leder** n *shagreen* **≃los** a *unscarred* **n·arbig** a *scarred, cicatrized* ‖ (Leder) *grained*

N·arde f ~/~n ⟨bot⟩ *spikenard* ‖ ~nöl [n], ~nsalbe [f] *nard*

N·arew m (recht. Nebenfluß des Bug)

N·arg·il·eh f ~/~ & n ~s/~s *narghile*

N·arko- ... *phoria* ‖ in der ~ *under the anaesthetic* | **~assistent** m, **~schwester** f *anaesthetist* **Nark·otikum** n ~s/–ka *narcotic*(*s* pl) ‖ ⟨sl⟩ *dope* **Narkot·in** n ~(e)s/ ⟨chem⟩ *narcotine* **nark·otisch** a *narcotic* **narkotis·ieren** vt *to narcotize* **N.-·ierung** f ~/~en *narcotization*

Narr m ~en/~en *fool*, ⟨fam⟩ *stupe, stupid* ‖ er ist ein ausgemachter ~ *he is as mad as a hatter* ‖ blöder ~ *imbecile* ‖ (v Beruf) *jester, buffoon, zany* ‖ v Geburt *born fool* ‖ ⟨theat⟩ *fool* ‖ ⟨sl⟩ *silly*; ⟨Am⟩ *mutt, sap, string* ‖ (Mode≃) *fop* ‖ [in comp] *fan, fiend* (*film f.*) | jedem ~en gefällt s–e Kappe ⟨fam⟩ *all his geese are swans*; z ~en m *or* h *to pull a p's leg*; *to make a fool of*; *to dupe, befool* ‖ ich wurde z ~en gehalten *I was being made the goat* ‖ (irreführen) *to mystify* ‖ e–n ~en gefressen h an [dat] *to be foolishly fond of, to be infatuated with* ‖ sich z ~en m *or* hergeben *to be made a laughing-stock of* ‖ sei kein solcher ~ *don't be a ghastly idiot* ‖ sich [acc] nicht f jdn z ~en hergeben *to be nobody's fool* ‖ den ~en spielen *to tomfool* | ⟨prov⟩ die alten ~en sind die schlimmsten *there is no fool like an old one* **N·ärrchen** n ~s/~ (Kosewort) *silly* ‖ (Mädchen) *silly little goose* od *th* **n·arren** vt [h] *to make a fool of*; *to dupe, mock*; (z besten h) *to chaff* **N·arren-** **~doktor** m *mountebank* ‖ → Fastnacht **~fest** n (1. April) *All Fools' Day* **~freiheit** f *privilege of fools* **~futter** n ⟨fam⟩ *flapdoodle* **~gang** m *fool's errand* **~hände** [f pl] beschmieren Tisch u Wände *white walls are a fool's writing-paper* **~haus** n *mad-house, lunatic asylum* **~jacke** f *fool's dress*; ⟨hist⟩ *motley* **~kappe** f *fool's cap*; ⟨hist⟩ *cap and bells* **~literatur** f *folly literature* **~possen** f pl *foolery, buffoonery* ‖ ~ treiben *to play the fool* ‖ laß die ~! *stop that tomfoolery*! ‖ ~! *nonsense*!, *pshaw*! **~seil** n; jdn am ~ führen *to make a fool of a p* **≃sicher** a *foolproof* **~stock** m *slapstick* **~streich** m *foolish trick*

Narret·ei f ~/~en *tomfoolery, buffoonery*; *piece*

od *act of folly*; ~en m *to play the fool* **N·arrheit** f ~/~en *foolishness*, (*piece of*) *folly* || *tomfoolery* **N·ärrin** f ~/~nen *fool, foolish woman* **n·ärrisch** a *foolish, comical* || dein ~er Bruder *your fool of a br.* || ~es Wesen *buffoonery* || (sonderbar) *odd, strange* || (lustig) *merry* || (verrückt) *mad* || *funny* (*ideas* Einfälle) || *eccentric* (*old fellow* Kauz); *silly* (*goose* Ding) | ~ auf *crazy about* || ~ w (vor [dat]) *to go mad* (*for, with*); *to lose one's head* (*over*) || es ist um ~ z w *it is enough to drive a p mad* | [adv] sich [acc] ~ aufführen, benehmen *to make a fool of o.s.*; ~ verliebt *head over heels* od *dotingly in love* (in *with*) || *frenziedly* (*clinging to him*) || wie ~ *like Bedlam, like blazes*

N·arwal m ~(e)s/~e *narwhal*

Narz·isse f ~/~n ⟨bot⟩ *narcissus* || gelbe ~ *daffodil* || weiße ~ *pheasant's eye* **Narz·ißmus** m ~/ *narcissism* || **nas·al** → unten

N·asch- **~katze** f ⟨fig⟩ *sweet-tooth* **~lust** f *fondness for sweet ths, greediness* **~maul** n *sweet-tooth* **~werk** n *sweets, dainties, delicacies, titbits* pl **n·aschen** vt/i [h] *to nibble* (*secretly*) (von *at*), *to eat on the sly* || *to eat* od *pilfer titbits* || gern ~ *to have a sweet tooth, to enjoy pleasures* **N·äscher** m ~s/~ *nibbler* od *lover of dainties, sweet-tooth* **Näscher·ei** f ~/~en *sweetmeat-eating, nibbling of dainties on the sly* || ~en [pl] = Naschwerk **n·aschhaft** a *fond of dainties* || ~ s *to have a sweet tooth* | ~**igkeit** f ~/ *love of titbits, fondness of dainties* **n·äschig** a = naschhaft

nas·al a ⟨gram⟩ *nasal* | ~(laut) [m] ~(e)s/~e *nasal* (*sound*) **N·as-** ~**führen** vt [h] *to lead* (*a p*) *by the nose, to bamboozle, dupe*, ⟨Am⟩ *guy, kid*; ⟨mil sl⟩ *to carry .. about* **~horn** n ⟨zoo⟩ *rhinoceros* | ~käfer [m] *rh.-beetle*; ~vogel [m] *rh.-bird* **N·ase** f ~/~n **A.** *nose*, ⟨sl⟩ *pecker* → Gurke || (e–s Tiers) *snout* | ⟨aero⟩ (Bug) *nose* || °(e–s Rohrs, e–r Röhre) *spout* || (e–s Hobels) *horn* || (e–s Pflugs, Schiffs etc) *beak* || *crocket* (*of a tile*) || (Mitnehmer) *cog, catch* || ⟨arch⟩ (Blatt) *foil* | ⟨übtr⟩ (Geruchssinn) *nose, scent*, feine ~ *flair* (*for*) | ⟨fig fam⟩ (Tadel) *rebuke, reproof, wigging* | aufgeworfene ~ *turnedup n.* || gebogene ~ *Roman n.* || schiefe ~ *lopsided n.* || stumpfe ~ *snub-n.* || ulkige ~ *puckish n.* **B.** ⟨fig⟩ °alle ~(n)lang *every few steps* **C.** wer sich die ~ **abschneidet,** verschandelt sich's Gesicht: *he cut off his nose to spite his face* || °daß du die ~ im Gesicht **behältst**! *Keep your hair* (⟨Am⟩ *shirt* od *pants*) *on*!; ⟨Am stud sl⟩ *don't blow your top*! || °sich [dat] die ~ begießen *to wet one's whistle*; *to souse*; *to fly high*; er hat sich die ~ begossen *he's basted* || e–e ~ bek *to get a wigging, to be snubbed* (*rebuked*) || mir **blutet** die ~ *my nose is bleeding* || e–m e–e ~ drehen *to make a fool of a p*, ⟨fam⟩ *to bamboozle a p* || immer der ~ nach **gehen** *to follow one's nose* || e–e feine ~ h *to have a keen sense of smell*, ⟨fig⟩ *to smell a rat from afar* || e–e ~ f etw h ⟨übtr⟩ *to have a scent for a th* || °ich **hab** die ~ (gestrichen) voll *I'm* (*rather*) *sick of it, I'm fed up* (*with it* davon) || e–m e–e lange ~ m *to cock a snook, to thumb one's nose at a p* || sich die ~ **putzen** *to blow one's nose* (in *on*) || die ~ rümpfen *to turn up one's n.* (über ⟨a.⟩ *to sneer* od *snuff at*); (verächtlich) *to pooh-pooh* (*a th*) || s–e ~ in etw (alles) **stecken** *to pry into a th*; *to bury one's nose in one's book*; (*to poke one's n. into everything*; *to have an oar in every boat*) || die ~ hoch tragen *to be stuck-up*; *to get above o.s.*; *to be high in the instep* || °die ~n **zählen** *to count n.s* || sich die ~ zuhalten *to hold one's n.* || man hielt sich die ~ zu *there were holdings of n.s* **D.** °e–m (etw) **an** der ~(nspitze) ansehen *to see* od *tell by a p's look* od *face* || faß dich an die eigene ~! *sweep before your own door* (*mind your own business*)! || ⟨fig⟩ an der ~ herumführen *to lead by the n.* || e–m etw **auf** die ~ binden (weism) *to hoax a p*; .. nicht .. (verraten) *not to blab a th out to a p* || auf die ~ fallen *to come a smeller* || auf der ~ liegen *to have fallen down*, ⟨fig⟩ *to have come to grief*, (krank s) *to be laid up* || e–m auf der ~ sitzen *or* tanzen *to humbug a p, to make game of a p* || er blutet **aus** der ~ *his n. is bleeding*; er trieft aus der ~ *he snivels* || °e–m die Würmer aus der ~ ziehen *to worm a secret out of a p* || **bei** = an der ~; sich bei der ~ nehmen *to pull o.s. by the n.* || **durch**: *to breathe, speak through the n.* (→ näseln); .. ausstoßen *to send smoke through the nostrils*; .. einziehen *to sniff up* || **in** der ~ bohren → popeln; in die ~ bek *to smell*, ⟨hunt⟩ *to scent* || der Geruch steigt in die ~ .. *is perceptible* || das sticht in die ~ *it makes his mouth water* || **mit** langer ~ abziehen *to be the loser* || mit der ~ rennen gegen .. *to run one's head against ..* || e–n mit der ~ auf etw stoßen *to rub a p's n. on a th* || immer der ~ **nach** *or* ⟨fam⟩ **lang** *follow your nose*; *go ahead and you hit it* || **um**: → Wind || e–m etw **unter** die ~ reiben *to rub a th in*(*to a p*); ⟨Am⟩ *to throw it up to a p*; (ständig) *to cast a th in a p's teeth* (*to bring it home to him*) || **vor**: *to put the handkerchief to one's n.*; *to lie right under a p's n.* || du siehst nur was direkt vor d–r ~ liegt *you never look further than your n.* || °jdm direkt vor der ~ sitzen, tun .. *under a p's* (*very*) *n.*; .. wegnehmen, -schnappen .. *to snatch a th away from under a p's n.*; .. zumachen *to slam the door upon a p* od *in a p's face* || der Zug fuhr ihm gerade vor der ~ weg *he missed the train by the skin of his teeth* **N·ase-** ~**weis** a *pert, saucy, smart*, ⟨Am⟩ *sassy* || *inquisitive* || *impertinent* || Jungfer ~ *Miss Pert* || Herr *or* Musje ~ *Master Jackanapes* **~-weisheit** f *p.ness, s.iness, i.ness, i.nence* **n·äseln** vi [h] **1.** *to speak through the nose, to have a nasal twang, to snuffle* **2.** (schnüffeln) *to sniff* **3.** ~ [n] ~s/ *nasal twang*; ⟨med⟩ *rhinolalia* **4.** ~d (Laut) *nasal*, ~de Aussprache (*nasal*) *twang* **N·asen-** **~affe** m *kahau* **~bär** m *coati* **~bein** n *bridge of the nose*, ⟨med a.⟩ *nasal bone* **~bluten** n *bleeding from* od *at the nose, n.-bleeding* || ~ h *to bleed at* od *from the n.* **~bremse** f ⟨hors vet⟩ *twitch* **~flügel** m *side* od *wing of the n.* **~höhle** f *cavity of the n.* **~klemmer, ~kneifer** m *eye-glasses* pl **~knorpel** m *cartilage of the n.* || um e–e **~länge** ⟨a. fig⟩ *by a short head*: *to win, lose by a neck*; es ging um ~ ⟨a. fig⟩ *it was a photofinish* **~laut** m ⟨gram⟩ *nasal* (*sound*) **~loch** n *nostril*; (of whale) *spout-hole* **~-polyp** m ⟨med⟩ *nasal polypus* °**~popel** m *nose-dirt*, ⟨fam⟩ *sweep* **~riemen** m *n.-band* **~ring** m *n.-ring* **~rücken** m *bridge of the n.* **~rümpfen** n *sneering*, verächtliches ~ *sniff of contempt* **~schleim** m *nasal mucus* | ~haut [f] *mucous membrane* **~spitze** f *tip of the n.* (→ Nase D. an) **~stoßkonferenz** f *n.-to-n. c.* **~stüber** m *fillip*, ⟨fam⟩ *n.r* || jdm e–n ~ geben *to f.* (⟨fig⟩ *snub*) *a p* **~wärmer** m *comforter* || (Pfeife) *n.-warmer*

N·aß n N·asses/ *fluid, liquid*; *flow* (*of tears*) || ⟨fam⟩ *liquor, beverage, damp* | ~schlamm [m] *wet sludge* **n·aß** a *wet* (a. v Regen) || (feucht) *moist* (*eyes*), *damp* (*walls*); (*the snow looks*) *sodden*; ⟨scient⟩ *humid* (*analysis*) || *watery* (*grave*) || nasser Bruder *tippler* | durch u durch ~ *wet through* (od *to the skin*); ~ bis auf die Knochen ⟨hum⟩ *soaked to the bones* || *soaking* (*shoes*) || *wringing wet* (*clothes*) || ~ wie e–e Katze (P) *like a drowned rat* || (sich) ~ m *to wet* (*o.s.*) || ~ w *to become* (⟨fam⟩ *get*) *wet*; durch u durch ~ w *to get a soaking* || nasse Füße bek *to get one's feet wet* ~**dampf** m *wet steam* ~**fäule** f *wet rot* **~kalt** a *damp and cold*; *raw*; ⟨sl⟩ *drizzerable* [*drizzly* + *miserable*] ~**reinigung** f *wet purification* ~**sumpf-anlage** f ⟨mot⟩ *wet sump system* ~**wäsche** f *bag-wash* (zurück) **N·ässe** f ~/ *wet*(*ness*) || *moisture*, ⟨scient⟩ *humidity* || vor ~ zu schützen! *to be kept dry* **n·ässeln** vi imps [h] *to be* od *to get slightly wet* **n·ässen** **1.** vt [h] *to wet*; *moisten* **2.** vi imps [h] *to be wet*; *to drop, drizzle* || ⟨surg⟩ *the wound discharges*;

~d *weeping* (*eczema*) **N·asse(r)** m ~n/~n *anti--prohibitionist*, ⟨Am⟩ *wet*

Nashv·ille [næʃ'vil] n (Stadt) (*Tenn., U.S.A.*)

N·assau n ⟨Ger⟩ (Stadt); → Hessen-~

°**N·assauer** m ~s/~ ⟨fig⟩ **1.** *sponge(r), parasite*; ⟨fam⟩ *deadhead, heel, chiseler, sucker*; ⟨Am⟩ *freeloader* **2.** *drencher* (*of rain*) **n·assauern** vi [h] *to sponge* (bei *on*)

nasz·ierend a *nascent* (Wasserstoff)

Natal 1. N·atal (Provinz der Südafr. Union) **2.** Nat·al (Hptst. v. Rio Grande do Norte)

Nati·on [–ts–] f ~/~en *nation* ‖ Konferenz der Vereinten ~en *United N.s Conference* ‖ der ~ vorlegen *to take .. to the people* | ≗·**al** a *n.al*(*ist*) ‖ (Zustand der) ~e(n) Einheit, ~es Leben *n.hood* ‖ ~e Gesinnung *n.alism*; ~er Notstand *domestic emergency* **Nation·al-** ~**anleihe** f *national loan* ~**charakter** m *n. character* ~**farbe** f *n. colour*(*s* pl) ~**flagge** f *n. flag*; ⟨engl⟩ *Union Jack*; ⟨Am⟩ *Stars and Stripes* pl; Tag der ~ ⟨Am⟩ *Flag Day* ~**gefühl** n *feeling for one's country* ≗**gesinnt** a *n. thinking* ~**hymne** f *n. anthem* ≗**liberal** a *n.-liberal* ~**marsch** m *n. anthem* ~**ökon·om** m (*political*) *economist* ~**ökonomie** f *political economy* ≗**-politisch** *n.-political* ≗**sozialistisch** a *n.--socialist*; ~ m *to nazify* ~**staat** m *nation-state* ~**stolz** m *national pride* ~**verein** m *n. league* ~**versammlung** f *n. assembly* **Nation·ale** [–ts–] n **1.** ~s/~s *statement of personalities* **2.** *form for the statement of a p's personalities* **nationalis·ieren** vt [h] *to nationalize* **Nationalis·ierung** f ~/ *nationalization* **National·ist** m ~en/~en *nationalist*; (Irland) *die-hard* **Nationalit·ät** [–ts–] f ~/~en *nationality*; *national status* ‖ mehreren ~en angehörend *multi-national* | ~skennzeichen [n] ⟨mot⟩ *country's identification sign* od *letter*; (Schild) *nationality plate* **Nativit·ät** f ~/~en *nativity, horoscope* ‖ jdm die ~ stellen *to cast a p's horoscope*

N·ato → Abk | ~-Kriegsakademie *Nato Defence College*

N·atrium n ~s/ ⟨chem⟩ *sodium* | ~**fluor·id** n *s. fluoride* ~**sulfat** n *sulphate of s., Glauber's salt*(*s* pl) **N·atron** n ~s/ ⟨chem⟩ *natron*, (*carbonate of*) *soda* ‖ (doppelt)kohlensaures ~ (*bi*)*carbonate of s.* ~**alaun** m *s.-alum* ~**lauge** f *caustic s.*; *potash* od *s. lye* ~**salpeter** m *sodium nitrate* ~**seife** f *s.-soap* ~**zellulose** f *soda cellulose*

N·atter f ~/~n *adder, viper* ‖ ⟨fig⟩ *serpent, snake* ~**biß** m *bite of a v.* ~**kopf** m ⟨bot⟩ *v.'s bugloss* ~**wurz** f ⟨bot⟩ *adder's wort* ~**zunge** f ⟨bot⟩ *adder's tongue* ‖ ⟨fig⟩ *viper* (*slanderer, backbiter*)

Nat·una-Inseln f pl (westl. v Borneo)

Nat·ur f ~/~en **A. 1.** *nature*, (*Mother*) *N.* ‖ (Körperbeschaffenheit) *constitution* ‖ (Gemütsart) *disposition, temperament*; *mould* (*of a character*); (Art) *ch., n.* (*a matter of private ch.* od *n.*) ‖ ~ u Pflege ⟨biol⟩ *n. and nurture* **2.** [konkr] (*natural*) *scenery* ‖ in Gottes freier ~ *in the open fields* pl, *in the realms* [pl] *of n.* ‖ °bei ihr ist alles ~ *she's got what it takes* **3.** [konkr] *person, being, creature* ‖ hitzige ~en *hot* od *fiery n.s, hot-tempered people* **B.** das Buch der ~ *the book of n.* ‖ Gegenstände der ~ *ths natural* ‖ die ~en sind verschieden *ch.s differ* ‖ solche ~en sind selten *such ch.s are rare* **C.** (un)**belebte** ~ (*inanimate*) *animated n.* ‖ erwachende ~ *growing n.* ‖ e–e **gesunde,** gute, starke ~ h *to have good health, a good, healthy, strong constitution* ‖ e–e **glückliche** ~ h (⟨fam⟩ s) *to have a happy disposition* ‖ die gr ~ *the macrocosm, N. in general* ‖ Fragen grundsätzlicher ~ .. *of a fundamental ch.* ‖ **lachende** ~ *smiling n.* ‖ leichter ~ [gen] (*a wound*) *of a light ch.* ‖ **schwache** ~en *weak ch.s* ‖ jds **wahre** ~ durchschauen ⟨sl⟩ *to get a p's number* **D.** (etw) der ~ **abringen** *to win from n.* ‖ s–r ~ berauben *to denaturalize* ‖ v der ~ **gegeben** *natural* ‖ der ~ s–n Tribut *or* Zoll zahlen *to pay the* od *one's debt of n., to go the way of all flesh* ‖ zur ~ zurückkehren *to return to the bosom of N.* **E.** das ist **gegen** *or* wider die ~ .. *contrary to n.* ‖ es liegt **in** der ~ der S *it is only natural, in the nature of ths* ‖ **nach** der ~ (gezeichnet) *from n.* od *life* ‖ s–r ~ **nach** kalt *cold by n., naturally cold* ‖ s–r innersten ~ nach *inherently* ‖ s–r ~ nach gehören zu *to be in its n. among* ‖ **von** ~ *constitutionally, temperamentally, naturally* (*indolent*), (*indolent*) *by n.*, etc ‖ es ist mir v ~ zuwider *I have a natural aversion to it* ‖ ein v ~ fester Platz *a natural stronghold* ‖ es geht mir **wider** (gegen) die ~ *it goes against the grain* ‖ wider alle ~ *perversely* ‖ zurück **zur** ~! *back to n.*! ⟨Am fam⟩ *let's go native* ‖ e–m zur zweiten ~ w *to become second n. with a p, to grow on a p* ‖ *it was s. n. to her* ‖ jds innerster ~ **zuwider** *contrary to a p's real n.* ~**anlage** f *n., disposition, temper*(*ament*) ‖ *talent* ~**arzt** m *n.-doctor* ~**aufnahme** f ⟨phot⟩ *n. view* ≗**bedingt** a *n.l* ~**begebenheit** f *n.l phenomenon* ≗**belassen** a *unadulterated* ~**beschreibung** f *n.l history* ~**bild** n *n.l scenery* ~**bursche** m *unceremonious fellow, hearty* od ⟨Am⟩ *cave-man* ~**dichter** m *people's poet, self-taught poet* ~**dichtung** f *n.-poetry* ~**dienst** m *worship of n.* ~**erscheinung** f *phenomenon* ~**erzeugnis** n *n.l produce* ≗**farben** a *self-coloured*; (*of unbleached and undyed dress-material*) *beige*; *brownish* (*paper*) ~**forscher** m *n.list, student of n.l science, scientist* ‖ *n.l philosopher* ~**forschung** f *n.l science* ~**freund** m *lover of n.* ~**gabe** f (*n.l*) *talent, gift of n.* ≗**gemäß** a [adv] *n.l*[*ly*] ~**geschichte** f *n.l history* ≗**geschichtlich** a *physical*; *n.l history* (*museum*) ~**gesetz** n *law of n., n.l law* ≗**getreu** a *faithful* (*reproduction*); *true to n.* od *life, lifelike*; *realistic* ‖ ⟨mus rec⟩ *hi(gh)-fi(delity)* (*records* Platten) ~**gewalt** f = ~kraft ~**heil-** ~kunde [f] *physiatrics*; *treatment by n.l remedies*; ~kundige(r) [m] *n. cure practitioner*; ~verfahren [n] *cure effected by n.l methods* ~**historiker** m *n.list* ~**kind** n ⟨fig⟩ *unsophisticated p* ~**kraft** f *force* od *power of n., n.l power* ≗**kräftig** a *elemental* ~**kunde** f = ~forschung; ⟨school⟩ *n. study* ~**kundige(r)** m *n.l philosopher* ~**landschaft** f *virgin country, n.l landscape* ~**lehre** f *n.l philosophy, physics* pl ~**leistung** f *payment in kind* ~**mensch** m *child of n., man in a state of n.* ≗**nachahmend** a *n.-imitating* (*art*) ≗**nahe** a *close to the soil* ~**notwendigkeit** f *physical necessity* ~**papier** n *unbleached paper* ~**pflicht** f *n.l duty* ~**philosophie** f *n.l philosophy* ~**produkt** n *n.l product* ~**raum** m *n.l region* ~**recht** n *n.l right* ‖ ⟨jur⟩ *Law of N.* od *Reason* ~**reich** n *n.l kingdom*, (*kingdom of*) *n.* ≗(**rein**) *unadulterated, n.l* (*wine*) ~**schätze** m pl *resources* ~**schönheiten** f pl *beautiful scenery*; durch ~ ⟨rail⟩ *sceneric*(*al*); reich an ~ *scenic* (*railway*) ~**schutz** m *preservation* od *conservation of n.l beauty* | ~gebiet [n] *wild-life reserve*; ~park [m] *park reservation* (*Luneburg Heath P. R.* [*Society*]) ~**seltenheit** f *n.l curiosity* ~**spiel** n *sport* od *freak of n.* ~**stein** m ⟨arch⟩ *stone* ~**studien** f pl *studies from n.* ~**theater** n *outdoor theatre* ~**treue** f *truth to n.* ~**trieb** m *instinct, n.l impulse* ~**volk** n *primitive race* ≗**wahr** a *true to n.* ~**wahrheit** f *trueness to n.* ≗**widrig** a *contrary to n., unn.l* ~**widrigkeit** f *unn.lness* ~**wissenschaft** f *n.l science* od *philosophy* ‖ die ~en [pl koll] (*n.l*) *science* ‖ (die einzelnen ~en) *the n.l sciences* | ~ler [m] *student of N.l Science*; *naturalist*; *man of science*; ≗liche Abteilung *Faculty of N.l Sc.* (*including mathematics*); ~ Sammlung *n.l history collection* ~**wolle** f *native wool* ≗**wüchsig** a *original* ‖ (ungezwungen) *spontaneous* ‖ (derb) *racy, blunt* ~**wunder** n *prodigy* ~**zustand** m *n.l* od *primitive state* **Natur·al-** ~**abgabe** f *payment in kind* ~**kosten** f pl *charges* pl *in kind* ~**leistung** f = ~abgabe ~**restitution** f ⟨jur⟩ *compensation in kind for damage suffered* ~**verpflegung** f ⟨mil⟩ *supply of provisions* ~**zins** m *rent paid in corn*, etc **Natur·alien** f pl **1.**

natural curiosities pl **2.** (Nahrung) *food, n.l products* [pl] od *produce* **~kabinett** n, **~sammlung** f *n.l history collection, collection of n.l curiosities* **Natural- ~isati·onsgesuch** [–ts–] n *petition for naturalization* **≃is·ieren** vt [h] *to naturalize* || sich ~ l *to become naturalized* **~is·ierung** f ~/ *naturalization* **~·ismus** m ~/ *naturalism* (*e. g.* Zola, G. Hauptmann, Farrell); *natural religion* **~·ist** m ~en/~en *naturalist*

Natur·ell n ~(e)s/~e (*natural*) *disposition, nature, temper*(*ament*) **nat·urhaft** a *unsophisticated* (*p*) || *untutored* (*instincts*) || *elemental* (*forces*) || die ~e Seite s–s Wesens *the instinctive and physical compounds of his being* **nat·ürlich I.** [a] **1.** *natural* || (angeboren) *innate, constitutional* || e–e ~e Eigenschaft *a property of n.* (*in a man*); ~e Größe *actual size*; in ~er Größe ⟨arts⟩, in ~em Maßstab ⟨tech⟩ *full size*; ~e Kraftreserven [f pl] *n.l resources* || *it was n.l in* (bei) *a lawyer* || ~e P ⟨jur⟩ *n.l p* || ~e Beschaffenheit *the n.* (*of a th*) | es ging ganz ~ zu *there was nothing strange about it* || das ging nicht mit ~en Dingen zu *there was sth uncanny* (⟨fam⟩ *fishy*) *about it* || es war ~, daß er .. war *it was n.l that he should be* .. || e–s ~en Todes sterben *to die a n.l death* || auf ~e Art erklären *to give a rational explanation of* **2.** (einfach) *simple* || (ungekünstelt) *unaffected, artless, unsophisticated* (*p, speech, manner*) || *unstudied* (*pose, graces, sentiment*) || *unstrained* (*mirth*) || (echt) *genuine* (*humour*) **3.** (unehelich) *illegitimate* **II.** ~ [adv], ~erweise [adv] *of course, n.lly* || ~ spreche ich F. *I do speak French* || aber ~! *but there! to be sure! rather!* ⟨Am⟩ *you bet!* || sich ~ geben *to have a n.l manner; not to show off* **≃keit** f ~/ *n.lness* || *unaffectedness* || *simplicity*; *ingenuousness*; *unsophistication*

N·autik f ~/ *nautical science* **N·autilus** m ~/~ ⟨zoo⟩ *nautilus* **~pokal** m *n.* **n·autisch** a *nautical* || ~es Jahrbuch *N. Almanac* **Navigati·ons- ~akte** f *Navigation Act* **~karte** f *n. map* **~licht** n *n. light* **~-L·ogblätter** n pl *N. Log* **~offizier** m *n.ing officer* (= "*the navigator*"); ⟨aero mar fam⟩ *navvy*; ⟨hist⟩ *sailing-master* **~raum** m *chart-room* **~-schule** f *naval school* **navig·ieren** vt [h] *to navigate*

Nav·arra n (†Königreich) (span. Prov.)

Naw·âb m ~s/~ ⟨Arab⟩ *nawab* → Nabob

N·axos n (Insel der Zykladen); Bewohner(in) v ~ *inhabitant of Naxos, Naxian*

Nazar·ener m ~s/(~) **1.** *Jesus of Nazareth* **2.** *early christian* **3.** ⟨Ger paint⟩ *member of the early 19th c. school* **4.** *Nazarene* (*a member of the Church of Nazarene*)

°**N·azi** m ~s/~s *Nazi*; die ~s ⟨hum⟩ *the Nasties*

Ne·anderthaler m ⟨Ger ["Gr"]⟩ *Neanderthal man*

Ne·apel n ⟨It⟩ (Stadt) *Naples* **Neapolit·aner** m, **~in** f, **neapolit·anisch** a *Neapolitan*

ne·arktisch a (betr nördl. N.-Am.) *Nearctic*

N·ebbich m ~(e)s/~e [österr] (unbedeutender Mensch) *small fry,* ⟨Am⟩ *small potatoes*

n·ebbich adv [Hebr] → leider, schade!

N·ebel m ~s/~ (dicht) *fog* || (gelb, dicht, Londoner) *pea-soup fog* || (leicht, dünn) *mist* ⟨a. fig⟩; *gauze* || (sehr dünn) *haze*; (fallend) *drizzle* || ⟨fig⟩ *cloud*; *fogginess* (*of his brain*) || (künstlich) (*artificial*) *smoke* (*screen*) || ⟨astr⟩ *nebula* | in ~ hüllen *to befog* ⟨a. fig⟩ in ~ ge–t *fog-shrouded* || ~ kam auf *mist closed in* || in ~ gehüllt *mist-hidden, wrapped in fog* || ~ geht nieder *it is misting* **~anlage** f *smoke plant*; *sm.-generating gear* **~bank** f *fog-bank* **~beschlag** m *damp moisture*; ~ entfernen an *to defog* **~bild** n *misty apparition* **~-decke** f = ~schleier **~ferne** f *hazy distance* **~fleck** m ⟨astr & path⟩ *nebula* **~gebilde** n *airy vision, misty form* **~gerät** n *sm. screen apparatus* **~geschoß** n, **~granate** f *sm.-shell* **~glocke** f *fog-bell* **≃grau** a *grey like fog* **≃haft** a *foggy, misty* ⟨a. fig⟩ || ⟨fig⟩ *nebulous, hazy, smoky*; *vaporous* (*argument*), *vague* (*hope*), *dim* (*future* Ferne) || mir ist es ~ *I find it obscure* **~horn** n *fog-horn* **~kammer** f ⟨phys⟩ *cloud chamber* **~kanone** f ⟨mar⟩ *fog-gun* **~kappe 1.** (e–s Berges) *hood of mist* **2.** ⟨myth⟩ = Tarnkappe **~krähe** f *hooded crow* **~land** n (England) *land of mist* **~mond** m (Nov.) *month of fogs* **~munition** f *smoke ammunition* **~regen** m *drizzle* **~scheinwerfer** m *fog lamp* **~schicht** f *fog-bank* **~schleier** m *misty veil*; ⟨mil⟩ *smoke blanket* **~schutz** m ⟨mil⟩ (*sm.-*)*-screen*(*ing*); e–n ~ legen *to lay a* (*sm.-*)*screen* **~schwaden** m *damp fog* **~signal** n *fog-signal* **~stern** m *nebula* **~stoff** m *sm.-producing agent* **~streif** m *streak of mist* **~topf** m *sm. producer* **~truppe** f *smoke generating unit*; ~n [pl] *chemical troops* **~vertilger** m ⟨aero⟩ (f Landestreifen) **F**og **I**nvestigation **D**ispersal **O**peration (*Fido*) **~vorhang** m, **~wand** f = –schutz ⟨mil⟩ (*smoke-*)*screen*(*ing*) **~wetter** n *foggy weather* **n·eb(e)lig** a *misty, hazy*; *foggy* (*weather*) || ⟨fig⟩ *filmy* || ~ u feucht *drizzly* **n·ebeln** vi **1.** imps [h] *to be misty* od *foggy* || es nebelt *there is a mist* **2.** ⟨mil⟩ *to lay a smoke-screen, to shoot smoke shells* **3.** ⟨fig⟩ *to float like a cloud* || (faseln) *to ramble*

N·ebelwerfer m (nach A. Nebel) ⟨Ger⟩ (W.W.II) *rocket-gun*

n·eben prep [dat & acc] **1.** *by, beside* (*the fire*); *by the side of* (*the sleeping child*); *near, close to* (*the house*); *side by side with, alongside* (*of*) (*the door*) || ~ mir (*walked*) *by my side*; (*sat*) *by me, next to me* | ~–e–a, eins ~ das andere (*she put them*) *side by side*; (zeitlich) *simultaneously with* **2.** (verglichen mit) *against, beside* → gegen **3.** (außer) *apart from, besides*; *in addition to* **N·eben-** [in comp] **acc**essory, **add**itional (*noise*), *adjoing* (*room*), *adjacent* (*sector*); **coll**ateral, **ex**tra, **inc**idental, **sec**ondary *sub-*, **sub**ordinate **~abdruck** m *information copy* **~absicht** f *sec. motive* od *object* **~achse** f *sec. axis* **~allee** f *by-walk* **~altar** m *side-altar* **~amt** n *sub-office*; im ~ *as a sec. occupation* || ⟨telph⟩ *branch* od *minor exchange* | **≃lich** [a] *part-time* (*employment, work, job*) **≃·an** adv *next door, in the next* od *adjoining room, close* od *hard by* **~angriff** m ⟨mil⟩ *sec. attack* **~anschluß** m ⟨telph⟩ *extension*(*-line*); (*branch*) *extension* N **~arbeit** f *ex. work, sec. work*; Mädchen für ~ *part-time girl* **~arm** m *lateral branch*; *backwater* **~artikel** m *sec.* od *sub. article, side-line* **~ausgaben** f pl *add.* od *petty expenses* pl, *extras* pl || (außerordentliche) *inc. expenses* pl **~ausgang** m *side-exit* **~-bahn** f ⟨rail⟩ *branch-* od *sec.* od *feeder-line* **~bedeutung** f *connotation*; *sec. meaning* od *signification* **~begriff** m *acc.* od *sub. notion* **≃b·ei** adv *adjoining, close by* || (außerdem) *besides* || (zeitlich) *meanwhile* || (beiläufig) *by the by, by the way, by way of parenthesis* || *inc.ly* (*a butler, first a man*) || ~ bemerkt *by the way, be it noted* || etw ~ erwähnen *to make passing reference to a th* || etw ~ m *to take a th in one's stride* **~beruf** m, **~beschäftigung** f *avocation*; *sec.* od *ex.-occupation, side-line* **≃beruflich** a *part-time* **~bestandteil** m *sec. ingredient* **~bewaffnung** f *sec. armament* **~beweis** m *coll. proof*; ⟨jur⟩ *adminicle* **~bild** n ⟨phot telv⟩ *ghost image* **~blatt** n ⟨bot⟩ *stipule*; Anordnung der ≃er *stipulation* **~buhler(in** f) m, **≃isch** [a] *rival*; ~schaft [f] *rivalry* **~bürgschaft** f *coll. security* **~ding** n *sec. matter* **≃ein·ander** adv *side by side, abreast* || ~ stehen *to stand s. by s.*; *to stand together* || ~ stellen ⟨fig⟩ *to compare, juxtapose* || dicht ~ *neck and neck* (*N. & M. were* ..) | (zeitlich) *simultaneous* || ~ bestehen *to coexist* || ≃fahren [n] *riding abreast* || (friedliches) ≃leben ⟨pol⟩ *co-existence* || ~stellung [f] *apposition, juxtaposition* **~eingang** m *side entrance* **~einkünfte, ~einnahmen** f pl (*ex.*) *perquisites, ex.s* pl, *casual emoluments* pl || *add.* od *ex.-income* **~erbe** m *coheir* **~fach** n ⟨univ⟩ *subsidiary* od *minor subject*; *minor* **~farbe** f *sec. colour* **~figur** f *subordinate* *figure* **~flügel** m ⟨arch⟩ *side wing* **~fluß** m *affluent, tributary* **~forderung** f *acc. claim* **~frage** f *sec. question* **~gang** m *by-way*; ⟨min⟩ *side lode* **~gasse** f *by-street, by-lane* **~gebäude** n *annex(e), wing (of a building), outhouse* ‖ (benachbartes) *neighbouring building* **~gebühren** f pl, **~gefälle** n pl *emoluments, ex.s* pl **~gedanke** m *sec. thought, simultaneous purpose* od *idea, by-motive* **~geleise** n, **~gleis** n *side-track, siding*; auf ein ~ schieben *to s.-tr.* vt **~gemach** n *side-chamber, closet* ‖ (benachbartes) *adjoining room* **≗geordnet** a *lateral* (⟨mil⟩ *unit*) **~geräusch** n *ambient noise*; ⟨wir⟩ *interference, jamming*; ⟨theat⟩ *noises off*, ⟨Am⟩ *off stage sound effects* | ~unterdrücker ⟨wir⟩ *x-stopper* **~gericht** n ⟨cul⟩ *side-dish* **~geschäft** n *ex. occupation* ‖ *branch establishment* **~geschmack** m *by-taste* **~gewinn** m *ex.* od *inc. profits* pl **~handlung** f *sub. action*; ⟨theat⟩ *episode, underplot, subplot* **~haus** n *outhouse* ‖ (benachbartes) *neighbouring house* **≗h·er** adv, **≗h·in** adv → ~bei **~h·ergehen** vi [s]: (er ging) n. s–r Mutter her *at the side of* od *side by side with* .. **~hode** f *epididymis* **~interesse** n *sub.* bzw *private interest* **~kanal** m *tributary canal* **~kirche** f *chapel of ease* **~kläger** m *co-plaintiff, intervener*; ⟨crim l⟩ *injured p who has the privilege of joining the public prosecutor* **~kosten** pl *inc.* od *ex. charges* pl, *ex.s* pl **~leiden** n ⟨demog⟩ *sec., contributory cause of death* **~leitung** f *by-line* **~licht** n ⟨theat⟩ *spilled light*; ⟨phot⟩ *false l.* **~linie** f ⟨geneal⟩ *coll. line* ‖ ⟨rail⟩ *loop-* od *branch-line* **~mann** m ⟨a. mil⟩ *next man* ‖ rechter ~ *right-hand man* **~meer** n *minor sea* **~mensch** m *fellow-creature* **~mond** m ⟨astr⟩ *paraselene, mock moon* **~niere** f *adrenal gland* **~nutzung** f *minor produce* **~ordnung** f *coordination* ‖ → Parataxe **~person** f (untergeordnete) *sec. character* **~pforte** f *side door* **~pleuel** m *auxiliary rod* **~postamt** n *branch post-office* **~produkt** n *by-product*; *derivative* **~punkt** m *sec.* od *acc. point* **~raum** m *side-, back-room*; ≗e [pl] *conveniences* pl; ⟨agr⟩ *outbuildings* pl **~redakteur** m *assistant editor* **~regierung** f *coll. government* **~rolle** f ⟨a. theat⟩ *sub.* od *minor part* | ~nspieler [m] *bit player* **~sache** f *inc. matter, sec. consideration* ‖ das ist ~! *that is a mere detail!* ‖ als ~ *non-essential, accidental* ‖ (Preis) ist ~ .. *counts for nothing*, ⟨Am⟩ *cuts no figure* ‖ Geld (ist) ~ *m. is no consideration* **≗sächlich** a *inc., sec., sub., negligible, unimportant, subsidiary* ‖ *irrelevant* (*ths* = *irrelevancies* pl); *minor* (*matters*) ‖ über ~e Dinge sprechen *to talk commonplaces* ‖ e–e ~e Rolle spielen *to be of sec. importance* | [pred] *beside the point* od *question*; *of sec. importance* | [adv] ~ behandeln *to set aside*; *to neglect* | ~keit [f] *triviality*; *minor point*; ~en [pl] ⟨a.⟩ *irrelevancies* **~satz** m ⟨gram⟩ *sub. clause* **~schalter** m *auxiliary switch* **~schluß** m ⟨el⟩ *shunt* **~sinn** m *connotation* **~sonne** f ⟨astr⟩ *mock sun, parhelion* **~speiseleitung** f *subfeeder* **~spesen** pl *add. charges* pl **≗stehend** *adjoining* (*column*); ⟨com⟩ *in the margin* ‖ ~ abgebildet *shown in the accompanying picture* **~stehende(r)** m *by-stander* **~stelle** f ⟨telph⟩ *private branch*; *satellite* (*radar*) *station* **~stimme** f ⟨mus⟩ *subsidiary melody* **~straße** f *offstreet*; *by-road, by-* od *side-street* ‖ e–e ~ der Oxf.-Str. *a street off Oxf. St.* **~strom** m ⟨el⟩ *induction current* **~tisch** m *next table* **~titel** m *sub-title* **~ton** m ⟨gram⟩ *sec. accent*; ⟨mus⟩ *second* **≗tonig** a (*syllable*) *having sec. stress* **~tür** f *postern, side-door* **~umstand** m *acc. circumstance* **~u Folgeerscheinungen** f pl *co-existences and sequences* **~ursache** f *coll. cause* **~verdienst** m *perquisites, ex. earnings* pl ‖ *add. merit* **~versicherung** f *coll. assurance* **~vorgang** m ⟨theat⟩ *side-show* **~vormund** m *ancillary guardian* **~weg** m *by-way* od *-road* **~werk** n *by-* (od *subordinate*) *work* **~wind** m *side-wind* **~winkel** m ⟨math⟩ *adjacent angle* **~wirkung** f ⟨chem, etc⟩ *sec. action* **~zeit** f ⟨mach⟩ *idle period* **~ziel** n (e–s Angriffs) *sec. target* N **~zimmer** n *adjoining* od *next room*; im ~ *next door* **~zweck** m *sec. object, subsidiary aim, by-end* **~zweig** m *side-branch* **n·ebst** prep [dat] (*together*) *with, besides, including*

Nebr·aska n (Staat der U.S.A.)

Necessaire [neseˈsɛːr] n ~s/~s *dressing-case*

N·eck m ~s/ = Nöck **~name** = Spitzname **~teufelchen** n *quiz(zer)*; ⟨cards⟩ *joker* **n·ecken** vt [h] *to tease* (getan z h *about doing*); *to chaff, rag, rally, rib, quiz*; ⟨Am⟩ *to jolly* ‖ sich ~ *to banter each other* ‖ ⟨fig⟩ *to pull a p's leg* ‖ sie neckt gern *she's a great teaser* ‖ er neckt sich mit ihr *he chaffs with her* **N·ecker** m ~s/~ *tease(r)*; *mocker* **Necker·ei** f ~/~en *teasing, chaff, banter*; *quiz(zing)*; *mockery* **n·eckisch** a (*fond of*) *teasing*, etc.; *quizzical* ‖ (drollig) *droll, comical, playful, sportive* ‖ (schalkhaft) *arch* ‖ (tückisch) *malicious*

N·eckar m (recht. Nebenfluß des Rheins)

nee [neː] ⟨fam⟩ = nein

N·effe m ~n/~n *nephew*

Negati·on f ~/~en *negation* **Negat·iv** n ~(e)s/~e ⟨scient, phot⟩ *negative* (dicht *dense*, schwach *thin*) | ≗ [a] *negative* (⟨el⟩ *pole*) | ~abstand [m] ⟨phot⟩ *pull-down*; ~einstellung [f] ⟨psych⟩ *negativism*; ~-P·ositiv-Verfahren [n] ⟨film⟩ *n.-p. process*; *reversal*; ~werte [m pl] ⟨math⟩ *minus terms*

N·eger m ~s/~ *negro* (f *negress*; *black woman*) ‖ ⟨dero⟩ *nigger*; ⟨hist⟩ *black-bird*; ⟨Am a.⟩ *colored (gentle)man* ‖ die ~ [pl] *the black population* ‖ schwarz wie ein ~ (*as*) *black as coal* **≗artig** a *n.-like* **~aufseher** m *n.-driver* **~ausdruck** m *negroism* **~handel** m *slave-trade* **~kind** n *pickaninny* **~knabe** m *n. boy* **~kuß** m ⟨cul⟩ *negrokiss* **~lied** n *n.-song* **~rasse** f *n.-race* **~tanz** m *n.-dance*

neg·ieren vt [h] *to deny, negate* ‖ *to ignore*

Negligé [ˈnegliʒeː] n ~s/ *négligé, undress, deshabille* Fr, *dishabille* ‖ ~haube *morning-cap*

Negozi·ant m ~en/~en ⟨com⟩ *wholesale merchant* **Negoziati·on** f ~/~en *negotiation, operation* **negozi·ieren** vt [h] *to negotiate*

n·ehmen vt [nahm/genommen] [h] **A. 1.** *to take* ‖ (ergreifen) *to seize, grasp*; *to lay hold of* ‖ (in Empfang) *to receive* ‖ ⟨exch⟩ *to call* **2.** (erzwingen) *to force*; ⟨mil⟩ *to take, capture, seize*; (im Sturm) *to storm*; *to gain* (*terrain*) **3.** (bezwingen) (Hindernis ⟨a. fig⟩) *to clear, negotiate, get over, dispose of* (*fence, obstacle, difficulty*); (Steigung ~) *to drive up a hill on* (im) *the third gear* ‖ ⟨ten⟩ (Ball) *to whip up* **4.** (anstellen) *to take* (*an apprentice*), *engage* (*an assistent, a tutor*); *to retain the services of* (*a lawyer*) **5.** (mieten, benutzen) *to take* (*a taxi, bus, train, the tram*), *to use* (*the train*), *to travel* (*by ship*) **6.** (an~) *to accept* (*a tip*) ‖ (entgegen~) *please accept our thanks* **7.** (ein~, zu sich ~) *to take* (*tea*) ‖ ~ Sie ..! *have* (*a cup of tea*)! ‖ (sich etw ~) *to help o.s. to* (*an egg, a cigar*) **8.** (fortschaffen) *to remove, to carry away* **9.** (stehlen) *to steal, pocket* ‖ jdm etw (weg)~ *to take a th from a p*; *to take away a p's* (*M. A. degree*) ‖ *to rob* (*a p of his honour, a book of its originality*); *to deprive a p* (*of his livelihood*) **10.** (machen) *to make* (*a copy*) ‖ (einschlagen) *to take* (*the way to*) **11.** (behandeln) er weiß sie zu ~ *he knows how to handle her* **12.** (befreien) *to free* (*a p from a difficulty*), *to take the weariness out of shopping* **13.** (verlangen) was ~ Sie f ..? *what do you want* od *charge for* (*these goods*)? **14.** (kaufen) *I'll have that* (*then*) **15.** (sich anmaßen) woher ~ sie das Recht? *what r. have they* (z tun *to do*)? → B. 2. **16.** (benehmen) (Aussicht) *to obstruct* **B. 1.** da ~ Sie!, ~ Sie nur! *there, take it!* ‖ woher ~ u nicht stehlen? *how to get hold of it without stealing it?* ‖ sie ~ sich beide nichts *the one is as good as the other* ‖ er ist v Stamme Nimm *he's a taker* (*no giver*) ‖ ⟨cul⟩ man nehme .. *take* .. ‖ ⟨sex⟩ *take her!* **2.** er will sich .. nicht ~ l *he won't give up* (*beer-drinking*) ‖ das (mein Recht) **lasse** ich mir nicht ∼ *I shall not be talked out of that*!, *I insist upon it*! (*I won't have my rights encroached upon*!) ‖ er läßt es sich nicht ∼ *he will go out of his way* (*to do*); → A. 15. **C.** das **Abendmahl** ∼ *to receive* .. ‖ → Abschied, Abstand, Anlauf, Anstoß etc ‖ s–n Anfang ∼ *to begin, commence* ‖ Anstand ∼ *to hesitate, pause* ‖ Anstoß, Ärgernis ∼ *to raise a scandal* (an *about*) ‖ alles ∼, wie es kommt *to take ths as they come* ‖ *to take a bath*; die **Bahn** ∼ .. *the train, to go by train* ‖ Ende ∼ *to* (*come to an*) *end, to finish*; kein .. *to go on endlessly*; das nimmt noch ein böses E. *that will lead to a bad end*; ein ehrenvolles E. ∼ (P) *to die an h. death*; die S nahm doch noch ein gutes E. *everything worked out all right in the end* ‖ beim Essen: → A. 7. ‖ *he helped h.s. freely* (reichlich) *to meat*, etc ‖ nochmals ∼ *to take a second helping of m.* ‖ ∼ Sie **es** wie es kommt *make the best of it*; wie man's nimmt *it all depends* ‖ ∼ wir den **Fall,** daß .. *let's suppose* od *assume that* .. ‖ ⟨chess⟩ *to take a piece* (Figur) ‖ e–e Frau ∼ *to marry* ‖ darauf kannst du Gift ∼! *bet your life*! ‖ *she caught John's hands in hers* ‖ Hindernis ∼ → A. 3. ‖ (Karten) *to draw* (*from the pack*) ‖ e–m alle Hoffnung ∼ *to deprive a p of all hope* ‖ sich das **Leben** ∼ *to take one's life* ‖ sich die Mühe ∼ *to take the trouble* ‖ Partei ∼ f *to side with, to espouse a p's cause* ‖ Platz ∼ *to take a seat*; ∼ Sie bitte Pl. *pray be seated, sit down please* ‖ Recht → B. 2. ‖ Rücksicht ∼ auf *to show consideration for* ‖ Schaden ∼ *to suffer damage* ‖ e–r S die Schärfe, Spitze ∼ → A. 12. ‖ den Schleier ∼ *to take the veil* ‖ e–m die Sicht ∼ *to spoil a p's view* ‖ ⟨cards⟩ e–n **Stich** ∼ *to win a trick* ‖ Stunden ∼ *to take lessons* ‖ sich zu Trinken ∼ → A. 7. ‖ Urlaub ∼ *to take one's holidays*, ⟨mil⟩ *to go on leave* ‖ Verkehrsmittel → A. 5. ‖ das Wort ∼ *to begin to speak* ‖ → Wunder ‖ sich (nicht) die Zeit ∼ *to take one's time* (*not to allow o.s. the t.*) ‖ Zigarre → A. 7. ‖ Zug ∼ → A. 5.; ⟨a.⟩ *by the night train he embarked for* **D.** [mit a & adv] **es ernst mit etw** ∼ *to be in earnest about a th* ‖ er war kaum ernst z ∼ *he was half a joke* ‖ im ganzen genommen *taking it all round* ‖ jdn richtig z ∼ wissen *to take a p the right way* ‖ ∼ Sie's nicht zu schwer! *don't worry*!, *take it easy*! ‖ jdn so ∼, wie er sich gibt *to take a p as you find him* ‖ wenn du's so ∼ willst *if you take it in that light* ‖ streng genommen *strictly speaking* ‖ als tauglich ∼: *he has been passed as fit* ‖ übel ∼ *to take amiss* ‖ den Mund voll ∼ ⟨fig⟩ *to talk very big* ‖ etw (nicht) zu wichtig ∼ (*not*) *to make much of a th*; sich wichtig ∼ *to think o.s. very important* ‖ wie man's nimmt! *according as you take it*!, *it depends*! ‖ die Art, wie er ihn nimmt *the way he takes him* **E.** etw **an** sich ∼ *to pocket, collect, recover*, ⟨sl⟩ *bag a th*; *to take care of a th* ‖ (wieder) *to retrieve* ‖ (gesetzlich) *to impound* ‖ (widerrechtlich) ⟨sl⟩ *to snaffle*; *to help o.s. to* (*a few pounds*) ‖ nimm ein Beispiel daran! *let it serve you as an example*! ‖ an die (*or* bei der) Hand ∼ *to take* (*a child*) *by the h.* ‖ jdn an s–n Tisch ∼ *to receive a p at one's t.* **|** (etw) **auf** sich [acc] ∼ *to undertake a th, to charge o.s. with* ‖ (Schweres) *to stand up to*; *to face* ‖ *to accept* od *shoulder* (*the responsibility, the troubles*) ‖ *to answer for, to take* od *bear* (*the consequences*) ‖ *I will take it upon me* (*to do*) ‖ etw auf s–e Kappe ∼ *to make o.s. responsible for a th* ‖ auf Kredit ∼ *to buy on credit* ‖ mehr auf sich ∼ als man leisten kann *to bite off more than one can chew* **|** ∼ **aus**: *to take one's hand out of one's pocket, a book from the book case, money from one's purse, the words out of a p's mouth* (e–m aus dem M.), *plants out of the ground* (Erde) ‖ *to abstract ths from a car* ‖ *to take* od *remove a boy from school* ‖ jdm den Wind aus den Segeln, die Trümpfe aus der Hand ∼ *to steal a p's thunder* ‖ aus–e–a ∼ *to undo* **|** e–n **beim** Kragen etc ∼ *to collar a p*; *to take a p by the hand, ears, forelock* (Schopf); .. beim Wort .. ..*at his word* **|** e–n **für** etw ∼ *to take a p for sth*; etw f ein gutes Zeichen ∼ .. *as a good omen*, f bare Münze ∼ .. *for gospel-truth* was ∼ Sie f ein Meter? *what will you charge* (⟨Am a.⟩ *tax*) *me for a m.* ‖ ∼ Sie es nicht f ungut, wenn *don't take it amiss* od *in ill part, don't think it unkind if* **|** sich manches **heraus** ∼ *to presume* **| in** Angriff ∼ *to commence* (*a job*), *to put in hand* ‖ in Arbeit ∼ *to start making* (*a dress*) ‖ (ein Land) gewaltsam in Besitz ∼ ⟨a.⟩ *to jump a land* ‖ ins Gebet ∼ *to take to task* ‖ im Grunde genommen *on the whole, when all is said and done* (*he is right*) ‖ in die Hand ∼ (zufällig) *to pick up*; ⟨fig⟩ *to take in hand* ‖ in Pacht ∼ *to lease* (*a farm*), *to rent* (*a house*) **|** etw **mit** sich ∼ *to take along with you, to carry away*; jdn .. *to make a p* (*to allow a p to*) *go with you* ‖ mit Gewalt ∼ *to take by main force* **| um**: *to put* (*a shawl*) *round one's shoulders* **|** die Beine **unter** die Arme ∼ *to walk briskly* → Bein **| von**: *to remove a th from the table* ‖ er nimmt's von den Lebendigen *he makes you pay a heavy price* **|** (etw) **zu sich** ∼ *to put into one's pocket* ‖ (Speise) *to partake of* (*wine*) ‖ *he can take no food* (→ genießen) ‖ ich möchte jetzt lieber nichts zu mir ∼ *I'd rather not partake now* ‖ jdn zu sich ∼ *to receive a p as a member of one's household, to take charge of* (*a child*) ‖ Gott hat ihn zu sich genommen *God called him to h.s.* **|** zur Ehe ∼ *to take in marriage, to marry* ‖ jdn zum Gehilfen ∼ *to engage a p as assistant*, zum Teilhaber *to take a p into partnership* ‖ zu Hilfe ∼ *to use* (*a tool*) **N·ehmen** n ⟨prov⟩ Geben ist seliger als ∼ *it is more blessed to give than to receive* **N·ehmer** m ∼s/∼ *taker* ‖ ⟨com⟩ *buyer*

N·ehrung f ∼/∼en *spit* (*of land separating a haff from the sea*): *bay-mouth bar*

N·eid m ∼(e)s/ *envy, grudge* ‖ aus ∼ (gegen) *from envy* (*of*) ‖ (Mißgunst) *jealousy* (*at, over*) ‖ Gegenstand des ∼es (*made her*) *the envy* (*of*) ‖ der blasse ∼ *green envy* (über *at*); *jaundice* **|** bei jdm ∼ erregen *to excite a p's envy* ‖ vor ∼ vergehen (⟨fam⟩ platzen) *to be eaten up, to die* (⟨fam⟩ *burst*) *with envy* ‖ das muß ihm der ∼ l *even the most envious must admit that* **≁erfüllt** a *envious* **∼hammel, ∼hart** m (P) ⟨fam⟩ *dog in the manger* **≁los** a *free from envy, ungrudging* **∼nagel** m (= Niednagel) *agnail* **n·eiden** vt [h] (jdm etw) *to envy* od *to grudge* (*a p a th*) **|** vi *to envy* **n·eidenswert** a *enviable* **N·eider** m ∼s/∼ *envious p, grudger* ‖ ⟨prov⟩ besser ∼ als Mitleider *better envied than pitied* **n·eidisch** a *envious, yellow*; *grudging, jealous* (auf *of*) ‖ ∼ s ⟨a.⟩ *to envy, grudge* ‖ mit ∼en Blicken *with jaundiced eyes*

n·eigbar a ⟨tech⟩ *tiltable, inclinable* **N·eige** f ∼/∼n *slope* ‖ auf der ∼ *aslant*; (v Faß) *atilt* **|** (Abnahme) *decline, decay* ‖ (Überbleibsel) *remnant, sediment, dreg*(*s* pl) ‖ (im Glase) *heel-tap* ‖ das Faß geht auf die ∼ .. *is nearly done* ‖ bis zur ∼ leeren *to drink to the dregs* ‖ auf die *or* zur ∼ gehen *to* (*be on the*) *decline, to run low, to wane* ‖ *the year, day draws to an end* ‖ *the money is running out* ‖ unser Wasser ging zur ∼ *we were running low on w., short of w.* ‖ ⟨bes com⟩ *to run short* (*of stock*) **∼kopf** m ⟨tech⟩ *tilt*(*ing*) *head* **n·eigen 1.** vt [h] *to incline, bow, bend, tilt* ‖ e–m, e–r S sein Ohr ∼ *to lend an ear to* .. **2. sich** ∼ [h] *to bow* (vor *to*) ‖ (mit e–m Knicks) *to curtsy* (*to*), *bend, incline* ‖ (v Abhang) *to slope* ‖ (v Nordnadel) *to dip* ‖ *the sun went down*; .. dem Westen zu .. *wore on due west* ‖ *the day is waning* od *departing* ‖ sich dem Ende zu ∼: *the day is drawing to a close, the festival is, the holidays are coming to an end* **3.** vi [h] (nach) *to lean* (*towards*) ‖ zu etw ∼ ⟨fig⟩ *to incline to, to feel i.d to, to be given* od *prone to* (*a th*) ‖ *to be liable* (*to do*) ‖ *to have a liking, weakness, propensity* (zum Trunk *for drink*); *to have a little way* (*of doing a th*) **| gen·eigt** *kind* (*reader*), ein ∼es

Ohr *a favourable hearing* **N·eigung** f ~/~en **1.** ⟨eig⟩ *slope* (*of a plain, of the ground*) ‖ (*a wall with a slight*) *lean* ‖ ⟨theat⟩ *rake* ‖ (Dach≗) *pitch, slope* ‖ ⟨min⟩ *dip, incline* ‖ ~ 1 : 3 *slope of one vertically to three horizontally* ‖ ⟨rail⟩ (Gefälle) *gradient* ‖ *dip* (*of the needle, in a road, of a ship*) ‖ *list* (*of a ship*) | *bending* (*of the head*), *bow, curtsy* **2.** ⟨fig⟩ *proneness* (zu *to quality, action, condition; to do*) ‖ *inclination* (*to, for; to do*) ‖ *propensity* (*to do, for doing*); *appetite, liking, preference, taste, turn* (*for*) ‖ allg ~ *leaning, tendency, trend* (*towards*) ‖ ⟨bes mot⟩ *sway* ‖ anormale ~ *twist* (*of mind, character*) ‖ ein Knabe mit ~en f Technik .. *with a technical bend* | ~ h *or* verspüren z tun *to feel up to doing; I don't feel inclined for work* ‖ er hat k–e ~ dazu *he has no bend that way* ‖ ~ jds z tun *tendency for a p to do* ‖ lasterhafte ~en *vicious proclivities* (zu *to*) ‖ *her Methodist, German proclivities* ‖ (*accident*) *proneness* (~ zu); *susceptibility* (*to*) ‖ *a pro-American slant* | ⟨com⟩ ~ z Fallen h *to show a downward tendency* **3.** ⟨fig⟩ (Zuneigung) *affection* (*for*), *inclination* (*towards*) ‖ e–e ~ erwacht .. *is awakened* ‖ e–e ~ fassen für *to take a fancy to* (*a p*); ., tiefe .. *to take a strong liking for, to conceive a great affection for* ‖ ~ zu–e–a fassen *to take to each other* **N·eigungs- ~- ~ebene, ~fläche** f *slope, incline*(*d plane*) **~heirat** f *love-match* **~kompaß** m *dipping-needle* **~messer** m (*in*)*clinometer*; ⟨aero⟩ *tiltometer* **~stabilität** f ⟨mot⟩ *cornering st.* **~winkel** m *angle of inclination*, ⟨min⟩ *dip* (*of a stratum*)

n·ein 1. adv *no* ‖ (*no*) *I don't* (*didn't*), *I am not* (*was not*), *I have not*, etc ‖ ~! *not I, he*, etc! ‖ ~ u abermals ~! *a thousand times no*! ‖ mit ~ antworten *to answer in the negative, to say no* ‖ ~ doch! *indeed not*! ‖ ~ sagen *to refuse*; zu jdm .. *to say a p nay*; (*I asked him whether he had* ..,) *he said not*; ich sage nicht ~ *I won't say nay, I don't mind* od *care if I do*, etc ‖ ~ so was! *well, I never*! ‖ ~ so'n Unsinn! (*well*,) *what nonsense*! **2.** [conj] zwei, ~ drei! *two, nay* od *rather three* **3.** ≗ [n] *no, denial* ‖ die mit ~ Stimmenden *the noes* pl

Neiße f (2 Nebenflüsse der Oder); Glatzer ~ mit Glatz u Neiße (Städte); Lausitzer ~ mit Görlitz u Guben (Städte)

Nekr- ~ol·og m ~(e)s/~e *obituary* (*notice*) **~om·ant** m ~en/~en *necromancer* | ~ıe [t] ~/ *necromancy* **~op·ole** f ~/~n *necropolis*(*es* pl) **~·ose** f ~/ ⟨med⟩ *necrosis*

N·ektar m ~s/ *nectar* | ≗haltig [a] *n.iferous* **n-·arisch** a *n.*(*e*)*ous* **N-·arium** n ~s/–ien ⟨bot & zoo⟩ (Organ) *n.y*

N·elke f ~/~n ⟨bot⟩ *pink, carnation, gillyflower* ‖ (Bart≗) *sweet-william* ‖ gefüllte ~ *double carnation* ‖ (Gewürz–) *clove* **N·elken- ~beet** n, **~flor** m *flowering bed of pinks* **~blüte** f *clove-blossom* **~duft** m *carnation scent* **~öl** n *oil of cloves* **~pfeffer** m *Jamaica pepper*; *pimento* **~stock** m *gilly flower plant* **~wurz** f *bennet*

N·elson R·iver m (Fluß in Kanada)

Nem·eisch [-'e:i–] a *Nemean* (*lion*)

N·enn- ≗bar a *mentionable* ‖ nicht ~ *unm., unexpressible, unspeakable* **~betrag** m *face amount* **~durchmesser** m *basic diameter* **~fall** m ⟨gram⟩ *nominative* **~form** f ⟨gram⟩ *infinitive* **~geld** n ⟨sport⟩ *entry-fee* **~leistung** f ⟨tech⟩ *rated output; power rating*; ⟨el⟩ *installed capacity* | ~shöhe [f] *rated altitude* **~wert** m *nominal* (od *face-*)*value* ‖ ⟨com⟩ mit ~ *par-value* (*stock*); zum ~ *at par*; ohne ~ *no-par* **~wort** n ⟨gram⟩ *noun, substantive* **n·ennen 1.** vt [nannte/genannt] [h] *to name, to call* (*by name*), *to christen* od *call a child after* (nach [dat]) *a p* ‖ sich ~ *to be named* od *called* | (benennen) *to term, denominate* ‖ er nennt sich N. N. *his name is N. N.* | genannt w *to be called, to go by the name of* | so ~ *to call so* | ~ Sie mir die Namen *tell* od *give me the names* (*he gave his n.*) | was man so .. nennt *as ths go*; (*a poet*) (*I've got a job*,) *of sorts* ‖ das nenne ich mir e–n Kerl *there's a man for you* ‖ das nenne ich schlafen *that's what I call sleeping* ‖ *he dubbed her the fairy* | (anführen) *to mention* (*a name*, etc) ‖ ich will k–e Zahlen ~ *I'll give no figures* ‖ *you need only call to mind* (~) *a few names* | ⟨sport⟩ *to enter* (zu *for*) | (betiteln) *to term, style* ‖ jdn e–n Schafskopf ~ *to call a p an ass* ‖ man nannte sie immer .. *it was always spoken of as N.-Road* | sich ~ als *to declare o.s. to be* | genannt *surnamed* (*the Just*); g. nach .. (*a ship*) *named after* (⟨Am⟩ *for*) *a state* ‖ oben genannt *above-mentioned* **2.** ≗ n *mention*(*ing*) ‖ ⟨sport⟩ *entry* **~swert** a *considerable, notable*; *worth mentioning*; *significant* (*increase*) ‖ nicht ~ *not to any extent, negligible* ‖ kein ~er Schlaf *no sleep to speak of* ‖ nichts ≗es ⟨fam⟩ *nothing to write home about* **N·enner** m ~s/~ ⟨math⟩ *denominator* ‖ gemeinsamer ~ *common d.* ..; *to bring to a c. d.* ⟨a. fig⟩ ‖ auf den kleinsten ~ bringen ⟨math⟩ *to reduce to the lowest terms* **N·ennung** f ~/~en *naming, mentioning, calling, denomination* ‖ ohne ~ der Quelle *without giving the source* ‖ (e–s Kandidaten) *nomination* ‖ ⟨sport⟩ ~(sliste f) *entry* | ~sformular [n] ⟨sport⟩ *entry form*

Neo- ~-G·otik f → Neugotik **~log·ismus** m ~/–men *neologism*

Neon- ~licht [n] *neon light*; ~röhre [f] *n. tube*; ~(leucht)schild [n] *n. sign*; ~tafel [f] ⟨comp⟩ *n. display unit*

Nep·al n (Land am Südhang des Himalaya) *Nepa*(*u*)*l* **Nepal·ese** m, **Nepal·esin** f *Nepaulese*

Nephr·it m ~s/~e *nephrite, jade*

Nepot·ismus m ~/ (Vetternwirtschaft) *nepotism*

°**N·epp(er·ei** f ~/~en) m (S) *cheat*(*ing*), *rooking* **~lokal** n ⟨Am sl⟩ *gyp-joint* **n·eppen** vt/i [h] *to cheat, fleece, vamp* ‖ geneppt w ⟨sl a.⟩ *to be stung* **N·epperin** f ~/~nen *vamp*, ⟨Am⟩ *gold-digger*

Nept·un m *Neptune* ‖ °⟨fig⟩ ~ [dat] opfern *to feed the fishes* | ≗**isch** a *Neptunian* (*stratum*) **~strabant** m ⟨astr⟩ *satellite of Neptune*

N·erfling m ~s/~e ⟨ich⟩ *ide, whitefish*

N·erv [–f] m [~(e)s & ~en/~en] [–f–] **A.** *nerve* (→ Bündel) | ⟨übtr bot⟩ *vein* (*of a leaf*) | ⟨fig⟩ [sg] *the sinews* pl (*of war, money*) **B.** es sind die ~ *it's n.s* ‖ eiserne ~en *a n. of iron*; starke, gute ~en *strong nerve*(*s*) ‖ die ~en angreifen, mitnehmen *to shake the n.s* ‖ die ~en behalten *to keep cool* ‖ sie bekam es mit den ~en z tun *her n.s began to go wrong* ‖ jdm auf die ~en fallen *or* gehen *to get, jar, grate on a p's n.s, to set a p's teeth on edge*; .. fallend *aggressive* ‖ ich bin mit den ~en herunter *my n.s have broken down* ‖ an den ~en leiden *to suffer from the n.s* ‖ jds ~en stark mitnehmen *to shake a p's n.s* ‖ ⟨fig⟩ im ~ treffen *to strike to the quick* ‖ er muß die ~en verloren h ⟨sl⟩ *his n.s must have gone phut* ‖ die ~en versagen *one's n.s break down* ‖ die ~en zermürbend *n.-racking* **N·erven- ~anfall** m *nervous fit* **~anstalt** f *nerve* od *mental hospital* **~anstrengung** f *nerve-strain* **~arzt** m *mental specialist* **~aufregung** f *nervous excitement* ≗**aufreibend** a *nerve-racking*, ⟨sl⟩ *nervy* **~bau** m *nervous texture* **~beschwerden** f pl *nervous troubles* **~bündel** n (P) ⟨fig⟩ *mass of n.s* **~elektrizität** f ⟨biol⟩ *neuroelectricity* **~entzündung** f ⟨med⟩ *neuritis* **~faser** f ⟨anat⟩ *nerve-fibre* **~fieber** n *nervous* (od *typhoid*) *fever* **~geflecht** n ⟨anat⟩ *plexus* **~heilanstalt** = ~anstalt **~inanspruchnahme** = ~anstrengung **~knoten** m ⟨anat⟩ *ganglion* | s–e **~kraft** verläßt ihn *his n. is gone* ≗**krank** a *nervous, neurotic, neuropathic* **~-kranke(r)** m *n.thic patient* [a. f] **~krankheit** f *nervous disorder* od *disease* **~krieg** m *war of nerves, nerve war* **~lehre** f *neurology* **~-leiden** n *nervous complaint* ≗**leidend** a *neuropathic* **~mittel** n ⟨med⟩ *neurotic* **~physiologie** f *micro- and macrophysiology of the central-nervous-system* **~probe** f *test of nerves* **~saft** m ⟨anat⟩ *nervous fluid* °**~säge** f *shake up*, *nerve racking* (*she's n.r.*; *she gets on my n.s*) **~-schmerz** m ⟨med⟩ *neuralgia* **~schock** m *shock* **≃-schwach** a *nervous, neurasthenic* **~schwäche** f *nervous debility* || ⟨scient⟩ *neurasthenia* **≃stärkend** a *neurotic, tonic* **~strang** m ⟨anat⟩ *nerve fibre*; ⟨übtr⟩ ≃e [pl] *control system* **~system** n *nervous system* **~überanstrengung** f = ~anstrengung **~überreizung** f *nervous strain* **~verlieren** n *vertigo* **~zelle** f *neuron* **~zentrum** n *nerve centre* ⟨a. comp⟩ **≃zerrüttend** a *nerve-racking* **~zuckung** f *twitching* **~zus-bruch** m *nervous breakdown*, ⟨fam⟩ *crack-up* **n·ervig** a *nervy, sinewy* || *strong* (*fist*), *vigorous* (*figure*) | ⟨bot⟩ *nerved, ribbed* (*leaves*) | ⟨fig⟩ *pithy, terse* (*style*) **nerv·ös** a **A.** *nervous* (⟨a. fig⟩ *n. bustle*) || (reizbar) *irritable, excitable* || (zappelig) *jumpy, fidgety, jittery*; ⟨sl⟩ *nervy* || sehr ~ *highly strung* || ⟨sl⟩ *windy* (über *about*), *edgy*; [pred] *on edge* (*with excitement*) | *skittish* (*horse*) **B.** jdn ~ m *to make a p nervous* od *irritable, to fidget* od *excite a p*; *to set a p's teeth on edge*; der Lärm macht mich ganz ~ .. *gets on my nerves* || ~ s *to suffer from one's nerves, to be nervous*, ⟨fam⟩ *to be on edge* od *end* (über *over*), *to be on the jump* || ~ w *to get nervous* (⟨fam⟩ *the fidgets* od ⟨sl⟩ *needle*) **Nervosit·ät** f ~/ *nervousness, nervous irritation*; ⟨sl⟩ *the jitters* pl

†**N·ervier** pl (gall.-germ. Volk) *Nervii* [L] pl

N·erz m ~es/~e ⟨zoo⟩ *mink* | ~cape, ~fell [n] *mink*

N·essel f ~/~n **1.** ⟨bot⟩ *nettle* (brennt *stings*) || ⟨tex⟩ *n. cloth*, ⟨bes theat⟩ *muslin* || ⟨fig⟩ sich in die ~n setzen *to get into hot water*; *to get o.s. into scrapes* pl (wegen *for*) **2.** **~n** pl ⟨path⟩, **~ausschlag** = ~fieber **~brand** m *pain inflicted by the sting of nettles* **~faser(n** [pl]) *n. filament* **~fieber** n ⟨path⟩ *nettle-rash* **~seide** f *dodder* **~sucht** f = ~fieber **~tier** n ⟨zoo⟩ *nematophore* **~tuch** n *grass-cloth, muslin*

N·est n ~es/~er **A.** *nest* (a. v Maus, Natter etc) || (Adler–) *eyrie* (Eichhörnchen–) *dray* | ⟨übtr min, mil⟩ *pocket* | ⟨fig⟩ *bed* || ⟨dero⟩ (Haus) *den, hole*; ⟨fam⟩ (Kleinstadt) *hole*(*-and-corner town*); ⟨sl⟩ *dump*, → Kaff **B.** ~er ausnehmen *to go bird's-nesting* || ~ ausheben ⟨fig⟩ *to raid a nest* (⟨Am⟩ *hang-out*) *of thieves* || das ~ leer finden ⟨fig⟩ *to find the bird flown* || ⟨fig⟩ ins ~ (Bett) kriechen ⟨fam⟩ *to go to roost* || sein eigenes ~ beschmutzen *to* (*be*)*foul one's own nest* **~ei** n *nest egg* **~flüchter** m *nidifugous bird* **~hocker** m *nidicolous bird* **~häkchen, ~küchlein** n *nest--chicken, nestling* || ⟨fig⟩ *mother's baby, pet* **~ling** m ~s/~e *nestling*; (Falke) *eyas* **~wärme** f ⟨fig⟩ *decent home, d. family life*; dem Kind fehlt die ~ .. *wants home life* od *family atmosphere* **N·estel** f ~/~n *lace, point, string* || (Stift) *tag* | **≃n** vt [h] *to* (*fasten with a*) *lace* || sich ~ (an jdn) = anschmiegen *to nestle* (*close*) *to*

nett a *neat, tidy* || ⟨Am⟩ *cute* (*hat, girl*) || (freundlich) *nice* (*simple girls*) || *be nice* od *kind to her*! || (hübsch) *pretty* || (gemütlich) *jolly* || ganz ~ *decent* (*cigar*) || rund u ~ *unambiguous* | ⟨iron⟩ ~es Früchtchen *fine sort of fellow*; ~er Kunde *nasty customer* || ~e Zustände *a nice state of affairs, a precious mess* | das ist (nicht) ~ v Ihnen! *that is* (*not*) *nice of you*! || ⟨iron⟩ das kann ja ~ w! *that may turn out a regular mess*! || zu jdm ~ s *to be pleasant to a p* **N·ettigkeit** f ~/ *neatness, tidiness, prettiness, niceness, jollity*, ⟨Am⟩ *cuteness*

n·etto adv ⟨com⟩ *at net price, net*; *clear* || ~ 10 Sch. *10 s net* **N·etto-** [in comp] *net* (*amount, weight, price*; *receipts* pl [Einnahme], *proceeds* pl [Ertrag], *assets* pl [Vermögen]) **~gewinn** m *clear gain* **~lohn** m ⟨fam⟩ *take-home pay*

Netz n ~es/~e **A.** ⟨eig⟩ *net* || ⟨hunt⟩ *toils* pl || enges, weites ~ *fine, wide meshed net* | (Auto≃ f Päckchen) *filet*; Ball·on≃ *network* od *netting of a balloon* || Einkaufs≃ *marketing net* || Eisenbahn≃ → B. || ⟨el⟩ *mains* || Fisch≃ *fishing-n.* || Gepäck≃ *luggage hold* || Grundschlepp≃ *trawl*(*-n.*) || ⟨cycl⟩ Kleider≃ *dress n.* || Spinnen≃ *cobweb, spider's* n. || ⟨mil⟩ Tarn≃, Schutz≃ *mask* || Treib≃ *drift*(*-n.*) || Wurf≃ *casting-n.* **B.** ⟨übtr tech⟩ Gitter≃ *reticule* ⟨a. opt⟩ || ⟨mil⟩ *grid reticule* || ⟨surv⟩ *triangulation* || ⟨tech, traffic, wir, el, etc⟩ *net*(*work*) (*of roads, rails, el. lines*); Eisenbahn≃ ⟨a.⟩ *grid*; ⟨el⟩ *tramway system* || ⟨anat⟩ *network* (*of veins, nerves*); Darm≃ *caul*, ⟨scient⟩ *omentum* | ⟨fig⟩ *web, network* (*of lies*) || *the tangled web* (*of complications*) **C.** ein ~ **aufstellen** *to put up* od *spread a net*; .. auslegen *to moor* ..; .. auswerfen *to cast* .. || im ~ **fangen** *to net, mesh* || ans ~ gehen ⟨ten⟩ *to go up to the n.*, am ~ spielen *to play up at the n.* || ins ~ gehen (Fische) *to be netted*, ⟨fig⟩ *to be trapped* (e–m *by*) || ins ~ locken *to entice, decoy* ⟨a. fig⟩ || ⟨ten⟩ (Ball) ins ~ schlagen *to net* || ein ~ **stellen** *to put out a n.* (⟨fig⟩ e–m .. *to set a trap for a p*) || sich im eigenen ~ verstricken *to be caught in one's own trap* **N·etz- ~anode** f ⟨wir⟩ *grid terminal, battery eliminator* **~anschluß** m ⟨com⟩ *current-supply*; ⟨wir⟩ *mains supply* | ~gerät [n] ⟨wir⟩ *mains operating set*; ~lampe [f] ⟨el⟩ *line-voltage lamp* **~antenne** f *mains aerial* **~arbeit** f *netting* **~ätzung** f *autotype*; *half-tone* **~auge** n ⟨ent⟩ *compound eye* **~ausschalter** m ⟨el⟩ *main limit switch* **~ball**! m ⟨ten⟩ *net*!; (Spiel) *net-ball* **~beutel** m, **~haube** f *purse-net* **~bruch** m ⟨path⟩ *epiplocele* **~empfänger** m ⟨wir⟩ *network-receiver* **~filter** m ⟨bes wir⟩ *hum eliminator* **~flügler** m pl ⟨ent⟩ *neuroptera* **≃förmig** a *retiform, reticular* **~gerät** n ⟨wir⟩ *network--set* **~gewölbe** n ⟨arch⟩ *reticulated vaulting* **~haut** f (Auge) *retina*; (Darm) *caul, omentum* **~hemd** n *cellular shirt* **~karte** f *runabout* od *rover ticket* **~kennung** f ⟨wir⟩ *net authentication* **~legung** f ⟨surv⟩ *triangulation* **~magen** m ⟨zoo⟩ *honeycomb*; *reticulum* **~melone** f *netted melon* **~nadel** f *netting--needle* **~plantechnik** f *network technique* **~planung** f *network planning* **~punkt** m ⟨surv⟩ *station* **~schalter** m ⟨el⟩ *mains switch* **~spannung** f *main voltage* **~sperrenleger** m ⟨mil⟩ *net layer* **~spiel** n ⟨ten⟩ *net-play* **~spinne** f ⟨ent⟩ *retilarian* **~steller** m *snarer* **~stickerei** f *darned netting* **~-stoff** m ⟨theat⟩ *net* **~störung** f ⟨tech⟩ *line disturbance* **~stricker** m *net-maker* **~strickmaschine** f *netting machine* **~strom** m ⟨el⟩ *line current* **~-strumpf** m *open-work stocking* **~teilung** f *squared graticule*, ⟨Am⟩ *retic*(*u*)*le* **~transformator** m *mains transformer* **~werk** n *net*(*work*); ⟨arch tech⟩ *reticulation*; ⟨fig⟩ *tracery, grid* **~zuleitung** f *mains lead*

n·etzen vt [h] *to moisten, wet, bathe*; → naß

Netzmittel n *wet*(*ting*) *agent*

n·eu I. a **A. 1.** *new* ⟨a. fig⟩ (*clothes, potatoes, wine, love, song, line* [Zeile], *hope, life, course, spirit, style, year, man* [Mensch a. ⟨bib⟩], *domestic*; *N. Testament, York, World*) **2.** *fresh* (*capital* ⟨com⟩, *play* ⟨theat⟩, *eyes, vigour, fuel, herrings, troops*) **3.** (erneut) *further* od *more* (*difficulties*) **4.** (~artig) (*this treatment is novel*) || *novel* (*features*); *original* **5.** (~ entdeckt, erfunden) *lately discovered* **6.** (~zeitlich) *modern* **7.** (im Entstehen) *rising* **8.** (kürzlich geschehen) *recent* **B.** ganz ~ *brand-new* || noch wie ~ *as good as new* | das ist mir ~ ⟨fam⟩ *that's a new one* | ~er Gast *arrival* || Ein glückliches ~es **Jahr**! *A happy New Year* (*to you*); e–m .. wünschen *to wish a p a h. N. Y.* || ~e Sachlichkeit ⟨arts⟩ *modern objectivity* || sich v e–r ganz ~en **Seite** zeigen *to show o.s. from quite a different side* || dadurch bekommt die S e–n ganz ~en Sinn *this gives the affair quite a different appearance* || e–e ihm ~e **Welt** *what was to him a strange world*, → A. 1. || ~e Wendung *neologism* | **~e(re)** Geschichte, Sprachen, *modern history, languages* || in ~er(er) Zeit *of late years, in modern* od *recent times* pl | **~(e)ste(r)** *latest* (*fashion, novel, patterns* pl, *news* od *intelligence*, *song-hit*) || ~ester Bauart *of the most modern type* || die ~sten Ereignisse *the most recent events* || auf den ~sten Stand bringen *to update*; mit der ~esten Mode gehend, bis in die ~este Zeit *up-to--date* | ~en Mut **fassen,** schöpfen *to take, gain fresh courage* || ~e Kräfte gewinnen *to recover* (*one's strength*) || ~ m *to renovate* || das **ist** mir ganz ~ *that is news to me*; ⟨fam⟩ *that's a new one on me* || mir ist die S ~ *I am unused to it* || in etw ~ s *to be a beginner in a th* | **C.** [**adv**] angek *just arrived*; ~ **aufgelegt** *reprinted* || ~ beleben ⟨fig⟩ *to rekindle* ~ **benennen** vt [h] *to relabel*; ⟨theat⟩ ein Stück ~ besetzen *to re-cast a play* || ~ beziehen *to re-cover* || ~ einkleiden *to dress up anew* | (Gesetz, Liste etc) ~ fassen *to re-edit, reword*; *new--born* (*child*); *new-won* (*freedom*); ~ gründen *to refound* | ~-möbliert *newly furnished* (*room*); ~ überziehen *to re-cover* ~ **zurichten** *to dress anew* **II. 1. das** ≃**e,** (≃(e)ste [Nachricht]) *the latest* || etw, nichts ≃es *sth, nothing new, no new th* || wenig ≃es *little of novelty* || was gibt es ≃es? *what* (*is the*) *news*? || alles ≃e *everything that is new* || ⟨com⟩ etw ganz ≃es *the latest novelty* || das ist jetzt das ≃este *that is now all the fashion, the last word* od *th* (in *in*); das ≃ste über jdn hören *to have the latest news of a p*; (gibt's) was ≃es? ⟨fam⟩ *anything doing*? **2. ein** ≃**er** *a new-comer* || → Neuling || die ≃eren [compr] *the moderns* **III.** adv **1.** → I. C. **2.** (kürzlich) (a. ≃**estens**) (*quite*) *recently* od *lately*; *of late* **3. aufs ~e, v ~em** *afresh, anew*; *newly* (*won freedom*) || stets aufs ~e herbeigesehnt *yearned and y. for* || etw aufs ~e beginnen *to start a th from the beginning* || v ~em anfangen *to begin the world anew*; v ~em füllen *to refill, to fill again* **N·eu-** [in comp] *new*(*-laid eggs, -born babe*) || *newly* (*appointed general, constructed bridge*) || ⟨scient mst⟩ *neo-*(*gothic, -Hegelian*) || [mit verbs & nouns oft] *re-*(*name*) (*reanimation*) **~angekommene(r)** m (*new*) *arrival* **~·anreicherung** f *re-enrichment* **~anschaffung** f *acquisition*, (Buch) *new purchase*; ⟨library⟩ *accession* ≃**artig** a *original*; *new-type* (Hut etc); *new kind of* (*fabric*) **~aufnahme** f ⟨film⟩ *retake* ≃**aufgelegt** a *reprinted* **~auflage** f, **~ausgabe** f *re-edition*; *new ed.* **~auftreten** n ⟨theat⟩ *come-back* ≃**backen** a *new-baked, fresh* || ⟨fig⟩ *brand-new* || ⟨dero⟩ *new-fangled* (*ideas*) **~bau** m *new building* || [abstr] *reconstruction* | ~land [n] *addition*; ~wohnung [f] *new flat* **~bauten** m pl *new buildings* **~bekehrte(r)** m *proselyte,* (*new*) *convert* **~besetzung** f ⟨theat⟩ *recast* **~beurteilung** f *reappraisal* **~bewaffnung** f *rearmament* **~bewertung** f *revaluation* **~bildung** f *new formation* od *growth* || *neologism* || ⟨path⟩ *neoplasm* **~bruch** m ⟨agr⟩ *virgin land*; *ground newly broken* **~druck** m *reprint* **~eichung** f *recalibration* ≃**einstellen** vt [h] ⟨tech⟩ *to readjust* ≃**englisch** a *modern English* ≃**entdeckt** a *recently discovered* **~entdeckung** f *rediscovery* **~entwerfen** n → -planung **~entwicklung** f [konkr] *novelty* **~erscheinung** f *new publication* **~erwerbungen** f pl *accessions* pl; ~ eintragen *to accession* **~fassung** f *new* (od *re-edited, amended*) *version* ≃**form·ieren** vt [h] *to re-form* **~f·undländer** m *inhabitant of Newfoundland* || (Hund) *Labrador* od *Newfoundland dog* ≃**gebacken** a → -backen || ⟨fig iron⟩ *upstart* (*nobility*); *newly fledged* (*doctor*) ≃**geboren** a *new-born* || sich wie ~ fühlen *to be feeling first--rate* **~geschaffen** a *newly created* ≃**gestalten** vt [h] *to reform, reorganize, redesign* **~gestaltung** f *reordering, reorganization*; *redesign*(*ing*); (Änderung) *modification*; *redirection* (*of economy*) ≃**gewählt** a *elect* (*the Viceroy-elect*) **~gewinnung** f *reclamation* (*of land*) **~gier(de)** f *curiosity, inquisitiveness*; *anxiety* || °(P) *rubberneck* || aus ~ *out of curiosity* || jds ~ erwecken *to intrigue a p* ≃**gierig** a *curious* [nur pred:] *he is c. to know* [auf a th], *inquisitive* (*an i. girl*) || ⟨sl⟩ *nos*(*e*)*y* || ich bin ~, ob *I wonder whether* od *if* || e–n ~ m *to arouse* od *stimulate a p's curiosity* | ≃e(r) *inquisitive p,* ⟨Am sl⟩ *rubberneck*; ~e [pl] sterben bald *curiosity killed the cat* **~glanzpolitur** f ⟨paint⟩ *refresher* ≃**gliedern** vt [h] *to reorganize* ⟨a. mil⟩ **~gotik** f ⟨m. m.⟩ *National Gothic* (*cf. House of Parliament*) **~grad** m ($^1/_{400}$ Kreis) *grad*(*e*) **~-grammatiker** m *neo-grammarian* **~griechisch** n *Romaic* **~heide** m *neo-pagan* **~herausgabe** f (Buch≃) *revival* ≃**hochdeutsch** a *modern High--German* **~jahr** n → neu I. B. || seit ~ *since the N. Y.* **~jahrs-** [in comp] *New Year's* (*Eve, Day, present*) | ~geschenk [n] *han*(*d*)*sel*; ~wunsch [m] *N. Y. card* od *greeting* || *good wishes for the N. Y.* **~land** n *untouched ground* ⟨a. fig⟩; ⟨fig⟩ ~ betreten *to break new ground* ≃**modisch** a *fashionable*; *new-fangled* (*contraption*) **~mond** m *new moon* || es war ~ .. *the moon was new* (*on the following day*) **~ordnung** f *reorganization, rearrangement, reordering*; ≃**orientiert** a ⟨eth, physiol⟩ ~e Bewegung *redirected activity* **~orientierung** f ⟨bes pol⟩ *new course*; ⟨eth⟩ *reorientation* **~philologe** m *student* od *teacher of modern languages* | ~ntag [m] *meeting of the Modern Language Association* (= ~nverband) **~plat·oniker** m *Neoplatonist* **~profilierung** f (e–s Reifens) ⟨mot⟩ *cap* **~regelung** f *rearrangement* ([gen] *for*) ≃**reiche(n)** m pl *arrivistes*; *nouveaux riches* pl Fr, *new men with plenty of money* ≃**s·eeländisch** a *Zelanian* **~siedlung** f *modern quarter*; *housing estate* **~silber** n *German silver*; *nickel silver* **~sprachler** m = ~philologe **~stadt** f *new town*; *addition* ≃**testamentlich** a *new testamental* **~unterbringung** f *rehousing* ≃**verheiratet,** ≃**verm·ählt** a *newly married* (*couple*) **~verm·ählte(r)** m *bridegroom* **~verm·ählte** f *bride* **~wahl** f *new* od *second election*; bei ~ im Amt Bleibende [pl] ⟨pol⟩ *holdovers* ≃**wertig** a *practically new*; [pred] *as new* **~zeit** f; die ~ *modern times* pl ≃**zeitlich** a *modern*; *present-day* (*leaders*); ~ ausbauen *to modernize* **n·euerdings** (⟨a.⟩ **neuerlich**) adv *newly, lately, recently*; *not so long ago* || (wieder) *again* **N·euerer** m ~s/~ *innovator* || Sprach≃ *neologist* | ~methode [f] ⟨SBZ⟩ *new method* **N·euerung** f ~/~en *innovation* || (Änderung) *change, reform* || ~en abhold s ⟨a.⟩ *to stand pat* | ~sstifter [m] *innovator* ~ssucht [f] *mania for innovation*; ≃s-süchtig [a] *fond of* (*making*) *innovation*(*s*); *new--fangled* **N·euheit** f ~/~en *newness, novelty, recentness* || [konkr] ⟨com⟩ *novelty,* ⟨sl⟩ *the last word* (*in*); ⟨tech fam⟩ *contraption*; modische ~en *novelty items* **N·euigkeit** f ~/~en (e–e *a piece of*) *news*; || ~ des Tages *event of the day* || (Buch etc) *novelty* | ~skrämer [m] *newsmonger, quidnunc* **n·eulich** adv *the other day*; *newly, lately, of late, recently* || ~ abends *the other evening* **N·euling** m ~(e)s/~e *novice, new hand, beginner, tyro* od *tiro* || ⟨fam⟩ *greenhorn,* ⟨Am⟩ *John Raw,* ⟨sl⟩ *rookie*

Neu- ⟨geog⟩ [in comp] *New*

Neubr·aunschweig n ⟨Can⟩ *New Brunswick*

Neuchât·el n → Neuenburg

Neue Hebr·iden f pl (Inselgruppe v. Melanesien) *New Hebrides*

N·euenburg n (Kanton u Stadt der westl. Schweiz) *Neu*(*f*)*châtel* **~er See** m *Lake of N.*

Neu·england n *New-England* (U.S.A.)

Neufchatel n → Neuenburg

Neu- ~f·undland n (Insel vor Labrador) *Newfoundland* **~f·undländer** m *N.er*; **~guin·ea** n [–gi–] *New Guinea* **~h·ampshire** n (Staat der U.S.A.) *N. H.* **~h·olland** n (†Name für ⟨Aust⟩) *N. H.* **~j·ersey** n (Staat der U.S.A.) *New Jersey* **~·irland** n (= Neumecklenburg, → d.) **~kaled·onien** n (franz. Inseln im Stillen Ozean) *New Caledonia* **~m·ecklenburg** n (†Insel des Bismarckarchipels) seit 1920 *New Ireland* **~m·exiko** n (Staat der U.S.A.) *New Mexico* **~·orleans** n (Stadt am Mississippi) *New Orleans* **~sch·ottland** n (Prov. Kanadas) *Nova Scotia,* ⟨poet⟩ *Acadia* **~s·eeland**

n *New Zealand* **~südwales** [–weilz] n *New South Wales* **~y·ork** n *New York* **~y·orker** m, **~in** f *inhabitant of New York, New Yorker*

neun 1. a *nine* || (Kegel) alle ~e schieben *to throw all the ninepins* || alle ~e! *the whole nine!, a floor(er)!* || ⟨fig⟩ *bang!* **2.** ≗ f ~/~en *nine* **N·eun- ~auge** n *(river-)lamprey* **~eck** n *nonagon* **≗eckig** a *nine-angled* **≗fach** a *n.fold* **≗h·undert** a *n. hundred* **≗h·undertste** a *n.hundredth* **≗jährig** a *n. years old* (→ jährlich) **≗mal** adv *n. times* **≗malig** a *n. times repeated* **~malweise** m ⟨iron⟩ *sapient; wiseacre* **~pfünder** m *n.-pounder* **≗seitig** a *n.-sided* **≗stündig** a *n. hours'* .. **≗tägig** a *n. days'* ..; *n. days old*; ~e Andacht ⟨R C⟩ *novena*; ~e Trauer *Novendial* **~töter** m ⟨orn⟩ *n.-killer; red-backed shrike* → *sh.* **~uhrfrühstück** n *second breakfast* **≗zehn** a *n.teen*; ~ Uhr ⟨Ger⟩ *7 o'clock p. m.* **≗zehnte** a *n.teenth* **≗zehntel** a *n.teenth (part)* **N·euner** m ~s/~ *novenary, the number nine* || *soldier of the 9th regiment*; → acht | ~jause [f] *second breakfast* **neunerl·ei** a *of nine different sorts* **n·eunte** a *ninth* || der 9. Januar *the ninth of J.* (geschrieben: *January 9th*) **n·euntehalb** a *eight and a half* **N·euntel** n ~s/~ *ninth (part)* **n·euntens** adv *ninthly, in the 9th place* **n·eunzig** a *ninety* (→ dreißig) || die ≗ erreichen *to live to the age of n.* **N·eunziger 1.** m ~s/~ *nonagenarian* || ⟨mil⟩ → Neuner || (Pikettspiel) *repique* **2.** ≗ a; in den ~ Jahren *in the nineties* **n·eunzigste** a *ninetieth* **N·eunzigstel** n ~s/~ *ninetieth (part)*

Neur- ~alg·ie f ~/~n ⟨path⟩ *neuralgia* **≗·algisch** a *neuralgic* **~asthen·ie** f ~/~n ⟨path⟩ *neurasthenia* **~asth·eniker** m ~s/~; **≗asth·enisch** a *neurasthenic* **~olog·ie** f *neurology* **≗-op·athisch** a = nervenleidend **~·ose** f ~/ *neurosis, nervous disorder* **~·otiker** m ~s/~ *neurotic*

neutr·al I. a **1.** *neutral* ⟨a. chem, pol, fig, etc⟩ || ~ bleiben, sich ~ [adv] verhalten *to remain neutral* **2.** ⟨gram⟩ *neuter* **II.** **≗e** m [der ~, ein ~r] *neutral(ist)*; *neutral country* od *party* **≗isati·onsmittel** n *antacid* **~is·ieren** vt [h] *to neutralize* || *to counteract (magnetic mines)* **≗it·ät** f ~/~en *neutrality*; wohlwollende ~ *benevolent n.* || ~sakte [f] *N. Act (1939)* | ~sbruch [m] *infringement of the neutrality*; ~serklärung [f] *declaration of n.*; ~sgesetzgebung [f] *n. legislation* **N·eutron** n ~s/–·onen ⟨at⟩ *neutron*, → d.; **N·eutrum** n ~s/–ra & –ren ⟨gram⟩ *neuter (word)*

Nev·ada n (Staat der U.S.A.)

N·ewark ['n(j)u:ək] n (amerik. Industriestadt westl. v New York)

N·ewcastle [nju:'ka:sl] n ⟨Engl⟩

N·exus m ~/ *connexion; nexus; bond*

Niag·arafälle m pl *Niagara Falls*

N·ias n (Insel bei Sumatra)

N·ibelungen- ~lied [n] *Lay of the Nibelungen*; ~strophe [f] *stanza (since Kürenberg, 1160) of the N.lied: 4 lines, each of 6 stressed syllables except the last which has 7*

†**Nic·äa** [–ts–] n **1.** (alte bithyn. Stadt) *Nicæa* **2.** alter Name v Nizza, → d.

Nicar·agua n (mittelamerik. Staat) **~holz** n *peach-wood* **~see** m *Lake Nicaragua*

n·icht adv **A. 1.** *not* **2.** [ell] ~? *is it not?*, ⟨fam⟩ *isn't it?* **3.** [pleonastisch] wie schön sind ~ diese Rosen! *how beautiful are these roses!* (*are they not?*) **4.** ~ .., ~ .. *neither .. nor ..* **5.** → mit ~en, zu ~e **B.** (verstärkt) **absolut** ~ → durchaus ~; ich verstehe abs. ~ *I fail to understand* || **auch** ~ *not either; neither; nor* || ich auch ~ *not I either*; (*my wife had never seen them,*) *nor had I* || ich glaube das auch ~ *I don't believe it either* || ~ **doch** (–‿) *certainly not* || (abwehrend) *don't!, oh, but (George)!, oh, come (you must stay)!* || **durchaus** ~, (ganz u) **gar** ~ *not a bit, not in the least; on no account* od *condition; not at all, by no means; in no way*; ⟨Am⟩ *I guess not* || (*you will leave that alone*) – *Oh no, we will not* || *never*: *I n. know how*; *he would n. believe that* || man muß gar ~ erst sagen *it goes without saying, it is needless to say* || ~ **eben** *scarcely* || ~ einmal *not even*; (*he*) *not so much as (looked at it)* || ~ **einmal** wieder *I can't ever even smoke again* || **lieber** ~! *I wouldn't!* || ~ **mehr** (→ E. 3.) *no longer, no more, not any more* od *longer*; .. lange u *soon* || **noch** ~ *not yet* || **nur** ~ ängstlich! *never fear!*, (→ E. 3.) || nur ~ verzagen! *never say die!* || nur das ~! *anything but that!* || .. **oder** ~ (*whether he would*) *or no*; ehrenvoll oder ~ *honour or no h.* || **sicher**(lich) ~ *surely* od *decidedly not* || **überhaupt** ~ *little (he l. knows)*; ich s·ah ihn übh. ~ *I did not so much as see him* || ~ **um** Haaresbreite *not by so much as a hair's breadth* || ~ um die Welt *not for the life of me* || ~ viel *scarcely any* || ~ **wenig** *not a little* || ~ wenige *not a few* || ~ weniger als 1 M (als du) *not less than* .., .. als 100 *no fewer than 100* || ~ weniger interessant *no less interesting* || ~ **wie** *not like (a little boy)* || **wo** ~ *if .. not, unless ..* **C.** ~ genehmigen *to disapprove*; ~ k *to fail to come*; ~ alle kamen *not all came*; [Stellung!] alle kamen ~ *none of them came*; ~ zurückkehren *to fail to return* || || [ell] sie ~! *not she!*; das ~! *no such th, that's not the case* || ~ ·ein Mal *not once* || .. ~ ein Wort .. *never a word, not so much as a word* **D. [vor Adj oft:]** *in-, im- (incommunicative); un- (unfaithful* ~ wortgetreu; *unsolicited* ~ erbeten; *unconfirmed, unimproved); non- (nonresident)*; ~ abfärbend *nonstaining*; *-less (heedless [of])* || ~ einwandfrei *objectionable* || ~ durch e–n ·einzigen Blick *never by so much as a glance* || ~ leicht *not easy*; ~ leichter *no easier* || [ell] ~ **wahr**? *is it not so?*, ⟨fam⟩ *isn't that so* || (*it's nice of him,*) *isn't it?*; *eh, George?* || (*You are of my opinion,*) *are you not?* || (*you will do it,*) *won't you?* || (*there is nothing like old oak,*) *is there?* || (*we needn't let him know,*) (*or*) *need we?* || (*we will go to him now,*) *shall we?* || (*shut the door,*) *will you?* **E. 1.** er **arbeitet** ~ *he does not work* || arbeitet er ~? *does he not work?*, ⟨fam⟩ *doesn't he work?, is he not working?* | ich hatte es ~ *I had it not*, ⟨fam⟩ *I didn't have it* | **[imp]** glaubt es ~! *don't* od *never believe it!* **2.** .. *out of*: ~ betreten *to keep out of* | *dis-*: ~ berücksichtigen *to disregard*, ~ glauben *to disbelieve*, ~ fortfahren *to discontinue* | ~ aufhören *to be unceasing* | sie ließ sich ~ überzeugen *she refused to be convinced* || die Tür wollte ~ schließen .. *refused to close* | ~ tun etc *to fail to do, return, understand, come*, etc **3.** er raucht ~ **mehr** *he has given up smoking* (→ B.) || wenn er **nur** ~ krank wäre *but* (od *if it were not*) *for his illness* (→ B.) || er las ~ **weiter** *he read no further, he did not read any further* **4. [vor inf]** *not to appreciate*, ⟨Am⟩ *to not appreciate* | ~ **zu** zählen *past counting* || entscheiden, warnen ~ zu tun *to decide, warn against doing* || das Gift ist ~ zu finden .. *baffles detection* **5.** es **gibt k-n, der** ~ wüßte *there is nobody but knows, everyone knows* **6.** ~, **daß** ich wüßte, **so viel** ich weiß ~ *not so far as I know, not that I know of* || ~, daß mich das wunderte *not that it astonishes me* **N·icht-** [in comp] mst *lack* od *want of (sympathy)* || *non- (non-Aryan, non-Asiatic, non-Russian; non-acceptance,* ⟨el⟩ *non-conductor; non-resident, etc.)* **≗achtend** a *slighting*; ~ behandeln *to slight* **~achtung** f *disregard* (vor *of, for*), *lack* od *want of respect*; jdm ~ zufügen *to put a slight on a p* **~addition** f ⟨comp⟩ *non-adding* **≗alkoh·olisch** a *soft (drink)* **≗amtlich** a *unofficial* **~·anerkennung** f *disavowal*; ⟨contr⟩ *repudiation; non-recognition (of debts)* **~·angriffspakt** m *non-aggression pact*; gegenseitiger ~ *pact of mutual non-aggression* **~annahme** f *non-acceptance* **~anwesenheit** f *absence*; (fortgesetzte) *absenteeism* **≗-arbeitend** a *(population) outside of the labo(u)r force* **~arzt** m *nonmedical man, layman* **≗ausschließlich** a *non-exclusive (license)* **~beachtung, ~befolgung** f *non-observance; neg-*

lect **~beantwortung** f *non-response* **~behaltenkönnen** n *irretention* **≃berechtigt** a *not entitled* **~bestellbarkeit** f ⟨post⟩ *non-delivery* **~bezahlung** f *non-payment*; (e–s Wechsels) *dishonouring* (*of a bill*) **~dasein** n *non-existence* **~duldung** f *intolerance* **≃eidlich** a *unsworn* (*statement*) **≃einlaufend** a *unshrinkable* **~einmischung** f *non-interference*; *non-intervention* | Politik der ~ *hands-off policy* **≃eintreibbar** a *uncollectable* (*tax*, etc) **~·eisenmetalle** n pl *non-ferrous metals* **≃·endenwollend** a; ~e Hurrarufe [pl] *round after round of cheers* pl **~erfolg** m *unsuccess*, *failure* **~-erf·üllung** f *non-compliance*, *non-performance*; sich auf ~ .. berufen *to set up a breach of contract* **~erscheinen** n (Buch) *non-publication* || ⟨jur⟩ *non-appearance*, *default*; wegen ~s verurteilen *to default*; ~de(r) [m] *defaulter* **~erwerbspersonen** f pl *unoccupied population* **~fachmann** m *outsider*, *layman* **≃fertig** a *unready* **≃gelernte** Arbeiter [pl] *unskilled labour* **~gelehrte(r)** m *unlearned p* **~gelingen** n = ~erfolg **~gewöhnung** f *want of habit* **~handeln** n *inaction* **~jude** m *gentile* **~kämpfer** m *noncombatant* **≃knüllend** a *wrinkleproof* **≃kommerziell** a ⟨aero⟩ ~e Landung *stop for nontraffic purposes* **≃kred·itgebend** a *non-credit* (*society*) **≃kriegführende** Staaten *nonbelligerent states* **~leiter** m ⟨el a.⟩ *insulator* **~militär** m *civilian* **~mitglied** n *non-member* **≃organis·iert** a; ~er Arbeiter [m] *non-unionist*; *non-society man* **~-raucher** m *non-smoker* || für ~! *smoking forbidden*! | ~abteil [n] ⟨rail⟩ *non-smoking compartment* **≃rostend** a *stainless* od *rustproof* (*steel*) **~s·achverständige(r)** m *non-expert* **~-schwimmer** m *non-swimmer* **~sein** n *non-existence*, *nonentity* **≃stubenrein** a ⟨fig⟩ *off-colo*(*u*)*r* (*joke*) **~treffer** m *miss* **~übereinstimmung** f *conflict* (*of evidence*, etc) **≃übertr·agbar** a *non-negotiable* (*receipt*), ⟨med⟩ *not contagious* [nur pred] **~ver-·antwortlichkeit** f *irresponsibility* **~verb·indlichkeit** f *immunity* **~(weiter)verbreitungsvertrag** m ⟨at⟩ *non-prolification treaty* **~vorh·andensein** n *absence* || ⟨philos⟩ *non-existence* **~weitergabe** f (v Kernwaffen) *non-prolification* **≃wiedergutzumachend** a *irreparable* (*loss*) **~wissen** n *ignorance*, *want of knowledge* **~wollen** n *unwillingness* **≃zahlend** a *defaulting* (*customer*) **~zahlung** f *non-payment* **~-zur Kenntnis-Nehmen** n ⟨psych⟩ (v Unangenehmem) *defence*, *-se mechanism* **≃zutreffend** a *inapplicable*

N·ichte f ~/~n *niece*

n·ichten adv; mit ~ *by no means*, *not at all* **n·ichtig** a (leer) *null*, *void* || (wertlos) *nugatory* || (ungültig) *invalid* || (eitel) *vain*, *airy* (*hopes*) || (nichtssagend) *empty*, *futile*, *flimsy* (*pretext*, *excuse*) || (wirkungslos) *ineffectual* || (vergänglich) *transitory*, *perishable* || für (null u) ~ erklären, ~ m *to annul*, *quash*, *abolish*; *to declare* (*null and*) *void* | **≃keit** f ~/ *invalidity* || *nullity* || *vanity*, *futility*, *nothingness*; ⟨fig⟩ *froth* || ~en [pl] *trifles* pl || die ~ alles Irdischen *world-worthlessness* **N·ichtigkeits- ~beschwerde** f ⟨jur⟩ = ~klage **~erklärung** f *nullification*, *annulment*, *invalidation* || ⟨jur⟩ *quashing a verdict*; *decree of nullity* (e–r Ehe) **~klage** f ⟨jur⟩ *plea of nullity* **~klausel** f *defeasance clause* **N·ichts** n ~/(~e) *nothingness* || ⟨philos⟩ (a. ⟨fig⟩ P) *nonentity* | (Geringfügigkeit, Einbildung) *insignificance*, *trifle*, *shadow*; *a mere nothing* | **aus** dem ~ (*raised*) *from utter obscurity*; aus dem ~ schaffen *to create .. from scratch* od *thin air* || **vor** dem ~ stehen *to be faced by complete ruin* **n·ichts A. 1.** [indef pron] *nothing*, *not anything*, *nought*, *naught*, *zero*; ⟨Am fam⟩ *nix* || er tat ~ *he did n.*, *he did not do anyth.* **2.** [adverbiell] *not at all*; *nowise*; *in n.* **B.** es ist ~ v **Belang** *it is of no consequence* || ~ Besseres *n. better* || ~ Genaueres *n. more precise* || °~ Genaues weiß man nicht *n. is known for certain* || es ist ~ **Gutes** an ihm *there is no good in him* || ~ Näheres *no particulars* od *details* pl || ~ Neues *n. new*, *no new th* || wissen Sie ~ Neues? *have you no news*? || es wird ~ **Rechtes** aus ihm w *he will never do any good* **C. absolut** ~ = durchaus ~ || ~ (anderes) als Sumpf *n. but bog*, *just a bog*, *a mere bog* || ~ als (*or* ×wie) *n. but*; *just* (*an ordinary man*); *mere* (*words*); ihr .. war ~ als .. *flirtation was her one occupation* || ~ **anderes** *n. else* || ~ außer *n. short of* || ~ da! *n. of the kind*! || ~ der Art, ~ dergleichen *no such th* || **durchaus** ~, (ganz u) gar ~, rein ~, ~ in der Welt *n. at all*, *n. whatever*, *n. in the world*, *not a th* || **fast** ~, nahezu ~ *next to n.* || ~ mehr *not any more*, *no*(*thing*) *more* || **mir** ~, dir ~ *quite coolly*, *as bold as brass*, *without so much as asking leave* || alles **oder** ~ *neck or n.* || sonst ~? ⟨a. iron⟩ *n. more* od *else*?, *is that all*?, *a.th. else*? || so viel wie ~ *next to n.* || ~ **weniger** als (das) *anything but* (*that*) || weiter ~ (?) *n. further* (*is that all*?) || ~ wert *of no value*; *no good* (*n.g.*) || ×~ **wie** los! *let's hop it*! → ~ als **D. 1.** das ist ~ **für** .. *that is not for* (*tender ears*); **für** (um) ~ u wieder ~ *without any cause* od *reason* (*whatever*), *for n.* (*at all*), *for no reason at all*, *for no earthly reason*, ⟨fam⟩ *for sth and n.* || (*he led us*) *gratuitously* (*into trouble*); sich **in** ~ auflösen (Wolke) *to break up* || es unterscheidet sich in ~ v *it cannot be distinguished from* || **mit** ~ anfangen *to start from scratch* od *on a shoe-string* || **um** ~ *for n.*; (*to play*) *for love* || um ~ besser (*he returned*) *none the better* || wir sind um ~ besser daran durch .. *the machine has not brought about any improvement* || **zu** ~ z gebrauchen *good for n.* **2.** es ist ~ **an** ihm *there is n. to him* || es ist ~ an der S daran *there's no truth in it*; ich kann daran ~ tun *there is n. I can do about it* || es ist ~ **damit**! *there is n. in it*!, *it is no go*! || ~ **davon** *none of it*; *she wouldn't have any* || ..! *not a word of that*! || das ist ~ **für** mich *that's not in my line*, *it's of no use for me* || ~ f ungut *don't take it amiss*, *don't think me rude* || ~ **von** .. *none of* (*that modesty*) || ~ v dem *no such th* || ~ **zum** Lachen *no laughing matter* **E.** für ~ **achten** *to think n.* od *little of* || ~ ahnend *innocent*(*ly*), *unsuspecting*(*ly*), *without any forebodings* || nach ~ **aussehen** *to look nohow* || es bleibt nichts übrig als zu tun *there is n. for it but to do* || es bleibt ihm ~ weiter übrig *he cannot do a.th. else* || ~ eintragend *unproductive* ⟨a. fig⟩ || zu ~ **führen**: *his success vanished into n.ness*; zu ~ führend *blind* (*reasoning*) || es geht ~ über *there is n. like* (*a swim*) || sie **h** ~ *they haven't got anyth.* || sie h ~ dagegen *they have no objection* || für ~ z h s *to be no good for anyth.* || er **kann**, leistet ~ *he is capable of n.* || er kommt zu ~ *he will succeed in n.* || es läßt sich ~ m (daran ändern) *there's n. to be done* (*that cannot be altered*) || es liegt mir ~ daran *it is n. to me* || das **macht**, schadet, tut ~, hat ~ zu sagen *that does not matter*, *is of no consequence* || ich mach mir ~ daraus *it is a matter of indifference to me*, ⟨fam⟩ *I don't care a pin* od *fig* || ~ z m, ~ los *n. doing* || **sein**: wenn es weiter ~ ist! *if that's all*! || er ist ~ weniger als reich *he is a.th. but rich* || es ist ~, wenn man alt wird *all is vanity when ..* || Sie brauchen sich um ~ z **sorgen** *there is n. for you to worry about* || das **tut** ~ zur S *that has n. to do with the matter* || ~ tun ⟨fig⟩ *to sit tight* || ~ mehr z tun h *to be out of work* || ~ Besseres **verlangen** *to ask no better* || das verschlägt ~ *that does not signify* || (zu) ~ w (v S) *to fall through*; *to fail*, *to come to nought* || es kann aus der S ~ w *n. can come of it*; *it can't be done* || aus ihm wird ~ w *he is a dead failure* || aus ~ wird ~ *from n. n. comes* || mit ~ **zufrieden** *never satisfied* **N·ichts- ≃bedeutend** a *insignificant* °**≃destotrotz**, **≃destow·eniger** adv *nevertheless*, *notwithstanding*, *after all*, *anyway*, *nonetheless* || [nachgestellt] *though* || ⟨Am⟩ *same time* **~könner** m *ignoramus* L; ⟨Am sl⟩ *nitwit* **~nutz** m *rotter*, *good-for-n.*, ⟨Am sl⟩

scalawag, beat ≃**nutzig** a *graceless, naughty, good-for-n.* **~nutzigkeit** f *naughtiness, gracelessness* ≃**sagend** a *futile, empty, void* ‖ *insignificant, inexpressive, meaningless, unmeaning* (*words, features*), *vain* (*pleasure*): ‖ *vague* (*promise*) ‖ *trivial, pointless* (*remark*), *colourless* (*girl*) ‖ ∼ aussehen *to look no-how*; (*his words*) *ring hollow* **~tuer** m *idler, loafer* ≃**tuerisch** a *idle* **~tun** n *idleness, inaction, supineness* **~wisser** m = ∼könner ≃**würdig** a *contemptible, vile, worthless, infamous, base* ‖ ∼er Mensch *villain* | ∼keit [f] *w.ness, villainy, b.ness*

N·ickel m ∼s/∼ *cad; nasty fellow* ‖ *tomboy*

N·ickel n ∼s/∼ **1.** n ⟨min⟩ *nickel* ‖ ≃plattiert *n.-plated* **2.** m ⟨Ger num⟩ *n. coin, small change* (10–50 Pf) ≃**haltig** d *n.ous* ∼**münze** f *n. c.* **~stahl** m *n. st.*

n·icken I. vi [h] **1.** (P) *to nod* (mit dem Kopf *one's head*), (zustimmend) .. *assent, one's agreement* ‖ (wiederholt) *to nid-nod* ‖ (winkend) *to beckon* ‖ (grüßend) *to bow* ‖ (schlummern) *to* (*take a*) *nap, to drop one's head* **2.** (v Pflanzen etc) *to droop, bend* **II.** ≃ n *nod*(*ding*), etc | ⟨a.⟩ **N·ickerchen** n (*cat*)*nap; snooze; forty winks*; ein ∼ m *to snooze, to take an easy* **N·ickhaut** f ⟨orn⟩ *nictitating membrane* ‖ ⟨hors⟩ *haw*

n·id [obd prep] (∼ dem Berg) *below*

Nidati·on [–ts–] f ∼/∼en ⟨physiol⟩ *nidation*

n·ie adv *never, at no time* ‖ fast ∼ *hardly ever* ‖ ∼ mehr *n. again* ‖ ∼ u nimmer *n. in all one's life* ‖ °wie noch ∼! *with a vengeance* | ∼ h wir .. gesehen *we have n. seen such magnificent breakers* ‖ ein noch ∼ gesehenes F. *fireworks of unrivalled beauty* ‖ e–e ∼ wiederkehrende Gelegenheit *an opp. that will n. recur*

n·ieden [adv] ⟨poet⟩ = unten; hie∼ = auf Erden

n·ieder I. [attr a] *low* (*standard, extraction, opinion, propensities*) ‖ *lower* (*nature; civil servants, ranks, courts of law*) ‖ *lower* od *lowest* od *humbler* (*classes*) ‖ *minor, inferior* (*official*) | (gemein) *vulgar* (*manners*), *common* (*people*); *base, mean* (*character*) | *menial* (*work*) | ∼er Adel, ∼e Geistlichkeit *lower grade of nobility, of the clergy* ‖ v ∼er Geburt, aus ∼em Stande *of humble, mean, low birth, descent, origin; low-born* ‖ ∼e Jagd (*shooting*) *small game* **II.** [adv] *down, low* ‖ der Mond etc ist ∼ *the m. has gone down, the fire has burnt out, the house has burnt down* ‖ auf u ∼ (*he walked*) *up and down* (*the room* im Zimmer) ‖ ∼ mit der Presse! *down with the Press!* **III.** [pref] **~|beugen, ~|biegen** vt [h] *to bend, bow* (a. sich), *turn down* ‖ ⟨fig⟩ jdn **~|beugen** *to depress, discourage a p; to damp a p's courage* **~|brechen** vt [h]/vi [s] *to break down* **~|brennen** vt [h]/vi [s] *to burn down* **~|bringen** vt [h] *to floor* (*a p*) **~|bücken,** sich [h] *to bow down, to stoop* **~deutsch** a *Low German* ≃**deutsche(r)** m *North German* ≃**deutschland** n *Lower Germany* **~|donnern** vi [h] *to come down with a crash* ‖ vt ⟨fig⟩ *to talk down* ≃**druck** m ⟨tech⟩ *low-pressure* **~|drücken** vt [h] *to press* od *weigh down* ⟨a. fig⟩ ‖ (unterdrücken) *to oppress* ‖ (Stimmung) *to sour* ‖ *to deaden* (*the flame*) ‖ (mutlos m) *to depress, grieve, distress* **~|ducken,** sich [h] *to squat down, to cower* (*down*) **~|fahren** vi [s] *to come* od *shoot down* ‖ *to descend* ⟨a. bib⟩ ≃**fahrt** f *descent* ≃**fall** m *downfall* **~|fallen** vi [s] *to fall down* od *prostrate* ‖ (auf .. herab) *her hair streamed over her shoulder* ‖ tot ∼ *to drop down dead* ‖ *his fist came down on the table* ‖ vor e–m ∼ *to throw o.s. at a p's feet* ≃**frequenz** f ⟨el⟩ *low frequency* ≃**gang** m (Mond) *setting*; (Westen) *West* ‖ ⟨mach⟩ *down-stroke* ‖ *descent* (*of a balloon*) ‖ ⟨fig⟩ *fall* (*of a regime*); *decline, decadence* **~gedrückt** a *dejected, depressed; dashed* (*look*) ‖ [pred] *down in the mouth* **~|gehen** vi [s] *to go* od *come down*(*ward*) ‖ (Vorhang) *to fall, drop* ‖ (Abhang) *to slope* (nach *to*) ‖ *her eyes drooped* ‖ (Sonne) *to set* ‖ (Gewitter etc) *to burst; to come down* ‖ ⟨aero⟩ *to land, alight; to dive* (*on a fleet*) **~geschlagen** a *downcast* (*eyes*) | ⟨fig⟩ *dejected, low-spirited, desponding, cast-down, downhearted; cut up* (über *about*) ‖ sich ∼ fühlen *to feel flat* | ≃heit [f] *despondency, dejection, low*(*ness of*) *spirits* pl **~gestreckt** a *prone, prostrate* **~|hageln** vi [s]: *blows fell in showers on them* ‖ ∼ l *to hail* (*blows*) (auf *on*) **~|halten** vt [h] *to hold down* ‖ *to keep* (*a fire*) *under* ‖ (Preis) *to keep down* ‖ ⟨fig⟩ *to suppress* (*indignation, a rebellion*); *to keep in hand, to curb, subdue* ‖ (durch Furcht) *to overawe* ‖ ⟨mil⟩ (Feind) *to neutralize* (*by fire*); *to bind .. in place* **~haltungsfeuer** n *neutralization fire* **~|hangen, ~|hängen** vi [h] *to hang down, to droop* ‖ mit ∼dem Haar *with loosely-flowing hair* **~|hauen** vt [h] *to hew* od *to cut down* ⟨a. mil⟩ **~|hocken** vi [s] (a. sich .. [h]) *to cower* **~|holen** vt (Flagge) *to haul down, to lower* ‖ *to bring down* (*a plane*) ≃**holz** n *underwood* **~|kämpfen** vt [h] *to outfight* ‖ *to fight down* (*feelings*) ‖ *to subdue, overcome* ‖ *to get the better of* ≃**kämpfung** f ⟨mil⟩ *reduction* N, *neutralization* **~kauern** vi [s] *to hunch up* **~|klappen** vt [h] *to flap* od *fold, turn down* °**~|knallen** vt [h] *to shoot* (*down*) ‖ e–m mit ≃ drohen *to hold a p up at the pistol-point* **~|knien** vi [s] *to kneel down* **~|k** vi [s] (auf die Erde) *to come to earth* ‖ *to lie in, to be brought to bed; to be confined* od *delivered* (mit *of*); *to give birth* (*to*) ‖ vor der Zeit ∼ *to miscarry* ≃**kunft** f *delivery, childbirth, child-bearing; lying-in, confinement* ‖ unzeitige ∼ *miscarriage* ‖ Zahl der ≃e ⟨stat⟩ *confinement order* od *rank* **~|krachen** vi [s]: *the pot threshed down* ≃**lage** f **1.** ⟨mil⟩ *reverse; overthrow, defeat* ⟨a. fig⟩ ‖ ⟨sport⟩ *defeat, licking*; ⟨fam⟩ *upset* ‖ ⟨fig⟩ gr ∼ *knock-out* ‖ jdm e–e ∼ beibringen *to bring about* od *to inflict a decisive victory over* ‖ e–e ∼ erhalten, erleiden ⟨pol⟩ *to take a beating, to suffer a defeat* (durch *at the hands of*) ‖ völlige ∼ *discomfiture* **2.** ⟨com⟩ *depot, warehouse* ‖ *branch establishment* **~|lassen** vt [h] *to let down* ‖ *to drop* (*a burden, curtain*) ‖ *to lower* (*a flag*) | sich ∼ *to sit down, to take a seat,* .. auf e–n Stuhl *to settle o.s. in* (od *lower o.s. into*) *a chair, to drop into a chair*; (behaglich) *to ensconce* ‖ ⟨com⟩ *to set up shop* ‖ (S) *to descend* ‖ ⟨orn⟩ *to alight* ‖ ⟨fig⟩ *silence closed over the house* (auf [dat]) ‖ *to install o.s.* (*at an inn*) ‖ (auf die Erde) *to come to earth* ‖ ⟨com⟩ *to set up* (*in business*), *to establish o.s.* (als *as*) ‖ (of doctor) *to set up* ‖ (sich ansiedeln) *to settle* (*down*) ⟨a. übtr & fig⟩ ≃**lassung** f *office, establishment* ‖ *domiciliation* ‖ (Kolonie) *settlement, colony* | ∼srecht [n] *right of domicile* **~|legen** vt [h] *to lay* od *put down* ⟨a. übtr⟩ (*rules*) ‖ *to formulate* (*thoughts*) ‖ *to ground* ‖ (etw) *to deposit* ⟨a. com⟩ (*money*) ‖ *to warehouse* (*goods*) ‖ *to place* od *lay* (*a wreath* [an] *on a grave*) ‖ *to put .. to bed* ‖ *to take* od *pull down* (*a house*) ‖ (die Waffen) *to lay down* (*arms*) | *to resign* (*an office*); ⟨fam⟩ *to send one's book, to throw up*; (Krone) *to abdicate* (*the throne*) ‖ *to give up* (*the command*) ‖ ⟨parl⟩ *to vacate* (*one's seat*) ‖ (Geschäft) *to retire from* ‖ (die Arbeit) *to down tools, to go on strike* | sich ∼ *to lie down* (auf *on*), *to go to bed* od *rest* ≃**legung** f *laying down* ‖ *abdication, retirement, resignation* **~|liegen** vi [h] *to lie down, to be in bed* (an *with influenza*); ∼d ⟨bot⟩ *decumbent* **~|m** vt [h] *to stab, kill* ‖ *to cut down* **~|mähen** vt [h] *to mow down* (*troops*) **~|metzeln** vt [h] *to massacre, slaughter, butcher* ≃**metzelung** f *massacre, slaughter* ≃**moor** n *fen* **~|prallen** vi [s]: *the sun beat down upon them* **~|prasseln** vi/t [s] (of rain) *to pelt; to patter down* ‖ ⟨fig⟩ *to pour* (*over*) ‖ er läßt Schläge ∼ *he rains blows* **~|reden** vt [h] *to talk* od *argue down* **~|reißen** vt irr [h] *to pull, take, tear, sweep down* (*a house*), *to demolish; to break down* (*barriers*) ‖ ⟨mil⟩ *to raze* **~reißung** f *pulling down, demolition* **~|reiten** vt [h] (jdn, etw) ∼ *to gallop* (*a p, a th*) *down* **~|ringen** vt

[h] *to overpower*; ⟨übtr⟩ *to get under control* ‖ ⟨fig⟩ *to wear down* (*a p*) ‖ *I can wrestle anyone* **~|säbeln** vt [h] *to cut down, to sabre* **~|schießen** vt [h] *to shoot* (⟨Am a.⟩ *gun*) *down, to shoot* (*at sight*) **|** vi [s] *to rush down* ‖ (of eagle) *to pounce* od *swoop* (*down*) **≗schlag** m ⟨chem⟩ *precipitate*; *deposit* ‖ *sediment* ‖ (Regen) *moisture*, ⟨a.⟩ ≗e pl *rain*(*fall*); *precipitation* ‖ ⟨at⟩ *fall-out deposits* ⟨Lit⟩ *literary expression, result, issue, echo* ‖ ⟨mus⟩ *thesis* **~|schlagen** vt [h] *to strike* od *to beat down* ‖ *to fell* (*trees*) ‖ *to knock* (*a p*) *down*, ⟨Am sl⟩ *to sand-bag* ‖ ⟨box⟩ *to knock down* **|** ⟨fig⟩ *to discourage, dispirit, dishearten* ‖ ⟨fig⟩ –ge– (durch) *stunned, depressed, dejected* (*by*) ‖ (Hoffnung) *to disappoint* ‖ *to calm down* (*feelings*) ‖ (e–e S) *to hush up* (*a matter*) ‖ (e–n Prozeß) *to stop, quash*; *to put an end to*; ⟨Am⟩ *to nolle-pros* **|** (Angriff) *to defeat* ‖ (Bewegung) *to smash* ‖ (Widerstand) *to bear, beat, put down*; *to crush, suppress* ‖ *to stamp out, to quell* (*a revolt*) **|** ⟨chem⟩ *to precipitate* **|** die Augen ~ *to cast down* od *to lower one's eyes* **|** sich ~: *the mist fell* ‖ ⟨fig⟩ *to be represented* od *reflected, to find shape* (*in poetry*) ‖ *to be realized* **|** vi [s] *to fall* od *tumble down*; → –ge– **~schlagend** a *disheartening* ‖ ⟨chem⟩ *precipitant* ‖ ⟨med⟩ *sedative, calming* **≗schlags-** ~gefäß [n] *precipitation-vessel*; ~messer [m] *rain ga*(*u*)*ge*; ~verteilung [f] ⟨at⟩ *fall-out pattern* **≗schlagung** f *striking down* ‖ *felling* ‖ *quashing* ‖ *suppression* ‖ *precipitation* **~|schlucken** vt [h] *to swallow down* **~|schmettern** vt [h] *to dash to the ground* ‖ ⟨fig⟩ *to overwhelm, crush* **‖** ~d [a] (P) ⟨a.⟩ *depressing* **~|schreiben** vt [h] *to write down*; *to take, note, put down* (*in writing*); *to pen* (*a description*); *to endite* (*a poem*) ‖ –geschrieben w (*everything must*) *go down* **~|schreien** vt [h] *to shout down* (*a p*) ‖ *to howl down* (*a play*) **≗schrift** f *record, copy* **~|senken** vt [h] *to let down, to lower* ‖ sich ~ *to sink down*; (Nacht) *to set in* **~|setzen** vt [h] *to deposit*; *to set* od *put down* ‖ *to install* (*a p*) *on a chair* ‖ sich ~ *to sit down* (an e–n Tisch *to a table*); ⟨orn⟩ *to perch down* ‖ (wohnhaft) *to settle* **~|sinken** vi [s] *to sink* od *drop down*; (im Wasser) *to go to the bottom* **|** ⟨met⟩ *descent* **≗spannung** f ⟨tech⟩ *low-tension* **|** ~smotor *l.-t. motor* **~|stechen** vt [h] *to stab* **~|steigen** vi [s] *to descent* (*a mountain*; *from heaven*), *to step* od *come down* (*the stairs*) **~|stoßen** vt [h] *to knock* od *strike down, to stab* ‖ vi [s] *to pounce down* (auf *upon*) **~|strekken** vt [h] *to knock* od *bring down*; *to floor* ⟨a. fig⟩ ‖ *to ground* (*arms*) ‖ (töten) *to lay down, to slay* **~|stürzen** vi [s] *to tumble* od *fall down* ‖ vt [h] *to hurl down* **~tor** n (Schleuse) *aft gate* **≗tracht** f *meanness* ‖ *dirty trick* **~trächtig** a *base, sordid, dirty, vile, low, mean*; *disgraceful* ‖ *cowardly* (*lie*), *dastardly* (*invention*), *wretched* (*intrigue*), *scurvy* (*treatment*) ‖ ⟨fam⟩ *beastly, disgusting* (*affair*) ‖ *awful* (*pain*) ‖ adv *beastly, horribly* (*cold*); ~ handeln ⟨a.⟩ *to play it* (*rather*) *low down* **|** ≗keit [f] *baseness, meanness, vileness* ‖ ⟨fam⟩ *beastliness* ‖ [konkret] *base action*; *villainy* **~|treten** vt [h] *to tread* od *to trample down* ‖ *to run down* (*one's heels*) **~wärts** adv *down*(*wards*) **~|werfen** vt [h] *to throw, fling, cast, slam down* ‖ ⟨fig⟩ (jdn) *to down*; *to lay a p on his back* ‖ *to crush* (*a rising*) ‖ (of storm) *to prostrate* (*trees*) ‖ sich ~ *to drop down, to prostrate o.s., to fall prostrate* (vor *before*) ‖ –geworfen w *to be laid low* od *stricken down* (*by grief*) **≗werfung** f *overthrow* ‖ *suppression* (*of a rising*); völlige ~ ⟨mil⟩ *debellation* **~wild** n *ground game* **~|ziehen** vt [h] *to drag* od *draw down* **N·iederung** f ~/~en *low ground, lowland, flat* ‖ *depression* ‖ ⟨Am⟩ *bottom land, piedmont* ‖ ⟨fig⟩ *lower ranks* (*of society*) **~smoor** n *fen*; *flat bog*

N·ieder- ⟨geog⟩ [in comp] **~deutschland** n *Lower* (od *North*) *Germany* **~lande** n pl; die ~ *the Netherlands* **≗ländisch** a *Dutch* (*Literature*); *Netherlands* (*the N. Minister*) ‖ ~ m *to Dutchify* **~österreich** n *Lower Austria* **~rhein** m *Lower Rhine* **~sachsen** n *Lower Saxony*

n·iedlich a *neat, nice* ‖ (zart) *dainty, delicate* ‖ *elegant* (*verses, compliments, jokes*) ‖ (hübsch) *pretty*; ⟨Am⟩ *cute*, ⟨fam⟩ *cunning* (*little baby*) ‖ °das ist ja ~! *that's a pretty state of ths!* **| ≗keit** f ~/ *neatness, delicacy* ‖ *prettiness*

N·iednagel m ~s/≗ *agnail, hang-nail*, → Neid

n·iedrig a *low* (→ hoch) **|** ⟨fig⟩ *base, mean, vile* (*character*) ‖ *menial, dirty* (*work*) ‖ *conservative* (*figure*) ‖ *cheap* (*place*) ‖ *inferior* (*race*) ‖ ⟨com⟩ *short* (*premium*) ‖ *low*(*ly*), *humble* (*birth, descent*) ‖ *vulgar* (*passions*) ‖ *bad* (*taste*) ‖ ~er w (of tide) *to neap*; ~ster Niederwasserstand (NNW) *minimum* od *lowest water level* **| adv** (Ort) ~ liegen *to lie at a low level*; (Kopf) *to lie low* ‖ ~ fliegen, brennen *to fly, burn low* ‖ ~ geschätzt *conservatively valued* (auf *at*) ‖ den Preis ~ stellen *to charge a low price* ‖ ~ geboren *of humble birth* ‖ jdn ~ schätzen *to have a low estimation of a p* ‖ sehr ~ stehen ⟨fig⟩ *to stand at a minimum* ‖ ~ halten *to keep down* (*prices*); möglichst ~ *to keep* (*requests*) *as few as possible* ‖ ~er stimmen *to lower* (*the pitch*) **| ≗keit** f ~/ *lowness* ‖ ⟨fig⟩ *baseness, meanness, lowliness, humbleness* ‖ *vulgarity* ‖ ⟨com⟩ *moderateness, lowness* **≗mietenbezirk** m *low rent area* **≗preisland** n *low wage country* **≗stand-** *low-level* (*warning light*) **~stehend** a *low-class* (*theatre*) **≗wasser(stand** m) n *low water* (*level*); kleinstes ~ *minimum flow at low water*

niell·ieren vi/t [h] *to* (*work in*) *niello*

n·iemals adv *never, at no time* ‖ [abs] *I should think so* od *not* **n·iemand** pron *nobody, no one, no man, not .. anybody* ‖ *nobody prevents you, do they*? (oder doch?) ‖ ~ als *none but* ‖ ~ anders *nobody else* (als *as*) ‖ ~ Fremdes *no stranger* ‖ ~ mehr? *anybody else*? **|** ≗sland [n] *no man's land*

N·iere f ~/~n ⟨anat⟩ *kidney* ‖ ⟨min⟩ *nodule, pocket* ‖ wandernde ~ *floating k.* ‖ ~n [pl] ⟨arch a.⟩ *reins* pl; zu den ~n gehörig *renal* ‖ ⟨fig⟩ es geht ihm auf die ~n *that cuts him to the quick* ‖ → Herz **N·ieren- ~baum** m ⟨bot⟩ *cashew*(*-tree*) **~beckenentzündung** f *pyelitis* **~beschwerden** f pl = ~krankheit **~braten** m *roast loin* **~entzündung** f ⟨med⟩ *nephritis*; durch ~ entstanden *nephritic* (*changes*); (mit Bezug auf harnabsondernde Zellen) *nephrotic* **~fett** n *suet* **≗förmig** a *k.-shaped*; ⟨minr⟩ *drusy* **~grieß** m ⟨med⟩ *gravel in the k.s* **~kartoffel** f *k. p.* **≗krank** a *suffering from the k.s* **~krankheit** f *disease of the k.s, nephritic disorder* **~schmerz** m *nephralgy* **~schnitt** m ⟨surg⟩ *nephrotomy* **~stein** m ⟨med⟩ *k.* od *nephritic stone, gravel*, ⟨scient⟩ *renal calculus* ‖ ‖ ⟨min⟩ *jade* **~stück** n *loin of veal with the k.s* **~talg** m *suet* **~tisch** m *k. t.* **~weh** n ⟨path⟩ *nephralgy* **≗weise** adv ⟨min⟩ *in nodules*

N·ies- ~krampf m *spasmodic sneezing* **~mittel** n *sternutatory* **~pulver** n *sneezing-powder* **~wurz** f *hellebore* **n·ieseln** vi [h] *to snuffle* ‖ (fein regnen) *to drizzle* **N·ieselpriem** m ~s/~e *empty braggart*

n·iesen vi [h] *to sneeze* ‖ °ich werde dir was ~ *you may whistle for it* ‖ ≗ [n] ~s/ *sneezing*; ein ~ *a sneeze* ‖ ~ erregend *sternutatory*

N·ieß- ~brauch m ⟨jur⟩ *usufruct* ‖ lebenslänglicher ~ *life-interest*; (an Grundstück) *estate for life* **~braucher** m *usufructuary*

Niet m ~(e)s/~en *rivet*; mit ~ u Nagel *lock and stock* **≗- u n·agelfest** *clinched and r.ed*; was nicht .. (*everything*) *that is* (*was*) *not red hot or nailed down* ‖ ~er Gegenstand [m] *fixture* **~hammer** m, **~kluppe** f *r.ing-hammer* **~kolben** m *holding-up tool* **~nagel** m *rivet* **~schweißung** f *rivet welding* **~stärke** f *diameter of a r.* **~stift** m *pin* **n·ieten** vt [h] *to rivet, to clinch* **≗hose** f (*blue*) *jeans* pl

N·iete f ~/~n *blank* ‖ (*the play was a*) *failure*; ⟨sl⟩ *lemon, washout*; ⟨mil⟩ *total loss* ‖ e–e ~ ziehen *to draw a blank* ‖ ⟨fig⟩ (P) *flop*; *dead nut*

N·iger m (Fluß & Staat in W.-Afrika)

Nig·erien n *Nigeria* (W.-Afrika); → Biafra

Nihil·ismus m ~/ *nihilism* **Nihil·ist** m ~en/~en *nihilist* **nihil·istisch** a *nihilist(ic)*

Nikob·aren f pl (hinterind.) *Nicobar Islands* pl

Nikot·in n ~(e)s/ *nicotine* ‖ mit ~ vergiften *to nicotinize* **~herz** n *smoker's heart* **~säure** f *nicotinic acid* **~vergiftung** f *nicotine-poisoning*

N·il m ~s/ *Nile* **~delta** n *delta of the Nile* **~messer** m *nilometre* **~pferd** n *hippopotamus*; ⟨fig⟩ (P) *grampus* **~pferdpeitsche** f *sjambok*

N·imbus m ~/~se *nimbus, halo* ‖ ⟨fig⟩ *prestige* ‖ *authority* ‖ s–n ~ verlieren *to suffer an eclipse* ‖ jdn s–s ~ entkleiden *to strip a p of his nimbus*; ⟨fam⟩ *to debunk a p* ‖ sich in e–n ~ hüllen, sich mit e–m ~ umkleiden *to clothe o.s. with a halo*

Nîmes n (Stadt) (Südfrankreich)

nimm([s]**t**) imp ([2.] 3. sg pres) v nehmen (→ B.)

n·immer(mehr) adv **1.** *never (again)* (→ nie) ‖ (nicht mehr) *not any longer* **2.** (ganz u gar nicht) *by no means* ‖ nie u ~! *never more*; nun u ~ *never, never* **(St.)** **≗leinstag** m (am) *(on) the Greek Kalends*, ⟨Am⟩ *the 31st of February* **~müde** a *tireless*; *unsleeping*; *unflinching* **≗satt** m ~(e)s/~e *glutton* ‖ ~ a *insatiable* **≗w·iedersehen** n; auf ~ *never to meet again*, ⟨fam⟩ *on the never*; er verschwand auf ~ *he .. and was never seen again*

N·imwegen n (holländ. Stadt) *Nimeguen*

Ningpo n (chines. Stadt)

†**N·inive** [–fe:] n (Hptst. v Assyrien) *Nineveh*

N·iob n ~s/, Ni·obium [n] *niobium*

N·ipp[1] m ~(e)s/~e *sip* ‖ e–n ~ tun *to take a sip* **~flut** f *neap-tide* **n·ippen** vt/i [h] *to (take a) sip* (an *of*, aus *from*)

N·ipp[2] **~sachen** f pl (a. **N·ippes** pl) *fancy ware, trinkets*; *objects of virtu* **~tisch** m *what-not, fancy-table*

N·ippel m ~s/~ ⟨tech⟩ *nipple*

n·irgend(s), ~wo(h·in) [adv] *nowhere, not anywhere* ‖ ich komme ~ mehr hin *I never go anywhere* ‖ *we couldn't find a trace* (od ⟨fam⟩ *hide nor hair) of him* ‖ bei ihm will es ~ reichen *he can never make both ends meet* **≗land** n *utopia*; *Erewhon* (= *nowherE*) **~wohin** [adv] *nowither*

N·ische f ~/~n *niche, recess, bay*

°**N·ischel** m ~s/~ (Kopf) *noodle, nut, pannikin*

†**N·ischni N·owgorod** n ⟨Russ⟩ (Stadt an der Wolga) *Nijni Novgorod*; → Gorki

N·isse f ~/~n ⟨ent⟩ *nit* **n·issig** a *full of nits*

N·ist- ~kasten m *breeding-cage* **n·isten** vi [h] *to (make one's) nest* ‖ ⟨fig⟩ *to nestle*; ⟨scient⟩ *to nidificate, nidify* | ≗ [n] ~s/ *nestling*

ˣ**nit** = nicht (trink aber ~)

Nitr·at n ~(e)s/~e ⟨chem⟩ *nitrate* **nitr·ieren** vt [h] *to nitrate* **nitr·ierhärten** vt [h] *to nitride* **N·itro- ~glyzer·in** n *nitroglycerine* **~lack** m (Zellulosenitratlack) *nitrocellulose lacquer* **~zellul·ose** f *nitrocellulose*

Niveau [ni'vo:] n ~s/~s *level* (⟨a. fig⟩ *moral l.*) ‖ ⟨arts⟩ *standard* ‖ ⟨fig⟩ ~ h *to be above the average* ‖ (etw) auf das gleiche ~ bringen, stellen *to level, equate* ‖ (jdn) auf sein eigenes ~ herabdrücken *to bring .. down to one's level* **≗los** a *of a very low standard* **~regulierung** f ⟨tech⟩ *levelling control*; [konkr] *l. c. device* **~schema** f *level scheme* **~trennung** f ⟨rail⟩ *grade separation* **~übergang** m ⟨rail⟩ *level-crossing* **Nivell·ier- ~instrument** n *levelling-instrument* **~latte** f *l.g staff* **~waage** f *level* **nivell·ieren** vt [h] *to level* ‖ ≗ [n], **Nivell·ierung** f *levelling, levelment* ‖ ⟨fig⟩ *levelling process*

n·ix dial & fam → nicht(s)

Nix m ~es/~e *water-sprite, nick, nix, merman* **~chen** n *little merman* od *mermaid* **N·ixe** f ~/~n *water-sprite, -fairy, nymph, nixie, mermaid, undine*

N·izza n ⟨Fr⟩ (Stadt) *Nice*

Nj·assa- ~land n *Nyasaland* **~see** m *Nyassa*

N·j·emen, Niemen m (in †Ostpreußen Memel)

Nob·elpreis(träger) m *Nobel prize(-winner)*

n·obel a *noble* ‖ (vornehm) *smart, swagger* ‖ *stylish, elegant, grand* ‖ (freigebig) *free-handed, munificent, liberal* ‖ *generous (tips)*; *expensive (hobbies)* | sich ~ zeigen *to show generosity* ‖ immer ~! *always play the gentleman!* ‖ ~ geh' die Welt zugrunde! *the world must go down proudly!* ‖ *elegantly (dressed)* ‖ **N·oble(r)** m ~n/~n *noble* ⟨a. Eg hist⟩ **nobilit·ieren** vt [h] *to ennoble* **Nobl·esse** [–'es] f ~/ *nobility* ‖ *smartness* ‖ *generosity*

noch[1] conj *nor*; → weder .. noch

n·och[2] adv **1. (zeitlich)** *still, (as) yet* **A.** ~ am selben Tage *the very same day* ‖ ~ bis jetzt *to this very hour* ‖ ~ eben *or* gerade .. *(escaped) by the skin of one's teeth*; *N., so recently an atheist, became ..* ‖ erst ~ vorige Woche *no longer ago than* (od *as recently as*) *last week* ‖ das müssen wir ~ erst abwarten! *wait and see!* ‖ er soll erst ~ fertig m *he is to finish his work yet* ‖ ~ gestern *only* od *but y.* ‖ ~ heute *this very day* ‖ ~ immer *still (no letter!)* ‖ (selbst) ~ im 19. Jh. *as* (od *even so*) *late as the 19th century* ‖ ~ jetzt *even now* ‖ ~ vor kurzem *until recently* ‖ ~ vor 2 Tagen (e–r Woche) *only 2 days (as recently as a week) ago* **B.** du wirst es ~ **bereuen** *you will rue it yet* ‖ er erreichte ~ gerade .. *he just managed to catch the train* ‖ ⟨iron⟩ das fehlte nur ~! *that would be the limit!* ‖ er hat ~ Geld *he has still some m.* ‖ du hast ja ~ welche! *you have some!* (wozu neue?) ‖ er hat nur ~ .. *he has but 5 s left* ‖ das mag ~ hingehen *that may pass muster* ‖ er wird (schon) ~ k *he will come yet* ‖ er kommt ~ an den Galgen! *he'll live to be hanged!* ‖ ~ **leben**: *he may still live many years*; (⟨Am⟩ *he lived*) *back (in '65)* ‖ *before he had well left the house* ‖ ~ ist k–r *or* als er ~ ein Kind war *when quite a child* ‖ was war's doch ~ *what was it now* ‖ er ist ~ gewachsen *he has grown still more* ‖ **C. [mit compr]** *even (better, larger, less [than])* ‖ ~ 5mal **größer** *five times as large* ‖ ~ lieber hätte ich *still more should I like, I should even prefer* ‖ 100 oder ~ mehr *100 or even more* ‖ das wäre ja ~ schöner *that would be the limit* ‖ es war ~ nicht (später als) 10 Uhr *it was not more than 10 o'clock* ‖ nur ~ seltsamer: *the happiness was made the stranger by ..* ‖ ~ stärker *stronger still* **D. [neg]** er war ~ **kaum** .. *before he had well left the house* ‖ ~ ist k–r *or* niemand da *as yet no one has turned up* ‖ ~ **nicht** *not yet*; ⟨ten⟩ *not ready*; ~ nicht 40 Jahre *on the sunny side of 40* ‖ ~ lange nicht *not by a long way* ‖ bis jetzt ~ nicht: *hitherto he has never known what want means* ‖ wenn er schon älter ist, ist er ~ (lange) nicht .. *though he is older than I he is far from being my superior* ‖ ~ nichts *nothing yet* ‖ ~ nie *never (yet)* **2. (außerdem)** ~ (dazu) *in addition (to that), further, besides* ‖ auch ~ *also, moreover, into the bargain, on the back* od *top of it* ‖ ~ ein .. *another (word, hour, cup of tea)*; ~ e–e M. *one mile more* ‖ er u ~ einige *he and some others* ‖ ~ einmal *once more* od *again*; *yet* od *over again* ‖ ~ einm·al so viel (gr) *as much (tall) again* ‖ ~ eins, ~ etw *one th more*; *someth. else* ‖ ~ etw? *anything else?* ‖ ~ etw! *just another matter* ‖ ~ etw Pudding? *a second helping of p.?* ‖ ~ **u** ~ *(he had money, time, etc) to burn*; [abs] ~ **u** ~! *without end! plenty (of money)!* ‖ ~ obendrein = ~ dazu; *over and above that* ‖ wer, was, wo ~? *who, what, where else?* ‖ was wollen Sie ~? *what more do you want* **3. [concess]** ~ **so**: **sei es ~ so wenig** *be it ever so little* ‖ Berge ~ so hoch *mountains however* (od *ever so*) *high* ‖ wäre er ~ so reich *though he may be ever so rich, if he were as rich again* ‖ wenn auch ~ so kl *no matter how small*; *however (old it might be)*; *(will-power) however (great)* ‖ u wenn du (auch) ~ so (sehr) bittest .. *and however much you beg*; *if he works* *ever so hard; he might look as imploring as he liked* **⁓geschäft** n ⟨com⟩ *call for more* **~mal** adv **1.** *once more;* ⟨theat⟩ *encore!* **2.** ~m·al so viel *twice as much, as much again* || ⟨emph⟩ zum Kuckuck (~m·al)! *hang it (all)!* **~malig** a ⟨oft⟩ *re-(examination)* || *repeated, reiterated; renewed (thanks)* || bei ~er Prüfung *on re-examination* || bei ~er Überlegung *on second thoughts* **~mals** adv *once more* od *again*

N·ock 1. n ~s/~s (äußerstes Ende) ⟨naut⟩ *peak (of a gaff)* || *yard-arm* || *wing (of the bridge)* **2.** m *rocky hill-top*

N·öck m ~s/~e = Nick *water-sprite*

N·ocke f ~/~n, [dim] **~rl** n ~rls/~rl(n) *dumpling*

N·ocken m ~s/~ ⟨mech⟩ *cam* **~steuerung** f *cam control; cam-gear* **~welle** f *cam shaft*

°**n·ödeln** vi [h] *to tarry, loiter, linger*

No·etik f ~/ (Erkenntnislehre) *noetics* pl

°**N·ölpeter** m *dawdler, slow-coach,* ⟨Am⟩ *-poke*

Nom·ade m ~n/~n *nomad* | ~nleben [n] *n.ic life, wigwam way of life* **nom·adisch** a *n.ic* **nomadis·ieren** vi [h] *to lead a n.ic life*

N·omen n ~s/-mina ⟨gram⟩ *noun (substantive* od *adjective)* **~klat·ur** f ~/~en *nomenclature; terminology* **Nomin·al-** ~betrag, ~wert [m] *nominal value;* ~gewicht [n] *standard weight;* ~satz [m] *normal price* **~·ismus** m ~/ ⟨philos⟩ *nominalism* **N·ominativ** m ~s/~e ⟨gram⟩ *nominative* **nomin·ell** a ⟨com⟩ *nominal* || *titular (ruler)* || *token (resistance, strike,* etc) **nomin·ieren** vt [h] *nominate*

N·omo- **~gramm** n *nomogram* **~graph·ie** f *-graphy*

Non- **~chal·ance** [nɔ̃ːʃaˈlɑ̃ːs] f *carelessness, inconsiderateness, languor* **⁓chal·ant** [nɔ̃ːʃaˈlɑ̃ː] a *careless, inconsiderate; languid* **~flam-** *nonflammable, safety (film)* **~konform·ist** m ~en/~en ⟨pol⟩ *dissenter*

N·one f ~/~n ⟨R. C. & ant⟩ *none* || ⟨mus⟩ *ninth* **N·onius** m ~/~ *vernier*

N·onne f ~/~n **1.** *nun* **2.** ⟨orn⟩ *nun* **3.** ⟨ent⟩ *nun (moth)* **4.** ⟨arch⟩ *concave tile* **N·onnen-** **~kloster** n *nunnery, convent* **~leben** n *convent-* (od *nun's) life* **~weihe** f *taking the veil* **~zelle** f *nun's cell*

Nonpar·eille f ~/ (Schriftgrad v 6 Punkten) *nonpareil (6-point body size)*

Nonplus·ultra n ~/ *height (of folly)* || *acme*

Nonst·opflug m ⟨aero⟩ *non-stop flight;* (den Ozean) **nonstop** [adv] überqueren ⟨aero⟩ *to span*

N·opp- ~eisen [n] *burling iron;* ~zange [f] *tweezers*

N·oppe f ~/~n ⟨weav⟩ *pile, nap* **n·oppen** vt [h] *to nap (-ped material)* **N·opper** m ~s/~ *burler*

N·ord m ~(e)s/~e *north* || mw = mißweisend ~ *magnetic N.* || geographisch *or* rw = rechtweisend ~ *true N.* || aus ~ *from the N.* || (Wind) *north wind* || ⟨naut⟩ ~ m *to make northing* | ~, Süd, Ost, West – tohus (= zu Hause) is best *I am under my vine and fig-tree* **~abschnitt** m ⟨mil⟩ *northern sector* **~·afrika** n *North Africa* **~armee** f ⟨mil⟩ *army of the North* **~atlantikpakt**-Organisation [f] *North Atlantic Treaty Organization (NATO)* | ~rat [m] *N. A. Council* N **~kap** n *North Cape* **~länder** m *Northman, inhabitant of the north, northerner* **~landreise** f *northern trip* || *arctic expedition* **~licht** n *northern light(s* pl), *aurora borealis* **~ost** m *north-east* (zu Nord *by north*) || (Wind) *north-east wind,* ⟨naut⟩ *north-easter* **⁓östlich** a *north-eastern, north-easterly* **~·ostwärts** (⟨mil⟩ = –östlich); ~ v .. *to the n.e. of* **~-Ostsee-Kanal** m *N.-Sea-Baltic Canal* **~pol** m *north-pole, arctic pole* **~pol·armeer** n Nördliches Eismeer *Arctic Ocean;* **~polfahrer** m *arctic explorer* **~polfahrt** f *arctic expedition* **~rand** m *northern outskirts (of a town)* **~schein** m *northern light* **~see** f *North Sea, German Ocean* **~seite** f *north side* || an der ~ *on its north* **~staaten** m pl *Northern States* pl ⟨a. Am⟩ **~stern** m *North Star* **⁓wärts** adv *northward(s)* **~w·est** m *north-west* **⁓w·estlich** a *north-western (corner), northwest(erly)* (v *of)* **~w·estwind** m *north-west wind, north-wester* **~-wind** m *north wind* **N·orden** m ~s/ *north;* die Berge im ~ *the northern m.s;* im ~ v *(B.lies) to the north of (L.)* || ⟨übtr⟩ *people living in northern parts,* etc || (ge)gen *or* nach ~ *to(wards) the N., northward, in a northerly direction* || der gemäßigte ~ *the moderate northern zone* || der hohe ~ *the extreme northern latitude* || der nebelige ~ *the foggy northern regions* **n·ordisch** a **1.** *northern (sky, forests, culture)* **2.** ⟨hist⟩ *Norse (language)* || ~e Völker *Scandinavians* pl **3.** ⟨ethn⟩ *Nordic (race)* || ~er Mensch *Nordic* || ⁓er Rat (Dänemark, Finnland, Island, Norwegen und Schweden) *Northern Council* **n·ördlich** a; [nur attr] *northern (hemisphere, coast, course), north (wind)* || [pred] ~ v *(to* od *in the) North of* || [a & adv] *northerly (wind)* || 30° ~er Breite *30 degrees north latitude* || das ⁓e Eismeer *the Arctic Ocean* || [adv] ~ steuern *to steer in a northern direction* || [compr] ~er *farther to the N.*

Nord(-) ⟨geog⟩ [in comp] ~albanische Alpen f pl *North Albanian Alps* **~-Dak·ota** n (Staat der U.S.A.) *North Dacota* **~deutsche T·iefebene** f *(Northern) German Lowlands* pl **~erney** [-ˈai] n ⟨Ger⟩ (Nordseeinsel) **~häuser,** ~ Korn [m] ⟨Ger⟩ *whisky from Nordhausen* **~kap** n *North Cape* **~karolina** n (Staat der U.S.A.) *North Carolina* **⁓liche Eismeer,** das *the Arctic Ocean* **~ostseekanal** m (in Holstein) → Nord **~pol** m *north-pole, arctic pole* **~pol·argebiet** n *arctic region(s* pl) **~pol·armeer** n → Nördliches Eismeer **~see** f *North Sea, German Ocean* **~westterrit·o-rien** n pl (v Kanada) *Northwest Territories*

N·orfolk [ˈnɔːfək] n ⟨Engl⟩ **~inseln** f pl (im Stillen Ozean) *N. Islands*

n·örgeln vi [h] *to grumble, cavil* (an [dat] über *at, about)* || *to nag, carp (at a p)* || ~de Kritik *fault-finding critique* **Nörgel·ei** f, **n·örgelig** a *nagging, grumbling, querulous* **N·örgler** m *grumbler, grouser, nagger;* alter ~ *old crab* || ⟨Am sl⟩ *kicker, knocker*

†**N·oricum** n (Land zw. Donau, Inn, Karn. Alpen u Wiener Wald)

N·orische Alpen pl *Noric Alps*

N·orm f ~/~en *norm, standard, rule, size* || Strahlungs⁓ ⟨at⟩ *st. of radiation;* Sicherheits⁓ *safety st.* || ⟨typ⟩ *signature* || als ~ gelten *to serve as a st.* **⁓gebend** a *n.ative* **~leistungen, ~werte** pl *st.s* pl **~vorschrift** f *st.ization regulation* **⁓widrig** a *irregular, abnormal* **~zeile** f ⟨typ⟩ *direction-line* **norm·al** a *normal (measurements, conditions)* || *regular (way)* ⟨a. tech⟩, *normal, standard* (Drehzahl) | er ist nicht ~ *he is not quite right in the head* | ~er Weise *normally* || unter ~er Größe *undersized* || Abweichung v ⁓en *twist* || wieder ~ w *to fall into pattern again;* alles ist wieder ~ *everything is back to normal;* das ist ganz ~ ⟨a.⟩ *that's par for the course* ⟨golf fig⟩ **Norm·al-** *standard, regular, normal, ordinary* **~aktendeckel** m *st. file cover* **~arbeitstag** m *o. working day* **~-ausführung** f *st.* (⟨rail⟩ *gauge) design* **~bahn** f ⟨rail⟩ *main line* **~bedingungen** f pl *st. specifications* pl **~beschleunigung** f *n. acceleration* **~buchstabe** m ⟨typ⟩ *st. letter* **~drehzahl** f → normal **⁓erweise** [adv] *n.ly, in an o. way* **~fixpunkt** m *datum point* **~format** n *st. size* **~geschwindigkeit** f ⟨tech⟩ *proper* (od *allowed) speed* **~gewicht** n *st. weight* **~größe** f *n. size, st. size* | in ~ ⟨a.⟩ *full-scale* [attr] **~klasse** f ⟨ten⟩ *scratch* **~lehre** f, **~maß** n *st. ga(u)ge* **~lehrplan** m *n. routine* **~leistung** f *rated output, n. rated power, st. capacity* **~lösung** f ⟨chem⟩ *st. solution, test-liquor* **~maß** n *st. (measure)* **~null** n ⟨surv⟩ *(mean) sea-level; datum l.* **~papier** n *st. paper* **~preis** m *(price) st.* **~satz** m *limit(ed price)* **≃sichtig** a *orthoptic* **~spielplatte** f *st. record* **~spur** f, **≃spurig** a ⟨rail⟩ *st. gauge* **~stab** m *st. bar* **≃stark** a (*solution*) *of st. strength* **~ton** m *reference tone, reftone*; ⟨Am⟩ *equivalent loudness level* | f **~- u Atomsprengkörper-** *dual-purpose* [attr] (Geschütz, Waffe, Rakete) **~uhr** f *st. clock* **~verbrauch** [m] an Kraftstoff *level road fuel consumption* **~weingeist** m *proof-spirit* **~zeile** f ⟨typ⟩ *direction line* **~zeit** f *st. time* **normalis·ieren, n·ormen, norm·ieren** vt [h] *to standardize, normalize* ‖ –rt [a] ⟨a.⟩ *unitary* **Normalit·ät** f ~/ *normality* **Normen-** ~vorschrift [f] *standard specification* **Norm·ierung, N·ormung** f ~/~en *normalization, standardization*

Normandie, die *Normandy* **Norm·anne** m, **Norm·annin** f, **norm·annisch** a *Norman*

Norm·annische Inseln f pl = Kanalinseln

Northamptonshire [nɔːˈθæmptənʃə] n ⟨Engl⟩

North·umberland [nɔːˈθʌmbələnd] n ⟨Engl⟩

N·orwegen n *Norway* **N·orweger(in** f) m, **n·orwegisch** a *Norwegian* ‖ das ≃e *Norse* (*in N.*)

Norwich [ˈnɔridʒ] n (Stadt) ⟨Engl⟩

N·ot f ~/≃e **A. 1.** *need, want* ‖ (Armut, Dürftigkeit) *indigence* ‖ (Mangel) *great privation* ‖ (Elend) *adversity*; *misery*; *distress* [a. pl: *-es*] **2.** (geistige, seelische) *anguish, anxiety, agony* **3.** (Mühsal) *trouble* ‖ (Sorge) *sorrow, care* ‖ (Kummer) *affliction, grief* ‖ ≃e *woes, stresses* (*of life*), *the stress* (*of war*) **4.** (Schwierigkeit) *difficulty, trouble* **5.** (Gefahr) (*imminent*) *danger* od *peril*; *distress* ⟨bes. mar⟩ **6.** (Zwang) *compulsion, necessity* ‖ (Dringlichkeit) *exigency, emergency, urgency* **B.** ~ u Elend *destitution and misery* ‖ im Falle der ~ *in case of need, on* od *in an emergency* ‖ es ist ~ am Mann *it is urgent*; wenn .. ist *in the last resort, when the worst comes to the w.* ‖ in der Stunde der ~ *in my* etc *hour of great need* ‖ für die Zeit der ~ *for a rainy day* **C. äußerste** ~ *extremity, utter destitution* ‖ bittere ~ *bitter distress* ‖ dringende ~ *urgencies, exigencies* pl ‖ drückende, höchste *or* größte ~ *pressure of want*; *oppressive, abject* od *deepest distress* ‖ er ist mit knapper ~ entk ⟨fam⟩ *he has had a close shave* ‖ schwere ~ → liebe ~ h; ⟨med⟩ *epilepsy* ‖ was, schwere ~, ..? *what the devil* (*do you want*)? ‖ (schock)schwere~! *damnation*! ‖ unerbittliche ~ *relentless want* od *need* **D. aus** ~ (gezwungenermaßen) *from necessity* od *compulsion* ‖ aus der ~ retten *to help .. in distress* ‖ **durch** die ~ der Umstände *under stress of circumstances* ‖ **in** der ~ *at a pinch* ‖ in ~ befindlich *distressed* (*aircraft*); Holland in ~! *there we are*! *we are in a fine mess*! ‖ in gr ~ *under the harrow* | in ~ bringen *to distress* ‖ jdm in der ~ beistehen *to help a p in distress* ‖ in ~ geraten *to come to poverty, to become destitute, to fall on evil times*, ⟨fam⟩ *to get low* | in ~ s, sich in ~ befinden *to be in distress, trouble, want*; (.. gr ..) *to be in want of common necessities* (⟨fam⟩ .. *in great straits*); *to be destitute, to be hard pressed* od *up, .. down on one's luck* ‖ in 1000 ≃en s *to be worried to hell* ‖ **mit** ~ *scarcely* ‖ mit Müh' u ~ *barely, with* (*great*) *difficulty* ‖ mit genauer *or* knapper ~ *narrowly, only just, with great difficulty, by a narrow margin, by the skin of one's teeth*; .. dem Tode entk: *they had narrow escapes from death* ‖ **ohne** ~ (Grund) *unnecessarily, needlessly*; *without cause* ‖ **über** ~ *more than necessary, required, needful* ‖ **vonnöten** h *to want, require*; *to be in need of* ‖ vonnöten s *to be needful, necessary, a matter of necessity* ‖ **zur** ~ *just* (*good enough*); *on an emergency*; *if need be*; *at the worst*; es reicht z ~ *it will do at a pinch* ‖ das läßt sich z ~ hören *that doesn't sound quite bad* **E.** die ~ **drängt** *help is urgent* ‖ ~ erfahren *to experience want* ‖ wenn es die ~ erfordert *if need be* ‖ wir müssen der ~ gehorchen *we must submit to need* ‖ ~ **h** *to be in trouble* od *difficulty*; ~ h zu tun *to be scarcely able to do*; ~ h mit *to labour under*, mit jdm *to have trouble with a p* ‖ s–e **liebe** ~ h *to be greatly troubled* od *bothered* (mit *about*); wir h unsere l. ~ mit ihm *he gives us no end of trouble, he is a handful*; wir h unsre l. ~, um zu *we have much ado to*; sie h ihre l. ~ mit .. *they have great difficulty in spelling* | die S hat ~ *the case is urgent* ‖ es hat ~ (hält schwer) *it is a difficult task* (, daß .., zu tun *to do*) ‖ es hat k–e ~ damit *it isn't urgent*!, *never fear*!, *don't worry* | sie h ~ auszuk *they find it difficult to make both ends meet* ‖ wenn die ~ an dich **herantritt** *at a pinch* ‖ jdm s–e ~ klagen *to complain to a p about one's troubles* ‖ ~ **leiden** *to suffer want, to famish, to go short*, ⟨fam⟩ *to feel the pinch*; .. an [dat] *to be short of* ‖ ⟨com⟩ e–n Wechsel ~ leiden l *to dishonour a bill* ‖ die Arbeit **macht** ihm gr ~ .. *gives him great trouble* ‖ er macht uns viele ~ *he causes us much anxiety* **F.** ⟨**prov**⟩ ~ kennt kein Gebot, ~ bricht Eisen *needs must when the devil drives, n.y has no law* ‖ in der ~ frißt der Teufel Fliegen *any port is good in a strom*; *beggars can't be choosers* ‖ aus der ~ e–e Tugend m *to make a virtue of n.y* ‖ Freunde in der ~ gehn 100 auf 1 Lot *a poor man has no friends* ‖ ein Freund in der ~ ist ein Fr. im Tod *a fr. in need is a fr. indeed* ‖ ~ macht erfinderisch *n.y is the mother of invention* ‖ ~ ist der Liebe Tod *when poverty comes in at the door love flies out at the window* ‖ ~ lehrt beten *sorrow draws us nearer to God* ‖ wenn die ~ am größten, Hilfe (Gott) am nächsten *man's extremity is God's opportunity* **n·ot** a [nur pred] *necessary, needful, wanting* ‖ eins ist ~ *one thing is needed* | Ruhe ist *or* tut mir ~ *I need rest, I badly want a rest* ‖ es täte ~, ich machte es selbst *I had better do it m.s.* ‖ wenn es ~ tut *in case of necessity* **N·ot-** [in comp oft:] *temporary* (*axle-tree, bridge, dike, structure*) od *emergency* (*address, rope, light, axe, exit, landing, measures, quarters, ramp*) **~anker** m *sheet-anchor* ⟨a. fig⟩ **~arbeit** f *e.y work* **~aufnahme** f *e.y reception* (*of refuges*) **~ausbesserung** f *e.y repair* ⟨a. mot⟩ **~ausgang** m *e.y door* od *exit*, ⟨Am⟩ *fire exit* **~ausrüstung** f *e.y equipment*; *survival kit* **~ausstieg** m (Rakete) *escape hatch*; ⟨aero⟩ *e.y exit* | ~kapsel [f] ⟨a–n⟩ *e. capsule* **~auswurf** m ⟨mar⟩ [abstr] *jettison*; [konkr] *jetsam* **~behelf** m (*make-*)*shift*; *a mere apology* (*for a dinner*) ‖ als ~ aufstellen, errichten *to rig*; *to set up as e.y* ‖ dürftiger ~ ⟨sl⟩ *contraption* **~behelfs-** *make-shift* (*hospital*) **~beleuchtung** f ⟨bes theat⟩ *secondary* (⟨Am⟩ *e.y*) *lighting* **~betrug** m *petty fraud due to need* **~bremse** f *safety* od *e.y brake, communication-cord* (ziehen *to pull*) **~dienst** m *incident/damage control* **~durft** f *want*, (*pressing*) *need*; *necessaries* pl (*of life*) ‖ s–e ~ verrichten *to ease o.s., to relieve nature* **≃dürftig** a *scanty, needy, poor*; ~ geleimt etc *mended to go on with* | ~keit [f] *scantiness, need, indigence* **~entwendung** f *pilfering due to need* **~erbe** m *legitimate heir* **~fall** m *e.y, exigency*; *case of necessity* od *need* | ≃s [adv] *or* im ~ *in case of need, in an e.y, if need arise, if necessary*; ⟨fam⟩ *at a pinch* od *push*; im äußersten ~ *at last need*; nur im ~ *except for e.y* **~fenster** n *e.y w.* **~feuer** n *alarm-fire* **~flagge** f *flag of distress* **~frequenz** f ⟨wir⟩ *distress fr.* **~frist** f *peremptory term* **≃gedr·ungen** a *compulsory, necessary, forced* ‖ adv *from sheer necessity*; *perforce*; *enforcedly*; *needs* [nur bei *must*] **~geld** n *e.y* od *token money* **~gemeinschaft** f *E.y Society* (*for German Sciences*) **~geschrei** n *cries* [pl] *of distress* ‖ ein ~ erheben *to raise an alarm* **~gesetz** n *e.y law* **~groschen** m *nest-egg* (→ ~pfennig) **~hafen** m *harbour of refuge*; *shelter* **~helfer** m *helper in need* od *distress*; ⟨RC⟩ *the 14 Auxiliary Saints* **~hilfe** f *help in need* ‖ *make-shift* ‖ Technische ~ *E.y Technical Corps, Organization for the Maintenance of Supplies* **~jahr** n *year of scarcity* **~knopf** m *panic b.* **~lage** f *need, misery,* *distress(ed condition), e.y; quandary, predicament, dilemma; plight;* ⟨fam⟩ *squeeze, fix, jam* ‖ in äußerster *in the last ditch* (v der *Steeple Chase*) **~lager** n *shake down* **≗landen** vi [s] ⟨aero⟩ *to be forced down; to force-land;* ⟨sl⟩ *to ditch* **~landeplatz** m *e.y landing ground* od *field* **~landung** f *forced* od *e.y landing* | nicht **≗leiden** l *not to impair* | **~d** a *needy, indigent; distressed, necessitous, destitute, poor; suffering distress;* ⟨com⟩ (Wechsel) *dishonoured* **~leidende(r)** m *p in distress; sufferer, needy p* ‖ die ~n *those suffering from want; the needy, the distressed* (*among them*) **~leine** f *communication-cord, bell-cord* (od *-pull*) **~leiter** f *fire escape* **~lösung** f *t. solution* **~lüge** f *shift; white lie; fib* **~maßnahme** f *rush measure* **~mast** m *jury-mast* **~mittel** n *expedient, shift* **~nagel** m ⟨fig⟩ *last shift* **~opfer** n *e.y aid* **≗p·einlich** a *penal, criminal* **~pfennig** m *spare-money, savings* pl ‖ e–n ~ aufsparen *to put money by for a rainy day* **≗reif** a ⟨bot⟩ *forced* **~reparatur** f *t. repair* **~ruder** n *preventer-* od *jury-rudder* **~ruf, ~schrei** m *cry of distress* **~rufnummer** f ⟨m. m.⟩ *emergency telephone code* **~schlachtung** f *e.y slaughter(ing)* **~schuß** m *shot of distress* **~sender** m ⟨wir⟩ *e.y transmitter* **~signal** n *signal of distress; d. s.;* (⟨mar⟩ *S.O.S.*); *distress-gun* od *-rocket* ‖ ⟨rail⟩ *danger signal* **~sitz** m ⟨mot⟩ *folding* od *occasional, auxiliary seat;* ⟨aero⟩ (mit runder Lehne *bucket s.*; ⟨sl⟩ *dickey* **~stand** m (*state of*) *distress* od *e.y; need; critical state* ‖ *urgent case* | ~sarbeiten [f pl] *relief-works* pl; ~sgebiet [n] *stricken* od *special, distressed, depressed area;* ~sgesetz [n] → ~verordnung | –gebung [f] *e.y* (*defence, -se plan*) *legislation* | Ausschuß [m] f ~splanung [f] (Zivilsektor) *Senior Civil E.y Planning Committee* N **~stativ** n *makeshift stand* **~strom-** ~aggregat [n] ⟨el⟩ *e.y power generating set;* ~versorgung [f] *standby electric power supply;* [konkr] *e.y power source* **~taufe** f *private baptism* **≗taufen** vt [h] *to baptize privately* (*in case of necessity*) **~treppe** *e.y staircase* **~tür** f *e.y door; fire-escape* **~unterkunft** f ⟨mil⟩ *shelter billets* pl **~verband** m *provisional dressing;* ⟨mil⟩ *rough bandage; field-dressing* **~verordnung** f *e.y decree; crisis bill* ‖ *e.y powers act;* ⟨engl⟩ *orders in council* **~visier** n ⟨mil⟩ *direct fire sight* **~wasserausrüstung** f ⟨aero⟩ *flo(a)tation gear* **≗wassern** vi ⟨aero⟩ *to force-water;* ⟨sl⟩ *to ditch* **~wasserung** f *forced landing on water;* ⟨sl⟩ *ditching* **~wehr** f *self-defence* (aus ~ *in s.*; ⟨jur⟩ *se defendendo* L) **≗w·endig** [a] *essential* (*books*) ‖ *necessary* (*time*) ‖ *needful, necessary* (*that .. should*) ‖ dringend ~ *imperative,* (logisch ~) *logical* ‖ (unumgänglich ~) *inevitable, indispensable* ‖ absolut ~ *mandatory* (*that .. should*) ‖ es war dringend ~, daß er tat *it was urgent for him to do* ‖ .. nicht mehr als ~ .. *we won't waste more of your time than we can help* ‖ etw ~ brauchen *to find sth indispensable* ‖ ~ m *to necessitate* ‖ die f das Gelingen des Plans ~en Schritte ergreifen *to take the steps necessary for the plan to succeed* ‖ das ≗ste, die ~sten Bedürfnisse *the requisites, necessaries* pl, *the most indispensable wants* pl | [adv] ich muß ~ verreisen *I must of necessity make a journey* **≗wendigenf·alls** adv *in case of need, if need be* od *arise* **≗wendigerw·eise** adv *of necessity, necessarily; needs* (*we must n. exercise restraint*) **~w·endigkeit** f *necessity* (gebieterisch *imperative*, dringend *pressing*); *need(fulness)* ‖ [konkr] *requirement* ‖ in die ~ versetzt *compelled* (zu *to*) ‖ es bestand k–e ~, daß er blieb *there was no need for him to stay* ‖ ⟨mil⟩ ~en [pl] *exigencies* pl ‖ dringende ~ *urgency; a life and death necessity* ‖ .. als die ~ sich einstellte *as the occasion arose* **~wohnung** f *alternative flat,* etc **~wurf** m ⟨aero⟩ = ~auswurf ‖ (Bomben) im ~ abwerfen *to jettison* **~zeichen** n *signal of distress* **~zucht** f *rape, violation* **≗züchtigen** vt [h] *to ravish, violate;* ⟨jur⟩ *to assault* **~züchtiger** m *ravisher* **~züchtigung** f = ~zucht

N·ota f ~/~s *note, bill* ‖ ⟨com⟩ (*short*) *memorandum* ‖ (Faktura) *invoice* | in ~ nehmen *to book* ‖ sich etw ad notam nehmen *to take note of a th* | ~ bene! L *be it noted; take notice, mind! nota bene!* L (abbr *N. B.*) **Not·abeln** m pl *notabilities, notable people* pl **Notabilit·ät** f ~/ [abstr] *notability* | ~en [pl] [konkr] = Notabeln **Not·ar** m ~s/~e *notary;* (als Verfasser v Urkunden) *solicitor;* (für Übereignungen) *conveyancer* **Notari·at** n ~(e)s/~e *notary's office, Notariate* ‖ v ~s wegen *by order of a notary* **~sgebühren** f pl *notary's fees* pl **~sinstrument** n *solicitor's deed* od *document* **~svertrag** m *deed* **notari·ell** [a] *notarial; attested before a notary* ‖ ~e Vollmacht [f] *power of attorney* | [adv] ~ beglaubigen *to notarize,* ~ b.gt *signed by a notary* (*public*) **N·ote** f ~/~n **1.** (Anmerkung) *note;* ⟨liter⟩ *annotation* **2.** ⟨com⟩ (Nota) *memorandum* ‖ (Rechnung) *bill, account* **3.** (Banknote) *bank-note* **4.** ⟨pol⟩ (*diplomatic*) *note* **5.** ⟨school⟩ *mark;* gute ~, die ~ „gut" *a good report, high marks* pl; schlechte ~ *poor m.s* (in *for*) **6.** (Zeichen) *mark* ‖ ⟨fig⟩ persönliche ~ *personal trait, feature, touch* ‖ *the case has its points* **7.** ⟨mus⟩ *note* ‖ ~n [pl] *music,* ⟨Am a.⟩ *sheet m.* ‖ ganze ~ *semi-breve,* halbe ~ *minim,* Viertel≗ *crotchet,* Achtel≗ *quaver* ‖ erhöhte ~ *sharp,* verminderte ~ *flat* ‖ ~n in Handschrift *manuscript m.* ‖ ~n abschreiben *to copy m.* ‖ in ~n setzen *to set to m.* ‖ ohne ~n (spielen) *without a copy of the m.* ‖ v ~n spielen (= v Blatt) *to play at sight* ‖ nach ~n *with the m. before one, from m.* ‖ ⟨fig fam⟩ *with a vengeance, thoroughly* **N·oten- ~ausgabe** f *issue of* (*bank-*)*notes* **~austausch** m ⟨pol⟩ *exchange of notes* **~bank** f *bank of issue, issuing bank* **~beilage** f *m.al supplement* **~bezeichnung** f *m. notation* **~blatt** n *sheet of m.* **~buch** n *m.-book* **~druck** m *printing of notes* bzw *m.* **~gestell** n *m.-stand* **~halter** m *m.-clamp* **~heft** n = ~buch **~inhaber** m ⟨com⟩ *bearer, holder* **~lesen** n *reading of m.* **~linie** f *m.-line;* ~n [pl] *staff* (⟨a.⟩ *stave*) **~papier** n *m.-paper* **~pult** n *m.-desk* **~schlüssel** m *clef* **~schrank** m *canterbury* **~schreiber** m *copier of m.* **~ständer** m *m.-stand* **~stecher** m *m.-engraver* **~system** n *staff* (⟨a.⟩ *stave*) **~type** f *m.-type* **~umlauf** m *circulation of* (*bank-*)*notes* **~wechsel** = ~austausch **~zeichen** n ⟨mus⟩ *note* **not·ieren** vt [h] *to note* (*down*), ⟨com⟩ *to book* ‖ *to make a memorandum* od *note of* ‖ (schnell) *to jot down* ‖ ⟨st exch⟩ *to quote* (*prices*), nicht notiert *unquoted* | die Anleihe notiert 83 *the loan is quoted at 83* **Not·ierung** f ~/~en *noting,* etc ‖ ⟨com⟩ *quotation* ‖ erste ~ *first call* **notifiz·ieren** vt [h] *to notify* **Notifiz·ierung** f ~/~en *notification*

ˣ**n·otig** a [obd] = arm, in Not **n·ötig** a **A.** *necessary, needful, needed, required* ‖ unumgänglich ~ *indispensable* **B.** ~ h *to want, require, need, have n. of, stand in n. of* ‖ es ~ h zu tun *to have occasion to do;* er hat es nicht ~ z arbeiten *he doesn't have to work* ‖ er hielt es nicht f ~ zu antworten *he didn't deign* (*to reply* od) *an answer* **C.** es **ist** nicht ~, daß du antwortest *there is no need for you to answer;* das war aber nicht ~ *that was uncalled for;* wäre es ~ geworden *had the n. arisen* ‖ ⟨fam⟩ ein neuer Rock ist *or* tut ihm sehr ~ *he is in great n. of* (od *he badly wants*) *a new coat* **D.** klüger **als** ~ *too clever by half* ‖ .. nicht länger als ~ (*don't stay*) *longer than you can help* (→ notwendig) **E.** ⟨fam⟩ wir brauchen ~ Regen *we want rain badly* ‖ das **≗e** *the necessary, necessaries* pl; *needful, wherewithall, all that is necessary* ‖ das **≗ste** *bare necessities* pl **~en** vt [h] **1.** *to necessitate, compel, force, coerce, constrain, oblige* **2.** (einladen) *to invite, ask* ‖ jdn ins Zimmer ~ *to ask a p in* **3.** (dringend bitten) *to urge, press* **4.** (zum Essen ~) *to press* (*a guest to help h.s.*), *to ply* (*a p*) *with food;* sich ~ l *to stand upon ceremony;* l Sie sich nicht ~! *don't wait to be asked, help y.s.!*; ich lasse mich nicht (lange) ~ *I require no pressing*, ⟨Am⟩ *I need little coaxing* **5.** sich **ge~t** sehen *to be put to* (od *to be under*) *the necessity* (zu tun *of doing*) ‖ *I feel compelled* (*to warn you*) **~enfalls** adv *in case of need, if need be* **≃keit** f ~/ *necessity*, (dringende) *urgency* **≃ung** f ~/~en *compulsion, force* ‖ *constraint* ‖ (freundliche) *invitation, pressing*; *urgent request* ‖ ⟨jur⟩ *duresse* (durch ~ *under d.*) | e–e ~ ausüben *to apply compulsion* ‖ ich empfand es als ~ *it felt very much like c.*

Not·iz f ~/~en **1.** (Vermerk) *note, memo(randum)* ‖ ~en ⟨a.⟩ *jottings* pl ‖ ~en m *to take n.s* (über *of*, ⟨Am⟩ *on*) ‖ sich e–e ~ m *to make a n. of sth*; *to jot* od *take down a n.* (über *of, about* ⟨Am⟩ *on*) **2.** (Zeitungs≃) *announcement* **3.** (Kenntnis) *notice* ‖ ~ nehmen v *to take notice* od *cognizance of* ‖ k–e ~ n. v *to ignore* **~block** m *scribbling block*, ⟨Am⟩ *pad* **~buch** n *n.-, pocket-, m.-book* **~heft** n *waste book* **Notoriet·ät** f ~/ *notoriety* **not·orisch** a *notorious* (*swindler*), *arrant* (*nonsense*)

Nov·ara n ⟨It⟩ (Stadt in der Lombardei)

Nov·elle f ~/~n **1.** *novelette*, (*long*) *short story* **2.** ⟨parl⟩ *supplementary* od *amending law*; *amendment* **≃nartig** a *in the form of a short story* **Novell·ist** m ~en/~en *novelist* | **~ik** f (*works of*) *fiction* | **≃isch** a *fictional*

Nov·ember m ~s/~ *November* ‖ im ~ *in N.*

Novit·ät f ~/~en *novelty* ‖ (Buch) *new publication* ‖ ⟨theat⟩ *new play* **Nov·ize** m [~n/~n] & f [~/~n] *novice* **Novizi·at** n ~(e)s/~e *novitiate* **N·ovum** n ~s/–va *unheard-of fact*, etc

N·owaja Semlja n ⟨Russ⟩ (Doppelinsel im nördl. Eismeer) *Novaya Zemlya, Nova Zembla*

N·owgorod n ⟨Russ⟩ (Stadt) *Novgorod*

Nowosib·irsk n ⟨Russ⟩ (Stadt) *Novosibirsk*

N·oxe f ~/~n ⟨med⟩ *morbific agent*; *noxa*, pl *-ae*

Nu m & n *moment* ‖ im ~, in e–m ~ *in a twinkling, flash, trice*, ⟨fam⟩ *jiff(y)*; *in no time* ‖ (*he was off*) *like a shot*; *before you could say Jack Robinson*; (*hours passed*) *like lightning* **nu**! intj *well*! ‖ ~ also! *well then*

Nuance [ny'ɑ̃:sə] f ~/~n *shade, tint, nuance* Fr (*art of the delicate n.* [Nuancen]) **nuanc·ieren** [s] vt [h] *to shade off* ‖ ⟨mus⟩ *modulate*

N·ubien n (nordafrik. Landschaft) *Nubia*

N·ubier m, **~in** f, **n·ubisch** a *Nubian*

n·üchtern a **1.** *fasting, empty* ‖ auf ~en Magen *on an e. stomach* ‖ mit ~em M. *e.* ‖ ich bin noch ~ *I have not broken my fast*; ~ bleiben *to go e.*; nicht (mehr) ganz ~ *the worse for drink* **2.** (mäßig) *sober* (& ⟨fig⟩ v Urteil), *temperate* ‖ *abstemious* (*life*) ‖ *level-headed* ‖ ~en Sinnes *with s.ness of mind* ‖ [adv] ~ denkend *uneffusive, level-headed* ‖ ~ w, wieder ~ denken *to come back to earth, to s. down* **3.** (besonnen) *calm, cool(-headed), prudent, sensible*; (etw) in ~en Zahlen ausdrücken *to put .. in cold figures* ‖ etw ~ [adv] betrachten *to take a sensible view* (od *cold survey*) *of a th*; ~ betrachtet *in cold fact* ‖ *staid* (*character, looks*) **4.** (schwunglos) *matter-of-fact, prosaic, prosy, unromantic, unimaginative, unemotional* ‖ *common(place), ordinary, plain, insipid, vapid, dull* ‖ (geistlos) *jejune, dryasdust* (*p*), *dreary* (*landscape*) ‖ *hard-headed* (*p, thought*) ‖ *dry* (*facts*) **5.** ⟨cul⟩ *insipid, stale* (*dish*) ‖ ⟨fig⟩ *dry, vapid* (*style*) | **≃heit** f ~/ *emptiness* ‖ *sobriety* ‖ *temperance* ‖ *prosiness* ‖ *unimaginativeness, jejuneness* ‖ ⟨fig⟩ *dryness* ‖ *common sense* ‖ *plainness, flatnes, vapidity, dullness*

°**N·ucke, N·ücke** f ~/~n **1.** *whim, crotchet* **2.** *malice* **n·uckisch,** ≃ a *stubborn*, ⟨*hors*⟩ *restive*

°**N·uckel** m ~s/~ → Schnuller **~pinne** f ⟨mot⟩ *tin lizzy, pip-squeak* °**n·uckeln** vi/t [h] *to suck*

N·udel f ~/~n; *noodle* ‖ (Faden≃n) *vermicelli* pl | (Gänse≃) *fatterning ball* | ⟨fig⟩ ulkige ~ *funny fellow* | ≃dick [a] *plump as a partridge*; ~holz [n] *rolling pin*; ~suppe [f] *vermicelli-soup* **n·udeln** vt [h] *to cram* (*geese*) ‖ ⟨fig⟩ *to cram* (*with food*)

Nudit·ät f ~/~en *nudity, nakedness*; *obscenity*

N·ugat m ~s/~s *nougat*

Nukle·ar- ~physik [f] *nuclear physics* [sg konstr]; ~waffen [f pl] *nuclear weapons*

null a *zero, nought, nil*; 1 – 1 = 0 *one minus one leaves nought*; gleich ~ (*the effect is*) *practically nil*; (*its value is*) *a mere nothing* od *next to n.*; (*supplies are*) *as good as non-existant* 0,3 (~ Komma 3) = *.3* (*point three*) ‖ in ~ Komma nichts *in* (*less than*) *no time* ‖ ⟨telph⟩ *0* [ou] z. B. *405* [fɔ: ou faiv] ‖ ⟨sport⟩ 1 zu ~ *one to nil*; ⟨ten⟩ ~ 30 *love 30*; x zu ~ schlagen *to beat hollow* ‖ wir h ~ Grad *the thermometer stands at zero* ‖ ~ u nichtig *nil*; *null and void* ‖ ~ u nichtig erklären *or* m *to annul* **Null** f ~/~en (Ziffer) *cipher, nought* ‖ (auf Skalen) *zero* ‖ auf, über, unter ~ *at, above, below zero* ‖ ⟨crick⟩ *duck's egg*; *blob* ‖ ⟨cards⟩ ~ ouvert *open nullo* It ‖ ⟨fig⟩ (P) *nonentity, mere cipher*; ⟨bes mil⟩ *bad bargain*; e–e gr *or* aufgeblasene ~ *a stuffed shirt*; e–e ~ s *to be no great shakes*; (Geschütz, Apparat) auf ~ stellen *to zero*; .. wieder *to reset .. to zero* ‖ ⟨aero⟩ Ruder auf ~ stellen ⟨a.⟩ *to neutralize* ‖ .. in ~ Komma nichts *in* (*less than*) *no time* ‖ ~- ⟨phys, el⟩ **n***eutral* **~ableitung** f ⟨gram⟩ *zero-derivation* (z. B. *service*/*to s.*) **~ablesung** f *z.-reading method* **~achse, ~linie** f *n. axis* **~form** f ⟨gram⟩ *z.form* (ohne Artikel: *to go to church, market, prison, school*, etc) **~geschütz** n *directing gun* **~kontrolle** f ⟨comp⟩ *line proof*; .. je Buchung *l.-by-l. zero proof* **~leiter** m ⟨el⟩ *n. conductor* **~partie** f ⟨ten⟩ *love-set* **~punkt** m *zero, freezing-point*; absoluter ~ (– 273,15° C) *absolute z.* ‖ ⟨mil⟩ geplanter ~ *desired ground z.* ‖ ⟨wir⟩ *n. point* ‖ ⟨fig⟩ *vanishing point*; *zero-mark* **~serie** f ⟨tech⟩ *zero-initial series* (*of manufacture*) **~stellung** f ⟨tech⟩ *home position* **~zeit** f *z.-hour* **n·ullen** vt [h] ⟨el⟩ *to neutralize* **N·ullen-** ~anschrift [f] ⟨comp⟩ *printing of ciphers* **~zirkel** m *bow compasses*

N·um- ~er·ale n ~s/–lien (Zahlwort) *numeral* **≃er·ieren** vt [h] *to number, to ticket, to label* ‖ –rierter Platz *reserved seat*; fortlaufend –riert *consecutively numbered* **≃·erisch** a *numerical* **~ero** n ~s/~s *number* **~erus** m ~/–ri ⟨gram & math⟩ *number* ‖ ~ clausus ⟨univ⟩ *numerus clausus*

†**Num·idien** n (altes Königreich in Nordafrika) *Numidia* **Num·idier(in), num·idisch** a *Numidian*

Numism·atik f ~/ *numismatics* pl [a. sg konstr] | **~er** m ~s/~ *numismatician* **numism·atisch** a *numismatic*

N·ummer f ~/~n **A.** *number*; Haus mit (un)gerader ~ (*un*)*even numbered h.* ‖ Fabrik≃ *serial n.* ‖ welche Handschuh–, Schuh≃ h Sie? *what size do you take* (*in gloves, shoes*)? ‖ gr *or* Haupt≃ ⟨theat⟩ *big* od *star act* ‖ laufende ~ *serial number* ‖ Probe≃ *specimen copy* ‖ ⟨school⟩ gute, schlechte ~ *high, poor marks* (in *for*) ‖ Sonder≃ *special edition* ‖ ⟨sport⟩ Programm≃ *event* ‖ ⟨telph⟩ ~ besetzt! (*n.*) *engaged*! ⟨Am⟩ *line busy*! ‖ Zeitungs≃ *copy, issue* **B.** ~ 12 *n. 12* ‖ eingetragene ~ *registered n.* ‖ in einzelnen ~n *serially, in serial parts* ‖ (fort)laufende ~n *series* sg, *successive* od *running n.s* pl ‖ in (monatlichen) ~n *in* (*monthly*) *parts* **C.** ⟨fig⟩ e–e ~ unter vielen *one among many* ‖ e–e bloße ~ *a mere figurehead* od *cipher* ‖ sich nur als ~ fühlen *to think o.s. a mere n.* ‖ ⟨fam⟩ auf ~ Sicher bringen *to put under lock and key*; auf ~ S. gehen! *to play it safe*; *safety first*! **D.** ⟨hot⟩ ~ 5 **haben** *to stay in room n.* (*No.*) *5* ‖ °⟨fig⟩ Sie h k–e ~ *you are of no consequence* ‖ °e–e gr ~ h *to hold a high position* ‖ °bei e–m e–e gute ~ h *to be in high favour with a p* **E.** ⟨fig⟩ **sein**:

°er ist e–e ~ ⟨fam⟩ *he is a card* || ⟨iron⟩ °e–e dufte ~ *a smart customer* || °e–e feine, saubere ~ *a nice sort, a ne'er-do-well*; ⟨Am⟩ *she is a hot little number* || °e–e schwere ~ *a hard case*, ⟨sl⟩ *a tough nut* | °⟨sex vulg⟩ *a turn, a short time*; e–e ~ schieben *to do a push* od *put* || °sie ist *or* schiebt e–e gute ~ *she's a bit of goods, she's a good bang* | (hübsches) **~mädchen** ⟨theat⟩ *show girl* **~marke** f *ticket* **~pfahl** m ⟨surv, rail⟩ *number-post* **~ndruck** m ⟨comp m. m.⟩ *end printing* **~nscheibe** f ⟨telph⟩ *dial*; Lochkranz der ~ *finger plate* **~nschild** n ⟨mot⟩ *licence-, -se, n.-plate*

nun I. [adv] **1.** (jetzt) *now, at present* || **als ~** *now when* || **~ endlich, ~ erst** *now at last* || bist du ~ (endlich) zufrieden? *are you satisfied at last* || ~ erst gab er nach *it was only then that he gave in* || ~ u **nimmer**(mehr) *never*; *never more*; *by no means* || **u** ~ *and now* || v ~ **ab** *or* **an** (in Zukunft) *henceforth, henceforward, in (the) future* || (Vergangenheit) *(ever) since then, from that time (forth)* || **was** ~? *what next*? **2.** *under present circumstances*; *then*; *as things (now) stand* od *(then) stood* || (also) *therefore* || ~ gerade! *all the more so*! **II.** [Füllwort] **1.** es ist ~ **(ein)mal** so! *as ths stand, as it is, well, it can't be helped*! || da es ~ mal so ist *since ths are as they are* || ich möchte ~ **freilich, daß** .. *I should wish indeed that* .. || sei es ~ wahr oder nicht *whether it be true or no* || ob er ~ kommt oder nicht *whether he comes or not* || **wenn** ~ *now if* **2.** (anschließend) ~ **aber** .. *but then* .. || da ~ aber *now since* **III.** [intj] **1.** *well*! ~ **also**: *why*!, *well now*!, *well then*! || ~ **ja**! *yes, indeed*! || ~ **gut**! *all right then*!, *never mind*! || ~ in der Tat! *upon my word*! ~ ich geh!, ~ meinetwegen! *well*, .. || *well* od *come, (that's better)* || je, ~! *here*! || ~, da waren wir *so there it was* **2.** (anspornend) *now then*! || ~ los! *come, hurry up*!, *now, go it*! **3.** (begütigend) *well then*!, *that's settled*! || ~ ~! *come, come*!, *gently*! **4.** (fragend) *well*? || ~, und? *well, and then*? || ~, was gibt's? *yes, what is it*? || ~, wie geht's? *then, how are you*? **IV. [conj]** (= als, da) ~ er darüber nachdachte *now that he came to think of it* || ~ es einmal so ist *since it is so* **nunm·ehr** adv & conj *now, by this time* **nunm·ehrig** a *present* || (Vertrag) in s–r ~en Fassung *as it stands* bzw *stood*

Nunti-, -zi- ~at·ur f ~/~en *nunciature* **~us** m ~/–en *nuncio*

nur I. [adv] **A.** (einschränkend) **1.** [vor (!) subst. pron, a, adv, inf] *only, solely, just, merely* (→ bloß) || *merely a dream* || *my mother alone* || *no one but she* || ~ Gutes *nothing but kindness* || ~ ein Nachgeben *nothing short of giving way* || ~ ein Narr von Staatsmann *no statesman but a fool* || *so far the poet's character has been discussed alone* [nicht *only*!] | *only natural* || *just tacky (not wet)* || *but small* | *only here* || *only moderately* | wir h ~ einen Sohn *we have but one son* || ~ wenige *but few* || für ~ *or* ~ für 3 J. *just for 3 years* | ~ schlafen! *to sleep, no more*; *just* od *only to sleep* **2.** [nach (!) verbum finitum] sie lächelte ~ *she simply* od *only smiled* || er arbeitet ~ *he does nothing but work* || ich konnte ~ staunen *I could only* (od *couldn't but*) *feel surprised* || das beweist es ~ *it merely, solely, only proves it* || Sie brauchen ~ .. zu verlangen *just ask for a form* || er öffnete ~ die Tür (trat nicht ein) *he did no more than open the door* **3.** [neg] **nicht** ~ Brötchen *not just rolls (for breakfast)* || .. ~ er nicht *all died (but he* od*) except him* || (alles,) nur das nicht *anything (rather than* od*) save that* (od *that alone excepted*), *everything but that* | **nicht** ~ .., **sondern auch** *not only* .., *but also* **B. bevor** er (auch) ~ d. Str. gekreuzt hatte *before he had so much as crossed the street* || (er ist reicher,) ~ **daß** wir k–e Kinder h .. *except we have no ch.* || ~ **eben** *scarcely*, (zeitlich) *a moment ago, but just*; *just for today* || ~ **etwa** *only about* || ~ **noch** (⟨fam⟩ ~ **mehr**) *barely*; *only just* || *just (another 2 minutes)* || *only (one page) more* || ich will ~ n. hinzufügen .. *I will merely add* .. || *(I have) only (10 s) left* || fast ~ noch *hardly any(thing) but* || [~ noch + compr]: *(he will be) still more arrogant* || *(he looked) the more helpless* || **oder auch** ~ *or even* || **ohne** .. auch ~ *without so much as (looking at her, a word)* || [~ **so** + verb] *admirably, fast, first-rate, like a house on fire, with a vengeance* || die Zeit flog ~ so *time just flew* || .. daß es nur so krachte .. *with a bang* || er tut ~ so *he's just* od *only pretending* || ~ **um so** mehr *all the more* || ~ **während** *not* .. *except during* || **wenn** ~ *if only, provided (that)* || **wenn auch** ~: *think of me, though at the station* || ~ **zu** (bald, geneigt) *all too (soon, apt)* || ~ zu sehr *only too well* od *much* || ~ zu wahr *(that's) true enough, (it proved) only too true* || du weißt ~ zu gut *you know well enough* **C.** ⟨emph⟩ **1.** (Aufforderung) [mst imp] sieh ~! *just look*! || sieh das ~ an! *look at that, now*! || sag mir ~! *do tell me*! || denke ~ (ja) daran! *be sure you think of it*! || na warte ~! *just wait*! || laß' mich ~ m! *leave everything to me*!, *(do* od *just) let me manage*! || er soll es ~ versuchen *he'd better try, that's all* | glaub es ~ ja nicht *don't believe it on any account* | (Bedingung) hier hast du's, ~ schweige! .., *but not a word*! | [ell] ~ nicht ängstlich! *no fear*! || ~ gemach! *gently*! || ~ her damit! *give it me*! || laß ~! *don't trouble y.s.*! || ~ so weiter! *go on the same way*! || ~ weiter!, ~ zu! *at it*!, *go on*! **2.** (Einwilligung) geh ~! *do go*! || ~ zu! *do as you please*! || ich will's ~ gestehen *well, I confess* || er mag ~ gehen *let him go by all means*! **3.** (Wunsch) daß *or* wenn wir ~ den Brief bek! *if only we receive the l.*! || er mag ~ k! *let him come, now*! **4.** (Frage) **warum** reist man ~? *why does one ever travel*? || warum sprichst du ~ nicht? *why don't you ever talk, now*? || **was** will er ~? *what ever does he want*? || *who ever can it be*? || was denkst du ~? *what on earth are you thinking of* || was er ~ denkt? *I wonder what he thinks* || was du ~ hast? *what's up with you*? || **wie** kann ich ~? *how can I possibly*? || wie können Sie das ~ denken? *how is it possible that you should think that* || wie kann er's ~ getan h? *but how can he have done it*? **5.** (Verallgemeinerung) [nach: was, wer, wie, wo] *(so)ever*; *possibly, in any way* || wo ~ *where(so)ever* || wohin ~ *wherever* || .. und anständig wie ~ **einer** *and ever so decent*; ⟨fam⟩ *and decent as they come* || er, der wie ~ **irgend**–e–r *he who as much as any* || wie ~ 2 Frauen *(eagerly) as any two women* || **so sehr** *or* **viel** ich ~ kann *as much as ever I can* || *the best wines one could possibly imagine* || (Frage → 4) **II.** [conj] (= aber) .. ~ nicht zu sehr *(be lenient) but not too lenient* || .., ~ müßte sie .. .., *but she should be slimmer* || ~ **daß** *only* **N·urd·üsenflugzeug** n *straight jet* **Nurfl·ügelflugzeug** n *flying wing*

N·ürnberg n ⟨Ger⟩ (Stadt) *Nuremberg, Nürnberg*, → Trichter | **~er** *Nuremberg* (Naziprozeß)

°**N·üschel** m ~s/~ **1.** = Maul **2.** = Stirn

n·uscheln vi/t [h] **1.** *to mumble* **2.** *to dawdle*

N·uß f ~/Nüsse **A. 1.** *nut* || welsche ~, Wal≃ *walnut* || → Hasel≃ etc || taube ~ *empty nut* || in die Nüsse gehen *to go a-nutting* || Nüsse auskernen *to shell nuts* **2.** = Kopfnuß *blow* **3.** Kalbs≃ ⟨cul⟩ *cushion* **B.** ⟨fig⟩ k–e taube ~ wert *not worth a straw* || harte, bittere ~ *hard nut (to crack)*, *large* od *tall order*; ⟨fam⟩ *teaser, stumper, poser (a tough proposition)*; ⟨Am⟩ *sticker* || jdm e–e ~ z knacken geben *to give a p a nut to crack* || → Muß || das hat Platz in e–r ~ *that would go in a nutshell* | (P) taube, °doofe ~ *zany*; *damp squib* || er ist e–e taube ~ *he's dead from the neck up* **~baum** m *(wal)nut-tree* | ~holz [n] *walnut* **~beißer** m ⟨orn⟩ *jay, nutcracker* **~bohrer** m ⟨ent⟩ *nut-weevil* **≃braun, ≃farben** a *nut-brown*; *hazel (eyes)* **~häher** m = ~beißer **~kern** m *kernel (of a* *nut)* **~knacker** m (*nut-)crackers* pl ‖ ⟨fig⟩ *old fogey* **~kohlen** pl *nuts* **~öl** n *nut-oil* **~schale** f *nut--shell* (⟨a. fig⟩ = Kahn) **~strauch** m = Hasel–

N·üster f ~/~n ⟨hors⟩ *nostril*; → Nase(n-flügel)

N·ut(e) f ~/~en *groove* → Falz ‖ ~falz [m] *recess*; ~hobel [m] *grooving-plane*; ~ u Feder *gr. and tongue*; ~- u -Federhobel [m] *matching plane*, .. –holz [n] *match-boarding* **n·uten** vt [h] *to groove*

N·utria f ~/~s (Biberratte) *nutria* (⟨a.⟩ Fell)

ˣ**N·utsch** m ~(e)s/~e = Schnuller ≗**en** vt [h] *to suck*

°**N·utte** f ~/~n *tart* (→ Dirne) ‖ [dim] N·uttchen [n] *good girl, good one*

Nutz m ~ens/ *utility, profit* ‖ zu jds ~ u Frommen *for a p's benefit, for a p's profit and advantage* ‖ *for the good of mankind* ‖ sich zu ~e m *to profit by*; *to turn to account*; .. jds Vorteile .. *to steal a p's thunder*; .. jds ungünstige Lage *to take a p at a disadvantage* **nutz** = nütze **N·utz-** [in comp oft] *useful* (*length, weight, effect, value*); ⟨el⟩ *net* (–energie, –last, –leistung) **~anwendung** f (*practical*) *application* (auf *to*), *utilization*; *moral* **~bremsung** f ⟨el⟩ *regenerative braking* ≗**bringend** a *profitable* **~effekt** m ⟨tech⟩ *efficiency* **~fahrzeug** n *utility* od *commercial vehicle* od *car* **~garten** m *kitchen-garden* **~gefälle** n *useful head* **~holz** n *timber* **~last** f *carrying capacity* (*of a vehicle*); *working, pay-, commercial load*; höchstzulässige ~ *maximum l.*; effektive ~ *effective payload* **~leistung** f ⟨mach⟩ *effective power* od *capacity*; *service capacity* od *output* ≗**los** a *of no use* ‖ *useless* (*attacks*); *unavailing* (*attempts*), *unprofitable* (*undertakings*), *needless* (*advice, ballast*) ‖ ~ s *to go for nothing* ‖ ~ s bei jdm (of suggestion) *to be wasted on a p* ‖ ~ zu fragen (*it was*) *no good asking* **~losigkeit** f ~/ *uselessness, futility* ≗**nießen** vt [h] ⟨jur⟩ *to usufruct* **~nießer** m *user, beneficiary*, ⟨jur⟩ *usufructuary*; ⟨dero⟩ *profiteer* **~nießung** f *use*, ⟨jur⟩ *usufruct* | ~srecht [n] *freedom* (v *of*) **~strom** m ⟨el⟩ *useful current* ≗- **u zwecklos** a ⟨emph fam⟩ *as useful as the fifth tit on a cow* **~wert** m *efficiency* **n·utzbar** a *useful, profitable* ‖ *effective* (*h. p.*) ‖ besser ~ m *to revitalize* ‖ etw e–r S ~ m *to put a th to the uses of a th* ‖ sich etw ~ m *to utilize, to turn to account* od *to one's advantage, to lay a th under contribution* ‖ *to mobilize* (f *for*) ‖ *to harness the trade to the wheels of a plan* | ≗**keit** f ~/ *usefulness*, etc ≗**-machung** f *utilization* **n·ütze** a *useful, of use* ‖ nichts ~ *of no use* ‖ zu nichts ~ s *to be good for nothing, to be no good* **N·utzen** m ~s/~ **A.** *use* ‖ (Nützlichkeit) *utility* ‖ (Vorteil) *profit, gain, advantage, benefit* ‖ ⟨com⟩ geringer ~ ⟨a.⟩ *small returns* pl **B. mit** geringem ~ anwenden *to turn to little account*; .. lesen *to read unprofitably*; .. verkaufen *to sell at a small profit* | **von** ~ f e–e S s *to be of advantage* od *use to a cause*; .. f jdn *to be useful for a p* ‖ v gr., geringem ~ s: *money would do much, little good* ‖ nicht mehr v ~ s: *he was no longer any use* ‖ nicht v ~ s *to be unhelpful* ‖ *it was of no particular good* (f *to*) ‖ *it won't do any good* | jdm **zum** ~ gereichen *to do a p much good, to turn to a p's advantage* **C.** bei diesem Geschäft **bleibt** nur ein geringer ~ *this b. only shows a small profit* ‖ ~ **bringen** *to yield* (*a*) *profit*; e–m .. *to benefit a p* ‖ ~ h v *to gain by, to take advantage of* ‖ ~ v etw h *to stand to profit from* .. **~ ziehen** aus *to derive advantage* od *profit from, to benefit by*; *to cash in on*; *to make capital out of* **n·utzen,** ≗ **I.** vt [h] *to utilize, use*; *to put to account* ‖ nütze den Tag! *make the best use of the day*! ‖ die Gelegenheit ~ *to improve the occasion, to avail o.s. of the opportunity* ‖ ⟨for⟩ (e–n Wald) zu wenig (viel) ~ *to underwork* (*overwork*) **II.** vi [h] [dat] *to be of use, to be useful* (*to*); *to serve* (*for*) **A.** etw, viel ~ *to be of some, great use* ‖ nichts, wenig ~ *to avail nothing, little*; *to do little good* ‖ das wird nicht viel ~ *that won't* (*help much* od) *do any good* | **was** nützt es, daß ..? *what avails it that* ..? ‖ was nützt das alles? *what's the use* od *good of it all*? ‖ wozu nützt das? *what good is that*?, *what is the good of that*? | wenn's nicht nützt, schadet's auch nichts *even if not useful, it can do no harm, that does nothing one way or another* **B.** [dat] das kann uns wenig ~ *that won't help us much, that will do us little good, we shall be none the better for it* ‖ wem nützt das? *who will profit by that*? ‖ es soll der Allgemeinheit ~ *it is intended for the public good* ‖ das nützt dir gar nichts *that doesn't get you anywhere* **n·ützlich** a *useful, conducive, profitable, advantageous, beneficial, helpful* ‖ *serviceable* (*gifts*) ‖ *a useful* (*member of society*) ‖ bei, in, zu etw ~ s *to be useful in, for a th* ‖ sich ~ m *to make o.s. useful, to make good*; sich ~ erweisen *to come in useful* | etw ~ [adv] verwenden *to use a th to good advantage* | das Angenehme mit dem ≗en verbinden *to combine pleasure with utility* od *business with pleasure* | ≗**keit** f ~/ *usefulness, utility, advantageousness, profitableness* ‖ *serviceableness* | ~sprinzip [n] *utilitarian principle*; ~srücksicht [f] *consideration of utility*; ~ssystem [n] *utilitarianism* **n·utzlos** a *bootless* | [adv] ~ arbeiten *to plough sand*(*s*) **N·utzung** f ~/~en *using*; *beneficial use*; *utilization* ‖ ⟨at⟩ friedliche ~ *peaceful uses* pl ‖ ⟨jur⟩ *usufruct* ‖ (Ertrag) *revenue, produce* | ~s(vor)anschlag [m] *estimate of revenue*; ~recht [n] *easement*; *beneficial interest*; ~swert [m] *value of produce*

N·ylon ['nai–] n ~s/~s *nylon* ‖ Netz≗ *mesh n.*; Streck≗ *stretchable n.* | ~pelz [m] *n.-fleece*; ~strümpfe [m pl] *n.s*; ~tanker [m] ⟨mar⟩ *flexitainer*; ≗verstärkt [a] *n.-reinforced*

Nymph·äum n ~s/–äen, (Nymphenbad) *grotto*

N·ymphe f ~/~n *nymph* ‖ ⟨ent⟩ *naiad, chrysalis, nymph* ≗**nhaft** a *nymphlike* **Nymphoman·ie** f ~/ *nymphomania*

Nyst·agmus m ~/ (Augenzittern) *nystagmus*

O

O, o [n] ~/~ *O, o*; **o!** [intj] (→ ⟨a.⟩ oh) **1.** *O*! *oh*! ‖ o ja (nein)! *oh yes* (*no*)! *to be sure*!, ⟨fam⟩ *rather*!; (*far from it*!, *not at all*) ‖ o Gott! *good heavens*!, o–la–la! *ô là, là* Fr, o weh! *alas*!, *oh dear*! **2.** o **daß** .. doch .. (*how*) *I wish* (*that*) (*I had gone*) **3.** o **wie** herrlich! *how splendid*! ‖ o welche Freude! *what a pleasure*! **O-Beine** n pl *bow* od *bandy legs* ‖ ‖ o-beinig [a] *bandy-legged*; O-Beinigkeit [f] ⟨med⟩ *valgus* **O-Bus** m → Bus (f Oberleitungsbus) *trolly-bus* **O-Wagen** m ⟨rail⟩ *platform-car*

·**Oakland** ['ouklənd] n (Stadt in Kalifornien)

O·ase f ~/~n *oasis* ‖ ⟨fig⟩: *like a gleam of light*

·**ob**[1] [conj] **1.** *if, whether* ‖ *she asked if he had arrived* ‖ es fragt sich, ~ .. *I wonder whether* .. ‖ *I do not know whether* (*there will be time*) ‖ ich weiß überhaupt noch nicht ~ .. *I don't know that I'm going at all* ‖ zweifeln: *I doubt* (od *there is doubt, it is doubtful*) *whether* .. | [ell] (ich frage mich,) ~ sie wohl kommt *I wonder if* od *whether she will come* ‖ ~ ich gehe? *should I go*? ‖ ~ wir wohl auch ..? *were we like that, I wonder*? ‖ ~ er wohl .. *will he come, do you think*? **2.** [neg] ~ ..

nicht *who knows but she thought of him still, .. but (what) he may be ill!* **3.** (Fragewiederholung) (*you know her of course*) ∼ ich sie kenne? *Do I not!* ‖ ∼ ich Sie .. *Did you say, would I marry you?* **4.** (Antwort) (na) **und ob!**: (*does he fence, then?*) u ∼! *Does he fence! He's a marvellous fencer* ‖ ⟨emph⟩ *know it! don't I!* ‖ *of course I do!* (*most*) *certainly!, definitely!, delighted!, every time* ‖ ⟨fam⟩ *rather!, I should just* od *rather think so!* ‖ (*does it hurt?*) *you bet it hurts! not half!* ‖ wurde getanzt? – u ∼! *rather; and we made a night of it* ‖ (*he was a fool*) *all right* **5. als** ∼ *as if, as though* ‖ *I feel as if I could* (möchte) *cry* ‖ er tut so, als ∼ er was täte *he pretends to be working* ‖ ⟨Am⟩ *it looks like it's going to rain* od *like it might rain* ‖ so tun, als ob man nicht verstände *to play at cross-purposes* | **nicht** als ∼ ich es nicht bedauerte *not that I am not sorry for it* | ∼ .. **auch** (*or* schon, wohl) *although, even though* (*he may be right*) | ob .. **oder nicht,** .. *whether or not we share his opinion* .. ‖ *whether it be true or not* | s–e Art ∼ angenehm oder **(ob)** unangenehm *his manners, good or bad*

·ob[2] [prep] **1.** [dat] (*up*)*on, above* ‖ *over* ‖ Rothenburg ob der Tauber (abbr o. T.) *R. above the T.* ‖ [dat] = *because of; for,* → **2.** [gen] .. ob (= wegen) ihres Irrtums *he scolded her for* (od *on account of*) .. **·Ob-**[2] **~acht** f *heed, care* ‖ ∼ geben *or* h (auf acc) *to pay attention* (*to*); *to give, take, pay heed* (*to*) ‖ in ∼ nehmen *to take care of* ‖ ∼! (*be*) *careful!* **≗bemeldet, ≗benannt, ≗besagt** (alle obs) a *above-mentioned, -said* **~dach** n *shelter* ‖ ⟨fig⟩ *lodging, dwelling, home* ‖ jdm ∼ geben, gewähren *to harbour a p, to give shelter to a p* ‖ kein ∼ h *to be homeless* ‖ unter ∼ bringen *to place, put, get under shelter* | ≗los [a] *unsheltered, homeless* ‖ ∼ m *to unhouse*; ∼lose(r) [m] ∼n/∼n *casual* (*poor*) ‖ die ∼n [pl] *the homeless* ‖ ∼losenasyl [n] *casual ward*; in ein ∼ aufnehmen *to ward*

Obdukti·on [–ts–] f ∼/∼en *autopsy; post mortem* (*examination*) **obduz·ieren** vt *to hold an inquest on*

Obedi·enz f ∼/ ⟨ec R. C.⟩ *obedience*

Obel·isk m ∼en/∼en *obelisk*

·oben adv **A.** (höher *or* weiter zurückliegend) *above* ‖ (hoch ∼) *aloft, on high*; ⟨typ⟩ *above*; ganz ∼ *top*; v ∼ nach unten *above from top, top to bottom* ‖ (im Hause) *upstairs* ‖ (außen) *on the surface* ‖ ⟨fig⟩ (bei Vorgesetzten) *in high quarters* **B.** da, dort ∼ *up there* ‖ mehr, weiter ∼ *higher* od *further up* ‖ (im Buche) *hereinbefore* ‖ ⟨fig⟩ ∼ hui, unten pfui *nothing but outside show* ‖ mir steht die S bis hier ∼ *I'm sick and tired of the whole matter* **C.** etw ∼ **ab**schneiden *to cut a piece off from the top* ‖ etw ∼ abschöpfen *to skim the surface of a th* ⟨a. fig⟩ ‖ ⟨fig⟩ den Kopf ∼ behalten! *keep your head!, never say die!* ‖ ∼ **er**wähnt *mentioned above* ‖ der ∼ liegt (Kampf) ⟨sl⟩ *top-dog* ‖ ∼ gelegen *upstairs* (*room*) ‖ ∼ **sitzen** *to sit at the top, at the head of the table* **D.** → **~an** ‖ e–e M. entfernt ∼ am Berge *a mile up the hill* ‖ ∼ **auf** *on top of* (*a tower*) ‖ *at the top of* (*a mountain*) ‖ *to sit atop a car* ‖ dort ∼ auf .. *there above on the roof* ‖ *at the head* od *top of the list* ‖ ∼ **drüber** *overhead* ‖ ∼ **im** Hause *on the upper floor* ‖ ∼ im 1. Stock *up on the first floor* ‖ (hoch) ∼ in *up in* (*the air, the wood*) ‖ **nach** ∼: *to go upwards, to go upstairs* ‖ (Kräfte) nach ∼ bringen *to bring into the ascendant* ‖ **von** ∼ *from above* ‖ (*orders*) *of the leader; the order comes from headquarters* ‖ v ∼ geführt *guided from on high* ‖ v ∼ bis unten ansehen, mustern *to measure with one's eye, to examine from head to foot* ‖ ⟨Am⟩ *to give a p the once over*; → A. ‖ v ∼ herab *from on high, from above* ‖ ⟨fig⟩ *haughtily, condescendingly, superciliously* ‖ jdn v ∼ herab ⟨fig⟩ *on the high ropes*; .. ansehen *to look down one's nose at* (od *down upon*) *a p; to high-hat a p*; .. behandeln *to treat .. contemptuously* ‖ v ∼ nach unten *downward*; .. kehren *to turn over from top to bottom* ‖ alles Gute kommt v ∼ *all blessings come from above* **·oben-** **~·ab** adv *from the top* od *surface* **~·an** adv *at the top* od *head* (*of the table*) ‖ *in the first place*; ⟨fig⟩ *at the top of the tree* **~·angegeben** a *above-named* **~·anstehend** a *chief*; *most* (*interesting*, etc) **~·auf** adv *above, uppermost, on the surface, atop* ‖ ⟨fig⟩ *in good health, in high spirits, up*(*pish*); (der Lump) sitzt ∼ .. *is top-dog*; er ist wieder ∼ *he is again h.s.* **~·aus** adv = ∼hinaus **~dr·ein** adv *besides, into the bargain, over and above; to boot; on the top of it* ‖ Sünde und Schande ∼ *sin and shame added* **~erw·ähnt** a *above-mentioned* **~gen·annt** a *said* **~h·in** adv *superficially, carelessly, slightly, airily; anyhow* ‖ ∼ tun *to half-do, to botch* ‖ ∼geworfen: *their off-hand "so longs"* **~hin·auf** adv *up to the top* **~hin·aus** adv *out above*; ∼ wollen ⟨fig⟩ *to give o.s. airs, to have high notions* od *high-flying ideas* ‖ sie geht leicht ∼ *she is hasty-tempered* **≗-ohne** n [invar] *topless* (*bikini, girl*), *mono-kini; no-bra* (*bather*) **≗öl** n ⟨mot⟩ *upper cylinder lubricant*

·ober a *higher* (*clouds, rank, form, notes*); *top* (*shelf*) ‖ *upper* (*storey, Nile*) ‖ ⟨fig⟩ *chief, superior* ‖ *supreme* (*authorities*) ‖ ∼e Grenze *upward limit* ‖ *supreme* (*authorities*) ‖ ∼e Grenze *upward limit*; am ∼en Ende [gen] *at the top of* (*the street*); ∼e Seite, Fläche etc *top*; ∼er Seitenrand (Buch, Zeitung) *head margin*; die ∼en 10000 *the upper classes*, ⟨Am⟩ *the upper crust* | ˣprep [dat] [österr] = über **·Ober** m ∼s/∼ ⟨cards⟩ *trump knave* ‖ Herr ∼! *waiter!* **~admiral** m *high admiral* **~äg·ypten** n *Upper Egypt* **~·älteste(r)** m *senior master* (*of a guild*) **~·amtmann** m *high bailiff* **~-appelati·onsgericht** n *High Court of Appeal* **~arm** m *upper* (*part of the*) *arm* **~arzt** m *senior physician* **~aufseher** m *principal inspector, inspector general, chief-surveyor, superintendent* **~aufsicht** f *chief inspection, superintendence* | ∼sbehörde [f] *central office* **~bau** m *overhead construction; building above ground* ‖ (Brücke) *superstructure* ⟨a. fig⟩ ‖ ⟨rail⟩ *permanent way* **~beamte(r)** m *superior functionary, head-clerk* **~befehl** m *supreme command* (führen *to have*) **~bef·ehlshaber** m *commander-in-chief, General officer c.ding-in-ch., c.-ding g.* ‖ ∼ des Heeres (der Flotte) *Chief of the Army Command* (*Naval Operations*) **~begriff** m *wider concept; category* **~beleuchtung** f *top* od *sky, overhead lighting* **~b·erg-** ∼amt [n] (*Superior*) *Board of* (*the*) *Mines*; ∼hauptmann [m] *Inspector General of* (*the*) *Mines* **~bett** n *coverlet* **~bibliothekar** m *chief librarian* **~boden** m *upper-loft, garret* °**~bonze** m *chief boss* **~bramsegel** n ⟨mar⟩ *royal* (*sail*) **~bürgermeister** m *chief burgomaster*; ⟨engl⟩ *Lord Mayor* **~deck** n ⟨mar⟩ *upper deck* **≗deutsch** a *Upper-German* ‖ ∼deutsche Hochebene [f] *Upper German Plain* **~einnehmer** m *receiver-general* **~fähnrich** m *aspirant officer* °**≗faul** a *fishy*, ⟨Am⟩ *phon*(*e*)*y* **~f·eld-** ∼herr [m] (*supreme*) *commander-in-chief*; ∼webel [m] *sergeant first class*; ∼zeugmeister [m] *master of the ordnance* **~f·euerwerker** m ⟨mil⟩ *chief artificer* od *gunner* **~fenster** n (e–r Tür) *transom* **~fläche** f *surface*, matte ∼ *dull finish*; weiche, wollige ∼ *nap*; nur die ∼ berühren *to skim the s.*; ⟨math⟩ *superficies, area*; an der ∼ *on the outside*; .. schwimmen *to float on the surface* ‖ mehr als nur an der ∼ *more than meets the eye* ‖ an die ∼ k *to break surface*; ⟨mar⟩ *to surface*; ⟨fig⟩ *to leap to* (od *to force*) *the s.* ‖ ⟨geol⟩ an die ∼ treten *to outcrop* ‖ | ∼nbeschaffenheit [f] *s. conditions* pl; ∼nentwässerung [f] ⟨geog⟩ *s. drainage*; ∼ngeschwindigkeit [f] (U-Boot) *s. speed*; ∼ngestaltung [f] ⟨geog⟩ *topography*; ∼nhärtung [f] *casehardening*; ∼qualität [f] ⟨tech⟩ *s. finish, s. quality*; ∼nreibung [f] *skin friction* **≗flächlich** a *superficial*; (*beauty is but*) *skin-deep*; *but s.-d.* (*wound*) ⟨a. fig⟩;

⟨fig⟩ *cursory, passing* (*attention*); (P) *flippant, flimsy, shallow* ‖ ~e Kenntnis *a smattering*; (*but a*) *bowing* (*acquaintance*) (mit *with*); nach ~er Schätzung *at a rough estimate* | [adv] *in a fashion, perfunctorily*; ~ mit–e–a bekannt *on speaking terms* ‖ ~ behandeln *to skim over, to treat cursorily, to scratch merely the surface of*; *to tinker with* ‖ ~ betrachtet *superficially considered*; *seen on the surface*; *at a surface inspection*; nur ~ kennen *to know .. but slightly* | ~keit [f] *superficiality, futility, levity, frivolity, shallowness* **~förster** m *head forester* **~f·ürsorgerin** f *senior woman social worker* **≈gärig** a *top-fermenting* **~gärtner** m *head-gardener* **~gärung** f *surface* od ⟨brew⟩ *high fermentation* **~gefreite(r)** m *corporal*; *private first class*; ⟨artill⟩ *acting bombardier* **~gericht** n *High Court of Judicature, Supreme Court*; *superior court* (*of justice*) **~geschoß** n *upper storey* **~gewalt** f *sovereignty, supreme authority, supremacy* **~gewand** n ⟨ec⟩ *cassock* **~gurt** m *head arch* **≈halb** adv (& prep [gen]) *on the upper-side, above* **~hand** f *upper hand, superiority* ‖ die ~ bek, gewinnen *to win* od *gain the upper hand, to prevail, to win the day* ‖ (über [acc]) *to get the whip-hand* (*of*), *to conquer*; .. über jdn *to get the better* (⟨Am⟩ *best*) *of a p*; .. behalten *to remain supreme*, ⟨fam⟩ *to carry it*; die ~ h *to be uppermost* (a. S); *to have the best of it, to be top dog*; *predominate, prevail* **~haupt** n *head, chief, lord* ‖ (Schleuse) *head bay* **~haus** n *Upper Chamber* ‖ ⟨engl⟩ *House of Lords* ‖ ⟨Am⟩ *Senate* **~haut** f *epidermis, cuticle* **~hefe** f *high fermentation yeast* **~hemd** n *day-shirt, dress-shirt* | ~einsatz [m] *sh.-front*, ⟨Am⟩ *bosom* **~herr** m *supreme lord, sovereign* | ≈lich [a] (*belonging to the*) *sovereign*; ~lichkeit [f] *sovereignty*; ~schaft [f] *sovereignty, supremacy, hegemony* **~hirt(e)** m ⟨ec⟩ *bishop, prelate* **~h·of-** ~gericht [n] *Supreme Court of Justice, High-Court*; ~marschall [m] *Lord High-Marshal*; ~meister [m] *Steward, Lord High Steward*; ~meisterin [f] *Mistress of the Robes*; ~prediger [m] *First Chaplain* (*in ordinary*) **~hoheit** f = ~gewalt **~hütten-** ~amt [n] *chief board of superintendence* (*of a foundry*); ~meister [m] *director of a foundry* **~ingenieur** m *chief engineer* **≈irdisch** a *overground*; ~e Leitung ⟨el⟩ *overhead conveyance* (od *lead* od *wire*); *surface* [attr] (*shelter*) **≈italienische Seen** m pl *Lakes in Upper Italy* **~jäger** m *first huntsman* ‖ ⟨mil⟩ *corporal* (*of rifle-men*) | ~meister [m] *Grand Master of the Huntsmen* **~kammer** f *Upper-Chamber* | ≈er [m] *master of the robes, Lord High Chamberlain*; ~herr [m] *Groom of the Stole* **~kante** f *top edge* **~kaplan** m *High Chaplain* **~kellner** n *head-waiter* **~kiefer** m *upper jaw* **~k·irchenrat** m (Versammlung) *High-Consistory* ‖ (Mitglied) *member of the H.-C.* **~klasse** f *upper class* (*of society*) ‖ ⟨Ger⟩ *upper forms* (*in a higher secondary school*) **~kleid** n *upper garment* **~koch** m *master-cook* **~kommando** n *high command* ‖ ⟨Ger⟩ das ~ der Wehrmacht (des Heeres *Army*) *High C.*; *General Headquarters* ‖ .. der Kriegsmarine *the Supreme Naval C.* **~konsistorium** n *High-Consistory* **~körper** m *upper* (*part of the*) *body* **~k·üchenmeister** m *master* od *clerk of the kitchen* **~kurs** m ⟨univ⟩ *advanced course* **~lafette** f *upper carriage*; ⟨mar⟩ *u. mounting* **~land** n *up-country, upland, highland, upper country* ‖ Berner ~ *Bernese Oberland* ‖ das ~ im südlichen Schottland *the Uplands* **~länder** m *highlander* **~l·andesgericht** n *Superior Provincial Court*; *Supreme Court of the country* | ~srat [m] *Councillor of the Superior Provincial Court* **≈lastig** a *top-heavy* **~lauf** m (e–s Flusses) *upper course* od *reaches*; *headwaters* **~leder** n *uppers* (*of boots*) **~l·ehnsherr** m *Sovereign Lord, Lord Paramount* | ~schaft [f] *paramountcy, suzerainty* **~lehrer** m *senior master* **~leib** m *upper-body* **~leitung** f *chief-management, supreme direction* ‖ ⟨el⟩ (*conduction by*) *overhead wires* | ~sträger [m] ⟨el⟩ *o.h. bearer* od pl *framework* ~sbus → O-Bus **~leutnant** m *first lieutenant*; ⟨aero⟩ *flying officer*; ⟨mar⟩ ~ zur See ⟨engl⟩ *lieutenant* (*R. N.*) **~licht** n *skylight, overhead l.*(*ing*); ⟨theat⟩ (*l.ing*) *batten*; (e–r Tür) *fan-l.* (a. Fenster), ⟨Am⟩ *transom*; mit ~ *sky-lighted* **~liga** f ⟨ftb, etc⟩ *major-league* **~lippe** f *upper-lip* **~lotse** m *chief pilot* **~lyzeum** n *highest secondary school for girls* **~macht** f *predominance, supreme authority, supremacy* **~mast** f ⟨for⟩ *mast proper* **~matrose** m *leading seaman* **~meister** m *chief master* °**~motz** m ~es/~e *king, king pippin*; ⟨fam⟩ *sachem* ⟨Am⟩ *boss*; ~ s *to boss* **~mus·ikmeister** m ⟨mil⟩ *trumpet-major* **~pfarre** f *rectory*; *rectorship* **~pfarrer** m *head-minister*, ⟨engl⟩ *rector* **~p·ost-** ~amt [n] *general post-office* (*G. P. O.*); ~direktion [f] *administration of the G. P. O.*, *Regional Postal Directorate* **~präsident** m ⟨Ger; etwa⟩ *Lord Lieutenant of a province* **~priester** m *high-priest* | ≈lich [a] *pontifical* **~prim·aner** m *Upper VI-boy* **~quart·iermeister** m *Quarter-master-General* **~rabb·iner** m *chief rabbi* **~rang** m *superiority* **~re·alschule** f ⟨Ger⟩ *higher modern school* **~r·echnungskammer** f *Exchequer and Audit Department* **~richter** m *chief justice* **~rheinische Tiefebene** f *Lowlands of the Upper Rh.* **~rinde** f *upper crust* **~rock** m *greatcoat, overcoat* **~satz** m *major* (*premise*) **≈schächtig** = –schlächtig **~schaffner** m *head guard* **~schale** f *cup* ‖ ⟨cul⟩ *buttock-steak, round*; ⟨Am⟩ *r.-steak* **~sch·atzmeister** m *Lord High Treasurer* **~schenk** m *head cup-bearer* **~schenkel** m *thigh* **~schicht** f ⟨geol & fig⟩ *upper stratum* ‖ die geistige ~ *the intellectual leaders* **≈schlächtig** a (Mühle) *over-shot* **~schreiber** m *head-clerk* **~schule** f *upper-school* **~sch·ulrat** m *senior inspector of schools* **~schwelle** f ⟨arch⟩ *summer, lintel* **~schwester** f *senior sister*, ⟨Am⟩ *chief nurse* **~schwingung** f *harmonic* | ~sfrequenz [f] *h. fr.* **~see** m *Lake Superior* **~segel** n *upper-sail, top-sail* **~sekund·aner** m *Upper V-boy* **~staatsanwalt** m *director of public prosecution*; **~st·absarzt** m *surgeon-major*; ⟨mar⟩ *surgeon commander* **~st·absveterinär** m *Major of the* (*Royal*) *Army Veterinary Corps* **~st·adtdirektor** m *town clerk* **~st·allmeister** m (*Lord Grand*) *Master of the Horse* **~steiger** m ⟨min⟩ *master-miner* **~stenge** f ⟨mar⟩ *top-gallant mast* **~st·euereinnehmer** m *Receiver-General of Taxes* **~st·euermann** m ⟨mar⟩ *first mate* **~stimme** f ⟨mus⟩ *treble, soprano, discant* **~stübchen** n ⟨fig fam⟩ *garret, attic*; *upper story*; nicht richtig im ~ *a little cracked*; ⟨sl⟩ *off one's chump* **~stube** f *upper room* **~st·udiendirektor** m *head master* (*of a secondary school*) **~stufe** f *higher grade*; *upper school* ⟨engl⟩ *remove*; *lower and upper sixth* **~tasse** f *cup* (u Untertasse *and saucer*) **~teil** m *upper part* **~terti·aner** m *Upper IV-boy* **~ton** m *harmonic* (*tone*) **~verdeck** n ⟨mar⟩ *upper deck* **~verwalter** m *agent* **~v·ormund** m *chief guardian* **~vorstellung** f *dominant idea* **~wachtmeister** m *squadron sergeant-major* **≈wärts** *upward*(*s*) **~wasser** n *upper* od *upstream*; *headwater* ‖ (oberschlächtig) *overshot water* ‖ ~ bek ⟨fig⟩ *to get the upper hand*, ⟨Am sl⟩ *to get the bulge* (über .. *on a p*) **~welt** f *upper world* **~w·erftdirektor** m *Admiral Superintendent of Dockyard* **~zählbezirk** m *census area* **~zähler** m ⟨demog⟩ *inspector, supervisor* **~zahn** m *upper tooth* **~z·ollamt** n *general custom house* **~z·ollinspektor** m → Zollober– **·Obere** m [der ~, ein ~r] *superior* ‖ ⟨ec⟩ (*Father*) *Superior* ‖ das ~ *the top* ‖ Oberer See [m] *Lake Superior* (*U.S.A.*) → Obersee **·Oberin** f ~/~nen *matron*, (*lady*) *superior* **·Obers** n ~/ [österr] (süße Sahne) *cream* **·oberst** a [sup v ober] *uppermost, topmost* (*bottle*), *highest* ‖ *top* (*deck, floor, 200, layer*) ‖ ⟨fig⟩ *chief, principal*; *supreme* (*law*) ‖ ⟨school⟩ er ist der ~e *he is head of his form* ‖ ~e Gewalt *supremacy* || ~er Schüler *head boy* || ~e Heeresleitung [f] *general headquarters* | [adv] z ~ *uppermost, atop* ·**Oberst** m ~en/~en *colonel* **~arzt** m *surgeon-c.* **~l·eutnant** m *lieutenant-c.*; ⟨aero⟩ *wing commander* **~enstelle** f *colonelcy* ·**obgedacht** a *above-mentioned* (→ ob-)

obgl·eich conj (*al*)*though* (*she is fair* od *she may be fair*) || *fair as she is* || *presumptious though it may appear* || ~ er steif u fest das Gegenteil behauptete *in spite of his bray to the contrary*

·**Obhut** f ~/ (Verwahrung) *keeping* (*in God's k.*) || (Fürsorge) *care* || (Schutz) *protection, guard* || sich in jds ~ begeben *to place o.s. under the protection of a p*; *to put o.s. under a p's care* || in jds ~ geben *to give into a p's charge* || in s–e ~ nehmen *to take charge of*

·**obig** a *above, former, fore-going, above-said, above-mentioned* || → obengenannt etc

Obj·ekt n ~(e)s/~e *subject* ⟨a. phot⟩; ⟨micro⟩ *specimen*; *object* ⟨a. gram⟩ (e–s Satzes *in a sentence*); gefährdete ~e [pl] ⟨mil⟩ *likely targets* | ~mikrometer [n] *stage m.*; ~sprache [f] (Ggs Meta–) *object l.*; ~schutz [m] ⟨mil⟩ *vulnerable point protection*; ~sicherung [f] ⟨mil⟩ *target defense* N; ~träger [m] *slide* (*of a microscope*); *specimen holder* **~·iv** n ~(e)s/~e *object-glass* od *-lens* | ~revolver [m] ⟨micro⟩ *multiple nosepiece*, –kopf [m] ⟨phot⟩ *lens turret*; ~ring [m] *lens adapter*; ~satz [m] *lens combination* **≃·iv** a *objective* || (unparteiisch) *impartial*; *detached* (*consideration*) **≃iv·ieren** vt [h] *to objectify* **~ivit·ät** f ~/ *objectiveness* || *impartiality, detachment*

Obl·ate f ~/~n *wafer*; ⟨ec⟩ *host*; *communion wafer*

·**ob|liegen** vi [h] **1.** (S) (jdm) ⟨jur⟩ *to lie on* od *fall to* (*a p*) || es liegt mir ob *or* obliegt mir *I am responsible for it*; *I am in duty bound, it devolves on me, it is incumbent on me* (z tun *to do*); ⟨fam⟩ *it is up to him* (*to do*) **2.** (P) (e–r S) *to apply* od *devote o.s. to, to study* (*a th*), *to attend to* || **≃heit** f ~/~en *responsibility*; *incumbancy, duty*; *obligation, function, office*

oblig·at a & adv *indispensable* || (üblich) *regulation* [attr]; *obligatory, customary* || ⟨univ⟩ *required* (*subjects*); ⟨mus⟩ *obligato* (*flute*) **≃i·on** f ~/~en *obligation* || ⟨bank⟩ *bond, debenture*; Industrie≃ ⟨m. m.⟩ *corporate b.*; Inhaber≃ (*non-registered* od) *coupon b.*; Klein≃ *baby b.* **≃i·ons-** **~gläubiger** m *bond-creditor, obligee* **~-schein** m *bond* **~schuld** f *bond-debt* **~schuldner** m *bond-debtor, obligor* **~·orisch** a (für) *obligatory* (*on*), *compulsory* (*instruction, subject, attendance*) ⟨jur⟩ *mandatory*; ⟨tech⟩ *enforced* ·**Obligo** n ~s/~s *engagement* || ohne ~ *free from liability, without prejudice* od *recourse*

·**Obmann** m (Vorsitzender) *chairman* || (der Geschworenen) *foreman* || (Schiedsmann) *umpire* || ⟨school⟩ *class spokesman*

Ob·oe f ~/~n *hautboy, oboe*

·**Obolus** m ~/~ & –len *obol* || ⟨fig⟩ *mite*

·**Obrigkeit** f ~/~en *authorities*, ⟨bib⟩ *powers* pl || *government, magistracy* || die ~ ausüben *to carry on the executive power* | ~sgeist [m], ~sdenken [n] *subservience to authority* od *authoritarianism*; ~sstaat [m] *authoritarian state* | **≃-lich** a *by* (*high*) *authority, magisterial* || ~es Amt [n] *magistracy* †**Obr·ist** m = Oberst

obsch·on conj = obgleich

Observ·anz f ~/~en *observance, custom, usance*

Observat·orium n ~s/–rien *observatory*

·**obsiegen** vi [h] *to be victorious, to gain one's cause, to carry the day* || [dat] *to triumph over* || (e~r S) *to conquer*

obsk·ur a *obscure* ⟨a. fig⟩ || ~e Größe (P) *nonentity* **≃·ant** m ~en/~en *obscurant*(*ist*) **≃an-t·ismus** m ~/ *obscurantism*

obsol·et a *antiquated*; *obsolete*

Obst n ~es/ *fruit* || *a variety of fruits* || (als Nachtisch) *dessert* || (abnehmen *pluck*, auflesen *pick up*, einmachen *preserve*, kochen *stew*, ziehen *cultivate*) || bei ~ u Eis *taking fruits and ices*; (ich) danke für ~! *thank you for nothing*! **~bau** m *fruit-culture* od *-growing*; *orcharding* **~baum** m *f.-tree* **~boden** m *store-room for f.* **~branntwein** m *f.-brandy* **~brecher** m (P & Werkzeug) *f.-gatherer* **~darre** f *f.-kiln* **~ernte** f *f.-crop* **~fleck** m *stain of f.* **~frau** f *f.-woman, coster*(*-monger*) **~garten** m *orchard* **~gärtner** m *f.-grower, orchardman* **~-händler,** **~höker** m *f.erer, coster*(*-monger*), *f.-seller* **~händlerin,** **~hökerin** f = ~frau **~jahr** n *f.-year* **~kammer** f *f.-chamber, f.-loft* **~keller** m *f.-cellar* **~kelter** f *f.-press* **~kenner** m *pomologist* **~kern** m *stone, kernel* || (Apfel, Birnen etc) *pip* **~konserven** f pl *tinned* od *canned f.* **~korb** m *f.-basket* **~kuchen** m *f.-tart* **~kultur** f = ~bau **~kunde** f *pomology* **~lese** f *f.-gathering* **~markt** m *f.-market* **~messer** n *f.-knife* **~most** m *cider, perry* **~mus** n *jam*, (v Apfelsinen) *marmalade* **~pflanzung** f *f.-grove* **≃reich** a *abounding in f.* **~saft** m → Frucht– **~salat** m → Frucht–, *mixed fruit, fr. salad* **~schale** f *fr.-dish* **~sorte** f *kind of fr.*; ~n [pl] *fruits* pl **~stand** m *f.-stall* **~törtchen** n *tartlet*; *turnover* **~torte** f *fruit tart* **~- u Gemüseladen** m *greengrocery* **~wein** m *f.-wine, perry, cider* **~zeit** f *f.-season* **~zucht** f *f.-culture* **~züchter** m *f.-grower*

obstin·at a *obstinate* **Obstipati·on** f ~/ *constipation* **obstru·ieren** vt [h] ⟨parl⟩ *to obstruct* || ⟨med⟩ *to constipate* **Obstrukti·on** f ~/~en *obstruction*; ⟨Am sl⟩ *filibuster*(*ing*) || ~ treiben *to practise obstr., to stone-wall*; ⟨Am sl⟩ *to filibuster* **~s-politik** = ~ || **~spolitiker** m *obstructionist*, ⟨Am sl⟩ *filibuster*

obsz·ön a *obscene* **Obszönit·ät** f ~/~en *obscenity*

·**ob|walten** vi [h] **1.** (P) *to rule over, to control* **2.** (S) *to exist, prevail* || unter den ~den Umständen *under the* (*prevailing*) *circumstances, as matters stand* od *stood*

obw·ohl, obzw·ar conj = obgleich

·**Ochse** (a. Ochs) m ~n/~n *ox* [pl *oxen*]; *bullock*; junger ~ *steer* || ⟨fig fam⟩ *blockhead, fool, boor* || der ~ brüllt .. *bellows* || (er steht da) wie der ~ am Berge .. *in great embarrassment* || v e–m ~n kann man nicht mehr verlangen als Rindfleisch *you can't make a silk purse out of a sow's ear* °·**ochsen** vi [h] *to cram*, ⟨sl⟩ *to swot, mug, stew*; *to grind* (an *at*); ⟨Am sl⟩ *to bone*; *crack* (*a book*) | ≃ [n] *cramming* etc ·**Ochsen-** **~auge** n ⟨bot⟩ *ox-eye, bull's eye* || ⟨arch⟩ *porthole light, bull's eye*, (oval) *dormer-window* || ⟨bot⟩ *ox-eye* || ⟨cul⟩ *fried egg* **≃äugig** a *ox-eyed* **~braten** m *roast beef* **~fleisch** n *beef* **~frosch** m *bull-frog* **~galle** f *ox-gall* **~geschlecht** n ⟨scient⟩ *bovine genus* **~gespann** n *team of oxen* **~handel** m *cattle trade* **~-händler** m *dealer in bullocks, drover* **~haut** f *ox-hide, neat's hide* **~hirt** m *neat-herd* **~kalb** n *bull-calf* **~karren** m *ox-wagon* od *-cart* **~knochen** m *ox-bone* **~kopf** m *bull's head* (a. fig ⟨hors⟩) || ⟨vulg⟩ *blockhead* **~kraut** n ⟨bot⟩ = Hauhechel **~leder** n *neat's leather* **~markschnitte** f *spline of beef* **≃mäßig** a *ox-like* || ⟨fam⟩ *blockish, rude, coarse* **~maulsalat** m *ox-muzzle salad* **~schwanzsuppe** f *oxtail soup* **~stall** m *neat-* od *cow-house* **~treiber** m *drover* **~wamme** f *dewlap* **~zaun** m *ox-fence* **~ziemer** m *cowhide*; dazu: *to c.h.* **~zunge** f *neat's tongue* || ⟨bot⟩ *ox-tongue, bugloss* || ⟨mil hist⟩ *ox sword* || ⟨arch⟩ *flat tile* ·**ochsig** a *ox-like* || ⟨fig⟩ *lubberly*, (*huge, enormous*)

·**Öchsle** n ~s/ *specific weight of must*: 90° ~

·**Ocker** m ~s/ *ochre* **≃farben** a *ochreous*

Odal·iske f ~/~n *odalisque*

·**Ode** f ~/~n *ode* (*Sappho, Anacreon, Pindar, Horace*)

·öde a *desert, deserted, desolate* || (kahl, trübe) *bleak* || (unbebaut) *waste* (a. ⟨fig⟩ *w. period*) || (trübselig) *dreary* (*life*) || ⟨fam⟩ (langweilig) *dull* (*speech*), *boring* (*talk*) **·Öde** f ~/~n *desert(edness), wilderness, solitude* || ⟨fig⟩ *dreariness, desolation* **·Öd- ~feld** n *barren field* **~land** n *waste land; barren* (⟨a.⟩ Ödung [f])

·Odem m ⟨poet⟩ = Atem *breath, breathing*

Öd·em n ~s/~e ⟨path⟩ *œdema*

·öden vt [h] *to bore* || sich ~ *to feel bored*

·Odenwald m ⟨Ger⟩ (rechtsrheinisches Gebirge)

·Oder f ⟨Ger⟩ (Fluß)

·oder conj *or* || ~ aber *or else, or again, otherwise* || ~ auch *or rather* || eins ~ das andere *either* (od *alternatively*) *one th or the other* || .., ~? .., *or do* od *are you? or am I mistaken?* || ..~! (wehe!) .., *or defend y.s.*, .., *or you'll see!*

·Odermennig m ⟨bot⟩ *agrimony*

Od·essa n ⟨Russ⟩ (Stadt)

·Odium n ~s/ sich mit dem ~ belasten zu tun *to incur the odium of doing*

Odyss·ee f ~/ *Odyssey*

·Ofen m ~s/≗ *stove* || (zum Schmelzen) *furnace* || (zum Brennen) *kiln* **A.** B·ack≗ *baker's oven* || B·ade≗ *bathroom st.* || Br·enn≗ *firing k., calcining f.* || Br·ut≗ *incubator* || D·auer≗ ⟨tech⟩ *continuous working k.* || Emaill·ier≗ *enamel f.* || Fl·amm≗ *reverbatory(-f.)* || G·as≗ (Zimmer) *gas st.* || G·asr·äucher≗ *gas curing apparatus* || Gl·as≗ *glass f.* || Gl·üh≗ *tempering* od *annealing f.* || H·och≗ *blast f.* || K·achel≗ *tiled st.* || K·alk≗ *lime k.* || K·ammer≗ *retort f., chamber f.* || K·ipp≗ *tilting f.* || Kn·ochenverk·ohlungs≗ *bone carbonizing oven* || K·och≗ *kitchener* || K·ühl≗ *annealing oven* || Kup·ol– *od* K·uppel≗ *cupola* (od *smelting*) *f.* || L·öt≗ *brazing f.* || M·uffel≗ *muffle f.* || Sch·acht≗ *shaft k.* || Schm·iede≗ *f. forge* || Str·eck≗ (Glas) *flattening k.* || Tr·ocken≗ *drying k.* || W·assermantel≗ *water jacket f.* || Zem·entbrenn≗ *cement f.* || Z·iegel≗ *brick k.* od *f.* || Z·immer≗ *stove* | °⟨fig sex⟩ *oven* **B.** e–n ~ abstechen *to tap a f.*; .. anheizen *to light a st., to heat a f.* || ausgeblasener ~ *f. out of blast* || e–n ~ beschlagen *to arm a f.*, .. in Betrieb setzen *to set a f. to work* || ⟨bib⟩ feuriger ~ *fiery f.* || e–n ~ kühlen *to slacken the fire*, kehren, setzen *to sweep, fit a st.*; übersetzen *to overcharge a f.* **C. am,** beim ~ sitzen *to sit near the st.* || **hinterm** ~ hocken *never to stir from one's chimney corner, to be a stay-at-home* || **nach** dem ~ sehen *to see to the stove* || ⟨fig⟩ er weiß den Hund **vom** ~ zu locken ⟨fam⟩ *he's up to snuff* **~aufsatz** m *cornice of a st.* **~bank** f *bench by the st.* || ⟨fig⟩ *chimney-corner* **~blech** n *plate in front of a st.*, (Back≗) *oven-tin* **~bruch** m *tutty* **~gabel** f *poker*; *o.-fork* **~hocker** m *stay-at-home* **~kachel** f *Dutch tile* **~klappe** f *register* **~loch** n *o.-mouth* **~rohr** n *st.-pipe* **~röhre** f (f. Speisen) *o.* || ⟨fig fam⟩ *st.-pipe hat* **~ruß** m *o.-soot* **~sau** f ⟨met⟩ *f.-pig* **~schaufel** f *fire-shovel* **~schirm** m *fire-screen* **~schwärze** f *powdered black-lead* **~setzer** m *st.-fitter* **~tür** f *o.-* (od *st.-*)*door* **~vorsetzer** m *fender* **~wäscher** m *scovel* **~wisch** m *malkin*

·Ofen-P·est n *Budapest*

·offen a **A. 1.** *open, unclosed, not shut* || *open* (*door, carriage, question, shop, secret; vowel, syllable*; ⟨mil⟩ *town,* ⟨pol⟩ *door*); *policy of the open door* || *to have an open ear, hand* || (of buildings, etc.) *to be open* (f *to*) || die Halle ist an den Seiten ~ *the sides of the hall are open* | *on* (*the switch* [Hahn] *is on*) | ⟨for⟩ *denuded* (*soil*) **2.** (öffentlich) *public* | ⟨mil⟩ (nicht geheim) *unclassified* N; ⟨telg⟩ (Ggs *in code*) *plain* **3.** ⟨fig⟩ *frank, candid, sincere; downright,* ⟨Am sl⟩ *flat-footed* || *unaffected* (*cordiality*); *outspoken* (*novel*) || ~ u ehrlich *fair and square*; *open and above-board* **4.** (geöffnet) ⟨aero⟩ *extended* (*formation*) **B.** ~e **Absage** *point-blank refusal* || ⟨eth⟩ *outright, downright* (*aggression*) || e–e ~e Antwort *straightforward answer*; .. auf e–e ~e Frage *a clear a. to a clear qu.* || mit ~en Augen *with open eyes*: (*he rushed*) *headlong* (*to his destruction*) || ~e Beine *legs with open sores* || ~er **Blick** *frank look, open face* || ⟨fig⟩ ~er Brief *open letter* || mit ~er Brust *frankly* || auf ~er Bühne *on the open stage* || ~es **Eis** *loose ice* || in ~er Empörung *out in revolt* || in ~er Feldschlacht *in open battle* || bei ~em **Fenster** (mit ~em Munde) schlafen *to sl. with the w.* (*m.*) *open* || ~e Flamme etc *unshielded flame, fire, etc* || ⟨tact⟩ *exposed* (Flanke) || ~e Fragen *unsolved qu.s*; (e–e Frage) ~ l *to leave open* || ~es **Gelände** *open ground* || ~e Geräte [n pl] *open-type apparatuses* || ~es Geschäft *retail business* || ~es Geständnis *frank admission* || ~er Güterwagen ⟨rail⟩ *truck, lorry* || ~e Handlungsweise *square dealing* || ~e Handelsgesellschaft (OHG) ⟨com⟩ *unlimited partnership* || ein ~es Haus h *to keep open house* od *table* || mit ~en **Karten** spielen *to place one's cards face up on the table* || ~er **Knopf** *unfastened b.* || ~es Konto = ~e Rechnung || ~er Kopf *clever* od *shrewd man, clear intellect* || ~er Kredit *blank cr.* || ~er Leib *open bowels* || ~er **Mensch** *candid p* || mit ~em Munde dastehen *to stand gaping* || ~e **Police** *floating p.* || in ~er Rechnung stehen mit *to have a current account with* || ⟨com⟩ ~er Posten *uncovered amount* || ~e **See** *high sea*; auf ~er See *on the* (*open sea* od) *main* || ~e **Stadt** *undefended, open, unfortified t.* || ~e Stelle *gap* || *vacant post*; *vacancy*; (besetzen *to fill up a v.*) || auf ~er Straße *in public, in the o. st.* || ⟨rail⟩ auf ~er Strecke *on the o. tr.* || ~e **Türen** einrennen *to force an o. d.*; *to carry coals to Newcastle*; *to flog a dead horse* || ⟨fig⟩ mit ~em **Visier** kämpfen *to speak openly* || ~er Vokal *slack v.* || ⟨com⟩ ~er **Wechsel** *blank cheque* || ~er Wein *w. from the cask* || in ~en Worten *in uncertain w.s* || ⟨hunt⟩ ~e **Zeit** *o. shooting season* **C.** [adv] *to keep a shop o.* || *the child's mind is* (liegt) *o. to* (vor) *the teacher* || die Teilnahme .. *part. is o. to all* || *the question remains o.* | ~ **auftreten** gegen *to come out in the o. against* || etw ~ **bekennen** *to make a candid conf.* || .. ~ gesagt *or* gestanden ..: *candidly* od *frankly speaking I ..* || jdm e–e Tür ~ **halten** *to hold a d. o. for a p* || ~ u ehrlich (handeln) .. *above board* || ~ heraus *point-blank* || (Frage) ~ l *to leave undecided* od *open*; (*to leave many loose ends*); k–e Möglichkeit ~ l *to leave no opening* (f *for*); e–e Zeile ~ l *to l. a line blank* || s–e E. **liegen** ~ vor aller Welt *his decisions are plain to the whole w.* || ~ **reden** *to sp. candidly, explicitly, plain*; *to come out in the open* || s–e ~e M. sagen *to express one's opinion candidly*, etc; ~ gesagt *as a matter of fact*; *I confess ..* ~ **stehen** *to stand o.*; halb ~ st *to be ajar*; ⟨com⟩ noch ~ st. *to be still owing* od *outstanding*; weit ~ st. *to gape o.*; die Wahl steht Ihnen ~ *you have the choice*; es steht dir ~ z tun oder .. *it is to you either to do or ..*; ihm steht die Welt ~ *he has the w. before him* || ~ vor jdm **tun** .. *under a p's nose* || ~ **zugegeben** *to admit openly* || zur Schau getragen ⟨fig⟩ *undisguised* || ~ zutage liegen *to be evident* od *obvious* **·offen- ~|halten** vt [h] *to reserve* **~herzig** a *candid, free, outspoken, open-hearted, sincere, frank* || ⟨fig⟩ (Kleid): *his coat is more holy* (torn) *than righteous* || zu ~ s *to wear one's heart upon one's sleeve* | ⟨hum P⟩ *décolletée* **≗keit** | *candidness, cando(u)r, frankness, sincerity* | ⟨hum fig⟩ *décolleté* || ~en [pl] *home truths* **~kundig** a *notorious, public*; *spectacular, flagrant, blatant*; *barefaced* (*lie*), *glaring* (*error*) || ~ w l *to allow to become known* | **≗keit** [f] *notoriousness, publicity* **~leibig** a *with open bowels* **~sichtlich** a *obvious* (*error*); *apparent, manifest*; *rank* (*nonsense*), *patent* (*blunder*) **~stall** m *open shed* od *stall*

·offenb·ar a (→ eindeutig) *open, obvious, manifest*

(*want*), *evident* (*sin*), *apparent* ‖ *downright* ‖ ~ w *to become known* | [adv] (*to be*) *obviously* (*mistaken*) ‖ er ist ~ v Lande *he is an obvious countryman* **offenb·aren** vt [h] *to make known*; *to disclose, bespeak, reveal, manifest* | **sich** ~ *to become known* od *obvious* ‖ (P) *to lay bare one's soul*; *to show one's intentions* ‖ (jdm) *to unbosom o.s., to open one's heart* (*to a p*); 〈rel〉 *God manifested h.s. to man* ‖ .. als 〈dero〉 *to betray o.s. as* | (ge)offenbart *open* (*secret*), *revealed* (*religion*) **Offenb·arung** f ~/~en *revelation, manifestation* ‖ 〈fig〉 *eye-opener* ‖ ~ Johannis *Revelation, Apocalypse* **~seid** m *oath of manifestation* od *disclosure*; *pauper's oath* **~sglaube** m 〈ec〉 *belief in revealed religion* **·Offenheit** f ~/~en *frankness, candour, openness, candidness, directness, unreserve* ‖ freimütige ~ *candid fr.* ‖ 〈Lit〉 *sincerity* ‖ in aller ~ *in all honesty*

offens·iv a (a. ≃-) *offensive* (*alliance, war*) **≃e** f ~/~n *offensive* ‖ die ~ ergreifen *to take the o.*

·öffentlich a *public* (*opinion, secret, scandal, announcement, authority, building, fund*) ‖ *civil* (*right, law*) ‖ *disorderly* (*house*) ‖ ~es Aufsehen *publicity*; ~er Auftrag *government contract*; ~e Bekanntmachung *proclamation*, 〈pol〉 *manifesto* ‖ ~er Dienst, Unternehmen der ~en Hand *public utility*; ~e Meinungspflege *public relations*; ~e Versorgung *public utilities* ‖ *in* (vor) *open court* ‖ *in* (auf) *the open street* | [adv] (*to appear, speak*) *in p.* ‖ (*to sell*) *by p. auction* | **≃-keit** f ~/ *p.ity*; breite ~ *general public*; in aller ~ *in p., openly* ‖ an die ~ dringen *to transpire*; an die ~ treten *to appear* (*in p.* od) *p.ly* ‖ in die ~ ziehen *to drag to the light of day* ‖ im Licht der ~ *in the limelight*; *public* (*man*) ‖ der ~ unterbreiten *to give p.ity to* ‖ im Brennpunkt der ~ stehen *to be in the p. eye* ‖ sich in die ~ flüchten *to rush into print* ‖ vor der ~ verbergen *to keep from the p.* ‖ sich v der ~ zurückziehen *to withdraw to one's tent* | 〈jur〉 die ~ ausschließen *to exclude the p.* ‖ die ~ wiederherstellen *to restore p.ity* | ~s-arbeit [f] *public relations*

offer·ieren vt [h] *to offer, tender* **Off·erte** f ~/~n *offer, tender*; 〈Am〉 *bid* (f *for*)

Off·ice [ɔ'fis] n ~/~s Sw = Büro, Anrichteraum

Offizi·al m ~(e)s/~e *official* **Offizi·ant** m ~en/~en *civil officer*; 〈ec〉 *officiating priest* **offizi·ell** a *official*; *on record* ‖ [adv] er hat ~ gesagt *he's on r. as saying* **Offiz·ier** m ~s/~e 〈mil & mar〉 **A.** *officer* ‖ 〈mar〉 1. ~ *second-in-command*; 2., 3. ~ *two-o, three-o*; die ~e [pl] *the quarter deck*; (Schach) *the best men* **B.** abgedankter ~ *retired o.* ‖ aktiver ~ *serving o.* ‖ ältester ~ *senior o.* ‖ höherer ~ *superior o.* ‖ ~ aus dem Mannschaftsstand *ranker* (*to rise from the ranks*) ‖ pensionierter ~, zur Disposition (z. D.) gestellter ~ *half-pay o.* ‖ ~ v Dienst *o. in charge, duty-o.* N; ~ v Ortsd. *o. of the guard*; ~ v Stabsd. *staff d.-o.*; ~ v Tagesd. *o. of the day* **C.** z ~ ernennen *to commission* ‖ z ~ befördert w *to obtain a comm.* ‖ z ~en h *to be o.ed by* ‖ mit ~en versehen *to o.* (*a troop*) **~anwärter** m *o. candidate, c. for commission* **~korps** n *body of o.s* **~sch·ulungsanstalt** f 〈engl〉 *cadet college* **~verein** m *army-and-navy club* ‖ *a.-a.-n. stores* pl **Offiz·iers- ~besprechung** f *conference*, 〈aero〉 *briefing*, 〈fam〉 *powwow* **~bursche** m *batman, orderly* (*to*) **~ehre** f; bei m–r ~ 〈engl〉 *on the honour of an officer and a gentleman* **~heim, ~kasino** n *o.'s mess* od *club* **~laufbahn** f *o.'s carreer* **~ledigenheim** n *bachelor o.s' quarters* (*BOQ*) **~messe** f 〈mar〉 *ward-room* **~nachwuchs** m *cadets* pl **~-patent** n 〈mil〉 *commission* **~rang** m *com.ed rank* **~stand** m *military profession, o.s* pl **~stelle** f 〈mil〉 *o.ship, com.* **~st·ellvertreter** m *warrant o.* **~zelt** n *marquee*

Offiz·in f ~/~en *laboratory* ‖ (Apotheke) *dispensary, chemist's shop* ‖ (Druckerei) *printing-office* od *-house* **Offizin·alpflanze** f *medicinal herb* **offizin·ell** a *officinal* **offizi·ös** a *semi-official, officious*

·öffnen vt [h] *to open* ‖ (Brief) mit Dampf ~ *to steam .. open*; *to untie* (*a package*); (Schloß) gewaltsam ~ *to pick*; (Schublade) *to unlock* ‖ weit ~ *to set wide, to throw open* ‖ das Mädchen öffnete (die Tür) .. *answered the door* ‖ 〈med〉 *to lance* (*an abscess*), *to relax* od *open* (*the bowels*), *to dissect* (*a body*) ‖ das Visier ~ 〈fig〉 *to show one's intentions* ‖ [ell] hier ~! *open here*! | jdm die Augen ~ 〈fig〉 *to undeceive a p* ‖ jdm die Tür ~ *to open the d. to* od *for a p*; 〈fam〉 *to open a p the d.* ‖ e–e Tür zu ~ suchen *to try a door* ‖ sich [dat] selbst ~ *to let o.s. in* ‖ 〈fig〉 [dat] Tür u Tor ~ *to give full license* (*to vice*); *to invite* (*disaster*); dem Bösen Tür u Tor ~ 〈fig〉 *to let the evil in* | geöffnet w (of shops) *to open*; → offen A. 4. | **sich** ~ [h] *to open, to be opened*; nach außen *to open out*; (weit) *to widen* ‖ (*of fist*) *to undouble itself* ‖ 〈fig〉 *to expand* (*to a p's devotion*) **·Öffner** m (*patent*) *opener*; *lever-knife* **·Öffnung** f ~/~en *opening, aperture* ‖ *gap* ‖ *mouth, orifice* ‖ *hole* ‖ (Lichtung) *glade* ‖ 〈tech〉 *nozzle, vent, notch* ‖ (Briefkasten≃) *slot* ‖ 〈med〉 *stool*; k–e ~ h 〈med〉 *to be costive* **~smittel** n 〈med〉 *aperient* **~sstromstoß** m 〈el〉 *break pulse* **~swinkel** m *aperture*

·Offset- ~druckfarben f pl *offset printing inks* pl **~folie** f *o. foil* **~(hochdruck)maschine** f *o. duplicator*

·oft adv *often, frequently, many times* ‖ ich habe sie ~ gesehen *I've seen a great deal of them* ‖ ebenso ~ wie *as often as* ‖ noch ~ (*he will*) *often* (*have to wait*) ‖ schon ~ *often* (*read*) ‖ schon so ~ *often enough* ‖ sehr ~ *very often* ‖ so ~ du kommst *every time* od *whenever you come*; 〈fam〉 *any time you are passing* ‖ so ~! *so often, again and again* ‖ wie ~? (!) *how many times*? (!) ‖ nur zu ~ *only* od *all too often* **·öfter** a *frequent, repeated* (*visits*) ‖ [adv] *oftener* ‖ je ~ ich ihn sehe *the more I see of him* **·öfter(s)** adv (a. des öfteren) *frequently*, (*pretty*) *often, as often as not, more often than not* **·oftmalig** a *frequent, reiterated, repeated* **·oftmals** adv *often* (*and often*), *repeatedly, frequently*

·Oger m ~s/~ *ogre*

·oh! intj *oh*! 〈Am〉 *gee*! → o

·Oh(ei)m m ~(e)s/~e *uncle*

Oh·io [o'haiou] (Fluß & Staat der U.S.A.)

·Ohm n ~(s)/~ 〈el〉 *ohm* **~meter** n *ohmmeter* **~sches Gesetz** *Ohm's law*

Öhmd n ~es/ [swd] 〈agr〉 *aftergrass*, → Grummet

·ohne I. [prep] **A.** *without* (*end*) ‖ *without any* (*sense of shame*) ‖ *innocent of* (*panes*) ‖ 〈com〉 *ex* (*dividend*) ‖ 〈fam〉 *minus*: (*a chair m. its legs*) ‖ ‖ *-less*: (*spouseless*) ‖ 〈jur〉 *for want of* (*advice*) ‖ (außer) *besides*; *apart from*; *not to speak of*; *but for* (*his help*); *except*; *save* | sein Mund war selten ~ Z. *a cigar was rarely out of his m.* ‖ .. nicht ~ sie s (*he cannot*) *bear her out of his sight* ‖ *had it not been for* (*a breakdown he would have reached L. in time*) **B.** ~ **Absicht** *unintentionally* ‖ ~ Arbeit *out of work* ‖ ~ jede Anstrengung *quite free from strain* ‖ auch ~ Auftrag 〈mil〉 *even in the absense of a mission* ‖ ~ Bedeutung *of no consequence* ‖ sie ist ~ Falsch *there is no guile in her* ‖ ~ Frage *doubtless, undoubtedly* ‖ ~ Furcht *void of fear* ‖ wenn es ~ Gefährdung des Verkehrs geschehen kann *if this does not endanger other traffic* ‖ ~ **Geist** *lacking in wit* ‖ ~ Geld *hard up for m.* ‖ ~ **mich**! *count me out*; (*count-me-out policy*) ‖ wir sind schon ~ Kohlen *we are out of coal* ‖ sei ~ Sorge (*have*) *no fear*! ‖ ~ das Testament *intestate* ‖ ~ mein Wissen *without my knowledge, unknown to me* ‖ ~ **Zweifel** = ~

Frage **C.** ~ **alle** Zwischenfälle, ~ jeglichen Zw.fall *without any incidents* ‖ ~ auch nur *without so much as* ‖ .. ~ dies! .., *now we are without!* ‖ ~ e–n *wanting one* ‖ ~ viel Federlesens tun *to make short work of doing* ‖ ~ weiteres *without more ado* **D.** [ell] (Rum) ~ (Wasser)! *plain, neat,* ⟨fam⟩ *due north,* ⟨sl⟩ *neaters* ‖ **nicht** ~! *not half bad!, not to be sneezed at!* ‖ *there is sth in it!* ‖ *that's a capital cigar!* **II.** [conj] **1.** ~ **daß** er es weiß *without his knowing it* ‖ ~ daß jd ihn sah *with no one seeing him* ‖ ~ daß ich es wußte = ~ mein Wissen → I. B. | (außer wenn) *unless* (*I see it*) **2.** [bei gleichem Subjekt: ~ **zu** + inf] ~ .. z sagen *without saying a word, unanswering* ‖ ~ je z unterbrechen *with never a break* ‖ ~ das Gericht in Anspruch z nehmen (*to settle*) *out of court* ‖ ⟨mil sl⟩ ~ mit der Wimper z zucken *unblinkingly, unshirkingly* **~dies, †~dem, ~hin** adv *without that, as it is* ‖ *otherwise* ‖ (*I should have done that*) *anyhow, at any rate*; ~ nicht reichlich *far from ample* (*money*); (*we are short enough of ..*) *already* **~gl·eichen** a *matchless, unequalled, unparalleled*; *unique* **~h·altflug** m *nonstop flight* ≃**-h·osen** m pl ⟨hist⟩ *Sansculottes* pl **~m·aßen** adv *exceedingly, beyond measure* **~s·orge** m p *without a care,* ⟨fam⟩ *happy-go-lucky chap* **·Ohnmacht** f ~/~en **1.** ⟨eig⟩ *powerlessness, impotence* **2.** ⟨path⟩ (a. ~sanfall) *fainting-fit* ‖ in ~ fallen *to faint, swoon* ‖ es wandelte mich e–e ~ an *I felt faint* **·ohnmächtig** a **1.** ⟨eig⟩ *powerless, impotent* (*rage*) ‖ *weak, helpless* ‖ [adv] ~ schimpfen *to bark at the moon* **2.** *faint*(*ing*), *in a faint* ‖ ~ w *to faint away, to feel faint* ‖ ~ s *to lie in a faint*

oh·o! intj *oho! hoity-toity* ‖ (*small but*) *great!*

·Ohr n ~(e)s/~en **A. 1.** ⟨eig⟩ *ear* (abstehend *protruding, bat* od *lop* [attr]; anliegend *close-lying*) **2.** ⟨übtr⟩ (Gehör) *hearing*; (*musical*) *ear, ear* (*for music*) ‖ (feines *fine,* äußerst feines *exquisite,* schlechtes ~ *dull ear* [f *for*]) **3.** ⟨fig tech⟩ *handle* ‖ (im Buch) *dog's ear*; ein ~ einschlagen *to turn down a leaf* **B.** ⟨fam⟩ **abschneiden** *to cut off* ‖ → aufmachen 1. a. ‖ das ~ **berauscht** sich .. *is entranced* (an *by*) ‖ jds ~ besitzen *to enjoy a p's confidence* ‖ ein offenes etc ~ **finden** *to find a willing ear*; taube ~en f. *to fall on deaf ears* ‖ (S) *to fall on ready ears* ‖ bei e–m *to obtain a favourable hearing from a p* ‖ taube ~en finden *to meet a dead wall* ‖ jds ~ **haben** *to have won a p's attention* ‖ die ~en bei etw h *to be all attention* ‖ ein ~ h f *to have an ear for* ‖ kein ~ h f: *he would not listen to it* ‖ Wände h ~en *walls have ears* ‖ **halt** die ~en auf! (.. steif!) *keep a watchful ear!* (*keep a stiff upper lip!* ⟨bes Am⟩ *take it on the chin*) ‖ die ~en hängen l *to look crest-fallen* ‖ mit hängenden ~en ⟨fig⟩ *down in the mouth* ‖ geneigten ~es **hören** *to listen with a friendly ear* ‖ mir klingen (noch) die ~en *my ears* (*still*) *tingle* ‖ klangen dir nicht die ~en? ⟨fig⟩ *didn't your ears burn?* ‖ jdm sein ~ **leihen** *to lend a p one's ear, to give ear to a p*; ⟨übtr⟩ *to be influenced by a p*; (e–r S) *to listen to*; jdm (e–r S) ein geneigtes ~ l. *to turn an attentive ear to a p* (*to a talk,* etc) ‖ lange ~en m = ~en spitzen ‖ tauben ~en **predigen** *to preach to unwilling ears, to talk to a brick wall* ‖ die ~en **sausen** mir *I have a buzzing noise in my ears* ‖ es schmeichelt dem ~ *it flatters one's ears* ‖ die ~en schmerzen mir *I have ear-ache* ‖ ganz ~ s *to be all ears* od *attention* ‖ die ~en **spitzen** *to prick* (*up*) od *cock one's ears*; *to listen intently* ‖ e–m Hunde die ~en stutzen *to crop a dog's ears* ‖ mein ~ hat sich getäuscht *my ears must have deceived me* ‖ jdm sein ~ **verschließen** *to refuse to listen to a p* ‖ jdm die ~en volljammern *to din lamentations into a p's ears,* .. vollschreien *to deafen a p with shouting* ‖ sich die ~en zuhalten *to stop up one's ears* **C.** bis **an** *or* hinter die ~en erröten *to blush to the eyes, to one's shoulders* ‖ am ~ befindlich *parotid* (*gland*) ‖ e–n am ~ zupfen *to pull a p's ear for him* ‖ ans ~ nehmen, halten *to put, hold to one's ear*; *to cup one's* (*hand to the*) *ear* ‖ ⟨fam⟩ sich **aufs** ~ legen *to take a nap, to go to bed,* ⟨sl⟩ *to go between the sheets* ‖ er sitzt auf den ~en *he doesn't hear* ‖ auf e–m ~ schlecht hören *to be deaf on one ear* ‖ e–n bei den ~en fassen *to collar a p* ‖ sich (= e–a) **bei** den ~en kriegen *to be* od *fall* (*together*) *by the ears* ‖ sich **hinter** den ~en kratzen *to scratch one's ear* ‖ es faustdick hinter den ~en h *to look as if butter wouldn't melt in one's mouth,* ⟨fam⟩ *to be up to snuff*; ⟨sl⟩ *to be a deep one* ‖ hinter den ~en noch nicht trocken s ⟨sl⟩ *to be still wet behind the ears* ‖ *to be but a greenhorn* od *like an unlicked cub, to be still in leading strings, to be a regular milksop* ‖ sich [dat] etw hinter die ~en (→ Löffel) schreiben *to make a* (*particular*) *note of a th* ‖ **in** m–n ~en klingt noch s–e Stimme *I can't get the sound of his voice out of my ears* ‖ e–m (mit etw) **in** den ~en liegen *to keep dinning* (*sth*) *in*(*to*) *a p's ear,* e–m etw ins ~ flüstern *to whisper a th in*(*to*) *a p's ear* ‖ e–m e–n Floh ins ~ setzen ⟨fig⟩ (beunruhigen) *to sow doubts in a p's mind* ‖ etw **mit** gespanntem (halbem) ~e anhören *to listen to a th with great attention* (*with half an ear*); mit den ~en wackeln *to wiggle one's ears* ‖ **über** → Fell ‖ eins übers ~ bek ⟨fam⟩ *to get one's ears boxed* ‖ e–n übers ~ hauen *to swindle, cheat, dupe, gull,* ⟨sl⟩ *to dope a p, to do a p in the eye*; übers ~ geh. w *to get slogged*; er hat mich damit übers ~ geh. *he planted it on me* ‖ **bis über** die ~en *over head and ears* (*in debt*; verliebt *in love* [in *with*]), *up to one's eyes* od *chin* (*in work*); *to be in .. right up to one's neck*; .. in e–m Plan stecken *to be in the thick of a scheme* ‖ **um** ein geneigtes ~ bitten *to ask for favourable attention* ‖ viel um die ~en h *to be in a rush* ‖ die Nacht um die ~en schlagen *to make a night of it* ‖ **vor** m–n ~en *in my hearing* ‖ vor tauben ~en reden *to talk to the air* ‖ e–m etw **zu** ~en bringen *to inform a p of a th* ‖ es ist mir zu ~en gek *it has come to my ears* od *knowledge*; *I understand*; *I have been told* ‖ zum e–n ~ hinein, zum andern wieder heraus *in at one ear and out at the other* ‖ ⟨fam hum⟩ e–m den Kopf **zw** die ~en setzen *to box a p's ears* **Öhr** n ~(e)s/~e **1.** (Nadel≃, Hammer≃) *eye* **2.** *axe-hole* **3.** (Haken u ~) *catch* (*and hook*) **4.** (Bolzen≃) *eyelet* **5.** (Henkel) *handle* **·ohren** vt [h] *to provide with handles* **·öhren** vt [h] *to perforate* (*needles*) **·Ohr-** °**~bammel** = ~gehänge **~eule** f *horned owl* **~feige** f *box on the ear* ‖ e–e ~ bek v *to have one's ears boxed by*; jdm e–e ~ geben *to slap a p's face* ≃**feigen** vt [h] (jdn) *to box* od *cuff a p's ears* ‖ ich könnte mich ~, daß *I could kick m.s. for having done* **~gehänge** n *ear-pendants* pl **~höhle** f *cavity of the ear* **~kissen** n *cushion, pillow* **~läppchen** n *flap* od *lobe of the ear* **~loch** n *ear-hole* ‖ sich ≃er stechen l *to have one's ears pierced* **~löffel** m *ear-pick*(*er*) **~muschel** f ⟨anat⟩ *auricle* **~ring** m *ear-ring* **~schwindel** m ⟨path⟩ *auditory vertigo* **~sp·eicheldrüse** f ⟨anat⟩ *parotid gland* | ~nentzündung [f] *mumps, parotitis* **~trommel** f ⟨anat⟩ *tympanum, drum of the ear* **~trompete** f ⟨anat⟩ *Eustachian tube* **~wurm** m *earwig* ≃**zerreißend** a ⟨fig⟩ *ear-splitting* (*noise*) **·Ohren- ~arzt** m *aurist, ear-specialist* **~beichte** f *auricular confession* ≃**betäubend** a *deafening, ear-shattering, -splitting, -piercing* (*noise*) **~bläser** m *tale-bearer, scandal-monger* ‖ (Kriecher) *sycophant* **~bläser·ei** f *tale-bearing* ‖ *sycophancy* **~brausen** n = ~sausen **~brille** f (mit Hörgerät) *hearing-aid* od *ear-glasses* **~drüse** f ⟨anat⟩ *parotid gland* **~entzündung** f ⟨med⟩ *inflammation of the ear,* ⟨scient⟩ *otitis* ≃**fällig** a *striking the ear*; *catching* (*tune*) **~fluß** m ⟨path⟩ *running from the ear* **~heilkunde** f *otology* **~höhle** f *cavity of the ear* **~kitzel** m *tickling in one's ears*; ⟨fig⟩ *curiosity* **~klingen** n *singing in the ears* **~klinik** f *ear hospital* **~kunde** f ⟨med⟩ *otology* **~leiden** n *ear-complaint,*

⟨scient⟩ *aural disease* **~reißen** n = ∼schmerz **~sausen** n *buzzing in the ear*, ⟨med⟩ *tinnitus* L **~schmalz** n *ear-wax* | ∼pfropf [m] *impacted cerumen* **~schmaus** m *treat for the ears* **~schmerz** m *ear-ache* **~schützer** = ∼wärmer **~spiegel** m ⟨med⟩ *auriscope* **~spritze** f *ear-syringe* **~wärmer** m *ear-flap*, ⟨Am⟩ *-muff* **~zeuge** m *ear-witness* **~zeugnis** n *auricular evidence* **~zwang** m *otalgy* .. **ohrig** a; l·ang∼ *long-eared* ‖ ⟨hors⟩ *flap-eared*

oj·e(mine)! intj *dear me!*, *good gracious!*, *my!*, ⟨vulg⟩ *lor!* ‖ ∼, ∼! *dear, dear!*

Ok·api n ∼s/∼s (kl Giraffenart) *okapi*

Okklu-si·on f ∼/∼en ⟨meteor⟩ *occlusion* | ∼sfront [f] *occluded front* **–s·ivpessar** n ⟨med⟩ *diaphragm pessary*

Okkult·ismus m *occultism* **–t·ist** m *occultist*

Okkup·ant m ∼en/∼en *occupant*, ⟨demog⟩ *squatter* **Okkupati·on** f ∼/∼en *occupation* **okku-p·ieren** vt [h] *to occupy*

Oklah·oma n (Staat der U.S.A.)

Öko- ~log·ie f ∼/ *ecology* **~̂l·ogisch** a *ecological* (Wert *function*) **~n·om** m ∼en/∼en *economist* ‖ (Landwirt) *gentleman-farmer*, *agriculturist* ‖ (Verwalter) *manager*, *housekeeper* ‖ (Wirtschaftsleiter e–s Kasinos etc) *steward* **~nometr·ie** f ∼/ *econometrics* [sg konst] **~nom·ie** f ∼/∼n (Verwaltung, Sparsamkeit) *economy*; (*art of*) *housekeeping* ‖ (Landwirtschaft) *agriculture* | ∼gebäude [n] *farm-building*; ∼verwalter [m] *steward* **~̂n·omisch** [a] *economical* ‖ [adv] ∼ umgehen mit *to economize*

Okt- ~a·eder n ∼s/∼ *octahedron* **okta·edrisch** a *octahedral* **~·an** n ∼s/ *octane* | ∼zahl [f] ⟨mot⟩ *knock-rating* **~·ant** m ∼en/∼en *octant* **~·av** n ∼s/∼e, (**~̂·av** a) *octavo* | ∼band [m] *octavo* (*volume*); ∼flöte [f] *flageolet*; ∼format [n] = ∼ **~·ave** f ∼/∼n ⟨mus⟩ *octave* | ∼ngänge [m pl] *successions of octaves* **~·ett** n ∼s/∼e ⟨mus⟩ *octet*, ⟨pros⟩ *octet* (8 Verse bes in 2 *quatrains* It Sonett) **~·ober** m ∼(s)/∼ *October* ‖ im ∼ *in O.* **~tog·on** n ∼(e)s/∼e *octagon* **~op·ode** m ∼n/∼n ⟨zoo⟩ *octopus*; *poulp*(*e*)

oktroy·ieren vt [h] *to dictate* ‖ jdm etw (auf)∼ *to force a th on a p*; (zu)∼ *to confer a th on a p*

Okul·ar n ∼s/∼e ⟨opt⟩ *eyepiece*, *ocular* | ∼auszug [m] ⟨phot⟩ *e.p. slide*; ∼blende [f] *diaphragm*; ∼inspektion [f] *ocular inspection* **okul·ieren** vt [h] *to inoculate*, *graft* **Okul·ier- ~messer** n *grafting-knife* **~reis** n *g.-twig*

ökum·enisch a *ecumenical* (*council* Konzil)

·Okzident m ∼s/ (Westen, Abendland) *occident*

·Öl n ∼(e)s/∼e *oil* ‖ ätherisches ∼ *essential oil* ‖ gehärtetes ∼ *hydrogenated oil* ⟨bes cul⟩; → *harden* ‖ heiliges ∼ *chrism* ‖ Roh~̂ *crude oil* ‖ rostlösend *penetrating* ‖ Schmier~̂ *lubricating oil* ‖ Treib~̂ *gas oil* | in ∼ malen *to paint in oils* ‖ mit ∼ schmieren *to* (*lubricate with*) *oil* ‖ mit ∼ tränken *to anoint with oil* ‖ ⟨fig⟩ ∼ auf die Wogen gießen *to pour oil on troubled water*; ∼ ins Feuer gießen *to add fuel to the fire, to blow the coals, to fan the flame* **~abdichtung** f *oil seal* od *packing*, *retainer, retaining ring, gasket* **~ablaßschraube** f *oil drain plug* **~abscheider** m *oil separator* od *collector*, *trap* **~abweiser** m *oil deflector* **~anstrich** m *coat of oil-paint* **~antrieb** m; mit ∼ *oil-driven*, *-burning* (*ship*) **~anzug** m *oil cloth* **~̂artig** a *oily*, *oleaginous* **~bad** n ⟨chem⟩ *oil-bath* **~bauer** m *grower of olive-trees* **~baum** m *o.-tree* ‖ wilder ∼ *oleaster* **~beere** f *olive* **~behälter** m *oil-tank* ‖ ⟨mach⟩ *-cup* **~beize** f *mordant of oil* **~berg** m *Mount of Olives* **~bild** n *oil-painting* **~̂bildend** a *olefiant* (*gas*) **~bilderdruck** m *oleography* **~blatt** n *olive-leaf* **~blau** n *o.-blue* **~bohranlage** f *oil boring plant* **~bohrung** f *oil-well* **~büchse** f *-cup* **~dampfer** m *tanker* **~druck** m *chromo-lithography* ‖ (Bild) *ch.-l.ph*, *oleograph* | ∼bremse [f] ⟨mot⟩ *hydraulic brake*; ∼messer [m] *oil pressure gauge*; ∼ventil [n] *oil surge valve* **~drüse** f *oil-bag* **~düse** f *oil atomizer* **~einlauf** m *oiling of new engines* **~farbe** f *-colour*, *-paint* ‖ in ∼n *in oils* **~feuerung** f *oil fire*; *oil* (*fired*) *furnace* **~firnis** m *oil-varnish* **~fläschchen** n *phial*, *ampulla* **~flasche** f *oil-bottle* ‖ (mit eingeschliffenem Stöpsel) *-cruet* **~fleck(en)** m *-stain*, *-patch* **~förderanlage** f *oil conveying plant* **~förderung** f *bringing oil out of the earth* **~früchte** f pl *-seeds* pl °**~funzel** f ⟨dero⟩ *oil lamp* **~̂gar** a *oiled* (*leather*) **~garten** m *olive-garden*, *-yard* **~gemälde** n *oil-painting*; pl *oils* **~geschmack** m *oily taste* **~götze** m ⟨fam⟩ *dunce*, *lubber*, *blockhead* **~̂haltig** a *oil bearing* **~handel** m *oil-trade* **~händler** m *-man* **~hefe** f *dregs* [pl] *of oil* **~heizapparat** m *-heater* **~heizung** f *oil firing* **~hut** m ⟨mar⟩ *tarpaulin* **~kammer** f ⟨tech⟩ *oil-box* **~kanne** f *oil-can*, *-tin*, *oiler* **~kessel** m *oil fired boiler* **~kuchen** m *oil-cake*, *linseed cake* **~kühler** m *oil-cooler* **~lager** n pl *oil dumps* pl **~lampe** f *oil-lamp*, *colza-lamp* **~leitung** f ⟨mach⟩ *oil lead* od *piping*; über Land *pipe line*, *oil duct* **~lese** f *gathering of olives* **~maler·ei** f *painting in oil*; *oils* pl **~meßstab** m *oil* (*dip* od) *ga*(*u*)*ge stick*; *oil dipper* **~mühle** f *oil-mill* **~müller** m *-miller* **~papier** n *oil*(*ed*) *paper* **~porträt** n *portrait in oils* **~presse** f *oil-press* **~quelle** f *-well*, ⟨Am⟩ *gusher*; unergiebige ∼ *dry hole* **~reiniger** m *-separator* **~rock** m *-coat* **~same(n)** m *oilseed*(*s*) **~sardine** f *sardine* (*in oil*) °**~sauce** f (Meer) glatt wie e–e ∼ *flat as a mill-pond* **~säure** f ⟨chem⟩ *oleic acid* **~schalter** m ⟨el⟩ *oil-switch* **~seife** f *yellow soap* **~(sprüh)nebel** m ⟨tech⟩ *atomized oil* **~stand** m *oil level* | ∼anzeiger [m] *o.-l. ga*(*u*)*ge*; ∼kontrollmarke [f] *o.-l. mark* **~stein** m *-rubber* **~tonne** f *-cask* **~trester** pl *olive-husks* pl **~sumpf**, **~trog** m, **~wanne** f ⟨tech⟩ *sump* **~tuch** n *oilskin* **~übernahme** f *oil fuelling* **~̂umspült** a *oil-immersed* **~wanne** f *-well* od *-container*; *save-oil* **~wechselzeit** f *oil change period* **~weide** f *oleaster* **~zeug** n ⟨mar⟩ *tarpaulin*; *oil-skins*, *oils* pl **~zuführung** f *oil feed* **~zweig** m *olive-branch*

·Oldenburg n ⟨Ger⟩ (Stadt & †Land)

Ole·ander m ∼s/∼ ⟨bot⟩ *oleander* **Ole·aster** m ∼s/∼ ⟨bot⟩ *wild olive*, *oleaster* **Ole·in** [–ˈi:n] n ∼s/ ⟨chem⟩ *olein*(*e*) ‖ ∼säure [f] *oleic acid*

·ölen vt [h] *to oil* ‖ ⟨tech⟩ *to lubricate* ‖ (salben) *to anoint* ‖ °⟨fig⟩ er hat gut geölt *he is well lubricated* od *oiled* (drunk) ‖ °geölt! (angeführt) ⟨fig fam⟩ *taken in!* **·ölig** a *oily*, *oleaginous* ‖ ⟨fig⟩ *smarmy* | **~keit** f ∼/ *oiliness*

·Olifants R·iver (in S.-Afrika)

Olig- ~arch·ie f ∼/∼n *oligarchy* **~̂·archisch** a *oligarchical* **~ozän** n (oberste Alttertiärstufe) *oligocene*; → –zän

·Olim (L ~̂ = einst) zu ∼s Zeiten ⟨fam⟩ *in the olden days, in the days of yore*

Ol·ive f ∼/∼n *olive* **~nbaum** m *o.-tree* **~̂nbraun** n, **~nfarbe** f *o.-colour* **~̂ngrün** a *o.-green* **~nhain** m *o.-grove* **~nöl** n *o.-oil*

·oll (öller, öllst) a **1.** ⟨dial⟩ = alt **2.** ° = häßlich, böse °**·Ollsche** f ∼/∼n = die Alte

·Olm m ∼(e)s/∼e ⟨zoo⟩ *proteus*

·Ölung f ∼/∼en *oiling*, *lubrication* ‖ ⟨ec⟩ *anointment* ‖ letzte ∼ ⟨ec⟩ *extreme unction* ‖ °(das war die) ∼! *taken in!*, → °ölen (anführen)

Ol·ymp m ∼(e)s/ *Olympus* ‖ ⟨fig theat⟩ auf dem ∼ (*a seat*) *among the gods*, ⟨Am⟩ *in the nigger-heaven* **~i·ade** f ∼/∼n *Olympiad* **~ier** m ∼s/∼ *Olympian* (*god*) | ∼in [f] *O.* (*goddess*) **~̂isch** a (göttlich) *Olympian* ‖ *Olympic* (*games*)

·Oma(ma) f ∼/∼s (a. Omi) *grandma*, *gran*(*ny*, *-nie*)

·Omaha n (Stadt) (*Nebr.*, *U.S.A.*)

Om·an n (arab. Staat)

·Ombrometer n ∼s/∼ (Regenmesser) *rain-ga*(*u*)*ge*, *ombrometer*

Omel·ett(e f ∼/∼n) n ∼s/∼e *omelet*; ∼ natur *plain o.*; ∼ confiture *o. with preserves*; ∼ mit Pilzen *mushroom o.* ‖ ein ∼ m *to make an o.*

·Omen n ∼s/Omina *omen, foreboding* **omin·ös** a *ominous*; (*name*) *of dark foreboding*

Ommat·idium n ∼s/–dia & –dien ⟨ent⟩ *ommatidium* [pl *–dia*] (*of a compound eye*)

·Omnibus m ∼ses/∼se *omnibus*, mst *bus*; ⟨bes Can⟩ *limousine*; ∼ mit el. Oberleitung *trolley-bus* ‖ mit dem ∼ fahren *to go by bus, to take a bus*, ⟨fam⟩ *to bus it* **∼fahrgast** m *bus-passenger* **∼fahrt** f *bus-ride* **∼führer** m *bus-driver* **∼schaffner** m *bus--conductor*

Omsk n ⟨Russ⟩ (Stadt)

Onan- **∼·ie** f ∼/ *onanism, masturbation* **≗·ieren** vi [h] *to masturbate* **∼·ist** m ∼en/∼en *onanist*

ondul·ieren 1. vt [h] (Haar) *to wave* **2.** ≗ n, **Ondulation** f *waving*; *wave* ⟨a. cosm⟩

On·egasee m ⟨Russ⟩ *Onega Lake*

·Onkel m ∼s/∼ *uncle* ‖ ⟨fig Am fam sex⟩ *sugar daddy* ‖ Rat e–s ∼s *avuncular advice* | ∼-Doktor-Ton [m] *good bedside manner*; ∼ehe [f] *uncle--marriage, pension-concubinage*

Önolog·ie f ∼/ (Wein[bau]kunde f) *oenology*

onomato- **∼po·etisch** [–o'e:–] a *onomatopoetic* **≗pö·ie** [–'i:] f *onomatopœia*

Ont·ario n ⟨Can⟩ Prov. u (See) (*Lake*) *Ontario*

Onto- **∼log·ie** f ∼/∼n *ontology* **≗l·ogisch** a *o.logical*

·Onyx m ∼(e)s/∼e *onyx*

Ool·ith m ∼s/∼e *oolite* **≗isch** a *oolitic*

Op·al m ∼(e)s/∼e *opal* ‖ ∼glas [n] *opal-glass, opaline* **opalis·ieren 1.** vi [h] *to opalesce* ‖ ∼d [a] *opalescent* **2.** ≗ n ∼s/ *opalescence*

·Opa(pa) m ∼s/∼s *gran(d)-dad*; ⟨vulg⟩ *gramp*

·Op-art f ∼/ ⟨Am⟩ *op(tical) art*; → optisch

Opat·ija n (jugoslaw. Seebad) → Abbazia

·Oper f ∼/∼n **1.** *opera* ‖ e–e ∼ geben *to give* od *perform an o.* ‖ in die (gr) ∼ gehen *to go to the* (*grand*) *o.* **2.** *opera-house* ‖ die Kroll-∼ *the Kr. O.-H.* **3.** [in comp] → ∼n- **∼ateur** [–'tø:r] m ∼s/∼e ⟨film⟩ *operator*, → d. ‖ ⟨med⟩ *operating surgeon* **∼ati·on** [ts] f ∼/∼en *operation* ⟨a. mil⟩; ⟨mil⟩ planmäßig verlaufende ∼ *set-piece encounter* ‖ ∼ am Hals *o. to the neck* ‖ ∼ e–r P *o. on a p*; mißlungene ∼ *operative failure* ‖ sich e–r ∼ unterziehen müssen *to undergo an o.* (*she was to have a serious o.*) | ∼sbasis [f] ⟨mil⟩ *base of o.s* N; ∼sbefehl [m] *o. order* N; ∼sbereich [m] *processing section* ⟨a. comp⟩; ∼sforschung [f] *Scientific Computation of Optimum Programs* (*SCOOP*); *o.al* (od ⟨Am⟩ *o.s*) *research*; *o.s analysis* od *evaluation*; ∼sfreiheit [f] *o.al freedom of action*; ∼sgebiet [n] *theater of o.s* N; Befehlshaber e–s ∼s *th. of o.s commander*; ∼skostenversicherung [f] *surgical fee insurance*; ∼slinie [f] ⟨mil⟩ *base of o.*; ∼splan [m] ⟨mil⟩ *plan* od *object of o.*; ∼ssaal [m] *operating-room*, (Hörsaal) *operating-theatre*; ∼stisch [m] *operating table*; ∼sziel [n] ⟨mil⟩ *objective* **≗at·iv** a ⟨med & mil⟩ *operative* (*result*) ‖ ⟨mil⟩ *operational* (*success, reserve* ‖ ∼e Behandlung *o.ve treatment, operation* ‖ ∼er Eingriff ⟨surg⟩ *operation* **∼·ette** f ∼/∼n *operetta, musical comedy*; *comic opera* **≗·ierbar** a [nicht] ∼ [*in*]*operable* (*cancer*) **≗·ieren** vt/i [h] ⟨med & mil⟩ *to operate* (*upon*) ‖ vi ⟨mar⟩ *to operate* (v *from*) ‖ sich ∼ l, operiert w *to undergo an operation, to be operated* (*up*)*on* (*for gall-stones*); ⟨Am a.⟩ *to come in for surgery* | ∼d ⟨mil⟩ *operational*

Operm·ent n ∼(e)s/ *orpiment*

·Opern- **∼abend** m *opera-night* **≗artig** a *operatic* **∼dichter** m *librettist* **∼glas** n, **∼gucker** m *opera--glass(es* pl) **∼haus** n *opera-house* **≗mäßig** a *operatic* **∼musik** f *opera-music* **∼sänger** m, **∼sängerin** f *opera-singer* **∼tenor** m *operatic tenor* **∼text** m *libretto*; *word-book*

·opernhaft a *operatic*

·Opfer n ∼s/∼ **A. 1.** [abstr] *offering, sacrifice*; ⟨poet⟩ *oblation, immolation* ‖ (un)blutiges ∼ *a bloody s.* (*a s. without bloodshed*) ‖ ewiges ∼ ⟨RC⟩ *oblation* **2.** [konkr] (das Geopferte gen) *he was the victim of inertia, of an avalanche, to drunkenness, to his passions*; *a prey to circumstances*; *a martyr* (der W.) *in the cause of science* ‖ (an Toten) *toll* (Kriegs≗ pl *war toll*) ‖ (e–s Schwindels) ⟨Am⟩ *fall-guy* **B.** ein ∼ **bringen** (etw z ∼ br.) *to make an offering* (*of a th to a god*), ⟨fig⟩ *to s. a th, to make a s. of a th* (*to* od *for*) ‖ sein Leben z ∼ br. *to make the supreme s.* | **unter** schweren ∼n an *at a heavy cost in* (*time, lives, money*) | (e–r S, P) z ∼ **fallen** *or* w *to be, become, fall a v., m., prey* (*to*) ‖ der Seuche fielen sehr viele z ∼ *many fell v.s to this e.* ‖ das Gebäude fiel e–m Brande z ∼ *the b. was destroyed by fire* ‖ dem Abwurf e–r Bombe fielen mehrere Zivilpersonen z ∼ *a bomb caused several civilian casualties* | kein ∼ **scheuen** *to spare no s.* (f. *for*) ‖ ich würde kein ∼ scheuen es zu finden *I would give anything to find it* **∼altar** m *sacrificial altar* **∼bereitschaft** f *spirit of s.* **∼binde** f *fillet* **∼flamme** f *flame consuming the v.* **≗freudig** a *willing to make s.s, self--sacrificing, devoted* **∼gabe** f *o.* **∼gebet** n ⟨R. C.⟩ *offertory* **∼gebrauch** m *sacrificial rite* **∼gefäß, ∼gerät** n *s.l vessel* **∼geld** n *money-o.* **∼herd** m *altar* **∼kasten** m *poor-box* **∼lamm** n *s.l lamb* ‖ ⟨bib⟩ *the Lamb* (*of God*) ‖ ⟨fig⟩ *v.* **∼messer** n *s.l knife* **∼priester** m *s.l priest* **∼schale** f *o.-cup* **∼schmaus** m *s.l repast* **∼stätte** f *place of s.* **∼stock** m *poor-, alms-box* **∼tag** m nationaler ∼ *flag-day*, ⟨Am⟩ *tag-day* **∼tier** n *v.* **∼tod** m *s. of a p's life*, ⟨rel⟩ *expiatory death* **∼trank** m *libation* **∼wein** m *sacramental wine* **≗willig** a = ∼freudig **·Opferer** m ∼s/∼ *sacrificer* **·opfern** vt/i ⟨a. fig⟩ (sich) *to sacrifice* (*o.s.*) ‖ ⟨fig⟩ *to make s.s* (*to Venus*); wem wird hier ge–rt? *who* od *what stands to benefit from this s.?* ‖ (T) *to immolate* [nur vt] ‖ sein Leben ∼ *to immolate o.s., to lay down one's life, to make the supreme s.* (f. *for*) **·Opferung** f ∼/∼en *sacrifice, sacrificing*; ⟨bib [arts]⟩ Isaaks ∼ *S.e of Abraham* ‖ (v Tieren) *immolation*

Ophiolatr·ie f ∼/ *ophiolatry*; *serpent-worship*

Ophthal- **∼mi·atrik** f ∼/ = Augenheilkunde **∼mie** f = –entzündung **∼mol·oge** m ∼n/∼n = –arzt

Opi·at n ∼(e)s/∼e *opiate* **·Opium** n ∼s/ *opium*, ⟨sl⟩ *dope* **∼esser** m *o.-taker* **≗haltig** a *opiated*, ∼es Mittel [n] *opiate* **∼handel** m *opium--trade* **∼mißbrauch** m, **∼sucht** f *o. habit*; *o.ism* **∼tinktur** f *laudanum* **∼wein** m *yen shee suey*

Op·orto n (portug. Stadt) *Oporto*

·Oppeln ⟨†Ger⟩ (Stadt a. d. Oder, Oberschlesien)

Opp- **∼on·ent** m ∼en/∼en *opponent, adversary* **≗on·ieren 1.** vt [h] [dat] *to oppose, resist* **2.** vi *to offer opposition, to resist* **≗ort·un** a *opportune, expedient* **∼ortun·ist** m *opportunist*, ⟨pol⟩ *trimmer* ‖ *timeserver* **∼ortunit·ät** f ∼/∼en *opportuneness, expediency* ‖ ∼spolitik treiben *to trim with the times* **∼ositi·on** [ts] f ∼/∼en *opposition* ⟨a. astr⟩ ‖ ⟨engl parl⟩ *His, Her Majesty's most loyal O.* [pl konstr] ‖ gegen etw ∼ m *to oppose a th* ‖ in ∼ stehen *to be in o.* (zu *to*) ‖ in ∼ treten *to go into o.* (*to*), ⟨Am sl⟩ *to buck the machine* ‖ → aufräumen ‖ die ∼ vertreiben *to clear the field of o.* | ∼sblatt [n] *o. paper*; ∼sgeist [m] *spirit of o.*; ∼smacher, ∼smann [m] *oppositionist, member of the opposition*; ∼spartei [f] *opposition* (*party*)

Opt- **∼at·iv** m ∼(e)s/∼e ⟨gram⟩ *optative* (*mood*) **≗·ieren** vi [h] **1.** (wählen) *to choose* **2.** (für etw) *to decide for a th* od *in favour of a th* **∼i·on** f ∼/∼en *option*

·Opt- **∼ik** f ∼/ *optics* pl [sg konstr] ‖ °⟨fig⟩ = Betrachtungsweise **·∼iker** m ∼s/∼ *optician* **≗isch** a *optic(al)* ‖ ∼e Täuschung [f] *optical* od *visual illusion*; *glass* (*sight* Visier); *visual* (*signal*); ∼e Kunst *op(tical) art* | [adv] ∼ übermitteln *to pass by visual signals*

Optim- **≗·al** a *optimum* [attr] | [adv] ∼ gestalten ⟨scient⟩ *to optimize* **∼·at** m ∼en/∼en

⟨Roman hist⟩ *optimate aristocrat* ‖ ~enherrschaft [f] *oligarchy* **~·ismus** m ~/ *optimism* **~·ist** m ~en/~en *optimist*; *sanguine p* ‖ unverbesserlicher ~ *confirmed o.* **≃istisch** a *optimistic, sanguine*; zu ~ *oversanguine* ‖ ~ s *to look at the sunny side of ths, to see a silver lining, to hope for the best, to be of good heart*; ~ s betreffs *to be opt. of*; *rosy* (*outlook*) | [adv] ~ aussehen (S): *his chances are looking up*

optomot·orisch a *optomotor* [attr] (*reaction*)

opul·ent a *opulent*; *wealthy* (*p*) ‖ *sumptuous* (*meal*) **Opul·enz** f ~/ *opulence, wealth*

Op·untie [–tsiə] f ~/~n ⟨bot⟩ *Indian fig*

·Opus n ~/·Opera *work* ‖ ⟨mus⟩ *opus* (abbr op.)

Or·akel n ~s/~ *oracle* ⟨a. fig: P⟩ ‖ in ~n sprechen *to sp. in riddles* ‖ (ein ~) befragen *to consult* .. **~blume** f *marguerite* **≃haft** a *oracular* **~spruch** m *oracle*; *oracular decree* **or·akeln** vi [h] ⟨fam⟩ *to speak oracularly*

Or·an n (Stadt in Algerien)

Or·ange [ɔ'raŋʒə] f ~/~n **1.** ⟨bot⟩ *orange* ‖ bittere ~ *Seville o.*; Blut≃ *blood-o.* **2.** ≃ [nur attr], ≃farben, ≃gelb a *orange*(*-coloured*) ‖ *her dress was a brilliant o.* **~ade** [oran'ʒɑ:də] f ~/~n *orangeade* **~·at** [–'ʒɑ:t] n ~(e)s/~e *candied orange-peel* **Or·angen-** ~baum [m] *orange-tree* ~blüte [f] *o.-blossom* ⟨a. cul⟩; ~saft [m] *o. juice* ~schale [f] *o.-peel* **~r·ie** [oraŋʒə'ri:] f ~/~n [i:ən] *orangery*

Orang-·Utan m ~s/~s ⟨zoo⟩ *orang-outang*

Or·anien n (nassauisches Geschlecht) *Orange*

Or·anje, ~fluß m *Orange River* †**~freistaat** m *Orange Free State*

orat·orisch a *oratorical* **Orat·orium** n ~s/–rien **1.** ⟨mus⟩ *oratorio* **2.** (Kirche) *oratory*

Orch·ester [–'k–, (–ç–)] n ~s/~ *orchestra, band* [pl konstr] ‖ ~- [in comp] *orchestral* (*accompaniment, concert, piece, society*) | ~-einrichtung [f] *orchestration, instrumentation*; ~musiker [m] *member of orchestra*; ~raum [m] *o. pit* **orchestr·ieren** vi [h] *to score, to orchestrate* **O-str·ierung** f ⟨mus⟩ *scoring* **O-strion** n *orchestrina*

Orchid·ee [–ç–] f ~/~n ⟨bot⟩ *orchid* **·Orchis** [–ç–] f ~/~ (Knabenkraut) *orchis*

Ord·al n ~s/–lien (Gottesurteil) *ordeal*

·Orden m ~s/~ **1.** ⟨ec⟩ (*religious*) *order* ‖ in e–n ~ eintreten *to join an o., to enter* (*into*) *religion* ‖ ⟨hist⟩ der Deutsche ~ *the Teutonic O.* ‖ Ritter e–s ~s *knight of an o.* **2.** (Ehrenzeichen) *order, decoration*; *badge, medal* ‖ der B. E.-Orden *the order of the British Empire* (Titel der Besitzerin: *Dame Mary N.*) ‖ e–n ~ erhalten *to receive a distinction* ‖ jdm e–n ~ verleihen *to bestow an o. on a p* ‖ e–m e–n ~ anheften *to decorate a p with an o.* **·Ordens- ~band** n *ribbon* (gr *broad*) ‖ ⟨ent⟩ *underwing* **~bruder** m *member of an o.*, ⟨ec⟩ *friar, monk* **~burg** f, **~schloß** n *castle of the* (*Teutonic*, etc.) *O.* **~geistliche(r)** m *regular* **~geistlichkeit** f *regular clergy* **~gelübde** n *profession, vow* ‖ das ~ ablegen *to take the vows* **~gesellschaft** f *chapter* **~jäger** m *medal hunter* **~kette** f *collar distinguishing an o.* **~kleid** n *monastic garb*, ⟨obs⟩ *habit* **~kreuz** n *cross of an o.* **~regel** f *rule of an o.* **~ritter** m *knight of an o.* **~schleife** f *decoration bow* **~schnalle** f *dec. clasp* ‖ gr ~ *o.s* pl, kl ~ *ribbons* **~schwester** f ⟨ec⟩ *nun, sister* **~stern** m *star of an o.*; mit ~ geschmückt *starred* (*general*) **~tracht** f ⟨ec⟩ *monastic habit* **~verbrüderung** f *confraternity* **~verleihung** f *conferring* (*of*) **~zeichen** n *badge of an o.* **~zucht** f *monastic discipline*

·ordentlich a **A.** *orderly, tidy, methodical, neat* ‖ (regelrecht) *regular* ‖ *square* (*meal*) ‖ (gewöhnlich) *ordinary* (*court, jurisdiction*) ‖ (anständig) *respectable, decent, steady, of orderly habits* ‖ er war soweit ganz ~ *he was all right in his way* ‖ (tüchtig) *good, sound* **B.** ein ~es Gericht *a r. court of law* ‖ ~er Kerl *decent fellow* ‖ ~e Mahlzeit *proper meal*; ~es Mitglied *ordinary member*; ~er Professor [m] *professor in o.y* ‖ ein ~er Schimpf *quite a disgrace* ‖ ~e Schläge bek *to get a sound beating* ‖ ~er Schluck *a good pull* (*at the bottle*) ‖ ~e Schlacht *pitched battle* **C.** **[adv]** *fairly, downright*; *tremendously*, ⟨fam⟩ *awfully* ‖ er war ~ grob *he was fairly rude* ‖ *I could not see properly* ‖ mach d–e S ~ *do your job nicely* ‖ lang nur ~ zu *help y.s. well* | mir ist ~ warm dabei geworden *it made me quite hot* ‖ etw ~ tun *to do a th properly* ‖ ~ gehalten *well kept* ‖ ~ froh s *to be truly glad* **D.** etw **(nichts)** **≃es** zu essen bek *to get* od *have a* (*no*) *regular meal* | **≃keit** f ~/ *orderliness*; *good* od *proper order*; *methodicalness* ‖ *regularity* ‖ *steadiness, respectability*

·Order f ~/~n *order, command* ‖ ~ erteilen *to give o.s* ‖ ~ parieren *to obey o.s* | ⟨com⟩ (für mich) an die ~ v *pay to the o. of* ‖ an ~ stellen *to endorse* (*a document*) ‖ Ihrer ~ gemäß *in obedience* od *conformity to your o.s* **~buch** n *o.-book* **~geber** m ⟨com⟩ *drawer* **~hafen** m *port of call* **~papier** n, **~scheck** m ⟨com⟩ *cheque to o.*

Ordin- ~·alzahl f *ordinal number* **≃·är** a *common, ordinary*; *regular* (*price*) ‖ *petty* (*average* Havarie) | ⟨dero⟩ *vulgar, mean* ‖ *inferior* (*quality*) ‖ ~er Mensch *cad*; *vulgar fellow* **~ari·at** n ~(e)s/~e ⟨school⟩ *form-mastership* ‖ ⟨univ⟩ *professorship* **~·arium** n ~s/ (*ordinary*) *budget* **~·arius** m ~/–rien ⟨school⟩ *form-master* ‖ ⟨univ⟩ *professor in ordinary*; ~ f. engl Philologie *professor of English philology* ‖ ⟨ec⟩ *ordinary* **~·ate** f ~/~n ⟨math⟩ *ordinate* | ~nachse [f] *axis of o.s* **~ati·on** [–ts–] f ~/~en ⟨ec⟩ *ordination* ‖ ⟨med⟩ *prescription* **≃·ieren** vt [h] **1.** ⟨ec⟩ *to ordain* (e–n z Priester *a p pr.*) ‖ sich ~ l *to take* (*holy*) *orders* **2.** ⟨med⟩ *to prescribe* **≃·iert** a *in* (*holy*) *orders* ‖ ~ w *to take* (*holy*) *orders*

·ordnen vt [h] *to order* ‖ *to arrange* (*documents*) ‖ *to settle, regulate, adjust, dispose, organize* ‖ *to put* od *set in order* od *to rights*; *to break down*; *rank, class*(*ify*), *grade* ‖ ⟨mil⟩ *to marshal* (*troops*; ⟨a. comp⟩ *into the right order*) ‖ ⟨gram⟩ *to construe* (*a sentence*) | alphabetisch ~ *to arrange alphabetically*, der Größe nach *according to size* ‖ systematisch ~ *to systematize* | s–e Angelegenheiten selbst ~ *to attend to one's affairs o.s.* ‖ in geordneten Verhältnissen (leben) .. *in easy circumstances* ‖ geordnete Zustände *proper* od *decent state of affairs* | **sich** ~ (S) *to settle itself*; die S läßt sich leicht ~ *that's easily settled* | (*the people*) *took their places* (*for the procession*) **·Ordner** m ~s/~ *organizer, regulator* ‖ (Fest≃) *steward* ‖ (Ordnungsschüler) *monitor* ‖ (Brief≃) *file*, ⟨Am⟩ *filer* **·Ordnung** f ~/~en **A. 1.** *putting in order* **2.** (Zustand) *order* ‖ ~ muß s *good o. is essential* ‖ (*the army retreated*) *in good o.* ‖ richtige ~ *trim* **3.** (Eigenschaft) *tidiness, tidy habits* pl **4.** (Richtigkeit) in (der) ~ s *to be in order* ‖ der ~ halber *for the sake of regularity* **5.** (Regelmäßigkeit) häusliche ~ *domestic arrangements* **6.** (Anordnung) *arrangement, disposition, regimentation* ‖ bestehende ~ *present regime* ‖ *Regulation* (*of Labour*) ‖ Gesellschafts≃, soziale ~ *order of society*; *social system* ‖ die politische ~ Englands *the English polity* | (Liste) Lohntarif≃ *wage schedule* **7.** (Klasse, Stand) (→ erste C.) *class, rank, division*; ⟨bot, zoo⟩ *order* (→ Art, Gattung, Klasse, Familie) ‖ Straßen erster ~ *roads of the first grade* ‖ ⟨ec⟩ Festtag erster (zweiter) ~ *red-* (*black-*)*letter festival* **8.** ⟨arch⟩ = Säulenordnung **9.** ⟨mil⟩ *formation* **B.** die ~ in der Welt aufrechterhalten *to police the w.* ‖ ~ in die Welt bringen *to bring order to the w.* ‖ e–e ~ festsetzen *to lay down an ordinance* (→ A. 6.) ‖ ⟨mil⟩ geöffnete (geschlossene) ~ *open* od *extended* (*closed*) *order* ‖ zerstreute ~ *scattered formation* ‖ hier herrscht ~! *good o. prevails here!* (→ A. 2.) ‖ ~ schaffen *to establish o.*, in e–m Hause *to bring a house to*

discipline || die ~ verletzen *to break square(s)* **C. aus** der ~ *out of o.* || aus der ~ bringen *to disarrange, disturb, derange* || aus der ~ k *to get out of o.; to be unsettled* (→ A. 5.) || **außer** ~ *amiss* || verstößt **gegen** die ~ *is contrary to good o., is an offence against divine o.* (→ A. 6.) || **in** ~ *in key, in good trim* od *condition* || in bester, schönster ~ *in excellent condition* od *trim* (→ A. 4.), ⟨fam⟩ *in apple-pie o.* || in ~! *all right!* ⟨sl⟩ *okay!, right-o.! Roger!* || ganz in der ~ *ordinary* || vollkommen in ~ *(I am) as right as a trivet* | in ~ **bringen** *to (reduce to) o.; to put (some) o. (in a room); to put* od *get right; to rectify, adjust; to put straight; to put, set to rights* || *to settle (a th)* || *to patch up* | *to straighten out (matters), to get (ths) square* || *that did the trick* || (Apparat) *to put right, to repair* || *to do (the flowers, one's hair)* || (Haar) *to groom, arrange* || s–e Finanzen .. *to balance one's budget* || e–e S mit jdm .. *to make it all right with a p* || **etw wieder** .. *to set straight* od *right, to straighten out; to recondition, rearrange* || jds Gesundheit wieder .. *to set a p up*; jdn wieder .. ⟨Am⟩ *to fix a p up* || ⟨com⟩ um unsere Bücher in ~ z br. *for the purpose of reconciling our books* || **nicht** alles war in schönster ~ *everything was not all right* | ich **finde** das ganz in der ~ *I think it quite right*; das ist g. in ~ *there is nothing wrong with that* od *about it* || Scheck **geht** in ~ .. *is in o.* || °geht in ~ ⟨sl⟩ *okay; it's jake* || in ~ **k** *to come (out all) right*; (allmählich) *ths are straightening out* | alles wird in ~ **s** *all will be well* (od *as it should be*) || es ist alles in ~ *all is settled* || der Wein ist ganz in ~ *there is nothing the matter with ..* | **nicht** in ~ *wrong, amiss* || (S) *not up to the mark; out of whack* || ist etw nicht in ~ mit ..? *do you see anything amiss with ..?* || da ist etw nicht in ~ *there's a screw loose somewhere* || etw ist mit ihm nicht in ~ *sth is the matter with him* || der ~ **nach** *in due o.* || ⟨parl⟩ **zur** ~ rufen *to call to o.* **·Ordnungs- ~begriff** m ⟨comp⟩ *logical consequence, pre-determined stage in processing* **⁓halber** adv *for regularity's sake*; ⟨a.⟩ *(let me mention,) just for the record, ..* **⁓gemäß** a = ~mäßig **~liebe** f *love of order, tidiness* **⁓liebend** a *orderly, tidy* **⁓los** a *disorderly* **~maschine** f ⟨comp⟩ *arranging m.* **⁓mäßig** a *orderly, regular* | [adv] *duly, r.ly* **~nummer** f ⟨off⟩ *current n.* **~partei** f ⟨parl⟩ *party of o.* **~ruf** m ⟨parl⟩ *call to o.* || jdm e–n ~ erteilen *to call a p to o.* || e–n ~ erhalten *to be called to o.* **~strafe** f ⟨jur⟩ *administrative* od *disciplinary penalty; fine* **~verhältnis** n ⟨scient⟩ *scaling relationship* **⁓widrig** a *contrary to* (od *out of*) *o., irregular, illegal* | ~keit [f] *infraction of regulations* (→ Vorschrift) **~zahl** f ⟨gram⟩ *ordinal number*; ⟨at⟩ *atomic n.* **Ordonn·anz** f ~/~en (Befehl) *order, ordinance* || ⟨mil⟩ (P) *orderly* | ~dienst [m] *o.ly duty* || ~ h *to be on o.ly duty* **~offizier** m *o.ly officer; assistant adjutant* **~zimmer** n *o.ly-room*, ⟨mil sl⟩ *Bow Street*
·Ordre f ~/~s Fr = Order

Ore·ade f ~/~n ⟨myth⟩ (Bergnymphe) *oread*

·Oregon n (Staat der U.S.A.)

Org·an n ~(e)s/~e *organ* ⟨a. pol⟩ || Sinnes⁓ *sense-o.* || Bewegungs⁓ ⟨anat⟩ *locomotor system*; ⟨micro⟩ *flagellum* || (Stimme) *voice* || ⟨phrenologisch⟩ *bump, understanding* (f *for*) || ~e der Meinungsäußerung *o.s* od *media of opinion* || ⟨off⟩ leitendes (Verwaltungs-)~ *governing body*, ständiges ~ *standing, permanent b.* **~isati·on** f ~/~en *organization* || ⟨pol⟩ *caucus*, ⟨Am⟩ *machine* || Verbraucher⁓ *cooperative society* || ~ der Vereinten Nationen *United Nations O. (UNO)* | ~sfehler [m] *faulty o.*; ~szwang [m] *compulsion to form* od *join an o.* **~is·ator** m ~s/–·oren *organizer* || ein glänzender ~ *an o. par excellence* **⁓isat·orisch** a *organizational* **⁓isch** a *organic* || *structural (disease)* **⁓is·ieren** vt [h] *to organize, arrange* || *to launch (a campaign for)*; (Produktion) *to pre-plan* || *to line up (meeting)* || (nicht) –rter Arbeiter *(non-) unionist* || °⟨fig⟩ („finden", stehlen) *to organize, wangle, win*, ⟨sl⟩ *to scrounge, liberate*; ⟨Am sl⟩ *to finagle* || sich ~ *to organize* (in, zu *into*) **~·ismus** m ~/–men *organism; system* **~·ist** m ~en/~en *organist* **·Orgel** f ~/~n *organ* || (bauen *to build*, aufstellen *to instal*) || ~ spielen *to play the o.* **~balg** m *o.-bellows* pl **~bauer** m *o.-builder* **~chor** n *o.-loft* **~dreher** m *o.-grinder* **~konzert** n *o.-recital* **~pfeife** f *o.-pipe* || die ~n abstimmen *to voice the pipes* || Kinder wie die ~n *little steps* **~pult** n *o.-desk* **~punkt** m ⟨mus⟩ *pause* **~register** n *stop of an o.; rank* **~solo** n ⟨ec⟩ *voluntary* **~spieler** m *o.-player* **~treter** m *o.-blower* **~werk** n *works* pl *of an o.* **~zug** m *range* od *row of pipes of an o.* || (Register) *o.-stop* **Orgel·ei** f ~/ *incessant* od *bad organ-playing* od *-grinding* || ⟨fig⟩ *dull music* **·orgeln** vi [h] *to play (on) the organ* || (auf der Drehorgel) *to grind a barrel-o.* || ⟨fam⟩ *to strum* || ⟨hunt⟩ (of stags) *to bell* **·Orgie** [–iə] f ~/~n *orgy* || ~n feiern ⟨fig⟩ *to run riot* || ~n w gefeiert *orgies are going on*

Org·asmus m ~/–men *orgasm* **org·astisch** a *orgasmic* || ~e Manschette [f] *orgasmic platform*

·Orient m ~(e)s/ *Orient, East; Eastern countries* pl || im ~ *oriental* || ~teppich [m] *turkey-carpet* || ~expreß [m] ⟨rail⟩ *Oriental Express* **~·ale** m ~n/~n **1.** *Oriental* **2.** ⟨fam⟩ *Jew* | **⁓·alisch** a *oriental, eastern* || die ~e Frage [f] *the Eastern Question* || ~es Seminar *school* od *class for O. languages* **~al·ist** m ~en/~en *Oriental scholar* **⁓·ieren** vt [h] (Karte etc) *to orient(ate)* (nach *towards*), *to set right* || s–e Politik ~ *to fix one's policy* (nach Grundsätzen *on principles*) || (belehren) *to inform* | **sich** ~ *to take one's bearings; to find one's way, to orient(ate) o.s.* || ⟨fig⟩ *to take soundings* || (sich erkundigen) *to inquire, to find out* (über [acc] *about*) || sich nicht mehr ~ können *to be all at sea, to have lost one's bearings* | ⟨fig⟩ gut **⁓iert** *well informed* || religiös orientiert s *(of book) to have a religious tendency* || nach dem Diesseits orientiert *worldly-minded* **~·ierung** f *orientation* (nach *towards*) || ⟨arch⟩ *eastering* ⟨fig⟩ *stock-taking* || ich habe die ~ verloren *I have lost my bearings* pl || zu Ihrer ~ *for your guidance* || nur zur ~ dienen *to be for reference only* | ~spunkt [m] *land-mark; guide* od *locating mark* | ~ssinn [m], ~svermögen [n] *instinct for direction; ability to find one's way*; ~szeichen [n] *bearings* pl

origin·al 1. [a] *original* **2.** ⁓ [n] ~(e)s/~e *o.l text; autograph letter* || (P) *o.l; queer character; (quite a) character; oddity* | ⁓ausgabe [f] *first edition*: ~aufnahmen [f pl] ⟨wir, telv⟩ *spot pick-ups* pl; ~band [m] *o.l binding*; ~beleg [m] *o.l medium*; ~druck [m] *o.l print*; ~gemälde [n] *o.l painting*; ⁓maß [n] *standard-measure*; ~negativ [n] *master n.* | höchste ~treue [f] ⟨wir⟩ *high fidelity (hifi)*: ~übertragung [f] *live broadcast*; ~unterlage [f] *document*; ⟨comp⟩ *o.l medium* **Originalit·ät** f ~/~en *o.lity (consists in the mode of treating a subject* [Scott]) || ⟨fig⟩ *oddity, peculiarity* **origin·ell** a *ingenious (device)* || *o.l (character)* || *peculiar*; (seltsam, spaßhaft) *funny, rum, strange, queer* || ein ~er Mensch *an odd sort of fellow*

Orin·oko, der (S.-Am. Fluß) *the Orinoco*

Ork·aden pl (= Orkneyinseln) *Orcades*

Ork·an m ~s/~e *hurricane, typhoon* | ~gebiet [n] zw 40° u 50° nördl. Br. *the roaring forties* pl

·Orkneyinseln f pl *Orkney Islands, Orkneys*

·Orkus m ~/ *Orcus, Hades* || in den ~ versenken *to cast into Hades* || zum ~ hinabfahren *to pass into the infernal regions*

·Orléans n ⟨Fr⟩ (Stadt an der Loire)

·Orlogschiff n ⟨hist mar⟩ *man-of-war*

·Orlopdeck n ⟨mar⟩ *orlop*

Ornam·ent n ~s/~e *ornament*; kombiniertes ~ *built up flower pattern* od *rosette* ⁓·**ieren** vt [h] *to ornament* **~ik** f ~/ *ornamentation* **~iker, ~·ist** m ⟨arts⟩ *decorator* **Orn·at** m ~(e)s/~e ⟨ec & jur⟩ *robe(s* pl), *the long robe, vestments* pl (→ Domherrn⁓) ‖ in vollem ~ ⟨fam⟩ *in full fig*

Ornith- **~ol·og(e)** m ~en/~en *ornithologist* **~olog·ie** f ~/ *ornithology* ⁓**ol·ogisch** a *ornithological*

·**orphisch** a *Orphean* ‖ *melodious* **Orph·ismus** m ~/ ⟨rel⟩ *orphism* (⟨a. arts⟩ *Delaunay 1912*)

·**Orplid** n ~s/ (Mörike) ⟨poet⟩ *dream-island*

Ort A. 1. m ~(e)s/~e & ⁓er *place, spot, locality,* ⟨Am⟩ *point* ‖ ⟨mar⟩ *position* (bestimmen *to fix*) ‖ (Gegend) *region* ‖ ⟨min⟩ n *working place*; *head* od *end of the gallery, forehead* ‖ ⟨math⟩ geometrischer ~ (*geometrical*) *locus* ‖ ⟨astr⟩ mittlerer ~ *mean place* **2.** (Ortschaft) *place, town* **3.** m & n (Schusterahle) *awl* **B.** *place* (*of peace, misery*) ‖ [dat] (S) e–n ~ an-, zuweisen *to locate, situate* ‖ ~ u Stunde *or* Zeit *place and time* ‖ ~ der Handlung (des Verbrechens) *scene of action* (*locality of the deed*) ‖ *this is not the place for* .. ‖ der ganze ~ spricht davon *it is the talk of the town* | .. **des** ~es *local* (*hotel, worthy*) ‖ die Einheit des ~es u der Zeit ⟨liter⟩ *the unity of time and place* ‖ aller⁓s, –orten *everywhere* **C. angenehmer,** berühmter, geschützter ~ *pleasant, celebrated, sheltered spot* ‖ elender, gr. kl ~ *wretched, large, small place* ‖ geweihter ~ *consecrated ground* ‖ ⟨euph⟩ gewisser ~ *lavatory,. W. C.* ‖ offener ~ *open town* ‖ öffentliche ~e *public places* | geeigneten **~(e)s** (empfehlen) *to the proper p, in the proper quarters* ‖ hiesigen ~s *of this place* ‖ höheren ~(e)s *in higher quarters,* (*approved of, ordered*) *by the authorities* ‖ ich m–s ~es *I for my part* **D. am** ~ *local* (*industry*); **an** e–m ~e *in a place* ‖ am ~ *locally* ‖ sehr am ~ *very appropriate* ‖ am unrechten ~ *in the wrong* (od *out of*) *place, misplaced* ‖ an welchem ~? *where* | an ~ u **Stelle** *on the* (*very*) *spot*; *in situ* L; ⟨film⟩ *on location*; .. gelangen *to reach one's destination*; .. an ~ u St. *field* ([attr] *study*); (nur) an .. (Ausschank) *on the premises*; an ~ u St. bleiben *to stay put*; *to stop in one's tracks* | an dem ~e, **wo** (*near*) *where* | an **allen** ~en (u Enden) *everywhere* ‖ am **angegebenen** ~e (a. a. O.) *at the stipulated place* (*l. c.* od *loc. cit.* = *loco citato*) ‖ an e–m ~ auftretend *endemic* (⟨zoo⟩ *enzootic*) (*disease*) ‖ am **dritten** ~ *somewhere away from home* ‖ fehl am ~ *misplaced* ‖ bin ich am rechten ~ *or* recht am ~? *am I at the right place?* ‖ an verschiedenen ~en *in several places* ‖ am ~e wohnend *resident* | er ist **aus** m–m ~ *he comes from my native place* | **in** bestimmten ~en, im ~e *locally* | **v** ~ **zu** ~ *from place to place* | ⟨min⟩ **vor** ~ *in the drift, at the face*; .. arbeiten *to drive the head of a gallery, to cut the rock* **~band** n *chape* (*of a scabbard*) **~scheit** n, *swing-bar, s.(le)-tree* **~schicht** f ⟨arch⟩ *barge-course* °·**Örtchen** n *W. C.*; ⟨hum⟩ *parliament*

·**orten** vt [h] (Karte) *to set* ‖ ⟨mil⟩ *to find the position of* | vi [h] *to take one's bearings* ·**Orter** m ~s/~ ⟨aero⟩ *navigator, observer* | ~raum [m] *n.'s compartment* ·**örtern** vt [h] ⟨tech⟩ *to chamfer* → örtlich

·**Ortho-** **~chromas·ie** f ~/ *orthochromatic sensitivity* **~dont·ist** m *orthodontist* ⁓**d·ox** a *orthodox*; *professing* (*Jew*) **~dox·ie** f ~/~n *orthodoxy* **~ep·ie** f ~/ *orthoepy* **~gen·ese** f ~/ ⟨biol⟩ *orthogenesis* **~gr·aph** [–f] m ~en/~en *orthographer* **~graph·ie** f ~/~n *orthography, correct spelling* ⁓**gr·aphisch** a *orthographic(al)* ‖ ~er Fehler *spelling mistake*; *m. in sp.*; *misspelling* | [adv] ~ schreiben *to spell correctly*; nicht .. *to be a bad speller* **~k·ieselsäure** f ⟨chem⟩ *silicic acid* **~kl·as** m ⟨min⟩ *orthoclase* **~p·äde** m *orthopædist* **~päd·ie** f *orthopædy, -dics* pl ⁓**-p·ädisch** a *orthopædic(al)* **~ps·ie** f *orthoptics* [sg konstr]

·**Ortler** m ~s/ (Berg in Tirol) | ~alpen [pl] *Ortler Alps*; ~gruppe [f] *group of the O. Alps*

·**örtlich** a *local* (*arrangements, news, campain* Werbung) ‖ ⟨med & tech a.⟩ *topical* ‖ ~e Beschaffenheit *local topography* ‖ [adv] ~ zuständiger Befehlshaber *commander on the spot* ‖ ~ verschieden s *to differ in different localities* | ⁓**keit** f ~/~en *locality, locale, place*

·**Orts-** oft *local* (*butcher*) **~adverb** n ⟨gram⟩ *adverb of p.* **~angabe** f *indication of p.*; *address*; ⟨bes mar⟩ *location* ⁓**ansässig** a *resident, local* **~ansässige(r)** m *l. man* ⁓**anwesend** a *actual, enumerated, present-in-area* (*population*) ⁓**bedingt** a *environmental* **~behörde** f *l. authorities* pl **~beschaffenheit** f *l. topography*; *nature of a l.ity* **~besichtigung** f *local survey, site inspection* **~beschreibung** f *topography* **~bestimmung** f *position-finding* | ~srecht [n] (über Schankgerechtigkeit) *l. option* **~bewohner** m pl *l. people*; *inhabitants* ⁓**fest** a *fixed, stationary* (*mount*) ⁓**fremd** a *visiting* (*man*) ⁓**gebunden** a *confined to a* (*certain*) *place* od *location* **~gedächtnis** n *memory for p.s* **~geistliche(r)** m *l. minister* **~gespräch** n ⟨telph⟩ *l. call,* ⟨post off⟩ = Ferngespräch **~gruppe** f *l.* (*branch*) **~kenntnis** f *knowledge of a p.* ‖ –nisse h *to know a p.*; über gute ~ verfügen *to have a good knowledge of the local area* **~klassenzulage** f *weighting* **~kommandant** m *town major* | ~ur [f] *post* od *garrison headquarters* pl **~krankenkasse** f *l. sick-fund* ⁓**kundig** a *having knowledge of a p.* **~mißweisung** f (*magnetic*) *variation* **~nachrichten** f pl *topical news* **~name** m *place(-)name* ‖ pl ~n *names of places* **~netz** n ⟨telph⟩ *l. plant* **~pfarrer** m *l. parson* **~polizei** f *l. police* **~sinn** m *sense* od *bump of l.ity*; *space sense* **~statut** n *by(e)-law,* ⟨Am⟩ *ordinance* **~teil** m *quarter* ⁓**üblich** a *customary in a p.* **~unterkunft** f ⟨mil⟩ *cantonment* **~veränderung** f *change of p.* (od ⟨med⟩ *of scenery*) ‖ (Fähigkeit der ~) .. *locomotion* **~verkehr** m *l. traffic* **~vorsteher** m *chief magistrate of a p.* **~zeit** f *local* od *zone-time*; mittlere ~ (MOZ) *local meantime* (*LMT*); scheinbare ~ *local apparent time* (*LAT*) ·**Ortschaft** f ~/~en *place, village, borough, locality* ‖ kl ~ *small town*; geschlossene ~ *built-up area* ·**Ortung** f ~/~en *position finding,* ⟨mil a.⟩ *fix, detection* ‖ Funk⁓ *wireless p. f.* ‖ Schall⁓ *sound locating* **~sgerät** n *detecting gear, position finder, radar* **~sleuchtkugel** f *navigation flare* **~s- u Leitdienste** pl *locator and guidance activities*

Ortol·an m ~(e)s/~e ⟨orn⟩ *ortolan,* → *bunting*

Os·aka n (japan. Stadt)

·**Öse** f ~/~n *ring, loop*; *eye* (*of a tool*) → Haken | **~n-** ~schraube [f] *eye screw*

·**ösen** vt [h] ⟨mar⟩ (ausschöpfen) *to bail*

·**Öser** m ~s/~ ⟨geol⟩ (glaz. Kieslager) *eskar*

·**Oskar** m ~s/ *Oscar*; °frech wie ~ (*as*) *bold as brass*

·**Oslo** n (Hauptstadt v Norwegen)

osm·anisch a *Ottoman*

Osm·ose f ~/~ ⟨phys⟩ *osmosis* L **osm·otisch** a *osmotic* (*pressure*)

Ost m ~es/~e; **~en** m ~ens/ *east,* → Norden | [nur ~en] Mittlerer ~ *Farther East*; im mittleren ~ ⟨a.⟩ *in the Middle East*; (e–r Stadt) *the East End,* ⟨Am⟩ .. *Side*; Bewohner des ~ens *East-Ender,* ⟨Am⟩ *-Sider* | [nur ~] (Wind) *east wind* ‖ aus ~ *from the east* **~afrika** n *East Africa* **~angeln** n *East Anglia* (Engl) **~·asien** n *Eastern Asia, the Far East* **~block** m (*communist*) *East bloc* **Ostende** n (belg. Stadt) *Ostend* ‖ (–teil) *East End* **~fr·iesland** n ⟨Ger⟩ (Küstenland zw Ems & Weser) **~gote** m *East Goth* **~·indien** n *India, the East Indies* pl **~·indienfahrer** m *East Indiaman* **~j·aken** pl (uralisches Volk in Sibirien) *Ostiaks* pl **~jude** m *Eastern Jew* **~mark** f *Austria* **~nord**⁓ (ONO) *E.-North-E.* **~preußen** n *East(ern) Prussia* **~see** f *Baltic* (*Sea*) ⁓**wärtig** a = östlich ⁓-

wärts adv *eastward* **~-West-Handel** m *East-West Trade* **~wind** m *east wind* **~zone** f *Eastern* od *Russian Zone* **·osten** vt [h] *to orient(ate)*

ostentat·iv a *ostentatious, defiant, challenging* | [adv] ~ tragen etc *to affect*

Osteolog·ie f ~/ (Knochenlehre, –forschung) *osteology*

·Oster- ~abend m *Easter eve* **~blume** f ⟨bot⟩ (gelbe) *daffodil*; (weiße) *wood anemone* **~ei** n *E.-egg* **~fest** n = Ostern **~hase** m ⟨Ger⟩ *E.-bunny (that lays the E.-eggs)* **~kerze** f *paschal candle* **~-lamm** n *p.l lamb* **~luzei** f ⟨bot⟩ *birth-wort*, → d. **~messe** f *E.-fair* **~monat, ~mond** m *E.-month, April* **~m·ontag** m *E. Monday* **~semester** n ⟨univ engl⟩ *Trinity Term* **~tag** m *E. day* **~woche** f *E.-week* **~zeit** f *Eastertide* **·österlich** a *Easter, Paschal* **·Ostern** pl *Easter* || (der Juden) *Passover* || diese ~ *this E.* || ⟨hum⟩ wenn ~ u Pfingsten auf einen Tag fallen *when Good Friday falls on a Thursday, when two Sundays come in a week, once in a blue moon, not in a month of Sundays*

·Österreich(er m) n ~s/ *Austria(n)* | †~-Ungarn [n] *A.-Hungary; the Austro-Hungarian Empire*

Ost·itis f ~/ → Knochenentzündung

·östlich a *eastern, easterly, Oriental* || ~er Kurs, *easting* || ~e Länge *East Longitude* || [adv] ~ von Berlin, ~ des Rheins *(to the) east of B., the Rh.* | **~st** sup *easternmost* **·Ostung** f ~/ *orientation*

Ostraz·ismus m ~/–men *ostracism*

Oszill·ator m ~s/–t·oren *oscillator, generator* **oszill·ieren** vi [h] *to oscillate* || ⟨mach⟩ *to hunt*

Ottaver·ime f ⟨pros⟩ → *ottava rima*

·Ottawa 1. (Nebenfluß des St. Lorenzstroms) 2. (Hauptstadt v Kanada) **~fluß** m *Ottawa River*

·Otter 1. m ~s/~ (Fisch~) *otter* **2.** f ~/~n (Natter) *adder, viper* (* = 1.) **~bau** m *holt* **~gerät** n ⟨mar⟩ *paravane* **·Ottern- ~balg** m *otter's skin* **~biß** m *bite of an adder* **~fang** m *catching of otters* **~gezücht** n ⟨fig⟩ *generation of vipers* **~gift** n *poison of a viper*

·Otto- (nach N. ~ †1891) **~m·otor** m *spark ignition motor; Otto engine* **~verfahren** n *Otto cycle*

Oudh n [aud] (vorderind. Landschaft zw Ganges u Himalaja)

outr·iert a *excessive, outré* Fr

Ouvert·üre [u:vɛr'ty:rə] f ~/~n *overture*

Ov·al n ~(e)s/~e *oval* | ⁓ a *oval* || ~er Platz *oval* | ~drehbank [f] *oval lathe* **Ov·arium** n ~s/–rien ⟨biol⟩ *ovary* **ovip·ar** a ⟨biol⟩ *oviparous* (Ggs *viviparous*)

Ovati·on [–ts–] f ~/~en *ovation* || jdm ~en bereiten *to give a p enthusiastic welcome* od *applause*

Ow·ambo pl (Bantuvolk in Afrika)

Ox·alsäure f *oxalic acid*

·Oxford n ['ɔksfəd] ⟨Engl⟩ (Universitätsstadt)

·Oxhoft n ~(e)s/~e (Maß = 1,5 Ohm = 238,54 l) *hogshead*

Ox·id, †Oxyd n ~(e)s/~e *oxide* || ~beschlag [m] *film of o.* **~ati·on** [–ts–] f ~/~en *oxidization* | ⁓sfähig [a] *oxidizable*; ~smittel [n] *oxidizer* ⁓**·ieren** vt [h] & vi [s] *to oxidize* **~·ierung** f *oxidation* **~·ul** n ~(e)s/~e ⟨chem⟩ *protoxide* || K·upfer⁓ *cuprous oxide* (Kupfer/I/-oxid) **Oxygen** n ~(e)s/ *oxygen*

·Ozarkberge m pl *Ozark Mountains (U.S.A.)*

·Ozean m ~(e)s/~e *ocean* || Gr *or* Stiller ~ *Pacific O.* || ⟨fig⟩ *sea (of pleasure); gallons and gallons (of ink)*; ~·arium [n] ~s/–rien *seaquarium*; ~dampfer [m] *transatlantic steamer*; ~flug [m] *transoceanic flight*; ~kabel [n] *submarine line*; ~ograph·ie [f] *oceanography*; ⁓ogr·aphisch [a] *-graphic*; ~reise [f] *ocean voyage*

Oze·anien n (Mikronesien, Melanesien, Polynesien) *Oceania, Australasia* **Oze·anier** m *South Sea Islander* **oze·anisch** a *Oceanic*

Oz·on n ~s/ *ozone* || in ~ verwandeln *to ozonify* | ⁓erzeugend [a] *ozoniferous*; ~gerät [n] *ozonizer, ozonator*; ⁓haltig [a] *ozonic*; ~messer [m] *ozonometer* ⁓**is·ieren** vt [h] *to ozonize*

P

P, p [pe:] n ~/~ *P, p,* ⟨telph⟩ *pip*

P·aalstek m ⟨mar⟩; (laufend *running*) *bowline*

Pä·an m ~(e)s/Pä·ane *pæan*

P·aar n ~(e)s/~e ([dim] Pärchen) **A. 1.** ein, zwei ~ *a* (od *one*) *pair* [pl konstr], *two pair(s) (of eyes, shoes, trousers, carriage-horse, pigeons)*; ⟨fig⟩ das sind zwei ~ Stiefel *that's another pair of shoes* **2.** *couple* [pl konstr]; 10 ~e *ten couples (danced)* || ein glücklich liebend ~ *a loving couple* || ein ~ w *to make a couple* (⟨fam⟩ .. *a match of it*), *to become man and wife* || sie w wohl ein ~ w *it looks like a match* **3.** ⟨hunt⟩ (S, T, ⟨dero⟩ P) *brace* [pl *brace*] *(two brace of pistols, partridges)* **4.** ⟨agr⟩ *a yoke (of oxen)* **B.** ~ **bei** *or* **um** ~, ~ u ~, bei *or* zu ~en *in couples, in pairs, by twos, two and two* | schön in ~en zus–setzen *to pair off nicely together* || diese Schuhe sind nicht **vom** selben ~ .. *are not fellows, are odd* || **zu** ~en *in couples*; z ~en treiben *to rout (completely), to put to flight* **p·aar I.** [a] (zus–gehörig) **1.** *matching, like; forming a pair* || diese Schuhe sind nicht ~ .. *are not a pair, .. do not match, .. are odd; these are odd shoes* **2.** *even (numbers)* || ~ oder un~? *odd or even?* **II.** [unbest. Zahlwort] (einige) *some, a few (cases)*; ein ~ hundert Menschen *some hundreds of people*; in ein ~ Tagen *in a few days* || nach ein ~ Tagen *after a day or two*; die ~ Dollar! *those few dollars!*; d–e ~ lumpigen Kröten! *what few paltry marks you have!*; die ~ Groschen Verdienst *a profit of a few pence*; ein ~mal *several times*; alle ~ Stunden *every few hours*; ein ~ Worte *a word or so* od *two*; mit ein ~ Worten *in* od *with a few words, in a nutshell*; ein ~ Zeilen schreiben *to write a line or two, (drop me a line!)*; sich mit ein ~ Zeilen bedanken *to write a few words of thanks* **P·aar-~hufer, ~zeher** m ⟨zoo⟩ *even-toed animal, artiodactyl* ⁓**weise** adv *in pairs, in couples, by pairs, by twos, two and two* || ~ gehen *to walk two and two* || ~ ordnen ⟨a.⟩ *to pair* || ~ hinter–e–a *in double file* **~zeit** f *pairing time* **p·aaren** vt & sich ~ *to pair, couple* || *match (socks, teams)* || sich ~ ⟨a.⟩ *to mate, copulate* | **gepaart**: *reserve coupled with pride* || *appetite and weakness were mated in him* || (paarweise vorhanden) *in twos, twinned* || ⟨bot⟩ *geminous* || ⟨math, anat, etc⟩ *conjugate* **p·aarig** a *in pairs, in couples; paired; geminate, geminous* | [adv] ~ gefiedert ⟨bot⟩ *paripinnate* **p·aarmal** adv; ein ~ *several times, a few times* **P·aarung** f ~/~en *pairing, coupling* || (Begattung) *copulation* || vor der ~ stattfindend *precoital (courtship)* **~sakt** m *coition* **~szeit** f *pairing time*

P·acht f **A. 1.** *lease, tenure, tenancy* **2.** (Geld) *rent* (billig *low*, mäßig *moderate*, hoch *high*) **B.** die ~ aufheben, kündigen *to cancel the lease, to give notice* || die ~ läuft ab *the l. runs out* | **in** ~ geben *to put out to l.; to farm* (od *let*) *out* || in ~ nehmen *to take on l., to farm* | ⟨fig⟩ die Wissenschaft angeblich in ~ h *to claim to be the only true representative of sc.* **~anschlag** m *estimate of a l.* **~bauer** m *tenant* **~besitz** m *l.hold* **~brief** m *l.* **~geld** n (*farm-*) *rent* **~gut** n *farm*; *holding*; bäuerliches ~ *peasant h.*; *l.hold-estate* **~herr** m *owner* (*of a farm*) **~hof** m *farm, barton* **~inhaber** m *tenant* **~jahr** n *year of a l.* **~kontrakt, ~vertrag** m *l.* **≃weise** adv *on l.* **~wert** m *rental value* **~zeit** f *term of l.* ‖ nach Ablauf der ~ *when the l. expires, at the expiration of the l.* **~zins** m *rent* **p·achten** vt [h] *to farm, rent* ‖ ⟨jur⟩ *to* (*take on*)*lease, to take a l. of* ‖ ⟨fig⟩ als hätte sie die Schlauheit gepachtet *as if she were the only p with a little commonsense* **P·achter,** ≃ m ~s/~ *tenant* ‖ *farmer* ‖ ⟨jur⟩ *leaseholder* ‖ ⟨Am sl⟩ (*share-*) *cropper* **P·achtung** f ~/~en **1.** [abstr] *taking on lease, farming, tenancy* **2.** [konkr] *farm, estate, l.hold, tenement*

Pack 1. [m (n) ~(e)s/* ~e & ≃e] *pack, bundle* ‖ ⟨pap⟩ (500 etc Blatt) *packet* (*of writing paper*) ‖ (Ballen) *bale* ‖ *packet* (*of letters, of sandwiches,* etc); (*wage*) *packet* ‖ *pile* (*of letters, books,* etc) *parcel* (*of washing*) ‖ mit Sack u ~ *with bag and baggage* **2.** [n] ~(e)s (niederes Volk) *rabble* ‖ so ein ~! *such a pack of cads!, this lot!* ‖ ~ schlägt sich, ~ verträgt sich *dog will not eat dog* **P·äckchen** n ~s/~ *small parcel*; ⟨post⟩ *packet* ‖ *sheaf* (*of notes*); ⟨Am sl⟩ *wad* (*of bills*); *packet* (*of cigarettes*) ‖ ⟨fig fam⟩ sein ~ tragen *to do one's bit* **P·ack-** °**~an** m ~/ ⟨fam⟩ *copper* (= policeman) ‖ (dog) *Holdfast* **~bindfaden** m *cord, twine* **~eis** n *pack*(*-ice*) **~esel** m *sumpter-mule* ‖ ⟨fig⟩ *drudge, fag*; ⟨mil⟩ *Joe Soap*, ⟨Am⟩ *stooge* **~haus** n, **~hof** m *packing-room, -yard* ‖ (*bonded*) *warehouse, custom-house* **~hofslager** n *bonded store* **~kammer** f *packing-room* **~knecht** m *packer* **~korb** m *hamper, pannier* **~leinwand** f *pack-cloth* **~material** n *packing* **~meister** m *p.g-master* **~nadel** f *p.g-needle* **~papier** n *p.g-sheet, wrapping paper*; (*strong*) *brown-paper* **~pferd** n *sumpter*(*-horse*), *pack-horse* **~presse** f *baling press* **~raum** m ⟨mar⟩ *stowage* ‖ (e–s Wagens) *boot* **~riemen** m *p.g-strap* **~sattel** m *pack-saddle* **~stock** m *p.g-stick* **~stoff** m *p.gs* pl **~tier** n *pack animal* **~tisch** m *wrapping table* **~träger** m *porter* **~tuch** n *pack-cloth* **~wagen** m ⟨mil⟩ *baggage-wag*(*g*)*on* ‖ ⟨rail⟩ (*luggage-*)*van*, ⟨Am⟩ *baggage-car* **~zellstoff** m *cellulose p.gs* pl **~zettel** m *docket* **~zwil(li)ch** m *drill* **P·acken** m ~s/~ (*large*) *bale, bundle, parcel, packet* ‖ *pack* od *pile* (*of books*); *hand-, armful* (*of snow*) **p·acken** vt [h] **1.** *to pack* (*up*) (*one's ths*) (*clothes in a trunk*) ‖ zu Haufen ~ *to pile up* (*books*) ‖ Waren vom Wagen ~ *to unload* .. ‖ (befördern) *to bundle* (*a p into a lift*) ‖ in–e–a ~ *to nest* (*boxes*, etc) **2.** s–e Koffer ~ *to pack one's trunks*; ⟨fig⟩ *to clear out, to be off* ‖ sich [dat] die Taschen voll ~ *to cram one's pockets* **3.** (greifen) (→ fassen) *to seize, grip, grab* ‖ (fest) *to clamp* ‖ (krampfhaft) *to clutch* ‖ (schnell) *to swoop* (*up*) ‖ am *or* beim Kragen ~ *to collar* ‖ *he took him by* (an) *the throat* (Kehle) ‖ *he gripped, grabbed him by the arm* ‖ .. mit den Händen an der Kehle *his hands closed upon her throat* ‖ mit den Krallen *to claw* ‖ v Raubvögeln *to pounce upon* **|** ⟨übtr⟩ *a norther* (Nordwind) *hit us* ‖ *the fever got him* ‖ es hat mich gepackt *I've caught it badly* ‖ hat's dich sehr gepackt? *were you very much smitten?* (*by love*) ‖ Angst packte ihn *fear gripped his heart, he was seized by fright* ‖ *the gaiety that was on him now* ‖ wir können es (zeitlich) noch gerade ~ *we can just manage it* **|** ⟨fig⟩ *to grip* (*the imagination*); die **Zuhörer** ~ *to impress* od *grip the audience* ‖ *it appealed to us with an irresistible charm* ‖ ⟨theat⟩ *the play grips, thrills* (*one*); *I was very much taken by it*; ⟨fam⟩ *the film flipped me* **| packend**: *a powerful play, touching scene, thrilling adventure*; *trenchant picture*; *stirring words* **|** [adv] *in a striking manner* **4.** °**sich** ~ *to get out*; *to decamp*; ⟨fam⟩ *to bundle off* od *out* ‖ pack dich! ⟨fam⟩ *get along with you! clear out! out you go!* ‖ pack dich z Teufel! *go to the devil! go to blazes!*

P·acker m ~s/~ *packer*; *moving-man, removal-man* ‖ ⟨hunt⟩ *boar-hound* **~lohn** m *charges* [pl] *for packing, package* ‖ *packer's wages* **Packer·ei** f ~/~en *packing* (*-up*) ‖ ⟨dero⟩ *bad packing* **P·ackung** f ~/~en [abstr] *packing* ‖ [konkr] *package, packet*; verlorene ~ (Behälter) *throw-away container* ‖ ⟨med⟩ (*wet*) *pack*(*ing*), *cataplasm, poultice* ‖ ⟨tech⟩ (Liderung) *packing*(*-tow*) ‖ ⟨ftb⟩ e–e ~ kriegen *to get a good licking* (= *be badly beaten*)

Pädag·og(e) m ~en/~en *pedagogue, educator* ‖ ⟨dero⟩ *pedant* **~ik** f ~/ *pedagogics* pl [a. sg konstr] **≃isch** a *pedagogic*(*al*), *educational* **~ium** n ~s/–gien *boarding-school*

×**P·adde** f ~/~n [niedd] *toad*; *frog*

P·addel f ~/~n (Ruder) *paddle* **~boot** n *canoe* **p·addeln** vi [h] *to paddle, to canoe*

Päder·ast m ~en/~en *pederast* **~·ie** f ~/ *pederasty* **pädom·orph** a *p*(*a*)*edomorphic* **| ≃e** m & f *p.ph*

P·adua n (Stadt in Oberitalien)

paff! I. [intj] *bang! pop!* (→ piff) ‖ ~ ging der Schuß los *off went the gun* ‖ ⟨fam⟩ ganz ~ *knocked silly*; *flabbergasted*; *struck all of a heap* **II.** ≃ [m] (Knall) *report*; ≃ m *to report* **|** (Zug des Rauchers) *whiff, puff* **p·affen** vi/t [h] *to puff*; *to blow a cloud* ‖ drauflos ~ *to puff away at one's cigar*; (schießen) *to pop away* (nach *at*) ‖ ⟨fam⟩ daß es (nur so) pafft *with a vengeance*

P·age ['pɑːʒə] m ~n/~n *page*, ⟨hist⟩ *varlet* ‖ ⟨hot⟩ *boy in buttons, button-boy* ‖ jdn durch e–n ~n holen l *to page a p* **~nkopf** m *bobbed hair* (*with fringe*) **~nschnitt** m ⟨cosm⟩ *pageboy*

P·agina f ~/~s *page* (*of a book*) ‖ ⟨typ⟩ *folio* **pagin·ieren** vt [h] *to page, paginate* ‖ nicht –rt *unpaged*

Pag·ode 1. f ~/~n *pagoda* **2.** m ~n/~n [a. f] (Nickfigur) *pagoda*

p·ah! intj *pooh! pah! pshaw! tut! tush!*

P·ahang n (Vereinigte Malaien-Staaten)

Pair [pɛːr] m ~s/~s *peer* [f *peeress*] **~schaft** f ~/ *peerage* **~skammer** f *House of Lords* **~sschub** m *creation of peers* **~swürde** f *peerage*

P·ak f ~/~ (= **P**anzer**a**bwehr**k**anone) → d.

Pak·et n ~(e)s/~e *parcel, packet, package*; *bundle* ‖ *paper* (*of needles*) ‖ (Reisig & ⟨met⟩) *fagot* ‖ in ~en *packaged* (*goods* pl); in ~e packen *to parcel* **~adresse** f = Begleitadresse **~ausgabe, ~beförderung** f *p.l-delivery* **~boot** n *mail-steamer, packet*(*-boat*), *mailboat* ‖ (atlantisches etc) *liner* **~fahrtgesellschaft** f *p.l* (*delivery*) *company*, ⟨Am⟩ *express company* (dazu: *express-office, -wagon, -man*) **~karte** f *dispatch-note* **~post** f *p.l-post* **~satz** m ⟨typ⟩ *piece work* **~setzer** m *piece hand* **~wagen** n *p.l-delivery van* **~zustellgesellschaft** f ⟨Am⟩ *express company*

Pakist·ani m ~(s)/~(s) Bewohner v P·akistan *do*

Pakot·ille [–'tiljə] f ~/~n Fr = Beilast

Pakt m ~(e)s/~e *agreement*, (*com*)*pact* ‖ ⟨pol⟩ *pact*; Beistands≃ *Mutual Assistence P.*, Dreimächte≃ *Tripartite P.*) ‖ ⟨parl⟩ (*to refuse any*) *compact* (*with Labour*) **pakt·ieren** vt/i [h] *to agree, to come to terms* (über *about*), *to make a compact* od *agreement* (*on*) ‖ *to consort, compound* (*with*) **|** (ausbedingen) *to claim, stipulate*

Palad·in m *paladin*; ⟨dero⟩ *stable companion*

Pal·ais [–lɛː] n ~/~ *palace*

Palank·in m ~s/~e (Sänfte) ⟨Ind⟩ *palankeen*

Paläo- ~gr·aph m ~en/~en *palæographer* **|** ~·ie [f] ~/ *palæography*; ≃isch [a] *palæographic*(*al*) **≃l·ithisch** a *palæolithic* **~ntol·og(e)** m ~en/~en *palæontologist*; –gie [f] *palæontology*; –gische Geographie *palæogeography* **~z·än** n ⟨geol⟩ (unterste Alttertiärstufe) *palæocene*; → –zän **~z·oikum** m **≃z·oisch** a *palæozoic*

Pal·ast m ~es/≃e *palace* **|** ≃artig [a] *palatial*; ~dame [f] *lady in attendance*; ~revolution [f] *palace revolution* ⟨a. fig⟩

Paläst·ina n *Palestine*; p–nisch [a] *Palestinian*
Palatsch·inke f ~/~n [österr] *stuffed omelette*
Pal·aver n ~s/~ *palaver*; ⟨sl⟩ *hot air*
Pal·embang n (Stadt Sumatras)
p·alen vt [h] [ndd] *to shell* (*peas*, etc)
Paleo-, paleo- → Paläo-, paläo-
P·aletot [–to:] m ~s/~s *overcoat*, ⟨mil⟩ *greatcoat* **~marder** m *stealer of*.. **~stoff** m *cover-coating*
Pal·ette f ~n/~n *palette*; ⟨cul⟩ *spatula*
Palimps·est m & n ~es/~e *palimpsest* **Palin-~dr·om** n ~s/~e *palindrome* (rück- wie vorwärts lautend) (z. B. Otto, Reliefpfeiler) **~gen·ese, ~-genes·ie** f ~/~n *palingenesis*
Palis·ade f ~/~n *palisade* ‖ ⟨fort a.⟩ **~nzaun** m *stockade* **palisad·ieren** vt [h] *to palisade*; *to stockade*
Palis·anderholz n *rosewood*; *palisander*
P·all m ~(e)s/~en ⟨mar⟩ *pawl* | ~kranz [m] *p. rim*
P·allasch m ~es/~e ⟨mil⟩ *broadsword*
Palliat·iv 1. n ~s/~e *palliative* **2.** ≈ a *palliative*
P·alm- ~baum m *palm-tree* **~kätzchen** n ⟨bot⟩ *catkin* **~kern** m *p.-nut* **~kohl** m *p.-cabbage* **~lilie** f ⟨bot⟩ *yucca* **~mehl** n *sago* **~öl** n *p.-oil* **~s·onntag** m *P. Sunday* **~wedel** m, **~zweig** m *p.-branch* **~-weide** f ⟨bot⟩ *sallow*, *goat-willow* **~woche** f *Passion Week* **P·alme** f ~/~n ⟨bot⟩ *palm* ‖ die ~ des Sieges erringen (zugestehen) *to carry off* (*to yield*) *the p.* (e–m *to a p*) ‖ → Schatten≈ | °jdn auf die ~ bringen *to get a p's shirt out* od *off*, *to blow a p up*; *to get a p's goat*; zum Auf-die-~-Klettern *enough to drive one up the wall* | **≈n** vt [h] ⟨mar⟩ *to haul* (*a cable*) *hand oder hand* **P·almen-** ≈artig [a] *palmaceous*; ~dieb [m] ⟨zoo⟩ *coco-nut crab*; ~hain [m] *grove of palm-trees*; ~haus [n] *palmery*; ≈reich [a] *palmy* **Palm·ette** f ~/~n ⟨arch⟩ *p.ette*, *p.-leaf* **Palm·ettopalme** f ⟨bot⟩ *fan-palm*, *palmetto* **®Palm·in** n ~s/~e *coconut butter* **~säure** f *palmitic acid*
Pam·ir m (ein Gebirgsstock Innerasiens)
P·ampa f ~/~s (Weidensteppe Südamerikas) *pampa* **~hirt** = Gaucho **~shuhn** n (Pampastinamu) ⟨orn⟩ *tinamou*
P·ampelm·use f ~/~n *grape-fruit*, ⟨a.⟩ *pomelo*
Pamphl·et n ~(e)s/~e (Flugschrift) *pamphlet* ‖ (Schmähschrift) *lampoon* ‖ **~·ist** m ~en/~en *pamphleteer* ‖ *lampoonist*, *lampooner*
ˣ**p·ampig** = breiig; ⟨übtr⟩ = frech **P·am(p)s** m ~es/~e *pap*
P·anama n; Landenge *or* Isthmus v ~ *Isthmus of Panama* **P·anama-** *Panama* (*hat*); *P. canal*, *P. bark*
P·an-, ≈- (= all) [in comp] *Pan* (*slavist*), *pan*(*chromatic*) **~athen·äen** pl ~/ *Panathenæa* pl **~chromas·ie** f *panchromatism* **~däm·onium** n ~s/–nien *pandemonium* **~d·ekten** pl *pandects* pl; ⟨engl⟩ (*the*) *Digest* | ~reiter [m] ⟨fam⟩ *student of law*; ~mix·ie [f] ⟨demog⟩ *panmixia* **~d·orabüchse** f *Pandora's box* **~eg·yrikus** m ~/–ken (auf [acc]) *panegyric* (*upon*) **≈eg·yrisch** a *panegyric*(*al*) **~kreas** n ~/ *pancreas* | ~saft [m] *pancreatic juice* **~·optikum** n ~s/–ken *panopticum* **~or·ama** n ~s/–men & ~s *panorama* | ~- *panoramic*; ~-Anzeigegerät [n] *plan position indicator*; ~bild [n] ⟨film⟩ *wide screen picture*; ~gerät [n] *radar landscape scanner*; ~scheibe [f] ⟨mot⟩ *bevelled windscreen*; ~wand [f] *cinerama* **≈or·amisch** a *panoramic* **~the·ismus** m ~/ *pantheism* **~the·ist** m ~en/~en *pantheistic* | ≈isch [a] *pantheistic*
Pandsch·ab m → Fünfstromland
p·äng! [intj] *a puncture*! ⟨a. fig⟩
Pan·ier n ~(e)s/~e *banner*, *standard*, *flag*
pan·ieren vt [h] ⟨cul⟩ *to crumb*, *dredge*
P·anik f ~/~en *panic*, *stampede*, *scare* ‖ in ~ versetzen *to stampede* ‖ das Ausbrechen e–r ~ verhindern *to prevent p.*; in e–e ~ ausbrechen *to panic* [vi] ‖ in ~ davonlaufen *to stampede* ‖ v e–r ~ ergriffen w *to be seized with a panic* **≈artig** a ⟨fam⟩ *panicky* **~mache** f *spreading of panic*, *scaremongering* **p·anisch** a *panic* (*fear* Angst) ‖ ~er Schrecken *panic*
P·ankow n (Stadtteil v Groß-Berlin)
P·ankreas etc → Pan–
P·anne f ~/~n *break-down* ⟨a. mot⟩ ‖ ⟨übtr⟩ *hitch* ‖ ⟨mot⟩ *failure*; (Reifen-) *burst*, *puncture* ‖ ⟨mach⟩ *failure* ‖ ⟨tech⟩ *trouble*, *puncture* ‖ e–e ~ h *to break down* (*we* [od *our car*] *broke down*)
†**Pann·onien** n (röm. Donauprovinz) *Pannonia*
p·anschen vt [h] = manschen ‖ (verfälschen) *to adulterate*, *water* ‖ im Wasser *to paddle* **P·anscher** m ~s/~ *adulterator*
P·ansen m ~s/~ *paunch*, *rumen* ‖ ⟨fig⟩ *belly*
P·ans- ~flöte, ~pfeife f *syrinx*, *Pan's pipe*
P·antalon [ˈpantalɔŋ] m ~s/~s *pantaloon*(*s*)
Panthe·ist etc → Pan–
P·anther m ~s/~ *panther* **~katze** f *ocelot*, *jaguar*, etc; → d.
Pant·ine f ~/~n *patten*, *clog* **Pant·offel** m ~s/~ & ~n *slipper*; gewirkter ~ *carpet sl.* ‖ in ~n schlappen *to hang about in slippers* ‖ (dem Papste) den ~ küssen *to kiss the Pope's toe* | ⟨fig⟩ unter jds ~ *under a p's thumb* ‖ sie schwingt den ~ *she wears the trousers* ‖ unter dem ~ stehen ⟨fam⟩ *to be hen-pecked* od *wife-ridden*; *to be tied to apronstrings*; *she hen-pecks her husband* **~blume** f *calceolaria* **~held** m *hen-pecked husband*; *home-bird*: ⟨sl⟩ *jerry-sneak* | ~ntum [n] *uxoriousness* **~holz** n *cork-wood* **~regiment** n *petticoat government* **~ritter** = ~held **~tierchen** n ⟨zoo⟩ → Wimpertierchen
Panto- ~kr·ator m ⟨ec arts⟩ *Christ in Judgment* **~m·ime** f ~/~n *dumb show* ⟨a. theat⟩ ‖ ⟨theat⟩ *pantomime* **≈m·imisch** a *pantomimic* | [adv] ~ darstellen *to act in dumb show*
p·antschen = panschen **P·anzen** m = Pansen
P·anzer m ~s/~ *armo*(*u*)*r*, *mail*, *cuirass*; [koll] ⟨mil⟩ *amo*(*u*)*r* ‖ ⟨hist⟩ *breast-plate* ‖ *shell* (*of a tortoise*) ‖ *armour*(*-plat*)*ing* (*of a ship*) | (~wagen) *tank*, [Ger] *panzer* ‖ schwerer ~ *cruiser tank*, leichter ~ *whippet* ‖ hindernisräumender ~ *wire-cutting tank* ‖ mit ~n ausgestattet, v ~n geschützt *a.ed* ‖ ⟨mil sl⟩ stur wie ein ~ (*as*) *pigheaded as a mule* **~abschuß** m *tank-busting* **~abwehr** f = Kampfwagenabwehr | ~kanone [f] (abbr Pak) *anti-tank gun*, leichte Pak ⟨engl⟩ *Piat* (*projector and infantry anti-tank*) **~ärmel** m *vambrace* **~attrappen** f pl *tank mockups* **~aufklärer,** –rung(s-) *armored cavalry* N **~auto** n *armoured car* **~batterie** f *a.ed battery* **~befehlsfahrzeug** n *a.ed command car* **~bombe** f *a.-p. bomb* **~brechend** a *a.-piercing* N **~deck** n ⟨mar⟩ *a.ed deck* **~division** f *tank division* **~dr·ehturm** m *revolving a.ed turret* **~durchschlag** m *a. penetration* **~echse** f ⟨zoo⟩ → Krokodil **~fahrzeug** n *a.ed car* **~faust** f *mailed fist*; (Waffe) *panzer-fist* (*recoilless antitank grenade launcher*); ⟨mil fam⟩ *bazooka* **~flotte** f *fleet ironclads* **~fort** n *a.ed fort* **~gewölbe** n *strong-room* **~glas** n *a.-plate* od *bullet-proof glass* **~grabenstellung** f *tank ditch position* **~-(spreng)granate** f *a.-piercing shell* **~grenadiere** m pl *a.ed infantry* **~handschuh** m *gauntlet* **~hemd** n *ring-mail*, *shirt* od *coat of mail* **~höcker** m (Hindernis) *dragon's tooth* **~hosen** f pl *breeches* [pl] *of mail* **~jäger** m (auf SFL) *tank destroyer* | ~truppe [f] *antitank artillery* **~kabel** n ⟨telph⟩ *a.ed cable* **~kampfwagen** m (*fighting*) *tank* **~kan·onenboot** n ⟨mar⟩ *monitor* **~kette** f (Uhr) *curb-chain* ‖ ⟨mil⟩ *tank track* **~knacker** m *t. killer* **~kolonne** f *tank column* **~kompanie** f *t. troop* **~kopf** m ⟨mil⟩ *a.ed head* **~korps** n *t.* od *a.ed corps* **~kräfte** f pl *a.ed forces* pl; ~ bekämpfen *to contend with a.ed forces* **~kraftwagen** m *a.ed car*, *tank* **~kreuzer** m *a.ed cruiser*; °⟨fig⟩ (Frau) *old battle-cruiser* **~-kuppel** f *a.ed cupola* **~macher** m *a.er* **~mann** m *trooper* **~munition** f *tank ammunition* **~nahab-**

wehrkanone → –abwehr- **~platte** f *a.-plate* **~reiter** m *cuirassier* **~ring** m *ring* od *link* (*of chain-mail*) **~schiff** n *ironclad* (*ship*), *a.-plated vessel*, ⟨Ger⟩ *pocket battleship* **~schlacht** f *tank battle*, **~spähwagen** m *a.ed patrol* od *scout car* N **~sperre** f *antitank obstacle* **~spitze** f *tank spearhead* **~spur** f *t. track* **~stärke** f *thickness of a.* **~tier** n *armadillo* **~truppe** f *tank force* **~tür** f (*army*) *bulkhead* **~turm** m ⟨mar⟩ (*a.ed*) *turret* **~verband** m *a.ed group* od *force* **~waffe** f *a.* **~wagen** m *tank*, *a.ed car* | ~abt·eilung [f] *a.ed car detachment* **~wangen** f pl ⟨ich⟩ *mailed cheeks* pl **~weste** f *body armo(u)r* **~zerstörer** m *tank-buster* **~zug** m *a.ed train* **p·anzern 1.** vt [h] *to* (*furnish* od *arm with a coat of*) *mail* ‖ ⟨mar⟩ *to armour* ‖ ⟨tech⟩ *to hard-face* (*by welding*) ‖ sich ~ *to put on mail*, ⟨fig⟩ *to arm o.s.* ‖ gepanzert *mail-clad, armoured* ‖ ⟨fig⟩ *armed, steeled* ‖ gepanzerte Faust *mailed fist* ‖ *to plate, armour(-plate)* (*a ship*) ‖ gepanzerte Schiffe *ironclads* **2.** ≈ n ⟨mar⟩ = **P·anzerung** f ~/~en (stark *heavy*) *a.(-plat)ing, a. protection*

Pä·onie f ~/~n ⟨bot⟩ *peony*

Pap·a m ~s/~s *papa*, ⟨fam⟩ *pa* ‖ (⟨fam⟩ *bes.* Anrede) *dad, daddy*

Papag·ei m [~en & ~(e)s/~e(n)] *parrot, parakeet* ‖ wie ein ~ schwätzen *to chatter* od *prate like a p.* **~enkrankheit** f ⟨med⟩ *psittacosis* (⟨a.⟩ *ornithosis*) **≈mäßig** a *stereotyped* **~taucher** m ⟨orn⟩ *puffin* **~weibchen** n *female parrot*

†**Paphlag·onien** n (in Kleinasien) *Paphlagonia*

°**P·api** m ~s/~s *pa*; ⟨fam⟩ *dad(dy)*, ⟨Am⟩ *pop*

Pap·ier n ~(e)s/~e **A. 1.** *paper* **2.** (Wert≈) *stock, share, bond* **3.** ~e [pl] *documents, papers* pl; (Ausweis≈e) *passport*; *identity papers* pl **B.** ·Abzug≈ *stock*; ·Alt≈ *waste paper*; Asb·est≈ *asbestos p.*; B·anknoten≈ *currency p.*; bitum·iertes ~ *bituminized p.*; Br·ief≈ *letter p.*; B·ütten≈ *hand-made p.*; B·utterbrot≈ *grease-proof* od *sandwich p.*; Druck≈ *stock*; dünnes, durchsichtiges ~ *onionskin*; D·urchschlag≈ (weißes) *thin typewriting p.*; D·urchschreibe≈ *duplicating p.*; ·Einschlag≈, ·Einwickel≈ *wrapping p.*; endloses ~ *p. in reels*; ein wertloser Fetzen, w.es Stück ~ *a dead p.*; Filter≈ *filter(ing) p.*; geglättet *glazed*; stark geleimt *hard-sized* ‖ gerippt *laid*; geschöpft *hand-made*; gewachst *wax*; Glas≈ *glass p.*; glatt *glazed*; Granit≈ *jaspe p.*; halbgeleimt *soft sized*; holzfreies ~ *p. without wood pulp*; kartenstarkes ~ *card p.*; Kreide≈ *enamelled p.*; Kr·epp≈ *crape p.*; L·einen≈ *linen p.*; liniiert *ruled*; maschinenglatt *mill-finished*; maßhaltig *nonshrinking* ‖ Öl≈ *oil p.*; Pergam·ent≈ *parchment p.*; ~ aus Reis *rice p.*; ~ in Rollen *p. in reels*; Sack≈ *wrapping p.*; satiniert *glazed*; Seiden≈ *tissue p.*; Staats≈e [pl] *government securities*; stumpfes ~ *foil*; ~ mit Trauerrand *black-edged p.*; Vorsatz≈ *fancy p.*; ~ mit Wasserzeichen *filigreed p.*; wasserdicht *waxed*; ~ z Zeichnen *drawing p.* **C.** das ~ beschneiden *to edge ..* ‖ mit ~ durchschossen ⟨bookb⟩ *interleaved* | ⟨com⟩ mündelsichere ~e *gilt-edged securities* pl ‖ auf den Namen lautendes ~ *registered share* ‖ die ~e fallen, steigen *the stocks go down, up*, leiden Not .. *are very weak* ‖ stehen gut (schlecht) *are high* (*low*) | zu ~ bringen *to commit to paper*; *to set down in black and white*, (schnell) *to jot down* ‖ ⟨fig⟩ nur ein Fetzen ~ *nothing more than a scrap of p.* ‖ es steht nur auf dem ~ *it exists only on p.*; nur auf dem ~ stehend *nominal* (*fee*); *p.* [attr] (*neutrality*) ‖ ⟨prov⟩ ~ ist geduldig *p. doesn't blush* **~abfälle** m pl *trimmings* pl, *scraps of paper*; *waste p.* **~ableiter** m ⟨typewr⟩ *p. deflector* **~adel** m = Briefadel **~ausschuß** m *broke* → –abfälle **~ausstattung** f *p. fancy* **~bahn** f ⟨print⟩ *web* **~bereitung** f *p. manufacture* **~beschneider** m *trimmer* **~beschwerer** m *p. weight* **~beutel** m *p. bag* | farbiges **~bild** ⟨phot⟩ (Ggs Dia) *colo(u)r print* **~bindfaden** m *p. twine* **~blume** f ⟨bot⟩ *immortelle, xeranthemum* ‖ (künstliche) *artificial (p.-)flower* **~bogen** m *sheet of p.* **~brei** m *p.-pulp* **~drache(n)** m (*p.-*)*kite* **~drucker** m *p.-stainer* **~durchlaß** m ⟨typwr⟩ *p. feed* (⟨a.⟩ ~breite) **~einwerfer** m ⟨typwr⟩ *p. injector* **~fabrik** f *p.-mill* **~fabrikant** m *p.-manufacturer* **~faser** f *p. fibre* **~fetzen** m *scrap of p.* **~form** f *p.-mould* **~format** n *size of p.* **~geld** n *p.(-money), notes*, ⟨Am⟩ *bills*; ~ ohne Deckung *p. m. not based on coin or bullion* **~gewicht** n (Boxen) *p. weight* **~girlande** f *p. garland* **~großhandlung** f *p. wholesale trade* bzw *business* **~grund** m *p.* (*raw*) *base* **~handel** m *p.-trade* **~(Klein)händler** m *stationer* **~handlung** f *st.r's* (*shop*), ⟨Am⟩ *st.ry-store* **~härtegrad** m *p. grade* **~holz** n *pulpwood* **~hülse** f *p. tube* **~kabel** n *p. insulated cable* **~kasten, ~korb** m (*waste-*)*p. basket*, ⟨Am⟩ *w.-b.* ‖ (etw) dem ~ übergeben *or* in den ~ befördern *to pass .. into* (od *to relegate .. to*) *the w.-p. b.*; im ~ enden *to find its ultimate home in the w.-p. b.*; in den ~ wandern *to go limbo* ‖ ~! *rubbish*! **~klemme** f *p. clip* **~kragen** m *p. collar* → Kragen **~krieg** m *bumf*; der ~! ⟨mil⟩ *snowed under with b.* **~laden** m = ~handlung **~laterne** f *p.-lantern* **~leim** m *size* **~leimer** m *sizer* **~lieferung** f *stationery supply* **~locher** m *p. punch* **~lumpen** m pl *rags* [pl] *for making p.* **~mach·é** n [papi:rma'ʃe:] *papier-mâché* **~macher** m *p.-maker* **~maschine** f *p.-m.ing m.* **~masse** f *p.-pulp* **~messer** n *p.-knife* **~mühle** f *p.-mill* **~müller** m *p.-maker* **~rolle** f *roll of p.* | ~nhalter [m] ⟨comp⟩ *roll p. holder* **~sammelaktion** f *w.-p. drive* **~schere** f *p.-shears* pl **~schirm** m *p.-screen* **~schlange** f (*coiled-up*) *p. ribbon*; *streamer* **~schneidemaschine** f *p.-cutter* **~schnitzel** n *scrap of p.* ‖ [pl] *shavings* **~sorte** f *type* od *grade of p.* **~stärke** f *thickness of p.* **~staude** f *papyrus* **~streifen** m *strip of p.* **~stütze** f ⟨typwr⟩ *p. support* **~tapete** f *p.-hangings* pl, *wall-p.* **~tiger** m ⟨pol⟩ *p. dragon* od *tiger* **~ton** m ⟨phot⟩ *p.-base tinge* **~tüte** f *p. bag* **~umlauf** m *p.-circulation* **~unterlage** f *p.* (*raw*) *base* **~valuta** f *p.-value* **~versprechen** n *p. pledge(s)* od *promise(s* pl) **~vorschub** m ⟨comp⟩ *p.feed* (*device*) **~währung** f *p.-currency* **~ware(n)** f pl *stationery* **~warenhandlung** f = ~handlung **~wäsche** f *p. linen* **~wickel** m *curl-p.* **~zeichen** n *water-mark* ‖ (f 250 Bogen) *token* **pap·ieren** a (*of*) *paper* ‖ ⟨fig⟩ *imaginary* ‖ *prosy* (*style*) ‖ papiernes Zeitalter "*paper*" *age*

Papill·ardrüse f *papillary gland* **Pap·ille** f ~/~n ⟨anat & bot⟩ *papilla*

Papill·ote [papil'jɔtə] f ~/~n *curl-paper*

Pap·ist m ~en/~en *papist* | **~er·ei** f ~/ (a. Papismus [m]) *popery, papistry* | **≈isch** a *papistical, popish*

P·app n ~s/ (Brei) *pap* ‖ (Kleister) *paste, size* **~arbeit** f *cardboard* od *p.b. work* **~band** m *p.b. binding*, (*book in*) *boards* pl; geleimter ~ *paperback* **~deckel** m *p.b., millboard* **~dia** n *card-mounted slide* | feste **~einlage** f *stiffener* (= *piece of paperboard*) **~kamerad** m (Klappschild) ⟨mil sl⟩ *bobbing-bastard*, (*aiming silhouette*) **~kasten** m, **~karton** m, **~schachtel** f *cardboard-box* ‖ (Hutschachtel) *bandbox* **~schädel** m *blockhead* **~waren** f pl *p.b. board articles* pl **P·appe** f ~/~n *paste* ‖ (Karton) *pasteboard, cardboard* (dick, voluminös *high bulking*); starke ~ *millboard* ‖ Dach≈ *building paper, roofing-felt, tar-board* ‖ ⟨fig⟩ nicht v ~ (P) *not made of sugar*; (S) *not to be sneezed at, not half bad* **p·äppeln** vt [h] *to feed with pap* ‖ ⟨fig⟩ *to coddle* ‖ (Ball) *to tiddle*; ⟨hockey⟩ *to nurse* (*a puck*); ⟨mot⟩ *to prime* **p·appen 1.** a *pasteboard* **2.** vt [h] *to* (*stick with*) *paste* | vi *to stick* | vt/i ⟨fam⟩: *to feed* **P·appen- ~fabrik** f *board mill* **~heimer** m pl *soldiers of General Pappenheim* (*30 years' war*) ‖ ich kenne m–e ~ ⟨fam⟩ *I know my man! I've got your* (*his*) *number!* **~stiel** m ⟨fam⟩ *trifle*; *this was no peanut* ‖ für *or* um e–n

~ *for a song, dirt-cheap* || nur e–n ~ wert *worthless* || 1000 M ist doch kein ~ .. *are not to be sneezed at* **p·appicht, p·appig** a *pappy, pasty* || *sticky* || *heavy* (*bread*) || *wet* (*snow*)

P·appel f ~/~n *poplar* **~allee** f *avenue of p.s* **~weide** f *black p.* **p·appeln** a *of p. wood* **p·appeln** vi/t [h] *to babble* **papperlap·app**! *fiddlesticks! rubbish!*

P·aprika m ~s/ *Cayenne pepper; red p.* || ⟨bot⟩ *capsicum* L | **~schote** f *green* (*red*) *pepper* od *paprika*; zwei ~n *two paprika*

P·apst m ~es/ ⁓̈e *Pope, Holy Father, Pontiff* || ⟨fam⟩: *W. C.*; den ~ zum Vetter *a friend at court*; ein Mann der .. hat *a name to conjure with* || **~anhänger, -gläubiger** m *Papist* **~krone** f *triple crown, tiara* **~nase** f ⟨cul⟩ *pope's* od *parson's nose* **~wahl** f *election of a pope* **~würde** f *papal dignity, pontificate* **P·äpstler** m ~s/~ *Papist* | **-·ei** f *Popery* **p·ästlich** a *papal, pontifical* || ⟨dero⟩ *Popish* || ~er Stuhl [m] *Holy See* || → Papst– || ~er s als der Papst *to overdo it* **P·apsttum** n ~(e)s/ *papacy, pontificate* || ⟨dero⟩ *Popedom*

Pap·ua, Pap·uaneger(in f) m (Urbevölkerung Neuguineas u Neupommerns) *Papuan*

Pap·yrus m ~/–ri *papyrus* **~rolle** f *p.* (*scroll*) **~staude** f ⟨bot⟩ *p.(-plant)*

Par·a n (brasil. Staat) *Para*; → P·aranuß

Par·abel f ~/~n *parable* || ⟨geom⟩ *parabola* || ~kurve [f] *parabolic curve* **-b·olantenne** f *parabolic dish* **p-b·olisch** a *parabolic(al)* || *figurative, symbolical* || ~er Spiegel *parabolic projector*

Par·ade f ~/~n **A. 1.** *parade* || ⟨fig⟩ *display* (⟨aero⟩ *air d.*) || ⟨mil⟩ *review* **2.** ⟨fenc⟩ *ward, parry* **3.** ⟨hors⟩ *rein(ing) up, pull-up* **B.** bei e–r *or* der ~ *on p.e* || die ~ abnehmen *to take the salute, to hold a r.*; .. (über) *to r.* (*troops*) || ~ anlegen ⟨mar⟩ *to dress ship* || ~ m *to make a show, to cut a figure*; mit jdm *to show a p off* || ⟨fig⟩ jdm in die ~ fahren *to upset a p's plans, to interfere with a p* **~anzug** m *full-dress,* **~aufstellung** f *r. order* **~beispiel** n *paragon* **~bett** n *bed of state*; auf dem ~ liegen *to lie in st.* **~flug** m ⟨aero⟩ *fly-past* **~marsch** m *march-past*, ⟨fam⟩ *goose-step* **~pferd** n *p.e-horse* || ⟨fig⟩ *show-boy, -object* **~platz** m ⟨mil⟩ *reviewing ground* **~schritt** m ⟨mil⟩ *p.e-step,* °*goose-step* (im ~ *at the* ..) **~stückchen** n *show-piece* **~tag** m *fieldday* **~uniform** f *full dress* **~zimmer** n *state apartment* **parad·ieren** vi [h] *to parade, flaunt*; *to make a show* (mit *of*), mit etw ~ *to exhibit a th, to show a th off*; *to flaunt a th*

ˣ**Parad·eis** m ~/~er, **~er** m ~s/~, **~apfel** m = Tomate **Parad·ies** n ~es/~e *paradise* ⟨a. fig⟩; (e–r Kirche *parvis*) || das Verlorene ~ *P. Lost* || wie im ~ *as if in p.* **~apfel** m *apple-john* || *tomato* °**~gärtlein** n ⟨paint⟩ *Garden of P.*; ⟨sex⟩ *garden* **~jungfrau** f → Huri **~vogel** m *bird of p.* **parad·iesisch** a *paradisi(a)c(al)* || ⟨fig⟩ *heavenly, delightful*

Paradent·ose f ~/~n → Parodont·itis

Para- ~d·igma n ~s/–men & ~ta *paradigm* **⁓̈digm·atisch** a *paradigmatic(al)* **⁓̈d·ox** a *paradoxical* || es war ~, daß .. *p.ly no one needed him* || so ~ es klingen mag, er hatte .. *p.ly enough he had* .. **~dox·ie** f ~/~n *paradoxicalness, paradoxy* **Par·adoxon** n ~s/–xa *paradox*

Paraff·in n ~(e)s/~e *paraffin(e)*; mit ~ behandeln *to p.* **-·iermaschine** f ⟨pap⟩ *waxing machine* **~öl** n *paraffin oil*

Para- ~gr·aph m ~en/~en → *paragraph, section, clause*; ⟨jur typ⟩ *article* (§) || in ~en einteilen (⟨a.⟩ –·ieren) *to p.* || (Symbol §) *section-mark* | ~enreiter, ~enwächter [m] *red-tapist, pedant* **⁓̈ll·aktisch** a *parallactic(al)* **~llaxe** f *parallax* | –·axsekunde [f] *parsec* (Entfernung v 3,26 Lichtjahren); –·axverbesserung [f] ⟨artill⟩ *displacement correction*; –·axwinkel [m] *azimuth diference* **⁓̈ll·el** a *parallel* ([dat] *or* mit, zu *to, with*) (laufen *to run*, stehen *to be*) || ⟨fig⟩ *to run on p. lines with* | ⁓̈fall [m] *p. case*; ⁓̈flach [n] *p.epiped(on)*; ⁓̈kreis [m] ⟨astr⟩ *p.*; ⁓̈leitung [f] ⟨mach⟩ (*cross-head*) *guides* pl; ⁓̈lineal [n] *p. rule(r)*; ⁓̈schaltung [f] ⟨el⟩ *shunt connexion*; ⁓̈stelle [f] ⟨liter⟩ *p.* (*passage*); ~träger [m] *braced girder*; ⁓̈trapez [n] *trapezium*; ~versammlung [f] *overflow-meeting* **~ll·ele** f ~/~n *parallel* (*line*) || ⟨fig⟩ *p.* (*passage*) || *comparison* || e–e ~ bilden *to form a p.* (*case*) || für diese Tat gibt es k–e ~ ⟨fam⟩ *there is nothing on all fours with this act* || e–e ~ nicht weiter verfolgen *to follow the p. no closer* || e–e ~ ziehen *to draw* od *establish a p.* (mit *with*, zwischen *between*) **~llel·ismus** m ~/ → *parallelism* ⟨a. pros & rhet⟩ || ⟨AT & NT⟩ *typology* **~llelogr·amm** n ~(e)s/~e *parallelogram* || ~ der Kräfte *p. of forces* || Wattsches ~ *Watt's parallel motion* **~l·yse** f ~/~n ⟨med⟩ *paralysis* **⁓̈lys·ieren** vt [h] *to paralyse* **~l·ytiker** m *spastic* **⁓̈l·ytisch** a *paralytic, paralysed* **~meter** m ⟨stat⟩ *population p.* **~phr·ase** f ~/~n *paraphrase* **⁓̈phras·ieren** vt [h] *to p.* **⁓̈phr·astisch** a *paraphrastic* **~psychologie** f *parapsychology* **~s·it** m ~en/~en *parasite* || ⟨fig⟩ *sponger, free-loader* | ~enbefall [m] *parasitization* ⁓̈isch a *parasitic(al)* ~olog·ie f *parasitology* **~taxe** f ⟨gram⟩ *parataxis*, asyndetische ~ *asyndeton* (*e. g. tacent: satis laudant*) **~typhus** m ~/ ⟨med⟩ *paratyphoid* **~zahl** f ⟨stat⟩ *all births to the mother*; → Parasol etc

P·arapluie m [–ply], °P·araplü n ~s/~s *brolly* || das Paraplü zumachen (sterben) *to pop out*, ⟨Am⟩ *to cash in*

Paragu·ay m (Fluß) (*River*) *Paraguay*

Paran·a m (Strom in Südamerika) *Parana*

P·aranuß f *Brazil-nut*; → Para

Par·aphe f ~/~n *paraph, flourish* **paraph·ieren** vt [h] *to initial*; *to sign* (*with a flourish*)

Paras·ol m [österr s] ~s/~s = Sonnenschirm

Parästhes·ie f ~/~n ⟨med⟩ *parœsthesia, -thesis*

par·at a *ready, prepared* || (*he answered*) *pat*

P·ärchen n ~s/~ (*loving*) *couple*

pard·auz! *flop*! (*ker-*)*bang*! *crash*! *wump(h)*

P·ardel, P·arder m ~s/~ *panther, leopard*

Pard·on [–dɔŋ] m ~s/ *pardon, forgiveness* || *remission* (*of offenses*) || ⟨mil⟩ *quarter* || ~! (⟨obs⟩ = Verzeihung) (*I*) *beg* (*your*) *p.*! || um ~ bitten ⟨mil⟩ *to ask for* od *cry q.* od *mercy* || ~ geben ⟨mil⟩ *to give q.* || k–n ~ geben *to show no m.* || ~ erhalten ⟨mil⟩ *to receive q.* **⁓̈·ieren** vt [h] *to p.* || ⟨mil⟩ *to give q. to*

Pard·une f ~/~n ⟨mar⟩ *backstay*

Parench·ymvolumen n *volume of the parenchyma*

Parenth·ese f ~/~n *parenthesis* **parenth·etisch** a *parenthetical* || [adv] ~ (*or* in Parenthese) ⟨a.⟩ *by way of parenthesis* **Par·ese** f ~/ ⟨med⟩ *paresis*

Parf·orce- [–'fɔrsə] **~hund** m *staghound* (→ Hund A. 2.) **~jagd** f *hunt(ing)* (*on horseback*), *coursing* **~kur** f *violent cure* **~reiter** m *cross-rider* **~ritt** m *steeplechase*; ⟨fig fam⟩ *mad career*

Parf·üm n ~(e)s/~e *perfume, scent* **~er·ie** f ~/~n *scents* pl || *scent-shop, perfumery* | ~beutel [m] *sachet*; ~händler [m] *perfumer*; ~fläschchen [n] *scent-bottle* **⁓̈·ieren** vt [h] *to perfume, to scent* || stark –iert *strongly scented up*

p·ari n ~s/ & adv *par* || (al) ~ stehen *to be at par(ity)* || über (unter) ~ *above* (*below*) *par* | zum ~kurs [m] *at par*; ⁓̈wert [m] *par value*; ~-Wetteinsatz [m] *even money* **⁓̈t·ät** f ~/ *equality* || (Währung) *parity* | ~sprüfung [f] aller Übertragungen ⟨comp⟩ *checking of all transfers* (*to and from the storage units*) | ⁓̈isch [a] *on a footing of equality* || *undenominational* (*school*) || (*state*) *with absolute religious equality* || ~e Vertretung *representation in equal numbers*

P·aria m ~s/~s ⟨Ind⟩ (Rechtloser) *pariah*

par·ieren 1. vt/i [h] ⟨fenc etc⟩ *to parry, to keep* od *ward off* || ⟨hors⟩ *to* (*draw*) *rein* od *pull up, to stop* || ⟨cul⟩ *to dress* (*meat*), *trim, pare* || (wetten) *to bet* (mit *with*), *to wager*, *lay* **2.** vi [h] [dat] *to obey* **Par·ierstange** f ⟨fenc⟩ *cross-guard* od *-hilt*

p·arisch a *Parian* (*marble*)

Par·iser 1. m ~s/~ *Parisian* **2.** a *Parisian* || ~ Mode *Paris(ian) fashions* pl || ~ Schrift ⟨typ⟩ *ruby*, ⟨Am⟩ *agate* || °⟨sex⟩ *French letter* ⟨sl⟩ *johnny* **~ Becken** n ⟨geol⟩ *Basin of Paris* **~blau** n *Paris blue* **P. Bluthochzeit** f (*Massacre of*) *St. Bartholomew's Eve* (1572) **par·isisch** a *Parisian*

P·arisurteil n ⟨myth⟩ *Paris awarding the apple*

P·ark m ~(e)s/~e ⟨hort, mil, mot⟩ *park*; ⟨mil⟩ *depot* N **|** ~anlage [f] *park*; ~aufseher [m] *p.-keeper*; ~automat [m], ~uhr [f] *p.ing meter*; ~dienst [m] ⟨mil⟩ *p. service*; ~garage [f], ~haus [n] *p.ing g.*; *autosilo*; ~h·ochhaus n *multi-storey car park*; *autosilo*; ~instandsetzung [f] ⟨mot⟩ *heavy maintenance*; ~platz [m] ⟨mot⟩ *p.ing place* od *ground*, ⟨Am⟩ *p.ing lot*; (an Autobahn) *p.ing area*; –kino [n] *carena*; ~streifen [m] *lay-by*; *roadside resting-place*, ⟨Am⟩ *emergency r.s. parking*; ~verbot(sschild [n]) [n] *No P.ing* (*sign*); ~verbotzone [f] ⟨Am⟩ *tow-away zone*; ~wache [f] ⟨mil⟩ *guard to a p.* (*of guns*, etc.) **|** **≃en** vt/i [h] *to park* **|** ≃ [n] nach der Uhr *metered p.ing*; ~ verboten *no p.ing any time* **|** **~·ett** n ~(e)s/~e *parquet(ed floor)*, *p.ry* || ⟨theat⟩ *stalls* pl || erstes ~ *orchestra* (*stalls*) || zweites ~ *pit* (*stalls*) **|** ~besucher [m pl] *people in the stalls*; ~fußboden = ~ || ~platz [m] *stall* (→ ~) **≃ett·ieren** vt [h] *to parquet*, *inlay* (*a floor*)

Parlam·ent n ~(e)s/~e *parliament* (auflösen *to dissolve p.*) || Auflösung des ~s *dissolution of p.* || das ~ u sein Dienst *P. and her service* || das ~ einberufen *to convoke the p.* || im ~ sitzen *to sit in p.* || ⟨arch⟩ ~(gebäude [n]) *P.* [ohne Artikel] **|** **~·är** m ~(e)s/~e *officer with a flag of truce* **~·arier** m ~s/~ *parliamentarian*, *member of parliament* || ein alter ~ *an old parliamentary hand* **≃·arisch** a *parliamentary* (*debater*) || ⟨hist⟩ *parliamentarian* (*army*) **~ar·ismus** m ~/ *parliamentary system* od *government* **≃·ieren** vi [h] *to parley* **| ~s- ~akte** f *Act of P.* **~anhänger** m *p.arian* || ⟨hist⟩ [pl] *Roundheads* **~bericht** m ⟨engl⟩ *Hansard* **~beschluß** m *vote of p.* **~dauer** f *session* **~ferien** pl *recess* (*of p.*) **~gebäude** n pl (*houses of*) *p.* **~mitglied** n *member of p.* (*M. P.*) **~ordnung** f *p.ary regulations* pl **~rede** f *p.ary speech* **~redner** m *speaker in p.* **~sitzung** f *sitting of p.* **~tagung** f *p.ary session* **parl·ieren** vt/i [h] *to chatter* || ein wenig F. ~ *to have some smattering in French*

P·arma n ⟨It⟩ (Stadt u †Herzogtum)

Parmes·ankäse m *Parmesan cheese*

†Parn·aß m ⟨Gr⟩ (Gebirge in Phokis, jetzt Liakura) *Parnassus*

Parochi·alkirche f *parish-church*

Parod·ie f ~/~n *parody* (auf *of*) → d. || leichte ~ *skit* (*on*) || ~nschreiber [m] *parodist* **| ≃ren** vt [h] *to parody*, *burlesque* || ⟨fam⟩ *to take off* **| -d·istisch** a *parodic*

Parodont·itis, Parodont·ose f ~/~n (Zahnfleischerkrankung) *paradentosis*

Par·ole f ~/~n ⟨mil⟩ *password* || ~! *friend or foe!* || ⟨fig⟩ *parole*, *cue*, *catchword slogan*, *watchword* (*make efficiency your w.w.*); die ~ des Tages ist .. *the order of the day is ..* || die ~ ausgeben *to pass the w.w.* **~befehl** m *order* (*given at the muster*) **~buch** n *o.-book* || *p.w. register* **P·aroli** n ~s/~s ⟨cards⟩ *double stakes* || ⟨fig⟩ ein ~ bieten *to pay back* (*in kind*); (e–m) *to challenge* (*a p*)

Parox·ysmus m ~/–men *paroxysm*

Pars·ek n (→ Parall·axsekunde) *parsec*

P·arsen pl (Nachkommen der Parther) *Parsi*

Part m & n ~(e)s/~e *part*, *share*, *portion* || ich für mein ~ *I for one*, *as for me* **P·arte** f ~/~n [österr] → Todesanzeige **Part·ei** f ~/~en *party* ⟨a. parl⟩, ⟨parl oft dero⟩ *faction* || ~en in e–m Hause ⟨fam⟩ *parties*, ⟨mst⟩ *families*, *households* || die Regierungs≃ u die Opposition *the ins and outs* pl || ⟨sport⟩ die spielende ~ *the ins* pl || ⟨jur & cards⟩ *side* **|** streitende ~en *opposing parties* || von jds ~ s *to be on a p's side* || ~ s *to be prejudiced* || ~ ergreifen *or* nehmen f *to side with*; .. gegen *to take sides against*; jds ~ ergr. *to take the part of a p* || sich zu k–r ~ bekennen *or* schlagen *to steer clear of any party*, *to sit on the fence* || es mit k–r ~ halten *to remain neutral* **~abzeichen** n *p. badge* **~anhänglichkeit** f *partisanship* **~apparat** m *p. machine* **~clique** f *caucus* **~disziplin** [f] halten *to follow the p. line* **~eifer** m *partisan zeal* **≃eifrig** a *factious* **~ergreifung** f (f e–e S) *espousal* (*of a cause*) **~feinde** m pl *antiparty elements* **~-führer** m = ~haupt **~gänger** m *partisan*, *follower*, ⟨Am⟩ *partyliner* **~geist** m *party* od *faction spirit* **~genosse** m *political friend*, (*fellow-*)*member of a party*, *adherent of the same p.* **~grundsatz** m *plank* **~hader** m *p.-squabbles* pl **~haupt** n *p.-chief*; *leader* od *head of a p.* || Führer der Arbeiter≃ *labour leader* **~herrschaft** f *p. hierarchy* **~kampf** m *p.-strife* **~kasse** f *p.-funds* **~leitung** f *p. headquarters* **~linie** f *p. line* **≃los** a *impartial*, *neutral* || ⟨pol⟩ *independent* || *non-party* (*interests*) **~losigkeit** f *impartiality*, *neutrality* **~mann** m *partisan*; starrer ~ *intransigent* **~-nahme** f (für) *partisanship* (*for*, *with*); *espousing of a cause* **~organ** n *p. organ* od *mouthpiece* **|** ~isati·on [f] *p. machinery* **≃politisch** a ⟨mst dero⟩ *political* (*motives*) **~programm** n ⟨parl⟩ *platform*; ⟨Am⟩ *ticket*; Punkt des ~s *plank* **~regierung** f *p. government* **~rücksichten** f pl *p. considerations* pl **~schulung** f *indoctrination* (⟨a.⟩ ~sarbeit) **~streit** m *p. strife* **~sucht** f *factious spirit*, *factiousness* **≃süchtig** a *factious* **~tag** m *p. convention*, *congress*(*-day*); ⟨nazi⟩ (Reichs-)~ *Reich P. Rally* **~treiben** n *factious agitation* **~verfahren** n *purge* (*procedure*; einstellen *to drop* od *squash*) **~-wesen** n *p. doings*, *methods*, *concerns* pl, *work* **~wirtschaft** f ⟨mst dero⟩ *partisanship*, *partisanry* **~wut** f *frenzy of* (*contending*) *parties* **~zwecke** m pl *p. purposes* **part·eien** vt [h] (sich) ~ *to split into parties*, *to form cliques* **part·eiisch, part·eilich** a *partial*, *biassed*, *prejudiced*; *factious*, *taking sides*; *one-sided*; *partisan* (*passion*) **| ≃keit** f ~/~en (gegenüber) *partiality* (*for*), *bias* (*towards*) **Part·eiung** f ~/~en **1.** *faction*, *party*, *clique* **2.** *division into*, *formation of parties*

P·artenreederei f ⟨mar⟩ *joint ownership*

part·erre adv; ~ wohnen *to live on the ground-floor* **|** ≃ [–'tɛr] n ~s/~s *ground-floor*, ⟨Am⟩ *first floor* (im ~ *on* ..) || ⟨theat⟩ *pit*, ⟨Am⟩ *parterre*; erstes ~ *stalls* pl || ⟨hort⟩ *flower-bed* **≃loge** f ⟨theat⟩ *pit-box* **≃publikum** n *the pit*, *pitsters* pl **≃vordersitze** m pl ⟨theat⟩ *stalls*, ⟨Am⟩ *orchestra seats* **≃wohnung** f *apartments* [pl] *on the g.-f.*

†Parther m, **~in** f (asiat. Volk) *Parthian*

†P·arthien n (in NO-Persien) *Parthia*

Part·ie f ~/~n **A.** (Gesellschaft) *party*, *company* || (Teil) *part* (⟨a. theat & mus⟩ = Rolle) || *passage* (*in a book*) **|** ⟨com⟩ *parcel* (~ Hemden *of shirts*), *pile* (*of books*), *line* (*in stockings*) **|** (Wettspiel, Heirat, zu heiratende P) *match* **|** (Spiel) *rubber* (*of whist*, *bridge*, etc) || game (~ Schach etc *of chess*, *cards*, *at billards*) **|** (Tennis) *set* **|** (Land-) *outing*, *excursion*, *trip* **B.** sie ist e–e **gute** (schlechte) ~ *she is a good* (*bad*) *match*; e–e glänzende ~ *a splendid catch* || e–e ~ (Heirat) **ausschlagen** *to refuse an offer* **|** e–e ~ m *to play a game*; *to have an outing*, *to go on an excursion* || e–e gute ~ m *to marry well* **|** ⟨com⟩ *lot*: **in** ~n v or z 10 St. *in lots of ten pieces* || in ~n billiger *in larger quantities cheaper* || ([mit] **von** *or*) **bei** der ~ s *to be one* (*of the company*), *to take part in it* **~artikel** m (Bücher) *remainder* **~geld** n *charges for the use of the* (*billard-*)*table* **~preis** m (f. Bücher) *special terms* **~ware** f *dead stock* **part·ienweise** adv ⟨com⟩ *in lots* od *parcels* **parti·ell** [partsi'el] a *partial* (*eclipse*, *paralysis*) || [adv]

partly, partially **Part·ikel** f ~/~n ⟨gram⟩ *particle* **~chen** n *speck, atom* || pl *tiny pieces*

Partikul·ar- ~bestrebung f ⟨pol⟩ *separatist movement* **~recht** n *special law* **~·ismus** m ~/ *particularism, sectionalism, separatism* **~·ist** m ~en/~en *regionalist* **≃·istisch** a *particularist*

Partis·an m ~s/~s, **~e** m ~n/~n *partisan; irregular* || ~en [pl], ~enbewegung [f] ⟨a.⟩ *maquis* Fr; ~enkrieg [m] *guerilla warfare*

Partis·ane f ~/~n *partisan, halberd*

part- ~it·iv [–'ti:f] a ⟨gram⟩ *partitive* (*article*) **≃it·ur** f ~/~en ⟨mus⟩ *score* **≃iz·ip** n ~(e)s/~e ⟨gram⟩ *participle* || (*present p.*; *past p.*) **~izip·ie·ren** vi [h] (an [dat)] *to participate* (*in*)· **≃ner** m ~s/~ *partner* || ~ in e–r S s *to be a party to a th* | ~schaft [f] *p.ship*; ~wahl [f] ⟨ad⟩ *match-making*

par- ~tout [par'tu:] adv *by all means* || ~ nicht *by no means* **≃venü** [parvə'ny] m ~s/~s *upstart; parvenu*; "*new*" *man* || ~s [pl] "*new*" *people*

P·arty f ~/~s [„engl"] *party/–ties* (geben *to give*) | ~keller [m], ~zimmer [n] *rumpus room*

P·arze f ~/~n *Fatal Sister, one of the Fates*

Parz·elle f ~/~n *allotment, lot, plot* (*of land*) || in ~n aufteilen *to plot* **p-ll·ieren** vt [h] *to divide into lots, to parcel out, to plot*

Pasch m ~es/~e & ≃e ⟨dice⟩ (ein ~ *a pair of*) *doublets* pl (od *triplets* pl) **p·aschen**[1] vi [h] *to throw doublets; to play at dice*

P·ascha m ~s/~s *pasha* | ~wirtschaft *arbitrary rule*

pasch- ~en[2] vt/i [h] *to smuggle* **≃er** m ~s/~ *smuggler, contrabandist* **≃handel** m *smuggling--trade*

pasch·oll! [Russ] → pack dich!, vorwärts!

P·aspel m ~s/~ & f ~/~n *braid, piping, edging* | **≃n, ≃·ieren** vt [h] *to pipe, braid; to trim with piping*

Pasqu·ill n ~(e)s/~e *lampoon; piece of satire*

Pasquill·ant m ~en/~en *lampooner*

paß adv *fit* || e–m zu paß s *to fit a p well* || e–m zupaß *or* zupasse k *to serve one's turn* | **≃**form- [f] *fully fashioned* (*stockings*)

Paß m Passes/Pässe (Berg-) *pass, defile, col* (→ Eng≃) || (Durchgang) *passage, thoroughfare,* ⟨mar⟩ *narrows* pl | (Reise≃) *passport,* ⟨bes pol⟩ *papers* pl (auf jds Namen *in a p's name*) || ⟨mot⟩ internationaler ~ *triptych; triptyque* Fr || e–n ~ ausstellen *to make out* (⟨Am⟩ *issue*) *p.p.* (f *for*) | ⟨hors⟩ (a. ~gang) *amble*; im ~ reitend ⟨a.⟩ *ajog* || ~ gehen *to amble* | ⟨arch⟩ *foil* **~amt, ~büro** n *passport-office* **~gang** m *amble, rack; ambling pace* || im ~ gehen *to amble, rack* **~gänger** m *ambler, ambling horse* **~glas** n *graduated glass* **~höhe** f *head of a pass* **~karte** f *passport; sea-chart* || ⟨cards⟩ *bad cards* pl **~kontrolle** f, **~revision** f *examination of p.p.s* **≃recht** a & adv *fitting exactly* **~stelle** = –amt **~straße** f *pass* **~wesen** n *p.p.-concerns* **~zwang** m *obligation to have a p.p.* **pass·abel** a *passable, tolerable* **Pass·age** [pa'sɑ:ʒə] f ~/~n *passage* || ⟨arch⟩ *arcade, gallery* || ⟨mus⟩ *run, passage* || ⟨hors⟩ *passage* || ⟨film⟩ *sequence* **Passag·ier** [pasa'ʒi:r] m ~(e)s/~e *passenger* || (Fahrgast e–s Mietwagens) *fare* || blinder ~ *deadhead;* ⟨mar⟩ *stowaway* **~beförderung** f *p.r service* **~dampfer** m *p.r-steamer, liner* **~flugzeug** n *air-liner* ⟨bes gr⟩; ⟨fam⟩ *sky-bus* **~geld** n *fare;* ⟨mar⟩ *passage* **~gut** n *baggage, luggage* **~kajüte** f ⟨mar⟩ *state-room* **~liste** f *way-bill* **~luftschiff** n *air-ship* **~schiff** n *liner* **~zettel** m *way-bill* **Pass·ant** m ~en/~en *passer-by* [pl *passers-by*]; *pedestrian* || *chance guest;* ⟨hot⟩ *transient* od *casual guest* **~enhotel** n *transient hotel* **Pass·at** m [illegible] **~wind** | ~strömung [f] *equatorial current;* ~wind [m] *trade-wind* °**passé** a Fr *old-fashioned;* [pred] *off* (.. *is off*)

P·assah(fest) n ~(e)s/ *Passover* (Exodus XII)

p·assen I. vi [h] **A.** [abs] **1.** (Kleider) *to fit* (*well*) (wie angegossen *to a T; like a glove,* ⟨mil iron⟩ .. *a sentry box*) || das paßt! *that will do!* || wie gut das paßt! *how nicely that suits!, how convenient!* || nicht ~ *to be a misfit* od *bad fit* || genau *or* knapp ~ *to be a tight fit* || nicht hierher ~ (S) *to have nothing to do with the matter;* (P) *to feel out of place* **2.** *to wait* || *to watch, to lie in wait* **3.** ⟨cards⟩ *to pass* (*I p.*) → Paß **4.** *to agree, harmonize; to go well together* od *with* .. **B.** (Kleider) ~ **jdm** *to fit a p* || (zusagen) *to suit a p, to be convenient for a p* || *that will do for me, that suits me fine* od *down to the ground;* ⟨Am fam⟩ *that's just what the doctor ordered,* ⟨sl a.⟩ *that hits me* || es paßt zur Rolle *it is proper to the role* || ⟨fam⟩ *suits my books* (*to do*) || wann es e–m gut paßt *in one's own good time* || °das könnte dir so ~ ⟨fam iron⟩ *you have got a hope* || wenn es dir nicht paßt, kannst du's blei-ben l *if you don't like it you can lump it* || jetzt paßt es ihm nicht mehr (in den Kram) *now the shoe is on the other foot* || .. wenn es ihnen paßte (*they came*) *when they felt like it* || wie es ihnen gerade paßt *as it suits their convenience* || warten, bis es jdm paßt *to wait a p's convenience* **C.** sie paßt **an** diesen Ort wie die **Faust** aufs Auge *she is a square peg in a round hole in this place* || ~ **auf** [acc] *to fit, to be applicable to* || *the lid does not fit the pot* || auf die Pl. paßt e–e K. *on the plate fits a jar* || ⟨fig⟩ die Beschr. paßt auf ihn *he answers to the description* || *many features in R.'s career fit in with Lord D.'s* | (warten) *to wait for; to watch, notice; to be attentive to* || e–m auf den Dienst ~ *to watch a p closely* | paß auf (*or* acht)! *look out!, take care!* || ~ **für** *to be suited to, to do for* || *the name fits him exactly* || *it matches each room* || ~ **in** *to fit* (*a hole*) || *to be fit for* (*a society*) || *to suit* (*a p's purpose* Plan, ⟨fam⟩ Kram); *to fit in* ([*with*] *a p's plan*); *to be suited to* (*an occasion*) || ~ **zu** (of key) *to fit* (*a door* od *lock*) || *to fit into* (*a background*) || *to go with* (*another colour*); *to dovetail into* (*a scheme*); (clothes) *go with* (*her face*) | ⟨fig⟩ *to fit* od *attune with* || *to suit* (*a part*) || *to be worthy of* (*a p's office*) | genau ~ zu *to dovetail into* || schlecht ~ z *to go amiss to, to chime* od *go ill with* | **nicht** zur S ~ *to be beside the question* || er paßt nicht z (Gelehrten) *he is not fit to be* (od *cut out* od *suitable for*) .., *he will never* (*do for* od) *make* (*a scholar*) | (P) **zu-e-a** ~ *to be suited to each other, to suit e. o.* || *to harmonize* || *to be well matched* || ⟨fam⟩ *to jog on* (od *gee in*) *well together;* ⟨sex⟩ *to get off* || (S & Farben) nicht zu–e–a ~ *to clash, not to blend well* || **zus-~** *to harmonize, tally* (*with*); *to square to* od *with* || nicht .. (P) *to be ill matched,* ⟨fam⟩ *not to hit it off well* **II.** vt [h] *to adjust; to fit on; to measure;* an *or* auf etw ~(d m) *to adapt to a th* **III.** v/refl [h] **sich** ~ (sich ziemen) *to be fitting* (f *in, for*), *to be fit* od *proper* (*for*) || *to be befitting, meet, convenient* || das paßt sich nicht *that is not becoming* od *proper* (*for a girl*), *does not become* (*a g.*) **p·assend** a **A.** *fit*(*ting*), *harmonizing, suitable, convenient; opportune; to the purpose;* (schicklich) *becoming* (f jdn *a p*), *fitting* (*for*); *seemly; adapted* || *in keeping* (*with*) || genau in–e–a ~ *dovetailing* (⟨a. fig⟩ *details*) || sich etw ~ einrichten *to arrange a th to suit o.s.* **B.** *apt* (*reply*), *timely* (*remark*), *right* (*word*), *appropriate* (*means*), *seasonable* (*time*) (f *for*) || *well-fitting* (*clothes*) || *well-matched* (*couple*) || ~e Farbe *colour to match* | [attr] (*a prayer*) *appropriate for* (f) | [neg] k–e ~e E. *not a proper* od *fitting excuse* || (in sich) schlecht *or* nicht ~ *out of proportion, ill proportioned* od *matched* || nicht ~es Stück *misfit* **C.** f ~ halten *to think proper, suitable, fit* || ~ m *to adjust* **D.** ~ **auf, zu** *applicable to* || [illegible] (*a coat*) *to match* (*this frock*) || *cut a piece to fit this hole* || dazu ~ (*a frock with a hat*) *to match* || können Sie mir hierzu ~e Seide geben? *can you match me this silk?* | [neg] nicht ~ zu *incongruous with; alien to* (*village life*)

Passepartout Fr [paspar'tu:] n ~s/~s **1.** *masterkey* **2.** ⟨arts, phot⟩ (*overthrow-*) *mount* || ~(billet n), ~(karte f) ⟨theat, etc.⟩ (*free*) *pass* **Pass·ier- ~gewicht** n (*mint-*)*allowance* **~schein** m *pass, permit* **~sieb** n ⟨cul⟩ *passe-vite* Fr **~tuch** n *tammy cloth* **~zettel** (Zoll≗) *permit,* ⟨engl⟩ *docket* **pass·ierbar** a *passable, traversable* | **~keit** f *passableness, traversableness* **pass·ieren 1.** vt [h] *to pass, cross, see* (*rivers, frontiers, towns*) || *to clear* (*a fence*) || *to pass* (*the censor* Zensur) || ⟨cul⟩ *to strain, colander*; *to pass through a sieve* | vi [s] zollfrei ~ *to go through free of duty* || ~ l *to let pass* (f etw *as, for a th*) || das mag ~ *that will just do* **2.** vi [s] *to happen, occur*; *to take place, to come to pass* || das *or* es kann leicht ~ *it can* od *may easily happen* || ist etw passiert? *is anything the matter*? *is sth wrong*? || was ist p.? *what's the matter*?, .. hier? ⟨fam⟩ *what's up here*? || daß nur nichts p. *that no accident happens* || wenn etw ~ sollte *if anything should go amiss* | [+ dat] *to happen to* || wenn mir etw ~ sollte *if I should meet with an accident* || dem kann nichts ~ *nothing will hurt him* **p·assim** L (→ da u dort zerstreut) *passim*

Passi·on f ~/~en ⟨a. mus, fig⟩ *passion* || *P.* (*of Christ*) || Jäger v ~ *passionately fond of hunting* | **~s-** → Leidens- **~betrachtung** f *Lenten meditation* **~blume** f *p.-flower* **~buch** n ⟨ec⟩ *p.ary* **~geschichte** f *P. of Christ* **~kreuz** n *p.-cross,* ⟨her⟩ *Latin c.* **~predigt** f *Good Friday sermon* **~prediger** m *preacher in P. week* **~spiel** n *P. play* **passio·n·ieren** v/refl; sich f etw ~ *to be passionately fond of a th* **passion·iert** a (für) *impassioned, passionately interested* (für *in*) || *inveterate* (*smoker, gambler*) **pass·iv** a *passive* (*resistance, member, corruption*) || ⟨a. gram, chem⟩ || ⟨com⟩ *passive* || → ≗um **≗geschäft** n *debit-transaction* **≗handel** m *passive* od *import-trade* **≗legitimation** f ⟨jur⟩ *capacity to be sued* **≗schuld** f *passive debt* **≗seite** f *left side* (*of the ledger*) **≗vermögen** n *indebtedness* **≗zinsen** m pl *interest to be paid* **P·assiva,** –ven [pl] ⟨com⟩ *debts, liabilities* pl; → Aktiva **passi·v·ieren** vt [h] ⟨com bal⟩ *to post on the liabilities* **pass·ivisch** a *passive* || adv *in the p.* **Passivit·ät** f ~/ *passiveness, passivity* **Pass·iv(um)** n ~s/–va & –ve(n) ⟨gram⟩ *passive voice* od *verb* || im ~ stehen *to be in the p.*

p·aßlich a *convenient* **P·assung** f ~/~en ⟨mach⟩ ~ h *to fit* [vi] || ~ geben *to fit* [vt]

P·assus m ~/~ ⟨liter⟩ *passage*

P·asta, P·aste f ~/–ten *paste* || ⟨tech⟩ (jewels) *paste* **Past·ell** (Farbstift) m, (Bild) n ~(e)s~e; (Farbstift) *crayon* (in ~ *in c.*) || (Bild, Farbe, Malerei) *pastel* **~farbe** f *crayon* **≗farben** a *pastel* [attr] **~maler** m *p.-painter, p.(l)ist* **~maler·ei** f *p.-painting* **~stift** m *crayon* **~zeichnung** f *c. study* **Past·etchen** n ~s/~ ⟨cul⟩ *patty* **Past·ete** f ~/~n *pasty, pie* || Obst≗ *tart* || ⟨cul⟩ *vol-au-vent* Fr || (*lobster*) *patty* || ⟨fig⟩ da h wir die ~! *that's a pretty mess* (od *kettle of fish*) **Past·eten- ~bäcker** m *pastry-cook* **~bäcker·ei** f *p.-c.'s* (*shop*) **~deckel** m *pie-crust* **~fleisch** n *mince-meat* **~händler** m *pie-man* **~kruste** f *pie-crust* **~werk** n *pastry* **Past·ille** f ~/~n *lozenge, pastil(le)*

Past·eur- ≗is·ieren [–tæ–] vt [h] *to pasteurize* || –rt *heat-treated* (*milk*) **-sch** a *Pasteurian, Pasteur*

Pastin·ake f ~/~n ⟨bot⟩ *parsnip*

P·astor, Past·or m ~s/–t·oren, ≗e *pastor, parson,* (*Anglican*) *vicar*; (*Protestant*) *minister* **≗·al** a *pastoral* | ≗brief [m] *p.* (*letter*); ≗konferenz [f] *clerical conference*; ≗theologie [f] *pastoral divinity* **~·ale** n ~/~ 1. ⟨ec⟩ *pastoral* (*letter*) 2. ⟨liter⟩ *idyll* || ⟨mus⟩ *pastoral* **~·at** n ~(e)s/~e (Haus) *parsonage, vicarage* || (Amt) (*clerical*) *living, appointment, office*

past·os a ⟨paint⟩ *blottesque*

Patag·onien n *Patagonia* **Patag·onier** m, **~in** f, **patag·onisch** a *Patagonian*

Pat·ate f ~/~n ⟨bot⟩ *batata*

P·atchen n ~s/~ *godchild, -son, -daughter* **P·ate** m ~n/~n *godfather,* [f] *-mother, sponsor* || ~ stehen bei *to stand godf.*, etc. *to a p*; ⟨fig⟩ *to be behind* (*a th*); *to be at the back of an event* || z ~n bitten *to ask a p to stand godf.* || (Kind) = Patchen **~nfirma** f; ~ e–r Reklamenummer ⟨Am wir⟩ *sponsor* **~ngeld, ~ngeschenk** n *christening-present* **~nkind** n = Patchen **~nstelle** f *sponsorship* || ~ vertreten bei = Pate stehen bei

Pat·ene f ~/~n (Hostienteller) *paten*

°**pat·ent** a *fine, smart, dashing* (*fellow, girl*) || *elegant, spick and span* || → umgänglich || ein ~er Kerl *quite a young buck*; ⟨Am sl⟩ *a good egg* || *well-contrived,* ⟨fam⟩ *patent* (*device*) | ≗ n ~(e)s/~e **A. 1.** *patent* (auf *for*) (zusätzlich *additional*; unabhängig *independent*); nicht durch ~ geschützt *in the public domain* **2.** ⟨mil⟩ (*officer's*) *commission* || (*major's*) *brevet* **3.** (Freibrief) *charter, license* **B.** ein ~ anmelden *to apply for, file a p.*; ~ –ge–det *p. pending*; besitzen *to hold*; erlangen *to obtain*; erteilen *to grant* (jdm *to a p*); nehmen *to take out* (auf *for*) || ihm wurde das ~ e–s Majors verliehen *he was breveted a m.* **~amt** n *patent office* **~anker** m *stockless anchor* **~anmeldung** f *application for a p.* **~anwalt** m *p.-agent* ⟨Am⟩ *p. attorney* | mißbräuchliche **~benutzung** *abuse of p.* **~beschreibung** f *p. specification* **~brief** m *letters* [pl] *patent*; *license* **~bruch** m *infringement of* (*a*) *p.* **~dauer** f *p. life* **~erteilung** f *issue of letters p.* **~fähigkeit** f *p.ability* °**~fatzke** m *dandy* **~gebühr** f *p.-fee, royalty* **~gesetz** n *p. law* **~inhaber** m *p. holder, p.ee* **~lösung** f *push-button way* **~mittel** n *p. medicine* (*for unhappiness*) **~register** n *p.-rolls* pl **~schutz** m *protection of p.s* **~schutzgesetz** n *p.-law* **~sucher** m *applicant for ..* **~träger** m *patentee* **~verleiher** m *patentor* **~verletzung** f *p. infringement* **~verschluß** m *p. stopper* **patent·ierbar** a *patentable* | **≗keit** f *patentability* **patent·ieren** vt [h] *to patent, license* || *to grant a p.* (*to*) || ~ l *to take out a patent for* || –tiert *patent(ed), registered* || –tierter Artikel ⟨a.⟩ *proprietary article* **Patent·ierung** f *patenting*

P·ater m ~s/~ & P·atres *father* || pater peccavi sagen *to confess,* ⟨fam⟩ *to cry peccavi* **Patern·oster** n ~s/~ **1.** *paternoster, the Lord's Prayer* **2.** *rosary, chaplet, beads* pl **3.** ⟨arch⟩ *paternoster* **~autzug** m *p. lift*, ⟨Am⟩ *continuous elevator* **~baum** m *bread-tree* **~draht** m *Bologna wire* **~erbse** f ⟨bot⟩ *jequirity* **~kraut** n *wild liquorice* **~kunst** f, **~werk** n ⟨tech⟩ *chain-pump*; *paternoster*

path·etisch a *exciting emotion* od *passion* || *with emotion*; *passionate* || *dramatic, theatrical* || ⟨derog⟩ *pompous* || (feierlich) *solemn*; *lofty*; *elevated* || **das ≗e** ~n/ ⟨rhet⟩ *passion, emotion* || *theatricality*; *dramatical emphasis*; ⟨derog⟩ *pompousness* || → Pathos **Patho- ≗g·en** a *pathogenous* **~l·og(e)** m ~en/~en *pathologist* **~log·ie** f ~/~n *pathology* **≗l·ogisch** a *pathological* **P·athos** n ~/ (*deep*) *emotion*; *solemn attitude* od *language* || *passionateness*; *vehemence*; *impulsiveness*; *excitement, excitation* || falsches ~ *bathos*

Patience Fr [pasi'ɑ̃s] f ~/~n ⟨cards⟩ *patience* || (e–e) ~ legen *to play solitaire* **Pati·ent** [–'tsient] m ~en/~en *invalid* || (e–s Arztes) *patient* || ~ s *to be under* (*medical*) *treatment,* ⟨fam⟩ *under the doctor*

P·atin f ~/~nen = Pate

P·atina f ~/ *patina* **patin·ieren** vt [h] *to patinate*

Patri·arch m ~en/~en *patriarch* **≗·alisch** *patriarchal* | **~·at** n ~(e)s/~e; (als Ggs zu Matriarchat) *patriarchy* | ~enwürde [f] *patriarchate*

Patri- ~moni·algericht n *patrimonial jurisdiction* **~m·onium** n ~s/–nien *patrimony* **Patri·ot** m ~en/~en *patriot* **≗isch** a *patriotic, public-spirited* **~·ismus** m ~/ *patriotism* || in ~ m *to set up for a patriot* || ~ der Hurrahrufer *jingoism* **Patr·istik** f ~/ *patristic learning, patristics* **Patr·ize** f ~/~n ⟨tech⟩ *punch(eon), counter-die*

Patrizi·at n ~s/ *patriciate* **Patr·izier** m ~s/~ (*Roman*) *patrician* | ⟨Ger⟩ *member of the* (*late Middle Ages*) *city aristocracy* | **≃haft** a *patrician* **~tum** n ~s/ [abstr] *patricianism* || [konkr] *patricians* pl **patr·izisch** a *patrician, upper class* (*privilege*) **Patr·on** m ~(e)s/~e **1.** ⟨eig⟩ *patron* (~in [f] *patroness*), *protector* (f *protectress*) || ⟨mar⟩ *owner of a ship* || (Schutzherr) ⟨ec⟩ *advowee* || (Schutzheiliger) ⟨ec⟩ *patron-saint* **2.** ⟨fam⟩ lustiger ~ *jolly blade* || komischer ~ *funny fellow* || liederlicher ~ *loose fish* || schlauer ~ *artful dodger* || ⟨dero⟩ richtiger, sauberer, schlimmer ~ *a rude fellow, an ugly customer* **Patron·at** n ~(e)s/~e *patronage* || (e–r Pfründe) *advowson* **~sherr** m *patron* (⟨ec⟩ *of a living*) **~spfarre** f *living in the gift of a patron* **~srecht, ~sverhältnis** n *patronage* **Patr·one** f ~/~n **A. 1.** (Muster) *pattern, model* || (Maler≃) *stencil* || (Füllhalter≃) *barrel* || ⟨phot, film⟩ (light-tight *magazine*) *cassette* **2.** (Schieß≃) *cartridge, bullet* || blinde ~, Platz≃ *blank c.* (⟨Am⟩ *bl. b.*) || Exerzier≃ *dummy* od *drill c.* || scharfe ~ *ball c.* || Spreng≃ *planted bomb* **B.** mit ~n drucken *or* malen *to stencil* || bis zur letzten ~ *to the last cartridge* **Patr·onen- ~auswerfer** m (Apparat) *ejector* **~-bandelier** n *cartridge-bandoleer* **~gurt, ~gürtel** m (*c.-*)*belt*; ⟨hist⟩ *cross-belt* **~hülse** f *c.-case, c.-shell* **~kammer** f (im Gewehr) *magazine* **~kasten** m *c.-box* **~lager** n *c. chamber* **~lehre** f *cartridge-gauge* **~munition** f ⟨artill⟩ *fixed ammunition* **~-rahmen** m *clip, charger* **~streifen** m *c. band* od *strip* **~tasche** f *pouch* **~trommel** f *c.-drum* **Patro·n·ymikum** n ~s/–ka; **patron·ymisch** a *patronymic*

Patrouille [pa'truljə] f ~/~n *patrol* | (Mannschafts-)~nlauf [m] ⟨ski⟩ (*team*) *p. race* **p-ll·ieren** vi [h] *to patrol*

patsch! *swash*!, *slap*!, *splash*!, *dash*! **P·atsch** m ~es/~e ⟨fam⟩ *clap, smack, pat, slap* || (Schnee≃ etc) *mire, mud, slime*; ~hand [f], ~händchen [n] ⟨fam⟩ (*little*) *paw*; ≃naß [a] *soaked to the bones, pouring wet* °**P·atsche** f ~/~n (S) *beater, swat*(*ter* ⟨Am⟩) || ⟨fam⟩ *paw* || (Pfütze) *puddle* || (Schlag) *smack* | ⟨fig⟩ *mess, jam, pickle, fix*, → Klemme || °e–e verfluchte ~ ⟨vulg⟩ *a bloody mess* || in die ~ k *or* geraten *to get into a scrape* od *into hot water* || schön in der ~ sitzen *to be in the soup, in a nice mess* od *pickle* od *in hot water, to be in for it*, ⟨Am fam⟩ *on the spot* || jdn in der ~ l *to leave a p in a fix* **p·atschen** v [h & s] ⟨fam⟩ (*of rain*) *to patter down* || (im Wasser) *to splash* (durch *through*) || vt/i (klatschen) *to slap, smack, pat* **p·atschert** a [österr] (P) *clumsy* **p·atschig** a *splashy* (*road*) || (P) *clumsy*

P·atschuli n ~s/~s ⟨bot⟩ *patchouli* || *p.* (*scent*)

Patt 1. n ~s/~s ⟨chess⟩ *stalemate* **2.** ≃ a; ~ m *or* setzen *to stalemate* || ~ s *or* w *to be stalemated*

P·atte f ~/~n ⟨tail, a. mil⟩ *flap*; *lapel*

°**p·atzen** vi [h] ⟨theat sl⟩ *to* (*do a*) *fluff*

°**p·atzig** a *saucy, pert* || ⟨fam⟩ *cheeky* || komm' mir *or* sei nicht so ~! *don't be insolent* od *impertinent* | **~keit** f *sauciness, pertness* || *insolence, impertinence* || ⟨fam⟩ *cheek*

°**P·auk- ~arzt** m *surgeon attending students' fencing* **~brille** f *f.g goggles* **~boden** m *f.g floor* **~handschuh** m *f.g gauntlet* **~zeug** n *rapiers* pl; → pauken 3, °**Pauk·ant** m ~en/~en *fencing student* **P·auke** f ~/~n **A. 1.** ⟨mus⟩ *bass* od *kettle-drum* **2.** ⟨anat⟩ *tympanum* **3.** ⟨fig fam⟩ *lecture, rebuke, jaw* **B.** mit ~n u Trompeten *with drums beating and trumpets sounding*, ⟨fig fam iron⟩ *utterly, ignominiously* || ⟨fig⟩ der ~ ein Loch m *to break off a th abruptly*; die ~ hat ein Loch *their intimacy has come to a sudden end*; e–m e–e ~ halten *to haul a p over the coals*; e–e ~ kriegen *to get a scolding*; auf die ~ hauen *to go to town, to paint the town red*; zu laut .. *to come it too strong* **p·auken 1.** vi [h] *to beat the kettle-drums* || *to strum* (*on the piano*) **2.** vt [h] (schlagen) *to bang out* || die Kanzel ~ *to thump the pulpit* || jdn tüchtig ~ *to give a p a sound thrashing* **3.** vt/i *to speechify, rant* || ⟨fam⟩ *to sputter* || Moral ~ *to talk morality* || ⟨sl⟩ (= büffeln) *to cram, grind*, ⟨sl⟩ *swot* | (sich) (mit e–m) ~ *to fence, to* (*fight a*) *duel* (*with a p*) **P·auken- ~fell** n ⟨mus⟩ *skin of a kettle-drum* || ⟨anat⟩ = Trommelfell **~klöppel** m *k.-d. stick* **~schall, ~schlag** m *sound of a k.-d.* **~schläger** m *k.-d.mer* **~wirbel** m *roll of the k.-d.* **P·auker** m ~s/~ *kettle-drummer* || ⟨fig fam⟩ (Lehrer) *kid-walloper*; *crammer*, (*gerund-*) *grinder*; ⟨sl⟩ *beak* °**Pauker·ei** f ~/~en **1.** *thrashing* || *row* || *duel*(*ling*), *fencing* **2.** ⟨sl⟩ *cramming, grinding*

P·aul- ≃·inisch a *Pauline* || ~e Briefe [pl] *epistles* pl *of St. Paul* **~skirche** f *St. Paul's* (*Cathedral*) **~us** m npr.; wie ~ auf die Korinther *with a vengeance*

Pauper·ismus m ~/ *pauperism*

P·aus- ~back m *chubby face* **~backen** f pl *ch. cheeks* pl **≃backig** a *ch.*(*-faced*); *blowsy, -zy* || (→ Pause[2]) **~leinwand** f *tracing cloth* **~papier** n *t.g* (*paper*) **~pulver** n *pounce* **~zeichnung** f *t.g, calking*

Pausch·al- ~entschädigung f *lump-sum indemnity* **~fracht** f *l.-s. freight* **~gebühr** f *flat rate* **~-kauf** m *wholesale purchase* **~police** f *global* od *blanket policy* **~preis** m *lump price* od *sum*; *flat rate*; *inclusive terms* **~reise** f *incl. tour* **~satz** m *flat rate* **~quantum** n, **~summe** f, (**~e**) f ~/ *lump sum* **~tarif** m *lump tariff* **~versicherung** f *all risks floater, fl. insurance*

P·ausche f ~/~n (Sattel≃) *pad*

P·ause[1] f ~/~n *pause*, (Unterbrechung) *stop, rest*; (*coffee*) *break* || *interruption, suspension* || *interregnum* (*of silence*) || ⟨school⟩ (*time*) *break, play time*, ⟨Am⟩ *intermission, recess*; in, während der ~ *at recess* || ⟨theat⟩ *interval*; ⟨Am⟩ *intermission* || (in, während der ~ *at the i.*) || ⟨Lit⟩ *pause* || ⟨mus⟩ *rest*; ganze ~ *semibreve rest*, halbe ~ *minim rest*, viertel ~ *crotchet rest* || e–e ~ m *to* (*make a*) *pause* od *stop* || *to* (*take a*) *rest* || ⟨fam⟩ *to stand down* || e–e ~ einlegen *to call* od *order a break*; *to adjourn* || nach e–r kurzen *or* verlegenen ~ *after a moment's hesitation* || e–e ruhige ~ hat sich eingestellt *a lull has settled down* (*over* ..) **≃n-los** a *ceaseless*; *non-stop* (*raids*) | adv *without let-up*, etc **~nglocke** f ⟨theat⟩ *bar-*, ⟨Am⟩ *intermission bell* **~nzeichen** n ⟨wir; m. m.⟩ *signature* **paus·ieren** vi [h] *to* (*make a*) *pause, to stop* || *to lay* od *lie off*

P·ause[2] ~/~n *tracing, pouncing* || *traced design, blue print* **p·ausen** vt [h] ⟨arts⟩ *to trace* (*over*), *to calk* || (mit Pauspulver) *to pounce*

Pav·ia n (Stadt in Oberitalien)

P·avian m ~(e)s/~e *baboon* || ⟨fig⟩ *duffer* || *fop*

P·avillon ['paviljɔŋ] m ~s/~s *pavilion*

Pax f ~/ (S) *osculatory* **paz- ~·ifisch** a; der ≃e Ozean *the Pacific* **≃if·ismus** m ~/ *pacifism* **≃i-f·ist** m ~en/~en *pacifist* **~ifiz·ieren** vt [h] *to pacify* || vi ⟨jur⟩ *to come to terms*

P·ecan-Nuß a *pecan-nut*

P·ech n ~(e)s/~e **1.** *pitch* || (Schuster≃) *cobbler's wax* || mit ~ abdichten (überziehen) *to pitch* (*wax*) || klebt wie ~ *sticks like glue* (an *to*) ⟨a. fig⟩ || ⟨prov⟩ wer ~ anfaßt, besudelt sich *who touches pitch will be defiled* **2.** ⟨fig fam⟩ (misfortune) *ill* od *bad luck*; *hard lines*; ⟨Am fam⟩ *jinx*, ⟨sl⟩ *tough* (*rough, rotten, lousy*) *break* od *luck* || ⟨sport⟩ *rot* || °verteufeltes ~! ⟨sl⟩ *dashed hard luck* (f *on*)!, ⟨sl⟩ *hard cheese*! | ~ h *to be out of luck, to strike a bad patch, to be down on one's luck* || ⟨Am sl⟩ *to fall down* (in *in*, mit *on*) || ~ wie immer! *just my luck*!; ekelhaftes ~ *sickening luck* || e–m ~ bringen *to bring misfortune upon a p* **≃artig** a *p.y* **~blende** f ⟨min⟩ *p.-blende* **~brenner** m *p.-maker* °**~bringer** m ⟨Am⟩ *jinx* **~draht** m *wax-end* **~erde** f *bituminous earth* **~fackel** f *torch* **~faden** m *p.ed thread* **≃finster** a ~e Nacht *p.-*

-dark night **~finsternis** f *pitchy blackness*, → stockfinster **~hütte** f *p.-hut*; ⟨fig⟩ *Abaddon, bottomless pit* || bis in die aschgraue ~ *till hell freezes over, to the end of the last chapter, until the arrival of that day of Greek Calends* **~kiefer** f *pitch-pine* **~kohle** f *soft* od *bituminous coal* **~kranz** m *p.-ring* **~krücke** f *p.-scraper* **~kugel** f *p.-ball* **~nase** f ⟨hist fort⟩ *murder-hole* **~nelke** f ⟨bot⟩ (*viscous*) *catch-fly* **≗schw·arz** a (*as*) *black as p., jet(-black)*; *p.y* **~sieder** m *p.-maker* **~stein** m *p.stone* **~strähne** f *run of bad luck* (reißt nicht ab *continues*); e–e ~ h *to be down on one's luck*, ⟨sport⟩ *to strike a bad patch* **~tanne** f ⟨bot⟩ *spruce*, (*American*) *p.-pine* **~tonne** f *p.-barrel* **~torf** m *black peat* **~vogel** m ⟨fig fam⟩ *ill-starred fellow*, ⟨Am fam⟩ *flop* || ein ~ s *to have bad luck* **p·echig** a *pitchy* °**pechik·ös**! a = °(verteufeltes) Pech! **P·echler** m ~s/~ *pitch-maker*

Ped·al n ~(e)s/~e ⟨mus & cycl⟩ *pedal* || (in) die Pedale treten *to pedal*; *to work the pedals* | ⟨fig fam⟩ (Füße) *trotters, paddles* pl | mit **~antrieb** [m] *pedal driven* **~harfe** f *pedal harp* **~taste** f (der Orgel) *p.-key*

Ped·ant m ~en/~en *pedant, precisian*; *prig*; *stickler*; ⟨sl⟩ *square-toes* pl [sg konstr] **~er·ie** f ~/~n *pedantry* **≗isch** a *pedantic* || adv; ~ genau *meticulous, literal*; *scrupulously* (*correct*)

Ped·ell [m] ~(e)s/~e ⟨jur⟩ *beadle* || ⟨school⟩ *attendant* || ⟨univ⟩ *proctor's man*, ⟨sl⟩ *bulldog*

Pedik·üre, f ~/~m *pedicure, chirupody* **Pedik·eur** [ø] m ~s/~e *chiropodist*; *foot specialist*

P·eersschub m *batch of Peers, wholesale creation of P.s*

P·egasus [m] ~/; den ~ besteigen *to mount P.*

P·egel m ~s/~; **Peil** m ~s/~e *depth ga(u)ge, water mark, water-* od *tide-gauge* || *flood measuring post* | ~gleichheit [f] ⟨rec⟩ *volume equalization*; ~stand [m] *water-level* **p·egel** vt/i [h] *to sound*

P·eil- **~anlage** f *sounding device* **~antenne** f ⟨wir⟩ *direction finding* (*D/F*) *aerial* **~bake** f ⟨aero⟩ *radio-beacon* **~feld** n *r. range* **~funk** m ⟨wir⟩ *d.-f.*; ~einrichtung [f] *d.-finder*; ~stelle [f] *d.-f. station* **~gerät** n *s. device, d.-f. apparatus* **~holz** n *gauge-rod* **~kompaß** m *bearing-compass* **~lot** n *s.-lead, plummet* **~rahmen** m ⟨wir⟩ *loop-antenna, D/F-frame* **~rohr** n (e–r Pumpe) *s.-pipe* **~sender** m *radio tracking beacon, d.al transmitter* **~stab** m *level rod* **~stange** f = ~holz **~scheibe** f *bearing disc* **~station** f *fixing* od *b. station* || *radio beacon* **~strahl** m ⟨aero⟩ *wireless beam*; mit ~ fliegen *to ride the b.* **~verfahren** n *d. f.* (*D/F*) *system* **p·eilen** **1.** vt [h] ⟨mar⟩ (Wasserstand) *to sound, gauge* || *to take the bearings of* (*the coast*), .. *the altitude of* (*the sun*) || (messen) *to measure* || ⟨radar⟩ *to ascertain a bearing* **2.** ≗ n, **P·eilung** f ~/~en *sounding* || (*taking a* [*the*]) *bearing*(*s* pl) (rechtweisend *true*); *direction finding* **P·eiler** m *direction finder* || *D/F-apparatus*

Pein f ~/ *pain* || *torment, agony, torture* || *sufferings* pl; ewige ~ ⟨rel⟩ *everlasting t.ts* || sich das Leben zur ~ m *to make l. a hell for o.s.*

p·einigen vt [h] *to torment, torture* || *to rack, harrow* || ⟨fig⟩ *to harass, distress, tantalize* || gepeinigt w *to be racked* (*by* od *with gout*) || ~d *excruciating* **P·einiger** m ~s/~ (P) *tormentor, torturer* || (S) *torment* **P·einigung** f ~/~en *torment(ing), torture*, etc **p·einlich** (a. peinvoll, ⟨fam⟩ peinsam) **A.** [a] **1.** *painful*; ⟨adv⟩ ~ echt *painfully real* || ⟨jur⟩ *penal* (*law*); *capital* (*offence*), *criminal* (*charge, trial*) || ~e Frage *torture*; in e–r ~en Lage (P) ⟨sl⟩ *up a tree* | ⟨fig⟩ *painful* || *agonizing* || *worrying, tormenting* || *awkward, embarrassing* || *sore* (*subject*) || ein ~er Auftritt *an unpleasant fuss*; ~e Lage *scrape*; *tight corner*; ~e Situation, ~e Stille *awkwardness* || es war mir ~ *I was embarrassed* **2.** (genau) *strict, punctilious, precise, scrupulous, meticulous* || ⟨fam⟩ *squeamish*; [pred] *pernickety, fidgety* (betr. *about*) **B.** [adv] ~ achten auf *to be very particular about, to be nice* (*in doing*) || ⟨jur⟩ ~ befragen *to torture, rack* || jdn ~ berühren *to jar on* od *to embarrass a p* || ~ berührt w *to be pained* (*to discover*) || ~ sauber *scrupulously clean* || ~ untersuchen *to examine thoroughly* || ~ vermeiden *carefully to avoid* || ~ wirken *to produce a painful impression* | **≗keit** f ~/ *painfulness* || *criminality* || *agony* | *strictness* | *preciseness, scrupulousness* || ⟨fam⟩ *squeamishness, fidgetiness*

P·eipus-See m ⟨Russ⟩ *Peipus*; *Lake Peipsi*

P·eitsche f ~/~n *whip* || (Strafe) *lash* || (Geißel) *scourge* || Reit≗ *horsewhip* || mit der ~ knallen *to crack, snap the whip* **p·eitschen** vt [h] *to* (*horse*)*whip, flog*; *lash, scourge* ⟨a. fig⟩, || ⟨fig⟩ *to beat*; (Gesetz) *to rush* (*through the House*) || (Regen) *to slash, pelt* || *to sweep along* || v Schneestürmen ge–t *blizzard-ridden* **≗hieb** m *lash* **≗knall** m *crack of a whip* **≗riemen** m *thong* **≗schmitze**, **≗schnur** f *lash, whip-cord* **≗stock** m *whip-handle*

Pek·esche f ~/~n *frogged* od *lace coat*

P·eking n *Peking, Pekin*

pekuni·är a *financial, pecuniary* (*profit*)

°**pekz·ieren** vt [h] *to be up to* (*mischief*)

Pelarg·onie f ~/~n ⟨bot⟩ *pelargonium*

†**Pel·asger** m pl *Pelasgians* pl

Pelem·ele [pæl'mæl] n ~/ *medley, hodge-podge* | ≗ [adv] *pell-mell*

Peler·ine f ~/~n *cape, pelerine* || (*fur-*)*tippet*

P·elikan m ~(e)s/~e ⟨orn⟩ *pelican* ⟨a. tech⟩ | **~·ol** ® n ~s/ *paste*

P·elle f ~/~n *peel, husk, skin* || ⟨fig⟩ e–m auf die ~ rücken *to press a p hard* **p·ellen** vt *to skin, peel* || wie aus dem Ei gepellt *spick and span, as if she came out of a band-box* **P·ellkartoffeln** f pl *potatoes* [pl] *in their skins* od *jackets*

Peloponn·es m, ⟨scient⟩ f *Peloponnesus* **~ier(in** f) m, **≗isch** a *Peloponnesian*

Pel·ote f ~/~n *pad* Pelot·on [–tɔŋ] n ~s/~s ⟨obs mil⟩ *file, platoon* **~feuer** n ⟨mil⟩ *p.* od *f. fire* od *firing*; *p.-volleys*

P·elz m ~es/~e **A.** *fur*, ⟨a.⟩ *pelt*; ~e [pl] ⟨a.⟩ *peltry* || (Mantel etc) *furs* pl | ⟨übtr⟩ *skin, furring* (*on liquids*) | ⟨fig fam⟩ *back, skin* **B.** mit ~ besetzen, füttern *to fur* || ⟨fig fam⟩ e–m den ~ ausklopfen *to give a p a good thrashing* od *hiding* || jdm auf den ~ brennen *to fire pointblank at a p* || jdm auf den ~ rücken *to press a p hard* || (jdm) den ~ waschen *to give .. a good scolding, to blow .. up* | °ihr brennt der ~ *she itches*, ⟨vulg⟩ *she's dripping for it* **~art** f *species of fur* **~aufbereitung** f *fur-dressing* **~besatz** m *f.-trimming* || °⟨sex vulg⟩ *f.*(*below*), *fud, fleece, plush, fluff* **≗besetzt** a *lined* od *trimmed with f.* **~flatterer** m ⟨zoo⟩ *flying lemur* **~fresser** m ⟨ent⟩ *mallophagan*; Gattung der ~ *mallophaga* pl **~futter** n *f.-lining* **~handel** m *f.-trade* **~händler** m *f.rier* **~handschuh** m *f.red glove* **~jäger** m *f.-trapper* **~kragen** m *f.-cape, f. collar* od *tippet*; Damen≗ *stole, neckpiece* **~mantel** m *f.red cloak, f.s* pl **~mütze** f *f.-cap*; ⟨engl⟩ (Husaren≗) *busby*, (Garde≗) *bearskin* **~rock** m *f.red coat, f.-coat* **~schuh** m *f.-shoe* **~stiefel** m *f.-boot* **~tier** n *f.-bearing animal* **~verarbeitung** f *fur-dressing* **~verbrämung** f *f. trimming* **~ware** f, **~werk** n *f.s* pl, *f.riery* **p·elzen** **1.** vt [h] ⟨hort⟩ *to graft* || *to fur*; ⟨fig fam⟩ *to drub* **2.** [a] *furred, of fur* **p·elzig** a *furry, like fur* || ⟨bot⟩ *cottony, nappy* || (Rettich) *stringy* || (*liquid*) *covered with furring* || ⟨fig fam⟩ *numb* (*feet*); ~es Gefühl (*sensation of*) *formication*

P·en-Club m ~s/ *pen-club* (**p**oets, **e**ssayists, **n**ovelists)

Pen·aten pl *Penates, household gods* pl

Pendant [paŋ'daŋ, pɑ̃:'dɑ̃:] n ~s/~s *counterpart, companion, complement, parallel* **P·endel** n ~s/~ *pendulum* || [in comp] *oscillating* od *p.* od *shuttle* **~achse** f *o. axle* **~ausschlag** m *p. deflection*

~bus m *sh.-bus* **~bewegung, ~schwingung** f *oscillation* **~fräsen** n *reciprocal milling* **~linse** f *p.-bob* **~stange** f *p.-rod* **~tür** f *swinging door* **~uhr** f *p.-clock* **~verkehr** m *sh.-traffic* od *-service* **~zug** m ⟨rail⟩ *relay-, sh.-train* **p·endeln** vi [h] *to oscillate, swing, sway* (mit den Armen *one's arms*) ‖ ⟨fig⟩ *to saunter about* ‖ *to go backwards and forwards; to commute; to walk* etc *to and fro* ‖ ⟨fig⟩ *to hover (between two extremes)* | ≃ n ⟨mach⟩ *hunting* **~d** a *p.-like* **P·endler** m *commuter* | ~gebiet [n] *commuting belt* **Pendüle** [pɑ̃ːˈdyːlə, paŋˈdyːlə] f ~/~n *chimney-clock*

penetr·ant a *penetrating* **-tr·ieren** vt [h] *to penetrate*

pen·ibel a *painful* ‖ *particular, fastidious, fussy*

Penizill·in n ~s/ (⟨scient⟩ –cill–) *penicillin*

Penn·al n ~(e)s/~e **1.** *pen-case* **2.** °*school* °≃**er** m ~s/~ *schoolboy* | ~liebe [f] *calf-love*

P·ennbruder m ~s/–brüder ⟨fam⟩ *vagabond, homeless tramp* °**P·enne** f ~/~n **1.** *doss-house;* ⟨Am⟩ *flophouse, jungle* **2.** = Pennal 2. °**p·ennen** vi [h] (schlafen) *to snooze, doss*

Penn·inische Alpen pl *Pennine Alps* pl

Penn·inische K·ette f (Zentralgebirge in N.-England) *Pennine Chain*

Pennsylv·anien n (U.S.A.-Staat) *Pennsylvania*

P·enny m ~s/–ies *penny* ([pl] *pence*); $1^1/_2$ ~ *three half-penny* ‖ für e–n ~ Z. *a p.worth of sugar*

Pensee [ˈpɑ̃ːseː] n ~s/~s ⟨bot⟩ *pansy*

Pensi·on [pɑ̃ːsˈjoːn] f ~/~en **A.** ⟨jur⟩ *pension,* ⟨mil⟩ *retired pay, half-pay* ‖ (Kostgeld) *board;* halbe ~ *bed, breakfast and one meal; demi-p.;* tägliche ~ 10.– DM *inclusive terms 19 s a day* ‖ volle ~ *or* Ganztages≃ [abstr] *room and board* ‖ (Kosthaus) *boarding-house* ‖ (Anstalt) *b.g-school* ‖ die ganze ~ *all the boarders* pl **B.** e–e ~ beziehen *to draw a p.* ‖ in e–e ~ bringen *to send to a b.g-school* ‖ sich in ~ geben bei *to board (out) with* ‖ in ~ gehen *to retire (on a p.)* ‖ mit voller ~ mieten, volle ~ nehmen *to take full board and lodgings* ‖ in ~ s bei *to board with* ‖ mit ~ verabschieden *to p. off* **Pensi·ons- ~alter** n *retirement age* **~anstalt** f *b.g-school* **~beitrag** m *superannuation-money* ≃**berechtigt** a *superannuable (post)* **~berechtigung** f *right to a p.* ‖ ~ h *to be entitled to a p.* **~berechtigt, ≃fähig** a *p.able (age)* **~gast** m *resident* **~inhar(in** f) m *keeper of a b.-h.* **~kasse** f *retirement* od *p.* od *s.tion fund* **~liste** f *retired list* **~preis** m *board* **~stand** m; in den ~ treten *to be p.ed off, to retire on a p.* **~versicherung** f *retirement p. insurance* **~vorsteher(in** f) m *principal of a b.g-school* ‖ *owner of a b.g-house* **Pension·är** m ~(e)s/~e *pensioner, pensionary* ‖ (Kostgänger) *boarder* | **~in** f ~/~nen *pupil at a boarding-school* **P-·at** n ~(e)s/~e *boarding-school (for young ladies)* ‖ °~sschlange [f] (b. Ausgang) *crocodile* **p-·ieren** vt [h] *to superannuate; to pension off* ‖ ⟨mil⟩ *to put on half-pay* ‖ sich ~ l *to sell out and go upon half-pay, to retire* **p-·iert** a *retired (officer)* **P-·ierung** f *retirement; pensioning off; superannuation* | ~salter [n] *retiring age* **P-·ist** m ~en/~en *pensioner* **P·ensum** n ~s/–sen & –sa *task, lesson* ‖ *curriculum* ‖ *course*

P·enta- ~·eder n ⟨geom⟩ *pentahedron* **~gr·amm** n ~s/~e *pentacle* **~meter** [·'··] m ~s/~ *pentameter* **~t·euch** m ~(e)s/ *Pentateuch* **Pent·omdivision** f ⟨mil⟩ *pentomic d.*

Pepini·ere f ~/~n *army medical college*

Pep- ~s·in n ~s/ *pepsin* ‖ ~drüse [f] *peptic gland* **~t·on** n ~(e)s/ *peptone* ‖ ≃erzeugend [a] *peptogenic*

per prep [acc] *by (rail, train, ship, express, road* = Achse, *post)* | *per (annum, month, pound, balance, procuration);* (Saldo) ~ 30. 6. *.. made up to 30 June* | per pedes L = *on foot* ‖ ~ Stück *apiece* ‖ zweimal ~ Jahr *twice a year* ‖ ~ sofort *at once* ‖ ~ Kassa *for cash* | ~ Adresse Herrn N. N. *care of (c/o) Mr. N. N.* | ~ „du" s *to call each other "thou"* **~eat** L, **~eant** pl intj ~! *confusion!* ‖ [mit dat] *(three) groans to* od *for* **~emt·orisch** a *peremptory* ≃**·enne** f Staude **~enn·ierend** a ⟨bot⟩ *perennial* **~f·ekt** a *perfect (cook; in shorthand)* ‖ *accomplished (young lady)* ‖ *concluded, settled (arrangement)* **~fekti·on** f ~/ (Vollendung) *perfection* | ~·ismus [m ~/] (⟨philos⟩ als sittliches Ziel; ⟨allg⟩ übertriebenes Vollkommenheitsstreben) *perfectionism* ≃**f·ekt(um)** n ~s/–ta ⟨gram⟩ *perfect (tense)* **~f·id** a *perfidious* ≃**fid·ie** f ~/~n *perfidy* | (seitliche) ≃**forationsreihe** f *row of (marginal) perforations* **~for·ieren** vt [h] *to perforate* ‖ perforiert [a] *rouletted (stamp)* ≃**for·iermaschine** f *perforator*

Pergam·ent n ~(e)s/~e *parchment;* (Kalbs≃) *vellum* L; in Kalbs≃ gebundenes Buch *vellum-bound book* ‖ *old document* ≃**artig** a *p.-like* **~band** m *volume bound in p.* ‖ *p. cover* **~ersatz** m *imitation p.* ≃**farben** a *p.-coloured* **~papier** n **1.** *vellum* (od *p.) paper* ‖ ⟨pap⟩ echt ~ *pure p.* **2.** *grease-proof* od *sandwich paper* **~rolle** f *scroll of p.* | ≃**en** a *(made of) parchment* **Pergam·in** ® n ~s/ *glassine*

†**P·ergamon, P·ergamum** n (Stadt in Kleinasien) *Pergamos*

P·ergel n ~s/~ [südd] *vine-arbour*

perhorresz·ieren vt [h] ⟨jur⟩ *to challenge (a judge* od *witness)* ‖ ⟨fig⟩ *to reject, deprecate (with horror)*

P·eri- ~g·äum n ~s/ ⟨astr⟩ *perigee* **~h·el(ium)** n ~s/ (Ggs Apo–) *perihelion* **~k·ope** f ⟨bib-pros⟩ *pericope,* → d. u Ev. Johannis 8, 1ff. **~l·un** n ~(e)s/ ⟨a–n⟩ (mondnächster Punkt) *perilune* ≃**nat·al** a *peri-natal (mortality)*

Peri·ode f ~/~n *period* ⟨a. gram & Lit hist⟩ ‖ *spell (of fine weather)* ‖ ⟨tech⟩ *period* ‖ ⟨biol⟩ *periods, menses* pl ‖ ⟨math⟩ *repetend; repeating figures* pl *(of a decimal)* ‖ ⟨astr, chem⟩ *figures* pl ‖ ⟨el⟩ *pole* ‖ ⟨phys, wir⟩ volle ~ *reversal* ‖ ⟨fig⟩ s–e ~ h *to have one's spells* **~nbau** m ⟨gram⟩ *structure of periods* **peri·odisch** a *periodic(al)* ‖ ~e Dezimalzahl *recurring* od *circulating decimal* ‖ ⟨chem⟩ ~es System *periodic law* ‖ ~e Veröffentlichung *serialization* ‖ ~e Zeitschrift *periodical* **Periodizit·ät** f *periodicity*

P·eri- ~öken m pl *Periæci* pl **~pat·etiker** m *Peripatetic* **~pet·ie** f ~/~n [iːən] *peripeteia, unravelling of plot* ≃**ph·er** a *peripheral* ⟨a. comp⟩ *(unit)* **~pher·ie** f ~/~n *perimeter; circumference* ‖ ⟨fig⟩ (an *on*) *the outskirts* [pl] *of a town* | ~-winkel [m] *angle at the c.* ≃**ph·erisch** a *peripheral* **~phr·ase** f ~/~n *periphrasis* **~sel·enum** n ~s/ (mondnächster Punkt) *perilune* **~sk·op** n ~s/~e *periscope,* ⟨fam⟩ *look-stick* od *-see* **~st·altik** f ⟨med⟩ *peristalsis* ≃**st·altisch** a *peristaltic* **~st·yl** n ~s/~e ⟨arch⟩ *peristyle*

Per- ~kussi·on f ~/~en *percussion* ⟨a. med⟩ | ~sgewehr [n] *p.-gun;* ~shammer [m] *p.-hammer;* ~szünder [m] *p.-fuse;* ~szündhütchen [n] *p.-cap* ≃**kut·an** a *percutaneous* ≃**kut·ieren** vt [h] *to percuss* **~kut·ierhammer** m ⟨med⟩ *plexor*

P·erl- ~asche f *pearl-ash* **~auster** f *p.-oyster* **~boot** n *p.y-nautilus* **~druck** n *nonpareil, pearl* ≃**farben** a *p.-coloured* **~fang** m, **~fischerei** f *p.-fishery* **~fischer** m *o.-fisher* od *-diver* **~gerste** f, **~graupen** f pl *(p.-)barley* ≃**grau** a *p.-grey* **~händler** m *dealer in p.s* **~hirse** f ⟨bot⟩ *gromil* **~huhn** n *Guinea-fowl* **~muschel** f *p.-oyster* **~m·utt(er** f) n *mother-of-p., nacre* | **~-** ⟨cosm⟩ *p.y (pastels);* ≃artig [a] *nacreous;* mit ~effekt *frosted;* ≃n [a] *mother-of-p.;* ~schnecke [f] *p.-cowry* **~rand** m ⟨num⟩ *border of dots; engrailed ring* **~schrift** f ⟨typ⟩ *pearl* **~stab** m ⟨arch⟩ *pater-noster* **~spat** m *p.-spar* **~sticker** m *embroiderer with p.s* **~sticke·r·ei** f *bead-(mat) work* **~sucht** f ⟨vet⟩ *bovine tuberculosis* **~tee** m *gunpowder tea* ≃**w·eiß** a *as white as p.;* [n] *p.-powder* **~zwiebel** f *p.-onion* **P·erle** f ~/~n *pearl* ‖ (Glas≃) *bead;* (hängende) *drop* ‖ ⟨fig⟩ *pearl, jewel, gem, treasure;* unsre „~"

(Dienstmädchen) *our one-er* || ~n bilden *to p.* || Schweiß stand in dichten ~n auf s–r Stirn *sweat was beaded thickly on ..., sweat beaded his f.* || s–e ~n vor die Säue werfen *to cast (one's) p.s before swine* **p·erlen** vi [h] *to rise in pearls, to bubble (up), to sparkle (sparkling wine)* || ~d [adv] spielen ⟨mus⟩ *to pearl* [vt] **P·erlen- ~aloe** f ⟨bot⟩ *pearl-aloe* **≗artig** a *beady, p.y* **~besatz** m *p.-edging* **~schmuck** m *ornament* od *set of p.s* **~schnur** f *string of p.s* **≗weiß** a *p.-white*

per- ~man·ent a *permanent* **≗man·enz** f ~/ *permanence, -cy* **~mut·ieren** vt [h] ⟨math⟩ *to permute, exchange* **~nizi·ös** a *pernicious (anaemia)* **~or·ieren** vi [h] *to speechify*; ⟨fam⟩ *to rant* **≗pen·d·ikel** m & n ~s/~ *pendulum* || *perpendicular (line)* **p-kul·ar** a *perpendicular* (auf *on*) | **≗-** *p.* ⟨arch⟩ *(style)* **~petu·ell,** perpetu·ierlich a *perpetual* **P–p·etuum** m·obile n ~/ *(a th in) perpetual motion* °**~pl·ex** a *amazed, disconcerted, embarassed, confused*; [pred] *all of a heap* || ~ m *to flummox; to knock (a p) cold*

†**Perr·on** [–'rɔŋ] m ~s/~s ⟨rail⟩ *platform*

Pers·enning f ~/~en *tarpaulin*

P·erser(in f) m *Persian* **P·ersien** n *Persia* → Iran

Persev·ant n ~en/~en ⟨engl her⟩ *pursuivant*

Persi·aner m ~s/~ *broadtail; Persian lamb*

P·ersiko m ~s/~s *peach-brandy*

Persim·one f ~/~n *(date-plum) persimmon*

P·ersischer M·eerbusen *Persian Gulf*

Pers·on f ~/~en **A.** *person* || *the p. of the Queen* || *p.al appearance* || die ~en ⟨a.⟩ *the p.nel* || ⟨theat⟩ *figure, rôle, character* | e–e ~, die *somebody who* || k–e ~ *nobody* || *if I was Woman as a whole* (alle Frauen in e–r ~) **B.** beteiligte ~ *party* || die eigene ~ *one's self*; ⟨fam⟩ *number one* || einzelne ~ *individual* || fähige ~ *capable body* || gefährliche ~ *dangerous p* || die handelnden ~en *the dramatis personae* L || hervorragende, hochgestellte (wichtige) ~ *p.age (of importance)* || juristische ~ *artificial p, body politic* od *corporate, corporation, entity, legal party* || lächerliche ~ *ridiculous figure* || natürliche ~ *natural p* || stattliche ~ *portly figure* || stumme ~ *dumb part* **C.** (nur) f 1 ~ ⟨a.⟩ *individual*; ich **für** m–e ~ *I for one, I for my part, p.ally I, I p.ally* || **in** ([höchst] eigener) ~ *in p* || *(the devil) incarnate* || die Redlichkeit in ~ *honesty itself, the p.ification of h.*; (so: *a picture of good humour*) || in ~ kennen *to know p.ally* || 1.– DM **je** *or* die (*or* pro) ~ *1 s a head* || klein **von** ~ *of short stature* || v ~ (kennen) .. *by sight* **D.** der Anblick m–r ~ *the sight of me* || ohne Ansehung der ~ *without respect* od *disinction of p.s* | als ~en auftreten *to appear in the form of p.s* || ~en kamen nicht um *no lives were lost* **Person·al** n ~(e)s/~e *p.nel, (office-)staff* || *employees, servants* pl || ⟨aero⟩ *(flying) p.nel (= aircrew)*; *(ground) staff* || ~ halten *to keep servants, a staff* **~abbau** m *reduction of staff* **~abteilung** f *staff department* **~akte** f *record sheet; personnel/personal file* **~amt** n ⟨mil⟩ *drafting office; Record Office* **~angaben** f pl *p.al data* pl **~auswahl** f *staff selection, s. of the appropriate st.* **~ausweis** m *identity card; identification* **~beschreibung** f *description of a p* | übermäßige **~besetzung** *featherbedding* **~bestand** m *officials, staff; manpower* **~büro** n *p.nel office* **~chef** m *p.nel manager* **~frage** f *p.al question* **~mangel** m; ~ h *to be shorthanded* **~papiere** n pl → –ausweis **~pronomen** n ⟨gram⟩ *p.al pronoun* **~steuer** f *p.al tax* **~union** f ⟨pol⟩ *p.al union* | ~monarchie [f] *Dual M.* **~vertretungsgesetz** n ⟨Ger⟩ *Staff Delegates' Act* **Person·alien** pl *particulars* pl, *identification of a p; p.al data* **Pers·önchen** [dim] n *little (wo)man* || gutartiges ~ *not a bad little sort* **Pers·onen- ~aufnahme** f ⟨phot⟩ *portrait* **~aufzug** m *lift for p.s,* ⟨Am⟩ *passenger elevator* **~bahnhof** m *pass. station* **~beförderung** f *pass. service, conveyance of pass.s* **~dampfer** m *pass.-boat* **~frage** f *question of p.ality* od *p.nel* **~fuhrwerk** n *pass.-vehicle* **~gedächtnis** n *memory for faces* **~hehlerei** f *conceiling fugitives* **~kraftwagen** m *pass.-, motor-car* **~kreis** m *group* od *categary of p.s; section of the population* **~kult** m *p.ality cult* **~luftverkehr** m *air pass. service* **~name** m *p.al name*; ⟨gram⟩ *p.al noun* **~post** f *stage-coach* **~schaden** m *p.al damage* od *injury* **~stand** n *status; state of population (births, deaths, marriages)*; Ihr ~? *your name and occupation?* | ~sregister [n] *register of vital statistics* **~steuer** f *poll-tax* **~verkehr** m (öffentlicher *public*) *pass.-traffic* **~verzeichnis** n *register of p.s* || ⟨theat⟩ *(list of) dramatis personae* L **~wagen** m ⟨rail⟩ *pass.-carriage* || *coach* || (Pkw) *private* ⟨Am⟩ *pass. car* **~wechsel** m *p.al changes* **~zug** m ⟨rail⟩ (Ggs Schnellzug) *slow* od *stopping* od *local train,* ⟨Am⟩ *accomodation train* || (Ggs Güterzug) *pass.-train* **Personifikati·on** f ~/~en *personification* || (Verkörperung) *embodiment* **p-fiz·ieren** vt [h] *to impersonate, personify, personalize* || die p–rte Bosheit *the incarnation* od *embodiment of wickedness* **persönlich A.** [a] *personal (insult, remark, reasons, pleasure, acquaintance, pronoun)* || *chief (bodyguard* Adjutant) || ~e Angriffe *personalities* || ~es Auftreten ⟨film⟩ *personal* || *individual (equipment)* || *private (opinion)*; m–r ~en Meinung nach *in my opinion* || (Briefaufschrift) *private* || ~ w *to indulge in (to take to) p.alities, to make p.al remarks* **B.** [adv] *in p; p.ally* || es ~ auffassen: *he took this up as a p.al matter* || sich ~ bemühen *to exert o.s. p.ally* || ~ erscheinen .. *in p* || ~ glauben: *I p.ally* od *p.ally, I think* || ~ haften *to be individually answerable* || *(to cook ..) with one's own hands* || *he insisted on going h.s.* || ~ interessiert *peculiarly interested* || ~ kennen: *I know him p.ally* || ~ kennenlernen *to come into p.al contact with a p* || alles ~ nehmen *to take everyth. p.ally* | **≗keit** f ~/~en (⟨psych⟩ Doppel≗ *multiple) p.ality* || *(the leading) figure* || angesehene ~ ⟨a.⟩ *worthy*; hochstehende ~ *distinguished p*; s–e ganze ~ einsetzen *to devote one's whole p.ality; to throw o.s. wholeheartedly into each situation* | *(to discover a p's) identity* || *p.al appearance* || *individuality* || → Person B. | ~sbeurteilung, ~sbewertung [f] *merit rating*; ~szerfall [m] ⟨psych⟩ *disintegration of p.ality*

Perspekt·iv [–f] n ~s/~e *telescope* || ⟨hist⟩ *field-glass* **~e** [–i:və] f ~/~n *perspective* || ⟨fig⟩ *prospect, issue* || neue ~n *new possibilities* od *aspects* || in der ~ *in pr.* | **≗isch** a ⟨paint⟩ *perspective* || ⟨theat⟩ *scenographic(al)* || [adv] *in perspective, in prospect*

P·erstoff m (Gas) *diphosgene, green cross*

Pertin·enz f ~/~ien ⟨jur⟩ [abstr] *accessoriness* || [konkr] (a. ~stücke) pl *appurtenances* pl

Per·ücke f ~/~n *wig,* ⟨hist⟩ *periwig* (tragen *to wear*) || ⟨fig⟩ alte ~n *old fogies* **~nmacher** m *wig-maker, hairdresser* **~nschachtel** f *wig-box* **~nstock** m *barber's* od *wig-block*

P·eru- ~balsam m *b. of P.* **~rinde** f *P.vian bark*

Per·u-Ch·ile-Graben ⟨mar⟩ *Peru-Chile-Trench*

perv·ers a ~er Mensch *sexual pervert* || **≗it·ät** f ~/~en *(sexual) abnormality*

Pesch·aur n (West-Pakistan) *Peshawar*

°**p·esen** vi [s] [du pest] (rennen) → wetzen

P·ess·ar n ~s/~e ⟨med⟩ *pessary*

Pessim·ismus m ~/ *pessimism* **Pessim·ist** m ~en/~en *pessimist* | **≗isch** a *pessimistic* || *to take a dim view of ths*

P·est f ~/~en *plague, pestilence* || wie die ~ *like hell* || (jdn) meiden wie die ~ *to avoid* od *shun .. like the pl.* || es stinkt wie die ~ .. *like a pigsty* || v der ~ befallen *pl.-stricken* | ~! *a pl. upon it! confound it! damnation!* | ⟨fig⟩ (Plage) *pest, nuisance* **~artig** a *pestilential* **~beule, ~blatter** f ⟨path⟩ *pl.-boil, pl.-ulcer* || ⟨fig⟩ *canker, pl.-spot* **~geruch** m *pestilential smell* **~hauch** m *p.tial vapour, miasma* **~haus** n *pest-house* od *-hospital* **≈krank** a *pl.-stricken, infected with the pl.* | ≈e(r) [m] *pl.-sufferer* || **~luft** f *pestiferous air* od *atmosphere* **~mal** n *pl.-mark* **~ordnung** f *regulations* [pl] *for pl.-stricken districts* **~ratte** f *bandicoot* **~schutzheilige(r)** m *pl.-saint* **~stoff** m *pestilential matter* od *virus* **~wurz** f *pestilence-wort* **~zeit** f *time of pl.* **p·esthaft** a *pestilential* **Pestil·enz** f ~/~en *pestilence* **≈i·alisch** a *p.tial, pestiferous*

Pet·arde f ~/~n *petard* **-d·ier** m ~s/~e *petardeer*

Pet·ent m ~en/~en *petitioner*; → Petition

P·eter m [npr] *Peter* || alberner ~ *foolish duffer* || dummer ~ *simpleton* || langweiliger ~ *slow-coach, bore* || Sankt ~ *St. P.* || ⟨Ger cards⟩ schwarzer ~ *Black P.* †**~sburg** = Sankt ~ (*St.*) *Petersburg*, → Leningrad **~skirche** f *St. P.'s* (*church*) **~spfennig** m *P.'s-pence* **Peters·ilie** f ~/ ⟨bot⟩ *parsley*; mit ~ bestreuen *to sprinkle with chopped p.* || ⟨fig⟩ (b. Tanz) sie pflückt ~ *she finds no partner* || ihm ist die ~ verhagelt *it snowed!* (man sieht es ihm an: *he looks like a duck in a thunderstorm*) **~nwein** m ⟨bot⟩ *p.-leaved vine*

Pet·it [-ti] f ~/ ⟨typ⟩ *brevier*

Petiti·on f ~/~en [-tsi'o:n] *petition* **~sweg** m; auf dem ~e *by way of p.* **≈·ieren** vi [h] (um, für) *to* (*submit a*) *petition* (*for*)

Petref·akt n ~(e)s/~e(n) ⟨geol⟩ *fossil, petrifaction* **~enkunde** f *palæontology* **Petro-~chem·ie** [f] *petrochemistry*; **≈ch·emische** Produkte [pl] *-chemicals* **Petr·oleum** n ~s/ *petroleum, rock-oil* || (rohes) *crude* od *mineral oil* || (Leuchtöl) *illuminating oil* **~felder** n pl *oil-fields* pl **~kocher** m *p.-stove* **~lager** n ⟨geol⟩ *oil-deposit* **~lampe** f *p.-lamp* **P·etrus** m Petri/ [npr] *Peter* || ⟨fig⟩ *Clerk of the weather*; ~ meint's gut *the weather god means well* || Petri Heil! *good luck at fishing!*

P·etschaft n ~(e)s/~e *seal, signet, s.-s.* **~ring** m *signet-ring* **~stecher** m *seal-engraver* **petsch·ieren** vt [h] *to seal*

P·etticoat [-ko:t] m ~s/~s (Halbunterrock) *petticoat*

°**p·etto** It: in ~ h *to have .. up one's sleeve*

Pet·unie f ~/~n ⟨bot⟩ *petunia*

Petz m ~es/~e; Meister ~ (Bär) (*Master*) *Bruin* **~e** f ~/~n *bitch* || *she-bear* || ⟨fam⟩ = Petzer(in) °**p·etzen** vt/i [h] ⟨fam⟩ (über [acc]) *to tell tales* (*of, about*), ⟨fam⟩ *to peach* (*on, against*) || ⟨school sl⟩ *to sneak* (*against*) | ⟨dial⟩ (= pfetzen) = zwicken, kneifen °**P·etzer** m ~s/~ (~in f) *tell-take*; ⟨sl⟩ *sneak*, ⟨Am⟩ *snitch*

pex·ieren vt [h] = pekz·ieren

Pfad m ~(e)s/~e *path, track*, ⟨hors⟩ *piste* Fr || ~ der Freude *the primrose path* || ⟨fig⟩ krumme ~e *crooked ways* pl **~finder** m *path-finder*; *boy-scout* (älterer) *rover*; (f *girl guide*) || ⟨fig⟩ *pioneer* | internationales ~lager *World Rover Moot*; ~treffen [n] (regional) *camporee*; Welt≈ ⟨Am⟩ *Jamboree* | ~tum [n] *scouting* **≈los** a *pathless*; *trackless* || *inaccessible*

Pfaff(e) m ~n/~n *priest* || ⟨fam⟩ *parson* || ⟨dero⟩ *shaveling* || ⟨pol⟩ *clerical* **Pf·affen- ~gewalt** f *pr.ly power* **~gezücht** n *clerical band* || ⟨sl⟩ *black brigade* **~holz** n *wood of the spindle-tree* **~hütchen** n ⟨bot⟩ *spindle-tree* **~knecht** m *slave of pr.s, pr.-ridden p* **~latein** n *monkish Latin* **~stück** n ⟨cul⟩ *Pope's eye* **~trug** m *pr.craft* **~wesen** n, **~wirtschaft** f *clerical doings* **Pf·affentum** n ~(e)s/ *pr.hood, clericalism* || *Popery* **pf·äffisch** a *clerical, pr.-like* || ⟨dero⟩ ~ gesinnt *pr.-ridden*

Pfahl m ~(e)s/≈e *pale, stake, pile*; [koll pl] ⟨a.⟩ *paling* || (Stange) *pole* || (Stütze) *prop* || (Pfosten) *post* || ⟨surv⟩ *picket, rod* || Schand≈ *pillory* | ≈e einrammen *to drive in* od *ram down piles* || (Tier) an e–n ~ binden *to stake*; durch ≈e gestützt *staked down* (*tent*) | ⟨fig⟩ ein ~ im Fleisch *a thorn in the flesh* od *in one's side* || in *or* zw s–n vier ≈en *within one's four walls* **~bau** m ⟨arch⟩ *pile-work*, ⟨hist⟩ *lake-dwelling* | **~-** *lacustrine* (*age*) **~brücke** f *pile-bridge* **~bürger** m *suburban citizen*; ⟨dero⟩ *cit* || ⟨fig⟩ *Philistine* **~bürgertum** n *Philistinism* **~graben** m *palisaded ditch* **~hecke** f *paling, palisade* **~muschel** f *toredo* **~ramme** f *pile-driver* **~rost** m *pile grating*; *grillage* **~werk** n *timber-work*; *pile-work, paling*; ⟨mil⟩ *stockade, palisade* **~wurm** m ⟨zoo⟩ *shipworm* **~wurzel** f ⟨bot⟩ *tap-root* **~zaun** m *palisade, paling*; ⟨Am⟩ *picket fence* **pf·ählen** vt [h] *to fasten* od *fence with stakes* od *pales* || ⟨arch⟩ *to drive in* od *ram down piles* || *to tie up, to train* (*on stakes*), *to prop* (*up*) || *to enclose with a paling* | (als Strafe) (jdn) *to impale* (*a p*) **Pf·ählung** f *impalement*

Pf·alz f ~/~en *palace* || ⟨geog⟩ *Palatinate*; Kurfürst v der ~ *Elector Palatine* **~gericht** n *imperial court of justice* **~graf** m *Count Palatine* **≈gräflich** a *belonging to a C. P.* **~grafschaft** f *Palatinate, County Palatine* **Pf·älzer 1.** m *inhabitant of the Palatinate* || *wine grown in the P.* **2.** ≈ a, **pf·älzisch** a *Palatine*

Pf·and n ~(e)s/≈er **p**l*edge*, **p***awn* (Flaschen≈ *b. refund*; Hinterlegung *deposit*) || (Spiel) *forfeit* || (Bürgschaft) *security* || (Hypothek) **m***ortgage* | ein ~ einlösen *to redeem a pl.* || ein ~ geben *to give security* od *a pl.* (f *for*); (Spiel) *to pay a forfeit* || etw als ~ geben *to give a th as security* || gegen *or* auf ~ leihen *to lend against security, upon p.* || zum ~e setzen *to* **p***awn*, **m***ortgage*; *to pl.* (*one's word, honour*) || ≈er spielen *to play at forfeits* || was soll das ~ in m–r Hand? *what shall he do to whom this belongs?* || ein ~ verfällt *a pl. expires* **~brief** m ⟨com⟩ *m.*(*-bond*), (*m.*) *debenture* || ⟨jur⟩ *m.-deed*; Hypothekenbank≈ ⟨m. m.⟩ *m. bond* **~bürge** m *hostage* **~darlehen** n *loan on s.* **~geber** m *m.r, pl.r* **~gebühr** f *interest on m.* **~gläubiger** m *m.e, hypothecary* **~haus** n *p.-broker's shop, p.shop*; ⟨Am⟩ *loan-office* **~hinterlegung** f *deposit* **~holz** n ⟨min⟩ *repair-timber* **~inhaber** m *holder of a pl.*; *pawnee, m.e, pl.e* **~lehen** n *fees m.d* **~leihe** f = ~haus **~leiher** m *p.broker* || s–e Uhr ist beim ~ .. *is in p.*, ⟨fam⟩ *up the spout* **~lösung** f *taking out of p.* **~nehmer** m *p.ee* **~objekt** n *p.ed article, pl.* **~recht** n ⟨jur⟩ *lien* | ~sgläubiger [m] *lienor* **≈rechtlich** a *hypothecary* **~schein** m *p.-ticket* **~schilling** m *money received on a p.ed subject* **~schuld** f *hypothecary debt, m.* **~schuldner** m *m.r*, ⟨jur⟩ *mortgagor* **~sicherheit** f *hypothecary security* **~stall** m ⟨jur⟩ *pound*; in den ~ sperren *to pound* **~stück** n *pl.* **~verleiher** m *p.broker* **~verschreibung** f, **~vertrag** m = ~brief **≈weise** adv *by way of pl., by m.* od *p.* **pf·andbar** a *mortgageable* **pf·ändbar** a *distrainable, seizable* **pf·änden** vt [h] *to levy distress* od *execution*; ⟨jur⟩ *to seize* || (jdn or etw) *to distrain* (*upon*), *to attach* (wegen *for*) || *the beds cannot be distrained on* || (Vieh) *to pound, to impound* || jdn ~ l ⟨jur⟩ *to levy a distress upon a p* **Pf·änder** m ~s/~ *distrainer, executor, bailiff* **Pf·änderspiel** n (*game of*) *forfeits* pl || ~ spielen *to play at f.s* pl **Pf·ändung** f ~/~en ⟨jur⟩ *seizure, attachment, distraint, distress* **~sbefehl** m *warrant of distress*; ⟨engl jur⟩ *distringas* L **≈sfreier** Betrag *minimum amount exempt from execution* **~protokoll** n ⟨jur⟩ *fieri feci* L

Pf·anne f ~/~n *pan* || ⟨cul⟩ (aus *in*) (*frying-*) *pan* || (Kohlen≈) *brazier* || ⟨mach⟩ *brass, pillow* || (gr Siede≈ in Brauereien etc) *copper* || (Gelenk≈) ⟨anat⟩ *socket* || ⟨arch⟩ *pantile* || (Gewehr≈) *priming-* od *powder-pan* | Pulver auf die ~ schütten *to prime a gun* || auf der ~ h ⟨fig⟩ *to have on the stocks* || in der ~ braten *to fry* || in die ~ hauen ⟨fig⟩ *to put to the sword, to cut down* od *to pieces*, ⟨fam⟩ *to chop into mince-meat* || schnell (Eier) in die ~ schlagen *to knock up* (*omelets*) || (Gold) in der ~ waschen *to pan* **Pf·annen- ~dach** n *pan tiling* **~deckel** m *cover of a pan* || ⟨hist⟩ *hammer* (*of a gun*) **~flicker** m *tinker* **~geld** n *brewing-*

-tax **~haus** n *salt-works* pl **~meister** m *inspector of salt-works* **~schloß** n *hammer* (*of a gun*) **~-schmied** m *pansmith* **~stiel** m *handle of a pan* **Pf·änner** m ~s/~ *salt-maker* || *owner of salt--works* | **~schaft** f [abstr] *ownership of s.-w.*; [konkr] *owners of s.-w.* **Pf·annkuchen** m *pancake* || (mit Obst) *fritter* || (Berliner) (*filled*) *doughnut*, ⟨Am⟩ *sinker* (backen *to make*) | °platt wie ein ~ *all of a heap*

Pf·arr- **~acker** m *glebe*(*-land*) **~amt** n, **~dienst** m ⟨allg⟩ *cure of souls* || *parsonage, office of a parson* || *benefice, incumbency* || ⟨C. E.⟩ *rectory* || *pastorate* || (v. Dissidenten) *ministry* **≈amtlich** a *parochial* **~bezirk** m *parish* **~buch** n *parochial register* **~dorf** n *parochial village* **~gebühren** f pl *parson's fees* pl **~gehilfe** m *curate* **~gemeinde** f *parish* | ~mitglied [n] *parishioner* **~gut** n *parochial estate* **~haus** n *parson's house, parsonage* || ⟨C. E.⟩ *rectory, vicarage* || ⟨scot⟩ *manse* **~herr** m *parson* || ⟨C. E.⟩ *rector, vicar* **~kind** n *parishioner* **~kirche** f *parish-church* **~land** n *glebe*(*-land*) **~le-h(e)n** n *advowson* **~schule** f *parochial school* **~-sprengel** m = ~bezirk **~stelle** f (*church*) *living, parsonage* **~wohnung** f *parson's house, parsonage* **~zehnte** m *parochial tithe* | **Pf·arre** f ~/~n = Pfarramt, ~bezirk, ~gemeinde, ~haus, ~stelle || erst die ~, dann die Quarre *first a living, then wiving* **Pfarr·ei** f ~/~en *parsonage* **Pf·arrer** m ~s/~ ⟨allg⟩ *parson, clergyman* || ⟨C. E.⟩ *rector* (mit allen Einkünften), *vicar* (ohne diese) || (bei Dissidenten) *minister, pastor* || °unter uns ~s-töchtern *between you and me and the bed-post*

Pf·au m [~(e)s⟨poet⟩ ~en/~e(n⟨poet⟩)] *peacock* || junger ~ *peachick* || ⟨her⟩ *pawn* || ~en [pl] *peafowl* || der ~ schlägt (ein) Rad .. *spreads out its train* **~fasan** m *argus-pheasant* **~hahn** m *peacock* **~henne** f *peahen* **Pf·auen-** **~auge** n ⟨ent⟩ (Tag≈) *peacock butterfly* || (Nacht≈) *eyed hawk--moth* **~feder** f *peacock's feather* **~schwanz** m *peacock's train* od *tail* **~taube** f *fantail*(*-pigeon*)

Pf·effer m ~s/ *pepper* || ganzer ~ *corn* od *round p., p.corns* pl || gestoßener ~ *ground p.* || spanischer ~ *red* od *Cayenne p., cayenne*; ⟨bot⟩ *capsicum* | ⟨fig⟩ *pep* | im ~ s *to be in a pickle* || das ist starker ~ *that's a bit too strong* || wo der ~ wächst ⟨fam⟩ *at Jericho, a thousand miles off*; jdn dahin wünschen, wo .. *to wish a p at the bottom of the* (⟨Am⟩ *Red*) *Sea* || ~ u Salz (Anzug) *a p. and salt suit* **~baum** m *p.-tree* **~büchse** f *p.-box* **~-fresser** m *p.-bird, toucan* **~gurke** f *gherkin* **~korn** n *p.corn* **~kraut** n ⟨bot⟩ *p.-grass, savory* **~kuchen** n *gingerbread* **~küchler** m *g.b.-baker* **~lilie** f *tiger--flower* **~m·inze** f ⟨bot⟩ *p.mint* **~minz-** ~likör [m] *crème de menthe*; ~plätzchen [n] *p.mint*(*--drop*); ~soße [f] *mint sauce*; ~tee [m] *m. tea* **~-nuß** f *ginger*(*bread-*)*nut* **~rohrstock** m *p.-tree cane* **~sack** m *p.-bag* || ⟨fig cont⟩ (P) *oof-bird* ⟨sl⟩; *shop-keeper* **~schote** f *chilli* **~strauch** m *p. plant* **~-streuer** m *p.-pot* **pf·eff(e)rig** a *peppered, peppery* || ⟨fig fam⟩ *peppy* **Pf·efferling** = Pfifferling **pf·ef-fern** vt [h] *to pepper*, ⟨fam⟩ *devil* °⟨a. fig⟩; *to season* || (werfen) *to pelt, to let fly* (auf *at*) || ge–rt ⟨fig⟩ *sharp*; *spiced*; *spicy* (*jokes*); *strong* (*words*); *exorbitant* (Rechnung)

Pf·eife f ~/~n (*blow-*)*whistle* || ⟨mar⟩ *pipe* || *organ-pipe* || (Quer≈) *fife* || ⟨hunt⟩ *bird-call* || ⟨phys⟩ (*sounding*) *tube* | (*tobacco-*)*pipe*; e–e gute ~ Tabak *a good p. of t.* | e–e ~ (sein Pfeifchen) rauchen *to smoke a pipe* (*to puff away at* od *to enjoy one's pipe*) || e–e ~ anrauchen (stopfen) *to season* (*fill*) *a pipe* | ⟨fig⟩ nach jds ~ tanzen *to dance to a p's music, pipe, piping, tune*; alles tanzt nach s–r ~ *he always plays first fiddle* || ⟨prov⟩ ~n schneiden, während man im Rohre sitzt! *make hay while the sun shines*! | °⟨sex⟩ sich die ~ verbrennen *to burn one's poker*, .. verbrannt h *to have a bad cold* **pf·eifen I.** vi/t [pfiff/gepfiffen] [h] **1.** ⟨eig⟩ *to whistle* (a. v Wind) || ⟨mus⟩ *to* (*play the*) *fife, to pipe* || ⟨hunt⟩ *to call* || (*mice*) *squeak* || (*thrushes*) *sing* || (*bucks*) *whistle* || (*bagpipes*) *skirl* || (v Geschossen, Wind) *to whiz*, (Wind) *to howl* || sein Atem pfeift *he breathes with a whistling noise* || ⟨theat⟩ *to hiss* || ⟨telv⟩ *to sing*; ⟨wir⟩ *to howl* | [dat] ~ *to whistle* (*to a dog, for a child*), ⟨mar⟩ *to call away* (*a boat*) | sich [dat] (fröhlich) eins ~ *to whistle to o.s.* **2.** ⟨fig⟩ (*of spies*, etc) → gestehen || °auf etw [acc] ~ ⟨fam⟩ *not to care a pin for, to snap one's fingers at a th* || (*you can have your fine old world*!) || → tanzen, trommeln || das soll anders ~! *I will lead you a nice dance*! || pfeift der Wind daher? ⟨fam⟩ *the wind's in that quarter, eh*? || aus dem letzten Loche ~ ⟨fig⟩ *to be on one's last legs* | sich eins ~ *to simulate unconcern* || e–n ~ (trinken) *to wet one's whistle* || wir ~ ihm was! *he may whistle for it*! *I'll see him further first* **II.** ≈ n ~s/ *piping*, etc. || ⟨wir⟩ *howl* **Pf·eifen-** **~anzün-der** m *pipe-light* **~beschlag** m *mounting of a p.* **~-deckel** m *p.-lid* || °~! *you may whistle for it*! **~ge-stell** n, **~halter** m *stand for tobacco-p.s* **~kopf** m *p.-bowl* **~räumer** m *p.-clenaer* **~rohr** n *p.-tube, -stem* **~satz** m (Schlamm) ⟨bes Am sl⟩ *goo* **~-spitze** f *p.-tip, mouthpiece of a p.* **~stiel** m *p.-stem*; das ist k–n ~ wert *I won't give a button for it* || ⟨fig⟩ ~e (dünne Beine) *broom-sticks* pl **~stopfer** m *p.-stopper* **~strauch** m ⟨bot⟩ *hogweed* || (falscher Jasmin) *mock orange*; *syringa* **~stummel** m *cutty* **~ton** m *p.-clay* **~werk** n (Orgel) *reed-stops* pl **Pf·eifer** m ~s/~ *whistler* || *fife-player, piper*

Pf·eil m ~(e)s/~e *arrow* ⟨a. traffic⟩; *dart, bolt* || den ~ auflegen *to fix* .., abschnellen *to shoot* .. || .. verschießen *to miss the mark* || mit ~en schießen *to shoot ar.s* || ~e des Spottes *jeers and gibes* **~-form** f ⟨aero⟩ *sweep back* **≈ger·ade** (geschw·ind: **≈schn·ell**) a *straight* (*swift*) *as a bolt* (*an ar.*) **~-kraut** n ⟨bot⟩ *ar.-head* **~naht** f ⟨anat⟩ *sagitta* **~(reifen)profil** n ⟨mot⟩ *herring-bone profile*: *h.-b.-tread* (*tyre*) **~regen** m *shower of ar.s* **≈-schnell** [adv] ~ fliegen ⟨a.⟩ *to arrow*; → –gerade **~schuß** m *ar.-shot* **~schütze** m *archer* **~spitze** f *ar.-head* | ~naufstellung [f] *V-formation* **~stellung** f ⟨aero⟩ *swept-*(*back*) (*wing*) **~tragfläche** f *ar.-type wing* **~wurfspiel** n *darts* pl **~wurm** m ⟨zoo⟩ *ar.--worm* **~wurz** f (~mehl [n] ⟨cul⟩) *ar.-root*

Pf·eiler m ~s/~ *pillar*; ⟨a.⟩ *column* (Säule) || (Brücken≈ etc) *pier* || ⟨arch⟩ (Grund≈) *foundation*; Mittel≈ *bearing shaft*; (Stütz≈) *prop, support, buttress* || (Pfosten) *post* || ⟨fig⟩ *fundamental principle* **~abbau** m ⟨min⟩ *panel work* **~bogen** m ⟨arch⟩ *pier-arch* **~brücke** f *br. resting on piers* **~haupt** n *starling*; *cut-water* **~säule** f *stele* **~spie-gel** m *pier-glass* **~tisch** m *pier-table* **~weite** f *intercolumniation*

Pf·ennig m ~(e)s/~e (abbr ₰) (= $^1/_{100}$ Mark, $^1/_5$ *penny*) || ohne e–n ~ Geld *penniless* || k–n ~ h *to have not a p. to bless o.s. with* || nicht e–n ~ mehr *not a farthing more* || mit ~en rechnen *to think of p.ies* || wer den ~ nicht ehrt, ist des Talers nicht wert *who needs not a p. shall never have* (*m*)*any*, (vgl.) *take care of the pence, and the pounds will take care of themselves*; *p.es make pounds* **~fuchser** m *scrape-* od *pinch-p.* **~fuchser·ei** f *niggardliness, mean economy* **~kraut** n *money-wort* || *p.cress* **≈weise** adv *by p.-worths, in driblets*

Pf·erch m ~(e)s/~e *fold, pen*; ⟨Am a.⟩ *corral* | ~hütte [f] *shepherd's cot*; ~lager [n] *sheep fold*; ~schlag [m] *penning* (*of cattle*) **pf·erchen** vt [h] *to pen, to fold* || ⟨fig⟩ *to cram*

Pferd n ~(e)s/~e **A. 1.** *horse* (→ Roß etc) || ⟨poet, rhet⟩ *steed* || ⟨fam⟩ *nag*, ⟨Kindersprache⟩ *gee*(*-gee*) || ~ u Wagen *carriage and pair*; ⟨Am⟩ *rig* **2.** ⟨chess⟩ *knight* **3.** ⟨gym⟩ *vaulting-horse*; Übungen am ~ *vaults over* od *on the horse* **4.**, ⟨mar⟩ *foot-rope, horse* **B.** Arbeits≈ *farm-, work--horse*; *dobbin*; ⟨fig⟩ *sloghorse* || leicht bockend *skittish* || H·and≈ *led h.* || K·utsch≈ *carriage-, cab-, shaft-h.* || L·ast≈ *cart-, dray-h.* || R·enn≈

racing h. ‖ R·eit∼́ *mount* ‖ leicht scheuendes ∼ *shier* ‖ S·ee∼́(chen ⟨ich⟩) ⟨myth⟩ *sea-h.* ‖ ·Übungs∼́ → A. 3. ⟨a.⟩ *wooden h.* ‖ Z·ug∼́ *draught-h.* **C. alt** *crock*; bockig *bucker, buck--jumper*; edel *well-bred*; feurig *high-mettled*; gescheckt *piebald*; hartmäulig *hard-mouthed*; kl ∼ ⟨a.⟩ *pony*; kl dick *cob* ‖ leicht, schwer *light, heavy h.* ‖ linkes, rechtes ∼ (im Gespann) *near h., off-h.*; schlecht *jade* ‖ schnittig *stylish* ‖ (kl) schweres Zug∼́ (*punch*) *dobbin* ‖ das Trojanische ∼ *the wooden h.* ‖ wildes (kalifornisches) ∼ *bronco* **D.** das ∼ **schlägt aus,** schnaubt, wiehert .. *lashes out, snorts, neighs* | die ∼e sind gesattelt *the horse are ready saddled* ‖ ⟨mil⟩ mit ∼en versehen *to horse* ‖ ein ∼ besteigen *to mount a h.* **E.** ⟨mil⟩ **an** die ∼e! *stand to your h.s!* ‖ **aufs** ∼ steigen *to mount a h.* od *on h.back* ‖ sich aufs ∼ schwingen *to swing o.s. into the saddle* ‖ °**nach** den ∼en sehen *to do the gentleman, to shoot the lion* ‖ **vom** ∼e absitzen *or* steigen *to dismount* ‖ (Gegner) v ∼e stechen *to unsaddle* ‖ v ∼en gezogen ⟨a.⟩ *h.-drawn* ‖ **zu** ∼e sitzen *to be on h.back*; (*how charmingly she sits her h.*) ‖ zu ∼e steigen *to get on h.back, to mount* ‖ Jäger, Wettkampf zu ∼e *mounted rifle, contest* ‖ 800 Mann zu ∼e *800 horse* **F.** ⟨fig⟩ mit e–m Gesicht **wie ein** ∼ .. *like a horse's* ‖ ⟨mil sl⟩ immer sachte mit die [statt: den] jungen Pferde(n)! *steady, steady!, don't bully the troops! come off the grass* | er **arbeitet wie** ein ∼ .. *like a h.* ‖ das ∼ beim Schwanze aufzäumen *to put the cart before the h.* ‖ nicht *or* k–e 10 ∼e bringen mich dahin *wild h.s will not persuade me (to do), .. won't drag me into (doing)* ‖ °ihm gingen die ∼e durch *he flew off the handle* ‖ das hält kein ∼ aus *that's beyond endurance* ‖ mach mir nicht die ∼e scheu *don't try to make me uncertain* ‖ mit dem kann man ∼e stehlen *he's game for anything,* ⟨bes Am⟩ *he's up to snuff* | **auf hohem** ∼e sitzen (sich aufs hohe ∼ setzen) *to ride (mount) the high h.* ‖ aufs falsche ∼ setzen *to back the wrong h.* ‖ die ∼e **hinter** den Wagen spannen *to put the cart before the horse* ‖ **vom** ∼ auf den Esel k *to go from bad to worse* **Pf·erdchen** n ⟨a.⟩ *pony* ‖ pl ⟨racing⟩ *ponies* **Pf·erde-** °**∼äpfel** m pl *h.-droppings* **∼arbeit** f ⟨fig⟩ *collar-work, drudgery* **∼́artig** a *horsy* **∼arzt** m *h.-doctor, vet(erinary surgeon)*; ⟨mil⟩ (*N.C.O.*) *farrier* **∼-ausfuhrverbot** n *law prohibiting the export of h.s* **∼ausstellung** f *h.-show* **∼bahn** f *(h.-)tramway* | ∼wagen [m] *(h.-)tramcar* **∼bändiger** m *h.-breaker* **∼behang** m *trappings* **∼beschlag** m *h.shoeing; h.shoes* **∼bestand** m *actual stock* (⟨mil⟩ *force*) *of h.s* **∼betrieb** m *h.-traction* **∼bohne** f ⟨bot⟩ *h.-bean* **∼box** f *loose-box* **∼bremse** f *h.-fly* **∼decke** f *h.-rug, -blanket, -cloth*; die ∼ auflegen *to put the blanket* **∼dieb** m *h.-thief; rustler* **∼droschke** f *(h.-)cab* **∼egel** m ⟨zoo⟩ *h.-leech* **∼fleisch** n *h.-flesh* od *-meat* **∼fuhrwerk** n *h. and cart; h.-drawn vehicle* **∼fuß** m ⟨übtr⟩ *club-foot*; ⟨fig⟩ da zeigt sich der ∼ *that shows the cloven hoof*; Ritter v ∼ (Teufel) *cl. h., Old Scratch,* ⟨hum⟩ *old gentleman* **∼futter** n *fodder, provender* **∼gasmaske** f *h. mask* **∼geschirr** n *harness, gear* **∼getrappel** n *tramping of h.s* **∼-gurt** m *h.-girth* **∼haar** n *h.hair* **∼hals** m *neck and shoulders* [pl] *of a h.* **∼halter** m *keeper (of h.s)* ‖ *groom,* ⟨mil⟩ *batman* **∼handel** m *h.-dealing* **∼-händler** m *h.-dealer* **∼haut** f *h.-hide* **∼heilkunde** f *veterinary art*; ⟨mil⟩ *farriery* **∼huf** m *h.'s hoof* **∼junge** m *stable-boy* **∼kamm** m *curry-comb* **∼kastanie** f *h.-chestnut* **∼kenner** m *judge of h.-flesh* **∼knecht** m *groom, footman, lackey* ‖ (im Wirtshaus) *ostler* **∼kopf** m *h.'s head* **∼koppel** f *paddock* **∼kraft** f = ∼stärke **∼krippe** f *h.-crib, manger* **∼kumt** n *h.-collar* **∼kur** f ⟨med⟩ *drastic treatment* **∼länge** f *h.-length* ‖ ⟨sport⟩ um 2 ∼n *by 2 lengths* **∼last** f *h.-load* **∼lazarett** n *veterinary hospital* **∼lenker** m ⟨hist⟩ *charioteer* **∼liebhaber** m *h.--fancier* | ∼·ei [f] *fancy for h.s; horsiness* **∼makler** m *h.-broker, -dealer* **∼markt** m *h.-market, -fair* **∼́mäßig** a *h.like* ‖ °⟨fig⟩ *excessive* **∼milch** f *mare's milk* **∼mist** m *h.-dung* **∼narr** m *horsy (wo)man* | er hat e–e **∼natur** *he's as strong as a h.* **∼netz** n *h.-net* **∼omnibus** m *h.-omnibus* **∼pflege** f *h. attending* **∼pfleger** m *groom,* ⟨mil⟩ *batman*; ⟨Am⟩ *wrangler* **∼putzzeug** n ⟨mil⟩ *h.-kit* **∼rennbahn** f *racecourse* **∼rennen** n *h.-race, -racing* **∼sattel** m *saddle* **∼-schau** f *h.-show* **∼schlitten** m *h.-sleigh, -sledge* **∼-schwanz, ∼schweif** m *h.'s tail* ‖ ⟨übtr cosm⟩ *pony tail* **∼schwemme** f *h.-pond* **∼stall** m *stable* **∼-stammrolle** f ⟨mil⟩ *muster-roll of h.s* **∼stärke** f (abbr PS) *metric h.-power (HP)*; errechnete ∼ *indicated h.-p. (IHP)*; → Bd. I S. 1120 | ∼leistung [f] *h.-p. output* **∼striegel** f *curry-comb* **∼tränke** f = ∼schwemme **∼(transport)wagen** m ⟨rail⟩ *h.--box* **∼verleiher** m *livery-stable keeper* °**∼verstand** m *little intelligence* **∼wagen** m *h. carriage* **∼wechsel** m *relay of h.s* **∼wurm** m ⟨zoo⟩ *bot(t)* **∼zucht** f *h.-breeding* **∼züchter** m *breeder of h.s*

Pf·ette f ∼/∼n ⟨arch⟩ *purlin*

pf·etzen vt [h] *to pinch, twitch, tweak (a p)*

Pfiff m ∼(e)s/∼e **1.** *whistle,* ⟨rail a.⟩ *shriek* ‖ e–n ∼ tun *to blow a wh.* **2.** ($^1/_8$ l = $^1/_4$ pint) *a sip (of wine)* ‖ ⟨fig⟩ *a mere nothing,* (zeitlich) *a twinkle* **3.** ⟨fig⟩ *trick* ‖ *a drop (of spirits)* ‖ mit ∼ *with a crunch*; Modernität mit ∼ *with-it-ness* ‖ den ∼ heraus h, verstehen *to know the tricks, to have the knack of a th*; → pfeifen **pfiff** 1. & 3. sg pret v pfeifen **pf·iffig** a *cunning, crafty, artful, casuistic(al)* ‖ *wide-awake* ‖ *sly* (*dog* Bursche) ‖ ⟨sl⟩ *downy* (*old bird*); *fly* (*customer*) ‖ ⟨Scot⟩ *pawky* ‖ [pred] *up to snuff,* ⟨sl⟩ *all there* | **∼́keit** f ∼/ *cunning, artfulness, craftiness* **Pf·iffikus** m ∼/–usse *cunning fellow, artful dodger* ‖ ⟨fam⟩ *sly-boots*

Pf·ifferling m ∼(e)s/∼e ⟨bot⟩ *chanterelle* ‖ ⟨fig⟩ *trifle, fig, straw* ‖ ich mache mir k–n ∼ daraus *I don't care a fig*; ⟨bes Am⟩ *I couldn't care less* ‖ (*not worth a*) *rush, bean, rap, leek* ‖ (*I wouldn't give a*) *farthing (for it)* ‖ .. k–n ∼ genützt *that's done us no earthly good*

Pf·ingst- **∼abend** m *Whitsun eve* **∼b·este(s)** n: mein ∼s (Kleid) *my Sunday best* **∼blume** f *peony* **∼feiertag** m *Whitsuntide holiday* **∼fest** n das ∼ *Whitsuntide,* ⟨ec⟩ *Pentecost* **∼m·ontag** m *Whit Monday* **∼ochse** m *ox adorned at Whitsuntide*; °geputzt wie ein ∼ ⟨sl⟩ *dressed up like a plush horse* **∼rose** f *peony* **∼(s·onn)tag** m *Whit Sunday* **∼vogel** m *yellow thrush* **∼woche** f *Whitsun week* **∼zeit** f *Whitsuntide* **Pf·ingsten** n & f [mit art. pl konstr] *Whitsuntide,* ⟨ec⟩ *Pentecost*; ⟨Am a.⟩ *Pinkster* **pf·ingstlich** a *of* od *for Whitsun,* ⟨ec⟩ *Pentecostal*

Pf·irsich m ∼(e)s/∼e *peach* **∼blüte** f *p.-blossom* **∼blütfarbe** f *p.-colour* **∼́blütfarben** a *p.--bloom* [attr]; *p.-coloured* **∼branntwein** m *p.--brandy* **∼garten** m *peachery* **∼kern** m *p.-stone* **∼ Melba** ⟨hot cul⟩ *pêche* Fr od *p. melba* **∼rost** m ⟨bot⟩ *p.-blight*

Pfl·anz- **∼eisen** n *dibble* ‖ mit dem ∼ arbeiten *to dibble* **∼holz** n *planting-stick*; *dibble* **∼ort** m *settlement* **∼reis** n *scion* **∼schule** f *nursery* ‖ ⟨fig⟩ *seminary* **∼staat** m *colony* **∼stadt** f *colonial town* **∼stätte** f ⟨fig⟩ *nurse(ry), seedbed, seminary* **∼-stock** n = ∼holz **∼volk** n *colonial people* **pfl·anzbar** a *plantable* **Pfl·änzchen** n ∼s/∼ *little plant* ‖ ⟨fig⟩ *tender plant*; junges ∼ *chit of a girl* ‖ leichtsinniges ∼ *fly-away, flighty fellow*; nettes ∼ *bad lot* **Pfl·anze** f ∼/∼n **1.** ⟨eig⟩ *plant* ‖ Humus∼́ *saprophyte* ‖ Luft∼́ *epiphyte* ‖ schmarotzende ∼ *parasite* **2.** ⟨fig⟩ *shoot, plant* **3.** ⟨fam⟩ Berliner ∼ *regular Berlin girl* **4.** ⟨fam & iron⟩ e–e saubere, nette ∼ *a nice article* ‖ ⟨dero⟩ *trollop, bad lot* **pfl·anzen** vt [h] *to plant, set, dibble* ‖ *to pot* | ⟨fig⟩ *to plant* ‖ ⟨mil⟩ *to mount* (*cannon* Geschütze) ‖ e–m etw ins Herz ∼ *to implant a th into a p* | °jdn ∼ (narren) [österr] pflanz d–e Großmutter! *tell* *that to the horse-marines* **Pfl·anzen-** [in comp oft] *vegetable* (*v.ble*) **~abdruck** m *impression of a plant* **~anatomie** f *phytotomy* **~art** f *species of plants* **~̊artig** a *v.ble* **~asche** f *v.ble ashes* pl **~bau** m *agricultural botany* **~beet** n *bed* (*of plants*) **~beschreibung** f *phytography, descriptive botany* **~-buch** n *herbal* **~chemie** f *phytochemistry* **~entst·ehungslehre** f *phytogenesis* **~erde** f *v.ble mould* **~ernährungslehre** f *agrobiology* **~esser** m *vegetarian* **~farbe** f *v.ble dye* **~faser** f *v.ble fibre* **~fett** n ⟨cul⟩ *v.ble fat* od *shortening* **~forscher** m (*expert*) *botanist* **~̊fressend** a *graminivorous* **~geographie** f *botanical geography* **~gesellschaft** f *plant association* **~gewächse** n pl *v.bles* pl **~gift** n *v.ble poison* **~kenner** m *botanist* **~kost** f *v.ble diet* od *food* **~-krankheit** f *disease in plants* **~kunde** f *botany* **~leben** n *vegetation, v.ble life* ‖ ein ~ führen *to vegetate* **~lehre** f *phytology, botany* **~natur** f *v.ble nature* **~öl** n *v.ble oil* **~physiologie** f *v.ble physiology* **~presse** f *botanist's press* **~reich** n *v.ble kingdom, flora* **~̊reich** a *rich in plants* **~saft** m *sap* ‖ ⟨pharm⟩ *juice of plants* **~sammeln** n *collecting plants, botanizing* **~sammlung** f *herbal* **~säure** f *v.ble acid* **~schleim** m *mucilage* **~schutz(dienst** m) m *phytopathological service* | ~mittel [n] *pesticide,* ⟨chem⟩ *agrochemical* **~stoff** m *v.ble matter* **~symbolik** f *symbolic meaning of plants* **~system** n *classification of plants* **~tier** n *zoophyte* **~veredelung** f *plant breeding* **~wachstum** n *vegetation, v.ble growth* **~welt** f = ~reich **~wuchs** m *vegetation*; grüner ~ *verdure* **~zelle** f *v.ble cell* **~zucht** f *cultivation of plants* **Pfl·anzer** m ~s/~ **1.** *planter, cultivator* **2.** *colonist, settler* **3.** *owner of a plantation, planter* **4.** *dibble* **pfl·anzlich** a *vegetable* (*oil*); ⟨scient⟩ *vegetal* **Pfl·änzling** m ~(e)s/~e ⟨bot⟩ *seedling-plant, young plant, set* ‖ ⟨fig⟩ *foster-child* **Pfl·anzung** f ~/~en *plantation* ‖ (Kolonie) *colony, settlement*

Pfl·aster n ~s/~ **A. 1.** ⟨med⟩ *plaster* ‖ englisches ~ *court pl.* ‖ (Not~̊) *adhesive* (*tape*) **2.** ⟨übtr⟩ *patch* (*on a shoe, vest*) ‖ *beauty-patch* **3.** ⟨fig⟩ *salve, compensation* | ein ~ auflegen, anbringen *to put on* od *apply a pl.*; ⟨fig⟩ *to heal a sore* ‖ ⟨fig⟩ ein ~ bek *to get a compensation* ‖ ein ~ schmieren, streichen *to spread a pl.* ‖ das ~ zieht *the pl. draws* **B. 1.** (Straßen~̊) *pavement* (*p.t*) **2.** (an Böschungen) *pitching* **3.** ⟨arch⟩ *paved floor, flagging* = **eingelegtes** ~ *tesselated p.t* ‖ holperiges ~ *pebble p.t* ‖ ⟨fig⟩ ein **teures** ~ *an expensive place to live in* | das ~ **aufreißen** (besetzen, rammen) *to take up* (*ram*) *the p.t* ‖ ~ legen in, auf *to pave* ‖ ⟨fam⟩ ~ treten *to saunter, loaf about* ‖ ⟨fig⟩ aufs ~ werfen *to turn* (⟨fam⟩ *chuck,* ⟨soc⟩ *lock*) *out* **~arbeit** f *paving, paver's work* **~brecher** m *p.g-breaker* **~einfassung** f *border of a p.t* **~fliese** s *p.g tile* **~geld** n *pavage* **~kasten** m *plaster-box* ‖ ⟨fam fig⟩ (P) ⟨surg⟩ *sawbones* **~meister** m *master paviour* **~probe** f ⟨med⟩ (z. Allergiediagnose) *patch test* **~ramme** f *p.g-beetle* **~setzer** m *paviour* **~stein** m *p.g-stone* **~straße** f *paved road* **~treter** m ⟨fam⟩ *loafer, idler, lounger* **~ziegel** m *p.g-brick* **~zoll** m *excise* **Pfl·ästerchen** n **1.** = kl Pflaster **2.** *beauty-patch* **3.** ⟨fig iron⟩ *soft sawder* **Pfl·asterer** m ~s/~ *paver, paviour* **pfl·astern** vt **1.** *to pave, cobble, flay* **2.** *to patch* (*up*) (*boots*) **3.** ⟨med⟩ *to plaster* **4.** ⟨übtr allg⟩ *to pitch* (*s.th. s.where*)

°**Pfl·äumchen** n ⟨sex⟩ (*her*) *fig* **Pfl·aume** f ~/~n **1.** ⟨eig⟩ *plum* ‖ gedörrte ~ *prune* ‖ geschmorte ~n *stewed prunes* pl **2.** °⟨fig⟩ *biting remark*; ⟨fam⟩ *leg-pull* | (P) ⟨fam⟩ *dope, dummy* **~nbaum** m *pl.-tree* **~̊nförmig** a *pruniform* **~̊nkern** m *pl.-stone* **~̊nkuchen** m ⟨Ger⟩ *pl.-tart* **~̊nmus** n *pl.-jam* **~schlehe** f ⟨bot⟩ *bullace* **~̊ntorte** f ⟨engl⟩ *pl.-tart* **~̊nweich** a *soft as a ripe pl.* ‖ ⟨fig⟩ *weak*; ⟨pol⟩ *wavering, without backbone*

Pfl·ege f ~/ **A. 1.** (Behandlg.) *care* (*of books, hands, hair*) ‖ *culture* (*of the body*) ‖ *bringing up, rearing* (*of children & animals*) **2.** (Kranken~̊) *nursing* **3.** *cultivation* (*of flowers, gardens, health, arts*) ‖ *encouragement* (*of arts*); Vertrauens~̊ → Kontakt– **4.** *guardianship, tutelage* **5.** *administration* ‖ *superintendence, direction* | ⟨tech⟩ *keeping, maintenance*; ~ u Wartung *preventive m.*; aufmerksame ~ *care and attention* **B.** in ~ *at nurse* ‖ (jdm) gute ~ angedeihen l *to take great care of, to nurse well* ‖ gute ~ h *to be well looked after, to have good nursing* ‖ in ~ geben *to put* (*out*) *to nurse* ‖ in ~ nehmen *to take charge of* **~amt** n *board of guardians* ‖ *guardianship* **~̊bedürftig** a *needing care* **~̊befohlen** a *committed to* (*a p's*) *charge* **~befohlene(r** m) f *charge* **~dienst** m *service trade*; *s.g*; „~̊" ⟨mot⟩ *s. station* **~eltern** pl *foster-parents* pl **~heim** n *charity* ‖ ⟨med⟩ *nursing-house,* ⟨Am⟩ *-home* **~hieb** m ⟨for⟩ *improvement cutting* **~kind** n *nursling, foster-child* ‖ (Mündel) *ward* **~̊los** a *neglected* **~mutter** f *f.-mother* ‖ ⟨fig⟩ *protectress* **~plan** m ⟨tech⟩ *maintenance schedule* **~sohn** m *f.-son* **pfl·egen I.** vt [reg] [h] **A.** *to wait upon, to nurse* (*a sick p*); gesund ~ *to n. .. back to health* ‖ (of nurse) *to attend* ‖ *to look after, take care of* (*a child*) ‖ *to care for* (*one's hair, nails*) ‖ *to train* (*one's beard*) ‖ *to tend* (*flocks, invalids, machines, one's nails*) ‖ ⟨mot⟩ *to service*; ~ l: *can I leave my car with you for s.g*? ‖ *to cultivate* (*flowers, gardens, habits, a p's friendship*) ‖ *to cultivate, foster, encourage* (*arts & sciences*) ‖ *to foment* (*a sentiment*) | (achten auf) *to attend to* | etw bes ~ *to make a speciality of* (*a subject*) | **sich** ~ *to take care of o.s.* **B.** s–n Bauch ~ *to cherish one's stomach* ‖ Rücksprache ~ mit *to have a talk with* ‖ Umgang ~ mit *to associate* (*to have* od *keep up intercourse*) *with* ‖ Unterhandlungen ~ *to be in treaty* **C.** [oft mit altem gen] vt [reg] (*or* [irr] [pflog/gepflogen]) *to carry on, to exercise a th, to apply o.s. to a th* ‖ ⟨bib⟩ er pflegte sein [gen] *he took care of him* ‖ (verwalten) *to administer* | s–s Amtes ~ *to perform the duties of one's office* ‖ s–s Leibes ~ *to coddle, pamper o.s.* ‖ der Liebe ~ *to enjoy the pleasures of love* ‖ sie pflogen Rats (mit–e–a) *they took counsel* (od *due deliberation*) (*together*) ‖ der Ruhe ~ *to* (*take a*) *rest, to take one's ease* **D. gepflegtes** Äußere *cultured appearance* ‖ (sorgsam) gepflegte Hände *well-cared for* (*exquisitely kept*) *hands; her hands were meticulously tended* **gepflogene** Unterhandlungen *negotiations conducted* **II.** vi [h] [reg] **(z tun)** (oft mit pleonastischem „häufig, immer, oft") *to be wont, used, accustomed to*; *to be given to, in the habit of* ‖ *to wont* od *tend* (*to do*) ‖ *to use* ([nur pret] *he used* [ju:st] *to say* = *he would say*) ‖ er pflegt .. *he usually sleeps long, he is in the habit of sleeping long, it is his custom to sleep long* ‖ *dogs will scratch* | **so** pflegt es (meist) z gehen *it generally happens like that, that is usually the case, such is life!, that is the way of the world!* ‖ .. **soweit** Ehen gl. z s ~ (*his m. is happy*) *as m.s go* ‖ **wie** man zu sagen pflegt *as the saying is* ‖ wie er zu tun pflegte *as his wont was* ‖ wie es so zu geschehen pflegt *as it generally happens* ‖ .. wie .. z s ~ *he was, as policemen go, honest* **Pfl·eg- ~er** m ~s/~ *fosterer* ‖ ⟨med⟩ *nurse* ‖ ⟨jur⟩ *guardian*; (Verwalter) *curator, trustee, administrator*; ⟨jur a.⟩ *committee* (*of a p* od *an estate*) → Vermögens– ‖ ⟨fig⟩ *promoter, patron*(*ess* ~in f) **~̊lich** a *careful, gentle* **~ling** m *foster-child* ‖ = Pflegesohn **~schaft** f ~/~en ⟨jur⟩ *guardianship* **~ung** f ~/~en *attendance, fostering, nursing* **Pfl·icht** f ~/~en **A.** *duty* (gegen *to*(*wards*)) ‖ (Verpflichtung) *liability, obligation* ‖ (Amt) *office* | eheliche ~ *conjugal duty* ‖ .. heilige ~ *it is your bounden duty* ‖ s–e (°verdammte) ~ u Schuldigkeit tun *to keep* od *hold one's end up* (⟨sl⟩ *to do one's damnedest*) | (Aufgabe) *it is up to Mr. S. to show* **B.** jdm die ~ **auferlegen** *to make it incumbent upon a p* (*to do*) ‖ s–e ~ (voll u ganz) erfüllen, tun *to do* (*fulfil*) *one's d.* (*to the utmost*) (an *by a p*), *to play one's part* (*in a th*); *to do one's bit, to keep up one's end*; ⟨mil⟩ *to discharge one's d.* (*to the bitter end*) ‖ e–r ~ nachgehen *to tend to a d.* ‖ die erste ~ gilt der W. *the first allegiance must be to truth* ‖ wie es ihre ~ war *as in d. bound* C. **auf** ~ u Gewissen *conscientiously* ‖ es **für** s–e ~ halten *to deem* od *think it one's d.* ‖ **in** ~ nehmen *to bind by oath* ‖ jdn **zu** s–r ~ anhalten *to urge a p to perform his d.* ‖ es sich zur ~ m *to make it one's d., to make a point of it* ‖ e–m etw zur ~ m *to urge a th on a p* **~anker** m ⟨mar⟩ *sheet-anchor* **~anteil** m *quota* **~arbeit** f *compulsory work* **~beitrag** m *contingent*; *quota* **~̈bewußt** a *conscious of one's d.* **~bewußtsein, ~gefühl** n *sense of duty* **~dienst(zeit** f) m (*period of*) *compulsory service* **~eifer** m *zeal* **~̈eifrig** a *zealous* **~en-** ~ethos [n] *ethics of duty*; ~-konflikt [m] *collision*; ~kreis [m] *responsibilities* pl; ~lehre [f] *deontology* pl; **~erfüllung** f *performance of one's d.* **~exemplar** n *presentation copy* **~fach** n *required subject* **~̈frei** a *exempt of d.* **~gebot** n *moral obligation* **~̈gemäß** [a] *incumbent, due*; [adv] *as in duty bound, loyally* **~gesetz** n *moral law* **~̈getreu** a *dutiful, conscientious, loyal* **~jahr** n *compulsory service* **~kommandierung** f *mandatory assignment* **~landung** f *comp.y landing* **~leistung** f *performance of a d.*; *oath of allegiance* | über das **~maß** hinausgehend *supererogatory* **~̈mäßig** a *dutiful* (vgl. **~̈gemäß**) **~̈schuldig** [a] *in duty bound* ‖ [adv] *duly* **~teil** n *legal portion* ‖ e–n aufs ~ setzen *to give a p merely his l.-p.* **~̈treu** a *dutiful, devoted* **~treue** f *dutifulness, devotion* **~̈vergessen** a *unmindful of one's duty, undutiful*; (untreu) *disloyal*, ⟨Am⟩ *derelict* | ~heit [f] *dereliction* (*of duty*); *delinquency*, aus ~ verlassen *to desert* | *disloyalty* **~verletzung** f *violation* od *neglect of d.* **~versäumnis** f *lapse* od *neglect of d.*; *shortcoming* **~versicherung** f *obligatory* od *compulsory insurance*, **~wert** m *specification* od *contract value* **~̈widrig** a *contrary to duty, undutiful*; *disloyal* **pfl·ichtig** a *obliged, in duty bound* .. **pflichtig** suff .. able: melde~ *repartable*

Pfl·ock m ~(e)s/~̈e *plug, peg*; kl ~ *pin*; *tent--peg*; Anbinde~̈ *picket*; Ruder~̈ *thole* ‖ mit e–m ~ befestigen *to peg* ‖ ⟨fig⟩ e–n ~ zurückstecken *to come down a peg or two* ‖ wie ein ~ *like a block of wood* **~ahle** f *pegging-awl* **~holz** n ⟨carp⟩ *pegwood* **pfl·öcken** vt [h] *to peg, plug, picket*

pflog 1. & 3. sg pret v pflegen → C.

Pfl·otsch m ~es/, **Pfl·üder** m ~s/ Sw (= Schneematsch) *sludge*

pfl·ücken vt [h] *to pick* (*cotton, hops, flowers*) ‖ *to gather* (*fruit, salad, a bunch of flowers*) ‖ (rupfen) *to pluck* (*a goose*, etc.) ‖ v ihr selbst gepflückt *picked by her own hands* ‖ [dat] *he picked her a posy* od *a p.. for her*

Pfl·ug m ~(e)s/~̈e *plough*, ⟨Am⟩ *plow* ‖ hinter dem ~e gehen *to follow the p.* ⟨a. übtr⟩; unter dem ~ *arable* (*land*); *under crop*; unter den ~ bringen *to put to the p.* ‖ der ~ nährt, das Schwert wehrt *the p. traces the furrow, but the sword defends it* **~arbeit** f *p.ing* **~balken** m *p.-beam* **~eisen, ~-messer** n *coulter* **~karren** m *p.-truck* **~kette** f *p.--trace* **~schar** f *p.share* **~schmied** m *p.wright* **~sterz(e** f) m *p.-handle* **pfl·ügbar** a *arable* **pfl·ügen** vt/i [h] *to plough* (⟨fig⟩ Sand *the sands*, mit fremdem Kalb *with another man's heifer*) ‖ zum erstenmal ~ *to break up* **Pfl·üger** m ~s/~ *ploughman*

Pf·ort- ~ader f ⟨anat⟩ *portal vein* **~luke** f ⟨mar⟩ *dead-light, port* **Pf·örtchen** n ~s/~ *little gate* od *door, wicket* **Pf·orte** f ~/~n *door, gate* ‖ ⟨geog⟩ *gate*; *low pass*; ⟨mar⟩ *port*; *gate* (*the Golden G.* [*Frisco*]) ‖ ⟨hist⟩ die Hohe (Ottomanische) ~ *the Sublime Porte* **Pf·örtner** m ~s/~ *porter, door--keeper* ‖ ⟨anat⟩ *pylorus* ‖ ~haus [n] *keeper's lodge* ‖ ~klappe [f] ⟨anat⟩ *pyloric valve*

Pf·osten m ~s/~ *post* ⟨a. ten⟩ ‖ (Pfahl) *stud*; *pale, stake* ‖ (Tür~̈, Fenster~̈) *jamb*, (steinern) *mullion* ‖ (Treppen~̈) *newel* ‖ ⟨min⟩ *puncheon*

Pf·ote f ~/~n *paw, claw* ‖ (of fox) *pad* ‖ ⟨fam⟩ (Hand) *fist* (*give me your f.*); *paw, flapper*; ⟨Am⟩ *mitten*; ⟨sl⟩ *bunch of fives* ‖ ⟨fig fam⟩ (Handschrift) *scrawl* ‖ e–e schlechte ~ schreiben *to write an ugly fist* ‖ e–m eins auf die ~n geben *to give a p a rap on the knuckles* ‖ gib Pfötchen! *give your paw!* ‖ ⟨fig⟩ sich die ~n verbrennen *to burn one's fingers*

Pfriem m ~(e)s/~e, **~e** f ~/~n *punch, awl, pricker* ‖ ⟨typ⟩ *bodkin* **~̈en** vt [h] *to punch* **~en-~gras** n ⟨bot⟩ *matweed* **~ginster** m, **~kraut** n ⟨bot⟩ *broom*

Pfr·opf m ~(e)s/~e & ~̈e; **~en** m ~s/~ *cork, stopper* ‖ die ~en knallen l *to drink* (*a lot of*) *champagne* ‖ ⟨allg⟩ *plug* ‖ ⟨mil⟩ (Gewehr~̈) *wad*, (Geschütz~̈) *tampion* ‖ *clot* (*of blood*), ⟨path⟩ *thrombus* ‖ ⟨med⟩ *tampon, wad* (*of cotton*) ‖ ⟨fig⟩ *chubby man* **~bastard** m *graft-hybrid* **~-messer** n *grafting-knife* **~reis** n *graft, scion* **~spalt** m *slit for grafting* **~wachs** n *grafting-wax* **pfr·opfen** vt [h] (stopfen) *to cram*; (*the hall was crammed full*) ‖ ⟨hort⟩ *to graft* (*in the rind, in the slit*); *to engraft* (auf *upon*, in *into*) ‖ (Flaschen) *to cork* **~̈geld** n *corkage* **~̈zieher** m *corkscrew* **Pfr·opfer** m ~s/~ *grafter*

Pfr·ünde f ~/~n *benefit*, ⟨ec⟩ *prebend* ‖ (Pfarrstelle) *living, benefice*; fette, magere ~ *fat, poor living* ‖ (ohne Seelsorge) *sinecure* ⟨a. fig⟩ **~nbesetzungsrecht** n *advowson* **~besitzer, ~inhaber** m = Pfründner 1. **~gut** n *glebe lands* **~handel** m *simony* **Pfr·ündner** m ~s/~ ⟨ec⟩ **1.** *beneficiary* **2.** (Domherr) *prebendary* **~haus** n **1.** = Pfarrhaus **2.** *hospital, almshouse*

ˣ**pf·üdi** (= behüt dich) (Gott) *God speed you*

Pfuhl m ~(e)s/~e *pool, puddle*; ⟨fig⟩ *cloaca, cesspool* ‖ ⟨fig⟩ Sünden~̈ *sink of corruption* ‖ Höllen~̈ *bottomless pit* | ~schnepfe [f] ⟨orn⟩ *bar-tailed godwit*

Pfühl m (& n) ~(e)s/~e **1.** *bolster, pillow, cushion* **2.** ⟨arch⟩ *torus*

pfui! *fie! shame!* ‖ *pish! tut!* ‖ (vor Ekel) *ugh! faugh!* ‖ ~ schäme dich! *for shame!* ‖ ~ über dich! *fie upon you!* ‖ ~ Spinne! *how nasty!* ‖ ~ Teufel! *faugh!* ‖ ~ rufen über [acc] *to cry out at*

Pf·und n ~(e)s/~e (Gewicht → Bd. 1. S. 1115) *pound* (*2 p.s of butter*) | (Geld) *pound*; ⟨sl⟩ *quid* (100 *q.*) ‖ ~ Sterling *p. sterling* ‖ fünf ~ *five p.s* (abbr £ 5) ‖ 1 Pfd in Silber *a p.'s worth in silver* ‖ fünf ~ u 10 Schilling *five p. ten* (*shillings*) | nach dem ~ *by the p.* ‖ ich wiege 162 Pfd *I weigh 11 stones 8 lbs* ‖ sein ~ vergraben *to hide one's talents* **~birne** f *large pear* **~geld** n *p.age* **~gewicht** n *p.-weight* **~hefe** f *German yeast* **~leder** n *sole--leather* **~note** f *p.-note* **~̈weise** adv *by the p.* **~-zoll** m *p.age* **..pfünder** m ⟨mil⟩ Zehn~ *ten--pounder* °**pf·undig** a ⟨sl⟩ *ripping, wizard, slashing, rattling*; → knorke **pf·ündig** a *of one pound* ‖ fünf-~ *weighing five pounds* ‖ ein 10-~es Geschütz *a ten-pounder* °**pfunds**! intj (°a. a) *screaming, scrummy, smashing, slashing, slap-up*

°**Pf·unds-** [in comp] ⟨sl⟩ *ripping, rattling*; *thumping* (*dinner*) **~bemerkung** f *scorcher* **~ding** n *topper* **~k·erl** m ⟨sl⟩ *rattler, brick, topper, slasher*; (P) *regular fellow*, ⟨Am⟩ *r. guy*, ⟨sl⟩ *stunner* **~mädel** n *smatterer*; °⟨sex⟩ *bit of jam* **~sache** f *slasher* **~verpflegung** f ⟨mil sl⟩ *snifty conner*

Pf·uscharbeit f = Pfuscherei **pf·uschen** vt/i [h] **1.** ⟨agr⟩ *to peel off the turf* **2.** ⟨fam⟩ *to bungle, botch*; ⟨sl⟩ *to foozle* ‖ in etw [dat] ([acc] hinein) ~ *to dabble in, to tamper with a th* ‖ jdm ins Handwerk ~ *to trespass on another's preserves* **3.** es pfuscht *it hisses* **Pf·uscher** m ~s/~ *bungler, botcher*, ⟨Am sl⟩ *dub* ‖ ⟨fig⟩ *dabbler*; ⟨bes phot⟩ *smudger*; (Arzt) *quack* **~·ei** f ~/~en *bungling* (*work*), *scampwork, blunder* ‖ ⟨arch⟩ *jerry-*

-building || ⟨sl⟩ *foozle* **≗haft** [a] *like a bungler*, etc || [adv] *in a bungling manner*

Pf·ütze f ~/~n **1.** *puddle, pool, slough, plash* || ⟨min⟩ *pool* (*of water*) **2.** ⟨min, mar⟩ *bailing-pail* **pf·ützen** vt [h] ⟨min⟩ *to pump out water* **≗wasser** n *puddle* od *stagnant water* **pf·ützig** a *plashy, slushy, muddy*; *full of puddles*, etc.

Ph.. [f–] siehe auch F ..

Ph·aeton [ˈfaetɔn] m ~s/~s *phaeton*

Ph·alanx f ~/Phal·angen ⟨mil hist⟩ *phalanx*

Phanerog·ame f ~/~n ⟨bot⟩ *phanerogam*(*ous plant*) **Phänom·en** n ~s/~e *phenomenon*, pl *-ena* **≗·al** a *phenomenal* **phänot·ypisch** a *phenotypic* (*characteristics*) | P–typus [m] ⟨biol⟩ *phenotype*

Phantas·ie f ~/~n **1.** *fancy, fantasy*; *imagination* || mit einiger ~ *with a stretch of i.*, → überlassen; **2.** ⟨liter⟩ *fiction, tale* || ⟨mus⟩ *reverie, fantasia* **3. ~n** pl *fantastic ideas, fancies, visions*, (*day-*) *dreams* pl **4.** (Übertreibung) *embroidery* **5.** (e–s Kranken) *wanderings, ravings* pl **≗arm** a *unimaginative* **≗begabt** a → –voll **~bild** n *vision*; *mind-picture* **~gebilde** n pl *figments* pl **~kostüm** n *fancy dress* **≗los** a = –arm **≗mensch** m *fantast* **~preis** m *fancy price* **~stück** n ⟨mus⟩ *fantasia* || ⟨arts⟩ *arabesque* **≗reich,** **≗voll** a *fanciful, imaginative* **phantas·ieren** vi [h] *to indulge in fancies, to dream* || ⟨med⟩ *to rave, wander*; *to be delirious* || ⟨mus⟩ *to extemporize, to improvise* **Phant·ast** m ~en/~en *fantast*(*ic*), *visionary, visionist* | **~er·ei** f ~/~en *fantasy, fantasticalness, visionariness* || *fancy* || *fantastic ideas* pl || ~en [pl] *vagaries* pl || sich in ~en einlassen *to throw one's cap over the windmill* **≗isch** a *fantastic* (*idea, speed*); *fanciful* || ⟨fam⟩ *excellent, first-rate*; *fantastic*; ⟨Am sl⟩ *swell* || °~e Angelegenheit *wildcat matter*; ~e Idee, Geschichte ⟨sl⟩ *dream*; ~e Preise *fancy prices*; ~es Wesen *fantasticalness, quaintness* **Phant·om** n ~(e)s/~e *phantom, vision* || *ghost* || ⟨fenc⟩ *dummy*, ⟨hist⟩ *Turk's head, quintain* (am ~ fechten .. *against* ..) || ⟨anat⟩ *anatomical model*

Ph·arao ~(s)/–ra·onen *Pharaoh* || ⟨cards⟩ *faro* **~ratte** f *ichneumon* **phara·onisch** a *Pharaonic*

Pharis·äer m ~s/~ *Pharisee* **~tum** n *Pharisaism* **pharis·äisch** a *Pharisaic*(*al*), *sanctimonious*

Pharma- ~kol·og(e) m ~en/~en *pharmacologist* **~kop·öe** f ~/ *pharmacopœia* **~z·eut** m ~en/~en *pharmaceutist* || (Apotheker) *pharmaceutical chemist* || *chemist's assistant* || *student of pharmacy* **~z·eutik** f *pharmaceutics* pl **≗-z·eutisch** a *pharmaceutic* **~z·ie** f ~/ *pharmacy*

Ph·arus m ~/~ & ~se *pharos, lighthouse*

Ph·ase f ~/~n *phase* ⟨a. el⟩ || (Stufe) die letzte ~ *the final stages* pl || ⟨sex⟩ Erregungs≗ *excitement ph.*; Plateau≗ *plateau ph.*; Orgasmus≗ *orgasmic ph.*, (⟨a.⟩ *melting period*); Rückbildungs≗ *resolution ph.* | **~n-** ≗falsch [a] *misphased*; ≗gleich [a] *similar phased* (*waves*); ~raum [m] ⟨stat, commun⟩ *ph. space*; ~schieber [m] *ph. modifier*; ≗verschoben [a] *out-of-ph.* (*waves*); ≗weise [a & adv] *ph.-by-ph.* | **≗nhaft, phasisch** a *phasic*

Phen·ol n ~s/ *phenol*; *carbolic acid*

Phi·ale f ~/~n *phial, vial*

Phil- ~adelphia n (Stadt) (*Penn*[*sylvania*] *U.S.A.*) **~anthr·op** m ~en/~en *philanthropist* | ≗isch [a] *philanthropic* | –ismus [m] ~/ *philanthropism* **~atel·ie** f ~/ *philately* **~harmon·ie** f ~/~n *Philharmonic Hall* **~·ippika** f ~/–ken ⟨a. fig⟩ *philippic* **~ipp·inen** f pl *Philippine Islands* (auf .. *in* ..) **~ipp·opel** n ⟨Bulg⟩ *Philippopolis*

Phil·ister m ~s/~ ⟨a. stud sl⟩ *Philistine* || ⟨fig⟩ *cit*, ⟨fam⟩ *muff, fog*(*e*)*y* || ⟨univ⟩ *townsman*; ~ u Studenten *town and gown* **≗haft** a *Philistine, narrow-minded, prosaic* **~haftigkeit** f, **~tum** n *Philistinism, narrow-mindedness, fogyism* °**-t·erium** n ~s/ ⟨stud⟩ *ordinary citizen's life* || [koll] *ex-student members of a student's corporation* (= Alte Herren) **philistr·ös** a = philisterhaft

Philo- ~d·endron n ⟨bot⟩ (gelappt *cut-leaf*) *ph.n* **≗g·yn** a (Ggs miso–) *philogynous* **~l·og(e)** m ~en/~en *philogist* || Alt≗ *classical scholar, student of classics* || Neu≗ *teacher* od *student of modern languages* | ~entag(ung [f]) [m] *philological congress* | ~enverband [m] ⟨Ger⟩ *association of teachers* **~log·ie** f ~/~n *philology*; klassische ~ *Humanities* pl **≗l·ogisch** a *philological* || ~-historische Disziplinen *humanities* **~s·oph** m ~en/~en *philosopher*; ~ der Landstraße ⟨Am⟩ *hobo* || als ~ (betrachten) .. *philosophically* | ~·aster [m] *philosophist*; ~·em [n] ~(e)s/~e *theorem*; ~·ie [f] ~/~n *philosophy*; ≗·ieren [vi h] *to philosophize* (über *on*); ≗isch [a] *philosophic*(*al*), ⟨Am univ⟩ *academic* (Fakultät *department*)

Phi·ole f ~/~n *phial, vial*

Phl·egma n ~s/ *phlegm* || *indolence* **-m·atiker** m ~s/~ *phlegmatic* od *indolent* od *lazy person*

..phob·ie f [suff] z Bildung v Subst. m. d. Bedeutung v „Angst vor, Abneigung gegen" ..-*phobia*

†**Phok·äa** n (alte Stadt in Lydien) *Phocæa*

Phon n ~s/~e *phon* **~·em** n ~(e)s/~e *phoneme*; Variation e–s ~s (= Allophon) (z. B. k in Koch & Küche) *v. of a ph.* | ~- *phonematic* **~·etik** f ~/ *phonetics* pl [mst sg konstr] **~er** m *phonetician* **≗·etisch** a *phonetic* (*transcription*) || ~es Lautzeichen *ph. symbol* **~messungen** f pl: ~ m *to take decibel readings* **~stärke** f *noise level*

†**Phön·ikien,** †**Phön·izien** n (Küstenlandschaft Vorderasiens) *Phœnicia* †**Phön·izier** m, **~in** f, **phön·izisch** a *Phœnician*

Ph·önix m ~es/~e (ein *the*) *phœnix, phenix* ⟨a. fig⟩

Ph·ono- ≗g·en a *phonogenic* (*p* ⟨film, telv⟩) **~gr·aph** m ~en/~en *phonograph* **~schrank** m, **~truhe** f *radiogram*, ⟨Am⟩ *radio-phonograph* **~super** m ~s/~ *superheterodyne with turn-table*

Ph·os- ~ph·at n ~(e)s/~e ⟨chem⟩ *phosphate* **~phor** m ~(e)s/~e *phosphorus* | ≗haltig [a] *-phoric*; ~metall [n] *-phide*; ≗sauer [a] *-phorous*; ≗saurer Kalk [m] *-phate of lime*; ≗saures Salz [n] ⟨chem⟩ *-phate*; ~verbindung [f] *-phide* **~esz·enz** f ~/ *-phorescence* **~esz·ieren 1.** n ~s/ *-phorescence* **2.** ≗ vi [h] *to -phoresce* || ≗d [a] *-phorescent* **phosph·orig** a *-phorous* || ~e Säure ⟨chem⟩ *-phite*

Ph·oto n ~s/~s *photo* **~album** *-graphic album* **~chem·ie** f *-chemistry* **~ecken** f pl *-fixers* **≗-el·ektrisch** a *-electric*(*al*) **≗g·en** a ⟨film, telv⟩ *-genic* (*p*) **~geschäft** n *-graphic-materials shop* **~grammetr·ie** f ⟨a-n⟩ *photogrammetry* **~grav·üre** f *heliogravure* **~kop·ie** f *-stat* | ~ranstalt [f] *-finisher* **~kopieren** n *document copying* **~korrespondent** m *assignment -grapher* **~-MG** n *gun camera* **~modell** n (P) *pinup girl* **~mont·age** [–ɑʒe] *composite picture*; (*photo*)*montage* || ~n [pl] *overlays and inserts* **~narr** m ⟨fam⟩ *shutter-bug* **~reporter** *press -grapher* **~satellit** m *picture-taking s.* **~scheinwerfer** m *-floodlight* **~-setzmaschine** f ⟨typ⟩ *-setter*, ⟨Am⟩ *photon* **~-thek** f *print library* **~therap·ie** f ⟨med⟩ *sunray treatment* **~zelle** f *-electric cell, photocell* **Photogr·aph** m ~en/~en *photographer* | **-·ie** f ~/~n [i:en] (Kunst) (bewegter Objekte *action*) *-graphy* || (Bild) *-graph, photo*, ⟨fam⟩ *snap*(*shot*) || [in comp] → Photo .. | **~·ier-** [in comp] *-genic* (*face*) | **≗·ieren** vt/i [h] *to-graph* || sich ~ l *to be -graphed, to have one's photo*(*graph*) *taken* || sich gut ~ l *to take well* (*a woman takes better standing*) ich lasse mich schlecht ~ *I always -graph badly* | **≗isch** [a] *-graphic* || e–e ~e Aufnahme v sich m l *to have one's photo taken* || [adv] *by photography*

Phr·ase f ~/~n *phrase* || wie die ~ lautet *as the ph. goes* || ~n [pl] *windy rhetoric, claptrap* ||

(leere) ~n m *or* dreschen *to make ph.s, to indulge in claptrap, to give out mere vapourings* ‖ k–e bloßen ~n *no mere words* **~ndrescher, ~nmacher** m *ph.-monger* **~drescher·ei** f *claptrap* **≗nhaft** a *rhetorical*, ⟨fig⟩ *claptrap, windy* | ~igkeit [f] *claptrap*, ⟨sl⟩ *bromidity* **~olog·ie** f ~/~n *phraseology* **phras·ieren** vt [h] ⟨mus⟩ *to phrase* ‖ Phrasierung [f] *phrasing*

phren·etisch a *phrenetic* ‖ ⟨fig⟩ *frantic* (*applause*) **Phrenol·og(e)** m ~en/~en *phrenologist* | **~·ie** f ~/~n *phrenology* | **≗isch** a *phrenologic*(*al*)

†**Phr·ygien** n (Landschaft in Kleinasien) *Phrygia* **Phrygier(in** f) m, **ph–isch** a *Phrygian*

Phth·alsäure f *phthalic acid*

Phys·ik f ~/ *physics* pl [sg konstr]; *natural philosophy* ‖ Assistent der ~ *physics assistant* | ~stunde [f] *physics lesson*; ~unterricht [m] *physics lesson*(*s*); *science-teaching* **≗·alisch** a *physical* (*law, map*) ‖ *philosophical* (*instrument*) ‖ ~e Anstalt [f] *physical laboratory* **Ph·ysiker** m ~s/~ *physicist, natural philosopher, teacher* od *student of physics* **Ph·ysikum** n ~s/ ⟨Ger⟩ *preliminary* (*medical*) *examination* **Ph·ysikus** m ~/~se *district physician* **Physio- ~gnom** m ~en/~en *physiognomist* | ~·ie [f] ~/~n *-gnomy, countenance*, ⟨fam⟩ *phiz* | ~ik [f] *-gnomics* | ≗isch [a] *-gnomic*(*al*) **~kr·at** m ~en/~en *-crat* | ~·ie [f] *physiocracy* **~l·og(e)** m ~en/~en *-logist* | ~·ie [f] ~/~n *-logy* | ≗isch a *-logic*(*al*) **ph·ysisch** a *physical* ‖ (körperlich) *somatic*

Piac·enza [pia'tʃɛntsa] n (oberital. Stadt)

Pi·affe f ~/~n ⟨hors⟩ *piaffer* | **≗n** vi [h] *to piaffe*

Pian- -·ino n ~s/~s *cottage* od *upright piano* **~·ist** m ~en/~en; ~in [f] ~/~nen *pianist* **~o-(f·orte)** n ~s/~s *p.*(*f.*) **~·ola** n *pianola*

Piass·ava f ~/–ven ⟨bot⟩ (*Bahia*) *bast-palm* | ~besen [m] *piassava broom*; ~faser [f] *Bahia bast*

P·iccolo f ~/~ 0,2 l *quarter bottle* (0,35 pt.)

°**p·icheln** vt/i [h] *to tipple*, ⟨fam⟩ *booze* **Pichel·ei** f *tippling* **P·ichler** m *tippler, boozer, tosspot*

p·ichen vt [h] *to pitch* ‖ (Schuhe) *to wax*

pick intj *pick, tick* ‖ ≗ [m] *prick, picking*; ⟨orn⟩ *peck* ‖ ⟨fig⟩ e–n ~ h auf *to have a secret grudge against* | ~fein [a] *smart*, ⟨sl⟩ *spiffy*; *dandy*; ≗napf [m] ⟨mil fam⟩ *porringer* **P·icke** f ~/~n *pick* (*axe*) | [österr] = Leim, Klebstoff **P·ickel** m ~s/~ **1.** *pimple, whelk* **2.** *ice-axe* **3. ~flöte** f *piccolo* **~haube** f *spiked helmet* **~hering** m ⟨theat hist⟩ *Merry Andrew* **p·ick(e)lig** a *pimpled, pimply* **p·icken** vi/t [h] *to pick* (a. P) ‖ ⟨orn⟩ *to peck* **P·icknik** n ~s/~e & ~s *picnic*, ⟨Am⟩ *basketdinner* ‖ ein ~ veranstalten *to get up a picnic* | ~korb [m] *luncheon-b.*

P·idgin ['pidʒin] → Pigeon

Piedest·al [pje:des'tɑ:l] n ~s/~s *pedestal* ‖ auf ein ~ erheben *to p.*

P·iek f ~/~en ⟨mar⟩ (Raum & Gaffel) *peak* ‖ → a. pick, Pik **~fall** n ⟨mar⟩ *peak halyard*

p·ieken vt [h] **1.** *to prick* **2.** ⟨mar⟩ *to toss* (*oars*)

Piem·ont n ⟨It⟩ (Landschaft) *Piedmont* **~·ese** m, **~·esin** f, **≗·esisch** a *Piedmontese*

p·iep intj *peep* ‖ nicht ~ sagen *not to utter a word* | (du) hast'n ≗! *you're mad*! °**~e, ~eg·al** a [pred] das ist mir ~ ⟨sl⟩ *I don't care a hoot, damn, fig* **~(s)en** vi [h] *to pule*, (of mice) *squeak* ‖ ⟨orn⟩ *to chirp, cheep, peep, pipe* | °bei dir piept's wohl? *you are a bit dotty* ‖ es ist zum Piepen *it makes me hoot* | °**≗en** pl (Geld) ⟨sl⟩ *dough*, → Pinke **≗er** m ~s/~ ⟨orn⟩ *titling*; *pipit* **~p(s)ig** a **1.** *piping*, etc.; *reedy* (*voice*) **2.** ⟨fig fam⟩ *peaky, weakly* ‖ *sickly, poorly* **≗matz** m *dicky-bird* ‖ ⟨Ger hum⟩ *order of the Red Eagle* ‖ *bat in the belfrey* (⟨a.⟩ –vogel) **~stimme** f *squeaking voice*

P·ier m ~(e)s/~e **1.** ⟨mar⟩ *pier* **2.** *lobworm*

°**p·iesacken** vt [h] *to pester, torment, vex*

Piet·a f ~/ *Our Lady of Pity* **Piet·ät** f ~/ *piety* ‖ *reverence* ‖ *filial love* **≗los** a *irreverent* **~losigkeit** f *impiety*; *want of reverence* | aus **~sgründen** *for sentimental reasons* **~swert** m *s.al value* **≗voll** a *reverent* **Piet·ismus** m ~/ ⟨ec Ger hist⟩ *pietism* (*Protestant Reformation*; *17th c*) ‖ *bigotry* **Piet·ist** m ~en/~en *pietist* ‖ *devotee, bigot* | **-er·ei** f ~/ *bigotry* | **≗isch** a *pietistical* ‖ *bigoted*

°**P·ietzen** f pl *charms* pl, ⟨vulg⟩ *bubbies* pl

p·iffp·aff!, piff! paff! (puff!) intj *ping*! ‖ *bang*! ‖ *puff, puff*!

P·igeon- ['pidʒin] ~-Englisch n *pigeon* od *pidgin English*

Pigm·ent- ~druck m *pigment-printing* **~fleck** m ⟨bot, zoo⟩ *p.-spot*

Pik m ~s/~s **1.** (Berg) *peak* **2.** (Groll) *grudge, rancour* ‖ e–n ~ h auf *to bear a gr. against*, ⟨fam⟩ *to have an edge against* **3.** n ~s/ *spade*(*s* pl) **~-b·ube** m (**~d·ame** f) *knave* (*queen*) *of spades* **≗-f·ein** a *smart, tiptop, stylish* **pik·ant** a *piquant, pungent* ‖ ⟨cul⟩ *highly seasoned*; *hot* ‖ ⟨fig⟩ (*highly*) *piquant, spicy, risky, suggestive* (*jokes*) ‖ *saucy, racy* (*girl*) ‖ **das ≗e** n *piquancy, pungency* **Pikanter·ie** f ~/~n *piquant* od *spicy story* ‖ [abstr] *piquancy* [pl *-cies*]

Pikard·ie f (ehem. franz. Prov.) *Picardy*

pikar·esk a *picaresque* (*novel*)

P·ike f ~/~n *pike* ‖ → a. Pik 2. ‖ von der ~ auf dienen *to start at the bottom of the ladder*; ⟨mil⟩ *to rise from the ranks*, .. gedienter Offizier ⟨fam⟩ *ranker* ‖ v der ~ auf ⟨Am⟩ *the hard way* **Pik·ee** m ~s/~s (Stoff) *piqué, quilting* **Piken·ier** m ~(e)s/~e ⟨mil, hist⟩ *pikeman* **Pik·ett** n ~(e)s/~e ⟨cards⟩ *piquet* ‖ ~ spielen *to play piquet* ‖ ⟨mil⟩ *picket, outpost* **pik·ieren** vt [h] *to nettle, pique, offend* ‖ ⟨hort⟩ *to plant out* | **sich** auf etw ~ *to pique o.s. on a th*; *to be set on doing* **pik·iert** a *piqued, huffy* ‖ gegen *or* auf jdn ~ s *to take a pique against a p* | **≗heit** f *pique* (über *at*)

P·ikkolo m ~s/~s **1.** *boy-waiter* **2.** (Flöte) *piccolo* **3.** → Piccolo

Pik·ör m ~s/~e ⟨hunt⟩ *whip*; *whipper-in*

Pikr·insäure f *picric acid*; *trinitrophenol*

P·ikten m pl *Picts* pl **~wall** m *Picts' Wall*

Pil·aster m ~s/~ ⟨arch⟩ *pilaster* **P·ile** n ~s/~n ⟨phys⟩ *nuclear pile* (erstellen *to set up*; lief an .. *went into operation*)

Pil·atus m (Bergstock am Vierwaldstätter See) (*Mount*) *Pilatus*

Pil·au, Pil·aw m ~s/ ⟨Turk cul⟩ *pilaf*(*f*), *pilav*

P·ilger m ~s/~ (a. P·ilgrim) *pilgrim* **~fahrt** f *p.age* **~hut** n *p.'s hat* **~kleid** n *p.'s garb* **~leben** n *earthly p.age* **~muschel** f *scallop* **~schaft** f = ~fahrt **~schar** f *troop of p.s* **~stab** m *p.'s staff* **~tasche** f *p.'s scrip* **p·ilgern** vi [s] *to make* (od *go on*) *a pilgrimage, to wander* ‖ ⟨fig⟩ *to flock, stroll* ‖ *long lines of travellers wound into the place*

Pil·iermaschine f *soap mill*

P·ille f ~/~n *pill* (⟨a. anti-baby⟩ die ~ *the* [*contraceptive*] *pill*) kl ~ *pellet* ‖ ~n drehen *to make p.s* | ⟨fig⟩ e–e bittere ~ *a bitter p. to swallow* ‖ die ~ schlucken ⟨fig⟩ *to take one's medicine* ‖ e–e ~ überzuckern *to sugar* od *gild a p.* **~ndose, ~nschachtel** f *p.-box* °**~ndreher** ⟨fam⟩ *p.-monger* **~nfarn** m *pillwort* **~nkäfer** m *p.-beetle* °°**P·ille-Paul** m ⟨anti-baby⟩ *Pope Paul*

Pil·ot m ~en/~en *pilot* ‖ **~in** f ~/~nen *woman p.*

P·ilsen n (Stadt in Böhmen) **P·ils(ner)** n ~s/~ (helles Bier) *pilsner*

P·ilz m ~es/~e ⟨bot scient⟩ *fungus* ‖ (eßbarer) *mushroom* ‖ (nicht eßbarer) *toadstool* ‖ in die ~e gehn, *to m.*; *to go m.-gathering*; ⟨fig fam⟩ *to go to the dogs*; *to run away* ‖ wie ~e aus der Erde schießen *to shoot up like m.s* **≗ähnlich** a *fungoid* **~befall** m *fungoid growth* | ≗en [a] *fungused* **≗förmig** a ⟨scient⟩ *fungiform* **~hütchen** n ⟨bot⟩ *pileus* **~kenner** m ⟨scient⟩ *fungologist* °**~köppe** (–pfe) m pl *beatles, mods, rockers* **~krankheit** f *mycosis* **~sauce** f *mushroom sauce* **~säure** f ⟨chem⟩ *fungic acid* **~spore** f *fungus-spore* **~stiel** m ⟨bot⟩ *stem of a fungus* **≃tötend** a *fungicide* **~vergiftung** f *m. poisoning*

Pim·ent m & n ~(e)s/~e *pimento, Jamaica pepper, allspice*

ˣ**p·impe** a [nd] = schnuppe **≃l·ei** f ~/~en **1.** *effeminacy; pampering* **2.** *complaining* **| ≃l- ~-fritze** m, **~liese** f *coddle; delicate* od *sickly p* **~lig** a *pimping, peaky, sickly, delicate* ‖ (weichlich) *effeminate* ‖ *fussy* **~ln** vi [h] **1.** *to be peaky* etc. **2.** *to complain, whine* **P·impernuß** f *pistachio-nut*

Pimpf m ~(e)s/~e (P) (*wolf-*)*cub* ⟨fig, a. nazi⟩

Pimpin·elle f ~/~n; Pimpern·ell m ~(e)s/~e *pimpernel, shepherd's clock, burnet*

Pinakoth·ek f ~/~en *picture-gallery*

Pin·asse f ~/~n *pinnace*

°**Pind** m ~(e)s/~e *pen*(*is*); ⟨vulg⟩ *cock, pintle*

ˣ**p·ingelig** a = pimpelig ‖ ⟨bes⟩ *fussy* (kleinlich); *niggling*

Pingu·in m ~(e)s/~e *penguin* ‖ ⟨aero⟩ *tail--sitter*

P·inie ~/~n ⟨bot⟩ *stone-pine* | ~ninseln [f pl] → Pityusen; ~nnuß [f] *p.-kernel*; ~zapfen [m] *p.-cone*

pink intj ~, ~! *ping, ping*! °**P·inke(p·inke)** f ~/ ⟨sl⟩ *oof, dust, pelf, brass; chinkers* pl, *jink* (*cash*) ‖ ⟨cards, dice⟩ *stake* °**P·inkel** m ~s/~ *smarty, dandy, tiger, toff, spiv, swell*; ⟨Am sl⟩ *dude* °**p·inkeln** vi [h] ⟨fam⟩ *to piddle, pee* **p·inken** vi [h] **1.** *to cling-clang on an anvil* **2.** ⟨orn⟩ *to warble*

P·inne f ~/~n (Zwecke) *peg, plug* ‖ (Zapfen) *pivot* ‖ (Stift) *tack* ‖ (Nagel) *pin* ‖ ⟨mar⟩ *tenon, spindle* ‖ (Kompaß≃) *centre-pin* ‖ (Ruder≃) *tiller* **| ~n** vt *to pin* (*fast*), *to fix with pegs* etc

P·inscher m ~s/~ *kind of terrier* (→ Schnauzer) **|** °**≃n** vi [s] *to beetle* (*let's b. off*)

P·insel m ~s/~ **1.** ⟨paint⟩ *brush*; ⟨cul⟩ *pastry-b.* ‖ (feiner ~) *pencil* ‖ er malt mit kühnem ~ .. *with a bold hand* **2.** *tuft of hair* **3.** ⟨vulg⟩ *pizzle* **4.** °⟨fig⟩ (P) *simpleton, duffer*, ⟨fam⟩ *ninny*, ⟨sl⟩ *flat, goof* **~äffchen** n → Seidenäffchen **~druck** m, **~führung** f *handling of the brush; touch* **~schimmel** m *b. mould* **~stiel** m *brush-handle* **~strich** m *dash* od *stroke of the brush* ‖ ⟨paint⟩ *touch* **~züngler** m ⟨orn⟩ *lory* **Pinsel·ei** f ~/~en *daub*(*ing*) ‖ ⟨fig fam⟩ *stupidity* **P·inseler** m ~s/~ *dauber*, ⟨fam⟩ *knight of the brush* **p·inselhaft, p·inselig** a *silly, foolish, like a duffer*, etc **p·inseln** vt/i [h] *to paint, b.* ‖ (schmieren) *to daub* **|** vi [h] *to handle the b.*

°**Pint** m ~s/~e (*penis*) ⟨vulg⟩ *pintle*, → Pind

P·inte f ~/~n *pint* (= $^1/_2$ *quart*) → d.

Pinz·ette f ~/~ (*pair of*) *pincers, tweezers*

Pion·ier m ~s/~e ⟨mil⟩ *engineer* ‖ (Soldat) *sapper* ‖ ⟨fig⟩ *pioneer, trailblazer; captain* (*of industry*); ⟨SBZ⟩ Junge ~e *Young P.s* | ~leiter [m] *Y. P.s' organizer* **~arbeit** f *spade-work* ‖ ⟨fig⟩ *pioneer* od *missionary work* ‖ ~ leisten *to blaze a trail* **~aufgaben** f pl *e.r missions* **~(bau)bataillon** n *construction battalion* **~gerät** n *pioneer's tools* **~k·ampfmittel** n pl *e.r combat items* **~korps** n *corps of e.rs* **~leben** n ⟨Am⟩ *frontier life* **~offizier** m *e.r officer* **≃technisch** a *technical e.r* (*measures*) **~truppe** f *e.r corps*; ~n [pl] *e.r troops* **~·übesetzmittel** n pl *e.r crossing* od *ferrying equipment*

P·ipe f ~/~n **1.** *long cask* **2.** (*tobacco-*)*pipe*

p·ip(p)e(r)le vt/i [h] [österr] *to tipple; booze* vi

°**P·ipi** n ~/ *urine*; ~ m *to piddle, pee*; (*do*) *wee-w.*

Pips m -ses/ ⟨orn⟩ *pip* ‖ ⟨fig⟩ *weak constitution*; ⟨sl⟩ d ~ h *to be dotty*

Pir·at m ~en/~en *pirate* ‖ ~enflagge [f] *jolly Roger* **| ~er·ie** f *piracy*

Pir·äus m (Hafen v Athen) *Piræus*

Pir·oge f ~/~n ⟨mar⟩ *pirogue*

Pir·ol m ~(e)s/~e ⟨orn⟩ *yellow thrush; oriole*

Pirou·ette f ~/~n (Tanz) *pirouette, spin*

P·irsch f ~/ ⟨hunt⟩ auf die ~ gehen *to go deer--stalking*, ⟨Am⟩ *still-hunting* **~jäger** m *deer--stalker*, ⟨Am⟩ *still-hunter* **p·irschen** vt/i [h] *to stalk* (*deer, a stag*)

P·isa n (Stadt in Oberitalien)

P·isang m ~s/~s *plantain, banana tree*

p·ispern vi/t [h] *to whisper*

°**P·isse** f ~/ ⟨vulg⟩ *piss* ⟨a. fig (Bier)⟩ **p·issen** vi [h] ⟨vulg⟩ *to piss, piddle* **P·isser** m *P-maker* **Pissoir** [pis'wɑ:r] n Fr ~s/~s *urinal, lavatory*, °**P·ißpott, P·ißtopf** m ⟨fam⟩ *pot, jerry*

Pist·azie f ~/~n ⟨bot⟩ *pistachio*(*-nut*)

P·iste f ~/~n *piste; caravan trail* (*motorable c.t.*) ⟨ski⟩ *course, piste*; (Zirkus) *ring fence*; ⟨aero⟩ *runway*

Pist·ill n ~s/~e *pestle* ‖ ⟨bot⟩ *pistil*

Pist·oia n ⟨It⟩ (Stadt der Toskana)

Pist·ole 1. f ~/~n; **Pist·ol** n ~(e)s/~e *pistol*, ⟨Am a.⟩ *gun* ‖ (Selbstlade≃) *automatic*; mit gezogenen ~n *a.s cocked* ‖ jdm die ~ auf die Brust setzen *to put a p. to a p's head*; ⟨fig⟩ *to force a p by threats*; als ihm die ~ auf die B. gesetzt wurde *at the p.'s point* ‖ wie aus der ~ geschossen ⟨fam⟩ *like a shot* **2.** ⟨num⟩ *pistole* **| ~n- ~duell** n *duel* (*fought*) *with pistols* **~forderung** f *challenge to a duel with p.s* **~kappe** f *cover for a p.* **~lauf** m *p.--barrel* **~schuß** m, **~schütze** m *p.-shot* **~schußweite** (in *within*) *p.-shot* **~stand** m *p.-gallery* **~tasche** f *holster*

Pist·on [–'ɔŋ] n ⟨mus⟩ *cornet* (*a pistons*) **| ~-bläser** [m] *cornettist*

P·itch-Kontrolle f ⟨rec⟩ *pitch control*

P·itchpineholz n ['pitʃpain–] → Pechkiefer

p·itschnaß a *wet through, soaked to the bones*

pittor·esk a *picturesque*

P·ittsburg n (Stadt) *Pittsburgh* (*Penn.*)

Pity·usen f pl (span. Inselgruppe) *Pityusæ*

p·itzelig a [österr] → übelnehmerisch

Piv·ot [–'vo:] m, n ~s/~s *pivot* **|** ~geschütz [n] *p.-gun*; ~lager [n] *p. bearing* **≃·ieren** vt [h] *to p.*

Plac·et [–ts–] n L; *consent* (geben *to give*)

plac·ieren [–s–] vt [h] *to place* (*a p, a ball*)

pl·acken[1] vt [h] **1.** *to beat down, to flatten* **2.** *to patch* **3.** *to stick* **Pl·acken** m ~s/~ *patch* ‖ *blot*

pl·acken[2] vt [h] *to plague, pester* ‖ (das Volk) *to oppress* ‖ sich ~ [h] *to toil, drudge, grub, slave, plod* ‖ sich ~ u plagen *to toil and moil* **Pl·acker** m ~s/~ *pesterer* ‖ *oppressor* **| ~·ei** f ~/~en *toil, drudgery, worry, grind* ‖ ~en [pl] ⟨Am⟩ *travails*

°**pl·addern** v [h] *to pour* (*down*) ‖ *it's p.ing* (*with rain*)

pläd·ieren vi [h] ⟨jur⟩ *to plead*; ⟨fig⟩ (f *for*)

Plädoyer [–dwɑ'je:] n ~s/~s ⟨jur⟩ *final pleading* (*of the defense attorney* od *of the public prosecutor*)

Plaf·ond [–'fɔŋ] m ~s/~s *ceiling* (⟨a.⟩ *credit c.*)

Pl·age f ~/~n (Qual) *plague, torment* ‖ *trouble, trial, vexation* ‖ (Insekten≃) *pest, infestation* **|** *nuisance, calamity* ‖ *harrow* ⟨fig⟩ ‖ ⟨prov⟩ jeder hat s–e eigene ~ *we all have our troubles* ‖ jeder Tag hat s–e ~ *sufficient for the day is the evil thereof* ‖ e–n durch ~n zu (um) etw bringen *to worry a p into* (*out of*) **~geist, ~teufel** m ⟨fig⟩ *nuisance; tormentor, bore, troublesome p, pest* **pl·agen** vt [h] *to plague, pester, worry, bother, trouble, torment, vex, harass* ‖ (necken) *to tease* ‖ der Teufel plagt ihn .. *drives him* ‖ geplagt v ⟨a.⟩ *racked by, a martyr to, troubled with* (*gout*, etc) ‖ es–gte mich immer wieder ⟨Am sl a.⟩ *it kept riding me* ‖ sich ~ [h] *to toil*, etc → placken[2] ‖ sich ~ mit *to take trouble about*

Pl·agge f ~/~n ⟨agr⟩ *sod* (*of turf*) **| ≃n** vt [h] *to cut sods, to take up turf* **~npflug** m *sod knife*

Plagi·at n ~(e)s/~e *plagiarism* ‖ ein ~ begehen, **plagi·ieren** vt [h] *to p.rize* **P-giator** m ~s/–oren *p.rist*

Pl·aid [ple:t] m & n ~s/~s *plaid* ‖ (Reisedecke) *rug* **~riemen** m *rug-strap* **~rolle** f *hold-all*

plaid·ieren = plädieren **Plaidoyer** = Plädoyer

Plak·at n ~(e)s/~e *poster, placard, bill* || (Aufstell≃) (*show*)*card* || ~e anschlagen, ankleben verboten! *stick* (⟨Am⟩ *post*) *no bills*! || mit ~en bekleben, durch ~e bekannt m *to placard* **~anschläger** m *bill-sticker* **≃farbig** a *poster-* (⟨zoo a.⟩ *flag-*)*coloured* **~säule** f *advertisement-pillar* **~-schrift** f *poster-type* **~träger** m *sandwich man* **~wirkung** [f] erzeugen *to posterize* **Plak·ette** f ~/~n *plaque*(*tte*), *badge* **plak·ieren** vt [h] (mit Gold etc) *to plate*

Pl·an I. [m] ~(e)s/≃e **1.** [abstr] *plan* ⟨a. mil⟩: ~ f die Gefechtsführung *operation plan* || *project, arrangement* || *design, intention* || (geheimer) *plot* || *scheme, idea* || ⟨pol a.⟩ *game* (*what's the g.*?) | Ausbildungs≃, Lehr≃ *syllabus* L || durchdachter ~ *carefully thought-out scheme* || ehrgeiziger ~ *ambition* || entgegengesetzte ≃e *cross--purposes* || fester ~ *schedule* || f Feuereinsatz ⟨artill⟩ *schedules of fire* || gedruckter ~ *prospectus* | nach neuem ~ *under a new plan*; ohne festen ~ *at a loose end*; ⟨SBZ⟩ *economic plan* | es war im ~ *it was planned* | e–n ~ aufschieben *to shelve*, .. durchkreuzen (vereiteln) *to thwart* (*upset*) *a plan*, .. fallen l *to abandon a scheme* || er faßte den ~ *the plan came to him*, .. formen, schaffen f *to form a mold for* (*a th*) || (s–e) ≃e schmieden *to scheme* (–d *scheming* [*mind*]), *to make plans* (*to lay one's plans*); dunkle .. *to put* (*lay, knock*) *heads together* || (jds) ≃e zunichte m *to upset the applecart* **2.** (Grundriß) *ground-plan* || (e–r Stadt) *plan*; *map* || ⟨mil⟩ *topographical map* || ⟨tech etc⟩ *layout* ⟨a. übtr crim⟩; Schmier≃ *lubrication schedule* **3.** (Ebene) *plain*; *battlefield, tilt-yard* || ⟨fig⟩ auf den ~ rufen (treten) *to call up*; *involve*; *call* od *bring forth* (*to make one's appearance*) **II. 4.** ≃ [a] *plain, level* [1]**~abweichung** f *deviation from the plan* ⟨a. comp⟩ **~disziplin, ~erfüllung** f ⟨DDR⟩ *fulfilment of the economic plan* [3]**≃drehen, ≃fräsen** vt [h] *to face* [1]**~feuer** n ⟨artill⟩ *plotted* od *prearranged fire*; → –schießen [1]**≃gemäß** adv ⟨mil⟩ *according to plan* [2]**~gerät** n ⟨mil⟩ *plotting tools* **≃konk·av** a *plano-concave* **~kontrolle** f ⟨DDR⟩ *control of pl. f.t* [3]**~kreuzung** f ⟨rail⟩ *level crossing* [1]**≃los** a *planless, aimless, unsystematic, unmethodical, wandering, purposeless, desultory* (*fire*), *indiscriminate* (*bombing*) | [adv] *without a fixed plan*; (aufs Geratewohl) *at random* || ~ (an)ordnen *to randomize*; ~ abwerfen *to jettison* **~losigkeit** f *aimlessness, go-as-you-please, desultoriness* **~macher** m *schemer, projector* **≃-mäßig** a *designed, well planned, according to* (*a fixed*) *plan*; *systematic*; ⟨mil⟩ *regular*; *numerary* (*p & th*); ⟨rail⟩ *compulsory* (*stop*); *on* od *to schedule* ⟨aero, a-n⟩ *controlled* (*landing*); → programm– || [2]*to scale* [1]**~mäßigkeit** f *methodicalness*; *systematic arrangement* [2]**~pause** f *traced chart*; *overlay* **~quadrat(zahl** f) n ⟨surv mil⟩ *map square* (*coordination*) **~schießen** n (verbessert *corrected*) *map fire*; *scheduled fire* [3]**~schnitt** m *facing cut* [1]**~soll** n *target, quota* [3]**~sortierer** m ⟨tech⟩ *flat screen* **~spiegel** m *plane mirror* [2]**~spiel** n *indoor manœuvre*; *map exercise* N [1]**~stärke** f *establishment* [1]**~stelle** f *permanent established post* | ~nnachweis [m] ⟨mil⟩ *table of organization*; ~nsoll [n] *allotment* | [adv] ~ geführt *carefully planned* [3]**~übergang** m ⟨rail⟩ *level crossing* [2]**übung** f ⟨mil⟩ *map exercises* pl **≃voll** a *systematic, well-planned, methodical* **~wagen** (→ Plane) *covered wag*(*g*)*on* [1]**~wirtschaft** f *systematized* od *planned economy*; *dirigism*; ⟨bes Am⟩ *scientific management* [2]**~zeichnen** n *plotting* **~zeichner** m *designer* **~zeiger** m ⟨mil⟩ *field plotter* **~zeit** f *scheduled time* [1]**~ziel** n (Soll) ⟨eco⟩ *target* [1]**pl·anen** vt/i [h] *to plan, project, scheme, conceive, devise, target*, ⟨tech⟩ *design*, ⟨com⟩ *budget* || (heimlich) *to plot* || was ~ Sie? *what are your intentions*? || (vorhaben) *to be bent on*, (jds Vernichtung) *to compass*; ~ f *to plan against* (*an event*) **Pl·aner** m ~s/~ *designer, etc*; → Planung

Pl·ane f ~/~n *awning, canvas, cover, tilt* || (geteerte) *tarpaulin* || mit e–r ~ versehen *to tilt*

Plan·et m ~en/~en *planet* **≃·arisch** a *planetary* **~·arium** n *planetarium*, ⟨hist⟩ *orrery* **~enplanetary** (*chart, space, system, year*) **~bahn** f *orbit* **~getriebe** n ⟨tech⟩ *epicyclic* (⟨Am⟩ *crypto*)-*gear*; *planetary transmission, pl.y gearing system* **~stand** m *position of the planets* || ⟨astrol⟩ *aspect* **~o·ide** m ~n/~n *planetoid, asteroid*

Pl·ani- ~glob m *planisphere* **~metr·ie** f *plane geometry* **≃m·etrisch** a *planimetric*(*al*)

Plan·ier- ~amboß m *planishing-anvil* **~bagger** m *skimmer* **~bank** f *smoothing lathe* **~hammer** m *pl.-hammer* **~kolben** m *planisher* **~löffel** m *skimmer* **~maschine** f *grader* **~presse** f ⟨bookb⟩ *size.press* **~raupe** f ⟨tech⟩ *bulldozer* [dazu: *to b.ze*] **~schaufel** f *trenching shovel* **~vorrichtung** f *levelling arrangement* **plan·ieren** vt [h] ⟨tech⟩ *to plane, level* || (Wege) *to grade*, ⟨Am⟩ *to graduate* || ⟨met⟩ *to planish* || ⟨bookb⟩ *to glue, size*

Pl·anke f ~/~n *plank, board* || ~n [pl] ⟨a.⟩ *boarding, planking* **~nbeschlag** m *sheeting* **~n-boot** n ⟨mar⟩ *pirogue* **~ngang** m ⟨mar⟩ *strake* **~n-gerüst** f *scaffolding* **~nrost** m ⟨arch⟩ *apron* **~n-weg** m *board-walk* **~nverkleidung** f, **~nwerk** n, **~nzaun** m *boarding* **pl·anken** vt [h] ⟨tech⟩ *to board*

Plänkel·ei f ~/~en *skirmish*(*ing*) **pl·änkeln** vi [h] *to skirmish* **Pl·änkler** m ~s/~ *skirmisher*

Plansch- ~becken n *wading pool* | **≃en** vt/i [h] *to splash, dabble, paddle*

Pl·ansche f ~/~n ⟨tech⟩ *ingot*

Plant·age [–ʒə] f ~/~n *plantation* || dazu: *planter*

Pl·anum n ~s/ *prepared track* (*of road*, etc)

Pl·anung f ~/~en *planning* (*of traffic*); ⟨demog⟩ *layout*; ⟨pol⟩ *policy making* || in der ~ s *to be being planned*; → Plan I. 1. | ~sausschuß [m] *planning-committee*; ~sforschung [f] ⟨tech com⟩ *operations research*; → planen

Pl·apper- ~maul n, **~tasche** f, **~er** m ~s/~ *prattler, chatterbox* **~·ei** f ~/~en *babble, babbling, prattle* **≃haft** a *babbling* || *talkative, loquacious, voluble, garrulous* | **≃igkeit** [f] *talkativeness, volubility, loquacity, garrulity* **pl·appern** vt/i [h] *to prattle, prate, babble, chat*(*ter*) || ⟨sl⟩ *to flap* (über *about*) || (Gebet) *to patter* **pl·ärren** vi/t [h] *to babble* || (weinerlich) *to boohoo, blub*(*ber*), ⟨fam⟩ *snivel* || (belehrend) *to rant* || (leiernd) *to rattle off* || (singend) *to bawl*

Pläs·ier n ~(e)s/ *pleasure* | **≃lich** a *amusing*

Pl·astik f ~/ [abstr & konkr] *sculpture* | ⟨ind, tech⟩ *plastics* pl, *plastic material* | ⟨fig⟩ *illusion of depth*; *plasticity* || *clearness* (*of expression*, etc); *graphic power and beauty* | ⟨med⟩ *plastic surgery* | ~- *squeezable, squeeze* [attr] (–flasche); ~führungen f pl ⟨bes comp⟩ *plastic* (*form*) *guides*; ~überschuhe m pl *pl. boots* **Plasti·lin** n ~s/ *plasticine* **pl·astisch** a *plastic*, ⟨fig⟩ *graphic* (*description*) || ⟨film⟩ *three-dimensional*; *widescreen* (*picture*); ⟨ac⟩ *binaural* | [adv] ~ hervorheben *to bring out*; *to place* od *throw into relief*; ~e Landkarte *relief map* || ~e Masse *plastics* pl **Plastizit·ät** f ~/ *plasticity*

Plat·ane f ~/~n *plane-*(*tree*); (Arten → plane)

Plateau [plɑ'to:] n ~s/~s *plateau, table-land*

Pl·atformbenzin *platinum-refined gasoline* **Pl·atin** n ~(e)s/ *platinum* **~blase** f *pl. retort* **~blech** n *pl. foil* **~blondine** f *pl.-* od *straw-blonde* **~chlor·id** n *platinic chloride* **~chlor·ür** n *platinous chloride* **~draht** n *pl.-wire* **~druck** m *platinotype* **≃haltig** a *platiniferous* **~schwamm** m *spongy pl.* **~verbindung** [f] *platinous compound*

Platit·üde f ~/~n (Seichtheit ⟨fig⟩) *platitude*; ⟨Am a.⟩ *bromide*

Plat·oniker m ~s/~ *Platonist* **p-isch** a *P.ic* (*love*)

Pl·atsch m ~es/~e *dash, flounce, splash* **platsch**! *dash! splash!* **~n·aß** a *wet through* **pl·atschen** vi [h] *to splash, squash, dash*; (Regen) *patter* || *fall plump* (in *into*) || ~des Geräusch [n] *splash* **pl·ätschern I.** vi [h] *to splash, paddle, dabble* (*in the water*) | (of water) *to murmur, ripple, lap*, ⟨poet⟩ *babble* || *to wash* (*against the shore*) || ⟨fig⟩ (Unterhaltung) *to be carried on in a light manner* **II.** ≈ n *lap*(*ping*) || *hubble-bubble* || *drip* (*of the rain*)

platt I. [a] **1.** *flat* (*roof, tile, face, nose, feet*) || *plain, level, even* (*ground*) || *flat, open* (*country*) | ~ drücken *to flatten* || auf der ~en Erde liegen *to lie on the bare ground* | sich ~ [adv] auf die Erde legen *to lie down flat on the ground* (⟨fam⟩ *on one's belly*) **2.** ⟨fig⟩ *downright* (*contradiction*) || *vulgar, low* (*joke*) || *boorish* (*manners*) || *flat* (*refusal*) || *plain, naked* (*truth*) || das ~e Gegenteil *quite the contrary* | (nichtssagend) *commonplace, trite, trivial* || *insipid* (*p*) || *dull* (*discourse*) | [adv] ~ heraussagen *to tell frankly, speak out plainly, speak straight out* **3.** ⟨fam fig⟩ (erstaunt) *wonder-struck* || (glücklich) *amazed* || (verblüfft) *taken aback, flabbergasted, dumbfounded*; da bin ich ~ ⟨fam⟩ *that knocks me* || ⟨sl⟩ *slewed*; *bowled over* **II. Pl·att** n ~s/ *Low German* (*dialect*[*s* pl]) || Hamburger ≈ *Hamburg d.* || ≈ sprechen *to talk in one's d.* **~boot** n *barge, lighter* **~decke** f ⟨arch⟩ *plain ceiling* **≈deutsch** a, **~deutsch(e)** n *Low German* **~fisch** m ⟨ich⟩ *flat-fish, plaice* **~form** f *platform* || ⟨a–n⟩ ~ für den Abschuß [bes Russ] *launch pad* || ⟨übtr pol⟩ *platform* (⟨a.⟩ Parteiprogramm etc) || Zement≈ *apron* | ~wagen [m] ⟨rail⟩ *flat* **~deck** n ⟨mar⟩ *orlop* **~fuß** m *flat foot*; °⟨mot, cycl⟩ *flat* **≈füßig** a *flat-foot*(*ed*) **~fußeinlage** f *instep-raiser, foot easer* **≈hufig** a *flat-hoofed* **~kopf** m *flat-head* **~menage** f *cruet-stand* **~mönch** m ⟨orn⟩ *black cap* **~schiene** f ⟨tech⟩ *plate-rail* **~schote** f ⟨bot⟩ *flat pea* **≈schwänzig** a ⟨scient⟩ *platurous* **~stich** m *broad* od *satin-stich* **~stickerei** f *plain embroidery* **≈w·eg** adv *flatly, downright* ≈|**werfen** vt ⟨mar⟩ *to feather* (*the oars*) **~wurm** m *flat worm* **≈z·u** = ~weg **Pl·ätt- ~brett** n *ironing-board* || ⟨fig fam⟩ ~ (mit 2 Erbsen) *regular straight Jane* (*flat-chested woman*) || (platt) wie ein ~ *flat as a board* **~eisen** n (*laundry*) *iron* **~frau** f *ironer* **~ofen** m *stove for heating the irons* **~stahl** m *heater* **~tuch** n *ironing-cloth* **~wäsche** f, **~zeug** n *linen to be ironed, ironed linen* **Pl·ättchen** n ~s/~ *small plate* || ⟨bot⟩ *lamella* L || ⟨arch⟩ *fillet*

Pl·atte f ~/~n ⟨allg⟩ *plate* **A.** ⟨arch⟩ *abacus, plinth, acroterion* [Gr]; kl ~ *ledge* || ⟨dent⟩ *dental plate* || ⟨for⟩ *glade, clearing* || ⟨geog⟩ *small plateau*; *ledge* || ⟨mar⟩ *sand-bank* || ⟨met⟩ *plate, sheet, planch* || ⟨mus⟩ → E., Schall≈ || ⟨arts, phot⟩ *plate* (Format in Zoll *half-~, quarter-~*) || ⟨rail⟩ → E., Haken≈ **B.** (**Fliese**) *flag* || (Kachel) *tile* || (Tablett) *tray, salver* **C. dünne** ~ *foil, sheet* || kalte ~ *mixed cold meat*; *cold collation*; schwedische ~ *Swedish c.* **D.** °⟨fig⟩ *head*; *pate*, (*bald head*); *tonsure* || ~n [pl] *dust, pelf* (Geld) **E. Abstell**≈ (f Bügeleisen) *iron-stand* || Anreiß≈ *marking-off table* || Auszug≈ (*pull-out*) *slide* || Bettungs≈ ⟨artill⟩ *bed plate* || Braten≈ *dish* || Elfenbein≈ *ivory sheet* || Druck≈ *stereotype plate* || ⟨typ⟩ Druckgegen≈ *plat*(*t*)*en* || Fels≈ *slab, shelf, smooth slope of rock*; (kl) *ledge* || ⟨ski⟩ Fuß≈ *footplate* || Fußboden≈ *tile* || Glas≈ *glass plate* || Grab≈ *tablet, memorial slab, monumental brass* || Grammophon≈ → u. Schall≈ || Haken≈ ⟨rail⟩ (*rail-*)*chair* || (Holzschnitt-) Hirnholz≈ *crossgrain-leaf* || Holz≈ *wooden sheet* || Kuchen≈ *cake plate* || Lafetten≈ *mount* || Langholz≈ *grain-wood leaf* || Loch≈ *swage block* || ⟨glass⟩ Marbel≈ *marver* || Präsentier≈ *tray, salver* || Ramm≈ *rammer slab* || Richt≈ *straightening plate* || Schall≈ *record, disk* || Schiefer≈ *slab* || Schlicht≈ *smoothing plate* || Schreib≈ *desk flap* || Sockel≈ *plinth* || Stein≈ *flag, slab* || Tanz≈ *dance record* || Taxi≈ ("*for hire*") *flag* || Tisch≈ *board, top*; (z Einlegen *leaf*); (z Klappen) *flap* || Wachs≈ *wax mould* || Zier≈ (Metall, Porzellan) *plaque* **F. immer die alte** ~! .. *harping on the same subject!* || mit ~n **belegen** *to flag*; *to lay .. with flags* || °e–e ~ **bek** *to become bald* || in ~n brechen *to flake off* || °das kommt nicht **auf** die ~! *that's out of the question!* **Pl·attefluß** m *Platte River, Nebraska River* (*U.S.A.*) **Pl·atteißе** f ~/~n ⟨ich⟩ *plaice* **pl·atten** vt [h] *to flatten* (a. sich ~) || *to level, plane* **pl·ätten** vt [h] *to iron, press* (*linen*) || *to flatten, laminate* (*wire*) **Pl·atten- ~abstrich** m ⟨bact⟩ *streak* **~abzug** m *stereotyped proof* **~archiv** n *record cabinet* **~aufnahme(gerät** n) f (*phonograph*) *record*(*er*) **~bahn** f ⟨tech⟩ *plate-conveyor* **~belag** m *slab covering* **~dat·ei** f ⟨rec⟩ *disc file* **~druck** m *stereotypy* **~-einheit** f ⟨rec⟩ *disc drive* **~erhitzer** m *plate-type heater* **≈förmig** a *plated, lamelliform* **~gießerei** f ⟨met⟩ *plate-moulding* || ⟨typ⟩ *stereotype-casting* **~halter** m ⟨phot⟩ *plate-holder* **~hammer** m *flatting h.* **~-Jockey** m ⟨wir, telv⟩ *disc-jockey* **~kamera** f *camera for plates* **~kassette** f, **~magazin** n ⟨phot⟩ *plate sheath* od *holder* od *carrier*; *dark slide* **~korrektur** f ⟨typ⟩ *stereo-correction* **~kröpfmaschine** f *plate-joggling m.* **~kupfer** n *sheet-copper* **~leger** m ⟨rec hum⟩ *disc-* od *disk-jockey* **~-lift** m *record lift* **~panzerung** f *plate-armour* **~-schrank** m *record cabinet*; (in) **~schrift** (drucken) (*to*) *stereotype* **~see** m (Ungarn zw Donau u Drau) *Lake Balaton* **~spieler** m *record player*; ⟨wir⟩ *playback*, Radio mit ~ *phonograph-radio* **~spieltisch** m (im Senderaum) *transcription turntable* **~teller** m *t.t. platter* | ~belag [m] *t.t. mat* **~-wechsel** m ⟨rec⟩ *changer operation* **~wechsler** m (*record*) *auto-changer* **Pl·ätter** m ~s/~ *flattener* | **~in** f *ironer* **pl·atterdings** adv *decidedly, absolutely, positively, utterly, by all means* || *altogether* (*impossible*) **Plätter·ei** f *ironing* || *ironing establishment* **Pl·attheit** f ~/~en *flatness* || ⟨fig⟩ *insipidity, dul*(*l*)*ness, staleness, triviality, banality* | (Ausspruch) *platitude, trivial talk, triviality* **platt·ieren** vt [h] *to* (*gold-*)*plate* || –rtes Blech *bi-metal plate*; –rte Ware *plated dishes, etc*; nicht –rt *unclad* **Platt·ierung** f ~/~en *plating* **Platt·ierer** m *plater* **Pl·atting** f ~/ ⟨mar⟩ *sennit, sinnet* **Pl·attner** m ~s/~ ⟨hist⟩ *armourer* [1]**Platz** m → ≈chen

[2]**Platz** m ~es/≈e **A.** (Ort, Stelle) *place, locality, post* || (Stadt) *town, place, city* || (Fleck) *spot* || (Stellung) *position* || (Lage) *site* || ⟨sport⟩ *ground*; ⟨ten⟩ *court* || (Raum) *room, space* || [ell] ~! (to dog) *down!* **B. Bau**≈ *site* || Exerzier≈ *drill* (od *parade, training-*) *ground* || → Flug≈ || ⟨racing⟩ Führ≈ *parade ring* || Holz≈ *woodyard* || Liege≈ ⟨mar⟩ *berth* || Sammel≈ *rallying point* || ⟨racing⟩ Sattel≈ *paddock* || Stand≈ (f Wagen) *stand* || Sitz≈ *seat* || Waffen≈ *place of arms* **C.** der **erste** ~ (Rang) ⟨a.⟩ *the primacy* (*of a p*); ⟨theat⟩ erster ~ *pit* || fester, befestigter ~ *fortified place* od *position*; *fortress* || eigener ~ ⟨sport⟩ *home ground* || freier ~ *open space* (f *for*), *esplanade*; (Stellung) *vacancy* || ⟨theat⟩ *reserved seat* || runder ~ *circus* || viereckiger ~ *square* || viel ~ *lots of room* || ⟨com⟩ wichtiger ~ *centre* **D.** e–m e–n ~ **anweisen** *to show a p to his seat* || e–n ~ angewiesen bek *to be accommodated with a seat* || s–n ~ ausfüllen *to fill the bill* (od *one's position well*); jds .. *to take a p's place* || ~ behalten *to keep one's seat* || s–n ~ behaupten ⟨fig⟩ *to maintain one's position* || der ~ ist belegt .. *engaged* || ~ bieten f .. *to have room for* (*30*) || e–n ~ einnehmen *to take station*; jds .. *to take a p's place* || den ersten (dritten) ~ einnehmen *to take the first place* (⟨sport⟩ *to come in third*) || e–m s–n ~ einräumen *to give a p one's seat* || e–n ~ freihalten *to keep a seat/place* (*for*) || (jdm) den rechten ~ geben *to position* || ⟨typ⟩ *to give space* (*to reviews*) || ⟨fig⟩ ~ greifen *to take root* od *effect*; (eintreten) *to*

take place, to come to pass ‖ ich habe ~ *I've room enough*; es h alle ~ *there is room for all* ‖ e–n ~ herunter! *go down one!* ‖ ~ l (im Heft) *to leave space* ‖ ~ m *to clear off*; [dat] *to make room* od *way for a p, to a th* ‖ ~ gemacht! [ell] ~ da! *clear the way!, make way (room) please!* ‖ ~ nehmen *to take one's place (in a boat)* ‖ *to sit down, to take a seat* ‖ wollen Sie ~ n. *will you be seated, won't you sit down; take a seat, will you not?* ‖ ~ n.! *be seated!, take your seats!*; bei *or* neben jdm ~ n. *to sit down beside a p*; jdn ~ n. l *to ask a p to sit down*, etc; *to sit a p down* ‖ es war ~ genug *there was room enough* ‖ hier ist kein ~ mehr *there is no more room here* ‖ kein ~ für ⟨fig⟩ *no place for* ‖ er verlor s–n ~ .. *his berth, position* ‖ laß uns die ~̈e wechseln *change places with me* ‖ ⟨racing⟩ ~ wetten *to back (a horse) for a place* **E.** (hier) **am** ~ (Stadt) *on the spot; in this place, here*; ⟨fig⟩ *apposite, suitable, opportune; in point; fit (to do); not amiss, in order* ‖ nicht am ~ *out of pl.*; ⟨fig⟩ *in the wrong box; unwanted; uncalled for; irrelevant; impertinent; having no application (in); it does not do (to do)* ‖ am falschen ~e stehen: *he is rather wasted here* ‖ am (un)rechten ~ *in the right (wrong) pl.*; ⟨a.⟩ *(to be) in pl.*; *the right man in the right pl.* | ein Wort mag **am** ~ s .. *might be in order* | ~ **an** der Sonne *pl. in the sun*; **an** s–m ~ bleiben *to keep one's pl.* ‖ an s–m gewöhnlichen ~ s *to be in its usual pl.* ‖ (jdn) an den rechten ~ stellen *to position* ‖ wieder an s–n ~ tun *to put back, replace* ‖ an öffentlichen ~̈en *in public pl.s* | **auf** [dat]: *in Trafalgar square* ‖ auf die ~̈e, fertig, los! *on your marks, get set, go!* ‖ auf Straßen u ~̈en *in the streets and public squares* ‖ geh an *or* auf d–n ~ *go to your seat* ‖ auf dem ~e bleiben ⟨mil⟩ *to fall in (the) battle, to be slain* ‖ auf gegenüberliegenden ~̈en *in facing seats* ‖ bis auf den letzten ~ besetzt *full to overflowing* | **immer** auf dem ~ s *to be always (on the alert* od) *ready; to be ready* (⟨fam⟩ *game*) *for anything* | sich **von** den ~̈en erheben: *they rose from their pl.s* ‖ sich nicht vom ~e rühren *not to move from the spot* ‖ er sprach von s–m ~e aus .. *from where he stood* ‖ jdn v s–m ~e verdrängen *to supplant a p* ‖ nicht v ~e weichen *to stand one's ground* **~angst** f *agoraphobia* **~anweiser(in** f) m *usher*; ⟨theat⟩ *attendant*; (f *usherette*) **~aufschlag** m *extra charge for position* **~bedarf** m *local wants* pl **~bestellung** [f] (rückgängig m *to cancel a*) *booking* **~einflugzeichen** n ⟨aero⟩ *boundary marker* **~einheit** f ⟨golf⟩ *bogey* **~ersparnis** f *space saving* **~flugverkehr** m *traffic pattern* **~geschäft** n *local business* | als **~halter** eingesetzt ⟨mil⟩ *appointed to hold the fort* **~karte** f ⟨rail⟩ *ticket for a reserved seat* | ~n-bestellung f ⟨rail⟩ *reservation of seats*, ⟨Am⟩ *s. r.* **~kenntnis** f *local knowledge* **~kommandant** m ⟨mil⟩ *commandant* **~major** m *town-major* **~mangel** m *lack of (sufficient) room* **~patrone** f (→ platzen) *blank cartridge* **~randbefeuerung** f ⟨aero⟩ *boundary lights* **~regen** m *pelting rain*, ⟨fam⟩ *downpour* **~reisende(r)** *m town-traveller* **~runde** f ⟨aero⟩ *traffic pattern*; *(to fly a) circuit* **~stoß** m ⟨ftb⟩ *place-kick* **~transport** m *local tr.* **~verein** m ⟨sport⟩ *home team* **~verkauf** m *sale on the spot* **~wart** m ⟨sport⟩ *ground(s)man* **~wechsel** m ⟨com⟩ *local* od *town-bill* **Pl·ätze- ~tauschen, ~wechseln** n (Spiel) *general post*; vgl Platz C. (am Ende)

Pl·ätzchen n ~s/~ **1.** *(snug) little place* od *seat* **2.** (v Zucker etc) *pastil, drop; lozenge* | (Gebäck) (a. Platz [m]) *(fancy) biscuit; bun*; ⟨Am⟩ *cookie*

pl·atz! intj *smash! crash!* °**Pl·atze** f: die ~ kriegen *to burst with envy, fury* **pl·atzen I.** vi **1.** [s] (→ bersten) *to burst, explode* (⟨a. fig⟩ vor .. *with envy, fury, laughter*) ‖ °da war er geplatzt *that did him, he was done for* ‖ *to blow out*; ⟨fam⟩ *to go bung* ‖ (of bubbles) *to break* ‖ ⟨fig⟩ *(of check) to bounce* ‖ (P) *to brim (with envy)* ‖ ich platze, wenn ich nicht rede *I'm bursting with talk* ‖ (reißen) *to crack, rip, split* ‖ (v Luftreifen) *to puncture*; uns ist der Reifen geplatzt *we had a p.* ‖ auf jdn ~ *to come flush on a p*, ⟨fam⟩ *to barge into a p* ‖ auf–e–a| ~ ⟨fig⟩ *to clash* ‖ ins Zimmer ~ *to burst* (⟨fam⟩ *barge*) *into the room* ‖ °geplatzt ⟨Am fam⟩ *rubber (check)* | °~ Sie! (= nehmen Sie Platz) *take a pew, sit you down*; ⟨vulg⟩ *park your stern* **2.** vi [h] (krachen) *to crack* ‖ *(of fire) to crackle* ‖ es platzt *it's pouring with rain* **II.** vt/i [h & s] (mit) etw heraus ~ *to burst out with (to blurt out) a th* **III.** ~̈ n *bursting*, etc. ‖ *puncture* ‖ ⟨med⟩ *rupture* ‖ z ~ satt *or* voll *f. t. b.* (= *full to bursting*) ‖ die S z ~ bringen *to prick the bubble*

pl·ätzen vt/i [h] **1.** *to smack, pop* **2.** *to patch* **3.** ⟨hunt⟩ (of stag) *to scratch (the ground)* **4.** ⟨for⟩ *to blaze, spot, mark (trees)*

Pl·auder- ~ecke f *cosy corner* **~̈haft** a *talkative, chatty* **~hans** m, **~liese** f, **~maul** n, **~tasche** f *chatterbox* **~stündchen** n *(an hour's) cosy chat* **~ton** m *conversational vein* od *tone* **Plauder·ei** f ~/~en *(cosy chit-)chat* ‖ (geistlose) *small talk; tittle-tattle* ‖ ~ am Kamin *fireside chat* **Pl·auderer** m ~s/~, Pl·auderin [f] *chatterer, prattler, talker, chatterbox* ‖ ⟨oft dero⟩ *gossip* ‖ ⟨dero⟩ *scandalmonger* **pl·audern (pl·auschen)** vi [h] *to chatter, prattle, yarn; to talk small* ‖ *to talk, chat* (mit *to*) ‖ ⟨Am a.⟩ *to visit* (⟨sl⟩ *chin*) *(with)* ‖ lange ~ *to have quite a chat* (⟨sl⟩ *chin*) *(with)* ‖ ⟨dero⟩ *to gossip* ‖ weiter ~ *to ramble on* | ⟨fig⟩ aus der Schule ~ *to tell tales (out of school)* | ~d *in gossip*

Pl·auen n ⟨Ger⟩ (Stadt)

Pl·ausch m ~es/~e (→ Schwatz) *chat* | **~̈en** vi [h] *to chat* | ×**~erl** n ~s/~ ⟨fam⟩ *chin-way*

plaus·ibel a (~ m *to make*) *plausible*; *that makes (good) sense* klingt ~ ‖ [dazu:] *plausibility*

Pl·auz m ~es/~e *bounce* | ~̈ intj *bang!*

°**Pl·auze** f ~/~n *belly; bow-window* ‖ auf der ~ liegen *to be laid up* ‖ sich die ~ vollschlagen *to cram (one's belly)* | **~̈n** vi [s] *to fall down with a bang*

Pleb·ejer m ~s/~ *plebeian*; ⟨fig sl⟩ *bounder* **~tum** n *the plebeians* pl, *the populace* | [abstr] *plebeianism* **pleb·ejisch** a *plebeian; low, vulgar* **Plebisz·it** n ~s/~e *plebiscite* **Plebs** f ~/; m ~es/ *mob, rabble* ‖ ⟨hist⟩ *plebs*

Pléi·ade f ~/ ⟨Lit⟩ (Kreis v 7 franz. Dichtern [mit Ronsard] um 1550) *Pleiad*, → d.

Pl·eistozän n ~s/ ⟨geol⟩ (Am-meisten-neu = oberes Diluvium = untere Abteilung des Quartärs) *pleistocene*; → –zän

°**Pl·eite** f ~/~n *bankruptcy*; ⟨Am sl⟩ *bust* ‖ ⟨fig⟩ *failure, fizzle*; ⟨sl⟩ *wash-out* ‖ ~ m, gehen *to go bankrupt* (⟨fam⟩ .. *broke*), *to fail*, ⟨Am sl⟩ *to (go) bust, to bosh up*; das wird ihn wohl ~̈ gehen l *or* m *I'm afraid that'll do for him* | ~̈ [a] *bankrupt* ‖ ~ s *to be on the rocks* (⟨Am fam⟩ *hog*); *on one's back, to be (dead, stone) broke, cracked, stony* | ~geier [m] *misfortune* (krächzt über .. *dogs* ..)

Plej·aden pl ⟨astr⟩ (Siebengestirn) *Pleiads* pl

°**Pl·empe** f ~/~n **1.** *sword* **2.** *slops* pl; *slipslop, swill* | **~̈rig** a = fade ⟨fig⟩ | **~̈rn** vi [h] **1.** *to splash* **2.** *to lounge about*

°**plempl·em** a *barmy*, ⟨mil⟩ *batty*; ⟨Am⟩ *daffy*

Plen·arsitzung f *plenary meeting* **Pl·enum** n ~s/ ⟨parl⟩ *plenum*, ⟨com⟩ *full assembly* ‖ ⟨jur⟩ in pleno *in full court*

Plenter- ⟨for⟩ **~betrieb** m *selection system* **~-durchforstung** f *s. thinning* | **~̈n** vt [h] (Wald) *to select*

Pleon·as- ~mus m ~/–men *pleonasm* **~̈tisch** a *pleonastic*

Pl·euel m ~s/~ *connecting* od *piston rod* **~lager** n *bottom end bearing* (läuft aus *runs out*) **~-schaft** m *connecting-rod blade* **~stange** f ⟨tech⟩ *c. r.* | ~sausschlag [m] *angle of c. r.*

Pleur·itis f ~/ (Rippenfellentzündung) *pleurisy*

Pl·exiglas® n ⟨m. m.⟩ (Acrylglas) *perspex*; *lucite*
Pli m ∼s/∼s *polish* ⟨fig⟩; *pluck* ‖ *envelope*
ˣ**pl·ieren** vi [h] *to peer* **pl·inkern** vi [h], (mit) ∼ *to blink* (*one's eyes*)
Pl·inse f ∼/∼n *fritter, pancake*; ⟨Am⟩ *blintzer*
Pl·inthe f ∼/∼n ⟨arch, arts⟩ *plinth*
Plioz·än n ∼(e)s/ ⟨geol⟩ *pliocene*; → –zän
Pliss·ee n ∼s/∼s *pleating* **pliss·ieren** *to pleat*
Pl·ombe f ∼/∼n *lead, seal* ‖ ⟨dent⟩ *stopping, filling*, (gegossen) *inlay* **p-bieren** vt [h] *to seal* ‖ ⟨dent⟩ *to plug, stop*; ⟨Am⟩ *fill*
Pl·ötze f ∼/∼n ⟨ich⟩ (Rotauge) *roach*
pl·ötzlich a *sudden, sharp* ‖ ∼er Ausbruch *rush* ‖ ∼er Befehl *rush orders* pl | adv *suddenly, all of a sudden, in* (*less than*) *no time, like a shot* (od *bolt from the blue*; *with a jerk, unexpectedly, abruptly, sharply* ‖ ∼ ein Lied anstimmen *to break into a song* ‖ ∼ eintreten, stattfinden *to spring up*; (*to turn*) *short*; sich [acc] ∼ verfinstern *to leap* od *spring to darkness* | [ell] ∼! *hurry up!, get a move on!*; *make it snappy!* ‖ nicht so ∼! *don't be in a hurry!* | ∸**keit** f ∼/ *suddenness*
Pl·uderhosen f pl *wide breeches* pl, *trunk hose*
Plumeau [ply'mo:] n ∼s/∼s *eiderdown quilt*
plump a (ungeschlacht) *clumsy, lumbering, heavy-handed*; *lumpish, unwieldy, burly* ‖ ein Paar ∼e Hände *two fat hands* ‖ *blunt* (*manners*) ‖ *gross* (*flattery*) ‖ *barefaced* (*fishing for compliments*) ‖ *heavy, ponderous* (*style*) ‖ *flat* (*lie*) ‖ *rank* (*swindle*) ‖ (ungeschickt) *awkward* ‖ etw ∼ geraten *on the plump side* ‖ (unfein) *crude, gross, coarse, rustic* ‖ plumpe Vertraulichkeit *familiarity* | so e–e ∼e Lüge, Schmeichelei *that was laid on with the trowel* | ∸**heit** f ∼/∼en *clumsiness*, etc ‖ *awkwardness* ‖ *crudity, grossness*, etc **Plumps** m ∼es/∼e & ∸ intj *plump, plop, flop, bang, thump, wump(h)* **Pl·umpsack** m *knotted handkerchief* ‖ ⟨fig⟩ *clumsy* od *coarse fellow* **pl·umpsen** vi [h & s] *to plump, plunk, plop, flop* | vt [h] *to dump*
Pl·under m ∼s/ *trash, trumpery, lumber, riff--raff, junk, rubbish*; ⟨Am sl⟩ *plug* ‖ (Lumpen) *rags* pl ‖ ⟨fig⟩ *bagatelle* **∼kammer** f *lumber-room* **∼kram** m *trumpery, frippery, lumber* **∼markt** m *rag-fair* **∼teig** m *flaky paste* **Plünderer** m ∼s/∼ *plunderer, pillager*; ⟨mil a.⟩ *marauder* **pl·ündern** vt [h] *to plunder* ‖ (Land) *to harry, ravage, raid, pillage, despoil* ‖ *to ransack, loot* (*a house*) ‖ *to sack* (*a shop*) ‖ (*put to*) *sack* (*a town*) ‖ *to rob, strip* (*a traveller*) ‖ *to rob* (*a train*) ‖ ⟨mil⟩ *to loot* | ⟨fig⟩ *to despoil, strip* (*a tree*, etc.) ‖ *to rifle* (*a book, pocket, cupboard*) ‖ ⟨cards⟩ *to bleed, fleece* (*a p*) **Pl·ünderung** f ∼/∼en *plundering, pillage, sack*(*ing*), *spoliation*; *robbery* ([gen:] *at a house*); (Raub) *rapine* ‖ der ∼ preisgeben *to allow to be sacked, looted*
Plur·al m ∼(e)s/∼e ⟨gram⟩ *plural* (*number*) | ∸**isch** a (*in the*) *plural* **∼wahlrecht** n *plural vote*
°**Pl·ürre** f *husband's tea*; *cat-lap*; (*wish-*)*wash*; (Tee) *mere water bewitched*
Pl·us n ∼/ (Betrag) *surplus* ‖ → ∼zeichen ‖ ⟨fig⟩ *asset* ‖ *advantage* (⟨a.⟩ *moral a.*) ‖ als ∼ buchen *to book as a plus* (f *for*) | ∸ [adv] *plus* **∼macher** m *financial schemer, profit-hunter* °∸|**machen** vt [h] ⟨sl⟩ *to make* ∸/**minus** ⟨comp⟩ *d*(*ebito*)*r or c*(*redito*)*r* **∼pol** m ⟨el⟩ *positive pole* °**∼punkt** m *a feather in one's cap*; e–n ∼ f ihn *chalk up one for him* **∼quamperfektum** n ⟨gram⟩ *pluperfect* **∼vorgabe** f ⟨ten⟩ *received odds* pl **∼-zeichen** n *plus-sign*
Pl·üsch m ∼es/∼e *plush*; ⟨Am fam⟩ *shag* ∸**-artig** a *plushlike* **∼möbel** n pl *plush-covered furniture* **∼samt** m *silk-plush* **∼sofa** n *plush-sofa* **∼teppich** m *Wilton* (*carpet*)
pl·usterig a *ruffled* (*feathers*) ‖ *baggy* (*trousers*) ‖ *puffed out* (*cheeks*)
Plutokr·at m ∼en/∼en *plutocrat* ‖ ⟨dero sl⟩ *gold-bug* | **-at·ie** f ∼/ *plutocracy* **plut·onisch** a *Plutonic* ⟨a. geol⟩; *igneous, plutonic* (*rocks*)
Pl·ymouth ['plimәθ] n (Hafenstadt) ⟨Engl⟩
Pneum·atik f ∼/ **1.** (Lehre) *pneumatics* pl **2.** m ∼s/∼s, (⟨obs⟩ Pneu [pnø:]) ⟨cycl⟩ (*pneumatic*) *tyre*; ⟨med⟩ *pneumothorax* **pneum·atisch** a *pneumatic* (*trough, brake*)
Po, der ⟨It⟩ (Fluß) *the* (*river*) *Po*
°**Po** m ∼s/∼s *butt*(*ock* [*s* pl]); *bum*; ⟨Am⟩ *fanny*
P·öbel m ∼s/ *mob, rabble, populace*; *rag and tag, tag and bobtail* | **∼·ei** f ∼/∼en *vulgar ways* od *doings* pl | ∸**haft** a *vulgar, low, plebeian* **∼haufe** m *mob, rabble* **∼herrschaft** f *ochlocracy*; *mob-rule*, ⟨fam⟩ *mobocracy* **∼justiz** f *lynch-law* **∼wort** n *vulgarism, low word*
P·och- ∼brett n ⟨cards⟩ *scoring-board* (*for poker*) **∼eisen** n ⟨min⟩ *stamp-head* **∼erz** n *ore to be stamped* **∼hammer** m **1.** *ore-hammer* **2.** = ∼-mühle **∼mehl** n *pulverized ore* **∼mühle** f, **∼werk** n *stamping-mill* **∼spiel** n ⟨cards⟩ *poker* **∼stempel** m ⟨min⟩ *stamp* **p·ochen** vt/i [h] **A. 1.** *to knock, beat, rap* ‖ mir pocht das Herz *my heart beats, throbs, thumps* ‖ mit dem Fuß ∼ *to stamp one's foot* **2.** ⟨tech, min⟩ *to stamp, break, pound, batter* **3.** ⟨cards⟩ *to play poker* **B. es, man pocht** *there is a knock at the door, somebody is knocking* **C. auf** etw [acc] ∼ ⟨fig⟩ *to boast of, brag about, presume on* ‖ auf sein (gutes) Recht ∼ *to stand on one's rights* pl ‖ .. **aus** dem Schlaf ∼ *to knock up the landlord* **P·ocher** m ∼s/∼ *knocker* ‖ ⟨tech⟩ (P) *pounder* ‖ → Poch– ‖ (Prahler) *braggart, boaster* ‖ ⟨cards⟩ *poker* **Pocher·ei** f ∼/ *repeated knocking* ‖ ⟨fig⟩ *boasting*
poch·iert [–ʃ–] a ⟨cul⟩ *poached* (*egg*), → verloren
P·ocke f ∼/∼n *pock*(*-mark*) ‖ ∼n [pl] *smallpox* | **∼n-** ∸**artig** a *resembling smallpox* ‖ ⟨bot, ent⟩ *variolate* **∼gift** n *s.p. virus* **∼impfung** f *vaccination* ∸**krank** a *down with s.p.* **∼lymphe** f *variolo-vaccine* **∼narbe** f *pock-mark* ∸**narbig** a *marked by s.p., pock-marked* **P·ockholz** n *pockwood* **p·ockig** a = pockennarbig
P·odagra n ∼s/ ⟨med⟩ *gout, podagra* **pod·agrisch** a *gouty* **Pod·est** m ∼s/∼e ⟨arch⟩ **1.** (*staircase-*)*landing* **2.** *podium, platform* ‖ ⟨theat⟩ *rostrum*, ⟨Am⟩ *parallel*
°**P·odex** m ∼es/∼e (*posterior*), *sit-upon*; → Po
Pod·olien n (Ukraine-Landschaft) *Podolia*
Poes·ie f ∼/∼n *poetry* | *poem, piece of poetry* ∸**los** a *unpoetical* ‖ ⟨fig⟩ *prosy, matter-of-fact* | *common-place, dull* **Po·et** m ∼en/∼en *poet* ‖ schlechter ∼ *poetaster* | **∼ik** f ∼/∼en *poetics* pl **∼in** f ∼/∼nen *poetess* ∸**isch** a *poetical* (*style, taste*) ‖ *poetic* (*vein, diction, spirit, justice*)
ˣ**P·ogge** f ∼/∼n *frog*
Point [pw'ɛŋ] m ∼s/∼s ⟨cards⟩ *point* ‖ → Punkt ‖ ⟨mil⟩ (bei Paraden) *field-colours* pl
Pointe [pw'ɛ̃tә] f ∼/∼n *point* (*of a joke*); ⟨Am fam⟩ *punch line* ‖ die ∼ vermasseln *to blunder the point* **point·ieren 1.** vt *to bring to the point*; *to express* (*an idea*) *pointedly*; –rt *trenchant* (*expression*) **2.** vi ⟨cards⟩ *to punt* **pointill·ieren** vt/i ⟨paint⟩ *to prick*
Pok·al m ∼(e)s/∼e *large cup, goblet* ‖ ⟨sport⟩ *cup*, ⟨fam⟩ *pot* ‖ ∼e [pl] *plate* [koll]
P·ökel m ∼s/∼ *pickle, brine, souse* **∼faß** n *salting-tub* **∼fleisch** n *salt meat*, ⟨Am⟩ *jerky*, ⟨mar⟩ *junk, corned beef*; *pickled pork* **∼hering** m *pickled herring* **∼lake** f *pickle* **p·ökeln** vt [h] *to pickle*, (*dry*)*salt, souse* ‖ ⟨Am⟩ *to jerk*
pokul·ieren vi [h] *to carouse*, ⟨fam⟩ *booze*
Pol m ∼(e)s/∼e ⟨geog, astr, el⟩ *pole* ‖ über den ∼ *transpolar* (Flug) ‖ ⟨el⟩ *terminal* (*point*) **∼draht** m *electrode wire* **∼ende** n ⟨el⟩ *electrode* **∼gehäuse** n *pole box* **∼höhe** f *latitude* (**∼kette** f [v Pole ⟨tech⟩] *pile-warp*) **∼klemme** f (*pole-*)*terminal* **∼prüfer** m *polarity indicator* **∼schuh** m *pole-piece* | ∼fläche [f] *p.-face* **∼stange** f *pole* **∼stein** m *loadstone* **∼umschalter** m *throw-over switch* **∼-wechsler** m *polarity reverser*

Pol·ack m ∼en/∼en ⟨dero⟩ *Pole*

pol·ar a ⟨math, geog, astr⟩ *polar* ‖ ⟨fig⟩ ∼e Gegensätze h *to have directly opposite ideas, to be in direct opposition* (mit *to*) **Pol·ar- ∼achse** f *polar axis* **∼fahrt** f *polar expedition* **∼flug** m *transpolar flight* **∼fuchs** m ⟨zoo⟩ *arctic fox* **∼gegenden** f pl *arctic regions* pl **∼kappe** f ⟨geog⟩ *ice-cap* **∼kreis** m *polar circle* ‖ (südl.) nördl. ∼ (*ant*)*arctic circle* **∼stern** m *Pole-star*, ⟨poet⟩ *lodestar* **∼strom** m *arctic current* **∼zone** f *frigid zone* **Polarisati·on, -s·ierung** f ∼/∼en *polarization* **∼sbrille** f *viewer, viewing spectacles for 3-D-film* **∼sebene** f *plane of p.* **polaris·ieren** vt [h] *to polarize*; linear –rtes Licht *plane-polarized l.* **Pol·arisflotte** f (Tauziehen [n] um die) ∼ (*discussion about the*) *Polaris-equipped submarine force* **Polarit·ät** f ∼/ *polarity*

P·older m ∼s/∼ *polder* | ∼mühle f *drain-mill*

P·ole f ∼/∼n ⟨weav⟩ **1.** *pile, nap* **2.** *bar*

P·ole m ∼n/∼n *Pole*, → Polen, Polack

P·olei m ∼s/ ⟨bot⟩ *penny-royal*

Pol·emik f ∼/∼en *polemics* pl [a. sg konstr], *controversy* ‖ *literary feud* **∼er** m ∼s/∼ *controversialist* **pol·emisch** a *polemic*(*al*) **polemis·ieren** vi [h] (gegen [acc]) *to controvert* [vt], *to enter into* (od *carry on*) *a controversy with a p*

P·olen n *Poland* ‖ °noch ist ∼ nicht verloren *you may be down but not out*

°**Pol·ente** f ∼/ (Polizist) ⟨sl⟩ *cop*, ⟨Am⟩ *flatty*

Pol·essje f (Landsch. in Rußland) *Polesia*

Police [–'li:sə] f ∼/∼n ⟨ins⟩ *policy* → offen *floating p.* | ∼inhaber [m] *p. holder*

Pol·ier m [v Parleur] ∼s/∼e *foreman*

Pol·ier- ∼bank f *polishing bench* **∼drücken** n *die-burnishing* **∼feile** f *smoothing-file* **∼papier** n *sand-paper* **∼rad** n, **∼scheibe** f ⟨met, dent⟩ *lap* **∼stahl** m *burnisher, p.g-steel* **∼stein** m *p.g-stone* **pol·ieren** vt [h] *to polish, furbish, burnish*; mit Leder *to buff* ‖ ⟨fig⟩ *to polish up* (*an essay*) ‖ sich blank ∼ l *to take a high polish* **Pol·ierer** m ∼s/∼ **1.** *polisher, furbisher* **2.** = Polier

Polikl·inik f ∼/∼en (*welfare*) *clinic*(*al hospital*); *health-centre*; *out-door patients department* **Polit·ik** f ∼/ (Staatswissenschaft, –kunst, –angelegenheiten) *politics* pl [sg konstr]; *national policy*; ∼ v oben *stateway* ‖ *to study politics* | (Welt-, Staatsklugheit, eingeschlagene Richtung) *policy* ‖ abwartende ∼ *waiting policy* ‖ *policy of the open door* ‖ freundnachbarliche ∼ *good-neighbour policy*; gefährliche ∼ *brinkmanship* | (Staatswissenschaft) *political science* ‖ äußere (innere) ∼ *foreign* (*home*) *affairs* pl | in ∼ m *to politic* | im eigenen Interesse ∼ m *to gerrymander, to politick* ‖ über ∼ sprechen *to talk politics* ‖ ∼ spielen *to play at politics* **Pol·itiker** m ∼s/∼ *politician* **pol·itisch** a *political* (*party, book, leader, offender, refugee, colouring, sense*) ‖ ⟨fig⟩ *politic, sagacious, prudent* (*p*) ‖ *politic, judicious, expedient* (*action*) ‖ ∼es Leben, ∼e Welt *politics* pl [sg konstr] ‖ ∼er Einfluß ⟨Am sl⟩ *pull* ‖ in ∼er Hinsicht *politically* ‖ ∼e Manipulationen ⟨fam⟩ *wire-pulling* | adv (*to think, act*) *politically* ‖ ∼ tätig s *to be engaged in politics* ‖ ∼ unerfahren *inexperienced in politics* **politis·ieren 1.** vi [h] *to talk politics* pl **2.** vt [h] *to politicize* **3.** ≃ n *political argument*

Pol·itbüro n (= politisches B. in allen kommunistischen Staaten) *politburo, -bureau*

Polit·ur f ∼/∼en ⟨a. fig⟩ *polishing*, (*to need polishing*) ‖ (Glanz) *gloss* ‖ ⟨fig⟩ *refinement*

Poliz·ei f ∼/ *police* [= Polizisten: pl konstr.: *the p. are on the alert*; = Amt: sg konstr: *the p. takes measures*] ‖ dümmer als die ∼ erlaubt *too silly for words* **∼amt** *p.-station* **∼beamte(r)** m *p. officer*; *constable* **∼behörde** f *p.-authorities* pl **∼bericht** m *charge sheet*, ⟨Am⟩ *p. blotter* **∼bezirk** m *p.-precinct* **∼bureau** n *p.-office* **∼aufsicht** f *p. supervision* **∼beamte(r)** m *p.-officer, constable, p.man* **∼behörde** f *p.* **∼diener** m *p.man, constable*, ⟨fam⟩ *bobby*, ⟨sl⟩ *copper* **∼direktor** m *chief commissioner of p.* **∼falle** f ⟨mot⟩ *p.-trap* **∼gefängnis** n *lock-up* **∼gericht** n *p.-court* **∼gewalt** f *p. power* **∼hauptmann** m ⟨Am⟩ *p. captain* **∼hilfe** in Anspruch nehmen *to ask the p. for help* **∼hund** m *p.-dog* **∼knüppel, ∼knüttel** m *truncheon*; ⟨Am⟩ *espantoon* **∼kommando** n *detail of p.* **∼kommissar** m *inspector of p.* **∼kontrolloffizier** m ⟨Am⟩ *roundsman* **∼leutnant** m ⟨Am⟩ *lieutenant* **∼ordnung** f *p. regulations* pl **∼präsident** m *Chief Constable*, ⟨Ger⟩ *P. President* **∼präsidium** n *p.-headquarters* **∼revier** n *p.-station*; *p.-precinct* **∼richter** m *p.-magistrate* **∼sache** f *p.-matter* **∼spitzel** m *p.-spy, stool-pigeon* [dazu: *to stool*]; ⟨sl⟩ *nark, noser* **∼staat** m *p. state* **∼streife** f *raid, beat*, ⟨Am⟩ *patrol* | ∼nwagen [m] *prowl car* **∼stunde** f *closing-time*; nach der ∼ *after hours*, um die ∼ *by c.g-t.* **∼truppe** f *military p.-force* **∼vergehen** n *offence against the p.* **∼verordnung, ∼vorschrift** f *p. regulation*(*s* pl) **∼wache** f *p.-station*, ⟨Am⟩ *station-house* **∼wachtmeister** m *p.-sergeant* **∼wesen** n *p.-department, p.-administration* ≃**widrig** a *contrary to p. regulations*; ∼es Gesicht [n] ⟨fam⟩ *ugly mug* ⟨sl⟩ **∼wirtschaft** f *doings* pl *of the p.* **poliz·eilich** [a] (*of the*) *police* ‖ *p.* (*regulations, investigations, intervention*) ‖ ∼e Meldepflicht *obligatory registration* ‖ ∼e Anmeldung (Abmeldung) *report of* (*change of*) *address to the p.* ‖ unter ∼er Bedekkung *in the care of p.men* ‖ unter ∼er Aufsicht stehen *to be under p. supervision* | [adv] ∼ bekannt s *to have a p. record*; ∼ verboten *contrary to p. regulations* ‖ ∼ einschreiten l *to cause intervention of the p.* **Poliz·ist** m ∼en/∼en *policeman, constable* (→ Polyp), ⟨Am a.⟩ *patrolman* ‖ ∼ in Zivil *plain-clothes man* ‖ 50 ∼en *50 police* ‖ berittener ∼ *mounted p.man*, ⟨Am⟩ *state trooper* **∼in** f *p. woman*

Pol·izze f ∼/∼n [österr] → Police ⟨ins⟩

P·olka f ∼/∼s *polka* ‖ ∼ tanzen *to dance a p.*

°**p·olken** vi [h] → bohren, klauben, stochern

P·ollen m ∼s/ ⟨bot⟩ *pollen* **∼träger** m *anther*

P·oller m ∼s/∼ ⟨mar⟩ *bollard*

p·olnisch a *Polish* †**P·olnischer K·orridor** m *Polish Corridor* **Polon·äse** f ∼/∼n *polonaise*

P·olo(spiel) n *polo* (urspr. Ind) | ∼schläger [m] *p.-stick*

P·olster n ∼s/∼ *cushion* ‖ Kopf≃ *bolster* ‖ (z Knien) *hassock* ‖ Stuhl≃ *stuffed seat* ‖ ⟨anat⟩ *pad* ‖ ⟨tech⟩ *bolster, pad*(*ding*) ‖ *stuffing* (*of chairs*, etc.) | die ∼ ausbürsten ⟨mot⟩ *to brush the cushion and seats* **∼arbeit** f *upholstery* **∼bank** f *cushioned bench* **∼bett** n *divan, ottoman* **∼möbel** n pl *upholstery* **∼sitz** m (niedriger) *humpty* **∼stuhl** m *stuffed* od *easy chair* **∼watte** f *carded cotton* **P·olsterer** m ∼s/∼ *upholsterer* **p·olstern** vt [h] *to bolster, upholster* (*sofas*) ‖ *to stuff* (*cushions*) ‖ *to pad* (*saddles*, etc.) **P·olsterung** f ∼/∼en *padding, stuffing*; *quilt-work*; *upholstery, upholstering*

Polt·awa n ⟨Russ⟩ (Provinz) *Poltava*

P·olter- ∼abend m ⟨Ger⟩ *wedding-eve* **∼geist** m (*hob*)*goblin* **∼kammer** f *lumber-room* **P·olterer** m ∼s/∼ *blusterer, noisy fellow, roisterer* **p·oltern 1.** vi [s] (fallen) *to roll, thump, tumble* | [h] *to make a rumbling noise*; *to rumble, lumber, rattle, knock* ‖ *to rap hard* (*at a door*) | heute wird gepoltert *today is the eve of the wedding* ‖ es poltert *there are ghosts* (*in the room*) ‖ (Fasan) *to clutter* | ⟨fig⟩ (schreien) *to bluster, roister, grumble, to kick up a row* ‖ ∼d *rumbustious*; ∼d äußern *to rap out*; ∼de Worte *blustering* (*words*) **2.** ≃ n *thump*(*ing*), etc. ‖ *the clutter of a pheasant* ‖ (P) *grumbling, blustering*

Poltr·on [–trɔ̃] m ∼s/∼s Fr *poltroon*

P·oly- ≃**·andrisch** a *polyandrian* ≃**chr·om** a *-chrome* **∼gam·ie** f ∼/∼n *-gamy* ≃**g·amisch** a *-gamous* ‖ ∼e Pflanze *-gam* **∼gl·otte** f ∼/∼n *-glot work* **∼g·on** n ∼(e)s/∼e *-gon* ≃**gon·al,**

≃g·onisch a *-gonal* **≃g·yn** a *-gynous* **≃meris·ieren** vt [h] ⟨chem⟩ *to polymerizate* **~n·esien** n ~s/ (Inselwelt im Stillen Ozean) *Polynesia* **~n·om** n *-nome* **≃n·omisch** a *-nomial* **~ph·on** a *-phonic* **≃t·echnisch** a *-technic* (Unterricht *training*) **~-t·echniker** m ~s/~ *-technician* **~t·echnikum** n ~s/–ken *-technic school* **~the·ismus** m ~/ *-theism* **~the·ist** m ~en/~en *-theist* **≃the·istisch** a *-theistic*

Pol·yp m ~en/~en ⟨zoo⟩ *polyp, octopus* ‖ ⟨med⟩ *polypus* L; Nasen≃en [pl] *adenoids* pl | °⟨fig⟩ (Polizist) ⟨fam⟩ *bobby*; ⟨sl⟩ *cop(per), catchpoll, slop*; (Detektiv) ⟨sl⟩ *busy*, ‖ ⟨Am sl⟩ *dick, bull, flatfoot, blue-coat* **~enstock** m *polypary* **~qualle** f ⟨zoo⟩ *jelly-fish*

p·ölzen vt [h] [österr] (Mauer) ~ *to prop*

Pom·ade f ~/~n *pomade*; *fixature* ‖ mit ~ einreiben *to pomade* ‖ °⟨fig⟩ *calm, ease* ‖ das ist mir ~ ⟨fam⟩ *it's all one to me* | ~nbüchse [f] *pomatum-pot*; ~nstange [f] *stick of p.* **pom·adig** a *greasy* ‖ °⟨fam⟩ *slow, lazy, phlegmatic, indolent*

Pomer·anze f ~/~n (*bitter Seville*) *orange* ‖ ⟨fig fam⟩ *country-miss* | **~n- ~baum** m *o.-tree* **~blütenöl** n *neroli* **~essenz** f *essence of o.s* **~farbe** f *o.* (*colour*) **≃farben** a *o.* **~öl** n *o.-oil* **~saft** m *o.-juice* **~schale** f, eingemachte ~ *candied o.-peel* ‖ *marmelade* **~wasser** n *o.ade*

P·ommer m, **~in** f, **≃(i)sch** a *Pomeranian*; P.sche Bucht *P.n Bay*; P.sches Haff n → Stettiner Haff | **~n** n *Pomerania*

Pommes frites ['pɔm 'frit] pl Fr ⟨cul⟩ *French fried potatoes*; ⟨Am fam⟩ *French fries*

Pomp m ~(e)s/ *pomp, splendour* ‖ ⟨a.⟩ *trappings* pl ‖ (Schaustellung) *ostentation*; (*brilliant*) *display* **p·omphaft** a *pompous, grandiose, spectacular, showy*; *large* (*talk*); *orotund* (*speech*) | adv ~ sprechen *to talk large, to mouth one's words* **pomp·ös** a *magnificent, splendid*

P·ompadour [–u:r] m ~s/~e & ~s *reticule*

†Pomp·eji n ⟨It⟩ (†Hafenstadt) *Pompeii* | pompej·anisch [a] *Pompeian* (Rot)

P·ompelm·use f ~/~n (gr) *shaddock*, (kl) *grape-fruit*

Pön f ~/~en *penalty* | **~·ale** n ~/ *fine*

p·onceau a, ~rot a *bright red*; *scarlet*

Pondich·éry [pɔdi'ʃeri] ⟨Fr⟩ (Siedlung an der Koromandelküste) *Pondicherry*

Pongé-Seide ['pɔ̃ʒe:] f *pongee*

P·onies ['pɔni:s] (Frisur) mit ~ *with a bang*

P·ontifex m ~/–fizes *pontiff* **-fik·alamt** n, **-l-messe** f *episcopal high mass* **-fik·at** n ~(e)s/~e *pontificate*

Pont·inische S·ümpfe ⟨It⟩ *Pontine Marshes* pl

P·ontius m npr; ⟨fig⟩ v ~ zu Pilatus (*to be driven* [geschickt]) *from pillar to post*; (*to be given the roundabout*) **Pont·on** [pɔn'tɔŋ] m ~s/~s ⟨mil⟩ *pontoon* | ~brücke [f] *p. br.*; ~kran [m] *floating cr.*; ~wagen [m] *p. carrier*; ~zug [m] *p. platoon*

†P·ontus m ~/ (Königreich) *Pontus* | ~ Eux·inus [m] ⟨Gr, L⟩ (Schwarzes Meer) *the Euxine* (*Sea*), *Black Sea*

P·ony ['pɔni] n ~s/~s *pony* **~frisur** f *bang*

P·op-art f ~/ (Pop-Kunst) *pop*(*ular*) *art*

P·opanz m ~es/~e *bugbear, bogey* ‖ (Vogelscheuche) *scarecrow* ‖ nur ein ~ *a mere dummy* ‖ wie ein ~ aussehen ⟨fam⟩ *to look a fright*

P·ope m ~n/~n ⟨Gr ec⟩ *pope*, ⟨mil sl⟩ *padre*

°**P·opel** m ~s/~ *nose-dirt*, ⟨fam⟩ *sweep* | **≃n** vi [h] *to pick one's nose* | ≃ n ⟨vulg⟩ *winkle fishing*

p·oplig a *poor* ‖ *stingy*

Popel·ine f ~/ *poplin*, ⟨Am⟩ *broadcloth*

°**Pop·o** m ~s/~s *backside, posterior*, → Po

popul·är a *popular* ‖ ~ m ⟨a.⟩ *to put* (*a th*) *over, to sell widely*, ⟨Am fam⟩ *to plug* ‖ sich ~ m *to ingratiate o.s. with the people* | [adv] ~ gehalten *popularity-phrased* (*account*) **~wissenschaft** f *public science* | ~lich [a] *near-scholarly*, ~liche Vorlesung *scientific lecture for the general public* **popularis·ieren** vt [h] *to popularize* **Popularit·ät** f ~/ *popularity* (genießen *to enjoy*); sich laufender ~ erfreuen *to be in the swim*; auf ~ bedachte P *glad-hander*

P·ore f ~/~n *pore*; aus allen ~n schwitzen *to sweat from* od *at every p.* (vor *from*) **p·orig, por·ös** a *porous, spongy* **Porosit·ät** f ~/ *porosity*

P·orphyr m ~(e)s/~e *porphyry* | **≃n** a *porphyritic*

P·orree m ~s/ ⟨bot⟩ *leek*

P·orst m ~es/ ⟨bot⟩ (*marsh-*) *rosemary*

P·ort m ~(e)s/~e *port, harbour* | ~wein [m] *port* **Port·al** n ~(e)s/~e *portal, entrance, porch*

Port: ~ ·Arthur n (auf Kwantung-Halbinsel); ~ D·arwin n (in N.-Australien); ~ El·izabeth n (im Kapland, Afrika); ~ Said (in Ägypten am Sues-Kanal)

Porte- ~chaise [–ʃ'ezə] f *sedan chair* **~feuille** [–'føij] n ~s/~s ⟨a. parl⟩ *portfolio* ‖ sein ~ zur Verfügung stellen *to resign office* ‖ M. ohne ~ *minister without a seat in the cabinet*; ~träger [m] *cabinet m.* **~monnaie** [port(ə)mɔ'ne:, 'pɔrt–] n ~s/~s *purse* **~p·ee** n ~s/~s *sword-knot* ‖ ⟨mil⟩ ohne ~ [attr] *non-commissioned* | ~fähnrich [m] *ensign* **P·orter** m ~s/, P·orterbier [n] *porter*; starker ~ *stout* **Portier** [pɔr'tje:] m ~s/~s *porter, doorkeeper* ‖ (e–r Firma) *commissionaire* ‖ Hotel≃ *doorman*; ⟨Am⟩ *baggage-man* ‖ stiller ~ *tablet with the names of the occupants* | ~loge [f] *porter's lodge* **Porti·ere** f ~/~n *portière, curtain hung over door*(*way*)

P·ortikus m ~/~ ⟨arch⟩ *portico, porch*

Porti·on [–ts–] f ~/~en *portion, share* ‖ (Anteil) *allowance* | (bei Tisch) (Gericht) *dish*; (auf dem Teller) *help*(*ing*), *plateful*; zwei ~en Kaffee etc *coffee, salad, etc for two*; e–e ~ Kaffee .. *a pot of c.* (*and two cups*) | ⟨mil⟩ *ration* ‖ knappe ~ *pittance* | ⟨fig⟩ e–e gr ~ Geduld (Mut, Frechheit) *great patience* (*a lot of courage, effrontery*) ‖ e–e gute ~ dicker *a lot fatter* ‖ °halbe ~ (P) *half-bit, -portion*; *molly-coddle*

P·ortland 1. ⟨engl⟩ (Stadt in Dorset) → Zement **2.** (Stadt) (*Oreg., U.S.A.*)

P·orto n (portug. Stadt) *Oporto* | ~ Al·egre n (in Brasilien) | **~r·iko** n (westind. Insel) *Puerto Rico*

P·orto n ~s/~s & –ti *postage* ‖ (für Pakete) *carriage* **~auslage** f *p. expenses* **~buch** n *book of p.es* **~einnahme** f *p. and revenue* **~ermäßigung** f *reduction of p.* **≃frei** a *post-paid, carriage paid, prepaid* ‖ *post-free* ‖ ~e Dienstsache ⟨engl⟩ *O*(*n*) *H*(*er*) *M*(*ajesty's*) *S*(*ervice*) (⟨Ger⟩ † frei durch Ablösung) ‖ (durch Namenangabe) ~ m *to frank* (*a letter*) **~freiheit** f *exemption from p.e* **~gebühr** f *p.e* **≃pflichtig** a *liable* od *subject to p.e* **~satz** m *rate of p.e* **~tarif** m *postal tariff* **~vergütung** f *refunding of p.e*; unter ~ *repaying p.e* **~zuschlag** m *additional p.e*

Portr·ät n ~(e)s/~e **Portrait** [–'trɛ:] n ~s/~s *portrait, likeness*; ~ en face *full-face p.t*; ~ in ganzer (halber) Figur *full-length p.t* (*p.t to the waist*); ~ in natürlicher Größe *full-, life-size picture*; ~ im Profil *side-face p.t*; ~ in Halbprofil *three-quarter face p.t* ‖ treffend hingehauenes ~ *thumb-nail p.t* ‖ ~ in Lebensgröße *full-length* (*p.t*) | jdm ~ sitzen *to sit for a p* | **≃-**ähnlich [a] *as like as a picture*; ~maler [m] *p.t-painter*; ~maler·ei [f] *p.t-painting*; ~photographie [f] *portraiture* **porträt·ieren** vt [h] *to portray*

P·ortsmouth ['pɔ:tsməθ] n (Hafen) ⟨Engl⟩

P·ortugal n *Portugal* **Portug·iese** m, **portug·iesisch** a *Portuguese*

P·ortulak m ~(e)s/ ⟨bot⟩ *purslain, purslane*

Porzell·an n ~(e)s/~e *china, porcelain* ‖ Delfter ~ *Delft ware* ‖ Meißner ~ *Dresden china* ‖ unglasiertes ~ *biscuit* ‖ unechtes ~ *earthenware*

|| ~ brennen *to bake p.* || ⟨fig⟩ unnötig ~ zerbrechen *to cause unnecessary trouble* **~erde** f *p. clay*; (chinesische) *kaolin* **~fabrik** f *ch. factory* **~gefäß** n *ch.-vase* **~geschirr** n *ch. ware; crockery* **~glas** n *glass-p.* **~glasur** f *enamel of ch.ware* **~händler** m *ch.-dealer* **~handlung** f, **~laden** m *ch.-shop* || wie ein Elefant im ~ *like a bull in a ch.-shop* **~malerei** f *painting on ch.* **~masse** f *p.-mass* **~ofen** m *p.-kiln* **~schnecke** f ⟨zoo⟩ *cowry* **~service** n *set of ch.* **~tasse** f *ch. cup* **~tiegel** m *p. crucible* **~ware** f *ch.-ware* **~ziegel** m *glazed brick* **porzell·anen** a (*of*) *porcelain* od *china*

Posam·ent n ~(e)s/~e(n) *lace, galloon* | **~en** pl *lace-(work), trimmings* pl, *haberdashery* || ⟨Am⟩ *notions* pl; Abteilung f ~en *notion department* **~·ier** [–'tje:] m ~(e)s/~e *lace-maker* || (Kurzwarenhändler) *haberdasher* **~arbeit** f → –en

Pos·aune f ~/~n *trombone, trumpet* ⟨a. fig⟩ || (Orgel≗) *trombone-stop* || ⟨bib⟩ die letzte ~ *the trump of doom* || (in) die ~ blasen *to sound the trumpet* ⟨a. fig⟩ | **≗n** vi [h] *to play* (*on*) *the trombone* || ~ vt [h] ⟨fig⟩ *to trumpet* || s–n eigenen Ruhm ~ *to sound one's own trumpet* | **~n- ~bläser** m *trombonist* **~engel** m *chubby-cheeked angel* od *baby* || beim letzten **~klang** ⟨bib⟩ *at the last trumpet-call* **~stoß** m *flourish of a trombone*

Pose[1] f ~/~n (Feder) *quill* || *feather* || in die ~n! *to Bedfordshire*! || raus aus ~n! *get up*!

P·ose[2] f ~/~n (Haltung) *attitude, pose* || ~n annehmen (*to assume*) *or* m = **pos·ieren** vi [h] *to attitudinize, posture, pose*; *to strike up an attitude*; *to assume airs* **Positi·on** f ~/~en *position* (*weak, lucrative p.*) || ⟨com, parl⟩ *item* || auf ~ *in station* **~s- ~geschütz** n *heavy ordnance* **~lichter** n pl ⟨mar, aero⟩ *position-lights*, ⟨Am aero⟩ *navigation lights* (→ Bug, Heck, Back-, Steuerbord) **~schiff** n *marker vessel* **~stange** f ⟨mot⟩ *steering indicator* **Posit·iv** [–f] **1.** n ~(e)s/~e [–və] ⟨phot⟩ *positive* (*picture*); ⟨film⟩ (Probe≗e [pl]) *rushes* **2.** ⟨mus⟩ *chamber-organ* **3.** m ~(e)s/~e ⟨gram⟩ *positive* (*degree*) **posit·iv** [a] ⟨phot, el, etc⟩ *positive* (⟨a. fig⟩ = *certain*) || (Antwort) *affirmative* || (Kenntnisse, Wissen) *solid* || *constructive* (*critism*) || *dead* (*certainty*) || nichts ≗es wissen *to know nothing p.e* || ~es Elektron *positron* | [adv] es ganz ~ behaupten *to be most p.e about it* || ~ elektrisch *p.ely electric*(*al*) **Posit·ur** f ~/~en *posture* || sich in ~ setzen *to strike an attitude, to attitudinize* || sich in ~ stellen ⟨fenc⟩ *put o.s. on guard* || ⟨fig & box⟩ *to square up, to square one's shoulders*

†**P·osen** n (†⟨Ger⟩ Stadt u Provinz) (→ [1]Pose) *Posnania*

P·osse f ~/~n *buffoonery, tomfoolery, drollery* || ⟨theat⟩ (derbe *broad*) *farce*; *antic*; (Gesangs≗) *vaudeville* || (Spaß) *fun, joking* || **~n!** pl *stuff*!, *rubbish*! || ~n reißen *to play antics* || ~n reden *to make jokes* || laß die ~n! *stop that fooling*! **P·ossen** m ~s/~ *trick, prank* || ~ treiben *to play tricks*; *to fool* (*about*) || jdm e–n ~ spielen *to play a p a trick* || jdm etw zum ~ tun *to do a th to spite a p* **≗haft** a *droll, farcical, sportive, clownish, comical, waggish* **~reißer** m *buffoon, mime, clown* **~reißer·ei** f *buffoonery* **~spiel** n ⟨theat⟩ *farce* || ⟨fig⟩ *mockery* (*of a trial*) **~spieler** m *low comedian* **~stück** n = Posse & Possen **poss·ierlich** a *droll, funny, comical, ludicrous* || *odd, queer* | **≗keit** f ~/~en *ludicrousness, comicalness, clownishness*

post L nach, hinter || **~ festum** = nachträglich **~datieren** vt [h] *to postdate* **~glazial** a *after-glacial* **~numerando** adv *cash on delivery* (*C.O.D.*); ~ bezahlen *to pay after receipt, at the end of term, month*, etc **~skr·iptum** n (P. S.) *postscript* **-·um** a *posthumous*

P·ost f ~/~en **A.** (Briefe) *post, mail; letters* pl || (Amt) *post*(*-office*); Haupt≗(amt) [n] *main post office*, ⟨engl⟩ *General Post Office* (*G.P.O.*); Neben≗ *station*; *branch p.-o.*, (in Geschäften) *postal substation* || (Kutsche) *mail-coach* || ⟨hist⟩ (Station) *relay, stage* || (Nachricht) *news, intelligence* **B.** Brief–, Paket≗ *letter-, parcel-p.* || Hiobs≗ *evil tidings* **C.** mit **besonderer** ~ u eingeschrieben *under separate and registered cover* || fahrende ~ *p.-* od *m.-coach*; *travelling post office* (*T. P. O.*) || gute, traurige *or* schlimme ~ *good, bad news* || reitende ~ *horse-m.* **D.** die ~ **austragen,** bestellen, zustellen *to deliver letters* || ~ bek, erhalten *to receive m.* od *letters* (mit .. *by the first p.*) || die ~ fährt *the m.-c. runs*, .. auch ohne dich *we can manage without you* || die ~ kommt an *the m. comes in* || es kommt noch e–e ~ *there's another p. in* (*at seven*) || die ~ nehmen *to take p.-horses* od *the m.-c., to travel by m.-c.* || ist ~ f mich da? *are there any letters for me*? || ist die ~ schon da? *is the m. in already*? **E. auf** die *or* **zur** ~ gehen *to go to the p.*; auf, bei der ~ (*the letter got lost*) *in the p.* || auf die *or* zur ~ geben *to* (*send to the*) *p., to drop in*(*to*) *the letter-box* || zur ~ tragen *to take* (*letters*) *to the p.*; ⟨Am a.⟩ *to mail* || auf der ~ aufliefern *to post*, ⟨Am⟩ *to mail* || **durch** die ~, v der ~ *postally* || durch die ~ versenden *to post* || Versendung durch die ~ *p.ing* || **mit** gewöhnlicher ~ *by surface m.*; mit getrennter ~ *under separate cover*; mit der ~ fahren *to travel by m.-c.*; .. schicken .. *by p.* || mit der ersten ~ *by the first delivery* od *p.* || mit nächster (umgehender, wendender) ~ *by the next m.* (*by return of* (*the*) *p.*) || mit heutiger ~ *by to-day's p.* || **ohne** ~ *letterless* || per ~ senden *to mail* || kurz **vor** Abgang der ~ *just before p.-time* **F. ~abfertigung** f *m. dispatch* **~adreßbuch** n *p.-o. directory* **~amt** n *p.*(*-o.*) || auf dem ~ *at the p.-o.* **~angestellte**(**r**) m *p.al servant* **~annahme** f *receiving-house* (*for parcels*, etc.) **~anschluß** m *p.al connexion* **~anschrift** f *p.al address* **~anstalt** f *p.-o.* **~anweisung** f *money-order, p.-o.* od *postal order* **~arbeiter** m *p.al worker* **~auftrag** m ⟨a-engl⟩ *order to the p. to collect money* **~auto** n ⟨Ger⟩ *P.-O. omnibus* **~beamte**(**r**) m *p.-o. clerk* **~beförderung** f *m.-service* || *carriage by p.* || Zug mit ~ *train with m.-van* **~befragung** f *p.al inquiry*; *mail survey* **~behörde** f *p.-o. authorities* pl **~bote** m *p.man*; ⟨Am⟩ *carrier, mail-man* **~chaise** f ⟨hist⟩ = ~kutsche **~dampfer** m *m.-steamer* od *-boat* **~diebstahl** m *p.-o. theft, m. robbery* **~dienst** m *p.al service* **~direktion** f *general p.-o.* **~direktor** m *p.master* **~einlieferungsschein** m *p.-o. receipt* **~fach** n *employment in the p.al service, situation at the p.-o.* | *p.-o. box*, ⟨a.⟩ *private b.* **≗fähig** a *mailable* **~flugzeug** n *mail-plane* || mit ~ *by air-m.* **≗frei** a *prepaid, post-free* **~freiheit** f *exemption from p.age* **~gebühr** f *p.age*; ~en [pl] *p.al rates* **~gefälle** n *p.age and revenue* **~gehilfe** m *p.-o. assistant* **~geld** n = ~gebühr || *fare* (*for the m.-coach*) **~gut** n *goods* pl *conveyed by p.* **~halter** m ⟨hist⟩ *keeper of p.-horses* **~halter·ei** f ⟨hist⟩ *p.-house station* **~haltestelle** f *stage* **~haus** n *p.-house* **~hilfsstelle** f *branch p.-o.* **~horn** n *p.*(*illion's*) *horn* **~karte** f (f Ausland *foreign*, mit Ansicht *pictorial* od *picture*, mit Rückantwort *reply*, ⟨Am⟩ *double postcard*; (mit eingedruckter Marke) ⟨Am⟩ *p.al card* **~kasten** m (*letter-*) (⟨engl⟩ *pillar-*)*box* **~kraftfahrzeug** n = ~auto **~kutsche** f → Post A.; Zeit der ~ *age of the m.-coach*; e–e ~ zu spät *a day after the fair* **≗lagernd** adv *to be* (*left till*) *called for, poste restante* Fr ⟨Am⟩ *General Delivery* **~leitzahl** f ⟨Am⟩ *zip* (= *Zone Improvement Plan*) *code number* **~liste** f *m.ing list* **~marke** f *stamp* **~meister**(**stelle** f) m *p.master*(*ship*) **~minister** m *Postmaster General* **~nachnahme** f ⟨a-engl⟩ *money* (*to be*) *collected by the p.* || gegen ~ *cash on delivery C.O.D.* **≗neu, ≗frisch** a *mint* (Briefmarken *stamps*) **~note** f *p.al order* **~ordnung** f *p.-o. regulations* pl **~ordonnanz** f ⟨mil⟩ *p.man* **~ort** m *p.-town* **~paket** n (*p.al*)

package || als ~ *by parcel-p.* **~paketadresse** f *parcel's direction* **~papier** n *note-paper* **~pferd** n *p.-horse* **~praktikant** m *learner at the P.-O.* (*qualifying for a higher appointment*) °„**~rat**" ⟨hum⟩ *postie* **~recht, ~regal** n *p.al monopoly* **~reisende(r)** m *m.-passenger* **~reiter** m *p.illion, p.rider, courier* **~route** f *stage-line* **~sache** f *p.al matter*; ~n [pl] *letters*; *mailed goods* pl **~sack** m *mail-bag* **~schaffner** m ⟨rail⟩ *m.-guard* **~schalter** m *p.-o. counter* **~scheck(amt** n) m ⟨Am⟩ *p.al cheque* ⟨Am⟩ *check* (*office*) | ~konto [n] *p.al ch. account* **~schein** m *p.-o. receipt* || *ticket for a mail-coach* **~schiff** n *paquebot* ⟨a. philately⟩ (a. ~stempel [m]) | ~umschlag [m] *p.b. cover* **~schließfach** n *lock-box* **~schluß** m; vor ~ *before closing time* (*of the p.-o.*); *before the m. goes out* | ~porto [n] *late-fee* **~sekretär** m *p.-o. clerk* **~sendung** f *mail*(*s* pl) **~sparkasse** f *p.-o. savings bank* **~sperre** f ⟨mil⟩ *stoppage of p.al services* **~station** f *p.-town, p. station*; ⟨hist⟩ *stage* **~stempel** m *p.mark* (mit ~ versehen *to p.mark*); Datum des ~s *date of p.mark* **~straße** f *p.-* od *high-road* **~streuversand** m ⟨Am⟩ *p.al m.ing* **~stube** f *p.-o.*; *waiting-room* **~stück** n *p.al parcel* **~stunden** f pl *p.-o. hours* pl **~tag** m *p.* od *m.-day*; e–n ~ zu spät *a day after the fair* **~überwachungsstelle** f ⟨mil⟩ *p.al censor's office* **~verbindung** f *p.al communication* **~verein** m Welt~ *Universal Postal Union* **~verkehr** m *p.al traffic*; im ~ s (of stamps) *to be used p.ally* **~vermerk** m *official note by the p.-o.* **~versandgeschäft** n ⟨Am⟩ *m.-order house* **~verwalter** m *postmaster* **~verwaltung** f *p.al administration* **~wagen** m *stage-coach, m.-coach* || ⟨rail⟩ *m.-van* **~wechsel** m *change of p.-horses* **≗w·endend** a & adv *by return of p.* **~wertzeichen** n *stamp* **~wesen** n *p.al matters, affairs* pl, *system* **~zeitungsdienst** m *p.al newspaper service* **~zensur** f *p.al censorship* **~zug** n ⟨rail⟩ *mail-train*
post·alisch a *postal*

Postam·ent n ~(e)s/~e *base, pedestal* **P·östchen** n ~s/~ (→ folg) || sauberes ~ (Anstellung ⟨a. mil⟩) *soft number* od *job*, ⟨mil⟩ *bobby's job*; *snip, graft* **P·osten** m ~s/~ **A.** *post, station, place* || (Anstellung) *post, situation, berth* || ⟨com⟩ *item, sum, amount* || *entry* || (Ware) *line, parcel, lot* || ⟨mil⟩ *outpost, sentry, sentinel* || ⟨hunt⟩ *buckshot* || ⟨crick⟩ *square-leg* || ⟨mar⟩ *quarters* **B. berittener** ~ *vedette*; *mounted sentry* || bequemer ~ *cushy job* || eingetragener Buchungs≗ *entry* || einträglicher ~ *remunerative post, snug berth* || gehobener ~ ⟨fam⟩ *high-level job* || ruhiger ~ ⟨mil sl⟩ *soft job* || starker ~ ⟨mil⟩ *strong picket* || ⟨fig⟩ verlorener ~ *forlorn hope* (= ⟨holl⟩ *hoop* = Haufe) **C.** ~ [pl] **ablösen** *to relieve sentries* || e–n ~ aufgeben *to resign a position* || ~ aufstellen (ausstellen) *to post* (*throw out*) *sentries* || ~ besetzen *to fill posts* || ~ stehen ⟨mil⟩ *to stand* od *keep sentry* || ~ stellen *to go on guard* || e–m ~ gewachsen s *to be equal to one's duties* || die ~ wechseln *to change guards* **D. auf** s–m ~ ausharren, bleiben *to stick to* (*to remain at*) *one's post* || auf dem ~ s ⟨fig⟩ *to be on deck*; seid auf dem ~! ⟨mar⟩ *keep good quarters* || ⟨fig⟩ auf dem ~ s *to be on the alert* || nicht recht auf dem ~ s *to be out of sorts* || wieder auf dem ~ (wohlauf)? *up to the mark again*? || auf verlorenem ~ kämpfen *to fight on a forlorn hope, to play a losing game* || auf ~ ziehen *to mount a guard* **~gang** m *sentry-go* **~jäger** m *office-hunter*; ⟨fam⟩ *job-jockey*, ⟨Am⟩ *carpet-bagger, spoilsman* | ~ei [f] *job-hunting*, ⟨Am sl⟩ *ratrace* **~kette** f ⟨mil⟩ *cordon of sentries*; *sentry-line, chain* od *line of posts* **~mantel** m *watch coat* **≗weise** adv ⟨com⟩ *in lots, parcels* **post·ieren** vt [h] *to post, place* **P·ostillion** m ~(e)s/~e *postillion, post-boy* **P·osto** n, ~ fassen *to post* od *station o.s.*

Post·ille f ~/~n *collection of sermons*

Postu- ~l·at n ~(e)s/~e *postulate* **≗l·ieren** vt [h] *to p.*

post(h)·um a *posthumous* (*child, book, edition*)

Pot·emkinsche D·örfer pl ⟨fig⟩ *cardboard façade*

pot·ent a ⟨biol⟩ *fecund* **≗·at** m ~en/~en *potentate, monarch* **~i·al** [–ts–] a, ≗ n ~s/~e *potential* ⟨a. mil, el⟩ (*war-p.l*) | ≗ der Arbeitskräfte *work-force* || Linie des gleichen ≗s ⟨phys⟩ *equip.l line* | ~ [a] ⟨mech⟩ *virtual* | **≗gefälle** n *p.l gradient* **Pot·enz** f ~/~en *power* ⟨a. math⟩ || die 2. ~ *the square*; die 3. ~ *the cube*; die 4. ~ *the fourth power*; 6. ~ *cubo-cube*; 9. ~ *cubo-cubo-cube* || Unsinn in der höchsten ~ *nonsense to the nth power* || Erhebung in e–e ~ *involution* | ⟨biol⟩ *fecundity* **≗·ieren** vt [h] *to raise* (*to a higher* [z. B. *the fifth*] *power*), *to involve* || ⟨fig⟩ *to intensify* | ≗ n, **~·ierung** f ⟨math⟩ *involution*; *raising to a power*; *potentiation*

P·otpourri [–u–] n ~s/~s ⟨mus⟩ *selection, medley, potpourri* || ⟨fam⟩ *olio* ×°**P·ott** m ~(e)s/ ≗e *pot*; ⟨mil⟩ *dixie, dixy* || ⟨cards⟩ *pot, kitty* || ⟨mar sl⟩ *man-of-war* **~asche** f *potash* **~fisch, ~wal** ⟨zoo⟩ m *cachalot, sperm-whale*

P·otsdam n ⟨Ger⟩ (Stadt in der Mark Brandenburg)

potzt·ausend! *great Scot*! *good gracious*! *the deuce*!; ⟨vulg⟩ *my* (*eye*)! || (anerkennend) *I say*!

Poul·arde f ~/~n ⟨cul⟩ *fattened pullet*; *fat* od *Surrey fowl*

°**Pouss-** °**~age** [pu'sɑʒə] f (P) ⟨bes mil⟩ *skoosh*; ⟨Am sl⟩ *crush* °**≗·ieren** vi/t *to sweetheart, to go sweethearting*; ⟨sl⟩ *to spoon, snog*; ⟨vulg⟩ *to moll* ⟨Am⟩ *to fuss*, ⟨sl⟩ *to crush* | (ein Mädchen) ~, (mit e–m M.) ~ *to flirt* od *spoon with .., to be spoony on ..*, ⟨sl⟩ *to crooky, moll* (*a girl*) || ⟨fig⟩ *to court the favour* (*of a superior*) | ~ [n] *carrying*(*s*)*-on* **~·ierstengel** m ⟨vulg⟩ *moll-hunter*

°**Prä** n; das ~ h *to rank* (*first* od) .. vor .. *before*

Präb·ende f ~/~n ⟨ec⟩ *prebend*

Pracht f ~/ *splendo*(*u*)*r, brilliance, magnificence, glory, grandeur, sumptuousness, elegance* || (Luxus) *luxury, luxuriousness* || (Staat) *state, pomp* || (*rich*) *array* || königliche ~ *panoply of royalty* || ~ entfalten *to display splendour* || das war e–e ~! *it was splendid*! **~aufwand** m *extravagant expenditure*; *gorgeous display*; *sumptuousness* **~aufzug** m *pageant* **~ausgabe** f *edition de luxe* **~bau** m *magnificent building* **~bett** n *state-bed* **~einband** m *splendid, choice, elaborate binding* **~exemplar** n *splendid specimen*, ⟨bookb⟩ *spl. copy* || ⟨sl⟩ (P) *ripper, topper*; ⟨Am⟩ *peach* **~finke** m ⟨orn⟩ *weaver-finch* °**~gaul** m ⟨sl⟩ *clinker* **~gesetz** n *sumptuary law* **~himmel** m *canopy* **~käfer** m *metallic beetle* **~junge, ~kerl** m *splendid fellow, regular brick*, ⟨sl⟩ *crackerjack, clinker, stunner* **~kleid** n *gala-dress* **~liebe** *love of splendour* **~liebend** a *sumptuous*; *splendour-loving* **~mädel** n *splendid girl, brick of a girl*; ⟨Am⟩ *queen, peach, cutie* **~mensch** m *trump, brick* **~stück** n *choice piece, show-piece*, ⟨sl⟩ *fizzer, crackerjack* **~sucht** f *ostentation* **≗süchtig** a *ostentatious, pompous, fond of show* **≗voll** a *magnificent, fine, splendid, gorgeous*; *glorious*; ein ~er Kerl *a dashed good sort* || das ist ja ~! *I like that*! **~wagen** m *state-carriage* **~werk** n ⟨bookb⟩ *edition de luxe* **~zimmer** n *state-room* **pr·ächtig** s *superb*; *splendid* (*town*) || *sumptuous, delicious* (*dish*) || *magnificent* (*clothes, works of art*) || *gorgeous* (*women, appearance*) || *charming* (*girl*) || *stately* (*style, building*) || *grand* (*weather*) || *colourful* (*excuse*) || *jolly* (*joke*) || *capital* (*fun*) | ⟨fam⟩ *showy, rattling* || (*mighty*) *fine* (*fellow*) | ⟨sl⟩ *posh* (*shoes*) || ⟨Am⟩ *bully* (*fire*) || ~er Kerl *sound egg*; *topper*; sie ist ein ~er Kerl *she's swell*

Prä- ~destinati·on f ~/~en *predestination* **~dik·ant** m ~en/~en *preacher* **~dik·at** n ~(e)s/ ~e ⟨gram⟩ *predicate* || (Titel) *title* || (Zeugnisnote) *mark* **≗dispon·ieren** vt [h] *to predispose* **≗domin·ieren** vi [h] *to predominate* **~f·ekt** m

~en/~en *prefect* | –·ur [f] ~/~en *prefecture* ~**fig·ieren** vt [h] *to pref·ix* **~f·ix** n ~es/~e ⟨gram⟩ *prefix*

Prag n *Prague* **Pr·ager(in** f) m *inhabitant of P.*

Pr·äg(e)- **~anstalt** f *mint* **~druck** m ⟨typ⟩ *die-stamping*; *raised printing* **~ort** m *place of coinage* **~presse** f *coining press* **~satz, ~schatz** m *mintage* **~stanze** f *embossing die* **~stätte** f *stamping-room* || → ~ort **~stempel** m *die, coin-stamp* **~stock** m *die, matrix, stamping-press* **~werk** n *coining press* **Pr·ägen** n ~s/ *stamping*; *embossing*; *coinage*; *coining* (⟨a. übtr⟩ *of a word*) **pr·ägen** vt [h] *to stamp, mint* || *to coin* (*gold*) || *badly stamped coins* | ⟨fig⟩ *to coin* (*words*); ge–gtes Wort *verbal coin* || *to imprint*; *to identify, characterize*; *to be the highlight* (od *distinguishing feature*) *of* | **sich** ~ in: *the words drove into the audience* || sich [dat] etw ins Gedächtnis ~ *to impress a th on one's memory* | geprägte Form *cast, mould* **Pr·äger** m ~s/~ *stamper, coiner* **Pr·ägung** f ~/~en *coinage, stamping*; *imprint*(*ing*) ⟨a. übtr⟩ | ⟨fig⟩ (*sharp*) *definition* (*of ideas*) || *coinage* (*of a word*) || (*souls of a noble*) *stamp* || (*democracy of a Swiss*) *character* || *pattern*

pragm·atisch a *pragmatic* (Geschichtsschreibung *history*)

prägn·ant a *pregnant* ⟨fig⟩; *pithy, full of meaning*; *concise, terse*; *precise, exact*; *significant*; *sententious* **Prägn·anz** f ~/ *pithiness, terseness*

Pr·ahl- **~hans** m *boaster, John Boaster, braggart, swaggerer* || ⟨sl⟩ *buckstick, stuffed shirt*, ⟨Am⟩ *blowhard* **~sucht** f *boastfulness* **pr·ahlen** vi [h] **1.** (P) [abs] *to show off*; *to swagger*; *to talk big* | laut ~ *to bluster, swank* | *to brag, vaunt, boast* (mit *of*) || *to talk big* (getan z h *about having done*) || (wie geht's? –) Man kann nicht ~ .. *Not much to boast of* **2.** (S) ~d *loud, gaudy* (*colours*); *attracting attention*; *shining, glittering* (*with splendour*) **Pr·ahler** m ~s/~ *braggart, boaster, swaggerer, blusterer, vapourer, ruffle* **Prahler·ei** f ~/~en *braggardism* || *boast*(*ing*), *brag*(*ging*), *bluff*(*ing*) || *bravade* Fr || (Gebärde) *swagger* || ~en *vapourings* pl (über *about women*) || (Prunken) *ostentation* || (Aufschneiden) *exaggeration* || → flunkern **pr·ahlerisch** a *boasting, boastful, bragging* || *showy, ostentatious* || ⟨Am⟩ *spread-eagle* (*article*)

Prahm m ~(e)s/~e *barge, pra*(*a*)*m, lighter, scow, pontoon*; ⟨Am⟩ *flatboat* **~geld** n *lighterage*

Prä- **~jud·iz** n ~es/~e (Vorurteil) *prejudice* || ⟨jur⟩ (Vorentscheidung) *precedent* **~judiz·ieren** vt [h] *to prejudice* || ⟨jur⟩ *to prejudge* **~klud·ieren** vt [h] *to exclude* || ⟨jur⟩ *to foreclose* (*a mortgage*) **~klusi·on** f ~/~en ⟨jur⟩ *foreclosure*

Praktik f ~/~en *practice* || ~en *tricks, dodges, practices, machinations, contrivances* pl **~·ant** m ~en/~en *trainee, probationer, assistant* || ⟨med⟩ *practitioner* | **~er** m ~s/~ *practician* || *practical man* || *expert* | **~um** n *practical course* || ⟨med⟩ sein ~ m *to walk the hospitals* **~us** m ~/–usse *practitioner* || ein alter ~ ⟨fam⟩ *an old stager, hand, soldier* **pr·aktisch** [a] *practical* (*man, christianity, training*) || *pragmatic* (*consequences*) || *working* (*knowledge of French*) || *rule of thumb* (*mathematics*) || *field* (*study*) | (geübt) *practised, sensible, business-like*; ⟨fam⟩ *hard-headed*, ⟨sl⟩ *hard-boiled* (*p*) | ~er Arzt (wenn a. Chirurg *general*) *practitioner* (*G.P.*); ~er Mensch *practician*; ~e Prüfung ⟨fam⟩ *practical*; ~er Sinn *p.ity* | (nützlich) *useful, serviceable*; ~es Wissen *know-how* || etw ~es schenken *to give a useful present* | [adv] *virtually*; *practically* (*minded*) || (*to learn*) *by practice* || ~ (genommen) *for all practical purposes, to all intents and purposes* || *technically* (*possible*) || .. hat ~ mit nichts angefangen *made his way up from next to nothing* || sich ~ bewähren *to prove useful* **praktiz·ieren** **1.** vi [h] *to practise* (*medicine, at the bar*) || *to undergo practical training* **2.** vt *to slip cleverly* ([*from*] *somewhere*)

Prä- **~lat** m ~en/~en *prelate* | ~enwürde [f] *prelacy, prelature* **~limin·ar-** ~friede [m] *preliminaries* pl *of peace*; ~verhandlungen [f pl] = ~ien [pl] *preliminaries* pl

Pral·ine f ~/~n, **Pr·aline** [–e:] n ~s/~s *chocolate-cream* || ⟨fig fam⟩ *billy-cock, bowler, pot-hat*

prall a *tense, tight*; *stuffed out*; *elastic, bouncing, springy* || *tight*(*ly fitting*) (*sweater*) || *plump* (*cushion*) || *tightly stretched* (*sails*) || ⟨mar⟩ *taut* (*rope*) | *strong, well-formed* (*legs, muscles*) || *well-rounded* (*arms, breasts*) || *chubby* (*cheeks*) | *glaring* (*sun*[*shine*]) | adv *tightly* (*filled*) || sich ~ anfühlen *to feel plump* **Pr·all** m ~(e)s/~e *shock, impact, bounce, bound*; *collision* || ⟨el⟩ *back-stroke* || *rebound, recoil* **~brecher** m *impact crusher* **~gefüllt** a *billowing* (*sail*) **~hang** m (e–s Flusses) *undercut slope*, → Gleit– **~heit** f *tightness, tension, plumpness, roundness* **~kraft** f *elasticity* **~licht** n *reflected light* **~luftschiff** n *non-rigid airship* **~schuß** m *rebounding shot, ricochet* **~stoß** m (Billard) *backstroke* **~triller** m *mordent* **~winkel** m *angle of reflection* **~wirkung** f *impacts* pl **~zerkleinerung** f *impact crushing* **pr·allen** vi [h & s] (auf [acc]) *to bounce, bound* (*against*) || *the sun beat down on them* || ab|~ ⟨artill⟩ *to ricochet* || zurück|~ *to rebound, recoil*; ⟨phys⟩ *to be reflected*

prä- **~lud·ieren** vi [h] *to prelude* **~l·udium** n ~s/–ien *prelude* **~medit·iert** a *premeditated* **~mie** f ~/~n (Preis) *award*, ⟨school⟩ *prize* || (Aufgeld) *premium* || ⟨exch⟩ *value above par* || ⟨ins⟩ periodische ~ *p.m paid periodically*; (gleich bleibend *level*) *p.m*; ⟨mst⟩ *insurance money* || ⟨eco, mil⟩ *bounty* || (Zollrückzahlung bei Wiederausfuhr) *drawback* || (Dividende) *bonus*; ⟨comp⟩ ~n *b. earnings* | e–e ~ setzen auf [acc] *to put a prize upon* **~n-** ~abrechnung [f] *p.m statement*; ~anleihe [f] *lottery-loan*; ~befreiung [f] *exemption of p.m*; ~frei [a] ⟨ins⟩ *paid-up* (Police *p.m*); ~geschäft [n]; ~handel [m] ⟨com⟩ *option-business*; ~nachzahlung [f] *supplementary p.m*; ~rechnungen [pl] *p.m notices*; ~schein [m] *p.m bond* || *lottery-bond*; ~zuschlag [m] ⟨ins⟩ *additional p.m* **~mi·ieren** vt [h] *to award a prize, to grant a premium* **~mi·iert** *prize* (*cock, novel*) **~m·isse** f ~/~n *premise* **~mol·ar** m ⟨dent⟩ *biscupid, premolar*

pr·angen vi **1.** (P) *to look fine* || *to shine forth* || *to be dressed up* (*in costly garments*) **2.** (S) *to make a* (*fine*) *show*; *to shine, glitter* || (of trees, etc) *to look beautiful* (*in their rich foliage*) **3.** ⟨mar⟩ *to carry a full press of sail, to crowd all sails*

Pr·anger m ~s/~ *pillory* || an den ~ stellen *to p.* ⟨a. fig⟩; ⟨fig⟩ *to expose, ridicule, gibbet*

Pr·anke f ~/~n *claw* || *clutch*, (*fore-*)*paw*

prä- **~numer·ando** adv *paid in advance* od *beforehand* || ~ bezahlen *to prepay* **~par·and** m ~en/~en *candidate* || ~enschule f ⟨Ger⟩ *training-college for teachers* **~par·at** n ~(e)s/~e ⟨chem etc⟩ *preparation* || ⟨übtr cont⟩ *concoction* || medizinisches ~ *patent medicine* **~parati·on** f ~/~en *preparation* **~par·ator** m *tachodermist* **~par·ieren** vt [h] *to prepare* (auf *for*) || (Prüfungsthema etc) *to get up* || (Skelett) *to skeletonize* || *to press* (*plants*) || *to stuff* (*birds*) || sich ~ ⟨school⟩ *to prepare one's lessons* | (nachgesetzte *deferred*) **~positi·on** f ~/~en *preposition* **~rapha·elisch** a *pre-Raphaelite* **~rogat·iv** [–f] n ~(e)s/~e, **~e** [–ve] f ~/~n *prerogative*

Prair·ie, Prärie f ~/~n *prairie* **~hund** m *barking squirrel* **~wolf** m *coyote*

Pras, Pr·asem, Pr·asen m ⟨minr⟩ *prase*

Pr·äsens n ~/–s·entia ⟨gram⟩ *present* **Präs·ent** n ~(e)s/~e *present, gift* || etw z ~ geben *to give a th as a pr.* **~·ieren** vt [h] ⟨allg⟩ *to offer* || *to present* (⟨a. com⟩ *draft*) || ⟨mil⟩ *to present arms*; –rt das Gewehr! *present arms!* | **sich** gut ~ *to have a good address* od *appearance* **~·ierteller** m *salver, tray* ‖ wie auf dem ~ sitzen *to sit in an exposed position* **Präs·enz- ~bibliothek** f *reference library* **~liste** f *list of persons present* ‖ ⟨mil⟩ *roll* **~stärke** f ⟨mil⟩ *effective strength, e. force*; *e.s* pl

Pr·ä- ~servat·iv n ~(e)s/~e ⟨sex⟩ *contraceptive* **~ses** m ~/ Präs·iden; **~sid·ent** m ~en/~en *president, chairman* ‖ ⟨parl⟩ *speaker*! ‖ → wählen; die Gattin des ~en ⟨Am⟩ *Mrs. N., the first lady* (*of the land*) **~sid·enten-** ~stelle [f] *presidentship, presidency*; ~stuhl [m] *presidential chair*; den ~ besteigen *to take the chair*; ~wahl [f] *presidential election* **⁓sid·ieren** vi [h] *to preside* (*over*), *to be in the chair* **~s·idium** n ~s/–ien *presidency* ‖ das ~ antreten (abgeben) *to take* (*leave*) *the chair* **~skripti·on** f ⟨jur⟩ (*statutory*) *limitation* (*of actions*)

pr·asseln vi [h] (of fire) *to crackle* ‖ (of rain) *to rattle, patter, pelt* | vi [s] *to fall with a rattling noise* ‖ ⟨fig⟩ (of words) *to scorch* (*from a p's lips*)

pr·assen vi [h] *to live in luxury* ‖ *to debauch* ‖ *to lead a gay, dissipated life* | ⟨eig⟩ *to gorge and guzzle*; *to revel, feast, riot, carouse* **Pr·asser** m ~s/~ *glutton* ‖ *spendthrift* ‖ *reveller* ‖ *rake* ‖ ⟨bib⟩ *the Rich Man of the Gospel* | **-·ei** f ~/~en *gluttony, debauchery, luxury, dissipation*

pr·ä- ~sum·ieren vt [h] *to presume* **⁓sumti·on** f ~/~en *presumption* **⁓sumt·iverbe** [–f–] m *heir presumptive* **⁓tend·ent** m ~en/~en (Thron⁓) *pretender* ‖ (Titel⁓) *claimant* **⁓tenti·on** f ~/~en *pretension, claim* **~tenti·ös** *pretentious* **⁓t·eritum** n ~s/–ta ⟨gram⟩ *preterite*; *past* (*tense*) **⁓tor** m ~s/–t·oren *prætor* **⁓t·ur** f ~/~en *prætorship*

°**Pr·atze** f ~/~n *paw, fist*, ⟨sl⟩ *duke*

Prä- ~varikati·on f ⟨jur⟩ *champerty* **~vent·iv-** [–v–f–] ~krieg [m] *preventive war*; ~maßnahmen, ~mittel [pl] *pr. measures* pl

Pr·axis f ~/–xen **1.** *practice*; *technique*; Mann der ~ *practical man, m. of affairs*; in der ~ stehen *to stand in practical life* ‖ für die ~ *for practical purposes* **2.** *experience* (*e. will show*) ‖ nur in der ~ zeigt sich die Bewährung *the proof of the pudding is in the eating* **3.** (Brauch) *custom* **4.** (Übung) *exercise* ‖ **5.** ⟨med⟩ *patients* pl, *practice* ‖ ⟨jur⟩ *clients* pl ‖ ~ ausüben *to carry on a pr.* ‖ die ~ geht gut *the pr. goes well* od *is good*

Präzed·enz f ~/ *precedence*; ohne ~ *unprecedented* **~fall** m ~(e)s/~̈e *precedent*; *example*; *leading case* ‖ e–n ~ schaffen *to set a pr.t* **~streit** m *the pr.ce question*

Präz·eptor m ~s/–t·oren *teacher, tutor*

präz·is a *precise, exact* ‖ (pünktlich) *punctual* ‖ ~ um 2 Uhr *at two o'clock sharp* ‖ [adv] e–e Frage etc ~er fassen *to narrow down an issue* **präzisieren** vt [h] *to define exactly* **Präzisi·on** f ~/ *precision, exactness, accuracy* ‖ ~ bringt e–e Art Entmenschlichung des Abenteuers mit sich *precision has a way of dehumanizing adventure* **~sarbeit** f *pr. work* **~sbombenwurf** m *pr.* (⟨mst⟩ *pin-point*) *bombing* **~sgewehr** n *pr. gun* **~sinstrument** n *pr. tool* **~skleinbildkamera** f *pr. miniature camera* **~smechanismus** m *pr.-built mechanism* **~s-Radaranfluggerät** n *pr. approach radar element* **~swaage** f *pr. balance*

pr·edigen vi/t [h] *to preach* (*morals*) ‖ Buße ~ *to call to repentance* | ⟨übtr⟩ *to rant, discourse*; *to hold forth* (über *about*) | (scheltend) *to lecture, sermonize* | Gelehrten ist gut ~ *a word to the wise is enough* **Pr·ediger** m ~s/~ *preacher* ‖ (Geistlicher) *pastor, clergyman* ‖ Feld⁓ *chaplain* ‖ Methodisten⁓ ⟨hum⟩ *ranter* ‖ ~ in der Wüste *one crying in the wilderness* ‖ ~ Salomo ⟨ec⟩ *Ecclesiastes* **~mönch** m *preaching friar* **~seminar** n *college of divinity* ‖ *pastors' college* **Pr·edigt** f ~/~en *sermon, homily* ‖ *discourse, address* ‖ (⟨fig⟩ e–m) e–e ~ halten *to preach a sermon* (⟨fig⟩ *to give a p a good lecture, to hold forth to a p* [*about women*]) **~amt** n *ministry* **~amtskandidat** m *candidate for holy orders* **~buch** n *book of sermons* **~stuhl** m *pulpit*

pr·eien vt [h] ⟨mar⟩ *to hail* (*a ship*)

Preis m –ses/–se **A. 1.** **(Lohn)** *prize, reward*, ⟨sport a.⟩ *plate*; erster ~ *first prize*; den 1. ~ davontragen ⟨fam⟩ *to take the biscuit* (*p.*) (bek, m *to get*); s–n ~ bek **in** .. *to get one's cap in* .., ⟨Am⟩ *to win one's letter in* (*baseball*); den ~ davontragen, erhalten, erringen, gewinnen *to carry off, win, take the p.*, ⟨fam⟩ *to take the cake, to ring the bell*; die ~e verteilen *to present* od *distribute the p.s*; jdm den ~ zuerkennen *to confer the p. on a p* | e–n ~ **auf** etw setzen *to offer a p. for a th*, → D. | **mit** e–m ~ auszeichnen *to distinguish with a p.* ‖ **um** den 1. ~ gebracht w ⟨racing, golf⟩ *to be a runner-up* **2.** **(Wert)** *price* (*p.*), *rate, value, cost* (f *of*) ‖ Brutto⁓ *gross p.* ‖ Friedens⁓ *pre-war p.* ‖ Fahr⁓ *fare* ‖ (Gebühr) *fee* ‖ gebundene ~e *controlled p.s*; geforderter ~ *charge*, → D. ‖ Grund⁓ *base rate* ‖ Pauschal⁓ *flat rate* ‖ Schleuder⁓ *ruinous price* **3.** **(Lob)** *praise, glory* ‖ Gott sei ~! *glory to God*!; jds ~ singen *to sing a p's praises* **4.** **(Blüte)** *jewel* (*among women*) ‖ *prince* (*among poets*) ‖ *best* (*of all violins*) **B.** (*price*) → A. 2.: **äußerster** ~ *cut rate, lowest p.* ‖ ~ bei Barzahlung *cash p.* ‖ erhöhte ~e *special p.s*, feste ~e *fixed p.*; feste ~e! *no abatement*! ‖ ein gewaltiger ~ ⟨sl⟩ *a thumping p.* herabgesetzte, reduzierte ~e *reduced p.s, short rates* ‖ *to have a high p.* ‖ (*how much would you say*?) jeden ~! *Oh, anything*! ‖ ortsübliche ~e *customary p.s* ‖ zivile ~e *reasonable, fair p.s*; *moderate charges* **C.** **[subj]** die ~e erholen sich *p.s are recovering*; geben nach *are weakening*; halten sich *are well maintained, keep steady*; klettern (schnell) *are going up, are rising* (*rapidly*); liegen hoch *are high*; ziehen an *are hardening* ‖ ~ Nebensache!, (der) ~ spielt k–e Rolle *p.* od *money* (*is*) *no object* ‖ die ~e steigen schnell (schwindelnd) *p.s skyrocket* **D.** **[obj]** die ~e abbauen *to reduce p.s*; was den ~ angeht *when it comes to costs*; den ~ ansetzen f *to price* ‖ den geforderten ~ bek *to get one's own p.* ‖ die ~e drücken (herabsetzen) *to bring down* (*to lower*) *p.s* ‖ e–n ~ erzielen *to fetch a p.* ‖ sie verstehen ~e z m .. *how to put it on* ‖ e–n ~ notieren, veranschlagen *to quote a p.* ‖ e–n ~ auf jds Kopf setzen *to put a p. on a p.s head* ‖ die ~e in die Höhe treiben *to rig up the p.s* ‖ den ~ [gen] veranschlagen *to cost* [*a th*] | die ~e verderben *to cut p.s* ‖ e–n ~ vereinbaren *to agree on a p.* | ‖ abschreckende ~e verlangen *to p. o.s. out of the market* **E.** **auf** ~ halten *to stick to p.s* ‖ es kommt nicht auf den ~ an *it's not a matter of cost* ‖ nicht auf den ~ sehen *not to consider the p.* | **im** ~ v *at the p. of* ‖ hoch im ~ *dear*, .. stehen *to be at a high rate* ‖ im ~ fallen: *the p.s* (*of the goods*) *are falling* ‖ etw sinkt, steigt im ~ *a th falls, rises in p.* od *goes up* ‖ im ~ zurückgehen *to be on the decline* | **mit** dem ~ heruntergehen *to reduce the p.* ‖ mit e–m ~ versehen *to price* ([a] *priced*) | **nach** dem ~ e–r S fragen *to p. a th* | **um** diesen (jeden) ~ *at this* (*any*) *rate* od *price* ‖ um jeden ~ *at all costs*, .. h wollen *to want* (*a th*) *no matter what it costs*, .. losschlagen *to sell at any sacrifice* | um k–n ~ (der Welt) *not at any p., on no account* od *consideration* (*whatever*), (*not for all the world, not for the life of me*) | **unter** dem ~ *below cost* od *the value*; bedeutend unter ~ kaufen *to buy at a considerable saving* | **zum** ~ v *at the rate of* ‖ zu festem ~ *at an appointed p.* ‖ zu billigem ~ ⟨fam⟩ *at a low figure* ‖ zu mäßigem ~ *at moderate charges* ‖ zum niedrigsten ~ *at the rock-bottom p.*; *dirt-cheap* **Pr·eis-** [in comp] ⟨sport⟩ *champion* .. ‖ (Wettbewerb) *prize* .. **~abbau** m *reduction of prices* **~abschlag** m *marking-down*; *abatement* **~angabe** -, **~angebot** n, **~ansatz** m *quotation*; reduzierte ~̈e *cut-price figures* | ohne **~angabe** f *not priced, not marked* **~arbeit** f *prize-paper* **~auf-**

gabe f *prize-subject, -essay*; *competition* **~aufschlag** m *marking-up*; *extra charge* **~anstieg,** **~aufstieg** m *rise in prices*, plötzlicher ∼ *jump* **~ausschreiben** n *(prize-)competition* **~bericht** m *market-report* **~bewerber** m *competitor* **~bewerbung** f *competition* **≂bewußt** a *price-conscious* **~bindung** f (der 2. Hand) *resale* od *retale price maintenance* **~drücker** m *price-cutter* ‖ (Feilscher) *haggler, screw* **~erhöhung** f *raising of price, rise in price* | ∼en [pl] *price rises*; bei ∼en mittun ⟨bes Am⟩ *to get aboard the price-rise wag(g)on* **~ermäßigung** f *reduction of* od *in prices, abatement* **~fall** m *price decline* **~fixierung** f ⟨off eco⟩ *valorization* **~frage** f *prize-subject* ‖ **~gabe** f [v It *presa* = Prise] *abandonment*; *disclosure, give-away* (*of a secret*); *sacrifice* (*of terrain*) **≂|geben** vt [h] *to give up*; *to part with*; *to abandon, surrender, sacrifice* ‖ *to give away, betray, reveal* (*a secret*) | (aussetzen [dat]) *to expose*; (der Schande) *to prostitute* ‖ dem Gelächter ∼ *to hold up to ridicule*; [dat] –ge– s *to be at the mercy of*; Wind u Wetter –ge– ⟨mar⟩ *adrift* | **sich** ∼ (v Frauen) *to prostitute o.s.*; sich e–r S ∼ *to submit to a th* **~gebung** f *surrender, abandonment* | *prostitution* ‖ **≂gekrönt** a *prize-winning* **~gekrönte(r)** m (*prize*) *winner* **~gesang** m *song of praise* ‖ *prize song*, ⟨Am fam⟩ *hit song* **≂gestoppt** a *price-controlled* (Miete) **≂günstig** a *priceworthy*, ⟨bes Am⟩ *budget-, economy-, thrift-priced*; *cut-rate* od *-price* (Angebot) | ∼st [pred] *at the best hand* **~herabsetzung** f *markdown of prices* **~kommissar** m ⟨Ger⟩ *price commissioner* **~kontrollamt** n *office of price administration* (*OPA*) **~kontrolle** f *price control* **~kurant** m, **~liste** f *rate-card, price-list, list of p.s* **~lage** f *cost*; in welcher ∼ etwa? *about what price* ‖ °⟨fig⟩ so in der ∼ *(s)he is about my type of man* (*girl*) **~liste** f *rate-book* **~medaille** f *prize-medal*; Inhaber e–r ∼ *medal bearer* **~nachlaß** m *allowance* | normales **~niveau,** n.r **~spiegel** *standard of prices* **~prüfung** f *price control* **~rätsel** n (Zeitungs≂) *competition* **~regulierung** f *price adjustment* **~richter** m *umpire, judge, arbiter*; ⟨liter⟩ *adjudicator*; als ∼ fungieren *to adjudicate* | ∼ausschuß [m] *panel of judges* **~schießen** n *rifle-competition* **~schraube** f ⟨com⟩ *spiral* **~schildchen** n *tag* **~schrift** f *prize-essay* **~schwankung** f *fluctuation of prices* **~senkung** f *cut in prices* | (staatliche) ∼saktion [f] *roll-back* **~spanne** f *zw* Ex- u Import *term of trade* **~spiel** n ⟨sport⟩ *event* **~spitze** f *price ceiling* **~steigerung** f = ∼erhöhung **~stopp** m *pegging*; ∼ durchführen *to freeze prices* **~sturz** m (*sudden*) *fall of* od *in prices*; ⟨Am a.⟩ *break* **~tafel** f *tariff* **~träger** m *prize-winner*, zweiter ∼ *runner-up* **~treiber·ei** f *rigging the market-corner*, ⟨sl⟩ *boost* **~treue** f *rigid price* **~überwachung** f; Amt f ∼ *Office of Price Administration and Supply* **~unterbietung** f *dumping* **~veränderungsanalyse** f *deviation analysis* **~verderber** m *cutting tradesman* **~vergünstigungen** f pl *price discounts* ⟨a. cust⟩ **~verteilung** f *prize-giving*; ⟨school⟩ *prize day*; *distribution of prizes*, **~verzeichnis** n = ∼liste **~vorbehaltsklausel** f *clause reserving price* **≂wert,** **≂würdig** a *worth the money, worth its price*; *cheap* ‖ *praiseworthy*; *low cost* [attr] **~wettkämpfer** m ⟨box⟩ *prizefighter* **~wucher** m *profiteering* **~zuschlag** m *additional* od *extra charge*

Preiselbeere (-ß-) f ⟨bot⟩ *cranberry, bilberry*

pr·eisen vt [pries/gepriesen] [h] *to praise, glorify* (*God*) ‖ Gott sei gepriesen! *glory* (*be*) *to God*! | *to extol, laud, praise*; *to exalt* (°über den grünen Klee *to the skies*); laut ∼ *to cry* (*write*) *up* ‖ (empfehlen) *to commend* ‖ jdn, (sich), etw glücklich ∼ *to call a p happy* (⟨a.⟩ *to bless o.s.*), *to bless* (*a day*)

prek·är a *precarious, equivocal* (*position*) ‖ in e–r ∼en Situation ⟨sex⟩ *in a somewhat vulnarable position*

Prell- **~bock** m ⟨rail⟩ *buffer-block, bulk-head, fender, bumper* **~pfahl** m *fender* **~schuß** m *ricochet* **~stein** m *guard stone, kerb(-stone)*; *post, bound* **~stoß** m ⟨ftb⟩ *drop-kick*; e–n ∼ m *to drop* **~tuch** n *tossing-blanket* **pr·ellen I.** vt [h] **1.** *to make rebound* ‖ *to* (*toss in a*) *blanket*; ⟨school⟩ *to court-martial* **2.** (betrügen) *to cheat, defraud, dupe, gull*; ⟨fam⟩ *to take in*, ⟨sl⟩ *to do in the eye*; *to bamboozle, spoof* | e–n um (etw) ∼ *to trick* od *do a p out of* .. **3.** ⟨path⟩ *to bruise* **II.** ≂ n *court martial* **Pr·eller** m ∼s/∼ *tosser* ‖ *bilk, cheat* ‖ = Prallschuß *rebound, ricochet* | **~·ei** ∼/∼en *cheat(ing), fraud, imposition, dupery* ‖ ⟨fam⟩ *sell, take-in, bilking* **Pr·ellung** f ∼/∼en ⟨path⟩ *bruise*

Premi·ere [prəm'je:rə] f ∼/∼n ⟨theat⟩ *first-night* ‖ (Stück) *first-nighter* **Prem·ier-** [prəm'je:] **~leutnant** m † (*first*) *lieutenant* **~minister** m *prime minister, premier*; Amt, Würde des ∼s *premiership*

Pr·esbyter m ∼s/∼ *elder*, ⟨a.⟩ *presbyter* **≂i·al** a *presbyterian* **~i·aner** m, **≂i·anisch** a *Presbyterian* **-t·erium** n *presbytery*

pr·eschen vi [h & s] *to hurry, scurry*; *to tear along*

press·ant a *urgent* **pr·eßbar** a *compressible* **Pr.eß-** **~balken** m ⟨typ⟩ *press-cheek* **~baum** m *p.-beam* **~bengel** m ⟨typ⟩ *p.-jack* **~brett** n *p.ing-board* **~eis** n *cake-ice* **~filter** m *filter press* **~flügel** m ⟨spin⟩ *p.er-flyer* **~form** f *stamping die* **~futter** n *comp.ed forage* **~gang** m *p.-gang* **~gas** n *comp.ed gas* **~glanz** m *gloss from the p.* **~hefe** f *German, p.-yeast* **~kohle** f *briquette* **~kolben** m *piston* **~kopf** m ⟨Ger⟩ *large round sausage* **~leder** n *embossed leather* **~luft** f *comp.ed air* **~lufthammer** m *pneumatic hammer* **~luftkammer** f *air-vessel* **~matrize** f → –form **~muster** n *tuck pattern* **~platte** f *p.ing-plate* **~profil** n *extruded shape* **~schiene** f ⟨typ⟩ *p.-hoop* **~schraube** f *p.ing-screw* **~schweißung** f *p.ure welding* **~sitz** m ⟨tech⟩ *force fit* **~span** m *p. span, p.* od *glazed board*, ⟨pap⟩ *gloss-b.* **~stempel** m *extrusion die* **~stoff** m (Kunstharz) *molded plastic*[s pl] **~stück** n *p.ing stamping* **~walze** f *p.-roll* **~wasserantrieb** m *hydraulic drive* | hydraulischer **~zylinder** m *h. cylinder* **Pr·esse** f ∼/∼n **1.** ⟨typ etc⟩ *press* ‖ Flachdruck≂ *flat-p.* ‖ Rotations≂ *rotary p.* ‖ eben aus der ∼ *fresh from the p.* ‖ in die ∼ gehen *to go to p.* ‖ in, unter der ∼ *in the p., printing, being printed* | ⟨übtr⟩ *the Press, journalism*; *the fourth estate* ‖ bezahlte ∼ *kept p.* ‖ e–e gute ∼ h *to have a good p.* ‖ sensationslüsterne ∼ *the yellow p.* ‖ Vertreter der ∼ *p.-man, newspaper man, reporter* ‖ die ∼ knebeln *to muzzle the p.* ‖ Tages≂ *daily p.*; Skandal≂ *gutter p.* **2.** ⟨tech⟩ (Appretur) *lustre, gloss, dressing* **3.** ⟨fig school⟩ *coaching-college, cramming-classes* **~abteilung** f *Public Information Division* N **~amt** n *public relations office* **~ausweis** m *p. card* **~bericht** m *p. report* **~büro** n *p.-department, editorial office*; → –amt **~chef** m *p. chief, publicity agent*; ⟨Am a.⟩ *p.-secretary* **~erzeugnis** n *publication* **~fehde** f *journalistic war, p.-feud* **~feldzug** m *p. campaign* **~freiheit** f *liberty of the p.* **~gesetz** n *p.-law* **~knebelung** f *muzzling of the p.* **~konferenz** f (abhalten *to hold a*) *p.* od *news conference*, (e–s Ministers etc) *P. C.* **~leute** pl *newspaper men* **~loge** f ⟨theat⟩ *p. box* **~mann** *p.man* **~notiz** f *p. notice*; geheime ∼ *dope* **~offizier** m *public relations officer* **~ordnung** f *p.-regulations* **~photograph** m *p. photographer* **~stelle** f → –amt **~prozeß** m *action against a newspaper* **~revision** f ⟨typ⟩ *revise* **~schau** f *p. review* **~sprecher** m → –offizier **~stimme** f *voice of the p.* **~telegramm** n *p. message* **~- u Informationszentrum** n *information center* N **~verein** m (*Anglo-American*) *P.-Association* **~vergehen** n *offence against the p.-laws* **~vertreter** m → –offizier **~zensur** f *p. censorship* **~zwang** m *restriction* od *suppression of the freedom of the p.*, ⟨fam⟩ *gagging of the p.* **pr·essen** vt [h] **I. 1.** *to press* (a. keltern) ‖ *to squeeze* (an *against*), *to pinch* ‖

jdn an sich ~ (umarmen) *to strain a p to one* || (zus~) *to compress* || ⟨tech⟩ *to force, form*; fließ-, kalt-, strang~ *to extrude* || (Öl) *to crush* || (Tuch, Papier) *to calender* || (Tuch) *to gloss* || (Glas etc) *to mould* || heiß ~ *to hot-press* || in Falten ~ *to goffer* || durch ein Tuch ~ *to strain* **2.** ⟨fig⟩ (Matrosen, Soldaten) *to (im)press, crimp*; ⟨mar⟩ *to shanghai* || (Land, Untertanen) *to oppress* || (drängen) *to urge* || jdn durch Drohungen zu etw ~ *to blackmail a p into [doing] a th* || ⟨mar⟩ den Wind ~ *to sail close to the wind* || das preßte ihr Tränen aus den Augen *that drew tears from her eyes* | **gepreßt** voll (Saal etc) *overcrowded*; *crammed full* || er macht s–m ~en Herzen Luft *he gave vent to his pent-up feeling*; mit ~er Stimme *in a choked voice*; ~er Stimmung s *to be depressed, dejected* **II.** ≈ n beim Stuhlgang *straining at stool* **Pr·esser** m ~s/~ *presser* || *oppressor* || (v Matrosen) *press-man* **press·ieren** vi [h & s] *to be urgent* || es pressiert (nicht) *it is most urgent* (*[there is] no hurry*) || ich bin pressiert *I am in a hurry* **Pressi·on** f ~/~en *pressure* **Pr·essung** f *pressure, pressing* || *compression* || *oppression* || *impression* || *squeeze, squeezing, crowding* (*of people*)

Prest·ige [prɛ'stiːʒə] n ~/ *prestige*; ~ bewahren *to save one's face* | ~- *token* [attr] (*raids*); **~-verlust** m *loss of face* **~werbung** f *pr. advertising* **~wiederherstellung** f ⟨fam⟩ *face-lifting*

Preti·osen [–ts–] f pl *valuables, jewelry*

Pret·oria n (Hauptstadt v Transvaal)

Pretze(l) f = Brezel

Pr·eugo → Abk.

Pr·euße m, **Pr·eußin** f *Prussian* **Pr·eußen** n *Prussia* **preußisch** a *Prussian* **Pr·eußenfeind** m *Prussophobe*

prezi·ös a **1.** † *precious* **2.** *affected, studied* | adv *with affectation* **Prezi·osen** → Pretiosen

Pr·icke f ~/~n ⟨ich⟩ *lesser lamprey*; *prick*

pr·ickeln vi [h] *to tickle* || *to prick(le)* || (of limbs) *to tingle* (vor *with*) || (jucken) *to itch* || (v Senf) *to be hot*; (v Sekt) *to effervesce* || es prickelt mir im Munde *it pricks my mouth* | ~d *tickling* etc; *hot, sharp, piquant, pungent*

Pr·iel m ~s/~e *tidal gutter* od *inlet, slough*

Pr·iem m ~s/~e *quid, plug, fig* (*of chewing--tobacco*), ⟨Am vulg⟩ *cud* || ⟨a-n⟩ *plug of rubber* **pr·iemen** vi [h] *to chew tobacco*

pr·ies, (priese) 1. & 3. sg pret (subj) v preisen

Pr·iese f ~/~n (Hemden~) *neck-band* || *hem*

Pr·iester m ~s/~ *priest*, ⟨Am⟩ *pastor* **~amt** n *priestly office, priesthood* **~beffchen** n *clergyman's bands* **~binde** f ⟨hist⟩ *fillet* **~ehe** f *marriage of (the) clergy* **~gewand** n *vestment, priestly garb* od *garment* **~habe** f ⟨bib⟩ *offering* **~hemd** n *alb, surplice* **~herrschaft** f *hierarchy* **~hut** m *clerical hat* **~käppchen** n ⟨R. C.⟩ *calotte* **~rock** m *cassock* **~seminar** n ⟨R. C.⟩ *seminary* (*for priests*) **~staat** m *hierarchical state* **~stand** m *priesthood, sacerdotal order* **~stolz** m *sacerdotal pride* **~weihe** f *consecration, ordination* **~würde** f *sacerdotal dignity* **Pr·iester- ~in** f ~/~en *priestess* **≈lich** a *priestly, sacerdotal, clerical* **~schaft** f ~/ **1.** *body of priests, clergy* **2.** = **~tum** n ~s/ *priesthood, priestcraft*

Pr·im f ~/~en ⟨fenc⟩ (*cut in*) *prime* **~geld** n ⟨mar⟩ *primage* **~zahl** f ⟨arith⟩ *prime* (*number*) **Pr·ima 1.** f ~/–men *highest form* od *class* || ⟨engl⟩ *sixth form* **2.** ≈ a [invar] *A one, A 1,* (*of best quality*) || ⟨fam⟩ *splendid, luscious, gorgeous*; *crushing*; *peachy*; *ace-high*; *champion* [attr] | ⟨sl⟩ *posh, immense, top-notch, tophole, topping, slap-up, spiffing, spiffy, crack, corking*; ⟨bes mil⟩ *quiff* ⟨Am⟩ *bully* || das ist ja ~ *that's a bit of all right, that's a pippin that's in the groove*; → knorke || ~ Kerl, S ⟨Am fam⟩ *darb* **~d·onna** f ⟨theat⟩ *prima donna* **~n·ota** f *day-book* **~qualit·ät, ~s·orte** f *prime* od *first quality* **≈v·ista** It [adv] ⟨mus & com⟩ *at first sight* **~w·are** f *first-rate goods*; *firsts* pl **~w·echsel** m ⟨com⟩ *first of exchange, gilt-edged bill* **Prim·aner** m ~s/~ *pupil of the highest form* || ⟨engl⟩ *six-former* | ~liebe [f] *calf-love* **prim·är** a *primary* | ≈farbe [f] *p.y c.*; ~n [pl] ⟨a.⟩ *primaries*; ≈netz [n] ⟨el⟩ *p.y network* (*of high-tension current*); ≈schule [f] *p.y school*: ~strom [m] ⟨el⟩ *p.y current*; ~takt [m] ⟨comp⟩ *p.y cycle*; ~wicklung [f] ⟨el⟩ *p.y winding* **Pr·imas** m ~/Primasse *primate* || ~ *Germaniae* (Salzburger Erzbischof) vgl *P. of (all) England* (*archbishop of York/Canterbury*) | **-m·aten** = Menschenaffen; ~forschung, ~kunde [f] *primatology* **Prim·at** n ~s/~e *primacy, primateship* **Pr·ime** f ~/~n **1.** ⟨fenc.⟩ = Prim **2.** (Stunde) ⟨ec⟩ *prime* **3.** ⟨typ⟩ *first page* **Pr·imel** f ~/~n ⟨bot⟩ *primrose, cowslip* **primit·iv** a *primitive* || ⟨fig⟩ *rough,* (*c*)*rude*; *simple* || das ≈e (z. B. Nietzsches „Blonde Bestie") *primitivism* **Prim·iz** f ~/~en ⟨R. C.⟩ (*priest's*) *first mass* °**pr·imstens** adv (→ prima) *galoptiously* **Pr·imus** m ~/~se ⟨school⟩ *top-, head-boy* (*of a form*), ⟨Am⟩ *top man* || *captain* (*of the school*) **Prinz** m ~en/~en *prince* | ~gemahl [m] *Prince Consort*; ~metall [n] *prince's metal*; ~regent [m] *Prince Regent* **Prinz-Eduard-Insel** f *Prince Edward Island* **Prinz·eß** f ~/–ssen = ~in | ~bohnen [f pl] *stringless* (*string-*)*beans* **Prinz·essin** f ~/~nen *princ·ess* || (*Pr·incess ·Ann*) **Prinz·ip** n ~(e)s/~e & ~ien *principle* || belebendes ~ *spirit* || aus ~ *on pr.* || im ~ *virtually, in pr.* || ⟨tech⟩ nach dem ~ v *to operate on the pr. of* | es sich [dat] z ~ m *to make a point* (*of doing* zu tun) | ~ienfrage [f] *question of pr.*; ~ienreiter [m] *dogmatist, pedant, doctrinarian,* ⟨fam⟩ *stickler* (*for pr.s*); ~ienstreit [m] *wrangling about pr.s* **Prinzip·al** m ~(e)s/~e *principal, head, chief* || ⟨fam⟩ *governor, boss* || (Brotherr) *master employer* **prinzipi·ell** adv *on principle* **pr·inzlich** a *princely* | ≈keiten [f pl] *princes* pl || ⟨engl⟩ *Royalties* pl

Pr·ior m ~s/Pri·oren *prior* **~·at** n ~(e)s/~e *priorship* **~·ei** f ~/~en *priory* **Pri·orin** f ~/~nen *prioress* **Priorit·ät** f ~/~en *priority, precedence, preference* | **~en, ~saktien** f pl *preference shares* pl **~sanleihe** f *mortgage-loan* **~sanspruch** m *priority claim* **~sobligation** f *preference-bond, debenture* **~spapiere** n pl *preference stock* **~sstreit** m *dispute about precedence* od *priority*

Pr·ise f ~/~n **1.** ⟨mar⟩ *prize, capture* || ⟨fig⟩ *he laid off his little prize* || für gute ~ erklären ⟨mar⟩ *to condemn as a lawful prize* || e–e ~ m *to take a prize* **2.** *pinch* (⟨a.⟩ *smack*) (*of snuff, salt, sugar*) || e–e ~ nehmen *to take a pinch of snuff* **Pr·isen- ~anteil** m *share in a prize* **~besatzung** f *p. crew* **~geld** n *p.-money* **~gericht** n *p.-court* **~kommando** n *p. detail*; *p. crew* **~meister** m *p.-master* **~offizier** m *boarding-officer* **~recht** n *prizage*

Pr·isma n ~s/–men *prism* **Prismenglas** n *prismatic binocular(s pl)* **prism·atisch** a *prismatic* (*colours*)

Pr·itsche f ~/~n **1.** *plank bed,* ⟨mil⟩ *guard-bed* **2.** (*harlequin's*) *slap-stick* || (Reit≈) *crop* **3.** *bat* || *rod* || jdm die ~ geben *to cane a p* **4.** *back-seat* (*of a sledge*) **~nmeister** m *harlequin* (*organizing a fête*) **~nwagen** m *light carriage* (*with plank seat*); ⟨mot⟩ *platform-truck* || ~ f den Huckepackverkehr *pick-a-back* (od ⟨fam⟩ *piggiback*) *trailer* **pr·itschen** vt [h] *to swish, slap, drub* || ⟨fig⟩ *to dupe*

priv·at [–v] a *private* (*entrance, affair*) || *confidential* (*talk*) **Priv·at-** ⟨oft⟩ *privately owned* (*car*), ⟨mst⟩ *private* (*p.e*) **~abmachung** f *private arrangement* **~angelegenheit** f *p.e affair* **~anschluß** m ⟨telph, el⟩ *p.e connection* **~archiv** n; Königliches ~ *the king's archives* pl **~bad** n *p.e bathroom* **~besitz** m; in ~ *p.ely owned* **~bühne** f *p.e theatre* **~-büro** n *p.e office* **~dozent** m ⟨univ Ger⟩ (*unsalaried*) *p.e lecturer* **~druck** m *p.ely printed edition* **~eigentum** n *personal property* **~entnahmen** f pl ⟨com⟩ *drawings* **~erziehung** f *home-education* **~-**

fliegerei f *civilian flying* **~gebrauch** m *p.e use* || (im Haus) *domestic consumption* **~gelehrte(r)** m *p.e scholar* **~interesse** n *p.e interest* **~kasse** f *privy purse* **~klage** f *civil action* (*criminal proceeding* [*in minor matters*] *instituted by the injured party*) **~klinik** f *nursing home* **~leben** n *p.e life*; unsauberes ~ *shady life* **~lehrer** m *p.e tutor* **~leute** pl *p.e individuals* **~mann** m, **~person** f *p.e p* od *gentleman* od ⟨mil⟩ *individual* **~meinung** f *individual opinion* **~patient** m ⟨med⟩ *p.e* od *pay(ing) patient* **~recht** n *civil law* **~rücksichten** f pl, aus ~ *on personal grounds* **~sache** f, sich in ~n mischen *to intrude on privacy* **~schatulle** f *privy purse* **~schule** f *p.e school* **~sekretär** m *confidential secretary* **~sektor** m *p.e sector* **~stand** m *p.e life* **~stunde** f *p.e lesson* **~unternehmen** n *p.e* (*economic*) *enterprise* **~unterricht** m *coaching* **~vorlesung** f ⟨univ Ger⟩ *p.e lecture(s* pl) (*which must be paid for*) **~zentrale** f ⟨telph⟩ *p.e* (mit Handbetrieb *manual*) *exchange* (*PMX*) **Privati·er** [–'tje:] m ~s/~s *p.e gentleman* **priv·at- ~im** adv *privately, confidentially* || ⟨univ Ger⟩ ~ *or* **~·issime** lesen *to lecture to a limited number of students* **~is·ieren** vi [h] *to live on one's own income* || ⟨fig fam⟩ *to eat the bread of idleness; not to take interest in ths one should* **≗·issimum** n ~s/–ma ⟨univ Ger⟩ *private lecture* (→ privatim) **privi- ~leg·ieren** vt [h] *to privilege* ⟨a. jur⟩ || –rt [a] *chartered* (*bank, company*, etc) **≗leg·ierte** m [ein ~r, der ~] ~n/~n *grantee, patentee* **≗l·eg(ium)** n ~s/–gien *privilege, license, patent* || auf Grund e–s ~s des K.s *under a patent granted by the king* || –gien [pl] *vested interest* od *rights*

pro L prep *for* || ~ K·opf (⟨fam⟩ Nase) *per head* || ~ M·ille *per thousand* || ~ St·ück *s piece* | ~ Mann u Tag *per*/*a man per*/*a day* → Kontra

prob·at a (*ap*)*proved, tried, tested* || *excellent* (*remedy*) **Pr·obe** f ~/~n **A.** (Versuch) *trial, experiment, try-out* | (kritische Untersuchung) *test* | ⟨met⟩ (Feingehaltsprüfung) *assay*; (auf dem Prüfstein) *touch* | ⟨arith⟩ (Beweis) *proof* | (Erprobung e–r P) *probation, ordeal* || (Theater≗) *rehearsal* | ⟨com⟩ (Warenmuster) *specimen*; ⟨chem⟩ (a. v Wein etc) *sample*; (Stoff≗) *pattern* || (Stempel etc) *brand, stamp, trade-mark*; (Gold) *hall-mark* | ⟨fig⟩ *sample* (*of handwriting*) || *example* (*of devotion*) || *exhibition* (*of skill*) || ⟨fam⟩ nicht die ~! *not a bit* (*of it*)! **B.** ⟨theat⟩ ~ **abhalten** *to rehearse*; e–e (die) ~ abhalten *to hold a* (*take the*) *rehearsal* | e–e ~ ablegen (v) *to give a proof* (*of*), *to show* (*to prove one's*) (*courage*) | e–e ~ mit etw anstellen, vornehmen *to give a th a trial* | die ~ aushalten *to stand fire* | die ~ bestehen, halten *to stand trial* (od *the test*); .. glücklich .. *to have a successful trial* | ~n aus e–m Behälter entnehmen *to sample a tank* | e–e ~ v Mut geben *to furnish proof of c.* | e–r ernsten ~ [dat] gegenüberstehen *to face a serious challenge* | es gilt die ~! *let's try*! | ⟨theat⟩ ~ halten *to have a rehearsal* | ⟨arith⟩ die ~ m *to do the proof*; *to prove* (auf etw *a th*); .. auf e–e Rechnung .. *to check an invoice*; die ~ aufs Exempel m ⟨fam⟩ *to put* (*a th*) *to the test* od *trial*; e–e ~ m mit (P & S) *to try, test*; *to give a trial to* || mit jdm die ~ m *to put a p to the test* || mit e–r S e–e ~ m *to experiment with* (*a medicine*) **C. auf** ~ (v P) *on probation* || auf ~, zur ~ anstellen, kaufen .. *on trial* || jdn auf die (harte) ~ stellen *to put a p to the* (*severest*) *test*; *to try, test*; jds Geduld auf e–e h. ~ st. *to grate on a p's p.* || auf die ~ gestellt w ⟨a.⟩ *to have a test, to be tried* (*and come out pretty well* u sie bestehen) || jds Geduld, Tugend auf e–e harte ~ stellen *to tax a p's .. to the utmost, to try a p's patience sorely*; jds Energie, Mut .. *to try a p's mettle, to put a p up to* od *on his m.* | **bei, in** e–r ~ schlecht bestehen *to pass a test badly* | **laut** ~ *as per sample* | **nach** ~ ⟨com⟩ by sample; nach ~ kaufen *to buy to s.* | **zur** ~ *on* od *for trial* || *as a sample, on approval* || zur ~ spielen ⟨theat⟩ *to be on trial* **D. ~abdruck, ~abzug** m ⟨typ⟩ *pull*; *rough proof* **~alarm** m *practice alarm* **~anbaufläche** f ⟨agr⟩ *sample plot* **~anwärter** m *probationer* **~arbeit** f *specimen*, ⟨Ger school⟩ *test* (*of work*) **~belastung** f *test load* **~bestellung** f *trial order* **~bild** n ⟨phot⟩ *proof*; ~er [pl] ⟨film⟩ *rushes* **~blatt** n, **~bogen** m ⟨typ⟩ *proof-sheet* **~bühne** f ⟨theat⟩ *rehearsal room* **~druck** m ⟨typ⟩ *proof-impression* **~entnahme** f ⟨tech⟩ *sampling* **~erhebung** f *pre-test*, ⟨stat⟩ *pilot survey* **~exemplar** n *specimen copy* **~fahrt** f *maiden trip, trial(-trip)*, ⟨Am mot⟩ *road test* **~fall** m *test-tube event* **≗fest** a *proof* **~flug** m ⟨aero⟩ *trial* (*flight*), *test* **~gewicht** n *standard weight* **~hahn** m ⟨mach⟩ *test-cock*; (am Faß) *sample-spigot* **≗haltig** a *proof, genuine*, (Gold) *sterling* **~haltigkeit** f *excellence* **~jahr** n *year of probation* **~kandidat** m ⟨school⟩ *probationer* **~kiste** f *samplebox* **~ladung** f *test-charge* **~last** f *test load* **~lauf** m *test-run* ⟨a. mot⟩ **~lektion** f *trial lesson* **~nehmer** m *sampler* ⟨a. cul⟩ **~nummer** f *specimen number* **~papier** n ⟨chem⟩ *test-paper* **~predigt** f *trial sermon* **~rennen** n ⟨sport⟩ *heat, trial* **~ritt** m *trial ride* **~rolle** f ⟨theat⟩ *beginner's part* **~schießen** n *trial shooting* **~schrift** f *specimen of handwriting* **~schuß** m *sighting-shot* **~seite** f *specimen page* **~sendung** f *sample sent on approval* **~statist(in** f) m *stand-in* **~stück** n (*test*) *specimen, sample*; *pattern*; *trial* **~untersuchung** f *test examination* od *investigation* **≗weise** [adv] *on probation* od *trial*; *as a specimen* || ~ aufführen ⟨theat⟩ *to give* (*a play*) *a trial run* **~zeichen** n *mark of assay* **~zeit** f (*period of*) *probation* **pr·oben** vt [h] ⟨theat, mus⟩ *to rehearse* || ⟨met⟩ *to mark* **≗buch** n ⟨typ⟩ *specimen copy* **≗karte** f *card of samples* **≗nehmer** m *sampler* **Prob·ier- ~fräulein** n, (**~mamsell** f obs) *mannequin, trier-on* **~glas** n *test-glass* **~hammer** m *assayer's hammer* **~korn** n *assay-grain* **~nadel** f *touch-needle* **~ofen** m *assay furnace* **~röhre** f *test tube* **~stein** m *touchstone* **~tiegel** m *cupel* **~waage** f *assay-balance* **prob·ieren 1.** vt [h] *to try, to test* || ⟨met⟩ *to assay* || (kosten) *to taste*; (Getränk) ⟨a.⟩ *to sample* || ⟨theat⟩ *to rehearse* || es noch einmal ~ ⟨sl⟩ *to try it on again* || °zu oft ~ *to try it once too often* **2.** ≗ n: ⟨prov⟩ ≗ geht über Studieren *the proof of the pudding is in the eating* **Prob·ierer** m *tester* || ⟨met⟩ *assay-master*

Pro- ~bl·em n ~(e)s/~e *problem* || ⟨comp⟩ *operation* || geschlechtliche ~e *sex* || das ~, vor dem die Welt stand *the pr. before the w.* | ~analyse [f] ⟨comp⟩ *evaluation*; ~kreis [m] *complex of pr.s*; ~stück [n] ⟨liter⟩ *thesis-play* **~blem·atik** f ~/ *the uncertainties* pl **≗blem·atisch** a *problematic* (*natures*) || (*the situation is*) *problematical, uncertain* **~d·ukt** n ~(e)s/~e *product* ⟨a. math⟩ || ⟨agr geol com⟩ *produce* || ~en [pl] *produce* (*of the soil*) || ⟨liter⟩ *product(ion)* || *figment* (*of the imagination*) || ~e der Arbeit *works* | ~register [n] *product* (*PROD*) *register* **~d·ukten-** ~börse [f] *commodity* od *produce-exchange*; ~handel [m] *trade in agricultural products, produce-trade* || (Altmaterial) *junk goods trade*; ~markt [m] *produce market* **~dukti·on** f *production* (*p.n*) || (Menge) ⟨min etc⟩ *output* || (Ertrag) ⟨agr⟩ *yield* **~dukti·ons-** ~abgabe [f] *payment in kind*; ~ausfall [m] *p.n loss*; ~einschränkung [f] *cut-back*: ~genossenschaft [f] *co-operative association*; ⟨agr SBZ⟩ (LPG) *p.n co-operative*; ~kapazität [f] ⟨el⟩ *producibility* (*of a power station*) ~höhe, ~leistung [f] *manufacturing efficiency*; ~leiter [m] *p.n supervisor* od *manager*; ~leitung [f] *Office of the Chief of P.n*; ~menge [f] *output*; ~mittel [n pl] *capital goods*; ~preis [m] *cost of pr.n*; ~programm [n] *range*; *p.n spectrum*; ≗reif [a] m *to develop .. to the p.n stage*; ~steuer [f] *tax on the p.n* (*of wine* etc.); ~übersicht [f] *statistics of p.n*; ~unternehmen [n] *productive undertaking*; ~-

wert [m] *productive value*; ~wirtschaft [f] *producing industry* **⁓dukt·iv** a *productive, fecund* ‖ ⟨übtr⟩ *prolific* (*writer*) **⁓genossenschaft** f *Workmen's Co-operative Production Society* (*bearing the risk*) **~duktivität** f ~/ *productiveness, productivity*; *efficiency* | Tafel der ehelichen ~ *marital fertility schedule* **~duz·ent** m ~en/~en *producer* ‖ ⟨com⟩ *manufacturer* ‖ ⟨agr⟩ *grower* **⁓duz·ierbar** a *producible* **⁓duz·ieren** vt [h] *to produce* | ⟨jur⟩ *to furnish* (*evidence*) | ⟨agr⟩ *to grow*; (*of soil*) *to yield* ‖ ~d (*wheat-*)*growing*, (*gold-*)*bearing*, (*coal-*)*producing* | ⟨fig⟩ (schnell) ~ *to turn out, to churn out* (*propaganda*) | **sich** ~ *to perform*; *to show* od *exhibit o.s.*; *to do one's bit*; ⟨dero⟩ *to make an exhibition of o.s.* ⟨Am⟩ *to put it on*; (v Pferd) *to go through its paces*; .. zum erstenmal .. *to appear for the first time* **~·emium** n ⟨Lit⟩ *proem* **⁓f·an** a *profane* (*writer, history*); *secular* (*music, building, arts*); *stereotyped*; ⟨derog⟩ *vulgar, common*(*place*) **⁓fan·ieren** vt [h] *to profane, to desecrate* **~f·eß** f ~/–sse *vow* ‖ ~ tun *to take vows* od *the veil* **~fessi·on** f ~/~en (studierter Beruf) *profession*; der ~ nach *professionally* ‖ (Handwerk) *trade, business* ‖ v ~ *by trade, profession* **⁓fession·ell** a *professional* (*gambler, rogue*) **~f·essor** m ~s/Profess·oren ⟨univ⟩ *professor* (*of theology* etc.) ‖ ⟨Ger⟩ außerordentlicher ~ *lecturer*; *assistant pr.*, ⟨Am⟩ *adjunct pr.* ‖ ⟨Ger⟩ ordentlicher ~ *pr. in ordinary*, ⟨Am⟩ *full pr.*, ⟨engl⟩ *Professor* (an der Univ. C. *in the university of C.*) ‖ jdn als ~ an die U.C. berufen *to appoint a p pr. at the univ. of C.* ‖ das ~chen *that Professor chap* **~fess·oren-** ~gehalt [n] *faculty salary*; ~titel [m] *title of pr.* ~stelle [f], **Profess·ur** f ~/~en *professorship* ‖ germanistische ~ *chair of German* ‖ jdm e–e ~ übertragen *to appoint a p to a pr.ship* **Prof·il** n ~(e)s/~e *profile* ⟨a. geol⟩ ‖ im ~ *in profile* ‖ im ~ zeichnen *to profile* ‖ ⟨tech⟩ Walz⁓ *rolled section* **~bild(nis)** n *pr.-likeness* **~eis** n ⟨aero⟩ *impact ice* **~eisen** n = –stahl **~fräser** m *profiled cutter* **~reifen** m ⟨mot⟩ *grip rubber* **~schnitt** m *longitudinal section* **~sohle** f *commando sole* **~stahl** m *structural steel* **~träger** m *st.l beam* **profil·ieren** vt *to profile*; ⟨mot⟩ (Reifen) neu ~ *to recap* | –rt (P) → markant **Prof·it** m ~(e)s/~e *profit, gain* ‖ s–n ~ ziehen *to make a p.* (aus *by*); ⟨Am sl⟩ *to have a rake-off* (*on*) ‖ auf ~ aus s *to think a lot of making a p.* **⁓·abel, ⁓lich** a *p.able, lucratice, advantageous* **⁓gierig** a *hungry for p.* **⁓·ieren** vt/i [h] (von) *to profit, benefit* (*by*), *to take advantage* (*of*) **pro f·orma** [L] [adv] *proforma, for form's sake, as a matter of form* **Prof·orma-** ~rechnung [f] *proforma invoice*; ~wechsel [m] ⟨com⟩ *accomodation bill* ‖ ⟨sl⟩ *kite* **Pro- ⁓f·und** a *profound* (*statesman, inquiry, treatise*) **~gester·on** n ~s/ ⟨med⟩ (Hormon) *progesterone* **~gn·ose** f ~/~n *prediction, prognosis* ‖ (Wetter⁓) *forecast* **~gn·ostikon** n ~s/–ken & –ka *prognostic* **⁓gnostiz·ieren** vt [h] *to prognosticate, forecast, predict* **Progr·amm** n ~(e)s/~e ⟨theat, mus⟩ *programme bill, card* ‖ (e–r Partei) ⟨a.⟩ *ticket* ‖ (Schule) *prospectus* ‖ ⟨ind, etc⟩ *plan* ‖ ⟨wir⟩ eigentliches ~ *sustaining program* (Ggs *commercial pr.*) ‖ ⟨comp⟩ *computer program*; neue ~e [pl] *new routines*; Bedienungs- u Unter⁓e *utility and sub-routines* | ⟨comp⟩ Lader f absolute ~e *absolute-program loader*; ~ wieder anlaufen l *to back up a program* ‖ ⟨parl⟩ *platform* ‖ ein ~ aufstellen *to put* od *draw up a program*(*me*) **~ablauf** m ⟨comp⟩ *routine*; während des ~s *at object time* **⁓atisch** a *according to* (*the*) *pr.*; [dazu:] *to pr.* **~aufbau** m ⟨comp⟩ *realization* **~austausch** m ⟨telv⟩ *link-up* **~bibliothek** f ⟨comp⟩ *pr. library* **~einheit** f ⟨comp⟩ *pr. unit* **⁓gemäß** a *pr.med* (*meeting*); ⟨comp⟩ *as defined by a pre-determined pr.* **~generator** m ⟨comp⟩ *compiler* **~gestaltung** f ⟨bes wir, telv⟩ *pr.ming* **⁓gesteuert** a ⟨comp⟩ *pr.med* **~leiter** m ⟨wir⟩ *editor* **~linie** f ⟨comp⟩ *pr. step* **⁓mäßig** adv *according to plan, as arranged*; ⟨Am⟩ *according to schedule* ‖ ⟨fig⟩ *without a hitch* **~musik** f *programme music* **~planer** m ⟨comp⟩ *pr.mer* **~rede** f ⟨pol⟩ *keynote speech* **~redner** m ⟨parl Am⟩ *keynoter* **~satz** m ⟨comp⟩ *sentence* **~schalttafel** f ⟨comp⟩ *pr. control panel* **~schleife** f ⟨comp⟩ *loop* **~schreibung** f ⟨comp⟩ *pr. writing* **~schritt** m ⟨comp⟩ *step of a pr.* **~setzer** m *assembler* **~sprung** m ⟨comp⟩ *repetition of selected pr. steps* **~taster** m ⟨el tech⟩ *power dial* **~umsetzer** m ⟨comp⟩ *compiler, assembler* **~versammlung** f ⟨Am pol⟩ *caucus* **~wahlknopf** m ⟨comp⟩ *pr. selector knob* **~wechsel** m ⟨comp⟩ *changing from one pr. to another* **programm·ieren** vt [h] (neu ~ *to re-*)*program* ⟨a. comp⟩ **P-ierer** m *programmer* **~sprache** f *programming language* (bestimmte) ⟨comp⟩ *autocoder*; **P-ierung** f *pr.ming*, vereinfachte ~ ⟨comp⟩ *ease of pr. preparation* | Unterstützung [f] bei ~sarbeiten *pr.ming assistance*; ~smöglichkeiten [f pl] *pr.ming facilities*

Pro- ~gressi·on f ~/~en ⟨math⟩ *progression* | ~ssatz [m] ⟨ins⟩ *rate of bonus increase* **⁓gress·iv** [–f] a *progressive* | ⁓ität [f] [–v–] *progressiveness, progressivity* (*of taxation*); ⁓steuer [–f–] f *progressive duty* od *tax* **~gymnasium** n ~s/–sien *lower part of a grammar school* **Prohibit·iv-** [–f] ~gesetze [n pl] *prohibitory laws* pl; ~system [n] *prohibitionism*; ~zoll [m] *prohibitive duty* **Prohibit·orium** n ~s/–rien *writ of prohibition* **Proj·ekt** n ~(e)s/~e (~e m *to*) *project, design, scheme, plan*; ~e m ⟨a.⟩ *to make plans* | ~enmacher [m] *projector, schemer* **⁓·ieren** vt [h] **1.** ⟨math⟩ *to project* **2.** = Projekte m | **~·il** n ~(e)s/~e *projectile* **~i·on** f [–ts–] ~/~en *projection* ⟨a. psych⟩ | ~sapparat [m] *p.n apparatus*; tragbarer ~ *p.n kit*; ~slehre [f] *projective geometry*; ~s-Persönlichkeitstest [m] (ohne Wissen der P) *p.n test*; ~sschirm [m] *screen* | **~or** m ~s/–·oren (Dia⁓ *slide*) *projector* | **~lampe** f *projection lamp* **projiz·ieren** vt [h] *to project* **Pro- ~klamati·on** f ~/~en *proclamation* (an *to*) **⁓klam·ieren** vt [h] *to proclaim* **~kr·ustesbett** n *procrustean bed*; aufs *or* ins ~ spannen *to stretch on the bed of Procrustes* **~k·ura** f ~/ ⟨com⟩ *right of signing per pro*; *procuration* (erteilen, h *to give, have the p.*) ‖ per ~ *per procuration* (abbr. *per pro*(*c*), *p. p.*) ‖ (Vollmacht) *power of attorney* **~kur·ator** m ~s/–at·oren ⟨hist⟩ *procurator* ‖ ⟨jur⟩ *attorney*; *proxy* **~kur·ist** m ~en/~en ⟨com⟩ *confidential* (*signing, chief, head*) *clerk* ‖ *proxy* **Prol·et** m ~en/~en ⟨cont⟩ *cad, grub, bounder*; ~ der Autobahn *road hog* **-tāri·at** n ~(e)s/~e *proletariat*(*e*); geistiges ~ *white collar pr.* ‖ ⟨cont⟩ *rabble* **-t·arier** m ~s/~ *proletarian* | **⁓·arisch** a *proletarian* | **⁓aris·ieren** vt [h] *to proletarianize* **Pro- ~l·og** m ~(e)s/~e *prologue* ‖ den ~ sprechen *to prologize* **~longati·on** f ~/~en *prolongation* ‖ ⟨st exch⟩ *carry*(*ing*)*-over* | ~sgebühr [f] ⟨st exch⟩ *contango rate*; ~sgeschäft [n] *contango-business* **⁓long·ieren** vt [h] *to carry over, to prolong, renew* (*bills*); *to extend* (*time*) **~mem·oria** n ~s/~s *memorial, memorandum* **~men·ade** f ~/~n (Weg) *promenade*; gr ~ ⟨fam⟩ *grand strut*; (Gehen) *walk* | ~nanzug [m] *day-suit*; ~nkleid [n] *walking gown*; ~ndeck [n] ⟨mar⟩ *pr.e deck*; ~nkonzert [n] *outdoor* od *park concert*, ⟨engl fam⟩ *prom*; °~nmischung [f] (Hund) *pug, mongrel*, ⟨Am sl⟩ *mutt* **⁓men·ieren** vt [s] *to take a walk* od *a stroll* **~m·esse** f ~/~n ⟨com⟩ *promissory note* **~m·ille** n ~/~ (abbr $^0/_{00}$) *per thousand* **⁓min·ent** a *prominent* (P); ~e P, ⁓e(r) V.I.P. (*very important p*); ~e Bürger [pl] *notabilities*; *civic heads* pl, ⟨Am sl⟩ *headliners* pl; ~e Pn [pl] *local celebrities* ‖ ~est [sup] *predominant* | ~enjäger [m] *lion* hunter -**miskuit·ät** f ~/ ⟨sex; zoo⟩ promiscuity ~**moti·on** [–ts–] f ~/~en ⟨univ⟩ graduation ‖ taking a (⟨Ger⟩ doctor's) degree | ~sschrift [f] dissertation; doctor's thesis ≗**mov·ieren** 1. vt [h] to graduate, to confer a degree on ‖ he was graduated at Oxford (⟨Am⟩ from O.) 2. vi [h] to graduate; to take a (⟨Ger⟩ doctor's) degree (in at, ⟨Am⟩ from), ⟨engl a.⟩ to commence M. A.

pr·ompt a prompt (answer, attendance); ready, quick (at hand) | [adv] with dispatch | ≗**heit** f promptness, promptitude

Pro- ≗**mulg·ieren** vt [h] to promulgate ~**n·omen** n, ~s/~ & –mina ⟨gram⟩ pronoun ~**päd·eutik** f ~/ propædeutics pl [sg konstr] ~**pag·anda** f ~/ propaganda (m, treiben to make p.; f for); marktschreierische ~ ⟨bes Am⟩ build-up ‖ ⟨pol⟩ ~ m to canvass (for) ‖ ⟨com⟩ advertising, ⟨Am⟩ publicity; ⟨fam⟩ boost ‖ ⟨dero⟩ [in comp] mongering ‖ Feind≗, Flüster≗ enemy, whispering p. | ~abteilung [f] ⟨pol⟩ Publicity Department; ~feldzug [m] p. campaign; ~kompanie [f] p. company ⟨fam⟩ loudspeaker and leaflet c.; ~krieg [m] mind campaign; ~leiter [m] press-agent; ~ministerium [n] ⟨Ger⟩ Ministry of P., ⟨engl⟩ M. of Information; ~spezialist [m] agitprop; ~trick [m] p. bluff od trick; ~wert [m] p. value ≗**pagieren** vt [h] to propagandize ~**p·eller** m ~s/~ airscrew, ⟨Am⟩ propeller ‖ Dr·uck≗ (Z·ug≗) pusher (tractor) airscrew | °~putzer [m] ⟨aero sl⟩ (Mechaniker) flying K.P. (= Kitchen Police); ~turbine [f] turboprop

pr·oper a neat, smart, clean, tidy

Proph·et m ~en/~en prophet (f prophetess) ‖ ⟨bib⟩ die gr. (kl.) ~en the major (minor) prophets ‖ ⟨fig⟩ °Moses u. die ~en ready cash ‖ ⟨prov⟩ der ~ gilt nichts in s–m Vaterlande a pr. is not without honour save in his own country ~**entum** n prophetic mission ≗**isch** a prophetic (soul, gift), mantic; mit ~er Kraft begabt fatidic(al) **prophez·eien** vt [h] to prophesy ‖ ⟨allg⟩ to foretell, predict ‖ jdm Gutes ~ to pro. well of od for a p **Prophez·eiung** f ~/~en prophecy | ⟨allg⟩ prediction **Pro-** ≗**phyl·aktisch** a preventive, prophylactic ‖ ~e Maßnahme, ~es Mittel prophylactic | [adv] by way of prevention ~**phyl·axe** f ~/ prophylaxis ≗**pon·ieren** vt [h] to propose ~**porti·on** f ~/~en proportion | ≗·al [a] pr.al; ⟨tech a.⟩ equivalent; ≗ale Aufteilung apportionment ‖ umgekehrt ≗al inversely pr.al; ~·ale [f] ⟨math⟩ (mittlere ~) (mean) pr.al; ~·alwahlrecht [n] pr.al representation; ≗·iert [a] pr.ate; ~**srechnung** f ⟨arith⟩ (rule of) pr.

Propriet·ät f ~/~en → Eigentum proprietary

Propst m ~es/≗e dean; prior; ⟨R.C.⟩ provost ~·**ei** f ~/~en pr.ship ‖ pr.'s jurisdiction, residence

Propyl·äen pl the Propylæa pl

Pr·or·ektor m ~s/–·oren prorector ‖ ⟨univ⟩ vice-chancellor ~·**at** n ~s/ pr.ate, pr.'s office

Pr·osa f, ~ prose; ~gedicht [n] ⟨m. m.⟩ free verse -·**aiker** m ~s/~ pr.-writer **p-·aisch** a prosaic, matter-of-fact, prosy; down-to-earth; unromantic, unimaginative ~·**ist** m ~en/~en pr.-writer

Pro- ~**sektor** m ~s/–·oren ⟨anat⟩ demonstrator ~**sel·yt** m ~en/~en proselyte ‖ ~en m to pr.e vi, to make converts | ~enmacher [m] proselytizer; ~enmacher·ei [f] proselytism, redegewandte ~ ⟨fam⟩ high pressure Christianity ≗**s(i)t!** (⟨fam a.⟩ prösterchen) your health! here's to you! ‖ ⟨sl⟩ chin-chin! ‖ ⟨Am fam⟩ here's looking at you! here's how! ‖ ⟨sl⟩ (here's) mud in your eye!; down the hatch! ~ Neujahr! a happy New Year to you! ‖ ⟨iron⟩ °ja ~!, °prost(e) Mahlzeit! you may whistle for it!, fiddlesticks!, ⟨Am sl⟩ applesauce! | ein ≗ dem Gastgeber here's to the health of our host ~**skripti·onsliste** f list of proscribed persons

Prosod·ie f ~/~n [–i:ən] prosody (Lehre u Buch) **pros·odisch** a prosodia(ca)l, –dic

Pro- ~**sp·ekt** m ~(e)s/~e (Aussicht) prospect; ⟨theat⟩ back-cloth, ⟨Am⟩ b.drop ‖ (Werbeschrift) prospectus; (ausführliche) folder, booklet, pamphlet, leaflet ≗**sper·ieren** vi [h] to prosper, flourish, thrive ‖ (P) to get along well (in business) ~**stata** f ~ ⟨anat⟩ 1. prostata (gland) 2. [in comp] prostatic 3. ⟨mil sl⟩ °~! = prosit! ≗**stitu·ieren** vt [h] (sich) ~ to prostitute (o.s.); to offer (o.s.) to anybody ~**stitu·ierte** f ~n/~n prostitute, call-girl, streetwalker ~**stituti·on** [–ts–] f ~/ prostitution; social evil ~**sz·enium** n ~s/–nien proscenium | ~sloge [f] stage box; ~srahmen [m] pr. border

Protagon·ist m ~en/~en ⟨hist-theat⟩ protagonist (⟨a. fig⟩ = Vorkämpfer)

prot·eisch a Protean; → Proteus [npr]

Pro- ≗**teg·ieren** [–ʹʒi:rən] vt [h] to protect, patronize, favour ~**tekti·on** [–ts–] f ~/ protection, patronage | ~swirtschaft [f] protectionism ~**t·ektor** m ~s/–tekt·oren protector (f protectress) ~-**tektor·at** n ~(e)s/~e protectorate ‖ unter m–m ~ under my patronage ~**t·est** m ~(e)s/~e protest (a. Wechsel≗) ‖ remonstrance (gegenüber to a p) ‖ e–n ~ beschließen to pass a resolution of pr. ‖ einlegen to pr. (bei to a p), to enter a pr. (gegen against); ‖ ~ mangels Annahme pr. for non-acceptance ‖ mit ~ zurückkommen to be returned dishonoured ‖ unter ~ verlassen to leave (a room) under pr. ‖ zum ~ to be pr.ed ‖ zu ~ gehen l to pr. (a bill), to get (it) pr.ed ‖ zum Zeichen des ~s as a gesture of pr. | ~frist(ablauf [m]) [f] (expiration of) protest period; ~kundgebung [f] remonstrance; ~ der Neger sit-in, swin-in, apply-in, etc (demonstration) → Bd. I –in; ~kosten, ~spesen [pl] pr.-charges; ~marsch [m] ⟨Am⟩ parade; ~versammlung [f] indignation-meeting

Protest·ant m ~en/~en Protestant | ≗**isch** a Protestant; ~ erziehen to bring up in the Protestant faith | ~·**ismus** m Protestantism **protest·ieren** vt/i [h] to (make) protest (to a p); to remonstrate; wegen etw ~ to expostulate with a p about a th; laut gegen jdn ~ to cry shame upon a p (sich verwahren gegen) to object to (a th) ‖ ⟨parl⟩ to take exception (gegen to) | e–n Wechsel ~ l to let a bill go to protest **Proth·ese** f ~/~en ⟨surg⟩ prosthesis; artificial limb; (Zahn≗) dental plate

Prot·ist m ~en/~en (noch ungeklärt ob bot? od zoo?) ~en [pl] protista

Proto- ~**k·oll** n, ~(e)s/~e ⟨pol⟩ protocol ‖ record; ⟨dipl⟩ agreed min·utes pl ‖ ⟨jur⟩ register ‖ das ~ aufnehmen to make minutes (of a meeting) ‖ ein ~ aufnehmen to take down evidence; e–e Erklärung ins ~ aufnehmen ⟨parl⟩ to note a statement ‖ das ~ führen to record, protocol; to keep the minutes, etc. ‖ zu ~ geben (to make an application, etc by oral statement to be recorded) to place (od go) on record, ⟨jur⟩ to depose ‖ zu ~ nehmen to record (officially); ⟨jur⟩ to take down (evidence) | ~buch [n] minute-book; ⟨parl⟩ Hansard, the Journals pl; ~eintragung [f] minute; entry; ~führer, (Protokoll·ant) [m] recorder, clerk ⟨jur mst⟩ stenographist ‖ p who keeps the minutes ‖ registrar; ≗mäßig [a] according to evidence od the minutes **protokoll·arisch** a recorded, entered in the minutes | [adv] by the minutes **p-ll·ieren** vt [h] to protocol, enrol, record, minute, register ‖ to take down on record ‖ ~ l to leave on record ‖ bitte nicht ~ this is off the record **P-llierung** f ~/~en registry, registration, entry | ~**n** (**Pr·oton** n ~s/–·onen = einwertiger H-Kern) proton; Kerne mit ungleicher ~en- u gleicher Neutronenzahl ⟨at⟩ odd-even nuclei ~-**pl·asma** n ~s/–men (proto)plasm ~**t·yp** m ~(e)s/~e prototype

Protuber·anz f ~/~en protuberance

Protz m ~en/~en snob, swell; puffed up fellow; swank, braggart, ⟨a.⟩ upstart, ⟨Am⟩ shoddy **Pr·otz-** (v Protze) ~gestell [n] limber-body; ~haken [m] l.-hook; ~kasten [m] ammunition box;

~nagel [m] *pintle*; ~öse [f] *trail-eye* **Pr·otze** f ~/~n ⟨mil⟩ *limber, gun-carriage* || ~n auf|≃n vt [h] *to limber*, ab|≃n *unlimber* **pr·otzen** vi [h] (mit) *to vaunt* [vt], *to make a show* (*of*); *to put on airs*; ⟨fam⟩ *to blow* **≃tum** n ~(e)s/ *snobbery, snobbism*, ⟨Am⟩ *shoddy* **Protzer·ei** f ⟨sl⟩ *swank, puff* **pr·otzig** a *pretentious*; *pompous, pursy, purse-proud, ostentatious, snobbish*; *flaring* (*advertisement*) || ⟨fam⟩ *stuck-up*; *ritzy, snooty, show-off* [attr]; ⟨sl⟩ *swank* | **≃keit** f *flare, snobbishness*

Pr·ovence [prɔ'vɑ̃s], die ~ *Provence*, → –nz·ale

Proveni·enz f ~/–en *origin, provenance*

Provenz·ale m, **–lin** f *native of Provence*; *Provençal* **p.lisch** a *Provençal*

Provi·ant m ~(e)s/~e *provisions, stores, victuals*, ⟨Am⟩ *commissaries* pl; *supply*; (Futter) *forage* || mit ~ versehen *to provision, supply, forage* **⁓amt** n *store-office, commissariat*, ⟨Am⟩ *commissary, supply depot* **⁓beamter** m *commissariat officer* **⁓fahrzeug** n ⟨mar⟩ *victualling vessel* **⁓haus** n *store-house* **⁓kolonne** f *supply column* **⁓magazin, ⁓lager** n, **⁓niederlage** f ⟨mil⟩ *supply depot*; ⟨a.⟩ *magazine* **⁓meister** m *storeman*, ⟨mil⟩ *commissariat-officer*, ⟨Am⟩ *commissary* || ⟨mar⟩ *purser* **⁓raum** m ⟨a-n⟩ *stores-cargo* **⁓sack** m *haversack* **⁓schiff** n *victualling* od *store-ship* **⁓wagen** m *supply-waggon* **⁓wesen** n *commissariat*(*-department*) **⁓zug** m *supply train* **provian·t·ieren** vt [h] *to provision, victual*; *to supply with provisions*, etc

Prov·inz f ~/~en *province* || die ~ (Ggs Hauptstadt) *the p.s* pl, *the country*(*side*); hinterste ~ ⟨Am sl⟩ *the sticks* || aus der ~ *provincial* [a & subst] || nach ~ riechen, schmecken *to be countrified* **⁓ial·ismus** m ~/–men *provincialism* **⁓i·al-, ≃i·ell** a *provincial, of a province* **⁓ler** m ~s/~ *provincial*

Pro- ⁓visi·on f ~/~en (Vorrat) *provision* || (Vermittlergebühren) *commission*; *factorage*; ⟨Am⟩ (*illegal*) *f.* || (Maklergebühren) *brokerage, percentage* | ≃sfrei [a] *free of c.*; ~skonto [n] *c.-account*; ~sreisende(r) [m] *travel*(*l*)*ing salesman on c.*; ≃sweise [adv] (z. B. *payment*) *on c.* **⁓v·isor** m ~s/–·oren *dispenser, chemist's assistant* **≃vis·orisch** a *provisional, temporary*; *tentative* (*agreement*) **⁓vis·orium** n *p*, od *t. state* od *arrangement*; [abstr] *tentativeness* **⁓vokati·on** f ~/~en *provocation* **≃voz·ieren** vt [h] *to provoke, challenge* **⁓zed·ur** f ~/~en *procedure, practice*; ⟨jur⟩ *proceeding* **⁓z·ent** n ~(e)s/~e (abbr $^0/_0$) *per cent* || ~e [pl] *per-cents* pl, *percentage, poundage, royalty* || zu 5 ~ *at 5 per cent.*, ⟨engl⟩ *a shilling in the pound*, ⟨Am⟩ *5 cents on the dollar* || zu wieviel ~? *at how much per cent.*? *at what percentage*? || hohe ~e [pl] *a high percentage* | ~rechnung [f] *interest account*; ~satz [m] *percentage*; *rate of interest* || ein gewisser ~ *a good part of it* || (so:) *only a small proportion of* (*the members*), *to a large extent* ..≃z·entig a [in comp] z. B. (*three*) *per cent.* (*stock*) **≃zentu·al** a *percental* || ~e Zunahme *percentage of increase* | [adv] *percentagewise* **Proz·eß** m, –esses/–esse *process* (*of refinement*) || *proceeding* | ⟨jur⟩ (*law*)*suit, action* || (Verfahren) *procedure, proceedings* pl; *trial* || gegen jdn e–n ~ anstrengen *to open court pr.gs against a p*; mit jdm e–n ~ h *to have a lawsuit with a p* || den ~ gewinnen *to gain one's case* || der ~ wurde zu s–n Gunsten entschieden *judgement was given in his favour* || e–n ~ anstrengen (führen) *to lay* (*conduct*) *a case* || in e–m ~ unterliegen *to lose a case* || es zum ~ k l *to let a matter come to legal proceedings* || jdm den ~ m *to put a p on trial* || der ~ schwebt *the case is pending* | ⟨fig fam⟩ kurzen ~ m *to act quickly*; *to pull no punches*; .. mit *to make short work of, to deal summarily with, to give* (*a p*) *short shrift*; *to shortshrift* (*a th*) **⁓akten** f pl *records* pl *of a lawsuit, minutes* (*of a case*) **⁓aufkauf** m ⟨jur⟩ *champerty* **⁓führer** m *litigant, plaintiff* (*'s counsel*) **⁓führung** f *management* od *conduct of a case* **⁓kosten** pl *lawcosts* pl | ~versicherung [f] *legal expenses insurance* **⁓liste** f *docket* **⁓ordnung** f *rules* pl *of the court* **⁓pfleger** m *guardian ad litem* L, e–s Minderjährigen ⟨jur⟩ *next friend* **⁓recht** n *adjective law* **⁓sache** f *legal case* **⁓standschafter** m → Verfahrens– **⁓sucht** f *litigious disposition* **≃süchtig** a *litigious* **⁓vollmacht** f *letter* od *power of attorney* **⁓verfahren** n *procedure* || ein ~ gegen jdm einleiten *to proceed against a p* **⁓wesen** n *legal procedure* **prozess·ieren** vi [h] *to carry on a lawsuit, to litigate, to be at law* (*with*) || gerne ~ *to be fond of going to law* **Prozessi·on** f ~/~en *procession* || e–e ~ veranstalten *to go in a pr.* | ~saltar [m] *temporary altar*; ~sspinner [m] ⟨ent⟩ *processionary caterpillar*

pr·üde a *prudish, stuffy*; *squeamish*; *strict*; *straight-faced, -laced* || „Frau ≃" (öffentl. Meinung) *Mrs Grundy* **Prüder·ie** f ~/~n [–iːən] *prudishness, prudery* || [pl] *acts of pr.*

Pr·üf- ~bürste [f] ⟨el⟩ *pilot brush*; ~frequenz [f] *sampling fr.*; ~glasständer [m] *test-tube rack*; ~lesen [n] ⟨comp⟩ *auto-correction checking*; ~maschine [f] *verifier*; ~messung [f] *control test*; ~schrank [m] *test board*; ~stand [m] *t. bench*; ~stein [m] ⟨fig⟩ *criterion*; *acid t.*; ~versuch [m] *test*; ~vorschrift [f] *test specification*, → –ungsordnung; ~zeichen [n] *check*; ein ~ setzen *to check* **pr·üfen** vt [h] **A.** *to try* (*a p's obedience*); *to test* (*safety, capacity*) || ⟨met⟩ *to assay* || ⟨chem⟩ *to analyse* || *to inspect* || ⟨bib⟩ *to prove* | etw ~ *to study* || *to check* (*up*) (*accounts, lists*) || *to check* (*statements, the correctness of*) || *to look into* (*a th*) (*we have been into the matter again*); *to give attention to* | (jdn) ~ *to probe*, ⟨Am⟩ *to quiz* || ⟨school etc⟩ *to examine* (*a p*) (in *in*) (⟨a. fig⟩ *o.s.*) || (heimsuchen) *to afflict* **B.** (Bücher) *to audit* || (Frage) *to ventilate, air* || (Herz) *to search* || (Kenntnisse) *to test* || (Listen) *to scan* || (Lage, Maschine) *to go over* || (Notizen) *to consult* || (Waren) *to sample* || (Wein) *to taste* **C.** etw durch und durch ~ *to put a th through its paces*; erneut ~ *to look into a matter afresh* || *to review again* || flüchtig ~ *to give* (*a p*) *the once-over* || gründlich ~ *to scrutinize, canvass, sift* (*to the bottom*) || kritisch ~ *to scan* (*a p's face*) || ständig ~ *to have under constant examination* **D.** (über~) *to screen* (**auf** *for*) ⟨fig⟩; etw **auf** Richtigkeit ~ *to verify a th* || jdn auf s–e Tauglichkeit ~ *to verify a p's fitness* (etc.) || jdn auf Herz und Nieren ~ ⟨bib & fig⟩ *to try the heart* (*and reins*) **E. ⁓d** *scrutinizing*, etc. || *speculative* (*look*) || *analytic* (*mind*) || ~d abschätzen *to assess* || ~ ansehen *to search a p, to look a p over* || etw ~d betrachten *to scrutinize* || ~der Blick *appraising, searching glance* **F. geprüft** (→ A–D) (*examined and*) *approved* || *certificated* (*teacher, electrician*) || ~ u f richtig befunden *audited and found correct* | (heimgesucht) *visited*; schwer geprüft ⟨fig⟩ *severely tried*; *sorely afflicted* (*father*) **G.** ≃ n ⟨comp⟩ *checking*: ~ der Karten *proving the accuracy of the punching* **Pr·üfer** m *tester, examiner*; ⟨met⟩ *assayer*; ⟨comp⟩ *automatic verifier* **Pr·üfling** m ~s/~e *examinee, candidate* **Pr·üfstein** m *touchstone* ⟨a. fig⟩, ⟨fig⟩ *test* (für *of*) **Pr·üfung** f ~/~en **A.** *examination, examining* || *probation* || *investigation*; ⟨tech⟩ *inspection* (*of material*); ⟨theat, film⟩ (Vor≃) *preview*; ⟨mil⟩ ~ der Einsatzbereitschaft f d. Alarmfall *operational readiness inspection* od *test*; ⟨com jur⟩ ~ der Insolvenz *solvency t.* || (Probe) *trial, test*(*ing*) || *proof* || (Versuchung) *temptation* || (Schickung) *affliction, visitation, trial* **B.** eingehende ~ *scrutiny* || mündliche ~ *oral* od *viva voce exam.*, ⟨fam⟩ *viva* (*voce*); ⟨Am a.⟩ *quiz* || schwere ~ *hard exam.*; *severe* od *hard trial*; ⟨fig⟩ *ordeal, racket* || wohlwollende ~

favourable consideration | Abnahme≃ *acceptance test* ‖ ⟨univ⟩ Aufnahme≃ ⟨Oxf.⟩ *responsions*; ⟨fam⟩ *smalls* pl; ⟨Cambr⟩ *little-go* **C.** e–e ~ anstellen, vornehmen *to inquire into a th* ‖ etw e–r ~ unterziehen *to submit* (od *subject*) *a th to severe scrutiny* .. (od *to a test*); .. erneut .. ⟨a.⟩ *to reconsider* | e–e ~ ablegen *or* m, in e–e ~ steigen, sich e–r ~ unterziehen *to go in for* (od *to sit for*) *an exam.*; etw e–r flüchtigen ~ unterziehen ⟨fam⟩ *to give a th the once-over* ‖ e–e ~ bestehen *to pass an exam.*; .. mit Auszeichnung *to be distinguished in an ex.* ‖ sich durch e–e ~ qualifizieren *to qualify o.s., to get qualified* ‖ in e–r ~ durchfallen, ⟨fam⟩ durchrasseln *to fail in an ex.*, ⟨fam⟩ *to be ploughed* od *plucked* | s–e **~sarbeit** abgeben *to turn in one's ex. papers* **~sattest** n *testing certificate* **~saufgabe** f (schriftliche) *paper*(*s* pl) **~sausschuß** m, **~skommission** f *examining board* od *body*; ⟨Am⟩ *review board*; dem ~ angehören *to be on the e. b.* **~serinnerung** f *observation* **~sexperte** m *ex. expert* **~skandidat** m *examinee* **~smaßstab** m *test* **~sordnung** -, **~sbestimmungen** f pl *regulations for the conduct of an ex.* **~sstelle** f *control office* ⟨a. tech & off⟩ **~sstück** n *test piece* **~ssystem** auf Ehrenwort ⟨Am⟩ *honor-system* **~szeit** f *testing time*; *time of ex.* od ⟨fig⟩ *of sore trial* **~szeugnis** n *certificate, diploma* | zu **~szwecken** m pl [dat] *for checking* ⟨a. comp⟩

Pr·ügel m ~s/~ **1.** *stick, cudgel* **2.** [pl] ⟨fam⟩ *thrashing* ‖ (tüchtige) ~ bek ⟨fam⟩ *to get a* (*sound*) *thrashing, belting*; *to get a thr.g for one's pains* ‖ e–e Tracht ~ *a good licking* od *drubbing*; ⟨sl⟩ *socks* [pl] (*to give a p socks*) ‖ e–e Tracht ~ verdienen *to want the stick* **~knabe** m ⟨hist⟩ *whipping-boy* ‖ ⟨fig⟩ *scapegoat*; ⟨Am⟩ *fall-guy* **~strafe** f *corporal punishment*; *caning*; *lash*; jdm ~ erteilen *to flog a p* **Prügel·ei** f ~/~en *scuffle, brawl, row, fight* **pr·ügeln** vt [h] *to cudgel, beat, flog, belabour, thrash, spank, baste, pommel*; ⟨Am⟩ *to paddle* ‖ ⟨sl⟩ *to hide* ‖ tüchtig durchgeprügelt w *to get a fine whipping* ‖ e–n beinahe zu Tode ~ *to thrash a p within an inch of his life* ‖ **sich** ~ *to fight*; *to come to blows*

Prün·elle f ~/~n ⟨bot⟩ *prunello*

Prunk m ~(e)s/, → Luxus *splendour, magnificence,* ‖ *pomp, ostentation, display, show* **~bett** n *bed of state* **~entfaltung** f *ostentation* **~gemach** n *state-room* **~harnisch** m ⟨hist⟩ *parade armo*(*u*)*r* **≃liebend** a *splendour-loving* **≃los** a *unostentatious, simple* **~losigkeit** f *unostentatiousness, simplicity* **~stück** n *show-piece* **~sucht** f *ostentation, love of display*; *luxury, pomposity* **≃süchtig** [a] *ostentatious, pompous* **≃voll** a *splendid, spectacular, gorgeous* | [adv] ~ überladen *pompous, showy* **~zimmer** n *state-room* **pr·unken** vi [h] *to exhibit great splendour* ‖ (mit) *to make a parade* od *show* (*of*); *to parade, flaunt* (mit) [vt]; *to boast* (*of*) ‖ ⟨fam⟩ *to show off* ‖ **~d** *gaudy, glaring, showy, ostentatious* **pr·unkhaft** a *showy, pretentious, ostentatious, luxurious*

pr·usten vi [h] *to puff out, to snort*; *to sneeze violently*; ich prustete los *I burst out laughing* ‖ °ich pruste dir was! *you may whistle for it!*

°**Prutsch** f ~/ *pouting mouth*; e–e ~ m *to pout*

pr·utzeln vi/t [h] *to frizz, sizzle*

Psalm m ~(e)s/~e *psalm* | **~·ist** m ~en/~en *ps.ist* **Ps·alter** m ~s/~ (Buch) *psalter* ‖ ⟨mus⟩ *psaltery* **~spiel** n *playing on the psaltery*

Pseudon·ym **1.** n ~s/~e *assumed name, pseudonym* **2.** ≃ a *pseudonymous*

pst! *hush! hist! stop!* ‖ (z Kellner) *here!*

Ps·yche f ~/~n **1.** npr **2.** *soul* **3.** *mentality* **Psychi·ater** m ~s/~ *alienist, psychiatrist* **Psychiatr·ie** f ~/ *psychiatry* **ps·ychisch** a *psychic* (*pressure, process*); *psychical* (*health, inhibition*) **Ps·ycho-** **~anal·yse** f ~/ *psycho-analysis* **~anal·ytiker** m *psycho-analyst* **~kin·ese** f ⟨occ⟩ *psychokinesis* **~l·og(e)** m ~en/~en *psychologist* **~log·ie** f ~/ *psychology, psychics* pl **≃l·ogisch** a *psychological* ⟨a. mil⟩ (*warfare*): **PSK-Zug** m *psywar platoon* ‖ ~-menschliche Faktoren [pl] *human relations* in ~er Hinsicht *psychologically*; *ps.l* (*warfare*); nach ~er Methode *subjective*; **~es** Moment *ps.l moment*; ~er Vorteil *ps.l advantage* **~neur·ose** f *psychoneurosis* **~pathologie** f *abnormal ps.y* **≃-som·atisch** a *psychosomatic* (Medizin) | (Affekt-) **Psych·ose** f (*affective*) *psychosis*

Pubert·ät f ~/ *puberty*; *adolescence* | ~s-~alter [n] *puberty*; ~erscheinung [f] *puberty phenomenon*

p·ublice [–tse] adv *publicly* **publ·ik** a *public* **≃-ati·on** [–ts–] f ~/~en *publication* **P·ublikum** n ~s/ **1.** *public* ‖ ⟨theat, etc.⟩ *audience* ‖ *readers* ‖ das große ~ *the public at large* ‖ das feinste ~ *the finest circles of society* **2.** (öffentliche Vorlesung) *public lecture* **3.** ≃wirksam a *human-interest* [attr] **P·ublikumsfang** m *crowd-catch*(*ing*); → Bauernfängerei **publiz·ieren** vt [h] *to publish* ‖ (verkünden) *to promulgate* **Publiz·ist** m ~en/~en *journalist, publicist* **~ik** f ~ *journalism* | **≃isch** a *journalistic* ‖ adv *in the Press* **Publizit·ät** f ~/ *publicity*

°**P·uckel** m ~s/~ (= Buckel) *back*

p·uckern vi [h] *to throb*

P·uddel- **~eisen** n ~s/ *puddled iron*; *muck bar* (⟨a.⟩ –stahl) **~hütte** f *forge* **~maschine** f *puddler* **~ofen** m *puddling furnace* **~roheisen** n *forge pig iron* **p·uddeln** vt [h] ⟨met⟩ *to puddle*

P·udding m ~(e)s/~e & ~s *pudding* (→ Güte)

P·udel[1] m ~s/~ (dog) *poodle* | ⟨fig fam⟩ *fault, blunder* ‖ (P) *drudge* ‖ wie ein begossener ~ *quite dumbfounded* od *abashed*, .. dastehen *to look a damned fool* ‖ des ~s Kern ⟨fig⟩ *the gist* od *very essence of the whole matter, the sum and substance of it, the whole th in a nutshell*; *the crux* **~mütze** f *furred cap* **≃n·ackt** a *stark naked* **≃n·ärrisch** a *very droll* **≃naß** a *soaked* (*to the bones*) **~schnitt** m ⟨cosm⟩ *bubbly* od *poodle cut* **≃w·ohl** a; ~ s *to feel awfully jolly* **p·udeln** vi [h] *to miss* ‖ ⟨fig⟩ *to blunder*

°**P·udel**[2] f ~/~n (Pfütze) *puddle, slough*

P·uder m ~s/ *powder*; ⟨cosm⟩ (*face-*)*p.* **~beutel** m *p.-bag* **~dose** f *p.-box*, ⟨Am a.⟩ *compact* **~mantel** m *peignoir* **~quaste** f *p.-puff* **~stein** m *cake* **~zucker** m *p.ed* od *castor sugar*; *confectioner's sugar* **p·udern** vt [h] (sich) *to powder*

puff! *puff!, bang!, pop!* | ≃–≃ f (Kindspr) ⟨rail⟩ *puff-puff*; ≃-~-Eisenbahn [f] ⟨bes Am⟩ *choo-choo-train* **Puff** m ~(e)s/~e & ≃e **1.** (Stoß) *cuff, punch, thump, buff* ‖ ⟨fam⟩ *dig, poke* (*in the ribs*); jdm e–n ~ geben *to take a p. at a p*; er (es) kann e–n guten ~ vertragen *he can stand a good deal* (*it will bear some rough handling*) **2.** (Bausch, Rauchwölkchen) *puff* **3.** (Knall) *pop, report* ‖ ⟨fig⟩ *fraud*; (Reklame) *puff* **4.** (Puffspiel) *backgammon* **5.** *round cushion* ‖ *basket* (*for dirty linen*) **6.** ⟨vulg⟩ (Bordell) *whore-, knocking-shop*; *nanny-house* **~ärmel** m *puffed sleeve* **~bohne** f *horse-bean* **~brett** n *backgammon-board* **~mais** m ⟨Am⟩ *pop-corn*; (gezuckert) ⟨fam⟩ *crackerjack* **~mutter** f *madame* **~reis** m *puffed rice, rice-crispies* pl **~spiel** n *backgammon* **p·uffen** **1.** vt [h] *to cuff, poke, thump*; (wiederholt) *to pummel, buffet* ‖ *to poke*; *to give a dig* (*in the ribs*) | *to puff up* (*one's hair*) | *to puff* (*o.s.*) *out* **2.** vi [h] *to puff*; (of engines) *to chuff* ‖ vorbei~: *a train chugged past* ‖ (schießen) *to pop, to bang away* ‖ ⟨fig⟩ daß es (nur so) pufft *thoroughly, awfully, with a vengeance* ‖ ~d zerplatzen *to detonate* **P·uffer** m ~s/~ **1.** ⟨rail⟩ *buffer*, ⟨Am⟩ *bumper* **2.** (Kartoffel~) *potatocake* **3.** ⟨tech el⟩ *dashpot* **4.** *pocket-pistol, pop-gun* **5.** = Puff 1. **~batterie** f ⟨el⟩ *balancing battery* **~scheibe** f ⟨rail⟩ *buffer-disk* **~staat** m *buffer state* **~zone** f ⟨aero⟩ *Bufferzone* (vor der ADIZ [*air defence identification zone*])

puh! [intj] *pish!, phew!, hoots!*

°**p·u(h)len** vi [h] *to pick* (in .. *one's teeth, nose*)
°**P·ulk** m ~(e)s/~ ⟨mil⟩ *group* (*of vehicles, planes*, etc); *collection*; *unit* || ⟨racing⟩ *ruck*
°**P·ulle** f ~/~n *bottle* (Sekt *of ch.*) || e–e ~ trinken (mit) *to crack a b.* (*with*) || °die ~ reinschieben ⟨aero sl⟩ (Gas geben) *to go through the gate*
p·ullen vt [h] **1.** *to row* || (of horse) *to bore* || *to pull in* (*a horse*) **2.** ⟨vulg⟩ *to piddle*
°**P·ulli** m ~s/~ = Pull·over m ~s/~ *pullover*, ⟨Am⟩ *sweater* || (ärmellos, lang) *jerkin*; (Kurzärmel≃) *sweat-shirt*
P·ulpa f ~/–pen ⟨dent⟩ *pulp*
P·uls m –ses/–se *pulse* || erhöhter ~ *high p.* || fliegender ~ *fast beating, hammering p.* || leichter ~ *weak p.* || ⟨übtr & fig⟩ *beat* (*the inner beat of hope*) || der ~ geht (setzt aus, stockt) *the p. beats* (*stops*) || jdm den ~ fühlen (zählen) *to feel* (*take*) *a p's p.* **~ader** f *artery*; (große) *aorta* | ~öffnung [f] *arteriotomy*; ~geschwulst [f] ⟨path⟩ *aneurism* **~ati·onsstrahlmotor** m *pulse jet* **~hammer** m ⟨phys⟩ *pulse-glass* **~schlag** m *pulsation*; ⟨fig⟩ *rhythm* **~schreiber** m *sphygmograph* **~stockung** f *stoppage of the pulse* **~uhr** f *pulse-glass* **~wärmer** m *cuff, mitt(en), wristlet* **~zähler** m *pulsation counter* **puls·ieren** vi [h] *to pulsate* || ⟨fig⟩ *to pulse, throb*; *to hum, to be vibrant* (*with life*)
Pult n ~(e)s/~e *desk, writing-table* || (*speaker's, teacher's*) *desk* || (*writing-, marking-*)*desk* || Dirig·enten≃ *conductor's desk* || L·ese≃ *podium, rostrum, lectern* || ⟨tech⟩ *console*, ⟨wir⟩ *control c.*; M·isch≃ *mixing table* || N·oten≃ *music-rest* || Sch·alt≃ *switch* od *control desk* || St·eh≃ *high desk* **~dach** n *pent-, shed-roof*
P·ulver [-f-] n ~s/~ **A.** *powder* ⟨a. pharm⟩ || ⟨fig⟩ (Geld) *brass* **B.** fein-, grobkörniges ~ *coarse-, fine-grained p.* || rauchloses ~ *smokeless p.*; *cordite*, ⟨Am⟩ *indurite* || Schieß≃ *gunp.* || mit ~ u Blei *with p. and shot* || ein Schuß ~ *a charge of p.* **C.** ein ~ **bereiten** (einnehmen, verreiben) *to prepare* (*take, grind*) *a p.* || ⟨fig⟩ er hat das ~ nicht erfunden *he's only twelve and six in the pound, he'll never set the Thames on fire, he's no conjurer* od *great light* || er hat ~ gerochen *he has seen service* (*smelt p.*) || noch kein ~ gerochen h *never to have been under fire* || er kann kein ~ riechen (ist feige) *he doesn't like the smell of p.* || sein ~ unnütz verschießen *to waste one's p.* (*to labour in vain*) || ⟨fig⟩ er hat sein ~ verschossen *he has shot his bolt, he has spent his substance*; ⟨sex⟩ *he has no money in his purse*; .. noch nicht .. *has still shot in the locker* || zu ~ u Blei verurteilt *condemned to be shot* || ⟨fig⟩ kein Schuß ~ **wert** *not worth p. and shot* od *one's salt* **≃artig** a *p.y, pulverous* **~dampf** *p.-smoke* **~explosion** f *gunp. explosion* **~fabrik** f *p.-mill* od *-works* pl **~faß** n *p.-barrel*; ⟨fig⟩ auf e–m ~ sitzen *to sit on the top of a volcano* **~flasche** f *p.-flask* **~form** f; in ~ *pulverized* **~gas** n *explosion gas* **~horn** n *p,-horn* **~kammer** f ⟨mar⟩ *p.-room* || (des Gewehrs) *exploding chamber* || (e–r Mine) *p.-chamber* **~körnchen** n *grain of p.* **~ladung** f *gunp. charge* **~magazin** n *p.-magazine* **~masse** f *p.-composition* **~mühle** f *p.-mill* **~probe** f *p.-test* **~prober** m *p.-prover* **~qualm, ~rauch** m *p.-smoke* **~rückstand** m *residue of p.* **~sack** m *p.-sack* **≃-scheu** a *timorous, cowardly* **~schlag, ~schwärmer** m *cracker* **~schleim** m *residue of p.* **~schnee** m *p.y snow* **~tonne** f *p.-barrel* **~turm** m *p.-magazine* **~-verschwörung** f *Gunpowder Plot* **~wagen** m *gunp. cart* **p·ulverig** a *powdery* **pulveris·ieren, p·ulvern** vt [h] ⟨pharm, chem⟩ *to levigate* || *to pulverize* (*charcoal*) || *to* (*reduce to*) *powder* (*cinnamon*, etc) || ⟨fam⟩ es wurde viel gepulvert *there was a lot of random shooting*
P·uma m ~s/~s ⟨zoo⟩ *puma, cougar*
°**P·ummel** m ~s/~ *roly-poly* | **≃ig** a *plump*, ⟨sl⟩ *crumby, crummy, cobby*
°**Pump** m ~(e)s/~e ⟨fam⟩ *tick*, (*credit*) || ⟨sl⟩ *touch* (*he attempted a t.*) || auf ~ *on tick* || e–n ~ anlegen, aufnehmen *to get a loan* || e–n tüchtigen ~ m *to run up a big bill* **~brunnen** m *pump-well* **~fix** m *plunger* **~haken** m *pump-hook* **~hose** -, (e–e *a pair of*) *plus-fours* pl, *knickerbockers* pl || (f Damen) *bloomers* pl **P·umpe** f ~/~n *pump* ⟨a. sex⟩, eiserne ~ ⟨a.⟩ *stanpipe* || die ~ faßt .. *draws, sucks* || .. ist verstopft *is choked* || e–e ~ ansaugen l *to fetch a p.* | ·Abteuf≃ *sinking p.* || Dr·uck- u S·aug≃ *pressure and suction p.* || Einspritz≃ *injection p.* || Motor≃ *motor p.* || Kreisel-, Rotations≃ *rotary p.* || ·Umlauf≃ *circulating p.* **p·umpen** vt [h] **1.** *to pump* **2.** *to buy, take, go on tick* || Geld v jdm ~ *to borrow money from a p*; *to touch a p for m.* || (leihen) *to* (*give on*) *tick*
P·umpen- ~antrieb m *pump drive* **~gatt** n *side hole of a p.* **~gehäuse** n ⟨mot⟩ *torus cover* **~geschirr** n *p. gear* **~gestänge** n *p. spears* **~heimer** m *Adam's ale* **~kolben** m *sucker* (*of a p.*) **~rad** n ⟨mot⟩ *driving torus* **~schwengel** m *p,-handle* **~stange** f *p.-rod* **~stiefel** m *p.-barrel* **~stock** m ⟨mar⟩ *p.-staff* **~ventil** n *clack* **~werk** n *p.ing plant* **~zylinder** m = ~stiefel ˣ**p·umperlges·und** a (as) *sound as a bell*
P·umpernickel m ~s/~ *Westphalian rye bread*
P·unier m, **~in** f *Carthagian* **p·unisch** a *Punic, Carthaginian*
Punkt I. m ~(e)s/~e **A. 1.** ⟨geom, geogr⟩ *point* (*p.*): ~e darüber hinaus ⟨rail, aero⟩ *p.s beyond*; höchster ~ e–r Steigung ⟨mot⟩ *brow* **2.** (zeitlich) *p.* (*when*) **3.** (Interpunktion) *full stop*, ⟨Am⟩ *period* **4.** ⟨mus-typ⟩ *dot* **5.** ⟨telg, wir⟩ *dot* (Ggs *dash*) **6.** (I-~) *dot* **7.** ⟨typ⟩ (Einheit) *p.*; ein ~ gesperrt *one p. letter-spaced* **8.** Aussichts≃ *p. of view* (⟨a. fig⟩ Gesichts≃) **9.** (Posten) *item, article, head* || ⟨jur⟩ (e–r Anklage) *charge* **10.** (Stelle) *spot* **11.** (Thema) *topic, p.*; *respect, order* **12.** (*examination*) *mark*; (*to obtain full marks*); ⟨Am⟩ *p*, **13.** ⟨dice⟩ *pip* || (e–r Zielscheibe) *bull's eye* || ⟨crick⟩ *run* **14.** Brenn≃ *focal p.* || Dreh≃ *pivot* **B.** ⟨fig⟩ **dunkler** ~ *shady p.* (*in his life*) || empfindlicher ~ *sore spot*, ⟨mil⟩ (*EP*) *vulnerable point* || ⟨parl⟩ *item*; erster ~: *the bill should be first order* || der fragliche ~ *the p.* || kein so günstiger *or* vorteilhafter ~ wie *no p. of advantage so good as* || heikler ~ *difficult p.* || ⟨fig⟩ höchster ~ *acme, climax, highest pitch* || e–n kitzligen ~ berühren *to approach a delicate matter* || der springende ~ *the* (*main* od *chief*) *p.*; (*that is*) *half the battle* || strittiger ~ *bone of contention* || toter ~ *dead centre* od *p., deadlock, hitch* || wichtiger ~ *important p.* od *item* od *matter*; der wichtigste ~ *the p.* || wunder ~ *bad spot*; *crux, rub*; *difficulty*; e–n w.n ~ berühren ⟨fig⟩ *to skate* od *be on thin ice* **C.** ⟨parl⟩ e–n ~ **erledigen** (erörtern) *to settle* (*discuss*) *a p.* || ⟨ten⟩ mit dem Aufschlag e–n ~ gewinnen *to serve an ace* || e–n ~ m *to put a full stop*; ⟨fig⟩ nu mach aber 'nen ~! *now shut up!*, *stop!* || ⟨sport etc⟩ wenig ~e m *to score low* || den ~ aufs I setzen *to dot one's i's* pl **D. an** einzelnen ~en *at some p.s* ⟨a. mil⟩ || an ~en übertreffen *to outpoint* || den wichtigsten ~ übersehen *to miss the p.* (daß *that*) || bis **auf** den letzten ~ (*to prove*) *to the hilt* || das trifft auf den ~ zu *that is right to a T, that is exactly the case* || auf dem ~ s (zu tun) *to be on the p.* (*of doing*) || auf dem ~, wo die S steht *as matters stand* || ⟨fig⟩ **auf** den toten ~ gelangen *to come to a deadlock* || ~ **f** ~ *p. by p.*; *in detail* | **im** ~e Geld *in money matters* || im ~e der Ehre *on questions of honour* || in allen ~en schuldig *guilty on all counts* || in vielen ~en *on many p.s, in many respects* || in diesem ~e *on this head* || **mit** 21 ~en Sieger s *to win by 21 p.s* || **nach** ~en siegen *to win on p.s* || ohne ~ u Komma schwatzen *to talk nineteen to the dozen* || **um** e–n ~ besser s *to go one better* || jdn um viele ~e schlagen *to score off a p* || der ~, um den sich alles dreht *the pivot on which everything turns* || **von** ~ zu ~

from p. to p. ‖ bis **zu** e–m gewissen ~e *to some* od *a certain extent, up to a p.* **II. punkt** [adv] ~ 2 Uhr *on the stroke of two*; ⟨fam⟩ *at two o'clock sharp, on the very tick of two* **P·unkt- ~abwurf** m ⟨aero⟩ *precision* od *pinpoint bombing* **~auge** n ⟨zoo⟩ *ocellus* L **~ball** m ⟨box⟩ *small punch ball* **~feuer** n ⟨mil⟩ *point* od *converging fire*; (MG) *single rounds* **^~förmig** a *punctiform*; *point* [attr] (*source, lamp*) **~haus** n ⟨rail⟩ *point-block* **~linie** f *dotted line* **^~los** a/adv ⟨sport⟩ ~ schlagen *to blank* **~roller** m *massage suction-roller* **~schießen** n *map firing* **~schweißen** n *spot welding* **~sieg** m ⟨box⟩ *winning on points* **^~weise** adv *point for p.* | [a] ~ Berührung *p. contact* **~zahl** f *score*; .. mit gleicher ~ *even-runner(s)*; mit jdm gleiche ~ h *to tie with a p* **~ziel** n *pinpoint target* | ~angriff [m] *p.p. attack*; ~bombenwurf [m] *precision bombing* | **~·allinse** f *toric lens* **Punktati·on** [ts] f ~/~en *draft of a treaty* **P·ünktchen** n ~s/~ *dot, jot*; ⟨bib⟩ *tittle* **Punkt·ier- ~feder** f *dotting pen, wheel pen* **~kunst** f *geomancy* **~manier** f ⟨arts⟩ *stipple* **~-nadel** f *stippler* **~rädchen** n *dotting wheel* **punkt·ieren** vt [h] **1.** *to point, dot* ‖ ⟨gram⟩ *to punctuate* ‖ (mit Löchern) *to prick* ‖ (Haut) *to tattoo* ‖ ⟨med⟩ *to tap* ‖ ⟨arts⟩ *to stipple* ‖ ⟨mus⟩ *to dot* ⟨typ⟩ punktiert *dotted* (*line* od *rule*) **2.** ⟨fig⟩ den Fr. ~ *to stipulate the conditions of peace* **Punkt·ierung** f ~/~en *pointing, dotting* ‖ ⟨gram⟩ *punctuation* ‖ ⟨med⟩ *tapping* (a. **Punkti·on**) ‖ e–e ~ vornehmen an jdm *to tap a p* **p·ünktlich** a *punctual* (*employee*) ‖ allzu ~ *over-p., precise, exact, accurate* (*worker*) ‖ *strict* (*obedience*) ‖ *right on schedule*: ~ wie ein Uhrwerk *like clockwork*; *as regular as c.w.* | [adv] *up to* od *on* od *in time* (wie immer *as usual*): ~ um 10 *at ten* (*o'clock*) *sharp*; etw ~ tun *to be punctual in doing* .. ‖ aufs ~ste erledigen *to do .. with a vengeance, to carry out to the letter* ‖ (*to pay*) *promptly* **^~keit** f *punctuality, strictness, accuracy*, etc. **punktu·ell** adv *point for p.* ‖ ~e Aufmerksamkeit *concentrated attention* **P·unktum** n ~s/–ta ⟨gram⟩ *point, full stop* | ⟨fig⟩ hinter e–e S ein ~ m *to put an end* (*to a th*) ‖ und damit ~! *and there's an end of it!, so there!, that's enough!, that's all!* **Punkt·ur** f ~/~en ⟨surg⟩ *puncture* ‖ ⟨typ⟩ *points* pl **~spitze** f *point-spur* **~zange** f *pincers* pl

Punsch m ~es/~e *punch*; *toddy* ‖ e–n ~ ansetzen, brauen *to brew a bowl of p.* **~bowle** f *p.-bowl* **~essenz** f *essence of p.* **~löffel** m *p.-ladle*

P·unzarbeit f *embossing* **P·unze** f ~/~n, **~n** m ~s/~ *punch*; *stamp*; ⟨print⟩ *counter* | **^~n** vt [h] *to punch*; *stamp*; ⟨met⟩ *hallmark* | **ge–zt** ⟨arts⟩ *embossed* (Goldgrund)

°**p·upen** vi [h] (*to break wind*) ⟨sl⟩ *to poop, fart*

pupill·arisch a ⟨jur⟩ *pupillary*

Pup·ille f ~/~n *pupil* (*of the eye*) | ~nabstand [m] *interpupillary distance*: ~nstarre [f] ⟨med⟩ *fixed pupil*

P·üppchen n *doll*; (Anrede) *popsy* **P·uppe** f ~/~n *doll* (⟨a. fig⟩ Frau) (Marionette & fig) *puppet*; ⟨fig⟩ *affected p* ‖ ⟨fig⟩ (a. Püppchen) *darling* ‖ ⟨ent⟩ *chrysalis, pupa* ‖ ⟨agr⟩ *stack* (*of sheaves*) ‖ °*wench* ‖ °das ist ~! ⟨fam⟩ *that's splendid*; °einfach ~! *that's the bee's knees*; ⟨Am sl⟩ *yummy!* | das geht bis in die ~n *that goes on till doomsday* ‖ *that beats all* ‖ über alle ~n *beyond all bounds*: *exceedingly* **P·uppen- ~bildung** f *pupation* **~gesicht** n ⟨fig⟩ *doll's features* pl, *doll's face* **~haus** n *doll's house* **~klinik** f *dolls' hospital* **~kram** m *toy-shop* ‖ (Spielzeug) *dolls, playthings* pl **~spiel** n *puppetshow*, ⟨engl⟩ *Punch-and-Judy show* **~spieler** m *P.-&-J. man* **~stube** = ~haus **~theater** = ~spiel **~wagen** m *doll's pram* **~zustand** m ⟨ent⟩ *chrysalis-state*

p·uppern vi [h] (*of heart*) *to throb*

p·uppig a *elegant but insipid* ‖ ⟨fam⟩ *jolly*

pur a *pure, genuine, mere*; (*a whisky*) *straight* ‖ *unvarnished* (*truth*); *tommy* (*rot* ⟨sl⟩) ‖ aus ~em Eigensinn *out of sheer obstinacy*

Pür·ee n ~s/~s *mash purée* Fr: *mashed potatoes*

Purg·anz f ~/ **Purgat·iv** n ~s/~e ⟨med⟩ *purgative, aperient* ‖ *purge* **Purg·ier- ~gurke** f *colocynth* **~körner** n pl *croton-seeds* pl **~kroton** m ⟨bot⟩ *croton* **~mittel** n = Purganz **~wurzel** f ⟨bot⟩ *scammony* **purg·ieren** vt/i [h] ⟨med⟩ *to purge*

purifiz·ieren vt [h] *to purify* **Pur·ismus** m ~/ *purism* **Pur·ist** m ~en/~en *purist* **Purit·aner** m ~s/~ *Puritan* **purit·anisch** a *Puritan, P.ic* (*simplicity*); ⟨dero⟩ *P.ical*

P·urpur m ~s/ *purple* ‖ (Gewand) *purple* (*gown*, etc.) ‖ in ~ geboren *born in the p.* **~farbe** f, **~röte** f *p.* (*colour*); sein Gesicht hatte (bekam) e–e ~ *his face was* (*went*) *a p. c.* **^~farben, ^~farbig** a *p.*(*-coloured*) **~friesel** m & n ⟨med⟩ *p.s* pl, *p.-fever* **~huhn** n ⟨orn⟩ *p. gallinule* **~hut** m *cardinal's hat* **~kleid** n *p. robe* **~maul** n ⟨Am ich⟩ *grunt* **^~rot** a *purple*; *scarlet*; *crimson* **~schnecke** f ⟨zoo⟩ *purple* **~weide** f ⟨bot⟩ *red osier* **p·urpurn** a *purple*; *petunia* (*cushion*); *red* (*wine*)

p·urren vt [h] **1.** *to poke, stir* (*the fire*) **2.** ⟨mar⟩ *to wake the watch* **3.** *to purr*

Pürsch = Pirsch **p·ürschen** = pirschen

P·urzel m ~s/~ *whipper-snapper*, ⟨fam⟩ *shrimp, Punch* **~baum** m, e–n ~ m (schießen, schlagen) *to turn* (*throw*) *a somersault* **~taube** f ⟨orn⟩ *tumbler* **p·urzeln** vi [s] *to tumble, topple* (*down*), *to trip* (über *over*)

P·uschel f ~/~n *tassel* ‖ ⟨fig⟩ *slavey* ‖ *hobby*

P·ussel(spiel n) n ~s/~ *puzzle* | **^~n** vi [h] *to potter about* od *around*

°**P·uste** f ~/ *puff* ‖ ihm ging die ~ aus *he ran short of breath*, ⟨fam⟩ *he bust his bellows* ‖ er verlor die ~ *he lost his breath* ‖ er lief, daß ihm die ~ ausging ⟨a.⟩ *he ran fit to burst*; e–m die letzte ~ aus dem Halse treiben *to flog a willing horse* **~-blume** f *blow-ball*; *dandelion* (*flower & ripe head*) °**~kuchen**! *the devil a bit!*, → °Kuchen! **~rohr** n *pea-shooter* **p·usten** vi [h] ⟨fam⟩ (blasen) *to blow, puff* ‖ (durch die Nase) *to snort*; (schwer atmen) *to wheeze* | (Damespiel) *to huff* ‖ ich werde dir was ~ *you may whistle for it, I'll see you further first* ‖ darauf puste ich was! *I don't care a straw about it*

P·ustel f ~/~n *pimple, pustule*; kl ~ *pimplet* **^~artig** a *pustular* **~bildung** f *pustulation*

p·ut(t)-put(t) [intj] *chick, chick!, chuck, chuck!*

P·utchen n → folg. ‖ ⟨fig⟩ mein ~! *duckie!*

P·ute f ~/~n *turkey-hen* ‖ ⟨fig⟩ *haughty woman* ‖ dumme ~ ⟨fig⟩ *goose* **P·uter** m ~s/~ *turkey cock* (kollert *gobbles*) **~braten** m *roast turkey* **^~r·ot** a (*she turned*) (*as*) *red as a beet* od *a turkey-cock* ‖ *his face* (wurde ~) *flushed a rich brick-red, turned scarlet* **P·uthahn** m = Puter, **P·uthenne** f = Pute

P·utsch m ~es/~e *putsch*; *coup de main* ‖ *riot* ‖ *insurrection* | **^~en** vi [h] *to* (*raise a*) *revolt*; *to riot* ‖ auf~ *to goad on*, (*to incite*) | **~·ist** m *rioter*

P·utte f ~/~n ⟨arts⟩ *putto* [It] ‖ ~n *putti* pl

p·utten vi ⟨golf⟩ *to putt* | **^~** n *putting*

P·üttings pl ⟨mar⟩ *chains, futtock-shrouds* pl

°**P·üttjer** m ~s/~ *pedant*; *fussy p* | **^~n** vi [h] *to potter about* | **^~ig** a *fussy, pedantic*

P·utz m ~es/ **1.** *dressing, toilet* ‖ (Schmuck) *ornaments* pl ‖ *millinery* ‖ (auffallend) *finery* ‖ (Kleidung) *dress, attire*, ⟨fam⟩ *rig* ‖ *articles* pl *of dress* ‖ im ~ *in full dress*, ⟨fam⟩ *in full fig* **2.** ⟨arch⟩ (gefurcht *rusticated*) *plaster*; (*rough*) *casting* ‖ mit Roh^~ versehen *to rough-cast* **~arbeiten** f pl ⟨arch⟩ *plaster-work* **~artikel** m pl *millinery* **~baumwolle** f *cotton waste* **~dämchen** n *dressy lady* **~frau** f *charwoman*, ⟨Am⟩ *cleaning w.* | ⟨theat⟩ ~en [pl] *cleaners* **~geschäft** n *milliner's shop* **~händlerin** f *milliner* **~kästchen** n *toiletbox, dressing-case* **~kram** m *millinery, finery* **~lappen** m *rubber, rag for cleaning* **~leder** n *wash-leather* **~macher·ei** f *millinery* **~macherin** f *milliner* **~pulver** n *polishing powder* **~schere** f (eine *a pair of*) *snuffers* pl **~sucht** f *vanity; love of finery, passion for dress* **≈süchtig** a *fond of finery* **~tisch** m *dressing-* od *toilet-table* **~tuch** n *polishing cloth* **~- u Flickstunde** f ⟨mar, mil⟩ *make and mend* **~-waren** f pl *millinery, articles of dress* **~werk** n *ornaments* pl **~wolle** f *wool* od *cotton-waste* **~zeug** n *cleaning utensils* od *tools* pl; ⟨mil⟩ *brush bag, stable bag* **p·utzen I.** vt [h] **1.** (reinigen) *to clean* ‖ *to wipe* ‖ ⟨cul⟩ *to pick* (*salad* etc) *to trim out* ‖ *to wash* (*dishes*) **2.** *to prune, lop* (*trees*) **3.** (blank~) *to furbish; polish* (*up*) **4.** (schmücken, kleiden) *to dress* (*smartly*); *to attire; adorn* ‖ *to smarten up* (*a dress*); *to tidy a p* (*up*); geputzt wie ein Pfingstochse *dressed up to the nines* | **sich** ~ ⟨a.⟩ *to prettify o.s.; to shine o.s. up; to doll* ‖ sie putzt sich gern *she likes to wear smart dresses* ‖ sich ~ ⟨orn⟩ *to preen o.s.* **5.** (Stiefel) *to black, polish,* ⟨Am⟩ *to shine* ‖ *to brush* (*clothes*) **6.** *to trim* (*a lamp*) ‖ *to snuff* (*a candle*) **7.** (Pferd) *to groom* **8.** ⟨arch⟩ *to plaster* **9. sich** [dat] den Bart ~ *to trim one's beard* ‖ *to blow* od *wipe* (*one's nose*) ‖ *to polish,* etc (*one's shoes*) ‖ *to wash* od *clean* (*one's teeth*) **10.** → ab-, herunter-, weg-~ **II.** [abs] (*of diamonds* etc.) *to be ornamental* od *dressy* **P·utzer** m ~s/~ **1.** *clean*(*s*)*-er* ‖ ⟨mach⟩ *fettler* ‖ ⟨mil⟩ *batman, orderly;* ⟨sl⟩ *mucko* **2.** = Putzlappen **3.** ⟨fig fam⟩ *snub, rebuff*

P·ütze f ~/~n ⟨mar⟩ *bucket*

p·utzig a ⟨fam⟩ *quaint, funny, queer*

Puzzol·anerde f *puzzolana*

Pyelogr·amm n ~(e)s/~e ⟨med⟩ intravenös(es) ~ *intravenous pyelogram,* –graph (I. V. P.) (*roentgenogram made by pyelography* [*i. e. roentgenographic visualization of the kidney pelvis*] → Becken, *pelvis*

Pygm·äe m ~n/~n *pygmy* **≈nhaft** a *pygmean*

Pyj·ama m ~s/~s (ein ~ *a suit of*) *pyjamas* pl

p·yknisch a ⟨biol⟩ *pycnomorphic, pycnic*

P·ylon n ~s/~e ⟨ant arch⟩ *pylon*

pyramid·al a *pyramidal* ‖ ⟨fam⟩ *immense, enormous, huge;* ⟨fig fam⟩ *stunning* **≈zahl** f ⟨math⟩ *pyramidal number* **Pyram·ide** f ~/~n *pyramid* ‖ ⟨mil⟩ Gewehr≈ *piled arms* **≈nförmig** a *pyramid, pyramid-shaped* **~npappel** f *Lombardy poplar*

Pyren·äen pl *Pyrenees* pl **~halbinsel** f *Iberian Peninsula*

Pyr·it m ~s/~e ⟨minr⟩ *pyrites* [sg] **Pyro-~gall·ol** n ~s/ *pyrogallol* | **~p** m ~(e)s/~e ⟨minr⟩ *pyrope* **~t·echnik** f, *pyrotechnics* pl | ~er [m] *pyrotechnist* **≈t·echnisch** a *pyrotechnic*(*al*)

P·yrrhussieg m *pyrrhic victory*

pythagor·eisch a *Pythagorean* ‖ ~er Lehrsatz *Pythagorean proposition* od *theorem*

p·ythisch a *Pythian* (*oracle*)

Q

Q, q n ~/~ *Q, q*

Qu·abbe f ~/~n *wen; fatty growth; jelly* | **~l** f ~/~n **1.** *flabby mass* **2.** *bog*(*gyland*) **≈lig** a *flabby, wobbling* ‖ (P) *podgy* ‖ ⟨fam⟩ mir ist ganz ~ *I feel qualmy,* (*sick*) **≈ln** vi [h] *to wobble, to shake like jelly* ‖ (fettes, welkes Fleisch) *to be flabby* ‖ (Morast) *to quake*

°**Quacke** f ~/ *rot, rubbish* **~l·ei** f ~/~en *quacking* ‖ *foolish talk, nonsense;* ⟨fam⟩ *rubbish, rot* **~l- ~fritze** m, **~liese** f *grumbler* **≈ln** vt/i [h] *to quack, babble, jabber, chatter*

Qu·acksalber m *quack, mountebank,* ⟨sl⟩ *faker,* ⟨Am a.⟩ *fakir* | ~medizin [f] *nostrum* **~·ei** f *quackery* ‖ *quack medicine* | **≈n** vi [h] *to quack* (an e–m herum *a p*)

Qu·addel f ~/~n *wheal;* ⟨med⟩ *urtica*

Qu·ader m ~s/~; f ~/~n **~stein** m *ashlar, square hewn stone, freestone* | **~-** *ashlar* (*facing*) **~werk** n *bound masonry, freestone work; rustic work* **qu·adern** vt [h] *to hew, dress* (*stones*) **Quadr·ant** m ~en/~en *quadrant* **Quadr·at** n ~(e)s~e *square* ‖ ins *or* zum ~ erheben ⟨math⟩ *to sq.* ‖ drei im ~ (3^2) *three sq.d* ‖ 5 Fuß im ~ *5 feet sq.* | Methode der kleinsten ~e ⟨demog⟩ *method of least squares* | ⟨mus⟩ *natural* (♮) | ⟨typ⟩ *quadrat;* Quadrätchen [n] *M-qu.,* halbes .. *N-qu.* **~fläche** f *sq.* **≈förmig** a *sq.* **~fuß** m *sq. foot* **~karte** f *sq.d map, patrol chart;* ⟨mar⟩ *sq.d chart* °**~latschen** f pl ⟨sl⟩ *beetle-crushers* **~meile** f *sq. mile* **~meter** n *sq. metre* ‖ ~gewicht [n] ⟨pap⟩ *substance* **~-netz** n *grid net* **~pflanzung** f *sq.-planting* **~schädel** m *sq.head, blockhead* **~wurzel** f ⟨math⟩ *sq. root* **~zahl** f ⟨math⟩ *sq. number* **quadr·atisch** a ⟨math⟩ *quadratic* ‖ ⟨allg⟩ *square* ‖ ~es Abstandsgesetz ⟨phot-phys⟩ *inverse square law* (*of lighting*) ‖ ~e Gleichung *quadratic* (*equation*); Lehre v dieser *quadratics;* ~er Mittelwert *root mean square value* **Quadr- ~at·ur** f ~/ *quadrature, squaring* ‖ die ~ des Kreises berechnen ⟨fig⟩ *to square the circle* **≈·ieren** vt [h] ⟨math⟩ *to square* **~·iga** f ~/–gen ⟨hist⟩ *quadriga, four-in-hand* **~·ille** f ~/~n [ka'drilјə] *quadrille* ‖ (e–e) ~ tanzen *to dance a qu.* **~·upel-** [in comp] *quadruple* (*alliance*) **~upl·ik** f ~/~en ⟨jur⟩ *rebutter*

Quai m (→ Kai) *quay, wharf; jetty*

quah! ⟨intj⟩ (*raven's*) *croak!* **Quak** m ~(e)s/~e *croak* | **≈en** vi [h] (v Fröschen) *to croak* ‖ (v Enten) *to quack* ‖ ⟨fig⟩ ≈e nicht! *shut up!* **qu·äken** vi [h] *to squeak*

Qu·äker m ~s/~ *Quaker* (f *Quakeress*) **~-bund** m *Society of Friends* **~gemeinde** f *congregation of Quakers* **~speisung** f *food supply* (*for German children after 1918*) **Quäker·ei** f ~/ *Q.ism*

Qual f ~/~en *torment, pain, agony, torture* ‖ (Seelen~) *anguish, agony; distress, affliction, pang* ‖ große ~en erleiden *to suffer great pain,* etc ⟨fam⟩ *a martyrdom* **≈beladen** a *full of pains* etc **≈voll** a *very painful* (*death*): *excruciating* (*pains*); *full of anguish; distressing, racking; agonizing; tormenting* (*uncertainty*) **qu·älen** vt [h] *to plague, torment, rack, vex, tantalize, agonize; bedevil* ‖ (foltern) *to torture* ‖ ~ mit *to torment with* (*reproaches*) ‖ *tormenting thoughts* ‖ gequält *tormented* (*expression of face*), *bored* (*mode of expression*) | (⟨fam⟩ = belästigen) *to bother, bore* | den Motor ~ *to labour the engine* | v Furcht ge–lt *wrung with terror* | jdn zu Tode ~ *to kill a p by slow torture;* ⟨fig⟩ *to worry a p to death,* sich .. *to work o.s. to death, to agonize* (durch *with*) ‖ sich umsonst ~ *to labour in vain* ‖ sich mit Schülern ~ *to go through the drudgery of teaching* **Qu·äler** m ~s/~ *tormentor, torturer* ‖ ⟨fig⟩ *bore* **Quäler·ei** f *tormenting* ‖ *torments* pl ‖ ⟨fig⟩ *vexation, worry*(*ing*) **Qu·älgeist** m ⟨fam⟩ *bore, blighter, torment, plague, nuisance*

Qualifikati·on f [–ts–] *qualification; capacity; ability;* berufliche ~ *skill* **qualifiz·ieren** vt [h] *to qualify* ‖ *to modify* ‖ *to fit* ‖ jdn f etw ~ *to certify a p for a th* | **sich** ~ zu *to qualify for* | –rt *competent, eligible; qualified* (*craftsman, majority*); (*crime*) *with aggravating circumstances* **Qualit·ät** f ~/~en *quality* ⟨a. sport⟩ ‖ erste ~ *best qu.;* ⟨Am sl⟩ *class;* erster ~ *first-rate, of finest grade* (→ erste(r) C); bester ~ [gen] *first-qu.* [attr]; v genau gleicher ~ wie *entirely equal to* (*the sample*) ‖ das ist ~! *that's sth like qu.!* ‖ (Art) die geringeren (mittleren) ~en *the inferior (medium) sorts* pl || ⟨chess⟩ ~ opfern *to sacrifice the exchange* | **~s-** *high grade (lotion)* ~begriff [m] *symbol of qu.; hallmark*; ~erzeugnis [n] *quality product*; ~forderung [f] *qu. specification*; ~leistung [f] *achievement of high qu.*; ~marke [f] *mark of qu.*; ~verbesserung [f] *upgrading*; ~ des Endprodukts *improvement of the finished product qu.*; ~ware [f] *good value; article of high qu.* || ~n [pl] *superior articles* ⟨fam⟩ *firsts* pl **qualitat·iv** a *qualitative*

Qu·alle f ~/~n *jelly-fish; medusa* || °⟨fig⟩ *gob*

Qualm m ~(e)s/ *smoke* || *vapour, damp, mist* || ~ v Öl *oil smoke*

qu·almen vi [h] *to steam, fume* || *the cigarette smoked in his fingers* || ⟨fam⟩ bei ihm qualmt's *he's bursting with rage* | vi/t [h] *to smoke* || *(chimneys) smoke; (engines) puff (up clouds of smoke)* || (Raucher) ⟨fam⟩ *to blow a cloud* | vt [h] er qualmt s–e Pfeife *he puffs away at his pipe* °**Qu·almer** m ~s/~ (P) *inveterate smoker* **qu·almig** a *smoky* || *vaporous, misty* || *steaming* || *full of smoke*

°**Qu·alster** m ~s/~ *phlegm, spittle* | ≗**ig** a *viscous*

Qu·andel m ~s/~ *chimney in a kiln*

Qu·ant n ~s/~en (klster Skalenabstand) ⟨math, stat⟩ *quantum* || °~en [f pl] *shaggy feet* | ~äquivalenzgesetz [n] ⟨phys⟩ *quantum equivalence law*; ~theorie [f] *quantum theory* **~·il** n ~s/~e ⟨stat⟩ *quantile* **~it·ät** f ~/~en *quantity* ⟨a. pros⟩ || *amount* || in kl ~en *in small lots; in little bits; in driblets* ≗**itat·iv** a *quantitative (analysis)* || [adv] *as to quantity* **~um** n ~s/–ten *quantum, quantity* || *ration (of bread)* || ein gehöriges ~ Alkohol h (P) *to have a jag on* || *dole (of opium)* || ⟨Am a.⟩ *grist* | ~ausbeute [f] ⟨phys⟩ *quantum efficiency* od *yield*; ~gewicht [n] *statistical weight*

Qu·appe f ~/~n *eel-pout* || (Kaul≗) *tadpole*

Quarant·äne f ~/~n *quarantine* || ~ halten *to pass qu.* || ~ halten müssen *to be subject to qu., pass qu.* || in ~ legen, unter ~ stellen *to qu.* || (of ships) in ~ liegen ⟨a.⟩ *to ride at qu.* **~arzt** m *health surgeon* **~beamte(r)** m *qu.-officer* **~haus** n *qu.-hospital* **~vorschriften** f pl *qu. regulations* pl

Quark m ~(e)s/ *curds* pl | ⟨fig⟩ = Quatsch || *trifle* || da liegt der ~! *there's a mess* || alten ~ aufrühren *to stir up some old tale* || er mischt sich in jeden ~ *he puts his finger in everywhere* || kümmere dich nicht um jeden ~ *don't bother your head about every little matter* || du verstehst e–n ~ davon *you haven't the slightest idea about it* **~käse** m *cottage-cheese* **~kuchen** m *curd-cake*

°**Qu·arre** f ~/~n *squalling child*; → Pfarre | ≗**n** vi [h] *to squall* **qu·arrig** a *squalling, fretful*

Qu·art 1. n ~(e)s~e (Maß) *quart* || ⟨typ⟩ in ~ *in quarto* **2.** f ~/~en ⟨fenc⟩ *quart, carte* || Hoch-, Tief≗ *cut in high, low carte* || ⟨mus⟩ *fourth* | ~band [m] *(volume in) quarto*; ~blatt [n] *quarter of a sheet*; ~flasche [f] *quart-bottle*; ~format [n] *quarto* (in ~ *in qu.*); ~heft [n] *copybook in quarto* | **~a** f ~/–ten ⟨Ger⟩ *fourth form* (⟨engl⟩ *3rd)* | **~·al** n ~(e)s/~e *quarter (of the year)*; ⟨mst⟩ *three months* pl || [in comp mst] *quarterly (notice, bill, balance)* | ~geld [n] *quarterly allowance*; ~miete [f] *quarter's rent*; ~tag [m] *quarter-day*; ≗weise [adv] *quarterly* **~·aner(in** f) m ~s/~ ⟨Ger⟩ *boy of the fourth class* || ⟨engl⟩ *third-form boy (girl)* **~·anfieber** n *quartan ague* | **~te** f ~/~n ⟨fenc, cards⟩ *quart* || ⟨mus⟩ *fourth* **~·ett** n ~(e)s/~e *quartet(te)* | ~abend [m] *quartet-concert*; ~lied [n] *four-part song*; ~musik [f] *music for four (string) instruments* **~·ier** n ~(e)s/~e **1.** *district* || ~ [kar'tieː] *Latin* [la'tɛ̃] Fr *Latin Quarter* **2.** *quarters (q.s)* pl, *lodging* || ⟨mil⟩ *q.s, billets (b.s)* pl, *(he saw the brigade into b.s), (to march out into b.s)* || ⟨übtr⟩ *to take up* (aufschlagen, beziehen) *one's q.s in a village*: ~ m *to prepare q.s; to have free q.s*; ein ~ nehmen *to take lodgings* || ~ m *to prepare q.s* | **in** ~ liegen bei *to be q.ed* od *b.ed upon*; ins ~ rücken *to move into q.s*; jdn ins ~ bek *to have a p q.ed on one* **3.** ⟨mar⟩ *watch* | ~amt [n] *b.ing office*: ~geber [m] *host*; ~geld [n] *b.-money*; ~macher [m pl] *b. party*: ~meister [m] *q.master*; ~meistertruppe [f] *Quartermaster Corps* N; ~schein [m] *billeting slip*: ~wirt [m] *host*; ~zettel [m] *billet* ≗**·ieren** vt [h] *to q., b.* | vi [h] *to be q.ed* (bei *on, with*) **~il** n ~s/~e ⟨stat, demog⟩ *quartile*

Quarz m ~es/~e *quartz*; ⟨wir⟩ *crystal* **~druse** f *q.y druse* **~fels** m *q.ite* **~haltig** a *q.iferous, q.ose* **~lampe** f ⟨med⟩ *q.-lamp* **~mühle** f *q.-crusher* **~-sand** m *arenaceous q.; q. sand* **~steuerung** f ⟨wir⟩ *q. control* **~uhr** f *q.-controlled clock* **Quarz·it** m ~(e)s/~e *quartzite*

Quas·ar m ~s/~e (quasistellare Radioquelle) *quasar = quasistellar source of radiation*

qu·asi [adv L] *as it were, so to say, in a way* | ≗- [oft] *would-be (lover, poet)* ≗**modog·eniti** *Quasimods, Low Sunday*

°**qu·assel- ~n** vi [h] *to prattle; to talk foolishly* od *nonsense*; ⟨fam⟩ *to talk rot, to drivel, dodder*; ⟨Am sl⟩ *to chin; to chew the rag* ≗**strippe** f **1.** (P) *dodderer* **2.** ⟨telph⟩ *phone*; ⟨fam⟩ *buzzer*; ⟨vulg⟩ *blower* (a. P)

Qu·assia f ~/ ⟨bot⟩ *quassia*

Quast m ~es/~e; **~e** f ~/~n *tassel, tuft, knot, (sword-knot); pompon* Fr || (gr Pinsel) *brush* || mit ~en schmücken *to tassel* | ≗**ig** a *tasselled*

Qu·ästor m ~s/–t·oren *questor*; ⟨univ⟩ *bursar*

Quäst·ur f ~/~en *questorship*; ⟨univ⟩ *bursary*

Quat·ember m ~s/~ ⟨R. C.⟩ (vierteljährliche strenge Fasttage) *ember-days* pl **Quatro- ~cent·ist** [–tʃen–] m ~en/~en It *artist of the* **~c·ento** n ~s/ *15th century*

Quatsch 1. m ~es/ *squash* || ⟨fig⟩ ~ (mit Sauce) *rubbish, (nonsense), twaddle*; ⟨sl⟩ *(tommy) rot; bosh, piffle, drivel, swosh, tripe, wash* || ⟨Am fam⟩ *baloney, bunk, blah*; ⟨sl⟩ *guff, hooey* **2.** ≗! [intj] *squash!* || ⟨fig fam⟩ → 1.; *shucks! my foot! it's all my eye* || Genius? ~! *a fiddlestick about genius!* **3.** ≗ [a] (dumm) *silly, stupid* | ≗**en** vi [h] *to squash, plash* || ⟨fig °fam⟩ *to talk nonsense* (⟨fam⟩ *rot*, ⟨sl⟩ *moonshine*), *to piffle, twaddle; drivel* [a. vt] || ⟨sl⟩ *to chew the rag*, ⟨Am⟩ *to chin* || (Geheimnis verraten) *to split* **~kopf** m *twaddler* ≗-**naß** a *wet-through, soaking-wet*

Qu·ecke f ~/~n; **~ngras** n ⟨bot⟩ *couch-, quick-grass* **Qu·ecksilber** n ⟨chem⟩ *quick-silver, mercury* || sie ist das reinste ~ *she is (like q,-s,* od) *awfully fidgety, terribly restless* | ~belag [m] *quicking*: ~gefäß [n] *m.y-bulb*; ≗haltig [a] *mercurial*; ~kuppe [f] *mercury meniscus (in capillary tubes)*; ~kur [f] ⟨med⟩ *m.l treatment*; ~legierung [f] *amalgam*; ~nitr·at [n] *nitrate of m.y*; ~oxid [n] *mercurous oxide*; ~oxid·ul [n] *mercuric oxide*; ~pille [f] *blue pill*; ~salbe [f] *mercurial ointment*: ~säule [f] *mercury column*; ~vergiftung [f] *mercurial poisoning*; ~vergoldung [f] *quick-water gilding* | ≗**n** a ⟨a. fig⟩ *mercurial* || ⟨fig fam⟩ *fidgety*

Qu·eensland n ['kwiːnzlənd] (N.-O.-Australien)

Quell m ~(e)s/~en = Quelle | ~bezirk [m] *head-water region*; ~bottich [m] *steeping-vat*; ~brunnen [m] *fountain-head, springwell*; ~fassung [f] *tapping of a source*: ~fluß [m] *source*; ~gebiet [n] = ~bezirk; *sources* pl; ~horizont [m] *spring level*; ~kuppe [f] *lava dome*; ~moos [n] *water-moss*: ~mulde [f] *valley head*; ~sand [m] *quick-sand*: ~schüttung [f] *delivery of a spring*: ~tablette [f] *foam tablet*; ~wasser [n] *spring-water* **Qu·elle** f ~/~n *spring, fountain; source* ⟨a. commun⟩; *well-head (of a river)*; pulsierende ~ *intermittent* od *periodic, pulsating spring* || (Brunnen) *well* | ⟨fig⟩ *source, origin (of strength)* || *(never-failing) fountain* || *sources (of*

information) ‖ (*well-*)*spring* (*of affection, actions*) ‖ *well-head* (*of truth*) ‖ ⟨liter⟩ *authority* ‖ aus sicherer ~ *on good authority* | neue ~n erschließen *to open up new sources* ‖ ~n wieder zum Fließen bringen *to give a fresh impulse to* (*religious feelings*) ‖ an der ~ kaufen *to buy at first hand* ‖ aus erster ~ ⟨fam⟩ *from the horse's mouth* **qu·ellen** vi [quoll/gequollen] [s] (aus) *to well, gush, spring* (*from*) ‖ (of tears) *to flow* ‖ ⟨fig a.⟩ *to originate* | (schwellen) *to swell* ‖ (*eyes*) *start* (*from their sockets*) | vt [h] *to cause to swell*; *to soak* (*hides*), *to steep* (*beans*, etc) **Qu·ellen-** **~angabe** f *mention of one's authorities* **~austritt** m *cropping out of a source* **~finder** m *water-finder* **~forscher** m *investigator of the sources* **~forschung** f *original research, study of the sources* **≈mäßig** a *according to the best authorities* od *sources*; ⟨allg⟩ *authentic* **~nachweis** m *acknowledgments* pl *indication of authorities used* **≈reich** a *abounding in springs*
Qu·eller m ~s/ ⟨bot⟩ *glasswort*

Qu·endel m ~s/ ⟨bot⟩ *wild thyme*

qu·engel- **≈·ei** f ~/~en *nagging, fault-finding* ‖ *grumbling, wrangling* ‖ *lamentation* **≈fritze** m *grumbler*; ⟨Am⟩ *kicker* | **~ig** a *fretful, querulous, fussy, complaining*, etc | **~n** vi [h] *to grumble* (über *about*); *to nag* (*at*) ‖ *to find fault* (*with*) ‖ *to whine* ‖ *to lament* (*over*) ‖ *to worry about trifles* ‖ *to be querulous* ‖ *to fret, grizzle*; ⟨Am⟩ *to grouch*

Qu·ent n ~(e)s/~e; **~chen** n ~s/~ (†Gewicht = 1,66 g) etwa: *drachm, dram* (= $^1/_{16}$ *oz*) ‖ ⟨fig⟩ ohne ein ~ Stolz *without a grain of pride*

quer a *cross* ⟨a. fig⟩ (*cross ways*) ‖ *transverse, oblique, slanting* ‖ *diagonal* | [adv] *across* ‖ *obliquely*; *athwart* (*to lie a., a. the bows*) ‖ (*to put*) *crosswise* ‖ *diagonally* ‖ ⟨fig⟩ *perversely* ‖ ~ hindurchgehend *transversal* ‖ ~ gesetzt *set across* (*the corner*) ‖ sich ~ setzen *to square* (*in one's saddle*) ‖ e–n ~ anblicken *to look askance at a p* ‖ kreuz u ~ *this way and that, criss-cross* ‖ ~ durch *right across* ‖ **(S)** ~ gehen *to go wrong* ‖ ⟨com⟩ ~ schreiben → ~|schreiben ‖ die S kommt ~ *that thwarts me, puts me out, crosses my plans* **Quer-** **≈·ab** [adv] *abeam*; *abreast* (v *of*) **~abstand** m *distance at right angle*(*s*); .. *cables apart* **~achse** f *transverse* (*axis*) **~addition** f ⟨comp⟩ *cross-adding* **~ader** f ⟨min⟩ *cross-lode* **~aufnahme** f ⟨phot⟩ *horizontal view* **~axt** f *twibill* **~balken** m *rood-, cross-beam, joist* ‖ (an Tür) *transom* ‖ *architrave* ‖ (an Fenstern) *cross-bar* ‖ ⟨her⟩ *bar, fesse* **~bau** m ⟨min⟩ *cross-working* **~baum** m (*horizontal*) *bar* ‖ ⟨mar⟩ *cross-tree* **~bild** n *oblong picture* **~binder** m *bowtie*; ⟨Am a.⟩ *four-in-hand* **~bruch** m ⟨surg⟩ *transversal fracture* **~damm** m *cross-dike, traverse* **~draht** m *cross-span* **≈d·urch** [adv] *right* od *straight across* **~fäden** m pl *weaving* **≈feld·ein** [adv] *across country, by the string rather than by the bow* | **~fahrt** [f] ⟨mot⟩ *moto-cross*; ~rennen [n] *cross country race* **~flöte** f *German flute* **~flügel** m ⟨arch⟩ *cross-aisle* **~folio** n *oblong folio* **~form** f *cross size* **~format** n (Ggs Hoch-) *oblong* od *landscape shape* **~frage** f *cross-question* **~gang** m *cross-passage*, ⟨fort, min, mountain⟩ *traverse* **~gasse** f *cross-street* **~gäßchen** n *cross-lane* **~gefälle** n (der Fahrbahn) *crossfall* **~gestein** n *stones crossing a stratum* **~haupt** n ⟨tech⟩ *yoke* **~hieb** m *cross-cut* **≈h·in** [adv] *crossways* **~holz** n *cross-bar*; *gibbet*; *traverse* ‖ ⟨mar⟩ *toggle* **~kopf** m ⟨fam⟩ *fuss-pot, crank* **≈köpfig** a *wrong-headed, pig-headed, cross-grained, cranky* **~köpfigkeit** f *wrongheadedness* **~lage** f ⟨aero⟩ (starke *steep*) *bank* | ⟨med⟩ (des noch ungeborenen Kindes) *cross-birth* **~lähmung** f ⟨path⟩ *paraplegia* **≈laufend** a *transversal* **~leiste** f *crosspiece, cleat* **~linie** f *cross-line* ‖ ⟨ten⟩ *service-line* **~naht** f *cross-seam* ‖ ⟨anat⟩ *transverse suture* **~neigung** f ⟨tech⟩ *sidewise bending* | ~s- ⟨aero⟩ *banking* [attr]; ~winkel [m] *angle of bank* **~paß** m ⟨ftb⟩ *cross*(*pass*) **~pfeife** f *fife*; ~ blasen *to fife* **~profil** *cross-section* **~richtung** f *transverse direction* **~riegel** m (Fenster≈) *shutter-bar*; ⟨rail⟩ *cross-brace, -rail* **~rinne** f *gully*; *open ditch*; ⟨for⟩ *catch-water*; *break* **~rippe** f (Rind) *fore rib* **~sack** m *wallet* **~ruder** n ⟨aero⟩ *aileron*; *wing flap* | ~ausgleich [m] *a. balance*; *a. boost*; ~ausgleichsklappe [f] *a. tab*: ~hinterkante [f] *a. trailing edge* **~säge** f *cross-cut saw* **~sattel** m *side-saddle* **~|schießen** vi [h] *to throw a spanner into the works*; jdm ~ *to kipper a p* **~schiff** n ⟨arch⟩ *transept* **≈schiffs** [adv] *athwartships* **~schlag** m ⟨min⟩ *cross-cut* **~schläger** m *obliquely striking projectile* **~schnitt** m *cross-cut, cross section* ‖ (Fläche) *sectional area transverse sectional view* | ~sbelastung [f] *cross-section load*; ~tafel [f] ⟨stat⟩ *current table*; ~Umfrage [f] *public opinion poll*; ~ziffer [f] *c. rate* **~schott** n *transverse bulkhead* **≈|schreiben** vi [h] *to put one's name to paper* (*bill*) **~schwelle** f ⟨rail⟩ *traverse sleeper* **~schwung** m ⟨ski⟩ *christiania* **~spant** n *transverse frame* **~sprung** m *cross-jump* **~stab** m ⟨crick⟩ *bail* **~stabilität** f *crosswise stability* **~stange** f *cross-bar* **~steuerung** f ⟨aero⟩ *aileron control* **~stollen** m ⟨min⟩ *lateral gallery* **~straße** f *cross-street, cross-road*; *intersecting r.* ‖ *turn* (*the first t. to the left*) **~streifen** m *cross-stripe* **~strich** m *diagonal line, cross-l., bar* ‖ ⟨fig⟩ *impediment, disappointment* ‖ e–n ~ durch etw machen *to thwart* od *cross a th* **~summe** f *total of the digits of a number* **~tal** n *transversal valley* **~träger** m *cross-arm* **~treiber** m *obstructionist* **~treiber·ei** f *obstruction* **≈·über** [adv] *diagonally opposite* **~übertragung** f ⟨comp⟩ "*total rolling*" *feature* **~verbindung** f ⟨mil⟩ *intercommunication along the line, grid connection*; ⟨telph⟩ *lateral line*; ⟨tech, el⟩ *cross-connection*; ⟨wir⟩ *liaison communication* **~verkehr** m *lateral traffic* **~verweisung** f *crossreference* | ~sstraße [f] *transversal route* **~wand** f *cross-wall* **~weg** m *cross-way, cross-road* **~wind** m *lateral wind* **Qu·ere** f ~/ *cross* od *transverse* od *oblique direction* ‖ *diagonal* ‖ (in) die ~, (in) der ~ *crossly, athwart, crosswise, criss-cross, across*; *transversely*; *aslant, slantwise* | (S) der ~ gehen *to take a wrong turn* ‖ es ist ihm etw in die ~ gek *sth has gone wrong with him* ‖ jdm in die ~ k *to cross a p's path*; ⟨fig⟩ *to put a spoke in a p's wheel, to balk* (*thwart, cross*) *a p's design, plans* ‖ jdm in die ~ lauten *to run across a p*

Querul·ant m ~en/~en *querulous* od *litigious p*; *grumbler*; ⟨fam⟩ *old crab* **querul·ieren** vi [h] *to grumble*; *to be qu.* od *lit.*

Qu·ese f ~/~n *blister* | **≈n** vi = quengeln

Qu·etsche f ~/~n ⟨tech⟩ *crusher*, ⟨fam⟩ *crush* ‖ ⟨fig⟩ *dilemma, fix* ‖ ⟨dial⟩ = Zwetsche ‖ ⟨fam⟩ *small business, farm, place* **qu·etschen** vt [h] *to squeeze* (*one's nose against the pane*) ‖ *to crush* (*berries*) ‖ *to bruise, pinch, roll* ‖ ⟨path⟩ *contuse* ‖ ⟨mil⟩ (Mine) *to kill* ‖ ⟨billiards⟩ (an die Bande) *to cushion* (*a ball*) ‖ **sich** ~, gequetscht w *to get a bruise*; (v S) *to squash* (*the fruit will squash*) ‖ wir mußten uns arg ~ *we had to squeeze together* ‖ sich [dat] den Arm ~ *to bruise one's arm, to get one's arm jammed* **Qu·etsch-** **~hahn** m ⟨chem⟩ *pinch-cock* **~kartoffeln** f pl *mashed potatoes* pl °**~kommode** f (Akkordeon) ⟨hum⟩ *stomach Steinway, squeeze-box* **~laut** m ⟨phon⟩ *affricate* ([tʃ] in *chop*; [dʒ] in *jam, age*; [ts] in zehn) **~mine** f *killmine* **~stelle** f *pinch*, ⟨Am⟩ *stem press* **~wunde** f, **Qu·etschung** f ~/~en *bruise, contusion*; *contused wound*

Queue [kø:] n ~s/~s (Billard) *cue* ‖ ⟨hors⟩ die ~ bilden *or* übernehmen *to bring up the rear* ‖ ⟨theat⟩ ~ bilden *to stand in file*

quick a *quick* ‖ ⟨fig⟩ *brisk, lively, alert* **≈beutel** m *amalgamating skin* **≈born** m *fountain of youth* **≈brei** m *amalgam* **≈erz** n *quicksilver ore* **≈gold** n *goldamalgam* **~leb·endig** a *alive and kicking*; *spicy* **≈sand** m *quick-sand* **≈wasser** n *quick-water*

Qu·idam m ~/ *somebody, a certain p, so-and-so*

quiek [intj] *squeak!* **~(s)en** vi [h] (of mice, pigs) *to squeak* **qu·ietsch- ~en** vi [h] (of doors, chairs) *to creak, squawk* ‖ (v P) *to scream out* ‖ (of child) *to squeal* **~vergnügt** a (*as*) *cheerful as a sandboy*

quillt 3. sg pres v quellen, ⟨poet⟩ quillen

quin·är a *quinary* **Qu·int- ~a** f ~/–ten ⟨Ger⟩ *fifth* (⟨engl⟩ *second*) *form* **~t·aner** m ~s/~ ⟨Ger⟩ *fifth-* (⟨engl⟩ *second-*)*form boy* **~(e)** f ~/~n ⟨mus⟩ (reine, verminderte *perfect, imperfect*) *fifth, quint; E-string*; leere ~n [pl] *incomplete fifths* ‖ ⟨cards⟩ *quint* ‖ ⟨fenc⟩ *quinte* ‖ ⟨fig⟩ *trick, prank, whim* **~essenz** f ~/~en *quintessence, pith* **~·ett** n ~(e)s/~e *quintet*(*te*)

Qu·ipu ['ki–] n ~(s)/~(s) [Peru] *quipu* (= *knot*)

Quirl m ~(e)s/~e *whisk, twirling-stick*; ⟨tech⟩ *agitator* ‖ ⟨bot⟩ *whorl, verticil* ‖ ⟨for⟩ *shoot* (*of conifers*); die Fichten stehen im 8. ~ .. *are 8 years old* ‖ ⟨fig⟩ (P) ⟨fam⟩ *fidget* | **≗en** vt [h] *to twirl* ‖ ⟨cul⟩ *to whisk*; *to beat up* (*eggs*) ‖ gequirlter Satz ⟨typ⟩ *broken matter, squabble* **≗förmig, ≗ständig** a ⟨bot⟩ *whorled* **≗ig** a (P) *mercurial, restless, fidgety* ‖ ⟨bot⟩ *verticillate*; ~e Blattstellung *verticil, whorl*

Qu·isling m ~(e)s/~e *quisling*

Quisqu·ilien pl L→Abfall, Kleinigkeiten

quitsch-quatsch adv *squeakety-squash*

quitt a [nur pred] (gleich) ~ s *to be quits, square, even* (mit *with*); ~ w (sich rächen) ⟨fam⟩ *to get one's own back* ‖ sich [acc] f ~ erklären *to call quits* ‖ (ledig) e–r S ~ s *to be quit* od *rid of a th* **~·ieren** vt [h] *to receipt* (*a bill*) ‖ (dankend *with thanks*) ‖ (für) *to sign* (*for*) | (aufgeben) *to cut, quit, abandon, leave* (*service*) **≗ung** f ~/~en *receipt*, ⟨a.⟩ *voucher* ‖ e–e ~ ausstellen *to* (*make out* od) *give a receipt* ‖ gegen ~ *on* od *against receipt* ‖ gegen ~ abgeben ⟨a.⟩ *to check* ‖ ⟨fig⟩ *answer* | ~sbuch [n] *receipt-book*

Qu·itte f ~/~n *quince* ‖ japanische ~ *japonica* **Qu·itten- ~apfel** m *quince-apple* **~baum** m *qu.-tree* **~birne** f *qu.-pear* **≗g·elb** a *yellow as a qu.* **~gelee** n *qu. marmalade* **~kern** m *qu.-kernel* **~saft** m *qu.-juice* **~schleim** m *emulsion of qu.s* **~wein** m *qu.-wine*

Quiv·ive [ki'vi:v] n [Fr] auf dem ~ s *to be on the alert*; ⟨fam⟩ *to be on one's toes*

Quiz n ~/~ *quiz*; ~master [m] *quizzer*, Gefragte(r) *quizzee*

†**Qu·odlibet** n ~s/~s *medley, farrago*

quoll pret v quellen

Qu·orum n ~s/ Sw ⟨parl⟩ *quorum* [pl ~*s*] (*fixed number*)

Qu·ote f ~/~n *quota, share, part, portion, contingent, dividend; percentage* | ~nstichprobe [f] *quota sampling*; ~nverteilung [f] (b. Konkurs) *rat*(*e*)*able distribution dividend* **Quoti·ent** m ~en/~en ⟨math⟩ *quotient* **quot·ieren** vt [h] ⟨com⟩ *to quote* (*prices*)

R

R, r n ~/~ *R, r* ‖ das R rollen *to trill* od *roll the r* ‖ ein kehliges R sprechen *to burr the r* ‖ ⟨telph⟩ bitte ein **R-Gespräch** (zu Lasten des Angerufenen) *reversed-charge call*: *please reverse the charge*, ⟨Am⟩ *I would like to call .. collect*

Ra(a) = Rahe

rab·anzen, rab·antern, rab·astern, rabauzen vi [h] *to busy o.s.* ‖ *to potter about noisily*

Rab·at n (Stadt in Marokko)

Rab·att m ~(e)s/~e *abatement*; (f Wiederverkäufer *trade*) *discount; allowance, concession, deduction; rebate* (*a 40 per cent. r.*) ‖ wieviel ~ geben Sie? *what disc. is there* ‖ ~ gewähren *to allow disc.* (auf *on*) ‖ 3% ~ bei Barzahlung *3% disc. for cash* (.. geben *to allow* ..) | ~geschäft [n] *discount house*; ~marke [f] *discount ticket*; ⟨Am a.⟩ *trading stamp*; ~rechnung [f] *discount* (*rate*) | ⟨comp⟩ ~betrag [m] *di.t rate*: ~schlüssel [m] *di.t code* | **~e** f ~/~n ⟨hort⟩ *ridge; border bed* ‖ ⟨tail⟩ *facing* **≗·ieren** vt [h] *to discount, allow, deduct*

°**Rab·atz** m ~es/ = Krach, Unfug ‖ Getümmel, Tumult

Rab·au m ~s/~e, **~ke** m ~n/~n *rowdy* | ~ntum [n] (handfestes *downright*) *rowdyism* **≗zig** a *rip-roaring*

R·abbi, -·iner m ~s/~ *rabbi* **r-·inisch** a *rabbinical*

R·abe m ~n/~n *raven* (krächzt *croaks*) ‖ ein weißer ~ ⟨fig⟩ *a white crow, a rare bird, a black swan* ‖ (P) *pickpocket*, ⟨Am fam⟩ *digger* ‖ du ~! du Räbchen! *you unnatural child!* ‖ (stehlen) wie ein ~ .. *like a magpie* **R·aben- ~aas** n ⟨a. fig⟩ *carrion* ‖ ⟨fig⟩ *gallows-bird* **~art** f ⟨fig⟩ nach ~ *like unnatural parents* **~artig** a ⟨scient⟩ *corvine* **~bein** n ⟨zoo, anat⟩ *coracoid bone*; ⟨fig⟩ *unnatural parent* **~feder** f *r.-* od *crow-quill* **~gekrächz(e)** n *croaking of r.s* **~haar** n *r.-black hair* **~krähe** f *carrion-crow* **~mutter** f ⟨fig⟩ *unnatural mother* **~schlacht** f *battle of Ravenna* **≗schnabel**förmig [a] *coracoid*; ~fortsatz [m] ⟨anat⟩ *coracoid process* **≗schw·arz** a *raven*, (*as*) *black as a crow, raven-hued, coracinous; jetblack* **~stein** m *place of execution* **~vater** m ⟨fig⟩ *unnatural father* **~vögel** m pl ⟨scient⟩ → *corvidae*

†**R·aben** n *Ravenna*

rabi·at a *furious, rabid raving*

Rab·itz- ~bau [m] *R.z wire netting construction*; ~wand [f] (*R.z*) *plaster fabric wall*

Rabul·ist m ~en/~en *pettifogger* **~er·ei** f *pettifogging*

R·ach- ~begierde, ~gier(de) f *revengefulness, thirst* od *desire for revenge, vindictiveness* ‖ **≗erfüllt** a *full of resentment* **~gefühl** n *r.t* **≗gierig** a *revengeful, resentful, vindictive* **~lust, ~sucht** f = ~gier **≗süchtig** a = ≗gierig **R·ache** f ~/ (mst Akt) *revenge* (*r.e*); (mst Art Strafe) *vengeance* (*v.e*) ‖ bittere, grimmige ~ *bitter, ferocious r.e* | ~ brüten *to plan v.e*; *to chew r.e*; geloben an jdm ~ z nehmen *to vow v.e on a p* ‖ ~ nehmen (an [dat]) *to take r.e* (*on*), blutige .. *to wreak dire v.e* (an *upon*); (f *for*) ‖ ~ schnauben *to breathe v.e* ‖ ~ schwören *to vow r.e* | **s-e** ~ ausüben *to execute v.e* (an *upon a p*), .. befriedigen, kühlen, stillen *to satisfy, cool one's v.e* | **auf** ~ sinnen *to meditate r.e*; **nach** ~ dürsten, schreien, verlangen *to long, call for v.e* **~akt** m *act of r.e* **~durst** m = Rachgier **≗durstig** a = rachgierig **~engel** m *avenging angel* **~gelüste** pl *ranco*(*u*)*rs* **≗schnaubend** a *r.eful* **≗schreiend** a *calling for v.e* **~schwert** n *sword of r.e* **~schwur** m *oath to r.e o.s.* **r·ächen** vt [h] **1. (P)** *to avenge* (*p, violated right*) (an [dat] [*up*]*on*) ‖ e–e Beleidigung ~ *to take revenge for an insult* | **sich** an jdm ~ *to take one's change out of a p*, .. wegen e–r S, f e–e S *to take* od *have* (*one's*) *revenge* (od *to revenge o.s.*) *on a p for a th, to wreak one's vengeance upon a p for a th*; *to be revenged* .. ‖ ⟨fam⟩ *to get quits with a p, to take it out of a p*, ⟨Am⟩ *to get back at* od *on a p* **2. (S) sich** ~ *to be atoned for, to meet with punishment* ‖ es rächte sich *it had to be paid for*, .. an ihm *he had to suffer for it, it came home to him*; es wird sich bitter *or* schwer ~ *there will be a heavy penalty to pay for that* **R·ächer** m ~s/~ *avenger*

R·achen m ∼s/∼ (T) *jaws* pl, *mouth* ‖ (P) *chops* pl ‖ (Schlund) *throat* ‖ ∼ der Hölle *jaws of hell* | ⟨fig a.⟩ *maw* (*death's m.*); *yawning abyss*; *chasm* | aufgerissener ∼ *open jaws* | °halt den ∼! ⟨vulg⟩ *hold your jaw*! ‖ °jdm in den ∼ laufen, rennen *to bump, run, butt into a p* ‖ jdm den ∼ stopfen *to yield to the exorbitant demands of a greedy p* ‖ er kann den ∼ nicht voll genug kriegen *he is insatiable* | **aus** dem ∼ des Todes befreien *to save from the jaws of death* ‖ jdm etw **in** den ∼ werfen *to cast sth in a p's teeth* **~bräune** f ⟨med⟩ *croup, quinsy* **~höhle** f *pharynx*; *fauces* pl **~-katarrh** m *cold in the throat*, ⟨scient⟩ *pharyngitis* **~lehre** f ⟨tech⟩ (S) *horseshoe gauge* °**~putzer** m *hearty* (Schnaps)

Rach·itis f ∼/ ⟨path⟩ *rickets* [sg *or* pl]; ⟨scient⟩ *rachitis* **rach·itisch** a *rickety*

Rack n ∼s/∼e ⟨naut⟩ *truss*

R·acke f ∼/∼n ⟨orn⟩ *roller*

R·acker m ∼s/∼ ⟨fam⟩ (*little*) *rascal, rogue*; *young scamp* od *devil* **r·ackern** vi [h] (a. sich) *to drudge*; *to toil* (*and moil*); ⟨fam⟩ *to fag*

Rad n ∼(e)s/∼̈er **A.** *wheel* ‖ (Rolle) *trundle*, ⟨el⟩ *trolley* | ⟨fig⟩ *the wh.* (*of time, history*), *the wh.s of evolution* (stehen .. *are never still*) ‖ das 5. ∼ am Wagen s *to be the fifth wh. to the cart* ‖ nur ein ∼ im Getriebe *only a cog in the machine*; ⟨mot⟩ montiertes ∼ *road wheel* **B. Antriebs**∼̈ = Treib∼̈; Bug∼̈ *nose-wh.*; Drahtspeichen∼̈ *wire wh.*; Ersatz∼̈ *spare wh.* **Fahr**∼̈ (*bi*)*cycle, machine*; ⟨fam⟩ (*push-*)*bike*, ⟨Am⟩ *wheel*; Geschäfts∼̈ *delivery bicycle*; Glücks∼̈ *wh. of fortune*; Hinter∼̈ *back* od *hind wh.*; Kamm∼̈ *cog*(*ged*) *wh.*; Kegel∼̈ *bevel* od *conical wh.*; Ketten∼̈ *sprocket wh.* ‖ Lauf∼̈ *roller*, (an Standuhr) *runner*; Lauf-∼schaufel [f] *wh. vane* (*of a turbine*); Meß∼̈ *measuring wh.*; Motor∼̈ *motor-cycle* **Mühl**∼̈ *mill-wh.*; Planetenhaupt∼̈ *sun wh.*; Richt∼̈ ⟨artill⟩ *laying wh.*; Riesen∼̈ (Jahrmarkt) *Ferris wh.*; Schaufel∼̈ *paddle-wh.*; Schellen∼̈ ⟨ec⟩ *wh. of bells*; Schnekken∼̈ *worm wh.*; Schnur∼̈ *band-wh.*; Schrauben-∼̈ *helical wh.*; Schwung∼̈ *balance-* od *fly-wh.*; Spinn∼̈ *spinning-wh.*; Sporn∼̈ *rowel*; Spul∼̈ *spooling wh., hand reel*; Steuer∼̈ *steering wh.*; Treib∼̈ *driving wh., driver, impeller*; Vorder∼̈ *front-wh.*; Wellen∼̈ *wh. and axle*, Zahn∼̈ *cog*(*ged*) *wh.*, kl ∼ *pinion*; ⟨arts⟩ *roulette*; Zwischen-∼̈ *idle wh.* **C. sich drehen** *to turn* ‖ ∼ fahren = radfahren ‖ bei ihm (fehlt ein Rädchen *or*) ist ein ∼ locker *he's got a screw loose* ‖ die ∼̈er gingen über ihn hinweg .. *went over him* ‖ das ∼ laufen l ⟨cycl⟩ *to coast* ‖ rollen *to revolve* ‖ sausen, surren *to whiz*(*z*) ‖ (ein) ∼ schlagen *to turn cart-wh.s, to throw hand-springs* pl; (vor Freude) *to turn* od *throw a somersault*; der Pfau ..: ein (stolzes) ∼ *shows off* od *spreads his* (*magnificent*) *tail* | ⟨mot⟩ ein ∼ schlägt .. *is loose*; die ∼̈er stehen ungleich .. *are out of line* **D. auf's** ∼ binden, flechten *to bind to the wh.* ‖ sich auf's ∼ schwingen, setzen *to jump on the bicycle* ‖ **in** die Räder k *to be caught in the wh.s* (*of a machine*) ‖ **mit** dem ∼e davon fahren *to go off on one's bike* ‖ er kam **unter** die Räder *he fell under the wh.s*; *was crushed beneath the wh.s* ‖ ⟨fig⟩ *he has gone under* ‖ **zum** ∼e verurteilen *to condemn to* (*be broken on*) *the wh.* **E.** (weiter) **~abstand** (*long*) *wh.-base* **~abzieher** m ⟨mot⟩ *puller* **~achse** f *axle-tree* **~antrieb** m *final* od *wh. drive* **~auflagepunkt** m ⟨mot⟩ *centre of tyre impact* **~ausschlag** m *wh. deflection* **~balken** m ⟨mar⟩ *paddle beam* **~bogen** m (Uhr) *rim* **~bremse** f *wh. brake* **~buchse** f *chair of the wh.* **~büchse** f *wh.-box* **~dampfer** m *paddle-steamer*, ⟨Am⟩ *side-wheeler* ‖ ⟨fig⟩ *enormous woman* **~fahr**-abteilung [f] ⟨mil⟩ *cyclist section*; ∼hose [f] (f Frauen) *pantalettes* pl; ∼kompanie [f] *bicyle company*: ∼weg [m] *cycle path* ∼̈|**fahren 1.** vi [h & s] *to cycle, to* (*ride a*) *bicycle*; ⟨fam⟩ *to bike, wheel*; (sausend) *to scorch*; wir sind –ge– *we went for a cycle ride* **2.** ∼̈ n (Katzbuckeln) *bobbing* **~fahrer** m *cyclist*, ⟨fam⟩ *wheelman* ‖ ⟨fig⟩ *cringing p* | ∼bahn [f] *cycling-track*; ∼verein [m] *cyclists' touring club* **~felge** f *felloe, felly* | ∼nkranz [m] *rim* **~fenster** n ⟨arch⟩ *rose-window* ∼̈**förmig** a *wh.-shaped*, ⟨bot⟩ *rotate* **~gehäuse** n, **~kasten** m ⟨mar⟩ *paddle-box*; ⟨tech⟩ *wh.-case* **~geleise** n *track, rut* **~gestell** n *wh.-frame*; (bewegliches) *bogie*, ⟨Am⟩ *truck* **~gürtel** m ⟨mil⟩ *wh. belt* **~-kamm** m *cog* **~kappe** f *hub-cap*, ⟨Am⟩ *wh. hub* **~kranz** m (*b*)*rim* **~lafette** f *wheeled carriage* (*of a gun*) **~landung** f ⟨aero⟩ *two-point landing* **~lauf** m *rotation* **~linie** f *cycloid* ∼̈**linig** a *cycloidal* **~macher** m *wheelwright* **~mantel** m *cape* **~melder** m *bicycle messenger* **~nabe** f *wh.-nave, hub, boss* **~-nagel** m *wh.-nail* **~polo** n *cycle polo* **~reif(en)** m *tyre*, ⟨Am⟩ *tire* **~rennbahn** f *cycling ground, race track* **~rennen** n *cycling race* **~satz** m *wh. set* **~-schaltung** f *wh. escapement* **~schaufel** f *paddle-board*; (Mühle) *sweep* **~scheibe** f *roll in a pulley*; *disk wh. centre* **~schiene** f *wh.-band* **~schlagen** n → C. ‖ ⟨fig⟩ das ist rein zum ∼! *that's enough to drive one mad!, that makes me hoot!* **~schlepper** m *wh.ed tractor* **~schuh** m *skid*; *brake* **~speiche** f (*wh.-*)*spoke* **~sperre** f *drag-chain* **~sporn** m ⟨hors⟩ *rowel* **~sport** m *cycling* **~spur** f *rut, cart-* od *wh.-track*; *print of wh.* **~stand** m *wheel base*; ⟨mil⟩ schiefer ∼ *oblique wh. b.* **~stern** m *wh. spider* **~-steuerung** f *wh.-stearing* **~sturz** m *camber* **~-umfang** m *circumference of a wh.* **~wechsel** m *wh. changing* **~weg** m *cycle path* **~welle** f *wh.-tree* od *-shaft, axle* **~zahn** m *cog* **~zapfen** m *pivot, spindle*

R·adar m ∼s/∼ *radar* (*radio detecting and ranging* [*apparatus*]); mit ∼ ausgerüstet *r.-equipped*; aktiver, passiver ∼ *secondary, primary r.*; was ist im ∼ z sehen? *what's on the r.?*; mit ∼ erfaßt (*aircraft*) *picked up by r.* **~abwehr-** ∼gerät [n] *anti-r. detection device*; ∼netz [n] *defence r. network* **~·anflugverfahren** n → G.C.A.- **~apparat** m *r. set* **~auffanggerät** n *lobe* **~bake** f *radar beacon* **~blindlandeanlage** f *ground-controlled approach* (*G.C.A.*) *plant* **~bombenzieleinrichtung** f *r. bomb sight* **~feuerleitung** f *r. fire control*; Flak mit ∼ *r.-directed anti-aircraft gun* **~flugzeug** n *r. plane* | ∼warnnetz [n] *r. aircraft network* **~funk-peilung** f *radiolocation* ∼̈**gelenkt** a *r.-directed* (*bomber*) **~gerät** n *r.-set* ∼̈**gesteuert** a *r.-guided* (*bomb, rocket*) | mit **~hilfe** f (*aircraft*) *r.* (*bombed bridge*) **~höhenmesser** m *r. altimeter* **~kenngerät** n *r. identification unit* | Ziel mit kontinuierlicher **~kennung** f *ramark* **~lenkung** f ⟨a–n⟩ (e–s Raumschiffs) *skin tracking* **~leuchtschirm** m *r. screen* **~mann** m *r. operator* od *man*, ⟨Am sl⟩ *Mickey* **~navigation** f ⟨aero⟩ *oboe*, Langstrecken∼̈ *loran* (*long range navigation*) **~netz** n *r. network* **~ortungsgerät** n *r.-detection device* **~schirm** m *r. screen*; ∼bild [n] *r. scope* **~sonde** f *r.-sonde* | e–e **~station** ausfindig m *to locate a*(*n enemy*) *r. station* **~steuerung** f *r. guiding* (*of missiles*) **~störer** m *r. jammer* **~störmaßnahmen** f pl *r. countermeasures* **~such-** ∼antenne [f] *r. search antenna*; ∼gerät [n] *s. r.* **~techniker** m *r. operator* **~überwachung** f *r. monitoring* **~visier** n ⟨aero-mil⟩ *r. sight*; .. mit ∼ *r. sighted* (*cannon*) **~vorpostenboot** n *r. picket ship* **~wagen** m *GCA r. truck* N **~warn-** ∼gerät [n] *r. picket*; ∼-ermittelte Wettermeldung [f] *r. plotted weather information*; ∼netz [n] *r. warning network*; ∼schirm [m] *r. w. screen*; ∼station [f] *r. w. station* **~zeichen** n (auf dem Schirm) *r. trace* | aktives **~ziel** n *ramark*; ∼ballon [m] *r. target balloon*

Rad·au m ∼s/ ⟨fam⟩ *row, shindy, racket, uproar*; ⟨sl⟩ *rag, row-de-dow, ruction* ‖ ∼ m ⟨sl⟩ *to rag*; ⟨Am sl⟩ *to whoop it up* **~bruder** m *rowdy, tough* **~komödie** f *slapstick comedy* **~posse** f *knock-about farce* **~versammlung** f *uproarious meeting*

R·ädchen n ~s/~ *dot-wheel, pricker* ‖ (unter Möbeln) *castor, roller* ‖ (des Sporns) *rowel*

R·ade f ~/~n ⟨bot⟩ *corn-cockle*

r·adebrechen vt [h] (→ Rad) *to jabber; to murder, torture (a language)*; Englisch ~ *to speak (a little* od) *broken E.; to mangle the King's E.* **r·adeln** vi [h] *to (ride on a bi)cycle* ‖ ⟨fam⟩ *to bike, wheel* **r·ädeln** vt [h] *to mill; to rim* **R·ädelsführer** m *ringleader* **R·äder-** [in comp] *wheeled (carriage)* **~antrieb** m *wheel drive* **~fahrzeug** n mit Verbrennungsmotor *wheeled fuel consuming vehicle* N **~flattern** n ⟨mot⟩ *shimmy* **~gehäuse** n (Uhr) *case, frame* ‖ ⟨mar⟩ *paddle-box* **~getriebe** n *transmission gear* **~schneidemaschine** f *teeth cutting machine* **~schutz** m ⟨mach⟩ *gear-guard* **~tierchen** n pl *rotifers, wheel-animalcules* pl **~-vorgelege** n *wheel* od *transmission gear* **~werk** n *gear(ing), works; (gear) train; (clock-)work* | ~-getriebe [n] *train of gears* **r·ädern** vt [h] *to break on the wheel* ‖ wie gerädert s *to be quite knocked* (od *done*) *up* ‖ gerädert u gevierteilt *drawn and quartered*

Radi·al- **~·achslagergehäuse** n *radial axle-box housing* **~b·ohrmaschine** f *r.l drilling machine* **~-druck** m *r.l pressure* **~laufring** m (Kugellager) *r.l raceway* **~spiel** n *r.l play* **~turbine** f *r.l flow turbine* **~verteilung** f ⟨el⟩ *r.l system* **Radi·an** m ~s/ (Winkelmeßeinheit) *radian*

Radi·ator m ~s/–·oren *radiant heater* **Radia·t·oren-** **~fräsmaschine** f *radiator milling machine* **~gewindeschneidemaschine** f *radiator tapping machine* **R·adien** m pl v Radius

Rad·ier- **~auflage** f *eraser table* **~grund** m *etching-ground* **~gummi** m *india-rubber* **~kunst** f *etching* **~messer** n *erasing-knife, eraser, scraper* **~nadel** f *et.g-needle; dry needle* **~schablone** f *erasing shield* **rad·ieren** vt [h] *to erase* ‖ ⟨arts⟩ *to etch* ‖ ⟨mot⟩ (Reifen) *to erase*; ≃ n *wearing action* **Rad·ierung** f ~/~en *erasure* ‖ ⟨arts⟩ *etching*

Rad·ieschen n ~s/~ *red radish* ‖ °er besieht sich die ~ v unten *he's (under the daisies* od) *daisy-pushing* **radik·al** a *radical (disagreement); sweeping (measures)* ‖ ⟨pol⟩ *extreme* | [adv] *radically (different)* **≃kur** f *radical cure* **Radik·ale** m [der ~, ein ~r] ~n/~n *radical, extremist* ‖ ⟨fam⟩ *rad*

R·adio n ~s/~s **1.** [abstr] (Rundfunk) *broadcasting (b.c.g)* **2.** [konkr] (Apparat) *wireless (w.l.), radio (r.)*; ~ mit eingebautem Plattenspieler *r.-record combination* ‖ das ~ ab-, einschalten *to switch off/on* (auf *to*); (etw im) ~hören *to listen in (to a th); to pick up .. by r.* ‖ im ~ singen *to sing on the w.l.* od *r.* ‖ mit ~ ausgestattet *w.l.-fitted* ‖ durch das ~ *through the microphone, over the r.* ‖ was gibt's heute abend im ~ *what's on the air this evening?* **≃akt·iv** a *r.active* (Elemente *isotopes*); Schutzmaßnahmen gegen ~e Bestrahlung *r.-logical defence, -se* ‖ ~ m *to activate*; ~er Indikator ⟨at-med⟩ *tracer* | ~ität *r.activity*; Lehre v der ~ *r.logy* **~amateur** m ⟨fam⟩ *ham* **~apparat** m, **~-anlage** f *w.l. (receiving) set*, ⟨Am⟩ *radio set* **~antenne** f *w.l. aerial* **~bastler** m *b.c* od *r. amateur, r.-fan* **~durchsage** f *spot announcement*, ⟨Am⟩ *spot* **~freund** m *r.fan* **~gehäuse** n *r. cabinet* **≃g·en** a *r.genic* **~gerät** n *r. set* **~gramm** n *r.gram, w.l. telegram* **~hörer** m [pl] *listener[s]-in* **~kennmelodie** f *signature* **~konzert** n *w.l. concert* **≃l·ogisch** a *r.logical (warfare)* **~mechaniker** m *r. mechanic*, ⟨Am⟩ *r.trician* **~musik** f etc ⟨fam⟩ *canned music* **~nachricht** f *r.gram* **~nukle·id** n *(r.active) tracer* **~nukl·id** n *r.nuclide* **~ortung** f *r. location* **~ortungsgerät** n *r. direction finder* **~peilung** f *r. homing* **~phon** n *r.gram* **~-Plattenspieler** m *radiogram* **~röhre** f *r. tube* **~sendung** f (gespendete) ~ *(sponsored) b.c.* **~werbesendung** f *commercial r. announcement*, ⟨Am⟩ *r. commercial* **~werbung** f: ~ betreiben *to sponsor r. b.c.s. (through commercials)* **~wesen** n *b.c.g; electronics* [sg konstr]

R·adium n ~s/ ⟨chem⟩ *radium* **~emanation** f *rays emanating from r.* **≃haltig** a *containing r.* **~h·eilverfahren** n *radiotherapy* **~kapsel** f ⟨med⟩ *implants* **~l·euchtartikel** m *radium luminous article* **~s·olbad** n *spa with radio-active spring* **R·adius** m ~/ R·adien *radius* ‖ ⟨übtr⟩ künstlerischer ~ *artistic range* **~lehre** f (S) *radius gauge*

radiz·ieren vt [h] ⟨math⟩ *to extract the root of*

R·adler m ~s/~ *cyclist*, ⟨Am⟩ *wheelman* | **~·ei** f ~/ *cycling* .. **rädrig** a *wheeled (two-wh.)*

R·adon n (Radiumemanation) *radon*, → Emanation 2.

R·adsch- **~a** m ~/~ *Raja(h)* **Radschput·ana** n (vorderind. Landschaft) *Rajputana* **Radschp·ut(a)** m, **Radschp·utin** f *Rajput, Rajpoot* **-p·ute** m ~n/~n *Rajpoot*

R·affel f ~/~n *iron rake* ‖ (Flachs≃) *hatchel* ‖ (Fisch≃) *raffle-net* ‖ ⟨fig⟩ (Mund) *potato-trap* **r·affen** vt [h] *to snatch up* ‖ *to sweep together* ‖ ⟨sl⟩ *to hog* ‖ (Kleid) *to gather up*; ⟨tail⟩ *to drape; to take up* ‖ (Segel) *to reef*; 1-, 2-, 3-mal gerafft *single-, double-, treble-reefed* **R·affer** m ~s/~ (P) = Raffke, ⟨Am fam⟩ *go-getter* **R·aff-** **~gier** f ~/ *greediness, rapacity* **≃ig** a *rapacious, grasping*; ~ s ⟨sl⟩ *to hog* **~gut** n *stolen articles* pl **~holz** n *gathered wood* **~zahn** m *snag-tooth* °**R·affke** m ~s/~s *profiteer; money-grubber*

Raffin- **~·ade** f ~/~n *refined sugar* **~ati·on** f *refinement; refining* **~ement** [-fi:n'mã] n ~s/~s *elaborateness* ‖ (Schlauheit) *cunning, shrewdness; refined, exquisite cruelty* **~er·ie** f ~/~n *(re)finery* **~·esse** f ~/ *refinement, elaboration* | *shrewdness, cunning* **~·eur** [ør] m ~s/~e *refiner* **≃·ieren** vt [h] *to refine (oil, sugar)* ‖ ⟨met⟩ *to try (out)* | **-rt** a *elaborate, refined* ‖ *studied (malice)* ‖ *exquisite (cruelty)* ‖ (schlau) *artful, crafty, wily, cunning, shrewd; slick* ‖ *skilful (trick)* | ≃heit [f] = Raffinement ‖ *smartness, shrewdness; cunning, craftiness, artfulness; cleverness* **~ierung** f *(re)fining*

R·age ['ra:ʒə] f ~/ in ~ k. *to fall into rage* ‖ in der ~ *in one's excitement*

r·agen vi [h] *to tower, soar; to be prominent*

Ragi·one [ra'dʒo:nə] f ~/~n It - Sw ⟨com⟩ → Firma

R·aglan(mantel) m *slipper*

R·agnarök f ~/ ⟨Norse myth⟩ *end of the world*

Ragout [ra'gu:] n ~s/~s ⟨cul⟩ *ragout*, (weißes *white*) *stew; hotchpotch; salmagundi*

†**Rag·usa** n (in Dalmatien) → Dubrovnik

R·ah(e) f ~/~n ⟨mar⟩ *yard* | Bram≃ *gallant y.*; Fock≃ *fore y.*; Groß≃ *main y.*; Kreuz≃ *mizzen y.*; Mars≃ *top y.*; Oberbram≃ *top gallant y.* | mit bloßen ~n *under bare poles* ‖ e–e ~ brassen, (heißen) *to brace, (hoist) a y.* **~liek** f *head rope* **~nock** f *arm of a y.* **~schiff** n *square-rigged vessel* **~schuner** m *brigantine* **~segel** n *square* od *yard sail* **~tau** n *head-line*

Rahm m ~(e)s/ (Sahne) *cream*; in ~ ⟨cul⟩ *cr.ed* ‖ den ~ abschöpfen *to skim the cr.* ⟨a. fig⟩ ‖ ~ ansetzen *to form cr.* **~apfel** m *custard apple* **~eis** n *ice cr.* **≃farben** a *cr.-coloured* **≃ig** a *cr.y* **~käse** m *cr. cheese* **~kelle** f *cr.-skimmer* **~löffel** m *cr.-spoon, cr.-ladle* **~messer** m (Gerät) *cr.ometer* **~topf** m *creamer* **~torte** f *cr.-tart*

Rahm, ≃ m ~s/~e ⟨carp⟩ (⟨a.⟩ ~stück) *breastsummer* **R·ahmen** m ~s/~ **A.** *frame (fr.)* ⟨a. am Klavier & cycl⟩, *(embroidery-, picture-, shaft-, mining-, window-,* (Pulver-) *shaking-fr.)* | ⟨allg⟩ *edge, border, rim* | ⟨fig⟩ *fr., setting (for a meeting); ambience, -ance* ‖ ⟨mil & mar⟩ *skeleton* ‖ (Grenze) *limit, bound* **B.** Auto≃, Fahrzeug≃ *chassis* ‖ Flügelfenster≃ *casement* ‖ Form≃ ⟨typ⟩ *chase* ‖ Kopier≃ ⟨phot⟩ *printing fr.* ‖ Lafetten≃ *chassis* ‖ Passepartout≃ *mount* ‖ Patronen≃ ⟨mil⟩ *clip* ‖ Scher≃ ⟨weav⟩ *warping-mill* od *-fr.* ‖ Schiffskreisel≃ *casing* ‖ Schließ≃ ⟨typ⟩ *chase* ‖ Schuh≃ *welt* ‖ Spann≃ ⟨bookb⟩

vice || (runder) Stick∸ *tambour* **C. auf** ~ arbeiten *to welt* (*shoes*) | ⟨fig⟩ **aus dem** ~ fallen *to be out of place*; *there was sth incongruous in him* || ⟨fig⟩ **in** engem ~ *within a narrow* od *close compass, within narrow bounds* || im ~ e–s Aufsatzes *within the scope of an essay* || im ~ des Möglichen *in the measure of the possible*; im ~ der Vereinbarungen, .. der gesetzl. Bestimmungen *within the framework of the agreement, .. of law*; im ~ der gesamten Volkswirtschaft *in the national economy* || (P) sich in e–n ~ einfügen *to fit into one's surroundings* || sich im ~ v etw halten *to confine o.s. to a th* || (Bild) **mit** e–m ~ versehen *to fr., mount* → B. || mit ~ sticken *to tambour* **~antenne** f *loop* od *fr. aerial*; (z Orten) *direction finding aerial* **~-arbeit** f (Schuhe) *welted work* **~bau** m ⟨arch⟩ *fr.work construction* **~erzählung** f *frame* || ~en [pl] *stories within a story* **~gesetz** n *skeleton law* **~lafette** f *slide carriage* **~lizenz** f ⟨com⟩ *open* (*export-*)*licence* **~oberlicht** n ⟨theat⟩ *proscenium batten*, ⟨Am⟩ *No. 1 light pipe* **~police** f ⟨ins⟩ *master policy* **~rohr** n ⟨cycl⟩ *tube* **~säge** f *fr.-saw* **~schuh** m *welted shoe* **~sohle** f *welted sole* **~stikker·ei** f *fr.-* od *tambour-work* **~sucher** m ⟨phot⟩ *fr. finder*; *iconometer* **~übung** f ⟨mil⟩ *cadre manœuvre*; *skeleton drill*; *command post exercise* **~vertrag** m *skeleton* od *basic agreement*

ˣ**R·ahne** f ~/~n [sd] ⟨bot cul⟩ *red beet*(*root*)

R·aiffeisengenossenschaft f ⟨Ger⟩ *agricultural* (*R.*) *co-operative association*

R·aigras n *rye-grass*

Rain m ~(e)s/~e (Ackergrenze) *balk, ridge*; ⟨for⟩ *bank* || ⟨fig⟩ *border, limit* **~farn** m ⟨bot⟩ *tansy* **~kohl** m ⟨bot⟩ *nipplewort* **~stein** m *boundary-stone* **~stufe** f *lynchet* **~weide** f ⟨bot⟩ *privet*

Raison Fr → Räson || **raj·olen** → rig·olen

R·ake f ~/~n ⟨orn⟩ *roller* || → Racke, Blau∸

r·äkeln → r·ekeln

Rak·ete f ~/~n *rocket* (*r.*) (.. abbrennen *to let off* ..) || Feuerwerks∸ *squib, fire-cracker*; Signal∸ *sky r.*; ballistische ~ *free r.*; ⟨a-n⟩ mehrstufige ~ *step r.*; Brand∸ *carcass r.*; → Leucht∸ || Boden-Boden-~ *surface-to-s. missile* (*SSM*) || ⟨a-n⟩ Brems∸ *braking r.*; e–e Brems∸ zünden ⟨a-n⟩ ⟨a.⟩ *to retrofire* || Dreistufen∸, dreistufige ~ *three-stage rocket* || Erkundungs∸ *patrol r.* || Flak∸ *surface-to-air missile* N || ⟨a-n⟩ Lenk∸, Steuer∸ *guide-r.* || ~ mit Pulverantrieb *dry-fuel r.*; ~ mit flüssigem Treibstoff *liquid-fuel r.* || ⟨a-n⟩ Rückfeuerungs∸ (f Raumforschung) *retro-r.*; Träger∸ *carrier r.* | mit ~n beschießen *to r.-bomb* **Rak·eten-** **~abflug** m *r.-assisted take-off* **~abschuß** m *blast-off*; *shoot* | ~basis [f] *r. launching site* **~abwehr-** ~anlage [f] *anti-missile defence*; ~rakete [f] *anti-missile* **~antrieb** m [abstr] *r. propulsion*; [konkr] *thermodynamic duct*; *thermojet*; mit ~ *r.-driven* **∸artig** [adv] verbrennen ⟨chem⟩ *to fuse* **~auto** n *r.-propelled car* **~bahn** f *rocket path* || ~ vermessen ⟨a-n⟩ *to skin-track* **~basis** f *r. base* **~bunker** m *silo* **~düse** f *r.-jet nozzle* **~fähre** f *ferry r.* **~feuer** n *r. trail* **~flugzeug** n *r.-plane* **~forscher** m *r.eer* **~gerät** n *r. apparatus* **~geschoß** n *flying r.*; (*remote-controlled*) *ballistic missile* **∸getriebenes** Überschallflugzeug *supersonic r. aircraft* **~hülse** f *r.-case* **~jäger** m *r. fighter* **~kapsel** f *r. capsule* **~raumschiff** n *r.-propelled space-ship* **~satz** m *r.-composition*; *r.-stage* **~schiff** n *r. ship* **~schleudersitz** m *r. ejection seat* | mit **~schub** [m] *r.-drive* [attr] **~stab, ~stock** m *r.-stick* **~start** m ⟨a-n⟩ *shoot*; ⟨aero⟩ *r.-assisted take-off* **~stoß** m *r. burst* **~-stufe** f *r. stage* || Abstoßen [n] e–r ~ *staging* **~technik** f *r.ry*, ⟨scient⟩ *r. engineering, r. technology* **~treibstoff** m *r. propellant* **~triebwerk** n *r. engine*; ~ mit Ionenantrieb *ion propulsion engine* **~typ** m *r.-type* (z. B. *Saturn V*) **~werfer** m *r. launcher* N **~zeichen** n *r.* od *flare signal* **~zünder** m *squib*

Rak·ett n ~(e)s/~s ⟨ten⟩ *racket* || (Federball) *battledore*

R·alle f ~/~n ⟨orn⟩ *ralline bird,* (*water-*) *rail*

R·amie f ~/~n (Bœhm·eria) ⟨bot⟩ *China grass* || ~garn [n] *ramie yarn*

R·amm- **~arbeit** f *piling* **~bär, ~bock** m *ram*(*mer*), ⟨fam⟩ *monkey* °**∸dösig** a → benommen, überreizt **~jungfer** f, **~klotz** m *pile-block* **sporn** m ⟨mar⟩ *ram* **~strahlmotor** m *ram jet* **~tau** n *lifting rope* **R·amme** f ~/~n ⟨tech⟩ *rammer* || (*paving-*)*beetle* || *pile-driver* || ⟨fam⟩ *monkey*

Rammel·ei f ~/~en *lustfulness*; °*shag, ram*

r·ammeln 1. vi [h] *to ram* || ⟨zoo⟩ *to buck* || °⟨sex⟩ *to shag* **2.** ∸n *shag*, ⟨mar⟩ *fore-and-aft*

R·ammelzeit f *bucking-time* **r·ammen** vt [h] *to ram*, (Beton) *tamp*; *to drive in, to beat down* || ⟨aero, mar⟩ *to ram* **R·ammler** m ~s/~ *buck*, (*male hare* od *rabbit*) || °⟨sex⟩ *shag*

R·ampe f ~/~n *sloping terrace*; *slope* || *platform* || *ramp, ascent* || ⟨fort⟩ *slope* || ⟨theat⟩ *footlights* pl ⟨a. fig⟩ (vor .. *before* ..) || ⟨fig⟩ °ran an die ~! *get to work*! **~nlicht** n ⟨theat⟩ *footlights* pl || ⟨fig⟩ (der Öffentlichkeit) *limelight*, ⟨Am⟩ *spotlight* (im .. *under* ..); mitten im ~ stehen *to be plumb center of the stage* ⟨a. fig⟩; er rückte ins ~ ⟨pol, etc⟩ *he was brought into the l.l.* || das ~ scheuen ⟨theat⟩ *to suffer from stage-fever*; ⟨fig pol⟩ *to dread publicity* **~nscheinwerfer** m ⟨theat⟩ *float* (⟨Am⟩ *footlight*) *spot* **~nzufahrt** f *elevated approach*

rampon·iert a *injured, shattered, damaged* || *disabled* (*ship*) || *crumpled, crushed, creased*

Ramsch m ~es/~e *refuse, rubbish, jumble,* || ⟨com⟩ *rummage, job lot*; *catchpenny article* || im ~ *in the lump* **~geschäft** n *junk-shop* **~händler** m *slaughterer* **~verkauf** m *r.age* od *jumble sale* **~ware** f *job lot, job* od *junk goods*; *trumpery* || ~n [pl] ⟨a.⟩ *oddments* pl

°**ran** (= heran [pref & adv]) nun aber ~ (an'n Speck)! *now for it*! || immer ~! *come along*! ⟨sl⟩ *jump to it*! °**~|gehen** vi [s] *to be hep* ⟨sl⟩ || an etw ~ ⟨fam⟩ *to jump to a th*

Rand m ~(e)s/∸er **A.** *edge, border, brink*; *periphery* || ⟨arch⟩ *cant, edge, arris* || ⟨astr⟩ (Sonnen-, Mond∸) *limb* || ⟨min⟩ (Tagebau) *ridge* || ⟨tech⟩ *edge, ledge, border, fringe* || ⟨typ⟩ *margin* (an *in*); mit schwarzem ~ *black-bordered* (*paper*) || unterer ~ *tail* (*of a page*) || ⟨mil⟩ vorderer ~ der Bereitstellung *line of departure*, .. der Verteidigung *main l. of resistance* N || ⟨poet⟩ *margin* (*of a river, glacier*) (an *on*) **B.** (~ e–s **Abhanges**) *brink, brow* || (Brot∸) *crust* || (Brunnen∸) *brink* || (Dorf∸) am ~ *on the outskirts* || (Fels∸) *ledge, lip* || (Gefäß∸) *rim, lip* || (Hut∸) *brim* || (Münz∸) *edge* || (Schraub∸) *screw rim* || (Teller∸) *rim* || (Ufer∸) *edge, bank* || (Wald∸) *border* || (~ e–r Wunde) *lip* **C.** als ~ **dienen** f etw *to fringe a th* || (v Tropfen, Töpfen) e–n ~ hinterlassen *to leave a mark* **D.** °**halt** den ~! *shut up*! **E. angestauchter** ~ *staved end* || äußerer ~ *outskirts* pl || blaue, dunkle Ränder unter den Augen *blue, dark rings* od *circles under* od *round one's eyes* || eingelassener ~ *faucet joint* || genähter ~ (am Schuh) *welt* || gewebter ~ *selvage* || hervorspringender ~ *flange* (*on the f.*) || schwarzer ~ (in Zeitung) *black border* || Papier mit schwarzem ~ *black-edged paper* || umgekrempelter ~ ⟨met⟩ *flanged rim* **F. am** ~e *on the edge* (*of starvation, of a precipice*), *on the brink* od *verge* (*of ruin, destruction, of the grave = at death's door*); *on the edge of the circle* || am ~ befindlich ⟨typ⟩ *marginal* || ⟨fig⟩ am ~e bemerken *to remark in passing* || am ~e bemerkt *by the by* || am ~e umgeben (of dust) *to rim* (*a bottle*) || das versteht sich am ~e *that's understood, that's a matter of course* || am ~e des Gesetzes *skirting the outer fringe of the law* || e–n **an** den ~ (e–r S) bringen *to bring a p to the verge* (*of despair, destruction, ruin*), *to the brink* (*of war*) || bis an den ~ → bis zum ~ || **aus** *or* **außer** ~ u Band *wild* (vor *with*), *out of joint* od *hand, out of all control* od *hand* od *bounds* pl; *as mad as a March hare* || **bis zum** ~ *up to the brim* od *edge*, .. voll *full to the brim, brimful* || °(mit etw) zu ~e k *to finish off, to manage* (*a th*); *to bring it about*; voll → Platzen **G.** **~bemerkung, ~erklärung** f *side-note, m.al note, gloss* **~bevölkerung** f *fringe population* **~gebiet** n *outskirts* pl; e–r Großstadt *subtopia* **~einstellung** f ⟨typwr⟩ *m.-stop* **~feuer** n ⟨aero⟩ *boundary lights* pl **~gebirge** n *highland rim* **⁓genäht** a *welted* (*shoes*) **~glosse** f *m.l gloss* || ~n [pl] *m.lia* L pl; ~n [m] → Glosse **~härchen** n pl *cilia* L pl **~landschaft** f *transitional zone*; *marginal region* **~leiste** f *ledge, cornice* **~lochung** f *row of m.al perforations* **~los** a *rimless* **~löser** m ⟨typwr⟩ *m. release* **~schicht** f ⟨aero dyn⟩ *outer layer* **~schleier** m ⟨phot⟩ *edge fog* **~schrift** f *inscription* od *legend* (*of coins*) **~siedlung** f *settlement on the outskirts* (*of a town*) **~spur** f ⟨rec, etc⟩ *m. track* **~staaten** m pl *Border States* **⁓ständig** a *m.al* **~stein** m *curb-stone* **~steller** m ⟨typwr⟩ *m. stop* **~stellung** f ⟨tact⟩ *perimeter position* **~streifen** m ⟨mot⟩ (nicht befahrbarer *soft*) *shoulder*; *verge* **~verteidigung** f *peripherical strategy* **~verzierung** f *ornamental border* od *edge*; ⟨typ⟩ *border, flourish, vignette* || ⟨arch⟩ *cartouche* **~wirbel** m *boundary vortex* **~zeichnung** f *m.al drawing* **r·ändeln, r·anden, r·ändern** vt [h] *to edge, ring, rim, border* || *to mill, edge*(*-raise*) (*coins*); ⟨phot⟩ *mount* **R-lung** f ⟨num⟩ *milled edge*

°**Rand·al** m ~s/~e *row, brawl* || ~ schlagen = **⁓·ieren** vi [h] *to kick up a row* **~macher** m *rowdy*

R·änftchen n ~s/~ *crust* (*of bread*); (v 2 Broten, die an–e–a hingen) *kissing-crust*

rang 1 & 3. sg [pret] (ränge subj) v ringen

Rang m ~(e)s/⁓e **A. 1.** *rank* ⟨a. mil⟩, ⟨mar⟩ *rating* || *grade, degree* || (*social*) *position*, (hoher) *station* || *dignity* || *quality, rate* || *class, order* || ⟨mil⟩ höherer ~ *more exalted rank*; genügender ~ *enough rank* **2.** ⟨theat⟩ *tier* (*of boxes*), *row* (*of seats*); erster ~ *dress circle*, ⟨Am⟩ *balcony*, zweiter *or* oberer ~ *upper*, ⟨Am⟩ *second b.* **B.** ersten ~es *of the first order*; (*scholar*) *of the first rank*; ⟨com⟩ *first-rate, -class, A 1* || niederer ~ (*a man of*) *low degree* **C.** jdm den ~ **ablaufen** *to outrun, outdo, outstrip*; *to cut out*; *to get the better of*; *to steal a march on a p*; (jdm, e–r S) den ~ –zu–suchen *to challenge* || e–n hohen ~ bekleiden, einnehmen, innehaben *to occupy a high position*, ⟨mil⟩ *to hold a high rank*; e–n mittleren (den zweiten) ~ einnehmend *middle-grade* (*second-ranking*) (*officer*) || den ~ über, unter jdm h *to be of higher, lower rank than a p* || s–n ~ jdm gegenüber geltend m *to pull rank on a p* || [dat] den ~ streitig m *to compete* (*with*) (*for position*) || jdm e–n ~ verleihen *to bestow a dignity upon a p*; .. höheren .. *to upgrade* **D.** **im** ~ e–s Fürsten *in the rank of a pr.*, .. e–s Hauptmanns stehen *to hold the rank of c.*; im gleichen ~ stehen wie jd *to take rank with a p* || jdm dem ~e **nach** untergeordnet s *to be inferior in rank to a p* || mit jdm **um** den ~ streiten *to compete with a p* || **vom** ersten ~e *of the highest eminence* **~abzeichen** n pl *badges* od *insignia* pl *of rank* od *grade* **~älteste(r)** m *senior officer* **~erhöhung** f *elevation in rank* **~folge** f *series* [a. pl] *of grades* **~klasse** f *class*, ⟨mar⟩ *category* **~liste** f *army* (*navy, airforce*) *list* || ⟨sport⟩ *ranking list* **~loge** f *tier-box* **⁓los** a *without rank* **⁓-mäßig** a *according to rank* **~ordnung** f *gradation, hierarchy, social scale*; ⟨mil⟩ *order of precedence* od *rank*; ⟨zoo eth⟩ *pecking order* **~streit(igkeit** f) m *quarrel* od *contention about precedence* **~stufe** f *degree, grade* || zu e–r höheren ~ befördert w *to be promoted* **~unterschied** m *distinction of rank*

R·ange 1. m ~n/~n *urchin, pickle, naughty boy*, || wilder ~ *tartar*, ⟨Am⟩ *hellion, pickle* **2.** f ~/~n *tomboy, romp, minx, hoity-toity, hoyden* **r·angeln** vi [h] → ringen II.

°**r·angehen** vi [s] → ran; *to go at* (*a th*)

Rang·ier- [raŋ'ʒiːr] **~bahnhof** m ⟨rail⟩ *shunting-yard* **~berg** m ⟨rail⟩ *hump* **~geleise** n ⟨rail⟩ *siding* **~lokomotive, ~maschine** f *sh.g-engine*; ⟨Am⟩ *switcher* **~meister** m *yardmaster* **~schiene** f (parallel beweglich) *switch* **~strecke** f ⟨rail⟩ *switching route* | **⁓en** [raŋ'ʒiːren] vt [h] *to rank, class* || ⟨rail⟩ *to shunt*, ⟨Am⟩ *to switch* || sich ~ *to settle one's debts* | vi [h] *to* (*have, take*) *rank* (vor *before*) || *to be ranked* (mit *with*) || *to take precedence* (vor *of*) || ~ als *to range as* || (S vor etw) *to come ahead of* || ⟨fig⟩ *to rank* (*foremost among*) **Rang·ierer** m ⟨rail⟩ *truck setter*; *yardman, shunter*

Rang·un n (Hauptstadt v Burma) *Rangoon*

rank a *slim, slender* || (topplastig) *crank*

R·anke f ~/~n *tendril, runner*; *bine* || *shoot* (*of a vine*) **⁓nartig** a *cirrous* **~nfüßer** m ⟨zoo⟩ *cirriped* **~ngewächs** n *creeper, climber* **~nwerk** n ⟨arch⟩ *scroll* **r·anken** [h & s] sich ~ *to climb* (*by the help of tendrils*), *to creep* || *to shoot* || *to ramble* || ⟨fig a.⟩ *to cluster* (um *round*) **r·ankig** a *with tendrils* || *creeping, rambling* etc

Ränke m pl *intrigues, artifices, dodges, machinations, tricks* pl; verwerfliche ~ *foul practices* || *to use* (anwenden) *all sorts of tricks and dodges*; ~ schmieden, mit ~n ·um|gehen *to hatch* (*dark*) *plots*; *to intrigue* || auf ~ sinnen *to plot cunning devices* **~schmied** m *plotter, schemer, trickster, machinator, intriguer* | ~er·ei [f] ⟨pol⟩ *cabal* **~spiel** n *intrigue*(*s* pl); ⟨Am sl⟩ *frame-up* **~sucht** f *intriguing spirit* **⁓süchtig, ⁓voll** a *intriguing, scheming, plotting, designing* || *tricky, artful*; ⟨Am⟩ *political*

rann 3. sg [pret] (ränne [subj]) v rinnen

r·annte 1. & 3. sg [pret] v rennen

Ran·unkel f ~/~n ⟨bot⟩ *ranunculus, buttercup*

R·änzel n, **R·anzen** m ~s/~ *knapsack, wallet* || ⟨mil⟩ *valise, kitbag* || ⟨school⟩ *satchel*; ⟨Am⟩ *school-bag* | sein ~ schnüren ⟨fig⟩ *to say good-bye*; ⟨fam⟩ *to pack off* | °(Bauch) *belly*, ⟨Am sl⟩ *breadbasket*; °sich den ~ füllen *to eat one's fill, to fill one's belly*

°**R·anzer** m ~s/~ *rebuke, wigging, blow up*

r·anzig a *rancid, rank* (*butter*) || etw ~ *rankish* || ~ w *or* ranzen *to turn rancid* | **⁓keit** f *r.ness*

Ranzi·on f ~/~en *ransom* | **~·ieren** vt [h] *to ransom, redeem* || *to demand a ransom*

R·änzlein n **1.** = Ränzel **2.** ⟨fig⟩ sich ein ~ anmästen *to fill one's belly* od *paunch*

rap·id a *rapid* || [adv] *fast, quickly, steeply*

Rap·ier n ~(e)s/~e (Schläger) *rapier*; (stumpfes Florett) *foil*; (modernes) *small-sword* || ein gutes ~ führen *to fence well*

rap·iert a *ground* (*snuff* etc.)

R·appe 1. m ~n/~n *black* (*horse*) || auf Schusters ~n reiten *to ride on shanks's mare* **2.** f ~/~n (Pferdekrankheit) *malanders* pl **~nantilope** f *sable-antelope*

°**R·appel** m ~s/ *whim*; *fit of madness* || den ~ h ⟨fam⟩ *to be crack-brained* **~kopf** m *cross-patch, madcap* | r⁓isch, (r·appelig) [a] *hot-headed, irritable* || *crack-brained, crazy*; ⟨fam⟩ *cracked* | **⁓n** **1.** vi [h] *to rattle* (⟨a. fig⟩ = darauf losschwatzen, *to r. on, away, along*) **2.** vi [imps] [h]; bei ihm ~lt's ⟨fam⟩ *he's off his block* **3.** °**sich** [acc] wieder in die Höhe ~ ⟨fam⟩ *to get on one's pins again*

R·appen m ~s/~ †*Swiss centime*

Rapp·ort m ~(e)s/~e ⟨mil⟩ (*formal*) *report* || zum ~ erscheinen *to muster*, ⟨sl⟩ *to be up for a spin*; z ~ gemeldet ⟨Am sl⟩ *wheeled up*; z ~ melden *to put .. on the peg* || ~ m = **⁓·ieren** vt [h] ⟨mil⟩ *to report*

Raps m –ses/ *rape*(*-seed*), *colza* | **~glanzkäfer** m *blossom beetle*

°**R·aptus** m ~/ = Rappel, ⟨med⟩ *seizure*

Rap·ünzchen n, **Rap·unzel** m ~s/~ ⟨bot⟩ *lamb's lettuce*

rar a *rare, scarce* || (vorzüglich) *exquisite* || °sich ~ m *to make o.s. sc.* || ~ w *to grow sc.* **≈ität** f ~/~en *curiosity*, ⟨fam⟩ *curio* [pl –*s*] || (Wert) *rarity, value* | ~enkabinett [n] *cabinet of c.ties*; ~enladen [m] (*old*) *c.y shop*

ras·ant a ⟨mil⟩ *sweeping, flat* (*trajectory*); *flat tr.y* (*fire*) **Ras·anz** f ~/ ⟨mil⟩ *flat*(*ness of*) *trajectory* || = rasende Geschwindigkeit

r·asch a *quick, swift* || ⟨com⟩ ~er Absatz *ready sale*; → u. || *ready* (*answer, apprehension*); *quick* (*repartee*); (brieflich) *prompt* od *speedy* (*reply*) || *brisk, nimble* (*feet*) || *nimble* (Kopf *brain*) || *hasty* (*decision*) || *fleet* od *swift* (*horse*) || ⟨com⟩ ~er Umsatz *quick returns* | [adv] ~ auffassend, begreifend *apt* (*pupil*); ~ auf–e–a–folgend *in rapid succession*; *rapidly alternating*; ~ eingreifen *to intervene quickly*; ~ erledigen *to rush* || sich ~ besinnen .. *in a hurry* || nicht so ~: *he won't do that in a hurry* || er muß ~ zurück *he must hurry back*; er eilte ~ herbei *he hurried here* | **~eln** vi **1.** [h] *to rustle, whisper, murmur* **2.** [s] (sich ~d bewegen) *to rustle, whiz along* od *off* **3.** ≈ n *frou-frou* (*of silk*); *susurration* (*of trees*) **R·aschheit** f ~/ *quickness, swiftness, briskness, fleetness* || *haste* (→ rasch, schnell)

r·asen vi [h] **1.** (wüten, zornig reden) *to storm, rage* (über *at*, gegen *against*) || ⟨fig⟩ *the storm* (*fire*) *raged over* (*through*) *the town* **2.** (krankhaft) vor Liebe ~ *to be madly in love* || (irre reden) *to rave* (gegen *about, against, at*) **3.** (eilen) *to race madly along* || *to rush* (*through*); *to tear* (*round the curve, after a p*) || *to dash* (an e–r Türe vorbei *past a door*; e–e [auf e–r] Straße entlang *along a road*) || *to whisk, whip* (*into, out of*) || *to take a wild dive* (*into*) || ⟨mot, etc⟩ *to scorch, tear, dash* (*along*) || *to barge, lunge* (*against*) || (T ⟨a.⟩) *to skitter* || (of water) *to swirl* **r·asend** a **1.** *raging, furious* || *raving, frantic, phrenetic*(*al*) || *towering* (*rage, frenzy*) || ⟨path⟩ *out of one's senses, delirious* | jdn ~ m *to send a p out of his mind*; m mich ~ *make me livid*, .. vor L.w. .. *to bore a p to distraction*; zum ≈-w *agonizing, maddening* || ~ w *to see red* || e–n ~ m *to enrage a p, to drive a p mad* || das macht mich ~ *that makes me wild* od *frantic* || ich möchte darüber ~ w *I shall go out of my mind about it* || es ist um ~ zu w *it's enough to drive one mad* **2.** ⟨fig⟩ *hot* (*haste, worker*), *terrible*; ⟨mot⟩ *scorching* (*speed*); *tearing* (*hurry*); ~e Fahrt *rush* ⟨a. a-n⟩; in rasender Geschwindigkeit *at a tearing* od *headlong pace* || *hell-for-leather* (*charge*) || *ravenous* (*appetite*) || *splitting* (*headache*) || *raving* (*jealousy*) || *agonizing* (*pain*) | [adv] ⟨fam⟩ *like blazes* || *desperately* (*in love*) || *furiously* (*hungry*) || (*to love*) *to distraction* || ~ schnell ⟨a.⟩ *meteoric* **Raser·ei** f ~/~en **1.** *madness, frenzy, rage* || *fury* **2.** *mad*(*man's*) *act* **3.** ⟨mot⟩ *crazy* od *reckless driving* | (jdn) zur ~ treiben *to drive .. mad* od *to distraction*

R·asen m ~s/~ *turf, sward, lawn* || *grass* (*keep off the* –!) || (Grassode) *sod* || ~ abheben, ausstechen *to cut sods* || ihn deckt der grüne ~ *he lies under the green turf* **~abdeckung** f (Tarnung) *layer of sods* **~bank** f *turf* od *grassy seat* **~bekleidung** f ⟨fort⟩ *sod-revetment* **~bleiche** f *bleaching on grass* || *bleaching-ground* **~decke** *turf* **~einfassung** f *grass-verge* **~·eisenerz** n, **~·eisenstein** m ⟨minr⟩ *bog-, meadow-ore*; *limonite* **~hügel** m *grassy hill* **~m·ähmaschine** f *lawn-mower* **~platz** m *grass-plot, green, lawn* **~spiele** n pl *out-door games* pl **~sprenger** m (S) *water-sprinkler* **~stechen** n *cutting of* (*green*) *turf* **~stecher** m *turf-cutter* **~stück** n *grass-plot* || *sod of grass* **~teppich** m *velvet lawn*; ⟨theat⟩ *grass cloth* **~weg** m *turf-walk*

Ras·ier- ~apparat m *safety razor*; *shaver* **~becken** n *shaving-basin* **~messer** n *razor* (.. schleifen *to grind* .., abziehen *to set* ..) **~pinsel** m, **~seife** f *sh.g-brush, -stick* **~zeug** n *sh.g case, -tackle, -things* pl **ras·ieren** vt [h] *to shave* || ⟨mil⟩ *to raze* || bitte ~! *a shave please!* | ⟨fig⟩ °rasiert s *to be done for*; ⟨hum⟩ du wirst gleich rasiert *it will soon be your turn* | sich ~ l *to get shaved*, ⟨fam⟩ *to have a shave* **Ras·ierer** m *barber*

Räs·on [rɛːˈzɔ̃] f ~/ *reason* || ~ annehmen *to listen to r.* **~·eur** [rezɔˈnøːr] m ~s/~e *grumbler* **~nem·ent** [–ˈmɑ̃] n ~s/ *reasoning* **≈·ieren** vi [h] *to argue, reason*; (schimpfen) *to grumble*; (sich streiten) *to litigate, quarrel, wrangle* (über *about*) **≈ierend** a *argumentative, litigating*

R·aspel ~/~n *rasp* || *grater* | ~brot [n] *grated bread*; ~feile [f] *rasp*; ~späne [m pl] *raspings* pl | **≈n** vt [h] *to rasp* || *to grate* (*bread*) || *to scrape* (*horn, leather* etc.) | ⟨fig⟩ Süßholz ~ *to spoon, flirt*; *to talk soft nonsense* (*to a woman*)

R·asse f ~/~n **A. 1.** (*yellow, white, red, black*) *race* **2.** (Zucht) *breed, blood, stock* **B. alpine** etc ~ *homo alpinus* etc || edle, gute ~ *noble, good blood* || gekreuzte ~ *cross-breed* || ⟨nazi⟩ v echt germanischer ~ *of the true Teutonic breed* || die jüdische ~ ⟨engl hum⟩ *the Jewish persuasion* || e–e reine ~ *a pure race* || v reiner ~ *thoroughbred* || semitische ~ *Semitic race* || ⟨hum⟩ ~ mit Schlappohren .. *quite out of the common* || Beschreibung u Einteilung der ~n *anthropography* || Menschentyp verschiedener ~n *interracial type of humanity* || ⟨zoo⟩ geographische ~ *subspecies* **C.** e–r fremden ~ angehören *to be of a foreign race* || ⟨nazi⟩ e–e ~ aufarten (aufnorden) *to introduce new* (*northern*) *blood* || ~ h (P) *to come from a good stock*, ⟨hors, etc.⟩ *to be thoroughbred* || das liegt in der ~ *that runs in the blood* || in der Musik liegt ~ *this music is racy* | [in comp → a.] ~n– | **~angehörige**(**r**) m *coracialist* **≈bewußt** a *race-conscious* **~bewußtsein** n *racialism, pride of race* | → Doktrin **≈echt** a *true-bred* (*German*); *thoroughbred* (*dog*) **~hund** m *hound of breed* **≈mäßig** a *racial* **≈rein** = ~echt; sich ~ vermehren *to breed true* **≈schädlich** a *dysgenic* **R·assen-** [in comp oft] *racial* (*feeling, law*); *phyletic* (*development*) (→ a. Rasse–) **ausrottung** f = –mord **≈bewußt** a *race-conscious* | ≈sein [n] *racial sense* **~diskriminierung** f = –grenze **~dünkel** m, **~fanatismus** m *raci*(*ali*)*sm* **~fanatiker** m *racist* **~grenze** f *colo*(*u*)*r line* **~haß** m *race-hatred* **~hygiene** f *eugenics* pl **≈hygienisch** a *eugenic*; in ~er Hinsicht *eugenically* **~ideal** n *racial image* **~kampf** m *racial conflict* od *violence*; *struggle of races* **~kreuzung** f *cross-breeding* **~kult** m *cult of a race* **~kunde** f *ethnology* **~mischung** f *miscegenation* **~mord** m *genocide* **~pflege** f *eugenics, race-culture* **~politik** f *racial policy* **~politiker** m *racist* **~politisch** = –hygienisch, ⟨a.⟩ *ethnological*; ~es Amt ⟨nazi⟩ *Eugenics Office* **~schande** f *race defilement* **~schranke** f = –grenze **~selbstmord** m *racial suicide* **~theorie** f *racial theory* **~trennung** f *segregation*; ⟨SAfr⟩ *apartheid* (⟨a.⟩ ~spolitik) || Anhänger der ~ *segregationist* (⟨a. ~s- [attr]); Aufhebung der ~ (*racial*) *integration* **~vermischung** f *integration* **~vorurteil** n *racial prejudice* **r·assig** a *thoroughbred* (*dog*) || *racy* (*girl, style*) || *smart* (*car*); (T) *of good breed*, ⟨hors a.⟩ *spicy* || ~ u hoch~ *highbred and in-bred* (*dogs*) || (P) ⟨a.⟩ *earthy*; v ~em Temperament *high-mettled* (*p*) || ⟨mot⟩ *having sweeping lines*; *thorough* || (*English*) *with a flair* od ⟨sl⟩ *crunch* | **das ~e** *raciness* **r·assisch** a *racial, national* (*decay, relationship, substance*) || *clannish* (*spirit*) | [adv] *racially* (*limited phenomena*, ⟨nazi⟩ *r. valuable families*) **Rass·ist** m ~en/~en *racist*

R·assel f ~/~n *rattle* | ~geräusch [n] ⟨path⟩ *rhonchus* | **≈n** vi **1.** [h] (*machines, carts*) *rattle* || (klirrend) *to clank* (mit den Ketten .. | .. *one's chains*); (bes v Waffen) *to clash*; (bes v Geschirr) *to clatter*; (v Wagen) *to hurtle* **2.** [s] *to come rattling along* || °er ist (in der Prüfung) ge–lt *he has been plucked* od *ploughed* .., ⟨Am⟩ *he failed*, ⟨sl⟩ *flunked* **3.** ≗ n *rattling, rattle* **4. | ≗nd** a *rattling* (*noise* ⟨a. med⟩, *râle* Fr)

Rast f ~/ **1.** *rest, repose* ‖ ⟨mil⟩ *halt*, ⟨fam⟩ *breezer*; ~ m *to take a rest*; ⟨mil, etc⟩ kurz ~ m *to make a short halt*, ⟨fam⟩ *to take an easy* ‖ ohne ~ u Ruh *restlessly* **2.** *halting-place*; *station, stage*; ⟨mil⟩ *rest area* **3.** ⟨cycl⟩ *foot-rest* **4.** ⟨tech⟩ *notch*; *spring catch* ‖ in die ~ einspringen *to jump into the groove* **5.** (e–s Hochofens) *boshes* pl **~buchse** f *guide bushing* **~enscheibe** f ⟨tech⟩ *star wheel* **~feder** f *stop spring* **~haus** n ⟨mot⟩ *road-house*, ⟨Am⟩ *pull-in, dinette*; f Fernfahrer *transport café* **~hebel** m ⟨mil⟩ *engaging lever* **≗los** a *restless* (*spirit*) ‖ *endless* (*anxiety*) ‖ *indefatigable* (*worker*) ‖ (zappelig) *fidgety* **~losigkeit** f *restlessness, indefatigableness* ‖ *fidgetiness* **~ort, ~platz** → ~ 2. **~stätte** f = –haus **~tag** m *day of rest*; ⟨mil⟩ *a day's halt* **~winkel** m (Hochofen) *angle of boshes* **r·asten** vi [h] *to* (*take one's*) *rest*; ⟨mil⟩ *to halt* ‖ v der Arbeit ~ *to lie by* ‖ ⟨sport⟩ *to be bye* | vt (⟨a.⟩ **sich** ~) *to rest, repose* ‖ ⟨tech⟩ *to engage* (*a lever*) | ⟨prov⟩ rast' ich, so rost' ich *resting is rusting* | **≗blende** f ⟨phot⟩ *click stop* **≗scheibe** f ⟨tech⟩ *slotted disc*

R·astelbinder m [österr] (*itinerant*) *tinker*

R·aster m ~s/~ ⟨phot, arts⟩ *screen, grid* | ~druck [m] *autotype*; ~tiefdruck [m] ⟨Am typ⟩ *rotogravure* | **≗n** vt [h] ⟨telv⟩ *to scan* | **~ung** f *screening*

Ras·ur f ~/~en 1. (paper) *erasure, rubbing-out* 2. (Bart) *shave*

Rat m ~es/ **A. 1.** [pl: Ratschläge] *advice, counsel* | (Ausweg) *means, remedy, expedient* ‖ ~ u Tat *advice and assistance* **2.** (Körperschaft) [pl: Räte] (*town-*) *council* ‖ ⟨Russ⟩ *soviet* ‖ Arbeiter≗ *workers' council* **3.** [pl: Ratsversammlungen] *meeting of a council* etc., *assembly, senate* **4.** [pl: Räte] *counsellor, adviser* ‖ ⟨jur⟩ *legal adviser*; *counsel* **5.** [pl: Ratsherrn, Räte] *councillor, alderman, senator* ‖ Frau ~ N. *Mrs. N.* ‖ Vortragender ~ ⟨Ger⟩ *Reporting* (⟨engl⟩ *Privy*) *Councillor* **6.** [pl: Beratungen] *deliberation, consultation* **B. ein arger,** böser ~ *a bad piece of advice* ‖ guter ~ kommt über Nacht *good advice comes over night* ‖ guter ~ kommt nie zu spat *though old and wise, yet still advise* ‖ da *or* nun ist guter ~ teuer *that's a difficult case* od *thorny matter, that's a critical situation*; guten ~ teuer m *to darken counsel* ‖ → Zeit **C.** ~ **annehmen** *to take* od *follow advice* ‖ jds ~ befolgen *to take a p's advice* ‖ folg m–m ~ *be advised* (*by me*) ‖ jdm (e–n, s–n) ~ erteilen *or* geben *to advise* od *counsel a p* (betr., über *on*), *to give a p advice, to tender advice to a p*; e–n überflüssigen ~ geben ⟨Am sl⟩ *to teach a dog to bark* ‖ ~ halten *to consult* ‖ halt ~ vor der Tat *look before you leap* ‖ jds ~ einholen (über) *to take a p's advice* (*about*) ‖ sich [dat] bei jdm ~(s) (er)holen *to turn to a p* (wegen *for*), *to consult a p, to come to a p* (od *to ask a p*) *for advice* ‖ auf jds ~ hören *to take a p's advice* ‖ ~(s) pflegen *to consult* od *deliberate* (mit *with*) ‖ ~ schaffen *to devise* od *find* (*ways and*) *means*; .. für etw *to provide for an emergency* ‖ ~ suchen *to ask for advice* ‖ ~ wissen *to know what to do* ‖ sich k–n ~ mehr wissen *to be at one's wits' end* **D. auf** jds ~ *at a p's suggestion, by* od *on a p's advice* ‖ auf e–n ~ hören *to listen to reason* ‖ **in** den ~ gehen *to attend the council* ‖ jdm **mit** ~ u Tat (an die Hand gehen *or*) beistehen *to assist a p by word and deed* ‖ es geht **nach** s–m ~ .. *according to his suggestion* ‖ jdn **um** ~ fragen *to ask a p's advice, to consult a p* (⟨a.⟩ *a doctor*), *to see* (*a doctor*) ‖ mit jdm **zu** ~e gehen *to consult with a p*; mit sich .. *to deliberate with o.s.*; mit sich selbst .. *to take stock of one's soul*; wenn ich mit mir zu ~e gehe .. *in my secret councils* (*I feel* ..) | jdn zu ~e ziehen *to take counsel's opinion*; (Arzt, Anwalt, Buch) *to consult*; .. wieder .. *to reconsult* | **etw** zu ~e halten *to be sparing* od *careful with* od *of*; *to economize, husband a th* **~geber** m *adviser, counsellor*; ⟨fam⟩ *tipster*; schlechter ~ *poor hand at advice* **~haus** n *town-hall*, ⟨Am⟩ *city-hall* **≗los** a *helpless, beat, perplexed* ‖ ~ s *to be at the end of one's tether, to be at sea* **~losigkeit** f *helplessness, perplexity* **≗sam** a *advisable, commendable* | (heilsam) *wholesome* ‖ (förderlich) *useful, expedient* [dazu: *expediency*] ‖ (geeignet) *fit* ‖ es wäre ~, wenn du .. *you had better* (*do it*) ‖ das ~ste wäre, wenn er .. *the best he can do is to wait* **~schlag** m *advice, counsel* **≗schlagen** vi [h] [–schlagte] *to deliberate, consult*; *to take counsel* **~schlagung** f *deliberation* **~schluß** m *decree, decision*; *resolution* ‖ ~ Gottes, der Vorsehung *the ways* pl *of God, the decree of Providence* ‖ nach Gottes ~ *by God's appointment* **rät(st)** 3. (2.) P sg [pres] v raten **R·äte** [pl v Rat m] **~regierung** f ⟨Russ⟩ *Soviet Government* **~republik** f ⟨Russ⟩ *Union of Soviet Socialist Republics* pl (abbr *U.S.S.R.*), ⟨a.⟩ *Soviet Union* **r·aten I.** vt/i [riet/ge~] [h] **1.** (vermuten) *to guess* (*a riddle*) ‖ ~ Sie mal, wie .. *guess how* (*old I am*) ‖ ~ Sie mal! *give a guess*! ‖ geraten! *right*! ‖ an e–m Rätsel ~ *to guess about the answer to a r.* ‖ hin u her ~ *to make random guesses* ‖ e–m etw zu ~ aufgeben *to give a p a nut to crack* ‖ gut ~ *to have a good guess*; *this was a shrewd g.* **2. (jdm)** *to advise, counsel* (*a p*) (zu etw *on a th*, in etw *respecting a th*); *to warn* .. (vorsichtig z s) ‖ ich riet ihm es zu tun *I advised him to do it*; ich riet ihr gut *I gave her good advice* ‖ (die Verhältnisse) ~ es .. *make it advisable* ‖ ich halte es für ge~ *I think it advisable* | .., das rate ich dir! *take my advice* ..; .. *if you are wise* ‖ das wollte ich dir auch ge~ h! *it's lucky for you that you did it* ‖ das will ich dir nicht ge~ h! *you had better not*! ‖ es ist ihm z ~ z gehen *he will do well to go* | **sich** [dat] ~ l *to be advised, to take advice, to listen to reason, to be ruled* ‖ er läßt sich v niemand ~ *he takes nobody's advice, he will take no advice from anyone* | ⟨prov⟩ wem nicht z ~ ist, ist nicht z helfen *who will not listen to reason cannot be helped* | **was** *or* wozu würden Sie mir ~? *what would* od *do you advise me to do*?, *what do you think I had better do*? **3.** (= **helfen**) ich wußte mir nicht mehr z ~ *I didn't know what to do, I was at my wits' end, at the end of my tether* ‖ damit ist mir nicht ge~! *that does not help me*! **II.** ≗ n ~s/ *guess*(*work*) ‖ *advice*; ≗ ins Blaue *blind guess* **R·ätin** f ~/~nen *councillor's wife* **R·ater** m ~s/~ **1.** *guesser* **2.** = Ratgeber | **~·ei** f, ~ *guesswork*

R·ate f ~/~n *rate* ‖ ⟨com⟩ *instalment* ‖ (e–r Konkursmasse) *dividend* ‖ in ~n *by instalments* **R·aten- ~einzug** m **u -Überwachung** f *hire purchase collections and control* **~kauf** m *instalment purchase* **≗weise** [adv] *by instalments* **~-zahlung** f *payment by instalments* **~zahlungs-system** n *hire purchase system* **Ratifikati·on** [–ts–] f ~/~en *ratification* **ratifiz·ieren** vt [h] *to ratify* ‖ nicht ratifiziert *unratified* **Rati·on** [–ts–] f ~/~en *ration, allowance, share* ‖ ~ Brot *ration of bread* ‖ kl ~en *short r.s* ‖ eiserne ~ *iron* od *emergency r.* | **≗·ieren** vt [h] *to ration, allowance, point* ‖ (nicht) –iert [*to be*] *on* (*off*) *points* od (*un*)*rationed* **rational** a *rational* | **≗is·ator** m ⟨SBZ⟩ *r.izer* | **~is·ieren** vt [h] *to r.ize, streamline* (⟨a. übtr⟩ Verwaltung ~) | **≗isierung** f *r.l development*; ⟨off⟩ *office productivity* | **≗ismus** m ~/ *r.lism* | **≗·ist** m ~en/~en *r.list* | **~·istisch** a *r.list*(*ic*) **ration·ell** a *rational, reasonable*; *economic*; *systematic* (Ausnutzung *employment*) | [adv] ~ betreiben *to carry* .. *on rational lines* ‖ ~ verfahren *to act reasonably*; *to rationalize* **Ration·ierung** f *rationing* (⟨a. [attr]⟩ ~svorschriften *r.g regulations*); (nach Notstand) *austerity* **Rations-** ~satz [m] *scale of rations*

..rath suff (= Rodung) z Bezeichnung von Ortsnamen (z. B. Benrath, Wülfrath) vgl. ..reuth, ..rode

R·atibor n ⟨†Ger⟩ (Stadt an der Oder in Oberschlesien)

R·ätische Alpen pl *Rhætian Alps* pl

rätlich a *advisable, expedient* **r·atsam** → Rat-

rätorom·anisch a *Romansh* ‖ das ~e *Romansh*

R·ats- **~beschluß** m *decree of the senate* etc **~bote** m *messenger of the s.te* **~diener** m *beadle* **~herr** m *s.tor, councillor, alderman,* ⟨Scot⟩ *bailie* **~herrlich** a *s.orial* **~keller** m *cellar (restaurant) of a town-hall, rathskeller* **~kollegium** n *board of c.ors, towncouncil, s.te* **~leute** pl *(town-)c.ors* pl **~memorandum** n *Council Memorandum* ⟨a. N.⟩ **~mitglied** n, **~person** f *member of the s.te* etc. ‖ *c.or*; ⟨Am⟩ *councilman* **~schreiber** m *town-clerk* **~sitzung** f *session* od *meeting of the council* **~stelle** f *place in the c.l* **~stube** f *c.l-chamber* **~tag** m *meeting-day of the s.te, day of sitting* **~versammlung** f *meeting of the s.te,* etc **~waage** f ⟨Ger⟩ *municipal (stamped) scales* pl **~wahl** f *election of s.tors,* etc **~zimmer** n *c.-chamber*

R·atsche, ~ f ~/~n **1.** *rattle, ratchet* **2.** (Verletzung) *scratch* **r·atschen 1.** vi [h] *to rattle* **2.** vt [h] ([sich] verletzen) *to scratch [o.s.]* **R·atscher** m ⟨artill⟩ *whizz-bang; pip-squeak*

R·ätsel n ~s/~ *riddle, puzzle, enigma, mystery*; ⟨Am fam⟩ *brain twister* ‖ ⟨fig a.⟩ *problem (it is a .. how)*; jdm ein ~ aufgeben *to set a p a riddle* ‖ ein ~ ergründen *to plumb a mystery* ‖ in ~n sprechen *to talk in enigmas* ‖ sie ist ein ~ *she is a puzzle* ‖ man steht vor e–m ~ *one stands before an e.a* ‖ das ist mir ein ~ ⟨fig⟩ *that puzzles* od *beats, baffles me* **~aufgabe** f *problem* **~frage** f *conundrum; puzzling question* **~haft** a *e.atical, mysterious, puzzling*; e–e ~e S = Rätsel | ~erweise [adv] *miraculously* **~raten** n *guess(ing)*; *guessing game* ⟨a. fig⟩; reines ~ *a shot in the dark* **r·ätseln** vi [h] *to talk in riddles; to rack one's brains* **~voll** a *e.atical* **~wort** n *e.a(tical saying)*

R·atte f ~/~n *rat* (→ *vole, rat*) ‖ v ~n heimgesucht *rat-infected (jail)* ‖ (wie) v ~n zernagt *rat--gnawn* ‖ leben wie die ~ im Speck *to live like fighting cocks, to be* od *live in clover* ‖ wie e–e ~ schlafen *to sleep like a top* ‖ ⟨fig⟩ (Ballet ~) e–e niedliche ~ *a neat little filly* **R·atten-** **~falle** f *rat--trap* **~fänger** m *rat-catcher*; ~ v Hameln *Pied Piper of Hamelin* ‖ (Hund) *rattler* **~gift** n *rat--poison; ratsbane* ⟨a. fig⟩; *rodonticide, raticide* **~jagd** f *rat-hunting*; auf die ~ gehen *to go ratting* **~könig** m ⟨fig⟩ *tangle, whole string (of ..)* **~nest** n *rat's nest* **~pulver** n = ~gift **~schwanz** m *rat's tail*; (Haarzopf) *pigtail, queue; rat-tail(ed file)*; ⟨fig⟩ *whole string (of ..)*

R·ätter m ~s/~ ⟨tech⟩ *ridar, grate, shaking sieve* ‖ ⟨agr⟩ *screen, riddle, sifter* ‖ ⟨min⟩ *ratter* | **~n** vt *to ridar* ‖ *to sift* **r·attern I.** vi [h] *to rattle, rumble, chatter, hurtle* ‖ an der Tür ~ *to rattle the door* ‖ gegen etw ~ *to fulminate against a th* **II.** ~ n *crunch, clack and clatter*

Ratz m ~es/~e **1.** *rat* (schlafen → Ratte) **2.** *firchet, fitchew* **3.** *hamster* **4.** (Kegelspiel) *miss,* ⟨fam⟩ *boss* **R·atze** f ~/~n *rat* **~k·ahl** [adv] (statt: radikal) *totally* ‖ jdn ~ essen *to eat a p out of house and home*

Raub m ~(e)s/ [pl ~taten] **A. 1.** *robbery* (⟨a.⟩ *of Colonies*); *robbing* ‖ ⟨poet, rhet⟩ *rape, rapine* ‖ (Jungfern~) *rape (of the Sabine women)* ‖ (Kinder~) *kidnapping* ‖ (Straßen~) *highway robbery* **2.** (Plündern) *plunder(ing), pillage, sacking,* ⟨mil a.⟩ *looting*; ~ u Plünderung *rapine and pillage* **3.** (Beute) *prey* ⟨a. zoo⟩; *booty, spoil(s* pl); (Geld) *loot* ‖ ⟨übtr⟩ Verteilung des „~es" (Gewinns) ⟨sl⟩ *mellon-cutting* **4.** (⟨mar⟩ & Verletzung des Urheberrechts) *piracy* **B.** gewaltsamer ~ *theft with violence* | e–n ~ begehen *to commit a robbery* | jds ~ w (e–m *or* e–r S **zum** ~e fallen) *to fall a victim* od *prey to ..* ‖ das Haus wurde ein ~ der Flammen .. *was destroyed by fire* | **auf** ~ ausgehen *to go plundering, thieving; to go to plunder*; ⟨zoo⟩ *to prowl (about)*; ⟨zoo⟩ ~ m auf *to be predatory upon* ‖ etw **durch** ~ bek *or* an sich bringen *to burgle a th* ‖ zum ~e geben *to hand over to be plundered* **~adel** m *robber barons* pl **~anfall** m *predatory attack* ‖ *highway robbery* **~ausgabe** f *pirated edition* **~bau** m *exhausting the soil; over-cropping; robber-farming*; ⟨min, etc⟩ *wasteful* od *ruinous exploitation*; ⟨for⟩ *destructive lumbering; rapine* ‖ ⟨fig⟩ *outrage (on health)* ‖ ~ treiben (an) *to exhaust (the soil), to rob (a mine), to cut down (woods) carelessly* **~begierig** a *rapacious* **~druck** m *pirate print* **~fisch** m *fish of prey* **~geschwader** n *pirate fleet* **~gesell** m *highwayman* **~gesindel** n *pack* od *gang of robbers, thievish vagabonds* pl **~gier** f *rapacity; lust for booty* **~gierig** a *rapacious, ravenous* ‖ ~er Mensch ⟨fig⟩ *shark, harpy* **~gut** n *stolen goods* pl; *booty* **~krieg** m *predatory war* **~lustig** a = –gierig **~mensch** m ⟨fig⟩ *cave man* **~mord** m *murder with robbery* **~mörder** m *robber who commits murder; cutthroat*; ⟨Ind⟩ *thug* **~nest** n *den of thieves* **~politik** f *grab policy* **~ritter** m *robber-knight, -baron* **~schiff** n *corsair, privateer* **~schiffer** m *pirate* **~schloß** n *robber-knight's castle* **~schütz(e)** m *poacher* **~staat** m *piratical state* ‖ ~en [pl] *Barbary States,* ⟨hum⟩ *Balkan States* **~sucht** f *rapacity* **~süchtig** *rapacious, predacious* **~tat** f *robbery with violence* **~tier** n *beast of prey, predacious animal*; ~e [pl] (Zirkus) *big cats (tigers, lions)* | ~augen [n pl] ⟨übtr⟩ *rapacious eyes* **~überfall** m *robbery (with violence), armed attack*; ⟨Am⟩ *holdup* **~vogel** m *bird of prey* **~wirtschaft** f = –bau **~zeug** n ⟨hunt⟩ *vermin* **~zug** m *raid, predatory excursion* **r·auben 1.** vi [h] *to rob (and murder), to commit robberies* ‖ *to go plundering,* etc **2.** vt [h] (jdm etw) *to rob, plunder (a p of a th), to take (a th) by force (from a p)*; jdm das Leben ~ *to take a p's life* ‖ *to steal* (⟨a.⟩ *a kiss)* ‖ (Kinder) *to kidnap* ‖ jdm den Glauben an etw ~ *to make a p lose faith in a th*; jdm die Unschuld ~ *to deflower a p* ‖ ⟨fig⟩ *to spoil (a view)*; *to rob (a p's hope, rest)*; *to take up* od *kill (4 hours out of the day)* ‖ es raubt mir den Atem *it takes my breath away* ‖ jdm die Ehre ~ *to defame* od *to calumniate a p* **R·äuber** m ~s/~ (Straßen-) *highwayman,* ⟨Am sl⟩ *hijacker*; (zu Fuß ⟨a.⟩) *footpad* ‖ (Dieb) *thief, brigand, robber* ‖ (⟨mar⟩ & Nachdrucker) *pirate* ‖ (Plagiator) *plagiarist* | er ist der ~ m–s Glücks *he has robbed me of my happiness* ‖ er fiel ~n in die Hände *he fell into the hands of brigands* ‖ unter die ~ fallen *to fall among thieves* **~bande** f *gang* od *race of robbers* **~geschichte** f *penny dreadful; sensational* od *invented story* ‖ (unglaubliche) *cock-and-bull story* **~h·auptmann** m *robberchief, captain of brigands* **~höhle** f *den of thieves* od *robbers* **~natur** f *predatory nature* **~pack** n *gang of robbers* °**~pistole** f (Lüge) *stretcher* **~roman** m *picaresque* **~unwesen** n *banditry* **~volk** n *predacious people, crew of robbers* **~(un)wesen** n *brigandage* **Räuber·ei** f ~/~en *robbery, brigandage* ‖ *depredation, pillage* **r·äuberisch** a *rapacious, predatory*

rauch a [obs, in comp] *shaggy* **~füßig** a *rough--footed*; ⟨orn⟩ *plumiped* **~waren** f pl, **~werk** n *furs* pl **~warenhändler** m *furrier*

Rauch m ~(e)s/ *smoke (s.)* ‖ (Dunst) *vapour* | beißender, scharfer ~ *biting, acrid s.* ‖ der ~ beißt in die Augen .. *makes my eyes smart* ‖ ~ u Qualm *dense s.* | (Fleisch) in den ~ hängen *to s.* ‖ nach ~ schmecken *to have a smoky taste* ‖ ~ annehmen (of milk) *to be s.d* ‖ v ~ geschwärzt *s.--stained* ‖ in ~ aufgehen *to be consumed by fire* ‖ ⟨fig⟩ *to come to nothing, to end in s.* ‖ ⟨fig⟩ lauter ~ u Trug *so much s. and sham* **~abteil** m ⟨rail⟩ *smoking compartment* **~altar** m *incense-altar* **~**-

becken n → ≈erpfanne **~belästigung** f *inconvenience from s.* **~bombe** f *s.-ball* °**~d·use** (= ≈ du sie [sc die Zigarre]) *toby* **~entwicklung** f *production of s.* **~fahne** f *trail* od *feather, plume of s.* **~fang** m *chimney, hood, cowl, flue* | ~-kehrer [m] *ch.-sweep(er)* **~faß** n ⟨ec⟩ *censer* | ~engel [m] *incense-bearer*; ≈schwingend [a] ⟨arts⟩ *censing (angel)* **~fleisch** n *s.d meat, hung beef* **~gas** n *stack* od *flue gas* **≈geschwängert** a *s.-laden (room, air)* **≈geschwärzt** a *s.-stained* **~kammer** f ⟨tech⟩ *s.-box*; ⟨rail⟩ *s.-arch* **~kasten** m ⟨theat⟩ *s. box*, ⟨Am⟩ *s. pot* **~kater** m *s.r's (hangover* od*) morningafter feeling* **~klappe** f ⟨teath⟩ *s. outlet*, ⟨Am⟩ *skylight* **~lokal** n *smoking-saloon* **~los** a *s.less* **~mantel** m *chimney-hood* **~ofen** m *s. producer*, ⟨Am⟩ *smudge fire* **~pilz** m ⟨mil⟩ *cloud mushroom* **~plage** f *s.-nuisance* **~reiniger** m ⟨el⟩ *arrester* **~säule** f *pillar of s.* **~schleier** m *smoke haze* **~schrift** f (Himmelsschrift) *sky writing* **~schutz** m ⟨mil⟩ *smoke-screen* **~schutzschleier** m ⟨mar, aero⟩ *s. screen* **≈-schwach** a ⟨mil⟩ *s.less (powder)* **~schwalbe** f ⟨orn⟩ *chimney-swallow* **~spurgeschoß** n ⟨mil⟩ *tracer* **~-streifen** m; schwacher ~ *thread of s.* **~tabak** m *tobacco* **~tisch(chen** n) m *smoking table* | ~-garnitur [f] *s.g set* **~topas** m ⟨min⟩ *smoky topaz* **~verbrennung** f *consumption of s.* **≈verzehrend** a *s.-consuming* **~verzehrer** m *s.-consumer, air-wick*; ⟨el⟩ *arrester* **~vorhang** m ⟨mil⟩ *s.-creen* **~waren** etc → rauch || *tobacco and t. products; t., cigars, cigarettes*; (Firmenschild) *Tobacconist* **~wolke** f *cloud* od *puff of s.* **~zimmer** n *smoking-room* **r·auchbar** a *smokable (cigar)* **R·auchen** n ~s/ *smoking* || (das) ~ (ist hier) verboten *no smoking allowed (here)* **r·auchen** vi/t [h] **A. 1.** *to smoke*, ⟨liter obs⟩ *to use the weed* || *the fire fumes* || *the chimney s.s* || es raucht *there's s. (in the kitchen)*; *there is a s. (rising)* || (dampfen) *to reek*; ⟨chem⟩ ~de Salpetersäure *fuming nitric acid* **2.** (P) *to (have a) s.*; *to s. away (at one's pipe)* || gern ~ *to be fond of smoking* od *of one's pipe, of a cigar* || ~ wie ein Schlot *or* kl Bäcker *to s. like a chimney* || kalt ~ *to suck a cold pipe* || stört es Sie, wenn wir ~? *do you mind our s.g*? || darf hier geraucht w? *is s.g allowed here*?; nicht ~! *no s.g*! **B.** ⟨fig⟩ heute raucht's *there'll be trouble today* || daß e–m der Kopf raucht .. *with a vengeance*, .. *to make one's head split*; arbeiten, daß .. ⟨fam⟩ *to swot* | ≈ [n] verboten! *s.g prohibited* **R·aucher** m ~s/~ (P) *smoker* (starker, eingefleischter *great, confirmed, inveterate*); sind Sie ~ *do you smoke* **~(abteil** n, = **wagen** m) m ⟨rail⟩ *smoking-compartment, -carriage*; ⟨fam⟩ *smoker* **R·äucher- ~aal** m *smoked eel* **~apparat** m *fumigator* **~büchse** f *incense-box* **~essenz** f *fragrant essence* **~faß** n ⟨ec⟩ *censer* **~hering** m *s.d* od *red herring, kipper(ed herring)* **~kammer** n *s.g-chamber* od *house* **~kerzchen** n, **~kerze** f *pastil for fumigation, fumigating candle* **~pfanne** f *perfuming-pan, perfume-box, -burner* **~pulver** n *fumigating powder* **~werk** n *perfume(ry), scents* pl; ⟨ec⟩ *(frank)-incense* **r·äucherig** a *smoky* **r·äuchern 1.** vt [h] *to smoke(-dry) (meat)* || *to cure, bloat (fish)* || *to perfume*; (desinfizieren) *to fumigate (rooms)* || ⟨tech⟩ (Farbtöne dunkeln) *to fume* || ⟨ec⟩ *to cense* || *to s. out (hives)* || geräucherter Hering = Räucherhering **2.** vi [h] *to burn incense* ⟨a. fig⟩ **R·äucherung** f ~/~en *fumigation, smoking* || ⟨ec⟩ *burning of incense* **r·auchig** a *smoky*

R·aude, ≈ f ~/~n (Krätze & Schorf) *scab* || (Hunde≈) *mange* || (Schaf≈) *rubbers* pl **r·äudig** a *mangy, scabbed, scabby* || ~es Schaf *scabby sheep*, ⟨fig⟩ *black sheep* | **≈keit** f ~/ *manginess, scabbiness*

R·audi m (⟨a.⟩ Rowdy) ~s/~s *rowdy, fire-eater*

rauf (= herauf) e–n Platz ~! *go up one*

Rauf- ~bold m *brawler, rough, rowdy, ruffian, bully*, ⟨Am sl⟩ *tough, scrapper, fire-eater* **~degen** m **1.** *rapier* **2.** = ~bold **~händel** m pl *affray* ⟨a. jur⟩; *brawl, scuffle* [sg] **~sack** m = ~bold **~-sucht** f *brawling disposition, pugnacity* **≈süchtig** a *brawling, quarrelsome, pugnacious* **~wolle** f *dead--wool* **R·aufe** f ~/~n *rack* (Futter–, Gewehr≈) || (Flachs≈) *hackle* **r·aufen 1.** vt [h] *to pull, pluck* || sich [dat] die Haare ~ *to tear one's hair* **2.** vi & **sich** ~ [h] *to struggle, scuffle, scramble, fight* (mit *with*, um *for*) || gerauft muß w! *we will* od *must have a scuffle* od *tussle* **R·aufer** m ~s/~ = Raufbold | **~·ei** f ~/~en *brawl, scuffle, row, tussle*; *free fight* **R·augraf** m ⟨Ger⟩ *raugrave*

rauh a **A.** *rough (r.)*; mit ~er Oberfläche versehen *to granulate*; ~e Stelle ⟨a.⟩ *r.ness*; ⟨ten⟩ ~ oder glatt? *r. or smooth*? | *sore (throat)*; *hoarse, throaty, raucous (voice)* **B.** ⟨fig⟩ *rugged (man)*; *gruff (Scotsman)*; ~er, aber biederer Mann *r. diamond*; *r., rugged (life)*; *hard (facts)*; *rude (times)*; *raw, unfinished (piece of work)* || ~ [adv] verputzt *r.-cast (wall)* || *harsh, gruff (voice, tone)*; *harsh treatment)*; ~es Benehmen *unceremonious ways*; *rude, rugged, coarse (manners, nature* v P), *austere (virtue)*; *rugged (path)*; *wild, bleak (country)*; *bitter, biting (cold)*; *bleak (wind, season, night)* || *inclement, surly, raw (weather)* | hier herrscht ein ~er, aber herzlicher Ton *here one finds a r. but hearty tone* || jdn mit ~er Hand anfassen *to handle a p r.ly* || jdn ~ [adv] anreden, anfahren *to speak harshly to a p* || ⟨fam⟩ in ~en Mengen *in enormous quantities* **C.** aus dem **≈en** arbeiten *to r.-hew* **R·auh- ~anstalt** f *workshop for teaseling* **~bank** f ⟨carp⟩ *trying-plane* **~bein** n ⟨fig fam⟩ *blackleg, churl, blackguard* || *ruffian, bully, bounder, rough, tough, rowdy* || ⟨hum⟩ *hedgehog, rough-neck, rough diamond sort of fellow*; ⟨engl⟩ *a rough, foxhunting, hard-drinking man* **≈beinig** a ⟨fig⟩ *hairy-heeled; tough, rough, rude, churlish, unmannerly* || ~ w *to cut up rough* **≈blätterig** a *asperifolious* **~frost, ~reif** m *hoar--frost*; ⟨poet⟩ *rime* **~futter** n ⟨agr & °cul⟩ *roughage* **~graf** m ⟨Ger⟩ *raugrave* **≈haarig** a *hirsute* **~maß** n ⟨for⟩ *nominal measure* **~reiter** m *rough--rider* **~waren** pl, **~werk** n *furs* pl **~wolle** f *skin--wool* **r·auhen 1.** vt [h] *to make rough, to roughen* || ⟨tech⟩ *to tease(l), card*; *to nap (cloth)* **2.** vi & **sich** ~ [h] ⟨orn⟩ *to moult* **R·auheit** f, **R·auhigkeit** f ~/ (→ rauh) *roughness* || *hoarseness* | ⟨fig⟩ *harshness, rudeness* || *ruggedness, wildness* || *inclemency, rawness, bleakness* || *sternness* || *coarseness* || *thorniness* || *the rough and tumble (of life)*

R·auke f ~/~n ⟨bot⟩ *rocket; hedge-mustard*

Raum m ~(e)s/≈e **A. 1.** *room*; *space* (a. → Welt≈ & ⟨arts⟩) | (~teil) *place* || *expanse*; *compass* || *(ship's) hold, space* || (Spiel≈) *scope, margin* || (Hohl≈) *capacity* | ⟨fig⟩ *occasion, accomodation* || ⟨typ⟩ *space* **2.** *room, chamber* || *locality* || *cabin, compartment* || ≈e [pl] ⟨a.⟩ *quarters, conveniences* pl (→ a. ≈lichkeiten) **3.** ⟨mil, geogr, arch⟩ *area (the European ar.*, der ~ v B. *the Berlin ar., rectangular ar.*, ⟨Am⟩ *block)* || ⟨mil pol⟩ *zone*; *the area assigned to it* **B. abgegrenzter,** eingefriedeter ~ *close* || abgeschlossener, beschränkter ~ *enclosed, limited space* || nicht eingesehener ~ ⟨mil⟩ *area in defilade* || enger ~ *narrow space* in engem ~ *within narrow compass* od *limits* pl || freie ≈e ⟨mil⟩ *unoccupied areas* || ⟨typ, etc⟩ *to leave* od *make a blank* || *(gas-filled) space* || Angst vor geschlossenen ≈en *claustrophobia* || gewaltige ≈e *tremendous spaces (of unsettled territory)* || Kampf≈ ⟨tact⟩ *forward area* || ⟨tech⟩ hohler ~ *chamber* || leerer, weißer ~ *blank* || luftleerer ~ *vacuum*; luftverdünnter ~ *rarified air space*; toter ~ ⟨mot⟩ → Kompressions≈ **C. aussparen** ⟨mil⟩ *to deny* || *there was space for many more* || **~ bieten** für *to accomodate (40 persons)*; ich brauche viel ~ *I want a lot of room* e–n geringeren ~ einnehmen: *songs bulk less largely in the book*; wenig ~ –d *compact* | e–r S

~ **geben**: *to entertain* (*a proposal*); *to live* od *indulge in* (*a hope*); *to follow* (*one's bent*); *to give way to* (*an idea*); *to trust* (*reason*); *to have* (*an intuition*); *to grant* (*comply with, yield to*) (*a request*) || ⟨mil⟩ ~ gewinnen *to gain territory* od *ground*; ⟨fig⟩ *the suspicion deepens that* .. || am Rande ~ l ⟨typ⟩ *to leave a margin* || ~ m *to make room* od *way, to clear a space* (f *for*) || es **ist** kein ~ f .. ⟨fig⟩ *there is no place for* .. || ein weiter ~ trennt uns *a wide gap* .. || s–n ~ überschreiten (in Wort oder Schrift) *to exceed one's space* **r·aum** a ⟨mar⟩ *open* (*sea*) || ~er Wind *quartering wind* || ⟨for⟩ *open*, → licht **R·aum-** ~**angst** f *claustrophobia* ~**anker** m ⟨mar⟩ *spare anchor* ~**anzug** m ⟨a-n⟩ *space suit* ~**aufteilung** f ⟨arts⟩ *articulation of space* ~**balken** m ⟨mar⟩ *hold-beam* ~**bedarf** m *space occupied* od *required* ≗**bedingt** a *space-induced* ~**bestimmung** f *determination of volume* ~**bewußtsein** n → –gefühl ~**bild** n *three-dimensional* (*3-D-*) *presentation*; *stereoscopic picture* | ~aufnahme [f] ⟨phot⟩ *3-D-photograph, stereophot.*; ~betrachter [m] *stereoscope*; ~entf·ernungsmesser [m] *stereoscopic range-finder*; ~-messung [f] *stereo photo-surveying* ~**deck** n ⟨mar⟩ *platform* od *orlop deck* ~**dichte** f *volumetrical density* ~**effekt** m *stereoscopic effect* ~**einheit** f *unit of space* ~**ersparnis** f *economy of sp.*; der ~ wegen *to save* od *gain room* od *sp.* ~**fahrer** m *space voyager* ~**fahrt** f *astronautics*; *sp. travel, rocketship voyage*; *interplanetary travel* | ~technik [f] *sp. navigation*; *astronautics* ~**fahrzeug** n *sp.craft* || Tätigkeit außerhalb e–s ~s *extravehicular activity* (*EVA*) ≗**fest** a ⟨a–n⟩ *inertial* (*frame of reference*; *platform*) ~**film** m *stereofilm*, ⟨sl⟩ *deepie* | ~verfahren [n] *cinerama* ~**flug** m *astronautics* | ~zeug [n] *stratocruiser* ~**forscher** m *sp. explorer* ~**forschung** f ⟨geog, demog⟩ *area research* | *interplanetary exploration*; *space research* | ~sinstitut [n] *Sp. Institute* ~**fracht** f *freight by volume* ~**gefühl** n *sense of sp.*; ⟨arts a.⟩ *awareness of sp.* ~**gehalt** m ⟨for⟩ *stacked measure* ~**gestaltung** f *the art of architectorial planning* ~-**gewicht** n *density*; *volumetrical weight*; *w. per unit volume* ~**gewinn** m *gain of ground* ≗**greifend** a *ground-gaining* (*exploits*) ~**größe** f *geometrical quantity* ~**inhalt** m *volume, capacity*; *solid* od *cubic contents* pl; ⟨mar⟩ *tonnage* ~**kapsel** f ⟨a–n⟩ *space capsule* ~**klang** m *stereophonic sound* | ~box [f] ⟨rec⟩ *stereo-box* | → ⟨a.⟩ Raumton ~**kunst** f *art of interior decoration* ~**lehre** f *geometry* ~**licht** n ⟨telv⟩ *ambient light* ≗**los** a *spaceless* ~**mangel** m *want* od *lack of room* od *space, pressure on space* ~**maß** n *solid measure, measure of capacity* ≗**mäßig** adv *spatially* ~**meßbild** n *stereogram* ~**meter** n/m (⟨for⟩ *stacked*) *cubic metre*; ⟨for⟩ *1 cbm of wood with interspaces* = *.7 – .8 cbm of piled wood* = *ca. .45 cbm of trunk timber* ≗**orientierte** Bewegung [f] ⟨eth⟩ *taxis* ~**ordnung**, ~**planung** f ⟨demog⟩ *area planning* ~**pendelschiff** n *space shuttle* ~**pflegerin** f *maid, charwoman, daily woman* ~**schiff** n *sp. ship* od *vehicle*; ~ zweiter Stufe *second-stage sp. sh.* | ~besatzung [f] *sp.-sh. crew*; ~fahrt [f] *astronautics*; ~kabine [f] *sp.-sh. cabin* ~**schiffer** m *sp.man* ~**simulator** m *sp. chamber, outer sp. simulator* ~**sonde** f *sp. probe* od *sonde* ≗**sparend** a *commercial* od *economical* [od *sp.-saving*] *loading* | adv (*packed*) *to save sp.* ~**spaziergang** m ⟨a–n⟩ *space walk* (Aussteigemanöver) ~**station** f ⟨a–n⟩ *sp. station* ~**teil** m/n *part of volume* | normale ~**temperatur** *standard room t.*, → Zimmer- ~**ton** m *stereophonic* od *spherical sound*; *binaurality* ~**tonne** f ⟨mar⟩ *measurement ton* ≗**überwindend** a *sp. conquering* ~**überwindung** f *conquering of sp.* ~**verminderung** f *contraction of volume* ~**verteilung** f ⟨eth⟩ *spacing out* ~-**Volumengeschwindigkeit** f *volume-sp. velocity* ~**wahrnehmung** f *sp.-perception* ~**winkel** m *solid angle* | ~maß [n] *steradian measure* ~**wirkung** f *3 D-effect* ~**wissenschaft** f ⟨geog⟩ *chorology, chorography* ~**zeichnung** f ⟨arts⟩ *spatial design* ~**zeitalter** n *sp. age* ~-**Zeitausbeute** f *sp.-time yield* ≗**zentriert** a *sp.* od *body centered* **Räum-** ~**boot** n *mine-sweeper* ~**eisen** n ⟨carp⟩ *puncher chisel*; ⟨met⟩ *tapping bar* ~**gerät** n ⟨mar⟩ *mine sweeping gear* ~**nadel** f *wire-riddle* ~**pflug** m *bulldozer*; kl ~ *calf-dozer* || mit ~ planieren *to bulldoze* ~**trupp** m *demolition squad* ~**zahn** m (e–r Säge) *raker* **r·aumen** vi [h] (*of wind*) ⟨mar⟩ *to veer aft* **r·äumen I.** vi [h] *to tidy up* || (umziehen) *to quit, move, leave* || es wird viel geräumt *there are many removals* || ⟨com⟩ *to sell off* || mit Beständen ~ *to clear out one's stock* || .. um damit zu ~ (*reduction of 10%*) *to clear* **II.** vt [h] **A. 1.** *to clear, empty* || (Haus, Zimmer, Stadt, Stelle) *to vacate* **2.** (aufgeben) ⟨mil⟩ *to give up* (*a place*); *to abandon* (*the field*); *to evacuate* (*a town, fort, position*) || ~ l *to evacuate* || das Lager ~ *to decamp* **3.** (verlassen) *to quit, leave, remove* || e–e Wohnung ~ *to remove from a flat, house*; *to quit*; ⟨mil⟩ (Gebiet) *to abandon* **4.** ⟨com⟩ *to clear off* (*goods, stocks*) **5.** *to remove* (*mines*; *a th from a th*) || das Geschirr v Tisch ~ *to clear the table* **6.** (säubern) *to clean up*; *to dredge* (*rivers, harbours*) **B. beiseite** ~, aus dem Wege ~ (S) *to push aside, to put out of the way* || *to clear away* (⟨a. fig⟩ *apprehensions*), *to remove* (*obstacles, difficulties*) || *to make away with* (*a p*), *to despatch, remove* (*a p*), *to finish* (*a p*) *off* **III.** ≗ n ⟨a.⟩ *clearance* **R·äumer** m ~s/~ *cleanser* **r·äumig** a = ge~; ⟨for⟩ *undercrowded, roomy* **r·äumlich** a (*of*) *space*; *relating to space*; *spatial* (Ggs *temporal*) || ⟨opt⟩ *stereoscopic* (Sehen *vision*); ~e Wirkung *relief* || [adv] *spatially* (*remote from*) || ~ gr Erfolge erzielen *to achieve substantial territorial gains* ~**keit** f [abstr] *spatiality* || *extent, space* || *spaciousness* || [konkr] = Raum || [pl ⟨a.⟩] *premises* pl; ⟨engl⟩ *accomodation*(*s* pl ⟨Am⟩) **R·äumte** f ~/~n **1.** *offing, main sea, main* || die ~ gewinnen (suchen) *to gain* (*to make for*) *the offing* **2.** (*ship's*) *tonnage, capacity* **R·äumung** f ~/~en *clearing* (*off*) || *removing, removal, quitting* || ⟨com⟩ *clearance* || ⟨mil⟩ *evacuation* (→ räumen) **R·äumungs-** ~**ausverkauf** m *clearance-sale* ~-**frage** f *question of evacuation* ~**hieb** m ⟨for⟩ *final cutting* ~**öffnung** f *manhole* (*of a cesspool*, etc.) ~**schlag** m ⟨for⟩ *final stage*

r·aunen vi/t [h] *to murmur*; *to whisper* (jdm ins Ohr *in*[*to*] *a p's ear*) || man raunt *there is a rumour* (daß *that*)

°**r·aunzen** vi [h] *find fault with everything*

R·aupe f ~/~n **1.** ⟨ent⟩ *caterpillar* || ~n [pl] ⟨fig fam⟩ *whims, maggots* pl; *high* od *funny notions, great plans* || jdm ~n in den Kopf setzen *to put silly ideas into a p's head* **2.** ⟨tail⟩ *chenille* || ⟨mil⟩ (Helm≗) *crest*; (Generals–, Majors-≗n) *thick fringes* pl *of the epaulettes* **3.** ⟨tech⟩ *crawler track* **r·aupen** vt *to clear of caterpillars* **R·aupen-** ~**antrieb** m ⟨mot⟩ *crawler-drive* ~**artillerie** f *c. artillery* ~**band** n ⟨tech⟩ *creeper-band* ~**fahr-** ~werk [n] *tractor-type undercarriage* ⟨a. aero⟩, ⟨aero a.⟩ *track landing gear*; ~zeug [n] *t.-t. vehicle, crawler-truck* ~**fliege** f *bristle-, larva-fly* ~**fraß** m *damage done by c.s.* ~**helm** m *padded helmet* ~**kette** f *creeper-chain, -track* | ~n-Löffelbagger [m] *mechanical shovel running on tracks* ~**krad** n *full-track mobike* ~**leim** m ⟨hort⟩ *insect paste* ~-**Lkw** m *full-track vehicle* ~**nest** n *nest of c.s* ~**rad** n *crawler-wheel* ~**schlepper** m *crawler-tractor*; *tank* || ⟨fig, fam, mil⟩ *brass-hat* (= *major, colonel*, etc.) (→ Raupe 2) ~**töter** m ⟨ent⟩ *ichneumon-fly* **r·aupig** a *full of caterpillars*

°**raus** = heraus; etw ~ h *to have the knack of a th, to know a th or two* || ~ damit! *spit it out!*

Rausch m ~es/≗e **1.** *inebriation, intoxication*; *drunken fit, drunkenness* || kl ~ *tipsiness* || im ~

in one's cups || sich [dat] e–n ~ antrinken *or* kaufen *to get drunk*, ⟨fam⟩ *tipsy, fuddled* || s–n ~ ausschlafen *to sleep* (*o.s. sober* od) *off the drink* || e–n kl (gehörigen, schweren) ~ h *to be a little fuddled* (*regularly intoxicated, completely drunk*), *to be half-seas-over* **2.** ⟨med⟩ (*slight*) *narcosis* **3.** ⟨fig⟩ *intoxication* (*of wealth*), *ecstasy* (*of success*) || *frenzy, transport, delirium*, ⟨fam⟩ *mad fit* || ~ der Begeisterung *frenzied applause* || ~ der Liebe *passionate love* || im ersten ~ *in the first excitement* **~beere** f *cranberry* || schwarze ~ *crowberry* **~faktor** m ⟨wir⟩ *noise ratio* **~gelb** n *orpiment* **~gift** n *narcotic, drug*, ⟨sl⟩ *dope* || ~en frönen *to drug* | ~angew·öhnung [f] *drug-habit*; ~handel [m] *drug-trafficking*; ~händler [m] *drugster, dope-pedlar*, ⟨sl⟩ *pusher* ⟨a. teens⟩; ~giftnehmer [m] *drug-addict*; ~schieber [m] → –händler; ~süchtige(r) [m] ⟨sl⟩ *dope-fiend*; ⟨sl⟩ *junkey* ⟨a. teens⟩, ⟨Am⟩ *hophead*; Bett, Couch, Treffpunkt der –n ⟨sl⟩ *pad* **~gold** n *tinsel* **~pfeife** f (Orgel) *loud alto* **~silber** n *leaf-silver* **~spannung** f ⟨wir⟩ *noise potential* **R·äuschchen** n ~s/~ (*slight*) *intoxication* || ein ~ h *to be slightly elevated* **r·auschen I. 1.** vi [h] (laut) (Wind, Wogen etc) *to roar* || (Wasser) *to rush* || (Beifall) *to ring* | (sanft) (Bach) *to murmur, purl, whisper, gurgle*; (Blätter) *to rustle, sough, whisper*; (Flügel, Seide, Wind) *to rustle* | (*of boar*) *to be ruttish* **2.** vi [s] ⟨wir⟩ *to rustle* || vorbei~ *to rush* od *dash past, to pass quickly* || hinein~ (P) *to sweep* od *sail in* **3.** vt [h] wach~ = –rufen **II.** ≃ n *rush*(*ing*), *roar* || *rustle* ⟨a. rec, commun⟩; *murmur, susurration* (*of trees*), *frou-frou* (*of silk*) **III.** ≃**d** a *roaring*, etc. || *susurrant* (*trees*) || *plangent* (*waves*) || *rustling* (*scythe*) || *swelling* (*music*); *sonorous* (*finale*) || *thundering, deafening* (*applause*) | ⟨fig⟩ *orgiastic* (*feasts*) || *uproarious* (*company, festivities*) || *exuberant* (*pleasures*)

r·äuspern I. vi [h] *to hem and haw* | **sich** ~ *to clear one's throat, to hawk* || (aus Verlegenheit) *to hem* **II.** ≃ n *the clearing of the throat*

°**Raus- ≃geschmissen** w ⟨fam⟩ *to get the kick* od *knock* **≃haben** → raus **≃schmeißen** vt [h] ⟨sl⟩ *to can a p, to give a p the brushoff* **~schmeißer** m (P) ⟨sl⟩ *chucker-out*, ⟨Am⟩ *bouncer* || (Tanz) = Kehraus ⟨Am fam⟩ *chaser*

R·aute f ~/~n ⟨bot⟩ *rue* || ⟨math⟩ *rhomb, square* || ⟨arch⟩ *quarrel* || ⟨her⟩ *lozenge* || (am Edelstein) *facet* **R·auten- ~diamant** m *brilliant* **~feld** n ⟨her⟩ *lozenge* **~fläche** f *rhomb, facet* **≃förmig** a *rhombic, rhomb-shaped* **~fries** m *lozenge-moulding*; *diamond-fret* **~glas** n *glass lozenge* **~kranz** m *lozenged chaplet* od *wreath* **~öl** n *rue oil* **~spat** m ⟨min⟩ *rhomb spar* **~stab** m *lozenge moulding* od *fret* **~stellung** f *lozenge-like arrangement* **~verband** m (f Pflaster) *diamond bond* **≃weise** a *lozengewise, in facets*

Ray·on [rɛ'jɔ̃] m ~s/~s ⟨fort⟩ *radius* || district || ⟨com⟩ *department* || (Bereich) ⟨artill⟩ *range*

R·azzia f ~/–ien *round-up, raid, razzia* (auf *on*); *dragnet raid*; ⟨pol a.⟩ *swoop* || e–e ~ halten *to make a raid*, ⟨Am fam⟩ *to crack down* | ~abteilung [f] (gegen Rauschgift–) *vice-squad*

Reag- ~·ens n ~/–·enzien ⟨chem⟩ *reagent, test*; [pl] *reactive means* **~·enzglas, -gläschen** n *test-glass, -tube* **~papier** n *test-paper* **≃·ieren** vi [h] ⟨chem & fig⟩ (auf [acc]) *to react* (*upon*) || ⟨fig⟩ auf etw sehr positiv ~ *to be responsive to a th as litmus paper to acid*; auf etw sauer ~ *to respond with a surly look, not to respond, to be irresponsive to a th* || **~d** a *reactive* (auf *to*) **Reakti·on** f ~/~en ⟨chem & fig, pol⟩ *reaction* || ⟨eth⟩ kritische ~ *critical r.* || ⟨fig⟩ *response* (auf *to*) | **~·är** m ~(e)s/~e *reactionary, reactionist* | **≃·är** a *reactionary, rightist*; *die-hard, Colonel Blimp* | **~s-** ~bremse [f] ⟨at⟩ *moderator*; ≃fähig [a] *reactive, responsive* (auf *to*); ~papier [n] *reactive paper* || ⟨at⟩ ~kette [f] *reaction chain*; ~kern [m] *r. core*; ~weg [m] *r. channel, r. path* **~losigkeit** f ⟨psych⟩ *stupor* | Weg während der **~zeit** f ⟨mot⟩ *thinking distance* **reaktiv·ieren** vt [h] ⟨mil⟩ *to recommission*, ⟨fam⟩ *to dig out* || –rter Offizier *dugout* **Reaktiv·ierung** f ⟨soc⟩ *return to active employment* **Re·aktor** m ~s/–·oren | ⟨at⟩ *pile*; *reactor* || Forschungs≃ *research r.*; Kern≃ *nuclear r.*; Leistungs≃ (f Krafterzeugung) *power r.* | ~graphit [m] *graphite of nuclear quality* **2.** ⟨eth⟩ *reactor*

Re·al f ~/ ⟨typ⟩ *eight-line pica* **re·al I.** a (wirklich) *real* || (gegenständlich) *substantial, material* || (tatsächlich) *actual* **II.** das ≃e *reality*; *true fact*; aufs ≃e eingestellt *objective* (*mind*) **~ denkend** a *objective* (*mind*), ⟨Am a.⟩ *hard-boiled* (*fellow*) **Re·alien** n [pl] **1.** *real facts, realities* **2.** *facts* od *studies bearing on the institutions and customs of a nation* **3.** *exact sciences* **Re·al- ~-enzyklopädie** f (*en*)*cyclopædia* **~gymnasium** n *secondary school for Latin, modern languages, and sciences* **~hypothek** f *mortgage on landed property* **~injurie** f ⟨jur⟩ *assault and battery* **~kenntnis** f pl *knowledge of useful facts*; *scientific knowledge* **~konkurrenz** f ⟨jur⟩ *actual coincidence of offences* **~kredit** m *credit on real property* **~lexikon** n (*en*)*cyclopædia* **~lohn** m *real wages, take-home pay* **~politik** f *realistic politics* [sg & pl konstr] **~schule** f *non-classical secondary school, central school* **~servitut** n *real property mortgage* || ⟨jur⟩ *easement* **~teilung** f *division of real estate* (*among the heirs*) **~wert** m *actual* od *true value* **~wörterbuch** n (*en*)*cyclopædia* **realis·ierbar** a, leicht ~ *liquid* (*securities*) || nicht ~ *frozen* (*assets*) **realis·ieren** vt [h] *to perform, to execute* | (zu Gelde m) *to realize, to convert into money* || *to raise* (*sums*) || *to effect* (*a sale*) **Real·ismus** m ~/ *realism*; ⟨Lit⟩ (–19. Jh) *descriptive naturalism*: "*it is*" (Flaubert etc); (20. Jh) *self-assertion of the artist*: "*I am*" || *psychological r.* (Dostojewski, etc) **Real·ist** m ~en/~en *realist* **≃isch** a *realistic*; *slice-of-life*, ⟨Am sl⟩ *hard-boiled* (*play*) || ~ denkend = realdenkend **Realit·ät** f ~/~en *reality* | österr = Immobilie: ~envermittlung [f] *real estate agency* **re·aliter** [adv] *in reality*

R·eaumur ['re:omyr] 20 Grad ~ *20 degrees R.*

R·eb- ~gewinde n *festoon of vine-branches* **~huhn** n *partridge*; ~jagd [f] *p.-shooting* **~land** n *land planted with vines* **~laus** f *phylloxera, vine-louse* **~messer** n *pruning-knife* **~pfahl** m *vine-prop* **~schoß** m *vine-shoot* **~stock** m *vine* **R·ebe** f ~/~n **1.** *vine* **2.** *shoot, tendril* **R·eben- ~auge** n *vine-bud* **~blatt** n *vine-leaf* **~blut** n = –saft **~gelände** n *vine-clad country* **~geländer** n *vine-trellis* **~holz** n *wood of the vine* **~laub** n *vine-leaves* pl **~messer** = Rebmesser **~pfahl** m *vine-prop* **≃reich** a *rich in vines* **~saft** m *grape-juice*, ⟨poet⟩ *wine* **~stab** m ⟨myth⟩ *thyrsus* **~stecher** m ⟨ent⟩ *vine-weevil* **≃umsponnen** a *vine-clad* **~züchter** m *vine-grower*, ⟨scient⟩ *viticulturist*

Reb·ell m ~en/~en *rebel, mutineer, insurgent* **≃·ieren** vi [h] *to rebel, mutiny, revolt* **~·i·on** f ~/~en *rebellion, insurrection, mutiny* **≃isch** a *rebellious, mutinous, revolutionary* || *seditious* (*speech*)

R·ebus m & n [~/~(se)] *picture-puzzle, rebus*

R·echen m ~s/~ **1.** *rake* | ~anlage [f] ⟨tech⟩ *screening plant*; ~gut [n]; ~rückstand [m] *screenings*; ~stiel [m] *handle of a rake* **2.** (Kleider-≃) *rack, peg-board* **3.** *grate* (*of a weir*) **4.** °(Frau) *lemon* **5.** ≃ vt/i [h] *to rake* **R·echen-** → rechnen **~anlage** f *computer* **~aufgabe** f *sum, arithmetical problem* || ~n stellen *to set sums* **~automat** m *computer*; elektronischer ~ (*automatic*) *electronic c.* **~befehl** m ⟨comp⟩ *arithmetic instruction* **~brett** n *abacus* **~buch** n *a.c book*; nach dem ~ (fechten, küssen) *by* (*the*) *book* **~dose** f ⟨mar⟩ *computer* **~einheit** f ⟨comp⟩ *a.c unit*; (*electronic*) *calculating unit* **~ergebnis** n ⟨comp⟩ *results of computing operations* **~exempel** n = ~aufgabe

⟨a.⟩ a matter of a.c **~fehler** m miscount; mistake, miscalculation **~funktion** f ⟨comp⟩ a.c function (⟨engl⟩ decimal od/& sterling) **~gerät** n ⟨artill⟩ data computer | hohe **~geschwindigkeiten** ⟨comp⟩ fast input and output **~größe** f ⟨comp⟩ operand **~heft** n sum-book **~kammer** f audit-office **~knecht** m = –tabelle **~kunst** f a.c **~künstler** m a.cal genius **~lehrer(in** f) m teacher of a.c **~locher** m ⟨off⟩ multiplier **~maschine** f calculating-machine || ⟨school⟩ abacus || computer | ~nschreiberin [f] keypunch operator **~meister** m a.cian **~operationen** durchführen ⟨comp⟩ to carry out the sequence of calculations **~pfennig** m counter, marker; token money **~register** n ⟨comp⟩ (a.c) register **~roboter** m = Rechenanlage **~scheibe** f ⟨phot⟩ disc calculator, ⟨Am⟩ rotodial **~schieber** m slide rule, ⟨Am⟩ slipstick **~schritt** m ⟨comp⟩ step of computation **~schule** f ciphering-school **~stanzer** m ⟨off⟩ computer **~stunde** f a.c-lesson | elektronisches **~system** n electronic computing system **~tabelle** f ready reckoner **~tafel** f counting-board; (squared) black-board od slate || (Einmaleins) multiplication-table; → rechnen **~tisch** m ⟨mar⟩ plotting board od table **~werk** n ⟨comp⟩ a.c unit **~zentrum** n processing centre ⟨a. sport⟩ **R·echenschaft** f ~/ account || ~ ablegen (v, über) to give od render an acc. (of); to acc. for || ~ ablegen müssen to have to answer for one's conduct; jdm .. to be acc.able od responsible to a p || sich der ~ entziehen to shirk the responsibility || zur ~ ziehen to call to acc. (wegen for), to bring to book; to haul (drag) a p over the coals **~sablage** f giving of an acc. **~sbericht** m statement (of acc.s), acc. rendered, report, audit **≗pflichtig** a accountable **r·echnen I.** vt/i [h] **A.** to count; to do sums od ciphering || (zus~) to reckon, to sum od cast up || (aus~) to calculate, compute || (veranschlagen) to value, esteem, estimate || (einordnen) to class, rank **B.** e–e Aufgabe ~ to do sums, to work out a problem || im Kopf ~ to reckon in one's head, [vt] to work out mentally || mit Buchstaben ~ to calculate in letters | jdm etw ~ to charge a p a price | auch die Zeit ~ to take into acc. also .. || ohne die Mühe zu ~ not to mention the pains || nicht ~ to discount || nicht ~d ⟨a.⟩ barring || Nebengelasse nicht ge–net excluding .. **C. falsch** ~ to miscalculate || gut or hoch ge–net ist es .. it is (an hour's walk) at the (ut)most || knapp ge–net closely reckoned || richtig ge–net properly calculated **D.** gut ~ **können** to be good od quick at reckoning, sums, arithmetic, figures || ~ lernen to learn a.c || sie weiß zu ~ she knows how to economize **E.** etw **für** nichts ~ to take no acc. of a th || eins **fürs** or **ins** andere ge–net taking one th with another || **gegen** e–a ~ to balance, compare || alles **in** allem ge–net taking all in all | ⟨übtr⟩ er r–net = man r–net ihn **unter** .. he is counted among (the best) || die Zinsen ~ = w ge–net the interest will run (from April 1.) | es sich (e–m) **als** or **zur** Ehre ~ to look on a th as a great h. (→ an~) || eins zum andern ~ to sum od add up || mit dazu~ to include, .. ge–net inclusive | ~ **zu** [vi] to be reckoned among .. || (etw) ~ zu to reckon in (with); to class, include in **II.** [vi] **an** e–r Aufgabe ~ to work at a problem | ~ **auf** [acc] to count, rely, depend (up)on; to look to a p (wegen for) || rechne nicht darauf or damit, daß er zahlt don't reckon on his paying; I count on your coming || darauf ~ befördert z w to expect to be .. || kann ich auf 5.– M ~? are you good for 5 s? || zuversichtlich auf etw ~ to trust to a th, to have sanguine hopes of a th | ~ **mit** to reckon with od on; to consider, contemplate || to face (a possibility) || to calculate on (fine weather) || to count on (support) || to budget od bargain for a th || damit ~ z tun to figure on doing || es ist damit z ~ it can be od is to be expected || er mußte mit jeder Feder ~ he had to make every pen count || er muß mit (s–n Kräften) den Tatsachen ~ he must (think of his strength) reckon with the actual facts || wir müssen damit ~, daß er .. we must take into account that he (may not come) || es ist damit z ~, daß .. it is to be hoped that .. || fest, bestimmt, sicher mit etw ~ to count od rely upon; nicht sicher ..: we cannot reckon on our trip as a certainty **III.** ≗ n reckoning etc || calculation, computation || kaufmännisches ~ commercial a.c **≗können** n numeracy **R·echner** m ~s/~ (P) reckoner, accountant, calculator, a.cian; computer || (S) computer | ~bediener(in [f]) [m] keypunch operator | **~·ei** f ~/~en long od endless reckoning, etc. **≗isch** a arithmetic, mathematical; ~er Wert book value || [adv] ⟨a.⟩ analytically; by computation **R·echnung** f ~/~en **A. 1.** (Berechnung) reckoning, account, computation || ⟨bes school⟩ calculation, sum(s pl), arithmetic **2.** ⟨com⟩ bill, account; (Begleit≗) invoice || memorandum || (Beleg) voucher || ⟨hot⟩ bill; m–e ~! my b. ⟨Am a.⟩ check!; (Restaurant-≗) ⟨a.⟩ check; (Wirtshaus≗) score **3.** ⟨sport⟩ score **4.** ⟨fig⟩ opinion, supposition, reckoning **B.** laufende ~ current account || gemeinsame or halbe ~ half-share, joint acc. || m wir getrennte ~ let's go Dutch || ⟨fig⟩ die ~ war falsch it was a failure od washout **C.** e–e ~ aus–, **begleichen** to clear od settle an acc., to strike a balance; ⟨fig⟩ (sich rächen) to square acc.s; alte ~en .. to wipe up old scores || jds ~ belasten mit to debit a p with, to put a th to a p's debit || e–e ~ **bezahlen** to pay a bill || die ~ bezahlen to foot the bill || ⟨fig⟩ s–e ~ (nicht) finden to make a profit (to lose, to be the loser) (bei by) || ~ führen to keep acc.(s pl) || geben Sie mir die ~! ⟨hot⟩ the bill, please || die ~ geht nicht auf the calculation does not work out || ~ **legen** (über [acc]) to render (an) acc. (of) || e–e gr ~ m to run up a big bill od acc. || ⟨fig⟩ die ~ ohne den Wirt m to count od reckon without one's host; s–e letzte ~ m ⟨sl⟩ to pass in one's cheques (and die) || e–e ~ saldieren to settle an acc.; .. schließen to close (od wind up) an acc.; .. **schreiben** to make out an invoice || ⟨fam⟩ → Schornstein || die (s–e) ~ stimmt nicht the acc. does not square (he is wrong in his calculation) || [dat] ~ **tragen** to make allowance for a th, to take a th into acc.; to accommodate o.s. to circumstances; to comply with a p's wishes; (Geschmack) to consider; to cater (to taste) **D. auf, für** eigene ~ on one's own acc. (od ⟨fam, fig⟩ hook) || auf (jds) ~ u Gefahr for acc. and risk (of) || auf ~ bestellen to order against invoice || das geht auf m–e ~ that goes to my debit od acc.; ⟨fam⟩ this is on me; auf ~ des Wirts on the house || (the item) is to be entered on the acc. of .. || auf ~ kaufen to buy on credit || auf jds ~ schreiben or setzen, stellen to charge to a p, to place to a p's acc., to book to the debit of a p's. acc.; ⟨fig⟩ auf ~ setzen v .. to ascribe to a th || auf ~ senden .. on acc. || auf m–e ~: (drink a glass) at my cost | **außer** ~ l to overlook || jdm e–n Strich **durch** die ~ m ⟨fig⟩ to thwart a p's projects od plans; to put a spoke into a p's wheel | **für** e–s dritten ~ kaufen to buy for acc. of a third party | **in** ~ bringen ⟨fig⟩ to take into acc.; jdm etw .. = auf ~ stellen || in feste ~ liefern to supply and charge to acc. || (S) in ~ stehen mit 10.– M to be charged 15 s; (P) to have an open acc. with (a p) || (etw) in ~ stellen to put .. down to "expenses"; jdm etw .. to pass, debit, put down, place, charge a th to a p's acc.; to enter a th to a p's debit || the the book is charged to you (mit .. at 5.– M) || ⟨fig⟩ etw in ~ stellen to provide for a th, to respect a th, to take a th into consideration, to take acc. of (the claims of other nations) || etw nicht in ~ ziehen to leave a th out of one's calculations | **laut** ~ as per acc.; laut beiliegender, eingesandter ~ (according) to acc. rendered || das stimmt nicht **mit** m–r ~ that does not agree with my calculation || **nach** m–r ~ *according to my c.s* || .. **v** .. absetzen *to knock an amount off the bill* **R·echnungs- ~ablegung** f *rendering of acc.s* **~abnahme** f *audit(ing)* **~abschluß** m ⟨com⟩ *account agreed upon* || *balancing* od *closing of acc.s* **~amt** m *audit-office* **~art** f *manner* od *method of reckoning* || die vier ~en *the four species* **~artikel** m ⟨com⟩ *item, entry* **~aufstellung** f *rendering of an acc.* **~auszug** m ⟨com⟩ *acc. rendered, abstract of acc.-current* **~beamte(r)** m *acc.ant* **~beleg** m *voucher* **~buch** n *acc.-book* **~datum** n *date of invoice* **~einheit** f *acc.g unit* (*5 million European Monetary Agreement acc.g u.s*) **~fehler** m *mistake, miscalculation* **~führer** m *book-keeper, acc.ant; pay clerk,* ⟨mil⟩ *pay sergeant; agent (finance) officer* **~führung** f *keeping of acc.s* **~hof** m, **~kammer** f *Court of Audit* **~jahr** n *fiscal* od *financial year* **~legung** f *rendering of acc.s* **≗mäßig** a ⟨ins⟩ *expected* (*mortality*) **~posten** m *entry, item* **~prüfer** m *auditor, controller; certified acc.ant* **~prüfung** f *audit(ing)* | ~samt [n] *audit office*; ~sausschuß [m] *public acc.s committee*; ~skommission [f] *board of audit* **~saldo** m ⟨com⟩ *rest* **~überschlag** m *rough estimate* **~unterlage** f *accounting* od *supporting document* **~wesen** n *acc.s* pl, *acc.antship*

Rech·erche [reˈʃɛrʃə] f ~/~n Fr ⟨off⟩ *investigation*

Recht n ~(e)s ⟨jur a.⟩ ~ens/~e **A. 1.** (subjektiv) *right* || ~ oder Un≗ *right or wrong* (*my country*) || (Vor≗) *privilege* || (Anspruch) (auf [acc], zu [dat]) *claim* (*on*), *title* (*to* ⟨a. jur⟩) || *a right to happiness, freedom* || Sachen≗ (an körperl. Dingen) *real right* **2.** (Gerechtigkeit) *justice* **3.** (Rechtsstudien) *jurisprudence, law*; (⟨a.⟩ ~e [pl]) *legal science* **4.** (Gesetz) ⟨engl⟩ *the law* || Gesetzes≗ *statute-law*; Ggs: Präzedenz≗ *case-law* || Gewohnheits≗ *prescriptive law* || Natur≗ *law of nature* **5.** (Gewalt) *power* (*over life and death*) **6.** (Berechtigung) *right* (*to assume the r.*) **7.** ⟨golf⟩ das ~ zuerst z schlagen *honour* **B.** ~ u Billigkeit *right and equity* | Student der ~e *law-student* || Doktor der ~e *doctor of law* (*L.L.D.* = *doctor legum*) | das ~ des Stärkeren *the rights of the strongest, club-law* **C.** ⟨jur⟩ **~ens s** *to be lawful, to be according to law* || den Weg ~ens beschreiten *to take legal proceedings* || im Wege ~ens *by legal means* od *proceedings* **D. angestammtes** ~ *birthright* || ausschließliches ~ auf *monopoly of* || bürgerliches ~ *civil law* od *code* || der bürgerlichen ~ verlustig *infamous* || ⟨engl⟩ dingliches ~ *real right*, .. erster Ordnung *legal estates and interests* pl || formelles ~ *adjective law* || gegenwärtiges ~ *vested estate* || gemeines ~ *common law* || geschriebenes ~ *statute-law* || sein gutes ~ *what is his by right*; es ist sein ~ = er hat das ~ || materielles ~ *substantive law* || öffentliches ~ *public law* || Körperschaft des öffentl. ~s *statutory corporation* || Römisches ~ ⟨m. m.⟩ *civil law* || unbedingtes ~ *vested r.* || uneingeschränktes ~ ⟨a.⟩ *unfettered discretion* (*to do*) || ungeschriebenes ~ *unwritten law* || ⟨Am⟩ (jdm) verbliebenes ~ *equity* (auf *in*) || verbrieftes ~ *vested right* **E.** das dingliche ~ (an e–r S) **aufgeben** *to derelict* || ≗ **behalten** *to carry one's point, to be right in the end* || das ~ beugen *to deviate from justice*, → Rechts–; das ~ brechen *to warp* od *pervert j.* || ein ~ erwerben *to acquire a right* || sein ~ fordern *to claim one's rights* || e–m ≗ **geben** *to acknowledge a p's views* || ich kann ihm nicht ≗ geben *I cannot concur* od *agree with him* || jdm das ~ geben *to empower a p* (*to do*) || das gibt uns kein ~ zu *that is no warrant for us* (*to believe*) || selbst dem Teufel sein ~ geben *to give the devil his due* || ihm ist ≗ geschehen *it served him right* || ≗ h *to be right* || das ~ h *to be justified* (*to do*) || kein ~ h *to have no business* od *standing* (*to do*) || jdm alles ≗ **m** *to suit a p's mind fully* || ~ **sprechen** *to administer justice*; ⟨hist⟩ *to speak the law* || dem ~ Hohn sprechen *to scoff at right* || die ~e studieren *to read law, to study the laws* || ⟨prov⟩ tue ≗ u scheue niemand! *be just and fear not*! || sich [dat] selbst ~ verschaffen *to take the law into one's own hands* || alle ~e vorbehalten! *all rights reserved*! || ihm **wird** sein ~ *he finds his rights* || sein ~ muß ihm w *justice must be done him* || e–m ≗ widerfahren l *to do a p justice* || das ~ steht ihm zu *he has the right* (*to do*); *it shall be in his power* (*to do*) **F. aus** eigenem ~ *on one's own right* || **außerhalb** des ~s gestellt *outlaw* (*p, state*) | **im** ~ s *to be in the right*; *it was legitimate in them* (*to do*) | **mit** ~ *legitimately, justifiably, with justice*; *rightly* (*proud, disputed*), *deservedly* (*punished*) | mit dem gleichen ~ *on equal terms* || wir können mit gleichem ~ dasselbe tun *we have just as much right to do the same* || mit größerem ~ *with greater reason* || mit gutem ~ *in reason* || mit vollem ~ *for good reasons, very rightly* || ob mit ~ oder Un≗ *whether rightly or wrongly*; *by hook or by crook* | .. und das mit ~ .. *and very rightly so,* .. *as well he might,* .. *and with reason,* (*he thought there was* ..) *of course there was* | **nach** geltendem ~ *de lege lata* || nach zukünftigem ~ *de lege ferenda* || → Rechte | **ohne** ~ *unjustly* || **von** ~s wegen *in justice, according to justice* od *law, by right(s)*; *as a matter of law* || **zu** ~ bestehen *to be* od *continue* (*legally*) *valid*; (Verordnung) *to be in force* || zu ~ erkennen *to find, according to law* || zu s–m ~e k *to come into one's* (S: *its*) *own* od *rights* ⟨a. fig⟩ || (*recreation must also*) *be granted its rights* |

recht I. [a] **A. 1.** (Ggs link) *right*; ⟨her⟩ *dexter* **2.** ⟨math⟩ *right* (*angle*), *straight* **3.** (gerecht) *right, just*; ~ u billig *just and fair*; → Recht E. **4.** ⟨mst⟩ *real, genuine, true*; *legitimate, lawful* **5.** (geziemend) (*be*)*fitting, proper, suitable, convenient* || (schuldig) *due* **6.** (richtig) *correct, accurate*; *right* [*way, key moment* (*for*)] **7.** (angenehm) *agreeable* **8.** (tüchtig, gehörig) *thorough, solid* **B.** das geht nicht mit ~en **Dingen** zu *there's sth queer, wrong,* ⟨fam⟩ *fishy somewhere* (od *about that*) || (Ehefrau) *lawful* || (Erbe) *legitimate* || er hat k–n ~en Erfolg gehabt *he has not been very successful* || (Herz) auf dem ~n **Fleck** .. *in the right place* || auf dem ~en Flügel stehen ⟨pol⟩ *to be on the Right* || (Freude) *great* || (Glaube) *true* || (Gleise) *right* ⟨a. fig⟩ || (Halunke) *regular, right-down* || (Hand) *right* ⟨a. fig⟩, ⟨a.⟩ *fugleman*; ~er H. *to the right* || (Licht) *proper* ⟨a. fig⟩ || k–e ~e Lust *no great liking* (*for work*) || der ~e **Mann** *the right man,* ⟨fam⟩ *sort*; an den ~en M. k *to meet one's match* || (Mühe) *great* (*pains*) || m–e ~e Mutter *my own m.* || (Nachbar) *right-hand* (*n.*) || *real* (*name*); das Kind beim ~en Namen nennen *to call a spade a spade* || am ~en **Ort** *in the proper, right place* || (Schande) *regular* (*disgrace*) || ⟨fam⟩ vor die ~e Schmiede k *to come to the right shop* || (Schwester) *full* od *own* || (Seite) *right* (*side*) ⟨a. tail⟩; ⟨hors⟩ *off-side*; (das Bild) ~e Seite oben .. *at the top of the right-hand page* || (Vorderrad) *off-front* (*wheel*) || (Winkel) *right* (*angle*) || (genau) zur ~en Zeit *punctually, in due* od *good time,* (*in the very nick of time*) **C. [mst adv]** wenn ich es ~ **bedenke** *when I come to think about it properly* | ~ behalten *to prove o.s. to be* (*in the*) *right*; du sollst ~ b. *all right, have it your way* | bitte ~ sehr! *don't mention it*; ich bitte ~ sehr um Verzeihung *please, excuse me*; (vorwurfsvoll) ich muß doch ~ sehr bitten *I beg your pardon*! | jdn ~ führen *to guide a p aright* || ~ gehen → ~ sein || das **geschieht** ihm ~! (*that*) *serves him right*!; .. dir ganz ~ *you deserve all you get*! | ~ **geben**: (*common sense*) *is on his side* || nicht ~ glauben: *they don't believe it quite* || ~ **h** *to be* (*in the*) *right* (in, mit *about*); du hast ~! *you've hit it,* .. ganz ~! *I should say so*! | ~ handeln *to act rightly* || nicht ~ geheilt *not healed properly* || du **kommst** mir (gerade) ~! *just what I expected*! (*you have come just when I wanted you*) || komme ich (Ihnen) recht? *I'm not disturbing you, am I*? || Sie k zu jeder Zeit ~ ⟨fam⟩ *anytime you're passing*; es kam ihm gerade ~ *it came pat to his purpose* | nichts ~ **m** *to do nothing right* || es e–m ~ m *to do a th to a p's satisfaction* || es jdm nicht ~ m können *to be unable to please a p* (*there is no pleasing him*) || °es ihr ~ m ⟨sex⟩ *to do a woman's job for her* | wenn man ihn ~ zu **nehmen** verstand *if you took him the right way* || → schlecht | ~ **sein**: was ~ **ist,** muß ~ bleiben ⟨m. m.⟩ *a fair th is a fair th* || .., ist es Ihnen ~? (*let's take a walk*), *shall we*? || ist es ~ so? *will that do*?, *is that all right*? || es ist schon ~ *that's all right* || das ist ~, so ist's ~! *that's right*! (→ D.) || so wird's ~ s *that will do*! || alles was ~ ist, aber .. *that's all well and good, but* .. || es war nur ~ u billig *it was no more than just* (*and reasonable*), *it was only fair* || bin ich hier ~ nach N.? *is this* (od *am I*) *right for N.*? || es war ~ (v dir), daß du es tatest *it was right of you to have done it, you were right in doing it* || *it's not nice of you to speak like that* | **jdm ~ s** *to suit a p* (*that would just suit me*) || mir ist's ~, mir soll's ~ s *I don't mind, it's all the same to me, it doesn't matter to me*, ⟨fam⟩ *I am agreeable*; ihm ist alles ~ *nothing comes amiss* od *wrong to him* || es war ihm nicht ~ *he did not like it* || wenn mir's ~ ist *if I'm not mistaken* || wenn es Ihnen ~ ist *if it is agreeable to you, if you agree* (*to it*), *if you don't mind*; → o. || mir ist (schon) alles ~ *I agree to everything* (*I put up with anything*) || mir ist nicht ~ (wohl) *I feel queer*, ⟨fam⟩ *I'm feeling a bit off colour* || alle Mittel sind ihm ~ *all means are good to him* || was dem e–n ~ ist, ist dem andern billig *sauce for the goose is sauce for the gander* | ~ **tun** *to do the right th* (→ Recht tun) || er hat ~ (daran) getan *he did well*; *small blame to him* | wenn ich dich ~ **v**erstehe *if I understand you correctly* || ich kann es nicht ~ verstehen, daß .. *I can't quite understand that* (*he should* ..) | ich **weiß** nicht ~, ob (wie) .. *I don't quite know, I hardly know whether* (*how*) ..; *I'm not sure* (*that*) *he will come* **D. [ell]** ~ (so)! *right you are*! *quite* (*so*)! *all right*!, ⟨sl⟩ *right-ho*!, *a good job too*! || ⟨mar⟩ ~ so! *right ahead*! || ganz ~! *precisely, exactly, certainly, just so, quite* (*so*)!, *true*! ⟨fam⟩ *rather*! **II. [adv]** (→ a. I. C.) **A. 1. [vor a]** *well, very, greatly* (*pleased*) || *downright* (*angry*) || *right* (*aware*) || *rather* (*hungry*) || *quite* (*good, upset*) || ⟨fam⟩ *jolly* (*good*), *precious* (*little*) || ⟨Am a.⟩ *real* (*soon*); er sieht ~ blaß aus *he looks kind of pale*; sie vertragen sich nicht ~ *they hardly get on together*; ~ gut wissen *to know well enough* **B.** ~ **achteraus** ⟨mar⟩ *right aft* || ~ freundlich *very nice* (*of you*) || du bist wohl nicht ~ gescheit *or* ~ bei Trost? *are you crazy*? || ich werde nicht ~ **klug** aus .. *I can't make heads or tails of* .. || es tut mir ~ leid *I am truly sorry* || ~ schade! *what a pity*!, *a great pity*! || ~ tüchtig *first-class* (*actor*) || ~ **viel** .. *a lot* || ⟨mar⟩ ~ voraus *right ahead* **C.** nun **erst** ~! *now more than ever, now all the more* (*so*) || gerade ~ *pat* (f *to*), *just in time* (*for*) || **so** ~ in s–m Element *just in his e.* || so ~ (als ob *or*) wie wenn *just* od *quite as if* **R·echt- ~eck** n *rectangle, oblong* °~**eckig** a *rectangular, oblong*; *flat* (*wire*); ~ beschneiden ⟨phot⟩ *to trim .. square* °~**fertigen** vt [h] *to justify, excuse, warrant, exculpate* || *to defend, vindicate* | **sich** ~ *to clear, exculpate o.s.*; ⟨jur⟩ *to plead* || nicht zu ~ *unjustifiable, indefensible* || sich vor jdm ~ *to put o.s. right with a p* || sich ~d *apologetic* **~fertigung** f *justification, exculpation, vindication* || e–e ~ finden f etw vor jdm *to justify a th to a p* || zu m–r ~ *in justification of* od *in justice to m.s., in my defence* || er kann nichts z s–r ~ vorbringen *he has nothing to say for h.s.* | ~sschrift [f] *apology* °~**gläubig** a *orthodox*; ~e(r) [m] *true believer* | ~keit [f] *orthodoxy* **~-haber** m *dogmatic p* od *arguer*, (*self-willed*) *dogmatist* | ~·ei [f] *dogmaticalness, obstinacy*; °~-isch [a] *dogmatic, obstinate, captious, positive, quarrelsome, cantankerous*; *self-assertive*; *arrogant*; *argumentative* (*retort*) °~**läufig** a ⟨astr⟩ *of normal course* **~lautung** f *orthoepy* °~**liebend** a *fair-minded* °~**linig** a *rectilinear* °~**los** a *illegal, unlawful*; (vogelfrei) *lawless, outlawed*; ein ~er *an outlaw* **~losigkeit** f *illegality* || *lawlessness* || *outlawry* °~**mäßig** a *lawful, legitimate, legal*; *rightful* (*heir, owner*) | [adv] *of right* | ~keit [f] *lawfulness, legitimacy, legality* °~**schaffen** a *upright, honest*; ⟨bes rel⟩ *righteous, straight*; sich ~ halten *to keep straight* (*as a die*) | etw °~es lernen *to learn some honest trade* | [adv] *righteously* || (tüchtig) *thoroughly, downright* || ~ müde *worn out, dead-tired* || ~ dumm, hungrig *awfully stupid, hungry* || sich ~ freuen *to take great pleasure* (über *in*) || sich ~ plagen *to work hard* | ~heit [f] *uprightness, honesty, righteousness, probity, integrity* **~schreibung** f *orthography*; (er ist) in ~ gut .. *a good speller* °~**sprechend** a *judicial* **~sprechung** f ⟨jur⟩ *jurisdiction, administration of justice*, ⟨Am⟩ *judiciary* °~**weisend** a: ~er Kartenkurs ⟨mar⟩ *true track*; ~e Peilung *true bearing*; ~er Wind *true course* °~**wink(e)lig** a *rectangular* || ~es Dreieck *right-angled triangle* || ~ zu *square to, at right angles to*; (*branching*) *at r. angle* °~**zeitig** [a] *opportune, timely, well-timed, seasonable*; ~e Geburt *confinement* od *delivery at term* | [adv] *in* (*good*) *time, at the right time*; (*to announce*) *sufficiently early*; ⟨com⟩ *in due course, duly* || ~ geborenes Kind *birth at term, full term b.* || ~ bevor .. *well before* .. **~zeitigkeit** f *opportuneness* || ⟨rail⟩ *punctuality*

R·echte m, f, n ~n/~n **I. 1.** der ~ (= der rechte Mann) *the right* od *very man, the right one* || du bist mir der ~ *or* ein ~r! ⟨iron⟩ *you are a nice one, you are a pretty sort of fellow, indeed*! || an den ~n geraten *or* k *to meet one's match*; ⟨iron⟩ *to come to the wrong shop* **2.** ⟨math⟩ *right angle* **3.** ⟨box⟩ *right-hander* **II.** die ~ **1.** (= Hand) *right hand* || zu m–r (s–r) ~n *at* od *on my right hand* (*on the right of him*) || sein Nachbar zur ~n *his n. on the right, his right-hand n.* **2.** ⟨pol⟩ *the Right, the Conservative side* || auf der äußersten ~n *on the extreme R.* **III.** das ~ *the right th* || das ~ treffen *to hit the mark* || etw (nichts) ~s (= Gehöriges) *sth* (*nothing*) *to be proud of*, (*nothing worth mentioning*) || er hat etw ~s gelernt, er kann etw ~s *he possesses sound knowledge, he understands his job* || ⟨iron⟩ das ist mir (auch) was ~s! *is that all*?, *aren't you proud of it now*!, *that won't help us, I'm afraid*!, *that's a fine go*! || er dünkt sich etw ~s *he thinks h.s. somebody* | nach dem *or* zum ~n sehen *to see* od *attend to a th*; *to see that everything is* (*going*) *well*; *to see fair-play*; *to put ths right* **r·echten** vi [h] *to dispute, argue* (über *about*); *to haggle* (*over*) || ⟨jur⟩ *to plead* **R·echtens** [gen] v Recht C. **r·echtlich** a **1.** *legal, lawful, legitimate, valid* || ⟨jur⟩ *judicial, juridical* || ~er Beistand [abstr] *legal aid*; (P) *counsel* **2.** (redlich) *honest, righteous* | °~**keit** f *legality, lawfulness* || ⟨jur⟩ *judicialness* || *validity* || *honesty, rectitude*

rechts I. [adv] *to the right* (*hand*), *at the r. h., on the r.* || ~ fahren *to drive on the r. side*; „~ vor links" ⟨m. m.⟩ *r.-hand car gives way to left-h. car* || ⟨theat⟩ *opposite prompt side*, ⟨Am⟩ *stage r.* || ~ v ihnen steht N. *to the r. of them is N.* || sich ~ halten *to keep to the r.* || das Bild ~ unten .. *at the lower r.* || gleich ~ um die Ecke *the first turning to the r.* || (linksfahrend) *offside* .. || nach ~ *to the right* || nach ~ u links (*he struck*) *r. and left*; (*not to look*) *to r. or l.* || ⟨pol⟩ ~ stehen *to be a conservative* | ⟨mil⟩ Augen ~! *eyes right*! || Gewehr ~! *trail arms*! || ~ um! *r. turn* od *face* || ~ schwenkt marsch! *r. wheel*! || v ~ (z vieren) abzählen *from the r., number*! (.. *tell off by fours*!);

nach ~ anschließen *close up on the r.* **II.** prep [gen] ~ des Rheins *on the r. bank of the Rhine* || ~ v Eingang *to the r. of ..* **Rechts-** [[1] gen v Recht ⟨oft⟩ *legal* (*l.l*), *lawyer* (*l.r*)] [[2] adv ⟨mst⟩ *right* (*r.*)] [1]**~abtretung** f ⟨jur⟩ *cession, assignment* **~-altertümer** n pl *l.l* (od *law-*)*antiquities* pl **~änderung** f *change of title* **≈anhängig** a *pending at law* **~anspruch** m *legitimate claim, demand*; *title* ⟨a. ins⟩ (auf *to*) **~anwalt** m *attorney, l.r, solicitor*; ⟨Am⟩ *attorney and counsellor-at-law*; ⟨Scot⟩ *advocate* || ⟨engl⟩ (plädierender) *barrister*(*-at-law*); als solcher zugelassen w *to be called to the bar* | ~gebühren [f pl] *l.r's fees*; ~schaft f **1.** *l. profession* **2.** *solicitorship* **3.** ⟨engl⟩ *the Bar* [2]**~·außen(stürmer)** m ⟨ftb⟩ *outside r.* [1]**~beflissene(r)** m *law-student, l.r* **~befugnis** f *competence* **~behelf** m *benefice of the law* **~beistand** m [abstr] *l.l assistance* || (P) *counsel, l.l adviser* **~belehrung** f *l.l information, summing-up*; (der Geschworenen) *charge* **~berater** m *l.r* (e–r Firma *to a firm*), *judicial adviser*; obskurer ~ ⟨Am fam⟩ *John Law* **~beratung** f *l.l advice* **~bestand** m *validity* **≈beständig** a *valid* **~beugung** f ⟨jur⟩ *miscarriage of justice*, → Recht E. [2]**~bewegung** f ⟨mil⟩ *movement to the r.* [1]**~brecher** m *criminal* [2]**~drall** m ⟨mil, tech⟩ *r.-hand twist* **≈drehend** a *dextrogyrate, -rous* **~drehung** f *clockwise rotation* [1]**~eingriff** m *encroachment upon a p's rights* **~einwand** m ⟨jur⟩ *demurrer* || ~ erheben ⟨jur⟩ *to traverse, demur* **~einwendung** f *plea of confession and avoidance* **~entziehung** f *depravation of r.* **≈erfahren** a *versed in law* **~erheblich** a *ultimate* (*facts*) **~erlöschung** f *extinction of r.* **≈fähig** a *competent*; *incorporated* (*company*); ⟨jur⟩ *personable* **~fall** m *case in law*; *suit*; (vorliegend) *c. at bar* **~folger** m *sucessor in business* **~form** f *form of law* **≈förmig** a *juridical, legal, in due form* **~frage** f *law-question, issue of law* **~-friede** m *peace based on justice* **~gang** m *proceedings at law, legal proceeding* od *procedure, lawsuit* **≈gängig** a (im Uhrzeigersinn) *clockwise* **~gefühl** m *sense of justice* **~gelehrsamkeit** f *jurisprudence* **≈gelehrt** a *learned in the law* **~gelehrte(r)** m *jurist, l.r* [2]**≈gerichtet** a ⟨pol⟩ *r.ist* [attr] (Kreise) [1]**~geschäft** n *law-business* [2]**~gewinde** n *r.-hand thread* [1]**~gleichheit** f *equality of law* **~grund** m *l.l ground* od *argument* **≈gültig** a *valid* od *good in law, l.l*; *regular* (*marriage*); für ~ erklären *to validate* | ~keit [f] *l.l force*; *l.lity, lawfulness, validity* **~gutachten** n *Counsel's opinion* **~handel** m *lawsuit, action, case* [2]**~händigkeit** f *ri.-handedness* [1]**≈hängig** a *pending* [2]**≈herum** [adv] *clockwise* [1]**~hilfe** f *l.l aid* od *redress*; ~ nachsuchen *to pray* (*in*) *aid* | ~ersuchen [n] *letters rogatory*; ~verkehr mit dem Ausland in Strafsachen *International L.l Aid in connection with punishable acts* **~irrtum** m *mistake in law* **~kniff** m *chicane, l.r's trick* **~kollege** m *coworker in the law* **~konsulent** m *l.l adviser* **~kraft** f (*res judicata*); *l.l validity* od *force*; ohne ~ *obsolete* || [dat] ~ erteilen *to make valid* **≈kräftig** a *l.l, valid*; ~ w *to become final* **≈kundig** a = ≈gelehrt [2]**~kurve** f *r.-hand curve* od *turn* **≈läufig** a *r.-h.ed* (Gewinde) [1]**~lehre** f *jurisprudence, l.l science* **~lehrer** m *professor of law* [2]**~lenkung** ⟨mot⟩ *r.-h. drive* [1]**~mangel** m *infirmity of title* **~mißbrauch** m *abuse of r.s* **~mittel** n *l.l* od *review remedy* od *measure*; e–m ~ stattgeben *to uphold an appeal* | ~frist [f] *time for a.*; die ~ ist abgelaufen *the a. has elapsed* **~nachfolger** m ⟨jur⟩ *assignee* **~nachteil** m *prejudice* **~ordnung** f *law* **~-person** f *body corporate* **~pflege** f *administration of justice* [2]**≈radikal** a, **≈e** m [der ~, ein ~r] *r.ist* [1]**~regel** f *l.l rule* **~sache** f *law-suit* **~satz** m (*thesis in*) *law, l.l axiom* **~schule** f *law-school*; → *inn* **~schutz** m *l.l protection* **~sitz** m *l.l domocile* **~sprache** f *l.l terminology* **~spruch** m *l.l decision* || (im Zivilprozeß) *judgement* || (im Strafprozeß) *sentence, verdict* **~staat** m *state in which the rule of law* (*is observed* od) *prevails*; *civilized* od *lawful st.*; ⟨Can⟩ *government based upon the rule of law* | ≈lich [a] *lawful-st.* [attr] || ≈lichkeit [f] *principles of a law-adhering st.* **~stellung** f *l.l status* **~streit** m *litigation, l.l contest,* (*law*)*suit, action* **~system** n *l.l system* **~titel** m *title* (auf Grund v Intestaterbfolge *by descent*) | ~urkunde [f] *t. certificate*; ~versicherungsschein [m] *t. policy* [2]**≈um** [adv] *r.-about*; ~ kehrt *r.-about face*!; ~ marsch! *r. turn quick march* | [1]Beseitigung der **~ungleichheit** f *introduction of uniform laws* **≈ungültig** a *void, illegal, invalid* **≈unwirksam** a *without l.l force* **~urkunde** f *l.l document* **~verdreher** m *pettifogger, chicaner* **~verdrehung** f *pettifogging, l.l quibble* || *l.l trickery, chicanery* **~verfahren** n *judicial proceeding, l.l procedure* **~verfassung** f *judicature* **~verhandlung** f *l.l* od *judicial proceedings* pl **~verletzung** f *infringer* | (absolute) **~vernutung** (*ir*)*rebuttable presumption* **≈verständig** a *skilled in law* **~verständige** m [der ~, ein ~r] *jurist, l.l authority* **~vertreter** m *proxy* **~verweser** m *administrator of justice* **~vorschrift** f *law* **~wahrer** m (Richter, Staats-, Rechtsanwalt etc) *l.er*; die ~ [pl] *judiciary*, ⟨engl a.⟩ *the Bar* **~weg** m *course of law* || unter Ausschluß des ~s *admitting of no appeal* || auf dem ordentlichen ~e *in due course of law* || den ~ beschreiten *to go to law, to take l.l measures* od *steps* **≈wegen** → Recht F. **~wesen** n *judicature, jurisdiction*; *judiciary* **≈widrig** a *contrary to law, against the law*; *illegal* | ~keit [f] *illegality* **~-wirksamkeit** f *l.l effect* **~wirkung** f *l.l effect* **~wissenschaft** f *law*; *l.l science, jurisprudence*, Student der ~ *student of law* | ≈lich [a] *jurisprudential, juridicial* **~wohltat** f *benefit of law, legal remedy* **~zuständigkeit** f *competence* **~-zwang** m *l.l compulsion*

R·ecke m ~n/~n *hero*; *valiant warrior, knight at arms* || *vassal, retainer, thane*; → rächen

Reck n ~(e)s/~e ⟨gym⟩ *horizontal bar* || ~turner [m] *gymnast on the h. b.* **r·ecken** vt [h] *to extend* (*one's hand*) || *to stretch* (*leather, one's limbs*) || *to crane* (*one's neck*), *to raise* od *toss* (*one's head*) || ⟨met⟩ *to rack, draw* || ⟨fig⟩ *to rise* || in die Höhe ~ *to lift up, to point .. into the air* || **sich** ~ *to stretch* od *straighten o.s., to give a stretch* || sich auf die Fußspitzen ~ *to strain on tiptoe*

Redakteur [–'tø:r] m ~s/~e *editor* || Haupt≈ *managing e.*; zweiter ~ *sub-e.*, ⟨Am⟩ *copy--reader* || ~ f Nachrichten *news e.*; ~ f Wirtschaftsnachrichten *city e.*, ⟨Am⟩ *financial e.*; ~ des Finanz- u Handelsteils ⟨engl⟩ *city e.*; des Unterhaltungsteils *features e.* **Redakti·on** f ~/~en (Tätigkeit) *editing, editorship* || (Büro) *editor's office* || (Personal) (*editorial*) *staff* || (Fassung, *wording, draft*(*ing*) | ≈·**ell** a *editorial* (Text *matter*)

R·ede f ~/~n **A. 1.** *speech* (*sp.*) (an *to*) [Teile der ~ → speech]; programmatische ~ *keynote sp.* od *address* || (künstlerische *or* ⟨fig⟩ lange) *oration*; langatmige ~ *screed* || (Vortrag) *sp.* || (Ansprache) *address*, ⟨ec⟩ *allocution*; ~ u Gegen≈ *address and rejoinder* || ⟨school, univ⟩ Abgangs≈ *valedictory* **2.** (~weise) *language* (*l.e*) **3.** (Gespräch) *discourse, talk, conversation* (*c.n*) **4.** (Gerücht) *rumour* **5.** (Rechenschaft) *account* **B. alltägliche ~** *common parlance* (in der gewöhnlichen ~ *in c. p.*) || ⟨gram⟩ (in)direkte ~ (*in*)*direct l.e*; halbdirekte, verschleierte, **erlebte** ~ *represented sp.* (Jespersen), *inward* od *silent monologue* (Bühler), *semi-direct sp.* (Spitzer) || ⟨parl, etc⟩ erste ~ *maiden-sp.* || fließende ~ *eloquent address* || **gebundene** ~ *poetry, verse* || gehobene ~ *lofty l.e, elevated* bzw *poetic style* || hochtrabende ~ *grandiloquent address* || sich in langen ~ ergehend *expatiatory*; der langen ~ kurzer Sinn *the long and the short of it* (*is*) || leere

~n hollow phrases, empty words || lose ~n führen to engage in loose talk || schwülstige ~n big talk, bombastic sentences || ungebundene ~ prose C. jdm die ~ abschneiden to cut a p short || die ~ fiel auf = kam auf || die ~ bringen auf .. to bring the conversation round to .. || die ~ geht, daß .. people od they say, it is (being) reported, said, rumoured that .. || e–e ~ halten to make a sp., to deliver an address, a discourse || ~n halten ⟨a.⟩ to hold forth (über about, on); gr ~n halten to talk big (über of); lange ~n halten ⟨fam⟩ to orate || die ~ kam auf .. the c.n turned on .. | sein: das war immer m–e ~ that's what I have always said || es ist die ~ v .. somebody, sth is the subject of the c.n; es war v ihm die ~ his name came up; es ist oft die ~ davon it is often mentioned; .. in den Zeitungen viel die ~ davon gewesen there has been a good deal about it in the papers || es ist die ~ davon zu tun there is talk of doing || es war die ~ v s–n Abenteuern it was the question of .. | v ihm ist in den Zeitungen viel die ~ gewesen he has been in the news | wovon ist die ~? what are you talking about?; what is the point in qu.?; .. in dem Abschnitt what is the subject of the paragraph? | davon kann k–e (or nicht die) ~ s that's out of the qu. || davon ist nicht die ~ that is not the qu. || v e–m Mord konnte gar nicht die ~ s there could be no qu. of m. | nicht der ~ wert negligible; .. ! not worth speaking of od mentioning, (don't mention it!) | e–m ~ (u Antwort) stehen to give a p an account (über of), to (have to) answer to a p for .. || jds ~ unterbrechen to interrupt a p in his sp. || vergiß d–e ~ nicht! don't forget what you were going to say D. sich nicht an die ~e der Leute kehren to pay no regard to what people say | nichts auf die ~n der Leute geben not to listen to idle rumours, not to go by talk | bei s–r ~ bleiben to stick to one's opinion | jdm in die ~ fallen to interrupt a p || die in ~ stehende P the p in qu. || in e–r ~ stecken bleiben to get stuck in the middle of a sp. | nach s–n ~n according to what he says | jdn zur ~ k l to let a p speak || zur ~ stellen to take to task (über for), to call to account (for; with regard to), ⟨fam⟩ to have it out with (a p) ~begabt a eloquent ~bild n figure of sp. ~blüte, ~figur, ~floskel, ~form f form of sp. ~erguß m, ~strom m tirade, rant, verbosity ~fluß m (her easy) flow of talk, sp., words; volubility (über about); (plötzlicher) torrent, burst of eloquence ~freiheit f liberty of sp. ~gabe f gift of sp.; eloquence ~gewandt a eloquent; ⟨dero⟩ voluble; ~ s to be a good speaker | ~heit [f] eloquence; fluency; command of language ~kunst f rhetoric ~künstler m orator, rh.cian ~lustig a talkative, loquacious ~scheu a shy of speaking, silent from shyness ~schmuck m ornament of style ~schwall m flood of words; rant, loquacity, verbosity ~schwulst f grandiloquence, bombast ~sucht f overtalkativeness, logomania ~teil m ⟨gram⟩ part of speech ~ton m rh.cal accent ~übung f exercise in speaking od declamation od debating ~weise f diction, parlance; mode of speech ~wendung f phrase; figure of sp., turn of expression r·eden I. vt/i [h] A. 1. to speak (sp.), talk (mit to; von of) || was ~ Sie da? what are you talking about?; ~ Sie doch nicht! come now! || to converse (with); (plaudern) to chat (with) || °~ wie ein Wasserfall to talk nineteen to the dozen, ⟨Am⟩ to talk a blue streak 2. to discourse (über of, upon) 3. ⟨jur⟩ to plead B. °Blech, Kohl etc ~ to talk rubbish, etc || Gutes (Schlechtes) v jdm ~ to speak well (evil) of a p || ein langes u breites über etw ~ to discuss a th at great length || k–e Silbe ~ to speak not a word || tot u wieder lebendig ~ to talk (a p) deaf, dumb, and blind || die Leute ~ viel people will talk || sehr or zu viel ~ to have a long tongue || (jdm, e–r S) das Wort ~ to defend, recommend; to take (a p's) side od part || ein Wörtchen mit jdm ~ to take a p to task (wegen for) C. sich heiser ~ to talk o.s. hoarse || sich in Wut ~ .. into a rage || sich um Hals u Kopf ~ to talk away one's life | sich [dat] den Mund fusselig ~ to talk one's head off || sich e–n Prozeß an den Hals ~ to bring a law-suit upon o.s. by one's talk D. mit jdm z ~ h to have sth to say to a p || Sie h gut or leicht ~! it's easy for you to say that od to talk; talk is cheap! || er konnte nie besonders ~ he was never much at talking || laß die Leute nur ~! let them od people talk! || mit sich ~ l to listen (od to be amenable) to reason, to be open to conviction || darüber läßt sich ~ we shall be able to come to an understanding about it || v sich ~ m to make o.s. notorious, to cause a great stir; to be in the news; ⟨fam⟩ to cut a dash od figure; viel .. ⟨oft dero⟩ to give rise to much comment; du weißt nicht, was du redest ⟨Am sl⟩ where do you get that stuff? E. jetzt redet er ganz anders! he talks in quite a different tone now || mit jdm deutsch ~ to talk plainly with a p || eintönig ~ to drone || fesselnd ~ ⟨Am pol⟩ to spellbind || gut (schlecht) v jdm ~ to speak well (evil) of a p || gut → D. || hochtrabend ~ to rant || klug ~ to play the wiseacre || offen ~ to speak openly, to be outspoken || nicht offen ~ to sp. with one's tongue in one's cheek || öffentlich ~ to sp. in public, ⟨fam⟩ to spout (über about) || rasch u munter ~ to rattle (off, out, over, away) || schwärmend ~ to rave || überschwenglich ~ to gush over || unsinnig ~ to talk wild || unverständlich ~ to babble || unzus–hängend ~ to ramble || weise ~ to talk wisdom || weiter ~ to go on (talking), (do go on!) || wie ein Buch, wie gedruckt ~ to sp. like a book || wie geschmiert ~ können to have a smooth od glib tongue F. jdm etw aus dem Sinn ~ to talk a p out of a th || aus ihm redet der Wahnsinn his is the language of madness | in einem fort ~ to talk voluble || in Gemeinplätzen ~ to use commonplace expressions || jdm ins Gewissen ~ to appeal to a p's conscience || in den Tag hinein ~ to talk at random || (etw) in den Wind ~ to preach to deaf ears || in Wortspielen ~ to play (up)on words | um mit dem Dichter zu ~ to use the words of the poet || mit den Händen ~ to gesticulate | jdm nach dem Munde ~ to humour a p, to chime in with a p | über (etw, jdn) ~ to discuss, (etw ausplaudern) ⟨sl⟩ to split about || über Politik ~ to talk politics | von → A. 1. || v etw anderem ~ to change the subject || v s–m Geschäft, Fach ~ ⟨fam⟩ to talk shop || es wurde davon geredet there was some talk of it; das ganze Dorf redete davon it was the talk of the whole village || wir ~ besser nicht davon we better keep it to ourselves || ~ wir nicht mehr davon forget it, will you! | jdm zu Gefallen ~ to talk to please a p || zur Menge ~ to harangue the mob II. ~ n speaking, talking etc.; speech, talk || → kläffen || das ~ fällt ihr schwer she speaks with difficulty || sie überließ ihm das ~ she left him to do the talking || all sein ~ war umsonst he was wasting his words || das viele ~ macht den Kopf warm so much talking provokes one || (nicht) viel ~s v etw m to make a great fuss about a th, (not) to attach much importance to a th || ⟨prov⟩ ~ ist Silber, Schweigen ist Gold speech is silver, silence is golden III. ~d a 1. speaking etc || ~de P speaker, interlocutor || ⟨her⟩ canting (arms) 2. (S) ~de Beweise, Gebärden, Zeugnisse speaking proofs, significant gestures, convincing evidence || (ausdrucksvoll) expressive || ~de Künste rhetorical arts; poetry, eloquence, and music R·edensart f A. phrase, expression, locution || (Spracheigenart) idiom || (sprichwörtliche) saying B. abgedroschene ~en well-worn phrases || eigentümliche ~ peculiar od idiomatic phrase || derbe ~ coarse, crude expression || e–e gewöhnliche, alltägliche ~ a common expression || feste ~ stock phrase; tag || geläufige ~ familiar term ||

höfliche ~en *compliments* || nur k–e ~en! *no ceremony, no fuss, please!* || e–e bloße ~ *a formula* || k–e bloße ~ *no mere figure of speech* || ein paar nichtssagende ~en *a few nothings* || das sind nur so ~en *these are but empty phrases, that's merely a polite way of putting it* || jds ständige ~ *a p's refrain* **C.** lange ~en m *to spin a long yarn* || jdn mit ~en abspeisen *to put a p off with fine phrases* || °jdn mit ~en besoffen m *to overwhelm a p with words* || → sich bewegen **Reder·ei** f ~/~en *empty talk, nonsense; oratorical drivel* °**Rede·r·itis** f ~/ *verbiage* **r·edlich** [a] *honest, upright* (*man*); *sincere, honourable* (*confession*); *candid* (*efforts*) | [adv] ⟨fam⟩ *on the square*; ~ handeln *to play it straight*; er meint es ~ *he means well* || sich ~ mühen *to take great pains* | ≈**keit** f ~/ *honesty, probity, integrity* || *uprightness* || *frankness* || *candour* || *sincerity*; *truth* **R·edner** m ~s/~ *speaker, orator* || ⟨ec⟩ *preacher*, ⟨dero⟩ *ranter* || ⟨pol a.⟩ *platform-speaker*; (faszinierender) ⟨Am⟩ *spellbinder*; ein gewandter ~ s *to have a ready tongue* **~bühne** f *platform, tribune*; ⟨Am⟩ (auf Straßen) ⟨a.⟩ *soap-box* (dazu: *to soap-box*) **~gabe** f *eloquence, gift of speech* **~künste** f pl *tricks* pl *of oratory* **~stuhl** m *chair* **~talent** n *oratorical gift* od *power* **~ton** m *oratorical tone* **R·ednerin** f ~/~nen *speaker, oratress* **r·ednerisch** [a] *oratorical, rhetorical, elocutionary* || ~e Darstellung *elocution* || [adv] ~ vollendet *eloquent* (*address*) **r·edselig** a *talkative, loquacious*; *non-reticent*; *chatty*; ⟨Am, sl⟩ *gabby*; nicht ~ *not given to speech*; *silent* || ~e P *copious* od *great talker* ≈**keit** f *talkativeness, loquacity, chattiness*

redig·ieren vt [h] *to edit* (*a newspaper, etc*)

R·edisfeder® f *script pen*

Redoute [re'du:tə] f ~/~n (Schanze) *redoubt* || (Maskenball) *masquerade*

Red·oxpotential n ⟨chem⟩ *oxidation-reduction potential*

Redukti·on [ts] f ~/~en ⟨math, chem, met⟩ *reduction*; ~en [pl] *cut-backs* (*in production*) **~stabelle** f *table of reductions* **~steilung** f (Meiose) ⟨biol⟩ *reduction division* **~szirkel** m *proportional compasses* pl **Reduz·ier-** ~anlage [f] ⟨phot⟩ *adapter*; ~stück [n] (Rohr≈) *reducing fitting* **reduz·ieren** vt [h] (auf [acc]) *to reduce* (*to*) || *to cut back* || *to limit* (*a number*) | **sich** ~ *to diminish, decrease* | ⟨fig⟩ (P) reduziert *shabby*

Redund·anz f ~/ *redundancy* ⟨a. comp⟩

R·eede f ~/~n *road*(*s* pl), *road-stead* || auf (der) ~ liegen *to lie in the ..* || vor der ~ kreuzen *to cruise in the ..* **R·eeder** m ~s/~ *shipowner* **Reeder·ei** f ~/~en *shipping-business, shipping* (*-trade*); ~ betreiben *to be in the sh.-tr.* || (Tätigkeit) *equipment, fitting-out* (*of ships*) || (Firma) *shipowner's firm, shipping company* od *line* **~betrieb** m *shipping-trade* **~flagge** f *house-flag*

Reef n ~(e)s/~e ⟨mar⟩ *reef* | ~bändsel [n] *r. point*; ~leine [f] *r. line*; ~talje [f] *r. tackle* **r·eefen** vt [h] *to reef*

re·ell I. [a] (zuverlässig) *respectable, honest, reliable* || (Gewinn) *clear, solid* || (Firma) *sound, solid*; ~er Kaufmann ⟨Am fam⟩ *square shooter*; (Preis, Bedienung etc) *fair* || (Ware) *good, sound* || (Offerte) *bona fide, real* | [adv] ~ bedient w *to get* (*fair dealing* od) *good value for one's money* **II.** **etw** ≈**es** *sth genuine* ≈**it·ät** f ~/ *respectability, honesty* || *soundness, solidity* || *fairness* || *soundness, good quality* || *bona fides*

Reep n ~(e)s/~e *rope* | **~erbahn** f *rope-walk*

Refa-Mann m (→ Abk.) *efficiency expert*

Ref·aktie f ~/ ⟨com⟩ *abatement, reduction* || *breakage* **refakt·ieren** vt [h] *to abate, deduct* **Refekt·orium** n ~s/–rien *refectory*

Refer- **~·at** n ~(e)s/~e *report* || ⟨univ⟩ *paper* (*to be read*), kurzes ~ *lecturette* || *review* (*of a book*) **~end·ar** m ~(e)s/~e (*law* od *teacher graduate in his first year*(*s*) *of practical training*) ⟨jur⟩ *junior barrister*, ⟨school⟩ *junior teacher* **~·endum** n ~s/ *plebiscite* || ⟨dipl⟩ *referendum* **~·ent** m ~en/~en *reporter, speaker, referee, official adviser*; (*personal*) *assistant*; *head of sub-department* || (Kritiker) *reviewer* || ⟨univ⟩ *student reading his paper* **~·renz** f ~/~en *reference* || *information* ≈**·ieren** vt [h] *to report* || *to read a paper*

Reff n ~(e)s/~e **1.** (Tragkorb) *dorser, dosser* **2.** ⟨mar⟩ *reef* || ⟨fig⟩ altes ~ (*old*) *hag* | ≈**en** vt [h] ⟨mar⟩ *to reef*; → reefen

Refl- ≈**ekt·ieren 1.** vt [h] ⟨opt, etc⟩ *to reflect* **2.** vi [h] ⟨com⟩ (auf [acc]) *to intend to purchase, to think of buying, to have* (*a th*) *in view* || *to have in mind*; *to reflect* (über *upon*) || [abs] *to turn ths over in one's mind* **~ekt·ant** m ~en/~en *intending purchaser*, ⟨Am⟩ *prospect* || *inquirer, applicant* **~·ektor** m ~s/–·oren *reflector* **~·ex** m ~es/~e *reflexion*; ⟨physiol⟩ angeborener ~ *unconditioned reflex* | ~bewegung [f] ⟨phys⟩ *reflex action*; ~empfänger [m] ⟨wir⟩ *r.x receiver*; ~kette [f] ⟨eth⟩ *r.x chain*; ~visier [n] *reflex sight* **~exi·on** f ~/~en *reflection, reflex*; ⟨bes wir⟩ *re-radiation* | ~sfaktor [m] *standing wave ratio* N; ~sgitter [n] ⟨op⟩ *grating*; ~swinkel [m] *angle of reflection* ≈**ex·iv** a *reflexive* (*pronoun*) | ≈um [n] ~s/–va *reflexive pronoun*

Ref·orm f ~/~en *reform* | ~bestrebungen [f pl] *reformatory efforts* pl; ~haus [n] *diet* od *health shop* (⟨Am⟩ *.. store*); ~hose [f] *bloomers* pl; ~kleidung [f] (*lady's*) *rational dress, rationals* pl; ~partei [f] *party of reformers* **~ati·on** f ~/~en ⟨a. ec⟩ *reformation*; ~ an Haupt u Gliedern *radical r.* | ~sfest [n] ⟨ec⟩ *celebration of the R.*; ~szeit [f] *time of the R.* **~·ator** m ~s/–at·oren *reformer* ≈**·ieren** vt [h] *to reform* **~·ierte** m [der ~, ein ~r] ~n/~n ⟨ec⟩ *member of the Reformed Church, Calvinist*

Refrain [re'frɛ̃] m ~s/~s *refrain, burden*, ⟨fam⟩ *chorus* **Refr·aktor** m ~s/–t·oren ⟨phys⟩ *refractor, refracting telescope*; → Fragment

Reg·al n ~(e)s/~e **1.** (Büchergestell) *shelf, shelves* pl || (f Briefe) *pigeon-holes* pl || ⟨typ⟩ *frame*, ⟨Am⟩ *stand* | (Hoheitsrecht) *royal prerogative, royalty* **2.** **~ien** pl ⟨hist, jur⟩ *regalia* L

regal·ieren vt [h] *to regale, entertain*; *to treat* (mit *to*) || sich ~ *to feast* (an *on*)

Reg·atta f ~/–ten *regatta, boat-race* || (Segel≈) *sailing* (= *yacht*) *race*; → **Regal** 1. [It riga], Reihe

r·ege a *stirring, astir, stirred up, intense, alert* || (tätig) *industrious*; *vigorous* (*activity*); *active*(*-minded*) (*nation*) || *active keen* (*mind*) || *quick* (*imagination*) || *brisk* (*business, demand*) || *animated traffic*) || *lively* (*p*) || *nimble* (*mind, hands*) || *vigilant* (*care*) | ~ m *to stir up, to excite, rouse, incite* | ~ s *to be up and doing* | ~ w *to be stirred up, to become awake* od *alive*; Zweifel wurde ~ *doubt has arisen* || in uns wurde der Wunsch ~ *we were seized with a desire* (*to do*); → regen

R·egel f ~/~n *rule* (⟨gram⟩, *of poetry, games, society*) || (Grundsatz) *principle* || allgemeine ~ *universal rule*; feste ~ *code*; *definite* od *set rule*; nicht d. herkömmlichen ~n entsprechend *unorthodox*; strikte ~ *hard and fast rule*; unfehlbare ~ *unvarying rule*; k–e ~ ohne Ausnahme *no rule without exception* || (Vorschrift) *regulation, precept* | ⟨physiol⟩ *menstruation, menses* pl | an → gebunden | **in** der ~ *as a rule, in general, usually* | ⟨fig⟩ **nach** allen ~n der Kunst *very effectually*, ⟨sl⟩ *up hill and down dale*, (*to beat a p*) *hollow* || ~n aufstellen *to lay down, make rules*; beachten, befolgen *to obey, observe* | (etw) zur ~ m, z ~ w l *to make a routine of*; die ~ s *to be r.* (etw) wird zur ~ *is becoming a* **r**egula**r** *custom* ⟨oft⟩ *standard* (*st.*) (*metal*) **~anlasser** m ⟨el mot⟩ *adjusting starter* **~bar** a *adjustable*; *controllable*; *variable* **~bau** m *st. design* **~detr·i** f

~/ *rule of three* **~getriebe** n *variable speed transmission* **~kompaß** m *st. compass* **≈los** a *irr.r, lawless, without rule*; ~e Flucht [f] *rout* **~losigkeit** f *irr.rity* **≈mäßig** a *r.r* (*publication; features, verbs*), *well regulated* (*system*) || *r.rly shaped* (*figure*) | *orderly* (*mode of life*) | [adv] *always, generally* || ~ jeden Morgen *each and every morning* **~mäßigkeit** f *r.rity, orderliness* ⟨Am a.⟩ *normality* **~motor** m *adjusting-speed motor* **≈recht** a *r.r, correct, consistent, methodical* (*investigation*) || *downright, unqualified* (*liar*) | adv ⟨a.⟩ *duly*; ~ verlaufen *to run true to form* **~ventil** n *control* od *throttle valve* **~widerstand** m ⟨el⟩ *rheostat* **≈widrig** a *contrary to rule, irr.ar, abnormal* || ⟨sport⟩ *foul* **~widrigkeit** f *irr.rity, abnormality*; ⟨sport⟩ *foulness* **r·egeln** vt [h] *to regulate* (*the traffic*) || *to control, manage* || (gesetzlich) *to regularize* || (bestimmen) *to arrange* (*things*) || (ordnen) *to put* (*one's affairs*) *in order*; *to wind up* (*one's a.s*) || *to adjust* (*a torpedo, one's finances*) || *to settle* (*the spelling*) || ich werde das mit ihm ~ *I'll arrange that with him* || **sich** ~ nach *to be ruled by* | **ge-lt** (*well*) *r.d* (*circumstances*) || *systematical, systematized* (*work*) || *orderly* (*life*) **R·egelung** f ~/~en *regulation, ordering, adjustment* | ⟨mach⟩ *control* || *settlement, arrangement*, || einstweilige ~ *interim*; eindeutige ~ ⟨a.⟩ *unequivocal designation*; gesetzliche ~ *regularization* | ~stechnik f (*automatic*) *control, c. engineering*; → Reglung

r·egen vt [h] (→ rege) *to stir, rouse, move, agitate* || *to beat* (*its wings*) || die Hände ~ *to get a move on* || sie regte k–n Finger *she didn't stir a f.*; kein Glied ~ können *to be unable to move a f.* | **sich** ~ [h] *to stir, quicken, move*; *to be stirring, alive, active, astir, moving*; *to bestir o.s.*; *to show activity*; ⟨fam⟩ *to stir one's stumps* | (S) *to be afoot* || (Herz) *to beat* || (Wind) *to be astir* || (Gefühl) *to spring up, to be roused* || ⟨fig⟩ er hat sich nicht geregt (hat nicht geschrieben, bezahlt) *he has not made a move of any sort*

R·egen m ~s/~ *rain* (*r.*) (anhaltender *steady*, leichter *light*, starker *heavy r.*) || strichweise ~ *r. in places*; zeitweise ~ *r. at times* || kurzer ~ *a short spell of r.* || strömender ~ *a regular downpour* | künstlicher ~ *cloud seeding* | der ~ prasselt, pladdert, rauscht .. *patters down* || der ~ läßt nach *it stops r.ing* || ob ~ oder Sonnenschein *wet or fine* | ⟨prov a. fig⟩ auf ~ folgt Sonnenschein *every cloud has its silver lining*; *after a storm comes a calm*; *life has its ups and downs* | ⟨fig⟩ *flight* (*of missiles*), ein ~ v Blumen ergoß sich *flowers r.ned down*; vor dem ~ unter Dach k ⟨sl⟩ *to just save one's bacon* || aus dem ~ in die Traufe k *to fall out of the frying-pan into the fire, to go from bad to worse* | automatische **~anlage** f ⟨theat⟩ *drencher*, ⟨Am⟩ *sprinkler* **≈arm** a, .. ~es Land *Spain is a semiarid country* **~auslaß** m *r.-outlet, storm-overflow* **~bach** m *torrent* **~be-** → –kleidung **~bogen** m *rainbow* | ~farben [f pl] *colours* pl *of the r.b*; in den ~ schillernd *iridescent*; ~färbung [f] ⟨phys⟩ *iridescence*; ~haut [f] (des Auges) *iris* **~brachvogel** m *whimbrel* **≈bringend** a *r.y* (*clouds*) **~dach** n *eaves* pl, *penthouse* **~decke** f (geteerte) *tarpaulin* **≈dicht** a *waterproof* **~entlastungskanal** m *stormwater discharge channel* **~fall** m *r.fall*, starker ~ *downfall* || reichlicher, schwerer ~ *abundant, torrential r.s* pl **~faß** n *water-butt* **~fluten** f pl *freshets* pl **~guß** m *torrent, downpour*; *violent shower*, ⟨fam⟩ *drencher* **~haut®** f *plastic r.coat* **~jahr** n *r.y year* **~karte** f *r.-chart* **~kleidung** f *weatherwear* **~leder** n *cornice* **~luft** f *r.y* od *misty air* **~mantel** m *r.-coat, waterproof, mackintosh*; (lang, lose) *slicker* **~menge** f *r.fall* **~messer** m *r.-gauge* **~messung** f *rain-ga(u)ging*; [abstr] *pluviometry* **~nacht** f *r.y night* **≈naß** a *r.y* **~periode** f *r.-spell* **~pfeifer** m ⟨orn⟩ → *plover* **≈reich** a *wet*; *well-r.ed-on* (*country*) **~schatten** m *r. shadow*, *r.less side* **~schauer** m *shower of r.*, *r.storm* **~schirm** m *umbrella*; gr. unordentlicher *gamp* || gespannt wie ein ~ *on the tiptoe of expectation* | ~gestell [n] *u.-frame*; ~ständer [m] *u.-stand* **~schutz** m ⟨tail⟩ *weatherwear* **≈schwanger, ≈schwer** a *full of r.* **~strich** m *tract of r.* **~sturm** m *storm of r.* **~tag** m *r.y day* **~tropfen** m *r.-drop* **~überfall,** –lauf m → –auslaß **~vorrichtung** f → –anlage **~wasser** n *r.-water*; ⟨geol⟩ *storm w.* | ~abfluß [m] *r.w., st.w. flow*; ~becken [n] *r.w., st.w. basin*; ~kanal [m] *storm-(water) drain* **~wetter** n *r.y weather* || ein Gesicht wie 14 Tage ~ *a sour face*; hübsches ~! *fine w. for ducks*! **~wind** m *wind that brings r.* **~wolke** f *r.-cloud* **~wurm** m *earth-* od *dew-worm* **~zeit** f *r.y season, the r.s* pl **~zone** f *r. belt*

Reg·encestil m [re'ʒɑ̃s–] *regency style*

Regener·atgummi m *regenerated rubber* **regene-r·ierbar** a *reconditionable, recoverable* **regene-r·ieren** vt *to regenerate* | –rt *reclaimed* (*rubber*) **Regener·ierung** f *regeneration, reclamation* (*of rubber*)

R·egensburg n ⟨Ger⟩ *Ratisbon, Regensburg*

Reg·ent m ~en/~en *regent* || *sovereign, ruler* | **~schaft** f ~/~en *regency* **Regie** [re'ʒiː] f ~/~n *public administration* || in eigener ~ *under one's own management* od *adm.* || e–e Arbeit in ~ geben *to put out a job on commission* || (Geschäftskosten) *working-expenses* pl || (Monopol) *state* od *government monopoly, régie* || ⟨theat⟩ (*stage-*) *m.t* od *-direction* (ungeschickte *bad*) || die ~ h *to have the m.t* **~anweisung** f *producer's direction* **~assistent** m *assistant producer* **~mikrophon** n ⟨film⟩ *director's m.* **~pult** n ⟨wir⟩(Ton) *mixing table* **~raum** m ⟨wir⟩ (Ton) *control room* **~verschluß** m, unter ~ *in bond* **reg·ierbar** a *governable* **reg·ieren** vt [h] *to rule* ⟨a. fig⟩, *to reign over, to govern* ⟨a. gram⟩; ⟨gram⟩ *to take* (*an object*) || (ein Pferd) *to manage* || ⟨mot⟩ nicht mehr ~ können *to lose control of ..* | vi [h] *to reign, rule* || (v Ministern) *to be at the head of affairs* || ⟨fig⟩ *to prevail, to predominate* | ≈ n *government* (*all g. is difficult*) **reg·ierend** a *ruling, reigning* (*sovereign*) *governing* (*body, power*, ⟨gram⟩ *noun*) **Regierer·ei** f ~/ *misgovernment* **Reg·ierung** f ~/~en **1.** [abstr & konkr] *government*, ⟨engl⟩ *the National Gov., His/Her Majesty's Gov.* || ⟨teens⟩ m–e ~ *my parents*; ohne Einwilligung der ~ *without gov. consent* || .. an der ~ (*the party*) *in power* || .. tritt ab *a gov. goes out of power* || in der ~ folgen *to succeed on the throne* | v der ~ geliefert *Gov.-furnished* (*material*); (P) ⟨Am sl⟩ *GI = Gov. Issue* | zur ~ gelangen (Fürst) *to come to the thr.*; (Partei) *to come into power* **2.** (~szeit) *reign* || unter s–r ~ *during* (*under, in*) *his r.* | **~s- ~antritt** m *accession to the thr.* **~art** f *mode of gov.* **~beamte(r)** m *gov. official, civil servant* **~beihilfe** f *subsidy* **~bezirk** m *gov.al* od *administrative district* **~blatt** n *official paper* **~chef** m *head of the gov.* **~dienst** m *gov. service* | mit **~förderung** f *gov.-sponsored* (*program*) **~form** f *form* od *system of gov.* **≈freundlich** a *gov.al* **~gebäude** n *gov. offices* pl **~gegner** m *member of the opposition* **~gewalt** f *supreme power*; die ~ übernehmen *to take over the reins of gov.* **~jahre** n pl *regnal years* **~kanzlei** f *gov. chancery, public office* **~koalition** f *gov. coalition* **~konferenz** f *intergov.al c.* **~kreise** m pl *gov.al circles* **~partei** f (*the*) *ins* pl **~paß** m *gov. passport* **~politik** f *gov. policy* (⟨Am⟩ *p.cies*) **~präsident** m ⟨Ger⟩ *president of an administrative district* **~rat** m *Councillor to the gov.* (⟨Ger⟩ title) **~sache** f *matter of state* **~sekretär** m *secretary to the gov.* **~stelle** f *government agency*; v allen ~n *from all levels of government* **~system** n *political system* **~truppen** f pl *gov. forces* **~unterstützung** → –förderung **~verordnung** f *executive order* **~viertel** n *Gov. section* **~wechsel**

m *change of gov.* od *ruler* **~zeit** f *reign* **Regim·ent 1.** n ~(e)s/~e *rule, government* ‖ ⟨ec⟩ *administration* ‖ ⟨dero⟩ *despotism* | ⟨fig⟩ *reign* (*of fashion*) ‖ das ~ h *or* führen *to rule, to command* ‖ der Winter führt ein strenges ~ *winter's sway is severe* ‖ sie führt das ~ im Haus *she wears the trousers* **2.** n ~(e)s/~er ⟨mil⟩ *regiment* (feudales ~ ⟨fam⟩ *crack r.*) ‖ ein ~ führen *to command a r.* ‖ bei e–m ~ stehen, dienen *to serve in a r.* ‖ in ein ~ eintreten *to join a r.* ‖ ~er aufstellen *to raise r.s.* ‖ das ~ betreffend *r.al* ‖ zw ~ern *inter-r.al* (*tournament*) ‖ ≗erweise [adv] *in r.s.* | **~s-** ⟨mil⟩, **~arzt** m *surgeon* **~befehl** m *r.al order* **~gefechtsstand** m *r.al command post* **~inhaber** m *honorary colonel of a r.* **~kamerad** m *brother officer* **~kasse** f *r.al chest* **~kommandeur** m *commander of a r.*; *r.al c.* **~kapelle** f, **~musik** f *r.al band* **~marsch** m *r.al march* **~quartiermeister** m *quartermaster-major* **~schreiber** m *r.al corporal major*; *r.al chief clerk* °**~spieß** m ⟨fam⟩ (P) *Reggie* **~stab** m *r.al staff* **~tambour** m *drum-major* **~tisch** m (*officers'*) *mess* **~uniform** f *r.als* pl **~unkosten** pl; auf ~ *at the general cost*; ⟨fig, fam⟩ *at other people's expense* **Regi·on** f ~/~en *region, district, area* ‖ ~ der Träume *or* Phantasie *cloudland* ‖ in höheren ~en schweben *to be in the clouds* | ~·alprogramm [n] ⟨wir, telv⟩ *closed-circuit program* **Regisseur** [reʒiˈsøːr] m ~s/~e ⟨theat⟩ *stage- director* od *manager*; *producer*, ⟨Am & film⟩ *production, stage m.* od *director*

Reg·ister n ~s/~ **1.** *register, record* **2.** (e–s Buches) *index*; *table of contents* ‖ *list, catalogue* | etw ins ~ eintragen *to* (*make an entry in the*) *register, to enter in the r.* ‖ ⟨fig⟩ ins alte ~ gehören ⟨fam⟩ *to be on the shelf* ‖ im schwarzen ~ stehen *to be on the black list* ‖ ⟨fam⟩ altes ~ (Weib) *back-number* **3.** (Ofenklappe) *damper, register* | ⟨comp⟩ *register* **4.** (Orgel≗) *r.* ‖ ein ~ ziehen *to pull out a stop* | ⟨fig⟩ *we can pull out the national stop*; alle ~ ziehen *to leave no stone unturned*; andere ~ ziehen *to adopt sharper measures* (gegenüber *with*); das sentimentale ~ ziehen *to play on sentimental feelings* **~mark** f *r.ed mark* **~ofen** m *r.-stove* **~papier** n *stout writing-paper* **~stimme** f = ~ 4. **~schiffsraum** m *r.ed tonnage* **~tonne** f *r. ton* **~zug** m = ~ 4. **Registr·ator** m ~s/–·oren *registrar, recorder*; ⟨Am⟩ *filer* | (S) (*letter*) *file* **Registrat·ur** f ~/~en [abstr & konkr] *registry* ‖ [konkr] *record-office*; *filing department* **Rigstrat·urnummer** f ⟨off⟩ *file number* **Registr·ier- ~apparat** m *recording apparatus, recorder* **~ballon** m *sounding balloon* **~einrichtung** f *recording attachment* **~kasse** f *cash register* **~papier** n *chart* od *recording p.*; *recorder ch.* **streifen** m *index strip* **~thermometer** n *self-registering thermometer* **registr·ieren** vt [h] *to register, to record* (a. v Apparaten) ‖ den Betrag ~ ⟨Am⟩ *to ring up the sale* ‖ ⟨fig⟩ die Presse registrierte nur ..., *..confined itself to a simple statement* (*of*) ‖ (Waren) *to tally* ‖ (Arbeitsbeginn, -schluß) *to clock in, out* ‖ (Ankunft u Abgang e–r P) *to clock a p* **Registr·ierung** f ~/~en *record*(*ation*) ‖ ~ der Bombentreffer durch Radar *radar bomb scoring*

Reglement [regləˈmã] n ~s/~s *regulations* pl ‖ *by-law* | ≗**·arisch** [–ent–] a *according to rules* od *r.s* ≗**widrig** a *contrary to r.s* od *r.s* | ≗**·ieren** vt [–ent–] *to order, regiment* | **~·ierung** f *r.ation* | **~ierer·ei** f *red-tape* **R·egler** m ~s/~ ⟨el⟩ *regulator*, ⟨mach⟩ *governor*; automatischer ~ *automatic controller* ⟨Am⟩ *control*; Wärme≗ ⟨el⟩ *damper* ‖ ⟨artill⟩ *corrector, deflection leaf* | ~bügeleisen [n] *thermostatic iron*; ~ventil [n] *check valve* **Regl·ette** f ~/~n ⟨typ⟩ *reglet, space-line* **R·eglung** f (Einstellung) *timing*; *adjustment, regulation*; *control* | ~sgerät [n] *adjusting device*; → Regelung

r·egnen vi [imps] [h] *to rain* ‖ fein ~ *to drizzle* ‖ es wird zur F. ~ *it will rain for the festivity* ‖ es wird gleich ~ *it's going to r.* ‖ heute regnet's nur einmal! *some r.!*, *fine* od *great weather for ducks!* ‖ es –nete heftig *heavy r. fell* ‖ es regnet Bindfäden *or* in Strömen *it's streaming with r.*, *it's r.ing in torrents*; *the r. is coming* (*down*) *in sheets*; *it's r.ing pitchforks*; ⟨fam⟩ .. wie mit Eimern .. *cats and dogs* | ⟨fig⟩ es regnete Püffe, Vorwürfe *it came to a regular shower of blows, of reproaches*; es regnete Briefe *the letters came thick and fast* **r·egnerisch** a *rainy, drizzly*

Regr·eß m –sses/–sse *recourse, remedy* ‖ ~ nehmen zu *to recur, to have recourse to*; (gegen jdn) *to come* (*upon a p*) **~nehmer** m *claimant, recoverer* ≗**pflichtig** a *liable to remedy*; e–n ~ m gegen .. *to have recourse against a p* **~recht** n *right of recovery*; ohne ~ *without recourse*

r·egsam a *quick, alert, active*(*-minded*) ≗**keit** f ~/ *quickness, alertness, activity*; *keenness* (*of mind*) ‖ geistige ~ *mental activity*; → rege

Regul- ≗**·är** a *regular* (*army*) ‖ ~e Truppen ⟨engl⟩ *regulars* pl **~arit·ät** f ~/ *regularity* **~at·iv** [–f] n ~s/~e [–və] *regulation* **~·ator** m ~s/–·oren ⟨a. tech⟩ *regulator, reducer*; ⟨mach⟩ *governor*; (Durchfluß≗) *baffle* | (Uhr) *regulator* **~hebel** m *controlling gear* **~·ier-** *regulating* (*machine*) **~apparat** m *regulator* ≗**bar** a → regelbar **~hahn** m ⟨tech⟩ *regulating cock* **~schraube** f *adjusting screw* **~stange** f *r.r* **~widerstand** m ⟨el⟩ [abstr] *r.ing resistance*, [konkr] *rheostat* ≗**·ieren** vt [h] *to regulate* (*river, clock*; ⟨a. el⟩); ⟨tech⟩ *to adjust*; ⟨mach, etc⟩ *to operate, govern* ‖ ⟨el, sl⟩ *to boost* ‖ ⟨fig⟩ *to square* (nach *with, by*) ‖ *to settle* (*insurance claims*) **~·ierung** f ~/~en *regulation* ‖ *operation, adjustment* ‖ ⟨com⟩ *settlement*

R·egung f ~/~en *movement, motion, stirring* | (innere) *rising* (*of feelings*); *emotion* (*of the heart*) ‖ *impulse* (*of pity*); *stirrings* pl (*of ambition*) ‖ menschliche ~ *humanity* ‖ aus e–r menschlichen ~ geschehen *to come from the heart* ‖ (heftige) *agitation* **r·egungslos** a *still*; *motionless, unmoving, immovable*; → regen

Reh n ~(e)s/~e *deer, roe*; ⟨cul⟩ *venison* ‖ (weibliches) *doe* ‖ ein Rudel ~e *a herd of deer* **~blatt** n *shoulder of a roe* **~bock** m *roe-buck* **~braten** m *roast venison* ≗**farben** a *fallow*; *fawn*(*-coloured*) **~geiß** f (im 2. Jahr) *pricket's sister* **~haut** f *doeskin* **~kalb** n, **~kitz** n *roe-calf*, ⟨hunt⟩ *kid*, weibl. *fawn* **~keule** f *haunch* od *leg of venison* **~leder** n *doeskin* **~ling** m *young deer* **~pfeffer** n ⟨cul⟩ *jugged venison* **~posten** m pl *buck-shot* **~rücken** m = ~ziemer **~schlegel** m = ~keule **~wildbret** n *venison* **~ziege** f (*young*) *doe* **~ziemer** m *loin* od *saddle of venison*

Rehabilitat·ion f ⟨jur⟩ *restoration*; ⟨med⟩ *rehabilitation* **rehabilit·ieren** vt [h] *to whitewash* (*a p*); *rehabilitate* (⟨a.⟩ sich *o.s.*) ‖ sich ~ *to recover one's reputation* | –rt *certificated* (*bankrupt*)

Reh·aut [rəˈoː] m ~s/~s ⟨paint⟩ *highlight* ‖ ~ geben *to h.l.*

R·ehe f ~/ ⟨vet⟩ *founder*

Reib- ~ahle f ⟨met⟩ *trib*(*o*)*let*, ⟨carp⟩ *reamer* **~antrieb** m *yielding drive* **~eisen** n *grater* ‖ ⟨fig⟩ *quarrelsome p* **~holz** n ⟨mar⟩ *spar fender* **~keule** f *grinder* **~schale** f *mortar* **~scheit** n *splinter bar* **~stein** m ⟨paint⟩ *grinding-stone* ‖ ⟨typ⟩ *ink-block* **~zeug** n ⟨el⟩ *cushion rubber* **R·eibe** f ~/~n ⟨tech, cul⟩ *grater* ‖ *rasp* **~keule** f *pestle* **~kuchen** m ⟨a. [pl]⟩ = Kartoffelpuffer ⟨a. [pl]⟩ **~lappen** m *rubber* **~laut** m ⟨phon⟩ *fricative* **r·eiben I.** vt [rieb/gerieben] [h] **A. 1.** *to rub* (*linen*) (an *upon, against*), *to give* (*a th*) *a rub* (mit *with*) ‖ *to massage* (*limbs*) ‖ sich [dat] vergnügt die Hände ~ *to rub one's hands for pleasure* **2.** (zerkleinern) *to grate* (*bread, cheese*) ‖ (mahlen) *to grind* (*colours*) **3.**

⟨fig⟩ e–n Salamander ~ ⟨stud⟩ *to drink a general toast* **B.** blank|~ *to polish up* (*metal* etc) ‖ klein|~ *to bray, powder, pulverize* ‖ warm, wund|~ *to chafe* ‖ sich wund|~ *to chafe* od *gall o.s.* ‖ sich [dat] die Haut wund|~ *to chafe one's skin* **C. an**: *she wiped her hands on her apron; to rub o.s. against a wall* | ⟨fig⟩ sich an e–m (etw) ~ *to tease, provoke a p, to carp* od *gird at a p* (*to complain of*) | **aus**: *to rub the sleep out of one's eyes* ‖ *to wipe the tears from one's eyes* | **mit** dem Knie ~ **gegen** *to scrape one's knee against* ‖ sich ~ mit *to scrub o.s. with* | **über** etw (Platte) ~ *to rub a th over* (*with a cloth*) | ⟨fig⟩ jdm etw **unter** die Nase ~ *to tell a th to a p's face, to throw* od *cast a th in a p's teeth, to bring a th home to a p* | **zu** Brei (Pulver) ~ *to grate, grind to a paste* (*a powder*) **II.** vi [h] *the collar chafes* **III. gerieben** ⟨fig⟩ *cunning*, ⟨fam⟩ *deep* ‖ *artful* (*dodger*) ‖ *smart* (*businessman*) **R·eiber** m ~s/~ **1.** (P) *p who rubs*, etc. ‖ (Farben≂) *grinder* **2.** (S) *brayer, rubber* | ⟨typ⟩ *plug* | **~·ei** f ~/~en ⟨fig⟩ *friction, provocation*, ⟨fam⟩ *tiff*, ⟨Am⟩ *spat* **R·eibsel** n ~s/~ *gratings* pl **R·eibung** f ~/~en **1.** *rub*(*bing*) etc.; *friction* **2.** *pulverization, trituration* **3.** ⟨fig⟩ *friction, clash, collision* ‖ *difference, dissension* ‖ zu ~en neigend *abrasive* (*character*) | **~s-** **≂arm** a ⟨tech⟩ *friction-free* **~bremse** f *fr.-brake* **~elektrizität** f *fr.al electricity* **~fläche** f ⟨el⟩ *striking surface* ‖ ⟨el⟩ *surface of contact* **~koeffizient** m *adhesive values* pl; *index of fr.* **~kuppelung** f *fr. clutch* **≂los** a *fr.less, smooth, quiet, easy* (*settlement*) ‖ *unexciting* (*life*) ‖ ~e Umstellung *smooth change-over* (auf *to*) | adv ~ ablaufen *to run smooth* ⟨a. fig⟩ | ~er gestalten *to streamline* **~punkt** m ⟨fig⟩ *point of fr.* **~widerstand** m *fr.al resistance; fr. and drag* **~verlust** m *loss due to fr.*

Reich n ~(e)s/~e **1.** *empire* (*British E.*) ‖ ⟨hist, Ger⟩ das Dritte ~ *the Third Reich* (1933–1945); das Großdeutsche ~ *Greater Germany, the Great-German Reich* ‖ das Heilige Römische ~ *the Holy Roman E.* ‖ (*the Indian*) *state* ‖ das ~ der Mitte (China) *the Celestial E.* **2.** (Gottes≂, König≂, Natur≂) *Kingdom* (*the K. of Heaven* etc) **3.** ⟨rhet, jur, fig⟩ *realm* (*of Satan, music* etc) ‖ *the r.s* (*of thought* etc), → Fabel ‖ *the three r.s of nature* ‖ *the kitchen is her r.* **reich I.** [a] **A.** ⟨allg⟩ *rich* ⟨a. fig⟩ (an [dat] *in*) **1.** (begütert) *rich* (*man*) ‖ er ist ein ~er Mann .. *a man of property*, ⟨Am, fam⟩ *he's on easy street* ‖ (wohlhabend) *wealthy* (*people, town*); *affluent* (*society*) | ⟨fam⟩ schwer, klotzig ~ *extremely rich* **2.** (umfassend, überströmend) *copious, exuberant* (*language*) **3.** (wertvoll) *rich* (*seam, brine, yield, harvest, mineral treasures*); *high-grade* (*ore*) ‖ (kostbar) *fine* (*jewelry*); *rich* (*clothing*) ‖ (fruchtbar) *fertile* (*soil*) **4.** (groß, vielfältig) *large* (*number*); *fine* (*collection*); *good* (*selection*); *rich* (*store*); *great* (*blessings*); *wide, ample* (*experience*) **5.** (reichlich) *abundant; generous* (*applause, measure of whisky*); *bountiful* (*harvest*; ⟨fig⟩ *heart*) **B.** e–e ~e **Erbschaft** m *to come into a fortune* ‖ ~er Farbenschmuck *a wealth of colo*(*u*)*r* ‖ ~e Gaben *bountiful gifts* ‖ ~es Gemüt *kind feelings* pl, *exuberant emotions* pl ‖ e–e ~e Heirat m *to marry an heiress* ‖ ~e Jahre *years of plenty* ‖ ~es Mahl *sumptuous repast* ‖ in ~em Maße *richly, in a high degree* ‖ ~e Partie *good match* **C.** ~ m *to enrich* ‖ ~ s **an** *to be rich in* (*ideas* etc); *rich, abounding in* (*game* etc) ‖ schnell ~ w wollen *to seek a quick fortune* **II.** [adv] **~ ausstatten,** entschädigen *to equip, recompense well*; ~ belohnen *to reward richly* ‖ ~ beschenken *to load with gifts* ‖ ~ heiraten *to make a wealthy marriage* ‖ ~ gekleidet *richly clothed* **III. ein ≂r** (e–e ≂e) *a rich* (*wo*)*man* ‖ die ≂en [pl] *the rich; the well-to-do* (*classes*); ⟨bib⟩ der ≂e *the Rich Man of the Gospel* ‖ die ehemaligen ≂en *the ex-rich* ‖ ~ u arm, ≂e u Arme (*the*) *rich and* (*the*) *poor* **~begütert** a *owning large estates* **~besch·enkt, ~ges·egnet** a *richly endowed* **~bes·etzt** a (Tisch) *well-spread* **~bl·ühend** a *multiflorous* **~gedeckt** a ⟨cul⟩ *groaning* (*board* Tafel) **~haltig** a *rich, abundant, copious, comprehensive*; (von Büchern) *full of matter* | ≂keit [f] *richness, abundance, copiousness* **~illustr·iert** a *richly illustrated* **~verz·iert** a *profusely decorated*

Reich- **~weite** f *reach; effective radius*; ⟨phot⟩ *action radius* | ⟨mil⟩ *range* ⟨a. fig⟩; gr, günstigste ~ *long, optimum range* | wie es die ~ der Scheinwerfer erlaubt ⟨mot, etc⟩ *within the limit of your lights* | ⟨wir⟩ *transmission distance* | ⟨aero⟩ *normal range* | **außer** ~ *on the windy side of* (*the law*) | **in** ~ bleiben *to remain within call* **r·eichen I.** vt [h] (jdm etw) *to reach, pass, hand, offer, give; present* ‖ (Mahlzeit) *to serve* (*lunch is served at ..*) ‖ (bei Tisch) *to help a p to a th*; darf ich Ihnen noch einmal ~? *would you like a second help*? reichen Sie mir bitte ..! *would you kindly hand me ..?, may I trouble you for ..?, would you pass the .., please*? | das **Abendmahl** ~ *to administer the sacrament* ‖ [dat] die Brust ~ *to suckle* (*a baby*) ‖ jdm die Hand ~ *to give one's hand to a p, to shake hands with a p*; ⟨fig⟩ *to marry a p* ‖ jdm die Wange z Kusse ~ *to offer one's cheek for a kiss* ‖ ⟨fig⟩ er kann ihm nicht das Wasser ~ *he is not a patch on him* **II.** vi [h] **1.** (bis) *to reach, to extend to* ‖ soweit das **Auge** reicht *as far as the eye can see* ‖ soweit der Blick (die Stimme) reicht *within sight* (*hail*); (of voice) *to carry* (*far*) ‖ **mit** dem Kopf bis an die Decke ~ *to touch the c. with one's h.* ‖ (das Wasser) reichte bis hier .. *came up to here*; .. bis an .. *was thigh-deep* ‖ *the wood came down to the lake*; *she came only to his shoulder* (ihm zur) ‖ *with this he could reach to the back of the oven* (hinter *acc.*) | (zeitlich) ~ v .. bis *to range from .. to ..*; *the scope of the book is from .. to ..* **2.** (ausreichen) *to be sufficient* (f *for*), *to suffice* ‖ das Geld reichte nicht .. *did not last out*; das Seil .. *was not long enough* ‖ soweit der Vorrat reicht *as long as the p. will last* | **~ für** *to cover* ‖ **damit** w wir ~ *that will do for us*; Reichweite → o. **r·eichlich I.** a **A.** *copious, abundant, plentiful* (*hair, evidence*); *ample* (*time, food, opportunity*); *plenteous* (*produce, profit, yield*); *bountiful* (*opportunity*); *liberal* (*gifts*); *rich* (*presents*) | sehr ~ *profuse, in profusion* **B.** sein ~es **Auskommen** h *to be well off, to make a good living* ‖ e–e ~e Mahlzeit zu sich nehmen *to make a square* od *hearty meal, to partake of a spacious meal* **C.** [abs] das ist etw ~ (= zuviel des Traurigen) ⟨iron⟩ *that's a bit too much of a good th* ‖ es gab ~ z tun *there was plenty to do* ‖ ich habe ~ gehabt *I've had a hearty meal*; .. nachgedacht .. *a good deal* **II.** [adv] **1.** ~ **genug** *full enough*, .. h *to have* (*enough and to spare* od) *plenty* ‖ *very* (*short*) ‖ *awfully* (*tedious job*) ‖ ~ so gr *quite* od *fully as large* ‖ *very* (*late*) ‖ *thoroughly* (*awkward*) | (ziemlich) *rather, fairly*; [pred] *flush*, ⟨Am fam⟩ *kind of* (*tattered*) **2.** ~ **beschenken** *to give* (*a p*) *presents in profusion* ‖ (*pockets were*) *freely* (*picked*) ‖ *amply* (*paid for; calculated*) ‖ etw ~ ersetzen *to make ample compensation for a th* ‖ (*to eat*) *largely* ‖ ~ versehen mit *to provide* (*a p*) *amply with* **3.** vor ~ **Jahresfrist** *more than a year ago* ‖ ~ Platz *plenty of room* ‖ *full* (*300 years*) ‖ *fully* (*1000 £*) ‖ ~ Zeit h *to have plenty of t.* | **~keit** f ~/ *plentifulness, plenty, abundance, copiousness, profusion*

Reichs- ⟨**Ger hist**⟩ (bis 1918) *Imperial, of the Empire*; (nach 1918) *National*, (*of the*) *Reich* **~abschied** m ⟨hist⟩ *recess of the Imperial Diet* **~acht** f ⟨hist⟩ in die ~ erklären *to put under the ban of the E.* **~adel** m ⟨hist⟩ *nobility of the E.* **~adler** m *Imp. eagle* **~angehörige(r)** m Deutscher ~r *German*; ~ [pl] *German nationals* pl **~anleihe** f *national loan* **~anstalt** f → physikalisch

~anzeiger m *National Herald* **~apfel** m (*Imp.*) *orb, mound* **~·arbeitsdienst** m ⟨nazi⟩ *National Labour Service* **~·arbeitskammer** f ⟨nazi⟩ *Reich Chamber of Labour* **~·arbeitsminister** m *R. Minister of L.* **~archiv** n *archive(s* pl) *of the E.* **~archiv·ar** m *Master of the Rolls* **~armee** f *Imp. army* **~·autobahn** f *State arterial motor-road*; *autobahn* **~bahn** f *German railway* **~bank** f *German Reichsbank* ‖ *Bank of England* **~banner** n *republican association of ex-service men* **~-b·auernführer** m ⟨nazi⟩ *R. Leader of Farmers* **~b·auerntag** m ⟨nazi⟩ *R. Farmer's Congress* **~ber·ufswettkampf** m ⟨nazi⟩ *R. Apprentices' Competition* **~bund** m [gen] *National League* (*of*) **~bürger** m = ~angehörige(r) m **~deutsche(r)** m *German belonging to the R.* **~drucker·ei** f *R. Printing-Office* **~·ehrenmal** n *cenotaph of the R.* **~exekution** f *execution of federal orders by force* **~feind** m *national enemy* **~flagge** f *national colo(u)rs* **~finanzminister** m *R. Minister of Finance* **≈frei** a *immediate* **~freiherr, ~fürst** m *baron, prince of the* (*Holy Roman*) *E.* **~gebiet** n *territory of the R.* **~gericht** n ⟨Ger⟩ *Supreme Court of Justice* | ~srat [m] *judge of the Supreme Court* **~geschichte** f *history of the E.* **~gesetz** n *law of the E., Federal Law* | ~blatt [n] *National Gazette* **~ges·undheitsamt** n *Ministry of Health* **~grenze** f *frontier of the E.* **~gr·undgesetz** n *fundamental law of the E.* od *R., constitutional law* **~hauptstadt** f *capital of the E.* od *R.* **~haushalt** m *budget of the R.* **~hilfe** f *aid* (*in money* etc) *granted by the E.* od *R.* **~innenminister** m ⟨Ger⟩ *Home Secretary of the R.*, ⟨engl⟩ *Secretary of State for Home Affairs* **~jägermeister** m ⟨nazi⟩ *R. Master of the Hunt* **~kabinett** n *German Cabinet* **~k·ammergericht** n *Imp. High Court of Justice* **~kanzlei** f *R. Chancery* **~kanzler** m *Chancellor* (*of the E.* od *R.*) **~karte** f *ordnance survey map* **~kasse** f *National treasury* **~kleinodien** n pl *Imp. crown-jewels* pl **~kommissar** m *Federal Commissioner* **~kontingent** n *Imp. contingent* **~kr·ankenversicherung** f ⟨engl⟩ *National Health Insurance* **~krone** f *Imp. crown* **~kult·urkammer** f ⟨nazi⟩ *R. Board of Arts and Culture* **~k·ursbuch** n ⟨Ger⟩ *general railway guide* **~land** n *territory of the E.*; ⟨Ger hist⟩ (1871–1918) die ~e *the Imp. Provinces* (*of Alsace and Lorraine*) **~lehen** n *Imp. fief* **~marine** f *navy of the R.* **~mar·ineamt** n ⟨Ger⟩ *Naval Board*, ⟨engl⟩ *Admiralty* **~mark** f *R. mark* (*monetary unit after* 1924) **~minister** m *Minister of the R.*; ~ des Auswärtigen (Innern) *R. Min. of Foreign Affairs* (*of the Interior*) **~n·ährstand** m *the R. Agricultural Estate* od *Board* **~notopfer** n (1920) *Capital levy* **~oberhaupt** n *supreme head of the E.* **~pair** m *peer of the realm* **~part·eitag** m (*annual*) *Nazi Congress* **~p·ostverwaltung** f *federal administration of Post* **~postministerium** n ⟨Ger⟩ *General P. Office*, ⟨engl⟩ *the Postmaster-General's Office*, ⟨Am⟩ *the P.-O. Department* **~präsident** m *President of the R.* **~pr·essestelle** f *R. press bureau* **~rat** m *Reichsrat* **~regierung** f *German Government* **~ritter** m *knight of the E.* | ~schaft [f] *nobility of the E.* **~r·undfunkgesellschaft** f *R. Wireless Company Ltd.* **~sache** f *Federal affair* **~sch·atzamt** n *Imp. Treasury*, ⟨Am⟩ *Treasury Department* **~-schluß** m *Imp. decree* **~sender** m ⟨wir⟩ *government station* **~siegel** n *Imp. seal* **~sp·arkommissar** m *commissioner for public economy* **~sportführer** m ⟨nazi⟩ *the R. sport Leader* **≈städtisch** a *belonging* od *relating to a free town* od *city of the R.* **~stände** m pl *estates* pl *of the E.* **~tag** m *Reichstag* (⟨a.⟩ –sgebäude); *Imp. Parliament, Diet* | ~s·abgeordneter [m] *Member of the R.t.* **~truppen** f pl *Imp. troops* pl **≈·unmittelbar** a *directly subject to the E., immediate* **~·unfallversicherungsgesetz** n *accident-insurance act* **~verband** m [gen] *R. Association* (*of*) **~verfassung** f *constitution of the E.* **~verteidigung** f ⟨engl⟩ oberste Behörde der ~ *Committee of Imp. Defence* (*C.I.D.*), *War Cabinet* (*W.C.*) **~verweser** m *Imp. administrator, regent* **~währung** f *standard currency* **~wappen** n *Imp. arms* **~wehr** f *defensive* (*land and naval*) *forces* | ~minister [m] *Minister of National Defence* **~werft** f *Naval* (*Royal* od *State*) *Dockyard* **~w·irtschaftsministerium** n *R. Ministry of National Economy* **~zepter** n *Imp. sceptre* **R·eichtum** m ~(e)s/≈er *riches* pl, *wealth, opulence* ‖ (Überfluß) *profusion, abundance, fulness* ‖ die ≈er des Landes *the wealth of the c.* | ⟨fig⟩ (an [dat]) *wealth, richness* (*of*); ~ an geistigen Gütern *intellectual wealth* | ~ ist vergänglich *riches have wings* ‖ ~ macht nicht immer glücklich *wealth does not ensure happiness*

Reif m ~(e)s/~e **1.** (Frost) *hoar-frost* ‖ voll ~ *rimy* | ⟨übtr⟩ (auf Obst) *bloom* **2.** = ~en

reif a *ripe* (⟨a. fig⟩ *understanding*) | ⟨fig⟩ *mature* (*age, judgement, woman*); *mellow* (*age, judgement*; [pred] °*ripe* (*drunk*) ‖ *fully developed* (*girl*), *full-blown* (*woman*) ‖ die ~ere Jugend *the rising generation* ‖ in ~(er)en Jahren *middle-aged* ‖ *in the fulness of years* ‖ ~ w *to season, ripen*; (f) *to become ripe* (*for*) ‖ die S ist ~ geworden ⟨fig⟩ *the pear is ripe* ‖ das Geschwür ist ~ *the boil has come to a head* ‖ noch nicht ~ *green* (*cheese*); der Plan ist noch nicht ~ *has not yet matured* ‖ er ist ~ f das Tollhaus *he is a candidate for ..* **R·eife** f ~/ *ripeness* (*of fruit, thought*) ‖ *maturity* (*of youth*) ‖ zur ~ bringen *to ripen*, (*make*) *mature, bring to maturity* ‖ zur ~ k *to ripen*, (*become*) *mature* ‖ mangelnde ~ *unripeness* | Zeugnis der mittleren ~ ⟨m. m.⟩ *certificate of general education at ordinary level* (*G.C.E.* "*O*" *level*) **~prüfung** f *final examination* **~teilung** f ⟨biol⟩ *maturation division* **~zeugnis** n *school-leaving certificate*; *c. of g. e. at advanced level*; *c. of maturity* **r·eifen I.** vt [h] **1.** (⟨a.⟩ ~ [vi] l) *to ripen, mellow, mature, to bring to maturity* **2.** (ein Faß) *to hoop* **II.** vi [h] **1.** *to ripen* (⟨a. fig⟩ *into conviction*), *to grow ripe* od *to maturity* ‖ (Geschwür) *to come to a head* ‖ **zum** Mann ~ *to grow to man's estate* ‖ zur Jungfrau ~ *to attain the age of womanhood* ‖ v gereifter Jugend *in the flush of youth* ‖ ⟨fig⟩ ~ zu *to become* (*a certainty*) **2.** ⟨meteor⟩ *to rime* ‖ es hat gereift *there is hoarfrost* od *white frost* **III.** ≈ n ⟨biol⟩ *maturation*; seelisches ≈ *spiritual m.* **r·eiflich** a *mature* (*consideration*) ‖ nach ~er Überlegung *upon careful consideration* ‖ sich e–e S ~ [adv] überlegen *to think a matter over well* **R·eifung** f ~/ ⟨eth⟩ *growth*

R·eifen m ~s/~ (Faß≈) *hoop, ring* ‖ ⟨mot⟩ *tire, tyre*; (Ballon≈) *lowpressure tire* ‖ (Schmuck) *circlet* ‖ (Schnee≈) *snow-shoe, racket* (→ S + M) | e–n ~ aufziehen *to fit on a t.*; treiben, schlagen (Spiel) *to trundle* od *bowl a hoop* **~abnehmer** m *tire remover* **~auflagepunkt** m ⟨mot⟩ *centre of t. impact* **~decke** f ⟨mot⟩ *cover* **~druck** m *inflation pressure* **~geschäft** n *shop selling t.s* **~gewebe** n ⟨mot⟩ *ply* **~heber** m *tire-lever* **~montage** f *fitting of t.s* **~panne** f *puncture*, ⟨Am, sl⟩ *blowout* **~prüfer** m *tire-gauge* **~schaden** m ⟨mot⟩ *burst* **~schulter** f *side wall* (*of tire*) **~spiel** n *hoop game, trundling a hoop* **~springen** n *skipping through a hoop* **~wächter** m *kerb feeler* **~wechsel** m *changing of t.s* **R·eifrock** m *crinoline*; ⟨hist⟩ *hoop-skirt hoop*(*ed*) *petticoat, farthinggale*

R·eigen (Reihen) m ~s/~ (*round* od *ring*) *dance* ‖ *row of dancers* | ⟨mus⟩ *song, dance* ‖ ⟨fig⟩ *a round* (*of* ..) ‖ den ~ eröffnen *or* führen *to lead the dance* ‖ ⟨fig⟩ *to lead off, to take the lead* ‖ *he opened, closed the series of addresses* **~führer** m *leader in a round dance* **~gesang** m *roundel*(*ay*) **~tanz** m *round dance*

R·eihe f ~/~n **A. 1.** *row* (*of trees, houses, books, seats*); *rank* (*of vehicles*; ⟨a. chess⟩ waagerecht); *line* ⟨a. math⟩, *file* (⟨a. chess⟩ senkrecht)

|| *string* (*of pearls*) || *series* (*of types*, ⟨exch⟩ *issues*) | *queue* (*of people*), *squad* (*of 4 men*) | ⟨theat⟩ *row*; *tier* (⟨a. sculp⟩ e–s Frieses, Tympanons); die ~n der Opposition ⟨parl⟩ *the o. benches* || (Hügel~) *range* **2.** (Auf–e–a–folge) *rotation*; *succession* (*of villages*) || *set*, *suit* (*of rooms*); *set* (*of tables*); *hail* (*of blows*) || *chapter*, *series* (*of accidents*) || *round* (*of days*) || *train* (*of thought*) **3.** (Reihenfolge) *turn* **4.** (Anzahl) *number of* .. **5.** (Ordnung) *order* **6.** ⟨crick⟩ *innings* pl **7.** ⟨mil⟩ *single-file column*; ~' u Glied *closed ranks* pl **8.** ⟨tech⟩ (Stufe) *rank* **9.** ⟨aero⟩ *echelon* od *trail formation* **B.** (*algebraical*) *progression* || (*arithmetical*) *series* || **ausgeglichene** ~ ⟨demog⟩ *graduated* od *smoothed series* || **bunte** ~ m *to pair off*, (bei Tisch) *to arrange ladies and gentlemen in couples* || dichte ~n *close* od *serried ranks* || ⟨fig⟩ erste ~ *foremost rank* (*of novelists*) || ⟨fam⟩ e–e **ganze** ~ v .. *a host of*; *a great number* (*of poets*) || gehäufelte ~ (Kartoffeln) *bank* || fest geschlossene ~ *phalanx* || imposante ~ *array* | **lange** ~ *string* (*of cars*, *children*), *long line* (*of ancestors*), *stream* (*of buses*), *queue*, ⟨Am⟩ *line* (*of women*); ~n, die nach Brot anstehen *bread lines* || lange ~n v Gestellen mit Röhren *racks upon racks of tubes* || lange, wirre ~ v .. *a wilderness of* (*houses*, *streets*) | lockere ~n *open ranks* || lückenlose ~ *unbroken line* || **senkrechte** ~ *column* || ⟨math⟩ steigende, unendliche ~n *rising*, *infinite numbers* || ununterbrochene ~ *run*, ⟨scient⟩ *continuum* L || ⟨racing⟩ vorderste ~ *first flight* (⟨a. fig⟩ *of great musicians*), ⟨fig⟩ *forefront* (*of a movement*) **C.** e–e ~ **eröffnen** (schließen) *to be the first* (*last*) *in a line* || die ~ öffnen (schließen) *to open* (*close*) *the ranks* ⟨a. fig⟩ **D.** ~ **an** ~ *row upon row* || an die ~ k (P) *to get one's turn*, (*of law-cases*) *to come on* || *then comes your turn*; *this is where you come in*; *when it came to N.'s turn* || jetzt komme ich an die ~ (zu sprechen) *it's my say now* || warten, bis man an die ~ kommt *to wait one's turn* | an der ~ s *to have one's turn* || wer ist an der ~? *whose turn is it?* die ~ ist an mir *it is my turn* || an die ~ k (= sterben) *to kick the bucket* | **aus** den ~n (des Adels etc) *from within* (*the nobility*, *the democratic ranks* [⟨Am⟩ *column*]) || e–r aus ihren ~n *one of their number* || aus den eigenen ~n (*criticism*) *from one's own friends* | aus der ~ k *to get out of order*; .. tanzen *to play one's own game*; .. treten *to break rank* | **außer** der ~ *out of turn*; .. fragen ⟨school⟩ *to dodge* || außer der ~ dran k *to come in*, *play* etc *out of one's turn* | **für** e–e ~ v *for many* (*years*) | **in** e–r ~ *in a row* od *line* || ⟨mil⟩ in ~n *in file* || ⟨fig⟩ in erster ~ *first and foremost* | in ~n angelegt, mit ~ versehen *tiered* || in 2 ~n angeordnet ⟨bot⟩ *distichous* || sich in e–r ~ anstellen *to line up in a queue* || in ~n aufstellen *to line*, sich .. *to file* (*along*) || in der ~ bleiben *to keep in regular succession* || ⟨fig⟩ etw in die ~ bringen *to get s.th into order again* || in ~n hergestellt *produced by series* || ⟨fig⟩ mit jdm in die ~ k *to come to an understanding with a p* || in ~ (ab-, vorbei)marschieren *to file* (*off*, *past* [an e–m *a p*]), *to march* (*single file* od) *in f.s* (zu Vieren *of 4 men*) || ⟨hort⟩ in ~en setzen *to bench* || in e–r ~ mit jdm stehen *to stand in line with a p* || in derselben mit .. *to rank with* || ⟨fig⟩ in dieselbe ~ stellen mit *to place in the same category with* || in die ~ der Kulturstaaten treten *to be ranked among* .. | in ~' **u Glied** *in rank and file*, .. bleiben *to keep rank*, (sich) .. stellen *to draw up* [vt/i], .. treten *to fall into ranks* || **nach** der ~, der ~ nach (⟨a.⟩ reih·um [adv]) *in*, *by turns*; *in file*, *in rows*; *turn and turn about*, *alternately*, *in succession*, *successively* || der ~ nach behandeln *to deal with one after another*; .. dran k *to take it in turns*; .. mit: *I'll take my turn with my comrades* | e–e ~ **neben** der anderen *row upon row* **r·eihen I.** vt/refl [h] **1.** *to rank*, *file*, *range*; *to put in a row* od *line* **2.** *to string* (*pearls*) **3.** ⟨tail⟩ *to baste*, *stich* **4. an** etw ~ *to add*, *join* (*to a th*) || an–e–a|~ *to link*, *to tack* (*material*) *together*; *to connect* **5. sich** ~ *to form a row*; *to file*, *rank* (hinter–e–a *along*); ⟨fig a.⟩ gereiht w *to rank* (unter *with*) || eins reiht sich ans andere *one th falls into sequence with another* **II.** ≃ n ⟨orn⟩ *pursuit flight* (*of ducks*) **R·eih- ~faden** m *tacking thread* ≃**·um** [adv] *in succession* **R·eihen-** ⟨oft⟩ *serial* (*s.l*), *series* (*s.s*) **~absprung** m *stick* (*of parachutists*) **~anlage** f ⟨telph⟩ *intercommunication set* **~anordnung** f *tandem arrangement* **~arbeit** f *repetition w.* **~bild** n *successive* od *s.l photographs* | ~aufnahme [f] *overlapping photography*; ~kamera [f] *s.s topographic camera*; ~stelle [f] *mass radiography unit*; ~untersuchung [f] *m.r.*; ~bombenwurf m (versetzter ~) *pattern bombing* **~dynamo** m *s.s dynamo* **~entwicklung** f ⟨math⟩ *development into s.s* **~fabrikation** f = –arbeit **~(an)fertigung** f *s.l production*, .. im gr *large scale production* **~folge** f (*consecutive*) *sequence*; *s.s*; *order of succession*; (*alphabetical*) *order*; in beliebiger ~ ⟨comp⟩ *irrespective of sequence*; in *or* nach der ~ *in succession*; ~ der Gespräche ⟨telph⟩ *turn of calls*; ohne die ~ des Restes z ändern *leaving the sequence of the remainder undisturbed* **~haus** n *terrace h.* **~häuser** n pl *s.l houses* **~kolonne** f ⟨mil⟩ *file* **~marsch** m *march*(*ing*) *in file* **~motor** m *s.s motor*; *in-line engine* **~sämaschine** f *ridge-drill* **~schaltung** f ⟨el⟩ *s.s-connection* **~schlußmaschine** *s.s dynamo* **~tanz** m *round dance* **~untersuchung** f ⟨surv⟩ *mass survey* **~verbundmaschine** f *tandem compound engine* ≃**weise** [adv] (⟨fam a.⟩ [a]) *in rows*, *by turns*; ~ geordnet *s.l*; ~ besetzen *to line* **~wurf** *stick* (*of bombs*); *volley bombing*

R·eihen m ~s/~ **1.** = Reigen **2.** = Rist

R·eiher m ~s/~ ⟨orn⟩ → *heron* || kl ~ *egret* **~beize** f *h. hawking*; *flying at h.s* **~busch** m *h.'s feathers* pl **~ente** f ⟨orn⟩ *scaup*(*-duck*) **~schnabel** m ⟨bot⟩ *stork's bill* **~stand**, **~horst** m *h.y* °**r·eihern** vi [h] (kotzen) *to shoot the cat*

Reim m ~(e)s/~e → *rhyme* || ~e m *or* schmieden *to make rh.s*, *to write poetry* **~chronik** f *rh.d chronicle* **~geklingel** n *jingling of rh.s* **~kunst** f *art of rhyming* ≃**los** a *rh.less*, *blank* (Verse [pl] *verse* [sg]) **~schmied** m *rhym*(*est*)*er* **~silbe** *rh.ing syllable* **~wörterbuch** n *rh.ing-dictionary* **r·eimen 1.** vt [h] *to rhyme* || *to make* (*a word*) *rhyme* (*with another*) || gereimt *rh.ed* (*fable*) | **sich** ~ [h] (mit) *to rhyme* (*with*) | ⟨fig⟩ *to agree*, *square* (*with*); sich nicht ~ *not to make any sense* **2.** vi [h] *to make rhymes* **R·eimer** m ≃s/~ *rhym*(*est*)*er*, *versifier* || ⟨dero⟩ *would-be poet* | **~·ei** f ~/~en *rhyming*; *making* (*bad*) *verses* || (Reimgeklingel) *jingling of rhymes*

Reims [raims od rẽs] n ⟨Fr⟩ (Stadt) *R*(*h*)*eims* **R·eimser** a *Rhemish*

rein I. [a] **A. 1.** (→ sauber) *clean* (*face*, *linen*) **2.** (klar) *pure* (*skin*, *air*, *water*, *tone*); ⟨mus⟩ *accurate* **3.** (unverfälscht) *unadulterated*; *pure* (*wine*, *silk*); *genuine*; (unverdünnt) *neat*, *straight* (*whisky*); ⟨fig⟩ *quintessential* (*toryism*) || ⟨met⟩ *unalloyed* || ⟨fig⟩ *arrant* (*nonsense*); *downright* (*lie*); der ~ste Othello *a regular O.*; wie die ~sten Kannibalen *like so many c.s* **4.** (ordentlich) *tidy*, *neat*, *proper* **5.** (unbeschwert) *unencumbered*, *clear* **6.** (fleckenlos) *faultless* (*marble*), (fehlerlos) *correct*, *faultless* (*pronunciation*) **7.** (⟨fig⟩ unbefleckt) *untarnished* (*fame*), *unsullied* (*honour*) || *free* (*from all blame*) || (keusch) *chaste*, *pure* (*as newly fallen snow*) **8.** ⟨fig⟩ (bloß) *mere*, *empty* (*forms*); *rank*, *plumb* (*nonsense*) **B.** ~e **Arbeit** mit etw m *to make a clean job of sth* || ~e Aussprache *good accent* || ~e Bahn m *to clear the way*, *to make a clean sweep* || ~e Bilanz *clear b.* || ~er Bogen Papier *blank sheet* (*of paper*) || aus ~ster Dummheit getan *done from sheer stupidity* || ~e Freude *pure* od *unadulterated pl.* || ~es Gemüt *pure* od *untainted mind* || ~e Gesichtsfarbe *clear complexion* || ~er Gewinn *net* od *real profit* od *gain* || ein ~es Gewissen h *to have a clear c.* || das **~ste** Glück ⟨fig⟩ (Zufall) *sheer* od *mere luck* || mit ~en Händen dastehen *to be blameless* || ~es Herzens *with a pure h.*, ⟨bib⟩ *pure in h.* || der ~e Hohn *bitter mockery* || **~ste** Metalle etc. *high-grade metals, etc.* || die **~ste** Komödie *a regular c.*; ~ster Barock *sheerest b.*; ~ste Musik ⟨fig⟩ *sheer m.* (*to a p's ear*); (*to die*) aus: *with sheer envy*; .. *by sheer horror* || ~e Lehre ⟨rel⟩ *true teachings* pl || ~es Löschpapier ⟨fam⟩ *innocent* .. || ⟨fig⟩ die Luft ist ~ *the coast is clear* || *downright* (*lie*) || *pure* (*mathematics* pl) || aus ~em Mitleid *out of sheer c.* || der ~ste Mord *nothing better than murder* || ~en Mund halten *to hold one's tongue*; ..! ⟨sl⟩ *don't split* || ~en Tisch, ~e Wirtschaft m *to make a clean sweep of ths* || .. ja die ~ste Torheit *that's rankest folly* || ~er Überschuß *net profit* || **~ster** Unsinn *the* (*most arrant* od) *veriest n.* || ~er Verlust *dead loss* || ~e Vernunft *pure reason* || ~er Wahnsinn *sheer madness* || ~e Wahrheit *plain* od *absolute t.* || Diamant (Diplomat) v ~stem Wasser .. *of the first water* (*of the finest character*) || ⟨fig⟩ jdm ~en Wein einschenken *to tell a p the plain truth* || er hat e–e ~e Weste *he can show a clean slate* || ~e Wirtschaft → ~en Tisch || ~es Wunder *absolute miracle* || ~er Zufall *merest accident, quite an a.* **C.** ~ **ab|schlagen** *to refuse flatly* || ~|**halten** *to keep* (*the home*) *clean* || ~ heraus|sagen *to tell plainly* || ~ m *to clean* (*clothes*) || ~ singen *to sing in tune* || ~ sprechen *to speak* (*English*) *purely* od *with a pure accent* || sich das Gesicht ~|waschen *to wash one's face clean* || ⟨fig⟩ ~|waschen *to wash* (*a p*) *pure, to exculpate*; sich .. *to clear o.s.* **II.** [adv] *purely, quite, entirely, plainly* || (geradezu) *absolutely* | ⟨fam⟩ ~ **alle** *clean gone* | etw **auf** ~ geschäftliche Basis stellen *to put .. on a strict business footing*; es ist ~ **aus** mit ihm *it's all over with him*, .. damit *it's all up with that* | das hat er ~ aus der Luft gegriffen *that is a pure invention of his* || ~ aus Neid, Schrecken → I. B. aus ~stem Neid | ~ nichts *nothing whatever* od *at all, absolutely n.*; (kein Brot) ~ gar nichts .., *no nothing* | ~ des Teufels *gone crazy* | ~ toll *stark mad; absolutely ridiculous* | ~ unmöglich *sheerly, quite, clean imp.*; es ist mir .. *I cannot possibly* | ~ vergessen *clean* od *completely forg.* | er ist ~ weg .. *enraptured* od *gone* | ~ wollen *all wool* (*material*) | das ist ~ **zum** Tollwerden *that is maddening* od *the very devil* **III.** [subst] **dem** ≗**en** ist alles ~ *to the pure all ths are pure* || (e–e S) **ins ~e** bringen *to straighten* (*a matter*) *out*; *to clear, square, settle, arrange*; *to set in order*, e–e Rechnung .. *to clear an account* || mit jdm ins ~e k *to get even, to arrange, to come to an understanding with a p*; mit sich selbst .. *to make up one's mind* (über *about*); mit sich selbst ins ~ k *to come to terms* (*to settle a th*) *with o.s.*; versuchen, mit sich ins ~e z k *to debate with o.s.* || ins ~e schreiben *to make a fair copy of*, (Akten) *to engross* || mit etw im ~en s *to be clear in one's mind about a th* **R·ein- ~darstellung** f *production in pure condition* **~druck** m ⟨typ⟩ *clean impression, fair proof* **~erhaltung** f *purification* **~ertrag** m *net proceeds* pl ≗**g·eistig** a *intellectual* **~gewinn** m *net profit* od *gain* **~halten** n, **~haltung** f *conservation* (*of waters*) **~kultur** f *bacilli-culture* || ⟨fig⟩ *pure culture* || Kitsch in ~ *the very essence of trashy work* **~machefrau** f *charwoman* **~machen** n *cleaning, scouring* **~rasse** f ⟨biol⟩ *clone* ≗**rassig** a *pure-bred, pure blood*; ⟨fig mil⟩ *straight armor*, etc (*formation*) **~schiff** n ⟨mar⟩ *clean ship* **~schrift** f *fair copy* ≗|**waschen** vt [h] *to whitewash* (*a p*); *to clear, vindicate* °**~(e)weg** [adv] *totally, completely, altogether, absolutely, clean* (⟨Am⟩ *plumb*) (*forgotten*); ⟨fam, hum⟩ *absoballelutely*; → Reinheit

°**rein** ⟨fam⟩ = herein ≗**fall** m *failure, fiasco*; *piece of ill luck*; *flash in the pan*; ⟨hum⟩ (⟨a.⟩ bei Schaffhausen) ⟨fam⟩ *let-* od *come-down*; ⟨sl⟩ *wash-out, frost, flop, sell* (*what a s.!*) || übler ~ *bad take-in, nasty cropper* **~|fallen** vi [s] *to fail, to come down*, ⟨fam⟩ *to be* (*badly*) *left*; ⟨Am, sl⟩ *to fall for*; –ge– s ⟨Am fam⟩ *to be sewed up* **~|legen** vt [h] *to deceive*; *take in*; *let down*; *to have, to do*

Reineclaude [rɛːnˈkloːdə] f ~/~n *greengage*

R·eineke m ~s/ *fox, Reynard*; ⟨fam⟩ *Charlie*

R·einheit f ~/ *clean*(*li*)*ness* || *purity* ⟨a. fig⟩ (*of wine, heart*) || *tidiness, neatness* || *chastity, innocence* || *clarity* (*of sounds, diamonds*) || *genuineness* (*of a cause*) **reinigen** vt [h] *to clean*(*se*); *purge, clear* || v oben bis unten ~ *to clean down*; *to tidy* (⟨Am⟩ *slick*) *up* || (Stall) *to clean out* || ⟨met⟩ *to refine*; *to try* (*out*) || ⟨chem⟩ *to purify* || ⟨fig⟩ *to purify* (*soul, heart*); *purge* (*of* ..) || ⟨med⟩ *to cleanse* || ge–gt w müssen *to need cleaning* | **sich ~** ⟨fig⟩ *to clear o.s.* (*of a crime*) | ~des Abreagieren ⟨eth⟩ *catharsis* **R·einiger** m ~s/~ *cleanser, purifier*; (Getreide≗) *smut-mill* || *refiner* || *reformer, purist* **R·einigung** f ~/~en *purification* (⟨a. fig⟩ *of the heart*) || *purging, washing, clean*(*s*)*ing* || ⟨met⟩ *refining* || ⟨chem⟩ *rectification* || *purgation* (*of the language*); chemische (organische) ~ *dry* (*solvent*) *cleaning*; ⟨hist, jur⟩ (durch Eid) *compurgation* | (Mariä) ~ ⟨ec⟩ *Purification* || monatliche ~ ⟨med⟩ *monthly courses* pl, *menses* pl | **~s- ~anlage** f *purification plant*; ⟨pap⟩ *cleaning plant* **~eid** m *oath of purgation* **~emulsion** f ⟨cosm⟩ *cleansing lotion, e., milk* **~flüssigkeit** f *cleansing fluid* **~krem** m *clean-up cream* **~maschine** f (Korn) *cleaner*; (*wool*) *cleaning machine* **~mittel** n *cleaner*; *cleansing agent*; ⟨med⟩ *detergent* || (Abführmittel) *purgative* **~opfer** n ⟨hist⟩ *lustration* **~pfanne** f *purifying pan* **~prozeß** m ⟨tech⟩ *cleansing process* **~vermögen** n (des Wassers) *purification efficiency* **r·einlich** a *clean* (*street, clothing*) || *cleanly* (*p*) || *neat* (*maid, houses*) || *tidy* (*room*) | ⟨fig⟩ *complete* (*separation*) | [adv] sich ~ halten *to keep o.s. clean and tidy* || *neatly* (*dressed*) | ≗**keit** f ~/ *clean*(*li*)*ness* || *neatness* || *tidiness*

r·einvest·ieren [reːinv–] vt [h] *to reinvest*, ⟨fam⟩ *to plow back*

Reis 1. n ~es/~er ⟨bot⟩ *twig, sprig, shoot* || (Ableger) *scion* || (z Feuern) [pl] *faggots* pl, *brushwood* **2.** m ~es/ → *rice* (geschält *husked*, mit Spelzen *paddy r.*) [1]**~besen** m *birch-broom* [2]**~brei** m *r.-pap* [1]**~bund** m, **~bündel** n *faggot* **~holz** n *brushwood* [2]**~mehl** n *r.-flour* **~papier** n *pith paper* **~pudding** m *r.-pudding* **~schleim** m *r.-milk* **~star** m ⟨orn⟩ *r.-bird* **~stärke** f *r.-starch* **~suppe** f *r.-soup* **~wein** m *sake*; *r. wine*

R·eise f ~/~n **A.** (kurze ~, Rund≗) *tour* || (kl) *trip* || (Auslands≗, Forschungs≗) *travels* pl || (~ z Lande) *journey* (*on land*), (⟨a.⟩ *river j.* den Fluß hinab *or* hinauf) || (~ z Wasser) (*sea*) *voyage* || (Überfahrt) *passage* | (*cycling & motoring*) *tour* || (im Wagen) *trek* || (z Fuß) *tramp*; *journey on foot* || .. mit der Bahn etc *by rail, bike, ship, aeroplane*; ⟨a.⟩ *train journey* | **~ durch** den Kontinent *crossing of the c.* || **~ in** Geschäften *business j.* || e–e ~ ins Ausland m *to travel abroad* || **nach**: ⟨a.⟩ *to move upon London* || e–e ~ **über** Land *an overland j.* || .. **um** die Welt m *to take a trip around the w.* || .. zur Erholung *travelling for health* **B. glückliche** ~! *a pleasant j.* (od *voyage*) *to you*! || lange abenteuerliche ~ ⟨fig⟩ *Odyssey* || die letzte ~ *the last long j.* (= *death*) || e–e tüchtige ~ *quite a jaunt* **C.** e–e ~ **antreten** *to start on a j.* || der Lachs tritt die ~ ins Meer an .. *finds its way to the sea* || jdm die ~ erleichtern *to frank a p through* || e–e ~ fortsetzen *to proceed on a j.* || wohin geht die ~? *where are you off to*? || wir wissen nicht, wohin die ~ geht .. *where we are* *going*; ⟨fig⟩ .. *how matters will develop* ‖ e–e ~ m *to go on a j.*, *to make a j.*; *to tour* (*through*); *the letter has travelled a long way* ‖ .. unternehmen *to undertake a j.* **D. auf** der ~ *whilst travelling* ‖ *on his j.* od *v.* ‖ auf ~n gehen *to go on a j.* ‖ auf ~n s *to be travelling*; immer .. ⟨fam⟩ *to be always on the go* ‖ was man auf ~n erlebt *one's experiences when travelling* | **von** der ~ ermüdet *wayworn* | **zu** e–r ~ aufbrechen *to start on a j.* **~abenteuer** n *adventure* **~andenken** n *travel(l)ing souvenir* **~antritt** m ⟨bes aero⟩ *embarkation* **~anzug** m *travelling-suit* **~apotheke** f *first-aid kit* **~barometer** n *portable b.* **~bedarf** m *travel(l)ing-necessaries* pl **~begleiter** m, (~begleitung f) *t.ing-companion(s* pl) **~bekanntschaft** f *t.ing acquaintance(ship)* **~bericht** m *travelogue* **~beschreibung** f *book of travels*, *itinerary*, ⟨Am a.⟩ *travelogue* **~bett** n *t.ing-bed* **~buch** n *guide*, *itinerary* **~büro** n *t.ing agency*, *tourists' office*, ⟨Am⟩ *travel a.* **~decke** f *t.ing-rug*; *lap robe* **~diäten** pl *t.ing-fees* pl **≗fertig** a *ready to start* **~fieber** n *excitement preceding a journey*, *t.ing spirits* **~flug** m *cruising* (*flight*) | ~geschwindigkeit [f] *c.g speed*; ~höhe [f] *c.g altitude*; ~leistung [f] *c.g power* **~führer** m *guide*(*-book*) **~gebühren** f pl *t.ing-expenses* pl **~gefährte** m *t.ing-companion*, *fellow-traveller* **~gefolge** n *suite* **~geld** n *t.ing-allowance* od *expenses* pl, ⟨a.⟩ *j.-money* **~gepäck** n *luggage*, *traps* pl **~gerät** n *travel requisites* ⟨a. cust⟩ **~geschwindigkeit** f ⟨mar, mot, aero⟩ *cruising speed* **~gesellschaft** f *party of travellers*, *fellow-t.s* pl **~grammophon** n *portable g.* **~handbuch** n = –führer, ⟨a.⟩ *road-book* **~hut** m *t.ing-hat* **~kappe** f *t.ing-cap* **~karte** f *t.ing-map* **~kleid** n *t.ing-dress* **~koffer** m *t.ing-trunk*, *-box*; (kl) *suit-case* **~korb** m *dress-basket* **~kosten** pl *t.ing-expenses* pl | ~rechnung [f] *t.ing claim*; ~vergütung [f] *t.ing allowance* **~küche** f *portable k.* **~leiter** m *travel cruise director*; *guide*; *tour conductor* **~lektüre** f *reading material for the j.* **~lust** f *spirit of t.ing*, *delight in t.ing* **≗lustig** a *fond of t.ing* **~mantel** m *t.ing-cloak* **~marschall** m *cicerone*; (*prince's*) *courier* **~mütze** f *t.ing-cap* **~necessaire** n *t.ing-* od *dressing-case* **~onkel** m ⟨fam⟩ *great traveller* ‖ (*commercial*) *t.er*, ⟨Am⟩ *drummer* **~papiere** n pl *travel documents* **~paß** m *passport*; (f Wanderburschen) *way-bill* **~pläne** m pl *plans for a j.* **~prediger** m *itinerant preacher* **~rock** m *t.ing-coat* **~route** f *route*, *itinerary* **~scheck** m *travel(l)er cheque*, (⟨Am⟩ *t. check*) **~schreibmaschine** f *portable* (*typewriter*) **~schreibzeug** n *portable writing-desk* **~sperre** f *travel ban* **~spesen** pl *t.ing-expenses* pl **~stab** m *t.ing-staff* **~stipendium** *n t.ing scholarship* **~tagebuch** n *diary of travel* **~tasche** f *t.ing-bag*, (zus–legbare) *hold-all*, ⟨Am⟩ *gripsack*, *valise* **~toilette** f *dressing-case* **~vergütung** f *t.ing allowance*, ⟨Am⟩ *mileage* **~verkehr** m *tourist traffic* **~wagen** m *Berlin*, *t.ing-carriage*; ⟨mot⟩ *caravan* **~wecker** m *t.ing alarm clock* **~weg** m *route* **~wetter** n *fine weather for t.ing* | ~versicherung [f] *rain-check* **~zeit** f *tourist season* **~ziel** n *destination* ‖ was ist Ihr ~? *where are you bound for?* **r·eisen** vi [s] *vt [h] **A. 1.** *to travel*, *journey*, *to be touring* od *on one's travels* ‖ er ist *or* hat viel gereist *he is a great traveller* | ⟨com (off)⟩ ~ *to tr. on* (*official*) *business*, ⟨Am a.⟩ *to commute* (*between*); *to go places* | ⟨com⟩ ~ l *to employ travellers* **2.** ~ **(nach)** *to travel*, *journey*, *go* (*to*); *to be bound* (*for*) **3.** (ab|~) **(nach)** *to set out*, *start*, *leave* (*for*) ‖ nächste Woche ~ wir *we* (*shall*) *start next week* **4.** [vt] e–n Weg, e–s Wegs, e–e Route, Strecke ~ *to travel by a line*, *route* | sich müde ~ *to tire o.s. with t.ing* ‖ in Belgien reist es sich gut *it is pleasant t.ing in B.* **B. aufs** Land ~ *to go into the c.* ‖ ⟨fig⟩ auf etw ~ *to trade* (*up*)*on a th* ‖ durch e–n Ort ~ *to pass a place* | **in** die Ferien ~ *to go for one's holidays* ‖ in Urlaub ~ *to go on leave* ‖ ins Gebirge ~ *to go to* .. ‖ in Geschäften (Seife) ~ *to travel on business* (*in soap*) | **mit** der Bahn etc ~ *to go by rail* od *train* etc | **über** Köln ~ *to go via*, *over*, *by C.* ‖ über Land ~ .. *overland* ‖ **von** Ort zu Ort ~ *to pass* od *move* (⟨fam⟩ *flit*) *from p. to p.* ‖ v London nach Bristol ~ *to leave L. for B.* | **zu** Fuß ~ *to go on foot*, ⟨fam⟩ *to tramp* (*it*) ‖ zu Land ~ .. *on land* ‖ zu Pferde ~ *to ride on horseback* ‖ zu Schiff ~ *to tr. by boat* ‖ zum Vergnügen etw ~ *to tr. for pleasure*, *to take a pl. trip* ‖ zur See ~ *to go by sea* **C. reisend** a *travelling* (*artisan*), *itinerant* (*preacher*); .. *on one's travels* **D.** ein weit **gereister** Mann *a great traveller*; weit gereiste Leute *travelled people* **R·eisende** m [der ~, ein ~r] ~n/~n *traveller*, ⟨Am⟩ *traveler*; (z See) *voyager* ‖ ⟨com⟩ *commercial traveller*, ⟨Am⟩ *salesman*, ⟨fam⟩ *drummer* | die ~n w gebeten *travellers are requested* ‖ armer ~r *destitute wayfarer* ‖ ein ~r f Sch. & Co *a traveller for* .. ‖ er ist ~r in Seife *he travels in soap* **R·eisige** m [der ~, ein ~r] ~n/~n ⟨hist⟩ *trooper*, *horseman*

R·eisholz n, **R·eisig** n ~s/ *brushwood* **~flechtwerk** n *hurdle* | Reisigbündel [n pl], –faschinen [f pl] *fascines*

R·eiß- ~ahle f = ~nadel **~·aus** m; ~ nehmen ⟨fam⟩ *to take to one's heels* ⟨sl⟩ *to make tracks*, *to decamp*; *to take o.s. off* **~blei** n *black-lead* **~brett** n *drawing-board* **~feder** f *line-dr.g-pen* **≗fest** a *snag-proof* (Strumpf etc.) **~festigkeit** f *tensile* od *tearing*, *breaking strength* **~kasten** m *box of compasses* **~kohle** f ⟨arts⟩ *black chalk* **~längenprüfer** m (S) *breaking length tester* **~leine** ⟨aero⟩ *rip*(*ping-*) od *release cord* **~nadel** f *scribe*(*-awl*); ⟨arts⟩ *graving needle*; *scriber* (*for graticules*) **~nagel** m *drawing-pin*; → –zwecke **~pflug** m *scarifier* **~schiene** f *dr.g-rule*, *T-square* **~schnur** f = –leine **~stift** m *tracing pencil* **~verschluß** m *zipper*, *zip-fastener* ‖ mit dem ~ öffnen *to unzip*, schließen *to zip up* ‖ Innenfutter mit ~ *zip-in*, *-out lining*; Tasche mit ~ *zipper*; mit ~ versehen *or* geschlossen *zipped* (Anorak) **~wolf** m *willow* **~wolle** *f shoddy* **~zahn** m (Raubtier≗) *carnassial* (*tooth*) **~zeug** n *drawing set* **~zirkel** m *dr.g-compasses* **~zwecke** f *dr.g-pin*, ⟨Am⟩ *thumb-tack* **R·eißen** n ~s/ *bursting*, *tear*(*ing*), *rending* ‖ ⟨pap⟩ *break in the web* ‖ bis z ~ gespannte Saite *almost breaking string* ‖ ⟨arts⟩ *graving*; *scribing* (*of graticules*) | ⟨path⟩ *tearing*; *acute pains* pl; *rheumatism* ‖ (Leib≗) *colic*, ⟨fam⟩ *gripes* pl ‖ (das) Sich-~ *scramble* (um *for*) **r·eißen I.** [vt] tung), *to corner* (*cotton* etc) ‖ (gierig) ⟨sl⟩ *to hog*; [riß/gerissen] [h] **A. 1.** *to tear*, *rend* **2.** (zerren) *to drag*, *tug*, *pull* (*along*) ‖ ⟨fig⟩ → gerissen **B. (ab-, los-)** ~ *to tear* od *pull off* | etw **an** sich [acc] ~ *to seize upon*, *to snatch*, *grasp*, *engross a th*; *to lay one's hands on a th* | ⟨fig⟩ *to seize*, *usurp* (*the power*), ⟨com⟩ *to monopolize* (⟨a. übtr⟩ Unterhaltung), *to corner* (*cotton* etc) ‖ (gierig) ⟨sl⟩ *to mop* (*profits*); die Führung an sich ~ *to take the lead* ‖ (Begeisterung) *to capture* ‖ (Gesetz des Handelns) *to take the situation into one's hands* ‖ *to grasp* (*success*) | (etw) **aus** e–r S ~ *to wrest*, *snatch*, *out of*, *from*; *to wrench*, *rive from*, ⟨Am, sl⟩ *to yank from* ‖ *he whipped the pistol from his pocket* ‖ aus den Angeln reißen *to fling* .. *off its hinges* ‖ *to tear o.s. from a p's arms* ‖ *to arouse a p from his contemplation* ‖ jdn aus allen Himmeln ~ *to destroy a p's illusions* ‖ *the sound shocked her out of her thoughts* | aus–e–a|~ ⟨a.⟩ *to prize apart* | **in** die Höhe ~ *to hoi(c)k* (*an aeroplane*) ‖ *to plunge a nation into war* ‖ *she was swept into the crowd* ‖ in Stücke *or* entzwei|~ *to tear up*, *to t. in two* od *to pieces* ‖ ins Verderben ~ *to ruin* (*a p*); in den Wirbel gerissen w *to be swept into the maelstrom* | **hin-** u her|~ *to drag backwards and forwards*; .. zw *torn between* (*two feelings*) | jdn **mit** sich ~ *to whisk a p off* | **nach** dem Faden ~ *to tear* (*linen*) *the right way of the material* | **von** etw (ab-, weg)|~: *to tear a button from a coat*, *one's eyes from a picture*; *the shock brought the plaster down from the ceiling* ‖ ⟨a.⟩ *to whip off*, *to rip from* | **zu** Boden ~ *to pull down*; *to floor a p* **C.** [Objekt] **1.** (Federn) *to split* ‖ (Fisch) *to draw*, ⟨cul⟩ *to gut* ‖ (v Raubtier) *to tear* (*a lamb*) (*to pieces*) **2. sich an** e–m Nagel ~ *to scratch o.s. with a nail* ‖ sich **um** etw ~ *to struggle*, *scramble*, *fight*, (*compete*) *for* ‖ man riß sich um .. *there was a rush for* (*a th*); *he was very much sought after* ‖ tu nicht so, als ob sich alles um dich risse *don't play hard-to-get* ‖ er reißt sich nicht um die Arbeit *he is no glutton for work* **3.** (als Ergebnis) **(Loch)** *to tear a hole in one's trousers*; *the bomb blew a hole in the wall* ‖ (Lücke) *his death made a great gap* ‖ sich [dat] e–e Schramme ~ *to scratch o.s.* | ⟨fig⟩ (Possen) *to play the buffoon* ‖ *to make* (*grimaces*, *faces*) ‖ *to crack* (*jokes*) ‖ (Zoten) *to talk smut* **II.** [vi] **1.** (of thread, lace) *to break*, *snap* ‖ (of material) *to tear* ‖ (of cord, rope) *to sever*, *seperate* ‖ (of clothes) ⟨fam⟩ *to get torn* ‖ (sich spalten) *to split*, *rip*, *chink*, *crack*; *to burst* ‖ (of water) *to flow rapidly* | ⟨fig⟩ mir reißt die Geduld *I'm losing all p.*, *I'm getting out of p.* ‖ wenn alle Stränge ~ *if nothing else avails*, *if the worst comes to the worst* **2. an** (etw) ~ *to pull*, *wrench*, *strain at* | ⟨fig⟩ *to grate on* (*the nerves*) | ⟨fig⟩ **ins** Geld ~ *to run into m.* **3.** [v/imps] **es** reißt nicht ab *it goes on for ever* ‖ es reißt mir in den Knien *I have shooting pains in my knees*, .. mich im Leibe ⟨fam⟩ *I have got the gripes* **r·eißend I.** [a] **1.** *rapid* (*flow*, *progress*), *racing* (*current*) ‖ (ungestüm) *impetuous* ‖ *tremendous* (*rapidity*) ‖ ~er Strom *torrent* **2.** ⟨path⟩ *acute*, *violent*, *racking* (*pains*) **3.** ⟨zoo⟩ *ferocious*, *rapacious*, *ravenous* ‖ *carnivorous* ‖ ~es Tier *beast of prey* **4.** ⟨fig, com⟩ ~en Absatz finden *to meet with a quick* od *rapid sale* **II.** [adv] ~ abnehmen *to decrease by leaps and bounds*, *rapidly* ‖ ⟨com⟩ ~ abgehen (*the goods*) *sell quickly*, ⟨fam⟩ *go off like wild-fire* **R·eißer** m ~s/~ ⟨journ⟩ *feature*; ⟨theat⟩ *thriller*, *good draw*; *phrase that brings the house down* ‖ (Buch) *bestseller* ‖ ⟨for⟩ *bark-blaze scratcher*

Reit- **~anzug** m *riding-dress* od *-habit* **~bahn** f *r.g-school*; *manège*; *r.g-track* **~gamaschen** f pl *leggings* pl **~gelände** n, glattes *or* gutes ~ *flying country* **~gerte** f *r.g-whip*, *horsewhip* **~gurt** m *r.g-girth*, *r.g-belt* **~handschuh** m *r.g-glove* **~haus** n *r.g-ground*, *manège* **~hengst** m *stallion* **~hose** f (e–e ~ *a pair of*) *breeches* pl (lange) *Jodhpurs* pl **~jacke** *r.g-jacket* **~kissen** n *pillion* **~kleid**, **~kostüm** n (Damen≃) *r.g-habit*; im ~ *dressed for r.g* **~knecht** m *groom* **~krawatte** f ⟨hors⟩ *ascot tie*, ⟨com⟩ *plastron-binder* **~kunst** f *horsemanship*, *equitation*; hohe ~ *horse-mastership* **~mantel** m *r.g-cloak* **~peitsche** f *horsewhip*; e–m die ~ geben *to h. a p* **~pferd** n *r.g-*, *saddle-horse*; ⟨fam⟩ *mount*, ⟨Am⟩ *saddler* **~platz** m *r.g-ground* **~post** f (*mail sent by a*) *courier* **~rock** m *r.g-coat* **~schule** f *r.g-school*, *manège*, ⟨mil⟩ *cavalry school* | *equestrianism* **~sport** m (Rennsport) *horse-racing*, *the turf* **~stall** m *stable for saddle-horses* **~stiefel(n)** m pl *r.g-boots*, *top-boots* pl **~stock** m (mit Schlaufe) *crop* ‖ (an Drechselbank) *tail stock* **~strümpfe** m pl *stirrup-stockings* pl **~tier** n (Kamel) *mount* **~- u Fahrturnier** n *equestrian contest*, *concours hippique* Fr **~wechsel** m ⟨com⟩ *accomodation-bill*, ⟨sl⟩ *kite* **~unterricht** m *instruction in r.g* **~weg** m *bridle-path*, *ride*, *riding* **~zeug** n *r.g equipment*, *r.g outfit*, *r.g-ths* pl; ⟨mil⟩ *harness of a saddle-horse* **~zug** m *cavalcade* **r·eiten I.** [vi] [ritt/geritten] [h & s] wir h heute ger. / wir sind nach Pl. ger. **1.** *to ride*, *to go on horseback*, ⟨Am⟩ *to go h.b. riding* ‖ ⟨fig, sex⟩ *to horse* ‖ gut ~ *to sit a horse well*, *to be a good rider*; waghalsig ~ *to ride for a fall*; geritten k *to come on h.b.*; spazieren ~ *to take a ride* | (im) Schritt, Trab, Galopp ~ *to* (*r. at a walking*) *pace*; *to trot*, *gallop* ‖ Hals über Kopf ~ *to r. whip and spur* ‖ Parade ~ *to ride in parade-step* ‖ (im) Tournier ~ *to r. in a t.* **2. auf** e–m Kamel ~ *to r. a camel* ‖ auf e–m Besen ~ *to r. on a broom* ‖ auf Schusters Rappen ~ *to go on Shanks's mare* ‖ auf e–m Schreibsessel ~ *to be a quill-driver* ‖ ⟨fig⟩ auf e–m herum|~ *to nag at a p* ‖ auf etw herum|~ *to be always harping on a subject* | **durch,** über e–n Ort ~ *to pass* (*through*) *a place on h.b.* | ~ **über** *to override* (*the country*), *to r. about* (*the fields*) | Schiffe ~ **vor** Anker .. *r. at a.* | **zu** zwei ~ *to r. double* **II.** [vt] **1.** *to ride*, *bestride*, *mount* (*a horse*) ‖ e–n (e–s) Weg(es) ~ *to r. along a road* ‖ ich habe *or* bin 80 km g. *I have ridden 80 kms* | ⟨fig⟩ ich will dich schon ~! *I'll tame you yet*! ‖ den Pegasus ~ *to be inspired by the muses* ‖ Prinzipien ~ *to have fads* ‖ sein Steckenpferd ~ *to have a hobby* ‖ Wechsel ~ ⟨sl⟩ *to fly kites* **2.** ein Pferd **ins** Freie ~ *to give a h. outdoor exercise* ‖ jdn in die Tinte ~ *to get a p into a scrape* | e–n **über** den Haufen *or* **zu** Boden ~ *to r. a p down* ‖ ein Pferd lahm *or* zuschanden ~ *to founder*, *overwork*, *override a h.* **3. sich** müde (steif) ~ *to become tired* (*get stiff*) *from r.g* ‖ sich wund (*or* sich [dat] e–n Wolf) ~ *to chafe o.s. in r.g* **4.** ⟨fig⟩ der Alp *or* Mahr reitet ihn *he has the* (od *suffers from*) *nightmare* ‖ Armut, Not etc reitet ihn *poverty* etc *follows him* ‖ ihn hat wohl der Teufel geritten *he must have had the very devil in him* **III.** ≃ n *riding*; *equitation*; ⟨sport, fam⟩ *equestrian* **r·eitend** a *mounted* (*post*, *police*, *riflemen*); *on horseback* ‖ ~ auf *mounted on* ‖ ~e Artillerie *horse-artillery* ‖ ⟨bot⟩ *equitant* (*leaf*) **R·eiter I.** m ~s/~ **1.** *rider*, *horseman* [pl *horsemen*] ‖ [kollekt] (leichte) ~ [pl] (*light*) *horse* ‖ schwerer ~ *trooper* ‖ (*regiment of*) *cavalry* **2.** ⟨über, tech⟩ (Laufgewicht) *rider* | (Kartei≃) *tab* | ⟨fort⟩ *cavalier* | ⟨mil⟩ spanischer ~ *cheval* (pl *chevaux*) *de frise* **II.** f ~/~n ⟨dial, agr⟩ *coarse sieve*, *riddle* [1]**~aufzug** m *cavalcade* **~bildnis** n *equestrian portrait* **~degen** m *c.y-sword* **~dienst** m *c.y-service*; *trooper's duty* **~fahne** f *standard* **~fähnrich** m *cornet* **~fest** n *c.y fête* **~gefecht** n *c.y-fight* **~haufen** m *troop of horse* **~heer** m *host of c.y* **~künste** f pl *equestrian feats* **~pferd** n *trooper's horse* **~pistole** f *horse-pistol* **~regiment** n *horsed* od *c.y-regiment*, *r. of horse* **~standbild** n *equestrian statue* **~stückchen** n ⟨mil⟩ *daring feat of a horseman* **~streife** f *mounted patrol* **~zug** m *cavalcade* **Reiter·ei** f ~/~en **1.** *cavalry*, *horse*(*men*), *mounted men* ‖ ⟨mil⟩ leichte ~ *light horse* **2.** (*inferior*) (*style* od *mode of*) *riding* **R·eiterin** f ~/~nen *female rider*, *horse-woman*; *lady on horseback* **R·eiterschaft** f ~/~en *body of horsemen* **R·eitersmann** m = Reiter I.

Reiz m ~es/~e **A. 1.** (Anziehung, Anmut) *charm*, *attraction* ‖ *grace*(*fulness*), *winningness*, *attractiveness*, *fascination* ‖ *magnetism* = *power to charm*, *charisma of a p* **2.** (Lockung) *enticement*, *lure*, *allurement*, *appeal* **3.** (Erregung) *excitement*, (*violent*) *irritation* ⟨a. path⟩ ‖ (Kitzel) *tickling*, *itching* ‖ (Anreiz) ⟨chem, mech⟩ *stimulus* ‖ ⟨physiol⟩ *impulse* ‖ auf innere (→ körpereigene) ~e ansprechendes Sinnesorgan ⟨eth⟩ *proprioceptor* **B.** der ~ der Neuheit *the charm* od *lure of novelty* ‖ die weiblichen ~e *charms of woman* ‖ *sport has great attractions* ‖ *the fascination of the mystical* ‖ persönlicher ~ ⟨a.⟩ *magnetism* (*of a p*) ‖ *the lure* (*of a language*) ‖ *the amenities* (*of country life*) **C.** s–n eigenen ~ h *to have a charm all one's own*; es liegt ein eigener ~ in: *there is a sort of fascination in it*; e–n ~ ausüben auf: *the light has an irritating affection on the eye* ‖ an *or* den Reiz f jdn verlieren *to pall on a p* ‖ *the thrill had gone out of it* (war verschwunden) ‖ sie l ihre ~e spielen *they turn on their charms* ‖ sie geht mit ihren ~en hausieren *she flashes her charms*, ⟨fam⟩ *airs the dairy*, ⟨vulg⟩ *hawks her meat* ≃**bar** a *sensitive*, *touchy*, *testy*, *nervy* ‖ (leicht erregbar) *fretful, irritable* ‖ (jähzornig) *irascible, short-tempered* ‖ ⟨fig, hum⟩ *waspish, peppery* **~barkeit** f *sensitiveness, touchiness; edginess* ‖ *irritability* ‖ *irascibility* **~gas** n ⟨mil⟩ *sternutatory* **~gift** n *irritant poison* **~-kampfstoff** m ⟨mil⟩ *irritant agent*; ⟨chem⟩ *irritant* **~körpertherapie** f *irritation* od *stimulation therapy* **~̂los** a *unprepossessing; destitute of charms, charmless*; ⟨arts⟩ *tasteless unattractive, unlovely* ‖ (fade) *insipid, uninviting, tame*; ⟨bes Am a.⟩ *homely* **~mittel** n *incentive, incitement; irritant, stimulus* ‖ ⟨med⟩ *stimulant* **~stoff** m *irritant gas* **~̂voll** a *attractive, charming* ‖ *enticing, fascinating* ‖ *tempting* (*offer*) **~strom** m ⟨physiol⟩ *stimulating current* **~summenregel** f ⟨eth⟩ *law of summation of heterogeneous stimuli* **~überflutung** f *excessive stimulation* **~wirkung** f *irritation* ‖ ⟨sex⟩ *appeal* **r·eizen** vt [h] **A. 1.** (anreizen) *to sharpen, stimulate* (*one's appetite*) ‖ *tickle* (*the palate*); *edge* (*the appetite*); *produce* (*thirst*) ‖*incite; stir up* (*eagerness to fight*) ‖ *pique* (*curiosity*) ‖ *egg* (*a p*) *on* (*to do*) ‖ *instigate, rouse, whet* (*a p to do*) ‖ *challenge* (*contradiction* zum W.) | ⟨cards⟩ *to bid* (*against a p*), *to call*; doppelt so hoch ~ *to redouble* **2.** (→ aufreizen) *to irritate* (*a p, the eyes*), *to provoke, annoy, chafe, worry* (*a p*) ‖ *excite* (*a dog, curiosity*) ‖ *to work up* (*a p*), *to raise* (*a p's anger*) ‖ *it rouses me* (*to contradict*) ‖ zur Wut ~ *to exasperate* ‖ (Körper) *to affect* **3.** (entzücken) *to charm* ‖ (verlocken) *to entice, allure* ‖ *to have charm* (*for*), *to attract, interest* (*a p*) ‖ es reizt mich ⟨Am, sl⟩ *it gets my goat* ‖ (in Versuchung führen) *to tempt* **B.** er ist **gereizt** *he is irritated, angry* (*about*); ⟨fam⟩ *his back is up*; *he is nettled* (über *at*) ‖ gereizter Stimmung [gen] *in an irritable* od *savage mood* **r·eizend** a *stimulant, irritant, exciting* ‖ *charming, taking; lovely, attractive; delightful, delicious; bewitching* ‖ *tempting* ‖ ⟨path⟩ *inflammatory* ‖ ⟨fig⟩ ~e P *a duck of a p, a perfect duck* od *peach* ‖ ⟨Am⟩ *cunning baby* ‖ ⟨iron⟩ *nice* (*state of ths*) **R·eizker** m ~s/~ ⟨bot⟩ (*orange*) *agaric* ‖ giftiger ~ *poisonous lactarius* L **R·eizung** f ~/~en *irritation, provocation* ‖ *stimulation, instigation* ‖ *incitement* ‖ ⟨path⟩ *inflammation* ‖ (Lockung) *enticement, allurement* ‖ (Reiz) *charm*

Rekapitulat·ion [ts] f ~/~en *recapitulation* (*recap*) | ~stheorie [f] ⟨biol⟩ *biogenesis, biogeny* **rekapitul·ieren** vt [h] *to recapitulate* ‖ um kurz zu ~ *briefly to r.*

°**Rekel·ei** f ~/~en *coarse and illmannered conduct* ‖ *lolling about; sprawling* **r·ekeln** vt [h] *to stretch* (*one's limbs*) *in a lubberly way* ‖ sich ~ *to loll about, to sprawl* (*on a sofa*)

Reklam- **~·ant** m ~en/~en *claimant* **~ati·on** [–ts–] f ~/~en *reclamation, claim* ‖ (Klage) *complaint, protest* ‖ ~sabteilung [f] *claim department* **Rekl·ame** f ~/~n (→ Werbung) *advertising, publicity* (*the book was given a large p.* f. d. B. wurde .. gemacht) ‖ (Inserat) *advertisement* [⟨sl⟩ *ad*(*s* pl)], *puff*; ⟨sl⟩ *boost* ‖ ~ m f *to advertise, pressagent; to cry up; to puff, boom*; ⟨Am a.⟩ *to publicize* ‖ (Buch) ⟨a.⟩ *blurb* ‖ gegenseitige ~ ⟨Am⟩ *log-rolling* **~ansager** m ⟨wir, Am⟩ *Master of Ceremony*, ⟨fam⟩ *emcee* **~artikel** m *a.g article* **~auto** n *admobile* **~büro** n *a.g office, publicity bureau* **~chef** m *publicity manager; public relations counsel*, ⟨Am⟩ *press agent* **~fachmann** m *publicity agent, ad-man* **~fernsehen** n *commercial TV* **~fläche** f *a.g space*; (*house*) *boarding* **~feldzug** m *p.y campaign* **~gerüst** n ⟨Am⟩ *signboard* **~held** m *p.y expert* **~konzertpate** m ⟨Am, wir⟩ *sponsor* **~kosten** pl *advertising expenditure* **~kunst** f *commercial art* **~marken** f pl z Aufkleben *advertising stickers* **~prospekt** m *dodger* °**~rummel** m *ballyhoo* **~sachen** f pl *dealer* *expenditure* **~kunst** f *commercial art* **~prospekt** m *dodger* °**~rummel** m *ballyhoo* **~sachen** f pl *dealer* *aids* pl **~schild** m *sign*, ⟨Am, fam⟩ *ad-card*; (Licht-~̂ auf Dach) *sky sign* **~schlager** m *stunt* **~schlepp** m *air poster towing* **~schrift** ⟨typ⟩ *display lettering* **~streifen** m ⟨bookb⟩ *blurb* **~trick** m ⟨sl⟩ *stunt; sell* **~verkauf** m *opening sale* **~wagen** m *a.g van* **~zettel** m *handbill*, ⟨Am⟩ *dodger* **~zeichner** m *designer of advertisements* **~zettel** m *bill* **reklam·ieren** vt [h] *to* (*re*)*claim; to ask for* ‖ ⟨mil, Ger⟩ (jdn) ~ *to claim back, to retain* (f *for*) | vi [h] (gegen) *to protest* (*against*), *to complain* (*about*)

Rekog- **~niti·on** f ~/~en *acknowledgment* | ~sschein [m] ⟨com⟩ *bill* od *receipt ad interim* **~̂nosz·ieren** vt [h] [obs]: *to reconnoitre* **~nosz·ierung** f ~/~en [obs] *reconnoitring* ‖ ⟨mil⟩ *reconnaissance*, ⟨fam⟩ *recon* | ~sabteilung [f], ~s-detachement [n] [obs]: ⟨mil⟩ *reconnoitring-party*; ⟨mil sl⟩ *recon party*

Rekonvalesz·ent m ~en/~en *convalescent* **Rekonvalesz·enz** f ~/ *convalescence*

Rek·ord m ~es/~e *record* (aufstellen, erzielen *to make* [*set up, establish*] *a r.*; brechen *to cut, break*; einstellen ⟨sport⟩ *to equal*; schlagen *to beat, cut*; verbessern *to improve*) ‖ ⟨fig⟩ ~ der Gemeinheit *r. in vulgarity* **~leistung** f *r. performance* **~saison** f; es war e–e ~ *the season was a r. one* **~versuch** m *attempt to beat the r., r. attempt* **~zeit** f *r. time*

Rekr·ut m ~en/~en ⟨engl⟩ *recruit*, ⟨a-engl⟩ *conscript* ‖ ⟨sl⟩ *colt, rookie* | **~en-** ~annahmestelle [f] *reception center* N; ~ausbildung [f] *initial training*; ~depot [n] *recruit depot*; ⟨Am⟩ *replacement center* N; ~unteroffizier [m] *drill-sergeant* **~̂·ieren** vt/i [h] *to recruit* ‖ sich ~ ⟨fig⟩ (aus) *to be recruited* (*from*) od *composed* (*of*) **~·ierung** f ~/~en *r.ing* | **~s-** ~quote [f] ⟨Am⟩ *draft intake*; ~swesen [n] *r.ing service*

Rekt- **~aszensi·on** f ~/~en ⟨astr⟩ *right ascension* **~ifikati·on** [ts] f ~/ *rectification* **~̂ifiz·ieren** vt [h] *to rectify* ‖ (Spiritus) *to try* **~i·on** ~/~en f ⟨gram⟩ *government, regimen* **R·ektor** m ~s/Rekt·oren (e–r Bürgerschule) *head-master*; ⟨Am⟩ *principal* ‖ (e–r Universität) *rector*; ⟨engl⟩ *Chancellor*, ⟨Scot⟩ *Lord Rector*; ⟨Am⟩ *rector* | **~·at** n ~(e)s/~e *headmastership, rectorship* **~·atsrede** f *rectorial* od *chancellor's address* **~·atswechsel** m *rotation in rector's office* **~·orenkonferenz** f ⟨Ger univ⟩ *rectors' meeting*

Relais [re'lɛ:] n ~/~ ⟨mil, el⟩ *relay* **~einheit** f ⟨comp⟩ *control unit* **~schrank** m *r. frame* **~system** n *r. combination* **~übertragung** f ⟨telg⟩ *repeater* **~zahlengeber** m *r. sender*

Relati·on [ts] f ~/~en *relation* **relat·iv** a *relative* ⟨a. gram⟩; *r.* (*humidity* ⟨meteor⟩); *comparative* | adv ⟨a.⟩ *fairly* (*large*) **~̂pronomen** n *rel. pronoun* **~̂satz** m *rel. clause*

Relegati·on f ~/~en *expulsion* ‖ ⟨engl, univ⟩ (zeitweilige) *rustication* **releg·ieren** vt [h] *to expel* ‖ *to send down* ‖ ⟨engl, univ⟩ *to rusticate* ‖ *he was expelled* (*from*) *the school*

Reli·ef n ~s/~s ⟨arts⟩ *relievo, relief* ‖ [dat] ~ geben *to set off* **~druck** m ⟨typ⟩ *surface-printing* **~karte** f, **~plan** m *embossed map* **~stickerei** f *raised embroidery* **~w·alzendruck** = ~druck

Religi·on f ~/~en *religion*; ⟨school⟩ Scripture ‖ e–e ~ annehmen *to embrace a faith; to turn* (*Christian*) | **~s-** **~bekenntnis** n (*religious*) *profession* **~duldung** f *toleration* **~edikt** n *edict concerning r.n* **~eid** m *r.ous oath, test* **~eifer** m *r.ous zeal* **~fanatiker** m *devotee, fanatic* **~freiheit** f *r.ous liberty* **~gebräuche** m pl *rites* **~gemeinschaft, ~gesellschaft** f *r.ous community* od *corporation* **~geschichte** f *history of r.n* **~gesellschaft** f *r.ous association* od *society* **~krieg** m *war of r.* **~lehre** f *r.ous instruction*, ⟨univ⟩ *divinity*, ⟨ec⟩ *doctrine* **~lehrer** m *teacher of r.n* ‖ *divine* **~̂los** a *irr.ous* **~partei** f *r.ous party* **~schwärmer** m *fanatic* **~schwärmer·ei** f *fanaticism* **~stat·istik** f *r.ous* *statistics* **~stifter** m *founder of a r.n* **~streit** m *r.ous controversy* **~stunde** f *Bible lesson* **~system** n *r.ous system* **~trennung** f *schism* **~übung** f *r.ous worship*; ~en [pl] *r.ous exercises* pl **~wechsel** m *conversion* **~wissenschaft** f *divinity, theology*; vergleichende ~ *science of comparative r.n* | ≈lich [a] *scientific-r.ous (book)* **~zwang** m *intolerance, r.ous compulsion* **religi·ös** [a] *religious* || (fromm) *pious*, ⟨sl⟩ *pi* || sein ~es Herz entdecken ⟨bes Am fam⟩ *to get religion* || in ~er Beziehung *r.ously* | [adv] nicht ~ veranlagt s *to have no r.ous instincts* **Religiosit·ät** f ~/ *religiousness* || *piety*

Rel·i- ~kten m [pl] ⟨geol⟩ *relics* || ⟨jur⟩ *heirs* **~quie** f ~/~n *relic* | ~ndienst [m] *adoration of r.s*; ~nkasten, ~nschrank [m] *shrine, reliquary* –nstück [n] *relic*

R·eling f ~/~e ⟨mar⟩ *rails* pl, *railing* || ~ um den Hauptmast *fife-rail*

R·ellmaus f ⟨zoo⟩ *large dormouse*

Reman·enz f ~/ *lag in the magnetic force*

Rem·arkdruck m ⟨engr⟩ *remarque, remark*

Remed·ur f ~/ [obs] *remedy* || ~ schaffen *to remedy matters*

Remilitaris·ierung f *remilitarization*

Reminisz·enz f ~/~en *reminiscence, recollection*

Remin·iszere m ~/ *second Sunday in Lent*

rem·is [rəˈmiː] a Fr ⟨chess⟩ *(the game is) drawn; there is a draw* | ≈e [reˈmiːzə] f ~/~n *coach-house* **Remitt- ~·enden** f [pl] (im Buchhandel) *remainders* pl **~·ent** ~en/~en ⟨com⟩ *payee* || (Wechselnehmer) *remitter* ≈**·ieren** vt [h] *to remit, return*, ⟨bes Am⟩ *to remainder; to send back* | ~d ⟨med⟩ *remittent (fever)*

Remonstrat·ion f ~, ~en *remonstrance* **remonstr·ieren** *to remonstrate*

Rem·onte f ~/~n ⟨hors-mil⟩ *remount* || **~depot** n *r.ing-depot* **~reiter** m *rough-rider* **~wesen** n *r.s* pl **Remont·ierung** f *r.ing* **remont·ieren** vt *to remount* **Remontoiruhr** [remɔ̃nˈtwaːr–] f *keyless watch*, ⟨Am⟩ *stem-winder*

Remoul·ade f ~/~n *salad-cream*

Rempel·ei f ~/~en *jostling* | [dazu:] *to jostle*

R·emter m ~s/~ *refectory*

remuner·ieren vt [h] *to remunerate* **Remuner·ierung**, Remunerat·ion f *remuneration*

Ren n ~s/~s & ~e ⟨scient⟩ → ~ntier

Renaissance [rənɛˈsɑ̃ːs] f ~/ *Renaissance, Renascence*; 18. Jh. *neo-classicism* **~stil** m *R. style*

Rend·ant m ~en/~en *accountant, treasurer* | **~·ur** f ~/~en *acc.'s post* bzw. *office* **Rendezvous** [rɑ̃ːdeˈvuː] n ~/~ *rendezvous, assignation, appointment*; ⟨Am⟩ *date* (verabreden *to arrange*, einhalten *to keep an app.*); sich mit jdm ein ~ geben *to arrange a meeting with a p*; mit jdm ein ~ h ⟨bes Am⟩ *to date* | ~manöver n ⟨a–n⟩ *rendezvous manœuvre*; ~platz [m] *love nest* **Rend·ite** f ~/~n *yield*

Reneg·at m ~en/~en *renegade*

Ren·ette f ~/~n ⟨bot⟩ *rennet, queenapple*

renit·ent a *refractory, obstinate* **Renit·enz** f ~/ *refractoriness, obstinacy*

R·enke f ~/~n ⟨ich⟩ *vendace*

r·enken vt [h] *to wrench, bend, turn, twist*

R·enn- ~arbeit f ⟨met⟩ *direct extraction from the ore* **~bahn** f *race-course*, ⟨Am⟩ *r.-track*; ⟨fam⟩ *oval* || (Leichtathletik) *(cinder-)tr.* || ⟨mot⟩ *speedway* **~bericht** m *Racing Notes* **~boot** n *r.g-boat, racer* **~fahrt** f ⟨mot⟩ *race* **~fahrer** m *r.g driver* **~hund** m *whippet* **~jacht** f *r.g yacht* **~kraftstoff** m *ternary fuel* **~pfahl** m *distance-post* **~pferd** n *r.horse, r.r* **~platz** m *r.-course*; die ≈e [pl] *the turf* | ~besucher [m] *turfite* **~reiter** m *jockey* (dazu: *to j.*); *turfite* **~saison** f *r.g season* **~schlitten** m *bobsleigh* **~schuhe** m pl *spike shoes* **~sport** m *r.g, the turf* **~stall** m *r.g* od *training--stables* pl **~strecke** f *distance*; ⟨mot sl⟩ *drag strip* **~termin** m *r.g fixture* **~tier** n *reindeer* | ~flechte [f] *r.-moss* **~vogel** m *courser* **~wagen** m ⟨hist⟩ *chariot* || ⟨mot⟩ *r.g-car, racer* **~wettsteuer** f *pari--mutual tax* **~wolf** m *Swedish sleigh* **~ziel** n *winning-post* **R·ennen** n ~s/~ *running* | ⟨bes sport⟩ *race (r.), racing, course*, ⟨sl⟩ *lope* || Einzel≈ *heat* || Flach≈ *flat r.* || Hindernis≈ *steeple--chase* || Jagd≈ (v Ziel z Ziel) *point-to-point r.* || totes ~ *dead heat* | ~ abhalten *to arrange r.s* || ein ~ laufen *to run a r.* || das ~ m *to make the running* ⟨a. fig⟩ || das ~ aufgeben *to give up the race* ⟨a. fig⟩; ⟨fig⟩ *to throw up the sponge* || alle ~ .. besuchen *to race at all the meetings* **~besucher** m *race-goer* **~reiten** n *r.-riding* **r·ennen I.** vi [rannte/gerannt] [s] *to run, race, rush* || **an,** gegen, wider (etw) ~ *to dash, bump*, ⟨fam⟩ *cannon*, ⟨sl⟩ *slump, barge, against* (in *into*) || (of car) *to collide with* | mit dem Kopf gegen die Wand ~ *to run one's head against a stone wall* || mit voller Wucht .. *to run full tilt (at, into)* || **hinter** e–m her|~ *to clash off in pursuit of a p* || die Straße hinunter|~ *to tear along the road* || **in** sein Unglück ~ *to rush to one's own ruin* || geradewegs ~ **in** ⟨fam⟩ *to rip into*; .. ins Verderben ~ *to rush headlong into destruction*; jdn ins V. ~ l *to give a p plenty of rope to rush headlong into destruction* | ~ **nach** *to hunt for* od *after (a th)* | mit jdm **um** die Wette ~ *to race a p for a wager* | **vorwärts** ~ *to rush forward* | er rennt wie ein Wiesel *he's as quick as a weasel* || (Pferd) ~ l *to race, run* **II.** vt [h] **1.** [obs] ⟨met⟩ *to smelt* **2.** sich [dat] ein Loch in den Kopf ~ *to knock a hole in one's head* || jdm den Degen in, durch den Leib ~ *to run one's sword into, through a p's body* || jdn über den Haufen ~ *to run a p over, to overturn a p* || zu Boden ~ *to turn over* **3. sich** außer Atem ~ *to run o.s. out of breath* || sich fest|~ *to get stuck fast* **R·enner** m ~s/~ *race-horse, racer*; *spanker*

Rennes [ren] n ⟨Fr⟩ (Stadt)

Renomm- ~·age [reːnɔˈmaːʒə] f ~/ *brag(ging), swagger(ing), bluff* **~·ee** n ~s/ *renown* || *common repute*; *reputation* || per ~ *by repute* || in gutem ~ stehen *to stand in good repute* ≈**·ieren** vi [h] *to brag, boast* (mit *of*), *swagger*, ⟨sl⟩ *to swank* || *to talk big*; *to ruffle it* || mit etw ~ *to make a show with a th* || um zu ~ *for show* ≈**·iert** a *renowned, famous* (wegen *for*) **~·ier-** [in comp] *showy, paraded, gorgeous*; *worn* (etc) *for show* **~·ist** m ~en/~en *boaster, braggart*; ⟨Am fam⟩ *fire-eater, bully* **~ierer·ei** ~/~en *boasting, bragging, bluff*

Ren·once [reˈnɔ̃ːsə] **1.** f ~/ *renounce* || *renouncing, revoking (a suit)* **2.** m ~en/~en ⟨Ger, univ⟩ *freshman of a "Corps"*

r·enovaskul·är a ⟨med⟩ *renovascular*

Renov- ~ati·on f ~/~en *renovation, redecoration* ≈**·ieren** vt [h] *to renovate, renew, redecorate*; *restore* ⟨a. arts⟩ || (Fassade) *to refront (a house)* || ⟨fam⟩ *to re-do*

Rent- ~amt n, **~kammer** f *board of revenue* || *r.e-office* **~meister** m *receiver of the r., treasurer* || (Verwalter) *steward* **rent·abel** a *lucrative, profitable, profit-earning* || *paying (business)*; knapp ~ *marginal*; nicht mehr ~ *submarginal* | ~ **m** *to put .. on a paying basis* **-bilis·ieren** vt [h] → rationalisieren **R-bilitätsgrenze** f *profit margin* **R·ente** f ~/~n *revenue, income*; *benefits* pl || *pension*; ~n [pl] *p.s* || (Miete) *rent* || (Zinsen) *interest* || ~ (aus Kapital- u Grundbesitz) *annuity* || ~n [pl] *stocks* pl || er lebt v s–n ~n *he lives on his private income* od *means* | **~n-** ~ablösung [f] *liquidation of an a.y*; ~bank f *a.y office*; ~bescheid [m] *p. decision* od *adjudication, award, note*; ~einmaleinlage [f] *single premium payment*; *annuity purchase*; ~empfänger [m] *old-age pensioner*; ⟨ins⟩ *beneficiary*; = Rentner; ~mark f *the Rentenmark*; ~titel [m] *annuity bond*; ~versicherung [f] *pension scheme* **Rentier** m = Rentner

Rentier n = Ren **rent·ieren** vi [h] & sich ~ *to yield a profit, to be profitable* || ⟨com⟩ *to pay, to leave a margin* **R·entner** m ~s/~ *person living on his private income, person of private* od *independent means; indep. gentleman; pensioner* || *annuitant*

reorganis·ieren vt [h] *to reorganize*

Repar- **~ati·onen** pl, **~ationszahlungen** pl *reparations* pl || ~ leisten *to make reparations* **~at·ur** f ~/~en *repair(ing)* || in ~ *under r.* | ≃bedürftig [a] *in need of r.*; ~dienst [m] ⟨mot⟩ *maintenance service*; ~grube [f] *working pit*; ~-kosten [pl] *r.ing-expenses* pl; ~werkstatt [f] *r.(ing)-shop* **≃·ieren** vt [h] *to repair, mend* || (Haus) ⟨a.⟩ *to do up* || (Uhr) *to repair,* ⟨Am a.⟩ *to fix* **~·iert** a *fixed* N

Repart- **≃·ieren** vt [h] *to distribute equally, to share, to go shares* || *to have a Dutch treat* (*let's go D.*) **~·ierung, ~iti·on** [ts] f ~/~en *repartition, division* || → Zuteilung

Repatri·ierung f *repatriation*

Repertoire [–'twa:r] n ~s/~s, (–t·orium [n] ~s/–rien) *repertoire, repertory* **~stück** n *stock-piece*

Repet- **~·ent** m ~en/~en *private tutor, coach* || *repeater* **~ier-** ~gewehr [n] *magazine rifle, repeating rifle, repeater*; ~uhr [f] *repeating watch, repeater* **≃·ieren** vt [h] *to repeat* **~iti·on** [ts] f ~/~en *repetition* **~·itor** m –oren/–oren ⟨univ⟩ *coach* **~it·orium** n ~s/–rien *survey of lectures*

Repl·ik f ~/~en *reply, retort* || ⟨jur⟩ *rejoinder, counterplea* **R·eplika** f ~/–ken ⟨arts⟩ *second version* **repliz·ieren** vt [h] *to reply*

Rep·ort m ~(e)s/~e ⟨com⟩ *carrying-over business; contango* | **~·age** f *rewrite* s; *news-reporting* od *-gathering* (*work*) | ~film [m] *newsreal, news film*; ~fotografie [f] *news photography* **~er** m ~s/~ *reporter* (bei .. *on a paper*); ⟨Am, fam⟩ *leg man* | ~ in [f] ⟨Am sl⟩ *news hen*

Reposit·orium n ~s/–rien *repository* || (*set of*) *bookshelves* || *music-stand*

Repräsent- **~·ant** m ~en/~en *representative, exponent* | ~enkammer [f] Fr *Chamber of Deputies,* **≃at·iv** [f] a *dignified; representative* || *gentlemanly* || *state* (*portrait*) || *impressive* (*car that looks like sth*) **≃·ieren** vt [h] *to represent; to stand for* (*a th*) | vi [h] *to act the host* od *hostess* || *to cut a dignified figure* **~ati·on** f ~/~en *representation* | ≃sfähig a *presentable*; ~sfigur [f], ~sstück [n] *figure-head*; ~sgelder [n pl] *official expenses* pl; ⟨mil, mar⟩ *table-money*

Repress·alien f pl *reprisals* pl, *retaliation* || ~ ergreifen, ausüben *to make reprisals* (gegen *on*)

Repr·ise f ~/~n ⟨film⟩ (Neuaufnahme) *retake* | ~nkino [n] ⟨a-engl⟩ *repertory cinema*

reprivatis·ierem vt [h] *to denationalize*

R·epro f ~/~s = **~dukti·on** f ~/~en *reproduction* || reine ~ ⟨demog⟩ *net replacement* (~s-ziffer [f] *net r.t rate*; ~sz. nach Heirats- u Ehelösungshäufigkeit *nuptial net r.t rate*) **≃-duktiv** [–f] *performing* (*artist*) **~duz·ierbarkeit** f *reproducibility* (*of measured values* od *results* od *measurements*) **≃duz·ieren** vt [h] *to reproduce* **~film** m *bibliofilm* **~graph·ie** f *reprography*

Rept·il n ~(e)s/~e & ~ien *reptile*

Republ·ik f ~/~en *republic*; Deutsche Demokratische ~ (DDR) *German Democratic R.* **~·aner** m ~s/~; **≃·anisch** a *republican* **~flucht** f ⟨SBZ⟩ *defection*

Reput- **~ati·on** [ts] f ~/ *repute, reputation, renown* **≃·ierlich** a *reputable, respectable* || nicht ~ *disreputable*

R·equiem n ~s/~s *requiem*

Requi- **≃r·ieren** vt [h] ⟨mil⟩ *to requisition* **~s·it** n ~(e)s/~e(n) *requisite* || ~en [pl] ⟨theat⟩ *properties* pl; ⟨fam⟩ *hand props* | ~enliste [f] *property-plot,* ⟨Am⟩ *prop list*; ~enmeister [m] *property-man, -master* **~sit·eur** [–ør] m ~s/~e *p.-m.* **~siti·on** f ~/~en ⟨mil⟩ *requisition* | ~sschein m *r. order*

resch a **1.** = knusprig **2.** *tough* (*meat*) **3.** *acid, sour* **4.** *lively, alert*

Re·seda f ~/~s; **Res·ede** f ~/~n ⟨bot⟩ *mignonette*

Reserv·at n ~(e)s/~e *reservation* | ~recht [n] *reserved right* **~i·on** f ⟨demog⟩ *native reserve; reservation* **Res·erve** f ~/~n *reserve* || ⟨com⟩ *capital r.*; (Mehr-) Minderbedarf **≃en** (*in*)*-adequate r.s*; stille ~ *inner r.*; s–e ~n angreifen *to draw on one's resources* ⟨mil⟩ *r.s* pl, ⟨engl a.⟩ *Territorial Army*; ~ hat Ruh *the r.s have been discharged* || ⟨fig⟩ in ~ *on ice* ⟨a. fig⟩ etw in ~ h ⟨fam⟩ *to have .. up one's sleeve* || sich k–e, zuviel ~ auferlegen *to have no r., to be excessively r.d* **~anker** m *spare anchor* **~behälter** m ⟨mot⟩ *emergency* od *stand-by tank* **~bestände** m pl *r. stocks* od *supplies*; ⟨mil⟩ ~ bei der Einheit *unit r.s* **~einheiten** f pl ⟨tact⟩ *r. echelon* **~fonds** m, **~kapital** n *r.-fund* **~mann** m *reservist* **~offizier** m *reserve officer* | ~anwärter [m] (R.O.A.) *r. o. candidate* **~rad** n *spare* od *extra wheel* **~tank** m *r. container* **~teil** m *spare part* **~truppen** f pl *reserves* **reservieren** vt [h] 1. *to reserve, book; to set .. apart* 2. = ausbedingen **reserv·iert** a *reserved* (*seat*) | ⟨fig⟩ *reserved* (*nature*) || ⟨fam⟩ *stand-offish* || sich ~ verhalten *to practise reserve* || ⟨Am⟩ den Indianern ~er Bezirk *reservation*; ~e Haltung *standoffishness* | **~heit** f *aloofness* **Reserv·ierung** f *reservation; booking* **Reserv·ist** m ~en/~en ⟨mil⟩ *reservist* **Reservoir** [–'vwa:r] n ~(e)s/~e *reservoir, tank*

Resid- **~·ent** m ~en/~en *resident* (*ambassador* od *minister*) | ~·ur [f] ~/~en ⟨pol⟩ = Außenstelle, Filiale **~·enz** f ~/~en (*royal* etc.) *residence,* ⟨Am⟩ (des Präsidenten) *the White House* | ~ler [m] *inhabitant of a capital*; ~stadt [f] *capital* (*town*); *place of residence* **≃·ieren** vi [h] *to reside* **Res·iduum** n ~s/–duen ⟨chem⟩ *residue*

Resignati·on [ts] f ~/ *resignation* **resign·ieren** **1.** vi [h] *to resign* (auf etw *a th*); ⟨fam⟩ *to step down* **2.** vt [h] *to resign* (*a th*) **3.** sich in etw ~ *to resign o.s. to a th* **resign·iert** a ⟨fig⟩ *resigned*

resist·ent a (*drought*) *resistant* (*plant*) **Re-sist·enz** f ~/ (passive) (*passive*) *resistance*

Reskr·ipt n ~(e)s/~e *rescript*

resol·ut a *resolute, determined* | **≃i·on** [ts] f; e–e ~ fassen ⟨pol⟩ *to pass a resolution* **resolv·ie-ren** vt [h] (⟨a.⟩ sich ~) **1.** (beschließen) *to resolve* **2.** (auflösen) *to resolve*

Reson·anz f ~/~en *echo, reverberation, resonance* || ⟨übtr theat etc⟩ *impact*; k–e ~ finden *to find no response* **~boden** m *sounding-board* || ⟨übtr⟩ = Widerhall **~kasten** m *sounding-box* **~loch** n *sound-hole* **~platte** f ⟨theat⟩ *baffle*

Resp·ekt m ~(e)s/ *respect, regard* || ⟨fam⟩ (vor [dat] *awe* (*of*) || ~ abringen *to draw respect*; e–m ~ einflößen *to inspire a p with awe* || allen ~ vor jdm h *to hold a p in great r.*; *to stand in awe of a p* || sich ~ verschaffen *to make o.s. r.ed* || ~ zollen *to pay r.s* | es **an** jedem ~ fehlen l *to lack all r.* (*for*) || **mit** ~ zu sagen ⟨fam⟩ *to put it mildly, saving your presence* | ~blatt [n] ⟨typ⟩ *fly-leaf; half--title*; ≃heischend [a] *redoutable; commanding respect*; ≃los [a] *irreverent*; ~sperson [f] *p held in respect; notability*; ⟨engl, univ⟩ *don* || ~en [pl] *elders and betters* pl; ~tage [m pl] ⟨com⟩ *days of grace*; ≃voll a *respectful, deferential*; ≃widrig(keit [f]) [a] *disrespectful*(*ness*), (*irreverence*) **≃·abel, ≃·ierlich** a *respectable, honourable* **≃t·ieren** vt [h] *to respect*; ⟨a. com⟩ (nicht) *to* (*dis*)*honour* (*a bill*) **≃·ive** [–və] [adv] *respectively* || 2 Schiffe v 25 resp. 20 t *two ships resp. of 25 and 20 tons*

Resp·iro n ~/ ⟨com⟩ *respite, delay*

Respons·orium n ~s/–rien ⟨ec⟩ *responses* pl || ⟨mus⟩ *antiphon*

Ressentim·ent [rɛsãti'mã] n ∼s/∼s Fr ⟨m. m.⟩ *resentment*; *secret grudge* (*chiefly due to an inferiority complex*)

Ressort [–'sɔ:r] n ∼s/∼s *department* ‖ (*administrative*) *province* ‖ das ist (nicht) mein ∼ *that is in* (*beyond*) *my province* **≈mäßig** a *departmental*

Rest m ∼es/∼e & ∼er **A.** *rest*; *scrap* ‖ *remains* pl (*of a meal*) ‖ (Spur) *vestige*; ⟨math⟩ *remainder* ⟨a. com⟩ ‖ *butt-end* ‖ letzter ∼ *fagend*, (im Glase) *heel-tap* ‖ ⟨chem, jur⟩ *residue* ‖ kl ∼e [pl] (*odds and*) *ends*; *trifles* pl ‖ sterbliche ∼e (*a p's*) *earthly remains* ‖ ⟨mil⟩ *balance* N ‖ ⟨fig a.⟩ *survival*, ⟨Am⟩ *hangover*; die letzten ∼e *the last shreds* (*of a conception*) ‖ ∼e ⟨Am⟩ *leftovers* ‖ der schäbige (traurige) ∼ *what's left in the basket* (⟨bes Am⟩ *the shambles*) **|** (Stoff≈) [∼er pl] *remnant* ¦ (e–r Rechnung) *remainder*; *balance* (⟨Am a. fig⟩: *of his life*); *arrears*, *debt* **B.** ⟨fig⟩ s–n ∼ bek *to receive the finishing stroke* ‖ in ∼ bleiben *to be in arrears* ‖ jdm den ∼ geben *to finish a p* (*off*), *to ruin a p*, *to do for a p*; das gab ihm den ∼ ⟨fam⟩ *that was the last straw for him* ‖ e–r S den ∼ geben: *the final touch was put to her disgust by ..* ‖ das gibt der S den ∼ *that settles it* ‖ ⟨stud, sl⟩ ∼ weg! *put* od *knock it back*!, *sink it*! **∼bestand** m *remaining stock* (*of books*); ≈e [pl] *remain(der)s*, *remnants*; *vestiges* pl **∼betrag** m *remainder*, *residual*; den ∼ bezahlen *to pay the balance* **∼empfänger** m ⟨jur⟩ *residuary legatee* **∼guthaben** n *balance* **∼kaufhypothek** f *purchase money mortgage* **≈lich** a *remaning* ‖ ∼er Teil *residue* ‖ ⟨fig⟩ *vestigial* (*democracy*) die ∼en 50 Pfd *the balance of* £ *50* **≈los** a *complete*, *final*, *without a remainder* **|** ⟨fig⟩ [adv] (gründlich) *thoroughly*, *completely*; (*paid*) *in full*; (*expelled*) *to the last man* ‖ ∼ vernichten *to rout* **∼nachlaß** m ⟨jur⟩ *residuary estate* **|** ∼empfänger = –empfänger **∼staat** m *remnant of a state* **∼waren** [pl] ⟨com⟩ *rummage* **∼zahlung** f ⟨bank⟩ *payment of the balance*; *final p.* **Rest·ant** m ∼en/∼en **1.** *p in arrears* **2.** **∼en** pl *arrears* pl; = Ladenhüter

Restau- **∼rant** [rɛsto'raŋ] n ∼s/∼s *restaurant* ‖ ⟨engl⟩ S.s ∼ *Simpson's*, so: *Frascati's*, etc ‖ ∼ mit Selbstbedienung *cafeteria*; ⟨Am a.⟩ *coffee-shop* **|** ∼chef [m] *r. manager*; ∼direktor [m] *dining-room supervisor*; unzufriedener ∼gast *waiter baiter* **∼rateur** [rɛstora'tø:r] m ∼s/∼e *r.t-keeper*, *publican*; ⟨Am⟩ *saloon-keeper* **∼ra·ti·on** f ∼/∼en *r.t*, *dining-rooms* pl, ⟨rail⟩ *refreshment room* ‖ ⟨fig⟩ *restoration* **|** ∼sessen [m] *meal at a r.t* **≈r·ieren** vt [h] *to restore*, *renovate* ‖ (Bild) *to touch up* ‖ sich ∼ *to partake of refreshments*

R·ester- [pl v Rest) **∼handlung** f *shop of remnants* **∼verkauf** m *remnant sale*

rest·ieren vi [h] *to be in arrears* ‖ (übrigbleiben) *to be left*, *to remain* ‖ ∼d (*debt*) *still owing*

restitu·ieren vt [h] *to restore* **Restituierung, Restituti·on** [ts] f ∼/∼en *restitution*

restrikt·iv [–f] a *restrictionist* [attr] (*politics*)

Result- **∼·ante** f ∼/∼n *resultant*

Result·at n ∼(e)s/∼e *result*; *issue*; *the showing*, *finding* ‖ ⟨sport⟩ *score* ‖ ⟨math a.⟩ *answer* ‖ das ∼ davon war .. *the upshot of it was* ..; das entgegengesetzte ∼ zeitigen *to achieve the exact opposite*; → Ergebnis **|** ∼druck m ⟨sport⟩ *printing of results* **≈ieren** vi [h] *to result*

Resüm·ee n ∼s/∼s *resumé*, *summary* **resüm·ieren** vt [h] *to make a resumé of*, *to summarize*, *recapitulate* ‖ sich ∼ *to sum up*

Ret·abel n ∼s/∼ ⟨ec⟩ *reredos* **|** ∼flügel [m] *wing-panel*

retabl·ieren vt (sich) ∼ *to re-establish* (*o.s.*)

retard·ieren vt [h] *to impede*, *check* ‖ ∼des Moment *obstruction in the dénouement*

Retenti·onsrecht [ts] n ⟨jur⟩ *lien*; *right of r.*

Retir·ade f ∼/∼n *retreat* ‖ (Abort) *urinal*, *water-closet* (*W.C.*) **retir·ieren** vi [s] (⟨a.⟩ sich ∼) *to retire*, *to make one's retreat*

retoil·ieren [–twa–] vt [h] *to reback* (*a canvas*)

Ret·orte f ∼/∼n ⟨chem⟩ *retort*

retour [re'tu:r] [adv] *back* **≈billet** n [obs] *return ticket* **≈kutsche** f ⟨fig⟩ *comeback*

retrogr·ad a ⟨geol⟩ *headward* (*erosion*)

°**R·ettchen** n (⟨mil sl⟩ f Ziga≈) *gasper*

r·ettbar a *savable* **r·etten** vt [h] *to save* ‖ *to preserve* ‖ (befreien) *to rescue*, *deliver*, *free* (*a th*, *a p* von *from*) ‖ jdm das Leben ∼ *to save a p's life* ‖ nicht zu ∼ *lost* ‖ (aus dem Wasser) *to retrieve* ‖ (Gegenstand) *to salvage*, *recover* ‖ s–e Ehre ∼ *to vindicate one's honour* ‖ sein Leben ∼ ⟨a.⟩ *to run for one's life* ‖ *the play was redeemed by this actor* ‖ ∼der Engel *good* od *guardian angel*, ⟨fig⟩ *deliveress* **| sich** ∼ [h] *to save o.s.*, *to make one's escape* ‖ sich aus der Umzingelung ∼ *to free o.s. from being surrounded* ‖ rette sich wer kann! *sauve qui peut*!, *each one for himself*!
R·etter m ∼s/∼ *rescuer*, *deliverer* ‖ (Heiland) *Saviour*, *Redeemer* ‖ ⟨fig a.⟩ *he was the salvation of his country*

R·ettich m ∼(e)s/∼e ⟨bot⟩ *large radish*

r·ettlos a ⟨mar⟩ = unrettbar **R·ettung** f ∼/∼en *rescue*, *deliverance*; *salvation*, *saving* ⟨a. rel⟩ ‖ (Entkommen) *escape* ‖ (v Gütern) *recovery*, ⟨mar⟩ *salvage* ‖ ⟨fig⟩ die einzige ∼ *any port in a storm* ‖ m–e letzte ∼ *my sheet-anchor* ‖ ohne ∼ *past help* **R·ettungs-** **∼anker** m ⟨a. fig⟩ *sheet-anchor* **∼anstalt** f *station of the Humane Society* **∼apparat** m *life-saving apparatus* ‖ (bei Feuerbrünsten) *fire-escape* ‖ ⟨mar⟩ *mortar* od *rocket app.* ‖ (Sauerstoff≈) *pulmotor* **∼boje** f *life-buoy* **∼boot** n *life-boat* **∼dienst** m *life-saving service* **∼floß** n *life raft* **∼flugzeug** n *search and rescue pl.* **∼gerät** n *escape* (*rope-escape*) **∼gesellschaft** f *Humane Society*; *Ambulance Brigade* **∼gruppe** f *salvage group* **∼gürtel** m *life-belt* **∼haus** n *house of refuge*, *asylum* **∼jacke** f *life jacket* **∼kolonne** f *search party* **∼leine** f (Taucher≈) *life-line* **∼leiter** f *fire-escape* **≈los** a *irrecoverable*, *irretrievable*, *irremediable*, *past help* **∼losigkeit** f *hopeless state* **∼mannschaft** f *rescue party*, ⟨mot⟩ *breakdown gang* **∼maschine** f *fire-escape* **∼medaille** f *medal* (*awarded*) *for saving life* **∼mittel** n *remedy*, *expedient* **∼rakete** f ⟨a–n⟩ *escape tower* **∼-schlauch** m *canvas chute* **∼stelle** f *first-aid post* **∼schwimmer** m *life-guard* **∼station** f = ∼anstalt; *emergency* (od *first aid*) *station* **∼-versuch** m *attempt at rescue* **∼wache** f (in Bädern) *life-guard* **∼werk** n *work of rescue* od *salvage*

Ret·usche f ∼/∼n ⟨phot⟩ *retouch*(*ing*) **retusch·ieren** vt [h] *to retouch*, *to touch up*

R·eu- **∼geld** n *forfeit*(*-money*), *smart-money* ‖ (Steuer) *conscience-money*; ⟨Am fam⟩ *wise m.* **∼kauf** m *forfeit* **∼mütig** a *repentant*, *contrite*, *penitent* ‖ in dieser ∼en Verfassung *in this frame of repentance* **R·eue** f ∼/ *repentance*, ⟨rel⟩ *penitence*, *compunction* ‖ ∼ empfinden über etw *to feel rep.* od *pen.* ⟨a.⟩ *remorse at a th*, *to repent* od *regret a th*; aktive ∼ zeigen *to actively make amends* **∼gefühl** n *remorse* **≈los** a *impenitent*, *remorseless* **≈voll** a *repentant* **reuen** vt [imps] [h] die Tat reut mich *I repent having done it*, *I feel sorry for it* ‖ es reut mich *I regret* (,daß *that*); (e–r [gen] Tat) *I repent* (*of*) *a th*, *I am sorry* (*for a th*) ‖ er wird es sich noch ∼ l *he will be sorry for it yet* ‖ es hat ihn gereut *he has repented it* **r·euig** a *repentant*, *penitent*, *contrite*

R·euse f ∼/∼n *eel-basket*, *eel-buck* ‖ *bow-net*, *drum-net*, *weir*

R·eußen pl (= Russen) Herrscher aller ∼ *Czar of all the Russias*

..reut(h) *suff* (= Rodung) z Bezeichnung v Ortsnamen (z. B. Bayreuth, Höllriegelskreuth) vgl → ..rath, ..rode

R·eut- ~feld [n] *land newly cleared, virgin soil;* **~hacke** [f] *mattock* **R·eute** f ~/ *clearing* (= Roden) **r·euten** vi [h] **1.** *to root up* od *out* **2.** ⟨agr⟩ *to clear;* → roden

Revan- ~che [rəˈvãːʃə, ⟨vulg⟩ reˈvaŋʒə] f ~/~n *revenge* ‖ ⟨fig⟩ *return* ‖ jdm ~ geben *to give a p his* → ~partie [f], ~spiel [n] *return-match, -game* ≃**ch·ieren,** sich [h] (an [dat]) *to have one's revenge (on), to get one's own back* ‖ *to repay (a service),* für *to make up for, to make (a present) in return* **~ch·ist** m ~en/~en *r.e seeker*

Reverber·ier- *reverberatory (furnace* etc)

Rever·enz f ~/~en **1.** *reverence* ‖ jdm s–e ~ erweisen *to do* od *show r. to a p* **2.** *bow, obeisance* ‖ e–e ~ m *to make a b.;* (Knicks) *to make* od *drop a curtsy*

Rev·ers [–s] m ~es/~e (Kehrseite) *reverse* ‖ (Schein) *reciprocal obligation* od *bond* ‖ e–n ~ ausstellen *to give a written declaration* | [rəˈvɛə] ~/~s ⟨tail⟩ *lapel*

Rev·ier n ~(e)s/~e *district, quarter, estate, manor, environs* pl; *part, section* ‖ ⟨mil⟩ *(unit's) sick room* ‖ (Polizei≃) *district, station; beat* ‖ *(postman's) round* ‖ ⟨hunt⟩ *preserve, shooting--ground* ‖ ⟨min⟩ *country* ‖ waldiges ~ *woodlands* | ein ~ abgehen ⟨hunt⟩ *to beat a cover, to shoot over an estate* ‖ ~ bek ⟨mil⟩ *to be put on the sick--list* **~förster** m *district-ranger* ≃**krank** a *sick in quarters* **~kranke(r)** m ⟨mil⟩ *soldier confined to the unit's sick room* **~stunde** f ⟨mil⟩ *sick parade* od *call* ≃**verteidigend** a ⟨zoo⟩ *territorial* (Art)

Revi- ≃d·ieren vt [h] ⟨typ⟩ *to revise* (⟨a. fig⟩ *one's opinion), to overhaul* ‖ ⟨com⟩ *to audit, check* ‖ (Entscheidung) *to reconsider,* ⟨jur⟩ *to review* **~si·on** f ~/~en ⟨jur⟩ *review, revision, revisal; appeal; proceeding in error* ‖ e–r ~ unterziehen *to review* ‖ ⟨com⟩ *audit(ing), checking* ‖ (Zoll≃) *examination* (dazu *to examine*) ‖ ⟨typ⟩ *revise; final proof* **~si·ons- ~befehl** wegen Formfehlers ⟨jur⟩ *writ of error* **~bogen** m ⟨typ⟩ *revise* **~forderung** f ⟨pol⟩ *demand for revision* **~hof** m ⟨jur⟩ *court of revision* **~jahr** n ⟨com etc⟩ *audit year* **~politik** f *revisionism* **Rev·isor** m ~s/–s·oren *reviser, auditor; examiner, controller*

Revokati·on f ~/~en *revocation, repeal*

Rev·olte f ~/~n *revolt* **revolt·ieren** vi [h] *to rise, revolt, riot* **Revoluti·on** f ~/~en ⟨pol, astr, fig⟩ *revolution* ‖ ⟨Am⟩ Zeit vor der ~ *colonial time* | **~·är** m ~(e)s/~e *revolutionist* | ≃**·är** a *revolutionary* ⟨a. s⟩; = *revolutionist* (°⟨a.⟩ –l·uzzer "*revolutioner*") | ≃**·ieren** vt [h] *to revolutionize* **Rev·olver** m ~s/~ *revolver* (⟨a.⟩ *six-shooter)* ‖ mit gezogenem ~ *at the point of the p.l, at p.l-p.t* **~attentat** n; ein ~ gegen jdn ausüben *to attack a p with a r.* **~bank** f ⟨tech⟩ *r.-lathe* **~blatt** n *blackmailing newspaper; yellow journal* **~blende** f ⟨phot⟩ *rotary diaphragm* **~drehbank** f *capstan lathe* **~held** m *gunman,* ⟨fam⟩ *gunslinger* **~kanone** f *Hotchkiss gun, revolving cannon* **~kopf** m ⟨tech⟩ *turret head;* ⟨opt⟩ *lens turret* **~presse** f *blackmailing-press* °**~schnauze** f ⟨vulg⟩ *jaw,* ⟨fig⟩ *habit of impudent repartee;* e–e ~ h *to be shooting off one's mouth* **~tisch** m (e–r Presse) *dial feed*

revoz·ieren vt [h] *to recall, revoke, retract*

Revue [reˈvyː] f ~/~n [yːən] *review* ‖ ⟨theat⟩ *revue* ‖ ~ passieren (l) *to pass in review,* ⟨mil⟩ *to pass muster* | ~girl [n] *showgirl,* ⟨fam⟩ *hoofer*

Reykjav·ik [rai–] n (Hauptstadt v Island)

Rey·on [rɛˈjɔ̃] m/n [invar] (Kunstseide) *rayon*

Rezens·ent m ~en/~en *critic, reviewer* **rezens·ieren** vt [h] *to review, to criticize* **Rezensi·on** f ~/~en *critique, review* **~sexemplar** n *r.er's* od *press-copy*

Rez·ept n ~(e)s/~e ⟨med⟩ *prescription, recipe* ‖ ein ~ m (schreiben) *to make up (write) a presc.* | ⟨cul⟩ *recipe* | ⟨fig⟩ *prescription (against boredom)* ‖ e–m das ~ verderben *to spoil a p's plans* | ~optiker [m] *dispensing optician* ≃**iv** [–f] a *receptive* | **~ivit·ät** [–v–] f ~ *receptivity* **~or** m ~s/–·oren *receiver, collector* **~·ur** f ~/ **1.** = Steuereinnahme **2.** ⟨pharm⟩ *dispensing*

Rez·eß m –sses/–sse *agreement, recess, treaty* **r-ss·iv** [–f] a *recessive* (Merkmal)

Rezid·iv [f] n ~(e)s/~e [və] ⟨jur, path⟩ *relapse*

Rezipi·ent m ~en/~en *container, tank* ‖ ⟨chem⟩ *recipient*

rezipr·ok a ⟨gram, math⟩ *reciprocal* **Reziprozit·ät** f ~/ *reciprocity*

Rezit- ~ati·on f ~/~en *recitation, recital* **~at·iv** n ~(e)s/~e ⟨mus⟩ *recitative* ≃**·ieren** vt [h] *to recite*

Rhab·arber m ~s/ ⟨bot⟩ *rhubarb*

Rhaps·ode m ~n/~n *rhapsodist* **Rhapsod·ie** f ~/~n *rhapsody* **rhaps·odisch** a *rhapsodical*

Rh·ein m ⟨Ger⟩ (Fluß) *Rhine* **~land** n *Rhineland* ≃**isch** a *Rhenish*

Rhein m ~s/; Wasser in den ~ tragen *to carry coals to Newcastle* **~brücke** f *bridge across the Rhine* **~bund** m ⟨hist⟩ *the Rhenish Confederation* **~dampfer** m *Rh.-steamer* **~fahrt** f *trip on the Rh.* **~fall** m *Falls* pl *of the Rh.* **~gau** m ⟨Ger⟩ (Landschaft) **~graf** m *Rh.-grave* **~hessen** n *Rhenish Hessia* **~kiesel** m *rhinestone* **~land** n *the Rh.land* **~länder(in** f) m *Rhinelander* ≃**ländisch** a *Rhenish; of the Rhineland* **~pfalz** f *Palatinate* **~preußen** n *Rhenish Prussia* **~provinz** f ⟨hist⟩ *Rhenish Prussia* **~schiffer** m *Rh. boatman* **~schiffahrt** f *navigation on the Rh.* **~tal** n *Rhine valley* **~wein** m *Rh. wine, hock*

Rh·esus- ~affe m *rhesus* **~faktor** m *RH.-factor*

Rh·etor m ~s/–·oren *rhetor* **-t·orik** ~/ *rhetoric* | ~er [m] *rhetorician* **rhet·orisch** a *rhetorical;* ~e Frage *erotesis*

Rh·euma n ~/ *rheumatism,* ⟨fam⟩ *rheumatics* **rheum·atisch** a *rheumatic* **Rheumat·ismus** m ~/ –men *rheumatism* ‖ Gelenk≃ *articular rh.* ‖ an ~ leiden *to suffer from rh., to be afflicted with rh.*

Rhin·ozeros n ~/–rosse *rhinoceros*

Rhiz·om n ~s/~e *rhizome, root-stock*

Rhode Island n (Staat der U.S.A.)

Rhod·esien n (Gebiet in S.-Afrika) *Rhodesia*

Rh·odos n (Insel im Ägäischen Meer) *Rhodes*

Rhodler m *inhabitant of Rh., Rhodian*

Rh·omb- ≃isch a *rhombic* **~o·eder** n ~s/~ ⟨geom⟩ *rhombohedron* ≃**o·edrisch** a *rhombohedral* **~us** m ~s/–ben ⟨geom⟩ *rhomb(us); diamond* ‖ ⟨her⟩ *lozenge* | ~antenne [f] *d.-shaped aerial*

Rhön f (Gebirge); **~rad** n ⟨gym⟩ *gyro-wheel*

Rh·one f ⟨Fr⟩ (Fluß)

Rhotaz·ismus m ~/–men ⟨phon-hist⟩ *rhotacism (s > r)*

Rh·yth- ~mik f ~/ *rhythmics* pl | ~er [m] *rhythmist* ≃**misch** a *rhythmical* ‖ ~e Gymnastik *eurhythmics* pl ‖ ~ gebaut *rhythmic (body);* ~-automatischer Reiz ⟨biol⟩ *automatic generation of rhythmic stimuli;* ~e Prosa ⟨m. m.⟩ *prose rhythm,* → d. **~mus** m ~/–men → *rhythm; lilt (of a song)* ‖ in e–m ~ *on a rh.;* in verschiedenem ~ *with varying pulse*

R·ibisel f ~/~n [österr] *(red, black) currant*

R·icht- ~amboß m *straightening anvil* **~ansatz** m ⟨mil⟩ *sight mount* **~antenne** f *beam* od *directional aerial,* ⟨Am⟩ *d. antenna* **~aufsatz** m ⟨artill⟩ *gun sight* **~bake** f ⟨aero, mar⟩ *land mark* **~balken** m *traverse beam* **~bar** a *adjustable* **~baum** m *pulley-beam* ‖ ⟨artill⟩ *hand-spike, traversing lever* **~beil** n *executioner's axe* **~blei** n *plummet* **~block** m *executioner's block* **~ebene** f ⟨mil⟩ *lining plane* **~eisen** n *straightening-rod* **~empfänger** m ⟨wir⟩ *direction-finder (D/F)* **~fehler** m ⟨mil⟩ *error of direction* **~fest** n *builder's; roof-raising ceremony treat* **~feuer** n ⟨mar⟩ *transit light,* ⟨Am⟩ *range light* **~funkbake** f *radio beam* **~gerät** n *laying gear* **~höhe** f ⟨mil⟩ *elevation* **~kanonier** m ⟨mil⟩ *(gun-)layer; pointer* **~kreis** m ⟨artill⟩ *arc sight, director; aiming circle* | ~verfahren [n] *circle aiming;* ~zahl [f] *d. reading* **~kreisel** m *directional gyro* **~latte** f ⟨artill⟩ *aiming post;* ⟨surv⟩ *guiding rod* **~linie** f *aiming line;* ⟨math⟩ *axis;* ⟨theat⟩ *setting l.* | ~n [pl] *lines* pl (nach .. *on cooperative lines*) ‖ *rules* [pl] *of conduct; outlines; regulations* pl; *code of standard* ‖ *terms of reference; guiding principles* od *policy; general instructions* od *directions* | den ~n anpassen ⟨pol, com⟩ *to bring into line* **~lot** n *plumb-line* **~maschine** f, **~mittel** n ⟨artill⟩ *laying gear, sighting device* **~maß** n *gauge, standard* **~meister** m *fitter* **~platte** f ⟨met⟩ *straightening-plate* **~platz** m *place of execution* **~preis** m *standard price* **~punkt** m ⟨mil⟩ *aiming* od *reference point* | ~verfahren [n] ⟨artill⟩ *indirect laying* **~satz** m *guiding rate* **~schacht** m ⟨min⟩ *vertical shaft* **~scheit** n *ruler, level, plumb-rule* ‖ ⟨tech⟩ *jointing-rule* ‖ ⟨typ⟩ *justifier* **~schnur** f *(plumb-)line* ‖ ⟨fig⟩ *guiding line; rule(s* pl*); guidance, precept* **~schütze** m (MG) m *gunner No 1* **~-schwert** n *sword of execution, headsman's sword* **~sendung** f ⟨wir⟩ *beam emission* **~sitz** m *layer's seat* **~spant** m ⟨mar⟩ *main frame* **~stab** m *pointing-rod* **~stange** f *scaffold-* od *pointing-pole* **~statt, ~stätte** f = ~platz **~steig** m *footpath* **~strahl** (→ Leit-) m ⟨aero wir⟩ *beam;* auf dem ~ fliegen ⟨fam⟩ *to ride the b.* ~-Anflugverfahren [n] *b. procedure;* ~-Landefunkfeueranlage [f] *b. approach beacon system (BABS)* **~antenne** [f] *beam aerial,* ⟨Am⟩ *b. antenna* **~strahler** m ⟨wir⟩ *beam aerial; beam station;* [dazu:] *b. transmission, to beam: program beamed at France; b. system* **~übungs-** ~gerät [n] *practice sight;* ~gestell [n] *aiming training stand* **~verbindungen** f pl ⟨mil⟩ *directional communications* **~verfahren** n *laying process* **~vorrichtung** f *laying gear,* (am Gewehr) *peep sight* **~waage** f *level* **~weg** m *short cut (through),* ⟨Am⟩ *cut-off* **~wert** m *reference value* **~zahl** f ⟨com⟩ *target* ***R·ichte** f ~/ *straight direction* od *line; proper order; right position* | etw in die ~ bringen *to put a th straight* od *right, to adjust a th* ‖ in die ~ gehen *to take the shortest cut, to go as the crow flies* ‖ aus der ~ k *to lose one's way;* (S) *to get out of order* **r·ichten I.** vt [h] ((a.) sich, → II.) **A.** (ordnen) *to arrange, fit; to set (right); align; adjust* (nach *to*) **1.** (her~) *to make (a bed), to lay (a table), to put (a room) in order* **2.** (zu~) (Fell) *to dress* **3.** (an~) ⟨cul⟩ *to dress* **4.** (auf~) *to put up (an aerial)* ‖ (Haus) *to set up the roof of a h.* **5.** (aus~) *to put a th straight,* ⟨met⟩ *to straighten;* (Bleche) *to level* ‖ *to regulate, set (a clock* etc) ‖ *to trim (sails)* ‖ *to dress, point (a telescope)* ‖ *to lay, train,* seitwärts *to traverse (a gun);* direkt ~ *to lay directly* ‖ ⟨arch⟩ *to lay out by a line* **6.** ⟨jur⟩ *to judge, try, sentence;* ((a.) über) *to pass sentence on* ‖ Gott richtete sie streng *the judgment of G. was harsh (up)on them* **7.** (hin~) *to execute* **8.** ⟨mil⟩ richt euch! *dress!* **B.** (lenken, wenden) ~ **an**: (Brief) *to send .. to a p;* (Rede etc) *to address .. to a p* ‖ (Aufforderung, Bitte *to direct .. to a p* ‖ e–e Frage an jdn ~ *to put a qu. to a p, to ask a p a qu.* ‖ das Wort an jdn ~ *to address a p* | ~ **auf** [acc]: (Angriff) *to direct .. against* ‖ (Aufmerksamkeit, Augenmerk) *to turn one's (draw a p's) attention to;* .. auf sich ~ *to collect the a. of the people* ‖ (die Augen, den Blick) *to fix one's eyes upon; his eyes were on her;* (fest) *all eyes were glued* od *riveted on him;* (ganz) *his eyes were all for the girl* ‖ *she bent her glance on the table* ‖ sein Begehren auf etw ~ *to covet a th* ‖ (Denken u Trachten) *all his scheming and striving were directed to ..* ‖ (Erwartung) *to place one's expectations in ..* ‖ (Gedanken) *to give one's mind to ..* ‖ (alle Hilfsmittel) *to concentrate all one's resources on an object* ‖ (Kräfte) *to this task she bent all her energies* ‖ (Lichtstrahlen) *to train* od *turn on* ‖ (Tätigkeit) *to aim at ..* ‖ (Waffe) *to present a pistol at; to level, aim, point a rifle at* ‖ *to lay* od *train a gun on* ‖ (s–e Wut) *to direct .. against, to vent .. upon a p* | ⟨fig⟩ *to bring to bear upon* ‖ *the goal towards which his policy had pointed* (gerichtet war) ‖ die Politik sollte darauf ge–tet s *the object of policy should be (to find ..)* | ~ **gegen**: (Anklagen) *to level .. against* ‖ (Augen, Blick) *to turn* od *cast one's eyes (up to* od*) towards Heaven* (gen H.) ‖ (Bemühungen) *to aim one's efforts at* ‖ (Kritik) *to level at* ‖ das ist gegen Sie gerichtet *that is intended for you* | den Blick **in** die Ferne ~ *to turn one's eyes to distant objects* ‖ in die Höhe ~ *to raise; to lift up, to throw (one's head) up* ‖ etw ins Werk ~ *to accomplish a th* | **nach** der Setzwaage ~ *to level, plumb* | ~ **nach**: (Blicke um etw zu erlangen) *to look (to a p, for a th)* ‖ *he brought his gaze to the terrace* ‖ (Kurs) *to shape .. to a given object* ‖ (Pläne) *to work out .. to fit in with* ‖ (Schiff) *to steer a ship northwards; to give the ship a course to the north* ‖ *the ship takes a course to the north* ‖ die Segel nach dem Winde ~ *to trim one's sails to the wind* (a. fig), ⟨fig⟩ *to be a timeserver* ‖ (Tun, Wünsche) *to accomodate one's actions, wishes to a th* ‖ (Weg) *to direct one's course to ..* ‖ **zugrunde** ~ *to ruin (a p), to destroy (a th)* **II. v refl sich** ~ **1.** *to stand erect, to dress (in line)* ‖ ⟨mil⟩ richt euch! *(right) dress!* **2.** sich selbst ~ *to pass judgement on o.s., (to commit suicide)* ‖ die Worte ~ sich selbst .. *stand self-condemned; the book is directed to the laity* **3.** sich ~ **an** *to appeal to; to turn to (a p* um *for)* | sich ~ **auf**: *to keep ready for a th* ‖ *the conversation, all eyes turned on him; his malice concentrated upon ..* | sich ~ **für** *to prepare for* | sich ~ **gegen**: *the play is all against ..* | sich **in** die Höhe ~ *to raise o.s., to rise* | sich ~ **nach** [dat]: *to accommodate o.s. to a p('s wishes), to take one's cue from a p* ‖ *to follow (the regulations)* ‖ *to act upon, to conform to (a p's advice)* ‖ sich nach jdm (e–m Muster) ~ *to model o.s. on a p (a th), to go by (what the doctor says, one's feelings)* ‖ *to be guided by (to act according to) circumstances;* (nach dieser Uhr) *they took the time (from this clock)* ‖ (P) *to conform with; to carry out the instructions* | (S) *to be determined by* ⟨a. com⟩; ⟨com⟩ (Preis, Qualität) *to depend on;* ⟨gram⟩ *to be dependent on, to agree with* ‖ *the magnet points to the pole* ‖ das richtet sich ganz danach, ob *that depends entirely on whether ..* **III.** vi *to judge, condemn, criticize* ‖ (ge)recht ~ *to judge justly* ‖ gnädig ~ *to pass a merciful sentence* (über *on*) ‖ in e–r S ~ *to pronounce sentence in a process* **R·ichter** m ~s/~ **A.** *judge, justice* ‖ der ~ N. *Judge N.* ‖ ~ [pl] [koll] *judicature,* ⟨Am⟩ *judiciary,* ⟨bib⟩ Buch der ~ *Book of Judges* ‖ ⟨engl⟩ Lord Ober≗ *Lord Chief Justice* ‖ oberster ~ *supreme judge* ‖ ⟨engl hist⟩ Reise≗ [pl] *Justices in Eyre* ‖ Polizei≗ *police-magistrate,* ⟨Am⟩ *Sheriff* ‖ der die Verhandlung führende ~ *the sitting judge* ‖ ⟨Am⟩ Testaments≗ *surrogate* **B.** sich z ~ **aufwerfen** *to constitute o.s. judge* (über *over*) ‖ jdn als ~ ablehnen *to reject a p as j.* ‖ z ~ ernannt w *to be called to the Bench* ‖ jdn vor den ~ bringen *or* schleppen *to bring a p to justice* od *before the court* | ⟨prov⟩ wo kein Kläger ist, ist auch kein ~ *no accuser, no judge* **~amt** n *judgeship, judicature,* oberstes ⟨a.⟩ *the ermine* **~bank** f ⟨engl⟩ *bench;* (höher) *banc* **~kollegium** n *jury; body of judges,* ⟨engl a.⟩ *the Bench* **~recht** n *judge-made law* **~spruch** m *judgement, sentence* (→ Entscheidung) **~stand** m *judiciary; judicial calling,* ⟨engl a.⟩ *the Bench,* ⟨Am⟩ *the Judicature* **~stuhl** m *tribunal;* ⟨bib⟩ *judg(e)ment-seat (of God)* ‖ das gehört nicht vor s–n ~ *that is not within his jurisdiction* **~tracht** f, **~würde** f *stuff;*

(höhere) *silk*; (höchste) *ermine* (bekleiden *to wear the e.*) **r·ichterlich** [a] *judicial* (*capacity*) ‖ (gerichtlich) *judiciary* ‖ ∼es Urteil *judg(e)ment, sentence*; jdm durch ∼es U. zusprechen *to adjudge* (*a th*) *to a p* | [adv] *judicially, as a judge* **r·ichterisch** a *magisterial, censorious, like a judge* **r·ichtig I.** [a] **A. [attr] 1.** *right* (*way, track*) ‖ (genau) *exact, accurate* ‖ (gerecht) *just, fair* | (wirklich, echt) *genuine*; *real* (*winter*); (*his real father*); *own* (*his own children*), *true-born* (*Englishman*), (*a Londoner*) *bred and born* ‖ *orthodox* (*democrat*) ‖ *good* (*money*) ‖ *good straight* (*novelist*) ‖ *proper* (*weight, measure, payment*) | (wahr) *correct* (*answer, information, solution, assumption*); *true* (*time, balance, copy, presentiment*) ‖ *just* (*distance*) | *regular* (*hero, rascal*); *perfect* (*cad*) | (geeignet) *suitable* | ⟨fig⟩ *plumb* **2.** ⟨**fig**⟩ im ∼en Fahrwasser *on the right way* ‖ im ∼en Lichte *in the right light* ‖ der ∼e Mann ⟨Am fam⟩ *the r. guy*, .. am ∼en Platz *the r. man on the r. place*; (nicht) der ∼e M. s (*not*) *to be the type* ‖ das ∼e Maß halten *to keep within bounds* ‖ am ∼en Ort, Platz, an ∼er Stelle *in place* ‖ ein ∼es Urteil h *to have a sound judg(e)ment* ‖ den ∼en Zeitpunkt abpassen (verpassen) *to hit upon* (*to miss*) *the r. moment* **3. [intj]** (tatsächlich) **a.** (als Antwort) [ell] ∼! (*that's*) *right*!, *exactly*!, *just so*!, *quite so*!, *quite*!, *sure enough*! **b.** (ich sagte: „Er kommt gleich",) und ∼, (da war er) .. *and behold* .., .. *and sure enough* .. ‖ [ell] ∼! *oh yes*! **B. [pred]** (in Ordnung) **1. (S)** *in order, arranged* ‖ etw ∼ m *to set a th to r.s*; *to settle, arrange a th, to settle ths r.*; ⟨com⟩ *to clear off* (*a debt*, etc) (vgl II. 2) | ist alles ∼? *is it settled?, is it all r.?* ‖ die S ist ∼ *it's all r.!* | es f ∼ halten *to find that .., to see fit* (*to do*) ‖ ich finde das **nicht** ∼ *that does not seem to me to be the r. th* ‖ es ist hier nicht ∼ *there's sth wrong here*; *this place is haunted* ‖ das ist nicht ∼! *that's not as it should be* ‖ zw ihnen ist etw nicht ∼ *sth has gone wrong between them* | **so ist's** ∼! *that's the way*, ⟨sl⟩ *cheese*, ⟨Am⟩ *Limburger* **2. (P)** der ist ∼! *he's all r.!* ‖ die ist ∼ ⟨sex⟩ *she's h. s.* (= *hot stuff*) *all r.* ‖ er ist nicht ganz richtig *he is cracked*, im Oberstübchen *he's* (*a little wrong* od) *not quite r. in the upper storey* **II. [adv]** *right(ly)*; (*as r. as a trivet*); (*to sing, hear, to do a sum*) *r.*; (*to think, act*) *r.ly*; (*to understand*) *properly* **1.** ∼ **böse** *really angry*, ⟨vulg⟩ *regular angry* **2.** (*to pronounce, write, calculate*) *correctly* ‖ (*to measure, think, judge*) *fairly* ‖ (*to pay* ..) *properly* od *in full* | ⟨com⟩ wir h ∼ empfangen *we duly received* | (Uhr) ∼ **gehen** *to be r., to go r.* od *correctly*; *to tell the r. time*; *to keep good time* ‖ das geht nicht ∼ zu *there's sth queer going on, there's sth wrong about it* (→ recht B.) ‖ es ist bei s–m Tode nicht ∼ (= natürlich) zugegangen *there was sth queer about his death* ‖ → ∼gehend ‖ nicht ∼ hören *to hear amiss* | etw ∼ m *to do a th properly* (vgl I. B. 1.) ‖ mach's diesmal ∼! *make good this time* ‖ wenn man es ∼ nimmt *if it comes to the point* | es **ist** nicht ganz ∼ mit ihm *he is not quite r. in the upper storey* | ∼ stellen *to adjust* (*the scales*) | ∼ **vergessen**: *I had clean forgotten* (*it*); *just as I thought he has forgotten it* ‖ ∼ würdigen *to appreciate* **III. der Richtige** (= ≗ Freier) *the r. man*; *he's just the sort of man for this job* ‖ das ist **das** ∼! *that's the th, stuff, sort, ticket, card* ‖ ⟨Am sl⟩ *it is the goods* ‖ das ∼ treffen *to hit upon the r. th*; (nicht) ganz das ∼ treffen (*not*) *to get it quite right* ‖ das ∼ tun *to do the r., correct, proper th* ‖ etw ∼s lernen .. *sth useful* ‖ es ist genau das ∼ *it suits me to the ground* od *a T* **r·ichtig- ≗befinden** n: nach ∼ ⟨com⟩ *if found correct* **∼gehend** [a] (Uhr) *keeping good time* ‖ ⟨fig⟩ *full-scale* [attr], *perfect* (*cad*), *regular* (*winter*), *thorough* (*philosopher*) | [adv] *actually* **≗machung** f *arrangement, settlement*; *putting in order* **∼|stellen** vt [h] *to set* od *put right, to rectify* **∼stellung** f *rectification* ‖ ⟨pol⟩ *dementi* **R·ichtigkeit** f ∼/ *rightness* ‖ *accuracy* (⟨a. comp⟩ & *of expression*); *exactness* (*of a contention*) ‖ *regularity* ‖ → bestreiten ‖ die ∼ e–r S beweisen ⟨a.⟩ *to prove that it is so* | etw in ∼ bringen *to arrange, settle*; *to set a th r.* od *to r.s* ‖ die ∼ e–r S nachprüfen *to verify a th*; ⟨bes Am⟩ *to check up on a th* | damit hat **es** s–e ∼ *that is all r.* od *correct, it is a real fact* ‖ es wird schon s–e ∼ h *it will be found quite correct* | für die ∼ (abbr f. d. R.) *certified correct* ‖ Angaben, deren ∼ der Käufer nicht bestreiten kann ⟨contr⟩ *and shall be accepted as accurate by the purchaser* **R·ichtung** f ∼/ ∼en **A. 1.** *direction* ‖ *aim, bent, drift, turn* ⟨a. fig⟩ ‖ (Weg) *course, route, way* ‖ (Kurs) *tack* (*on the right t., try another t.*) ‖ *line* (*of policy*) ‖ (Bewegung) *movement, tendency*; *drift* (*of clouds, thoughts*) **2.** ⟨mil⟩ *alinement, dressing*; ∼ nehmen *to correct the d.* ‖ ⟨mar⟩ *bearings* pl **3.** ⟨fig⟩ (Hang) *tendency, trend, drift, stream, ply* ‖ *line* od *school of thought* (*in a science*, etc) ‖ *respect* (*that's wrong in every r.*) ‖ ⟨rel, ec a.⟩ *persuasion* ‖ ⟨pol⟩ *line of policy* **B.** e–e **bestimmte** ∼ h *to trend* (*towards*) ‖ herrschende ∼ *turn* ‖ e–e extreme ∼ vertreten *to hold extreme views* ‖ neue ∼ *new departure* ‖ neuere ∼en *modern methods* ‖ (*political*) *opinion, views* pl, *course* ‖ radikale ∼ *radicalism* ‖ (*religious*) *twist* (*given to a movement*) **C.** die ∼ **ändern** *to change one's course*, (of ball) *to twist* ‖ ‖ e–e ∼ an–, einnehmen, einschlagen *to adopt a course, to turn* (auf *toward*) ⟨fig⟩ *to take a ply* ‖ ∼ halten *to keep in line* ‖ ∼ nehmen nach *to head for* ‖ die ∼ nehmen auf: *his ideas were directed to* ‖ die ∼ suchen, verlieren *to take, lose one's bearings* **D. in** der ∼ auf, nach *in the direction of*, .. nach Westen *westbound, westwards* ‖ in derselben ∼ weiter gehen *to pursue the same course* ‖ in dieser ∼ *this way* ‖ .., der in dieser ∼ gemacht wurde (*the first attempt*) *in this direction* ‖ ⟨fig⟩ (*to apply pressure*) *on that head* ‖ alle in ·einer ∼ geneigt *all aslope one way* ‖ in e–e andere ∼ zeigen (S) *to look the other way* ‖ in (gerade) entgegengesetzter ∼ *in an opposite direction*, (*directly opposite*); Trieb in .. (Rakete) *opposite action* ‖ in gerader ∼ *in a straight line, straight on*; .. liegen, verlaufen ⟨fig⟩ *to be the other way* ‖ in welcher ∼? *which way?* | **nach** (*or* in) allen ∼en *in all directions, to the four winds*; nach ·einer ∼ hin *unidirectional*; nach beiden ∼en *both ways, either way, on either side* ‖ nach e–r bestimmten ∼ laufen (of currents) *to set that way* ‖ nach irgend e–r ∼ *one way or the other* ‖ nach jeder ∼ *every way* ‖ sich nach k–r ∼ hin festlegen *not to bind o.s. to any given course* **R·ichtung- ∼anzeiger** m ⟨mot⟩ *trafficator*; *direction indicator* (*gives the signal intended, is cancelled*) **∼blinker** m ⟨mot⟩ *flashing indicator* **∼finder** m ⟨wir⟩ *direction-finder* **≗gebend,** **≗weisend** a *directive, constitutive*; *heuristic*; ∼es Organ *policy-making body*; ∼ s f *to guide, direct* **∼geber** m ⟨aero⟩ *turn-control* **R·ichtungs- ∼fahne** f ⟨surv, mil⟩ *field-colours* pl **∼fehler** m ⟨mil⟩ *line error* **∼-hörer** m = Horchgerät; (Fla) *sound locator* N **∼kontrolle** f ⟨aero⟩ *directional control* **∼-linie** f *line of direction* | (grüner) **∼pfeil** ⟨mot⟩ (*green*) *arrow filter signal* **∼schild** n ⟨rail⟩ (*coaches*) *destination board*; (*station*) *route indicator* **∼sucher** m ⟨wir⟩ *direction-finder* **∼telegraphie** f *directional W/T* (= *wireless telegraphy*) **∼verfahren** n *method of direction-finding* **∼weiser** m *pointer gear* **∼winkel** m *angle of elevation* **∼zeichen** n ⟨cycl⟩ *left* (*right*) *turn signal*

R·icke f ∼/∼n ⟨hunt⟩ *doe*

Ridik·ül, Retik·ül m & n ∼s/∼e *reticule, lady's handbag*

rieb 1. & 3. sg pret v reiben

Riech- ~essig m *aromatic vinegar* **~fläschchen** n *scent-* od *smelling-bottle* **~kissen** n *scent-bag* °**~kolben** m *bottle-nose* **~mittel** n *perfume* **~nerv** m ⟨anat⟩ *olfactory nerve* **~salz** n *smelling-salts* pl, *sal volatile* **~wasser** n *scent* **~werkzeug** n ⟨anat⟩ *olfactory organ*; ⟨hum⟩ *bottle-nose, snout* **r·iechbar** a *smellable, perceptible* **r·iechen I.** vi [roch/gerochen] **A. 1.** [h] (P) *to smell* ‖ *the cheese smells* ‖ sein Atem riecht, er riecht aus dem Munde *he has bad breath, his br. is offensive* **2.** (verwesend) *to smell faint*; ⟨vulg⟩ *to stink, whiff*; *to be rank, tainted, putrid* ‖ zu ~ beginnen ⟨cul⟩ *to get high* **B.** ~ **nach**: *he smells of brandy*; *it smells of* od *like garlic* | v/imps **es** riecht (hier) nach Gas *there is a smell of gas* | (S) **to be redolent* (*of leather*) ‖ ⟨fig⟩ *to smack* od *reek of* ‖ (of book) *to smell of* (*the lamp*) **C. angebrannt** ~ *to smell burnt* ‖ (un)angenehm, berauschend ~ *to have a*(*n un*)*pleasant, intoxicating odour* od *smell* ‖ es riecht gut (schlecht) *it smells good* (*bad*), köstlich *it has a delicious scent* ‖ (of rooms) schlecht ~ *to be fetid* ‖ sengerig ~ *to smell of burning* ‖ scharf, stark, streng, süß ~ *to have a pungent, strong, sharp, sweet smell* (*the cheese smells loudly* stark) ‖ widerlich ~ → stinken ‖ es riecht **wie** angebrannt *it smells of burning* **II.** vt/i (wahrnehmend) **A. 1.** *to smell* (*gas, fire*) **2.** (wittern) *to scent* ‖ scharf ~ *to have a keen scent* **3.** (schnüffeln) *to sniff* **4.** °⟨fig⟩ *to find out, foresee* ‖ °das konnte ich doch nicht ~! *How should I have known*? ‖ °jdn nicht (mehr) ~ können *to be sick of* (*seeing*) *a p*; *I can't stick him*! **B.** ⟨mst fig⟩ **Lunte,** den Braten ~ *to smell a rat* ‖ er kann Moschus (⟨fig⟩ Pulver) nicht ~ *he can't stand* od *bear the smell of musk* (*powder*) ‖ °ich kann ihn nicht ~ *I can't bear* (*the sight of*) *him, I have a down on him, I can't stand him* (→ fressen B. 2.) **C. 1. an** etw ~ *to* (*take a*) *smell at* (⟨Am⟩ *of*) *a th* ‖ an e–r Blume ~ *to smell* od *sniff* (*at*) *a flower* **2.** °⟨fig⟩ du darfst mal dran ~ (kriegst aber nichts) *you can have a smell at it* ‖ da kannst du dran ~ (merk es dir!) *you can put that in your pipe and smoke it* **III. riechend** (S) *redolent* ‖ (v Fleisch) *touched, too high* | wohl–end *fragrant, scented, odor*(*ifer*)*ous* °**R·iecher** m ~s/~ **1.** feiner ~ *keen-scented*, ⟨fam⟩ *nosy p* **2.** ⟨fam⟩ (Nase) *smeller, snout* ‖ ⟨fig⟩ e–n guten ~ h f .. *to have a good nose for* ..

Ried n ~(e)s/~e **1.** ⟨bot⟩ *reed*(*-grass*) **2.** *fen, moor* **~bock** m *reed-buck* **~gras** n **1.** *reed*(*-grass*) **2.** *sedge* **3.** *bent* **~land** n *bent*

rief 1. & 3. sg pret v rufen

R·iefe f ~/~n ⟨arch⟩ *flute, channel, chamfer*, ⟨carp⟩ *groove* ‖ (im Gewehr) *rifle* **r·iefe(l)n** vt [h] *to flute*, etc ‖ (Papier) *to rib*

R·iege f ~/~n ⟨gym⟩ *row, section*; ⟨ftb⟩ *team*

R·iegel m ~s/~ **A. 1.** ⟨carp⟩ (*cross-*)*bar* **2.** ⟨arch⟩ *transom* **3.** *sliding bar,* (*key-*)*bolt, slot* **4.** (*clothes-*)*rack* **5.** *stick, bar,* ⟨Am⟩ *piece* (*of chocolate*); *cake* (*of soap*) **6.** ⟨tact⟩ *cut off* **B.** den ~ vorschieben *to shoot the bolt* ‖ ⟨fig⟩ e–r S den ~ vorschieben *to check* od *stop a th, to put a stop* (*an end*) *to a th, to make an end of a th* ‖ → Schloß **~bohrer** m *bar-wimble* **~bolzen** m *latch-pin* **~feder** f *bolt-spring* ≗**fest** a *bolted* **~form** f *ingot mould* **~holz** n ⟨carp⟩ (*cross-*)*bar* **~schloß** n *stock-lock* **~sicherung** f ⟨tech, phot⟩ *safety catch* **~stellung** f ⟨tact⟩ *cutting-off* od *barrier, bolt position* **~verschluß** m *bolting* **~wand** f *wooden partition*

R·iemen[1] m ~s/~ **A.** *strap*, (starker) *thong* **B.** Antriebs≗ *driving-belt* ‖ Gewehr≗ *sling* ‖ Keil≗ ⟨mot⟩ *fan-belt* ‖ (Schuster) Knie≗ *knee-strap* ‖ Leib≗ *belt* ‖ Schnür-, Schuh≗ *boot-lace, shoe-string* ‖ Schulter≗ *belt-support* ‖ Streich≗ (f Messer) *strop* ‖ Sturm≗ *chin strap* ‖ Trag≗ *carrying strap* ‖ Transmissions≗ *belt-gearing, driving-belt* **C.** ⟨hors⟩ Hals≗ *neck-strap* ‖ Kehl≗ *throat-band* ‖ Nasen≗ *nose-band* ‖ Rücken≗ *crupper*(*-strap*) ‖ Schweif≗ *crupper-dock* ‖ Stirn≗ *frontlet* **D.** mit ~ binden *to strap*, peitschen *to lash* ‖ ⟨fig⟩ den ~ enger schnallen *to tighten one's belt* ‖ ~ schneiden aus *to profit by* **Riemen**[2] m ~s/~ ⟨mar⟩ *oar* ‖ (f 1 Hand) *scull* ‖ die ~ klar m (pieken) *to ship the* (*to toss*) *oars* ‖ die ~ platt werfen *to feather* ‖ klar bei ~! *ship your oars*! *oars ready*! ‖ ~ bei! *oars out*! ‖ ~ ein! *unship your oars*! *way enough*! ‖ °(sich) am ~ reißen *to keep one's end up* | ⟨carp⟩ (Fußboden-≗) *match-board* **R·iemen-**[1] **~blume** f *loranth* **~antrieb** m *beltdrive* **~boot** n *rowing boat* [2]**~auflage** f *thole* [1]**~ausrücker** m *belt shifter* **~blatt** n ⟨bot⟩ *clivia, caffre lily* **~fisch** m *band-, ribbon-, oar fish* **~gabel** f *belt fork* **~halter** m *strap-clamp* [2]**~kunst** f *watermanship* [1]**~leiter** m *strap-guide* **~leitung** f *belting* [2]**~parkett** n *herring-bone parquetry* [1]**~peitsche** *cat-o'-nine-tails* **~pferd** n *leader* **~scheibe** f *belt-pulley* [2]**~schlag** m *stroke* [1]**~schlaufe** f *keeper* **~schneider** m *strap-cutter, saddler* **~schuh** m *sandal* **~tang** m ⟨bot⟩ *sea--tangle* **~welle** f *strap-rod* **R·iemer**[1] m ~s/~ *saddler, belt-, harness-, strap-maker* **..r·iemer**[2] m ~s/~ [in comp] z. B. Acht~ ⟨univ sl⟩ (*an*) *eight*

Ries n –es/–s(e) ⟨pap⟩ *ream* ≗**weise** adv *in r.s*

R·iese[1] m ~n/~n *giant* ‖ (i. Märchen) *ogre* ‖ ⟨fig⟩ (P & S) *colossus*, ⟨fam⟩ *whacker*, → ~n–

R·iese[2] f ~/~n (Rinne) *timber-slide*; → rieseln

Riese[3] npr: nach Adam ~ *according to Cocker*

R·ieseler m ~s/~ (f Abwässer) *irrigator, percolator* **r·ieseln 1.** vi [h & s] *to murmur, babble, purl* ‖ (of sweat) *to run, trickle* ‖ ⟨fig⟩ (of feeling) *to ripple* **2.** v/imps [h] (Regen) es rieselt *it drizzles*; → krachen **R·iesel- ~anlage** f ⟨tech⟩ *dripping installation* **~feld** n *sewage-field* ‖ *irrigated field* **~regen** m *drizzling rain* **~werk** n = Gradierwerk

R·iesen- *giant* (*g.t*), *gigantic* (*g.c*), *super* (*s.*) [1]**~ameise** f ⟨ent⟩ *great black ant* **~arbeit** f ⟨fam⟩ *tremendous piece of work* **~·aufschwung** m ⟨gym⟩ *upward circle* **~bau** m *g.c.* (⟨fam⟩ *tremendous*) *building* ‖ ⟨a.⟩ *noble pile* **~erfolg** m *howling success* **~felge** f ⟨gym⟩ *grand circle* **~farn** m ⟨geol⟩ *megaphyton* **~faultier** n ⟨geol⟩ *megatherium* **~feuer** n *great fire* **~flugzeug** n *g.t machine* od *plane* **~gebirge** n ⟨geog⟩ (zw Schlesien u Böhmen) *R.* **~geist** m *powerful intellect* **~geschlecht** n *race of g.ts* **~gestalt** f *colossal figure, colossus* **~grab** n *g.t's grave, cairn, barrow* ≗**groß** a *g.c*, ⟨fam⟩ *whacking great* **~größe** f *g., g.c size*; *outsize* (*bottle*) **~hai** m *basking shark* **~hirsch** m ⟨geol⟩ *megaceros* **~konzern** m *mammoth undertaking* **~kraft** f *Herculean strength* **~mäßig** a *g.c, colossal* **~menge** f *mammoth crowd*; ⟨übtr⟩ *a power* (*of work*) **~rad** n *Ferris wheel* | mehrstufige **~rakete** f *multi*(*ple*)*-stage* od *step* (od *multispeed*) *giant rocket*; → Rakete **~(luft)reifen** m *s.-balloon tyre* **~salamander** m *g.t salamander*, ⟨Am⟩ *hellbender* **~schlagzeile** f ⟨Am sl⟩ *screamer* **~schlange** f *boa constrictor, anaconda* **~schritt** m *g.t* od *g.c stride* **~schwung** m ⟨gym⟩ *g.t swing* | e–n **~skandal** m *to raise the roof* **~stadt** f *immense* od *huge town*; *megalopolis* **~stimme** f *stentorian voice* **~summe** f *immense amount of money* **~tanne** f ⟨bot⟩ *sequoia* **~tier** n *huge beast* **~welle** f ⟨gym⟩ *grand circle*; ⟨fam⟩ *slobber-swing* **r·iesenhaft** a *g.c* (*achievement*) *colossal* (*building*), *immense, huge, enormous* (*elephant*) **r·iesig** [a] = riesenhaft ‖ ⟨fam & fig⟩ *stupendous, awful, formidable* ‖ ~er Lärm ⟨sl⟩ *a hell of a noise* | [adv] *extremely, like hell, awfully* ‖ (*she likes him*) *a lot*; *devilish* (*uncomfortable*) ‖ *jolly* (*good*) ‖ *frightfully* (*decent*) ‖ *mighty* (*fine*) ‖ *thumping* (*great*) | ich habe mich ~ gefreut *I was awfully glad* **R·iesin** f ~/~nen *giantess*

R·iester m ~s/~ *patch* | **~n** vt [h] *to patch*

riet 1. & 3. sg pret v raten

Riet n ~s/~e ⟨weav⟩ *reed*

Rîf, das (Gebirge in Marokko) *the Riff*
Rîfi·ote, R·îfkabyle m *Riff*; → vor.
Riff n ~(e)s/~e *reef* ‖ **~auster** f ⟨zoo⟩ *reefer* **~piraten** m pl *Riff Arabs* od *Pirates* pl
R·iffel f ~/~n *flax-comb, ripple* ‖ ~ m ~s/~ ⟨theat⟩ *ripple effect* **~eisen** n *riffler* **~maschine** f ⟨tech⟩ *fluting-machine* **r·iffeln** vt [h] *to chamfer, to flute* ‖ (Flachs) *to ripple* **R·iffelung** f *corrugation*
R·iga n (Hauptstadt v Lettland) **R·igaischer Meerbusen** m *Gulf of Riga*
Rig·ole f ~/~n (Pflug m) *trench-plough* | **≃n** vt [h] ⟨agr⟩ *to turn up the ground, to t.-pl.*
rigor·os, ≃ a *rigorous, strict* | **≃um** n ~s/–sen & –sa *oral examination for a doctor's degree*
Rik·ambio m ~s/~s *re-exchange, re-draft*
Rikosch·ett m ~s/~e ⟨mil⟩ *ricochet* (*shot*) **~feuer** n *ricochet-fire* **≃·ieren** vi *to ricochet*
R·ille f ~/~n *rill* ‖ (e–r Säule) *chamfer* ‖ (*small*) *furrow* od ⟨carp⟩ *groove* ‖ ⟨arch⟩ *flute, chamfer* ‖ ⟨agr⟩ *drill* | **≃n** vt [h] *to groove, flute, chamfer, channel* **~nflanke** f ⟨rec⟩ *wall of a groove* **~nzieher** m ⟨for⟩ *drill-hoe* **r·illig** a *marked with rills*, etc.; *fluted*, etc.
Rim·esse f ~/~n ⟨com⟩ *remittance* ‖ ~ m *to remit* ‖ ~ per Saldo *remittance to square*
Rind n ~(e)s/~er *neat* ‖ *bullock, ox, cow* ‖ ~er [pl] (*horned*) *cattle* ‖ 20 ~er *20 head of cattle* ‖ einige ~er *a few cattle* (*were grazing*) **~fleisch** n *beef*; (gesalzenes) *bully-beef* **~fleischbrühe** f *beef-tea* **~stück** n *beefsteak* **~vieh** n *cattle* pl ‖ ⟨vulg, fig⟩ (P) *blockhead, duffer, ass, idiot* **~viehzucht** f *cattle-breeding* **R·inder- ~braten** m *roast beef* **~bremse** f ⟨ent⟩ *gadfly* **~brust** f ⟨cul⟩ *brisket of beef* **~herde** f *herd of cattle* **~hirt** m *neat-herd, cowherd*, ⟨Am⟩ *cowboy* ‖ Pony des ~en *cow-pony* **~pest** f *rinderpest, cattle-plague* **~pökelfleisch** n *corned beef* **~talg** m *beef-suet* **Rinds- ~auge** n ⟨bot⟩ *Ox-Eye* **~blase** f *bullock's bladder* **~fell** n (ganzes gegerbtes) *crop* **~fett** n *beef-suet* **~keule** f (vordere) *shin*, (hintere) *round of beef* **~leder** n *neat's leather* **≃ledern** a *of neat's leather* **~lende** f ⟨cul⟩ *fillet of beef, tenderloin* | ~nstück [n] *steak* **~mark** n *beef-marrow* **~roulade** f *collared beef* **~zunge** f *neat's tongue*
R·inde f ~/~n ⟨bot, med⟩ *cortex*; (Baum≃) *bark* ‖ (Brot≃) *crust* ‖ (Käse≃) *rind* ‖ e–e ~ bek *or* bilden *to crust* **≃nartig** a *cortical* **~nboot** n *pit pan* **~nkoralle** f ⟨zoo⟩ *fan-coral* **~nlaus** f ⟨ent⟩ *psocid* **~nschicht** f *cortical layer* **r·indig** a *crusty, crusted*
R·ing m ~(e)s/~e **1.** *ring* ⟨a. box⟩ ‖ *coil* (*of wire*) ‖ (e–r Kette etc) *link*, ⟨arch⟩ (Säulen≃) *astragal* ‖ ⟨tech⟩ (Dichtungs≃) *washer* ‖ Dreh≃ *swivel* ‖ Feder≃ *spring washer* ‖ (Zwinge) *ferrule* ‖ (Aufhalte≃) ⟨hors⟩ *choke-strap* ‖ (am Schlüssel) *bow*; (Schlüssel≃) *key-ring*; (Straße) *orbital road*; kl ~, ~lein [n] *ringlet, circlet, annulet*, ˣdu hast ja noch's ~ele vom Häfele am Ärschle! ⟨mil sl⟩ *I cut barbed wire when you were cutting your teeth* ‖ (Tor b. Ballspiel) *hoop* ‖ ⟨artill⟩ Führungs≃ *driving band* **2.** (um die Augen) *dark circle* (*round the eyes*) ‖ ⟨orn⟩ (Hals≃) *ruff* ‖ ⟨ent⟩ (Bauch≃) *segment* ‖ (des Mondes) *halo* ‖ (des Saturn) *ring* ‖ ⟨anat⟩ *areola* ‖ ⟨racing⟩ Führ≃ *parade-ring* **3.** (P) *circle* ‖ ⟨com⟩ *ring, trust, corner, pool, combine* ‖ sie bildeten e–n ~ um ihn *they ringed themselves round him* **~alkohol** m *cyclic a.* ¹**~amsel** f ⟨orn⟩ *ring-ousel* **≃artig** a *annular* **~bahn** f *circular* (od *belt-*)*railway* **~bolzen** m *eyebolt* **~finger** m *ring-finger, third* od *fourth finger* **≃förmig** a *annular, ring-shaped*, ⟨scient⟩ *orbicular*, ⟨anat⟩ *cricoid*; fast ~ *penannular* **~gewölbe** n ⟨arch⟩ *annular vault* **~harnisch** m *brigandine* **~kammer** f ⟨mot⟩ *annular chamber* ²**~kampf** m [→ ringen] *wrestling-match* **~kämpfer** m *wrestler* ¹**~knorpel** m ⟨anat⟩ *cricoid cartilage* **~kolben** m ⟨tech⟩ *annular piston* **~kragen** m ⟨hist⟩ *gorget* **~leitung** f ⟨tech⟩ *circular* od *ring main* | ~kabel [n] *perimeter c.* **~mauer** f *town-wall, circular wall*; ⟨hist⟩ *precinct* **~mitglied** n ⟨com⟩ *ringster* **~ofen** m *annular brick-kiln* **~panzer** m ⟨hist⟩ *ring-mail* **~reiten** n *tilting at the ring* **~richter** m ⟨box⟩ *referee* **~scheibe** f *rifle* (*ring*) *target* **~schmierlager** n *r. lubricating bearing* ²**~schule** f ⟨hist⟩ *palæstra* **~straße** f *circular road, boulevard* Fr; ⟨aero⟩ *perimeter* (*track*) **~tennis** n *deck-tennis* **~wall** m *rampart* **~wechsel** m ⟨ec⟩ *exchange of rings*
R·ingel m ~s/~ *small ring* ‖ ⟨weav⟩ *mail* **~blume** f ⟨bot⟩ *marigold, calendula* **~flechte** f ⟨med⟩ *ringworm* **~gans** f ⟨orn⟩ *brent-goose* **~haar** n *curled hair* **~locke** f *ringlet* **~natter** f *ring-snake* **~panzer** m *ring-mail* °**~pietz** m ⟨aero⟩ *ground loop* **~spinner** m ⟨ent⟩ *lackey moth* **~stechen** n *tilting match* **~reihen, ~tanz** *round dance* **~taube** f *wood-, ring-dove* **~wurm** m ⟨zoo⟩ *ringed worm, annelid* ˣ**R·ingele** n ~s/~ → Ring 1. (gegen das Ende hin) **ringelig** a *resembling a ring* ‖ *annular* ‖ *coiling, curling* **r·ingeln I.** vt [h] *to furnish with rings, to ring* ‖ *to curl* **II. sich ~** *to curl* ‖ (of smoke) *to wreathe* ‖ (schlängelnd) *to wriggle, wind* **III. geringelt** *curled, in ringlets* ‖ mit ~em Hals *ring-necked*
r·ingen I. vt [rang/gerungen] [h] **1.** (Wäsche, die Hände) *to wring* (über *over*) ‖ jdm etw aus der Hand ~ *to wrest a th from a p's hand* **2.** jdn zu Boden ~ *to throw a p in wrestling* **II.** vi [h] ⟨a. fig⟩ *to wrestle, struggle, grapple* (gegen mit *with*), ⟨a.⟩ *to try a fall with a p* ‖ *to wrestle* [a. vt] (*I can wrestle anyone*) ‖ mit jdm um etw ~ *to contend with a p for a th* | ⟨fig⟩ (innerlich) schwer ~ mit *to be in travail with, to tussle with*; (*he had a hard time of it*) | **mit** dem sprachlichen **Ausdruck** ~ *to wrestle with the diction* ‖ mit e–m Entschluß ~ *to strive after a decision* ‖ *to grapple with a problem* ‖ mit dem Tode ~ *to be in the last agonies, to be in the throes of death* ‖ mit den Tränen ~ *to struggle against one's tears* | **nach** etw ~ *to strive for* od *after, to contend for a th* ‖ nach Atem ~ *to gasp, fight, sob for breath* ‖ nach Ausdruck, Fassung, Worten ~ *to struggle for expression, composure, words* | **um** etw ~ *to fight, strive, labour for a th* ‖ um die Palme ~ *to struggle for the palm of victory* **III.** v/refl: ein Seufzer rang sich ihm aus der Brust *he heaved a sigh* **IV.** ≃ [n] *twisting* etc ‖ *wrestling*; freies ~ ⟨Am⟩ *catch-as-catch-can* od *all-in wrestling*; sich im ~ messen *to try a fall* (mit *with*) ‖ ⟨fig⟩ *fight, struggle* (*for*), *grappling* (*with*), *tussle* (über *over*) ‖ *scramble* (um *for places*) ‖ ~ mit dem Tode *last agony*
rings [adv] *around* ‖ ~ umgeben v *entirely surrounded by* ‖ ~ um *around* ‖ **~·um, ~her·um, ~umh·er** *all* od *right round, round about*, ⟨bes Am⟩ *all around*
R·inne f ~/~n *furrow* ‖ (Gosse) *gutter, kennel, channel* ‖ ⟨met⟩ *casting gutter* ‖ ⟨geog⟩ *gully* ‖ ⟨geol⟩ *trough* ‖ (Wasserabfluß≃) *sewer* ‖ ⟨arch⟩ *chamfer, flute, groove* ‖ (Röhre) *pipe* | **≃n** vi [rann/geronnen] [s] **1.** *to run, to flow* ‖ *water drips, brooks gush, tears flow, wine runs from the cask* ‖ *money runs through one's fingers like water* **2.** (v Fässern etc) *to drop, leak* **R·inn- ~leiste** f *drip moulding, cyma* **~stein** m (Straßen≃) *kerb, curb*; *gutter* (⟨a. fig⟩ *to end in the gutter*) ‖ (Küchen≃) *sink, sewer* ‖ ⟨arch⟩ *culvert* **~steinkehrer** m *sewerman* **R·innsal** n ~(e)s/~e, **R·innsel** n ~s/~ *channel, water-course, streamlet, rivulet, rill, trickle*
R·io de Janeiro [ʒaˈneːro] n (Stadt in Brasilien)
R·io m ~ de la Pl·ata *River Plate, Plate River, Rio de la Plata*; ~ de Oro n (Landschaft in W.-Afrika); ~ Grande del Norte m (nordamerik. Strom zw Mexiko u U.S.A.); ~ Gr·ande do

N·orta (Staat in Brasilien); ~ Gr·ande do Sul (Staat in Brasilien); ~ Magdal·ena → Magdalenenstrom; ~ N·egro (Nebenfluß des Amazonas)

R·ipp- ~sam(me)t [m] *ribbed velvet*; ~seide [f] *corded silk*; ~speer [m] ⟨cul⟩ *spare-rib* **R·ippchen** n ~s/~ ⟨cul⟩ *cutlet* ‖ (Rinds≗) *ribs* pl (*of beef*) ‖ (*mutton-*)*chop* **R·ippe** f ~/~n **1.** *rib* ‖ falsche ~ *short, false, floating rib*; hohe ~ (Rind) *sirloin* ‖ zwischen den ~n liegend *intercostal* ‖ e–m alle ~n im Leibe zerschlagen *to break every bone in a p's body* ‖ e–m den Dolch durch die ~n jagen *to thrust a dagger between a p's ribs* ‖ °ich kann's mir nicht aus den ~n schneiden *where do you expect me to take it from* ‖ e–m in die ~n stoßen *to give a p a dig in the ribs* ‖ bei ihm kann man alle ~n zählen *you can count every rib in his body* **2.** (Blatt≗) *nerve, rib* | ⟨arch⟩ *rib, groin*; Neben≗ *lierne*; Diagonal≗ *ogive* ‖ *slat* (*of a blind*) | ⟨mar⟩ (Spante) *frame*, ~n [pl] *frame-work*; ⟨mot⟩ (Schaufel) *vane*; (Kühler≗) *gill* ‖ (Schokoladen≗) *bar, piece*, ⟨Am⟩ *strip, section* ‖ ⟨fig⟩ (P) *wench*; falsche ~! *crooked rib*! **~lmarken** f pl ⟨geol⟩ *ripple marks* **r·ippen** vt [h] *to rib* ‖ *to plait* (*a frill*) **gerippt** *laid* (*paper*) ‖ *groined* (*ceiling*) ‖ ~er Stoff = Rips **R·ippen~braten** m *roast ribs* pl **~fell** n ⟨anat⟩ *pleura* **~fellentzündung** f ⟨path⟩ *pleurisy, pleuritis* **~gegend** f *costal region* **~gewölbe** n *rib-vaulting* **~halter** m ⟨anat⟩ *scalenus* L **~kühler** m ⟨mot⟩ *ribbed cooler* **~speer** m *spare-rib* **~stoß** m *nudge, thrust* (⟨fam⟩ *poke, dig*) *in the ribs* ‖ ≗e austeilen *to deal out blows* ‖ jdm e–n ~ geben *to nudge a p* **~stück** n ⟨cul⟩ *sirloin, top-cut* **~weh** n ⟨path⟩ *pleuralgia* **R·ips** m –es/–e *rep* **~seide** f *ribbed silk, faille* Fr ×**R·ipserle** n (Streichholz) ⟨sl⟩ *twig* **r·ipsraps** [adv] *quickly, at a hurry*

ripu·arisch a *Ripuarian* (*Franks*)

Risal·it m ~(e)s/~e ⟨arch⟩ *projection, set-off*

risch a **1.** *quick* **2.** *straight*

R·isiko n ~s/~s *risk* (gr *big*, wohlkalkuliert *calculated*) ‖ *peril* ‖ dem ~ ausgesetzt *exposed to r.*; ein ~ eingehen (tragen) *to take* (*bear*) *a r.*; auf eigenes ~ *at one's own r.* ‖ es geht auf sein ~ *it's for his account and r.* | ⟨ins⟩ ~beginn [m] *Terminus a quo* L, *attachment of r.*; ~ende [n] *T. ad quem* L, *cessation of r.*; ~deckung [f] *coverage*; ~verteilung [f] *spread of r.s*; ~zuschlag [m] *premium loading for abnormal r.* **risk·ant** a *risky, perilous* ‖ *touch-and-go* (*business*); ⟨fam⟩ *sporting* (*chance*) ‖ ~e Lage *touch-and-go* **risk·ieren** vt [h] *to risk* (*one's life*), *to run the r. of* ‖ man muß auch mal was ~ *one must sometimes take r.s* ‖ °e–n ~ *to take a drop* (*of sth short*); Sie ~ nichts dabei *you are quite safe in doing it*; etw ~, es ~ *to take a risk*

R·ispe f ~/~n *panicle* **≗nförmig** a *panicled* **~ngras** n ⟨bot⟩ *meadow-grass*

R·iß m –sses/–sse **A.** *tearing, rending* | *rent, rift, break, tear, split, cleft, scission, scissure* ‖ *leak* (*the shoe had a l.*) ‖ (Bruch) *fracture* ‖ (Spalt) *crevice, chink, fissure* ‖ (Sprung) *flaw, crack* (*in a rock, glass*) ‖ e–n ~ h *to have a flaw* ‖ (Ratsche) *scratch* ‖ (Hautschrunde) *chap* | ⟨**fig**⟩ *schism, breach, disunion, difference* ‖ *gulf* ‖ *shock* ‖ *gap* | (Skizze, Plan) *sketch, design, plan, draft*; *orthography* **B.** Risse bek *to tear*, ⟨fig⟩ *to get a good hiding* ‖ v Rissen durchzogen *seamed with cracks* ‖ e–n ~ hinterlassen (v Tod) *to leave a great blank* ‖ in den ~ treten *to step into the breach* **~bildung** f *cracking* **~wunde** f *lacerated wound* **R·isser** m ~s/~ ⟨for⟩ = Reißer **riß** 1. & 3. sg [pret] v reißen **r·issig** a *cracked, flawed, split, chinky*; *full of rents*; *shaky* (*timber*); *rimose, rimous* ‖ ~ w *to crackle*

Rist m ~(e)s/~e (Fuß) *instep* ‖ (Hand) *wrist* ‖ (Wider≗) *withers* pl **~griff** m ⟨gym⟩ *overgrasp*

R·iste f ~/~n *bundle of raw fibre*

Rist·orno n ⟨ins⟩ *cancellation of a contract*

r·ite [L adv] *in due form* ‖ ~ bestehen ⟨univ⟩ *to pass with decent credit*

°**R·ititi** m; e–n ~ h *to have got a screw loose*

Ritorn·ell n ~s/~e ⟨mus⟩ *ritornello, burden*

Ritr·atte f ~/~n *redraft, re-exchange*

r·itschr·atsch [intj] *slish, slash*!, *slap, bang*!

ritt 1. & 3. sg [pret] v reiten **Ritt** m ~(e)s/~e *ride* ‖ in e–m ~e *in one ride*, ⟨fig, fam⟩ *at one go* od *pull* ‖ kurzer, schneller ~ *sprint* ‖ Gelände≗ *or* ~ querfeldein *cross-country ride* ‖ e–n ~ m *to take* (od *to go for*) *a ride* **R·itter** m ~s/~ **1.** *knight*, ⟨fig⟩ *cavalier*; *companion*; *paladin* ‖ fahrender *or* irrender ~ *kn.-errant* ‖ bewaffneter ~ *kn.-at-arms* ‖ ~ v der Ahle (Elle, Feder) *kn. of the awl* (*thimble, pen* od *quill*) ‖ ~ des Glücks *soldier of fortune* ‖ v der traurigen Gestalt (Don Quixote) *kn. of the woeful countenance* ‖ ~ ohne Furcht u Tadel (Bayard) *kn. without fear or reproach* ‖ der letzte ~ ⟨Ger⟩ *Maximilian I* | ~ des Deutschordens *kn. of the German Order* | ~ der Ehrenlegion *kn. of the L. of Hono(u)r* | jdn zum ~ schlagen *to dub a p a kn., to knight a p* ‖ er war ihr ~ *he was her kn.* ‖ er warf sich zu ihrem ~ auf *he proclaimed h.s. her champion* ‖ an jdm zum ~ w *to win one's spurs by overthrowing a p* **2.** ⟨cul⟩ arme ~ [pl] *fritters* **~akademie** f *academy* od *boardingschool for young noblemen* **~brauch** m *k.ly usage* **~burg** f *k.t's castle* **≗bürtig** a *of noble descent* **~dienst** m *k.-service*; ⟨fig⟩ *k.ly service, chivalrous wooing*; (jdm) ~e leisten *to squire* vt **~epos** n *chivalrous epic* **~geist** m *spirit of chivalry* **~gut** n *manor, manorial estate* **~gutsbesitzer** m *lord of the manor* **~kreuz** n ⟨Ger mil⟩ *k.t's cross*; mit dem ~ ausgezeichnet w *to be awarded the k.hood of the Iron Cross* **~kreuzträger** m *k. of the I. C.* **~lehen** n *k.t's fee* **~orden** m *Order of K.hood*; deutscher ~ *Teutonic Order* ‖ Angehöriger des niedrigsten Grades e–s ~s *companion* (*C. of the Bath*) **~pflicht** f *k.ly duty* **~roman** m *romance of chivalry* **~saal** m *baronial hall* **~schaft** f *k.hood* ‖ [koll] *k.s* pl **~schlag** m *accolade, k.ing, dubbing* ‖ den ~ bek *to be dubbed a k.* ‖ jdm den ~ erteilen *to dub a p a k.* **~sitte** f *chivalrous manners* pl, *courtesy* **~sitz** m *k.ly residence* **~spiel** n *tournament, joust* **~sporn** m ⟨bot⟩ *larkspur, Delphinium* **~stand** m *gentry*; ⟨hist⟩ *k.hood* **~tat** f *feat of chivalry* **~wesen** n *chivalry* **~wort** n *word of a k.* od *gentleman* **~würde** f *k.hood, dignity of a k.*; die ~ empfangen *to receive the accolade* **~zeit** f *age of chivalry* **~zug** m *k.ly expedition* **r·itterlich** a *knightly, chivalric, chivalrous* ‖ ⟨fig⟩ *gentlemanly, ch.s, sporting, sportsmanlike, fair*; *playing the game* ‖ (tapfer) *valiant, gallant* (*conduct*) | [adv] (*he helped her*) *ch.sly*; (*he*) *gallantly* (*offered her his arm*) | **≗keit** f ~/ *knightliness, chivalry* ‖ *gentlemanliness, ch.sness* ‖ *valour, gallantry*; *fairness* **R·itterling** m ~s/~e ⟨bot⟩ *Tricholoma* L **R·ittertum** n ~s/ *knighthood, chivalry* **r·ittlings** [adv] *astraddle, astride* **R·ittmeister** m ~s/~ ⟨mil⟩ *captain* (*of cavalry* od *of horse*), *cavalry captain*

Ritu·al n ~(e)s/~e ⟨ec⟩ *ritual* | ~kleidung [f] *r. garb* **~isierung** f ⟨a. eth-physiol⟩ *ritualization* **ritu·ell** a *relating to rites*; *ceremonial* **R·itus** m ~/–ten ⟨ec⟩ *rite* ‖ nach religiösem ~ getauft w *to be b. with the rites of religion*

Ritz m ~es/~e; **R·itze** f ~/~n *chink fissure, cleft, crack, crevice*; ⟨min⟩ *scar* ‖ (Schramme) *scratch* **R·itzel** n ~s/~ ⟨tech⟩ *pinion* **~antrieb** m *pinion-drive* **r·itzen** vt [h] *to scratch* ‖ *to carve* (*one's name on a th*) **r·itzig** a *crannied, cracked, flawed* **R·itzung** f ~/~en *scratch*(*ing*)

Riv·al m ~en/~e(n) *rival* **≗is·ieren** vi [h] (mit jdm) *to rival* (*a p*); *to compete* (*with a p*) ‖ ~d *rival* [nur attr] **~it·ät** f ~/~en *rivalry, rivalship, competition*

Rivi·era, die *the Riviera* (*of Genoa*)

R·izinus m ~/ ⟨bot⟩ *castor-oil plant* **~öl** n ⟨med⟩ *castor-oil*

..rl, (e)rl [dim suff] ⟨bes österr⟩ z. B. Kalbshaxe(rl n); Korb/Körberl; Kraut/≈erl; Flicken/Flickerldruck ⟨tail⟩ *patchwork*

R·obbe f ~/~n ⟨zoo⟩ → *seal* | **≈n** vi [h] *to crawl* | **~n** n ~s/ flaches ~ *leopard's crawl* **~fang** m *s.-hunt, s.ling* **~fänger** m *s.er* ‖ ⟨mar⟩ *s.ing--vessel* **~fell** n *s.skin* **~speck** m *s.-blubber*

R·obber m ~s/~ ⟨cards⟩ *rubber*

R·obe f ~/~n *robe, dress, gown*; → Raub

Rob·inie f ~/~n ⟨bot⟩ *locust-tree, Robinia*

Robinson·ade f ~/~n ⟨Lit⟩ *robinsonade*; ⟨ftb⟩ *full-length save*

Rob·ot f ~/~en; m ~(e)s/~e *statute-labour* ‖ ⟨fig⟩ *drudgery* **R·oboter** m ~s/~ *robot* | **~flugzeug** n (Zieldarstellung) ⟨fam⟩ *drone*

rob·ust a *stout, robust, sturdy*; *rude* (*health*); ⟨Am⟩ *rugged*; ⟨fam⟩ *whacking, strapping* (*wench*)

Roch m ~s/~e **1.** ⟨myth-orn⟩ *roc* **2.** ⟨chess⟩ *castle* **≈·ieren** [–ʃ–] vi [h] *to castle*

roch 1. & 3. sg [pret] v riechen

R·oche(n) m ~n/~n ⟨ich⟩ *ray*

r·öcheln vi [h] *to rattle in one's throat*; ⟨mil hum sl⟩ (schlafen) *to hog it* | ≈ n *rattling* ..; Todes≈ *death-rattle*

R·ochester n [ˈrɔtʃəstə] ⟨engl⟩ (Stadt in Kent)

Rock m ~(e)s/≈e **A. 1.** Damen≈ *skirt, frock*; sehr enger ~ *hobbled s.*; Glocken≈ *flared s.*; Hosen≈ *divided s.*; Rad≈ *circular s.* ‖ die ≈e ⟨übtr fam⟩ (Frauen) *the skirt* **2.** Herren≈ *coat, jacket* **B.** Amts≈ ⟨bes jur, univ etc⟩ *gown* ‖ Geh≈ *frock-coat* ‖ des Königs *or* den bunten ~ anziehen *to don the king's colours*; .. tragen ⟨hist⟩ *to wear the king's coat* ‖ Morgen≈ *dressing-gown* ‖ Plissee≈ *pleated skirt* ‖ → Reif≈ ‖ roter ~ ⟨hunt⟩ (*to hunt in*) *scarlet* ‖ Staats≈ *robe* ‖ Über≈ *frock-coat* ‖ Unterrock *petticoat* ‖ Waffen≈ *tunic* ‖ Wappen≈ *tabard* **C.** ⟨fig⟩ jdm den ~ ausklopfen ⟨fam⟩ *to dust a p's jacket* ‖ → Hemd **~aufschlag** m *lapel* **~schoß** m *front of a skirt*; (*coat-*)*skirt, coat-tail*; sich an jds ≈e klammern *to hang on to a p's coat-tails* **~stoff** m *coating* **~zipfel** m *lappet* (*of a coat*); der Mutter am ~ hängen *to be tied to one's mother's apron--strings* **R·öckchen** n ~s/~ (*baby's, child's*) *frock* ‖ ⟨engl mil⟩ (Sch·otten≈) *kilt* .. **röckig** a (*short-*)*-coated* od *skirted*

R·ocken m ~s/~ *distaff* **~bolle** f ⟨bot⟩ *rocambole*

..rode suff (= Rodung) z Bezeichnung v Ortsnamen (z. B. Walsrode, Wernigerode)

R·ode- **~hacke** f *mattock* **~land** n *woodland turned into arable land* **r·oden** vt [h] *to grub* od *stub up, to root out* ‖ *to clear* (*land*) ‖ *to lift* (*potatoes*) **R·odung** f = Rodeland ‖ (Baum≈) *uprooting*; → Urbarmachung

R·odel- **~bahn** f *toboggan shoot* od *slide, track, chute* **~schlitten** m *toboggan*; ⟨Am⟩ *coaster*; (mit Steuer) *bobsleigh*; (kl) *luge* **r·odeln** vi [h] *to toboggan, luge, coast*

R·ödelbalken m (Brückenbelag) *ribband* **r·ödeln** vt [h] *to ribband*

Rog·ate; Sonntag ~ ⟨ec⟩ *Rogation Sunday*

R·ogen m ~s/~ *roe, spawn* **~fisch** m *spawner* **~stein** m *oolite* **R·og(e)ner** m ~s/~ *spawner*

R·oggen m ~s/ ⟨bot⟩ *rye* **~stroh** n *rye-straw*; (z Dachdecken) *thatch*

roh I. [a] **A.** (S) **1.** *raw* (*fruit, meat, ham, egg*) | ⟨fig⟩ jdn wie ein ~es Ei behandeln *to treat a p with great delicacy and consideration* **2.** *crude* (*ore, oil, metal*); *virgin* (*alumin*[*i*]*um*) ‖ *unwrought* (*iron, copper*) ‖ *native* (*lime, sulphur*) ‖ *rough* (*diamond*) ‖ ⟨stat⟩ *crude, general* (*death rate*) **3.** *brown, unbleached* (*linen*) ‖ *raw* (*material, silk, cotton*) ‖ *untanned, undressed* (*hide, skin*) **4.** ⟨bookb⟩ *in sheets, unbound* **5.** ~es Bauwerk *building in the rough* **6.** ⟨com⟩ *gross* **7.** in ~em Zustand *in the raw* **B.** ⟨hors⟩ *untrained, unbroken, fresh* (*horse*) **C.** ⟨fig⟩ **1.** (P) *rough, rude, brutal* ‖ *vulgar, ill-bred, uncultured, unpolished* ‖ *truculent* (*people*), *barbarous* (*nation*) ‖ (ungeschult) *raw, crude* ‖ ~er Bursche, Geselle *dragoon*; *brutal fellow* ‖ ~er Kerl *lout* ‖ ein ~er Mensch *a brute* **2.** [v abstr] (derb) *coarse, unrefined* (*desires, customes, manners*) ‖ *brute* (*force*) **II.** [adv] (etw) ~ ausarbeiten *to block out*; *to rough-hew*; ein ~ gezimmerter Tisch *a roughly made table* ‖ jdn ~ behandeln *to roughhouse*; *to maul a p about, to ride rough-shod over a p* ‖ ~ verputzen *to rough-cast* **III.** n; etw aus dem ≈en arbeiten *to work sth up from the raw material* ‖ im ≈en schnitzen *to rough-hew* (aus *from*) **R·oh-** **~arbeit** f ⟨met⟩ *raw smelting* **~bau** m *unfinished building*; ⟨arch⟩ *frame*; *brick--work*; ⟨fig⟩ *frame, skeleton* ‖ im ~ darstellen (vorbereiten) *to skeleton*(*ize*) **~baumwolle** f *raw c.* **~bilanz** f ⟨com⟩ *rough b.* **~dachpappe** f *roofing felt base* **~einnahme** f *gross receipts* pl **~eisen** n *pig-iron* **~eiweiß** n *crude protein* **~entwurf** m *rough drawing* od *sketch* **~ergebnisse** n pl ⟨stat⟩ *basic data* **~ertrag** m ⟨com⟩ *gross income* **~erz** n *crude ore* **~erzeugnisse** n pl *raw produce* [sg] **~faser** f (v Gemüse) *roughage*; ⟨agr/chem⟩ *crude fibre* (⟨Am⟩ *fiber*) **~film** m *rawstock* **~gewicht** n *gross w.* **~gewinn** m *gross p.* **~gummi** m *crude r.*; *unvulcanized r.* **~häute** f pl *raw skins* **~kohle** f *run of the mine* **~kost** f *uncooked food* **~köstler** m *fruitarian* **~kupfer** n *raw c.* **~material** n ⟨com⟩ *raw m.* **~metall** n *crude m.* **~öl** n *crude oil* **~papier** n *base p.* **~petroleum** n *native naphtha* **~produkte** n pl *raw p.s* pl **~putz** m *rough cast*(*ing*) **~schiene** f ⟨met⟩ *puddle-bar* **~schwefel** m *native s.* **~seide** f *raw s.*; *hackle* **~spaltbenzin** n *straight-run gasoline* **~stahl** m *raw st.* **~stahleisen** n *steel-pig* **~stoff** m *raw material* | ≈erzeugend [a] *primary* (*industries*); ~gebiet [n] *district yielding raw m.s*; ~industrie [f] *basic i.*; ≈verarbeitend [a] *processing* (*industries*) **~walzwerk** n *puddle rolling-mill* **~ware** f *basic commodity* **~zelluloid** n *celluloid base* **~zucker** m *unrefined s.*; *muscovado* **R·ohheit** f ~/~en *rawness*; *raw* od *crude state* | *truculence*; *rudeness*; *coarseness*; *roughness, ill--breeding* ‖ *crudeness* ‖ *brutality, savagery* | *brutal act*(*ion*) ‖ *rude expression* | e–e ~ begehen *to commit a brutal action* **R·ohling** m ~s/~e *brute, rowdy*, ⟨Am a.⟩ *yahoo* ‖ ⟨tech⟩ *raw wood* (*for tanning*); ⟨met⟩ *slug*

Rohr n ~(e)s/~e **A. 1.** ⟨bot⟩ (a. Schilf≈) *reed* ‖ Bambus≈ *cane* ‖ Peddig≈, spanisches ~ *rat*(*t*)*an* **2.** ⟨tech⟩ *tube, pipe* | Abfluß≈ *waste-p.* ‖ Auspuff≈ *exhaust p.* ‖ Blas≈ *blowpipe, blowtube*; (indianische Waffe) *sarbacand*; ⟨mus⟩ *reed* ‖ Druck≈ *pressure p.* ‖ Fahrrad≈ *tube* ‖ Fall≈ *gutter-p.* ‖ Fern≈ *telescope* ‖ Futter≈ *liner* ‖ Gas≈ *gas-p.* ‖ Geschütz≈, Gewehr≈ *barrel* ‖ Heiz≈ *flue* ‖ Hör≈ *stethoscope* ‖ Minenwerfer≈ *bore* ‖ Ofen≈ *stove-p., flue* ‖ Pfeifen≈ *stem* .. ‖ ⟨cycl⟩ Rahmen≈ (oberes, unteres) (*top, down*) *tube* ‖ Resonanz≈ *resonance tube* ‖ Schlüssel≈ *stem, body* .. ‖ Schutt≈ *chute tube* ‖ Seh≈ *periscope* ‖ Sprach≈ *speaking-tube*; *megaphone* ‖ ⟨cycl⟩ Steuer≈ *head tube* ‖ Teleskop≈ (*telescopic*) *chute* ‖ Torpedo≈ *t.-tube* **B.** durch ~e leiten *to pipe* ‖ mit ~ beziehen *to cane* (*a chair*) ‖ ~e legen in .. ⟨tech⟩ *to p.* (*a house*) ‖ gezogenes ~ *solid drawn tube*; ⟨mil, tech⟩ *rifle-barrel* ‖ sich auf ein schwaches ~ stützen *to trust to a broken reed* ‖ schwankendes ~ *trembling r.* ⟨a. fig⟩ ‖ schwankend wie ein ~ *as uncertain as a r.* ‖ ⟨prov⟩ wer im ~e sitzt hat gut Pfeifen schneiden *he that sits among r.s cuts pipes when he pleases* **~ammer** f ⟨orn⟩ *r. bunting* **~ansatz** m ⟨tech⟩ *socket* **~bruch** m *p. burst* **~dach** n *r.-thatch* **~decke** f *r.-mat* **~dommel** f ⟨orn⟩ *bittern* **~durchlaß** m *pipe culvert* **~erhöhung** f ⟨artill⟩ *elevation* **~flansch** f *p.-flange* **~flechter** m *caner*

~flöte f *r.-pipe*; (Orgel-) *r. flute* **≃förmig** a *tubular*; ~er Gegenstand (z. B. Schlangenkörper) *barrel* **~gebüsch** n *r.-plot*; *cane-brake* **~geflecht** n *c.-work* od *-plaiting* **~halter** m ⟨artill, tech⟩ *breech lug* **~halm** m *r.* **~huhn** n ⟨orn⟩ *moor-cock, -hen* **~kabel** n *pipe-type c.* **~kanal** m = –stollen **~klaue** f ⟨artill, tech⟩ *guide ring* **~kolben** m *r.-mace*; breitblättriger ~ *bulrush* **~krepierer** m *burst in the bore, barrel burst* **~krümmer** m *p.-bend* **~legen** n *p.-laying* **~leger** m *p.-fitter, plumber* **~leitung** f *p.s* pl, *piping, p.-line, conduit* **~matte** f *cane-mat* **~muffe** f *connecting sleeve, pipe-bell* **~mündung** f ⟨artill⟩ *muzzle* **~netz** n *piping*; *service system* **~palme** f *rat(t)an, calamus* [L] **~pfeife** f *r.-pipe* **~post** f *pneumatic post* od *dispatch* (od *tube* [*plant*]); ⟨fam⟩ *letter shoot* | ~karte [f] *pn.c* od *tubular p.-c.* **~r·ücklauf** m ⟨artill⟩ *barrel recoil* | ~bremse [f] *buffer*; ~geschütz [n] *recoil-barrel gun* **~sänger** m ⟨orn⟩ *r.-warbler* **~schelle** f *p.-clip* **~schlange** f *pipe coil* **~schmied** m *gun-barrel maker* **~schelle** f *p.-clip* **~schraubstock** m *p.-vice* **~spatz, ~sperling** m *r.-sparrow*; ⟨fam⟩ schimpfen wie ein ~ *to swear like a trooper* **~sitz** m *cane seat* **~stock** m *c.(-stick)*, ⟨Am⟩ *switch*; mit dem ~ schlagen *to c., switch* **~stollen** m *pipe tunnel* od *gallery* **~stuhl** m *c.-(seated) chair* **~- u** Verbundmühlen [f pl] *tube and compound mills* **~verbindung** f *p.-joint* **~verzweigung** f ⟨tech⟩ *manifold* **~wagen** m ⟨artill⟩ *gun carriage* **~weih(e** f) m *moor-hawk* **~weite** f *bore, calibre, diameter* **~werk** n (Orgel≃) *reed-stop* **~wiege** f ⟨artill⟩ *sleigh* **~wischer** m (S) *slush brush*; *sponge*; *scovel* **~zange** f (e–e ~ *a pair of*) *p.-grips* **~zerspringer** m ⟨artill⟩ *premature bursting* **~zucker** m *cane-sugar* **R·öhre** f ~/~n **A.** *pipe*, ⟨bes Am⟩ *tube*; *channel*; *nozzle*; *socket*; *cylinder* ‖ kl ~ *tubule* ‖ ⟨anat⟩ *duct* ‖ ⟨bot⟩ *tube* ‖ ⟨hunt⟩ (Fuchs≃) *warren, earth*; e–e ~ verlegen ⟨hunt⟩ *to put to an e.* **B.** Bein≃ (Rüstung) *jamb(e)* ‖ Bestrahlungs≃ *X-ray tube* ‖ Brat≃ *oven* ‖ Brunnen≃ *pipe* od *barrel* .. ‖ ~ der Dachrinne *spout* ‖ Drän≃ *drain-pipe* ‖ Dreh≃ (Drechsler-≃) *turning gouge* ‖ Kamin≃ *funnel, shank* ‖ kommunizierende ~n *communicating tubes* ‖ Ofen≃ *oven* ‖ Pilz≃ *tube, canal* ‖ Pumpen≃ *pump-barrel* ‖ Radio≃ *valve*, ⟨Am⟩ *tube* ‖ Saug≃ *siphon* ‖ Schütt≃ *chute tube* ‖ Verbindungs≃ *connector* ‖ Verstärker≃ ⟨wir⟩ *amplifying valve* **r·öhren** vi [h] sd = schreien, weinen, ⟨hunt⟩ = rören **r·ohren** vt [h] *to cover* od *line with reeds* **r·ohren** a *made of reeds* **R·öhren- ~anlage** f *tubing, piping* **~apparat** m ⟨wir⟩ 5-~ *five-valve set* **~bestückung** f ⟨rec⟩ *tube complement* **~blitz** m *electronic flash* (*unit*), ⟨Am⟩ *strobe fl.* (*u.*) **~brücke** f *tubular bridge* **~brunnen** m *tube-well*; *running-fountain* **~embargo** n *pipe(-line) e.* **~falte** f ⟨arts⟩ *tubular fold* **≃förmig** a *tubular* **~hose** f *drain-pipe trousers* od *slacks*, ⟨fam⟩ *d.-p.s* **~kessel** m *t.r boiler* **~knochen** m *hollow cylindrical bone* **~kupplung** f ⟨tech⟩ *union-joint* **~legung** f *pipe-laying* **~leitung** f *conduit p.s* pl, *water-duct* **≃los** a *ductless* (*gland*) **~meister** m *conduit-maker* **~pilz** m ⟨bot⟩ *boletus* **~pulver** n *t.r* (⟨sl⟩ *macaroni*) *powder* **~schrank** m *valve* (⟨Am⟩ *tube*) *bank* **~sender** m ⟨wir⟩ *tube* od *valve transmitter* **~sicherung** f ⟨el⟩ *tube fuse* **~walzwerk** n *pipe mill, tube-rolling mill* **~werk** n *conduit*; *drain* **~wurm** m *tubiculous worm* **~ziegel** m *hollow-brick*; *tubular brick* **R·öhricht** n ~(e)s/~e *reed-bank, -plot*; *reeds* pl; *cane-brake* **R·öhrling** m ~s/~e ⟨bot⟩ *boletus* ‖ Familie der ~e *Boletaceae*

r·ojen vi [h] –jete/gerojet ⟨mar⟩ *to row*

Rok·aillearbeiter [rɔ'kai–] m *grotto-maker*

R·okoko n ~s/, **~stil** m *rococo*

R·oll- *r.*(*oll*[*ing*]) **~bahn** f ⟨aero⟩ *runway, airstrip, taxi-strip* ‖ zementierte ~ ⟨Am⟩ *tarmac* **~bahre** f *wheel stretcher* **~band** n *conveyor belt*; (f P) ⟨urspr Am⟩ *travolator* **~bett** n *truckle-bed* **~brett** n *mangling-board* **~brücke** f *turning bridge* **~feld** n ⟨aero⟩ *landing ground* od *strip*; *manœuvring area* | ~ringstraße [f] *perimeter* (*track*) **~fenster** n *sash-window* **~film** m *r.-film* | ~spule [f] *film cartridge* **~fläche** f ⟨aero⟩ *movement area* **~fleisch** n *collared beef, rolled roast* **~fuhr-** | ~dienst [m] *cartage*; ~geschäft [n], ~wesen [n] *carrier's business*; *moving company, transportation firm*; ~mann [m] *carter, drayman, carrier* **~fuß** m (Möbel≃) *castor* **~geld** n *carriage*; *delivery charges* ‖ *money paid for mangling* **~gut** n *r.ing freight*; *casks and cases* pl **~handtuch** n *jack-towel, roller* **~heilige** m pl (Sekte) ⟨Am⟩ *holy r.ers* pl **~hilfe** f ⟨aero⟩ *aid to taxying* **~holz** n *r.er*; *r.ing pin* **~kasten** m ⟨met⟩ *ore chest* **~kloben** m *pulley* **~knecht** m *carter's man* **~kommando** n *raiding squad*, ⟨Am sl⟩ *necktie party* **~kreis** m *r.ing circle* **~(l)aden** *roll* od *sliding shutter, roller blind* **~material** n ⟨rail⟩ *r.ing stock* **~mops** m *collared herring r.-mops* **~pult** n *roll top desk* **~rädchen** n (an Möbeln) *castor* ‖ ⟨engr⟩ *roulette* **~salve** f ⟨mil⟩ *r. of fire, r.ing volley* **~scheibe** f *sheave* **~schinken** m *r.ed ham* **~-schnecke** f ⟨zoo⟩ *butterfly-shell* **~-Scooter** m *r.-scooter* **~schrank** m *r.-fronted cabinet* **~-schreibtisch** m *r.-top desk, tambour-table* **~-schuhe** m pl *r.er-skates* pl **~schuhbahn** f (*skating-*) *-rink* **~schuß** m *ricochet* **~schutzschicht** f ⟨phot, rep⟩ *backcoat* **~schwanzaffe** m *sapajou* **~siegel** n ⟨bes ant⟩ *seal-cylinder* **~sitz** m (im Boot) *sliding-seat* **~söckchen** n (P) ⟨Am fam⟩ *bobby--soxer* **~splitt** m *loose chippings* pl **~stein** m *erratic block, boulder* **~straße** f ⟨aero⟩ *taxitrack* **~stuhl** m *Bath-*, ⟨Am⟩ *wheel-chair* **~tabak** m *twist(ed tobacco)* **~tendenz** f ⟨phot⟩ *tendency to curling* **~tisch** m *table on castors* **~transport** m *drayage* **~treppe** f *escalator*, → –band **~vorhang** m *r.er-blind* **~wagen** m *dray, truck* ‖ ⟨rail⟩ *lorry, trolly* ‖ (*children's*) *go-cart* **~werk** n ⟨arch⟩ *cartouche* [Fr] **~widerstand** m *r.ing resistance* **R·öllchen** n pl *detachable cuffs* pl **R·olle** f ~/~n **A. 1.** *roll, coil, twist, bundle* ‖ ⟨tech⟩ *r.er, pulley, cylinder*; *mangle, calender, trundle, truckle*; *castor*; *round log of wood*, (Walze) *r.er* ‖ ⟨el⟩ *coil* | ~ Klosettpapier *toilet r.*; e–e ~ Garn etc *a reel* (⟨Am⟩ *spool*) *of thread, wire*; *a roll of paper, money, tobacco* **2.** (als Maß) *a bolt* (*of canvas*) **3.** (Register) *roll, list, register* **4.** ⟨anat⟩ *trochlea* **5.** ⟨theat⟩ *part, character, rôle, lines* pl; → C. **6.** ⟨mar⟩ *station* ‖ Berge≃ *abandon ship stations*; Feuer≃ *fire station bill*; Klarschiff≃ *action stations* **7.** ⟨aero⟩ *roll, wing-over*, ⟨Am⟩ *barrel roll*; langsame ~ *hesitation* od *aileron r.*; gerissene *abrupt*, (un)gesteuerte (*flick*) *slow r.* **8.** ⟨gym⟩ *neck-r.* **B.** Andruck≃ ⟨telg⟩ *pad roller* ‖ Angel≃ *reel, spool* ‖ Aufhänge≃ (⟨a.⟩ ganze Vorrichtung) *pulley* ‖ Bindfaden≃, Garn≃ *reel of string, thread* ‖ Flaschenzug≃, Gardinen≃ *pulley* ‖ Gleit≃, Lauf≃ *roller, pulley* ‖ ⟨el⟩ Kontakt≃ *trolley* ‖ Kurven≃ (Bergbahn) *curve pulley* ‖ Lenk≃ *guide wheel* ‖ Möbel≃ *castor* (*chairs* auf .. *on castors*) ‖ Papier≃, Pergament≃ *scroll* (*of* ..) ‖ Rollschuh≃ *roller* ‖ Schlauch≃ *hose reel* ‖ Schlummer≃ *bolster cushion* ‖ Schrift≃ *scroll* ‖ Spann≃ *tension pulley* ‖ Stamm≃ *muster roll* ‖ Trossen≃ ⟨mar⟩ *wire reel* ‖ Wäsche≃ *mangle*; die Wäsche wird auf der ~ geglättet .. *is passed through the mangle* ‖ Zeichnungs≃ *drawing roll* **C.** ⟨theat & fig⟩ **W.'s** ~ im 30jährigen Kriege *the part played by W. in* .. | **effektvolle** ~ *fat* (*part*); führende ~ *lead*; heitere ~ *comedy role*; tragende ~ *leading part*; e–e umfangreiche ~ *a big part*; verpatzte ~ ⟨sl⟩ *fluff* | er hat s–e ~ **ausgespielt** *he is played out* ‖ e–e ~ besetzen mit *to cast a rôle* (.. *Hamlet*) *with* (*a p*) ‖ e–e ~ darstellen *to take a part, to fill a rôle* ‖ s–e ~ genau im Kopf h *to be letter-perfect* ‖ s–e ~ **lernen** *to learn one's part* od *lines* ‖ e–e ~ übernehmen *to play a p.* ‖ e–e doppelte ~ *or* zwei ~n übernehmen *to double a p.* or *p.s* ‖ die ~n vertauschen *to change p.s* ‖ ~n **verteilen** *to cast* (od *assign the p.s*) ‖ mit verteilten ~n lesen *to read in alloted characters* | e–e ~ **spielen** *to enact a p.*; *to figure* | ⟨fig⟩ *to cut a* (*great*) *dash*; k–e ~ sp. ⟨fig⟩ *to have no effect, to count for nothing*; die ~ des Liebhabers sp. *to play the juvenile lover*; .. ausgezeichnet .. *he was ideal in* ..; ⟨fig⟩ nicht die beste ~ sp. *to play a somewhat doubtful* od *shady p.*; ⟨fig⟩ gesellschaftlich eine (ge)wichtige ~ sp. *to be a p of* (*great*) *social importance*; e–e gr ~ sp. *to act an important p.*, ⟨fig, fam⟩ *to do the swell*; (S) *to figure largely* od *prominently* (*in a p's thoughts*); e–e klägliche ~ sp. *to cut a poor figure*; e–e lebenswichtige (untergeordnete) ~ sp. *to play a vital* (*only a minor*) *rôle* (in *in*) ‖ **Geld** spielt (bei ihm) k–e ~ *money* (od *expense is*) *no object* (.. *is no consideration for him, cost doesn't mean anything to him*); .. geringe .. *is of minor importance*; es spielt k–e ~, ob .. oder ob .. nicht .. *may or may not* | ⟨fig⟩ jd, der einst e–e ~ gespielt hat *a has-been* ‖ e–e ~ zugeteilt bek *to be cast for a role* | **aus** der ~ fallen *to forget one's p.*, *to act out of character, to show one's real face*; *to diverge from the norm*; ständig .. *to kick over the traces*; fall nicht aus .. *mind your P's and Q's* ⟨urspr theat⟩ **r·ollen I.** vt/i [h & s] *to roll, revolve, trundle* **II.** vt [h] *to r.* (*a barrel, one's eyes*) ‖ *to r. up* (*paper, a carpet*) ‖ *to mangle* (*linen*) ‖ *to calender* (*cloth*) ‖ *to wheel* (*a p in a Bath-chair*) ‖ °jdn ~ *to beat a p* ‖ *to trill the r* ‖ **aus**–e–a ~ *to unroll, unfold* | **gerollt** *money in rolls*; *hair in curl-papers* ‖ den Mantel gerollt tragen *to carry one's cloak slung over one's shoulder* **III. vrefl**: **sich** ~ *to roll* (*on the lawn*) ‖ *the snake coils itself up* ‖ (v S) *to roll up, to curl* ‖ sich ~ l *to be on castors* od *wheels,* (*the chair can be wheeled*) **IV.** [vi] (*wheels, balls, carts*) *run* ‖ (*trains*) *trundle* (weiter *on*) ‖ (*ships*) *lurch* ‖ (*waves*) *surge* ⟨a. übtr v P⟩ ‖ *the sea is rolling* ‖ (of thunder) *to* (*g*)*rumble, roll, growl, roar* | °(schlafen) *to hog it* ‖ ~der Angriff *ever-recurrent* od *wave-by-wave attack* ‖ ~des Geräusch *rumbling* ‖ ~des Material ⟨rail⟩ *rolling stock* | **auf** die Erde ~ *to lurch to the floor* ‖ ⟨aero⟩ auf der Erde ~ *to taxi* ‖ **durch**: *the whisky coursed through his veins* ‖ **in**: *noble blood flows in his veins* ‖ **mit** den Augen ~ *to roll one's eyes*; (*his eyes rolled*) ‖ **über**: *tears rolled down her cheeks* ‖ **um** [acc]: *the coach rumbled round the corner* **V.** ≃ n *rolling* (a. v der See & in der Luft) ‖ ≃ der See ⟨a.⟩ *heavy swell* ‖ ⟨aero⟩ *taxying* | ins ≃ bringen *to bowl a th over* ‖ ins ≃ k *to start rolling,* (*the matter gets going*) **R·ollen- ~bahn** f ⟨tech⟩ *roller race* **~besetzung** f ⟨theat⟩ *cast*(*ing of parts*) **~blei** n *sheet-lead* **~boden** m ⟨theat⟩ *barrel-loft* **~exerzieren** n ⟨mar⟩ *general drill* **~fach** n ⟨theat⟩ *kind of character* **~kreis** m ⟨aero⟩ *gyro-roll* **~lager** n *roller bearing* **~papier** n *endless web of p.* **~stromabnehmer** m ⟨el⟩ *trolley-pole* **~tabak** m *pigtail* **~verteilung** f = ~besetzung **~zug** m *block-and-pulley* **R·oller** m ~s/~ **1.** ⟨mot⟩ *scooter*; Einkaufs≃ *shopping trolley* od *cart* ‖ dazu: *to scooter* **2.** *calenderer* **3.** *rolling sea* **4.** ⟨orn⟩ *roller canary* | ~braut [f] ⟨mot hum⟩ *pinion bride*; ~mobil [n] *cycle-car* **R·ollo** n ~s/~s *blind,* ⟨Am⟩ *shade*

Rom npr *Rome* ‖ alle Wege führen nach ~ *there are many ways leading to the same goal* ‖ Los-von-~-Bewegung [f] *modern tendency to desert the church of Rome* **Rom·an** m ~(e)s/~e → *novel,* (*work of*) → *fiction* ‖ Abenteuer≃ *n. of adventure*; ~ aus dem Leben *romance in real life*; Familien≃ *domestic n.*; technische ~e [pl] *science-fiction*; Tendenz≃ *n. of purpose*; (Ritterroman & ⟨fig⟩) *romance* ‖ erzähl' k–e langen ~e! *cut it short!* **~dichter** m *romancer* **~held** m *hero of a n.* **~leser(in** f) m *n.-reader* **~literatur** f *fiction* **~schreiber, ~schriftsteller** m *n.-writer, n.ist* **~zeitung** f *fictional magazine* **Rom·ane** m [~n/~n] *a Latin* ‖ pl *the Latins, the Romance people*(*s*), *the Latin nations* **romanähnlich, –haft** a *romantic* **rom·anisch** a ⟨arch⟩ *Romanesque* ‖ (Völker, Sprachen) *Romance, Romanic* ‖ (Mensch) *Latin* **Roman·ist** m ~en/~en; der Marburger ~ *the Marburg professor of French etc* **Rom·antik** f *romanticism*; *romantic poetry* ‖ ⟨übtr⟩ *romance* (*of a town*), ⟨a.⟩ *quaint* (od *old-world*) *character of a city* **~er** m *romanticist* **rom·antisch** a *romantic* (*opera, soul, country*) ‖ (romanhaft) *fictitious* ‖ die ~e Schule [f] *the* → *Romantic School* **Rom·anze** f ~/~n *romance, ballad, archaic romaunt* **Rom·aunsch** n ~/ *Romansh* = *Rhaeto-Romanic* **r·ömeln** vi [h] ⟨ec⟩ *to lean to Rome* **R·ömer** m ~s/~ *Roman* ‖ (Pokal) *rummer*; *hock-glass* **~brief** m *Epistle to the Romans* **~zug** m *expedition to Rome* **r·ömisch** a *Roman* (*numerals, law*) ‖ *of Rome* ‖ der Römische Stuhl *the Holy See* ‖ ~e Kamille *large c.* **~-kath·olisch** *Roman catholic* **R·ömling** m ~(e)s/~e *papist*

Rommé n ~s/ ⟨cards⟩ *rummy, euchre*

R·onde f ~/~n ⟨mil⟩ *round* ‖ (auf) ~ gehen *to go rounds* **~boot** n *guard boat* **Rond·ell** n ~(e)s/~e (Beet) *round bed* ‖ ⟨mil⟩ *round bastion*

r·öntgen vt [h] *to x-ray, to Röntgen*(*ize*) | **≃-appar·at** m *X-ray unit* **≃arzt** m *radiologist* **≃assistent** m *radiographer* **≃aufnahme** f, **≃bild** n *röntgenogram, radiograph, -gram*; *X-ray*; dazu: *to X-ray*; **≃durchleuchtung** f *radioscopy, Röntgenoscopy*; (*X-ray*) *screening* **≃kater** m *X-ray sickness* **≃ol·oge** m ~n/~n *radiographer* **≃-strahlen** m pl *Röntgen-* od *X-rays*; ≃durchleuchtung [f] *radioscopy*

r·ören (r·oren) vi (of stag) *to bell, bellow, troat*

rösch a *crisp* (*roll*) → knusprig ‖ ⟨pap⟩ *free* (*stuff*)

r·osa I. a [invar] *rose-coloured, pink* ‖ ~rot färben *to dye .. a rosy pink* ‖ Brustwarzen mit ~ Spitzen *pink-tipped nipples* **II.** ≃ n [invar] *pink* ‖ ≃ centifolia [f] *cabbage-rose* **R·ös|chen** n ~s/~ *little rose* **R·ose** f ~/~n **1.** *rose* ‖ hochstämmige ~ *standard* ‖ wilde ~ *brier*; *dog-r.* ‖ gelbe ~ *Austrian brier* ‖ Letzte ~ *Last R. of Summer* ‖ Pflücke die ~, eh sie verblüht *gather ye r. buds while ye may* (*Herrick*) er ist nicht auf ~n gebettet *it is not all honey with him* ‖ ⟨prov⟩ k–e ~ ohne Dorn *no r. without a thorn* **2.** ⟨med⟩ *St. Anthony's fire, erysipelas* **3.** ⟨hunt⟩ (am Geweih) *burr, coronet* **4.** ⟨arch⟩ *r.-window* **Ros·é** m ~/~ *rosé* (*wine*) **R·osen- ~apfel** m *r.-apple* **~baum** m *r.-tree* **~beet** n *bed of r.s* **~blatt** n *r.-leaf* **~blütler** m pl *Rosaceae* **~busch** m *r.-bush*; (wilder) *wild brier* **~dorn** m ⟨bot⟩ *dogrose, wild r.* **~duft** m *fragrance, perfume, scent of r.s* **~essenz** f *attar* (*of r.s*) **~essig** m *r.-vinegar* **~farbe** f *r.-colour* **≃farben, ≃farbig** a *r.-coloured, rosy* **~fenster** n *r.-window* **~fest** n *feast of r.s* **≃fingerig** a ⟨poet⟩ *rosyfingered* **~garten** m *rosary* **~hecke** f *r.-hedge* **~holz** n *r.-wood*; (indisches) *sisso* **~honig** m *r.-honey* **~käfer** m *r.-beetle,* ⟨Am⟩ *r.-bug* **~kavalier** m *R.-bearer* **~knospe** f *r.-bud* **~kohl** m *Brussels sprouts* pl **~kranz** m *garland of r.s* ‖ ⟨ec⟩ *rosary, chaplet* (*of beads*) ‖ den ~ beten *to tell one's b.s* **~kreuzer** m ⟨ec⟩ *Rosicrucian* **~kriege** m pl ⟨engl⟩ *Wars* pl *of the Roses* (1455–85) **~lippe** f *rosy lip* **~lorbeer** m ⟨bot⟩ *oleander* **~malve** f ⟨bot⟩ *hollyhock* **~monat** m *month of r.s, June* **~montag** m *Shrove Monday* (→ rasen) **~mund** m *rosy mouth* **~öl** n *attar* (*of r.s*) **~pappel** f ⟨bot⟩ *r.-mallow* **~pfad** m *path strewn with r.s* **~pomade** f *r. lip-salve* **~quarz** m ⟨min⟩ *r.-quartz* **≃rot** a *r.-coloured, rosy, as red as a r.*; *rose tinted* (Brille) | ⟨fig⟩ → rosig **~salbe** f *r.-liniment* **~schwamm** m *r.-gall* **~sonntag** m *Shrove Sunday* **~star** m ⟨orn⟩ *r.-coloured starling* **~stein** m ⟨min⟩ *r.-diamond* **~stock** m *r.-tree* **~strauch** m *r.-bush*; (wilder) *wild brier* **~strauß** m *bunch of r.s* **~wange** f *rosy cheek* **~wasser** n *r.-water* **~wurz** f ⟨bot⟩ *r.-root* **~züchter** m *r.-grower* **Ros·ette** f ~/~n *rosette* ‖ ⟨arch⟩ *rose*; (am Schlüsselloch) *rose, escutcheon* ‖ (Schmuck) *rose-diamond* **~n-fenster** n *Catherine-wheel* **r·osig** a *pink, rosy, roseate* (*lips*, etc.) (⟨a. fig⟩ *r.y prospects, account*); *like a r.*; *ruddy* (*face*), *florid* (*ruddy*) (*complexion*); ⟨scient⟩ *rubicund* (*complexion*) | ⟨fig⟩ *buoyant* (*optimism*); *bright* (*temper*); *high* (*spirits, glee*); *merry* (*humour*) ‖ alles andere als ~ *anything but promising, not all r.s* ‖ etw ~ ansehen *to look at a th* (*through r.-coloured glasses* od) *from the bright* od *best side* ‖ *to see* (*everything*) *in a r.y light* ‖ in ~en Farben schildern *to paint .. in its brightest colours*

Rosin·ante f ~/~n *Rosinante, jade*

Ros·ine f ~/~n *currant* ‖ (große) *raisin* ‖ (im Pudding, Kuchen) *plum* ‖ (kernlose) *sultana* | ⟨fig⟩ ~n [pl] (das Beste) *plums*; sich [dat] die ~n herauspicken *to pick out the sugar plums*; °gr ~n h *to have high notions, to think a great deal of o.s., to talk big* °**~nkacker** m = °Klugscheißer, Kleinigkeitskrämer **~nkuchen** m *plum-cake* **~n-wein** m *straw* od *raisin-wine*

Rosmar·in m ~(e)s/ *rosemary*

Roß n –sses/–sse, ˣRösser *horse* (feurig *high-mettled*) ‖ ⟨poet⟩ *steed, charger* ‖ ~ u Reiter *man and h.* ‖ hoch zu ~ *mounted on h.back* ‖ sich aufs ~ schwingen *to mount a h.* ‖ ⟨fig⟩ sich aufs hohe ~ setzen *to mount the high h.* | ⟨fig⟩ das größte ~ *the biggest ass*; so'n ~! *what a fool* od *duffer!* **~arznei** f *h.-physic* **~arzn·eikunde, ~arz-n·eikunst** f *science of farriery* **~arzt** m *h.-doctor, veterinary surgeon, farrier* **~bändiger** m *h.-breaker* **~breiten** f pl ⟨geog⟩ *h.-latitudes* pl **~bremse** f *h.fly, gadfly* **~egel** m *h.leech* **~haar** n *h.hair* **~haarmatratze** f *hair mattress* **~handel** m *h.-trade* **~händler** m *h.dealer* **~haut** f *h.hide* **~käfer** m *dung-beetle* **~kamm** m **1.** *curry-comb* **2.** *h.dealer* **~kastanie** f *h.-chestnut* **~kümmel** m ⟨bot⟩ *hemlock* **~makrele** f ⟨ich⟩ *blue-fish* **~markt** m *h.-market, -fair* **~schlächter** m *h.-butcher* **~-schweif** m *h.'s tail* **~täuscher** m *h.dealer* **~trappe** f ⟨myth⟩ *mark of h.'s hoof* ‖ → Pferde- **R·osse-~bändiger** m *h.-breaker* **~lenker** m ⟨hist⟩ *charioteer* ‖ ⟨fam, hum⟩ *cabby* **R·össel** n ~s/~ ⟨chess⟩ *knight* **~sprung** m *knight's move* ‖ (Rätselaufgabe) *problem on the knight's moves* **r·ossen** vi [h] (of mares) *to be in heat* **r·ossig** a *in heat*

Rost 1. m ~es/ (an Metallen) *rust* ‖ vom ~ befreien *to clean from ru.* ‖ (am Getreide) *blight, smut* **2.** m ~es/~e (Bratrost) *grate, gridiron, grid rack, grill* ‖ auf dem ~ braten *to roast, grill, broil*; vom ~ *grilled*, etc **3.** ⟨arch⟩ *grating*; *pile-work* **4.** ⟨met⟩ *roasting* ‖ (Erz) *ro.g-charge* ‖ garer ~ *sufficiently ro.ed ore* [1]**~angriff** m *ferrous corrosion* [1]**~ansatz** m; auf ~ prüfen *to examine for rust* [2]**~balken** m *fire bearer* **~beschickung** f *stoking* ‖ ~sanlage [f] *bunker plant* [1]**~beständigkeit** f *rust-resisting quality* **~beständigmachen** n *r.proofing*; *r.-preventing* [2]**~braten** m *roast joint*; *grill(ed meat)* **~bratwurst** f *grilled sausage* [1]**≗-br·aun** a *rusty-brown* **~farbe** f *rusty colour* [2]**~-fläche** f *grate-area* [1]**~fleck** m *iron-mould*; (auf Papier) *yellow damp-spot*; *foxing* **≗frei** a *rust-proof*; *stainless* (*steel*) [2]**~pendel** n *gridiron pendulum* [1]**~pilz** m ⟨bot⟩ *uredo* **~schutz** m *anti-rust* | ~farbe [f] *rust-proof colour*; ~mittel [n] *rust preventive* [2]**~spalt** m ⟨mill⟩ *grate opening* **R·öst- ~arbeit** f ⟨met⟩ *ro.g-process* **~kaffee** m *roast(ed) c. beans*; 1 Pfund ~ *a pound of c. French* od *Continental roast* **~ofen** m *ro.g-furnace* **~pfanne** f *frying-pan* | gemischte **~platte** ⟨cul⟩ *mixed grill* **R·öste** f ~/~n *roasting, ro.g-place* | *steeping* (*of flax*); *flax-hole, flax retting* **~flachs** m *red flax* **~schnitte** f *toast* [1]**r·osten** vi [s] *to rust, to grow rusty*; ⟨chem⟩ *to oxidize* ‖ alte Liebe rostet nicht *old love is not soon forgotten* [2]**r·östen** vt [h] (Brot) *to toast*; geröstetes Brot *toast* ‖ braun ~ *to crisp, brown* ‖ *to roast, burn* (*coffee*) ‖ *to fry* (*potatoes*) ‖ *to bake* (*fruit*) ‖ (Fleisch) *to roast, grill*; (sautieren) *to sauté*; ge–tet *sauté(ed)* ‖ (Mais) ⟨Am⟩ *to pop* ‖ (Erz) *to roast* | (Flachs) *to rot, ret, steep* | sich in der Sonne ~ l *to lie roasting in the sun* **R·öster** m ~s/~ *roaster* [1]**r·ostig** a *rusty* ‖ ~ w *to grow rusty, to rust* | ⟨fig⟩ alt u ~ *old and rusty*

R·ostock n ⟨Ger⟩ (Universitätsstadt)

Rot n ~es/ (⟨mot⟩ = Halt!) *red colour, ruby*; bei ~ auf die Tube drücken ⟨mot fam⟩ *to run the red* ‖ ⟨mil⟩ *orange* (*forces*) ‖ ⟨cosm⟩ ~ auflegen *to apply rouge* ‖ ⟨her⟩ *gules* **rot** a **A. 1.** *red* (*rose, nose*) ‖ *ruddy* (*face*) ‖ ⟨hunt⟩ (*to hunt in*) *pink* ‖ ⟨scient⟩ *rubicund* (*complexion*) ‖ hoch ~ *vermilion* ‖ knallig ~ *blowzy* (*face*) ‖ fuchs~ *bay* (*horse*) ‖ hell~ *ginger* (*hair*) ‖ brennend ~ *carroty* (*hair*) **2.** ⟨her⟩ *gules* **B. Rot ..** *Soviet* (*Army*); *Red* (*Cross*; Meer, *Sea*) → C. **C.** ~es **As** *ace of hearts* od *diamonds* ‖ mit ~en Backen ⟨fam⟩ *rosy about the gills* ‖ ~e Beete *beet-root* ‖ die ~e Erde *the red ochreous soil of Westphalia* ‖ sich wie ein roter Faden durch etw ziehen *to run like a red thread through ..* ‖ ~e Grütze *pudding made of red fruit and groats* ‖ ~e **Haare** h *to have red(dish)* (⟨fam⟩ *carroty*) *hair*; *to be red-haired, carroty* ‖ e–m den ~en Hahn aufs Dach setzen *to set a p's house on fire* ‖ ~er Heller *brass farthing* ‖ ~e Internationale *the International League of Anarchists* ‖ ≗e-Kreuz-Schwester *Red-Cross nurse* → B. ‖ er bekam e–n ~en Kopf *he flushed* (*with anger*, etc) ‖ ~e Presse *radical press* ‖ ~e Rasse *red race* ‖ ~e Ruhr (*attack of*) *dysentry, bloody flux* ‖ ~er Titelkopf (Gedrucktes) *rubric(ated matter)* ‖ .. wirkt auf ihn wie ein ~es **Tuch** .. *acts on him as a red cloth on a bull*; ein ~es Tuch s (f) *to be a perpetual red flag* (*in the faces of the police*), .. *a red rag* (*to a p*) **D.** e–n Tag im Kalender ~ **anstreichen** *to mark a red-letter day in the c.* ‖ ~ m *to dye* od *paint red* ‖ ~ w *to pink, crimson, redden*; *blush* (bis über die Ohren *up to one's eyes*); *to flush* (*a dark red*), *to become black* (*with anger*); ein wenig ~ w *to go a little pink* **E.** ≗e m [der ~, ein ~r] ⟨pol⟩ *red* ‖ die ~en *the Reds* **R·ot- ~alge** f ⟨bot⟩ *dulse* **~auge** n ⟨ich⟩ *red bream*; *roach* **≗bäckig** a *red-, cherry-cheeked, ruddy, blowzy* **~barbe** f, **~barsch** m *red mullet* **~bart** m *red b.*; Kaiser ~ *Barbarossa* **≗bärtig** a *red-b.ed* **~blindheit** f *protanopia* **≗blond** a *sandy, auburn* **≗braun** a *reddishbrown, russet, puce*; *sorrel, bay* (*horse*) **≗-brüchig** a *red-short* (*iron*) **~buche** f ⟨bot⟩ *red beech, copper-b.* **≗bunt** a *red-and-white* (Vieh) **~dorn** m *red-blowing hawthorn*, ⟨pop⟩ *the May* **~drossel** f ⟨orn⟩ *redwing* **~eiche** f *red-oak* **~eisen-** ~erz [n] *red iron-ore*; ~ocker [m] ⟨min⟩ *red ochre*; ~stein [m] *blood stone, h(a)ematite* **~empfindlichkeit** f ⟨phot⟩ *sensitivity to red* **~erle** f ⟨bot⟩ *common alder* **≗farbig** a *red-coloured* **~feder** f ⟨ich⟩ *rudd* **~fink** m ⟨orn⟩ *chaffinch, bullfinch* **≗fleckig** a *red-spotted* **~forelle** f *char* **~fuchs** m **1.** *fox* **2.** *sorrel* od *bay horse* **≗gelb** a *orange-coloured, reddish-yellow* **~gerber** m *tanner* **~gießer** m *brazier* **≗glühend** a *red-hot* **~glut** f *red-heat* **~güldenerz** n *ruby silver-ore* **~guß** m *red brass*; *bronze*; *copper goods* **≗haarig** a *red-haired*, ⟨fam⟩ *carroty* **~hänfling** m ⟨orn⟩ *redpoll* **~haut** f *redskin, Red Indian* **~hirsch** m *common stag, red deer* **~holz** n *camwood, Guinea red-wood, Brazil-wood* **~käppchen** n *Little Red Riding-Hood* **~kehlchen** n ⟨orn⟩ *robin* (*redbreast*) **~kabis** m Sw, **~kohl** m *red cabbage* **~kopf** m *carroty p*, ⟨fam⟩ *carrots* pl [sg konstr], *sandy* **~kreuzschwester** f *Red Cross nurse* **~kupfer** n *red c.* **~lauf** m ⟨med⟩ *erysipelas, St. Anthony's fire* ‖ ⟨vet⟩ *red murrain* **~lichtüberwachungsanlage** f *red-light control system* **~liegende(s)** n *lower new* *red sand-stone* **~pause** f *red print* **~rock** m ⟨engl mil fam⟩ *redcoat* **~schimmel** m *roan* (*horse*) **~schmied** m *coppersmith* **~schwanz** m ⟨orn⟩ *redstart*; ⟨ent⟩ *tussock-moth* **≃seiden** a *red silk* (*kerchief*) °**~spon** m = ∼wein, *ruby* **≃stichig** a ⟨phot⟩ *red tinged* **~stift** m *red pencil* **≃streifig** a ⟨bot⟩ *red-striped* **~strumpf** m ⟨fig⟩ *bishop* **~tanne** f ⟨bot⟩ *red* od *spruce fir* **~tannenholz** n *red deal* **~verschiebung** f ⟨opt⟩ *red shift* **≃wangig** a = ≃backig **~wein** m *red w.*; *claret* | ∼bowle [f] *cl.-cup*; ≃farben [a] *cl.-coloured*; ∼nase [f] *brandy nose*, ⟨fam⟩ *rosy drop* **~welsch** n *thieves' cant*; *gibberish* **~wild** n *red deer* [pl konstr] **~wurst** f *black pudding* **~-zunge** f ⟨ich cul⟩ *lemon sole*

Rotati·on [–ts–] f ∼/∼en *rotation* || (Umdrehung) *revolution* **~sbestrahlung** f *rotating irradiation* **~smaschine** f ⟨typ⟩ *rota*(*to*)*ry machine* **~s-verschluß** m ⟨phot⟩ *rotary shutter*

R·öte f ∼ **1.** *redness*, *red* od *rosy colour*; (leuchtende) *vermilion*; *flush* (*a fl. spread over her cheeks* = *she coloured up*) || *blush* (*of shame, shyness*) || ihm stieg die ∼ ins Gesicht *the colour rose to his face* || → Färber≃ **2.** = Rotlauf **R·ötel** m ∼s/∼ *red chalk, ruddle* | ∼erde [f] ⟨min⟩ *Adamic earth*; ∼stift [m] *red chalk pensil* **R·öteln** pl ⟨med⟩ *German measles* pl **r·öten I.** vt [h] *to redden*; *to paint in red*; (of blood) *to stain* **II.** v/refl (of cheeks) *to flush, to colour up* || *to turn* od *grow red*; *to redden* || mit gerötetem Gesicht (*a man*) *red in the face* **r·ötlich** a *reddish, ruddy* || *carroty, ginger* (*hair*) | adv ∼ angehaucht ⟨fam pol⟩ *pink*(*o*) **~br·aun** a *bay*

R·ote Meer, das ∼ ∼ *the Red Sea*

rot·ieren vi [h], *to rotate, revolve* **~d** [a] *rotatory*; *rotary* (*engine*) **R·otor(schiff** n) m ∼s/Rot·oren *rotor*(*-ship*)

R·otte f ∼/∼n **1.** *gang, troop* (Arbeiter *of workmen*), *band* (*of musicians*) **2.** *party, faction* **3.** ⟨dero⟩ *gang, horde* (*of robbers*) || *set, ring, clique* **4.** (Pöbel) *mob, rabble* || die ∼ Korah *the company of K.* **5.** ⟨mil hist⟩ *battalion* || (Reihe) *file*; (Trupp) *squad* || blinde ∼ *blank file* || in ∼n links! *left, file*! **6.** ⟨aero⟩ *sub-flight, element*; *two-plane formation* **7.** ⟨hunt⟩ *pack* (*of wolves*); *herd* (*of wild swine*) **~marsch** m *march in file* **r·otten**: **sich ~** [h] *to form a faction* || *to flock, troop, band together*; *to assemble* | *to collect in a mob* || *to conspire, plot* **R·otten- ~arbeit** f *gang labour* **~aufmarsch** m *deployment in file*(*s*) **~feuer** n *file-firing* **~führer** m *file-leader, corporal* || (Vorarbeiter) *foreman, ganger* **~geist** m *factious spirit* **~marsch** m ⟨mil⟩ *file-marching* **≃weise** adv *in gangs*, etc.

r·ötten vt [h] *to rot, ret, steep* (*flax*)

R·otterdam n ⟨holl⟩ (Stadt)

Rot·unde f ∼/∼n (⟨arch bes⟩ *Palladio's*) *rotunda*

Rot·üre f ∼/ (*Fr roture*) *sine nobilitate* (= *snob*)

R·otz m ∼es/ *mucus*, ⟨fam⟩ *snot, nosedirt*; ⟨übtr aero⟩ (aus MG) *confetti* || °das sitzt wie ∼ am Ärmel *that was laid on with a trowel* || ⟨hors vet⟩ *glanders* pl °**~fahne** f *nose-*, (⟨vulg⟩ *snot-*)*rag* **~junge, ~lümmel** m ⟨vulg⟩ *snot-nose*; *snotty* od *saucy stripling* **≃krank** a = rotzig **~krankheit** f *glanders* °**~kerl** m *snivel of a chap* **~nase** f ⟨vulg⟩ *snot-nose*; *cheeky boy* od *girl* **≃näsig** a *snotty* **r·otzig** a *snotty* || ⟨hors vet⟩ *glandered*

Rouen [ru:'ã] n ⟨Fr⟩ (Stadt)

Roué [ru'e:] m ∼s/∼s *roué* Fr, *rake* **Roul·ade** f ∼/∼n *collared beef*; *meat-roll* **Rouleau** [ru'lo:] n ∼s/∼s & ∼x *sun-blind, roller-blind*, ⟨Am⟩ *shade*; ⟨theat⟩ *roller drop* (aufziehen *to pull up*; herunterlassen *to let down*) **Roul·ett** [ru'let] n ∼s/∼e & ∼s; **Roul·ette** [ru'let] f ∼/∼n *roulette*; *wheel*

Route ['ru:tə] f ∼/∼n *route* || auf dieser ∼ *by this r.* || Dampfer ohne feste ∼ *tramp* || die ∼ kennzeichnen an *to r.* (*a ticket*) || die ∼ .. legen durch *to r.* (*a procession*) *through* (*a town*) **Rout·ine** [ru–] f ∼/ *routine*; *experience*; *daily practice*; *rut* ⟨fig⟩ **Routin·ier** [–'nje:] m ∼s/∼s *routinist, old-hand* **routin·iert** a *smart*; *practised, experienced, versed*; ⟨fam⟩ *well up*

Rowdy m *rowdy, hooligan, rough*(*neck*); ⟨Am sl⟩ *bohunk, plug-ugly, hoodlum, though* **~tum** n ∼s/ *hooliganism*

Royal·is- ~mus m ∼/ *royalism* **≃tisch** a *royalist*

R·üb- ~öl n *rape*(*-seed*) *oil* **~saat** f, **~samen** m *r.-s.* **R·übe** f ∼/∼n ⟨bot⟩ *rape* || (gelbe) *carrot* || (rote) *Red Beet, beetroot* || schwedische ∼ *swede* || (weiße) *turnip* | °⟨fig⟩ *noddle, pate* || (P) alte ∼! *old bean*! | e–m ein Rübchen schaben *to taunt* od *tease a p* || → Kraut **~zahl** m npr ∼s/ "*turnip--tailed*" *mountain ghost*, → Zagel **R·üben- ~blattwespe** f *t.p fly* **~bau** m *cultivation of t.ps*, etc **~ernte** f ⟨agr⟩ *root-crop* **~feld** n *t.p-field* **~fliege** f *beet--leaf miner* **≃förmig** a *t.p-shaped* **~kohl** m *t.p--rooted cabbage* **~kraut** n *t.p-tops* pl || ×∼ *treacle* **~rettich** m *large black radish* **~stecher** m *t.p--scoop* **~zucker** m *beetroot sugar*

R·ubel m ∼s/∼ ⟨Russ⟩ *rouble, ruble*

°**r·über** adv = herüber

†**R·ubikon** m ⟨It⟩ (Fluß) *Rubicon*

Rub- ~·in m ∼(n)s/∼e ⟨minr⟩ *ruby* || (Uhr) mit 12 ∼en .. *with 12 stones* | ≃farbig, ≃rot [a] *ruby*; ∼fluß [m] *mock-ruby* **~r·ik** f ∼/∼en *rubric, title, heading* || (Kategorie) *category* || (Spalte) *column* **≃rizieren** vt [h] *to arrange in columns* (*with headings*) **~rum** n ∼s/–ren *caption, title*

R·übsen m ∼s/ *rape*(*-seed*); *colza*

r·uchbar a (→ Ruf A. 3.) *notorious, manifest, known* || ∼ m *to divulge, to spread about* (*the crime was noised abroad*) || ∼ w *to take air*; *to become known*; *get abroad* od *out, to transpire* **≃keit** f ∼/ *notoriousness, publicity*

R·uch m ∼(e)s/≃e ⟨poet⟩ = Geruch **~gras** n *vernal grass* **≃los** a *odo*(*u*)*rless*

r·uchlos a (→ Ruf A. 3.) *profligate, wicked, vile, malicious, reprobate*; ∼e P *reprobate* **≃igkeit** f ∼/∼en *profligacy, wickedness, malice* || *iniquity* || (Tat) *vicious action*

Ruck m ∼(e)s/∼e *pull, jolt, jerk, hitch, start* || ⟨pol⟩ *movement, shove* (*to the left*) | auf einen ∼ ⟨fam⟩ *at one go* || mit e–m ∼ *with a jerk, spasmodically*; .. herausziehen *to yank* (aus *out of*) || (e–r S) e–n ∼ geben *to give a start to, to jerk at* || mit e–m ∼ losfahren *to jerk off* || e–n ∼ tun *to give a wrench*, etc || er gab sich e–n ∼ *he pulled h.s. together* || mit ∼ u Zuck *with a smart effort* || ⟨mar⟩ h·aur·uck! *yo-* (*heave-*) *ho*! **≃artig** a *jerky, snappy* || e–e ∼e Bewegung mit dem Kopfe m *to jerk one's head* (nach *at*) | adv *with a jerk* **~frei** a ⟨mot⟩ *jerkless* | **ruck, zuck**! hau-ruck! *heave ho*! **≃weise** adv *by jerks, by fits* (*and starts*) || ∼ gehen ⟨mach⟩ *to hunt* || ∼ hin- u herbewegen *to bob, jig*

R·ück-[1] (v Rücken), **R·ück-**[2] (v zurück) [2]**~abtretung** f *retrocession* [1]**~ansicht** f *back view* [2]**~anschrift** f *return address* [2]**~anspruch** m *counter--claim* **~antwort** m *reply*; die ∼ e–s Telegramms bezahlen *to prepay the reply to ..* || ⟨telg⟩ ∼ bezahlt *reply paid* **~beorderungsrecht** n *right of stoppage* **~berufung** f *recall* **~bewegung** f *retrograde movement* **≃bezüglich** a *reflexive* (*pronoun*) **~bildung** f ⟨biol⟩ *involution* || ⟨gram⟩ *back--formation* || ⟨med⟩ *disappearing of symptoms* | ∼spsychologie [f] *involutional ps.* **~bleibsel** n *rest, remnant, residue, remainder* **~blende(n** n) f ⟨film⟩ *cutback, flashback* **~blick** m *retrospect*(*ive view*), *glance backward* (auf *at*); ⟨film, Lit⟩ *flash--back* || e–n ∼ werfen auf *to cast a retrospective glance at, to pass .. in review* **~blickspiegel** m ⟨mot⟩ *rear-view mirror* **~buchung** f ⟨com⟩ *storno* **~bürge** m, **~bürgschaft** f *counter-security* **≃datieren** vt [h] *to postdate* **~datierung** f *dating back* **~einfuhr** f *reimportation* **~entladung** f *back* *discharge* **~erinnerung** f *reminiscence* **≚erstatten** vt [h] *to refund* **~erstattung** f *restitution, refund* | Oberstes ~sgericht *Supreme Restitution Court* **~fahr-** ~karte [f] *return* (*-ticket*), ⟨Am a.⟩ *round-trip ticket*; ~scheinwerfer [m] ⟨mot⟩ *backing* od *back-up lamp* od *light*; ~sucher [m] ⟨mot⟩ *reversing spotlight* **~fahrt** f *return* (*-voyage*) ‖ sich auf die ~ m *to start back* ‖ auf der ~ *on the return, on the way home* **~fall** m (in Krankheit, Untugend etc) *relapse, new fit*; ⟨fig⟩ *throw-back* (*to barbarity*) ‖ (Heimfall ⟨jur⟩) *reversion* ‖ e–n ~ bek ⟨med⟩ *to have a relapse* | ⟨jur⟩ *recidivism*; *third or subsequent offence* (.. im ~ .. *of*) | ~fieber [n] *relapsing fever* **≚fällig** a *relapsing* ‖ *recidivous* (*criminal* = *recidivist*) ‖ ⟨jur⟩ *revertible* ‖ ~ w *to* (*have a*) *relapse*, ⟨jur⟩ *to revert*; ~er Verbrecher *recidivist* | ≚keit [f] *recidivism* **~flug** m ⟨aero⟩ *homing*; *flight home*; Hin- u ~ *outward and return flight*, ⟨Am⟩ *round trip* **~fluß** m *reflux, flowing back* **~förder-** ~pumpe [f] ⟨mot⟩ *scavange pump* **~forderung** f *counter-claim* | ~sklage [f] *action of reclaim* **~fracht** f *back-* od *return*(*ing*)-*freight*; Aus- u ~ *freight out and home* **~frage** f *counter-question* ‖ (zusätzliche Anfrage) *further inquiry*; bei e–m ~ halten *to inquire* (*again*) *of a p* **~fuhre** f *return conveyance* **~führung** f ⟨tact⟩ *rearward movement* ‖ ~ in den Kreislauf ⟨tech⟩ *recycling* | (P) *repatriation* **~gabe** f *return, restitution* ‖ ⟨jur⟩ *retrocession* (an *to*) ‖ bei der ~ *on returning it* | ~schein [m] *turn-in slip* **~gang** m *retrogression, regress* ‖ ⟨astr⟩ *retrogradation*; *retrocession* (*of the Celtic speech*) ‖ ⟨fam⟩ *falling--off* (*in his later works*) ‖ (v Preis) *decline*, ⟨sl⟩ *slump* ‖ ~ v Verkäufen *drop in* (*our*) *sales* ‖ ⟨eco⟩ *recession* ‖ *reduction* (*of traffic*) ‖ (Rückweg) *return* **≚gängig** a *retrograde* ‖ *falling, drooping* (*prices*) ‖ *declining* (*business*) ‖ ~ m *to annul, cancel, rescind, withdraw, retract, undo*; *to break* od *call off*; (Rechtsgeschäft) *to disaffirm* ‖ ⟨mil⟩ *to revoke* N | ~ w *to come to nothing, to be broken off* | ~machung [f] melden! *report corrective action taken* N **~gewinnungsanlage** f *adsorber* **~gliederung** f *reincorporation* [1]**~grat** n & m ⟨anat⟩ *backbone* (P ⟨a. fig⟩), *spine*, (of animal) *chine* ‖ ⟨fig⟩ *main stay* (*of the business*) ‖ ⟨fig⟩ jdm das ~ stärken (brechen) *to strengthen* (*weaken*) *a p's resistance, to back up a p* ‖ ~ h *to be stiff in the back* **≚gratlos** a *invertebrate* ⟨a. fig⟩ ‖ ⟨fig⟩ *weak, limp, spineless, boneless, lacking backbone* **~grats-** ~verkrümmung [f] *curvature of the spine*; ~nerv [m] *spinal nerve*; ~wirbel [m] *vertebra* [2]**~griff** m *recourse* **~gut** n *goods returned, returns* pl **~halt** m ⟨mil⟩ *reserve* ‖ (Stütze) *support* ‖ ohne ~ *unreservedly, without restraint* ‖ ohne jeden ~ [+ gen] *without having an organisation behind it* | ⟨fig⟩ *mainstay*; e–n ~ h an jdm *to have someone to fall back upon* ‖ k–n ~ finden bei jdm *to find no backing from a p* ‖ ~ suchen an *to have recourse to* ‖ (*moral, financial*) *reserves* pl **~haltebecken** n *retardation* od *retaining basin* **≚haltlos** a *unreserved, frank* ‖ adv = ohne ~halt, ⟨a.⟩ *roundly*; ⟨Am a.⟩ *straight* **~haltlosigkeit** f *unreservedness* **~haltungsberechtigte(r)** m *lienor* **~händer** m ⟨ten⟩ *backhander* **~hub** m *return stroke* **~handschlag** m ⟨ten⟩ *backhand* (*stroke*) **~hol-** ~feder [f] *recuperator* od *rebound spring*; ~taste [f] ⟨rec⟩ *back-space control* **~kauf** m *repurchase, redemption*; ⟨fam⟩ *come-back* | ~srecht [n] *equity of redemption*; ~swert [m] *r.e-value*; ⟨ins⟩ *surrender-value* **~kehr, (~kunft)** f *return*(*ing*) (auf den Thron *to* ..); ⟨bes Am⟩ *comeback* | ⟨biol⟩ *reversion* | bei m–r ~ .. *on my returning home I found* ‖ es gab k–e ~ *there was no r.g*; nach m–r ~ nach M. *back again in M.* **~kohlung** f *recarburization* **~kopplung** f ⟨wir⟩ *reaction, back-coupling, feedback*; ⟨el⟩ *regeneration* | ~sspule [f] *reaction* (⟨fam⟩ *tickler*) *coil* ‖ .. mit ~ *heterodyne* (*receiver*) **~ladung** f ⟨mar⟩ *return-cargo* **~lage** f *reserves* pl, *reserve fund* ‖ der ~ [dat] zuweisen ⟨bal⟩ *to transfer to r. f.* **~lauf** m *return*, ⟨fig⟩ *recurrence* ‖ ⟨artill⟩ *recoil* (*of a gun*) ‖ ⟨astr⟩ *retrogradation* | ~bremse [f] *recoil-brake*; ~sicherung [f] ⟨mot⟩ *sprag*; ~wasser [n] *return* od *recirculated w.* **~läufer** m *dead letter* **≚läufig** a *recurrent, retrograde* **~lehne** f *back* (*of a chair*) **~leiter** m ⟨el⟩ *negative return* **~leitung** f ⟨el⟩ *return* (*-wire, -line, -current*) **~licht** n ⟨mot⟩ *tail* od *rear light* od *lamp* **~lieferung** f *redelivery* ‖ *restitution* | ~skommission [f] *commission for the restitution of property* (*seized during a war*) **~marsch** m ⟨mil⟩ (Rückzug) *retreat, countermarch*; e–n ~ m *to c., r.* ‖ (Rückweg) *march back* od *home* **~meldeglocke** f ⟨rail⟩ *reply bell* **~meldung** f *reply*; ⟨mil a.⟩ *repetition* **~nahme** f *taking back* **~ordnung** f ⟨comp, etc⟩ *refiling* **~porto** n *return-postage* **~prall** m *recoil, repercussion, rebound* | ~atom [n] *recoil atom* **~prämie** f *return of premium* ‖ *put-option* **~reise** f *journey* od *voyage back, return* ‖ auf der ~ *on the r.n-j.y, on one's way back* ‖ auf der ~ s *to be homeward bound* **~ruf** m *recall* **~schau** f ⟨fig⟩ *retrospect* (über *of*), *looking-back* (*to*); ~ halten *to run back over the past* **~schauend** a *retrospective, in retrospect*(*ion*) **~schein** m *reciprocal bond, obligation, acknowledgment of receipt*; *return receipt*; gegen ~ *r. r. requested* ‖ ⟨opt⟩ *reflexion* **~schicht** f ⟨phot⟩ *backing* **~schlag** m *back-stroke rebound, recoil kick* ‖ ⟨ten⟩ *first-stroke* ‖ *recoil* (*of a gun*) ‖ ⟨biol⟩ *throwback* | ⟨fig⟩ *reaction, pull-, set-back, reverse, let-down* ‖ der ~ kam *the reaction set in* ‖ [dat] e–n ~ versetzen *to set* (*a p, etc*) *back* ‖ ⟨biol⟩ *throwback, atavism* ‖ ⟨med⟩ *turn* ‖ ~ geben (Gewehr) *to recoil, kick* | ~ventil [n] *return* od *check valve* **~schläger** m ⟨ten⟩ *striker out* **~schluß** m *conclusion a posteriori* ‖ –schlüsse m *to gather* (*from*), *to draw a conclusion* (*from*); vorschnelle ≚e ziehen *to jump to quick c.s* **~schreiben** n *reply, rescript* **≚schreitend** a ⟨geog⟩ *headward* (*erosion*) **~schritt** m *step backward, retrograde step, retrocession* ‖ ⟨fig⟩ *set--back, regress* ‖ ⟨pol⟩ *reaction* ‖ ~e m *to retrocede* | ~ler [m] *Mr. Stuck-in-the-mud*; ≚lich [a] ⟨soc⟩ *retrograde* | ~spartei [f] *retrograde* od *reactionary party* [1]**~seite** f *back*; *wrong side* ‖ (of coins) *reverse, tail* ‖ ~ des Mondes *far side of the moon* ⟨a. a–n⟩ ‖ ⟨bookb⟩ *left-hand page* ‖ siehe ~! *over-leaf*! **~sendung** f *return*; wir bitten um ~ *will you kindly r. it* [2]**~sicht** f *regard, consideration, respect* ‖ aus ~ gegen *in deference to* ‖ nicht aus ~ auf [acc] *not from any cons. for* (*a p*) ‖ in ~ auf *in cons.* od *view of, in respect to* ‖ mit ~ auf *with an eye to* ‖ ohne ~ auf *without any cons. of* od *for, irrespective of*; *regardless of* (*expense*); *no matter what* (*the consequences*); *in spite of, unmindful of*; k–e ~ in Worten etc kennen *to let o.s. loose* | ~ nehmen auf [acc] *to take notice of, to consider, to have regard for* ‖ k–e ~ nehmen auf *to be regardless of*; *to take no count of* ‖ (schonend) *to allow for, to make allowance for* ‖ ~ zeigen für *to show regard for* **~sichtlich** prep [gen] *concerning, regarding, as regards, as to, with regard to* **~sichtnahme** f (auf [acc]) *regard, thoughtfulness, consideration* (*to*) ‖ mit e–r ~ *with a reference* (*to*) **≚sichtslos** a *unfeeling, merciless, harsh, grim, rough-shod* (*persecution*); ⟨ftb⟩ *rough* (*play*); *reckless, inconsiderate, regardless* (gegen *of*), *thoughtless*, (*it is th.less of you*) ‖ *rude* (*conduct*) ‖ *ruthless* (*exploitation*) ‖ ~er Fahrer ⟨mot⟩ *speed merchant* | [adv] sich [acc] ~ einsetzen f *to go for a th bald-headed*; ~ auf s–n Vorteil bedacht s *to drive a hard bargain*; ~ fahren ⟨mot sl⟩ *to hog*; ~ spielen *to play rough*; sich [acc] ~ eindrängen *to muscle in* **~sichtslosigkeit** f *recklessness, inconsiderateness, lack of consideration* **≚sichtsvoll** a *attentive, considerate, regardful* (gegen *of*); *thoughtful* (*it was th.ful of* *you*); ⟨mot⟩ *courteous* (*driving*) **~siegel** n *counter-seal* **~sitz** m *back seat* ‖ (klappbar) ⟨mot sl⟩ *dicky*, ⟨mot cycl⟩ *pillion*, ⟨sl⟩ *flapper-bracket* ‖ auf dem ~ fahren *to pillion* **~spiegel** m ⟨mot⟩ *driving* (⟨Am⟩ *rear vision*) *mirror* **~spiel** n ⟨sport⟩ *return match* **~sprache** f *conference*, *consultation* (nach ~ mit *on c. with*) ‖ ohne ~ *without reference back* ‖ ~ h mit *to interview a p*, *to get speech to a p* ‖ ~ nehmen (mit) *to consult*, *to confer* (*with*) ‖ bitte ~! *please discuss this with me*! **~sprung** m *leap-back* | ~gipfel [m] ⟨arch⟩ *set-back*; (⟨Am⟩ *s.-b. skyscraper*) **~spul-** *reversing* (*button*); *rewind* (*crank*) **~stand** m ⟨com⟩ (*tax*, etc) *arrears* pl, ⟨bes chem⟩ *residue* ‖ im ~ bleiben mit *to be back in*, *to fall behind with* (*one's rent*); in ~ geraten *to get behindhand* (mit *with*) ‖ im ~ s *to lag behind*; .. (mit) *to be in arrears* (*with*), *to be behind in*; *to delay in* (*making payment*); mit e–r Rate im ~ s *to be one instalment b.h.*; ⟨Am⟩ *way b.h.* (mit .. *in planting*), ⟨min⟩ *backlog* **~stände** pl *outstanding debts* ‖ ⟨tech⟩ *residue*, *remains* pl; (of a gun) *fouling*; ⟨min⟩ *tailing*(*s*) **~ständig** a (unerledigt, überfällig) *outstanding*, *overdue*, *still due*, *in arrears* (mit *with*) ‖ ⟨Am⟩ *back* (*salary*, *number*, *tax*) ‖ (P) (unmodern) *old-fashioned*, *antiquated*, *backward*; ⟨fam⟩ *slow* ‖ ~ s *to be behind the times* ‖ ~e Arbeit *overdue work*; ⟨Am min⟩ *backlog* ‖ ~er Betrag *overdue amount* ‖ ein ~er Mensch *an old-timer*; ⟨fam⟩ *backnumber* ‖ ~e Zinsen *arrears* pl *of interest* ‖ ⟨fam⟩ *stuffy* (*views*) ‖ ⟨tech⟩ *under-developed* (Land) **~ständigkeit** f *backwardness*, (*cultural*) *lag*; *leeway* (*to make up the l. in*) ‖ geistige ~ *infantilism*, ⟨Am a.⟩ *backlog* (*of public opinion*); *cultural lag* **~stands-** ~öl [n] *residual fuel*; ~strahlung [f] ⟨at m.m.⟩ *radioactive fallout* **~start** m *homing st.*; den ~ zünden ⟨a–n⟩ *to retrofire* **~stau** m *damming-up* **~stellfeder** f *restoring spring* **~(stell)taste** f ⟨typwr⟩ *resetting key* **~stellung** f ⟨com⟩ *transfer to reserve*; e–e ~ bilden ⟨bal⟩ *to make provision* (*for income tax*, etc) **~stoß** m (Schußwaffe) *recoil*, *kick* | ≗frei [a] *recoilless*; ~motor [m] *jet engine*; ~kraft [f] *energy of recoil*; ~verstärker *muzzle attachment* **~strahler** m ⟨mot⟩ *rear reflector* **~stromkreis** m ⟨el⟩ *reverse current relay* **~taste** f ⟨typwr⟩ *back-spacer* **~tratte** f *redraft* **~trift** f *lag*; ⟨aero⟩ *air lag* **~tritt** m *withdrawal*, *retreat* (v *from*) ‖ *resignation* (*of an office*) ‖ um s–n ~ einkommen *to tender one's r.* ‖ (v Ministern) *going out of office* | ~bremse [f] *back-pedalling brake*; ~sklausel [f] *escape clause* **~übersetzung** f *retranslation* **~vergrößerung** f ⟨rep⟩ *re-enlargement* **≗vergüten** vt [h] *to refund* **~vergütung** f *refund*, *repayment*, *rebate* **~versicherung** f ⟨ins⟩ *reinsurance* | ~s-vertrag [m] *R. Treaty* (1887) **~wand** f *back-wall*, *back-board*; ⟨ec⟩ *reredos* **~wanderung** f *re-* od *return migration* **~wärtig** a *rear* (*communications*) | ⟨mil⟩ *rear* (*area*; *combat zone*); ~es Korpsgebiet *corps r. a.* (*CRA*) | ~es Armeegebiet *base*, *communications* pl ‖ ~e Dienste [pl] *r.* (*supply*) *services*; ~es Gebiet *communications zone*, *rear area* N, ⟨tact⟩ *service area*; ~e Kampfzone [f] *rear combat zone* (*RCZ*) N; ~es Kriegs- *or* Versorgungsgebiet (rückwärts der rückwärtigen Grenze des Korps) *comm.s zone* N; ~es Nachschubdepot *base depot* N ‖ ~e Linien [pl] *rear* ‖ ~e Verbindungen *lines* [pl] *of c.s in the rear* ‖ ~e Zimmer *rooms at the back* ‖ ⟨aero⟩ *back* (Leitstrahl *beam*) **≗wärts** adv *back*(*wards*) ‖ ~ fahren [vi] *to back up*; [vt] *to back* (*a car*), *to reverse* ‖ ~ fahren! ⟨mar⟩ *back water*! ‖ ~ feuern *to fire to the rear* ‖ ~ gehen (v Geschäften) *to fall off* ‖ ~ gerichtet .. *backward* (*glance*) ‖ ~ rudern *to back oars* ‖ ~ sehen *to look back* ‖ ~ sitzen *to have one's back to the engine*, *horses* ‖ ~ u vorwärts *backwards and forwards*, ⟨Am⟩ *back and forth* | ≗gang [m] ⟨mot⟩ *reverse speed*, den ~ einschalten *to go into reverse*; ≗kipper [m] *rear dump*; ~lagerung (der Gebärmutter) *retroversion*; ~sitz [m] *rearward-facing seat*; ~turbine [f] *astern-turbine* **~wasser** n ⟨tech⟩ *back water* **~wechsel** m ⟨com⟩ *re-exchange*, *redraft*; *cross-bill* **~weg** m *way back*, *return-journey* | (jdm) den ~ abschneiden *to block* (*the enemy's*) *route of withdrawal*; den ~ antreten *to start back* ‖ jdm den ~ verlegen *to obstruct a p's return* ‖ auf dem ~ *on one's way back* **≗wickeln** vt [h] *to rewind* **≗wirken** vi *to react* (auf *on*) | ~d [a] *retrospective*, *retroactive*, *reacting* (auf *on*) ‖ ⟨gram⟩ *reflective* ‖ *back* (*pay*); ~der Antrag *application in retrospect* (ab 1. 1. 68 *as from .. r.tively*) ‖ Gesetz mit ~der Kraft *ex post facto law* **~wirkung** f *re*(*tro*)*action*, *repercussion* (auf *on*) **~zahlung** f (*loan*) *repayment*, *refund*, *reimbursement* | ~stag [m] *day of redemption* **≗zedieren** vt [h] *to re-assign* °**~zieher** m; e–n ~ m *to climb down*; *to draw* od *pull in one's horns*; *to crawfish* (*about a th*) **~zoll** m ⟨com⟩ *drawback* | ~güter [n pl] *debenture goods* **~zug** m ⟨bes mil⟩ *retreat* ‖ (Rückkehr) *return*; ⟨rail⟩ *back-train*; ⟨glacial⟩ *recessian* ‖ ⟨fig⟩ *climb-down* | (schnell) den ~ antreten *to* [*beat a* (*hasty*)] *retreat*; .. geordnet .. *to withdraw one's forces in good order* ‖ zum ~ blasen *to sound the retreat* | **~s-** ~bewegung [f] *retreat*; *retrograde movement*; ~gefecht [n] *running fight*; ~straße [f] *route of retreat*; *withdrawal route* **~zündung** f ⟨mot⟩ *backfire*

r·uckedigu intj (of pigeons) *coo*, *coo*

R·ücken m ~s/~ **A.** *back* (⟨a.⟩ *of a book*, *knife*, *hand*); *spine* (*of a book*) ‖ (e–s Gebirges) *ridge*, *crest*, ⟨a. übtr meteor⟩ *ridge* (*of a high pressure*) ‖ (der Nase) *bridge* ‖ *chine* (*of beef*); *saddle* (*of mutton*) ‖ ⟨mil⟩ (e–s Heeres) *rear* **B.** den ~ **beugen** = krumm m ‖ jdm den ~ decken *to cover a p's rear*, *to back up a p*, *to support a p* ‖ ⟨fig⟩ ich habe e–n breiten ~ *I can stand a lot* ‖ sich den ~ frei halten *to secure one's retreat*; (*never commit yourself*!) ‖ ⟨fam⟩ dir juckt wohl der ~? *you want a good beating*! ‖ [dat] den ~ **kehren** *to turn one's b.* (*upon*), *to retire* (*from a club*) ‖ ⟨fig⟩ *to desert a p* (*luck has deserted him*) ‖ den ~ krumm m, e–n krummen ~ m *to stoop*, ⟨dero⟩ *to cringe* (vor *before a p*); (er macht .. *he has a cringing manner*) ‖ als N. den ~ gewendet hatte *when N.'s b. was turned* ‖ sobald ich den ~ wende .. *as soon as I turn my b.* .. ‖ jdm (dem Feind) den ~ zeigen *to give a p the cold shoulder* (*to show one's b. to* ..) ‖ er **wandte** uns den ~ **zu** *his b. was to us*, *he stood with his b. to us*, *he had his b. turned on us*; ⟨fig⟩ *he turned his b. on us* **C.** ~ **an** ~ *b. to b.*; ⟨her⟩ *addorsed* ‖ am (*or* auf dem) ~ befindlich *dorsal* | [acc] **auf** den ~ nehmen *to lift .. on one's b.* ‖ die ganze Arbeit liegt auf s–m ~ *he has .. on his shoulders* ‖ auf den ~ fallen ⟨fig⟩ *to be taken-aback* ‖ auf m–n ~ geht viel *I can stand a lot* ‖ auf dem ~ liegend *prostrate*, ⟨scient⟩ *supine* ‖ .. schwimmen *to swim on one's b.* ‖ die Hände auf dem ~ verschränkt .. *with his hands clasped behind his b.* ‖ ⟨aero⟩ auf den ~ gelegt *inverted*, *in dorsal position* | ~ **gegen** ~, mit dem ~ gegen e–a = ~ an ~ ‖ **hinter** jds ~, jdm hinterm ~ *behind a p's b.*, *on the sly* ‖ hinter jds ~ reden *to backbite* ‖ jdm **in** den ~ fallen *to attack a p in* od *from the rear*; ⟨fig⟩ *to get* (*at*) *the back of*, *to stab a p in the b.*, ⟨Am⟩ *to knife a p* ‖ mit der Sonne im ~ angreifen ⟨aero⟩ *to fly out of the sun* ‖ ⟨mil⟩ im ~ u in der Flanke *in rear and flank* ‖ **mit** breitem ~ *broad-backed*; mit dem ~ gegen .. *with one's b. to* (*the light*) ‖ mit dem ~ liegen nach .. (of houses) *to have their backs to* .. ‖ etw mit dem ~ ansehen müssen *to have to give a p a th* ‖ es läuft e–m heiß, halt **über** den ~ *it makes* (*one shiver* od) *one's flesh creep* ‖ **zum** ~ gehörig *dorsal*

r·ucken vi [h] **1.** *to coo* **2.** *to jerk*, *to give* od *send a jerk* (durch *through*) **3.** = rücken vi

r·ücken I. vt *to (re)move; to shove (a chair* an .. *into place, to the fire); to hitch (to)* || *to push (along), to jerk* || *to regulate (a watch)* | **an** sich heran ~ *to draw towards one; to bring nearer, closer* || fort ~ *to remove; to push away* || etw vom Feuer ~ *to take .. off the fire* **II.** vi [s & h] **A. 1.** [s] *to move, push along* **2.** °[s] (heimlich ausziehen) ⟨fam⟩ *to shoot the moon* **3.** [h & s] rück ein wenig! *make a little room!*, .. hierher! *move a little this way!* **B.** [s] höher ~ *to rise (in rank)* || näher ~ *to draw near, to approach* || vor~ *to advance, to march on* || weiter~ *to proceed* **C. 1.** [h] **an** etw ~ *to remove a th; (he touched his cap)* **2.** [s] an jds Stelle ~ *to take a p's place* || dicht an–e–a ~ *to draw close together* || jdm **auf** den Leib (°die Bude) ~ *to press a p hard* || **aus** [dat] ~ *to move out of (the light),* ⟨mil⟩ *to leave, quit (a town)* || **durch** [acc] ~ *to march through (a town)* || **in** ein Land ~ *to invade a country* || ins Feld ~ *to take the field* || nicht **von** der Stelle ~ *not to stir* (⟨fam⟩ *budge) (an inch)* || **vor** e–e Stadt ~ *to lay siege to a town* || e–m **zu** Leibe ~ = auf d. L. ~ **R·ücken- ~aufzug** m ⟨gym⟩, den ~ m *to skin the cat* **~blatt** n *back of an altar-piece* **~dekkung** f *backing, cover, support* **~fallschirm** m *back-type parachute* **~federn** pl, **~haare** n pl *hackles* pl **~flosse** f *dorsal fin* **~flug** m ⟨aero⟩ *upside-down flight; inverted flying* od *flight* | ~lastfall [m] *i. flight condition* **~lage** f *supiness* **~lehne** f *back(-rest) (of a chair)*; ohne ~ *backless (bench)*; Sessel mit runder ~ *bucket seat* **~mark** n *spinal cord* °**~märker** m, **~marks-** ~leidende(r) *m spinal patient* ~schwindsucht [f], ~auszehrung, ~-darre [f] ⟨path⟩ *spinal consumption, dorsal tabes* **~muskel** m *dorsal muscle* **~peilung** f *back bearing* **~säge** f *backsaw* **~schild** m ⟨zoo⟩ *carapase* **~schlag** m *blow on the back* **~schmerz** m *pain in the back, back-ache* **~schwimmen** n *back-stroke* **~schwimmer** m *back-swimmer* ⟨a. ent; (ent a.⟩ *water-boatman)* **~steifung** f *backing, support (of a p)* **~stück** n *back-piece* || ⟨cul⟩ *chine (of beef), saddle (of mutton)* **~stütze** f *back rest* **~wehr** f ⟨fort⟩ *parados* **~wind** m *following* od *tail wind,* ⟨Am⟩ *rear-on wind* **~wirbel** m ⟨anat⟩ *vertebra* **rück-** ~gängig [a] m *to reverse*; ~lings [adv] *backwards* || *on one's back* || (v hinten) *from behind* **R·ucksack** m ~(e)s/~̈e *knapsack, haversack, rucksack,* ⟨Am⟩ *carryall, holdall*; → Ruck

R·üde m ~n/~n **1.** *large (boar-) hound* **2.** *male dog, fox, wolf* || ~mann [m] *huntsman*

rüde a *rude, rough* || *coarse* || *vulgar, low, brutal*

R·udel n ~s/~ **1.** ⟨hunt⟩ *flock, wisp (of birds)* || *herd (of deer)* || *pack (of wolves)* **2.** ⟨übtr⟩ *troop, crowd (of people)* || ⟨mar⟩ ~ U-Boote *U-pack* || in ~n *in large numbers*; .. gehen *to be gregarious* ~̈**weise** [adv & a] *in flocks,* etc

R·uder n ~s/~ *oar* || kurzes ~ *skull, paddle* || (Steuer~̈) *rudder, helm* || ⟨aero⟩ *rudder*; ~ u Flossen *control surfaces and fixed planes* | ~ an! *give way together* || (gut) ~ gehorchen *to answer the helm* (well) || nicht ~ gehorchen *to be unmanageable* | **am** ~ sitzen, das ~ führen *to be at the helm;* ⟨fig⟩ *.. at the head of affairs, .. in power* || am ~ ⟨parl⟩ *(the parts) in power* || schon lange am ~ s ⟨parl⟩ *to have had a long innings* || am ~ bleiben *to remain in office* || jdn **ans** ~ bringen *to put a p in office*; ans ~ k ⟨fig⟩ *to get at the head of affairs, to come into power, to get a chance*; wieder .. ⟨pol fam⟩ *to stage a comeback* || ⟨fig⟩ sich **in** die ~ legen *to carry on energetically* || ⟨mar⟩ das ~ umlegen *to shift the helm* **~anlage** f *steering gear* **~apparat** m *rowing-machine, -tackle* **~bank** f *rower's seat, thwart* **~blatt** n *rudder blade* **~boot** n *row(ing)-boat; racing b.* **~dolle** f *thole-pin* **~fahrt** f *row* || e–e ~ m *to go for a row* **~fuß** m ⟨zoo⟩ *webbed foot* **~füß(l)er** m *remiped* **~gänger,** **~gast** m *helmsman* **~gatt** n *oar-lock* **~haus** n *wheel-house* **~jacke** f *yachting-jacket* **~joch** n *cross-head* **~klampe** f *rowlock* **~kommandos** n pl *helm orders* **~klub** m *rowing-club* **~kunst** f *watermanship* **~knecht** m *oarsman, rower* **~leitung** f *stearing-leads* **~loch** n *hole for an oar, rudder-hole* **~pflock** m *thole(-pin)* **~pinne** f *tiller* **~rad** n *steering wheel* **~schaft** m *rudder-post* **~schaufel** f *paddle* **~schiff** n *galley, row-barge* **~schlag** m *stroke of the oar* **~schnecke** f *pteropod* **~sperrung** f *control-gear* **~spieker** m *rudder-nail* **~sport** m *rowing-sport* **~stand** m *steering position* **~stange** f *oar, puntpole* **~steven** m *stern post* **~verein** m *rowing-club* **~wettfahrt** f *rowing-match* **~wettkampf** m *boat race*; ⟨univ⟩ (in Achtern) *the Eights* pl **~zeiger** m *helm indicator* **R·uderer** m ~s/~ *rower, oarsman* **..ruderer** m Drei~ *trireme* **r·udern** vi/t [h & s] **1.** *to row (a boat); to pull (on the river); to paddle (a canoe)* || (gut) ~ *to pull* od *ply an (a good) oar* || tüchtig ~ *to pull (one's weight* od*) a swinging stroke* || schnell ~ *to row up* || allein, zu vieren ~ *to row a single-, four-oared boat* **2.** ⟨übtr⟩ *to paddle (with the arms)* || (of duck) *to swim (with its feet)* || ⟨fig⟩ beim Gehen mit den Armen ~ *to swing one's arms when walking* **3.** ~̈ n *rowing,* etc || (Kunst) *watermanship* || durch ~̈ erschöpft *rowed out*

R·üdesheim n (Weinort am Rhein)

Rudim·ent n ~(e)s/~e *rudiment* ~̈**·är** a *rudimentary, vestigial*

Ruf m ~(e)s/–e **A. 1.** *call* || (Schrei) *cry, shout*; ~ e–r Stimme *(he heard a) voice crying* || *call (of the bell)* || (Trompeten~̈) *signal, sound* || ⟨orn⟩ *call(ing), note* || *(owl's) hoot* **2.** (Beruf) *calling, vocation* || (Berufung, Aufforderung) *summons,* ⟨univ⟩ *call* → B. **3.** (Gerücht) *report* || (Ansehen) *repute; reputation,* guter ~ *credit*; (verbreiteter) *renown, fame* || ⟨com⟩ *standing, credit* **B.** besser als sein ~ *not so black as he is painted* | ~ **bek** *to acquire fame, to rise into public notice* || e–n ~ als Professor bek (nach ..) *to be invited to fill a pr.'s chair (at ..); (he was offered a professorship* od *chair at a univ.)* | e–n guten ~ **besitzen,** genießen, h *to bear a good character, to be of good report*; .. wegen *to have a name for*; s–n ~ bewahren (*or* nicht preisgeben) *to save one's face* | jdm den ~ **eintragen** .. z s *to bring a p the reputation of being* .. || an Professor H. erging ein ~ nach .. *has received a call to ..* || e–n gr ~ erlangen *to rise into fame* || ein ~ **ertönt** *a cry is heard* || sich den ~ e–s tüchtigen Arztes **erwerben** *to acquire fame as a clever doctor* || dem ~ des Herzens (Schicksals) **folgen** *to obey the voice of the heart (the call of fate)* || den ~ [gen] herabsetzen, schädigen *to let (a business,* etc*) down* || s–m ~ (Ehre m *or*) gerecht w, treu bleiben *to live up to one's reputation* **C. in** ~ bringen *to bring into vogue, repute*; in üblen ~ br. *to defame; to bring disrepute upon, to cry* (⟨fam⟩ *run) down (a p's character)*; ⟨Am⟩ *to gum up a p's rep.n* || in üblen ~ geraten *to get a black mark* || in ~ k *to become famous* || in gutem (schlechtem) ~e stehen *to be well (ill) reputed, (to be in evil repute)* (bei *with*), *(to be in a p's good books)*; im ~e e–s Strebers (*or* des Geizes) st. *to have the character of a place-hunter (of being a miser)*; im ~e e–s Frühaufstehers st. *to enjoy the reputation of an early-riser*; im ~e der Gelehrsamkeit st. *to have a rep.n for learning*; in gutem ~ stehend *reputable*; im ~e st.d zu tun *believed to do* || dem ~e **nach** *by rep.n* || .. **von** ~ *(a writer, school) of (high) standing, (an artist) of high repute; a famous, noted, wellknown man; a man of great distinction; a distinguished author* | drahtlose **~anlage** *wireless intercom(munication)* **~fall** m ⟨gram⟩ *vocative* **~mord** m *defamation* **~name** m *Christian name (by which a p is called)* **~nummer** f ⟨telph⟩ *call-number* **~pfeife** f *bird-call* **~taste** f ⟨telph⟩ *call-button* **~weite** f, in ~ *within call* od *hail* **~zeichen** n ⟨telph⟩ *ring*; ⟨wir⟩ *(address) call-sign(al)* **r·ufen** [rief/gerufen] [h] **I.**

vi **A.** *to cry* (*out*), *shout*; ⟨bes Am⟩ *holler* ⟨a. zoo⟩ || *to call* ⟨a. orn⟩ || (mit Zeichen) *to beckon* || laut ~ ⟨a.⟩ *to sing out* | *duty, the hour, death calls* | e–m ~ (ihn k l) *to call for a p*; (warnend) *to call to a p* | ich höre „Feuer!", „Hilfe!" ~ *I hear a call of fire, for help* **B.** .. **hinter** jdm her~ *to shout* ("*witch*") *after a p* || wie du rufest **in** den Wald, so es dir entgegenschallt *you get as good as you give* || ~ **nach**: *to call to* od *for a p* (→ A.); *it calls aloud for remedy*; *to be clamorous for* (*food*) || **um** Hilfe ~ *to call* (laut *cry, shout*) *for help* || die Glocke ruft **zum** Essen, Gebet, Gottesdienst *dinner is announced, the dinner bell rings, the church bell summons to prayers, calls to divine service* || das Horn ruft zur Jagd .. *calls the huntsmen* **II.** [vi/t] ins *or* unters Gewehr, zu den Waffen ~ *to call to arms* **III.** vt **A. 1.** *to call* (*a p*); *to beckon* (→ A.) || telephonisch ge~ w zu *to be summoned by telephone to* (*a man*) || (jdn) ~ l *to send for* | Beifall ~ *to acclaim* ([dat] *a p*) **2.** sich [acc] heiser ~ *to shout o.s. hoarse* || e–n wach|~ *to rouse a p from his sleep* **B.** jdn **beim** *or* **mit** Namen ~ *to call a p by name* || **beiseite** ~ *to call aside* || jdm etw **ins** Gedächtnis ~ *to recall a th to a p*(*'s mind*), *to remind a p of a th*; sich .. *to recover* (*the episode*) || ins Leben ~ *to beget, start, to call a th into being*; .. wieder *to restore, recall a p to life, to resuscitate* || ~ **nach**: *business took him to Berlin*; jdm etw .. *to say, write sth in memory of a dead p* || jdn **zu** sich [dat] ~ *to bid a p come* (*near*), *to call a p to join one*; (feierlich) *to summon a p* (*into one's presence*); (v Gott) *to call a p to himself* || jdn zu Hilfe (⟨parl⟩ zur Ordnung) ~ *to call for a p's help* (*to call a p to order*) **C.** ⟨fig⟩ **wie** ge~ k *to be as welcome as sunshine*; ⟨Am⟩ *to come very handy*, ⟨sl⟩ *to come up a p's alley* || (*that*) *fits the occasion*; (*that, he*) *comes in the nick of time*; *you have come at the right moment*!, *well met*!; *to come pat* (für *to*) **R·ufer** m ~s/~ *shouter, caller, crier* || ⟨el⟩ *alarm-bell*

°**R·üffel** m ~s/~ → Riffel ⟨fam⟩ *wigging, jobation*; *rap on the knuckles*; *scolding* (= *reprimand*); ⟨sl⟩ *raspberry* °**r·üffeln** vt [h] ⟨fam⟩ *to call over the coals, to blow up* (= *to scold, reprimand*)

R·üge f ~/~n **1.** *blame, reproof* || (öffentliche) *censure* || e–e ~ bek *to be reprimanded* || e–m e–e ~ erteilen *to reprove a p* (f *for*) **2.** ⟨jur⟩ [obs] *denunciation* **r·ügehaft** [adv] sich ~ benehmen *to show o.s. a bad sort* **r·ügen** vt [h] **1.** *to find fault with*; *to reprehend, reprimand, blame, reprove* (wegen *for*) | (öffentlich) *to censure, denounce* **2.** ⟨jur⟩ [obs] *to denounce* | *to punish* **≃gericht** n (*inferior*) *court of justice*; *police-court* **~swert** a *deserving a reprimand*

R·ügen n ⟨Ger⟩ (*isle of*) *Rugen* od *Rügen*

R·uhe f ~/ **A. 1.** (Ausruhen) *rest* (*R. on the Flight into Egypt*); *repose*; (Erholung) *recreation* || ⟨fig⟩ *sleep* (→ Ferien) **2.** (Stille) *quiet* (*of peace, winter, a house*); *stillness, tranquility calmness*; *placidity* || *peace* (*descended on his soul*); (*to live in*) *peace*(*fulness*) || *silence* (*in a church*) || *tranquillity* || *peace* (*in nature, of the grave*) || *calm* (*before the storm*) **3.** (Nichtbewegung) *quiescence* **4.** (Gemüts-, Seelen≃) *composure, imperturbability, serenity, placidity*; *balance* || (innere) *nonchalance, nerve* || *peace* **5.** (Gemächlichkeit) *leisure* **6.** ⟨mil⟩ *rest* (*of a gun*) **B.** angenehme ~! *sleep well*! || ewige ~ (Tod) *everlasting rest*; letzte ~ *last long rest* || nächtliche ~ *night's rest* || öffentliche ~ *public peace* **C.** ~! *order*!; *silence*! || nur ~! *cheer up* || ~ s–r Asche! *peace be with him* || ~ ist die erste Bürgerpflicht! *to keep the peace* (⟨fig, fam⟩ *to keep calm*) *is the first duty of a citizen*! **D.** → **ausbitten** || s–e ~ bewahren *to maintain one's self-composure, to keep calm*, ⟨fam⟩ *to keep one's hair on* || °nur die ~ kann es bringen! *cheer up*!; *nothing can upset my, his composure* || ~ finden: *now I have a few moments of respite*; (innere) *to find peace* (*in*) || gebt ~! *be quiet*!; *silence*!, *hush*!; (endlich) *let the matter rest*! || jdm ~ geben *to reassure a p* || dem Geiste ~ gönnen *to rest one's mind* || jdm k–e ~ gönnen *to be for ever bothering a p* || ~ h vor *to be undisturbed by*; keine: *she gives us no peace* || er hatte k–e ~ *he could find no rest* etc || °nun hat die liebe Seele Ruh! *he's satisfied at last*!, *that's all* (*he* od *I wanted*) || ~ **halten** *to keep quiet* || e–m k–e ~ l *to be constantly bothering a p, not to allow a p a moment's respite*, ⟨com⟩ *to press a p hard*; das läßt mir k–e ~ *that plagues me continually* || nimm uns nicht die ~! *do sit down a minute*! || der [gen] ~ **pflegen** *to take one's ease, to enjoy one's rest* || jdm die ~ rauben *to upset a p* || ~ schaffen *to quieten ths down* || „m–e Ruh ist hin" *my peace is flown* || ~ suchen *to seek rest* || die ~ verlieren ⟨sl⟩ *to get the needle*; *to lose one's hair* (.. nicht .. *to hold* ..) || ~ u Ordnung wahren (wiederherstellen) *to maintain* (*restore*) *law and order* || e–m angenehme ~ wünschen *to wish a p a good night's rest* **E.** sich [acc] aus der ~ bringen l *to lose one's temper* || nicht **aus** der ~ z bringen .. *imperturbable, not easily put out* (*nothing disturbs his equanimity*); wir l uns durch so was doch nicht aus der ~ br. *I* (*we*) *can't be bothered* || **für** ~ u Ordnung sorgen *to maintain law and order* || **in** ~ u Frieden *in peace and quietness* || in aller ~ *very calmly, quietly*; *confidently* || etw in ~ fertigstellen, überlegen .. *at one's leisure* || in ~ l *to let* od *leave alone, to leave* (*in peace* od) *quiet, to let* (*a p*) *be* || laß mich in ~! *don't bother me* || l Sie mich damit in ~ *don't bother me with that* || in ~ ⟨mil⟩ *at half-cock*, .. setzen *to half-cock* (*a gun*), ⟨mach⟩ *to ungear, stop* || **mit** (aller) ~ (*he bore the blow*) *with* (*perfect*) *amenity, with* (*great*) *composure* od *self-possession* || °immer mit der ~ *take it easy*; (⟨mil sl⟩ la rue [*ry*] Fr die ~!) *keep cool*!, ⟨sl⟩ *keep your wool* (⟨Am⟩ *shirt*) *on*! || etw **in aller** ~ erzählen *to tell a th without getting emotional*; in aller ~ schließen *to finish quite quietly* || **ohne** Rast u ~ *restless*(*ly*), *without any rest or peace* || sich **zur** ~ begeben *to go to bed* od *rest* || e~n z letzten ~ begleiten, bestatten *to lay a p to rest* || z ~ bringen *to quiet, hush, calm, pacify*; Kinder .. *to put children to bed*; durch Schrecken .. *to terrify into silence*; z ewigen ~ eingehen *to go to one's eternal home*; z letzten ~ gehen *to pass away*; z ~ k (P) *to come to rest, to settle down*; (S) *to level off*; nicht .. *I shall be on thorns* (*until I know*); nirgends .. *he cannot stay* od *rest anywhere*; nicht z ~ k l: *his conscience would not let him alone*; *the thought bored into him* || z ~ setzen *to pension off, to superannuate*; sich .. *to retire from business, office, active life* || z ~ gesetzt *retired, emeritus* **~altar** m ⟨RC⟩ *temporary altar* **~bank** f *seat, bench* **≃bedürftig** a *in want of rest* **~befehl** m ⟨mil⟩ *rest order* **~bett** n *couch, lounge* **~gehalt** n (*retiring*) *pension, retirement pay* | ~salter [n] *r.g age*; ~sansprüche [m pl] *pension rights*; ~sempfänger [m] *retired pensioner* **~kissen** n *pillow* || ein gutes Gewissen ist das beste ~ *a good c. is a soft pillow* **~kontakt** m ⟨el⟩ *open circuit* **~lage** f ⟨tech⟩ *normal, neutral* od *off-position*; ⟨mil⟩ *steady p., rest area* **~lager** = -bett **≃los** a *restless, unquiet* (*age*) || in ~er Bewegung s *to be on the fidget* **~losigkeit** f *restlessness* **~ort, ~platz** m *resting-place*; (auf e–r Treppe) *landing* || ⟨fig⟩ *retreat* **~pause** f *pause, respite, intermission*; ⟨fam⟩ *breather* || ⟨meteor & fig⟩ *lull* || ⟨school⟩ *recreation-time* || e–e ~ halten *to take an easy* **~perioden** f pl ⟨fam⟩ *times out* **~posten** m ⟨fig⟩ *sinecure* **~punkt** m *resting-point* || ⟨mus⟩ *pause* || ⟨tech⟩ (Hebel-) *fulcrum* L **~quartiere** n pl *restbillets* pl **~raum** m ⟨mil⟩ *rehabilitation area* **~sessel** m *lounging-chair* **~sitz** m *bench, seat*;

(Wohnsitz) *country-seat* **~stand** m **1.** *state of repose* **2.** *retirement* ‖ im ~ *pensioned off, ex--(bank-manager)* ‖ ⟨mil⟩ *on half-pay*; .. lebend *retired* ‖ in den ~ versetzen *to pension off, to superannuate* ‖ ⟨mil⟩ *to put on half-pay* od *on the retired list* ‖ in den ~ treten *to retire from active life* **~ständler** m *retired p*; *retiree*; er ist ~ *he is r.* **~statt, ~stätte** f *place of rest, resting-place* ‖ *retreat* ‖ ⟨mar⟩ s–e ~ aufschlagen *to make one's berth* ‖ ⟨fig⟩ die letzte ~ *the grave* **~stellung** f → –lage; ⟨drill⟩ *original position*; ⟨tech⟩ in ~ *inoperative* ‖ ⟨phot⟩ *p. at rest*; ⟨el⟩ *off-p.* **~stifter** m *peace-maker* **~störer** m *disturber of the p.* **~störung** f *breach of the p., disturbance, riot(ing)*; ⟨jur⟩ *affray* **~stunde** f *hour of rest, leisure-hour* **~tag** m *day of rest*; ⟨fam⟩ *day off* **~wert** m ⟨scient⟩ *quiescent value* **~zeit** f *(time of) rest* **~zustand** = ~stand 1.; *quiescent state* **r·uhen I.** vi [h] **A. 1.** *to rest* (⟨a. mil⟩ of arms); *to repose, to take (one's) rest* ‖ ⟨fig⟩ *to sleep* ‖ (ich) wünsche wohl z ~ (geruht z h) *I wish you a good night (I hope, trust you have [slept well* od*] had a good night's rest)* ‖ Hier ruht .. *Here lies* .., ⟨Am a.⟩ *In Memory of .., To the Memory of ..* | ⟨fig⟩ *I shall not rest until ..* ‖ ⟨prov⟩ nach der Arbeit ist gut ~ *rest is pleasant after work* **2.** (aufhören) *to cease working* ‖ (of negotiations) *to have been interrupted* ‖ (of business, work) *to have come to a standstill* ‖ (of thunder) *to have ceased* ‖ die Schlacht ruht *there is a pause in the battle* ‖ *all work ceases on the 1st of May* ‖ (of contracts) *to remain out of force* ‖ (of fields) *to remain untilled, to lie fallow* **B.** ~ **lassen** *to leave alone, to leave to rest*; *to give rest (to the body), to give (the mind) a rest* ‖ *to leave (a task) unfinished* ‖ *to let a matter rest* ‖ *to drop (a quarrel, legal process)* ‖ *Let's drop the matter! Let bygones be bygones!* ‖ *Let the dead be!* **C.** ~ **auf** [dat] (liegen, lasten) *to lean on*; *to be based, founded on*; *to be supported by (pillars)*; *to rest on (a pedestal,* (of work) *on a p's shoulders)* | ⟨fig⟩ *to ride a th* ‖ *the evening falls o'er woods and meadows* ‖ *suspicion points to him* ‖ *God's hand rests heavily on him* ‖ *there is a blessing, a curse on it* | ~ **in** *to reside in, to be resident in* ‖ *to rest (in the soil of Flanders)* ‖ im Grabe ~ *to sleep in peace, to be at peace* ‖ Hier ruht in Frieden *or* Gott *Here Rests in Peace, Here Sleeps in Jesus* | nach, von der Arbeit ~ *to rest after work* **II.** vt [h] *to rest (one's mind)* | **sich** ~ *to take one's rest, to rest o.s.* ‖ hier ruht sich's gut *here you will find sweet rest* **III.** ≈ n *repose, rest(ing)* ‖ ⟨jur⟩ *suspension* **IV. ~d** (nach Arbeit) *quiescent*; *(Venus) in repose* ‖ *static (pressure)* ‖ ⟨com⟩ *dead, uninvested (capital)* ‖ ⟨tech⟩ ~de Belastung *permanent* od *dead load* ‖ ⟨fig⟩ ~d in *inherent in* **r·uhig I.** [a] **A. 1.** *quiet* (a. v Farben) ‖ *tranquil (mind, scene)* ‖ *at rest* ‖ *staid (p, colours, habits)* ‖ *quiet (p, conversation, life, town, flat)* ‖ *peaceful (tenant)* ‖ *imperturbable (p)* | *composed (countenance, thoughts)* ‖ *serene (eye)* | *calm (glance)* ‖ *even (voice)* | *good (conscience)* ‖ *kind (disposition)* | *retired (life, valley)* ‖ *calm (landscape, days, weather)* ‖ *smooth, calm, unruffled (water, temper, brow)* | *peaceful, settled (times)* ‖ *halcyon (days)* **2.** (beruhigt) *reassured* **3.** (bequem) *easy, at ease* **4.** (unbewegt) *quiescent* **5.** (kaltblütig) *cool, steady* **6.** (nicht gesprächig) *silent, taciturn* **7.** ⟨com⟩ *quiet, dull, lifeless* **8.** ⟨mil⟩ *deliberate (fire)* **9.** ⟨mach⟩ *soft, smooth (action)*; *quiet (running)* **B.** ~e Augenblicke [pl] ⟨a.⟩ *silences* pl ‖ ~ Blut bewahren *to keep cool*, ⟨fam⟩ *to keep one's feet on the ground* ‖ nur ~ Blut! *keep your temper!, steady, steady!* ‖ ⟨mar⟩ ~e Fahrt *calm run, smooth steering* (nach *to*) ‖ ~er Geschäftsgang *still business* ‖ in ~em Schritt *at an easy pace* ‖ bei ~er Überlegung *if calmly considered, on reflection, on cool consideration*; *in cold blood* ‖ ein ~es Wort reden mit *to speak calmly with* **C.** [**pred**] *(to be, keep, remain) quiet, still, collected* ‖ *at peace* ‖ ~ bleiben ⟨fam a.⟩ *to keep one's hair on*; ganz ~ **bl.** ⟨fig fam⟩ *not to get one's wind up*; bl. Sie ~ ⟨sl⟩ *don't get jittery* ‖ das läßt mich ganz ~! *that doesn't trouble me!* ‖ ~ m *to calm, appease* ‖ ~ w ⟨fam a.⟩ *to feel one's legs*; (of wind) *to calm down* ‖ ~er w *to quiet(en) down* | alles ~ *all serene* ‖ sei deswegen ganz ~! *don't worry about that!* ‖ du magst ~ s ⟨fig⟩ *rest easy* ‖ sei endlich mal ~! *can't you keep quiet!* ‖ ~! *silence!, hush!* **II.** [adv] *quietly* etc; *cooly*; *at ease* ‖ *(you can go) all right* ‖ ⟨exch⟩ ~ liegen: *securities are easy* ‖ *(the fowls picked) staidly* ‖ *(he said) evenly* ‖ man kann ~ sagen *it is safe to say*; .. *without fear of contradiction, .. without any hesitation*; *I thought him – I may as well say so – an imposter*; l Sie ~ das W. aus *it does not matter if you omit the word* ‖ ich kann es Ihnen ~ erzählen *there is no reason why I shouldn't tell you* ‖ *(to sleep) soundly* ‖ sich ~ verhalten *to keep quiet, passive, inactive*; *to hold one's peace*; *to remain neutral* ‖ [[ell] ~! *steady*, ⟨Am⟩ *easy*!; nur ~! *there, there!* ‖ ~ zusehen *to sit by*

Ruhm m ~(e)s/ **A. 1.** *glory* ‖ *fame* ‖ *renown* ‖ *honour* **2.** **reputation* **3.** (Preis) *praise* **4.** ⟨rel⟩ (Lob) *thanks-giving* **B.** eitler ~ *vain g.* ‖ gr., hoher ~ *celebrity, great f.* od *r.* ‖ unsterblicher ~ *eternal g.* | auf Fittichen des ~s *on the pinions of f.* ‖ flüchtiger ~ ⟨fam⟩ *flash in the pan* ‖ der Gipfel des ~s *the meridian of (a p's) f.* ‖ .. s–s ~es voll *(the press is) full of his pr.s* **C.** ~ davontragen *to cover o.s. with g.* ‖ ~ ernten *to win celebrity* ‖ s–n ~ genießen *to enjoy one's f.* ‖ den ~ muß man ihm l *it must be said to his credit* ‖ *his celebrity hardly lets him sleep* ‖ ~ in etw suchen *to seek g. in a th* **D.** sich **mit** ~ bedecken *to win great f.* ‖ °sich nicht mit ~ bekleckern: *he didn't cover h.s. with g.* ‖ **zu** ~ u Ehre gelangen *to attain f. and h., to leap into f.* ‖ jdm zum ~e gereichen *to redound to a p's h.* od *credit* ≈**bedeckt** a; ≈**bekränzt,** ≈**gekrönt** a *covered, crowned with g.* **~begierde,** ~gier [f] *desire* od *thirst of g., love of f.* ≈**(be)gierig** a *desirous of g., ambitious, eager* od *anxious for g.* ≈**los** a *inglorious, obscure* **~losigkeit** f *ingloriousness* ≈**redig** a *boastful, vainglorious* **~redigkeit** f *boastfulness, vainglory* **~reich** a *glorious* **~sucht** f *love of f., greediness of g., thirst* od *passion for g.* **~süchtig** a *thirsty for g., eager after f.* ≈**voll** a *glorious* ≈**würdig** a *praiseworthy* **~würdigkeit** f *praiseworthiness* **r·ühmen I. 1.** vt [h] *to speak highly of*; *to praise, glorify*; *to sing the praises of* ‖ (verhimmeln) *to celebrate, extol* ‖ (empfehlen) *to commend*, ⟨com⟩ *to advertise, puff*; *to cry up* | man rühmt ihn als tapfer *he is said* od *reputed to te brave* ‖ ~d erwähnen *to mention with praise, to make honourable mention of, to speak in high terms of* **2. v/refl sich** ~ [h] [gen] *or* wegen *or* mit *to glory in, to boast of, to speak proudly of*; *to pride, praise, plume o.s. on a th* ‖ ohne mich z ~ *without boasting* ‖ ich rühme mich, sein Freund z s *I am proud to call m.s. his fr.* ‖ ich erinnere mich, daß er sich rühmte, daß *I remember his boast that* | sich ~ **können** etw zu besitzen *to boast of a th* ‖ er konnte sich ~ ein F. abgeschossen z h *he had to his credit a plane shot down (he had heroic deeds to his credit)* **II.** ≈ n *praises* pl ‖ *glorification* ‖ viel ~s v e–r S m *to speak in the highest terms of a th*; ⟨fam⟩ ohne viel ~s davon z m *without making any fuss about it* | **~swert** a *praiseworthy* ‖ nicht ~ *not much to boast of* **R·uhmes- ~blatt** n *roll of fame*; es ist ein ~ [gen] *it is a credit to, it does (him) credit* **~glanz** m *prestige* **~halle** f *pantheon* **r·ühmlich** a *laudable, creditable*; *glorious* ‖ *honourable (end)* ‖ *that was not very praiseworthy of him* | jds ~ [adv] gedenken *to make honourable mention of a p* ≈**keit** f *laudability gloriousness, praiseworthiness*

Ruhr f ⟨Ger⟩ (Nebenfluß des Rheins)

Ruhr f ~/~en ⟨path⟩ *flux, dysentery* ‖ rote ~ *bloody flux* ‖ weiße ~ *diarrhoea* ‖ ~- [in comp oft] *dysenteric* **~anfall** m *attack of d.y* **≃artig** a *d.c* **≃krank** a *suffering from d.y* **~kranke(r)** m *d.c patient* **~kraut** n *cud-weed* **R·ühr- ~arm** m ⟨tech⟩ *stirring arm* **~ei** n *scrambled eggs* pl **~faß** n *churn* **~kelle** f, **~löffel** m (*pot-*)*ladle* **~kitsch** m *sobstuff* **~kuchen** m *plain cake*; ~ mit Rosinen *fruit-cake* **~löffel** m → –stab **~maschine** f *stirring m.* **~michnichtan** n ⟨bot⟩ *touch-me-not* **~scheit** n *mash-stick* **≃selig** a *sentimental, emotional, maudlin, soppy*; *lacrymose*; bes ~ *two-handkerchief* [attr]; *sob* (*story*) | **≃**keit [f] *sentimentality* **~stab** m ⟨cul⟩ *muddler* **~stock** m ⟨tech⟩ *dolly, puddle* **~stück** n ⟨theat⟩ *melodrama, sentimental piece*; ⟨wir Am fam⟩ *soap opera* **~szene** f *touching scene*; e–e ~ spielen ⟨a.⟩ *to do a mammy act* **~werk** n *agitator, stirring device* | ~system [n] *stirrer system* **r·ühren I.** vi [h] **1.** *to stir, move* **2.** ~ **an** *to touch* (*on*), *to flick*; an etw (lieber) nicht ~ *to let sleeping dogs lie* | ~ in *to stir in* ‖ v (= her~) *to originate from, to be attributable to* ‖ daher r.t (der Gebrauch) *hence* (*the custom*); *to this is due, by this is caused* (*the mistake*) **II.** vt [h] **A.** *to stir* ⟨a. cul⟩; *move* ‖ (be~) *to touch* ‖ (treffen) *to strike* ‖ (innerlich) *to touch, affect, to go to* (*a p's*) *heart*; *to move* (zu Tränen *to tears*) **B.** das r.t mich nicht *that's nothing to me* ‖ wie v Donner g.t *as if thunderstruck* ‖ ihn hat der Schlag g.t *he has had a*(*n apoplectic*) *stroke* ‖ v Schlag g.t *struck with apoplexy* **C.** die **Beine** ~ *to use one's legs, to put one's best leg foremost, to trot along* | *to beat* (*eggs*) ‖ k–n F. ~ *not to wag a finger* ‖ (Glieder) *to move* ‖ *to touch* od *play* (*the harp, lute*) ‖ *to temper, mix* (*mortar*) ‖ (Sahne) *to whip* .. ‖ (e–e Saite) *to touch* .. ‖ (die Trommel) *to beat* .. **III.** v/refl **sich** ~ *to* (*be a*)*stir, move,* ⟨fig⟩ *to be up and doing,* ⟨Am⟩ *to get a move on* | *to make a move* od *sign* ‖ sich nicht ~ ⟨com⟩: *the banks sit tight* ‖ er r.te sich nicht mehr (war tot) *he no longer made the slightest movement* ‖ rühr dich nicht v Platz *stay where you are* ‖ sich nicht ~ können ⟨a. fig⟩ *to be unable to bestir o.s.* ‖ sich nicht genug ~ *to lack energy* ‖ **es** r.t sich nichts (kein Lüftchen) *everything is quiet* (*there is not a breath of air*) ‖ sein G. r.t sich *his conscience pricks him* | ⟨mil⟩ *to stand* (*at ease* od) *easy* (⟨engl⟩ Hände auf Rücken); r–t euch! (*at parade*) *rest*! R–t–euch-Stellung [f] *ease*; (im Marsch) *easy*!, *as you were*! | rühr' dich ein bißchen! *look alive*! ‖ *don't move from the spot* (v Fleck)! **IV.** ≃ n – Rührung ‖ ein menschliches ≃ fühlen *to feel a touch of human sympathy* ‖ ⟨hum, fam⟩ *to feel hungry, sick*, etc **V. ~d** a *moving, touching, affecting*; *emotional, heart-stirring, thrilling, pathetic, pitiable* **R·ührer** m ⟨tech, pap⟩ *paddle* **r·ührig** a *active*(*-minded*), *alert, busy, lively* ‖ *pushing, pushful* ‖ *nimble* | [pred] ⟨bes Am⟩ *on the go, on one's toes* | **≃keit** f ~/ *activity, nimbleness, alertness, stir* **R·ührung** f ~/~en **1.** unter ~ der Trommeln *with drums beating* **2.** *emotion, feeling* (gr *deep*), *compassion, sympathy* ‖ mit ~ ⟨a.⟩ *touchingly* ‖ übertriebene ~ *unctuosity* ‖ vor ~ nicht sprechen können *to be too deeply moved to speak, to have a lump in one's throat*

Ru·in m ~(e)s/ *ruin* (*economic, moral r.*) (aufhalten *to stave off*) ‖ das ist sein ~ *that means his r.* ‖ du bist noch mein ~ *you are my evil fate* ‖ unmittelbar vor den ~ gestellt *faced with ruin* ‖ zum ~ führend *ruinous* ‖ dem ~e nahe s *to be nearly ruined*, dem ~ entgegengehen *to be on the way to destruction* od *ruin* ‖ den ~ über sich bringen *to draw one's own ruin on o.s.* | (Verfall) *decay* ‖ (Sturz) (*down*)*fall, undoing* ‖ ⟨fig⟩ *bane* **Ru·ine** f ~/~n *ruin*(*s* pl) ‖ ⟨fig⟩ (P) *wreck* **≃nhaft** a *ruinous, in ruins, decayed* | [attr] *dilapidated, tumble-down* **ruin·ieren** vt [h] *to ruin, mar, destroy* ‖ *to be ruinous to*; (etw) ~ *to dilapidate* ‖ *to cause* (*a p's*) *ruin*; ⟨vulg⟩ *to do a p's job for him* ‖ sich ~ ⟨a.⟩ *to come a cropper* ‖ (Kleider etc) *to spoil* **ruiniert** [pred] ⟨com⟩ *broken,* ⟨fam a. fig⟩ *broke, done for, smashed, up the tree, down and out* ‖ er ist –rt ⟨Am, fam⟩ *his goose is cooked* **ruin·ös** a *ruinous*

°**Rülps** m –es/–e *belch*(*ing forth*), ⟨Am⟩ *burp* ‖ ⟨scient⟩ *eructation* ‖ ⟨fig⟩ *lout* | **≃en** vi [h] *to belch,* ⟨fam⟩ *to gurk,* ⟨Am⟩ *burp* ‖ ⟨scient⟩ *to eruct*(*ate*) | **~er** m ~s/~ 1. = Rülps 2. (P) *belcher*

Rum m ~s/~s & ~e *rum*; (Tee) mit etw ~ ⟨fam⟩ *with* (*a*) *lacing*, ⟨Am⟩ *with a stick in it*

°**rum** [adv] = herum ‖ ~ u num *all over the place*; *upside down* ‖ ~ wie num *so or so*

Rum·änien n *Roumania* **-er** m *Roumanian*

r·um-bidi-plum! [intj] *rataplan*!, *rub-a-dub*

†**Rum·elien** n (Balkanlandschaft) *Rumelia*

R·ummel m ~s/ ⟨fam⟩ **1.** *racket, hubbub, row* **2.** = Gerümpel **3.** *swindle* **4.** (Vergnügungs≃ etc) *revelling, revel*(*s* pl), ⟨Am, sl⟩ *shivaree* ‖ ⟨com⟩ der ganze ~ *the whole lot* ‖ im ~ *in the lump* ‖ er kennt *or* versteht den ~ *he knows all about it, he has the knack of it*; *he knows* (*what's what* od ⟨sl⟩) *the ropes* ‖ *he's up to snuff, he knows a trick or two* **~platz** m *amusement park*; *fair* **rumms**!, ≃ m *wumph*(!) **Rum·or**(**en** n) *m* ~(e)s/ *noise, bustle, hubbub* ‖ (Lärm) *uproar,* ⟨fam⟩ *rumpus* **rum·oren** vi [h] *to make a h.b, to bluster* ‖ *to kick up a row* ‖ es –rt in m–m Leibe (Kopfe) *I have rumbling* (*buzzing*) *noises in my stomach* (*head*) **Rum·orer** m ~s/~ *bustler* **R·umpel- ~kammer** f *lumber-room, limbo* ‖ in die ~ k ⟨fig⟩ *to be laid on the shelf, to go to limbo*; (etw) in die ~ werfen *to relegate .. to the limbo* **~kasten** m *lumber-box* ‖ ⟨fam⟩ (Kutsche) *rattle-trap* **r·umpeln** vi/t [h & s] *to rumble, rattle, lumber* ‖ es rumpelt *it's thundering* | [vt] alles durch e–a ~ *to toss everything upside down* ‖ (jdn) ~ (abreiben) *to rub down* ‖ (Wäsche) *to toss*

Rumpf m ~(e)s ≃e *body, trunk* ‖ (*of horse, cow*) *barrel* ‖ mit ~ u Stumpf *root and branch, altogether* ‖ (Schiffs-, Flugboots≃, ⟨a–n⟩) *hull*; (abgetakelt) *hulk* ‖ (e–r Mühle) *hopper* ‖ (e–s Flugzeugs) *body, fuselage* ‖ (e~s Luftschiffs) *hull* ‖ (e–r Statue) *torso* **~abwurfbehälter** m ⟨aero⟩ *ventral drop tank,* ⟨fam⟩ *belly t.* **~behälter** m *fuselage tank* **~baum** m (e–r Mühle) *trimmer* **~beugen** n ⟨gym⟩ *trunk bending* **~bug** m ⟨aero⟩ *nose* **~ebene, ~fläche** f ⟨geol⟩ *peneplain* **~ende** n ⟨aero⟩ *tail* **~gebirge** n *uplifted peneplain* **~(längs)-holm** m ⟨aero⟩ *longeron* **~parlament** n ⟨engl hist⟩ *the Rump* **~querschnitt** m ⟨aero⟩ *fuselage section* **~scholle** f ⟨geol⟩ *truncated fault rock* **~spant** m *frame*

r·ümpfen vt [h] *to turn up* od *wrinkle* (*one's nose*) (über [acc] *at*) ‖ *to pucker up* (*one's mouth*)

R·umpsteak n ⟨cul⟩ *sirloin* od *rump steak*

rums-r·ums! [intj] *rataplan*!

rund I. a **A.** *round* (*table* etc, *cheeks, numbers*) ‖ (abgerundet) *r.ed* (*column*) ‖ (kreisförmig) *circular* ‖ (walzenförmig) *cylindrical* ‖ (kugelig) *globular, spherical* ‖ ⟨scient zoo bot⟩ *rotund*(*ate*) ‖ ⟨fig⟩ *plain* | [pred] hübsch ~ u drall *nice and plump* | ~ m *to r.* (*off*); (vollständig m) *to complete* ‖ ~ w *to grow stout, plump, fat* **B.** *plain* (*answer*) ‖ *well-r.ed* (*arms* etc) ‖ ~e Augen m *to make big eyes* ‖ (Gesicht) *a r. red freckled face* (ohne Komma!) ‖ ~er Griff *crook-handle* ‖ (Säule) *r.ed* ‖ *good r.* (*sum, dozen*) ‖ *full-voiced* (*tone*) **II.** [adv] *about* (*4000*) | ~ abschlagen *to refuse flatly, to give a flat denial* | ~ um .. *r.* (*the world*) ‖ ~ um etw her(um) *r. about a th* | ~ heraus *plainly, flatly, r.ly* ‖ – ~ heraus gesagt – *in plain terms,* – *to speak plainly,* – *to tell it you openly, frankly*; ..! *out with it*! | ~ herum *all r., right r., r. and r., r. about* | 5 Meilen ~ umher *for five miles r.* | ~ u nett *plainly and bluntly*; .. 1000

a good r. thousand; ⟨Am⟩ *a cool $ 1000* **III.** ~̊ n [abstr] *r.ness* (*of cheeks*) ‖ das ~ der Erde *the globe* | *[konkr] ein ~ *a r.* **R·und-** ⟨oft⟩ *circular* (*c.r*) **~alarm** m (of police) *all-stations call* **~̊bäkkig** a *chubby-*, *r.-cheeked* **~bau** m *rotunda*; *c.r building* **~beet** n ⟨hort⟩ *r. bed* **~bild** n *panorama* (*picture*); ⟨paint⟩ *roundel* **~̊blätt(e)rig** a *r.-leaved*, ⟨scient⟩ *rotundifolious* **~blick** m *view all r.* | ~fernrohr [n] *panoramic sight* od *telescope*; *director* **~bogen** m *Roman*, *Norman*, *r. arch* | ~stil [m] *Roman* od *Norman style* **~̊bogig** a *arched* **~boot** n (aus Weidengeflecht u Leder) ⟨Ir⟩ *coracle* **~brenner** m *r. burner* **~brief** m *c.r letter*, ⟨Am⟩ *form l.* **~bühne** f *amphitheatre* **~dorf** n = ~ling **~eisen** n *r. bar-iron*, *r. i. b.* **~̊erhaben** a *convex*, (beiderseitig) *biconvex*; dazu: (*bi*)*convexity* **~erlaß** m *c.r* (*notice*) **~̊erneuern** vt [h] ⟨mot⟩ *to retread* (*tyres*) **~erneuerung** f *r.ing*; *full cap* **~fahrauto** n *motor-coach*, *char-a-banc* **~fahrt** f *drive r. a town* etc.; (gr) *c.r tour* (nach, zu *of*) | ~wagen [m] *sightseeing car* **~flug** m *air-tour*, *circuit* (*flight*) (~ m *to fly a c.*), ⟨fam⟩ *s.s.g flight*, *joy-ride* **~form** f *c.r form* **~funk** m → u. **~gang** m [abstr] *tour* (durch *of*) ‖ ⟨mil⟩ *r.* (durch *of*) ‖ den ~ m durch *to go the r. of* ⟨a. übtr⟩; (festgesetzter) *beat* (*of a policeman*) ‖ ⟨astr⟩ *rotation* | [konkr] *corridor*, *balcony*; *circuit* (um *of the city walls*) **~gebäude** n *rotunda* **~gemälde** n *panorama* **~gesang** m *glee*; *song with a chorus*; (komischer) *catch* **~̊her·aus** [adv] **~̊her·um** [adv] → rund II. **~höcker** m ⟨geog⟩ *roche moutonnée* Fr **~̊hohl** a *concave*, (beiderseits) *biconcave*; dazu: (*bi*)*concavity* **~holz** n *uncleft wood*; *scaffold pole*; *r. timber*; ⟨mar⟩ [koll] *spars*, *masts*, *gaffs* pl **~horizont** m ⟨theat⟩ *cyclorama* **~kipper** m *all-r. dump car* **~kirche** f *r. church* **~kopf** m *bullet head*; ⟨biol⟩ *r. head*; ⟨hist⟩ *R. H.* | ~stativ [n] *tripod with r. head* **~lauf** m *rotation*, *c.r motion* ‖ ⟨gym⟩ *giant('s)-stride*, *r.-trip* **~maschine** f ⟨tech⟩ *r.er* **~maul** n ⟨ich⟩ *cyclostome* **~reim** m *refrain*, *burden* **~reise** f *c.r tour*, *circuit*, ⟨Am⟩ *r. trip*, *belt-line tour* ‖ (zeremonielle) *progress*, ⟨jur⟩ *circuit* | ~billet [n], –(fahr)karte [f] *c.r* od *tourist's ticket*; ~zug [m] (internat.) *cruise train* **~rücken** m *humpback*, ⟨med⟩ *kyphosis* **~säule** f *cylinder*, *r. column* **~schaber** m *r. scraper* **~schau** f *panorama* ‖ (Zeitung) *review* **~schild** n *r. shield* **~schreiben** n *c.r* (*c.r letter*); (*Pope's*) *encyclical l.*; durch ~ bekannt geben, benachrichtigen *to c.rize* **~schrift** f *r.hand* **~sein** n *r.ess* **~̊|senden** vt ⟨wir⟩ *to broadcast* **~sichtverglasung** f ⟨bes mot⟩ *panorama windscreen* **~spitzfeder** f *c.r-pointed pen* **~stab** m ⟨arch⟩ *roundel*; *astragal* ‖ ~̊e [pl] *beadings* **~strahler** m ⟨wir⟩ *omni-directional aerial* **~stück** n ⟨hort⟩ *c.r lawn* ‖ ⟨cul⟩ *steak*; *bun*, *roll* **~such-** ~radargerät [n] *surveillance radar* (*element*) N; ~verfahren [n] *c.r scanning* **~tanz** m *r.* od *ring dance* **~teil** n *r.*(*el*) **~trunk** m *drinking all r.* **~̊·um** [adv] *r. about*, *all-*(⟨Am⟩ *a*)*r.* | ~verteidigung *all-r. defence* **~̊w·eg** [adv] *plainly*, *flatly*, *squarely*, *bluntly*, *point-blank*, *plump* **~weg** m *circular path* **~zange** f (*a pair of*) *r.nosed pliers*
R·unde f ~/~n *round* ⟨a. mil⟩; ⟨police⟩ *beat* ‖ (P) *party*, *company*; (Tanzende) *ring* ‖ ⟨sport, golf, box⟩ *round*; ⟨baseball⟩ *inning*; (Bier~̊) *round* ‖ ⟨racing, aero⟩ *lap* (*a ten-lap race*) ‖ in der ~ *around* | **die ~ m** *to go the round* (zw, unter Leuten *of people*); (v Pokal) *to be passed r.* ‖ (v Wächtern etc) *to patrol* od *to make* od *go one's r.s* ‖ der .., der die ~ hatte *the policeman on beat* ‖ (Nachricht, Witz etc) *to go the r.* ‖ (Mode) *to spread* (*all over the world*) | e–e ~ (Bier) geben, ⟨fam⟩ schmeißen *to pay drinks r.*; die erste ~ zahlen ⟨mar⟩ *to push out the boat* ‖ m–e ~! *it's my shout this time* ‖ s–e ~ bestellen *to put one's hand down* | ⟨sex⟩ e–e ~ m *to break a lance* (*with a woman*), *faire la noce* Fr ‖ (Blick) **in** die ~ *circular* (*glance*) **R·ünde** f ~/ *r.ness* ⟨a. fig⟩, *rotundity* ‖ ⟨arch⟩ *curve of an arch*; *vault* **r·unden**, ***ründen** vt [h] *to r.*; ⟨fig⟩ *to finish* ‖ sich ~ *to grow r.*; *to r. off* | vt [h] ⟨comp⟩ *to round off* **Runden-** ~führer [m] *officer inspecting sentries*; ~gang [m] → Wehr- | ⟨sport⟩ *lap* (*gain*, *arrears*, *lead* [Vorsprung], *judge*, *status*) **R·undfunk** m ~s/ *broadcasting*, *wireless*, *radio* ‖ ~ auf Kurz-, Mittel-, Langwelle *short wave*, *standard*, *long wave b.t* ‖ was gibt es im ~? *what's on the air?* ‖ dem ~ angeschlossen s, im ~ singen, sprechen etc *to be on the air* ‖ ~ hören *to listen in* ‖ durch ~ senden *to flash* ‖ im ~ *on the air* od *radio* (*his hearers on the w.*); ⟨Am⟩ *over the air*; im ~ übertragen *to put on the air*; .. spricht .. im ~ *will be on the air* (*at 5*) ‖ im ~ berichtet w *to be* (*told in a*) *b.t* ‖ (etw) im ~ hören *to hear .. on the w.* **~anlage** f *w. installation* **~aufnahme** f *recording from r.* **~beamte(r)** m *w. operator* | f **~empfang** m *for r. pick-up* **~erfasser** m *monitor* **~gebühr** f *charges for w.*; *w. licence* **~genehmigung** f *receiving licence* **~gerät** n *r. apparatus* od *set*; (tragbares) ⟨fam⟩ *portable*, ⟨sl⟩ *walkie-talkie* **~gesellschaft** f *b.ting company*; Britische *B.B.C.* **~gespräch** n *panel discussion* **~hörer, ~teilnehmer** m *b.t listener*, *l.-in* **~kommentar** m *commentary b.t* **~musik** f *w. music* **~orgel** f *theatre organ* **~programm** n *w. programme* **~reklame** f *r. advertising*; ⟨fam⟩ *plug* ‖ ⟨Am⟩ *commercial(s)* (*broadcast during sponsored radio or TV program or between programs*) **~sender** m *r. b.ting station*; *w. transmitter* | ~netz [n] *network* **~sendung** f *b.ting*; k–e ~ geben *to be off the air* **~seriensendung** f *radio serial* **~sprecher** m (etc) *b.ter* **~stelle** f *b.ting station* **~studio** n *r. studio* **~übertragung** f *b.t*(*ing*) **~wesen** n (*world of*) *w.*; staatl. ~ *subscription r.* **rund·ieren** vt [h] *to make round*, *to r. off* **r·undlich** [a] *r.ish* ‖ *plump* (*cheeks*) ‖ (P) *rotund*, *plump* ‖ (gebauscht) *sinuous*, *swelling*, *well-r.ed* (*arm*) ‖ ⟨tech⟩ *cambered* ‖ ~e Erhöhung *knob* | [adv] ~ geschliffen *ground r.* **~̊keit** *r.ishness*, *plumpness*, *sinuosity*
R·undung f ~/~en *r.ness*, *r.ing*, *swelling* ‖ zierliche ~ *bulge* ⟨a. arts⟩ | ~sfehler [m] ⟨comp⟩ *rounding error*

R·une f ~/~n *rune*; **~nschrift** f *runic writing* od *characters* pl, *runes* pl **~nalphabet** n *futhark* **~nstab** m *runic wand* **~nstein** m *rune-stone*

R·unge f ~/~n *pin*, *bolt*, (e–s Wagens) *standard* ‖ (e–s Karrens) *support* ‖ ⟨rail⟩ *stanchion*, *stake* ‖ (Lkw~̊) *stanchion* | ~nanhänger [m] *flat-bed trailer*; ~nhalter [m] *stake socket*; ~nwagen [m] ⟨rail⟩ *platform-car*

R·unkel- **~rübe** f *White Beet*, *beetroot*; ~n [pl] *beetroot*, ⟨Am⟩ *beets* **~rübenzucker** m *beet-sugar*

°**R·unken** m ~s/~ **Runks** m ~es/~e *a thick'un*, *a hunk* (*of bread*) ‖ ⟨fig⟩ (P) *a regular boor*

R·unse f ~/~n (Wildbachbett) ⟨for⟩ *rill*, *rivulet*

°**runter** [adv] = herunter

R·unzel f ~/~n (Stirn~̊) *wrinkle* ‖ (Mund~̊) *pucker* ‖ (Augen~̊n [pl]) ⟨fam⟩ *crow's feet* pl ‖ ~n bek *to wrinkle*; *to get w.s* ‖ (v Obst) *to shrivel* **r·unz(e)lig** a *w.d*, *puckered* (*old face*) ‖ *rugose* | ~keit [f] *rugosity* **r·unzeln** vt [h] *to w.* ‖ die Stirn ~ *to purse one's brow*; .. nachdenklich .. *to scowl in thought* ‖ sich ~ ⟨bot⟩ *to shrivel up*

R·üpel m ~s/~ ⟨fam⟩ *bounder*, *clown*, *lout*, *ruffian*, *yokel* | **~·ei** f *horseplay* **~̊haft** a *rude*; *coarse*; *clownish*, *loutish*; *vulgar*; *brutal*

R·upfen m ~s/~ *sack cloth*; *canvas*; ⟨theat⟩ *Hessian*, ⟨Am⟩ *burlap*

r·upfen vt [h] (ein Huhn etc) *to pluck* ‖ (ausreißen) *to pick*, *to pull* (*up*) ‖ ~ an .. *to pull* (*a p's hair*) | ⟨fig, fam⟩ *to skin*, *fleece*, *shave* (*a p*)

R·upie ['ru:piə] f ~/~n *rupee*

r·uppig a *unkempt*, *scrubby*, *ragged* ‖ *coarse*, *rough-looking*, *r.*(*-and-tumble*) ‖ ⟨fig⟩ *shabby*, *tattered* ‖ *paltry* ‖ *rude* | **~̊keit** f *raggedness*;

coarseness; *shabbiness*; *rudeness* **R·uppsack** m = Rüpel

R·uprecht m [npr] *Rupert* ‖ Knecht ~ *Santa Claus* **~skraut** n *herb-robert*

Rusch m ~es/~e ⟨bot⟩ *rush*

R·üsche f ~/~n *ruche*; *ruching* ‖ Hals≗ *frill*

r·uschelig a *fidgety* ‖ *scamped* (*job*) **r·uscheln** vi [h] *to rustle*, *fidget*; *scamp* vt

Ruß m ~es/ *soot* ‖ mit ~ bedecken *to soot*, *smut* **~abdruck** m ⟨engr⟩ *smoke proof* **≗artig** a *fuliginous* **~braun** n *bistre* **~bütte** f *soot-box* **~fleck** m *smut* **~kohle** f *sooty coal* **~kreide** f *black-chalk* **~schreiber** m *carbon-recorder* **~-schwarz** n *bistre wash* | **≗en 1.** vi [h] (of lamp) *to smoke* **2.** vt *to soot*, *blacken* **r·ußig** a *sooty*, *smutty* ⟨scient⟩ *fuliginous*

R·usse m ~n/~n ⟨fig⟩ *black beetle*

R·usse m, **R·ussin** f *Russian* **r·ussisch** n *Russian* ‖ ~er Bauer *moujik* ‖ ~-japanisch [a] *Russo-Japanese* (*war*) **R·ußland** [n] *Russia*

R·üssel m ~s/~ (v Schwein) *snout* ‖ (v Elefanten, Tapir) *trunk* ‖ ⟨ent⟩ *proboscis* **≗förmig** a *trunk-shaped* **~käfer** m *weevil* **~tiere** n pl *proboscidians* pl | **≗ig** a *snouted*, *trunk-shaped*

Rußni·ake m *Russniak*

R·üst- ~anker m *sheet-anchor* **~balken** m *put-log* **~baum** m *scaffolding-tree* **~gewicht** n ⟨aero⟩ *structural weight* **~haken** m ⟨hist⟩ *lance-rest* **~haus** n *arsenal* **~holz** n (*wooden*) *prop* ‖ ⟨mar⟩ *shore* **~kammer** f *armoury* **~loch** n *beam-hole* **~material** n *scaffolding* **~knappe** m, **~meister** m *armourer* **~platz** m *place of arms* **~seil** n ⟨mar⟩ *shroud* **~stange** f *scaffolding-pole*; (kurz) *putlog*, (lang) *ledger* **~tag** m *eve* (*of a feast*) **~woche** f *holy week* **~zeit** f *time of recreation*, *holidays* pl **~zeug** n (Rüstung) *armour*; *panoply* ⟨a. fig⟩ ‖ (⟨mil⟩ *accoutrement* ‖ (Werkzeug) (*set of*) *tools* ‖ ⟨fig⟩ *bastion*; stattliches ~ *panoply* (*of rights*) ‖ ⟨fig⟩ (Ausstattung) (a. geistiges ~) *equipment* ‖ *plant* ‖ ⟨bib⟩ auserwähltes ~ *chosen vessel* (*of the Lord*) | °⟨sex⟩ *gear* **R·üste 1.** f ~/~n *roost*, *rest* ‖ die Sonne, der Tag, das Jahr geht zur ~ *the sun is setting*; *the end of the day*, *year is approaching*; → Rast **2.** ⟨mar⟩ *chain-wale*, *channel* **r·üsten I.** vt [h] *to prepare*; *provide* (*a meal*); *lay* (*the table*) ‖ ein Haus ~ *to raise scaffolding for a house* ‖ ⟨mil⟩ *to arm*, *equip*, *mobilize* ‖ ⟨mar⟩ *to fit out*, *to equip* ‖ ⟨fig⟩ f alle Fälle gerüstet *armed at all points* ‖ ⟨fig⟩ gerüstet ⟨a.⟩ *ready* **II.** vi [h] & sich ~ *to prepare*, *to get ready* (auf, zu *for*) ‖ *to lay o.s. out* (*for Xmas*) ‖ ⟨mil⟩ *to mobilize*; *to arm* (*o.s.*) **R·üster** m ~s/~ (Schuh≗) *patch* ‖ ⟨aero⟩ *rigger* **r·üstig** a *stout*, *vigorous*, *robust*; *able-bodied*) ‖ *hale* (*and hearty*) ‖ ⟨fam⟩ *lusty*, *spry* ‖ f sein Alter sehr ~ *well preserved* ‖ (schnell) *quick*, *alert*, *nimble* | **≗keit** f *vigour*, *stoutness*, *strength*, *haleness*, etc **R·üstung** f ~/~en **1.** [abstr] *preparation* ‖ ⟨mil⟩ *equipment* ‖ *armament* ⟨a. psych⟩ ‖ *mobilization* **2.** [konkr] (Harnisch) *armour* (⟨a. fig⟩ *his moral a.*); in prächtiger ~ *clad in shining a.*; volle ~ *panoply* (*of war*) (a. modern) ‖ ⟨fig⟩ *implements*, *utensils*; ⟨mar⟩ *tackling* ‖ ⟨arch⟩ *scaffold*(*ing*) ‖ ⟨min⟩ *light timbering* **~sapparat** m ⟨Am⟩ *Supply Priorities & Allocations Board* (1941) **~sbetrieb** m *war factory*; *arms* od *armament* od *munitions works* ‖ ⟨aero⟩ *aircraft plant* **~sindustrie** f *armaments industry* **~sminister** m *M. of M.s* **~sprogramm** n *defence pr.* **~srennen** n *arm*(*ament*)*s race* **~swerk** = ~sbetrieb **~szentrum** m *arms centre*

R·üster f ~/~n ⟨bot⟩ *elm* ‖ Berg≗ *wych-elm*

R·ustika f ~/ *rustic work*; ⟨typ⟩ *r. capitals*

R·ute f ~/~n **A. 1.** *rod*, *verge*, *wand*, *twig*, *switch*, *birch* → Wünschel≗ **2.** ⟨hunt, zoo⟩ *brush*, *tail*; (of hound) *stern* **3.** ⟨anat, vet⟩ *pizzle* | °⟨sex⟩ *rod*, *horny*, *pizzle* **4.** (Maß) *perch*, *pole*, *rood* **B.** die ~ bek *to get the rod* ‖ der ~ entwachsen *too old to be whipped* ‖ *to rule with a rod of iron* ‖ e–m (sich selbst) e–e ~ binden *to have a rod in pickle for a p* (*to make a rod for one's own back*) ‖ jdm die ~ *or* etw mit der ~ geben *to whip*, *birch*, *flog*, ⟨Am⟩ *to switch a p*; *to give a p a whipping* ‖ ⟨bib⟩ wer die ~ spart, verzieht das Kind *spare the rod and spoil the child* **R·uten- ~bündel** n *bundle of rods* ‖ (des Liktors) *fasces* pl L **~gänger** m *dowser* **~hieb**, **~streich** m *lash* od *stroke with a rod* **~schwinger** m ⟨school⟩ *wielder of the cane*

Ruth·ene m, **Ruth·enin** f *Ruthenian* **Ruth·enien** n *Ruthenia* **ruth·enisch** a *Ruthenian*

Rutsch m ~es/~e **A. 1.** *glide*, *slide*; *slip* (*of the earth*), *landslip* ‖ ⟨geol⟩ *creep* **2.** ⟨fam⟩ (kl Reise) *trip*; guten ~! *a happy New Year to you*! **B.** im ~ *in a twinkling* ‖ in einem ~ *in one go* **~bahn** f ⟨rail⟩ *switchback* ‖ *slide* ‖ (*water-*)*chute* ‖ (*fire-*)*chute* **~fläche** f ⟨geol⟩ = Harnisch 2. a. **~kupp(e)lung** f *slipping-clutch*; die ~ einschalten *to slip the cl.* **~partie** f *slide* ‖ ⟨fam⟩ *little trip* **≗sicher** a *skid-proof* **R·utsche** f ~/~n *slide*; *chute*; *shoot* ‖ (Kohlen≗) *hurry* **r·utschen I.** vi [s] **1.** *to glide*, *slide*, *slip*, *slither* ‖ ⟨mot, cycl⟩ *to skid*; *the brake* (rutscht) *will not hold*, *the chutch is slipping*; ⟨met⟩ *to sink* | *the necktie has slipped up* (in die Höhe) ‖ ~ l *to slide* (*wood*) ‖ das Essen will nicht ~ *I am not able to swallow my food* ‖ vor jdm auf den Knien ~ *to crawl on one's knees before a p* ‖ er muß erst auf den Knien gerutscht k *he must first go down on his knees* **2.** ⟨fig, fam⟩ aufs Land ~ *to pay a flying visit to the country* ‖ die S rutscht *the matter is making headway* **II.** ins ≗ k *to slither* ‖ ⟨fig⟩ er ist ins ≗ gek *he is slipping downwards* ‖ ⟨mot⟩ *skid*

R·üttel- ~beton m *vibrated concrete* **~fischer** m ⟨orn⟩ *ceryle* **~herd** m ⟨met⟩ *percussion frame* **~meister** m (Sekt) *shaker* **~sieb** n *vibrating sieve* **~stroh** n *litter* **r·ütteln** vt/i [h] *to shake* (*up*), *to toss* (*up*) ‖ (leicht) *to jiggle*, *joggle* ‖ *to winnow*, *sift* (*corn*) ‖ e–n aus dem Schlafe ~ *to rouse a p by shaking* ‖ ⟨fig⟩ ein gerütteltes Maß (voll) *full measure*; *a generous portion* (*of*) | (v Vögeln) *to hang*, *hover* (*in the air*) ‖ (v Wagen) *to jog*, *jolt* [vt/i] | **~ an** *to rattle at* (*a door* etc) ‖ ⟨fig⟩ *to attack*, *undermine* ‖ *to throw doubt on* ‖ *to upset the existing order* ‖ daran ist nicht zu ~ *that is unalterable*; *that is a well established fact*; ..! *I will not permit any modifications* **R·üttler** m ~s/~ ⟨tech⟩ *vibrator*

S

S, s [n] ~/~ *S*, *s* ‖ °das gr S [es] (Syphilis) ⟨fam⟩ *the pip* ‖ mach s-s! [s s] (z Kind) *do number one*! **S.-A.-Mann** m ⟨nazi⟩ *storm-trooper* **S-Haken** m *ess* **S-Kurve** f ⟨mot⟩ *S-curve*, *double corner*, (scharfe) *d. haipin*(*-bend*) SS(-Mann) f *body-guard*

's = es ‖ **..s**: fürs = für das, ins = in das

Saal m ~(e)s/Säle *hall* ‖ (Empfangszimmer) *drawing-room* ‖ (Kranken≗) *ward* ‖ (Operations-≗) *operating theatre* ‖ Speise- etc ≗ *dining-* etc *room* ‖ (Tanz≗) *ball-room* ‖ (Vor≗) *entrance hall* ‖ (Vorlesungs≗) *lecture-room* **~beleuchtung** f ⟨theat etc⟩ *house lights* pl **~diener** m *usher* **~tochter** f Sw = Kellnerin

S·aale f ⟨Ger⟩ (Nebenfluß der Elbe)

Saar f ⟨Ger⟩ **1.** (Fluß) **2.** = ~land **~br·ücken**

n ⟨Ger⟩ (Stadt) **~land** n *Saar district*

Saat f ~/~en **A. 1.** (das Säen) *sowing* (*the seed*) **2.** *seed* (*s.*) **3.** (junges Getreide) *green corn, standing crops* pl **4.** (Ernte) *crop* **B.** die ~ in die Erde bringen *to s. the land* ‖ die ~ geht auf *the young crops are coming up*, ⟨fig⟩ *the results are beginning to make themselves felt* ‖ die ~ steht gut *the crops look well* ‖ in ~ schießen *to run to s.* **~beize** f *dressing* **~bestellung** f *sowing* **~egge** f *s.-harrow* **~feld** n *field sown with corn, corn-field* **~gans** f ⟨orn⟩ *bean-goose* **~gut** n *seed(-corn)*; als ~ zurückhalten *to keep as* od *for s.* **|** ~beize [f] *s. desinfection*; ~hammer [m] ⟨for⟩ *dibble-mallet* **~huhn** n *golden plover* **~kartoffeln** f pl *s. potatoes* **~korn** n *s.-corn* **~krähe** f ⟨orn⟩ *rook* **~lerche** f ⟨orn⟩ *skylark* **~pflug** m *drilling-, s.ing-plough* **~reihe** f *drill* **~wechsel** m *rotation of the crops* **~wucherblume** f *yellow ox-eye daisy* **S·aaten-~anerkennung** f *seed certification* **~stand** m *condition of the* (*young*) *crops* **~standbericht** m *crop report* **s·äbar** a *sowable*

S·aba n ⟨bib⟩ (in S.-Arabien) *Sheba*

S·abbat m ~(e)s/~e *Sabbath*; ⟨ec, poet⟩ *Sunday, the Lord's day* ‖ den ~ heiligen (brechen) *to keep* (*break*) *the S.* **~feier** f *keeping the S.* **~jahr** n *Sabbatical year* **~ruhe** f *Sabbath* od *Sunday rest* **~schänder** m *Sabbath-breaker* **~schändung** f *breaking of the S.* **s·abbatlich** a *Sabbatarian*; *of the Sunday* **|** adv *on a Sabbath*, etc

S·abbel- ~fritze m, **~liese** f *babbler* **s·abbeln** vt/i [h] ⟨fam⟩ *to babble, drivel* **S·abber** m ~s/ *slaver, drivel* ⟨a. fig⟩ **~·ei** f *slavering* **~fritze** m, **~liese** f *slaverer, driveller* **s·abbern** vi [h] ⟨fam⟩ *to slaver, drivel* ‖ °~ Sie sich aus! *stop that drivelling talk*

S·äbel m ~s/~ *sabre, sword* ‖ ⟨Ger fenc⟩ *basket-handled sabre* ‖ krummer ~ *falchion, scimitar* ‖ (blank *bare*; ziehen *to draw*, zücken *to flourish*) ‖ mit dem ~ rasseln *to rattle one's s.d* ‖ (jdn) mit dem ~ hauen *to sabre* (*a p*) ‖ auf ~ fordern *to challenge to a duel with s.ds* **~beine** n pl *bow-legs* pl **≗beinig** a *bow-legged* **~duell** n *duel with s.ds* **~fechten** n *sabre fighting, s.d-play* **~fisch** m *s.d-fish* **~gefäß** n *sabre-hilt* **~halter** m *frog* **~herrschaft** f *s.d-law* **~hieb** m *sabre-cut* **~klinge** f *blade of a sabre* **~korb** m *knuckle-bow* **~koppel** n *sabre-belt* **~rasseln** n *rattling of s.ds*; *provocative chauvinism*; ⟨Am pol⟩ *big stick* **~raßler** m *chauvinist, jingo(ist), swashbuckler* **~scheide** f *sabre-sheath, scabbard* **~schnäbler** m ⟨orn⟩ *avocet* **~tasche** f *sabretache, frog* **~troddel** f *s.d-knot* **s·äbeln** vi/t [h] *to sabre* ‖ ⟨fig⟩ *to cut* od *carve awkwardly*

Sab·ine f ~/~n ⟨bot⟩ *savin*

†**Sab·iner** m, **~in** f (mittelital. Volk) **sab·inisch** a *Sabine* **Sab·inergebirge** n *Sabine Mountains*

Sabotage [–'tɑːʒə] f ~/ *sabotage, rattening* **|** ~trupp [m] *s. team* N **sabot·ieren** vt [h] *to s.*

Sachal·in n ⟨Russ⟩ (Insel) *Sakhalin*

Sa(c)char·in n ~(e)s/ *saccharine*

S·ach- ~angabe f *statement of facts* **~arrest** m *arrest of goods* **~aufnahme** f ⟨phot⟩ *object view* **~bearbeiter** m *p, official, clerk competent for a certain subject* od *department*; *appointed agent*; ⟨soc, med⟩ *case worker* **~begriff** m ⟨jur⟩ *conception* **~beschädigung** f *wilful destruction*; *damage to property* (vorsätzlich *malicious*) **~beweis** m *objective proof* **~bezüge** m pl *allowances* od *payment in kind* **~buch** n, ≗er [pl] *non-fiction* **≗dienlich** a *suitable, to the purpose*; *practical*; *proper*; *relevant*; *pertinent* (*to*) **~einlage** f *contribution not consisting of money* → Apport **~erklärung** f *definition* **~führer** m *appointed agent* od *representative* **~gedächtnis** n *memory for facts* **≗gemäß** a = –dienlich **≗gerecht** adv ~ beschlagen *soundly shod* (*horse*) **~gruppe** f *branch, line, department* **~güter** n pl *material goods* od *ths* **~katalog** m *catalogue raisonné* **~kenner** m, **~kundige** m [der ~, ein ~r] *expert, connoisseur* **~kenntnis** f *knowledge of the subject, experience, special* od *expert k.*; mit ~ *expertly*; °ein durch ~ ungetrübtes Urteil abgeben ⟨sl⟩ *to talk through one's hat* **~konto** n *real account* **~kunde** f *expertise* **≗kundig** a *experienced, versed, expert* **~lage** f *state of affairs* od *ths*; ⟨Am a.⟩ *lay of ths* ‖ wie die ~ ist *as matters are* ‖ er durchschaute die ~ *he saw how the land lay* **~leistung** f *payment* od *performance, service in kind* **~mangel** m *defect of quality* **~name** m *generic term* **~pfändung** f *attachment* **|** ~sverfahren [n] *a. proceedings* pl **~register** n *subject index*; *glossary* **≗reich** a *full of facts*; *copious* **~schaden** m; (ziviler) ~ *damage done to* (*civilian*) *property*; *material damage* **~umfang** m *range of subject matter* **~verhalt** m *bearings,* (*statement of*) *facts, circumstances* pl *of a case*; *factual situation*; wahrer ~ *actual state of affairs* ‖ den ~ darlegen *to explain how matters stand* ‖ Darlegung des ~s ⟨jur⟩ *brief* **~versicherung** f *property insurance* **~verständnis** n *knowledge of the subject, expert kn.*; *experience* **≗verständig** a *expert* **~verständige(r)** m *expert* (*in at, in*; [auf dem Gebiet] e–r S *on a th*); *authority, specialist* (*on*); ⟨Am sl⟩ *clackerjack* ‖ durch e–n ~n begutachten l *to expertize* ‖ ~ [pl] z Rate ziehen *to call in experts* **|** ~ngutachten [n] *expert opinion* **~walter** m ⟨jur⟩ *counsel, solicitor, attorney, legal adviser* **|** ~honorar [n] (*solicitor's*) *costs*; (*barrister's*) *fees*; *retainer* **~waltung** f *management, administration* **~wert** m *actual, true, real value*; ~e [pl] *capital goods* **~wort** n ⟨gram⟩ *common name, appellative* **~wörterbuch** n (*en*)*cyclopædia* **~zwang** m *compulsion by the object in question* **S·ache** f ~/~n **A. 1.** (Gegenstand) *thing, object*; ~n [pl] *material* **2.** (Angelegenheit) *matter, affair, object, concern* → Ding **3.** (Ereignis) *event*; das ist schon 'ne ~! *it's quite an e.!* ‖ (Tatsache) *fact, point* ‖ (Umstand) *circumstance* **4.** (Geschäft) *business, job*; zwecklose ~ *bad job* **5.** ⟨jur⟩ *action, case, lawsuit* **6. ~n** [pl] (Habseligkeiten) *ths, clothes, effects, belongings* pl; *furniture* ‖ (Gepäck) *luggage* ‖ (Güter) *goods* pl **7.** °⟨mot⟩ mit 80 (1000) ~n *sixty miles per* (*sc hour*), (⟨bes aero⟩ *full bore* [adv]) (*sc hour*) **8.** °[ell] (das ist) ~! *top stuff!* (*it's*) *all the go! the bee's knees! quite an event! nuts!*; *a honey, a peach, an eagle! that's It*; ⟨Am sl⟩ *hot stuff*; ⟨vulg⟩ *bit of fat!*; ⟨aero⟩ (Flugzeug, Leistung) *smashing job* **9.** °⟨sex⟩ *thing*; die ~ in die Hand nehmen und sehen, wie sie ausläuft °*to shake hands with an old friend* (urinieren) **B. [mit subst]** die ~ hat folgende Bewandtnis *the matter is as follows* ‖ in der Natur der ~ *in the nature of ths* ‖ den Hergang der ~ erzählen *to recount the course of events* ‖ das ist ~ des Herzens (Vertrauens) *that is an affair of the heart* (*a matter of confidence*) ‖ das ist e–e ~ von vielen Jahren .. *a work* od *matter of* ‖ es ist allein ~ der Regierung, wie .. *it is a matter for the government how they treat ..* ‖ ~ der Truppe selbst (*is a*) *unit responsibility* ‖ *it is a question of will* **C. [mit a]** abgekartete ~ *put-up job*, ⟨fam⟩ *regular plant* ‖ allerhand ~n *all kinds of ths* ‖ alte ~n [pl] *junk* ‖ das ist e–e andere ~ *that is another th,* (*it would be a different story*), *that's quite a new aspect*, ⟨Am⟩ *a different proposition* ‖ (ich weiß) noch ganz andere ~n .. *better ths than that* ‖ ausgemachte ~ *foregone conclusion* ‖ °bessere ~ z 15 ⟨fam⟩ *worth a guinea a box* ‖ bewegliche ~n *personal property* ‖ dumme ~ *silly business* ‖ k–e einfache ~ *not all plain sailing* ‖ das ist e–e fatale ~! *here's a job!* ‖ °e–e ganz faule ~ ⟨sl⟩ *a real bad egg* ‖ die ganze ~ *the whole business* ‖ mit jdm gemeinsame ~ m *to make common cause, to sail in the same boat with a p* ‖ ehrliche, gefährliche ~ *genuine, dangerous affair* ‖ gerechte, verzweifelte ~ *just, desperate matter* ‖ nur e–e geringfügige ~ *but a* *small point* || e–e gr ~ *quite an affair*; es ist k–e gr ~ (nicht d. Rede w.) *it's nothing* || e–e kinderleichte ~ *a boy's job* || k–e leichte ~ *no slight matter*, ⟨sl⟩ *no snap* || körperliche ~n *tangible property* || tolle ~! *absurd affair, nice goings-on!* || unverrichteter ~ heimkehren *to come home with empty hands* ⟨a. fig⟩ → A. 4. **D. [mit pron pers]** Denken ist nicht jedermanns ~ *it is not everybody who has the gift of reflexion* || das ist d–e ~ *that's your concern, business* (⟨fam⟩ *look-out*); *that is for you* (*to find out*); ⟨fam⟩ *that's your pigeon* (⟨sl⟩ *funeral*); *it's up to you* || du hast d–e ~ gut gemacht *you have done fine*; .. *done a good job*; kümmere dich um d–e ~n! *mind your own business*! || nicht m–e ~ ⟨fam⟩ *not my funeral* || s–e ~ gut, schlecht m *to acquit o.s. well, ill*; *to manage well* || s–e ~n packen *to pack up*; (heimlich) *to decamp* | das ist s–e ~ *that is his concern, affair, business, own look-out*; .. gerade .. *that just suits him*; .. nicht .. *he has no business to do that* || es ist nicht s–e ~ .. *he is not given to* (*drinking*), *it is not his way to do such a th* || s–e 7 ~n *his goods and chattels, all his belongings* | s–r ~ gewiß s *to feel sure about the matter, to know what one is about* || er trug s–e eigenen ~n vor *he played compositions* (*read poetry*, etc) *of his own* || s–e ~n zus halten *to keep one's belongings together* **E. [mit verb]** wenn er die ~ nur richtig **anfaßte** *if he would but play his cards well* || e–e ~ anhängig m *to take legal proceedings in a matter* || es als e–e ~ bezeichnen *to call it a th* || e–e ~ deichseln *to wangle a matter* || e–e ~ führen ⟨jur⟩ *to plead a cause* || ~n gibt's! *there are all sorts of ths under the sun* || die ~ geht noch schief *ths look bad* || jede ~ hat zwei Seiten *there are two sides to every question* || **mach** k–e ~n! *you don't say so*! || die ~ macht sich *the matter is progressing* || die ~n müssen zur Post *these ths must be posted* || e–e ~ in Angriff nehmen *to take a job on* || e–e ~ schmeißen *to pull a th off*; die ~ schm. *to do the trick* || die ~ schwebt *the matter is in abeyance* || darf ich wissen, wie die ~ **steht**? *may I see how the land lies*? || die ~ steht gut (schlecht) *the matter looks well* (*it's a bad outlook* [*for a p*]) || so steht die ~! *that's how matters stand*! || s–e ~n stehen gut *his affairs are going on well, he is doing well* || °⟨stud⟩ die ~ steigt *the matter is coming to a head* || s–e ~ auf nichts gestellt h *to let ths take their chance* || e–r ~ überdrüssig s *to be sick of a matter* || e–e ~ verfolgen *to push on an object* || die ~ **verhält** sich so *the matter stands thus* || e–e ~ verfechten *to defend a cause* || e–e ~ verlieren *to lose a case* || s–e ~ verstehen *to know one's business* od *job* | die ~ **ist** die, daß .. *the fact is that* .. || die ~ ist doch die, daß .. *the point is that* .. || A. 8. || das ist e–e ~ f sich *that's a th* od *matter for itself* **F. [mit prep]** sich **an** die ~ selbst halten *to keep to facts* || es ist etw Wahres an der ~ *there is a shred of truth in the matter*; .., was an der ~ ist *I must know what is the truth of the m.* | sich **aus** der ~ ziehen *to draw out of the affair*, vgl. F. in | **bei** der ~ bleiben *to keep* (stets *to stick*) *to the point* (od *business in hand*); ⟨fam⟩ *to sit tight*; nicht .. *to go* od *be woolgathering* || bei der ~ s *to pay attention to the matter in hand*; sei b. d. ~! *put your mind to it*!; (*a woman is always much more single-minded about it*); nicht .. *to be absent-minded*; mit Leib u Seele .. *to be heart and soul in a th*; *his full heart was in the game* | **für** e–e gute ~ kämpfen *to fight for a good object* | hinter der ganzen ~ stecken *to be at the bottom of the matter* | nichts **mit** der ~ zu tun h *to have nothing to do with the subject* od *matter* || wie steht's mit der ~? *how are matters getting on*? | **in** ~n des Geschmackes *in matters of taste*; .. läßt sich nicht streiten *tastes differ* || ⟨jur⟩ in ~n A gegen B *in re* (od *the case, lawsuit*) *A versus B* || er half ihm in die ~n *he helped him to get dressed* || sich in fremde ~n mischen *to meddle* od *interfere with other people's affairs* || in e–r ~ klar sehen *to see clear into a matter* | **über** der ~ stehend *above concern with the th* | es steht schlecht **um** die ~ *the affair is in an unsatisfactory state* | **von** der ~ abschweifen *to stray from the subject* | aus Liebe **zur** ~ *for the sake of the cause* || zur ~! (*come* od *keep*) *to the point* (od *business*)!; ⟨parl⟩ *Question*! || das gehört nicht zur ~ *that has nothing to do with it*; *that's beside the question* || (nicht) zur ~ gehörig [a] (*ir*)*relevant*; [adv] *to* (*off*) *the point* || zur ~ k *to come to the basic essentials, to facts, to the point*, ⟨fam⟩ *to get down to business*, ⟨fam a.⟩ *brass-tacks*, ⟨Am a.⟩ *to get down to cases* || etw zu e–r besonderen ~ m *to make a point of a th* || das tut nichts zur ~ *that's irrelevant, it is of little consequence* **S·ächelchen** n ~s/~ *little thing* **S·achenrecht** n ⟨jur⟩ *law of real property* **s·achlich I.** [a] *pertinent, relevant* || *material* (*difference, aim, motive*) || ⟨arch⟩ *functional*; ~es Bauen *practical building* || *objective, non-personal, impersonal, unbiassed* (*opinion*); *detached* (*manner of looking at ths*); streng ~ *realistic* | (P) *matter-of-fact* || ⟨jur⟩ *real* | ~ bleiben *to keep to the subject* **II.** [adv] *to the point* || (*to treat*) *practically* || ~ auswerten *to evaluate soberly* || ich habe ~ nichts einzuwenden *I have no positive* od *essential objections to raise* || ~ zuständig s ⟨jur⟩ *to have jurisdiction ratione material* (*irrespective of* ..) **III.** das ≃-Zweckmäßige ⟨arch⟩ *objective fitness* **s·ächlich** a ⟨gram⟩ *neuter* (*gender, noun*) **S·achlichkeit** f ~/ *reality, essentiality, objectivity, impartiality, detachment* || (*business-minded*) *matter-of-factness* || ⟨arch⟩ *utility, practicality* || *appositeness* || ⟨arts⟩ die neue ~ *neo-* od *modern objectivity* od *functionalism*; ⟨Am fam⟩ *debunking*

Sachs m ~es/~e ⟨hist⟩ *knife* | **~e** m ~n/~n, ≃**in** f ~/~nen f *Saxon, Saxonwoman* | **~en** n *Saxony*; (†preußische) Provinz ~ *Prussian Saxony* †~-Altenburg [n] *Saxe-Altenburg*; †~-Coburg und Gotha [n] *Saxe-Coburg-Gotha*; †~-M·einingen [n] *Saxe-Meiningen*; †~-Weimar(-Eisenach) [n] *Saxe-Weimar*; S·ächsische Schweiz [f] *Saxon Switzerland*

s·acht(e) [a] *soft* (*steps*); *cautious* (*hands*) || *slow, gentle* (*movement*) || (geräuschlos) *quiet* | [adv] (*to walk*) *softly* || (*to handle*) *gingerly, cautiously* || *gently* (*rising roads*) || ~, ~! *well, well*; *there, there*; *come, come*; *steady*; *gently*; *gently does it* || nur man *or* immer ~! *help*!, *go easy*! *don't flurry y.s.* || immer ~ mit die [statt: den] jungen [P]ferde[n] ⟨fig⟩ *hold your horse*(*s*)! *draw it mild*! *help*!

S·ack m ~(e)s/≃e **A. 1.** *sack, bag* || ≃e voll Geld *pots of m.* || ein ~ (voll) Kohlen *a sack*(*ful*) *of coal* || vier ~ .. *four sacks of* .. **2.** ⟨fam⟩: *pocket, purse* **3.** *pucker* (*in a dress*) **4.** Aal~ *eel-trap* || Fuß~ *foot-muff* || ⟨mil⟩ Futter~ *wallet* || ⟨mar⟩ Kleider≃ *kit* || Sand≃ *sandbag* || Zelt≃ *sleeping-bag* **5.** (Maß = 280 Pfd) *pack* (*of wool*) **6.** *budget* (*of news*) **7.** ⟨anat, zoo⟩ *sac* **8.** ⟨mil⟩ = Ausbeulung **B.** **(auf)** den ~ schlagen u den Esel meinen *to strike one p through another* | **aus** → Katze | die Faust **im** ~ ballen *to bear a secret grudge against a p* || in ~ u Asche (gehen etc) (*to mourn*, etc) *in sackcloth and ashes* || etw im ~ h *to hold sth securely* || Lachen u Weinen in einem ~ h *to laugh and cry in one breath* || e–n im ~ h *to hold a p in one's clutches* || er redet e–n in den ~ *he talks nineteen to the dozen* || ⟨fig⟩ alles in einen ~ stecken *to bulk everything in one class* || jdn in den ~ stecken *to outwit, overmatch a p, to get the better of a p*; .. zweimal .. *to be worth two of a p* || in ≃e verladen *to sack up* || ihr habt wohl ≃e vor der Tür! *were you born in a barn*? | **mit** ~ u Pack (*with*) *bag and baggage*, (*to throw a p out*) *neck and crop* || alles zus mit ~ u P. *the whole th, lock,* *stock and barrel* **C.** schlafen **wie** ein ~ .. *like a top* od *log* ‖ voll wie ein ~ *drunk as a lord* | ⟨prov⟩ viele ~̊e sind des Esels Tod *it's the last straw that breaks the camel's back* **~̊artig** a *baggy* **~bahnhof** m ⟨rail⟩ *terminus* **~band** n, **~bändel** n *sack-string, purse-string* **~flug** m ⟨aero⟩ *stalling flight* | ~geschwindigkeit [f] *st. speed* **~garn** n *sack-thread* **~gasse** f *cul-de-sac* Fr; *blind alley*; *dead-end street*, ⟨fig a.⟩ *side-track* ‖ ⟨fig⟩ in e–e ~ geraten *to come to a dead-end, to reach a dead-lock* ‖ ⟨fig⟩: (*a way out of the*) *impasse*; jdn in e–e ~ treiben *to corner a p* **~geschwulst** n ⟨path⟩ *cyst* **~hüpfen** n *sack-race* **~jackett** n *loose jacket* **~karre** f *trundle, track* **~kleid** n ⟨tail⟩ *sheath dress* **~landung** f ⟨aero⟩ *pancake landing* **~leinwand** f *sack-cloth, sacking* **~nadel** f *packing-needle* **~netz** n *bag-net* **~pfeife** f *bagpipe* | ~nmelodie [f] *pibroch* **~pfeifer** m *bagpiper* **~rohr** n *closed-end pipe* **~rutsche** f *sack shooter* **~̊siedegrob** a *exceedingly rude* **~spinner** m ⟨ent⟩ *bagworm* **~träger** m *sack-heaver* ‖ ⟨fig⟩ *ass* ‖ harmloser ~ *silly prick* ‖ ein Esel schilt den andern ~ *the pot calls the kettle black(-arse)* | ⟨ent⟩ *case-bearer moth* (*coleophoridae*) **~tuch** n *sack-cloth, sacking* ‖ (grobes indisches) *gunny* ‖ ⟨fam & dial⟩ *hanky* (*pocket-handkerchief*) **~̊weise** adv *by the bag* **~zwilch** m *bagging, sacking* **~zwirn** m *sack-twine* **S·äckchen** n ~s/~ *little bag* ‖ ⟨scient⟩ *saccule* **S·äckel** m ~s/~ *purse* ‖ ⟨übtr⟩ *treasury* **~wart** m *treasurer* **s·acken** vt [h] **1.** *to bag* ‖ *to put into sacks* ‖ *to pocket* | sich ~ *to* (*form a*) *bag, to bulge out, to be baggy* ‖ sich [dat] die Tasche voll~ *to cram one's pocket* ‖ sich [acc] ([dat] den Wanst) voll~ *to fill one's belly* **2.** vi [s] (sinken) (sich ~) *to sink, give way, sag* ‖ ⟨arch⟩ *to settle*; dazu: *settling, settlement* ‖ ⟨mar, arch⟩ *to subside* ‖ ⟨mar⟩ *to founder*; achteraus ~ *to drop astern* **s·äcken** vt [h] *to drown in a sack*

sackerl·ot! sackerm·ent! *by Jove! the deuce! bother(ation)* **~̊er** m ~s/~ *devil of a fellow*

Sacram·ento (River) m (in Kalifornien)

Sadduz·äer m ~s/~ *Sadducee* **s-äisch** *-cean*

S·adebaum m ⟨bot⟩ *savin-tree*

Sä(e)- **~mann** m *sower* **~maschine** f *sowing-machine, drill* **~pflug** m *drill-plough* **~tuch** n *seed-cloth, seed-bag* **~zeit** f *sowing-time* **s·äen** vt/i [h] *to sow* (*corn*) (⟨a. fig⟩ *discord, hatred*, etc) ‖ *to seed* (*the land*) ‖ mit der Hand *to sow broadcast* ‖ mit der Maschine *to drill, dibble* ‖ gesät *grown from seed* ‖ wie gesät *lying thickly* ‖ dünn gesät *scarce, sparse*

Safe [seif] m & n ~s/~s *safe, strong-room*

Saffi·an m ~(e)s/~e *Morocco(-leather)* **~(auf)bereitung** f *morocco-dressing* **~einband** m ⟨bookb⟩ *m.-binding* **~papier** n *m.-paper*

Safl·or m ~(e)s/ ⟨bot⟩ *safflower*

S·afran m ~(e)s/ ⟨bot, tech⟩ *saffron* ‖ ⟨bot⟩ *crocus* **~̊farben, ~̊gelb** a *saffron(-coloured), saffrony*

Saft m ~(e)s/~̊e **A. 1.** (*Obst*~̊) *juice* (*grape-, lemon-* etc *j.*) ‖ (eingekochter) *syrup* **2.** ⟨bot⟩ *sap* **3.** (des Fleisches) *gravy* **4.** ⟨physiol hist⟩ *humour* **5.** °⟨sex⟩ *spunk* **6.** °⟨aero⟩ (Benzin) *gravy* **7.** °⟨el⟩ (Strom) ⟨sl⟩ *juice* **B.** im ~ *in sap* ‖ voll ~ *juicy, succulent* | ⟨fig⟩ ohne ~ u Kraft *without strength or flavour, insipid, marrowless, stale* ‖ im eigenen ~ ⟨cul⟩ *with gravy*; °.. schmoren ⟨fig⟩ *to stew in one's own juice* **~abscheider** m ⟨cul⟩ *catchall* **~beere** f *acinus* **~behälter** m ⟨bot⟩ *nectary, honey-cub* **~braun** n ⟨tech⟩ *soluble brown* **~farbe** f *sap-colour* **~̊führend** a *succiferous* **~fülle** f *juiciness* ‖ ⟨bot⟩ *abundance of sap* **~̊grün** a *sap-green* **~̊los** a *juiceless* ‖ ⟨bot⟩ *sapless* ‖ ⟨fig⟩ *pithless, insipid, stale*; *wishy-washy*, ⟨Am⟩ *pussyfoot* (*soup*) **~losigkeit** f *juicelessness* ‖ *saplessness* ‖ ⟨fig⟩ *pithlessness, insipidity* **~mischung** f ⟨med hist⟩ alte, fehlerhafte ~ *dyscrasy, -sia* **~schinken** m *juice ham* **~̊reich, ~̊strotzend, ~̊voll** a *juicy, rich in juice, succulent* **~zeit** f *spring-time* **s·aftig** [a] *juicy, succulent* (*pear*) ‖ ⟨bot⟩ *sappy, succulent* (*tree*); *lush* (*plant, grass*) | [adv] ~ süß *meltingly sweet* | ⟨fig fam⟩ *high-seasoned, spicy, fruity, juicy* (*joke*) ‖ *salty, fruity* (*remark*) ‖ *luscious* (*style*); ⟨Am⟩ *husky* (*smack*) **~̊keit** f ~/ *juiciness, succulence* ‖ *sappiness* ‖ *spiciness* ‖ *lusciousness*

S·age f ~/~n *fable, myth* ‖ (altnordische) *saga* ‖ ⟨mst rel⟩ *legend* ‖ Helden~̊ *heroic story* ‖ (Überlieferung) *tradition* ‖ es geht die ~ *it is rumoured, the story goes, people say, they say* (*that*) → ~̊n

S·äge f ~/~n (→ ~̊n) *saw*; Ast~̊, Baum~̊ *pruning s.*; Band~̊ *band s.*; Blatt~̊ *pad s.*; Brett~̊ *pitsaw*; Bügel~̊ *bow s.*; Fuchsschwanz~̊ *hand s.*; Kapp~̊ *oscillating s.*; Kreis~̊ *circular s.*; Laub~̊ *fret s.*; Loch~̊ *lock saw*; Mauer~̊ *stone saw*; Metall~̊ *hack saw*; Quer~̊, Trumm~̊ *cross-cut saw*; Schrot~̊ *ripping saw* **~bank** f *saw bench* **~barsch** m ⟨ich⟩ *squirrel-fish* **~blatt** n *saw-blade* (mit enger Zahnteilung *fine pitch blade*) **~bock** m *sawing-jack, saw-horse*; *buck* **~dach** n *shed-roof* **~fisch** m *saw-fish* **~̊förmig** a ⟨scient⟩ *serrate*; ~ gezähnt *dentate-s.e* ‖ ~er Schnabel ⟨orn⟩ *saw-bill* **~gatter, ~gestell** n *saw frame* **~grube** f *sawpit* **~maschine** f *sawing-machine, bench-saw* **~mehl** n *sawdust* **~messer** n *serrated knife* **~mühle** f *saw-mill* **~schlitten** m *travel(l)er* **~späne** m pl *scobs, shavings* **~werk** n *sawmill*; ⟨Am⟩ *lumber mill* ‖ ⟨fort⟩ *indented line* **~zähne** m pl *sawteeth* pl **~̊zähnig** a ⟨bot⟩ *serrate(d)*

s·agen vt/i [h] **A. 1.** (e–m etw) *to say* (*sth to a p*) (mechanisch *automatically*; sanft *blandly*); (mitteilen) *to tell* (*a p sth*) **2.** (ausdrücken, meinen) *to express, mean* **3.** (behaupten) *to declare, say* (daß *that*) **4.** (zugeben) *to admit* **5.** (e–m befehlen) *to order a p about* ‖ (etw bestimmen) *to say* **6.** (bedeuten) *to mean* ‖ (v Bedeutung s) *to signify* **7.** (schätzungsweise) [eingeschoben] ~ wir 20 (*let's*) *say 20*; *say* od *perhaps* (*ten times*) **8.** (beteuernd) sage u schreibe *actually*; *just imagine*! → F. **9.** [dat] (Eindruck m) *to make impression on* **10.** (raten) *to advise a p* (*to come*) **B.** *Homer says* ‖ *my heart tells me that* .. | er sagte: „Ja." *he said*: "*Yes.*", *he answered in the affirmative* ‖ auf e–e Bitte Nein ~ *to refuse a request* ‖ ich sage: du warst dort! *I say you were there* ‖ sag mal, kennst du ihn? *tell me if you know him*; ⟨vulg⟩ [interpolated] nun, sag ich, .. *well, says I*, .. ‖ er sagte, er habe *he said that he had* ‖ sie ~ (sagten) ihm, es sei so *they tell* (*told*) *him it is* (*was*) *so* ‖ er sagte, ich solle .. *he told me I should wire*, ⟨Am⟩ *he said to wire* ‖ ~, daß *to convey that* ..; der Name sagt gar nichts .. *conveys nothing* ‖ ~ Sie ihm, daß er es tun soll *tell him to do it* | ich sage **nicht,** daß *I don't want to say that* .. | **sich ~, daß** *to tell o.s. that* ..; *to reflect that* ..; er s–te sich, die Zeit sei noch nicht gek *he felt time had not yet come* | | sag, wer du bist *tell me who you are* | **man** sagt, es sei so *they say* (*that*) *it is so* | **das** sagt viel *that's saying plenty* od *a lot* | *sth tells me that* .. **C. 1.** niemandem wurde **gesagt** *none were told* (*that* ..) ‖ hast du etw g.? ⟨euph⟩ (= gefurzt) *did you make a noise*? es ist nicht g. .. *that does not mean* (*that he will not return*), *I do not say* (*that* ..) ‖ es ist nicht zu viel g., daß *it is not saying too much to declare that* ..; ich hab es doch gleich g. *didn't I tell you*? *you know I told you* | g., getan *no sooner said than done*; *adapting* od *suiting his action to his word* od *text* ‖ leichter g. als getan *easier said than done* | aus dem G.en folgt *from what has been said it follows* (*that*) **D. 1. jdm Dank** ~ *to thank a p* ‖ das Gegenteil ~ v *to contradict* ‖ jdm Grobheiten ~ *to abuse a p* ‖ s–e Gründe ~ *to give one's reasons* ‖ jdm s–e Meinung ~ *to give a p a piece of one's mind* ‖ (jdm) Lebewohl (gute Nacht) ~ *to bid* (*a p*) *good-bye* (*good night*), *to say farewell* (*g. n.*) || jdm Schmeicheleien ~ *to flatter a p* || die (volle) **Wahrheit** ~ *to tell, speak the* (*plain*) *truth* || (du darfst) *k–m* ein Wort ~! *don't say a word to anybody*; *you must not tell anybody anything* **2. das** ~ Sie! (aber ..) ⟨fam⟩ *says you*!; **das** ~ Sie **mir**! **wem** ~ Sie das?! das brauchen Sie mir nicht z ~! *you're telling me*! *don't tell me*! | ~ Sie das nicht! *don't make any mistake*! || das (*or* so etw) sagt man nicht *you shouldn't say such a th, that's not the proper th to say* || das sagt mir (gar) nichts *that's meaningless to me* | er sagte **es** mir *he told me* (*of it*) [NB. nur so!] || ich sag's, wie's ist *I call a spade a spade, I don't mince matters* | sag's nur, wenn du mich brauchst *please feel free to holler* | man sagte **ihn** tot *he was said to be dead* | (gar) **nichts** ~ *to make no comment, to keep o.s. to o.s.* | **was** Sie nicht ~ *you don't say so*!; *I say*! *well, really*! || was sagte ich noch? *what was I saying*? **E. zu ~ haben**: *he had nothing to say* (*in his own house*) || *if I had anything to say in the matter* || wenig oder nichts z ~ h in *to have little or no say in* (*a matter*) | .. bei uns .. *he has no influence with us* || .., was man z ~ hatte *to have said one's say* || Sie h mir gar nichts z ~ *I won't be ordered about by you* | **das** *or* **es**, hat nichts z ~ *that means nothing, it is of no consequence, it is not dangerous*; *it doesn't matter* od *signify*; *never mind*! | .. das **kann** man wohl ~ *you may well say so*; *I should just think so*! *I dare say*! || das kann ich dir ~! *I'm telling you*! *I can tell you*! || (*she had a good heart*) *he could tell that* || Sie können *or* w ~, was Sie wollen *you won't convince me whatever you say* || .., das kann man nicht anders ~ *I must admit* (*that he was generous*) || (man könnte es vielleicht) so ~ .. *put it this way* | jdm ~ **lassen** *to send a p word* od *a message* (*that*) || ich ließ ihm ~ *I had him told* (*that*) | wir h uns ~ l *we have heard* (*that*); so h wir .. *we have been told so* | **laß** dir (offen) v mir ~ *take it* (*straight*) *from me* || das l Sie sich gesagt s! *take it from me*! *take my word for it*! *let it be a warning to you*! *believe me*! *take the hint*! ⟨fam⟩ *get it straight*! *put that in your pipe and smoke it*! | das Publikum möge sich gesagt s l *let the public be told* od *reminded* | er läßt sich [dat] nichts ~ *he won't listen to reason, you can't tell him a th, he will listen to no* (*advice* od) *one* || er läßt es sich nicht zweimal ~ *he doesn't wait to be told a second time* | **es** läßt sich nicht ~ *it is inexpressible, beyond words, there is no saying* || es läßt sich nichts dagegen ~ *there is no objection to it* || es läßt sich viel ~ f *there is a case for* | das **muß** ich ~ *indeed*!, *well*!, *I declare*, (*I don't know*) || das muß man ~ *that must be admitted* || Sie müssen sich [dat] ~, daß *you must realize that* .. || das mußte einmal gesagt w *it was high time to say that* | man pflegte z ~ *it used to be said* | z ~ **sein**: es ist nicht z ~, wie ich .. *I can hardly express how I* ..; *there is no telling* (*if, when*) | da **soll** nun e–r ~ *you never can tell*; *there, who will say* (*that* ..); wie soll ich ~? *how shall I put it*? | ~ **wollen** *to mean* (*to say*) (mit *by*, daß *that*); wollen Sie damit ~ ..? *do you suggest by that* ..?; will das ~ ..? *does that suggest* ..? || was wollte ich noch ~? ⟨fam⟩ *where was I*? || was ich ~ wollte ..: *I was going to say* .. || ⟨Am⟩ *come to think of it* ..; .. noch .. *as I was about to say* || das wollte ich eben ~ *that's just what I* .. || ich wollte bloß ~ .. *all I wanted to say was* .. || jetzt sehe ich, was Sie ~ wollen *now I see your point* || (*that was not my point*) || als wenn er ~ wollte (*he* ..) *as much as to say* | ich will **nicht** gerade ~ *I won't say as much as that*; *I don't intend to imply* (*that*) || das will ich nicht gesagt h *I didn't mean that* || ich will nichts gesagt h *don't tell anybody I said so, I don't want to imply anything* | **das** will nichts ~ *that's nothing, there is n. in that* || das will viel ~ *that is saying a lot* od *a great deal* || ⟨fam⟩ und das will was ~ *that makes all the difference* **F. [parenthetic]** → A. 7. || ich **kann** sogar ~ *I might even venture to say* || hübsch, ich **möchte** fast ~ schön *pretty, I might as well say b.* || .., ich **wollte** ~, .. *or rather* | erfreut, **was** sage ich, begeistert .., *nay I may say* .. || **wenn** ich so ~ darf *if I may say so, if I may so express m.s.* || **wie** man sagt *or* z ~ pflegt *as the saying is* || sie hat so was – wie soll ich ~ *she has a certain air* || – wie sagt man? – *we should be–how do you say it–thrown out* || .. das mindeste **zu** ~ *to say the least of it*, (*he* ..) || mit Verlaub z ~ *begging your pardon*; *if I may say so*; *with due deference to you* || sozu~ *so to speak*; *as it were* | beiläufig **gesagt** *by the by* || kurz g–t *to cut a long story short* || offen g–t *to put it plainly*; *in plain language* || richtiger g–t *properly* (od *more exactly*) *speaking* || unter uns g–t *between you and me* || im Vertrauen g–t *in confidence* || zu unserer Schande sei es g–t *I must confess that we* .. || **es** wird v ihm g–t *it is said of him, he is said* (daß *to* ..) **G. [mit adv]** ich hätte **bald** etw gesagt *I wasn't far off saying sth* || ich hatte es **beinahe** g–t *I had it on the tip of my tongue* || das ist wirklich **genug** g–t *that is putting it very clearly* || das ist **leicht** g–t u schwer getan *easier said than done* || er sagt nur **so** *he doesn't mean it really*; *it's just his way of putting it* || das kann ich nicht **vorher** ~ *I can't say in advance* || wenn Sie es nur e–n Tag vorher ~ *even at a day's notice* || **wie** ich Ihnen sage *as I tell you* || wie g–t *as I* (*have already*) *said* **H. [mit prep]** er weiß **auf** alles etw z ~ *he has an answer ready to everything* | **für** etw gut ~ *to be security* od *to go bail for a th* || was man f (gegen) das Stück ~ kann *the case for* (*against*) *the play is* (*that* ..) || dagegen ist nichts z ~ *there is no gain-saying that* | **ins** Gesicht ~ *to tell* (*a p*) *to his face* || jdm etw ins Ohr ~ *to whisper sth in a p's ear* || was wollen Sie da**mit** ~? *what do you mean to say by that*? || damit ist nichts g–t *that means nothing* | **über** jdn z ~ h *to have authority over a p* || darüber wäre viel z ~ *there is much to be said about that* | ich kann dasselbe **von** mir ~ *I can apply the same to me*; ⟨fam⟩ *same here*! || davon hat er nichts g–t *he has said nothing about that* || er kann v Glück ~ *he can thank his lucky star* | er sagte **zu** mir *he said to me* || was soll man dazu ~? *what can one say to that* || was sagst du dazu? ⟨sl⟩ *how is that for high*? ⟨Am fam⟩ *how does it listen to you*?; .., wenn wir gingen *what do you say to going* || er sagte nichts dazu *he made no comment*; es **zur** Ehre, zugunsten jds ~ *to say it for a p* **S·agen- ~buch** n *collection of sagas* od *legends* **~dichtung** f *legendary poetry* **~forscher** m *student of popular l.ds, folklorist* **~forschung** f *l.y research, study of popular l.ds, investigation of popular traditions, folklore* **~geschichte** f *history of traditions, mythical history, folklore* **≈haft** a *mythical, fabulous, traditional, l.y* | [adv] °*immensely* (*beautiful*); *excessively* (*bad*) **~kreis** m *l.y* od *epic cycle* **~kunde** f *mythology, folklore* **≈reich** a *rich in traditions* od *l.ds* **~schatz** m *folklore* **≈-umwoben** a *wrapt in l.ds* **~zeit** f *fabulous age, heroic* od *l.y era, mythological period*

s·ägen (→ Säge) vt [h] *to saw* (längs *along the grain*) || ⟨fig fam⟩ (schnarchen) 10 Klafter Holz ~ *to drive one's hogs to market* **≈schmied** m *maker of saws* **S·äger** m ~s/~ *sawer, sawyer* || ⟨orn⟩ *sawbill* **S·ägetaucher** m ⟨orn⟩ *goosander*

S·ago m & n ~s/ ⟨bot⟩ *sago, tapioca* **~mehl** n *sago-powder* **~palme** f *s.-palm, s.-tree*

Sag·unt n (⟨hist⟩ in Spanien) *Saguntum* L

sah 1. & 3. sg pret v sehen

S·ahara, Sah·ara f, die (Wüste) ~ *the Sahara*

Sah·ara- *Saharan* (*Oases, Atlas*)

S·ahne f ~/ *cream* **~-Baiser** n *cream-meringue* (*Chantilly*) **~bonbon** m *toffee* **~eis** n *ice-cream* **~(n)gießer** m *cream-jug* **≈haltig** a *creamy* **~(n)-kanne** f *creamer* **~karamelle** f *toffee* **~käse** m *cream-cheese* **~törtchen** n pl *French cakes* **~torte** f *cream-tart* **s·ahnig** a *creamy*

S·aibling m ~s/~e ⟨ich, cul⟩ *char*

Saim·iri m ~s/~s ⟨zoo⟩ *squirrel-monkey*

Saint Louis n (Stadt am Mississippi)

Sais·on [sɛːˈzɔ̃, ⟨vulg⟩ zeˈzɔŋ] f ~/~s *season* ‖ stille ~ *dead* od *off-s. doldrum's s.* ‖ Blumen der jeweiligen ~ *flowers in their s.* ‖ es ist jetzt (nicht) die ~ f .. *are in* (*out of*) *s.* ‖ die ~ ist eröffnet *the s. has begun* **~arbeit** f *s.al work* **~arbeiter** m *s.al worker* od *labourer* **~artikel** m pl *s.al goods* pl **~ausverkauf** m *end of s. sale* **≗bedingt** a *s.al* (*factors*); *dependent on the s.* **~bereinigung** f ⟨stat⟩ *s.al adjustment* **~geschäft** n *s.al business* **~gewerbe** n *s.al trade* **~karte** f *s. ticket* **≗üblich** a *s.al* (Gewerbe) **~wanderung** f *s.al migration* **~werbung** f *s.al advertising*

S·aite f ~/~n *string, chord* ‖ (anschlagen *to touch* od *strike*; bloß *naked*) ‖ ~n aufziehen *to put on strings* ‖ mit ~n beziehen *to string* ‖ über die ~n streichen *to run over the strings* ‖ e–e ~ reißt *or* platzt .. *breaks* | ⟨fig⟩ andere ~n aufziehen *to take a new line*; *to sing another tune* ‖ gelindere ~n aufziehen *to come down a peg* (*or two*), *to sing small*; *to draw in one's horns* ‖ .. noch nicht z Erklingen gek .. *still untouched* ‖ s–e ~n zu hoch spannen *to aim too high, to assume too much* ‖ die gleichgestimmten ~n verwandter Seelen *the harmony between kindred souls* | **~n-~bezug** m *set of strings* **~draht** m *music wire* **~instrument** n *stringed instrument* **~spiel** n *string--music* ‖ ⟨poet⟩ *lute, lyre, harp* **~spieler** m *lute-*etc *player* .. **saitig** a [in comp] (*four-*)*stringed*

S·akko m ~s/~s *sack coat, lounge jacket* od *c.* **~anzug** m *lounge suit*, ⟨Am⟩ *business suit* **~hemd** n *abbreviated* od *jacket shirt*

×°**s·akra** ⟨intj⟩ *damn*! **sakr·al** a *sacral, sacred* **Sakram·ent** n ~(e)s/~e ⟨ec⟩ *sacrament* (→ Abendmahl) ‖ das ~ empfangen *to partake of the Lord's Supper* ‖ zum ~ gehen *to attend Sacrament* **~·ar** n ~s/~e (Meßbuch) *s.ary* | ~shäuschen [n] ⟨ec⟩ *pyx, tabernacle* | **≗·al** a *sacramental* ×**s·akrisch** a *damned* **Sakrist·an** m ~(e)s/~e *sacristan, sexton* **Sakrist·ei** f ~/~en *vestry, sacristy*

Säkul·ar- ~feier f *centenary* **~klerus** m *secular clergy* **~isati·on** f ~/~en *secularization* **≗is·ieren** vt [h] *to secularize*

Sal- ~band n ⟨min⟩ *wall, rider* **~band** n, **~leiste** f ⟨weav⟩ *selvage, border* **~hof** m *freehold farm* **~weide** f ⟨bot⟩ *sallow*; *goat's willow*

Sal·am n ~s/~e [Arab] *salaam* | **≗lek**! *s. to you*!

Salam·ander m ~s/~ *salamander* ‖ ⟨stud⟩ e–n ~ reiben *to drink a round toast* (auf *in a p's honour*)

Sal·ami(wurst) f *salame* | ~taktik [f] *S. tactics* **Sal·är** n ~(e)s/~e *salary* **salar·ieren** vt [h] *to salary* **Sal·at** m ~(e)s/~e ⟨cul⟩ *salad* (anm *to dress*) ‖ ⟨bot⟩ *lettuce* ‖ Feld≗ *lamb's l.*; italienischer ~ *salmagundi* ‖ ⟨fig⟩ da h wir den ~! *a pretty kettle of fish* **~besteck** n *wooden* od *plastic spoon and fork* **~blatt** n *l.-leaf* **~kopf** m *head of l.* **~öl** n *s.-oil* **~platte** f ⟨cul⟩ *mixed s.* **~sauce** f *s.--dressing* **~schüssel** f *s.-bowl*

Salb·ader m ~s/~ *twaddler, bore* **~·ei** f ~/~en *twaddle, slobber, rigmarole* **salb·adern** vi [h] *to preachify, twaddle, to talk foolishly*; ~d *slobbery*

S·alb- ~gefäß n ⟨arts⟩ *phial* **~öl** n ⟨ec⟩ *consecrated oil* **S·albe** f ~/~n *salve, ointment, unguent* ‖ *pomade* ‖ (duftende) *scented oil*; *balm* ‖ abwaschbare ~ ⟨cosm⟩ *vanishing cream* ‖ (Rheuma≗) *liniment* ‖ ⟨mar⟩ *coating for a ship's bottom* **~nbüchse** f *salve-box* **~ntopf** m *gallipot* **s·albig** a *greasy* ‖ ⟨fig⟩ *unctuous* **s·alben** vt [h] *to oil* (*one's hair, skin*) ‖ *to embalm* (*a dead body*) ‖ jdn zum Priester, Könige ~ *to anoint a p king*, etc. ‖ ⟨mar⟩ *to coat* (*a ship's bottom*) ‖ ⟨fig⟩ e–m die Hände ~ *to bribe a p* **S·albung** f ~/~en *anointing* ‖ ⟨fig⟩ *unction, unctuousness, unctuosity* **≗svoll** a *sententious*; *unctuous*; (P) *mealy-mouthed* ‖ adv *with unction*

S·albei f ~/~en ⟨bot⟩ *sage, salvia* L

S·älbling m ~(e)s/~e ⟨ich⟩ *char*

Salden- ~karte [f] *new balance card* ⟨a. *comp*⟩; ~liste [f] *trial b.* **sald·ieren** vt [h] ⟨com⟩ *to balance, to clear* (*an account*), *to settle* **Saldierwerksperre** f ⟨comp⟩ *crossfooter non-clear lock* **S·aldo** m ~s/~s & S·aldi ⟨com⟩ *balance* ‖ per ~ *on b.* ‖ ~ zu Ihren Gunsten *your credit-balance* ‖ e–n ~ aufstellen, ziehen *to strike a b.* ‖ ~ ausgleichen *to b. an account* ‖ als ~ ergibt sich .. *a b. of .. is shown* ‖ e–n ~ auf neue Rechnung vortragen *to carry forward a b. to new account* ‖ per ~ quittieren *to receipt in full* **~auszug** m *balance* **~betrag** m (*amount of*) *b.* **~bilanz** f *net b.*; *b. of payment* **~karte** f ⟨comp⟩ *blank* od *trailer card* **~konto** n *current account sheet* **~rimesse** f *remittance in full settlement* **~übertrag** m *transfer of b.* **~vortrag** m *b. forward* **~wechsel** m *b.-bill* **~zahlung** f *settlement, balancing of an account*

S·alep m ~s/ **S·alepwurzel** f ⟨bot⟩ *saloop*

Sal·erno n ⟨It⟩ (Stadt)

Sal·ett(e)l n ~/~[n] It [bay-österr] = Laube, Pavillon

†**S·alier** pl (fränkischer Volksstamm) *Salians* **s·alisch** a *Salic, Salian*

Sal·ine f ~/~n *salt-pit, salt-works* pl [sg konstr]

s·alisch a ⟨hist⟩ *Salic* (*law*)

saliv·ieren vi [h] *to salivate*

Saliz·yl n ~s/ ⟨chem⟩ *salicyl* **≗·ieren** vt [h] *to impregnate with salicylic acid* **~säure** f ⟨chem⟩ *salicylic acid* **≗saure(s) Salz** n *salicylate*

Salm m ~(e)s/~e **1.** ⟨ich⟩ → *salmon* **2.** (= Psalm) *rigmarole* ‖ k–n ~! *no sermonizing*!, *to the point*! | **~ling** m ~(e)s/~e ⟨ich⟩ *char*, ⟨cul⟩ *botcher*

S·almiak m ~(e)s/ ⟨chem⟩ *sal-ammoniac* **~geist** m *liquid ammonia*

S·alomoninseln f pl *Solomon Islands* pl

Salon [zaˈlɔ̃ŋ] m ~s/~s *drawing room, lounge*, ⟨Am⟩ *parlor* ‖ ⟨hot & mar⟩ *saloon* ‖ Friseur≗, Herren≗ *hairdressing saloon*, ⟨Am⟩ *barber-shop* **~bolschewist** m ⟨Am fam⟩ *pink* [s] **~dampfer** m *saloon steamer* **≗fähig** a *presentable*; ~ s *to be "good form"* ‖ (Witz) [pred] *out of the top drawer* ‖ nicht ~ ⟨Am fam⟩ *off-color* **~held, ~löwe** m *carpet-knight, lady's man*, ⟨Am sl⟩ *tea hound, lounge-lizard* **~kunststück** n *parlour trick* **~politiker** m *armchair politician* **~soldat** m *c.-k.* **~sozialist** m *parlour socialist* od *pink* **~tiroler** m *sham Tyrolese* **~wagen** m ⟨rail⟩ *saloon-car*(*riage*), *Pullman car*

Salon·iki n ⟨Gr⟩ (Stadt) *Salonica, Saloniki*

sal·opp [a] *careless, slovenly* ‖ [adv] er schreibt ~ *he writes in a slovenly style*

Salp·eter m ~s/ ⟨chem⟩ *nitre, saltpetre* ‖ flammender ~ *ammonium nitrate* **≗artig** a *nitrous* **~bildung** f *nitrification* **~blumen** f pl *wall-saltpetre* **~dampf** m *nitric fumes* pl **~erde** f *nitrous earth* **≗führend** a *saltpetrous* **~geist** m *spirits of nitre* **≗haltig** a *nitric, nitrous* **~grube** f *s.e mine* **~hütte** f *s.e house* od *works* pl [sg konstr] **~lauge** f *s.e lye* **≗sauer** a; –saures Salz [n] *nitrate* **~säure** f *nitric acid* ‖ rauchende ~ *strong fuming nitric acid* **~sieder** m *s.e-maker* **~siederei** f *s.e manufactory* | **≗ig** a ⟨chem⟩ *nitrous* ‖ ~saures Salz *nitrite*

S·alto mort·ale m ~/Salti mortali *somersault, break-neck leap* ‖ e–n ~ m *to somersault*

Sal·ut m ~(e)s/~e *salute* ‖ ~ schießen *to fire a s.* | **≗·ieren** vt/i [h] *to salute* ‖ ~ mit .. *to fire a s. of .. guns*; ~schießen [n] *salute, saluting* **S·alve** f ~/~n *volley, discharge, round, salvo* ⟨a. fig⟩ ‖ (Ehrengruß) *salute* ‖ e–e ~ abgeben *to fire a salute*, ⟨mil⟩ .. *a volley*, ⟨mar⟩ *to deliver a broadside* ‖ in ~n feuern *to fire by volleys* ‖ 10 ~n *a volley of ten shots* | ~nfeuer [n] *salvo--fire, volley-firing, firing volleys* | verlangsamte ~nfolge *deliberate fire* **salv·ieren** vt [h] *to save* ‖ **sich** ~ *to secure o.s.*; *to get off without a loss*; *to be on the safe side*

Salvad·or n (mittelamerik. Staat)

Salz n ~es/~e **1.** *salt* ‖ ~e [pl] *salts* | ~ u Brot (das Nötigste) *bread and butter* od *cheese* ‖ man verdient dabei nicht das ~ z Suppe *it brings in next to nothing* ‖ er hat nicht das ~ z Brot *he is in dire want* | basisches ~ *subsalt* ‖ englisches ~ Epsom salts ‖ (Riech~̂) *smelling-salts* ‖ ~ sieden *to make salt* ‖ in ~ legen *to pickle* **2.** ⟨fig⟩ (Witz) *wit* ‖ attisches ~ *Attic salt* ‖ ohne ~ u Schmalz *without seasoning*; *tasteless, insipid* ‖ bei jdm noch e–n Schinken im ~ h *to have a rod in pickle for a p* **~ader** *salt-vein* **~amt** n *s.-office* **~arbeiter** m *s.-maker* **~̂artig** a *saline* **~berg** m *s.-hill, s.-mountain* **~bergwerk** n *s.-mine* **~̂bildend** a *halogenous* **~bild(n)er** m *halogene* **~bildung** f *halification* **~blumen** f pl *flowers of s.* **~brühe** f *pickle, brine* **~brunnen** m *s.-spring* **~burger** m *p*, [pl] *people of Salzburg* **~faß** n *s.-box* od *-pot*; (Tisch~̂) *s. cellar*; ⟨com⟩ *barrel of s.* **~fäßchen** n pl ⟨anat⟩ *salt cellars* **~fleisch** n *s. meat, corned beef*; ⟨mar⟩ *s.-horse*, ⟨sl⟩ *s.-junk* **~fluß** m ⟨med⟩ *s.-flux* **~frei** a *s.free* (*diet*) **~gehalt** m *proportion of s.* **~geist** m ⟨chem⟩ *muriatic acid* **~geschmack** m *salt(i)ness, briny* od *salt taste, brackishness* **~grube** f *s.-mine* **~gurke** f *pickled* od *salt(ed) gherkin* od *cucumber* **~̂haltig** a *saline, saliferous* | ~keit [f] *salinity* **~handel** m *s.-trade* **~händler** m *s.-dealer* **~haus** n *s.-magazine* **~hering** m *s.* od *pickled herring* **~kartoffeln** f pl *boiled potatoes* **~korn** n *grain of s.* **~kote** f *s.-cote* **~kraut** n ⟨bot⟩ *s.wort* **~krebs** m ⟨zoo⟩ *brine-shrimp* **~krücke** f *s.-stirrer* **~kuchen** m ⟨chem⟩ *s.-cake* **~lake** f, **~lauge** f *pickle, brine* **~lecke** f ⟨agr⟩ *s.-lick* **~lösung** f *s. solution* **~messer** m ⟨tech⟩ *salino-meter* **~monopol** n *s.-monopoly* **~näpfchen** = –fäßchen **~niederschlag** m *saline deposit* **~pfanne** f *salt-pan* **~pflanzen** f pl ⟨bot⟩ *halophytes* pl **~probe** f *s.-test* **~quelle** f *s.-spring*; *brine-pit* **~reich** a; ~es Uferland *salting(s* pl) **~̂sauer** a ⟨chem⟩ *muriatic* **~säule** f ⟨bib⟩ *pillar of salt* **~säure** f ⟨chem⟩ *hydrochloric* od *muriatic acid* **~schaufel** f *s.-shovel* **~schreiber** m *clerk to the s.-works, s.-clerk* **~see** m *s.-lake* **~sieder** m *s.-maker, s.-boiler* **~siederei** f → –werk **~sole** f *s.-spring, s.-water, brine* **~steuer** f *s.-duty, s. tax* **~streuer** m *s.-shaker* **~tonne** f *s.-barrel* **~tropfen** m (im Käse) *tear* **~waage** f *s.-gauge* **~wasser** n *s.-water, brine* | ~teich [m] *brine-pond* **~werk** n *s.-works* [sg konstr] **~wirker** m *s.-maker* **~zoll** m *s.-tax* **s·alzen** vt [h] **1.** *to salt, season* (*dishes*) ‖ *to pickle* (*gherkins*) ‖ die Suppe ist nicht ge~ *there is no seasoning in the soup* ‖ ge~ *corned* (*beef*), *salt* (*butter*) **2.** ⟨fig⟩ *to enliven* (*a speech*) *with spicy remarks* ‖ *to season* (*a conversation*) *with wit* ‖ jdm den Buckel ~ *to give a p a good thrashing* | **ge~** *salt, heavy* (*blows*), *smart* (*box on the ears*), *witty* (*words*), *spicy* (*joke*), *stiff* (*letter*); *exorbitant* (*invoice, price*) ‖ ge~er Seemann *old salt* **s·alzig** a *salty* (*tears*) ‖ *briny* (*water*) ‖ *brackish* (*backwater*) ‖ *saline* (*substance*) ‖ etw ~ *saltish* ‖ ~ schmek-ken *to taste salty* **~̂keit** f ~/ *saltness*

S·alz- ~burg n (österr. Stadt) **~kammergut** n (österr. Landschaft) **~see, der (Große)** *the Great Salt Lake* (*Ut., U.S.A.*) **~seestadt** f *Salt Lake City*

†**Samar·iter** m, **~in** f *Samaritan*

Samar·iterin f ⟨bib, arts⟩ *the Samaritan Woman*

Samark·and n ⟨Russ⟩ (Stadt & Gebiet)

Samb·esi m (Fluß in S.-Afrika) *Zambesi*

S·ame(n) m ~ns/~n **A.** ⟨bot⟩ *seed*; (*vine-*)*buds*; (T & P) *sperm, semen* ‖ ⟨ich⟩ *spawn, fry* ‖ °⟨sex vulg⟩ *mettle, milk, letch-water* | ⟨fig⟩ *descendants*, ⟨bib⟩ *offspring, s.* **B.** ⟨bot⟩ aufgehen *to come up*; treiben *to spring up* ‖ ⟨biol⟩ sich ergießen *to pour out* ‖ in ~n schießen ⟨bot⟩ *to run to s.* ‖ aus ~ ziehen *to raise from s.* ‖ ⟨fig⟩ *to sow the s. of one's own ruin* **~ader** f *sp.atic vein* **~anlage** f *ovule, gemmule* **~baum** m *s.-tree* **~behälter** m *s.-vessel* ‖ ⟨bot⟩ *pericarp* **~beständigkeit** f *growing true to type* **~blatt** n *seminal leaf* **~bruch** m ⟨surg⟩ *sp.atocele* **~drüse** f *sp.atic gland* **~ergießung** f, **~erguß** m *pollution* **~̂erzeugend** a *seminific*, ⟨biol⟩ *sp.atic* **~faden** m *sp.atozoon* **~fluß** m **1.** *sp.atorrhoea* **2.** *gonorrhoea* **~flüssigkeit** f (Erguß) ⟨sex⟩ *ejaculate* **~gang** m *sp.aduct* **~ge-fäß** n ⟨anat⟩ *sp.atic vessel* **~gehäuse** n ⟨bot⟩ *s.--vessel, pericarp* **~handel** m *s.-trade* **~händler** m *s.sman* **~haut** f *s.-coat* **~hügel** m ⟨anat⟩ *colliculus seminalis*; *verumontanum* **~hülle** f *s.-case*; *aril* **~hülse** f *pod, husk, hull* **~kapsel** f *boll, capsule* **~kelch** m ⟨bot⟩ *s.-cup* **~kern** m *sp.-nucleus* **~korn** n *grain of s.* ‖ (Saatkorn) *s.-corn* **~krone** f ⟨bot⟩ *down, pappus* **~lappen** m ⟨bot⟩ *cotyledon* **~lehre** f *sp.atology* **~leiter** m *sp.atic duct* **~pflanze** f *phanerogam* **~perle** f *s.-pearl* **~schule** f ⟨hort⟩ *nursery, s.-plot* **~staub** m *pollen* **~stengel** m ⟨bot⟩ *s.-stalk* **~strang** m ⟨anat⟩ *spermatic cord* **~tier-chen** n *sp.atozoon* **~̂tötend** a *spermicide* **~̂tragend** a *seminiferous* **~zellen** f pl *sp.atozoa* **~zwiebel** f *seed-bulb* **Sämer·eien** f pl *seeds* pl, *grain* .. **samig** a [in comp] .. *–seeded* **S·ämling** m ~s/~e ⟨bot⟩ *seedling*

s·ämig a *thick, viscid* | **~̂keit** f *viscidity*

s·amisch a *Samian* → Samos

S·ämisch- *chamois* (*-dresser, -leather*)

S·amland n (Landsch. in †Ostpreußen)

S·ammel- *collect..*, *reservoir* .. (*r.r*) **~anschluß** m ⟨telph⟩ *party-line*; *private branch exchange line* **~anstrengung** f *combined effort* **~apparat** m ⟨tech⟩ *c.or* **~ausgabe** f ⟨Lit⟩ *collected edition of works* **~band** m *omnibus volume, miscellany, anthology* **~becken** n *r.r*; *storage basin*; ⟨geog⟩ *catchment area* **~begriff** m *collective* **~behälter** m **~gefäß** n *collector*; *starage tank* etc; *reservoir* ‖ ⟨mot⟩ *sump* **~bestellung** f *omnibus order* **~buch** n *scrap-book* **~büchse** f *c.ing-box* **~fahr-schein** m *collective* od *party ticket* **~fleiß** m *indus-try in compiling* od *c.ing* **~frucht** f *c.ive fruit, syncarp*(*ous fruit*), *sorosis* **~gefäß** n ⟨chem⟩ *re-ceiver* **~kasten** m *r.r* **~gut** n *groupage traffic* **~ladung** f *c.ive consignment* od *shipment*; *com-bined* od *consolidated carload* **~lager** n *assembly centre* **~linse** f *positive* od *collecting lens* **~mappe** f *file* **~meldung** f ⟨mil⟩ *consolidated report* N **~name** *c.ive noun* od *name* **~paß** m *joint passport* **~platz** m (S) *c.ing depot* ‖ (P) *meeting-place, place of m.g* od *appointment*; ⟨tact⟩ *rallying point*; ⟨mil mar⟩ *rendezvous* **~produkt** n *cumulative product* **~punkt** m ⟨mil⟩ *rallying-point* ‖ ⟨fig⟩ *hive* (*of workers*); *head-quarters* (ein ~ *a h.*) **~raum** m *receiver* **~ruf** m ⟨mil⟩ *assembly*; (Zei-chen) *collective call* **~schaltung, ~verbindung** f ⟨telph⟩ *bunched circuit* **~scheibe** f ⟨tech⟩ *c.or* **~schiene** f ⟨comp⟩ *trunk* **~stelle** f (*central*) *depot, c.ing station*; ~ f. Gefechtsmeldungen *combat information center* N ‖ ⟨allg⟩ *centre* **~s·urium** n *omnium-gatherum* **~tag** m *flag* od *tag day* **~teller** m *collection plate* **~transport** m *c.ive transport* **~trieb** m *c.ing instinct* **~urlaub** m ⟨mil⟩ *block leave* **~verzeichnis** n *summary* **~werk** n *compilation*; (*en*)*cyclopædia* **~wort** n ⟨gram⟩ *c.ive noun* **~wut** f *rage of collecting ths* **~zylinder** m *accumulator*

s·ammeln I. vt [h] **A. 1.** *to gather* (*herbs*, etc); (ernten) *to gather, pick, harvest* **2.** *to collect* (*stamps*, etc) **3.** (anhäufen) *to heap, store, treasure up* ‖ (Reichtümer) *to accumulate* (*wealth*), *to amass* (⟨Am fam⟩ *to lay up*) (*riches*) **4.** *to compile* (*words*, etc) (aus .. *from books*) **5.** ⟨opt⟩ *to focus* (*rays*) **6.** ⟨mil⟩ *to mass, concentrate* (*troops*) ‖ *to* *rally* (*scattered troops*) **7.** ⟨fig⟩ *to store* (*knowledge*) ‖ *to canvas* (*votes*) ‖ *to gather* (*strength*) ‖ *to concentrate* (*one's thoughts*) **B.** Auskünfte ~ ⟨Am a.⟩ *to check up on information* ‖ (Beiträge) ⟨a.⟩ *to bag* ‖ (Erfahrung) *to glean* ‖ Pflanzen ~ ⟨a.⟩ *to botanize, herborize* ‖ (Schmetterlinge a.) *to bag* **| ge-lt** *collected* (⟨liter⟩ *works*) **II.** vi *to collect money* (f *for*), *to make a collection, to send round the hat* **| an** etw ~ *to collect* [vt] **III.** v/refl **sich** ~ **1.** *to gather, collect, accumulate* ‖ (sich ver~) *to meet, assemble*; *to flock together, to cluster* (um *round*) ‖ *tears grew in her eyes* **2.** ⟨chem⟩ *to collect* **3.** ⟨mil⟩ sich wieder ~ *to rally*; ~! *the Assembly*! **4.** ⟨fig⟩ *to collect one's thoughts, o.s.*; *to concentrate* ‖ *to compose o.s.* ‖ (wieder) *to regain one's composure*; *to recover, recollect* (*o.s.*) **IV.** ≃n *collecting*, etc ‖ ⟨mil⟩ z ≃ blasen *to sound the recall*; → Sammler etc

S·am(me)t m ~(e)s/~e *velvet* ‖ Rippen≃ *corduroy* ‖ Wasch≃ *v.een* ‖ sich in ~ u Seide kleiden *to dress in silks and satins* **≃artig** a *v.-like, velvety*; *v.* [attr] **~band** n *v. ribbon* **~blume** f ⟨bot⟩ *amaranth, v.t-flower* **~bürste** f *v.t-brush* **~handschuh** m, ⟨fig⟩ jdn mit ~en anfassen *to try the suède glove with a p* **~jacket** n *v. jacket* **~manchester** m *v.een* **~nelke** f ⟨bot⟩ *red rose-campion* **~pappel** f ⟨bot⟩ *marsh-mallow* **~pfötchen** n: ~ m *to draw in the claws* ⟨a. fig⟩ **≃-schwarz** a *v.-black* **~stoffe** m pl *v.ings* pl **~teppich** m *Brussels carpet* **~weber** m *v.-maker* **≃weich** a (*as*) *soft as v.*; *v.ed* **s·amten** a *v.y*

S·ammler m ~s/~ **1.** *collector, gatherer, gleaner* ‖ *amasser, hoarder* (*of wealth*) ‖ *compiler* (aus *from books*) **2.** ⟨el⟩ *accumulator* **3.** (Dampf≃) *steam drum* **~batterie** f *acc.r, storage b.y* **~wagen** m *b.y motor car* **S·ammlung** f ~/~en **1.** *collection* (*of stamps*, etc., *of money*) ‖ *selection* (*of scientific material*) ‖ *compilation* ‖ ⟨Lit⟩ *anthology*; (v Aussprüchen etc) *ana*, → Tischgespräche **2.** *gathering*, etc **3.** ⟨mil⟩ *assembly* **4.** ⟨fig⟩ *concentration, composure, equanimity*; *collectedness, balance of mind*; *recollection*; → sammeln

Sam·oa-Inseln f pl (im Stillen Ozean) *Samoan Islands* pl, *Samoan Archipelago, Samoa*

Samoj·ede m, **Samoj·edin** f (ural-altaischer Volksstamm) *Samoyed, Samoide*

S·amos n ⟨Gr⟩ (Sporaden-Insel); ~- *Samian*

S·amstag m ~(e)s/~e *Saturday*; ~s *on S.s*

samt I. adv; ~ u sonders *jointly and severally*; (*all together*); *each and all*; *the whole lot*; ⟨dero sl⟩ *the whole lot* od *caboodle* **II.** prep [dat] *together with*; *as well as*; ~ allem Zubehör, ~ allem Drum u Dran *and lock and key* **sämtlich I.** a (*all* od *each and*) *every*; *all* (*together*) ‖ *entire* ‖ *complete* (⟨liter⟩ *works*) ‖ ~e Glocken *all the bells* ‖ ~e Anwesenden *all present* **II.** adv *in a body, to a man*

S·amum m ~s/~e ⟨Arab meteor⟩ (Sandsturm) *simoom*

Sand m ~ (e)s/~e *sand* ‖ grober ~ *grit, gravel* ‖ (Schwemm≃) *quicksand* **|** wie ~ am Meer *as the sand of the sea* **|** den ~ v den Füßen schütteln *to shake off the sand off one's feet* ⟨a. fig⟩ ‖ ⟨fig⟩ streu ~ darauf! *enough* (od *no more*) *of that*! ‖ ~ in die Augen *eye-wash*; jdm ~ in die Augen streuen *to throw dust in a p's eyes*; *to dust, hoodwink, eye-wash* (*the public*); ⟨Am sl⟩ *to pull wool over a p's eyes* **|** ⟨fig⟩ **auf** ~ bauen *to build on sand* ‖ ⟨mar⟩ auf den ~ laufen *to run aground* ‖ jdn auf den ~ setzen *to floor, unhorse*, ⟨fig⟩ *to nonplus a p* ‖ auf dem ~ sitzen *to be stranded* ⟨a. fig⟩, ⟨fig⟩ *to be in great distress, to be left in the lurch* **|** ⟨fig⟩ **in** ~ geschrieben *written in water* ‖ im ~e verlaufen (of rivers) *to be s.ed up*, ⟨fig⟩ (S) *to peter* od *fizzle out, to drop*; *to come to nothing*; (*of conversation*) *to lapse* .. l *to let* (*a th*) *slide* **| mit** ~ bestreuen *to s.* **~aal** m ⟨ich⟩ *s.-eel, grig* **≃artig** a ⟨scient⟩ *arenose* **~bad** n *s.-bath* ⟨a. chem⟩ **~bahn** f ⟨mot⟩ *dirt-track* **~bank** f *s.-bank, s.s, shelf*; *reef*; *cay*, ⟨Am⟩ *key*; (vor Flußmündung) *bar* **~berg** m *s.-hill* **~blatt** n (Zigarre) *shrub* **~boden** m ⟨agr⟩ *s.y soil* **~büchse** f *s.-box* **~burg** f *s. castle* **~dorn** m ⟨bot⟩ *sallow-thorn*; *sea buckthorn*; ⟨Am⟩ *fire thorn* **|** ~beere [f] *sallow thorn berry* **~dünen** f pl *s.s* pl **~ebene** f *s.y plain, s.s* pl **~erze** n pl ⟨min⟩ *s.-ores* **~fang** m ⟨pap⟩ *s. trap*; (Abwässer≃) *grit chamber* **~feld** n *s.y field* **~fläche** f = ebene **~floh** m *s.-flea*, ⟨Am⟩ *beach-flea* **~form** f ⟨tech⟩ *s.-mould* **|** ~verfahren [n] ⟨met⟩ *sable mould process* **≃führend** a *sabulous* **~gebäck** n *s. cake* **~gebirge** n *s.-hills, s.-mountains* pl **~gebläse** n *s.-jet* **~gegend** f *s.y country* **~grieß** m *grit*; *fine gravel* **~grube** f *s.-pit* **~grund** m = ~boden **~hase** m **1.** *hare* (*living*) *in a s.y country* **2.** ⟨mil⟩ *foot-soldier*; ⟨mil sl⟩ *mud-crusher, foot-slogger*, ⟨Am⟩ *doughboy*, ⟨mar⟩ *boot-neck* **3.** *miss* (*at nine-pins*); e–n ~n schieben *to miss* **~haufen** m *heap of s.* **~hose** f *s.-spout* **~hügel** m *s.-hill* **~huhn** n *s.-grouse* **~junge** m *s.-boy* **~käfer** m ⟨ent⟩ *tiger-beetle* **~kasten** m *s.-box*, ⟨mil⟩ *s. table* **~korn** n *grain of s.* **~kraut** n *s.-wort* **~kuchen** m *sponge* (⟨Am⟩ *pound*) *cake* **~läufer** m ⟨orn⟩ *strand-plover* **~loch** n *s.-pit*, ⟨golf⟩ *bunker* **~mann** m *s.-man* ‖ der ~ kommt ⟨fig⟩ *the dustman's in your eyes*; → „Schlaf" A. 4 **~massen** f pl *sands* **~meer** n *s.y desert* **~nelke** f *s.-pink* **~papier** n *s.-paper* **~pulver** n ⟨med⟩ *gravel-powder* **~rücken** m *s.-ridge* **~sack** m *s.-bag* **~schaufel** f *s.-shovel* **~schicht** f *layer of s.* **~schimmel** m *roan-horse* **~schmirgeln** n *sanding* **~schwalbe** f ⟨orn⟩ *s.-martin* **~stein** m *s.stone, freestone* **~strahl**-~gebläse [n] *s.blast* **|** ≃en vt [h] *to s.b.* **~strahler** m *s.-jet* **~strand** m *s.y beach* **~streubüchse** f *s.-box* **~strudel** m *quicksand* **~sturm** m *s.-storm* **~torte** f → –kuchen **~ufer** n *s.y bank* **~uhr** f *s.-, hour-glass, egg-boiler, -timer* **~waschtrommel** f *drum gritwasher* **~weg** m *s.-walk* **~wehe** f *drift of s.* **~wurm** m *s.worm*, (Köder) *lugworm* **~wüste** f *s.*(*y*) *desert, s.s* pl **s·andig** a *s.y*; *gritty* (*powder*)

Sand·ale f ~/~n *sandal* ‖ mit *or* in ~n *sandalled* **|** Sandal·ette [f] *strip sandal*

S·andarach (-ak) m ~s/ ⟨min⟩ *sandarac*(*h*)

S·andel m ~s/ *sandal* (*wood, oil*)

S·ander m ~s/~ **1.** ⟨ich⟩ *pike* **2.** ⟨geol⟩ *outwash* **|** ~ling [m] ⟨orn⟩ *sanderling*

San Di·ego n (Stadt) (*Cal., U.S.A.*)

San Dom·ingo (auf Haiti)

s·andte 1. & 3. sg pret v senden

sanforis·ieren vt [h] (Stoff) ~ *to sanforize*

San Franz·isko n (Stadt) *San Francisco* (*Cal.*)

sanft I. [a] *soft* (*light, red, rain*); *gentle* (*breeze*); *mild* (*wind*) ‖ *light* (*blow, touch, rain, wind*) ‖ (glatt) *smooth* **|** *gentle, low* (*voice*) ‖ *easy* (*gait, riding* Fahren) **|** (ruhig) *calm* (*sleep, nature*); *placid* (*feelings*) ‖ *sensitive* (*heart*) ‖ *sweet* (*character*) ‖ *bland* (*temper, persuasion*) ‖ *gentle* (*nature*) ‖ *good natured* (*p*) ‖ *peaceful* (*as a lamb*) **|** *wheedling* (*diplomacy*) **|** *gentle* (*slope, hand, pressure*) **|** e–s ~en Todes sterben *to die an easy death* ‖ ~er w *to mellow, relent, soften* **II.** [adv] ~ ansteigend *gently rising* (*hill*) ‖ ~ ausdrücken .. *blandly, mildly*; ⟨Am a.⟩ *to soft-pedal* (*a th*) ‖ (*to smile*) *gently*; (*to sleep*) *peacefully* **≃heit** f, **≃mut** f *softness, smoothness*; *gentleness*; *sweetness of character* **~mütig** a *soft, gentle, sweet, mild* ‖ ⟨bib⟩ *meek* **≃mütigkeit** f = –mut **S·änfte** f ~/~n *sedan*(*-chair*); *stretcher* ‖ (*horse-*)*litter* **|** ~nträger [m] *chairman, sedan-bearer* **s·änftigen** vt [h] *to soften, mitigate* **s·änftiglich** adv *softly, gently, mildly*

sang 1. & 3. sg pret v singen **Sang** m ~(e)s/≃e *song* ‖ *singing, chanting* ‖ mit (ohne) ~ u Klang *with singing and bands playing* (*without a sound*, ⟨fig⟩ *quietly, unceremoniously*), ohne .. (= **≃los**) abziehen *to sneak off*, .. abtreten *to retire quietly*; *to die obscurely* **s·angbar** a *singable, fit for* *singing*; *cantabile* It ≃**keit** f *melodiousness* **S·änger** m ~s/~ *singer, vocalist* ‖ ⟨orn⟩ *songster,* → *warbler* ~**bund** m *choral society, saengerbund* ~**fest** n *choral festival* ~**krieg** m *bard's contest* **S·ängerin** f ~/~nen (*female*) *singer* ‖ ⟨poet⟩ *songstress* | (Wiener) **S·ängerknaben** pl (*Vienna*) *Boys Choir* **S·ängerschaft** f, **S·ängertum** n **1.** *singers, poets, minstrels* pl **2.** *singer's vocation* **3.** *art of singing* **S·anges-** ~**bruder** m *member of a singing club* ≃**froh** a *fond of singing*

Sangu·iniker m ~s/~ *sanguine p* **s-nisch** a *s.e*

Sanhedr·in m ~s/ ⟨Hebr jur⟩ (Synhedrion) *Sanhedrim, Sanhedrin*

°**S·ani** m ~s/~s (~t·äter) ⟨mil sl⟩ *poultice wallah* **san·ieren** vt [h] (S) *to sanitate*; (P) *to cure* ‖ *to sanify* (*towns*), *clear* (*slums*) ‖ ⟨com⟩ *to reconstruct, reorganize* ‖ *to restore* (*currency*) | operativ saniert *operated on and cleared* **San·ierung** f ~/~en *restoration* (*to health*) ‖ *reconstruction, reorganization*; *clearance* (*of slums*) | (S) *sanitation* ‖ *restoration* (*of currency*) | ~sabteilung [f] *department of sanitation*; ~sstelle [f] ⟨sex med⟩ *pro*(*phylactic*) *station,* ⟨mil⟩ *army control facilities* pl **sanit·är** a *sanitary* ‖ ~e Einrichtungen [pl] *sanitation*; *hygienic* od *sanitary facilities* pl ≃**keramik** f *s.y ceramics* **Sanit·ät** f ~/ *health, sanitation* °**Sanit·äter** m ~s/~ (*first-*)*aid man,* ⟨sl⟩ *pill-roller* | ~korps [n] ⟨mil⟩ *bearer--corps*; → Sanitätssoldat **Sanit·äts-** ~**beamte(r)** m *sanitary officer* ~**behörde** f *Board of Health* ~**depot** n ⟨mil⟩ *medical stores* ~**dienst** m (⟨Engl⟩ *Royal*) *Army Medical Service* (*R.A.M.S.*) ~**einrichtung** f *medical support installation* ~**flugzeug** n *ambulance plane* ~**gast** m ⟨mar⟩ *sick berth attendant* ~**hund** m *amb.-dog* ~**kasten** m *first-aid kit* ~**kolonne** f ⟨mil⟩ *amb. corps* ~**kompanie** f *clearing* od *amb. company* ~**korps** n (⟨Engl⟩ *Royal*) *Army Medical Corps* ~**kraftwagen** m → Sanka ~**-mannschaften** pl *hospital orderlies* ~**materi·al** n *medical supplies* pl ~**offizier** m (leitend *chief*) *medical officer* ~**offizierskorps** n *med. staff* ~**personal** n *med. personnel* ~**polizei** f *sanitary police, health-office* ~**rat** m ⟨Ger⟩ (Titel) *Member of the Board of Health* ~**soldat** m *hospital* od *med. orderly* ~**stelle** f ⟨sex path⟩ *prophylactic* (⟨fam⟩ *pro-*)*station* ~**truppe** f *Medical Corps* N; ~ des Heeres *army m. service* ~**unteroffizier** m *first-aid corporal* ~**wache** f *sanitary station, first-aid st.* od *post, amb. st.* ~**wagen** m *amb.*(*-van*), ⟨mil a.⟩ *med. stores wagon* ~**wesen** n *sanitary matters* od *arrangements* pl, ⟨mil⟩ *med. service* °**S·anka** m ~s/~s ⟨mil sl⟩ *motor amb.*

sank 1. & 3. sg pret v sinken

Sankt a (abbr St.) *Saint* (*St*) ~**-·Elmsfeuer** n *St Elmo's fire* ‖ ~ Nikolaus [m] *Santa Claus* ≃**ifizieren** vt [h] *to sanctify* ~**i·on** [–kts–] f ~/~en: ~ finden ⟨parl⟩ *to be sanctioned* ‖ ~en [pl] *sanctions*; *coercive measures* ‖ ~en erlassen *to put s.s into motion* ‖ ~en durch führen *to push s.s* ≃**ion·ieren** vt [h] *to sanction* ~**u·arium** n ~s/~rien *sanctuary*

Sankt- ~ B·ernhard [m] (*Mount*) *St. Bernard* **1.** der Große S. B. *Great St. B.* **2.** der Kleine S. B. *Little St. B.* ~ Chr·istoph [n] (westind.) *St. Christopher* ~ Gallen [n] ⟨Swiss⟩ (Kanton & Stadt) *Saint Gallen* ~-Georgs-Kanal [m] *Saint George's Channel, South Channel* ~ G·otthardt [m] (*Mount*) *St. Gotthard* ~ Helena [n] (Insel im Atlant. Ozean) *Saint Helena* ~-Lorenz-Golf [m] *Gulf of Saint Lawrence* ~-Lorenz-Strom [m] *Saint Lawrence River, the* (*river*) *St. Lawrence* ~ Mor·itz [n] (Wintersportplatz in der Schweiz) *Saint Maurice* † ~ Petersburg [n] → Petersburg u Leningrad

San Mar·ino n (Freistaat in Mittel-Italien)

sann 1. & 3. sg pret v sinnen

San Salvad·or n **1.** (e–e der Bahamainseln) *Watling Islands* **2.** (Hauptstadt v. El Salvador)

S·ansibar n (Insel bei O.-Afrika) *Zanzibar*

Sanskr·it n ~(e)s/ *Sanscrit* ≃**isch** a *Sanscritic*

S·anta Cathar·ina n (brasil. Staat)

S·anta-Cruz-Inseln f pl (in Melanesien) *Santa Cruz* od *Queen Charlotte Islands* pl

Santand·er n (Stadt u Prov. in Spanien)

Santi·ago n **1.** ~ de Chile (Hauptstadt) **2.** ~ de Compostela ⟨Span⟩ (Stadt) **3.** ~ de Cuba

S·äntis m (Alpenberg) *Säntis, Sentis*

S·antos n (Stadt in Brasilien)

Saône ['so:nə] n ⟨Fr⟩ (Nebenfluß der Rhone)

São Paulo n (brasil. Staat & Stadt)

Saph·ir [–f–] m ~(e)s/~e (blauer, weißer) *sapphire* ‖ (grüner) *green corundum* ‖ (roter) *oriental ruby* ≃**en** a *sapphirine*

sapi·enti sat (L) *a word to the wise is sufficient*

S·appe f ~/~n ⟨fort⟩ *sap, mine* ‖ .. anlegen *to sap* **Sappeur** [zɑ'pør] m ~s/~e ⟨mil⟩ *sapper, pioneer* **sapp·ieren** vt/i [h] *to sap, undermine*

sapperl·ot! sapperm·ent! ⟨intj⟩ *by Jove!, the deuce!* | ≃**er** m = Sackerloter

Sarag·ossa n ⟨Span⟩ (Stadt) *Zaragoza*

Saraj·evo n (†Hauptstadt v Bosnien u Herzegowina) *Sarajevo, Serajevo*

Sar·atow n ⟨Russ⟩ (Stadt) *Saratov*

Saraz·ene m, **Saraz·enin** f ([bes. arab.] Mohammedaner) *Saracen*

Sard·elle f ~/~n ⟨ich⟩ *anchovy* ‖ °sich (über d. Glatze) ~n kämmen °*to quiff the bladder* ~**n-butter** f *anchovy-paste* **Sard·ine** f ~/~n ⟨ich⟩ *sardine, pilchard* ‖ ~n [pl] in Öl *tinned sardines* pl

S·arder m ~s/~ ⟨minr⟩ *sard*

Sard·inier m, ~**in** f, **sard·inisch** a *Sardinian*

Sard·inien n *Sardinia* **S·arde** m → Sard·inier

sard·onisch a *sardonic, spasmodic* (*smile*)

Sarg m ~(e)s/≃e *coffin* (⟨mar a. fig⟩ = altes Schiff), ⟨Am a.⟩ *casket* ‖ (→ Nagel) ‖ in e–n ~ legen *to coffin* ~**beschlag** m *c.-mounting* ~**gestell** n *catafalque* ~**nagel** m *c.-nail* (⟨a. fig⟩ Zigarette) ~**träger** m *pall-bearer* ~**tuch** n *pall*

Sarg·assomeer n (zw d Kanarischen u Westindischen Inseln) *Sargasso Sea*

Sark·asmus m ~/–men *sarcasm* **sark·astisch** a *sarcastic, biting* ‖ ~e Bemerkung *dig* (über *at*)

Sark·om n ~(e)s/~e ⟨path⟩ *sarcoma*

Sarkoph·ag m ~(e)s/~e *sarcophagus*

†**Sarm·ate** m, **Sarm·atin** f (v skyth. Stamm am Schwarzen Meer) *Sarmatian*

S·arraß m –sses/–sse *heavy sabre, broadsword*

S·arsche → **1.** = Serge **2.** = Zarge

Sarsen·ett m ~(e)s/~e ⟨weav⟩ *sarcenet*

Sask·atchewan m (Fluß & Prov. in Kanada)

saß 1. & 3. sg pret v sitzen **Saß, S·asse 1.** m –ssen/–ssen *freeholder, tenant* **2.** f ~e/~en ⟨hunt⟩ *seat* (*of hare*)

S·atan m ~(e)s/~e *Satan* ‖ ⟨fig⟩ ein wahrer ~ *the veriest devil, the d. incarnate* ~**sbraten,** ~**skerl** m *d. of a fellow* ~**spilz** m *satanic bolete* ~**sweib** n *d. in petticoats* **sat·anisch** a *satanic, diabolic*(*al*)

Satell·it m ~en/~en *satellite* ‖ Nachrichten≃ *telecommunication satellite* | ~enbahn [f] *orbit*; ~enstaat [m] *puppet state*

Satin [zɑ'tɛ:ŋ] m ~s/~s (Seide) *satin* ‖ (Baumwolle) *sateen* | ~papier [n] *glazed paper* ~**·ett** m [–i–] ~(e)s/~e ⟨weav⟩ *satinet*(*te*) ≃**·ieren** vt [h] *to press, glaze, satin, calender*; scharf –t *high--glazed* (*paper*) ~**·ier-** ~**presse** f *rolling-press* ~**werk** n *calender*

Sat·ire f ~/~n *skit*; *satire* (beißend *biting*, auf *on*) ~**ndichter** m *satirical poet* **Sat·iriker** m ~s/~ *satirist, satirical writer*; dazu: *to satirize*

Satisfakti·on [–ts–] ~/; ~ fordern, geben *to demand, give satisfaction* ≃**sfähig** a *qualified to give s.*

S·atladsch, S·atledsch m (Indusnebfl.) *Sutley*

Satr·ap m ~en/~en *satrap* ~**·ie** [f] *satrapy*

satt [a] **A. 1.** *satiate*(*d*), *satisfied with food* etc, *full to satiety, sated* ‖ *full* (*stomach*) ‖ (*to make a*) *well-satisfied* (*impression*) ⟨a. fig⟩ **2.** ⟨fig⟩ (zufrieden) *satisfied* (v *with*) **3.** (v Farben) *dark, deep, rich, saturate, intensive* **4.** ⟨chem⟩ *saturated* **B.** ~ u selig ⟨fam⟩ *gloriously full* | [adv] ~ u genug *enough and to spare, more than amply* **C. etw ~ bek,** kriegen → e–r S ~ w ‖ nicht ~ z bek *insatiable* ‖ man kriegt es ~ *it's too much of a good th* (wenn man .. *to do*) ‖ e–n ~ m *to give a p enough to eat* ‖ nicht ~ z m *always hungry* ‖ das macht ~ *that is very satisfying* | er hat nicht einmal ~ z essen *he does not even get enough to eat* ‖ ~ s *to feel satisfied* ‖ ich bin v der Portion nicht ~ .. *was not enough for me* | ⟨fig⟩ jdn, etw ~ h, e–r P *or* S [gen] ~ s *to have had enough of ..., to be weary* od *tired of ..., of doing*; ⟨fam⟩ *to be sick* (*to death*) *of ..., to be fed up* (*to the teeth*) *with ..* ‖ es ~ s *or* h *to have had enough of it* | er wird nie ~ *he can never get enough* ‖ e–r S ~ w *to grow* od *get tired* (⟨fam⟩ *sick*) *of a th* ‖ er wird nicht ~, ihn z loben *he cannot praise him enough* **D. sich** ~ essen, trinken, weinen *to eat* od *take*, etc *one's fill, to eat*, etc *to one's heart's content*; *to get enough of laughing*; *to laugh, cry to the top of one's bent* | ich kann mich nicht ~ sehen *I never weary of seeing*, .. daran .. *I cannot take my eyes off it*; *they could not have their fill of staring* ‖ sich ~ gesehen h *to have seen enough* (an *of*), *to have had enough of sight-seeing* | **~dampf** m *saturated steam* **S·attheit** f ~ *satiety* ‖ *fullness* (*of the stomach*) **s·ättigen** vt [h] **1.** *to satisfy a p's hunger*; *to sate, satiate* ‖ (v Speisen) *to be satisfying* ‖ **sich** ~ an *to appease one's hunger with*, (übermäßig) *to glut o.s. on* **2.** ⟨fig⟩ *to satisfy* (*one's desires*) **3.** ⟨chem⟩ *to saturate* **4.** ⟨tech⟩ *to impregnate* | **gesättigt** *satisfied, saturated* ‖ ⟨com⟩ *the market is glutted with goods* **S·ättigung** f ~/ *satiation, sating*; (Gefühl) *feeling full up* ‖ *repletion* (*with food*) ‖ *glutting* (*of the market*) | ⟨arts⟩ *ful(l)ness* ‖ ⟨chem⟩ *saturation* | ~sfähigkeit [f] *satiability*; ~punkt [m] *s. point, limit of s.*; → sattsam

S·atte f ~/~n *milk-pan, -bowl*

S·attel m ~s/≃ **A. 1.** *saddle*, ⟨sport a.⟩ *pigskin* ‖ Damen~ *side-s.*, ⟨hist⟩ *pillion* ‖ deutscher ~ *heavy dragoon s.* ‖ englischer ~ *English s.* ‖ ~ u Zeug *s. and harness* **2.** ⟨anat⟩ *bridge* (*of the nose*) ‖ ⟨arch, tech⟩ *cross-beam* ‖ ⟨cycl⟩ *s.* ‖ Feder≃ *spring pivot seat* | ⟨geogr⟩ *s.*; *ridge* (*of a hill*); *depression*, ⟨a.⟩ *pass* (*between two peaks*); *s.back* ‖ ⟨geol⟩ *s.*; *anticline* ‖ ⟨mar⟩ (Klüverbaum≃) *jib-boom s.* ‖ ⟨min⟩ *s.* ‖ (Mühlen≃) *collar beam* ‖ ⟨mus⟩ *upper s.* (*of a violin*, etc) ‖ ⟨tech⟩ *s., backfall* ‖ ⟨typ⟩ *gallows* pl **B.** ⟨hors⟩ ~ auflegen, abschnallen, festschnallen *to put .. on, take .. off, to tighten up the s.* **C. aus** dem ~ heben, werfen *to unhorse, dismount, throw*; ⟨fig⟩ *to unseat, oust, supplant, supersede, to take* (*a p's*) *place*; ⟨fam⟩ *to put a p's nose out of joint* | **in** allen Sätteln gerecht *ready for anything*; *versatile*; *all-round* (*man*) | ⟨fig⟩ sich im ~ halten *to be firmly established* ‖ jdn in den ~ heben ⟨a. fig⟩ *to help a p up* ‖ ich habe ihn in den ~ gehoben, reiten muß er selbst *you can lead a horse to water but you cannot make it drink* | den ganzen Tag im ~ s *to ride the whole d.* | sind Sie fest im ~? *can you stick on a h.* | gut im ~ sitzen ⟨hors⟩ *to sit one's horse well, to have a firm seat, to be firm in the s., to keep in one's s.*, ⟨fig⟩ *to be safely settled, to master one's subject* od *the situation, to know a th thoroughly, to be on safe ground*; *to have a toe hold in it, to be soundly established*; *to sit tight* **~anhänger** m ⟨mot⟩ *semitrailer* **~band** n ⟨tech⟩ *s.-band* **~baum** m *s.-tree* **~bildung** f ⟨geol⟩ *anticlinal formation* **~blech** n *ridge-lead, wither-band* **~bogen** m *s.-bow* **~braut** f ⟨mot⟩ *pillion-rider* **~bügel** m *tree of a pack-s.* **~dach** n *s.-roof* **~decke** f *s.-cloth* **~druck** m ⟨vet⟩ *s.-gall* **≃fertig** a *ready to mount* **≃fest** a *s.-fast*; ~ s ⟨a.⟩ *to sit one's horse well* ‖ ⟨fig⟩ *all-round* (*singer*), nicht ~ *shaky*; ~ s *to know one's business* **~gurt** m *s.-girth* **~holz** n ⟨hors⟩ *s.-beam*, ⟨carp⟩ *bolster* **~kissen** n *pillion*, (f Kutschpferde) *pad* **~knecht** m *groom* **~knopf** m *pommel* **~lage** f ⟨hors⟩ *saddle*; mit tiefer ~ *s.backed* **~nase** f ⟨anat⟩ *saddle nose* **~pausche** f *cantle* **~pferd** n *s.-* od *near horse* **~pistole** f *horse-pistol* **~platz** m *paddock* **~polster** n *bolster, pillion* **~protze** f *limber without chest* **~riemen** m *girth-leather* **~schlepper** m *tractor truck*; ⟨Am⟩ *dolly* **~seite** f *near side* **~steg** m ⟨min⟩ *cross-beam of a s.* **~stück** n ⟨cul⟩ *s.* (*of mutton*, etc) **~stütze** f ⟨cycl⟩ *seat-pillar* **~tasche** f *s.-bag* **~trunk** m *stirrup-cup* **~wagen** m ⟨artill⟩ *platform-carriage* **~wunde** f ⟨vet⟩ *s.-gall* **~zeug** n *s.ry, s. and harness* **~zugmaschine** f → –schlepper **s·atteln I.** vt [h] *to saddle* (*a horse*) ‖ sich ~ *to prepare* (*for an examination*), ich bin gesattelt *I'm ready* (*for any emergency*) **II.** ≃ n *saddling* ‖ zum ≃ blasen *to sound the boot-and-saddle* **S·attler** m ~s/~ *harness-maker*, ⟨Am⟩ *saddler* **~arbeit** f *s.'s work* **~handwerk** n *s.'s trade* **~messer** n *s.'s knife* **~waren** f pl *s.y* **Sattler·ei** f ~/~en *harness-maker's* (⟨Am⟩ *s.'s*) *trade* od *workshop*

s·attsam a [& adv] *sufficient*[*ly*], *abundant*[*ly*] | [adv] *enough* ‖ (*to criticize*) *severely* ‖ (*to discuss*) *amply* ‖ ~ durchhecheln *to pull to pieces*

Satur·ei f ~/ ⟨bot⟩ *savory*

satur·ieren vt [h] ⟨chem⟩ *to saturate*

S·atyr m ~s & ~n/~n *satyr* **~drama** n *satiric drama* **~huhn** ⟨orn⟩ *trag*

S·atz m ~es/≃e **A.** (Gruppe) **1.** ⟨gram⟩ *sentence* (einfach *simple*, erweitert *expanded*, zus–gesetzt *complex*), zus-gesetzter ~ *period* ‖ verkürzter ~ *phrase*; längerer ~ *passage* ‖ abhängiger, beigeordneter ~ *subordinate clause* ([beigeordnet *co-ordinate*] Haupt≃) (*main*) *clause*; (bilden *to form*, konstruieren *to construct, analyse, construe*) **2.** ⟨mus⟩ (Vertonung) *composition* ‖ (Teilstück) *movement, phrase* **3.** ⟨ten⟩ *set* **4.** (S) *set* (*of stamps, tools, weights, tables, skittles, pans*) ‖ *nest* (*of cups, boxes* etc) ‖ *pile* (*of wood*) ‖ (*galvanic*) *pile* | (Menge) *batch* (*of bread, ore*) | ⟨com⟩ *parcel, assortment* (*of goods*) **5.** ⟨hunt⟩ *breeding* (*of hares*), *nest* (*of rabbits*), *fry* (*of fish*) **6.** ⟨print⟩ Hand≃ *hand-set, type*; (Maschinen≃ *mechanical*) *composition*; (durchschossen *leaded*, kompreß *solid*) *matter*; *setting*; **7.** ⟨comp⟩ *record* ‖ Programm(ierungs)satz ⟨comp⟩ *sentence* **B.** (Glaubens-, Grund-) **1.** *articel* (*of faith*) ‖ ⟨ethics⟩ *tenet* ‖ ⟨log⟩ *proposition, thesis* ⟨a. math⟩ ‖ (Grundmotiv) *theme, subject* ‖ (Lehr≃) *theorem, tenet*; Leit≃ *maxim, axiom* ‖ kurzer Grund≃ *aphorism* | e–n ~ annehmen *to accept a dogma* ‖ e–n ~ aufstellen *to lay down an article of belief* ‖ s–n ~ behaupten *to maintain one's point* **2.** (festgesetzte Menge, Summe) *rate, limit* (*2 glasses that is about the limit for me*) ‖ ⟨com⟩ *fixed sum, amount, price*; (Tarif) *rate* ‖ *sum agreed upon* | zu hohen ≃en *at high rates* ‖ m–n ~ überschreiten: *the price is higher than I intended to go* **3.** (Einsatz) ⟨cards⟩ *stake* **4.** °e–n ~ geben *to stand a treat* **C.** ⟨typ⟩ (Arbeit) *setting* ‖ (zu Setzendes) *copy* ‖ (Gesetztes) *matter*; → A. 6. ‖ Abdruck *pull* ‖ gequirlter ~ (*printer's*) *pie* | sich im ~ befinden: *the book is being set up* (*in type*) ‖ (*to correct*) *the proofs* ‖ den ~ stehen l *to leave the type set up* **D.** (Boden≃) *sediment, deposit* ‖ *dregs* (*in wine*) ‖ *grounds* (*in coffee*) **E.** (Sprung) *leap, bound*; *start, dash*; *jump, vault* | e–n ~ m *to take a leap, make a jump, dash forward*, .. über *jump over* ‖ *he gave a bound towards the door* | **in** Sätzen *by leaps and bounds* ‖ in e–m ~e *at* od *with one bound, leap, jump*; ⟨fig⟩ (*he emptied the glass*) *in a single pull* **~akzent** m ⟨gram⟩ *tonic* od *sentence accent* **~anordnung** f ⟨typ⟩ *lay-out* **~anweisungen** pl *instruction for the compositor* **≃artig** a *sedimentary* **~ausführung** f mit Setzmaschine *foundry type* **~ball** m ⟨ten⟩

match-, set-ball **~bau** m, **~bildung** f *construction; formation of sentences* **~brett** n ⟨typ⟩ *composition board* **~fehler** m *misprint* **~fräser** m ⟨tech⟩ *gang cutter* **~gefüge** n ⟨gram⟩ *period; complex sentence* **~glied** n = ~teil **~gegenstand** m *subject* **~höhe** f *depth of type* **~lehre** f ⟨gram⟩ *syntax* **~rhythmus** m *prosody* ⟨a. poet⟩ **~spiegel** m ⟨typ⟩ *type area; page-proof* **~teich** m (f Fische) *stock-pond* **~teile** m pl *parts* pl *of speech* **~umfang** m ⟨typ⟩ *volume;* den ~ schätzen *to cast off* **~-** (u Bild)**entwurf** m *lay-out* **~verbindung** f *sentence* **~waage** f *spirit-level* **≃weise** adv *sentence by sentence* ‖ (sprungweise) *by leaps* (*and jumps*) ‖ (unregelmäßig) *by fits and starts* **~zeichen** n *punctuation-sign* **~zeit** f ⟨hunt⟩ *breeding-time* **S·ätzchen** n ~s/~ *short sentence* od *leap* **S·atzung** f ~/~en *statute; standing rule* ‖ ⟨rel⟩ *dogma* ‖ ⟨ec⟩ *ordinance* ‖ (Einrichtung) *institution* ‖ (Gesetz) *law* ‖ (Vorschrift) *precept* **≃sgemäß** a *according to the articles* **≃smäßig** a *statutory* **≃widrig** a *contrary to the articles*

Sau f → Save (Nebenfluß der Donau)

Sau f ~/≃e **A. 1.** *sow,* grobe ~ (Keiler) *tusker* ‖ schwitzen wie e–e ~ *to be in a heavy sweat* ‖ schreien wie e–e gesengte *or* gestochene ~ *to cry like a stuck pig* **2.** ⟨hunt⟩ [pl: Sauen] *wild sow, hog, boar* ‖ die ~ hetzen *to hunt the wild hog* **B.** ⟨fig⟩ **1.** *ink-blot* ‖ ⟨met⟩ *sow of melted iron* ‖ (Versehen) *blunder* **2.** °⟨fig⟩ (P) (weibl.) *slut, trollop* ‖ (männl.) *smutty fellow* **3.** °unter aller ~ (*that is*) *a regular mess* od *below contempt* **4.** °~ h *to be lucky,* ⟨cards⟩ *to be in luck* **5.** °zur ~ m *to make a muck of, to mess* (*up*) (*ths*), ⟨fam⟩ *to pig* ‖ *to devastate, undo, destroy* ‖ (Buch etc herunter|m) *to slate;* ⟨vulg⟩ *to knock the shit out of* (*a p*); ⟨Am fam⟩ *to shellac* (⟨sl⟩ *ride*) *a p* **~arbeit** f *filthy work,* ⟨fig⟩ *drudgery, hard graft; rotten job; miserable workmanship* **~bär** m *boar* **~beller** m → –hund **≃b·illig** a *dirt-cheap* **~bohne** f ⟨bot⟩ *broad, horse-bean* **~borste** f *hog's bristle* °**~buch** n *putrid book* **~distel** f ⟨bot⟩ *sow-thistle* **≃dumm** a *daft;* er ist ~ *he's a damned fool, a silly ass;* → dumm **~fang** m *stockade trap* **~feder** f ⟨hunt⟩ *hog-spear* **~fenchel** m ⟨bot⟩ *sow-fennel* °**~fraß** m *dirty* od *very bad food* **~garten** m ⟨hunt⟩ *preserve for wild boars* °**~glück** n *undeserved good luck* **~hatz** f *boar-hunt; pig-sticking* °**~hieb** m ⟨fenc⟩ *irregular cut* **~hirt** m *swine-herd* **~hund** m *boar-hound* ‖ °*swine, blackguard* °**~igel** m *filthy fellow* **~jagd** f *wild-boar chase* **~**°**kerl** m *blackguard* **~koben** m → –stall **~lache** f *pool for swine* **~leben** n *beastly* od *disgusting life* **~magen** m *hog's paunch* °**≃mäßig** [a & adv] *infamous, beastly, rotten, filthy* ‖ er hat es ~ [adv] gemacht *he has made an awful mess of it* °**~mensch** n (!) *bad wench* **~nest** n *dirty place* °**~pech** n *rotten luck* **~rüde** m → –hund **~rüssel** m *swine's snout* °**≃schl·echt** a ⟨mil⟩ *breamy* **~spieß** m *boar-spear* **~stall** m *pigsty;* ⟨fig⟩ *filthy hole* °**~trank** m *hog's wash* **~trog** m *hog-trough* °**~wetter** n *filthy weather;* ⟨mil & aero⟩ *soup, muck* °**~wirtschaft** *dirty household, filthy surroundings* pl ‖ *wretched, filthy management* °**≃wohl** a (*to feel*) *awfully jolly, top-hole;* (*to be*) *as cheerful as a sandboy* °**~zucht** f: verdammte ~! *damn it all!*

s·auber I. [a] **1.** (rein) *clean* (*face, shirt*) ‖ ~ m *to clean, wash* ‖ *speckless, spotless* (*glass*) ‖ *they were neat and cleanly* od *spick and span* **2.** (charakterlich) *square;* ~er, junger Mensch *young hopeful* ‖ *neat, orderly* (*mind*) **3.** (ordentlich) *tidy* (*room*); ~ m *to tidy* ‖ *neat* (*clothing*) ‖ *good, careful* (*work*[*ing*]) ‖ *legible, clear* (*writing*) ‖ *fair* (*copy*) ‖ *lucid, clear* (*style*) **4.** (schmuck) *fine, elegant, smart, pretty* (*girl*) ‖ *promising young scamp* (Bub) ‖ *trim, spruce, natty* (*appearance*) **5.** ⟨fig⟩ *tidy* (*penny*) **6.** ⟨iron⟩ (Bürschchen, Früchtchen) *young scamp* od *scapegrace* ‖ (Freund) *nice sort of friend* ‖ (Gesellschaft) *nice set* ‖ (Patron) *bad lot* ‖ (v S) *rare, fine, nice* ‖ (Bescherung) *fine mess* ‖ (Dinge, Treiben) *fine doings, nice goings-on* **II.** [adv] (*to do a th*) *square and proper;* ~ abschreiben *to make a fair copy of* ‖ ~ abräumen *to clear the table tidily* ‖ (behutsam) *to handle carefully* ‖ *properly* (*shaved*) ‖ ~ halten *to keep* (*the house*) *tidy;* sich .. *to dress neatly;* (*to look*) *trig* **III.** die **≃ste** *the prettiest girl* | **≃halten** [n] v *protecting* (*foodstuffs*) | **≃keit** f *clean*(*li*)*ness, pureness, neatness* ‖ *fineness, elegance, prettiness* ‖ *clearness, lucidity* **s·äuberlich** a *clean* ‖ *gentle, soft, careful* ‖ *proper, decent* ‖ fein ~ *very neat and proper* etc | [adv] → sauber ‖ *neatly* (*packed*) fein ~ eingeordnet *pigeon-holed in apple-pie order* ‖ (*to handle carefully*) **s·äubern** vt [h] *to clean*(*se*), *purge* ‖ *to clear* (*the table*) ‖ *to tidy* (*a room*); (Stall) *to clean out* | etw v Schmutz ~ *to give a th a clean-up* | v Unkraut ~ *to weed* | *to clear* (*the country of the enemy*), ⟨mil⟩ *to mop up,* ⟨mar⟩ *to sweep* (*the seas*); die Straße v .. *to sweep the insurgents from the street* | ≃ n *mopping-up* **S·äuberung** f ~/~en *clean*(*-up*) ⟨a. pol⟩; *clearing; purification* ‖ *mopping-up* (*of an area*) ‖ (P ⟨pol⟩ *political*) *purification, purge* **~saktion, ~soperation** f *mopping-up operations* pl **~skomitee** n ⟨pol⟩ *action committee* od *group* **~sprozeß** m *tidying process, clean-up, cleansing, purging* **~swelle** f ⟨pol⟩ *cleaning-up action; purge*

S·auce ['zo:sə] f ~/~n *sauce* ‖ (Braten≃) *gravy* ‖ (pikante) *dressing, ketchup* ‖ (Pudding≃) *dip* | ~nlöffel [m] *s.-, g.-ladle* **Sauci·ere** [so:'sierə] f *sauce-, butter-, gravy-boat* **Sauc·ischen** [so'-si:sçən] n ~s/~ *small sausage*

°**s·auen** vi/t [h] (→ Sau) *to mess* ‖ (sudeln) *to daub* | sich voll~ *to mess o.s. up* °**Sauer·ei** f ~/~en *dirtiness, nastiness, beastliness* ‖ (Zote) *obscenity*

s·auer I. a **A. 1.** *sour* (*milk, beer, wine, fruit*) ‖ *acid* (*drops*) ⟨a. chem⟩ ‖ (essig~) *acetous* ‖ etw ~ *acidulous* (*drops, salts*) ‖ *pickled* (*cucumber*) **2.** ⟨fig⟩ (verdrossen) *cross, morose, peevish, crabbed* **3.** ⟨fig⟩ *hard* (*work, earnings*), *painful* (*work*), *harassing* (*office*), *worrying* (*duty*), *laborious* (*care*) **B.** in den ~en **Apfel** beißen *to swallow the bitter pill* ‖ ~es Aufstoßen *flatulency* ‖ (Boden) *sour, marshy* (*land*) ‖ ein ~es Gesicht m *to put on a sour face, to look surly* od *cross,* zu etw .. *to pull a long face over a th* ‖ mit ~er Miene *sour-faced* ‖ ~er Schweiß *sweat of the brow* ‖ ~e Trauben! *sour grapes, said the fox, when he could not reach them* **C. ~ erworben** *hard-earned, -gotten* ‖ das kannst du dir ~ kochen! *you can put that in your pipe and smoke it* ‖ das kommt ihm ~ an *he finds it troublesome* ‖ ~ m *to sour; to turn* (*milk*); ⟨chem⟩ *to acidify* ‖ mach mir das Leben nicht ~ *don't worry the life out of me* ‖ °⟨fig⟩ ~ reagieren *not to respond to a th;* °er ist ~ *he took it in ill part,* ⟨sl⟩ *he is peeved* ‖ ~ w *to turn sour;* (*of milk*) *to turn* ‖ e–m ~ w *to find it trying* (*it fatigues me greatly, walking is becoming a trouble to him, he finds it a worrying task*) ‖ es sich ~ w l *to take great pains, to toil and moil, to drudge* **II.** ≃e(s) n *goose-giblets* ‖ °gib ihm ~es! *give him beans! make it warm for him!* **S·auer- ~ampfer** m ⟨bot⟩ *sorrel,* kl ~ *sheep-s.* **~braten** m (*beef soaked in vinegar and cooked in a stewpan*) *sauerbraten* **~brunnen** m *mineral* od *acidulous spring* od *water* **~dorn** m *barberry-shrub* **~kirsche** f *morel*(*la cherry*) **~klee** m *wood-sorrel;* → *oxalis* **~kleesalz** n ⟨chem⟩ *oxalate* **~kraut** n *pickled cabbage, sauerkraut* **~land** n ⟨Ger⟩ (südl. Westfalen) Landschaft **~milch** f *curdled milk* **~stoff** m *oxygen;* flüssiger ~ *lox* (= *liquid ox.*) ‖ dem Blut ~ zuführen *to oxygenate the blood* ‖ mit ~ behandeln *to oxygenate;* mit ~ angereichert *oxygenerated;* mit ~ verbinden *to oxidize* | ~atmungsgerät [n] *pulmotor; oxygen breathing apparatus,* ⟨Am⟩ *oxygen respirator;* ~aufnahmefähigkeit [f] *oxygenation capacity;* ~behälter [m] *oxygen cylin-*

der; ~bleichmittel [n] *o.ated bleaching compound*; ~entzug [m] *deoxygenation*; ≗haltig [a] *oxygenated, oxidized*; ~hunger [m] *oxygen starvation*; ~mangel [m] im Blut *anoxemia*; im Gewebe *anoxia*; -erkrankung [f] ⟨aero⟩ *anoxia*; ~messer [m] *eudiometer*; ~pol [m] *anode*; ~schwund [m] ⟨biol⟩ *oxygen depletion*; ~verbindung [f] *oxide*; ~versorgung [f] *supply of oxygen*; ≗**süß** a ⟨a. fig⟩ *bitter-sweet* **~teig** m *leaven, sauerteig*, ⟨Am⟩ *sourdough* **~topf** m ⟨fig⟩ *ill-tempered p* ≗**töpfisch** a *morose, peevish, sour*; *crabby* **~wasser** n = ~brunnen **~wein** m *verjuice* **Sauere-G·urken-Zeit** f *dull* od *silly season, cucumber-time* **s·äuerlich** a *sourish*, ⟨chem⟩ *acidulous* ‖ *sourish, tartish* (*wine*) | ~ m *to acidulate* | ≗**keit** f *sourishness* **S·äuerling** m ~s/~e *acidulous water* od *spring* ‖ *sourish wine* **s·auern** vi [h & s] *to turn sour, to curdle* **s·äuern** vt [h] *to (make) sour*; *to acidulate*; ⟨chem⟩ *to acidify*; (Teig, Brot) *to leaven* **S·äuerung** f ~/ ⟨chem⟩ *acidification*; *acidulation* ‖ (des Brots) *leavening*

°**S·auf- ~aus, ~bruder** m *tippler, boozer, toper*; = -genosse **~bold** m *drunkard* **~gelage** n *drinking-bout*, ⟨fam⟩ *booze*, ⟨Am sl⟩ *bat, jamboree, tear, razzle-dazzle* **~genosse** m *boon-companion* **~gesellschaft, ~kompanie, ~kumpanei** f *party of boozers* **~lied** n *bacchanalian song* | auf **~tour** gehen *to paint the town red* **s·aufen I.** vi/t [soff/gesoffen] [h] (T) *to drink* ‖ °(P) *to drink hard*; *to booze* [vi], *tipple* [vi/t]; *to go on the booze* ‖ ⟨sl⟩ *to swizzle, soak, swig, lush* [vi/t] ‖ ~ wie ein Loch *to drink like a fish* ‖ [dat] zu ~ geben *to water* | [vt] *to imbibe* (*spirits* etc) ‖ e–n unter den Tisch ~ *to drink a p under the table* ‖ sich tot ~ *to drink o.s. to death* ‖ sich voll ~ *to get boozed* **II.** ≗ n *hard drinking*, ⟨fam⟩ *tippling* °**S·äufer** m ~s/~ *drunkard*, ⟨fam⟩ *tippler, toper*, ⟨sl⟩ *boozer, sot*, ⟨Am⟩ *soak* ‖ unverbesserlicher ~ *hard* od *heavy drinker*; *alcoholic*; ⟨path⟩ *dipsomaniac* ‖ stiller ~ *wet Quaker* ‖ alter ~ ⟨Am fam⟩ *booze hound* **~nase** f *tippler's* od *brandy, copper nose* **~stimme** f *gin voice* **~wahnsinn** m *delirium tremens*, ⟨fam⟩ *the junjams* pl **Saufer·ei** f ~/~en *hard drinking* ‖ (Gelage) *drinking-bout*, ⟨sl⟩ *booze(-fight), binge*

S·aug- ~ader f ⟨anat⟩ *absorbent* (*blood-*)*vessel* **~bagger** m *aspirating dredge(r)* ≗**fähig** a *absorbative*; *absorbent* (*paper*) | ~keit [f] *absorbency* **~filter** m *vacuum filter* **~flasche** f (*baby's*) *sucking-bottle, feeder* ‖ ⟨tech⟩ *aspirator* **~füßchen** n ⟨zoo⟩ *sucker-foot* **~heber** m *syphon* **~höhe** f *head of suction* **~hub** m ⟨mot⟩ *intake stroke* **~hütchen** n (e–r Babyflasche) *nipple*; (bei Brustentzündung) *n.-glass* **~kanal** m *induction port* **~kolben** m *valve-piston* **~kreis** m ⟨telv⟩ *absorption circuit* **~luft** f ⟨aero⟩ *inflow* | ~anlage [f] *vacuum plant*; ~bremse [f] *vacuum brake* **~lüfter** m *exhaustor* **~maschine** f *exhauster* **~napf** m ⟨zoo⟩ *sucking disc, sucker* **~öffnung** f *s.g-port* **~papier** n *absorbent paper* **~pfropfen** m (*baby's*) *rubber teat*; *dummy* **~platte** f ⟨dent⟩ *suction plate* **~pumpe** f *s.n* od *s.g-pump* **~rohr** n *s.n-pipe, sucker* **~röhrchen** n (Strohhalm) *straw-pipe* **~rüssel** m *suctorial organ*, ⟨ent⟩ *proboscis* **~scheibe** f *s.n-disk, sucker* **~stutzen** m (*pump*) *intake* **~ventil** n *s.n-valve* **~warze** f *nipple* **~walze** f *s.n couch roll* **~werk** n *s.g-pump* **~werkzeug** n *suctorial organ* **~windkessel** m ⟨mot⟩ *vacuum tank* **~wurm** m ⟨zoo⟩ *fluke* **~zone** f *s.n zone* **~zug** m *induced draught* **S·äug(e)- ~amme** f *wet-nurse* **~ferkel** n *s.l.g* **~fläschchen** n, **~flasche** f *s.g bottle*; *feeder* **~kalb** n *s.g-calf* **S·äuge- ~tier** n *mammifer, mammal* [pl ~ia] **~zähne** m pl *milk-teeth* pl **~zeit** f *s.g-period*, ⟨scient⟩ *lactation* **S·augen** n ~s/ *suction* **s·augen** vt/i, reg & irr: [sog/gesogen] [h] **A.** *to suck*; ~des Fohlen *unweaned* od *sucking foal*; *suckling* ‖ Staub ~ *to suck up dust* **B. an** etw ~: *baby sucks* od *takes the breast*; *the bear sucks its claws* ‖ ⟨fig⟩ an den Klauen ~ *to live in great misery, to be starving* ‖ (etw) an sich ~ *to suck up* ‖ Milch **aus** der Brust ~ *to suck the breast* ‖ Saft aus e–r Beere ~ .. *from* .. ‖ Feuchtigkeit aus der Erde ~ *to absorb .. in the soil* ‖ Honig aus allen Blüten ~ *to gather h. from every fl.* ⟨a. fig⟩ ‖ ⟨fig⟩ es ist nicht aus den Fingern gesogen *it has not been made up* (= *invented*) ‖ **in** sich ~ *to suck in, to imbibe* (*with one's mother's milk*) **C. sich** fest|~ *to attach o.s. by sucking* ‖ sich satt *or* voll|~ *to suck one's fill*; *the sponge has sucked itself full of water* **s·äugen I.** vt *to suckle, nurse*; *to give* (*baby*) *the breast* | **~d** (*mare*) *with an unweaned foal, giving suck*; *sucking* (*foal, lamb*) **II.** ≗ n *suckling, nursing*, ⟨scient⟩ *lactation* **S·auger** m ~s/~ ⟨zoo⟩ *suckling*; (*pig, whale*) *sucker* (⟨a.⟩ P) **S·äugling** m ~s/~e *suckling* (*baby*); *baby*; *child in arms*; *infant* (*child*); gestorbene ~e ⟨stat⟩ *infant deaths* | ⟨fig⟩ *sucker, cub* (*c. reporter*) **~salter** n *babyhood*; *infancy* (im ~ *in inf.*) **~sflasche** f *baby bottle* **~sfürsorge** f *infant welfare* (*services*) **~sheim** n *baby farm*; *infant home, crèche* Fr **~ssterblichkeit** f *infant mortality* | ~sziffer [f] *i. m. rate*

säuisch a *piggish* | ⟨fig⟩ *obscene*; → Sau

S·äule f ~/~n ⟨allg⟩ *column* (*c.*) ‖ Bündel≗ *bundle-c.*; gewundene ~ *spiral c.*; Halb≗ *imbedded c.*; Ring≗ *banded c.*; vorgesetzte Voll≗ *detached shaft* ‖ ⟨arch⟩ *pillar* (⟨a. fig⟩ *of society*), (*the P.s of Hercules*); ⟨a.⟩ *upright, support, prop* ‖ (Pfosten) *post, jamb* ‖ ⟨cryst⟩ *prism* ‖ ⟨mil⟩ *column* ‖ ⟨el⟩ (*voltaic*) *pile* | (Anschlag≗) *poster pillar* ‖ Steuer≗ *steering column* | wie e–e ~ dastehen *to stand like a post* **S·äulen- ~apostel** m = ~heiliger **~bau** m *building supported by c.s* ‖ *c.ar architecture* **~briefkasten** m *pillar-box* **~bündel** n *clustered column* ≗**förmig** a *c.ar* **~fuß** m *base, plinth* **~gang** m *colonnade, peristyle, portico*; (gedeckter) *hypostyle*; (e–s Tempels) *peridrome* ≗**gerade** a (*as*) *straight as pillars* od *as a p.* **~halle** f *pillared hall* od *arcade*; ⟨Eg⟩ *hypostyle*; *h. hall* **~hals** m *neck-mould, necking* **~heilige(r)** m *stylite, pillar-saint* **~hof** m *pillared court* **~knauf** m *capital* **~koppel** f *coupled columns* pl **~kranz** m *astragal* **~kuppelung** f *grouping of c.s* **~laube** f *portico*, → Vorhalle **~laubwerk** n *acanthus* **~ordnung** f *order* (*Doric o.*) **~platte** f *plinth, abacus* **~reihe** f *row of c.s, colonnade*; *peristyle*, (runde) *monopteron* **~schaft** m *shaft of a pillar* **~schwellung** f *entasis* Gr **~stativ** n ⟨phot⟩ *pillar stand* **~stellung** f *disposition of pillars* **~stumpf** m *truncated c.* **~trommel** f *barrel, tambour* **~weite** f *intercolumniation* **~werk** n *colonnade* **s·äulig** a = säulenförmig ‖ [in comp] *with* (*four*) *columns*

Saum[1] m ~(e)s/≗e (*to sew a*) *seam*; *hem* (*of a dress*); (Rand) *border, margin, edge*; *narrow line* ‖ ⟨bot, zoo⟩ mit fransigem, behaartem ~ *fimbriate(d)* ‖ ⟨weav⟩ *selvage* ‖ ⟨arch⟩ *fillet* ‖ *doubling* (*of sails*) ‖ ⟨übtr⟩ (Wald≗ etc) (*out*)*skirts* pl; *lip* (*of a harbour*) **~holz** n *curb-beam* **~naht** f *hem* **~riff** n *fringing reef* **~schlag** m ⟨for⟩ *strip cutting* **~schwelle** f ⟨arch⟩ *raising-piece* **~stich** m *hemming stitch*

Saum[2] m ~(e)s/≗e *burden, mule-load* **~pfad** m *bridle-path, mule-track* **~pferd, ~roß** n *sumpter-* od *pack-horse* **~sattel** m *pack-saddle* **~steig** m = ~pfad **~tier** n *beast of burden, sumpter-mule*

s·äumen 1. vt *to hem, border, edge* ‖ (mit Fransen) *to fringe* **S·äumung** f ~/~en (Einsäumen) *hemming in* **2.** vi (zögern) *to delay, tarry* ‖ (zaudern) *to hesitate* ‖ (zurück bleiben) *to linger* od *lag behind* **S·äumer** m ~s/~ **1.** *lingerer* **2.** *driver of pack animals* **3.** *hemmer* **s·äumig** a *tardy* (*to do*); *slow* (*payer*); *defaulting* (*tenant*); *dilatory* (*debtor*); ~e Partei *defaulter* ‖ [pred] *in default*; *behindhand* (*with the delivery*), *remiss* **S·äumnis** f ~/-nisse; ~ n -nisses/-nisse *delay, delatoriness* | ~zuschlag [m] *extra charge on over due payment*

s·aumselig a = säumig || *lagging behind, hanging back* || (lässig) *lazy, heedless* || (nachlässig) *negligent; dilatory (correspondent)* **≃keit** f *tardiness, procrastination, dilatoriness, negligence*

S·auna(bad n) f ~/~s *sauna(bath)*

S·aurach m ~(e)s/~e ⟨bot⟩ *barberry*

S·äure f ~/~n **1.** [abstr] *sourness* || *acidity (of wine, of the stomach)* || ⟨fig⟩ *sourness, moroseness* ⟨fam⟩ *crabbiness* **2.** [konkr] ⟨chem⟩ *acid (a.)* **~ballon** m *carboy* **≃beständig** a *a.-proof* **≃bildend** a *a.ifying, a.ific* **~bildner** m *a.ifier* **~bildung** f (im Blut) *a.osis* **~haltig** a *a.iferous* **~messer** m *a.imeter* **~schutzfett** n *acidproof grease* **~verätzung** f *acid burn*

S·aurier m ~s/~, **S·aurier-** ⟨zoo⟩ *saurian*

Saur·oktonos m ~/ ⟨ant arts⟩ *Lizzardkiller*

S·aus m ~es/ *noise*; ⟨fig⟩ *whirl of pleasure, revel, riot* || in ~ u Braus leben *to live high* (od *a wild life*); *to revel, riot*; *to indulge in riotous living* | **~e- ~fahrt** f *race*, ⟨fam⟩ *scorching* **~laut** m ⟨gram⟩ *sibilant* **~wind** m *blustering wind* || ⟨fig⟩ *giddy, heedless, impetuous p*; *roaring* od *flighty young blade*; *harum-scarum* **s·äuseln I.** vi **1.** [h] (Blätter, Wind) *to rustle* || (Wind) *to whisper* || ⟨fig⟩ *to lisp, whisper* **2.** [s] *to buzz along* || **~d** *humming (voice), murmuring (tones)* **II.** vt *to hum, whisper* || jdn in den Schlaf ~ *to lull a p to sleep* **s·ausen I.** vi **1.** [h] (Wind) *to whistle, sough* || (Wasser) *to swish, rush* || (Kugel) *to swish, whiz* || (Blut) *to buzz* || (Zug) *to whirl* || (Räder) *to whiz* | mir saust der Kopf *my head is in a whirl* || mir ~ die Ohren *I have a singing noise in my ears* || es saust *the wind sighs* etc **2.** [s] (S) *to hurtle, rush, bluster, swoop (along, through, into, out of, from, down on)* || *to whiz (round)* | (P) *to rush, dash*, ⟨fam⟩ *hurtle, whisk, whip*, ⟨sl⟩ *snip* **II.** ≃ n *rumbling* etc; *r.g noise*; *sough* || *humming* od *singing (in the ears)*

Sav·annah 1. m (Fluß in Nordamerika) **2.** n (Hauptstadt Georgias, U.S.A.)

Sav·anne f ~/~n *savanna*; ~nfieber *prairie-fever*

S·ave f → Sau (Nebenfluß der Donau)

Savoy·arde m, **Savoy·ardin** [savwa-] f *Savoyard, inhabitant of Savoy* ⟨Fr⟩ **savoy·ardisch, Sav·oyen** n [-oi-] *Savoy* **Sav·oyerkohl** m *savoy cabbage* **sav·oyisch** [sa'voiiʃ] a *Savoyard, (of) Savoy*

S·ax- ~horn n *saxhorn* **~oph·on** n *saxophone*

Scapa Flow [-'flou] (brit. Flottenstützpunkt auf den Orkney Inseln)

sch! [intj] *sh! hush! shoo!* || ~ m *to hush, shoo*

Sch·abe f ~/~n *cockroach*; *blackbeetle*

Sch·ab(e)- ~b(l)ock m, **~brett** n *(hide-)dresser's horse*; *trestle*; *scraping-block* **~eisen** n *rasper, scraper* **~fleisch** n *scraped meat* **~hobel** m *scraping-plane* **~klinge** f *scraper* **~kunst, ~manier** f ⟨arts⟩ *mezzotint-engraving* || in ~ ausführen *to (engrave in) mezzotint* **~messer** n *paring knife*; *scraping-knife*, ⟨med⟩ *scalping-iron* **~pol·ierstahl** m *scraper-burnisher* **~wolle** f *glover's wool* **sch·aben** vt **1.** *to scrape (carrots*, ⟨sl⟩ *o.s.* sich rasieren) || *to shave (skins)* || *to shred, mince (meat)* || (kratzen) *to scratch* || (auf dem Reibeisen) *to rasp, grate* | jdm den Bart ~ *to shave*, ⟨hum⟩ *to scrape a p* **2.** ⟨arts⟩ *to (engrave in) mezzotint, to etch* **3.** ⟨fig⟩ ~ u kratzen *to save and scrape* || e–m Rübchen ~ *to make game of a p* **Sch·aber** m ~s/~ (P & S) *scraper* ⟨a. praeh⟩ || ⟨pap⟩ (Werkzeug) *doctor* || ⟨fig⟩ (P) *skinflint* **~nack** m ~s/~e *trick*; *practical joke* || e–m e–n ~ spielen *to play a p a nasty trick, to play a practical joke on a p* || mit jdm s–n ~ treiben *to pull a p's leg* || zum ~ *out of mischief* || jdm zum ~ *to a p's annoyance, to spite a p* || zu allerlei ~ bereit *up to all kinds of devilry* **sch·äbig** a *shabby (dress)*; *scrubby (room)* || ⟨fig⟩ *sh.y, mean, stingy, dirty* **≃keit** f *sh.iness* ⟨a. fig⟩ || ⟨fig⟩ *meanness, dirtiness, filthiness*

Schabl·one f ~/~n *model, mould, pattern* || *cutting shape (for prints)* || ⟨tech⟩ *loam-board* || ⟨arts⟩ *stencil* || ⟨fig⟩ nach der ~ *by rote* od *routine* || nach der ~ arbeiten *to work mechanically* | **~n- ≃haft, ≃mäßig** a *mechanical, after a certain pattern* || ⟨fig⟩ *routine-like, conventional, stereotyped, cut and dry* od *dried* **~malerei** f *stencil-work*; *slapdash work* **~mensch** m *stereotyped figure* || ~ s *to be in a groove* **~wesen** n *routine* **~zeichnung** f *stencil drawing* **schablon·ieren** vt/i ⟨arts⟩ *to stipple*

Schab·otte f ~/~n *anvil block*

Schabr- ~·acke f ~/~n *saddlecloth*; ⟨hist⟩ *caparison*; ⟨decor⟩ *pelmet* **~·unke** f *decorated cloth*

Sch·absel n ~s/~ *scrapings, shavings* pl

Schach n ~(e)s/ *chess (c.s)* || ~! *check (c.k)* || ~ durch Abzug *discovered c.k* | ~ bieten *to (give) c.k* || ⟨fig⟩ (jdm) *to defy (a p)* || maskiertes ~ bieten *to discover c.k* || ~ decken *to cover the king* || ~ spielen *to play c.s* || in ~ halten ⟨fig⟩ *to keep in c.k* (od *at bay*; *under*); den Feind in ~ halten ⟨mil⟩ *to contain the e.* || mit der Pistole *to cover with a p.* || *to restrain, curb* || ~ u matt! *c.kmate!* **~aufgabe** f *c.s-problem* **~brett** n *c.s-board* | **≃artig** [a] *chequered; checkerlike; tesselated*; ~blume [f] *fritillary*; ~system [n] ⟨arch⟩ *gridiron s.* **~feld** n *square* **~figur** f *c.k-man* || ~en [pl] (sämtliche) *a set of c.s-men* **≃förmig** a *chequered* **≃m·att** a (Spiel) *(c.k)mate* ⟨a. fig⟩ || ⟨fig⟩ *tired out*, ⟨fam⟩ *dead-beat* || ~ m *to c.kmate* || ~ s *to be c.kmated* || ⟨fig⟩ *to be exhausted* **~meisterschaft** f *c.s-championship* **~partie** f *game of c.s* **~spiel** n *c.s-playing* || (Partie) *g. of c.s* || (Brett u Figuren) *c.s-board and set of c.smen* **~spieler** m *c.splayer* **~stein** n *c.sman* **~turnier** n *c.s-match* **~zug** m *move* || ⟨fig⟩ geschickter ~ *dexterous move, well-timed measure*

Sch·achen m ~s/~ obd *coppice*; Sw *lowland*; *littoral*

Sch·acher m ~s/ *chaffer(ing), haggling, higgling* || ⟨pol⟩ *political jobbery* || ~ treiben *to huckster* **~handel** m = ~ || **~jude** m *old-clo'man*, ⟨übtr⟩ *haggler, huckster* **Schacher·ei** f ~/~en = Schacher **sch·achern** vt/i [h] *to chaffer*; *to barter (away)*; *to haggle* (um *about, over*)

Sch·ächer m ~s/~ ⟨bib⟩ (Übeltäter) *robber, murderer* || der ~ am Kreuz *the thief on the cross* | ⟨fig⟩ armer ~ *poor wretch*

Schacht m ~(e)s/≃e ⟨min⟩ *shaft, pit*; blinder ~ *wince* | ⟨allg⟩ *opening, hollow, depression* || *gorge, ravine* | ⟨tech, met⟩ *fire-room* || ⟨arch⟩ *lift* (⟨Am⟩ *elevator) pit* od *well* || (Licht≃) *light-room, well* || Luft≃ *uptake*; *ventilating shaft* || e–n ~ befahren *to descend into a sh.* **~abdeckung** f ⟨arch⟩ *man-hole cover* **~abteufung** f *sinking of a sh.* **~arbeiter** m *pitman*; *sh. sinker* **~brunnen** m *dug well* **~bühne** f *landing stage* **~einfahrt** f *pit-mouth* **~feld** n *bay of a sh.* **~förderung** f *sh.-hoisting* **~futter** n *lining of a sh.* od *of a furnace* **~loch** n *manhole* **~meister** m *overseer of a pit*; ⟨rail⟩ *foreman of navvies* **~ofen** m *cupola, pit-furnace* **~scheider** m ⟨min⟩ *brattice* **~verkleidung** f *sh.-lining* **sch·achten** vt [h] *to sink, to excavate*

Sch·achtel f ~/~n *box* || (Hut≃) *bandbox* || e–e ~ Soldaten *a box of soldiers* | ⟨fig⟩ alte ~ *old maid* od *spinster* od *woman*; ⟨fam⟩ *hay-bag, hen-wife, frump* | nett wie aus der ~ *as if straight from a bandbox* **~deckel** m *cover of a box, box-lid* **~halm** m ⟨bot⟩ *pewter-grass, horse-tail* **~karton** m *box board* **~macher** m *bandbox-maker* **~männchen** n *Jack-in-the-box* **~pappe** f *box board* **~satz** m ⟨gram⟩ *involved period* **~wort** n *portmanteau word (e.g. brunch = breakfast + lunch)*; → *acronym* **Schächtelchen** n ~s/~ *little box* **sch·achteln** vt [h] *to put in a box*; *to pack* || *to polish with pewter-grass* || in–e–a–~ *to nest (boxes*, etc)

sch·ächten vt [h] ⟨Hebr⟩ *to kill, butcher* **Sch·ächter** m ~s/~ *Jewish butcher* **Sch·ächtung** f ~/ *kosher butchering*

Sch·adchen m ~s/~ [Hebr] *marriage-broker*

sch·ade I. [a & adv] ~! *what a pity!*, ⟨Am a.⟩ *too bad!* || es ist recht *or* sehr ~! *it is a great pity!* ([*that*] *you were late,* [*that*] *he should have died*) || wie ~, daß ..! *and to think I've lost it!* || es ist nur ~, daß *the pity is that*; ~ drum! *the pity of it!*; es ist ewig ~! *it is a thousand pities!* || ~ um ihn *it's a great pity for him* || um den ist's nicht ~ *he's not much of a loss, that serves him right* | zu ~ [a] **für** *too good for* **II.** → ≗n

Sch·ädel m ~s/~ *skull, brain-pan,* ⟨scient⟩ *cranium* || (*to hit a p on the*) *head* || ⟨sl⟩ *sconce, noddle* || mit kurzem ~ *blunt-headed* || jdm den ~ einschlagen *to dash a p's brains, to beat* od *kick a p's skull* od *brain in* || sich blutige ~ holen *to get broken heads* || ⟨fig⟩ sich den ~ einrennen *to run one's head against a brick wall* **~basisbruch** m *basal fracture of the skull* **~beschreibung** f *craniography* **~bohrer** m ⟨surg⟩ *trepan* **~bruch** m *fracture of the skull, fractured skull* **~brummen** n *a* (*sore*) *head* (*to have a h.*) **~haut** f *pericranium* **~höhle** f *cranial cavity* **~index** m ⟨biol⟩ *index* **~kappe** f ⟨a–n⟩ *skull-cap* **~lehre** f *craniology, phrenology* **~messung** *craniometry* **~naht** f *coronal suture* **~stätte** f ⟨bib⟩ *Calvary, Golgatha* .. **schäd(e)lig** a (*narrow-* etc)*skulled*

Sch·ade(n) m ~ns/≗n **A. 1.** *damage* (*d.*); Brand≗ *d.* (*caused*) *by fire*; Flur≗, Gebäude≗ *d. to crops, buildings*; Nutzungs≗ *d. through loss of use*; Sach≗ *d. to property*; See≗ *d. by sea*; Vertrags≗ *d. for breach of contract* **2.** (körperlich) *harm, hurt*; *injury* (*to health*) || (Gebrechen) *infirmity*; ⟨fig⟩ *handicap* **3.** (Verlust) *loss* **4.** (Unheil) *mischief, harm, wrong* **5.** ⟨fig⟩ (Abbruch) *detriment, prejudice, disadvantage*; ⟨jur⟩ *tort* **6.** ≗n [pl] (Verheerung) *ravages* pl || (Mängel) *evils, nuisances* pl **7.** mehr ~ als Nutzen *more harm than good* **B.** dein **eigener** ~ *your own loss* || eingewurzelter ~ *deeply rooted evils* pl || empfindlicher ~ *a serious loss* || geringer ~ *a slight injury* || innerer ~ *internal injury* od *disease* od *complaint* || offener ~ *open sore* || nicht wiedergutzumachender ~ *irreparable injury* **C.** gr ~ **anrichten** *to do great harm* od *d.* || sich ~ antun: *lest he should do h.s. a mischief* || ~ beseitigen *to counteract d.* || ~ bringen, stiften, tun *to do harm, mischief* || e–n ~ am Bein davontragen *to suffer an injury to one's leg* || ein ~ entsteht, erwächst *a loss results* || ~ erleiden *to suffer d.*; .. durch .. *to be d.d by*; *to be a loser in a th*, k–n .. *to be none the worse for a th* || den ~ ersetzen *to make good the loss*; ⟨ins⟩ jeder ~ z ers. *all average recoverable* (*a. a. r.*) || h Sie ~ dabei? *are you a loser by it?* || er hat an s–r Gesundheit ~ gelitten *his health has suffered* || was kostet der ~? *what's the d.?* || ~ **nehmen** *to become impaired*; (k–n) ~ n. *to come to* (*no*) *harm*; *to suffer d.*, ohne ~ an s–r Seele z n. *without harm to his soul* || den ~ regeln *to settle for losses* || es wird dein ~ s *it will be the worse for you*, .. nicht .. *you shall not regret it* || den ~ tragen *to bear the loss* || *the loss hit* (traf) *him hard* || ~ **tun** *to do prejudice*; vgl ~ bringen || das wird s–r Gesundheit ~ tun *that will injure his h.* || sich [dat] e–n ~ tun *to do o.s. an injury, to hurt o.s.* || ~ verhindern, verhüten *to prevent injury*; bemüht ~ z v. *d. conscious* || ~ verursachen *to cause d.* || er will d–n ~ nicht *he means no harm to you* || jdm ~ zufügen *to harm, hurt, wrong a p, to inflict d.* od *injury upon a p* || *to bring harm to a country* || *to do d. to a th* | **sich** [dat] ~ z. *to injure o.s.* ⟨a. fig⟩ **D. gegen** ~ versichert *insured against loss* || jdn **in** ~ stürzen *to bring losses upon a p* || **mit** ~ verkaufen *to sell at a loss* od *sacrifice* od *below cost price* || fort *or* weg mit ~! *let it go!*, *'tis a good riddance* || sich **von** s–m ~ erholen *to recover one's loss*(*es*) || (nicht) **zu** ~ k *to come to* (*no*) *harm*; **zum** ~ v *to the belittlement of* || zu m–m ~ *at my cost* od *expense*; *to my detriment* || ob zum ~ oder zum Vorteil *for better for worse* || es wird ihm zum ~ gereichen *it will be the worse for him* || zu ~ k *to sustain losses, to be hurt, to come off a loser, to come to grief* (a. v S), ⟨Am sl⟩ *to fall down* (bei *in*) **E.** ⟨**prov**⟩ **durch** ~ wird man klug *bitten once, twice shy*; *bought wit is best, a burnt child dreads the fire* || wer den ~ hat, braucht für den Spott nicht z sorgen *losers are always in the wrong*; *that's adding insult to injury*

sch·aden vi [h] **A. 1.** jdm ~ *to harm, hurt, injure, prejudice*; *to do harm to a p*; *to do a p injury*; *to be damaging a p* | jdm bei e–m andern ~ *to prejudice a p against a p* || jdm weder ~ noch nützen *neither to make nor mar a p* || du schadest dir selbst *you will only be standing in your own light* | [**abs**] *to be harmful* **2.** jdm, e–r S ~ *to derogate from a p, a th* **3.** e–r S ~ *to damage, prejudice a th, to be prejudicial to a th* || *to injure* (*one's health*) **B.** e–e Frage kann nicht ~ *there is no harm in asking* || Bürsten würde dem Hut nichts ~ *the hat would be none the worse for a brushing* || Vorsicht kann nicht ~ .. *never comes amiss*, .. *will never do any harm* || blinder Eifer schadet nur *more haste less speed*; *hasty speed does not oft succeed* || zuviel kann nie ~! *the more the merrier!* **C. 1. das** schadet nichts *there is no harm in that, that won't hurt, it doesn't matter, never mind* || das schadet fast gar nichts *that doesn't signify much* | das schadet ihm nicht(s!)! *that will do him no harm* (*that serves him right!*) **2. es** kann nicht ~ *it can do no harm* (*to write to him*) || es könnte nicht ~ .. *it mightn't hurt* (*to check up*), *it wouldn't be amiss, it would be none the worse for it* (wenn *if*); *his hands would all be better for a wash* **3. was** schadet es? *what harm can it do?*; *what harm is there, what does it matter* (wenn *if*)?, ⟨fam⟩ *what of it?*, *what's the odds?*

Sch·aden- **~abrechnung** f ⟨ins⟩ *claim statement* **~anzeige** f *notification of loss* **~aufmachung** f ⟨mar ins⟩ *statement of average* **~aufwand** m ⟨ins⟩ *claim expenses* **~bearbeitungskosten** pl *unallocated claim adjustment expenses* **~begutachtung** f *loss assessment* **~bekämpfung** f *d. control* **~bericht** m *d. report* **~beseitigung** f *d. repair* **~besichtigung** f *d. survey* **~betrag** m *damage* **~ermittlung** f: Aufwendungen f ~ *direct claim adjustment expenses* **~ersatz** m *indemnity, indemnification, compensation* || (Geldsumme) *d.s* pl (*liable to d.s*); vereinbarter ~ *liquidated d.s* || ~ erhalten *to recover d.s* || ~ leisten *to make amends, to pay d.s*; *to allow compensation* (*for*) || auf ~ verklagen *to sue for damages* pl | ~anspruch [m] *right to claim for d.s*; ⟨jur⟩ *claim in tort*; ~klage [f] *action* od *proceedings* pl *for d.s* **~fall** m ⟨ins⟩ *claim* **~festsetzung ~feststellung, ~schätzung** f (tatsächlich) *d. ascertainment*, (wertmäßig) *d. assessment* **~feuer** n *destructive fire* **~freude** f *malice*; (*malicious*) *joy at a p's misfortunes*; *malignity*; *grim enjoyment of a p's discomfiture* (Shaw); *malicious relish of a p's defeat* (Thackeray) ≗**froh** a *malicious, mischievous, mischief-loving, gloating* **~haftung** f *liability for d.s* **~klage** f ⟨jur⟩ *action for d.s* **~rückstellung** f *claim reserves* pl *remaining* **~satz** m *claim percentage* **~untersuchung** f *d. survey* **~verlauf** m *claim development* **Schadens-** **~andienung** f ⟨ins⟩ *notification* **~bearbeiter** m *appraiser* **~kammer** f *indemnity commission* **~lagekarte** f ⟨mil⟩ *d. situation chart* **schadhaft** a *damaged, injured*; *defective, faulty*; *spoiled*; *worn out*; *carious* (*tooth*); ~e Wegstrecke! ⟨mot⟩ *Bumps!*; *dilapidated, ruinous*; ⟨Am⟩ *hurt* (*book*) || ~ w *to decay*; *to get spoilt* od *damaged* | ≗**igkeit** f ~/ *damaged condition, damaged state, faultiness, defectiveness*

sch·ädigen vt [h] *to wrong, impair* (*a p*) || *to prejudice* (*a p, a th*), *to let* (*a p, a th*) *down* | der

Ge–gte *the aggrieved party* | **~d** *prejudicial (influences)* **Sch·ädigung** f ~/ *damage* ([gen] *done to*), *prejudice, detriment* (*to*); *impairment* (*of rights*); *derogation, detraction* (*from a th*) ‖ ~ verursachend *tending to injure* (*the voice*) **sch·ädlich** a *injurious, hurtful* ‖ *mischievous* (*beetle, work*) ‖ *deleterious, bad* (*effect*) ‖ (nachteilig) *prejudicial, detrimental* ‖ (bösartig) *noxious, pernicious* ‖ *damaging* (*to trade*) ‖ *injurious* (*to health*), (ungesund) *noisome* ‖ ⟨fig⟩ *unwholesome* (*book, influence*); ~er Einfluß *blight* ‖ e–r S ~ s ⟨a.⟩ *to be a foe to a th*; ~e Substanz *injurant* | **≃keit** f, ~ *injuriousness* ‖ *malignity, harmfulness* ‖ *noxiousness, perniciousness, noisomeness* **Sch·ädling** m ~s/~e *noxious p*; *misfit* ‖ *waster* ‖ *injurant* ‖ ⟨bot⟩ *pest* (~sbekämpfer *insect and rodent controller*; ~sbekämpfung *p. control, disinfection*; –gsmittel *p.icide, insecticide, exterminant*) ‖ (T) *n. animal*; *infestant*; ⟨a.⟩ *vermin* | ⟨fig⟩ *blighter, pest*; *mischief* (*to*) **sch·adlos** a *indemnified* ‖ (harmlos) *without hurt*; *harmless* ‖ ~ halten *to indemnify, to compensate* (f *for*) ‖ sich ~ halten *to indemnify, repay, reimburse, recoup o.s.*; .. bei jdm *to take* (*one's change* od) *it out of a p, to hold a p responsible* (*for*); .. f .. *to recover expenses, damages* **≃haltung** f *indemnification, indemnity, compensation*; *recoupment* **≃igkeit** f ~/ *harmlessness, hurtlessness*

Schad·uf m ~s/~s [Arab] (Schwingbrunnen) *shadoof*

Sch·af n ~(e)s/~e *sheep* [pl *sheep*] ‖ (Mutterschaf) *ewe* ‖ (nach der 1. Schur) *shearling* ‖ (im 2. Jahr) *teg* ‖ (wild) *bighorn, moufflon, argali* ‖ ⟨fig fam⟩ *goose, simpleton, blockhead, oaf* ‖ *to seperate the sheep from the goats* (v d. Böcken) **~blattern** f pl *chicken-pox* **~bock** m *ram* **~darm** m *sh.-gut* **~fäule** f *sh.-rot* **~fell** n *sh.skin*; *fleece* **~fleisch** n *mutton* **~garbe** f ⟨bot⟩ *milfoil*; *common yarrow* **~gesicht** n *stupid* od *sh.'s face* **~halter** m ⟨Am⟩ *sh.man* **~haltung** f *the keeping of sh.* **~haut** f (Embryohülle) *caul* **~herde** f *flock of sh.* **~hirt** m *shepherd* **~hürde** f *sheepfold, -cot*; *pen* **~husten** m *dry cough* **~hütte** f *shepherd's cot* **~käse** m *sheep's-milk cheese* **~knecht** m *shepherd's man* **~(s)kopf** m ⟨fig⟩ = ~ ‖ *mutton-head, dunderhead, fool, numskull, dolt, nitwit, noodle* ‖ ⟨fam⟩ *mutton-head*, ⟨Am sl⟩ *mutt, dub* ‖ ~! *ass*! **~köpfig** a *sh.like* (*face*) **~lamm** n *ewe-lamb* **~leder** n *sh.skin*; °ausreißen wie ~ *to take to one's heels* | ~einband [m] *sh.skin binding* **≃mäßig** a ⟨fam⟩ *stupid* **~meister** m *sh.-master* **~milch** f *sh.'s* od *ewe's milk* **~mist** m *sh.'s dung* ‖ ⟨fig⟩ ~! *rot*!; ein netter ~! *what a mess*! **~mutter** f *ewe* **~snase** f = –kopf **~pelz** m *sh.skin coat* **~scherer** m *sh.-shearer* **~schere** f (e–e *a pair of*) *sh.-shears* pl **~schur** f *sh.-shearing* **~schwemmen** n *sh.-washing* **~seuche** f *sh.-rot* **~stall** m *sh.-fold* **~stand** m *stock of sh.* **~sterben** n ⟨path⟩ *sh.-rot* **~trift, ~weide** f *sh.-walk, -run* **~wolle** f *sh.'s wool, fleece* **~zecke** f *sh.-louse* **~zucht** f *sh.-rearing, -breeding* **~züchter** m *sh.-breeder* **Sch·äfchen** n ~s/~ *lamb, lambkin* ‖ ⟨fig⟩ *kid(dy)* ‖ [nur pl] (Wolken) *dappled* od *fleecy clouds* pl, ⟨meteor⟩ *cirrocumulus* sg ‖ sein ~ ins Trockene bringen, sein ~ scheren ⟨fig⟩ *to feather one's nest* **Sch·äfer** m ~s/~ *shepherd* **~dichtung** f *pastoral poetry* **~gedicht** n *pastoral* (*poem*), *idyll, eclogue* **~gespräch** n *pastoral dialogue* **~hund** m *shepherd's dog*, deutscher ~ *Alsatian*, schottischer ~ *collie* **~hütte** f *shepherd's cot* **~junge, ~knecht** m *sh.d's boy* **~karren** m *sh.d's cart* **~lied** n *pastoral song* **~mädchen** n *young sh.dess* **~pfeife** f *sh.d's pipe* **~roman** m; **~spiel** n *pastoral romance*; *p. play* **~szene** f *pastorale* **~stab** m *sh.d's staff, crook* **~stunde** f *hour of love* **~tasche** f *sh.d's pouch* **Schäfer·ei** f ~/~en *sheep-farm* | ~knecht [m] *sheep-herder* **Sch·äferin** f ~/~en *shepherdess*

Schaff n ~(e)s/~e [obd] *tub, vat* ‖ *cupboard*

Sch·affen n *creating* ‖ *creation* ‖ *work, productions* pl (*poetic p.s*) **sch·affen** vt/i **I.** [schuf/ge~] [h] **1. (erschaffen)** *to make, produce, create, provide*; *to bring forth* od *about, to call into life* od *existence*; *to form, fashion*; *to put together*; *establish, found*; *devise*; *organize*; *contrive, set up*; ⟨fam⟩ *concoct* ‖ (im Geiste) *to conceive* | *to cause* (*a vacancy*) ‖ *to constitute* (*a position*) ‖ *to afford* (*pleasure*) ‖ *to brew* (*a situation*) ‖ *to breed* (*a spirit of* ..) **2. ~ zu**: *he turned them out good citizens* **3.** neu **geschaffen** *newly created, recently produced* ‖ das Geschaffene *the creation* | **wie** ihn (sie) Gott g. hat *in nature's garb* | (wie) g. f .. (P) *just cut out for, most fitted for, the very man for*; (S) *made, destined for*; f jdn: *this position is just what will suit him*; *a peach of a part for him* **II.** [reg] [h] **A. 1. (verschaffen)** *to procure*; *furnish, provide* (⟨a.⟩ *with*) | (e–e Aussteuer) *to collect* ‖ (etw z Essen): *let me have* od *find me* .. ‖ Geld ~ *to procure, provide supplies, funds, to find the money*; jdm .. *to provide a p with m.* ‖ Hilfe ~ *to procure help, to render assistance* ‖ Linderung ~ *to soothe* ‖ Rat ~ *to devise means*; (*he knows how*) *to find a way out*; .. schon .. *he will see to that*; .. immer .. *he is never at a loss* ‖ sich Recht ~ *to secure one's right*; (Ruhe) *to procure* ‖ sich gute Tage ~ *to arrange for a good time* **2. (bewirken)** ~ Sie, **daß** Sie fertig w *see that you get ready* **3.** (S) das schafft (= fördert)! *that helps a lot*!, ⟨fam⟩ *that's a lift*! ‖ die Arbeit schafft *the work is progressing well* **B. 1. (arbeiten, wirken)** *to do, work, make, act* ‖ tüchtig ~ *to be a good worker* ‖ viel ~ *to do a lot, to get through much work* ‖ nichts ~ *to effect nothing* ‖ fertig ~ *to finish* ‖ er schafft am besten, wenn .. *he does best when* .. **2. (beschäftigt s)** *to be busy, occupied, active* **3. es** ~ (= **fertig bringen**) *to manage it, to get along*, ⟨Am⟩ *there*; *to succeed*; *to achieve one's object* ‖ wir h es aber noch geschafft *we made it in time, we have run it fine*; (*I wonder if he'll*) *do it*; *we've done it* **C. 1. e-m z ~ geben** [vi] *to give a p plenty to do, work, occupation* **2. z ~ h** *to have sth* od *a lot to do, to be engaged* ‖ was **hast** du hier z ~ *what business have you here* ‖ ich will nichts z ~ h mit *that is no concern of mine, I will have nothing to do with* od *to say to, I wash my hands of it*; *I have done with him* ‖ das hat nichts damit z ~ *that is irrelevant to it* **3.** jdm (gehörig, viel, schwer) **z ~ m** *to cause* od *give a p* (*great*) *trouble* od (*much*) *anxiety*; *to be a charge upon a p*; *to lead a p a dance* ‖ *that will get him into trouble* (*into no end of troubles*); ⟨sport⟩ *to punish a p*; (S) *to trouble a p* (*a great deal*) | **sich** [dat] z ~ m *to set to work, to find work, to busy o.s.*; .. an *or* mit *to be busy about* od *with, to tamper* od *struggle with, to apply o.s. to* (*a th*); *to fiddle at a th* ⟨fig⟩ *to nurse* (*one's stick*) **D.** (bringen, befördern) **1.** *to convey, transport* ‖ (her~) *to bring* (*to*) ‖ (fort~, hin~) *to take* (*to*), *to run* (*goods to an island*) **2. an** Ort u Stelle ~ *to bring to the spot* | **auf** den Boden ~ *to put in the attic* ‖ auf die Seite (*or* **beiseite**) ~ *to put aside*, (betrügerisch) *to embezzle* | **aus** [dat]: *to remove from* (*the house*) *to send out of* (*the town*) ‖ aus dem Wege ~ *to remove, to get* (*a th*) *out of the way*; ⟨fig⟩ *to make away with* (*a p, a th*) ‖ jdn aus der Welt ~ *to dispatch a p*; etw ..: *does that put the matter right*?, *that does not blot the matter out*, (durch gute Führung) *he lived it down* | wir –ten es **bis** N. in e–m Tag *we made N.* .. | **in** [acc]: *get him into that room* | **nach** Hause ~ *to take home* | sich jdn **vom** Halse, Leibe ~ *to get rid of a p, to shake a p off* | **zur** Bahn ~ *to bring to the station* ‖ zur Stelle ~ *to produce* **sch·affend** a *working* (*man*) ‖ *creative* (*spirit*) ‖ *active* (*nature, forces*) ‖ *productive* (*trades*) ‖ (*iron-*)*producing* (*industry*) **≃e(r)** m *maker*; *man of work* **Sch·affens- ~drang** m *desire to create, creative instinct* **~kraft** f *creative power* **~lust** f *delight in creating* **≃lustig** a *creative*; *desirous of* *producing* **~zeit** f *floruit* L (*of an author*) **Sch·affer** m ~s/~ **1.** *worker* ‖ *creator* ‖ *hard-working man* **2.** ⟨mar⟩ *steward* | **~·ei** f ⟨mar⟩ *bread-room* **Sch·affner** m ~s/~ *steward, housekeeper, manager* ‖ ⟨rail⟩ *guard*, ⟨Am⟩ *conductor* (*on a train*) ‖ (Schlafwagen~̈) *porter* ‖ (Straßenbahn–, Autobus~̈) *conductor* **Sch·affnerin** f ~/~en *housekeeper* **Sch·affung** f ~/ *creation*; *production*

Sch·äffler m ~s/~ [bayr] *cooper*; dazu: ~tanz (München) → Schaff

Schaf·ott n ~(e)s/~e *scaffold* (besteigen *to mount*) ‖ auf dem ~ enden *to end on the gallows*

..schaft f [suff] **1.** [abstr] (*member*)*ship*; Lehrer~ *teacher's vocation* ‖ Eigen~ *property* ‖ Wissen~ *knowledge* **2.** (Stand) Leibeigen~ *serfdom* **3.** [koll] Lehrer~ *body of teachers* **4.** (Ort) Graf~ *county*, Ort~ *township, village*

Schaft m ~(e)s/~̈e *shaft* (*of a lance, column etc*) ‖ (e–s Gewehrs) *stock* ‖ *stick* (*of a flag*) ‖ (e–s Taues) *strand* ‖ ⟨weav⟩ erster (zweiter) ~ *back* (*front*) *shaft* ‖ *bolt* (*of a crew*) ‖ (e–s Stiefels) *leg* ‖ (e–s Pfeilers, Werkzeugs, Schlüssels, Ankers) *shank* ‖ (e–r Radiernadel) *handle* ‖ ⟨cycl⟩ *handlebar stem* ‖ (*valve-*)*stem* ‖ *main-piece* (*of the rudder*) ‖ (e–s Baumes) *trunk, bole* ‖ (e–r Blume) *scape, stalk* **~fräser** m *end mill* **~leisten** m *boot-tree* **~litze** f ⟨weav⟩ *heddles* pl **~ring** m (e–r Säule) *annulet* **~rinne** f (e–r Säule) *groove* **~stiefel** m pl *Wellingtons* pl, *high* od *top boots* pl, ⟨Am⟩ *boots* **sch·äften** vt [h] *to provide with a shaft*, etc ‖ (ein Gewehr) *to stock, mount* ‖ (Stiefel) *to leg* **geschäftet** a *stocked* ‖ ⟨for⟩ gut geschäfteter Wald *wood with fine trunks*

Schah m ~s/~s *shah* (*of Persia, Iran*)

Sch·akal m ~(e)s/~e ⟨zoo⟩ *jackal*

Sch·ake f ~/~n, **Sch·äkel** m ~s/~ ⟨mar⟩ *shackle*

Sch·äker m ~s/~ *joker, wag, jester* ‖ *flirt* | **~·ei** f ~/~en *playfulness, dallying, jest, joke* ‖ *flirting, flirtation* | **~̈haft** a *playful, dallying, waggish, roguish* | adv *flirtingly* **sch·äkern** vi [h] *to jest, joke* ‖ *to dally, philander, flirt*, ⟨Am⟩ *neck* (*with*) | ~d [a] *sportive*

Schal m ~(e)s/~e & ~s *shawl, comforter, scarf, wrap* ‖ e–n ~ umlegen, umbinden *to put on a sh.*

schal a *stale, flat* (*beer*) ‖ *vapid* (*pleasures*) ‖ *insipid, shallow* (*talker*) ‖ *dull, spiritless*; → reizlos **~̈heit** f *staleness* ‖ *vapidity* (*of life*) ‖ *shallowness*

Schal- [v Schale] **~brett** n *slab, outside plank*; *shuttering board* **~holz** n *outside of a tree* **~kragenkleid** n *scarf-skimmer* **~muschel** f *bivalve shell-mussel* **~tier** n *testaceous* od *crustaceous animal, shell-fish* **~tierkunde** f *conchology* **~tierlaich** m *spat* **Sch·äl-** **~kur** f ⟨cosm⟩ *skin-up* **~maschine** f *barker, sheller* **~wald** m *tan-bark coppice* **Sch·älchen** n ~s/~ *little cup, small dish* ‖ ˣein ~ Heeßen (= Heißen) *a cup of coffee* **Sch·ale** f ~/~n **A. 1.** ⟨bot⟩ *skin, peel, rind, bark* (*of a fruit*) ‖ ~n [pl] *parings* | (Apfelsinen~̈) *skin* ‖ Kartoffeln in der ~ kochen *to boil p.s in their jackets* ‖ (Kleie) *bran* ‖ (Nuß~̈) *shell* ‖ Samen~̈ *hull, husk, capsule*; (Schote) *pod* ‖ *cup* (*of an acorn*) **2.** ⟨zoo⟩ (v Mollusken) *test, crust, shell* ‖ (Chitin~̈) *chitin* ‖ (v Rädertierchen) *lorica* [pl *loricae*] | Auster–, Eier~̈ *shell* ‖ Hummer~̈ *chitin* ‖ Muschel~̈, Schildkröten~̈, Schnecken~̈ *shell* **3.** ⟨hunt⟩ ~n [pl] *cloven hoofs* pl **4.** ⟨fig⟩ nicht ganz aus der ~ .. *not quite hatched* ‖ *beneath a chitinous shell of his exterior beats a gentle heart* ‖ → Kern **B.** ⟨tech⟩ **1.** *basin, bowl, vase, vessel, dish, tray* ‖ e–e ~ Milch *a cup of milk* **2.** Aschen~̈ *ash-tray* ‖ Aussaat~̈ *seed-pan* ‖ (Wecker) Glocken~̈ *bell dome* ‖ Guß~̈ ⟨met⟩ *chill* ‖ Lager~̈ ⟨tech⟩ *bush, brass, pillow* ‖ (Löffel~̈) *bowl* ‖ ⟨mar⟩ Mast- etc ~̈n [pl] *fishes* pl ‖ ~n um e–n Mast legen *to fish a mast* ‖ (Messer~̈n) *scales, plates* pl ‖ Obst~̈ *fruit dish* ‖ Opfer~̈ *sacrificial bowl* ‖ Reib~̈ *mortar* ‖ Sekt~̈ *champagne glass* ‖ Unter~̈ (Tasse) *saucer* ‖ Waag~̈ *scale* ‖ Wasch~̈ *wash-basin* **3.** ⟨fig⟩ die (Waag-)~ senkt sich .. *the scale falls in his favour* ‖ die ~ des Zorns ausgießen *to pour out the vials of wrath, to vent one's anger* (über *upon*) **sch·alen** vt [h] *to line with planks* **sch·älen I.** vt [h] **1.** (Erbsen etc) *to shell, husk* ‖ (Bäume) *to bark*, ⟨scient⟩ *to decorticate* ‖ (Obst, Kartoffeln) *to peel, pare* ‖ (Pilze) *to turn* ‖ (Mandeln) *to skin, blanch* ‖ die Schale v Obst schälen *to pare the skin off fruit* ‖ Eier ~ *to remove the shells of eggs* **2.** ⟨agr⟩ *to plough fleet*; *to peel off the turf* **3.** ⟨fig⟩ → Ei A. 3. b. **II. sich** ~ v/refl *to shell* ‖ die Haut schält sich *the skin peels* od *comes off* ‖ *the tree sheds its bark* ‖ ⟨fam⟩ sich aus den Kleidern ~ *to undress*; *strip* **Sch·alen-** **~bauweise** f (f Rakete) *monocoque* ‖ ⟨aero⟩ *stressed skin construction*; verstärkte ~ *semi-monocoque c.* **~beton** m *shell concrete* **~eisen** n ⟨met⟩ *sow-iron* **~form** f *shell of a mould* **~gehäuse** n ⟨zoo⟩ *shell* **~guß** m *chilling, chill-casting* ‖ *chilled iron castings* pl **~̈hart** a ⟨met⟩ *chilled* **~kalk** m ⟨min⟩ *aragonite* **~kreuz** n *cross with cups* (= *cup anemometer*) **~kupplung** f *split-coupling* **~sessel** m *shell-shaped chair* **~ständer** m *basin stand*; → Schaltier **~wild** n *hoof*(*ed*) *game*

Sch·äl- ~hengst [m] *stallion*; ~messer [n] *peeling* od *paring knife*; ~pflug [m] *paring plough* ⟨Am⟩ *plow* **Schäler** m ⟨cul⟩ *peeler* **sch·alig** a *shelled, shelly* ‖ ⟨zoo⟩ *crustaceous* ‖ ⟨bot⟩ *tunicated* | [in comp] (*thick-*) *skinned*; (*delicate*) *shelled* (*egg*)

Schalk m ~(e)s/~e & ~̈e **1.** [obs] *servant* **2.** (*little*) *rogue* od *rascal* **3.** (Spottvogel) *wag* **4.** ⟨dero⟩ *knave* **5.** ⟨fig⟩ den ~ im Nacken h *to be a sly-boots* ‖ der ~ lacht ihr aus den Augen *she looks a little rogue* (*in porcelain* Meredith) **sch·alkhaft** a *sly, cunning, arch* (*fellow*); *roguish* (*smile*) ‖ (neckisch) *waggish* (*trick*) **~̈igkeit** f ~/ **Sch·alkheit** f ~/ *archness, roguishness* ‖ *roguery* (Schalkheit) ‖ *waggishness* ‖ *cunning, slyness* ‖ ⟨bib, dero⟩ *villainy, guile, knavery* **Schalks-** **~auge** n *roguish eye* **~freund** m *false friend* **~-knecht** m *deceitful fellow* ‖ ⟨bib⟩ *unfaithful servant* **~narr** m *jester, buffoon* **~streich** m *sly trick*

Schall m ~(e)s/~e, ~̈e *sound, clang* ‖ *noise* ⟨a. fig⟩ ‖ *ring*(*ing*) (*of bells*) **~becken** n *cymbal* **~boden** m *sound*(*ing*)*-board* **~brechung** f *refraction of sound* | ~slehre [f] *diacoustics* pl **~dämpfer** m *silencer*; *muffled wall*; *baffle*(*-board*); ⟨mus⟩ *sourdine*, ⟨mot⟩ *muffler* **~dämpfung** f *sound-proofing*; *silencing*; *noise reduction*; ⟨wir⟩ *acoustical damping*, mit ~ ausstatten *to dampen* | ~swand [f] *sound baffle board, s. damping wall* **~deckel** m ⟨ec/arch⟩ *sound-board* **~̈dicht** a *sound-proof*; ~ m *to s.p.*; *s.p.ed* (*booth*), ~e Wand *baffle-wall* **~dose** f *sound-box* **~druck** m *sound pressure* **~erreger** m *sound-producer* **~explosion** f *sonic boom* **~fänger** m *ear tube* **~fenster** n ⟨ec/arch⟩ *louver-window* **~ferne** f *earshot* **~frequenz** f *acoustic frequency* **~gefäß** n *harmonical vase* **~geschwindigkeit** f *sound velocity*; *Mach*; über ~ *supersonic*; unter ~ *subsonic*; mit ~ *at* (od *with*) *s. v.*; Beanspruchung bei Nahezu-~ *shock stall* | **~s-** *speed-of-sound* (*aircraft*) **~gewölbe** n *acoustic vault* **~grenze** f *sound* od *sonic barrier* **~hemmung** f *sound-shadow* **~höhenmessung** f *air sounding*; *echometry* **~kammer** f ⟨telph⟩ *screen* **~kasten, ~körper** m ⟨mus⟩ *body* **~lehre** f *acoustics* pl [a. sg konstr] **~loch** n *sound-hole* **~mauer** f *sound barrier* (durchstoßen *to rip through*); beim Durchstoßen .. *transonic* **~meß-** ~batterie [f] *s.-ranging b.*; ~gerät [n] *s. locator* **~messer** m *phonometer* **~meß-** ~trupp [m] *sound-ranging section*; ~uhr [f] *phonete-*

lemeter **~mine** f *sonic mine* **≃nahe** a *transonic* **~platte** f (*phonographic*) *record* (bespielen *to cut*); etw auf ∼ bringen *to record, to put on r.s* **~platten-** ∼aufnahmegerät [n] *recording equipment*; ∼bar [f] *discotheque*; ⟨mst sl⟩ *disco*; ∼geschäft [n], ∼laden [m] *record* od *disc shop* ∼hülle [f] *sleeve*; ∼musik [f] *recorded music*; *recording*; ⟨fam⟩ *canned music*; ∼parade [f] *r. round-up*; ∼rille [f] *microgroove*; ∼teller [m] *turn-table*; ∼verzeichnis [n] *discograph*; ∼-wechsler [m] *automatic record changer*; ∼wiedergabe [f] ⟨wir⟩ *recorded broadcast* **~rohr** n *speaking-trumpet*; *megaphone* **~schluck-** ∼hülle [f] *blimp*; ∼platte [f] *acoustic tile* **~schutz** m *sound protection* **|** ∼verfahren [n] *s.-proofing method*; *noise-control technique* **~schwingung** f *acoustic vibration* **~spiegel** m *s. level* **~stärke** f *volume of s.* **|** ∼nmesser [m] *phonometer* **~trichter** m ⟨mus⟩ *bell-mouth*, ⟨rec⟩ *megaphone*; durch ∼ sprechen *to m.* ‖ (des Grammophons) *horn, trumpet* **~- u Lichtmeß-** *sound and flash* [attr] N **~verstärker** m *amplifier* **~wand** f ⟨mot⟩ *splash wall* **~welle** f *sound-wave* **sch·allen** vi [h] *to resound* ‖ (v Glocken) *to peal* ‖ *to ring* (vor *with*) ‖ laut ∼ *to thrill, boom* ‖ *the sound came to my ears, still rings in my ears* ‖ es schallt hier sehr *there is a strong echo here* **| ~d** *sounding* (*box on the ear*), *ringing* (*applause*), ∼des Gelächter *loud peal of laughter*; in ∼es G. ausbrechen *to burst into* (*a boohoo of*) *laughter*

Sch·allern m ∼s/∼ ⟨hist⟩ (Helm) *salade*

Schalm·ei f ∼/∼en *shawm*; *reed-pipe*

Schal·otte f ∼/∼n ⟨bot⟩ *shallot, scallion*

schalt 1. & 3. sg pret v schelten

Sch·alt- ~anlage f *switch-gear*, ⟨telph⟩ *-board* **~bild** n ⟨el⟩ (*wiring*) *diagram* **~brett** n *s.-board*; ⟨comp⟩ *plugboard* **~draht** m ⟨telph⟩ *jumper wire* **~folie** f ⟨rec⟩ (*automatic*) *stop foil* **~gabel** f *gear shift fork* **~getriebe** n; automatisches ∼ *self--changing gear* **~haken** m ⟨mach⟩ *catch* **~hebel** m *gear-lever, control lever*; *s. key* od *arm* **~jahr** n *leap-year* **~karte** f ⟨comp⟩ *small board*; vgl Stammkarte **~klinke** f *click* **~kupplung** f *clutch coupling*; *shifting clutch* **~monat** m *intercalary month* **~organisation** f *switching o.* **~plan** m *diagram of connections* **~pult** n ⟨el⟩ (*control*) *desk* **~rad** n ⟨telph⟩ *stepping wheel*, ⟨mach⟩ *star blade*; ⟨typewriter⟩ *escapement wheel* **~raum** m (*main*) *control room* **~schema** n = –bild **~schnur** f ⟨comp⟩ *flexible pluggable connector* **~steuerung** f *feeder control* **~tafel** f ⟨el⟩ *s. board, s.-panel*, ⟨mot⟩ *instrument* od *dash board*; ⟨wir⟩ *control board*; ⟨comp⟩ *c. panel*, mit ihren Schnüren *interchangeable c. p.*; ⟨theat⟩ *dimmer board* **|** ∼personal [n] ⟨theat⟩ *switchboard operators* **~tag** m *intercalary day* **~ventil** n *pilot valve* **~vorrichtung** f ⟨el⟩ *s.* **~wort** n *interpolated word* **sch·alten I.** vi/t [h] *to act, command, direct, rule* ‖ ⟨mot⟩ *to shift gears* (zügig *smoothly*) ‖ ⟨wir⟩ wir ∼ (uns) um auf *we now join* (*the B.B.C.*); *we now take you* (*over*) *to*; wir ∼ zurück z .. *we return you to* (*the studio*) **|** ∼ u walten *to manage, command*; frei .. *to do as one likes*, (mit *with*); .. mit *to deal with* ‖ e–n ∼ u w. l *to give a p rope, free rein, full power* **|** ⟨fig hum⟩ (P) spät ∼ ⟨sl⟩ *to do a double take* **II.** vt ⟨el⟩ *to switch, connect*; parallel ∼ zu *to shunt to*; *to connect in parallel to* ‖ ⟨comp⟩ (verdrahten) *to wire*

Sch·alter m ∼s/∼ **1.** ⟨arch⟩ *wing, wicket*; *shutter* ‖ *sliding window* ‖ ⟨cul, hot⟩ *service hatch* ‖ ⟨bank, post⟩ *counter*, ⟨Ger⟩ *window* ‖ Auskunfts≃ *inquiry office* **|** ⟨aero⟩ *ticket counter*; ⟨rail⟩ *booking-*, ⟨Am⟩ *ticket-office*, ⟨Ger⟩ *ticket window* **|** am ∼ aufgeben *to post at the counter* **2.** ⟨el⟩ *switch* (eingebaut *flush*, aufgebaut *surface*; mit Sicherung *sw. and fuse*) ‖ *contact* od *circuit closer* od *breaker* ‖ den ∼ anstellen *to* (*turn* od) *press down the sw.* **|** Dreh≃ *rotary sw.* ‖ Fahr≃ *controller*; *starting sw.* ‖ Haupt≃ *mains sw.* ‖ ⟨hot⟩ *two-way sw.* ‖ Kipp≃ *tumbler sw.* (anknipsen *to flip*) ‖ Messer≃ *knife-sw.* ‖ Serien≃ *parallel sw.* ‖ Trenn≃ *separating sw.* ‖ Wechsel≃ *two-way sw.* ‖ Wellen≃ *change-over sw.* ‖ Wipp≃ *rocker sw.* **3.** ⟨tech⟩ (Umschalter) *reversing valve* **|** ⟨comp⟩ (*auto/manual*) *sw.* **~beamte(r)** m *booking clerk, counter attendant* **~bezeichnung** f *name of the counter* **~dienststunden** f pl *hours of posting* etc **~fenster** n *ticket window*; (vergittert) *wicket* **~halle** f *booking hall* **~öffnung** f *opening of the booking-office*, etc **~raum** m *b.-* etc *office* **~stop** m ⟨comp⟩ *breakpoint* **Sch·altung** f ∼/∼en ⟨el⟩ *connexion, connection* ‖ Dreieck≃ *delta c.*; Gruppen≃ *series-parallel circuit*; Hinter–e–a–≃ *series conn.* **|** ⟨mot, mech⟩ *gear--change*; *gears* ‖ ⟨mot⟩ automatische ∼ *automatic transmission*; ohne ∼ *gearless* (*car*) **|** ⟨rec–el⟩ *circuitry* **|** jeweilige ∼ *form of plugging* **|** ⟨typwr⟩ *escapement* **|** ⟨comp⟩ *circuit*

Schal·uppe f ∼/∼n *sloop*; *jolly-boat*; gr *long--boat*

Scham f ∼/ **A. 1.** [abstr] *shame*; *modesty, bashfulness* ‖ ohne ∼ *unashamed* **2.** ⟨anat⟩ *privy parts, genitals* pl ‖ m: *penis*; f: *pudenda* **3.** ⟨bib⟩ *nakedness* **B.** aller ∼ bar *past sh., devoid of all sh.* ‖ vor ∼ erröten, vergehen *to blush, die with sh.* **~bein** n *pubic bone* **~bug** m ⟨anat⟩ *groin* **~drüse** f ⟨anat⟩ *inguinal gland* **≃erregend** a *filling with sh.* **~gefühl** n *sense of sh.*; *modesty*; kein ∼ h *to be incapable of sh.* **~gegend** f *pubic region* **~haar** n *pubic hair* **~hügel** m *mons Veneris* **~lippen** f pl *wings of the vulva* **≃los** a *shameless, impudent* **|** [pred] *devoid of shame* **|** ⟨fig⟩ *unblushing, unabashed, barefaced*; *immodest* (*publication*) → Jugendgefährdung; *flagrant, glaring, scandalous* (*offence, offender*) **~losigkeit** f *sh.lessness, impudence* **~ritze** f *vulva* **~rot** a *blushing* ‖ ∼ w *to blush*; *to colour up* **~röte** f *blush*(*ing*) ‖ jdm die ∼ ins Gesicht treiben *to bring blushes to a p's cheeks* ‖ *she blushed for shame* **~teile** m pl = ∼ 2 **~verletzer** m *exhibitionist*; –tzung [f] *–nism* **sch·ämen**: **sich ~** [h] ([gen] *or* über) *to be* od *feel ashamed* (*of*); *to feel small* ‖ *to blush* (*at*); sich zu Tode ∼ → weiter u. ‖ ∼ Sie sich! *for shame!, out upon you!* ‖ du solltest dich was ∼! *you should be ashamed of y.s.!* ‖ ich schäme mich so *I'm frightfully ashamed of m.s.* ‖ ohne sich zu ∼ *unashamedly* ‖ sich nicht ∼, etw z tun *not to mind doing a th*; Sie brauchen sich **deshalb** *or* deswegen nicht z ∼ *there is no reason for you to be* (od *you need not be*) *ashamed of it* ‖ sich **in** Grund u Boden ∼ *to be thoroughly ashamed* ‖ sich ∼ **vor** *to be ashamed to stand before* (*a p*) ‖ sich **zu** Tode ∼ *to die of* od *with shame* **sch·amhaft** a *bashful, modest, shamefaced* ‖ (keusch) *chaste* ‖ (scheu) *shy, coy* **≃igkeit** f ∼/ *bashfulness, modesty* ‖ *chastity* ‖ *shyness, coyness*

Scham·ade f ∼/∼n *chamade, parley* ‖ ∼ blasen, schlagen *to sound, beat a parley*

schamf·ilen vt/refl ⟨mar⟩ *to chafe*

Scham·otte f ∼/ *fire-clay* **~stein** m *fire-brick*

schampun·ieren vt [h] *to shampoo*

°**Schampus** m ∼/ *champagne*, ⟨fam⟩ *fizz, sham*

Sch·an- ~deck n, **~deckel** m ⟨mar⟩ *gunwale, gunnel*

Sch·and- ~blatt n *scandalous paper*; *rag* **~bube** m *wretch, scoundrel, villain* **~buch** n *infamous book* **~fleck** m *stain, blemish, brand*; *eyesore*; *slur* (*on a p's name*) ‖ *blot*; *dark spot* ‖ ⟨übtr⟩ *disgrace* (f *to*); *taint* (*of insanity*); (*moral*) *taint*; (*without taint of commercialism*) **|** (P) *discreditable, disreputable relation* (*in the family*) **|** e–n ∼ beschönigen ⟨fig⟩ *to whitewash a dark spot* **~gedicht** n *lampoon* **~geld** n *money got by infamy* ‖ *scandalous price, paltry sum* ‖ für ein ∼ ⟨fam⟩ *dog-cheap, dirtcheap* **~gemälde** n *obscene picture* **~geschichte** f *scandalous history* **~leben** n *dis-*

graceful life **~lied** n *obscene, ribald, bawdy song* **~lüge** f *infamous lie* **~mal** n *stigma; mark* od *badge of infamy, brand of shame* °**~mäßig** a *infamous* **~mauer** f (*Berlin*) *Wall of Shame* °**~maul** n *scandalous tongue* || ⟨fig⟩ *slanderer, foul-mouthed p* **~pfahl** m, **~säule** f *pillory* °**~schnauze** f *black mouth*; er hat e–e ungewaschene ~ *he is hard-mouthed* **~schrift** f *lampoon, libel* **~streich** m *villainous trick* **~tat** f *iniquity; shameful* od *infamous action; crime* || ~en [pl] *evil doings* **~vertrag** m *infamous treaty* (*of the peace of Versailles*) **~volk** n *infamous people* **~weib** n *vile woman* **~worte** n pl *obscenities* pl **sch·andbar** a *ignominious, infamous; abominable, scandalous* (*book*) | **~keit** f ~/~n *infamy* **Sch·ande** f ~/ **A.** *shame, disgrace, infamy* || *ignominy, outrage* || größte ~ *deep disgrace, abject dishonour* || *an outrage* (f *to his house*) || °e–e Affen~ *a wicked shame* | pfui ~!, ~ über dich! *shame on you, you disgrace y.s.* **B.** jdm ~ **antun,** bringen *to disgrace a p, to bring disgrace on a p*; tu mir diese ~ nicht an *spare me this d.* || jdm ~ einbringen *to bring* od *cast reproach upon a p* || ~ auf sich laden *to draw down disgrace upon o.s.* || es macht ihm ~ *it brings discredit on him* || er macht s–r Familie ~ *he is a disgrace to ..* || es würde mir wenig ~ m *it would be little shame to me* || jds ~ auf sich nehmen *to take the blame for a p's infamy* || er ist die ~ s–r Familie *he is the black sheep of ..* || es ist e–e ~, daß *it's a shame that* (*he should ..*) | ⟨prov⟩ (*poverty is no*) *sin* **C. in** ~ bringen *to dishonour, disgrace, debauch* || um das M. nicht in ~ z bringen *to avoid ruining the girl's reputation* || in ~ geraten, s, leben *to come to disgrace, to be in d., to live in infamy* | **mit** ~ abziehen *to retire ignominiously* || mit ~ beladen *completely discredited* | **zu** m–r ~ *to my shame* (*I must confess, it must be said*) || zu ~n = zu~n || zur ~ gereichen *to be disgraceful* **sch·änden** vt [h] *to disfigure, spoil, deform* | (e–e Frau) *to violate, deflower, ravish* | ⟨fig⟩ *to dishonour, disgrace; to desecrate* (*a grave*); *to bring disgrace upon* (*a good name*); *to break* (*the sabbath*) || es –det nicht, zuzugeben *it is no reproach on a p to own* **schande(n)halber** [adv] *to save appearances* **Sch·änder** m ~s/~ *ravisher, violator* || ⟨fig⟩ *defamer, detractor, slanderer* **sch·ändlich** a *shameful, disgraceful* (*fellow*), *infamous* (*life*) || *vile, low, base, shameless, atrocious, foul* (*plot, crime,* etc) || *scandalous* (*lies, intentions, swindle*) || *abominable* (*deed*) | ⟨fig⟩ *awful* (*weather*) | [adv] *infamously*; ⟨fig⟩ *extremely, exceedingly,* ⟨fam⟩ *awfully* (*annoying*) **~keit** f ~/~en *baseness, iniquity, infamousness, shamefulness, atrociousness* || *ignominiousness* || *disgrace*(*fulness*) || ~en begehen *to act disgracefully* **Schändung** f ~/~en *violation* (*of ..*), *ravishing* (*a woman*), *rape* (durch *at the hands of*) || *disfigurement* || *profanation, desecration, sacrilege* || *breaking* (*of the sabbath*) || ⟨fig⟩ *prostitution* (*of talents*)

Sch·anghai n (chin. Stadt) *Shanghai*

Schank m ~(e)s/~stätten **1.** *tap-house,* ⟨fam⟩ *pot-house* **2.** *retail of alcoholic beverages* **3.** = **~berechtigung, ~gerechtigkeit** f *publican's licence, licence for selling liquor* || (f Lokal) *on-licence*; (f Straßenschank) *off-licence* **~bier** n *beer from the tap* **~mädchen** n *barmaid* **~stätte** f *licenced premises* pl **~tisch** m *bar*; ⟨bar⟩ *buffet, counter* **~wirt** m *licenced victualler; publican*; ⟨Am⟩ *bartender* **~wirtschaft** f *tap-house, public house,* ⟨fam⟩ *beer-shop, pub* || e–e ~ h *to keep a ..* **~zimmer** n *tap-room*

Sch·anker m ~s/~ ⟨path⟩ *chancre* (weich *soft*)

Sch·ansi (chin. Prov.) *Shansi*

Sch·anstaaten m pl (in Burma) *Shan States*

Sch·antung n (chin. Prov.) *Shantung*

†**Schaumburg-Lippe** n ⟨Ger⟩ (Land)

Schanz- ~arbeit f *throwing-up of earth work* || ⟨mil⟩ *entrenching, digging*; ⟨a.⟩ *fatigue*(*-work*) **~arbeiter** m *pioneer, sapper, trencher* **~bau** m *construction of field-works* **~bekleidung** f *gabionnade* **~gerät** n = ~zeug **~gräber** m = ~arbeiter **~kleid** n ⟨mar⟩ *bulwark* **~korb** m *gabion* **~pfahl** m *palisade* (dazu: *to palisade*) **~werk** n *earthwork, entrenchment* **~zeug** n *sappers' tools* pl, *entrenching implements* pl **Sch·anze** f ~/~n *redoubt, entrenchment, fieldwork* || *bulwark* || *ski-jump* || (beim Kinder-Fangenspiel) *home* (⟨a.⟩ [intj]) ~! ⟨mar⟩ *quarter-deck* || e–e ~ aufführen, aufwerfen *to make trenches, to throw up earthworks* || in die ~ schlagen ⟨fig⟩ *to risk, hazard, venture; to risk* (*one's life*) **sch·anzen** vt/i [h] *to entrench, dig, fortify; to throw up entrenchments* | vi [h] ⟨fam⟩ *to work hard, to drudge*; ⟨sl⟩ *to sap, fag, sweat* **Sch·anzer** m ~s/~ = Schanzarbeiter || ⟨fam⟩ *plodder*

Schapp m & n ~s/~s [ndd] = Schaff

Schar f ~/~en *troop, band; school* (*of fish*) || *flight* (*of swans*) || *flock* (*of geese*) || *lot* (*of children*) || *large number* (*of rabbits,* etc) || *troop* (*of horse*) || *squad* (*of riders*) || *crowd* (*of people*) || glänzende ~ *galaxy* || in ~en *in crowds* || in ~en wandern nach *to crowd to* | → Pflug~; Vier~-pflug [m] *four-furrow plough* **~wache** f *watch guard; patrol* **~wächter** m *watch-man* **sch·aren** vt [h] & sich ~ *to assemble, collect; to flock* (*together*); *to rally* (*around* od *to a p, to a p's aid*) || sich ~ um *to cluster about* od *round* **sch·arenweise** [adv] *in bands, crowds, troops,* etc

Schar·ade f ~/~n *charade, dumb crambo* || ~n aufführen, spielen *to act charades*

Sch·arbe f ~/~n ⟨orn⟩ *cormorant*; → *shag*

Sch·arbock m ~(es/ ⟨path⟩ *scurvy* || mit dem ~ behaftet *scorbutic* **~skraut** n ⟨bot⟩ *figwort*

Sch·äre f ~/~n *skerry, reef, cliff; rocky island*

scharf I. [a] [~er/~ste] **A. 1.** (**Ggs: stumpf**) *sharp* (*blade, axe, teeth, sand*) || *cutting* || *sharp-edged* (*sword*) || ⟨fig⟩ *cutting* (*remark*); *acute, keen* (*understanding*) | (spitz) *pointed, acute,* ⟨bot⟩ *acuminate* || ⟨fig⟩ *sharp* (*corner, edge, bend, curve, line*) **2.** (**Ggs: sanft**) *harsh, rough* || *ferocious* (*dog*) || ⟨gram⟩ *acute* (*accent*) | (ätzend) *corrosive* (*liquid*) || *caustic* (*substance*) || *acrid, pungent* (*taste, smell*) | (stark) *strong* (*vinegar, mustard, poison, spectacles*) || *powerful* (*field-glass*) | (gepfeffert) *hot, peppered* | ⟨fig⟩ *sharp, keen* (*air*) || *acute, biting* (*cold*) || *piercing* (*noise, wind, tone*) || *shrill* (*voice, tone*) | *biting* (*tongue, remark*) || *caustic, satirical* || *bitter* (*mockery*) || *slashing* (*criticism*) || schneidend ~ *biting, bitter* | *hot* (*discussion*) || *hot, smart* (*fight*) || *violent* (*speech, article*) || *strong* (*resistance*) || *heavy* (*artillery fire*) | *stringent* (*measures, law, test*) | *severe* (*rebuke, reprimand*) || *severe, rigorous, searching* (*examination*) **3. (rasch, lebhaft)** *quick* (*pace, fire*), *sharp* (*trot*) || ~er Ritt *a ride at full speed* || *hard-fought* (*race*) || ⟨mil⟩ ~es Nachdrängen *close pursuit* **4.** ⟨mil⟩ *live* (*mine, grenade*); (Zünder) ~ m *to activate* **5. (schroff)** *steep, abrupt* **6. (hervortretend)** *salient* || (ausgesprochen) *pronounced* **7. (wahrnehmend)** *acute, keen, shrewd* (*observer*) || ~es Auge *acute eyesight* || *good* (*eyes*) || *quick, sharp* (*ears*) || *penetrating* (*sight*) || *incisive, shrewd* (*mind*) || *sound* (*judgement*) || *faithful* (*memory*) **8. (genau)** *exact, precise* || *close* (*calculation, scrutiny*) || *beady-eyed* (*control, supervision*) || *strict* (*investigation*) **9.** °⟨sex⟩ (*red-*)*hot*; ~e S! ⟨sl⟩ *she's h.s.* (= *hot stuff*) *all right,* ⟨vulg⟩ *she's a hairy bit* || ⟨sex⟩ *salacious, sexy*; ⟨vulg⟩ *cockish, coming,* ~ wie ein Rasiermesser s *to feel sexy all over*; (Frau) *juicy, hot, on heat*; (Mann) *nutty, fuckish, horney; on for one's greens*; ⟨euphem⟩ ~ s *to feel gay* **B.** ~e **Beweismittel** *actual proofs* od *facts* || mit ~em Blick *with a keen eye* || in ~em Ggs z *in strong opposition to* || ein ~es Gesicht h *to be keen-sighted* || ~e Gesichtszüge *sharply cut fea-*

tures; mit .. *sharp-faced* ‖ ~er Hieb *barbed thrust* ‖ ~e Kritik üben *to critisize severely* ‖ ~e Kurve *sharp truning, hairpin bend* ‖ ~es Objektiv ⟨phot⟩ *high definition lens* ‖ ~e Patrone *live cartridge, ball-c.* ‖ ~e Prägung *sharply cut coinage* ‖ ~en Protest einlegen *to protest strongly* ‖ ⟨fig⟩ ~ wie ein Rasiermesser ⟨fam⟩ *as keen as mustard*; → a. A. 9. ‖ ⟨med⟩ ~e Säfte *acrid humours* pl ‖ ~er Schuß *shot with ball* od *bullet* ‖ in ~em Tempo reiten ⟨a.⟩ *to ride greatly* ‖ in ~en Umrissen *in bold relief* ‖ in ~en Worten *sharply* ‖ ~e Zucht *rigid* od *iron discipline* **C.** ⟨prov⟩ allzu ~ macht schartig *a bow long bent at last grows weak* **II. [adv] 1.** (*to work, ride*) *hard* ‖ (*to drive, walk*) *fast* ‖ jdn ~ **anfassen** *to pull a p up sharply* ‖ jdn ~ ansehen *to look at a p hard, to have a close look at a p* ‖ ~ aufpassen *to give close attention, to look out like a lynx* ‖ um es nicht ~̈er auszudrücken .. *not to put too fine a point on it ..* ‖ ~ ausspähen nach .. *to keep a sharp outlook for ..* ‖ sich ~ auswirken *to become effective* ‖ *smartly* (*built ship*) ‖ ~ beobachtend *sharp-eyed; perceptive* ‖ er blickte ~̈er auf *his eyes sharpened* ‖ ~ durchgreifen *to take sharp measures* ‖ [dat] ~ entgegentreten *to oppose* (*an opinion*) *energetically* ‖ ~ entgegnen *to give a sharp reply*, ⟨fam⟩ *to shoot back* ‖ ~ erfassen *to grasp* (*a question*) *thoroughly* ‖ ~ fahren *to go* od *drive* (*at*) *a good* od *sharp pace* ‖ ~ gehen *to go at a quick pace* ‖ ~ herausarbeiten *to work out* (*an idea*) *closely* ‖ es geht ~ her *it goes hard, it is hot work* od *a hot fight* ‖ ~ hören *to have a quick ear* ‖ ~ **laden** *to load with ball*; ~ gel. *loaded* (*rifle*) ‖ ~ m *to sharpen* ‖ *to fuse* (*a shell*) ‖ ⟨fig⟩ *to excite* (*a p*) (gegen *against*) ‖ (e–n, etw) ~ nehmen *to be very strict* (*with a p, about a th*) ‖ ~ schießen *to use ball-cartridge* ‖ ~ **sehen** *to be keen-sighted, to have a quick eye* ‖ ~ umreißen *to define clearly* ‖ ~ verfolgen *to pursue closely* ‖ e–n ~ zurechtweisen *to give a p a good talking to* **2.** °~ **auf** etw s *to want a th badly*, ⟨fam⟩ *to be as keen as mustard on ..*, *to be crazy for* od *about*, ⟨sl⟩ *to be nuts on ..* | ~ **hinter** e–r S her s *to pursue a matter eagerly*; (*to be keen on making money*) | e–m ~ **zu** Leibe gehen *to press a p hard* **3.** ~ **ausgeprägt** *chiselled out, clean-cut* ‖ *strictly* (*limited*) ‖ *well* (*defined*) ‖ ~ hervortretend *standing out* **Scharf-** **~blick** m *penetrating glance*, ⟨fig⟩ *penetration, observation, clear-sightedness, perspicacity, acuteness* **⁓blikkend** a = –sichtig **⁓gebaut** a ⟨mar⟩ *clipper-built* (*ship*) **~geladen** a *loaded with ball* od *bullet* **~geschliffen** a *sharp-ground*, ⟨fig⟩ *clean-cut* **~gezeichnet** a *clearcut* (*lines*) ⟨a. phot⟩ **⁓kantig, ⁓wandig** a *sharp-edged* **~macher** m ⟨fig⟩ *alarmist, panic--monger, firebrand*; (*political*) *agitator*; pl ⟨fam⟩ *ginger-group* | ~ei [f] *agitation, intriguing* **~richter** m *hangman, executioner* **~schießen** n *firing with ball, bullet, shot* **~schuß** m *ball-shot* **~schütz(e)** m *rifleman, sharp-shooter, sniper*, (*distinguished*) *marksman* **⁓sichtig** a *sharp-sighted, quick-sighted* ‖ ⟨fig⟩ *perspicacious, acute, penetrating* | ~keit [f] *sharp-sightedness* ‖ ⟨fig⟩ *penetration* **~sinn** m *acuteness, brilliance, apprehensiveness; sagacity, penetration, ingenuity; powers of discernement; discrimination* **⁓sinnig** a *acute, sagacious, ingenious; apprehensive, penetrating, discerning; perceptive; sharp-eyed; sharp*(*-witted*), *subtle, shrewd; deep* (*mind*) | ~keit [f] *acuteness, sagacity* **Sch·ärfe** f ~/~n *sharpness* | ⟨fig⟩ *edge* (*of voice*); *pointedness, trenchancy* (*of style*); (geistige) *brilliance; keeness, acuteness*; mit aller ~ durchsetzen *to use sharpness and severity in achieving* ‖ *point* (*of epigrams*) ‖ beißende ~ *pungent criticism; asperity; animosity* | *pungency, acridness, acridity; corrosiveness; mordacity; causticity* | *piercingness* ‖ *harshness, severity, rigour* (*of confinement*), *stringency* (*of regulations*) | ⟨tech⟩ *exactness*; ⟨phot⟩ *poignance, -cy; sharpness, clearness, definition, rendition* | (Schneide) *edge* | ⟨mar⟩ (am Bug) *entrance* | ⟨cul⟩ *high seasoning* | e–r S die ~ nehmen ⟨fig⟩ *to take the edge of a th* **~einstellung** f ⟨phot⟩ *focusing* **sch·ärfen I.** vt [h] *to sharpen*, (*re*)*set, whet* (*a knife*) ‖ (zuspitzen) *to put an edge on ..., to point* ‖ *to fresh-cut* (*a millstone*) ‖ *to point, cut* (*a pencil*) ‖ → scharf beschlagen | ⟨fig⟩ *to sharpen, strengthen, intensify, quicken* ‖ *to increase, raise* ‖ *to put into relief* ‖ *to rouse* (*a p's conscience*) ‖ e–m den Blick ~ *to open a p's eyes* | sich ~: (Geist) *to become keener; senses become more acute* **II.** vi (betrügen) ⟨sl⟩ *to sharp*

Sch·arlach m ~(e)s/~e *scarlet* (*colour, cloth*) ‖ ⟨med⟩ *s.-fever* **~farbe** f *s.* (*colour*) **⁓farben** a *s.* **~färber** m *s.-dyer* **~kraut** n ⟨bot⟩ *clary* **⁓rot** a (*red as*) *s.*; *vermeil, vermilion* ‖ ~er Jagdrock *hunting pink* **sch·arlachen** a *scarlet*

Sch·arlatan m ~(e)s/~e *charlatan, humbug, quack*(*-doctor*), *mountebank* **~er·ie** f ~/~n *charlatanry, humbug, quackery*

Scharl·ei m ~(e)s/ ⟨bot⟩ *clary*

Scharm m ~(e)s/ *prettiness, charm* **⁓·ant** a *charming, pretty* ‖ *fine* (*that you have come*) **⁓·ieren I.** vi [h] (mit) *to flirt* (*with*) **II.** vt *to charm*

Scharm·ützel n ~s/~ ⟨mil⟩ *skirmish, bicker* | **⁓n** vi [h] *to sk.* **⁓utz·ieren** vi [h] **1.** (mit) *to flirt* (*with*) **2.** ⟨mil⟩ *to skirmish*

Scharn·ier n ~(e)s/~e *hinge, joint* ‖ mit ~en verbinden *to hinge together* **~band** n *j.-frame* **~deckel** m *h.d cover* **~eisen** n *j.-tool* **~gelenk** n *h.-joint*, ⟨anat⟩ *ginglymus* **~klemme** f *hinge clip* **~säge** f *j.-saw* **~stift** m *j. pin* **~ventil** n *leaf* od *flap valve* **~zange** f *j.-plyers* pl

Sch·ärpe f ~/~n *scarf, sash; full dress belt*

Scharp·ie f ~/~n *lint* ‖ ~ zupfen *to shred lint* **~bausch** m *roll of lint* **~pfropf** m *tampon*

×**Sch·ar(re)n** m ~s/~ *shambles* pl [oft sg konstr]

Sch·arre f ~/~n *scraper, raker* **sch·arren** vt/i [h] *to scrape, rake, scratch; to scrabble* ‖ (v Pferden) *to paw* | **auf** e–n Haufen ~ *to rake into a heap* | **in** die Erde ~ *to bury* (*in the ground*) | **mit** den Füßen ~ (P) *to scrape one's feet*; ⟨hors⟩ *to paw the ground*; ⟨orn⟩ *to scratch the gr.* **Sch·arr-** **~eisen** n ⟨for⟩ *scraper* **~netz** n *dragnet* **~tier** n *meerkat* **~vogel** m *scratcher*

Sch·arte f ~/~n *notch, jag* ‖ (Riß) *fissure* ‖ (Einschnitt) *dip* ‖ (Schieß⁓) *loophole* ‖ die ~ auswetzen ⟨fig⟩ *to repair a fault, to wipe out a mistake, to make amends* **Sch·arten-** **~backe** f ⟨fort⟩ *merlon* **~kraut** n ⟨bot⟩ *saw-wort* **~mauer** f *loopholed wall* **sch·artig** a *jagged, full of notches, notchy, notched* **⁓keit** f *jaggedness, notchiness*

Schart·eke f ~/~n *old* od *worthless book, trashy volume* ‖ *trash* ‖ ⟨fig fam⟩ (P) *old frump* **~njäger** m *curio-hunter*

Scharw·enzel m ~s/~ *flunkey, toady* | **⁓n** vi [h] *to bow and scrape* ‖ *to dance attendance; to cringe* (*to*), *fawn* (*upon*)

°**sch·assen** vt [h] *to expel; to give* (*a p*) *the sack*; ⟨mil⟩ *to cashier* | **-ss·ieren** *to chassé*

sch·atten vi [h] *to cast a shadow* (auf *upon*) | **⁓** m ~s/~ (kühlend) *shade*, (*to sit in the sh.*) ‖ (e–s Körpers) *shadow*, (*a shadow crossed her face*) ‖ ⟨fig⟩ nicht ein ~ v *not a trace, vestige, bit of* ‖ (P) *shadower* ‖ nur ein ~ *a mere semblance* (*of proof*) ‖ nicht der ~ e–s Verdachts *not the slightest suspicion* ‖ ⟨arts⟩ Licht u ~ *light and shade* ‖ tiefe (tote) ~ ⟨phot⟩ *heavy* (*lifeless*) *shadows* ‖ ⟨astr⟩ *umbra* ‖ ⟨fig⟩ *background* ‖ *shady side* (*of life*) ‖ (Gespenst) *spectre, shade, spirit* ‖ e–m ~ m *to stand in a p's light* | **in** den ~ stellen *to place in the shade* ‖ ⟨fig⟩ *to eclipse, overshadow, obscure, efface; to take the shine out of* (*a th*); *to cut out* (*a p*), *to put* (*other dresses*) *to shame* ‖ in den ~ gestellt w *to suffer an eclipse* ‖ alles in den ~ stellend *crowning* (*victory*) ‖ e–n ~ werfen auf [acc] ⟨fig⟩ *to reflect upon, to throw discredit on* ‖ ⟨fig⟩ dunkle ~ [pl] .. h .. *dark lines* (*under one's* *eyes)* **~autor** m *ghost writer* **~bild** n (Schattenriß) *outline, silhouette* || ⟨fig⟩ *simulacrum; shade, phantom;* (*poetic*) *fiction* od *fancy* **~blümchen** n *bifoliate lily of the valley* **~dasein** n *shadowy existence; limbo-twilight* **~fabrik** f *dummy works* [sg konstr] **~farbe** f *umber* **~figur** f *figure in a shadow-play* **~geben** n ⟨paint⟩ *shading* **~gestalt** f *phantom* **~gitter** n ⟨fig⟩ *chequered shade* **~kegel** m ⟨astr⟩ *umbra* || (Röntgen) *radiopacity* **~könig** m *sham* (od *puppet, mock*) *king, kinglet* || *phantom-king* **~morelle** f *morello* (*cherry*) **~palme** f ⟨bot⟩ *talipot* **~pflanze** f *plant thriving in the shade* **≏reich** a *shady, umbrageous* **~reich** n *realm of shades; Hades* **~riß** m *shadow(-figure)* || (Bild) *silhouette* || ⟨her⟩ *umbration* || sich wie ein ~ abheben *to silhouette* (gegen *against, upon*) **~seite** f *shady side* ⟨a. fig⟩ || ⟨fig⟩ *dark side* || ⟨fig⟩ *drawback, reverse, seamy side* (*of* od *to a th*) || er sieht an allem nur die ~ *he always looks but on the dark side of ths* || das Junggesellenleben hat s–e ~n *it's not all jam being a bachelor* **~spender** m *sunshade* **~spiel** n *shadow show, Chinese shades* pl || ⟨fig⟩ *phantasmagoria* **~stufe** f *graduation of shade* **~verteilung** f *distribution of lights and shades* **~vogel** m *umber-bird* **≏werfend** a *casting a shadow, giving shade, umbriferous* **~werk** n ⟨aero⟩ *shadow factory* **~wesen** n *phantom, vision* **~zeiger** m *hand of a sundial* **sch·attenhaft** a *shadowy, shadowlike* || ⟨fig⟩ *like a mere shadow; vague* **schatt·ieren I.** vt [h] *to shade (off), to tint, to adumbrate* || (abstufen) *to graduate* **II.** vi [h] (v Farben) *to harmonize, to blend well* **Schatt·ierung** f ~/~en *shade(s pl), nuance, tinge, tint* || um e–e ~ zu hell *a shade too light* || ⟨fig⟩: *the press of all shades* || (das Schattieren) *shading, shadowing* **sch·attig** a *shady, umbrageous* || ⟨paint⟩ *shaded* || ⟨her⟩ *umbrated*

Schat·ulle f ~/~n *casket* || ⟨a.⟩ ~ngelder n pl *privy-purse* (*of a prince*, etc) **~ngüter** n pl *private estates* (*of a pr.*)

Schatz m ~es/≃e *treasure* || ⟨fig⟩ (P) *gem,* ⟨fam⟩ *brick* || (vergrabener, aufgefundener ~ unbekannter Herkunft) *treasure trove* || ≃e [pl] *riches* pl, *wealth* | ⟨fig⟩ *hoard* (*of songs, facts*); *fund* (*of informations*); *find, quarry, stock* || ⟨fig⟩ (e–r Sprache) *the* (*American*) *bonanza* || (Vorrat) *store* (⟨a. fig⟩ *of knowledge*) | ⟨fam⟩ *sweetheart, love sweetie,* ⟨Am⟩ *gal* || (*her*) (*young*) *man,* (*his*) *best girl,* (*his*) *lady love* || (Anrede) *darling, honey, treasure* || ⟨vulg⟩ (z Frau) *my tart,* ⟨mil⟩ *bird;* (z Mann) *my bloater* | e–n ~ heben *to dig up a t.* **~amt** n *exchequer, Treasury* || Präsident des ~s *First Lord of the T.y;* Generalzahlmeister des ~s *Paymaster-General* **~anweisung** f *ex.r* (od *t.y*) *bill* od *bond* **~fund** m *t.-trove* **~gräber** m *digger for t.s, t.-seeker* **~haus** n *t.y, storehouse* **~kammer** f *t.y, ex.r;* ⟨bib⟩ *t.y-house* || ⟨fig⟩ *storehouse* (*of a language*, etc) | ~schein [m] *ex.r-bill* **~-kästchen, ~kästlein** m *money-box, jewel-box* || ⟨fig⟩ *collection of gems* **~kasten** m *t.-box* **~meister** m *t.r,* ⟨univ⟩ *Bursar* (*of a college*) **≏pflichtig** a *tributary* || *taxable* **~schein** m *t.y-bill* **sch·ätzbar** a *valuable* (*services*) || *estimable* || *esteemed, worthy* (*friend*) **≏keit** f *valuability, estimableness* || *worthiness* **Sch·ätzchen** n ~s/~ → Schatz || (T) ~ [pl] *beauties* pl **sch·atzen** vt [h] *to tax, assess* **sch·ätzen I.** vt [h] *to estimate* (*a bequest, a distance, the value of* ..) || (zur Besteuerung) *to assess* | (taxieren) (auf [acc]) *to value, compute* (*at*); (Ms.-Umfang) *to cast* || (Entfernung) *to judge* || *the house is rated at* .. || ⟨fam⟩ *to size up* || wie hoch (= teuer) ~ Sie es? *what would you put it at?* | ⟨fig⟩ *to prize* (*experience*) || *to value* (*freedom more* [höher] *than life*) | (jdn) ~ *to esteem, to think much of* || sie ~ sich nicht *there's no love lost between them* || wie alt ~ Sie ihn *how old do you take him?* || wir ~ ihn auf 65 *we judge him to be 65* | (etw) sehr ~ *to like very much; to be keen on* (*cherries*) || *to set great store by,* ⟨Am⟩ *to be very choice of* | im voraus ~ *to forecast* || zu hoch ~ *to overestimate, overrate* || zu ~ wissen *to appreciate* | **sich** ~ f *to consider o.s.* (*an expert*) || sich glücklich ~ *to count* od *think o.s. lucky* || sich [dat] etw als *or* zur Ehre ~ *to regard it as* (*to deem it*) *an honour* (*to do*) | **geschätzt** *highly esteemed* (*scholar*), *worthy, dear* (*friend*) | ⟨com⟩ Ihr Geschätztes *your esteemed favour* || wir ~ Sie im Besitz .. *we trust you are in receipt of* .. **II.** vi *to think, guess* || *I reckon there will be 100* || wir ~, du wirst kaum .. *we hardly think you will* .. **sch·ätzenswert** a *estimable, worthy of esteem* **Sch·ätzer** m ~s/~ *valuer, appraiser* **Sch·atzung** f ~/~en *taxation, tax, assessment; imposition of taxes* **Sch·ätzung** f ~/~en (*e*)*valuation, rating, estimate* || *gauge of the value of* .. || bei roher ~ *at a venture* || nach m–r ~ *by my computation* || nach ungefährer ~ *at a rough guess* || (Meinung) *estimation* || (Hochachtung) *esteem* || (Hochschätzung) *appreciation* **≏sweise** adv *approximately* **~swert** m *estimated value*

schau a *attractive, taking,* ⟨Am⟩ *taky* (*girl*); ein ~er Anblick! *she's very easy on the eye*

Sch·au f ~/~en *way of looking at ths; view, sight* || ⟨mil⟩ *review* || (~spiel) *show, spectacle,* Mode≏ *fashion parade* od *show* || (Ausstellung) *exhibition* | (geistige, innere) *vision, vista* | nur **zur** ~ *only for show* || zur ~ stehen (S) *to be on view* || zur ~ stellen *to show, display, feature, parade, exhibit;* (bes. ostentativ) *to sport, flash, flaunt; to show .. off; to make a great parade of* || **sich** z ~ st. ⟨vulg⟩ *to flourish it* || das Sich–z–~–st. (*self-*)*display* || *she made play with her beauty* || zur ~ tragen *to wear* (*a sour look*); *to air* (*one's feelings*); *to bear* (*a perfect*) *demeano*(*u*)*r;* Manieren etc zur ~ tragen *to affect manners;* s–e Gefühle nicht .. *not to wear one's heart upon one's sleeve;* (heucheln) *to put on; to feign, sham;* absichtlich z ~ getragen .. *laborious* (*incompetence at games*) **~bild** n *diagram* (*of a motor*); ⟨tech⟩ *operational chart* **~brot** n *sh.-bread* **~bude** f *sh.-booth* | ~nbesitzer [m] *sh.man* **~bühne** f *stage, theatre* **~burg** f *picture-palace* **~ende** n *sample, pattern, sh.-end* (*of cloth*) **~fenster** n *shop-, sh.-, display-,* ⟨Am⟩ *store-w.* (ansehen *to go w.-shopping;* dekorieren *to dress*) im ~ ausstellen *to display in the w.* | ~auslage [f] *w. display;* ~bummel [m] *w. gazing;* e–n ~ m *to w.shop;* ~dekorateur [m] *w. dresser;* ~dekoration [f] *w.-dressing* **~fliegen** n *flying display; exhibition flying* | im **~funk** *on television* **~gefecht** n *sham-fight* **~gepränge** n *pageantry* **~gericht** n ⟨cul⟩ *sh.dish, table ornament* **~gerüst** n *scaffold, stage, stand* **~geschäft,** –gewerbe n *show business* **~glas** n *sight* od *gauge glass* **~haus** n *mortuary,* Fr *morgue* **~kampf** m *exhibition match* od *bout* **~kästchen** n *sh.-case* **~kasten** m *display case* **~loch** n *spy-hole;* ⟨comp⟩ *dial* | ~deckel [m] *inspection cover* **~lust** f *curiosity* **≏lustig** a *curious* **~lustige(r)** m *sight-seer;* ⟨Am fam⟩ *rubberneck* **~münze** f *medal* **~packung** f *dummy* **~pfennig** m *medal* **~platz** m *scene* || *theatre* (⟨a.⟩ *of war*) || ⟨liter⟩ *setting;* e–n Ort z ~ e–s Romans m *to lay in a place the scene of a novel* **~prozeß** m *mock* od *sh. trial* **~seite** f *front, face* **~spiel** n *spectacle, exhibition* || ⟨übtr⟩ *sight* || ⟨theat⟩ *play, dramatic piece, drama* | ≏-artig [a] *theatrical, dramatic;* ~dichter [m] *dramatic poet, dramatist, playwright;* ~dichtung [f] *dramatic poetry;* ~direktor [m] *manager;* ~schule [f] *acting* od *drama school* **~spieler** m *actor, player, dramatic professor* || (verächtlich) *play-actor* || ⟨fig⟩ *poseur* || ~ kleinster Rollen *utility actor* || ~ s (w) *to be* (*to go*) *on the stage* || umherziehender ~ (*strolling* od) *touring player;* ⟨sl⟩ *busker* | ~gabe [f] *flair for acting;* ~gesellschaft, ~truppe [f] *company* (*of actors*); ~gewerkschaft [f] ⟨Am⟩ (seit 1912) *Equity* **~spieler·ei**

f *acting*; ⟨fig⟩ *affectation* **~spielerin** f *actress* **≈spielerisch** a *histrionic*; *mimic* (*action*) **≈spielern I.** vi [h] *to* (*play*)*act*; ⟨fig⟩ *to sham, to feign*, ⟨fam⟩ *to put it on* **II.** ≈ n *acting, mimicry* **~spielhaus** n *play-house, theatre* **~spielkunst** f *dramatic* od *scenic art* ‖ (e–s Schauspielers) *play-acting* ‖ ⟨fig⟩ *theatre* **~stellung** f *exhibition*; *show*; *display*; verschwenderische ∼ ⟨Am⟩ *splurge* **~steller** m *exhibitor* ‖ (Budenbesitzer) *showman* **~stück** n *sh.-piece*, prunkvolles ∼ *pageant*(*ry*) **~tür** f ⟨tech⟩ *inspection door* **~turnen** n *gymnastic display* **~vorstellung** f *display* **~zeichen** n *visual* od *telltale sign*

Schaub m ∼(e)s/∼e *sheaf*; *wisp of straw*

Sch·aube f ∼/∼n ⟨hist tail⟩ *houppelande*

Sch·auder m ∼s/∼ *shudder, shiver* ‖ ⟨fig⟩ *horror, terror* (vor *of*) ‖ ein ∼ ergriff ihn *a shudder took him* ‖ kalter ∼ *the creeps* (*to give a p the c.s*) ‖ ein kalter ∼ packte ihn *it made his flesh creep*; *horror overcame him*; *a shudder ran through him* °**≈bar**; **≈erregend, ≈haft** a *horrible, terrible* (*cold*), *awful* (*weather, handwriting*), *dreadful* (*feeling*) ‖ ⟨fig⟩ *atrocious, tremendous, awful* **~haftigkeit** f *horribleness, horror* ‖ ⟨fig⟩ *atrociousness, awfulness* **~geschichte** f *horror yarn*, ∼n [pl] *horrors* pl **~szene** f *horrible scene* od *sight* **≈voll** a *horrible* **sch·audern** vi [h] (vor [dat]) *to shudder, shiver* (*at*) ‖ sie schauderte vor ihm *she had a horror of him* ‖ **es** schaudert mich, **mir** schaudert (die Haut) *I shudder, my flesh creeps* | ich denke **mit** ≈ *I shudder to think* (daß *that*) ‖ jdm ≈ verursachen *to give a p the shivers* **schaudernd** a (*she stared*) *in horror*

sch·auen I. vt [h] *to see, observe* ‖ *to look, gaze, peep at* **II.** vi [h] *to look* (vorwärts *forwards*) (um sich *round*) (zur Seite *to one side*) ‖ jdm ins Auge ∼ *to look a p in the face* ‖ Habgier schaut ihm aus d. Augen *greed looks through his eyes* | ⟨fig⟩ auf etw, jdn ∼ *to take .. as model* ‖ schau, schau! *well, well!* ‖ schau, daß *take heed that* (*you do it*) ‖ ∼ Sie, daß Sie weiter k *get along with you* ‖ ˣgelt, da schaust (du)? *there you are looking* | sich [dat] in den Hals ∼ l *to have one's throat examined*

Sch·auer m & n ∼s/∼ *barn* ‖ *shed*; *sheltering roof*

Sch·auer m ∼s/∼ (*shivering-*)*fit, paroxysm, attack, thrill, shiver*; kalter ∼ *the shivers* pl | (*mad*) *fit* ‖ (*bodily*) *fear* ‖ (*secret*) *horror* ‖ (*sacred*) *awe, sublime* (*thrill*) | (Regen≈) *shower*, ⟨Am⟩ *flurry* (*of rain*) ‖ in ∼n herunter k *to shower down* **~bad** n *showerbath* **~drama** n *thriller* **~fieber** n ⟨path⟩ *trembling fever, ague* **~film** m ⟨fam⟩ *shocker* **~gefühl** n *feeling of horror* ‖ es überfiel sie ein ∼ *she felt a sense of horror creeping over her* **~geschichte** f *hair-raiser* **~roman** m ⟨Lit⟩ *Gothic novel* (*H. Walpole, W. Scott*); ⟨mod⟩ (*shilling*) *shocker, penny dreadful, thriller*, ⟨Am sl⟩ *goose-flesher* **~tat** f *atrocity, awful crime, atrocious deed* **≈voll** a *horrible, dreadful* **sch·auerig** = schaurig **sch·auerlich** a *awful, thrilling, horrible, ghastly, rotten* ‖ *weird, gruesome* **≈keit** f *awfulness*, etc ‖ *atrociousness, gruesomeness* **sch·auern** vi & imps [h] (stark regnen) *to shower, pour* (*with rain*) ‖ (schaudern) *to shudder, shiver* ‖ es schauert mich *or* mir, mir schauert *I tremble*; *I shiver* (*with cold*); *I shudder* (*for fear, horror*)

Sch·aufel f ∼/∼n *shovel* | Anker≈ *palm* ‖ ⟨hunt⟩ Geweih≈ *shovel, palm* ‖ Kalk≈ *lime rake* ‖ Kehricht≈ *dust-pan* ‖ Kohlen≈ *coal-shovel* ‖ Kuchen≈ *cake server* ‖ Raddampfer≈ *paddle* ‖ ⟨mar⟩ Riemen≈ *blade* ‖ Schöpf≈ *scoop* ‖ Tisch≈ *crumb tray* ‖ Turbinen≈ *blade* ‖ Wasserrad≈ *float, wing* | e–e ∼ voll *a shovelful* (*two shovelfuls* Kohlen *of coal*) **~bagger** m *shovel dredger* **~blatt** n *vane* **~bohrer** m *bung-hole borer* **~brett** n (Mühlrad≈) *float, ladleboard* **~fuß** m *root of the blade* **~geweih** n *palmed antlers* pl **~hirsch** m *fallow-buck* (*over two years old*); kapitaler ∼ (Damhirsch im 7. Jahr) *great buck* **~kasten** m *paddle-box* **~löffel** m *ladle* **~pflug** m *moulding-plough* **~rad** n *blade-wheel* (am Raddampfer) *paddle-wheel* **~rotor** m ⟨aero⟩ *paddle-wheel rotor* **~teilung** f ⟨turbo⟩ *spacing of blades* **~zahn** m *broad incisor* **sch·aufelig** a *shovel-shaped* **sch·aufeln** vt/i [h] *to shovel* ‖ *to scoop* (*a hole*), *to dig* (*a grave*) **Sch·aufler** m ∼s/∼ *p who shovels* ‖ ⟨hunt⟩ = Schaufelhirsch

Sch·aukel f ∼/∼n *swing* ‖ (Wippe) *seesaw* ‖ russische ∼ *swing-boats* pl, *ferris wheel* **~couch** f *swing c.* **~pferd** n *rocking-horse* **~politik** f *policy of vacillation* ‖ ∼ (be)treiben) *to balance one's policy* **~reck** n *trapeze* **~stuhl** m *rocking-chair* **~system** n ⟨pol⟩ *temporizing, fence-riding* **sch·aukeln I.** vi & sich ∼ [h] *to swing, rock, toss* ‖ (wippen) *to see-saw* ‖ (wackeln) *to wobble, waddle* ‖ mit dem Stuhle ∼ *to rock the chair* ‖ sich auf dem Stuhle ∼ *to balance o.s. on the chair* ‖ im Schaukelstuhl ∼ ⟨Am⟩ *to teeter* ‖ (v Schiffen) (rollen) *to roll* ‖ (stampfen) *to pitch* **II.** vt *to dandle*; *to rock* (*a child on one's knees*) ‖ ⟨fig⟩ °wir w das Kind *or* die S schon schaukeln *we will manage to put the matter in order* (⟨sl⟩ *pull the job, swing the th*); *we'll swing it* ‖ (e–e S) ∼ ⟨sl⟩ *to wangle*

Schaum m ∼(e)s/≈e (Meeres≈) *foam, spray* ‖ ⟨zoo path⟩ *foam*; der ∼ stand ihm vor dem Munde *he foamed at the mouth* (*with anger*) ‖ (Bier–, Sekt≈) *froth* ‖ (Seifenwasser≈) *lather* ‖ (Gär–, Abschaum) *scum* ‖ ⟨cast⟩ *sullage* | zu ∼ schlagen *to whip* (*cream*); *to beat up* (*an egg*) | ⟨fig⟩ eitel ∼ *froth*; zu ∼ w *to vanish* ‖ ⟨prov⟩ Träume sind ≈e *dreams are mere shadows* ‖ °er schlägt nur ∼ *everything he does comes to naught* **≈artig** a *foamlike, frothy* **~bad** n *bubble* od *foam bath* **~beton** m *f. concrete* **~bildung** f *frothing* **~blase** f *bubble*, (im Wein) *pearl*; ⟨fig⟩ *delusion*; ⟨tech⟩ *bell* **~feuerlöscher** m *fire-extinguisher, foam-e.* **~gebäck** n *meringue* **≈geboren** a ⟨myth⟩ *risen from the sea-foam*, die ∼e *Venus* (od *Aphrodite*) *Anadyomene* **~gemisch** n ⟨tech⟩ *emulsion* **~gold** n *tinsel* **~gummi** m *foam*(*ed*) *rubber* od *latex* **~kalk** m *aphrite* **~kämme** m pl (der Wellen) *white horses* pl **~kelle** f, **~löffel** m *skimmer*; *skimming ladle* **~kraut** n ⟨bot⟩ *cardamine*; *lady smock* **~krone** f *white crest* (*of a wave*) **≈los** a *without foam*, etc; (Bier) *without a head*; *flat* **~löschgerät** n *foam-extinguisher* **~schläger** m *whisk*; ⟨fig⟩ *maker of empty compliments*; *puffing trader*; *humbug, quack*, ⟨fam⟩ *swash-buckler*, ⟨sl⟩ *squirt* | ∼ei [f] ⟨pol, Am⟩ *bunk*(*um*) ‖ *swash-buckling*; *squirtism, froth, frothiness* | ≈isch [a] *charlatanic*(*al*) **~ventil** n *scum-valve* **~verhütungsmittel** n *anti-froth preparation*; *foam-inhibitor* **~wein** m *champagne*; *sparkling wine* **≈weiß** a *white as froth* **~zirpe** f ⟨ent⟩ *frog-hopper* **sch·äumen I.** vt [h] (ab∼) *to scum, skim* **II.** vi [h] *to foam* (*the surf foams, the waves are foamy*); (of milk etc) *to cream* ‖ ⟨fig⟩ *to foam* od *froth at the mouth, to boil, seethe* (vor *with*, über *about*) ‖ (Wein) *to froth, sparkle, effervesce* ‖ (Seifenlauge) *to lather* | **~d** *spumescent, spumous, spumy, foaming, frothy*; (heftig) *barmy*; (Getränk) *effervescent* ‖ *sparkling* (*wine, cup*) **III.** ≈ n *effervescence, frothiness* ‖ zum ≈ bringen *to froth* **sch·aumig** a *foaming, frothy*

sch·aurig a *awful, horrid, horrible, weird, unearthly*; → Schauer

Scheck m ∼s/∼e & ∼s *cheque*, ⟨Am⟩ *check* ‖ Blanko∼ *blank ch.*; durchkreuzter ∼ *crossed ch.*; falscher ∼ *forged* (⟨sl⟩ *stumer-*, ⟨Am⟩ *rubber-*) *ch.*; offener, an den Überbringer zahlbarer ∼ *open ch., ch. to bearer*; Post≈ *postal ch.*; Reise≈ *travel*(*l*)*er's ch.*; ungedeckter ∼ ⟨a.⟩ *bad cheque*, ⟨Am⟩ *check*; Verrechnungs≈ *negotiable ch.* | e–n ∼ ausstellen *to draw a ch.* (über *for*) ‖ e–n ∼ einlösen *to cash a ch.* ‖ mit ∼(s) bezahlen *to pay* *by ch.* (*in ch.s*) **~abschnitt** m *counterfoil*, ⟨Am⟩ *stub* **~buch** n *ch.-book* **~fälscher** m *ch. forger* **~formular** n *blank ch.* **~inhaber** m *bearer* **~konto** *ch.(ing* ⟨Am⟩) *account* **~verkehr** m *ch. transactions* pl **~zahlung** f *payment by ch.*

Sch·eck(e f) m ~(n)/~n *piebald* od *dappled horse*; ⟨Am a.⟩ *pinto* **sch·ecken** vt [h] *to streak, to dapple* **sch·eckig** a *spotted* ‖ *piebald, dappled* (*horse* etc) ‖ °sich ~ lachen *to split with laughing*

scheel a *squinting, squint-eyed* ‖ ⟨fig⟩ *envious, jealous*; etw mit ~en Blicken betrachten *to fret and frown at a th* | [adv] *askance, awry* (*to look a.* od *a. at*) ‖ jdn ~ ansehen ⟨fig⟩ *to look at a p with an envious* od *evil eye* **~äugig** a *squint-eyed* **≗sucht** f *jealousy, envy* **~süchtig** a *jealous, envious*

Sch·effel m ~s/~ *bushel* ‖ ⟨fig⟩ sein Licht unter den ~ stellen *to hide one's light under a b.* **~sack** m *sack holding a b.* **~(macher)ware** f *hollow ware* **≗weise** [adv] *by the bushels*; *abundantly* ‖ ~ Geld ausgeben *to squander money*; *to go on a spending spree* | **≗n** vt/i [h] 1. *to heap up, amass* (*money*) 2. vi ⟨agr⟩ *to yield abundantly*

Sch·eibe f ~/~n **A.** *disk*; *sheet*; *plate* ‖ ⟨astr⟩ *orb, disk* ‖ *cake* (*of wax*), *coil* (*of rope*) ‖ (Schnitte) *slice, cut* ‖ ⟨hockey⟩ *puck* **B. Antriebs**(stufen)≗ *driving* (*cone*) *pulley*; Brems≗ *brake pulley*; Brot≗ *slice* od *round of bread*; Butzen≗nfenster *window of bull's eye glass*; Dichtungs≗ *washer*; Dreh≗ *revolving disk*; Exzenter≗ *eccentric sheave*; Fenster–, Glas≗ *window-, glass-pane*; Honig≗ (*honey*) *comb*; Hub≗ *eccentric sheave*; Kompaß≗ *card*; Papp≗ *piece of pasteboard*; Polier≗ *burnishing wheel*; Putzmaurer≗ *hawk*; Riemen≗ *sheave*; Schleif≗ *grindstone, grinding wheel*; Schnur≗ (Seilerei) *band pulley*; Signal≗ *signalling disk*; Spann≗ *tension disk*; Töpfer≗ *potter's wheel*; Tünch≗ *hawk*; Transmissions≗ *transmissing pulley*; Trieb≗ *slow motion tangent screw*; Uhr≗ *face, dial*; Umlenk≗ *reversing sheave* ‖ Verschluß≗ *stopping washer*; Windschutz≗ *wind-screen*; Winker≗ *signal disk* ‖ Wurf≗ *discus*; Ziel≗ *target* **C. in** ~n schneiden *to slice* (*potatoes, apples*) ‖ nach der ~ schießen *to shoot at a target* **D.** ~ u Tau *whip* ‖ zwei ~n u Taue *whip upon whip* **E.** ⟨fig⟩ °bei dem kannst du dir noch 'ne ~ von abschneiden *take a lesson from his book, you connot hold a candle to him* | **~n-** **≗artig** a *disk-shaped* **~bank** f (Drahtzieherei) *drawing-bench* **~blei** n *glazier's lead* **~bremse** f *puck type brake* **~büchse** f *rifle for target--shooting* **~dichtung** f *sheet gasket* **~egge** f *disk--harrow* **~elektrisiermaschine** f *plate machine* **~floß** n *target raft* **≗förmig** a *orbicular* **~fräser** m *side milling cutter* **~gardine** f *casement curtain* **~gatt** n ⟨mar⟩ *sheave-hole* **~glas** n *sheet-glass, pane-glass* **~hantel** f *disk-loading bar-bells* **~hitzer** ⟨mot⟩ *wind-screen heater* **~honig** m *honey in combs*; °⟨fig euph⟩ = Scheiße **~klärer** ⟨mot⟩ *demister* **~kleister** m *target paste*; °⟨fig euph⟩ = Scheiße *mess*! **~kommando** n *marking party*; *pit detail* **~könig** m *best shot of a rifle-club* **~kupplung** f *plate-coupling* **~pflaster** n *paster* **~rad** n *disk-wheel* **~schießen** n *target-practice* od *-shooting* **~schleifmaschine** f *grinding wheels* pl **~-schlepper** m *target sled*; ⟨mar⟩ *t. towing tug* **~schütz(e)** *m marksman* **~spüler** m ⟨mot⟩ *screen-washer* **~übersetzung** f *sheave ratio* **~stand** m *butts* pl, *shooting-range* | ~deckung [f] *pit* **~- und Seilwerk** n *sheaves* pl *and cordage* **~wachs** n *cake--wax* **≗weise** [adv] *in slices* **~werfen** n *playing at throwing disks* **≗wischer** m ⟨mot⟩ *wind-screen wiper* **sch·eibig** a *in slices*

Scheich m ~s/~s *sheik(h)* ‖ °⟨hum⟩ *fellow*

..scheid [suff] (z Bildung v Ortsnamen), [urspr] (Wasser-)Scheide (z. B. Rem≗, Lüden≗); → folg.

Scheid- ~bogen [m] ⟨ec arch⟩ *pier-arch*; ≗ pl ⟨a.⟩ *nave arcades* **sch·eidbar** a *separable* ‖ ⟨chem⟩ *analysable*; → folg.

Sch·eide f ~/~n **A. 1.** *sheath, scabbard* **2.** ⟨anat⟩ *sheath, vagina*; ⟨vulg⟩ *cockalley, -lane, concern, cunny*; (*poke-*)*hole* **3.** (Trennung) *parting* (*of the ways*); *separation*; *border-line* **B.** in die ~ stecken *to put up*; *to sheathe*, aus der ~ ziehen *to draw, unsheathe* (*one's sword*) **~anlage** f (*magnetic*) *screening device* **~anstalt** f *parting--work* **~bank** f ⟨min⟩ *sorting-table* **~blick** m *parting look* **~brief** m *letter of separation, farewell l.* ‖ ⟨jur⟩ *bill of divorce* **~erz** n *culled ore* **~feuer** n ⟨min⟩ *refining furnace* **~flüssigkeit** f ⟨chem⟩ *separating liquid* **~gruß** m *farewell* (*greeting*) **~kunst** f *analytical chemistry* **~kuß** m *parting kiss* **~linie** f *line of demarcation, dividing line* **~mauer** f = ~wand **~münze** f *small coin*; *change*; *fractional currency* **~punkt** m *point of separation* od *divergence* **~stunde** f *hour of parting* od *death* **~wand** f *partition*(*-wall*) ‖ ⟨zoo, bot, anat⟩ *septum* ‖ Nasen~ *dissepiment* ‖ ⟨mar⟩ *bulkhead* ‖ ⟨el, tech⟩ *diaphragm* **~wasser** n ⟨chem⟩ *aqua fortis* **~weg** m *cross-road* ‖ am ~e stehen *to be at the parting of the ways*, ⟨fig⟩ *at the cross-roads*; Herkules am ~e s *to have the choice of Hercules* **Sch·eiden** n ~s/ *parting* ‖ e–e Bemerkung beim ~ *a parting remark* ‖ vor s–m ~ *previous to his death*; *before leaving* ‖ ~ tut weh *partings are grievous* **sch·eiden** v/irr [schied/geschieden] **I.** vt [h] **1.** *to divide*; *separate, part* (v *from*) ‖ ⟨chem⟩ *to analyse, refine* ‖ ⟨met⟩ *to try* (*out*) ‖ (gewaltsam) *to sever* ‖ (zerlegen) *to decompose* ‖ (Rübensaft) *to defecate*; (Zucker) *to clarify* **2.** jdn (v Tisch und Bett) ~ *to divorce a p*, (Eheleute *a married couple*), (e–e Ehe *a marriage*, ⟨a.⟩ *to dissolve a m.*) | **sich** ~ l *to divorce* (v jem a p); sie h sich ~ l *they have been d.d* | **geschieden** *divorced* (⟨a. übtr⟩ *art d. from religion*) ‖ wir sind durch gegensätzliche Ansichten g. *our opinions are antagonistic* ‖ ⟨fig⟩ wir sind g.e Leute *we have finished with each other* | hier ~ **sich** die (⟨fig⟩ unsere) Wege *here the roads part* (*here we go different ways*) ‖ (of milk) *to curdle* | sich ~ l (wollen) *to obtain* od *get a divorce* od *a judicial separation* (*to sue for a d.*) ‖ sich von jdm ~ l *to divorce a p* ‖ sie sind v–e–a geschieden *they are divorced* **II.** vi [s] *to separate, depart, withdraw* ‖ *to come away* (v *from*) | **als** Freunde ~ *to part friends* ‖ **aus** dem Amte ~ *to resign* (od *retire from*) *office* ‖ aus dem (diesem) Leben ~ *to die* (*to depart this life*) ‖ sie ~ **v-e-a** *they part* (*company*), *they separate, they take leave of one another* ‖ **~d** *closing* (*year*), *passing* (*day*) ‖ es muß **geschieden** s *a parting is inevitable* **Scheiden-** ⟨sex⟩ ~injektion [f] *douche*; ~schwamm [m] *sponge*; ~tampon [m] *tampon* **Sch·eider** m ~s/~ *a p who divides*; *separator* ‖ *sorter* (*of ore*) ‖ *refiner* (*of metals*) **Sch·eidung** f ~/~en *separation* ‖ (Erze≗) *spalling* ‖ ⟨met⟩ *refining* ‖ (Zucker≗) *clarifying* ‖ ⟨chem⟩ *analysis* ‖ (Ehe≗) *divorce* (v *from*); ~ v Tisch u Bett *judicial separation*; ~ beantragen *to sue for a d.*; ~ erlangen *to get a d.*; sie liegt mit ihm in ~ *she has taken divorce proceedings against him* ‖ ⟨fig⟩ ~ der Geister *differences of opinion* **Sch·eidungs-** **~grund** m *cause for divorce* **~klage** f *action for divorce, divorce, divorce-suit* **~urteil** n *divorce decree*; (endgültiges) *decree absolute*; (vorläufiges) *decree nisi*

Schein m ~(e)s/~e **1.** *shine*; *gleam* (*of arms*); [*subdued*] *light* (*of the sun* [*a lamp*]); (*no glimmer of hope*); *sheen* (*on silk* ⟨a. poet⟩) ‖ *lustre*, ⟨Am⟩ *luster, splendo(u)r, brillancy*; greller ~ *glare*; heller ~ *glitter* (*of gold*); *refulgence* ‖ leerer ~ *make-believe* ‖ Heiligen≗ *halo, glory*; der letzte ~ v .. *the last shreds of ..* **2.** ⟨fig⟩ (Anschein) *semblance, make-believe*; *appearance* ‖ (Aussehen) *air, look* ‖ äußerer ~ *outward look, mere show*; *appearances* pl (*are against him*), (*to save a.s*);

der ~ trügt *a.s are deceptive* || (Verstellung) *make-believe, sham* (⟨fam⟩ *it's all (a) sham*) || fauler ~ ⟨sl⟩: *all was fake* || (Vorwand) *pretence* | den ~ **erwecken** *to create the appearance (of doing)* || sich den ~ [gen] geben *to assume the pose (of ..)*, .., als ob *to pretend as though* || es hat den ~ als ob *it looks as if* || den ~ (..) wahren *to keep up appearances (the illusion of ..), to save one's face* ⟨Am a.⟩ *to put up a front* | dem ~e **nach** *apparently* nach dem ~ urteilen *to judge by appearances* | **unter** dem ~ [gen] *under the mask* od *colour, cloak, show of ..* | nur **zum** ~ *for form's sake, pro forma, only for show*; (*it's all pretence*) **3.** (Zeugnis) *attestation, certificate* || (Quittung) *receipt* || (Rechnung) *bill* || (Geld≈) *banknote*, ~e *paper money* || (Schuld≈) *I.O.U.* || (Formular) *form* | Durchfuhr≈ *transit-bond* || Entlassungs≈ *ticket of discharge* || Erb≈ *certificate of heirship* od *inheritance* || Erneuerungs≈ *certificate of renewal* || Flieger≈ *flying certificate* || Führer≈ *driving licence* || Geburts–, Tauf–, Toten≈ *baptismal, birth, death certificate* || (Gepäck– etc ≈) *check* || Hundertmark≈ *hundred mark note* || kl ~ *tally* || Lager≈ *warrant* | e–n ~ **ausstellen** *to make out a receipt*, etc || er besteht auf s–m ~ *he claims his pound of flesh* **Schein-** [in comp] *false, sham, ficticious, delusive, pseudo(-), mock, imaginary, dummy, pro forma* [attr], ⟨Am⟩ *phony* **~amateur** m ⟨sport⟩ *shamateur* **~angriff** m ⟨mil⟩ *m.* od *sh. attack*, ⟨fenc⟩ *feint* **~anlage** f *d.y works* **~batterie** f *d.y battery* **~bewegung** f ⟨mil⟩ *deceptive movement* **~beweis** m *d.e proof, fallacy* **~bieter** m (Auktion) *by-bidder* **~bild** n *illusion; simulacrum; phantom* **~blüte** f ⟨fig⟩ *apparent prosperity* **~christ** m *false* od *lip-Christian* **~ding** n *f.s object* **~ehe** f *pretended marriage* **~ehre** f *m. honour* **~einwurf** m *specious objection* **~farben** f pl *accidental colours* pl **~flugplatz** m *decoy airfield* **~friede** m *hollow peace* **≈fromm** a *hypocritical* | ≈igkeit [f] *hypocrisy* **~frucht** f *collective fruit*, ⟨scient⟩ *pseudocarp, sorosis* **~gebot** n ⟨Am⟩ *straw bid* **~gelehrsamkeit** f *sciolism, would-be* od *apparent learning* od *erudition* **~gericht** n *m. trial* **~geschäft** n *sh. transaction* **~glaube** m *pretended faith* **~glück** n *fool's paradise* **~gold** n *false gold* **~größe** f *sh. greatness* **~grund** m *apparent reason* || *pretext, pretence, sophistry* **~handel** m *sh.-transaction* **≈heilig** a *hypocritical, sanctimonious*, ⟨fam⟩ *goody-goody* || ~e Sprache, ~es Wesen *cant* || etw ~ preisen *to pay lip-service to a th* || ~ tun *to snivel* **~heilige** m [der ~, ein ~r] *hypocrite*; ⟨fam⟩ *goody* **~heiligkeit** f *hypocrisy, sanctimoniousness, snivel; cant* **~hoffnung** f *d.e hope* **~kampf** m *m. fight* **~kauf** m *sh. purchase* **~könig** m *m. king, sh.-king, kinglet* **≈krank** a ⟨mil, mar⟩ *malingering* | ~heit [f] *ficticious sickness, malingering* **~krieg** m *mimic warfare* **~leben** n *half-life, empty life* **~manöver** n ⟨mil⟩ *demonstration* **~parlament** n *sh. parliament* **~quittung** f *sh. receipt* **~sendung** f ⟨wir⟩ *deceptive* od *simulated (electronic) transmission* **~stellung** f ⟨mil⟩ *sh.* od *d.y position* **~tablette** f ⟨med⟩ *dummy* od *placebo* [L] *tablet* **~tod** m ⟨path⟩ *asphyxia, (cataleptic) trance, state of suspended animation, apparent death* **≈tot** a *seemingly dead* **~tote(r)** m *a p apparently dead* **~tugend** f *sh. virtue* **~verhör** n *m. trial* **~verkauf** m *pro-forma sale* **~wechsel** m ⟨com⟩ *accommodation-bill* **~welt** f *world of visions* **~werfer** m *reflector, search(ing)light* ⟨bes mil, mar⟩ || ⟨theat⟩ *spot(light)*, Klein≈ *baby spot*; Parab·ol≈ *pageant lantern*, ⟨Am⟩ *parabolic reflector floodlight*; Proszeniums≈ *perch* (⟨Am⟩ *tormentor*) *spot*; Prunklicht≈ *pin spot*; Streu≈ *diffused floodlight*, ⟨Am⟩ *jelled flood*; Verfolgungs≈ *follow spot*; Vorbühnen≈ *proscenium spot* || ~leuchten! *switch on search-lights* || ⟨mot⟩ *(dazzle) headlight, headlamp* | ~halter [m] ⟨theat⟩ *spot bar*, ⟨Am⟩ *light pipe* | ~licht [n] ⟨theat⟩ *spotlight, flood-light(ing)* ⟨a. übtr⟩; im ~ *floodlit*; ~stellung [f] (Fla≈) *s.l. station*; ~zug [m] *s.l. section* **~werk** n *dummy works* [sg konstr] **~wesen** n *appearances* pl, *show, pretence* **~widerspruch** m *paradox, seeming contradiction* **~widerstand** m ⟨el⟩ *impedance* || ~ leisten *to offer token resistance* **~zahlung** f *feigned payment* **~ziel** n ⟨mil⟩ *dummy* **sch·einbar** a *specious (pretext)* || *plausible (reason)* || *likely (motive)* (→ anscheinend) *apparent (horizon), ostensible (object), seeming* || ⟨phys⟩ *virtual (focus)* || *fictitious (wealth)* | adv (nur) ~ *seemingly, on the surface*; ⟨jur⟩ *prima facie* **sch·einen** vi [schien/geschienen] [h] **1.** (glänzen) *to shine: the sun shines* od *is shining, (there is a sunshine)*, .. heiß .. *is hot* || *to glitter, gleam (the house was gleaming white from the dark)* || nieder~ auf *to blaze down upon* || zum Fenster herein~ *to shine in through the panes* || ein Licht ~ l durch *shine a l. through (a slit)*, .. auf *to flash a l. upon ..* **2.** (den Anschein h): ~ z s: *they seem (to be) happy, they appear to be h.* || sie ~ .. z s, es scheint, sie sind .. *or* als ob .. *it seems as though (they were happy)* || *they are richer than they seem* (als sie ~ *or* als es scheint) || mir scheint *it strikes me (that)* || er scheint ein ehrlicher Kerl (z s) *he looks an honest fellow, (a man who, by his dress, should be a parson)* || er schien ungläubig *he sounded incredulous* || ~ .. z s ⟨Am⟩: *they look to be able* | es scheint **nicht,** daß .. *they are not likely to be there* | das scheint **nur** so *it's only an illusion* | **mir** scheint: *it seems to me (that ..), he seems to me (to be ..), it looks to me (as if ..)* || das will mir nicht ganz ~ *I don't quite see that* || **wenn** es Ihnen recht scheint *if you think it proper, if you like, if it seems advisable to you* || **wie** es scheint *as it seems* || wie scheint dir das? *what do you think of it* | ⟨prov⟩ ein anderes ist ~, ein anderes ist s *ths are not always what they seem*

°**Sch·eiß-** [in comp] °*fucking, fuggin* **~angst** f *blue funk* (e–e ~ h *to be in a ..*) || er hat e–e z gr ~ ⟨Am⟩ *he's too fuggin yellow* **~dreck** m; ~! *shit!* || über jeden ~ beklagt er sich *.. about every trifle* **~haus** n *privy* **~kerl** m *shit(-bag); cad; perisher* **~wetter** n *muck, shit* °**Sch·eiße** f ~/ *excrements* pl, ⟨vulg⟩ *shit, turd*; ⟨Am⟩ *crap* || ~! *shit* || jdn aus der (durch die) ~ ziehen *to give a p a lift out of mud (to drag a p through) the mud* || er sitzt in der ~ *he is regularly in the soup* **sch·eißen** vt/i [h] [schiß/geschissen] *to shit* || scheiß! *rot* || scheiß drauf! *to hell with it* **Scheißer·ei** f ~/~en *shitting; excrements* pl || ⟨fig⟩ *paltry matter* || ⟨path, vulg⟩ *the shitters*

Scheit n ~(e)s/~e *block* od *piece of wood; billet, log* || *little board* || Holz in ~e hacken *to chop wood into billets* **~holz** n *logwood; split fire-wood* **Sch·eitel** m ~s/~ **1.** *top* od *crown of the head, vertex* || vom ~ bis zur Sohle *from top to toe, from head to heel* **2.** ⟨geom⟩ *vertex (of an angle, curve, arch); crest (of a curve)* || *apex; zenith; summit* **3.** (des Haares) *parting*; den ~ ziehen *to make the p.* (in der Mitte *down the middle*) **~abstand** m ⟨astr⟩ *zenith-distance* **~bein** n *parietal (bone)* **~linie** f *vertical line* **~punkt** m ⟨geom⟩ *vertex*, ⟨ball⟩ *summit*, ⟨astr⟩ *zenith; point of culmination*, ⟨artill⟩ *apex of trajectory* **≈recht** a *vertical* **~rippe** f ⟨arch⟩ *ridge-* od *tie-rib* **~winkel** m *opposite angle; vertical angle* **sch·eiteln** vt [h] *to part (one's hair)* || das Haar gescheitelt tragen *to wear the hair parted* || das Haar scheiltelt sich .. *parts* od *forms a parting* **Sch·eiterhaufen** m *stake* (besteigen *to mount*) || z ~ verurteilen *to condemn .. to burn at the st.* || (für Leichen) *funeral pile* od *pyre* || ⟨praehist crem a.⟩ *sepulchral bonfire* **sch·eitern I.** vi [s] *to run aground, to split, to be wrecked* (an *on*); *to become a wreck* | ⟨fig⟩ *to come to naught; to get nowhere; to fall to the ground* || *to miscarry, fail* (an *owing to*), *to go to pieces* od ⟨fam⟩ *to smithereens, to go fut*;

(of negotiations) *to break down* | ~ **an** *to founder* od *split on*; daran scheitert m–e ganze Kunst *that's beyond me, that baffles me*; viele ~ an: (*slang*) *is the great pitfall* | **gescheitert** ⟨fig⟩ *broken down* (*existence*), *abortive* (*attempt*), *frustrated* (*scheme*), ⟨Am⟩ *failed* (*enterprise*) **II.** ≗ n *shipwreck* ‖ ⟨fig⟩ *breakdown* ‖ etw zum ≗ bringen *to make a th abortive*; z ≗ bringen, ~ l ⟨lit & fig⟩ *to wreck* ‖ z ≗ verurteilt *doomed to failure* od *miscarriage*, .. s *to spell failure*; *the venture could never have succeeded*

Sch·elde f (belg. Fluß) *Scheldt*

Sch·elf m ~(e)s/~e ⟨geog-mar⟩ *shelf* [pl *shelves*] | ~meer [n] *epicontinental sea*

Sch·elfe f ~/~n *husk, shell* **sch·elfern** vt/refl [h] *to peel* (*off*) ‖ ⟨anat⟩ *to exfoliate*

Sch·ellack m ~(e)s/~e *shellac, French polish*

Sch·elle f ~/~n **1.** (Klingel) *bell*; *dinner-b., hand-b., school-b.* ‖ ⟨bib⟩ klingende ~ *tinkling cymbal*; ⟨fig⟩ jeder hat s–e ~ *everyone has his own pecularities* ‖ der Katze die ~ umhängen *to bell the cat*, ⟨fig⟩ *to call a spade a spade* **2.** (Fessel) *manacle, handcuff* **3.** ⟨tech, el⟩ *clamp, clip*, Rohr-≗ *coupling strap* **4.** *box on the ear* **5.** ⟨cards⟩ ~n [pl] *diamond*(*s* pl) **sch·ellen** vt/i [h] *to ring* (*the bell*) ‖ es hat geschellt *there was the bell* ‖ (**nach**) e–m ~ *to ring for a p* **Sch·ellen-** ⟨cards⟩ *diamonds* **~baum** m ⟨mil⟩ (*Turkish*) *crescent, Chinese* od *military bells*, ⟨fam⟩ *Jingling Johnnie* **~ente** f ⟨orn⟩ *garrot* **~geläute** n *tinkling* od *ringing of bells* ‖ [koll] (*set of*) *bells*, (e–s Pferdes) *bell-harness*, (am Schlitten) *sleigh-bells* **~kappe** f (*fool's*) *cap and bells* **~klang** m *sound of bells* **~könig** m ⟨cards⟩ *king of diamonds* ‖ e–n über den ~ loben *to praise a p to the sky* ‖ das geht noch übern ~ *that's a bit too silly* **~schlitten** m *sledge with bells* **~trommel** f *timbrel* **~zeug** n *bell-harness* **~zug** m *bell-pull*

Sch·ell- ~fisch m ⟨ich⟩ *haddock* **~hengst** m *stallion* **~kraut** n ⟨bot⟩ *common celandine*

Schelm m ~(e)s/~e **A. 1.** [obs] ⟨dero⟩ *knave, villain, rascal, scoundrel* **2.** ⟨mod⟩ *rogue, urchin* ‖ armer kl ~ *poor little rogue* (od *devil, fellow, wretch, scamp*) **B.** ein ~, der Schlechtes dabei **denkt** *hon*(*n*)*i soit qui mal y pense* ‖ jdn z ~ m *to say evil of a p* ‖ der ~ **schaut** ihm aus den Augen *you can see the artful dodger in his eyes* ‖ ich will ein ~ s, wenn .. *if .. you may call me a knave* ‖ den ~ im Nacken (sitzen) h *to be a rogue* ‖ an e–m z ~ w *to betray a p, to play a p a dirty trick* **C.** ⟨prov⟩ ein ~ gibt mehr als er hat *you cannot give more than you have* ‖ auf e–n ~ gehören anderthalb *you must set a thief to catch a thief* od *pay rogues in their own coin* ‖ ein ~, der mehr tut als er kann *you must not expect impossibilities* **Sch·elmen- ~gesicht** n *roguish face* ‖ *roguish-looking p* **~lied** n *frivolous song* **~roman** m *picaresque novel* (*e.g. Le Sage, Gil Blas*) **~sprache** f *thieves' slang* **~streich** m, **~stück** n *roguish prank* od *trick, piece of roguery* ‖ [obs] *villainy* **Schelmer·ei** f ~/~en *roguery* ‖ [obs] *knavery, villainy* **Sch·elmin** f ~/~nen *female rogue, vixen*; ⟨fam⟩ *huzzie* **sch·elmisch** a *roguish, sly*; *wanton*; *teasing* ‖ *waggish* (*trick*), *quizzical, arch* (*look*); ~e Miene *air of mischief* | [adv] *elvishly, mischievously* ‖ ~-boshaft *impish*

Sch·elte f ~/~n *scolding, wigging*; ⟨fam⟩ *talking-to* ‖ ~ bek *to be scolded*; *to get a sc.g* (⟨fam⟩ *a jaw*) ‖ er fürchtete sich vor ~ *he was afraid of a reprimand* | ≗**n I.** vi/t [schalt/gescholten] [h] *to scold, chide* ‖ auf jdn ~ *to run a p down* ‖ über etw ~ *to grumble about a th* | *to inveigh against a custom* | jdn ~ ⟨a. fam⟩ *to tonguelash a p*; e–n wegen s–s Betragens ~, j–s Betragen ~ *to scold, rebuke, blame, reprimand a p for his conduct* ‖ ein Schurke schilt den andern *the pot calls the kettle black* | jdn e–n Esel ~ *to call a p a duffer*; sich e–n I. ~ *to curse o.s. for an idiot* **II.** ≗ n *scolding, reprimand*; *setdown* **Sch·elt- ~name** m *opprobrious name* **~rede** f *philippic* **~wort** n *invective, reproachful term, abusive word* ‖ jdm ~e an den Kopf werfen *to call a p names*

Sch·ema n ~s/~s & ~ta (Plan, Entwurf) *schema, scheme, system, diagram* (a. Schaltschema ⟨wir⟩), *sketch* ‖ (Formular, Tabelle) *schedule* ‖ ~ F *redtape*; nach ~ F *by rule of thumb*; *conventional, usual, orthodox* (*warfare*); nach ~ F verlaufen *to run to pattern* ‖ (Muster) *model, plan, pattern* **sch–·atisch** a *schematic*; ~e Darstellung *diagrammatic view, plan* od *layout*, .. im Durchschnitt *d. section* ‖ *in accordance with a certain pattern* (od *plan, model, formula*); *to a letter* ≗**tis·ieren** vt [h] *to schematize* **~t·ismus** m *schematism, officialism*

Sch·emel m ~s/~ (*foot*)*stool*

Sch·emen m ~s/~ *shadow, phantom, delusion*; (⟨bib⟩ *vain show*) | ≗**haft** a *sh.y, like a sh., delusive*

Schenk m ~en/~en (Mund≗) *cupbearer* ‖ (Wirt) *bar-, alehouse-keeper*; *publican* **~gerechtigkeit** f *licence to retail* od *sell beer and liquor* **~kanne** f *tankard, can* **~kellner** m *barman* **~mädchen** n, **~mamsell** f *barmaid* **~stube** f *tap-room, bar*(*-room*) **~teller** m *salver, waiter* **~tisch** m *side-board, bar* **~wirt** m *tavern-keeper, publican* **~wirtschaft** f *public-, ale-house, tavern* **sch·enkbar** a *fit to be given away* (od *to be retailed* [Getränk]) **Sch·enke** f ~/~n *inn, ale-, public-house, tavern*; ⟨fam⟩ *pot house, pub* **sch·enken** vt [h] **A. 1.** (ein|~) *to pour out* (in Gläser *into glasses*) **2.** *to retail* (*liquor*) **3.** jdm etw ~ *to give a p a th, to make a present of a th to a p* ‖ *to bestow a th upon a p* ‖ *to oblige a p with a th* ‖ *to endow a p with* (*a quality*) ‖ *to confer* (*benefits upon mankind*) ‖ ⟨Am⟩ *to donate a th to a p* **4.** (erlassen) *to acquit* (*a p of a th*) **B.** diese **Arbeit** wird dir nicht ge–kt *you will not be spared this work* ‖ e–r S Aufmerksamkeit ~ *to give a thought to a th*, jdm .. *to pay attention to a p* ‖ e–r S ernstlich **Beachtung** ~ *to give a th one's careful consideration* ‖ jdm Beifall ~ *to applaud a p* ‖ e–m die **Freiheit** ~ *to bestow freedom upon a p, to give him his liberty* ‖ jdm s–e Freundschaft (Gunst) ~ *to show a p one's fr.* (*favour*) ‖ jdm e–n Augenblick Gehör ~ *to listen to a p for a moment*; e–r Propagande G. ~ *to fall victim to a pr.* ‖ (**Geschenke**) *to give, to make a present of, to present* (*a p*) *with a th*, .. z Geburtstage (etc) *to give a p a birthday-present* ‖ ein Glas voll|~ *to fill a glass* ‖ [dat] Glauben ~ *to put faith in, to give credence to* ‖ jds Worten Glauben ~ *to take a p's word* ‖ jdm sein **Herz** ~ *to give a p one's heart* ‖ jdm Kinder ~ *to bear .. to ..* ‖ jdm das Lben ~ *to spare* od *grant a p his life*, (e–m Verurteilten) *to pardon a p* ‖ wenn Gott mir das L. schenkt *if God grants me life* od *spare me* ‖ *she gives all her love to her husband* ‖ (den **Rest**): *I will spare you the rest of it* ‖ (ewige Ruhe): *may God grant him everlasting peace* ‖ (Schuld, Strafe) *to remit*; *to let a p off without punishment for a th* ‖ schenkt Wein! *pour out wine*! **C.** sie schenkte **sich** ihm ganz *she surrendered h.s. to him entirely* | sich [dat] selbst etw ~ *to treat o.s. to a th* ‖ °sich ~ *to cut* (*the last act*) ‖ das kannst du dir ~ *you need not bother about going there* od *doing that* **D.** wir h es **geschenkt** bek *it was given to us, we got it as a present*, .. zur Hochzeit .. *as a wedding-present* ‖ beinahe, fast g. *almost given away*, (*I bought it*) *for next to nothing* ‖ das ist g. zu teuer *I wouldn't have* od *take it as a gift* ‖ es soll dir diesmal g. s *I'll let you off this time* | es soll ihm **nicht** g. w *he shall pay for it yet, he shall not come off with impunity* ‖ es wurde ihm nichts g. *he got his due* ‖ °nicht geschenkt [sc: nehme ich's] *not as a gift* | ⟨prov⟩ ˣeinmal g'schenkt bleibt g.'t, bis die Welt untersenkt! *Indian giver*! **Sch·enker(in** f) m ~s/~ *donor, giver* **Sch·enkung** f ~/~en *donation*, (m *to give*); *presentation, bequest* (*to make*) ‖ ⟨hist⟩ reiche

~en *rich gifts, largess* (an *to*) **~sbrief** m, **~surkunde** f *deed of gift* **≈sweise** [adv] *as a gift, by way of donation* **~swiderruf** m *revocation of g.*

Sch·enkel m ~s/~ ⟨anat⟩ (Ober≈) *thigh*; er schlug sich auf den ~ *he smote his th.* ‖ (Unter≈) *shank* ‖ ⟨allg⟩ *leg* (*thin legs*) ‖ ⟨hors⟩ (Pferd) dem ~ weichen l *to passage* | ⟨tech⟩ *leg, shank* ‖ *side* (*of pliers*); (e–r Lehre) *arm* ‖ ⟨geom⟩ *side* (*of an angle*) ‖ (e–s Zirkels) *foot* ‖ ⟨arch⟩ (Bogen-, Gewölbe≈) *haunch* ‖ ⟨carp⟩ *post, standard, stud, upright* ‖ (e~s Hebezeugs) *pry pole of the triangle gin* ‖ *arm* (*of a horseshoe magnet*) ‖ ⟨mar⟩ (Tau) *pendant* **~ader** f *femoral vein* bzw *artery* **~bein** n, **~knochen** m *thigh-bone* **~bruch** m ⟨surg⟩ *fracture of the th.*(*-b.*) ‖ ⟨path⟩ *femoral hernia* **~druck** m *pressure of the thigh*(*s*) **~hilfen** f pl ⟨hors⟩ *action of the legs*; ~ geben *to keep a horse in thigh-leading* **~muskel** m *crural muscle* **~schiene** f *thigh-armour*; *cuishes* pl **~schlagader** f *femoral artery* **~weite** f *stretch of compasses* **~zirkel** m (*pair of*) *compasses* pl

sch·eppern vi [h] *to tinkle*

scher, scher(s)t → sch(i)er etc

Sch·er- ~baum m ⟨weav⟩ *thread-beam* ‖ (Wagenbau) *shaft* **~beanspruchung** f *shearing-stress* **~becken** n *shaving-basin* **~blatt** n *shear-blade* **~block** m (Seilerei) *warping-block* **~eisen** n ⟨tan⟩ *flesh-knife* **~festigkeit** f *shearing strength* **~gang** m ⟨naut⟩ *sheerstrake* **~kopf** m *shaving head*; Doppel≈ *bi-ax sh. h.* **~leine** f ⟨mar⟩ *hauling-line* ***~messer** n *razor* ‖ ⟨oft: tan⟩ *shaving-knife* **~rahmen** m *warper* ‖ *shearing-frame* **~spannung** f ⟨tech⟩ *shearing-stress* **~versuch** m *shear-test* **~wolle** f *shearings* pl **Sch·ere** f ~/~n **A. 1.** (gr) *shears* pl (*sh.*[*s*]) ‖ kl (*a pair of*) *scissors* pl (Wagen≈) *shafts* pl **3.** (Waagen≈) *cheeks* pl **4.** (Krebs≈) *claw* **5.** ⟨hors⟩ (Kandare) *curb* **6.** ⟨hunt⟩ (Birkhahnschwanz) *forked tail* **7.** (Drehbank≈) *adjustment plate* **8.** ⟨gym⟩ *sh.s* **B.** Achs≈ (am Ackerwagen) *shaft-bar* ‖ Baum≈ *tree--pruner* ‖ Blech≈ *plate-sh.s*; *plate sh.ing-machine* ‖ Draht≈ *wire-cutters* pl ‖ Geflügel≈ *game dividers* ‖ Hecken≈ *hedge sh.s* ‖ Knochen≈ *bone forceps* [sg & pl] ‖ Papp≈ *cardboard guillotine* ‖ Schaf≈ *sheep sh.s* ‖ Schiefer≈ *slater's sh.s* ‖ Stabeisen≈ *bar sh.ing-machine*

sch·eren I. vt/i [schor/geschoren] [h] **A. 1.** *to cut* (*a p's hair*) ‖ *to shear* (*sheep*) ‖ *to clip* (*poodles*) ‖ e–m den Bart ~, e–n ~ *to shave a p* ‖ sich den Kopf glatt ~ l *to have a close crop* ‖ kurz geschoren *close-cropped*; glatt g. *close-shaven* ‖ *to mow* (*the lawn*) ‖ *to clip* (*the grass*) ‖ *to prune* (*hedges*) ‖ *to cut* (*skins, carpets, velvet*) **2.** (ausspannen) ⟨tech⟩ *to warp* (*threads*) **3.** ⟨mar⟩ *to reeve* (*a rope*); (of ship) *to yaw*; *to fall off* vi **4.** ⟨fig⟩ *to tease, vex* **B.** ⟨fig⟩ sein Schäfchen ~ *to feather one's own nest* ‖ alles über e–n Kamm ~ *to treat everything alike* **II.** [reg] **sich** ~ [h] *to be off, to cut and run* ‖ scher dich ins Bett! *clear off to bed*! ‖ scher dich zum Teufel *or* Henker *get you gone*!, *go to hell*!, *go and be hanged*! **2.** sich [acc] um etw ~ *to trouble* (*o.s.*) *about a th* ‖ sich um nichts ~ *to be reckless* ‖ sich (k–n Deut *or*) den Teufel um etw ~ *not to care a pin for a th*, ⟨fam⟩ *to let a th go hang* ‖ was sch(i)ert mich das? *what's that to me*? ‖ er hat sich den Teufel g–t um .. *he didn't give a damn for* .. **Sch·eren- ~armleuchte** f *extending wall lamp* **~fernrohr** n *scissors telescope* **~kran** m *shear-legs* (*crane*) **~schleifer** m *knife-grinder* ‖ ⟨fig, fam⟩ *mongrel* (*dog*) **~schnabel** m ⟨orn⟩ *scissors bill*; (schwarzer) *skimmer* **~schnitt** m *paper-, scissor-cut* **~stuhl** m *x-chair* **Sch·erer** m ~s/~ *shearer* ‖ ⟨weav⟩ *warper* **Scherer·ei** f ~/~en *vexation, trouble, bother*(*ation*) ‖ e–m ~ m *to give a p trouble, to bother a p* ‖ ~en verursachend *bothersome*

Sch·erbe f ~/~n, **~n** m ~s/~ *potsherd, shard* ‖ *fragment* (*of china* etc) | *flower-pot* | ⟨sl⟩ (monocle:) *window-pane, quiz*(*zing glass*) | **~n** [pl] *débris* [sg & pl], *shivers* pl ‖ in ~n schlagen *to shiver*; *to smash* (*to shivers*); *to dash to pieces* ‖ es geht in ~n *it goes to pieces*; **~ngericht** n *ostracism* °**sch·erbeln** vi [h] *to foot it* (= *to dance*) **Sch·erflein** n ~s/ *mite* ‖ sein ~ beitragen *to give one's mite*; *to contribute one's share* (zu *to*), *to do one's bit*; ⟨Am⟩ *to put in one's two cents worth*

Sch·erge m ~n/~n ⟨obs *or* dero⟩ *beadle, constable* ‖ *catch-poll, tipstaff* | *executioner* | ~n [pl] *myrmidons* (*of the law*) **~namt** n *beadle's office* **~ndienste** tun *to execute a tyrant's orders*

Sch·erz m ~es/~e *jest*(*ing*), *joke, joking*; *pleasantry*; *fun, sport*; *pranks* pl; ⟨fam⟩ *larks* pl ‖ (grober) *horseplay* ‖ (frivoler) *levity* ‖ ⟨stud⟩ *rag* ‖ ⟨theat⟩ *gag*; (improvisiert) *wheeze* ‖ ~ beiseite! *joking apart*! ‖ aus, im, zum ~ *for fun, in jest, jestingly* ‖ ~ m (mit) *to make fun* (*of*) ‖ rüpelhafte ~e treiben ⟨sl⟩ *to horse around*; s–n ~ treiben mit *to make merry with, to play on, to make game* od *sport of* (*a p*) ‖ sich [dat] auf jds Kosten ~e erlauben *to indulge in witticism at a p's expense*; e–n ~ über jdn m *to break a joke on a p*; auf e–n ~ eingehen *to understand a joke* ‖ mach k–e ~e *without joking*! *you don't say so*! ‖ ist das ~ oder Ernst *is that meant as a joke or in earnest* **~artikel** m pl *articles for amusement* **~frage** f *quiz* **~gedicht** n *humorous* od *comic poem* **≈haft** a *playful, facetious, jocose, jocular, droll, sportive, waggish* ‖ die ~e Seite e–r S *the humour of a th* ‖ ins ≈e ziehen *to make joke of* ‖ ~e Bemerkung *pleasantry* | [adv] man sagt ~, daß *the joke goes that* ‖ *archly* **~haftigkeit** f *facetiousness, jocoseness, jocularity* **≈liebend** a *jocular, jovial* **~lied** n *comic song* **~lüge** f *white lie* **~macher** m *joker, jester* **~name** m *nickname* **~rede** f *pleasantry, facetious speech* **≈weise** [adv] *jestingly, by way of jest, in jest, for fun* **~wort** n *jesting* od *facetious word, witticism* **sch·erzen I.** vi [h] *to jest, joke* (über [acc] *at a th*) ‖ *to quip*, ⟨Am fam⟩ *to josh* | (über etw *or* jd) *to make fun* (*of*) ‖ (mit) *to have fun, to play, sport* (*with a p*) | er scherzt gern *he likes his little joke* ‖ Sie ~! *you don't say so*! *you are only joking*! ‖ er läßt nicht mit sich ~ *there is no nonsense about him, he won't stand a joke, he is not to be trifled with* **II.** ≈ n; es ist wahrlich nicht z ≈ *it is past joke* **Sch·erzer** m ~s/~ *jester, joker*

Scheu f ~/ *shyness, nervousness, timidity*; *coyness, reserve* ‖ ehrfurchtsvolle ~ *awe*; v ~ ergriffen *awe-struck* ‖ (vor [dat]) *aversion* (*to*); ~ vor der See *sea-shyness* ‖ *to start sth with a certain nervousness* ‖ ohne ~ *without the least fear*; (schonungslos) *unsparingly* ‖ heilige ~ *awe*; ~ h vor *to stand in awe of* **~klappe** f, **~leder** n *blinkers* pl, ⟨Am⟩ *blinders* pl ⟨a. fig⟩; er trägt –klappen *he's got a bear-trap mind* **scheu** a *shy* (*deer, glance*) ‖ ⟨hors⟩ *starting, skittish, shying* ‖ (furchtsam) *timid*; (schüchtern) *coy, bashful* ‖ scheu s vor *to be timid of* (*horses*) ‖ (menschen~) *retired* ‖ ~ m *to frighten, startle* ‖ ~ w *to take fright, to shy* ⟨hors⟩ **Sch·euche** f ~/~n *scare--crow* ⟨a. fig⟩ ‖ ⟨fig⟩ *bugbear* **sch·euchen** vt [h] *to scare, frighten*; *chase away* **sch·euen I.** vt [h] *to shun*; *be afraid of*; *eschew, avoid, fear* ‖ die Kosten ~ *to grudge the cost* ‖ weder Mühe noch Geld ~ *to stint neither trouble nor m.* ‖ k–e Mühe, Kosten ~ *to spare no pains, expense* ‖ tue recht u scheue niemand *tell truth and shame the devil* ‖ s–e Taten ~ das Licht *his deeds will not bear the light of day* **II. sich** ~ [h] *to be bashful* od *shy* ‖ (vor [dat]) *to be afraid* od *timid* (*of horses*) ‖ *to dread* (*a job*) ‖ (*she is not afraid of work*) ‖ ⟨fam⟩ *to fight shy* (*of*) ‖ sich ~ zu tun *to be afraid to do, to be diffident in,* (*shrink from*) *doing* (*I should be reluctant to say*); .. ein wenig *to be a* little hesitant to do; .. nicht .. to make no bones about doing **III.** vi [h] to shy (⟨Am hors a.⟩ scare) (vor [dat] at), to (take) fright

Sch·euer f ~/~n shed, barn **~tor** n barn-door

Sch·euer- ~besen m mop **~bürste** f scrubbing-brush **~faß** n scouring-tub **~fest** n scouring-day **~festigkeit** f rub (od scuff, abrasive) resistance **~frau** f charwoman, scourer; ⟨Am⟩ scrubwoman **~lappen** m scouring-clout, mop (dazu: to mop); gr ~ swab; (Geschirrtuch) dish-clout **~leiste** f skirting-board; ⟨mar⟩ rubbing strake **~magd** f charwoman **~marke** f abrasion mark ⟨a. phot⟩, stressmark **~mittel** n scouring powder **~sand** m sc.g-sand **~spur** f abrasion mark **~stein** m ⟨mar⟩ holy-stone **~tuch** n slop-cloth **~wirkung** f abrasive action; abrasive effect **~wisch** m = ~lappen **sch·euern I.** vt [h] to scour, scrub ‖ es muß tüchtig gescheuert w it wants a good scrub ‖ to wash up (china) | (Haut) to chafe; to rub off | to rub (the pig rubs its back) | ⟨tech⟩ to polish, rub; tumble (iron), (reiben) to chafe **II.** vi [h] mein Kragen scheuert: .. chafes my neck

Sch·eune f ~/~n shed; barn, hay-loft; byre **~ndrescher** = Drescher ‖ er frißt wie ein ~ he eats like a wolf **~ntenne** f thrashing-floor **~ntor** n barn-door ⟨a. fig⟩

Sch·eusal n ~(e)s/~e ⟨a. fig⟩ monster, ⟨fam⟩ fright, beast (he is a b. [of a fellow]), °(Weib) lemon ‖ ein richtiges kl ~ a perfect little horror **sch·eußlich** a frightful, dreadful, abominable, hideous, atrocious, monstrous, execrable, vile, villainous | ⟨fam⟩ beastly (weather), awful (cold) ‖ das ist ja ~! that's terrible | [adv] awfully (cold) exceedingly (unpleasant) | **≈keit** f ~/~en frightfulness, abominableness, horribleness, hideousness, atrociousness | [konkret] abomination, horror | (Tat) atrocity; beastliness

Schi m ~s/~er = Ski ski

Schi- ~baum m ⟨bot⟩ shea **~butter** f sheabutter

Schibb·oleth n ~s/~s [Hebr] (Zeichen) shibboleth

Schicht f ~/~en, **~e** ([österr] ⟨geol⟩) **I. A.** layer (of sand ⟨a. min⟩), slab (to split into slabs) ‖ bed ⟨a. min⟩ ‖ ⟨geol, min, zoo, bot⟩ stratum; ~ mit Wasserführung ⟨min⟩ water st.m ‖ (Erz≈) ledge ‖ ⟨arch⟩ course (of stones) ‖ (Holz≈) pile, stack ‖ tier (t.s of cable) ‖ ⟨phot⟩ coating, emulsion ‖ region (of the air) ‖ mass (of fog) **B.** **dicke** ~ thickness (of gravel) ‖ dünne ~ coating, film (of oil); mit e–r ~ bedecken to film ‖ ⟨anat⟩ oberste ~ der Haut epidermis, .. des Zellgewebes epithelium ‖ untere ~ substratum ‖ unterhalb liegende ~ underlay **C.** ⟨fig⟩ ⟨soc⟩ rank, class, set ‖ breite ~n .. great masses (of the population) ‖ in den höchsten ~n in the highest walks of life ‖ die unteren ~n the lower classes; Angehöriger der führenden ~ Establishmentarian **II. A. 1.** (Arbeits≈) shift, turn; task, job ‖ (to work a shift), (in three shifts) ‖ day's work **2.** pause, rest, break **3.** [koll] gang (of miners, etc), shift **B.** in einer ~ without a break, uninterruptedly ‖ ~ arbeiten to work staggered hours; auf ~ arbeiten to work by stint ‖ halbe or kz ~ arbeiten to work short time ‖ (Feierabend) ~ ist's knock off (work)! ‖ ~ halten to work ‖ ~ m to make a break, to leave off working, to close down | ⟨fig⟩ ~ m mit etw to put an end to a th, to have done with a th **~ablösung** f ⟨phot⟩ peeling off **~arbeit** f day-work, shift **~arbeiter** m day-worker **~aufnahme** f (Röntgen) stratography **~betrieb** m relay-system **~fuge** f joint (in a stratum) **~gestein** n sedimentary od stratified rocks pl **~holz** n stacked wood **~käse** m ⟨Ger⟩ three-tiered cheese (curd and creamcheese) **~kuchen** m layer cake **~linie** f = Höhenlinie **~lohn** m pay for day-work **~machen** n → ~ II. B. **~meister** m foreman, overseer; ⟨min⟩ purser **~sattel** m anticline **~seite** f ⟨phot⟩ emulsion side **~streichen** n ⟨geol⟩ trend of beds **~stufe** f cuesta | ~nlandschaft [f] c. topography **~torte** f layer cake **≈weise** [adv] in layers, piles, tiers; by strata **~wolke** f stratus ‖ (federige) cirrostratus **~zahn** m milk-tooth **schichten** vt [h] to dispose od put in layers; to stack (wood, bricks); to pile up ‖ ⟨geol⟩ to stratify | ⟨fig⟩ to arrange, distribute, divide; ⟨mar⟩ to stow (the cargo) | (nach Klassen) to classify | ⟨met⟩ to charge (the furnace) | sich ~ to dispose o.s. (on conquered tribes) **sch·ichtig** a ⟨geol⟩ laminated **Sch·ichtung** f ~/~en strata (of the air, of clouds) ‖ arrangement in layers; etc. ‖ ⟨geol⟩ striation, stratification ‖ classification ‖ die soziale ~ the social classes **Schick** m ~(e)s/ (stilvolle Eleganz) chic, elegance ‖ jd, etw hat s–n ~: .. is quite shipshape ‖ (Geschmack) taste, stylishness, smartness; ~ h to by stylishly dressed ‖ (Takt) tact ‖ (Geschicklichkeit) skill, adroitness, dexterity; fitness ‖ (Verstand) er hat s–n rechten ~ nicht he is not quite h.s. ‖ (Ordnung) fitness, order ‖ aus dem ~ ⟨fig⟩ out of gear od order ‖ wieder in ~ bringen to put to rights **schick** a stylish (young lady); smart, swell, ⟨Am a.⟩ swank (young fellow) ‖ elegant (coat) ‖ [pred] fashionable, chic Fr; ⟨fam⟩ nobby ‖ das ist aber ~! that's smart! | [adv] (she dresses) elegantly **sch·icken I.** vt [h] **A.** to send, dispatch (letters, parcels to a p) ‖ to send (a p greetings, an invitation; a messenger to a p, to a place) | ich schicke Ihnen .. I'll let you have .. ‖ er hatte es geschickt bek he had it sent, it had been sent to him | (jdn) dorthin ~ to send along there ‖ (jdn) **her**|**~** to send along ‖ (jdn) hin u her ~ to order about ‖ **nach** (jdm, etw) ~ to send for (the doctor) ‖ mit etw zus ~ to send .. along with .. **B.** der Zufall –kte es it chanced, it so happened ‖ (**Geld**) to remit m. to a p ‖ Gott –kt den Menschen Freude (Krankheiten) God sends man joys (afflicts man with sickness) ‖ (Nachricht) to send a p word ‖ (Vertreter) to send one's agent **C.** jdn **auf** Reisen ~ to s. a p on his travels, on a tour ‖ auf die Weide ~ to put (cattle) out to grass ‖ .. schlafen or **ins** Bett ~ to s. .. to bed ‖ ins Elend ~ to exile, banish ‖ ins Parlament ~ to return a p to P. ‖ ein Buch in die Welt ~ to publish a b. ‖ (jdn) **nach** .. ~ to dispatch a p to Scotland; .. nach Hause ~ to s. .. home; **zur** Schule .. to school; .. zum Kuckuck ~ to tell a p to go to the devil **II.** vrefl [h] **sich ~ A.** (sich ereignen) to come to pass; to happen; (unerwartet) to chance ‖ je nach dem es sich –kt (just) as the case may be ‖ wenn es sich gerade –kt if ths so shape themselves ‖ es –kt sich wohl noch it will probably go well **B.** (geziemen) das –kt sich **nicht** it won't do, that's not the proper th to do, that is not proper (at table) | sich ~ **für** to be proper for, to be becoming in; it ill-behoves him, it is not the th for him, it does not do for you to do that ‖ eines ~kt sich nicht f alle every shoe does not fit all feet, one man's meat is another man's poison **C.** (eignen) to suit; to be fit, suitable (**für, zu** for); to go well, to agree (with) ‖ (he is well suited for this work) ‖ es –kt sich f mich it behoves (⟨Am⟩ behooves) me **D.** sich **in** e–e S ~, sich **darein** ~ to resign o.s. to, to become reconciled, to put up with, to conform to a th ‖ to yield to (the inevitable) ‖ sie kann sich nicht darein ~ she cannot accommodate h.s. to that ‖ er –kt sich in alles he adapts h.s. (od gets accustomed) to everything ‖ sich in die Leute ~ to know how to get on with people ‖ sich in die Zeit ~ to go (well) with the times, ⟨dero⟩ to be a time-server **sch·icklich** a becoming, seemly, decent, proper ‖ suitable, convenient ‖ appropriate (answer) | [adv] .., wie er am ~sten ..: how he could best get out of it **≈keit** f ~/ becomingness, seemliness, propriety, decorum, decency ‖ suitability, convenience | ~sgefühl [n] tact **Sch·icksal** n ~(e)s/~e **1.** fate, destiny ‖ (the hand of f.) ‖ das Gewebe des ~s the vicissitudes of life ‖ d. calls ‖ to oppose f. ‖ s–m ~

mit Ruhe entgegensehen *to meet one's f. calmly* **2.** *fortune, lot* (*a sad lot*) ‖ sonderbare ~e *strange adventures* | *he was left to his fate* ‖ *to quarrel with one's fate* ‖ sich in sein ~ fügen *to dree one's weird*; *to believe in kismet*; *he knew his doom*; sein ~ knüpfen an das v *to cast one's lot among* od *with* ‖ *she is my fate*; *it's my destiny*! ‖ *the dice were loaded against me*; *to thank one's star*; *to turn the tide against a p* ‖ das ~ wollte es, daß er .. *it fell to his lot to do* ‖ *his fate is sealed* (*to* od *for damnation*) ‖ das gleiche ~ erfahren *to fare alike* ‖ sein ~ erreichte ihn *he met his doom* ‖ durch ~ *providentially* **≈haft** a *fateful* | **~s-** **~fügung** f *divine ordinance*; *providence* **~gemeinschaft** f *common d.* **~genossen** m pl *companions in misfortune* **~glaube** m, **~lehre** f *fatalism* **~gewalt** f *destiny* **~göttinnen, ~schwestern** f pl *Fates*; *Weird Sisters* pl **~jahr** n *fatefal y.* **~linie** f (der Hand) *line of Fate* **≈mäßig** [adv] *providentially* **~prüfung** f *ordeal, visitation* **~schlag** m *heavy blow* **~schläge** pl ⟨a.⟩ *buffets* pl *of fate*; *reverses* **≈schwanger** a *big with destiny*; *portentous* **~-schwer** a *catastrophic* (*death*) **~tragödie** f *fate tragedy*; *t. of circumstances* **~tücke** f *tricks* pl *of fortune* **~wechsel** m *change of fortune, vicissitude*(*s* pl) **~weg** m *march of* (*one's*) *destiny* **~wort** n *decree of fate* **Sch·ickung** f ~/~en *divine will* (od *dispensation, decree*) ‖ *Providence*

°**Sch·ickse** f ~/~n, **~l** n ~s/~ [Hebr] **1.** *shickster* **2.** *wench, gal* (= *girl*); °*bit, bird*

Schieb- ~fenster m *sash-window* **~karren** m *wheelbarrow* **~lade** f *drawer* **~lehre** f *cal(l)iper rule* **~ventil** n ⟨tech⟩ *slide-valve* **~zeug** n *cog--work* (Säge) **Sch·iebe-** *sliding* (*s.g*) **~barriere** f ⟨rail⟩ *s.g barrier* **~blech** n *sliding screen*, (Rost–, Kamin≈) *blower* **~bleistift** m *s.g-pencil* **~bock** m *wheelbarrow* **~brett** n *slip-board, slide, slider* **~brücke** f *s.g-bridge* **~bühne** f ⟨rail⟩ *traverser, s.g platform*; ⟨tech⟩ versenkte ~ *trench type tr.r*; ⟨theat⟩ *rolling* od *sliding stage*; ⟨bes film⟩ *s.g platform* **~fenster** n *sliding w.* | ~gegengewicht [n] *mouse* **~lehre** f (Feinmeß≈) *vernier cal(l)iper* **~leuchter** m *slide-candlestick* **~maß** n *s.g-rule* **~rahmen** m *sash-frame* **~ring** m *s.g ring* **~schachtel** f *slide* **~schalter** m *slide switch* **~sitz** m *pull--out seat* **~taste** f (f Plattengröße) ⟨rec⟩ *record indexing size selector* **~tür** f *s.g door* **~vorrichtung** f *slide, shifter* **~wand** f *s.g partition* **~welle** f ⟨tech⟩ *spline shaft* **~widerstand** m ⟨el⟩ *slider dimmer* **schiebbar** a *sliding* **sch·ieben I.** vt/i [h] **A.** *to push, shove* ‖ (*to push a p out of the room*) ‖ (*to give a th a push*) ‖ er muß (immer) geschoben w (sonst tut er nichts) *he must be shoved along* **B.** (gleitend) *to slide, slip* ‖ (ruckweise) *to jab, jam* ‖ (schnell) *to pop* (zur Tür herein *in at the door*) **C.** *to push* (*a pram*) ‖ *to wheel* (*a barrow*) ‖ ⟨aero⟩ *to drift* | ⟨mil⟩ °Dienst, Wache ~ *to go on duty, guard* ‖ sein F. ~ *to walk, wheel one's bicycle* ‖ Kegel ~ *to play* (*at*) *skittles*, alle neun(e) ~ *to throw all nine* ‖ Kugel ~ *to bowl* ‖ (Brettspiele) (Dame, Mühle) Stein etc ~ *to move a piece, man* | °⟨com⟩ *to work a swindle*; Ware ~ *to sell goods illicitly* **D.** ~ **an** *to push, shove against* (*the wall*) ‖ an die Stelle v *to put into the place of* | etw **auf** die lange Bank, auf das tote Gleis ~ *to shelve* od *table a th, to put it off* (*from day to day*) ‖ ⟨rail⟩ auf ein Nebengleis ~ *to shunt* (*a train*) ‖ den Fehler auf etw ~ *to lay the blame for the fault on sth* ‖ die Schuld auf jdn ~ *to put the blame upon a p* | **beiseite** ~ *to put* od *thrust aside* od *out of the way*; *to elbow* (*a p*) (aus *out of*) | **in**: *he slipped his car into the garage* ‖ *he slipped* od *put it into his mouth* ‖ *to put bread into the oven* ‖ *he shoved* (*jammed*) *his hand, slipped sth into his pocket* ‖ jdm etw in die Schuhe ~ *to lay the blame at a p's door* | **über** die Grenze ~ *to send* (*tramps*) *out of the country* | **von** sich ~ *to shuffle off* ‖ vorwärts ~ *to push along* **II. sich** ~ [a. °vi ~] *to shuffle along*; *to shift, move* ‖ (schlurrend) *to scuff* ‖ (S) sich in die Höhe ~ *to shift* od *move up* ‖ sich in–e–a–|~ ⟨rail⟩ (Zus–stoß) *to be telescoped* ‖ (P) sich weiter ~ *to proceed slowly* | sich ~ **lassen** *to slide, drift* **III.** (vgl I. C.) vi ⟨aero⟩ *to drift* ‖ ⟨cycl⟩ *to wheel* ‖ ⟨com⟩ *to be smart*; *to job, shift*, ⟨sl⟩ *wangle*, ⟨Am sl⟩ *to graft* **IV.** ≈ n ⟨aero⟩ (bei Seitenwind) *crab* **Sch·ieber** m ~s/~ **A. 1.** *shover, pusher, bowler* **2.** ⟨com⟩ *profiteer, jobber, smuggler, blacketeer*; ⟨sl⟩ *spiv, wangler*, ⟨Am sl⟩ *grafter, racketeer* **3.** (Riegel) *bolt, bar* **4.** ⟨Ger⟩ "*shover*" (dance) **5.** ⟨tech⟩ *slide*(*r*) ‖ ⟨mach⟩ *sliding valve* ‖ ⟨mar artill⟩ *deflection bar* **B.** Absperr≈ *stop valve* ‖ Bleistift≈ *sliding ring* ‖ Brot≈ (*baker's*) *peel* ‖ Devisen≈ *currency smuggler* ‖ Kolben≈ *piston valve* ‖ Mühlen≈ *slide-plate* ‖ Ofen≈, Rauch≈ *damper* ‖ Rechen≈ *slide-rule* ‖ Schirm≈ *runner* ‖ Schnallen≈ *slide-loop* ‖ Seiten≈ ⟨mar artill⟩ *deflection bar*: ~ links 8 *deflection 8 left* ‖ Stoff≈ (Nähmaschine) *feed* ‖ Türschloß≈ *safety bolt* ‖ ⟨typ⟩ *pusher* ‖ Visier≈ ⟨mil⟩ *backsight slide* ‖ Wind≈ ⟨met⟩ *blast valve* **~blende** f ⟨theat⟩ *barn-door shutter*, ⟨Am⟩ *b.-d.*; ⟨phot⟩ *sliding diaphragm* **~geschäft** n *profiteering job*; ~e m *to profiteer* **~kasten** m *steam-chest, slide box* **~schleuse** f *sash sluice* **~stange** f (*slide-*)*valve rod* **~verbesserung** f ⟨mar artill⟩ *correction for deflection* **~weg** m *travel of the slide valve* **sch·ieberhaft** a *profiteering*, ⟨sl⟩ *wangling* ‖ ~e Gewinne ⟨Am sl⟩ *scoop* **Sch·iebung** f ~/~en ⟨com⟩ *job, profiteering*, ⟨fam⟩ *setup job*, ⟨sl⟩ *wangling, skul(l)duggery*; ⟨Am sl⟩ *graft, racket* ‖ ⟨pol⟩ *pull*, ⟨Am⟩ *spoils* pl ‖ ~! ⟨hum⟩ *jiggery-pokery*! *hanky-panky*!, *put-up job*! ‖ ~en m *to profiteer, job*; durch ~ ⟨fam⟩ *on the cross*

schiech a [bay.-österr] → häßlich, furchterregend, zornig

schied 1. & 3. sg pret v scheiden **sch·iedlich** adv *by arbitration* ‖ ~ u friedlich *amicably, peacefully* **Sch·ieds- ~gericht** n *court of arbitration*; *tribunal*, ⟨sport⟩ *a.n committee* ‖ e–m ~ angehören *to sit upon a tr.* | ~shof [m]: Haager ~ *the Hague Tr.* (1899 u 1920); ~klausel [f] *a.n clause*; ~spruch [m] *award of a.tors* **~klausel** f *a.n clause* **~mann** m *conciliatory officer*; = ~richter **~mauer** f *partition-wall* **~richter** m *judge, arbitrator, arbiter*; ⟨pol⟩ *amiable compositeur* ‖ ⟨sport⟩ *umpire, arbiter, referee* ‖ ⟨mil⟩ *umpire* ‖ ~ s bei *to referee* od *umpire* (*a match*) | ~amt [n] *umpirage*; ~besprechung [f] ⟨mil⟩ *umpires' convention*; ≈lich [a] *by arbitration, arbitrational* | **≈n** [vi/t] [h] ⟨sport⟩ *to referee* **~spruch** m *arbitration, award*; *arbitrament* (durch Krieg *of war*) ‖ e–n ~ tun *or* fällen *to arbitrate* ‖ durch ~ beilegen *to settle by arbitration* **~urteil** n *arbiter's sentence* od *award* **~vertrag** m *a.n agreement*

schief I. [a] **A.** *slanting oblique, wry* ‖ (geneigt) *inclined, sloping* (*the table is sl.*) ‖ (krumm) *one-* od *lop-sided*; *crooked* (*the wall is cr.*) ‖ ⟨arch, math, tech⟩ *skew* (*bridge, chisel, wheel, curve*) ‖ ⟨fig⟩ *distorted, incorrect, inexact, inaccurate* **B.** ~e **Absätze h** *to be down at heel* ‖ ~e Ansicht *erroneous view* ‖ ~e Behauptung *distorted statement* ‖ ⟨fig⟩ ~es Bild *false figure of speech* ‖ ~e **Ebene** *inclined plane*; ⟨rail⟩ *gradient*; auf die ~e E. geraten *to go off the straight path*; auf ~er E. *or* Bahn s ⟨fig⟩ *to be going bad* ‖ ~e Fahrt *oblique sailing* ‖ etw aus e–m ~en Gesichtswinkel sehen *to regard sth from a wrong angle* ‖ ~e **Lage** *tilt*, in e–r ~en L. *at a t.*, ⟨fig⟩ *in a false position*; das bringt mich in e–e ~e L. *that puts me in a bad spot* ‖ das wirft ein ~es Licht auf ihn *that puts him in a false l.* ‖ *to see sth in a wrong light* ‖ (e–m) ein ~es **Maul** m *to make a wry face* (*at a p*) ‖ *wry* (*mouth*) ‖ *sloping* (*shoulder*) ‖ *leaning* (*tower of Pisa*) ‖ ~es Urteil *distorted judgement*; *bad opinion* ‖ ⟨math⟩ ~er Winkel *oblique angle* **C. sich** [acc] (krumm u)

~ lachen *to split one's sides (with laughter)* **II. A.** [adv] *obliquely, awry, askew, on the skew* ‖ *(to wear one's hat) at an angle* ‖ *(to judge, think) erroneously* ‖ *across, crosswise* **B.** ~ **anfangen** *to begin at the wrong end* ‖ bei jdm ~ ank, anlaufen *to meet with a setdown at a p* ‖ ~ ansehen *to look askance (at a p), to look (at a p) wryly* | ⟨fig⟩ °~|**gehen** (S) *to come off* od *turn out crabs* ‖ bei ihm geht alles ~ *everything goes wrong with him*; mir geht heute alles ~, ⟨Am⟩ *this is my off-day* ‖ ⟨hum⟩ nur Mut, die S wird schon ~ gehn *buck up, ths will end all right* od *in a glorious mess* ‖ ~ **halten** *to tip (a platter), to hold (one's head) aslant* ‖ °⟨fig⟩ sie h ~ geladen *they have taken a drop too much* ‖ (etw) ~ legen *to (give a th a) tilt* ‖ (P) völlig ~ liegen ⟨fig⟩ *to be right off the beams* ‖ °~ (übel) **nehmen** *to take amiss* ‖ *(to write) crooked* bzw *slantingly* ‖ ~ segeln *to tack* ‖ ~ sitzen: *his tie was crooked* ‖ ~ stehen *to (be* od *stand on the) slant*; ⟨fig⟩ es steht ~ darum *there is sth wrong about it* ‖ ~ **treten** *to run* od *tread (one's boots) down on one side* od *down at the heels* ‖ ~ urteilen *to judge wrongly* ‖ ~ **gewachsen** *deformed* ‖ ~ w (of wood) *to warp* | °⟨fig⟩ ~ gewickelt *on the wrong track* (mistaken); ~ gew. s ⟨a.⟩ *to bark up the wrong tree* ‖ ~ stehender Schneidezahn *crooked front tooth* ~**beinig** a *bandy-, bow-legged* ≂**blatt** n *begonia* ≂**führung** f *bending (of a chimney)* ~**geladen** a *tipsy* ~**kantig** a *bevel-edged* ≂**kopf** m *wrong-headed p* | zum ≂**lachen** n *side-splitting* ~**liegend** a *on the slant* ~**mäulig** a *wry-mouthed* ~**rund** a *oval* ≂**sehen** n ⟨path⟩ *strabismus* ≂**steg** m ⟨typ⟩ *inclined quoin* ≂**stehen** n *inclination (of letters)* ≂**stellung** f ⟨tech⟩ *inclination* ≂**werden** n ⟨ceram⟩ *warping* ~**wink(e)lig** a *oblique(-angled)* **Sch·iefe** f ~/ *obliqueness, obliquity*; *inclination*; *crookedness*; *slope, slant* ‖ *one-sideness* ‖ ⟨fig⟩ *wrongness, erroneousness, perversity*

Sch·iefer m ~s/~ ⟨min⟩ *slate* ‖ ⟨geol⟩ *schist* ‖ ⟨arts⟩ *(lithographic* od *Solnhofen) stone* ‖ mit ~ decken *to slate* ~**abdeckung** f (Außenwand≂) *sl. hanging* ~**arbeiter** m *slate-cutter* ≂**artig** a *slaty, schistous* ~**bank** f *bed of slate* ≂**blau** a *sl.-coloured* ~**bruch** m *sl.-quarry, sl.-pit* ~**dach** n *sl.(d) roof*; mit e–m ~ bedecken *to slate* ~**decker** m *sl.r* ~**farben** a *sl.-coloured* ~**formation** f *schist-formation* ~**gebirge** n *sl.-mountains* pl ≂**grau** a *sl.-gray* ≂**grün** a *dark-green* ~**griffel** m *sl.-pencil* ~**hammer** m *sl.r's hammer* ~**kohle** f *slaty coal* ~**mergel** m *slaty marl* ~**nagel** m *sl.r's nail* ~**öl** n *shale oil* | ~gewinnung [f] *sh. distillation* ~**papier** n *sl.-paper* ~**pergament** n *sl.-coloured parchment* ~**platte** f *sl.-slab* ~**schicht** f *schistous stratum* ≂**schwarz** n *sl.-black* ~**spat** m ⟨min⟩ *schistous-spar* ~**stein** m ⟨min⟩ *schist, slaty stone* ~**stift** m = ~griffel ~**tafel** f *slate* ~**teer** m *shale tar* ~**ton** m ⟨min⟩ *shale* ~**wand** f *rock of sl.* ~**weiß** n ⟨theat⟩ *flake white* **sch·ief(e)rig** a *slaty* ‖ ⟨min⟩ *schistous*; ⟨geol⟩ *laminated* **sch·iefern,** (sich) [h] *to peel off in scales, to scale off, to exfoliate* **Sch·ieferung** f ~/~en *exfoliation*

Sch·iel- ~**auge** n *squint-eye* ≂**äugig** a *squint-eyed* ~**brille** f *glasses* pl *for strabismus* ~**operation** f *strabotomy* **Sch·ielen** n ~s/ *squinting*; ⟨med⟩ *strabismus* **sch·ielen** vi [h] *to (have a) squint* auf .. *in one eye*; *to have a cast in one's eye*; *to look two ways to find Sunday* ‖ ~ auf, nach *to skew, squint at*, (lüstern, boshaft) *to leer at*; *to look at a th surreptitiously* ‖ ⟨fig⟩ *to cast enquiring, longing glances, sly looks at*; *to hanker after ..* **sch·ielend** a *squint-eyed, walleyed, squinting* ‖ *furtive (glance)* **Sch·ieler** m ~s/~ *squinter, squint-eye*

Sch·iemann m ⟨mar⟩ *boatswain's mate* | ~sarbeit [f] *working up junk*; ~sgarn [n] *spun yarn* | ~**en** vi [h] *to overhaul the rigging*

schien 1. & 3. sg pret v scheinen

Sch·ienbein n ⟨anat⟩ *shin(-bone)*, ⟨scient⟩ *tibia* ‖ (jdn) vor das ~ treten *to shin* ‖ sich mit dem ~ stoßen an *to shin o.s. against* ~**schutz** m ⟨sport⟩ *(shin-)pad* **Sch·iene** f ~/~en **A. 1.** ⟨surg⟩ *splint* ‖ in die ~ legen *to sp., to put .. in a sp., to put sp.s to* **2.** ⟨met⟩ *bar* **3.** ⟨weav⟩ *lease rod* **4.** ⟨arch⟩ *iron hoop* od *band*; *tire* **5.** ⟨rail⟩ *rail*; pl ⟨a.⟩ *metals, track(age)* ‖ auf ~n *(to run) on rails* **B.** ausgebauchte ~ *fish-bellied rail* ‖ breitbasige ~ *flat-footed rail* ‖ ohne ~n *trackless* ‖ lückenlos verschweißte ~n *continuous welded rails* | Anschluß≂ *junction rail*; Bein≂ *greave, leg-guard*; Block≂ *filled section rail*; Führungs≂ *table track* od *slide*; Jalousie≂ *slat*; Kreuz≂ ⟨weav⟩ *lease (bar)*; Kreuzungs≂ *frog*; Lauf≂ *runners* pl, (am Schlittschuh) *blade*; Prell≂ *side-walk guard* ‖ (am Rade) *iron band, rim, clout*; Reiß≂ *T-square*; Roll≂ (am Rudersitz) *runners* pl ‖ (am Schirm) *rib*; T-~ *T-rail*; Zahnradbahn≂ *rack-rail* **C.** ~-Straße-Verkehr *combined rail and road transport* **D.** ~n **abrichten** (aufreißen) *to bend (tear up) rails* ‖ ~n ausrichten *to set and straighten rails* ‖ ~ **legen** *to lay (down) rails* ‖ **aus** den ~n springen *to run off the rails* od *metals* **sch·ienen** vt [h] ⟨surg⟩ *to splint, to put into splints* | (Räder) *to clout, shoe* **Sch·ienen-** ~**bahn** f *track* ~**dräsine** f ⟨mil⟩ *rail jeep* ~**eisen** n *iron in bars* ~**fahrzeuge** n pl *rail vehicles, v.s running on r.s* ~**fuß** m *bottom flange* ≂**gleicher** Übergang ⟨rail⟩ *level* (⟨Am⟩ *grade) crossing* ~**kopf** m *rail-head* ~**kreuzung** f *crossing of rails*; *level c.g* ‖ (Weiche) *points and c.g* ~**lärm** m *track sounds* pl (gedämpft *muffled)* ~**leger** m *plate-layer*, ⟨Am⟩ *trackman* ~**lücke** f *track joint* ~**netz** n *system of railroads* ~**pflug** m *sweeper* ~**rad** n *velocipede trolley* ~**räumer** m ⟨rail⟩ *safeguard*, ⟨Am⟩ *cow-catcher* ~**reibung** f *rolling friction* ~**rükker** m *rail shifter*, ⟨fam⟩ *Jim-Crow* ~**spur** f *track of rails* ~**stoß** m *(rail) joint* ~**strang,** ~weg [m] *railway, track* ~**strecke** f *line* ~**träger** m ⟨rail⟩ *support* ~**stuhl** m ⟨rail⟩ *chair* ~**verbindung** f (durchlaufend *continuity*) *bond* ~**verkehrsmittel** n *rail transportation* ~**-Wasser-** (Transport) *rail-water* N ~**weg** m ⟨mil⟩ *rail route* ~**weite** f *gauge*

schier a *sheer (impossibility)*; *pure (kindness, butter)* ‖ *complete, utter (nonsense)* ‖ ~es Fleisch *all meat (without bones)* | [adv] (fast) *almost, very nearly* ‖ ~ unmöglich *clearly impossible* ≂**tuch** n *fine linen*

sch(i)er imp, sch(i)er(s)t (2.) 3. sg pr v scheren

Sch·ierling m ~(e)s/~e ⟨bot⟩ *hemlock* ~**sbecher** m *cup of h.* ~**stanne** f *h. (-spruce)* ~**strank** m *h.-potion*

Schieß- *shooting (sh.g) (affair)* ~**arbeit** f ⟨min⟩ *blasting-work* ~**aufgabe** f ⟨artill⟩ *firing problem* ~**ausbildung** f *rifle training*; ⟨artill⟩ *gunnery-drill* ~**baumwolle** f *gun-cotton, nitrocotton* ~**bedarf** m *ammunition* ~**befehl** m *order to fire* ~**bereich** m *range* ~**buch** n *score-book* ~**bude** f *miniature rifle-range* | ~nfigur [f] ⟨fig hum⟩ *scarecrow*; *comic figure* °~**eisen** n (Pistole etc) ⟨sl⟩ *rod, stick*; ⟨Am⟩ *shooting iron*, ⟨sl⟩ *hardware* ~**gerechtigkeit** f *right of sh.g over a preserve* ~**gewehr** n *fire-arm, gun* ~**gezähe** n ⟨min⟩ → –zeug ~**graben** m *sh.g-trench* ~**haus** n *sh.g-gallery* ~**hund** m *pointer* ‖ ⟨fam⟩ aufpassen wie ein ~ *to watch like a lynx* ~**hütte** f *sh.g-lodge, sh.g-box* ~**kunst** f *marksmanship* ~**lehre** f *ballistics* pl, ⟨mil⟩ *gunnery* ~**loch** n *loop-hole, embrasure* ‖ ⟨min⟩ *blast-hole* ~**mal** n *mark to shoot at*; *white* ~**platz** m *sh.g-place, -grounds* pl, *rifle-range*, ⟨artill⟩ *gunnery range* N °~**prügel** m ⟨fam⟩ *Brown Bess* ~**pulver** n *gun-powder* ~**recht** n *right to shoot* ~**regeln** f pl *firing rules* ~**scharte** f *port(-hole)*; ⟨fort⟩ *archery window, arrow slit*; = ~loch ~**scheibe** f *target* ~**schule** f *school of musketry* od *artillery* ~**stand** m *sh.g-gallery*; *rifle-range*; ⟨fam⟩ *butts* pl ~**tasche** f *huntsman's pouch* ~**übung** f *rifle* bzw *artillery* *practice* **~übungsplatz** m *practice ground* **~verfahren** n *firing system*; *type of fire-control* **~vorschrift** f *sh.g regulations* pl; *gunnery manual* **~zeug** n ⟨min⟩ *shooting tools* pl **~zeit** f *sh.g season* **sch·ießen I.** vt/i [h] [schoß/geschossen] **1. vt A.** *to shoot* (*arrows, hares*), (*with harpoons, spears*) ‖ .. *or I fire*! ‖ ⟨min⟩ *to blast* ‖ ⟨phot⟩ *to shoot*; ⟨ftb⟩ *to score* (*a goal*) **B.** (Panzer) bewegungsunfähig, (jdn) kampfunfähig ~ *to disable* ‖ e–n **lahm** ~ *to lame a p* (*with a shot*) ‖ jdn tot| ~ *to shoot a p dead*; *to kill a p* (*with a shot*) **C.** den **Ballast** ins Schiff ~ *to ballast the ship* ‖ Blicke ~ *to dart glances* ‖ auf: *to cast* od *throw a swift glance at* ‖ ⟨fam fig⟩ e–n Bock ~ *to make a gross mistake, to blunder* ‖ Bresche ~ *to make a breach* (in *in*) ‖ Brot in den Ofen ~ *to shove a batch of bread into the oven* ‖ jdm e–e **Kugel** durch die Brust (ins Herz) ~ *to send a bullet through* .. (*to a p's heart*); sich [dat] e–e K. vor den Kopf ~ *to blow out one's brains* ‖ ein **Loch** in die Luft ~ *to make a miss* ‖ e–n Purzelbaum ~ *to throw a s.* ‖ ⟨mar⟩ die Sonne ~ *to take the sun's altitude* ‖ Sperrfeuer ~ *to put up a barrage* ‖ viel Wild ~ *to bring down a lot of game* **D.** wie **aus** der Pistole geschossen *like a shot* ‖ e–n Vogel **im** Fluge ~ .. *on the wing* ‖ in Grund u Boden ~ *to batter down*, ⟨mar⟩ *to sink* (*by firing*) ‖ .. **mit** Schrot ~ *to shoot* (*hares*) *with shot* ‖ .. **vom** Baum .. *to shoot* .. *down from a tree* ‖ von der Stange ~ *to bring down* (*with a shot*) ‖ e–n **zum** Krüppel ~ *to cripple a p* (..) **2. vi** [h] **A.** *to shoot*; *to fire* (*off*); *to discharge a gun* od *an arrow* **B. blind** (scharf) ~ *to shoot with blank* (*ball-*)*cartridges* ‖ ⟨übtr⟩ daneben ~ *to make a bad shot*; fehlgeschossen! *wrong*! ‖ gerade drauf los ~ *to fire point-blank* ‖ **gut,** unfehlbar sicher ~ *to be a good, dead shot*; *the gun shoots well* ‖ °schieß los! ⟨fig⟩ *go ahead*!, ⟨fam⟩ *fire away*! *shoot*! ‖ unaufhörlich ~ *to keep up an incessant fire* ‖ weit ~ *to carry far* **C. auf** jdn ~ *to shoot* (od *to aim a shot*) *at a p*; aufs Blatt ~ *behind the shoulder* | **aus** dem Hinterhalt ~ *to snipe* ‖ daneben, vorbei ~ *to miss* (*one's aim*) | **ins** Schwarze ~ *to hit the bull's eye* ‖ e–m in die Schulter ~ *to shoot a p in the sh.* ‖ blindlings in die Menge ~ *to fire into the brown* ‖ ⟨ftb⟩ ins Tor ~ *to shoot* | **mit**: *to shoot with a gun* | **nach** = auf: *to shoot at* (*a p, the target, clay pigeons*) ‖ ⟨fam⟩ *to have a pop at* ‖ nach Spatzen mit Kanonen ~ *to break a fly on the wheel* | ⟨hunt⟩ **vor** Hunden ~ *to shoot over dogs* **II. vi** [s] ⟨übtr⟩ **A.** *to shoot dash, dart, run, rush, hurry*; *to burst forth* ‖ (Blut, Wasser etc) *to gush* ‖ wie ein Pfeil dahin|~ *to arrow ahead* ‖ *to sweep* (über *across*) ‖ (Flammen) *to streak* (*out of the window*) ‖ (surrend) *to whir*(*r*) ‖ (= auf|~: v Pflanzen) *to spring* (*up*) (⟨fig⟩ wie Spinat *like Jack's Beanstalk*) ‖ *the lettuce is shooting up* **B. auf** .. herab|~ *to swoop* od *pounce down upon* .. | wie Pilze **aus** der Erde ~ *to shoot up like mushrooms* | **durch**: (den Kopf), **in**: (den Sinn) *a thought, an idea shot* od *flashed into* od *through* od *across my mind* (od *crossed my m.*) ‖ es schoß mir durch den K. *it* (*suddenly*) *struck me* | **in**: *tears* (*the blood*) *rushed to her eyes* (*to her face*); *terror stabbed him in the heart* ‖ in die Höhe ~ *to shoot* od *spring up* (a v. Pflanzen); *to spring to one's feet*; *to be growing very quickly* ‖ in Ähren ~ *to ear* ‖ ins Blatt, Kraut, in Saat ~ *to run to leaf, weeds, seed* | **in herum**: *his eyes darted wildly about the room* | schieß **los**! *shoot*! → I. 2. B. | **nach**: *to have a pop at* | **um**: *he shot round the corner* | **zur** Erde ~: ⟨aero⟩ *to dive to the ground* **C.** (e–m Pferd) die Zügel ~ **lassen** *to give* (*a horse*) *the rein*(*s* pl), ⟨fig⟩ *to give rein to* (*one's feelings*) ‖ den Leithund ~ l: *to let go* od *loose*; Kabel: *to pay out* ‖ ⟨fig⟩ (etw) ~ l *to give up* **III. sich mit jdm** ~ *to fight a pistol duel with a p* **IV.** ≈ n *shooting match*; *target* od *artillery practice* ‖ *musketry-fire, artillery-fire* ‖ *discharge* od *report of guns* ‖ das ~ beginnen *to open fire* ‖ die S geht aus wie das Hornberger ≈ *the matter comes to nothing* ‖ ⟨fam⟩ das ist ja **zum** ≈! *it is a scream*!, *it is too funny for words*!, *it makes me hoot*!, *what a lark*! **schießend** a (*unit*) *of fire* N **Sch·ießer** m ~s/~ *shooter* ‖ *blasting miner* ‖ *oven-peel* **~·ei** f ~/~en (*incessant*) *shooting* ‖ *sh.g affray* ‖ ⟨dero⟩ *bad* od *useless sh.g* od *firing*

Sch·iet m & n ~s/ [niedd] → Scheiße, Dreck; ~ näch!? (= nicht wahr?) *bother*! → Schitt

Schiff n ~(e)s/~e **A. 1.** *ship, vessel* ‖ (kl) *craft* [pl *craft*] **2.** ⟨ec/arch⟩ (Mittel≈) *nave*; Seiten≈ *aisle*; Quer≈ *transept* **3.** ⟨weav⟩ *shuttle* **4.** (im Herd) *boiler* **5.** ⟨typ⟩ (Setz≈) *galley* **6.** ⟨fig⟩ *the ship of the state*, .. *of life*, (Kamel) .. *of the desert* **B.** Begleit≈ *escorting vessel* ‖ Bergungs≈ *salvage v.* ‖ Feuer≈ *light v.* ‖ Fracht≈ *freighter* ‖ Großkampf≈ *capital s.* ‖ Handels≈ *merchant v.* ‖ Kohlen≈ *collier* ‖ Kriegs≈ *warship* ‖ Schluß≈ *rear s.* ‖ Segel~ *sailing s.* ‖ Spitzen≈ *leading v.* ‖ Tank≈ *tanker* ‖ Unterwasser≈ *submarine* ‖ Voll≈ *fullrigged s.* ‖ Vorposten≈ *patrol v.* ‖ Wach≈ *guard s.* ‖ Werkstatt≈ *repair v.* ‖ Ziel≈ *target v.* **C.** alleinfahrendes ~ *single cruising v.* ‖ aufgebrachtes ~ *prize* ‖ außer Dienst gestelltes ~ *laid-up v.* ‖ manövrierunfähiges ~ *s. not under control* ‖ nach .. bestimmtes ~ *s. bound for* .. **D.** ein ~ **abtakeln** *to unrig*, aufbringen *to bring up*, ausrüsten *to fit out*, besteigen *to go on board a s.*; außer(in) Dienst stellen *to pay off* (*to commission*); klar m *to clear a s.* (*for action*) | wie heißt das ~? *what s.*? **E. auf** dem ~ *on board the s.* ‖ durch ~e befördern *to ship* (nach *to*) ‖ direkt hinter dem ~ *in the wake of the s.* ‖ in e–m ~ *in a s.* ‖ **zu** ~e gehen *to go on board*; *to embark*; *to take s.* ‖ zu ~e s *to be on board* ‖ zu ~e versenden *to send by boat* | **~bau** m *ship-building* | ~kunst [f] *naval architecture*; ~meister [m] *naval architect*; ~platz [m] *s.-building yard* **~bauer** m *s.-builder, s.wright* **~bruch** m (*ship*)*wreck*; ⟨fig⟩ *failure* ‖ ~ leiden (& fig) *to be* (*ship*)*wrecked*, ⟨fig⟩ *to fall down* (bei *on*) **≈brüchig** a *shipwrecked, castaway*; ein ≈iger s ⟨a. fig⟩ *to be stranded* **~brücke** f *floating bridge, pontoon-bridge* **~gerippe** n *hulk* **~leine** f *tow-rope* **≈reich** a *rich in ships, filled with ships* **~schaukel** f *swing-boat* **Sch·iffahrer** m *navigator, seaman* **Sch·iffahrt** f *navigation*; *maritime commerce* | ~sgesellschaft [f] *shipping company*; ~skunde [f] *nautics, art of navigation*; ~slinie [f] *shipping line*; ≈treibend [a] *seafaring*; ~sweg [m] *shipping route* **sch·iffbar** a *navigable*, nicht ~ *unnavigable* | ≈keit [f] *navigability* **Sch·iffchen** n ~s/~ *small* od *little vessel, craft, boat*; *skiff* | ⟨tech⟩ *shuttle* ‖ ⟨bot⟩ *carina* | ⟨fig, mil sl⟩ (*side*) *cap* | ~ werfen *to make ducks and drakes* **~arbeit** f *tatting* °**Sch·iffe** f ~/ *piss* (⟨a. fig⟩ Bier), *piddle* **sch·iffen 1.** vi [s] *to navigate, sail, ship*; *to steer* (*one's way*) **2.** vt [h] *to convey by ship* **3.** °vi [h] *to make water*, ⟨vulg⟩ *to pump ship* **Sch·iffer** m ~s/~ *sailor, mariner, seaman* ‖ (Schiffsführer) *navigator, sailing-master* ‖ (Schiffskapitän) *skipper* ‖ (Bootsvermieter, Führer des Mietsboots) *boatman* ‖ (Fluß≈) *bargee* **~ausdruck** m *nautical* (od *sea-*)*term*; *sailor's expression* **~hosen** f pl ⟨fam⟩ *slops* pl **~klavier** n *concertina*, ⟨sl⟩ *squiffer* **~knabe** m *boatman's boy* **~knecht** m *bargee* **~knoten** m *sailor's knot* **~mütze** f *s.'s cap* **~sprache** f *nautical language* **Sch·iffs-** *shipping* (*s.g*) **~abgaben** f pl *s.g dues* pl **~angelegenheiten** f pl *s.g affairs* pl **~ansammlung** f *s.g concentration* **~artillerie** f *naval ordnance* **~arzt** m *ship's surgeon* od *doctor*; ⟨mil⟩ (*principal*) *medical officer* (*of a s.*) (*P.M.O.*) **~ausrüstung** f *ship's gear* **~aufzug** m *shiphoist* **~bau** etc = Schiffbau etc **~bedürfnisse** n pl *s.'s stores* ‖ (Geschäft für Tauwerk etc) *s.-chandlery* **~bemannung, ~besatzung** f = ~mannschaft **~bergung** f *s. salvage* **~bewegung** f *movement* od *manœuvre of a s.* **~boden** m *s.'s bottom* od *hold* **~bohrwurm** m *teredo* **~boot** n ⟨zoo⟩ *pearly nautilus* **~breite** f *beam* **~brot** n *s.-bread* **~brücke** f = Schiff– **~disponent** m *s.'s husband* **~eigner** m *s.-owner* **~flagge** f *flag of a s.*, ⟨mil⟩ *ensign* **~fracht** f *freight* | ~brief [m] *bill of lading* **~führung** f *conduct of a s.* **~gebäude** n *body of a ship*; *hull* **~geschütz** n *s.'s gun*, ~e pl *armament* ‖ im Bereich der ~e *within gunfire of the ships* **~glocke** f *s.'s bell* **~haken** m *grappling-iron* **~halter** m ⟨ich⟩ = Schildfisch **~händler** m *s. chandler* **~heizer** m *s.'s stoker* **~herr** m *s.-owner* **~hinterteil** n *stern*, *poop* **~journal** n *log-book* **~junge** m *cabin-boy* **~kammer** f *cabin* **~kapitän** m *captain*, (v kl. S) *skipper* **~kellner** m *steward* **~kessel** m *marine boiler* **~knecht** m *bargee* **~koch** m *ship's cook* **~kompaß** m *mariner's compass* **~körper** m ⟨aero⟩ *body* od *hull* **~kreisel** m (*gyro*[*scopic*]-) *stabilizer* **~küche** f *galley*, *caboose* **~ladung** f *cargo*, *s.load* (*of* ..) **~last** f *freight of a s.* ‖ (Maß = 2 t) *last* **~laterne** f *s.'s lantern*, *poop-lantern* **~lauf** m *course* **~lazarett** n *sick-bay*, ⟨mil⟩ *s.'s hospital* **~lieferant** m *chandler* **~maat** m *s.mate* **~makler** m *s.-broker*; *s.builder's-husband* **~mannschaft** f *crew* **~marketender** m *chandler* **~maschine** f *marine engine* **~maschinist** m *s.'s engineer* **~meldedienst** m *s. registration service* **~motor** m *marine motor* **~nachrichten** f pl *s.g news* pl **~offizier** m *naval officer* **~ort** m *location*; den ~ bestimmen *to determine the s.'s position* **~parkett** n *herring-bone parquetry* **~part** m *share in a s.* **~partner** m *partner in a s.* **~paß** m *passport* **~patron** m *skipper*, *master of a s.* **~personal** n (ohne Offiziere) *ratings* pl **~planke** f *gangplank* **~pumpe** f *s.'s pump* **~ration** f *allowance*, *rations* pl **~raum** m *hold of a s.*; *tonnage*, *s.g space*; 10000 BRT feindlichen ~s *10000 tons of enemy s.g* **~raummangel** m *lack of tonnage*, gr ~ *s.g bottle neck* **~reaktor** m *nuclear reactor for s.s* **~reeder** = Reeder **~rumpf** m *hull*, ⟨mil⟩ den ~ treffen *to hull a s.* **~schnabel** m *prow*, *head of a s.* **~schraube** m (*srew-*) *propeller* **~soldat** m *marine* **~spiegel** m *stern* **~spur** f *wake* **~tagebuch** n *log-book*; ins ~ eintragen *to enter in* .. **~taue** n pl anziehen *to heave short* **~taufe** f *ducking* **~teer** m *pitch and tar* **~treppe** f *companion* (*ladder*) **~trümmer** m pl *wreck of a s.* **~verkehr** m *s.g traffic* **~volk** n *s.'s company*, *crew* **~vermieter** m *charterer* **~vorderteil** n *fore-castle*, *prow* **~wanten** f pl ⟨mar⟩ *shrouds* pl **~werft** f *s.yard*, *dockyard*, ⟨Am⟩ *navy yard* **~wesen** n *s.g* **~winde** f *capstan* **~zimmermann** m *s.'s carpenter* **~zertifikat** n *certificate of registry*; *navicerts* pl **~zwieback** m *s.'s biscuit*; *hard chuck*; *sea bread* **~zoll** m *freightage* **~zubehör** n *equipment of a s.*

Schik·ane f ~/~n *vexation*, *bullying* ‖ *underhand work* ‖ ⟨fig⟩ mit allen ~n (*outfitted*) *with all conveniences* od °*the frills* (= sumptuously) **s-n·ieren** vt [h] *to annoy*, *vex*, *victimize*; ⟨Am⟩ *to haze* ‖ *to play tricks upon*; ⟨school sl⟩ *to rag* **s-n·ös** a *vexatious*

Schild 1. m ~(e)s/~e *shield* ⟨a. zoo, bot, tech; geol⟩ *continental sh.*) ‖ (kl) *buckler* ‖ ⟨mil hist⟩ *targe*; Setz≈ *large sh.* ‖ ⟨her⟩ (*e*)*scutcheon*; *coat of arms* ‖ e–n Löwen im ~e führen *to bear the lion in one's c. of a.*; etw im ~e führen ⟨fig⟩ *to harbour a design*, *to be up to* ..; .. gegen jdn *to have designs on a p*; Unfug im ~e f. *to be up to mischief*, *to mean m.f* ‖ ⟨fig⟩ jdn auf den ~ (er)heben *to select a p as one's leader* ‖ ⟨fig⟩ *to keep the shield of one's honour bright* ‖ mit blankem ~ hervorgehen *to come through with flying colours* **2.** n ~(e)s/~er (Laden≈) *sign-board*, *sign*, *board* ‖ ⟨com⟩ das ~ aushängen *to open shop* ‖ (Tür≈) *door-plate* ‖ Dach≈ *sky sign* ‖ Fahnen≈ *sign* ‖ Flaschen≈ *etiquette* | Straßen≈ *road sign*, (für Straßennamen) *name-plate* | (Dienstabzeichen) *badge* (a. v Trägern) | Preis≈ *price-ticket* ‖ *label* ‖ Rücken≈ ⟨bookb⟩ *title-panel* ‖ Wahl≈ *election placard* ‖ Anhänge≈ *luggage tag* ‖ (auf Heften, Dosen, Kisten etc) *label* | Mützen≈ *peak* **~abteilung** f ⟨her⟩ *quartering* **~assel** f ⟨zoo⟩ *shield-centipede* **~bogen** m *arcaded arch* **~buckel** m *umbilicus* **~bürger** m *duffer*, *Gothamite* | ~streich [m] *silly action*; ~tum [n] *folly* **~dach** n ⟨hist mil⟩ *tortoise* **~drüse** f ⟨anat⟩ *thyroid gland* | ~n-überfunktion [f] *hyperthyroid condition* **~erhebung** f *rising in arms*, *insurrection* **~fessel** f *sh.-loop* **~fisch** m *remora* **~förmig** a *scutiform*, ⟨bot⟩ *scutate* **~halter** m ⟨her⟩ *supporter* **~klee** m *sainfoin* **~knappe** m *shield-bearer*, *squire* **~kraut** n *thyssum* **~krot**, **~patt** n *tortoise-shell* | ≈artig [a] *testudineous* **~kröte** f (See≈) *turtle* ‖ (Land≈) *tortoise*; Riesen≈ *giant to.*; Süßwasser≈ *to.* | ~ninseln [f pl] → Gal·apagosinseln; ~n-schale [f] *tortoise-shell*; ~nsuppe [f] (*real*) *turtle-soup* ‖ (unechte) *mock-turtle soup* **~laus** f ⟨ent⟩ *shield-louse* **~mauer** f *curtain-wall* **~patt** n *tortoise-shell* | ~dose [f] *tortoise-shell box*; ~kamm [m] (*tortoise-*)*shell comb* **~träger** m **1.** = ~knappe **2.** (Plakatträger) *sandwich man* **~wache** f *sentinel*, *sentry* ‖ ~ stehen *to stand sentry*, *to be on sentry-go* **~zapfenlager** n *trunion bearing* **Sch·ilder-** **~haus**, **~häuschen** n *sentry-box* **~maler** m *sign-painter* **~wald** m *forest of signs*

Schilder·ei f ~/~en ⟨hist⟩ *painting*, *picture* **Sch·ilderer** m ~s/~ *limner*, *portrayer*; *descriptive writer* **sch·ildern** vt [h] *to paint* ‖ ⟨fig⟩ *to delineate*, *describe*, *depict* (in lebendigen Farben *in vivid tints*) ‖ anschaulich ~ *to portray*, *to draw a portrait of* .. ‖ ~ als *to represent* (*a th*) *as* (od *to be*) **Sch·ilderung** f ~/~en *painting* ‖ ⟨fig⟩ *delineation* (*of character*); *description* ‖ *picture*, *sketch* ‖ *portrait*(*ure*) ‖ *representation* ‖ lebhafte ~ *portrayal* **~skraft** f *descriptive power*

Sch·ilda n *Gotham*; → Schildbürger

Sch·ilf n ~es/~e *reed*, *rush*, *sedge* ‖ Rohrkolben≈ *club-rush* | ~decke [f] *rush-mat*; ~gras [n] *reed-grass*, *sedge*; ~klinge [f] *two-edged hollow-ground blade*; ~meer [n] *reedy sea*; ⟨bib⟩ *Red Sea*; ~rohr [n] *reed*; ~sänger [m] = Teichrohrsänger **sch·ilfig**, **sch·ilfreich** a *rushy*

Schill m ~s/~e ⟨ich⟩ *giant pike-perch*

Sch·iller m ~s/ *iridescence* ‖ *rose-colo*(*u*)*red wine*; ⟨minr⟩ *schiller*; (~farbe [f], ~glanz [m]) *shot colour*, *lustre*, *splendour*; *iridescence*; *iridescent colour* **~eidechse** f *chameleon* **~falter** m ⟨ent⟩ *Purple Emperor* **~spat** m ⟨min⟩ *schiller-spar* **~taf(fe)t** m *watered taffeta*, *shot silk* **~(wein)** m *wine made of red and white grapes*

Sch·iller ⟨Ger poet⟩ **~kragen** m *broad*, *soft collar worn open and outside coat-collar* **~locke** f *type of cream-filled pastry* | *smoked haddock roll*

sch·illern vi [h] *to change colour*(*s*), *to play from one c. into another*, *to opalesce* ‖ in allen Farben ~ *to play in all colours* ‖ ins Grünliche ~ *to have a greenish tinge* **sch·illernd** a *iridescent*; (v Stoffen) *shot* ‖ in allen Regenbogenfarben ~ *playing in a thousand colours*; *iridescent*, *opalescent* ‖ ⟨fig⟩ *ambiguous*, *equivocal* (*expression*) ‖ (*an attitude*) *hovering* (*between seriousness and mockery*)

Sch·illing m ~(e)s/~e (Münze) *shilling*

sch·ilpen vi [h] ⟨orn⟩ *to chirp*, *cheep*

schilt(st) 3. (2.) sg pres v schelten

Schim·äre f *chimera* **schim·ärisch** a *chimerical*

Sch·immel 1. m ~s/ (a. ~pilz) *mould*, *mustiness*, *mildew* **2.** m ~s/~ (Pferd) *white* od *grey horse*; ⟨typ⟩ *recto and verso banks* pl **~reiter** *rider on a wh. h.* **sch·imm(e)lig** a (a. sch·immelfleckig) *mouldy*, *musty* ‖ *mildewed* (*paper*) ‖ ~ w *to mould*, *mildew* ≈**keit** f *mouldiness*, *mustiness* **sch·immeln** vi [s] *to get mouldy*, *to mould* **Sch·immer** m ~s/~ *brightness*, *glitter* (*of gold*) ‖ *glimmer* (*of stars*) ⟨a. fig⟩, *faint light* ‖ ⟨fig⟩ *glimpse* | ⟨fig⟩ erborgter ~ *borrowed pomp* | ⟨fam⟩ ⟨fig⟩ kein ~ *not the slightest trace* (*of feeling*, *hope*); *not the ghost* (*of a chance*); *not the* *faintest idea* od *notion* (von *about*) ‖ nur ein ~ *just a flicker* (*of hope*), *a glint* (*of a jest*) ‖ (ich hab) k–n ~! ⟨fam⟩ *search me!*, *ask me another!* **≗los** a *lustreless* ‖ ⟨fig⟩ *utterly ignorant*; ⟨mil sl⟩ ~ wie e–e Heeresgruppe *clueless* **sch·immern** vi [h] *to glitter, glisten, glimmer, glint, gleam, twinkle* ‖ kaum ~ *to loom* (*in the distance*) ‖ ~d *bright*; *gleaming* (*silk*)

Schimp·anse m ~s/~n *chimpanzee*

Schimpf m ~(e)s/~e *affront, insult*; *outrage* | (Ehrenkränkung) *contumely* ‖ e–m e–n ~ antun *to insult a p*; e–n ~ einstecken *to pocket an i.* | er wollte diesen ~ nicht auf sich sitzen l *he would not put up with this i.* | (Schande) *dishonour, disgrace* ‖ ~ u Schande *opprobrium* ‖ jdm ~ u Sch. antun *to affront a p* ‖ mit ~ u Sch. *ignominiously* ‖ ~ u Sch. v etw h *to be disgraced by a th* **~lied** n *lampoon* **~name** m *abusive name* **~rede** f *abusive* od *insulting speech* **~reden** f pl *abusive language* od *remarks* pl **~wort** n *swear-word, abusive word*; *invective*; *term of abuse*; *violent epithet* ‖ ~e gebrauchen *to use bad language* ‖ ≗er *abusive words* **sch·impfen** vi/t [h] *to scold* [vi], höllisch ~ *to make the air blue with abuse* ‖ ⟨zoo⟩ *to swear, squawk* ⟨a. fig⟩, *to insult* (*a p*), *to rail against, to call* (*a p*) *names* | **jdn** e–n Narren ~ *to call a p a fool, to curse him for a f.* | [vi] *to be abusive*; *to curse, swear, rail* (über, auf [acc] *at, against*) (tüchtig *lustily*); hemmungslos ~ *to indulge in bad language*; ~ wie ein Rohrspatz ⟨sl⟩ *to bitch*; ~ auf *to inveigh against* ‖ ~ über *to grumble about* **Sch·impfer** m ~s/~ *grumbler, reviler* **~·ei** f ~/~en *abuse, abusive language, reviling*; *scolding* **sch·impflich** a *disgraceful, dishonourable, discreditable, abusive*; *outrageous, ignominious* (f *to*) ‖ ~e Behandlung *indignity, scandalous treatment* | [adv] *with ignominy* **≗keit** f ~/ *disgracefulness*

Schind- **~aas** n *carrion* **~anger** m = Abdeckerei **~luder** n *carrion* ‖ ~ treiben mit *to play* (*billy, the devil, the very deuce* od) *fast and loose with* (*a p, one's health*), *to do* (*a p*) *dirt* od *the dirty* **~mähre** f *knacker, dobbin, screw*; *sorry jade*; ⟨Am sl⟩ *plug* **sch·inden I.** vt [schund/geschunden] [h] *to flay, skin, excoriate* | ⟨fig⟩ *to treat* (*a horse*) *badly, to oppress, grind* (*one's subjects*), *sweat,* (*one's workmen*) | °Eindruck ~ (*to try*) *to make o.s. conspicuous* od *to look big*; *to put on a show*; um E. z ~ *for show* ‖ °er hat gr E. geschunden ⟨Am fam⟩ *he went over big* ‖ Einlaß ~ ⟨sport⟩ *to crash the gate* ‖ Kolleg ~ *to attend lectures without paying* ‖ Lokal ~ *to sit in a restaurant without consuming anything* ‖ Wärme ~ *to sit for warmth by somebody else's fire* ‖ ⟨allg⟩ *to do sth on the cheap* **II. sich** ~ *to slave, drudge*; *to keep one's nose to the grindstone* ‖ sich ~ u plagen *to slave one's life out, to fag o.s. to death* **III.** [vi] ~ u schaben *to scrape, to be a skinflint* **Sch·inder** m ~s/~ **1.** *flayer, knacker* **2.** ⟨fig⟩ *extortioner, sweater, oppresser, grinder* **3.** ⟨mil sl⟩ = Schindmähre **~·ei** f **1.** = Abdeckerei **2.** ⟨fig⟩ *oppression, grinding, sweating, extortion* **3.** ⟨fig⟩ *slavery, drudgery, sweating* | ~betrieb [m] *sweatshop* **~grube** f *flaying-pit* **~karren** m *flayer's* od *knacker's cart* **~knecht** m *flayer's man* **≗mäßig** a ⟨fig⟩ *oppressive, extortionate, harsh, cruel, grinding*

Sch·indel f ~/~n *shingle* ‖ ⟨her⟩ *billet* | ~beil [n] *shingling-hatchet*; ~dach [n] *shingle-roof*; ~decker [m] *shingler*; ~macher [m] *shingle-splitter*; ~wand [f] *wall covered with shingles* **sch·indeln** vt [h] *to shingle* (*a roof*)

Sch·inken m ~s/~ **1.** *ham*; geräuchert (ohne Knochen) *gammon*; Knochen≗ *daisy ham* ‖ Ei mit ~ *ham and eggs* ‖ ein Brötchen mit ~ belegen *to make a ham-sandwich* ‖ für jdn e–n ~ im Salz h *to have a rod in pickle for a p* ‖ die Wurst nach dem ~ werfen *to throw a sprat to catch a whale* **2.** ⟨fam⟩ *leg, buttock* **3.** °*old book* ‖ *huge picture*; *smearing, daub* **~bein** n, **~knochen** m *knuckle of ham* **~brötchen** n *ham-sandwich*; ⟨Am⟩ *ham on rye* **~fabrikant** m *ham-curer* **~klopfen** n (Spiel) *hot-cockles* pl **~schnitte** f *slice of ham*, (dünne) *rasher* **~speck** m *g. of bacon, breakfast b.*

Schinn m ~(e)s/~e; **~e** f ~/~n *scurf, dandruff*

Sch·ippchen n ~s/~ (*child's*) *pout* **Sch·ippe,** Sch·üppe [f] ~/~n *scoop, shovel* ‖ (Spaten) *spade*; °(jdn) auf die ~ nehmen ⟨bes Am sl⟩ *to string* ‖ ~n [pl] ⟨cards⟩ *spades* pl ‖ ⟨fam⟩ e–e Schüppe *or* ein Schüppchen m *or* ziehen *or* aufwerfen *to pout* **~könig** m *king of spades* **sch·ippen** (= schaufeln) vt/i [h] *to shovel* **Sch·ipper** m *navvy* **~bruch** m *shovel(l)er's fracture*

Sch·iras n (pers. Stadt) *Shiraz, Sheeraz*

Schirm m ~(e)s/~e *screen, shade* ‖ (Regen≗) *umbrella*, ⟨sl⟩ *brolly* ‖ den ~ aufspannen *to put up one's u.* ‖ (Sonnen≗) *parasol, sunshade* ‖ (Mützen≗) *peak*; *visor* ‖ (Lampen≗) *screen, shade* ‖ ⟨aero⟩ *parachute canopy* | ⟨fig⟩ *shelter, shield, protection* ‖ unter s–m Schutz u ~ *under his patronage or protection* | ⟨bot⟩ *umbel* **~antenne** f ⟨wir⟩ *umbrella aerial* **≗artig** a *umbellate* **~bildphotographie** f (Röntgen) *photofluorography* **~dach** n *penthouse, shed, tilt*; ⟨mar⟩ *awning* **≗förmig** a ⟨scient⟩ *umbelliform* **~futteral** n *umbrella-case* **~gestell** n *u.-frame* **~händler** m *u.-man* **~herr** n *protector* (f *protectress*), *patron*(*ess* f) **~herrschaft** f *protectorate, aegis, sponsorship*; unter der ~ v *under the auspices of, sponsored by* **~hülle** f *u.-case* **~hut** m *shade-bonnet* **~lafette** f *shielded gun-carriage* **~los** a *defenceless* **~macher** m *u.-maker* **~mütze** f *peaked cap* **~palme** f *u.-palm* **~pilz** m *parasol mushroom* **~ständer** m *u.-stand* od *-rack, hall-stand* **~tanne** f *umbrella pine*, → *pine* **~überzug** m *u.-cover* **~vogt** m *patron* **~wand** f *folding-screen* **~zwinge** f *u.-tip* **sch·irmen** vt [h] *to guard, shield, shelter* ‖ ⟨fig⟩ (vor [dat]) *to protect* (*against, from*) **Sch·irmer** m ~s/~ = Schirmherr

Schir·okko m ~s/ [Arab] (Südwestwind) *sirocco*

Schirr- **~holz** n (*carriage-*) *timber* **~kammer** f *harnessroom* **~macher** m *cartwright* **~meister** m *conductor, guard*; *head ostler* ‖ ⟨mil⟩ *headman, foreman, harness keeper* | ~·ei [f] ⟨mil mot⟩ *harbo(u)r* **sch·irren** vt [h] *to harness* (an, vor *to*)

Sch·irting m ~s/~e *shirting*; ⟨theat⟩ *transparency linen*

Sch·isma n ~s/–men & ~ta *schism* **-·atiker** m ~s/~ *schismatic* **s-·atisch** a *schismatic(al)*

°**Schiß** m ⟨fam⟩ *shit(ting)* ‖ ⟨fig⟩ *funk* ⟨sl⟩; ⟨aero⟩ *the shits* ‖ ~ bek *to get the wind up*; da bekam er ~ ⟨a.⟩ *that gave him the jitters* ‖ ~ h *to funk, to be yellow* ‖ gewaltigen ~ h *to be in a blue funk* (vor *of*), *to show the white feather* °**schiß** 1. & 3. sg pret v scheißen °**Sch·isser** m ~s/~ ⟨übtr⟩ *shit(-bag)* ×°**Schitt!** *bother!* → Schiet

schizophr·en a *schizophrenic*, ~ s *to suffer from a split personality* | **≗·ie** f ~/ ⟨path⟩ *schizophrenia, split p.y*

schl·abbern vi [h] (geifern) *to slabber* ‖ (plappern) *to chat, prattle, jabber* ‖ (schlappen) *to lap* **-rig** a *prating, talkative* ‖ (fade) *insipid, tasteless*

Schlacht f ~/~en *battle* (blutig *sanguinary*, regelrecht *pitched*; schlagen *to fight*) ‖ wie ein Turm in der ~ *like a rock in the midst of the b.* ‖ die Prager ~ *the b. of Prague*, an der Marne *of the M.* ‖ e–e ~ liefern *to give b.* (*to*) ‖ die ~ gewinnen *to carry the day* ‖ damit ist die ~ halb gewonnen *that's half the b.* ‖ es kam zur ~ *a b. was fought* ‖ an e–r ~ teilnehmen *to see action* (bei *at*) ‖ in die ~ ziehen *to go into action* **~bank** f *shambles* pl, *slaughter, butchery* ‖ zur ~ führen ⟨fig⟩ *to slaughter, sacrifice* **~beil** n *butcher's axe*; *pole-ax(e)* **≗bereit** a *ready for b.* **~feld** n *b.field* **~fest** n *pig-sticking*; *killing-day* **~flieger** m *b.-*

plane; pl *b.-aircraft* **~flotte** f *b.-fleet* **~flugzeug** n (*ground-*)*attack* (od *g.-strafing*) *plane* **~geld** n *butcher's pay* **~gemälde** n = ~stück **~gesang** m *war-song* **~geschrei** n *b.-cry* **~getümmel** n *din of b., thick*(*est*) *of the fight, mêlée* **~gewicht** n *dead meat* od *weight* **~haus** n, **~hof** m *slaughterhouse, abattoir* (Fr) **~kreuzer** m *b.-cruiser* **~lied** n *warsong* **~linie** f *line of b.* **~messer** n *slaughtering-knife, butcher's knife* **~ochs** m *stalled ox* **~opfer** m *victim, sacrifice* **~ordnung** f *b.-array, order of the b.* ‖ in ~ aufstellen *to embattle, to draw up in order of b., to array for b.*; sich .. *to place o.s. in b.-array* **~pferd, ~roß** n *b.-, war-horse*; *charger* **≗reif** a *ready for killing* **~ruf** m *war-cry*, ⟨mst übtr⟩ *slogan* **~schiff** n *b.ship, major combat sh.* **~schwert** n *broadsword* **~steuer** f *tax on killing cattle* **~stück** n ⟨arts⟩ *b.-piece* **~tag** m *killing-day* ‖ ⟨mil⟩ *day of b.* **~vieh** n *animals for slaughter*(*ing*), (Rind) *beef cattle*, (Schwein) *pig*(*s*) *for sl.*, (Geflügel) *market* od *meat poultry* ‖ Mast≗ *fattened beasts* pl, ⟨Am⟩ *killers* pl; ⟨agr⟩ *fat stock* **schl·achten I.** vt/i [h] *to kill, butcher, slaughter* ⟨a. fig⟩; ⟨fam⟩ *to knock off* (*chicken*[*s*]) ‖ ⟨rel⟩ *to immolate, sacrifice* | morgen wird geschlachtet *we kill to-morrow* **II.** ≗ n *the killing* ⟨a. übtr⟩ **Schl·achten- ~bummler** m *camp-follower* **~glück** n *fortune of war* **~gott** m *god of battles* **~lenker** m *God of hosts* **~maler** m *battle-painter*

Schl·achter, ≗ m ~s/~ *butcher* ‖ *she went to the b.'s* (*shop*) **~·ei** f *b.'s* (*shop* od) *trade* ‖ ⟨fig⟩ *b.y, slaughter* **~jäger** m *pot hunter* **~laden** m *the b.'s* **Schl·achtung** f ~/~en *slaughter*(*ing*)

Schl·acke f ~/~n ⟨met⟩ *dross* ⟨a. fig⟩, *slag, scoria* ‖ *cinder* ‖ (*coal-*) *clinker*(*s* pl) ‖ *sediment* | ~ bilden *to slag* **schl·acken** vi [h] *to give off scoria* ‖ ⟨met⟩ *to be drossy* **Schl·acken- ≗artig** a *slaggy, scoriaceous*; ⟨met⟩ *drossy* **~bad** n *bath of scoria* **~bildung** f *scorification* **~erz** n *glassy silver-ore* **~förmig** a *scoriform* **≗frei** a *drossless* **~halde** f *dross-heap* **~ofen** m *slag-furnace* **~stein** m *slag-stone* **~wolle** f *mineral wool* **~(ziegel)stein** m *scoria brick* **~zinn** n *block-tin* **schl·ackig** a *slaggy*, ⟨met⟩ *drossy*; *clinkery* (*cinders of coal*)

Schl·acker- ~regen m *continuous rain making the roads heavy* **~wetter** n *slushy* od *rainy weather* **schlackerig** a *sloppy, slushy* (*weather*) **schl·ackern** vi [h] *to hang* od *move limply* ‖ ⟨mar⟩ (of sail) *to flap* | [imps] **es** schlackert *it is slushy weather*

Schl·ackwurst f *German sausage*

Schlaf m ~(e)s/ **A. 1.** *sleep* (*light, heavy, leaden*; tief, fest *deep, sound,* unruhig *uneasy*), ~ vor Mitternacht *beauty s.*; magnetischer ~ *hypnotism* | 6 Stunden ~ *6 hours s.* | ⟨fig⟩ letzter, ewiger ~ *last long s.* ‖ das Reich des ~es *the Land of Nod* **2.** (Ruhe) *repose, rest* **3.** ⟨poet, dial⟩ [pl ≗e] *temple* **4.** „~" (Schmutz) *sleepy seeds*; *dust* **B. leichter** ~ *dog's sleep*; e–n leichten *or* leisen (festen, schlechten) ~ h *to be a light* (*sound, poor*) *s.er* ‖ der ~ befällt, überfällt, übermannt e–n *s. overcomes a p* ‖ die ganze Nacht ist kein ~ in m–e Augen gek *I have not slept a wink all night* ‖ jdn im ~ stören *to break a p's s.*; e–m ~ verschaffen *to make a p s.* ‖ e–n ~ tun *to s. a s.* ‖ sich des ~es nicht erwehren können *not to be able to keep awake* ‖ den ~ des Gerechten ≗en *to sleep the s. of the just*; *to be sound*; sich zum ~ zurückziehen *to retire* **C. aus** dem ~ erwachen *to awake from s.* ‖ sich aus dem ~ raffen *to drag o.s. awake* ‖ **im** ~e *asleep* ‖ etw im ~ können *to know a th backwards* ‖ sein V. verfolgt ihn in jedem ~ *his crime haunts all his s.s* ‖ in tiefem ~e liegen *to be* (*in a deep s.* od) *fast asleep* ‖ in (e–n tiefen) ~ fallen, sinken *to fall asleep, to drop off to s.* (*to fall into a profound s.*) ‖ in ~ singen (wiegen) *to lull* (*rock*) *to s.* ‖ im ~e reden *to talk in one's s.* | ⟨fig fam⟩ das fällt mir nicht im ~e ein *I should never dream of* (*doing*) *such a th* **~abteil** n *s.ing-compartment* **≗ähnlich** a *dormant* (*state*) **~anzug** m *night-clothes*, ⟨Am⟩ *n.-robes* pl; (ein *a pair of*) *pyjamas*, ⟨Am⟩ *pajamas* pl **~baracke** f *bunk-house* **~bedürftig** a *drowsy, sleepy*, ⟨scient⟩ *comatose* **≗bringend** a *soporific, somniferous* **~bursche, ~gänger** m *night-lodger* **~gast** m *traveller who sleeps at an inn* **~gefährte, ~genosse, ~geselle** m *bed-fellow* **~geld** n *lodging-money* **~gelegenheit** f; jdm e–e ~ bieten *to sleep a p* **~gemach** n *bedroom, bedchamber* **~gewand** n *night-dress* od *-gown* **~haube** f *night-cap* **~kabine** f *bunk, berth*; (in Klöstern etc) *cubicle* **~kamerad** m = ~geselle **~kammer** f *bedroom* **~koje** f *berth, bunk* **~krankheit** f *sleeping-sickness*, afrik. ~ *trypansomiasis* **≗los** a (P) *sleepless* ‖ *wakeful* (*night*) **~losigkeit** f *s.lessness, insomnia* **~maus** f *dormouse* **~mittel** n *soporific, hypnotic*(*um*), *opiate* **~mütze** f *night-cap* ‖ ⟨fig⟩ *drowsy fellow, s.y-head, dullard, dawdler, milksop, slow-coach, a slow sort of a fellow, stick-in-the-mud* **~pelz** m *night-fur* **~platz** m ⟨aero⟩ *s.er, berth* **~quartier** n *s.ing quarters*; Arbeiter≗ *bunkhouse* **~ratz**(**e** f) m ⟨fam⟩ *sound* od *great s.er* **~raum** m (kl) *cubicle* **~reden** n *somniloquence* **~rock** m *dressing-* od *morning-gown, wrapper*; ⟨Am a.⟩ *bathrobe* ‖ japan. ~ *kimono* **~saal** m *dormitory*, ⟨mar⟩ *bunk-room* **~sack** m *s.ing-bag*; ⟨mil sl⟩ *flea-bag* **~sofa** n *sofa-bed*(*stead*) **~stelle** f *s.ing-place*, ⟨mar⟩ *berth* ‖ *lodging* (*-house*) | ~nvermieter [m] *lodging-house keeper* **~stube** f *bedroom* **~sucht** f *somnolency, coma, stupor, lethargy* **≗süchtig** a *somnolent, lethargic, drowsy*; *comatose* **~trunk** m *soporific potion, s.ing-draught* ‖ ⟨fam⟩ *night-cap* **≗trunken** a *overcome with s.*; *s.y, drowsy*; *drugged* od *drunk with s.* **~trunkenheit** f *s.iness, drowsiness* **~wachen** n *somnambulism* **~wagen** m ⟨rail⟩ *s.ing-car*, ⟨Am⟩ (*Pullman*) *S.er* | ~bett [n], ~liege [f] *berth* **~wandeln** n *s.-walking, somnambulism* **≗wandeln** vi [h & s] *to walk in one's s.* **~wandler**(**in** f) m *s.-walker* **~zeit** f *s.ing-time, bed-time* **~zimmer** n *bedroom*, ⟨Am a.⟩ *s.-room* ‖ (mit zwei Betten) *double bed-room* **~zustand** m (künstlicher) *hypnosis* L **Schl·äfchen** n ~s/~ *nap, slumber, short sleep, snooze*; ⟨Am fam⟩ *cat nap* ‖ ein ~ m *or* halten *to take* (*a nap* od) *forty winks, to snooze*

Schl·äfe f ~/~n ⟨anat⟩ *temple* → Schläfen–

schl·afen vi [schlief/geschlafen] [h] **A.** *to sleep* (8 Stunden *8 hours*) ‖ (fest) *to be* (*fast*) *asleep*; *to sleep* (*hard*); (ganz fest *or* tief *intensely*); ⟨fam⟩ *to doze, snooze* ‖ ⟨sl⟩ *to doss* ‖ (ruhen) *to repose, to* (*take one's*) *rest* ‖ (v Angelegenheiten) *to lie dormant* **B. gut,** fest, tief ~ *to be a good s.er, to s. soundly, to have a deep s.* ‖ leise, unruhig ~ *to s. uneasily* ‖ schlaf gut!, ~ Sie **wohl** *good night!*, *s. well*; °gute Nacht, s. sacht *g. n., s. tight* ‖ ich wünsche (Ihnen) wohl zu ~ *I trust you may have a good night's rest* ‖ zu lange ~ *to oversleep* | **wie** ein Dachs etc ~ *to s. like a top*, (*we slept like logs*); ⟨sl⟩ *to hog it* **C.** ~ **gehen,** sich ~ legen *to go to bed, to retire to rest*, ⟨fam⟩ *to bunk* ‖ ⟨fig⟩ (S) ~ gehen *to die out* ‖ (Angst etc) ließ ihn nicht ~ .. *robbed him of s.* ‖ ~ **legen** (schicken) *to put* (*send*) *to bed* ‖ e–e S ~ l *to let a matter rest* ‖ jdn nicht ~ l *to prevent a p from s.ing* **D. außer** dem Hause ~, auswärts ~ (= übernachten) *to s. out* ‖ bei, mit jdm ~ *to spend the night with a p* ‖ ~ Sie noch darüber! *s. on it!* ‖ **unter** freiem Himmel ~ *to spend the night in the open* ‖ zu zweit ~ *to s. double* **E.** in diesem Bett schläft **es** sich gut *this is a comfortable bed to s. in* **Schl·äfen-** [in comp] *temporal* (~ader *t. vein*, ~bein *t. bone*, ~gegend *t. region* **Schl·afenszeit** f *bed-time* ‖ es ist ~ *it is time to go to bed* **Schl·äfer**(**in** f) m ~s/~ *sleeper* **schl·äfern** vt [imps] mich schläfert *I am* od *feel sleepy* **schlaff** [a] *slack* (*rope*), *flabby* (*balloon, muscles*); *sagging* (*face*) ‖ *loose* ‖ (herabhängend) *limp, drooping* | ~ m, ~ w *to slacken, relax* | ⟨fig⟩ *lax* (*principles*), *loose* (*morals*) ‖ (träge) *indolent* ‖

|| (lau) *half-hearted, languid* || (nachlässig) *negligent, remiss* || *enervated (character)* | [adv] ~ gespannt *loosely stretched* || ~ herabhängen *to hang down slack* od *limply* od *lazily* **Schlaffheit** f ~/~en *slackness, flabbiness, looseness* | ⟨fig⟩ *laxness, laxity* || *indolence* || *half-heartedness, languor* || *negligence, remissness*

Schlaf·ittchen n; am *or* beim ~ nehmen *to get .. by the short hairs; to (seize by the) collar;* ⟨fig⟩ *to call to account*

schl·äfrig a *sleepy, drowsy; somnolent* || ~ m *to make s.y* || ~ s *to drowse, to have dust in the eyes;* sehr ~ ⟨fam⟩ *rare and s.y* || noch ganz ~ *still half asleep* || ⟨fig⟩ *slow, indolent* | ≈**keit** f ~/ *s.iness, drowsiness, somnolence* || ⟨scient⟩ *oscitancy* || ⟨fig⟩ *indolence, slowness*

Schlag m ~(e)s/≈e **A.** *blow* ⟨a. fig⟩; *kick, bounce* | (Uhr, Schwert, Trommel, Ruder, Kolben etc; ⟨golf, ten⟩ *stroke* | *beat* ⟨a. mus⟩ || ⟨fam⟩ *buff, bounce,* ⟨Am⟩ *biff,* ⟨sl⟩ *sock* || *rap (on the knuckles)* || *jab (on the head)* || *smack;* heftiger ~ ⟨Am fam⟩ *(s)wipe* || ⟨tech⟩ *excentricity, beat* || ⟨for⟩ *cutting, felling;* [konkr] *f.g area,* Kahl≈ *clear f.g;* → D. || ⟨path⟩ *apoplexy,* → ~anfall | ≈**e** [pl] *beating, flogging, thrashing, whipping* | ⟨fig⟩ *knock (I got* od *had a bad k. after the war), coup* Fr **B. ausholend** *swipe* || derb, heftig, kräftig *heavy blow; thwack, whack;* ⟨fam⟩ *purler;* ⟨sl⟩ *settler, smeller* (bes. auf die Nase) || **dumpf** *thud, thump,* ⟨Scot⟩ *dunt* || entscheidend *knock-out, settler;* ⟨fam⟩ *haymaker* || (Spiel) erster *toss throw; start;* ⟨fam⟩ *first go* | ⟨fig⟩ ein harter *or* schwerer ~ *a hard* od *terrible blow* || **laut** *bang* || leicht, leise *tap(ping), snick,* ⟨Am⟩ *spat* || sanft *chuck (under the chin)* || schwer *hard knock* || tief (mit Axt) *chop* || treffend *hit* || ⟨box⟩ unerlaubt *foul,* tötlich, vernichtend *deadly blow* **C. Donner**≈ *clap of thunder;* kalt *lightning not attended with ignition* || Faust≈ *cuff, punch* || (mit der flachen Hand) *slap* || **Herz**≈ *beat(ing), palpitation, pulsation, throb(bing) of the heart* || zwei Herzen u ein ~ *they are hand and glove* || (v Huf) *kick; the snap-snap of horses' hoofs* || Pendel≈ *oscillation* || Peitschen≈ *lash* || **Puls**≈ *beat* || (mit dem Stock) *whack,* ⟨sl⟩ *wallop (to aim a w. at a p)* || (der Taschenuhr) *tick* || Taubenschlag *cote* || **Tor**≈ *bar (of a gate);* Trommel≈ *beat* || (der Vögel) *song, warbling, carol(ling), trill(ing)* || (Wagentür) *carriage-* od *coach-door* || *tone (of the zither)* **D.** ⟨**agr**⟩ *parcel, strip (of land); tilled field;* in ≈e teilen *to parcel the crops* || die ≈e der Fruchtfolge *the rotation of crops* | ⟨el⟩ *(electric) shock* od *stroke* | ⟨for⟩ *block;* → ⟨a.⟩ A. ⟨for⟩; *cut (of timber* od *in the wood), clearing* | ⟨golf⟩ (→ Einheit) || der erste ~ *the drive* || ~ aus schwerer Lage *recovery* || schneller ~ ins Loch *goby* || gewöhnliche Zahl guter ≈e *bogey,* ohne Vorgabe *par* | ⟨hort⟩ *clump (of strawberry bushes)* | ⟨mach⟩ *knocking* | ⟨weav⟩ *pick* | ⟨mar⟩ (e–s Taues) *coil, turn* (ganzer *round,* halber *half turn)* || (Knoten) *hitch* || ⟨sailing⟩ *tack, board* | ⟨med⟩ *(paralytic) stroke; apoplectic fit,* (bek *to have*) || v ~e gerührt *struck by apoplexy* || z ~e geneigt *apoplectic* (→ F.) | °⟨mil cul⟩ *helping* | ⟨min⟩ *horizontal works* | ⟨mus⟩ *measure, rhythm* | ⟨weav⟩ *lath; beat-up; lay* **E.** (**Art,** Geschlecht) *sort, kind, stamp, type, race, calibre, cut (you are of the same cut as he)* || Leute s–s ~es *the like of him* || alt: *(a man of the) old stock* od *stamp* || v e–m anderen ~e *cast in a different mould* || der gewöhnliche ~ *the common run of men* || v gutem ~e *of the right sort* || ⟨hors⟩ *breed* (gut *fine*) **F.** e–n ~ **ausführen** *to strike a blow;* austeilen: *to deal out blows, (blows were struck)* || austauschen: *to exchange blows* || e–n ~ beibringen *to get in* [adv], *to plant a blow* || ≈e **bek,** erhalten *to receive blows;* e–n: *he had stopped one from her* || *to be flogged, whipped, to have a whipping, to get a (sound) beating* od *drubbing* || e–m Pferde e–n leichten ~ geben *to flick a h.* || der ~ hat ihn gerührt *he had a fit of apoplexy* (→ E.) || °„landen" ⟨sl⟩ *to plant* || ≈e sausten auf s–n R. *blows fell on his back* || ohne e–n ~ z tun *without striking a single blow* || [dat] e–n ~ versetzen *to catch a p a blow* od *smack, to strike a blow at ..;* ⟨fam⟩ *to fetch a p a purler; to give a check to a th;* mit e–m Stock .. auf .. *to hit a p with a stick over the head* || der ~ wirkte *the shot told* **G. auf**: *a cut over the buttocks* | **in**: *a slap on* od *in the face; a facer* ⟨a. fig⟩; ⟨fig⟩ ins Kontor *a smack in the eye, a pretty mess, a nasty affair, a serious setback* || ⟨fig⟩ ins Wasser: *a blow in the air, flash in the pan, wild-goose chase;* es war .. *it failed, it fell flat* | **mit**: *(20 strokes) of the cat, rod* **H.** (**auf** den, **mit** dem) ~ 10 Uhr *(at) ten sharp; (on the stroke of ten)* || auf den ~ *punctually, to the minute* || auf einen ~ *at one fell sweep* || ~ auf ~ *blow after* od *upon bl.,* ⟨fig⟩ *one after the other, in rapid succession* || zwei Fliegen **mit** e–m ~ *(to kill) two birds with one stone* || ⟨mar⟩ mit langen ≈en aufkreuzen *to beat up by long boards* || mit e–m ~ *at one blow* ⟨a. fig⟩, *at one sweep;* ⟨fig⟩ *in a trice, suddenly, all at once, straightway* || sich mit e–m ~ ändern *to undergo a sudden change* || wie **vom** ~e getroffen w *to get the shock of one's life* || **zum** ~e ausholen *to strike (a blow)* **~abraum** m ⟨for⟩ *slashings* pl **~ader** f ⟨anat⟩ *artery* | ~geschwulst [f] *aneurism* **~anfall** m → ~ D.; leicht *strokelet* (×Schlägle) ≈**artig** a *sudden; spontaneous;* ⟨path⟩ *apoplectic* | [adv] *instantaneously; all of a sudden* **~ballspiel** n ⟨Ger⟩ *rounders* pl; *trap-ball* **~baum** m *turnpike* **~bolzen** m ⟨mil⟩ *striker* **~brücke** f *draw-bridge* **~elemente** n pl ⟨mill⟩ *percussion studs* **~feder** f *striker spring* ≈**fertig** a *ready for battle, r. to fight* || ⟨fig⟩ *quick--witted, q. in* od *at repartee,* ⟨Am fam⟩ *q. on the draw* od *trigger* || *(it is very ready of you)* || ~e A. *pert answer* || ~ s *to have a ready wit at one's fingertips;* er ist nicht bes ~ *he is not good at repartee* | ≈keit [f] *readiness for battle* || ⟨fig⟩ *ready wit, acuteness, patness; (quickness of) repartee* ≈**fest** a *shockproof* | ≈igkeit [f] *resistance to shocks* **~flügelflugzeug** n *ornithopter* **~fluß** m → ~ D. ≈**flüssig** a *apolectic* **~gewicht** n (Uhr) *striking-weights* pl **~hammer** m *hammer* **~härteprüfung** f *impact hardness test* **~holz** n *wood fit for felling* || ⟨sport⟩ *mallet, bat, club* **~instrument** n ⟨mus⟩ *percussion instrument* **~kraft** f *percussive force* || *striking power;* ⟨bes mil⟩ *effectiveness* || ⟨Am fig⟩ *punch* | ≈ig [a] *powerful, effective* **~leine** f *chalk-line;* ⟨theat⟩ *throwline,* ⟨Am⟩ *lashline* **~leiste** f *rabbet-ledge* **~licht** n ⟨paint⟩ *strong light* | ≈artig [adv] *at a stroke* **~loch** n ⟨mot⟩ *pot-hole;* schlechte Straße mit ≈ern *wash-board road* **~lot** n *hard solder; spelter* **~mallinie** f ⟨sport⟩ *crease* **~mann** m (Ruderer) *stroke* **~maschine** f ⟨tech⟩ *batting-machine, blower* **~mechanismus** m ⟨weav⟩ *picker-stick* **~mühle** f *desintegrator* **~nase** f ⟨mill⟩ *percussion stud* **~netz** n (z Ballspiel) *racket* || (z Vogelfang) *clap--net* || (z Fischen) *seine(-net)* **~regen** m *pouring rain* **~ring** m *knuckle-duster* || ⟨mus⟩ *plectrum, quill* **~röhre** f ⟨mill⟩ *percussion fuse* **~sahne** f *whipped cream* **~schatten** m *deep* od ⟨arts⟩ *cast shadow* **~schatz** m *mintage* **~seite** f ⟨mar⟩ *list, lopside* || ~ bek ⟨mar⟩ *to heel over* || ~ h *to (have) list;* ⟨fam, fig⟩ *to be a bit over the line* (= tipsy) **~stock** m (Ballspiel) *bat* **~tot** m ⟨fam⟩ *tall, hulking fellow* **~trommel** f *gong, tom-tom* **~uhr** f *striking clock* **~wasser** n ⟨mar⟩ *bilge-water* **~weite** f ⟨el⟩ *striking-distance* **~welle** f *billow* **~werk** n *clock-work, striking work(s pl)* **~wetter** n ⟨min⟩ *fire-damp* **~wort** n *slogan,* ⟨derog⟩ *catchword, commonplace, cliché* **~worte** n pl *claptrap* **~zeile** f *catch-phrase* od *-line;* (Zeitung) *(splash-) -headline;* in grellen ~n *in flaring headlines* || ⟨Am⟩ *banner* || Riesen≈ *screamer* **~zeug** n ⟨mus⟩

percussion (*instrument*); [koll] *battery* **~zeuger** m ⟨Am⟩ *drummer* **~zither** f *dulcimer* **~zünder** m *p. fuse* **~zündung** f *p. priming* **schl·agbar** a *fit for felling* **Schl·ägel** etc → Schlegel etc **schl·agen** [schlug/ge~] **I.** vt [h] **A.** *to beat, strike, knock, dash; to buffet, punch, cuff; to pat, tap, clap, slap, slat, bang* ‖ (treffen) *to hit* ‖ (v Pferd) *to kick* | ⟨mach⟩ *to hammer* ‖ (Glocke, Uhr) *to strike* → III. B. | ⟨sport⟩ *to score a p off; to beat, worst*; ⟨sl⟩ *to out a p* ‖ (vernichtend) *to beat .. hollow* od *into a cocked hat* od *into fits* | ⟨mil⟩ *to defeat* | ⟨pol⟩ *to rout*, ⟨Am⟩ *to slaughter* **B.** (**heftig**, tüchtig) *to lam, whang*; ⟨fam⟩ *to clump, slosh, slog*, ⟨Am⟩ *slug* ‖ (klatschend) *to smack* ‖ (leicht) *to tip* ‖ (sanft) *to flick*; *chuck* (*a p under the chin*) ‖ (strafend) *to spank* ‖ (wiederholt) *to belabour, pummel* ‖ (zerrend) *to knock about* **C.** e–e **Ader** ~ *to open ..* ‖ Alarm ~ ⟨mil⟩ *to sound the a.* ‖ (e–n **Ball**) *to strike, hit*; den B. gut ~ *to bat well* ‖ (Bäume) *to fell* ‖ jdm Beulen in den Kopf ~ *to raise bruises on a p's h.* ‖ (Beute) ⟨orn⟩ *to strike, kill; to pounce upon* ‖ (e–e Brücke) *to build, make, throw* ‖ (**Eier**) *to whisk*; .. in die Pfanne ~ *to fry* (*eggs*), in die Suppe *to stir .. into ..* ‖ (Fäden) *to lay* ‖ Falten ~ *to wrinkle, crease* ‖ *to whip the enemy* ⟨Am fam⟩ ‖ Feuer ~ *to stroke a light* ‖ (Geld) *to coin* ‖ (Holz) *to fell, hew; chop* ‖ (die Harfe etc) *to play* (*on*) ‖ e–e gute Klinge ~ *to be a good swordsman*, ⟨fig⟩ *to play a good knife and fork* ‖ (e–n Knoten) *to tie* ‖ (e–n Kreis) *to draw, describe* ‖ (e–e Kurve) *to make* ‖ (**Lärm**) *to make* (*a n.*) ‖ e–m ein Loch in den Kopf ~ *to break a p's head* ‖ (Öl) *to press* ‖ (e–n Reifen) *to trundle* ‖ (Saiten) *to touch* ‖ Schaum → E. ‖ e–e Schlacht ~ *to fight a* (od *give*) *battle* ‖ Schnee → E. ‖ den **Takt** ~ *to beat time* ‖ (ein Tau) *to lay* ‖ ⟨fenc⟩ e–e Terz ~ *to thrust in tierce* ‖ (die Trommel) *to beat* ‖ (die Tür) *to bang* ‖ (**Wellen**) *to throw up* ‖ das Meer schlug hohe Wellen *the waves* (*of ..*) *ran high* ‖ e–n Wirbel ~ *to beat a roll* (*on the drum*) ‖ jdm Wunden ~ *to wound* (*to inflict wounds to*) *a p*; ⟨fig⟩ (e–r S) *to cause serious difficulties* (z. B. *in trade*) ‖ (Wurzel[n]) *to strike*; ⟨fig⟩ ich hätte hier bald W. ge~ *I was very nearly settling down here for good* **D. an**: *to nail* od *fix to* (*the cross* = to crucify) ‖ ⟨univ⟩ ans schwarze Brett ~ *to announce on the board* | [dat] **auf** [acc]: *to hit* (*a p*) *on* (*the head*), *to rap* (*a p*) *on* (*the knuckles* Finger) ‖ (den Feind) aufs Haupt ~ *to conquer .. completely* ‖ ⟨com⟩ *to charge* od *clap* (*the expenses*) *on* (*the goods*) | [dat] **aus** [dat]: *to knock .. out of* (*a p's hand*); ‖ (Staub) *to pound .. from* ‖ jdn aus dem Felde *or* in die Flucht ~ *to put .. to flight* ‖ *to strike* (*fire*) *from* (*a flint*), *water out of* (*a rock*) ‖ *to knock* (*the bottom*) *out of* (*a cask*); ⟨fig⟩ das schlägt dem Faß den B. aus *that puts the lid on it* ‖ *to make* (*capital*) *out of* (*a matter*) ‖ sich etw aus dem Kopf, Sinn ~ *to dismiss .. from one's thoughts* od *mind, to put .. out of one's mind* | **durch** (ein Sieb) ~ *to pass through ..* | **in** (→ E.): die Arme (Hände) in–e–a ~ *to cross one's arms* (*to clasp one's hands*) ‖ in Fesseln ~ *to put .. in irons* od *chains* ‖ *to cut* (*holes*) *into* (*the ice*) ‖ in die Höhe ~ *to knock up*; die Augen ..: *to look up* ‖ in Papier ~ *to wrap up in p.* ‖ *to drive* (*a nail, a post*) *into* (*the wall, the ground*) ‖ (*the eagle drove its fangs into its prey*) ‖ ⟨fig⟩ in den Wind ~ *to ignore, disregard* (*advice*) | **mit**: *to hit .. with* (*the hand*), *to beat ..* (*with a stick*) (= to cane) ‖ mit der Faust ~ *to cuff* ‖ zwei Fliegen mit e–r Klappe ~ *to kill two birds with one stone* ‖ mit Schwung ~ *to swipe* (*a ball*) ‖ mit der Peitsche *to cut with .., to whip* ‖ *to afflict* (*with sorrow*) | **nach** hinten ~ *to comb back* (*one's hair*) | **über**: *to hit .. over* (*the head with ..*) ‖ *to put* (*boots*) *on* (*the last*) ‖ über–e–a: *to cross* (*one's legs*) | **um**: *to throw* (*one's arms*) *around* (*a p*); .. (*a shawl*) *over* (*one's shoulders*), *to wind .. about* od *round ..* ‖ *to put* (*a cover*) *on* (*a book*) ‖ dem Schüler das Heft um die Ohren ~ *to hit .. over the head with his ..* ‖ sich [dat] die Nacht, (Welt) um die Ohren ~ *to make a night of it*, (*to knock about the world*) | (mit den Fäusten) um sich ~ *to lunge about* | **von**: *to knock* (*a fly*) *off* (*one's hand*), (*the helmet*) *off* (*a p's head*) | wie **vor** den Kopf ge~ *nonplussed* ‖ sich vor die Stirne ~ *to smite one's f.* ‖ die Hände weinend vors Gesicht ~ *to cover one's face with one's hands to hide one's tears* | **zu** Boden ~ *to knock down, to strike to the ground*; *to cast down* (*one's eyes*) ‖ *to add* (*the interest*) *to* (*the capital*) ‖ zum .. → E. **E.** (**Wirkung**): e–n **blau**, grün u gelb ~ *to beat a p black and blue* ‖ e–n krumm u lahm ~, e–n windelweich ~ *to beat a p to a jelly* ‖ gerade ~ *to straighten*; glatt ~ *to flatten* ‖ klein|~, **in** Stücke ~ *to hack, cleave, split, break into small pieces*; kurz u kl ~, in Trümmer ~ *to knock to smithereens, to smash up*; alles .. ~ *to s. ths up* ‖ tot ~ *to beat to death, to kill with a blow* ‖ ich lasse mich tot ~, (es ist so)! *I stake my life on it* ‖ die Zeit tot~ *to waste one's time* ‖ sich den Bauch voll~ *to gorge o.s.* ‖ (Eier etc **zu**) **Schaum** *or* Schnee ~ *to whisk* ‖ ⟨fig⟩ Schaum ~ *to talk idly* ‖ zum Krüppel ~ *to beat to a cripple* ‖ zum Ritter ~ *to knight* **F. geschlagen**: (*a*) *broken* od *ruined* (*man*); (*a*) *full* (*hour*); (*ten*) *mortal* (*hours*): den ge~en Tag *all day long, the livelong day* ‖ ich bin ge~ *that beats me, I'm nonplussed* od *nowhere* ‖ sich ge~ geben *to admit one's defeat* **II. 1.** [v/refl] [h] **sich** ~ *to hit o.s.* **2.** [v/recip] sich ~ *to fight* (*a duel with*) *a p* (auf Säbel *with sabres*, gut *bravely*) ‖ sich links ~ *to turn* od *strike to the left* **3.** sich **an** die Brust, Taschen, Stirn ~ *to beat one's breast, to slap one's pockets, to smite o.s. over the forehead* ‖ sich auf den F. ~ *to hit one's finger* ‖ sich auf jdes Seite ~ *to take a p's part, to join a p* od *his party* ‖ sich **durch** die Welt ~ *to make one's way*, .. schlecht u recht: *he just manages to make a bare living* ‖ **in** → Busch ‖ sich ins Mittel ~ *to interpose, intervene* ‖ sich ~ **um** *to fight for* ‖ sich zu e–r Partei, zu jdm ~ *to side with, go over to, to join ..*; ⟨fig⟩ *to throw in one's lot with ..* **III.** vi [h & s] **A.** [h] *to beat, strike* ‖ (dröhnend): *a clock boomed ten* ‖ (dumpf) *to* (*give a*) *thud, thump* ‖ (heftig) *my heart is throbbing* ‖ (leicht) *to flip* (über *over*) ‖ (krachend gegen) *the car caught the wall with a smash* **B.** [h] ⟨chess etc⟩ *to take pieces* ‖ (v **Fenstern**) *to rattle* ‖ *the gun kicks* (*heavily* stark) ‖ sein Gewissen schlägt ihm *his conscience pricks him* ‖ ⟨fig⟩ wissen, was **es** (*or* die **Glocke**) ge~ hat *to know what's what* od *the clock*; du weißt, was .. *you know what you are in for* ‖ sein Herz schlug warm für .. *he had a warm heart for the poor* ‖ (Nachtigall) *to sing* ‖ (Rad) *one of the wheels is loose* ‖ (Segel) *to flap* | (**Stunde**): (*the hour*) *strikes* ‖ (*his hour*) *has come* ‖ sein letztes Stündlein hat ge~ *his last hour has struck* ‖ dem Glücklichen schlägt k–e St. *a happy man does not hear the clock strike* ‖ (**Uhr**): *the clock strikes, chimes, booms* (*ten*) ‖ **es** schlägt zehn *it is striking ten o'clock*, .. ein Viertel *the quarter*, halb *the half-hour*, voll *the hour* ‖ jetzt schlägt's aber dreizehn! *that beats all!* | (**Vögel**) *to warble, sing, carol, trill*; (Wachtel) *to call* **C.** [s] der Kahn schlägt voll Wasser .. *fills with water* ‖ durch etw ~ *to pass through* **D. an**: *the rain beats* od *patters against the window* ‖ *a noise came to* (*smote on, fell on* od *struck*) *his ear*(*s*) ‖ *waves dash against the shore* | **auf**: *to beat* od *strike a th* ‖ (P) *to bounce upon the floor*, ⟨sl⟩ *to slump to the fl.* ‖ *the fumes settle on the chest* ‖ bei jdm auf den Busch ~ *to pump a p* ‖ jdm auf die Finger (den Mund) ~ *to give a p a rap on the knuckles* (*to hit a p on the m.*) ‖ *to slap one's knees, a p's shoulder* ‖ *to bump a p on the head* ‖ *to bang, thump the table* | **aus**: aus der Art ~ *to degenerate* ‖ *flames leaped through the window* ‖

smoke rose from the chimney || sein Herz schlug ihr **entgegen** *his h. went out to her* | **gegen**: (of waves) *to lap* || *the rain slashed the panes* || (S) *to flop, flap against* || mit dem Kopf: *to knock,* ⟨fam⟩ *run one's h. against* .. | **gen** Himmel: *flames shoot, leap, flash up to heaven* | jdm **hinter** die Ohren ~ *to box a p's ears* | **in** [acc]: *the lightning has struck the tree* || das schlägt nicht (gerade) in mein Fach *that is not (much) in my line* || jdn ins Gesicht ~ *to slap a p's face, to hit him in the f.* || ⟨fig⟩ .. schlägt der Gerechtigkeit ins Ges. .. *is a mockery of all justice* || es ist mir in die Glieder ge~ *I feel it in every limb* | **mit**: *to strike with a sword* || *to bang on the table with the fist* || *to flap one's wings* || er schlug mit dem Kopf auf den Boden *in falling his h. struck the g.* | **nach** [dat]: *to hit out at* .. || sie ~ sehr dem Vater nach *they very much take after their father* | **über**: (of waves) *to sweep* | hintenüber (kopfüber) ~ *to fall backward (headlong)* | **um** sich ~ *to lash, strike, hit out; to lay about one; (to lay on with the sword)* | zu Boden ~ *to lay low* **IV.** ≈ n *beating, striking,* etc || *thrash (of rain,* etc) || *felling (of trees)* || *song (of birds)* || *construction (of a bridge)* || *action, palpitation (of the heart)* || *pulsation* || *kicking (of horses)* || *fighting* **schl·agend** a || ⟨crick⟩ *batting,* nicht ~ *fielding (side)* || ⟨fig⟩ *striking (remark)* || *convincing, cogent (proof)* || ~e Erwiderung ⟨Am, fam⟩ *nifty* | [adv] *(to repudiate) forcibly* **Schl·ager** m ~s/~ ⟨theat, mus⟩ *hit song, s.-h.*; *music hall song, popular tune*; ⟨sl⟩ *draw* ⟨a. com⟩, *hit, rage* || (Buch) *bestseller, thriller* || ⟨mus⟩ unsterblicher ~ *evergreen* || ⟨theat, film⟩ *hit, draw*; *hit show*; Kassen≈ *box-office draw,* ⟨Am sl⟩ *b.-o. attraction*; Presse≈ *topliner,* ⟨Am⟩ *headliner* **~bezirk** m (London) ⟨sl⟩ *Tin-pan Alley* **~gruppe** f *pop group* **~musik** f *pop music* **~sänger** m *crooner; pop singer* **Schl·äger** m ~s/~ **1.** (P) *fighter, duellist, swordsman; brawler*; ⟨crick⟩ *batsman, batter* || harter ~ ⟨baseball Am fam⟩ *slugger* **2.** *rapier, sword; mallet*; ⟨golf⟩ *putter; iron*; ⟨ten⟩ *racket* **3.** ⟨orn⟩ *warbler* **4.** ⟨hors⟩ *kicker* **5.** ⟨tech⟩ *breaking hammer* **~mensur** f ⟨stud⟩ *fencing with rapiers* **Schläger·ei** f ~/~en *fray, scuffle, brawl, row; fight*; ⟨fam⟩ *set to*; (im Suff) *drunken brawl*; (allg) ⟨Am a.⟩ *free-for-all*

°**Schlaks** m –ses/–se *hobbledehoy* ≈**ig** a *gawky*; *(to be) all legs*

°**Schlam·assel** n ~s/~ [Hebr] ⟨mil⟩ *box-up, muck-up* || (allg) *jam, mess, scrape, fix*; ⟨sl⟩ *packet*

Schlamm m ~(e)s/ *mud, mire; sludge* || ⟨met⟩ *slime* || Pfeifen≈ ⟨Am⟩ *goo* || im ~ gehen, pantschen *to slosh* **~bad** n *mud-bath* **~beißer** m *mud-fish* **~boden** m *muddy soil* **~fänger** m *gully(-hole)* **~grube** f *sink* **~netz** n *drag-net* **~packung** f *mud-pack* **~peitzger** m ⟨ich⟩ *pond loach* **~springer** m ⟨ich⟩ *mud-skipper* **~ventil** n *sludge valve* **~vulkan** m *mud-volcano* **~wurm** m *pond blood-worm* **~ziegel** m ⟨Eg⟩ *mud-brick* **Schlämm- ~faß** n *dolly-tub* **~kreide** f *precipitated chalk; whit(en)ing* **~vorrichtung** f *cleansing apparatus* **~werk** n *washing-mill* **schl·ämmen** vt [h] *to wash, clean (ore, chalk)* || *to dredge (a lake)* || *to whitewash* **schl·ammig** a *muddy, slimy, miry*

Schl·ämmung f ~/ ⟨tech⟩ *elutriation*

°**schlamp·ampen** vi [h] *to feast; to gorge o.s.*; *to lead a jolly life* **Schl·ampe** f ~/~n *slut, slattern, dowdy, rag-bag, draggle-tail; trapes* [sg] || ⟨agr⟩ *swill* **~r·ei** f *sluttishness, slovenliness; mess; inefficiency*; das ist e–e verfluchte ~ *you made a hopeless muddle of it* || [konkr] *slovenly job* **schl·ampen** vi [h] *to lap* **Schl·ampian** m ~s/~e ⟨fam⟩ *litter-bug* **schl·ampig** a *slovenly, frowsy, sluttish, dowdy, sloppy, slouchy; sleezy; draggle-tailed* || (Weg, Tisch, Arbeit) *sloppy* || ~es Weib *slut, slattern, drab*; → Schlampe | ≈**keit** f *grubbiness*, → Schlamperei

schlang 1. & 3. sg pret v schlingen **Schl·ange** f ~/~n **1.** *snake* (⟨a. fig⟩ P), falsche ~! (Frau) *cat!*; *serpent* (zischt, *hisses*) || ⟨fig⟩ e–e ~ am Busen nähren *to cherish a viper on one's bosom* **2.** ⟨tech⟩ (Rohr) *coil, worm* **3.** ⟨fig⟩ ~ bilden (P) *to form up* (od *join on to*) *a queue*; ~ stehen *to wait in line, to queue up,* ⟨Am⟩ *to line up*; die ~ überspringen *to jump the q.* **4.** (Pensionats≈) *crocodile* **schl·ängeln I.** vt [h] *to coil* || ge–lt *winding (road)* **II. sich** ~ [h] *to wind, meander, snake, twine, twist, wriggle*; sich durch den Verkehr ~ *to weave in and out of traffic* || ⟨fig⟩ sich aus der Affäre ~ *to twist o.s. out of the affair* **schl·ängelig** a *sinuous (line), winding (path), meandering (river)* **Schl·angen- ≈ähnlich, ≈artig** a *serpentine (s.t[ine]) snaky* **~anbeter** m *s.-worshipper* **~balg** m *slough of a s.e* **~beschwörer** m *s.-charmer* **~biß** m *s.-bite* **~brut** f ⟨a. fig⟩ *brood of s.s, generation of vipers* ≈**förmig** a *s.tine, meandering* °**~fraß** m ⟨fig⟩ *slush* **~gang** m *s.tine walk* **~gift** n *s.e-poison* **~haar** n *s.y locks* pl **~holz** n *s.e-wood* **~kraut** n ⟨bot⟩ *s.e-weed* **~linie** f *s.tine line* **~mensch** m *dis* .. od *contortionist* **~rohr** n *winding tube* od *pipe* **~stab** m *caduceus* **~stein** m ⟨min⟩ *s.tine* **~stich** m (Stickerei) *s.tine stitch* **~weg** m *winding path* **~windung** f *s.tine, winding, meander* **~zunge** f ⟨bot⟩ *adder's tongue* ≈**züngig** a *adder-t.d*; → *serpent* & *snake*

schlank a *slender (deer), slim, svelte* [Fr] *(figure)*; ⟨Am a.⟩ *rangy* || ⟨fig⟩ *fast (trot)* || die ~e Linie *the slimming (waist)line* || ~ m, auf ~e L. halten *to slim* || ~ wie e–e Tanne *slim as a young sapling* || ~er w *to be reducing* **~w·eg** [adv] *downright, flatly, point-blank* **Schl·ankheit** f ~/ *slenderness, slimness*

schlapp a = schlaff || (P) *weak*; ein ~er Kerl *a sloppy sort of fellow* || °~ m [vi] ⟨mil sl⟩ *to flag* || nicht ~ m *to stay the course* || ich bin ~ *I'm done up* ≈**hut** m *flapped* od *floppy hat, slouchhat* ≈**ohr** n *flap-ear* ≈**schuh** m *old slipper*; ⟨mil sl⟩ *frog* °≈**schwanz** m ⟨fam⟩ *milksop, slacker* **Schl·appe** f ~/~n *check, blow, reverse* || ⟨mil⟩ *set-back; defeat* || *loss* || e–e ~ erhalten *or* erleiden *to meet with a reverse* || ⟨fig⟩ *to be discomfited* **schl·appen** vt/i [h] **1.** *to lap* **2.** *to flap; to shuffle*; *to slip-slop*

Schlar·affe m ~n/~n *lubber, sluggard* **~nland** n *land of milk and honey, lotus-land, Cockaigne* **~nleben** n *life of idleness and luxury*

schlau a *sly, cunning (caution), crafty, sly, knowing*; ⟨fam⟩ *deep (fellow)*; *artful (idea)* || wir w nicht recht ~ daraus *we don't quite take it into our heads* ≈**berger,** ≈**fuchs,** ≈**kopf,** ≈**meier** m ⟨fam⟩ *slyboots, shiner, artful dodger* || ein ~ s *to know a th or two,* .. *what's what* **Schl·äue, Schlauheit** f ~/ *slyness, cunning, wiliness, archness, artfulness, craftiness; astuteness,* → Bauern-

Schlauch m ~(e)s/≈e (T) *skin*; (Wein≈, Ölbehälter) *(leather-)bag* || ⟨cycl⟩ *(inner) tube* || ~ geplatzt! *tire gone!* || (Feuerwehr≈, Garten≈) *hose* || Füll≈, Zapf≈ *filling hose* | ⟨fig⟩ *drunkard, belly-worshipper* | *drudgery* | Gas≈ *gas-tube* | *long narrow room* **~boot** n *rubber-boat, life-raft*; ⟨fam⟩ *pneumatic*; ⟨sl⟩ *rubber dinghy* **~frucht** f ⟨bot⟩ *utricle* **~leitung** f *hose pipe* **~löffel** m *tire-lever* ≈**los** a ⟨mot⟩ *tubeless* **~schoner** m ⟨mot, etc⟩ *chafing strip* **~verbindung** f *hose clamp* od *coupling* **schl·auchen** vt [h] *to put into casks,* etc; *to hose* | °(jdn) ~ *to torment, fag, overstrain; to give it a p well*; ⟨Am univ⟩ *to haze* || *to get (riding soon gets me)*

Schl·aufe f ~/~n *runner, loop, noose*

Schlaw·iner m ~s/~ [bes österr] (Nichtsnutz) *rotter,* ⟨Am sl⟩ *scalawag*; (Herumtreiber) *loafer*

schlecht I. [a] **A.** *bad* [compr: *worse,* sup: *worst*] *(food, humour, state, business, man, habits, name)* || *imperfect (combustion)* || [pred a.] *amiss*; ~ s gegen *to behave badly toward (a p)* || *worthless* (*book*); *inefficient* (*teacher*) ‖ *poor* (*health, workmanship, reputation*); ⟨Am fam a.⟩ *ornery* (f *ordinary*) ‖ (gemein) *common, vile, low* ‖ (erbärmlich) *wretched* ‖ (böse) *wicked* | äußerst ~ *desperate* (*night*) ‖ ~ u billig *cheap and poor quality* ‖ ~ (= schlicht) u recht *plain and honest*, → II. ‖ nicht ~! *not* (*so* od *half*) *bad* od *dusty*! (joke) *that's a good one*! ‖ wie ~! *bad show*! ‖ ziemlich ~ *very indifferent* **B.** (**Absatz**) ⟨com⟩ *heavy* ‖ ~e Aussichten *poor prospects* ‖ ~e Behandlung *illtreatment* ‖ ~es Benehmen *misconduct* ‖ ~es Deutsch sprechen *to sp. G. indifferently* ‖ ~er Einfluß *infection* ‖ *lame* (*excuse*) ‖ (**Geld**) *base* ‖ v ~em Geschmack *bad tasting* (*medicine*); (*a man*) *of false taste* ‖ (*house*) *of ill-fame* ‖ (Hirsch) .. *with poor antlers* ‖ ~er Laune [gen] s *to be out of h.* ‖ ~er Leiter ⟨phys⟩ *non-conductor* ‖ (**Luft**) *foul* ‖ (Papiere) *worthless* ‖ *poor* (Patient) ‖ (Schulden) *dubious* ‖ v der ~esten Seite sehen *to see .. at his* (*its*) *worst* ‖ (Sicht, Trost) *poor* ‖ ~e Verdauung *indigestion* ‖ ~e Verteilung *maldistribution* ‖ ~e Verwaltung *misconduct* ‖ (Ware) *inferior* ‖ (Wetter) *bad, foul, vile* ‖ (Zeiten) *hard* **II.** [**adv**] *badly* (*weighed, lit*) ‖ (*to hear*) *badly* ‖ *ill-*(*assorted, fitting, tasting*) | ~ **angeschrieben s** *to be in bad odour* (bei *with*), .. bei .. *to be in a p's bad books* ‖ ~ aufgelegt s *to be in a bad temper* ‖ ~ ausfallen *to miscarry, to turn out badly* ‖ jdn ~ behandeln *to maltreat, mistreat a p* ‖ sich [acc] ~ benehmen *to misbehave*, (großtuerisch) *to play up* ‖ ~ denken v *to think ill of* ‖ von jdm ~ denken *to think evil of a p* ‖ ~ u recht *after a fashion*; sich [acc] ~ u recht durchschlagen *to crack a crust* ‖ es wird ihm ~ **ergehen** *it will go hard with him* ‖ (v Schiff) ~ fahren *to be a poor sailor* ‖ ~ führen *to mismanage* ‖ (Uhr) ~ gehen *to keep bad time* (→ gehen) ‖ ~ gezielte Schüsse *ill-directed bullets* ‖ etw f sehr ~ halten, als ~ hinstellen *to make the worst of it* ‖ ~ laufen **können** *to be bad at running* ‖ ⟨aero⟩ ~ landen *to make a bad landing* ‖ (jdn) ~ m *to slander, backbite* ‖ nicht so ~ wie sein Ruf *not so black as he is painted* ‖ mir **ist** ~ *I feel poorly* od *ill* ‖ ~ **s** in etw *to be poor at* (*drawing*) ‖ ~ daran s wegen *to be the worse for* ‖ ~ singen *to sing out of tune* ‖ er staunte **nicht** ~ *he was not a little surprised* ‖ jdn ~er stellen *to worsen a p* ‖ sich ~ unterhalten .. *poorly* ‖ ~ **w** *to turn bad*, (Bier) *to go off*, (Zahn) *to decay*; (P) *to go to the bad*; *to lose one's temper* ‖ dabei kann es e–m ~ w *it upsets one* ‖ ~er w *to deteriorate* | (nicht) **~er** daran s als *to be* (*no*) *worse off than* **III. der, die** ≃e *the wicked p* od *one* ‖ **das** ≃e *the bad th* ‖ *evil ths* ‖ das ≃e daran *the bad side of it* ‖ alles ≃e reden v *to say everything bad about* od *of* | **~denkend** a *evilminded* **~erdings** [adv] *positively, absolutely, by all means* ‖ ~ nicht *by no means* ‖ ich muß ~ *I must needs* (*do it*), *I'm bound to* (*do it*), *I can't help* (*doing*) *it* **~h·in, ~w·eg** [adv] *simply, plainly*; (*science*, etc) *as such in any case* ‖ ein A. ~ *a plain agnostic* ≃**wetter** n *adverse w.* | ≃-Landeverfahren [n] *instrument landing system* (*ILS*); ≃lage [f] *adverse w.*; ≃-Versicherung [f] *weather insurance* **~wüchsig** a ⟨for⟩ *unthrifty*

schl·echter- ≃stellung [f] *discrimination, being placed in a worse position*; ~gestellt [a] (*economically*) *handicapped* | **Schl·echtigkeit** f ~/~en **1.** *meanness, baseness*; *wickedness, iniquity* **2.** *vile action, base* od *evil deed*

schl·ecken etc = lecken etc

Schl·egel m ~s/~ ⟨tech⟩ *flapper, maul, mallet, beetle* ‖ ⟨min⟩ *sledge*; ⟨sculp⟩ *s.*(*-hammer*); ~ u Eisen ⟨min⟩ *mallet and gat* ‖ ⟨mus⟩ *drumstick* ‖ ⟨sport⟩ *bat* ‖ ⟨cul⟩ *leg*

Schl·eh- **~dorn** m ⟨bot⟩ *sloe-tree, blackthorn* ≃**w·eiß** a *white as sloe-blossoms* **Schlehe** f ~/~n *sloe, wild plum* **Schle·hen-** **~blüte** f *sloe-blossom* **~busch, ~strauch** m *sloe-tree* **~likör** m *sloe-gin*

Schl·eich- **~fieber** n *slow fever* **~gut** n *contraband, smuggled goods* pl **~handel** m *black marketing* ‖ ⟨allg⟩ *illicit* (od *sneak-*)*trade* ‖ ~ treiben *to s.le* **~händler** m *black marketeer*, → Schieber A 2 **~katze** f = Ichneumon, Mungo, Palmenroller, Zibetkatze **~patrouille** f *secret patrol* **~propaganda, ~werbung** f *covert, suggestive p.* **~treppe** f *backstair* **~ware** f *smuggled merchandise* **~weg** m ⟨fig⟩ *secret way, crooked path*; *subterfuge* ‖ auf ~en *furtively, stealthily* **schl·eichen** vi [schlich/geschlichen] [s] *to sneak, slink, creep, catfoot* ‖ *to slip, sidle* ‖ (T) *to prowl* ‖ (Fluß, Zeit, Uhrzeiger) *to crawl, drag* ‖ sich davon|~ *to steal away* od *off* ‖ sich hinein|~ *to steal in* ‖ im Finstern ~ *to prowl in the dark* ‖ umher|~ *to skulk* ‖ geschlichen k *to come sneaking along* **schl·eichend** a *sneaking, creeping* ‖ *prowling* (*steps*) ‖ ⟨fig⟩ *lingering* (*disease*) ‖ (heimlich) *furtive* ‖ ⟨med⟩ *slow* (*poison*), *low* (*fever*), *subtle* (*poison*) **Schl·eicher** m ~s/~ *creeper*; ⟨fig⟩ (P) *weasel* ‖ *sneak*(*ing fellow*), *sneaker, intriguer* **~·ei** f ~/~en *sneaking, clandestine practice* **Schl·eie** f ~/~n ⟨ich⟩ *tench*

Schl·eier m ~s/~ *veil* (⟨ec⟩ nehmen *to take*) ‖ *film, haze, mist* ‖ ⟨phot⟩ *fog, halo* ‖ ⟨glass⟩ *blur* ‖ ⟨übtr⟩ (Schützen≃, Sicherungs≃, Rauch≃) *screening* ‖ ⟨fig⟩ unter dem ~ [gen] *under the guise of* ‖ den ~ lüften ⟨fig⟩ *to lift the lid* [nur abs] **~eule** f ⟨orn⟩ *barn-owl* **~flor** m *crape* ≃**haft** a *like a veil* ‖ ⟨fig⟩ *mysterious, obscure* ‖ das ist mir ~ *that beats me, it's a mystery to me* **~haube** f *crape cap* **~lehen** n *petticoat hold* **~tanz** m *skirt-dance* **~tuch** n *lawn* **~wolke** f *scarf cloud*

Schl·eif- **~antenne** f ⟨wir⟩ *trailing antenna* **~bahn** f *slide* **~band** n ⟨tech⟩ *sand belt* **~bank** f *grinding-lathe* **~bügel** m ⟨el⟩ *sliding-bow* **~feder** f ⟨el⟩ *earth-terminal* **~holz** n ⟨pap⟩ *pulp wood* **~knoten** m *slip-knot*, ⟨mar⟩ *running k.* **~kontakt** m ⟨el⟩ *sliding c.* **~lade** f (der Orgel) *sounding-board* **~maschine, ~scheibe** f *grinding machine, g.g wheel* **~mühle** f *grinding-mill* **~note** f ⟨mus⟩ *slurred note* **~papier** n *abrasive p.* **~paste** f *emery-p.* **~rad** n *polishing-wheel* **~sand** m *fine s.* **~schritt** m (Tanz) *glissade* **~spur** f *trail* (*of a slug*); ⟨bes mot⟩ *drag mark* **~stahl** m *sharpening st.* **~stein** m *whetstone*, (drehbarer) *grindstone* **~zeug** n *grinding* od *polishing tools* pl **Schl·eife** f ~/~n (gebundene ~) *slip-knot* ‖ (Band≃) *bow, knot* ‖ (Schlips) *tie* ‖ (Schlinge) *noose* ‖ (Kurve) *horseshoe bend*; *loop* ⟨a. aero⟩: e–e ~ m *to loop the loop* ‖ (Öse) *eye* ‖ (Schlitten) *sledge, drag* ‖ ⟨tech⟩ *loop*(*-line*) ‖ ⟨comp⟩ *automatic iteration*; *cycle, loop* **Schl·eifen** n ~s/ *grinding* ‖ (Fein≃) *polishing* ‖ *setting* ‖ ⟨mot⟩ ~ der Kupplung *slipping of the clutch* **schl·eifen I.** vt/i [h] *to draw, drag*(*gle*), *trail* ‖ (Festung) *to dismantle, raze* ‖ (Zügel) ~ l *to slacken* ‖ ⟨mus⟩ *to slur, tie* | vi [h] *to slide, glide* ‖ ⟨hunt/orn⟩ *to dance* ‖ mit den Schuhen ~ *to shuffle one's boots* **II.** vt [schliff/geschliffen] [h] *to whet, grind* ⟨a. fig⟩ ‖ (fein ~) *to polish* ⟨a. fig⟩; (matt ~) *to rough* ‖ (Edelstein, Kristall) *to cut* ‖ (Rasiermesser abstreichen) *to set, hone* ‖ (Holz) ⟨pap⟩ *to grind* | ⟨fig⟩; (P) *to polish*, ⟨fam⟩ *to lick into shape* ‖ er muß geschliffen w *he wants polish* od *bullying* ‖ ⟨übtr⟩ scharf g. *sharpedged* (*tongue, words*), *delicately polished* (*verses*) **Schl·eifen-** **~fahrt** f, **~flug** m *loop, looping* (*the loop*) **~schaltung** f ⟨el⟩ *loop connection* **~vorbereitung** f ⟨comp⟩ *setting* **Schl·eifer** m ~s/~ *grinder, polisher* ‖ (v Edelsteinen) *cutter* ‖ ⟨mus⟩ *slurred note, colorature* ‖ (Walzer) *slow waltz* **~·ei** f [abstr] *grinding* (*-trade*) ‖ [konkr] *grinding mill* ⟨a. pap⟩ **~krankheit** f *silicosis* **Schl·eifung** f ~/~en **1.** *grinding* **2.** *slur*(*ring*) **3.** ⟨fort⟩ *dismantling* **Schl·eifsel** n ~s/ *shreds, clippings* pl

Schleim m ~(e)s/~e *slime* ⟨a. sex⟩ ‖ ⟨med⟩ *phlegm*; *mucus* L ‖ ⟨chem, bot⟩ *mucilage* **~absonderung** f ⟨med⟩ *mucous secretion* ≃**artig** a *mucous* **~auswurf** m *expectoration* **~drüse** f ⟨anat⟩ *mucous gland, glandule* **~fieber** n *mucous fever* **~fisch** m *blenny* **~fluß** m *blennorrhoea* **~haut** f ⟨anat⟩ *mucous membrane* | ~entzündung [f] *mycodermitis*; ~gewebetumor [m] ⟨path⟩ *myxoma* **~höhle** f ⟨anat⟩ *mucous cavity* **≃lösend** a *expectorant* [a. subst] **~säure** f ⟨med⟩ *mucic acid* **~suppe** f *thick gruel* **~zucker** m *glucose* **schl·eimen** vi [h] **1.** *to cause slime* od *phlegm* **2.** *to grow slimy* od *viscous* **schl·eimig** a *slimy* ⟨a. fig⟩ ‖ ⟨med⟩ *mucous* ‖ ⟨chem⟩ *mucilaginous* | **≃keit** f ~/ *sliminess* ‖ ⟨med⟩ *mucosity*

Schl·eiße f ~/~n **1.** *splint(er)* **2.** *quill* (*of a feather*) **schl·eißen I.** vt [schliß/geschlissen] [h] *to slit, to split* ‖ *to strip* (*quills, the bark of trees*) **II.** vi [s] *to be worn out by use, to wear out* | ~d *abrasive* (Material), ~des M. *material with abrasive character* **schleißfest** a *wear-resisting*

Schlemm m ~s/~e ⟨cards⟩ ≃ m *to make a slam*

schl·emmen vi [h] *to levigate, carouse, gormandize, revel* **Schl·emmer** m ~s/~ *gormandizer, glutton, reveller*; *stodger*; *good* od *high liver, free-liver*; (verweichlicht) *sybarite* ‖ **~-** *gastronomic* **~·ei** f ~/~en *gormandising, revelry, gluttony* **~lokal** n *lobster palace* **Schl·empe** f ~/~n **1.** ⟨agr⟩ *mash, slops* pl **2.** *refuse, swill* (⟨a.⟩ Gesöff) **3.** *distiller's wash* **4.** (Gärungs≃) *vinasse*

schl·endern vi [s] *to saunter, lounge, loiter* (herum *about*), dahin ~ *to jog along* ‖ ~ nach *to amble to* **Schl·endrian** m ~(e)s/ (alter *familiar*) *routine, old custom, old jog-trot, beaten track* ‖ (amtlicher) *red-tapism* ‖ in den alten ~ verfallen *to fall into the old groove*

schl·enkern vi/t [h] *to shamble, dangle* | vi (P) *to roll* ‖ die Beine *or* mit den Beinen ~ *to swing one's legs* | vt *to shake off, to fling, toss, jerk* | ~d *jerky* (*gesture*)

Schlepp m ~(e)s/ ⟨aero⟩ *glide-towing*; ⟨mar⟩ in ~ nehmen ⟨a. fig⟩ *to take in tow* ‖ im ~ h ⟨a. fig⟩ *to have in tow* **~antenne** f ⟨aero⟩ *drag* od *trailing aerial* **~boot** n *tug(-boat)* **~dampfer** m (*steam-*)*tug* **~degen** m *sabre* **~flug** m *towed flight* **~flugzeug** n *tug* (*for gliders*), *tow plane* **~jagd** f *drag-hunt* **~kahn** m *towed boat* **~kasten** m ⟨min⟩ *sledge* **~kette** f *drag-chain* **~kleid** n *dress with a train* **~kraft** f ⟨tech⟩ *tractive force, drawing power* **~laternen** f pl *towing lights* pl **~lift** m ⟨ski⟩ *skimobile* **~lohn** m ⟨mar⟩ *towage* **~netz** n *drag-net*; *seine* ‖ (Grundnetz) *trawl(-net)*; dazu: *to trawl*; *trawling* | ~fischer [m] *dragger, trawler* **~pflug** m *drag-plough* **~säbel** m *cavalry sabre*; ⟨fam⟩ *dangler* **~sack** m ⟨mar⟩ *drogue*; ⟨aero⟩ *sleeve-target* **~schiff** n *tug(-boat)* | ~(f)ahrt [f] *navigation with tugs* **~seil, ~tau** n, **~trosse** f **1.** [act Bdtg] ⟨aero, mar⟩ *drag-rope, tail* od *tow(ing)-rope*; ⟨artill⟩ *drag-rope*; ⟨mot⟩ (Ab≃) *tow-rope* **2.** [pass Bdtg] (am Freiballon) *guide-, trail-rope*; ins ~ nehmen ⟨a. fig⟩ *to take in tow*; sich ins ~ n. l *to be taken in tow* **~wagen** m *truck* **~zielbeschuß** m *towed target firing* **~zug** m ⟨mar⟩ *train of barges* **Schl·eppe** f ~/~n *train* (*of a dress*), *trail* **schl·eppen I.** vt/i [h] *to drag* (a. sich *o.s.*); (S) *to drag, to trail* ‖ ⟨mar⟩ *to tow, tug* (*barges*); ~ in *to nurse into*; *to draw* (*nets*); *to drag* (*the anchor*) ‖ (v Kleid) *to draggle on the ground* ‖ (jdn) *to lug*; sich mühsam ~ *to plod along* ‖ ⟨com⟩ (Kunden werben) *to tout* ‖ sich ~ **mit** *to be burdened* (⟨fig⟩ *troubled*) *with* ‖ sich **müde** ~ *to tire o.s. with dragging* ‖ **vor** den Richter ~ *to haul a p before ..* | sich ~ zu .. *to crawl to ..* **II.** ≃ n ⟨mar⟩ *towing, towage* **schl·eppend** a ⟨fig⟩ *languid, heavy*; *flagging, halting* (*gait, style*) ‖ ⟨bes a. com⟩ *lagging, dilatory* ‖ (Sprache) *drawling* (dazu: *drawl, to drawl*); *slow* (*conversation*) ‖ *wearisome* (*method*) ‖ ⟨com, mus⟩ *dragging, slow* **≃e(s)** n *drag* **Schl·eppenträger** m *train-bearer* ‖ ⟨fig⟩ *henchman* **Schl·epper** m ~s/~ **1.** ⟨mar & aero⟩ *tug* **2.** ⟨mot⟩ (*haulage*) *tractor*; *trail, truck* **3.** (Kunden≃) *tout*; (Gaunerspr.) *tout, shill* **4.** ⟨min⟩ (P) *hauler, hurrier* | **~·ei** f ~/~en *dragging* ‖ ⟨fig⟩ *drudgery, toiling*; *burden* **Schl·eppung** f ~/~en ⟨geol⟩ *drag, bending*

Schl·esien n ⟨†Ger⟩ *Silesia* **Schl·esier** m, **~in** f, **schl·esisch** a *Silesian*

Schl·eswig n ⟨Ger⟩ (Stadt) *Slesvic, Sleswick, Schleswig* **~er(in** f) m *inhabitant of Sleswick, Sleswicker* **~-H·olstein** n ⟨Ger⟩ (Land)

Schl·euder f ~/~n *sling(shot* ⟨Am⟩), *catapult* ‖ Wäsche≃ *dryer* **~artikel** m, **~ware** f ⟨com⟩ *catch-penny article* **~gefahr** f ⟨mot⟩ *danger of skidding* **~geschäft** n *cutting trade* **~guß** m *rotary process* **~honig** m *strained h.* **~kraft** f *centrifugal force* **~maschine** f *centrifuge, separator* (*of milk*); ⟨mil, aero⟩ *catapult* **~preis** m *ruinous* (od ⟨sl⟩ *knock-out*) *price* ‖ zu ~en *dirt cheap*, (Ausfuhr) *dumping* **~sitz** m ⟨aero⟩ *ejector seat* **~spur** f ⟨mot⟩ *skid mark* **~start** m ⟨aero⟩ *catapult take-off* **~stein** m *slingstone* **~trommel** f *rotating drum* **~versuch** m *centrifuging test* **Schl·euderer** m ~s/~ *slinger* ‖ ⟨fig⟩ *underseller*; (ins Ausland) *dumper* **schl·eudern I.** vt [h] *to sling, throw, toss, fling, hurl, shoot* ‖ hoch|~ *to toss up* | ⟨fig⟩ *to fling away, to sell at ruinous prices*; *to undersell, dump* **II.** vi [h] *to swing* ‖ ⟨mot⟩ *to skid, fling, side-slip* ‖ ⟨mach⟩ *to shake*

schl·eunig a *quick, speedy, prompt* ‖ [adv] *in all haste* ‖ aufs ~ste *with the utmost expedition* od *dispatch, as quickly as possible* **≃keit** f ~/ *speed, quickness, swiftness, promptness*

Schl·euse f ~/~n *sluice* ⟨a. fig⟩, *lock*; *water gate*; (Luft≃ ⟨a–n⟩ *air lock*) ‖ (im Krematorium) ⟨crem⟩ *transfer chamber* ‖ (unter der Straße) *drain* ‖ ⟨fig a.⟩ *flood-gates* pl ‖ die ~n öffnen (weinen) *to turn the tap on* **schl·eusen** vt [h] *to lock* (*a canal, a ship*) **Schl·eusen- ~geld** n *sluice-dues* pl, *lock charges* pl **~flügel** m *flood-gate* **~meister** m *lock-keeper, locksman, sluice-master* **~räumer** m *cleanser of a sluice* od *drain* **~tor** n *flood-gate*; hinteres ~ *tailgate*, unteres ~ *aft gate* **~wärter** m *lockman* **~wehr** n *lock-weir* **~werk** n *lock, lockage*

schlich 1. & 3. sg pret v schleichen **Schlich** m ~(e)s/~e **1.** *the ins and outs* (*of a house*) **2.** ⟨fig⟩ *trick, dodge, game, artifice* ‖ ⟨fam⟩ *hanky-panky* ‖ ~e [pl] *guile* (*of policy*) ‖ die ~e kennen *to know a move or two* ‖ jds ~e durchschauen *or* kennen *to be up to a p's tricks* ‖ hinter jds ~e k *to find out a p('s tricks, wiles), to see a p through* **3.** (= Schlick) ‖ ⟨met⟩ *slick*

schlicht [a] *plain, simple* (*dress, p*), *homely, unpretentious* (*manners*); *quiet* (*dress*) ‖ *unvarnished* (*truth*) ‖ *unpretentious* (*people, speech*) ‖ *plain, straightforward* (*man*) ‖ ~er Menschenverstand *common sense* | (glatt) *smooth, sleek* (*hair*) ‖ ~er Abschied (*curt*) *dismissal* | ~e Schönheit (e–r Frau, ⟨arts, etc⟩) *beauty unadorned* | [adv] ~ um ~ *free board and lodging for work done* **≃beil** n ⟨carp⟩ *chip-axe* **≃feile** f *smooth(ing)-file* **~gleitsitz** m ⟨tech⟩ *plane sliding* **≃hammer** m *planishing-hammer* **≃hobel** m *jointing-, smoothing-plane* **~passung** f ⟨tech⟩ *medium fit* **≃stahl** m *finishing tool* **Schl·ichte** f ~/~n ⟨weav⟩ *glue, size, dressing* ‖ *facing material* ‖ ⟨met⟩ *black-wash* **schl·ichten** vt [h] *to plane, level, smooth(e)* ‖ ⟨met⟩ *to planish, polish* ‖ ⟨weav⟩ *to size, dress* | ⟨fig⟩ *to arrange, adjust* ‖ (e–n Streit etc) *to compose, adjust, settle, to make up*; ⟨jur⟩ *to compromise* **Schl·ichter** m ~s/~ *arbitrator, referee*; ⟨jur⟩ *conciliatory officer* **Schl·ichtheit** f ~/~en *smoothness* ‖ *plainness, simplicity, homeliness* ‖ *unpretentiousness* **Schl·ichtung** f ~/~en *smoothing* ‖ ⟨fig⟩ *composition, settlement, compromise* **~samt** n *arbitration board*, ⟨soc⟩ *B. of A. and Conciliation* **~sausschuß** m *arb. committee, Court of conciliation* **~sbestimmungen** f pl (im Tarifvertrag) *conciliation provisions* **~sinstanzen** f pl *facilities for settling differences* **~swesen** n *system of arbitration*

Schlick m ~(e)s/~e *silt, slime, mud*; ⟨mar⟩ *ooze* **≗erig** a *muddy, oozy* **~grund** m ⟨mar⟩ *oozy bottom* **~laufen** n *walking on the mud-flat* (*between coast and island*) **~watt** n *oozy beach*

Schl·ickermilch f *curdled milk*

schlief 1. & 3. sg pret v schlafen

schl·iefen vi [schloff/geschloffen] [s] ⟨hunt⟩ *to crawl, creep, glide* **Schl·iefer** m ~s/~ ⟨hunt⟩ *terrier*; *badger*; → Klipp≗

Schl·iere f ~/~n *streak* ⟨a. phot, geol⟩ ‖ ~n ⟨glass⟩ *schlieren* **schl·ierig** a ⟨phot⟩ *streaky*

Schl·ieß- **~anker** m *brace, cramp-iron* **~band** n *hasp* **~baum** m *bar, barrier, beam*; ⟨mar⟩ *boom* **~fach** n *post(-office)* od *private box* ‖ *safe*; *locker* **~feder** f (Tür) *spring-bolt*; (Uhr) *locking-spring* **~geviert** n ⟨typ⟩ *M-quadrate* **~haken** *catch* (*of a lock*); ⟨bookb, tail⟩ *clasp* **~kette** f *barring-chain* **~klappe** f *boltlock*; (Buch≗) *staple* **~kontakt** m ⟨el⟩ *make c.* **~korb** m *hamper with lock* **~muskel** m ⟨anat⟩ *contractor, sphincter* **~rahmen** m ⟨typ⟩ *chase* **~riegel** m *dead-bolt* **~säge** f *sash saw* **schl·ießbar** a **1.** *capable of being shut* od *locked* **2.** ⟨log⟩ *inferable, deducible* **Schl·ieße** f ~/~n *fastening-pin* od *-bolt*; *buckle* ‖ ⟨bookb, tail⟩ *clasp* **schl·ießen** [schloß/geschlossen] [h] **A. I.** vt **1.** *to shut, close* (*door, eyes*) ‖ (mit Schloß) *to lock* ‖ (wieder) *to relock*; ⟨tech⟩ *to lock* **2.** *to finish, end* **3.** *to form* (*an alliance*) **II.** sich ~ *to shut, close* ‖ (Wunde) *to heal up* ‖ sich an–e–a ~ *to draw closely together, to crowd* **III.** vi **1.** *the door shuts* (v selbst *by itself*) ‖ (Buch) *to end* ‖ (Rede) *to end, close, terminate, to wind up* (mit *with*) ‖ (Markt) *to close* ‖ (Parlament, Schule) *to break up* ‖ (Geschäfte, Wirtshäuser) *to close* (*down*) ‖ indem ich schließe *in conclusion*, (*I* ..) **2.** *to fit* od *join well* ‖ *the key does not fit the lock* **3.** (folgern) *to conclude* (daß *that*) **B.** (vt) die **Augen** vor etw ~ *to blink a th* ‖ (Betrieb) *to close down* ‖ die Beweisaufnahme ~ ⟨jur⟩ *to rest one's case* ‖ (Brief) *to conclude* ‖ (**Debatte,** Geschäft, Versammlung) *to close* ‖ (Ehe) *to contract, conclude* ‖ *to contract a friendship* = *to make friends* (*with*) ‖ **Frieden** ~ *to make* (od *conclude a*) *peace* ‖ (Handel) *to conclude* od *strike* (*a bargain*) ‖ ⟨gram⟩ (Klammer) *to close* ‖ ⟨fig⟩ (Kluft) *to bridge over* ‖ (Konto) *to balance* ‖ (Kreis) *to form* ‖ den **Laden** ~ *to shut up shop* ‖ ⟨parl⟩ (Debatte) *to closure* ‖ (Reihen, ⟨el⟩ Stromkreis) *to close* ‖ (Vereinbarung, Vertrag) *to conclude* ‖ e–n Vergleich ~ *to come to an agreement* ‖ ⟨mil⟩ den Zug ~ *to bring up the rear* **C.** [vt/i] **an**: *to add* (*a remark*) *to* ‖ *to press to* (*one's heart*) ‖ sich ~ an *to be followed by*; *following the lecture a dinner took place* ‖ ~ l **auf** *to infer* (*a th*); *to suggest* (*a th*; *that*); *to point to* | **aus**: *to conclude, infer, judge, reason, gather, deduce, assume from* .. (daß *that*) | **hinter**: *the door closed on him* | jdn, etw **in** [acc] ~ *to lock .. up in* ‖ *to clasp in one's arms* (= *to embrace*) ‖ ins Herz ~ *to take a fancy* od *liking to* ‖ in **sich** ~ *to comprehend, include, involve, imply, implicate, encompass, connote, entail* | **mit**: (in Reden) *to wind up with*; *he concluded by asking* ‖ ⟨exch⟩ *stocks closed at 98* | **von** .. auf: ⟨philos⟩ *to argue from a th to a th*; *to judge of a th from a th* ‖ *I infer* od *deduce her character from her dress* | v **sich** auf andere ~ *to judge others by o.s.*; *to argue from o.s. to the general*; *to measure another's foot by one's own last* **D. geschlossen**: *complete, absolute* (*whole*) ‖ *complete* (*personality*) ‖ *private* (*party*) ‖ *serried* (*ranks*) ‖ ⟨hunt⟩ *close* (*season*); g–ne Jagd *preserve* | [adv] *in a body* ‖ g–n für etw s *or* stimmen *to go* od *be solid for* **schl·ießend** a ⟨mil⟩ *supernumerary* (*officer*) ‖ ⟨hors⟩ e–n ~en Sitz h *to have a firm seat, to sit one's horse well* | ≗**e(r)** m ⟨mil⟩ *trail officer* **Schl·ießer** m ~s/~ *doorkeeper* | *jailer, turnkey* **~in** f ~/~nen *doorkeeper* | (Schaffnerin) *house-keeper* **schl·ießlich** [adv] *lastly, finally, in conclusion, in the end* od *event, at last, ultimately*; ⟨fig⟩ *after all* ‖ *he ended by doing it h.s.*; *in the long run eventually*; ~ zu etw gelangen *to end* od *wind up in*; ~ m Sie es sowieso, warum nicht jetzt? .. *eventually, why not now*?; ~geraten in *to end up in* (*prison*, etc) **Schl·ießung** f ~/~en *shutting, closing* ‖ ⟨fig⟩ *conclusion* ‖ (e–r Versammlung) *breaking-up, rising* ‖ ⟨parl⟩ (der Debatte) *closure*

Schliff m ~(e)s/~e ⟨a. fig⟩ [abstr] *polish* ‖ (v Edelsteinen) *cut*; *grinding* (*of lenses*) ‖ [konkr] ⟨pap⟩ (*mechanical*) *wood pulp* | e–r S den letzten ~ geben *to put the final touch to a th* | ~e [pl] ⟨geol⟩ *polish* **~stopfen** m *ground-in stopper* **schliff** 1. & 3. sg pret v schleifen

schlimm I. [a] **A. 1.** *bad* [compr: *worse*, sup: *worst*], *sad, evil* **2.** (krank) (P) [pred] *ill, bad, low* ‖ *bad* (*finger*), *sore* (*eyes, throat*) **3.** (heftig) *severe* (*cold*), *serious* (*wound*) **4.** (übel) *sick, unwell* **5.** (unangenehm) *disagreeable, annoying, unpleasant* (*news, experiences*), *troublesome* (*cough*) | *disquieting* (*omen, conditions*) **6.** *naughty* **7.** *wicked, malicious* **8.** ⟨fam⟩ *desperate* (*night*; *fear, fool*) **B.** noch ~er *worse yet*; immer ~er *worse and worse* ‖ um so *or* desto ~er *all* (od *so much*) *the worse*; *worse luck*! ‖ am ~sten *worst* | ~er **m** *to aggravate* ‖ das ist nicht (so) ~ *it doesn't* (*much*) *matter* ‖ es ist ~ f ihn *it is hard on him* ‖ immer ~er **w** *to go from bad to worse* ‖ es wird ~ w, wenn nicht *it will go hard but* **C. Dinge:** ⟨fig⟩ *to say bad ths of a p* ‖ im ~sten Fall, ~stenfalls *at* (*the*) *worst, if the worst comes* (*came*) *to the worst* ‖ Geschichte ⟨fig⟩ *a bad job* ‖ **Geselle**: *ugly customer, nasty fellow* ‖ Lage: *in great straits, in a sorry plight* ‖ v der ~sten Seite: *to see the dark side* (*of everything*) ‖ (Verbrecher) *desperate* ‖ e–e ~e Wendung nehmen *to take a turn to the worse* ‖ (Zeiten) *hard*; die letzte Zeit war ~ *it's been tough going lately* ‖ Zustände: *a bad state of ths* **II.** [**adv**] *I cut m.s. badly* ‖ die S steht ~ *the matter looks bad* ‖ es steht ~ um ihn *he is in a sorry plight* ‖ treibt's so ~ ihr wollt! *do your worst*! es geht ihm ~, er ist ~ dran *he is in a bad way, he is badly* (am ~sten *the worst*) *off*, ⟨fam⟩ *he's up a tree* ‖ ⟨fam⟩ *I don't look too foul, do I*? ‖ ⟨fam a.⟩ = sehr: °~ hinter etw her s *to be mad after a th* **III.** ≗**es** [n] *erleiden* ⟨fam⟩ *to go through the hoop* ≗**eres:** *worse followed*; *worse befell them* **IV. der, das** ≗**ste**: er ist nicht der ≗ste *he is not one of the worst sort* | das ≗ste daran *the worst of it* ‖ das ist das ≗ste! *that's where it is*! ‖ aber das ≗ste v allem *but worst of all* (*was* ..) **~stenfalls** adv *if the worst comes to the worst*

Schl·ing- **~beschwerden** f [pl] *difficulty in swallowing* **~gewächs** n, **~pflanze** f ⟨bot⟩ *creeper, climbing plant, climber, rambler* **~stich** m *close stitch* | ~borte [f] *scallops* pl **Schl·inge** f ~/~n *loop, bight* (*of rope*) ‖ (Schleife) *running knot*; (z Tragen) *lanyard* ‖ (z Auf- & Zuziehen) *noose, slip-knot* ‖ ⟨hunt⟩ *wire, snare* (legen *to lay*), (Vogel≗) *springe* ‖ ⟨skating⟩: *loop-change-loop* ‖ ⟨surg⟩ *sling* ‖ in der ~ fangen *to snare* ‖ ⟨fig⟩ jdm in die ~ gehen *to fall into a p's trap*; jdm aus der ~ helfen *to get a p off*; sich aus der ~ ziehen *to have a lucky escape*, ⟨fam⟩ *to get off the hook, to slip the collar*

Schl·ingel m ~s/~ *rascal, rogue, jackanapes* ‖ *naughty boy* ‖ (kl) *pickle*; fauler ~ *lazy-bones* **~·ei** f *rascality, impudence* ‖ *roguish trick* **schl·ingen** vt/i [schlang/geschlungen] [h] **1.** *to swallow greedily*; *to devour, gulp, gorge, raven* ⟨fam⟩ *gobble, bolt* **2.** (winden) *to wind, twist, loop*; *fling* (*one's arms round a p*) | **sich** ~ (um) *to wind* od *twine* (*round*), ⟨bot⟩ *to creep* (*round*) **Schl·inger-** [in comp] ⟨mar⟩ *anti-rolling* **~blech** n ⟨mot⟩

baffle plate, ⟨aero⟩ *baffle* **~dämpfeinlage** f *stabilizer(s)* **~kiel** m *bilge keel* **~kreisel** m *gyroscopic stabilizer* **~wülste** m [pl] *a.-r. bulges* pl
schl·ingern vi [h] ⟨mar⟩ *to roll, lurch* | ≗ n *lurch*; Schiff z ~ bringen *to set .. rolling*
°**Schl·ippchen** n ⟨sex fam⟩ *judy; slut,* ⟨sl⟩ *broad*
Schl·ippe f ~/~n *narrow passage* od *lane*
schl·ippen vt [h] ⟨mar⟩ *to slip (a cable)*
Schlips m ~es/~e *(neck-)tie, scarf* ‖ (Querbinder) *bow* **~halter** m *tie-rack*
schl·itteln vt [h] (Holz ~) *to sledge,* ⟨Am⟩ *to sled* **Schl·itten** m ~s/~ **1.** *sledge* ‖ (für Lasten) *sled* ‖ (Pferde≗) *sleigh* ‖ (Rodel≗) *toboggan, luge* ‖ (Einsitzer) ⟨Am⟩ *cutter* ‖ ~ fahren *to luge; to go in a sledge;* ⟨Am⟩ *to coast down a hillside on a sled* ‖ °mit jdm ~ fahren *to ride roughshod over a p; to haul a p over the coals* ‖ ⟨fig⟩ unter dem ~ *under the harrow* ‖ unter den ~ k *to come to grief* | ⟨übtr hum⟩ = Auto **2.** ⟨tech⟩ *slide, sliding-carriage* ‖ ⟨mar⟩ (z Stapellauf) *ways* pl ‖ ⟨typewr⟩ *(paper-)carriage* **~bahn** f *sledge-course, -road; slide* ‖ es gibt bald ~ *there will soon be sledging* ≗|**fahren** vi [s] *to sledge* ‖ °mit jdm ~ ⟨fig⟩ → ~, jdn schurigeln **~fahrt** f *sleigh-ride, sledge-drive* **~führung** f ⟨tech⟩ *slide rail* **~geläute** n *sleigh-bells* pl **~kufe** f *runner* **~partie** f *sleighing-party* **~pferd** n *sledge-horse* **Schl·itt-** **~erbahn** f *slide,* ⟨Am⟩ *shoot* | ≗**ern** vi [h & s] *to slide, slither* ‖ ⟨fig⟩ ~ in *to slide into* ≗**erig** a *slithery* **~schuh** m ~(e)s/~e *skate* ‖ ~ laufen *to skate* | ~bahn [f] *skating-ground* | ~laufen [n] *(ice-)skating* (Ggs *roller-sk.*); ~läufer [m] *skater*
Schlitz m ~es/~e *slit, slash* ‖ (Geld–, Brief-Einwurf) *slot* ‖ (Spalt) *cleft, rift* ‖ (im Frauenrock) *placket-hole* ‖ °⟨sex⟩ *slit, gap, crevice; cunny* ‖ ⟨tech⟩ *(discharge,* etc) *opening* ‖ mit e–m ~ versehen *slotted* **~auge** n *slit eye* ≗**äugig** a *s.-e.d* **~blende** f ⟨phot⟩ *slotted diaphragm* **~fenster** n *gap-w.* **~flügel** m pl ⟨aero⟩ *slot(ted) wings* **~messer** m ⟨surg⟩ *lancet* **~mutter** f *slotted nut* **~rock** m *slit-skirt* **~verschluß** m ⟨phot⟩ *roller blind shutter* **schl·itzen** vt/i [h & s] *to slit, slash* ‖ geschlitzt *slit (eyes)* ‖ *slashed (sleeves)*
schl·ohweiß a *white as snow*
Schloß n ~sses/≗sser **1.** (Tür≗, Gewehr≗) *lock* ‖ (Vorhänge≗) *padlock* ‖ (Zylinder≗) *Yale lock* ‖ (Bücher≗, Handtaschen≗) *clasp* ‖ (Gürtel≗) *buckle* ‖ (Halsband≗) *snap* | ein ~ erbrechen *to pick a lock* ‖ hinter ~ u Riegel *behind bars, under lock and key; in durance vile* ‖ der Schlüssel steckt im ~ *the key is in the door* ‖ (die Tür) fällt ins ~ *.. clicks shut* ‖ er hat ein ~ vor dem Mund *his lips are sealed* **2.** ⟨zoo⟩ *hinge (of shells)* **3.** (Gebäude) *castle, château, palace; manor-house* (Gutshaus) **schloß** 1. & 3. sg pret schließen **~abzug** m *Château wine* **~aufseher** m *castellan* **~beamte(r)** m *officer in the castle* **~beschläge** m [pl], **~blech** n *lock-furniture, -plate, escutcheon* **~feder** f *spring of a l.* **~freiheit** f *(privileged) precincts* pl *of a c.* **~führung** f *l.-guide* **~garten** m *c.-garden* **~hauptmann** m *captain* od *governor of a c.* ‖ (bei Hofe) *Deputy-Master of the household* **~herr** m *lord* od *proprietor of a c.* ‖ (Gutsherr) *squire* **~herrin** f *lady of a c.* **~hof** m *c.-yard* **~kirche** f *c.-church* **~platz** m *c.-yard* **~riegel** m *bolt of a l.* **~tor** n *c.-gate* **~turm** m *c.-tower* **~vogt** m *keeper, castellan* **Schl·osser** m ~s/~ *locksmith* **~·ei** f *l.'s workshop* od *trade* **~arbeit** f *l.'s work* **~gesell(e)** m *journeyman l.* **~handwerk** n *l.'s trade* **~herberge** f *meeting-house for journeymen l.s* **~meister** m *master-l.* **~werkstatt** f *l.'s workshop* **Schl·ossern** n *lock-making*
Schl·oße (Hagel) f ~/~n *hail-stone* ‖ ~n [pl] *hail* sg | ≗**n** vi [imps] [h] *to hail* | **~n-** **~korn** n *hail-stone* **~wetter** n *hail-storm*
Schlot m ~(e)s/~e *chimney* ‖ ⟨rail, mar⟩ *funnel* | ⟨fig fam⟩ (P) *bounder* ⟨sl⟩; (Zylinderhut) ⟨sl⟩ *plug-hat* **~baron** m *cotton-lord* **~feger** m *chimney-sweep(er)*
Schl·otte f ~/~n *hollow stalk* ‖ ~n [pl] *leek-stalks*
schl·ott(e)rig a *shaking, shaky* ‖ *loose, flabby, limp* ‖ (nachlässig) *slovenly, slipshod* ‖ ~ gehen *to slouch* od *shuffle along* **schl·ottern** vi [h] *to wobble, totter, dodder; to hang loose;* vor Angst ~ *to quake* (über, vor *at*) | **~d** *shaky (limbs); shaking, wobbling (knees); jolting (carriage); slouching, shuffling (gait)* ‖ innerlich ~d *quaking inside*
Schlucht f ~/~en *gully, gorge, ravine; glen;* ⟨mil⟩ *defile* ‖ *canyon,* ⟨Am a.⟩ *coulee*
schl·uchzen vi [h] *to sob,* ⟨sl⟩ *snivel* | ≗ n, **Schluchzer** m *sobbing*
Schl·uck m ~(e)s/~e & ≗e *sup, mouthful* ‖ (kräftiger) *gulp, swig, quaff* ‖ (zu Trinken) *draught,* (kl) *sip, nip;* ⟨sl⟩ *tot (of whisky);* ~ Schnaps ⟨Am sl⟩ *a short one;* gr ⟨fam⟩ *a tall one;* e–n gr ~ tun aus *to drink deep(ly) of;* schnell *a quick one* ‖ (~ Wasser hinterher) ⟨Am⟩ *chaser* ‖ e–n ~ (übern Durst) nehmen ⟨fam⟩ *to have* od *take a drop (too much)* **~auf** m = –en **~impfung** f *oral vaccination* ≗**weise** adv *by* od *in sips, sip by sip; by mouthfuls,* etc | **Schl·ückchen** n ⟨übtr⟩ *tot*
Schl·ucken m ~s/~ *hiccup, hiccough* ‖ den ~ h *to hiccup* (⟨a.⟩ Schluckser) | ≗**en** vt/i [h] *to gulp* od *drink (down), to swallow* ‖ ⟨fig⟩ *to absorb; to pocket (an insult, the receipts)* ‖ dabei gibt's nicht viel zu ~! *(there is) not much money in that!* ‖ mehr ~ als man verdauen kann *to bite off more than one can chew* **Schl·ucker** m ~s/~ **1.** ⟨fig⟩ armer ~ *pauper; poor wretch; starveling* **2.** (⟨a.⟩ Schluckser) = Schlucken
°**Schluder·ei** f *sloppiness* **schl·uderig** a *floppy (style), slipshod (p)* | [adv] ~ ausführen *to scamp*
schl·udern vt/i [h] *to bungle*
Schluft f ~/≗e obd = Schlucht
schlug 1. & 3. sg pret v schlagen
Schl·ummer m ~s/ *slumber,* ⟨sl⟩ *snooze* ≗**betäubt** a *dulled, stupefied, stupid, numbed; torpid with* od *by sleep* **~kissen** n *head-rest* **~körner** n pl ⟨bot⟩ *poppy-seeds* pl **~lied** n *lullaby* **~punsch** m ⟨fam⟩ *nightcap* **~rolle** f *bolster, sofa-roll* **~trunk** m ⟨fam⟩ *sundowner, nightcap* | ≗**n** vi [h] *to slumber, doze, snooze, drowse* ‖ *to take one's forty winks* ‖ ⟨fig⟩ *to lie dormant* | ≗**nd** *latent (power)*
Schl·umpe f ~/~n ⟨vulg⟩ *slut, slattern* ≗**n** vi [h] *to hang* od *drag loosely* **schl·umpig** a *draggle-tailed, sluttish, slovenly,* → Schlampe, schlampig
Schl·und m ~(e)s/≗e ⟨anat⟩ *throat, gorge, gullet* | ⟨fig⟩ *maw (of death)* ‖ (Abgrund) *gulf, abyss* **~kopf** m ⟨anat⟩ *pharynx* | ~schnitt [m] ⟨surg⟩ *pharyngotomy* **~sonde** f ⟨surg⟩ *probang*
Schlupf m ~(e)s/≗e **1.** *slip(ping)* **2.** *running knot* **3.** *cover, refuge* **~hafen** m ⟨mar⟩ *creek, cove* **~hose** f *(a pair of) knickers, drawers* **~loch** n *loop-hole, lurking-place* **~wespe** f ⟨zoo⟩ *ichneumon(-fly)* **~winkel** m *recess; den; lurking-, hiding-place; sneak-hole, bolthole* ‖ ⟨dero⟩ *haunt* **schl·üpfen** vi [s] *to slip* (in *into* od *on* [adv] *a garment*) ‖ *to glide, slide* ‖ ⟨ent⟩ *to emerge* (aus *from*) **Schl·üpfer** m ~s/~ **1.** (Mantel) *ulster* **2.** (Hose) *(ladies') knick(er)s, drawers;* ⟨fam⟩ *panties;* (eng) *tighties;* (dünn) *scanties, nixies;* (kurz) *briefs* pl **3.** *jumper*
schl·üpf(e)rig a *slippery, slithery, eely* | ⟨fig⟩ *prurient, obscene, indecent; bawdy, ribald;* ⟨Am⟩ *slimy* ‖ *racy (joke); ticklish, precarious* | ~ m *to lubricate* ≗**keit** f ~/~en *slipperiness; lubricity* ⟨a. fig⟩ ‖ ⟨fig⟩ *pruriency, obscenity* ‖ *raciness* ‖ *ticklishness*
°**Schl·urf** m ~s/~e 1. → Geck 2. *loafer* 3. *beatnik* **schl·urfen,** ≗ vt [h] *to sip, lap,* ⟨Am⟩ *to slurp* | vi (a. schlurren) *to shuffle along* ‖ mit den Füßen ~ *to drag one's feet* | **-rig** a *slovenly* → schlampig

Schluß m –usses/–üsse **A. 1.** (Schließen) *shutting* etc **2.** (Passen) *fittingness* **3.** *end, conclusion*; ⟨school⟩ *breaking up* **4.** [konkr] *butt-end* ‖ ⟨arch⟩ *keystone* **5.** ⟨parl⟩ (Debatten≈) *closing*, (auf Antrag) *closure*, (vorher festgesetzt) *guillotine* ‖ ~ beantragen *to put the question* ‖ ~! *time*! **6.** Redaktions≈ *press date* **7.** (e–r Rede) *winding up*; *end*; *conclusion*; ⟨rhet⟩ *peroration*; *close* (*of a period*) **8.** ⟨telph⟩ ~! *that's all*! **9.** (e–s Vertrags) *conclusion* **10.** (Folgerung) *inference, conclusion*; *consequence* ‖ ⟨log⟩ *syllogism*; *induction, deduction*; *illation* **11.** (Entschluß) *resolution* **B.** den ~ **bilden** *to bring up the rear* ‖ ~ folgt *to be concluded* ‖ guten ~ h *to close, shut, fit properly*; ⟨hors⟩ *to have a firm seat, to sit one's horse well* ‖ **mach'** ~!, .. damit! *stop it*!, *have done*!; ~ m mit *to wind up with*; ~ m bei *to draw the line at* ‖ e–n ~ **ziehen** *to infer, conclude* (aus *from*), *to draw the conclusion* (*that*); allgemeinen: *to generalize*, aus e–r S: *to put two & two together*, übereilt: *to jump to quick conclusions* **C. am** ~ *at the end*; (räumlich a.) *at the tail*; am ~ s–r Rede erklärte er *he ended his speech with the declaration* | **bis** z ~ *to the last*, (*right*) *to the finish* od *end* | ~ **mit** [dat] m *to have done with* ‖ ~ (damit)! *no more*! ‖ ~ mit ..! *a truce to* (*jesting*)! ‖ ~ damit! *that will better finish*! | **nach** ~ der Redaktion *before going to press*; ⟨fig⟩ *at the last moment* | ~ **von** .. auf ..: *deduction of .. from ..* | **zum** ~ (..) *finally, in conclusion* (*he finished by* ..) ‖ z ~ bringen *to settle, terminate* ‖ zu dem ~ k *to argue* od *decide, to come to the conclusion* (*that*) **Schl·uß-** [in comp] *final* (*act*), *concluding, closing* (*scene, address*), *terminal* (*examination*), *last* (*line*) **~abrechnung** f ⟨com⟩ *final account* **~akt** m ⟨school⟩ *speechday* **~akte** f *final act* **~antrag** m ⟨parl⟩ *motion for closure*; *putting the question* **~balken** m ⟨arch⟩ *top-girder* **~band** m *completing volume* **~bemerkung** f *final o.* **~bilanz** f *f. b.* **~bild** n ⟨theat⟩ *apotheosis* **~choral** m *recessional* **~effekt** m, **~ergebnis** n *upshot* **~examen** n ⟨univ⟩ *finals* pl **~feier** f *breaking-up* **~folge(rung)** f *argument*; *reasoning process*; ⟨a.⟩ = Schluß 10. **~kampf** m: mit in den ~ k *to be in at the finish* **~kurs** m, **~notierung** f *closing quotation* od *prices* pl **~leuchte** f, **~licht** n ⟨rail, mot⟩ *rear* (od *tail-*)*light, marker lamp* od *light* **~liste** f *summary* **~mann** m ⟨Rugby⟩ *full-back* **~marsch** m ⟨mus fam⟩ *chaser* **~offizier** → Schließender **~prüfung** f *finals* pl **~punkt** m *last point*; ⟨gram⟩ *full-stop* **~rechnung** f *final balance* **~rede** f *epilogue* **~reim** m *end-rhyme* **~rennen** n ⟨sport⟩ *final heat*; dazu: *finalist* **~runde** f *final*; Teilnehmer an der ~ *finalist* **~satz** m ⟨log⟩ *consequent* ‖ ⟨mus⟩ *finale* **~schiff** n *rear ship* **~schein** m ⟨com⟩ *contract-note* **~schrift** f ⟨print⟩ *colophon, imprint* **~seite** f *concluding page* (*of a book* **~sprung** m *standing jump* **~stein** m *keystone* | den **~strich** ziehen unter .. *to put paid to* .. **~tag** m ⟨com⟩ *closing date* **~termin** m ⟨jur⟩ *final hearing* **~verkauf** m (*seasonal*) *closing-out sale* **~vignette** f ⟨typ⟩ *tail-piece* **~wort** n ⟨theat⟩ *tag line*; *epilogue* **~zeichen** n ⟨telph⟩ *clearing signal* **Schl·üssel** m ~s/~ *key* (zu .. *of a room*) (⟨a. fig⟩ *to the political situation*; *for the distribution*) ‖ (falscher) *skeleton-k., picklock* ‖ ⟨übtr⟩ *cipher* (*-code*) ‖ ⟨mus⟩ *clef* | den ~ umdrehen *to turn the k.* ‖ den Code-~ entziffern *to break the k.*; Entzifferung bei unbekanntem ~ *cryptanalysis*

Schl·üssel- ⟨übtr⟩ **c***rypto*(*graphi***c**) **~anschrift** f *codress* **~bart** m *k.-bit* **~bein** n *collar-bone* **~blume** f ⟨bot⟩ *cowslip* ‖ (gelbe ~) *primrose* **~brett** n *k.-rack* ⟨a. Am & hot⟩ **~bruch** m *crypto-security violation* **~bund** n *bunch of k.s* **~burg** f *k.-fortress* **≈fertig** a: ~es Haus (*new*) *h. ready for moving in* **~gerät** n *c.c device*; Instandsetzungsdienst [m] f ~ *c.c repair facilities* N **~gewalt** f ⟨jur⟩ *authority of wife to act in name of husband within range of her domestic activities*; ⟨ec⟩ *power of the k.s* **~haken** m *k.-swivel* **~kind** n *latchkey child* **~liste** f ⟨mil⟩ (Hauptnachweis f Bekleidung, Ausrüstung u Bewaffnung) *Master Equipment Authorization List* N **~maschine** f *crypto-mechanism*; *code converter* **~mittel** n (Code≈) *crypto-aid* **~loch** n *k.hole* | ~schild [n] *k.h.-cover, escutcheon* **~reiz** m ⟨eth⟩ *sign stimulus* **~ring** m *k.-ring* **~roman** m *k.-novel, roman à clef* **~schrift** f *code* (*in c.*) **~stellung** f ⟨tact⟩ *k. position* **~unterlage** f *encoding and decoding chart* **~verleihung** f *Christ's Charge to Peter*, ⟨arts⟩ *Delivery of the Keys* **schl·üsseln** vi/t [h] *to* (*code in*) *cipher, to* (*en*)*code* **schl·üssig** a *resolved, determined, certain* ‖ ⟨jur⟩ *well-grounded, conclusive* ‖ sich [dat] ~ w *to resolve, to make up one's mind* (über [acc] *on*; ob *whether*) ‖ (sich) ~ s *to be decided*

Schmach f ~/ *blemish, ignominy, disgrace, dishonour*; ~ u Schande *dirty shame* ‖ (Beleidigung) *insult* (antun *to offer*) **≈bed·eckt** a *covered with ignominy* **≈voll** a *disgraceful, ignominious*

Schm·acht- **~blick** m *languishing look, sheep's eye, come-hither look* **~fetzen** m ⟨fam⟩ *sentimental song* **~lappen** m ⟨fam⟩ *love-sick swain* **~locke** f (*ear-lock*) *lovelock, kiss-me-quick*; *bow-*(für *beau*) *catcher* **~riemen** m ⟨fam & fig⟩; den ~ umschnallen *to tighten one's belt*; .. enger schnallen! *a subaltern's luncheon*! . **≈en 1.** vi [h] *to languish* (*with*), *to pine* (*under*) ‖ *to be parched* (*with thrist*) ‖ ~ nach *to hanker after*; *to languish, yearn, ache, pine*; *to be dying for* .. od *to do*; *to ache* (*to do*) ‖ ~ l *to tantalize* **II.** ≈ n *languor* | **≈end** a *languishing, languorous, yearning, wistful* (*look*) **schm·ächtig** a *slender, slim slight* (*figure*); (P) ⟨fam⟩: *a little slip of a th* **≈keit** f ~/ *slenderness, slimness* **Schm·ächtling** m ~(e)s/~e *slender p*

Schm·ack(e) f ~/~en ⟨mar⟩ *smack*

schm·ackhaft a *savo(u)ry, palatable, flavo(u)rful, delicious, sapid, toothsome, appetizing*; ~ finden *to relish* ‖ nicht, wenig ~ *flat, insipid*; (etw) ~ m ⟨fig⟩ *to sugar-coat*; jdm ein Projekt ~ m *to sell a p a p.* **≈igkeit** f ~/ *savouriness*, etc, *daintiness, delicacy*

°**Schm·adder** m ~s/ *mud* **≈n** vt [h] *to soil*

Schm·äh- [in comp] *defamatory* **~rede** f *abuse, invective, diatribe*; *philippic* **~schrift** f *lampoon, libel* **~schriftsteller** m *libeller* **~sucht** f *love of scandal, abusiveness, slanderous disposition* **≈süchtig** a *slanderous* **~wort** n *insulting word, abusive expression* **schm·ähen** vt/i [h] (schelten) (⟨a.⟩ auf, gegen, über) *to revile, abuse* [vt] ‖ ⟨fam⟩ *to run down* | vi *to scold*, ⟨hunt⟩ *to bleat* | vt (verleumden) *to slander, insult, calumniate* **Schm·äher** m ~s/~ *reviler, detractor, calumniator* **schm·ählich** a *ignominious, disgraceful, discreditable, abusive* | [adv] ⟨fam⟩ *outrageously, immensely, awfully* **Schm·ähung** f ~/~en *abuse, abusing* ‖ *invective* ‖ *libel, slander*

schmal a *narrow, slim, thin* | (knapp) *scanty* (*meal*), *small* (*morsels, income*), *poor* (*fare*); ~e Kost *short allowance* ‖ ~e Bissen h *to be on short commons* ‖ ~ w *to narrow*; der Weg wird ~ .. *dwindles* ‖ auf der ~en Seite *edgewise* | es geht bei ihm ~ her *he is poorly off* ‖ ~ gehalten *kept on a small pittance* **~bäckig** a *hollow-cheeked* **≈beet** n ⟨gard⟩ *border* **≈film** m *narrow*(*-gauge*) od *substandard film* | ~verleih [m] *renting agency for narrow gauge* **≈hans** m; bei ihnen ist ~ Küchenmeister *they are on short commons in this house* **~lippig** a *thin-lipped* **~randig** a *narrow-marginated* **≈rillen-** *microgroove* (*record*) **≈spießer** m (Hirsch im 2. Jahr) *knobb*(*l*)*er, bullock* **~spur-** ⟨rail⟩ *narrow-gauge* [attr] ‖ °⟨univ⟩ ~lateiner *taking L. but as a minor subject*; ⟨Am sl⟩ *small-time* [attr] **~spurig** a ⟨rail⟩ *narrow-gauge* (*line*) **≈tier** n (Hirsch) *young hind*, (Damwild) *y. doe* **≈vieh** n *small cattle, sheep* pl

schm·älen vt/i [h] *to chide, scold* (auf *against*) ‖ ⟨hunt⟩ *to bleat* **schm·älern** vt [h] *to lessen, diminish, curtail, impair, belittle* ‖ *to encroach upon, to prejudice* (*a p's rights*), *to derogate from* .. **Schm·älerung** f ~/~en *lessening, diminution, curtailment, impairment*

Schmalk·alden n ⟨Ger⟩ (Stadt) *Schmalkalden*

Schm·alte f ~/ ⟨chem⟩ *smalt(-blue)*

Schmalz n ~es/ *grease, lard, fat* ‖ (Braten≃) *dripping* ‖ ⟨fig⟩ im ~ *as a bug in a rug* ‖ ⟨fig fam⟩ *sentimentalism*, ⟨mus, lit, film⟩ *schmal(t)z* **~birne** f *butter-pear* **~gebackene(s)** n, **~kuchen** m [pl] *fritters* pl, *doughnuts* **~öl** n *lard oil* **schm·alzen** vt [h] *to butter, lard* **schm·alzig** a *greasy* ‖ ⟨fig hum⟩ *sentimental*

×**Schmant** m ~(e)s/~e (Sahne) *cream*

schmar·otzen vi [h] *to sponge on others*; ⟨fam⟩ *to toady* **Schmar·otzer** m ~s/~ *sponger, flunkey, hanger-on* ‖ ⟨bot, zoo⟩ *parasite* ‖ ⟨fam⟩ *toady* ‖ ⟨mil sl⟩ *heel* ‖ ⟨Am fam⟩ *dead beat* | ~flora [f] *commensal fl.* **~·ei** f ~/~en *sponging* **≃isch** a *parasitic(al), sponging* **~tum** n *parasitism, toadyism*

Schm·arre f ~/~n *slash, gash* (*in the face*) ‖ (Narbe) *scar* **schm·arrig** a *scarry*

Schm·arr(e)n m ~s/~ **1.** *scrambled pancake* ‖ Grieß≃ *mashed semolina omelette*; Kaiser≃ *scrambled o.* ‖ ⟨fig⟩ mit ungelegten Eiern ist nicht gut ~ m *you cannot make an o. with unlaid eggs* **2.** ⟨fig⟩ *trifle, trash, rubbish*; ⟨Lit⟩ *shilling shocker* | über jeden ~ weinen *to cry about every peanut*; wegen jedes ~s geht er gleich hoch *every fiddle-faddle gets his monkey* od *dander up*; das ist e–n ~ wert *that's good for the birds*; du weißt e–n ~ *you know a fat lot*; ~! *fiddlesticks*!, ⟨Am sl⟩ *boloney*!; ein Streit um e–n ~ *a row over a little th* **3.** → Kitsch, Schund

°**Schmatz** m –es/–e & ≃e *hearty kiss, smack*; ⟨Am sl⟩ *smooch* **schm·atzen** vi [h] *to give a smacking kiss, to kiss heartily* ‖ (beim Essen) *to smack one's lips, to munch* **Schm·ätzer** m ~s/~ ⟨orn⟩ *chat*

Schmauch m ~(e)s/ *smoke* | **≃en** vt/i [h] *to smoke* ‖ e–e Zigarre ~ *to puff away at a cigar*

Schm·aus m ~es/≃e *feast, banquet, junket, regale* ⟨fam⟩ *tuck*; ⟨fam a.⟩ *spread* | ⟨fig⟩ *treat* | **≃en** vi [h] *to feast* (von *upon*), *to junket, banquet* | **~er** m ~s/~ *feaster, banqueter* **~·ei** f ~/~en *feast(ing), banquet(ing), junket(ing)*

schm·ecken I. vt [h] (kosten) *to taste* ‖ ⟨fig⟩ (erdulden) *to undergo, experience* **II.** vi [h] *to taste* (*sweet*; *burnt* angebrannt), (⟨dial⟩: *to smell*) ‖ es schmeckt (gut) *it tastes good*; das schmeckt! *that hits the spot*! ‖ man soll aufhören, wenn es am besten schmeckt *you should leave off with an appetite* | **nicht** ~ *to have no taste* od *flavour*; *the cigar loses its relish when you are ill*; schlecht ~ *to be unpleasant to taste*; schlecht ~d *unpalatable* | es (der Wein) schmeckt **mir** *I relish it*, (*I like, enjoy this wine*) ‖ wie schmeckt es (dir)? *how do you like it* (⟨a. fig⟩: *your caning*?) ‖ ihm will nichts (die Arbeit nicht) ~ *nothing is to his taste, he has no appetite* (*he doesn't like work*) ‖ er ließ es sich ~ *he ate with a good appetite, he enjoyed his meal* | .. schmeckt **durch, vor** [adv] *it tastes of* (*baking powder*), *the predominating flavour is* (*marjoram*) ‖ ~ **nach** *to taste of* (*the cork* = *the wine is corked*) ‖ ⟨fig⟩ *to smack* od *savour of, to look like* (*treachery*) ‖ nach mehr ~ *to taste "morish"* **Schm·ecker** m ~s/~ *taster* ‖ (Fein≃) *gourmand* ‖ er ist ein ~ *he has a fine palate* | ⟨hum⟩ *palate*

Schm·eichel- ~katze f *wheedler, flatterer* ‖ *puss* **~rede** f, **~worte** n [pl] *flattering speech* ‖ ⟨fam⟩ *soft sawder* od *soap* **Schmeichel·ei** f ~/~en *flattery, cajolery* ‖ (sanfte) *coaxing*; (grobe) ⟨fam⟩ *blarney*; (plumpe) ⟨fam⟩ *butter*; ⟨dero⟩ *wheedling, fawning, adulation* ‖ ~en sagen *to say nice ths* **schmeichelhaft** a **1.** *flattering, complimentary* ‖ ⟨dero⟩ *adulatory* **2.** (P) *full of flattery* **3.** jdm etw sehr ≃es sagen *to pay a p a great compliment* **schm·eicheln I.** vi [h] jdm *to flatter* (*this portrait flatters her*); (sanft) *coax* ‖ *to caress* (*a dog*) (*a p*); *to tickle a p*; *to play* od ⟨fam⟩ *butter a p up*; ⟨dero⟩ *to adulate* (*a p*), *fawn* (*upon a p*); *to* (*be a*) *toady to a p* ‖ **sich** mit (etw) ~ *to flatter o.s.* (*to buoy o.s. up*) *with* ‖ **es** –lte ihr *or* sie *she was flattered* ‖ sich ge–lt fühlen *to feel flattered* (durch *at*) ‖ (den Sinnen) ~ *to cater for* .. ‖ (jds Leidenschaft) ~ *to pander to* .. **II.** vt [h] sie –lte es ihm ab *she coaxed him out of it* **Schm·eichler** m ~s/~ *flatterer* ‖ *coaxer* | ⟨dero⟩ *cringer, wheedler, adulator* (f *adulatress*) **≃isch** a **1.** *flattering* **2.** *fawning, adulatory*

Schmeiß m ~es/ *fly-dirt* **≃en** vi [h] ⟨ent⟩ *to lay eggs* (*on*) **~fliege** f *bluebottle, blowfly* | **~en I.** vt/i [schmiß/geschmissen] [h] *to throw* (⟨a. fig⟩ *a party*); *to fling, cast, hurl* ‖ *to slam, bang* (*the door*) | (nachlässig *or* verächtlich) *to chuck* | (⟨fam⟩ = meistern) *to run* od *boss* (die S *the show*); *to pull* (*the matter*) *off*; *to do* (*the trick*); *to get* (*it*) *across*; es ~ *to manage it, to turn the trick*, ⟨fam⟩ *to swing it* | jdm etw ~ *to stand a p a drink*; ⟨Am fam⟩ *to throw* (*a party*) **II.** vi [h] mit dem Gelde um sich ~ *to squander one's m.* ‖ (v Pferd) *to lash out, to kick*

Schmelz m ~es/~e *enamel* (*e.l*) (a. Zahn≃); *smalt, glazing* ‖ ⟨fig⟩ *bloom, glow* (*of youth*) ‖ ⟨arts⟩ Gruben≃ (Zellen≃) *champlevé* (*cloisonné*) *e.l* ‖ ⟨mus⟩ *mellowness, sweetness*; *patina* (*of a voice*) ‖ ⟨paint⟩ *soft brightness* **~arbeit** f *e.l(ing)* **~arbeiter** m *e.ller* ‖ ⟨met⟩ *smelter* **~butter** f *oiled butter*; *shortening* **~farbe** f *e.l* od *vitrified colour* **~fluß** m (geschmolzenes Metall) *fused mass*; *melt* **~glas** n *e.l* **~herd** m ⟨met⟩ *ore hearth* **~hütte** f *foundry, smelting-house, -works* pl **~käse** m *processed ch.* **~löffel** m *s.g -ladle* **~maler(ei** f) m *e.l-painter* (*painting*) **~masse** f *fusion* **~mittel** n ⟨met⟩ *flux* **~ofen** m *furnace* ⟨a. fig⟩ **~perle** f *e.l--pearl* **~punkt** m *melting-point* **~schupper** m ⟨ich⟩ *ganoid* **~stahl** m *German st.* **~tiegel** m *crucible* **~topf** m *melting-pot* | latente **~wärme** *latent heat of fusion* **~wasser** n *melted snow* od *ice* | ~ebene [f] *outwash plain*; ~rinne *glacial spill way* **schm·elzbar** a *fusible* ‖ schwer ~ *refractory* **≃keit** f ~/ *fusibility* **Schm·elze** f ~/ *melting* | ⟨met⟩ *smelting, fusion*; [konkr] *charge* | *foundry* **Schm·elzen** n ~s/ *melting* ‖ *reduction, diminution* **schm·elzen I.** vt [h] [reg] *to melt* ‖ (Erze) *to smelt, fuse* **II.** vi [s] [–olz/ge–olzen] *to melt, dissolve*; *to* (*begin to*) *run* ‖ ⟨fig⟩ *to soften* | (schwinden) *to diminish, decrease*; *to be reduced*; *to melt away* | **geschmolzen** *melted* (*snow*), *molten* (*metal*) **schm·elzend** a ⟨fig⟩ *languishing* ‖ ⟨mus⟩ *sweet, melodious* ‖ (Stimme, Ton) *mellow* **Schm·elzer** m ~s/~ *smelter, founder* **~·ei** f ~/~en *foundry* **Schm·elzung** f ~/~en *smelting*

Schmer m & n ~(e)s/ *grease, animal fat* **~bauch** m ⟨fam⟩ *big belly, paunch, corporation*; *bay-, bow-window* ‖ mit ~ *big-bellied, b.-w.ed* **≃ig** a *greasy* **≃en** = schmieren: wer gut schmert, der gut fährt *money makes the mare go*; *let's grease the gills* (= *drink*)!

Schm·ergel [obs] = Schmirgel

Schm·erle f ~/~n **1.** ⟨ich⟩ *loach* **2.** ⟨orn⟩ *merlin*

Schmerz m ~es/~en **A. 1.** *pain, smart, ache* ‖ heftiger (stechender, [aufwühlender]) ~ *terrible* (*racking, smarting* [*throbbing*]) *pain* **2.** ⟨fig⟩ *pain, grief, sorrow, anguish*; *pang*(*s of love*) ‖ ungeheurer ~ *mortal agony* ‖ Trennungs≃ *wrench* **B.** jdm ~ **bereiten,** verursachen *to give a p pain* ‖ ~ empfinden *to be* (*deeply*) *grieved* (über *at*) ‖ ⟨hum⟩ (h Sie) sonst noch ~en? *anything else*? **C.** ⟨fig⟩ **mit** ~en (erwartet) *with great regret* (*anxiously waited for*) ‖ **von** ~en gequält *racked with pain* ‖ **zu** s–m ~ *to his distress* **≃betäubend** a, ~es Mittel *analgesic* [a & subst] **~betäubung** f *analgesia* **≗erfüllt** a *grief-stricken* **≗durchfurcht** a (*face*) *lined with pain* **~gebrüll** n *howl of p.* **≗gequält** a (*a heart*) *torn with anguish* **≗haft** a *painful* ‖ *angry* (*wound*) ‖ *sore* (*spot*) ⟨a. fig⟩ ‖ ⟨fig⟩ *grievous, distressing, afflicting* **~haftigkeit** f *painfulness* ‖ ⟨fig⟩ *grievousness* **≗lich** a *aching, painful* ‖ ⟨fig⟩ *grievous, distressing, painful* (*experience*) ‖ *sad* (*smile*) ‖ *cruel* (*fate*) | [adv] ~ entbehren *to miss badly* od *sadly* **≗lindernd** a *soothing*; ⟨med⟩ *lenitive* **≗los** a *painless* ‖ ⟨med⟩ *indolent* (*ulcer*) **~losigkeit** f *painlessness* **≗stillend** a *soothing* ‖ ⟨med⟩ ~es Mittel *pain-killer*; *analgesic*; *anodyne* **≗verzerrt** a *pain-racked* (*face*) **≗voll** a *painful* ‖ sehr ~ *agonizing* ‖ *it was agony* (f *to*) **schm·erzen** vt/i [h] *to hurt, pain, smart* ‖ *to afflict, distress* | (nur körperlich) *to ache* [vi] | (nur seelisch) *to grieve* | mich –zt der Kopf *my head aches*; *her shoulder hurt her*; *the place was smarting* | –zte **es**? *did it hurt*?; *where does it feel painful*? ‖ es –zt mich tief *it grieves me to the heart* (*to say*); *I am pained* (*to think*); *it wrings my heart* | **~reich** a *deeply afflicted* ‖ ~e Mutter ⟨ec⟩ *our Lady of Sorrows* **Schm·erzens- ~bezeigungen** f [pl] *regrets* pl **~geld** n *smart-m.*; ⟨jur⟩ *damages* od *compensation for pain and suffering*; ⟨fam⟩ *dole-bob*, ⟨Am⟩ *wise money* **~kind** n *ch. of sorrows* **~lager** n *bed of suffering* **~mad·onna** → Vesperbild; K. der ~ *Church of the M. of the Dolours* **~mann** *Sorrowing Christ, Man of Sorrows* **~schrei** m *wail* od *cry of pain* (⟨fig⟩ *of distress*) **~ton** m *doleful accent*

Schm·etterling m ~(e)s/~e *butterfly* **~sblüte** f, **~sblütler** m *papilionaceous flower* **~sfang** m *b.ly-catching* **~skunde** f *lepidopterology* **~snetz** n *ring-net* **~sammlung** f *collection of b.lies*

Schm·ettern n ~s/ *flourish, braying, blare* (*of trumpets*) ‖ *warbling* (*of birds*) | ≗ **I.** vi **1.** [h] (Trompete) *to bray, blare* ‖ (Vogel) *to warble* ‖ (Stimme) *to ring* (*forth*) **2.** [s] *to come down with a crash* **II.** vt [h] **1.** *to smash* (*a ball*), *to dash* (in Stücke *to pieces*) ‖ *to hurl down* **2.** ⟨fam⟩ e–n ~ *to wet one's whistle, to knock one back* **3.** (Worte, Lieder) *to blare* (jdm entgegen *at a p*) ‖ eins ~ *to sing a song* **Schm·etterschlag** m ⟨ten⟩ *smash* **Schm·icke** f ~/~n *whip-lash*

Schmied m ~(e)s/~e (Grob–) (*black*)*smith* ‖ ⟨fig⟩ *founder* **schm·iedbar** a *malleable annealed* (*cast iron*) **≗keit** f ~/ *malleability* **Schm·iede** f ~/~n *forge, smithy* ‖ Huf≗ *farrier's shop* ‖ ⟨fig⟩ vor die rechte ~ gehen *to apply to the right quarter*, ⟨fam⟩ *to go to the right shop* ‖ vor die unrechte ~ k *to catch a Tartar* **~amboß** m *anvil* **~arbeit** f *forging* ‖ *iron work, wrought i.* **~balg** m *smith's bellows* pl **~eisen** n *forge* od *wrought iron* ‖ (z Schmieden) *forging* (od *low carbon*) *steel* **≗eisern** a *of w. i.* **~esse** f, **~feuer** n, **~herd** m *forge* **~gesell(e)** m *journeyman smith* **~gesenk** n *forging die* **~hammer** m *smith's* od *sledge-h.*; *forging drop* **~handwerk** n *smith's trade* **~kohle** f *blacksmith's coal* **~meister** m *master-smith* **~rohling** m *forged blank* **~technik** f *forging practice* **~waren** f pl *forgings* pl **~werkstatt** f *smithy, forge* **~zange** f (e–e *a pair of*) (*black*)*smith's tongs* pl **schm·ieden** vt [h] *to forge* (⟨a. fig⟩ *friendship*) ‖ ⟨fig⟩ *to plan, devise, scheme*, ⟨dero⟩ *concoct* | *to make* (*schemes, plans*) ‖ Ränke ~ *to intrigue* ‖ *to concoct* (*verses*) | **in** Eisen ~ *to put in chains* | schmiede das Eisen, solange es heiß ist *make hay while the sun shines*

Schm·iege f ~/~n ⟨tech⟩ (*angle*) *bevel, rule* **schm·iegen** vt [h] **1.** *to bend gently* ‖ *to bevel* **2. sich** ~ *to bend, yield*, ⟨dero⟩ *crawl, cringe* (vor [dat] *to*) ‖ sich ~ u biegen *to bow and scrape* (*before*) | sich **an** jdn ~ *to cling, snuggle, nestle to a p* ‖ **in**: *to nestle, cuddle, in a p's arms*; in die Hand ge–gt (*chin*) *in cupped hand*(*s*) **um**: *to wind round* ‖ ge–gt *snuggled up* **schm·iegsam** a *pliant, flexible, supple* ‖ ⟨fig⟩ *submissive* **≗keit** f ~/ *flexibility, pliancy* ‖ ⟨fig⟩ *submissiveness*

Schm·iele f ~/~n ⟨bot⟩ *hair-grass*

Schm·ier- ~achse f *plain axle* **~anstich** m ⟨tech⟩ *oil hole* **~apparat** m *oil-feeder, lubricator* **~block** m *scribbling pad* **~buch** n *waste-book* **~büchse** f *oil-cup, grease-box, oiler* **~bürste** f *dauber* **~fähigkeit** f *unctuousness*; ⟨tech⟩ *lubricity* **~fett** n ⟨tech⟩ *grease* **~fink** m ⟨fam⟩ *mudlark* ‖ (Schlechtschreiber) *srawler, scribbler* **~geld(er** pl) n ⟨fam⟩ *palm-oil, grease*, ⟨Am⟩ *slush-money*; ⟨vulg⟩ *flip*; ⟨Am pol⟩ *slush fund* **~käse** m *soft cheese* **~leder** n *curried leather* **~loch** n ⟨tech⟩ *oil hole* °**~max(en** pl) m ⟨aero sl⟩ *grease monkey*(*s*), *ground wallah*(*s*); *penguin*(*s*) **~mittel** n *lubricant* ‖ ⟨med⟩ *unguent* **~öl** n *lube* **~(öl)vorrichtung** f *lubricator* **~plan** m *lubrication schedule* od *diagram* **~presse** f ⟨tech⟩ *grease gun* **~salbe** f *salve* **~seife** f *soft soap* **~wolle** f *greasy wool* **Schm·iere** f ~/~n *grease*; ⟨fam⟩ *squish* ‖ (Salbe) *salve* ‖ ⟨mar⟩ *stuff* | ⟨fig fam⟩ *bribe, bribing* ‖ *the old story*! ‖ (Prügel) *thrashing, flogging, lick* ‖ (Bande) *gang* ‖ ⟨theat⟩ *strolling company*; ⟨sl⟩ (*penny-*)*gaff* | °~ stehen *to stall*, ⟨school sl⟩ *to keep cave* **~nschauspieler(in** f) m *strolling player*; ⟨fam⟩ *barn-stormer*, ⟨Am⟩ *ham* **~steher** m *back-stall* **schm·ieren** vt/i [h] (→ schmeren) **1.** *to smear* (*ointment, clay*) ‖ (Butter) *to spread* ‖ (Brotscheibe) *to butter* ‖ (Leder) *to liquor* ‖ (Wein) *to doctor* | (ölen) *to grease, oil, lubricate* ‖ (salben) *to salve* ‖ (sudeln) *to scrawl, scribble*; *to sling* (*a book*) ‖ ⟨bes. paint⟩ *to daub* **2.** ⟨fig⟩ (bestechen) *to grease*, ⟨Am⟩ *sweeten* ‖ jdn ~ *to grease a p's palm*; ⟨sl⟩ *to square a p* | **jdm** e–e ~ *to box a p's ears*; ⟨Am sl⟩ *to paste* ‖ wie ge–rt *swimmingly*; *like greased lightning* | e–m Brei *or* Honig ums Maul ~ *to buoy a p up with vain hopes*; ⟨fam⟩ *to soft-soap a p* ‖ das ~ Sie mir nicht aufs Brot *tell that to the horse-marines* ‖ sich die Kehle ~ *to wet one's whistle* ‖ e–m alles ins Maul ~ *to put the words in a p's mouth* | **(nicht-)~d** (*non-*)*smudgeable* **Schm·ierer** m ~s/~ *lubricator* ‖ ⟨fig⟩ *scrawler, scribbler* ‖ ⟨paint⟩ *dauber* ‖ ⟨liter⟩ *scribbler, writer of pot-boilers* | **~·ei** f ~/~en *smearing, scrawl, scribbling* ‖ ⟨paint⟩ *daub* ‖ ⟨liter⟩ → vor. ‖ ⟨übtr⟩ *mess* **schm·ierig** a (fettig) *greasy* ‖ (schlammig) *muddy* ‖ (schmutzig) *dirty, grubby* ‖ ⟨fig⟩ *sordid, stingy, dirty, mean* ‖ ~ m *to besmear* ‖ sich ~ m *to muck o.s. up* **Schm·ierung** f ~/~en *lubrication*; Druck- *forced*, Mischungs- *petroil*, Oben- *upper cylinder*, Tauch- *splash*, Umlauf- *circulatory*, Zentral≗ *chassis l.*

schmilzt 3. p sg ind pres v schmelzen II.

Schmink- ~bohne f *kidney-bean* **~büchse** f *paint-box* **~läppchen** n *paint-rag* **~mittel** n *cosmetic* **~pflästerchen** n (*beauty-*)*patch* **~topf** m *paint-, rouge-pot* **~wasser** n (*cosmetic*) *wash* **~weiß** n *pearl-powder* **Schm·inke** f ~/~n (*grease*) *paint*; *make-up* ‖ rote ~ *rouge*, weiße ~ *ceruse* **schm·inken** vt [h] *to paint* ‖ (rot) *to rouge* ‖ ⟨übtr⟩ (Bericht) *to touch up, cook* ‖ sich ~ *to paint*; *to* (*wear* od *use*) *rouge* ‖ ⟨bes theat⟩ *to make* (*o.s.*) *up*

Schm·irgel m ~s/ *emery* **~leinwand** f *emery-, glass-cloth* **~papier** n *emery-paper* | **≗n** vt [h] *to polish* od *rub with emery*; *to sandpaper*

Schmiß m –sses/–sse *stroke, blow, gash* ‖ –sse bek *to get a thrashing* ‖ (Narbe) *cut, scar* ‖ (⟨fig⟩ = Schwung) *smartness, verve*, ⟨sl⟩ *fizz, dash* (*with d.*); *go* (*there's no go in it*); ⟨Am⟩ *pep*; (*this th has got to have*) *sock*!; ⟨sport fam⟩ *smoke*; **schm·issig** a *brisk, sprightly, smart, dashing*; *saucy* (*hat*); ⟨fam⟩ *zippy*; ⟨sl⟩ *peppy* **schmiß** 1. & 3. sg pret v schmeißen

Schmitz m ~es/~e *cut, lash* ‖ *blot, spot, mackle* | **~e** f ~/~n *whip-lash* | **≗en** vt/i [h] *to lash, whip* ‖ ⟨typ⟩ *to mackle, blur*

Schm·öker m ∼s/∼ *old volume, trashy book* ‖ (billig) *yellowback* ‖ ⟨school⟩ *crib*, ⟨Am⟩ *trot* **schm·ollen I.** vi [h] *to pout, sulk* ‖ (*her mouth went sulky*) ‖ (*she made a little face* [od *up a lip*]) ‖ *to look glum* (mit *at*) **II.** ∼̈ n *sulks* pl, *pout, tiff* **Schm·ollwinkel** m *sulking-corner, growlery* **Schm·ollis** n ⟨univ sl⟩ ein ∼ [dat]! *good health to ..!* ‖ ∼ trinken mit jdm *to drink to a p's health, proposing to use* „du" *in mutual address; to fraternize with a p*

Schm·onzes n *invar* [Hebr] → Geschwätz; leeres Gerede; Vorspiegelungen ‖ ∼ mit Lakritzen ⟨Am sl⟩ *apple-sauce* ⟨fig⟩

Schm·or- ∼**braten** m *braised meat; braisé* Fr; *pot roast* ∼**hitze** f *broiling-heat* ∼**pfanne** f, *saucepan, braising pan* ∼**topf** m *stew-pot* **schm·oren** vt/i [h] *to braise* ‖ ⟨fig⟩ *to be parched with heat, to swelter* ‖ ⟨fam⟩ laß ihn ∼! *let him stew in his own fat!*

°**Schmu** m ∼s/ *unfair profit; swindle* ‖ ∼ m *to swindle, to make an unfair profit*

schmuck a *neat, spruce, dapper* (*p*); *nifty* (*girl*); *trim* (*house*); *smart* (*as fresh paint*) ‖ *saucy* (*hat*) ‖ *smart* (*costume, youngster, couple*) ‖ (hübsch) *handsome* (*young man*), *buxom* (*lass*) **Schmuck** m ∼(e)s/∼e *ornament, trappings* pl ‖ (Juwelen etc) *jewelry; jewels, gems* pl ‖ (Putz) *finery* ‖ *the beauty* (*of flowers*) ‖ ⟨fig⟩ *flowers* (*of speech*) ∼**arbeit** f *jewellery* ∼**arbeiter** m *working jeweller* ∼**feder** f *plume* ∼**kästchen** n *casket* ‖ ⟨fig⟩ *gem* (*of a house*) ∼**leiste** f *swag border* ⟨a. theat⟩ ∼̈**los** a *unadorned, undecorated; void of ornament, unornamental; plain, unvarnished* (*truth*); *austere, severe* (*style*); ⟨arch⟩ *functional* | ∼̈igkeit [f] *plainness, severity*, etc ∼**nadel** f *breast-pin* ∼**sachen** f pl *ornaments* ‖ *jewels* ‖ *trinkets* ∼**stück** n *ornament* ‖ *piece of jewelry* ∼**voll** a *ornate* ∼**waren** f pl *jewelry* **schm·ücken** vt [h] *to adorn, trim* ‖ (kleiden) *to attire, dress* ‖ *to decorate* (*a room*) ‖ *to lard* (*a speech .. with*) ‖ *to bespangle* (*with stars*) ‖ ⟨theat⟩ *to swag* ‖ reich ge–kt *enriched* (*with gems*) | sich ∼ ⟨a.⟩ *to deck o.s. out* **Schm·ückung** f ∼/∼en *decoration* ‖ *tiring, dressing*

Schm·uddel m ∼s/∼ 1. = Unsauberkeit 2. = schmutzige P (m & f) ∼·**ei** f ∼/∼en = Sudelei **schm·udd(e)lig** a = unsauber, ⟨a.⟩ *draggled, shabby* **schm·uddeln** vi [h] = sudeln

Schm·uggel m ∼s/, ∼·**ei** f ∼/∼en *smuggling* ‖ ∼ treiben *to run contraband* | ∼̈**n** vt/i [h] *to smuggle* ‖ ⟨sl⟩ *to bootleg* ∼**ware(n** pl) f *smuggled goods* pl, *contraband* **Schm·uggler** m ∼s/∼ *smuggler* ∼**bande** f *gang of smugglers* ∼**boot** n *smuggler* ∼**nest** n ⟨Am⟩ *plant*

schm·unzeln I. vi [h] *to smirk, chuckle, grin* **II.** ∼̈ n ∼s/ *grin, smirk*

°**Schm·us** m –es/, ∼**er·ei** f ∼/∼en *soft soap* od *sawder; blarney* | ∼̈**en** vi [h] *to wheedle, smoodge* ‖ mit jdm ∼ *to cuddle a p*

Schm·utz m ∼(e)s/ *dirt, filth; garbage* ‖ ⟨a. fig⟩ *ordure, soil* ‖ ⟨fam⟩ *mess*; ∼ m *to make a m.* | ⟨fig⟩ *smut, mire* ‖ *obscenity* ‖ in den ∼ ziehen *to drag through the mud; to smear* ∼**blech** n ⟨cycl⟩ *mud-guard* ∼**abstreifring** m *sludge scraper* ⟨a. tech⟩ ∼**bogen** m ⟨typ⟩ *set-off sheet* ∼**farbe** f *dirty* (od *mud-*)*colour* ∼̈**farben** a *drab* ∼**fink** m ⟨fam⟩ *mudlark, brock; brother smut* ∼**geier** m *Egyptian vulture* ‖ (Verleumder) *mud-slinger* ∼**fleck** m *smear, spot, smudge, stain* ‖ ⟨typ⟩ *mackle* ‖ ⟨fig⟩ *blemish* ∼**kerl** m *blighter* ∼**kittel** m *overall*; ⟨agr⟩ *smock-frock* ∼**konkurrent** m *dumper* ∼**konkurrenz** f *undercutting, dumping*, [konkr] *dumpers* pl ∼**lappen** m ⟨fig⟩ *draggle-tail* ∼**literatur** f *pornography* ∼**loch** n *mud-hole*; ⟨fig⟩ *dirty hole* ∼**papier** n *waste-paper* ∼**presse** f *gutter press* ∼**rinne** f *waste water gutter* ∼**schicht** f *smear* ∼**stoff** m *polluted* od *-ting matter* ∼**titel** m ⟨typ⟩ *bastard t., half-t.* ∼**- u Schundgesetz** n *dirt and trash law* ∼**wasser** n *slops* pl | ∼kanal [m] *foul* od *waste water sewer* od *drain* ∼**winkel** m *dirty corner* **schm·utzen** vi [h] *to get dirty* | *to give off dirt, to soil* **Schmutzer·ei** f ∼/∼en *filthiness* **schm·utzig** a **1.** *dirty* (*linen*) ‖ *grubby* (*sweater*); *grimy* (*hands*); *soiled, squalid; filthy* ⟨a. fig⟩; ⟨fig a.⟩ *dingy, slimy* ‖ *drab, dull* (*colour*) | es ist ∼ auf der Straße *the streets are muddy* ‖ ∼ m, ∼ w *to soil* **2.** ⟨fig⟩ (geizig) *sordid, niggardly, shabby* (*fellow*) ‖ *scatological* (*literature*); *obscene, smutty* (*novel*) ‖ *sordid, nasty* (*affair, desires*) ∼̈**keit** f ∼/∼en *dirtiness, filthiness* ‖ ⟨fig⟩ *nastiness* ‖ (Geiz) *sordidness*

Schn·abel m ∼s/∼̈ *bill, beak*, ⟨Scot, Am⟩ *neb* ‖ (e–r Feder) *nib* ‖ (e–r Kanne) *spout, snout* ‖ (des Schiffs) *beak, prow* | ⟨fam⟩ halt' den ∼! *shut up! stop your gap* od *jaw! cut the cackle! can it!*; den ∼ halten ⟨fam⟩ *to keep one's lip buttoned*; ⟨Am sl⟩ *to pipe down*; er spricht wie ihm der ∼ gewachsen ist ⟨fam⟩ *he doesn't mince matters, calls a spade a spade, speaks plain English* ∼**flöte** f *flûte-à-bec* Fr ∼̈**förmig** a *beak-shaped, beaked, bill-headed* ‖ ⟨bot⟩ *rostriform* ∼**schuh** m *beaked shoe* ∼**spitze** f *tip of a bill* ∼**tier** n ⟨zoo⟩ *duck-bill* °∼**weide** f *delicacy, titbit* ∼**zange** f ⟨surg⟩ *rostrum* **schnabel·ieren, -bul-** vt/i [h] *to grozzle*, (*eat with relish*), *to peg away* **schn·äbeln** vt [h] *to furnish with a beak* ‖ ge–lt *beaked* ‖ sich ∼ *to bill* ‖ ⟨fig⟩ *to bill and coo*

Schn·ack m ∼(e)s/ *nonsense, drivel, chit-chat* ‖ dummer ∼ *silly twaddle* **schn·acken** vi/t [h] *to prattle, to chatter* ∼**erlohn** m [österr] ⟨dero⟩ *paltry pay* **schn·ackig, -isch** a *chatty* ‖ *droll* ‖ *funny*

Schn·adahüpfe(r)l n ∼s/∼ (→ Schnitter) *extempore* (*alternate*) *Alpine ditty of one stanza*; *e.g.* Die Vögel ham (= h) Kröpferl und singen damit / Mei Alte hat an Kropf, aber singen kanns nit! *Wee birdies have cropsies and use them in song / My missus has a crop, but her singing's all wrong*

°**schn·afte, schn·aftig** a *snorting, nifty* → prima

Schn·ake f ∼/∼n **1.** *gnat, midge; crane-fly* **2.** *drollery, joke* **schn·akisch** a *droll, funny*

Schn·alle f ∼/∼n **1.** *buckle, clasp* **2.** *door-latch* | ∼̈**n** vt [h] *to buckle* ‖ *to strap* ‖ enger ∼ *to tighten*; länger ∼ *to lengthen* | ∼**n-** ∼**bügel,** ∼**dorn** m *catch, tongue of a buckle* ∼**haken** m *chape* ∼**riemen** m *bucklestrap* ∼**schuh** m *buckled shoe*

schn·alzen vi [h] (**mit**) *to click* od *smack* (*one's tongue*) ‖ (verächtlich) *to snap* (*disdainful fingers*); *to crack* (*a whip*) **Schn·alzer** m ∼s/∼ *smacking* **Schn·alzlaut** m (der Kaffern) ⟨phon⟩ *click*

schnapp! I. *snap! before you can say "Jack Robinson"!* **II.** mit e–m ∼̈ *at one bite* od *gulp* ∼̈**feder** f *catch-spring* ∼̈**deckel** m *snap-fastener* ∼̈**hahn** m *highwayman* ∼̈**messer** n *flick knife* ∼**riegel** m *spring bolt* ∼̈**sack** m *knapsack* ∼̈**schloß** m *spring-lock*; Tür mit ∼ *self-locking door* ∼̈**schuß** m ⟨phot⟩ *snapshot* (m v *to take .. of*), e–n ∼ m *to shoot a picture* ∼**verschluß** m ⟨phot⟩ *snap-catch* ∼**stativ** n ⟨phot⟩ *self-erecting tripod* **schn·appen I.** vi [h] *to snap* ‖ (of lid) *to slip off* ‖ (of lock) *to catch* ‖ (of board) *to tip up* | **nach** etw ∼ *to snatch* od *catch at a th* ‖ nach Luft ∼ *to gasp for breath* ‖ °jetzt hat's geschnappt! *now, I've had enough of that*; bei ihm hat's g. *he's in for it*; °bei ihr .. ⟨sex, vulg⟩ *she caught, she's up the spout* **II.** °vt [h] *to catch, grab*; ⟨fam⟩ *nail* (*a p, a th*), ⟨sl⟩ *to pinch, nail* (*a p*) ‖ °schnapp dir .. ⟨vulg⟩ *just you fist* (*the brush and ..*); es hat ihn ge–pt ⟨aero sl⟩ *he's had it* **Schn·äpper** m ∼s/∼ **1.** ⟨tech⟩ *snap, catch* **2.** (des Gewehrs) *trigger* **3.** ⟨surg⟩ *fleam, lancet* **4.** ⟨orn⟩ *fly-catcher*, → *fly* | e–n **Schnapper** m *to give a gasp*; das letzte ×∼l tun (sterben) ⟨fam⟩ *to snuff it* od *out*

Schnaps m –es/∼̈e *booze, swizzle*, ⟨Am⟩ *liquor*, ⟨sl vulg⟩ *licker; schnap(p)s* ‖ (*whisky*, *brandy, gin*) ‖ ein Glas ~ *a dram*, ⟨fam⟩ *a drop of sth* (*out of the bottle*) ‖ e–n ~ trinken *to take a drop* **~brenner(ei** f) m *distiller(y)* ‖ heimlicher –brenner ⟨Am sl⟩ *moonshiner* **~bruder** m *tippler* ‖ er ist ein ~ *he is fond of his drops* **~bude, ~destille** f = ~laden **~flasche** f (leer) *gin-*, etc *bottle*; (voll) *bottle of gin*, etc **~glas** n *nog-gin* (bes 1/4 *pint*) **~idee** f → Kateridee **~-kneipe** f, **~laden** m *gin-shop, tippling-house*, ⟨Am⟩ *grocery*, ⟨sl⟩ *gin-mill* **~nase** f (*p with a*) *copper nose* **~trinker** = ~bruder **Schn·äpschen** n ~s/~; ein ~ *a little drop* od *sth*; *a nip*, ⟨fam⟩ *a peg, a pick-me-up*; ⟨Am⟩ *an eye-opener* ‖ ein ~ trinken ⟨a.⟩ *to take a horn*; ich könnt' ein ~ vertragen *I'm so frisky* ⟨rhyming sl⟩ (zu whiskey) **schnapsen** vi [h] *to take nips, to drink gin*; *to tipple, booze, swizzle*; *to sling a pot* °**Schn·äpser** m ~s/~ ⟨mil⟩ *lance-corporal*

Schn·arch- ~klappe f ⟨tech⟩ *blast-pipe regulator* **~ratze** f *snorer* **~ventil** n *sniffle-valve* | **≈en I.** vi [h] *to snore*, ⟨fig⟩ *snort* **II.** ≈ n *snoring, snore(s* pl) | **~er** m ~s/~ *snorer* | **~er·ei** f *snor(t)ing* **Schn·arr- ~baß** m *drone* **~drossel** f *missel-thrush* **~laut** m *rattling* od *strident sound* **~pfeife** f *drone-pipe* **~wecker** m ⟨telph⟩ *trembler* **~werk** n (der Orgel) *reed-work* **Schn·arre** f ~/~n *rattle* | ⟨orn⟩ *missel-thrush* | **≈n** vi [h] ⟨rhet⟩ *to snarl, burr*; *to speak with a twang* ‖ (Uhrwerk etc) *to rattle* ‖ ⟨ent⟩ *to stridulate*; ~d *stridulant, rasping*

Schn·atter- ~er m ~s/~; **~gans** f, **~hans** m *prattler, chatterer, chatterbox* **~haft** a *prattling, chattering, chatty* **schn·attern I.** vi [h] (v Gänsen, Enten) *to cackle* ‖ ⟨fig⟩ *to chatter* (⟨a.⟩ *with cold*), *to prattle* ⟨a. zoo⟩ ‖ (Worte) *to gabble* **II.** ≈ n *cackle, cackling* ‖ *prattle, prattling*

schn·auben vi/t [h] *to puff* (*and blow*), *to pant*, ⟨zoo⟩ *to snort* ‖ ⟨mach⟩ *to wheeze* | **nach** Luft ~ *to gasp for breath* ‖ (nach) Rache ~ *to breathe* (*pant for*) *revenge* ‖ **vor** Zorn ~ *to fret and fume, to foam with rage* | sich ~, sich [dat] die Nase ~ *to blow one's nose* **schn·aufen** vi [h] *to breathe hard* od *heavily, to blow, snort* ‖ er schnaufte: .. *he wheezed out*: .. ‖ ~d *stertorous* (*breathing*) **Schn·aufer** m ~s/~ *breath* (*up to one's last b.*) | °**~l** n ~s/~ ⟨mot⟩ *snorting* od *wheezy car*; ⟨sl⟩ *hippo*

Schn·auzbart m *long moustache* ‖ ⟨fig⟩ *impolite person*; *old soldier* **Schn·auze** f ~/~n (of dog) *nose* (⟨a. aero⟩ Rumpfbug); *muzzle* ‖ (of pit) *snout* (⟨fam⟩ a. P), (P a.) *mug* ⟨sl⟩ ‖ (v Kannen etc) *spout* ‖ (am Blasebalg) *nozzle* | °e–e tüchtige ~ h *to have plenty of jaw* ‖ °die ~ voll h *to be fed up* (mit *with*) (*to one's teeth*) ‖ °halt die ~! *shut up! hold your jaw!* ⟨mil⟩ ~! *chuck it! choops!* → Schnabel ‖ jdm über die ~ fahren *to tell a p where to get off* °**schn·auzen** vi/t [h] ⟨fam⟩ *to snarl* (vt/i), *scold, curse*, ⟨fam⟩ *jaw* **≈bauart** f (e–s Lkw) *normal control* †**schn·äuzen** etc = schneuzen etc **Schn·auzer** m ~s/~ (dog) *schnauzer*

Schn·ecke f ~/~n *snail* ‖ (Nackt≈) *slug* ‖ ⟨cul⟩ *escargot* Fr ‖ ⟨tech⟩ Förder≈ *endless screw, gear worm* ‖ *scroll* (*of a violin*) ‖ Uhr≈ *fusee* ‖ ⟨übtr⟩ *spiral* ‖ ⟨arch⟩ *volute, helix* ‖ ⟨anat⟩ *cochlea* ‖ °⟨sex⟩ *periwinkle* | ⟨fig⟩ wie e–e ~ gehen *to walk a snail's pace* **Schn·ecken- ~antrieb** m *worm-drive* **~auge** n ⟨arch, geom⟩ *centre of a volute* od *helix* **~bohrer** m *screw-auger* **~feder** f *volute-spring* **≈fett** a *as plump as a partridge* **~förderer** m *auger* (od *screw, worm*) *conveyor* **≈förmig** a *spiral, helical* **~fraß** m *damage done by snails* **~gang** m *spiral walk*; *winding alley* ‖ ⟨fig⟩ im ~ *at a snail's pace* **~gebläse** n *screw-blower* **~getriebe, ~gewinde** n *worm-gear* **~gewölbe** n *spiral vault* **~haus** n *snail-shell* **~horn** n *spiral horn* ‖ (Fühlhorn) *feeler* **~kegel** m (Uhr) *fusee* **~klee** m ⟨bot⟩ *snail-clover* **~linie** f *spiral, helix* **~muschel** f *conch* **~post** f, **~tempo** n ⟨fig⟩ (*to go a*) *snail's gallop* od *pace* **~trieb** m *endless screw* **~rad** n ⟨tech⟩ *screw-wheel, snail-wheel* ‖ (Uhr) *balance-wheel* **~treppe** f *winding staircase* **~ventilator** m *propeller fan* **~windung** f *spiral turning*; *volution*

Schnee m ~s/ **1.** *snow* (ewig *perpetual*) ‖ frisch gefallener ~ *virgin snow* ‖ (Matsch) *slush* ‖ es war viel ~ gefallen *there had been a heavy snowfall* ‖ der ~ liegt 30 cm hoch, es liegt 30 cm hoher ~ *the snow is a foot deep* ‖ im ~ stecken bleiben *to be snowed up* (⟨Am⟩ *in*) **2.** ⟨cul⟩ *whipped cream, whipped whites* pl; zu ~ schlagen *to whisk until stiff* **3.** ⟨radar⟩ *grass* **4.** (Cocain) *snow* **~ammer** f ⟨orn⟩ *snow-bunting* **≈arm** a *open* (*winter*) **~bahn** f *s.y path, s.-road* **~ball** m *s.ball* ‖ ⟨bot⟩ *guelder-rose, viburnum* ‖ (sich) mit ~en werfen, (sich) ≈balle(r)n *to s.ball* (*each other*); wie ein ~ wachsen *to* (*have a*) *s.ball* (*effect*) | ~brief [m], ~system [n] *s.ball*; *system of cumulative returns*; ~schlacht [f] *s.b. fight* **≈bedeckt** a *s.-clad, s.-capped* **~beere** f *s.-berry* **~besen** m ⟨cul⟩ *whisk* **≈blind** a *s.-blind* **~brille** f (e–e *a pair of*) *s.-goggles* pl **~dach** n *s.-shed* **~decke** f *blanket* od *layer of s.* **~eule** f *s.-owl* **~fall** m *s.-fall* **~flocke** f *s.-flake* **~gans** s *s.-goose* **~gebirge** n *s.-clad mountains* pl **~gestöber** n *s.-storm* **~glöckchen** n ⟨bot⟩ *s.drop* **~grenze** f (*perpetual*) *s.-line* **~hase** m *Alpine hare* **~haufen** m *heap of s.* **~hemd** n (*camouflage*) *ski-smock, parka* **~huhn** n ⟨orn⟩ *s.-grouse* **~hütte** f *igloo* **~kette** f ⟨mot⟩ *non-skid* od *tire chain* **~könig** m ⟨orn⟩ *wren* ‖ er freut sich wie ein ~ *he is as merry as a grig, as happy as a king, as pleased as Punch* **~koppe** f (Riesengebirge) (*Mount*) *Schneekopp* **~kufe** f ⟨aero⟩ *landing skid* **~landschaft** f *snowscape* **~lawine** f = Lawine **~luft** f *s.y wind* **~mann** m *s.-man* **~massen** f pl *snows* **~matsch** m → ~ 1. **~mensch** m (*the*) *abominable snowman* **~pflug** m (mit Schaufeln *revolving*) *s.-plough* ⟨a. rail⟩ **~regen** m *sleet* [koll] **~reifen** m *racket* ⟨mot⟩ **~schipper** m *s.-sweeper* **~schläger** m ⟨cul⟩ *whisk* **~schlamm** m *slush* **~schmelze** f *thaw* **~schuh** m *s.-shoe, ski*; ~ laufen *to go skiing*; mit ~en ausgerüstet ⟨mil⟩ *ski-borne* (Truppe) | ~läufer [m] *skier* **~teller** m *racket* **~traktor** m *snowmobile* **~treiben** n *s.-storm*, (stark) *blizzard* **~verwehung** f *cover of drifted s.* **~wächte** f *s. plume* **~wasser** n *s.-water* **~wehe** f *s.-drift* **≈w·eiß** a *s.-white* **~wetter** n *s.y weather* **~w·ittchen** n (*Little*) *Snow-white* **~wolke** f *s.-cloud* **schn·eeig** a *snowy, snow-clad, snow-white*

Schneid m ~(e)s/ (f ~/) *resoluteness, determination*; ⟨fam⟩ *go, push, dash, pluck, snap* (*to begin with a* ~), ⟨Am⟩ *sand* ‖ ⟨sl⟩ *ginger, guts*, ⟨Am⟩ *pep* **≈bar** a ⟨bes minr⟩ *sectile* **~brenner** m *cutting blow pipe, c. torch, c. burner* **~flüssigkeit** f *cutting fluid* **~haltigkeit** f ⟨tech⟩ *edge-holding property* **~öl** n *cutting oil* **Schn·eide** f ~/~n (*cutting*) *edge* ‖ (e–s Geräts) *bit* **~bank** f *chopping-bench* ‖ *cooper's bench* **~bohnen** f pl *French beans* pl **~bohrer** m *screw-tap* **~brett** n *carving* od *flat board* **~hobel** m *slitting-plane* **~maschine** f *cutter*; ⟨phot⟩ *edger*, (*print*) *trimmer* **~mühle** f *saw-mill* **~tisch** m ⟨film, rec⟩ *editing t.* **~werk** n ⟨met⟩ *slitting-mill* **~(werk)zeug** n *cutter, edge-tool* **~zahn** m *incisor* **~zeug** n *cutting-tools* pl **~zirkel** m *cutting-compasses* pl **schn·eiden I.** vt/i [schnitt/ge–en] [h] (→ ab–, be–, ein–, zurecht~) **A. 1.** *to cut*; *to scissor, snip* (an *at*, zu *into*); kl ~ *to mince* | ⟨film⟩ *to trim* (*ready-trimmed film*); ~ u betiteln *to edit* ‖ in 2 Teile ~ *to cut in two* | (hacken) *to chop, shred* ‖ (schnitzen) *to carve* ‖ *to engrave* ‖ (spalten) *to split, cleave* **2.** (das Messer) –det **nicht** .. *won't cut* od *has no edge* **3. (jdn)** ~ *to cheat, overcharge, fleece* ‖ (nicht grüßen) *to cut* od *freeze a p* (*dead* total); *to send .. to Coventry*; ⟨Am sl⟩ *to go by* ‖ ostentativ .. *to give a p the cut direct* | er muß ge–en w *he has to be operated on* **B. (Bälle)** ⟨ten⟩ *to cut, twist, screw* ‖ (Bäume) *to prune* || (Braten) *to carve* || (Bretter) *to saw* || (jdm) die Fahrbahn ∼, Fahrzeuge ∼ ⟨mot⟩ *to cut in sharply* (*in front of the vehicle overtaken*) || (e–e **Feder**) *to mend* || ihm das Fleisch ∼ *to cut his meat for him* || ⟨fig⟩ (**Geld**, Gesichter, Grimassen) *to make* || (Gewinde) *to thread* || (Gras) *to mow* || (**Haare**) *to clip*; sich die Haare (den Bart) ∼ l *to have one's hair cut* (*beard trimmed*) || (Holz) *to saw* || (**Korn**) *to reap* || sich die Nägel ∼ *to cut, pare one's nails* || (Schrauben) *to thread* || e–n Stempel ∼ *to sink a die* || e–m den Stein ∼ ⟨surg⟩ *to operate on a p for the stone* || (Stroh) *to chop* || (T) *to castrate* || ⟨fig⟩ (Wein) *to adulterate*, ⟨fam⟩ *to doctor* **C. sich** ∼ *to cut o.s.*; ⟨fig⟩ *to be mistaken* bzw *disappointed* (gewaltig *grievously* bzw *greatly*) || (v Linien, Straßen) *to cross, intersect* (in W.n *at angles*) **D. sich an** etw ∼ .. *on* .. || s–m Vater wie **aus** dem Gesicht ge–en *the very image of his f.* | **durch, in** etw ∼ *to cut a th* | **in**: *to carve a figure in wood* || *to cut lines in stone* || ins lebendige Fleisch ∼ *to cut to the quick* || das –det mir durchs *or* ins Herz *that cuts me to the quick* od *heart, pierces my heart* || sich in den Finger ∼ *to cut one's f.* | **in** Streifen ∼ *to shred* ⟨a. cul⟩ || in Stücke ∼ *to cut up* | **mit** der Dame ∼ ⟨cards⟩ *to finesse the queen* **II.** ∻ n *cutting* etc || ⟨path⟩ ∼ im Leib *sharp pain in the stomach, colic*, ⟨fam⟩ *the gripes* || ⟨surg⟩ *incision* || ⟨geom⟩ *intersection* (*of lines*) **III. ∼d** a *cutting sharp* || ⟨fig⟩ *piercing, nipping* (*wind, cold*) || es ist ∼d kalt *it's bitterly cold* || *sharp* (*pain*) || *shrill* (*whistle*) || *glaring* (*colours*) || *biting* (*mockery*) || *sarcastic* (*remark*) || *ironical* (*speech*) || *keen* (*intellect*) || *marked* (*contrast*) **IV. geschnitten** a fein ∼ *finely cut* od *chiselled* (*profile*) || griechisch ∼e Nase *Greek profile* || mandelförmig ∼ *almond-shaped* (*eyes*) **Schn·eider** m ∼s/∼ **1.** *cutter* **2.** *tailor*, ⟨sl⟩ *snip* || Damen∻ *ladies' t.* || Maß∻ *bespoke t.* **3.** ⟨fig⟩ *poltroon*; *weakling* **4.** ⟨ent⟩ *daddy-long--legs* **5.** ⟨cards⟩ ∼ w (aus dem ∼ heraus s) *to score less* (*more*) *than 30 points at* Skat; (⟨fig⟩ *to be on the shady side of thirty*) **∼arbeit** f *t.'s work* || ([a. attr] v Kleidern) *t.-made* **∼gesell(e)** m *journeyman-t.* **∼handwerk** n *t.'s trade* od *business* **∼herberge** f *house of call for t.s* **∼karpfen** n ⟨hum⟩ *herring* **∼kleid** n *t.-made, costume* **∼kreide** f *French chalk* **∼lehrling** m *t.'s apprentice* **∼mamsell** f *t.ess* **∻mäßig** a *t.-like* **∼meister** m *master t.* **∼puppe** f *t.'s dummy* **∼rechnung** f *t.'s bill* **∼schere** f (eine *a pair of*) *t.'s shears* pl **∼seele** f ⟨fig⟩ *grovelling creature* | **im ∼sitz** (*to sit*) *t.-fashion* **∼tisch** m *t.'s shop board* **∼werkstatt** f *t.'s workshop* **∼zunft** *f t.s' company* **Schneider·ei** f ∼/∼en *t.ing, t.'s business* || *dressmaking* || (Hausarbeit) *needle--work* || ⟨fig⟩ *cheating, fleecing* **Schn·eiderin** f ∼/∼en *dressmaker, ladies' t.* **schn·eidern** vi [h] *to make clothes, to tailor* (für .. *a p*) **schn·eidig** a *sharp, cutting* || (mutig) *spirited, plucky*, ⟨fam⟩ *full of go* || *resolute* (*character*) || (fesch) *dashing, smart, snappy* || (schnell) *rattling* (*pace*) || ⟨mus⟩ (*a march*) *with plenty of go in it* || ⟨fam⟩ *zippy* | [adv] *with a flourish* | **∻keit** f ∼ *pluck, dash, smartness*, ⟨fam⟩ *go*

schn·eien vi **1.** [h] → Schnee; es schneit (heftig) *it snows, it is snowing*, (*the snow is falling fast*) **2.** [s] er kam *or* ist uns ins Haus ge–t *he unexpectedly popped in*

Schn·eise f ⟨for⟩ (*straight*) *glade*; *fire line* || *vista, aisle* || ⟨aero⟩ *runway funnel*; → Schneide

schnell A. a (Bewegung, Puls, Bote, Blick, Auffassung, Entschluß) *quick* || (Lauf, Fuß, Vogel, Flug) *swift* || (Pferd etc) *fleet* || (ohne Aufschub erfolgend) *speedy* || (Zug, Flugzeug, Schiff) *fast*; *fast moving* (*troops*) || (Strömung, Schritte, Gewehrfeuer, Wuchs) *rapid* || (Antwort, Zahlung) *prompt* || (Verkauf) *ready, brisk*; Umsatz (*quick*) || (plötzlich) *sudden* || (hastig) *rash, hasty* | ⟨übtr⟩ *fast* (*girl*) | → Blitz **B.** [adv] (*to act*) *promptly* || (fortschreiten *to go on*) *apace* || ∼ fahren ⟨Am a.⟩ *to make good time* || sehr ∼ fahren ⟨bes mot⟩ *to speed* || das **geht** ∼ *that's quickly done* || ∼ gehen *to go fast, to put one's best leg forward* || so ∼ **wie** .. *fast as* od *like* (*a thunderbolt, a streak of lightning, a blue streak, a bat out of hell*) || so ∼ wie möglich ⟨contr, etc⟩ *with all speed* | **∼er** gehen *to hasten one's step*, .. als jd *to outmarch a p* || es ging ihm ∼ v der Hand *he was quick about it* || so ∼ er **konnte** *at his best pace* || ∼ laufend *high--speed* (*engine*) || **mach'** ∼! *be quick!, hurry up!, look sharp!* || man kann **so** ∼ k–n Ersatzmann finden *a s. cannot be found at this short notice*; nicht so ∼! *gently!, steady!* || etw ∼ überblicken *to run one's eyes over a th* || er **will** ∼ .. *he is in a hurry to do it* | ∼ **in** Tränen u Zorn (s) .. *given to tears and furies* | **∼er** reiten als (die anderen) *to outride* .. | **∼stens** *at full speed, with the utmost speed, with a rush* **Schn·ell-** [in comp oft] *speed-*(*boat, skating*) || *high-speed* (*railway, press, engine*) || *portable* (*bridge*) || *instantaneous* (*fuze*) || *q.-acting* (*mechanism*) **∼ablaß** m ⟨tech⟩ *q.-release* | ∼ventil [n] *q. damp valve* **∼arbeit** f *hustle* **∼bleiche** f *chemical bleaching* **∼boot** n *motor* (⟨mil⟩ *torpedo*) *boat*, ⟨mil⟩ *assault b.* **∼brief** m *express letter* **∼dampfer** m *fast steamer, express liner*; *clipper* **∼drehstahl** m *h.-s. steel* **∻fassend** a ⟨psych⟩ *sharp, q.* **∼feuer** n ⟨mil⟩ *running* od *rapid fire* | ∼geschütz [n] *q.-firing gun, q. firer* (*Q.F.*); automatisches ∼ *pom-pom* (*gun*); ∼waffe [f] *automatic weapon* **∼frage** f ⟨wir⟩ *q.y* **∻füßig** a *fleet* od *swift* (*-footed*) **∼gaststätte** f *q.-service restaurant* **∼hefter** m (*rapid*) *letter-file, q. file* **∼imbiß** m *snack*, e–n ∼ nehmen *to s. up* | ∼halle [f] = –gaststätte; ∼stube [f] *snack-bar*, ⟨bes Am⟩ *cafeteria* **∼käfer** m *elator*; *click-beetle* | ∼larve [f] *wire-worm* **∼kaffee** m *instant c.* **∼kocher** m *q. cooker* **∼kochtopf** m *pressure cooker* **∼kopie** f *quick print* **∼kopierverfahren** n ⟨rep⟩ *rapid copying* **∼kraft** f *elasticity, spring* **∼küche** f *instant-cooking* **∼kupplung** f *bayonet c.* **∼kurs** m *accelerated course* **∼(l)ade** f ⟨weav⟩ *fly-shuttle lathe* **∼(l)ader** m *q.-loading* od *automatic gun* **∼(l)auf** m ⟨sport⟩ *s.-running*; im ∼ *at full s.* **∼(l)äufer** m *racer*; ⟨fam⟩ *skip-jack* **∼(l)ot** n *tin-solder* **∼messer** m ⟨surv⟩ *tachymeter* **∼photographie** f *instantaneous ph.y*, (Bild) *snap-shot* **∼post** f *diligence, express mail*(*-coach*) **∼presse** f *fly-press, steam-p.* || ⟨typ⟩ *mechanical p.* **∼rechner** m *h.-s. electronic computer* **∼richter** m *judge of summary court* **∼rücklauf** m ⟨rec⟩ *fast rewind* **∼rührer** m ⟨cul⟩ *impeller* **∼schaltkabel** n ⟨el⟩ *q. link c.* **∼schleppscheibe** f *fast-towing target* **∼schluß** m *q.-action closure* **∼schreiber** m (Gerät) *tachygraph* || (P) *shorthand writer, stenographer* **∼schrift** f *shorthand, stenography*; ⟨tech & hist⟩ *tachygraphy* **∼schritt** m *q. march*; im ∼ marschieren *to double* **∼schußkamera** f ⟨phot⟩ *quick-fire c.* **∼schütz(e)** m ⟨tech⟩ *flying shuttle* **∼segler** m *fast sailer, clipper* **∼speicher** m ⟨comp⟩ *rapid memory* **∼sperre** f ⟨mil⟩ *hasty obstacle* **∼straße** f *express street* (abbr. E) **∼test** m *spot t.* **∼triebwagen** m *rail-car* **∼trockenleine** f *seccotine* **∼urteil** n *snap judgment* **∼verband** m ⟨med⟩ *adhesive bandage* od *tape* **∼verhör** n *rapid trial* **∼verkehr** m ⟨rail⟩ *fast service*, ⟨Am⟩ *rapid transit* | ∼straße [f] *speedway* **∼waage** f *steel--yard*; *h.-s. balance, self-indicating, scale* **∼weg** m *speedway* **∻wüchsig** a *fast-growing* **∼zeichner** m *lightning artist* **∼zug** m *express* (*train*), *fast train* || ⟨Am a.⟩ *flyer* **∼z·ugriffspur** f ⟨comp⟩ *fastband* **∼zünder** m *q. match* **∻züngig** a *voluble* **∼züngigkeit** f *volubility* **schnellen I.** vt [h] *to let fly* od *rebound*; *to jerk, whip, flick*; *to toss* (*up*); (prellen) *to toss* **II.** vi [s] *to spring, jerk* || *to fly off* || *to kick* od *bound* (*up*) | (P) hoch|∼ *to start up*; *to shoot* od *snap erect* (*in salute*) || **mit** dem Finger *to flick a f.* **Schn·eller** m ∼s/∼ *flick* || (Nasenstüber) *fillip* ||

(am Gewehr) *hair-trigger* **Schn·elligkeit** f ~/ *quickness* (a. *of pulse*), *speed, swiftness, celerity, hurry; promptness, rapidity; dispatch* (*of the law*) || ⟨tech⟩ *velocity* || *suddenness* || mit großer ~ *at a quick rate* **~srekord** m *speed record*; → Rekord

Schn·epfe f ~/~n ⟨orn⟩ (→ *godwit*) → *snipe* (~n [pl] *snipe*), *woodcock* || ~n schießen *to snipe* | ⟨fig, vulg⟩ (*streetwalker*) *nightingale, owl, pheasant* | **~n-** **~dreck** m ⟨cul⟩ *roast giblets* (pl *of s.*) **~jagd** f *s.-shooting* **~strauß** m ⟨orn⟩ *kiwi* **~strich** m *passage of wood-cocks* || auf den ~ gehen *to s.* **~zug** m *flock of s.s* **Schn·eppe** f ~/~n **1.** (an Kannen) *spout* **2.** ⟨vulg⟩ *streetwalker*; → Schnepfe **Schn·epper** = Schnäpper

schn·euzen vt [h]; sich *or* die Nase ~ *to snot* (*to blow one's nose*); mit den Fingern .. *to sling a snot* || (e–e Kerze) *to snuff* °**Schn·euztuch** n *snot-rag*

Schn·ickschnack m ~(e)s/ *chit-chat, tittle-tattle, twaddle* || *trash* || ~! *nonsense*!

schn·ieben, schniefen vi [h] = schnauben

schn·iegeln vt [h] *to trick* od *fig out*; *to dress up*; *to smarten, prink* || ge–lt u gebügelt *spick and span* °**schn·ieke** a (fesch) *smart*, ⟨sl⟩ *spiffy*

°**Schn·iepel** m ~s/~ (Frack) *swallow-tail(s* pl); ⟨sl⟩ *full waiters*

schnipp! **1.** *snap*! ~ schnapp! *snip-snap* **2.** n (Schneider) *nip-shred, Mr Snip* **≈chen** n ~s/~ *snap* || jdm ein ~ schlagen *to snap one's fingers at a p* || ⟨fig⟩ *to play a trick on a p, to overreach* (*one's pursuers*) **≈(s)el** m & n ~s/~ *scrap, snip* (*of paper*) || ~ [pl] *snippets* pl **schn·ippeln** vt/i [h] *to cut into snips, to cut up, to snip* (an *at*, zu *into*) **~(s)en I.** vt [h] *to snip, snap* (mit .. *a th*) **II.** vi [h] *to snap one's finger, to flip* **~isch** a *pert, perky, snappish, airy* || ~ erwidern *to snap*

schnitt 1. & 3. sg pret v schneiden **Schnitt** m ~(e)s/~e *cut(ting)* ⟨a. film⟩; ⟨film a.⟩ *editing*; ⟨phot⟩ *section*; *snip* (*of the scissors*) || ⟨bookb⟩ *cut, fore-edge* || (Kerbe) *notch* || (Wunde) *cut, gash, flesh-wound* | ⟨surg⟩ *incision, operation* | ⟨agr⟩ *harvest(ing), reaping, crop* | ⟨geom⟩ (*inter*)-*-section*; goldener ~ *golden section*; Kegel≈ *conic section* || (Quer–, Längs–, Schräg– *horizontal, longitudinal, oblique*) *section*; *profile* | ⟨arts⟩ *cut, engraving*; *silhouette* | ⟨tail⟩ *cut, make, shape*; *build* (*of a coat*); nach dem neuesten ~ *up-to-date* [a. attr], *in the latest fashion*; schräger ~ (*cut on the*) *bias* || (~muster) *pattern, model* | ⟨bookb⟩ *edge* | (Scheibe) *slice*; (Stück) *piece*; (Bier) *small glass* | ⟨fig⟩ (Übervorteilung) *unfair profit*; s–n ~ m (*to do a fine stroke of business*), *to feather one's nest, to cut a large melon*, ⟨Am⟩ *to make one's pile*, e–n gr ~ m ⟨fam⟩ *to cut a large melon*; .. bei etw *to make a large profit over a th* | im ~ = Durch≈ **~ansicht** f ⟨tech⟩ *cutaway drawing*; *exploded view* **~aufnahme** f ⟨phot⟩ *sectional exposure* **~ball** m ⟨ten⟩ *twister* **~bild** n *sectional view* **~blumen** f pl *cut flowers* **~bohne** f *French bean* **~brot** n *sliced br.* **~fläche** f *cut*; ⟨geom⟩ *plane of intersection* **~gut** n *loose material* **~hobel** m *paring-knife* **~holz** n (*sawn*) *timber* **~kohl** m *cabbage* **~lauch** m *chives* pl **~linie** f *line of intersection* **~meister** m *film cutter* **~messer** n ⟨surg⟩ *bistoury*; ⟨agr⟩ *pruning knife* **~modellzeichnung** f *phantom view* **~muster** n *pattern* **~punkt** m (*point of*) *intersection* **~rand** m *sectional edge* **≈reif** a ⟨agr⟩ *ready for cutting* **~salat** m *lettuce* **~waren** f pl *drapery, mercery, dry-goods*; *piece goods* | ~-händler [m] *mercer, draper* **≈weise** [adv] *in slices* **~wunde** f *cut, gash* **~zeichnung** f *sectional drawing* **Schn·ittchen** n ~s/~ ⟨cul⟩ *canapé* **Schn·itte** f ~/~n *slice* (*of bread, meat*); *cut* (*of meat, pork*); *rasher* (*of bacon*) || ⟨cul⟩ (v Fisch u Fleisch) *steak* | **~r** m ~s/~ *reaper, harvester, mower* | **~rin** f ~/~nen (*female*) *reaper* **schn·ittig** a *smart(-looking), racy, brisk, lively, sprightly*; ⟨mot⟩ → rassig; *trim* (*sailboat*) **Schn·ittling** m ~(e)s/~e ⟨hort⟩ *cutting, slip* || = Schnittlauch || *recently gelted ox*

Schn·itz m ~es/~e *slice, chop, cut* | ~arbeit [f] (*wood-*)*carving*; ~bank [f] *cooper's* bzw *carver's bench*; ~messer [n] *carving-knife*; *whittle*; ~-werk [n] *carved work* | ~el [n] ~s/~ *cutting, snip, chip* || *scrap* (*of paper*) || ⟨cul⟩ *scallop, escalop*; Wiener ~ (*breaded*) *veal cutlet*; ⟨Am a.⟩ *schnitzel* || ~ [pl] (Abfälle) *shavings, parings*, ⟨hunt⟩ *scents* pl → **~jagd** f *paper-chase*, ⟨sl⟩ *bumf*; → Klopapier **~maschine** f *slicer*; Bohnen≈ *shredder* | **~el·ei** f ~/~en *cutting, carving* | **≈e(l)n** vt/i [h] *to whittle, chip, cut*; *to carve* || ⟨fig⟩ aus demselben Holz geschnitzt *a chip of the same block* | **~er** m ~s/~ **1.** (P) *wood-carver*; *cutter* **2.** *cooper's* etc *knife* **3.** ⟨fam, fig⟩ *blunder, slip*, ⟨Am⟩ *boner*; lächerlicher ~ *howler*; Sprach≈ *solecism*; in der Gesellschaft e–n ~ m *to make a break, a faux pas* Fr | **~er·ei** f ~/~en *wood-carving*; *carved work* | **≈ern** vi [h] *to blunder, bungle, botch*

schnob 1. & 3. sg pret v schnauben, schnieben

schn·odderig a *cheeky, saucy*, ⟨Am a.⟩ *sassy* **≈keit** f *cheek, sauciness* **schn·öde** a **1.** (geringschätzig) *disdainful, scornful, contemptuous* **2.** (rücksichtslos) *inconsiderate* || jdn ~ behandeln *to use a p badly* **3.** (verächtlich, schändlich) *contemptible, despicable, base, heinous, mean* || ~er Gewinn *vile profit*; ~er Mammon *filthy lucre* || ~en Undank ernten *to meet with black ingratitude* **Schn·ödigkeit** f ~/ *scornfulness* || *baseness, heinousness, vileness*, etc

schn·opern vt [h] = schnuppern

Schn·orchel m ~s/~ ⟨mar⟩ *snorkel*

Schn·örkel m ~s/~ ⟨arch⟩ *scroll, volute* || Schrift≈ *flourish, twirl*, ⟨Am fam⟩ *curlicue* || ⟨mus⟩ *ornamentation* || ⟨rhet⟩ *euphuistic expression*; *embroidery* ⟨fig⟩ **~schrift** f *flourishy handwriting* | **≈n** vi [h] *to make flourishes* | vt ⟨arch⟩ *to adorn with scrolls* || ge–lt ⟨a.⟩ *twisted*, ⟨rhet⟩ *euphuistic* | **~·ei** f ~/~en *superfluous ornaments*

schn·orren vt/i [h] ⟨fam⟩ *to cadge* **Schn·orrer** m ~s/~ *cadger*, ⟨bes Am⟩ *freeloader*

°**Schn·ösel** m ~s/~ *dandy, fop, coxcomb*; ⟨Am⟩ *show-off*

Schn·ucke f ~/~n *small sheep* || ⟨fam⟩ mein Schnuckchen *my pet*

schn·üffeln vi/t [h] *to snuffle, sniff(le)* || (T) *to nuzzle, nose* | ⟨fig⟩ *to smell, pry*; *to* (*act the*) *spy* || ⟨fam⟩ *to nose* (*at, in, about*) | *to speak through the nose* **Schnüffel-** **~nase** f ⟨sl⟩ *nosey* **~ventil** n *blow-valve* **Schn·üffler** m ~s/~ *snuffer* || ⟨fig⟩ *spy, snooper*

Schn·uller m ~s/~ (*baby's*) *dummy, comforter*, ⟨Am⟩ *pacifier*

Schn·ulze f ~/~n *soap-opera, gasser*, ⟨sl⟩ *hokum* || *tear-jerker*

Schnupf- **~tabak** m *snuff* **~tabakdose** f *snuff-box* **~tuch** n (*pocket-*)*handkerchief* **Schn·upfen** m ~s/ *cold* (*in the head*), *catarrh* || den ~ h *to be troubled with a cold* || den ~ bek *to catch cold* | ~fieber [n] *influenza* | ≈ vt/i [h] *to snuff* | vi [h] *to take snuff* **Schn·upfer** m ~s/~ *snuff-taker, snuffer* **schn·upfig** a *having a cold* **Schn·uppe** f ~/~n (Licht≈) *snuff* || (Stern≈) *falling* od *shooting star* °**schn·uppe** a = egal

schn·uppern vi [h] *to smell, snuffle, nose*

Schnur[1] f ~/~en ⟨bib⟩ *daughter-in-law*

Schnur[2] f ~/~en u ≈e *twine, cord* || *whip-cord* || ⟨el⟩ *flex* || ⟨hunt⟩ *leash* || ⟨tail⟩ *lace*; *tape, trimming* || ⟨mil⟩ *aiguillette* | *string* (*of pearls*) | **mit** ~ besetzen *to braid*, ⟨tail⟩ *to trim with cord*; mit ≈en befestigt *corded* (*weight*) || **nach** der ~ *by the line* || **über** die ~ hauen ⟨fig⟩ *to kick over the traces, to overshoot the mark*; einmal .. *to break the rule for once* **~besatz** m *braid trimming, piping*; (verschlungen) *frog* **≈ger·ade** a *straight, as the crow flies* **~stracks** [adv] *directly* || *by the string rather than by the bow*; ~ gehen nach *to make a beeline for* | (sofort) *immediately, on the* *spot*, ~ zuwider *diametrically opposed* **~zugfeder** f *turned-up point nib* | ≈- **~band** n (*stay-* od *boot-)lace* **~boden** m ⟨mar⟩ (*mould-)loft* || ⟨theat⟩ *drawing-, rigging-loft*; *grid* | ~anschluß [m] *fly--plug*; ~mann [m] *flyman* **~brust** f *stays* pl, *corset* **~kette** f *lacing-chain* **~latz, ~leib(chen** n) m *stays* pl, *corset* **~loch** n *eyelet* **~nadel, ~nestel** f *bodkin* **~riemen** m = ~band **~rock** m *frogged coat* **~schalter** m ⟨el⟩ *line cord* **~schuhe** m pl *lace boots* **~senkel** m (*shoe-)lace* || ~ [pl] *lacings* pl **~stiefel** m pl *lace-boots* pl **Schn·ürchen** n ~s/~; etw am ~ h ⟨fig⟩ *to have a th at one's fingers' ends* || es geht wie am ~ *it goes like clock-work* od *one o'clock* || etw am ~ können *to know a th off pat* **schn·üren I.** vt [h] *to lace* (⟨a.⟩ *a corset*) || *to string* (*pearls*) || (zubinden) *to tie* (*up*), *to* (*fasten with a*) *cord* || ⟨med⟩ *to underbind* (*a limb*) | **sich** ~ *to wear stays* | ⟨fig⟩ das Bündel ~ *to cut one's stick*, (*to prepare for departure*) || es schnürt mir das Herz (die Kehle) zu *it makes my heart ache* (*a lump rises in my throat*) **II.** vi [s] (Fuchs) *to trot*

schnurr! *buzz*!, *whir*! **≈bart** m *moustache* (englischer *toothbrush m.*) || sich [dat] e–n ~ wachsen l *to grow a moustache* | ~spitzen [f pl] *waxed moustaches* **~bärtig** a *moustached* **Schn·urre** f ~/~n ⟨obs⟩ *rattle*; *spinning-wheel*; ⟨fig⟩ *old hag* | (Posse) *drollery, droll story, buffoonery, funny tale* || *jest* || *piece of nonsense* || *freak, whim* **schn·urren** vi [h] *to rattle* || ⟨ent⟩ *to hum, to buzz* || (Räder) *to whir(r)* || (Katze) *to purr* ⟨fig⟩ a. mot⟩ || = schnorren **schn·urrig** a *droll, funny* || (wunderlich) *queer, odd*; ⟨sl⟩ *rum* **≈keit** f ~/ *drollery* **Schnurrpfeifer·ei** f ~/~en *drollery* || *trifle, trash* || ~en [pl] *rattletraps, odds and ends* **schnurz** a; das ist mir ~! *much I care*!; ⟨bes Am⟩ *I couldn't care less* °**Schn·ute** f ~/~n *pouting lips* pl || ⟨sl⟩ *mug* || ⟨fig⟩ e–e ~ m *to be in the pouts*

schob 1. & 3. sg pret v schieben **Sch·ober** m ~s/~ *stack, heap, mow, rick* || *shock* (*of sheaves*) || *shed* **sch·obern** vt [h] *to stack, to heap up* **Schock** n ~(e)s/~e **1.** *sixty, threescore* || ⟨fig⟩ *a whole crowd* (*of children*) **2.** ⟨path⟩ *shock* (erleiden *to get*) || jdm e–n ~ versetzen (S) *to come as a sh. to a p*; (P) *to sh. a p* **sch·ocken I.** vt [h] *to dispose in heaps* od *bundles of sixty each* || *to shock* (*corn*) | (stoßen) *to thrust* **II.** vi [h] *to yield much* **schokk·ieren** vt [h] *to outrage, shock* **Sch·ockschwerен·ot**! *damn it all*! **sch·ockweise** [adv] *by three scores*

°**sch·ofel(ig)** a ⟨fam⟩ *paltry, worthless*; ⟨sl⟩ *trashy* || *miserly* || *mean* (*fellow*), *shabby* (*conduct*) || [adv] ~ aussehen *to look shabby*; → Schuft

Sch·öffe m ~n/~n ⟨jur⟩ *juror, juryman* **~ngericht** n *jury-court*; ⟨engl⟩ *court of aldermen*

Schoff·ör m ~s/~e → Chauffeur

Schokol·ade f ~/~n; ⟨hot a.⟩ **Sch·ok** [invar] *chocolate* **~nfabrik** f *ch.-works* [sg konstr] **~nfabrikant** m *ch.-manufacturer* **~geschäft** n *sweet--shop* **~nkanne** f *ch.-pot* **~plätzchen** n pl *ch.-drops* pl **~ntafel** f *cake* (od *square* od *block*) *of ch.* **~ntasse** f *ch.-cup*

Schol- **~·ar** m ~en/~en ⟨Ger⟩ *medieval* (*itinerant*) *student* **~·astik** f ~/ *scholasticism* | ~er [m] ~s/~ *scholastic, schoolman* **≈·astisch** a *scholastic* **~i·ast** m ~en/~en *scholiast, commentator* **Sch·olie** f ~/~n *scholium, commentary*

scholl 1. & 3. sg pret v schallen

Sch·olle[1] f ~/~n ⟨ich⟩ *plaice* [a. pl]

Sch·olle[2] f ~/~n *clod* || *lump* (*of ice* = *floe*) || ⟨geol⟩ *block* || an die ~ gebunden *deeply rooted in the soil*; an der ~ hängen *to love* (*to stay in* od *cling to*) *one's native soil* od *country* || auf eigener ~ *on one's own soil* **~nbrecher** m *clod-crusher* **~ngebirge** n *block mountains* **sch·ollig** a *cloddy, lumpy*

Sch·öllkraut n ⟨bot⟩ *celandine*

sch·ölte 1. & 3. sg subj pret v schelten

schon [adv] **A.** *already* (~ $^{1}/_{2}2$ *half past one a.*) || ~ 3 Jahre tot *dead now 3 years* || ~ 1893 *as far back as 1893* | ~ **als** Kind *when a ch., from childhood* | ~ **am** nächsten T. *the very next day* || als ob ~ **einmal** gesehen *as though previsited* || **in**: *as early as* (od *already in*) *the tenth century*; *so long ago as last May* || ~ im Frieden *in peacetime* || ~ in den 20er Jahren ⟨bes Am⟩ *back in the twenties* | **nach**: *within a month* || ~ **vor** 1875 *so long ago as 1875* || ~ **zu** Cäsars Zeiten *as far back as the age of C.* **B.** (**bis jetzt**) (*he should be here*) *by this time* || (*have you been abroad*) *yet*? || ~ **damals** *even at that time* || ~ früher *long before this* || ~ immer *always* || ~ **jetzt** *already* || ~ lange *long ago, long since*; *I had planned it a long time ago* || ~ längst *a very long time ago* **C.** nicht .., ~ **gar nicht** *not .., not .. anyway*; *not .., to say nothing of ..*; *let alone ..* || ich werde es dir ~ **noch** sagen *I won't forget to tell you in time* || **nun** ist es aber ~ so *well, what is, must be*; was nun ~ wieder *what is it again*? || **so** ~ genug .. *enough .. as it is* || ~ **über** 1 Stunde (*she had been gone*) *this hour and more* || .. überhaupt ~? .. *at all*? || ~ **weil** (wegen) *just* (od *if only*) *because* (*of*) || **wenn** ~! *well, that's no odds*! || wenn .. nur ~ ..! *if it were only time now*! *if he would only come*! | wenn es ~ wahr ist *even if it is true*, (*al*)*though it be true* || wenn ~, dann gründlich *if at all, then properly* || wenn ~, denn ~! *as well be hung for a sheep as for a lamb*! **D.** ~ der **Anblick** *the bare* od *very sight* || ~ anstandshalber *for mere courtesy* || ~ der Gedanke (*even*) *the very idea, the mere thought* **E.** ~ **ganz** erwachsen *quite grown-up* || ~ **gut**! *all right, very well, that'll do*!, *quite right* (aber *but*) || das ist (alles) ~ **richtig,** aber .. *that is* (*all*) *very well, but ..* || ~ **wahr**: *that's true enough*!, *it is certainly quite true, but ..* **F.** (**futurisch,** tröstend) *surely* (*it will be all right*) || *I trust* (od *never fear*) (*he will be in time*) || *no doubt* (*he will know*) || (*they will put him up*) *all right* || er **wird** ~ k *he will be sure enough to come* || (*we'll find them*) *soon enough* || (*he will prove all right*) *in the end* || das wird er ~ m *wait and you will see him doing it* || das wird ~ stimmen *that is probably quite true* **G.** ~ **denken**: *I thought it was at least a thief* || ich gehe ~ *I'm just going* || ~ glauben: *he did not disbelieve it, but ..* || genug h: *he has already enough* || das **kenne** ich ~ *that's an old story* || wir k ~! *coming*! || mach' ~! *now, hurry up*! || was macht es ~! *what does it matter*? || müssen: *after all I had to give in* || nun rede doch ~! *say sth*! || da sind wir ~! *here we are*! ⟨fam⟩ das ist ~ ein Bild! *that's sth like a picture*! || wie lange **warten** Sie ~? *how long have you been waiting*? || wissen: *you know well enough what I mean* || zugeben müssen: *I cannot help admitting it* || (*it may*) *indeed* (*be in one of them*) **schön I.** a **A. 1.** ⟨allg⟩ *beautiful*; ⟨poet a.⟩ *beauteous*; ⟨Scot⟩ *bonnie* **2.** (gut) *excellent* (*butter* etc) **3.** ~ **von** Gesicht *good-looking* || ~ v Gestalt *well built* od *made* || **zum** Malen ~ *a perfect picture* || ~ anzusehen *beautiful to see* **B.** ~! *that's right*!, *right you are*! *all right*! || *nice going*!, *there*! || *certainly*! | das ist alles recht *or* ganz ~ u gut *that's all very well*, (*but*); *right enough*, (*but*); ~ u gut! *so far, so good*! || das ist (nicht) ~ v dir *it is very kind* (*not nice*) *of you* || das wäre ja noch **~er**! *that would be the limit*!, *certainly not*! || das wäre ~ gewesen *now, that would have been nice* **C.** (**Alter**) *fine old* (*age*) || e–m ~e Augen m *to flirt with a p* || (Charakterzug) *fine* || ~en Dank! *many thanks* || (**Frau**) *beautiful, lovely, fair*; ~e Frau, ~es Mädchen *or* Kind! ⟨fam⟩ *pretty*! || (Gelegenheit) *good* || ein ~es Geschäft m *to do a fine stroke of business* || ~e Geschichte! ⟨fam⟩ *fine th* od *doings*! || (Geschlecht) *fair* (*sex*) [*a lover of the sex*] || (Gesicht) *good-looking* || ~e Grüße *kind regards* || (**Hand**) (zu Kindern) *the right hand* || (Handlung) *noble (action)* || (~ste Harmonie) *perfect* || sich in die ~sten Kleider werfen *to dress in one's finest* || (Konzert) *magnificent* || (Künste) *fine* || (Literatur) *polite* || manch ~es **Mal** *many a time* || (Mann) *handsome*; ⟨iron⟩ *precious* || e-s ~en Morgens *one fine m.* || in ~ster Ordnung *in apple-pie order* || du bist mir e-e ~e Hilfe! ⟨derog⟩ *you're a hell of a helper*! || das sind mir ~e **Sachen**! *pretty* od *fine doings indeed*!; ~e Sn sagen *to make pretty speeches* (*to*) || (Seele) *beautiful, fair* || (Spaziergang) *pleasant* || ein ~es Stück Geld *a lot of m.* || (Summe) *nice round* || (**Tag**) *fine* || (Tod) *easy* || (Tracht Prügel) *a jolly good thrashing* || (Vermögen) *handsome* || e-n ~en Vortrag h *to have a fine delivery* || *the fashionable world* || *lovely, fine weather* || ~e Wissenschaften *belles lettres* || ~e **Worte** m *to make flattering speeches* || (Zeiten) *fine* || das war kein ~er Zug v ihm *that was not nice of him* **D.** ⟨emph⟩ sei ~ **brav**! *now, be good*! || ~ schlecht *or* mies! *pretty bad*! || ~ warm *nice* od *lovely and warm* || sich ~ wehe tun *to hurt o.s. badly* **E.** sich ~ **anfühlen** *to have a good feel* || sich f etw ~stens bedanken *to decline decidedly* || **bitte** ~! *don't mention it*! ⟨Am⟩ *you are welcome* || ich bitte ~ *please* || das werde ich ~ bleiben l *I shall take good care not to do that* || **danke** ~! *thank you very much* || da sind wir ~ daran *we are in a nice fix* || sich ~ erschrecken *to get a nice fright* || ~ geformt *beautifully shaped* (*hands*) || ~er gestalten *to beautify* || ~stens **grüßen** *to send one's kindest regards* || ~ heraus s *to be a lucky fellow* || ~ klingen *to sound nice* || Sie h ~ lachen *it's very well for you to laugh* || sich ~ langweilen *to find it awfully slow* || ~ m *to make fine, to clean up*; (of dog) *to beg* || etw ~ m *to manage sth well* || sich ~ m *to adorn, prettify, glamo(u)rize o.s.*, ⟨fam⟩ *to smarten o.s. up* || ~ **reden** *to talk soft sawder* || ~ riechen (schmecken) *to have a pleasant smell* (*taste*) || ~ schreiben *to write a good hand* || ~ **tun** *to* (*play the*) *gallant* [gəˈlænt], *to flirt* (*with a p*); ⟨Am fam⟩ *to polish apples* || jdm *to court a p* **II. 1. die** ≃**e** f ⟨poet⟩ = ≃heit **2.** e-e ≃e *a beautiful woman*, ⟨fam⟩ *a belle, a beauty* || die ≃e *the fair one*, (Liebchen) *sweetheart* || die ≃ste *the fairest* od *queen* (*of all*), *the belle* (*of the ball*); die ~ste Zeit des Jahres *the pick of th y.* **III. das** ≃**e** n *the beautiful*; *the beauty* (*of this poem*) || das ≃e u Gute *all that is good and beautiful* || die Welt des ≃en *the w. of beauty* || etw ≃es anrichten *to make a pretty mess of ths* || Sie w was ≃es v mir denken! *you will have a nice opinion of me*! || das ≃ste war, daß *the best of the joke was that ..* **Sch·ön-** ~**bartspiel** [eig Schem–] n *mummery* || ~**blatt** n ⟨bot⟩ *poon* ~**druck** m ⟨typ⟩ *primer* ≃**färben** vt *to gloss over* ~**färber** m *dyer in high colo(u)rs*; ⟨fig⟩ *optimist* | ~·ei [f] *dying in fast colours*; ⟨fig⟩ *optimism, window-dressing* ≃**geb·aut,** ≃**gef·ormt** well-built, shapely ~**geist** m *man of sensibility and taste wit, bel-esprit* Fr, *aesthete* | ~er·ei [f] *aestheticism*, ⟨dero⟩ *priggishness*; ≃ig [a] *aesthetic, belletristic*; ~ige Literatur *belles-lettres*; ~ler [m] *snob, high-brow* ≃**-geschnitten** a *well-featured* (*face*) ≃**redend** a *fine-spoken* ~**redner** m *rhetorician, fine talker* | ≃risch [a] *rhetorical* ~**schreibekunst** f *calligraphy* ~**schreiber** m *calligrapher* ~**tuer** m *flirt* | ~·ei [f] *gallantry, flattery, flirtation, coquetting* ≃**tun** vi → I. E. ~**wissenschaftlich** a *belletristic, literary* **Sch·on-** ~**gang** m ⟨mot⟩ *cruising gear* ~**kost** f ⟨med⟩ *diet, regimen* ~**zeit** f ⟨hunt, ich⟩ *fence-time, close(d* ⟨Am⟩) *time* od *season* **sch·onen** vt [h] (P) *to spare*; *to reduce the strain on* (*a p*); *to rest* (*eyes, men*) || ⟨hunt, for⟩ *to preserve* || *to treat with consideration* || *this soap preserves the linen* || (Bein) ⟨fam⟩ *to favour*; (Stimme) *to nurse* || schone d–e Lunge *save your breath* | (sparen) *to save, husband*; *s. your eyes*!; nicht ~ *to lavish* | **sich** ~ *to take* (*good*) *care of o.s.*; *to look after* (*one's health* od) *o.s.* || er muß sich ~ *he must be careful* | ~**d** a *tender, careful* || (rücksichtsvoll) *considerate* || (nachsichtig) *indulgent, forbearing*; *lenient* (*to, with*) **sch·önen** vt [h] *to clarify*, (*re*)*fine* (*wine*)

Sch·öneberg n (Stadtteil v Groß-Berlin)

Sch·onen n (schwed. Landschaft) *Scania*

Sch·oner m ~s/~ **1.** (Möbel≃) *antimacassar, tidy, covering* || (Ärmel≃) *oversleeve* **2.** (Mehrmaster mit Gaffeln) *schooner* | ~brigg [f] *brigantine* **Sch·önheit** f ~/~en *beauty, handsomeness* || *good looks* || *loveliness* || ⟨fig⟩ *fineness* | (Frau) *beautiful woman*; *beauty*, ⟨fam⟩ *belle*, ⟨Am⟩ *glamour girl*, (in Zeitschrift) *pin-up girl*, ⟨fam a.⟩ *beaut*; abgetakelte, gewesene ~ *faded beauty* | (P) andersgeschlechtliche ~ *epicene beauty* | ~**en** [pl] (der Natur) *beauties, beauty spots*; *attractions, amenities* pl || (Artigkeiten) *civilities* pl | ~**s-** ~**fehler** m *mar* ~**gefühl** n *taste* ~**königin** f *b. queen* ~**konkurrenz** f *b.-contest* ~**lehre** f *aesthetics* [sg konstr] ~**linie** f *line of b.* ~**mittel** n *cosmetic, b. aid* ~**pflästerchen** n *b.-spot, patch* ~**pflege** f *b. care* ~**(pflege)salon** m *b.-parlour*; dessen Inhaber *b. specialist* ~**reparaturen** f pl ⟨contr⟩ *repairs of ordinary wear and tear* ~**sinn** m *sense of b., taste*; *aesthetic sense* ~**wasser** n *cosmetic*, (*beautifying*) *wash* od *lotion* ~**wettbewerb** m *b.-contest* **Sch·onung** f ~/~en *forbearance, indulgence* || mit ~ behandeln *to treat* (*a p*) *with considerateness* || bei ~ der eigenen Kräfte *while conserving one's own forces*; um ~ bitten *to beg for mercy*; ⟨mil⟩ *to ask for* (od *cry*) *quarter* || ([gen] S) *husbanding, sparing* | [konkr] ⟨for⟩ *plantation of young trees* || (Baumschule) *nursery* | ≃**s-** ~bedürftig a: ~ s *to have to save one's strength* ~**los** a *unsparing, relentless, merciless* | adv ~ offenherzige Meinungsäußerung *home truths* pl ~**voll** a *full of consideration*; → schonend

Schopf m ~(e)s/≃e *top* (⟨a.⟩ *of trees*), *tuft* || ⟨agr⟩ *shed* || ⟨orn⟩ *crest* || ⟨fam⟩ *head of hair* || jdn (die Gelegenheit) beim ~e fassen *to catch hold of a p by the hair* (*to take time by the forelock*) ~**lerche** f *crested lark* ~**wachtel** f *helmet-quail*

Schöpf- ~**brunnen** m *draw-well* ~**eimer** m *well-bucket, pail* ~**gefäß** n, ~**kelle** f *scoop, dipper* ~**löffel** m (*basting-*)*ladle* ~**maschine** f *chain-pump* ~**papier** n *vat paper* ~**rad** n *scoop-wheel, Persian wheel* ~**rahmen** m ⟨pap⟩ *deckle* ~**werk** n *water-engine* **Sch·öpfe** f ~/~n *place for drawing water* | ≃**n** vt [h] *to draw* (aus *from*), *to scoop* (*up*); Flüssigkeit ~ aus *to dip liquid from* (od *out of*); mit Kelle *to ladle* (*food*) || ⟨fig⟩ *to obtain, get*; *learn, hear, gather*; *to borrow from* (*a book*) || in etw ~ *to fill .. into* || leer ~ *to empty* (*a cask*) | **Argwohn** ~ *to conceive a suspicion* || (Atem) *to draw*; tief *to fetch a deep breath*; wieder *to recover one's breath* || neue Hoffnung ~ *to gather fresh hope* || frische Luft ~ *to take the air* || Mut ~ *to take heart* od *courage* || → voll **Schöpfer** m ~s/~ *creator* || (f *creatress*) || ⟨Lit⟩ *author*(*ess* f); *coiner* (*of a new phrase*) ~**geist** m *creative genius* od *mind* ~**kraft** f *creative power*; *creativity* ~**wort** n *fiat* **sch·öpferisch** a *creative, productive* (an *of*); *constructive* || *fertile, inventive, fecund* || ⟨arts⟩ *original* || ~e Kraft *ingenious ability* **Sch·öpfung** f ~/~en [abstr & konkr] *creation* (*the wonders* (⟨iron⟩ *the lords*) *of c.*) || [konkr] *production*; *the universe*; *offspring* || ⟨arts⟩ *production* ~**sgeschichte** f *history of* (*the*) *creation*; *Genesis* ~**skraft** f *creativity, creativeness*; *power of invention* **Sch·öppchen** n ~s/~ ⟨dim⟩ (→ folg) *small glass* (*of beer* etc) **Sch·oppen** m ~s/~ *pint* (*-pot*) || °auf 7 ~ *three sheets in the wind*; *muggy* ≃**weise** [adv] *by pints* **sch·öppeln** vt *to tipple*; gern ~ *to like one's little drop* (*of wine*)

Schöps m ~s/~e *wether* || ⟨fig fam⟩ *donkey, simpleton*; ~! *silly kipper* | ~**en-** ~**braten** m *roast-mutton* **~fleisch** n *mutton* **~keule** f *leg of mutton*

schor 1. & 3. sg pret v scheren

Sch·ore f ~/~n ⟨carp, mar⟩ *shore,* (*prop*)

Schorf m ~(e)s/~e (Wund≃, Apfel≃) *scab*; ⟨med a.⟩ *eschar* || (Kopf≃) *scurf, dandruff* **≃ig** a *scabby, scurfy*

Sch·örl m ~(e)s/~e ⟨min⟩ *schorl*

Sch·orlem·orle f ~/~ (*white*) *wine soda*

Sch·ornstein m ~(e)s/~e *chimney* || ⟨mar, rail⟩ *funnel* || hoher ~ *stalk* || ⟨Am rail⟩ *smoke--stack* || ⟨fam⟩ das kannst du in den ~ schreiben *you may whistle for it,* ⟨Am⟩ *you can put that on the ice, you won't see the colour of your money* || *put your opinion in your pipe and smoke it* **~aufsatz** m *chimney-pot, -cowl* **~brand** m *ch. on fire* **~feger** m *ch.-sweep* **~gruppe** f ⟨engl⟩ *stack* **~kappe** f *ch.-top*; (bewegliche) *cowl* **~röhre** f *ch.-pipe* od *-flue*

Sch·ose f ~/~n ⟨fam⟩ = Sache, Angelegenheit

schoß 1. & 3. sg pret v schießen

Schoß[1] m [–ɔ–] –osses/–osse & –össe ⟨hist⟩ (Abgabe) *scot* || (Reis, Schößling) *sprig, shoot, sprout* **Schoß**[2] [–o:–] m ~es/≃e **A.** *lap* (auf .. *in* ..) | (Mutterleib) *womb* || ⟨fig⟩ *the bowels* (*of the earth*) | ⟨tail⟩ *skirt, tail, flap* **B. auf** jds ~ *on a p's knee*(*s* pl) || (T) auf den ~ nehmen *to take up on to one's lap* || **in** Abrahams ~ *on A.'s bosom* || .. mir in den ~ gefallen .. *come to me over night* || die Hände in den ~ legen *to fold one's arms* ⟨a. fig⟩, ⟨fig⟩ *to rest upon one's oars* || im ~e .. *in the bosom* (*of one's family*), *in the arms* (*of fortune*), *within the pale* (*of the Church*); im ~e der Zukunft *on the knees of the gods* **~hund** m, **~hündchen** n *lap-dog* **~kind** n *darling, pet* (*child*) **~leder** n *apron* **~sünde** f ⟨theol⟩ *pet sin* **~tasche** f *tail--pocket* **Sch·ößling** [œ] m ~s/~e ⟨bot⟩ *shoot, sprig,* ⟨scient⟩ *stolon* || (Wurzel≃) *runner* | ⟨fig⟩ *stripling* || *new growth*

Sch·ötchen [ø] n ~s/~ ⟨dim⟩ → **Sch·ote**[1] f ~/~n *pod, shell, hull, husk* || ~n [pl] *green peas* pl || ~n ansetzen *to pod* **Sch·ot(e)**[2] f ~/~n ⟨mar⟩ *sheet* **~(en)gat** n *eyelet-hole* **~horn** n *clew* °**Sch·ote**[3] m ~n/~n *fool* **Sch·oten**[1]**- ~dorn** m ⟨bot⟩ *thorny acacia* **~erbsen** f pl *green peas* **≃förmig** a *pod--shaped*; ⟨bot⟩ *siliquose* **~frucht** f *legume, pod* **≃früchtig** a *leguminous, poddy* **~gewächse** n pl *leguminous plants* **~klee** m ⟨bot⟩ *bird's foot trefoil* **≃tragend** a *pod-bearing*

Schott n ~(e)s/~e; **Sch·otte** f ~/~n **1.** (*wooden*) *partition wall* **2.** ⟨mar⟩ *bulkhead* || ~en dicht! *close the bulkheads!* | ~endeck [n] *bulkhead deck*

Sch·otte m *Scot, Scotchman* || (Spitzname) *Sandy* || die ~n [pl] *the Scotch*; ⟨hist a.⟩ *the Scots* (*Mary Queen of Scots*) **~nmütze** f *glengarry* (*cap*), *Balmoral* (*cap*); runde ~ *tam-o'--shanter* **~tuch** n *tartan*

Sch·otter m ~s/ *road-metal, slag, stone-work*; *broken stones* pl; ⟨rail⟩ *ballast* || ⟨geol⟩ (fluvioglazial) *valley train* | ~straße [f] *metalled* od *macadamized road* | **≃n** vt [h] *to gravel, macadamize* **~ung** f *macadamization*; ⟨rail⟩ *ballasting*

Sch·ottin f ~/~nen *Scotchwoman* **sch·ottisch** a *Scotch* (*language, plaid, whisky*) || *Scottish* (*people*) || *Scots* (*guards*) | das ≃e *the Scotch language* || der ≃e *the Scotch reel* || das ≃ [inv] *tartan* **Sch·ottland** n ~s/ *Scotland*

Schr·affe f ~/~n *hatch* || ~n [pl] *hatching* | **≃n, schraff·ieren** vt [h] ⟨arts⟩ *to hatch* || (kreuzweise) *to cross-h.* **Schraff·ierung** f ~/~en ⟨arts⟩ (*cross-*)*hatching*

schr·äg(e) a *oblique* (*lines*), *sloping* (*order of battle*), *slanting* (*mast, direction*) || *diagonal, transversal* || ⟨sl⟩ *hot* (*music*) || ⟨tech⟩ *outswept* | [adv] ⟨a.⟩ *slantwise, aslant* || ~ bearbeiten *to bevel* || ~ einfallend *oblique incident* (*light source*) **Schr·äg- ~balken** m ⟨her⟩ *bend* || linker ~ *bar sinister* **~fläche** f *slope* **≃gelegt** a *uptilted* **~heck** n ⟨mot⟩ *outswept tail* **~hobel** m *bevelling-plane* **~kante** f *chamfer* **~kreuz** n *St. Andrew's cross,* ⟨her⟩ *saltire* **~lage** f ⟨mot⟩ *side sway* **~lauf** m ⟨comp⟩ *skew* **~legen** n ⟨mot⟩ *sway* **~maß** n *bevel-rule* **~sitzventil** n *Y-valve* **≃stellen** vt [h] *to tilt* **~stellung** f ⟨tech⟩ *inclination* **~strich** m ⟨print, etc⟩ *oblique stroke* **≃·über** [adv] *aslant* **~wind** m (v achtern) ⟨mar⟩ *quartering w.* **~zahnrad** n *helical gear* **Schr·äge** f ~/~n *obliquity, slope, slopingness* || ⟨tech⟩ *bevel*; *chamfer* || ⟨theat⟩ *ramp* || ~ der Fensterlaibung *splay*; *pitch* (*of a roof*) **Schr·agen** m ~s/~ *trestle* | ~tisch [m] *tr. t.* **schr·ägen** vt *to bevel* **Schr·ägung** f *bevelling*; *skew, cant*

schrak 1. & 3. sg pret v schrecken

schr·alen vi [h]: der Wind schralt *the wind is scanting and changing*

Schr·amme f ~/~n *scratch, abrasion* || (Narbe) *scar*; ⟨geol⟩ ~n [pl] *striae* pl | **≃n** vt/i [h] *to scratch, graze*; *you grazed the gatepost* **schrammig** a *scarred*; *full of scratches*

Schr·ammelmusik f (nach Joh. Schrammel) *popular music of violins, guitars, and concertina*

Schrank m ~(e)s/≃e *cupboard* || (Akten≃) *roll-top cabinet* || (Bücher≃) *bookcase* || (Geschirr≃) *sideboard* || (Geld≃) *safe* || (Glas≃) *cabinet* || (Kleider≃) *clothes-press, wardrobe,* ⟨Am a.⟩ *armoire* || (Spiel≃) (b. d. Orgel) *console* || (Wäsche≃, Wand≃) *press* || (Reliquien≃) *shrine* **~fach** n *shelf, compartment* || (Bank≃) *safe* **≃fertig** a *fluffy-dry* (Wäsche) **~koffer** m (*wardrobe*) *trunk* **Schr·anke** f ~/~n *barrier* ⟨a. fig⟩ || ⟨rail⟩ *gate* || ⟨parl, jur⟩ *bar* | (Turnier≃n) [pl] *lists* || ⟨fig⟩ *bounds, limits* pl || in ~n halten *to restrain*; *to hold in check*; *to keep within bounds* || sein Ehrgeiz kennt k–e ~n *there is no limit to his a.* || [dat] ~n setzen *to set bounds to*; *to keep within bounds*; *to limit, check* || in die ~n treten *to enter the lists* || in *or* vor die ~n fordern *to challenge*; jdn in s–e ~n weisen *to put a p in place, to show him his place* **schr·änken** vt [h] (Beine) *to cross,* (Säge) *to set* **Schr·anken- ≃los** a *boundless, unlimited*; *unbounded* (*egoism*) || ⟨fig⟩ *licentious* **~losigkeit** f ~/ *boundlessness* || ⟨fig⟩ *licentiousness* **~wärter** m ⟨rail⟩ *gateman* **Schr·änker** m ~s/~ ⟨sl⟩ *safe-blower*

Schr·anze m ~n/~n *sycophant, toady, flunkey* **~nart** f *cringing ways* **≃haft** a *flunkey-like, toadying, cringing*

Schrapn·ell n ~s/~s *shrapnel* **~granate** f *shr.--shell* **~schuß** m *round of case-shot*

Schr·ap(p)e(r m ~s/~) f ~/~n *scraper* || ⟨hors⟩ *curry-comb* **Schr·ap(p)eisen** n *scrap-iron* || **schr·ap(p)en** vt/i [h] *to scrape* **Schr·ap(p)sel** n ~s/ *scrapings* pl

Schrat m ~(e)s/~e *hobgoblin*; *faun, satyr*

Schr·aub- ~deckel m *screw-top* (Dose *tin*) **~fassung** f ⟨el⟩ *screwed lamp holder,* ⟨Am⟩ *sc.d l.socket*; *Edison* **~knecht** m ⟨tech⟩ *cabinet clamp* **~öse** f *eye bolt* **~sicherung** f *sc.-fuse* **~stollen** m ⟨hors⟩ *sc.-cap* **~stock** m *vice,* ⟨Am⟩ *vise* || ⟨übtr⟩ am ~ stehen *to stand at the workman's bench* **~verschluß** m *sc. top* (*jar,* etc) **~zwinge** f *clamp frame* **Schr·aube** f ~/~n *screw* (anziehen *to tighten*) ⟨a. mar⟩ || ~ u Mutter *nut and bolt* || ⟨mar, aero⟩ *propeller* **A.** ⟨aero⟩ **Druck**≃ *pusher--propeller* || Holz≃ *wood screw* || Klemm≃ *connecter*; *terminal s.* || Kopf≃ *cap-s.* || Laschen≃ ⟨rail⟩ *track bolt* || Schlitz≃ *slotted s.* || Senk≃ *countersink* || Sechskant–, Stell≃ *set s.* || Stein≃ *stone bolt* || Vierkant≃ *square head s.* **B. dreiflügelige** ~ *three-bladed s.* || drei–, eingängige ~ *triple-, single-thread s.* || endlose ~ *worm* || hochköpfige ~ *raised s.* || linksgängige ~ *left--hand s.* || männl., (weibl. *fe*)*male s.* **C.** ~n **schneiden** *to cut screws* **D.** °⟨fig⟩ verdrehte ~ *queer fish, old frump* | bei ihm ist e–e ~ los *he has* *a screw loose* **schr·auben** vt/i *to screw* | ⟨fig⟩ *to chaff, banter* || *to cheat* | fest(er), loser ~ *to tighten, slacken the screw(s)* || höher ~ *to turn up (a lamp)* | ⟨fig⟩ höher (niedriger) ~ *to raise (lower) (one's demands, hopes); to boom (the market)* || s–e Worte ~ *to speak* od *write in a stilted way* | ⟨fig⟩ ge–bt *strained, forced, affected; stilted (style)* **Schr·auben- ~blech** n *screw-plate* **~bohrer** m *s.-tap, -auger, twist drill* **~dampfer** m ⟨mar⟩ *s. steamer (S. S.)* **~dreher** m ⟨mod⟩ = ⟨obs⟩ –zieher *s. driver* **~feder** f *coil spring* **~flügel** m *propeller-blade* **~flugzeug** n *helicopter, gyroplane* **≃förmig** a *screw-shaped* **~gang** m, **~gewinde** n *worm* od *thread* od *furrow of a screw* **~gebläse** n *helical blower, propeller fan* **~kopf** m *s.-cap* **~kreis** m ⟨aero⟩ *propeller disc* **~linie** f *spiral line* **~muffe** f *screw(ed)* od *threaded socket* **~mutter** f *female s.; nut* **~rad** n *worm-wheel* **~rahmen** m ⟨typ⟩ *s.-chase* **~schloß** n *jack lock* **~schlüssel** m *(s.-) wrench, spanner*; (englischer) *monkey-wrench* **~schneidebank** f *s.-cutting lathe* **~spindel** f *male s.* **~strahl** m ⟨aero⟩ *propeller slipstream* **~welle** f *p.-shaft* **~winde** f *s.-jack* **~windung** f *turn of a s.* **~zieher** m (⟨mod⟩ –dreher) *s.-driver* **~zwinge** f *vice-pin*

Schr·ebergarten m ⟨hort⟩ *allotment, a. garden*

Schreck m ~(e)s/~e; → **~en** m ~s/~ *fright, alarm, shock; terror* (vor *of*) || *the horrors of war* || *the terrors of death, the sea* | [konkr] *dread* | **ach** du mein ~!, ~ laß nach! *good heavens!* | e–n ~ **bek** *to be frightened* || der ~ fuhr mir in die Glieder *I was terror-stricken* od *paralysed, seized with fright* (→ vor ~) || jdm e–n (schönen) ~en einjagen *to strike terror into a p, to give him a (pretty) fright* od *start* (mit *with*); *to send a shock across (the country)* | jdn **in** ~en jagen, (ver)-setzen *to scare, terrify, dismay, frighten a p* || im ersten ~ *in the sudden dismay* | ein Ende **mit** ~en nehmen *to come to a sad end* || mit dem ~en davonk *to be more frightened than hurt; to get off with a fright* | **von** ~en befallen *awe-* od *terror-stricken* || er konnte **vor** ~ nicht sprechen *he could not speak in fright*; ich wäre vor ~ fast umgefallen *you would have knocked me down with a feather*; außer sich vor ~ *frightend out of one's senses; (he opened his mouth) in horror* **~bild** n *bugbear, fright* **≃erfüllt** a *terrified* **~gespenst** n *night-mare, phantom, bugbear* **~mine** f ⟨mil⟩ *booby mine* od *trap* **~mittel** n *scarecrow* **~schuß** m *shot in the air* || ⟨fig⟩ *false alarm; bluff* **~neurose** f *fright neurosis* **~sekunde** f ⟨mot⟩ *thinking* od *reaction time*; Weg in der ~ *reaction distance* **schr·ecken I.** vt [h] *to frighten, startle, dismay, alarm*; (sehr) *to terrify* | ⟨fig⟩ *to chill; to take the chill off (water)* **II.** vi [h] *to become frightened* | das Reh schreckt .. *gives the alarm* **III.** ≃ m → Schreck || jdm e–n ~ einjagen, ihn in ~ versetzen *to panic a p*; .., daß es ihm eiskalt den Rücken hinunterläuft *to chill a p's spine* | **mit** ~ feststellen *to be scared when noticing, to his dismay he noticed*; [stärker] *he was alarmed/frightened noticing, when he noticed fright seized him, n.g .. he was struck by terror*; sich mit ~ erinnern *to remember with alarm; he ran a frightened eye over it* | **in** ~ geraten vor *to take fright at (a shadow)*; jdn **in** ~ versetzen ⟨fam⟩ *to make a p sit up* || **~erregend** a *terrific, horrific* [adv *-ally*] **~voll** a *terrible* **Schr·eckens- ~bild** n *dreadful sight* **~bote** m *bearer of alarming news* od *scare-news* **~herrschaft** f *Reign of Terror* **~jahr** n *terrible year* **~kammer** f *Chamber of Horrors* **~mann** m *Terrorist* **~nacht** f *night of horrors* **~nachricht** f *fearful piece of news* **~ruf** m *wail of terror* **~schreie** m pl ausstoßen *to cry one's terror* **~system** n *terrorism* **~tat** f *atrocious deed* **~verbreiter** m *alarmist* **schr·eckhaft** a *easily frightened; nervous, fearful, shy, timid* **≃igkeit** f *nervousness, timidity* **schr·ecklich** a *terrible, horrible, fearful, awful, dreadful* (alle a. fam & fig), *frightful* ⟨a. fig sl⟩ | ~! *ugh!* | *atrocious (deed); morbid (details); cruel (fate); shocking (language)*; ⟨fam⟩ *unholy (row)* || *ghastly (crime, noise); grim (tusk, death); formidable (weapon), dire (tragedy)* | [adv] ⟨fam⟩ (sehr) *awfully, terribly; dreadfully, (to look) ghastly* || ein ~ langweiliger Mensch *a fearful bore* || ⟨fam⟩ geradezu ~ *(I suffer from ..) something awful* **≃keit** f ~/ *terribleness, horror, dreadfulness* **Schr·ecknis** n –nisses/–nisse *horror, terror, fright* || *the horrors of war*

Schrei m ~(e)s/~e *cry*; ⟨orn⟩ *note* || (gellend) *yell(ing), shriek* || (Angst≃) *scream* || ~ der Entrüstung *(a universal) outcry* || e–n ~ v sich geben *to give a cry, scream*, ausstoßen *to utter a scream* | ⟨fig⟩ der letzte ~ *the latest craze, the cry of the day* **~hals** m ⟨fam⟩ *squaller* || kl ~ *crybaby* °**~pudding** m (mit wenig Rosinen) *hooting pudding* **~stimme** f *yelling voice* **~vogel** m *screecher*

Schr·eib- *writing (w.g)* **~apparat** m ⟨el⟩ *indicator* **~arbeit** f *deskwork, paperwork* **~art** f *style* od *manner of w.g*; (Orthographie) *spelling* **~bedarf** m *w.g-materials* pl, *stationery* **~block** m *w.g-pad* **~(e)buch** n *w.g-book, copy-book* **~empfänger** m *recording* od *teletype receiver* **≃faul** a *disinclined for corresponding; lazy about w.g* **~feder** f *pen*, ⟨fam⟩ *nib* **~fehler** m *slip of the pen, mistake in spelling; misspelling* || ⟨typ⟩ *error* || *clerical error* **≃fertig** a *ready with the pen* | ~keit [f] *penmanship* **≃freudig** a *fond of w.g* **~freund** m *pen pal* **~gebühr** f *w.g-fees* pl **~gerät** n = –bedarf; ⟨tech⟩ *recorder* **~griffel** m *style* **~heft** n *exercise--book* ⟨bes school⟩ **~kalender** m *diary* **~kräfte** f pl *clerical staff* **~krampf** m *writer's cramp* **~kunst** f *art of w.g, calligraphy; penmanship* **~künstler** m *w.g-master* **~lehrer** m *w.g-master* **~lust** f *love of w.g* **≃lustig** a *fond of w.g* **~mappe** f *w.g-kit, blotting-case; portfolio* **~maschine** f *typewriter*; (auf der) ~ schreiben *to type(-write)* | ~nbüro [n] *type-w.g office*; ~nfarbband [n] ⟨typewr⟩ *ribbon*; ~ngummi [m] *typewriter eraser*; ~nmanuskript [n] *typewritten copy; typescript*; ~nwalze [f] *roller*; ~npapier [n] *typing paper*; ~nschreiber(in [f]) [m] *typist*; ~nschrift [f] *typescript*; ~nwagen [m] *paper-carriage* **~materalien** n pl, etc = –bedarf, –waren, etc **~meßgerät** n *recorder* **~papier** n *note* od *w.g-paper* **~pergament** n *vellum* **~pult** n *(w.g-) desk* **~rad** n ⟨comp⟩ *print(ing) wheel* **~schrift** f *script (-type; handwriting* **≃selig** a = –lustig | 120 **~stellen** f pl mit je 50 Zeichen ⟨comp⟩ *printing positions 120, each of 50 (numeric and alphabetic) characters* **~stift** m *stylus, style* **~stube** f *office*; ⟨mil⟩ *orderly room* **~stunde** f *w.g-lesson* **~sucht** f *passion for w.g* | s.≃ig [a] *infected with a p. f. w.g* **~tafel** f *tablet (for w.g)* || (Wandtafel) *blackboard* || (Schiefertafel) *slate* **~taste** f ⟨typwr⟩ *finger--form fitting key*; 5 ~n *5 characters* **~tisch** m *desk, w.g-table; bureau* | ~arbeit [f] *writing* || (Beruf) *desk job*; ~flieger [m] *arm-chair pilot*; ~garnitur [f] *desk set* | ~lampe [f] *desk lamp*; ~sessel [m] *desk arm-chair*; ~stratege [m] *swivelchair* od *arm-chair strategist* **~übung** f *practice in w.g* **≃unkundig** a *ignorant of w.g* **~unterlage** f *blotting-pad* **~unterricht** m *w.g--lessons* pl **~vorlage** f *copy* **~waren** f pl *stationery* sg | ~händler [m] *stationer* | ~handlung [f] *st.r's shop*, ⟨Am⟩ *stationery store* **~weise** f *style* || *spelling (of a word)*; ⟨comp⟩ *notation* **~werk** n ⟨comp⟩ *print unit* **~zeug** n *ink-stand, writing case* **Schr·eibebrief** m ⟨fam⟩ *(long) epistle* **Schr·eiben** n ~s/~ *writing* || *letter, epistle* || wichtiges ~ *document* || kurzes *or* diplomatisches ~ *note* || ⟨com⟩ Ihr geehrtes ~ *your favour* || in m–m letzten ~ *in my last* || unser ~ v .. *our respects of May 12* **schr·eiben** vt/i [schrieb/ge–en] [h] *to write* ([dat] *to*) || ~ Sie! ⟨fam⟩ *take a letter; take down (please); to t. d. a l.* (nach jds Diktat *at a p's* *dictation*) ‖ (orthographisch) *to spell* ‖ (wie) die Zeitung schreibt (*according to* ..) .. *says*; *we read in* .. ‖ ⟨comp⟩ *to print* **A. 1. Aufsätze** ~ *to write essays*, ⟨school⟩ *to do composition* ‖ *to sign* (*one's name*) ‖ Noten ~ *to copy music* ‖ e–m ein paar Zeilen ~ *to drop a line to a p* **2.** jdn krank ~ *to certify a p ill* **3.** (Datum) den wievielten ~ wir? *what date is today*? ‖ man (wir) schrieb(en) 1914 *it was, we were in the year 1914* **4.** ⟨bib⟩ wie ge–en steht *it is written* **B. falsch** ~ *to misspell* ‖ groß ~ *to write with a capital letter* ‖ gut ~ *to write a good hand*; ⟨liter⟩ *to be a good writer*; (v Federn) *those are good pens* ‖ richtig ~ *to spell correctly*; er kann nicht richtig ~ *he is a bad speller*; schnell ~ *to write off*; wie ~ Sie sich *or* Ihren Namen? *how do you spell y. n.*? **C. an** (jdn): *to write to* ‖ an etw ~: *he is working on his play* ‖ **auf** (→ ~ mit): (Rolle) [dat] auf den Leib ge–en *just cut out for* .. ‖ etw auf Rechnung [gen] ~ *to debit* od *credit a p with a th*; ⟨fig⟩ *we must put that down to his stupidity* ‖ man –bt uns **aus** Genf *we hear from* .. ‖ sich [dat] etw hinters Ohr ~ *to take note of a th* | **in**: *to write in a book* ‖ in e–e Liste ~ *to book, enter* ‖ in Maschinenschrift ~ *to type* (*out*) (auf *on*) ‖ ins (Unreine) Reine ~ *to make* (*a rough draft*) *a clean copy, to type out* | **mit**: *to spell with k* ‖ *to write in ink, with a pencil, on a typewriter*, **nach** Diktat *from dictation* | **über**: *about* (*a p, a th*) ‖ darunter: *to put one's name to a th, to sign one's name* | **zur** Last ~ *to debit with* **D. sich** mit jdm ~ *to be in correspondence with a p* ‖ wie ~ Sie sich? *how do you spell your name*? *what's your name*? ‖ wo ~ Sie sich her? *where do you hail from*? ‖ wo –bt es sich her? *where does it come from*? ‖ es –bt sich von .. her *we inherited it from* .., *it dates from* .. ‖ das –bt sich daher, daß .. *that's the outcome of* (*there having been* ..) **E. Geschr·iebene(s)** n *writing*; *written matter* **Schr·eiber** m ~s/~ *writer* (*of a letter*); *author* (*of a play*) | (Abschreiber) *copyist* | (Angestellter) *clerk, secretary*; ⟨hist⟩ *scribe*; ⟨mil⟩ *staff-sergeant*, etc | (S) *graph*(*ic instrument*), *recorder* **~schule** f ⟨hist⟩ *scribal school* **~seele** f *quill-driver* **~stelle** f *clerk's place, clerkship* **~stuhl** m *office-stool* **Schreiber·ei** f ~/~en *writing, scribbling, copying* **Schr·eibung** f ~/~en *spelling*

schr·eien I. vt/i [schrie/geschrien] [h] **A.** *to cry, shriek* (→ rufen) ‖ (laut) *to roar, bawl* (*out*) ‖ (schrill) *to squeak, yell*; ⟨orn⟩ *to squawk* ‖ ⟨sl⟩ *to blaze*, ⟨Am⟩ *to yip, holler* ‖ (wie e–e gestochene Sau) *to scream* (*like a stuck pig*) | *don't bawl so, I'm not deaf* ‖ *they don't sing, they yell* **B.** (Baby) *to squall, howl* ‖ (Elefant) *to clamour* ‖ (Esel) *to bray* ‖ (Eule) *to hoot, screech* ‖ (Hahn) *to crow* ‖ (Hase) *to cry out* ‖ (Hirsch) *to bell, troat* ‖ (Krähe) *to caw* ‖ (Menschenmenge) *to clamour* ‖ (Papagei) *to scream* ‖ (Schnee) *to crackle* ‖ (Vieh) *to low* (nach *for*) ‖ (Vögel) *to squawk* ‖ (Wildgans) *to honk* ‖ (Zinn) *to creak* **C. weh** u **ach** ~ *to set up a pitiful cry* ‖ Zeter u Mord(io) ~ *to cry murder* ‖ sich [dat] die Lunge aus dem Halse ~ *to scream one's lungs out* ‖ e–m die Ohren voll ~ *to deafen a p with one's shouting*; jdm etw in die O. ~ *to din .. into a p's ears* ‖ jdn wach ~ *to waken a p with shouting* | **sich** heiser ~ *to shout* od *shriek o.s. hoarse* **D. aus** vollem Halse ~ *to bawl with all one's might* | ~ **nach**: *to clamour for* (*food*) ⟨a. übtr⟩ ([of land] *for ploughing*); *to call for vengeance* | **über** [acc]: *to cry out against* | **um**: *to call out for help* | **vor**: *to scream with pain, fright, laughter*; *to yell with pain, anger, fright*; *to shout with joy*; *to crow* | ⟨fig⟩ **zum** Himmel ~ *to cry aloud to Heaven* **II.** ≃ n ⟨fam⟩ das ist zum ≃! *that's screamingly funny*! *that's a scream*! **III. ~d** a *crying*, etc ‖ *loud, flashy, glaring, clashing, strident, jazzy* (*colours*); *an aggressive shade of red*, etc; ~de Ungerechtigkeit *injustice calling loudly for redress*; *blazing* (Buchstaben) ‖ ~es Unrecht *crying shame*; *flagrant* (*disparity, injustice*) ‖ *direct* (*contradiction*) ‖ *glaring* (*contrast*) ‖ *screaming* (*absurdity*) **Schr·eier** m ~s/~ *crier* ‖ (**Schreihals**) *bawler*, (Kind) *cry-baby* ‖ ⟨pol⟩ *grumbler* ‖ (Lärm–, Streitmacher) *brawler* **~·ei** f ~/~en *crying, bawling, hullabaloo*

Schrein m ~(e)s/~e Reliquien≃ *shrine*; (Kiste) *chest*; (Schrank) *cupboard, cabinet* **Schr·einer** m ~s/~ *joiner* ‖ (Kunst≃) *cabinet-maker* **~arbeit** f *j.'s work, joinery* **~gesell(e)** m *journeyman-j.r* **~handwerk** n *j.r's trade* **~meister** m *master j.r*

schr·eiten vi [schritt/ge–en] [s] *to walk, stride, step* (über *across*) ‖ auf u ab ~ *to pass to and fro*, im Zimmer .. *to pace the room* ‖ *death stalks through the streets* | ⟨übtr⟩ **zu** etw ~ *to proceed to* .. ‖ zur Abstimmung ~ *to vote*, ⟨parl⟩ *to divide* ‖ zum Äußersten ~ *to take extreme measures* ‖ zu Werke ~ *to set to work*

schrie(b) 1. & 3. sg pret v schrei(b)en

Schrift f ~/~en **1.** *writing* **2.** (Hand≃) *hand* (*-w.g*), *script* ‖ ausschreibende ~ *longhand* (Ggs *shorthand*) **3.** (~zeichen) *character*; ⟨print⟩ *type* ‖ **in**: *in German, Roman* (= lateinischer) *ch.*(*s*) | ⟨typ⟩ *type, printing*; *letters, characters* pl ‖ fett *fat* (*type*, etc) ‖ **gotisch** *Gothic, German* (*type, print*); magere ~ *light type* ‖ in schräger ~ *in italics* pl ‖ Pariser ~ *ruby*, ⟨Am⟩ *agate* | ⟨telg⟩ in gewöhnlicher ~ (nicht chiffriert) *en clair* Fr ‖ ~ u Buchmalerei v .. *written* od *lettered and illuminated by* .. **4.** (~stück) *document, record, deed*; ⟨jur⟩ *writ* ‖ e–e ~ abfassen *to draw up a document* ‖ e–e ~ einreichen *to submit a petition* | (Abhandlung) *paper* ‖ (Veröffentlichung) *book, publication* ‖ die Heilige ~ *Holy Writ, the Scripture*(*s* pl) ‖ die ~ auslegen *to interpret the text* | Poes sämtliche ~en [pl] *Poe's complete works* ‖ vermischte ~en *ana*(*s*) ‖ *philosophical w.gs* **5.** (Inschrift) *text* (*on a tombstone*) **~abschnitt** n *versicle* **~art** f *type, fount*; ~en [pl] *type styles* **~auslegung** f *exposition of the Scriptures, exegesis* **~band** n ⟨paint⟩ *scroll* **~bild** n *type face* **~blase** f *balloon* (*in comic strip*) **~deutsch** n *literary German* **~druck** m *autography* **~fach** n ⟨typ⟩ *box of a type-case* **~führer** m *secretary* **~gelehrte(r)** m ⟨bib⟩ *scribe* **~gießer** m *typefounder* | ~·ei [f] *type-foundry* **~grad** m *size of type* **~graphik(er** m) f *lettering* (*man*); *type designer* **~guß** m *type casting*; *fount*, ⟨Am⟩ *font* **~kasten** m *type-case* **~kegel** m ⟨typ⟩ *body of a letter* **≃kundig** a *well versed in the Scriptures* **~leiter** m *editor*; *type director* [a. f] **~leitung** f *editorial staff* bzw *supervision, editorship* **~liebhaber** m *typophile* **≃mäßig** a *scriptural* | ≃keit [f] *conformity to the Scriptures* **~metall** n *type-metal* **~probe** f *specimen of type*; *sample of handwriting* **~rolle** f ⟨paint⟩ *scroll* **~satz** m ⟨jur⟩ *pleadings* pl; (des Anwalts) ⟨m. m.⟩ *brief*; ⟨print⟩ *type setting*; *finished page of print* **~schneider** m *form-cutter* **~seite** f *page*; ⟨num⟩ *tail* (*of a coin*) **~setzer** m *compositor, typesetter* **~sprache** f *literary language* **~stelle** f *passage from the Scriptures* **~steller(in** f) m *author*(*ess*), *writer, publicist, penman* | **~·** *w.g* (*life*) | (fruchtbar *prolific*) ‖ elender ~ *penny-a--liner* ‖ kein ~: *he was not of the w.g world* | ~·ei [f] *w.g for the press, authorship*; *author's trade*; *pen and ink, penmanship*, elende ~ *penny--a-lining* | ≃isch [a] *literary* ‖ ~ [adv] *as an author*; ~name [m] *pen-name* **≃stellern** vi [h] *to write* **~stempel** m ⟨print⟩ *punch* **~stück** n → ~ **4.** ‖ ⟨typ⟩ *packet* **~text** m *Biblical text* **~verdreher** m *distorter of the Scriptures* **~verfälschung** f *forgery* **~wart** m *secretary* **~wechsel** m, **~wesen** n *correspondence* **≃widrig** a *unscriptural* **~zeichen** n *letter, character*; *type* **~zettel** m ⟨typ⟩ *bill of a fount* **~zug** m *duct, stroke*; *character* ‖ (Schnörkel) *flourish* **Schr·iftchen** n ~s/~ *pamphlet* **schr·iftlich** [a] *written*; *letter* [attr], (Befehl) *l. of* *instruction* || ~e Arbeit *exercise*; *examination paper* || ~e Entschuldigung .. *in w.g* || ~e Arbeiten *paperwork* || ~e Aufforderung ⟨jur⟩ *writ* || ~er Auftrag *order in w.g* || ~es Zeugnis *testimonial* | [adv] *in w.g*, *in black and white* || (brieflich) *by letter* || ~ abfassen *to write down* || ~ anfragen *to write and ask* || das kann ich dir ~ geben *I give you my word for it* **Schr·ifttum** n ~s/ *literature*; *letters* pl

schrill a *shrill*, *strident*, *reedy*, *acute* (*noise*) || *grating* (*laughter*) **schr·illen** vi [h] *to utter a shrill sound* || *to resound in shrill tones*

schr·inden vi/t [s & h] *to chap*, *crack* || **sich** ~ *to scratch o.s.*

Schr·ippe f ~/~n (*French*) *roll*

schritt 1. & 3. sg pret v schreiten **Schritt** m ~(e)s/~e **A. 1.** *step*; *pace* (a. als Maß = *30 in.*) (*50 paces*) || zwei ~ v *within a stone's throw of* || drei ~ v Leibe! *keep your distance*! **2.** (hörbar) *footfall*, *footstep* **3.** ⟨tail⟩ *perinée* Fr, *cf. perineum*; im ~ zu kurz (of trousers) *too short in the leg* **4.** ⟨hors⟩ *walk*(*ing-pace*) **5.** ⟨fig⟩ (Maßregel) *step*, *move*, *action*; *measures* pl **B. diplomatischer** ~ *diplomatic action*; *démarche* Fr || ⟨fig⟩ **erster** ~ *initiative*, *gambit*; *the first*, *preliminary*, *initial step* (zu *to*, *towards*); *the thin end of the wedge* (*for*) || der erste ~ ist der schwerste *the difficulty is at the beginning* || gemessenen ~es gehen nach, zu *to stalk* (*off*) *to* || gr, **langer** ~ *lope*, *stride* || Politik der kleinen ~e *policy of gradualism* || langsamen ~es *with slow steps* || schneller ~ vorwärts *bound* || (m–e) 1000 ~e *constitutional* s **C.** ~ **fahren** *to drive slowly* || zehn ~(e) gehen *to walk ten paces* || ⟨fam⟩ e–n guten ~ am Leibe h *to walk a good pace* || ~ **halten** *to keep* (*in step* od) *up* (mit *with*); (*to keep abreast of*); (*to pull in double harness with*); mit der Zeit ~ h. *to move with the times* || s–e ~e lenken nach *or* zu *to make* od *wend one's way to*, *to bend one's steps towards* || die ersten ~e m *to learn to walk* || e–n falschen ~ tun ⟨fig⟩ *to put a foot wrong* || gr ~e m *to take long strides*, *to stride* || kl ~e m *to take little steps* || dem Ziele e–n gr ~ näher k *to advance a long way towards ..* || ~ reiten *to go at a walk* | ~e **tun** *or* unternehmen *to take action* od *measures*, *steps* pl; *to press the button*; ⟨jur⟩ *to take legal proceedings*; .. in etw *to move in a th* || den ersten ~ tun *to make the first move* (zu *towards*), *to take the initiative*, *to break the ice* || den gefährlichen ~ (Heirat) wagen: *I've been and gone and done it*; ⟨mil⟩ *he went over the top* || den ~ **wechseln** *to change foot* od *step* || s–e ~e wenden *to turn one's steps* (nach *towards*) || e–n ~ **zulegen** *to put one's best leg foremost* **D. auf** ~ u Tritt *at every step*, *everywhere* || jdm auf ~ u Tritt folgen *to stick to a p's heels*, *to dog a p's steps*, (heimlich) *to shadow a p* | **aus** dem ~ *out of step* | **bei** jedem ~ *at every turn* || ~ f ~ *step by step*, *inch by inch* | (→ A. 3) **im** ~ gehen *to go at a foot's pace*, ⟨a. hors⟩ *at a walk*; ⟨hors⟩ *to pace* || mitten im ~ *in mid-stride* || in gleichen ~ k mit *to fall into step with*; mit jdm in gleichem ~ gehen *to keep one's step in time to a p's* || in langen ~en k *to come striding along* || in *or* **mit** schnellen ~en *fast-paced*; *at a quick pace*, *at his quickest pace* **~gänger** m ⟨hors⟩ *good stepper* **~gerät** n ⟨phot⟩ *planetary camera* **~macher** m ⟨sport⟩ *pace-maker*; ~ s *to set the pace* (*for*), ~ s f jdn *to pace a p* **~messer** m *pedometer* **~stein** m *stopping stone* ⟨a. fig⟩ (Schlüsselwort beim Dolmetschen) | im **~(t)empo** fahren ⟨mot⟩ *to crawl* **~wechsel** m *change of step* **~weise** [adv] *step by step*, *by steps*; *progressively* **~weite** f *stride* **~zähler** m = ~messer

Schr·ubel m ~s/~ ⟨tech⟩ *fine-tooth card* **~n** vt [h] *to comb*, *card*

schroff a *steep*, *precipitous* || ⟨fig⟩ *gruff*, *rough*; *harsh* || ~e Erwiderung *tart rejoinder*, *tart retort* || (unvermittelt) *abrupt* (*transition*) | in ~er Weise *in a tart manner* | adv ~ zurückweisen *to turn* (*a request*) *down unceremoniously* **~heit** f *steepness* || ⟨fig⟩ *gruffness*, *tartness*, etc **Schr·offen** m ~s/~ *steep* od *towering rock*, *cliff*

Schr·öpf- ~eisen, ~gerät n *cupping-instrument* **~glas** n, **~kopf** m *c.g-glass* **~schnepper** m, **~zeug** n = ~eisen **schr·öpfen** vt [h] *to cup* || ⟨fig⟩ *to fleece*, *skin*, ⟨Am⟩ *to soak* (*a p*) (um etw: *he soaked me $ 10*); ge–ft w ⟨fig⟩ *to get skinned* **Schr·öpfer** m ~s/~ *cupper*

Schr·oppstahl m *roughing tool*

Schrot m & n ~(e)s/~e **1.** ⟨hunt⟩ *hail-shot*, (*small*) *shot* **2.** (Grütze) *groats* pl, *crushed* od *bruised grain* || ⟨brew⟩ *grist*; *crushed malt* **3.** ⟨num⟩ *due size and full weight*; *standard* || ~ u Korn *weight and alloy*, *alloy and standard* || ein Mann von altem ~ u Korn *a man of the old stamp* od *of sterling character* od *probity* **~axt** f *wood-cutter's axe* **~beutel** m ⟨hunt⟩ *shot-pouch* **~brot** n *whole-meal* (od *Hovis*) *bread* **~büchse** f *shot-gun* **~eisen** n *chisel* **~flinte** f *shot-gun*, *fowling-piece* **~gießer·ei** f *shot-foundry* **~hobel** m *horse-plane* **~kleie** f *very coarse bran* **~korn** n *groats* pl || ⟨hunt⟩ *shot* **~kugel** f *pellet* **~leiter** f *pulling-ladder*, *pulley*, *drag-ladder* **~mehl** n *coarse meal*, *groats* pl **~meißel** m = ~eisen **~mühle** f *bruising-mill* **~säge** f *large saw*, *pit-saw* **~schere** f (e–e *a pair of*) *large shears* pl **~seil, ~tau** n *parbuckle* **~waage** f *plummet*, *level* **Schr·ote** f ~/~n *cutting-knife* **schr·oten** vt [h] **1.** [pp geschroten] (Malz) *to bruise* || (Korn) *to rough-grind*, *to shred* || ⟨met⟩ *to rough-plane* || (durchschneiden) *to cut*, *saw* || (nagen) *to gnaw* **2.** [pp geschrotet] || (Fässer etc am Schrotseil herablassen) *to lower*, *shoot*, ⟨mar⟩ *parbuckle* **Schr·öter** m ~s/~ **1.** (P) *drayman*, *porter*, *packer* **2.** *wood-cutter* **3.** (Käfer) *stag-beetle* **Schr·ötling** m ~(e)s/~e ⟨num⟩ *blank for coining*; *disc*

Schrott m ~(e)s/ *junk*; *scrap-metal* | ~platz [m] *s.* od *junk yard*; ~wert [m] *salvage value*

Schr·ubb- ~en vt/i [h] *to scrub* || ⟨mar⟩ *to swab* || ⟨tech⟩ *to rough-plane* **~er** m ~s/~ *scrub*(*ber*) || ⟨mar⟩ *swab* **~hobel** m *large plane*, *jack-plane*

Schr·ulle f ~/~n [abstr] *crotchet*, *fad*, *whim*, *freak*, *kink*; ~n [pl] *oddities*; *vagaries* | [konkr] (Frau) *crotchety old hag* **~nhaft** a *crotchety*, *whimsical*; *queer*, *faddy* | schrulliger Mensch *curmudgeon*; *eccentric*

°**schrumm**! *done*! *finished*!

Schrump- °~el f ~/~n *wrinkle* || ⟨fig⟩ *withered old woman* | **~ig** [a] *wrinkled* || *crumpled* **~fen** vi [s] *to shrink*, *shrivel* **~fig** a *shrivelled*, *crumpled*, *wrinkled* **~friß** m *contraction crack* **~fsitz** m ⟨tech⟩ *shrink fit* **~fung** f ~/~en *shrinking*, *shrinkage*; ⟨tech⟩ *contraction*

Schr·unde f ~/~n *cleft*, *chink*, *crevice*, *fissure*, *crack* || ~n [pl] (Haut~) *chaps* pl **schr·undig** a *cracked*, *cleft* || (Haut) *chapped* || ~ m, ~ w *to crack*; *to chap*

Schub m ~(e)s/~e **1.** *shove*, *push*, *thrust* (*with one push*, *at one go*; *to give a p a shove* etc) **2.** ⟨tech⟩ *shear* **3.** *batch* (*of bread* & ⟨fig⟩ *of books*, *letters*, *petitions*, etc) **4.** *throng*, *push*, *set*, *lot* (*of people*): *I got in with the first lot* || (Völker~) *wave* **5.** (polizeilich) *compulsory conveyance of tramps*; auf den ~ bringen *to pass* (*tramps*) *to their domicile* **6.** (Kegelspiel etc) *throw*(*ing*) || mein ~! *my turn*! || auf einen ~ *with one throw* | [pl ~] *set* (*of ninepins*) **7.** ⟨aero, a–n⟩ *thrust* **8.** ⟨path⟩ *attack*, *spell* (*of jaundice*); *flare-up* **~beanspruchung** f ⟨tech⟩ *shear-stress* **~belastung** f *thrust loading* **~düse** f ⟨aero⟩ *discharge nozzle* **~fach** n, **~kasten** m, **~lade** f *drawer*; kl ~ *pigeon-hole* **~fenster** n *sash-window* **~karren** m *wheelbarrow*, (kl) *pushcart* **~kärrner** m *w.b. man* **~kraft** f ⟨tech⟩ *shearing force*; ⟨aero, a–n⟩ *thrust*(*ing power*) °×**~lädle** n ⟨sex⟩ *front door* od *parlour*

~lehre f *slide-gauge* **~rakete** f ⟨a–n⟩ *booster* **~riegel** m *bolt* **~schraube** f ⟨aero⟩ *pusher air--screw* **~spannung** f ⟨tech⟩ *shear-stress* **~stange** f ⟨mach⟩ *connecting-rod; push-pull rod* **~ventil** n *sliding-valve* **~verstärker** m ⟨turbo⟩ *thrust-boosting device* **~weise** [adv] *by shoves, in batches* od *sets*, etc ‖ *little by little* ‖ (polizeilich) *by compulsory conveyance* | [a] ~ Verarbeitung ⟨comp⟩ *batch-mode* °**Sch·ub(b)jack** m ~s/~s *scaramouch, blackguard, cad, tike* ‖ *skinflint, miser* °**Schubs** m –ses/–se = Schub 1. **sch·ubsen** vt [h] *to push*

sch·üchtern a *shy, slow, bashful* (*lover*), *timid* (*attempt* ‖ *diffident* ‖ *shy* ⟨a. hunt⟩; (P) *retiring*, ⟨fam⟩ *sheepish*; *slow* (Liebhaber) ‖ ~ m *to intimidate* ≗**heit** f ~/ *bashfulness, timidity* ‖ *diffidence* ‖ *shyness* ‖ e–m die ~ nehmen *to put a p at his ease*

schuf 1. & 3. sg pret v schaffen

Schuft m ~(e)s/~e *blackguard, scoundrel, rascal, rogue*; ⟨sl⟩ *rotter*, ⟨fam⟩ *son of a gun*; ⟨Am⟩ *mucker, scal(l)awag* ‖ ein ~, wer Böses dabei denkt *honi soit qui mal y pense* ‖ ein ~ schimpft den andern *the pot calls the kettle black* | ≗**en** vi [h] *to drudge, toil, plod, graft, slave* (an *at*) (wie ein Pferd *like mad*) ‖ sich zu Tode ~ *to slave o.s. to death* **~er·ei** f ~/ *knavery* ‖ (Arbeit) *sweat*; ⟨Am fam⟩ *grind*, ⟨sl⟩ *elbow grease* | ≗**ig** a *blackguardly, rascally* ‖ *shabby* (*fellow*) ‖ *mean* (*behaviour*) | ≗keit [f] ~/ *rascality, roguery* ‖ *shabbiness* | *mean trick*

Schuh m ~(e)s/~e **A. 1.** *shoe* **2.** ⟨obs⟩ (Längenmaß, pl ~) *foot* **3.** ⟨poet⟩ *horse's shoe* **4.** ⟨tech⟩ *socket, ferrule*; ⟨phot⟩ *clip* **B. derber** ~ *stout shoe*; *clog*; ⟨Ir, Scot⟩ *brogue* ‖ eng *tight* ‖ genagelt *hobnailed* ‖ halbhoher ~ *boot* (a. = Stiefel); ⟨obs⟩ *high-low* ‖ ~ mit hohen Absätzen *high--heeled shoe* **C. Bade**≗ *bathing slipper* ‖ Filz≗ *felt s.r* ‖ Gleit≗ (der Lafette) *buffer guide* ‖ Halb≗ (*low*) *shoe* ‖ Holz≗ *clog* ‖ Horn≗ ⟨hors⟩ *coffin* ‖ Kabel≗ ⟨el⟩ *cable shoe* ‖ Lauf≗e *shoes that can be walked in* ‖ Pol≗ ⟨telg⟩ *pole piece* ‖ Schnabel≗ *pointed shoe* ‖ Schnür≗ *lace boot* ‖ Strapazier≗e *heavy-duty shoes* ‖ Tanz≗, Turn≗ *pump* **D. an**: (*white shoes*) *on her feet* | **mit** (guten) ~en bekleidet *shoed* (*well-shod*) ‖ mit abgetretenen ~en *down at heels*; ⟨fam⟩ (*down*) *on one's uppers* | **ohne** ~e *unshod*; 2 m ohne ~ *six feet high in one's stockinged feet* **E.** ⟨fig⟩ jdm etw in die ~e schieben *to lay* (*a fault*) *at a p's door*, ⟨Am⟩ *on a p's d.step*; ⟨sl⟩ *to plant* od *stick a th on a p*; .. alles .. *to put it all unto a p* ‖ das habe ich mir längst an den ~en abgelaufen *that's nothing new to me* ‖ da drückt der ~ *that is where the shoe pinches* ‖ ich möchte nicht in s–n ~en stecken *I should not like to change places with him* ‖ umgekehrt wird ein ~ daraus *do the contrary and you'll be all right* **~absatz** m *heel* **~ahle** f *shoemaker's awl* **~anzieher** m *shoehorn* **~auszieher** m *boot-jack* **~band** n *shoe-lace* **~bürste** f *shoe-brush* **~creme** f *polish* **~draht** f *shoemaker's thread* **~einlage** f *instep-raiser*; *arch support* | jdn wie e–n **~fetzen,** ~lappen behandeln *to wipe one's boots on a p* **~flicker** m *cobbler* **~geschäft** n *boot--shop*, ⟨Am⟩ *shoe store* od *saloon*; *bootery* **~knöpfer** m *shoe-buttoner* **~leisten** m *last* (*of a shoe*) **~macher** m *shoemaker, bootmaker* | ~bedarf [m] *grindery*; ~gesell(e) [m] *journeyman-shoemaker*; ~handwerk [n] *shoemaking*; ~innung [f] *the Cordwainer's Company*; ~meister [m] *master shoemaker* **~maß** n *shoe-measure, size* **~nagel** m *hobnail* **~pflock** m *wooden peg* **~plattler** m *foot--slapper* (*Alpine clog-dance*) **~putzer** m (P) *shoe--black*, ⟨fam⟩ *boots*; ⟨Am⟩ *bootblack, shoe-shine boy*; wie e–n ~ behandeln *to treat like dirt* **~putzladen** m ⟨Am⟩ *shoe-shine parlor* **~reparaturanstalt** f *shoe repair shop* **~riemen** m *shoe-lace*, ⟨bib⟩ *latchet* ‖ ⟨fig⟩ nicht wert s, jdm die ~ aufzulösen *not to be fit to black a p's boots* | ~spitze [f] *anglet* **~-Röntgenapparat** m *foot--ga(u)ge* **~schmiere** f *grease for boots* **~schnalle** f *shoe-buckle* **~schrank** m *boot-cabinet* **~schwärze** f *blacking* **~sohle** f *sole of a shoe* **~werk** n *footgear, footwear* (fest *stout*); *boots and shoes* pl **~wichse** f *blacking, shoeblack, polish* **~zeug** n = ~werk **~zwecke** f *shoe-peg, brad*

Sch·uko- (= Schutzkontakt) ⟨el⟩ | ~material [n] *earthed plugs and sockets* pl; ~stecker [m] *earthed plug*, ⟨engl⟩ *Home Office plug*

Sch·ul- **~abgänger** m *leaver* **~akt** m *speech--day* **~alter** n *school-age* **~amt** n *teacher's office* od *post, teaching* **~anstalt** f *school*, ⟨engl a.⟩ *college* **~arbeit** f *work, task* ‖ s–e ~en m *to do one's lessons* **~arrest** m *detention* **~aufgabe(n** pl) f *home-work* **~aufseher** m *school-inspector* **~ausgabe** f *s.-edition* **~bank** f *form* **~behörde** f *S.-board* **~beispiel** n *test case* **~besuch** m *attendance at s.*; *years of schooling* **~betrieb** m *s. activities* pl bzw *management* **~bildfunk** m *educational TV* **~bildung** f *s.ing, education*; (of girls) *accomplishments* pl **~buch** n *s.book* **~bücherverlag** m *educational publishers* **~diener** m *s. porter* **~direktor(in** f) m *head master* (f *head mistress*) **~englisch** n *s.-boy English* **~entlassungszeugnis** n *leaving certificate* **~erziehung** f *education at s.* **~fall** m = ~beispiel **~ferien** pl *holidays*; die ~ beginnen *the s. is breaking up* **~fernsehen** n *TV teaching system* **~fest** n *s.-fête, s.-treat* **~film** m *white blackboard* **~flug** m *training flight* | ~zeug [n] *t.g plane*; (*ab initio*) *trainer* ≗**freier Tag** m *holiday*; ~freier Nachmittag *half-h. afternoon* **~freund(in** f) m *s.-mate, s.fellow*; (bester) *chum* **~freundschaft** f *s.-friendship* **~fuchs** m *prig, pedant* **~fuchser·ei** f *pedantry* **~funk** m *educational radio program* **~gebäude** n *s.house* **~geld** n *s.-fees* pl, *s. bill(s* pl); *tuition* **~gelehrsamkeit** f *book-learning, erudition* ‖ ⟨dero⟩ *pedantry* **~gelehrte(r)** m *scholar* **~genosse** m = ~freund ≗**gerecht** a *proper for schools*; *methodical, in due form* ‖ *well-trained* (*horse*) **~gesetz** n *s.-regulation* **~globus** m *ed.l globe* **~haus** n *s.(-house* od *-premises* [pl]) **~heft** n *exercise-book* **~hof** m *play-ground* **~inspektor** m *inspector of s.s* **~jahr** n *scholastic year* ‖ ~e [pl] *s.-days* **~jugend** f *s.-children* pl **~junge, ~knabe** m *s.boy* **~jungenscherz** m *s.boy joke* **~kamerad** m = ~freund **~kenntnisse** f pl *knowledge acquired at s* **~klasse** f *form*, ⟨Am⟩ *grade* **~kollegium** n *staff* (*of teachers*) **~kommission** f *s.-committee* **~konferenz** f *meeting of the teachers of a s.* ≗**krank** a *shamming* **~krankheit** f *sham illness* **~landheim** n *boarding-s. in the country* **~lehrer** m *s.master, teacher* **~lehrerin** f *s.mistress* **~leiter** m *headmaster*, ⟨Am⟩ *superintendent* **~mädchen** n *s.girl* **~mann** m *educationist, pedagogue* ⟨Am⟩ *s. man* ‖ mit dem ~ (Übersetzung) arbeiten ⟨sl⟩ *to ride hobbies* **~mappe** f *school bag* ≗**mäßig** a *scholastic* **~meinung** f *ism* **~meister** m *s.master* ≗**meisterisch** a *pedantic* ≗**meistern** vi/t [h] *to teach* | vt [h] *to censure* **~ordnung** f *s.-regulations* pl **~pause** f *recess*, kl *break* **~pferd** n *trained horse* **~pflicht** f; allg. ~ *compulsory education* ≗**pflichtig** a *of s. age*; *s.able*; Kind im ~en Alter ⟨demog⟩ *s.child* **~programm** n *prospectus* **~prüfung** f *s.-examination* **~rat** m *inspector of s.s*, ⟨Am⟩ *supervisor* **~reiten** n *equestrianism* **~rektor** m *headmaster* **~sache** f *s.-matter, s.-affair* **~schießen** n (*record*) *service practice*; *classification firing* **~schiff** n *training ship* **~schluß** m *break-up* **~schritt** m ⟨hors⟩ *short pace* **~schwänzer** m *truant* **~speisung** f *feeding of s.-children*; [konkr] *children's lunch(es* pl) **~sprache** f *s.-slang* **~sprecher** m ⟨Ger⟩ *head boy* od *prefect* ⟨engl⟩ **~statistik** f *current s. statistics* [a. sg konstr] **~stube** f *s.room* **~stunde** f *s.--hour, lesson* **~tag** m *s.-day* ‖ 1. ~ (nach den Ferien) *Black Monday* **~tasche** f *school bag* **~theologie** f *scholastic divinity* **~übung** f *s.-exercise* **~unterricht** m *s.ing*; (*s.-*)*instruction* **~verein** m *s.*

association **~versäumnis** f *absence from s.* **~vorstand** m *s. committee* **~vorsteher** m *head master, principal* **~weg** m *way to s.* **~weisheit** f *philosophy* **~wesen** n *s.-affairs* pl, *s.-management, education(al matters* pl); höheres ~ *secondary education* **~wissenschaft** f *s.-learning, humanities* **~witz** m *s.master's* od *s.boy's joke* **~zeugnis** n *s.-certificate, report* **~zeit** f *s.-days* pl **~zimmer** n = ~-stube **~zucht** f *s.-discipline* **~zwang** m = ~pflicht || → Schule

Schuld f ~/~en (ˣ~ → B. ˣ~ s) **A. 1.** (Ursache, Fehler) *fault, blame* **2.** (Vergehen) *guilt, offence, sin*; ⟨bib⟩ (*forgive us our*) *trespasses* pl; ⟨crim l⟩ *guilt* || ~ u Sühne *wrong-doing and atonement* || ⟨liter⟩ tragische ~ *tragic flaw, fatal action of the hero*, (ihre Sühnung *the Nemesis*) **3.** (Geldˣ~) *debt* (drückend *heavy*; faul *bad*; schwebende *floating*) || *money owing* (*by a p* bzw [Außenstände] *to a p* = *assets*; *outstanding debts*) || ~en [pl a.] *liabilities* pl, *indebtedness* || wer s–e ~en bezahlt, vergrößert sein Vermögen ⟨prov⟩ *short reckonings make long friends* || ~ u Gegenˣ~ *debts active and passive* **4.** (Verpflichtung) *obligation* **B.** e–e ~ **abtragen** *to pay off a debt* || die ~ auf jdn abwälzen, jdm die ~ zuschieben, zuschreiben *to shift the blame on to a p* || e–e ~ **begleichen,** bezahlen, tilgen *to settle, pay a debt*; *to pay off* (od *settle*) *old scores*; (*she discharged his debts*) || [dat] die ~ beimessen, → ~ geben || die ~ bek *to get the blame* || s–e ~ bemänteln *to cover one's guilt* || sich [dat] k–r ~ bewußt s *not to feel o.s. to blame* || e–e ~ **büßen,** sühnen *to suffer for a wrong* || die ~ drückt ihn sehr *the debt is heavy upon him* || *he feels very guilty* || e–e ~ einklagen *to take legal proceedings for the recovery of a debt* | *the blame fell on him* | [dat] die ~ **geben** *to ascribe, impute, attribute the fault to .., to set the blame down to*; *to lay it down to*; *to blame* (*a p*) || s–e ~ gestehen *to own up* || die ~ h, tragen *to be to blame* (an *for*) || mehr ~en h als Haare auf dem Kopf *to be head over ears in debt* || e–e schwere ~ auf sich **laden** *to make o.s. guilty of a great wrong* || s–e ~ leugnen *to plead not guilty* || an wem liegt die ~?, wer ist ˣ~?, wessen ~ ist es? *who is to blame for it?*; *whose fault is it?*; *the blame lies on the ruling conditions* || **~en m** *to run into debt*; *to contract, incur debts*; *to run up a score* od *bills*; ⟨fam⟩ *to go on tick* || die ~ auf sich nehmen *to take the blame* od ⟨fam⟩ *the rap* || jdm die ~ in die → Schuhe schieben *to pin the blame on a p* || ˣ~ **s,** die ~ tragen, (ˣes in ~ s) *to bear the blame, to be responsible* od *to blame* (*for*); *this was all the fault of the war*; *the weather was the cause of it*; *it was all his doing*; *it is my fault, the f. is mine*; es ist alles s–e ~ *it is all his doing*; *I was at f.* || ihn trifft k–e ~ *no blame attaches to him* **C. aus** den ~ herausk *to get into the black* || ~ **auf** ~ häufen *to add fault on fault* | nicht **durch** eigene ~ *through no fault of one's own* | **in** ~en geraten *to fall, get, run into debt*; *to incur debts* || ˣetw in ~ s = an etw ˣ~ s || in jds ~ s or stehen *to owe a p* (*some repayment*) *for a th, to be in a p's debt*; ⟨fig⟩ *to be* (*deeply*) *indebted to a p* || (tief) in ~en stecken *to be* (*up to the neck*) *in debt* || tief in jds ~ stehen *to owe a p a deep d.* || jdn (sich) in ~en stürzen *to run a p into debt* (*to run up debts*) | **mit** ~ beladen *steeped in crime* || **ohne** m–e ~ *through no fault of mine* | frei **von** aller ~ *exonerated from all blame* || (Haus) frei v ~en *unincumbered* || ich fühle mich nicht frei v ~ *I am open to criticism* || sich etw **zu**ˣ~en k l *to make o.s.* (*to become*) *guilty* (*of*); *to commit a fault, misdemeanour* (ein Verbrechen *a crime*), .. e–n Übergriff .. k l *to trespass*; .. nichts *I have not given cause for complaint* **anerkennung** = ~verschreibung **~arrest** m = ~haft ˣ~**befleckt** a *stained with guilt* **~bekenntnis** n *confession of guilt* ˣ~**beladen** a *laden with crime, guilt-laden, guilty* ˣ~**bewußt** a *conscience-stricken, conscious of guilt* | ~sein [n] *conscience of guilt* **~brief** m *bond*; *instrument of debt* **~buch** n *account-book, ledger*; ⟨pol⟩ *Debt Register* || unser ~ sei vernichtet *let bygones be bygones* **~erlaß** m ⟨jur⟩ *release* **~erlassung** f *remission of a debt* **~forderung** f *claim*, (*active*) *debt, demand* **~frage** f *question of fact*; Verneinung der ~ *verdict of not guilty* **~gefangene(r)** m *prisoner for debt* **~gefängnis** n *debtors' prison* | (erwachtes) **~gefühl** *the conviction of sin*; krankhaftes ~ *morbid feeling of guilt* **~haft** f *imprisonment for debt* **~herr** m *creditor* **~klage** f *action for debt* ˣ~**los** a *innocent, guiltless, blameless* || ~ erklären *to exculpate* | [adv] (*divorced*) *without guilt* **~losigkeit** f *innocence, guiltlessness* **~posten** m *sum* (*of money*) *owing, debt, item* **~saldo** m *debit balance* **~schein** m = –verschreibung | –darlehen [n] ⟨jur⟩ *loan by private treaty* **~spruch** m (bes der Geschworenen) *conviction*; (der *jury*) *verdict of guilty*, bei Jugendlichen *finding of guilt* **~turm** m *debtors' prison* **~überweisung** f *delegation* **~verpflichtung** f *obligation, liability* **~verschreibung** f *bond, note of hand, I.O.U.* (*I owe you*) (*to give a p one's I.O.U.*) || (öffentliche) *debenture, bond* || (Wandelˣ~) *convertible bond* || (Ablösungsˣ~) *refunding b.* || (vorzeitig kündbar) *redeemable* od *callable b.* || (nicht zurückzahlbar) *perpetual* od *irredeemable b.* || durch 1. (nachstellige) Hypothek gesicherte) ~ *first* od *senior* (Ggs *junior*) *mortgage b.*; durch Hypothek gedeckte ~en [pl] *collateral mortgage b.s* || Namensˣ~ (mit Inhaber-Zinsschein) *registered* (*coupon*) *b.* ˣ~**voll** a *guilty*

sch·ulden vt [h] *to owe* (*I owe you, I owe it to him*) || ⟨fig⟩ *to be indebted* (*to a p for a th*) || geschuldet ⟨Am⟩ (*the amount*) *due him* **Sch·ulden-**ˣ~**belastet** a *burdened* od *crippled with debts*; *deep in debt* ˣ~**frei** a *free from debt, unencumbered* ˣ~**halber** [adv] *owing to debts* **~last** f *burden of debt, liabilities* pl || (e–s Hauses) *encumbrance* **~macher** m *contractor of debts* **~masse** f *aggregate liability* **~tilgung** f *discharge, redemption, liquidation*, ⟨pol⟩ *sinking of debts*; Staatsˣ~ *amortisation* | ~sfonds [m], ~skasse [f] ⟨pol⟩ *sinking-fund* **~wesen** n *liabilities* pl **sch·uldig** a **A. 1.** (strafbar) *guilty* (e–r S *of a th*) || *culpable* || ~e Partei ⟨contr, etc⟩ *party in default* **2.** (Geld) *owing, due* **3.** (gebührend) *fitting, due* (*respect*); (*respect*) *due* (*to*) || *just* (*punishment*) || die ~e Pflicht der D. erfüllen *to fulfil the duties of gratitude* **B.** des Mordes (überführt) f ~ **befunden** w *to be convicted on a charge of m.* || sich ~ bekennen *to acknowledge one's guilt*; *to plead guilty* (*to a charge*) || ~ **bleiben**: *I must remain in his debt for .., he still owes me ..* || jdm die Antwort .. *to give a p* (*to return*) *no answer*; .. nicht .. *to give a smart a.* || e–m nichts ~ bleiben *to give a p tit for tat* || auf „~" **erkennen** *to bring in a verdict of guilty* || f ~ erklären *to pronounce* (*bring in*) *guilty* || sich ~ fühlen *to feel o.s. to blame* || sich [gen] ~ m *to make o.s. guilty* (*of a great wrong*) || ~ **sein** *to be* (*in duty*) *bound, to be obliged* od *under obligations* (*to do*) || wie (ich) ~ (bin) *duly, as I ought to* || jdm etw ~ s *to owe a p a sum*; ⟨fig⟩ *to be indebted to a p for a th* || beim Bäcker ~ s *to owe money to the b.* || das ist man ihm ~ *that is due to him* || das ist er s–r Stellung ~ *that is due to his p.* || das bist du ihm ~ *that you owe to him* || e–m nichts mehr ~ s *to be quits with a p* | jdm **Achtung** ~ s *to be bound to show a p respect* || jdm gr Dank ~ s *to be under a great obligation to a p* || jdm Rechenschaft ~ s *to owe a p an explanation* || des **Todes** ~ s *to deserve to be hanged* || e–s Verbrechens ~ s *to be guilty of a c.* || die Ware ~ s *to owe for the goods* | ~ **geschieden** *divorced and declared the guilty party* || jdn ~ sprechen *to find, pronounce a p guilty* **Sch·uldige** m [der ~ | ein ~r]; f [die ~ | e–e ~] ~n/~n; **~r** ~s/~ m *culprit, delinquent* || der ~

e–s Unfalls *the party at fault in an a.* | ⟨bib⟩ *as we forgive* (unsern ~rn) *them that trespass against us* **Sch·uldig- ~erklärung, ~sprechung** f *verdict of guilty* || nach ~ *upon conviction* **sch·uldigerm·aßen** [adv] *duly, as in duty bound* **Sch·uldigkeit** f ~/ **1.** *debt; the fee due* || was ist m–e ~? *how much do I owe (you)?* **3.** *duty (to do one's d.); obligation* || nur jds Pflicht u ~ *not more than one's bounden duty*: s–e Pflicht u ~ tun *to keep up one's end* **sch·uldigst** [adv] *most duly; as is due and proper* **Sch·uldner** m ~s/~; **~in** f *debtor*; ⟨jur⟩ *obligor*, ⟨Am⟩ *obligator*; im Verzug *defaulter*

Sch·ule f ~/~n [in comp Schul–] **A.** *school* || (Gebäude) *school (-house)* | (Lehrmeinung) *school* | (Buch) ⟨mus⟩ (*violin*) *school, school* (*of* ..) | ⟨hort⟩ *nursery* | (Schulung) *training, teaching, schooling* || (Schüler pl) (*boys an girls of a*) *school* | ⟨hors⟩ (hohe) ~ *haute école* Fr **B.** Aufbau≗ ⟨Ger⟩ *special school for advanced elementary school children* || Elementar≗ = Volks≗ || Fach≗ *professional s.* || Fortbildungs≗ *continuation s.* || gelehrte ~ *college; public s.* || gemischte ~ *coeducational s.* || Gewerbe≗ *technical s., trade-s.* || **Grund**≗ *primary s.* || Handelshoch≗ *commercial academy* || Handwerker≗ *mechanics' institute* || Hoch≗, [obs] hohe ~ *university* || höhere ~ *high* od *secondary s.* || höhere Mädchen–, Töchter≗ *high s. for girls*, ⟨Scot⟩ *academy*; höhere ~ (staatlich) [*modern*] *secondary s.*; höhere ~n pl *institutions of higher learning* || höhere Internats≗ ⟨Am⟩ *academy* || Internats≗ *boarding s.* || Kinder≗ *infant s.* || Knaben- u Mädchen≗ *mixed s.* ⟨Am⟩ *co-educational s.* || Latein≗ (Gymnasium) ⟨engl⟩ *grammar-s.* || ⟨mil⟩ *training center* N || **Mittel**≗ *intermediate s.* || Privat≗ *private s.*; (exklusiv) *public s.*, ⟨Am⟩ *high s.* || Simultan≗ *s. for children of different confession* || Staats≗ *state s.* || Technische Hoch≗ *polytechnic academy* || → Volks≗; (mehrklassige) ⟨Am⟩ *graded s.* || staatl., städtische ~ ⟨Am⟩ *public s.* || Volks≗ *primary* od *elementary s.*, ⟨Am⟩ *public s.*; (mehrklassig) ⟨Am⟩ *graded s.*; (öffentlich) *board s.*; Unter-/Oberstufe *junior/senior (high) s.*; → Volkshoch≗ || Vor≗ *primary* od *preparatory s.*; ⟨Am⟩ *public s.* **C.** die ganze ~ *the whole s.* || ~ **abhalten** *to keep (a) s.* || die ~ wird abgehalten, findet statt *the s. sits (in the Palace)* || er hatte nie e–e ~ besucht *he never went to s. at all* || die ~ mit Ach u Krach durchm *to scrape through the s.* || der ~ entwachsen s *to have left one's s.days behind* || heute **fällt** die ~ aus, ist k–e ~ *there are no lessons today, today is a holiday* || die ~ ist aus *s. is over* || die ~ fängt um 8 an *s. hours begin at 8 a. m.* || wann h wir wieder ~?, wann fängt die ~ wieder an? *when does the s. reopen?* || ~ m *to find adherents, to be imitated*, ⟨arts⟩ *to form a s.* || die hohe ~ **reiten** *to put a horse through its paces* || die ~ schwänzen *to play truant* **D. auf**, in der ~ *at s.* | **aus** der ~ genommen w *to be withdrawn from school* || aus der ~ plaudern, schwatzen (*to tell tales out of s.*) *to let out stable secrets*; ⟨sl⟩ *to split* | **durch** die ~ gelaufen s *to have a smattering of knowledge* || durch e–e harte ~ gehen (schicken) *to go (put) to the mill, to stand a severe test* | **hinter**, neben die ~ gehen *to play truant* | **in** die ~, zur ~ gehen *to go to s.*; mit jdm ..: *he was at s. with* ..; ⟨fig⟩ bei jdm ..: *to learn much from a p* || jdn in die ~ nehmen *to take a p in hand* | **nach** der ~ dableiben *to stay in after s. hours* | mit jdm **zur** ~ gehen *to be at s. with a p* **sch·ulen** vt [h] *to teach, school, discipline, tutor, instruct* || seine Stimme ~ *to train one's voice* || (Schwerverletzte) f e–n (anderen) Beruf ~ *to rehabilitate* | jdn politisch ~ *to give a p a political education* || **sich** ~ *to go through a good s.(ing)* | ⟨sport⟩ *to train* ⟨a. fig⟩ | ⟨hors⟩ *to train, to break in, to put (a horse) through its paces* | **geschult** *trained (eye, mind, staff, voice)*; *experienced (speaker)* || bestens g. *highly trained (crew)* **Sch·üler** m ~s/~ *school-boy, pupil* (⟨obs & vulg a.⟩ *scholar*) || ⟨engl⟩ (Stipendiat e–r Public School or e–s Univ. Coll.) *scholar* || (Jünger) *disciple* ⟨rel & philos⟩ || (Anfänger) *novice* | im 1. Jahr *freshman*; ⟨Am⟩ im 2. *sophomore*, 3. *junior*, 4. *senior* | ein alter ~ v mir *a former pupil of mine* || ehemaliger ~ der Anstalt *old boy* || fahrender ~ *itinerant scholar* || ~ e–s Gymnasiums *grammar--school boy* || ~ der unteren (oberen) Klassen *lower (upper) form boy* || ~ der Prima *sixth-form boy* | *a scholar of Dürer, Röntgen; he follows the school of Dürer* | *there are ten boys in this form* **~arbeit** f *pupil's task* **~austausch** m *exchange of p.s* **~bibliothek** f *library for p.s* **~lotse** m *school safety patrol, traffic monitor*; ⟨fam⟩ *lollipop-man* | ~ndienst [m] *sc. p.* **~material** n *school-children* **~spiel** n *boys' game* **~szene** f (im „Faust") *student scene* **sch·ülerhaft** [a & adv] *boyish, schoolboy-like* || ⟨fig⟩ *bungling, blundering* ≗**igkeit** f *boyishness; lack of experience; blundering ways* pl **Sch·ülerschaft** f ~/ **1.** *discipleship* **2.** [koll] ([pl] ~en) *all the pupils* etc → Schüler **Sch·ülerin** f ~/~nen *schoolgirl* || (Jüngerin) *disciple* || ~ e–r gemischten Schule ⟨Am fam⟩ *co-ed* [pl *co-eds*] **sch·ulisch** a *scholastic*; → Schulung

Sch·ulp m ~(e)s/~e, **~e** f ~/~n *cuttle-bone*

Sch·ulter f ~/~n *shoulder* || breite ~n h *to be broad-sh.ed* || er straffte s–e ~n *he squared his shoulders*; jdm die kalte ~ zeigen *to show a p the cold sh.* | ~ **an** ~ *side by side, touching s.s, serried, sh. to sh.* ⟨a. fig⟩ || (hoch) **auf** den ~n *sh.-high* || jdm auf die ~ klopfen *to tap a p on the sh.* || auf die ~ nehmen *to sh.* || ⟨fig⟩ etw auf die leichte ~ nehmen *to make light of a th* || auf beiden ~n tragen *to make one boot serve for either leg, to run with the hare and hunt with the hounds* | eng **in** den ~n *narrow in the chest*; in den ~n breiter w *to fill out* | (jdn) **mit** der ~ anstoßen *to give a sh.-shove* || mit der ~ zucken *to (give a) shrug (of) one's sh.* || e–n **über** die ~ ansehen *to look down upon a p*, ⟨fam⟩ *to look down one's nose at a p* **~band** n ⟨anat⟩ *humeral ligament* **~bein** n *sh.-bone* **~blatt** n *sh.-blade* **~blech** n *sh.-piece* **~decker** m *semihighwing (mono)plane* ≗**frei** a ⟨tail⟩ *bare-topped; strapless (gown)* **~gehenk** n *sh.-belt* **~klappe** f ⟨mil⟩ *sh.-strap* **~riemen** m *sh.-strap* **~stück** n ⟨tail⟩ *yoke (of blouse, shirt, coat)*; ⟨mil tail⟩ *sh. knot, loop, mark*; ⟨cul⟩ (Schwein) *hock*, (Rind) *brisket* **~tuch** n *scapulary*; *R.C.* ⟨a.⟩ *humeral* **~verrenkung** f *dislocation of the sh., sh.-wrench* **~wehr** f ⟨fort⟩ *épaulement* Fr **sch·ultern** vt [h] *to shoulder (arms)* || mit geschultertem Gewehr *with arms shouldered*

Sch·ultheiß m ~en/~en; **Sch·ulze** m ~n/~n *(village) mayor*

Sch·ulung f ~/ *schooling*; ⟨pol⟩ (*party*) *indoctrination* || ⟨fig⟩ *training* **~sarbeit** f ⟨SBZ⟩ *indoctrination* **~skurs** m *ind. course*; ⟨engl⟩ *refresher course* **~slager** n *training camp* **~swoche** f *one week's course (of instruction)*

°**Schum** m ~s/ (Sekt) *fiz(z), sham*

°**sch·ummeln** vi [h] ⟨fam⟩ *to cheat*

Sch·ummer m ~s/ *dusk* **~stunde** f *twilight, dusk* | ≗**ig** a *dusky, dim* | **~ung** f ⟨cart⟩ *hatching*

schund 1. & 3. sg pret v schinden **Schund** m ~(e)s/ *refuse, offal* || ⟨fig⟩ *trash, junk*; (Buch) *rubbish*; (Ware) *trumpery* || ⟨sl⟩ *tripe* **~bau** m *jerry-building* **~blatt** n *rag* **~literatur** f *trash(y books* od *literature)*; *shoddy literature* **~roman** m *pulp; penny-dreadful, shilling-shocker* **~ware** f *catch-penny* od *slop-made goods* pl **~zeug** n *trash, refuse*

°**sch·unkeln** vi/t [h] *to see-saw, sway*

Schupf, Schupp m ~(e)s/ = Schups

Sch·upo f ~/ (abbr f Schutzpolizei) *police* || ~ m ~s/~s (abbr f Schutzpolizist) ⟨sl⟩ *bobby* **~mann** [pl Schupoleute] m = ~ [m]

Sch·üppchen n ⟨dim⟩ **1.** v Schuppe **2.** v Schüppe: ein ~ m *to pout (and snivel)* **Sch·uppe** f ~/~n ⟨zoo⟩ *scute, scale* ⟨a. fig⟩; ⟨bot, zoo⟩ *squama* ‖ ~n [pl] (P) *dandruff*; mit ~n bedeckt *scutate* **Sch·üppe** f ~/~n *scoop, shovel* ‖ ⟨cards⟩ *spades*

Sch·uppen m ~s/~ *barn* ‖ *shed, coach-house*; ⟨rail⟩ *engine-house*; ⟨mot⟩ *garage*; ⟨aero⟩ *hangar*

sch·uppen vt [h] **1.** (Fische) *to scale* **2.** (sanft stoßen) *to shove, to push* **Sch·uppen-** **~baum** m *lepidodendron* **~eidechse** f *scaly lizard* **~flechte** f ⟨path⟩ *psoriasis* **~fisch** m *scaly fish* **≈förmig** a *squamiform* **~kette** f *scaly chin-strap (of helmet)* **~muster** n *scallops* pl **~panzer** m *scale-armo(u)r, splint a.* | ~(jacke [f]) *brigandine* **~tanne** f ⟨bot⟩ *monkey-puzzle* **~tier** n *scaly ant-eater* ‖ *pangolin* **≈weise** [adv] *in scales* **~wurz** f *tooth-wort* **sch·uppig** a *scaly, squamous*; *tegular* ‖ *with (red) scales*

°**Schups** m –ses/–se *shove, push* **sch·upsen** vt [h] *to shove, push*

Schur f ~/~en *shearing* ‖ (Wolle) *fleece* | ⟨hort⟩ *mowing (of grass)* ‖ *clipping (of hedges)* | ~wolle [f] (rein *pure*) *virgin* od *new wool*

Schür- **~eisen** n *poker* **~haken** m *fire-hook, (furnace-)rake* **~loch** n *stoke-hole* **~zange** f (e–e *a pair of*) *fire-tongs* pl **sch·üren** vt [h] *to stir, poke, rake, mend; to kick up (the fire), to add fuel to ..* ⟨a. fig⟩ ‖ das Feuer ~ *to give the fire a stir* | ⟨fig⟩ *to stir up; to fan, incite, agitate* **Sch·ürer** m ~s/~ *poker, raker* ‖ ⟨fig⟩ *agitator, fomenter*

Schurf m ~s/ ⟨min⟩ *prospect, opening, bore-hole* **Schürf-** **~arbeit** f *prospecting* **~befugnis** f *p.g rights* pl **~bohrer** m *p.g drill* **~loch** n *test* od *trial pit* **~schein** m *grant* **~stelle** f, **~ung** f *p.g place* **sch·ürfen** **1.** vt [h] *to scratch, cut, graze* | ⟨min⟩ *to explore, prospect* (nach *for*) ‖ *to uncover (a mine)* **2.** ≈ n *searching operations* pl; *exploration* **Sch·ürfer** m ~s/~ *prospector*, ⟨Am⟩ *cruiser* **Sch·ürfung** f ~/~en [abstr] *cut, abrasion* ‖ ⟨min⟩ *prospecting* | ~svorhaben [n] *p.g activities* pl

sch·urigeln vt [h] ⟨fam⟩ *to plague, vex, bully, ride (a p)*; ich laß mich nicht ~ *you can't boss me* **Sch·urke** m ~n/~n *scoundrel, blackguard, rogue, knave, cad, villain*; ⟨film sl⟩ *heavy* ‖ ⟨vulg⟩ *sod* ‖ aalglatter ~ *slick scamp* ‖ diese ~n! *these scum!* **~nstreich** m *knavish* od *scurvy trick*; *devilry* | **~r·ei** f ~/~en *roguery, knavery, rascality* **Sch·urkin** f ~/~nen *rascally woman* **sch·urkisch** a *knavish, rascally, villainous, vile, scoundrelly*

Sch·urre f, ~/~n *slide* ‖ ⟨tech⟩ *escape gate* **sch·urren** vi [h & s] *to shuffle, slide (along)* • **Sch·urrmurr** m ~s/ *medley, hodge-podge*

Schurz m ~es/~e *apron* ‖ ⟨Scot⟩ *kilt* ‖ (Kaminmantel) *mantelpiece* | ~fell [n] *leather apron* | **≈e** f ~/~n *apron* (vorbinden *to put on*) ‖ (Kinder≈) *pinafore* | ⟨übtr theat⟩ *house border*; *proscenium pelmet*, ⟨Am⟩ *grand drapery* ‖ ⟨decor⟩ → Überfall | ⟨fig⟩ *placket, wench*; ⟨sl⟩ *(bit of) skirt* ‖ hinter jeder ~ her s *to run after every petticoat* ‖ °⟨sex⟩ *front-door mat* **sch·ürzen** vt [h] *to tie (truss, tuck, pin) up (a skirt)* ‖ *to tie (a knot)* ‖ *to shorten (a dress)* ‖ *to purse (one's lips)* ‖ ⟨liter⟩ den Knoten ~ *to weave the plot* | **sich** ~ *to tuck up one's dress*; ⟨fig⟩ *to prepare, to get ready* ‖ der Knoten –zt sich *the plot thickens* **Sch·ürzen-** **~band** n *apron-string* **~herrschaft** f *petticoat government* **~jäger** m *womanizer, snake, moll-hunter, dangler after petticoats; a rascal of a Lovelace*, ⟨Am fam⟩ *wolf* **~latz** m *bib* **~volk** n (Weiber) *skirts* **~zipfel** m (Mann) an ihrem ~ *tied to her apron-strings* **Sch·ürzung** f ~/~en ⟨Lit⟩ (des Knotens) *twisting*; *point of attack (e.g. Hamlet I. 5)*

Schuß m Schusses/Schüsse, (als Maß pl) ~ **A. 1.** *shot* ‖ ⟨fam⟩ *pop* ‖ ~! *fire*; ⟨mil comm⟩ *on the way!* ‖ 30 ~ Patronen *30 rounds of cartridges* | (Knall) *report* ‖ (Ladung) *charge* ‖ (~weite) *range* ‖ (~wunde) *shot-wound* | **blinder** ~ *blind round*; scharfer ~ *live shot* ‖ ⟨artill⟩ erster (Richtungs–) ~ *sighting shot*, ⟨Am⟩ *witness shot* **2.** ⟨min⟩ *blasting* **3.** ⟨weav⟩ *weft, woof* **4.** ⟨bot⟩ (Treiben) *shooting*; (Trieb) *shoot, sprout* **5.** (Bewegung) *rush, swoop, swing; shooting along* od *ahead* ‖ ⟨hors⟩ *career* | ⟨ski⟩ *schuss* **6.** ⟨fig⟩ *batch (of bread)* ‖ *dash (of brandy, recklessness, French blood)* ‖ Bier mit ~ *shandy* ‖ *milk with a dash* (Kaffee) ‖ ein ~ Wasser (hinter dem Schnaps her) ⟨Am sl⟩ *chaser* ‖ ~ (Schnaps) dazu: *(would you like a) little sth in it* **B.** ~ **aufs** Geratewohl *wild shot* ‖ ~ aus dem Hinterhalt *sniping s.*; aus der P. *from a pistol* | ~ **ins** Blaue *random s.* ‖ ein ~ ins Schwarze *a bull's eye* ‖ ⟨ftb⟩ ~ ins Tor *(s. at the) goal* | ~ **vor** den Bug *shot over* od *across the bows* ⟨a. fig⟩ **C.** e–n ~ **abgeben,** tun *to fire a s.* ‖ ein ~ fiel, (ging los) *a s. went off, was fired* od *heard* ‖ ~, der nicht losgeht *miss-fire* ‖ jeder ~ saß *or* traf .. *went home, told* **D. auf** den ersten ~ *at the first s.* | **im** ~ *at full speed, in full swing*; ⟨fam⟩ *on the move* ‖ ⟨fig⟩ (gut) im ~ *in good condition* od *order*; (gut) im ~ s ⟨fam⟩ *to be going strong* | etw **in** ~ bringen, kriegen *to set a th going* ‖ in ~ k *to dart off; to get into swing, into working order, into the proper spirit* ‖ e–m in den ~ laufen *to run across a p* | der ~ geht nach hinten los ⟨fig⟩ *the matter, etc boomerangs* | fern **vom** ~ *out of harm's way* | sich **zum** ~ fertig m *to make ready to fire* ‖ dreimal zum ~ k *to get in three shots* **E.** ⟨fig⟩ e–n ~ h *to be a bit crazy* ‖ ich möchte nicht zwei ~ dran wenden *I wouldn't spend a farthing on it* ‖ k–n ~ Pulver wert *not worth powder or shot* **~bahn** f *range* **~be·obachtung** f ⟨artill⟩ *spotting* **~bereich** m *(effective) range*; *zone of fire* **≈bereit** a *ready to fire* ‖ .. ~ halten *to hold the guns at the ready* **~ebene** f *plane of fire* **~elemente** n pl *ballistic elements* pl | wirksamste **~entfernung** f *optimum range* **~feld** n *zone of fire*; ~ frei m *to set free the range* **~fertig** a *at the ready*; *cocked (rifle)*; (Munition) *prepared for firing* **≈fest** a *bullet-, shot-proof* **≈frei** a *out of range* **~garbe** f *cone of fire*; (MG) *burst* **~garn** n *weft-thread* **≈gerecht** a *within gunshot* ‖ *true (gun)* ‖ ⟨hors⟩ *trained to stand fire* **~kanal** m ⟨med⟩ *track of gunshot wound* **~leistung** f *firing efficiency, marksmanship* **~linie** f, **~richtung** f *line of fire, firing line* **~loch** n ⟨min⟩ *shot hole* **≈scheu** a *gun-shy* **~schweißung** f *shot-welding* **≈sicher** a *shell-proof* **~spule** f *bobbin* **~tafel** f *range* od *elevation, firing table*; graphische ~ ⟨artill⟩ *(graphic) firing t., trajectory chart* od *diagrams* pl **~träger** m ⟨weav⟩ *shuttle-carrier* **~waffe** f *fire-arm* **~weite** f *range*; größte ~ *maximum r.*; wirksame ~ *efficient r.* ‖ auf ~ *within r.* od *shot*; ⟨artill⟩ *within shelling r.* ‖ in (außer) ~ *within (out of) shot* od *r.* **~wert** m: ~e pl ⟨artill⟩ *data* | ~eberechner [m] (S) *firing data computer*; ~rechenzettel [m] *data sheet*; ~verbesserung [f] ⟨artill⟩ *adjustment* **~wunde** f *gun-shot-* od *bullet-wound*

Sch·ussel m ~s/~, f ~/~n **1.** [f] *sloven, slut, slattern* **2.** [m & f] *fidget(y p)*; *harum-scarum* | **≈ig** a **1.** *slovenly* **2.** *giddy, fickle* **≈igkeit** f *slovenliness, sluttishness* ‖ *giddiness, fickleness*

Schüssel f ~/~n *dish* (a. Gericht); bunte ~ (Gericht) *made dish* ‖ (hölzerne) *platter* ‖ (irdene) *pan*, (Napf) *basin* ‖ *(salad-)bowl* ‖ *(sauce-)boat* ‖ Sitzbade≈ *bidet* ‖ Suppen≈ *tureen* ‖ e–e ~ **mit** Wasser *a dish of water* **~brett** n *shelf for plates* ‖ *plate-drainer* **~deckel** m *plate-cover* **~glocke** f *dish-cover* **~schrank** m *sideboard* **~trage** f *tray* **~wärmer** m *dish-heater* **~wäscherin** f *scullery-maid*

Sch·usser m ~s/~ *marble*; → Klicker

Sch·uster m ~s/~ *shoemaker* ‖ (Flick≈, ⟨a. fig⟩) *cobbler* ‖ auf ~s Rappen *on Shank's mare* ‖ ~, bleib bei deinen Leisten! *the cobbler must stick to his last; mind your own business!* **~ahle** f *awl* **~arbeit** f *shoemaker's work* **~draht** m *twine* **~junge** m *s.m.'s apprentice* **~gang** m *fool's errand* **~karpfen** m (Hering) ⟨sl ich⟩ *soldier, sea-pheasant* **~laden** m *s.m.'s shop* **~messer** n *shoe-knife* **~pappe** f *s.m.'s paste* **~pech** n *cobbler's wax* **~pfriem** m *c.'s punch* **~schwärze** f *s.m.'s blacking* **~werkstatt** f *c.'s workshop* **~zwecke** f *s.m.'s peg* od *brad* **Schuster·ei** f ~/~en *shoemaking trade, shoe-making* **sch·ustern** vi [h] *to cobble*; *to make* od *mend boots and shoes* | ⟨fig⟩ **1.** *to potter* **2.** *to bungle* **3.** *to fawn* | etw zus-~ *to put a th together*

Sch·ute, (⁓) f ~/~n **1.** *barge* **2.** *scoop-bonnet*

Schutt m ~(e)s/ *rubbish, refuse* || (Stein⁓) *rubble, débris* ⟨a. geol⟩ || ⟨geol⟩ (Gehänge⁓) *scree* || ⟨arts⟩ *ruins* || ~ abladen *to shoot rubbish*; .. verboten *no r. to be shot here*; *no dumping* || in ~ u Asche liegen *to be all rubble* **~abladeplatz** m → Müll– *dump(ing-ground), trash-dump* **~ablagerung** f ⟨geol⟩ *detritus* **~decke** f ⟨geol⟩ *mantle rock* **~fächer** m *alluvial fan* **~halde** f *spoil-bank*; ⟨geol⟩ *screes* pl, *talus* **~haufen** m *rubbish-heap* || in e–n ~ verwandeln *to lay in ruins* **~karren** m *dust-cart, tumbrel, –il* **~ramme** f *bulldozer*, dazu: *to bulldoze* **Sch·ütt-boden** m *corn-loft, granary* **~gut** n *bulk goods* od *cargo* **~kasten** m (Bomben-⁓) *trough* **~stein** m Sw *kitchen-sink* **~trichter** m *hopper* **~verlust** m *spillage* **Sch·ütte** f ~/~n *granary* || (Stroh⁓) *bundle, truss* || (Kohlen⁓) *coal-scuttle* **~(krankheit)** f ⟨for⟩ *blight* **Sch·üttel-~bewegung** f *tremulous motion* **~fieber** n, **~frost** m *the shivers* pl **~reim** m *spoonerism* **~rinne** f *shaking gutter* **~rost** m *oscillating* od *rocking grate* **~rutsche** f *shaking chute* **~sieb** n *shaker screen, shaking sifter* **~sortierer** m *oscillating strainer* **~speiser** m *shaking feeder* **~vorrichtung** f *shake* **sch·ütteln** vt [h] *to shake, toss* | vi (rütteln) *to jolt* | vor Gebrauch zu ~ *to be shaken before taken* || durch–e–a|~ *to scramble* || *to pass (flour through a sieve)* || den Kopf ~ *to shake one's head* || jdm die Hand ~ *to shake hands with a p, to shake a p by the hand* | jdm **aus** dem Schlafe ~ *to rouse a p by shaking him* || °jdn aus den Lumpen ~ *to call a p over the coals* || **von**: *to shake the dust off one's feet* | das Fieber schüttelte **mich** *I shivered with fever* || **es** schüttelt mich *it makes me shiver* | **sich** ~ *to shiver* (vor .. *with disgust*) **sch·ütten I.** vt [h] *to throw, shoot (corn)* || (Getränke) *to pour (out, into)* ⟨a. fig⟩ || Futter ~ *to feed*; *to deal out fodder* || leer (voll) ~ *to empty (fill)* | **auf**: *to pour, spill on (the floor)* || auf e–n Haufen ~ *to heap up*; *to throw on a heap* | **aus**: *to empty out of* (**in** *into*) || **über**: *to pour over*; *to upset (a kettle) over* **II.** vi das Korn schüttet gut .. *shows up well* || der Baum schüttet .. *throws off its needles* | **es** schüttet *it's pouring (with rain)* **schütter** a *thin, sparse (hair)*; *scanty (eyebrows)* || ⟨bot⟩ *straggling* | ⁓zone [f] ⟨geol⟩ *seismic zone*; ⟨geopol⟩ *shatter z.* **sch·üttern I.** vi [h] *to tremble, shiver, shake, quake* **II.** vt *to shake*

Schutz m ~es/ **A.** *protection, defence* (gegen, vor *against, from*); ~ gegen Staubentwicklung! *No dust nuisance*! || (Obdach) *shelter* || (Obhut) *custody* | *safety* || *support* | (Bedeckung) *safeguard* (gegen *against*), ⟨mil⟩ *escort* | ⟨mil⟩ *cover, shelter*; Feuer⁓ *protective fire* || jds persönlicher ~ ⟨a.⟩ *bodyguard to a p* | ⟨hunt⟩ (T) *cover(t)* | (Ort) *shelter, refuge* **B.** *the grounds are recommended* (**anempfohlen**) *to the care of the public* || e–m Wechsel gebührenden ~ bereiten *duly honour a bill* || ~ **finden** ⟨a.⟩ *to gain cover (in a house)* || jdm ~ gewähren *to give* od *afford a p shelter* od *refuge (against)* || ~ suchen unter *to (seek) shelter, to take refuge* od *cover under* || ~ z·usichern *to promise safety* **C. in**: *in the hands of God, in God's holy keeping* || ⟨a.⟩ *in* od *under lee of a tree* | **in, unter**: *under cover of darkness, of the guns* || *in the shelter of the Church* | **unter**: *under a p's wing*; *(bombers) protected by* || unter dem ~ u Schirm *under the protection* od *auspices (of)* | **zu** ~ u Trutz *defensive(ly) and offensive(ly)* **D. sich in** jds ~ **begeben** *to take refuge* od *seek shelter with a p* || (jdn) in [s–n] ~ nehmen *to defend, support, champion (against), vindicate (from)* [*to take under one's protection*], e–n Wechsel: *to honour a bill* | **unter** s–m ~ **einführen** *to patronize* **Sch·utz-** [in comp oft] *p(.rotectiv)e, p(.rotecto)r, p(.rotectio)n* **~amt** n *p.rship, guardianship* **~anstrich** m *p.e coat*, ⟨mil⟩ *dazzle paint* **~anzug** m *protective clothes*; ⟨mil⟩ *p.e uniform* | Zubringer der ⁓e ⟨a–n⟩ *big swimmer* **~ärmel** m *p.r, saving sleeve* **~ausrüstung** f *protective equipment* **~befohlene(r)** m *charge, protégé(e f)*, (Mündel) *ward* **~bereich** m *restricted* od *reserved area* **~blattern** f pl *cow-pox* **~blech** n *guard-plate, screen*; ⟨cycl⟩ *mud-guard*; ⟨mot⟩ *dash-board* **~brett** n *flood-board, water-gate* **~brief** m *safe-conduct* **~brille** f *eye-preservers* pl; e–e gute ~, f Damen ⟨mot⟩ *a god pair of lady's goggles* **~bündnis** n *defense alliance* **~bunker** m *bomb shelter* **~dach** n *shed*; *shelter*; *awning* **~damm** m *(inner) dike*; ⟨Am⟩ *levee* **~deckel** m ⟨bookb⟩ *wrapper, (protective) jacket, slip* || (Uhr) *hunting case* **~engel** m *guardian angel* **~färbung** f ⟨zoo⟩ *p.e colo(u)ring* **~fenster** n ⟨hort⟩ *frame* **~frist** f *term of copyright* **~frucht** f *cover crop* **~gatter** n *portcullis* || (Wasser⁓) *flood-gate* **~gebiet** n *protectorate, colony*; ⟨fig⟩ *preserve* **~geist** m *(tutelary) genius* **~geländer** n *guard rail* || vgl Schutzgitter **~geleit** n *safe-conduct*, ⟨mil⟩ *escort*, ⟨mar⟩ *convoy* **~gerechtigkeit** f *right of (claim to) p.n* **~gesetz** n ⟨zoo⟩ *Conservation Act* **~gitter** n *grid*; *guard rails* pl **~glas** n *shatter-proof glass* **~gläser** n pl *eye-goggles* pl **~gott** m (**~göttin** f) *tutelary god(dess)* **~hafen** m *harbour of refuge* **~haft** f *p.e custody (to take into .., to be under ..)* **~haube** f *hood*; ⟨tech⟩ (Ventil⁓) *petticoat* **~heilige(r)** (m &) f *patron saint* **~heiligtum** n *palladium* **~herr** m *p.r, patron* **~herrschaft** f *p.rate* **~hülle** f ⟨bookb⟩ *cardboard case* || ⟨el⟩ *casing p.rate* **~hütte** f *(Alpine) refuge* **~impfung** f *vaccination*; *preventive inoculation* **~insel** f (auf der Straße) *island, refuge* **~karton** m ⟨bookb⟩ *carton* **~kette** f *cordon* **~kind** n *charge*, (Mündel) *ward* **~körper** m *antibody* **~leder** n *apron* ⟨a. min⟩ **~leistung** f *p.n* ⁓**los** a *defenceless, unprotected*; *helpless* **~lösung** f ⟨mot⟩ *antifreeze solution* **~mann** m [pl **-leute**] *policeman, constable*; berittene –leute *mounted police* **~mannschaft** f *constabulary, police* **~mantel** m ⟨tech⟩ *serving*; ⟨R.C. art⟩ *cloak of p.n* | ~madonna [f] *Virgin of Mercy* **~marke** f ⟨com⟩ *trade-mark* **~maske** f *respirator* **~maßnahmen** f pl *precautions* pl *(against)* **~mauer** f *defensive wall, rampart* || ⟨fig⟩ *bulwark* **~mittel** n *preservative* (gegen *against*), *preventive (of)* **~papier** n *backing paper* ⟨a. phot⟩ **~patron(in** f) m ⟨ec⟩ *patron saint* **~plane** f ⟨mil⟩ *manta* **~pocken** f pl *cow-pox* | ~impfung [f] *vaccination*; ~-stoff [m] *vaccine* **~polizei** f (abbr Schupo) *security police* **~polizist** m = ~mann **~raum** m *shelter* ([ober-] unterirdisch [*surface*] *underground sh.*) **~recht** n ⟨ind⟩ *p.e right* (Sammelbegriff) **~schicht** f *safety coating* **~schild** m ⟨artill⟩ *shield* **~sperre** f ⟨pol⟩ *p.e tariff* **~staat** m *protected state* **~staffel** f ⟨aero⟩ *defence squadron* || ⟨nazi⟩ (abbr SS) *Black Shirts* pl **~streifen** m (Verkehr) *refuge* **~suchende(r)** (m &) f (Luftschutz) *shelterer* **~truppe** f *colonial troop* od *force* **~umschlag** m *book jacket, dust jacket* **~- u Trutz-** ~bündnis [n] *defensive and offensive alliance*; ~waffen [f pl] *defensive and offensive arms* **~verordnung** f *p.e statute* **~vorrichtung** f *safety-device, guard* **~wache** f *escort, safeguard* **~waffe** f *defensive weapon* **~wagen** m ⟨rail⟩ *safeguard-wag(g)on* **~wall** m ⟨fort⟩ *rideau* [Fr], ⟨fig⟩ *dike* **~wand** f *screen* **~wanne** f ⟨mot⟩ *drip tray*; *mud-shield* **~weg** m (auf der Straße) *safety zone* **~wehr** f *fence*, ⟨mil⟩ *bulwark* ‖ ⟨fig⟩ (P) *the only defence, -nse of their mother* **~zaun** m ⟨sport⟩ (*solid*) *backstop* **~zoll** m *protective duty*; *protection* | ≈ner [m] ⟨pol⟩ *protectionist*; ~politik [f] *protectionism*; ~system [n] *p.e system, protectionism*

Schütz(e) m ~en/~en → schießen *shot, marksman* | ⟨mil⟩ *rifleman* (pl ⟨a.⟩ *Rifles, rifles*); ausgezeichneter ~ ⟨bes mil⟩ *expert* ‖ ⟨aero⟩ (Bord≈) *gunner* ‖ MG-~ *machine-gunner* ‖ (Dienstgrad) *private* | (Ballspiel) *shooter* | ⟨astr⟩ *Archer, Sagittarius* | ein guter (sicherer) ~ *a good* (*dead*) *shot*

Sch·ütze 1. m ~n/~n ⟨weav⟩ *shuttle* **2.** f ~/~n (Schleuse) *flood-gate, sluice* ‖ (Wasserbau) f *sluice-board* | ~nschleuse [f] *sash sluice*

sch·ützen vt [h] → Schutz (gegen, vor [dat]) *to shelter* (*from*) ‖ *to screen* (*from the wind*) ‖ *to shade* (*from light*) | ⟨com⟩ *to protect* od *honour* (*a draft*) ‖ ⟨tech⟩ (Wasser, Mühle, Rad) *to shut off the water* od *a mill-dam* | ⟨fig⟩ *to protect, defend, shelter, guard* (gegen *against*; vor [dat] *from*); vor Nässe ~! *keep dry*!; .. *keep out of sunlight* ‖ *to secure* (*against losses*) ‖ (Recht) *to vindicate* ‖ *to maintain* (*in possession of*) | **sich** ~ *to guard* (*o.s.*) (*against*); *to protect o.s.* (*from danger, against the cold*) ‖ **~d** [a] *tutelary* ‖ *protective* (*clothing*); die Hand ~ halten *to put out a protective hand* ‖ **geschützt** [a] *safe* (*from attacks*); *sheltered* (*harbour, corner*); *armoured* (*cruiser*); gesetzlich g. *patented, registered* ‖ nicht g. *in the public domain*; **Sch·ützen-** *r*(*ifle*), *f*(*ire*) **~auftritt** m *fire-step* **~bataillon** n *r. battalion* **~brigade** f *r.-brigade* **~bruder** m *fellow-sharpshooter* **~fest** n *r.-meeting, shooting-match*; *schuetzenfest* **~feuer** n ⟨mil⟩ *running f.* **~gesellschaft** f, **~gilde** f *Sharpshooter's Company, r.-association* **~graben** m *trench* (*tr.*) *r.-pit* ‖ ≈ [pl a.] *entrenchment* ‖ mit ≈ versehen *to* (*en*)*trench* ‖ die ≈ beziehen *to mount the tr.es* ‖ ≈ ausheben *to open the tr.es, to tr.* ‖ im ~ liegen *to be stationed in* .. | ~neur·ose [f] ⟨psych⟩ *shell shock* **~gruppe** f *infantry section*, ⟨Am⟩ *i. squad* **~haus** n *house of the Sharpshooters' Company* **~joppe** f *shooting-jacket* **~kette** f = ~linie **~kompa(g)nie** f = ~gesellschaft **~könig** m *champion shot, prize-winner* **~korps** n *r.men, r.s* pl; ⟨mil⟩ *r.-corps* **~linie** f ⟨mil⟩ *skirmish* od *extended order* od *line* **~loch** n ⟨mil⟩ *r.-pit* **~meister** m *master of the Sharpshooters' Company* **~mine** f → Tret- **~nest** n *nest of r.men* **~panzer** m (SP) *combat vehicle* N **~platz** m *shooting-place* **~posten** m *sniper* **~regiment** n *r.-regiment* **~reihe** f *squad column* N **~schleier** m ⟨mil⟩ *screen* **~verein** m *r. club*

Sch·ützer m ~s/~ *protector, guardian* **Sch·ützling** m ~(e)s/~e *protégé*(*e f*) ‖ (Schutzbefohlene[r]) *charge*

Schw·abacher f ~/ ⟨Ger typ⟩ *Schwabacher*

schw·abb- ~eln vi/t [h] *to babble* ‖ *to wobble* ‖ ⟨tech⟩ *to buff* °≈**el·ei** f ~/ *babble*, ⟨Am⟩ *gas* **~(e)lig** a *shaky, wobbly, flabby* ≈**elscheibe** f *buff* (*wheel*) ≈**er** m ~s/~ *mop* ‖ ⟨mar⟩ *swab* **~ern** vt/i [h] *to squill* | ⟨mar⟩ vt *to swab*

Schw·abe m, (Schwäbin [f]) *Swabian* | **~n** n *Swabia* | ~alter [n] ⟨fig⟩ (*of p being 40*) (*late*) *years* pl *of discretion*; ~streich [m] *tomfoolery* | **s**≈**ln** vi *to talk with a Swabian accent* | **s**≈**bisch** a *Swabian* ‖ ~es Zeitalter *time of the Hohenstaufen*

Schw·abe f ~/~n ⟨ent⟩ *cockroach*

schwach a **A.** *weak, feeble* ‖ ⟨physiol⟩ *debilitated* (*constitution*); *sapless, impotent, powerless, gone soft, frail*, sehr ~ *weak as water, as a cat, baby, as a rained-on bee* ‖ (matt) *languishing* ‖ (entkräftet) *effete* ‖ (gebrechlich) *frail* (⟨a. fig⟩ *frail ladies*) ‖ (*ill and*) *feeble* ‖ (alters~) *infirm*; (*old and*) *decrepit* ‖ (dünn) *thin, slight, slender* ‖ *light* (*breeze*) ‖ (mäßig) *moderate* (*musician, dose*) ‖ (kaum sichtbar, hörbar) *faint, dim* ‖ (willens~) *weak* (*as water*), *feeble-minded* **B.** *weak* (*child; thread; eyes, heart, nerves, voice*); ⟨fig⟩ *father, government*, ⟨mil⟩ *forces*; *tea*; *hope*; ⟨gram⟩ *verb*) ‖ *feeble* (*picture, impressions, consolation, achievement, intellect, attempt*) | *delicate* (*chest*); *low* (*pulse*); *bad* (*memory*) | *poor* (*hearing, soup*; ⟨racing⟩ *field*; ⟨sport⟩ *players*) | *dim* (*light*) ‖ *faint* (*glimmer, praise*) ‖ *dull* (*sound*) | *small* (*dose, proof*) ‖ *sparse* (*population*) ‖ *slight* (*signs, applause, success*) | ⟨arts⟩ *inferior* (*work*) ‖ ⟨com⟩ *low* (*exchanges*); (*business, the market was*) *slack* ‖ ⟨hunt⟩ *partly-grown* (*buck*) **C.** e–n ~en **Abglanz** h v *to have* (*but*) *slight traces of* ‖ auf ~en Beinen stehen ⟨fig⟩ *to stand on flimsy foundations* ‖ das ~e Geschlecht *the gentle sex* ‖ m–e ~en **Kräfte** *my insignificant services*; was in .. steht *my little best* ‖ ~er Magen *poor digestion* ‖ *we feeble people* ‖ ~ **Seite** *foible, hobby*; *blind side, weak point* ‖ ~e Stelle, ~er Punkt ⟨Am⟩ *soft underbelly* ‖ ~e Stunde *unguarded moment* **D.** er **war** so ~, daß *he had the weakness to* .. ‖ ≈er s als *to be inferior* (*in strength*) *to* ‖ ~ w *to grow weak*; (Herz, Augenlicht) *to fail* ‖ ≈er w *to lose* (*in*) *strength*; ⟨path⟩ *to sink* ‖ sich ~ zeigen *to betray weakness* **E.** ~ **auf** der Brust *weak-chested*; ⟨hum⟩ *short of money* ‖ auf ~en Füßen *on a slender basis* ‖ ~ im Glauben *of little faith* ‖ ~ im Kopf *a bit of a fool* ‖ er ist ~ v Begriff(en) *he is a slowcoach* **F. [adv]** ⟨mus⟩ *softly, piano* ‖ ~arbeitend ⟨phot⟩ *low-energy* (*developer*) ‖ ⟨mar⟩ ~ bemannt *short-handed* ‖ *sparsely* (*populated*) ‖ ⟨theat etc⟩ *poorly* (*attended*) ‖ (*to burn*) *low* ‖ der Puls geht ~ .. *is weak* od *low* ‖ mir wird ~ *I am feeling faint* ‖ es wurde ihr ~ *she fainted* (*away*) **Schw·ach-** ≈**äugig** a *weak-eyed* ≈**beleuchtet** a *dimly lit* **~gas** n ⟨mot⟩ *weak* od *lean gas* ≈**gläubig** a *weak in faith* **~herzig(keit** f) a *faint-hearted*(*ness*) **~-kopf** m *simpleton, nit*(*wit*); ⟨fam⟩ *lame-brain* ≈**köpfig** a *weak-headed, silly, soft* °**~m·atikus** m ⟨hum⟩ = Schwächling ≈**sichtig** a *dimsighted* **~sinn** m *weakness of mind* | ≈ig [a] *feeble-minded, imbecile, soft-headed, soft-witted*; ~ige(r m) f *mental deficient*; *imbecile*; ~igkeit [f] *imbecility* **~strom** m ⟨el⟩ *low current* **~stromkabel** n *w.-c. cable* **Schw·äche** f ~/~n **1.** *weakness, feebleness, frailty*; *languor*; *debility, infirmity*; *faintness, dimness, lowness, thinness* ‖ *feebleness* (*of intellect*) ‖ vor ~ umfallen *to faint away* **2.** (männliche) *impotence* **3.** (moralische) *foible* ‖ ~n [pl] *faults, failings, imperfections* pl **4.** ⟨fig⟩ (*music is my*) *weak side* od *point*; (*clothes are*) *my biggest weakness* ‖ *I have a fancy* od *weakness for stamps* ‖ *I have a soft spot for him* **~gefühl** n *sinking sensation* od *feeling* **~zustand** m *feeble condition*; *asthenia* **schw·ächen** vt [h] *to weaken, debilitate, enervate, enfeeble* ‖ (vermindern) *to diminish, lessen* | *⟨bib⟩ *to deflower, ravish* (*a virgin*) | ⟨tech, arts, phot⟩ *to tone down* (⟨a. fig⟩ *an expression*) **Schw·ächere,** der ~ [m] *the under-dog* ‖ leicht sich an e–m ~n z vergreifen *an easy th to find a stick to beat a dog* **Schw·ächerwerden** n *loss of vital power*; *enfeeblement* ‖ *failure* (*of sight*) ‖ (Verminderung) *diminution* **Schw·achheit** f /~en *weakness* ‖ (Gebrechen) *infirmity* ‖ (moralische) *frailty* ‖ (Willensschwäche) *weakness* ‖ ⟨fig⟩ °bilde dir k–e ~en ein! *don't deceive y.s.* **schw·ächlich** a *infirm, sickly, feeble* ‖ (zart) *delicate, frail* ≈**keit** f ~/ *feebleness, infirmity, sickliness* ‖ *frailty, delicacy* **Schw·ächling** m ~(e)s/~e, °**Schwachm·atikus** m ~/ *weakling* **Schw·ächung** f ~/~en *weakening, debilitation* ‖ *enervation* ‖ *diminution* ‖ *⟨bib⟩ *rape, defloration* **~swiderstand** m *potentiometer*

Schw·aden m ~s/~ **1.** ⟨agr⟩ *swath* **2.** (Dampf, Rauch) *water vapo*(*u*)*r*; *damp, fire-damp* ‖ *wind* *row* || ⟨min⟩ *choke-damp* **~gras** n ⟨bot⟩ *gromwell* **~rechen** m (hay) *side rake*

°**schw·adern** vi [h] *to prate, prattle*

schw·adern vi [h] [sd] = plätschern; schwatzen, schnattern **Schwadroneur** [–'nø:r] m ~s/~s *swaggerer, ranter, braggart,* ⟨fam⟩ *gas-bag*; ⟨mil⟩ *buzz-nagger* **s-n·ieren** vi [h] *to brag, swagger*; *to talk big*; ⟨fam⟩ *to gas*; ⟨Am sl⟩ *to shoot one's mouth off*

Schwadr·on f ~/~en *squadron* **~̈(s)weise** [adv] *by* od *in squadrons*; → Batterie

Schwafel·ei f *padding*; ⟨sl⟩ *hot air* **schw·afeln** vi [h] *to jabber* **Schw·afler** m *gas-bag,* ⟨Am sl⟩ *gasser*

Schw·ager m ~s/~̈ *brother-in-law* || ⟨obs⟩ *postilion, friend* | **~̈in** f ~/~nen *sister-in-law* **~̈schaft** f ~/ *affinity/relations by marriage* || **Schw·äher** m ~s/~ ⟨obs⟩ *father-in-law* | **~in** f ~/~nen ⟨obs⟩ *mother-in-law*

Schw·aige f ~/~n, **Schw·aighof** m = Sennhütte

schw·ajen ⟨mar⟩ **I.** vi *to swing round* **II.** vt *to to swing* (*the ship*) [*before the anchor*]

Schw·albe f ~/~n *swallow* (zwitschert *twitters*) → *pranticole, tern, martin, swallow, petrel* || ⟨prov⟩ eine ~ macht noch k–n Sommer *one swallow does not make it spring* | **~̈n** vt [h] → verzinken | **~n-** **~nest** n *swallow's nest* || ⟨mil⟩ *bandsman's epaulette* **~schwanz** m ⟨ent⟩ *swallow--tail* || ⟨carp⟩ *dovetail* || ⟨hum⟩ (Frack) *swallow(s pl)* **~wurz** f ⟨bot⟩ *swallow-wort* || *celandine*

Schwalch m ~(e)s/~e ⟨met⟩ *furnace-flue* || *gullet*

Schwall m ~(e)s/ (Sw Schwalm) *swell, surging*; *flood* (⟨a. fig⟩: .. *of words*) || ⟨fig⟩ *deluge, profusion* || ⟨fig⟩ *crowd* (*of people*); *volley* (*of abuse*)

Schwamm m ~(e)s/~̈e **1.** (Bade~̈) *sponge* || mit dem ~ abwischen *to sponge*; .. über etw hinfahren *to pass the sp. over a th* || er kann sich mit dem ~ frisieren *he can do his hair with a sp.* || °~ drüber! *let bygones be bygones*! ⟨fam⟩ *let's wipe it off the slate*; *skip it*! *kiss and make up*! **2.** (eßbar) *mushroom, fungus* **3.** (Feuer~̈) (*German*) *tinder* **4.** (Haus~̈) *dry rot* **5.** ⟨path⟩ *fungus* **6.** ⟨fig⟩ °der ganze ~ ⟨sl⟩ *the whole caboodle* **~fischerei** f *sp.-fishing* **~gummi** m *foamed latex*; *sponge rubber* **~kuchen** m *sp.-cake* **Schw·ammchen** n ~s/~ **1.** *mushroom* **2.** ⟨path⟩ *fungus* || da kann man ja die ~ kriegen! *it's enough to drive one mad*! || ˣnarrische Schwammerl gegessen h *to have cut a folly tooth*; → –rl **schw·ammig** a *spongy, fungous* **~̈keit** f ~/ *sponginess*

schwamm 1. & 3. sg pret v schwimmen

Schwan m ~(e)s/~̈e *swan*; männl. ~ *cob*, weibl. ~ *pen*; junger ~ *cygnet*; → *swans* **schw·anen** **I.** vi imps [h]; es schwant mir (etw) *my heart misgives me* (*about a th*), *I have a presentiment* (*of a th*); mir –nt nichts Gutes *I have misgivings*; das hatte mir schon lange ge–nt *I have long had m.s about that* **II.** ~̈ n *presentiment, misgiving(s pl)* **Schw·anen-** **~bett** n *swan's-down bed* **~busen** m *snow-white bosom* **~feder** f *swan's feather* **~fell** n *swan-skin* **~gesang** m ⟨a. fig⟩ *swan-song* **~hals** m *swan-neck* **~haut** f = ~fell **~kiel** m *swan's quill* **~lied** n = ~gesang **~ritter** m *Knight of the Swan* **~teich** m *swannery*

schwand 1. & 3. sg pret v schwinden

schwang 1. & 3. sg pret v schwingen **Schwang** m ~(e)s/ *swing* || ⟨fig⟩ im ~e s *to be in vogue* || in ~ k *to become the fashion*

schw·anger a *pregnant, expectant*; ⟨fam⟩ *in the family way*; *enceinte* Fr | ~ s *to be with child* || ~ w v *to conceive by* || Beratungsstelle f ~̈e [pl] *ante-natal clinic* | ⟨fig⟩ ~ gehen mit *to labour with* (*grand projects*) || mit Unheil ~ *big with ruin* | **s~̈n** vt [h] *to get .. with child*; *to get .. into trouble* || ⟨fig⟩ *to impregnate* || ⟨chem⟩ *to saturate* **~̈schaft** f ~/~en *pregnancy*; (*period of*) *gestation*; ⟨stat⟩ → *pregnancy* | ~sbeihilfe [f] *pre-natal allowance*; ~sunterbr·echung [f] ⟨med⟩ *therapeutic* [künstl. *induced, intentional*] *abortion*; ~szwischenraum [m] *inter-p.y interval* | **~̈ung** f ~/~en *getting with child* || ⟨fig⟩ *impregnation* || ⟨chem⟩ *saturation*

Schwank m ~(e)s/~̈e *droll story, merry tale, good joke* || (Spaß) *drollery* || ⟨theat⟩ *farce, slapstick* || (P) voller ~̈e *full of pranks* **schwank** a *slender, flexible, pliable* || *faltering* (*steps*); *frail* (*bridge*); *slack* (*rope*) || ⟨fig⟩ ein ~es Rohr im Winde *a reed shaken by the wind* | **~̈en** n ~s/ *staggering* || (der Preise) *fluctuation* || ⟨fig⟩ *hesitation, irresolution, vacillation* || (des Waggons) *tail-motion* || ins ~ k *to begin to waver* ⟨a. fig⟩ | **~en** vi [h] *to totter*; *rock* || (beim Gehen) *to waver, stagger* || (Zweige) *to wave to and fro* || (Boden) *to shake* || (Barometer) *to oscillate* || (Preise etc) *to fluctuate, vary* || (Schiff) *to toss, roll* || s–e Stimme –kte vor Erregung .. *trembled* od *was unsteady with emotion* | ⟨fig⟩ *to hesitate, waver, falter*; *to be irresolute* od *undecided* || *to vacillate, rock* | **~d** *tippy* (*boat*) || *tottering*, etc; ⟨fam⟩ (P) (*wibbly-*)*wobbly* (*from fatigue*) (⟨a. fig⟩ *irresolute*); *shilly-shally* (*unsteady*); *precarious* (*health*); *faltering* (*gait*) = ⟨med⟩ *titubation*; *wavering attitude* | *doubling* (*client*); *undecided, irresolute* (*in one's views*) || er ist ein ~des Rohr *he shakes like a reed in the wind* | **~̈ung** f ~/~en (→ Schwanken) ⟨bes phys⟩ *oscillation* || ⟨com⟩ *fluctuation, variation* || ~en *vacillations* (*in temper*) || ⟨astr, phys⟩ *deviation*; (der Erdachse) *nutation* || (Barometer~̈) *variation* → Frequenz~̈, Touren~̈ || ⟨mil⟩ Unempfindlichkeit gegen die ~en der Lage *steadfastness against the fluctuations of battle* | ~sbreite [f] *range of variation*

Schwanz m ~es/~̈e **A.** **1.** *tail* (*t.*) ⟨a. aero, astr, Noten~̈⟩; (*hound's*) *stern*; (Fuchs~̈, Hirsch~̈) *brush* || ⟨hors⟩ den ~ stutzen *to dock* (*a horse*) || (Rädertierchen~̈) *foot* **2.** *trail* (*of a gun*) **3.** (Anhang, Gefolge) *train* **4.** (Schnörkel) *flourish* **5.** ⟨vulg⟩ *tail, cock,* (*penis*) **B.** ⟨fig⟩ °kein ~ *nobody, nothing* || den ~ einziehen *to sneak away, to take to one's heals*; mit eingezogenem ~ *with his t. between his legs*; ⟨fig⟩ *t.s down*; jdm auf den ~ treten *to tread on a p's t.*, e–m den ~ streicheln *to coax a p* || ⟨stud, sl⟩ e–n ~ m *to pass the post mortem*; e–n ~ m müssen *to fail just in one subject* || °⟨sex⟩ sich den ~ verbrannt h *to have a bad cold* (= *gonorrhoea*) || °wenn e–m der ~ steht, ist der Verstand am Arsch ⟨prov⟩ *standing prick has no conscience* **~fächer** m (Hummer) *tail fin* **~feder** f *t.-feather* **~flosse** f *t.* od *caudal fin*; ⟨aero⟩ *t. f.* **~gesteuert** a ⟨aero⟩ *t. controlled* **~̈lastig** ⟨aero⟩ *t. heavy* **~meise** f ⟨orn⟩ *long-t.ed titmouse* °**~parade** f ⟨mil med vulg⟩ *small-arm inspection* **~quaste** f *tuft of the t.* **~riemen** m *crupper* **~schraube** f *t.-screw* || (am Gewehr) *breech-screw, plug* **~sporn** m ⟨aero⟩ *tail skid* **~stern** m *comet* **~steuer** n ⟨aero⟩ *rudder* **~stück** n *t.-piece* (*of a fish*); ⟨cul⟩ (Mittel–) *sirloin, aitch--bone*; (Eck–) *rump* **~wirbel** m *caudal vertebra* **s~̈eln** vi [h] (T) *to wag its tail* (⟨a. fig⟩: *one's t.*) || (P) *to strut* | ⟨fig⟩ *to flatter*, ⟨dero⟩ *to cringe*; *to fawn* (um jdn *upon a p*) **s~̈en** vi/t [h] *to idle about* || die Schule ~ *to cut classes, to play truant* od ⟨sl⟩ *hooky* || *to shirk* (*a lesson*) || *to cut* (*a lecture*) || *miss* (*the sermon*) | vt *to provide with a tail* | **ge~̈t** a *tailed, caudate* || ~e Note ⟨mus⟩ *crotchet* **Schw·änzer** m ~s/~ *truant* °**Schw·änzi** n (Kindersprr) ⟨sex⟩ *nippy*

schwapp(s)! *slap*! *dash*! *snap*! **schw·appeln** vi/t [h] **1.** *to spill, splash* (*from*) **2.** *to wabble* **schw·appen** vt/i [h] *to flap* || = schwappeln 1. || ~d voll *brim-full*

Schwäre f ~/~n ⟨path⟩ *ulcer, abscess* || voller ~n *covered with sores* od *ulcers* | **~̈en** vi [h]

⟨path⟩ *to fester, suppurate, ulcerate* ‖ ⟨fig⟩ *to break out, to rankle* **schw·ärig** a *ulcered, ulcerous*

Schwarm m ~(e)s/≃e (Bienen etc) *swarm, colony* ‖ (Insekten) *swarm, cluster* ‖ (Vögel) *flight*, ⟨hunt⟩ *skein* ‖ (Fische) *shoal* ‖ (Menschen) *crowd, multitude* ‖ (Rudel) *flock, pack, herd*; ⟨aero⟩ (6–8) *flight* | ⟨fig fam⟩ *ideal, fancy; lady love; pet, hero, idol*; ⟨fam⟩ *craze, rave* ‖ ich habe e–n ~ f sie, sie ist mein ~ *I admire* od *adore her*; *I'm gone on her* **~fische** m pl *schooling fish* **~geist** m *enthusiast(ic mind)*; ⟨rel⟩ *fanatic(al spirit)* **~linie** f ⟨mil⟩ *extended order* **≃weise** adv *in swarms, crowds*, etc | ≃- **~attacke** f *attack in extended line* **~sporn** f ⟨bot⟩ *swarm-cell* **~zeit** f *swarming-time* | **≃en** n ~s/ *swarming* ‖ ⟨mil⟩ *skirmishing* ‖ ⟨fig⟩ *revelling* ‖ (ideales) *enthusiasm* (f *for*) | s **≃en** vi **1.** [h & s] (*gnats, bees*) *swarm* ‖ (*butterflies*) *flutter* ‖ (*hounds*) *get off the scent* ‖ (P & T) *to wander, rove* ‖ ⟨mil⟩ *to sprawl*, ~ (l) *to extend* ‖ es schwärmt v Menschen *there are crowds of people about, the place is crowled with p.e* **2.** [h] *to revel, riot, to be on the loose, to lead a gay life*; (nachts) *to be* od *go on the tiles, to spend a gay night* | (geistig) *to dream, to be a dreamer* ‖ *to be full of enthusiasm* | **für**: *to be enthusiastic about* (*the theatre*) (= *to be stage-struck*); *to thrill at a th*; ⟨Am⟩ *to go overboard for a th* ‖ *to adore, admire, worship* (*a p*), *to be taken with, to dote on* (*a p*); ⟨fam⟩ *to go for a th*; *to be gone on* (*a p*) ‖ *to be in raptures about* (*a singer*) ‖ wir ~ nicht gerade für .. *we don't much care for* (*him,it*) | **von**: *to rave* od *gush about* (*a th, a p*) | **≃er** m ~s/~ **1.** *reveller, rioter* ‖ *fickle lover* ‖ (geistig) *dreamer; enthusiast; gusher* ‖ ⟨rel⟩ *fanatic* **2.** (Feuerwerk) *squib, cracker, serpent* **3.** ⟨ent⟩ → *hawk-moth* | **≃er·ei** f ~/~en *roaming* | *revelling, riotousness* ‖ (ideale) *enthusiasm* (f *for*) ‖ ⟨rel⟩ *fanaticism* ‖ *ecstasy; wild imaginings* ‖ *reverie* ‖ (Liebe) *passionate devotion* (f *to*) s **≃erisch** a *enthusiastic(ally* adv) ‖ *fanatical* ‖ *eccentric* ‖ *fanciful, wild, visionary*

Schw·arte f ~/~n **1.** *rind* (*of bacon*) ‖ *skin* (*of badger, boar*) ‖ (fur) *summer-skin* ‖ (Schwiele) *callosity* **2.** ⟨cul⟩ gebratene ~ *crackling* **3.** ⟨agr⟩ *sward, sod* **4.** ⟨carp⟩ *slab, flitch* ‖ ⟨min⟩ *plank* **5.** *pigskin binding*, ⟨fam⟩ *old volume* ‖ ⟨school sl⟩ *crib* **6.** ⟨fig⟩ daß die ~ knackt *vigorously, with a vengeance*; arbeiten .. *to work till the bones crack*; fressen .. *to overeat o.s.*, prügeln .. *to knock the stuffing out of* (*a p*) **~nmagen** m ⟨cul⟩ *collared pork* **schw·artig** a *thick-skinned*

Schwarz 1. n ~es/ *black colo(u)r, black*; Frankfurter ~ *German bl.*; reines ~ *neutral bl.* ‖ nichts ~es .. *nothing black* (*to put on*) ‖ das ~e im Auge *the pupil* ‖ ins ~e treffen ⟨a. fig⟩ *to hit the bull's eye*, ⟨fig⟩ *to make a hit* **2.** [inv] in ~ gehen *to dress in black, to be in mourning*; ganz .. *to wear full m.g* **3. ~e(r)** m *black, negro*, (f *negress*) ‖ *devil* ‖ *dark p; black horse* ‖ °ein ~er *a parson*; die ~en [pl] *the black brigade*, ⟨pol⟩ *the blacks* **schwarz** a **A.** *black* (⟨a.⟩ *pepper, tea*; ⟨a. fig⟩ *day, deed, art, market, thoughts*) ‖ (finster) *dark* (*scheme*), *gloomy* (*look*) ‖ *atrocious* (*crime*) ‖ *dirty* (*linen*) ‖ *brown* (*bread*) ‖ *swarthy, tanned* (*complexion*) | ⟨mil sl⟩ (überzählig) *buckshee* (*bike, juice* „Sprit") | ~ **auf** weiß *in bl. and white, in* (*cold*) *print* ‖ ~ **wie** die Nacht, ein Rabe (*as*) *bl. as coal pitch, a crow; jetblack* **B.** ~e **Blattern** *malignant smallpox* ‖ ~es Brett *blackboard*, ⟨univ⟩ *notice-board* ‖ *bl. diamonds* (= *coal*) ‖ (Fleisch) *red* ‖ ~e **Gefahr** *the negro danger* ‖ das ~e Gerüst *the scaffold* ‖ ≃: *the Black Continent, Death, Sea* (Meer) ‖ jdn auf die ~e Liste setzen *to put a p on the bl. list*; er steht auf der ~en L. *his name is on ..* ‖ der ~e **Mann** *the chimney-sweep* ‖ mit ~em Rand *black-edged* **C.** e–n bei jdm ~ **anschreiben** *to speak ill of a p to a p* ‖ bei jdm ~ –ge–rieben s *to be in a p's bad books* ‖ ~ behängt *hung with bl.* ‖ sich ~ ärgern *to worry o.s. to death* ‖ ~fahren *to ride free* ‖ ~ **färben** *to dye bl.* ‖ ~ **gekleidet** *dressed in bl.* od *mourning* ‖ ~ (kaufen) *on the bl. market* ‖ ~ m *to blacken* ‖ etw ~ **sehen** *to look at a th on the bl. side* ‖ ~ gerahmt *in a bl. frame* ‖ ⟨fig⟩ ~ s *to be very religious* ‖ ~ w *to turn bl.*, (Haut) *to tan*, ⟨cards⟩ *not to make a single point* ‖ du kannst warten, bis du ~ wirst .. *till you are bl. in the face* ‖ mir wurde ~ *I saw stars* **Schw·arz-** **~amsel** f ⟨orn⟩ *bl.bird* **~arbeit** f *illicit work*; ⟨vulg⟩ *graft* **≃äugig** a *dark-, black-eyed* **~beere** f *bilberry* **≃blau** a *very dark blue* **~blech** n *bl. sheet-iron; plate-iron* **~blei** n *bl.lead* **≃blütig** a *atrabilious* **≃braun** a *dark-brown*; ⟨hors⟩ *dun; tanned, swarthy, tawny* **~brenner** m (Alkohol) ⟨Am⟩ *moonshiner* | ~ei [f] *illicit still* **~brot** n *brown bread*, (*bl.*) *rye-bread* **≃bunt** a *bl.-and-white* (*cattle*) **~dorn** m ⟨bot⟩ *black-thorn, sloe* **~drossel** f *bl.bird* **~erle** f ⟨bot⟩ *alder-tree* **~fahrt** f ⟨mot⟩ *unlicensed* od *illegal driving*, ⟨fam⟩ *joy-ride* **~färber** m *dyer in bl.* ‖ ⟨fig⟩ *pessimist* **≃gallig** a *atrabilious, morose, melancholic* **≃gar** a *tanned* **~gebrannt** a Alkohol ⟨Am fam⟩ *moonshine*, ⟨sl⟩ *mountain dew* **≃gelb** a *tawny, bl.ish yellow* ‖ ⟨fig⟩ *Austrian* **≃grau** a *dark-grey* **≃grün** a *dark-green* **~guß** m *all-bl. malleable cast iron* **~handel** m *bl. marketing*; mit Alkohol ⟨Am⟩ *bootlegging*; ~ treiben *to bl.-market* | ~spreis [m] *under-the-counter price* **~händler** m *bl.eteer*, ⟨sl⟩ *spiv* **~-hemden** n pl ⟨pol⟩ *Bl. Shirts* **≃hören** vi ⟨wir⟩ *to tap* **~hörer** m ⟨wir⟩ *pirate* **~kauf** m *illicit sale* **~kiefer** f ⟨bot⟩ *bl. spruce* **~kümmel** m ⟨bot⟩ *fennel-flower seed* **~kunst** f *bl. art* **~künstler** m *necromancer, magician* **~markt** m *bl. market* **~meise** f ⟨orn⟩ *bl. titmouse* **~pulver** n *gun-powder* **~rock** m ⟨fig⟩ *parson; bl. coat* | **≃rotg·old(en** a) n *bl., red, and gold* **~schecke** f *bl.-pied horse* **~schimmel** m *dark-grey horse* **~schlachten** n *illicit killing* (*of cattle*) **~seher(in** f) m *pessimist*, ⟨Am fam⟩ *crêpe hanger* **~seherei** f *pessimism* **~sender** m ⟨wir⟩ *pirate* **≃streifig** a *bl.-streaked* **~wald** m *Bl. Forest* | ~uhr [f] ⟨m. m.⟩ *Dutch clock* **~w·eiß-** ~gemälde [n] *bl.-and-white drawing*; ~malerei [f] ⟨pol⟩ *extremist attitude*; ~negativ [n] ⟨phot⟩ *b.-a.-wh. negative* **~wild** n *bl.game, wild boars* pl **~wurz(el)** f ⟨bot⟩ *viper's-grass* ‖ *comfrey* **Schw·ärze** f ~/~n *blackness* ‖ ⟨fig⟩ *darkness* ‖ ⟨typ⟩ *printer's ink* ‖ (Wichse) *black(en)ing* ‖ *dark colour* (*of eyes*) **schw·ärzen** vt [h] *to black* ‖ ⟨fig⟩ *to blacken; to darken* (⟨a.⟩ *eyebrows*) ‖ ⟨typ⟩ *to ink* ‖ ⟨com⟩ *to smuggle* **schw·ärzlich** a *blackish, darkish* ‖ (Haut) *swarthy* **Schw·ärzung** f ~/ *black(en)ing*; ⟨phot⟩ (*optical*) *density*

Schwatz m ~es/ *prattle, chat, chatter(ing)*; *gossip* ‖ e–n ~ m *to gossip* | °~base [f], ~maul [n] *chatterbox, gossip*; ~sucht [f] *garrulity, loquacity; talkativeness; love of gossip*; ⟨psych⟩ *logorrhea*; ⟨fam⟩ *gift of the gab* | **≃en**, **≃en** vi/t [h] *to chat, chatter, prattle; gab*, ⟨Am sl⟩ *yap* ‖ ⟨mil⟩ (im Glied) *to natter* ‖ unablässig (ohne Punkt u Komma) ~ *to talk nineteen to the dozen* ‖ indiskret, aufdringlich ~ *to wag one's tongue* ‖ aus der Schule ~ ⟨fig⟩ *to tell tales out of school*, ⟨sl⟩ *to split* ‖ ins Blaue hinein ~ *to talk at random* od *foolishly* ‖ das Blaue v Himmel ~ *to talk the hind leg off a donkey* ‖ über dies u jenes ~ *to chatter discursively* **≃er(in** f ~/~en) m ~s/~ *chatterbox, prattler, babbler, gossip*; ⟨Am⟩ *gas-bag, rattlebrain* **≃er·ei** f ~/~en *babbling, tittle-tattle* **≃haft** a *talkative, garrulous, loquacious*; ⟨fam⟩ *gossipy, newsy*; ⟨bes Am⟩ *gabby*; ~ wie ein Papagei *parroty*; ~es Greisenalter *anecdotage* | **≃igkeit** [f] = ≃sucht **≃ler** m (Kasperle) ⟨m. m.⟩ *swatchel* (*Punch*)

Schw·eb- **~fliege** f ⟨ent⟩ *syrphus-fly* **~stoffe** m pl ⟨mil⟩ *gaseous agents* pl **Schw·ebe** f ~/ *suspense* ‖ in der ~ *in the air*, .. hängen *or* s *to be* *still undecided* od *in suspense, to tremble in the balance*; ⟨fam⟩ *to hang fire* ‖ in der ~ l *to leave .. at a loose end*; e–e S in der ~ lassend *pending a th* **~bahn** f *aerial tramway*; ⟨Am⟩ *suspended railroad* **~baum** m *horizontal bar* **~fähre** f *s.n ferry* **~fliege** f *hover-fly* **~flug** m *hovering flight* **~künstler(in** f) m *equilibrist* **~reck** n *trapeze* **~ruder** n ⟨mar⟩ *balance rudder* **~schiff** n *hovercraft* **~schritt** m *balance-step* **~stange** f *rope-dancer's pole* **~stoffe** m pl ⟨phys⟩ *suspended solids* od *matter* **~teilchen** n *s.ed particle* **schw·eben** vi [h & s] *to be suspended* ‖ (Ballon) *to float* ‖ *to hover* (*over an abyss*) ‖ *a smile hovers on her lips* ‖ ⟨dancing⟩ *to sway* ‖ ⟨orn⟩ *to hover, hang, soar* ‖ (P) (gleiten) *to glide* (*through a room*), *to sail* (*in* hinein) ‖ (S) ⟨a.⟩ *to swim* | ⟨fig⟩ *to be floating* (*in higher regions*) ‖ ⟨fig & jur⟩ *to be pending* | e–m vor **Augen** ~ *to wave, be, hang before one's eyes*; *to be present to one's mind* ‖ in **Gefahr** ~ *to be in danger*, (*jeopardy* Lebensgefahr) ‖ *to hover between fear and hope, life and death* ‖ in Ungewißheit ~ *to be kept in suspense* ‖ e–m auf der Zunge ~ *to be on the tip of one's tongue* **schw·ebend** a *floating, suspended* | ⟨fig a.⟩ *undecided* | ⟨phon⟩ *hovering, fluctuating* (*accent*); *level* (*stress*) ‖ ⟨jur⟩ *pending* (*action*) ‖ ⟨com⟩ *floating* (*debt*) ‖ ⟨pol⟩ *standing* (*differences*) ‖ ~e Brücke *suspension-bridge* ‖ *hanging* (*gardens*) ‖ *pending* (*negotiations*), *unsettled* (*question*), ⟨ins⟩ *outstanding* (*claim, loss*) ‖ *light, elastic* (*step*) ‖ ~e Strecke ⟨min⟩ *heading* | zw Leben u Tod ~ *hanging between life and death*; ⟨fig⟩ *poised on the brink of disaster* ‖ in ~em Zustand ⟨chem⟩ *in suspension* **Schw·ebung** f ~/~en *vibration* ‖ ⟨wir⟩ *surge* ‖ (Orgelregister) *tremor* | ~en bilden mit *to beat with* ‖ ⟨mus⟩ um e–e ~ *a very little* | ~sempfang [m] *heterodyne reception*; ~sfeuer [n] ⟨aero⟩ *oscillating beacon*; ~ston ⟨wir⟩ *beat note*

Schw·ede m ~n/~n *Swede* ‖ ~n [pl] *safety--matches* pl ‖ alter ~! ⟨fig fam⟩ *old boy* **Schweden** n *Sweden* **~punsch** m *smash* **schw·edisch** a *Swedish* (*gymnastics, language*) ‖ das ≗e, die ~e Sprache ⟨a.⟩ *S.* (auf ≗ *in S.*) ‖ hinter ~en Gardinen *in prison*

Schw·efel m ~s/ *brimstone, sulphur* ‖ gediegener ~ *native s.* ‖ ~ in Stangen *sticks of s.* **~ader** f *s.-lode* **≗artig** a *s.eous* **~äther** m ⟨chem⟩ *s.ic ether* **~bad** n *s.ated bath* ‖ (Ort) *s.(e)ous waters* pl **~bande** f *gang of ruffians*; ⟨hum⟩ *little devils* **~blumen, ~blüten** f pl ⟨chem⟩ *flowers* pl *of s.* **~dampf** m *s.(e)ous fumes* pl **~erde** f *s.eous earth* **~faden** m *s.ated match* **≗farben, ≗gelb** a *brimstone-coloured* **~geist** m ⟨chem⟩ *spirits* pl *of s.* **~grube** f *s.-mine* **≗haltig** a *s.(e)ous, s.ic*; ~e Drogen *sulphonamides* **~holz, ~hölzchen** n *match* **~hütte** f *brimstone-house* **~kies** m (*iron*) *pyrites* sg **~kohlenstoff** m *carbonic disulphide* **~leber** f ⟨chem⟩ *s.et of potass* **~milch** f *precipitated s.* **~pfuhl** m *hell-fire* **~phosphor** m ⟨chem⟩ *phosphuret of s.* **~pulver** n *powdered s.* **~quelle** f *s.--spring* **≗sauer** a *s.ic*; ~es Natrium *sulphate of sodium*; ~es Salz *sulphate* **~säure** f ⟨chem⟩ *sulphuric acid*; rauchende ~ *vitriolic acid* **~verbindung** f ⟨chem⟩ *s.et* **~wasserstoff** m *hydrogen sulphide* **schw·ef(e)lig** a *sulphurous* ‖ ~e Säure *sulphurous acid* ‖ ~es Salz *sulphite* **schw·efeln** vt [h] *to* (*impregnate, combine, treat with*) *sulphur, to sulphurate* ‖ (Fässer) *to fumigate, match*; (Kautschuk) *to vulcanize* ‖ → schwafeln

Schw·eidnitz n ⟨†Ger⟩ (Stadt in Schlesien)

Schweif m ~(e)s/~e *tail* ⟨a. astr⟩ ‖ ⟨fig⟩ *train* **~haar** n *tail hair*(*s* pl) **~reim** m *tail rhyme* **~riemen** m ⟨hors⟩ *crupper* **~säge** f *rip-saw* **~stern** m *comet* **≗wedeln** vi *to wag the tail*; ⟨fig⟩ *to fawn* (vor *upon*) **schw·eifen** vt [h] **1.** *to slant, slope, curve*; *camber* | *to rinse* (*washing*) | *to tail* | **geschweift** *curved* (*chair*) ‖ schön ~ ⟨hors⟩ *with a fine* od *full tail* **2.** vi [h] *to stray, ramble, rove*; *to stroll* (*through the town*), *to roam* (*through the woods*) ‖ *he let his thoughts* (*eyes*) *roam in the past* (*distance*) ‖ s–e Augen ~ über .. *his eyes travel over* .. ‖ s–e Gedanken ~ l *to cut o.s. adrift* **Schw·eifung** f ~/~en *curve, sweep, bend*(*ing*) ‖ *waist* (*of a bell*)

Schw·eige- **~geld** n *hush-money* **~geschütz** n *concealed gun* **~-MG** n *ambuscade m. g.* **~pausen** f pl *silences* **~pflicht** f *professional* od *business discretion*; ⟨allg⟩ *obligation to be silent* (über *about*); Verletzung der ~ *breach of* .. **~zone** f ⟨wir⟩ *skip zone*; ⟨mil⟩ *shadow region* **Schw·eigen** n ~s/ *silence* (eisig, frostig *stony*; bewahren *to keep*, gebieten *to impose*); seltsames ~ *queer hush* | in ~ versinken *to lapse into s.*; zum ~ bringen *to hush* ⟨a. fig⟩, *to tie a p's tongue*; (durch Bestechung) *to stop a p's mouth*, ⟨fam⟩ *to shut a p up*; ⟨übtr⟩ *to put down* od *quench*; ⟨mil⟩ *to silence* ‖ sich in ~ hüllen *to wrap o.s. in s.*, ⟨fam⟩ *to be mum* **schw·eigen I.** vi [schwieg/geschwiegen] [h] *to be silent, to hold one's peace* od *tongue* (**über, von** *about*); ~ über etw *to leave a th unsaid* ‖ *to keep silence* (vor Schreck *from terror*) ‖ nachdenklich ~ *to keep a pensive s.* ‖ (Gewissen) *to be hushed* ‖ **auf, zu**: *to make no reply to a question, reproach*; *to let sth pass without saying a word* ‖ ~ Sie! *silence!*, *be quiet!*, ⟨fam⟩ *shut up!* ‖ ~ Sie mir davon! *don't refer to it!* ‖ die Vögel ~ *no bird sings* ‖ der Donner, Lärm, die Musik –ieg .. *ceased* ‖ alles –ieg *there was a dead silence* ‖ da ~ alle Flöten *I'd better keep quiet altogether* ‖ darüber –gt des Sängers Höflichkeit *it's better to say nothing about that* ‖ ganz zu ~ v *to say nothing of* ‖ wer –gt, stimmt zu *silence gives consent* ‖ aber ~! *keep it dark* | **~d** *silent* (*submission, expectation*) ‖ der ~de Wald *the silence of the forest* ‖ ~d vor sich hinstarren *to stare in s.*; sie gingen ~d neben–e–a her *they had fallen silent as they walked along*; ~d zuhören *to listen in s.* **II.** vt (etw) tot|~ *to hush up*, ⟨arts⟩ *to kill by silence* **schw·eigsam** a *taciturn* **≗keit** f ~/ *taciturnity*

Schw·ein n ~(e)s/~e *pig, hog* (grunzen *to grunt*) ‖ ⟨zoo, agr, poet⟩ *swine* [pl *swine*] ‖ wildes ~ *wild boar* | ⟨fig⟩ °(Schmutzfink) *pig* ‖ (unmoralischer Mensch) *swine* ‖ ⟨fam⟩ kein ~ *nobody*; daraus wird kein ~ klug *I can't make head or tail of it* ‖ (Klecks) *blot* | °(Glück) *fluke, luck*(*y hit*); (gr, kolossales) ~ h *to click* (*good and proper*), ⟨mil sl⟩ *to be spawny, to fall on one's feet* | wir h nicht zus ~e gehütet! *don't hobnob with me!*; ⟨vulg⟩ *have we ever pigged it?* **~furter Grün** n *copper azetoarsenite* **~igel** m *hedgehog* ‖ °⟨vulg⟩ *sweep*; *filthy pig, dirty wretch* ‖ *obscene talker, swine* **~igel·ei** f ⟨vulg⟩ *filth, obscenity* **≗igeln** vi [h] *to talk smut* **Schw·eine-** ⟨scient⟩ *porcine* **~braten** m *roast pork* **~bucht** f *pigsty* ⟨a. fig⟩; ⟨Am⟩ *hog-pen* → –stall **~fett** n *hog's grease*; *lard* **~fleisch** n *pork* **~fraß** m *food for pigs* ⟨a. fig⟩ **~hirt** m *s.herd* **~hund** m *filthy fellow*; *smear* ‖ du ~! *dirty dog!* ‖ der innere ~ *one's baser feelings, the devil inside* **~koben** m → –stall **~mast** f *food for s.* **~nacken** m *spare rib* **~pest** f ⟨vet⟩ *s.-fever, s.-plague* **~pökelfleisch** n *salt pork* **~schlachten** n *pig-sticking* **~schmalz** n *lard* **~seuche** f = –pest **~stall** m *pigsty* ⟨a. fig⟩; ⟨Am⟩ *hog-pen* **~trank** m *hog-wash* ⟨a. fig⟩ **~treiber** m *pig-driver* **~volk** n *filthy people* **~wirtschaft** f ⟨°fig⟩ *regular scandal, beastly shame* **~zucht** f *pig-breeding, hog-rearing* **Schweiner·ei** f ~/~en *filth, dirtiness* | °⟨fig⟩ *mess* ‖ (Zote) *smut, obscenity* **Schw·einerne(s)** n [sd] = –fleisch **schw·einisch** a *piggish* ‖ (stärker) *swinish* **Schw·eins-** **~blase** f *hog's bladder* **~borste** f *hog's bristle* **~feder** f *boar-spear* ‖ (Borste) *bristle* ‖ (e–s Gitters) *spike* **~füße** m pl *pettitoes, pig's trotters* pl **~hamme, ~haxe** f ⟨cul⟩ → Eisbein **~jagd** f *wild-boar chase* **~keule** f *leg of pork* **~-**

knochen m pl *pig's pettitoes* pl **~kopf** m *boar's, hog's head* | ⁓sülze [f] *headcheese* **~kotelett** n *pork chop* **~leder** n *hogskin* ‖ ⟨bookb⟩ *pigskin* **≚ledern** a (*of*) *pigskin* **~magen** m *hog's paunch* **~rippchen** n *pork-chop*

Schweiß m ⁓es/ *perspiration*; ⟨allg⟩ *sweat* ‖ *moisture* (*on panes*) | ⟨hunt⟩ *blood* | sich den ⁓ abwischen *to wipe the s. from one's brow* ‖ (wie) in ⁓ gebadet, v ⁓ triefend *in a bath of persp.*; in ⁓ gebadet s *to swelter* ‖ der ⁓ brach ihm aus allen Poren *he was all of a s.* ‖ in ⁓ geraten *to break into persp.* ‖ der kalte (Angst–, Todes–) ⁓ trat ihm auf die Stirn *the cold persp. broke out of his brow* | ⟨bib⟩ im ⁓e d–s Angesichts *in the s. of thy brow* | ⟨fig⟩ das hat viel ⁓ gekostet *that meant a lot of hard work* ‖ mein saurer ⁓ *the fruit of my toil* **Schw·eiß-**¹ **~ausbruch** m *bursting out of persp.* **~bad** n *steam-bath* **≚befördernd** a *diaphoretic, sudorific* **~blatt** n *dress-preserver, -shield* **~drüse** f *perspiratory gland* **~fieber** n *sweating-sickness* **~fuchs** m *sorrel horse* **~fuß** m *sweaty* od *perspiring foot* | °ein ⁓ kommt selten alleine *it never rains but it pours* **~geruch** m *smell of sweat*, ⟨Am euph⟩ *B. O.* [*bi: ou*] (= *body odor*) ‖ Mittel gegen ⁓ *deodorant* **~hund** m *bloodhund* **~leder** n *sweat band* **~loch** n *pore* **~mittel** n *sudorific* **~perlen** f pl stehen auf s–r Stirn *his forehead has beaded with sweat* **~riemen** m ⟨hunt⟩ *leash* **≚treibend** a *sudorific, diaphoretic* **~triefend** a *running with sweat* **~tropfen** m *drop of sweat* **~tuch** n ⟨ec⟩ *sudarium*; ⁓ der hl. Veronika *vernicle*; *the Holy Shroud* od *Handkerchief* **~wolle** f *wool in the grease* **Schweiß-**² (→ folg) **~arbeit** f *welding* **~brenner** m *blow pipe, welding torch* **~kolben** m *electrode holder* **~naht** f *weld*(*ing-seam*) **~pulver** n *flux* **~stahl** m *weld*(*ed*) *steel* **~stelle** f *weld* **schw·eißbar** a *weldable* **≚keit** f *weldability* **schw·eißen I.** vt [h] *to weld* (*together*); (zus–)ge–ß-te Teile pl *weldment* **II.** vi [h] *to sweat* ‖ ⟨hunt⟩ *to bleed* ‖ ⟨met⟩ *to begin to melt* **Schw·eißer** m ⁓s/⁓ *welder* **schw·eißig** a *sweaty, perspiring* ‖ ⟨hunt⟩ *bloody* ‖ *greasy* (*wool*)

Schweiz, die ⁓ *Switzerland* (*in Switzerland*)

Schw·eizer(in f) m ⁓s/⁓ *Swiss* ‖ die ⁓ [pl] *the Swiss* ‖ (Stall≚) *dairyman* ‖ (Türsteher) *porter* ‖ ⟨mil-hist⟩ *Switzer* ‖ ⟨cul⟩ → ⁓käse **~bund** m *Helvetic* od *Swiss Confederation* **~degen** m ⟨typ⟩ *compositor and printer* **~deutsch** n *S. German* **~flöte** f *flageolet* **~garde** f *S. life-guard* **~haus** n *S. chalet* **~-Käse** m *S. cheese*; *gruyère* Fr; *schweizerkaese* | **~·ei** f ⁓/⁓en (*Swiss*) *dairy* | **≚isch** a *Swiss*; *of Switzerland*

Schw·el- **~anlage** f *carbonizing plant* **~teer** m *carbonization tar* **schw·elen I.** vi [h] *to smoulder* (⟨a. fig⟩ *smouldering hate*) ‖ (Lampe) *to smoke* **II.** vt *to burn slowly* ‖ *to distil* (*tar*) **Schw·elung** f *low temperature carbonization*

schw·elgen vi [h] *to luxuriate, wallow*; *to lead a luxurious life* ‖ ⟨a. fig⟩ *to revel* (in [dat] *in*) ‖ ⟨fig⟩ ⁓ in *to* (*take*) *delight in* ‖ im Überfluß ⁓ *to live on the fat of the land* ‖ beim Anblick v Geld ⁓ *to gloat over money* **Schw·elger** m ⁓s/⁓ *reveller, voluptuary, glutton*; *orgiast* | **~·ei** f ⁓/⁓en *revelry, feasting, gluttony* ‖ *debauch*(*ery*) **schw·elgerisch** a *luxurious*; *gluttonous*; *voluptuous* ‖ *given to luxury* ‖ *orgiastic* ‖ *sybaritic*

Schw·elle f ⁓/⁓n **1.** (Fenster≚) *sill*; (Tür≚) *threshold* (⟨a. fig⟩ *of negotiation* ⟨pol⟩) ‖ ⟨fig a.⟩ *brink* ‖ jds ⁓ betreten *to cross a p's thr.*; .. nicht mehr .. *not to darken a p's door again* ‖ an der ⁓ des Grabes *at death's door* ‖ Eintritts≚ ⟨eth⟩ *thr.*; Hör≚ ⟨ac⟩ *thr. of audibility*; Schmerz≚ ⟨ac⟩ *thr. of pain*; Unterschieds≚ *difference thr.* **2.** (Balken) *beam* ‖ ⟨rail⟩ *sleeper*, ⟨Am⟩ *tie* (.. legen *to lay down* ..) ‖ ⟨theat⟩ *scenic sill*, ⟨Am⟩ *saddle iron* **3.** ⟨geog⟩ *shelf*; ⟨mar⟩ *ridge* (*Atlantic R.*) **Schw·ellen-** ⟨biol⟩ *liminal* **~belichtung** f ⟨phot⟩ *exposure thr.* **~dosis** f ⟨pharm⟩ *liminal* od *threshold dose* **~holz** n *wood for sleepers* **~-reiz** m ⟨psych⟩ *lowest perceptible amount of sensation* **~stopfer** m (P) ⟨rail⟩ *packer* **~wert** m ⟨physiol, biol⟩ *thr.* (*value*)

Schw·ell- **~gewebe** n *spongy tissue* **~körper** m ⟨anat⟩ *corpus cavernosum* **~ton** m *crescendo* **~werk** n (Orgel) *swell* **schw·ellen I.** vi [schwoll/ge–en] [s] *to swell* ⟨a. mus⟩ ‖ (vom Wasser etc) *to rise* ‖ (anwachsen) *to increase* ‖ geschwollen *swollen* (*feet*) ‖ geschwollen reden *to talk big* **II.** vt [reg] [h] *to swell, bloat, belly*; *to puff up* ‖ (*courage*) *filled* (*his breast*) ‖ **~d** *bellying* (*sail*) **Schw·eller** m ⟨mus⟩ *swell* **Schw·ellung** f ⁓/⁓en *swelling, inflation* ‖ (des Bodens) *swell* ‖ (Zustand) *bagginess, puffiness*; *inflatedness* ‖ ⟨path⟩ *tumour* | ⟨fig⟩ *growth, increase*

Schw·emm- **~boden** m *alluvial soil* **~kanalisation** f *sewerage* **~klöße** m pl ⟨cul⟩ *light dumplings* pl **~land** n *alluvial land*; *wash* **~teich** m *horse-pond*; ⟨for⟩ *tank* **Schw·emme** f ⁓/⁓n **1.** *horse-pond* ‖ (für Vieh) *watering place* ‖ in die ⁓ reiten, treiben *to* (*ride, take to*) *water* **2.** °⟨fig⟩ *public bar*; *tap-room*, ⟨sl⟩ *dive* **3.** ⟨fig, com⟩ (Überangebot) *glut* (*of eggs, butter, milk*, etc) **schw·emmen** vt [h] (weg⁓) *to wash, carry, sweep off* ‖ (an⁓) *to deposit* ‖ (Vieh) *to water* (→ vor.) ‖ (berieseln) *to irrigate* ‖ (Felle) *to soak* ‖ (Holz) *to float*

schw·enden vt [h] ⟨for⟩ *to burn up, destroy*

Schw·engel m ⁓s/⁓ (Glocken≚) *clapper* ‖ (Pumpen≚) *handle, sweep* ‖ (Brunnen≚, Balg≚) *swipe* ‖ (Wagen≚) *swing-bar* ‖ (Brücken≚) *bascule* ‖ (Preß≚) ⟨typ⟩ *lever* **~brunnen** m *well with a swipe* **schw·enkbar** a ⟨tech, mil⟩ *swivel mounted* **Schw·enk-** *turning* (*arm*) **≚bar** a *pivoting* od *pivot-mounted* (*gun*) **~bereich** m ⟨rec⟩ *area of* (*tonearm*) *travel*; ⟨artill⟩ *total movement in traverse, extent of tr.* **~becken, ~faß** n *basin* od *tub for rinsing* od (Küche) *washing-up* **~einrichtung** f *swivel mechanism* **~kopf** m ⟨phot⟩ *panorama head* **~lafette** f *swivel* (*gun*) *mount* **~rahmen** m (f elektron. Bauelemente) ⟨comp m. m.⟩ *turret-gate extraction fans* **~säule** f *pivot column* **~schiene** f *traversing rail* **schw·enken I.** vt [h] *to swing* (*the censer*) ‖ ⟨cul⟩ *to toss, shake* (*potatoes*, etc) ‖ *to swing* (*one's arms*) *to and fro* ‖ *to swing* (*one's dancing partner*) *round* ‖ (Schwert etc) *to brandish, flourish* ‖ (Hut, Tuch) *to wave* ‖ ⟨film⟩ (Kamera) *to pan* ‖ (Geschütz) *to slew*, Geschütze nach l. ⁓ *to slew guns to the left* ‖ (Gläser etc) *to rinse* (*out*) | ⟨fig, fam⟩ *to expel* (*a boy* [*from*] *the school*) | **II.** vi [h] *to turn* (*about*) ‖ ⟨mil⟩ *to wheel round* (rechts *to the r.*); r. schwenkt – marsch! *r. wheel – march* | ⟨fig⟩ *to change one's mind*; ⟨pol⟩ *to change sides* **III.** ≚ n ⟨aero⟩ *castoring* **Schw·enkung** f ⁓/⁓en *swinging, waving, brandishing* ‖ ⟨hors⟩ *caracol*(*e*) ‖ ⟨mil⟩ *wheel*(*ing*), *evolution* (m *to carry out*); *change of front* ⟨a. pol⟩; ⟨tact⟩ *pivoting* od *wheeling manœuvre* ‖ ⟨artill⟩ *traversing motion* | ⟨fig⟩ *change of mind* ‖ ⟨pol⟩ *changing sides* **~spunkt** m *pivot*(*ing point*) **~swinkel** m *arc of traverse*

schwer I. [a] **A. 1.** *heavy* (*load, silk, tank*); *weighty* (*purse*) ⟨a. fig → 5.⟩ ‖ 5 g ⁓ *5 g in weight*, *weighing 5 g* ‖ oben zu ⁓ *top-heavy* ‖ ⁓sten Kalibers *superheavy* (*bomb, gun*) **2.** (schwerfällig) *ponderous*; *clumsy* (*gait*); mit ⁓en Gliedern *heavy-limbed*; ⁓ v Begriff *thick-witted* **3.** (schwierig) *difficult, hard* (*work*) **4.** (ernst) *grave, serious, grievous*; *severe* (*blow*); *strong* (*suspicion*) **5.** (gewichtig) *weighty* **6.** (kräftig) *full-bodied* (*sauce, wine*) **7.** (mühsam) *troublesome* ‖ (drückend) *oppressive, burdensome* ‖ (Amt) *onerous* ‖ (schlimm) *grievous* (*blunder*), *bad* (*sore*), *hard* (*times*) **8.** °⁓er Bursche ⟨crim⟩ *big shot* ‖ ⟨sex⟩ (*dead*) *easy* (*girl*) | [adv] ⁓ reich *rolling* ‖ ⁓ verliebt *bung in love* **B.** (Krankheit, Verletzung, Krise) *serious* ‖ (Verstoß etc) *grave* ‖ (Bier, Wein,

Zigarre) *strong* **C.** ~er **Abschied** *sorrowful parting* || ~e Angst *great a.* || ~e Arbeit *hard manual labour* || ~er Atem *short(ness of) b.* || ~e Artillerie *heavy ordnance* | ~ v **Begriff** *slow of conception; obtuse* | *thick blood* || ~er Diebstahl *great theft* || *deep* (*disappointment*) || ~er Fluch *strong c.* || ~e Frage *poser* || ~es Gehör *hard hearing* || ~es **Geld** *specie*; in ~em G. *in hard cash*; ~es Geld kosten *to c. a pot of m.* || ~(st)es Geschütz *heavy guns* pl, (*supergun*) || ~en Herzens *with a heavy h.*; *reluctantly* || e–m das Herz ~ m *to grieve a p* || ~er Junge *swift youngster, hard case* || ~er **Kampf** *hard struggle*; ⟨mil a.⟩ *serious engagement* || ~stes Kampfflugzeug *super-fortress* || ⟨jur⟩ *aggravated* (Kuppelei etc) || ~er Reiter *trooper*; ~e Reiterei *heavy horse* | *heavy, rough sea* || ~e Speise *heavy, rich food* || ~e (Geld)**Strafe** *severe punishment*, (*heavy fine*) || ~es Verbrechen *shocking crime* || ~e Zunge *heavy, slow, stammering t.* **II.** [adv] **1.** *heavily*, ⟨fig⟩ *grievously; extremely* (*rich*); *helplessly* (*drunk*); *seriously* (*ill*); *badly* (*damaged*); ~beschreibbar *nondescript*; ~ flüchtig *of low volatility*; *l.-v.* [attr]; ~ löslich *difficult to dissolve*; ~ verständlich *abstruse; hard to understand*; ~ v.e Behauptung *blind statement* || *severely* (*wounded*) || ~ **zu** besteigen, erlangen, verdauen, verstehen *difficult to climb* etc; ~ lenkbar (P) *trying, unwieldy* || das ist ~ z sagen *that is hard to say; who knows?*; es fiel mir ~ es z tun *I had a hard time doing it* **2.** sich ~ **ärgern** *to feel greatly vexed* || ~ beleidigen *to give great offence to* | ~ bepackter Rucksack *heavy-laden knapsack* || (etw) ~ bezahlen *to pay dearly* (*for ..*) || ~ darniederliegen *to be seriously* od *dangerously ill* || es **fällt** mir ~ *I find it hard* (*to do*), *I have some difficulty* (*in starting*); es wäre ihm ~ gefallen → Verlegenheit; es fiel ihm ~ sich z bücken *his difficulty was to bend down*, .. z tun *he had a hard time doing* || (zu) ~ gehen ⟨tech⟩ *to have* (*too*) *little play* || es ~ h *to have a hard life* || ~ hören *to be hard of hearing* || es kommt ihn ~ an *he finds it hard* || es **liegt** mir ~ in den Gliedern (im Magen), (auf der Seele) *my limbs feel heavy* (*it lies h. on my st.*), (*it weighs heavily on my mind*) | mir ist ~ ums Herz *I am sick at heart* || ~ verdauliches Gericht ⟨cul⟩ *stodgy food* || sich ~ versündigen an *to sin grievously against* || e–m ~ w *to come difficult to a p* || ~ wiegen *to be of great weight* ⟨a. fig⟩ **Schw·er-** ~**arbeiter** m *heavy worker* ~**athletik** f *heavy athletics* pl (= *boxing, wrestling, weight-lifting*) ≃**atmend** a *breathing hard* ≃**atmig** a *asthmatic* ≃**beladen** a *heavily laden* ~**benzin** n *heavy petrol*, ⟨Am⟩ *h. gasoline* ≃**betrübt** a *deeply grieved* ≃**bewaffnet** a *heavy-armed* ≃**blütig** a *thick-blooded* | ≃keit [f] *thickness of blood* ~**erde** f *heavy spar* ≃**errungen** a *hard-won* ≃**erworben** a *hard-earned* ~|**fallen** → schwer II. 2. ≃**fällig** a *heavy, slow* || (Stil) *labo(u)red, ponderous* || *ungainly, clumsy, awkward, dull* || *cumbrous, unwieldy* || ⟨fig⟩ *cumbersome and slow* (*administrative machinery*) || *dull* (*of comprehension*); *stodgy*, ⟨Am⟩ *logy* || ~ gehen *to lumber* || ~ s *to be a stick-in-the-mud* ~**fälligkeit** f *heaviness, unwieldiness, slowness* || ⟨fig⟩ *stodginess, dullness* ≃**flüchtig** a *persistent* (*gas*) ≃**flüssig** a *stubborn, viscous* **-flüssigkeit** f *heavy medium* (*ore dressing*) ~**gewicht** n ⟨sport⟩ *heavy-weight* (⟨box⟩ über 159 Pfd, ⟨engl⟩ *175 lbs*) || ⟨fig⟩ *chief stress, dominant factor, chief importance, full import, emphasis* | ~sanziehung [f] *gravitational attraction*; ~smeister [m] *heavy-weight champion* ~**gut** n *dead weight, heavy goods* pl ≃**hörig** a *hard of hearing, deaf* | ≃keit [f] *deafness* ~**industrie** f *heavy industry* ~**kraft** f *gravitation*, der ~ gehorchen *to gravitate* ~**kranke(r)** m *seriously sick p* ~**kriegsbeschädigte(r)** m (*seriously*) *disabled veteran* od *ex-serviceman* ~**lastwagen** m *h.-duty truck* ~**mut** f *melancholy, sadness, dejection, depression; somberness*; ⟨Am fam⟩ *blues* ≃**mütig** a *melancholy; dyspeptic* || *mournful; saturnine, somber* || *depressed* || *sad, dismal, pensive, moody, heart-sick*; (*face*) *of gravity*; ~e Töne *blue* od *melancholy chords* || ~ s *to feel dejected*; ⟨Am fam⟩ *to have the blues* ~**öl** n *h. oil* ~**ölmotor** m *h. o.* od *Diesel engine* ~**punkt** m *centre of gravity*; ⟨fig⟩ *focal point, central p. of interest; importance; emphasis, stress* (liegt auf *is on*); *interest was focus(s)ed on the economic situation*; ⟨mil⟩ (*attacks with their*) *focal point* (*S. W. of the town*), *centre of combat, principal attack; main effort*: e–n ~ bilden *to establish a point of m. e.*, den ~ verlegen *to shift ..*; den ~ legen auf *to mass one's e. on* || in ~en der ABC-Abwehr *in significant CBR-aspects* | ~-artillerie [f] *heavy ordnance*; ~bildung [f] ⟨tact⟩ (*main*) *concentration* (*of troops*); ~-programm [n] *key program* ~**spat** m *heavy spar; barytes* sg ≃**verständlich** a *difficult to understand* ≃**verwundet** a *severely* od *seriously wounded* ≃**wiegend** a *weighty, serious, pregnant; grave* (*suspicion, error*) **Schw·ere** f ~/~n *weight* (⟨a. fig⟩ *of a word*), ⟨phys⟩ *gravitational pull* || *heaviness*; (of wine) *headiness* || (Ernst) *seriousness* || (Strenge) *severity* || ⟨phys⟩ *gravity* (⟨a. fig⟩ *of a crime, insult*) || *body* (*of wine*) || *full import* (*of the proofs*) ~**feld** n *gr.l* od *gravity field* | ⟨a–n⟩ Kurskorrektur durch das ~ e–s Planeten beim Vorbeiflug (z. B. am Mars) *swing-by* ≃**los** a *weightless* ~**masse** f *gr.l mass* ~**messer** m *gravimeter, hydrometer* ~**n·ot** f ⟨path⟩ *epilepsy* || es ist um die ~ zu kriegen *it's enough to drive one mad* || ~! *hang it all!* || wer, ~, war es? *who the devil was it?* ~**n·öter** m *badmash, masher; gay dog; ladies' man, lady-killer; young rascal*; ⟨hum⟩ *sheikh*; ⟨Am sl a.⟩ *sugar daddy* **schw·erlich** [adv] *hardly, scarcely* **Schw·erst-** *extremely* ~arbeiter [m] *e. heavy worker, worker in h. industry*; ~beschädigte(r) [m] *e. disabled p*; ⟨m. m.⟩ *p with a full disability pension*

Schwer·in n ⟨Ger⟩ (Stadt & †Land)

Schwert n ~(e)s/~er *sword* || das ~ ziehen, zum ~e greifen *to draw* od *unsheathe the s.* || durch das ~ fallen *to fall to the s.* || mit dem ~e hinrichten *to behead* || mit blankem ~ *with s. drawn* || zum ~ verurteilen *to send* (*a p*) *to the block* ~**feger** m *s.-cutler, s.-maker* | ~arbeit [f] *s.-cutlery* ~**fisch** m *s.-fish* || *grampus* ≃**förmig** a *s.-like, s.-shaped* ~**griff** m *hilt* ~**jacht** f ⟨mar⟩ *centre-board yacht* ~**lehen** n *male lief* ~**leite** f *reception of a squire into knighthood* ~**lilie** f ⟨bot⟩ *flower-de-luce, orris, iris; gladiolus*; (gelbe) *s.-flag*, ⟨Am⟩ *spatterdock*; → *iris* ~**mage** m ⟨hist⟩ *male relation* ~**orden** m *Order of the S.* ~**ritter** m *knight of the Order of the S.* ~**schlag,** ~**streich** m *s.-blow, s.-stroke* || ohne ~ *without* (*striking*) *a blow* ~**träger** m *s.-bearer* ~**wal** m ⟨zoo⟩ *grampus; killer whale* **Schw·ertel** m ~s/~; gelber ~ ⟨bot⟩ *water-flag* **Schw·erter-** ~**geklirr** n *clashing of swords* ~**tanz** m *sword-dance*

Schw·ester f ~/~n *sister*; ~n im Herzen *s.s under the skin* || barmherzige ~ *s. of mercy, S. of Charity* || (Kranken≃) *hospital nurse* ~**firma** f *affiliated firm* ~**kind** n *s.'s child; niece, nephew* ~**kirche** f *affiliated church* ~**liebe** f *s.ly love* ~**mann** m *s.'s husband, brother-in-law* ~**nhelferin,** ~**nhilfe** f *junior nurse, nurse's aid* ~**nkleidung** f *nurse's dress* ~**npaar** n *two s.s* ~**schiff** n *sister ship*, ⟨Am⟩ *running mate* ~**sohn** m *s.'s son, nephew* ~**sprache** f *s. language* ~**tochter** f *s.'s daughter, niece* ~**waffe** f ⟨mil⟩ *related arm* **Schw·esterchen** n ~s/~ *little sister* **schw·esterlich** a *sisterly* || ~ [adv] *in a sisterly way* | ~**keit** f ~/ *sisterly feeling* **Schw·esterschaft** f ~/~en *sisterhood* || ⟨Am, univ⟩ *sorority*

Schw·ibbogen m ⟨arch⟩ *flying buttress; arch*

schw·ichten vt [h] ⟨mar⟩ *to snake* (*the riggings*) **Schw·ichtleine** f ⟨mar⟩ *snake, swifter*

schwieg 1. & 3. sg pret v schweigen

Schw·ieger- ∼**eltern** pl *parents-in-law* pl ∼**mutter** f *mother-in-law* ∼**sohn** m *son-in-law* ∼**tochter** f *daughter-in-law* ∼**vater** m *f.-in-l.*

Schw·iele f ∼/∼n *callosity* ‖ (Strieme) *wale* **s-lig** a *horny, callous*; ⟨a.⟩ *horned* (*hands like a labourer's*) ‖ (striemig) *full of wales*

°**Schwiemel** m ∼s/ **1.** *giddiness* **2.** *dissolute fellow* | ∼**er** m ∼s/∼ *tippler, rake* | ≗**ig** a **1.** *giddy*; mir ist ∼ *I feel g.* **2.** *rakish, gay* | ≗**n** vi [h] *to go on the spree*

schw·ierig I. [a] **A.** *hard* (*work*); *h. to accomplish* ‖ *difficult* (*climb, position, enterprise*) ‖ *arduous* (*task, mountain*) ‖ *delicate* (*matter*) ‖ *intricate* (⟨fam⟩ *pretty, knotty*) (*problem*) ‖ *tough* (*job*) ‖ *stiff* (*examination*) ‖ *complicated* (*negotiation*) ‖ *trying* (*circumstances*) | **zu** ∼ f ihn (*that was*) *one too many for him* **B.** ∼er **Fall,** ∼e Frage *thorny* od *knotty question*; ⟨fam⟩ *teaser, poser* ‖ ∼es Gelände *difficult* od *broken country*; bei ∼em G. *with difficulties of terrain* ‖ ∼e **Lage** *precarious* od *awkward position*; *difficulty, exigence, -cy*; e–r ∼en L. entgegensehen *or* gegenüberstehen *to face tough odds* ‖ ⟨m. m.⟩ *treacherous* (*road*) **C.** (P) *difficult to please* ‖ ∼ zu behandeln *difficult, fastidious*; *unmanageable, impractic, intractable*; *unaccomodating* (*fellow*) ‖ *rebellious, unwieldy* (*continent*) ‖ ∼ w *to begin* od *raise difficulties* **II.** ∼**er** [compr] (*the answer is*) *more complicated* **III. das** ≗**ste** h wir hinter uns *the worst is over* | ≗**keit** f ∼/∼en *difficulty* ‖ *arduousness* ‖ *intricacy* ‖ *precariousness* | ∼en [pl] ⟨a.⟩ *obstacles*, ∼en in der Versorgung *logistical d.s*; der Text bereitet gr ∼en .. *is full of d.s* | nicht ohne ∼ *not without some trouble*; ohne ∼en *in comfort*, ⟨Am sl⟩ *without a hitch* ‖ es ging ohne ∼en *it was plain sailing* ‖ in ∼en geraten *to get into trouble* od ⟨fam⟩ *hot water*; *to be in deep water* ‖ ∼en h mit etw *to have d.y in doing a th, to do a th with d.y* ‖ ∼en m *to raise difficulties*, unnötige .. *to make a fuss*, jdm .. *to put obstacles in a p's way*; macht es Ihnen ∼en, mich z verstehen? *have you any d.y in understanding me*? ‖ das macht k–e ∼ *there is no obstacle*, ⟨fam⟩ *that's simple as applepie* ‖ auf ∼en stoßen *to meet with difficulties*, unerwartet .. ⟨fam⟩ *to strike a snag* ⟨fig⟩ ‖ die (ersten) ∼en überwinden ⟨fig⟩ *to clear the hurdle* (*to break the ice*); ohne ∼(en) überwinden, tun *to take* (*a th*) *in one's stride*

Schw·imm- ∼**anstalt** f, ∼**bad** n *swimming-bath, s.-establishment*; *baths* pl ∼**aufbereitung** f ⟨tech⟩ *flotation* ∼**bassin** n *swimming pool* ∼**becken** n *basin*; *s.-pool*; (im Freien) *Lido* ∼**blase** f *s.-bladder* ‖ ⟨ich⟩ *sound* ∼**dock** n *floating dock* ∼**ente** f *surface-feeding duck* ≗**fähig** a *able to float* ∼**fähigkeit** f = ∼kraft ∼**fest** n *s.-match*; *aquacade* ∼**feder,** ∼**flosse** f *fin* ∼**fuß** m *web-foot* ∼**füßer** m ⟨orn⟩ *palmiped* ∼**gestell** n ⟨aero⟩ *float* ∼**gürtel** m *life-belt* ∼**halle** f *s.-pool* ∼**haut** f ⟨orn⟩ *web* ∼**hemd**(e) n *cork-jacket* ∼**hose** f (e–e *a pair of*) *bathing-drawers* pl ∼**käfer** m ⟨ent⟩ *diving beetle* ∼**kampfwagen** m *amphibious tank* ∼**kapsel** f *flotation capsule* ⟨a. a–n⟩ ∼**körper** m *float* ⟨a. aero⟩; ⟨tech⟩ *floating body* ∼**kraft** f *floatage, buoyancy* ∼**kunst** f *art of s.* ∼**lehrer** m *s.-master* ∼**-Lkw** m (2,5 t) *duck wagon* N ∼**panzer**(**wagen**) m *amphibian tank* ∼**sack** m ⟨aero⟩ *floatation bag* ∼**sand** m ⟨geol⟩ *quick-sand* ∼**schicht** f, ∼**schlamm** m (*layer of*) *scum* ∼**schule** f *s.-school* ∼**stoffe** m pl *floating solids* pl od *matter*; *skimmings* pl ∼**stoß** m *stroke* ∼**tauchen** n (ohne Taucheranzug) *skin-diving* ∼**vogel** m *s.-bird, web-footed bird* ∼**werk** n ⟨aero⟩ *float landing gear* ∼**weste** f *air-, life-jacket*; ⟨aero⟩ *floatation* (*seat*) *cushion, life vest* **schw·immen I.** vi [schwamm/geschwommen] [h & s] **A. 1.** (v P) *to swim* (wie e–e bleierne Ente *like a rock*) ‖ auf dem Rücken ∼ *to float* ‖ auf der Brust (Seite) ∼ *to s. with a breast-*(*side-*)*stroke* ‖ im Freistil ∼ *to s. free style* ‖ im Kraul∼ *to crawl* ‖ Hand über Hand ∼ *to s. with the overhead-stroke* | ⟨cul prov⟩ (der) Fisch will ∼ (*the enjoyment of fish calls for wine*), *poisson sans boisson est poison* Fr **2.** (v S u Toten) *to drift, float* (*about*) ‖ *the moon floats* | (v Schiffen) *to be afloat* ‖ ∼ l *to sail* (*there are pools for sailing model boats*) **3.** ⟨fig, theat etc⟩ (s–e Rolle etc nicht wissen) *to be fluffy* od *at sea* ‖ (v Anblick) *to be hazy* **4.** ⟨übtr⟩ (v Boden etc) *to be under water* **B. 1.** ∼ **lassen** *to swim* (*a cork*); *to sail* (*a boat*) | ⟨fig⟩ laß es ∼! *let it go*! **2.** es –mt mir vor den Augen *I see everything as if in a haze* **3. sich** frei ∼ *to pass in s.ming* **C. ans** Land, Ufer ∼ *to s. to* (*the*) *shore* ‖ (v S etc) *to drift ashore* | **auf**: (→ A. 1.) (P) auf dem Meere ∼ *to be at sea* ‖ (Schiff) *to sail on the high sea* ‖ auf den Wellen ∼ *to ride the waves* | davon|∼ *to escape by s.ming* | **gegen** (⟨fig⟩ wider) den Strom ∼ *to strive against the current* ⟨a. fig⟩ | **in**: *to welter in one's blood* ‖ *to be s.ming in delight, to s. in a sea of black, in pleasure, in abundance* ‖ (im Gelde) *to be wallowing in m., to be simply rolling* ‖ (im Glück) *to be in luck's way* | *to be bathed in tears* ‖ ⟨cul⟩ *to be soaked* (*in wine*) | **mit** dem Strom ∼ *to float with the c.*, ⟨fig⟩ *with the tide* | **über** den K. ∼ *to s. the Channel* **D.** ∼**d** *floating* (*battery, mine*) ‖ *untrue* (Magnetnadel) ‖ (*goods*) *afloat* od *in transit* bzw *carried by water* | ⟨a.⟩ *adrift* | ∼er Blick *humid eyes* **II.** ≗ n **1.** *s.ming* etc ‖ ⟨fig⟩ ins ≗ k (→ A. 3.) *to get unsteady* ‖ zum ≗ gehen *to go s.ming*; *to have a s., a bathe* **2.** = Schwindel 1. **Schw·immer** m ∼s/∼ **1.** (P) *swimmer* **2.** (Fischfang, ⟨tech, aero, mot⟩) *float* **3.** ⟨tech⟩ *float chamber* (ersoffen *flooded*) ∼**flugzeug** n *float-plane* ∼**kasten** m *float-chamber* ∼**nadel** f *float-wire* ∼**ventil** n *float-gauge, floating valve* ∼**werk** n ⟨aero⟩ *float undercarriage*

Schw·indel m ∼s/ **1.** *giddiness, swimming*; (mit Übelkeitsgefühl *sick*) *dizziness* ‖ ⟨path⟩ *vertigo* ‖ ∼ bek *to turn giddy* **2.** ⟨fig⟩ (Täuschung, Betrug) *swindle* (ausgemacht *out-and-out*); *fraud, cheat, hoax, humbug, bubble, skin-game*; ⟨fam⟩ *take-on, frame-up* ‖ ⟨sl⟩ *do, moonshine, bosh, ramp, eyewash, racket*, ⟨Am⟩ *bunco, phon(e)y, make-up* ‖ (Unsinn) *twaddle*; ⟨sl⟩ *bunk*, ⟨Am⟩ *buncombe* | den ∼ kenn ich *I know that dodge* ‖ °der ganze ∼ *the whole lot* od *kit* ‖ den ganzen ∼ aufdecken *to give the whole show away* ‖ es ist alles ∼ *the whole th's a plant*; es ist der reine ∼ *it's a rank swindle*, ⟨sl⟩ *it's all bunkum* | auf jds ∼ hereinfallen *to be taken in by a p's tricks* **3.** ⟨fam⟩ *lot, caboodle*; was kostet der ∼? *how much the whole lot*? | ∼**-** [in comp] ⟨fig oft⟩ *bogus* (*bank, case, message*) ∼**anfall** m *vertigo* ∼**auktion** f *mock auction* ≗**erregend** a = ∼haft ∼**firma** f *long firm* ≗**frei** a *not liable to giddiness* ‖ nicht ∼ sein ⟨a.⟩ *to have no head for heights* ∼**gefühl** n *vertigo*; *giddy sensation* ∼**geschäft** n *swindle* ∼**gesellschaft** f ⟨com⟩ *bubble* od *bogus c.* ∼**kopf** m *hare-brained p*; *harumscarum* ‖ *swindler* °∼**meier** m *humbug*; *fibber, braggart*; *liar, boaster*; ⟨Am fam⟩ *gyp artist* ∼**methode** f *confidence trick* ∼**sucht** f *vertigo* ∼**unternehmen** n ⟨Am fam⟩ *wild-cat* (*enterprise*) **Schwindel·ei** f ∼/∼en *swindle, bubble, swindling, cheat* ‖ ⟨fam⟩ *sell*, ⟨sl⟩ *do* ‖ grobe ∼ *rank fraud* **schw·indelhaft, schw·ind(e)lig** a **1.** *causing dizziness*; *dazzling*; *making giddy*; *giddy, dizzy vertiginous* (*rapidity, height*) **2.** schwindelig w *to faint*; *to turn giddy*; mir wird ∼ *my head spins* **3.** *fraudulent, swindling* **schw·indeln 1.** vi [h] *to lie, fib*; *swindle, cheat*; *sharp* ‖ er –lt sich durchs Leben *he swindles his way through life* | (flunkern) *to humbug*; *to tell fibs* **2.** vi [imps] [h]; mir –lt der Kopf *I feel giddy, my head swims*; ⟨fig⟩ .. bei dem Gedanken *my brain reels at the idea* (*that .. should*), .. von Zahlen *with figures* ‖ ∼**d** = schwindelhaft 1. **schw·inden I.** vi [schwand/geschwunden] [s] (kleiner werden) *to dwindle, wane, shrink*; (ver~) *to evanesce*; ⟨met⟩ *to contract* || (v Kraft) *to waste away* || mir –det der Mut, die Hoffnung *I am losing courage, hope* | (ver~) *to disappear, vanish, lapse* || (of feelings) *to pass off* || *the colour faded from his face* || *his power was crumbling* || ihm ~ die Sinne *he is losing consciousness* || *I have lost all confidence in her* || *the name has escaped my memory* || *his reputation is failing* || *all my hope has deserted me* | ~ l *to give up, to abandon* **II.** ≗ n *dwindling* etc; *shrinkage*; *waste*; ⟨met⟩ *contraction* || *the passing* (*of feudalism*) **Schw·indler** m ~s/~ *swindler, humbug, cheat*; *crook, sharper*; gerissener ~ ⟨fam⟩ *slicker* || ⟨Am sl⟩ *come-on, phon(e)y* **~bande** f *gang of s.s* **~gesellschaft** f *bogus c.* **≗haft** a = schwindelhaft 3. **Schwind- ~maßstab** m *shrink rule* **~maßzugabe** f *shrinkage allowance* **~riß** m ⟨for⟩ *season-crack* **~sucht** f ~/ ⟨path⟩ *tabes*; (galoppierende *rapid*) *consumption*; ⟨scient⟩ *phthisis* || die ~ bek *to become consumptive* || sich die ~ an den Hals ärgern *to vex o.s. to death* | °~skandidat [m] *consumptive p* **schw·indsüchtig** a *consumptive*, ⟨scient⟩ *phthisical*

Schw·ing- ~achse f *jointed cross shaft axle*; *oscillating* od *floating, flexible axle, independent wheel suspension* **~arm** m *suspension arm* **~bank** f (f Flachs) *swingle-bench* **~baum** m ⟨weav⟩ *rocking tree* **~hebel** m *rocker arm* **~kolben** m ⟨ent⟩ *balancer* **~moor** n *quaking bog* **~sieb** n *vibrating screen* **~signal** n *wigwag signal* **~trog** m (f Goldwäscher) *washing-cradle* **~wanne** f *winnowing-fan* **Schw·inge** f ~/~en **1.** (Fittich) *wing* || ⟨poet⟩ *pinion* **2.** (Wanne) *fan, winnow* **3.** (f Flachs) *swingle* **4.** ⟨tech⟩ *oscillating lever* **Schw·ingel** m ~s/~ ⟨bot⟩ *fescue-grass* **schw·ingen** [schwang/geschwungen] [h] **I.** vi *to swing* || (wie ein Pendel) *to oscillate, sway* || *the ship swings* || (zittern) *to vibrate* | Sw ⟨a.⟩ = ringen **II.** vt *to swing* (auf *on*) || (Waffe) *to flourish, brandish*; e–e Keule über jds Kopf ~ *to wield a club over a p's head*; (Stock) *to whirl* || (Hut, Fahne) *to wave* || (Flachs) *to swingle, scutch* || (Korn etc) *to winnow* || geschwungen *curved* (*line*) | °⟨fig⟩ die gr Klappe ~ *to have the gift of the gab* || den Pantoffel ~ *to wear the breeches* || e–e Rede ~ *to make a* (*bombastic*) *speech* || das Tanzbein ~ *to foot it* **III. sich** ~ *to jump, vault* (auf *onto*; in *into* [*the air*]) || *to leap into the driving seat* || *to vault into the saddle* || *the eagle soars up* (in die Luft) || (auf Schaukel) *to have a swing* || (auf Balken) *to see-saw* || sich aufs Pferd ~ *to vault on horseback* || sich auf den Thron ~ *to take possession of the throne* || sich aus dem Sattel ~, sich vom Pferde ~ *to leap from ..* || sich ~ über *to swing o.s. over* (*a fence*) **IV.** ≗ n = Schwingung etw zum ≗ bringen *to get* od *set a th vibrating, swinging* etc **Schw·inger** m ~s/~ ⟨box⟩ *swing* | Sw ⟨a.⟩ = Ringer **Schw·ingung** f ~/~en *swinging*; *vibration*; *oscillation*; *pulsation*; ~en *cycles* (*per second*); ungedämpfte ~en ⟨phys⟩ *continuous osc.ns*; volle ~ ⟨phys⟩ *cycle, period* || ~en m = schwingen I. | **~s- ~achse** f *axis of oscillation* **~bewegung** f *vibratory motion* **~bild** n *oscillogram* **~bogen** m *arc of osc.* **~dämpfer** m ⟨mot⟩ *shimmy damper* **~dauer** f *time of osc., period* **~festigkeit** f *vibrator fatigue strength* **~knoten** m *nodal point* **~kreis** m *oscillatory circuit* **~lehre** f *kymatology* **~weite** f *amplitude* **~zahl** f ⟨phys⟩ *frequency*

schwipp I. [intj] *flip* (schwapp *flop*) **II.** [a] **1.** *flexible, pliant* **2.** *nimble, agile* | ≗schwager [m] *brother of a brother-* od *sister-in-law* **Schw·ippe** f ~/~n *whip-cord* || (Gerte) *thin switch* **schw·ippen I.** vt [h] *to whip, switch, jerk* **II.** vi [h & s] *to see-saw* **Schwips** m ~es/~e ⟨fam⟩ *tipsiness* || e–n ~ h ⟨sl⟩ *to be tight* od *moony, to be over the line*; ⟨Am⟩ *to be lit up*

schw·irren I. vi [h] *to whir, swish, whiz, scur* || (Insekt) *to buzz, stridulate* || umher ~ *to flit about* || herum|~ *to whirl round* | **es** –rt mir in den Ohren, vor den Augen *I feel a buzzing in my ears, I have a haze before my eyes* **II.** ≗ n (e–r Kugel) *zip*

Schwitz- ~bad n *sweating-bath, Turkish bath* **~bank** f: auf der ~ sitzen *to sweat over one's work* **~kammer** f *sudatorium* **~kasten** m *sweating--box* || °⟨fig⟩ (*arm-pit*): im ~ ⟨sport⟩ *in chancery* **~kur** f *sweating-cure* **~mittel** n *sudorific* **Schw·itze** f ~/~n **1.** ⟨cul⟩ *hot fat and flour* (*for soups*) **2.** ⟨tech⟩ Häute in die ~ bringen *to pile up hides* **schw·itzen I.** vi/t [h] *to sweat, perspire* (tüchtig *freely, profusely*; *to have a good sweat*) || am ganzen Körper ~ *to be bathed in sweat* || ~ wie ein Bär, Pferd *to be all sweat, to* (*be in an awful*) *stew*; *to sweat like a horse, pig*, ⟨Am⟩ *like a prize hog at a country fair* | (v Mauern etc) *to get* od *be damp, moist, wet* | ich –ze (⟨a.⟩ mich –zt) *I am perspiring* || jdn ~ l ⟨fig⟩ *to sweat a p* (*by questioning*, ⟨fam⟩) | [vt] ich kann's nicht durch die Rippen ~ *I can't sweat it out of my system* || Blut ~ *to sweat blood* || ⟨tech⟩ Häute ~ (l) *to sweat hides* || ⟨cul⟩ *to sweat* **II.** ≗ n *sweat*(*ing*), *perspiration* || ~ verursachen *to procure p.*

°**Schwof** m ~(e)s/~e ⟨fam⟩ *shilling-hop, skip*; ⟨sl⟩ *shindig* || ~ z Kennenlernen ⟨Am⟩ *stag dance* | ≗**en** vi [h] *to hop*, ⟨fam⟩ *to foot* od *hoof it, to sling a foot*

schwoll 1. & 3. sg pret v schwellen

schw·ojen vt/i [h] = schwajen

schw·ören vt/i [schwor & -ur/ge–oren] [h] *to swear* (**bei** *by God, on one's honour*); ich möchte ~ *I dare s.* || *to take an* (⟨jur⟩ *the*) *oath*; ⟨sl⟩ *to take one's dick* (*that*) || falsch ~ *to forswear o.s.* || e–n ~ l *to administer an oath to a p* | **Rache** ~ *to vow vengeance* || sie ~ sich Treue *they pledge their devotion* | ich könnte ~, **daß** es N. ist *I could swear to its being N.* | **sich** [dat] ge–n h *to have sworn to o.s.* (*that*) | **auf** etw ~ *to swear to a th*; ⟨übtr⟩ *to be sold on a th*; auf die Bibel *on the book* (⟨fam⟩ *to kiss the b.*) || ich möchte darauf ~ *I dare swear by it, I'll be bound* || auf e–e S ~ *to swear by* (*iodyne*); auf jdn ~ *to have absolute confidence in a p* || wir ~ darauf, daß *we are absolutely certain that* | **zur** Fahne ~ *to take one's military oath* || zum K. ~ *to embrace Catholicism* || **geschworen** *sworn* (*oath, adherent, enemy*) || die Ge–nen *the jury* **Schw·örer** m ~s/~ *swearer*

°**schwul** a *homosexual* **schwül** a *sultry* (*air*), *close* (*room*), *stifling* (*heat*) *sticky* (*weather*), *breathless* (*day*) || ⟨fig⟩ *uneasy* (*dreams*) || mir ist ~ zu Mute, ums Herz *I feel very uneasy* | °in **Schwulibus** ⟨hum⟩ *up a tree* **Schw·üle** f ~/ *sultriness, closeness*; *stifling heat* || *oppression* °**Schwulit·ät** f ~/~en ⟨fam⟩ *quandary, predicament, scrape, stew* || in ~en s ⟨fam⟩ *to stew*

Schwulst 1. m ~es/ *bombast, fustian, grandiloquence* | *pompousness* | ~stil [m] ⟨Lit⟩ *Baroque style* **2.** f ~/≗e *swelling, tumour* **schw·ülstig** a *bombastic* [*ally* adv], *turgid, grandiloquent, verbose* || *pompous* (*phrases*); *mouthy, ranting* || *high--flown* (*author*) | [adv] ~ reden *to rant*; → hochtrabend | ≗**keit** f ~/ *bombastic style, turgidity*; *flatulence*

×°**schw·ummerig** a: mir wird ~ *I'm feeling shaky*

Schwund m ~(e)s/ *dwindling*; *disappearance*; *decay, decline* || *loss in* od *of weight*; *wastage* || (Haar≗) *falling off* | (Eingehen) *shrinkage* || (durch Lecken) *leakage* || ⟨path⟩ *atrophy* || ⟨wir⟩ *fading* || ⟨gram⟩ *dropping* **~ausgleich** m ⟨wir⟩ *automatic volume control* **~regelung** f ⟨wir⟩ *anti-fade control* **~stufe** f ⟨gram⟩ *null-grade*

Schwung m ~(e)s/≗e *swing*(*ing*), *sweep* (*of arm, wheel*); *whisk*; *impetus*; *flourish, jerk* || (Auf≗) *leap, bound*; *rise, rising* | ⟨fig⟩ *verve, elan, impetus, stride*, → Temperament || ⟨mus⟩ *momentum*, *vigor* || ⟨mil⟩ *momentum* (*of attack*), (die Verfolgung) in ~ halten *to maintain the m. of* .. | (poetischer) *flight, soaring; loftiness; inspiration; ardour* || (v Versen) *noble* od *lofty diction*; ohne ~ *dull, dry* || ⟨arts⟩ ~ h *to have plenty of life* | (des Geistes) *buoyancy*; (Schneid) *snap* | die S hat k–n ~ *there is no go in it* (⟨fam⟩ *in the show*) || in ~ bringen *to set* (*a th*) *going, to put snap into a th* || in ~ k *to get going* od *in stride* || im ~e s *to be in full swing, to* (*be*) *run*(*ning*) *full tide*, ⟨fig⟩ *to be in vogue* || in ~ k *to swing into motion; to get into one's stride, to get thoroughly going*; voll .. *to hit full stride*; wieder .. k, bringen ⟨fig⟩ *to revive* || mit ~ aus .. werfen *to send flying from the house* **~bewegung** f *vibrating motion; oscillation* **~brett** n *spring-board* **~feder** f ⟨orn⟩ *pinion* **~gewicht** n *flyweight* **~kraft** f *momentum* (an ~ gewinnen *to gather m.*); *motor force; centrifugal power; flywheel force* || ⟨fig⟩ *energy, go* || (geistige) *buoyancy, verve* **~kreiselskala** f ⟨wir⟩ *spin wheel tuning* **≚los** a *without life* (⟨fam⟩ *go*); ⟨liter⟩ *dull, dry* **~masse** f *revolving mass* **~moment** n *flywheel action* **~rad** n *flywheel* **~riemen** m (am Wagen) *main braces* pl **~scheibe** f *fly-pulley* **≚voll** a *spirited, full of fire, energy, enthusiasm* || *daring* (*attack*); *smooth*, ⟨fam⟩ *snappy* (*music*) **schw·unghaft** a (Geschäft) *flourishing* || *roaring, brisk* (*trade*) || *stirring* (*speech, movement*) || ⟨liter⟩ *lofty* (*verse*), *lively* (*scene*)

schw·upp(dich)!, -diwupp! *slap! flip!*

schwur 1. & 3. sg pret v schwören **Schwur** m ~(e)s/≚e *oath*; ⟨pol, ec⟩ *vow* || e–n ~ ablegen, leisten *to take* od *swear an oath* || *to make a vow* **~formel** f *wording of an oath* **~gericht** n *jury, assizes* pl; *trial by jury* **~zeuge** m *sworn witness*

Schw·yz n ⟨Swiss⟩ (Stadt & Kanton) **~er(in** f) m *inhabitant of Schwyz*

Scilly-Inseln [sts–] f pl (vor Cornwall, England) *Scilly Islands*

S·eal-El·ektrik [si:l] m ~/ *electric seal*

Sec·ento n [–etʃe–] ~s/ It *17th century*(*'s art*)

Sech n ~es/~e (Pflugmesser) *coulter*

Sechs f [–ks] ~/S·echsen *the number six* **sechs** a *six* || mit sechsen (*or* sechse lang) fahren *to drive* (*in*) *a coach and six* || ~unddreißig *thirtysix* || → acht **Sechs-** **~·achteltakt** m *six-eight time* **≚blätt(e)rig** a *six-leaved* **~eck** n ⟨math⟩ *hexagon* **≚eckig** a *hexagonal* **~ender** m *stag with six antlers* **≚fach, ≚fältig** a *sixfold, sextuple* **≚füßig** a *of six feet, six-footed* **≚h·undertste** a *six hundredth* **≚jährig** a *six years old, sexennial* **~kammerrevolver** m *six-chambered r.*, ⟨Am fam⟩ *six-shooter* **~kant-** ~bolzen [m] *hexagonal bolt*; ~mutter [f] *hexagon nut*; ~-(schlüssel) [m] *hexagon spanner* **≚läufig** a *six-chambered* (*revolver*) **≚mal** [adv] *six times* **≚malig** a *six times repeated* **~männig** a ⟨bot⟩ *hexandrous* **≚monatig** a *lasting six months* **≚monatlich** a *six-monthly, semi-annual* | [adv] *every six months, every sixth month* **~pfünder** m *sixpounder* **≚reihig** a *in six rows* **~saitig** a *of six strings* **≚seitig** a *six-sided, hexagonal* **~spänner** m *coach and six* **≚spännig** a *drwan by six horses* **≚stündig** a *of six hours* **~t·agerennen** n ⟨cycl⟩ *six-day race* **≚tägig** a *of* od *lasting six days* **≚unds·echzig** a, *sixty-six* ⟨a. subst: Ger cards⟩ **≚wertig** a ⟨chem⟩ *hexavalent* **≚wöchentlich** a *six-weekly* | [adv] *every six weeks, every sixth week* **≚wöchig** a (*vacations*) *of* od *lasting six weeks* **~zyl·inder-** [in comp] ⟨mot⟩ *six-cylinder* (*car*) **S·echser** ~s/~ **1.** *six-pfennig* (od *-kreutzer*) *piece* || nicht f e–n ~ R. *not a pennyworth of romance* **2.** *the number six* **3.** *soldier of the sixth regiment* etc → acht **s·echserlei** a *of six sorts, six kinds of* **s·echste** a *sixth* || der ≚ (geschr. VI.) (*Edward*) *the Sixth* (*VI*) || → achte **~h·alb** a *five and a half* **S·echstel** n ~s/~ *sixth* (*part*) || fünf ~ (5/6) *five sixths* **s·echstens** [adv] *sixthly, in the sixth place* **s·echzehn** [seç–] a *sixteen* || ~ Uhr *four o'clock p. m.* **S·echzehn-** **~ender** m *stag with sixteen antlers* **≚fach** [a & adv] *sixteenfold* **≚jährig** [a] *16 years old* || ~e [pl] *16 year-old youths* pl **≚lötig** a *of eight ounces weight* || *unalloyed* (*silver*) **s·echzehnte** a *sixteenth* (→ sechste) **S·echzehntel** n ~s/~ *sixteenth part* (→ Sechstel) **~format** n ⟨typ⟩ = Sedezformat **~note** f ⟨mus⟩ *semiquaver* **~pause** f ⟨mus⟩ *semiquaver rest* **s·echzehntens** [adv] *in the sixteenth place* **s·echzig** a *sixty* → achtzig **~jährig** a *sixty years old*; → Sechziger **S·echziger** m ~s/~ *sexagenarian* || (im Pikett) *sixth*, → Achtziger **s·echzigste** a *sixtieth* → dreißig, achtzig

S·edan n ⟨Fr⟩ (Stadt) *Sedan* | ~tag [m] 2. September (1870)

Sedat·ivum n ~s/–va *sedative*

Sed·ezformat n ⟨typ⟩ *sedecimo, 16 mo*

Sedim·ent n ~(e)s/~e *sediment* **~ablagerung, ~bildung** f *sedimentation* **≚·är** a *s.ary* **~gestein** n *s.ary rocks* pl **≚·ieren** vt/i [h/s] *to settle to the bottom* **S·edisvak·anz** [–w–] f ~/~en *vacancy of the Papal See*

See 1. m ~s/~n *lake* (Wener-~ *L. Väner*), *mere*; (kl Berg≚) *tarn*; ⟨Scot⟩ *loch* **2.** f ~/~n *sea* (*Coral S., Tasman S.*); *ocean* || grobe ~ *rough s.* || die alles verschlingende ~ *Davy Jones's locker* || hohe ~ *high sea* || offene ~ *open sea; offing* (*to get the o.*) | schwere ~n (Wellen) *heavy seas* | **an** der ~ *by the sea*(*side*) || auf, zur ~ *at sea* (*to perish at sea*), (*he had never been to sea*) || in ~ gehen *or* stechen *to put* (*off* od *out*) *to sea, to set sail* || in ~ gehend *outward bound* || zur ~ *by sea* od *water* (*to France*) || zur ~ fahren *to follow the s.*; gehen *to go to sea, to take to the sea* || zur ~ gehörig *marine* (*m.*), *maritime* (*m.t.e*), *naval* (*n.*), *nautical* (*n.t.l*) **~aal** m *conger*; ⟨com, cul⟩ *flake*, ⟨Am⟩ *grayfish* **~ablagerung** f *sea-deposit* **~abrüstung** f *n. disarmament* **~adler** m *white-tailed eagle* **~alpen** pl *M.t.e Alps* pl **~amt** n *m.t.e court*; (*Court of*) *Admiralty* **~anemone** f ⟨zoo⟩ *sea-anemone* **~arsenal** n *n. dockyard* **~-aufklärer** m ⟨aero⟩ *naval patrol plane*, ⟨fam⟩ *fleet spotter* **~ausdruck** m *sea-term* **~bad** n (Ort) *seaside resort; spa* || (das Baden) *sea-bath* **~bär** m ⟨zoo⟩ *sea bear*, ⟨fig⟩ (P) *old salt, sea-dog*, ⟨Am⟩ *gob* **~bataillon** n ⟨mil⟩ *battalion of m.s* **~beben** n *seaquake*, ⟨Am⟩ (*submarine*) *t*(*r*)*emblor* **~dienst** m *n. service* **~einhorn** n ⟨zoo⟩ *narwhal* **~einsatzflugzeug(e** pl) *m.t.e aircraft* [*invar*] **~-elefant** m *sea-elephant* **≚fähig** a *seaworthy* | ~keit [f] *seaworthiness* **≚fahrend** a *sea-going; seafaring* (*nation*), *sailor* (*merchant*) **~fahrer** m *navigator, m.r, sailor* **~fahrt** f *navigation at sea*, christliche ~ *seafaring, seagoing profession, life of a sailor* || (Reise) *voyage* **≚fest** a *sea-worthy, sea-proof* || (P) *not subject to sea-sickness* || (nicht) ~ s *to be a good* (*bad*) *sailor* || ~ w *to get, find one's sea-legs* **~festigkeit** f ⟨fam⟩ *sea legs* **~festung** f *fortified n. base* **~feuer** n *sea-lights* pl **~fisch** m *salt-water fish* | ~er·ei [f] *deep-sea fishing* **~flieger** m *n. aviator* **~flug-** ~hafen [m] *seaplane base, m.t.e airport*; (ohne Land–) *seaplane anchorage*; ~wesen [n] *n. aviation*; ~zeug [n] *sea-plane* || –mutterschiff [n] *s.p. tender*; –träger [m] *s.p. carrier* **~frachtbrief** m *bill of lading* **~funk** m *m. radio* | ~stelle [f] *m. r. service station; ship r. st.* **~gang** m (*motion of the*) *sea* || es ist hoher ~ *a rough sea is running, there is a heavy swell on* || ~ kommt auf *a sea gets up* **~gebiet** n: überwachtes ~ *m.t.e. control area*; im ~ v Elba *in the waters off E.* **~gebrauch** m *n.t.l. usage, custom at sea* **~gefahr** f *sea-risk* **~gefecht** n *sea-fight, n. action* **~gegend** f *m.t.e. country* **~geltung** f *prestige at sea* **~gemälde** n *sea-piece* **~gericht** n = ~amt **~gesetz** n *m.t.e. law* **~gewächs** n *m. plant* **~gras** n ⟨bot⟩ *sea-weed*; ⟨com⟩ *sea-grass* **≚grün** a *seagreen* **~-**

gurke f ⟨zoo⟩ *s.-cucumber* **~hafen** m *harbo(u)r; seaport* (⟨a.⟩ Stadt) **~handbuch** n *sea manual* **~handel** m *m.t.e trade, oversea trade* **~hase** m ⟨ich⟩ *lump-fish* **~hecht** m *hake*, ⟨Am⟩ *snook* **~held** m *n. hero* **~herrschaft** f *control* od *command of the sea, n. supremacy* **~höhe** f *altitude above sea-level* **~hund** m ⟨zoo⟩ (männl., weibl. *bull-, cow-*) → *seal* | ∼sfell -n] *sealskin* **~igel** m ⟨zoo⟩ *sea-urchin* ‖ ⟨scient⟩ *echinus*; (fossiler) *echinite* **~jungfer** f *mermaid* **~kabel** n *submarine cable* **~kadett** m *n. cadet* **~kalb** n *sea-calf* **~kampfflugzeug** n *n. fighter plane*; *seaplane fighter* **~karte** f *chart* **~kompaß** m *m.r's compass* **~kennung** f *intelligence of the soundings* **≃klar** a *ready for sea* **~klima** n *m.t.e* od *m. climate* **~kohl** m *sea-kale* **~konferenz** f *n. c.* **~krabbe** f *sea-crab* **~kräfte** f pl *sea-forces* pl **≃krank** a *seasick*; leicht (nicht) ∼ w *to be a bad (good) sailor*; ∼ s *to feed the fishes* | ∼heit [f] *seasickness* ‖ an ∼ leiden *to be subject to s., to be a bad sailor* **~krieg** m *n. war, war at sea* | ∼führung [f] *n. warfare*; ∼skunst [f] *n. tactics* pl; ∼sleitung [f]; oberste ∼ ⟨engl⟩ *Board of Admiralty*, ⟨Ger⟩ *Supreme N. Command*; ∼srecht [n] *law of n. warfare*; ∼sstrateg·ie [f] *n. strategy* **~kuh** f *sea-cow* **~kunde** f *n. knowledge* **~küste** f *sea-coast, shore, beach, seabord* **~lachs** m *coalfish* **~land** n **1.** (größte dänische Insel) *Zeeland* **2.** holl. Zeeland (niederländische Prov.) *Zealand* **~landschaft** f *waterscape* **~leben** n *m.t.e life, m.t.e habits* pl **~leute** pl *seamen, mariners* pl **~liste** f *shipping list* **~löwe** m ⟨zoo⟩ *sea-lion* **~luft** f *sea-air* | ∼hafen [m] *seadrome*; ∼streitkräfte [f pl] *navy airforce* **~macht** f ⟨pol⟩ *naval* od *m.t.e power, power at sea*; ⟨mil⟩ *n. force*; (Flotte) *navy* **~mann** m *seaman, sailor, m.r*; ⟨fam⟩ *salt*; oller ehrlicher ∼ ⟨fam⟩ *true-penny* ‖ ∼ w *to go to sea* ‖ °Hein ∼ *Jack Tar* **≃männisch** a *sailor-like* ‖ (Fertigkeit etc) *n.t.l* | **~manns-** ∼amt [n] *sailors' registration-office*; ∼sausdruck [m] *sea-term*; ∼shaus [n] *sailors' home*; ∼jacke [f] *pea-jacket*; (zweireihig) *reefer*; ∼kunst [f] *seamanship*; ∼leben [n] *sailoring*; ∼ordnung [f] *regulations* pl *for seamen*; ∼schule [f] *n. school*; ∼weise [f] *sailor-fashion* **~mannschaft** f *ship's crew* ‖ *seamanship* **~marke** f *sea-mark* **≃mäßig** a *seaworthy (packing)*; *suitable for shipment* **~maus** f ⟨zoo⟩ *sea-mouse* **~meile** f *n.t.l mile, seamile, knot* (1852–55 m) ‖ mit 15 ∼ Geschwindigkeit *at a (steady) 15 knots* **~mine** f *n. mine* **~moos** n ⟨bot⟩ *sea-moss* **~möve** f ⟨orn⟩ *seagull, seamew* **~muschel** f *sea-shell* → **Seen-** **~nadel** f ⟨ich⟩ *pipefish* **~nebel** m *fog at sea* **~not** f *distress (at sea)* | ∼boot [n] *sea rescue launch*; ∼dienst [m] *s. r. service*; ∼flugzeug [n] *s. r. plane*; ∼frequenz [f] ⟨wir⟩ *distress fr.*; ∼ruf [m] *d. call*; ∼welle [f] *d. wave-length*; ∼rettungsdienst [m] *(air-) s. r. system* **~offizier** m *n. officer*; *executive officer* N **~otter** m & f ⟨zoo⟩ *sea-otter* **~paß** m *ship's passport* **~pferd** n ⟨myth⟩ *sea-horse* ‖ ⟨zoo⟩ *walrus* **~pferdchen** n ⟨ich⟩ *sea-horse*; ⟨scient⟩ *hippocampus* **~pflanze** f ⟨bot⟩ *(sub)marine plant* **~rabe** m ⟨orn⟩ *cormorant* **~ratte** f ⟨fig⟩ *old salt* **~räuber** m *pirate, buccaneer*; alter ∼! *(old) son of a gun!* | ∼flagge [f] *black jack* | ∼ei [f] *piracy* ‖ ∼ treiben *to pirate, buccaneer*; ≃isch [a] *piratical* **~raum** m *offing* **~recht** n *m.t.e law; law of the sea* ([⟨a.⟩ attr] *conference*) **~reise** f *voyage; cruise* **~rose** f ⟨bot⟩ *water-lily* **~route** f = ∼weg **~rüstung** f *n. armament* **~sache** f *n. affair, n.t.l matter* **~salz** n *bay-salt* **~sand** m *sea-sand* **~schaden** m *sea-damage*; *average* | ∼berechnung [f] *adjustment of averages* **~scharbe** f ⟨orn⟩ *shag* **~schiff** n *sea-going vessel* | ∼(f)ahrt [f] *sea-navigation*; ∼sreederei [f] *ocean shipping company* **~schildkröte** f *turtle* **~schlacht** f *n. battle* od *engagement* **~schlange** f *sea-serpent* ‖ ⟨fam⟩ (Zeitungsente) *mare's nest* **~schlick** m *sea-ooze* **~schule** f *n. school* ‖ ⟨engl Lit⟩ *the Lakists* pl **~schwalbe** f ⟨orn⟩ *sea-swallow, tern, scray* **~sieg** m *n. victory* **~soldat** m *m.* **~sprache** f *n.t.l language* **~staat** m *m.t.e power* **~stabilität** f *seaworthiness* **~stadt** f *seaport* od *seaside* od *m.t.e town* **~station** f *n. st.* **~stern** m *starfish* **~stille** f *calm at sea* **~strand** m *sea-shore, beach* **~straßenordnung** f *Regulations for Preventing Collisions at sea* **~streitkräfte** f pl *n. forces* od *units* **~strich** m *track of the sea* **~stück** n ⟨arts⟩ *waterscape, seascape, sea piece* **~stuka** m ⟨aero⟩ *n. dive-bomber* **~sturm** m *storm at sea* **~stützpunkt** m *n. base* **~taktik** f *n. tactics* pl **~tang** m *dulse, sea-weed* **~teufel** m ⟨ich⟩ *sea-devil; angler, monk* **~tier** n *sea-animal, m. animal* **~tonne** f *buoy* **~transport** m *n. transport* | ∼versicherung [f] *m. insurance* **~treffen** n *sea-fight* **~trift** f *articles washed ashore*; (Wrackgut) *flotsam and jetsam* **~trompete** f ⟨zoo⟩ *conch* **~truppen** f pl *m.s* **≃tüchtig** a *seaworthy (ship)* **~ufer** n *sea-shore; margin of a lake* (am *on the*) **~uhr** f *chronometer* **~ungeheuer** n *sea-monster* **~untüchtigkeit** f *unseaworthiness* **~verkehr** m *oceam-traffic* **~versicherung** f *m. insurance* **~vogel** m *sea-bird* **~volk** n *m.t.e nation*; ≃er [pl] ⟨ant hist⟩ *Sea Peoples* **~walze** f *sea-slug* **~warnung** f *stormwarnings* (erlassen *to raise*) **~warte** f *n. observatory* **≃wärts** [adv] *seaward(s)* **~wasser** n *sea-water* | ≃beständig [a] *s.-w. resistant* **~weg** m *sea lane; voyage* ‖ *sea-route* ‖ auf dem ∼e *by sea*; .. befördert *sea-borne*; auf dem Land- u ∼e ⟨post⟩ *surface mail* (Ggs aero) ‖ ∼ nach .. *passage by sea to India* ‖ ∼e [pl] → Verbindungswege **~wesen** n *n. affairs* pl, *navy* **~wetteramt** n *m. weather station* **~wind** m *sea-breeze; onshore wind* **~wissenschaft** f *n.t.l science* **~wolf** m ⟨ich⟩ *wolf fish, catfish* **~wurf** m (S) *jetsam*; [abstr] *jettison* **~zeichen** n *sea-mark* **~zug** m *n. expedition* **~zunge** f ⟨ich⟩ *sole*

S·eel- **~amt** n ⟨ec⟩ *requiem, office for the dead* **≃erquickend** a *refreshing the soul* **~sorge** f *cure of souls, ministry, ministerial office* **~sorger** m *pastor* **≃sorgerisch** a *pastoral*

S·eele f ∼/∼n **A. 1.** *soul* (gut *dear*; *good*, schön *beautiful*, stolz *proud*, arm *poor*, die deutsche ∼ *the German s.*) ‖ schöne ∼n finden sich *kindred spirits meet* | (seelischer Zustand) *mind* (edel *noble*, gr *great*, kl *small*, rein *pure*) ‖ verwandte ∼n *soulmates*; zwei ∼n u ·ein Gedanke *two minds with but one single thought* ‖ (P) treue ∼ *faithful soul* | [konkr] *the souls (of the blessed)*; *the spirits (of the righteous)* ‖ k e ∼ *not a (living) soul* ‖ 90 ∼n *90 souls* **2.** ⟨übtr⟩ (e–s Federkiels) *pith* ‖ (e–r Geige) *sounding-post* ‖ (e–s Herings) *bladder* ‖ (e–s Seils) *centre*; (e–s ⟨el⟩ Kabels, Taues) *core* ‖ (e–r Schußwaffe) *bore* **3.** ⟨fig⟩ *soul (of nature)* ‖ *spirit (of a landscape)* ‖ (⟨sc⟩ Geld) *sinews* pl (of war) ‖ die ∼ des Ganzen *the very (life* od *heart and) soul of it* (od *them*) *all* ‖ die ∼ aller Kampfführung *the gist of all combat operations* ‖ e–e ∼ v (e–m) Mann, Kind *a love of a man, a darling child* **B.** die ∼ aushauchen (hingeben) *to breathe one's last (to lay down one's life)* ‖ ihr Gesang hat k–e ∼ .. *lacks soul* ‖ sich die ∼ aus dem Leibe husten *to cough o.s. nearly to death* **C.** jdm **an** die ∼ gewachsen *very dear to a p* | jdm **auf** die ∼ binden *to give strict injunctions to a p (to do)* ‖ jdm auf der ∼ brennen [liegen] *to be (preying) on a p's mind* [*to weigh heavily upon a p*] | **aus** ganzer *or* tiefster ∼: *(to love) with all one's soul*; *(to thank) from the bottom of one's heart* ‖ mir aus der ∼ gesprochen! *you have guessed my inmost thoughts!* | **(bei)** m–r ∼! *upon my soul!* | das schneidet mir **durch** die ∼, tut mir **in** der ∼ weh, schmerzt mich .. *that cuts me to the quick* od heart ‖ sich in der ∼ freuen *to be as happy as a king* | in die Tiefe der ∼ schauen *to look into the very soul* ‖ sich in die ∼ hinein schämen *to be thoroughly ashamed of o.s.* || er ist mir in tiefster ~ zuwider *I detest him from the bottom of my heart* | **mit** ganzer ~; *to lend s. to a th* (*to throw o.s.*) *heart and soul* (*into a th*); (*to be*) *h. a. s.* (*in one's work*) || *with all one's might* | **von** ganzer ~ *candidly* **S·eelen-** **~achse** f *axis of the bore* **~adel** m *noble-mindedness, nobility of mind* **~amt** = Seelamt **~angst** f *mental anguish, a. of spirit*; *agony* **~arzt** m *curer of souls* **~brand** m *pangs* pl *of conscience*; *compunction* **~braut** f (*mystical*) *bride of Christ* **~bund** m *union of souls* **~durchmesser** m *caliber of a gun* **~forscher** m *psychologist* **~freund** m *soul-mate* **~frieden** m *peace of mind* **≈froh** a *heartily glad* **~gefährte** m *soul-mate* **~größe** f *greatness of soul* od *mind*; *magnanimity* **≈gut** a *kind-hearted* **~güte** f *kind-heartedness* **~haltung** f *mental attitude* **~heil** n *salvation, spiritual welfare* | ~kunde [f] *psychiatry* **~hirt** m *pastor* **~kampf** m *mental conflict* **~kraft** f *strength of mind* **~leben** n *mental life* **~lehre** f *psychology*; *psychics* pl **~leiden** n *mental suffering* od *trouble* **≈los** a *inanimate* || ⟨fig⟩ *unfeeling, cold, soulless* **~messe** f *requiem, mass for the dead* | ~nregister [n] ⟨RC⟩ *obituary* **~not, ~pein, ~qual** f *agony, anguish* **~rohr** n ⟨artill⟩ *A-tube* **~ruhe** f *tranquillity* (od *peace*) *of mind*; *calmness* **≈ruhig** adv *without turning a hair* **~stärke** f *strength of mind* **≈vergnügt** a *quite charmed* | [adv] *calmly* **~verkäufer** m *kidnapper* || ⟨mil⟩ *recruiting-sergeant* || ⟨mar fam⟩ *cockle-shell* **≈verwandt** a *congenial* (*in mind*) | ≈schaft [f] *congeniality of souls, mental affinity* **≈voll** a *soulful, full of deep feeling* **~wägung** f ⟨ant⟩ *weighing of souls* ⟨a. arts⟩ **~wallung** f *thrill* **~wanderung** f *transmigration of souls, transfiguration, metempsychosis* **~wärmer** m (*woollen*) *comforter* **≈zermürbend** a *soul-destroying* **~zustand** m *frame of mind* **s·eelisch** [a] *psychic*(*al*) (*excitement, equipoise, stagnation*) || *spiritual* (*life, doubts, suffering, cleansing* = Läuterung); *inner* (*sufferings*) || *psychological* (*status* = *state of soul*) | ~e Belastbarkeit *capacity to bear up under psychological stress*; aus dem ~en Gleichgewicht k *to lose one's psychic equipoise*; .. gek s *to have an unbalanced mind* || aus ~en Tiefen *from the depths of the soul* | [adv] ~ empfindsam *psyche-delicate*; ~ mitgenommen *spiritually affected, labouring under some mental indisposition* | **das ≈e** *the psychic*

S·een- ['ze:ən–] **-Distrikt** n (Teil des Kumbrischen Berglandes, → d.) *Lake district* **~platte** f *flat lake district*

S·egel n ~s/~ **A. 1.** *sail* || gr ~ *mainsail* || lose ~ [pl] *spare sails* pl **2.** ⟨fig⟩ (= Schiff) *sail*; 20 ~ *20 sail* pl **3.** (Windmühlen≈) *sail* **4.** ⟨bot⟩ *wing*, ⟨scient⟩ *ala* || ⟨zoo, anat⟩ *veil* **B.** alle ~ **beisetzen** *to crowd all sail* || ~ bergen *to take in the sails* || die ~ einziehen *to shorten sail*; *to reef the sails* || ~ setzen *to set sail* || die ~ streichen *to strike sail*; ⟨fig⟩ *to strike one's colours* (vor [dat] *to*), ⟨fam⟩ *to climb down* **C. mit** vollen ~n ⟨fig⟩ (*to throw o.s.*) *heart and soul* (*into a th*); .. fahren *to crowd all sail, to carry a full press of sail, to boom* | **unter** ~ *under canvas, with her canvas spread* || mit *or* unter vollen ~n *under full* (*pressure of*) *sail* || unter ~ gehen *to set sail, to put to sea* **~baum** m *mast* **~boden** m *sail loft* **~boot** n *sailing* (*s.g*) *boat* || ⟨sport⟩ *yacht* **~fahrt** f *cruise* **≈fertig** a *ready to sail*; *r. for sea* || sich ~ m *to get under sail* **~fläche** f *sail area* **~fliegen** n ⟨aero⟩ *gliding, soaring* **~flieger** m 1. (P) *glider* 2. *gliding machine, sail-plane* **~flug** m *soaring*; *gliding*; (einzelner) *glide* | ~kunde [f] *aerodonetics* [a. sg konstr] | ~schein [m] *g.g certificate*; ~verein [m] *g.g club*; → *feather* II. 1. ; ~zeug [n] = ~flieger 2.; –schlepp [m] *glide towing* **~garn** n *sail-twine* **~handbuch** n *Sailing Directions* **≈klar** a = –fertig **~klasse** f ⟨sport⟩ *rating* **~koje** f *sail locker* **~macher** m *sail-maker* | ~·ei [f] *sail loft* **~persenning** f *sail-cover* **~schiff** n *s.g.-vessel, s.g-ship*; gr ⟨fam⟩ *windjammer* **~schiffahrt** f *navigation by sail* **~schlitten** m *ice-yacht* **~schulschiff** n *s.g training ship* **~sport** m *yachting* **~stag** n *pier* **~stange** f *yard* **~tuch** n *sail-cloth, canvas*; || (geteertes) *tarpaulin*; (leichtes) *duck* | ~hose [f] *ducks* pl; ~plane [f] *canvas, parasol*; ~sack m ⟨Am mil⟩ *duffel bag*; ~schuhe [m pl] *duck shoes*, ⟨Am sl⟩ *sneakers* **~werk** n *sails and rigging* **~wettfahrt** f *regatta, s.g-match* **~wind** m *favourable wind* **s·egeln** vi [h & s] *to sail* (⟨a. orn⟩; *to plane*) || ⟨sport⟩ *to yacht, to go yachting* (v Wolken) *to float in the air* | wir h viel ge–lt *we have done a lot of sailing* || die Jacht segelt gut .. *is a good sailer* | sich fest ~ *to run aground* || .. tot ~ *to outstrip a boat* | **auf** etw los|~ *to head for a th* ⟨a. fig⟩ | **aus**: *to steer* (*one's way*) *out of* | ein Schiff **in** den Grund ~ *to run down* | **längs** der Küste ~ *to coast along* | **nach**: *to make sail for* (*Africa*), *to set sail* (*westwards*) | **um** ein Kap ~ *to double a cape* | ⟨fig⟩ **unter** fremden Namen ~ ⟨liter⟩ *to go under other names*

S·egen m ~s/~ ⟨ec⟩ *benediction* || *blessing* (*the bl.s of work*) || (Zauberformel) *spell* || (Ertrag) *yield*; *the produce* (*of mining*) || (Fülle) *abundance* || *children are the gift of God* | ein **wahrer** ~ *a great boon* (f *to*) || es ist ein wahrer ~ *it is quite a mercy* (daß *that*); *a perfect godsend* | es ist **kein** ~ dabei *it's a failure*; .. bei s–r Arbeit *he has no luck with* .. || das bringt k–n ~ *that will not bring* (*you*) *any luck* | Gott **gebe** s–n ~ dazu *God's blessing on it* || e–m s–n ~ geben, erteilen *to give a p one's blessing* || den ~ m *to make the sign of the cross* || den ~ sprechen *to give the benediction*, (Tischgebet) *to say grace* || ⟨iron⟩ m–n ~ h Sie! (*have it!*) *for what it is worth* | **an** Gottes ~ ist alles gelegen *God's blessing gained, all is obtained* **≈bringend** a *beneficial*; *bringing luck* **~erteilung** f ⟨ec⟩ *benediction* **≈spendend** a *benedictive, beneficial, blessing, blessed* || ⟨fig⟩ *fertile, abundant* **~sprecher** m = Segner **S·egens-** **≈reich** a *blessed* || *lucky, prosperous* **~spruch, ~wunsch** m *blessing, benediction*; [pl] *good wishes* pl

S·egge f ~/~n [ndd] (Riedgras) ⟨bot⟩ *sedge*

S·egler m ~s/~ (P) *yachtsman, cruiser* || (Schiff) *sailing-vessel*, (guter, schlechter, schneller etc *good, bad, fast* etc) *sailer* || ⟨orn⟩ → *swift* || (Wolken) *aerial travellers* **~in** f ~/~nen *yachtswoman* **~verein** m *sailing* od *yachting club*

Segm·ent n ~(e)s/~e *segment* **~bogen** m *s.al arch*

s·egnen vt [h] *to bless* | *to make the sign of the cross on*; *to cross* (⟨a.⟩ sich *o.s.*) || ⟨ec⟩ *to consecrate* | der H. segne .. *heaven speed* (*your efforts*) || wir ~ .. *we bless* (*the hour*), .. d–n Entschluß *your d. has our blessing* || ~d ⟨ec⟩ a *in blessing* | **gesegnet** *prosperous* (*New Year*); *blessed* (*country*), *blest* (*with children*), *sound* (*sleep*) || g.en Leibes, in g.en Umständen *in interesting circumstances*, ⟨fam⟩ *in the family way* || g.en Andenkens *of blessed memory* || ein G.er des Herrn *a man blessed by God* **S·egner** m ~s/~ *blesser*; *pronouncer of a blessing* od *of the benediction* **S·egnung** f ~/~en *benediction, blessing*

S·eh- *v.*(*isua*)*l*, *v.*(*isio*)*n*, *s.*(*ight*), **~achse** f *axis of s.* **~fehler** m *defect of v.n* **~feld** n, **~kreis** m *field of v.n* | im **~funk** m *on television* **~hilfen** f pl *aids to vision* **~hügel** m ⟨anat⟩ *optic thalamus* **~kraft** f *v.l faculty* od *power*; *s.* **~lehre** f *optics* pl **~linie** f ⟨phys⟩ *line of collimation* **~loch** n *pin-hole* **~nerv** m *v.l* od *optic nerve* **~organ** n *v.l organ* **~punkt** m *point of view* **~rohr** n (e–s Unterseebootes) *periscope* || (Fernrohr) *telescope* **~schärfe** f *s.*; auf ~ einstellen *to focus* **~schlitz** m *observation* od *vision slit* **~spalt** m *peep* (*-hole*); (Helm≈) *eye-slit* **~vermögen** n *v.l faculty* od *power strength of v.n* **~weite** f *range* od *field of v.n*, (*reach of*) *s.*; *visual range* ‖ in (außer) ∼ *within* (*out of*) *s.* od *eyeshot* ‖ in Seh- u Hörweite *within sight and sound* | ∼n-messer [m] *optometer* **∼werkzeug** n *v.l organ* **∼winkel** m *angle of s.* **S·ehen** n ∼s/ *seeing, looking* ‖ ⟨physiol⟩ *vision* ‖ (Sehvermögen) (*eye*)-*sight*; deutliches ∼ *distinct vision*; skotoptisches ∼ ⟨physiol⟩ *scotoptic* od *twilight vision*; räumliches ∼ *perception of depth* ‖ beim ersten ∼ *on* (*first*) *sight* ‖ vom ∼ (*I only know him*) *by sight*

s·ehen [sah/ge∼] [h] **I. vi** *to see, look* ‖ ⟨physiol⟩ *to be endowed with sight* ‖ wieder ∼d w *to regain one's sight* ‖ die Blinden ∼d m *to make the blind see* ‖ mit ∼den Augen blind s *to walk about with one's eyes shut* **A.** → **ähnlich** I. 2. a ‖ ernst drein|∼ *to look serious* ‖ gut (schlecht) ∼ *to have good* (*bad*) *eyes* ‖ ich sehe schlecht *my* (*eye*)*sight is bad* ‖ scharf ∼ *to be clear-sighted* **B.** [eingeschaltet] **1.** er ist, sehe ich (*or* wie ich sehe), nicht da *I see he is not here* **2.** ⟨fam⟩ haste (= hast du) nicht gesehn! *helter-skelter*; ⟨fam⟩ *before you could say Jack Robinson*; *like a shot* **3.** [imp] siehe oben (unten) [abbr s. o. (s. u.)] *see above* (*below*) **4.** [intj] und, siehe, .. *behold* od *lo* **C.** [imp] ∼ Sie mal! *just* od *do come and see*!, *look here*! ‖ ∼ Sie nur! *just, only look*! ‖ sieh, da hat er .. *see now, he has* .. ‖ sieh da! *look there*!, *bang*! ‖ ei sieh doch, ..! *what*! .., *well, I declare* ..! ‖ ⟨iron⟩ sieh mal an! *indeed*! sieh e–r (an)! *I say*! **D.** (bemerken) ∼ Sie, **wie** ..? *do you notice how* ..? | (erkennen) auf den ersten Blick ∼, **daß** *to see with half an eye that* .. ‖ ich sehe, daß Sie recht h *I see* (*that*) *you are right* ‖ ⟨fam⟩ da ∼ Sie, **wie** er ist! *that's the man he is*! ‖ da ∼ Sie's selbst *that goes to show you* | (erleben) hier ∼ wir, er .. *here he is risking his life* ‖ ich möchte doch ∼, **was** er an m–r Stelle täte *I should like to see him in my place* ‖ das möchte ich denn doch mal ∼! *I'd watch it*! | (dafür sorgen) ich werde schon ∼, **wo** ich bleibe *I shall look after m.s. all right*; *she would see that he did not do it* ‖ du wirst schon ∼, **wie** du damit fertig wirst *I dare say you will manage it* ‖ ∼ Sie, **daß** .. *take care that you don't lose it* | (versuchen) ∼, wie weit man bei jdm gehen kann *to try it on with a p* ‖ ich will ∼, daß *or* ob ich es kriege *I'll try to get it* (*for you*) (vgl. II. A.) **E. an** [dat]: *by her eyes I could see that* | **auf** [acc]: *to look at, to set eyes upon* ‖ *all eyes are upon her* ‖ ∼ Sie darauf! *look* od *see to it*! *of course she did not see to it h.s., but she saw to it that the butler should see to it* ‖ (daß *that*): *mind that* ..! ‖ e–m auf die Finger ∼ *to watch a p closely* ‖ auf Gehalt ∼ wir nicht *salary is no consideration* (*to us*), *we don't mind the s.* ‖ das war auf e–e Meile z ∼ ⟨a. fig⟩ *that stuck out a m.* | **aus** [dat]: *to look out of* od *at the window* ‖ ⟨fig fam⟩ *his toes peep out of his socks* ‖ ich kann kaum aus den Augen ∼ *I'm unable to open my eyes* ‖ daraus ist zu ∼, daß *hence it appears* (*to me*) *that* ‖ hinter e–m her|∼ *to gaze after a p* | **in** [acc]: *to look into* ‖ e–m ins Gesicht (Herz) ∼ *to look into a p's face*, (scharf) *to look a p in the f.* (*to read a p's heart*) ‖ *to glance in a mirror* ‖ *to look each other in the eyes*; er sah ihr ins Auge *he met her eyes*; jdm ins Gesicht ∼ *to face a p* ‖ in die Zukunft ∼ *to dive into the future*, weit .. *to look far ahead* | **mit** e–m Auge ∼ *to apply one eye*; ⟨übtr⟩ *to see with half an eye* | **nach**: *to look at* (*the clock, one's watch*) ‖ (suchend) *to look for*, (sorgend) *to look after*; *to see to* (*the oven*) ‖ (v Fenster, Zimmer) *to overlook the garden, to face the street* ‖ nach dem Rechten ∼ *to see that everything is done properly* od *is in order* | siehe **unter** „sanft"! *see at soft*! | **vor** sich hin|∼ *to face ahead, to fix one's eyes straight before one* **II. vt** *to see*; ⟨mst poet⟩ *behold* ‖ (wahrnehmen) *to perceive, notice* ‖ (betrachten) *to look at* **A.** nur **flüchtig** *to get but a glimpse of* ‖ gern ∼ *to approve of, to like* ‖ sähen Sie (es) gern, wenn ich es schickte? *would you like me to send it*?, *would you care for me to send it*? (vgl. I. D.) ‖ gut: *I had a good look at them* ‖ klar: *to see a th clearly* | sie ∼ in dem Ort ihre zukünftige H. *they look to the place for their future capital* | **sich** (in e–r Situation) ∼ *to visualize o.s.* .. ‖ **sich** ∼ **als** *to envisage o.s. as* ‖ **sich satt** ∼ *to feast one's eyes* **B.** (abwarten) das müssen wir erst ∼ *that remains to be seen* | (besichtigen) *would you like to walk over the library* | (ein∼) [oft ell] da ∼ Sie['s] *so there*!, *there now*!, *there you are*! | (bewirten) *to entertain some guests* (vgl G.) | (erleben) da sah man's wieder *but there it was* ‖ da ∼ Sie's selbst! *see for y.s.*; *that just goes to show you*; du sollst, wirst es ∼ (*you*) *see if I don't* ‖ ich möchte den ∼, der .. *I defy anybody to do it* ‖ hat man je so etw ge∼? *can you beat it*? | (leiden) sie kann ihn nicht ∼ *she can't bear the sight of him* | (treffen) *to meet*; sie ∼ sich (= e–a) selten *they meet seldom* od *infrequently*; sie tat, als ob sie ihn noch nie ge∼ hätte *she gave him no sign of recognition* | (Zeuge s v) *to witness* (*a ballot*) **C. als** er ihn (zuerst) sah *at the sight of him* (*on his first sight of him*) ‖ das letztemal, als *or* daß .. *the last he saw of them was* .. ‖ .. mehr als man sah *there was more than meets the eye* ‖ soviel wir ∼ *for aught we see* **D.** etw **nicht ∼ wollen** *to blink a th, to turn a blind eye to it, to pretend not to see it, to shut one's eyes on it*; *to blind o.s. to the facts* ‖ man will sie nirgends ∼ *no one will receive them*; ich will (ihn/es) noch einmal ∼ *I want a last look at* .. **E. ∼ lassen** *to show, display* ‖ l Sie mich ∼! *let me look* ‖ **sich** ∼ l *to be visible, to show o.s.*; ⟨com⟩ *to show the flag* ‖ ⟨dero⟩ *to make a show* (*of o.s.*) ‖ *to appear*, ⟨fig⟩ *to parade* ‖ (sich einführen) *to present o.s.*; sich nicht wieder ∼ l *not to show one's face again* ‖ etw, das sich ∼ l kann *sth to be proud* (*not to be ashamed*) *of*; das kann sich ∼ l, damit kannst du dich ∼ l! *not bad*! *you have no need to be ashamed of it*! ‖ er kann sich f Geld ∼ l *he is ripe for an exhibition of curiosities*, ⟨Am sl⟩ *he's a knock-out* | sich **nicht** ∼ l *to keep out of sight*; *he never shows up at balls* ‖ wir l uns (⟨sc⟩ f Besucher) nicht ∼ *we are not at home* ‖ *they won't be seen by anybody* (v niemandem), sie h sich nicht wieder ∼ l *they never turned up again* ‖ warum l Sie sich gar nicht mehr ∼? *why doesn't one ever see you now*? *you are quite a stranger* ‖ laß dich hier nicht wieder ∼! *don't show your face here again*! **F. zu ∼** s *to be visible* ‖ *only the roof showed over the hedge* ‖ *it was long on view* ‖ jdn (jds Gesicht ganz) z ∼ bek *to clap eyes upon a p* (*to get a full view of* ..) ‖ es ist f Geld z ∼ *it is exhibited* | **nicht** z ∼ s *to be out of sight* ‖ *nobody was in sight* ‖ es ist dort nichts z ∼ *there is nothing worth seeing there*; er bekam viel Neues z ∼ *he was shown many new ths*; die Dinge v e–r anderen Seite z ∼ bek *to be shown the other side of the picture* **G.** (oft) **Gäste** bei sich ∼ *to receive* (*a great deal of*) *company* (vgl B. & K.) ‖ das Licht der Sonne ∼ *to be in the land of the living* ‖ weiße Mäuse ∼ *to see snakes* ‖ er konnte es nicht aushalten, ohne **sie** z ∼ *he could not bear her out of his sight* ‖ wir ∼ **nichts** *we can't see anything* ‖ nun sieh mal diesen ..! *now here is a rascal*! ‖ sich ∼ **als**: *she saw h.s. a mother* **H.** [acc + inf] ich sah ihn k *I saw him come* (= daß er kam), *I saw him coming* (= wie er kam) ‖ wir h es k ∼ (= ge∼) *we knew it would happen* **I. sich** im Spiegel ∼ *to see o.s. in* .. | sich **blind** ∼ *to stare one's eyes out* (nach *after*) ‖ sich **satt** ∼ *to feast one's eyes* (an *on*) | [recip] (treffen) sie ∼ sich nicht oft *they don't see much of one another* ‖ wir ∼ uns recht oft *we see quite a lot of each other* ‖ wir h uns lange nicht ge∼ *it is such a long time since we have met* **K. auf** den Preis wird nicht (vor allem) ge~ [imps] *the price is no object* (*is the first consideration*) (vgl. I. E.) | er würde sich freuen, ihn bald einmal zu e–m (einfachen) Abendessen **bei** sich zu ~ *he requested the pleasure of his company at dinner on an early day*, (⟨hum⟩ *he hoped to have the pleasure of seeing him to cut mutton with him before long*) | alles **im** rosigsten Lichte ~ *to see the sunny side of everything*; sie ~ in ihm ihren Feind *they regard him as e.* | wir hören u ~ nichts mehr **von** ihm *we neither see nor hear anything of him now* | sich e–r Aufgabe gegenüber ~ *to be faced with a task* **L. ~d:** der, die ≃de (Ggs Blinde) *the sighted* (Ggs *sightless*) **M. gesehen:** agronomisch g. *agronomically speaking* ‖ g. w *to be seen* ‖ v jdm g. w *to catch a p's eye* ‖ v allen g. w *to meet all eyes* ‖ g. w können: *the hill is not to be seen at its finest from here* ‖ er ist überall gern g. *he is liked by everybody* od *welcome everywhere* ‖ sie w überall zus g. *they are always seen about together* **s·ehens- ~wert, ~würdig** a *sightworthy*; *worth seeing*; *remarkable*; *viewable* ⟨bes telv⟩ **≃würdigkeit** f *curiosity, sight, object* od *place of interest* ‖ ~en [pl] *sights* (*of a town*) ‖ die ~en besichtigen *to go sight-seeing, to see the sights*; ⟨Am⟩ *to go places*; ⟨sl⟩ *to see the lions* (⟨Am⟩ *the elephant*) **S·eher** m ~s/~ *seer, prophet* | **~in** f *prophetess* ‖ (Hellseher[in]) *clairvoyant*(*e*) **~blick** m, **~gabe** f *prophetic gift* | **≃isch** a *mantic*

S·ehne f ~/~n ⟨anat⟩ *sinew, tendon* ‖ (Bogen-≃) *string*; ⟨math⟩ *chord* ‖ mit e–r ~ beziehen *to string* (*a bow*) **~nband** n ⟨anat⟩ (*tendinous*) *ligament* **~nscheide** f *sheath covering a tendon* **s·ehnig** a *sinewy* (*arms*), *stringy, tough* (*meat*) ‖ *brawny, wiry, stringy* (*p*)

s·ehnen I. sich ~ [h] (nach) *to long, ache, hunger, languish* (*for*); *to yearn* (*for, after*) ‖ .., nach der er sich –nte ⟨a.⟩ *the longed-for* ‖ (schmerzlich) *to grieve* od *pine after* ‖ sich heim-~ *to be homesick* ‖ sich aufs Land ~ *to yearn to be in the country* ‖ *to wish for glory* ‖ *to wish to do*; → sehr A. 2. **II.** ≃ n ~s/ *longing, yearning* **s·ehnlich** a *sincere, earnest, eager, passionate, ardent, longing* | [adv] *anxiously* **S·ehnsucht** f ~/ *intense longing, ardent desire* (nach *for*), *yearning* (*for, after*) ‖ [konkr] *ideal* **~sgefühl** n *nostalgia* **≃svoll, s·ehnsüchtig** a *longing, yearning, wistful* ‖ *burning* (*desire*) ‖ [adv] (*to wait*) *anxiously* (*for*)

sehr [adv] **A. 1.** [vor a, a–part, adv] *very* (*good*; *interesting, pleased, celebrated*; *dearly, well*); das ist ~ nett v Ihnen *it is too kind of you* ‖ *greatly* (*proud*) ‖ *sadly* (*hampered*) | [vor mehrsilbigem a] ⟨a.⟩ *most* (*delightful*) | ≃ geehrter Herr N. *Dear Sir* ‖ ~ verehrte Anwesende *my esteemed hearers* **2.** [vor reinem pp u Verb] *much, very much, greatly, highly* (*annoyed, respected*) | (*to exert o.s.*) *to the utmost* | sich sehr nach e–r Beschäftigung sehnen *to want badly a th to do* **B.** ⟨fam⟩ *mighty, jolly, terribly, frightfully* | ich bin ~ in Eile *I'm in an awful hurry* | (bes v Frauen) *ever so* (*far, small, many*) ‖ (bes v Männern) *nothing if not* (*courageous*); ⟨Am⟩ *real* (*good time*) **C. danke** ~! *thanks very much*! – Bitte ~! *Not at all*!, *don't mention it*!, ⟨Am⟩ *you are welcome* ‖ ebenso ~ *just as much* ‖ ~ **gern** *most willingly* ‖ (*he knows*) *perfectly well* (*that* ..) | ~ **im** Rückstand *much behindhand* | ~ **mit** Unrecht glauben *to make a great mistake in believing* | ~ **oft** ⟨a.⟩ *as often as not* ‖ recht ~ *greatly* ‖ so ~, daß *so much* (od *to such a degree*) *that* .. | ~ **viel** *a good* od *great deal of* od *plenty of* (*money*) ‖ ~ viele *a great many* ‖ ~ wenig ⟨a.⟩ *little enough* | **wie** ~ auch [immer] *however much* od *much as* (*he may try*) | er wäre dazu ~ **wohl** imstande *he could easily manage it* | **zu** ~ *much too* (*cold*); (*it vexed him*) *too much* ‖ zu ~ Kind *too much of a child* ‖ nur zu ~ (*the play is Senecan*) *to a fault* ‖ zu ~ in Anspruch nehmen *to overstrain*

°**Seich** m ~(e)s/ **S·eiche** f ~/ **1.** *urine*, ⟨vulg⟩ *piss* **2.** ⟨sl⟩ *twaddle*; *hot air* °**Seichbeutel,** Seicher m *windbag*; er ist ein furchtbarer ~ ⟨vulg⟩ *he's all piss and wind* **s·eichen** vi [h] (v. Rindern etc) *to urine, piss*; *to make water* ‖ ⟨sl⟩ *to twaddle, palaver, vapour, platitudinize*; *to talk rubbish*

seicht a ⟨a. fig⟩ *shallow* ‖ ⟨fig⟩ *insipid* (*novel, conversation*); *superficial* (*character, p*); (leichtfertig) *flippant*; *wishy-washy* (*talk*); *flimsy* (*art*); ~e Redensarten *platitudes* **~köpfig** a *shallow-pated, -brained* **S·eichtheit, Seichtigkeit** f ~/~en ⟨a. fig⟩ *shallowness* ‖ ⟨fig⟩ *insipidity, superficiality*

S·eidel n ~s/~ (Maß) *pint* ‖ (Trinkgefäß) *mug*; (gr) *tankard, seidel*, ⟨Am⟩ *stein*

S·eidelbast m ⟨bot⟩ *spurge-laurel, daphne*

S·eide f ~/~n *silk* (roh *raw*) ‖ künstliche ~ ⟨Am⟩ *rayon* ‖ die beiden spinnen k–e ~ *those two don't hit it off well* ‖ er wird dabei k–e ~ sp. *he won't gain much by it* **s·eiden** a *silk* (*gown*), *silken* (*thread* ⟨a. fig⟩, *hair*) **S·eiden- ~abfall** m *waste-silk* **~äffchen** n *marmoset* **~arbeit** f *s.-work* **~arbeiter** m *s.-weaver* **≃artig** a *s.y, s.-like* **~bau** m *s.-culture*, ⟨scient⟩ *sericulture*; *rearing* od *culture of s.-worms* **~drucker** m *s.-*(*stuff*) *printer* **~ernte** f *yield of cocoons* **~fabrik** f *s.-factory* **~fabrikant** m *s.-manufacturer* **~faden** m *s. thread* **~färber** m *s.-dyer* **~flor** m = ~gaze **~garn** n *spun s., s. yarn* **~gaze** f *s. gauze* **~gehäuse** n *cocoon* **~glanz** m *s.y lustre* ‖ (dem Haar) ~ geben ⟨Am⟩ *to glamorize* **≃glatt** a *silkily smooth* **~haar** n *s.en hair* **~hase** m *Angora rabbit* **~haspel** m & f *s.-reel* **~kocherei** f *degumming of silk* **~krepp** m *georgette* **~lamp·as** m *figured silk*; *lampas* **~papier** n *tissue-paper* **~plüsch** m *s.-plush* **~raupe** f *s.worm* **~reiher** m ⟨orn⟩ *little aigrette* **~schnur** f *s.-lace* **~schwanz** m ⟨orn⟩ *s.-tail, waxwing* **~spinner** m (P) *s.-spinner* ‖ ⟨zoo⟩ *s.-moth* **~spinner·ei** f *s.-spinning mill* **~spitz** m *Pomeranian* (*dog*) *with s.y hair* **~-sticker** m *s.-embroiderer* | ~·ei [f] *s.-e.dery* **~stoffe** m [pl] *s.s* pl **~ware** f *s.-ware, s.-goods* pl | ~nhändler [m] *mercer* **~weber** m *s.-weaver* **~wickler** m ⟨tech⟩ *s.-reeler* **~winde** f *s.-winder* **~wirker** m *s.-weaver* **~wurm** m *s.worm* | ≃erzucht [f] *sericulture, s.*(*worm*)*-nursery* **~zeug** m *s.* (*cloth, goods, material*) | ~weber·ei [f] *broad-s. weaving* **~zucht** f *s.worm breeding* **~zwirn** m *s.-thread* **~zwirner·ei** f *s.-thread factory* **s·eidig** a *silky*; *sericeous*

S·eife f ~/~n **1.** *soap* ‖ grüne ~ *soft s.* ‖ ~ sieden *to boil s.* ‖ ein Stück ~ *a cake of s.* **2.** ⟨geol⟩ *placer* **3.** ⟨min⟩ *stream-works* [sg konstr] **s·eifen** vt [h] *to* (*smear* od *rub with*) *soap* ‖ ⟨min⟩ *to stream* **S·eifen- ≃artig** a *soapy*, ⟨scient⟩ *saponaceous* **~asche** f *soap-ashes* pl **~bad** n *s.-bath* **~bau** m *alluvial ore mining* **~baum** m *s.-tree* **~bildung** f ⟨chem⟩ *saponification* **~blase** f *s.-bubble*; ~n m *to blow bubbles* ‖ ⟨fig⟩ *bubble* **~erde** f *fuller's earth* **~flocken** f pl *soap flakes* **~kessel** m *s.-pan* **~kisten-** ~redner [m] *s.-box orator*; ~rennen [n] *s.-b. derby* **~kraut** n ⟨bot⟩ *s.wort, fuller's herb* **~kugel** f *s.-ball* **~lauge** f *s.-lye, s.-suds* pl **~näpfchen** n *s.-dish* **~pflaster** n *s.-plaster* **~pulver** n *s.-powder* **~riegel** m *s.-bar* **~schaum** m *lather* **~sieder** m *s.-boiler*; ⟨fam⟩ jetzt geht mir ein ~ auf *now it dawns upon me* | ~·ei [f] *s.-works* [sg konstr] **~spender** m *s. dispenser* **~spiritus** m ⟨chem⟩ *spirit of s.* **~stein** m ⟨min⟩ *s.stone*; *steatite* **~wasser** n *s.-suds* pl, *s.y-water* **~zäpfchen** n ⟨med⟩ *suppository* **~zinn** n *stream-tin* **s·eifig** a *soapy*, ⟨scient⟩ *saponaceous*

S·eiger m ~s/~ ⟨tech⟩ *plummet* ‖ (Sanduhr) *hourglass* | **≃n** vt [h] ⟨min⟩ *to sink a shaft* **≃(gerade)** [a & adv] *straight down, vertical* **s·eigern** vt [h] ⟨met⟩ *to refine, liquate* **S·eiger-**

~arbeiter m *refiner* **~herd** m *cupelling-furnace* **~hütte** f *refining-house* **S·eigerung** f ~/~en ⟨met⟩ *refining, liquation* | ~szone [f] *line of segregation*

S·eih- ~gefäß n *filtering-vessel* **~sack** m *straining-bag* **~trichter** m *colander* **~tuch** n *filtering-, straining-cloth, strainer* **S·eihe** f ~/~n *strainer, colander, filter* ‖ (Rückstand) *dregs* pl **s·eihen** vt [h] *to strain, filter*

Seil n ~(e)s/~e *rope* ‖ (Tau) *cable* ‖ schlaffes (straffes) *slack* (*tight*, ⟨mar⟩ *taut*) *r.* ‖ aus Betttüchern gedrehtes ~ *blanket rope* ‖ Draht≈ *wire r.* ‖ Förder≈ *winding c.* ‖ Halt(e)≈ *tether; picket line* ‖ Leit≈ *guide-r.* ‖ ⟨mount⟩ *rappel rope* ‖ Schlepp≈ *towing c.* ‖ Spring≈ *skipping-r.* ‖ Stroh≈ *binder, wisp of straw* | ~ springen *to skip* ‖ **am** ~ hoch-, (nach)ziehen *to hoist on* (*drag by*) *a r.* ‖ sich am ~e führen l *to be led by the nose* ‖ an einem ~ ziehen *to row in the same boat* ‖ **auf** dem ~ tanzen *to dance on the tight-r.* **~bahn** f *c. railway, r.way; funicular; overhead railway* **~bohren** n ⟨min⟩ *r.-boring* **~bremse** f *c. brake* **~brücke** f *c.-bridge* **~dreher** m *r.-twister* **~fähre** f *trail* od *c. ferry* **~fahrt** f ⟨min⟩ *descending by the r.* **~führungsrolle** f *c. pulley* **~geschirr** n *twister* **~hüpfen** n *skipping* (*the r.*) **~rettungsgerät** n *r. escape* **≈tanzen** n *to walk the tight r.* **~tänzer(in** f) m *r.-dancer* **~tänzerei** f *walking the tight r.*; ⟨pol⟩ *brinkmanship* **~trommel** f *c.-drum* **~winde** f (f Lkw) *truck winch* **~ziehen** n ⟨sport⟩ *tug of war* **~zug** m *c.-pull* | ≈e pl ⟨theat⟩ *track wires* **S·eiler** m ~s/~ *r.-maker, r.r* **~bahn** f *r.-walk* **~meister** m = Seiler **~rad** n *r.-maker's wheel* **~waren** f [pl] *cordage* **Seiler·ei** f ~/ *r.-making* ‖ (Werkstatt) *ropery* **S·eilschaft** f ~/~en ⟨mount⟩ *r.d party*

Seim m ~(e)s~e *mucilage, mucilaginous fluid* ‖ (Honig) *strained honey* | **≈en** vt [h] *to strain* (*honey*) | vi [h] *to yield* (*honey* etc.) | **≈ig** a *mucilaginous*

Sein n ~s/ *being* ‖ (Da-~) *existence*, ⟨scient⟩ *entity* | (So-~) *essence, true nature* ‖ ~ u Schein *reality and pretence* ‖ das Ende alles ~s .. *of all ths* ‖ ~ oder Nicht≈ .. *to be or not to be* (*that is the question*) **sein** [war/gewesen (gw)] **I. [v/aux]** [bei vielen vi] *to have* (*arrived, come, died, fallen*) ‖ [ell] wie weit sind wir (⟨sc⟩ gek)? *how far have we got*? **II. vi** [s] **A. [als Kopula]** ich bin's ⟨bib⟩ *it is I* (⟨fam⟩ *me*)! oh, Sie sind es! *oh, it's you*! ‖ er ist reich (ein Dichter) *he is rich* (*a poet*), .. 9 Jahre alt .. *9 years old* ‖ er ist 6 Zoll größer als ich *he stands 6 in. higher than I* od ⟨fam⟩ *me* ‖ *Punch is no longer* (nicht mehr) *what it used to be* (was es war)! – *Never was*! (war es nie!) so **war es denn** auch: der alte Herr hatte s–n Hut wieder und die Menge zog vergnügt vondannen ⟨fam⟩ *then the band played* ‖ N.s Ansicht war die richtige *N's was the accurate theory* | **sei(d** pl) still! *be quiet*; sei(d) nicht so dumm! *don't be so stupid*! | e–m gut (böse) ~ *to be fond of a p, to like a p* (*to be cross with a p*) | ⟨arith⟩ 3 mal 3 ist 9 *three times 3 is 9* ‖ 6 u 3 ist 9 *six and 3 are 9* | das **wäre** ein Gedanke! *that's a good idea* ‖ .. – Und das wäre? .. – *What's that*?; so das wär's *so that's that* ‖ erfolglos ~ *to prove abortive* | [ell] das ist aber doch (⟨sc⟩ stark)! *that's coming it rather strong* ‖ ei, das wäre (⟨sc⟩ noch schöner)! *well!, well, I never!, you don't say so*! | es ist **anzustreben** *a constant objective should be to* ..; sie ist **zu bedauern** *she is to be pitied* ‖ es ist nicht z befürchten, daß er .. *there is no fear of his being late* ‖ es war z erwarten, daß *it was to be expected that* .. ‖ (anordnend) .. ist geschlossen z halten *will be kept closed* ‖ ich bin nicht z sprechen *I'm busy* od *engaged* ‖ ist Herr N. z sprechen? *can I see Mr. N.*? ‖ das Haus ist z vermieten .. *is to let*; .. seit Jahren .. *has been to let for years* | ich bin **der Meinung** [gen], daß *it is my opinion that* .. ‖ du bist wohl ganz des Teufels! *I think you are mad*! ‖ des Todes ~ *to be a dead man* | **es ist** alles eins *nothing matters*; es ist weit, spät *it is far, late* ‖ es ist ein Jahr, daß .. *he left a year ago, it is now a year since he left* ‖ nun will es k–r gewesen ~ *and now no one admits having done it* ‖ hier ist('s) teuer leben *it is expensive living here* ‖ ich weiß nicht, ob es nicht besser wäre .. *not that it mightn't be better to leave* ‖ wie ist's? *how do matters stand*? ‖ es ist nun mal so *but there it is* ‖ es ist, als ob .. *it would seem as if* .. ‖ **es sei,** sei's drum! *granted*! ‖ es sei! *be it so*! ‖ x sei .. *let x be the unknown* ‖ es sei *or* wäre denn, daß *unless* (*it be thus*) ‖ sei es .. oder .. *whether .. or* .. ‖ sei es im Guten oder Bösen *for better* (*or*) *for worse* ‖ sei es auch noch so viel *be it ever so much* | (es) sei dem, wie ihm wolle *however this may be* | **mir ist('s)** warm (schlecht, übel) *I feel warm* (*sick*) ‖ was ist dir? *what's the matter with you* ‖ wie ist Ihnen? *how do you feel*?, *how are you*? ‖ es ist ihm nur ums Geld *he only thinks of* (*the*) *money* ‖ es war mir, als ob ich träumte *it seemed to me that I was dreaming*; mir war (so), als ob ich .. hätte *I felt as if I had, I fancied* od *thought I had* **B. (bedeuten)** was soll das ~? *what does that mean* ‖ ich dachte wunder, was es wäre *I expected sth wonderful* | **(vorhanden ~)** *to be there, to exist, live* ‖ wäre er nicht gw *but for him* (od *if it had not been for him*) ‖ das ist gw *that is at an end* ‖ alles was war u ist *ths past and present* ‖ was nicht ist, kann noch w *time will show* ‖ [ell] ⟨fam⟩ ist nicht! *nothing of the kind*! | **(stattfinden)** *to happen, to take place* ‖ die Schlacht war am 5. .. *was fought on the 5th* ‖ *the address will be given tonight* | **(sich befinden)** da wären wir! *and so here we are*! ‖ wie lange sind Sie (schon) hier? *how long have you been here*? .. waren Sie dort? *how long were you there* ‖ °das ist nicht drin *that won't pay*; *it is not worth my* (etc) *while*; *it's no use doing it* | **(sich verhalten)** so ist's *that's it, that's how it is* ‖ wäre das nicht so gw *if that had not been the case* ‖ wie wir gerade waren *as we stood* **C.** es **mag** ~ *granted it be so* ‖ das **kann** nicht ~ *that is impossible* ‖ kann ~ *perhaps*, ⟨Am⟩ *may be* ‖ etw ~ **lassen** *to leave a th alone* ‖ laß gut ~! *let it be*! laß das ~! *stop it*! **D.** es ist **an** ihm *it's* (*up to him* od) *for him to do it* ‖ gut daran ~ *to be well off* ‖ .., woran wir sind (*we know now*) *where we stand* | er ist **aus** der Schweiz *he comes from Sw.* | **bei**: *have you seen a doctor*? ‖ ⟨fam⟩ *Mr. N. has been to see you* ‖ bei Kasse ~ *to be in funds* | zuviel ~ **für**: *the blow had proved too much for him* ‖ dafür ~ zu gehen *to be for going* | **hinter** M. her ~ *to be gadding after girls* | **in** Genf ~ *to be at G.* ‖ **mit** ihm ist es dasselbe *he is in the same position* ‖ wie ist's damit? *what about it*? ‖ wie wär's mit ..? *what's wrong with a cup of tea*? | [ell] er ist **nach** Rom (⟨sc⟩ gefahren) *he has gone to R.* | er ist **von** hier *he belongs here*

Seine ['sɛnə] f ⟨Fr⟩ (Fluß) → Pariser Becken

sein I. [⟨poet⟩ gen v er & es (= ~er)] gedenke ~ *remember him* ‖ ~er nicht mehr mächtig s *to have lost control of o.s.* **II.** [pron poss] **A. 1.** m & n *his* (*father, book*) ‖ ~e [f & pl] *his* (*mother, children*) ‖ S–e Hoheit *His Highness* | e–r ~er Brüder *or* v s–n B.n *one of his brothers, a br. of his* ‖ mein u ~ Freund *my fr. and his* ‖ ~e vielen Freunde *his many friends* ‖ all ~ (bißchen) Geld *what* (*little*) *money he has* od *had* ‖ irgend welche ~er Geschäfte *any transactions of his* ‖ er kennt ~en Homer *he knows his H.* | ⟨pop⟩ m–m Vater ~ Hut (Sohn) *my f.'s hat* (*this child*) ‖ alles zu ~er Zeit *all in good time, all in due course* | [mit inf] (*to put on*) *one's* (*shoes*) **2.** (v e–m Land, Schiff, dem Mond) *her*

3. (v Dingen u kl Tieren) *its* ‖ es kostet ∼e 8, 9 M *it will cost 8 or 9 marks* **B.** [pred] alles was ∼ ist *everything he possesses* ‖ es ist ∼ *it is his* ‖ dies ist alles ∼ *all this is his* (*own*) od *belongs to him* **III.** **°∼er, °∼e, °∼es; der, die, das °∼(ig)e** *his, its* ‖ *his property, his own* ‖ *his duty* ‖ die °∼en [pl] *his people* od *family, kith and kin* (*he and*) *his* ‖ jedem das ∼e! *give every one his due* ‖ das ∼(ig)e (dazu) tun *to pull one's own weight, to do one's duty* od *best* ⟨fam⟩ *bit* ‖ jds Gedanken zu den ∼(ig)en m *to adopt a p's ideas* ‖ den ∼en gibt's der Herr im Schlaf ⟨fig fam⟩ *Fortune favours fools* **s·einer- ∼seits** [adv] *for* od *on his part; in his* (*its*) *turn;* er ∼ *he for one* **∼zeit** [adv] *in due course* (a. = später) ‖ *in his* od *its time* **s·einesgl·eichen** pron [inv] *his equals* pl ‖ er hat nicht ∼ *he has not his equal* od *like; he is without equal; no man* (*in the town*) *is his equal* ‖ es hat nicht ∼ *there is nothing like it; it is unparalleled* ‖ er u seinesgleichen *he and people like him* ‖ v ∼ gerichtet w *to be tried by one's peers* ‖ e–n wie ∼ behandeln *to treat a p like one's equal* **s·einet- ∼halben, ∼wegen,** um **∼willen** *on his account* od *behalf, for his sake* ‖ *for all he cared* (→ meinetwegen) **S·einige** n ∼s/ → sein III.

S·eising n ∼s/∼e ⟨mar⟩ *gasket*(*s* pl)

S·eismik f ∼/ *seismology* **s·eismisch** a *seismic;* ⟨geo-phys-min⟩ *seismical* (*prospecting*) **S·eismo- ∼gr·aph** m ∼en/∼en *seismograph* **∼log·ie** f *seismology* **∼m·eter** n *seismometer*

seit I. prep [dat] *since* ‖ (Zeitdauer) *for* **A.** ∼ **jeher** *from time immemorial* ‖ ∼ heute *since today* ‖ ∼ kurzem (langem) *of late, for a short* (*long*) *time* ‖ ∼ wann bist du hier? *how long have you been here?* ‖ *since 1911* (*I have lived* [lebe] *in L.*) **B.** ∼ s–r **Abreise** *since his d.* ‖ ∼ Anfang Juli *s. the beginning of J.* ‖ ∼ 2 M. *for the last two months* ‖ er ist ∼ 1 Jahr in A. *he has been in A. for a year* ‖ ∼ 3 Jahren *for* od *these 3 years;* ∼ vielen Jahren .. *it has not been seen for* (*many*) *years,* ⟨Am⟩ *in years* ‖ jeden Morgen ∼ 5 Jahren *e. m. for these 5 years;* .. ∼ über 50 J.n *for over 50 years* ‖ *these 3 days* ‖ *this 3 weeks* ‖ ∼ 4 **Uhr** warte ich *I've been waiting ever since 4 o'clock* ‖ *since last Xmas* ‖ ∼ einiger Zeit *for some time past* ‖ u ∼ dieser Zeit *since when* **II.** [conj] *since* ‖ .., ∼ sie .. hatte .. *since first meeting him* ‖ *it is 50 years since he appeared, .. since I have had it* ‖ ∼ er fort ist (*ever*) *since he left* ‖ ∼ ich weiß .. *ever since I have known .. I have not trusted him* | **∼d·em I.** [adv] *since then; from* (od [*ever*] *since*) *that time* | [bei pret] *ever after* (*he was ..*); in den ∼ verflossenen Jahren *in the years since* ‖ *thenceforward* (*there was no danger*) ‖ *it never was what it has since become* **II.** [conj] = seit II. | **∼h·er** [adv] *since* (*that time*) | *up to now* | ∼ig [a] *still in use* etc

S·eite f ∼/∼n **A.** *side* ⟨a. sport & fig⟩ ‖ (Richtung) *direction;* ⟨artill⟩ *azimuth;* Anzeige v ∼ u Höhe ⟨radar⟩ *azimuth and elevation* ‖ (Algebra) *member* ‖ ⟨geom⟩ *side;* (e–s Körpers) *face* ‖ ⟨mil⟩ *flank* ‖ ⟨mil, arch⟩ *wing* ‖ ⟨pol⟩ *side, party* ‖ ⟨fig⟩ *facet* (*of a p's character*); *aspect* (*of a problem*) **B. Bild°∼** *face* (*of a coin*) ‖ Buch°∼ *page,* ⟨com⟩ *folio* ‖ Anzeigen°∼ *advertising page* ‖ Lee°∼ (Wetter°∼) ⟨mar⟩ *lee* (*weather*) *beam* ‖ Speck°∼ *flitch of bacon* ‖ ⟨num⟩ Rück°∼ *reverse* ‖ Titel°∼ *front page* ‖ Vorder°∼ *face, front* **C.** die v .. **abgekehrte** ∼ *the s. away from* ‖ **alle** ∼n *the ins and outs* (*of a question*) ‖ beiden ∼n gerecht w *to cut both ways* ‖ besondere ∼ ⟨fig⟩ *note* ‖ v der falschen ∼ .. durchsehen *to look through the wrong end of a pair of field-glasses* ‖ **gute** ∼: *a good feature about him; good* (*bad*) *point in a p* (jds) ‖ ⟨fig⟩ lange ∼n h *to be a good eater* ‖ s. nächste ∼ *see over* ‖ obere (untere) ∼ *top* (*bottom*) ‖ rechte (linke) ∼ ⟨bookb⟩ *recto* (*verso*); ⟨tail⟩ *right* (*wrong*) *side;* ⟨hors⟩ *on* (*off*) *side* ‖ schwache ∼ *soft spot; arithmetic is his weak point; smoking is a weakness of his* ‖ starke ∼ *forte; his strong point* od *suit* ‖ ⟨fig⟩ unangenehme ∼ *seamy side* ‖ unbedruckte ∼ *blank* od *white p.;* → Schimmel ‖ zugewandte ∼ ⟨arch⟩ *hither side* **D.** die ∼ e–r Wand **ausfüllen** *to flank a wall* ‖ die Frage hat noch e–e andere ∼ *there is another side to the question* ‖ jedes Ding hat s–e zwei ∼n *there are two sides to every question; every cloud has its silver lining* ‖ sich die ∼n vor Lachen halten *to split one's sides with laughing* ‖ ⟨sport⟩ ∼n wechseln *to change* (*over*) **E. an** [dat]: *to wear a sword at one's side* ‖ (P) *at a p's side, beside a p, by the side of* ‖ with *Mr. N. by his side* ‖ *she sat on the other side of* ‖ *he fell into step beside me* ‖ an den ∼en *in the sides* (*of a wag*(*g*)*on*), *at the sides* (*of a car*) ‖ ∼ an ∼ (*to sit*) *elbow to e.;* (intim) *cheek by jowl;* (*of boats*) *alongside* ‖ an m–r °grünen ∼ *at my right s.* ‖ dicht an s–r ∼ *at his elbow* | [acc] *to step, to be called to a p's s.* ‖ an die ∼ treten *to step aside* ‖ ⟨fig⟩ e–n jdm an die ∼ stellen *to place a p on the same footing as a p* ‖ dem kann nichts an die ∼ gestellt w *nothing can be compared with it* ‖ **auf** [dat]: *on the one* (*other*) *side; on one hand .. on the other; on both sides* ‖ ⟨fig⟩ *on all hands* ‖ auf der l. ∼ (des Bildes, d. h. im Bilde) *on the left* (*of the p.*) ‖ auf beiden ∼n z tragen ⟨tail⟩ *reversible* ‖ (*to swim*) *with a side-stroke* ‖ auf der gleichen ∼ gelegen, die gl. ∼ betreffend *homolateral, ipsilateral;* auf jeder ∼ *on each* od *either hand;* (*they sat four*) *a side* ‖ .. – Ganz auf m–r ∼ (*Pleased to meet you*) – *The pleasure is mine* ‖ *at page 50; at pages 2–4; in the following pages* ‖ auf umstehender ∼ *overleaf* ‖ auf °∼n jds s *to side with a p* ‖ auf °∼n [gen] *on the part of* ‖ auf der faulen ∼ liegen *to lounge about* ‖ ⟨mar, mot⟩ auf der ∼ liegen, sich auf die [acc] ∼ legen *to have a list* | [acc] auf die ∼ bringen *to remove, to put aside* od *out of the way;* (heimlich) *to make away with* ‖ jdn auf s–e ∼ bringen *to bring a p over to one's party;* ⟨Am pol⟩ *to swing* (*a district*) ‖ *the horse fell on its side* (die ∼) ‖ auf die ∼ gehen *to go aside* ‖ jdn auf s–e ∼ kriegen *to get a p alongside one* ‖ (etw, sich) auf die ∼ legen *to cant* ‖ ⟨fig⟩ *to save money* ‖ (sich, im Bett) *to turn on one's side;* .. faule ∼ .. *to turn lazy* ‖ ⟨fam⟩ sich auf die ∼ m *to get out of the way* ‖ jdn auf die ∼ nehmen *to take a p aside* ‖ jdn auf die ∼ räumen *to do away with a p* ‖ auf die ∼ schieben ⟨fig⟩ *to pass up* ‖ auf jds ∼ stehen *to stand by one's friend* ‖ sich auf jds ∼ stellen *to take one's stand by a p* ‖ auf die ∼ treten: *he stood to one side* ‖ auf jds ∼ treten *to side with a p* | jdn **bei** s–r schwachen ∼ nehmen *to appeal to a p's weakness* | ⟨mil⟩ e–m **in** die ∼ fallen *to attack .. in the flank* ‖ die Hände in die ∼n gestemmt *akimbo* | etw **mit** der richtigen ∼ nach oben stellen *to set a th right s. up* | **nach allen** ∼n *in all directions; on all hands; all-round;* .. filmend *panning* ‖ .. betrachten *to look at a th from all sides, to consider every side of* (*a problem*); er sah sich .. um *he looked on every side of him;* nach beiden ∼n *to look each* od *either way;* nach der ∼ zu *away to* ‖ nach dieser ∼ ⟨a.⟩ *over this way* ‖ nach irgend e–r ∼ *one way or another* | jdn (kritisch) **von** der ∼ ansehen *to look at a p from the corner of one's eye* | **von °∼n** *at the hand of* ‖ v jds ∼ *at a p's hands* ‖ v °∼n des Herrn N. *on the part of ..* ‖ Unterstützung v °∼n der Regierung *Government support* ‖ v °∼n s–s Vaters *on* od *by his f.'s side* ‖ v °∼n [gen] wurde protestiert *the industry entered a protest* (*against*) | v **allen** ∼n: *on all sides, on every hand;* (*received, recognized*) *on all hands* ‖ *from all quarters* ⟨a. fig⟩ ‖ *all-round* ‖ .. filmend *panning* ‖ alle ∼n (e–r Frage) *the ins and outs;* allen ∼n gerecht w *to cut both ways* ‖ v der ∼ *askance; sideways* (*a s. glance*) ‖ See v der ~ ⟨mar⟩ *beam sea* ‖ *to cast sidelong glances at* ‖ v berufener ~ (*I have it*) *from good authority*, ⟨sl⟩ *straight from the horse's mouth* ‖ sich v der besten ~ zeigen *to put one's best foot forward*; v dieser ~ ⟨fig⟩ *in that light, from that angle, from that point of view* ‖ .. *whichever way one looked at it* ‖ man kann die Frage, S auch v e–r anderen ~ betrachten *there is another s. to the question* ‖ v k–r ~ bestritten *not disputed in any quarter* ‖ ich v m–r ~ *I, for my part* ‖ v m–r ~ aus *on my part* ‖ *from a well-informed source* ‖ ⟨fig⟩ *from various quarters*; v deutscher ~ *from a German q.* ‖ sich v der besten ~ zeigen *to put one's best foot forward* | jdn v der ~ ansehen *to look at a p contemptuously* ‖ alles v der guten ~ ansehen *to look on the bright side of ths* ‖ jdn v der schlechtesten ~ sehen *to see a p at his worst* ‖ jdm nicht v der ~ gehen *not to leave* od *quit a p's side, not to move from a p's side*; ⟨fam⟩ *to stick to a p* | **zur** ~ *aside, apart*; (*he stepped*) *to one side*; (*his arm fell*) *to his side* ‖ jdm z. ~ stehen *to stand by a p, to support a p* ‖ es stehen ihm gute Zeugnisse z. ~ *he can produce fine references* ‖ jdn [+ dat] z. ~ stellen *to rank a p among* .. ‖ sich jdm z. ~ stellen *to take a p's part* ‖ z. ~ treten ⟨a.⟩ *to make room*, ⟨fig⟩ jdm .. *to stand up for a p* **S·eiten-** *s*(*ide*), *l*(*atera*)*l* **~abriß** m = ~ansicht **~abstand** m *l.l distance* **~abweichung** f ⟨artill⟩ *drift, deflection, deviation*; (Rakete) *crab angle* **~achse** f *diagonal* **~allee** f *s.-walk* **~angriff** m *flank attack* **~ansicht** f *profile*; *l.l* od *s.-view*, ⟨phot⟩ *s.-face* **~ast** m *l.l branch* **~bahn** f ⟨rail⟩ *branch-line* **~balken** m *s.-beam* **~baum** m *cheek* (*of a gun--carriage*) **~begrenzer** m ⟨tech⟩ *traversing stop* **~blick** m *s.-look, -glance*; *leer*; e–n ~ werfen auf *to glance sideways at*, ⟨a. fig⟩ *to take a slant at* **~davit** m ⟨mar⟩ *quarter d.* **~deckung** f ⟨mil⟩ *flank-guard* **~druck** m *l.l pressure* **~einrichter** m ⟨typ⟩ *page setter* **~erbe** m *collateral heir* **~fehllage** f ⟨artill⟩ *l.l* od *deflection error* **~fenster** n (im Schiff) *port-light* **~fläche** f *flat s.*; ⟨minr⟩ *s. face*; ⟨geom⟩ *face* (*of a solid*) **~flosse** f ⟨aero⟩ *vertical* od *tail fin*; ⟨Am⟩ *v. stabilizer* **~flügel** m ⟨arch⟩ *s.-wing, -aisle* **~front** f ⟨arch⟩ *s.-face* **~führung** f *l.l guide* **~galerie** f (e–s Schiffes) *quarter-gallery* **~gasse** f *by-street* **~gebäude** n *wing* (*of a building*), *out-house* **~geleise** n *siding* **~gewehr** n *bayonet*, ~ pflanzt auf! *fix bayonets!*; *s.-arm, sword* | ~halter [m] *stud* **~grenze** f ⟨ftb⟩ *touch-line* **~hänger** m ⟨theat⟩ (*scenic*) *leg*, ⟨Am⟩ *leg drop* **~hieb** m *s.-cut, scorcher*; *smart crack*; ~ auf *slant on*; ⟨fig⟩ *innuendo, wipe, sly hi*(*n*)*t* **~korrektur** f *l.l correction* **~kraft** f *component* **~kulisse** f ⟨theat⟩ *wing, side-scene* **~lähmung** f *hemiplegia* **≃lang** a *pages long* **~lastigkeit** f *l.l trim* **~lehne** f *arm* **~leitwerk** n ⟨aero⟩ *rudder unit* od *assembly* ‖ doppeltes ~ *double fins and rudders* **~linie** f *s.-line* ⟨a. ten⟩; ⟨geneal⟩ *collateral line*; Erbfolge in der ~ *c.l descent*; ⟨ftb⟩ *touch*; ⟨rail⟩ *branch*(*-line*); ⟨ich⟩ *l.l line* **≃linig** a *c.l* (*descent*) **~locke** f *s.-lock* **~loge** f *s.-box* **~moräne** f *l.l moraine* **~neigung** f ⟨mot⟩ *l.l sway* **~parallaxabstand** m *l.l displacement* **~pfad** m *by-path* **~rand** m ⟨typ⟩ *margin* **~richten** n *laying for direction* **~richter** m ⟨ftb⟩ *touch-judge* **~richt-** ⟨artill⟩ ~feld [n] v 360° *all-round traverse*; ~kanonier [m] *azimuth setter*; *trainer*; ~maschine [f] *traverse*; ~rad [n] *training hand--wheel*; ~vorrichtung [f] *traversing gear*; **≃-richtig** a ⟨rep, etc⟩ *true sided, t. to sides, right-way-round* **~richtung** f ⟨artill⟩ *azimuth*; (e–m Geschütz) ~ geben *to traverse* **~riß** m *s. projection, profile* **~rolle** f ⟨aero⟩ *yawing* **~ruder** n ⟨aero⟩ *rudder* | ~fußhebel [m] *r. bar* od *pedal* **~schiff** n ⟨arch⟩ *aisle* **~schmerz** m *s.-ache* **~schritt** m *s.-step* **~schub** m ⟨arch⟩ *drift*; *s. thrust* **~schwimmen** n *s.-stroke* **~schwimmer** m ⟨ich⟩ *flat-fish* **~sprung** m *s.-leap, swerve*; ⟨hors⟩ *caracol*; (des Hasen) *double, doubling* ‖ ⟨fig⟩ *evasion* ‖ (leichtsinniger) *escapade* **~staffelung** f ⟨mil⟩ *deployment in width* **≃ständig** a ⟨bot⟩ *l.l* **~stechen** n ⟨path⟩ *stitch in the s.* **~steuer** n ⟨aero⟩ (*vertical*) *rudder* **~steuerung** ⟨aero⟩ *directional controls* pl **~stoß** m *thrust in the flank* **~straße** f *by-street* **~streifen** m ⟨mot⟩ = Rand- **~streuung** f *dispersion* | ~sbild [n] *deflection pattern* **~stück** n *s.-piece, counterpart* (*to*); *opposite number* ‖ (Pendant) *companion-picture, -piece* **~stürmer** m ⟨ftb, soccer, rugby, hockey⟩ *winger* **~takel** n *mast tackle* **~tasche** f *s.-pocket* **~teil** m *s.-part*, ⟨mach⟩ *cheek*, ⟨tail⟩ *flap* **~thema** n ⟨mus⟩ *subsidiary subject* **~trieb** m *s. growth* **~trumm** n *secondary lode* **~tür** f *s.-door* **~verbesserung** f ⟨artill⟩ *deflection* **~vergleich** m *comparison of one with the other* **~verhältnis** n *width to height ratio* **≃verkehrt** a (*l.lly*) *reversed* | schußtafelmäßige **~verschiebung** *theoretical deflection shift* **~verwandte(r)** m *collateral* **~verwandtschaft** f *cognation* **~verweis** m *paginal reference* **~vorhalt** m ⟨artill⟩ *l.l deflection* od *lead* **~weg** m *s.-way, by-way* **~wendung** f *turn* **~werk** n ⟨fort⟩ *flank*(*er*) **~wind** m *flank* od *s.-wind*; ⟨aero⟩ *cross-wind* ([attr] *landing*) **~zahl** f *page-number, folio*; *number of pages*; mit ~n versehen *to folio* od *paginate* **~zeiger** m *index* **s·eitens** prep [gen] *on the part of*; (*to receive*) *at a p's hands*; (*the use of phrases*) *by a p*; ⟨geneal⟩ *on* (*the mother's, father's*) *side* → aber: **seit-** .. **seitig** a [in comp] (z. B. *ten*)*-sided* ‖ ⟨tech⟩ rauchgas~e Verschmutzung *impurities caused by stack gas* **s·eitlich** a (*col*)*lateral, side-* .., *side* (*leaf*) ‖ ⟨artill⟩ *lateral* (Beobachtung); ⟨theat⟩ *off-stage* ‖ ~e Bewegung *twist* | ~ herumgehen um *to flank* .. **seits** [in comp]: m–r~ *for my part* **s·eitwärts** [adv] *sideways, aside*; *laterally* ‖ (*lying*) *edgeways* ‖ ~ ausweichend *l.y withdrawing*; ~ springen *to double*; ~ drehen *to traverse*; sich ~ nähern *to edge nearer*; ~ geneigt *aslant* ‖ durch ≃treten ausweichen *to side-step*

Sek·ante f ~/~n ⟨math⟩ *secant*

Sekr·et n ~ s/~ e *secretion*(*s* pl)

Sekret·är m ~(e)s/~e **1.** *secretary, clerk* **2.** *desk*; *writing table*; *bureau* | ~anlage [f] *executive telephone*, ⟨fam⟩ *execuphone* **3.** ⟨orn⟩ *secretary* **~in** f *lady clerk*; *secretary* **Sekretari·at** n ~(e)s/~e *secretary's office, secretariat*(*e*) ‖ *clerkship*

Sekt m ~(e)s/~e *champagne*; ⟨fam⟩ *sham* | ~frühstück [n] *ch. lunch*; ~kühler [m] *ch.--cooler*; ~quirl [m] *ch.-whisk*, ⟨fam⟩ *swizzle--stick*

S·ekte f ~/~n ⟨rel⟩ *sect*; ~ der Quäker *Q. persuasion* **-t·ierer** m ~s/~ *sectarian* | ~·ei [f] ~/ *sectarianism*; | ≃isch [a] *schismatic*(*al*) (adv *schismatically*) **Sekti·on** f ~/~en *section* ‖ ⟨med⟩ *dissection*, ⟨pop⟩ *post-mortem* **~ssaal** m *dissecting-room* **≃sweise** [adv] *in sections* **S·ektor** m ~s/-·oren ⟨math⟩ *sector* ⟨a. off⟩ ‖ ⟨com⟩ field ‖ ⟨mil⟩ in jedem ~ *on every s.*; auf .. → Bereich

Sek·und f ~/~en ⟨fenc⟩ *cut in seconde*

Sek·unda f ~/-den ⟨Ger⟩ *second class* od *form*; ⟨engl⟩ *fifth form* **~reife** f *second-form standard* **~wechsel** m ⟨com⟩ *second* (*bill*) *of exchange* **Sekund·aner** m ~s/~ (~in f) ⟨Ger⟩ *second-form boy* (*girl*) ‖ ⟨engl⟩ *fifth-form boy* (*girl*) **Sekund·ant** m ~en/~en *second* ‖ ⟨sport⟩ *bottle-holder* **Sekund·ararzt** m [österr] = Krankenhausarzt **sek·und·är** a *secondary* | ≃- [in comp oft] *secondary* **≃bahn** f (*narrow-gauge*) *branch-line* **≃element** n ⟨el⟩ *secondary cell* **≃erscheinung** f *attendant phenomenon* **≃schule** f Sw = höhere

Volksschule **Sek·unde** f ~/~n *second* ⟨a. mus⟩ || e–e ~! ⟨sl⟩ *half a mo*; ich blieb auch nicht e–e ~ stehen *I never stopped* **≗nlang** a *lasting s.s* | [adv] *for s.s* **~nliter** m *liter per s.* (*l/s*) **~npendel** n *s.-pendulum* | in ~nschnelle *in a matter of s.s* **~uhr** f *stop-watch* **~zeiger** m *s.-hand* | → Sekund **sekund·ieren** vi [h] (jdm) ⟨fenc⟩ *to second a p* || ⟨fig⟩ *to play up to a p*; ⟨mus⟩ *to accompany* **Sek·undogenit·ur** f ~/ ⟨jur⟩ *right of the younger son*

s·ela [intj] ⟨bib⟩ *selah*! || ⟨fam⟩ *done*!

S·eladongrün n *sea-green*

selb a *same* || noch am ~en Tage *that very day* || zur ~en Stunde *at* (*the same* od) *that very hour* **~·ander** [adv] *our* (*your, their*) *two selves, we two* **~dr·itt** [adv] *with two others*; die heil. Anna ~ *St. A.* (*with*) od, *the Virgin, and Child* **s·elber** = selbst **s·elbiger, s·elbige, s·elbiges** [obs pron] *the same, that very* || ⟨jur⟩ *such* **selbst I.** [pron] *self*; meine Freunde u ich selbst *my friends and self* || Herr N.? ~!.. *I'm the identical* || ~ ist der Mann *everyone must depend on h.s.* || ich ~ *I m.s.* || er ~ *he h.s.* || wir ~ *we ourselves* || wie geht's selbst? ⟨fam Am⟩ *how's y.s.*? || ~ Schuft! *rogue y.s.*; ~ e–r! *another*! || ~ k *to come personally* || er ist die Rechtschaffenheit ~ *he is the soul of probity*; Sie sind die Güte ~ *you are kindness itself* || er ist nicht mehr er ~ *he is no longer the same p* || ~ ist der Mann ⟨prov⟩ *do it yourself*! || selbst entscheiden *to decide for o.s.* || sich [dat] die Kleider ~ m *to make one's own clothes* || sich ~ erhaltend *s.-sustaining*; sich ~ erklärend, aus sich ~ z erklären(d) *s.-explanatory* || sich [acc] ~ so nennend *s.-styled* || *willing to burden no one, her or himself* || (in) sich ~ genug s *to be self-sufficent* | **in** sich ~ vertieft *s.-absorbed*; sich [acc] über sich ~ erheben *to rise above o.s.* || v sich ~ eingenommen *full of o.s.* | **von** ~ *of one's own accord, voluntarily, spontaneously, of itself, mechanically, automatically* || v ~ entstanden *spontaneous* || das versteht sich v ~ *it goes without saying* || **zu** sich ~ k *to come to one's senses* **II.** [adv] *even* || ~ nicht *not even* || ~ wenn *even if, even though* | ~ angebaut, gezogen *home-grown* **III.** ≗ n; mein besseres ≗ *my better self* || sein zweites ≗ *his second individuality* **Selbst- ~abholung** f *collection by the customer* **~achtung** f *self-respect, -esteem*; *proper pride* **~analyse** f *s. searching* **~anklage** f *s.-accusation* | → selbständig **~anlasser** m ⟨mot⟩ *automatic* (od *s.-*)*starter s.-starting motor* **~anschluß** m ⟨telph⟩ *automatic telephone* | ~anlage [f], ~betrieb [m] *dial system* **~ansteckung** f ⟨med⟩ *self-infection* **~aufopferung** f *s.-sacrifice* **~auslöser** m ⟨phot⟩ *s.-timer*; *delayed-action release* **~bauspielzeug** n *constructional toys* pl **~bedienung** f *s.-service* [a. attr]; ~ im Einzelhandel *s.-s. retailing*; Laden mit ~ ⟨Am⟩ *groceteria* | **~s-** ~Filialbetriebe [m pl] *s.-s. chain*; ~laden [m] *s.-s.*, (⟨Am a.⟩ *s.-y.s.*) *store*; gr ~ ⟨bes Am⟩ *retail supermarket*; ~ssystem [n] ⟨Am⟩ *help-y.s. plan* **~befleckung** f *onanism* **~befruchtung** f *autogamy* | zur **~behauptung** [f] *to maintain one's* (*its*) *existence* **~beherrschung** f *s.-command, s.-control*; mangelhafte ~ *intemperance*; ~ besitzen *to be marked by s.-c.*; die ~ verlieren *to lose one's temper*; s–e ~ wiedergewinnen *to recover one's temper* **~bekenntnis** n *voluntary confession* **~beköstigung** f *boarding o.s., s.-subsistence* **~beobachtung** f *introspection* **~bespiegelung** f *s.-adulation* **~bestäubung** f *s.-pollination* **~bestimmung** f *autonomy, independence, s.-determination* || ⟨rel⟩ *free agency* | ~srecht [n] *right of selfdetermination* **~betrachtung** f *s.-inspection* **~betrug** m *s.-deceit, s.-delusion, s.-deception* **~beurteilung** f *judgment of o.s.* **≗bewußt** a (*s.-*) *confident, s.-conscious*; (*s.-*)*assured*; er ist ~ *he has confidence in h.s.* || *assured* (*tone*) (aber: s–r selbst bewußt) || (stolz) *proud*; ⟨dero⟩ *s.-assertive* | ≗sein [n] (*s.-*)*confidence* | *s.-consciousness* ⟨philos⟩ || ⟨dero⟩ *s.-assertion*; Wiedererlangung des ~s *regaining of one's s.-assurance* **~beziehungsideen** [f pl] ⟨psych⟩ *ideas of reference* **~binder** m ⟨tail⟩ *bow*; *open-end tie* **~biographie** f *autobiography* **≗eigen** a (*one's*) *own* **~eingenommenheit** f *presumption* **~einschätzung** f *s.-assessment* **~einsicht** f ⟨psych⟩ *insight* **~einstellung** f ⟨mot⟩ *s.-alignment* **~entäußerung** f *s.-abnegation* **~entladung** f *s.-discharge*, ⟨Am⟩ *local action* **~entleibung** f *suicide* **≗entwickelt** a ⟨phot⟩ *user-processed* **~entzündung** f *spontaneous ignition*; (v Heu) *hay-burn* **~erhaltung** f *s.-preservation*; *survival* **~erhebung** f *s.-exaltation* **~erhitzung** f (v Heu) *hay-burn* **~erkenntnis** f *self-knowledge* **~erlösung** f ⟨rel⟩ *s.-redemption* **~erniedrigung** f *s.-abasement* **≗erwählt** a *s.-chosen, of a p's own choosing* **~fahr-** *s.-propelled* (*mount* Lafette [SFL]); auf SFL *s.-p.d* **~fahrer** m *owner-driver* | ~dienst [m] ⟨mot⟩ *hire service*; ~-Mietwagen [m] *drive-y.s. car*; ~geschütz [n] *s.-driving gun*; ~lafette [f] ⟨a.⟩ *gun motor carriage* (→ o.) **≗gebacken** a *home-made* **≗gebraut** a *home-brewed* **≗gefällig** a *s.-conceited, complacent, s.-satisfied, smug* || ~gefällige P *prig* | ≗keit [f] *conceit, complacency*; *smugness* **~gefühl** n *s.-confidence s.-reliance* **≗gemacht** a *home-made* (*maccaroni*) **≗genügsam** a (P) *self-sufficient* (*person*) **≗gerecht** a *s.-righteous* **~geschriebene(s)** n *autograph* **~gespräch** n *monologue, soliloquy*; ~e führen *to talk to o.s.* **~gewählt** a (*book*) *selected by a p o.s.* **≗gezogen** a ⟨agr⟩ *of a p's own growth* **~haß** m *hatred of o.s.* **≗herrlich** a [adv] *autocratic*[*ally*] **~herrschaft** f *autocracy* || *s.-command* **~herrscher** m *autocrat* **~hilfe** f *s.-help* || zur ~ greifen *to proceed to s.-aid, to take the law in one's own hands* **~kipper** m ⟨rail, mot⟩ *s.-tipping car* **~klebefolie** f *s.-adhesive film* **~kocher** m *s.-acting boiler* **~kosten** pl *prime* od *first cost* | ~beteiligung [f] ⟨ins⟩ *the deductile*; ~preis [m] *c. price* **~kühlung** f ⟨tech⟩ *natural cooling* **~lade-** ⟨mil⟩ *s.-chambering* || *automatic*; ~gewehr [n] *au.c gun*; ~pistole [f] *automatic pistol*; ~vorrichtung [f] *au.c loader* **~lader** m *autoloading rifle, au.c gun* **~laut** m ⟨gram⟩ *vowel* **≗leuchtend** a *s.-luminous* **~liebe** f *s.-love* **~lob** n *s.-praise* **≗los** a *unselfish, altruistic, disinterested* | adv ~ handeln *to forget o.s.* **~losigkeit** f *unselfishness, altruism* **~mord**(**versuch** m) m (*attempted*) *suicide* (⟨a. fig⟩ *sheer s.*) (begehen *to commit*) **~mörder** m *suicide* | ≗isch [a] *suicidal* °**≗murmelnd** a *of course, to be sure* **~oxidation** f *spontaneous oxidation* **~porträt** n *a portrait of o.s.* **~prüfung** f *s.-examination*; *introspection* **≗quälerisch** a *s.-tormenting*; ~es Verhalten (*desire for*) *s.-torture* **≗redend** [a & adv] = ~verständlich **~reflektant** m (*principal prospective buyer* od *tenant whishing to buy* od *rent in his own name*) *principal*; nur ~en! *only principals*!, *no agents*! **~regelung** f *automatic control* **~regierung** f *autonomy* **≗regulierend** a *s.-registering, s.-regulating* **~reinigung** f (Wasser≗) *s.-purification* **~retter** m ⟨mil⟩ (Gas≗) *aerophore* **~schuß** m *spring-gun* **~schutz** m *s.-protection* **≗sicher** a *s.-reliant*, (*s.-*)*assured*; ~e P *a man sure of h.s.* | ≗heit [f] *s.-reliance, aplomb* **~spanner** m (Waffe) *s.-cocker* **≗sperrend** a *irreversible* (*steering*) **~sperrung** f *au.c locking* **≗spielend**; ~es Klavier [n] *autopiano* **≗ständig** etc = selbständig etc **~steuergerät** n ⟨aero⟩ *automatic pilot*; *autopilot*; *au.c flight control* **~steuerung** f *automatic control* **~studium** n *private study* **~sucht** f *ego*(*t*)*ism, selfishness* **~süchtel·ei** f *selfishness* **≗süchtig** a *selfish, self-seeking ego*(*t*)*istic*(*al*) [adv *ego*(*t*)*istically*] **~süchtler** m *ego*(*t*)*ist* **≗tätig** a *spontaneous, independent* || (v Maschinen) *automatic, self-acting*;

⟨comp⟩ ~e Kontrolle *internal checking system* | adv (*to register*) *automatically* **~tätigkeit** f *spontaneousness, spontaneity; automaticity* **~-täuschung** f *s.-delusion, -deception* **≗tragend** a *integral* (Karosserie); ⟨aero⟩ *stressed* (*skin*) **~über-** ~hebung [f] *s.-importance; hybris* Gr, *presumption*; ~schätzung [f] *overrating of o.s.*; ~windung [f] *s.-victory* **~unterbrecher** m ⟨el⟩ *trembler* **~unterricht** m *s.-instruction* **~verachtung** f *s.-contempt* **~verarbeitung** f *home proceeding* ⟨a. phot⟩ **~verbesserung** f ⟨rhet⟩ *s.-correction* (*in six troubles*) **~verbrennung** f *spontaneous combustion* **≗vergessen** a *s.-forgetful, -forgetting* | ≗heit [f] *abandonment* **~vergötterung** f *idiolatry* **~verkäufer** m ⟨el⟩ *prepayment meter* **~verlag** m; im ~ *published by the author* **~verleugnung** f *s.-denial; s.-abnegation* **~vernichtung** f *s.-destruction; autocide* **~vernichtungssucht** f *self-destructiveness* **~verpflichtung** ⟨DDR⟩ *pledge* **~versenkung** f ⟨mar⟩ *scuttling* **~versicherer** m *own insurer* **~verschluß** m; mit ~ *automatic--closing* **~versorger** m *s.-supporter*; ⟨cul⟩ *s.-supplier* **~versorgung** f ⟨geopol⟩ *s.-sufficiency* **≗verständlich** a *s.-evident, obvious; axiomatic*; es ist ~, daß *it stands to reason that*; ~e Folgerung *implication* ‖ [adv] *of course; naturally; to be sure; that goes without saying* ‖ etw S.es h *to seem a matter of course* | ~keit [f] (jdm) e–e ~ w *to become second nature* **~verstümmelung** f *s.-mutilation; autotomy*; Verletzung durch ~ *s.-inflicted wound* **~verteidigung** f *s.--defence* **~vertrauen** n *s.-confidence, s.-reliance; s.-assurance*; mangelndes ~ *diffidence, s.-mistrust*; zu wenig ~ h *to be too diffident of o.s.* **≗vertrauend** a *s.-confident, s.-reliant* **~verwaltung** [f] *s.-government, autonomy* **~wähl-** ~anlage [f] ⟨telph⟩ *automatic exchange*; ~(er)dienst [m] *subscriber trunk dial(l)ing* (*STD*); ~ferndienst [m] (SWFD) *direct distance dial(l)ing* (*DDD*); ~vermittlung [f] *dial exchange* **~wille** m *s.-will, arbitrariness* **~zählung** f ⟨demog⟩ *household method* **~zerleger** m (Geschoß) *s.detonator* N **~zucht** f *s.-discipline* **≗zufrieden** a *s.-satisfied* ‖ *smug* | ≗heit [f] *s.-contentedness, s.-satisfaction* ‖ *smugness* **≗zündend** a *s.-igniting* **~zünder** m ⟨chem⟩ *pyrophorus* **~zündung** f *hypergolic ignition* (*of fluid rocket propellant*) **~zweck** m *goal in itself*

s·elbständig a *independent* ‖ *self-reliant, s.-sufficient* ‖ (Ggs angestellt) *s.-employed* ‖ ≗e(r) ⟨demog⟩ *employer*; ~er Berufsloser *s.-supporting p*; alleinschaffender ≗er *independent worker, w. on own account* | ⟨mil⟩ *separate* (*battery*); *s.-administering* (*unit*) | ⟨pol⟩ *autonomous* | (ohne Hilfe) *unaided, unassisted, original* | ~e Erwerbstätigkeit *non-wage-earning activity*; er ist ~er Schreiner *he is s.-employed as joiner*; ⟨mil⟩ die ~e Übernahme der Aufgabe *the automatic assumption of the tasks*; ~e Verwendung *independent employment* ‖ ~es Handeln *individual initiative* ‖ sich ~ m *to go into business for o.s.*; °(of car) *to run away* | [adv] *on one's own initiative*; ~ arbeiten *to perform duties without supervision, to work free lancing* ‖ ~ denken *to think for o.s.*; ~ denkender Soldat *the type of soldier who thinks independently* | **~keit** f *independence; initiative* ‖ ⟨pol⟩ *sovereignty* (*re-establishment of German sovereignty*)

s·elbstisch a *selfish, ego(t)istic* [adv] *e.ally*

s·elchen vt [h] *to smoke* (*meat*) ‖ Geselchte(s) [n] *smoked meat* **S·elcher** m ~s/~ *pork butcher* **S·elchkammer** f *smokehouse*

Seldsch·uken m pl (türk. Stamm) *Seljuks* pl

Sel·ekta f *special class* (*for senior pupils*) **Selekt·aner** m *senior pupil* **Selekt·ionstheorie** [–kts–] f (*Darwin's*) *theory of natural selection*

Sel·en n ~(e)s/ ⟨chem⟩ *selenium* ‖ [in comp] *selenic* (*acid*) **≗haltig** a *seleniferous* | **~·it** n ⟨minr⟩ *selenite* **~ograph·ie** f ~/ *selenography*

s·elig a *blissful* (*times*), *happy* (*smile*) ‖ *peaceful* (*end*) | (verstorben) *deceased, lamented, late* (ihr Vater ~ *her late father*) | ⟨ec⟩ *blessed*; ⟨fam⟩ ~en Angedenkens *of blessed memory* ‖ ⟨fig⟩ *delighted, in the seventh heaven of delight* ‖ ⟨fam⟩ (betrunken) *gloriously drunk* | die ≗en [pl] *the departed* ‖ die Gefilde der ≗en *the realms of bliss* ‖ m–e ≗e *my late wife* | [adv] ~ sterben *or* entschlafen *to die a Christian* ‖ Gott hab ihn (sie) ~! *may his soul rest in peace*; ⟨sl⟩ (*let her rip*! → *r. i. p.*) ‖ der Glaube macht ~ *faith is the means of grace* ‖ ~ sprechen *to canonize* ‖ ~ w *to go to Heaven*; ich will nicht ~ w, wenn *I'll be damned if* | die ≗en [pl] *the Saved* od *Elect* pl **S·elig-≗machend** a *beatific, soul-saving* **~macher** m *Saviour* **~machung** f *salvation* **≗|preisen** vt [h] *to call happy* **~preisung** f *glorification*; die 7 ~en *the Beatitudes* **≗ sprechen** vt ⟨ec⟩ *to beatify* **~sprechung** f *beatification* **S·eligkeit** f ~/~en *happiness, bliss, blissfulness* ‖ ⟨übtr⟩ ~en *pleasures* (*of life*) ‖ ⟨ec⟩ ewige ~ *salvation, beatitude, eternal bliss*

S·ellerie m ~s/~s ⟨bot⟩ *celery* **~salat** m *c. salad*

s·elten a *rare* (⟨a. fam, fig⟩ *r. bird*); ~er Mensch *one in a thousand*; Helden sind ~ *there are not many heroes* ‖ (knapp) *scarce* ‖ ⟨fig⟩ *remarkable, unusual* (*guest, gifts, case*) ‖ sich ~ m *to make o.s. scarce* ‖ was bei ihm sehr ~ ist *which, with him, is a very rare* od *unusual th* | [adv] *seldom, rarely* ‖ nicht eben ~ *pretty often* ‖ wir sehen ihn ~ *we see very little of him* ‖ ~ schön *exceptionally beautiful* ‖ ~ geeignet *qualified as few are* | **≗heit** f ~/~en *rarity, rareness, scarcity* | [konkret] [mit pl] *curiosity, rarity; curious* od *rare th* ‖ (Merkwürdigkeit) *remarkableness* | ~swert [m] *scarcity value*; (*to have*) *v. as rarity*

s·eltsam a *singular, strange, odd, curious*; ⟨fam⟩ *little* (*his l. ways*); ⟨sl⟩ *rum* | [adv] *unusually* (*soft*) ‖ mir war ~ *I felt queer* ‖ das berührt mich ~ *that offends my feelings* ‖ das ist mir ~ *that seems strange* ‖ so ~ es klingt .. *as strange as it may sound; str. though it m. s.; strange to say* ‖ wie ~! *the strangeness of it*! **≗keit** f ~/~en *strangeness, oddness, queerness* | [konkr] *oddity, curiosity*, persönliche ~ *quirk of personality*

S·elterwasser n *seltzer-, soda(-water)*

Semar·ang n (Stadt auf Java)

Sema- ~ph·or m ~s/~e *semaphore* **~siolog·ie** f ~/ *semasiology; theory of signs; semantics; sematology* **Semi·otik** f ~/ ⟨log, ling, math⟩ (Zeichentheorie) *semiotic*

Sem·ester n ~s/~ *half-year*, ⟨univ⟩ *term, half* ‖ ein erstes ~ (P) *a freshman* ‖ sein Kon-~ *his brother freshman* ‖ altes *or* hohes ~ *senior student; veteran* ⟨übtr a. allg⟩ **~schluß** m *close of term; term-end* **Semik·olon** n ~s/~s & –la *semicolon*

Semin·ar n (→ Samen) ~(e)s/~e & ~ien ⟨ec⟩ *seminary*; (Lehrer~) *training-college for teachers* ‖ ⟨univ, Ger⟩ *seminar,* (*advanced class*) **~arbeit** f ⟨univ⟩ (*student's*) *report on his research-work* | **~·ist** (~in f) m ~en/~en *seminarist* ‖ *pupil of a training-college* | **≗·istisch** [adv] gebildet *having passed through a t.-c.*

Sem·it m ~en/~en *Semite, Jew* | **≗isch** a *Semitic*

S·emmel f ~/~n *roll* (gestrichen *buttered*) ‖ belegte ~ *r. sandwich* ‖ ⟨fig⟩ wie warme ~n abgehen ⟨fam⟩ *to sell* od *go like hot cakes* **≗bl·ond** a *flaxen-haired*; ⟨fam⟩ *sandy* (*hair*) **~-kloß,** ×**~knödel** m ⟨Ger⟩ *r.-dumpling* **~kuchen** m *muffin* **~mehl** n *wheat-flour*

S·emmering m (österr. Paß)

Sen·ar m ~(e)s/~e (*iambic*) *verse of six feet*

Sen·at m ~(e)s/~e *senate*; ⟨jur⟩ *division* | ~spräsident [m] ⟨m. m.⟩ *chief justice*; ~ssitzung [f] *meeting of the s.* | **~or** m ~ors/–'oren *senator* | **≗·orisch** a *senatorial*

S·end- **~bote** m *emissary, messenger, envoy; apostle* **~brief** m, **~schreiben** n *epistle, missive, circular, circular letter* **S·ende-** ⟨wir⟩ [in comp] *transmitting (key, set, stage, station)* **~bereich** m *transmitter range* **≗bereit** a: ~ s *to stand by* **~folge** f *wireless programme* **~gerät** n *transmitter unit, radio tr.r* **~impuls** m *pulse* **~komplex** m *control room* **~leiter** m ⟨wir⟩ *production director* **~lizenz** f *broadcasting license* **~netz** n *b.c.g network* **~pause** f: ~ h, (m) *to be (go) off the air* **~raum** m *studio* **~reichweite** f = –bereich **~schluß** m: ~ m *to go off the air* **~spiel** n *transmitted play* **~stärke** f *transmitter energy* od *power* **~station** f = Sender **~stelle** f *transmitting station;* ⟨Am a.⟩ *outlet* **~text** m *script* **~- u Empfangsgerät** n *transmitter/receiver; two-way radio* **~welle** f *transmitting wave* **~zeit** f *b.c.g time, airtime;* ⟨telv⟩ *viewing hours* **s·enden** vt reg & [sandte/gesandt] [h] *to send* (nach *for*) ‖ *to address goods to* ‖ ⟨telg, wir⟩ *to transmit* ‖ ⟨wir⟩ *to broadcast, to take the air;* nicht ~ *to be off the air* ‖ ⟨telv⟩ *to screen* ‖ ~ Sie! *transmit!, go ahead* N **S·ender** m ~s/~ *sender* ‖ ⟨telg, wir⟩ *transmitter;* ⟨wir⟩ *broadcasting station* ‖ Geheim≗ *mystery station* ‖ Schwarz≗ ⟨wir⟩ *pirate sender* **~empfänger** m *transceiver* **~-zeichen** n *tuning signal, signature tune* **S·endling** ~(e)s/~e *emissary* **S·endung** f ~/~en *sending* | ⟨com⟩ [konkr] *parcel (of bulbs); shipment, consignment, cargo (of timber); dispatch (of letters)* | ⟨fig⟩ (Aufgabe) *mission* | ⟨telg, wir⟩ *transmission,* ⟨Am⟩ *radio-casting* ‖ ⟨wir⟩ *Life-*~ = Direkt≗ ‖ die ~ beginnen *to take to the air,* einstellen *to go off the air;* auf ~ s *to be on the air* ‖ ~ „fahren" *to balance the program, to be putting the p. on the air* ‖ die ~ wiederholen *to rebroadcast*

S·enegal **1.** m (Fluß in Afrika) **2.** n (Staat = Senegambien, Landschaft) in Afrika

S·enesbaum etc = Sennesblätter

S·eneschall m ~(e)s/~e *seneschal*

Senf m ~(e)s/~e *mustard* ⟨a. bot⟩ ‖ wilder ~ *common charlock* ‖ ⟨fig, fam⟩ s–n ~ dazu geben *to put in a word,* ⟨fam⟩ *to put one's oar in; to butt in with one's opinion;* er muß immer .. ⟨Am⟩ *he's always putting in his two cents* ‖ e–n langen ~ m (über) *to twaddle (about)* **~brühe** f *mustard-sauce* **~büchse** f *m.-pot* **~gas** n ⟨mil⟩ *mustard gas; (WW I) yperite* **~gemüse** n *vegetables* pl *pickled with m. (seed)* **~gurken** f [pl] *cucumbers* pl *pickled with m. (seed)* **~korn** n *grain of m.-seed* **~löffel** m *m.-spoon* **~mehl** n *m.-powder* **~pflaster** n *m.-plaster, sinapism* **~same** m = ~korn **~sauce, ~tunke** f *m.-sauce* **~teig** m = ~umschlag **~töpfchen** n = ~büchse **~umschlag** m *m.-poultice*

°**S·enge** f ~/ ⟨fam⟩ *licking (to get a l.)* ‖ jdm ~ geben ⟨sl⟩ *to give a p socks* **s·engen I.** vt/i [h] *to singe (fowls);* (v Plätteisen) *to scorch* ‖ *(the blazing* od *scorching sun)* ‖ (Schwein) *to scald* ‖ (Fuchs) *to smoke* ‖ ~ u brennen *to burn and fire, to lay waste (by fire)* ‖ ~e Hitze *parching heat* **II.** vi [h] *to burn, scorch; to get singed* etc **s·engerig** a ⟨fam⟩ = brenzlich ‖ die Sache riecht ~ ⟨fam⟩ *it's rather hot quarters here* ‖ es wird ~ *it's getting hot here*

S·enior m ~s/Seni'oren *senior* ⟨Ger a. stud⟩ ‖ ≗ [a] *senior* | **~·at** n ~(e)s/~e *seniority* **Seni·orenkonvent** m ⟨Ger⟩ (abbr S.C.) *assembly of heads of student's clubs*

S·enk- **≗bar** a *tiltable, inclinable* **~blei** n *plummet, sinker* **~fuß** m *flat* od *weak foot* | ~einlage [f] *arch-support, instep raiser* **~grube** f *cesspool, cesspit; draining well; gully hole* **~-haue** f ⟨min⟩ *sinker's pick* **~kasten** m *caisson* **~leine** f *fathom-line* **~nadel** f ⟨surg⟩ *probe* **~niet** m *flush rivet* **~rahmen** (f Wasserbau) m *sinking-frame* **~rebe** f *layer of a vine* **≗recht** a *vertical;* ⟨math⟩ *perpendicular* (nicht ~ *out of the perp.*) ‖ ~er Durchschnitt *profile* ‖ °das einzig S.e *the only right th to do* | adv ~ abfallen *to fall sheer* | ≗start [m] *vertical takeoff* **~reis** n ⟨hort⟩ *layer* **≗rückig** a ⟨hors⟩ *saddle-backed* **~schacht** m ⟨min⟩ *well* **~scharte** f ⟨hist fort⟩ *machicolation* **~schnur** f *plumb-line* **~schraube** f *countersink* **~stoffablagerung** f *silt of precipitates* **~waage** f *areometer, plumb-rule* **S·enke** f ~/~n *dell* (→ Senkung) **S·enkel** m ~s/~ *lace* | **≗n** vt *to lace* **~nadel** f *tag* **~schnur** f *plummet-line* **~stift** m *tag* **s·enken I.** vt [h] *to let down* ‖ *to lower (a sword, lance, coffin, one's voice, head)* ‖ *to lower, reduce (prices,* ⟨med⟩ *pressure)* ‖ (den Kopf ⟨a.⟩) *to incline, bow, bend* ‖ *to cast down (one's eyes)* ‖ *to drop (one's arms)* ‖ *to dip (a flag)* ‖ *to sink (a shaft, the number of ..)* ‖ *(trees) drive (their roots into the soil)* ‖ ⟨hort⟩ *to lay* ‖ mit Hilfe staatl. Subvention ~ *to roll back (prices)* ‖ halbge–kte Lider *drooped lids;* mit ge–ktem Kopf *with the head down* **II. sich ~** [h] *to sink, to go down* ‖ (of ground, buildings) *to give way, to subside* ‖ (of ground) *to fall away;* (of road) *to run downwards; to pitch down;* (of wall) *to sag* ‖ (sich neigen) *to dip, slope* ‖ (Fundament, Bodensatz) *to settle* ‖ ⟨aero, a–n⟩ (langsam) *to touch down* | **auf**: *to settle down on; night descended over (the earth); rest d.d on (his soul); silence fell upon him; sleep closed (his eyes)* | **unter**: *to sink under a load* **S·enker** m ~s/~ **1.** ⟨hort⟩ *layer, offshoot* **2.** ⟨min⟩ (P) *sinker* **S·enkung** f ~/~en *sinking, sag; pit* ‖ (bes. der Preise) *lowering, reduction* ‖ *subsidence* ‖ ⟨path⟩ *prolapse* ‖ (Vertiefung) *depression, dip, hollow* ‖ (Neigung) *inclination* ‖ ⟨pros⟩ *thesis* ‖ ~ (e–s Bauwerkes) *subsidence, sinking* | ~sblutfülle [f] ⟨med⟩ *congestion, hypostasis;* ~sküste [f] *sinking coast;* ~swinkel [m] ⟨artill⟩ *depression angle*

Senn m ~en/~en *Alpine herdsman* | **~e** f *pasture-land* **~er·ei** f *A. dairy* **~erin** f *A. dairy-(maid* od*)-woman* **~hütte** f *chalet; A. dairy*

S·ennes- **~blätter** n [pl] *senna-leaves* pl

†**Sen·onen** pl (gallische Völkerschaft) *Senones*

Sens·al m ~(e)s/~e *(sworn) broker* **Sensar·ie** f ~/~n *brokerage* **Sensati·on** [ts] f ~/ *sensation, thrill* ‖ (Trick) *stunt* ‖ ⟨fig⟩ *melodrama* ‖ e–e ~ s *to raise a s.* ‖ ~ erregen *to create a s.* ‖ e–e ~ z erwarten h ⟨sl⟩ *to be for the high-jump* | **≗·ell** a *s.al* ‖ (aufregend) *thrilling;* ⟨sl⟩ *blue fire* [attr], ⟨Am a.⟩ *yellow* | **~s-** *s.al* **~lust** f *s.-seeking, -mongering* **≗lüstern** a ⟨Am fam a.⟩ *yellow* **~mache** f *sensationalism* **~presse** f *yellow press* **~propaganda** f *propaganda stunts* pl **~roman** m *shocker, thriller* **~sucht** f *s.alism*

S·ense f ~/~n *scythe* (dengeln *to sharpen*) | ~! ⟨teens⟩ *not I! nothing doing!* | **~n-** **~mann** m *mower, reaper, scytheman* ‖ ⟨fig⟩ *Death* **~-schmied** m *scythe-smith* **~stein** m *whetstone* **~wurf** m *handle of a sc.*

sens·ibel a *sensitive, emotionally alive* ‖ ⟨dero⟩ *touchy* **S-bilisierung** f ⟨phot⟩ *sensitization* **S-bili·t·ät** f ~/ *sensibility, sensitiveness, sensitivity* **Sens·orium** n ~s/ ⟨anat⟩ *sensory* **Sent·enz** f ~/~en *maxim, aphorism* ‖ in ~en sprechen, **~i·ös** s *to be sententious, to speak in aphorisms* **sentiment·al** a *sentimental;* ⟨fam⟩ *mawkish; mushy;* ⟨sl⟩ *soppy* ‖ ~ w *or* reden *to sentimentalize* (über *about*) **~isch** a (bei Schiller Ggs zu naiv = realistisch in Harmonie mit der Natur); ~ = ohne diese, aber idealistisch danach strebend **≗it·ät** f ~/ *sentimentality* ‖ ⟨sl⟩ *sob stuff*

separ·at a *separate* **≗abzug** m *off-print* **~druck** m = Sonderdruck **≗eingang** m *private entrance* **≗·ist** m ~en/~en *separatist* | **S-or** m ~s/–'oren ⟨a. brew⟩ *grader* **separ·ieren** vt & sich ~ [h]

to separate || sich ~ ⟨pol⟩ *to secede*; ⟨com⟩ *to dissolve partnership*

S·epia f ~/–pien ⟨zoo⟩ *cuttle-fish* || (Farbe) *sepia* | ~zeichnung [f] *s. drawing*

Sept·ember m ~(s)/~ *September* → April

Sept·ett n ~s/~e ⟨mus⟩ *septuor* **Septim·aner** m ~s/~ ⟨Ger⟩ *seventh-form boy, preparatory pupil*

Sept·ime f ~/~n ⟨mus⟩ *seventh*

s·eptisch a *dirty* (*wound*), ⟨med⟩ *septic*

sepulkr·al a *funeral* (*art*)

S·equens m ~/–entes ⟨mst stud sl⟩ *the following* **Sequ·enz** f ~/~en ⟨cards⟩ *sequence*

Sequ·ester 1. m ~s/~ (P) *sequestrator* **2.** n ~s/~ (Beschlagnahme) *sequestration* **-trati·on** ~/~en ⟨jur⟩ *seq.tion, seizin* **s-tr·ieren** vt [h] *to put in trust* || ⟨jur⟩ *to sequester, sequestrate*

Serail [ze'ra:j] n [~s/~s & ~e] *seraglio*

S·eraph m [~s/~e & Seraph·im] *seraph* **ser·aphisch** a *seraphic* || ⟨fig⟩ *angelic*

S·erbe m, **S·erbin** f *inhabitant* (od *native*) *of Servia*; *Servian* **S·erbien** n *Servia* **s·erbisch** a *S.n*

Seren·ade f ~/~n *serenade* || dazu: *to s. a p*

Seren·issimus m ~/–mi *His Serene Highness*

S·erge, Sersche f ~/ ⟨tail⟩ *serge*

Sergeant [ser'ʒant] m ~en/~en ⟨mil⟩ *sergeant*

seri·al/parall·el a ⟨comp⟩ *s. p.* **S·erie** f ~/~n *series* || (Billard) *break* || ⟨com⟩ *issue* | **~n-~arbeit** f → Reihen **~artikel** m *mass produced article* **~durchleuchtung** f (v Pn) *mass radiography* **~fabrikation** f → Reihen– **~fertigung** f *series* od *quantity production* **~flugzeug** n (*mass*) *production aircraft* **~guß** m ⟨tech⟩ *duplicate casting* **~los** n *serial lottery-ticket* **≃mäßig** a/adv ~hergestellt *production-type* [attr] (⟨mot⟩ .. *car*) **~motor** m *engine currently in production* **~nummer** f *factory serial number, maker's number* **~schalter** m *multicircuit switch* **~schaltung** f ⟨el⟩ *series-* od *tandem-connection*; in ~ *in series* **~stanzen** n ⟨comp⟩ *gang punch*(*ing*) **~wagen** m ⟨mot⟩ *stock car*

seri·ös a *serious*; *well-reputed*; *respectable*; *reliable*

ser·ös a ⟨physiol⟩ *serous* → Serum

Serpent·ine f ~/~n *serpentine* (*line, road*)

Serpent·in- ~stein m ⟨min⟩ *serpentine-stone* || (edler) *jade* **~tanz** m *skirt-dancing*

S·erum n ~s/Seren ⟨med⟩ *serum*; → serös, ~ gegen Kinderlähmung *anti-polio vaccine*

Serv·ante f ~/~n = Kredenz

Servel·atwurst = Zervelatwurst

Service m ~/ ['sə:vis] (Bedienung, „Kunden"-„Dienst") *service* | S·ervic·enter [n] *servicenter*

Service [zer'vi:s] n ~s/~ (*dinner-*)*set*, (*china*) *service*; englisches ~ *silver service* | [abstr] ⟨hot⟩ *attendance* **Serv·ier- ~brett** n *salver, tray* **~schürze** f *pinafore*, ⟨fam⟩ *pinny* **~tisch** m *service-table, sideboard*; *dumb waiter* **~wagen** m *trolley*, ⟨Am⟩ *coaster* **serv·ieren** vt [h] *to serve* (*up*) || jdm ~ *to help a p* (*to fish*); jdm Tee ~ *to lay a p's tea* | vi [h] *to wait* (*at table*) **Servi·ette** f ~/~n *serviette*, (*table-*)*napkin* **~nkreppapier** n *creped s. paper* **~nring** m *n.-ring* **~ntasche** f *napkin-sachet* **s·ervil** a *servile, obsequious* | **≃it·ät** f *servility* **Servit·ut** f ~/~en (n ~s/~e) ⟨jur⟩ ⟨engl⟩ *easement*; ⟨Scot⟩ *servitude* || ~ des dienenden (herrschenden) Grundstücks *negative* (*positive*) *easement* **S·ervo-** ~bremse f *power* od ⟨bes mot⟩ *vacuum brake*; **~motor** m ⟨a-n⟩ *booster*

S·esam m ~s/ **1.** ⟨bot⟩ *sesame* **2.** ~, tu dich auf! *open, sesame!* | **~öl** n *benne oil*

S·essel m ~s/~ *arm-, easy-chair* || (ohne Lehne) *stool* **~bahn** f, **~lift** m *chair-lift* **~recht** n ⟨hist⟩ *right of sitting at Court* **~träger** m *sedan-chair man* **s·eßhaft** a *settled, domiciled, established, stationary* || (irgendwo ansässig) *resident*; ⟨zoo⟩ *sedentary* || *persistent* (*gas*) || ~ w *to settle* | **≃igkeit** f *settledness, stationariness* **S·ession** f ~/~en *session, sitting*

Sest·erz m ~(e)s/~e ⟨num⟩ *sesterce*

Sest·ine f ~/~n ⟨pros⟩ *sextain*

Set n ~s/~s ⟨tail⟩ (Pullover u Weste) *twin-set*

S·etz- ~angel f *trimmer* **~art** f *manner of composing* (*c–g*) **~brett** n ⟨typ⟩ *c–g-board* **~ei** n *fried egg* **~fehler** m *misprint* **~hase** m *doe hare* **~holz** n ⟨agr⟩ *dibble* **~kasten** m (*type-*)*case*, (*letter-*)*case* **~kunst** f ⟨mus⟩ *composition* | *type-setting* **~linie** f ⟨typ⟩ *setting-rule* **~maschine** f ⟨typ⟩ *c–g-* (od *type-setting*) *machine* **~rebe** f ⟨hort⟩ *layer of vine* **~reis** n ⟨hort⟩ *layer, shoot, cutting* **~schiff** n ⟨typ⟩ *galley* **~teich** m *store-, breeding-pond* **~waage** f *level* **~weide** f *wellow-slip* **~zeit** f *breeding-time* || ⟨ich⟩ *spawning-time*

s·etzen I. vt [h] **A.** *to seat* (*a p*) || *to set* (*a hen* [*on eggs*]) || ⟨hunt⟩ = gebären | mst *to put* (an *to*, auf *on*); *to place* (an *at*, auf *on*, in *in*[*to*]) | (wetten) [a. ell] *to stake money*; *to bet, wager* (auf *on*) | ~ wir, **daß** *let's assume that* || gesetzt es wäre so *supposing it were so* **B.** (**Denkmal** etc) *to erect, raise* (f *to*) || den Fall ~ *to suppose*; gesetzten Falls .. *suppose* ..! || [dat] Grenzen ~ *to limit* || Interpunktion ~ *to punctuate* || Junge ~ *to breed*, ⟨ich⟩ *to spawn* | *to put up* (*boundary-stones*) || *to place* (*one's feet*) || *to hoist* (*flags*) || *to apply* (*leeches*) || *to put in* od *up* (*a stove*) | ⟨hort⟩ *to plant* || ⟨sport⟩ *to seed* (*competitors*) | ⟨typ⟩ *to compose* ⟨a. mus⟩, *to set up* **C.** e–n **fest** ~ *to put a p in jail* || es wird hoch gesetzt *the stakes are high* || ⟨mus⟩ höher ~ *to raise the pitch of*; mehrstimmig ~ *to arrange for several voices* || ordentlich ~ *to arrange* || e–n warm ~ *to put a p in a warm place*, ⟨iron⟩ .. *into prison* **D. an**: alles daran ~ *to move heaven and earth* || sein Leben daran ~ *to risk one's life for it* || ⟨tail⟩ an–e–a–~ *to piece .. together* || ans Land ~ *to disembark* || jdn an die Luft *or* auf die Straße ~ *to turn* od *kick a p out* || an den Mund ~ *to raise to one's lips* || sich .. *to sit down to the typewriter* | **auf** den Thron ~ *to raise to the throne*, wieder .. *to restore to the thr.* || auf ein Pferd ~ (wetten) *to back a horse*, alles .. *to put one's shirt on a h.*, aufs falsche (richtige) .. *to back the wrong h.* (*to back the winner* ⟨a. fig⟩); auf Pferde ~ *to play the ponies* || den Punkt aufs „i" ~ *to dot the "i"* || Bier auf Wein ~ *to drink b. on the top of w.* | **außer** Gebrauch ~ *to put aside* (od *out of use, service*) || außer Gefecht ~ *to put out of action* | etw **gegen** etw anderes ~ *to compare one th with another* | **in**: **1.** *to sit a p in a car, chair*; *to set out carp in a pond* **2.** s–n Ehrgeiz darein ~, zu tun *to take pride in doing* || k–n **Fuß** mehr in das Haus ~ (*I'll*) *never again set foot in that h.* || **Hoffnung** ~ in *to set one's hopes upon* .. || (**Kinder**) in die Welt ~ *to beget* bzw. *bear* || s–n Stolz darein ~ *to take pride in it* || **Truppen** in Marsch ~ *to give orders to march* || **Vertrauen** in jdn ~ *to trust a p* **3. in Brand**, Flammen ~ *to set .. on fire* || ⟨fig⟩ in **Flammen** ~ *to incite, rouse* || in Galopp ~ ⟨hors⟩ *to put .. to a gallop* || in Gang ~ *to set going*, (Unternehmen) *to set on foot* || in das **Jahr** 1600 ~ *to assign to 1600* || in Schrecken etc ~ *to terrify, alarm* || ⟨theat⟩ in **Szene** ~ *to mount, stage*; neu .. *to revive* || in **Verlegenheit** ~ *to perplex* || in die **Zeitung** ~ *to insert in the paper, to advertise* | **über** [acc]: *to take .. across* (*the water*), [abs] *to ferry .. across* || ⟨fig⟩ *to place over* od *above, to prefer to* || jdn (als Verwalter) über etw ~ *to place a p in charge of a th* || den Fuß über die Schwelle ~ *to cross the thr.* | **um**: (Pn) *to range .. about* (*the table*), (Sn *to arrange .. about* ..) | e–n **unter** (die ersten) ~ *to rank a p among* .. || unter Wasser ~ *to flood, submerge* || e–n (*or* e–m den Stuhl) **vor** die Tür ~ *to turn a p out*; k–n Fuß .. *never to move out of the house* | **zum** Pfande ~ *to pawn* || zurecht ~ (S) *to set .. right*; (P [gehörig]) *to reprimand* ||

zum Richter ~ *to appoint .. judge* ‖ zur Ruhe gesetzt *pensioned off* **II. sich** ~ [h] *to sit down*; (formell) *to take a seat, to be seated* | ⟨orn⟩ *to perch* | (zu Boden gehen) *to sink* ‖ (Niederschlag, Haus) *to settle* | ⟨fig⟩ (P) *to settle down* | sich gerade ~ *to sit up (straight)* | sich **aufs** Pferd ~ *to mount* od *get on horseback* | sich gegen etw ~ *to oppose, resist a th* | sich bei jdm **in** Ansehen (Gunst) ~ *to acquire influence with a p* (*to ingratiate o.s. with a p*) ‖ der Staub setzt sich in die Kleider .. *clings to ..* ‖ sich in e–n Wagen ~ *to get into a car* | sich (nahe) **zu** jdm ~ *to sit down with a p*; *to sit near* (*close to*) *a p* ‖ sich zu Tische ~ *to sit down to dinner* ‖ sich zur Wehr ~ *to defend o.s.* **III.** vt/imps [h] **es setzt** .. *it causes* (*trouble*) ‖ es setzt etw (= Schläge) *you'll get it hot*; *they will come to blows* **IV.** vi [s & h] [→ I. A.] ‖ über etw ~ *to leap over, to jump, clear* (⟨hors⟩ *take*) (*a hedge*) ‖ (über den Fluß ~) *to pass* (*over*), *to cross* .. **V. gesetzt,** es wäre so *say that it is so* → gesetzt **S·etzer** m ~s/~ ⟨typ⟩ *compositor* ‖ ⟨racing⟩ *layer* **~fehler** m *compositor's error* **~saal** m, **~·ei** f *composing room* **S·etzling** m ~(e)s/~e ⟨hort⟩ *slip, young plant* ‖ ⟨ich⟩ *spawn, fry* **S·etzung** f ⟨arch⟩ *settlement, settling*

S·euche f ~/~n *contagious disease, epidemic* (⟨vet⟩ *epizootic*), *e. disease*; *pestilence* | ⟨fig⟩ *plague*; *contagion*; *scourge*; *infectious habit* ‖ v der ~ heimgesucht *plague-stricken* | **~n-** *epidemiological* (*statistics*) **~herd** n *centre of an epidemic*

s·eufzen vi [h] *to sigh* (nach *for*, über *at*) ‖ *to groan* (*under*) | **~d** ⟨a.⟩ *with a sigh* **S·eufzer** m ~s/~ *sigh, moan, groan* (ausstoßen *to give* od *heave a s.*; *to moan*; *to utter a g.*); (tiefes Atmen) *suspiration* ‖ der letzte ~ *the last breath* **~brücke** f *Bridge of S.s* **~spalte** f *agony-column*

Sev·illa [se'vi(l)ja] n ⟨Span⟩ (Stadt)

S·ex m ~es/ °**~biene** f *sexy girl* **~bombe** f *A-bomb*, ⟨sl⟩ *oomph-girl* | Frau mit **~krasit** m *A-bomb* **S·exibild** n ⟨Am⟩ *cheesecake* **Sex-Starkasten** m, **Sex-Sternenhimmel** m *sex stardom*

S·ex- ~ta f ~/ *sixth* (⟨engl⟩ *first*) *form* **~t·aner** m (~in f) *sixth* (⟨engl⟩ *first-*)*form boy* (f *girl*) **~t·ant** m ~en/~en ⟨astr⟩ *sextant* **~te** f ~/~n ⟨mus⟩ (kl *minor*, gr *major*) *sixth* ‖ ⟨ec⟩ *sext* **~t·ett** n ~s/~e ⟨mus⟩ *sextet* **~t·ole** f ~/~n ⟨mus⟩ *sextuplet*

Sexu·al- ~erziehung f *sexual education* **~roman** m *sex-novel* **~verbrechen** n *sex crime*; *sexual offense* **~it·ät** f ~/ *sexuality* ‖ intellektuelle ~ *high brows, low loins* **sexu·ell** a *sexual*

Sezessi·on f ~/~en *secession*

Sez·ier- ~besteck n (*case for*) *dissecting instruments* **~messer** n *scalpel* **~saal** m *dissecting-room* **sez·ieren** vt [h] *to dissect*

Se(y)sch·ellen pl (Inseln im Ind. O.) *Seychelles*

Sh·effield [ʃ–] n ⟨engl⟩ (Stadt)

Sh·etlandinseln f pl *Shetland Islands*

Sh·irting m → Schirting

S·iam, der Meerbusen v *the Gulf of Siam*

Sib·irien n *Siberia* **Sib·irier** m, **~in** f *Siberian, inhabitant of Siberia* **sib·irisch** a *Siberian*

Sib·ylle f ~/~n *sibyl* **sibyll·inisch** a *sibylline*

sich [dat & acc] **I.** [des pron refl] **A.** *oneself*; *himself, herself, itself* ‖ (*to free, injure, hate o.s.*) ‖ *don't hurt yourself*, pl: *yourselves* | *him etc* (*he looks about him*) (*the committee, audience* etc *had before them*) | [oft a. unübersetzt]: ~ (·an)-kleiden etc *to dress* (*o.s.*); *to hide* (*o.s.*), *to wash* (*o.s.*) = *to have a wash* ‖ ~ [dat] die Hände waschen *to wash one's hands* ‖ ~ [acc] hindurcharbeiten *to work one's way through* | [unübersetzt]: ~ trennen *to separate* [vi] | [durch pass] ~ schämen *to be ashamed* **B. es** macht (*or* ⟨fam⟩ tut) ~ [acc]! *pretty well!* ‖ hier lebt ~'s gut *it's pleasant to live here* | **das** findet ~ *time will show* ‖ das läßt ~ hören *that is sth like* ‖ das fragt ~ *that is questionable* **C.** [**Betonung** nach prep: das Ding an ·~; aber: etw ·an ~ nehmen ‖ in ·~ ruhen; aber: ·in ~ h | so: ·auf ~ nehmen; ·außer ~ s; b·ei, f·ür, h·inter ~ h; m·it ~ bringen, führen, nehmen; n·ach ~ ziehen; ·über ~ bringen; ·um ~ schlagen; ·unter ~ h; v·on ~ geben, weisen; v·or ~ h; z·u ~ k] **·an** ~ *on one's p* ‖ (S) *in itself* (⟨a.⟩ ·an u ·f ~); an ·~ ohne Wert *without intrinsic value* | (S) nichts ·auf ~ h *to be of no consequence* | **für** ·~ *individually, by itself* ‖ f ·~ betrachtet *considered on its own merits* ‖ f ·~ s *to be alone* ‖ das ist e–e S f ·~ [acc] *that's another story* | **z·u** ~ [dat] bitten *to invite ..* (*home* od *to one's flat*) **II.** (= e–a) (*they love*) *each other, one another* **III.** ≃**·androhen** n ⟨eth⟩ *threatening*; ≃**zursch·austellen** n *exhibitionism*

S·ichel f ~/~n *sickle, reaping-hook* ‖ (Mond-≃) *crescent* ≃**förmig** a *sickle-shaped*; ⟨bot⟩ *falcated*; ⟨scient⟩ *meniscal* **~messer** n ⟨hort⟩ *pruning knife* **~wagen** m ⟨hist mil⟩ *scythed chariot* **s·icheln** vt [h] *to cut with a sickle*

s·icher a **A.** (gewiß) *sure, certain, positive* ‖ (geschützt) *proof* (*against*), (*fire-* etc.) *proof* ‖ (außer Gefahr) *secure, safe* (vor [dat] *from*) ‖ (zuversichtlich) *confident, positive* ‖ (zuverlässig) *reliable* | ⟨fam⟩ so ~ wie nur was *or* wie das Amen in der Kirche (*as*) *safe as a house*; *as sure as eggs* (*are eggs*); *as sure as fate* ‖ ~ ist ~ *no harm being on the safe side*; *safety first*! | es kann **als** ~ gelten *it can be safely assumed* **B.** *steady* (*hand*) ‖ v ~er **Hand** (*I have it*) *on good authority*; mit sicherer H. *sure-handed* ‖ *confident* (*bearing*) ‖ *safe*(*-conduct*) ‖ *certain* (*death*) ‖ *good* (*money, debts*) ‖ *faithful* (*memory*) ‖ *sure* (*proof, method*) ‖ *safe* (*way*) ‖ *reliable* (*opinion*; *news* [sg]) ‖ *unfailing* (*remedy*) ‖ *trustworthy* (*result*) ‖ ⟨sl⟩ *dead* (*tip*) *good* (*marksman*) | ~es Auftreten *assurance* ‖ ~e S *cinch* ‖ ~e Tatsache *certainty* **C.** ~ s: *it is certain*; *I feel sure*, ⟨Am a.⟩ *I guess* ‖ *I am not sure that* (ob) .. ‖ e–r S ~ s *to be sure, positive* (⟨fam⟩ *dead certain*) *of a th* ‖ s–r S ~ s *to be sure of o.s., to be positive* (*that* ..), *to know what one is about* ‖ (das ist so) ~ wie ich hier stehe! *as sure as I live by bread, that's as sure as taxes and death* | *his election is regarded as certain* ‖ *success is assured* ‖ du kannst ~ s, daß .. *you bet I don't forget it* **D.** [adv] *I arrived safe*(*ly*) ‖ auf jdn ~ bauen *to put full confidence in a p* ‖ um ~ zu gehen *to be on the safe side*; (*in order*) *to avoid risks* ‖ ~ gewinnen *to be safe to win* ‖ er kommt ~ *he is sure to come* ‖ (*to count*) *confidently* (*upon a p*) ‖ (*to know*) *for certain* **E.** [adv] [objektiv] *certainly, for certain* ‖ [subjektiv] *surely, to be sure* | *he certainly did do it* | ~! *certainly*! *that's right*! ⟨Am⟩ *sure*! *sure th*! ‖ aber ~! *by all means*!; um ~ z gehen *in order to play safe*; er wird ~ gewinnen *he is sure to win* **F.** ⟨fam⟩ auf Numero ≃ *in prison* **~|gehen** vi [s] → D. **~|stellen** vt [h] *to secure, safeguard*; *to put in safe keeping*; ⟨übtr⟩ *to insure* (*success*); (*the guns were*) *seized* (*by the police*); ⟨hum fig⟩ *I got it nice and safe* ‖ sich ~ *to protect o.s.* (*against*) ≃**stellung** f ⟨ins⟩ *guarantee, cover* **S·icherheit** f ~/~en *certainty, security, safety* ‖ *safeguard* ‖ *trustworthiness, reliableness* ‖ *guarantee* ‖ *confidence, positiveness* ‖ ⟨jur, com⟩ *security* ‖ (des Auftretens) *assurance, self-possession, self-confident address* | (S) (nur) scheinbare ~ *rope of sand* | ~ geben, leisten f ⟨a.⟩ *to guarantee* [vt]; sich ~ verschaffen, daß *to insure o.s. that* | **auf** ~ bedacht s *to play for safety* ‖ **in** ~ bringen *to secure*; sich .. *to save one's skin* ‖ **mit** ~ behaupten *to affirm* ‖ mit ~ annehmen *to take for granted*; es kann mit ~ angenommen w *it can be safely assumed*; mit an ~ grenzender Wahrscheinlichkeit *in all probability* (vgl: *it is pretty safe to say, I expect it will prove true, it may well* *be true, it seems almost certain)* | es besteht k–e ~ *there is no assurance*; ~ leisten *to furnish a bond*, ⟨jur⟩ *to file a b. in court* | **~s- ~abkommen** n *s.c.y agreement* **~abstand** m ⟨bes mot⟩ *safe driving distance* **~archiv** n *s.c.y collection* **~aufhängung** f ⟨theat⟩ *secondary suspension*, ⟨Am⟩ *safety chain* **~ausschuß** m *committee of s.f.y*, ⟨Am⟩ *vigilance-committee* **~beamte(r)** m *s.c.y agent*, ⟨Am⟩ *vigilante* **~beanspruchung** f ⟨tech⟩ *safe stress* **~beauftragte(r)** m *adviser on s.c.y questions* **~behörde** f *police* | zusätzliche **~bestimmungen** f pl *s.f.y supplement* **~dienst** m *secret service* **~film** m *s.f.y film* **~fonds** m *s.c.y-fund* **~geleit** n *safe-conduct* **~glas** n *s.f.y glass* **~grenze** f ⟨stat⟩ *level of significance* **~gurt** m ⟨aero⟩ *seat belt* **~hahn** m *s.f.y cock* **≗halber** [adv] *for s.f.y* **~kette** f *s.f.y chain*; (f die Uhr) *watch-guard* **~klausel** f *safeguard* **~koeffizient** m ⟨tech⟩ *factor of s.f.y* **~lampe** f *Davy(-lamp)* **~leistung** f *s.c.y, bail* (gegen ~ *on b.*; gegen ~ aus der Haft entlassen ⟨jur⟩ *to admit to b.*) **~nadel** f *s.f.y-pin* **~polizei** f ⟨Ger⟩ *s.c.y police* **~schloß** n *s.f.y-lock* **~radius** m (*ABC*) *minimum safe distance* N **~rat** m *S.c.y Council* (UN) **~soll** n ⟨logist⟩ *s.f.y level of supply* **~ventil** n *s.f.y* od *emergency valve* **~vertrag** m *s.c.y treaty* **~wache** f *police* **~zündholz** n *s.f.y-match*

s·icherlich [adv] *certainly, surely, assuredly* || *I am sure* || *it is sure* (*to get warmer*); *he stands* (*to win, lose*); *he would be sure* (*to split*) || ⟨fam⟩ ~! *rather*!, *you bet*! **sichern I.** vt [h] *to secure* ⟨a. mil⟩, *to steady* || *guarantee* || *to stow away* || *to fortify, cover* (⟨a. mil⟩ *a hill, a bridge*) || *to safety* (*a gun*) | **sich** ~ *to look to* (*one's, its*) *security* ⟨a. mil⟩; sich selbst ~ *to provide one's own s.c.y*; sich ~ gegen *to provide* od *safeguard against*; sich [dat] etw ~ *to assure* (Vertrauen) | ge–rt ⟨com⟩ *covered* **II.** vi [h] ⟨hunt⟩ (of game) *to wind, scent* [vi] **S·icherung** f ~/~en *securing, safeguard(ing)*; *mil. protection* || ⟨el⟩ *fuse, cut-out*; e–e ~ durchbrennen *to fuse a f.*; *the f. is blown* || Seil≗ *belay* || (am Gewehr) *safety(-bolt)* || **~s- ~aufgaben** f pl ⟨mil⟩ *s.c.y missions* **~auftrag** m *covering* (*s.c.y, screening*) *mission* **~dienst** m *s.c.y* ⟨a. mil⟩ **~faktor** m ⟨tech⟩ *reserve factor* (*in materials*) **~feder** f *locking spring* **~flügel** m ⟨tact⟩ *protective flank* od *wing* **~gurt** m (Dachdecker≗) *s.f.y-belt*, ⟨aero⟩ *seat belt* **~gürtel** m ⟨tact⟩ *cover belt* **~hypothek** f *cautionary mortgage* **~linie** f ⟨tact⟩ *outpost line of resistance*; vorderste ~ *outpost line* N **~geschäft** n *covering transaction* **~kompanie** f *covering c.* **~streifen** m ⟨el⟩ *fuse strip* **~truppen** f pl ⟨tact⟩ *s.c.y forces*

Sicht f ~/ *sight*; *clearness*; *range of vision* | (die) ~ behindern auf .. *to obscure* (*a traffic sign, a pedestrian*) || (etw) der ~ entziehen *to screen .. from* (*enemy*) *vision* || jdm die ~ nehmen *to cut off a p's sight* | ~ unbegrenzt! *visibility unlimited*!; unbegrenzte ~ ⟨meteor⟩ *unl.d v.y*; ⟨aero⟩ *ceiling and v.y unl.d* (*CAVU*) || ungehinderte ~ auf Formulare ⟨comp⟩ *complete forms v.y* || volle ~ ⟨comp⟩ *full v.y* || wenig ~ *poor v.y* | **auf** (lange) ~, bei ~ ⟨com⟩ *at* (*long*) *sight*; auf l. ~ ⟨allg⟩ *for a long time to come*; Plan auf l. ~ *l.-t. plan*; Planen auf l. ~ *long range planning*; Vorhaben auf l., weite ~ *l.-term project* || auf l. ~ denken *to take a l. view* | **außer** ~ k *to drop out of sight* | **bei** schlechter ~ *during conditions of reduced* od *poor v.y* | ⟨mil⟩ Deckung **gegen** ~ *cover from view* | **in** ~ k *to come in sight*; in ~! ⟨mar⟩ *ahead*!; in ~ bek *to get view of* | **nach** ~ ⟨com⟩ *after sight* **~ausschnitt** m ⟨phot⟩ *section* **~begrenzung** f *optical limitation* **~behinderung** f *loss of v.y* **~bereich** m *visual range* **~beton** m ⟨arch⟩ *stripped concrete* **~fähigkeit** f ⟨mill⟩ *sifting properties* **~fenster** n *control window* **~flug-** ~regeln [f pl], ~vorschrift [f] *visual flight rules* (*VFR*) N **~linie** f *sight line* ⟨a. theat⟩ **~lochen**! n ⟨comp m. m.⟩ *operators can see the card while they are punching it* **~luke** f *peephole*; *control window* ⟨a. a–n⟩ **~navigation** f ⟨aero⟩ *terrestrial* od *contact n.* **~peiler** m *indicating direction finder* **~peilgerät** n *cathode-ray d. f.* **~schießen** n *seen fire* **~tage** m pl ⟨com⟩ *days of grace* **~verhältnisse** n pl *visibility* **~vermerk** m *initials* pl, *visé, visa* **~wechsel** m *sight-bill* **~weite** f *visibility*; *optical range*; ⟨mar⟩ *sighting distance*; außer ~ *out of sight* **~werbung** f *visual advertising* **~zeichen** n *visual signal, visible mark*; *marker*; ⟨aero⟩ *ground signal* **s·ichtbar** *a visible* || (deutlich) *conspicuous, marked* || (offenbar) *evident, manifest* || ~ m ⟨tech⟩ *to visualize* || ~ s ⟨a.⟩ *to show, to be showing* || ~ w *to heave in sight, to loom to be seen, to come clear* (*of a house* hinter [dat]) | adv (*to carry the pistol*) *in plain sight* | **≗keit** f ~/ *visibleness* || *conspicuousness* || *evidentness* | **~lich** [a & adv] *visibly, evidently* etc **≗machung** f *showing* **≗werden** n *appearance, loom(ing)* **s·ichten** vg [h] **1.** *to sight, spot* **2.** (sieben) *to shift, screen, winnow* | ⟨fig⟩ *to sort, sift, examine* **S·ichter** m ~s/~ *classifier* || Flügel≗ *whizzer cl.r*; Regulier≗ *regulating fine air separator* | ≗mittig [a] ⟨mill⟩ *centrally through the cl.r* **S·ichtigkeit** f ~/ (der Luft) *visibility* **s·ichtlich** [a & adv] → sichtbarlich **S·ichtung** f ~/~en *sifting, sorting, examination*; *classification*

S·icker- ~graben [m] *leaching trench*; ~grube [f], ~schacht [m] *dry well, seepage pit*; ~kanal [m] *drainage culvert*; ~wasser [n] *ground-w.* | **≗n** vi [h & s] *to trickle, ooze, drop, seep* || (Licht) *to filter* || (*barrels*, ⟨fig⟩ *news*) *leak*

sid·erisch a ⟨astr⟩ *sidereal* (*year*)

Sie 1. pron [sg & pl] (höfliche Anrede) *you* || ⟨fam⟩ ~ da! *I say*!, *you there*! **2.** f ~/~n (*it's a*) *she, female*; *hen bird* **sie** pron pers **1.** [f/sg] *she*; [acc] *her* || (S) ⟨mst⟩ *it* || (Schiff, Land) *she* || (*sun, Providence*) *he* **2.** [pl] *they*; [acc] *them* || ~ drei *three of them* || ~ h ⟨a.⟩ *theirs is*

Sieb n ~(e)s/~e *sieve* || (grobes) *riddle*; *coarse* od *preliminary sieve* od *screen*; Kies≗ *screen* || (f Flüssiges) *strainer* || ⟨tech⟩ *wire, colander* || Vor- u Feinsiebbespannung [f] *preliminary and fine sifting sieves* pl **Sieb-** ⟨tech⟩ *granulometric* (*analysis*) **~blech** n *perforated tray, slotted plate* **~druck** m ⟨typ⟩ *silk-screen process* bzw *picture* **~gut** n *screenings, sievings* **~kasten** m *box-riddle, cinder-sifter* **~kette** f ⟨wir⟩ *filter* **~korb** m ⟨mill⟩ *round screen* **~kreis** m ⟨wir⟩ *selectivity* **~leder** n ⟨tech⟩ *apron* **~lochung** f *screen perforation* **~mehl** n *coarse flour* **~mühle** f *bolting-mill* **~setzer** m ⟨min⟩ *jigger* **~staub** m *siftings* pl **~trommel** f *screening drum*; *rotary* od *revolving screen* **~tuch** n *straining-cloth* **~walze** f ⟨pap⟩ *dandy-roller* **s·ieben**[1] vt *to sift, riddle, screen*; auf Körnung ~ *to grade* || ⟨fig⟩ *to weed out* **Sieber·ei** f ~/~en *screen plant* **S·iebsel** n *siftings*

s·ieben[2] **I.** [a] *seven* → acht; ein Buch mit 7 Siegeln *a closed book*; das ist mir ein Buch mit ~ Siegeln *that's Greek to me* **II.** ≗ [f] *the number 7, card of 7* || böse ≗ *vixen, termagant*, ⟨Am fam⟩ *battle axe* **S·ieben-** **≗armig** a *seven-branch* (*candlestick*) **~bürge** m, –bürgin [f] *inhabitant* od *native of Transylvania* **~bürgen** n *Transylvania* **~eck** n *heptagon* **≗fach, ≗fältig** a *sevenfold* **~gebirge** n *Seven Mountains* pl **~gestirn** n *Pleiades* pl **~h·ügelstadt** f (Rom) *City of the Seven Hills* **≗jährig** a *of s. years, s. years old* || der ≗jährige Krieg *the S. Years' war* **≗jährlich** a *septennial, occuring every 7 years* **≗mal[ig]** a *7 times* [*repeated*] **≗männig** a ⟨bot⟩ *heptandrious* **~m·eilenstiefel** m pl *seven-league boots* pl **~m·onatskind** n *s.-months' child* **~punkt** m ⟨ent⟩ *lady-bird* **~s·achen** f pl ⟨fam⟩ *belongings* pl, *ths, goods and chattels*; s–e ~ packen *to pack up one's traps, to get one's kit together* **~schläfer** m ⟨zoo⟩ *fat dormouse*; (Tage) pl *the s. sleepers* ||

(⟨fig⟩ = Langschläfer) *lie-a-bed, sluggard* **~-Schmerzen-Madonna** f *M. of the S. Dolours* **≗-stündig** a *of 7 hours* **≗tägig** a *of* od *lasting 7 days* || *7 days old* **~undzw·anzig** *twenty-s.* **~zehn** ⟨obs⟩ = siebzehn **S·iebener** m ~s/~ *the number seven, card of 7* **≗l·ei** a *of seven different sorts;* → Achter **s·iebente** a *seventh* (vgl sechste) **~halb** a *six and a half;* → achte **S·iebentel** n ~s/~ *seventh (part)* **s·iebzehn** a *seventeen* (vgl sechzehn) | **≗er** m *the number 7* **s·iebzehnte** a *7th* **S·iebzehntel** n ~s/~ *seventeenth (part)* **s·iebzig** a *seventy,* → achtzig, dreißig | **≗er** m ~s/~ *septuagenarian* | **~ste** a *seventieth*

siech a *sick(ly), infirm* **≗bett** n *sick-bed* **≗(en)-haus** n *infirmary, hospital for incurables* **s·iechen** vi [h] *to be ailing, sickly* od *in bad health* || ⟨a. fig⟩ *to languish, to pine away,* ⟨fig⟩ *to go into a decline* **S·iechheit** f ~/, **S·iechtum** n ~(e)s/ *sick(li)ness; failing health* || *languishing* ⟨a. fig⟩ || ⟨fig⟩ *decline*

S·iede- ~beginn m ⟨phys⟩ *initial boiling point (I.B.P.)* **~ende** n ⟨phys⟩ *final boiling point (F.B.P.)* **~grad** m = ~punkt **~haus** n *boiling-house* **~hitze** f *boiling heat* **~kessel** m *boiler* **~-ofen** m *blanching-furnace* **~pfanne** f *boiling--pan; salt-pan; soap-pan* **~punkt** m *boiling-point* (⟨a. fig⟩ *to b.-p.*) **~verzug** m *delayed act of boiling* **≗warm** = siedendheiß **s·ieden** [sott/gesotten] & reg [h] **I.** vi *to seethe* ⟨a. fig⟩ || ⟨mst⟩ *to boil* || (gelinde) *to simmer* || das Wasser, mein Blut siedet .. *is* (tüchtig *quite*) *boiling* || vor Wut ~ *to be in a boiling rage* **II.** vt *to boil (eggs, potatoes, soap, glue)* || *to refine (sugar)* || *to make salt* || ⟨met⟩ *to blanch* **III.** ≗ n ⟨phys⟩ *ebullition* || stoßweises ~ *bumping* od *unsteady boiling* || ⟨fam⟩ (nahe) am ≗ *near the boil* **s·iedendheiß** a *seething hot* **S·ieder** m ~s/~ *boiler, seether; refiner* | **~·ei** f ~/~en *boiling-house; pan room*

ˣ**Siedel·ei, S·ied(e)lung** f ~/~en *settlement* **s·iedeln** vi [h] *to settle*; ich siedle um, wir siedeln um *I am, we are going to settle somewhere else*

S·iedler m (→ Ansiedler) *settler; homesteader; colonist* | ~stelle [f] *settler's homestead;* ⟨Am a.⟩ *claim;* ~stolz [m] ⟨hum fam⟩ *home-grown tobacco* **S·iedlung** f ~/~en *settlement; colony; housing estates* bzw *project; garden-city;* ⟨Am⟩ *(veterans') development;* Außenbezirks≗ e–r Großstadt *overspill town* | ~sbau [m] *housing estates* pl; pl ~ten ⟨Am⟩ *h.g development;* ~sfarm [f] ⟨Am⟩ *subsistence farm;* ~gemeinde [f] *neighbourhood unit;* ~sgesellschaft [f] *building-society;* ~sgrenze [f] ⟨Am⟩ *frontier;* ~s-planung [f] *layout;* ~sweise [f] ⟨demog⟩ *habitat, settlement;* ~swerk [n] *settlement scheme*

Sieg m ~(e)s/~e *victory* || *mastery (over passion)* || *success* (über *with women*) || leichter ~ *easy conquest,* ⟨parl⟩ *walk-over* ⟨a. sport⟩, ⟨Am⟩ *walkaway, landslide;* e–n leichten ~ davontragen *to win in a walk* || totaler ~ *all-out victory* || den ~ davontragen *or* erringen = siegen || ~ wetten, auf ~ setzen *to back the winner, to bet, back against the field;* ~ u Platz wetten *to bet both ways* || ~ Heil! *three cheers* || der ~ war ihm sicher *he was considered a sure winner* || Wille zum ~ *will to win* **~ball** m ⟨ten⟩ *match-ball* **≗gekrönt** a *crowned with v.* **≗gewohnt** a *accustomed to v.* **≗reich** a *victorious, triumphant; conquering (hero)* || ~ auf der ganzen Linie *victorious all along the line* | [adv] *as a victor* **s·iegen** vi [h] *to conquer* (⟨a.⟩ *o.s.* über sich selbst); *to win* od *carry the day; to come off conqueror* || *to gain the victory* || ⟨sport⟩ *to win* || ⟨fig⟩ *to prevail, flourish* || (über [acc]) *to be victorious, to triumph (over)* || schließlich doch ~ *to win through (over)* || ~ oder sterben! *death or victory!* || ⟨fam⟩ er siegte auf der ganzen Linie *he carried everything before him* **S·ieger** m ~s/~ *conqueror, victor* || ⟨sport⟩ *winner, scorer,* ⟨fam⟩ *top dog;* als ~ durchs Ziel gehen *to come in first (in a race)* || zweiter ~ *runner-up,* zw. ~ s ⟨hum fam⟩ *to come off second-best* **~kranz** m, **~krone** f *conqueror's laurels, crown* **~staat** m *victorious country* **S·ieges- ~aufzug** m *triumph* **~beute** f *trophy; spoils* pl **~bogen** m *triumphal arch* **~-d·ankfest** n *Te Deum* **~denkmal** n *monument in commemoration of a victory* **~feier** f, **~fest** n *celebration of a v.y* **~freude** f *joy over a v.y* **~fürst** m = Sieger **~gepränge** n *triumph* **~geschrei** ausstoßen ⟨fam⟩ *to crow* **≗gewiß** a *sure of v.y* **~-göttin** f *V.y* **~held** m *conquering hero* **~lauf** m, **~lied** n *triumphal progress, song* **~preis** m *prize* **~taumel** m *flush of v.y* **≗trunken** a *flushed with v.y* **~wagen** m *triumphal car* **~zeichen** n *trophy;* ⟨wir⟩ *V-sign* **~zug** m *triumphal march* od *procession* || *victorious campaign* **s·ieghaft** a = siegreich **S·iegwurz** f ⟨bot⟩ *sword-lily*

S·iegel n ~s/~ *seal* (erbrechen *to break*); sein ~ aufdrücken auf *to affix one's s. to* || Staats≗ *privy seal* || Brief u ~ *sign and seal* || **unter** dem ~ [gen] *under the s. (of secrecy)* unter ~ legen *to seal* | ⟨hunt⟩ (Tritt≗ = Fährte) *slot* **~amt** n *signet-office* **~bewahrer** m *keeper of the Seal* || geheimer ~ *Lord Privy Seal* **~bruch** m ⟨jur⟩ *s.-breaking* **~erde** f ⟨min⟩ *terra sigillata* L; *bole, Lemnian earth* **~kunde** f *sphragistics* [a. sg konstr] **~lack** m (~stange [f] *stick of*) *sealing-wax* **~-ring** m *signet-ring* **~stecher** m *seal-engraver*

s·iegeln vt [h] *to seal*

s·iehe! sieh(e) da! *see!* (→ sehen I. B. 3, 4; C)

Siel m & n [~(e)s/~e] (→ seihen) *sluice* || *dike-lock* || (Abzugsgraben) *drain, sewer* | **≗en** vt [h] *to drain* **~wasser** n *sewage*

S·iele f (e–s Karrenschiebers) *belt* || (e–s Pferdes) *breast-piece* || ⟨fig⟩ in den ~n *in harness* || in den ~n sterben *to die in one's boots* od *in the shafts, in harness* ⟨fig⟩ **~ngeschirr** n *breast--harness*

°**s·ielen** vrefl [h] sich ~ *to loll about, to sprawl* | *to loaf*

Si·erra Le·one n (westafrikan. Staat)

Si·erra Mor·ena f ⟨Span⟩ (Gebirge)

Si·erra Nev·ada 1. (Gebirge in Spanien) **2.** (Gebirge in Kalifornien)

Si·esta f [~/~s & Si·esten] *afternoon nap; siesta* || ~ halten *to have one's forty winks*

s·iezen vt [h] *to call a p* „Sie"

S·igel n ~s/~ *logogram, symbol*

Sign·al n ~(e)s/~e *signal* (geben *to give,* ⟨mot⟩ *to sound one's horn,* blasen *to sound,* ablesen *to take in*); ~e geben ⟨rail⟩ *to wigwag;* ⟨Am rail⟩ durch ~ stoppen *to flag (a train)* || Verkehrs≗ *beacon* | ⟨a–n⟩ ~ f Servomotoren zur Schwenkung der Antriebsdüsen *servo-motor input for swinging of thrust nozzles* || ⟨rail⟩ *semaphore;* das ~ auf halt stellen *to stop the block signal* **~apparat** m *s.ling apparatus* **~-brücke** f ⟨rail⟩ *signal gantry* od *bridge* **~buch** n *Code of S.s* **~feuer** n *s.-light, beacon* **~flagge** f *s.ling-flag, hand-flag* **~gast** m *s.man, s.ler,* ⟨fam⟩ *wigwagger* **~geber** m *s.ler* **~glocke** f *warning-bell* **~horn** n *bugle-horn* **~hupe** f *s.-horn* **~kladde** f ⟨mar⟩ *s. log* **~lampe, ~laterne** f ⟨rail⟩ *s.-lamp, s.-light;* ⟨phot⟩ *indicating lamp,* ⟨theat⟩ *cue light,* ⟨comp⟩ *check light* **~mast** m ⟨rail⟩ *semaphore* **~ruf** m *(bugle) call* **~scheibe** f *disk-s.* **~schuß** m *s.-gun* **~streifen** m *s. strip* **~tafel** f ⟨theat⟩ *cue board;* ⟨comp⟩ *display panel;* ⟨wir⟩ *code chart* **~tuch** n *panel* **~wärter** m *s.man,* ⟨Am⟩ *tower man* **Signalement** [–'maŋ] n ~s/~s *personal description* **signalis·ieren** vt/i [h] *to signal* **Signat·ar** m ~s/~e *signatory* || **~-** *s. (power)* **Signat·ur** f ~/~en *signature* ⟨a. typ⟩ || (Marke e–s Kollo) *mark, brand* || ⟨fig⟩ *mark, stamp* **sign·ieren** vt [h] *to sign* || (Kolli) *to mark, brand* || ⟨arts⟩ –rt *signed; inscribed (copy)* **Sign·ierung** f *label(l)ing* **Signifik** f ~/ ⟨Sprache u Denken⟩ *significs* [a. sg konstr]

Sigr·ist m ~en/~en [bes obd & Sw] *sexton*

Sik·ang m (chin. Fluß)

S·ikkim n (vorderindischer Staat)

Sil·age [–ʒə] f ~/~n ⟨agr⟩ (Gärfutter) *(en)-silage*; → Silo

S·ilbe f ~/~n *syllable* ‖ ⟨fig⟩ *word* ‖ lange ~ *long*; *l. s.* ‖ vorletzte ~ *penult*; drittletzte ~ *antepenult*; aus 3 ~n bestehend *trisyllabic*; *a four--syllable word* ‖ ~n verschlucken *to mumble one's words* ‖ mit k–r ~ erwähnen *not to mention a word about* ‖ ⟨fig⟩ ~n stechen *to quibble* **S·ilben- ~maß** n *metre, quantity* **≃mäßig** a *syllabic* **~messung** f *prosody* **~rätsel** n *charade* **~stecher** m *pedant, hair-splitter, petty critic* **~stecher·ei** f *pedantry, hair-splitting* **~stolpern** n *stammering* **~trennung** f *syllabication* **≃weise** [adv] *syllable by syllable*; → .. silbig

S·ilber n ~s/ *silver* ‖ (Geschirr) ⟨a.⟩ *plate* ‖ ~ in Stangen *bar-s.* ‖ mit ~ auslegen *to damask* ‖ mit ~ beschlagen [a] *s.-mounted* ‖ auf ~ essen *to dine off s.* ‖ mit ~ zahlen .. *in s.* ‖ ⟨fig⟩ das ~ des Mondes *the s.y moon* ‖ glänzt v ~ .. *has a s.y tinge* **~ader** f ⟨min⟩ *vein of silver* **~amalgam** n *argental mercury* **~arbeit** f *s.-work, work in s.* **~arbeiter** m *s.-smith* **≃artig** a *s.y, s.like* **~barre** f, **~barren** m *ingot* od *bar of s.* **~bergwerk** n *s.-mine* **~blatt** n *s.-leaf* **~blech** n *thin plate of s.* **~blende** f *sham s.-ore* **~blick** m ⟨min⟩ *flashing of s.*; ⟨fig⟩ *bright moment*; *squint* **~buche** f ⟨bot⟩ *white beech-tree* **~diener** m ⟨m. m.⟩ *butler* **~distel** f *carline thistle* **~dollar** m ⟨Am fam⟩ *(cart-)wheel* **~draht** m *s.-wire* **~erz** n *s.-ore* **~faden** m *s.--thread*; einige ≃ im Haar *a touch of grey in a p's hair* **~farbe** f *s.(-colour)* **≃farben** a *s.-coloured* **~felchen** n ⟨ich⟩ *s. trout* **~fischchen** n ⟨ent⟩ *sugar--mite* **~flittern** pl *s.-spangles* pl **~flotte** f *(Spanish) s.-fleet* **~folie** f *s.-foil* **~fuchs** m ⟨zoo⟩ *grey fox* **~gehalt** m *alloy of s.* **~geld** n *s. money, s. coin* **~gerät, ~geschirr** n *s. (plate)* ⟨Am⟩ *s.ware* ‖ v ~ essen *to dine off s.* **~glanz** m *brightness of s.* ‖ ⟨min⟩ *argentite, s. glance* **~glätte** f *litharge of s.* **≃grau** a *s.-grey* **~groschen** m *s. groschen (ca. = 1 d)* **~grube** f = ~bergwerk **~haar** n *s.-white hair* **≃haltig** a *containing s., argentiferous* **≃h·ell** a *s.y*; *s. (sky, tone)* **~hochzeit** f *s. wedding* **~kammer** f *plate-room* **~klang** m *s.y sound* **~klumpen** m *lump of s.* | mit **~knauf** *s.-headed (cane)* **~könig** m ⟨ich⟩ *tarpon* **~korn** n *grain of s.* **~lahn** n *s. tinsel* **~locke** f *s.y curl* **~lot** n *s.-stain* **~löwe** m *puma* **~möve** f ⟨orn⟩ *herring-gull* **~münze** f *s. coin* ‖ (Denkmünze) *s.-medal* **~papier** n *s.-paper, tin-foil* **~pappel** f *white poplar* **~platte** f *plate of s.* **~plattierung** f *s.-plating* **~probe** f *s.-test* **≃reich** a *rich in s., argentiferous, s.-bearing* **~putzer** m ⟨hot⟩ *s.-man* **~rubel** m *s.-rouble* **~rückstand** m ⟨chem, phot⟩ *residual s.* **~sand** m *s.-sand* **~schaum** m *(very thin) s.-leaf* **~scheibe** f *s.y disk* **~schimmel** m *s.-grey horse* **~schläger** m *s.-beater* **~schlacke** f *s.-dross* **~-schmied** m *s.-smith* **~schrank** m *plate-cupboard* **~service** n *service* od *set of plate* **~stange** f = –barre **~stickerei** f *embroidery in s.* **~stimme** f *s.y voice* **~stoff** m *s.-cloth, s.-brocade* **~streif** m *s.y streak* **~stück** n *piece of s.*; *s. coin* **~stufe** f *piece of s.-ore* **~tanne** f *s. fir* **~ton** m *s.y tone* **~tresse** f *s. lace* **~währung** f *s. currency, s. standard*; Anhänger der ~ ⟨Am⟩ *bimetallist* **~wäscher** m *plate--washer* **~weide** f *white willow* **≃w·eiß** a *s.--coloured, s.y-white* **~wurz** f ⟨bot⟩ *white dryas* **~zeug** n *s. (plate)* **S·ilberling** m ~s/~e *piece of silver*

s·ilbern a *(of) silver, made of silver* ‖ ~e Hochzeit [f] *silver wedding*; ⟨Am⟩ *s. anniversary*

..silbig a *syllable(d) (four-s.)*; → Silbe

Silhouette [zilu'ɛtə] f ~/~n *silhouette* ‖ ~n [pl] ⟨fig⟩ *outlines* **s-tt·ieren** vt [h] *to shade, silhouette*

Silik·at n ⟨chem⟩ *silicate* **Silik·onmasse** f ⟨rec⟩ *silicon cushion* **silikonis·iert** a *silicon-treated (paper)* **Silik·ose** f ⟨med⟩ *silicosis* **Sil·izium** n *silicon*

S·ilo m ~s/~s *silo* ‖ im ~ einlagern *to ensil(ag)e* | ⟨tech⟩ *bin* **~lagerung** f *ensilage*

sil·urisch a ⟨geol⟩ *Silurian*

Silv·ester m, **~abend** m (zu *on*) *New Year's Eve*

S·imandel m & n ~s/~ [bay–österr] *henpecked husband*

S·imili- ~diamant m *paste-diamond* **~steine** m pl *paste (stones* pl), *sham jewels* pl

Simon·ie f ~/ *simony* **sim·onisch** a *simoniac(al)*

S·impel I. m ~s/~ *simpleton* ‖ zum ~ w *to become a duffer* **II.** ≃ a *simple, plain* °**~fransen** f pl (Frisur) ⟨hum⟩ *idiot-fringe* | **≃haft** a *silly* | **≃n** vi *to behave* od *talk like a simpleton* **Simplicissimus** m ~/ ⟨Ger hist⟩ *(funny paper* ⟨a. pol⟩)

Simplizit·ät f ~/ *simplicity*

S·implonpaß m ⟨Swiss⟩ *Simplon*

Sims m & n [–es/–e] *ledge* ‖ ⟨arch⟩ *cornice, moulding* ‖ (Brett) *shelf* ‖ (Kamin≃) *mantelpiece* **~hobel** m *moulding-plane* **~träger** m *burden--bearer* **~werk** n *moulding*

S·imse f ~/~n ⟨bot⟩ *club-rush*

Simul·ant m ~en/~en *malingerer* **simul·ieren** vt [h] *to simulate, malinger, feign, pretend*; ⟨(mil) sl⟩ *to sham the doctor* | ⟨pop⟩ (auf, über etw) ~ *to brood (over a th)*

simult·an a *simultaneous* **≃schule** f *undenominational* bzw *co-ed(ucational) school* **≃verschränkung** f ⟨biol⟩ *combination of simultaneously linked components*

S·inai m *Mount Sinai* **~halbinsel** f (zw dem Golf v Sues u Akabah) *Sinaitic peninsula*

Sind, Sindh n (vorderindische Provinz)

Sinek·ure f ~/~n *sinecure*

S·ing- ~akademie f *singing-school* **~drossel** f ⟨orn⟩ *(common* od *song-)thrush* **~kränzchen** n *s.g-club, glee-club* **~kunst** f *art of s.g* **~lehrer, ~meister** m *s.g-master* **~sang** m *singsong*, ⟨fig⟩ *yaw-yaw* **~schar** f *glee-club* **~schule** f *singing--school* **~schwan** m *whistling swan* **~spiel** n *musical (comedy), operetta* **~spielhalle** f *music-hall* **~stimme** f *(s.g-)voice, vocal part* ‖ *pair of pipes* **~-stunde** f *s.g-lesson* **~talent** n *vocal talent* **~vogel** m *s.g-bird, song-bird* **~weise** f *melody, tune* **s·ingen** vt/i [sang/gesungen] [h] **A.** *to sing* ‖ (fröhlich) *to carol* ‖ (feierlich) *to chant* ‖ (of birds) *to warble* ‖ (leise) *to croon* ‖ (mit Schwung) *to lilt* ‖ (un)rein ~ *to sing in (out of) tune* ‖ (mehrstimmig) *to s. in parts* | mir ~ die Ohren *I have a buzzing in my ears* | (Gaunerspr) *to squeal* **B.** das hohe C ~ *to take the high C* ‖ Alt ~ *to have an alto voice, to take the alto part* ‖ solo, dem Herrn, nach (dem) Gehör, **nach** Noten, **vom** Blatt ~ *to sing solo, unto the Lord, by ear, from music, at sight* ‖ davon weiß ich ein Lied zu ~ *I could tell a tale about that* | ⟨fig⟩ sein eigenes Lob ~ *to praise o.s.*, ⟨fam⟩ *to blow one's own trumpet* ‖ immer dasselbe Lied ~ *to be always harping on the same string* ‖ das ward mir nicht an der Wiege gesungen *nobody thought I should ever come to this* ‖ ⟨prov⟩ wie die Alten sungen (= sangen), so zwitschern die Jungen *as the old cock crows the young ones learn* **C. jdn in** den Schlaf ~ *to lull .. to sleep* ‖ **sich** heiser ~ *to sing o.s. hoarse* **D.** das singt **sich** leicht *that is easy to sing* ‖ **es** singt sich schön im Wald *it is pleasant to sing in the woods* **E. ~der** Tonfall *sing-song voice* **S·inger** m ~s/~ ⟨hist⟩ *singing-master* | **~·ei** f *(poor* bzw *perpetual) singing*; *sing-song*

Singap·ur n (Staat, Stadt & Insel vor der Halbinsel Malakka) *Singapore*

Singhal·ese m, **Singhal·esin** f (Mischvolk im Süden Ceylons) *Cingalese, Singhalese*

S·ingrün n ~(e)s/ ⟨bot⟩ *periwinkle*

S·ingular m ∼s/∼e ⟨gram⟩ *singular (number)*

S·ink- ∼flug m ⟨aero⟩ *descent, let-down* **∼kasten** m *gully* **∼stoff** m *sediment, deposit; settlings* pl; *sludge* **∼ventil** n *sinking valve* **∼verfahren** n ⟨aero⟩ *let-down procedure* **s·inken** [sank/gesunken] **I.** vt [h] *to sink (a shaft)* **II.** vi [s] **A.** *to sink*; (v Schiffen a.) *to founder* || *to drop, fall, descend* || *to droop, sag* || *to give way, to go down* || (sich vermindern) *to diminish* || *(confidence, strength) decrease* || *his strength is failing* || *(reputation, influence) decline* || (verfallen) *to decay, to crumble away* | (v Erdboden) *to subside* || ihm sank der Mut *his heart sank* || (v Nebel, Wasser) *to fall* || (v Druck, Waagschale) *to drop* | (v Preis) *to fall; to come* od *go down; (stocks) decline; (the value of ..) is falling* | (zurückgehen) *to fall back* | (P) ⟨fig⟩ *to come down*, ⟨fam⟩ *to go to the dogs* **B. auf** [acc]: *to drop into a chair* || *to sink to (drop, fall on) one's knees* || *to drop on one's bed* || auf den (*or* **zu**) Boden ∼ *to fall, drop to the ground*, ⟨box⟩ *to go down* | **in** [acc]: *to sink into the grave; to subside into a chair; to fall into a p's arms, into a deep sleep* || *I nearly sank into the earth for shame* || in Ohnmacht ∼ *to faint, swoon away* | **in** [dat]: *to fall in a p's estimation; to sink in public opinion* || *to go down in price* || im Wert ∼ (bes Währung) *to depreciate* **C. ∼lassen**: *to let down* || *to let (one's hand) fall* || *to hang (one's head)* || *to lose (hope, courage)* || die Flügel ∼ l *to lose heart, courage* || *to lower, drop (one's voice)*; s–e Stimme nicht ∼ l *to keep one's voice up* **D. ∼d** *falling (twilight*; Abend *evening shadows)* || bis in die ∼de Nacht *till nightfall* || ∼de Fahne ⟨m. m.⟩ *the lowering of the flag* **E.** ≗ n *sinking* etc || *drop, fall (of prices)* || *diminution, decrease, decline* || *decay* || *lowering (of standards)* || *falling-off (of orders)* || (Schiff) zum ≗ bringen *to founder*

Sinki·ang n (Provinz Chinas)

S·inn m ∼es/∼e **A. 1.** *sense* || ∼ u Verstand ⟨Lit criticism⟩ *good sense*, → *sense*; ohne ∼ u Verstand *without rhyme or reason* || s–e 5 ∼e beisammen h *to have one's wits about one* || der ∼e beraubt *robbed of one's reason* || im Besitz s–r ∼e *in one's right senses* || s–r ∼e nicht mächtig s ⟨a.⟩ *not to be o.s.*; er hatte s–e 5 ∼e nicht beie–a ⟨fam⟩ *he was not all there*; s–e 5 ∼e zusnehmen *to gather one's wits about one* || scharfe ∼e *keen faculties* || gesunder ∼ *commonsense* || das hat k–n ∼ *there is no s. in that*; → B. **2.** *intellect, intelligence, mind, wit* | *memory* || *apprehension* || *tendency* | *intention, wish, will* | *thoughts* pl | *opinion* || freier ∼ *mental freedom* || viele Köpfe viele ∼e *many men many minds* **3.** *heart, soul* || *temper, nature, disposition* || *ways* pl | demütigen etc ∼es *humble-, noble-, high--minded* || *with an open mind* || leichten ∼es *light--hearted, easy-going* **4. (Vorliebe)** *taste, liking* **(für** *for*) || **(Empfänglichkeit)** *mind (for)* || ∼ h f .. *to have a taste, an eye for the beautiful; a love of nature; a sense of humour, of proportion* ⟨a. pol⟩; *historical, national feelings* pl; *clothes sense; social inclinations*; ∼ fürs Praktische *practicality* | ⟨fam⟩ *a bump of locality* || *to take an interest in literature* | **k-n ∼ h f ..**: *to have no inclinations for; my incl. do not run that way*; .. f Familie *I am no family man* **5. (Bedeutung)** *sense, import, signification, significance*; allg angenommener ∼ *acceptation* || *the purport* od *meaning of a book, word; tenor of a speech*; ⟨fam⟩ *hang of a subject* || tiefer ∼ *pregnancy*, tieferer ∼ *implication* || der ∼ des Ganzen ist, daß *the idea is that* .. was ist der tiefere ∼? ⟨fam⟩ *what's the big idea*? **B.** s–n ∼ **ändern,** anderen ∼es w *to change one's mind* || e–n ∼ ergeben *to make sense*; die Worte geben k–n ∼ .. *convey no s.* || k–n ∼ h: *there is no sense* od *point in doing it* || *it has no point* || was **hat** es für e–n ∼, daß wir ..? *what is the point* od *where is the good of our arguing*? || nimm d–e (5) ∼e zus *pull your wits together* || das **sagen** mir m–e 5 ∼e *my common-sense tells me that* || die ∼e schärfen *to sharpen (a p's) faculties* || eines ∼es s mit *to be of one mind with, to agree with, to be at one with* (über *on*) || ihr ∼ **steht** nach .. *her mind is bent on nothing but pleasure*, .. nach Höherem *she has more ambitious views* || ihm schwanden, vergingen die ∼e *he lost consciousness, his mind went black*; ⟨fam⟩ *he saw stars* || jdm den ∼ f Sch. wecken *to make a p beauty-conscious* **C. auf** s–m ∼ beharren *to persist in one's opinion* | e–m etw **aus** dem ∼ bringen *to talk a p out of a th* || der Gedanke geht mir nicht aus dem ∼ *the idea keeps running through my mind* || sich etw (f immer) aus dem ∼ schlagen *to put a th (definitely) out of one's head, mind*; .. e–n Gedanken .. *to banish a thought* || das kommt *or* will mir nicht aus dem ∼ *I cannot get it out of my head, my mind runs on the subject, I can't forget it* | **bei (von)** ∼en s *to be in (out of) one's mind, senses*; (nicht) ganz bei ∼ *in one's right mind* (⟨fam⟩ *not all there*); *he's not (quite) h.s.* | **durch**: *it flashed across my mind, it passed through my m.* = *it struck me* | **in** [dat]: im ∼e [gen] *in accordance* od *line with a th, with the intentions of a p* || in jds ∼e handeln *to enter into a p's ideas*; ich glaubte in Ihrem ∼e z handeln, wenn .. *I felt you would want me to say so* | *in a limited acceptation* || in bildlichem etc ∼e *figuratively; in the most literal sense* = *literally* || in diesem ∼e *with this in mind; (written) to this effect* || *in the proper* (eigentlichen) *sense* = *properly speaking* || *in every respect* || in gewissem ∼e ⟨fam⟩ *in a way* || im ∼e der Führung handeln *to act in line with the concepts of higher commands* || im ∼e des Ganzen handeln *to act in the light of the overall mission* || im ∼e des Gesetzes *within the purview of the law*; im ∼e des Grundgesetzes *as defined in the Basic Law* || im ∼e der Luftüberlegenheit *(invincible) in terms of air power* || im obigen ∼e *to the above effect* || im tiefsten ∼ *most profoundly* || im übertragenen ∼ *metaphorically* || im ∼e v *within the meaning of* .. || im weiteren ∼e *by extension* || im ∼ behalten *to bear in mind* || im ∼ h *to intend, contemplate, meditate*; .. zu tun *to think of doing, to be about to do*; .. mit jdm: *the gods had other purposes for him* || es liegt mir im ∼ *I bear it in mind; it occupies my mind*; wir h nichts Böses im ∼ *we don't mean any harm* | **in** [acc]: (bei Addition) (3 hin), 5 in'n ∼ *carry 5* || in den ∼ fallen(d) *to appeal to the senses, (striking)* | e–m gerade in den ∼ k *to cross a p's mind*; es kam mir in den ∼ *it occurred to me; it crossed my mind, it struck me; (a tune) got* od *came* (plötzlich: *rushed*, ⟨fam⟩ *popped) into my head, mind; it (suddenly) occurred to me; (the idea) suggested itself to me* || wie's ihr in den ∼ kam *as the fancy took her, as the spirit moved her* || laß dir's nicht in den ∼ k! *don't take it into your head*; es ist mir nie in den ∼ gek, daß er .. *I never supposed he would* | es will mir nicht in den ∼ *I don't wish* bzw *conceive it* | **nach** jds ∼ *in agreement with a p's views* || ein Gesetz dem ∼ nach erfüllen *to obey the spirit of a law* (→ Buchstabe) || er muß alles nach s–m ∼ h *he will have his own way* | **ohne** → A. 1. || **von** → C. bei || v ∼en *mad*; v ∼en sein *to have lost one's wits* pl **S·inn- ≗beraubend** a *blinding, deafening* **∼bild** n *symbol, emblem*; ⟨arts⟩ *allegory* || das ∼ e–r S darstellen *to symbolize a th* **≗bildlich** a *symbolic(al)* [adv *s.ally*], *emblematic* [adv *e.ally*]; ∼ darstellen *to symbolize*, ⟨arts⟩ *allegorize*; ∼e Darstellung *allegory* **∼deutung** f *inner meaning* (⟨rel⟩ *of the cross), semantic interpretation* **≗fällig** a *obvious, striking; spectacular* **∼gedicht** n *epigram* **≗gemäß** a *analogous* || ∼ verfahren wie bei *(the procedure) approximates that for* .. **≗getreu** a *faithful (rendering)* **≗los** a *senseless*; *brainless*; *meaningless*; *futile*; *pointless*; *devoid of sense*; *absurd*; etw ~ finden *to see no reason to* .. | [adv] ~ betrunken *blind* od *dead drunk* || (Geld) ~ vertun *to waste*, ⟨sl⟩ *to blue* **~losigkeit** f *pointlessness* (*of life*) **ˣ~reich** a *ingenious*, *clever*; *witty* **~spruch** m *sentence*, *device*, *motto*, *saying* **ˣ~verwandt** a *synonymous* **~verwirrend** a *bewildering* **ˣ~voll** a *significant*, *pregnant*, *suggestive*; *purposeful* (*cooperation*); *meaningful*; *useful*; *successful* **~widrigkeit** f *illogicallity* **s·innen** [sann/gesonnen] [h] **I.** vi *to meditate*, *brood*, *ponder*, *think* | (auf [acc]) ~ *to plan*; ⟨dero⟩ *to scheme*, *plot*, *contrive* vt || *to devise* (*new ways*) || (über [acc]) *to reflect*, *meditate* ([*up*]*on*) || *to ponder* (*over*) || (mit Muße) *to muse* ([*up*]*on*) | gesinnt *minded* || gesonnen s (zu tun) *to be inclined*, *disposed*, *to have a* (*good*) *mind*, *to intend* (*to do*) **II.** vt *to invent*, *plot*; *to meditate* (*revenge*) || *to think out* (*new ways*) || nichts Gutes ~ *to harbour ill designs* **III.** ˣ~ n *thinking*; *thoughts*, *meditations* pl; *planning* || in ˣ~ versunken *in a brown* od *blue study* || unser ˣ~ u Trachten *our aspirations* **IV.** **~d** a *musing*, *meditative*, *pensive* **S·innen-** **ˣ~freudig** a *sensuous* **~genuß** m, **~lust** f *sensual enjoyment*, *s. pleasure*; *s.ity* **~kitzel** m *itch of desire* **~mensch** m *s.ist*; *voluptuary* **~rausch**, **~taumel** m *intoxication of the senses* **~reiz** m *sensuous charm* **~welt** f *material world*; *world of sense* **S·innes-** **~änderung** f *change of mind* **~art** f *disposition*, *temper*, *charakter* **~eindruck** m *sensory impression*; ˣ~e h *to take* od *drink in through the senses* **~empfindung** f *sensory perception* **~reiz** m *stimulus* **~richtung** f *turn of mind* **~organ**, **~werkzeug** n *organ of sense*; auf äußere Reize ansprechendes ~ *exteroceptor* **~störung** f *mental derangement*; *delusion* **~taumel** m **~täuschung** f *deception* (*of the senses*); *illusion*, *mental delusion hallucination* **~wahrnehmung** f *apperception*; *sensory perception*; *sensation* **~wandel** m *change of heart* **~zentrum** n *sensory centre* **sinn·ieren** vi *to brood*, *ponder* **s·innig** a *contemplative* || *thoughtful* (*girl*) || *sensible* (*idea*, *girl*) || *judicious* (*interpreter*) || *ingenious* (*present*) || *graceful* (*verse*) **s·innlich** a ⟨philos⟩ *sentient*; *sensuous* (*impression*) || *material*, *physical* | *voluptuous* (*mouth*, *thought*), *sensual* (*eyes*, *love*), *carnal* (*desire*) || ~er Mensch *sensualist* | adv ~ wahrgenommen *sensed* | **ˣ~keit** f ~/ *sensuousness* || *material existence* | *sensuality*; *sensualism*

Sinol·og m ~en/~en *Chinese scholar*

*__sintem·al(en)__ [conj] (u alldieweil) *since*

S·inter m ~s/~ ⟨min⟩ *sinter*, *stalactite* || ⟨met⟩ *dross of iron* | **ˣ~n** vi [s] **1.** *to trickle*, *drop*, *ooze* | *to form stalactites* **2.** *to frit together*, *to slag*

S·intflut f *deluge*; ⟨bes fig⟩ *flood* **ˣ~lich** a *diluvian*

Sinto·ismus m ~/ *Shintoism*

S·inus m ~/~ ⟨math⟩ *sine* **~satz** m *sine theorem* | **~-** ⟨el⟩ *sinusoidal* (*current*, *wave*)

S·ioux [ziuks] pl (Indianerstamm in N.-Amerika) *Sioux* [su:]; **~frau** n *Sioux squaw*

S·iphon m ~s/~s *siphon*; ⟨tech mst⟩ *trap*

S·ippe f ~/~n *kin*(*dred*); *clan*; ⟨zoo⟩ *tribe* ⟨a. fig⟩; Heilige ~ *Holy Kindred* od *Kinship* **~nhaftung** f *liability of clan and kin*; *collective responsibility* **S·ippschaft** f ~/~en *consanguinity* || ⟨fam⟩ die ganze ~ *the whole lot*, *set*, *crew*, ⟨sl⟩ *caboodle* || mit der ganzen ~ *with kith and kin*

Sir·ene f ~/~n ⟨myth⟩ *siren* || ⟨tech⟩ *siren hooter*, *buzzer* **~ngesang** m *siren-song* **~ngeheul** n *hooting of sirens* **ˣ~nhaft** a *siren-like*, *seductive* **~nzeichen** n *siren*

S·irup m ~(e)s/~e *syrup* || (Zuckerˣ~) *treacle* **ˣ~artig** a *syrupy*

S·isal- **~faserplatte**, **~pappe** f *sisalkraft*

sist·ieren vt [h] ⟨jur⟩ *to inhibit*, *stop*, *nonsuit* (*an action*) | *to arrest* (*a p*) || *to summons* (*a p*)

Sist·ierung f ~/~en *cessation*, *inhibition* || *summons*

S·istrum n ~s/-ren ⟨Eg ant⟩ (Tanzrassel) *sistrum*

Sitkafichte f ⟨bot⟩ *blue spruce*

S·itte f ~/~n (Herkommen) *custom*, *habit*, *usage* || e-e alte ~ *a time-honoured custom* || mit der ~ brechen *to break away from habits* || das ist bei uns nicht ~ *we don't do such ths* || das ist so s-e ~ *that is his way* || das ist nicht mehr ~ *that is out of date* | ~n [pl] *morality*; (*good*) *manners*, (*loose*) *morals* pl || gegen die guten ~n *against decency*, .. verstoßen *to offend against the feeling of justice* od *fairness*; .. ~d *against public policy* | ~n u Gebräuche [pl] *manners and customs* pl **S·itten-** **~bild** n *common life picture* **~buch** n *book of morals* **~geschichte** f *social history* **~gesetz** n *moral law* **~komödie** f *comedy of manners*, → *comedy* **~lehre** f *moral philosophy*, *ethics* pl [a. sg konstr] **~lehrer** m *moralist* **ˣ~los** a *immoral*, *profligate*, *licentious* **~losigkeit** f *immorality*, *profligacy*, *licence* **~polizei** f *police department for* (*control of*) *prostitutes* **~prediger** m *moralizer* **~regel** f *rule of conduct*, *moral precept* **ˣ~rein** a *chaste* **~reinheit** f *chastity* **~richter** m *censor* **~spruch** m *maxim*; *moral sentence* **ˣ~streng** a *strict*, *straight-faced*, *austere*, *puritanical* **~strenge** f *austerity*; übertriebene ~ *Grundyism* **~verderbnis** f *corruption of morals* **~verfeinerung** f *refinement of manners* **~zeugnis** n *testimonial* (od *certificate*) *of* (*good*) *conduct* **~zwang** m *conventionalism* **s·ittig** a *well-mannered*, *well-bred* || *modest* || *polite* || *virtuous* **s·ittlich** a *moral* (*stability*), *ethical* (*views*) || ~e Haltung *morals* pl || ~er Lebenswandel ⟨a.⟩ *respectable life* || ~e Weltordnung *moral natural laws* pl | **ˣ~keit** f ~/ *morality*, *morals* pl **S·ittlichkeits-** **~gefühl** n *moral feeling* od *sense* **~verbrechen** n *indecent assault* **~vergehen** n *sexual offense* **s·ittsam** a *modest*, *demure* | *virtuous* | *proper*; *decorous* (*behavio*(*u*)*r*); *well-behaved* | *respectable*, *decent* | *bashful* | **ˣ~keit** f ~/ *modesty*, *demureness*, *decency* || *respectability*

S·ittich m ~(e)s/~e ⟨orn⟩ *parrot*, *parakeet*

s·itu L: in ~ ⟨film, etc⟩ *on location*

Situati·on f ~/~en *situation* || in derselben ~ *in the same position* (⟨fam⟩ *boat*) || je nach der ~ *according to how the land lay* || jeder ~ gewachsen *equal to any occasion* || die ~ bessern *to help matters* || die ~ ausnutzen *to make the most of the opportunity* **~skomik** f *comicality of queer situations* **~splan** m *plan of site*; ⟨mil⟩ *general situation* **~sstück** n ⟨theat⟩ *light comedy* **situiert** [a]; gut ~ *prosperous*, *in affluant circumstances*; *well off*; *well-to-do*; schlecht ~ *badly off*

Sitz m ~es/~e **A.** *seat* (⟨a. theat & fig⟩ *of a disease*, *of the Government*) || *place* || *chair* || erhöhter ~ *dais* || Kutscherˣ~ *box*, *dickey* || ⟨tech⟩ *seat* || ⟨orn⟩ *perch* | (Sitzen) auf einen ~ (*to finish*) *at a sitting without getting up* | (Wohnort) *residence* || (e-r Firma) *location*; *head office*, *headquarters* pl || (*episcopal*) *see* | ⟨hors⟩ *seat* (*a good*, *firm s.*); ⟨tail⟩ *fit*; e-n guten ~ h *to fit well*; ⟨hors⟩ *to sit one's horse well* **B.** s-n ~ in .. aufschlagen *to settle down at* .., *in a place*; s-n ~ h *to be located* || ~ u Stimme h *to have seat and vote* || mit e-m ~ versehen *to seat* (*a chair*) **~arbeit** f *sedentary work* **~bad** n *hip-bath*; *sitz b.* **~bank** f *bench*; (Ruderˣ~) *thwart* | ~breite [f] ⟨mot, etc⟩ *hip-room* **~bein** ⟨anat⟩ *ischium* **~bock** m *stool* **~fläche** f (e-s Stuhls) *seat* °**~fleisch** n: (kein) ~ h *to have* (*no*) *perseverance* (*to be fidgety*, *to be always on the go*; *to have ants in one's pants*) **~füßler** m ⟨orn⟩ *percher* **~gelegenheit** f *seating accomodation*; k-e ~ h *to have nothing to sit on* **~gurt** m ⟨aero⟩ *seat-belt* **~kasten** m *box* (*of a coach*) **~kissen** n *cushion*; ⟨hors⟩ *pad* **~knauf** m ⟨ec⟩ *misericord* **~krieg** m *sitz-krieg*

(1939/40) **~parterre** n ⟨theat⟩ *pitch* **~plan** m ⟨theat⟩ *seating plan* **~platz** m *seat* ⟨a. aero⟩ | ~bestellung [f] *reservation of seats* **~redakteur** m *dummy editor* **~reihe** f *row* (*of seats*) **~stange** f ⟨orn⟩ *perch* **~streik** m *sit-down strike*; (Farbiger im Bus etc) *sit-in*, ~e pl *sit-ins*; (vor Gebäuden) *sit-out* || *stay-down strike*; → *in* **~stufe** f ⟨theat⟩ *gradine* **~truhe** f *box-seat* **~vogel** m *percher* **~-waschbecken** n *hip bench for washing* **s·itzen I.** vi [saß/gesessen] [h], österr [s] **A. 1.** (P) *to sit, to be seated* (an *at*, auf *on*) | ⟨fig⟩ *to live, stay, dwell* | ⟨übtr⟩ [abs] *to hold a meeting* || (*of courts* etc) *to be sitting, to meet* || ⟨fam⟩ (in Haft) *to be doing time* **2.** (of birds) *to perch, to be p.ed* || (auf Eiern) *to be sitting* **3.** (v Orten) *to be situated* **4.** (S) (Rock etc) *to fit* (*well, badly*) || (e–m wie angegossen *a p to perfection*; ⟨fam⟩ *like a glove*, ⟨Am⟩ *like paper on the wall*) || (Nagel) *to be firmly in, to grip*; fest ~ ⟨tech⟩ *to be seizing* || ⟨fig⟩ da sitzt der Haken, Knoten *there's the rub* || das Übel sitzt tiefer *the trouble lies deeper* || *that blow, shot* (*went home* od) *told* || ⟨fenc⟩ sitzt! *a hit*! **5.** jetzt sitzt **es** *now I know my lesson, part* **6.** wo sitzt **dir's**? *where do you feel it*? **7.** (**jdm** [Modell]) ~ *to sit* (*to a p*) (*for one's portrait*), *to give* (*a p*) *a sitting, to model* (*for a p*) **B. allein,** einsam ~ *to sit all by o.s.* **bequem,** warm ~ in *to be ensconded in* || (fest) ~ an, auf *to cling to*; (kleben) *to stick*; (of ship) *to be aground* || **gut** ~ *to have good seats, places, to be comfortable*, ⟨fig⟩ *to be in a good position*; ⟨tail⟩ → A. 4. || etw locker [adv] ~ h *to be ready with* (*knife*, etc) müßig ~ *to sit at home* (= *to remain idle*) || sein Hut sitzt immer schief *he wears his hat tilted on one side* || **still,** weich ~ *to sit still, soft* || voll ~ v *to be full of* (*worms*) || ⟨fam⟩ warm ~ *to be well off* || vorgeneigt ~ *to sit forward* **C. an** (e–r Arbeit) ~ *to sit over* .. | **auf** e–a ~ *to sit on each other's laps* || auf Grund ~ ⟨mar⟩ *to have run aground* || auf e–m Hof etc ~ *to live on a farm, in a castle*; *to be settled on a farm* | **bei** den Karten ~ *to be playing cards* || beim Tee, bei Tisch ~ *to sit at tea, at table* | **im** Gefängnis ~ *to be in prison*, ⟨fam⟩ *to be doing time* || im Glücke ~, in der Wolle ~ *to be in luck's way, in clover* || im Grase ~ *to sit on* .. || in Prima ~ *to be a sixth-form boy* || im Rat etc ~ *to have a seat in parliament, the council*; *to be a member of c., p.*; *to be an M.P.* || °wie die Made im Speck ~ *to be as snug as a bug in a rug* || in der Tinte, Patsche etc ~ ⟨fam⟩ *to be cut up* **über** [dat]: *to have a work* (⟨fam⟩ *job*) *in hand* || *to be boring over one's books* || ⟨school⟩ *to top another boy* | über [acc]: **zu** Gericht ~ *to sit judgement on*; mit sich selbst .. *to be a court--martial on o.s.* | zu [dat]: *to sit at a p's feet* || immer zu Hause ~ *to be a regular home-bird* || zu Pferde ~ *to be mounted* od *on horseback*; gut .. *to sit* (*one's horse*) *well, to be a good horse*(*wo*)*man* || zu Rate ~ *to be assembled in council* **D.** ~ **bleiben** *to keep one's seat, to remain sitting*; bis z Ende des Essens ~ bl. *to sit out the dinner* | ~bl. ⟨school⟩ *not to get one's move*, ⟨Am⟩ *to be left behind*; ⟨com⟩ (auf der Ware) ⟨Am fam⟩ *to hold the bag* || e–n Tanz ~ bl. *to sit out a dance*; (ohne Partner) ⟨fam⟩ *to decorate the wall, to be a wallflower* || (nicht heiraten) ⟨fam⟩ *to be left on the shelf* | ~geblieben *soggy* (Kuchen) | °e–n ~ **h** (= betrunken s) *to be a bit over the line*; ⟨Am⟩ *to have a jag on* || **~ l** *to make* (*a p*) *sit down* || ⟨fig⟩ *to abandon, desert, to throw over*, ⟨fam⟩ *to leave in the lurch*; *to jilt* (*a lover, a girl*); ⟨fam⟩ *he left her high and dry*; ⟨Am fam⟩ *to ditch a p*; *he let her down*; *he left him holding the bag* (in der Patsche) || e–n Schimpf auf sich ~ l *to pocket an affront* || *to put up with* (*an accusation*) **E. sich** lahm etc ~ *to become stiff with sitting* || sitzt **es** sich nicht gut hier? *isn't it comfortable* (*aren't we snug*) *here*? **II.** ≃ n des ≃s müde *tired of sitting* || er kommt nie z ≃ *he is never able to sit down* || jdn z ≃ nötigen *to ask a p to take a seat* || nichts z ≃ h *to have nothing to sit on* **s·itzend** a *sitting* etc.; *seated* (*statue*) || *sedentary* (*life* Lebensweise) || ⟨bot⟩ *sessile* (*leaf*) **S·itzer** m *sitter* || [in comp] (*four-*)*seater* **s·itzlings** [adv] *sitting* **S·itzung** f ~/~en *meeting* (eröffnen *to open*, schließen *to close*) || *sitting* ⟨a. arts, parl, jur⟩ || (Tagung) *session* (⟨a. parl⟩ *in open s.*); ~ halten *to sit*; ⟨fam, übtr⟩ e–e lange ~ halten *to sit a long time over dinner* || die ~ wurde eröffnet *the chair was taken*; .. geschlossen ⟨H. C.⟩ *the House adjourned*, ⟨HL⟩ *Their Lordships rose* (*at* ..) || °er hat ~ (im W.C.) *he sits in parliament* || zu e–r ~ zus–treten *to gather for a meeting* | **~s- ~bericht** m, **~protokoll** n *record*; *minutes* pl *of proceedings* **~periode** f ⟨jur⟩ *session, term* **~saal** m *board-room, council-chamber* || ⟨parl⟩ im ~ *on the floor* **~tag** m *day of sitting*

Sixt·inisch a *Sistine* (*Chapel, Madonna*)

Sizili·aner m, **~in** f, **siz·ilisch, sizili·anisch** a *Sicilian* **Siz·ilien** n *Sicily* || auf ~ *in Sicily*

Skabi·ose f ~/~n ⟨bot⟩ *scabious* || wilde ~ *gipsy-rose*

Sk·agerrak n (Meeresarm nördl. v Jütland) *Skager-Rack* || im ~ *in the S.* || die ~schlacht *the Battle of Jutland, Jutland Day*

Sk·ala f ~/–len *scale* || bewegliche *or* gleitende ~ *sliding scale* || ⟨mus⟩ *gamut*; perlende –len *rippling scales* || ⟨wir⟩ (*tuning*) *dial* | ~einteilung [f] *graduation*

Sk·alde m ~n/~n *scald* **~ndichtung** f *s.ic poetry*

Skalp m ~(e)s/~e *scalp* | ≃**·ieren** vt [h] *to scalp* | **~·iermesser** n *scalping-knife*

Skalp·ell n ~s/~e ⟨surg⟩ *scalpel*

Skand·al m ~(e)s/~e (Ärgernis) *scandal* | (Tumult) *disturbance, noise, row, riot*; ⟨sl⟩ *roughhouse*, ⟨Am⟩ *ruckus* || ~ m *or* schlagen ⟨fam⟩ *to make* (od *to kick up*) *a row*, ⟨sl⟩ *to rag*; *to roughhouse*; *to raise the roof* || (aufrühren) *to search for muck to rake*; gegen .. *to rake up* (*against*) *a p* **~geschichte** f (*piece of*) *scandal* **~macher** m *rowdy, rioter* **~presse** f *gutter press* ≃**süchtig** a *fond of scandal*; ~e P *scandal-monger* **skandal·ieren** = Skandal m **skandalis·ieren,** sich ~ *to be shocked, scandalized* (über *at, by*) **skan-dal·ös** a *scandalous, shocking, outrageous, disgraceful*

skand·ieren vt [h] *to scan* (*verse*) **Skansi·on** f ~/~en *scansion, scanning*

Skandin·avien n *Scandinavia* **Skandin·avier** m, **~in** f, **skandin·avisch** a *Scandinavian*

Skapul·ier n ~(e)s/~e ⟨ec⟩ *scapulary*

Skat m ~(e)s/~e ⟨Ger cards⟩ *skat* || ~ spielen, °dreschen *to play at skat*

Sk·ating n ~s/ [–eit–] ⟨rec⟩ *skating*

Skelett n ~(e)s/~e *skeleton*; zum ~ abgemagert (P) *grown worn and thin* **~bau** m ⟨arch⟩ *sk. construction* **~schrift** f ⟨typ⟩ *sk.-type*

Sk·ep- ~sis f ~/ *scepticism* **~tiker** m ~s/~ *sceptic* ≃**tisch** a *sceptical* (in bezug auf *of*); *incredulous*

Sk·etch m ~es/~e **1.** = Skizze **2.** *skit*

Ski [ʃi:] m [~s/~s & ~er] (*snow-shoe*), *ski* || ~ laufen *to ski* **~anzug** m *skiing suit* **~ausrüstung** f *s-g equipment* **~bindung** f *ski binding* **~bruch-versicherung** f *ski-breakage insurance* **~fahrer, ~läufer** m *skier* **~gebiet** n *s-g area* **~gelände** n *ski slope* **~hase**(**rl** n) m ⟨hum⟩ *snow-bunny* **~lift** m *skimobile* **~springen** n *ski-jumping* **~-sprung** m *ski jump* **~stiefel** m pl *s-g boots* pl **~verhältnisse** n pl *s-g conditions* **~wachs** n *ski wax* °**~wasser** n *lemonade* **~wetter** n *s-g weather*

Sk·izze f ~/~n *sketch*; *rough draft* od *drawing*; *outline* || ⟨mil⟩ *croquis* || biographische ~ *profile* || e–e (flüchtige) ~ m *to* (*make a rapid*) *sk.* **~nbuch** n *sk.-book* ≃**nhaft** a *sk.y*; *thumbnail-*

[attr] **skizz·ieren** vt/i [h] *to outline sketch* || ⟨übtr⟩ flüchtig ~ *to jot down, to blueprint*; grob ~ *to block out*

Skl·ave m ~n/~n *slave* || z ~n m *to enslave* || ~ [gen] s *to be enslaved by* (*one's passions*), *to be a slave to* (*drink*) || wie ein ~ arbeiten *to slave, drudge*; *to work like a horse* | **~n- ~arbeit** f *slave-work* || ⟨fig⟩ *drudgery* **~aufseher** m *s.-driver* **~befreiung** f *emancipation of s.s* **~besitzer** m *s.-owner, s.-holder* **~dienst** m *s.ry* **≟gegnerisch** a ⟨Am hist⟩ *free-soil* [attr] **~handel** m *s.-trade*, ⟨sl⟩ *blackbirding* **~händler** m *s.-trader, s.-dealer* **~jagd** f *s.-hunting* **~joch** n *yoke of bondage* **~krieg** m ⟨hist⟩ *Servile War* **~leben** n *s.'s life* **~moral** f *s. morality* **~schiff** n *s.-ship, slaver* **~seele** f *slavish mind* **~staat** m *s.-holding state* **~züchter** m *s.-breeder* **Sklaver·ei** f ~/ *slavery* || ⟨fig⟩ *thraldom, servitude* **Skl·avin** f ~/~nen (*female*) *slave* **skl·avisch** a *slavish* || ⟨fig⟩ *servile*; sich ~ binden an *to enslave o.s. to*; alle Launen jds ~ erfüllen *to be subservient to all whims of a p*

Skl·avenfluß m (in N.-Amerika) **1.** (Großer ~) *Great Slave River* **2.** (Kleiner ~) *Little Slave River*

Skl·avenküste f (in W.-Afrika) *Slave Coast*

Skl·avensee (in N.-Amerika) **1.** (Großer ~) *Great Slave Lake* **2.** (Kleiner ~) *Lesser Slave Lake*

Sk·onto [m & n] ~s/ ⟨com⟩ *discount* || abzüglich ~ *less discount* **skontr·ieren** vt/i [h] ⟨com⟩ *to settle, pay, balance* || (abstimmen) *to check*

Skorb·ut m ~(e)s/ ⟨path⟩ *scurvy*; ~ bekämpfend *ascorbic* | **≟isch** a *scorbutic*

Skorpi·on m ~(e)s/~e *scorpion*; ⟨astr⟩ *Scorpio*

†**Sk·ote** m, **Sk·otin** f *Scot*; dazu: *Scotia, Scotland*

Skrib·ent m ~en/~en *writer, author* || ⟨dero⟩ *quilldriver* **Skript·uren** pl *papers, writings* pl

Skr·of- ~eln f pl, **~ul·ose** f ~/ ⟨path⟩ *scrofula* **~ul·ös** a *scrofulous*

Skr·upel m ~s/~ *scruple* (a. Gewicht) || sich [dat] ~ m *to scruple* (über *about*) **≟los** a *unscrupulous, sharp*; ⟨fam⟩ *stick-at-nothing* [attr] || *Machiavellian* **skrupul·ös** a *scrupulous*

Skrut·inium n ~s/Skrut·inien *scrutiny*

Skulpt·ur f ~/~en *sculpture*

skurr·il a *farcical*; *weird, whimsical*; *ludicrous*

Sk·ylla f ~/; zw ~ u Char·ybdis *between hell and high water*

†**Sk·ythe** m, **Sk·ythin** f, **sk·ytisch** a *Scythian*

†**Sk·ythien** n *Scythia*

Sl·alom m ~s/~s ⟨ski⟩ *slalom* | ~bretter [n pl] ⟨sport & Spiel⟩ *scate-boards*

Sl·awe m, **Sl·awin** f *Slav, Slavonian* **sl·awisch** a *Slavonic, Slavonian* **Sl·awentum** n *slavism* †**Slaw·onien** n *Slavonia* **Slow·ak, Slow·ake** m *Slovak* **Slowak·ei** f *Slovakia* **slow·akisch** a *Slovak* **Slow·ene** m *Slovene* **slow·enisch** a *Slovenian*

Smalte = Schmalte

Smar·agd m ~(e)s/~e, **≟en** a *emerald*

Sm·okarbeit f *smocking*; smoken vt [h] → *to smock*

Sm·oking m ~s/~s *dinner-jacket* bzw *dress-suit*; ⟨Am⟩ *tux*(*edo*) || °Smok ⟨sl⟩ *half waiters*

Sm·yrna n (Hafenstadt in Kleinasien)

Sn·ob m ~s/~s *snob*, ⟨Am fam⟩ *high-hat*

so I. [adv] A. 1. *so*; *like this, that*; *in this state, manner, way*; *in such a degree* || *thus* (*he spoke*) || ~ war's nicht i. *it hasn't always been that way*; ~ ist's eben *that's the way it is*; so ist das Leben *such is life* || so sind die Menschen *that's the way of the world*; vgl D. & E. || °u ~ war's denn auch *then the band played* **2.** (vergleichend) ~ .. wie .. *as* (*white*) *as* (*snow*); vgl E. ~ wie **3.** ~, (~)! *well,* (*well*)!, *you don't say so*! || ~! *there* (*you are*)! || ~, das reicht! (*there*), *that will do*! **4.** ~? *really*?, *indeed*?; (*it is true*), *is it*? || (*I have seen him.*) – *Have you*? || (*Exited*), *hey*? **5.** (ungefähr) ~ 500 *about 500*; ~ um 12 (*somewhere*) *about noon*; ~ ungefähr $^2/_3$ *sth like two thirds*; ~ um 7 *sevenish*, (*ring me up*) *about seven* **6.** (in e–m Grade .., daß) *he is so ill that he can't get up*; → E. **7.** ⟨emph⟩ er ist ~ reich! *he is s·o* (*very*) *rich*!; → C. || wir h ~ gelacht! *we h·ad such fun*!; vgl D. **8.** (zufällig) → E. bloß **9.** ⟨fam⟩ das gibt's ~ *you get it without paying* **10.** (sowieso) → ~ schon **11.** (Füllwort) ~ h·ören Sie doch! *do but listen*! || ~ m–e (s–e) Pläne *all sorts of plans* || er saß dort ~ in s–r Art *he would sit there* (*for hours*) || ~ für *or* vor mich hin *just for* od *by myself* **B.** ~ **ein** .. *such a* .. || ~ einer *such a one* (*are you*!), *a fellow like that* || .. ~ ein Schuft (*he is*) *such a cad* || ~ ein Sch.! *what a cad*! || ~ e–e Art Reisender *a com. tr. of sorts* || ~'n Ämtchen! *that's the sort of berth I'd like* || wir h ~ e–e Ahnung, daß .. *we have some presentiment that* .. || °~ 'ne Arbeit! *that's the kind of job I'd* (*I shouldn't*) *like*! || ⟨fam⟩ da ist ~'n Mann *there's a bloke* | ~ **mancher** *many a p* | ~ **etwas** *such a th, that sort of th* || ~ etw (Schönes) h wir noch nicht erlebt *we never saw anything of the sort* (*anyth. so beautiful*) || (nein *or* gibt's denn) ~ was! *the idea*! *really*! *can you beat it*? *well, I never*! || ~ etw v Frechheit! *such impudence* || .. – ja, ~ etw Ähnliches *yes, it amounted to that* || ihr Vetter oder ~ etw *her c. or sth* **C.** ein ~ **bek·annter** Dichter wie N. *as well known a poet as N.* || n·icht ~ d·umm .. *not fool enough* .. || ~ gr·oß .. *such were his merits* || s·eien Sie ~ **gut** es zu tun (*will you*) *be kind enough* (od *so kind as*) *to do it* || ein n·icht ~ guter Leiter .. *not as good a c. as metal* || ~ groß er war *tall as he was* || ein ~ (*or* ~ ein) großer Junge *so tall a boy, such a tall boy* || ~ l·ange kann ich nicht warten *I can't wait so* (⟨Am⟩ *that*) *long* || .. nicht ~ **l·eicht** *they never escape so easily as that* || ~ leicht! ⟨fam⟩ *that easy* || war es ~ schlimm? *was it as b·ad as th·at*? || das ist nicht ~ schlimm! *it's all right* || ~ seltsam es klingt *strange though it may sound* **D.** (*I felt*) *that way* || ~ **geht's,** wenn *that's what happens, when* || *that's the way it must go* || ~ kann ich's auch! *two can play that game*! || wie konnte sie nur ~ w? *how did she get that way* || ~ geht's nicht *that won't do* || ~ mußte es k *that was bound to happen* || ~ **macht** man's *that's the way how to do it* || aber es **schien** nicht ~ (*there might be some*) *but it seemed not* || ~ sein (P) *to be that way*; wer wird denn gleich ~ **s!** *don't fuss*! || ich will mal nicht ~ s *I won't be so hard on you* || ~ ·ist es! *that's it*!, *that's right*; *I mean it*; ~ ist es *that's about the size of it* || aber ~ ·ist es (nun mal) *but there it is, but there you are* || wie es oft ~ ist *as is often the case* od *way* || *it would not be like this in spring* || da dies ~ ist, ~ [conj → II.] erwarten wir *such being the case, we expect* || es war doch ~: .. *the point was this* .. || es ist mir ~, als ob *or* wie wenn *I feel as if* od *though*; *I have an idea* (*it was this*); *I am not sure it was not this* || ~ **steht's** *that's how it is* || wenn man es ~ versteht *if one takes it that way* || (*don't cry*) *like that* **E.** (**ach**) ~! *I see*! *of course*! || [concessive] ~ .. (**auch**) *poor as I am*; *however rich he may be* || ~ **bald** wie (*or* als) möglich *as soon as possible* || bald ~, bald ~ *now this, now that*; *different ths at different times, first one th, then another* || **bloß** ~ → nur ~ || ~ .., **daß** (→ ~daß) *so .. that*, ⟨Am⟩ *so hot* (*that*) *one can't eat it*; *near enough for me to see* || s–e Wünsche waren ~, daß *such were his wishes that* || es war doch ~, daß *the point was this, that* || ~ .. daß .. nicht *too ill to get up* || (nur) ~ **eben** reichen *to be barely sufficient* || .. liegt mir ~ **fern** .. *is so foreign to me*, (daß *that*) || u ~ **fort** → usf. || Sie h nicht ~ ganz Unrecht *you are not so far wrong* || ein **gar** ~ .. *such a very poor man* || schmeckt Ihnen Ihre Zigarette auch so **gut?** ⟨Am⟩ *does your cigarette taste this good*? || ~ **gut** wie *as good as*; *practically* (*nothing*), *next to* (*nothing*); ~ gut (wie *or* als) ich kann *to the best* *of my ability* || ~ gut wie beschlossen, (vergessen) *practically settled* (*almost* od *all but forgotten*) || ~ gut wie nichts (k–e Aussicht) *next to nothing* (*practically no chance*) || gut ~! *that's right* || **ja** ~! *ah*! || was tr·eibst du denn ~ **lange**? *what are you doing all this time*? → solange || ~ lange als *as long as*; ~ **lange** bis .. *until* (*he found it*) || ~ hin *or* **leidlich** (⟨fam⟩ lala) *so-so, middling* || wäre er **noch** ~ reich *were he* (*n*)*ever so rich*, mag er noch ~ bemüht s *try he never so much, whatever pains he may take* || alle noch ~ gr Unterschiede *all d.s however great* || ~, **nun** .. *there, now* (*I'm ready*) || das ist nun einmal ~ *it can't be helped* || **nur** (*or* bloß) ~ gesagt *only a casual remark* || er tut, sagt nur ~ *he doesn't mean it* || ich dachte, meinte nur ~ *it just struck me, it was only an idea of mine* | das g·eht (fl·utscht) nur ~ *it works well* || sauste nur ~ *went at a terrible speed* || *time just flew*; *conversation flowed freely* || ~ **oder** ~ *one way or* (*the*) *other* od *another*; *either way*; ⟨dero⟩ *by hook or by crook* || ~ **recht** nach m–m Sinn *just in my line* || recht ~! *quite right*!; *that will do*! || ~ (= ~wie~) **schon** *as it is, was* || ~ **sehr** *so much, to such a degree* || ~ sehr auch *however much* || ~ sehr sie auch K. s mag *child though she is*; *search his memory as he might* || ~ sehr .., **so** sehr *in the same degree* od *measure* as .., (*even so*) .. || ~ schnell .., ~ schnell *at the same speed as it grows it also decays*; *they disappear as quickly as they appeared on the scene* || ~ schnell .., ~ langsam *however fast it grows, it takes a long time to* .. || **~s·o** → ~lala || **um** so besser *so much the better* || .. um so .., als .. *he is all the more pleased as* (*it will be repeated*) || ~ **und** nicht anders *that's just how it is*, ⟨Am⟩ *thus and so* || → ~u~ || ~ **viel** (wie) *so* od *as much* (*as*) || ⟨fam⟩ nicht ~ viel *not .. th·at*: ⟨sl⟩ *I don't care th·at* (od *a hoot*) || ~viel ist sicher *one th is certain* || n·och ~ viel → n·och ~ || → ~viel || ~ viel Bücher *so many books* || n·icht ~ viele *not very many* || ~ **wahr** ich lebe (*as true*) *as I live* || nein, ~ was! ⟨fam⟩ *the idea*! || **weder** ~ noch ~ *not one way or another* || so **weit** wären wir! *here we are* || es ist ~ weit gek, daß *ths have reached the stage of* (*being* ..) || ~ weit gut *so far, so good*; ~ weit ganz gut *pretty well, considering* || es ~ weit treiben, daß .. *to go so far as to* .. || u ~ weiter → usw. || ~ .. **wie** .. *she is as tall as he* || *a pair of boots like* (od *such as*) *these* || *he is safer* (~ wie) *as he is* || m Sie es ~ wie ich *do as I do* || ~ wie er .., ~ hat er *just as he* .., *he* .. || ⟨mar⟩ ~ wie man ist *all standing* || nicht ~ .. wie .. *not so .. as* .. || wie der Herr ~ der Knecht *like master like man* || ~ **z·iemlich** *pretty* od *fairly well*; vgl ~ ~ **II. [conj] 1.** *if, in case* (*he says that, he lies*) || ~ Gott will *if it please God* **2.** *consequently*, (*and*) *therefore, so*; vgl so daß || *he wasn't there, so we didn't see him*; *as he wasn't there, we didn't* .. [oft unübersetzt] |[ell] ~ laß uns eilen *let's hurry up then* || ~ willst du nicht? *so you don't want to*? **3.** .., ~ kam er (*it wasn't long*) *before he came* || kaum war er fort, ~ .. (*he had scarcely left*), *when it rang again* **III. [rel pron]** ⟨poet, rhet, obs⟩ die, ~ mich lieben *those who* .. **IV.** [in comp] → dort **sob·ald** [conj] (~ als) *as soon as, directly*; *when*; *when first, the moment* od *instant* (*I saw him* ..) || ~ wie möglich ⟨a.⟩ *at your earliest convenience*; *let us hear the moment your plans are final*

S·öckchen n *anklet*; junges Mädchen in ~ ⟨Am⟩ *bobby soxer* **S·ocke** f ~/~n *sock* || ⟨fam⟩ sich auf die ~n m *to take to one's heels* **~nblume** f ⟨bot⟩ *barrenwort* **~nhalter** m *suspender*, ⟨Am⟩ *garter* **S·ockel** m ~s/~ *socle, base*(*ment*); ⟨min, mount⟩ *headstart*; ⟨tech⟩ *sole-plate* || ⟨arts, mil⟩ *pedestal* **~platte** f *plinth*

socket·ieren vt [h] ⟨golf⟩ (Ball) *to socket*

Sod m ~(e)s/~e *boil brew*

S·oda f ~/ & n ~s/ ⟨chem⟩ (*carbonate of*) *soda* **~seife** f *soft soap* **~wasser** n *soda-water*

sod·ann [adv] *then*; *after that*

ˣ**sod·aß** [conj] *so that*; *so as to* + inf → so E.

S·odbrennen n *heart-burn, brash, pyrosis*

S·ode(n m) f ~(s)/~n (Rasen⁓) *sod*

Sodom·it m ~en/~en *sodomite*; ⟨fam⟩ *bugger* | **~er·ei** f ~/ *sodomy* | **⁓isch** a *sodomitic*(*al*)

so·eben [adv] *but* od *just* (*now*) || *just* (*arrived*)

S·ofa n ~s/~s *sofa*; (kl) *settee* || *sleeperette* || ⟨Am⟩ *davenport* **~lehne** f *back of a s.* **~schoner** m *tidy*

sof·ern [conj] *if*; *in case*; *so*; *as far as* || (wenn nur) *provided that*; ~ nicht .. *except when* od *where* (*otherwise provided*)

soff 1. & 3. sg pret v saufen

S·öffel m ~s/~ ⟨vulg⟩ *tippler, boozer*

Soff·itte f ~/~n ⟨arch⟩ *soffit* || ⟨theat⟩ ~n [pl] *flies* | ~nlampe [f] *tabular* (od *strip, scaffold*) *lamp*

S·ofia n (Hauptstadt Bulgariens)

sof·ort adv *at once, immediately, directly, forthwith* || *straight* od *right away* || (als Antwort) *coming* || ~ tot *killed on the spot*; ~ wirkend *instantaneous* || notfalls ~ *will have to go .. at short notice* **⁓hilfe** f *Immediate Aid* (*I.A. Ordinance*) | **~ig** a *immediate, prompt* || ⟨com⟩ *spot*(*-cash*) || ⟨mil⟩ Bereitschaft zu ~em Gegenschlag *quick reaction alert* **~kaffee** m *instant coffee* **⁓maßnahmen** [pl] *immediate action*; *urgent measures* pl **~menü** n *straight away meal* **~programm** n ⟨bes Am⟩ *crash pr.*

S·og m *whirl* (*pool*); → Saug-; ⟨mar, aero⟩ *wake, suction*; *undertow* (*of waves*) || *whirl* (*of events*); *mysterious power of* (*destructive*) *alluring forces*; ⟨fig⟩ *maelstrom* **sog** 1. & 3. sg pret v saugen

sog·ar adv *even* || (*hundreds*) *nay* (*thousands*) || sogar die St. *the very stones* (*cry out*)

s·ogenannt a *so-called, as it is called* || *pretended* || (sich selbst so nennend) *would-be, pretended*

s·ogestalt a *so formed* **sogl·eich** adv → sofort

S·ohl- ~bank [f] ⟨arch⟩ *ledge, sill* **S·ohle** f ~/~n *sole*; auf leisen ~n *softly* || (Tal–, Graben–, Fluß–, Dock–, Ofen⁓) *bottom* || ⟨min⟩ *level*; *bottom* || (Pflug⁓) *foot* || das h wir uns an den ~n abgelaufen *we knew that long ago* || mir brennen die ~ *the floor burns under my feet* || m wir uns auf die ~ *let's clear out* || sich an jds ~n heften *to dog a p* || °e–e saubere ~ aufs Parkett legen ⟨fam⟩ *to shake a toe* **Sohl(en)- ~druck** m ⟨oil⟩ *bottom hole pressure* **~fläche** f (e–r Sperrmauer etc) *base* **~gänger** m *plantigrade* **~leder** n *soleleather* **~linie** f *level* **~platte** f ⟨mach⟩ *sole-plate* **~stein** m *bottom-stone* **s·ohlen** vi [h] **1.** *to sole* **2.** °⟨fam⟩ *to tell fibs* **..sohlig:** doppel~ *double-soled* **s·öhlig** a ⟨min⟩ *level*; nicht ~ *unlevelled*

Sohn m ~(e)s/⁓e *son* ⟨a. fig⟩ || der verlorene ~ *the prodigal son* || Gottes ~ *the Son of God* || des Menschen ~ *the Son of Man* || ⟨fam⟩ mein ~ *my lad* || °~ e–r räudigen Hündin, ⟨vulg⟩ *sonofabitch*, ⟨Am a.⟩ *sonuvabitch* **~espflicht** f *filial duty* **S·öhnchen** n ~s/~ *little son* || mein ~! *sonny*!; ⟨fig⟩ *youngster*! **S·ohnschaft** f ~/ *sonship*; ⟨jur⟩ *filiation*

Soiree [swa:ˈre:] f ~/~n *evening-party, soirée*

S·oja- ~bohne f *soy*(*a*) *bean* **~öl** n *soy*

S·ol- ~bad n *salt-water bath* **~ei** n *egg boiled in salt-water* **~quelle** f *salt-spring* od *-well*

sol·ange [conj] (~ als) *so* od *as long as*; (*the*) *while, whilst*; → so lange

Sol·ar- ~isati·on ⟨opt phot⟩ f *reversal* **~jahr** n *solar year* **~öl** n *solar oil*

S·olawechsel m ⟨com⟩ *sole bill, promissory note*

solch [~er, ~e, ~es] [pron] **1.** *such* (*a man*), (*a man*) *like that* || ~ e–r *such a one* || nur ein ~er Mann *but one such man* || ~e gute(n) Menschen *such good people* || ~e Äpfel *such apples* || ~e Sn *this sort of th* || ~e Sn, die *or* welche .. *such ths as* (*children love*) || es gibt ~e (Autos) u ~e *there are cars and cars* || als ~er *as such* || als ~es gefühlt *felt to be such* || ·auch ~ ein *just such another* (*pen*) **2.** ⟨emph⟩ wir h ~en Hunger *we are awfully hungry* **3.** [abs] ~e [pl] *some of these, that sort* **4.** [adv] → so C. so bekannt **s·olchenfalls** adv *in that* (od *such a*) *case* **s·olcher- ~gestalt** adv *in such a manner, to such a degree* | **~lei** a *of such a kind* | **~maßen** [adv] → .. maßen | **~weise** [adv] *in such a way* od *manner*

S·old m ~(e)s/ ⟨mil⟩ *pay* || ⟨allg⟩ *wages* pl (⟨a. bib⟩ *the wages of sin is death*) || *guerdon* (*of love*) || in ~ nehmen *to engage, hire* || im ~ jds stehen *to be in a p's pay* **~abzug** m *deduction from pay* **~buch** n *pay-book* **~einbehaltung** f *detention of pay* **~erhöhung** f *increase of* od *in pay* **~schreiber** m *literary hack*, ⟨sl⟩ *ink-slinger* **~truppen** f pl *mercenaries* pl **~zulage** f ⟨sl⟩ *buckshee*
Sold·at m ~en/~en *soldier* (unbekannt *unknown*) || aktiver ~ *regular* || altgedienter ~ *veteran* || ausgedienter ~ *ex-service man* || gemeiner ~ *private*, → Mannschaften || unbekannte(r) ~ *Unknown Warrior* || ~ zweiter Klasse *degraded private* || ~ zu Fuß (Pferde) *foot-soldier* (*horseman*) | ~(en) spielen *to play at soldiers* || ~ s *to soldier*; (im Kriege) ⟨fam⟩ *to do one's bit* || ~ w *to enlist*; *to enter the army, to join the ranks*; ⟨fam⟩ *to join up, to go soldiering* | des ~en Braut (Gewehr) *the s.'s best friend* || °ich war ~, als du noch in die Windeln machtest *I was cutting barbed wire while you were cutting your teeth* **Sold·aten- ~art** f: nach ~ *in military fashion* **~brauch** m *s.ly custom* **~eid** m *mil. oath* **~friedhof** m *military cemetary* **~geist** m *mil. spirit* **~handwerk** n *mil. profession*, ⟨fam⟩ *s.ing* **~heim** n *S.s' Home, leave centre* **~fieber** n *camp-fever* **~leben** n *mil. life* **~liebchen** n *garrison-hack* **~lied** n *s.'s song* **~mütze** f *foraging-cap* **~pferd** n *trooper's horse* **~rock** m *s.'s coat, uniform* **~sender** m ⟨Am⟩ *Armed Forces Network* **~sprache** f *army language* od *slang* **~stand** m *mil. state* od *order*; *s.y* **~tum** n *s.ship, s.liness* **~wesen** n *mil. concerns* pl, *s.y* **~zeit** f (*a p's*) *s.ing days* pl **Soldat·eska** f ~/ *the soldiery* **sold·atisch** a *soldierly* (*bearing*), *soldierlike, military*
Söldner m ~s/~ (a. Söldling [m] ~(e)s/~e) *mercenary, hireling* || ⟨Am, hist⟩ *Hessian* **~heer** n *army of mercenaries* **~truppen** f pl *mercenary troops* pl

S·ole f ~/~n *salt-water, brine* | ~leitung [f] *brine-tubing* od *-piping*; *b.-pipe*; → Sol-

sol·enn a *solemn* | ≗**ität** f *solemnity*

solfegg·ieren [–dʒ–] vi [h] *to sol-fa*

sol·id- ~(e) a *solid, strong* || (achtbar) *respectable*; (gesetzt) *steady*; (*of*) *sober* (*habits*) || ⟨com⟩ *good, safe, solvent* || ⟨com⟩ (*firm*) *of good standing* || ~e Konstruktion ⟨a.⟩ *ruggedness* ≗**·ar-** [in comp] *joint* (*debtor, security*) **~·arisch** [a] *jointly and separately liable, conjointly responsible* od *liable* || ~e Verbindlichkeit *joint liability* | [adv] *jointly and severally* || sich ~ erklären mit *to identify o.s. with, to throw in one's lot with* ≗**arität** f ~/ *solidarity* ≗**it·ät** f ~/ *solidity* || *respectability* ⟨a. com⟩ || *steadiness*

S·olingen n ⟨Ger⟩ (Stadt)

Sol·ist m ~en/~en *solo-player* || (Sänger) *solo-singer, soloist* **Solit·är** m ~(e)s/~e (Diamant & Spiel) *solitaire*

Soll n ~(s)/~(s) **1.** *command* **2.** *debit* || ~ u Haben ⟨com⟩ *debit and credit* **3.** ⟨com⟩ *target* (*export t.*) | **~-** *nominal* (*size*, etc) **~arbeitstunden** f pl *nominal man-hours* **~bestand** m *presumed assets* pl; ⟨mil⟩ = ~stärke **~bruchstellen** f pl ⟨tech⟩ *shear points* **~einnahme** f *supposed receipts* pl **~posten** m ⟨com⟩ *debit item* **~reichweite** f *rated coverage* **~saldo** n ⟨com⟩ *debit balance* **~seite** f (*debit-* od) *liabilities side* **~stärke** f ⟨mil⟩ *required strength*; *establishment, complement, paper strength* **~wirkungsgrad** m *declared efficiency* **S·ollen** n *duty, obligation*

s·ollen vi [h] **A. 1.** (**Gebot**) [mst 2. & 3. P] *you* (*he, they*) *shall go this instant* || *shall I open the window? – Yes, you shall* || *shall not = shan't* || *one must obey* || *you must not lie* || *he is to come at once* || *you are to wait* | ⟨bib⟩ *thou shalt not kill* || du sollst .. ehren *honour thy father and thy mother* **2.** (**Anordnung** [e–s Dritten], Vereinbarung) [bes 1. P indic, pres & pret] *I am, was* (*you are, were, he is, was*) *not to go there*; vgl B. || Sie ~ es tun (ich will es) *I w·ill have you do it!*; es soll nach Möglichkeit *it is axiomatic that .. should* **3.** (**Schicksal**) *to be destined* (*fated, decreed*) || .., was k sollte *I knew what was to come to pass* || es soll(te) nicht s *it is* (*was*) *not to be* ([pret a.] es hat nichts s ~ *or* ~ s) || es hat so ~ s *it had to happen* || 3 Jahre sollten vergehen, ehe *three years were to pass before I met him* || *she looked for him who* (*was to* od) *would return no more* → A. 12. **4.** (**moral.** *or* soziale Pflicht) *to be* (*in duty*) *bound, to be obliged to do* | [pres] *I am to leave*; *one should not rely upon others*; *little girls ought to be seen and not heard* (soll man sehen ..); *you never do what you ought* | [pret] (oft „eigentlich“) *he was to leave the next day*; *he was to have left at 6, now it is 9*; *you should not make such a row* || man sollte nicht .. *a fellow has no business* (*to laugh*) || Sie sollten ihm doch lieber schreiben *you had better write to him* | ich sollte es (nicht) getan h, ich hätte es tun ~ [statt „gesollt“] *I ought* (*not*) *to have done it*; *you were to have come earlier*; *I sh·ould have been more careful* || es hätte getan w ~ *it ought to have been done* **5.** (**Absicht**) [pres] dies soll .. ersetzen *this is intended to replace pepper* || das soll ·ich s *this portrait is meant for me* || hier ~ einige Worte gesagt w *here some remarks may* od *must be made* || dieser Brief soll .. *this is to tell you ..* || man soll nicht sagen können, daß *no one shall say that* | [pret] es sollte .. *it was meant in fun, .. to be like this* || *this was all that the declaration was meant, intended, designed to effect* **6.** (**Wunsch**) Gott soll mich bewahren *God help me* (*if ..*) || den soll der Teufel holen *he may go to hell* || er soll leben (– hoch)! *three cheers to him* **7.** (**Herausforderung**) soll e–r k u .. *now let any one come and ..* || er soll mir nur unter die Finger k *let me but get hold of him* **8.** (**Möglichkeit**) sollte er tot s? *can he be dead?, do you think he is dead?, do you think it could have been stolen?* || sollte das Ihr Ernst s? *are you in earnest?* | wenn es regnen sollte *if it should rain*; *if you should* (*happen to*) *see him* **9.** (**Vermutung**) soll das wahr s? *can it be true?* || man sollte meinen .. *one would* od *might think ..* || *I should think ..* || sollte er es getan h? *is it possible that he should have done it?* || den sollte ich doch kennen *I must have met him before* || *could I have been so much mistaken?* **10.** (**Gerücht**) er soll (reich s) *he is said, believed, supposed* (*to be rich*) || *they say he is ..* || *he is understood, reported, alleged* (*to have done it*) || er soll gesagt h, daß *he is reported as saying that* || *he is expected to arrive today* **11.** (**Erwartung**) ich sollte ihn verraten! *I betray him!* || es sollte mich freuen, wundern *it would give me much pleasure, I should be surprised* (*if ,,*) || da soll e–r .. *how is one expected to keep quiet?* **12.** (**Zukunft**) Sie ~ = w sehen *you shall* od *will see* || *we are to receive some money* || *it shall not happen again* || *I shall be very pleased* || *the rest will do me good* || das soll mich kalt l *that won't trouble me* || der soll erst geboren w, der das versteht *no man alive can understand that* | [pret] er sollte sie nie mehr sehen *he was never to see her again*; → A. 3. **13.** (**Einräu-**

mung) du sollst recht h! *now, you shall be right; let's say you are right* || *let him be right* **14. (Bedingung)** wenn er .. sollte *if he should happen to die* || *should he come yet, bring him along* || *if this be so, I'm all mistaken* || *if I should hear (in case of my hearing) from him I'll let you know* || *even though they should all fall* **B. (Frage) 1.** was soll es s (= was wollen Sie h)? *what's it going to be?* || *what am I (going) to do?; what shall I do now* || was sollte ich dagegen m? *how could I help it* || wie sollte ich da nicht lachen *how could I help laughing* **2.** [ell] was soll das? *what does that mean? how now?* || *what is that for?* || *what's the good of it?* || was soll das Weinen? *of what use is it to cry?* || was soll mir das (nützen)? *what is that to me?* || wohin soll ich? *where am I to go?* || ⟨fam⟩ wozu soll das? *what is it for?* **C.** [ell] dich soll der Teufel! *go to hell!* || der Brief soll auf die Post .. *must be posted* **D. (abhängig)** (ich weiß nicht), was ich tun soll .. *what to do*, .., was es bedeuten soll .. *what it means*, .., ob ich l. oder w. soll .. *whether to laugh or cry* || *he was told* od *desired to wait* || *he promised them that they should go with him* || *he said I was to ask you* || *where does he wish us to go?* (daß wir hin ∼) **E. sollend**: ernst s ∼d *would-be serious (tone)* || *with an attempt to be serious*

S·öller m ∼s/∼ *loft, garret* || *balcony*

S·olo [n] ∼s/∼s & Soli ⟨mus, cards⟩ *solo* | **≗** [adv] *alone*, ⟨mus⟩ *solo* **∼geiger** m *solo violinist* **∼gesang** m *solo* **∼maschine** f *solo (motor cycle)* **∼partie** f ⟨jazz⟩ *break* **∼stimme** f *solo part* **∼tänzerin** f *first (opera-* od *ballet-)dancer*; ⟨theat⟩ *ballerina*

S·olothurn n (Schweiz. Kanton u Stadt)

Solöz·ismus m ∼/–men *solecism*

S·olper m ∼s/ *brine*

Solst·itium [–ts–] n ∼s/–tien *solstice*

solv·ent a *solvent* **Solv·enz** f ∼/ *solvency*

Som·aliland n (Staat in O.-Afrika) *Somalia*

Somatis·ierung f (verdrängter Komplexe) ⟨psych⟩ *conversion*

som·it adv *therefore, consequently, so, thus*

Somme f ⟨Fr⟩ (Fluß mit Amiens [Stadt])

S·ommer m ∼s/∼ **1.** *summer* (⟨a. poet⟩ = Jahr) || ≗s, des ∼s im ∼ *in s., during the s.* || es will nicht ∼ w *the s. weather keeps back* || sie zählt erst 16 ∼ *she has seen but 16 s.s* || f den ∼ mieten *to summer-rent* **2.** fliegender ∼ = Sommerfäden **∼abend** m *s.-evening* **∼anzug** m *s.-suit* **∼aufenthalt** m = ∼frische **∼birne** f *s.-pear, early pear* **∼fäden** m pl *St. Martin's s., gossamer; air-threads* **∼fahrplan** m ⟨rail⟩ *s.-service* **∼ferien** pl *s.-vacation* **∼fleck** m etc = ∼sprosse etc **∼frische** f *health-, s.-resort* || in die ∼ gehen *to take an outing in the s.* **∼frischler** m *holiday-maker*, ⟨Am⟩ *vacationist* **∼frucht** f *s.-fruit* || (Korn) *s.-corn* **∼gerste** f *spring-barley* **∼getreide** n *s.-corn* **∼gewächs** n *s.-vegetable* **≗grün** ⟨for⟩ *with deciduous leaves* **∼haus** n *s.-house*, ⟨Am⟩ *cottage* **∼hitze** f *s. heat* **∼hut** m *summer hat* **∼kleid(ung** f) n *s.-dress* **∼korn** n *s.-corn, spring-rye* **∼leuchten** n ⟨meteor⟩ *s. luminescence* **∼linde** f *broad-leaved lime(-tree)* **∼monat** m *s.-month* **∼nachtstraum** m *Midsummer Night's Dream* **∼obst** n *s.-fruit, early fruit* **∼roggen** m *s.-rye* **∼saat** f *spring-corn* **∼schlaf** m ⟨zoo⟩ *aestivation*; ∼ halten *to aestivate* **∼seite** f *sunny side* **∼sonnenwende** f *s.-solstice* **∼sprosse** f *freckle* **≗sprossig** a *freckled* **∼stoff** m *s.-stuff, material for s.-wear, s. goods* pl **∼tag** m *s.-day* (an .. *on this fine s.-d.*) **∼tracht** f *summer flow of honey* **∼überzieher** m *light overcoat* **∼vogel** m *butterfly* **∼weg** m (e–r Landstraße) *soft shoulder; mud track, dirt carriage-way* **∼weizen** m *spring-wheat* **∼wetter** n, **∼witterung** f *s.-weather* **∼wohnung** f *s.-residence, s. home* **∼zeit** f *s.-time*, ⟨Am⟩ *daylight saving time* (⟨a.⟩ ∼verschiebung) **∼zeug** n = ∼stoff **s·ommerhaft, s·ommerlich** a *summer-like, summer(l)y*, ⟨scient⟩ aestival || sich ∼ kleiden *to put on summer clothes*

s·ommern I. vt [h] (Betten etc) *to air* || *to prune (trees)* || *to turn out (cattle)* || ⟨agr⟩ ein Feld ∼ *to sow .. for early crop* || sich ∼ *to bask* **II.** vi [imps] es sommert *summer is near*

somnamb·ul a *somnambulist(ic)* | **≗e** m ∼n/∼n; f ∼/∼n *s.list* | **≗·ismus** m ∼/ *s.lism*

son·ach [adv] *therefore, consequently*

Son·ate f ∼/∼n *sonata* **Sonat·ine** f ∼/∼n *sonatina*

S·onde f ∼/∼n ⟨surg⟩ *probe* || Schlund≗ *probang* | ⟨mar⟩ *plummet; sounding-lead*; → sondieren

s·onder prep ⟨obs, poet⟩ *without* **S·onder-** *sp(ecial), sep(arate)* **∼(ab)druck** m ⟨typ⟩ *off-print, sep. print* **∼abgabe** f *sp. rate, levy, tax, contribution* **∼abkommen** n *sp. agreement* **∼absicht** f *ulterior motive* **∼angebot** n *sp. offer; bargain*; ein ∼ m *to make a sp. feature*; „∼"! ⟨com⟩ *featured* **∼anfertigung** f *custom order*; ⟨mot⟩ *custom-built car* **∼antrieb** m *sp.* od *accessory drive* **∼aufbau** m ⟨mot⟩ *sp. body* **∼auftrag** m *sp. mission* **∼ausführung** f *sp. design* **∼ausgabe** f ⟨com⟩ *extras* pl || ∼n [pl] *particular charges* || ⟨typ⟩ (Buch) *sep.* od (Blatt) *sp. edition* **∼ausschuß** m ⟨parl⟩ *select committee* ∼ausweis m *sp. pass* **∼beauftragte(r)** *sp. representative* od *commissioner* **∼bedingungen** f pl ⟨ins⟩ *sp. policy conditions* **∼befehl** m *sp. order* **∼berater** m *sp. adviser* **∼berichterstatter** m *sp. correspondent* **∼besitz** m ⟨jur⟩ *severalty* **∼bestimmungen** f pl des Gesetzes *legal saving clause* **∼bestrebung** f *separatism, particularism* **∼bevollmächtigte(r)** m *plenipotentiary* **∼botschaft** f ⟨parl⟩ *sp. message* **∼botschafter** m *ambassador-at-large* **∼bund** m Sw ⟨hist⟩ *separatist league* **∼bündler** m Sw *member of Sonderbund*; ⟨Ger⟩ *separatist* **∼dienst** m *sp. duty* **∼druck** m *reprint* **∼eigentum** n *estate in severalty* **∼erzeugnisse** n pl *sp.ities* **∼fall** m *sp.* od *exceptional case*; ⟨comp⟩ *exc.l item* **∼genehmigung** f ⟨com⟩ (im GATT) (befristet *Hard Core*) *Waiver* **∼flug** m *extra flight* | **∼flugzeug** [n] *sp.-type aircraft* **∼fonds** m *sp. purposes fund* **∼formation** f *sp. auxiliary troop* **∼friede** m *sep. p.* **∼gelüste** n [pl] *particular desire(s* pl) **∼gericht** n *sp. court* od *tribunal* **∼geschwader** n ⟨aero⟩ *sp. task force* **≗gleichen** a *matchless, unequalled, unparalleled, unrivalled, unique* **∼interesse(n** pl) *sp., private, particular interest* **∼kampfverband** m *joint task force* N **∼klasse** f ⟨sail, racing⟩ *sonder-class* **∼leistung** f *extra (work)*; ⟨bes DDR⟩ *amenity* **∼marke** f ⟨post⟩ *sp. postage* (⟨a.⟩ *commemorative) stamp* || ⟨com⟩ *best quality sp.ly selected* **∼konto** n *sep. account* **∼meldung** f *sp. announcement* **∼nummer** f *sp. edition* **∼recht** n *privilege* **∼regelung** f *sep. settlement* **∼sitzung** f: zu e–r ∼ zus–treten *to meet in sp. session* **∼stab** m *sp. staff* **∼stahl** m *sp. steel* **∼stellung** f *exceptional position* **∼stempel** m ⟨post⟩ *sp. postmark* **∼unterhalt** m *sep. maintenance* **∼urlaub** m bei Sterbefall *compassionate leave* **∼vergütung** f *bonus* **∼verkauf** m *bargain sale* **∼vermögen** n *private fortune* **∼waffe** f *sp. w.* **∼zeichen** n ⟨comp⟩ *special character* **∼zug** m ⟨rail⟩ *sp.* od *extra, excursion train* **∼zulage** f *sp. bonus*; ⟨mil sl⟩ *buckshee* **∼zustellung** f ⟨post⟩ *sp. delivery* **∼zuteilung** f *sp. ration* **∼zweck** m *specific purpose*

s·onderbar a *strange, singular, peculiar, odd, bizarre; queer; unaccountable; little (his l. ways)* || *curious (coincidence)* || ∼! *how strange!* || ∼ v ihm, daß er es getan hat *strange of him to* (od *that he should) have done it* | **≗keit** f ∼/ *strangeness singularity oddness, oddity* | ∼en [pl] *strange* (etc) *ths, facts, habits* **S·onderheit** f ∼/ ⟨mst⟩: in ∼ *in particular; particularly, primarily, especially* **s·onderlich** [a] *(e)special, particular, peculiar,* *remarkable, extraordinary* || nichts ≗es *nothing remarkable* || kein ~er .. *no great* (*hero, scholar*) || kein ~es Vergnügen ⟨a.⟩ *not much of an amusement* | [adv] nicht ~ *not particularly* od *specially, not much* od *very*; es gefällt ihm nicht ~ *he doesn't like it so much*; interessiert? – nicht ~! *not very*! **S·onderling** m ~(e)s/~e *eccentric, freak; outsider* || *odd p* od *character, strange fellow*; ⟨sl⟩ *codger* **s·ondern** vt [h] *to separate, part, sift, sever* || (unterscheiden) *to distinguish, differentiate* (v *from*) || ⟨comp⟩ *to separate, select* **s·ondern** [conj] *but* || nicht nur .., ~ auch *not only .., but also* **sonders** → samt **S·onderung** f ~/~en *separation*

Sond·ier- ~stollen [m] ⟨min⟩ *trial* od *exploratory heading* od *tunnel* **sond·ieren** vt/i [h] ⟨allg⟩ *to study*; (e–e Wunde) *to probe* | (den Meeresgrund) *to sound, fathom* || ⟨fig⟩ *to sound*; *to approach cautiously* || jdn ~ *to pump a p*

Son·ett n ~(e)s/~e *sonnet*

S·onnabend m ~s/~e *Saturday* → Montag

S·onne f ~/~n *sun* [m] (aufgegangen *risen*) || untergehende (*or* sich neigende) ~ *westering sun* || (~nlicht) ⟨a.⟩ *sunlight* (bei strahlender ~ *in bright s.l.*) || an der ~ *in the sun*(*light*); an der ~ gedörrt, getrocknet *sun-baked*; zur ~ gehörig *solar* || v der ~ beschienen *sunlit* || v der ~ verbrannt *sunburnt* || die ~ scheint ⟨a.⟩ *there is sunshine*; sticht *is burning* || wir h die ~ im Gesicht *the sun is in our eyes* || die ~ bringt es an den Tag *murder will out* || er ist nicht wert, daß ihn Gottes ~ bescheint *he is not worthy of the sun shining on him* || ⟨prov⟩ es ist nichts so fein gesponnen, es kommt doch an das Licht der ~n *what snow conceals, the sun reveals*; ⟨fam⟩ *it all comes out in the wash* **s·onnen** vt [h] *to sun, to expose to the sun* || sich ~ *to sun*; *bask* (*in the sun*); sich an etw ~ *to delight in a th, to sun o.s. in* (*a p's favour*), ⟨iron⟩ *to gloat on* .. **S·onnen-** **~anbeter** m *sun-worshipper* **~aufgang** m *sunrise*, ⟨Am⟩ *sunup* (bei *at*) **~bad** n *sun-bath*; ein ~ nehmen *to sun-bathe* **~bahn** f ⟨astr⟩ *orbit of the sun* || *ecliptic* **~ball** m *orb of the sun* ≗**beschienen** a *sunlit*; (*road*) *in the sunshine, bathed in s.sh.* **~bestrahlung** f *insolation* **~blende** f ⟨phot⟩ *lenshood*; *sun-shade* **~blicke** m pl ⟨fig⟩ *snatches of sunshine* **~blume** f ⟨bot⟩ *sunflower* **~boot** n ⟨Eg rel⟩ *the sun's* (*heavenly*) *boat, solar b.* **~brand** m *broiling sun* || (der Haut) *sunburn* **~bräune** f *tan*; ⟨cosm⟩ *tan make-up* **~brille** f *sun-glasses* **~bruder** m *tramp* **~dach** n *sunblind*; ⟨mar⟩ *awning*; ⟨mot⟩ *sunshine roof* **~energie** f *solar energy* || durch ~ antreiben *to solar power* **~deck** n ⟨mar⟩ *sundeck* **~dienst** m *sunworship* ≗**durchflutet** a *flooded with sunlight*; ~er Raum *sunroom* **~energiekraftwerk** n ⟨el⟩ *solar power station* **~fackel** f *luminous spot on the sun* **~fächer** m *large fan* **~ferne** f ⟨astr⟩ *aphelion* **~finsternis** f *solar eclipse, eclipse of the sun* **~fleck** m *spot in the sun, sun-spot* ≗**gebräunt** a *sunburnt*; *tanned* || stark ~ w *to take on a deep sunburn* **~glanz** m *splendour of the sun* **~glut** f *blazing sun* **~gott** m *Helios, Phœbus, Apollo, Sol* ≗**haft** a *sunlike, sunny*; *radiant*; *akin to the sun* ≗**hell** a = ≗klar **~helligkeit** f *brightness of the sun* **~hitze** f *heat of the sun*; *solar heat* **~hochhaus** n *point-block* **~hof** m *solar corona* **~höhe** f ⟨astr⟩ *sun's altitude* **~hut** m *sun-hat* **~jahr** n *solar year* **~käfer** m ⟨ent⟩ *ladybird* ≗**kl·ar** a (*crystal*) *clear*; *sun-bright, sunny*; ⟨übtr⟩ *evident*; *clear as daylight*; ⟨fam⟩ *as plain as a pikestaff*; *as clear as* (*the sun at*) *noonday*, → Tinte, Kloßbrühe **~kraft-** ~maschine [f] *solar furnace*; ~werk [n] *solar power station* **~kreis** m *solar orb* **~kult** m *sun-worship* | ~- *heliolithic* **~lauf** m *course of the sun* **~licht** n *sunlight* ≗**los** a *sunless* **~messer** m *heliometer* **~mikroskop** n *solar microscope* **~monat** m *solar month* **~nähe** f ⟨astr⟩ *perihelium* **~regen** m *rain and sunshine together* **~rös|chen** n *Helianthemum* L **~scheibe** f *disk of the sun*; ⟨Eg arts⟩ *sun's disc* **~schein** m *sunshine* || ⟨fig⟩ nicht nur ~ *not all rose colo*(*u*)*r* | ~anzeiger [m] *sunshine recorder* **~schirm** m *sunshade* || (für Damen) *parasol* **~schutz** m *sun-blinds* pl; ⟨cosm⟩ *sun* (*protective*) *oil*; ⟨mot⟩ *glare eliminator* **~segel** n *awning* **~seite** f *sunny side* || ⟨astr⟩ die ~ e–s Planeten *the dayside of a p.* **~spektrum** n *solar spectrum* **~stand** m *sun's position* (od *altitude* ⟨a. phot⟩) **~stäubchen** n *mote*, ⟨*fig*⟩ *atom in a sun-beam* **~stich** m *sunstroke* (bek *to have*) || °er hat'n ~ *he's loony* (⟨mil⟩ *daty*) **~strahl** m *ray of sunshine, sunbeam*; der erste ~ *the first sun*; die ersten ~en *the first rays of the rising sun* **~strahlung** f *solar radiation* | ~smesser [m] *pyroheliometer* **~straße** f ⟨astr⟩ *ecliptic* **~system** n *solar system* **~tag** m ⟨astr⟩ *solar day* || (sonnig) *sunny day*; ⟨fig⟩ *day of happiness* **~tau** m ⟨bot⟩ *sundew* ≗**überflutet** a *sun-drenched* **~uhr** f *sundial*; *gnomon* **~untergang** m *sunset*, ⟨Am⟩ *sundown*; (bei .. *at* ..) **~veranda** f *solarium*, ⟨Am⟩ *sun parlor* ≗**verbrannt** a (*sun*)-*burnt, tanned* **~vorhang** m *sunshade* **~wärme** f *solar heat* **~wende** f ⟨astr⟩ *solstice* || (Wendekreis) *tropic* **~wendfeuer** n *St. John's fire* **~wind** m ⟨astr⟩ *solar wind* | ~-Empfangsgerät [n] *solar wind collector*; ~-Teilchen [n pl] *solar wind particles* pl **~zeit** f *solar time* **~zelt** n ⟨mar⟩ *awning* **s·onnig** a *sunny* ⟨a. fig⟩ **S·onntag** m ~(e)s/~e *Sunday* || → Montag || freier ~ (*his*) *S.y off* od *out* **~(nachmittag)ausgehanzug** m *one's best bib and tucker, S.-go-to-meeting clothes* **s·onntägig** a *S.y* **s·onntäglich** a *S.y* | [adv] *every S.y* || ~ gekleidet *dressed in one's S.y-best* **S·onntags** [adv], (des) ~ *on S.ys*, (*of*) *a S.y* **~andacht** f *S.y devotion* **~anzug** m *S.y-best* **~arbeit** f *S.y work* **~entheiliger** m *Sabbath-breaker* **~ausflügler** m (*p who makes a S.y excursion*) *week-ender* **~fahrer** m *S.y driver* **~fahrkarte** f *week-end ticket* **~heiligung** f *Sabbath observance* **~jäger** m ⟨fig⟩ *Cockney* od *would-be -sportsman* **~kind** n *S.y-child, p born on a S.y* || ein ~ s *to be born with a silver spoon in one's mouth* **~kleid** n *S.y-best*, ~er [pl] *S.y clothes* pl **~prediger** m *dominical preacher* **~reiter** m ⟨fig⟩ *unpractised rider* **~ruhe** f *S.y rest* || = ~heiligung **~schule** f *S.y-school* **~staat** m *S.y finery*, ⟨Am sl⟩ *gladrags* || s–n ~ anlegen ⟨fam⟩ *to put on one's best bib and tucker* || ⟨fig⟩ .. prangte im ~ (*the earth*) *had donned the garb of festival* **~-Unfallzahlen** f pl *holiday toll* **~vergnügen** n *S.y amusement*

son·or a *sonorous*

sonst [adv] **A. 1.** (andernfalls) *otherwise* (*he would have been lost*); *in the contrary case* || (*quickly*) *or* (*they will see us*), *else* (*I shall miss him*); (*you should eat*) *or* (*you will be hungry*) **2.** (im übrigen) *in other respects* || (*he suffers from .. but*) *otherwise* .. || (für gewöhnlich) *generally*; (*this*) *normally* od *ordinarily* (*bouncing girl*) || **wenn** ~ *if on the other hand*; *provided* **3.** (außerdem) *moreover, besides*; *independently of that, in addition to that*; ~ noch jd? *is there any other one*? *anyone else*? **4.** (zeitlich) *at other times* || *generally, usually* || **wie** ~ *as usual, as it was*; er war wieder lustig wie ~ *he was once more his gay self* || anders **als** ~ *different from what it used to be*; früher (schneller) als ~ *earlier* (*faster*, etc) *than usual* || ~ einmal *some other day, some time or other, on some other occasion* || du bist doch ~ nicht so *you are not usually so easily offended* || ~ u jetzt *once and now* || das ≗ u Jetzt (*the*) *past and present* **5.** (ehemals) *formerly* **B.** ~ **etw** *sth else* || ~ (noch) etw? *anything else*? || darf es ~ noch etw s? *what else can I show* (od *do for*) *you*? || ~ **jd** *or* °wer? *anybody else*? || ~ **k-r** *nobody else* || wenn's ~ **nichts** ist! *if that's all*! || ~ nichts als *nothing but* || u **was** ~ noch *and all the rest of it*; ⟨fam⟩ *and what not*! || ⟨iron⟩

~ noch was (gefällig)? *lie down and I'll fan you* || was (wer) ~? *what (who) else?* | ⟨fam⟩ wie ~ was *like anything* || wir w ~ was tun *we'll see you further first* || und **wer** ~ noch *and I don't know who all* || er denkt, er sei ~ **wer** *he fancies h.s. a great man* **s·onstig** a *other* || in ~er Hinsicht *otherwise* || (ehemalig) *former* **s·onst- ~wie** adv *in some other way* **~wo** adv *elsewhere, anywhere* od *somewhere (else)*

Soph·ist m ~en/~en *sophist, quibbler* | **~er·ei** f ~/~en *sophistry* | ≗**isch** a *sophistic(al)* [adv *s.ally*]

Sopr·an m ~(e)s/~e *soprano*; (Knaben≗) *treble* **~sänger(in f)** m *sopranist, soprano (singer)*

S·orbe m (Wende); **s·orbisch** a *Sorbian*

Sorb·ett n ~(e)s/~e *sherbet; sorbet*

Sord·ine f ~/~n ⟨mus⟩ (Dämpfer) *sordine*

S·orge f ~/~n (um, für) *care (of)* || (Leid) *grief, sorrow; distress, anguish* || (Besorgnis, Unruhe) *uneasiness, anxiety*; gr ~ *alarm* | (Gegenstand) *distress*, ⟨fam⟩ *headache* | (Sorgfalt) *care* | (Für≗) ⟨jur⟩ *custody* (⟨a.⟩ Recht der ~ f die P e–s Minderjährigen); *c. of the child was conferred on the mother* .. wurde der M. übertragen | andere ~n *to have other ths to think about* || etw mit ~ betrachten *to view a th with concern* | ~n [pl] *troubles, woes, worries* pl | in ~n s *to fear, apprehend* || jdm ~ bereiten *to worry a p* || jdm ~ m *to give a p trouble* || sich [dat] ~ m (um) *to bother* od *worry; to be anxious; to trouble o.s. (about); to view a th with concern*; unnötig .. *to borrow trouble*; mach dir k–e ~n *don't be alarmed*, .. k–e vorzeitigen ~n *never trouble trouble before it troubles you* || außer ~n s *to be unconcerned* od *easy* || frei v ~n *light (heart)*; er ist v gar k–r ~ beschwert *he hasn't a care in the world* || das wird ihn v dieser ~ befreien *that will relieve his mind in this matter* || ~ tragen f *to take care of; to attend to; to see (to it) that* (daß) || l Sie das m–e ~ s *leave that to me, never you mind* || das ist m–e ~ *that's my grief* od *look-out* .. nicht .. *it isn't my worry* (⟨sl⟩ *funeral*) | sich durch ~n zerrütten *to worry o.s. to death* || ~ zerstreuen *to cast away care* | die ~ **um** Angehörige *the concern for relatives, dependents* **s·orgen** vi [h] ~ f *to care* od *provide for; to take care of, to look after (the needs of ..)*; ⟨mil⟩ f s–e Truppen ~ *to look after the welfare of one's troops* || *to attend* od *see to (every detail)*; ⟨Am⟩ *to fix (the fire)* || dafür ~, daß .. *to ensure that*; .., daß etw geschieht *to see a th done, to arrange for a th to be done* || dafür z ~ h, daß .. *to make due provision, to assure that* .. || (erst mal) f sich ~ *to fend for o.s., to look after o.s.* (⟨fam⟩ *number one*) || f ihn ist gesorgt *he is provided for* || f jdn z ~ h *to have a p on one's hands* || (in Sorge s) *to fear, to be afraid* od *anxious* | **sich** ~ [h] (um) *to worry* od *grieve (about)* **S·orgen- ~brecher** m ⟨fig⟩ *care-expeller, th that drowns care* **~falten** f pl *lines of sorrow* od *care* ≗**frei,** ≗**los** a *free* od *exempt from care; carefree*; ≗**frei** a *unworried, secure, insouciant; without any worry* | adv *in unembarrassed circumstances* **~kind** n *problem child, (delicate) ch. causing anxiety*; ⟨fam⟩ *handful* ≗**schwer** a *weighed down with care* etc **~stuhl** m *armchair, easy chair* ≗**voll** a *uneasy, anxious, woeful, full of anxiety, troubled* **S·orgfalt** f ~/ *care(fulness)* || *attention* || *precision* || *conscientiousness* || *exactness* | gr ~ auf etw verwenden *to bestow great pains upon a th* || mit ~ *with care* | **s**≗**ig** [a] *careful, attentive, painstaking, precise, accurate* etc || (ausgeführt) *elaborate* | [adv] *with care* **s·orglich** a *careful* || (sorgenvoll) *anxious, solicitous* **s·orglos** a *carefree, happy-go-lucky* || *come-day go-day (fellow)* || (nachlässig) *careless, thoughtless, negligent* || (leichtfertig) *irresponsible* || (gleichgültig) *unconcerned, indifferent; care-for-nothing (fellow)* | [adv] ⟨a.⟩ *airily* ≗**igkeit** f ~/ *insouciance; airiness; carelessness, thoughtlessness, negligence* || *irresponsibility* || *indifference* **s·orgsam** a *careful, care-taking, heedful* || (vorsichtig) *cautious* | ≗**keit** f ~/ *carefulness*

S·orghum n ~s/ ⟨bot⟩ *sorgho, sorghum*; ⟨Am⟩ *broomcorn*

s·orren vt [h] ⟨mar⟩ *to seize, frap, moor* || *to lash up (hammocks)* **S·orrtau** n ⟨mar⟩ *lashing, seizing*

S·orte f ~/~n *sort, kind, species; description*; ⟨pap⟩ *grade* || (Zigarren etc) *brand* || feinste ~ *prime quality* || (P) ⟨hum⟩ *kidney* || übelster ~ *(a man) of the worst type* od *description* ≗**necht** a ⟨agr⟩ *true to seed* **~nzettel** m *list of specie* **sort·ieren** vt [h] *to (as)sort, grade* || (Wolle) *to break*; (auslesen) *to pick out* || ⟨comp⟩ *to sort, to re-arrange (data)*; mit der Maschine ~ *to machine-sort* **Sort·ierer(in f)** m (P) *sorter* || ⟨tech⟩ (S) *screen, strainer* **Sort·ier-** ⟨comp⟩ ~dat·ei [f] *sort file*; ~folge [f] *card sequence*; ~kriterium [n] *control data*; ~maschine [f] *sorter*, ⟨brew⟩ *barley separator* **~tisch** m *grading table* **Sortim·ent** n ~(e)s/~e *assortment; range (of suits); collection (of plants)* || (Satz) *set* | **~er** m ~s/~ *retail bookseller* | **~s- ~abteilung** f *new book department* **~buchhandel** m *retail book-trade* **~buchhändler** m *retail bookseller* **~buchhandlung** f *bookseller's shop*

s·o-so! ['sɔsɔ] adv, intj [bay] *is that so?*

°**sos·o** (–lala) [adv] *middling*

×**Soß** [sɔs] ~! (Soße) ⟨vulg⟩ *mind the grease!*

S·oße f ~/~n *sauce, gravy* || pikante ~ *ketchup* | ~nschüssel [f] *sauce-boat*

†**sot·an** a *this* || unter ~en Umständen *under the circumstances*

sott 1. & 3. sg pret v sieden

Sott·ise [s–] f ~/~n *foolishness* || (Grobheit) *rudeness* || ~n sagen *to make foolish remarks*

Soubr·ette [s–] f ~/~n *soubrette* (vgl *sober*)

Souffleur [su'flø:r] m ~s/~e *prompter* **~ecke** ⟨engl⟩ *prompt corner*, ⟨Am m. m.⟩ *stage left* **~kasten** m *prompt(er's) box* **souffl·ieren** vi [h]; jdm ~ *to prompt a p*

s·oundso I. [adv] ~ lange *for a certain length of time* || ~ oft *over and over again* || ~ viel *so much; a certain amount* od *quantity* || 100 u ~ Mark *a hundred odd shillings* || den ~vielten Mai *such and such a day of May* || ~viele ⟨sl⟩ *umpteen* **II.** ≗ [s] Herr (Frau) ≗ *Mr. (Mrs.) So-and-so* od *what's-his(-her)-name* **der ~vielte Teil** *such and such a part*

Souper [su'pe:] n ~s/~s *supper* **soup·ieren** vi [h] *to have one's supper* || es sollte erst .. soupiert w *supper was not to be until past midnight*

Sout·ane [su–] f ~/~n ⟨ec⟩ *cassock*

Souterrain [sute'rɛŋ] n ~s/~s *basement*

South·ampton [sau'θæmptən] n ⟨Engl⟩ (Hafen)

Souver·än [suvə–] **I.** m ~(e)s/~e *sovereign* **II.** ≗ [a] *sovereign* || *(the king was) supreme* || (etw) ~ [adv] beherrschen *to have absolute mastery of* | **~it·ät** f ~ *sovereignty*

sov·iel [a & adv] *so much* || ~ wie *or* als *as much as* || noch einmal ~ *twice as much* || ~ ich mich erinnere *at the best of my recollection* || ~ ich weiß (nicht) *as far as I know, for aught I know, (not so far as I know)* || → so viel **soweit** [conj] (→ sofern) *as* (od *so*) *far as* | *that* [rel pron]: *(there are none) that (I can see)* || *so far* || *in its* (etc) *way* || es ist ~ *it is on* || ·~ ging's *so far, so good* || ~ es bei ·mir liegt *as far as in me lies* || ganz gut *all right as far as (books* etc) *go* bzw *went; as far as it goes* || *(a good place) as places go* || ~ ganz nett *quite pretty*; das ist ~ ganz richtig *that's right enough* || gilt, ~ nicht ⟨contr etc⟩ *apply, save as* || ~ es .. zuläßt *to the extent that (the situation) permits* **sow·ie** [conj] *as well as* || (sobald) *as soon as, directly (he arrived ..)* **so-**

wies·o [adv] anyhow, anyway, as it is (was), any case, in any case ‖ ~ nicht not .. do what he etc. may **sow·ohl** [conj]; ~ .. als (auch) as well .. as; both .. and; not only .. but also

Sowj·et m ~s/~s (= Rat) Soviet; der oberste ~ the Supreme S.; **~anhänger** m s.ite **~armist** m red od S. soldier **≗feindlich** a anti-s. **≗isch** a s.(ist); unter ~em Einfluß S.-sponsored, S.-oriented **≗isieren** vt [h] to s.ize **~kongreß** m Union Congress of S.s **~republik** f S. Republic **~rußland** n S. Russia; ⟨off⟩ Union of S. Socialist Republics **~stern** m S. star **~system** n s.ism **~union** f (UdSSR) S. Union; ⟨off⟩ Union of S. Socialist Republics (U.S.S.R.)

°**S·ozi** m ~/~ & –zen = Sozialdemokrat, ⟨sl⟩ sosh [sɔːʃ] **sozi·al** a social (Einrichtungen, Nothilfe services) ‖ ~e Eingliederung socialization ‖ e–e ~e Gesellschaftsordnung a socially-orientated order of society; ~e Marktwirtschaft system of free competition with special regard for its social aspects; ~e Ökologie human ecology | **in** ~er Hinsicht s.ly | [adv] ~ unter jdm below a p s.ly **Sozi·al- ~abgaben** pl s. charges **~amt** n s. welfare office | zusätzliche **~aufwendungen** f pl ⟨com⟩ fringe benefits **~ausschuß** m s. committee **~beamte(r)** m s. (w.) worker **~beiträge** m pl s. insurance contributions **~demokrat** m s. democrat, s.ist **~demokratie** f s. democracy **≗demokratisch** a s.-democratic; die S~e Partei Deutschlands (SPD) the S.ist Party of Germany **~fürsorge** f s. security; s. services; s. (welfare) work; ⟨engl⟩ National Assistance; ~ beziehen to be in receipt of N. A. | ~r(in [f]) [m] s. welfare worker od officer **~gerichtsbarkeit** f s.-security jurisdiction **~gesetzgebung** f s. legislation **~lasten** f pl expenditure for welfare-work | zusätzliche **~leistungen** f pl ⟨Am⟩ fringe benefits **≗ökonomisch** a socio-economic **~paket** n train de mesures sociales Fr **~pfleger(in** f) m almoner **~politik** f s. politics [a. sg konstr] **≗politisch** a socio-political **~produkt** n gross national product; ~ je Kopf der Bevölkerung real n.l income per head **~psychiatrie** f s. psychiatry **~referent** m Labo(u)r Attaché **~rentner** m old-age pensioner **~versicherung** f s. insurance; s. security | ~sbeitrag [m] s. i. contribution **~werk** [n] f Kinderbeschränkung ⟨Am⟩ planned parenthood work (vgl birth control) **~wissenschaft** f s. economics; sociology **~wohnungsbehörde** f housing authority **sozialis·ieren** vi [h] to socialize, communize, ⟨engl⟩ nationalize **Sozial·ismus** m ~/ socialism, ⟨sl⟩ sosh [sɔːʃ] **Sozial·ist** m ~en/~en socialist **≗isch** a social-ist(ic) **~engesetz** n law against socialists **Soziol·og** m ~en/~en sociologist | **~·ie** f sociology **s·ozio-** ~-ökonomische Gruppe socio-economic group; ~-professionelle Gliederung s.-e. classification; social status categories pl **S·ozius** m ~/S·oziusse ⟨com⟩ partner; ⟨mot⟩ pillion-rider **~sitz** m ⟨mot⟩ pillion, ⟨fam⟩ flapper-bracket ‖ auf dem ~ fahren (mit) to ride pillion (to be a p's p.-rider)

sozus·agen adv as it were ‖ ⟨sl⟩ (I) sort od kind of (let him run my life) ‖ ⟨vulg⟩ (of a sudden) like

Sp·achtel f ~/~n spattle; spatula; ⟨typ⟩ slice | ~kitt [m] filler; ~masse [f] surfacer; ~messer [n] putty-knife, ⟨paint⟩ palette-knife [a. attr] | **≗n** vt [h] to prime, smooth ‖ °⟨übtr⟩ to play a good knife and fork ‖ → Spatel

Spag·at m ~(e)s/ It [obd] twine, string ‖ °⟨fig gym⟩ the splits pl

sp·ähen vi [h] (nach) to look out (for), to peer (at) ‖ (auf) to watch (for); ⟨mil⟩ to scout ‖ (spionieren) to spy | ≗ n espial **Sp·äher** m ~s/~ ⟨mil⟩ scout ‖ (Spion) spy; ⟨dero⟩ prowler **~blick** m searching glance **Sp·äh- ~schiff** n spy-boat, scout **~trupp** m ⟨mil⟩ (scouting od reconnaissance) patrol, scout party | ~tätigkeit [f] patrol activity **~wagen** m recon. vehicle, patrol od scout car

Sp·ake f ~/~n (Steuerrad≗) spoke; hand lever

Spal·ier n ~(e)s/~e ⟨hort⟩ trellis ‖ ⟨fig⟩ (P) lane; rows (of people) ‖ ~ bilden to form cordon od a lane, to line the street ‖ am ~ ziehen to train **~baum** m trained (fruit-)tree; wall-tree **~obst** n wall-fruit **spal·ieren** vt [h] **1.** to train (trees) **2.** to cover with trellis-work

Spalt m [~(e)s/~e], **~e** f [~e/~en] crack, rift, rent, split; cleft ⟨a. sex⟩; crevice ⟨a. geol⟩; fissure, chink ‖ (die Tür) ging e–n ~ weit auf .. opened a crack; e–n ~ weit offen l to leave (the door) open in a crack ‖ (f Geldeinwurf) slit, slot ‖ (Gletscher≗) crevasse ‖ ~e [f] ⟨typ⟩ column; ⟨comp⟩ card column **~algen** f pl ⟨bot⟩ diatomaceae **~axt** f, **~eisen** n cleaver **~blende** f ⟨phot⟩ slit diaphragm **~fläche** f cleavage **~flügel** m ⟨aero⟩ slot **~frucht** f ⟨bot⟩ schizocarp **≗früchtig** a schizocarpous **≗füßig** a cloven-footed **~füßler** m fissiped **~holz** n fire-wood **~keil** m wedge **~leder** n skiver **~messer** n cleaver **~öffnung** f ⟨bot⟩ stoma **~pfropfen** n ⟨hort⟩ slit-grafting **~pilz** m fission-fungus **~produkte** n pl ⟨biol, chem⟩ split products; ⟨at⟩ fission p.ts **~richtung** f line of cleavage **~ring** m ⟨tech⟩ split-ring **~zeugung** f fissiparism **sp·altbar** a cleavable; ⟨at⟩ fissonable **sp·alten** vt [h] to split, rive ‖ (Leder) to skive ‖ (Holz) to cleave, chop ‖ (e–e Feder) to slit ‖ ⟨fig⟩ Haare ~ to split hairs ‖ (Lichtstrahl) to decompose ‖ ⟨chem⟩ to crack (bes Öl) ‖ ~de Kräfte disruptive forces ‖ mit gespaltenem Huf cloven-footed | (teilen) to divide | **sich** ~ to divide, rip; (v Kristallen) to cleave; (P) to break up, to splinter, sunder ‖ (sich gabeln) to bifurcate **Sp·alten- ~anzeiger** m ⟨comp⟩ column (check) indicator **~breite** f width of c. **~satz** m ⟨typ⟩ setting up in columns **~steller** m tabulator **≗weise** adv in columns **sp·altig** a fissured, cracked ‖ ⟨typ⟩ (drei)~ in (three) columns **Sp·altung** f ~/~en cleaving, splitting ‖ ⟨phys⟩ decomposition; ⟨at, chem⟩ fission; ⟨chem⟩ scission, decomposition, separation, dissociation ‖ ⟨fig⟩ dissension, rupture, cleavage ‖ (der Meinungen) division ‖ (religiöse) schism ‖ ⟨pol⟩ split(-up), division (of Germany) | ~ begünstigend divisive **~sirresein** n split personality, schizophrenia **~sprodukt** n ⟨at⟩ fission product

Span m ~(e)s/≗e chip ‖ (Hobel≗e) chippings, shavings pl ‖ (Feil≗e) filings pl; (Metall–, Elfenbein≗e) scobs ‖ (Splitter) splinter | ⟨fig⟩ ≗e m to make a fuss ‖ e–n ~ h to be a bit crazy ‖ ⟨prov⟩ wo gehobelt wird, da fallen ≗e from chipping come chips; you cannot make an omelette without breaking eggs **~holz** n ⟨typ⟩ scale-boards pl **~korb** m chip-basket

Sp·andau n ⟨Ger⟩ (Stadt in der Mark Brandenburg)

spanen vt [h] to machine, cut

Sp·anferkel m sucking pig; sucker; ⟨cul⟩ roaster

Sp·ange f ~/~n clasp ‖ (Schnalle) buckle ‖ (Haar≗) slide ‖ (Arm≗) bangle, bracelet ‖ (Ordens≗) bar **~nschuh** m strap-shoe; anklet

Sp·aniel m ~s/~ (schwerer clumber) spaniel

Sp·anien n Spain **Sp·anier(in** f) Spaniard ‖ **sp·anisch** a Spanish ‖ ~e Fliege (Käfer!) Sp. fly; ⟨Am⟩ blister bug; ~e F.n [pl] cantharides pl ‖ ~er Pfeffer Cayenne pepper, cayenne ‖ ~e Reiter [pl] chevaux de frise pl ‖ ~es Rohr Bengal cane ‖ ~e Wand folding-screen ‖ ~er Wind = Meringe ‖ es kommt mir ~ vor I think it strange, how strange!

spann 1. & 3. sg pret v spinnen **Spann** m ~(e)s/~e instep **Sp·ann- ~ader** f sinew **~balken** m ⟨carp⟩ girder; straining beam **~band** ⟨tech⟩ tightening strap **~bereich** m ⟨tech⟩ reach **~beton** m prestressed concrete **~brett** n ⟨ent⟩ setting-board **~daumen** m, **~stück** n ⟨mill⟩ cogging cam

~dienst m *statute labour with teams* **~draht** m *bracing wire; tensioning cable* **~feder** f *spring* **~futter** n ⟨tech⟩ *chuck* **~haken** m *tenterhook* **~hebel** m *cocking lever* **~kette** f *tether* ‖ *drag* **~kraft** f *elasticity* ⟨a. fig⟩ ‖ ⟨physiol⟩ *tonicity*; ⟨med⟩ *tone* | ⟨fig⟩ *energy, buoyancy* **≃kräftig** a *elastic* ‖ ⟨übtr⟩ *resilient* (*personality*) **~muskel** m ⟨anat⟩ *tensor* **~nagel** m *large nail* **~rahmen** m *tenter(-frame)* **~riegel** m ⟨tech⟩ *strutting-piece*; ⟨arch⟩ *tie-beam* **~riemen** m *shoemaker's knee-strap* **~ring** m ⟨phot⟩ *cocking ring* **~rolle** f ⟨tech⟩ *tension pulley* **~säge** f *frame-saw* **~seil** n *tether* **~schraube** f *tension* od *adjusting screw, turnbuckle*; *clamp* **~verschluß** m ⟨phot⟩ *spring shutter* **~vorrichtung** f *tensioning device* **~weite** f *spread* ‖ ⟨aero, arch⟩ *span* **~wirbel** m (am Klavier) *tension-bar* **Sp·anne** f ~/~n *span* ‖ e–e ~ Zeit *a short space* ‖ die kurze ~ (unseres Lebens) *our brief span* (*of life*) ‖ (Gewinn≃) *margin* (*of profit*), ⟨Am⟩ *spread* ‖ ⟨eco⟩ *gap* (*inflationary g.*); zunehmende ~ zw Import- u Exportpreisen *deteriorating terms of trade* **sp·annen I.** vt [h] **A.** *to stretch* (*out*); *brace; strain; to stretch* (*a rope*) ‖ (Bogen) *to bend* ‖ (Nerven) *to brace; to strain* (*every nerve*) ‖ (Gewehr) *to cock* ‖ (Saite, Feder) *to tighten* ‖ die Schuhe ~ mich .. *pinch* (*me*) ‖ ⟨phot⟩ *to set the shutter* ‖ ⟨tech⟩ *to cock, set, tension*; (weiten) *to extend*; den Dampf ~ *to increase the tension* (*of steam*) ‖ ⟨mus⟩ *to stretch* (*an octave*) ‖ eng (weit) ~ *to tighten* (*loosen*) | (etw) **aufs** Äußerste ~ *to stretch .. to the rending point* | ⟨fig⟩ hoch ~ *to raise* (*a p's hopes*) *to a high pitch* ‖ aufs höchste ~ .. *greatly to excite* (*a p's curiosity*) ‖ s–e Forderungen zu hoch ~ *to make ridiculous prentensions* **B. auf** die Folter ~ *to put to the rack* ‖ ⟨fig⟩ *to keep a p on the rack of expectation* ‖ **ins** Joch ~ *to yoke* ‖ (Tuch) in den Rahmen ~ *to tenter* ‖ ⟨tech⟩ *to put .. in* (*a vice* etc) ‖ **über**: *to stretch an awning over a carriage* ‖ sich ~ über: *the rainbow stretches over us* ‖ **vor** den Wagen ~ *to put* od *harness to the carriage* | ⟨prov⟩ das Pferd hinter den Wagen ~ *to put the cart before the horse* **C. gespannt** (*steam*) *under pressure* ‖ (äußerst *severely*) *strained* (*situation, relations*), *close* (*attention*), *eager* (*curiosity*) ‖ fest g. halten *to keep a strain on* (*a rope*) ‖ auf g.em Fuß stehen mit *to be at loggerheads with* ‖ hochg. *high* (*expectations, hopes*) ‖ ich bin g., was wird *I'm anxious to know how it will turn out* ‖ ⟨fam⟩ ich bin gespannt wie ein Flitzebogen *I'm all* (od *on the tiptoe of*) *expectation* **II.** vi [h] *to be exciting* od *fascinating* | (of dress, etc) *to be tight* (*over the breast*) | **auf** etw ~ *to attend, listen eagerly to; to be anxious about ..* **sp·annend** a (Lektüre etc) (*deeply*) *interesting, thrilling, exciting* | *tense* (*moment*) | ⟨Am fam⟩ *juicy* (*story*) **sp·annenl·ang** a *span long* **Sp·anner** m ~s/~ **1.** ⟨anat⟩ *tensor* **2.** ⟨ent⟩ *geometer; measuring worm; looper* **3.** *tenter* (*for cloth*) **4.** ⟨cycl⟩ *spanner* **5.** *gaffle* (*of a cross-bow*) **6.** *boot-tree* **~raupe** f *looper, inchworm* **..spänner** m ~s/~: Ein~ *one-horse carriage* ‖ Zwei~ (= zweispänniger Wagen) *carriage and pair* ‖ Vier~ *c. and four* **Sp·annung** f ~/~en *tension* ⟨a. fig & el⟩ ‖ ⟨el⟩ *voltage*; unter ~ *energized* | *tightness, tautness* ‖ ⟨mech⟩ *strain* ⟨a. glass⟩, ⟨a. fig pol⟩ ‖ ⟨arch⟩ *span* | (Erwartung) *eager expectation*; Zeit nervöser ~ *keyed-up period* | mit ~ ⟨a.⟩ *agog* | (Neugier) *curiosity*; (Ungewißheit) *suspense* ⟨a. Lit⟩; (Aufmerksamkeit) *close attention* ‖ (Verdienst) ⟨com⟩ *margin* (*of profit*) ‖ (Entfremdung) *strained relations* pl, ~(en [pl]) (beträchtliche *acutely*) *strained* od *critical situation* od *condition*; *problem factors*, | **in** ~ halten *to hold* (*the audience*); *to keep* (*a p*) *in suspense* ‖ es herrscht ~ zw ihnen *they are on strained terms* ‖ in gr ~ s *to be very anxious* od *all agog* od *on tenter-hooks* | **unter** ~ ⟨el⟩ (*a*)*live* | die ~ lösen *or* vermindern *to ease* od *relieve the tension* ⟨a. fig⟩ | **~s- ~abfall** m ⟨el⟩ *loss in potential* (*in volts*) **~abnahme** f *relaxation of tension* ⟨a. fig⟩ **~anzeiger** m ⟨el⟩ *potential* (od *charge, voltage*) *indicator* **~entlastung** f *stress relief* **~erhöher** m ⟨el⟩ *booster transformer* **~frei** a ⟨el⟩ *non-tension* (*joint*) **≃los** a ⟨el⟩ *dead* ‖ ~e Trennstrecke [f] ⟨el⟩ *neutral section* **~messer** m ⟨mach⟩ *indicator* ‖ ⟨el⟩ *voltmeter* **~regler** m ⟨tech⟩ *variac* **≃reich** a *stressful* **~riß** m *tension crack* **~unterschied** m ⟨mot⟩ *potential difference* **~verhältnis** n *stretch ratio* **~wahlschalter** m ⟨rec, etc⟩ *voltage selector switch* **~zeit** f *time of tension* ⟨a. mil⟩

Spant n ~(e)s/~en ⟨mar aero⟩ *rib, frame, former*

Sp·ar- **~bank** f = ~kasse **~büchse** f *money-box, home-safe*, ⟨Am⟩ *coin-bank* **~deck** n ⟨mar⟩ *spar-deck* **~einlage** f *savings deposit* **~endchen** n *save-all* **~flug** m ⟨aero⟩ *flight at economical speed* **~geld** n, **~groschen** m pl *savings* pl **~gemisch** n ⟨aero, mot⟩ *economical* od *lean mixture* **~guthaben** n *savings(-bank* ⟨Am⟩) *account* **~herd** m *kitchen-range*, (*economical*) *kitchener* **~kasse** f *savings-bank* ‖ Geld auf die ~ tun *to put m. in the s.s-b.* | ~nbuch [n] *s.s-b. book*; ~nfonds [m] *s.s-b. fund* **~konto** n → –guthaben **~lampe** f *economical lamp* **~maßnahmen** f pl *economy measures; austerities, economics* **~meister** m *saving p; p adept at skimping* **~pfennig** m *nest-egg, spare money* ‖ (Notgroschen) *money put by for a rainy day* **~politik** f *policy of economy* **~rate** f *savings instal(l)ment* **~schweinchen** n *piggy-bank* **~sinn** m *thrift* **~strumpf** m *fat* od *long stocking* **~- u Darlehenskasse** f ⟨Am⟩ *Savings and Loan Association* **~ventil** n *economizer valve* **Sp·aren** n ~s/ *saving, economy*; prämienbegünstigtes ~ *bonus-issue savings deposit* **sp·aren** vt/i [h] **A.** (zurücklegen) *to save; to lay by* od *up* | (sparsam anwenden) *to spare, husband; economize* (*on forces*) **B.** *to save* (*time, trouble, strength*) | *to spare* (*neither trouble nor expense*) ‖ (*not*) *to consider* (*one's own life*) | ⟨fig⟩ *to keep* (*a matter*) *back* (*for ..*) ‖ *to keep* (*one's remarks*) *to o.s.* **C.** vi *to economize, to be economical*; streng ~ *to scrimp, to pinch pennies* ‖ ~e in der Zeit, so hast du in der Not! *put the penny away for the rainy day!* | **am** Essen ~ *to scrape on food* ‖ am unrechten Ende ~ *to be penny-wise and pound-foolish* ‖ mit dem Lobe (den Worten) ~ *to be sparing of praise* (*chary of one's words*) ‖ nicht ~ **mit** *to be profuse in* od *of* (*gifts, etc*) **D. gespartes** Geld *savings* pl | auf ≃ bedacht *economy-minded* **Sp·arer** m ~s/~ *economizer* **sp·ärlich** a **1.** (→ dürftig) *scant(y); scanty, frugal* (*meal*); *meagre* (*fare*); *slender* (*repast*) ‖ *scanty* (*booty, resources, vegetation*); ⟨bot⟩ *straggly* **2.** (verstreut) *sparse; thin* (*hair*) | [adv] *sparsely, thinly* (*populated*) ‖ ~ eingehen ⟨com⟩ *to come in slowly* ‖ ~ fließen *to be scare* ‖ ~ gesät ⟨fig⟩ *few and far between*; (vgl kärglich) **~keit** f *scantiness, sparseness; frugality* **sp·arsam** a *sparing, saving, economical* ‖ (kleinlich) *parsimonious* ‖ (genügsam) *frugal, thrifty* (vgl sparen) [adv] ~ austeilen *to dole out*; ~ leben *to lead a frugal life, to practise economy* ‖ ~ umgehen mit *to be sparing of* (*chary of one's words*); mit s–m Geld ~ umg. *to be close with one's m.* ‖ ~ verwalten *to nurse* ‖ ~ wirtschaften *to economize* | **≃keit** f ~/ *economy* (aus ~ *for e.*) (mit *of*), *parsimony* ‖ *frugality, thrift*(*iness*)

Sp·argel m ~s/~ *asparagus* (stechen *to cut*); Stangen≃ *a.* (*whole stalks*) Brech≃ *cut a.* **~abschnitte** m pl *a. cuts* **~bau** m *growing of a.* **~beet** n *a.-bed* **~essen** n *a. feast* **~kohl** m *broccoli* **~köpfe** m pl *a. tips* **~pflanzung** f *plantation of a.* **~salat** m *a.-salad* **~säure** f (Asparaginsäure) *aspartic acid* **~spitzen** f pl *a. tips, heads of a.* **~stecher** m *a.-knife*

~stoff m (Asparagin) *asparagine* **~zeit** f *asparagus season*

Sp·arren m ~s/~ *spar, rafter* || ⟨her⟩ *chevron* || ⟨fig fam⟩ *kink, spleen*; e–n ~ (zuviel) h *to have a bee in one's bonnet* (*about a th*); *to have a screw loose* **~kopf** m ⟨arch⟩ *corbel, bracket, modillion* **~werk** n *frame-, timber-work*; *rafters* pl; offenes ~ *wooden roof* **sp·arrig** a ⟨bot⟩ *squarrous*

Sp·arta n ⟨Gr⟩ (Stadt) **Spart·aner(in** f) m, **spart·anisch** *Spartan*

Spartak·ist m ~en/~en ⟨ant & mod hist⟩ *Spartacist* **spart·anisch** a *Spartan* (*simplicity*)

Sp·arte f ~/~n *sector, section*; *department*

sp·asm(·at)isch, sp·astisch a *spasmodic* **-mol·ytisch** a *antispasmodic* **-mus** m ~/–men *spasm*

Sp·aß m ~es/≃e *pleasantry, jest, joke, fun*; ⟨stud⟩ *rag* || (Unterhaltung) *sport, amusement, pastime,* || viel ≃! (*I*) *hope you'll enjoy y.s.* || ~ muß s *always a bit of fun* || derber ~ *practical joke* || (*this comedy is a great*) *lark* || (*it's no*) *joke* (*being a king*) || (*to get one's*) *fun* (*out of a th*) || **aus,** im, zum ~ *in* od *for fun*; °aus ~ an der Freud' ⟨fam⟩ *just for kicks* || ~ beiseite! *it's no joke*; *joking apart*; ⟨Am⟩ *no kidding*! || da fängt der ~ erst an *that's where the fun comes in* | (viel) ~ h *to enjoy o.s.* (*immensely*) || ~ h **an** etw [dat] *to enjoy a th* .. gr, diebischen, königlichen .. ⟨fam⟩ *to get a kick out of a th* || jdm (viel) ~ m *to amuse a p greatly* || ≃e m *to crack jokes* || es macht mir ~ *it gives me pleasure* || es machte ihm e–n diebischen ~ *he was as pleased as Punch* || sich e–n ~ m *to have a joke* || das wäre ein ~ *that would be fun* || etw **im** ~ sagen, tun *to say, do a th in sport* || ≃e treiben **mit** *to play tricks with, to make sport of*; mit jdm (s–n) ~ treiben ⟨bes Am⟩ *to kid a p* || ~ verstehen *to take* od *see a joke*; *he can see a joke* || k–n ~ verstehen ⟨a.⟩ *not to be trifled with* | zu ≃en aufgelegt (*in a*) *sportive* (*mood*) | **zum** ~ v *for the sport of* **~macher** m *jester, wag, joker, mime, buffoon* **~verderber** m *spoil-sport* **~vogel** m *wag*; *banterer* **sp·aßen** vi [h] *to joke, jest* (über *about*); *to make fun* || ich –e nicht (nie) *I mean what I say* (*I am always serious*) | Sie ~! *you are only jesting*! || nicht mit sich ~ l *to stand no nonsense* || mit ihm (damit) ist nicht zu ~ *he is not to be trifled with* (*it's no joking matter*; *it's nothing to play about with*) **sp·aßhaft, sp·aßig** a *funny, droll*; *jocose*; *ludicrous*; *waggish, comical, amusing* | e–r S das ≃e abgewinnen *to get one's fun out of a th*

Spat m ~(e)s/~e **1.** ⟨min⟩ *spar*; → ≃ig **2.** ⟨vet⟩ *spavin*; → ≃ig **~eisenstein** m *siderite, sparry iron-ore* ≃**lahm** a *spavined* (*horse*)

spät [a & adv] **A.** *late* (→ ~er) || wie ~ ist es? *what's the time*? || es wird ~ *it is getting late* || ⟨prov⟩ besser ~ als nie *better late than never* || es ist schon ~ **am** Tage (**in** der Nacht) *it is late in the day* (*night*), *the d.* (*n.*) *is far spent* || ~ am Nachmittag *in the late afternoon* || ~ nachts *late at night* || **bis** ~ in den Abend *well into the evening*, ⟨Am⟩ *till away late in the e.* || v früh bis ~ *from morning till night* **B.** ~ **aufstehen** *to get up late*, (stets) *to be a late riser* || immer ~ ins Bett k *to be accustomed to late hours* || jdn sehr ~ benachrichtigen *to give a p very short notice* (*about*) || (2 St.) **zu** ~ k *to be* (*2 hours*) *late* (zu *for*); ⟨Am⟩ *to be* (*2 hours*) *tardy for supper, to show up late* **C.** [attr] *belated* (*luck, repentance*) || ⟨fam⟩ ~es Mädchen *old maid* || *advanced*; *remote* || **am** ~en Abend *late in the evening, far on in the day* || **zu** ~er (Nacht-)Stunde *at a late hour* (*late at night*) | **z·u** ~e Erkenntnis! *wise after the event* | e–e Stunde zu|·~|k *to turn up an hour late* **Sp·ät-** **~abend** m *latter part of the evening* **~apfel** m *late apple* ≃**blühend** a *blossoming late* **~entwickler** m (P) *late developer* **~gotik** f ⟨arch⟩ *late Gothic*, ⟨engl⟩ *perpendicular style* **~heimkehrer** m *late returnee* **~herbst** m *latter part of autumn*; *late autumn* **~jahr** n *autumn* **~lese** f *mellow* od *late-vintaged wine, l. vintage* ≃**mittelalterlich** a *late medieval* **~obst** n *late fruit* ≃**reif** a ⟨hort⟩ *late* **~-Säuglingssterblichkeit** f *post-neonatal mortality* **~schaden** m ⟨at-path⟩ *latent* (*tissue*) *injury*; ⟨ins⟩ *delayed damage* **~schicht** f ⟨ind, Am fam⟩ *swing shift* **~sommer** m *late* od *Indian summer, St. Martin's summer* **~werk** n ⟨arts⟩ *late work* **~zerspringer** m ⟨artill⟩ *retarded burst* **~zündung** f ⟨mot⟩ *retarded ignition*; °⟨fam fig⟩ *slowness in comprehension,* °~! *slowcoach*! **Sp·äte** f ~/ *lateness* **sp·äter** a *later* (*years*) || (nachfolgend) *subsequent* (*events*) || *ulterior* (*plans*) | [adv] (a. **~hin**) (*this happened*) *later on*; (*we shall see*) *by and by* || *in after years* || *afterwards* || früher oder ~ *sooner or later* || etw f ~ l *to leave a th over* || ich sah ihn erst viele Jahre ~ *it was years before I saw him again* || sich auf ~ vertrösten *to console o.s. with the thought of later times*

sp·ätestens adv *at the latest*; ~ bis *by* (*tomorrow*); bis ~ in 8 Tagen *this day week at latest* **Sp·ätling** m ~(e)s/~e ⟨hort⟩ *late fruit* || ⟨zoo & fig⟩ *late-comer*

Sp·atel m ~s/~ ⟨med⟩ *spatula* || ⟨tech⟩ *spattle*; → Spachtel

Sp·aten m ~s/~ *spade* || mit dem ~ umgraben *to turn up, to sp.* || **~forschung** f *prehistory, excavation(s pl)* **~stich** m *spit* (*2 spit*[*s*] *deep*), *cut with a sp.* || den ersten ~ tun *to turn the first sod*; ⟨fig⟩ *to break ground*

sp·atig a **1.** ⟨vet⟩ *spavined* **2.** ⟨min⟩ *spathic*

Spation·ieren n ~s/ ⟨print⟩ *letter spacing* **spati·ös** a [–ts–] **Sp·atium** n ~s/–tien *distance* || ⟨typ⟩ *space* (*-line*) (dazu: *to space*); → Spazier–

Spatz m ~en/~en *sparrow* || die ~en pfeifen es v den Dächern *it is the talk of the town, it is common knowledge* || → Kanone || der ~ in der Hand ist besser als die Taube auf dem Dach *a bird in hand is worth two in the bush* **~enhirn** n *birdbrain* | ≃**le** pl (*Swabian*) *dumplings*

Spaz·ier- **~fahrt** f *drive* || *pleasure trip*; (zu Wasser) *sail, row* **~gang** m *walk, stroll*; Gesundheits≃ *constitutional*; ⟨mil, sport⟩ (leichter Sieg) ⟨fam⟩ *walkover*; *promenade* ⟨a. Ort & fig⟩ || *place to walk in* || e–n ~ m *to go for a walk*, ⟨fam⟩ *trot*; *to take a walk*; e–n kz ~ im Garten m *to take a turn in the g.* **~gänger** m *promenader, pedestrian, walker* **~ritt** m *ride* **~stock** m *walking-stick*, ⟨Am⟩ *cane* **~weg** m *walk* **~wetter** n *walking-weather* **spaz·ieren** vi [s] *to walk* (*leisurely*), *to stroll* || ~ fahren *to take a drive* || (jdn) *to drive out*; ⟨fam⟩ *to air* || (zu Wasser) *to go* (*out*) *in a boat* od *punting* od *for a sail* || ~ führen *to lead about, to take* (*out*) *for a walk* || ~ gehen *to go for a walk* od *run, to take a stroll, run, walk* || ~ reiten *to take a ride, to go for a ride* || ~ tragen *to sport* (*a th*) || → Spatium

Specht m ~(e)s/~e ⟨orn⟩ → *woodpecker*, ⟨Am a.⟩ *wake-up* **~meise** f ⟨orn⟩ *nutcracker, nutpecker*

Speck m ~(e)s/ (Schweine≃) *bacon* || (Wal≃) *blubber* || ⟨anat⟩ *fat* || gebraten *rasher of bacon*; durchwachsen *streaky bacon*; *gammon* || ~ ansetzen *to grow fat* || ~ auf den Rippen h *to be well off* || im ~ sitzen *to be in clover*; *to have one's bread well buttered* od *b.d on both sides* || 'ran an'n ~! *and now for it*! *here goes*! *lump into it*! ⟨Am⟩ *put your nose to the grindstone* || mit ~ fängt man Mäuse *good bait catches fine fish* **~artig** a *lardaceous* **~bauch** m *paunch* **~grieben** f pl *greaves* pl **~hals** m *bull-neck* **~händler** m *dealer in bacon* **~haut** f *fat membrane* **~keule** f *gammon of bacon* **~kuchen** m *larded cake* **~-scheibe, ~schnitte** f *rasher, slice of bacon* **~-schwarte** f *bacon-rind, skin of bacon, sward* **~schwein** n *bacon-hog, fat hog* **~seite** f *side* od *flitch of bacon*, ⟨Am a.⟩ *middling*; geräuchert

flitches pl **~stein** m ⟨geol⟩ *steatite, soapstone*
sp·eckig a *fat(ty), greasy*

sped·ieren vt [h] *to send (off), to forward, to dispatch (des-)* ‖ ⟨mar⟩ *to ship* ‖ °⟨fig⟩ ins Jenseits ~ *to launch into eternity* **Sped·ierung** f ~/~en *sending, dispatching (des-)* **Spediteur** [–'tø:r] m ~s/~e *shipping-, forwarding-agent, carrier; trucker* ‖ (Möbel≈) *(furniture) remover* **Spediti·on** f ~/~en *conveyance, forwarding, sending, dispatching (des-)* ‖ *forwarding-* bzw *shipping--agency;* ⟨Am⟩ *drayage* | **~s- ~gebühren** f pl, **~kosten** pl = ~spesen **~geschäft** n *forwarding--business* ‖ (Kontor) *forwarding-agency* **~gut** n *goods* pl *for transmission* **~handel** m (Geschäft) *forwarding-business* (od *-trade*) ‖ (Frachtfahrt) *carrying-trade* **~handlung** f = ~geschäft **~spesen** [pl] *forwarding-charges* pl

Speer m ~(e)s/~e *spear, lance* ‖ (leichter Wurf≈) *javelin;* (Fisch≈) *leister* ‖ jdn (wie) mit e–m ~ durchbohren *to spear a p* **~reiter** m *lancer* **~schleuder** f ⟨hist⟩ *propeller* **~stechen** n *spearing* **~stich** m *spear-wound* **~träger** m *spear-man* **~werfen** n ⟨sport⟩ *(throwing the) javelin*

Sp·eiche f ~/~n *spoke* ‖ ⟨anat⟩ *radius* | ⟨fig⟩ greif mit in die ~n! *give us a hand!* ‖ jdm in die ~n fallen *to put a spoke in a p's wheel;* f jdn .. greifen *to roll a log for a p* | **≈n** vt [h] *to spoke (a wheel)* **~nzapfen** m *end of a spoke*

Sp·eichel m ~s/ *spittle, saliva* ‖ (Geifer) *slaver* ‖ (Auswurf) *spit* **~bildung** f *salivation* **~drüse** f *salivary gland* **~fluß** m ⟨med⟩ *salivation;* den ~ h *to salivate* **≈lecken** vi [h] *to toady* **~lecker** m *toady, flunkey; sycophant;* ⟨Am sl⟩ *boot-lick(er), apple-polisher* **~lecker·ei** f *toadyism*

Sp·eicher m ~s/~ (Kornboden) *granary* ‖ *store, storage space;* Schnell≈ *immediate access store;* zum ~ *to store;* → leiten ‖ (f Waren, Möbel) *storehouse, warehouse* ‖ ⟨dial⟩ *loft* ‖ ⟨tech⟩ *accumulator;* (Heißwasser≈) *boiler* ‖ ⟨comp⟩ *store, memory,* ~ der Tabelliermaschine *tabulator counter;* akustischer ~ *acoustic memory* od *storage;* Großraum≈ *mass-mem.* Schnell-≈ *rapid mem.* in den ~ lesen *to read (data) into the store* **~anlage** f, **~becken** n *store--reservoir* | ⟨**comp**⟩ ~arten [f pl] *backing stores; filing system;* ~auszug [m] *(memory* od *storage) dump;* ~daten [pl] *file data;* ~einheit [f] *memory unit;* ~information [f] *filed information;* ~inhalt [m] *backing stores* pl; ~kapazität f *storage capacity, c. of an information store* | **~kraftwerk** n *storage power station* | ⟨**comp**⟩ ~mittel [n pl] *media of storage;* gebotene ~möglichkeit *bulk storage (of data)* | **~ofen** m *storage stove* | ⟨**comp**⟩ ~platzzuordnung [f] *allocation of storage;* ~stelle [f] *location;* ~-trommel [f] *memory drum;* ~verschiebung [f] *storage allocation;* | **~werk** n ⟨el⟩ *storage power station* | ⟨**comp**⟩ *storing mechanism, accumulating memory;* ~werkswahltasten [f pl] *pushbutton distribution;* ~zelle [f] *storage location* | ⟨el⟩ *accumulator;* ~zentrale [f] *central storage* **sp·eichern** vt [h] *to store, warehouse; to hoard, to accumulate; to deposit* ‖ ⟨comp⟩ *to record; store away* ‖ ⟨fig⟩ *to treasure up* | ≈ n ⟨comp⟩ ≈ gr Datenmengen *large-scale storage;* ≈ in verschiedenen Speicherstellen *multiple posting to a series of destinations* **Sp·eicherung** f ~/ *storing; storage* ⟨a. comp⟩ ⟨comp a.⟩ *accumulation, filing* **~sform** f *organization*

Sp·ei- ~becken n, **~napf** m *spittoon* **~gatt** n ⟨mar⟩ *scupper* **~tüte** f ⟨aero⟩ *sick cup* **sp·eien** vi/t [spie/gespie(e)n] [h] *to spit* ‖ (sich erbrechen) *to vomit;* ⟨sl⟩ *to (shoot the) cat* ‖ ⟨arts, fig⟩ *to throw up (water)* ‖ *to belch forth (fire)* | ⟨fig⟩ es ist zum ≈ *I'm sick of it*

Speik m ~(e)s/~s ⟨bot⟩ *bird's eye*

Sp·eiler m ~s/~ ⟨cul⟩ *skewer;* dazu: *to skewer*

Speis m –ses/ *mortar* ×**Speis** f ~/ *larder* **Sp·eise** f ~/~n **1.** *food* ⟨a. fig⟩, *nourishment, meal* ‖ ~ zu sich nehmen *to take food* ‖ (Gericht, Schlüssel) *dish* ‖ schnell zubereitete ~ *short order* ‖ (Kost) *fare* | ~n [pl] *provisions* | die ~n abtragen *to clear the table* | ~ u Trank *meat and drink* **2.** ⟨met⟩ *speiss; bell-metal* **~anstalt** f = ~haus **~bar(tisch** m) f ⟨Am⟩ *lunch-counter* **~brei** m ⟨physiol⟩ *chyme* **~eis** n *ice-cream* **~fett** n *edible* od *cooking fat* **~gast** m *guest, frequenter, customer,* ⟨Am a.⟩ *patron* **~haus** n *eating-house, restaurant* **~kabel** n ⟨el⟩ *supply cable* **~kammer** f *larder, pantry* **~karte** f (reichhaltige *rich*) *bill of fare; menu* Fr **~keller** m *underground restaurant* **~korb** m *hamper* **~leitung** f ⟨tech⟩ *feed pipe;* ⟨el⟩ *feeder* **~marke** f *voucher (for a meal)* **~meister** m *steward; chef* Fr **~öl** n *salad* od *edible -oil* | ~produkte [n pl] *oil foods* **~opfer** m *oblation* **~pumpe** f ⟨tech⟩ *feed-pump* **~punkt** m *input terminals* pl **~raum** m ⟨mil⟩ *canteen* **~reste** m pl *broken victuals* pl **~rohr** n ⟨tech, mot⟩ *feed(pipe)* **~röhre** f ⟨anat⟩ *gullet* ‖ ⟨scient⟩ *oesophagus* **~saal** m *dining-room;* (gr) *banqueting-hall* ‖ (Kloster≈) *refectory* ‖ *(officers') mess-room* ‖ ⟨mar⟩ *dining--saloon* ‖ ⟨univ⟩ *hall (to dine in h.)* **~saft** m ⟨physiol⟩ *chyle* **~schrank** m *cupboard, meat-safe* **~spannung** f ⟨el⟩ *feeding voltage* **~wagen** m *restaurant-, dining-car; diner* **~wärmer** m *meat--warmer* **~wasser** n ⟨tech⟩ *feed water* **~wirtschaft** f *eating-house, restaurant* **~zettel** m = ~karte **~zimmer** n *dining-room;* kl *dinette* **sp·eisen I.** vt [h] *to feed* ⟨a, tech & fig⟩: *the lake is fed from a stream* ‖ *to give meals* od *to eat* ‖ (bewirten) *to entertain* ‖ (verpflegen) *to board, maintain, keep* ‖ ⟨fig⟩ *to supply, provide (with); to nurture* mit e–r Batterie ~ ⟨el⟩ *to power by a b.* **II.** vi/t [h] *to take one's meals, to partake of food; to feed (with a p);* ⟨mil⟩ *to mess* ‖ (zu Mittag) *to lunch* ‖ (zu Abend) *to dine* ‖ auswärts ~ *to dine out* ‖ was wollen Sie ~? *what will you take to eat?* ‖ wünsche wohl z ~ (gespeist z h) *I wish you a good appetite (hope you've enjoyed your meal)* **Sp·eisenfolge** f ~/~n *bill of fare; menu* Fr **Sp·eiser** m ~s/~ ⟨tech⟩ *feeder;* Teller–, Schub–, Walzen≈ *shaking, jigging, cylinder-tipe feeder* **Sp·eisung** f ~/~en *feeding* ⟨a. tech⟩, *boarding, maintainance* ‖ *meal* ‖ die ~ der 5000 ⟨bib⟩ *feeding; the miracles of the loaves and fishes* **~sapparat** m ⟨tech⟩ *feeder*

Spekt·akel m & n ~s/~ *uproar, hubbub, noise* ‖ (Radau) *shindy, row, rumpus, racket; ruction* ‖ ~ m *to kick up a row* od *racket* | sich z ~ jds aufführen *to make o.s. a show for a p* **~macher** m *rowdy* **~stück** n *sensational play* **spekt·akeln** vi [h] *to kick up a row* **spektr·al** a *spectroscopic(al)* | ≈analyse [f] *spectral* od *spectrum analysis;* ~analytisch [a] *spectrometric;* ≈farbe [f] *spectral colo(u)r;* ~linie [f] *spectral line;* ≈photometr·ie [f] *spectrophotometry* **Spektrosk·op** n ~s/~e *spectrometer* | **~·ie** f *-try* **Sp·ektrum** n ~s/–ra & –ren *spectrum* (aussetzend *broken*)

Spekul·ant m ~en/~en *speculator,* ⟨com⟩ *operator,* ⟨st exch⟩ *bull,* ⟨Am⟩ *wild-catter* ‖ erfolgreicher ~ *money-spinner;* kl ~ ⟨exch⟩ *dabbler* **Spekulati·on** f ~/~en *speculation* ‖ auf ~ ⟨fam⟩ *on spec* **~serfolg** m (~ h *to make a) killing* **~sgeschäft** n *adventure* **~sunternehmen, ~s-objekt** n *venture,* ⟨sl⟩ *flutter* **spekulat·iv** [–f] a *speculative* **spekul·ieren** vi [h] (auf [acc], mit) *to speculate (on, with)* (auf Hausse, Baisse *on the rise, fall*) ‖ *to reckon (on an inheritance)* ‖ ⟨st exch⟩ *to gamble (in shares);* mit kl Gewinnen ~ *to dabble* ‖ ⟨philos⟩ *to speculate, theorize, ponder, ruminate* (über [acc] *on*)

Spelt m ~(e)s/~e ⟨bot⟩ *spelt; emmer*

Spel·unke f ~/~n *den* ‖ (Kneipe) *low pothouse* od *gin-shop, jerry(-shop)* ⟨Am sl⟩ *joint* **≈n-mäßig** a ⟨Am⟩ *honky-tonk*

Spelz m ~es/~e **1.** = Spelt **2.** = **~e** f ~/~n *chaff* ‖ ⟨bot⟩ *beard* ‖ ⟨scient⟩ *glume* **≃ig** a *chaffy* °**spend·abel** a *generous* **Sp·ende** f ~/~n *contribution* (~n gehen ein *c.s come* (*flow, pour*) *in*) | (Almosen) *alms* [mst sg], *charity*; (kleinliche) *dole* ‖ *donation, gift* | ⟨hist⟩ *libation* (⟨a. ~guß [m]) **sp·enden** vt [h] *to deal out, distribute* ‖ (beitragen) *to contribute* (zu *to*) ‖ reichlich ~ *to give generously* (zu *towards*); *to lavish*; *to be ungrudging in* (*praise*) ‖ *to bestow* (*alms*), kärglich ~ *to dole out* ‖ *to administer* (*the sacrament*) ‖ (Blut) *to donate* **Sp·ender** m ~s/~ *dispenser, contributor, giver* ‖ Herz- etc ≃ f Übertragung *heart- etc donor* | ~laune [f] *spending mood* **spend·ieren** vt [h] *to give liberally, to spend lavishly* ‖ jdm etw ~ *to treat a p to a th, to give a p a treat* ⟨fam⟩ *to stand a p a th* ‖ etw ~ ⟨sl⟩ *to loosen up*

ˣ**Sp·engler** m ~s/~ *tin-smith; edge-tool maker*

Sp·enzer m ~s/~ ⟨tail⟩ *spencer*

Sp·erber m ~s/~ ⟨orn⟩ *sparrow-hawk* **~baum** m *sorb, service*(*-tree*)

°**Sper·enzchen** [pl] *ado* ‖ k–e ~! *don't fuss*!

Sp·erling m ~(e)s/~e → *sparrow* (→ Spatz) (schilpen *to twitter*) | **~s-** **~schrot** n *small shot* **~weibchen** n *hen-sparrow* **~vögel** m pl *passerines*

Sp·erma n ~s/ ⟨biol⟩ *sperm* **~toz·oon** n ~s/–·oen *spermatozoon, -tozoid*

Sp·err- **≃angelw·eit** [adv] *wide, wide open* **~ballon** m *barrage balloon*, ⟨fam⟩ *flying elephant* **~baum** m *bar*(*rier*); (e–r Straße) *turnpike* **≃beinig** [adv] *astride* **~bolzen** m *locking bolt* **~druck** m *spaced type* **~feder** f *click-spring* **~feuer** n ⟨mil⟩ *barrage, curtain-fire*; ~ schießen, mit ~ belegen *to* (*lay down a*) *barrage* | ~linie [f] ⟨m. m.⟩ (*final*) *protective line* **~filter** m ⟨phot⟩ *suppression filter* **~flug** m ⟨aero⟩ *interception flight* **~fort** n *outer fort* **~frist** f (f Veröffentlichung) *embargo*; ~! *embargoed* (*for publication*) **~gebiet** n *reservation*; *restricted* od *reserved, danger, barred area*; *forbidden zone* **~geld** n *entrance money* **~gesetz** n *prohibition, law suspending rights* **~getriebe** n *locking mechanism*; *arresting gear* **~grenzbezirk** m *prohibited frontier zone* **~gut** n, **~güter** [pl] *bulky goods* pl **~hahn** m *stop-cock* **~haken** m *click, catch* ‖ *ratchet* ‖ *pick-lock* **~hebel** m *arresting, locking* od *ratchet-lever* **~holz** n ⟨tech⟩ *plywood* **~kegel** m ⟨tech⟩ *stay, stopper, ratchet, pawl* **~kette** f *drag-chain* ‖ *door-chain* **~klinke** f = ~kegel; *locking pawl*; *safety catch*; (Geschütz-≃ etc) *latch* **~knopf** m *stop knob* **~konto** n *blocked account* **~kreis** m ⟨wir⟩ *eliminator, wave trap*; ⟨aero⟩ *filter circuit* **~linie** f ⟨tact⟩ *obstacle line* **~mauer** f *barrage*; (*wall of a*) *dam* **~müll** m *bulky junk* **~objekt** n ⟨mil⟩ *barrier point* **~plan** m *barrier plan* **~(r)ad** n ⟨tech⟩ *cog-wheel*, ⟨weav⟩ *ratched-wheel* **~riegel** m *bolt* **~schraube** f *detent screw* **~schwerpunkte** m pl ⟨tact⟩ *main barrier positions* **~sitz** n ⟨theat⟩ *stall*, ⟨Am⟩ *orchestra seat* **~stange** f *ratch* **~stoffe** m pl *clogging constituents* **~trosse** f ⟨mar⟩ *wire boom* **~ventil** n *stop-valve* **~vermerk** m ⟨com⟩ *non-negotiability notice* **~vertrag** m ⟨at⟩ *non-proliferation treaty* **~vorrichtung** f *stop, stay, catch*; *locking* od *arresting device* **~zeit** f *closing-time* **~zoll** m *prohibitory duty* **Sp·erre** f ~/~n *shutting, closing, closure* ⟨a. parl⟩ ‖ (e–s Hafens) *closing*, ⟨mil⟩ *blockade*; *artificial obstacle, barrier* (schließen *to close*, lösen *to release*) ‖ (e–s Flusses) *block*; *barring* ‖ ⟨com, mar⟩ *embargo* | Ballon≃ *barrage* ‖ Devisen≃ *embargo on foreign exchange* ‖ Draht–, Netz≃ *wire apron* ‖ Gesundheits≃ *quarantine* ‖ Reise≃ *travel ban* | (Versperrung) *block*(*ing*) | (Vorrichtung) *stop, bolt, brake*; *arresting device* ‖ *barricade* ‖ ⟨rail⟩ *gate* ‖ (Sperrbaum) *bar*; ⟨mar⟩ Balken≃ *boom defence* ‖ (Rad≃) *drag* | ~ fliegen *to fly on defensive patrol* ‖ e–e ~ lösen ⟨tech⟩ *to free a lock* ‖ ⟨parl⟩ die ~ verhängen über *to closure* **sp·erren** vt [h] **1.** (öffnen) *to spread open* od *out* od *apart* ‖ (Beine spreizen) *to straddle* ‖ ⟨typ⟩ *to space* (*a word*); gesperrt drucken *to print in spaced type* ‖ gesperrt gedruckt *spaced out* **2.** (ver~) *to shut, close, lock* ‖ *to bar*(*ricade*), *obstruct* ‖ *to block up* (*a street, river*) ‖ *to bolt* (*a door*), *to lock up* (*a room, a p's fortune*) ‖ *to close* (*a frontier*) ‖ *to lock* (*a port*) ‖ *to trig* (*a wheel*) | (blockieren) *to blockade* **3.** *to forbid* (*an area*) ‖ *to ground* (*a plane* ⟨a. fig⟩ P) ‖ *to prohibit* (*exports*) ‖ (e–e Stadt) *to block the traffic to* (*a town*) ‖ (Konto) *to block* ‖ *to put a stop on, to lay an embargo on* (*commerce, goods*) | *to stop* (*a cheque*; *a p's credit, salary*) ‖ *to deny* (*terrain to the enemy*) ‖ *the fortress stops up the pass* ‖ *to suspend* (*a clergyman*) ‖ ⟨parl⟩ *to closure* (*a debate*) **4. aus** dem Hause ~ *to lock* (*a p*) *out, to shut the door in a p's face* | **in**: *to shut a bird up in ..*; *to lock a p up in .., to put a p in prison* **5.** jdm etw ~ *to cut off a p's gas* etc **II. sich ~ 1.** (P) *to bridle up* ‖ (gegen) *to resist, oppose*; *to fight, struggle* (*against*) **2.** die Tür sperrt (sich) .. *jams* | ≃- **~schaffner** m ⟨rail⟩ *gate-man*, ⟨Am⟩ *g.-keeper* **sp·errig** a **1.** *stretched out, spread*; (*tree*) *with wide-spreading branches* **2.** (P) *unmanageable* **3.** (S) *unwieldy, cumbersome* ‖ ⟨rail⟩ *bulky*; ⟨tech a.⟩ *awkward* **Sp·errung** f ~/~en *barring, stoppage*; *obstruction* ‖ (Verkehrs≃) *block* ‖ (Hafen≃) *blockade* ‖ (Handels≃) *embargo* ‖ (Verbot) *prohibition*

Sp·esen f pl *charges, expenses*; einschließlich ~ *all ex.s paid* ‖ (kl) *petties* ‖ ⟨Am fam⟩ *upkeep* ‖ verschiedene ~ *sundries* ‖ unter Nachnahme der ~ *charges forward* (*Chgs. fwd.*) **≃frei** a *free of charge* **~analyse** f (f Vertreter *salesmen*) *expenditure analysis* **~nachnahme** f *reimbursement for expenses* **~rechnung** f *note of ch.s* **~vorschuß** m ⟨com⟩ *expenses advanced*

Sp·eyer n ⟨Ger⟩ (Stadt) ⟨a.⟩ *Spires*

Spezer·ei f ~/~en *spices*; *groceries* pl (⟨a.⟩ ~waren) **~handel** m *grocery* **~händler** m *spicer, grocer*

ˣ**Sp·ezi** m ~s/~s [obd] *pal*, ⟨fam⟩ *crony* **spezi·al I.** a *special, particular* **II.** ≃ m ~s/~e **1.** *bosom friend* **2.** *half a pint* **Spezi·al-** **~arzt** m *sp.ist* **~begabung** f ⟨eth⟩ *localized learning* **~belastungen** f pl ⟨ins⟩ *particular charges* **~berichterstatter** m *sp. correspondent* **~fach** n *sp.ity*; als ~ betreiben *to sp.ize in*, ⟨Am⟩ *on* **~gebiet** n *sp. branch* **~geschäft** n *one-line* od *sp.ity shop* **~karte** f *local map* **~mittel** n *specific remedy* **~truppen** f pl *sp.* od *technical forces* N **~vollmacht** f *special power* | **~ien** n pl *details, particulars* pl **≃is·ieren** vt [h] *to specify*; *to specialize* ⟨a. sich⟩ **~is·ierung** f ~/~en *particularization, specialization* **~·ist** m ~en/~en *specialist* **~it·ät** f ~/~en *speciality* | ~entheater [n] *music-hall* **spezi·ell** [a] *special, particular* (*details, wishes, friend*) | [adv] *particularly*, (*you*) *of all people* | Ihr **≃es** ([sc] Wohl)! *your health*! **Sp·ezies** f ~/~ *species* ‖ ⟨math⟩ *rule* ‖ die 4 ~ *the first rules* [pl] *of arithmetic* **~taler** m *specie-dollar* **Spezifi-** **~kati·on** f ~/~en *specification*; ⟨jur⟩ *acquisition of title to a chattel by working it into new forms* **-·ifikum** n ⟨med⟩ **s-·ifisch** a (⟨zoo, biol⟩ inner~ *intra-*, außer~ *extra-*)*specific* [s & a] ⟨a. phys⟩ | [adv] *specifically* **s-ifiz·ieren** vt [h] *to specify*, ⟨a.⟩ *prettify*, ⟨Am⟩ *to itemize* | –rt *detailed*

Sph·äre f ~/~n *sphere* ⟨a. fig⟩; ⟨fig⟩ *domain*; *world*; *sweep* (*of influence*) **~nharmonie** f *celestial harmony*; *music of the spheres* **sph·ärisch** a *spherical* (*triangle*) ‖ (himmlisch) *spheric* **Sphäro·id** n ~(e)s/~e *spheroid*

Sphinx f (Eg m) ~/~e *Sphinx* ‖ (Schmetterling) *hawkmoth* **~gesicht** n ⟨Am fam⟩ *deadpan*

Sphrag·istik f ~/ = Siegelkunde

Sp·ick- ~aal m *smoked eel* **~gans** f *larded and smoked goose(-breast)* **~nadel** f *larding-pin* **~speck** m *larding-bacon* °**~zettel** m ⟨school sl⟩ *crib*; **sp·icken** vt [h] **1.** *to (inter)lard* ‖ ⟨fig⟩ *to fill (one's purse), to interlard (one's pouch with ..)* | gespickt *studded (with nails)*; *well-lined (purse)*; (stark *heavily) interspersed (with references)*; *crammed (with errors)*; *(walls) plastered (with pictures)* **2.** ⟨fam⟩ *to bribe, tip* **3.** ⟨school sl⟩ *to crib* (v *from*) **4.** ⟨sl⟩ *to gobble*

spie 1. & 3. sg pret v speien

Sp·iegel m ~s/~ **A.** *mirror, (looking-)glass* ‖ Pfeiler≃ *pier-glass* ‖ Rück≃ ⟨mot⟩ *rear view mirror* ‖ ⟨phys, med⟩ *speculum* ‖ ⟨tech⟩ *reflector* | ⟨übtr, mar⟩ *stern* ‖ ⟨hunt⟩ (des Rehs) *rump, escutcheon* ‖ ⟨mil⟩ (Scheiben≃) *bull's eye* ‖ ⟨mil⟩ (Kragen≃) *facings* pl, *(gorget) tab* od *patch* ‖ (am Gehrock) *lapel* ‖ (des Karpfens) *scale* ‖ *level, surface (of the sea)* | ⟨fig⟩ *pink (of politeness), model, paragon (of honesty)* ‖ *(medieval) law code* | ⟨übtr⟩ (Stand) *level (of prices,* etc) **B.** glatt wie ein ~ *smooth as glass* ‖ in den ~ sehen *to look in the glass*; s. Sie sich im ~ an *look at y.s. (in the mirror)* ‖ das wird er sich nicht hinter den ~ stecken *he will not boast of it*; das kannst du dir hinter den ~ stecken *put that in your pipe and smoke it* ‖ e–m e–n ~ vorhalten *to hold up a mirror to a p* **~becken** n *barber's basin* **~belag, ~beleg** m *m. coating*; *tinfoil of a m.* **~berg** npr: ~, ich kenne dich! (nach Schillers „Räuber") *I know your tricks!* **~bild** n *mirage*; *(reflected) image*; *reflex, reflection* | ~wiedergabe [f] (e–s Ausdrucks) *use-reversal (in a dictionary)* ≃**bildlich** a: ~e Wiedergabe [f] ⟨lexicography⟩ *use-reversal* ≃**bl·ank** a *glassy*; *m.ing like glass*; ⟨fig⟩ *spick and span* **~decke** f *m.ed ceiling* **~ei** n *fried egg* **~erz** n *specular iron-ore* **~fabrik** f *manufactory of l.-g.es* **~fabrikant** m *l.-gl. manufacturer* **~fechter** m *humbug* **~fechter·ei** f *mock-fight(ing)* ‖ ⟨fig⟩ *bluff, humbug, pretence, make-believe* ‖ ~ treiben *to fence* **~feld** n *panel of a m.* **~fenster** n *plate-gl. window* **~fernrohr** n *reflector* **~fläche** f *gl.y surface* **~folie** f *tinfoil* **~futteral** n *m.-case* **~galerie** f = –saal **~glas** n *plate-gl.*; ≃er [pl] (Sonnenbrille) *mirror sun-glasses* ≃**gl·att** a *(as) smooth as gl.*; mit ~er Oberfläche *m.-surfaced* ‖ (Wasser) *gl.y, unrippled* ≃**h·ell** a *as clear as a m.* **~hütte** f *l.-gl. works* pl & sg **~karpfen** m ⟨ich⟩ *m.r-carp* **~lehre** f *catoptrics* pl [a. sg konstr] **~metall** n ⟨tech⟩ *speculum-metal* **~mikroskop** n *reflecting microscope* **~optik** f *mirror optical system* **~pfeiler** m *pier* **~quadrant** m *quadrant with reflectors* **~rahmen** m *l.-gl. frame* **~reflexkamera** f *(m.) reflex camera* **~saal** m *hall of m.s* **~scheibe** f *plate-gl. pane* **~schiefer** m *specular schist* **~schiff** n *square-sterned vessel* **~schleifer** m *m. polisher* **~schliff** m ⟨tech⟩ *satin finishing* **~schrank** m *wardrobe with a m.* **~schrift** f *reflected face* **~sucher** m *reflector view-finder* **~tafel** f *m.-plate* **~telegraph** m *heliotrope* **~teleskop** n = ~fernrohr **~tisch(chen** n) m *pier-table*; *toilet-table* ≃**verkehrt** adv: ~ arbeiten .. *by m. inversion* od *with reversed values* **~zimmer** n *m.-room* **sp·iegeln** **I.** vi [h] *to glitter, shine, sparkle*; *to be bright* **II.** vt *to reflect* | *to dazzle with a mirror* | *to ice (cakes)* | **sich** ~ (in [dat]) *to be reflected* od *mirrored (in)* ‖ *the sun reflects in the lake* ‖ *to look at o.s. in the glass* ‖ ⟨übtr⟩ *there was disgust in his face* ‖ grün-~des Wasser *water with green reflection* ‖ ⟨fig⟩ *to take an example* (an *by*) | gespiegelt *dappled (horse)*; ⟨hum⟩ g.es Ei *fried egg*, ⟨Am hum⟩ *Sunnyside up* ‖ *specular (light)* | **~d** a → spiegelglatt **Sp·iegelung** f ~/~en *reflection* ‖ ⟨phys & mar⟩ *mirage* | ≃sfrei [a] *(glasses) free of reflection*; *antireflex (glasses)*

Sp·ieke f ~/ ⟨bot⟩ *spikenard, lavender* **Sp·ieker** m ~s/~ *large nail*; ⟨mar⟩ *tack, spike* | ≃**n** vt [h] ⟨mar⟩ *to spike*

Sp·iel n ~(e)s/~e **A.** *play(ing)* ‖ (Karten≃, Billard≃, Sport etc) *game* ⟨a. fig⟩ ‖ ⟨sport⟩ *performance (of a team)*; *play (is over)* ‖ ⟨ten⟩ ~ zu vieren *four-handed game* ‖ (körperliches) *sport* (⟨a. fig⟩ *to be a sp. of the winds*) | (Hazard≃) *gambling (bout)* | ⟨theat⟩ *(play-)acting*; *performance, style (of an actor)* | ⟨mus⟩ *(manner of) play(ing)* ‖ (Anschlag) *touch* ‖ *technique, execution* ‖ *military music* ‖ *carillon* | ~karten etc *pack of cards*, → Teufels≃ ‖ *set of ninepins*, etc | ⟨fig mach⟩ *play, motion, working*; *slack(ness) (of a gear), free* od *dead travel*; *free space* od *movement*; *latitude, allowance*; *stroke (of a piston)*; *throw (of a needle)* ‖ *play (of the eyes, hands, muscles, colours, waves)*; *(inter)play (of forces), play (with fire, death)*; *game (of life)* | ⟨orn hunt⟩ *tail(-feathers)* **B.** **abgekartetes** ~ *calculated gambit*, ⟨Am⟩ *frame-up* ‖ anständiges ~ spielen *to play the game* ‖ (un)ehrliches ~ *(foul) fair play* ‖ e–m freies ~ l *to give full scope to a p* ‖ **gewagtes** ~ *gambit*; spielen *or* treiben *to play a bold* od *risky game* ‖ e–m gewonnenes ~ (das ~ verloren) geben *to throw up the game* ‖ gewonnenes ~ h *to be sure of the game, to gain one's point*; halb gewonnenes ~ *half the battle* ‖ genug des grausamen ~s! *(let's) make an end of this cruel sport* ‖ hohes ~ *high play* ‖ *the profound inner workings of genius* ‖ **leichtes** ~ *walkover*; l. ~ h *to have an easy task (to do)*; l. ~ h mit *to have an easy th on with* ‖ leichtsinniges ~ ⟨fig⟩ *long shot* ‖ *(Olympian, knightly games)* ‖ stummes ~ ⟨theat⟩ *by-play, dumb-show* ‖ unentschiedenes ~ spielen *to draw game*; verlorenes ~ sp. *to play a losing game*; verteufeltes ~ sp. *to play merry hell* ‖ **volles** ~ *full organ* ‖ wechselseitiges ~ *interplay (of forces)* ‖ zweideutiges ~ treiben mit *to play fast and loose with (a girl)* **C.** das ~ **beginnen** ⟨ftb⟩ *to kick off* ‖ wie im ~ lernen *to learn easily* ‖ das ~ m *to take the call* ‖ das ~ hinwerfen *to throw up one's cards* (a. aufgeben) ‖ ⟨mil⟩ das ~ rühren *to beat the drum* ‖ es ist ein ~ *it's quite easy* ([dat] *for*) ‖ wie **steht** das ~? *what's the score?* ‖ ein dummes ~ treiben *to play a silly game* ‖ falsches ~ treiben *to play* od *act a part*, mit jdm *to juggle with a p*; sein ~ tr. mit *to make sport* od *game of (a p, a th), to trifle with, to play upon, to play a* (listiges *deep*) *game with a p* ‖ das ~ hat sich gewandt *the tables are turned* ‖ das ~ ist aus *the jig is up* ‖ ⟨rec⟩ *to interrupt play* **D.** ich bin **am** ~ *it's my turn* | **auf** dem ~ stehen *to be involved* od *at stake*; *my hono(u)r is concerned* ‖ aufs ~ setzen *to jeopardize, stake, venture, risk*; *to gamble with (success)*; *to compromise (the reputation)*; *to gamble with (one's life)*; *to expose a th (for a cause)* | **aus** dem ~ bleiben *to take no part in an affair*, ⟨fam⟩ *to keep one's finger out of the pie*; (S) *not to be counted* ‖ aus dem ~ l *to let alone*; *leave me out of the question* od *of this* | **beim** ~ *while* od *in playing*; b. ~ s *to be at play* ‖ *at the sound (of the flute)* ‖ bei ~ u Scherz *at play and sport* | die Hand **im** ~ h *to be mixed up with it*, ⟨fam⟩ *to have a finger in the pie* ‖ im ~ s *there are (influences) at work*; mit im ~e s *to be involved in it*; Ehrgeiz ist mit im ~e *it's a matter of a.* ‖ im ~ vergeuden *to gamble away* ‖ im ~ verlieren *to lose by gambling* | jdm **ins** ~ gucken *to look into a p's cards* ‖ sich ins ~ mischen *to interfere* | **mit** klingendem ~ *with drums beating (and trumpets sounding)* **~abend** m *play-night*; ⟨theat⟩ erster ~ *first-night* **~anweisung** f ⟨theat⟩ *stage directions* pl **~art** f *manner of p.ing*; ⟨mus⟩ *manipulation* ‖ ⟨bot, zoo⟩ *variety* ‖ (Züchtung) *strain* ‖ ⟨übtr⟩ *a sort of* **~automat** m *slot(ting) machine* **~ball** m ⟨bill⟩ *ball (in p.)* ‖ ⟨fig⟩ *p.thing, sport, puppet (of fortune* etc) **~bank** m gaming-table; g.g casino **~brett** n g.g-board, draught-board **~bruder** m gambler **~bude** f gambling-booth **~dauer** f ⟨rec⟩ playback time ⟨Am, film⟩ box-office life ‖ die ~ feststellen to time the picture **~dose** f musical box **~ecke** f children's corner ‖ (in Zeitungen) games-column **~einsatz** m stake **~ergebnis** n score **~feld** n ⟨sport⟩ cricket-field, ground ‖ ⟨ten⟩ court ‖ ⟨Am ftb⟩ grid **~film** m (abendfüllend feature-length) fiction film **~fläche** f ⟨theat⟩ acting area **~folge** f program(me) **~freiheit** f ⟨mach⟩ absence of play **~führer** ⟨ftb⟩ captain **~gebrauch** m rules pl of the game **~gefährte** = ~geselle **~geld** n p.-money; (Einsatz) stake, pool **~genosse**, **~gesell(e)** m p.fellow, p.mate **~gesellschaft** f party of p.ers ‖ card-party **~gesetz** n = ~gebrauch **~glück** n chance, run (of luck) **~grenze** f ⟨ftb⟩ dead-ball line **~handlung** f ⟨theat⟩ (stage) business **~hans** m gambler ‖ (Müßiggänger) trifler **~haus** n, **~hölle** f gambling-house, -hell **~kamerad** m = -gesell; ⟨sex⟩ playboy | ~in [f] playmate **~-karte** f p.ing-card ‖ ~n [pl] pack (⟨Am⟩ deck) of cards **~kätzchen** n p.ful kitten od ⟨fig⟩ girl **~kittel** m romper **~kränzchen** n card-club **~leidenschaft** f gambling **~leiter** m ⟨film⟩ producer, ⟨Am⟩ director, ⟨theat⟩ stage-manager **~leitung** f → Regie **~leute** [pl zu] **~mann** m musician, fiddler, street-pl.er; ⟨mil⟩ fifer, bandsman; [pl] ⟨mil⟩ drums and fifes ‖ ⟨hist⟩ minstrel **~mannszug** m regimental drummers pl **~marke** f counter, fish, chip **~material** n (spy's) false trail **~oper** f comic opera, opéra bouffe Fr **~partie** f game; (Gesellschaft) card-party **~plan** m ⟨theat⟩ repertory; ⟨sport⟩ fixture list **~partner** m partner **~platz** m p.ground, ⟨crick⟩ field, ⟨ten⟩ court; ⟨Am⟩ park (base-ball p.) ‖ ⟨sport⟩ den ~ betreten to take the field **~proszenium** n ⟨theat⟩ false proscenium, ⟨Am⟩ portal opening **~puppe** f doll **~ratte** f gambler **~raum** m ⟨tech⟩ (free) play, → Spiel; allowance; outlet, clearance ‖ ⟨mar⟩ berth ‖ (e–r P.) elbow-room ‖ ⟨fig⟩ scope, margin; latitude (to allow a certain l.) ‖ freien ~ h to have full scope ‖ geringen ~ l ⟨a. fig⟩ to draw it fine **~regel** f rule of the game; sich an die ~n halten to play the game **~sache** f toy, plaything **~schuld** f gam(bl)ing debt **~schule** f platoon-school, kindergarten **~stunde** f recreation-hour **~sucht** f passion for gambling **~tag** m play-day, ⟨sport⟩ fixture **~teller** m plate, pool **~teufel** m ⟨fig⟩ demon of play **~tisch** m card-table, gaming table ‖ ⟨wir⟩ turn-table **~trieb** m playing instinct od urge **~uhr** f musical box **~verbot** n ⟨sport⟩ playing ban (verhängt gegen placed upon) **~verderber** m spoil-sport; wet blanket; kein ~ s to be a good sport; ich will .. I don't want to be a meanie **~waren** f pl toys pl | ~händler [m] toy-merchant, ⟨fam⟩ toyman; ~handlung [f] toy-shop **~wart** m captain **~werk** n p.ths, toys pl ‖ (e–s Instruments) action ‖ ein leichtes ~ ⟨fig⟩ easy work, mere child's play **≈widriger** Ball no-ball **~wut** f gambling-passion, passion for g.g **~zeit** f playtime ‖ ⟨theat⟩ season; ⟨film⟩ screen time; ⟨crick⟩ innings **~zelt** n (Zirkus) big top **~zeug** n p.ths, toys pl ‖ ⟨fig⟩ bauble; sport (of the waves) **~zimmer** n games (od card) room, (Kinder≈) playroom **Sp·ielchen** n ~s/~ a quiet game ‖ sein ~ m to take a hand (at whist etc) **sp·ielen** vt/i [h] **A.** to play, ⟨a. mus⟩ .. an air, .. (einmal: on) the flute, .. Bach well | (v Kindern) to p. games | (tändeln) to dally | ⟨theat⟩ to p., act, perform (a drama) ‖ (8 Tage) gespielt w to be on (to be run for) a week ‖ heute wird nicht gespielt there will be no performance today | (heucheln) to assume, pretend; Erstaunen ~ to feign ast.t | (Hasard) to gamble ‖ er spielt he is a regular gambler | (S) to be in action ‖ (of gems) to glitter, sparkle ‖ a smile p.ed od flickered round od upon her lips ‖ die Natur spielt .. p.s tricks ‖ die Springbrunnen ~ the fountains play ‖ die Telegraphen ~ .. flash their messages **B.** **so** ~ wir nicht that's not (⟨fig⟩ p.ing) the game ‖ ausgezeichnet ge–lt ⟨mus⟩ in the groove (of jazz) ‖ **ehrlich** ~ to p. fair ‖ ernst ~ (f Geld) to p. for keeps ‖ falsch ~ to cheat at cards etc; ⟨mus⟩ to p. wrong notes ‖ hoch ~ to p. for high stakes ‖ laut ~ to bang out ‖ vierhändig ~ to p. a duet ‖ wundervoll ~ ⟨theat⟩ to give a wonderful performance **C.** **sich** arm ~ to ruin o.s. with gambling ‖ sich müde ~ to p. till one gets tired **D.** etw ~ (vorstellen) to assume a part ‖ to act (the fine [= gr] lady) ‖ to do (the polite) ‖ den Beleidigten ~ to sulk ‖ Verrückte ~ ⟨theat⟩ to act mad parts ‖ die Herrin, Königin ~ to queen it ‖ **Indianer** ~ to p. that we are I. ‖ **Karten** etc ~ to p. cards, tennis etc, to take a hand at piquet; to p. at ninepins ‖ Komödie ~ to act (on the stage od) a play; ⟨fig⟩ to make believe; to sham, pretend ‖ to p. at (robbers) ‖ e–e **Rolle** ~ ⟨theat & fig⟩ to p. a part; ⟨theat⟩ to act (Hamlet), to impersonate (Garbo); to do (the ghost); es wird Lear gespielt Lear is on; er sp. den L. he is on as L. ‖ ⟨übtr⟩ den Unschuldigen, Narren~ to play the innocent, the fool ‖ e–e klägliche Rolle ~ to cut a piteous figure; Geld sp. k–e R. m. is no object | → Streich | **gespielte** Bestürzung mock alarm; studied (calm) assumed (confidence); mit g.r Entrüstung with the pretence (⟨Am⟩-se) of indignation; mit g.m Gleichmut affecting an easy nonchalance **E.** etw ~ **lassen** to bring a th into play ‖ to direct (od fire off) (guns) ‖ to set going (musical boxes, waterworks) ‖ to spring (mines); to exhibit (one's talents) ‖ to run (one's eyes über over a th) ‖ sein Geld ~ l to use one's m. for bribery ‖ to put (one's charms) into action **F.** **an**: to speculate on change | **auf**: to strum (a piano) | **gegen-e-a** ~ to be opponents | **in**: to p. in (⟨Am⟩ on) a team ‖ to put in the lottery ‖ to flutter in the wind ‖ e–m etw in die Hände ~ to slip od smuggle a th into a p's hands, ⟨fig⟩ to help a p to a th; e–a .. to play into one another's hands ‖ ins Grüne ~ to have a greenish tint, to incline to green ‖ ⟨Ger bill⟩ ins Loch ~ to pocket a ball ‖ ⟨theat, Lit⟩ das Stück spielt in L. etc the (action of the) play, novel, the scene is set od laid in London; the action takes place in the spring of 1928, the time of the action is 1928 | **mit**: to p. with fire, with the idea (of doing) ‖ (tändelnd) to toy, fiddle with a ring; to dally with an idea ‖ to twiddle one's fingers; ⟨fam⟩ to monkey with .. ‖ to p. upon words ‖ (sein Spiel treiben mit) to trifle, sport, palter with ‖ wir l nicht mit uns ~ we won't be paltered od trifled with; we stand no nonsense | den Krieg **nach** Afrika ~ to carry the war into A. | **um**: to p. for money (= to gamble); um nichts, umsonst ~ to p. for love ‖ um die Ganzen ~ to p. a Pfennig a point (vgl A.) | **vom** Blatt ~ to p. at sight | **vor** Anker ~ to ride at anchor | **zus** ~ to be partners **sp·ielend** [part & a] playing | [adv] easily ‖ ~ gewinnen, siegen to win hands down, ⟨racing sl⟩ to romp home ‖ ~ durchk ⟨med⟩ to romp through the convalescence ‖ etw ~ erreichen to secure a th with utmost ease; etw ~ leicht tun ⟨fam⟩ to take ths in one's stride; e–e Stimme, die ~ alle Register beherrscht .. with a great versatility of range and control **Sp·ieler** m ~s/~ player ‖ ⟨crick⟩ bat ‖ (Glücks-≈) gambler, gamester ‖ ⟨theat⟩ performer actor, f actress ‖ ausübender ~ ⟨mus⟩ executant | falscher ~ blackleg, card-sharper ‖ guter ~ ⟨ftb⟩ a good kick ‖ hervorragender ~ swell (at tennis) ‖ vorsichtiger ~ ⟨Am sl⟩ piker | **~·ei** f ~/~en play, sport, child's p. ‖ ⟨fig⟩ trifle; ⟨fam⟩ breeze, pie, ⟨Am⟩ cinch; es ist e–e ~ f mich ⟨sl⟩ I can do it on my head ‖ ~en [pl] trivialities pl |

≈**isch** a *p.ful* **~abstandssumme** f ⟨Am⟩ *transfer-fee*

Spier m ~(e)s/~e *stalk* (*of grass*) **Sp·iere** f ~/~n; **Sp·iering** m ~(e)s/~e ⟨mar⟩ *spar, boom* **Sp·ierstaude** f ⟨bot⟩ → Spir·äe, *meadow-sweet*

Spieß m ~es/~e **A. 1.** *spear, lance, pike* ‖ (Wurf≈) *javelin* ‖ (Brat≈) *spit* (*to roast on the sp.*) **2.** ⟨hist⟩ *spearman* ‖ ⟨mil sl⟩ *sergeant--major*; ⟨fam⟩ *top sergeant*, ⟨Am⟩ *topkick* **3.** ⟨weav⟩ *skewer* **4.** ⟨hunt⟩ ~e [pl] *first year's antlers* **5.** ⟨typ⟩ *pick* **B.** den ~ umkehren ⟨fig⟩ *to turn the tables* (gegen *on*) ‖ schreien, als ob man am ~ stäke *to scream like a stuck pig* **~bock** m ⟨hunt⟩ *pricket* **~bürger** m *Philistine, commonplace fellow*, ⟨Am fam⟩ *Babbit*, ⟨sl⟩ *mossback* | ≈lich [a] *Philistine, narrow-minded*; *commonplace*; ~tum [n] ⟨Am⟩ *babbitry* **~dreher** m *turnspit* **~gesell(e)** m *companion, accomplice* **~glanz, ~glas** m ⟨min⟩ *antimony* **~hirsch** m = Spießer **~ruten** f pl; ~ laufen *to run the gauntlet* **~träger** m *spearman* **~chen** n ⟨cul⟩ *skewer* | ≈**en** vt [h] *to* (*pierce with the*) *spear* ‖ (durchbohren) *to run through*; *to spit, pierce* ‖ ~ auf *to fix on* (*a board*), *to stick on* (*a fork*) **Sp·ießer** m ~s/~ (Hirsch) *brocket* ‖ (Reh) *pricket* ‖ = Spießbürger **sp·ießig** a *Philistine*; *dowdy* (*woman, dress*) ‖ (unangenehm) *disagreeable* ‖ *badly tanned*

Spikes [–ˈaiks] pl ⟨sport⟩ *spike shoes*

Spill n ~(e)s/~e ⟨mar⟩ (stehend) *capstan* ‖ (liegend) *windlass* **~baum** m *c.-bar* **~haken** m *c.-pawl* **~mage** m *relative on the female side* **~spake** f *c.-bar*

Sp·ille f ~/~n *spindle, newel*; (Walze) *cylinder* | ˣ ≈**rig** a = schmächtig

Sp·illing m ~s/~e *egg-plum*

Spin m ~s/~s ⟨at phys⟩ *spin*

spin·al a *spinal* (*paralysis*); ~e Kinderlähmung *poliomyelitis*, ⟨Am fam⟩ *polio*

Spin·at m ~(e)s/ *spinach*; dazu *s.ceous*

Spind [n & m] ~(e)s/~e *cupboard, wardrobe* | ~foto [n] *pin-up girl*

Sp·indel f ~/~n *spindle*; ⟨bot⟩ *rachis* ‖ (Spinnrocken) *distaff* ⟨a. fig⟩ ‖ ⟨mech⟩ *axis* ‖ (Uhr≈) *verge* ‖ ⟨spin⟩ *bobbin* ‖ (Fräs≈) *milling sp.* ‖ (Zapfen) *pin* ‖ (Welle) *arbor, beam, shaft* ‖ (Schrauben≈) *worm* ‖ (Treppen≈) *newel* **~bank** f *bobbin and fly frame* **~baum** m *sp.-tree* ≈**beinig** a *sp.-shanked* **~buche** f ⟨bot⟩ *hornbeam, yoke-elm* ≈**dürr** a (*as*) *lean as a rake* ≈**förmig** a *sp.-shaped, fusiform, taper* [a] **~holz** n *sp.-tree wood, prick--wood* **~kasten** m *gear case* **~mage** = Spillmage **~öl** n *watchmaker's* **~presse** f *screw-press* **~rolle** f *sp.-roll* **~treppe** f *spiral staircase* **~welle** f *bobbin* **~zapfen** m *pivot*

Spin·ell m ~(e)s/~e ⟨min⟩ *spinel*

Spin·ett n ~(e)s/~e *spinet, harpsichord*

sp·innbar a *fit for spinning* **Sp·inn- ~faden** m *spider-thread*; (fliegender) *gossamer* ≈**gefärbt** a *spun-dyed* **~gewebe** n *cobweb* ‖ ⟨fig⟩ *rope of sand* **~haus** n *spinning-house* **~hütte** f *hut for silk-worms* **~maschine** f *sp.-machine, -jenny* **~mühle** f *sp.-mill* **~rad** n *sp.-wheel* **~rocken** m *distaff* **~stoff** m ⟨text⟩ *fabric* ~(f)abrik [f] *rayon mill* **~stube** f *sp.-room, sp.-party* **~stubenerzählung** f *old wives' tale* **~warze** f ⟨zoo⟩ *sp.-wart* ≈**web-**~artig [a] *cob-webby*; ~fein [a] ~es Gewebe ⟨Am a.⟩ *gossamer* **~webe** f = –gewebe **Sp·inne** f ~/~n *spider*; ⟨fig⟩ (Frau) *lemon* ‖ °pfui ~! *shocking*! ‖ „~" ⟨a–n⟩ (Mondfähre) *spider*; → Wanze (*bug*) ≈**feind** a; e–a ~ s *to hate each other like poison* **sp·innen** vt/i [spann/gesponnen] [h] *to spin* ‖ der Kreisel (die Katze) –t *the top s.s round* (*the cat purrs*) | e–n Gedanken weiter ~ *to follow up a thread* ‖ (ausdenken) *to hatch, to plot* (*treason*) ‖ ⟨sl⟩ du –st! *you are mad*! ‖ ⟨stud sl⟩ *to drink* | ⟨prov⟩ dabei ist k–e Seide z ~ *there is not much to be made by it* ‖ (→ Sonne) **Sp·innen- ~fisch** m *sculpin* **~kenner** m *arachnologist*

Sp·inner m ~s/~ *spinner* ‖ ⟨ent⟩ *bombyx*; (Weiden≈) *satin moth*; → *gipsy* | °(P) *fool* **Spinner·ei** f ~/~en *spinning* ‖ (Fabrik) *sp.g-mill* **spintis·ieren** vi/t [h] **1.** *to muse* (über *over*) **2.** *to subtilize*

Spi·on m ~(e)s/~e *spy* ‖ ⟨sl⟩ *nark*, ⟨Am⟩ *gum-shoe man*, ⟨fam⟩ *spotter* ‖ ⟨fig⟩ *plant* ‖ jdn als ~ aufstellen ⟨sl⟩ *to plant a p* | **~·age** [ʃpioˈnaːʒə] f ~/~n *spying, espionage*; ⟨mil⟩ *intelligence* | ~abwehrdienst [m] *secret service*; ~ring [m] *spy-ring, -network* **~enfurcht** f *spy-scare* | ≈**·ieren** vi [h] *to* (*play the*) *spy* (hinter jdm her *upon a p*) ‖ ⟨fig⟩ *to pry about* | **~ierer·ei** f = –age

Spir·äe f ~/~n ⟨bot⟩ *spiraea*

Spir·al- ~feder f *spiral* od *helical spring*; (Uhr≈) *balance s.l* ≈**förmig** a *s.l* ‖ ⟨bot⟩ *convolute* ‖ ~e Kurve, Verzierung *twist*; ~es Heizrohr *worm* **~linie** f *s.l line* **~nebel** m ⟨astr⟩ *s.l nebula* ≈**ständig** a *arranged in a s.l* **~sturzflug** m ⟨aero⟩ *s.l dive* **Spir·ale** f ~/~n *s.l* (*line*) ‖ ⟨tech⟩ *twist, worm, coil* **spir·alig** a *s.l, helical*

Spirit·ismus m ~/ *spirit*(*ual*)*ism* **Spirit·ist** m ~en/~en *spiritualist* ≈**isch** a *sp.listic* (*séance*) **Spiritualit·ät** f ~/ *spirituality* **spiritu·ell** a *witty* **Spiritu·osen** [pl] *alcoholic drinks* pl ‖ (*wine and*) *spirits* pl **Sp·iritus** m ~/~ & –tusse *alcohol, spirit*(*s* pl) ‖ denatur·ierter ~ *methylated s.* | ⟨gram⟩ *s.us* ‖ ~ (asper *rough*, lenis *soft*) *breathing* **~brennerei** f *distillery* **~gehalt** m *s.uosity* **~kocher** m *etna, s.-burner* **~lampe** f *s.-lamp* **~waage** f *alcoholmeter* ‖ (Libelle) *s.-level*

Spirom·eter n (Atemmesser) ⟨med⟩ *spirometer*

Spit·al n ~(e)s/≈er (a. Sp·ittel [n] ~s/~) *hospital, infirmary*, → Krankenhaus; *old people home* (*mostly for paupers*) **~fieber** n *h.-fever* **~kirche** f *h.-church* **~kostenversicherung** f *h. expenses insurance* **~prediger** m *h.-chaplain* **~-vorsteher** m *warden of a h.*

Spitz m ~es/~e **1.** *Pomeranian* (*dog*), *spitz* **2.** (Berg) *peak* **3.** ⟨fam⟩ e–n ~ (Rausch) h *to be slightly elevated, to be tipsy* **spitz** a *pointed* (*p.ed*) *conic*; ~es Ende *fine point* | ⟨fig⟩ *sarcastic, biting* (*remark*), *sharp* (*tongue*) ‖ (Winkel) *acute* ‖ mit ~en Fingern *with the tips of one's fingers* ‖ ~ zulaufen *to come* od *narrow to a point* ‖ ~ zulaufend *tapering* ‖ °⟨fig⟩ es ~ kriegen *to make it out* | ⟨fig⟩ *delicate*; *peaky* (*child*) **Spitz-** *point*(*ed*) **~ahorn** m *Norway maple* **~amboß** m *beaked anvil* **~axt** f *pickaxe* **~bart** m *p.ed beard, imperial, goatee* | s≈ig [a] *goateed* **~blattern** f pl = –pocken **~bogen** m ⟨arch⟩ *ogive*; *p.ed arch* **~bogen-** *ogival* [a]: ~fenster [n] *lancet-window*; ~stil [m] *pointed* od *Gothic style* **~bohrer** m *draw-p., centre-bit, joiner's awl* **~bube** (f –bübin) ⟨eig⟩ *thief, villain*; ⟨allg⟩ *rogue, rascal* ⟨a. fam⟩: ⟨sl⟩ *spiv* | ~n ~gesicht [n] *roguish face* od *look*; ~sprache [f] *thieves' cant*; ~streich [m], **~bübe-r·ei** f *roguery, knavery, rascality* ≈**bübisch** a *mischievous*; *roguishly*; *rascally* ([adv] *in a r.y way*) **~feile** f *taper-file* ≈**findig** a *subt*(*i*)*le, cunning, crafty*; *sharp, captious, sophistic*(*al*) **~findigkeit** f *quibbling, quillet*; *subtlety, craftiness, cunning, refinement, subtleness*; *captiousness, casuistry, sophistry* ‖ ⟨sl⟩ *quillit* **~geschoß** n *ogival* od *conical bullet* od *shell* **~glas** n *flute glass* **~hacke** f *pick*(*axe*) **~hammer** m *pick*(*hammer*) **~haue** f = –hacke **~hut** m *p.ed hat* **~kehre** f (e–r Straße) *hairpin* (*turn*) **~keimer** m ⟨bot⟩ *monocotyledon* **~kopf** m *long head* **~kugel** f = –geschoß **~kühler** m ⟨mot⟩ *V-fronted* od *angular radiator*; ⟨fam fig⟩ *belly, paunch* **~marke** f ⟨typ⟩ *head*(*ing*) **~mäulchen** n ⟨fam⟩ *button-mouth* **~maus** f *shrew*(*-mouse*); → *shrew* **~meißel** m *angular punch, cape chisel* **~name(n)** m *nickname*; jdm e–n ~ geben *to n. a p* **~nase** f *p.ed nose* ≈**nasig** a *sharp-n.d* **~pocken** f pl ⟨path⟩ *chicken-pox* **~säule** f *pyramid, obelisk, pinnacle* **~sieb** n *conical strainer* **~stahl** m *p.ed chisel* **~stein** m *p. diamond*

~tonne f *spar buoy* **~turm** m ⟨arch⟩ *spire*; *pinnacle* **~wegerich** m ⟨bot⟩ *rib-wort* **⁓wink(e)lig** a ⟨math⟩ *acute-angled*; (*branching*) *at an acute angle* **~zahn** m *dog-, eye-, ocular tooth* **Sp·itze** f ∼/∼n **A. 1.** (Dorn–, Nadel–, Degen⁓) *point* (⟨a. fig⟩ *of an epigram*) ‖ (Finger–, Nasen–, Zungen⁓) *tip* (⟨a. fig⟩ *of a flame*) ‖ *top* (*of a tree, house, gable*) ‖ ⟨bot, geom⟩ *apex*, *vertex* ‖ ⟨anat⟩ *apex* (*of the heart*) ‖ *peak* (*of a cone*, ⟨fig⟩ *breast*; *of sails*) **|** (Berg⁓) *top*, *peak*, *summit* ‖ (Pfeil) mit Bronze⁓ *bronze-tipped* ‖ (Feder⁓) *nib* ‖ (Pfeifen⁓) *mouth piece* ‖ Stock⁓ *spike* ‖ (Turm⁓) *spire* ‖ Zigarren⁓ *cigar-holder* ‖ (Zinke) *spike* **|** ⟨com⟩ *peak sum* (*of money*) **2.** ⟨fig⟩ (gegen) *p.ed allusion* (*to*) ‖ mit deutlicher ∼ *very p.edly* **3.** ⟨fig, mil, pol⟩ *head* ‖ ⟨tact⟩ (*advance guard*) *point*; *vanguard*; *head* (*of a column*) ‖ (Angriffs⁓) *spearhead* ‖ die ∼n der Behörden *the heads* od *chiefs of the State* od *of the administration, the* (*leading* od *foremost*) *authorities*; *the powers-that-be* ‖ *the leaders* (*of society*) **|** *the van* (*of a procession*) ‖ *the vanguard* (*of a movement*) ‖ *the sperhead* (*of an attack*) **4.** ⟨tail⟩ ∼n [pl] *lace*; Brüsseler ∼n *Brussels l.*; Erzgebirgische ∼n *Dresden l.*; geklöppelte ∼n *bone-l.*; genähte ∼n *p.-l.*; Seiden⁓ *blond lace*; Tüll⁓n *net-l.*; *tulle*; Valencienner ∼n *Valenciennes* pl Fr ‖ Zier⁓ *fancy edge* **|** ∼n klöppeln *to make* (*pillow-*)*lace* **B.** ⟨fig⟩ ∼n **austeilen** *to pass offensive remarks* ‖ [dat] die ∼ abbrechen *to break the neck of* (*a th*), *to take the sharp edge off* (*a painful situation*) ‖ [dat] die ∼ bieten *to make head* (od *stand out*) *against*; *to oppose*, *defy* ‖ (S) s–e ∼ richten auf *to be directed against* **C. an** [dat]: *at the top*; *at the head of* (*affairs*); *in the van of* (*the army, column, troops*); Wagen an der ∼ (e–r Reihe) *lead car* ‖ an s–r ∼ *atop it* **|** an die ∼ treten *to take the lead* **| auf** die ∼ treiben *to carry .. to extremes* od *too far*; *to reduce to absurdity*; ⟨fam⟩ *to put the lid on* (*a th*); auf die ∼ getriebener Gemeinplatz *overexpression of a. t.* **Sp·itzel** m ∼s/∼ *informer*; ⟨sl⟩ *trap*, *nose*(*r*); *private detective*, *police-spy*, ⟨sl⟩ *squeaker*; ⟨Am fam⟩ *gumshoe*; *stool pigeon*; ⟨sl⟩ *nark* **~tum** n *espionage*; *informer system* **sp·itzen** vt [h] **1.** *to point* ‖ *to sharpen* (*a pencil*); *to mend* (*a quill*) **|** ⟨fig⟩ das ist auf mich gespitzt *that's meant for me* **2.** ⟨fig⟩ *to pout* (die L. *one's lips*), *to prick up* (*one's ears*) **3.** ⟨fam⟩ **sich ~ auf** [acc] *to anticipate with eagerness*, *to be eager about a th* **| gespitzt** auf [acc] *anxious to know* ..; ⟨fam⟩ *agog* (*for, about*; *to do*) **Sp·itzen- ~arbeit** f *lace-work*, → –leistung **~behang** m *flounce*, *volant* **~belastung(s-zeit** f) f *peak period* **~besatz** m *l.-trimming* **~besetzung** f ⟨theat⟩ (nur .. *all*) *star cast* **~einsatz** m (im Kleidausschnitt) *modesty vest* **~entladung** f ⟨el⟩ *point discharge* **~geschwindigkeit** f *maximum speed* **~gesellschaft** f ⟨com⟩ *holding company* **~grund** m *l.-net*, *bobbinet* **~gruppe** f ⟨soc⟩ *jet-set* **~halstuch** n *l.-neckerchief* **~handel** m *l.-trade* **~kandidat** m *front runner* **~kleid** n *dress trimmed with l.* **~klöppel** m *l.-bobbin* **~klöppelei** f *l.--making* **~kompanie** f *vanguard c.* **~lagerung** f ⟨rec⟩ *pivots* pl **~lastenenergie** f ⟨el⟩ (je Stunde) *peak-load power* **~leistung** f *masterpiece*, *best achievement* od *production*, *masterly* od *top performance*; ⟨tech⟩ *peak capacity*/*output* **~lohn** m *maximum pay* **~personal** n *key personnel* **~schiff** n *leading ship* **~spannung** f *peak voltage* **~spieler** m ⟨sport⟩ *best string*, *swell-player* **~stickerei** f *l.--running* **~tank** m ⟨mil⟩ *leading tank* **~papiere** n pl ⟨exch⟩ *blue chips* **~tänzer(in** f) m *pirouetting ballet dancer* **~tuch** n *l.-scarf*, *l.-coif*; (f d. Busen) *tucker* **~verband** m *head organization* **~verkehr(szeit** f) m *rush hours* **~verrundung** f ⟨rec⟩ *type of stylus point* **~ware** f *l.-ware* ‖ *best produce* **~wein** m *vintage wine* **~werk** n *lacery* **~wert** m *peak value* **~zeit** f ⟨traffic⟩ *rush hours* **~zwirn** m *fine twisted thread for l.* **Sp·itzer** m ∼s/∼ (*pencil-*)*sharpener* **sp·itzig** a *pointed*, *sharp* ‖ ⟨fig⟩ *biting*, *poignant*, *sharp* **|** [adv] ∼ zulaufen *to taper*

Sp·itzbergen n (arktische Inselgruppe)

°**Spleen** [ʃpli:n] m ∼(e)s/ → Fimmel ‖ e–n ∼ h *to have a bee in one's bonnet* od *bats in one's belfry* **|** ⁓**ige** P *crank*

Spl·eiße f ∼/∼n *splinter*, *splint* **spl·eißen** vi/t [spliß/gesplissen] [h] *to split*, *cleave* **|** vt ⟨met⟩ *to refine* **spl·eißig** a *easy to split*

splend·id a **1.** *liberal*, *free-handed* **2.** *splendid*, *magnificent* **3.** ⟨typ⟩ *wide*(*ly-spaced*)

Spl·int m ∼(e)s/∼e ⟨bot⟩ *sap-wood*, *alburnum* ‖ (Splitter) *splinter* ‖ ⟨tech⟩ *split pin*, *forelock* **~(holz** n) ⟨for⟩ *sap* **~ring** m ⟨tech⟩ *split-ring* **~zange** f *key-pincers*

spliß 3. sg pret v spleißen **Spliß** m –sses/–sse *cleft* **~hammer** m *splicing-hammer* **spl·issen** vt [h] ⟨mar⟩ *to splice* (*ropes*) **Spl·issung** f ∼/∼en ⟨mar⟩ *splice* **Splitband** n ⟨film⟩ *magnetic split film*

Spl·itt m ∼(e)s/∼e *gravel*; *broken stone*; *stone-chip*(*ping*)*s*; (z Betonieren) *aggregate* **Spl·itter** m ∼s/∼ *splinter*, *chip* ‖ *sliver* (*of bone, glass, stone*) ‖ ⟨fig⟩ *fragment* (⟨a.⟩ Granat⁓) ‖ ⟨bib⟩ *mote* **|** sich [dat] e–n ∼ in den Finger reißen *to run a splinter into one's f.* **~bombe** *fragmentation* od *antipersonnel bomb* **~boxe** f ⟨aero⟩ *revetment* **~bruch** m ⟨surg⟩ *splintery fracture* **⁓(faser)-nackt** a *without a stitch on*, *stark* od *mother--naked*; ∼es Mädchen ⟨hum⟩ *bobby*(*-soxer*) *sans sox*, *wearing a smile* ‖ *in the buff* od *raw* od *altogether* **~frei** a *toughened*, *splinter-proof* (*glass*) **~gruppe** f ⟨pol⟩ *splinter group* **~kohle** f *slate-coal* **⁓n·ackt** a *mother-naked*, *stark naked*; *naked as a cuckoo*, *needle*, *one's nail* ‖ (sich) ∼ ausziehen *to strip* (*naked* od) *to the buff* **~partei** f *breakaway* od *splinter party* **⁓richten** vi [h] *to criticize minutely and uncharitably* **~richter** m *fault--finder*, *carper* **~schutz** m *s.r-protection* **~sicher** a ⟨mil⟩ *s.r-proof* ‖ ∼es Glas *safety-glass*; *shatter--proof* od *non-splintering glass* **~stein** m *chipped stone* **~wirkung** f *s.r effect* **spl·itt(e)rig** a *s.ry* **spl·ittern** vi/t [h] *to s.r*, *shiver*

Spl·ügen m (Paß oberhalb des Comer Sees)

Sp·odium n ∼s/ *spodium*, *bone-manure* **~fabrik** f *bone-mill*

ˣ**Sp·ökenkieker** m ∼s/∼ er ist ein ∼ *he has the second sight*

Sp·olien [pl] *spoils* pl

spond- ~·eisch a *spondaic* **⁓·eus** m ∼/–deen *spondee*

Spons- ~·alien ⟨obs⟩ [pl] *betrothal* **⁓·ieren** vi *to woo*, *flirt*

spont·an a *spontaneous* **⁓ab·ortus** m *spontaneous* od *unintentional abortus*; *miscarriage*

Spor·aden, die [f pl] (Inselgruppen im Ägäischen Meer) *the Sporades* **spor·adisch** a *sporadic* [adv *–ally*]

Sp·ore f ∼/∼n ⟨bot⟩ *spore*, *sporule* **Sp·oren** [pl] v Sporn & Spore **~behälter** ⟨bot⟩ *sporangium* **⁓förmig** a *spur-shaped*, *calcariform* **~frucht** f *sporocarp* **~kapsel** f *sporocyst* **~pflanzen** f pl *acotyledons* pl **~tiere** n pl *sporozoa* **~träger** m *sporophore* **Sp·orer** m ∼s/∼ *spurrier*, *spur-maker* **sp·orig** a *mouldy*, *musty* **Sporn** m ∼(e)s/Sporen *spur* ⟨a. zoo, mount, arch, & fig⟩ ‖ ⟨mar⟩ *ram* ‖ ⟨artill⟩ *spade* ‖ MG-⁓ *spike* ‖ ⟨aero⟩ *skid* (⟨a. –kufe [f]⟩) ‖ ⟨fig⟩ *stimulus*; *inducement*, *incentive* ‖ e–m Pferde die Sporen geben *to set* (*put, clap*) *spurs to* (od *to spur*) *a horse* ‖ ⟨fig⟩ sich [dat] die Sporen verdienen *to win one's spurs* ‖ mit dem ∼ verletzen *to spur-gall* **~blume** f *larkspur*, *red valerian* **~rad** n ⟨aero⟩ *tail wheel* (einziehbar *retractable*; schwenkbar *castoring*) **~rädchen** n *rowel* **~riemen** m *spur-strap*, *-leather* **⁓stätisch** a *restive* **~stich** m *spur*(*-gall*) **⁓streichs** [adv] *post-haste*, *at a gallop*; ⟨Am⟩ *hot-foot*; *at* *full speed, directly* **~träger** m *spur-bearer* **sp·ornen** vt [h] *to provide with spurs* || sich ~ *to put on spurs* || ⟨hors⟩ = Sporen geben || ⟨fig⟩ *to stimulate* || gespornt *spurred*

Sporogon·ie f ~/ *sporogenesis*

Sport m ~(e)s/ *sport* (vornehm *lordly*); ~ u Turnen *physical training* ⟨a. mil⟩ || Hallen≗ *indoor s.* || (Pferde≗) *turf* | ⟨übtr⟩ *pursuit* | guten ~ ergeben *to bring good results* pl || ~ treiben *to go in for s.s* **~abzeichen** n ⟨Ger⟩ *s.s badge* **~anzug** m *s.s clothes* **~ausdruck** m *s.ing-term* **~dame** f *s.s-woman* **~druck** m *s.ing print* **~fest** n *s.s festival*; ⟨Am⟩ *field day* **~fisch** m *game fish* **~flechte** f *athlete's foot* **~flieger** m *s. flier* **~freund** m *s.sman* **~funkreporter** m ⟨wir m. m.⟩ *race reader* **≗gemäß** a *s.ing* **~herz** n *athletic heart* **~jacke** f *blazer*; (Damen≗) ⟨bes Am⟩ *shirt jacket* **~kabriolett** n *s.s-car*, ⟨Am⟩ *roadster* **~kamera** f ⟨Am film⟩ *akeley* **~karikatur** f *sportoon* **~kleidung** f *s.s clothing, s. wear*; ⟨Am⟩ *s.swear* **~klub** m → –verein **~lehrer** m *coach, trainer* **~leistungsabzeichen** n ⟨DDR⟩ = –abzeichen **≗mäßig** a *s.smanlike* **~mütze** f *s.ing cap* **~nachrichten** f pl *s.ing news* **~platz** m *playing-field, s.s-ground* **~reportage** f ⟨wir⟩ *s.scast* **~reporter** m *s.caster* **~schule** f *physical training school* **~strümpfe** m pl *golf-hose* **~sucher** m ⟨phot⟩ *wire frame viewfinder, s.s finder* **~suspensorium** n *jock-strap* **~treibend** a *s.ing* **~verein** m *s.s* od *s.ing* od *athletic club* (od *association*) **~wagen** m (f [Klein-]Kinder) *folding pram*; *mail-cart*; [*carry--cart*, ⟨Am⟩ (*baby*) *stroller*]; ⟨mot⟩ *s.s-car* ⟨Am⟩ *roadster* **~warenhändler** m *s.s outfitter* **~wart** m *trainer, coach*; ⟨fam⟩ *flag marshal* **~welt** f *s.ing-world* **~zeitung** f *s.ing-paper* **~zweisitzer** m ⟨mot⟩ *roadster* **Sp·ortler** m ~s/~ = Sportfreund | **~in** f ~/~nen *s.swoman* | **≗isch, sp·ortlich** a *sportsmanlike, sporting*, ⟨Am⟩ *athletic* **Sp·orts-~mann** m *sportsman* || ⟨univ⟩ *hearty* || gr ~ *athlete* **≗männisch** a *sportsmanlike*

Sp·orteln [pl] *perquisites, fees*, (*legal*) *costs* pl

Sp·ott m ~(e)s/ **A.** (Hohn) *m(ockin)g, mockery, scorn, ridicule, scoffing, sneering*; *jape* || (Scherz) *jest(ing)* | *irony* || *derision* || *sarcasm* || gutmütiger ~ *banter* || wilder ~ *derisive fervidity* || ~ u Hohn *taunts and sneers*; *jibes and jeers* | Gegenstand [m] des ~es *laughing-stock* **B.** s–n ~ an jdm auslassen *to pour one's scorn on a p*; nur ~ eintragen *to gain, earn, reap nothing but ridicule*; dem ~ preisgeben *to expose to ridicule* || von etw nur ~ u Schande h *to derive nothing but shame and disgrace from a th* || ~ treiben mit *to mock, deride*; *to make sport* od *game of* || zum ~ dienen *to serve as a butt* || jdn z ~ reizen *to excite a p's ridicule* || zum ~ jds w *to become the scorn of a p* **~bild** n *caricature*; *cartoon* **≗b·illig** a *dirt-cheap*; [pred] *for a song* || ~e Ware *dead bargain* | adv ⟨sl⟩ *at a knock-out price* **~dichter** m *satirist* **~drossel** f ⟨orn⟩ *m.g-bird* **~gebot** n *ridiculous offer* **~geburt** f *monstrosity* **~gedicht** n *squib, satirical poem* **~gelächter** n *derisive laugh(ter)* **~geld** n *ridiculously low price, trifling sum, dead bargain* || um ein ~ *for a song*; *dirt-cheap* **~lied** n *satirical song* **~lust** f *flippancy* **≗lustig** a *flippant* **~name(n)** m *nickname* **~preis** m = ~geld **~rede** f *m.g speech* | **≗schl·echt** a *vile* **~schrift** f *satire, lampoon* **≗süchtig** a *fond of m.g, satirical* **~vogel** m ⟨orn⟩ *m.g-bird* || ⟨fig⟩ *wag, mocker*; *quiz* **≗weise** [adv] *ironically, m.gly* **Spöttel·ei** f ~/~en *sarcasm, mockery, sneer, jeer* || *derision, raillery* || (leichte) *banter* **sp·ötteln** vi [h] (über [acc]) *to mock, jeer, scoff, sneer (at)*; *to be flippant, to pass sarcastic remarks (about)* **sp·otten** vi [h] (über [acc]) *to mock (a p)* || *to scoff (at)* || *to (turn into) ridicule* | [gen] es –tet jeder Beschreibung *it baffles description* || *the door deluded all efforts to break it open* || aller Gefahr ~ *to see no danger* || Gott läßt s–r *or* sich [vt] nicht ~ *God is not mocked* | nicht **mit** sich ~ l *not to be trifled with* **Sp·ötter** m ~s/~ *mocker, scoffer* || ⟨rel⟩ *blasphemer* || alter ~! *you old cynic!* | **~·ei** f ~/~en *mockery, derision, raillery, jeering*, etc **sp·öttisch** a *satirical, derisive, ironical, scoffing, mocking*; *quizzical* (*look*) || *cutting, caustic, sarcastic, japish, sneering* (*words*) || [adv] *with a scornful* etc *air*; *ironically* etc; *in mockery*; in ~-feierlichem Ton *in mock-solemn tone*

sprach 1. sg 3. sg pret v sprechen **Spr·ach-** *linguist(ic), language (l.e)* **~ähnlichkeit** f *analogy of l.e(s)* **~armut** f *poverty of expression, in speech, of a l.e*; *lack of words* **~atlas** m *li.ic atlas* od *maps* pl **~ausgabe** f ⟨comp⟩ *audio response* **~begabung** f *gift of tongues* **~beherrschung** f *command of language* **~denkmäler** n pl *texts* pl **~eigenheit, ~eigentümlichkeit** f *idiom(atic peculiarity)* || deutsche, Fr, Engl, L ~ *Germanism, Gallicism, Anglicism, Latinism* **~fähigkeit** f *li.ic gift*; *faculty of speech* **~fehler** m *solecism* || *grammatical mistake* || ⟨path⟩ *defect of speech* **≗fertig** a; ~ s *to have a ready tongue*, ⟨fam⟩ *the gift of the gab* || (in Sprachen) *to be a good li.* | **≗keit** [f] *fluency of speech* || *proficiency in foreign l.es* **~form** f *l.e form* **~forscher** m *philologist* | vergleichende **~forschung** f *comparative philology* **~führer** m *colloquial guide* (*to a l.e*), *phrase-book* **~gebiet** n *district, country where a l.e is spoken* **~gebrauch** m *usage* (*of a l.e*) || der heutige ~ *modern English* (etc) *usage*; dem ~ folgend *dictional* **~gebräuchlich** a *idiomatic* **~gefüge** n *connected speech* **~gefühl** n *li.ic instinct* od *feeling*; *f.g for words* **~gelehrsamkeit** f *philology* **~gelehrte(r)** m *philologist, li.* **~geneinschaft** f *community speaking the same l.e* **≗gewandt s** *to be a good li.* **~gewandtheit** f *fluency of speech*; *felicity with tongues*; *language skills* pl **~insel** f *li.ic enclave* **~kenner** m *li.* **~kenntnis, ~kunde** f *li.ics*; *knowledge of l.es* **≗kundig** a *polyglot, versed in l.es* **~kundige(r)** m = ~kenner **~labor** n *l.e laboratory* **~lehre** f *grammar* **~lehrer** m *teacher of l.es* **≗los** a *speechless* (über *at*, vor with), *struck dumb* (*with*); *blank* (*astonisment*); *tongue-tied* || ~ dastehen *to be dumb-founded, to be struck dumb* || ~ (geworden) s *to have lost one's tongue* || ich bin ~! *you don't say so!, not really!* | **≗igkeit** [f] *sp.ness*, etc **~mittler** m → Dolmetscher **≗mündig** a *articulate* **~neuerer** m *neologist* **~organ** n *organ of speech* **~regel** f *grammatical rule, rule of grammar* **~reinheit** f *purity of speech, of a l.e.* **~reiniger** m *purifier of a l.e.* || ⟨dero⟩ *purist* **~reinigungseifer** m *purism* **≗richtig** a *correct, grammatical* | ~keit [f] *g.l correctness* **~rohr** n *speaking--trumpet, -tube*; ⟨mil⟩ *megaphone* || ⟨fig⟩ *mouth--piece, spokesman* **~schatz** m *vocabulary* **~schnitzer** m *g.l blunder, solecism* **~schule** f *school of l.es* **~stamm** m *family of l.es* **~störung** f *impediment of speech*; ⟨med⟩ *speech defect* **~studium** n *study of l.es* **~stunden** f pl, deutsche ~ *German lessons* **~system** n *l.e system* **~talent** n *talent for l.es* **~tonfrequenz** f *voice frequency* N; **~übung** f *g.l exercise*; *ex. in elocution* **~unterricht** m *instruction in a l.e.*; deutschen ~ geben *to give lessons in German* **~verbesserer** m *reformer of a l.e* **~verderber** m *corrupter of a l.e* **~verein** m *li.ic society* **~vergleichung** f *comparative philology* **~verlust** m *aphasia* **~vermögen** n *faculty of speech* **~verständnis** n *natural inclination for l.es* **~verwirrung** f; babylonische ~ *Babel of tongues* **~werkzeug** n *organ of speech* **≗widrig** a *incorrect, ung.al* **~wissenschaft** f *li.ic philology, science of a l.e.* **≗wissenschaftlich** a *philological*

Spr·ache f ~/~n **A. 1.** (Sprachfähigkeit) *speech, language* || (Verständigungsart) *l.* Augen≗ etc *l. of the eyes, l. of flowers, finger-l.* || (Landes≗) *l., tongue* || ~ des Umgangs *colloquial l.* || ~ gewisser Kreise *slang* (*technical, soldiers', students'* *sl.*) || (Kauderwelsch) ⟨fam⟩ *lingo* || *cant* (*of thieves*) **2.** (Ausdrucksweise e–r P) (*vulgar, bad, plain*) *l.*) || (Redeweise) *expression, diction, style* || (Vortrag) *elocution, delivery* || (Sprechweise) (*common, legal*) *parlance* || (Aussprache) *articulation, pronunciation, accent* **3.** ⟨fig⟩ *voice* (*of conscience*) **B. alte,** neuere ~n *ancient, modern l.s* || abgehackte ~ *staccato speech* || e–e begeisterte ~ reden *to speak enthusiastically* || blumenreiche ~ *flowery style* || derbe ~ *strong l.* || *the serious tone of his father* || (S) e–e erschütternde ~ sprechen *to speak in terrible tones* || e–e flüssige ~ *a good flow of l.* || gehobene ~ *elegant l., elevated diction* || gesprochene ~ *l. in action* || die gleiche ~ sprechen *to speak a common l.*; grobe, gemeine ~ ⟨engl⟩ *billingsgate* || e–e **kühne** ~ führen *to use bold words* || lebende, tote ~n *living, dead l.s* || mundartliche ~ *dialect*(*ic speech*) || rauhe ~ *rough voice* || e–e sarkastische ~ führen *to bite one's tongue* || scheinheilig, unaufrichtige ~ *cant* (dazu *to cant*) || e–e verletzende ~ führen ⟨fam⟩ *to speak daggers* || zögernde ~ *scamping speech* **C.** e–e ~ **beherrschen** *to know a l. thoroughly, to have a ready command of a l.* || e–m die ~ benehmen *to strike a p dumb* || der ~ beraubt *bereft of speech* || die ~ wiedergewinnen *to recover one's speech* **D. an** der ~ erkennen *to know* (*a p*) *by his voice* | heraus **mit** der ~! *speak up!, out with it!*, ⟨sl⟩ *spit it out!*; er wollte nicht mit der ~ heraus *he was evasive* || frei, offen mit der ~ herausgehen *to speak out freely, openly* || nicht mit der ~ herauswollen *to beat about the bush* | s–r ~ **nach** ist er .. *to judge by his way of speaking* .. | **zur** ~ bringen *to broach, mention, introduce* (*a subject*), *to track upon* .., *to bring a th up* || zur ~ k *to come up for discussion*; *to come under review* **spr·achlich** a *linguistic* [adv *-ally*], *of language, grammatical* || ~e Entgleisung *slip of the tongue*

sprang 1. & 3. sg pret v springen

Spr·ech- ~art = –weise **~brief(gebühr** [f]) m *phonopost* **~chor** m *speaking chorus* **~fehler** m *slip of the tongue* **~film** m *talking film*; ⟨sl⟩ *talkies*, ⟨Am⟩ *squawkies* pl **~freiheit** f *freedom of speech* **~frequenz** f *vocal frequency* **~funk** m *radiotelephony, voice radio* | ~er [m] *v. r. operator*; ~gerät [n] ⟨mil⟩ *walkie-talkie* **~gesang** m *recitative* **~muschel** f ⟨telph⟩ *mouthpiece* **~oper** f *comic opera* **~-Schreibmaschine** f *talking typewriter* **~rolle** f ⟨theat⟩ *speaking part* **~stelle** f *telephone station* **~stunde** f *calling-* (⟨com⟩ *office-*, ⟨med⟩ *consultation-*)*hour* **~stundenhilfe** f *receptionist* (*to a doctor*) **~taste** f *microphone switch, push-to-talk button* **~ton** m *speaking voice* **~trichter** m *mouthpiece* **~übung** f *exercise in speaking* od *conversation* **~weise** f *speech*; *manner of speaking, accent*; gedehnte ~ *drawl* **~zimmer** n *parlour*; ⟨med⟩ *consulting-room* **spr·echbar** a *utterable* **spr·echen** vt/i [sprach/gesprochen] [h] **I.** vi **A. 1.** *to speak* (mit *to*) || (über [acc]) *to sp., talk* (*of, about*) | spricht es schon? *can it talk yet?* || sprich! *sp. up!* || ⟨wir⟩ hier spricht .. *this is* .. (*calling*), *you are tuned to* .. || **als** Gäste w ~ .. *the guest sp.ers will be* .. | ~ **wie** .. *to talk like a book*; wie im Fieber: *he sp.s as if he were rambling* | ⟨a.⟩ *to give tongue* | ich brauchte nur z ~ (um .. z ..) *I had but to ask* (*to possess her*) | z ~ k auf *to touch* (*up*)*on* || nicht ~ können *to lose one's voice* (vor .. *with fright*); *to have a lump in one's throat* || ohne z ~ (*he nodded*) *speechlessly* **2.** (sich unterhalten) *to talk* (mit *to, with*; über [acc] *about, of, over*) || (plaudern) *to chat* || ohne z ~ *unspeaking* **B. affektiert,** gespreizt ~ *to mouth one's words* | allgemein, **bildlich** gesprochen *generally, figuratively sp.ing* || ausführlich ~ über *to discuss at some length* || mit e–m deutsch ~ ⟨fig⟩ *to give a p a piece of one's mind* | **frei** ~ *to sp. extempore* od *without notes*; *to speak off the cuff* || frei heraus ~ *to sp. openly* || gebrochen deutsch ~ *to sp. broken German* || hastig ~ *to sp*(*l*)*utter* || hoch ~ *to sp. in a high tone* | **kühl** ~ *to talk distantly* | **kurz ~ mit**: *can I have a word with him for a moment?* || laut(er) ~ *to sp. loudly* (*to sp. up*); so laut man ~ kann *at the top of one's voice* || leise ~ ⟨a.⟩ *to breathe* || stockend ~ *to struggle with one's speech* || unanständig ~ *to speak grossly* || undeutlich ~ *to mumble* || viel ~ *to talk a great deal* **C. auf** → II. A. die Bosheit spricht **aus** s–m Gesicht *his malice is written in his face*; aus s–m Brief spricht Entmutigung *his l. expresses d.* | **durch**: *to sp. on the radio, telephone, wireless* | **für** jdn ~ *to put in a good word for a p*; f etw ~ *to plead* (⟨Am⟩ [pret & pp] *plead*) *for*; (beweisen) *to argue, to go to prove* || das spricht f ihn (..) *that sp.s in his favour* (*for his innocence*) || .. dafür *there is much to be said for it* || die Wahrscheinlichkeit spricht dafür, daß *probability seems to indicate that* .. || die Sn ~ f sich selbst .. *tell their own tale* | der Schein spricht **gegen** ihn *appearances are against him*; vieles spricht **gegen** diesen Plan *there are many objections to this plan* | **in** Versammlungen ~ *to address meetings* | **mit** (→ A., B.): ⟨a.⟩ *to see a p* (über *about*); ⟨Am⟩ *to visit with a p* || wir h mit dir z ~ *we have sth to say to you* || mit **sich** ~ *to argue* od *commune with o.s.* || nicht mit sich ~ l *not to listen to reason* | mit jdm ~ **über** *to discuss* .. *with a p* || über P. ~ *to talk politics* || ~ wir nicht darüber *let's be* od *keep quiet about it* | **unter** uns gesprochen *between ourselves* | **von** etw anderem ~ *to change the subject* || ~ wir nicht davon *don't mention it* || ⟨Am fam⟩ *let's don't talk about it* || er sprach v ihm als e–m gr Gelehrten *he referred to him as a great scholar* || v etw kurz, beiläufig, nebenbei ~ *just to mention a th* || es wird viel davon gesprochen *it is much talked about* od *of*; *there's* (*election*, etc) *talk in the air* || alle Welt spricht davon *it is the general talk* | **vor** Gericht ~ *to plead* | zugunsten jds ~ *to hold a brief for a p*; Beweise ~ zur Vernunft *arguments appeal to reason* **II.** vt **A. jdn** z ~ wünschen: *I must have a word with you*; *that's what I wanted to see you about*; .. **in** e–r dringenden S *to want to speak to a p on an urgent matter* || ist Herr N. z ~? *can I see* ..; f jdn nicht z ~ s *to shut the door on a p*; er ist nicht z ~ *he is not at home* (*for* od *to anyone*); *he is not to be seen*; *he is busy*; *you cannot see him now* || (nicht) gut z ~ s auf [acc] *to feel pleasantly towards* (*to be angry with*); s–e Frau ist schlecht auf ihn z ~ ⟨bes Am fam⟩ *he is in the dog-house* | sie sprachen **sich** nur kurz *they had but a few words* || wir w uns (darüber) noch ~ *we'll see about that* (*we'll discuss that later*) **B. etw** ~ *to utter, speak* || über den Rundfunk *to broadcast* || *to say a prayer*; *to pronounce a benediction* (über *upon*); das Tischgebet ~ *to say grace*; ein, das U. ~ *to pronounce judgement* **C. frei**|**~** *to acquit* || heilig|~ *to canonize* || schuldig|~ *to find* od *pronounce guilty* **D. es** spricht **sich** herum *the news spreads about* **spr·echend** a *expressive*; *eloquent* (*eyes*); *speaking* (*likeness*); *living, breathing* (*likeness, portrait*); ein ~es Zeugnis v *a telling piece of evidence of* **Spr·echer** m ~s/~ *speaker* ⟨a. parl⟩ || *orator* | *spokesman* ⟨a. film⟩ | *foreman* (*of the jury*) | ⟨wir⟩ *announcer*

Spr·ee- ~athen n = Berlin an der Spree

Spr·e(h)e f ~/~n [nwd] = ⟨orn⟩ Star

Spr·eißel m [österr n] ~s/~ = Span, Splitter

Spr·eit(deck)e f *counterpane*; *bed-cover* **spr·eiten** vt [h] *to spread out* **spr·eizbeinig** a & adv *with one's legs apart* **Spr·eize** f ~/~n ⟨arch⟩ *stay, prop*; ⟨carp⟩ *strut* **~nkopf** m *stay-head* **spr·eizen** vt [h] **1.** *to spread open, to open* || die Beine etc ~ *to plant one's legs wide apart, to straddle* (*one's legs*); *to spread out* (*one's fingers*); (Lafette, Frequenzen) *to spread* || **sich** ~ *to sprawl*; ⟨fig⟩

to give o.s. airs || sich ~ mit *to boast of* || mit ge–zten Beinen *astraddle* (.. sitzen auf *to sit straddle-legged on*) || ge–zte Reden *high-flown speeches* **2.** ⟨arch⟩ *to prop* (*up*) || **sich** ~ gegen *to strive against* **Spr·eiz- ~kamera** f ⟨phot⟩ *strut c.* **~klappe** f ⟨aero⟩ *split type landing flap* **~lafette** f *spread trail carriage* **~ring** m ⟨mot⟩ *expander* **~schritt** m ⟨mount⟩ *straddle*

×°**Spr·eizen** f ~/~ *fag, gasper* (= *cigarette*)

Spr·eng- *sprinkling; blasting;* ⟨mil⟩ *demolition* (*bomb, detail, team*) **~arbeit** f *b.g operation* **~attrappe** f *booby trap* **~bombe** f *bomb-shell,* ⟨aero⟩ *high explosive bomb* **~boot** n *one-man torpedo* **~büchse** f *primer* **~faß** n *s.g-tub* **~geschoß** n *explosive shell* od *projectile* **~gräber** m *miner* **~granate** f (*high*) *explosive shell* **~höhe** f *bursting height* **~kammer** f *mine chamber;* (Brücken≗) *bridge ch.* **~kanne** f *watering-can, -pot* **~kapsel** f *detonator, primer; percussion-, blast-cap* **~kegel** m *cone of burst* **~kessel** m *s.g-pot;* ⟨ec⟩ *holy-water vessel* **~kommando** n *bomb disposal squad, demolition detachment* **~kopf** m ⟨mil⟩ *war-head* **~körper** m *melinite petard;* fliegender ~ *robot plane* **~kraft** f → Brisanz **~kugel** f *bomb, shell* **~ladung** f *explosive* od *demolition* (⟨min⟩ *b.g*) *charge;* (Raketenflugzeug) *destructor* **~loch** n *bore* **~meister** m *explosives expert* **~mittel** n = –stoff **~niete** f *explosive rivet* **~patrone** f *expl. cartridge, planted bomb* **~pulver** n *b.g powder* **~punkt** m ⟨mil⟩ *bursting point* | ~beobachtung [f] *burst spotting;* ~höhe [f] *height of burst* **~regen** m *drizzle* **~sachverständige(r)** m = –meister **~satz** m *ignition charge* **~schnur** f *quick match* **~schuß** m *blast* **~sicherungskommando** n *d.n guard* **~stoff** m *explosive* || ~attentäter [m] *dynamiter* **~stück** n **1.** *petard* **2.** *splinter* od *fragment of a shell* || ~e [pl] *shrapnel* [koll] **~trichter** m ⟨mil⟩ *mine-crater* **~trupp** m *demolition, firing party* **~- u Zündmittel** n pl *explosives and firing devices* **~wagen** m *s.g-machine, water-(ing)-cart;* ⟨Am⟩ *water wagon* **~wedel** m *sprinkler, s.g-whisk; aspergill(um* L) **~werk** n ⟨carp⟩ *strut-frame* **~werkzeug** n *b.g-tools* pl **~wolke** f *burst* **~zünder** m *b.g-fuse* **Spr·engel** m ~s/~ **1.** *diocese* **2.** = Sprengwedel **spr·engen I.** vt [h] **1.** *to break* od *burst .. open* bzw *asunder, to force* (*a gate*); *to disrupt; to burst* (*one's bonds*) || (of water) *to burst through* (*the ice*) || *to rupture* (*a blood-vessel*) | ⟨min⟩ *to blast* (*a rock*), *to spring* (*a mine*) || *to blow up* (*a ship*) || ⟨tech⟩ *to crack* (*glass*) || ⟨bill⟩ *to spring* (*a ball*) | (Hasard) *to break* (*the bank*) **2.** *to break up, dissolve* (*a meeting*) || *to scatter, disperse* (*a crowd*) | (S) ⟨fig⟩ *to break* (*a p's heart*) || *to go beyond* (*the scope of an essay*) **3.** *to drive* (*a p to a place*) || *to jump* (*one's horse across a hedge*) **II.** vt/i [h] *to sprinkle* (*water, linen*) || *to water* (*a street, garden*) **III.** vi [s] **1.** *to ride* (*at*) *full speed, to gallop* | auf [acc]: *to dash at the enemy* | aus: *to come galloping through* (*a gate*) | über: *to jump, take* (*a hedge*) **2. es** hat nur gesprengt *it only drizzled* **Spr·enger** m ~s/~ (Wasser≗) *sprinkler;* ⟨mil, min⟩ *blaster* **Spr·engung** f ~/~en *bursting open, blasting, demolition,* etc; *explosion* | *dispersal, break-up* | *sprinkling* **Spr·enkel** m ~s/~ **1.** (Falle) *springe, snare; noose* **2.** (Fleck) *speck, dot, speckle, spot* | ≗**ig** a *speckled* etc **spr·enkeln** vt [h] *to sprinkle, dapple, fleck, speckle, spot, dot; splash* (*paper*) || ⟨bookb⟩ *to marble* **Spreu** f ~/ *chaff* || wie ~ im Winde *like ch. before the w.* || die ~ v Weizen scheiden *to sift the chaff from the wheat* ⟨a. fig⟩ || ⟨fig⟩ *dead wood* (= *waste, refuse*) **~blättchen** n ⟨bot⟩ *palea* **~gebläse** n ⟨agr⟩ *chaff-blower* **~kasten** m *chaff-tub* **~sack** m *chaff-bag* ≗**tragend** a *paleaceous*

sprich [imp] v sprechen **Spr·ichwort** n *proverb, byword* || (gelehrtes) *adage,* (*proverbial*) *saying* || wie es im ~ heißt *as the saying is* || z ~ w *to become a by-word* || ≗er spielen *to act proverbs* od *charades* **spr·ichwörtlich** a *proverbial* || ~ s *to be a proverb* od *by-word* (wegen *for*)

Spr·iegel m ~s/~ *tarpaulin frame; cart-tilt holder* || *hoop, bow; reed-work* (*of walls*)

spr·ießen vi [sproß/gesprossen] [s] *to sprout,* ⟨a.⟩ ~ l, *shoot* || (keimen) *to germinate* || ⟨fig⟩ *to thrive* **Spriet** n ~(e)s/~e ⟨mar⟩ *sprit*

Spring m ~s/~e ⟨mar⟩ *sheer* (*of the deck*) (→ a. Sprung–) **~anker** m ⟨mar⟩ *kedge(-anchor)* **~ball** m (Spielzeug m. Griff od/u zum Draufsitzen und Hopsen) *jump ball; space hopper;* ⟨Am fam⟩ *hoppedy-hop* **~bein** n ⟨ent⟩ *saltatorial leg* **~bock** m ⟨zoo⟩ *springbok, Cape antelope* **~brunnen** m *fountain, water-spout* **~faden** m ⟨bot⟩ *elater* **~flut** f *spring-tide* **~fuß** m ⟨zoo⟩ *saltatorial foot* **~hase** m *jumping-hare* **~hengst** m *stallion* **~insfeld** m *whipper-snapper, giddy young fellow, kicker, harum-scarum* || (wildes Mädchen) *romp* **~käfer** m *leaping-beetle* **~körner** n pl *seeds* pl *of the caper-spurge* **~kraft** f *springiness, elasticity* **~kraut** n ⟨bot⟩ *touch-me-not* ≗**lebendig** a → quick– **~maus** f ⟨zoo⟩ *jerboa* **~pferd** n *jumper* **~prozession** f *dancing procession* **~quell(e** f) m *spring, fountain, well* **~schwanz** m ⟨ent⟩ *springtail* **~seil** n *skipping-*(⟨Am⟩ *jumping-*) *rope* **~spinne** f ⟨ent⟩ *saltigrade* **~stab** m, **~stange** f, **~stock** m (*jumping-*), *leaping-pole* **~tau** n = –seil || ⟨mar⟩ *slip-rope* **~übung** f *jumping-, vaulting-exercise* **~wasser** n *spring-water* **~wurzel** f ⟨bot⟩ *caper-spurge* **~zeit** f *coupling-time;* ⟨mar⟩ *springs* pl **spr·ingen** vi [sprang/gesprungen] [h & s] **A. 1.** *to spring, leap* || (in e–m Satz) *to jump, bound* || (hüpfen) *to skip* ⟨a. comp⟩ *frisk, gambol* || (mit Schwung) *to vault* | (tauchen) *to dive, plunge* | ⟨dial⟩ ~ *to run, hasten;* gesprungen k *to come running along* | **sich** müde ~ *to jump, run till one is tired* | ⟨fig⟩ ihr Herz sprang .. *gave a jump* (vor F. *with joy*) **2.** (v Wasser etc) *to gush, spout, flow* || die Wasser ~ l *to make the fountains play* **3.** *to copulate* || *to cover* (*the mare*) **4.** (bersten) *to burst, crack, break* || *a string has snapped* || *my bat is* od *has sprung* || *the glass flew* od *cracked* || *the mine exploded* || mir will der Kopf ~ *I have a splitting headache* **B.** etw ~ **lassen** ⟨fam⟩ *to stand treat* || *to spend* (*money freely*) || *to stand* (*a bottle of wine*) || *to spring* (*a mine*) || vgl A. 2. **C.** er sprang **an** ihre Seite *he fell in at her s.*; schleunigst an den Straßenrand ~ *to make a dash for ..* | **auf:** *to jump on to,* ⟨Am⟩ *to hop* (*a train*) || *a car mounted* (*the pavement*) || *to vault on* (*a horse*) | **aus**: *to leap out of* (*bed*) || *to jump down from* (*the saddle*) || *blood flowed from* (*his wound*) || *to fling o.s. out of* (*the window*) || aus dem Stein ~ Funken *sparks are struck from the st.* | **in**: *to get into* (*the saddle*) || ⟨fig⟩ *to leap to* (*the eye*) (= *to be obvious, self-evident*) || in die Höhe ~ *to bob* od *bounce up* | es springt nichts dabei **heraus** *there is not much in it* | **über**: *to jump, vault over, to leap, take* (*a ditch*), *to clear* (*a wall*) || über die Klinge ~ l *to put to the sword* | **von**: *to jump off* (*a horse*) (= *to alight*); (Preis etc) *to jump from .. to ..* | **zu**: *to drop to* (*earth*) || zur Seite ~ *to jump aside* || zu e–m hin|~ *to run up to a p* **spr·ingend** [pres. p. & a] *leaping,* etc || *bouncing* (*ball*), gut ~er Ball *good bouncer* || ⟨her⟩ *salient, rampant* || *the salient* (= *main*) *point* **Spr·inger** m ~s/~ *leaper, vaulter, acrobat;* ⟨a. hors⟩ *jumper* | ⟨chess⟩ *knight* | ~anzug [m], ~kombination [f] ⟨Ger-Zivil-aero⟩ *jump suit* ⟨a. Feind- mil⟩; → Kampfanzug ⟨Ger mil⟩

Sprint m ~s/~e ⟨sport⟩ *sprint*

Sprit m ~(e)s~e ⟨tech⟩ *spirit, alcohol;* ⟨mot⟩ *petrol;* ⟨Am⟩ *gas(oline)* || ⟨sl mot⟩ *juice,* ⟨aero⟩ *gravy* **~fabrik** f *distillery* ≗**haltig,** ≗**ig** a *alcoholic, spirituous, brandied* (*wine*) **~kanister** m ⟨sl⟩ *jerrycan*

Spr·itz- ~arbeit f *fireman's work* || ⟨bookb, etc⟩ *marbled work* **~bad** n *douche, shower-bath*

~beutel m → –sack **~bewurf** m ⟨arch⟩ *rough-cast* **~brett** n *dash-, splash-board* **~büchse** f *squirt, syringe* **~decke** f *canvas* **~düse** f (*rose-*)*spray*; ⟨mot⟩ *spraying nozzle* °**~fahrt** f *trip, jaunt, outing, junket*, ⟨mot⟩ *spin* **~feuer** n *spray-fire* **~flakon** n *scent-squirt* **~flasche** f ⟨chem⟩ *wash--bottle* **~fleck** m *splash* **~gebackene(s)** n ⟨cul⟩ *fancies* pl **≗gießen** vt [h] *to die-cast* **~kanne** f [bes Sw] *watering-can* **~kuchen** m *fritter*; ⟨bes Am⟩ *cruller* **~lappen** m ⟨mot⟩ *fender-* od *mud--flap* **~leder** n *splash(ing)-leather* **~loch** n (des Wals) *spout-hole* **~malerei** f *spatter-work* **~pistole** f *spray(ing* ⟨Am⟩) *gun* **~regen** m *drizzle* **~sack** m ⟨cul⟩ *piping-, forcing-bag* **~schutz** m ⟨mot⟩ = –lappen ‖ [abstr] *splash protection*, (S) *sp. guard* ⟨mot⟩ **~tour** f = –fahrt **~vergaser** m *spray--carburettor* **~wasser** n *spray*; *splash-water* **~-wässerung** f *washing with jets of w.* **Spr·itze** f ~/~n *squirt, syringe* ⟨a. med⟩; ⟨übtr med⟩ *injection*; ⟨fam⟩ *shot* ⟨a. übtr sex⟩ (*give her a shot*) ‖ (Feuer≗) *fire-engine, hose* ‖ (Luftschutz-≗) *stirrup pump* ‖ ⟨fam⟩ = Spritzfahrt | ⟨fig fam⟩ an der ~ *at one's post* ‖ *ahead* ‖ Mann an der ~ *ring-leader* **spr·itzen I.** vt [h] *to spirt, spurt, spout, syringe, squirt*; *sprinkle*; *flick* ‖ (mit Wasser, Schmutz) *to splash* | *to play* (mit .. *the fire-engine, with the hose*) | ⟨med⟩ *to inject* ‖ (Klistier) *to use the enema* **II.** vi [h & s] *to sp(l)utter* ‖ *to throw water* ‖ (of boiling water) *to spit* ‖ (v d. Feuerspritze etc) *to play* ‖ (Schmutz, Meer) *to splash* ‖ (Regen) *to spatter* ‖ (Feder) *to splutter* ‖ (Wal) *to spout* | **~dheiß** *piping hot* **Spr·itzen- ~haus** n *fire-station* **~ladung** f *syringe-*(etc)*ful* **~leute** [pl v folg.] *firemen* **~mann** m *fireman* **~meister** m *head fireman* **~röhre** f *tube of a fire--engine* **~schlauch** m *hose* (*of a fire-engine*) **Spr·itzer** m ~s/~ **1.** (P) *squirter* etc **2.** *splash* ‖ (Klecks) *dab* ‖ ⟨fam⟩ *spatter* (*of rain*) **spr·itzig** a *bubbling* ‖ *effervescent* (*wine*) ‖ *snappy*; *sparkling* (*dialogue*) ‖ ⟨fig⟩ *buoyant, jaunty* (*p*)

Spr·öde f ~n/~n *prude* **spr·öde** a *brittle* ⟨Am⟩ *brash*; *short* (*iron*) ‖ *parched, chapped* (*skin*); *rough* (*hair*) | *unyielding*; *stubborn* (⟨a.⟩ P) (⟨tech⟩ *material*) | (P) *demure*; *reserved, shy* ‖ *prim, prudish, coy* (*girl*) ‖ ~ tun *to affect shyness, to be prudish* | ≗ [f] (*to play the*) *prude*; ⟨mil sl⟩ *huffy* **Spr·ödigkeit** f ~/ *brittleness* ‖ *stubbornness* ‖ *reserve* ‖ *coyness* ‖ *shyness* ‖ *prudery*; *prudishness* | ~sverhalten [n] ⟨eth⟩ *coyness behavio(u)r*

Sproß m –sses/–sse ⟨bot⟩ *sprout, shoot*; *germ* | ⟨fig⟩ *offspring, descendant, scion* (*a lineal sc. of Otto I*) **~pilze** f pl *gemmiparous fungi* **~silbe** f *excrescent syllable* **sproß** 3. sg pret v sprießen **Spr·osse** f ~/~n (Leiter≗) *step, rung, round, rundle* ‖ (Fenster≗) *cross-bar* ‖ (Geweih≗) *prong, branch, tine, point* **spr·ossen I.** vi [h & s] = sprießen **II.** ≗ n ~s/ *pullulation* ⟨a. übtr⟩ **Spr·ossen- ~bier** n *spruce-beer* **~fichte** f *spruce--fir* **~kohl** m *broccoli* **~tanne** f *hemlock(-spruce)* **~tau** n *knotted climbing-rope* **≗treibend** a *proliferous* **~wand** f ⟨gym⟩ *wall-bars* **Spr·osser** m ~s/~ ⟨orn⟩ (*bastard*) *thrush-nightingale* **Spr·öß-ling** m ~(e)s/~e = Sproß; ⟨for a.⟩ *chat, browse* | ⟨fig⟩ *chip, sprout*; mein erster ~ *my first-born* ‖ ein hoffnungsvoller ~ *a young hopeful* **Spr·ossung** f *proliferation*

Spr·otte f ~/~n ⟨ich⟩ (Kieler) ~ (*Kiel*) *sprat*

Spruch m ~(e)s/≗e *saw, aphorisme* (*a.sm*), *saying, dictum*; *maxim*; *passage, text* | ⟨jur⟩ *sentence*; *verdict, judgment* | (*arbitrator's*) *award* | ≗e Salomonis *Proverbs* pl *of Solomon* | e–n ~ fällen *to pronounce a sentence, to give a verdict, to make an award* ‖ ⟨fam⟩ ≗e m *to brag* **≗artig** a *a.stic* **~band** n *streamer*; ⟨paint⟩ *banderol*; ⟨arch⟩ *scroll*; ⟨arts, etc⟩ *banner* ⟨a. pol⟩ **~be-hörde** f, **~kammer** f *Court of Arbitration*; *appeal board*; *denazification panel* **Haupt≗** *d. court* **~buch** n *book of a.sms* **~dichter** m *a.st, gnomic poet* **≗mäßig** a *a.stic sententious* **≗reich** a *sententious* **≗reif** a *ready* od *fit for judgment* ‖ noch nicht ~ *not yet fully investigated* **~reim** m *rhymed a.sm* **~weisheit** f *a.sms* pl *proverbial wisdom* od *philosophy*

Spr·udel m ~s/~ *bubbling source* ‖ ⟨fam⟩ *soda-water* ‖ ⟨med⟩ (*hot*) *springs* pl ‖ ⟨fig⟩ *overflow* (*of words* etc) **~bude** f ⟨Am fam⟩ *soda-jerk* **~kopf** m *hotspur* **~quelle** f *boiling* od *bubbling spring* **~salz** n *mineral salt* **~stein** m ⟨min⟩ *thermal tuff* **~wasser** n *bubbling water* **spr·udeln** vi **1.** [s] *to bubble*; *gush, spout* (*forth*) (aus *from*) ‖ es sprudelt v s–n Lippen *he is bubbling over* (*with mirth, wit*, etc) **2.** [h] *to boil up* ‖ (Getränk) *to effervesce*, ⟨fam⟩ *fizz* ‖ (im Sprechen) *to splutter* **3. ~d** *purling, murmuring* (*brook*) ‖ *bubbling* (*merriment*) ‖ *ebullient* (*personality*) ‖ *exuberant* (*spirits*) ‖ *fizzy* (*drink*) ‖ ~e Laune *flow of spirits*; in ~er L. *brimming over with good humour* **Spr·udler** m ~s/~ *splutterer* **Spr·üh- ~auge** n *flashing eye* **~feuer** n *sparkling fire* **~funke(n)** m *flying spark* **~regen** m *drizzling* od *mizzly rain*; *drizzle*; *Scotch mist*; ⟨mar⟩ *spray* **~teufel** m (Feuerwerk) *devil* ‖ ⟨fig⟩ *spitfire* **~trocknen** n *spray drying* **~welle** f *white-crested wave* **spr·ühen 1.** vt [h] *to shower, to sprinkle in small drops* ‖ *to spit* (*fire*) ‖ Geist ~ *to sparkle with wit* ‖ *her eyes flashed fire, scintillated anger* **2.** vi [s & h] *to emit sparks* ‖ ⟨fig⟩ *to flash, sparkle* (vor [dat] *with*) **3.** [imps] (of rain) *to drizzle* | **~d** a *coruscating* ‖ *brilliant* ‖ ~er Witz ⟨a.⟩ *blaze of wit*

Sprung m ~(e)s/≗e **A. 1.** (Riß) *chink, fissure* ‖ (in e–m Edelstein) *flaw* ‖ (in e–m Topf etc) *crack* ‖ ⟨min⟩ *fault* ‖ die Tasse hat e–n ~ .. *is cracked* **2.** *leap* ‖ ⟨comp⟩ *branch*; *transfer of control* ‖ (Satz) *bound, jump* ‖ aufs Pferd *vault* ‖ aus dem Stand *standing jump* ‖ *plunge* (in *into*) ‖ ⟨fig⟩ .. ins Dunkle *a leap in the dark*; den ~ in die Ehe wagen ⟨fam⟩ *to go over the top*, → *top* I. A. 2. ‖ mit Anlauf *running jump*; *flying bound*; ⟨sport⟩ Drei≗ *hop, step, and jump* ‖ Freuden≗ *caper* ‖ ⟨mil⟩ (z Angriff) *dash, rush*; ~ auf – marsch, marsch! *up, at the double!*; in gr ≗en ⟨tact⟩ *in longer moves* | ⟨übtr⟩ *spring* (*astonishing sp.s*); *sudden transition*; der ~ nach vorn *the great leap forward* ⟨a. pol⟩ ‖ ⟨gram⟩ *anacoluthon* ‖ ⟨mar⟩ *sheer* (*of a deck*) ‖ ⟨zoo⟩ *coition* ‖ ⟨hunt⟩ ~ Rehe *herd of deer* | ⟨fig⟩ [pl] *gambades* (eig ⟨hors⟩ Luft≗), *pranks* **B. nur** ein ~ (bis ..) *within a stone's throw* (*to* ..) ‖ e–n ~ m *to* (*make* od *take a*) *jump*; ⟨aero⟩ *to zoom* (*a plane* mit ..); ⟨fig⟩ *to have a big promotion* ‖ ≗e m *to frisk, gambol* ‖ d. N. **macht** k–e ≗e *Nature plays no tricks* ‖ gr ≗ m *to launch out* ‖ damit kann er k–e gr ≗e m *he can't allow h.s. any extravagances with that* ‖ den ~ in die Ehe wagen ⟨fam⟩ *to go over the top* ⟨eig mil⟩ **C.** jdn **auf** e–n ~ besuchen *to step round to a p, to pay a p a flying visit* ‖ ⟨fam⟩ jdm auf die ≗e helfen *to set a p right* od *on his legs, to give a p a lift, to assist a p's memory* ‖ ich komme auf e–n ~ mit durch .. ⟨sl⟩ *I'll lope you across the Park* ‖ wieder auf s–e alten ≗e k *to fall back into one's old ways* ‖ sich auf die ≗e m *to cut and run* ‖ auf dem ~e stehen *to be on the jump* od *point* (*of*), *to be ready* (*to*) | **hinter** jds ≗e k *to find out a p's tricks* | **im** ~e *leaping*; (in Eile) *all on a hop* ‖ ⟨mil⟩ in ≗en vorgehen *to leap-frog* ‖ in vollem ~e *at full speed* | **mit** e–m ~e *at one jump* ⟨a. fig⟩ | ⟨zoo⟩ es duckt sich **zum** ~e *it crouches for its leap* **~bein** *ankle-bone* **≗bereit** a *on the pounce* **~bock** m (Schafzucht) *ram* **~brett** n ⟨gym⟩ *spring-board*, ⟨swim⟩ *diving board* ‖ ⟨fig⟩ *stepping-stone* (z *to*) **~deckel** m *watch-cap* | ~uhr [f] *hunter* **~feder** f *spring* | ~matratze [f] *sp.-mattress* **~garten** m: durch den ~ nehmen *to put* (*a horse*) *through his jumps* **~gelenk** n *ankle joint*; ⟨hors⟩ *hock* **~riemen** m (Hosen≗) *strap*; ⟨hors⟩ *martingale*

~schanze f *ski-jump, spring-board* **~schlag** m ⟨ten⟩ *half-volley* **~stoß, ~tritt** ⟨ftb⟩ *drop-kick*; e–n ~ m *to d.-k.* **~taste** f ⟨comp⟩ "*set skip*" *key* **~tuch** n (Feuerwehr) *net* **≗weise** adv *by leaps* (*and bounds*); ⟨mil⟩ *by leap-frog movement*; ~ vorgehen *to l.-f.*; ~ vorziehen *to march by bounds* ‖ ⟨fig⟩ *by fits and starts* **~weite** f *leaping--range* | **≗elung** f ⟨ceram⟩ → Krakelee **spr·ung-haft** a *jumpy*; *volatile, jerky* (⟨a.⟩ *style*); *erratic* (*mind*); *scrappy* (*thinking*) | **~igkeit** f *jumpiness*; → plötzlich

Sp·ucke f ~/ *spittle, saliva* ‖ °da bleibt mir die ~ weg! *I'm flabbergasted* od *nonplussed, it fairly takes my breath away* **sp·ucken** vt/i [h] *to spit*; ⟨mot⟩ *to chug, stutter* ‖ °jdm auf den Kopf (in die Suppe) [ins Gesicht] ~ *to haul a p over the coals* (*to put grit in a p's oiler*) [*to spit a p in the eye*] ‖ °gr Bogen ~ ⟨sl⟩ *to shoot one's mouth off* ‖ °der ge–kte Vater *the very spit of his father* **Sp·ucknapf** m *spittoon*, ⟨Am⟩ *cuspidor*

Spuk m ~(e)s/~e (Aufruhr) *hubbub, uproar, confusion* | *witchcraft* | (Gespenst) *spook, ghost, spectre, apparition* ‖ es ist ~ dabei *there is sth uncanny about it* **~geist** m *hobgoblin* **~geschichte** f *ghost-story* **~stunde** f *witching hour* **sp·uken** vi [h] *to make* (⟨fam⟩ *kick up*) *a row* | *to appear*; *to haunt a place* (an, in) | ⟨fig⟩ der Gedanke spukt in s–m Kopf *he is haunted by the idea* | **es** spukt hier *this place is haunted* ‖ es spukt bei ihm im Kopfe *he is not quite right in his head* **Spuker·ei** f ~/~en *apparitions, ghosts* pl; *haunting* **sp·uk-haft** a *uncanny, ghostly*

Sp·ul- **~baum** m *spindle-tree* **~draht** m *spool--wire* **~maschine** f *bobbin-, jack-frame* **~rad** n *spool(ing)-wheel* **~vorrichtung** f = Spuler **~wurm** m *belly-worm* **~würmer** m pl ⟨zoo⟩ *ascarides* pl

Sp·ül- **~abort** m → –klosett **~anlage** f, **~ap-parat** m ⟨tech⟩ *rinser* **~bad** n ⟨tech⟩ *rinsing solution*; → Spülung **~becken** n *kitchen sink* **~bohrer** m ⟨min⟩ *scavengering drill* **~eimer** m *rinsing-tub, slop-pail* **~einrichtung** f *flushing de-vice*; *rinsing equipment* **~faß** n *r.g-t.* **~frau** f *scullery-maid* ‖ (in Gasthäusern) *washer-up* ‖ (Abort–) **~kasten** m (*flushing*) *cistern* (*of W. C.*) **~kessel** m *r.g-vessel* **~klosett** n *flush toilet* od *lavatory, water-closet* (*W. C.*) **~küche** f *scullery* **~lappen** m *dish-cloth* **~leitung** f *scavenging duct* **~magd** f *scullery-maid* **~napf** m *r.g-bowl* ‖ (für Teegeschirr) *slop-basin* **~öl** n *flushing oil* **~stein** m *sink* **~wasser** n *dish-water*; *rinsing w.* ‖ *water for r.g* ‖ *sloppy water* ‖ ⟨fig⟩ (Bier) *hog-wash, belly-wash* ‖ ⟨school sl⟩ (Tee, etc) *wash* **~wir-kung** f ⟨mot⟩ *washing action* **sp·ülen I.** vt [h] *to wash* (*up*) (*crockery*); *to rinse* (*glasses, linen, one's mouth*); *to cleanse* (*wool*) **II.** vi/t *to wash* (*against .., ashore*) **Sp·ülicht** n ~(e)s/~e *dish--water*; *rinsings, wastes*, ⟨fam⟩ *slops* pl ‖ (f Schweine) *swill* **Sp·ülung** f ~/~en *washing*; *rinsing*; *cleansing*; ⟨med, sex⟩ *irrigation* ‖ (W. C.) *flushing*; (S) *flush-pipe*

Sp·ule f ~/~n *reel*; ⟨weav⟩ *spool*; ⟨spin⟩ *bob-bin*; ⟨phot⟩ *spool* ‖ (Feder≗) *quill* ‖ ⟨el⟩ *coil* ‖ ⟨wir⟩ *honeycomb* | **~nabstand** m ⟨el⟩ *coil spacing* **~nkern** m *bobbin core* **sp·ulen** vt [h] *to spool, to reel* **Sp·uler** m ~s/~ ⟨weav⟩ (P) *winder* ‖ (d. Nähmaschine) *bobbin-winder*

Spund m ~(e)s/≗e *bung* ‖ *plug*; *vent-peg* ‖ ⟨carp⟩ *feather, tongue* ‖ ⟨met⟩ *shutter* **~aus-treiber** m *bung-starter* **~bohle** f (Wasserbau≗) *sheeting pile* **~bohrer** m *b.-hole borer* **~hobel** m *tongue-plane* **~lappen** m *b. flap* **~loch** n *b.-hole*; *vent* **~pfahl** m → –bohle **~wand** f *pile planking* | ~eisen [n] *steel pile*; ~kasten [m] *sh.g pile casing* **~zapfen** m *b.* **~zieher** m *b.-pick* **sp·unden,** ≗ vt [h] *to bung* ‖ ⟨carp⟩ *to groove, fit, join* | ≗ [n] ⟨carp⟩ *grooving and tonguing* **Sp·undung** f (mit Nut u Feder) *match-joint*

Spur f ~/~en **A.** *trace, footprint, footstep* ‖ (fortlaufende ~) *track* ⟨a. rec, comp⟩ ‖ (Fährte) *trail* ‖ ⟨hunt⟩ *scent* ‖ (Verbrecher≗) *lead* | (Wagen≗) *rut*; ⟨mot⟩ → Fahr≗; ⟨rail⟩ *track* ‖ ⟨mar⟩ *wake* | *remains* pl ‖ ⟨fig⟩ *trace, vestige, hint, tinge, mark, sign, shadow*; *a suspicion* (*of dust*) **B. frische** ~ *hot scent, warm trail* ‖ alte Fuchs≗ *stale line* ‖ falsche ~ *false scent, wrong track* ‖ Hasen≗ *trod* ‖ °**keine** ~! *not a bit!, not at all!* ‖ ⟨fam⟩ k–e ~ v *not an idea, trace* etc *of*; *nothing of* (*emotion*), *not a touch of* (*sense*); *no show of* (*a bud, of reason*); *no breath of* (*scandal*); *not a streak* (od *the ghost*) *of* (*humour*); *no .. whatever* ‖ **ohne** (die geringste) ~ v Erregung *without a trace of emotion* | ⟨mot⟩ linke (rechte) ~ *right-(left-)hand* (*traffic*) *lane* | die letzte ~ v *the last remnant of* **C.** e–e ~ **durchlaufen** l ⟨rec⟩ *to cover a track* ‖ jds **~ folgen** *to tread in a p's footsteps*; *to run in the wake of a car* ‖ **~ halten** ⟨mot⟩ *to stay in lane* ‖ Hinterlassen v ~en *tracking effect* ‖ jds ~ verfolgen *to track a p*; (Polizei) *to play the leads* ‖ tiefe ~en hinterlassen ⟨übtr⟩ *to have far-reaching repercussions* ‖ s–e ~en verwischen *to cover up one's tracks* **D. auf** die ~ bringen *to put on the scent*; (P) *to put a p on the trail* (*of*) ‖ jdm auf die ~ helfen ⟨fig⟩ *to give to a p a clue* ‖ [dat] auf die ~ k *to get on the track* (*of*); ⟨fig⟩ (e–r S) *to trace a th, to get wind* od *scent* (*of a th*), *to find a clue* (*to a th*) | jdm scharf auf der ~ s *to be hot on a p's trail* | **von** der ~ abbringen *to throw off the scent* ‖ von der ~ abk *to lose track* **~erweiterung** f *ga(u)ge widen-ing of track* **~haltigkeit** f ⟨mot⟩ *track-hold-ing properties* pl **~kranz** m *flange* **~lage** f ⟨rec⟩ *standards* **≗los** a *trackless* ‖ ~ an jdm vor-übergehen *to leave no mark upon a p* ‖ ~ ver-schwinden ⟨fig⟩ *to vanish* (*into space*), *to dis-appear without leaving a trace* **~planstellwerk** n ⟨rail⟩ *geographical circuitry* **~tafeln** f pl ⟨mil⟩ *treadway* N **~umschaltung** f ⟨rec⟩ *track change* **~weite** f ⟨rail⟩ *track ga(u)ge* **Sp·ür-** **≗bar** a *noticeable* ‖ ⟨übtr⟩ *considerable, marked* (*dif-ference*) **~gerät** n ⟨at, chem, biol⟩ *detector* **~hund** m *track-hound*; (P) ⟨fig bes Am⟩ *sleuth* ‖ (kl) *beagle* ‖ (Vorstehhund) *setter* ‖ ⟨fig⟩ *spy* **~sinn** m; **~nase** f *scent, flair* Fr; *tracking nose* °**-nase** ⟨fig⟩ *inquisitive p* **sp·üren I.** vt [h] (empfinden) *to feel, notice* ‖ ~ Sie Linderung? *do you feel easier?* ‖ (wahrnehmen) *to perceive*; *to find* (*little of ..*) ‖ ⟨hunt⟩ *to scent, trace, track* ⟨a. fig⟩; *to follow by the scent* ‖ zu ~ bek *to feel the pinch of ..* **II.** vi [h] (**nach**) *to track* (*game*); *to be in quest* (*of*), *to search* (*for*) **sp·uren** vi [h] ⟨ski⟩ *to lay a track* (*trail*) ‖ *to follow a* (od *the same*) *track, to keep track* ‖ °*to obey* | ≗ n (⟨aero⟩ & Rakete) (*automatic*) *tracking* **≗element** n *trace(r) element*; ⟨at a.⟩ *tracer* **≗finder** m ⟨at⟩ *radio(active) tracer* **sp·urenhaft** a *vestigial* **..spurig** a: schmal~ *nar-row-gauge* (*railway*)

Sp·urt m ~s/~e ⟨bes sport⟩ *spurt* | **≗en** vi [s] *to* (*make a*) *spurt*

sp·uten, sich [h] *to make haste, to hurry up*, ⟨fam⟩ *to look sharp*, ⟨sl⟩ *to get a move on*

Sp·utnik m ~s/~s [Russ] ⟨fam⟩ *baby moon*

Sp·utum n ~s/ [L] *expectoration*

st! *hush! hist! peace!*

Staat 1. m ~(e)s/~en *body politic*; *state* (oft: *S.*: der ~ N *the S. of N.* ‖ *S. and Church, the United States* [sg konstr]) *the U.S. follows its own policy* ‖ abhängiger ~ *client s.*; v ~s wegen *for reasons of s.* **2.** ~ [m] ~(e)s/ (Aufwand) *pomp, show, parade, state* ‖ *fine clothes* ‖ *best ths* ‖ ⟨fig⟩ *panoply*; *trappings* pl ‖ (Putz) *finery*; ⟨fam⟩ *toggery*; *war paint* | ~ m *to cut a dash, to show off, to live in great style* ‖ mit etw ~ m *to make a show* od *parade of a th, to parade a th* ‖ in vollem ~ *in full dress* (⟨fam⟩ *fig*) ‖ damit kann man nicht viel ~ m *there's not much to boast of* | es ist ein wahrer ~ *it is really splendid* **St·aaten-**

~beschreibung f *political geography* **~bund** m *confederation, confederacy* **~kunde** f *politics* **~los** a *without a nationality; stateless* (⟨a.⟩ ~e[r]) **~losigkeit** f *statelessness* **~system** n *political system* **st·aatlich** [a] *state* (*help*); *public* (*institutions*); *maintained* (*school*); *state-operated* (*industries*); *political* (*life*) || ~e Gesinnung *citizenship*; ~e Tugenden [pl] *good c.*; ~e Wohlfahrt *public assistance* | [adv] ~ unterstützt *state-assisted* (*theatre*) **~erseits** [adv] *on the part of the state* **Staats-** [in comp] *government, state; national, public* | ⟨fig, fam⟩ *prize .., egregious ..* **~abgaben** f pl *g.t taxes* **~akten** f pl *st. papers* od *records* pl **~aktion** f *st. proceedings* pl; (*to make a*) *federal case* (*out of a th*) **~allmacht** f (wirtschaftl.) *statism* **~amt** n *g.t appointment, public office* **~angehörige(r)** m *subject of a st.* || (deutscher) ~ *German subject* **~angehörigkeit** f *n.lity*; *n.l status* || die ~ erwerben (verlieren) *to become* (*de*)-*naturalized* **~angelegenheit** f *matter of st., st.-affair* **~angestellte(r)** m **~anleihe** f *g.t-loan*; konsolidierte ~ *consols* pl, ⟨fam⟩ *the Threes* (= *the three-per-cents*; später $2^1/_2$%) **~annuitäten** f pl *pub. annuities* pl **~anstellung** f *pub. appointment* **~anwalt** m *pub. prosecutor* | ~schaft [f] *pub. pros.'s office* **~anzeiger** m *official gazette* **~archiv** n *Record Office* **~aufsicht** f *st. control* **~auftrag** m *g.t contract* **~ausgaben** f pl *pub. expenditure* **~bahn** f *st. railway* **~bank(rott** m) f *n.l bank-*(*ruptcy*) **~beamte(r)** m *civil servant, st.-official* **~begräbnis** n *st. funeral* **~betrieb** m *st.-run factory* **~besitz** m; in ~ *st.-owned* **~besuch** m *st. visit* **~bibliothek** f *n.l library* **~bürger** m *citizen*; Heranbildung v guten ~n *development of good citizenship* | ~kunde [f] *civics* pl [a. sg konstr]; ~lich [a] *political, public, civic* (*rights*); ~schaft [f] *citizenship, n.lity* **~d·ame** f *fine lady* **~degen** m *sword of parade* **~diener** = ~beamte(r) **~dienst** m *civil service* **~eigen** a *st.-owned* **~eigentum** n *g.t* od *pub. property* **~einkünfte** f pl *pub. revenue* od *income, inland revenue* [sg] **~eisenbahn** f = ~bahn **~examen** n *g.t examination* **~feind** [m] No 1 *public enemy No 1* **~feindlich** a *subversive* **~finanzen** pl *finances* pl *of the St.* **~form** f *form of g.t; polity* **~gebäude** n *pub.* bzw *magnificent building* || *pol.l structure* **~gedanke** m *conception of* (*st.-idea* od) *a nation, st.-i.* od *c.* **~gefährlich** a *pernicious to the st.* **~gefangene(r)** m, **~gefängnis** n; **~geheimnis** n *st.-prisoner, -prison,* ⟨Am⟩ *penitentiary-secret* **~gelder** n pl *pub. money, st. funds* pl **~gerichtshof** m ⟨nazi⟩ *political tribunal* **~geschäft** n *state-affair, -business* || die ~e führen *to carry on the government* **~geschichte** f *pol.l history of a state* **~gesetz** n *law of a state, statute-law* **~gewalt** f *supreme power*; alle ~ geht v Volk aus *all st.-authority emanates from the people* **~gläubiger** m *pub. creditor* **~grundgesetz** n *pol. constitution* **~gut** n *pub. property* **~handbuch** n *red book, court calendar* **~handelsländer** n pl (Ostblock) *st. trade countries* **~haushalt** m *administration of revenue* || *finances* pl *of the state, ways and means* pl | ~anschlag [m] *budget* **~hilfe** f *state-aid* **~hoheit** f *sovereignty* **~interesse** n *pol. interest* **~kalender** m *state calendar* **~kanzlei** f *state chancellery* **~kanzler** m *Lord-Chancellor* (*of a state*) **~kapital** n *pub. funds* od *stocks* pl **~kasse** f *Treasury,* (*Public*) *Exchequer* **~kirche** f *state church*; ⟨engl⟩ *Established Ch., Ch. of England* **~kleid** n *robe of state* **~klug** a *politic, diplomatic* **~klugheit** f *policy, statecraft* **~körper** m *body politic* **~kosten** pl; auf ~ *at pub. expense, by state-funds* °**~krippe** f *state employment* **~kunst** f *statesmanship, politics* pl, *statecraft* **~kutsche** f *state-coach* **~leben** n *pol.l life* **~lehre** f *science of politics* **~mann** m *statesman, politician* **~männisch** a *statesmanlike*; ~e Befähigung *or* Kunst *statesmanship* **~maschine** f *state-machinery* **~minister** m *minister; Secretary of State* **~monopol** n *government monopoly* **~oberhaupt** n *head of the state, sovereign* **~ökonomie** f *pol.l economy* **~papier** n *government bond*; pl *pub. funds, stocks*; (konsilidierte) *consols* pl **~polizei** f, Geheime ~ ⟨nazi⟩ *secret police* **~polizist** m ⟨Am⟩ *trooper* **~prozeß** m *state-trial* **~prüfung** f *government examination* **~raison** f *reason of state* **~rat** m *Privy Council* [pl konstr] || (P) *Privy Counsellor* **~recht** n *pol.l law* | **~lich** [a] *relating to pol.l law* **~regierung** f *state administration; government* **~ruder** n *helm of the State* **~sache** f *state-affair* **~säckel** m *pub. purse* **~schatz** m *Treasury, Exchequer* **~schiff** n *ship of state*; das ~ lenken *to be at the helm of the st.* **~schrift** f *pol.l treatise* **~schuld** f *national* od *public debt* | ~buch [n] *Great Ledger* **~schule** f *State School* **~sekretär** m *Secretary of St.* **~siegel** m *Great Seal* **~steuer** f *government tax* **~streich** m (*military*) *coup, c. d'état* Fr **~theorie** f *pol.l theory, th. of the state* **~umwälzung** f *pol.l revolution* **~unterstützung** f *state aid* od *subsidy* **~verband** m *polity* **~verbrechen** n *pol.l crime* **~-verbrecher** m *state criminal* **~verfassung** f (*pol.l constitution* **~verleumdung** f ⟨jur⟩ *seditious utterances* **~vermögen** n *pub. property* **~versammlung** f *Constitutional Assembly* **~verwalter** m *regent, administrator* **-tung** f *administration of the St., government* **~visite** f *ceremonious* od *st. visit* **~wagen** m *St. landau* **~wesen** n *st. affairs* pl; *St.* **~widrig** a *hostile to the st.* **~wirtschaft** f *pol.l economy, economics* pl [a. sg konstr] | ~slehrer [m] *economist* **~wissenschaft** f *pol.l science* **~wohl** n *pub. weal* **~zimmer** n *room of st., st. apartment* **~zuschuß** m *st. grant* od *subvention*

Stab m ~(e)s/~e *staff, stick, rod* **A.** Amts~ *wand, mace* || = Daube || Geländer~ *banister, upright* || Gitter~ *bar* || (waagerechter) *rail*(*ing*) || (e–r Jalousie) *slat* || (Marschall~) *baton* || (Pilger~, Schäfer~) *staff* || (e–s Schirmes) *rib* || Sprung~ *pole* || Staffellauf~ *baton* || (Stütze) *support* || Turn~ *wand* || (Vogelsitz) *perch* || Zauber~ *magic wand* **B.** pl ~ ⟨hist⟩ = Meter **C.** ⟨arch⟩ *ledge*; (Leiste) *fillet*; (Rundstab e–r Säule) *astragal* || ⟨crick⟩ *stump* || ⟨ec⟩ (Krumm-~) *crosier, pastoral staff* || ⟨met⟩ *bar* || ⟨weav⟩ (Kreuz~) *lease bar*; (Strickholz) *mesh-pin* **D.** ⟨mil⟩ *staff*(*-officers* pl), *headquarters* (Bataillons-~ *battalion h.*) || Major (Offizier) beim ~e *staff-major* (*st. officer*) || b. ~e dienen *to serve on the st.* | ⟨übtr⟩ *corps* (*of assistants*); (*large*) *number* (*of experts* etc) **E.** über jdm den ~ **brechen** *to condemn a p* (*to death*); ⟨fig, hum⟩ *to give a dog a bad name and hang him* || den (Wander-)~ ergreifen *to set out on one's travels* || am ~e gehen *to walk with the help of a stick* || s–n ~ weiter setzen *to continue one's journey* **~alge** f *bacillaria* **~antenne** f ⟨wir⟩ *whip aerial* **~einguß** m *ingot-mould* **~eisen** n *bar* od *wrought iron* | ~walzwerk [n] ⟨tech⟩ *rolling-works* pl (od *-mill*) **~förmig** a ⟨scient⟩ *bacilliform, bacillary* **~gereimt** a *alliteral* **~gitter** n *bar screen* **~hammer** m *tilt-hammer* **~heuschrecke** f *stick insect* **~hobel** m ⟨carp⟩ *rabbet-plane* **~hochsprung** m *pole jump* od *vault*(*ing*) **~holz** n *staves* pl **~kirche** f *stave church* **~lampe** f ⟨el⟩ *flash light* **~reim** m ⟨pros⟩ *head rhyme; alliteration* **~springen** vi [s] *to pole-jump* **~sprung** m *p.-j.* **~tierchen** n ⟨scient⟩ *bacillus* **~träger** m *mace-bearer* **~wechsel** m ⟨sport⟩ *delivery* **~wicklung** f *rod winding* **St·äbchen** n ~s/~ *little wand* od *stick*; ~ [pl] (China ⟨cul⟩) *chopsticks* pl || ⟨anat⟩ (Netzhaut~) *rod*; ~ [pl] u Zapfen *rods and cones* || *long stitch* || Kragen~ *collar bone* | ⟨fam⟩ *gasper, fag*; ⟨sl⟩ *pill,* ⟨mil a.⟩ *snart* (= *cigarette*) || hast'n ~ f mich? ⟨mil sl⟩ *got a buckshee* (*fag*)? **~bakterie** f *rod-bacterium* **~diagramm** n *bar chart* **st·äbeln** vt [h] *to prop* (*flowers*) || *to stake* (*peas*)

stab·il a *stable, steady* || die Preise ~ halten *to*

keep .. on an even keel || ~e Zuwachsrate [f] *intrinsic* od *true rate of natural increase* **~is·atorstange** f ⟨mot⟩ *stabilizer bar* **~is·ieren** vt *to stabilize* || (Löhne, Preise) *to freeze* | **~d** *steadying (influence)* | kreisel–**rt** *gyro-stabilized* **~is·ierung** f *stabilization* | ~sflossen [f pl] *(anti-roll) stabilizers*; ~swulst [m] ⟨aero⟩ *stabilizer* **~it·ät** f ~/ *stability*; ⟨com⟩ *life*; Währungs~ *soundness of currency* || ~ e–s Amtes *fixity of tenure*

St·abs- *headquarters, staff* **~akademie** f *Armed Forces St. College* N **~arzt** m ⟨mil⟩ *captain*; *surgeon-major* || ⟨mar⟩ *st.-surgeon* **~batterie** f *h.s b.* **~chef** m ⟨mil, pol⟩ *chief of st.* **~kompanie** f *st.* od ⟨Am⟩ *h.s c.* **~offizier** m ⟨mil⟩ *st.* od *field-officer* **~quartier** n ⟨mil⟩ *headquarters* pl [a. sg konstr] | ~meister [m] *quartermaster-general* **~rahmenübung** f *command post exercise (CPX)* N **~schiedsrichter** m *headquarters umpire* **~trompeter** m *trumpet-major* **~veterinär** m *captain*; *staff veterinary*

stach 1. & 3. sg pret v stechen **St·achel** m ~s/~n ⟨ent⟩ *sting* || ⟨zoo⟩ *quill* || ⟨bot & fig⟩ *prick(le), spur, thorn* | (am Sporn) *point* || (e–r Schnalle) *tongue* || (unter Läuferschuhen) *spike* || (Sporn, Antrieb) *stimulus* | ⟨fig⟩ *pricks* pl *(of doubt), thorns (of injustice)*; *sting*; *keen edge (of pain* etc); e–n ~ hinterlassen *to leave a sting, dart behind* || das war ihm ein ~ *that was a thorn to him* || der bohrende ~ *the dragon (of his dissatisfaction)* || wider den ~ löcken *to kick against the pricks* **~beere** f *gooseberry* **~beer-** ~busch, ~strauch [m] *g.-bush*; ~spinner [m] *g.-moth* **~draht** m *barbed wire* **~flosse** f *fin-spine* **~flosser** m *spiny-finned fish* **~flügelig** a ⟨scient⟩ *acanthopterous* **~halsband** n *training-collar* **~häuter** m pl ⟨zoo⟩ *echinoderms* pl **~häutig** a ⟨scient⟩ *echinodermatous* **~rede** f *biting (satirical, caustic) speech*; *sharp words* pl **~roche** m *sting-ray*, ⟨Am⟩ *stingaree*; *thornback* **~same** m ⟨bot⟩ *acanthospermum* **~schnecke** f *murex* **~schwein** n *porcupine* **~stock** m *goad* **~zaun** m *barbed-wire fence* **st·ach(e)lig** a *prickly, thorny* || ⟨zoo⟩ *spiny* || *bristly (beard)* || (v Worten) *stinging, pungent, sharp, biting* **st·acheln** vt [h] *to sting, prick, goad* || ⟨fig⟩ *stimulate*

ˣ**St·adel** m ~s/~ *barn, shed, stall*

St·aden m ~s/~ *bank, embankment*

St·adion n ~s/–dien ⟨sport⟩ *stadium*

St·adium n ~s/–dien *stage*; erstes ~ *incipience* || ⟨path⟩ in vorgerücktem ~ *far-gone*

Stadt f ~/~e *town* || (Groß~) *city* || die ~ N: *the t.* od *city of N.* || *the Holy C.* || *the Free C. of Bremen* || auf die ~ begrenzt *c.-limited* || sie stammt aus dieser ~ *she is a local girl, a native of this t.* || in die ~ gehen *to go to t.*, ⟨Am⟩ *downtown*, in der ~ *d.t.* || nach (von) der ~ (London) *up (down)* || in der ~ erzogen *t.-bred* || die ganze ~ weiß es *that is all over the t.* **~abgabe** f *(t.-)rates* pl **~adel** m *patricians* pl **~amt** n *municipal office* **~anleihe** f *mun. loan*, ⟨engl⟩ *corporation loan* **~arzt** m *t.-physician* **~bad** n *mun. bath* **~bahn** f *c.-railway, metropolitan (r.w.)* **~bann** m *district of a t.* **~baumeister** m *mun. architect* **~beamte(r)** m *mun. officer* **~behörde** f *mun. authorities, municipalities* pl **~bek·annt** a *notorious, known all over the t.* **~bevölkerung** f *urban population* **~bewohner** m = Städter **~bezirk** m *urban district*; *ward* **~brief** m *local letter* **~bürger** m *citizen, townsman* | ~recht [n] *mun. franchise*; *civic rights* pl **~eigen** a *council (house)* **~feste** f *citadel* °**~frack** m (P) ⟨Am sl⟩ *dude*; *city slicker* **~gebiet** n *township*; *urban district* **~gemeinde** f *municipality, township* | ~rat [m] *borough council* **~gerede** n *(common) talk of the town, town-talk* **~gericht** n *mun.* od *city court* **~gespräch** n **1.** = –gerede **2.** ⟨telph⟩ *local call* **~graben** m *t.-moat* **~grenzen** f pl *city limits* **~hauptmann** m ⟨hist⟩ *captain of the t.-militia* **~haus** n *t. house*; (Rathaus) *t.-hall* | ~halt [m] *mun. budget* **~innere(s)** n = –mitte **~kämmerer** m *treasurer of the t.* **~kern** m *central city*, ⟨Am⟩ *inskirts* pl **~kind** n *t.sman*; *city-born* [attr] **~kirche** f *t. church* **~klatsch** m = –gerede **~kleidung** f *c. clothes, t. wear* **~koffer** m *attaché-case* **~kundig** a **1.** = –bekannt **2.** *knowing the t. well* **~leben** n *t. life* **~leute** pl *t.speople, t.folk* pl **~mauer** f *t. wall* **~miliz** f *t.-militia* **~mitte** f *t.-centre*, ⟨Am⟩ *mid-t. city* **~müde** a *(she felt very) sick and tired of t. life* **~musikanten** m pl ⟨fam⟩ *waits* pl **~musikus** m *t. musician* **~neuigkeit** f *t.-news* **~ordnung** f *city laws* **~park** m *mun. park* | ~verwaltung [f] *c. p. department* **~pfarre** f *t. parish* **~pfarrer** m *t. clergyman* **~pfeifer** m ⟨hist⟩ = –musikus **~physikus** m *t. physician* **~planung** f ⟨arch⟩ *urbiculture* **~post** f *t.-delivery* **~rand** *suburbia, exurbia, exurbs* pl; am ~ *on the edge* od *outskirts of the town* | ~siedler [m] *suburbanite*; ~siedlung [f] *suburb(an development)* **~rat** m *t.* od *mun.* od *common council*; (P) *t.-councillor, alderman*; ⟨Can⟩ *controller* **~recht** n *t.-* od *mun. by-law(s pl)*; *freedom of a city* **~richter** m *city-magistrate* **~schilderung** f *t.scape* **~schreiber** m *t. clerk* **~schule** f *mun. school* **~schulkommission** f *local school-board* **~schulrat** m *inspector of mun. schools* **~soldat** m *t.-militiaman* **~staat** m ⟨Gr ant⟩ *city-state* **~syndikus** m *syndic, city-recorder* **~teil** m = –viertel **~telegramm** n *local tel.* **~tor** n *t.-* od *city-gate* **~urlaub** m ⟨mil⟩ *local leave* **~väter** m pl ⟨fam⟩ *city-fathers* **~verordnete(r)** m *t.-councillor*, ⟨Am⟩ *selectman*, ⟨Can⟩ *alderman* | ~nversammlung [f] *(T.) Council*; ⟨Am⟩ *t. meeting*; ⟨Can⟩ *city council* **~viertel** n *quarter, ward* || in diesem ~ *in this part of t.* **~vogt** m *t.-bailiff* **~volk** n = –leute **~waage** f *public scales* pl; *weighing-house* **~wappen** n *city-arms* pl **~werke** n pl *public utilities* **~wohnung** f *t. residence, t.house, city apartment* **~zentrum** n = –mitte, ⟨Am⟩ *downtown* **St·ädtchen** n ~s/~ *small town* || ⟨prov⟩ andre ~, andre Mädchen *a sweetheart in every port* **St·ädte-** **~bau** m *town-planning* **~kampf** m ⟨sport⟩ *intertown match* **~ordnung** f *municipal statutes*; ⟨engl⟩ *Mun. Corporation Act* **~(schnellverkehrs)zug** m *interurban (train)* **~wiederaufbau** m *urban renewal* **St·ädter** m ~s/~ *townsman* (pl *townspeople*); *citizen*; *town-bred* **st·ädtisch** [a] *municipal, town(-)*; ~e Gemeinde f *urban district* || [adv] ~ gekleidet *dressed like a townslady*

Staf·ette f ~/~n *courier, express* | ⟨sport⟩ *relay* || ~nlauf [m] *relay-race*

Staff·age [–'fa:ʒə] f ~/~n ⟨arts⟩ *accessories, figures* pl || ⟨fig⟩ das ist nur ~ *that's all make-up*

St·affel f ~/~n *step, rundle, rung, round* || ⟨mil⟩ *echelon (= formation of troops, each with its front clear of that in advance)* || ⟨fig⟩ *degree* || (Stapel) *staple* || ⟨sport⟩ *relay* || ⟨aero⟩ *flight* (⟨engl⟩ 5 od 6; ⟨Ger⟩ 9 Flugzeuge), *squadron* (⟨engl⟩ 12 F.); 2 ~n (etwa 30 F.) *wing* || ⟨mil mot⟩ *wagon-line* **~aufstellung** f ⟨mil⟩ *echelon (order)* **~bild** n ⟨ec arts⟩ *prdella* **~feuer** n ⟨artill⟩ *searching* od *ladder fire* **~förmig** a ⟨mil⟩ *by* od *in echelons* **~führer** m ⟨aero⟩ *(acting) sq. commander* **~lauf** m ⟨sport⟩ *relay-race* **~methode** f ⟨bank, etc⟩ *balance method* **~salve** f *ladder salvo* **~tarif** m *sliding scale* || (Löhne, Preise etc) *differential* od *adjustable tariff*; *graded wage scale* | *graduated scale of charges* **~weise** a & adv *in echelon(s pl)* **Staffel·ei** ~/~en *easel* | ~bild [n] *e.-picture* **st·affeln** vt (abstufen) *to graduate* || ⟨aero⟩ *to stagger* (⟨a.⟩ Tage, Stunden ~) || ⟨mil⟩ *to echelon* || ⟨arch⟩ gestaffelt *stepped (gable)* **St·affelung** f ~/~en (v Steuern etc) *graduation* || ⟨mil⟩ *echelon* ⟨a. aero⟩, ⟨tact⟩ *echelonment*

staff·ieren vt [h] *to furnish, garnish, dress, trim* **Staff·ierung** f ~/~en *furnishing, garnishment, garnishing*

Stag n ~(e)s/~e ⟨mar⟩ *stay* ‖ über ~ gehen *to go about* **~fock** f *forestaysail* **~segel** n *staysail*

Stagnati·on [–ts–] f ~/~en *stagnation* **stagn·ieren** vi [h] *to stagnate, vegetate*; (*trade*) *seizes up*

stahl 1. & 3. sg pret v stehlen

Stahl m ~(e)s/~e & ≗e **1.** *steel* ‖ ⟨übtr⟩ (*whetting-*)*steel* ‖ *chisel* ‖ *dagger, sword* ‖ *heater* (*of an iron*) | ausglühen *to anneal*; härten *to temper*; glätten *to flatten*; vergüten *to refine* ‖ hochelastischer, zugfester ~ *high-tensile st*; legierter ~ *st. alloy* **2.** ⟨com⟩ *stamp* **3.** **~-** *chalybeate, steel* **~arbeit** f *st.-work* **~arbeiter** m *worker in st.* **≗artig** a *steel(y)* **~bad** n *ch. spa* od *bath* **~band** n (*steel*) *hoop* **~bau** m *steel construction* **~beton** m *steel concrete* → Eisenbeton ⟨obs⟩ | ~einzelteil [n] *pre-cast reinforced c. unit* **≗blau** a *st.-coloured, st.-blue, electric blue* **~blech** n *sheet-st.* **~brunnen** m *ch. spring* **~draht** m *st. wire* **~erz** n *sparry iron-ore* **~fachwerk** n *structural steelwork* **~fabrik** f *st. forge* **~feder** f *st. spring* ‖ (z Schreiben) *st. pen* **~frischen** n *st.-fining* **≗gepanzert** a *st.-clad* **~gerben** n *tilting* **≗gr·au** a *grey as st.* **~griffel** m → Reißnadel **~guß** m *cast st.* **~haltig** a ⟨scient⟩ *ch.* **~hammer** m *st. forge* **≗h·art** a (*as*) *hard as st.* **~härte** f *steeliness* **~härtung** f *tempering of st.* **~helm** m *st. helmet*; ⟨sl⟩ *tin hat, battle bowler* ‖ ⟨Ger ex-mil⟩ „Der ~" (Bund der Frontsoldaten) *the St. Helmets* (*Front Line Soldiers' League*) **~hütte** f *st. forge* **~kammer** f *strong--room* **~kerngeschoß** n *armo(u)r(-piercing) bullet* **~kette** f *st. chain* **~matratze** f *spring-mattress* **~panzer** m ⟨mil mar⟩ *st. armour* **~platten-Startbahn** f ⟨aero⟩ *pierced-steelplate runway* **~-quelle** f *ch. spring* **~(rohr)möbel** n pl, (sg *piece of*) *tubular furniture* **~roß** n ⟨cycl fam⟩ *iron steed*; *grid*; ⟨rail⟩ *iron horse* **~schnalle** f *st. buckle* **~schneider** m *st.-cutter* **~skelettbau** m *st.-frame(d) building* **~stecher** m *engraver on st.* **~stich** m ⟨arts⟩ *st. engraving* **~trosse** f (*st.*) *hawser* **~umgürtet** a ⟨poet⟩ *st.-girt* **~ware** f *hardware*; *cutlery* **~wasser** n *ch. water* **~werk** m *st.-works* pl [a. sg konstr] **st·ählen** vt [h] *to harden, temper* (*iron*) | ⟨fig⟩ *to brace up, to steel, fortify* **st·ählern** a (*made*) *of steel*; *steel* (*tools*) | ⟨fig⟩ *steely*; *iron* (*will*) **St·ählung** f ~/ *steeling*; *temper* ‖ ⟨fig⟩ *bracing, hardening*

stak 1. & 3. sg pret v stecken **St·aken** m ~s/~ **1.** *pole, stake* **2.** ⟨mar⟩ *boathook* **3.** ⟨agr⟩ *rick, stack* **st·aken I.** vt *to pole, punt* **II.** vi ⟨fam⟩ *to stalk along* **Stak·et** n ~(e)s/~e *fence, railing, palisade, paling*

Stalagm·it m ~(e)s & ~en/~e(n) *stalagmite*

Stalakt·it m ~(e)s & ~en/~e(n) *stalactite*

St·alingrad n ⟨Russ⟩ (Stadt) *Stalingrade*

Stall m ~(e)s/≗e (Kuh≗) *cow-house* ‖ (Pferde≗) *stable* ‖ (Schweine≗) (*pig*)*sty* ‖ (Hunde≗) *kennel* ‖ (Einzelstand) *stall* ‖ (Vieh≗) ⟨Am⟩ *barn* ‖ ⟨racing⟩ *stables* pl ‖ °(P) ⟨fam⟩ *hangout* | (f Holz etc) *shed, outhouse* | ⟨fig fam⟩ *pigsty* ‖ das beste Pferd im Stall *the best horse in the stable* **~baum** m *spring-tree*, (*stable-*)*bar* **~bedienstete(r)** m *equerry, groom* **~bursche** m *lad*; *stable-boy* **~bürste** f *horse-brush* **~decke** f *horse rug* **~dienst** m *stables* pl **~eimer** m *stable--pail* **~feind** m Sw = Maul- u Klauenseuche **~fütterung** f *stall-feed(ing)* ‖ [dat] ~ geben *to stall-feed* **~gasse** f *stallway* **~gefährte** m *stable--mate, -companion*, ⟨bes hors a.⟩ *team-mate* **~geld** n *stabling, stable-money, stallage* **~geruch** m *stable-smell* **~halfter** m *halter* **~hase** m *tame rabbit* **~junge** m *stable-boy* **~kittel** m *coachman's frock* **~knecht** m *stable-man, groom*; *ostler* (*at an inn*) **~laterne** f *stable-lantern*; ⟨fam⟩ jetzt geht mir e–e ~ auf *now it dawns upon me* **~leine** f *picket line* **~meister** m *equerry, master of the horse* **~mist** m *barnyard manure* **~wache** f *stable police* **~wirtschaft** f *animal husbandry* **St·ällchen** n (Kinder≗) *playpen* **st·allen I.** vt [h] *to stall, stable* **II.** vi [h] *to be stabled* od *housed* | (harnen) *to stale* **St·allung** f ~/~en *stabling* ‖ pl *stables*

St·ambul n *Constantinopel*; → Istanbul

Stamm m ~(e)s/≗e **1.** (Baum≗) *stem, trunk, bole* ‖ (Stengel) *stalk, stem* ‖ *tree* (*of the cross*) ‖ Holz auf dem ~ *standing timber* ‖ ⟨prov⟩ der Apfel fällt nicht weit v ~ *like father like son* **2.** (Geschlecht) *race, family, house*; ⟨Scot⟩ *clan* ‖ männl. ~ *male line* ‖ aus königlichem ~ *of royal blood* ‖ e–s ~es u Geschlechts *of one stock and family* **3.** (Volks≗) *tribe* (*the t. of Judah*) ‖ ≗e der Germanen *Teuton tribes* ‖ pl (e–s Volkes) *branches* .. ‖ zw verschiedenen ≗en bestehend *intertribal* **4.** ⟨biol⟩ *phylum* L ‖ ⟨agr⟩ (v Vieh) *breed* **5.** ⟨gram⟩ (Wort≗) *stem* **6.** (Grundstock) ⟨mil⟩ *skeleton, cadre, depot* | *the stock of regular guests* = *the regulars* pl; ⟨cul⟩ → 9. | ⟨agr⟩ *stock* (*of poultry, of a herd*); *swarm* (*of bees*) | ⟨fig⟩ *backbone* (*of a troop, an undertaking*); (P) *permanent staff* **7.** (Kapital) *principal*; *invested capital* **8.** ⟨cards⟩ *undealt pack*; (Einsatz) *stake* **9.** ⟨cul⟩ = ~gericht **~abschnitt** m ⟨for⟩ *butt-log* **~aktie** f *original* od *ordinary share*; ~n [pl] ⟨a.⟩ *capital stock* **~bataillon** n *home b.* **~baum** m (P & T) *genealogical table, family tree, ancestral* [(T) *blood*] *line* ‖ ⟨mst hors & dog⟩ *pedigree* **~besatzung** f *nucleus* od *skeleton crew* **~buch** n *album*; ⟨geneal⟩ *register*; ⟨hors & dog⟩ *studbook* **~buchstabe** m *radical letter* **~burg** f *ancestral castle* **~einheit** f *original* od *parent unit* **~eltern** pl *ancestors, progenitors*, ⟨rel⟩ *first parents* pl **~ende** n (e–s Baumes) *stump*; *butt* **~erbe** m *rightful heir* **~firma** f, **~haus** n *parent company* od *firm* **~folge** f *line of descent* **~form** f ⟨gram⟩ *radical form*; pl *principal parts* (*of a verb*) **~gast** m *regular* (*guest* od *customer*); *patron*; *habitué* Fr (⟨a. sport⟩: *of the turf*) **~geld** n *stock, capital* **~gericht** n *stand-by*; (*farmers'*)-*ordinary* **~gut** n *home-farm, family estate* **~halter** m (*first-born*) *son and heir* **~haus** n *ancestral mansion* ‖ (fürstliches Geschlecht) *dynasty, house* ‖ ⟨com⟩ *parent* od *original firm, head office* **~holz** n *trunk-wood, standing timber* **~kapital** n *original stock* od *capital* **~karte** f ⟨comp⟩ *large board*; vgl Schaltkarte **~karten- u -bändersätze** pl *initial card and magnetic tape files* °**~kneipe** f ⟨fam⟩ (*one's*) *usual pub* od *hangout*; ⟨teens⟩ *la-la* **~kultur** f ⟨bact⟩ *stock culture* **~kunde** m *regular* od *steady customer* od *patron* **~kundschaft** f *r. c.s*; Fr *clientele* **~leh(e)n** n *fee-simple, hereditary fee* **~leitung** f *trunk-line*; → Haupt– **~linie** f *line(age)* **~lode** f ⟨for⟩ *stem-sprout* **~(m)annschaft** f ⟨mil⟩ *skeleton body*, ⟨mar⟩ *sk. crew* **~mutter** f *ancestress* **~organ** n ⟨biol⟩ *parent body* **~police** f ⟨ins⟩ *master policy* **~prioritäten** f pl *preference shares* **~register** n *genealogical register* **~rolle** f ⟨mil & mar⟩ *rolls* pl, *muster--roll*; in der ~ *on the strength* od *m.-r.* | ~n-nummer [f] *official number* **~silbe** f *radical syllable* **~sitz** m *ancestral seat* **~sprache** f *original language* **~substanz** f ⟨chem, pharm, etc⟩ *parent substance* **~tafel** f *genealogical table* **~tier** n *sire* **~tisch** m (*table reserved for*) *regular guests* | ~-politiker [m] *armchair politician* **~truppenteil** m → –einheit **~vater** m *ancestor, progenitor*; (Adam) *First Parent* ‖ jds ~ s ⟨a.⟩ *to ancester a p* **~verbindung** f *clanship* **≗verbunden** a *clannish* **~vermögen** m = –kapital **≗verwandt** a *cognate, kindred*; *of the same race* ‖ ⟨gram⟩ *paronymous* | ~schaft [f] *identity of origin* **~vokal** m *stem vowel* **~volk** n *aborigines* pl, *primitive people* **~wort** n ⟨gram⟩ *root-word, primitive word, stem* **~würze** f ⟨brew⟩ *original wort* °**~zahn** m ⟨teens⟩ (Mädchen) *ja-ja* || hast du jetzt e–n ~? ⟨bes Am⟩ *going steady*? **~zeiten** f pl = –formen **st·ammen** vi [s] *to be descended* (⟨gram⟩ *derived*); *to spring, stem, originate, come* (v .. her *from*) || *to be* (aus *of good family*); er stammt aus Marburg *he is a native of M.* || ⟨Lit⟩ *to have been written by* (v) || *to date from* | ~d aus *originating in* **St·ammes-** [in comp oft] *tribal* (*chieftain, system*); *racial* (*peculiarity*); *clan* (*spirit*) **~gefühl** n *clan(nish)ness, tribalism* **~genosse** m *clansman, tribesman* **~geschichte** f ⟨biol⟩ *evolution* | sich **~̈geschichtlich** entwickeln *to evolve* (*independently*) **~häuptling** m *tribal leader* **~stolz** m *clannish pride* **~zugehörigkeit** f *inclusion in a race* **st·ämmig** a *stout, strong, sturdy, stocky, burly*; ⟨Am⟩ *husky* | *bouncing* (*girl*); *buxom, strapping* (*wench*) | (untersetzt) *thick-set* || **~̈keit** f ~/ *stoutness, strength* etc

St·ammeln n ~s/ *stutter* | ~̈ vt/i [h] *to stammer, stutter* || ⟨fig⟩ *to falter* **St·ammler** m ~s/~ *stammerer, stutterer*

St·ampe f ~/~n (= Kneipe) *pub*, ⟨Am fam⟩ *beanery* ×**St·amperl** n ~s/~ *gin-tumbler*; ⟨fam⟩ *snifter* || ein ~ trinken ⟨Am fam⟩ *to take a horn* **St·ampf-** [in comp] *stamping(-mill, -trough)* || *stamped* (*concrete, clay*) || *mashed* (*potatoes*) || *crushed* (*sugar*) || *stamp(-hammer)* **~asphalt** m *compressed asphalt* **~bewegung** f ⟨mar⟩ *pitching motion* **~klotz** m *piledriver* **~mauerwerk** n *rubble construction* **~moment** n ⟨aero⟩ *pitching moment* **~see** f *heavy sea over the bows* **St·ampfe** f ~/~n **1.** *stamp(ing)* **2.** (Werkzeug) *stamper, pounder, rammer, pestle, beater,* (*paving*) *beetle* **3.** (*short-stemmed*) *goblet*; → Stamperl **st·ampfen I.** vt [h] **1.** (zerstoßen) *to stamp, pound* (*ore*) || *to mash* (*potatoes*) || *to crush* (*grapes*) || *to bruise* (*corn*) || *to express* (*oil*) || ⟨hors⟩ *to paw* (*the ground*) **2.** (einstampfen) *to ram down* || kl ~ *to crush* || ⟨fig⟩ aus dem Boden ~ *to get .. out of one's hat*; *to conjure up* **II.** vi [h] **1.** *to stamp* (mit dem Fuß [⟨fam⟩ *to plank down*] *one's foot*) || (*of ship*) *to pitch* **2.** [s] *to tramp, thump, clump, pound, stump along* **St·ampfer** m ~s/~ **1.** (P) *stamper* etc. | *pawing horse* **2.** ⟨tech⟩ *rammer, stamper*; *pestle*; ⟨fam⟩ *dolly*; ⟨cul⟩ *pestle*; (f Abfluß) *plunger*

Stand m ~(e)s/~̈e **1.** **(Stehen,** P & S) *standing, upright position* || (des Jägers) *stand*; ⟨mount⟩ sicherer ~ *secure stance* od *footing* || festen ~ fassen ⟨fig⟩ *to take up a strong position* || Stoß **aus** dem ~ *standing-put* **2.** **(~ort)** *stand(ing-place), position* || ein geeigneter ~ *a convenient station* || ⟨golf, crick⟩ *stance* || ⟨astr⟩ *position* (*of a star*), *configuration* (*of planets*) | s–n ~ an e–m Ort h *to be posted in a place* || wir h hier k–n guten ~ *we are not well placed here* | **(Abteil)** *box, stand* (*in a stable*) || (Ablauf) ⟨racing⟩ *start* || Droschken~̈ *cab-stand* || Gefechts~̈ ⟨mil⟩ (*commanding officer's*) *observation post*, ⟨mar⟩ *action station* || (Geschütz~̈) *emplacement* || (Leit~̈) ⟨mar⟩ *fire control platform* || (Lokomotivführer~̈) *cab* || (Markt–, Meß–, Verkaufs~̈) *stall, booth*, ⟨Am⟩ *stand* || Zeitungs~̈ *kiosk*, ⟨Am⟩ *newsstand* || Zeugen~̈ *witness-box* **3.** **(~höhe)** *level* (*of the water, of prices, petrol*); nach dem ~e v 1. Jan. *as of January, 1st*; (Barometer– etc ~̈) *reading* (*the r. is 15°*) || ⟨exch⟩ *rate* || (Bestand) ⟨agr, com⟩ *stock* | hohe(r) ~ *splendour* (*of arts* etc) || e–n hohen ~ h (S) *to be advanced* || höchster ~ *culmination*; *culminating point*; *the highest peak* (*of ,,*); ⟨Am⟩ *high* (*a h. of 87*), (*to attain the*) *highest stand* || niedrigster ~ *low-water mark* || die Aufträge stehen auf höchstem ~ *orders are running at* (*an*) *all-time high*; auf vollen ~ bringen *to bring up to establishment* od *strength*; den tiefsten ~ erreichen *to touch bottom, to reach the lowest ebb* **4.** **(Zu~̈)** *situation, condition*; *state* (*of bondage, innocence, sin, affairs, a process*) | die Dinge auf dem **alten** ~ l *to let ths go* || ehelicher ~ *married state* || bei *or* nach dem gegenwärtigen ~ der Dinge *as matters* od *ths now stand* || in **gutem** ~, gut im ~ *in good condition* od *repair*, (P) *in a good state of health* || bei jdm e–n guten ~ h *to be in favour with a p* || k–n **leichten** ~ h *to have no easy time of it* || e–n schweren ~ h *to have much to contend with*, mit jdm .. *to have a great deal of trouble with a p* **5.** ⟨sociol⟩ *social position*; *rank, class, status, station, order* || (*the upper, lower classes*) || (Kaste) *caste* || (Beruf) *vocation* || s–s ~es .. (*a baker*) *by trade*, (*a teacher*) *by profession* || **gebildete** ~̈e *educated classes*; **gelehrte** ~̈e *learned professions* || geistlicher ~ *clergy, the cloth, holy orders* || weltlicher ~ *laity* | **aus**: *of all classes* || .. **unter** ihrem ~e .. (*she has married*) *beneath her* || **von** ~e: *a man of rank, quality, station* || v niedrigem ~e *of low degree* **6.** ⟨pol⟩ *estate* (*the third e.; the clerical, secular e.*); der **vierte** ~ *the working classes* pl | **die** ~̈e *the estates of the realm*, ⟨engl⟩ *the Three Estates* (*Lords Spiritual, Lords Temporal, Commons*), (Frankreich, Niederlande vor 1789) *the States General*, ⟨parl⟩ *the diet* [sg], *the representatives of a country* **7.** [in comp] → außerstande, imstande, instand, zustande **stand** 1. & 3. sg pret v stehen

St·and- ⟨zoo⟩ *sedentary* (*game, bird, insect*) **~anzeiger** m *gauge-glass* **~bein** n ⟨sculp⟩ *leg bearing main weight* **~bild** n *statue*; jdm ein ~ errichten *to raise a st. to a p* || ~er [pl] *statuary* || ⟨phot⟩ *inanimate picture* **~büchse** f *rifle for target-shooting* **~drehzahl** f ⟨aero-mot⟩ *bench revolutions per minute* **~entwicklung** f ⟨phot⟩ *tank development* | ~stank [m] *vertical processing tank* **~̈fest** a *sturdy, stable, firm* (Stativ) | ~igkeit [f] *stability, steadiness*; *endurance*; (*moral*) *stamina* **~flasche** f *show vessel* **~geld** n *stallage, stall-rent* || ⟨rail⟩ *demurrage*; ⟨mot⟩ *garage fee*; was verlangen Sie ~? *what is the g. f.*? **~gerät** n ⟨wir⟩ *radio console* **~gericht** n *drum-head court-martial* **~̈gerichtlich** a; ~ verurteilen *to court-martial* **~̈|halten** vi [irr] [h] [dat] *to stand* (*a test*), *to make a* (*strong*) *stand, to bear up* (*against*), *to keep* od *hold one's own* od *ground, to resist a p* || *to stand firm, to hold out* || bis zum Äußersten ~ *to die in the last ditch* || das hält nicht stand *that won't wash* ⟨fig⟩ **~krämer** m *stall-keeper* **~lager** n ⟨mil⟩ *permanent camp* ⟨bes hist⟩ **~laut** m ⟨hunt⟩ (des Hundes) *bay* **~licht** n ⟨mot⟩ *parking light* **~linie** f *base*; ⟨artill⟩ *datum line* **~motor** m *fixed* bzw *vertical engine* **~ort** m *stand, station, location*; ⟨bot⟩ *habitat*; ⟨com⟩ *local situation*; ⟨mil⟩ *post*; *garrison, headquarters* pl; e–n ~ bestimmen *to find a position* || ⟨demog⟩ *geographical* od *spatial distribution* | ~älteste(r) [m] *post commander*; ~anzeiger [m] ⟨aero⟩ *indicator* (*A. P. I.*); ~aufnahme [f] ⟨bot phot⟩ *photography in situ*; ~befehl [m] *garrison routine order*; ~bereich [m] *g. command*; ~dienst [m] *garrison duty*; ~kommandantur [f] *post headquarters* pl; ~lazarett [n] *station hospital*; ~meldung [f] ⟨aero⟩ *position report*; ~situation [f] ⟨com⟩ *local situation*; ~übungsplatz [m] *garrison training area*; ~verwaltung [f] *garrison administrative headquarters* pl; ~wachdienst [m] *interior guard duty*; ~wechsel [m] *change of station* N °**~pauke** f *calling down*; ⟨sl⟩ *pi-jaw*, jdm e–e ~ halten *to pi-jaw a p* **~punkt** m *standpoint, station* || ⟨fig⟩ *standpoint, point of view, views* pl; *angle*, ⟨Am⟩ *slant*; ⟨Lit⟩ *view-point* || jds ~ erkennen *to see a p's point* || überwundener ~ *exploded idea* || s–n ~ aufgeben (behaupten) *to retrace one's steps*, ⟨Am⟩ *to backtrack* (*to carry one's point*) || den ~ einnehmen *or* vertreten *to take the view* od *line* (*that*) || jdm den ~ klar m ⟨fig⟩ *to give a p a piece of one's mind* | v ~ [+ *gen*] *in terms of* (*progress*) **~quartier** n *fixed quaters* pl, *cantonment* **~recht** n *martial law* (verhängen *to impose*) ⩪**rechtlich** [a & adv] *according to martial law, by a sentence of court-martial* ~**rede** f *harangue* ~**riß** m ⟨arch⟩ *elevation, upright projection, sketch* ~**scheibe** f *fixed target* ~**sicherheit** f ⟨aero⟩ *stability* ~**sprung** m ⟨swim⟩ *heeler* ~**uhr** f *hall* od *French clock* ~**visier** n *block-sight* ~**wild** n *sedentary game* ~**wind** m *steady breeze* ~**zeit** f ⟨tech⟩ *endurance, service life* **St·ändchen** n ~s/~ *serenade* ‖ jdm ein ~ bringen *to s. a p* ‖ man hat ihm ein ~ gebracht *he was serenaded* **St·ände-** ~**haus** n *assembly-hall of the States* ~**staat** m *corporate state* ~**tag** m *meeting of a diet* ~**versammlung** f *assembly of the States; diet*

St·andard m ~s/~s *standard; criterion* ‖ Lebens⩪, ~ der Lebensführung *quality of life* | ~-abweichung [f] *st. deviation*; ~ausführung [f] *standard-type design* bzw *model, construction*; *normal* (⟨Am⟩ *conventional*) *design*; ~einrichtungen [f pl] *basic features*; ~kennsatz [m] ⟨comp⟩ *standard label*; ~-Leitstrahlanflug m *st. beam approach* (*SBA*); ~lösung [f] *test* od *st. solution*; ~typ [m] *st.* (⟨Am⟩ *conventional*) *type*; ~wert [m] *st. value*; ~e [pl] ⟨exch⟩ *blue chips* ⩪**is·iert** a *st.ized* ⟨a. stat⟩; ~es Wort *word type*; ~es Zeichen *sign type* | Internationale Gesellschaft f ~**is·ierung** f *International St.ization Association* N | ~sabkommen [n] *st.ization agreement* N

Stand·arte f ~/~n **1.** *standard, banner* **2.** ⟨hunt⟩ *brush* (*of a fox*) ~**njunker** m *cornet* ~**n-träger** m *standard-bearer*

St·ander m ~s/~ ⟨mar⟩ *pennant; burgee*

St·änder m ~s/~ (Hut–, Schirm–, Noten⩪) *stand* (*music-st.*) ‖ ⟨theat-el⟩ *standard* ‖ (Gewehr–, Kleider–, Pfeifen⩪) *rack* ‖ (Billardstock⩪ etc) *rest* ‖ Gewürz⩪ *cruet-stand* ‖ (Pult) *desk* ‖ zus-klappbarer ~ *folding frame* ‖ (im Stall) *stanchion* ‖ (f Fensterauslagen) *prop* | (Pfosten) *post, pillar* ‖ ⟨carp⟩ *upright* | °⟨sex⟩ *stand, pole, bar,* ⟨hum⟩ *star-gazer* ~**lampe** f *standard lamp* **St·andes-** ~**adel** m *nobility of birth* ~**amt** n *registry office* | ~sregister [n] *register* ⩪**amtlich** a *civil* (*marriage*); *by a registrar* ‖ ~ [adv] getraut *married at a registry* ~**beamte(r)** m *registrar* (*of vital statistics*) ~**bewußtsein** n *class-feeling, -consciousness* ~**dünkel** m *pride of place* ~**ehe** f *marriage of rank* ~**ehre** f *professional honour* ~**erhöhung** f *elevation of rank* ~**gebühr** f: nach ~ *in accordance with one's position* ⩪**gemäß** [a & adv] *suitable* od *conformable to one's station, in accordance with one's rank* ‖ ~ leben *to live up to one's station* ~**genosse** m *equal, compeer* ~**gleichheit** f *equality of rank* od *station* ~**herr** m *mediatized prince* od *count, baron* ‖ ~en [pl] *the aristocracy* ⩪**herrlich** a *baronial* ~**herrschaft** f *mediatized territory* ~**person** f *notable; p of quality, rank, distinction* ~**register** n **1.** *register of births* etc **2.** *book of the peerage* ~**unterschied** m *social difference* ~**vorurteil** n *class-prejudice* ⩪**widrig** a *contrary to one's rank*; ~es Verhalten *breach of professional etiquette* **st·andhaft** a *constant, firm, resolute, steady, pertinacious, persevering; unyielding; stalwart, stout* | [adv] ~ arbeiten *to persevere* ‖ (*to deny*) *flatly* ⩪**igkeit** f ~/ *steadfastness, firmness, constancy, perseverance* ‖ übermenschliche ~ *superhuman fortitude* **st·ändig** a *permanent; incessant; standing* (Ausschuß; ⟨mil⟩ *Group* N); *stationary, fixed* (*equipment*), *regular; continuous* (*use*); *chronic* (*doubt, invalid, complaint*) ‖ ~e Wachsamkeit *round-the-clock vigilance; continual* (*change, shouting*); ~er Wohnort *home* | [adv] *invariably*; ~ ausgestellt s *to be on permanent display, exhibit, view*; ~ wachsend *ever-growing* ‖ ~ wiederholen *to keep repeating* ⩪**keit** f ~/ *permanence* **st·ändisch** a *relating to the estates of the realm*, etc

St·ange f ~/~n **A.** *pole, stick; post* | *handle, shaft* | (eiserne) *bar, rod* | (Pfahl) ⟨bes hort, agr⟩ *stake*; durch ~n stützen, (T) an e–e ~ binden *to stake* ‖ (Spargel⩪) *spear* | ~ Pomade, Siegellack, Zimt etc *stick of ..*; ~ Rasierseife *shaving--stick* | ⟨met⟩ *ingot* ‖ ⟨fam⟩ e–e ~ Gold verdienen *to make a packet* ‖ ~ Gold gekostet! *gave a good figure for it*! .. *a mint of money, a pretty penny* **B.** (hohes **Bierglas**) *schooner* ‖ Gardinen⩪ *tringle* ‖ Kandaren⩪ *bit*; auf die ~ beißen *to champ the bit* ‖ (⟨mus⟩ Bogen⩪) *stick* ‖ ⟨hunt⟩ (Fuchsschwanz) *tail, brush* ‖ (Geweih⩪) *beam, main stem* ‖ Schutz⩪ *guard-rail* **Sitz**⩪ *perch, roost* ‖ Stoß⩪ ⟨mot⟩ *bumper* ‖ Stütz⩪ *prop* ‖ Zahnstange (Bergbahn) *rack* ‖ °⟨sex⟩ = Ständer **C.** ⟨fig fam⟩ **bei** der ~ **bleiben** *to keep to the rails, the point; to stick to business* ‖ jdm die ~ halten (als Freund) *to take up the cudgels for a p; to back, support a p, to take a p's part*; (als Gegner) *to be a match for a p* ‖ jdn bei der ~ halten *to bring a p up to* (*the*) *scratch* ‖ °Anzüge v der ~ *reach-* od *hand-me-downs*; v der ~ *off the peg*; e–n A. v d. ~ **kaufen** *to strip a peg* **St·angen-** ~**aufsatz** m ⟨artill⟩ *tangent-sight* ~**barriere** f ⟨rail⟩ *rod-barrier* ~**besen** m *long-handled broom* ~**bier** n *beer in schooners* ~**blei** n *bar-lead* ~**bohne** f *climbing* od *running* od *pole bean* ~**bohrer** m *auger* ~**eisen** n *bar-iron, rod-iron* ‖ ⟨hunt⟩ *fox-trap* ~**gebiß** n *bar-bit, cannon-bit* ~**gerüst** n *scaffolding of poles* ~**geschirr** n *wheel-harness* ~**gitter** n *grating* ~**handpferd** n *off-wheeler* ~**holz** n *poles* pl; *young copsewood,* ⟨for⟩ *pole-forest, -wood; -timber* ~**käse** m *rolls of cheese* ~**kelch** m *flute glass* ~**pferd** n *wheeler, shaft horse* ~**reiter** m *wheeler, pole driver* ~**sattelpferd** n *pole saddle horse* ~**schwefel** m *roll-brimstone* ~**seife** f *soap in bars* ~**silber** n *silver in ingots* ~**spargel** m *asparagus served whole* ~**stahl** m *bar-steel* ~**steuerung** f ⟨mot⟩ *push-pull control* ~**stromabnehmer** m ⟨el–rail⟩ *trolley*(*-contact*) ~**tabak** m *twist, pigtail* ~**visier** n ⟨artill⟩ *bar sight* ~**zaum** m *cannon-bit; curb-bridle* ~**zaun** m *pole-fence* ~**zinn** n *bar-tin* ~**zirkel** m *beam-compasses* pl ~**zucker** m *butter--scotch* ~**zug** m ⟨tech⟩ (z Kanalreinigung) *sewer rod*

Stank m ~(e)s/ *stench* ‖ ⟨fig⟩ = Stänkerei | ⩪ 1. & 3. sg prt v stinken **St·änker** m ~s/~ *stinking p* od *th*; ⟨fam⟩ *stinker* | ⟨fig fam⟩ *mar--plot, mischief-maker, quarreller* ‖ *prying* od *cantankerous fellow* | ~**·ei** f ~/~en ⟨fig fam⟩ *paltry dispute* od *quarrel* ‖ (schnüffelnde ~) *prying* **st·änkern** vi [h] *to smell*; ⟨fam⟩ *to stink* | ⟨fig fam⟩ *to pick quarrels, to quarrel* ‖ (schnüffeln) *to pry about*

Stanni·ol n ~(e)s/ *leaf-tin, tinfoil* | ~streifen [m pl] ⟨aero⟩ (f Radarstörung) *chaff*

st·antep·e(de) L adv ⟨fam⟩ *pretty damn quick, p.d.q.*; = & → stehend(en Fußes)

St·anze f ~/~n ⟨pros⟩ (8zeilige Strophe) *stanza*

Stanz- ~**automat** m *feed press* **St·anze** f ~/~n ⟨tech⟩ *punch*, (Blech⩪) *die, stamp*(*ing machine*) ‖ (Unterlage) *matrix* **st·anzen** vt [h] *to stamp, punch* **St·anzer** m ⟨comp⟩ *card punch*

St·apel m ~s/~ *pile, heap, stack* ‖ ein ~ Bücher *a p. of books* ‖ ⟨spin⟩ *staple*; v langem ~ *long-s.* (*wool*) | ⟨com⟩ (*stock*)*pile*; (~platz) *mart, emporium, branch, warehouse*; (bes im Freien) *dump* | (Gerüst) *scaffolding*; ⟨theat⟩ (*scenic*) *pack*, ⟨Am⟩ *stack* ‖ ⟨mar⟩ *stocks, slips* pl (*for a ship*) ‖ (Schiff) auf ~ legen *to lay*; vom ~ gehen, laufen *to be launched* ⟨a. fig⟩, *to leave the slips* ‖ vom ~ l *to launch* (*a ship*), ⟨fig⟩ *to let loose* (*a speech*), *to bring out* (*books*) ‖ in ~ setzen (S) → aufstapeln ⩪**bar** a ⟨a.⟩ *nesting* (*chairs*) ~**gerechtigkeit** f *staple-right* ~**gut** n *s.e-goods* pl, *s.e-ware* ~**handel** m *s.e-trade* ~**lauf** m *launch*(*ing*) ~**platz** m → ~ ‖ ⟨mil⟩ *dump* ~**recht** n *s.e-laws*

~ware f = –gut **st·apeln I.** vt [h] *to pile up* ‖ *to stockpile* ‖ (Stückgüter) *to palletize* **II.** ˣ vi [s] *to stalk* (*along*) **St·apelung** f (*stock*)*piling* etc; (v Müll etc) *dumping*

St·apfe f ~/~n *footstep* | **≃n** vi [h & s] *to stamp* ‖ *to plod* od *plug along, to trudge*; (mühselig) *to footslog* ‖ *to stump*

Star m ~(e)s/~e **1.** ⟨orn⟩ (⟨fam⟩ a.) **~matz** m *starling* **2.** ⟨theat⟩ („Stern") *star* **3.** ⟨path, → starr⟩ *cataract* ‖ (grüner) *glaucoma* ‖ (schwarzer) *amaurosis, gutta serena* ‖ jdm den ~ stechen *to couch a* (*p's eye for*) *cataract*; ⟨fig⟩ *to undeceive a p, to open a p's eyes,* ⟨Am⟩ *to put a p wise* **≃blind** a *blind with cataract* **~blindheit** f *blindness caused by c.* **~brille** f *spectacles* pl *for couched eyes* **~operation** f *operation for c.* **~reklame** f ⟨film, theat, bes Am⟩ *star-billing*

Stär m ~(e)s/~e (Widder) *ram, tup*

starb 1. & 3. sg pret v sterben

stark I. [a] **A. 1.** *strong* (*bones, nerves, soul; government, regimen*; ⟨gram⟩ *declension, verbs; string,* etc; *coffee, spirits, cigar*; [⟨a.⟩ *powerful*] *glasses*); die Butter ist ~ .. *is on the turn*; *short,* ⟨fam⟩ *humming* (*drink*) ‖ *heavy* (*drinker, smoker*) ‖ *mighty* (*God*) ‖ ziemlich ~ *fairish* (*shoulders*) ‖ *powerful* (*glasses, lamp, mind*) | (rüstig) *stout, robust*; ⟨fam⟩ *beefy,* ⟨Am⟩ *rugged, husky* (*fellow*) | *sturdy* (*nature*) **2.** (dick) (P) *stout, corpulent* ‖ ~ w *to put on flesh* od *weight*, sehr .. *to put on a good many pounds*; ~ m, ~ w *to stouten* ‖ er war stärker geworden *he had filled out* | (S) *thick* (*wall, branch*) **3.** (lebhaft) *keen* (*interest*) **4.** (heftig) *violent* (*perspiration, cold*); *high* (*wind*); *splitting* (*headache*); (Geruch) *strong breath*; **≃er** w *to tone up* ‖ der Sturm wird **≃er** *the storm stiffens* ‖ → B. **5.** (bedeutend) *considerable, great, abundant* | (groß) *large* (*family, army, demand*), *big* (*words*) ‖ ⟨pharm⟩ *stiff, high* (*dosis*); *heroic* (*drug*) **6.** *good* (*player, memory*) **7.** (willens~) *strong-minded*; sich ~ m etw (z tun) *to pledge* od *bind o.s.* (*to do*); darin ist er ~ *he's a a good hand* od *very skilful at that* **8.** ⟨mus⟩ *forte* **B.** → A. 1. (**Arm**) *vigorous,* ⟨poet⟩ *stark* (*arm of war*) ‖ ~e Auflage *large edition* ‖ (Band) *big* ‖ (Baum) *well-grown* ‖ ~e Dramatik *dramatic iron*; (Erkältung) *bad* ‖ (**Esser**) *hearty* ‖ (Familie) *large, numerous* ‖ (Fieber) *high* ‖ (Frost) *hard* ‖ (Geschlecht) *stronger* ‖ (Getränk) *strong, potent,* ⟨Am a.⟩ *hard* ‖ (Hirsch) *warrantable* ‖ (Husten) ⟨fam⟩ *blustering* ‖ (Kälte) *severe* ‖ (**Meile**) *good, long* ‖ (Papier) *thick* ‖ (Raucher) *avid* ‖ ~e Seite ⟨fig⟩ *strong point* ‖ (Strom) ⟨el⟩ *strong* ‖ (Stunde) *good* ‖ das ist (doch) zu ~, *or* ein ~es **Stück,** ⟨fam⟩ das ist ~er Tobak *that's a bit thick!, that is coming* od *going it too strong* ‖ in ~en Tagemärschen *by forced marches* ‖ (Trinker) *heavy* ‖ (Tuch) *strong* ‖ (Übertreibung) *great* ‖ (Verkehr) *heavy* ‖ (Wind) *high, strong* ‖ *extensive* (Zerstörungen [pl] *destruction*) ‖ (Zumutung) *rather too much of a good th* **C. 40000** Mann ~ *forty thousand strong* ‖ 100 Millionen ~ *100 million people strong* ‖ e–e 40 Mann ~e Bande *a band of 40 men* ‖ viele hundert Seiten ~ *containing many hundreds of pages*; → A. **D.** ⟨fig⟩ ein wenig **zu** ~; etw zu ~! *pretty thick* (→ ~es Stück) ‖ zu ~e Dosis *overdose* ‖ zu ~ betonen *to overstress* ‖ zu ~ braten *to overdo* **E. stärker** w → A. 2. 4. ‖ (Gefühl) *to deepen* ‖ (Fieber) *to increase* (in mir *on me*) ‖ **≃er** s als *to prevail against* od *over*; ~ vertreten s *to be more fully represented* **F.** ~ **an** Waffen *strong in arms* ‖ [adv] ~ **auf** 10 Uhr *nearly ten* ‖ **in**: *clever, skilful at* ‖ er ist ~ im Glauben, Denken *he is a strong believer, he is strong in thinking* ‖ darin ist er ~ *he is a good hand* od *great at that* ‖ ⟨fam⟩ er ist ~ [adv] in den Vierzigern *he is getting on for fifty* **II.** [adv] *very much, hard* (→ I. D., F.); *badly* ‖ *strongly* (*defended*) ‖ *heavily* (*diluted*) ‖ *well* (*attended lecture*) ‖ *strongly-brewed* (*beer*) ‖ *thickly* (*populated*) | (*to smell*) *loudly* ‖ (*to freeze, rain*) *hard* ‖ (*to gesticulate*) *freely, largely* ‖ (*to run*) *fast* ‖ (*to bleed*) *profusely* ‖ (*to work*) *hard* | *keenly interested* (an *in*) | ~ essen, trinken *to be a hearty eater, heavy drinker* ‖ er hinkt ~ *he walks with a pronounced limp* ‖ man spricht ~ davon *it is much talked of* | ~ beansprucht w *to be subject to strain and fatigue*; *their threngtth is greatly sapped* (*by movements*) | ⟨fig fam⟩ ~ benebelt *far-gone* | ~ gesucht *in great demand* ‖ ~ verschuldet *deeply in debt* ‖ ~ in Anspruch genommen *very much engaged* **III. der Starke**: dem ~n gehört die Welt *victory always goes to the strong* ‖ das Recht des Stärkeren *the rights of the stronger* **~bel·eibt, ~leibig** a *corpulent, stout* **~besetzt** a *well-attended, crowded* **≃bier** n *strong brown stout* **~gebaut** a *powerful* **~gläubig** a *staunch in faith* **~gliedrig** a *strong-limbed* **~knochig** a *well-boned* **≃strom** m ⟨el⟩ *power* (*current*) | ~kabel [n] *power-cable*; ~leitung [f] ⟨el⟩ *power-line*; ~sperre [f] ⟨mil⟩ *electrified obstacle* **≃ton** m *ictus* **~wirkend** a *powerful, strong* ‖ *efficacious*

St·ärke f ~/ **1.** *strength, force* ‖ (Rüstigkeit) *vigo*(*u*)*r, robustness* ‖ *intensity* (*of light*) ‖ *potency* (*of drinks*) ‖ ⟨mot, opt⟩ *power* ‖ ⟨mil⟩ *potential*; zur ~(nachweisung) gehörig *on the strength* ‖ (Dicke) *corpulence, stoutness* ‖ ⟨tech⟩ *ga*(*u*)*ge* ‖ (Heftigkeit) *violence* ‖ (Größe) *largeness, size* ‖ (Anzahl) *strength*; *density* (*of population*) | (starke Seite) *strong point*; ⟨cards⟩ *long suit* ⟨a. fig⟩ ‖ innere ~ *fortitude, virility, backbone*; s–e ~ liegt im Singen *he is good at singing* **2.** (Wäsche≃) *starch* **≃artig** a *s.chy* **~blau** n *blue s.ch* **~grad** m *strength* **~gummi** n *dextrine* **~kleister** m *s.ch-paste* **~mehl** n *s.ch-flour* **~meldung** f ⟨mil⟩ *morning report* N (*strength report* od *return*) **~nachweis(ung** f) m ⟨mil⟩ *table of organization* od *distribution* **~- u Ausrüstungsnachweis** m (*STAN*) *table of organization and equipment* (*TOE*) **~zucker** m *s.ch-sugar* **st·ärken** vt [h] **1.** *to strengthen* ‖ ⟨med⟩ *to give tone to* ‖ (Herz) *to stimulate* ‖ wieder ~ *to restore* ‖ (bestärken) *to corroborate* ‖ den Magen ~ *to recruit the inner man* ‖ (den Mut) *to brace up* ‖ jdm den Rücken ~ ⟨fig⟩ *to stiffen a p* ‖ (Wirtschaft, Plan etc) *to bolster* | **sich** ~ *to take some refreshment*; *to fortify o.s.* (mit *with*) **2.** (Wäsche) *to* (*clear-*)*starch* | **~d** a *strengthening* ‖ ⟨med⟩ *restorative* ‖ *nourishing* (*diet*) ‖ –des Mittel *tonic* **St·ärkung** f ~/~en *strengthening, invigoration, fortifying* ‖ (Erfrischung) *refreshment* **~smittel** n *restorative, tonic* ‖ ⟨fam⟩ *pick-me-up* ⟨a. fig⟩

St·arnberger See m (in Oberbayern)

Star·ost m ~en/~en [Polish] *starost*

starr a *stiff* (*limbs, silk*), *benumbed* (*limbs*) ‖ (unbeweglich) *rigid* ⟨tech⟩ *fixed* (⟨a. aero⟩ Fahrwerk) ‖ (Blick) *fixed*; *set* (*face, smile*); (im Tode) *glassy* ‖ (unbeugsam) *inflexible* (*laws*); *rigid* (*rules*) ‖ ⟨aero⟩ *rigid* ‖ (Sinn) *stubborn, unbending* ‖ (vor Entsetzen) *paralysed, transfixed* ‖ (Entsetzen) *paralysing* ‖ (vor Überraschung) *dumbfounded, flabbergasted, thunderstruck* ‖ *aghast* (über *at*); ~ vor Staunen *petrified with amazement* ‖ ~ w *to stiffen* (vor Angst *with terror*); s–e Augen w ~ *his eyes set* | [adv] jdn ~ ansehen *to stare at a p*; ~ blickend *walleyed* **St·arr-~flügler** m ⟨off⟩ = Flugzeug **~kopf** m *bullhead; stubborn fellow*; *headstrong, hard-mouthed, obstinate p* **~köpfigkeit** f = –sinn **~krampf** m ⟨path⟩ *tetanus* **~leinwand** f *buckram* **~schmiere** f *solid lubricant* **~sinn** m *stubbornness, obstinacy* **≃sinnig** a *stubborn, headstrong, obstinate* **~sucht** f ⟨path⟩ *torpor, catalepsy* **≃süchtig** a *cataleptic* **st·arren I.** vi [h] (mit den Augen) *to stare* (vor sich hin *in front of one*; ins Blaue *into vacancy*; ins Leere *into space*; vor Staunen *in astonishment*) | *to be numb* (*with cold*) ‖ ⟨fig⟩ (dicht besetzt s mit) *to bristle, to be crowded* od *studded* (vor [dat] *with*); *to be covered* (*with*); *to be begrimed* (*with dirt*) **II.** ≗ n (*vacant*) *stare, staring* **St·arrheit** f ~/ *stiffness, numbness, rigidity* || *fixedness* || *inflexibility* || *stubbornness, obstinacy*

St·art m ~(e)s/~e ⟨sport, mot, etc & fig⟩ *start*; fliegender ~ ⟨sport⟩ *running st.* || ⟨aero⟩ *take-off, taking-off*; (Raketen≗) *lift-off*; ⟨a–n⟩ *shoot*; ~ mit Raketenunterstützung *boosted take-off* | *starting-point* | ⟨fig⟩ guter ~ *head st.* | ⟨a–n⟩ 9′15″ bis zum ~ *9.15 to lift-off* | 6′56″ nach ~ *6.56 into mission* | vor ~ *before take-off*; (Rakete) *b. lift-off* || mit stehendem Motor *stall st.* **~antrieb** m (Raketen≗) *booster power* | ~s-phase [f] *boost-ph.* **~bahn** f ⟨aero⟩ *runway*; ⟨a–n⟩ *launching-site* **~band** n ⟨film⟩ *leader strip* **≗bereit** a ⟨aero⟩ *ready for t.-o.*; *in flying condition*; ~ m *to make ready for flight* (⟨a.⟩ sich ..), *to tune up* || ⟨sport⟩ *ready* (od *all keyed-up*) *to go* || ⟨fig⟩ *poised on the brink of action* **~bereitschaft** f ⟨aero⟩ *ground alert* **~dauer** f ⟨aero⟩ *time to t.-o.* **~deck** n *flight-deck* **~düse** f *easy-st. jet* **~erlaubnis** f *clearance to t.-o.* **~fenster** n ⟨a–n⟩ (zeitlich) (*start*) *window* **≗fertig** a ⟨aero⟩ *in running order* **~geld** n ⟨sport⟩ *entry fee* **~genehmigung** f = –erlaubnis; *permission to t.-o.* **~gewicht** n *initial* od *t.-o. weight* ⟨a. a–n⟩ **~grube** f ⟨sport⟩ *st.ing pit* | mit **~hilfe** f ⟨aero⟩ (*jet-*)*assisted* (*t.-o.*) **≗klar** a *ready for t.-o.* **~kontrollraum** m ⟨a–n⟩ *firing control room* **~kraft** f ⟨a–n⟩ *launching power* **~meldung** f ⟨aero⟩ *departure message* **~phase** f ⟨a–n⟩ *boost ph.* **~rakete** f ⟨aero⟩ *booster*; *b. rocket*; *r.-assisted t.-o. gear*; *launching r.* **~schleuder** f ⟨aero⟩ *catapult* **~schuß** m ⟨a–n⟩ *blast-off* **~seil** n (Segelflug) *l.g rope* **~/Stopeinrichtung** f ⟨comp⟩ *automatic stopping and st.ing* (*device*) **~/Stop-Taste** f ⟨rec⟩ *stop-start control* **~strecke** f ⟨aero⟩ *t.-o. distance* **~- u Landebahn** f ⟨aero⟩ *runway* N (befestigt *paved*) **~verbot** n *prohibition from flying*; ~ h *to be grounded* **~vorrichtung** f *catapult* **~wagen** m *launching trailer* **~zählung** f *count-down* **~zeichen** n *st.ing signal*; ⟨aero⟩ *t.-o. order*; ⟨traffic⟩ (grünes Licht) ⟨fam⟩ *go-ahead*

st·arten vi/t [s & h] *to start* (zu *for*), ⟨aero, a–n⟩ *to take off*; *to take the air* | ⟨sport⟩ *to start*; *to get off the mark*; *to take part in a race* | ⟨fig a.⟩ *to begin* || gestartet w *to be in course of preparation* **St·arter** m ~s/~ (P), ⟨mot⟩ (S) *starter*; (S ⟨a.⟩) *cranking motor* | ~klappe [f] *choke*; ~ritzel [m & n] *st.r pinion*; ~segment [n] *st.r quadrant*

stat·arisch a *slow and careful* (*reading*) **St·atik** f ~/~en *statics* pl [a. sg konstr] **Stati·on** f ~/~en ⟨rail⟩ *station* ⟨a. rel, scient, wir, mar⟩ || (Haupt≗) *terminus* || (Halte≗) *stopping-place* | ⟨med⟩ *ward* | freie ~ *board and lodging* (*found*), (⟨a.⟩ *all found*) | in kurzen ~en *by short* od *easy stages* || ~ m *to break one's journey* **station·är** a *stationary* || *static* (*population*) || ⟨phys⟩ *steady* (*state, flow*); ⟨med⟩ (Ggs ambulant) *in-patient* (*treatment*) **station·ieren** vt h *to station* || –rt s *to be stationed* **S–ierungsmächte** f pl (⟨Ger pol⟩ seit 5.5.1955) *Sender States* **Stati·ons-** ~arzt [m] *house* (*resident*) *physician*; ~chef [m] ⟨mar⟩ *commander-in-chief*; ~hilfe [f] ⟨med⟩ *ward-maid*; ~gebäude [n] ⟨rail⟩ *station*; ~vorsteher [m] ⟨rail⟩ *st.-master*, ⟨Am⟩ *st. agent* **st·atisch** a *statical* | [adv] ~ erproben *to static-test* **st·ätisch** a *restive* (*horse*) **Stat·ist** m ~en/~en ⟨theat⟩ *stand-in*; *extra*; *super*; ⟨fam⟩ *dummy* | **~en-** ~fach [n] *super line* || e–e ~rolle spielen *to have a walking-on part* | **~in** f ~/~nen ⟨theat⟩ *figurante* Fr **Stat·istik** f ~/~en *statistics* pl [a. sg konstr] (über *about*, ⟨Am⟩ *on*) [*st.s in its modern form*; *st.s are compiled*]; ⟨comp⟩ *statistical precedures*; ~ des Bevölkerungsstandes *current population st.s*; ~ der Geburten u Sterbefälle, ~ der natürl. Bev.sbewegung *vital st.s*; ~ des Gesundheitswesens *health st.s* | ~enlehre [f] *taxonomy, biotaxy* | **~er** m ~s/~ *statistician* **stat·istisch** a *statistical* || ~e Angaben, Ausweise (*st.l*) *returns* pl || staatl. ~es Amt *st.l department*; Leiter des ~en Amts *Registrar General* **Stat·iv** [–f] n ~(e)s/~e [–və] (ausziehbar *telescopic*, ⟨Am⟩ *folding*), ⟨theat⟩ *stand, support* || ⟨phot, film⟩ *tripod*

Statt f ~/ *place, stead* || = Stätte || an m–r ~ *in my place* || an Eides ~ *in lieu of an o.* || an Kindes ~ annehmen *to adopt* || an Zahlungs ~ *instead of p.* || → an≗, von≗en, zu≗en **statt** prep [gen] *instead of, in lieu of* || ~ meiner *instead of me, in my place* || ~ zu tun, ~ daß er tut *instead of doing* || ~ bei der Arbeit *instead of being at work* **St·ätte** f ~/~n *place* || bleibende ~ *abode*; *abiding home* || ⟨med⟩ (*treatment*) *facility* **st·att-** ~|**finden** vi irr [h], ~|**haben** vi irr [h] *to have* od *take place, to happen, to be* (*where the game was to be*), *to be on, to come off* ~|**geben** vi irr [h] [dat] *to give way to*; *to grant* (*a petition*), *to allow* (*a claim*) **~haft** a *admissable, allowable* || *lawful, valid, legitimate, legal* || *permitted* || *competent* (daß jd tut *for a p to do*) | ~igkeit [f] *permissibility* **≗halter** m ~s/~ *governor* || *viceroy* || ⟨hist⟩ *stad*(*t*)*holder* (*in Holland*) **≗halter·ei** f ~/~en; **≗halterschaft** f ~/ (Amt) *governorship* || (Bereich) *government* **st·attlich** a (→ Staat 2.) *stately* || (schön) *handsome, comely* || (prächtig) *splendid, grand, lofty*; *magnificent* || (würdevoll) *portly, personable, imposing, commanding, noble* || *pretentious* || *respectable* (*names*) || (wichtig) *considerable* || *tidy* (*sum*); *goodly* (*number*) | [adv] *sumptuously, luxuriously* (*fitted up*) | **≗keit** f *stateliness* etc **St·atue** f ~/~n *statue* || pl *statuary* **st·atuenhaft** a *statue-like, statuesque* **Statu·ette** f ~/~n *figurine* **statu·ieren** vt [h] *to decree, establish, enact, ordain* **Stat·ur** f ~/~en *stature, height, size* || *figure* || s–e kl ~ *his shortness of stature*; v kl ~ *on the small side* **St·atus** m ~/ *state, status* || ~ quo *actual state*; im ~ quo l *to leave* (*ths*) *as they are* od *were* **Stat·ut** n ~(e)s/~en *statute, regulations* pl || ~en ⟨com⟩ *articles* pl (*of an association*); (öffentl. rechtlich) *ordinances*; (privatrechtl.) *by-laws* **stat·uten-** **~gemäß,** (~widrig) a *according* (*contrary*) *to regulations* **≗kollision** f ⟨internat. law⟩ *conflict of laws* **~mäßig** a *statutory* **≗recht** n *statutory law*

Stau m ~(e)s/~e ⟨tech⟩ *pond*; *backwater*; [abstr] *ram*; *impoundage* || das Wasser ist im ~ *the tide is turning* || im ~ halten *to dam up* **~anlage** f *barrage* **~becken** n *reservoir* **~bereich** m *backwaterzone* **~damm** m *high* (*retaining*) *dam* **~druck** m *ram*; *pressure head*; ⟨phys⟩ *stagnation pr.*; ⟨aero⟩ *impact* od *dynamic pr.* | ~fahrtmesser [m] *dynamic air speed indicator*; ~fahrtschreiber [m] *pr. speed* (⟨Am⟩ *Pitot static air sp.*) *recorder* **~höhe** f *height of raised water*; *weight of swell* **~keil** m ⟨mar⟩ *chock* **~luft** f *ram air* **~mauer** f *impounding dam, retaining wall* **~raum** m ⟨mar⟩ *hold, stowage-room* **~rohrheizung** f ⟨aero⟩ *pitot-head heater* **~see** m *impounded reservoir* od *lake*; *dam reservoir* **~stoß** m ⟨el⟩ *rush of current* **~strahl(rohr** n) m, **~strahltriebwerk** n *aero-thermodynamic duct* N (*athodyd*); *ramjet* **~stufen** f pl *barrages* **~(ung** f) ⟨eth⟩ *damming-up* **~wasser** n *backwater* **~wehr** n *weir* **~wirkung** f *ram effect*; → stauen etc

Staub m ~(e)s/ *dust* || *powder* | viel ~ aufwirbeln ⟨fig⟩ *to raise a dust, to make a splash* || was f ~ würde es aufw.! *what a dust-up there would be*! || den ~ löschen *to settle the dust* || den ~ hinunterspülen (trinken) *to play off* od *to lay one's dust, to wet one's clay* | sich **aus** dem ~e m ⟨fam fig⟩ *to clear off*; *to bolt, decamp*; (schnell) *to skip it*; *to show a clean pair of heels* | **im** ~e baden ⟨orn⟩ *to pulverize* ‖ ⟨fig⟩ in den ~ sinken *to grovel in the d.* ‖ jdn in den ~ werfen *to throw a p to the ground* ‖ ⟨bib⟩ wieder **zu** ~ w *to return to dust* **~abscheider** m *dust separator; dust collector* **~besen** m *duster, dust(ing)-brush* **~beutel** (.. **tragend** a) m ⟨bot⟩ *anther(iferous)* **~bindungsmittel** n *road binder* **~blatt** n *stamen* **~blüte** f *male flower* **~brand** m *smut* **~brille** f ⟨mot⟩ *goggles* pl **~bürste** f *dust(ing)-brush* **~dicht, ~geschützt** a *dustproof* **~faden** m *filament* **~fänger** m *dust-catcher* **~filteranlage** f *dedusting filter* **~flocke** f *flue* **~geboren** a ⟨rel⟩ *of clay*; ⟨fig⟩ *baseborn* **~gefäß** n ⟨bot⟩ *stamen* **~hülle** f ⟨rel, poet⟩ *mortal coil* **~kamm** m *fine-tooth comb* **~kittel** m *smock-frock* **~kohle** f *small coal* **~korn** n *dust particle* **~lappen** m, **~tuch** n *duster* **~lawine** f *avalanche of dry snow* **~lunge** f *silicotic lungs* pl **~mantel** m *dust-cloak*, ⟨Am⟩ *duster* **~maske** f *dust respirator* **~mehl** n *mill-dust, dustings* pl **~perle** f *seed-pearl* **~pilz** m ⟨bot⟩ *puff-ball* **~plage** f *dust nuisance* **~regen** m *drizzling rain, Scotch mist* **~same(n)** m ⟨bot⟩ *pollen* **~sand** m *fine sand* **~sauger** m *vacuum-cleaner*, ⟨tech⟩ *dust-extractor* **~saugern** vi/t ⟨fam⟩ *to vacuum* **~sieb** n *dust-sieve* **~wedel** m *(feather-)duster, (f.-)whisk* **~weg** m ⟨bot⟩ *pistil* **~wolke** f *dust cloud, cloud of dust* **~zucker** m *sifted* od *castor* od *icing sugar* **St·äubchen** n ~s/~ *speck of dust; (dust-)mote, atom* **st·auben** vi [h & s] *to give off dust* ‖ **es** staubt (kolossal) *it is dusty*, ⟨stud sl⟩ *I'm parched* (= *thirsty*); ⟨mil⟩ *let's play off our* od *lay the dust* (= *drink*) **st·äuben** vt/i [h] *to raise* od *scatter dust* ‖ (abstäuben) *to dust* ‖ (spritzen) *to spray* **St·äuber** m ~s/~ *duster* ‖ (Spritze) *spray* **st·aubig** a *dusty, powdery* | **~keit** f ~/ *dustiness*

St·auche f ~/~n **1.** ⟨agr⟩ *heap, bundle; stook* (*of hemp* etc) **2.** (Pulswärmer, vgl Fr étui) *muffetee* | **~n** vt [h] *to toss, jolt* ‖ ⟨tech⟩ *to upset* ‖ ⟨agr⟩ *to stook (hemp)* | °⟨fig fam⟩ **1.** *to steal* **2.** *to rebuke, to call over the coals* | ~ n ⟨met⟩ *pressure forging* | °**~r** m ~s/~ **1.** ⟨fam⟩ *sweat, drudgery* **2.** *rebuke*

St·aude f ~/~n *hardy annual; shrub, brush, bush* ‖ *head (of lettuce)* | **~n** vi [h & s] *to grow into shrubs* ‖ *to (form a) head* **~nartig** a *shrubby* **~ngewächs** n *shrub* **~nsalat** m *headed lettuce, cabbage-lettuce* **~sellerie** m *celery sticks* **st·audig** a *shrubby*

st·auen vt [h] ⟨mar⟩ *to stow (away)* ‖ (Wasser) *to dam up* ‖ ⟨hum⟩ *to dispatch* (= *eat*) ‖ ⟨psych⟩ (Erregung) *to accumulate* | **sich** ~ [h] *to be jammed, stopped* od *congested; traffic piles up* ‖ (v Wasser) *to rise* **St·auer** m ~s/~ ⟨mar⟩ *stevedore* **~lohn** m *stowage*

Staufferfett n *cup grease*

St·aunen n ~s/ *astonishment, amazement* ‖ jdn in ~ versetzen *to astonish, surprise a p*; ⟨fam⟩ *to make a p sit up* ‖ voll ~ *in perplexity* ‖ ~ erregend *astonishing, disconcerting* ‖ etw mit ~ z Kenntnis nehmen *to arch one's eyebrows at a th* **st·aunen** vi [h] *to marvel; to be astonished, surprised*, (sehr) *amazed* (über [acc] *at*) (daß *that*) ‖ man staune! .. *of all amazing ths ..* ‖ ⟨fam⟩ da staunt der Laie! *that's a startler!* | ~d *wondering (eyes); in amazement* ‖ [adv] *astonishingly (cheap)* **~swürdig** a *astonishing, amazing*

St·aup- ~besen m *scourge, lash* **~säule** f *whipping post* **St·aupe** f ~/~n **1.** *flogging, scourging* **2.** ⟨vet⟩ (in dogs) *distemper*; (in horses) *strangles* pl ‖ ⟨fig⟩ *crisis; shower (of rain)* **st·äupen** vt [h] *to flog, whip, scourge*

St·auung f ~/~en ⟨mar⟩ *stowage* ‖ (des Wassers) *swell, rising*, (Aufstauen) *damming up* ‖ (Verkehrs~) *congestion, stoppage*; ~en [pl] *traffic hold-ups* ‖ ⟨med⟩ *engorgement, congestion* ‖ ⟨eth⟩ *damming up* ‖ (zusammengedrängte Masse) *jam*; → Stau, stauen

Stear·in n ~(e)s/ *stearin(e)* **~kerze** f, **~licht** n *stearin-* (od *composite*) *candle* **~säure** f ⟨chem⟩ *stearic acid*

St·ech- ~apfel m *thorn-apple* **~bahn** m *lists* pl, *tilt-yard* **~becken** n → Steck- **~beitel** m ⟨carp⟩ *ripping-chisel* **~bolzen** m *pointed arrow*; ⟨mar⟩ *reef-ear-ring* **~dorn** m *Christ's thorn* **~eiche** f *holm-oak* **~eisen** n *punch* ‖ ⟨met⟩ *tapping-bar* **~fliege** f *stinging* od *gad-fly*; → fly **~gabel** f *fish-spear* **~ginster** m *furze, gorse, whin* **~heber** m *plunging siphon; wine taster; pipette* Fr; ⟨fam⟩ *thief* **~helm** m ⟨hist⟩ *jousting* od *tilting helmet* **~karte** f *winning card* **~mücke** f *gnat, mosquito* **~nelke** f *rose-campion* **~palme** f *holly(-tree)* **~puppe** f *quintain* **~ring** m *tilting-ring* **~sattel** m *jousting-saddle* **~scheibe** f *target* **~schloß** n = Stecher ‖ im **~schritt** m *at the goose-step* **~uhr** f *attendance recorder* **~winde** f ⟨bot⟩ *smilax* **~zeug** n *punching-tools*; ⟨carp⟩ *chisels* pl ‖ ⟨hist⟩ *tilting armour* od *lances* pl **St·echen** n ~s/~ *tournament, tilt(ing), joust(ing)* ‖ ⟨arts⟩ *engraving* ‖ ⟨path⟩ *stitch (in the side), stinging pain*; ich habe ein ~ in der Haut *my skin prickles* ‖ ⟨sport⟩ (bei gleichen Punkten) *playing off the tie* **st·echen** vt/i [stach/gestochen] [h] **A. 1.** (Dorn, Nadel etc) *to prick* (sich *o.s.* mit *with*) [durch *through*, in *in(to)*], *to jab (into)* | jdn **tot**|~ *to stab a p* | (Insekt) *to sting*, (Floh, Schlange) *to bite* ‖ (Pflanze) *to urticate* ‖ die Sonne sticht .. *is beating down, scorching, burning* ‖ (Schmerzen) *to sting*, (nervöse) *to shoot* **B.** ⟨arts⟩ *to engrave* (in Kupfer *on* ..); (punktiert) *to stipple* | ⟨cards⟩ *to take, trump* ‖ ⟨whist⟩ *to ruff* ‖ ~ müssen *to be forced* ‖ die Karte sticht .. *takes the trick* | ⟨hist⟩ (ritterlich) *to joust* | ⟨med⟩ *to puncture* | ⟨sport⟩ (bei gleichen Punkten) *to play off the tie* | ⟨tail⟩ *to stitch* | ⟨tech⟩ *to prod* **C. (Tiere)** *to kill, slaughter* ‖ (Hirsch, Bär, Sau, Schwein) *to stick*; (Fische) *to leister* | (Rasen, Torf, Spargel, Petschafte) *to cut* | (Gewehr) *to pull the trigger* | e–n Kegel *to knock over* | die Kontrolluhr ~ *to check in* bzw *out* | **Wein** *to tap wine with the siphon* | **Löcher** *to pierce holes (in a p's ears)* | ⟨fig⟩ **Silben** ~ *to split hairs, to pick one's words* **D.** e–m den Degen **durch** den Leib ~ *to run one's sword through a p* ‖ durch u durch ~ *to pierce, perforate* | das stach ihr **in** die Augen *that dazzled her eyes*, ⟨fig⟩ *caught her eye, took her fancy; she covets that greatly* ‖ sich in den Finger ~ *to prick one's finger* ‖ jdm ein Messer in den Leib ~ *to run a knife into a p* ‖ *to stab a p in the arm* ‖ *to stab a weapon into ..* ‖ (v Farben) ins Rote ~ *to incline to red* ‖ in See ~ [s] *to put to sea, to set sail, to stand for the offing* ‖ in ein Wespennest ~ *to stir up a wasp's nest* | **mit** e–m Dolch ~ *to stab (with a dagger)*; mit dem Messer ~ *to knife* ‖ sich [acc] mit e–r Nadel in den F. ~ *to run a needle through one's finger* | ~ **nach** *to thrust at* (mit *with*) ‖ nach dem Ring ~ *to tilt* | **um** etw ~ *to cast lots for a th* ‖ **vom** Pferde ~ *to unhorse* **E. es** sticht mir *or* mich in der Seite *I have* od *feel a stitch* od *pain in the side* **F.** wie **gestochen** (*to write*) *like copperplate* ‖ Augen wie ein gestochenes Kalb *bulging eyes* **st·echend** a *stinging, pricking* ‖ *piercing (eyes)* ‖ *penetrating (glance)* ‖ *pungent (smell)* ‖ *sharp, burning (pains)* **St·echer** m ~s/~ *pricker* ‖ *tilter, jouster* ‖ *engraver* | (am Gewehr) *hair-trigger* ‖ (Feld~) *binoculars* pl ‖ (f Käseproben) *taster* **St·eck- ~amboß** m *stake* **~anschluß** m ⟨el⟩ *connector* **~becken** n ⟨med⟩ *bedpan* **~brief** m *warrant* od *apprehension (of arrest)* (erlassen *to take out*) **~brieflich** [adv] *by warrant* ‖ er wird ~ verfolgt *there is a warrant out against him* **~dose** f ⟨el⟩ *power-point; wall-socket; (socket) outlet* **~einheit** f ⟨comp⟩ *valve unit* **~kissen** n *pillow to carry a baby in* **~kontakt** m ⟨el⟩ *plug contact* **~ling** m ⟨bot⟩ *cutting* **~nadel** f *pin*; .. wie e–e ~ gesucht *we looked for it like* *for a pin in a haystack* | ~kissen [n] *pincushion*; ~spitze [f] *pin-point*; ~kopf [m] *pin's head* **~perlen** f pl ⟨tail⟩ *interlocking pearls* **~reis** n *slip, set, shoot* **~rübe** f *swede*; *turnip* **~schlüssel** m *socket wrench* **~schuß** m ⟨med⟩ *retained missile* **~vorrichtung** f ⟨el⟩ *plug-and-socket* **~zwiebel** f *bulb for planting* **St·ecken** m ~s/~ *stick, staff*: ⟨bib⟩ *rod* || er hat Dreck am ~ *he has stains on his waistcoat*; .. *a skeleton in his cupboard* (⟨Am⟩ *in the closet*) **~pferd** n *hobby-horse* || ⟨fig⟩ *hobby*; sein ~ reiten *to mount one's hobby-horse* **~zaun** m *stick-fence* **st·ecken I.** vt [h] **A.** (an, auf, in [acc]) *to stick* (*on*; *into*); *to put, fix, place* (*on*; *in*) || ⟨fam⟩ *to stuff, ram, tuck* [*in*(*to*)] || mit Nadeln *to pin*; fest~ (los~) *to* (*un*)*fix*, (*un*)*pin*, (*un*)*fasten* || (Nadel) *to stick* (*in*); (Papier) *to slip* (*in*) | °**es** jdm ~ *to give a p a piece of one's mind, to hit a p home*, → C. **B.** (**eilig**) *to huddle* (*into*) || (heimlich) *to slip* (*into*) || (schnell) *to pop* (*one's head* z Tür herein *in at the door*, um .. *round the door*) || (täppisch) *to fumble* (*into*) || wieder ~ *to return, restore* (*to*) **C.** (**Gardinen**) *to fix up* || Grenzen ~ *to set bounds* || [dat] das Haar ~ *to dress a p's hair* || jdm (e–e Neuigkeit) ~ *to tell a p .. secretly* || (**Pflanzen**) *to set, plant* || jdm ein Ziel ~ *to set a p a task*; *to keep a p in bounds* || °**es** e–m ~ *to hit a p home*, → A. | gesteckt voll *crowded* (*out*), *crammed full* **D. an**: *to stick .. on, to pin .. to* (*one's hat*); *to put .. on the spit* | **durch**: *to slip* od *pass .. through a th* | **sich hinter** e–n (etw) ~ *to shelter behind a p, to make a tool of a p* (*to work a th secretly*) | **in**: *slip it into your pocket*; *put it in your bosom*; *stick it into your mouth*; *insert it into the hole*; *he thrust his hands into his pocket* | **in** Brand ~ *to set on fire, to set fire to* || jdn ins Bett °~ *to confine a p to his bed* || in e–a ~ *to fit into each other* || ins Gefängnis, Kloster ~ *to shut a p up in p., in a m.* || *to invest money in a business*; *to put m. into a b.* || °sich [dat] e–e Zigarre ins Gesicht ~ *to light a c.*: °~ Sie sich das ins G.! *shove that in your face*! .. in den Mund .. *he put the cigar to his m.* || den Kopf in den Sand ~ *to hide one's h. in the s.* || in die Scheide ~ *to sheathe* (*one's sword*) || ⟨fig⟩ e–n in die Tasche ~ *to outdo a p* | **um**: *he poked his head round the corner* | **unter** die Soldaten ~ *to make a p a s.* | **zu** sich ~ *to put in one's pocket* **II.** vi [h] **A. 1.** *to stick* (*fast*) (*in, to*); *to be fixed* (*to*); *to be stuck fast* **2.** *to be* (*somewhere*) (a. P) || *the sword is in the sheath* || da ~ sie *there they are* || wo ~ Sie? *where have you been all this time*? **3.** *to hide, to lie hidden* || in ihm steckt was *there's some good stuff in him* **4.** *to be involved* (*in*) **B. es** steckt mir in allen Gliedern *I feel it in all my limbs* || hier steckt mir's *I've got it here* || da steckt's *there's the rub* || wo's mal nicht drin steckt –! *you can't spin silk from a pig's ear* **C.** ~ **bleiben** [s] *to stick* (*fast*), *to be stuck* (*in*); *to come to a dead stop* || (in der Rede) *to break down*; ⟨theat⟩ *to dry-up, to forget one's lines*; ⟨allg⟩ *the name caught in my throat* || (*of a bullet*) *to lodge* (*in*) || *to remain stuck* (*in the belief* ..); *the discussion got bogged down in trivialities* | ~ **lassen** [h] *to leave* (*in*), *to abandon* || *to leave a p in the lurch* || den Schlüssel ~ l *to leave the key in the door* **D.** (schreien), als ob man **am** Spieß stäke .. *as if one were going to be murdered* | **hinter** s–m Wissen steckt nicht viel *he has all his knowledge in the window*; h. all dem –kte sein Stolz *at the back of it all was his pride*; dahinter steckt was *there is more in that than meets the eye* || er steckt dahinter *he is at the bottom of it* || es steckt Betrug dahinter *there's some trickery about it* | tief **in** Arbeit (Schulden) ~ *to be up to the neck in work* (*up to the ears in debt*) || darin steckt (viel) Arbeit *it takes* od *took a lot of painstaking care* || in jds Haut ~ *to be in a p's shoes* || was steckt dir im Kopf? *what have you got into your head*? || e–e ziemliche Summe darin ~ h *to be in for a pretty sum* || **voller** Nadeln etc ~ *to be full of pins, vice, tricks, wit* | ⟨fam⟩ immer **zu** Hause ~ *to stick for ever at home* | **unter** → Decke **St·ecker** m ~s/~ ⟨el⟩ *plug*(*-top*), *adaptor*; ~ mit Schalter *switch-plug, switchsocket* **St·eckling** m ~s/~e ⟨hort⟩ *slip*

Steg m ~(e)s/~e *path* | (Brücke) *plank, foot-bridge* || *landing-stage, jetty, pier* || *platform* | (Geigen≃) *bridge* | ⟨typ⟩ *stick*, pl *furniture* | ⟨arch⟩ *fillet, frame* | ⟨el⟩ *cell connector* | (Hosen≃) *strap* | (Ketten≃) *stud* **~eisen** n *closed horseshoe* **~hose** f *strapped trousers* pl **~kette** f *stud-chain* **Stegreif** m ~(e)s|~e *stirrup* || aus dem ~ ⟨fig⟩ *ex-tempore, off-hand, on the spur of the moment* || aus dem ~ sprechen ⟨fig⟩ *to extemporize, to improvise*; ⟨bes Am⟩ *to speak off the cuff*, .. spielen *to vamp* **~dichter** m *ex-tempore poet*; *improvisatore* It **~dichtung** f *impromptu* **~komödie** f *commedia dell'arte* It **~witz** m *ad-lib gag*

St·eh- **~·auf(männ)chen** n *cork-tumbler*; *skip-jack* **~ausschank** m *refreshment room* **~bierhalle** f (*refreshment*) *bar* **~bus** m *standee bus* °**~fick** m ⟨sex⟩ *knee-trembler* **~gesellschaft** f ⟨sl⟩ *perpendicular* **~hose** f *pash* (= *passionate*) *pants* **~kragen** m *stand-up collar* || °⟨fig⟩ (auf Bier) → Feldwebel | ~-Beamte(r) [m] etc *white-collar-man* **~lager** n ⟨tech⟩ *plummer-block* **~lampe** f *standard* od *floor lamp* **~leiter** f (*pair of*) *steps* **~platz** m; ein ~ *standing-room*; nur ≃e *st.-r. only* | ≃ler [m] ⟨bes Am⟩ *standee* **~pult** n *st.g-desk, high desk* **~sprung** m ⟨swim⟩ *heeler* **~umlegkragen** m *turn-down* (*collar*) **~vermögen** n ⟨sport⟩ *stamina* [pl; sg konstr]; *standing-, staying-power* **st·ehen I.** vi (vt → E.) [stand/gestanden] [h & ˣs] **A. 1.** (P & S) *to stand* (*firmly, upright*) || *I can hardly stand* (vor .. *for fatigue*) || (*the audience that*) *stand up* || *here once stood an oak* || ich stehe schon .. *I have been an hour* | ⟨gram⟩ (Artikel etc) *to be used* | ⟨hunt⟩ (Hund) *to point, to hold fast* || ⟨min⟩ (v Schichten) *to be inclined more than 45°* || | **da** steht's *there you can read it* **2.** (sich befinden) *to be* (*situated*) || *to be* (*in one's tenth year*) **3.** (Bluten) *to stop* || ⟨mach⟩ *to stand still* || (Uhr) *to have stopped* **B.** [dat] ~ *to sit* (*to a painter*) | (Kleider etc) jdm (gut) [schlecht] ~ *to fit, suit, become a p well* [*ill*]; *that colour is very becoming to you*; der H. steht ihm gut *the hat looks well on him* || °⟨sex⟩ er stand ihm ⟨vulg⟩ *he was horney* **C.** hiermit steht es **anders** *with this it is otherwise* || sie ~ uns fern *they are strangers to us* || es steht fest, daß *it is certain that* || das steht mir frei *I am at liberty to do so* || die Saaten ~ gut *the corn looks well* od *promising* || die S steht gut *matters are in a fair way* || **hoch**: *the prices rule high* || leer: *the flat stands empty* || offen: *the door stands open* || s–e S steht schlecht *his affair looks bad*; *ths go badly* || es steht schlimm um ihn (s–e G.) *he is in a bad way* (*in poor health*) || **sicher**: *the money is safe*(*ly invested*) || **so** steht es *that's where it is*!, *that's how the matter stands*!, *well there we are*! || ~ die Sn **so**? *is the wind in that quarter*? || **still**: *to stand still* ⟨a. mach⟩ || steh doch still! *do keep quiet*!, *don't fidget* || da steht mir der Verstand still! *that beats me*! | zu ~ k *to cost*; das wird ihm **teuer** .. *he will have to pay dear*(*ly*) *for that*; *he will have to pay* (*the piper* od) *through the nose* || sehr traurig ~ *to be at a low ebb* || wie angewurzelt auf der Schwelle ~ *to be rooted to the floor* || (⟨fam⟩ wie geht's), **wie steht's**? *how are you* od *matters* (*getting on*), ⟨fam⟩ *how's the world with you*?; .. zu Hause? *how's your family*? || wie er (es) steht u geht *just as he is* ([*I buy it*] *lock stock and barrel*) || °wie steht's mit ..? *what about* ..?; → G. ~ mit | er weiß nicht, **wo** er steht ⟨fig⟩ .. *where he is* **D.** gesattelt ~ *to be saddled* || es steht geschrieben *it is written* **E.** [vt] °sich [dat] die **Beine** in den Leib ~ *to cool one's heels* || (als) Bürge ~ *to go security* || °ein Loch in die Erde ~ *to wait long enough to take root* || s–n **Mann** ~ *to hold one's own* (gegen *against*) || Modell ~ *to stand model* ([dat] *to*) || Rede ~ *to answer* | **sich** [acc] müde ~ *to tire o.s. with standing* || wie ~ sie sich? *how do they get on (with one another)*? (→ mit jdm ~) || sie ~ sich (pekuniär) gut *they are well situated*, .. dabei *they make quite a good deal of money by it* || sie ~ sich auf .. *they have $ 900 a year*; sich besser ~ *to be better off* || hier steht **es** sich besser, sicherer *here one can stand more comfortably, it's safer to stand here* **F. ~bleiben** [s] *to stop* **~ bleiben** [s] *to remain standing*, ⟨typ⟩ *to remain in type*; dies muß ~ bl. *this must stand; stet!* L || die Zeit –bt nicht ~ *time keeps going on* || *to (make a) stop; to stand still* || ⟨school etc⟩ *where did we leave off* od *stop*? || *she paused for a moment* || *to come to a halt* || ⟨mot⟩ *to conk*, ⟨Am⟩ *to stall* || (vollkommen) *to stop dead*; ⟨mach⟩ *to seize* || (P) ~ bl. bei *to stand fast on (the lessons of the past)*; (plötzlich) *to stop* (od *pull up*) *short* || nicht ~ bl.! *move on!* | ~geblieben *remnant (of walls)* | Geld ~ **haben** bei *to have placed m. with (a p)* || nichts mehr ~ h *to have paid up* || vier Pferde im Stall (zu) ~ h *to keep four horses* | ~ **lassen** *to let alone* || *to leave (one's tick)* ⟨fam⟩ || *to abandon* || e–n ~ l *to leave a p unnoticed*, ⟨fig⟩ *to give a p the slip*; (draußen) *to leave a p to cool his heels*; (in übler Lage) *to l. a p in the lurch* || (Speise) *to leave .. untouched*; die Sp. ~ l *to drop one's fork for good; to leave* od *refuse one's food* || *to leave a th (just) as it stands* od *is* || alles ~ u liegen l *to leave all at rack and manger, to drop everything* || (Geschriebenes) ~ l! *leave it!* || sich e–n Bart ~ l *to grow* (⟨Am⟩ *raise*) *a b.* || ~ **lernen** ⟨a. fig⟩ *to find one's legs* | **es** steht **zu** befürchten, .., daß .. *it is to be feared, expected, it may be hoped that* **G. auf**: *to be, figure, appear in a list* || *the barometer points to fair*; .. *stands at 38°* || ⟨com⟩ *the stocks are at 98 per cent* || das steht auf e–m anderen Blatt *that's up another street* || der Akk. steht auf die Frage „wen" *the acc. follows* od *answers the question "whom"* || auf die Beine zu ~ k *to fall on one's feet* || auf eigenen Füßen ~ *to play off one's own bat* (= *to be independent*) || *(a price) is set upon (his head)* || auf Diebstahl (Mord) steht Gefängnis (der Tod) *theft is punishable* od *punished with imprisonment (murder is a capital crime, a hanging-matter)* | **bei**: *to serve in (the artillery)* || bei s–r Meinung ~ *to adhere to ..* || es steht bei dir *it depends on you, it rests with you*, .. zu bleiben *you are welcome to stay* || es steht nicht bei mir .. *it is not within my power (to do it)* | das –ht **dahin** *it remains to be seen* | **für**: *to asnwer, stand, be responsible for* || (gut) ~ f *to vouch for* || sie ~ f einen Mann *they are all one, they rise like one man* || f den Schaden ~ *to make good all losses* || Aussage steht **gegen** A. *one statement contradicts the other* | **hinter** jdm ~ *to support, help a p* || wir ~ .. *he has our support* || hinter e–r S ~ *to be at the back of a th* || ⟨gram⟩ *to come after ..* | **in**: *to be garrisoned in N.* || in e–m Amt ~ *to occupy a post* || in Arbeit ~ *to be employed*, .. bei jdm *to be in a p's employ* || *tears stood in her eyes* || mit jdm in Beziehung (Briefwechsel) ~ *to be in touch (to correspond) with a p* || *it is to be found in the book* || ⟨fig⟩ wie er im Buch steht *typical* || im Feuer ~ *to stand under fire* || in schweren Kämpfen ~ *to be engaged in ..* || .., was in m–n Kräften steht *(I'll do) my utmost* od *all I can* || sich [dat] im Licht ~ *to stand in one's own l.* || Liste → ~ auf || im Mittelpunkt ~ v *to hold the center of (interest)*; .. steht im M. des Buches *the book focuses on (painting)* || im Rang [gen] ~ *to be in the rank of ..* || in schlechtem Ruf ~ *to be in bad repute* || in jds Sold ~ *to be in a p's pay* || im Verdacht ~ *to be suspected* || was steht in der Zeitung? *what do the papers say?* | er steht nicht allein **mit** s–r Meinung *he is not alone in thinking so* || gut (schlecht) ~ mit *to be on good (strained) terms with* (a. sich mit jdm stehen), *to be on a good footing with, to stand well with* || wie steht's mit ..? *what about (wine)?*; .. Ihnen? *how are you?, how is your health?* | **es** steht schlecht mit ihm (um ihn) *he is in a bad way* | **nach**: → trachten || *the weathercock points to the north* || mit der Deichsel nach: *the car faced the house* | **über** e–m ~ *to be above (superior to) a p*; (im Rang) *to rank above a p, to be a p's superior* | **um** [acc] herum ~ *to stand round ..* || → ~ mit | **unter**: *to be under water, arms* | jdm **vor** Augen ~: *it is present to my mind, I cannot forget it* || vor e–r .. Aufgabe ~ *to be up against a (hard) job* || vor dem Bankrott ~ *to be on the verge of b.* || vor s–r Beförderung ~ *to be down for promotion* (zum .. *to the rank of ..*) || vor Gericht ~ *to take one's trial* || vor dem Ruin ~ *to be faced with r.* || vor Schwierigkeiten ~ *to be confronted with d.* | **zu etw** ~ *to stand for a th* || **zu jdm** ~ *to be loyal to, to adhere to, to take a p's part* || wie ~ Sie dazu? *what do you think about it?* || wie –ht er zu ihr? *what is his attitude to her?* || die Haare ~ mir davon zu Berge *it makes my hair stand on end; his hair sticks up* || was steht Ihnen zu Diensten? *what can I do for you?* || fest zum Reich ~ *to stand firmly to the E.* || jdm zur Seite ~ *to help (stand by) a p* || zu s–m Worte ~ *to stand by one's words, to be as good as one's word* **II.** ≈ n *standing* | ⟨film⟩ (des Bildes) *steadiness* | das ≈ fällt mir schwer *I cannot stand long* | e–e **im** ≈ eingenommene Mahlzeit *a stand--up meal* | Platz z ≈ *standing-room* | z ≈ bringen *to make stand; to stop, stay; to halt (a rebellion)*; (Wagen) ⟨a.⟩ *to pull up*, ⟨Am⟩ *to stall*; (schnaufend) *to snort to a stop* | z ≈ k *to stop; to bring up (he brought up beside her)* || (Wagen) *to come* (quietschend *to squeal*) *to a stop*; schlagartig z ≈ gebracht w *to stop dead* **st·ehend** [pp & a] *standing* (auf *on*) || *upright (shaft)* || *standing* od *regular (army)* || *vertical (engine)* || *stock* od *hackneyed (phrase)* || *fixed (target, capital)* || *stagnant (water)* || *fast (colour)* || ⟨typ⟩ *standing (matter)* || ~en Fußes *on the spot* || (wiederkehrend) *periodical* | gut ~ *becoming (hat)* **St·eher** m ~s/~ ⟨cycl & hors⟩ *(long-distance racer) stayer*; (im Bus) ⟨fam⟩ *strap-hanger* || ⟨racing⟩ *stayer*

St·ehlen n ~s/ *stealing, theft*; ⟨fam⟩ *pilfering* | ≈ vt/i [h] *to steal* (wie ein Rabe *like a magpie*), *to thieve* || (mausen) *to pilfer*, ⟨sl⟩ *pinch, bone* | *to kidnap (children* etc) || ⟨sl⟩ *to snaffle (people's husbands)* | e–m etw ~ *to rob a p of a th; to conquer a p's heart* || *to abstract (a key from a bunch)* | ⟨fig⟩ dem lieben Gott die Zeit ~ *to idle away one's time* || sich [dat] die Zeit ~ müssen *to have to make time somehow* (f, zu *for*) || das [der] kann mir gestohlen w *I don't care two straws* (⟨sl⟩ *a damn) for it [I could worry along without him*, .. mit .. *he can go to the deuce with his plans]* | **sich** ins Haus ~ *to sneak, steal into the h.*; sich seitwärts ~ *to sidle along* || *a ray of light stole through the cleft* || *a sigh broke from her breast* **St·ehler** m ~s/~ *stealer, thief* **St·ehlsucht** f ~/ *cleptomania*

st·ei(e)risch a *Styrian* **St·eiermark** f (in Österr.) *Styria* ≈**er(in** f) m *Styrian*

steif a **A. 1.** *stiff (linen, paper, lining; neck; gait, bow; breeze)* || (erstarrt) *benumbed (limbs)* || ⟨phys⟩ *rigid* || ~er Hut *bowler* || *erect (penis)* || *thick (porridge)* || ~ von .. *stiff with sitting; set fast with rheumatism* **2.** ⟨fig⟩ (Grog) *strong*; e–n ~en G.! *a stiff glass of grog! a nor'-wester!*, etw ≈es *sth short* | (ungeschickt) *awkward, clumsy* || *wooden (fingers)* || °~er Bock *clumsy Dick* | (förmlich) *formal, prim, ceremonious (bow)*;

precise (*manner*) || (gezwungen) *starchy, strait-laced* **B.** ~ m *to stiffen, to dress* || ~ w *to grow stiff* od *rigid* || (v Muskeln) *to stiffen* || ~e Züge annehmen (of face) *to harden* || .. **wie** ~e Puppen (*they sat*) *like ramrods* || ~ wie ein Stock (Bock) *as stiff as a poker* (*as stubborn as a mule*) **C.** [adv] (*to sit*) *rigidly* || (*to nod*) *woodenly, starchily* || die Ohren ~ halten! *never say die! keep a stiff upper lip!* ⟨bes Am⟩ *to take it on the chin* || ~ u fest behaupten *to contend positively, to maintain obstinately* **St·eif-** **~leinen** n *buckram* || (Futter) *backing* **~̊leinen** a (*of*) *b.m* || ⟨fig⟩ *starchy, strait-laced* (*p*) **~̊nackig** a ⟨fig⟩ *stiff-necked* **~rock** m *stiff petticoat* **~werden** n *stiffening* etc || *rigor mortis* L || ⟨physiol⟩ *erection* **St·eife** f ~/~n *stiffness, consistency* | (f die Wäsche) *starch* || (Hutmacher~̊ etc) *dressing, size* || ⟨carp, min⟩ *support, stay* || ⟨arch⟩ *strut* | **~̊n** vt [h] *to stiffen* || (Wäsche) *to starch* || (Hüte) *to dress* || (Stoff) *to size* || ⟨carp, min⟩ *to stay, support* || jdm den Nacken ~ *to buck a p up* | **sich** ~ auf [acc] *to insist upon, to persist in* **Steifen-** ⟨theat⟩ ~gewicht [n] *brace weight*; ~öse [f] *br.-eye* **Steifheit** f ~/~en *stiffness, rigidity* || ⟨physiol⟩ *erection* | *thickness* | *awkwardness* | ⟨fig⟩ *formality, starchiness*

Steig m ~(e)s/~e *path* **~brunnen** m *artesian well* **~bügel** m *stirrup* || ⟨anat⟩ *stirrup-bone* **~eisen** n *climbing-iron; spur* || (z Gehen auf Eis) *crampon* **~fähigkeit** f ⟨aero⟩ *climb*(*ing capacity*) ; ⟨mot⟩ *gradability, grade-ascending ability* **~flug** m *climb* **~geschwindigkeit** f *rate of climb, climbing speed* | ~sanzeiger [m] *climb indicator* **~höhe** f *rise*; ⟨aero⟩ *ceiling*; größte ~ *climbing maximum*; kapillare ~ *capillary r.* od *elevation* **~leitung** f ⟨tech⟩ *standpipe, riser, feed pipe* **~rad** n (e–r Uhr) *balance-wheel* **~riemen** m *stirrup-leather* **~rohr** n *lifting tube* (Pumpe); *rising pipe*(*line*) **St·eige** f ~/~n *ladder* || (Treppe) *steep stairs* pl, *staircase* || (f Hühner) *coop* || ⟨agr⟩ (Zaun~̊) *stile* || (steiler Weg) *ascent* (*the Pfalzburg, Saverne a.*) || → Stiege **St·eigen** n ~s/ *rising, ascending* || (des Bodens) *gradient* || (der Preise) *advance, rise*; (plötzliches) *boom* | (Zunahme) *increase, growth* || *the rise* (*of unemployment*) || das ~ u Fallen *fluctuation* | ⟨com⟩ **auf** ~ spekulieren *to buy for the rise* || **im** ~ *on the upgrade*; im ~ s *to be on the increase, to be rising* || sein Stern ist im ~ *his star is in the ascendant* || ⟨com⟩ Neigung **zum** ~ *upward tendency* **st·eigen I.** vt [stieg/gestiegen] [s] *to climb* (*stairs*) **II.** vi [s] **A.** *to mount, ascend; to go up, climb* || ⟨hors & her⟩ *to rear* || schnell ~ *to zoom* || (Barometer etc, Wasser, Preise) *to rise* || (Wasser ⟨mar⟩) *the tide is coming in* | (Preis a.) *to appreciate*; ⟨com⟩ die Kurse ~ *the market is improving, advancing* || *wool is rising* || *prices, shares are going up*; schwindelnd ~ ⟨fam⟩ *to sky-rocket* | *the fever went higher* | (of feelings) *jealousy began to mount in her; her j. mounted* | ⟨aero⟩ (Ballon) *to go up*; (Flieger) *to climb up* | ⟨orn⟩ *to soar up* | ⟨fam⟩ (stolzieren) *to strut, stalk* || ⟨hors⟩ *to prance, rear* | °⟨fig⟩ *to take place*; ⟨theat⟩ *to be on*; (Lied) *to be sung*; (Rede) *to be delivered*; (Ball, Tanz) *to come off* || (anwachsen) *to increase* | ~ u fallen ⟨fig⟩ *to ebb and flow* | ~ **lassen** *to fly* (*a kite*), ⟨stud sl⟩ *to sing* (*a song*), *to deliver* (*a speech*) **B. abwärts** ~ *to descend, go down* **C. an(s)** Land ~ *to go ashore, to land* | **auf** [acc]: *to climb up on to* (*the railings*) || *to mount, ascend, climb* (*a hill, tree*); (mit e–r Leiter) *to scale* (*a wall*) || aufs Pferd, Rad ~ *to mount* (*a h., bicycle*); *to mount a ladder* || *to get on a table* || *ascend the throne* || (Zahl) *to rise to* || ⟨fig⟩ jdm aufs Dach ~ *to haul a p over the coals* | **aus**: *to alight from a taxi, train* || (Bus) *to debus*; ⟨mar⟩ *to disembark* || *to get out of bed* || *to go out at the window* | **bis zu**: ⟨com⟩ *to amount to* | **durch**: *to enter by the window* | **in** [dat]: *to advance in price* || *to go up* od *to rise in a p's opinion* | **in** [acc]: *to step into the bath* || *to get into bed* || ⟨Ger stud sl⟩ *to sit for* (*an examination*) || ins Flugzeug ~ *to emplane* || *to board* (*a train*) || *the blood raced into* (*flushed in*) *her face* || e–m in den Kopf ~ (of wine) *to mount* od *go to a p's head* | **über** [acc]: *to climb over a fence* | **von**: *to get off a chair* || *to descend from the throne* | (vom) **zu** Pferde ~ *to* (*dis*)*mount*; die Haare ~ mir zu Berge *my hair stands on end* **III.** ~̊ n *appreciation* (*of the* $) ; plötzliches, starkes ~ *steep jump* **st·eigend** [pp & a] *ascending, rising, mounting* etc || *advancing* (*age*); mit ~em Alter *as one grows older* | *growing, increasing* || ⟨a.⟩ *stiff* (*prices*); *mounting* (*popularity*) || ⟨com⟩ *upward* (*tendency*) || ⟨her⟩ (*lion*) *rampant* [Stellung!] **St·eiger** m ~s/~ *climber* || ⟨min⟩ *surveyor, overseer, overman, foreman, head miner* || (Pferd) *rearer* **St·eigerer** m ~s/~ *auctioneer* || ⟨exch⟩ *bull* **st·eigern** vt [h] *to raise* (*the price*) (jdn mit der Miete *to r. a lodger's rent*) || *to increase, expand* (*the output*) || *to aggravate* (*an illness*) || *to strengthen, enhance* (*forces*) || *to rouse* (*a feeling* bis zu .. *to boiling-point*) || *to enrich, intensify, heighten* (*a quality*); ⟨paint⟩ *to enliven* | ⟨bes pol⟩ *to escalate*, ⟨gram⟩ *to compare* | ⟨com⟩ (Auktion) *to outbid* (*a p*) || ⟨exch⟩ die Kurse ~ *to bull the market* | **sich** ~ *to increase, rise* || .. desto mehr steigerte sich .. *the greater was* (*his delight*) || *excitement beats up* || **sich ~d** ⟨a.⟩ *mounting* (*uneasiness*); *cumulative* (*tension*); *climactic* **St·eigerung** f ~/~en *raising* (*of the price*) || ⟨fig⟩ *development, increase, enhancement; expansion*, erhebliche ~ [gen] *sharp rise* (*in exports*) || ⟨path⟩*aggravation*; plötzliche ~ *paroxysm* || (allmähliche) *graduation* || ⟨gram⟩ *comparison* || ⟨Lit, rhet⟩ *gradation* || ⟨mus⟩ *leading* od *coming to a climax; progression; growing in intensity* **~sbetrag** m *increment* **~sformen** f pl *comparative forms* (*c. f. & superlative*) **~sgrad** m, **~sstufe** f *degree of comparison* **~sklausel** f *escalator clause* **St·eigung** f ~/~en *rise* (*of 10 degrees*) || *gradient, slope, ascent* || ⟨tech⟩ (Gewinde~̊) *pitch* (*quick p. thread*) || ⟨aero⟩ gr ~ *high* od *coarse p.*; kl ~ (bei gr Drehzahl) *fine p.* | beträchtliche ~en [pl] *steep grades* **~sregen** m *orographic rain* **~swinkel** m *angle of ascent; gradient angle*; in % *percentage of slope* || ⟨aero⟩ *pitch* (od *blade*) *angle*

steil a *steep* (*path, slope*) || ~es Ufer *bluff* || ~e Böschung *scarp* || *sharp* (*incline*) || *precipitous* (*rocks*) || *sheer* (*cliff*) | [adv] ~ auf|ragen: *the mountains stand out boldly* **~̊abfall** m ⟨geog⟩ *escarpment* **~̊dach** n *high-angled roof* **~̊feuer** n *plunging* od *high-angle fire* | ~geschütz [n] *h.-a. gun* **~̊flug** m *vertical flight* **~̊hang** m *steep slope* od *grade; precipice* | ~-Wald [m] *hanger* **~̊kurve** f *steep turn* **~̊küste** f *bluff* **~̊rohrkessel** m *vertical tube boiler* **~̊schrift** f *vertical writing* **~̊ufer** n *river bluff* **~̊vorlage** f ⟨ftb⟩ *upright pass* **St·eile** f ~/, **St·eilheit** f ~/ *steepness, precipitousness, abruptness* || ⟨el⟩ *transconductance*

St·ein m ~(e)s/~e **A. 1.** *stone* || Ziegel~ *brick* || → Läufer, Binder; halber ~ *half bat* || Straßen~̊e *road metal* **2.** (Fels) *rock* ⟨a. min, geol⟩ **3.** (Edel~̊) *gem*, ⟨vulg⟩ *ice* || echte ~e *genuine stones*; (Uhr) *jewels* (*a 12 jewel watch*) || geschliffene ~e *gems* || geschnittener ~ (versenkt) *intaglio*; (erhaben) *cameo* **4.** ⟨bot⟩ (Kern) *stone, kernel* **5.** ⟨path⟩ *stone, calculus* **6.** ⟨draughts⟩ *man*; ⟨chess⟩ *piece, chessman* **7.** (Maß) *weight, stone* **8.** ⟨fig⟩ ~ des Anstoßes, Ärgernisses *thorn; stumbling-block* (f *to*); ⟨sl⟩ *peeve* || ~ der Weisen *the philosopher's stone* **B. aus** ~ (*a bridge*) *in st.*, *a st.* (*bridge*) || **mit** e–m ~ polieren *to st.* || mit ~en ausgelegt, eingefaßt *st.-paved* (*hall*), *st.-lined* (*well*) || **zu** ~ m *to petrify* || zu ~ w *to turn into st.* **C.** e–n ~ **ansetzen** *to play a domino* || es blieb kein ~ auf dem anderen *not one st. was left unturned* ||

k–n ~ auf dem anderen l *to l. not a st. in place* | es fiel mir ein ~ vom Herzen *I had a weight taken off my mind* ‖ es **friert** ~ u Bein *there is a severe cold, it freezes as hard as can be* ‖ ich habe e–n ~ auf dem Herzen *my heart is weighed down* ‖ bei jdm e–n ~ im Brett h *to be in a p's good books,* ~ u Bein schwören *to swear by all that's holy* ‖ jdm ~e in den Weg legen *to put a spoke in a p's wheel* ‖ e–n ~ zur Dame m *to crown a king* | ⟨prov⟩ zwei harte ~e mahlen selten reine *two hard natures seldom agree well* **⁓acker** m *stony field* **⁓ader** f *rocky vein* **⁓adler** m ⟨orn⟩ *golden eagle* **≗·alt** a (*as*) *old as the hills* **≗arm** & **≗·arm** → –reich **≗artig** a *stone-like, stony* **⁓auster** f *rock-oyster* **⁓axt** f *stone-axe* **⁓bank** f *st.-bench* ‖ ⟨geol⟩ *st.-bed* **⁓bau** m *st. building* **⁓baukasten** m *box of bricks* **⁓beil** n *st. axe-hammer* **⁓beißer** m ⟨ich⟩ *st.-grig, spined loach* **⁓beschwerden** f [pl] *calculous disease* **⁓bild** n *statue* **⁓block** m *boulder* **⁓bock** m ⟨zoo⟩ *ibex, steinbock* ‖ ⟨astr⟩ *Capricorn* (im ~ *in C.*) **⁓boden** m *stony ground* ‖ ⟨arch⟩ *stone floor* **⁓bohrer** m ⟨zoo⟩ *st.-borer* ‖ ⟨min⟩ *trepan* **⁓brech** m ⟨bot⟩ → *saxifrage*; rankender ~ → Judenbart | ~widderchen [n] ⟨ent⟩ *sixspotted burnet* **⁓brecher** m (P) *quarryman*; (S) *st.-crusher* **⁓brocken** m *st.-chip* **⁓bruch** m *quarry* **⁓brücke** f *st. bridge* **⁓b·untdruck** m *chromolithography* **⁓butt(e** f) m ⟨ich⟩ *turbot* **⁓damm** m ⟨mar⟩ *jetty, pier, mole* ‖ (Straße) *paved road* **⁓druck** m (Bild) *lithograph* ‖ [abstr] *l.y* | ~farbe [f] *l.ic ink*; ~papier [n] *litho paper* **⁓drucker** m *l.er* **⁓druckerei** f *l.ic establishment* **⁓eiche** f ⟨bot⟩ *holm-oak* **⁓erbarmen** n ⟨fig⟩ das ist z ~ *that would melt a st.* **⁓falke** m ⟨orn⟩ *st.-falcon* **⁓farn** m ⟨bot⟩ *st.-fern* **⁓flachs** m *asbestos* **⁓flechte** f *rock-lichen* **⁓fliege** f *st.-fly* **⁓frucht** f *st.(-fruit)*; *drupe* **⁓galle** f ⟨min⟩ *st.-gall* ‖ ⟨vet⟩ *wind-gall* ‖ ⟨orn⟩ *kestrel* **⁓garnele** f *prawn* **⁓garten** m *rockery*; *rock-g.* | ~gewächs [n] *r. plant* **⁓geröll** n *shingle, rubble* **⁓geschirr** = ~gut **⁓grieß** m *gravel* **⁓grube** f *stone-pit* **⁓grund** m *stony ground* **⁓grab** n *barrow*; *dolmen, cromlech* **⁓gut** n *earthen-ware, crockery*; feines ~ *bone china* | ~topf [m] *crock* **⁓hagel** m *shower of st.s* **≗h·art** a *petrous* (*portion*); *stony, as hard as stone* **⁓haue** f *pickaxe* **⁓hauer** m *st.-cutter, st.-mason* **⁓haufen** m *heap of st.s* **⁓holz** n *xylolith* **⁓hügel** m ⟨Scot⟩ *cairn* **⁓inschrift** f *petroglyph* **⁓kabinett** n *cabinet of rare st.s* **⁓kalk** m *quick-lime* **⁓kauz** m ⟨orn⟩ *little owl* **⁓kenner** m *lithologist* **⁓kerze** f ⟨mot⟩ *porcelain plug* **⁓kitt** m *mastic-cement* **⁓klee** m ⟨bot⟩ *melilot* **⁓klippe** f *cliff* **⁓klopfer** m *st.-breaker* **⁓kohle** f (*pit-*)*coal, hard c.* | ~nbergwerk [n] *coalmine, -pit, colliery*; ~nformation [f] *carboniferous formation*; ~nlager [n] *coal-bed* ‖ (Niederlage) *coal-warehouse*; ~npech [n] *coal-pitch*; ~nteer [m] *coal-tar* **⁓kolik** f *calculous obstruction* **≗krank** a *suffering from st.* **⁓krankheit** f *stone* **⁓kraut** n *st.crop* **⁓krebs** m *crawfish* **⁓kreide** f *hard chalk* **⁓kreis** m ⟨praeh⟩ *st. circle* **⁓kresse** f ⟨bot⟩ *st.-cress* **⁓krug** m *st. jar* **⁓kruke** f *st. bottle* **⁓kugel** f ⟨mil⟩ *st. shot* | ~mörser [m] ⟨hist⟩ *swivel-gun* **⁓kümmel** m ⟨bot⟩ *cicely* **⁓kunde** f *lithology, mineralogy* **⁓lage(r** n) f *layer of stones*; (Uhr) *jewel bearing* **⁓leiden** n *stone* **⁓lerche** f ⟨orn⟩ *tit-lark* **⁓marder** m ⟨zoo⟩ *st.-, beech-marten* **⁓mauer** f *wall made of st.* **⁓mehl** n *st.-dust* **⁓meißel** m *st.-cutter's* od *brick chisel* **⁓messer** n *st. knife* ‖ ⟨surg⟩ *lithotome* **⁓metz** m = –hauer | ~zeichen [n] *mason's mark* **⁓moos** n *rock-lichen* **⁓mörtel** m *cement, concrete* **⁓nelke** f ⟨bot⟩ *little wild pink* **⁓obst** n *st.-fruit* **⁓öl** n *petroleum* **⁓operation** f ⟨surg⟩ *lithotomy* **⁓pappe** f *fire-proof pasteboard* **⁓pech** n *st.-pitch* **⁓periode** f = ~zeit **–pflaster** n (*st.*) *pavement* **⁓pilz** m ⟨bot⟩ *yellow boletus, flat mushroom* **⁓platte** f *slab, st. flag, flagstone* | (Natur-)~nbelag [m] *crazy paving* **⁓rabe** m ⟨orn⟩ *mountain-raven* **⁓reich** n *mineral kingdom* **≗reich** a *full of st.s* **≗r·eich** ⟨fig⟩ *made of money, st. rich, as rich as Crœsus* **⁓ring** m ⟨praeh⟩ *hut-circle* **⁓roche** m ⟨ich⟩ *thornback* **⁓rose** f *hairy alpenrose* **⁓säge** f *st.-(cutting)-saw* **⁓salz** n *rock-salt* **⁓same** m ⟨bot⟩ *gromwell* **⁓sammler** m ⟨geol fam a.⟩ *rock-hound* **⁓sammlung** f *collection of minerals* **⁓sarg** m *st. coffin* **⁓schicht** f *layer of st.* **⁓schlag** m *falling, rolling st.s rock-, st.fall*; ~! *loose st.s!*, ⟨Am⟩ *fallen rock zone!* **⁓schleifer** m *lapidary, st.-polisher* **⁓schleuder** f *st.-bow, sling* **⁓schloß** n *flint-lock* | ~gewehr [n] *fusil* **⁓schmätzer** m *fallow-finch*; → *wheatear* **⁓schmerzen** m pl *st.-evil, st.-colic* **⁓schneidekunst** f *glyptics* pl **⁓schneiden** n *gem-carving* ‖ ⟨surg⟩ *lithotomy* **⁓schneider** m *lapidary, cutter of gems*; *cameo-c.* **⁓schnitt** m ⟨surg⟩ *lithotomy* **⁓schotter** m *macadam* **⁓schraube** f *st.-bolt* **⁓schrift** f *lapidary characters* pl; ⟨typ⟩ *Grotesque* **⁓schüttungsdamm** m *rockfill dam* **⁓schwalbe** f ⟨orn⟩ *swift* **⁓setzer** m *paviour* **⁓sinter** m *stalactite* **⁓splitter** m *st.-chip* **⁓stoßen** n *putting the shot* **⁓topf** m *earthen pot* **⁓waffe** f *st.-weapon* **⁓wälzer** m ⟨orn⟩ *turnstone* **⁓wand** f *st. wall* **⁓weg** m *paved way* **⁓werfen** n *st. throwing* **⁓werkzeug** n *eolith*; *flint tool* **⁓wurf** m *st.-cast* ‖ e–n ~ weit *within a stone's throw* **⁓zeichner** m *lithographer* **⁓zeichnung** f *lithograph* **⁓zeit** f (ältere *palaeolithic*; jüngere *neolithic*) *st. age* **st·einern** a *stone*, (*built*) *of stone* ‖ (*of*) *earthenware* ‖ der ~e Gast *the marble statue* ‖ ~es Herz *heart of flint* **st·einig** a *stony, full of stones, rocky* ‖ ⟨bib, fig⟩ *shallow* (*ground*) **st·einigen** vt [h] *to stone* (*to death*) | ≗ n ~s/, **St·einigung** f ~/~en *stoning*

St·eiper m ~s/~ ⟨mar⟩ *stanchion*

St·eireranzug m *Styrian braided grey suit*

Steiß m ~es/~e *backside, rump* ‖ ⟨cul⟩ (Gans≗) ⟨fam⟩ *parson's nose* ‖ (P) *buttocks* pl, *posterior* **⁓bein** n ⟨anat⟩ *coccyx*; *rump-bone* **⁓feder** f *caudal feather* **⁓flosse** f *anal fin* **⁓fuß** m ⟨orn⟩ *grebe* **⁓geburt** f *pelvic presentation*

Stellage [ste'la:ʒə] f ~/~n **1.** *stand, frame* ‖ (Etagere) *whatnot* **2.** ⟨com⟩ *double option, put and call,* ⟨Am⟩ *straddle* **st·ellbar** a *movable, adjustable* **St·ell-** **⁓dichein** n *meeting, appointment, assignation*; *rendezvous* Fr, ⟨Am⟩ *date* ‖ ⟨sport⟩ *meet* ‖ (Ort) *place of meeting,* ⟨poet⟩ *trysting-place* ‖ e–m (sich) ein ~ geben *to make an appointment with a p* (*to meet*) **⁓eisen** n ⟨tech⟩ *adjustment plate* **⁓falle** f (Schleuse) *regulating gate* **⁓feder** f *stop-spring* **⁓garn** n (Fischerei) *stalker* **⁓geschäft** n = Stellage 2 **⁓haken** m *catch* **⁓hebel** m *switch lever* **⁓macher** m *wheelwright* **⁓motor** m *servomotor* **⁓mutter** f *adjusting nut* **⁓netz** n *anchored net* **⁓rad** n, **⁓scheibe** f *regulator* **⁓schlüssel** m *adjusting wrench* **⁓schraube** f *adjuster* od *regulator screw* **⁓stift** m *set pin* **≗vertretend** a *vicarious* ‖ ⟨off⟩ *acting* ⟨a. mil⟩, *deputy* (*director*) ‖ (e–s Bischofs) *surrogate*; ~er Kommandeur [m] *second-in-command, executive officer* N; ~er Ministerpräsident *Vice-Prime Minister*; ~er Vorsitzender *vice-chairman*; ⟨mil⟩ *deputy* (⟨Am⟩ *vice*) (*chief of staff*); *lieutenant* **⁓vertreter** m *alternate*; *representative*; ⟨off⟩ *deputy*; (Ersatzmann) *substitute*; (Bevollmächtigter) *proxy*; ⟨ec, med⟩ *locum tenens* L | als ~ wirken f *to stand proxy for* **⁓vertretung** f *representation, substitution* ‖ ⟨off⟩ *deputyship* ‖ in ~ *by proxy* **⁓wagen** m *stage-coach* **⁓werk** n ⟨rail⟩ *signal-box,* ⟨Am⟩ *switch-tower* **⁓zirkel** m *wing-compasses* pl **St·elle** f ~/~n **A. 1.** (Ort) *place, spot*; freie ~ *opening* **2.** (Standplatz) *stand, position* **3.** (Bau≗) *plot* **4.** (Buch- etc -≗ ⟨a. mus⟩) *passage* (angezogen *quoted*) **5.** (Fleck) *patch* (*of white*), (*white*) *spot* **6.** schadhafte ~ *flaw* **7.** (Körper≗) (*sore*) *spot* | ⟨fig⟩ schwache ~ *blind spot* ‖ jdn an der wunden ~ treffen *to flick a p on the raw* **8.** ⟨arith⟩ (e–r

[Dezimal-]Zahl) *figure, digit*; [*place*] **9.** (Amts- etc -≃) *department*; *station* || Dienst≃n [pl] *authorities*; führende ∼ ⟨a.⟩ *prime spot*; die maßgebenden ∼n *the powers that be*; zuständige ∼ *the proper quarter* **10.** (Anstellung) *situation, office, berth, place, post* || e–e gute (⟨fam⟩ saubere) ∼ h *to be in a good situation* (*to have a snug berth*) || freie ∼ *vacancy* || ⟨pol etc⟩ höchste ∼ *highest place* | die Stelle jds als Professor antreten *to succeed a p as pr.*; e–e ∼ **bekleiden** *to hold a post*, e–e ∼ bek *to get an appointment*, sich um e–e ∼ bewerben *to apply for a vacancy* || jds ∼ einnehmen *to take a p's place*, .. vertreten *to represent a p* **B. an**: *in another place* (= *elsewhere*) || an dessen ∼ *instead of that* || nahe an der ∼, wo *near where* || an dieser ∼ ⟨übtr⟩ *at this juncture*; an derselben ∼ *at the same spot* || an einigen, gewissen ∼n *in places* od *spots* || → erste C., an erster ∼ ⟨fig⟩ *in the first instance*, .. k vor *to take precedence of*, .. stehen *to stand foremost* od *first, to be pr(ed)ominent*, (als Kritiker) *to be at the top of the critical tree* || an dritter, fünfter ∼ *third-, fifth-ranked* | an sichtbarer, prominenter, exponierter ∼ stehen *to be posted prominently*; bei jdm an erster ∼ stehen *to be first with a p* || an Ihrer ∼ *if I were* (od *had been*) *you, in your place*; was hätten Sie an m–r ∼ getan? *what would you have done*? || an der (un)richtigen ∼ *in* (*out of*) *place* || *in the vulnerable spot* || an welcher ∼ etwa? *whereabout*? || an 2. ∼ stehen *to take second place* | **an ∼ von** *in* (*the*) *place of*, ⟨off⟩ *vice* (*v. Mr. N.*); an ∼ [+ gen] *in substitution of*; .. setzen ⟨a.⟩ *to substitute for, to replace*; .. treten *to replace* (*a p*), *to take the place of*; → anstatt, an≃ | **auf** der ∼ *on the spot, immediately, at once, there and then, right* od *straight away*; *offhand*; *outright* (*killed*); nicht ..; *I can't tell you straight off*; .. treten ⟨mil & fig⟩ *to mark time*; ⟨fig⟩ *to drag one's feet* (dazu [s]: *footdragging*) | (nicht) **von** der ∼ k *to make progress, to get on* (*to remain stationary, to mark time, to dawdle along*) || nicht v der ∼! *don't budge*!; (of car) *to fail to budge* (sich rühren); **zur** ∼! *present*!, *here*! || (*to come*) *on the scene* ⟨fig⟩ || (*to hurry*) *to the spot* || sich z ∼ melden *to report o.s. present* || z ∼ s ⟨a.⟩ *to be at* (⟨Am⟩ *on*) *hand* || z ∼ schaffen *to produce*
st·ellen I. vt [h] **A. 1.** *to set, lay, arrange* etc || (a. **sich** ∼, → II.) *to put, place, plant, post, locate* (*o.s.*) (auf *on*, an *against*) **2.** (aufhalten) *to stop* | (jdn) (anhalten) *to accost*; (bes Verbrecher) *to close in upon*; (⟨mil⟩ herausfordernd) *to challenge, fix*; (freundlich) *to buttonhole* || ⟨hunt & fig⟩ *to bring to bay* || ⟨mil⟩ (jdn abstellen) *to supply* **3.** (S & P beschaffen) *to supply* ⟨a. mil⟩, *find* (*everything* ⟨a.⟩ ∼ müssen); *to provide* (*a car*) **4.** (festsetzen) *to fix* (*a date*) **5.** (richten) *to regulate* || ⟨tech⟩ ([ein]stellen) *to set*; *to time* **B. aufrecht** ∼ *to put* od *set up*(*right*) || die Füße einwärts ∼ *to turn .. in* || es jdm frei|∼ *to leave it to a p's choice* || gut gestellt (P) *well off* || ⟨fig⟩ höher|∼ als *to put .. above ..* || (etw) kalt ∼ *to cool, ice* || richtig|∼ (berichtigen) *to put* od *set right*; *to rectify, correct* | richtig ∼ *to regulate* (*a clock*) || **so** gestellt s, daß . *to be so placed as to* (*do it*) || warm ∼ *to keep hot* || wieder ∼ *to put* etc *again, to reset* || (s–e Worte) zierlich ∼ *to arrange nicely* **C.** bescheidene **Ansprüche** ∼ *to have simple tastes*; gr Ansprüche ∼ *to advance large claims* || e–n Antrag ∼ ⟨jur⟩ *to bring an action*; ⟨parl⟩ *to bring forward a motion, to move* || jdm e–e Aufgabe ∼ *to set a p a task*; sich [dat] ..: *the functions they intend to fulfil* || (Bedingungen) *to make* || jdm ein Bein ∼ *to trip a p up* || (lebende Bilder) *to arrange* || e–n Bürgen ∼ *to find bail* || e–e **Falle** ∼ *to set a trap, to lay a snare* ([dat] *for*) || (Fragen) *to put, ask* (an *of*) || (Geiseln) *to furnish* || (Geschütze etc) *to aim, point, train* (richten) || (ein Gesuch) *to submit* || jdm das Horoskop ∼ *to cast a p's nativity* || 10 **Mann** ∼ *to find ten men* (f .. *for diking work*) || s–n Mann ∼ *to make one, to contribute one's share*; *to show a bold front* (*to a p*), *to assert o.s.*; *to be the right man for the job*, ⟨fam⟩ *to be up to the mark* || die Probleme, die e–m gestellt sind *the problems confronting one* || (Segel) *to trim* (nach .. *to the wind*) || (e–n Stellvertreter) *to provide, find, appoint* || e–n Termin ∼ *to fix a certain date* || (Truppen) *to furnish* || (**Uhr**) *to set* (nach .. *by* ..) || (Verbrecher) *to arrest* || (Zeugen) *to produce* || (Zünder) *to time* **D. auf** sich selbst gestellt s *to be dependent on o.s.*; (P) gestellt s auf *to be bent on* || s–e S auf nichts ∼ *to care for nothing in the world, to be non-carish* ⟨a. bib⟩ || wird v Hand auf null ge–llt *resets to zero manually* || jdn auf die Beine ∼ *to pull a p to his feet* ⟨a. fig⟩ || dies stellt uns Problemen **gegenüber** *this brings us up against problems* | **in** jds Belieben ∼ *to leave to a p* || ⟨mar⟩ in Dienst ∼ *to put into service* || (Kind) in die Ecke ∼ *to stand .. in the c.* || (Pferd) in den Stall ∼ ⟨a.⟩ *to stable* | jdm **nach** dem Leben ∼ *to attempt a p's life* || nach der Schnur ∼ *to aline* | jdn ∼ **über** *to place a p over* (*a p*) || die S über die P ∼ *to esteem the matter above the p* | (etw) **unter** Beweis ∼ *to prove* | gestellt w **vor** (of claims) *to take precedence of* || jdn vor bes Aufgaben ∼ *to raise special problems for* ..; sich [dat] (etw) vor Augen ∼ *to imagine* || jdn vor e–e Frage ∼ *to face a p with a question* || vor die Tatsache gestellt w *to be brought up against the fact* | **zur** Diskussion ∼ *to table* (*a motion*); *to open a discussion upon* .. **II. sich** ∼ **A.** (→ I. A. 1.) **1.** *to* (*take one's*) *stand, to take up a position* **2.** (v Sitz) *to stand* od *get up* **3.** *to come forward, to appear*; *to present o.s.* **4.** ⟨mil⟩ *to attend the muster, to join up, to enlist* **5.** sich (e–m Problem) ∼ *to face* (*up to*) ..; ⟨hunt & fig⟩ sich jdm ∼ *to stand at bay* **6.** ⟨jur⟩ *to give o.s. up* (*to the police*) || *to surrender* (*to the court*) **7.** sich ∼ (verstellen), als ob .. *to dissemble, feign, pretend, sham* (*repentence* etc); *to make a show of* (*doing*); sich nur **so** ∼ *to be only shamming*, °*to be putting it on*; *to play possum* | sich **dumm** ∼ *to pretend to know nothing* (*about it*); sich krank ∼ *to feign sickness, to malinger*; sich unschuldig ∼ *to put on an appearance of innocence*; sich verrückt *or* wahnsinnig ∼ *to feign o.s. mad*; sich wütend ∼ *to make a show of rage* **B.** sich **auf** die Füße ∼ *to lift o.s. to one's feet*; .. Hinterfüße .. ⟨fig⟩ *to put one's foot down* (gegen *against*); .. Zehen ∼ *to stand on tiptoe* || sich auf die Seite ∼ v .. *to range o.s. on the side of* .. || sich auf sich selbst ∼ müssen *to be obliged to rely upon o.s.* || der **Preis** stellt sich auf *the price is* || es stellt sich auf .. *it works out at, it comes to* (*£ 2 each*) || wie ∼ Sie sich **dazu**? *which line are you taking in it*? ich bin gespannt, wie er sich dazu ∼ wird .. *what he will say to it* || sich **dazw** ∼ *to interpose* || sich gegen etw ∼ *to oppose a th* || sich **hinter** jdn ∼ *to support a p, to back* (*up*) *a p*; .. geschlossen .. *to rally behind a p* || sich **in** den Dienst e–r S ∼ *to do one's best to promote a matter* || sich **mit** jdm gut ∼ *to be on good terms with a p, to put o.s. right with a p*; ⟨fam⟩ *to hit it off with a p* || sich **neben** jdn ∼ *to take one's place* od *stand beside* od *by a p* || sich **vor** jdn ∼ *to stand in front of a p*, ⟨fig⟩ *to enter the lists on behalf of a p* || sich **zu** den anderen ∼ *to take one's place with the others* || sich z Dienst ∼ ⟨mil⟩ *to report for duty* (bei *to*) || sich z Kampfe (Turnier), [Zweikampf] ∼ *to accept battle*, (*to enter the lists*), [*to accept a challenge to a duel*]; .. erneut .. *to resume a defensive attitude* || sich zu etw ∼ *to take an attitude to a th*
St·ellen- ∼angebot n *offer of a post*; ∼e [pl] *wanteds*, ⟨Am a.⟩ *want ad*(*vertisement*)*s* **∼anzeigen** *advertisements for positions* (*vacant or wanted*) **∼besetzungsplan** m

establishment: im ~ sind (3 Hauptleute) vorgesehen *the e. provides for* .. **~bewerber** m *applicant* **≗gerecht** a *after point (alignment)* ⟨a. comp⟩ **~gesuch** n *application for a post* ‖ ~e [pl] (Zeitung) *situations wanted*; ⟨Am a.⟩ *want ad* **~handel** m *traffic in public appointments* **~jäger** m *place-hunter* **≗los** a *unemployed, out of employment; out of (a) job* **~markt** m *employment market* **~nachweis** m *e. agency* **~suche** f *looking for a post* **~vermittlung(samt** n) f *(servants') registry (-office) e.-agency,* ⟨engl⟩ *Appointments Board* ‖ **≗weise** [adv] *here and there, in places, occasionally*; ein Buch ~ lesen *to read a book desultorily* **~zahl** f ⟨comp⟩ je Feld *number of columns per field* | **5-stellig** a *(number) of 5 digits, 5-digit (number)* ‖ ⟨comp⟩ *of 5 positions*; *(80-)column (sorter)* **St·elling** f ~/~e ⟨mar⟩ *gangway* **St·ellung** f ~/~en **1.** (das Stellen) *putting, placing* etc ‖ (v Zeugen) *producing*, (v Truppen) *furnishing* ‖ *pointing (of gun), regulation (of clocks)* ‖ (Ordnen) *arrangement* ⟨a. gram⟩ ‖ ⟨mil⟩ zur ~ (Musterung) gehen *to attend the muster* **2.** (das Stehen) *(kneeling) position* ‖ (Anordnung) *arrangement, disposition* ‖ *constellation* | ⟨fig⟩ *status* ⟨a. pol⟩ ‖ *(foot)hold* ⟨a. fig⟩ ‖ ⟨mar⟩ richtige ~ der Segel *trim* | ⟨a–n⟩ *position (in space)* **3.** (Haltung) *attitude* ⟨a. fig⟩, *line, posture* ‖ ~! ⟨mil⟩ *attention*, ⟨fenc⟩ *on your guard!* | ~en annehmen *to pose, to strike poses* od *an attitude* ‖ ~ nehmen *to take one's stand* ⟨a. fig⟩, .. zu .. *to face*, ⟨fig⟩ *to define one's attitude regarding, to adopt a definite attitude to*; .. gegen .. *to oppose*; .. gegen jds Ansicht *to challenge a p's view* **4.** *(social) rank, consequence, position, station, level, status, footing* ; P v hoher soz. ~ *p of consequence*; jd, der e–e gehobene ~ anstrebt *a status seeker* ‖ *(baronial) capacity* ‖ *character (as landlord)* ‖ amtliche ~ *official standing* ‖ bevorzugte ~ *prominence* ‖ führende, hervorragende ~ *pre-eminence* ‖ hohe ~ *pride of place* **5.** (Anstellung) = Stelle A. 10. | ~ im Beruf, Erwerbsleben *employment status* | (als) *the position of chief clerk, his job of professor* ‖ ⟨com⟩ *job*, ohne ~ *out of job*; (annehmen *to take*); e–e ~ aufschnappen, erreichen ⟨fam⟩ *to land a job*; leicht ~ finden ⟨a.⟩ *to be jumped at* ‖ in ~ gehen (of servants) *to go into* od *out to service* ‖ in welcher ~ bist du? *how do you rate?* **6.** ⟨mil⟩ *position*, ⟨fam⟩ *pozzy*; *line*; *trenches* pl | **befestigte** ~ *lodg(e)ment* ‖ beherrschende ~ *key* (über *to*) ‖ tiefgestaffelte ~ *pos. in depth* | Ausgangs≗ *original pos.* ‖ Batterie≗en *gun pos.s* ‖ Bunker≗ *pill-box pos.* ‖ Flak≗ *antiaircraft emplacement* | e–e ~ **ausbauen** *to consolidate a pos.*, .. bekleiden als *to function as*, .. beziehen *to take up* ..; die „~" halten ⟨fam fig⟩ *to hold the fort*, .. bis z äußersten .. *to stick to one's colours*; ~ nehmen gegen *to speak out against*, .. entschieden .. *to express o.s. one way or the other*; die ~ wechseln *to shift, move* | den Feind **aus** der ~ vertreiben *to dislodge the e.* ‖ (Geschütz) **in** ~ bringen *to emplace* ‖ in ~ gehen *to take a turn of duty in the front-line*; *to emplace* N, In-~-gehen [n] *emplacement* ‖ als die D. das 3. Mal in ~ lag *on the Division's third turn in the front line* **St·ellungnahme** f *attitude*; *point of view*; *opinion*; *comment* (zu *on*); ⟨mil⟩ (bei Beurteilung) *en-, indorsement*; ⟨com, etc⟩ wir sehen Ihrer ~ entgegen *your comments are awaited, will you please put forward your c.s* ‖ neue ~ zu .. *fresh approach to* .. **St·ellungs- ~bau** m *field fortification* ‖ (Tätigkeit) *digging-in* | ~stoffe [m pl] *defensive stores* **~befehl** m *order to present o.s.* **~kämpfe** m pl *trench warfare* **~krieg** m *stationary war*; *trench* od *stabilized warfare* **≗los** a *unemployed* **≗pflichtig** a *liable to conscription* **~wechsel** m *change of position*; ⟨artill⟩ *gun displacement*

St·elz- ~bein n, **~fuß** m *wooden leg*, (P) ⟨fam⟩ *peg-leg* **≗beinig** a *with stiff legs*; *wooden-legged* ‖ **≗füßig** a ⟨orn⟩ *grallatorial* ‖ **~vögel** m pl *grallatores* **St·elze** f ~/~n *stilt*; *wooden leg* ‖ auf ~n gehen ⟨a.⟩ *to stilt*, ⟨fig⟩ *to be stilted* ‖ *to stalk along* | °~n [pl] ⟨fig fam⟩ (Beine) *pins* pl

St·emm- ~axt f *woodman's axe* **~bogen** m ⟨ski⟩ *stem (christiania)*; dazu: *to stem* **~brett** n (im Boot) *stretcher* **~eisen** n *(two-bevelled) ripping chisel* **~leder** n *toe-piece* **~meißel** m *mortise- (-ce), caulking-chisel* **~nadel** f *closing-needle* **~ring** m *shoemaker's thimble* **st·emmen** vt [h] (stützen) *to prop, support* ‖ (gegen) *to plant (one's feet) firmly against* ‖ die Arme in die Seiten ~ *to set one's arms akimbo*; .. gestemmt *with arms akimbo* ‖ *to brace (one's feet against the floor)*; *to put (one's weight against a door)* ‖ (stauen) *to stem*; *to dam up* | (Gewichte) *to lift* | **sich** ~ gegen *to breast (waves)* ‖ ⟨fig⟩ *to turn restive against*; *to resist, oppose*; *to set one's face against*

St·empel m ~s/~ **1.** (Werkzeug) *stamp* (a. Post≗ etc) ‖ Präge≗ *die* ‖ Loch≗ *punch* | (Stößel) *pounder, pestle* | ⟨arch⟩ *prop* ‖ ⟨min⟩ *stemple* **2.** ⟨bot⟩ *pistil* **3.** (Zeichen) *stamp, (post)-mark, brand* ‖ ~ des Feingehalts ⟨met⟩ *plate--mark, hallmark* | ⟨fig⟩ den ~ e–r S tragen *to bear the impress (of a period), the stamp (of untruth)* ‖ e–r S den Stempel .. aufdrücken *to stamp a th with an equivocal character, to set one's stamp upon a th* ‖ *this alone stamps the story (as) a slander* ‖ e–r S s–n ~ aufdrücken *to put one's mark on a th*; *to give a th the impress of one's personality*; der Welt .. *to make some mark on the w.* **~amt** n *stamp-office* **~bogen** m *stamped sheet of paper* **~eisen** n *stamp*; *punch* **≗frei** a *free from*: **~gebühr** f, **~geld** n *stamp-duty* **~hammer** m *stamping-hammer* **~holz** n *prop timber* **~kissen** n *ink-pad* **~marke** f *fiscal stamp, duty--stamp* **~papier** n *stamped paper* **≗pflichtig** a *liable to stamp-duty* **~schneider** m *punch-, stamp--cutter, die-sinker* **~setzer** m ⟨min⟩ *timber man* **~zeichen** = Stempel 3. **st·empeln** vt [h] *to stamp* ‖ *to put* od *stick a stamp on* ‖ *to mark* | (als Arbeitsloser) ~ (gehen) *to go on relief*; *to be on the dole* od *Labour* | ⟨met & fig⟩ *to hallmark* ‖ zu etw ~: *to dub a p a liar, to stigmatize a word (as) a vulgarism, to stamp a story (as) a slander*

St·enge f ~/~n ⟨mar⟩ *topmast* **~nwanten** f pl ⟨mar⟩ *top-shrouds* pl **St·engel** m ~s/~ *stalk, stem*, ⟨bot⟩ *stipe* | °v ~ fallen ⟨sl⟩ *to fall off one's perch* **~bohne** f *runner* **~glas** n *wine-glass* **≗ständig** a *caulinar* **≗umfassend** a *amplexicaul*

St·eno °= ~graphie **~gr·amm** n ~(e)s/~e *shorthand notes* pl od *report* **~gr·aph** m ~en/~en *sh.writer*, ⟨Am⟩ *stenographer* | ~·ie [f] ~/~n *st.y, sh.*; ≗·ieren vt/i h *to write sh.*; *to take down in sh.*; ≗isch [a] *st.ical, sh.* | [adv] *st.ically, in sh.* **~typist(in** f ~/~nen) m ~en/~en *sh. typist*

Sten·ose f ~/~n ⟨path⟩ *stenosis* [pl *-ses*] **st-siert** a *stenosed*

St·entor- *stentorian (voice)* ‖ mit ~stimme *in st.n tones*

St·epp- ~decke f *quilt*, ⟨Am⟩ *comforter* **~naht** f *closing-, quilting-seam* **~ort** m *closing-awl* **~seide** f *stitching-silk* **~stich** m *q.g-stitch* ⟨mach⟩ *back-stitch, lockstitch* **st·eppen I.** vt [h] *to quilt*; *to stitch* **II.** vi [h] *to step-dance* **St·epper** m ~s/~ *quilter*

St·eppe f ~/~n *steppe(s pl)* (z. B. ⟨Russ⟩ *Bet-Pak-Dala St.*) ‖ Hartgras≗ ⟨SAfr⟩ *veldt* ‖ Kälte≗ *tundra* ‖ Trocken≗ *karoo* **~nantilope** f *saiga* **~nfuchs** m *corsac, caragan* **~nwolf** m *prairie-wolf* ‖ ⟨fig⟩ (P) *lone wolf*

×**St·eppke** m ~s/~ *youngster, lad*; → Dreikäsehoch

St·eptanz m *step dance, tap dance*

St·erbe- ~alter n (häufigstes *modal, normal*) *age at death* **~bett** n *d.-bed* **~buch** n *register of d.s* **~fall** m *death* | ~zählblatt [n], -karte [f]

⟨demog⟩ *d. certificate* **~geld** n *d. benefit* **~gesang** m *funeral dirge* od *hymn* **~gewand** n *shroud; winding-sheet* **~glocke** f *funeral bell* **~haus** n *house of mourning* **~hemd** n = –gewand **~hilfe** f *euthanasia* [L] **~jahr** n *year of d.* **~kasse** f *d. benefit fund* **~kleid** n = –gewand **~koeffizient** m = –ziffer **~liste** f *bills* pl *of mortality, register of d.s* **~sakramente** n pl *last sacraments* **~stunde** f, **~tag** m *dying-hour, -day, day of a p's d.* **~tafel** f = –ziffer; *life* od *mortality table*; abgekürzte ∼ *abridged l. t.*; allg ∼ *aggregate l. t.* **~szene** f *dying-scene* **~urkunde** f *d. certificate* **~wahrscheinlichkeit** f *probability of d.* **~ziffer** f ⟨demog⟩ (*central*) *d. rate*; reine ∼ *life table d. rate*; ∼ nach Geschlecht u Altersgruppen *sex-age-specific d. rate*; ∼ nach Todesursachen *cause-specific mortality r.* **~zimmer** n *d.-chamber* **st·erben I.** vi [s] **A.** *to die* (gehobene Sprache → entschlafen, einschlummern; veratmen, verhauchen; verscheiden, dahingehen, heimgehen; ⟨fam⟩ Armee .., Vater ..; drankommen, hinübergehen, abgehen, abtreten, ⟨sl⟩ abkratzen, abrutschen, abschnappen, krepieren, verrecken, totgehen) **B.** jung, arm ∼ *to die young, in poverty*; furchtlos *hard*, ⟨fam⟩ *game* ‖ sanft, schwer ∼ *to have an easy, a hard death* | **als** Bettler, Christ ∼ *to die a beggar, a Christian* | e–n (e–s) natürlichen [gewaltsamen] Tod(es) ∼ *to die a natural* [*violent*] *death, to die in one's bed* [*shoes*] | falls Mr. N. stirbt .. *failing Mr. N.* (*R. will be heir*) **C. ~ an** [dat]; **infolge** [gen] *or* **von**: *from* (*old-age, poison; a wound, stroke, broken heart*) ‖ *of* (*a malady*) ‖ am ersten Kinde *in her first childbed* | **aus**: *of* (*grief*) | **daran, davon** wirst du nicht gleich ∼! *that won't kill you!* | **durch**: *by* (*the sword, a p's hand*); durch, **infolge**: *through* (*teething*) | **im** Bett ∼ *to die of natural causes*; **in** den Sielen *in harness* | **über** etw ∼ *to die before the realization of* (*one's plans*) | **vor**: *with* (*laughter*), vor Langerweile ∼ *to be bored to death* **II.** ≗ n *dying, death* ‖ das gr ≗ *the Great Plague* | **im** ≗ *at the point of death*, .. liegen *to be dying* od *in the last agony*; *to be mortally ill* | es war **zum** ≗ langweilig *I was bored stiff* od *to death* ‖ z ∼ zu viel u z Leben zu wenig ⟨fam⟩ *just enough to keep the wolf from the door* ‖ e–i S z ∼ überdrüssig *dead-tired of a th* **III. gestorben** *dead, deceased* ‖ e–r, der an Ch. gest. war *a man dead of cholery* ‖ gest., verdorben *dead and gone* ‖ der kürzlich gest.e Mr. N. *Mr. N. who lately died* **St·erbens- ~·angst** f *mortal fear* od *terror* **≗b·ange** a *in mortal fear* **≗kr·ank** a *sick to death, dangerously ill* **≗l·angweilig** a *duller than cold roast mutton* **≗m·üde** a *tired to death* **~w·örtchen** n; kein ∼ *not a syllable*; .. verraten *not to breathe a word* **st·erblich** a *mortal* ‖ kein ≗er *no man alive* ‖ die ≗en *mortals* pl | [adv] ≗ verliebt in [acc] ⟨fam⟩ *desperately in love with* | **≗keit** f ∼/ **1.** *mortality* ‖ ⟨demog⟩ ∼ nach dem Alter *age-specific m.*; ∼ nach Todesursachen *cause m.*; Alters≗ *m. of old age*; Erwachsenen≗ *adult m.* **2.** ⟨fig, rel⟩ *this world of ours* | **~s-** → *mortality, death-rate*; ∼sformel [f] *law of m.*; ∼sziffer [f] *death-rate, mortality* **St·erbling** m ∼s/∼e *weakly creature whose days are numbered* **~swolle** f *pelt-wool*

St·ereo n ∼s/∼s ⟨fam⟩ = ∼typ·ie | ∼- *stereoscopic* (*camera, film, photo*) **~betrachter** m (S) *stereoviewer* **~kamera** f ⟨phot⟩ *binocular camera* **~meßbildkamera** f *stereophotogrammetric c.* **~meter** n *volumenometer* **~metr·ie** f ∼/ *solid geometry*, ⟨a.⟩ *stereometry* **≗m·etrisch** a *st.metrical* **~-Mikroskop** n *st.*(*scopic*) *m.* **~-schallplatte** f *st. record* **~sk·op** n ∼(e)s/∼e *st.scope* **≗sk·opisch** a *st.scopic* **≗t·yp** a ⟨typ⟩ *st.type*(*d*) (a. ⟨fig⟩) od [mst] *stock* (*phrases*); ∼e Wendung *st.-in-trade* **~typ·ie** f ∼/ *st.type-printing, st.typy* **≗typ·ieren** vt [h] *to st.type* **≗t·ypisch** a = stereotyp **~t·ypplatte** f ⟨typ⟩ *stereo*(*typeplate*)

ster·il a *barren, unfruitful* ‖ (T) ⟨biol⟩ *axenic* **≗is·ierapparat** m *sterilizer* **~is·ieren** vt [h] *to sterilize* **≗is·ierkasten** m *sterilizing tray* **≗it·ät** f ∼/ *barrenness, unfruitfulness* **≗milch** f *sterilized milk*

St·erke f ∼/∼n [niedd] *heifer*

St·erlet m ∼s/∼e ⟨ich⟩ *sterlet*

St·erlingzahlen f pl *sterling figures* ⟨a. comp⟩ (*10 s & 11 d*)

Stern m ∼(e)s/∼e (= Heck) ⟨mar⟩ *stern*

St·ern m ∼(e)s/∼e *star* ⟨a. fig (P), bot⟩ (erster Größe *of the first magnitude*) ‖ ⟨mil⟩ (Abzeichen) *pip* ‖ ⟨typ⟩ *asterisk* ‖ (der Nägel) *white spot* ‖ (Straßen≗) *circus* ‖ **mit** drei ∼en *threestar* (*brandy*) ‖ mit ∼en besät *bestarred, star-spangled* | ⟨fig⟩ er hat weder Glück noch ∼ *he has no luck, the fates are against him* ‖ der Hoffnung letzter ∼ *the last gleam of hope* ‖ sein ∼ ist erloschen *his star has set* ‖ sein guter ∼ *his good fortune* ‖ die ∼e v Himmel verlangen *to cry for the moon* | **an** s–n Stern glauben *to believe in one's luck* | °**nach** den ∼en sehen (urinieren) ⟨vulg⟩ *to do the gentleman* | sich nach den ∼en richten ⟨eig mar⟩; ⟨übtr a.⟩ (auf dem Marsche) *to steer by the stars* | **v** den ∼en nicht begünstigt *star-crossed* (*lovers*) **~anbeter** m *star-worshipper* **~anis** m ⟨bot⟩ *star-aniseed* **≗artig** *starlike, astral* **≗besät** a *starry; bespangled with stars* **~beschreiber** m *astrographer* **~bild** n ⟨astr⟩ *constellation* **~blume** f ⟨bot⟩ *starwort* **~blüter** m pl *stellates* **~deuter** m *astrologer* **~deuter·ei, ~deutung** f *astrology* **~dienst** m *star-worship* **~distel** m ⟨bot⟩ *star-thistle* **~dolde** f ⟨bot⟩ *large astrantia* **~fahrt** f ⟨mot⟩ *rally* **~flug** m ⟨aero⟩ *star flight* **≗förmig** a *starlike, stellar*, ⟨bot⟩ *stellate*(*d*) **~gewölbe** n ⟨arch⟩ *radial vault*(*ing*) **~gruppe** f ⟨astr⟩ *constellation* **~gucker** m ⟨hum⟩ *stargazer* **≗hagelv·oll** a ⟨fam⟩ *as drunk as a lord* od *as blazes; tight as a drum; stewed to the gills; soaked*; [pred] *whole-seas* **~haufen** m *cluster of stars* **≗h·ell** a *starry, starlit* ‖ es ist ∼ *the stars are out* **~himmel** m *starry sky* **~jahr** n *sideral year* **~kammer** f ⟨engl⟩ *Star-Chamber* **~karte** f *celestial chart* **~kenner** m *astronomer* **≗klar** = –hell **~koralle** f ⟨zoo⟩ *astraea* **~kreuzung** f *multiple crossing* **~kunde** f *astronomy* **~kundige(r)** m *astronomer* **≗kundlich** a *astronomical* **~lehre** f = –kunde **~leuchtkugel** f *star shell* **~licht** n *starlight* **~miere** f ⟨bot⟩ *starwort*; gr ∼ *adder's-meat* **~moos** n ⟨bot⟩ *starred moss* **~motor** m *radial engine* (4fach .. *four-row* ..) **~nudeln** f pl *star-macaroni* **~orientierung** f ⟨a–n⟩ *star orientation* **~rad** n *turnstile* **~schaltung** f ⟨el⟩ *R connection* **~schanze** f ⟨mil⟩ *star-redoubt* **~schnuppe** f *shooting star* **~schnuppenfall,** –regen [m] *fall, shower of meteors* **~-schreiber** m *plan position indicator* **~seher** m *astronomer* ‖ (Sterndeuter) *astrologer* **~stunde** f *sideral hour* ‖ ⟨fig⟩ ∼ der Menschheit *decisive moment in history* **~tafel** f *astronomical table* **~tag** m *sideral day* **≗übersät** a *studded with stars* **~uhr** f *sideral dial* **~wahrsager·ei** f *astrology* **~warte** f *observatory* **~zeichen** n ⟨typ⟩ *asterisk* **~zeit** f *sideral time* **St·ernchen** n ∼s/∼ ⟨typ⟩ *asterisk* ‖ [pl] ⟨cul⟩ *star-macaroni* **Sternen- ~all** n *stellar world* | mit **~augen** *star*(*ry*)*-eyed* **~bahn** f *orbit of stars* **~banner** n ⟨Am⟩ *star-spangled banner, stars and stripes* pl **~gefilde, ~gewölbe** n, **~himmel** m *firmament, starry sky* ‖ unter dem ∼ *under the stars* | ∼chen [n] ⟨Am ich⟩ *jewel fish* **~glanz** m, **~licht** n, **~schimmer** m *starry glitter, starlight* ‖ im ∼ *in the star-blink* **~heer** n, **~schar** f *starry host* **~zelt** n *starry canopy of heaven* **st·ernig** a *starry*

St·erz m ∼es/∼e *tail* ‖ ⟨agr⟩ *plough-handle* | **≗eln** vi (*of bee*) *to ventilate*

stet a *steady, constant; fixed, stable* **st·etig** a *continual, perpetual, constant; continuous* (*force*) ‖

(fest) *steady* || *undeviating* || *uninterrupted* **≈keit** f *constancy; steadiness; continuity* (⟨mil⟩ der Führung *of operations* **stets** [adv] *continually, constantly* || *always, at all times, every day* || ~ Ihr W. H. *ever yours W. H.*

Stett·iner Haff n ⟨Ger⟩ *Stettin Haff*

St·euer[1] n ~s/~ ⟨mar⟩ *rudder* ⟨a. aero⟩; *helm* || (Ruderpinne) *tiller* || ⟨mot⟩ *wheel* (*to be at the wh.*) | am ~ (*to be drunk*) *in charge of a car* | das ~ führen *or* halten *to steer* (*the vessel*); *to be at the helm* ⟨a. fig⟩ || das ~ herumwerfen *to throw over the helm* **St·euer**[2] f ~/~n (staatliche) *tax*; ⟨hist⟩ *impost*; (bewilligte) *grant*; (veranlagte) *assessment*; (indirekte) *duty*; (Zoll) *custom, duty* | (städtische) *rate* | erträgliche ~n *reasonable taxation* || ~n auferlegen, beitreiben *to impose, collect taxes* || jdm ~n auferlegen *to tax a p* || ⟨fig⟩ zur ~ der Wahrheit *for the sake of truth* [2]**~abgabe** f *levy* **~abstrich** m *tax cut* od *reduction* **~amt** n *inland-revenue office*; *board of assessment* od *i.-r.* **~anschlag** m *assessment* (*of taxes*) **~aufkommen** n *yield of a tax* **~aufschlag** m *surtax* (dazu: *to surtax*) **~aufsicht** f *tax supervision* **~band** n (Tabak) *r.-stamp* **~beamte(r)** m *r.-officer* **~befreiung** f *exemption from taxes* **~behörde** = –amt **~berater** m *tax expert* od *consultant* **~bescheid** m *assessment note*, ⟨Am⟩ *tax bill* [1]**~betätigung** f ⟨aero⟩ *actuation of the controls* [2]**~bewilligung** f ⟨parl⟩ *grant of supply* **~bezirk** m *tax-collector's district* [1]**~bord** n ⟨mar⟩ *starboard*; etw ~! *st. a little* || ~ Ruder an! *give way st.!* || streich ~! *back st.!* ~ voraus *off the st.* | ~swache [f] ⟨mar⟩ *starboard watch* **~einheit** f ⟨comp⟩ *program* od *command register*; *control unit* [2]**~-einnehmer** m *receiver of taxes, tax-collector* **~erhebung** f *levying of taxes* **~erklärung** f *tax return* **~erlaß** m, **~erleichterung, ~ermäßigung** f *abatement* od *remission of taxes*, → –abstrich; *tax concessions* pl; ⟨off⟩ *tax relief* od *rebate* || (Gemeinde≈) *derating* [1]**~feder** f ⟨orn⟩ *rectrix, rudder-feather* [2]**~flucht** f *flight from taxation* **≈frei** a (S) *tax-free, non-exisable* (Getränk); *free of duty, duty-free* || (P) *tax-free, exempt from taxes* **~freiheit** f *e.ion* od *freedom from taxes* od *taxation* [1]**~gehäuse** f *steering gear case* **~gerät** n (Kreisel) *gyro pilot* [2]**~gesetz** n *finance-bill* **~gutschein** m ⟨Ger⟩ *taxation credit certificate* [1]**~hahn** m ⟨mach⟩ *valve-cock* **~haus** n ⟨mar⟩ *wheel-house* **~hebel** m ⟨aero⟩ *control column* [2]**~hinterziehung** f *defraudation of the r.* **~inspektor** m *surveyor of taxes* **~kasse** f *tax-collector's office* **~kataster** m & n *tax-roll* [1]**~kette** f ⟨mot⟩ *timing chain* **~knagge** f *cam, catch, peg, tappet* **~knüppel** m ⟨aero⟩ *control column* od *stick*, (⟨sl⟩ *joy-*)*stick* [2]**~kraft** f *taxability, capacity for paying taxes* || [1]⟨mar⟩ *steerage-way* || ⟨aero⟩ *stick-force* [2]**~last** f *burden of taxation* [1]**≈lastig** a ⟨mar⟩ *down by the stern*; ⟨aero⟩ *control heavy* **~leine** f *tiller-rope* **~leistung** f ⟨mot⟩ *rating horse power* **≈los** a *rudderless* || ⟨fig⟩ *adrift* [2]**~liste** f *tax roll* **~-listen** u –forderungen f pl *rate books and demands* [1]**~losigkeit** f *lack of control* ⟨a. fig⟩ **~maat** m *second mate* [2]**~mahnzettel** m *demand-note* [1]**~mann** m ⟨mar⟩ *mate* || (am Ruder) *helmsman, steersman* || (Boots≈) *coxswain* **~mannskunst** f *art of navigation* [2]**~-marke** f *r.-stamp* **~minderung** f *reduction of taxation* [1]**~motoranlage** f (f Zielverfolgung) *aided tracking mechanism* [2]**~nachlaß** = –erlaß [1]**~organe** n pl ⟨tech⟩ *control* **~pferdestärke** f = –leistung [2]**≈pflichtig** a (P) *taxable, liable to duty* od *taxation* od *to pay taxes* || (S) *dutiable* (*goods*) **~ordnung** f *system of taxation* **~politik** f *fiscal policy* [1]**~programm** n ⟨comp⟩ *executive p.* **~pult** n ⟨comp⟩ (*display*) *console* **~quarz** n ⟨wir⟩ *quartz crystal* **~rad** n ⟨mot, mar⟩ (*steering-*)*wheel*; *timing gear* [2]**~recht** n *tax law* **~sachverständige(r)** m *tax expert* [1]**~röhre** f ⟨wir⟩ *control valve* **~ruder** n ⟨mar⟩ = Steuer[1] | [2]**~satz** m *tax rate* | [1]~ m ⟨comp⟩ (mit 4 Programmen *four-program*) *control unit* [1]**~säule** f ⟨mot⟩ *steering* (⟨aero⟩ *control*) *column* **~schalter** m ⟨el⟩ *controlling switch* [2]**~schein** m *tax collector's receipt* **~-schiebung** f ⟨fam⟩ *tax fiddle* **~schraube** f *oppressive taxation* **~schuld** *accrued taxes*; f *tax debt* | ~ner [m] *t. d.or* **~senkung** f *tax cut* [1]**~stand** m ⟨mach⟩ *operating stand* **~stange** f *tiller* **~symbol** n ⟨comp⟩ *control code* **~-tafel** f ⟨comp⟩ *operator controls* pl **~taste** f ⟨rec⟩ *operating switch* [2]**~veranlagung** f *assessment* **~vergünstigung** f *tax concessions* pl **~verkürzung** f *fiscal evasion* **~verweigerung** f *refusal to pay taxes*; ⟨parl⟩ *refusal to grant supplies* **~verweser** m *administrator of taxes* [1]**~walze** f *control cylinder* [2]**~wesen** n *taxes, finances* pl [1]**~werk** n ⟨aero⟩ *control drive* od *system, flying controls* pl | ⟨comp⟩ *control unit* [2]**~zahler** m (staatl.) *taxpayer*; (städt.) *ratepayer* **~zettel** m *tax-paper* **~zuschlag** m *supertax, surtax* **st·euerbar** a **1.** ⟨mar⟩ *manageable*; ⟨aero⟩ *controllable* **2.** *taxable*; *ratable* | **≈keit** f ⟨mar⟩ *handiness* **st·euern I.** vt/i [h & s] *to steer*, (lotsen) *pilot* || ⟨tech⟩ *to govern* ⟨a. comp⟩ || ⟨aero⟩ *to pilot, control, guide*; *to be at the controls* || fest u sicher ~ ⟨a–n⟩ *to steady .. in flight*; ⟨comp⟩ karten–, programmge–rt *controlled by card designation, .. by program*; streifenge–rt *tape-controlled* **II.** vi [h] (v Schiff) *to head, stand, ply, to be bound* (nach *for*) || ausgewogen, gleichmäßig ~ ⟨fig⟩ *to remain on an even keel* **III.** vi; e–r S [dat] ~ *to prevent, check, restrain, remedy a th* **St·eu(e)rung** f ~/~en ⟨mar, mot⟩ *steering* || ⟨mach⟩ *distribution* || (Wirkung) *steerage* | (Vorrichtung) ⟨mot⟩ *st.g-gear* || ⟨aero, wir, comp⟩ *control* || ⟨comp a.⟩ *adapter* (*control*), *c.* od *tape adapter* || ⟨mach⟩ *valve gear, distributing-regulator* || ⟨biol⟩ *regulation, control* | (Verhinderung) *prevention* || ⟨comp⟩ Kartenleser≈ / Lochstreifen≈ / Magnetband≈ / Simultan≈ / Stanz≈ / willkürliche ~ *card reader* / *paper tape* / *magnetic t.* / *simultaneous mode* / *card punch* / *manual control* **~(sanlage** f) ⟨aero⟩ *control system* **~sart** f *system of control* **~befehl** m ⟨comp⟩ *procedure branching statement* **~sdüse** f ⟨a–n⟩ *steering nozzle* **~shahn** m *distributing-cock* **~shebel** m ⟨rail⟩ *starting lever* **~srechner** m ⟨a–n⟩ *steering computer* **~sstange** f ⟨tech⟩ *reversing-lever* **~s- u Regelungstheorie** f ⟨cyb⟩ *theory of* (*automata* od) *control systems*

St·even m ~s/~ ⟨mar⟩ *stem* || (Hinter≈) *stern-post*

Steward·eß f ~/–ssen ⟨aero⟩ *cabin-attendant*; *air-hostess*; ⟨Am⟩ *stewardess*

°**Stib·itz- ~-Code** m ⟨comp⟩ *excess-three-code* | °**≈en** vt /i [h] ⟨fam⟩ *to pilfer, filch, purloin*; ⟨sl⟩ *to pinch, bone, snoop*, ⟨mil⟩ *to swipe*; ⟨Am sl⟩ *to snitch, scrounge*

stich imp v stechen **Stich** m ~(e)s/~e **A. 1.** (Bienen≈ etc) *sting*, (Floh≈) *bite* || (Nadel≈) *prick* || ⟨surg⟩ *puncture* || (Wunde) *stab* || ⟨fenc⟩ *thrust* || ⟨fig⟩ (Anspielung) *taunt*; *hit* (auf, gegen *at*); *jab* **2.** (Näh≈) *stitch*; (langer) *tack* ⟨a. bookb⟩ **3.** ⟨tech⟩ (Loch) *puncture* **4.** ⟨path⟩ (innerer Schmerz) *stitch, pang* **5.** ⟨arts⟩ *engraving, cut*; *engraved plate* **6.** ⟨mar⟩ *knot, hitch* **7.** ⟨cards⟩ *cut, trick* || e–n ~ m *to make a tr.* || ⟨whist⟩ k–n ~ m *to make a slam* **8.** (ins Grüne etc) *touch, tinge* (*of green*, etc) **B.** e–m e–n ~ **beibringen** *to stab a p* | ⟨fig⟩ e–n ~ h (Bier etc) *to turn sour*; (Fleisch) *to be high*; (P) a) *to be tipsy*, b) *to have a screw loose* | das war mir ein ~ ins Herz *that cut me to the quick* od *heart* | das ist ein ~ auf uns *that's meant for us* | ~ **halten** *to hold firm*, ⟨fig⟩ *to hold good, to stand the test, to hold water* | (jdn) im ~ **lassen** *to forsake, fail* (*a p*); *to leave in the lurch*; ⟨Am fam⟩ *to ditch*, *to throw a p over, to walk out on a p*; (Weib u Kind) *to desert, abandon*; *to jilt* (*a girl*); (of a girl) *to turn down*, ⟨sl⟩ *to plant*; (of a car etc) *to let down*; (of limbs etc) *to fail* ‖ im ~ gel w *or* s *to hold the sack* | **etw** im ~ l *to go back on*; *to chuck a th*; ⟨prov⟩ ein ~ z Zeit erhält das Kleid *a stitch in time saves nine* **~anker** m ⟨arch⟩ *iron tie* **~axt** f *mortise axe* **~bahn** f *branch railway*; *spur* **~balken** m ⟨tech⟩ *tie-piece*; ⟨arch⟩ *sole-piece, footplate* **~blatt** n (e–s Degens) *guard* ‖ ⟨cards⟩ *trump* ‖ (Ziel) *butt* ⟨a. fig⟩ **~entscheid** m ⟨parl⟩ *casting vote*; ⟨sport etc⟩ *playing* (etc) *off the tie* **≈fest** a *proof*; ⟨fig⟩ *airtight* (*argument*) **~flamme** f *flash*; *darting* od *pilot, blast, jet flame* **≈haltig** a *standing the test*; *valid, solid, sound*; (glaubhaft) *plausible* ‖ ~ s ⟨fam⟩ *to hold water*; *to wash* (*that won't w.!*) **~haltigkeit** f *validity, soundness, weight* (*of reasons*, etc) **~höhe** f ⟨arch⟩ *rising* (*of a vault*) **~loch** n *tap hole* **~mal** n *mark of a stab* **~ofen** m ⟨met⟩ *blast-furnace* **~presse** f *cold press* **~probe** f *assay of run metal* ‖ ⟨fig⟩ [konkr] *sample taken offhand* od *at hazard*; *random* (od *chance, grab*) *sample* ‖ [abstr] *chance control*; *random test*, ⟨Am⟩ *spot check* ‖ ⟨demog⟩ Flächen≈ *area sampling*; geschichtete ~ *stratified random s.g* ‖ ⟨tech⟩ *s. check*(*ing*) ‖ ~ bei Rechnungsprüfung *s. audit* | ~neinheit [f] *s.g unit*; ~nentnahme [f] *bulk s.g* ‖ ~nerhebung [f] *s. survey*; ~nfehler [m] *s. error* ‖ ~nkontrolle [f] ⟨pharm, etc⟩ *acceptance s.g* ‖ ~nnachschau [f] *selective inspection* **~säge** f *lock-, fret-saw* **~straße** f *side* od *feeder road* **~tag** m *term, settling-day*; den 1. 1. z ~ f etw m *to take Jan. 1st as the date fixing the ..* ‖ ⟨com a.⟩ *target date*; ⟨mil⟩ *effective date* **~waffe** f *foil*; *stabbing* od *thrusting weapon* **~wahl** f ⟨parl⟩ *second ballot*; entscheidende ~ *runoff election* **~wort** n ⟨theat⟩ *cue* (überhören *to miss*) ‖ ⟨typ⟩ *catchword*; in ~en *in outline form* | ≈erverzeichnis [n] ⟨print⟩ *index* **~wunde** f *stab, thrust* (*-wound*) **St·ichel** m ~s/~ *cutter*; ⟨arts⟩ (*en*)*graver* | ~name [m] *nick name*; ~rede [f] *taunt, sneer, gibe* **Stichel·ei** f ~/~en **1.** ⟨dero⟩ = Näherei **2.** *sneer*(*ing*), *innuendo*; *gibes, taunts* pl; ⟨Am⟩ *ribbing* **st·icheln** vt/i [h] *to stitch, prick* | ⟨fig⟩ (auf [acc]) *to taunt*; *to sneer, nag, gird at*; ⟨Am⟩ *to needle* **St·ichler** m ~s/~ *taunter, teaser* **St·ichling** m ~(e)s/~e ⟨ich⟩ → *stickleback, tittlebat* **sticht** 3. sg pres v stechen **St·ick-** **~arbeit** f *embroidery* **~fluß** m ⟨med⟩ *choking catarrh, angina pectoris* **~garn** n *e.ring-cotton* **~gas** n ⟨chem⟩ *nitrous gas* **~gaze** f *canvas* **~husten** m (*w*)*hooping-cough* **~luft** f *close* od *stiffy, stifling air* **~muster** n *pattern for e.ring, sampler* **~nadel** f *e.ry-, crewel-needle* **~rahmen** m *e.ry-frame, tambour*(*-frame*) **~schere** f *e.ry scissors* pl **~seide** f *e.ry-silk* **~stoff** m ⟨chem⟩ *nitrogen* | ~bindung [f] ⟨agr⟩ *nitrogen fixation*; ≈haltig [a] *nitrogenous*; ~lost [m] *nitrogen mustard* (*gas*); ~oxid [n] *nitric oxide* **~tuch** n *sampler* **~wolle** f *e.ry-wool* **~zeug** n *e.ry-materials* **st·icken** vt/i [h] *to embroider* ‖ mit Rahmen *to tambour* ‖ ge–ktes Bild *needlework p.* | ≈ n *e.y* **St·icker(in** f) m ~s/~ *embroiderer* **Sticker·ei** f ~/~en *embroidery* **st·ickig** a *suffocating* ‖ (Luft) *close* ‖ (Raum) *airless, stuffy* **St·ickluft** f *stifling air*

st·ieben vt/i [stob/gestoben] [h & s] *to fly about like dust* ‖ (Flüssigkeit) *to spray* ‖ aus–e–a ~ *to disperse*

St·ief- *step..* **~bruder** m *..brother, half-b.* **~eltern** pl *..parents* pl **~geschwister** [pl] *step-..brothers and ..sisters* pl **~kind** n *..child* **~mutter** f *..mother*, ⟨dero⟩ *cruel mother* **~mütterchen** n ⟨bot⟩ *pansy*; wildes ~ *love-in-idleness, hearts-ease* **≈mütterlich** a (*like a*) *..mother* ‖ ⟨fig *grudging, niggard* | [adv] ~ behandeln *to treat without kindness* **~schwester** f *..sister, half-sister* **≈väterlich** a (*like a*) *..father*

St·iefel m ~s/~ *boot* ‖ hochschäftige ~ *Wellington* od *top boots* pl | (e–r Pumpe) *tube, barrel* ‖ e–n guten ~ gehen *to walk a good pace* ‖ er redet sich e–n ~ zus *he talks nonsense* ‖ er kann e–n ~ vertragen *he can stand a great deal* (*of liquoring*), *he's a hard-drinking* od *five-bottle man* **~absatz** m *boot-heel* **~anzieher** m *b.-pulls* pl, *shoe-horn* **~bürste** f *blacking-brush* **~holz** n *b.tree* **~hose** f *pantaloons* pl **~knecht** m *b.jack* °**~lecker** m *b.-lick* **~putzer** m *shoeblack*; *shoe-shine boy*; ⟨hot⟩ *boots* sg **~schaft** m *leg of a b.* **~strippe** f *b.-strap* **~stulpe** f *top of a b.* **~wichse** f *blacking* **Stiefel·ette** f ~/~n **1.** *gaiter* **2.** *elastic-sided boot* **3.** *laced boot* **st·iefeln** **I.** vt [h] *to boot* | **sich** ~ *to put on one's boots* | der gestiefelte Kater *Puss-in-Boots* | gestiefelt u gespornt *booted and spurred* **II.** vi [s] *to stalk* (*along*) ‖ °wo ~ Sie hin? *where are you off to?*

stieg 1. sg 3. sg pret v steigen **St·iege** f ~/~n **1.** (Treppe) *staircase* **2.** (20 Stück) *score* **3.** (Kiste) *crate*

St·ieglitz m ~es/~e ⟨orn⟩ *goldfinch*

stiehlst 2. sg pres v stehlen

Stiel m ~(e)s/~e **A. 1.** (Griff) *handle, helve* | (Beil≈) *helve* (→ stielen) ‖ Besen≈ *stick* ‖ (Glas-≈) *stem* ‖ (Handgranaten≈) *stick* ‖ (Messer≈) *haft* ‖ (Nagel≈) *shank* ‖ (Pfeifen≈) *stem* **2.** ⟨aero⟩ *strut* **3.** ⟨carp⟩ *upright* **4.** ⟨bot⟩ *stem, stalk*; (Pilz≈) ⟨a.⟩ *stipe* ‖ ⟨scient⟩ (Blatt≈) *petiole*; (Blüten≈, Frucht≈) *peduncle*, (kl) *pedicle*; Eis am ~ *ice lolly* **5.** ⟨zoo⟩ *pedicle*, (der Entenmuschel) *stalk* **B.** den ~ umkehren *to turn the tables* (jdm *upon a p*) **~auge** n *stalked eye*; °⟨fig⟩ (P) *rubberneck*; ~n m *to r.* **≈äugig** a *stalk-eyed* **~besen** m *long-handled brush* **~blatt** n *petiolate leaf* **≈blütig** a *cauliflorous* **~brille** f *lorgnette* **~ende** n ⟨bot⟩ *base* **~glas** n *glass with a stem* **~handgranate** f *stick grenade* **~kloben** m ⟨tech⟩ *tail-vice* **≈los** a ⟨bot⟩ *stalkless*, ⟨scient⟩ *sessile* **~stich** m *stem-stitch* **st·ielen** vt [h] *to furnish with a handle*; *to helve, haft* | gestielt ⟨bot⟩ *pediculate* ‖ *petiolate* (*leaf*) ‖ *pedunculate* (*flower*) **..stielig** a *..-stalked* (*long-stalked*) ‖ °⟨fig⟩ = langweilig

Stier m ~(e)s/~e *bull* ‖ ⟨astr⟩ *Taurus* ‖ junger ~ *b.ock* ‖ den ~ bei den Hörnern packen (*to square up to difficulties*) *to grasp the nettle*; *to take the b. by the horns* **~hetze** *f b.-baiting* **~kalb** n *b.-calf* **~kampf** m *b.-fight* **~kämpfer** m *b.-fighter* **≈köpfig** a *with a b.'s head* **~nacken** m *b.neck* **≈nackig** a *broad-necked*; ⟨fig⟩ *obstinate* **st·ier** a = starr | **~en** vi [h] (auf [acc], nach) *to stare* (*vacantly*) (*at*) ‖ [abs] *to look vacant*

°**St·iesel**, -ßel m ~s/~ *lout, boor*; *dolt*

stieß 1. & 3. sg pret v stoßen

Stift m ~(e)s/~e **1.** *brad, nail*; *tack*; *pin* ‖ (Sicherungs≈) *cotter* ‖ (hölzerner) *peg* ‖ (Schnür-≈) *tag* ‖ ⟨mach⟩ (Zapfen) *pivot* ‖ (Zahnstumpf) *stump* **2.** (Zeichen≈) *pencil* ‖ (farbig) *crayon* ‖ bunte ~e *chalks* pl | ~zahn [m] *pin-tooth*; ~zeichnung [f] *crayon-drawing* **3.** °(Büro-Lehrling) *apprentice, office-boy* ‖ (Knirps) *youngster* ⟨fam⟩ *dot, whipper-snapper* **4.** °⟨sex vulg⟩ *pointer, pin, pencil*

St·ift n ~(e)s/~e(r) (*charitable*) *foundation* ‖ *religious establishment* od *endowment* ‖ *institution* (*for ladies of rank*) | *convent* ‖ *bishopric* ‖ (*theological*) *seminary* ‖ *chapter* (*of a cathedral*) | **≈en** vt [h] **A. 1.** ⟨rel⟩ *to endow* (*masses, candles*) ‖ (gründen) *to establish, found* **2.** (vermachen) *to bequeath* (*pictures*) | (schenken) *to subscribe to* od *for* ‖ ⟨fam⟩ *to make a present of* ‖ ⟨sl⟩ *to stand* (*a barrel of beer*) **3.** (ins Leben rufen) *to set on foot* ‖ *to bring about* (*a marriage*) ‖ (einsetzen) *to institute* ‖ (gründen) *to establish* (*towns, states*) ‖ *to found* (*schools*) ‖ *to start* (*a club*) | (schaffen) *to originate* ‖ *to make, establish* (*peace, an alliance*) ‖ *to create* (*order*) | *to make* (*friendship, mischief, a match*) ‖ *to do* (*good, harm*) | (anstiften) *to* provoke, excite (a quarrel) ‖ to cause (trouble, an accident) ‖ to sow (discord; Feindschaft the seeds of hatred) **B.** (wieder) Freundschaft ~ zw .. to make two people friends (to conciliate them, to reconcile them to one another) ‖ Nutzen ~ to be useful ‖ ⟨fam iron⟩ da h Sie was Schönes gestiftet! that's a fine bit of business you've done | °~ **gehen** to clear out **St·ifter** m ~s/~ founder, author, originator ‖ donor; ⟨jur a.⟩ settler **St·iftler** m ~s/~ inmate of an endowed establishment, foundation-scholar **St·ifts- ~amt** n canonicate, chapter-court **~amtmann** m vidame **~brief** m foundation-deed **~dame** f, **~fräulein** n canoness **~gebäude** n living quarters of Chorherren etc **~gemeinde** f congregation of a cathedral **~gut** n chapter estate **~herr** m canon, prebendary **~hütte** f ⟨bib⟩ tabernacle **~kirche** f cathedral; collegiate church **≈mäßig** a capitular **~pfarrer** m = –prediger **~pfründe** f prebend **~prediger** m chaplain of a collegiate church **~schule** f foundation-school, endowed school **St·iftung** f ~/~en establishment | (Gründung) foundation | (Anstalt) institution | milde ~ pious bequest; charitable foundation od institution; charity | originating, making, causing **St·iftungs- ~fest** n, **~tag** m anniversary; foundation-festival; commemoration- od founder's day ‖ ~ h °⟨sex vulg⟩ to tail, → Stift 4. **~fonds** m endowment-fund **~urkunde** f charter of foundation

stigmatis·ieren vt [h] to stigmatize

Stil m ~(e)s/~e **A.** ⟨arts & liter⟩ style ‖ ⟨fig⟩ manner; ⟨pol⟩ tact, finesse, diplomacy, savoir-faire Fr; scharfer ~ stiletto st. ‖ sein ~ his st. od manner ‖ im gotischen etc ~ in the Gothic st.; of the Victorian order | ⟨liter⟩ Meister des ~s stylist ‖ Unterricht im ~ teaching of composition | gekünstelter ~ mannerism ‖ geschraubter, hölzerner ~ stilted, clumsy st. | sich im ~ anlehnen an (S) to be in the st. of, (P) to follow the st. of ‖ dem ~ nach stylistically ‖ er schreibt e–n .. he writes (in) a pleasant st. **B.** üblicher ~ established usage ‖ Kalender alten, neuen ~s c. of old, new st. | Unternehmen gr Stils large-scale enterprise ‖ in gr ~e leben to live in a great st. ‖ ein Architekt in kl ~ a builder in a small way of business **~art** f style, turn **~blüte** f (Irish) bull, ⟨school, etc⟩ howler **~gefühl** n artistic taste **≈gerecht** a stylish; [adv] in style **~kleid** n period dress **~kunde** f composition, ⟨Am⟩ rhetoric **≈los** a without st., incongruous **~möbel** n pl period furniture **~übung** f exercise in composition **≈voll** a in good st., stylish, harmonious ‖ (geschmackvoll) tasty, classy, tony, ⟨Am sl⟩ nifty **Stil·ett** n ~(e)s/~e stiletto **stilis·ieren** vt [h] **1.** to compose, word, draft ‖ er stilisiert gut he writes well ‖ schlecht stilisiert written in bad style **2.** to touch up **3.** to stylise (movements, etc) **Stil·ist** m ~en/~en stylist; elegant writer **~ik** f ~/~en art od theory of style od composition **≈isch** a as regards style od composition ‖ ⟨Am⟩ rhetorical (rules) ‖ in ≈er Hinsicht stylistically

St·ilfser J·och n (am Ortler) Stelvio Pass

still I. a **A.** quiet (lodger, lodgings, place) ‖ (See, Luft, Gefühle) calm ‖ stagnant (pool) | ⟨com⟩ flat, dull | motionless | peaceful, peaceable | (zurückhaltend) undemonstrative | wordless, silent, taciturn; ⟨fam⟩ mum | (leise) low, soft **B.** Holy (Week) ‖ Good (Friday) ‖ Pacific (Ocean) **C.** (Beileid) unspoken; wir bitten um ~es B. no visits of condolence (desired) ‖ (Gebet) silent, private ‖ ⟨com⟩ (Gesellschafter) sleeping, ⟨Am⟩ silent (partner) ‖ ~es **Glück** peace and happiness ‖ (Hochzeit) quiet, private ‖ ⟨com⟩ (Jahreszeit) dead, dull, slack ‖ (Liebe) secret, unavowed ‖ (Luft) calm, tranquil ‖ (Mensch) calm, inoffensive ‖ ⟨R. C.⟩ (Messe) low ‖ in ~er Nacht → Stille ‖ ⟨com⟩ (Reserven) sleeping ‖ (Schmerz) dull ‖ dem ~en **Suff** ergeben given to drinking on the quiet od ⟨sl⟩ sly ‖ (Übereinkunft) tacit ‖ ~er Vorbehalt mental reservation ‖ (Vorwurf) silent ‖ (Wasser) smooth ‖ ~es Wetter calm weather, ⟨mar⟩ calm **D.** ~! hush!, silence! **~ doch!** do be quiet ‖ ~ davon! no more of that!, ⟨fam⟩ cut that! | **im** ~en silently, (heimlich) in secret, privately; ⟨sl⟩ on the sly **E.** ~ **bek** to silence ‖ sich ~ davon m to slink od sneak away ‖ ~ m to kill ‖ ~ s to be quiet ‖ es war ~ there was a lull ‖ **verhaltet** euch ~! keep quiet!, don't move od stir; sich ~ verhalten ⟨a.⟩ to lie low ‖ ~ w to hush, to grow silent etc, to dwindle into silence; (v Wind) to calm down; to abate, drop **F.** ⟨prov⟩ die Toten sind ~e Leute dead men tell no tales ‖ ~e Wasser sind or gründen tief still waters run deep **II. ein ≈er** a quiet p ‖ **die ≈en** im Lande the pious of the land **St·ill- ≈begl·ückt** a happy and at peace **~geld** n breast-feeding benefit **~halteabkommen** n standstill agreement **≈|halten** vi [irr] [h] to (make a) stop; to pause, to keep still ‖ den Mund ~ to hold one's tongue **~haltung** f respite from claims of creditors **~(l)eben** n retired life ‖ ⟨arts⟩ still-life; (Obst≈) fruit-piece **≈|(l)egen** vt (Betrieb) to shut down, to put out of operation, to phase out; –gelegt inactive (Anlage) ‖ (Wagen) to lay up **~(l)egung** f shutting down, shutdown **≈|(l)iegen** vi [irr] [h] to lie still ‖ to stop ‖ (Schiff) to lie to ‖ (Verkehr) to be suspended, to tie up ‖ ⟨tech⟩ to be out of action ‖ ⟨fig com⟩ to lie dormant **~periode** f lactation period **~schweigen** n silence ‖ e–m ~ auferlegen to enjoin secrecy on a p, to seal a p's lips; to muzzle a p ‖ ~ bewahren über etw to keep a th quiet; .. jdm gegenüber not to breathe a word to a p ‖ das ~ brechen to break si. ‖ sich in ~ hüllen to keep one's counsel ‖ mit ~ übergehen to pass in si. **≈|schweigen** vi [irr] [h] to be silent, to keep silence, to hold one's peace od tongue ‖ ~ zu to take no notice of **≈schweigend** a silent ‖ ⟨fig⟩ tacit, implied | [adv] (as if) by tacit agreement, tacitly; jdm ~ vertrauen to trust implicitly in a p **≈|setzen** vt [h] ⟨tech⟩ to switch off **~|sitzen** vi [h] to sit by **~stand** m standstill, (complete) stop(page); deadlock (of ths); ⟨com⟩ recession; ⟨tech⟩ inoperation; (Einstellen) stopping; (Pause) let-up; ⟨Am⟩ (infolge v Umständen) tie-up; (vorübergend) lull ‖ ⟨astr⟩ station ‖ ⟨fig⟩ stagnation ‖ z ~ bringen to stop (engines), to shut down (a factory), to halt (a rebellion); (Wagen) plötzlich .. to bring up sharply; .. gebracht arrested (tuberculosis) ; z ~ k to stop, to break down ‖ geistiger ~ backwater ‖ ⟨prov⟩ ~ ist Rückgang stagnation means recession **≈|stehen** vi [irr] [h & s] to stand still, to stop; ⟨tech⟩ to be out of action ‖ ⟨fig⟩ to be at a standstill ‖ ⟨mil⟩ to stand at attention; still gest·anden! attention!, ⟨fam⟩ 'shun! ‖ das Herz ~ l or m ⟨fig⟩ to stop the h. dead **≈stehend** a (Maschine) stationary ‖ (Gewässer) stagnant ⟨a. fig⟩ **≈vergnügt** a calm and serene; quietly happy **~wasser** n slack **~wein** m still wine **St·ille** f ~/ **1.** stillness, silence, hush; quiet(ness); tranquillity ‖ es trat e–e (vorübergehende) ~ ein there was a silence ‖ nächtliche ~ the silence of night ‖ (der Natur) calmness, peace ‖ (der See) calm(ness), lull | **in** der ~ silently, privately, in secret ‖ in aller ~ on the quiet, ⟨sl⟩ .. sly (→ still E.) ‖ in der ~ der Nacht in the dead od stillness of (the) night, at dead of night **2.** = Stillstand **st·illen I.** vt [h] to quiet, calm; to silence ‖ (Zorn) to appease | (Schmerz) to still ‖ (Kummer) to assuage ‖ (Frucht) to allay | (Blut) to stop, stanch | (Kind) to suckle, breast-feed, nurse | (Aufruhr) to quell | (sich [dat]) den Durst ~ to quench one's thirst ‖ (Hunger) to appease (⟨a. fig⟩ the appetite [for good books]); to stay the pangs of h. ‖ (Sehnsucht) to still, satisfy ‖ (Begierde) to satisfy, gratify **II.** ≈ n lactation

st·illend a *lenitive, allaying* **St·illung** f ~/~en *quieting* || *stanching* || *suckling, nursing* || *quenching* || *appeasing, appeasement*

St·imm- ~abgabe f *voting, vote* **~band** n ⟨anat⟩ *vocal c(h)ord* **~bandlähmung** f ⟨path⟩ *aphony* **≗berechtigt, ≗fähig** a *entitled to vote, enfranchised* **~berechtigte(r)** m *voter* **~bildung** f *phonation* **~bruch** m = –wechsel **~enthaltung** f *abstinence from voting* **~führer** m *leader; spokesman* **~führung** f ⟨mus⟩ *scoring* **~gabel** f *tuning-fork* **~geber** m *voter* **~gewirr** n *babel of voices* **≗haft** a ⟨phon⟩ *voiced* **~hammer** m *tuning-hammer* **~heilkunde** f *phoniatrics* [sg konstr] **~holz** n *soul (in a violin)* **~kreise** m pl *constituencies* **~lage** f *register* **~lippe** f ⟨anat⟩ *vocal c(h)ord* **≗los** a ⟨phon⟩ *voiceless, breathed* **~-mittel** [pl] *voice* **~pfeife** f *tuning-pipe* **~recht** n *right of voting, v.g r.* || allg ~ *universal suffrage* || gleiches ~ *equality of votes* || das ~ übertragen bek h, sich das ~ ü. l ⟨com⟩ *to act as proxy*; das ~ verlieren *to be disenfranchised* **~ritze** f ⟨anat⟩ *glottis* | ~ndeckel [m] *epiglottis* **~schlüssel** m *tuning-key* **~stock** m = –holz **~umfang** m *compass* od *range of voice* °**~vieh** n *herd of voters* **~wechsel** m *breaking of the voice, mutation* **~werkzeug** n *vocal instrument* **~zettel** m *voting-* od *ballot-paper* **~zimmer** n ⟨theat⟩ *band-* (⟨Am⟩ *musicians'*) *room* **St·imme** f ~/~n **1.**/*voice* | angegriffene ~ *strained throat*; schmetternde ~ *booming v.*; schwankende ~ *unsteady v.* || e–e außerordentlich umfangreiche u volle ~ *a voice of extraordinary range and volume* || e–e innere ~ sagt mir *I have a hunch* || e–e ~ ertönte *a voice came* || mit tiefer ~ *in a deep voice* || die ~ dämpfen *to drop the v.*; mit gedämpfter ~ *with bated breath*, → gedämpft; s–e ~ klang ernst *he spoke gravely*; s–e ~ über etw vernehmen l *to sound off on a th* || die ~n der Presse *press comments* pl **2.** ⟨mus⟩ *voice, organ*; (Noten) *part*; zweite ~ *alto* || (Orgelregister) *stop* | ⟨fig⟩ *tone (of joy)* || *call (of the blood, of nature, duty)* | die ~ ging ihm aus *his voice failed* || nicht bei ~ *not in voice* || (gut) bei ~ *in (good) v.* || die ~ an- u abschwellen l *to modulate the v.* **3.** (Wahl≗) *vote, suffrage* || s–e ~ abgeben *to (give one's) vote* || die abgegebenen ~n *votes polled, the ballot*; wobei sich F. der ~ enthielt *France not voting* || in e–r S k–e ~ h *to have no say in a matter* || mit 93 gegen 52 ~n *by 93 votes to 52* || ausschlaggebende, entscheidende ~ *casting-vote* || ~n sammeln, werben *to collect votes, to canvass* || ~n auf sich vereinigen *to poll .. votes* **st·immen I.** vt [h] (Geige etc) *to tune (up)* (nach dem Klavier *to the piano*) || höher, tiefer ~ *to raise, lower the pitch* | ⟨fig⟩ jdn günstig ~ *to put a p in a favo(u)rable mood*, .. f etw .. *to dispose a p to a th*; schlecht ges–mt *out of temper, illhumo(u)red*; es –mte ihn seltsam *it gave him a strange feeling*; jdn skeptisch ~ *to arouse scepticism in a p*; jdn traurig ~ *to make a p sad*; jdn ~ gegen *to prejudice a p against* **II.** vi [h] (bei Wahlen) *to vote, poll* (f *for*) || f jdn ~ *to give a p one's vote* || gegen jds Aufnahme ~ *to blockade a p* | ⟨fig⟩ (mit) *to accord, agree, tally (with)*; *to square* || etw stimmt nicht zw den beiden *sth is wrong* od *amiss between the two* || die Rechnung stimmt nicht .. *is incorrect* | **es** –mt beinahe aufs Haar *it is almost the exact truth*; **(das)** –mt (nicht)! *that is true* od *right*! (*that is not so*!); .. wie's Kirchenbuch *it's as right as rain* || irgend etw –mt da nicht *there's sth wrong (somewhere)*; irgendwo –mt etw nicht *sth is wrong somewhere*; –mt was nicht? *(is) sth wrong?*; mit ihm –mt etw nicht *sth is wrong with him* || –mt's? *is that so* od *it?*, .. oder hab ich recht? *isn't it so or am I right?* || **f (gegen)** e–n Gesetzesvorschlag ~ *to vote a proposal up (down)* || das –mt zu m–r Lage *that's just the th in my position* | ⟨mus⟩ *to be in tune* | ⟨fig⟩ schlecht ge–mt (P) *out of sorts; ill-tempered* **St·immen- ~abgabe** f *vote, voting* **~einheit** f *unanimity* **~gleichheit** f *tie* **~gewirr** n *jangle, babble, din* od *buzz of voices* **~mehrheit** f *majority (of votes)* || einfache ~ *simple* od *bare majority* **~prüfer** m *scrutator* **~prüfung** f *scruting (of votes)* **~sammlung** f *collection of votes* **~teilung** f *division; splitting of votes* **~werbung** f *canvass(ing)* **~zahl** f, erforderliche ~ *requisite number of votes* **~zählung** f *counting of votes* **St·immer** m ~s/~ *tuner* **..stimmig** a; vier~ *for four voices* **st·immlich** a *vocal (quality, power)* || ~ auf der Höhe *in good voice* || ~ behindert s *to have a vocal impediment* || ~ begabt s *to be a gifted singer* **St·immung** f ~/~en **1.** ⟨mus⟩ *tuning* **2.** (Höhe etc) *tonality; tune, pitch, key* || ~ halten *to keep in tune* **3.** ⟨fig⟩ (P) *humour, mood; frame of mind; disposition, temper* || (der Umgebung) *atmosphere* || die ~ im Volke *the national temper* || öffentliche ~ *public feeling* || ⟨com⟩ *tendency, tone* | jdn in **frohe** ~ versetzen *to put a p in a happy frame of mind, to exhilerate a p*; **gehobene** ~ *exaltation, elation*; in g–r ~ *buoyant, elate, in high spirits*, ⟨hum⟩ *in full feather*; sie kam in g–e ~ *her spirits rose high*; die ~ **drücken** *to cast a gloom on the mood*; in ged–ter ~ *in low spirits, depressed; her spirits were at a very low ebb*; in g–r ~ s ⟨fam⟩ *to have the blues* || in lustiger ~ *in capital humour* || niederdrückende ~ *blight (to cast a b. over a p)* | **gute ~ erhalten,** f gute ~ sorgen ⟨fig⟩ *to keep ths pleasant* | ~en gehen in–e–a über *mood shades into m.* | ~ m f *to roof for* | ~en unterworfen *addicted to moods* | **in** ~ bringen (durch Trunk) *to gin up*; **in der** ~ f, z etw *in the vein* od *humour for ..* || ich war nicht in (der) ~, es zu tun *I did not feel like* (od *feel up to*) *doing it* || wenn er in der ~ war *when the mood was on him, when he was in the m.* **St·immungs- ~bild** n ⟨paint, (liter)⟩ *picture (description) of a certain atmosphere* **~lokal** n *amusement bar* od *place* **~mache** f ⟨com⟩ *boom(ing), bull manœuvres* pl; *(patriotic) flag-waving* **~mensch** m *moody creature* **~schwankungen** f pl *fluctuations in mood* **≗voll** a *impressive; elated* **~wechsel** m *change of mood* (od ⟨com⟩ *tendency*)

St·imulans n ~/ Stimulantia ⟨med⟩ *stimulant* **stimul·ieren** vt [h] *to stimulate*

St·ink- °**~ad·ores** [pl] *stinking weeds (= cigars)* pl **~as·ant** m ~s/~e ⟨bot⟩ *asafetida* °**≗besoffen** a *dead drunk* **~bock** m *he-goat*; ⟨fig sl⟩ (P) *stinker* **~bombe** f, **~topf** m *stink-pot* **≗f·aul** a *dog-, bone lazy* °**~fingerchen m** ⟨sex vulg⟩ *to get one's hand on it, to play at stink-finger* °**≗gemütlich** a → gemütlich **~morchel** f ⟨bot⟩ *stink-horn* **~tier** n *skunk* (⟨a. fig⟩ P) **st·inken** vi [stank/gestunken] [h] (nach) *to stink (of), to be fetid (with)*, ⟨sl⟩ *to niff* || hier stinkt's *here's a nasty smell*, ⟨fig⟩ *there's sth fishy about it*; ~ wie ein Bock *to stink like a (he-)goat, polecat, monkey-house* || das stinkt z Himmel *that's a crying shame* | **~d** [a] *foul* (v *with*), ⟨bot⟩ *vile-smelling* || *gross (lie)* | [adv] ~ faul → stinkfaul; er ist ~ faul *he's as lazy as Hall's dog which lay down to bark* || ~ fauler Mensch *lazy dog* °**St·inker** m ~s/~ ⟨fig⟩ (P) *stinker, stink-pot, skunk* **st·inkig** a *stinking, smelling, fetid* || ⟨fig⟩ *vile (temper)* || ~es Geld *pelf*

Stint m ~(e)s/~e ⟨ich⟩ *smelt* || sich freuen wie ein ~ *to be as happy as a sandboy*

Stipendi·at m ~en/~en *stipendiary* || (an Schulen & Univ.) *foundation-scholar*; ⟨engl⟩ *fellow* **Stip-endium** n ~s/–dien *scholarship*; ⟨Scot⟩ *bursary* || (Jahres≗) *exhibition*

°**St·ipp- ~besuch** m, **~visite** f *flying visit* e–e ~ m *to drop in* **~fleck** m (Apfel≗) *bitter pit* **~milch** f *sweet curdled milk* **St·ippe** f ~/~n ⟨cul⟩ *dip* **st·ippen** vt [h] *to dip, steep* || (auf|~) *to soak up*

stirb(st) imp (2. P sg pres) v sterben

Stirn f ~/~en *forehead* → Stirne **~ader** f *frontal* (*f.l*) *vein* **~ansicht** f *front view* **~band** n, **~binde** f *head-band, fillet*; (*Jew's*) *frontlet* **~bein** n *f.l bone* **~blatt** n *facing, fr.let* **~bogen** m ⟨arch⟩ *f.l arch* **~brett** n ⟨carp⟩ *fascia-board* **~falte** f *wrinkle on the f.h.* **~fläche** f *f.l area*; ⟨übtr⟩ *face, front*; ⟨for, carp⟩ *end face* **~fräser** m ⟨tech⟩ *front-milling tool* **~gegend** f *f.l region* **~getriebe** n *spur gearing* **~haar** n *forelock*; *front hair* **~höcker** m *f.l eminence* **~fläche** f *front, face* **~höhle** f *f.l cavity* | ~nentzündung [f] *f.l sinusitis* **~holz** n ⟨carp etc⟩ *crosscut* od *endgrained wood* **~joch** n ⟨arch⟩ *front-truss* **~leiste** f *f.l ridge*; ⟨aero⟩ *leading edge* **~locke** f *forelock* (→ Schmachtlocke) **~mauer** f *front-wall* **~-moräne** f *f.l morain* **~muskel** m *f.l muscle* **~rad** n *spur wheel* **~riemen** m ⟨hors⟩ *headpiece, frontal* **~runzeln** n *frown*(*ings* pl); mit zornigem ~ auf jdn sehen *to frown angrily at a p* | ~̈d *frowning*; ~̈d vor sich hinblicken *to frown to o.s.* **~schutz** m *brow-pad* **~seite** f *front* **~wand** f (*fore*)*front* **~widerstand** m ⟨aero⟩ *head-resistance* **~wunde** f *f.l wound* **~ziegel** m *tile-end* **Stirn(e)** f ~/~en *forehead*; ⟨poet⟩ *brow* (hohe *lofty*) ‖ (Front) *frontage* ‖ [dat] die ~ bieten *to confront, face* ‖ die ~ runzeln, in Falten legen *to knit one's brow, to frown*; nachdenklich ge–lte ~ *meditative frowning* | ⟨fig⟩ die ~ h zu .. *to have the face, cheek* (= *insolence, impudence*) *to* .. ‖ jdm etw **an** der ~ ablesen *to see .. by the look of a p's face* ‖ ihm auf die ~ geschrieben *written on his brow* ‖ sich vor die ~ schlagen *to strike one's f.d*

stob 1. & 3. sg pret v stieben

st·oben vt [h] ⟨cul⟩ *to stew*

St·öber- ~hund m *retriever*; *cocker-spaniel* **~wetter** n *snow-drift*; *sleet*(*y weather*) **st·öberig** a *snowy* **st·öbern I.** vi [h] *to rummage, rake, hunt* **II.** vi imps [h] (of snow) *to drift* ‖ es stöbert *a fine snow is falling* ‖ in den Büchern ~ *to browse over* ..

stoch·astisch a Gr ⟨prob⟩ *stochastic* (*process*)

St·ocher m ~s/~ *poker* ‖ → Zahn~̈ | ~̈n vt/i [h] (das Feuer) *to stir, poke*; *to stoke* ⟨a. °fig = essen⟩ ‖ (stacheln) *to prick, goad* ‖ sich die Zähne ~ *to pick one's teeth* **Stock** m **I.** ~(e)s/~̈e **A.** *stick* ‖ ⟨bot⟩ *stem, stock* ‖ ⟨com⟩ *original capital* **B.** (**Amboß**~̈) *stock* ‖ (Anker~̈) *stock* ‖ Berg~̈ *alpenstock* ‖ Bienen~̈ *hive* ‖ Billard~̈ *cue* ‖ Blumen~̈ *flowerpot, pot-plant* ‖ Brems~̈ *brake-shaft* ‖ Druck~̈ ⟨typ⟩ *cliché* Fr ‖ Flagg~̈ *flagstaff* ‖ (Sattler–) Füll~̈ *rammer* ‖ Gebirgs~̈ *mass*(*if* Fr), *stock* ‖ (Gewehr~̈) *rod* ‖ (Granatwerfer~̈) *stick* ‖ *hockey-stick* ‖ Hut~̈ *block* (*to put on the b.*) ‖ Krokett~̈ *mallet* ‖ Kumt~̈ *horse-collar form* ‖ Lade~̈ *ramrod* ‖ Mal~̈ *maulstick* ‖ Opfer~̈ *poor-box* ‖ Prügel~̈ *rod, stick, birch* ‖ *polo-, ski-stick* ‖ Spazier~̈ *cane, walking-stick* ‖ Straf~̈ *stocks* pl (*to put in the st.*) ‖ Trommel~̈ *drumstick* ‖ Wein~̈ *vine* ‖ Wurzel-~̈ *stump, stub* (*of a tree*) ‖ (Zahn~̈) *body, stump* **C.** das Regiment des ~es *the rule of the rod* ‖ den ~ bek *to get thrashed* (od *the stick*) ‖ **am** ~ gehen *to use a stick* ‖ **mit** dem ~ bearbeiten *to use a stick on* (*a p*) ‖ **über** ~ u Stein *over bush and brake, over hedge and ditch* **II.** ⟨fig⟩ [pl ~̈er] *block, stupid* **III.** [pl ~] ([sd] 1. ~ = Erdgeschoß; 2. ~ = nordd 1. ~) *stor*(*e*)*y, floor* (→ erste C.) ‖ im 3. ~ (*living*) *on the third* (⟨Am⟩ *fourth*) *floor* od *up three pair of stairs* ‖ Zimmer im oberen ~ *upstairs room*(*s*) ‖ wieviel ~ hat es? *how many stories are there*? **St·ock-** [in comp fig mst] *thorough, quite, regular, to the backbone* **~amboß** m *anvil* **~amerikaner** m *th.gh Yankee* **~ausschlag** m ⟨for⟩ *stump-shoot*(*s*) **~ballspiel** n *bandy* (*-ball*) **~̈blind** a *stone-blind* **~börse** f *stock-exchange* **~degen** m *sword-cane* **~̈dumm** a *utterly stupid* **~dürr** a (as) *dry as a bone* **~eisen** n *pitching tool*, pl ⟨a.⟩ *stocks* pl **~engländer** m *true* od *thoroughbred Englishman* **~ente** f ⟨orn⟩ *mallard* **~fäule** f ⟨for⟩ *stock-rot* **~fechten** n *stick-fencing* **~̈finster** a *pitch-dark*, [pred] *dark as a pocket*; in ~er Nacht *at dead of night* ²**~fisch** m ⟨ich⟩ *dried cod* ‖ ⟨fig⟩ *dunce, blockhead* | ~fang [m] *cod-fishing* ²**~flecke** m pl *mildew, damp-stain, mould* ²**~fleckig** a *mouldy* ‖ (Papier etc) *mildewy, foxed, foxy* **~̈finster** a *pitch-dark* | ~̈nis [f] *p.y d.ness* **~flinte** f *cane-gun* **~̈fremd** a *quite strange* **~granate** f *rifle-grenade* **~händler** m *dealer in sticks* **~haus** n ⟨hist⟩ *jail* **~holz** n *stump-wood*; *roots and stumps* pl **~kampf** m *cudgel-play* **~knopf** m *knob of a stick* **~makler** m *stockbroker* **~meister** m ⟨hist⟩ *jailer* **~n·arr** m *arrant fool* **~presse** f *large press* **~prügel** m pl *cudgelling, thrashing, caning* **~rose** f ⟨bot⟩ *rose-mallow, hollyhock* **~schirm** m *umbrella in a walking-stick* **~schlagbetrieb** m ⟨for⟩ *coppice system* **~schläge** m pl = –prügel **~schnupfen** [v stocken²] m *chronic cold in the nose* **~schwämmchen** n ⟨bot⟩ *Agaricus* L **~spule** f *head-quill* **~ständer** m *umbrella-stand* **~stativ** n ⟨phot⟩ *cane tripod* **~̈st·eif** a *stiff as a poker*; ⟨fig⟩ *like a stick* **~̈st·ill** a *stockstill* **~̈t·aub** a *stone-deaf*, [pred] (*as*) *deaf as a post* **~uhr** f *French clock* **~werk** n = Stock III. | ~anzeiger [m] ⟨el⟩ *position and/or direction indicator*; ~schalter [m] *landing switch*; Zwei-~-Wohnung [f] *duplex apartment* **~zahn** m *grinder* **~zange** f (*a pair of*) *forge tongs* **~zwinge** f (*cane-*)*ferrule* **St·öckchen** n ~s/~ *little stick* od *cane* ‖ *switch* ‖ ⟨engl mil⟩ *swagger-cane* **St·öckel- ~absatz** m *Louis XV heel* **~schuh** m *high-heeled shoe*; *patten* **st·ocken**¹ vt [h] *to provide with a stick*, etc ‖ *to prop, stake* (*vines*) | *to roll* (*cloth*) **..stöckig** a *storey*(*ed*) (*4-st.d house*)

st·ocken² **I.** vi [h & s] **1. A.** *to stop* (*short*) ‖ *to come to* (*be at*) *a deadlock* od *stand*(*still*) ‖ *to get stuck* | (langsamer w) *to slacken* | **es** stockt *there's a hitch* **B.** sein **Atem** stockte *his breathing was arrested* | (**Blut**) *to cease to circulate, to run cold* ‖ (Feder) *to refuse to write* ‖ (Gespräch) *to flag* ‖ (Handel) *to be slack* ‖ (**Herz**) *to cease to act* ‖ ⟨mach⟩ *to be dogged* ‖ (P in der Rede) *to stumble, stammer, falter*; *to hum and haw*; *to break down* ‖ (**Pferd** etc) *to jib* ‖ *the pulse is irregular* ‖ (Verhandlungen) *to hang fire* ‖ (Verkehr) *to be* (*held up* od) *suspended* ‖ (Wasser & ⟨fig⟩) *to stagnate* ‖ ihm stockte die Zunge *he was tongue-tied* **2.** (zögern) *to hesitate* **3.** (gerinnen) *to thicken, congeal, coagulate* ‖ (Blut, Milch) *to curdle* **4.** (muffig w) *to turn mouldy* od *fusty* ‖ es stockt hier *ths become mouldy here* **5.** (Zahn) *to rot, decay* **II.** ~̈ n *stopping, stagnation* ‖ *catch in the breath*; *catch in the voice* | ins ~̈ geraten = stocken; (Angriff) *to bog down*; (Briefwechsel) *to be broken off* **St·ockerl** n ~s/~n [bay-österr] = Hocker

Stockh·olm n (Hptst. v Schweden)

st·ockig 1. = stöckisch **2.** = stocksteif **3.** *fusty, mouldy*; *smutted* (Holz) **st·öckisch** a *obstinate, stubborn* **St·ockung** f ~/~en (*coming to a*) *standstill, stoppage* ‖ ⟨com⟩ *dul*(*l*)*ness* ‖ ⟨med⟩ *congestion*; *stasis* ‖ ⟨tech⟩ *jam* ‖ ⟨mil⟩ *stoppage* N ‖ (Verkehrs~̈) *block*; *congested state* (*of the goods traffic*) ‖ (Wasser & ⟨fig⟩) *stagnation* ‖ (Zögern) *hesitation* (a. in der Rede) | ⟨fam⟩ *hitch* (*in*); → stocken² 1. A.

Stoff m ~(e)s/~e **1.** ⟨weav⟩ *material, stuff*; *cloth*; (*textile*) *fabric*; englische (Woll-)~e *British woollens* **2.** (Materie) *matter, substance* ‖ ⟨chem⟩ einfacher ~ *elementary body* | ⟨fig⟩ *mettle* (*of which he was made*) ‖ er ist aus anderem ~ gemacht *he is cast in a different mould* ‖ ⟨philos⟩ *hyle* | ⟨stud sl⟩ *stuff, tap* (*excellent st.* od *t.*), ⟨sl⟩ *booze* **3.** (Gegenstand) *subject*(*-matter*) (*of a speech* etc) ‖ *topic* (*for a speech*) ‖ *food* (*for conversation*) ‖ ~ z Lachen, Nachdenken *sth to laugh, think about* ‖ s–n ~ beherrschen *to master* one's subject || ~ sammeln ⟨liter⟩ to collect material ~bahn f (Ballon) panel ~bespannung f fabric covering ~(f)änger m ⟨pap⟩ save-all ~-gleichheit f isogeny ~gurt m web belt ≃haltig a substantial, material ~handschuh m fabric glove ~lehre f chemistry ≃los a immaterial ~losigkeit f ⟨philos⟩ immateriality ~mangel ⟨stud sl⟩ lack of beer ~muster n swatch ~name m concrete od material noun ~reste m pl scraps (of cloth) ~vergeudung f spilling of good stuff ~verwandtschaft f material affinity ~wahl f ⟨liter⟩ selection of a subject ~wechsel m change of matter; ⟨physiol⟩ assimilation, metabolism | ~-metabolic; ~-Grundumsatz [m] basal m.c rate (BMR), b.l m.sm; ~lehre [f] biostatics [sg konstr]; ~vergiftung [f] auto-intoxication

St·offel m ~s/~ booby, bumpkin (→ Flaps) ~·ei f boorish manners pl ≃ig a boorish

st·offlich a (→ Stoff) material (changes) || with regard to the subject-matter

st·öhle 1. & 3. sg pret subj v stehlen

st·öhnen vi [h] to groan, moan (über at, vor with) || (Wind) to howl || (Holz) to creak

St·oiker m ~s/~ stoic **st·oisch** a stoical

St·ola f ~/-len scarf; ⟨ec⟩ stole, surplice; ⟨hist⟩ stola **St·olgebühren** f pl ⟨ec⟩ s.e-fees

St·olle f ~/~n 1. loaf-shaped Christmas-(currant-)cake 2. ⟨dial⟩ = Stulle **St·ollen** m ~s/~ 1. ⟨min⟩ adit, gallery, (coal-)drift, tunnel, level; e–n ~ (vor)treiben in .. to tunnel down into ..; aufsteigender ~ headway 2. (Stütze) post, prop, standard 3. leg of a tallboy 4. (am Hufeisen) calk(in) || mit ~ [pl] versehen to sharpen (horse-shoes) 5. ⟨pros⟩ one half of an Aufgesang 6. = Stolle 1. ~bau m ⟨min⟩ tunnelling, gallery-driving ~first(e f) m head of an adit ~schrank m tallboy; side-table, dresser

St·olper(·ei f ~/en) m ~s/~ stumbling ~drahtmine f trip-wire mine | ~er m stumbler | ≃ig a uneven; stumbling **st·olpern** I. vi [s & h] to stumble ⟨a. fig⟩, to trip (über [acc] over) || ⟨fig⟩ to blunder, bungle, to make a faux pas, über (e–e Frage) ~ to slip up on .. II. ≃ n stumble; blunder

Stolz m ~es/ pride (auf in), haughtiness; arrogance; disdain; vornehm(tuend)er ~ airs pl; beleidigter ~ outraged pride || er hat auch s–n ~ he's not quite devoid of some pride either || s–n ~ setzen in to pride o.s. on, to take a pride in (doing); s–n ~ l etc to put one's p. into one's pocket || s–n ~ suchen in to glory in || jdn mit ~ erfüllen to do a p proud | ≃ trunken [a] ⟨sl⟩ tight with pride **stolz** a (auf [acc]) proud (of) || ~ wie ein Spanier (as) proud as a peacock || ~en Herzens with a proud heart || (hochmütig) haughty || arrogant || disdainful | darauf kann er ~ s it's a feather in his cap || jdn ~ m to make a p conceited; ⟨sl⟩ you do me proud | er ist zu ~ zu antworten he is above answering | ⟨fig⟩ (großartig) noble, stately, majestic || memorable (day) || fine (ship) || prancing (horse) || gallant (knight) | [adv] ~ einhergehen, –spazieren to walk with a swagger | ≃·ieren vi [s & h] to flaunt, strut, stalk; galumph; to walk tall || daher stolziert k to come strutting along; to sweep (hinein in)

St·opf- ~buchse f ⟨mach⟩ stuffing-box ~ei n darner ~garn n darning-yarn ~holz m stopper ~lappen m stopping-clout ~maschine f stuffer ~mittel n ⟨med⟩ astringent ~nadel f darning-needle ~naht f darn ~segel n drift-sail ~wachs n stop-wax ~werg n oakum **st·opfen** I. vt [h] A. 1. (polstern) to stuff || voll ~ to cram, fill || lose ge–ft loosely packed (cigarettes) | gestopft voll crammed full (v of), crowded (with) || etw in die Tasche ~ to cram a th into one's pocket 2. ⟨med⟩ to constipate 3. (verstopfen) to obstruct | (zu≃) to darn 4. ⟨mus⟩ to muffle, mute (horn, sounds) B. (Durchfall) to stop || ⟨mil⟩ das Feuer ~ to stop firing || (Gans) to cram, noodle; ⟨cul⟩ to stuff || ⟨mar⟩ (Leck) to plug || (Loch) to fill (up); ⟨tail⟩ to patch up, to mend, stop, darn || jdm den Mund ~ to stop a p's mouth od talk || (Pfeife) to load, fill || (Polster) to stuff || (Schiff) to caulk || (Strumpf) to mend, darn || (Würste) to make II. sich ~ (P) to stuff o.s., to gorge | (S) to be jammed (by crowding) || to crowd together || (Straße) to become blocked od obstructed III. vi [h] cocoa is binding od constipating (stopft) || ⟨med⟩ to cause constipation | ⟨fam⟩ (P) to gorge || (sättigen) to satisfy IV. ≃ m ~s/~ cork | ~geld [n] corkage

st·opfend a stopping etc | ⟨med⟩ astringent || (das Bluten) styptic || ~es Mittel astringent

St·opfer(in f) m stuffer; filler || darner | m = Stopfmaschine °**St·öpke** ~s/~ (P) dumpling; Duck's Disease **stopp**! (imp v stoppen) stop! **St·opp-** stop.. ~flugball m ⟨ten⟩ ..-volley ~licht n ⟨mot⟩ stop and tail light ~(p)reis m controlled price ~schild n ⟨mot⟩ halt sign ~straße f street ..ped for traffic ~uhr f ..-watch, timer; ⟨sl⟩ clock ~ventil n stop valve ~vorrichtung f counter gear ~wasser n ⟨mar⟩ ..-water

St·opp- ~ball [m] ⟨ten⟩ dropshot; ~licht [n] ⟨mot⟩ stop tail lamp, ⟨traffic⟩ red light; ~-signal [n] stop s.; ~uhr [f] stopwatch **st·oppen** vt/i [h] ⟨mot, mar⟩ to stop (plötzlich short) || ⟨sport⟩ to clock (mit at 42,7 minutes)

St·oppel f ~/~n 1. ⟨agr⟩ stubble 2. [pl] pin-feathers 3. (Bart≃n) bristles; bristly hair ~bart m bristly od stubbly beard ~butter f late butter ~feder f = Stoppel 2 ~feld n stubble-field ~gans f stubble-goose ~gedicht n patched up poem °~-hopser m (Landwirt) ⟨fam⟩ haykicker ~mast f stubble-grazing ~rübe f late turnip ~weide f after-grass, -pasture ~werk n ⟨liter⟩ patchwork, compilation ~zeit f gleaning season **st·opp(e)lig** a stubbly **st·oppeln** vt/i [h] to glean || ⟨fig⟩ to patch, compile **St·oppler** m ~s/~ gleaner || ⟨fig⟩ compiler

st·oppen vt/i [h] to stop | ⟨mot⟩ to pull up; ⟨comp⟩ to halt | vt ⟨a.⟩ to interrupt || (Zeit) to clock, stop || ⟨comp⟩ to halt **St·opper** m ~s/~ ⟨mar⟩ ring-rope, stopper

St·öpsel m ~s/~ (→ stopfen) stopper, cork || ⟨el⟩ plug | ⟨fig⟩ (P) humpty-dumpty, punch, pudge; pluggy, stumpy [s] | ~flasche [f] glass-stopped bottle; stoppered b. **st·öpseln** vt [h] to stopper, cork; plug ⟨a. °sex⟩

Stör m ~(e)s/~e ⟨ich⟩ sturgeon [a. pl]

ˣ**Stör** f ~/ auf die ~ gehen to hobo it ≃anfällig a susceptible to noise, disturbance ~angriff m harassing attack; ⟨aero⟩ h.g raid ~feuer n ⟨mil⟩ h.g fire ~flug m ⟨aero⟩ nuisance raid ~geräusche n pl disturbances, noises ~klappe f ⟨aero⟩ spoiler ~schutz m ⟨wir⟩ noise gate od suppressor; ⟨mot wir⟩ interference protection ~sender m jamming station ~spiegel m (Ton≃) interferential level ~stange f stick for stirring ~suchgerät n ⟨wir⟩ interference detector ~-zeichen n (Radar≃) clutter

Storch m ~(e)s/≃e ⟨orn⟩ → stork (klappert clatters) || v ~ gebissen (= schwanger) storked | da brat mir e–r 'nen ~! that beats me!, well, I never!, well, I'm blowed || wie der ~ im Salat (→ storchen) to strut about like a cock on a dunghill ≃beinig a spindle-shanked ~mode f maturity dresses pl ~nest n stork's nest ~schnabel m stork's bill || ⟨bot & surg⟩ crane's-bill || ⟨tech⟩ pantograph **st·orchen** vi [s] to walk as if on stilts

st·ören I. vt [h] to disturb, trouble, bother, discommode, inconvenience || to interrupt || to annoy || to be irritating to (a p) || ⟨mil⟩ to gall, harass; ⟨aero⟩ to spoil | ⟨wir⟩ to jam | (Frieden) to break || jdn in s–r Ruhe ~ to disturb a p's rest || jds Stundenplan ~ to throw a p off schedule || (Verkehr) to disorganize, ⟨fam⟩ jam | the light *worries my eyes* || stört Sie mein Rauchen? *do you mind my smoking?* || das stört mich nicht *I don't mind, I am not bothered* | **sich ~ l** *to inconvenience o.s.* || l Sie sich nicht (durch nichts) ~! *go ahead! don't put y.s. out!* ⟨oft iron⟩ *don't mind me!* | **gestört** (Schlaf) *broken*; (Verdauung) *out of order* || (geistig) *deranged, not o.s.*, ⟨fam⟩ *cracked, crazy* **II.** vi [h] *to be intruding* od *in the way* (*I hope I am not ..*) | **~d** *a inconvenient, troublesome, annoying* || *officious* || *disconcerting* (*thought*, etc) || *awkward* (*fact*) || etw als ~ empfinden *to resent a th* || ~ [adv] beeinflussen *to abrogate* **≃fried** m ~(e)s/~e *trouble-, mischief-maker, marplot, intruder*, ⟨vulg⟩ *mixer* **St·örer** m ~s/~ *disturber* ⟨a. wir⟩ || *intruder* || *meddler* || ~ des Friedens *peace-breaker* | **~ ei** f ~/~en *constant disturbance*, etc

storn·ieren vt [h] **1.** *to transfer from one account to another* **2.** *to cancel, annul* **St·orno** n ~s/~s *cross-entry, reverse e.*; *adjustment, cancellation*

St·orr(en) m, **St·orze(n** m) f *stump of a tree*

st·örrig, (st·örrisch) (→ starr) a *stubborn, obstinate*; *mulish* || *unruly, unmanageable* (*child*) || *perverse, intractable* || *wilful, headstrong, dogged* || *pigheaded, hard-mouthed* || *restive* (*horse*) **≃keit** f *stubbornness, obstinacy, intractability* || *wilfulness* || *doggedness*, etc

St·örung f ~/~en *disturbance, troubling, trouble; inconvenience; annoyance*; ⟨mil⟩ *stoppage*; ⟨comp⟩ *bug*; ⟨telv⟩ *breakdown* || (Betriebs≃) *breakdown*; (im Uhrwerk) *obstruction* ⟨a. el⟩ || (Verkehrs≃) *dislocation of traffic*, ⟨fam⟩ *hold-up* || ⟨fig⟩ *hitch* ⟨a. wir, tech⟩; ⟨wir⟩ *jamming, interference*; Fremd≃ *garble*; (atmosphärische) *atmospherics* pl; (magnetische) *perturbation* | frei v ~en *untroublesome* (*drug*) | geistige ~ *mental disorder* od *derangement*; atmosphärische ~ ⟨wir⟩ *static*; ⟨med⟩ *morbid disturbance of the balance of the mind*; nervöse ~ *neurosis* L | (Unterbrechung) *interruption* **St·örungs- ~befreiung** f ⟨wir⟩ *noise elimination* **~beseitigung** f *trouble-shooting* **~dienst** m ⟨telph⟩ *line fault service* **~fall** m ⟨tech⟩ *accidental breakdown* **~feuer** n ⟨mil⟩ *harassing fire* **≃frei** a *trouble-free; undisturbed; free from noise*, etc; ⟨wir⟩ *clear of strays* | [adv] ~ arbeiten ⟨mach⟩ *to work perfectly* **~stelle** f ⟨telph⟩ *trouble department* **~sucher** m ⟨telph⟩ *lineman, trouble-man, faultsman* **~suchtrupp** m *wire patrol, repair gang* **~widerstand** m ⟨phys⟩ *drag*

Stoß m ~es/≃e **I.** ⟨eig⟩ **A.** *thrust, push* || (Schlag) *blow, knock, hit; prod, poke; nudge* || (Ruck) *jerk, jog* || (Erschütterung) *percussion, bump, jostle* || ⟨phys⟩ *impact* || *jolt* (*on landing*) || ⟨ftb⟩ *kick*; Frei–, Straf≃ *free k.*; 11-m-~ *penalty* (*k.*) **B.** (**An≃** ⟨eig⟩) *impetus, impulse* || Dolch≃ *stab* || (Erd≃) *shock* || (Gewehrrück≃) *kick, recoil* || (des Herzens) *throb* || (**Rippen≃**) *dig, poke, prod, nudge* (*in the ribs*) || (Schwimm≃) *stroke*; *buffet* || (Trompeten≃) *blast, flourish* || (e–s Wagens) *jolting* || (**Wind≃**) *gust* || (Zus≃) *collision* (mit *with*), ⟨bes mech⟩ *impact* (*on, against*) **C. auf** den ~ (auf Hieb u ~) fechten *to fence with foils* (*swords*); auf e–n ~ legen *to pile .. up* | **~ gegen** (Wand etc) *bump* | ~ **in** die Luft *tilt at windmills* | ~ **mit** e–r S (gegen) *impingement* | **mit**: (dem Ellbogen) *nudge*, (Fuß) *kick*, (der Faust) *punch*, (Kopf *or* Hörnern) *butt* **D.** ⟨billards⟩ *stroke; impact, cannon*; ⟨fenc⟩ *thrust, pass; lunge* ⟨a. fig⟩ || ⟨ftb⟩ *kick*; (nach dem Auffallen) *dropkick*; (wuchtiger) *punt*; aufs Tor *shot* || ⟨mil⟩ *thrust* || ⟨sport⟩ (hoher) ⟨fam⟩ *balloon* **E.** e–n ~ **auffangen** *to absorb a shock*, ⟨fenc⟩ *to parry a thrust* || e–n ~ führen *to make a thrust* || e–m e–n (leichten) ~ **geben, versetzen** *to give a p a push, to push a p* (*to jog, nudge a p*) (so: *to jog a p's memory*) | ⟨fig⟩ das gab ihm (e–n schweren) den letzten ~ *that was* (*a great shock* od *blow to him*) *the end of him* || e–r S (jds Gesundheit) e–n ~ geben *to affect a th* (*to injure a p's health*) **II.** ⟨übtr⟩ [konkr] **1.** (Haufen) *heap, pile* (*of wood*); *pile* (*of plates*); ⟨fam⟩ *stack* || *batch, crop* (*of letters*) || *pile* (*of books*); in e–m ~ liegen *to lie piled* || (Akten) *bundle, file* || *sheaf* (*of notes*), ⟨Am⟩ *wad* (*of bills*) || *wad* (*of paper*) || *stack* (*of boards*) **2.** ⟨tail⟩ *seam, hem* **3.** ⟨carp⟩ *joint*; (auf Gehrung *mitre-j.*; stumpfer ~ *butt-j.*) **4.** ⟨artill⟩ *breech* (*of a gun*) **5.** ⟨min⟩ *side of a shaft; stope; end of a gallery* **6.** (Schwanzfedern v Habicht etc) *trains; tail-feathers* pl **~arbeit** f ⟨tech⟩ *work of impact* **~balken** m *joint* **~band** n, **~besatz** m ⟨tail⟩ (Hosen≃) *bottoms tape* **~bewegung** f *propulsion* **~brigade** f *shock br.* ⟨a. SBZ⟩ **~dämpfer** m ⟨mot⟩ *shock-absorber, bumper*; ölgefüllter ~ ⟨mot⟩ *oil dashpot* | ~stütze [f] ⟨a–n⟩ *sh.-a. leg* **~dämpfmatratze** f *sh.*(*-a.ing*) *couch* ⟨a–n⟩ **~degen** m *rapier, foil* **~dosis** f ⟨med-pharm⟩ *priming dose* **≃empfindlich** a *sensitive to shock* **~fest** a *impact* od *sh.-proof; sh.-resisting* (*steel*) **≃frei** a ⟨mot⟩ *smooth* (*steering*) | [adv] ~ anlaufen *to start without a jerk* **~fuge** f *butt joint* **~gebet** n *short and fervent prayer* **~hang** m = Prall– **~heber** m *hydraulic ram* **~hobel** m *cooper's jointer* **~ionisierung** f *ionization* (⟨Am⟩ –s–) *by collision* **~kante** f *hem, edge* **~keil** m ⟨tact⟩ *spearhead* **~kissen** n ⟨rail⟩ *buffer*(*-head*) **~klinge** f *thrust-blade* **~kraft** f *impetus, drive*, ⟨mech⟩ *impact, momentum*; *shock action*; ⟨mil⟩ *dash*; ⟨fam⟩ *kick* **~kurs** m (Rakete) m *collision course* **≃lindernd** a *shock* [attr] ⟨a–n⟩ (*sh.-couch*) **~linie** f ⟨tact⟩ *thrust line* **~moräne** f *push m.* **~naht** f *French seam* **~polster** n ⟨tech⟩ *buffer* **~riemen** m *jolting-strap* **~säge** f *handsaw* **~seufzer** m *sigh* **≃sicher** a *insentive to shock*; *sh.* [attr] (*mount* Aufhängung) **~stange** f = –dämpfer; *impact*, (od *buffer, bumper*) *bar*; ⟨fam⟩ *bumper* **~strahlung** f *impact radiation* **~strom** m ⟨el⟩ *impulse current* **~trupp** m ⟨mil⟩ *commando; raiding party; patrol* | ~tätigkeit [f] *patrol activity* **~verbindung** f ⟨rail⟩ *fishtail joint* **~verkehr** m *rush hours* **~vogel** m *bird of prey* **~waffe** f *stabbing-weapon* **≃weise** adv *by pushes, by fits and starts, fitfully*; (*to breathe*) *in lunges; throbbingly, pantingly* | [a] *intermittent* **~welle** f *shock* od *percussion wave* **~werk** n ⟨tech⟩ *escapement* **~widerstand** m *impact resistance* **~wind** m *gust of wind; squall* **~zahn** m *tusk* **~zeit(en)** f (pl) *rush hours* | ~stromabschaltung [f] *load shedding in peak hours* **St·ößel** m ~s/~ *beetle, rammer*, ⟨fam⟩ *dolly* || (Mörser-≃) *pestle* || ⟨mach, mot⟩ *tappet* **st·oßen** [stieß/ge~] **I.** vt [h] **A.** *to push; to give a kick to* | °⟨sex⟩ *to knock* [vt/i] | **(behutsam)** *to poke*; (schiebend) *to shove*; (schlagend) *to knock, strike, hit*; (schnellend) *to jerk* | **(im** Mörser) *to pound, bruise, bray* | **(mit)** (Ellbogen) *to nudge, elbow, jog, jostle*; (Faust) *to punch*; (Fuß) *to kick* ⟨a. ftb⟩; (Kopf *or* Horn) *to butt* (Stier: ⟨a.⟩ *to toss*); (Stock) *to poke*; (Waffe) *to thrust* | **fest** ~ *to batter down* || glatt ~ ⟨carp⟩ *to smooth* || kl ~ *to pound, crush, bray*; *to grind* (*sugar, pepper*) **B. (Ball)** *to kick* ⟨a. ftb⟩, (vor dem Aufschlagen) *to punt*, (vor sich her) *to dribble*, (hoch) *to balloon* || ⟨billards⟩ *to play*; (ins Loch) ⟨Ger⟩ *to pocket* (*a ball*) || **(Dolch)** *to plant ..* (*in a p's back*) || e–m den Dolch ins Herz ~ *to stab a p to the heart* || die Gläser an–e–a ~ *to touch glasses* || (Loch) *to make* (*a hole in the paper*), sich ein L. in den K. ~ *to break one's head* || sich e–n **Nagel,** Splitter in den Fuß ~ *to run a .. into one's foot* || *to drive, ram* (*a pole into the ground*) || *to grind* (*pepper*) || *to powder* (*sugar*) **C. an** [acc] *to kick, hack* (*a p's shin*) || *to knock a p against the wall* ⟨a. fig⟩ || ⟨carp, tail⟩ an–e–a~ *to join* | **auf**: (durch Zufall) *to happen on a th; to chance upon a p*; er stieß mich mit der Nase darauf *he put it under my very nose*

| aus dem Hause ~ *to turn out*; aus e–m Verein ~ *to expel from* .. || e–m den Degen durch den Leib ~ *to run one's sword through a p* **| gegen**: *to jostle push against* **| in**: *to jab, pitch into* || e–m das Messer in den Hals ~ *to thrust a knife in a p's throat* || jdn in die Rippen ~ *to prod a p's ribs, to give a p a dig in the ribs* || ins Gefängnis ~ *to thrust into pr.* **| über** den Haufen ~ *to knock .. down*; *to overthrow* (*a p, an institution*) **| von sich** ~ *to push away*, ⟨fig⟩ *to reject, repudiate, to turn adrift*, (Sohn) *to cut off with a shilling*; *to divorce* (*one's wife*); *she pushed that thought from her*; *to fling away* (*one's good fortune*) || vom Thron ~ *to dethrone* **| vor** den Kopf ~ *to offend, affront* || wie vor den Kopf gestoßen *flabbergasted* **| zu** Boden ~ *to throw down* **II. sich** ~ *to hurt o.s.* || sich lahm ~ *to lame o.s.* (*by a knock*) || sich ~ **an** [dat]: sich am Kopf ~ *to bump one's head*; *to knock, run strike against*; ⟨fig⟩ → Anstoß nehmen, ⟨a.⟩ *to take offence at, exception to, to mind* (*a th*), ⟨fam⟩ *to stick at* (*the price*) || wir ~ uns nur daran, daß *the only difficulty is that* .. **| an** [acc] *to knock, bang* (*one's head*) **III.** vi [h & s] **A.** [abs] (Biene) *to swarm* || ⟨billards⟩ wer stößt? *who plays*? || (Bock, Rind) *to butt, toss* || (Falke etc) *to swoop down* || ⟨fenc⟩ *to thrust* || (Gewehr etc) *to kick, recoil* || ⟨mot⟩ *to knock*; (of car) *jump*; || (Schiff) *to toss* || (Wagen) *to jolt, bump* || (Wind) *to blow in gusts* **B.** [h & s] **an** [acc]: ⟨aero⟩ *to strike* (leicht *to brush*) *a chimney* || an Land ~ *to land* || (grenzen) *to border* (*up*)*on, to be adjacent, adjoining, contiguous, next door to* **| auf** [acc]: [h] (Raubvogel) *to pounce on* **|** [s] *to come across, to stumble on* (*a th*) || *to come upon, to meet with*, (zufällig) *to run across, to fall in with* (*a p*) || ⟨mar⟩ *to run onto, dash against* (*a rock*); (direkt) *to hit off* (*the pier*) || *to discover* (*irregularities*) || *to come on* (*passages like* ..) || (plötzlich) *to come up against* (*opposition, a problem*); *to meet* (*with*), *to encounter* (*opposition*); *to strike* (*oil*) || (bei jdm) *to be met with opposition* (*from a p*) || *to face* (*resistance*) || *to fall upon, to experience* (*difficulties*) **| durch** [s]: ⟨mil⟩ *to smash through* (*the defences*) **| gegen**: *to jostle, hurtle, bump, strike, blunder against* **| in** [h]: *to blow* (*the trumpet*), *to sound* (*the horn*) **| mit** etw ~ **gegen**: *to knock one's knee, to run one's head*, (*to strike one's head a sharp blow*) *against* .. || *he jabbed with his finger at his leg* || mit etw nach vorn ~ *to shoot out* (*one's leg*) **| nach**: *to thrust at* || **vom** Lande ~ (Boot) *to shove off*, (Schiff) *to put to sea* **| zu** [s]: *to join* (*a p*) **St·ößer** m ~s/~ *hawk* || (Stößel) *pestle* **st·ößig** a *goring, butting* (*bull*)

°**St·otter-** (Abzahlungs-) *never-never* (-System) **Stotter·ei** f ~/~en *stuttering* **St·otterer** m *stutterer, stammerer* **st·otterig** a *stuttering* **st·ottern I.** vi/t [h] *to stammer*; *to* (*have a*) *stutter*; verlegen ~ *to hum and haw* || ⟨mach⟩ *to work by fits and starts*; ⟨mot⟩ *to sputter* **II.** ≏ n ⟨fam⟩ auf ≏ kaufen *to buy on tally*(*-system*)

St·övchen n ~s/~ *tea-pot warmer*

stracks adv **1.** (räumlich) *straight, direct* **2.** (zeitlich) *immediately, directly, straightway*

Str·af- **~änderung** f *commutation of sentence* **≏androhend** a *comminatory* **~androhung** f *threat of punishment*; jdn unter ~ vorladen *to subpoena a p* **~anstalt** f *penal institution*; *house of correction*; *penitentiory* || **~antrag** m *formal demand of injured party for punishment of accused* (*in minor criminal proceedings*); (§ 194 StGB) ⟨m. m.⟩ *procession for insult taking place* (*only*) *upon request* **~anzeige** f ⟨jur⟩ *accusation*; *penal report*; *charges brought against a p* || ~erstatten gegen .. *to lay an information against a p* **~arbeit, ~aufgabe** f *imposition*, ⟨fam⟩ *impo*(*t*); *lines* pl, *extra sums* pl **~arrest** m ⟨school⟩ *detention*; ⟨mil⟩ *cells* pl **~ausspruch** m ⟨jur⟩ *sentence* **~befehl** m *order to inflict punishment* od *fine*; *order of summary punishment* (*without trial*) **~befugnis** f *penal power* **~bestimmung** f *paragraph in the penal code* || ~en [pl] *penal provisions* **~buch** n ⟨mil⟩ *defaulter* od *back book* **|** ~auszug, ~eintrag [m] *d.* od *conduct sheet* **~dienst** m ⟨mil⟩ *fatigue-duty* **~erkenntnis** n *sentence* **~erlaß** m *remission of a punishment* od *penalty* || (allg) *amnesty* **~exerzieren** n *punishment* od *pack-drill* **|** ≏ vi *to do pack-drill* **~fall** m ⟨jur⟩ *criminal case* **≏fällig** a *punishable, culpable* || ~ w *to incur a penalty* **|** ≏keit [f] *punishableness, culpability* **~feuer** n ⟨mil⟩ *retaliation fire* **≏frei** a *exempt from punishment*; ~ ausgehen *to go scot-free* **|** ≏heit [f] *impunity* **~gefangene(r)** m *convict* **~geld** n *fine* **~gericht** n *punishment, chastisement* || (göttliches) *judgment* (*of God*) || (Gerichtshof) *Criminal Court* **|** ~sbarkeit [f] *criminal jurisdiction* **~gesetz** n *penal law* **|** ≏buch [n] *penal code*; *C. of Cr. Law* **~gewalt** f = –befugnis **~kammer** f *Cr. Court* **~kasse** f *penalty box* **~klage** f *cr. proceedings* pl **~kolonie** f *convict settlement, penal colony* **≏los** a = –frei || (unschuldig) *guiltless* **~mandat** n *penalty*; *summons* [sg konstr] [pl *–es*]: hat man ~ z befürchten? *is there any danger of a s.*?; ⟨Am traffic⟩ *ticket* **~maß** n *amount of punishment*; höchstes ~ *maximum penalty* **~maßnahmen** f pl *penalties* pl **~milderung** f *mitigation of a penalty*; *commutation of a sentence* **|** ~sgrund [m] *extenuating circumstance*(*s*) **≏mündig** a *of a responsible age* **|** ~keit [f] *age of discretion* **~nachlaß** m *abatement* **~porto** n *postage-due, surcharge, excess postage* **~prediger** m *censurer, rigid moralist* **~predigt** f *severe lecture, admonition* || ⟨fam⟩ jdm e–e ~ halten *to give a p a dressing down* **~prozeß** m *criminal case* od *proceedings* pl **|** ≏ordnung [f] (*code of*) *cr. procedure* **~punkt** m ⟨bes mot racing⟩ *bad mark* **~raum** m ⟨ftb⟩ *penalty area* **~recht** n *cr. law* **|** ≏lich [a] *cr., penal* || ~ verfolgen *to prosecute*; ~slehre [f] *criminology*; ~sverfahren [n] *criminal procedure*; ~swissenschaft [f] *penology* **~register** n *penal record* **|** ~auszug [m] *excerpt of the cr. records* **~richter** m *cr. judge* **~rute** f *rod* || ⟨fig⟩ *scourge* **~sache** f *cr. case* **~stoß** m (11 m) ⟨ftb⟩ *penalty-kick* **~summe** f *penalty, fine* **~tat** f ⟨jur⟩ *tort* **~tor** n ⟨ftb⟩ *penalty-goal* **~umwandlung** f *commutation of punishment* **~urteil** n *sentence, judgment*; ein ~ über jdn verhängen *to pass judgment upon a p* **~verfahren** n *criminal proceedings* pl; ein ~ einleiten *to launch a prosecution* **|** ~sordnung [f] *cr. procedure* **~versetzung** f *transfer for disciplinary reasons* **~verteidiger** m *trial lawyer*; *barrister* **~vollstreckung** f *execution of a sentence* **≏würdig** a *punishable, penal* **~zug** m *punitive expedition* **~zumessung** f ⟨jur⟩ *determination of the measure of a penalty* **~zuschlag** m (bei Steuern) *surcharge* **str·afbar** a *punishable, actionable* (*offence*); *criminal* (*deed*) || (*suicide is*) *against the law* **|** *culpable* **|** sich ~ m *to be subject to penalty*; *to be liable to prosecution*; Gefahr laufen .. zu m ⟨fam⟩ *to sail close to the wind* **≏keit** f ~/ *punishableness, criminality* || *culpability* **Str·afe** f ~/~n *punishment*, körperliche ~ *corporal pu.*; milde ~ *light pu.*; ⟨rel⟩ *visitation* (*of God*) || ⟨jur, sport⟩ *penalty* ⟨a. fig⟩ || (Geld≏) *fine*; ~e u Geldbußen *pains and penalties* || verhängte ~ ⟨bes jur⟩ *ordained sentence* **|** s–e ~ **abbüßen** *to undergo pu.* || s–e ~ absitzen *to expiate one's crime in prison*, ⟨fam⟩ *to do one's time* || s–e (verdiente) ~ bek *to be punished* (*to get one's deserts* pl) || der gerechten ~ entgehen *to cheat justice* || jdm die ~ erlassen *to let a p off* || die ~ kommt! *retribution will come* || darauf steht e–e harte ~ *it is severely punishhed* **|** ⟨fig⟩ es ist e–e ~ *it is an infliction* (*to listen to him*) **| bei** ~ v *on pain of* || Vorladung bei ~ *subpoena*, bei ~ vorladen *to s.* **| in** ~ nehmen *to punish, penalize*, *fine* || in ~ verfallen *to incur pu., to have to pay a fine* | (ihm) **zur** ~ *for a pu., in pu.,* (*in order to punish him*) **str·afen** vt [h] *to punish* (f *for*); ⟨mil aero⟩ *to strafe* || (tadeln) *to censure, rebuke* || (züchtigen) *to chastise, correct* || *God's hand afflicts us* | **an** der Ehre ~ *to disgrace, degrade* || am Leben ~ *to sentence to death* | **mit** Gefängnis, (Geld) ~ *to send to prison,* (*to fine*); mit Verachtung ~ *to p. with contempt* || mit Verlust s–r Güter ~ *to p. a p by confiscating his property* || ⟨fig⟩ gestraft s mit *to be cursed with* | e–n **um** Geld ~ *to fine a p*; e–n um ein Vergehen ~ *to p. a p for some misdeed* | so etw straft **sich** selbst *such doings meet with their due reward* **str·afend** a *punishing, punitive* || *corrective* || ⟨jur⟩ *penal* || *revengeful* || *reproachful* (*glance*) **str·äflich** a *punishable, criminal* || *culpable* || *censurable, blamable* || ⟨fig fam⟩ [mst adv] *severe(ly), awful(ly), enormous(ly)* **Str·äfling** m ~s/~e *convict; culprit; prison inmate* **~sfürsorge** f *welfare-work among convicts* **~sjacke, ~skleidung** f *convict's garb*

straff a *tight, tense*; ⟨mar⟩ *taut* (*rope*) | ⟨fig⟩ *rigid, austere* | *firm* (*breast*) || *well-filled* (*purse*) || *severe, strict* (*discipline*) || *tight* (*control*) || *straight* (*hair*) || *strictly conducted* (*organization*) || *stately* (*p*) || ~e Haltung *straight military bearing*; ~e H. annehmen ⟨mil⟩ *to come* od *stand to attention* || ein ~es Regiment führen *to rule with a firm hand* || e–n ~en Stil schreiben *to write succinctly, concisely* | [adv] ~ anliegen *to fit tightly* || die Schraube noch etw ~er anziehen ⟨a. fig⟩ *to tighten the screw one more turn* || ~ geführt *tightly controlled* || jdn ~ halten *to keep a tight rein on a p* || ~ ziehen, ~ w *to tighten* ⟨a. liter, film, theat⟩; ⟨mar⟩ *to tauten*; ⟨mus⟩ *to stretch* (*a string*) **(sich) str·affen** *to tighten, tense*; *to brace* (*o.s. up*) der Muskel –ft sich .. *sets* **Str·affheit** f *tightness*; *straightness*, etc

Strahl m ~(e)s/~en **A.** *beam*; *ray* (ausfallend *emergent*) || ⟨geom⟩ *radius* || (Milch≗) *jet* || (Wasser≗) *jet, spout* || (Blitz≗) *flash* || (im Pferdehuf) *frog* || ⟨bot⟩ (e–r Dolde) *spoke* **B.** ~en schießen *to flash forth* || ~en werfen(d) *to emit rays* (*radiant*), ⟨poet⟩ *to dart beams* **~bild** n *spray pattern* **~düse** f *jet nozzle* **~fäule** f ⟨vet⟩ *thrush* **~fliegen** n ⟨aero⟩ *flying on beam*; *riding the b.* **~gebläse** n *jet blower* **~motor** m *jet(-engine)*; mit ~ *jet-propelled* **~mühle** f *fluid-energy mill*; *jet-mill* | Flugzeug mit **~triebwerk** n *turbojet* **~turbine** f *turbojet* **~vortrieb** m *jet-propulsion* **str·ahlen** vi [h] *to emit rays*; *to radiate, beam, shine*; e–e Laterne –lte mir plötzlich ins Gesicht *I had a l. flashed in my f.* | ⟨fig⟩ vor Freude etc *to beam, glow* (*with joy*, etc) || vor Gesundheit ~ *to radiate health* || *courage gleamed in his eye* || ~d *irradiative*; *resplendent, lustrous, effulgent*; *aureate*; *raging* (*beauty*) || ~d ansehen *to beam at* **Str·ahlen- ~austritt** m ⟨at⟩ = –kanal **~bahn** f = –gang **≗brechend** a *refractive* **~brechung** f *refraction* **~bündel** n, **~büschel, ~kegel** m *luminous brush*; *cone, beam, pencil* (*of rays*); Breite des ~s *beam angle* ⟨a. theat⟩ **~chemie** f *radiation ch.* | Behandlung v **~erkrankungen** f pl *radiothermy* **≗förmig** a *radial* || sich ~ ausdehnen *to radiate* **~gang** m *path* od *track of rays* **~glanz** m *radiance* **~kanal** m ⟨at⟩ *beam hole tube* **~krankheit** f *radiation sickness* **~kranz** m, **~krone** f *glory, gloriole, halo, nimbus* **~pilz** m *rayed fungus*; *actinomyces* **~quelle** f *source of radiation* **~schaden** m *r.n injury* **~schutz-** ~mittel [n], ~stoff [m] *radioprotective agent* **~-spürtrupp** m *radiological survey team* **~stärkemesser** m ⟨at⟩ *intensitometer* **~therapie** f *radiotherapy* **~undurchlässigkeit** *radio-opacity* **~werfen** n *irradiation* **str·ählen** vt [h] *to comb* **str·ahlend** a *radiating, radiant, shining, luminous, brilliant* || *glorious* (*sunshine*) || *starry* (*eyes*) || *jetty* (*brightness of boots*) || vor Freude ~ *gleeful* || in, bei ~er Gesundheit *glowing with health* **Str·ahler** m *radiant heater*; ⟨at⟩ *radiator* **str·ahlig** a *radiant* || *star-shaped* || ⟨bot & phys⟩ *radiate* **Str·ahlung** f ~/ ⟨phys⟩ (radioaktiv *ionizing*) *radiation* | ~sablenkung [f] *radio wave deflection*; ~sdiagramm [n] *radiation characteristic*; ~senergie [f] *radiant e.*; ~sheizkörper [m] *r.t element*; ~skraft [f] *emissivity*; ~smesser [m] *radiac(tive) dosimeter*; ~sofen [m] ⟨el⟩ *electric radiator*, ⟨Am⟩ *el.c radiant heater*; Offizier f ~sschutz [m] *radiological defence* (⟨Am⟩*-se*) *o.* N; in ≗ssicherem Behälter ⟨at⟩ *shielded*; ~sthermometer [n] *radiation th.r*; ~stiefenmeßgerät [n] ⟨at⟩ *penetrometer*; ~svektor [m] *vector radiant*; ~svermögen [n] *radiance, -cy*; *radiating power* ~swärme [f] *radiant heat*

Str·ähne f ~/~n (Seil) *strand* || (Garn) *skein, hank* || (Wolle) *rove* || (Haar) *lock*

Straits S·ettlements [streits] (brit. Kronkolonie auf der Halbinsel Malakka)

Stram·in m ~(e)s/~e *canvas*

stramm a = straff || ⟨typ⟩ *stiff* (*ink*) | ⟨fig⟩ *robust* (*youth*); *sturdy* (*fellow*); *buxom* (*woman*); *strapping* (*wench*); *bouncing* (*girl*); *fine, smart* (*soldier*); *soldierlike* (*p*) || *strict* (*discipline*); ~er Dienst *strenuous training*; ~e Haltung annehmen *to spring* od *stiffen to attention*; *tight* (*organization*) | [adv] (*to go*) *smartly* || zu ~ aufgepumpt *overinflated* (*tire*) || er ist jetzt ~ daran *he is hard at it* || ⟨fam⟩ jdn ~ halten *to keep a p in hand* | ~ marschieren *to march strongly* ⟨a. mil⟩ **~|stehen** vi [h] ⟨mil⟩ *to stand* (*at*) *attention*; **~|ziehen** vt [h] *to tauten*; *to pull hard on* (*one's belt*); *to stretch* (*a boy's breeches*), *to dust* (*his jacket*) **str·ammen** vt [h] (a. sich ~) *to tighten*, etc

str·ampeln vi [h] *to move restlessly*; *to struggle, fidget* || mit den Beinen ~ *to fling one's legs about, to kick* || sich bloß|~ *to kick the* (*bed-*)*clothes off* **Str·amperle** n pl (Füße) ⟨Kinderspr⟩ *tootsie--wootsies*

Strand m ~(e)s≗e (*sea-*)*shore*; (flacher) *beach* || (steiniger) *shingle* || auf den ~ laufen *to run ashore*, .. laufen, setzen, werfen *to strand* || auf den ~ geworfen w *to be beached, to strand* || (Schiff) an den ~ ziehen *to beach* **~anzug** m *b.-suit* **~bad** n *bathing b.* **~batterie** f *sh.-battery* **~eis** n *sh.-ice* **~fischerei** f *sh.-fishing* **~floh** m *sh. jumper* **~gerechtigkeit** f = –recht **~gut** n *stranded goods* pl, *jetsam*; (schwimmendes) *flotsam* **~gutjäger** m *b.-comber* **~hafer** m *lymegrass* **~haubitze** → –kanone **~häuschen** *b. bungalow* **~hütte** f *cabana* **~kaffee** n *b.-café* **~kanone** f: ⟨fam⟩ voll wie e–e ~ *drunk as a piper, tight as a drum*; ⟨bes Am⟩ *drunk as a skunk* **~kies** m *shingle* **~kleidung** f *b.-wear* **~kohl** m *sea-kale* **~korb** m *wicker chair for the b.* **~kreuzkraut** n *maritime groundsel* **~läufer** m ⟨orn⟩ *strand-piper*, → *stint* **~promenade** f (*the*) *front*; (aus Holz) *boardwalk* **~raub** m *wrecking* **~räuber** m *wrecker* **~recht** n *right of salvage* **~schuhe** m pl *sand-shoes* pl **~see** m *lagoon* **~verdriftung** f *b. drifting* **~vogt** m *wreck-master* **~wache** f, **~wächter** m *coast-guard* **~wall** m *b. ridge* **str·anden** vi [s] *to strand*; *to be stranded, beached, wrecked*; *to founder* || ⟨nur mar⟩ *to run ashore* od *aground* | **gestrandet** *cast ashore*; ⟨mar⟩ *aground* | ⟨fig⟩ *on the beach*; *fallen* (*girl*)

Strang m ~(e)s/≗e *rope, cord* || (des Wagens) *trace* || (zum Hängen) *halter*; zum ~ verurteilen *to condemn to be hanged* || (Schienen≗) *track, rail* | ⟨fig⟩ alle ≗e anziehen *to do one's utmost* || wenn alle ≗e reißen *if the worst comes to the worst* || über die ≗e schlagen *to kick over the traces* ⟨a. fig⟩, ⟨fig⟩ *to kick up one's heels*; *to overshoot the mark*; *to break out*; gehörig .. *to have tremendous releases* || an demselben ~e ziehen

⟨fig⟩ *to pull together* **≈ul·ieren** [–ŋg–] vt [h] *to strangle*

Strap·aze f ~/~n *hardship, over-exertion, fatigue, toil* **Strapaz·ier-** [in comp] *knock-about* (*suit* etc), .. *for hard wear* **≈fähig** a *sturdy, hardwearing* (*dress*, etc), *high-duty* (höchst *superduty*) (*shoes*); *for hard wear*; *standing the hardest wear*; ⟨com⟩ *fair* (od *for*) *wear and tear* **~jacke** f *casual jacket* **strapaz·ieren** vt [h] *to knock up*; *to fatigue, tax, tire, harass* ‖ sich ~ *to exert o.s.* ‖ (ein Kleid) *to wear out* ‖ zum ≈ *for hard wear* ‖ strapaziert *battered* **strapazi·ös** a *harassing*, etc

Straß m –sses/–sse (Bleiglasschmuck) *strass*

straß-auf, straß-ab adv *up and down the street*

Str·aßburg n (Stadt im Elsaß) *Strasburg* **Str·aße** f ~/~n **A. 1.** (→ Land≈) *road*, (*high*)*way* ‖ ungepflasterte ~ *dirt-road* ‖ Gebirgs≈ *mountain road* **2.** (Stadt–, Dorf≈) *street* ‖ abgelegene ~ *back s.* ‖ (breit, gr) *thoroughfare*, ⟨Am⟩ *boulevard, avenue*; *broadway* ‖ belebt *lively*, ruhig *quiet* ‖ die Hohe ~ *High S.* ‖ die Oxforder ~ *Oxford S.* ‖ ~ der Freundschaft (zw Thailand & USA) *friendship highway* ‖ ~ 1. Ordnung *primary road*; ~n gleicher O. *streets* od *roads of equal priority*; ~ mit Halteverbot *clearway* ‖ ~ mit mehreren Fahrbahnen *multi-lane highway* **3.** (Meeres≈) *strait*: (*Straits of Gibraltar, Florida*; *Strait of Messina*) ‖ ~ v Calais *the* (*English*) *Channel*; *Yukatan Ch.* ‖ enge ~ *bottle-neck* ⟨a. fig⟩ **4.** (Seeweg) *route* **B.** ~ (ist) frei! *go ahead*!; ~ frei! *gangway*! ‖ die ~ ist freizumachen: *a clear road is to be conceded* (bei .. *upon the approach of police vehicles*); **gehen** Sie die 2. ~ links *take the second turning on your left* ‖ geh d–e ~! *be off*! ‖ s–e (⟨fig⟩ stille) ~ ziehen *to go one's* (*own*) *way* (*quietly*) ‖ die breite ~ des Herkommens ziehen *to beat the common track* (*of custom*) **C.** abseits der ~n marschieren *to march cross-country*; abseits v ~n *away from roads*; abseits der breiten ~ ⟨fig⟩ *off the beaten track* | **an** der ~ *by the roadside, wayside* | **auf** der ~ *in* (⟨Am⟩ *on*) *the s., on the r.* ‖ auf offener ~ *in a public thoroughfare* ‖ die ~ auf u ab *up and down the s.* ‖ auf der ~ liegen ⟨fig⟩ (arbeitslos) *to be on the stones*; immer .. ⟨eig⟩ *to be for ever knocking about the s.* ‖ auf die ~ gehen ⟨sex⟩ *to walk the s.s* ‖ °auf die ~ setzen ⟨sl⟩ *to chuck out, to give a p the sack*; .. gesetzt w (entlassen w) ⟨sl⟩ *to hit the pavement*, ⟨vulg⟩ *to get the hoof* ‖ ⟨fig⟩ auf die ~ werfen (Geld) *to squander*, (Arbeiter) *to turn out of doors, to give* (*a p*) *the sack* ‖ auf der ~ *out of work*, ⟨Aust⟩ *on the road* | **in** der Hohen ~ wohnen *to live in* (⟨Am⟩ *on*) *High Street* | **über** die ~ gehen *to* (*go* od *walk a*)*cross the s., to cross over* | ein Mädchen **von** der ~ *a street-walker* ‖ v der ~ aufgelesen s *to come from the gutter* ‖ ⟨fig⟩ der Mann v der ~ *the man in the street* | ⟨prov⟩ wer da bauet an der ~n, muß die Leute reden l *he who builds that all may see for criticism prepared must be* **Str·aßen- ~abbiegung, ~abzweigung** f *turn*(*ing*); *side-road*; kurvenförmige ~ *rounded turn-off in the r.* **~anlage** f *laying out of a street* od *road* **~anzug** m *walking-suit, lounge* od *business suit* **~arbeiten** f pl *r. repair*; ~! *r. under repair*! **~arbeiter** m *road-mender* **~aufbrecher** m (S) *scarifier* **~aufschüttung** f *r. embankment* **~ausbesserung** f *r.-mending* **~aufseher** m *r.-surveyor* **~bahn** m *tram*(*way*); ⟨Am⟩ *st.-car* | ~haltestelle *t.w. stop*; ~netz [n] *t.w. system*; ~wagen *tram*(*-car*); ⟨Am⟩ *street-car*, ⟨a.⟩ *surface-car* **~bau** m *r.-making* | **~befestigung** f *r. crust* | e–e **~bekanntschaft** f *a pick-up* | Dauer [f] der **~belegung** f ⟨mil⟩ *time en route* N **~beleuchtung** f *s.-lighting* **~bengel** m = –junge **~berührung** f *r. contact* **~beschaffenheit** f *r. conditions* **~biegung** f *r.-bend* **~damm** m *r.-way, carriage-r.* **~decke** f *r. metal, carpet, bed* **~dirne** f *s.-walker* **~dreieck** n *triangular r. junction* **~ecke** f *s.-corner* **~einmündung** f *r. junction* **≈fähig** a ⟨aero⟩ *roadable* **~falle** f *hidden speed check-point*; *h. traffic control p.* **~feger** m *r.* od *st. sweeper* od *cleaner* **~festigkeit** f *r. stability* °**~floh** m ⟨mot-cycl⟩ *pip-squeak* **~fluchtlinie** f *s. line* **~gabelung** f *fork* (*of a r.*) **~gesindel** n *mob of roughs* **~graben** m *roadside ditch* **~handel** m *s.*(*-vendors'*) *trade* **~händler** m *s.-vendor, costermonger, hawker*; ⟨sl⟩ *s.-pitcher* **~hobel** m *grader* **~inspektor** m *r.-surveyor* **~junge** m *s. arab, mud-lark, ragamuffin, gutter-snipe* od *-slush*; ⟨Am a.⟩ *dead-end kid* **~kampf** m *s.-fighting* **~kehrer** m = –feger **~kehricht** m & n *r.-sweepings* pl **~kehrmaschine** f *s.-sweeper* **~kind** n *urchin* **~kleid** n *walking-dress* **~kontakt** m *r. feel* **~kot** m *mud* **~kreuzer** m *r. liner*; *gasoline cruiser* **~kreuzung** f *cross r.s* [sg konstr] *crossing* **~lage** f ⟨mot⟩ *r.-holding capacity*; der Wagen hat e–e gute ~ .. *holds the r. well* **~laterne** f *s.-lamp* **~lümmel** m *rowdy, larrikin* **~mädchen** n *girl on the s.*; ⟨sex⟩ *s.-walker*; ⟨sl⟩ *tart* **~nagel** m *stud* **~netz** n *r.-system* **~oberfläche** f *r. carpet* **~pflaster** n *pavement* **~photograph** m ⟨fam⟩ *smudger* **~prediger** m *ranter* | am **~rand** m *on the roadside*; der linke [rechte] ~ (in links-[rechts-]fahrenden Ländern) *the near* [Ggs off] *side of the r.* **~raststätte** f *wayside inn* **~raub** m *highway-robbery* **~räuber** m *highwayman, footpad* ‖ ~ w *to take to the r.* **~redner** m *soapbox orator* **~reinigung** f *s.-cleaning, scaveng*(*er*)*ing* **~rennen** ⟨sport⟩ n *r.-race* **~rinne** f *gutter, gully* **~rowdy** m *r.-hog* **~schotter** m *metalling* **~sperre** f *barricade*; *r. block* **~sperrung** f *blocking of traffic* od *of a s.* **~spinne** f *multiple r. junction* **~tür** f *front door* **~überführung** f *viaduct*; *flyover* **~übergang** m (*s.-*)*crossing* **~- u Geländefahrt** f ⟨mot⟩ *on-and-off-the-r. operation* **~unterführung** f *subway* **~verkauf** m *hawking* **~verkehr** m (*s.-*)*traffic* | ~skarte [f] *traffic circulation map*; ~snagel [m] *stud*; ~sordnung [f] *R. Traffic Code*; *Highway Traffic Act* **~verzeichnis** n *s. directory* **~walze** f *steam-roller* **~zulassungsordnung** f *R. Licensing Code* **~zustandsbericht** m *r. condition report*; ⟨mil⟩ *r. reconnaissance report*

Strat·ege m ~n/~n *strategist* **Strateg·ie** f ~/ *strategy* **strat·egisch** a *strategic* ([adv] *-ally* ⟨a.⟩ in ~er Hinsicht); [adv] ~ wichtig *strategic*(*al*)

Stratosph·äre f ~/ *stratosphere* **~nkreuzer** m *stratocruiser, -liner*

str·äuben vt [h] *to ruffle, bristle* ‖ gesträubt *ruffled* (*plumage*) | **sich** ~ (Borsten) *to bristle* (*up*) ‖ (Haar) *to stand on end* ‖ ⟨fig⟩ (gegen) *to strive, rise, fight, fret, struggle, revolt* (*against*); *to resist, oppose* (*a th*); [abs] *to hang back* | die Feder sträubt sich, zu schildern .. *refuses to describe* ‖ wie sehr er sich auch ~ mochte *in spite of his resistance, reluctance* | (sich) sträubend *recalcitrant*

Strauch m ~(e)s/≈e(r) *bush, shrub* ‖ pl *undergrowth* **≈artig** a *shrub-like, shrubby* **~dieb** m *highwayman, vagabond, footpad* ‖ ~ w *to take to the bush* **~holz** n *brushwood* **~ritter** m *footpad* **~werk** n *bushes, shrubs* pl, *underwood*

str·aucheln vi [h & s] *to make a false step*; *to stumble, trip* ⟨a. fig⟩ ‖ ⟨fig⟩ *to make a faux pas* Fr | jdn zum ≈ bringen *to stagger a p* (*a staggering blow*) ‖ ⟨fig⟩ *to lead astray*

Strauß 1. m ~es/~e ⟨orn⟩ *ostrich* (*the o. sticks its head in the sand*) **2.** m ~es/≈e (Kampf [→ strotzen]) *fight, strife, struggle, combat, tussle* ‖ e–n ~ ausfechten mit *to have a fight with* **3.** ~es/≈e *bouquet, nosegay, bunch* ‖ e–n ~ binden *to make up a nosegay* ‖ e–n ~ pflücken *to gather/pick a bunch of flowers* **~binderin** f *flower-girl* **Str·äußchen** n ~s/~ *small bouquet*; (z Anstecken) *corsage* **Str·auß(en)- ~ei** *ostrich-egg* **~feder** f *ostrich-plume* **~gras** n ⟨bot⟩ *bent-grass*

~politik f *ostrich policy*; Vogel-~ treiben *to play the ostrich*

Str·azze f ~/~n ⟨com⟩ *waste-book*

Str·ebe f ~/~n ⟨min⟩ *prop*; ⟨aero⟩ *stay*; ⟨arch⟩ *spur, strut, buttress*; *truss* **~balken** m *brace, strut* **~bogen** m ⟨arch⟩ *flying-buttress* **~mauer** f *retaining wall* **~pfeiler** m *buttress, spur* **~stütze** f *prop*; *shore* **~system** n ⟨arch⟩ *abutment system* **Str·eben** n ~s/ *striving* (nach *after*), *aspiration* (*for, after*) ‖ (Anstrengung) *effort* (*for*), *endeavour* (*after*); *pursuit* ‖ (Neigung) *tendency, trend* ‖ ⟨fam⟩ *push* ‖ (Ehrgeiz) *ambition, aspiration*; sein ~ geht dahin *it is his object* od *aim*, etc (zu tun *to do*) **str·eben** vi [h] **(nach)** *to strive* (*after, for*); *to aspire* (*to*); *to seek* (*for*); *to aim* (*at*; ⟨Am⟩ zu tun *to do*) ‖ (S) *to gravitate, tend* (*towards*) ‖ (sich bemühen) *to endeavour* (*to do*) ‖ (erstreben) *to aspire* (*after, at, to*) ‖ (beanspruchen) *to lay claim to*, (begehren) *to covet* (*a th*) ‖ *to struggle* (*for*) | **(gegen)** *to oppose, resist* (*a th*) | [abs] *to be striving*, ⟨dero⟩ *to be a pushing fellow* ‖ ⟨univ sl⟩ *to swot* | **~d** ⟨a.⟩ *forward-looking* **Str·eber** m ~s/~ *pushing* od *ambitious p*; *place-hunter* ‖ (gesellschaftlicher) *tuft-hunter* ‖ ⟨fam⟩ *thruster, climber*; ⟨Am sl⟩ (elender *greasy*) *grind*; *pusher, hustler* ‖ ⟨univ sl⟩ *swot(ter)*, *(s)mug*; *bloke* **~tum** n ~s/ *pushing place-hunting*; *tuft-hunting* **str·ebsam** a *active, assiduous, strenuous*; ⟨fam⟩ *pushing, pushful* ‖ (ehrgeizig) *ambitious* **≗keit** f ~/ *activity, assiduity, strenuousness*, ⟨fam⟩ *push*

Str·eck- **~apparat** m ⟨med⟩ *extension apparatus* **~balken** m *sleeper, stretcher, strut, cross-beam* ‖ (Brücken≗) *road-bearer* **~bett** n *stretch-bed, orthopaedic bed* **~eisen** n *stretching-iron, stretcher* **~gesenk** n *fuller* **~grenze** f *yield-point* **~hammer** m *flattening-hammer* **~lage** f ⟨gym⟩ *stretched position* **~machine** f ⟨spin⟩ *drawing-frame* ‖ ⟨med-gym⟩ *stretching* od *orthopaedic machine* **~metall** n *expanded m.* **~mittel** n pl *stretching stuffs* pl; ⟨tech⟩ *filler* **~muskel** m ⟨anat⟩ *extensor* **~ofen** m *flattening-furnace* **~probe** f *tensile test* **~schiene** f ⟨med⟩ *extension-splint* **~strumpf** m *stretch stocking*; ≗e [pl] ⟨fam⟩ *stretchies* **~stütz** m ⟨gym⟩ *resting on one's hands* **~verband** m ⟨med⟩ *extension-bandage* **~walze** f *flatter*; *drawing-machine* ‖ ⟨mint⟩ *laminating roller* **~werk** n *rolling* ‖ *rolling-mill, plate-roller* **~werkzeug** n *stretcher* **str·eckbar** a *extendible* ‖ (dehnbar) *ductile* ‖ (hämmerbar) *malleable* **≗keit** f *extensibility, ductility, malleability* **Str·ecke** f ~/~n **A.** *extent, stretch* (a. Zeit≗); ⟨geom⟩ *straight line*; *reach* (a. Fluß≗) | (Entfernung, Lauf≗) *distance* | (Weg) *road*; *way*; *route*; (Länge) *length*; (Zwischenraum) *interval*; (Raum) *space* | ⟨rail⟩ *line*; *section*; *track*; ⟨Am⟩ *division*; auf freier ~ *on the open line* | glatte ~ *level stretch of road* | ⟨mar⟩ *route*; (gefahrene) *run*; (Kreuz≗) *leg* | ⟨aero⟩ *distance (flown)* | ⟨min⟩ *gallery, gangway, passage, tunnel, drift*; ~n treiben *to drive* | ⟨geom⟩ *straight line* | ⟨sport⟩ *distance*; gerade ~ *straight*; ⟨Am sport & voyage⟩ *leg* | e–e ~ Weges *some distance* | ⟨hunt⟩ *bag* (*of small game*) (*the b. consisted of 9 hares*); e–e gute ~ h *to make a good b.* **B.** e–e gr *or* **gute** ~ Weges *a long way* ‖ kl ~ ⟨a.⟩ *turn* (*round the square*) | **in** e–r ~ *at a stretch* ‖ ~ nach Hause *home-stretch* | ⟨fig⟩ e–e lange ~ *a far cry* (*from the days when*), *a run* (*of bad luck*) **C.** die ~ Berlin-Köln **fahren** *to go from B. to C.*; lange ~n d·urchfahren ⟨mot⟩ *to drive for long spells* | e–e ~ gehen *to walk for a little way* ‖ e–e ~ überbrücken *to span a distance*; e–e ~ zurücklegen *to cover a d.* | **auf** der ~ bleiben *to perish*: *to be finished off*; auf der ~ ist viel Verkehr *there is heavy traffic on that line* | **zur** ~ bringen *to hunt down*; ⟨hunt⟩ *to kill, shoot*; *to* (*bring to*) *bag*; *to run to earth*; ⟨fig⟩ *to bring* (*a p*) *down, to defeat, stretch, puncture* **str·ecken** vt [h] **A.** *to stretch* (*one's limbs*, ⟨med⟩ *a leg*, ⟨a.⟩ **sich** *o.s.*) ‖ *to extend, spread, draw* | ⟨met⟩ *to laminate, roll*; *to hammer out* | ⟨hunt⟩ *to bag, kill* **B.** **(Arbeit)** *to protract* ‖ (Arme) ⟨gym⟩ *to stretch out* ‖ *to raise* (*one's arms toward heaven*) ‖ die Bestände w ge–kt *inventories are drawn down* ‖ **(Eisen)** *to draw* (*into bars*), *to roll* ‖ (Glas) *to spread* ‖ alle viere v sich ~ *to lie down* (*at*) *full length*; *to sprawl* ‖ ⟨cul⟩ *to stretch* ‖ (Vorräte etc) *to eke out, to adulterate* ‖ die **Waffen** ~ *to lay down one's arms* (vor *to*); *to capitulate* ⟨a. fig⟩ ‖ die Zunge aus dem Munde ~ *to stick out one's tongue* **C.** **zu** Boden ~ *to knock down*, ⟨fam⟩ *to floor* ‖ *to shoot*; *to fell* (*to the ground*) **D.** **sich** ~ (wachsen) *to grow* od *shoot up* ‖ sich ins Gras ~ *to lie down on ..* ‖ sich nach der Decke ~ *to cut one's coat according to one's cloth* | **sich** ~ **l** *to stretch, flatten* **E.** **gestreckt** *rectilinear* (*angle*) ‖ *broad* (*glass*) ‖ in ~em Galopp *at full tilt* **Str·ecken-** **~arbeiter** m ⟨rail⟩ *plate-layer, lineman, navvy*, ⟨Am⟩ *section-hand* **~aufseher** m *track-walker* **~bau** m *railway construction* **~betrieb** m ⟨min⟩ *driving* **~einweisung** f *route familiarization* ⟨a. aero⟩ **~feuer** n ⟨aero⟩ *course light* **~förderung** f ⟨min⟩ *transport* **~führung** f ⟨traffic⟩ *routing* **~geschwindigkeit** f ⟨rail⟩ *speed* | -- höchst≗ *sp. limit over a section of track* **~markierung** f *itinerary signing* **~verkehr** m ⟨rail⟩ *local traffic* **~wärter** m ⟨rail⟩ *line-keeper, surface-man* **≗weise** [adv] *here and there* **~wettervorhersage** f ⟨aero⟩ *route forecast* **~zimmerung** f ⟨min⟩ *tubbing* **Str·ecker** m ⟨tech⟩ *stretcher* ‖ ⟨anat⟩ *extensor* **Str·eckung** f *stretching, dilution*, etc ‖ ⟨met⟩ *rolling, lamination* ‖ ⟨med, tech⟩ *extension*

Streich m ~(e)s/~e **A.** *stroke* (mit .. *of the axe*), *blow*; (leichter) *tap*; Peitschen≗ *lash* | ⟨fig⟩ *trick, turn*; *coup* Fr; *stroke* (*of business*) **B.** **betrügerische** ~e spielen *to run the rig* ‖ böse ~e *mischievous tricks* ‖ derber ~ *skylark(ing)* ‖ derber ~ *practical joke*, ⟨sl⟩ *booby trap* ‖ **dummer** ~ *stupid th to do, piece of folly, foolish prank* ‖ Jugend≗ *escapade* ‖ Lausbuben≗ *rag* ‖ lose *or* mutwillige ~e *pranks*, ⟨fam⟩ *larks* pl ‖ dumme ~e m *to commit follies* **lustiger** ~ *piece of fun* ‖ schlechter ~ *mean* od *dog's trick* ‖ übermütige ~e *roguish jokes* pl **C.** ~e **m** *to be up to tricks* ‖ tolle ~e m *to indulge in mad tricks* ‖ e–m e–n (bösen) ~ spielen *to play a p a* (*nasty*) *trick*; *to pull a fast one on a p*; ihm wurde ein ~ ge–lt *he was played a t.* ‖ ~e vollführen *to carry out practical jokes* **D.** **auf** einen ~ *at one blow*, ⟨fam⟩ *in one go* | **von** einem ~e fällt k–e Eiche *a single stroke won't fell an oak, Rome was not built in one day* | **zum** ~e ausholen *to strike out* **~bein** n (Falzbein) *folding-knife* **~brett** n *smoothing-board*, ⟨min⟩ *locking-sheet*; (Pflug≗) *earth board* **~bürste** f ⟨pap⟩ *spreading brush* **~eisen** n *smoothing iron* ‖ ⟨tan⟩ *shaving knife* ‖ (der Nadler) *rubber* **~feuer** n ⟨mil⟩ *flank fire* | ~zeug [n] *striker lighter* **~garn** n *carded yarn* ‖ (Schleppnetz) *dragnet* **~holz** n (*safety-*)*match* ‖ ein ~ anzünden *to strike* od *light a m.* | ~brief [m] *book of m.s, m.-b.*; ~schachtel *m.-box* **~instrument** n ⟨mus⟩ *stringed instrument* ‖ ~e [pl] *strings* pl **~kamm** m *carding-comb* **~kappe** f ⟨hors⟩ *hoof-pad* **~leder** n (*razor-*)*strop* **~maß** n *full measure* **~masse** f ⟨tech⟩ *coating* **~messer** n *paring-knife, spatula* **~musik** f *string-music* **~netz** n *drag-net* **~orchester** n *string-band* **~quartett** n *string-quartette* **~riemen** m (*razor-*)*strop* **~spatel** m *spatula* **~stein** m *hone* **~zeit** f ⟨ich⟩ *spawning-time* **str·eicheln** vt [h] *to stroke, nurse* (*a p's hand*) ‖ *to caress, cajole, fondle* (*a p*) **str·eichen** [strich/gestrichen] [h] **I.** vt **A.** **1.** *to pass softly over*; *to stroke, rub gently* (*with the hand*) **2.** (an~) *to paint*; (mit Wasserfarben) *to distemper*; weiß ~ *to paint white* **3.** (aus~) *to cross out*; *to cancel*, *delete, erase, obliterate, elide* **B.** (den **Baß**) *to play* ‖ (den Bogen) ⟨mus⟩ *to resin* ‖ (Butter) *to spread* ‖ (die Flagge) *to haul down, to strike* ‖ (Lerchen) ⟨hunt⟩ *to snare* ‖ (Messer) *to sharpen, whet* ‖ (Nichtzutreffendes) *to strike out* ‖ (Pflaster) *to spread* ‖ (Rasierklinge) *to strop, set* ‖ ⟨mar⟩ die **Riemen** ~ *to back-water*; streich überall! *back together*! ‖ (Satz etc) ~ *to kill* ‖ (Segel) *to lower, strike*; ⟨fig⟩ die S. ~ *to surrender* ‖ (Streichholz) *to strike* (an [acc] *against*) ‖ (**Wolle**) *to card* ‖ (Ziegel) *to make* **C. glatt** ~ *to smooth* ‖ Butter (Wurst) **aufs** Brot ~ *to butter* (*to put sausage on*) *one's bread* ‖ sich die Haare zurück (*or* **aus** dem Gesicht) ~ *to push one's hair back* (od *out of one's eyes*) ‖ **aus** *or* **von** e–r Liste ~ *to strike* od *cross off a list* **D. gestrichen**: (Maß) *full* ‖ (Note) ⟨mus⟩ *above* bzw *below the staff* ‖ (auf der Speisekarte) (.. *is*) *off*, ⟨Am⟩ *gone* **E. sich** ~ ⟨hors⟩ *to interfere* **II.** vi **A.** [h & s] **1.** (sich erstrecken) *to extend* ‖ (Gebirge) *to run*, ⟨geol⟩ *to trend*, (dazu: ≃ n *direction of trend*); ⟨min⟩ zutage ~ *to crop out* **2.** ⟨orn⟩ *to be on the wing, to fly, migrate* **3. an** [acc]: *to graze, touch* ‖ vorüber ~ an [dat] *to move* od *rush past* [acc] | **auf**: (Kleid) *to trail on* (*the ground*) **B.** [h] **1.** sich mit der Hand **durch** die Haare ~ *to run one's fingers through one's hair* | jdm **über** das Haar ~ *to stroke a p's hair*, sich .. *to pass one's hand over* (*one's face*) **2.** ⟨ich⟩ (= laichen) *to spawn* **3.** °e–n ~ **lassen** *to pass a wind* **C.** [s] ~ **durch, gegen, über** [acc] *to fly, run, sweep through towards, over* ‖ durch die Wellen ~ (of ships) *to plough the waves* ‖ **umher** ~ *to stroll* od *ramble about* **Str·eicher** m pl ⟨mus⟩ (*the*) *strings* pl **Str·eichung** f ~/~en *striking-out* ‖ *cancellation* ‖ *expurgation* (*of members*) | ⟨typ⟩ [abstr] *deletion*, [konkr] *deleted passage* **~srichtung** f ⟨geol⟩ *trend*

Str·eife f ~/~n (berittene *cavalry*, ⟨mar⟩ *naval*) [*roving*] *patrol* (P & [abstr]) ‖ (Pn) *detachment* ‖ [abstr] *beat* ‖ (Polizei≃) im Frack ⟨sl⟩ *Pansy Patrol* **Streif** m ~(e)s/~e; **Str·eifen** m ~s/~ *stripe, streak* ‖ (im Glas etc) *vein, cloud* ‖ (Papier, Tuch, Land etc) *strip* ⟨a. film⟩; ⟨film a.⟩ *scene*; ⟨Eg paint⟩ *register, row* ‖ ⟨mil⟩ *section*, Angriffs≃ *sector* N ‖ ⟨tail⟩ *braid, list* ‖ ⟨mil-tail⟩ *bar*; (Ärmel–, Hosen≃) *stripe*; Unteroffiziers≃ *chevron* Fr ‖ ⟨met⟩ *plate* ‖ ⟨arch⟩ *band, fillet* ‖ ⟨astr⟩ *belt* ‖ ⟨typ⟩ *slip-proof* ‖ (Mikroskop≃) *slide* ‖ ⟨film⟩ *film* ‖ ⟨telg⟩ *tape* | ⟨übtr⟩ (Abschnitt) *sector* ⟨a. mil⟩ | in ~ schneiden *to shred* **Str·eif- ~band** n *wrapper*; unter ~ *enclosed in a w.*; *by book-post* **~blick** m *glance* **~hieb** m *glancing blow*; *grazing cut* **~jagd** f *coursing* **~kolonne** f, **~korps** n *scouting-party*; *raiding-force* **~licht** n ⟨phot⟩ *glancing* od *skimming light*; ⟨arts⟩ *accidental light* ‖ ⟨theat⟩ *strip l.* ‖ ⟨fig⟩ *side-light* **~partie** f *ramble* **~patrouille** f *long-distance patrol* **~schuß** m *grazing shot, graze*; e–n ~ bek *to be grazed* **~wache** f *patrol* **~wunde** f *scratch, skin-wound* **~zug** m ⟨mil⟩ *inroad, raid*, (*roving*) *expedition, incursion* ‖ ⟨fig⟩ *ramble*; *r.g* (durch *through*), *excursion* (*into* **str·eifen I.** vt [h] **1.** *to stripe, streak* ‖ ⟨carp, etc⟩ *to channel, flute* **2.** *to graze, brush, shave, skim* ‖ leicht ~ *to brush up against* ⟨fig⟩ *to skirt* (*to deal briefly with*) *a subject* ‖ ⟨hunt⟩ mit dem Bauch das Gras ~d *belly to grass* **3.** (**ab~**) *to strip off* ‖ *to skin* (*a hare*) | (**hoch~**) *to tuck up* (*one's sleeves*) | (Decke) *to slip* (*over* **über**) ‖ **von**: *to strip leaves off* (*a bough*) (= *to strip a b. of its l.s*) ‖ v Finger ~ *to take off* (*one's ring*) **II.** vi [h & s] **A. 1.** *to ramble, rove, roam, stroll* **2.** *to make an inroad* od *incursion* **B. an** [acc]: *to touch in passing*; *to graze* od *brush* (*against*); ⟨fig⟩ *to border* od *verge* (*up*)*on* (*fiction*) | **auf** Kundschaft ~ *to reconnoitre* | **durch**: *to roam in* (*field and forest*), *to range* (*the woods*) | **über** [acc]: (of eyes) *to wander* od *glide over*; *to roam* (*a scene*) | ~ **lassen** über *to run over*

III. ≃ n gegenseitiges ~ (of 2 cars) *sidewipe* **Str·eifen- ~barbe** f ⟨ich⟩ *surmullet* **~farn** m ⟨bot⟩ *spleenwort* **≃gesteuert** a ⟨el⟩ *tape-operated* **~locher** m ⟨acc mach⟩ *paper tape punch, t. perforator* **~lochung** f ⟨comp m. m.⟩ *punched t.* **~pantoffel** pl *list slippers* **~polizist** m *roundsman* **~pulver** n ⟨mil⟩ *lamellar powder* **~wagen** m (*prowl, squad* od) *patrol car* **≃weise** [adv] *in stripes* **Str·eifer** m ~s/~ *ranger, rover, rambler*; *scout* **~·ei** f ~/~en *excursion, ramble* ‖ ⟨mil⟩ *raid, incursion* **str·eifig** a *striped, streaky*; *sprinkled*

Streik m ~(e)s/~e *strike*; organisierter ~ *walkout*; wilder ~ *wildcat st.* ‖ in den ~ treten *to go on st.* **~arbeit** f *scab-work* **~ausschuß** m *st.-committee* **~brecher** m *st.-breaker*, ⟨fam⟩ *black-leg*; ⟨Am⟩ berufsmäßiger ~ *fink*; ~ s *to scab on the strikers* **~kasse** f *st.-funds* pl **~lohn** m *st.-pay* **~posten** m *picket*(*s* pl); ~ stehen *to picket* **~recht** n *right to strike* **~verbot** n ⟨Am jur⟩ *injunction* **str·eiken** vi [h] *to* (*go* od *be on*) *strike*; *to strike work* **Str·eikende** m [der ~, ein ~r] ~n/~n *striker* ‖ die ~n ⟨Am fam⟩ *the walkouts*

Streit m ~(e)s/~e *dispute, row*; *quarrel*; *disagreement, difference*; *misunderstanding*; *inharmoniousness, disharmony, dissonance*; *disunity*; *altercation* ‖ kl *tiff*, ⟨Am⟩ *spat* ‖ (Kampf) *fight, combat* ‖ (Wort≃) *controversy, argument*; ⟨parl⟩ *debate* ‖ (wissenschaftlicher) *controversy* ‖ (Wider≃) *conflict* ‖ (Wett≃) *competition* ‖ (Rechts≃) *lawsuit* | Gegenstand des ~es s *to be at issue* | ~ **anfangen** *to pick a quarrel* ‖ e–n ~ beilegen *to settle a difference* ‖ darüber gibt's k–n ~! *that is agreed on all hands*! ‖ in ~ geraten *to fall out, to get into a dispute* ‖ mit jdm ~ h *to have words with a p*; .. in ~ k *to run up against a p* ‖ l wir den ~! *let's agree to differ* ‖ im ~e liegen mit *to be at variance with* ‖ mit jdm *to be engaged in a contest with a p* ‖ ohne ~ *undoubtedly* (*correct*) ‖ ~ suchen mit *to pick a quarrel with* ‖ den ~ verkünden ⟨jur⟩ *to interplead* ‖ (jdn) in ~ verwickeln *to embroil* (mit *with*) ‖ in den ~ ziehen *to go to battle* **~axt** f *battle-axe*; die ~ begraben *to bury the hatchet* **≃befangen** a ⟨jur⟩ *in dispute* | ~heit [f] *state of being in litigation* **~fall** m *matter* od *point in dispute* **~frage** f (*point of*) *controversy*, (*case at*) *issue*; *argument*; *contentions* pl; *question*; *query* **~genosse** m (aktiver) *coplaintiff* | passive ~schaft [f] *majority of defendants*, notwendige ~ *necessary parties* pl **~gespräch** n *dispute, controversy* ⟨a. pol⟩ **~hammel** m ⟨fam⟩ *squabbler* **~hammer** m *pole-axe, mallet* **~handel** m *quarrel* ‖ *law-suit* **~kolben** m *club, mace* **~kräfte** f pl ⟨mil⟩ *forces* pl | Angehörige(r) [m] der Streitkräfte *serviceman* **~lust** f *quarrelsomeness* ‖ *argumentativeness* **≃lustig** a *combative, pugnacious*; *quarrelsome*; *argumentative, aggressive, truculent* **~macht** f ⟨mil⟩ (*armed*) *forces* pl; feindliche ~ *enemy forces* **~punkt** m = –frage **~rede** f *dispute* **~roß** n *war-horse, steed, charger* **~sache** f = –punkt **~satz** m *thesis* **~schlichter** m *arbitrator* **~schrift** f *pamphlet, controversial* od *polemic*(*al*) *treatise* **~sucht** f *quarrelsomeness* ‖ ⟨jur⟩ *litigiousness* **≃süchtig** a *quarrelsome*; *bellicose, belligerent, contentious*; *argumentative*; *polemic*; ⟨jur⟩ *litigious* **~summe** f *amount in dispute, being argued about* **~verhältnis** ⟨jur⟩ n *issue* **~wagen** m *war-chariot* **~wert** m *value of claim*; *money involved*; *amount in litigation* **str·eitbar** a **1.** *warlike, valiant, martial* **2.** = streitlustig **≃keit** f ~/ *warlike spirit* ‖ *combativeness, aggressiveness* **str·eiten I.** vi [stritt/gestritten] [h] **1.** *to quarrel*; (mit Worten) *to dispute*, (prozessieren) *to litigate*; (kämpfen) *to fight* (über, um *about*) ‖ darüber läßt sich ~ *that's a matter of opinion*, ⟨Am⟩ *that's an open question*; laß uns nicht ~! *let's agree to differ*! **2.** (S) *to be at variance* (mit *with*) ‖ das streitet gegen die Vernunft *that's contrary to* *reason* **II. sich** (mit jdm) ~ *to quarrel* (*with a p*) (um *about*) **III. ~d** [a & pres p] *belligerent* (*powers*), *litigant* (*parties*) ‖ die ~e Kirche *the Church Militant* **Str·eiter** m ~s/~ *combatant, fighter, warrior* ‖ (Zänker) *disputant, quarreller* ‖ (Vorkämpfer) *champion* **str·eitig** a **1.** *disputable, debatable, doubtful, contested, disputed; at issue* ‖ ⟨jur⟩ noch ~ *still pending* **2.** jdm etw ~ m *to contest a p's right to a th, to contend with a p for a th* ‖ jdm den Rang ~ m *to compete with, to rival a p* ‖ mit jdm ~ s *to quarrel*, etc *with a p* (über *about*) ≗**keit** f ~/~en *difference, quarrel*

Str·elitz n → Mecklenburg **Strel·itze** m ⟨hist⟩ *Muscovite militia-man*

°**Str·emel** m ~s/~ ⟨allg⟩ *strip* ‖ *skein* (*of beer*) ‖ *journey* (= *term in prison*)

streng(e) I. [a] (→ gestreng) *severe, strict, exacting, rigorous, stern* ‖ *severe* (*ruler*) ‖ *uncompromising* (*critic*) | (bestimmt) *strict* (*teacher*) | (pünktlich) *strict, precise* | (hart) *harsh* | (sitten-~) *austere* (⟨a.⟩ *style*) | *stern* (*features*) ‖ *sharp, bitter, tart; acrid* (*taste*) ‖ *rigorous, stringent* (*law, measures*) ‖ *strict* (*holiday, rule*) ‖ *stiff* (*examination*), *close* (*confinement*) ‖ (Kälte) *biting, bitter, intense, severe, rigorous* ‖ im strengsten Winter *in the depth of winter* ‖ *inclement* (*weather*) ‖ ⟨for⟩ *stiff* (*soil*) | ~ s gegen *to be strict with* od *severe toward* (*a p*) ‖ ~en Ausdruck annehmen (of face) *to harden* ‖ ein ~es Regiment führen *to rule with a firm hand* ‖ im ~sten Sinne des Wortes *in the very strictest acceptation of the word* **II.** [adv] *strictly, scrupulously* (*scientific*) ‖ *devoutly* (*Catholic*) ‖ *top* (*secret*) N ‖ ~ gewissenhaft *religious* | **aufs** ~ste, ~stens *most severely* od *strictly; in the most rigorous manner* | es ~ **nehmen** *to take it strictly* (→ ~-) ‖ ~ schmecken *to have a sharp, acrid, pungent taste* | sich ~ **an** die Wahrheit halten *to adhere strictly to the truth* | ~ **nach** der Vorschrift *in strict accordance with instructions* **~flüssig** a *difficult to fuse* od *melt, refractory* **~genommen** [adv] *strictly speaking* **~gläubig** a *orthodox* | ≗e(r) [m] *true believer;* ≗keit [f] *orthodoxy* **Str·enge** f ~/ *severity, rigour* ‖ *austerity* (*of character*) ‖ *sharpness* (*of taste*) ‖ *strictness* ‖ *bitterness* ‖ *intensity* (*of cold*) ‖ *inclemency* (*of weather*) | ~ beobachten *to be strict* ‖ an ~ nachlassen gegen *to unbend toward* ‖ ~ zeigen *to be severe* | die ~ der Zucht *strict discipline*, .. des Geschmacks *the strong taste*

Strepto- **~k·okkeninfektion** f *streptococcal i.* **~kokkus** m *-coccus* **~mycin** n *-mycin*

Streu f ~/~en *litter* ‖ (Lager) *bed of straw; bedding* **~bereich** m ⟨ball⟩ *spread* **~büchse** f ⟨cul⟩ *castor* ‖ (für Mehl) *dredger* | *sandbox* **~düse** f *spray* od *sprinkler nozzle; sprinkler* **~feld** n ⟨phys⟩ *stray field* **~feuer** n ⟨mil⟩ *scattered* od *searching, traversing fire* **~gabel** f *stable-fork* **~garbe** f *cone of dispersion* **~gemeinde** f → Diaspora **~gold** n *gold-powder* **~kalk** m *agricultural lime* **~licht** n *diffused light* ⟨a. theat⟩; ~ abschneiden ⟨phot⟩ *to screen off straylight* **~pulver** n *sprinkling-powder* **~mehl** n *dredging-flour* **~mine** f *uncontrolled, stray mine* ‖ ~n [pl] *scattered mines* **~sand** m (*writing-*)*sand* ‖ ~ drauf! *enough of it!* ‖ ⟨traffic⟩ *grit* | ~büchse [f] *sand-box* **~schießen** n *area shooting* **~siedlung** f *scattered settlement* **~strahlung** f ⟨phys⟩ *scattered radiation* **~teller** m ⟨mill⟩ *distributing, spreading plate* **~zucker** m *powdered sugar, castor-sugar* **str·euen I.** vt [h] *to strew* (*flowers*; jdm *in a p's path*) ‖ *to scatter* ‖ *to spread* (*manure*) ‖ (Licht) *to flood* ⟨a. theat⟩ ‖ Zucker ~ auf *to sugar* | ge–ut ⟨comp⟩ *random* (*organization*) **II.** vi [h] (vom Gewehr) *to spread the shot* ‖ den Kühen ~ *to litter the cows* **Str·eusel** n ~s/~ *crumbs;* Schokoladen≗ *ch. chips* | ~kuchen [m] *crumb* od *streusel cake* **Str·euung** f ~/~en *strewing*, etc ‖ *spread, dispersion error* (*of guns*) ‖ ⟨artill a.⟩ *variation* ‖ ⟨phot, at⟩ *scattering* ‖ ⟨el⟩ *leakage* ‖ ⟨stat⟩ *variability, -ance* **~sindex** m ⟨stat⟩ *measure of dispersion* **~skegel** m ⟨mil⟩ *cone of spread* od *dispersion* **~sradius** m ⟨artill, at⟩ (*probable*) *circular error*

Strich m ~(e)s/~e **A.** *stroke* ‖ *line* ⟨a. ten⟩ ‖ *comma* ‖ ⟨opt⟩ *graticule* ‖ Kompaß≗ *point* ‖ *dash* ⟨a. telg⟩ ‖ Ablese≗ *gradation mark* | ⟨fig⟩ einige ~ [pl] höher stehend an Bildung als *several cuts above .. in education* ‖ nur ein ~ *a mere stripling* | (Maß) *millimetre* | (das Streichen, Gestrichene) ⟨theat⟩ *cut* | (Land) *region, stretch, district, tract;* ⟨mar⟩ *ocean-track;* Küsten≗ *coastline* ‖ (Zone) *belt* | (Streifen) *stripe* ‖ ⟨mot⟩ → Leitlinie ‖ ⟨orn⟩ *passage, flight, migration* ‖ (Rebhühner) *covey* ‖ ⟨ich⟩ *spawning-time;* (Brut) *young fry* | (des Holzes) *grain* ‖ ⟨min⟩ *trend, direction* ‖ ⟨meteor⟩ *direction* (*of the wind*), *flight* (*of the clouds*) ‖ ⟨mil fam⟩ (Ronde) *beat* ⟨a. vulg sex⟩ | (des Malers, Geigers) *touch* ‖ (mit der Bürste) *a* (stroke with the) *brush;* ⟨fig⟩ *characteristic, trait;* ⟨mus⟩ (Bogen≗) *bowing;* (Takt≗) *bar* | (Zitze) *teat, dug* **B.** er hat noch k–n ~ **gearbeitet** *he hasn't done a tap* od *stroke of work* ‖ ⟨aero⟩ ~ fliegen *to fly on a straight course;* ⟨mar⟩ den ~ halten *to keep the right course* ‖ e–n ~ m durch *to cross out, to run one's pen through*, e–n ~ m unter (etw) *to underline*, ⟨fig⟩ .. unter das Vergangene *to let bygones be bygones; to put an end to a th;* ~ drunter! *let's call it quits!* ‖ jdm e–n ~ durch die Rechnung m *to cross, disappoint, thwart a p, to upset a p's plans, to queer the pitch for a p* ‖ ⟨fig⟩ e–n ~ **ziehen** zw *to draw the line between* (*ths*), *to keep clear of* (*persons*) **C.** ich kann noch **auf** dem ~ gehn (noch nüchtern) *I'm still able to walk a chalk* | **auf** den ~ gehen ⟨hunt⟩ *to go out sniping;* ⟨fig⟩ *to walk the streets*, ⟨vulg⟩ *to go on the batter, to be on the bash, to hawk it;* (Mann) *to go after the girls*, ⟨fam⟩ *to do a grouse* ‖ jdn auf dem ~ h *to harbour a grudge against a p: I cannot stand him* | **in** *or* **mit** einem ~ *at one stroke* od *stretch* ‖ in groben ~en *in broad lines;* mit knappen ~en zeichnen *to give a short sketch of* ‖ **gegen** den ~ bürsten *to brush the wrong way* ‖ es ging ihm gegen den ~ *it went against the grain with him;* ⟨Am⟩ .. *against his grain* ‖ **nach** ~ u Faden *to every tune; properly, thoroughly* ‖ .. besiegen *to knock spots off a p* ‖ **unterm** ~ (Zeitung) *under the line, in the feuilleton* **~einteilung** f *graduated scale; graduation* **~feuer** n ⟨mil⟩ *enfilade* **~kreuzlinse** f ⟨opt⟩ *lens with ruled cross* **~linie** f *broken line* **~liste** f *tally* (*list*) **~marke** f *guide* od *locating mark* **~punkt** m ⟨gram⟩ *semicolon* | ~linie [f] *dash-dot line* **~regen** m *transient, passing* od *local shower* **~vogel** m *local* (→) *migrant; bird of passage* ≗**weise** [adv] *by strokes, by lines* ‖ *partially; here and there* ‖ ⟨hunt⟩ (of birds) *in flights, flocks* **~zeichnung** f *line drawing* **~zeit** f *migration-time* **str·icheln** vt/i [h] *to hatch, streak* ‖ kreuzweise ~ *to cross-h.* **Str·ichelung** f ~/~en ⟨cart, arts⟩ *hatching, hachures* pl Fr

Strick[1] m ~(e)s~ ~e *cord, line* ‖ (dicker) *rope* (⟨a.⟩ z Hängen) ‖ ⟨fig⟩ wenn alle ~e reißen *should all else fail; if the worst comes to the worst* ‖ (z Hängen) *halter, rope* ‖ ⟨fig⟩ jdm e–n ~ drehen *to sell a p;* er will mir e–n ~ daraus drehen *he wants to lay a trap for me* (od *to catch me out*, ⟨Am a.⟩ *to catch me off base* ⟨fam⟩; da kann ich gleich den ~ nehmen *then I might as well hang m.s.* | ⟨fig fam⟩ *scamp, mischief, scape-grace, good-for-nothing, young rogue* ‖ (Mädchen) *minx* **~leiter** f *rope-ladder* **~werk** n *ropes* pl; *cordage* **Str·ick**[2]**-** [stricken] **~arbeit** f *knitting(-work)* **~beutel** m 1. *reticule* 2. *k.g-bag* **~garn** n *k.g-yarn* **~gewebe** m *k.g* **~jacke** f *jersey; woolly* **~kleid** n *knitted dress* **~maschine** f *k.g-machine* **~muster** n *pattern for k.g* **~nadel** f *k.g-needle*

~strumpf m stocking which is being knitted **~zeug** n k.g(-things pl) **str·icken** vt/i [h] to knit (mit der Hand) by hand) ‖ links ~ to purl ‖ netzartig ~ to net **Str·icker(in** f) m knitter **~·ei** f ~/~en knitting

Str·iegel m ~s/~ curry-comb, horse-comb ‖ (P) flesh-brush **str·iegeln** vt [h] **1.** to curry, dress, clean **2.** ⟨fig⟩ to ill-use, to cut up

Str·ieme f ~/~n; **Striemen** m ~s/~ stripe, streak ‖ (auf der Haut) wale, weal; welt **str·iemig** a streaked, striped ‖ covered with wales

Str·iezel m ~s/~ plaited cake | = Lausbub

°**str·iezen** vt/i [h] to pilfer → mausen, stibitzen

strikt a strict | **~e** [adv] strictly, literally

Str·ippe f ~/~n band, strap, string ‖ °⟨telph⟩ cable

str·ippen vi [h] to do a striptease

str·itt 1. & 3. sg pret v streiten **~ig** a = streitig 1.: controversal, debatable; contentious (point), vexed (question) ‖ [pred] (questions) in dispute; open to argument; subject to dispute

Stroh n ~(e)s/ straw ‖ (Dach~̂) thatch ‖ mit ~ decken to thatch ‖ ⟨fig⟩ leeres ~ dead wood ‖ leeres ~ dreschen to beat the air, to waste one's words; ⟨fam⟩ to flog a dead horse, ⟨Am⟩ to chew the fat ‖ °~ im Kopf h ⟨fam⟩ to have no milk in the cocoa-nut **~arbeit** f straw-work **~̂artig** a s.y **~band** n s.-band **~bett** n bed of s. **~̂blond** a tow-headed **~blume** f ⟨bot⟩ immortelle, xeranthemum **~bund** n truss of s. **~butter** f winter-butter **~dach** n thatch(ed roof) ‖ ⟨fig⟩ (Haar) nob--thatch **~decke** f cover of s., s. mat **~decker** m thatcher **~̂dumm** a beef-witted **~farbe** f s.-colour **~̂farben, ~̂farbig** a s.-coloured **~feuer** n s.-fire ‖ ⟨fig⟩ short-lived zeal, transient ardour **~flasche** f bottle etc in a s.-case **~futter** n s. fodder **~geflecht** n s.-plaiting **~̂gelb** a s.-coloured **~halm** m (blade of) straw; ⟨cul⟩ st.(-pipe) ‖ nach e–m ~ greifen to catch at a s. ‖ über e–n ~ stolpern to swallow a camel **~hälmchen** ziehen to draw lots **~haufen** m heap of s. **~hülse** f bottle envelope **~hut** m s. hat; steifer ~ ⟨a.⟩ boater **~hütte** f thatched hut **~kopf** m ⟨fig⟩ numskull, dunce **~korb** m s.-basket **~kranz** m s.-wreath **~lager** n couch of s., s.-bed **~lehm** m mud plaster; cob **~mann** m scare-crow ‖ ⟨cards⟩ dummy ‖ ⟨fig⟩ man of s., dummy, cat's paw; ⟨pol fam⟩ front **~matte** f s. mat **~papier** n s.-paper **~sack** m s.-bed, s.-mattress, paillasse ‖ °heiliger ~! holy cow! **~schneider** m s.-chopper **~seil** n s. rope **~stoff** m ⟨pap⟩ mechanical s. pulp **~stuhl** m s. stool **~teller** m table mat **~ware** f s.--goods pl **~wein** m vin de paille Fr **~wisch** m wisp od whisk of s.; rubber **~witwe(r** m) f temporarily a bachelor [m]; grass-widow(er); ⟨Am⟩ California widow ‖ ich bin ~er my wife is away from home **str·ohern** a ([made] of) straw; s.-built ‖ ⟨fig⟩ empty, insipid; dull **str·ohig** a strawy

Strolch m ~(e)s/~e tramp, vag(abond) ‖ rowdy, hooligan; ⟨Am sl⟩ hoodlum, thug **~̂en** vi [h & s] to roam, to ramble, to loaf about

Strom m ~(e)s/~̈e (large) river ‖ (Berg~̂) torrent | ⟨allg⟩ stream, flood ‖ (im Meer) stream, current | ⟨el⟩ current ⟨a. fig⟩; galvanischer ~ voltaic od galvanic current; vagabundierende ~̈e ⟨el⟩ stray od vagabond, vagrant currents ‖ der ~ wird .. abgeschaltet w there will be a power cut (from 10 to 11); ~ eingeschaltet! power on! ‖ den ~ unterbrechen to break the c.; geschlossener ~ circuit; unter ~ live (wire) | ⟨at⟩ Neutronen~̂ flux, → Fluß | ⟨fig a.⟩ rush, throng, crowd (of people); flood (of tears); streams pl (of blood); flow (of words); floods pl (of rain) ‖ ~ der Ereignisse swim (to be in the s.) | **in** ~̈en in torrents ‖ es gießt in ~̈en it is pouring with rain | **mit** dem (**gegen,** wider den) ~ schwimmen to float with the current, ⟨fig⟩ to go with the tide (to swim against the tide od stream ⟨a. fig⟩) **Str·om-** [in comp] ⟨el-scient⟩ rheo.. (rheomotor, rheotome **~̂·ab(wärts)** [adv] down stream **~abgabe** f current output **~abnehmer** m ⟨el⟩ collector; troll(e)y contact | ~stange [f] tr.-pole **~abschaltung** f (in Stoßzeit) load shedding **~anker** m kedge **~anschluß** m ⟨el⟩ junction **~̂·auf(wärts)** [adv] up-stream **~ausfall** m power failure; current breakdown **~belastung** f ⟨el⟩ power load **~bett** n bed of a river **~brecher** m groin **~dichte** f ⟨el⟩ current density **~enge** f narrows pl of a river **~erzeuger** m generator; dynamo **~erzeugungsanlage** f ⟨el⟩ generating plant **~̂führend** a live (Draht) **~gebiet** n basin **~generator** m power (supply) unit **~karte** f river-chart **~kreis** m (offener broken) circuit **~leiter** m ⟨el⟩ rheophore **~leitung** f ⟨el⟩ circuit **~linien-** ~form [f] stream-line shape; dazu: to s.l.; ~wagen [m] ⟨mot⟩ s.-l. car; ~zug [m] ⟨rail⟩ s.l.er **~̂los** a ⟨el⟩ dead **~losigkeit** f absence of current **~messer** m ammeter; galvanometer **~netz** n network of electricity; power system od connections; mains pl **~prüfer** m circuit detector **~quelle** f ⟨el⟩ power source **~richtungsanzeiger** m polarity-indicator **~sammler** m storage-battery **~schiene** f live rail **~schiffer** m boatman **~schnelle** f rapid, shoot; chute Fr **~spannung** f voltage **~stärke** f ⟨el⟩ intensity of current; amperage **~stoß** m pulse, current impulse | ~dauer [f] impulse period **~unterbrecher** m interrupter **~verbrauch** m ⟨el⟩ current consumption **~versetzung** f drift **~versorgung** f power od electric supply | ~seinheit [f] ⟨comp⟩ p. s. [pl -lies] **~verteiler** m commutator **~waage** f electrodynamic balance **~wandler** m ⟨el⟩ transformer **~wechsel** m commutation **~̂weise** a in torrents **~wender** m ⟨el⟩ commutator **~zähler** m current-meter **~zuleitung** f ⟨el⟩ [abstr] supply of electricity ‖ [konkr] conduit **str·ömen** vi [h & s] to flow ⟨a. el⟩ ‖ to stream ⟨a. P⟩ ‖ (Regen) to pour ‖ (Tränen) to gush ‖ (Wasser) ⟨a.⟩ to dash ‖ (Blut) to rush (to a p's head), to gush (forth) | (sich drängen) to flock, crowd, swarm; to come trooping | **nach** einem Orte ~ (P) to pour into a place | ~der Dampf ⟨tech⟩ flowing stream

°**Str·omer** m ~s/~ vagabond, tramp, loafer; ⟨Am fam⟩ floater **~̂n** vi [h] to tramp it ‖ to rove

Str·ömling m ~s/~e ⟨ich⟩ small herring (in the Baltic) **Str·ömung** f ~/~en current, flow, flood, stream, drift ‖ (⟨meteor, el, geol⟩ [Materie~̂]) convection ‖ vorherrschende ~ ⟨fig⟩ mainstream ‖ ⟨fig⟩ trend, tendency; movement; ⟨arts etc⟩ neue ~en new forms, trends, influences **~sbild** n ⟨el⟩ flow diagram **~sgröße** f ⟨phys⟩ f.ing quantity **~smesser** m f. meter **~slehre, ~stechnik** f hydrodynamics [a. sg konstr] **~sspuren** f pl ⟨geol⟩ flute casts pl **~sverlauf** m flux plot

Str·ophe f ~/~n stanza, verse ‖ ⟨ant⟩ strophe **~nbau** m structure od scheme of verse **~nform** f stanzaic measure **..strophig** a [in comp] of (four) stanzas **str·ophisch** a strophic; in stanzas; consisting of stanzas

Stropp m ~(e)s/~e **1.** ⟨mar⟩ strop ‖ sling **2.** ⟨fig⟩ (P) (Stöpsel) punch ‖ (Strick) scamp **str·oppen** vt [h] ⟨mar⟩ to strop

Str·osse f ~/~e **1.** ⟨min⟩ stope **2.** ⟨anat⟩ windpipe

str·otzen vi [h] (vor or von [dat]) to overflow, bristle, teem, swarm, burst, exuberate od to be exuberant, littered, swelled (with); to abound (in) | to bubble with (new ideas, etc); (vor Gesundheit) **~d** a puffed (with pride) ‖ (vor Gesundheit etc) exuberant (with health etc), in the pink (of health) ‖ ~d voll crammed full

str·ubb(e)lig a dishevelled, shock(-headed)

Str·ubbelkopf m mophead, shock head

Str·udel m ~s/~ whirlpool, gulf, swirl, vortex, eddy ‖ ⟨cul⟩ (apple-)pancake; strudel | ⟨fig⟩ abyss; rush, crush (of business); whirl (of amusements), maelstrom (of pleasure), tumult (of distress), tide (of events) **~kessel** m ⟨geol⟩ pot-hole

~kopf m *hot-brained* (od *-headed*) *fellow, hotspur* **~loch** n, **~topf** m ⟨geog⟩ *pothole* **str·udeln** vi [h] *to spout, whirl, swirl, bubble* | ⟨fig⟩ *to bluster*

Strukt·ur f ~/~en *structure, make; fabric; texture* (*of glass*) || *architecture* (*of a speech*) || der ~ nach *structurally* | ~beschreibung [f] *structure-description*; ~formel [f] ⟨chem⟩ *structural, graphic formula*; ~viskosität [f] *intrinsic viscosity* ≗·**ell** a *structural* (Arbeitslosigkeit)

Strumpf m ~(e)s/≗e (wollener *woollen* od *worsted*) *stocking* (a. Geld≗) || Damen≗e ⟨com⟩ *hose* pl (halterlos *hold-up*) || Sport≗e *golf-hose* || (kurzer) *sock*, ⟨com⟩ *half-hose* pl | (Glüh≗) *mantle* | ⟨fig fam⟩ e–m auf die ≗e helfen *to give a p a lift* || sich auf die ≗e m *to hook it*; in ≗en *st.ged* (*feet*); *in one's st.g-feet* (*to walk in st.g-feet*) | °⟨fig⟩ aufgeblasener *or* vollgefressener ~ (P) *stuffed shirt* **~band** n *garter* **~fabrik** f *stocking-factory* **~fabrikant** m *s.-manufacturer* **~form** f *s.-leg* **~halter** m *suspender* **~händler** m *hosier* **~hose** f ⟨hist⟩ *hose* pl; ⟨mod⟩ *body s.* **~stricker** m *s.-knitter* **~waren** f pl *hosiery* | ~händler [m] *hosier* **~weber**, **~wirker** m *s.-weaver* | ~·ei [f] *s.-factory*; ~stuhl [m] *s.-frame* **~wolle** f *fingering; wool for stockings*

Strunk m ~(e)s/≗e (e–s Baums) *stump, stock, trunk* || (e–r Pflanze) *stalk, stipe* ≗**ig** a *stalky*

°**Str·unsel, Str·unze(l)** f ~/~n *slattern, slut* || ⟨fam⟩ *frump* °**str·unzen** vi [h] **1.** *to show off, to brag* **2.** *to loaf, loiter about*

str·uppig a *rough, unkempt, frowzy, dishevelled; patchy; bristly* (*beard*), *scrubby* (*beard, tree*) || *shaggy* (*dog*); *wiry* (*pony*)

Str·uw(w)el- ~kopf m *person with unkempt hair* **~peter** m *shock-headed Peter*

Strychn·in n ~(e)s/ *strychnia, strychnin(e)*

St·ubben m ~s/~ *stump* (*of a tree*)

St·übchen n ~s/~ *small room* || ~ vermieten [n] (Kinderspiel) *puss-in-the-corner* **St·ube** f ~/~n *room* ⟨a. mil⟩, *apartment*, ⟨poet⟩ *chamber* || ⟨fam⟩ gute ~ *parlour*, ⟨Am⟩ *parlor* **St·uben-~älteste(r)** *m senior*, ⟨mil⟩ *corporal* (*of the room*) **~arbeit** f *indoor work* **~arrest** m *confinement to one's own room*; ⟨mil⟩ *c.t to barracks* (abbr *C. B.*) || ~ h *to be under arrest in one's own room*; (Kind) *to be detained* || ⟨mil⟩ *to be confined to b.s* (abbr *C. B.*) **~dienst** m ⟨mil⟩ *room duties* pl **~fliege** f *common fly* **~gelehrsamkeit** f *book-learning* ≗**gelehrt** a *bookish* | St–te [m pl] *bookish people* **~gelehrte(r)** m *bookworm, bookman*; trockener ~ *dryasdust* **~genosse** m *fellow lodger* **~hocker** m *stay-at-home, home-bird*, pl *indoor people* | ⟨sl⟩ *fug* || ~ s *to stuff indoors* | ~leben [n] *sedentary life* **~luft** f *close air* **~mädchen** n *housemaid* || (im Hotel) *chambermaid* **~ofen** m *stove* ≗**rein** a *clean(ly), house-trained* (*dog*) || ⟨fig⟩ (P) [pred] *in the clear*; nicht ~ *off-colo(u)r* (*story*, etc) **~schlüssel** m *key of a room* **~uhr** f *clock* **~vogel** m *cage-bird*

St·über m ~s/~ **1.** ⟨num⟩ *stiver* (*not a s.*) **2.** *fillip* || jdm e–n ~ geben *to f. a p*

Stuck m ~(e)s/ *plaster* || ⟨arch⟩ *stucco*; → Stukkatur **~decke** f *stuccoed, floated ceiling*

Stück n ~(e)s/~e ⟨fam⟩ ~er 10 **A. 1.** [konkr] *piece* (a. als Maß) || (Bißchen) *bit* || (Teil) *part, portion* || (Bruch≗) *fragment* | ⟨theat⟩ *play* (*a p. by Sh.* od *of Sh.'s*); die Pn des ~es *dramatis personae* || ⟨mus⟩ *piece of music* || ⟨arts⟩ *work of art* || ⟨Lit⟩ *passage, extract*; (Aufsatz) *article* || (e–r Sammlung) *specimen* || (e–r Zeitschrift) *number* || ⟨Lit⟩ [pl ~] (Exemplar) *copy* [*copies*] || ⟨mil obs⟩ = Geschütz || ⟨bank⟩ ~e [pl] *stocks, shares, securities* | ein ~ **von** e–r Strunze *a piece* od *bit of a slut* | [pl] ~: 6 ~ Eier *6 eggs*; (wieviel?) 6 ~! (..) *6!* | °~**er** 50 *about 50* | **Ausstanz**≗ *cut-out* || Beleg≗ *voucher copy*, ⟨Am⟩ *tear sheet* || Drei-Penny≗ *threepenny bit*; Zweimark≗ *two-mark piece* || Repräsentations≗ *figure-head* || Verlängerungs≗ *lengthening piece* **2.** [abstr] *point, circumstance, matter, affair* || (Vorfall) *event* || (Tat) *piece, act, proof, mark* (*of villainy*) || (Teil) *part*, ⟨a.⟩ *wedge* (*of income*) **B.** (**Arbeit**) *job; piece of work*; schweres .. *difficult task* || (Brot) *piece, slice*; dickes .. *hunk* || (Butter) *pat* || (Fleisch) *cut* || ein hübsches, schönes ~ **Geld** *a pretty penny, a nice bit of m., a nice little sum* || (Kautabak) *fig* || (Land) *plot, tract*, ⟨Am⟩ *lot* || (Papier) *sliver, scrap* || ~ Rasen *sod* || (**Seife**) *cake* || (Tuch) *length* || ~ [a. pl] Vieh, Wild, Geflügel *head* [a. pl] *of ..* || ein (gutes) ~ (Weges) begleiten *to go* (*a good*) *part of the way, a little way, for some distance* (*with a p*) || (Wein) *butt* || (Zucker) *lump* **C. abgeschnittenes** ~ *cut, crop* || brennendes ~ Holz *brand* || fehlerhaftes ~ *faulty piece* || gr ~ ⟨fam⟩ *chunk, hunk* || das war kein hübsches ~ v ihm *that wasn't nice of him* || gr ~e auf jdn halten *to hold a p in high esteem, to make* od *think much of a p; to set great store by* (*one's hono(u)r*) ⟨a.⟩ *upon* (*one's work*); *to think the world of* (*a p*) || sich [dat] gr ~e einbilden *to think* (*too*) *highly of o.s.* || ein **gut(es)** ~ weiter als *a long way from, a lot farther than* || das ist ein **starkes** ~! *that's a bit thick* od *a tall order, a smart piece of work! the impudence!* || ein tüchtiges ~ z gehen *quite a walk* || ein gutes, tüchtiges ~ weiter gek s *to be far along the way* **D. auf** ~ arbeiten *to do piece-work* | **aus** einem ~ *integral; entire; all of a piece*; .. gearbeitet *made in one p.*; .. gepreßt *pressed out of one p.* | ⟨fig⟩ aus freien ~en *of one's own account* od *free will* | ~ **für** ~ *p. by p., bit for bit*; ~ f ~ 10 Pf. *a penny a p.* | **in** einem ~ gegossen *cast whole* || in ~en abbröckeln *to chip away in chunks* | in [1000] ~e fallen, (gehen), [schlagen] *to fall*, (*go* od *break*), [*break, knock, smash*] *to pieces* [⟨fam⟩ *smithereens*] || in ~e zerbrochen *in pieces* || in tausend ~en *in a thousand shivers* | ⟨fig⟩ **in** allen ~n *in all points* od *ths; in every respect* od *way* || in diesem ~e *in this particular instance* || in einem ~ fort *continuously; the whole* (z. B. *night*) *through* || in vielen ~en *in many points, respects, ths*; (*to agree*) *on many points* || in ~e gehen *to go to bits*, ⟨Am⟩ °*to go bla(h)*; in ~e schlagen ⟨fam⟩ *to knock into a cocked hat* | **nach** dem ~ v. *to* (*sell by*) *retail* | **ein** ~ **über** .. *a cut above* **~arbeit** f *piece-, job-work* **~arbeiter** m *p.-worker, jobber* **~butter** f *butter in lumps* **~faß** n *butt, large cask* **~gewicht** n *item* od *individual weight* **~gießer** m ⟨obs⟩ *cannon-founder* **~gut** n ⟨com⟩ *p.-goods* pl; ⟨mar⟩ *general cargo* | ~frachtsatz [m] *part-load rate*; ~ladung [f] *less-than-carload lot* || ~sendung [f] *less-than-truckload shipment*; ~verkehr [m] ⟨rail⟩ *smalls traffic, part-load tr.*; *less-than-c.l. freight* (LCL); ~waggon [m] *package car*; als ~ befördern *to send in single parcels* || ~ladung ⟨a.⟩ *mixed cargo* | ⟨obs⟩ *gun-metal* **~kalk** m *pebbled lime* **~kohle** f *large* od *lump coal*, [pl] ~en *cobbles* **~kuchen** m pl *cakes* **~kugel** f *cannon-ball* **~lohn** m *wages* pl *for p.-work*; ⟨comp⟩ *rate; piecework* || in ~ *paid by the p.* | ~karte [f] *wages* od *job card* **~maß** n *tally* **~meister** m ⟨obs⟩ *master gunner* **~möbel** pl (Ggs Einbau–) *free-standing furniture* **~pforte** f ⟨mar⟩ *port(-hole)* **~seife** f *bar soap* **~verkauf** m *retail-selling, -sale* **~wagen** m ⟨obs⟩ *artillery-waggon* ≗**weise** [adv] *p.meal, in p.s, by the p.* || ~ angeben *to specify*; ~ nachzählen *to tally* || *bit by bit* | ~ angeben *to specify*; ~ austeilen *to parcel out*; ~ nachzählen *to tally* **~werk** n *p.-work* || ⟨fig & cont⟩ *imperfect work, bungling work, patchwork* || unser Wissen ist ~ *we know in part* **~zahl** f *number of pieces; quantity* **~zeit** f *production time* **~zinsen** m pl *interest* [sg] *on shares* **~zucker** m *lump-sugar* **St·ückchen** n ~s/~ *small piece, spot, bit* || *morsel* (*of bread*) || *pat* (*of butter*); *end* (*of string*); *scrap* (*of paper*) ||

[pl] (Kuchen) *cakes* ‖ ⟨theat⟩ *short piece* od *play* ‖ ⟨mus⟩ *air, tune* ‖ ⟨übtr⟩ die Straße ein ~ hinauf *a little way up the street* ‖ *plot* (*of land*) ‖ ⟨fig⟩ *anecdote* ‖ jdm ein ~ spielen *to play a p a trick* **st·ücke(l)n** vt [h] *to cut in* od *to pieces* ‖ ⟨exch⟩ *to divide into shares* ‖ (flicken) *to piece* (*together*), *to patch up* **..stück(er)l** n [in comp] ⟨fam⟩ [österr] z. B. Kabin·ett~ *delightful piece of art*

st·ucken vi [h] [österr] ⟨sl⟩ *to bone* °**St·ucker** m ~s/~ ⟨fam⟩ *plug*(*ger*) **st·uckern** vi [h] *to jolt*

Stud·ent m ~en/~en (–in f) (f *woman*) *student*, (f *girl*) *undergraduate* (⟨Am fam a.⟩ *co-ed*) ‖ ⟨med [dent]⟩ vor dem Physikum ⟨fam⟩ *premed* ‖ ⟨engl⟩ *first-*, etc *year man* ‖ ⟨Am⟩ ~ im 1. & 2. Semester *freshman*, ⟨fam⟩ *yearling*; im 3. & 4. Sem. *sophomore*, im 5. & 6. Sem. *junior* ‖ graduierter ~ *graduate* ‖ viele ~en *many university youths* ‖ ewiger ~ *perpetual st.* ‖ ~ der Theologie *st. of divinity*, Medizin *medical st.*, Rechte *st. of law*, Philosophie ⟨Ger⟩ *st. of philosophy*, ⟨engl⟩ *st. of arts*; Mathematik *mathematical st.*, Naturwissenschaften *science st.*; ⟨agr fam⟩ *aggie* ‖ Philister u ~en *town and gown* **Stud·enten-~blume** f *French marigold, pheasant's eye* **~bund** m ⟨Ger⟩ *the St.'s League* **~(kostüm)fest** n (*fancy-dress*) *rag* **~futter** n *almonds and raisins* **~heim** n *hostel*, ⟨Am⟩ *dormitory* **~jahre** n pl *college-* (od *university-*)*years* pl **~jahrgang** m ⟨Am⟩ *class* **~kneipe** f *st.s' tavern* ‖ (Kneiperei) *convivial gathering* **~leben** n ⟨Ger⟩ *st.-life*, ⟨engl⟩ *undergraduate-life* **~mädel** n ⟨Am⟩ *college widow* **~mappe** f *document case* **~mütze** f *st.'s* (⟨engl⟩ *college-*)*cap* **~sprache** f *st.s' slang* **~streich** m *st.s' prank, college-trick* **~verbindung** f ⟨Ger⟩ *st.s' association*; ⟨Am⟩ *fraternity*, (entsprechend: *sorority*) **~viertel** n *st.s' quarter* **~zeit** f: in s–r ~ *in st. days* **Stud·entenschaft** f ~/~en *students*, ⟨Am⟩ *student-body* **Stud·ententum** n ~s/ *students' habits* [pl] od *life* **stud·entisch** a *student-like, undergraduate, academic*, ⟨Am⟩ *collegiate* **St·udie** f ~/~n ⟨arts⟩ *study* ‖ ⟨Lit⟩ *sketch, essay* ‖ ⟨a.⟩ *study* (über *of Poe*) **St·udien** n pl [sg Studium ~s/] *studies* pl, *reading, pursuit* ‖ s–e ~ abschließen *to finish one's st.s* ‖ s–n ~ eifrig obliegen, s–e ~ eifrig betreiben *to be a hard reader* **~assessor** m *assistant master* (*not yet appointed*) **~beratung** f *information about studies* **~direktor(in f)** m *head master* (*h. mistress*) (*of a secondary school*) **~gang** m *course of studies* **~gebühr(en pl)** f *fees* pl **~genosse** m *fellow-student* **~gruppe** f *study groop* **≗halber** adv *for the purpose of studying* **~jahre** n pl *years* pl *of study*; *schools* (*to get through s.s*) **~kopf** m ⟨arts⟩ *study of a head* **~plan** m *curriculum*; *syllabus* **~rat** m (f –rätin) *assistant master* (*mistress*) *at a secondary school* **~referendar(in f)** m *graduate teacher-trainer* **~reise** f *study trip* **~semester** n *school term* **~zeit** f *term* ‖ *student days* **Stud·ier- ~lampe** f *reading--lamp* **~stube** f, **~zimmer** n *study* **~zeit** f *hours* [pl] od *time of study* **stud·ieren** vt/i [h] **A.** *to study*; etw gründlich ~ *to st. up on a th*; etw als Hauptfach ~ ⟨bes Am⟩ *to major in*; etw f s–n Beruf ~ *to st. to enter a profession* ‖ (die Hochschule besuchen) *to go to college, to keep one's terms* ‖ ~ l *to send to college* ‖ (f ein Examen) *to read* (*for a degree*) | ⟨fig⟩ (über [acc]) *to reflect, meditate* (*upon*) **B. was** ~ Sie? *what is your special subject*, od *your branch of study*?, ⟨fam⟩ *what do you go in for*? – *I'm reading history* ‖ M. ~ *to study medicine* ‖ Jura ~ *to read law* ‖ ein Fachgebiet ~ *to read up on a special subject* ‖ **wo** h Sie studiert? *which university have you been to*? **stud·iert** a *educated*; (*man*) *of education* ‖ (gekünstelt) *studied, affected* **Stud·ierte** m [der ~, ein ~r] ~n/~n *educated* od *university man*; *scholar* **St·udio** n ~s/~s *studio* ⟨a. wir⟩ **Studi·osus** (⟨fam⟩ Studio) = Student **St·udium** n ~s/ → [pl] –dien ‖ sein jur. ~ beginnen *to take up law at the university*

St·ufe f ~/~n *step*; oberste u unterste ~n *top and bottom steps* ‖ ⟨arch a.⟩ *flier, flyer* ‖ (e–r Leiter) *rung* ⟨a. fig⟩ ‖ (vor der Haustür) *doorstep* | ⟨übtr⟩ Raketen≗ *stage* ‖ ⟨a–n⟩ 1. ~ *booster* ‖ Alarm≗ *alert phase* (*first phase*) ‖ ⟨Lit hist⟩ Entwicklungs≗ *period* ‖ ⟨school⟩ *class* ‖ (Farb≗) *hue, shade* ‖ ⟨mus⟩ *interval* ‖ ⟨gram⟩ *degree* (*of comparison*) ‖ ⟨min⟩ *step* (*cut in a rock*); (Erz≗) *specimen of ore* | ⟨fig⟩ *order, degree, footing, level, rank*; ⟨school⟩ *standard*, ⟨Am⟩ *grade* ‖ (Entwicklungs≗) *phase, stage* ⟨a. Lit⟩ | **auf** gleicher ~ wie *on a level* od *an equality with*; auf die gl. ~ stellen wie *or* mit *to equate with* ‖ e–e ~ über jdm stehen *to be a cut above a p* ‖ auf eine ~ stellen *to bracket* (mit *with*), *to* (*put on the same*) *level* ‖ auf e–e höhere ~ heben *to upgrade*; auf der höchsten ~ *at the top of the ladder*; .. des Glücks *at the height of one's fortune* | **in** einzelne ~n zerlegen *to phase* **St·ufen-≗artig** a *like steps* ‖ ⟨fig⟩ *gradual, gradational* **~berater** m *guidance counselor* **~breite** f (e–r Treppe) *tread* **~erz** n *ore in pieces* **~folge** f, **~gang** m *gradual progress, gradation, succession* **≗förmig** a *resembling steps* **~generator** m ⟨at⟩ *cascade generator* **~jahr** n *climacteric* (*year*) **~land** n *land rising in terraces* | ~schaft [f] *terraced landscape* **~leiter** f *step-ladder*; ⟨mus⟩ *scale* ‖ ⟨fig⟩ (*progressive*) *scale*; lange ~ *long rainbow* ‖ *gradation* [mst pl *-s*] **≗los** a *ridgeless*; *without stages*; *continuous*; *steady* | adv ~ regelbar *infinitely variable* (*gear*) **~mündung** f ⟨geog⟩ *discordant junction* **~pyramide** f ⟨Eg⟩ *step*(*sided*) *p.* **~schalter** m ⟨el⟩ *power dial* **~tarif** m ⟨a.⟩ Staffel- *differential tariff*; **≗weise** a ~ Erhöhung *escalation* (*of wages*, etc); ~r Schaltvorgang ⟨el⟩ *notching* | adv *by degrees, gradually, successively, progressively* ‖ ~ fortschreitend *gradual, graduated, gradatory*; ~ zunehmend *gradually-increasing* (⟨a–n⟩ *rocket bursts*) **..stufig** a [in comp] viel~ *with many steps*, etc ‖ neun~ (*school*) *with nine forms*

Stuhl m ~(e)s/≗e **A. 1.** *chair*; *seat* (*to get a s.*) **2.** = Stuhlgang **B. Beicht**≗ *confessional* ‖ Dach≗ *roof truss* ‖ Dreh≗ *swivel stool, revolving ch.* ‖ elektrischer ~ *electric chair* ‖ Glocken≗ *belfry* ‖ der Heilige ~ ⟨R C⟩ *the Holy See* ‖ Kirchen≗ *pew* ‖ Klapp≗ *camp-stool* ‖ **Kontor**≗ *stool* ‖ Korb≗ *wicker-ch.* ‖ Lauf≗ *babywalker* ‖ Lehn≗ *arm-* od *easy ch.* ‖ Lehr≗ ⟨univ⟩ *chair, professorship* ‖ Liege≗ *deck-ch.* ‖ Nacht≗ *night-stool* ‖ Orgel≗ *organ casework* ‖ Polster≗ *stuffed ch.* ‖ **Rohr**≗ *cane-ch.* ‖ Roll≗ *wheel-* od *Bath ch.* ‖ Schreibtisch≗ *desk-ch.* ‖ Walzen≗ (*series of*) *rollers* ‖ **Web**≗, Wirk≗ *loom, frame* ‖ Weiden≗ *wicker ch.* **C.** Meister v ~ *master of the Lodge* **D.** ⟨obs⟩ zu ~e gehen *to go to the closet* **E.** jdm e–n ~ **anbieten** *to motion a p to a ch.* | ⟨fig⟩ jdm den ~ vor die Tür setzen *to give a p the cold shoulder, to show a p the door*, (entlassen) *to give a p the sack* ‖ sich zw zwei ≗e setzen *to fall between two stools* **~bein** n *leg of a chair* **~bezug** m *ch.-covering* **~binder** m *ch.-mender* **~drang** m *urgent need of relieving* ‖ plötzlich ~ h *to be taken short* **~entleerung** f *relief* (*of the bowels*), *motion, dejection, evacuation, defecation* **~feier** f ⟨ec⟩ *St. Peter's Day* **~flechter** m *ch.-bottomer* **~gang** m *stool, evacuation* (*of the bowels*); *bowel movement*; ⟨med⟩ *dejection, stools* pl ‖ k–n ~ h *to suffer from constipation* ‖ regelmäßig ~ h *to have open bowels* **~geld** n ⟨ec⟩ *pew-rent* **~gericht** n *secret tribunal* **~gestell** n *frame of a ch.* **~kappe** f *ch.--cover* **~kissen** n *ch.-cushion* **~lehne** f *back of a ch.* **~richter** m *presiding judge* **~rohr** n *cane for chairs* **~rolle** f *chair-castor* **~schlitten** m *hand-sledge* **~sitz** m *bottom of a ch.* **~verhaltung** f *constipation* **~vermieter** m *p who lets* (*out*) *chairs*

⁓wagen m *basket-carriage* **⁓zäpfchen** n ⟨med⟩ *suppository* **⁓zwang** m ⟨med⟩ *tenesmus*; *obstruction of the bowels*

St·uka m ~s/~s (= Sturzkampfflugzeug) ⟨aero⟩ *stuka*, *dive-bomber* || mit ~s bombardieren *to d.-bomb* [vt] **⁓angriff** m *d.-bombing onslaught* || e–n ~ m *to d.-bomb* [vi] **⁓flugzeug** n = Stuka

Stukkat·eur [-ør] m ~s/~e *stucco-worker*, *plasterer* **Stukkat·ur-** **⁓arbeit** f *stucco-work*, *stucco* **⁓arbeiter** m = Stukkateur

St·ulle f ~/~n *slice of bread* (*and butter*)

Stulp, Stülp m ~es/~e *sth turned up* || *brim* (*of a hat*) **St·ulpe** f ~/~n (Stiefel≃) *top* || (Manschette) *cuff* **Stulp(en)-** **⁓handschuh** m *gauntlet*; *fencing* od *boxing-glove* **⁓hut** m *cocked hat* **⁓stiefel** m pl *topboots*, *turn-down boots* pl **st·ülpen** vt [h] *to cock* (*a hat*) || (umklappen) *to turn up* || (auf [acc]) *to put* od *lay* (*upon*) || (Hut) *to jam*, *slap* .. (*on one's head*) || auf–e–a ~ *to clap one above the other* **St·ülpnase** f *turn*(*ed*)*-up nose*, *pug-nose*

stumm a *dumb*, *mute* (a. *mute* [*salutation*]) || (still) *silent* (a. *film*), ⟨fam⟩ *mum* (*to sit mum*) || ⟨theat⟩ ~es Spiel *dumb-show*; *pantomime* || *dull* (*piano*) || *speechless* (*anger*) || *dumb* (*with astonishment*) || ⟨phon⟩ *silent* || ~ wie ein Fisch *as mute as a fish* || [adv] ⟨a.⟩ *without saying a word* **St·umme** m [der ~, ein ~r] ~n/~n; **Stumme** f ~n/~n *dumb person*; *mute* **St·ummheit** f ~/ *dumbness*, *muteness*

St·ummel m ~s/~ *stump*, *remnant* || (e–r Zigarre, Kerze etc) *end*, *stump*; ⟨fam⟩ *fag*(*-end*), *snipe* (*of a cigar*[*ette*]) || ⟨Am⟩ *butt* **⁓affe** m *colobin* **⁓mast** m *short m.* **⁓pfeife** f *cutty* **⁓welle** f *stub shaft* **St·umpen** m ~s/~ *hat-body* || Schweizer ~ *Swiss cheroot*; ⟨Am⟩ *stogy*, *-ie* (*without wrapper*) | ~rodemaschine f *uprooting m.* **St·ümper** m ~s/~ *bungler*, *botcher*; *duffer*; ⟨Am sl⟩ *dub*; *sad sack* **⁓·ei** f ~/~en *bungling*, *botching*; ⟨sl⟩ *foozle* **≃haft** a *bungling*, *botchy*, *clumsy* || ~e Kriegführung etc *prentice* [attr] *war*, *etc* **≃n** vt/i [h] *to bungle*, *botch*, ⟨sl⟩ *foozle*; ⟨Am fam⟩ *to muff*; ⟨mus⟩ *to strum* (auf .. *on a piano*, *guitar*, etc) **Stumpf** m ~(e)s/≃e *stump*, *trunk*; *stub* || ⟨math a.⟩ *frustum* L; mit ~ u Stiel *root and branch*, .. ausrotten *to destroy lock*, *stock*, *and barrel* **stumpf** a *blunt* || (Winkel) *obtuse* || (Kegel) *truncated* || *snub* (*nose*) || *mat* (*silk*); *subdued* (*colo*(*u*)*r*) || ⟨fenc⟩ *buttoned* (*foil*) | ⟨fig⟩ *dull*, *callous*, *apathetic*; *insensitive* || *flat*, *stupid*, *dense* || *worn-out* (*horse*) || *masculine* (*rhyme*; *ending of a line*) | ~ m *to blunt*, *dull*, ⟨fig⟩ *hebetate* || ~ w ⟨fig⟩ *to grow shaky*, ⟨fam⟩ *to grow rusty* **≃heit** f ~/~en *bluntness*, etc; (Nase) *flatness* | ⟨fig⟩ *dulness*, etc, *stupidity* || *apathy*, *lethargy* || *hebetude*, *stupor*, *torpor*, *torpidity* || *phlegm* **St·umpf-** **⁓gleis** n ⟨rail⟩ = Abstell- **⁓machen** n *obtusion* **⁓näschen** n *little turn-up nose* **⁓nase** f *pug-*, *snub-nose* **≃nasig** a *pug-*, *snub-nosed* **⁓schwanz** m *bobtail* **⁓schweißen** n *butt welding* **⁓sinn** m *stupidity*, *dulness* || (Blödsinn) *idiocy* **≃sinnig** a *stupid*, *slow-*, *dull*(*-witted*) || (blödsinnig) *idiotic* || ~er Mensch *dolt* || ~e Leute *stocks and stones* **⁓stoß** m *butt-joint* **⁓werden** n *obtusion* **≃wink(e)lig** a ⟨math⟩ *obtuse-angled*

stund ⟨poet⟩ = stand, ≃e subj pret v stehen

St·ündchen n ~s/~ *little hour* || ein ~ verplaudern *to have an hour's nice little chat* **St·unde** f ~/~n **A. 1.** *hour* **2.** (Zeitpunkt) *hour* (*of judgment*) **3.** in e–m Zeitraum v nur 12 ~n *in one twelve-hours* || Reise v 12 ~n *twelve-hour journey* || e–e ~ Wegs *an h.'s walk* (v *from*) || mehrere ~n im Umkreis *for miles around* || 3 ~n Schlaf *three hours' sleep* **4.** ⟨ec Lit⟩ ~n *Hours* (*of Devotion*) **5.** (Unterrichts≃) *lesson* **B. freie** ~n *leisure-*, *off-h.s* || ganze ~n lang *for whole h.s* || geschlagene ~ *whole h.*, fast e–e g. ~ *the best part of an h.* || 3 gute ~n *three good h.s* || e–e **halbe,** (Viertel–) ~ *half an h.*, (*a quarter of an h.*) || e–e knappe ~ *a short h.* || e–e kl ~ entfernt *hardly an h.'s walk* (*from here*) || normale (Arbeits)~ *actual time*; Überstunde *overtime* || ihre schwere ~ *her h. of travail*; *she was near her time* **C.** ~n **geben** *to give lessons*, ⟨Am⟩ *to teach school* || ~ halten *to have a class* || d–e ~ **kommt** noch *your time will come* || s–e ~ ist gek ⟨a.⟩ *his number is up*, *he is done for* || ~n nehmen *to take lessons* (bei *from*) || s–e (Todes-)~ (die ~) hat geschlagen *his last h.* (*the day*) *has come* **D.** ~ **für** ~ *h. after h.* | **in** e–r ~ *within an h.*; in letzter or zwölfter ~ *at the eleventh h.*, → Moment; in vorgerückter ~ *late at night* | ~ **um** ~ *h. after h.* || **von** Stund' an *from that very h.*, *from this time forth*, *ever since then* | **vor** e–r ~ *an h. ago* | **zur** ~ *at present*; (sogleich) *at once* || zur guten ~ *at the right time* || zu jeder ~ *any time* **st·unden** vt [h] *to grant a respite of* od *delay for* (*payment*) || *to give credit for* (*a sum*) **St·unden-** **⁓arbeitsleistung** f *man-hour* **⁓betrieb** m *one-h. duty* **⁓buch** n ⟨rel arts⟩ *Book of Hours* **⁓geben** n *giving lessons* **⁓gebet** n *horary prayer*; ~e *hours* **⁓geld** n *fee for lessons* **⁓geschwindigkeit** f *speed per hour* **⁓glas** n *hour-glass* **⁓hotel** n *convenience hotel* **⁓kilometer** m *kilometer hour* **⁓kreis** m ⟨astr⟩ *horary circle* **≃lang** [a & adv] *for hours* (*together*), *by the hour*; ⟨sl⟩ *any time you are passing* || *to talk by the hour* **⁓leistung** f *out per h.* **⁓lohn** m *wages* pl *per hour*; *h.ly wages* od *earnings* **⁓plan** m *syllabus*, *table of lessons*, *time-table*; ⟨bes Am⟩ *schedule* **⁓rad** n *hour-wheel* **⁓schlag** m *stroke of the hour* || mit dem ~e *on the stroke* (*of* ..), *as the clock struck* | ≃er [m] *Jack o' the clock* **⁓uhr** *clock that strikes the hours* (*only*) **⁓verzeichnis** n *table of lessons*, *syllabus* **≃weise** [adv] *by the hour* **⁓weiser, ⁓zeiger** m *hour-hand* **st·ündig** a *of an hour*(*'s duration*) | [in comp z. B.] drei~ *lasting three hours* || acht~e Fußtour *eight-hour walking tour* **St·ündlein** n ~s/~ ⟨dim⟩ → Stündchen **st·ündlich** [a & adv] *hourly*, *every hour*, *hour by hour* | [in comp z. B.] zwei~ *every two hours* **St·undung** f ~/~en *respite*, *extension*, *grace*, *delay*; *delay of payment* ⟨a. cust⟩ || zeitweilige ~ *moratorium* **⁓santrag** m *request for a respite* **⁓sfrist** f *delay granted for payment*

°**Stunk** m ~(e)s/~e *row*, *quarrel* || *mischief*

stup·end a *stupendous* (*structure*, *error*, *folly*)

Stupf m ~(e)s/~e *push* ×**St·upfer** m ~s/~ (*gentle*) *reminder* **st·upfen** vt [h] *to push*

stup·id a *stupid* **≃it·ät** f *stupidity*

Stups m ~es/~e ⟨fam⟩ *push*, *nudge* (geben *to give*) **⁓nase** f *pug-*, *snub-nose* || sie hat ein wenig ~ *her nose has a slight tiptilt*

°**stur** a *pig-headed* (⟨mil sl⟩ wie ein Panzer *as a mule*); *stubborn*, ⟨Am⟩ *logy*; *wooden* (*face*) | [adv] *obstinately*

Sturm m ~(e)s/≃e *storm* (⟨a. fig⟩: *st. of indignation*), *gale* || (Orkan) *hurricane* || ⟨mil⟩ *attack*, *assault*; ~! *charge*! || ⟨com⟩ *run* (*on the bank*) | ⟨nazi⟩ *storm* (= *company*) *of Brown* od *Black Shirts* | ⟨fig⟩ *rage*, *fury*, *passion* || *rough and tumble* (*of life*) || *tumult* || ~ u Drang ⟨Ger Lit⟩ *sturm u drang*; *storm and stress* || ein ~ im Wasserglas *a storm in a tea-cup* | den ~ **bestehen** *to weather the st.* ⟨a. fig⟩ || ~ blasen ⟨mil⟩ *to sound the attack* || ⟨fig⟩ im ~ gewinnen *to win* (*hearts*) *by st.* || e–n ~ heraufbeschwören *to raise a st.* ⟨a. fig⟩ || ~ laufen gegen ⟨mil⟩ *to storm*; *to make an assault on* || ~ läuten *to ring the alarm-bell*, ⟨fig⟩ *to ring with a vengeance* || im ~ nehmen ⟨mil & fig⟩ *to carry by assault*, *to take at the point of the bayonet* || v ~ gepeitscht *st.-ridden* (*ocean*) **⁓abteilung** f ⟨mil⟩ *commando*; ⟨nazi⟩ (abbr SA) (*detachment of*) *Brown Shirts* **⁓angriff** m *assault* **⁓artillerie** f *assault* od *breakthrough a.* **⁓ausgangsstellung** f ⟨mil⟩ *jumping-off* od *assault position* **⁓band** n (an

Mützen etc) *hat-guard* **~bann** m ⟨nazi⟩ *storm-troop* (= *battalion*) (→ ~ ⟨nazi⟩) **~bataillon** n *shock b.* **~bewegt** a *tempestuous* **~bock** m *battering-ram* **~boot** n ⟨mil⟩ *assault boat* **~dach** n ⟨fort⟩ *mantelet*, ⟨ant⟩ *tortoise* | **~- u Drangperiode** f ⟨Lit⟩ *Period of Storm and Stress* **~- u Jugendzeit** *adolescent turbulence* **~fahne** f *war-standard, banner* **~fest** a *tempest-proof* **~flut** f *storm tide* **~frei** a ⟨mil⟩ *unassailable* (*position*), ⟨stud sl⟩ *unmolested* (*diggings* pl) **~gasse** f ⟨mil⟩ *passage, lane* **~gepäck** n ⟨mil⟩ *skeleton equipment* **~glocke** f *tocsin*, ⟨bes fig⟩ *alarm-bell* **~haube** f, **~hut** m (*h*)*elmet*; ⟨hist⟩ *morion* ‖ ⟨bot⟩ *monk's hood* **~kolonne** f ⟨mil⟩ *storming-party* **~laterne** f *hurricane-lamp* **~lauf** m, **~laufen** n ⟨mil⟩ *assault* **~läufer** m *assailant* **~leiter** f *scaling-ladder, fire-ladder* **~lücke** f *breach* **~möwe** f ⟨orn⟩ *black-backed gull* **~pionier** m *combat engineer* **~reif** a *ready to be assaulted*; ~ m *to soften up*; ~ schießen *to fire a lane into* **~riemen** m *chin-strap* **~schaden** m *storm havoc* **~schritt** m ⟨mil⟩ *double-quick step* od *time* ‖ im ~ *at the double* **~schwalbe** f *storm petrel* **~segel** n *lugsail* **~signal** n *the "charge"*; ⟨mar⟩ *storm-signal*; ~e geben *to raise stormwarnings* **~trupp** m ⟨mil⟩ *storming party* **~versicherung** f *storm and tempest insurance* **~vogel** m *petrel* **~warnung** f *gale warning* **~welle** f ⟨tact⟩ *assault echelon* **~wetter** n *stormy weather* **~wind** m *storm, tempest*; *heavy gale* **st·ürmen I.** vt [h] *to rush, storm*; *to take by assault* ‖ *to charge into* (*a room*) | *to force* (*a door*) *open* | ⟨ec hist⟩ *to break* (*the* [*saints'*] *images*) **II.** vi [h] *to storm* (⟨a. fig⟩ = schelten), *to roar* ‖ ⟨mil⟩ *to make an assault* ‖ (Wind) *to rage, rush* ‖ **es** stürmt *it is stormy weather*; ⟨fig⟩ *the tocsin is ringing* **III.** vi [s] (schnell laufen) *to rush, sweep, tear, dash* (*along*) ‖ gestürmt k *to come rushing* | **nach**: *to dash for, to flounce to* (*the door*) **St·ürmer** m ~s/~ **1.** *hotspur, blusterer* **2.** ⟨ftb⟩ *forward*, ⟨Rugby⟩ die ~ [pl] *the pack* **3.** ⟨mil⟩ *assailant* **4.** ⟨stud⟩ *cocked cap* | **~ u Dränger** m *revolutionary* **st·ürmisch** a *stormy* ⟨a. fig⟩; *tempestuous, storm-swept* ‖ *rough, wild, turbulent* (*sea*) ‖ *blustering* (*wind*) ‖ *squally* (*weather*) | *boisterous, tumultuous, impetuous* ‖ *turbulent* (*meeting, passion*) ‖ *rousing* (*welcome*) ‖ *rapturous, frantic* (*applause*) ‖ ⟨mar⟩ *rough* (*crossing*) | ⟨fig⟩ *wild* (*youth*) | [adv] *greatly, deeply* (*moved*) ‖ ⟨sl⟩ *like blazes* ‖ nicht so ~! *now, now*! ‖ sich ~ vertiefen in *to plunge into*

Sturz m ~es/~e **A.** (*sudden, great*) *fall, tumble, rush*; ⟨aero & fig⟩ *nose dive* ‖ ⟨fam⟩ *purler* ‖ (Zus~) *collapse, crash* ‖ (ins Wasser) *plunge* | ⟨com⟩ *collapse* (*of prices*), ⟨fam⟩ *smash*, ⟨sl⟩ *slump* ‖ (Kassen~) *audit* | ⟨min⟩ *dumping-ground* ‖ (Halde) *precipice* | ⟨arch⟩ (Fenster–, Tür~) *lintel* (dachförmig *pedimented*) | (Glas~) *glass shade* (*over a clock*) | *waterfall* | (Wetter~) *sudden change* | ⟨fig⟩ (*a p's*) (*down*)*fall, come-down* ‖ *abolition* (*of the monarchy*) ‖ *overthrow*, ⟨Am⟩ *overturn* (*of the government*) ‖ (Ungnade) *disgrace* ‖ (Untergang) *ruin*, ⟨jur⟩ *failure* **B.** e–n ~ **tun** *to have a great fall*, ⟨fam⟩ *to come a purler* (⟨sl⟩ *cropper* bes. v Pferde); °e–n gewaltigen ~ drücken ⟨sl⟩ *to come a mucker* **C.** ein Glas **auf** einen ~ leeren .. *at one gulp* | **zu(m)** ~ bringen *to overthrow*; jdn **zu(m)** ~ br. *to cause a p's fall, to tumble a p* **~acker** m *new-ploughed field* **~angriff** m ⟨aero⟩ *nose-diving attack*; *dive bombing attack* **~bach** m *torrent* **~bad** n *shower-bath, plunge* **~bügel** m ⟨hors⟩ *safety-stirrup* **~bühne** f **~fliegen** ⟨aero⟩ *to dive* **~flieger** m *dive-bomber* **~flug** m (*nose-*)*dive*; ~ mit Vollgas *power dive* (ungestüm *headlong*) ⟨a. a–n⟩; im ~ ⟨a.⟩ *screaming downhill*, .. angreifen *to dive-bomb* ‖ e–n ~ m *to dive*; im ~ niedergehen *to swoop down, to dive* | ~(abfang)automatik [f] *automatic dive control*; ~bremse [f] *diving brake*; ~klappen [f pl] *speed brakes* **~furche** f *newly-ploughed furrow* **~güter** n pl ⟨com⟩ *bulk goods, goods loaded in bulk* **~helm** m ⟨mot & aero⟩ (*crash-*)*-helmet* **~kampfflieger** m *dive*(*-bombe*)*r* | ~einrichtung [f] f führerloses Flugzeug *ditching device* **~karren** m *tumbrel* **~kocher** m ⟨tech⟩ *plunging boiler* **~see** f *heavy sea* (*breaking over the deck*) ‖ e–e ~ bek *to ship a sea* (v achtern *to be pooped*) **~spirale** f ⟨aero⟩ *spin* **~welle** f *breaker, roller* **St·ürze** f ~/~n (*dish-*)*cover, pot-lid* ‖ (Licht~) *extinguisher* **st·ürzen I.** vt [h] **A.** *to throw, precipitate, hurl* (⟨a.⟩ *o.s.*) ‖ *to plunge* | (S) *to turn upside down* ‖ (Feld) *to plough* ⟨for, agr a.⟩ (Boden) *to turn up* ‖ (Glas [hinunter]~) *to toss off* ‖ (Karren) *to upset*, ⟨tech⟩ *to tilt*, ⟨min⟩ *to shoot* ‖ (Kasse) *to count, examine* ‖ (Kiste) nicht ~! *this side up! do not overturn!* ‖ ⟨cul⟩ *to turn out*; (Pudding) *to unmould* ‖ (Schutt) *to shoot, dump* ‖ (Topf etc) *to turn .. over* | ⟨fig⟩ *to ruin* ‖ *to subvert, overturn, upset* (*monarchy, principles, morality*) ‖ (Regierung) *to overthrow, topple* | (jdn) **aus** s–n Träumen ~ *to disenchant, disillusion* | **in**: *to plunge* (*into poverty*) ‖ *to land ..* (*in disaster*) ‖ ins Verderben ~ *to ruin* ‖ *to cast* (*into despair*) ‖ *rashness involved him in further misery* | **vom** Throne ~ *to dethrone, to sweep potentates from their seats* **B.** → ⟨a.⟩ II. **sich ~**: **auf**: *to plunge into*; *to pitch into* (*work*); *to go for*: *he went for* (*the tarts*) ‖ *to turn on* (*a p*) | **aus**: *to throw o.s. out of* (*the window*) | **in**: ⟨a–n⟩ *to launch o.s. into ..* ‖ ⟨fig⟩ *to plunge into* (*adventures, debt, licentiousness*) ‖ *to incur* (*expenses*) ‖ *to rush into* (*danger*) ‖ *to fling o.s. into* (*an undertaking*) ‖ sich in den Krieg ~ *to fly to arms* ‖ sich ins Schwert ~ *to fall upon one's sword* ‖ sich ins Wasser ~ **a)** *to drown o.s.* **b)** *to plunge into the water, to dive* | **von**: *to hurl o.s. from a rock* **II.** → a. I. B.; vi [s] & refl [h] (**sich**) ~ (auf; in [acc]) *to rush* (a. v Wasser) (*at, upon*; *into*) ‖ *to sink* ‖ *to gush, plunge, fall* (*upon, into*) | (Abgrund) *to descend precipitously* ‖ (of prices) plötzlich, stark ~, (of plane) kerzengerade ~ *to plummet* | **auf**: *to dart, whirl, pounce on*; *to make a rush for* ‖ *to rush at* (*the enemy*) ‖ ⟨Am⟩ *to break for* (*the barn*) | (sich) aus dem Zimmer ~ *to fling out of the room*; **hinter** .. her: *to dash after* | **in**: *to throw, fling* (*o.s.*) *into* (*a p's arms*) ‖ (sich) jdm zu Füßen ~ *to throw* (*o.s.*) *at a p's feet* **III.** vi [s] **A. 1.** *to* (*have a*) *fall*; *to tumble* (*down*) ‖ (gefährlich) ⟨fam⟩ *to come a fearful purler*, ⟨sl⟩ *mucker* ⟨a. fig⟩, *cropper* ‖ (v Pferde) (→B.) ⟨a.⟩ *to take a toss* | ⟨fig⟩ (Firma) *to fail*, ⟨fam⟩ *to go smash* **2.** (eilen) *to rush, whip, lunge, tear, bolt* ‖ gestürzt k *to come rushing* (*along*) **B. aus**: *to tumble, fall out of* ‖ (*tears*) *stream from* (*her eyes*) ‖ ⟨a.⟩ *to flounce out of* (*the room*) | **durch**: *to break through* ‖ **gegen**: ⟨sl⟩ *to slump against* (*a door*) | **in**: *to burst, scurry, barge into* (*a room*); (of plane) *to crash into* (*the sea*) | **mit** dem Pferde ~ ⟨sl⟩ *to come a cropper* (*horse and man*) | **nach**: *to plunge for, flounce to* (*the door*) | **über**: *to tumble over* | **vom** Pferde ~ *to fall off one's horse*, ⟨sl⟩ *to come a cropper* | **zur** Türe ~ *to* (*make a*) *break for the d.* **st·ürzende** Linien ⟨opt⟩ *sloping*, ⟨phot⟩ *convergent* od *distorted verticals* **St·ürzer** m ~s/~ (Welle) *breaker*

°**Stuß** m; (so'n) ~! (*stuff and*) *nonsense*! ⟨Am sl⟩ *hogwash, banana oil*!

Stute f ~/~n *mare* **~nfohlen, ~nfüllen** n *foal, filly* **~nmilch** f *mare's milk* **Stuter·ei** f ~/~en *stud*

St·uten m ~s/~ (*sweet*) *white bread*

St·uttgart n ⟨Ger⟩ (Hptst. v Württemberg)

Stutz m ~es/~e **1.** (Stoß) auf den ~ *all of a sudden* **2.** (der Pferde) *crop, dock* **3.** (Feder~) *tuft of feathers, plume* **~ärmel** m *short sleeve* **~bart** m *trimmed beard* **~büchse** f *carbine, short rifle* **~flügel** m ⟨mus⟩ *semi-grand piano, baby grand* **~glas** n *short-stemmed wineglass* ‖ (f

Wasser etc) (*low*) *tumbler* **~handschuh** m *mitten* **~kopf** m ⟨fam⟩ *short crop* **~ohr** n *cropped ear* **≗ohrig** a *crop-eared* (*dog, horse*) **~perücke** f *bob-wig* **~säbel** m *cutlass* **~schwanz** m *bob-tail*, ⟨fam⟩ *scut* **~uhr** f *French clock, timepiece*

Stütz- **~balken** m *shore* **~holz** n (am Kreuz Christi) *foot-rest* **~mauer** f ⟨arch⟩ *buttress*; *retaining wall* ‖ (Böschungs≗) *breast-wall* **~platte** f *backing plate* **~punkt** m *point of support, bearing surface* ‖ (des Hebels) *fulcrum* ‖ (Halt) *foot-hold, footing* ‖ ⟨hist & fig⟩ *stronghold*; ⟨mil⟩ *bastion*; *defended locality*; *strong-point*; *base*; ⟨aero⟩ *air base*; ⟨mar⟩ *fleet base*; *naval bastion* ‖ (Handels≗) ⟨Am⟩ *fort* | ~programm [n] ⟨comp⟩ ⟨hum⟩ *post-mortem pr.*; ~system [n] ⟨mil⟩ *web defence* **~schwimmer** m ⟨aero⟩ *wing-tip float* **~verband** m (→ Arm) *sling* **~weite** f *span* **~wort** n ⟨gram⟩ *propword* **St·ütze** f ~/~n *prop, stay* ‖ ⟨carp⟩ *post, shore, stanchion* ‖ ⟨theat⟩ *brace* ‖ ⟨fig⟩ *rock* ‖ (Kopf≗) *rest* ‖ ⟨fig⟩ *support, staff, mainstay* ‖ ~ der Hausfrau *lady help* ‖ *to have a strong backing in a town* ‖ k–e ~ finden bei *to find no support with* (*a p*) ‖ zur ~ *in support* (*of his contention*) **~moment** n ⟨mech⟩ *moment about the points of support* **~nwechsel** m *alternate order*; *alternation of columns and pillars* **st·ützen** vt [h] **1.** *to prop, stay, support* ⟨a. fig⟩ | *to retain* (*a bank*) ‖ *to shore* (*a wall*) ‖ ⟨fig a.⟩ *to back up, to countenance* ‖ *to shore up* (*currency*) ‖ nichts h, s–e Behauptung z ~ *not to have a leg to stand on* ‖ *to be* (*at the*) *back of a p* ‖ mächtig ~ ⟨Am fam⟩ *to boost* | **auf** den E. gestützt *propped on his elbow*; *to rest* (*elbows*) *upon* **2.** (gründen) (auf [acc]) *to base, found* (*on*) **3. sich** ~ *to steady o.s.* ‖ **(auf** acc) *to lean* od *rest* (*upon*); ⟨fig⟩ *to build upon* (*a th*); *to rely* (*on a p*) ‖ (*she stepped down*) *with a hand* (*from her father*) ‖ sich mit dem E. ~ auf .. *to rest one's elbow on* (*the cushion*)

St·utzen m ~s/~ **1.** *short rifle, car(a)bine* **2.** ⟨tech⟩ (Rohransatz) *nozzle* ‖ Abgas≗ *exhaust gas n.*; Anschluß≗ *connecting point*; Brüden≗ *vapo(u)r n.*; Staubabzugs≗ *dust extraction socket* **3.** [pl] ⟨m. m.⟩ *golf-hose* pl **4.** (Pulswärmer) *muffetee* **st·utzen** vt [h] *to truncate*; *to curtail* ⟨a. fig⟩ ‖ *to dock* (*tails*) ‖ *to crop* (*ears*) ‖ *to clip* (*wings*) ‖ *to trim* (*beard*) ‖ *to prune, lop* (*trees*) **St·utzer** m ~s/~ *masher, bean, dandy, exquisite, fop, buck, spark*, ⟨sl⟩ *swell, toff* **≗haft** a *dandified, foppish*; *doing the masher* etc **~tum** n *foppishness*

st·utzen vi [h] *to stop short, to be startled*; *to* (*give a*) *start, hesitate, blench* ‖ *to be taken aback* (bei, über *by*) **st·utzig** a *startled, puzzled*; *taken aback*; *sceptic* ‖ ⟨fam⟩ *flabbergasted* | ~ m *to disconcert, stagger, startle, puzzle* ‖ ~ w ⟨a.⟩ *to be nonplussed, to be all at sea, to pull up*

St·ützungsaktion f *holding operation*

st·ygisch a *Stygian* | **st·yptisch** a ⟨med⟩ *styptic*

Su·ade f ~/~n *flow of speech*, ⟨fam⟩ *gift of the gab* ‖ *power of persuasion*

Suah·eli m *Suaheli, Suahili*; **~frau** f *S. woman*

subalt·ern a *subordinate* ‖ ⟨mil⟩ *subaltern* **≗beamte(r)** m ~n/~n *subordinate official* **≗offizier** m *subaltern*

Sub- **≗atom·ar** a *subatomic* (Teilchen, Vorgang) **~diakon·at** n *subdeaconship* **~diakonus** m *subdeacon* **~hastati·on** [ts] f ~/~en *subhastation, public auction, forced sale* **≗hast·ieren** vt [h] *to sell by public auction* **~j·ekt** n ~(e)s/~e ⟨gram⟩ *subject* | ⟨dero⟩ (P) *fellow* ‖ ekelhaftes ~ *unpleasant wart* ‖ gemeines ~ *swine* ‖ liederliches ~ *sloven* ‖ schlechtes, verworfenes ~ *blackguard* **≗jekt·iv** [f] a *subjective* (*writer, e.g. Th. Wolfe*); *personal* ‖ ~es Verbum *neuter verb* **~jektivit·ät** [v] f ~/ *subjectivity* **≗kut·an** a *subcutaneous* (*injection*)

subl·im a **1.** *sublime* **2.** *subtle* **≗at** n ~(e)s/~e *sublimate* **~·ieren** vt [h] ⟨chem⟩ *to sublimate* ‖ ⟨fig⟩ *to sublime* **≗·iergefäß** n *aludel* (*sublimating-vessel*) **≗·ierung** f ~/~en ⟨chem⟩ *sublimation*

sub- **~lun·arisch** a *sublunary* **~mar·in** a *submarine* **~m·iß** a *submissive* **≗missi·on** f ~/ ⟨com, jur⟩ (*contract by*) *tender* ‖ in ~ geben *to invite tenders, to put out by contract* | ~sangebot [n] *tender*; ~slieferant [m] *contractor*; ~sstrich [m] *line drawn lengthwise from the foot of a petition to the signature*; im ~swege *by tender* **≗normale** f ~/~n *subnormal* **~ordin·ieren** vt [h] *to subordinate* **~sidi·arisch** a *subsidiary* ‖ [adv] ~ unterstützt *subsidized* **≗s·idien** [pl] *subsidies* pl ‖ zahlen f *to subsidize* **≗sist·enz** f ~/ *subsistence* **~sist·ieren** vi [h] *to subsist* **≗skrib·ent** m ~en/~en *subscriber* **~skrib·ieren** vi [h] (auf [acc]) *to subscribe* (*to*) **≗skripti·on** f ~/~en *subscription* ~sanzeige [f] *prospectus of a new publication*, etc: ~spreis [m] *pre-publication price*; *subscription* **~stanti·ell** [–ts–] a *substantial* **≗stant·iv** [–f] n ~(e)s/~e ⟨gram⟩ *substantive, noun* **~stantiv·ieren** [–v–] vt [h] *to use as a noun* **~stant·ivisch** *substantive* **≗st·anz** f ~/~en *substance, material* ⟨a. fig⟩ ‖ ⟨cul etc⟩ *ingredient* ‖ ⟨com⟩ *principal, capital* ‖ v der ~ leben .. *on one's capital* ‖ ⟨fig a.⟩ *stuff, body* | **≗los** [a] *vaporous* (*argument*) **~stitu·ieren** vt [h] *to substitute* (*one th* od *p for another*) **~stit·ut** m ~en/~en *substitute* **≗stituti·on** f ~/~en *substitution* ‖ ⟨poet⟩ (zweier Kürzen f e–e Länge) *resolution* | ~smethode [f] *s. method* **≗str·at** n ~(e)s/~e *basis, foundation* | ~osphäre [f] *substratosphere* (zw 5,5 u 11 km ⟨a. aero⟩) **~sum·ieren** vt [h] (unter [acc]) *to embrace, comprise, imply* (*in*) **~t·il** a *subtile, delicate* ‖ *subtle* ‖ *careful* (*treatment*) | [adv] ~ behandeln .. *with great caution*; jdn .. *to humour a p* **~tilis·ieren** vt [h] *to subtilize* **≗tilit·ät** f ~/~en *subtility* **~trah·ieren** vt [h] *to subtract* **≗traktionsaufgabe** f *subtraction sum* **~tropisch** a *semitropical* **≗venti·on** f ~/~en *subvention, subsidy, grant* (*-in-aid*) ‖ (Ausfuhr- etc Prämie) *bounty* ‖ staatliche ~ *government sponsorship* od *patronage* **~vention·ieren** vt *to subsidize* **~vention·iert** a *subsidised*; *bounty-fed* (*products*); *grant-aided* (*program*) | nicht ~ *unsubsidised* **~vers·iv** a (revolutionär) *subversive*; Bekämpfung ~er Elemente *counterinsurgency*

S·uch- **~anzeige** f *classified*, ⟨Am⟩ *want ad*(*vertisement*) **~dienst** m (internat. etc) *tracing* (od *missing persons*) *service* **~eisen** n ⟨surg⟩ *probe* **~gerät** n ⟨wir⟩ *locating equipment* **~glas** n ⟨astr⟩ *finder* **~kriterium** n ⟨comp⟩ *search argument*; *control data* pl **~leine** f ⟨mar⟩ *sweep wire* **~leitstelle** f *rescue coordination station* **~maske** f ⟨comp⟩ *scan control word* **~methode** f ⟨med⟩ *m. of finding out* **~mine** f *dummy mine* **~ort** m ⟨min⟩ *prospecting-shaft* **~programm** n ⟨comp⟩ *retrieval pr.* **~scheinwerfer** m ⟨mot⟩ *spotlight* **~sektor** m ⟨radar⟩ *searching s.* **~- u Rettungsdienst** m *search and rescue* N **S·uche** f ~/, **~n** n ~s/ *search* (nach *for*), *quest* (*of*); *inquiry* (*after*); ⟨hunt⟩ *tracking* ‖ vergebliche ~ *wild goose chase*; auf der ~ nach *in search* od *quest of*; (*to be*) *out to get* (*a th*); *on the lookout* od *hunt for*; auf die ~ gehen nach *to go in search of* **s·uchen** vt/i [h] **A. 1.** *to seek, search* (*after, for* ⟨a.⟩ nach vi]) ‖ *to look* (*out*) *for* ‖ *help me look*! ‖ *to feel for* ‖ *to hunt for* (.. *in one's bag*) ‖ nach Öl ~ ⟨Am⟩ *to posthole*; (eifrig) *to ferret about* (*in a book*) ‖ (forschend) *to go in quest* od *search of a th*; *to go questing* [vi] ‖ ⟨fam⟩ *to go in for* ‖ (jdn) ⟨Am sl a.⟩ *to page* | *to find*; such! *find it out*!, *catch him*! ‖ ⟨bib⟩ suchet, so werdet ihr finden *seek and ye shall find* ‖ wir h, was Sie ~ *we have* (*got*) *what you want*; man kann lange ~, bis man findet *you'd have to go a long way to find* (*it*) ‖ ⟨fig⟩ sie ~ ihresgleichen *they cannot be rivalled* ‖ was h Sie hier **zu** ~? *what business have you here*?; *I wondered what he did there* (→ C.) ‖ wo da wohl Geist zu ~ war? *where did the intellect come in*? **2. jdm etw** ~ *to* *find a p a th* od *a th for a p* (*he'll find us seats*) **3.** (Gefallen finden an, Wert legen auf) ~, es **zu tun** *to make it a point to do it* ‖ (sich bemühen) *to attempt, try, endeavour, seek to do it* ‖ (etw) zu erlangen ~ ⟨fam⟩ *to have a shot at*; zu bewältigen, erzwingen ~ *to attempt* (*a passage*, etc); ~, Vorteile z ziehen aus *to seek to turn .. to one's advantage* **B. (Abenteuer)** *to go in quest of ..* ‖ (Arbeit[er]) *to advertise for* ‖ Ausflüchte ~ *to use shifts; to fence, shuffle* ‖ (e–e Ausrede) *to try to find ..* ‖ (ein Darlehen) *to request* ‖ s–e **Ehre** in [dat] *to glory in* ‖ (Gott) *to seek* ‖ (ein Haus, Kunden, e–e Stelle) *to look for* ‖ den **Tod** *to court death* ‖ jds Verderben ~ *to plot a p's ruin* ‖ sich mühsam e–n Weg ~ *to pick one's way* (*through*) **C. an**: ⟨fig⟩ *to look for a th in a p* ‖ wir h **dabei** nichts **zu** ~ *we have nothing to do with it* ‖ das h wir nicht **hinter** ihm gesucht *we didn't think he could have done it* ‖ hinter, **in** allem etw ~ *to be* (*easily offended* od) *very suspicious* ‖ **in**: *to fish, hunt in* (*one's bag*) ‖ Sie ~ etw darin z .. *you make it a point to contradict* ‖ **nach**: *to be in search of* ‖ *to feel, fish, hunt for* ‖ *to seek for* (*a solution*) ‖ *to probe for* (*an answer*); *to study for* (*an excuse*) ‖ nach Worten ~ *to be at a loss for words* **D. gesucht** (*a doctor*) *much sought after* ‖ ⟨fig⟩ *far--fetched* (*excuse*) ‖ *trumped up* (*reason for divorce*) ‖ *affected* (*style*) ‖ (im Inserat) *wanted ..* ‖ *wanted* (*for crime; by the police*) ‖ der Zwist war nicht v ihm ~ .. *was not of his own seeking* ‖ ⟨com⟩ sehr ~ s *to be in keen demand* **|** das Gesuchte *what one is looking for, the th wanted* **S·ucher** m ~s/~ *seeker, searcher* ‖ ⟨surg⟩ *probe* ‖ ⟨wir⟩ *selector* ‖ ⟨mot⟩ *spotlight* ‖ ⟨opt⟩ *finder* ‖ ⟨phot⟩ *view-finder* (*erect-image v.f.; reversible v.f.* **|** ~einblick [m], ~okular [n] *v.f. eyepiece*; ~schuh [m] *accessory shoe* **Sucht** f ~/ **1.** *disease* ‖ fallende ~ ⟨path⟩ *epilepsy, falling-sickness* **2.** (Begierde) *mania, passion, rage* (nach *for*); *addiction* (*to*) ‖ die ~ nach Geld *the hankering after m.* ‖ ~ z stehlen *kleptomania* ‖ e–e ~ h, sich z putzen *to have quite a craze for dress*; zur ~ führend *addictive* (*drug*, etc) **s·üchtig** a **1.** *diseased* ‖ gelb~ *jaundiced* **2.** *having a mania for* ‖ kokain-~ *addicted to cocaine* **| ~e(r)** m *drug* od *dope addict* (⟨sl⟩ *fiend*), ⟨sl⟩ *junky* ⟨a. teens⟩

ˣ**s·uckeln** vi/t [h] = in kl Zügen saugen

Sud m ~(e)s/~e *boiling* ‖ *decoction* ‖ *brew-(ing)* **|** ~werk [n] *brew-house outfit*

S·üd m ~(e)s/ *south* ‖ (Wind) *s. wind* **~afrik·anische Union** *Union of South Africa* **~bahn** f *s.ern railway* **~breite** f ⟨geogr⟩ *s. latitude* **~-früchte** f pl *citrus and tropical* (od *exotic*) *fruit* **~fruchthandlung** f *Italian warehouse* **~italien** n *S.ern* (⟨poet a.⟩ *Midday*) *Italy* **~kreuz** n ⟨astr⟩ *S.ern Cross* **~küste** f *s.*(*ern*) *coast* **~länder(in** f) m *inhabitant of the s.; meridional, s.erner* [⟨a.⟩ f] **≗ländisch** aussehend ⟨a.⟩ *dark Latinical* (*man*) **~licht** n *aurora australis* **~ost** m *s.-east* ‖ (Wind) *s.-easter* **~ostasien-Organisation** f *S. East Asia Treaty Org.* (*SEATO*) **≗östlich** a *s.-east*(*ern*) **~pol** m *antarctic pole, S. Pole* **~see** f *Pacific* (*Ocean*), ⟨hist⟩ *S. Sea* **~seeinsulaner** m *kanaka* **~seeländer** n pl *Australasia* **~seite** f *s.* od *sunny side* **~staaten** m pl *S.ern States*; Krieg gegen die ~ der Union *War of Secession* (1861–65) **~ti-r·ol** n *Southern Tirol* **≗wärts** [adv] *s.ward* **~-w·est** m *s.-west* ‖ (Wind) *s.west wind, s.wester* **~w·ester** m *sou'wester* **≗w·estlich** a *s.-west*(*ern*) **~wind** m *s. wind*

Sud·an, S·udan, der (innerafrikan. Landschaft) *the Soudan* **Sud·anneger, Sudan·ese** m, **sudan·esisch** a *Sudanese*

S·udel- ~arbeit f = Sudelei **~koch** m *slovenly* od *dirty cook* **Sudel·ei** f ~/~en *scamped work*; *patchwork, patching* ‖ ⟨fig⟩ *filth* ‖ ⟨paint⟩ *daub*(*ing*) ‖ (Gekritzel) *scrawl*(*ing*) **s·ud(e)lig** a *slovenly, dirty, nasty, filthy*, ⟨fam⟩ *messy* **s·udeln** vi/t [h] *to mess about* **|** ⟨fig⟩ (pfuschen) *to botch, bungle* ‖ („malen") *to daub, smear* ‖ („schreiben") *to scribble* **S·udler** m ~s/~ *bungler* ‖ *dauber* ‖ *scribbler*

S·üden m ~s/ *south*, → Norden ‖ im ~ *in the south*, ⟨Am⟩ *down south* ‖ gegen ~, nach ~ *southward*, ⟨Am⟩ *down south* **s·üdlich** a [nur attr] *South, s.ern* ‖ das ~e Eismeer *the Antarctic Ocean* ‖ [pred] ~ von *to the S. of* ‖ [a & adv] *s.erly* (*wind*) ‖ ~st, am ~sten *s.ernmost*

S·üdersee f → Zuidersee (in Holland)

Sud·eten pl **1.** *Sudetic Mountains, Sudetes* (~-deutsche) *Sudeten Germans* ‖ ~land [n] *S.n Country*

S·ues, S·uez n (ägypt. Stadt) *Suez* **~kanal** m *Suez Canal*

†**Su·even** pl (ostgerman. Volk) *Suevi* [L] pl

°**Suff** m ~s/ ⟨fam⟩ *boozing, tippling*; ⟨sl⟩ *soak* ‖ sich dem ~ ergeben *to take to drink*; ⟨sl⟩ *to soak* ‖ stiller ~ *solitary drinking*; dem stillen ~ ergeben [a] *tippling on the sly* **|** (Getränk) (*vile*) *swill* °**s·üffeln** vi *to tipple, booze* °**s·üffig** a *tasty, palatable*; [pred] *nice to drink*

süffis·ant [syfiˈzant] a *disdainful* (*smile*), *supercilious* (*p*)

Suff·ix n ~s/~e *suffix*

Suffrag·anbischof m *suffragan*

sugger·ieren vt [h] *to suggest, to influence by suggestion* **suggest·ibel** a *suggestible* **suggest·iv** [–f] a *suggestive* **≗frage** f *leading question*

S·uhle f ~/~en ⟨hunt⟩ *wallow* **sich ≗n, sühlen** [h] *to wallow*

s·ühnbar a *expiable* **≗keit** f *possibility of being expiated* **S·ühne** f ~/~n *atonement, expiation* **Sühn(e)- ~bock** m *scapegoat* **~geld** n ⟨hist⟩ *blood-m.* **~maßnahme** f *sanction* **~opfer** n *expiatory sacrifice*, ⟨fig⟩ *atonement* **~termin** m ⟨jur⟩ *judicial conciliation; c. hearing* **~verfahren** n *c. proceeding* **~versuch** m *attempt at reconciliation* **s·ühnen** vt [h] *to expiate; to atone for* ‖ *to wash out* (*a shame*) **S·ühnung** f ~/~en = Sühne

Suite [ˈswiːtə] f ~/~n *train, retinue; suite* ⟨a. mus⟩ **|** ⟨stud sl⟩ ~n m *to play tricks* **Suitier** [swiˈtjeː] ~s/~s *fast fellow*

Suj·et n [syˈʒɛ] ~s/~s Fr *subject*

Sukk·ade f ~/~n *succades* pl; (Zitronat) *citronella*

S·ukkubus m ~/-ben *nightmare, incubus* L

sukzed·ieren vi [s] [dat] *to succeed a p* **sukzes-si·onsfähig** a *entitled to succession* **sukzess·ive** [–və] [adv] *little by little, bit by bit*

Sulf·at n ~s/~e *sulphate* **≗·ieren** vt [h] *to sulphate*, ⟨Am⟩ *sulfate* **Sulf·id** n ~(e)s/~e *sulphide* **Sulf·it** n ~(e)s/~e *sulphite* **Sulfonam·id(e** pl) n *sulphur drug*(*s*)

S·ülfmeister m *superintendent of saltworks*

Süll m [~(e)s/~e], f [~/~e] ⟨mar⟩ *sill*

S·ultan m ~(e)s/~e *sultan* **~·at** n ~s/~e *sultanate* **~in** f ~/~nen *sultana, sultaness* **~·ine** f ~/~n (Rosine) *sultana* **~swürde** f *sultanship*

S·uluinseln f pl (Inselgruppe der Philippinen) *Sulu Archipelago*

S·ülze f ~/~n **1.** *brawn* (*in jelly*); *aspic jelly* ‖ Kalbs≗ *calvesfoot jelly* **2.** (Lake) *brine* **≗n** vt [h] *to pickle, preserve* (*in jelly*) **S·ülzkotelett** n *cutlet in aspic*

S·umach m ~(e)s/ ⟨bot⟩ *sumac*(*h*)

S·umatra n (Sundainsel); Bewohner(in) der Insel ~ ⟨oft⟩ *Sumatran*

S·umba n (Sundainsel)

†**Sum·erer** pl (älteste Bewohner S.-Babyloniens) *Sumerian, Sumir*(*ian*)

summ, summ [intj] *buzz, buzz* **s·ummen I.** vt/i [h] *to hum, croon* (*a tune* etc) **II.** vi [h] (Biene) *to buzz*; (Kreisel, Kessel) *to hum* ‖ (Ohren) *to tingle, sing* ‖ ⟨aero⟩ *to zoom, drone*; ⟨mot⟩ *to purr* ‖ ⟨fig⟩ *his head buzzed* (vor .. *with* ..) **S·ummer** m ~s/~ ⟨telph⟩ *buzzer* ‖ ⟨el⟩ *vibrator*

S·umma f ~/ *sum* || ≃ summ·arum *sum total* || in ~ *altogether*; *in short*; *taking all in all* **-·and** m ~en/~en *item* **s-·arisch** a *summary* (*proceedings*) **S·ümmchen** n ~s/~: nettes, hübsches ~ *nice little sum of money*; ⟨fam⟩ *pretty penny* **S·umme** f ~/~n *sum, sum total, aggregate* || fehlende ~ *deficiency, deficit* || gr ~ *considerable amount* (*of money*); kl ~ *pittance*; schöne ~ *fine lump* (*of m.*) || höchste ~ *maximum* | **in** ~ *in short, taking all in all*; → (in) Summa **S·ummen-** ⟨comp, demog⟩ **~karte** f *summary* (*total*) *card* **~lochen** n *s.y punching* **~locher** m u Serienstanzer *gang s.y punch* **~speichern** n *store accumulatively* **~-stanzer** m ⟨comp⟩ *gang summery punch* **summ·ieren** vt [h] *to sum* od *add* od *cast up* | **sich** ~ *to run* od *sum up* **Summ·ierung** f ~/~en *summing* od *casting up*; *addition*

S·umpf m ~(e)s/≃e *swamp, marsh, bog*; *ooze* || ⟨a. fig⟩ *morass* || ⟨fig⟩ *pool, den, sink* (*of infamy*), *squalor* (*of big cities*) | e–n ~ trocken legen *to drain a marsh* || ⟨fig⟩ in den ~ geraten *to get into bad ways* || im ~e stecken (bleiben) *to stick in the mud* ⟨a. fig⟩ **~baldrian** m ⟨bot⟩ *marsh--valerian* **~beere** f *mossberry* **~bewohner** m *dweller in a fen country*, ⟨fam⟩ (Ir) *bog-trotter* **~boden** m *marshy ground*; *slash* **~d·otterblume** f *marsh marigold*; *kingcup* **~erz** n ⟨min⟩ *bog-iron ore* **~fieber** n *malaria, marsh-fever* **~heidelbeere** f *bog-vaccinium* **~huhn** n *moorhen* (→ *crake*) || ⟨fig⟩ *rake, boozer* **~lache** f *pool, quagmire* **~land** n *marshland, fen* **~moor** n *bog* **~otter** f *small otter* **~pflanze** f *marsh-*, od *paludial plant* **~porst** m *wild rosemary* **~schildkröte** f ⟨Am⟩ *terrapin* **~schnepfe** f *jack-snipe* **~vogel** m *wader* **~wasser** n *bog-water* **~weihe** f ⟨orn⟩ *marsh-harrier* **s·umpfen** vi [h] *to be boggy* || ⟨fig⟩ *to lead a fast life* || ⟨vulg & univ⟩ *to go on the bust* od *blow* **s·ümpfen** vt [h] **1.** ⟨min⟩ *to drain* **2.** *to knead clay* **s·umpfig** a *boggy, fenny, marshy*

Sums m ⟨fam⟩ (e–n) großen ~ m *to make a fuss* (*about*) **s·umsen** vi [h] *to hum, buzz*

Sund m ~(e)s/~e *strait*(*s* pl), *sound* || bes zw Seeland u Schweden *Sound*

S·undainseln f pl *Sunda Islands* pl (S.-O.-Asien)

S·undastraße f (Meerenge zw Sumatra u Java) *Sunda Strait, Strait of Sunda*

S·ünd- **~flut** f *deluge, the Flood* **≃los** a *sinless, impeccable* **~opfer** n *sin-offering* **S·ünde** f ~/~n *sin* (wider *against*), *trespass* || läßliche ~ *venial offence* || kl ~n *slight offences, petty misdemeanours* ⟨a, jur⟩; ⟨fam⟩ *peccadilloes* pl; alte ~n *sins long past* | e–e ~ begehen *or* auf sich laden *to commit an offence*; mit ~ belastet *weighed down by sin* || ich hasse ihn wie die ~ .. *like poison* || e–e (himmelschreiende) ~ u Schande *a wicked shame* || Gott verzeih mir die ~! *Heaven forgive me*! **S·ünden-** °**~abwehrkanone** f ⟨mil sl⟩ (Pfarrer) *God-botherer*; ⟨sl⟩ *sky-pilot*, ⟨Am⟩ *sin-buster* **~bekenntnis** n *confession of sins* **~bock** m *scapegoat*, ⟨Am⟩ *goat*; *fall-guy* || den ~ m, abgeben, spielen *to be the s.* || gut, daß wir e–n ~ h *it's nice to have a peg to hang ths on* **~erlaß** m ⟨R. C.⟩ *absolution* **~fall** m *fall of man*; ⟨arts⟩ *Temptation by the Serpent* **~geld** n *ill-gotten money* od *gains* pl || ⟨fam⟩ *exorbitant price, enormous sum* **~-knecht** m *slave of sin* °**~krüppel** = ~lümmel **~last** f *burden of sin* **~leben** n *sinful life* || ein ~ führen *to live in sin* **~lohn** m *wages* [pl] *of sin* || *starvation-wages* **~lümmel** m *wicked old sinner* **~lust** f *sinful pleasure* **~pfuhl** m *sink of iniquity* **~register** n *long list* (⟨fam⟩ *budget*) *of sins* **~schuld** f *trespasses* **~tilger** m *Redeemer* **~vergebung** f *forgiveness of sins*, ⟨R. C.⟩ *absolution* **≃voll** a *sinful* **S·ünder** m ~s/~ *sinner* || armer ~ *delinquent, criminal under sentence of death* || ⟨fig⟩ *poor wretch* || ein alter ~ ⟨fam⟩ *an old offender* **~bank** f *penitent-form* **~glöcklein** n *passing-bell for a p to be executed* **~hemd** n *garb of penitent* **s·ündhaft** a *sinful, iniquitous, wicked* || ⟨fig⟩ [adv] *disgracefully* (*expensive*) **das** ≃**e** *iniquity* **≃igkeit** f *sinfulness* **s·ündig** a *sinful*; *peccant* || *liable to sin* || wir ~en Menschen *we poor sinners* **s·ündigen** vi [h] *to* (*commit a*) *sin* || was h wir gesündigt? *what wrong have we done*? || an jdm ~ *to wrong a p* || wider Gott ~ *to sin against G.* **S·ündigkeit** f ~/ *sinfulness* **s·ündlich** a *sinful* || *unlawful* || *impious* **≃keit** f ~/ *sinfulness*

S·undgau m *southern part of Upper Alsace*

S·uomi n finnischer Name für Finnland

S·uper m ~s/~ ⟨wir⟩ *superheterodyne receiver* **≃fein** a *superfine, A 1* [ei wʌn] **~festung** f ⟨aero⟩ *superfort* **~intend·ent** · m ~en/~en ⟨ec⟩ *superintendent* | ~·ur [f] ~/~en *superintendency* **Sup·erior** m ~s/–i·oren *superior* **~it·ät** f ~/ *superiority* **S·uper-** **~k·argo** m ~s/~s *supercargo* **≃klug** a *sapient, priggish, pert, over-wise*, ⟨fam⟩ *too clever by half* | ~e(r) [m] ⟨fam⟩ *clever dick* **~lat·iv** [–f] m ~(e)s/~e [–v–] ⟨gram⟩ *superlative* (*degree*) || in ~en sprechen *to talk in s.s* || in den höchsten ~en schwärmen *to be excessively gushing* **~markt** m *supermarket* **~numer·ar** m ~s/~e *supernumerary* **~ox·id** n *peroxide* **~-phosph·at** n *superphosphate* **~p·orte** f = Supra– **~revisi·on** f *final revision*; ⟨typ⟩ *final proof*

Sup·inum n ~s/~na ⟨gram⟩ *supine*

S·üppchen n ~s/~ *nice soup* **S·uppe** f ~/~n *soup* || klare ~ *clear s.*; Creme-~ *cream-s.* | (Einbrenn≃) *thick s.*; Gemüse≃ *jardinière* Fr; schwarze (Sparta-)~ *black broth* || e–n Teller ~ mit jdm essen *to take pot-luck with a p* | ⟨fam fig⟩ *mud* || *pea-soup fog*, ⟨fam⟩ *pea-souper* || °rote ~ (Blut) ⟨fam⟩ *claret* | die ~ ausessen müssen *to have to face the music* || die ~ auslöffeln müssen, die man sich eingebrockt hat *to lie in the bed one has made, to stew in one's own juice* || e–m etw in die ~ brocken *to serve a p an ill turn* || er hat was in die ~ zu brocken *he's in clover* || jdm in die ~ spucken, jdm die ~ versalzen *to cook a p's goose*; *to spoil a p's game* || er fand ein Haar in der ~ *there was a fly in the ointment* **S·uppen-** **~anstalt** f *soup-kitchen* **~-fleisch** n ⟨cul⟩ *stock-meat* (*for making s.*); *boiled beef* **~kaspar** m *boy who would not eat his s.* **~kraut** n *pot-herb* **~löffel** m *table-spoon* || (Kelle) *s. ladle* **~napf** m *s.-bowl* **~schüssel** m *s.-tureen* **~schwab(e)** m *p fond of s.* **~teller** m *s.-plate* **~terrine** f *s.-tureen* **~topf** m *stock-pot* **~würfel** m *s.-cube* **s·uppig** a *soup-like*

Sup- **~ple·ant** m ~en/~en Sw ⟨off⟩ = Ersatzmann **~plem·ent** n ~(e)s/~e *supplement* ⟨a. math⟩ | ~band [m] *supplementary volume*, ~winkel [m] (*adjacent angle*) *supplement* **~pl·ik** f ~/~en *petition* | ~·ant [m] ~en/~en *petitioner* **≃pliz·ieren** *to petition* (um *for*) **≃pon·ieren** vt [h] *to presume, suppose* **~p·ort** m ⟨tech⟩ *tool carriage*; *slide, rest* **~posit·orium** n ~s/–rien ⟨med⟩ *suppository*

Suprap·orte f *picture above the door*

Suprem·at m & n ~(e)s/; ~·ie [f] ~/ *supremacy*

Surab·aja n (Stadt auf Java) *Surabaya*

S·ure f ~/~n (Koran≃) *sura*(*h*)

°**S·urius** m ~/–sse *sour wine*

Surre·altischchen n *kidney table*

s·urren I. vi [h] *to buzz, chug, hum, whir, whiz, zip* || ⟨mot⟩ *to burr, purr* **II.** ≃ n *buzz*, etc

Surrog·at n ~(e)s/~e *substitute*

Sus- **≃pend·ieren** vt [h] *to suspend* || *to abolish* (*institutions*) || *to stop* (*payment*) **~pend·ierung** f ⟨jur⟩ *abatement* (*of actions*) **~pend·ierungsbefehl** m ⟨jur⟩ *suspendeas* L **~pensi·on** f ~/~en *suspension* || *abolition* **~pens·orium** n ~s/–rien *suspensor*; *masculine support*

süß I. a **A.** *sweet* (⟨a. fig⟩ *girl, idleness, repose*) || ~e Speise *sweet*(*s* pl), *pudding* | ⟨übtr⟩ *fresh* (*butter, water*), *unleavened* (*bread*) || *honeyed, wheedling* (*words*) | ⟨fig⟩ *lovely, sweet* || *charming*, *enchanting* | (P) *dear* || ⟨sl⟩ dein Bräutigam ist aber ∼ .. *is a dear* || ⟨dero⟩ ein ∼es Herrchen *a young fop, a namby-pamby fellow* **B.** ∼ **m** *to sugar; sweeten* (⟨a. fig⟩ *life*) || e–m ∼e Worte m *to speak a p fair* **II. du** ≃e! *my sweetheart! darling love! own dear!* ⟨Am⟩ *sugar! hon(ey)!* || er ist **ein** ≃**er** *he has got a sweet tooth* **S·üß-** **∼futter** n *ensilage* (dazu: *to e.*) **∼holz** n *liquorice* || ⟨fam⟩ ∼ raspeln *to flatter (insincerely); to sweet-talk, to polish apples* **∼holzraspler** m *flirt,* ⟨Am⟩ *apple polisher* **∼l·iebchen** n *sweetheart,* ⟨fam⟩ *lady-love* °**∼maul** n *sweet-tooth* **∼milchkäse** m *cream-cheese* **∼mittel** n *edulcorating agent; sweetening* **∼most** m *(unfermented) fruit juice* ≃**sauer** a *bitter-, sour-sweet* ≃**sentiment·al** a *maudlin, mawkish, mushy, oversentimental* **∼speise** f; *sweet coarse* od *dish; dessert* **∼stoff** m *sweetening agent; saccharin(e)* **∼waren** f pl *confectionery, sweets, sweetmeats;* ⟨bes Am⟩ *candies* | ∼fabrikant [m] *sweet maker;* ∼geschäft [n] *sweetshop,* ⟨fam⟩ *tuck-shop* **∼wasser** n *freshwater* | ∼fisch [m] *f.w. fish;* ∼pflanze [f] *aquatic plant;* ∼kunde [f] *limnology* **∼wein** m ⟨mst⟩ *sherry* od *port;* ⟨hist⟩ *sack* °**s·usselig** a (= süßlich) *sloppy, soppy, sloshy* **S·üße** f ∼/ *sweetness, sugariness;* → süß II. **s·üßeln** vi [h] *to be nauseously sweet* || *to talk sweetly* od *fulsomely* **s·üßen** vt [h] *to sweeten, sugar* **S·üßigkeit** f ∼/∼en *sweetness* || ⟨fig⟩ *suavity* || ∼en [pl] *sweetmeats, sweets, succades, lollipops* pl, ⟨Am⟩ *candy, candies* pl **s·üßlich** a *sweetish* || ⟨dero⟩ *fulsome, mawkish, soppy, luscious* || *complacent (smile), suave (expression)* || ⟨Lit⟩ *pretty-pretty (sentimental stuff)* **S·üßling** m ∼(e)s/∼e *fop, coxcomb, ladies' man* || (Schmeichler) *cajoler*

S·ussex ['sʌseks] ⟨engl⟩ (Grafschaft)

S·ust f ∼/∼en Sw *penthouse* | *warehouse*

S·utre f ∼/∼n ⟨Ind Lit⟩ *Sutra*

Suzer·än m ∼s/∼e *suzerain* **∼it·ät** f ∼/ *s.ty*

Sw·asiland n (in Afrika) *Swaziland*

Sw·ing(tanz) m *swing;* nach –musik tanzen *to jive, jam* **∼-by** m [–'bai] ⟨a–n⟩ *swing-by (e.g. through the gravitational field of Venus on the way to Mars)* **∼enthusiast** m *jitterbug*

Sybar·it m ∼en/∼en *sybarite, sensualist* ≃**isch** a *sybaritic* [adv *-ally*]

S·ydney ['sidni] n (Hpst. v Neu-Süd Wales)

Syen·it m ∼(e)s/∼e ⟨min⟩ *syenite*

Sykom·ore f ∼/∼n ⟨bot⟩ *sycamore*

syl- **∼lab·ieren** vt [h] *to syllabize, to divide into syllables* ≃**lab·ierung** f ∼/∼en *syllabication* **∼l·abisch** a *syllabic(al)* ≃**log·ismus** m ∼/–men *syllogism* **∼log·istisch** a *syllogistic* [adv *-ally*]

S·ylphe, Sylph·ide f ∼/∼n *sylph*

Sylv·ester [–v–] m ∼s/∼ *New Year's Eve*

Sym- → a. Wörter im I. Teil des Wörterbuchs **∼bi·ose** f ∼/ *symbiosis* **∼b·ol** n ∼(e)s/∼e *symbol;* ⟨comp⟩ *character* || ∼ s f ⟨a.⟩ *to stand for* | ∼ik [f] ∼/∼en *symbolism;* ≃isch [a] *symbolic(al);* ∼e Handlung *token* (als .. v, f *in t. of*); ∼e Programmierung mit Buchstaben ⟨comp⟩ *mnemonic* | [adv *symbolically*]; ∼ darstellen *to represent;* ≃is·ieren [vt/i] *to symbolize* **∼me·tr·ie** f ∼/ *symmetry* ≃**m·etrisch** a *symmetric(al)* [adv *symmetriecally*]; ⟨bot⟩ radiär ∼ *regular (flower)* **∼path·ie** f ∼/∼n *sympathy; liking; attractiveness* || ∼ erwecken bei *to arouse sympathetic feelings in* || jds ∼ gewinnen *to win a p's s.* | ∼streik [m] *sympathetic strike* **∼p·ath·ikus** m ∼/–ka ⟨anat⟩ *sympathetic nerve* ≃**p·athisch** a *sympathetic (expression)* || (jdm) ∼ s *to be attractive, congenial (to a p), pleasant, to have a p.t personality* || er (das) ist mir ∼ *I like him, (that appeals to me);* .. sehr ∼ *I have a great affection for him* ≃**pathis·ieren** vi [h] (mit) *to sympathize (with), to feel (for)* **∼phon·ie** f ∼/∼n *symphony* **∼pt·om** n ∼(e)s/∼e *symptom;* objektives ∼ ⟨med⟩ *sign* || Lehre v den ∼en *semeiotics* pl | ≃·atisch [a] (für) *symptomatic (of); organic* (Psychose) || ∼engruppe [f] ⟨path⟩ *syndrome;* ≃los [a] *silent (stone,* etc)

Syn- → a. Wörter im I. Teil des Wörterbuchs **∼ag·oge** f ∼/∼n *synagogue* **∼·apse** f ∼/∼n ⟨biol⟩ *synapse* **∼är·ese** f ∼/∼n ⟨gram⟩ *synaeresis* ≃**-chr·on** [–kr–] a *synchronous* | ≃blitz [m] *synchroflash;* ≃getriebe [n] ⟨mot⟩ *synchromesh gear;* ∼chronisati·onsspur [f] ⟨comp⟩ *timing track;* ∼chronis·ator [m ∼s/–·oren] *synchronizer;* ∼chronis·iervorrichtung [f] *magslip* ||≃-is·ieren [vt h] ⟨film⟩ *to synchronize* | ∼isiert [a] *dubbed (film);* ≃is·ierung [f] ∼/∼en *synchronization;* ≃·ismus [m] ∼/–men *synchronism;* ∼·istisch [a] *synchronous;* ≃schwimmen [n] ⟨sport⟩ *coordinated group swimming* **∼chrotr·on** n ∼s/–·onen ⟨at phys⟩ (Elektronen-Teilchen-Beschleunigungsmaschine) *synchrotron* **∼dik·at** n ∼(e)s/∼e *syndicate, combine, trust* **∼dikus** m ∼/–diken & –dizi *syndic; corporation lawyer* **∼ekdoch·e** [f] *syn·ecdoche (e.g. 50 sail = 50 ships)* **∼klin·ale** f ∼/∼n ⟨geol⟩ *syncline* **∼k·ope** f ∼/∼n ⟨gram, mus, med⟩ *syncope* || ⟨med⟩ *fainting-fit* || *syncope* | ∼nmusik [f] ⟨sl a.⟩ *ragtime* ≃**kop·ieren** vt [h] ⟨mus⟩ *to syncopate* ≃**k·opisch** a *syncopated* **∼kr·etiker** m ∼s/∼ *syncretist* **∼od·al..** [in comp] *synodal (order, decision)* **∼·ode** f ∼/∼n *synod* (zu *of*) ≃**·odisch** a ⟨astr⟩ *synodical* **∼on·ym** n [∼(e)s/∼e & –·onyma] *synonym(ous word)* || *close; a s. for shut,* so: *bold, brave, reckless,* etc | ≃(isch) [a] *synonymous;* ≃isches Wörterbuch *dictionary of synonyms;* ∼ik [f] ∼/∼en *synonymy; study of* (bzw *book on*) *synonyms* **∼·optiker** m ∼s/∼ *synoptic, synoptist* **∼taktik** f (Syntaxforschung) → *syntactics* [a. sg konstr] ≃**t·aktisch** a *syntactic* [adv *-ally*]; ∼es System ⟨commun⟩ *s.al system* **∼tax** f ∼/∼en ⟨gram⟩ *syntax* **∼th·ese, ∼thesis** f [∼/–th·esen) *synthesis* **∼th·etiks** pl *synthetics* pl ≃**th·etisch** a *synthetic(al)* [adv *-ally*]; *reconstructed (ruby)* **∼thetis·ieren** vt [h] *to put .. together*

S·yphilis f ∼/ ⟨path⟩ *syphilis* **Syphil·itiker** m ∼s/∼ *syphilitic patient* **syphil·itisch** a *syphilitic*

Syrak·us n (Stadt auf Sizilien) *Syracuse*

S·yrien n *Syria* **S·yrier(in f)** m, **s·yrisch** a *Syrian*

Syringe f ∼/∼n ⟨bot⟩ *lilac*

S·yrte f, die Große (Kleine) ∼ (zwei Buchten der nordafrik. Küste) *the Great(er) (Lesser* od *Little) Syrtis; the Gulf of Sidra* bzw. *Gabès*

Syst·em n ∼(e)s/∼e *system* ⟨a. pol⟩ || *doctrine* || *school setup (press s.)* || ⟨biol⟩ *(natural) order* || ⟨pol⟩ das jeweilige ∼ *the establishment* || ⟨com, etc⟩ *plan (instalment p.)* || *(is this hotel European or American plan?* nach welchem ∼ wird es geführt?) || ⟨anat⟩ *tract (digestive t.)* || in der S liegt ∼ *there is method in it* || in ein ∼ bringen *to systematize* || nach e–m ∼ arbeiten *to operate a s.* **∼analyse** f *system analysis* **∼·atik** f *systematism* | ⟨scient⟩ (Methode) *systematics* [a. sg konstr] | ⟨bot, zoo⟩ *taxonomy* **∼·atiker** m ∼s/∼ *systematizer,* ⟨allg⟩ *systematic p* ≃**·atisch** a *systematic* [adv *-ally*], *methodical* ≃**atis·ieren** vt [h] *to systematize* **∼berater** m, **∼planer** m ⟨comp⟩ *system engineer* **∼programmierung** f ⟨cyb, comp⟩ *system programming* **∼zwang** m ⟨phil⟩ *levelling*

Sz·egedin [s–] n (Stadt in Ungarn) *Szeged*

Sz·ene f ∼/∼n, ⟨film⟩ *sequence; shot* || lärmende ∼ *commotion* | ungeheuerliche ∼ ⟨übtr⟩ *outrage* || e–e gr ∼ m *to make a song and a dance* || (jdm) e–e ∼ m *to make a sc., to carry on* || **auf** offener ∼ *during the act* || **hinter** der ∼ *behind the scene, off-stage;* ⟨Am⟩ *backstage* || **in** ∼ gehen *to be staged* || in ∼ setzen *to get up, to mount, to (put on the) stage* || ⟨fig⟩ *to start* || sich in ∼ setzen *to show off* **∼naufnahme** f ⟨film⟩ *take* **∼nbuch** n ⟨film⟩ *studio continuity sheet* **∼nfolge** f ⟨theat⟩ *running order* **∼nwechsel** m *shifting of scenes, change of scene* **~r·ie** f ~/~n *scenery,* ⟨übtr Lit⟩ *setting* **sz·enisch** a *scenic* [adv *-ally*]

Sz·epter n ~s/~ [österr] *sceptre, mace* ‖ ⟨fig⟩ das ~ führen *to do all the commanding*

Szetschwan n (Prov. Chinas) *Szechwan*

Sz·ylla f ~/ zw ~ u Charybdis *between the devil and the deep sea; between hell and high water* ‖ ⟨myth⟩ *Scylla*; → Skylla

†**Szythe** m, **sz·ytisch** s *Scythian*

T

T, t n ~/~ *T, t* ‖ ⟨telph⟩ *toc* **T-Antenne** f *T-antenna* **T-Dose** f ⟨el⟩ *branch-T* **T-Eisen** n *T-girder, tee-iron* **T-Klemme** f *tee-joint,* ⟨Am⟩ *Y-joint* **T-Schiene** f *T-rail* **T-Stoß** m ⟨welding⟩ *T-joint* **T-Stück** n *T(-piece)* **T-träger** m *T-iron* **T-Winkel** m *T-square*

Tabag·ie [–'ʒiː] f ~/~n [–'ʒiːən] ⟨obs⟩ *smoking-den* **T·abak** m ~(e)s/~e **1.** *tobacco* ‖ ⟨fam⟩ *baccy* ‖ pl *kinds of t.* ‖ leichter, schwerer ~ *mild, strong t.* ‖ ~ u Zigarettenpapier *makings* ‖ (Schnupf~) *snuff* ‖ Virginia~ *common t.* ‖ e–e Pfeife ~ *a pipeful of t.* ‖ ~ kauen (rauchen) *to chew (smoke) t.*; ~ schnupfen *to take snuff* **2.** ⟨fam fig⟩ das ist aber starker ~ *that's rather too strong; that's too much of a good th* **~asche** f *t.-ashes* pl **~bau** m *t.-growing, cultivation of t.* **~beize** f *sauce casing* **~blatt** n *t.-leaf* **~büchse** f *t.-canister* **~geruch** m *t.-smell* **~geschäft** n *t.nist business* **~handel** m *t. trade* **~händler** m *t.nist, t.-dealer* **~handlung** f, **~laden** m *t.-shop* **~kasten** m *t.-jar* **~monopol** n *t.-monopoly* **~pflanzung** f *t.-plantation* **~qualm** m, **~rauch** m *t.-smoke* od *-cloud* **~raucher** m *smoker* **~regie** f *government monopoly of t.* **~reibe** f *snuff-rasp* **~schnupfer** m *snuff-taker* **~spinner** m *t.-dresser* **~steuer** f *duty on t.* ×**~verschleiß** m *t.-shop* **~waren** f pl *cigars, cigarettes, tobacco*; ⟨fam⟩ *smokes* pl; (Firmenschild) *Tobacconist* **~zoll** m *duty (paid) on t.* **T·abaks- ~beutel** m *tobacco-pouch* **~dose** f (Schnupf~) *snuff-box, t.-box* **~kollegium** n ⟨hist⟩ *smoking-club* **~pfeife** f *pipe* **~rolle** f *tobacco-roll* **Tabatiere** [–'tjɛːrə] f ~/~n *snuff-box*

tabell·arisch a *in tables, tabulated, tabular* ‖ ~es Verzeichnis *schedule* | [adv] *in tabular form* **tabellaris·ieren** vt [h] *to tabulate* **Tab·elle** f ~/~n *table, schedule, tabulation, scroll, graph, diagram, chart (health-ch.)*; (Zahlen~ etc ⟨a.⟩) *synopsis* ‖ (Inhaltsverzeichnis) *index* ‖ Rechen~ *ready reckoner* ‖ in ~n anordnen, in e–e ~ aufnehmen etc *to tabulate, index* **~nförmig** a *tabular* **~nkopf** m *heading* **~nlesen** n ⟨comp⟩ *(table) look-up* **~nsatz** m ⟨typ⟩ *table-work* **~nwerk** n *tabular compilation* **tab·ell·ieren** vt [h] *to tabulate* ⟨a. comp⟩; –rte Listen [pl] ⟨comp⟩ *printed output* **Tabell·iermaschine** f *tabulator* ⟨a. comp⟩ **Tabern·akel** n ~s/~ *tabernacle* †**Tab·erne** f ~/~n *tavern* **Tabl·ar** n ~s/~e Sw *rack-board* **Tableau** [ta'bloː] n ~s/~s *tableau* ‖ ~! *tableau!* | ~vorhang [m] ⟨theat⟩ *blackout* **Table d'hôte** ['tabl 'doːt] f ~/~ *table d'hôte, ordinary* **Tabl·ett** n ~(e)s/~e *tray, salver, waiter* **Tabl·ette** f ~/~n *tablet, tabloid, lozenge*

tab·u 1. a *taboo* **2.** ~ n *taboo, anathema*

tabula rasa L machen *to make a clean sweep* (mit *of*) **Tabul·ator** m ~s/–'oren *tabulator* | ⟨comp⟩ ~sprung [m] *skip stop*; ~e pl *column skipping* **Tabulat·ur** f ~/~en ⟨mus⟩ *tablature* | ~taste [f] ⟨typwr⟩ *tabular key* **Tabul·ett** n ~(e)s/~e *pedlar's box* ‖ (Brett) *shelf* **~kram** m *pedlar's ware*

Tabur·ett n ~(e)s/~e *tabouret, (low) stool*

Tacho(m·eter) n ⟨tech, mot⟩ *speedometer,* ⟨sl⟩ *tac* **T·achy- ~graph·ie** f *tachygraphy, shorthand* **~kard·ie** f ⟨med⟩ *tachycardia*

t·ack-t·ack [intj], ~-~ n (M.-G.-Feuer) *ack-ack*

Tadd·edl, Tadd·ädl m ~s/~ [österr] → Weichling

T·adel m ~s/~ **1.** *blame, censure, reproach, reproof; critism*; ⟨school⟩ *bad mark* ‖ e–n ~ einstecken *to take a rebuke* ‖ jdm e–n ~ (Verweis) erteilen *to give a p a reprimand* ‖ ihn trifft kein ~ *he is not to be blamed* ‖ sich (jds) ~ zuziehen *to incur (a p's) condemnation, to get blamed (by)* **2.** (Fehl) **ohne** ~ *blameless; faultless; spotless (life)* ‖ ⟨hist⟩ (Ritter) ohne Furcht u ~ *without fear or reproach* **~frei, ~los** a *faultless, blameless* | *irreproachable, unexceptionable* | ⟨com⟩ *perfect, immaculate; flawless* ‖ ⟨fam⟩ *perfect, splendid* ‖ ein (ganz) -loser Kerl ⟨fam⟩ *a thoroughly good sort,* ⟨sl⟩ *a (regular) brick* | adv ~ rein *spotless clean*; sich ~ benehmen *to behave very well*; sich ~ kleiden *to dress spotlessly*; sich ~ unterhalten *to enjoy o.s. immensely* **~losigkeit** f *blamelessness,* etc **~sucht** f *censoriousness, censorious* od *fault-finding spirit* **t·adelhaft** a *faulty, blameworthy, censurable, blamable, reprehensible, objectionable* | [pred] *in fault* **Tadel·ei** f ~/~en *(constant) nagging, faultfinding* **t·adeln** vt [h] *to find fault with; to take exception to; to blame, censure, reprove* (wegen *for*) ‖ jdn ~ ⟨fam⟩ *to rap a p's knuckles* od *finger*; .. strenge .. *to haul a p over the coals*; ⟨Am⟩ *to call down*; .. wegen etw *to pull a p up for a th* ‖ an allem etw zu ~ finden *to find fault with everything*; → kritisieren **~d** *faultfinding, censorious (p), reproachful (look)* **t·adelns- ~wert, ~würdig** a = tadelhaft **T·adelsantrag** m ⟨parl⟩ *motion for censure* (stellen *to table a m. of c.*) **T·adler(in** f) m ~s/~ *fault-finder, censurer, carper*

T·afel f ~/~n **1.** *table, large board* ‖ (Platte) *plate,* (dünne) *slab* ‖ ⟨geog⟩ *plateau* | **Abfahrt~** *indicator* ‖ Anschlag~ *poster, hoarding,* ⟨Am⟩ *bill board* ‖ (Blech~) *sheet* ‖ (Brücken~) *panel* ‖ Gedenk~ *memorial t.t* ‖ (Glas~) *pane* ‖ ⟨com⟩ (Laden~) *counter* ‖ **(Leim~)** *bar* ‖ ⟨math⟩ *t.* ‖ Schalt~ *switchb.* ‖ (Schalter~) ⟨com, etc⟩ *counter* ‖ (Schau~) *diagram, graph* ‖ Schiefer~ *slate* ‖ (Schokolade) (⟨Ger⟩ 100 g, ⟨engl⟩ 57 g) *block* od *slab (of ch.)* gr *cake,* kl *bar* ‖ Schul~ *blackb.* ‖ ⟨mil⟩ **Schuß~** *range t.* ‖ Steigungs~ *gradient b.* ‖ (Stein~) *slab* ‖ (Tabelle) *diagram* ‖ ⟨typ⟩ *plate* ‖ Warnungs~ *notice-b.* **2. (Tisch)** *dinner-t.*; gedeckt *b.*; *t. set for the banquet*; gr (Hof-)~ *gala dinner, banquet* | die ~ aufheben *to make a move* ‖ offene ~ halten *to keep open t.* | **an** der ~ der Fürsten speisen *to dine with the gods* | **bei** ~ *at t., at* od *during dinner* | **zur** ~ heranziehen *to invite to dinner* ‖ ⟨engl univ⟩ (~ der *fellows*) *High T.* **~aufsatz** m *centre-piece* **~bai** f *T. Bay (near Cape of Good Hope)* **~berg** m *t. mountain* ‖ *tabular iceberg* **~besteck** n *knife, fork, and spoon* **~bier** n *dinner-ale, t.-beer* **~birne** f *dessert-pear* **~blei** n *sheet-lead* **~brötchen** n *dinner-roll* **~butter** f ⟨com⟩ *best fresh butter* **~decken** n *laying the t.* **~diener** m *footman* **~felsen** m *t.-rock* **~fertig** a *ready-to-serve* **~förmig** a *tabular* **~freuden** f pl *pleasures* pl *of the t.* **~freund** m *epicure* **~gedeck** n *t.-linen* **~gelder** n pl *t.-money* **~gemälde** n = –malerei **~geschirr** n *t.-plate, t.-, dinner-service*; *t.ware, crockery*; *t. utensils*; (silbernes) *silver*

~glas n *sheet-glass* || (Spiegelglas) *plate-glass* **~klavier** n *square piano* **~land** n *plateau, t.land* **~malerei** f *panel-, wood-painting* **~musik** f *dinner music* **~obst** n *fresh-fruit dessert* **~öl** n *salad-oil* **~runde** f *dinner guests* pl || (Artussage) (*King Arthur's*) *Round T.* **~salz** n *t. salt* **~schere** f *plate shears* pl **~schiefer** m *slate* **~service** n *dinner set* (*china*) **~tuch** n *t.cloth* **~waage** f *weighing machine* **~wagen** m *lorry, dray* **~werk** n *wainscoting* **~wein** m *dinner wine* **~zeug** n *t. linen, setting* **T·äfelchen** n ~s/~ *tablet*, etc → Tafel **t·afeln** vi [h] *to sit at table*; *to dine, banquet* || gern ~ *to be fond of the pleasures of the t.* **t·äfeln** vt [h] *to board, panel, wainscot* || (Fußboden) *to inlay, to floor* **T·äfelung** f ~/; **T·afelwerk** n ~s/ *panelling* etc (→ vor.)

T·aferlklasse f ⟨österr school⟩ = Elementarklasse

T·af(fe)t m ~(e)s/~e *taffeta* **~band** n *sarcenet ribbon* **t·af(fe)ten** a *made of taffeta*

Tag m ~(e)s/~e **A.** *day* || *date* (*publication d.*) || (*day*)*light* || ⟨min⟩ *surface* | 14 ~e *a fortnight*, ⟨Am⟩ *two weeks* || der ~ des Herrn *the Lord's Day* || ~ des Waldes ⟨Am⟩ *Arbor Day* || der Tag vor (nach) der Schlacht *the eve* (*morrow*) *of the b.* || das Ende aller ~e *the end of the world* || verschieden wie ~ u Nacht *different as chalk from cheese* || ⟨sex⟩ ihre ~e → Regel; ⟨vulg⟩ *the curse, Holy Week*; sie hat ihre ~e *she's got the painters in*; ich habe zweimal m–e ~e nicht gehabt *this is my second no go* **B.** (**grau** *dismal*, heiter *sunny*, herrlich *grand*, schön *fine*, trübe *dull, dreary*) | ein **denkwürdiger** ~ *a red letter day* || sich e–n freien ~ m *to take a holiday* (→ Ausgang D.) || die friedlichen ~e *the halcyon days* (*are over*) || e–n ganzen ~ fernbleiben *to make a day of it* || den geschlagenen ~ schlafen *to sleep the clock round* || ein gr ~ *a field-day*; sein gr ~ *his day of days* || **guten** ~ sagen *to say how do you do*, ⟨a.⟩ *to pass the time of day* (jdm *to a p*); 'n Tag! *How'd do?*, *Hello!* || gute ~e h *to have a fine time of it* || s–n (k–n) guten ~ h *to be in a good mood* (⟨a.⟩ *not to be at one's best*) || sich e–n g. ~ m *to take a holiday, to enjoy o.s.*, ⟨fam⟩ *to make a day of it*; [pl] *to enjoy life* || der **jüngste** ~ *the Day of Judgment*; ⟨a.⟩ *Doomsday* || ⟨prov⟩ auch der **längste** ~ hat sein Ende *it is a long lane that has no turning* || strahlend schöner Tag! *grand weather, isn't it?* **C.** s–e ~e **beschließen** (= sterben) *to close* od *end one's days*; *to pay the debt of nature* | jeder ~ **hat** s–e Plag' *each day brings its trouble* || einmal kommt der ~, wenn *the day will dawn when*; er kam den ganzen ~ nicht zurück *he didn't come back until late at night* || e–n ~ z spät k *to come the day after the fair* || er lebt k–n ~ mehr ⟨a.⟩ *his life is not worth a day's purchase* || man soll den ~ nicht vor dem Abend **loben** *don't halloo until you are out of the wood* || solange es noch ~ **ist** *before the day ends* || es **ist noch nicht** aller ~e Abend *there is always tomorrow, there is many a slip twixt the cup and the lip* || was ist heute f ein ~? *what's to-day?* || den ~ totschlagen *to beguile the time* || verschieden wie ~ u Nacht *different as midnight from noon* || dem lieben Gott den ~ wegstehlen *to waste one's time* || es **wird** ~ *day is breaking* || ⟨fig fam⟩ jetzt wird's ~! *well, I never!* **D.** [**gen**] **e-s** (schönen) **~es** *once*; *one day*, (Zukunft) *some day* (*eventually* od *or other*); *one fine morning* od *day*; *some of these days*; *in due time*; *sooner or later*; dieser ~e *lately*, (Zukunft) *shortly, soon, one of these days* || zweimal des ~es *twice a day* **E.** [**acc**] **alle ~e** *every day*; all' mein' ~e *in all my life* || (ganze) ~e lang *for whole days* || den ganzen ~ (über) *all day* (*long*); gestern den g. ~ *the whole of y.*; *throughout y.* || den geschlagenen ~ *the livelong day* || er sieht keinen ~ älter aus als 35 *he doesn't look thirty-five if he is a day* || den lieben langen Tag *as the day is long* || mehrere ~e *for several days* || e–n um den andern ~ *every other day, on alternate days* || ~ u Nacht hatte er k–e Ruhe *he couldn't rest by d. and n.* **F. am** ~e *during the daytime* || früh am ~e *early in the day* || am hell(icht)en ~ *in broad daylight* || am ~ danach *the day after* || **an** den ~ bringen *to bring to light*; *to get .. right out in the open* || es kommt alles an den ~ *everything comes to light at last* || an den ~ legen *to show, exhibit, disclose, evince, expose*; *to betray*; *to give evidence of* | genau **auf** den ~ .. (*50 years after*) *to a day* || auf s–e alten ~e *in his old days* | **bei** ~e *in the day-time, in* od *by daylight* | **bis** auf den heutigen ~ *to this day*; von da an .. *from that day to this* || bis in den hellen ~ *well into the day* || bis z Jüngsten ~ *till doomsday* || ×bis die Tage denn! *hope to see you again!* | ~ **für** ~ *d. by* od *after d.* | **in** s–n alten ~en *in his later days* || **in** diesen (unseren) ~en *nowadays* || in m–n ~en *in my time* || in wenigen ~en *in a few days* || in 14 ~en *in a fortnight*(*'s time*); in 8 ~en spricht kein Mensch mehr davon *it's all the same in a hundred years* || in guten u bösen ~en *for better for worse*; *through good and evil* || in den ~ hinein leben (reden) *to live in a happy way*; *to live at random*, (*to talk at large*) | mit jedem ~ *day by day* | ⟨min⟩ **über** ~e *above ground* || heute über 8, 14 ~e *to-day week, fortnight* | ⟨min⟩ **unter** ~e *underground*, .. gehen *to descend the shaft*; .. gewonnen *deep-mined* (*coal*) | **von** ~ zu ~ *with each day, from d. to d.* | **vor** 14 ~en *a fortnight ago* || ⟨min⟩ zu ~e ausgehen *or* treten *to crop out* || z ~e fördern *to unearth* || ⟨fig⟩ z ~e liegen *to be naked, manifest, to stand revealed* || → **zutage** **T·ag- ~-Abfangjäger** m ⟨aero⟩ *interceptor day fighter* **~angriff** m ⟨aero⟩ *daylight raid* **~arbeit** f *day-labour* **~·aus, ~·ein** [adv] *day by* od *after day, from day to day*; *daily, everyday* **~bau, ~blatt** → Tage.. **~blindheit** f *day-blindness*; *nyctalopia* **~bogen** m ⟨astr⟩ *diurnal arc* **~bombenangriff** m *day-time bombing raid* **~bomber** m ⟨aero⟩ *day bomber* **~dienst** m *day-service* **~falter** m *butterfly* **~hell** a *with the full light of the day* || ⟨fig⟩ (*as*) *light as day* **~j·agd** f *day interception* **~jagdgeschwader** n *fighter day wing* N **~jäger** m ⟨aero⟩ *day-fighter* **~pfauenauge** n ⟨ent⟩ *vanessa*; *peacock butterfly* **~scheu** a *shunning daylight* **~schicht** f *day-shift, -turn* **~schule** f *day-school* **~sichtigkeit** f *nightblindness* **~t·äglich** [adv] *every mortal day* **~traum** m *day-dream* | gleichzeitiger ~ **u Nacht Eindruck** ⟨a–n⟩ *day-and-night-together effect* **~- u Nachtgleiche** f *equinox* **~wasser** n *surface water* **T·age- ~arbeit** f *day's work* | ~er [m] ⟨min⟩ *surfaceman* **~bau** m ⟨min⟩ *open work*(*ing*); *open mining* od *pit* | ~- *open-cast, -pit* (⟨Am⟩ *-cut*) (*system, mining*) **~blatt** n *daily* (*paper*) **~buch** n *journal, diary*; ⟨com⟩ *daybook*; ⟨mar⟩ *log*, ⟨aero⟩ *air-log* || (ein) ~ führen *to keep a diary* **~dieb** m ⟨fig⟩ *idler, loiterer, time-waster*; ⟨fam⟩ *lazy-bones* **~geld**(**er** pl) n *daily allowance* **~lang** [adv] *for days* (*together*) **~lied** n ⟨Lit⟩ *morning-song, alba* **~lohn** m *day's wages* pl | ~arbeit [f] *chare*, ⟨Am⟩ *chore* **~löhner**(**in** f) m *day-labourer*, ⟨agr Am⟩ *hired man* (*charwoman*) **~löhnern** vi [h] *to work by the day*; *to chare*, ⟨Am⟩ *chore* **~reise** f *day's journey* || nur e–e ~ v E. entfernt *within a day's sail off England* **~weise** [adv] *by the day*; ~ abwechselnd *on alternate days*; *on each alternate day* **~werk** n *day's work*; *routine*; *round of duty* **T·agen** n ~s/ *daybreak* || ⟨poet⟩ *dayspring* **t·agen I.** vi imps [h] *to dawn* || es tagt *the day is breaking*; ⟨fig⟩ *it dawns* (ihm *upon him*) **II.** vi [h] (Tagung abhalten) *to meet* (od ⟨jur⟩ *be in session*), *to sit, deliberate* | ständig ~d *in permanent session*

T·ages- ~anbruch m (bei *at*) *day-break, dawn*;

vor ~ *before daylight* **~anfall** m, **~menge** f *daily (water) flow* **~angabe** f *date* **~arbeit** f *day's work* | ~er [m] ⟨theat⟩ *dayman*, ⟨Am⟩ *full time stage--hand* **~bedarf** m (*daily*) *ration* (an *of*); *daily necessities* pl **~befehl** m *order of the day* ‖ (f alle Dienstgrade) *general* [subst] **~bericht** m *daily report, bulletin* ⟨a. mil⟩ N **~billet** n ⟨obs rail⟩ *day-ticket* **~dienst** m *duty of the day* | ~plan [m] *daily schedule* **~dosis** f *daily dose* **~einflüsse** m pl (*ballistic*) *density and wind* | s–e eigene **~einteilung** m *to arrange one's own day* **~ereignis** n, **~gespräch** n *event/topic of the day* ‖ –ereignisse [pl] *current affairs* pl **~geld** n *call m.* | ~satz [m] *c. m. rate* **~grauen** = –anbruch **~heimstätte** f *day-care centre, center* **~helle** f *light of day* **~karte** f (Bus) *rover ticket* ‖ ⟨cul⟩ *day's bill of fare* **~kasse** f ⟨theat⟩ *box-office* ‖ *takings* pl *of the day* **~kleid** n *round-the-clock dress*; *walking d.*; ⟨fam⟩ *loungees* [sg konstr] **~kopfverbrauch** m *daily per capita consumption* **~kurs** m ⟨com⟩ *current* (*rate of*) *exchange*; *rate* (v Aktien *quotation*) *of the day* (⟨a.⟩ –notierung) ‖ zum ~ *at value* **~lauf** m *daily round* od *routine* **~leistung** f ⟨tech⟩ *daily output* **~licht** n *daylight*; gedämpftes ~ *subdued d.l.* ‖ ans ~ bringen ⟨fig⟩ *to exhume, unearth*; .. k *to come to light, to become known* ‖ bei hellem ~ *in broad d.l.* ‖ das ~ erblicken *to see d.l.*; *to be born*; (S) *to come to l., to transpire*, ⟨Am⟩ *to develop* ‖ er scheut das ~ *he shuns the l. of day* | ~aufnahme [f] *d.l. shot*; ~entwickeln [m] *d.l. developer*; (S) *d.l. developing machine*; ~farbfilm [m] *d.l. type colo(u)r film*; ~kassette [f] ⟨film⟩ *d.l. loading magazine*; ~lampe [f] *d.l. type lamp*; ~papier [n] ⟨phot⟩ *printing-out paper* (*P.O.P.*); ~patrone [f] ⟨phot⟩ *d.l. loading cartridge*; ~spule [f] *d.l.* (*l.g*) *spool* **~mädchen** n ⟨fam⟩ *daily* **~meldung** f *daily report* od *return* **~nachrichten** f pl ⟨wir⟩ *bulletin* **~ordnung** f ⟨parl⟩ *order of the day*; an der ~ s *to be the o. ..*; zur ~ *on a point of o.*; z ~ übergehen *to pass to the o.*; (*No. 5 on*) *the agenda* **~post** f *day's* od *daily mail* **~preis** m *current price* **~presse** f *daily press* **~satz** m *per diem equivalent*; ⟨logist⟩ *one day's supply*; *day of s.* N **~sehen** n *photopic vision* **~stempel** m *date-stamp*; (Gerät) *dater* **~stunde** f *hour of daylight*; die frühen ~n *the small hours* **~suppe** f *soup of the day* **~zeit** f *time of day* ‖ bei guter ~ *early*; zu dieser ~ *at that t. of d.*; zu jeder ~ *at any hour*; zur ~ *in the day-time* ‖ (jdm) die ~ bieten *to pass the t. of d.* **~zeitung** f *daily* (*paper*) **~ziel** n ⟨tact⟩ *day's objective*

t·äglich I. [a] *daily* ‖ ⟨scient⟩ *diurnal* ‖ ~es Geld ⟨com⟩ *call-money* ‖ ⟨com⟩ auf ~e Kündigung *at call* | (alltäglich) *every-day, ordinary* (*life*) **II.** [adv] *every day* ‖ ⟨com⟩ *per diem* ‖ ~ notwendige Dinge *daily necessities* ‖ zweimal ~ *twice a day* **t·ags dar·auf (zuv·or)** [adv] *the following* (*preceding*) *day* **t·ags(über)** [adv] *in the day-time* **T·agung** f ~/~en *meeting*, ⟨parl⟩ *session* ‖ *congress*; *conference*; *symposium*; ⟨Am⟩ *convention* ‖ ⟨sport⟩ *rally* ‖ ⟨pol⟩ *gathering* | ~steilnehmer [m] *conferee*

Tah·iti n (größte der Gesellschaftsinseln)

Taif·un m ~s/~e (Chin. Gr Wind) *typhoon*

T·aiga f ~/ (gr Nadelwälder Sibiriens) *taiga*

T·aijüanf·u n (chines. Stadt) *Taiyüanfu*

Taille ['taljə] f ~/~n; ⟨tail⟩ *waist*; *bodice* ‖ jdn um die ~ fassen *to put one's arm round a p's w.* | ~̈nfrei [a] (nabelfrei) ⟨fam⟩ *peek-a-boo* (*dress*)

T·ajo m (Fluß der Pyrenäenhalbinsel) *Tagus*

T·akel n ~s/~ ⟨mar⟩ *tackle* **~boden** m *rigging-loft* **Takelage** [takə'lɑːʒə] f ~/~n; **T·akelung** f ~/~en; **T·akelwerk** n ⟨mar⟩ *tackling, rigging*; *tackle* **t·akeln** vt [h] *to tackle, rig*

Takt m ~(e)s/~e **A. 1.** ⟨mus⟩ *time, measure* ‖ ¾-~ *three-four time* ‖ (Abteilung) *bar* (*in the middle of the bar*) **2.** ⟨mach⟩ *stroke* (*four-stroke engine*) **3.** ⟨fig⟩ (Feingefühl) *tact*; *delicacy and consideration*; *address*; *good feeling* **B.** den ~ **angeben** *to give the time*, ⟨fig⟩ *to lead* ‖ ⟨fig⟩ ~ h *to have great tact*, etc (→ A. 3) ‖ ~ halten *to keep time* ([b. Rudern] *stroke*) ‖ den ~ schlagen *to beat* (*the*) *time* ‖ mit dem Fuß den ~ zur Musik treten *to tap one's f. to the rhythm of the m.* | **aus** dem ~ bringen, [k] *to put*, [*get*] *out of time*, ⟨fig⟩ *to* [*be*] *disconcern*[*ed*] | **im** ~ marschieren *to march in time*; *to keep step* ‖ im ~ tanzen *to keep good time* **~art** f *time, measure* **~̈fest** a *keeping good time*; ⟨fig⟩ *firm, strong, fit*; ⟨hum⟩ *sober* | ~̈igkeit [f] *steadiness in keeping time*; ⟨fig⟩ *firmness, mastery* **~frequenz** f: ~ 1 MHz *1.000.000 cycles a second* (= *a megacycle*) **~geber** m ⟨comp⟩ = Zeit– **~gefühl** n *tact* (f *of*) **~generator** m ⟨comp⟩ *pulse g., computer clock* **~̈los** a *tactless, injudicious, indelicate, indiscreet*, (*in*) *bad taste* ‖ *ill-judged* (*action*); (P) *gauche* Fr **~losigkeit** f *tactlessness, indiscretion, injudiciousness, lack of tact* od *delicacy, indelicacy*; *solecism* ‖ e–e ~ begehen *to make a bad faux pas, bloomer* ‖ e–e plumpe ~ begehen ⟨a.⟩ *to blunder badly* **~̈mäßig** a ⟨mus⟩ *well-timed, rhythmical* **~messer** m ⟨mus⟩ *metronome* **~note** f ⟨mus⟩ *semibreve* **~pause** f *bar-rest* **~schlag** m *beat* **~stock** m *baton* **~strich** m ⟨mus⟩ *bar* **~teil** m *division of the bar* **~̈voll** a *tactful, diplomatic, judicious, discreet, delicate* (*mind*), (*man*) *of tact* etc **~vorzeichnung** f *time-signature* **~zeit** f ⟨comp⟩ *cycle time* **Takt·ier- ~stab, ~stock** m *baton* **takt·ieren** vi [h] ⟨mus⟩ *to beat* (*the*) *time*

T·aktik f ~/~en ⟨mil⟩ *tactics* pl [a. sg konstr] ‖ e–e kluge ~ *a clever stroke of t.* ‖ ⟨fig a.⟩ *fencing* ‖ ⟨pol⟩ *politics* **~er** m ~s/~ *tactician* **t·aktisch** a ⟨mil⟩ *tactical* (*unit*) ‖ ~e Annahme *assumed tactics* ‖ ~e Aufgabe *problem* ‖ ~e Führung, ~e Unterstellung [f] *operational control* ‖ ~e Luftflotte (*numbered*) *tactical air force* | adv ~ wichtig *tactical* (Gelände)

Tal n ~(e)s/~̈er *valley* ‖ ⟨poet a.⟩ *vale* ‖ (breites Fluß~̈) ⟨Scot⟩ *strath* ‖ (enges) *dingle*; *glen* ‖ (kl) *dale* ‖ (tief eingeschnittenes) *deep-, steep-sided valley*; *canyon* | **zu** ~(e) *down*(*ward*); (stromabwärts) (fahren *to go*) *down-stream* **~̈·abwärts** [adv] *down-stream, -hill* **~̈·aufwärts** [adv] *up the valley*; *up-stream* **~̈·aus** [adv] *out of the v.* **~brücke** f *viaduct* **~̈·ein** [adv] *entering the v.* **~enge** f *narrow part of a v.* **~fahrt** f **1.** ⟨mot, etc⟩ *descent* **2.** *downstream voyage* **3.** *d. navigation* **~kessel** m *basin* **~mulde, ~senke** f *coomb* **~schlucht** f *glen* **~see** m *finger lake* **~sohle** f *valley floor* **~sperre** m *barrage, river dam*; *catchment basin* **~weg** m *road through a v.* **~wind** m *upslope wind, v. breeze*

Tal·ar m ~(e)s/~e ⟨jur⟩ *robe* ‖ ⟨ec, school, univ⟩ *gown*

Tal·ent n ~(e)s/~e **1.** ⟨ant-num⟩ *talent* **2.** (Begabung) *talent*; *gift, aptitude* (zu *for*) ‖ ~ h *to be talented, gifted* (*with a th*); ~ zur Schauspielerin h *to have the t. to be* od *become an actress* ‖ gesellige ~e [pl] *accomplishments* pl **~̈los** a *untalented* **~̈voll** a (sehr *highly*) *accomplished, gifted, talented*

T·aler m ~s/~ *thaler, three-mark piece* ‖ ⟨fig⟩ *sum of money* ‖ blanke ~ [pl] *hard coins* pl

Talg m ~(e)s/ *tallow, suet* **~drüse** f ⟨anat⟩ *sebaceous gland* **~licht** n *tallow-candle* **~säure** f *stearic acid* **~stoff** m *stearin*(*e*) **t·algen I.** a (*of*) *tallow* **II.** vt *to grease* **III.** vi *to yield tallow* ‖ ⟨cul⟩ *to become covered with t.* **t·algig** a *tallowy, tallowish, suety*

T·alisman m ~(e)s/~e *talisman*; *mascot*

T·alje f ~/~n ⟨mar⟩ (*long-*)*tackle* **~reep** n ⟨mar⟩ *lanyard* **t·aljen** vt [h] ⟨mar⟩ *to hoist*

Talk m ~(e)s/~e ⟨min⟩ *talc*(*um*) **~̈artig** a *talcky*, ⟨scient⟩ *talcous* **~erde** f *magnesia* **~spat** m *magnesite* **~stein** m *talc, soap-stone*

T·alkum n -s *talcum powder*

T·almi n ~s/ *talmi* ‖ ⟨fig⟩ *pinchbeck, sham,* ⟨Am sl⟩ *gold-brick* | [in comp] ⟨Am⟩ *phon(e)y* [a] **talm·udisch** a *Talmudical*

Talon [ta'lɔŋ, ta'lɔ̃:] m ~s/~s ⟨com⟩ *counterfoil;* ⟨Am⟩ *stub* (*of a cheque-book*); *dividend warrant* ‖ (im Spiel) *talon*

Tamar·inde f ~/~n ⟨bot⟩ *tamarind(-tree)* **~nfrucht** f *t.* **~nmark** n *pulp of the t.*

Tamar·iske f ~/~n ⟨bot⟩ *tamarisk*

T·ambour ['–bu:r] m ~s/~e **1.** *drum* **2.** *drummer* **3.** ⟨arch, tech⟩ *tambour* **~major** m *drum-major* **~·ier-** ~nadel [f] *t.-needle*; ~rahmen [m] *t.* **Tambur·in** n ~(e)s/~e *t.ine, timbrel* **~schläger(in** f) m *player on the t.ine* **~stich** m *t.-stitch*

Tam·ilen, Tam·ulen m pl (drawidischer Stamm im südl. Dekkan; Vorderindien) *Tamul*

T·amp(e f) m ⟨mar⟩ *rope's end*

Tamp·on [tam'pɔ̃:] m ~s/~s ⟨surg⟩ *plug* **≈·ieren** [tampo'ni:rən] vt [h] *to plug*

Tamt·am n ~s/~s *tom-tom* ‖ ⟨fig⟩ ~ m *or* schlagen *to make a great fuss, to-do, noise*; ⟨com⟩ *to boom* → Reklame, Klamauk

Tand m ~(e)s/ *frills,* (*k*)*nick-*(*k*)*nacks* pl, *trumpery, trifles, baubles* pl; ⟨fam⟩ *doodad; gewgaw* ‖ *toys, playthings* pl ‖ irdischer ~ *earthly pomp* **Tändel·ei** f ~/~en *trifling, dallying, toying* ‖ ⟨fig⟩ *flirt(ing), flirtation,* ⟨fam⟩ *spooning* **t·ändelhaft, t·ändelig** a *trifling, dallying, playful* ‖ *frivolous* **T·ändel-** **~markt** m *rag-fair* **~schürze** f *fancy apron* **t·ändeln** vi [h] *to trifle, fribble, dally, toy* ‖ (herum~) *to fiddle-faddle; to fiddle* (mit *with a th*); *to potter* ⟨fam⟩ *fool about* ‖ ⟨fig⟩ *to flirt* **T·ändler** m ~s/~ (⟨a.⟩ Tandler = Trödler) | *trifler, dawdler*; ⟨fig⟩ *flirt* [a. f]

T·andem n ~s/~ ⟨hors, cycl⟩ *tandem* | ~-(bomben)träger [m] *t. rack*

Tang m ~(e)s/~e ⟨bot⟩ *seaweed,* ⟨scient⟩ *fucus* **~asche** f *kelp*

Tanganj·ika- ~see [m] (in O.-Afrika) *Lake Tanganyika* **~-Territorium** n *Tanganyika Territory*

Tang·ente f ~/~n ⟨math⟩ *tangent*; ⟨fig⟩ plötzlich in der ~ abspringen, abschweifen *to go* od *fly off at a t.* **Tangenti·al-** [in comp] *tangential* (*movement, force*) | ~wunde [f] *gutter wound* **tang·ieren** vt [h] *to touch* ‖ es ~rt ihn *it concerns him* ‖ das ~rt mich nicht! *what's that to me?*

T·anger n (Hafenstadt in Marokko) *Tangier(s)*

Tank m ~s/~s **1.** *tank* **2.** ⟨fam⟩ = Panzerwagen *tank*; leichter ~ *whippet* **~abwehr** f *anti-t. defence* | ~geschütz [n] *a.-t. gun* **~anhänger** m *tank trailer* **~anlage** f *fuel-storage depot* **~ausweis** m *fuel permit* **~dampfer** m *tanker* **~falle** f *tank trap* **~flugzeug** n *tanker* **~holz** n *producer-gas wood* **~landungsschiff** n *t.-landing craft* **~lager** n *fuel dump*; (*oil*) *storage tank* **~löschfahrzeug** n *fire-extinguishing tanker* **~raum** m *t. space*; ungenutzter ~ *ullage* **~säule** f *petrol-, gas-pump* (*pillar*) **~schalter** m ⟨mot⟩ *selector valve* **~stelle** f ⟨mot⟩ *filling-* ⟨Am⟩ *gas-* od *service--station* | ~nautomat [m] ⟨Am⟩ *gas-a-teria* **~uhr** f *fuel gauge* **~verschluß** m *filler cap* **~-wagen** m *fuel t.er* ⟨bes mot⟩; *cistern* od *t. wagon*; ⟨rail⟩ *t. car* **~wart** m *petrol-pump attendant*; ⟨mil⟩ *fuel point orderly* **t·anken** vt ⟨mot⟩ *to tank, to take in petrol* ‖ ⟨aero⟩ *to fuel* | ⟨fig⟩ (trinken) *to tank up* | voll ~! *fill her up* (*with shell*)! **T·anker** m ~s/~ ⟨mar⟩ *tanker*; Gr ≈ *bulk t.*

Tann m ~s/ *fir-wood* **~apfel** m *fir-cone* **T·anne** f ~/~n *fir(-tree)* ‖ Weiß≈ *silver fir*; Rot≈ *spruce fir* **t·annen** a (*made of*) *fir* **T·annen-** **~baum** m *fir-tree*; *Christmas-tree* **~brett** n *deal board* **~gehölz** n, **~hain** m *fir-grove* **~häher** m ⟨orn⟩ *nutcracker* **~harz** n *resin from fir-trees* **~(harz)-säure** f ⟨chem⟩ *abietic acid* **~holz** n *fir-wood, deal* **~meise** f ⟨orn⟩ *coal-mouse* **~wald** m *fir-wood* **~wedel** m ⟨bot⟩ *mare's tail* **~zapfen** m *fir-cone* **T·annicht** n ~(e)s/~e *thicket of young firs* **t·annig** a *grown with firs*

Tann·in n ~(e)s/ ⟨chem⟩ *tannin, tannic acid*

Tant·al n ~(e)s/ *tantalum* **≈haltig** a *columbiferous* **~säure** f *tantalic acid*

T·antalusqualen f pl *tantalizing torments* ‖ jdm ~ bereiten *to tantalize a p*

T·antchen n ~s/~ *auntie* **T·ante** f ~/~n *aunt* ‖ ~ Meier! *my aunt! aunt Jones*; ⟨Am⟩ *Widow* od *Mrs Jones*

Tantieme [tan'tje:mə] f ~/~n *royalty, percentage, share in profits*

Tanz m ~es/≈e **A. 1.** *dance* **2.** ⟨fig⟩ *row; quarrel* **B.** Gesellschaft ohne ~ *sit-still party* ‖ einen ~ aussetzen *to sit out a dance* ‖ z ~ auffordern *to ask* od *invite to dance* ‖ z ~ aufspielen *to strike up for a dance* ‖ darf ich um e–n ~ bitten? *may I have the pleasure of a dance?* **~abend** m (*evening's*) *dance, dancing-party*; [pl] ⟨Am a.⟩ *danceables* ‖ ⟨theat a.⟩ *ballet; dance* **~bär** m *dancing bear* **~bein** n; das ~ schwingen ⟨fam⟩ *to foot* (⟨sl⟩ *hoof*) *it* ‖ ⟨sl⟩ *to shake a toe* (⟨Am⟩ *hoof*) **~boden** m *d.g-room, ball-room* **~diele** f *d.g-saloon,* ⟨Am⟩ *dance-hall* **~fläche** f *dancing floor* **~gesellschaft** f, **~kränzchen** n *d.g-party,* [pl] ⟨Am a.⟩ *danceables* **~karte** f *memorandum, programme* **~kunst** f (*art of*) *d.g* **~lehrer** n *d.g--master* **~lokal** n (*restaurant,* etc *with*) *d.g-,* ⟨Am⟩ *dance-hall* **~lust** f *love of d.g* **≈lustig** a *fond of d.g* **~maus** f ⟨fig Am⟩ *pony* **~meister** m *d.g-master* **~musik** f *dance-music* **~ordnung** f *d.g-arrangement, programme* **~paar** n *d.g couple* **~partner** m *partner* **~pause** f (*dance*) *interlude* **~platz** m *d.g-ground* **~saal** m = ~boden **~schritt** m *d.g-step* **~schuh** m *d.g-shoe* ‖ (für Herren) *pump* **~schule** f *d.g-school* **~stunde** f *d.g-lesson* | ~nliebe [f] *calf-love* **~tee** m *thé dansant* Fr **~turnier** n *ballroom d.g tournament* **~vergnügen** n *merry dance*; (*lower-class*) *ball* **~wut** f *rage for d.g* **T·änzchen** n ~s/~ *carpet--dance,* ⟨fam⟩ *hop, spin* ‖ ⟨fig⟩ mit jdm ein ~ wagen *to try a fall with a p* **t·änzeln** vi [h] *to skip about*; *to trip, frisk* ‖ (Pferd) *to curvet, prance*

t·anzen I. vi/t [h] *to dance* (nach dem Klavier *to the piano*; [e–n] Walzer *a waltz*) ‖ (als Gigolo) ⟨fam⟩ *to hoof* ‖ auf dem Seil ~ *to walk on the rope* ‖ ⟨fig⟩ *to be rocked* (*on the waves*) ‖ man kann nicht gleichzeitig auf zwei Hochzeiten ~ *you cannot eat your cake and have it* ‖ ~ müssen, wie jd pfeift *to be at a p's beck and call* ‖ jdn über den Haufen ~ *to knock a p down in dancing* | **sich** müde ~ *to tire o.s. with d.g* | **es** (der Walzer) tanzt sich hier gut *it is nice d.g* (*the w. is nice to dance*) *here* ‖ mir tanzt alles vor den Augen *everything is swimming before my eyes* | .. ~ l *to dance* (*a child on one's knee*) | ⟨prov⟩ ~ wollen, wenn die Musik aufhört *to come a day after the fair* **II.** ≈ n *dancing* ‖ über das ≈ hinaus s .. *past one's d.g days* **T·änzer** m ~s/~ *dancer* (a. f: **~in**) ⟨theat⟩ *ballet dancer* ‖ (Ein≈) *professional* ‖ (Mit≈) *partner* ‖ (Ballett≈) *opera-dancer* ‖ (Pferd) *prancer* **Tanzer·ei** f ~/~en (*wild, bad*) *dancing, dances* pl, ⟨Am a.⟩ *danceables* pl **t·anzerlich** a: es war mir nicht ~ *I was not in a dancing mood* **T·änzerschaft** f **1.** *dancer's calling* **2.** [koll] *dancers; corps de ballet* Fr

t·aperig a → tapprig **T·apergreis** m *doddering old man, dodderer*

Tap·et n [nur:] am ~ *on the carpet*; aufs ~ bringen *to broach, start* (*a question*); *to bring .. on the tapis* od *into play* ‖ aufs ~ k *to come up for discussion* **Tap·ete** f ~/~n **1.** *wall-paper, paper--hangings* pl, *paper on the wall* **2.** (gewirkte) *tapestry* ‖ (aus Arras) *arras* **3.** °⟨fig fam⟩ woll'n die ~ wechseln! (in ein anderes Lokal gehen) *let's hop it and go somewhere else, let's have a change of scenery* **Tap·eten-** **~bahn** f *width of wall-paper* **~behang** m *t.y* **~borte** f *p.-border*

~fabrik m *w.-p factory* **~fabrikant** m *w.-p. manufacturer* **~händler** m *w.-p. dealer* **~leiste** f *room-border* **~muster** n *w.-p. pattern* **~nagel** m *tack* **~papier** n = Tapete 1. **~stickerei** f *t.y-work* **~stuhl** m *t.y-loom* **~tür** f *tapestried door, jib door* °**~wechsel** m ⟨fig⟩ *going to some other place* **~wirker** m *t.y-maker* **Tapez·ier** m ~s/~e; **~er** m ~s/~ *paper-hanger*, ⟨Am a.⟩ *decorator* ‖ (Möbelpolsterer) *upholsterer* **~bedarf** m *decorators' requirements* pl **~arbeit, ~ware** f *paper-hanging*; *upholstery* **tapez·ieren** vt [h] *to paper* ‖ neu ~ *to repaper* **Tapez·ierung** f ~/~en *papering*

t·apfer a *brave* ‖ *valiant, gallant* ‖ *courageous, manful*; *doughty*, ⟨fam⟩ *plucky* ‖ auch die ~ste Truppe *even the most valiant forces* pl | [adv] sich ~ wehren *to make a gallant stand* (*against*) ‖ halt' dich ~! *don't flinch*! ‖ ~! ⟨fam⟩ *go it*! ‖ ⟨fig⟩ (tüchtig) (*to work*) *hard, strenuously*; (*to walk*) *a good pace* **≈keit** f ~/ *valour, bravery, gallantry* ‖ ~ vor dem Feinde *conspicuous gallantry* ‖ mit verzweifelter ~ *with a courage of despair* ‖ ~sauszeichnung [f] *award for valour* ‖ ~smedaille [f] *medal for bravery*

Tapi·oka f ~/ Ind ⟨bot-cul⟩ *tapioca*

T·apir m ~(e)s/~e ⟨zoo⟩ *tapir*

Tapisser·ie f ~/~n [–i:ən] *tapistry(-work)* **~geschäft** n *fancy-workshop* **~waren** f pl *t.y goods*

tapp [intj] *tap* **T·appe** f ~/~n *paw* ‖ *footstep* **t·appeln** vi [h] *to trip* **t·appen** vi [h] *to grope*, ⟨fam⟩ *fumble, poke* (*about*) (nach *after*) | im Dunkeln ~ *to grope one's way*; ⟨fig⟩ *to be in the dark* .. ~d ⟨fig⟩ *benighted* **t·app(r)ig, t·äppisch, t·apsig** a *awkward, clumsy* **Taps** m ~es/~e **1.** *hobbledehoy* **2.** *pat* **t·apsen** vi [h] **1.** = tappen **2.** *to pat*

T·ara f ~/ ⟨com⟩ (reine *real*, usancemäßige *customary*) *tare* **~rechnung** f *tare-account* **~vergütung** *allowance for tare* **tar·ieren** vt [h] *to counterbalance* ‖ ⟨com⟩ *to* (*ascertain* od *deduct the*) *tare*

Tar·antel f ~/~n ⟨ent⟩ *tarantula* dazu: *-tella*

Tar·ent n [Gr] ⟨It⟩ (Stadt) *Taranto*

Tar·if m ~(e)s/~e ⟨com⟩ *tariff* (laut ~ *as per t.*) ‖ ⟨rail⟩ *table of fares* (P), *rates* (S) ‖ zeitbegrenzter ~ *restricted hours' t.* | e–n ~ aufstellen f *to t.* **~bestimmungen** f pl *t. regulations* **~erhöhung** f *increase in rates* **~ermäßigung** f *reduction in t.* **~lohn** m *standard wages* pl **≈mäßig** a *trade-union* (*rates* [*of pay*]) | [a & adv] *according to t., by the t.*(*-rate*) **~partner** [pl] ⟨ind⟩ *labour and management* **~satz** m *t.-r.* ‖ gewöhnlicher, voller ~ *full fare*; *normal t.* **~ordnung** f *t. agreement* **~staffel** f *rate* od *t. scale* **~vereinbarung** f *rating agreement* **~verhandlungen** f pl *collective bargaining* **~vertrag** m *t. treaty*, ⟨Am⟩ *collective agreement* **~wesen** n (*system of*) *t.s* pl **tarif·ieren** vt [h] *to t.* **Tarif·ierung** f ~/~en ⟨com⟩ *rating*

Tar·im m (Fluß Innerasiens) **~becken** n *T. Basin*

T·arn- **~anstrich** m *camouflage*; ⟨mil, mar⟩ *dazzle-paint*; ⟨fig⟩ *smoke screen* **~ausweis** m *c.d identity card* **~betrieb** m (z Umstellung auf Kriegsproduktion) *shadow factory* **~geräusch** n *screen noise* **~kappe** f *magic hood*, (*cap of invisibility*) **~licht** n *blackout light* **~netz** n ⟨mil⟩ *netting* **~scheinwerfer** m ⟨mot⟩ *blackout headlight* **~zeltbahn** f *c. cape* **t·arnen** vt [h] ⟨mil⟩ *to mask, hide, camouflage, screen, dazzle*(*-paint*) ‖ ⟨fig⟩ *to veil*; *to cover up* **T·arnung** f ~/~en *masking*; *screening*; *comouflage*; *smoke-screen* ⟨a. fig⟩

Tar·ock n ~(e)s/ ⟨cards⟩ *tarot, taroc*

Tarp·ejisch a *Tarpeian* (Fels)

Tart·ane f ~/~n ⟨mar⟩ *tartan*

Tart·ar → Tatar

T·artsche f ~/~n *target*

Tart·üff m ~(e)s/~e *Tartuf(f)e, hypocrite*

T·asche f ~/~n **A.** *pocket*; (im Frauenrock) *placket*; (Beutel) *bag, pouch* ⟨a. anat⟩, (kl) *purse* (⟨a.⟩ *under the eyes*); gr ~ *catchall*; ~ mit Reißverschluß *zipper bag*; ⟨Am⟩ (Damenhandtasche ⟨a.⟩) *purse*; *pocket book* **B.** Akten≈ *document wallet*; Besuchs≈ *handbag*, (mit Spiegel) *vanity bag*; (Bettler≈) *wallet*; Brust≈ *breast-pocket*; Geld≈ *purse*; (Hirten≈) *pouch*; Jagd≈ *game-bag*; ⟨mil⟩ Karten≈ *map-case*; Markt≈ *marketing bag*; Mundtuch≈ *serviette sachet*; Pack≈ *saddle-bag*; Patronen≈ *cartridge pouch*; Pilger≈ *scrip*; Schul≈ *school case*; (Schwert-, Seitengewehr≈) *frog*; (Uhr≈ der Reithose) *fob*; Umhänge≈ *satchel*; Visitenkarten≈ *card case*; Zigarren≈ *cigar-case* **C.** (sich [dat] die) *or* s–e ~n umstülpen *to turn one's pockets inside out*; ⟨fig⟩ die ~ zuhalten *to tighten one's purse-strings* | jdm **auf** der ~ liegen *to live at a p's expense* ‖ er liegt mir auf der ~ ⟨a.⟩ *I have him on my hands* B. wie s–e ~ kennen *to know Berlin like the back of one's hand* | **in** die eigene ~ arbeiten *to make one's own hay* ‖ in die ~ greifen *to thrust* od *put one's hand into one's pocket*; ⟨fig⟩ *to pay, to dip into one's purse*; ⟨sl⟩ *to fork over* ‖ Geld in der ~ h *to have m. to spend*; etw (so gut wie sicher) in .. ⟨fig⟩ *to have a th in the bag*; das h wir noch nicht in der ~ *there's many a slip between the cup and the lip* ‖ wir h ihn in der ~ *we have got him where we want him* ‖ in die ~ stecken *to pocket*, ⟨fig⟩ jdn .. *to be more than a match for a p* **T·äschelkraut** n *shepherd's purse* **T·aschen-** **~ausgabe** f *pocket-edition*; ⟨m. m.⟩ *paperback* °**~billard** spielen ⟨sex⟩ *to play pocket-billards* **~buch** n *note-, p.-book* ‖ (Führer) *vade-mecum* ‖ (Almanach) *annual* **~dieb** m *pickpocket*; ⟨Am a.⟩ *purse snatcher*; vor ~en wird gewarnt! *beware of p.p.s*! **~diebstahl** m *p.ing p.s* **~feuerzeug** n *pocket lighter* **~futter** n *p.-lining* **~geld** n *spending* od *p.-money, allowance*; er gab s-m S. das ~ ⟨a.⟩ *he tipped his son* **~kalender** m *p.-almanac* **~klappe** f *flap* **~kompaß** m *p.-compass* **~krebs** m ⟨zoo⟩ *common crab* **~lampe** f (*p.-*)*torch*, ⟨Am⟩ *flashlight* **~messer** n *p.-knife, clasp-knife*; (kl) *penknife* **~spieler** m *prestidigitator, juggler* | ~ei [f] *j.y* ⟨a. fig⟩, *sleight of hand*; ~künste [f pl] *juggling-tricks* pl **~tuch** n (*p.-*)*handkerchief* **~uhr** f *watch* **~wörterbuch** n *p.-dictionary* **T·äschner** m ~s/~ *pursemaker* ‖ (Koffermacher) *trunkmaker*

Taschk·ent n ⟨Russ⟩ (Stadt) *Tashkent, -nd*

Tasm·anien n (Insel südl. Australiens) *Tasmania* **Tasmanische See** f *Tasman Sea* **Tasm·anier** m, **~in** f, **tasm·anisch** a *Tasmanian*

T·asse f ~/~n *cup*, (mit Unter≈) *cup and saucer* ‖ (gr) *breakfast-cup* ‖ e–e ~ Tee einschenken *to pour out a cup of tea* ‖ kl ~ (Kaffee) *demitasse* Fr ‖ ⟨fig⟩ °trübe ~ *creep* | er (sie) hat nicht alle ~n im Schrank *he's a few pence short in the shilling* (*she hasn't all her buttons on*); ⟨mil sl⟩ *he's round the bend* | österr (Servier≈) *tray* **~nfertig** a *instant* (*coffee*)

T·ast- **~empfindung** f *sense of feeling* **~feld** n ⟨comp⟩ *keyboard* ‖ auf einmal ins ~ geben *to group into one k.b. entry* **~funk** m *keying* | ~verkehr [m] *continuous wave communacation* **~geräusch** n *key click* **~geschwindigkeit** f *keying speed* **~knopf** m *keying head* **~körperchen** n ⟨anat⟩ *touch-body* **~sinn** m *sense of t.* **~werkzeug** n *organ of t.* **~zirkel** m (ein ~) (*a pair of*) *cal(l)ipers* **Tastat·ur** f ~/~en ⟨mus⟩ *keyboard, keys* pl **t·astbar** a *palpable, tangible* **T·aste** f ~/~n ⟨mus⟩ *key* ‖ e–e falsche ~ anschlagen *to strike a wrong note* ‖ weiße ~ *natural note* od *key* | ⟨telg⟩ *sounder*, (*sending*) *key* ‖ ⟨typwr⟩ *stop* ‖ ⟨tech⟩ press key **t·asten I.** vt [h] *to feel, touch* ‖ ⟨telg⟩ *to transmit .. by key*; ⟨comp⟩ *to index*; *to key in* | sich vorwärts ~ *to feel one's way* **II.** vi [h] *to grope* (*about*), *to feel* (*for*), *fumble* (*after*) | **~d** ⟨fig⟩ *tentative* (*trial*), *groping* (*efforts*) ‖ ~d suchen *to fumble for* ‖ ~d vorgehen *to feel one's way* ⟨a. fig⟩ **T·asten-** **~anschlag** m *key depression*

~brett n *finger board* **~feld** n ⟨typwr⟩ *keyboard* **~instrument** n *keyed instr.* **~kalkulator** m *digital computer* **~lager** n ⟨mus⟩ *keyboard* **~satz** m *keyboard* **~tiefgang** m ⟨typwr⟩ *key depression* **T·aster** m ~s/~ ⟨ent⟩ *feeler, antenna* || ⟨el⟩ (*sending*) *key* **~schenkel** m *cal(l)iper leg* **~zirkel** m (*a pair of*) *c.r compasses* pl, *c.rs* pl

Tat f ~/~en *act* || (Handlung) *action* || (wichtige) *deed* || (rühmliche) *exploit* || (gr) *achievement* || (geschickte) *feat* || edle, schlechte, verruchte ~ *noble, foul, atrocious deed* || verbrecherische ~ *criminal act* | das ist e–e ~! *now there's a th!* || e–e gute ~ vollbringen *to do a good action* || die ~ leugnen *to deny the charge* || die ~ dem Worte folgen l *to suit the action to the word* || Mann der ~ *man of action* | **auf** frischer ~ ertappen *to catch* od *take a p red-handed* od *with the goods* od *in the act of crime* | **in** der ~ *in fact, indeed, actually, as a matter of fact* || in die ~ umsetzen *to put into action* od *execution*; ⟨a.⟩ etw in ~en umsetzen *to exercise a th* **tat** 1. & 3. sg pret v tun **T·at-** **≈bereit** a *ready to act* **~bericht** m *delinquency report* **~bestand** m (*statement of*) *facts* pl *of the case, matter of fact* || *state of affairs*; *set of circumstances*; festgestellter ~ *findings of fact* **~beweis** m *practical proof* **~einheit** f ⟨jur⟩ *unity of deed* **~form** f ⟨gram⟩ *active voice* **~handlung** f *deed of violence* **~kraft** f *energy, vigo(u)r*; *enterprise*; ⟨fam⟩ *pluck* **≈kräftig** a *active*; *energetic* [adv *-ally*] || sich ~ einsetzen f *to be vigorous in support of* **≈los** a *inactive* **~mehrheit** f ⟨jur⟩ *plurality of deed* **~mensch** m *realist* **~ort** m *scene of crime* **~sache** f (*matter of*) *fact* || nackte ~n *glaring facts* || gegebene ~n *data* || e–e anerkannte, feststehende, klare, unwiderlegliche ~ *an accepted, established, indisputable, inescapable, undeniable fact* | das sind die ~n *those are the facts* (*in* od *of the matter*), *this is the whole story*; vollendete ~ *fait accompli* Fr || sich mit den gegebenen ~n abfinden *to come round to facts* | den ~n entsprechend *exact* (*account*) || durch ~n nicht z überzeugen(d) *fact-proof* || sich **an** die ~n haltend *matter-of-fact* (Bericht); angesichts (*or* auf dem Boden) dieser ~n *against this background* | ~nfeststellung [f] *findings of fact*; offensichtlich wahre T.f.g. ⟨jur⟩ *truism*; ~nmaterial [n] *factual material*; ~nsinn [m] *factual sense, fact-facing mind* **≈s·ächlich** a *actual* (*time of arrival, departure* N); *real*; *true*; *virtual* (Wert); *de facto* (*separation*); ~e Fluggeschwindigkeit *air speed* || *founded on fact* | [adv] *in fact, as a* (*matter of*) *fact*; *in good earnest*; es ist ~ so, daß *it is an actual fact that .., there is no doubt that ..* **T·aten-** **~drang, ~durst** m *fervid activity*; *strenuousness* **≈durstig** a *energetic, strenuous* **≈los** a *inactive, idle* **≈reich, ≈voll** a *fruitful in achievements, strenuous*; *active* (*life*) **T·äter** m ~s/~ *doer* || (Übel≈) *perpetrator, culprit, delinquent*; ⟨civ l⟩ *tortfeasor* || (Urheber) *author* **~schaft** f *guilt* || die ~ nicht leugnen *not to deny having done it*, ⟨jur⟩ *to plead guilty* **t·ätig** a *active* ⟨a. gram⟩, *busy, up and doing, stirring*; *energetic*; *efficacious*; rastlos ~ *industrious* || ~ s (*of organs*) *to operate*; ~ s als *to act as* (*assistant*); ~ s f *to work for*; als Arzt ~ s *to practise medicine* | **~en** vt [h] *to carry out*; *effect* (*sales*); *to transact* (*business*); *to effect, reach, ratify* (*a treaty*); *to make* (*a compact*) | **≈keit** f ~/~en *activity*; *action, operation*; *occupation*; *profession*; *business*; ⟨fam⟩ *job* || (*barristers of 5 years'*) *standing* | ehrenamtliche ~ *service in an honorary capacity* | **außer** ~ setzen (P) *to suspend*; ⟨mach⟩ *to throw out of gear*; ⟨fig⟩ *to bring to a standstill* | **in** voller ~ *in full swing* od *play* || in (höchste) ~ setzen *to set going* od *working* (*to set in full blast*), *to put* od *bring into action*; (Muskel, Hirn) *to activate* || in ~ treten *to come into operation* | ~sbereich [m] *extent of action*; *range of activity*; ~sbericht [m] *action report*; ~sform [f] ⟨gram⟩ *active voice*; ~sfeld [n] *province*; ~swort [n] ⟨gram⟩ *verb* **t·ätlich** a *active, actual* || ~er Scherz *practical joke* || (gewaltsam) *violent* || ~ w *to come to blows* | adv ⟨jur⟩ ~ bedrohen, beleidigen *to assault*; ~e Beleidigung f *assault* (*and battery*) **≈keit** f ~ [oft pl ~en] *act of violence*, ⟨jur⟩ *assault* (*and battery*)

Ta(r!)t·ar m ~en/~en *tartar*; ~-Beefsteak [n] *t.-steak* **Tatar·ei** f, **Tat·arien** n ⟨Russ⟩ *Ta(r)tary* **tat·arisch** a *Ta(r)tar(ic)*

tat(a)u·ieren, tätow·ieren vt [h] *to tattoo* **Tätow·ierung** f ~/~en *tattoo(ing)*

T·atra f (in den Karpaten); die Hohe ~ *the High Tatras* pl; die Niedere ~ *the Low Tatras* pl

t·ätscheln vt [h] *to fondle, pat* °**T·atterich** m ~(e)s/ ⟨sl⟩ *tizzy*; er hat den ~ *he is all of a shake* od *dither* °**t·attern** vi [h] *to dodder, to be shaky* **T·atze** f ~/~n **1.** *paw, claw* || ⟨fig⟩ *fist*, ⟨Am sl⟩ *mitt*; in jds ~n s *to be in a p's clutches* **2.** *rap over the knuckles* **~lwurm** m ⟨Alp. myth⟩ *Grendel* (*cf.* Grindelwald) **~nhieb** m *stroke with a paw*

Tau[1] m ~(e)s/ *dew* || es fällt ~ (*the*) *d. is falling* || vor ~ u Tag *in the small hours* **~fall** m *d.-fall* **≈feucht** a *moist with d., bed.ed* **≈frisch** a *fresh with d.* **~luft** f *soft air* **~mantel** m ⟨bot⟩ = Frauenmantel **~messer** m *drosometer* **~perle** f *d.y pearl* **~punkt** m *thaw-point* || *d.-point* **~regen** m *mild rain* (*causing a thaw*) **~tropfen** m *d.-drop* **~wasser** n *thaw water* **~wetter** n *thaw* (*a ~ has set in*) **~wind** m *mild breeze*

Tau[2] n ~(e)s/~e ⟨allg⟩ *rope* || ⟨mar⟩ *cable*, (starkes) *hawser*; (→ Leine); ~e [pl] *rigging* || ⟨fig⟩ an einem ~ ziehen *to sail in the same boat* **~anker** m *drag-anchor, mooring-rope* **~brücke** f *r.-bridge* **~ende** n *slack* **~länge** f *c.'s length* **~schiffahrt** f *c.-towing* **~werk** n *r.s* pl, *cordage* || (laufendes, stehendes) (*running, standing*) *rigging* || (altes) *junk* **~verzierung** f ⟨arts⟩ *cable moulding* **~ziehen** n *rope-pulling contest*; *tug-of-war* ⟨a. fig⟩, ⟨parl⟩ *discussion*

taub a **A.** *deaf* (gegen, f *to*) (auf e–m Ohr *of* od *in one ear*) || ein **≈er** *a deaf man* **B.** ⟨fig⟩ (Ähre) *empty* || (Ei) *addled* || ⟨min⟩ (Gang) *dead, barren*, (mager) *mute*; ⟨geol⟩ *dead*; das Taube *deads* pl, *dead heaps* pl || (Nuß) *empty, hollow, deaf* **C.** (gefühllos) *benumbed, callous, unfeeling*; *obtuse*; *dead* (gegen *to*) || (Finger) *numb* (*with cold*) **D.** ~ m *to deafen* || ⟨fig⟩ ~ s gegen *to turn a deaf ear to* || ~en Ohren predigen *to talk to the winds* **≈feld** n *barren track* **~geb·oren** a *born deaf* **≈hafer** m *wild oats* pl **T·aubheit** f ~/ *deafness* || *numbness* || *emptiness, barrenness* **≈nessel** f ⟨bot⟩ *dead nettle* **~stumm** a *deaf and dumb* | **≈e(r)** *deaf-mute* m & f; **≈en-** [in comp] *d.-and-d.* (*alphabet, asylum, institute*; (*teacher*) *of the d. and d.*; *school, institute for the deaf-mute*) **≈heit** f *d.-and-d.ness*

T·äubchen n ~s/~ *little dove* || mein ~! *my love!*, ⟨fam⟩ *duckie* || ⟨iron hum⟩ unschuldiges ~ *sucking d.* **T·aube** f ~/~n *pigeon* (→ *dove*) || ⟨poet⟩ *d.* || ⟨Ger⟩ *type of aeroplane* | sanft wie e–e ~ (*as*) *gentle as a d.* || ein Flug ~n *a flight of p.s* || ~n gurren .. *coo* || Land der gebratenen ~n → Schlaraffenland || wo ~n sind, fliegen ~n zu *to him that hath shall be given* ⟨bib⟩ **T·auben-** **≈artig** a *columbine* **≈äugig** a *d.-eyed* **~ausstellung** f *p.-show* **~ei** n *p.'s egg* **~einfalt** f *d.-like simplicity* **~falke** m ⟨orn⟩ *p.-hawk* **~farbe** f, (**≈farbig, ≈grau** a) *shot-, d.-clour(ed)* **~fuß** m ⟨bot⟩ *p.-foot* **~habicht** m = –falke **~haus** n, **~schlag** m *d.-cote, p.-house*; ⟨fig⟩ → Hosenlatz || ⟨fig⟩ wie in e–m ~ *like in a transit-camp* **~liebhaber** m *p.-fancier* **~mist** m *p.'s dung* **~post** f *p.-express* **~schwanz** m ⟨ent⟩ *hawk-moth* **~stößer** m = –falke **~zucht** f *breeding of p.s* **T·auber,**

T·äuber (~ich [m]) m ~s/~ *cock p.* **T·äubin** f ~/~nen *hen-p.*

T·auch- **~batterie** f ⟨el⟩ *immersion-b.* **~boot** n *submarine* **~ente** f ⟨orn⟩ *diver, ducker* **~falte** f ⟨geol⟩ *plunging fold* **~färben** n *dip dyeing* ⟨a. phot⟩ **~helikopter** m (*Piccard*) *mesoscaphe* **~käfer** m *water-beetle* **~retter** m (S) *escape gear* **~sieder** m ⟨Ger el⟩ *immersion-heater*; ⟨engl⟩ *element liquid heater* **~stange** f ⟨tech⟩ *plunger* **~tank** m ⟨sub-mar⟩ *ballast tank* **t·auchen A.** vt [h] *to dip, duck*; ⟨mst tech⟩ *plunge* | vi [h & s] *to dive, plunge* || (Sonne) *to dip, sink* || (Wal) *to sound* || (U-Boot) *to submerge* **B.** die *or* **mit** der Hand ~ in *to dip one's hand into* | **in** Licht getaucht *flooded with, swimming* od *bathed in light* **T·aucher** m ~s/~ *diver* ⟨a. orn⟩ (→ *auk, grebe, diver, merganser, shearwater*) **~anzug** m *diving--dress* **~glocke** f *d.g-bell* **~helm** m *d.g-helmet* **~kunst** f *art of diving* **~leine** f *life-line* **~(sauerstoff)gerät** n *aqualung* **~schiff** n *d.g-ship* **~stuhl** m *ducking-stool*

t·auen[1] vt [h] *to tow* (*a boat*) **t·auen**[2] vt [h] *to taw* (*skins*) **t·auen**[3] vi **I.** [h & s] es taut *it is thawing* || der Schnee ist v den Dächern getaut .. *has melted off the roofs* **II.** [h] es taut *there is a dew* (*falling*) **III.** vt [h] *to melt*: *the sun melts the ice*

T·auern pl, Hohe ~ *Hohe* od *High Tauern*

T·auf- **~akt** m (*ceremony of*) *baptism* **~becken** n (*b.al*) *font* **~buch** n *parish-register* **~kapelle** f *baptistery* **~kleid** n *b.al robe* **~name(n)** m *Christian name* **~pate** m & f *godfather, godmother* **~register** n *b.al register* **~schein** m *certificate of baptism* **~schmaus** m *christening-feast* **~stein** m (*b.al*) *font* **~tag** m *ch.g-day* **~tuch** n *b.al cloth* **~wasser** n *b.al water* **~zeuge** m *godfather, sponsor* **~zeugin** f *godmother* **T·aufe** f ~/~n ⟨ec⟩ *baptism*; (v Erwachsenen *adult b.*); ⟨mst⟩ *christening* ⟨a. fig⟩ || die ~ empfangen *to be christened* od *baptized* || aus der ~ heben *to stand godfather* od *godmother to* || ⟨fig⟩ *to inaugurate* (*a club*) || über die ~ halten *to present at the font* **t·aufen** vt [h] *to christen* (a. v Schiffen, Glocken, Wein etc), *to baptize* (auf den Namen *to the name of*) || er wurde Ernst getauft *he was christened E.*; ge–er Jude *converted Jew* || sie l alle Jahre ~ *they have a new baby every year* || ⟨fig⟩ *to water* (*wine*); ⟨fam⟩ *to simpson* (*milk*) | getaufte Milch *simpson* || .. tüchtig getauft *we got soaked to the bones* **T·äufer** m ~s/~; Johannes der ~ *John the Baptist* **T·äufling** m ~(e)s/~e *child* (od *p*) *to be baptized*

t·augen vi [h] *to be worth* (*much, little*) || (zu) *to be fit, good, of use* (*for*) || gut ~ *to do, answer, serve well* || wir ~ nicht f Sänger *we never should have done for singers* || nichts ~ *to be no* (*earthly*) *good, to be good for nothing* || wenig ~ *to be not much good* (zu *at*) **T·augenichts** m ~ & ~es/~e *ne'erdo-well* (⟨Scot⟩ .. *weel*), *good-for--nothing, scape-grace, scamp, waster*; *rip*; ⟨Am⟩ *scal(l)awag*; ⟨fam⟩ *stuffed shirt* **t·auglich** a *good, fit, useful, apt, appropriate* (f, z *for*) || er ist z nichts ~ *he is no earthly good* || (fähig) *able* (*to do*) || ⟨mil, mar⟩ *able-bodied* || als ~ befunden w *to be passed fit* || *seaworthy* (*ship*) | **≃keit** f ~/ *ability* || *usefulness* || (*physical*) *fitness* ⟨a. com⟩ || *competence* | ≃snachweis [m] *certificate of qualification*

t·auig a *dewy, moist with dew*

T·aumel m ~s/ *reel(ing), staggering* || *giddiness* | ⟨vet⟩ *staggers* pl | ⟨fig⟩ *intoxication* (*to be in a state of i.*); *flush*; *ecxtasy, transport, exuberance* || (Vergnügungs≃) *racket* **~becher** m *intoxicating cup* **~käfer** m *whirligig* **~kerbel** m *hemlock--chervil* **~lolch** m ⟨bot⟩ *bearded darnel* **~scheibe** f ⟨tech⟩ *swash plate* **t·aum(e)lig** a (schwindlig) *giddy* || (schwankend) *reeling, staggering* **t·aumeln** vi [h & s] *to reel, lurch, stagger* (*into, against*); *to totter*; *to be giddy* || sie ~ vor Glück *their luck has turned their heads*

T·aunus m ⟨Ger⟩ (Gebirge)

†**T·aurien** n, **T·auris** n *Tauris, the Crimea* **Taurisch** †**~er Cherson·es** m, **~e H·albinsel** f *Tauric Chersonese* od *Peninsula*, jetzt: *the Crimea*

T·aurus m (Gebirge in Kleinasien)

Tausch m ~es/~e *exchange, barter, swap* || ein schlechter ~! *a poor exch.*!; z ~ f *in truck for* **~geschäft** n, **~handel** m *barter, truck*, ⟨Am⟩ *dicker* || ~ treiben *to truck, barter*; *dicker* **~händler** m *barterer, trucker* **~mittel** n *medium of exchange, circulating m.* **~verkehr** m *exch. of goods* **≃weise** [adv] *by way of exch.* **~wert** m *exch.able value* **t·auschen** vt/i [h] *to exchange* (gegen *for*) || (*to exch. glances*) || ⟨sl⟩ *to swap, swop* vt/i (*with a p*) || ⟨com⟩ *to barter, truck* | (die Rollen) ~ ⟨fig⟩ *to change places* (*with a p*) || sie ~ Küsse *they kiss* (*each other*) **t·äuschen** vt [h] (**sich**) *to deceive, delude* (*o.s.*) | *to disappoint*; *dupe*; *trick, cheat*; *hoodwink* || (Hoffnung etc) *to belie* | ⟨fam⟩ *to take in, to do* od *fox*; ⟨ftb⟩ *to sell* (*the dummy*) || es täuscht ⟨a.⟩ *it is misleading* || durch Worte ~ *to juggle with words* | **sich** ~ ⟨a.⟩ *to be deceived, deluded* (**durch** *by*), *mistaken* (**in** in) || sich (nicht) ~ l *to let o.s. be deceived,* (*not to be d.d*), *to be imposed on, duped, mocked* || ~ Sie sich nicht! *don't be mistaken*! ⟨Am sl⟩ *don't kid y.s.*!; jdn in s–n Erwartungen ~ *to frustrate a p's expectations* || in Hoffnungen (etc) getäuscht w *to be disappointed* || jdn **um** etw ~ *to trick a p out of a th* **t·äuschend** a *delusive, illusory, deceptive*; *false* || (Ähnlichkeit) *striking* | [adv] sie sind ihm ~ ähnlich *they are like two peas in a pod* || ~ nachgemacht *copied to the life* || ~ nachahmen *to imitate to a T* **T·auscher** m ~s/~ ⟨com⟩ *barterer* **T·äuscher** m ~s/~ *deceiver, cheat* || (Roß≃) *horse-dealer* **~·ei** f ~/~en *delusion, deception* **T·äuschung** f ~/~en *deceipt, deception, delusion*; (Bluff) *bluff* || alte ~ *outworn fallacy* || (arglistige) *fraud* || optische ~ *visual delusion* | (Selbst≃) *illusion* || sich e–r ~ hingeben *to mislead, deceive o.s.* (über *on*); sich k–r ~ h.g. *to have no illusion* (*about a th*); gib dich da k–r ~ hin *there must be no mistake about that* **~sangriff** m *feint attack* **~smanöver, ~sunternehmen** n *diversion*; *feint* **~sversuch** m *attempt to deceive*; ⟨fam⟩ *try-on*

Tausch·ier- ~kunst [f] *damaskeening* | **≃t** *inlaid* (*floor*)

t·ausend I. a (*a*) *thousand* || ~ u aber~ *th.s upon th.s* || ~ Jahre (Mann, Dank) *a th. years,* (*men, thanks*) || viel(e) ~ Mal, (Menschen) (*many*) *th.s of times,* (*of people*) || ~Schritte tun *to go for a constitutional* || ≃ u eine Nacht *The Arabian Nights* | **per** ~ *per mil* || nicht einer **unter** ~ *not one in a th.* **II.** ≃ n ~s/~e *thousand* || **im** ≃ *per th.* od *mil* || es geht **in** die ≃e *it runs into th.s* || (**bei** *or*) **zu** ≃en *by the th., by th.s*; (v Volksmenge) *in th.s* || (*they came*) *in their th.s* **III.** [intj] (ei) der ≃!, potz ~! *dear me*!, *good gracious*! | ≃schwerenot! *damn* od *hang it all*! **T·ausend-** **≃armig** a *th.-armed* **~blatt** n *water milfoil* **~eck** n *chiliagon* **≃fach, ≃fältig** a (*a*) *th.fold, a th. times* | [adv] *in a th. ways* **~fuß** m ⟨ent⟩ *milleped* **~g·üldenkraut** n *centaury* **~j·ahrfeier** f *millenary celebration* **≃jährig** a *of a th. years, a th. years old, millennial* || ~e(s) Reich ⟨ec & nazi⟩ *millenium* || ~e Lebensräume *living spaces with a history going back a th. years* **~korngewicht** n (v Saatgut) *1000 kernel weight* **~künstler** m *conjurer*; *Jack of all trades*; er ist ein ~ *he can turn his hand to anything* **≃mal** [adv] *a th. times, dozens of t.s*; ⟨fam⟩ (*thanks*) *ever so*; (*it's*) *a damned sight* (*better*) || ⟨Am fam⟩: *I'd heap rather go than stay* °**~sakram·ent** [intj] *damn* od *hang it all*! °**~sakram·enter, ~sasa** m *devil of a fellow*; *regular brick* **~schön(chen)** n ⟨bot⟩ *daisy* **≃weise** [adv] *by th.s* **T·ausender** m ~s/~ **1.** (*a*) *thousand* **2.** *banknote of th.*

marks **3.** *figure marking the th.s* | ~amt [n] ⟨telph⟩ *three-figure exchange* **t·ausenderl·ei** a (*of*) *a thousand* (*different*) *sorts* ‖ ~ z tun h *to have a hundred* (od *thousand*) *ths to do* ‖ auf ~ Art *in a th. ways* **t·ausendste** a, ≗l n *thousandth*; z ~n Mal *for the dozenth time* ‖ ein ≗l *a thousandth part* (*of it*) ‖ ein ≗l Sekunde *a millisecond*

Tautolog·ie f ~/~n *tautology* dazu: *tautological*

T·ax- ≗**frei** a *free from taxation* ~**gebühr** f *valuer's fee* ~**ordnung** f *scale of fees*; *assizement*; *tariff* ~**wert** m *estimated value* **Taxam·eter** m ~s/~ (Fahrpreisanzeiger) *taximeter* ‖ (Droschke) *taxi*(*cab*) **Taxati·on** f ~/~en *taxation, valuation, appraisement* **Tax·ator** m ~s/–t·oren *valuer*, (*sworn*) *assessor*; ⟨bes Am⟩ *appraiser* **T·axe** f ~/~n *rate, tariff* ‖ (Steuer) *tax* ‖ (Gebühr) *fee* ‖ (Fahrgeld) *fare* ‖ (Auto) (⟨a.⟩ Taxi [n] [pl –xen]) *taxi*(*cab*); ~ anhalten *to flag a car, to wave a car down* ([dazu]: *to taxi* vt/i; *taxi-rank* Stand) ‖ (Schätzung) *estimate* ‖ (Auktion≗) *knock-down price* | nach der ~ verkauft w *to be disposed of at a valuation* **T·axi-** (→ Taxe) ~chauffeur [m] *cabman*; ~fahrer [m] *taxi-driver*; ~stand [m] *taxi-rank* ⟨Am⟩ *-stand* ~tänzerin [f] *gigolette* **tax·ieren** vt [h] *to value, rate, estimate, appraise* (auf *at*); *to size a th up* ‖ (amtlich) *to tax, to assess* **Tax·ierer** = Taxator **Tax·ierung** = Taxation **taxon·omisch** a ⟨eth⟩ *taxonomic* (*determination*)

T·axus m ~/~ ⟨bot⟩ *yew* (*-tree*)

Tbc- u Bang-frei a *certified* (*milk*)

tcha! [intj] *hm*!; *well, well*!

T·eak [ti:k] m *teak* ~**holz** n *teak wood*

×°**T·ebs** m ~es/~e *din, racket, hubbub*; *rag*

T·echnik f ~/~en (Wissenschaft) *engineering* | (Anwendung; Fertigkeit) *technique* (*New T.*: ⟨at, a–n⟩); *practice*; *skill* ‖ (Ausführung) *execution* ⟨a. mus⟩, *workmanship* ‖ ⟨mus paint etc⟩ *technique*; ⟨arts⟩ *craftsmanship* ‖ (Einzelheiten) *technicalities* pl; *technical* od *constructional features* ‖ ⟨scient⟩ *technology* (*slaves of science and t.gy*) ~**er** m ~s/~ *engineer* ‖ ⟨arts⟩ *technician* ~**um** n ~s/ *technical school* **t·echnisch** a *technical*; ⟨a.⟩ *special* (*knowledge*) ‖ *engineering* (*process, sciences*) ‖ *industrial* (*asbestos, use*) ‖ ~e Ausbildung *mechanic training* ‖ ~er Ausdruck *t.l term* ‖ ~er Betriebsleiter *chief engineer* ‖ ~e Einzelheiten *t.lities* pl ‖ nach den letzten ~en Erkenntnissen (*constructed*) *in accordance with the most modern techniques* ‖ ~e Fortschritte *technological progress* ‖ ~e Gegenstände *mechanical accessories* ‖ ≗es Hilfswerk *T.l Aid Programme* (*of the United Nations*) ‖ in ~er Hinsicht *t.lly* ‖ ≗e Hochschule *t.l college*, (v B. Berlin) *Institute of Technology* ‖ ~es Können *t.l know-how* ‖ ~e Methode, ~er Handgriff *technique*; ~e Möglichkeiten *t.lities* ‖ ≗e Nothilfe *organization for maintenance of supply* **Technolog·ie** f ~/~n [–i:ən] *technology* **technol·ogisch** a *technological*

T·echtelm·echtel n ~s/~ (Liebelei) *romp*; (*nice little*) *intrigue, goings-on* pl

T·eckel m ~s/~ *dachshund*

T·eddybär m *teddy bear*

Ted·eum [–'e:um] n –s/–s *Te Deum*

Tee m ~s/~s **1.** *tea* (grün *green*, dünn *weak*); ~ ohne alles *raw t.* ‖ (den) ~ trinken, nehmen *to drink* (*take, have*) *t.* ‖ ⟨fig⟩ abwarten u ~ trinken! *wait and see*! ‖ er trinkt gern starken ~ *he likes his t. strong* ‖ der ~ muß noch ziehen *the t. must stand a little longer* **2.** (Mahlzeit) e–n ~ geben *to give a t. party* ‖ *that was where t. would be* ‖ *to invite a p to t.* ‖ zu jdm zum ~ gehen *to go to t. with a p* **3.** (Kräuteraufguß) *infusion* (*of herbs*) **4.** ⟨fig⟩ im ~ s *to be tipsy*; .. bei *to be in a p's good books* ‖ s–n ~ kriegen *to get the sack* ‖ ~ reiten *to curry favour* (bei *with*) ~**anbau** m *t.-growing* ~**arten** f pl *t.s* pl ~**blatt** n *t.-leaf* ~**brett** n *t.-tray* ~**büchse,** ~**dose** f *caddy* ~**ei** n *t.-infuser, t.-egg* ~**geschirr** n = –zeug ~**gesellschaft** f *t.-party* ~**händler** m *t.-merchant* ~**kanne** f *t.-pot* ~**kessel** m *t.-kettle* ‖ ⟨fig & fam⟩ *blockhead* ~**kind** n ⟨school⟩ *favourite* ~**klatsch** m *t. and scandal* ~**kuchen** m *t.-cake* ≗**löffelvoll** m (pl) *t.-spoonful*(*s* pl) ~**maschine** f *t.-urn* ~**mischung** f *blend of t.* ~**mütze** f *t.-cosy* ~**pause** f *break for tea* ~**prüfer** m *t.-taster* ~**rose** f *t.-rose* ~**satz** m *t. leaves* pl °~**schlacht** f ⟨hum sl⟩ *t. fight* ~**service** n *t.set* ~**sieb** n *t.-strainer* ~**strauch** m *t.-plant* ~**stunde** f *t.-time* ~**tasse** f *t.-cup* ~**tisch** m *t.-table*; den ~ decken *to lay the t.* ~**zimmer** n [sg] *t.-rooms* pl ~**wagen** m (*t.-*)*troll*(*e*)*y*, *t.-wagon* ~**wärmer** m = –mütze ~**zeug** n *t.-things* pl

Teer m ~(e)s/~e *tar* ‖ mit ~ anstreichen *to t.* ~**abscheider** m *detarrer* ≗**beschmiert** a *t.ry, t.red* ~**beton** m *t.-macadam* ~**brenner** m *t.-maker* ~**farben** f pl *aniline colours* pl ~**farbstoffe** m pl *coal-t. dyes* pl ~**hütte** f *t.-factory* ~**jacke** f *t.red jacket* ‖ ⟨fig⟩ *Jack T.*, ⟨Am sl a.⟩ *gob* ~**leinwand** f *t.paulin* ~**makadam** m *tarmac* ® ~**ofen** m *t.-kiln* ~**öl** n *t.-oil* ~**pappe** f *t.-board, bituminized b.* ~**schwelerei** f = –hütte ~**seife** f *t.-soap* ~**splitt** m *macadam* dazu: *to m.ize* ~**wasser** n *gasliquor* ~**werg** n *black oakum* **t·eeren** vt [h] *to tar*, ⟨mar⟩ *to pay* **t·eerig** a *smeared with tar, tarry*

T·egel m ~s/~ ⟨geol⟩ *green marl*

T·egernsee m (in Oberbayern)

Teher·an n (Hptst. v Iran)

Teich m ~(e)s/~e *pond, pool* ‖ e–n ~ bespannen *to stock a pond with fishes* ‖ ⟨fam⟩ er ging über den gr ~ (nach Amerika) *he crossed the Puddle* (od *big*) *pond* ~**binse** f ⟨bot⟩ *bulrush* ~**forelle** f *pond-trout* ~**gräber** m *pond-digger* ~**gras** n *sedge* ~**huhn** n *moor-hen* ~**kolben** m *reed-mace* ~**lilie** f ⟨bot⟩ *water-lily* ~**muschel** f *pond-mussel* ~**rohr,** ~**schilf** n *reeds* pl ~**rohrsänger** m ⟨orn⟩ *reed-warbler* ~**rose** f ⟨bot⟩ *water lily*; weiße ~ → *nenuphar* ~**schnecke** f *pond-snail*

°×**T·eifi**! (→ Teufel) *the deuce*!

Teig m ~(e)s/~e *dough* (kneten *to knead*); Bier≗ *batter*; Blätter≗ *puff paste*; Hefe≗ *leavened dough* ~**decke** f *dough crust* ~**mulde** f *kneading-trough* ~**rädchen** n *jagging-iron* ~**rolle** f *rolling-pin* ~**schaber** m *scraper* ~**waren** f pl *noodles*; *farinaceous pastes* (= *macaroni, spaghetti, vermicelli* = [It] *pasta*) **t·eigig** a **1.** *doughy*; *pasty, pulpy* **2.** *mellow, soft, sleepy* (*pear*)

Teil m & n ~(e)s/~e **A. 1.** *part* (*to spend p. of the day* ..), *piece* **2.** (An ≗) [mst n] *portion, share* **3.** (Ab≗ung) *division*; *section* (*of the population*) **4.** ⟨Lit⟩ *part, volume* **5.** (Partei) *side*, ⟨jur⟩ *p.y* (= *plaintiff* od *defendant*) **6.** (Bau≗) (*structural*) *member* ‖ (Bestand–, Einzel≗) *element* **7.** ⟨com⟩ *assortment* **8.** ⟨mil⟩ (*logistics is a*) *function* (*of command*); ~e *elements*; ~e des Feindes *enemy detachments* pl **9.** ⟨jur typ⟩ *part* **B.** der **bestimmte** ~ *the allowance* ‖ ⟨anat⟩ edle ~e [pl] *vital p.s* ‖ gebender (nehmender) ~ *giving* (*receiving*) *p.y* ‖ ein gr ~ *a great deal* ‖ der größere ~ *the bigger p.* (*of the business*) ‖ der **größte** ~ *the bulk, the greater p.*; *the best p.* (*of a year*) ‖ (die meisten) *most* (*of them*), *most* (*people*); ein **gut** ~ *a good deal* od *bit* (*of*); (*of this he had*) *a great p.* od *a fair share* ‖ kl ~ (*not without*) *some fraction* (*of the trouble*) ‖ kl ~e *bits* pl ‖ der (e–r S) zustehende ~ (*its*) *quota* | → andern≗s, e–s≗s, großen≗s **C.** 2 ~e (= $^2/_3$) *two thirds*, 3 ~e (= $^3/_4$) *three p.s*; der 4. ~ *the fourth p.* od *section* ‖ in 4 ~e teilen *to divide into four p.s* **D.** jdm e–n ~ s–r Arbeit **abnehmen** *to take some of the work off a p* ‖ e–n ~ abtrennen *to set a portion off* ‖ s–n ~ **beitragen, tun** *to put in, bear, contribute one's share*; *to take* od *play one's p.* (*by*; *in doing*); ⟨fam⟩ *to do one's bit* ‖ sein ~ bek *to get one's due, one's full share*, ⟨sl⟩ *one's gruel* ‖ **bilden**: *to form* od *be p. of* ‖

er sagt nichts, aber **denkt** sich sein ~ *though he says nothing, he thinks the more*; .. ich .. *I had my own notions about it* ‖ ⟨fig⟩ jdm sein ~ **geben** *to give a p a piece of one's mind* ‖ beide ~e hören *to listen to both sides* **E. aus** allen ~en Englands *from all over E.* ‖ aus 2 ~en bestehend: *a two--piece (suit)* | ich **an** m–m ~e, ich f mein ~ *as to* od *for me, I for my p., I for one* ‖ f e–n ~ .. *for p. of the season* | **in** ~en geschlagen w ⟨mil⟩ *to be defeated in detail* | **um** ein gut ~ größer *a good deal taller* | **zum** ~ (abbr. z. T.) *p.ly, in p., to some extent* ‖ sie sind z. T. krank *p. of them are ill* ‖ z. T. .. z. T. *p.ly .. p.ly; he is p. artist p. searcher* ‖ z gleichen ~n *share and share alike*, ⟨fam⟩ *fifty-fifty*; .. beteiligt s *to be equal p.ners* (an *in*) ‖ z größten ~ *for the greater* od *most p.*; .. gelesen h *to have read the greater p. of it* ‖ (meistens) *mostly* ‖ → zuteil **~belichtung** f ⟨phot⟩ *p.ial exposure* dazu: *partly exposed* **~besitzer** m *p.-owner* **~betrag** m *p.ial amount, instalment*; (Anteil) *quota* **~bevölkerung** f *sub--population* **~einbürgerung** f *denization* **~einheiten** f pl ⟨mil⟩ *elements of units* **~erfolg** m *p.ial success* **~gerät** n → -kopf **~|haben** vi [h] (an [dat]) *to (have a) share (in), to p.icipate (in), to p.ake (of)* **~haber** m *p.icipator*, ⟨com⟩ *p.ner, joint proprietor* ‖ stiller ~ *sleeping p.ner* **~haberschaft** f *p.nership* **~härtung** f *selection hardening* **~kerbe** f (Tabletten~) *breakscore; rupture notch* **~kreis** m ⟨mil etc⟩ *graduated* od *pitch circle* **~komponente** f *part; component* **~kopf** m *index center* **~ladung** f ⟨mil⟩ *separate charge* **~maschine** f ⟨opt⟩ *graduating m.* **~montage** f *subassembly* **~motorisiert** a *partly m.ized* **~nahme** f (an [dat]) *p.icipation (in); cooperation*; (an Verbrechen) *complicity* ‖ *attendance (at a meeting)* ‖ ⟨fig⟩ *sympathy (with), interest (in); concern (for), (to express one's deep c. [at])* | ~bezeigung [f] *condolence* **~nahmslos** a *unconcerned* ‖ *un-responsive, indifferent (to); listless* ‖ (gefühllos) *callous, impassible; impassive (face)* ‖ (vor Schwäche) *apathetic* [adv *-ally*] | **~igkeit** [f] *unconcern* ‖ *impassibility* ‖ *apathy* **~nahmsvoll** a *sympathetic; solicitous* ‖ sich ungemein ~ zeigen *to display extraordinary interest* **~|nehmen** vi [irr] [h] (an [dat]) *to p.icipate, take p., to share, cooperate (in); to be a p.y to a th* ‖ *to enter (into)* ‖ an etw ~ ⟨a.⟩ *to bear a hand in a th* ‖ *to be present (at)* ‖ *to attend ([at])* ‖ ⟨Lit⟩ *to contribute (to)* ‖ *to be involved (in a scheme, etc)* ‖ *to join (in a game)* ‖ *to be of the company* ‖ ⟨fig⟩ *to sympathize (with)* **~nehmer** m *p.icipator, member (of a trip)* ‖ ⟨sport⟩ *competitor*; ⟨Am⟩ *contestant* ‖ [pl] *those present; p.ies* pl ‖ ⟨telph⟩ *subscriber*; (~verzeichnis [n] *telephone directory*); ~ antwortet nicht *there's no reply* ‖ ⟨jur⟩ *accomplice* | ~quote [f] ⟨univ⟩ *student quota* **~programm** n ⟨comp⟩ *subroutine* **~ring** m *graduated ring* **~scheibe** f *g.ting-machine*; ⟨mil⟩ *g.ted dial, dialsight* **~strecke** f ⟨rail⟩ *section, stage* **~streitkraft** f *branch* N **~strich** m ⟨mil⟩ *scale* od *graduation mark; point, pitch* **~ton** m ⟨mus⟩ *p.ial* **~vorrichtung** f ⟨tech⟩ *spacing attachment* **~weise** a *p.ial* ‖ [adv] *p.ially, in p.*; ~ bezahlt *part-paid* **~wertversicherung** f *insurance for less than the full value* **~wohnung** f *converted flat* **~zahlung** f *p.-payment* ‖ monatliche ~ *payment by monthly instalments* ‖ auf ~ *on the instalment--plan* **~zirkel** m *divider* **t·eilbar** a *divisible, separable* ‖ ⟨math⟩ *commensurable* **~keit** f ~/ *divisibility*, etc **T·eilchen** n ~s/~ *particle, fleck* ‖ ⟨mach⟩ *gadget* ‖ ⟨bak⟩ *bun, scone* | ⟨at⟩ ~beschleunigung [f] *p.le acceleration*; ~nachweis [m] *p.le detection*; ~verschiebung [f] *p.le shift* **t·eilen 1.** vt [h] *to divide* ‖ (anteilig) *to share* ‖ (ver~) *to distribute; to split (the difference)* ‖ (ein~) *to graduate* ‖ (ab~) *to partition (off); to separate* | (teilhaben an) (Leid) [Freude] *to sympathize [rejoice] with a p*; (Gefühle) *to enter into a p's feelings* | **sich** ~ *to split* ‖ (sich gabeln) *to divide; to branch out, to fork* ‖ (P) sich **in** etw ~ *to share a th* ‖ (v 2 P) *to go halves* ‖ sich ~ l: . *can be divided by 3* ‖ sich **mit** jdm ~ in *to share with a p in (the vigils)*, (gleichmäßig) *to share and share alike* **2.** vi [h] *to go shares* od ⟨fam⟩ *snip* **T·eiler** m ~s/~ *divider* ‖ ⟨math⟩ *divisor*; größter gemeinsamer ~ *greatest common measure* (abbr *G. C. M.*) **t·eilhaft, teilh·aftig** a [gen] *partaking (of), sharing, participating (in)* ‖ e–r S ~ w *to partake of, to share, to get a part in*, ⟨fam⟩ *to come in for a th* **..teilig** a: fünf~ *in five parts* **teils** [adv] *partly, in part* ‖ ~ .., ~ *part(ly) (in cash), part(ly) (by instalments); some (open), some (shut); what (with his conduct), what (with his courage)*; [so:] *what (with ..), and (..), and (..)* **T·eilung** f ~/~en *division, separation, partition* ‖ *sharing* ‖ *(linear, circular) graduation* ‖ *dismemberment (of Poland)* ‖ *parcelling out (of lands)* ‖ ⟨her⟩ *quartering* ‖ ~ in 2 Teile ⟨pol, etc⟩ *dichotomy* **T·eilungs- ~artikel** m ⟨gram⟩ *partitive article* **~klage** f *partition action* **~linie** f *dividing line* **~punkt** m *point of division* **~vertrag** m *treaty of partition* **~zahl** f ⟨math⟩ *dividend* **~zeichen** n ⟨gram⟩ *mark of division; hyphen*

Te·in [te:ˈi:n] n ~(e)s/ ⟨chem⟩ *theine*

Teint [tɛ̃:, tɛŋ] m ~s/~s *complexion* ‖ e–n guten ~ h *to have a fine c.* ‖ mit dunklem ~ *dark-c.ed*

Tekt·onik f ~/ *tectonics* **tekt·onisch** a *tectonic; regarding (the) construction*

Tele- ~f·on = *-phon* **~gr·amm** n ~(e)s/~e *telegram, wire* ‖ ein ~ schicken *to (send a) wire* ‖ ein ~ aufgeben *to hand in a t.* ‖ (drahtloses) *wireless message* ‖ (überseeisches) *cablegram, cable* ‖ ~ zu Lasten des Empfängers *cash on delivery t.*, ⟨Am⟩ *collect t.* | (→ Draht–); ~adresse [f] *telegraphic address (T. A.)*; ~code [m] *cable--code*; ~formular [n] *telegraph-form*; ~schalter [m] *telegram-office*; ~stil [m] *telegraphic style; cablese, telegraphese*; im ~ *t.cally* **~gr·aph** m ~en/~en *telegraph* **~gr·aphen-** ~amt [n] *telegraph office* (~apparat [m] *tape-machine*) ~beamte(r) [m] *t.-clerk*; ~bote [m] *t.-boy*; ~draht [m] *t.-wire*; ~leitung [f] *t.-line*; ~netz [n] *t.-system*; ~stange [f] *t.-pole*; ~station [f] = -amt; ~wesen [n] *telegraphy* **~graph·ie** f ~/ (drahtlose) ~ *(wireless) telegraphy* | **~ren** [vt/i] [h] *to telegraph, to wire* ‖ (v, nach Übersee) *to cable*; ~rfrequenz [f] *dot fr.y* **~gr·aphisch** a *telegraphic* ‖ ~es Angebot *cable-offer* | ~e Nachricht [f] *telegram* ‖ [adv] *by telegraph, by wire* ‖ ~ übertragen ⟨wir⟩ *to pipe* ‖ jdm ~ 100 M anweisen *to cable a p £ 7* **~graph·ist** m ~en/~en *telegraphist, (telegraph[ic]) operator*, ⟨Am⟩ *telegrapher* **~kin·ese** f ~/ *telekinesis*; ⟨occ⟩ → a. Psycho- **~objektiv** n ⟨phot⟩ *long-distance lens; telephoto* **~olog·ie** f ~/ *teleology* **teleol·ogisch** a *teleological* **~p·ath** m ~en/~en *telepathist*; ~ie [f] ~/ *telepathy* **~ph·on** n ~(e)s/~e *(tele)phone* ‖ ~ mit Selbstanschluß *dial t.* ‖ wir h ~ *we are on the t.* ‖ das ~ abstellen *to disconnect the t.* ‖ ans ~ gehen *to answer the t.*, .. rufen *to call up* ‖ am ~ *on the phone*, .. verlangt w *to be wanted on ..* ‖ auf das ~ aufpassen *to listen to the t.* | das ~ ging, läutete .. *went, rang* | ~amt [n] *(t.) exchange*; ~anschluß [m] *t. connexion*, ~ h *to be on the (tele)phone* ‖ Haus mit ~ *wired house*; ~ h *to be on the wire*; (Luxus-)Freudenmädchen mit ~ *call girl*; ~aufnahme [f] *recording from t.*; ~automat [m] *public t.*; ⟨fam⟩ *pay phone*; ~buch [n] *t. directory*; ~fräulein [n] *operator*, ⟨fam⟩ *hello girl*; ~gespräch [n] *t. call* od *conversation*; ~leitung [f] *t.nic circuit* ‖ ~netz [n] *t. network*; ~ruf [m] *t. call*; ~schnur [f] *t.-flex*; ⟨Am⟩ *t. cord* ‖ ~stelle [f] *call-office*; ~verbindung [f] *connection*; ~vorwählnummer [f] *area* *code number*; ~zelle [f] *call-box, phone-booth* **≃phon·ieren** vt/i [h] *to telephone* (mit [*to*] *a p*) **≃ph·onisch** a *telephonic* ‖ [adv] *by telephone* ‖ jdn anrufen *to ring a p up* (*on the ph.*) ‖ jdn ~ erreichen *to get on to a p by phone* ‖ ~ zu erreichen s *to be on the ph.*; er ist unter Nr. .. z err. *he can be got by phone calling number* .. **~phon·ist(in** f) m ~en/~en *telephonist, operator*; *switch-board operator* **~sk·op** n ~(e)s/~e *telescope* | ~feder [f] *t.pic fork*; ≃isch [a] *telescopic* [adv *-ally*] ~stoßdämpfer [m] *t.pic shock absorber*

T·eller m ~s/~ *plate* (v silbernen ~n essen *to eat off silver p.*); flacher ~ *dinner-p.*; Mittel≃, kl ~ *dessert p.* ‖ °den ~ abschlecken ⟨fam⟩ *to clean up* ‖ hölzerner ~ *trencher* | ⟨tech⟩ *disk*; *table* (*of an air-pump*) ‖ ⟨anat⟩ *palm* (*of the hand*) **~brett** n *plate-rack* **~deckchen** n *doily* **~eis** n *pancake ice* **~eisen** n *spring-trap* **≃förmig** a *plate-shaped* **~gestell** n *plate-rack* **~knecht** m *dumb-waiter* **~muschel** f ⟨zoo⟩ *limpet* **~mütze** f *tam-o'-shanter, tammy* **~tuch** n (zum Abwischen) *dish-cloth* ‖ (Serviette) *napkin* **≃voll** m; ein ~ *a plateful* **~wärmer** m *plate-warmer*

Tell·ur n ~s/ ⟨chem⟩ *tellurium* **≃isch** a *tellurian* **~rium** n ~s/–rien (Planetarium) *orrery*

T·empel m ~s/~ *temple, sanctuary*, ⟨poet⟩ *fane* ‖ *synagogue* ‖ ⟨fig⟩ e–n z ~ hinauswerfen *to turn a p out* **~bau** m *construction of a t.* **~dienst** m *t.-service* **~gang** m Mariä *Presentation in the T.* **~herr** m (*Knight*) *Templar* **~hof** n (Stadtteil & Flughafen v Groß-Berlin) **~orden** m *order of the T., order of St. John of Jerusalem* **~raub** m, **~schändung** f *sacrilege* **~räuber, ~schänder** m *desecrator* **~ritter** m = –herr **≃schänderisch** a *sacrilegious*

T·empera- *t.(-painting)* **~farbe** f *distemper* **~malerei** f (*painting in*) *d.*; *tempera* **~manier** f: in ~ malen *to distemper* **Temperam·ent** n ~(e)s/~e *temper(ament), disposition*; *liveliness, spirit*; *animation, vivacity*; *life*; *ardo(u)r, fervo(u)r, fervency* ‖ ausgeglichenes ~ *equanimity*; hitziges ~ *hot temper* ‖ (Feuer) *mettle*, (*high*) *spirits* pl **~sausbruch** m *outburst of temper, emotional onslaught* **≃los** a *spiritless* **≃voll** a *full of spirits*; *impulsive, ebullient* **Temperat·ur** f ~/~en ⟨mus⟩ → temperieren **Temperat·ur** f ~/~en *temperature* (messen *to take*; h *to have*; heben *to raise*); erhöhte ~ h ⟨med fam⟩ *to run a t.* ‖ die ~ steht auf Null *the t. is at 0° C* → Bd I, S. 1115; *normal body t.*: *37° C = .8° F*; *boiling point*: *100° C = 212° F* ‖ Messung hoher ~en *pyrometry* ‖ bei e–r ~ v .. *at a t. of* .. **~abfall** m ⟨meteor⟩ *lapse rate* **~ausgleich** m ⟨tech⟩ *equalization of t.* **~erhöhung** f *rise in t.* **~grad** m *degree of t.* **~gradient** m ⟨meteor⟩ *vertical gradiant* **~regler** m *attemperator* **~schwankungen** f pl *fluctuating t.s*; *t. range* **~strahler** m ⟨phys⟩ *heat radiating light source* **~sturz** m *sudden fall of t.* **≃unempfindlich** a *refractory* (*ceramics*) **~wächter** m ⟨tech⟩ *temperature controller* **~wähler** m ⟨el⟩ *power dial* **~wechsel** m *change in t.* **Temperenzler** m ~s/~ *total abstainer*; *teetotaller*; *abstemious p.* | ~treffen [n] *teetotal meeting* **≃isch** a *teetotal(ly* adv) **T·emper-** **~guß** m *malleable cast iron* **~ofen** m *annealing furnace* **t·empern** vt [h] *to temper, anneal* **temper·ieren** vt [h] *to temper* (a. ⟨mus⟩; [hierzu:] Temperatur *temperament*) | ⟨allg⟩ *to control the* (od *to bring to the suitable*) *temperature* | ≃ n (e–s Bades) *t.ture control*

T·empler m = Tempelherr

T·empo n [~s/~s & Tempi] *pace*; *speed*, ⟨Am⟩ *gait* ‖ ⟨fenc, mus⟩ *time, measure*; **im** ~ *in time* ‖ in langsamem ~ *at a slow rate* ‖ in schnellem ~ *at a great, smart, good speed* ‖ in ganz anständigem ~ *at a very fair pace* ‖ in rasendem ~ ⟨sl⟩ *at a rare bat*, ⟨mot sl⟩ *at a scorch* | das ~ **angeben** *to set the pace* (od *stroke* ⟨a. fig⟩), *to make the running* ⟨a. fig⟩ ‖ das ~ beschleunigen *to hasten* od *force the pace* ‖ das ~ bestimmen ⟨fig⟩ *to set the pace* ‖ ~ fahren ⟨mot⟩ *to drive in double-quick time* ‖ ⟨fig⟩ (kein) (Lebens-)~ h *to be fast* (*slow*) **~taschentuch**® n *paper handkerchief*; ⟨Am⟩ *tissue* **tempor·är** a *temporary* ‖ [adv] ⟨a.⟩ *for the time being* **temporis·ieren** vt [h] *to temporize*

T·empus n ~/–pora ⟨gram⟩ *tense*

Ten·akel [m & n] ~s/~ ⟨typ⟩ *visorium, copy-holder* ‖ ⟨surg⟩ *tenaculum*

Tend·enz f ~/~en *tendency* ‖ ⟨Lit⟩ *propaganda* ‖ steigende ~ *uptrend*, fallende ~ *depressed trend* ‖ e–e bestimmte ~ h *to trend* (*towards*) **~roman** m *novel with a purpose* **tendenzi·ös** a *tendentious, prejudiced, biassed*; *having a marked tendency* ‖ ⟨theat⟩ *agitprop* (*play*)

T·ender m ~s/~ ⟨rail⟩ *tender*; ⟨mar⟩ *tender, advice-boat* **~lokomotive** f *tank-engine*

Tener·iffa n (größte der Kanarischen Inseln) *Tenerife*; Bewohner(in) v ~ *Tenerifian*

T·enne f ~/~n (*thrashing-, malting-*)*floor*

Tenness·ee [tene'siː] n (Staat der U.S.A.)

T·ennis n ~/ (*lawn-*)*tennis* **~kleidung** f (Herren) *flannels* pl **~platz** m *t.-court* **~schläger** m (*t.-*)*racket* **~spiel** n (*game of*) *tennis* | ein sehr guter ~spieler s *to play a very good game of t.*

T·enor[1] m ~s/ ⟨jur⟩ *tenor*; *order* (*dispositive portion of a decision*); *purport* **Ten·or**[2] m ~(e)s~e ≃e **1.** *tenor* **2.** = ~·ist **~geige** f *viola* **~partie** f *tenor part* **~schlüssel** m *t. clef* **~stimme** f *t. voice* od *part* **Tenor·ist** m ~en/~en *tenor(-singer)*

Tenuis f ~/Tenues ⟨gram⟩ *voiceless stop*; *tenuis* (*p, t, k are tenues*)

Tepp m ~s/~e *dunce* | ≃ert [a] ⟨sl⟩ *goofy*

T·eppich m ~(e)s/~e *carpet* ⟨a. fig⟩ ‖ (Wand-≃) *tapestry* ‖ (Kamin≃) *hearth-rug* ‖ (weicher) *pile-carpet* ‖ Brüsseler ~ *Brussels carpet* ‖ gewirkter ~ *arras* ‖ mit e–m ~ belegen *to carpet* ‖ (Bombenwurf) *saturation bombing* **~arbeit** f *tapestry-work* **~band** m *carpet-binding* **~beet** n ⟨hort⟩ *c.-bed* **~-Fußboden-Auslegeware** f *wall-to-wall carpet* **~bombenwurf** m *carpet bombing* **~kehrmaschine** f *c.-sweeper* **~(klopf)stange** f ⟨a–engl⟩ *cross-bar* **~legen** n ⟨aero⟩ *pattern bombing* **~schoner** m *drugget* **~stange** f *stair-rod* **~stift** m *c.-tack* **~unterlage** f *hair-cloth, drugget* **~wirker** m *c.-weaver* **~wirkerei** f *c.-manufacture* ‖ [konkr] *c.-manufactory*

Tereb·inthe f ~/~n ⟨bot⟩ *terebinth*

Term·in m ~(e)s/~e **A. 1.** (*appointed* od *fixed*) *time, day*; (letzter *latest, closing*) *date*; ⟨mil⟩ *due date* N; ⟨jur⟩ *term* **2.** *delay, respite* **3.** ⟨jur⟩ *summons* **4.** ⟨sport⟩ *fixture* **B.** äußerster ~ *final term* ‖ ~ (z mündl. Verhandlung) anberaumen ⟨jur⟩ *to fix a day*, (*to set down a case for hearing*) ‖ den ~ einhalten *to keep one's time*; *to meet the deadline* ‖ ~ festsetzen ⟨jur⟩ *to fix a day for the hearing* ‖ ich habe morgen ~ *I am* (*summoned*) *to appear* (*in court*) *to-morrow* ‖ noch e–n ~ Miete schulden *to owe a quarter's rent* ‖ e–n ~ setzen *to fix a time* ‖ in 4 ~en zahlbar *payable in 4 instalments* **~festsetzung** f ⟨jur⟩ *note of issue* **~geschäft** n, **~handel** m *time-bargain*; *option-business*; *futures* pl (⟨a.⟩ –waren) **~kalender** m *date-block*; ⟨jur⟩ *calendar of cases* **~lieferung** f ⟨exch⟩ *forward* od *future delivery* **~liste** f ⟨jur⟩ *cause-list*, ⟨Am⟩ *calendar* **~markt** m ⟨com⟩ *market for future delivery* **~tag** m *quarter-day* **≃weise** [adv] *by terms, by instalments, at stated times* **~zahlung** f *instalment* **Terminolog·ie** f ~/~n *terminology* ‖ ⟨chem, etc⟩ *notation* **T·erminus t·echnicus,** [pl] –ni–ci L *technical term*

Term·ite f ~/~en ⟨ent⟩ *white ant* **~nbaum** m *termitary*

Terpent·in n & m ~(e)s/ *turpentine* **~baum** m *t.-tree* **~geist** m ⟨chem⟩ *spirit of t.*. **~harz** n ⟨chem⟩ *abietin(e)* **~öl** n *oil of t.* **~pistazie** f *terebinth*

Terrain [te'rɛŋ, te'rɛ̃ː] n ~s/~s ⟨allg⟩ *ground* ‖

⟨mil⟩ *country* || *building site* || ⟨theat⟩ (*scenic*) *groundrow* || das ~ sondieren *to reconnoitre* od *survey the ground*, ⟨fig⟩ *to feel one's way* (*towards*) || ⟨mil⟩ ~ gewinnen *to gain ground* **~aufnahme** f *ground survey* **~beschaffenheit** f *conditions* pl *of the ground* **~kenntnis** f *local knowledge* **~skizze** f *topographical sketch* **Terrak·otta** f ~/–ten *baked clay* **Terr·asse** f ~/~n *terrace*; *platform* || ⟨arch⟩ *flat roof* || ⟨paint⟩ *foreground* **≗nförmig** a *in the form of a terrace, terraced* **~nland** n *country rising in terraces* **terrass·ieren** vt [h] *to terrace* || ⟨rail⟩ *to step* **terr·estrich** a ⟨astr⟩ *terrestrial* **Terr·ine** f ~/~n *tureen* || (Fleisch≗) *pot of potted meat* **Territori·al-** **~armee** f ⟨engl⟩ *territorial army* **~dienststellen** f pl *t.l defence, -se agencies* **~gerechtigkeit** f *t.l privilege, sovereignty* **~staaten** m pl ⟨hist⟩ *independent states* **~verbände** m pl *t.l d.e units* **~verteidigung** f *t.l d.e* **Territ·orium** n ~s/–rien *territory*

T·error m ~s/ **~·ismus** m ~/ *terrorism* **≗is·ieren** vt [h] *to terrorize*, ⟨fam⟩ *to bully*; ⟨sl⟩ *bulldoze* **~·ist** m ~en/~en *terrorist* **≗·istisch** a *terrorist* **~organisation** f *terror o.*

T·ertia f ~/Tertien **1.** *third* (⟨engl⟩ *fourth*) *form* **2.** ⟨typ⟩ *great primer* **~(wechsel** m) ⟨com⟩ *third of exchange* **Terti·al** n ~s/~e *term* **Tertianer(in** f) m ~s/~ *third-* (⟨engl⟩ *fourth-*)*form boy* (*girl*) **Terti·anfieber** n ⟨path⟩ *tertian ague* od *fever* **terti·är I.** a **II.** ≗ n ~s/ *tertiary* **T·ertie** f ~/~n ⟨R. C.⟩ *tierce* **Terz** f ~/~en ⟨fenc, cards⟩ *tierce*; ⟨fenc⟩ hohe (tiefe) ~ *cut in high* (*low*) *t.* || ⟨mus⟩ *third*; gr (kl) ~ *major* (*minor*) *third* **~engang, ~enlauf** m *run of thirds* | gr **~verwandte** f ⟨mus⟩ *major third relationship* **Terzer·ol** n ~(e)s/~e *pocket-pistol* **Terz·ett** n ~(e)s/~e ⟨mus⟩ *tiercet*, *trio* **Terz·ine** f ~/~n ⟨pros⟩ → *terza-rima*

T·esafilm® m *sellotape*®; ⟨Am⟩ *scotch tape*

T·esching n [~(e)s/~e & ~s] *small gun* od *rifle*

Tess·in 1. m ⟨It⟩ (Nebenfluß des Po) *Ticino* **2.** n (schweiz. Kanton) *Tessin* **Tess·iner Alpen** pl *Tessin Alps* pl

Test m ~es/~e (cf. Fr tête) ⟨chem⟩ *test*, *cupel* || ⟨psych⟩ *test* || ⟨engl hist⟩ (Beamteneid) *test*, [so:] **~akte** f (1673–1826) *t.-act* **~benzin** n *white spirit*; *painter's naphtha* **~eid** m *test* **~gelände** n *proving grounds* pl | oberster **~pilot** m ⟨a–n⟩ *senior test pilot* **~platte** f ⟨opt⟩ *t. plate* **~programm** n ⟨comp⟩ *diagnostic pr.* **~vorlage** f ⟨rep⟩ *t. object*

Testam·ent n ~(e)s/~e *testament*, (*last*) *will* || ⟨theol⟩ *Testament* | mit [ohne] ~ (*to die*) [*in-*] *testate* || ein ~ m *to make one's will* || nach jds ~ *under a p's will* **≗·arisch, ≗lich** a *testamentary* || [adv] *testamentarily*, *by will* || ~ bestimmen *to will* | **~s-** **~erbe** m, (**~erbin** f) ⟨jur⟩ *testamentary heir*(*ess* f) **~eröffnung** f *opening of the will* **~vollstrecker** m ⟨jur⟩ *legal representative*; *executer* **≗weise** [adv] *by will* **~zeuge** m *witness to a will* **~zusatz** m *codicil* **Test·at** n ~s/~e ⟨univ⟩ *certificate of attendance* **~or** m ~s/–·oren *testator* **t·esten** vt [h] *to test*; ⟨comp⟩ ≗ n *checkout*; ≗ des Programms *pr.m proving* || ≗ e–s Produkts *pr.t testing* **test·ieren I.** vt [h] (letztwillig) *to dispose* (*of* ..) *by will* || (bezeugen) *to testify*; ⟨univ⟩ *to certify* (vgl Testat) **II.** vi [h] *to make a will* **Test·ierfähigkeit** f *testamentary capacity* **Test·ierer** m = Testator **Test·ikel** m ~s/~ ⟨anat⟩ *testicle* **Testim·onium** n ~s/–ien *testimonial* || *certificate* **T·esting** f ~/~en *testing*

T·ete f ~/~n ⟨mil⟩ *head* (*of a column*, etc)

Tetra·eder n ~s/~ ⟨math⟩ *tetrahedron*

Tetr·arch m ~en/~en (Vierfürst) *tetrarch* **~·ie** f ~/~n [–i:ən] *tetrarchy*

t·euer a **A.** *dear*, *expensive*, *costly* (*oysters are c. ths*) | ⟨fig⟩ *dear*, *beloved*, *precious*, *cherished* || f ~es Geld kaufen *to pay a high price for* ..; teure Zeiten *dearth*, *famine* **B.** alles was uns ~ ist *all that is dear to us* || Kaffee ist ~ *c. stands high* || ihr ist nichts z ~ *nothing is too dear for her* || er ist sehr ~ *he charges a lot for his goods* || hier ist das Leben nicht ~ *living is not expensive here* || da ist guter Rat ~ *there we are* (*and don't know what to do*)! || **wie** ~ ist *or* kommt es? *how much* (*is it*)? *what does it cost*? **C.** [adv] (etw) ~ **bezahlen** *to pay dearly for* .. || sich etw ~ bez. l *to charge* (*a lot* od) *too much for sth* || er soll es ~ bez. ⟨fig⟩ *he shall sweat for it* || es war nicht **zu** ~ bezahlt *it had been worth it* | ~ **[ver]kaufen** *to* [*sell*] *buy dear*(*ly*); *to sell one's life dearly* || man kauft dort zu ~ *ths cost too dear there* || da hast du zu ~ gekauft *they've overcharged you* || jdn jdm ~ m *to endear a p to a p* || schwören, versprechen → hoch || das wird ihm ~ z stehen k *that will cost him dear*, ⟨fig⟩ *he will be sorry for it yet* | teurer w *to go up* **T·eu(e)rung** f ~/~en *scarcity of provisions*; *dearth*, *dearness* **~szulage** f *cost-of-living allowance* **~szuschlag** m *c.-o.-l. surcharge*

T·eufe f ~/~n ⟨min⟩ *depth* **≗n** vt/i [h] *to deepen*

T·eufel m ~s/~ **A.** *devil* || *fiend* || der ~ ⟨a.⟩ *Old Blazes*, *Scratch*, *Nick*, *Horny*, *Harry* **B.** **armer** ~ *poor devil*, *fellow*, *wretch* || eingefleischter, leibhaftiger ~ *devil incarnate*, *the Old Gentleman himself* || kl ~ *little fiend* || des ~s Bilderbuch ⟨cards⟩ *the d.'s books* **C.** ~ **auch,** ~ noch mal etc! *dash it* (*all*)! || pfui ~! *for shame*!; *the deuce*! || wie der ~ *like hell* od *blazes*, *like the deuce*, *like old gooseberry* od *boots* || (*to work*) *hell-for-leather* | (festhalten ..) *like grim death* || wie der ~ hinter der armen Seele *like a duck on* od *after a June bug* **D.** da soll der ~ arbeiten *it's the d.s own job to* ..; den ~ austreiben *to cast out the d.*; da soll der ~ (dreinfahren)! *damn* od *confound it* (*all*) || ich **frag** den ~ danach *I don't care a hang about it* || der **geht** dem ~ vor die Tür' *he's a hell-for-leather nature*, *he has a devil-may-care recklessness* || er (sie) hat den ~ im Leibe *he* (*she*) *is a devil of a fellow* (*woman*) (*she is a tomboy*) || **hol** ihn ('s) der ~ *curse him*!, *drat him*! (*confound it*) || hol mich der ~ (wenn) *I'm blessed*, ⟨sl⟩ *I'll be blowed* od *jiggered* (*if*) || (es) soll dich der ~ holen *or* frikassieren! *go to hell*! | den ~ **los l** *to let hell loose*, *to raise the very devil* || da ist der ~ los ⟨a.⟩ *there's the d. to pay*; *hell is broke loose* || man soll den ~ nicht an die Wand malen; wenn man den ~ nennt, kommt er gerennt *talk of the d. and he is sure to appear*; mal den ~ nicht an die W.! ⟨Am⟩ *don't start painting the d. on the wall*! || **reitet** dich der ~?, bist du des ~s *are you mad*? ⟨Am⟩ *you're crazy* || °der ~ scheißt immer auf den gr Haufen *money breeds money* || °den ~ in die Hölle treiben (Boccaccio) ⟨sex⟩ *to put the d. into hell* || sie w den ~ **tun** *I'll be damned if they do* || weiß der ~, wie etc *goodness*, *the d. knows how* || man möchte des ~s w *it's enough to drive one mad* || weiß der ~, (da ist's) *the deuce* .. **E. auf** ~ komm raus *like blazes* | **in** ~s Küche k *to get into the very d. of a mess*, *a hell of a scrape*; ⟨bes mil sl⟩ *to catch hooks*; da k–t er in .. *he'll be swimming against the stream* | **mit** dem ~ fertig w *to beat the Dutch*; das muß mit dem ~ zugehen *the d. is in it* | **vom** ~ besessen *possessed of the d.* || wenn man v ~ spricht .. *talk of the d. and he is sure to appear* | **zum** ~ *Oh, hell*!; *hang it all*!; ⟨sl⟩ *blast you*! | geh z ~, scher dich z ~ *go to the deuce*, *to Hell*, *blazes*, *Jericho*, ⟨Am⟩ *to Halifax* | (S) z ~ gehn *to go to rack and ruin*, *to pot*, *to the dogs* | jdn z ~ schicken *to tell a p to go to hell* | z ~ s *to be lost and gone* | z ~ mit .. *drat* (*that door*), *to blazes with* (*him*), *let him go to hell*, etc | wer, wie, wo z ~ .. *who*, etc *the deuce*, *dickens*, etc .., *why in hell* .. **~austreibung** f ⟨bib⟩ *casting out devils* **~chen** n *imp*, *devilkin* || kartesianisches ~

Cartesian devil **~·ei** f ~/~en *devilry, devilment, devilish trick* **~in** f ~/~nen *fiend* | **~s- ~arbeit** f *devilish hard work* **~balg** m ⟨fam⟩ *pickle* **~banner, ~beschwörer** m *exorcist* **~beschwörung** f *exorcism* **~braten** m ⟨fam⟩ *rake-hell, limb* **~braut** f *hag* **~brut** f *devil's brood, hellish crew* **~dreck** m ⟨bot⟩ *asafœtida* **~haar** n ⟨bot⟩ *dodder* **~junge, ~kerl** m *dare-devil, devil of a fellow* ‖ (Prachtkerl) *brick* **~kind** n *imp of Satan* **~krabbe** f ⟨zoo⟩ *spider-crab* **~kunst** f *black art* **~lärm** m *hell of a* (od *infernal*) *noise* **~list** f *diabolic cunning* **~-rochen** m ⟨ich⟩ *horned ray* **~spaß, ~spuk** m ⟨fam⟩ *devilment* **~spiel** n ⟨cards⟩ *the devil's books*; ⟨Am sl⟩ (Automat) *one-armed bandit* **~streich** m *diabolic trick* **~verehrung** f *demonolatry* **~weib** n *she-devil, d. of a woman* **~werk** n *piece of devilry* ‖ *fiendish action*; *sheer diabolism* **~zeug** n *damned nonsense* ‖ *devilry* **~zwirn** m ⟨bot⟩ *box-thorn* **t·euflisch** a *devilish, diabolical, infernal, fiendish* ‖ ~e Arbeit *the d.'s own job*

T·eutoburger Wald m ⟨Ger⟩ (Gebirge) *Teutoburg Forest* †**Teut·onen** pl (westgerm. Volk) *Teutons* †**teut·onisch** a *Teutonic* **teutsch** a = deutsch

T·exashose f (*blue*) *jeans* pl

Tex n ~es/~e (Garn-Numerierung →) *tex*

Text m ~es/~e *text* ‖ (Lieder≗) *words* pl ‖ (Opern≗) *book* ‖ ⟨jur⟩ *context* ‖ ⟨com⟩ *copy* (*on the package*) ‖ ⟨film⟩ *caption* ‖ ~ e–s Liedes ⟨a.⟩ *lyrics* pl ‖ ⟨typ⟩ (zu Bildern) *letterpress* ‖ redaktioneller ~ *editorial matter* ‖ verbesserter ~ *revise* | ⟨ec⟩ den ~ lesen *to read the lesson*; ⟨fig⟩ jdm .. ⟨fam⟩ *to read a p a lesson, to lecture a p*; .. väterlich .. *to talk to a p like a Dutch uncle* | jdn **aus** dem ~ bringen *to put a p out* ‖ aus dem ~ k ⟨a.⟩ *to break down* | weiter **im** ~e! *go on!* | mit unterlegtem ~ *titled* (*film*) **~abbildung** f *illustration of the letterpress* **~abfassung** f *drafting* **~anzeige** f *reader advertisement* **~ausgabe** f *text* **~band** m ⟨theat⟩ *prompter*; ⟨wir⟩ *teleprompter, telecue* **~buch** n (e–r Oper) *word-book, libretto* It **~dichter** m *author of a libretto* **~kritik(er** m) f *textual criticism* (*critic*) **≗mäßig** a *textual* **~-schreiber** m ⟨typ⟩ *copywriter* **~verdrehung** f *straining a text* **~vergleichung** f *collation* **~worte** n pl *original wording* **Text·il- ~industrie** f *textile industry* **~waren** ‖ [pl] *t. goods* od *fabrics*; *t.s* pl **Text·ur** f ~/~en *texture* ‖ ⟨typ⟩ *black letter*

T·ezett n ~/: bis ins *or* zum ~ *to* od *till the last*

Than m [~(e)s/~e & ~s] ⟨Scot⟩ *thane*

The·ater n ~s/~ **1.** *theatre* ‖ (Bühne) *stage* ‖ ⟨Am⟩ schwimmendes ~ *showboat* ‖ (Vorstellung) *performance* | **fürs** ~ schwärmend *stage--struck* | **im** ~ *at the theatre* od *play* ‖ ins ~ gehen *to go to* (oft: *to frequent*) *the th.* | **zum** ~ gehen (Schauspieler w) *to go on the stage* ‖ (*he left the law*) *for the footlights* **2.** ⟨fig⟩ *farce, mockery* (*of a trial*); ⟨Am⟩ *hugger-mugger* ‖ ein wahres ~ aufführen *to put on a terrific act* ‖ ~ m *to dissemble* ‖ mach kein ~ *don't fuss* **3.** ~ spielen *to go in for amateur theatricals* **~bericht** m *theatrical news* **~besuch** m *playgoing* **~besucher** m *playgoer* **~billett** n *ticket* **~coup** m *stage-trick* **~dekoration** f *stage-setting* **~dichter** m *dramatist, dramatic author, playwright* **~diener** m *attendant, usher* **~direktor** m *stage manager*, ⟨Am a.⟩ *producer* **~effekt** m *stage-effect* **~-enthusiast** m *stage-struck p* **~fieber** n *st.-fever* | typische **~figur** → *type* (der *commedia dell'arte* etc), *stock character* **≗freundlich** a *th.-minded* **~held** m *st.-hero* **~karte** f *ticket* **~kasse** f *booking-, box-office* **~leben** n *theatrical profession* **~maler** m *scene-painter* **~mantel** m *opera-cloak* **~manuskript** n *acting copy* **~park** m ⟨film⟩ *physical assets* pl **~portier** m *commissionaire*, ⟨Am⟩ *house doorman* **~spielen** n *play-acting*; ⟨fig⟩ *th.ls* **~stück** n *play* **~tischler** m (*stage*) *carpenter* **~vorstellung** f *th.l performance* **~wesen** n *th.l affairs* pl **~wissenschaft** f *dramatics* pl **~zeitung** f *th.l paper* **~zettel** m *play-bill* **theatr·alisch** a *theatrical, stag(e)y* | [adv] *with a th.l pose*, etc

Theat·iner(in f) m *Theatine monk* (*nun*)

Theb·ais f ~/ ⟨Lit⟩ *Thebaid* †**Th·eben** n ⟨Gr & Eg⟩ (Städte) *Thebes*

The·ismus m ~/ *theism* **the·istisch** a *theistic*(*al*)

Theiß f (Fluß)

Th·eke f ~/~n ⟨com⟩ *counter* ‖ (Wirtschafts-≗) *bar* (an *at*) °**~nhupser** m *counter-hopper, -jumper*

Th·ema n [~s/–men & –mata] *theme* ⟨a. mus⟩ ‖ ⟨mus⟩ *motif* ‖ ⟨Lit⟩ *subject* ‖ (Gesprächs≗) *topic* ‖ ~ Nummer 1 *leading article novelty* od *subject* ⟨a. sex⟩ ‖ ein heikles ~ berühren *to skate over thin ice* ‖ ständiges, übliches ~ ⟨fam⟩ *standing dish* | sich das ~ stellen *to take as one's t.* ‖ beim ~ bleiben *to stick to the point* ‖ z ~ h *to have for t.* **Themen-** ⟨mus⟩ ~aufschließung [f] *theme evolvement*; ~verflechtung [f] *thematic links between individual movements*

Th·emse f *Thames*; der ~bogen *the Thames loop*

Theo- (Gott) **~diz·ee** [–'tse:] f ~/~n *theodicy* **~gon·ie** f ~/~n *theogony* **~krat·ie** f ~/~n *theocracy* **≗kr·atisch** a *theocratic* [adv *-ally*] **~l·og(e)** m ~en/~en *theologian, divine* ‖ (Student) *student of divinity* **~s·oph** m ~en/~en *theosophist* | ~·ie [f] ~/ *theosophy*; ≗isch [a] *theosophic*(*al*) **~log·ie** f ~/~n *theology* ‖ Doktor der ~ *Doctor of Divinity* (*D. D.*) **theol·ogisch** a *theological* **~phan·ie** f ~/~n [–i:ən] *theophany*

Theo- (Sicht) **~dol·it** m ~(e)s/~e *theodolite* **~r·em** n ~(e)s/~e ⟨math⟩ *theorem* **~r·etiker** m ~s/~ *theorist* **≗r·etisch** a *theoretic*(*al*) (adv *-ally, in theory, in the abstract*) ‖ *pure* (*demography* ‖ ⟨tech⟩ *ideal* ‖ ⟨dero⟩ *bookish* **≗retis·ieren** vi [h] *to theorize* **~r·ie** f ~/~n *theory* (aufstellen *to evolve*) ‖ graue ~! *that's an -ism* (*without any scientific basis*)!

Therap·eut m ~en/~en *therapist* **~ik, Therap·ie** ~/ *therapeutics* pl [a. sg konstr] | ~resistenz [f] ⟨med⟩ *drug-fastness*

Th·eriak m ~(e)s/ *theriaca, treacle*

Th·erme f ~/~n *thermal spring* **Thermidor·ist** m ~en/~en ⟨pol⟩ *Thermidorian* **Th·ermik** f ~/ *thermic current* | ~flug [m] *th.c flight* **thermisch** a *thermal* (⟨at⟩ *radiation*) **Therm·it-** ~brandbombe [f] *incendiary bomb with thermite*; ~-handgranate [f] *th. grenade* **Th·ermo- ~element** n *thermocouple* **~m·eter** n ~s/~ *thermometer* ‖ Fieber≗ *clinical th.* ‖ das ~ steht 5 Grad über (unter) Null *the th. stands at 5 degrees above* (*below*) *zero* | ~säule [f] *thermopile* **≗m·etrisch** a *thermometric*(*al*) [adv *-ally*] **≗nuklear** a *thermo--nuclear* (Spaltung) **≗plastisch** a *thermoplastic*; ~e Kunststoffe *th.cs* pl **~p·ylä, ~p·ylen** pl (*the pass of*) *Thermopylæ* pl **~sflasche** f *thermos*(*-flask*) **~sk·op** n ~s/~e *thermoscope* **~stat** m ~en/~en *safety stat* **~st·atik** f ~/ *thermostatics* pl [a. sg konstr]

thesaur·ieren vt [h] *to store*

Th·ese, Th·esis f ~/–sen ⟨log⟩ *thesis*, (*Descartes'*) *proposition*; *assertion* | ⟨pros⟩ *thesis, unaccented syllable* **Th·esenanschlag** m (Luthers) *posting up of his theses*

Th·espiskarren m: mit dem ~ ziehen *to be a strolling actor*

Thess·alien n ⟨Gr⟩ (nordöstl. Landschaft) *Thessaly* **Thess·alier** m, **thess·alisch** a *Thessalian*

Thing [t–] n ~(e)s/~e ⟨hist⟩ *thing, meeting*

Th·omas- ~mehl n ⟨agr⟩ *Thomas meal* **~-schlacke** f *basic Bessemer slag* **~stahl** m *basic Bessemer steel* **~verfahren** n *production of steel by the Thomas process*

Thorn ⟨†Ger⟩, Geburtsort des Kopernikus

Thr·azien n (Landschaft im SO. der Balkanhalbinsel) *Thrace, Thracia* **Thr·azier** m, **~in** f, **thr·azisch** a *Thracian*

Thromb·ose f ~/~n ⟨path⟩ *thrombosis*

Thron m ~(e)s/~e *throne* || den ~ besteigen *to mount the t.* ⟨a. fig⟩ || auf den ~ setzen *to raise to the t., to enthrone* || (jdm) auf dem ~e folgen *to succeed to the t., .. (a p on the t.)* || vom ~e stoßen *to dethrone, depose* **~anwärter** m *heir to the t.* **~besteigung** f *accession to the t., enthronement* **~bewerber** m *claimant* od *aspirant to the t., pretender* **~bewerbung** f *pr.ship* **~entsagung** f *abdication* **~erbe** m, **~erbin** f *heir(ess f) apparent* **~erledigung** f *regal vacancy* **~folge** f *succession (to the t.)* **~folgegesetz** n *settlement* **~folger** m *heir* od *successor to the t.* **~himmel** m *baldachin, canopy* **~räuber** m *usurper* **~rede** f *Royal speech, speech from the t.* || ⟨parl⟩ *King's, Queen's speech* **~saal** m *presence-chamber* **~sessel** m *chair of state* **~wechsel** m *change of sovereigns* **thr·onen** vi [h] *to sit* od *to be enthroned* || ⟨fig⟩ *to reign*

Th·unfisch m ⟨ich⟩ *tunny*

Th·urgau m (schweiz. Kanton) *Thurgovia*

Th·üringen n ⟨Ger⟩ *Thuringia* **Th·üringer** m, **~in** f *Thuringian* **Th·üringer Wald** m *Thuringian Forest* **th·üringisch** a *Thuringian*

Th·ymian m ~(e)s/ ⟨bot⟩ *thyme*

Ti·ara f ~/–ren (Papstkrone) *tiara*

T·iber m ⟨It⟩ (Fluß)

T·ibet n (mittelasiat. Hochland) **Tibet·aner(in** f) m, **tibet·anisch** a *Tibetan*

T·ic m ~s/~s Fr ⟨med⟩ *tic* **Tick** m ~(e)s/~e **1.** *tap* **2.** *spleen; whim,* ⟨fam⟩ *fad* || e–n ~ h *to be whimsical* od *conceited* || e–n ~ h auf *to have a grudge against* **tick**! [intj] *tick*! (Uhr, Herz) *tick-tack*! || ~ m (Uhr) *to tick*; (Herz) *to go pit-a-pat* **~tack** f (Uhr) *tick-tick* **t·icken I.** vi [h] *to tick(-tock)* **II.** vt [h] *to tap* **T·icker** m ~s/~ ⟨wir⟩ *trembler*

T·ide f ~/~n *tide* **~nhub** m *tidal range*

Tief n ~(e)s/~e ⟨mar⟩ *deep water* || ⟨meteor⟩ *low, depression* || ⟨fig⟩ *minimum* | ⟨mar⟩ *deep (e.g. Tuscarora D.* vor Japans Ostküste) **tief I.** [a] **A. 1.** *deep (water, lines of battle. voice, red, shade, sigh, thinker, insight, swoon, grief* etc); unergründlich ~ *plumbless* **2.** (niedrig gelegen) *low (country, valley* etc) **3.** ⟨fig⟩ [+ abstr] *profound (secret* etc) **B.** 3 Fuß ~er Graben (Schnee) *ditch three feet deep (.. high)* **C.** *high (antiquity)* || aus ~ster **Brust** *with a full heart* || kein ~er Denker *superficial th.* || im ~sten Elend *in utter, extreme m.; in the depth of m.* || (Frieden) *complete*; im ~sten F. *in the lap of p.* || in ~(st)en Gedanken *deep in thought, in a brown study* || ~es Gefühl hegen *to feel deeply* (f *about*) || (Geheimnis) *profound* || (Gemüt) *serious* || **(Herz)** *innermost*; aus .. *from the bottom of one's h.*; im .. *in one's h. of h.s* || (Himmel) *dark (blue)* || (Lage) *low,* ⟨fig⟩ *inferior* || in ~ster **Nacht** *in the dead of n.* || (Norden, Süden) *extreme* || in ~(st)em Schlafe *fast asleep, (dead a.)* || (Stimme) *deep, bass* [a] || ~er **Teller** *soup-plate* || (Temperatur) *low* || in der ~sten ~e *in the very depth(s* pl) || in ~ster Trauer *deeply afflicted; in the deepest mourning* (Kleid) || (Verbeugung) *deep* || (Vertrauen) *strict* || (Weg) *sunken* || im ~sten Winter *in the depth of w.* **II.** [adv] **A.** ~ **(atmen)** *heavily*; (einmal) *to draw a deep breath* || etw ~er begründen *to give deeper reasons for ..* || aufs ~ste (bedauern) .. *extremely* || das läßt ~ blicken *that makes you think, that tells its own tale* || ~er blicken *to look deeper (into)* || ~ einbrechen (eindringen) in *to break (enter) deep into* || ~ empfunden *deep-felt* || sich ~ erniedrigen *to demean o.s., to stoop low* || (fühlen) *deeply, keenly* || ~ **gehen** (Schiff) *to draw much water* || ~ gekränkt *cut to the quick* || er ist sehr ~ gesunken *he is very low* || (Straße etc) ~er legen *to lower* || ~ liegend *sunken (eyes)* || ~er sehen ⟨fig⟩ *to see beneath the surface* || (seufzen → ~ atmen) || zu ~ (e–e Terz tiefer) **singen** *to sing flat (to go down a third)* || ~ gesunken ⟨fig⟩ *broken* || ~ stehen (Thermometer etc) *to be low* || ⟨mus⟩ ~er stimmen *to lower the pitch of ..* || *acutely (unhappy)* || sich ~ verbeugen *to make a deep bow*, etc || ~ verletzen = ~ kränken || *heavily (veiled)* || ~ wurzeln *to root deep* **B.** ~ **am** Boden liegen *to be flat on the floor* | ⟨fig⟩ ~ **auf** der Stufenleiter *on the bottom rungs of the social ladder* | **aufs** ~ste *deeply (I d. deplore), with all one's heart, (touched) to the very core* | **bis** ~ **in** .. *till autumn is well advanced,* ⟨Am⟩ *till late fall; deep into the night, the 17th century* | **in**: *to look deeply in a p's eyes*; er hatte ~ ins Glas geschaut *he was in his cups* || .. steckt ihm noch ~ in den Knochen *vice is yet ingrained with him* || ~ in der Patsche *in the soup* || ~ in Schulden stecken *to be over head and ears in debt* || hineinstecken in: *I shoved my hands deep into ..* || ~ im Wald *deep in the w.* | den Hut ~ **über** die Augen drücken *to pull one's hat over one's eyes* **C.** **~er als** *below* || ~ **unten** *low down* **T·ief- ~angriff** m ⟨aero⟩ *low-level* od *ground attack,* ⟨fam⟩ *groundstrafing* [Ger] **~aufschlag** m ⟨ten⟩ *underhand service* **~äugig** a *hollow-eyed* **~bahn** f *underground railway* **~bau** m *u.g. workings* || ⟨min⟩ *deep mining* || ~- ⟨a.⟩ *subterranean* **~betr·übt** a *(deeply) distressed* od *grieved* **~bettanhänger** m ⟨mot⟩ *low-loading trailer* → –lade– **~bew·egt** a *deeply moved* **~bl·au** a *dark* od *deep blue* **~blick** m ⟨fig⟩ *penetration* **~blickend** a *deep-sighted, penetrating* **~bohrer** m *mechanic auger* **~bunker** m *cave* od *underground shelter* **~decker** m *low-wing (mono)plane* **~denkend** a *profound* **~druck** m ⟨meteor⟩ *low-pressure; depression* (⟨a.⟩ ~gebiet) | ~ausläufer [m] *secondary d.*; ~rinne [f] *trough, col* | ⟨typ⟩ *intaglio; copper-plate printing; rotogravure* **~ebene** f *flat, lowhand, l. plain* **~empfunden** a *heart-felt* **~·ernst** a *solemn* **~flieger** m *low-flying plane; ground-attack aircraft* | ~angriff = Tiefangriff **~flug** m ⟨aero⟩ *low flying* || im ~ *from a low level* | ~bombenangriff [m] *low altitude bombing* **~gang** m ⟨mar⟩ *draught* (→ tief gehen); v geringem ~ *of light d.* || 5 F. ~ h *to draw 5 feet of water* || schiffbarer ~ *navigable depth (of a waterway)* **~garage** f *underground car-park* **~gebeugt** a *bowed down; deeply afflicted* **~gefrieranlage** f *sharp freezer* **~gefühlt** a *heart-felt* **~gegliedert** a ⟨tact⟩ *distributed in depth* **~gehend** a ⟨fig⟩ *profound, searching, deep (influence)* **~gekühlt** a *low-temperature cooled; deeply cooled; frozen; deep-freezed (food)* **~gestaffelt** a ⟨mil⟩ *deep (lines); echeloned in depth*; ~e Stellung *position in depth* **~greifend** a *radical* **~gründig** a ⟨agr⟩ *deep soil* | ⟨übtr⟩ *profound, deep; recondite (style)* **~kühl-** ~kost [f] *quick frozen foods* pl; ~truhe [f] *deep freezing chest; deep-freeze (chest); chest* od *home freezer* **~lade-** ~linie [f] *load-line*; ~wagen [m] ⟨rail⟩ *well (wag(g)on* **~lader** m *low loader* | in **~lage** f (Ruhr-Schnellweg) *constructed below street level* **~land** n *lowland(s* pl) **~liegend** a *deep-seated*, (Augen) *deep-set, sunken*; ⟨fig⟩ *basic* **~löffel** m (Bagger~) *backhoe* **~lot** n *deep-sea lead* **~ofen** m *soaking pit* **~punkt** m ⟨fig⟩ *nadir*; ⟨meteor⟩ *low point* || ⟨übtr⟩ den ~ erreichen *to hit bottom* **~schlag** m ⟨box⟩ *low blow*; e–n ~ versetzen *to hit below the belt* **~schürfend** a *thorough; most searching* **~-schwarz** a *deep* od *jet black* **~see-** ~forschung [f] *deep-sea sounding* od *research*; ~graben [m] *trench*; rinne [f] *d.-s. furrow*; ~tauchkugel [f] *bathysphere*; ~-Unterwasserschiff [n] *deep diver,* ⟨Am a.⟩ *d. quest* **~sinn** m *profoundness, thoughtfulness; depth, profundity* || (Schwermut) *melancholy* **~sinnig** a *thoughtful, pensive, melancholy, wistful* || (gründlich) *deep* **~stand** m *lowness*; ⟨fig⟩ *low state of relations; nadir; lowest ebb; low level* **~stehend** a ⟨print⟩ *inferior* | geistig ~e(r) *low-brow* **~tonlautsprecher** m *woofer* **~tönend** a *deep-sounding, -toned* **~wurzelnd** a *d.-*

-rooted **T·iefe** f ~/~n **1.** *depth* ⟨a. tact⟩; in die ~ gegliedert *organized in d.* || (Stimme) *deepness*; ⟨rec⟩ *bass* || *height* (*of snow*) || ⟨fig⟩ *profoundness, profundity* **2.** *deep*; *d. place*; *gorge, abyss, pit* || ⟨mar⟩ *soundings* pl || *bottom recesses* pl (*of the heart*) **t·iefen** vt/i **1.** *to deepen* **2.** ⟨mar⟩ *to sound* **T·iefen-** **~bombe** f ⟨aero, mar⟩ *depth charge* **~boot** n *bathyscaphe* **~einstellung** f ⟨phot⟩ *depth focusing* **~erosion** f ⟨geol⟩ *down cutting* **~feuer** n ⟨mil⟩ *searching fire* **≃gefrorene** Schicht *permafrost* **~gestein** n *plutonic rock* **~gliederung** f ⟨mil⟩ *distribution* od *disposition, formation in depth* **~linie** f ⟨mar⟩ *isobath* **~messer** m *fathometer* **~messung** f *sounding* **~psychologie** f *depth ps.* **~reiniger** m ⟨cosm⟩ *deep cleanser* **~rinne** f *deep channel* **~ruder** n ⟨aero⟩ *elevator control*; ⟨mar⟩ *hydrovane*; ⟨sub-mar⟩ *horizontal rudder* **~schärfe** f ⟨phot⟩ *depth of focus* od *field* **~staffelung** f ⟨tact⟩ *defence* od *deployment in depth*; → -gliederung **~streuung** f *longitudinal dispersion* || *ranging* **~wirkung** f *plastic effect*; *stereoscopic e.* ⟨a. film⟩; ⟨arts⟩ *appearance of 3-dimensional depth* (*in a print*, etc); *illusion of d.* **t·ieferstehend** a (im Rang) *inferior* **t·iefst** ([sup] v tief) *deepest*; *lowermost* (⟨cosm⟩ Haut)

T·iegel m ~s/~ ⟨cul⟩ *saucepan* || ⟨chem, met⟩ *crucible* **~druckpresse** f *plate-press* **~guß** m *c.-smelting* | ~stahl [m] *c.-steel*

T·iekholz n *teak*(*-wood*); → Teak

Tients·in n (chin. Hafenstadt)

Tier n ~(e)s/~e ⟨allg⟩ *animal*, (*dumb*) *creature* || (gr 4-füßiges) *beast* || (vernunftloses) *brute* | ⟨hunt⟩ *doe, deer, hind*; ⟨allg⟩ *game* || ⟨hors⟩ *mount* | ⟨fig⟩ (P) *beast, brute* || ein großes ~ ⟨fam⟩ *a swell*; *big bug* od *gun*; *bigwig, panjandrum* || ein gutes ~ *a kind soul* || hohes ~ *mogul*; ⟨mil sl⟩ *brass hat* || das schwarze ~ ⟨fig⟩ *the dumps* || ich hab's arme ~ *I've got the mopes* || sich durch Trunk z ~ m *to make a beast of o.s. drinking* **≃ähnlich** a *b.-like* **~anbeter** m *worshipper of a.s* **~art** f *species* **~arznei** f *veterinary medicine* | ~kunde [f] *v.y science* **~arzt** m *v.y surgeon*, ⟨fam⟩ *vet* **≃ärztlich** a *v.y* **~aufnahme** f *a.l photograph* **~ausstopfer** m *taxidermist, embalmer* | ~kunst [f] *t.my* **~bändiger** m *a.l trainer* **~beschreiber** m *zoographer* **~bildhauer** m *a.lier* **~bude** f *menagerie* **~epos** n *a.l* od *b. epic* **~fabel** f *a.l* od *b. fable* **~freund** m *lover of a.s* **~garten** m **1.** *zoological gardens* pl **2.** *deer park* || Gott hat e–n gr ~ *it takes all sorts to make up the world* **~gehege** n *preserve*; ⟨Am⟩ *state* od *national park* **~geographie** f *zoogeography* **~handel** m *trade in live stock* **~handlung** f *pet shop* **~heilkunde** f *veterinary medicine* **~hetze** f *baiting of b.s*; *a.l chase* **~klinik** f *pets' hospital* **~kohle** f *char* **~kreis** m ⟨astr⟩ *zodiac* | ~zeichen [n] *sign of z.* **~kunde** f *zoology* **~laute** m pl *a.l calls* **~leim** m *a.l size* **~maler** m *painter of a.ls*; *a.lier* **~mensch** m *abominable snowman* **~natur** f *brute-(like)* od *a.l nature*; die ~ in mir *the beast in me* **~ornamentik** f *a.l style* **~pflanze** f *zoophyte* **~pfleger** m ⟨im Zoo⟩ *keeper* **~präparator** m *embalmer* **~quäler** m *a.l teaser*; *tormentor of a.ls* | ~ei [f] *cruelty to a.ls* **~reich** n *a.l kingdom* **≃reich** a *rich in a.ls* **~schau** f *show of a.ls* **~-schutzverein** m (⟨engl⟩ **R**oyal) **S**ociety *for the* **P**revention *of* **C**ruelty *to* **A**.*ls* ([*R.*] *S. P. C. A.*); *Humane Society* **~stimmenimitator** m *a.l impersonator* **~stück** n ⟨arts⟩ *a.l-picture* **~versuch** m ⟨med⟩ *guinea-pig inoculation* **~wärter** m *keeper* (*of wild b.s*) **~welt** f *a.l world*; *fauna* **~wesen** n *a.l*; [abstr] *a.lity* **~zucht** f *a.l husbandry* **T·ierchen** n ~s/~ *little a.l*; ⟨Scot⟩ *b.ie* || (kleinstes) *a.lcule* **T·ierheit** f ~/ *a.l nature*; *a.lity* || ⟨dero⟩ *brutishness, bestiality* **t·ierisch** a *a.l* || ⟨dero⟩ *brute, brutal, bestial* | sich ~ betrinken *to make a b. of o.s. drinking* | das ≃e *the a.l part*; (⟨a.⟩ Tierhaftigkeit) *animality*

T·iflis n ⟨Russ⟩ (Hptst. Grusiens)

t·ifteln → tüfteln

T·iger m ~s/~ *tiger* (**~in** f *tigress*) **~decke** f, **~fell** n, **~haut** f *tiger-skin* **~hund** m *Dalmatian* (*dog*) **~pferd** n *zebra* **~schlange** f *spotted rock-snake* **~schnecke** f *tiger-cowry* **~weibchen** n *tigress* **~wolf** m *spotted hyena* **t·igern I.** vt [h] *to spot, speckle* **II.** vi [s] *to stalk* (*about*)

T·igris m (Fluß, Kleinasien & Mesopotamien)

T·ilde f ~/~n **1.** ⟨typ⟩ (*sign of repetition*) *tilde-(-mark)* **2.** (über n [ñ] [–nj–] z. B. cañon) *tilde*

t·ilgbar a *extinguishable* || (Schuld) *redeemable* **≃keit** f *e.ness, r.ness* **t·ilgen** vt [h] (auslöschen) *to extinguish* || (streichen) *to strike out* || (auswischen) *to wipe out, to efface* || ⟨typ⟩ *to delete* || (annullieren) *to annul, cancel* || (ausrotten) *to extirpate* || (vernichten) *to destroy, annihilate* || (e–e Schuld) *to pay, compound, discharge, cancel* || (e–e Anleihe) *to redeem* || (sühnen) *to make good* || .. aus s–m Gedächtnis ~ *to erase .. from one's m.* || *time was gradually expunging the unhappy th.* || (Makel) *to wipe out* **T·ilgung** f ~/~en *extirpation* || *striking out, obliteration* || *annulment, cancelling* || *payment* || *making good* || *redemption* || *amortization* (*of bonds*) || ~ der Wechselverpflichtung ⟨com, bank⟩ *discharge of a bill* **T·ilgungs-** **~kasse** f, **~fonds** m *sinking fund* **~plan** m *plan for gradual payment*; *program of redemption* **~schein** m *certificate of redemption*; *bill of amortization* **~zeichen** n ⟨typ⟩ *dele* (₰)

T·ingeltangel m & n ~s/~ (*low*) *music-hall*

Tinkt·ur f ~/~en *tincture* **T·inte** f ~/~n *ink* || ⟨paint⟩ *tint* || unauslöschliche ~ *undelible ink* || viel ~ (verschreiben) .. *floods of i.*; ⟨fam⟩ (*to sling*) *ink* || mit ~ beklecksen etc *to ink, blot* || mit ~ nach-, ausziehen *to i. in, over* || säuberlich mit ~ geschr. *set down in neat black ink* || ⟨fig⟩ in die ~ k *to get into a scrape, a pretty pickle* || tief in der ~ sitzen *to be right in the soup* || °klar wie dicke ~ (*as*) *plain as paint, mud* od *as a pikestaff* || °~ gesoffen h *to be off one's chump* | °⟨fig⟩ rote ~ (Blut) *claret* **T·inten-** **~faß** n *i.stand, i.pot* || (eingebaut) *i. well* **~fisch** m ⟨zoo⟩ *octopus*; *cuttlefish*, ⟨cul a.⟩ *squid* **~fleck** m *blot*(*ch*), *i.-spot* **~glas** n *i.-glass* **~gummi** m *i.-eraser* **~klecks** m *i.-blot* **~kleckser, ~kuli** m ⟨fam⟩ (P) *i.-slinger, hack writer*; *quilldriver*; (S) *ball-point* **~pulver** n *i.-powder* **~stift** m (*copying-*)*i. pencil* **~strich** m *line drawn with i.* **~wischer** m *pen-wiper* **t·intig** a *inky* (a. *taste*) | *stained with ink*

Tip m ~s/~s ⟨sport etc⟩ *tip, wrinkle, snip* (*to give the straight* [richtig] *t., w.*); ⟨Am sl⟩ *steer* || guter ~ ⟨Am fam⟩ *hot tip, straight dope* **≃p-tapp**! [intj] *pit-a-pat* °**≃-t·op**! [intj & pred a] *tip-top*; *elegant*; *swell* **~pelbruder** m *tramp* **≃peln I.** vt [h] = tüpfeln **II.** vi [s] *to tiptoe* || ⟨fam⟩ *to tramp* **≃pen** vi/t [h] *to touch gently, to tap*; ⟨mot⟩ (Vergaser) *to tickle* || ⟨fam⟩ *to type*(*-write*) || ⟨sport sl⟩ *to tip* || ⟨mil sl⟩ *to foot-(-slog), to frog, flog, pad it*; weiter ~ *to knock along* **~pfehler** m *error in typing* **~pfräulein** n ~s/~ (⟨fam⟩ a. Tipp(ö)se [f] ~/~n) (*girl*) *typist* **~schein** m ⟨ftb⟩ *coupon*

T·ippler m ~s/~ ⟨bes österr⟩ *drunkard*

Tir·ade f ~/~n *tirade, heroics* pl || sich in ~n ergehen *to fly off the handle*; ~n schreiben *to overwrite* **Tiraill·eur** [tiral'jør] m *skirmisher*

tiril·ieren vi [h] (Lerche) *to warble*

Tir·ol n (österr. Alpenland) *the Tyrol* **Tir·oler(in** f) m, **tir·ol(er)isch** a *Tyrolese* || die Tiroler pl *the Tyrolese* **Tir·olerland** n *Tyrolese homeland*

Tisch m ~(e)s/~e **A. 1.** *table*, (Tafel) *board* **2.** (Kost) *board* **3.** (Mahlzeit) *meal* **4.** (~gesellschaft) *table* (*the whole t.*) **B.** den ~ **(ab)decken** *to* (*clear*) *lay the t.*, (*to draw the cloth*) || ⟨hot⟩ e–n ~ bestellen *to reserve* od *book a t.* || ~ u Bett *bed and board*; Scheidung v ~ u B. *judicial separation* **C. Anrichte≃** *server*; *side t.* || ~ des

Herrn *Holy T.* ‖ Laden≗ *counter* ‖ Nacht≗ *commode*; ⟨bes Am⟩ *bedside table*; *night table* ‖ ⟨ski⟩ Schanzen≗ *take-off* ‖ Werk≗ *work bench* **D.** f den **feinen** ~ *for the epicure* ‖ am grünen ~ *at the round t.*; .. v grünen ~ *red-tape* (*ordinance*) ‖ e–n guten ~ führen *to keep a good t.* ‖ ⟨fig⟩ reinen ~ m *to make a clean sweep* (*of it*) ‖ hier wird ein schmackhafter ~ geführt *the cuisine is excellent here* **E. am** ~ sitzen *to be sitting at the t.* | ⟨parl⟩ **auf** den ~ des Hauses *on the t. of the h.* ‖ ⟨cul⟩ .. kommt bei uns nie auf den ~ *this food is never served by us* | **bei** ~ *at t.*; *during meal-time* ‖ **nach, vor** ~ *after, before dinner* | **.. über** den ~ (schieben) .. *along the t.* | ⟨fig⟩ **unter** den ~ fallen *to come to nothing, to pass unnoticed*; .. l *to overlook*; *to suppress* ‖ unter den ~ klopfen *to touch wood*, .. reden *to talk down*, .. trinken *to drink* (*a p*) *under the t.* ‖ er steckt die Füße unter fremden ~ *he has no roof to his head* | **vom** ~ aufstehen *to get* od *stand up from* (*the*) *t.* | **zu** ~ bitten (bleiben) *to invite to* (*to stay for*) *dinner* ‖ (Dame) zu ~ führen *to take in* (⟨Am⟩ *out*) ‖ z ~ gehen *to sit down to dinner*; ⟨univ⟩ *to go to hall* ‖ wo gehen Sie z ~? *whom do you board with*? ‖ z ~e des Herrn gehen *to partake of the Lord's Supper* ‖ Gäste z ~ h .. *at t.* ‖ bei jdm z ~ s *to break bread at a p's t.* ‖ sich z ~ setzen *to sit down to a meal* **~apparat** m *table-phone* **~besen** m *crumb-brush* **~blatt** n *t.-top* **~dame** f *lady taken in to dinner* **~decke** f *t.-cloth* **~einlage** f *t.-leaf* **~ende** n (oberes) *head*, (unteres) *foot of the t.* **~fernsprecher** m *portable telephone* **≗fertig** a ⟨cul⟩ *instant convenience* (*food*) **~gänger** m *boarder* **~gast** m *diner* **~gebet** n *grace* (*before, after dinner* [Tisch]) ‖ das ~ sprechen *to say grace*; (an Geistlichen:) *will you give us a grace* **~geld** n *board* **~genosse** m *companion at t.*, *fellow-guest* **~gerät, ~geschirr** n *t.-requisites* pl, *utensils* [pl] *for the t.* **~gesellschaft** f *company at t.*; *guests* pl; *dinner-party* **~gespräch** n *t.-talk*; ~e [pl] ⟨Lit etc⟩ *ana*(*s*) **~gestell** n *trestle* **~glocke** f *dinner-bell*; *hand-bell* **~karte** f *place card* **~kasten** m *t.-drawer* **~klappe** f *leaf of a t.* **~klopfen** n *t.-rapping* **~kochplatte** f ⟨el⟩ *t.-cooker* **~korb** m *plate-basket* **~lade** f *t.-drawer* **~lampe** f *t. standard* **~läufer** m *t.-centre* **~messer** n *t.-knife* **~leinen, ~linnen** n *napery* **~ordnung** f *order of the* (*guests at*) *t.* **~platte** f *t.-top*; *leaf* **~rechenmaschine** f ⟨comp⟩ *desk calculator* **~rede** f *toast, after-dinner speech* **~rücken** n *t.-tipping, -turning* **~schmuck** m *t.-garnish* **~tennis** n *t.-tennis* **~tuch** n *t.-cloth*; das ~ zw sich u jdm zerschneiden *to break off all relations with a p* **~versenkung** f ⟨theat⟩ *grave* (⟨Am⟩ *stage*) *trap* **~wäsche** f *t.-linen* **~wein** m *ordinary wine* **~zeit** f *meal-, dinnertime* **~zeug** n *t.-linen* **T·ischchen** n *end table* **~garnitur** f *range of 3 tables* **T·ischlein** n ~s/~ *small table* **~-deck-dich** n *magic table* **T·ischler** m ~s/~ *joiner* ‖ (Kunst≗) *cabinet-maker*; → Zimmermann *carpenter* **~arbeit** f *j.'s work, j.y* **~bank** f *j.'s bench* **~geselle** m *journeyman j.* **~handwerk** n *j.'s trade* **~leim** m *strong glue* **~meister** m *master j.* **~werkzeug** n *j.'s tools* pl **Tischler·ei** f ~/~en *j.y, j.'s trade* od *shop, cabinet-work* **t·ischlern** vi [h] *to do j.'s work*

Tit·an I. m ~en/~en (f ~in) *Titan*(*ess* f) **II.** n ~s/ *titanium* **~eisenerz** n *t.iferous iron-ore* **≗enhaft, ~isch** a *T.ic*

T·itel m ~s/~ **1.** *title* ‖ der ~ Professor *the t. of pr.* ‖ den ~ e–s Grafen führen *to have the t.* (*of*) *count* ‖ bloßer ~ *mere t.* ‖ sich e–n ~ beilegen *to assume a t.* ‖ viele ~ *strings of letters after one's name*; ~ vor dem N. *handle to one's name* **2.** (Anspruch) *claim* **3.** (Überschrift) *heading*; (e–s Abschnittes etc) *caption* ‖ (Buch≗) *title*; (Buch) *title*; Buch mit aufgedrucktem ~ *lettered book* **~auflage** f *edition having merely a new t.* **~bild** n *frontispiece, cover-photo* | ~mädchen [n] *covergirl* **~bildchen** n *vignette* **~blatt** n *t.-page* | ~-Schönheit [f] *covergirl, pin-up-g.* **~bogen** m *t.-sheet* **~brett** n (INRI) ⟨ec arts⟩ *titulus* **~halter** m ⟨sport⟩ *t.-holder* **~heilige(r)** m *titular* **~held** m ⟨theat⟩ *protagonist* **~kopf** m *catchword, headword, heading* **~kupfer** n *frontispiece* **~held** m *protagonist* **~mädchen** n *covergirl* **~rolle** f *name-part, t.-rôle*; ein Film mit N. in der ~ *a f. featuring N.* ‖ sie spielt ~n ⟨Am fam⟩ *she gets top billing* **~seite** f *front page* **~sucht** f *rage for* od *fondness of t.s* **≗süchtig** a *greedy after t.s* **~verteidiger** m ⟨sport⟩ *defender* **~wesen** n (*system of bestowing*) *t.s* **Titel·ei** f ~/~en *title-sheet*

titr·ierbar a ⟨chem⟩ *titratable* **titr·ieren** vt/i [h] *to titrate* **Titr·ieranalyse** f *titration*

T·ittelchen n: bis aufs ~ ausarbeiten *to work out to a nicety* ×°**T·itten** f pl *bubbies, titties* pl

Titul·ar- ~bischof m *titular b.* **~fürst** m *titular sovereign, nominal ruler* **~professor** m *honorary pr.* ‖ ⟨mil⟩ **~rang** m *brevet rank*; *brevetcy* **-lat·ur** f ~/~en *titles* pl **t-l·ieren** vt [h] *to title, call, style* ‖ jdn Herzog ~ *to give a p the title of duke*; *to call a p d.*

T·ivoli n ~s/~s (Spiel) *bagatelle, pinball*

Tixoband® n [österr] = Tesafilm®

°**tj·a** [intj] *hm!, well, well!*

Tj·ost m ~(e)s/~e ⟨hist⟩ *joust*

×°**tj·üs, tj·üssing!** [intj] → tschüß ⟨fam⟩ *tata!*

Toast [to:st] m ~es/~e **1.** (Röstbrot) *toast* | ~halter [m] *t.-rack* **2.** (Trinkspruch) *health, t.* ‖ e–n ~ ausbringen *or* halten *to propose a t.*; auf jdn *to t.* od *propose a p*(*'s health*) | **≗en** vi [h] **1.** *to t.* (Brot) **2.** *to t.* (auf jdn *a p*) | **~er** m ~s/~ (S) *toaster*

°**T·obak** m = Tabak, ⟨sl⟩ *baccy* ‖ das ist starker ~ *bit thick!* ‖ °seit Anno ~ *from time immemorial*

T·ob- ~sucht f *raving madness, frenzy, delirium* **≗süchtig** a *raving mad* **~suchtsanfall** m *fit of raving madness* **t·oben** vi [h] *to rave, roar, rage, storm, bluster* ‖ (Kinder) *to romp, rag* (→ lärmen) ‖ (Meer) *to rage, roar* ‖ (Sturm) *to roar* | **~d** a ⟨a.⟩ *furious, enraged*; *phrenetic*(*al*[*ly* adv]); (stürmisch) *tempestuous*; *uproarious* (*applause*)

T·ochter f ~/≗ *daughter* ‖ die ~ des Hauses *the d.* od *girl* od *young lady of the h.* ‖ ⟨fam⟩ höhere ~ *young lady* (*still at school*) **~anstalt** f *branch establishment* **~gesellschaft** f ⟨com⟩ *subsidiary* (*company*) **~kind** n *d.'s child* **~kirche** f *filial church* ‖ (für entfernt Wohnende) *chapel of ease* **~kompaß** m ⟨mar⟩ *master-c. indicator, repeater* od *auxiliary c.* **~liebe** f *d.'s love* **~mann** m *son-in-law* **~sprache** f *d.-language* **~staat** m *colony* **~stadt** f *colonial town* **t·öchterlich** a *daughterly* ‖ [adv] *in a daughterly way* **T·öchterschule** f *girls' school* ‖ höhere ~ *girls' secondary school, girls' college*

Tod m ~(e)s/~e **A.** *death*; ⟨arts⟩ ~ der Maria *Dormition of the Virgin* ‖ ⟨jur⟩ *decease* ‖ (Ableben) ⟨pol⟩ *demise* | der ~ als Sensenmann *the grim reaper* ‖ .. ein Kind des ~es (*you are*) *a dead man* (*if*) ‖ ⟨cards⟩ ~ u Leben → Bettelmann ‖ ~ u Teufel! *the deuce!, hang it all!* ‖ ⟨prov⟩ des e–n ~, des andern Brot *one man's meat is another man's poison* **B. bitter,** grimm *bitter, grim* (*d.*) ‖ bürgerlicher ~ *civil d. outlawry* ‖ e–n (e–s) elenden ~(es) sterben *to die a dog's d.*; gewaltsamer ~ *violent d.*; .. gewaltsamen ~es st. *to die in one's shoes* ‖ **langsam** *lingering* (*d.*) ‖ aussehen wie der leibhaftige ~ ⟨fam⟩ .. *like d. warmed up* ‖ **leiblich,** zeitlich *temporal* (*d.*) ‖ ⟨med⟩ leichter ~ *euthanasia* L ‖ e–s natürl. ~es sterben *to die a natural d.* od *in one's own bed*, ⟨jur⟩ *to die a natural d.*; .. schönen .. *to die a beautiful d., to die well* ‖ der schwarze ~ *the Black D.* ‖ ein seliger ~ *a Christian d.* **C.** den ~ **finden** *to meet one's d., to be killed* (*in an accident* bei); durch e–n Sturz *to fall to one's d.*; in den Wellen *to find a* *watery grave* (→ finden I. B. 2. b.) || sich den ~ **geben** *to kill o.s., to commit suicide* || den ~ herbeisehnen *to long for d.'s relief* || sich den ~ holen *to catch one's d.* || das wird sein ~ **sein** *that will be the d., ruin, end of him* || des ~es s *to be doomed* || ich will des ~es s *I will fall down dead* (*if*) || dem ~e nahe s *to be at d.'s door, to be sinking fast* || ⟨prov⟩ nur der ~ ist umsonst *everything costs money* || der ~ schloß ihre Augen *she closed her eyes in d.* || ihm steht der ~ vor der Tür *he is at d.'s door* || tausend ~e **sterben** *to die a thousand d.s* (→ B.) || den ~ am Galgen (durch Henkershand) sterben *to suffer d. by the gallows* (*by the hangman's noose*) || den ~ suchen *to ask for d.* || ~ verursacht durch .. *d. from diphtheria* || dem ~e geweiht *doomed* **D.** sich **auf** den ~ erkälten *to catch one's d. of a cold* || (etw) auf den ~ nicht ausstehen *not to be able to stand* od *tolerate* || Kampf auf Leben u ~ *mortal combat* || auf L. u ~ kämpfen *to strive to the bitter end* || auf den ~ krank *hopelessly ill*; .. verwundet *mortally wounded* | **bei** s–m ~e *at his d.* | getreu **bis** in den ~ *f. unto d.* || bis über den ~ hinaus *beyond the grave* || bis z ~e *till d., to one's dying day*; *to the bitter end* | **gegen** den ~ ist kein Kraut gewachsen *there is no cure for d.* | **im** ~e *in d.* || in den ~ gehen ⟨fig⟩ *to walk the plank* || Tausende in den ~ schicken *to send .. to their doom* || er ist mir in den ~ verhaßt, zuwider *I hate him like poison* | **mit** (dem) ~e abgehen *to pass away* || mit dem ~ bestraft w *to be under pain of d.* | **nach** dem ~e erfolgt etc *posthumous* (*award*) | **trotz** ~ u Teufel ⟨fam⟩ *roll, bowl, or pitch* | **vom** ~ umfangen s *to be in d.* | **zu** ~e beschämt *mortified*, betrübt *mortally grieved* || jdn v Leben z ~e bringen *to put an end to a p's life* || z ~e erschrocken *frightened to d.* || z ~e hetzen ⟨hunt⟩ *to run down*, ⟨fig⟩ *to hunt* (*a simile*) *to d., to run* (*a s.*) *off its feet* || jdn (durch Arbeit) z ~e hetzen *to work* od *slave a p to d.* || z ~e k *to come by* (*to meet*) *one's d.*; (durch Fall) *to fall to d.* || ⟨fig⟩ (Gefühl) z ~e reiten *to whip to d.* || z ~e verurteilt *sentenced to d.*; .. s ⟨a.⟩ *to lie under penalty of death* | **jdn zu** ~e ängstigen *to frighten a p out of his senses*, halb .. prügeln .. *within an inch of a p's d.* | **sich zu** ~e ärgern *to fret* etc *o.s. to d.*; zu ~e erschrecken *to* (*be*) *scare*(*d*) *to d.*, zu ~e erschrocken [a] *scared stiff, panic-stricken, terrified*; geängstigt [a] *mortally afraid*; .. grämen *to wear o.s. to d. by grieving*; .. hungern *to be starved*; .. lachen *to die with l.*; .. langweilen *to bore o.s. to d.*; ⟨hum⟩ .. reformieren etc *to reform*, etc *one's head off* || unmittelbar **zum** ~e führendes Leiden *immediate cause of d.* **~́ähnlich** a *death-like* **~́bringend** a *deadly, fatal* **~feind** m *mortal* od *deadly enemy* **~́f·eind** [pred a]: e–m ~ s *to be a p's sworn enemy* **~́geweiht** a *doomed* **~́krank** a *dangerously ill* **~́m·üde** a *tired to death*; *dead-tired, dead beat*; jdn ~ gehen l *to walk a p off his legs* **~́s·icher** a *as sure as a gun, cock-sure* || ⟨sl⟩ *dead* (*tip*) || e–e ~e S *a dead certainty* od ⟨sl⟩ *snip*, ⟨sl⟩ *cinch* **~sünde** f *deadly* od *mortal sin* **~́wund** a *mortally wounded* **T·odes-** **~ahnung** f *presentiment of d.* **~angst** f *hag-ridden fear*; *agony*; ⟨fig⟩ in ~ *in mortal dread*; e–e ~ h vor *to go in mortal terror of ..* **~anzeige** f *obituary* (*notice*) || (polizeiliche) *notice of d.* **~art** f *manner of d.* **~becher** m *fatal cup* **~́bleich** a *deadly pale* **~engel** m *angel of d.* **~erklärung** f ⟨Ger jur⟩ *declaration of d.* **~fall** m (*case of*) *d., decease*; ~́e [pl] *d.s*, ⟨mil⟩ *casualties*; Zahlen der ~́e [pl] *figures of d.*; ⟨ins⟩ eingetretene ~́e *actual d.s* **~falle** f *death-trap* **~furcht** f *fear of d.* **~gedanke** m *thought of d.* **~gefahr** f *deadly peril*; *danger* od *peril of a p's life* || Achtung! ~! *Danger to life*! || jdn aus ~ retten *to save a p's life* || in ~ schweben *to be in mortal danger* **~instinkt** m ⟨psych⟩ *d. instinct* **~jahr** n *year of a p's d.* **~kampf** m *agony* (*of d.*), *d.-struggle* °**~kandidat** m *p at d.'s door* **~keim** m *mark of d.* | er bekam die **~kugel** [f] *he was shot to death* **~́mutig** a *d.-defying* **~nachricht** f *news of a p's d.* **~not** f = –gefahr || in ~́en *struggling with d.* **~qualen** f pl *pangs of d., d.-throes* pl **~röcheln** n *d.-rattles* pl **~schauer** m *horror of d.* **~schlaf** m = Totenschlaf **~schreck** m; e–n ~ bek *to get the fright of one's life* || jdm e–n ~ einjagen *to frighten a p out of his wits* **~schweiß** m *cold sweat of d.* **~stoß** m (versetzen *to deal* od *deliver the*) *d.-, finishing-blow* **~strafe** *death penalty*; *capital punishment* || bei ~ *on pain of d.* || die ~ erleiden *to be executed* || Vollziehung der ~ *execution*, ⟨Am⟩ *electrocution* **~streich** m = –stoß **~stunde** f *hour of d., supreme hour* **~sturz** m *fall to d.* **~szene** f *d. scene* **~tag** m *day* od *anniversary* (200-jähriger ~ *bicentenary*, ⟨Am⟩ *bicentennial*) *of a p's d.* **~ursache** f *cause of d.* (primär *primary, principal*) **~urteil,** n (fällen *to pronounce*; vollstrecken *to carry out a*) *sentence of d.* **~verachtung** f *contempt of d.*; *utter disregard of d.* | ⟨fig⟩ mit ~ hinunterwürgen ⟨cul⟩ *to somehow manage to swallow* (*it*), *to get* (*it*) *down somehow or other* **~verbrechen** n *capital crime* **~vermutung** f *presumption of d.* **~vorbote** m, **~zeichen** n *d.-token, sign of d.* **~wunde** f *mortal wound* **t·ödlich** a *deadly* (*effect, boredom*) || *mortal* (*blow, wound*) || *fatal* (*accident, shot, poison, disease*) || ⟨at⟩ *lethal* (*radiation*) | ⟨fig⟩ *complete* (*certainty*) | [adv] *mortally*(*-wounded*); *deadly*(*-pale*) || (*to hate*) *like poison* od *with a deadly hate* || ~ verunglücken *to be killed in an accident, to have a fatal acc.* || sich ~ langweilen *to be bored stiff* **~́keit** f ~/ *deadliness*; *fatal nature*

T·öffel m ~s/~ *blockhead, dolt*

T·oga f ~/Togen *toga* || in der ~ *togated*

T·ogo n (⟨†Ger⟩ Kolonie in Afrika) *Togo*(*land*)

T·ohuwab·ohu n ⟨bib⟩ *tohu bohu, hubbub*

toi-toi-t·oi! [intj] (lautmalend = Ausspucken) ⟨m. m.⟩ *touch wood!, keep your fingers crossed*

Toil·ette [twɑˈlɛtə] f ~/~n *toilet-stand, -table* || (Klosett) *lavatory, W. C.*; *powder-room*; ⟨Am⟩ *bathroom, rest-room* | (Kleid) *toilet*(*te*), *dress*; gr ~ *dress-up for a party* || ~ m *to dress, to make one's toilet* || in gr ~ *in full dress* || sie ist bei der ~ *she is at her toilet* **~(n)-** **~artikel** m *toilet-requisite, -article* **~eimer** m *slop-jar* **~frau** f *lavatory attendant* **~garnitur** f *t.-set* **~gegenstand** m *article of dress* **~kasten** m *d.ing-case* **~kommode** f = –tisch **~necessaire** n *d.ing-case* **~papier** n *t.-* (od *sanitary*) *paper* od *roll* **~seife** f *t.-soap* **~spiegel, (~tisch)** m *d.ing-glass,* (*-table*, ⟨Am⟩ *dresser*) **~wässer** n pl etc *toiletries* (*in crystal jars*)

Tok·aier m ~s/ [*Hungary*] *Tokay*(*-wine*)

°**T·öle** f ~/~n (dog) ⟨dero⟩ *cur*

toler·ant a *tolerant*; *broad-, large-minded* **Toler·anz** f ~/ *toleration* || *margin* || ⟨tech⟩ (zulässige) *permissible limits* pl, *allowed variation* od *tolerance, allowance* | ~meßgerät [n] *electrolimit gauge*; ~tabelle [f] *table of limits* **toler·ieren** vt [h] *to tolerate*

T·okio n (Hptst. Japans)

Tol·edo n ⟨Span⟩ (Stadt)

toll a **A.** *mad* (*dog*) || (rasend) *furious, raving, frantic*; *phrenetic*(*al*); ⟨fam⟩ *scrumptious* || (wunderlich) *odd, strange, absurd* || (spaßig) *droll* | ⟨fam⟩ *wild, extravagant* (*plan, days*); *desperate* (*night*) | ⟨sl⟩ *ripping* (*performance*) || *infernal* (*noise*) || *amazing* (*th*) || *screaming* (*fun*) || ~e S, ~er Kerl ⟨fam⟩ *hot stuff* | ⟨arts sl⟩ *significant* | (sehr) *jolly* **B.** ~er **Bursche,** ~er Kerl *mad fellow* || ~es Jahr *wild* (⟨fam⟩ *crazy*) *year*; *y. of madness* || ~er Streich *mad prank* od *trick* || °~es Stück ⟨sl⟩ *tall order* || ~e Wirtschaft *loose state of affairs*, ⟨fam⟩ *terrible mess* || ~es Zeug *nonsense*, ⟨fam⟩ (*utter*) *rot* **C. wie** ~ *wildly, furiously*; *like Bedlam, as if one was mad*; (*to run, work*) *like mad* || ~ **auf** .. *mad after, about ..* || ~ u voll *dead drunk* || **je** ~er, desto besser *the madder the mer-*

rier || das ≃**ste** dabei *the funniest part of it* **D. es ging** ~ her *there was a great uproar* || es kommt noch ~er *the worst is to come yet* || es (zu) ~ treiben *to go all lengths,* (*to go too far*) **E. ~ machen** *to drive mad, to madden* | **bist** du ~? *are you mad,* ⟨Am⟩ *crazy?* || das ist doch ~ *there now!, isn't it absurd?* || das ist zu ~ *that's too much of a good th* | ~ w *to go* od *run mad* (⟨fig⟩ über *to become enraged at* ..) || zum ≃w ⟨fig⟩ *enough to drive you mad* **T·oll- ~apfel** m *mad-apple* **~beere** f ⟨bot⟩ *belladonna* || *deadly nightshade* **~dreist** = –kühn **~haus** n *madhouse, lunatic asylum* || ⟨fig⟩ *bedlam* **~häusler** m *lunatic, bedlamite* **~kirsche** f ⟨bot⟩ = –beere **~kopf** m *madcap* ≃**kühn** a *foolhardy, temerarious, rash*; ⟨Am sl⟩ *slap-happy* || *desperate* **~kühnheit** f ⟨a.⟩ *derring-do; dare-devilry* **~wut** f *canine madness* || ⟨vet⟩ *rabies* **t·ollen**[1] vi [h & s] *to frolic, rollick*; ⟨fam⟩ *to carry on* | (herum~) *to scamper, romp about* || *to romp* (*through the streets*) **T·ollheit** f ~/~en *madness, frenzy* || *fury, rage* || *piece of folly; mad prank* od *freak*

T·olle f ~/~n (P) *tuft, top-knot; long hair* | ⟨orn⟩ *crest, frill* **t·ollen**[2] vt [h] *to crimp* (*frills, the hair*)

T·olpatsch m ~es/~e; T·ölpel [m] ~s/~ **1.** *clumsy* od *awkward fellow, boob(y), dunce, dolt*; ⟨fam⟩ (Dummkopf) *duffer,* ⟨Am a.⟩ *yahoo*; ⟨sl⟩ *mutt, lout* || kl ~ *toddler* | ≃**ig** a ⟨sl⟩ *ham-fisted* **2.** ⟨orn⟩ **T·ölpel** m *gannet* | **~·ei** f ~/~en, **~haftigkeit** f *awkwardness, clumsiness; doltishness; boorish manners* pl, *ill-breeding* ≃**haft, -pisch** a *awkward, clumsy; clownish; oafish; dull; gawky* || ~es Spekulieren, Wetten *mug's game* || *ill-bred* || sich ~ benehmen ⟨sl⟩ *to play the giddy goat* | ≃**n** vi [h] *to be awkward,* etc *in one's manners*

Tom·ate f ~/~n ⟨bot⟩ *tomato* || ⟨fig fam⟩ treulose ~! *deceiver* | **~n-** *t.* (*juice, sauce, soup*); ~mark [n] *concentrated t.es* pl

T·ombak m ~(e)s/ *tombac, pinchbeck*

T·ombola f ~/–len *charity lottery; tombola*

Tomsk n ⟨Russ⟩ (sibirische Stadt)

Ton[1] m ~(e)s/~e *clay, potter's earth* || feuerfester ~ *fire-clay*

Ton[2] m ~(e)s/≃e **A. 1.** (Schall) *sound* || ⟨mus⟩ *tone,* (einzelner) *note*; die höchsten ≃e *topnotes*; ⟨fig⟩ sich in den höchsten ≃en ergehen über .. *to sing the* od *high praises of* .. | (~art) *key; strain* (a. der Sprache) | ⟨fig⟩ *tone, fashion* || (Klangfarbe) *timbre, tone* **2.** ⟨gram⟩ (Betonung) *accent, stress,* (e–s Wortes) *emphasis* (fällt, liegt auf *is on*) **3.** ⟨paint⟩ *shade* (*of colour*), *tinge, tint, tone* (ganze ≃e *full tones*) **B.** k–n ~ mehr! *not another word!* || der ~ macht die Musik *it isn't what you say, it's the way you say it* (*I object*) || ein ~ der Verstimmung *a note of ill-humour* **C. dumpfer** ~ *thud* || ⟨fig⟩ **feiner** ~ *politeness; mark of good-breeding*; es ist jetzt .. *it is now the fashion* || **große** ≃e reden *to show off, to boast* || ⟨fig⟩ **guter** ~ *good form* od *taste*; .. v gutem ~ *perfect* (*gentleman*) | ⟨mus⟩ **ganzer** ~ *tone, whole step* || halber ~ *semitone* || um e–n halben ~ erhöhen, erniedrigen *to sharp, flatten* | in **hohen** (höchsten) ≃en reden .. *in a lofty strain, loftily, in a rich chord,* (*in superlatives*), .. über *to gush about* || ein leidenschaftlicher ~ *a note of passion* || näselnder ~ *twang* || den **richtigen** ~ treffen *to touch the right note* || hier herrscht ein **rauher,** aber herzlicher ~ *there is a coarse but genuine atmosphere here* || in spöttischem ~ *jeeringly* **D.** den ~ **angeben** *to intonate,* ⟨fig⟩ *to set the fashion* od *tone; to lay down the law,* .. f etw *to set the tone of a th*; ~d ⟨fig⟩ *setting the tone*; es sich [dat] etw kosten l, den ~ –zu– *to pay the piper and call the tune* || e–n ~ anschlagen *to strike a note* || ⟨fig⟩ .. jdm gegenüber ⟨fig⟩ *to take a tone with a p*; e–n anderen .. *to sing another song* od *time; to change one's tune; to adopt a different attitude* || den ansprechenden ~ finden ⟨fig⟩ *to pull out the sympathetic stop* || e–n ~ v sich **geben** *to sound*; s–r Stimme e–n drohenden ~ geben *to put a threatening tone into one's voice* || °haste (= hast du) ≃e? *it struck me dumb! well, I never!* || ⟨mus⟩ den ~ **halten** *to keep in tune* || e–n ~ hervorbringen, (reden) *to utter a sound* (*a word*) **T·on-**[1]&[2] [in comp] [2]⟨wir⟩ *audio* (*frequency*) **~abnehmer** m ⟨wir⟩ *pick-up*; ⟨telv⟩ *sound head* | ~arm [m] *tone arm*; ~gegengewicht [n] *tone-arm balance weight*; ~kabel [n] *phono cable*; ~system [n] *cartridge*; ~s.träger [m] *c. holder* **~abstand** m *interval* **~abstimmung** f ⟨phot⟩ *balancing of tonal values* **~abstufung** f = –wert ≃**angebend** a *setting the fashion, fashionable, leading, rampant*; ~s ⟨a.⟩ *to rule the roost, to be a sort of Crichton* **~angeber** m *leader* [1]**~arbeiter** m *worker in clay* [2]**~art** f ⟨mus & fig⟩ *key, strain,* ⟨fig⟩ *vein* || ⟨fig⟩ in allen ~en *in every possible strain* [1]≃**artig** a *clayed* [2]**~aufnahme** f [abstr] *sound recording*; [konkr] *transcript* **~bad** n ⟨phot⟩ *toner, toning b.* **~band** n ⟨film⟩ *sound track*; ⟨rec⟩ (*magnetic*) *tape,* dazu: *to tape*; Einlegen des ~es ⟨rec⟩ *threading the t.* | ~aufnahme [f] ⟨rec⟩ *transcription*; ~gerät [n] *tape recorder* **~beschaffenheit** f ⟨mus⟩ *tonality* **~bild** n *musical tableau* | ~schau [f] *sound-slide show* [1]**~boden** m *clayey soil* [2]**~dichter** m (*musical*) *composer* **~dichtung** f *musical composition* [1]**~eisenstein** m ⟨min⟩ *argillaceous iron-stone* **~erde** f ⟨min⟩ *alumina; clay; argillaceous earth* || essigsaure ~ *alumin(i)um acetate* [2]**~fall** m ⟨pros⟩ *cadence* || (Sprache) *intonation, accent* **~farbe** f *timbre* [1]**~figur** f *clay figure* [2]**~film** m *talking-film,* ⟨fam⟩ *talkie*; ⟨Am a.⟩ *sound movie* | ~atelier [n] *sound stage* ≃**filmen** vt *to make sound pictures of* .. **~fixierbad** n ⟨phot⟩ *toning and fixing bath* **~folge** f *scale; tune, melody* **~frequenz** f *audio-fr.y* **~führung** f *modulation* **~fülle** f ⟨a.⟩ *plangency* **~gebung** f *intonation* [1]**~geschirr** n *earthenware, pottery* [2]≃**getreu** a ⟨wir⟩ *high fidelity,* ⟨fam⟩ *hifi* [attr]; ~e Wiedergabe *h. f.* [1]**~grube** f *clay-pit* [2]**~halle** f *concert-hall* [1]≃**haltig** a *clayey* [2]**~höhe** f *pitch of a note, musical pitch* | ~n-schwankungen [f pl] ⟨rec⟩ *wow and flutter* **~-holzschnitt** m *chiaroscuro woodcut* **~ingenieur** m *sound* od *audio engineer* **~kino** n ⟨fam⟩ *talky* [1]**~klumpen** n, **~patzen** m ⟨arts⟩ *dab* [2]**~kopf** m *reproducer*; (Grammophon-Schalldose) ⟨rec a.⟩ *sound-box* **~kunst** f *music, musical art* **~künstler(in** f) m *composer, musician* **~lage** f ⟨mus⟩ *compass, pitch* [1]**~lage(r** n) f ⟨min⟩ *clay-bed* [2]**~lampe** f ⟨el⟩ *exciter lamp* **~lehre** f *acoustics* **~leiter** f ⟨mus⟩ *scale, gamut* (⟨a. fig⟩ ganze ~) ≃**los** a *toneless* || ⟨gram⟩ *unstressed* **~losigkeit** f *absence of sound, stress* ≃**malend,** ≃**nachahmend** a *onomatopoetic* **~maler·ei, ~nachahmung** f *onomatopœia* **~messer** m *tonometer* **~mischer** m ⟨film⟩ (S) *mixer* **~meister, ~mixer** m (P) *sound man* **~optik** f *optical system of sound head* **~papier** n *toned* od *tinted paper* [1]**~pfeife** f *clay pipe* || (lange) *church-warden* **~röhre** f *earthenware tube; earth pipe* **~sandstein** m *argillaceous sandstone* [2]**~satz** m ⟨mus⟩ *composition; phrase* [1]**~schicht** f *clay-bank* **~schiefer** m *argillaceous schist* [2]**~-schwund** m ⟨wir⟩ *fading* [1]**~seife** f *soap earth* [2]**~setzer** m ⟨mus⟩ *composer* **~setzung** f = –satz **~silbe** f *accented syllable*; Haupt≃ *tonic* **~spur** f ⟨film⟩ *sound track* **~streifen** m ⟨film⟩ *sound band* **~stück** n *piece of music* **~stufe** f ⟨mus⟩ *pitch* **~system** n *musical system* [1]**~tafel** f *clay-tablet* **~taube** f ⟨sport⟩ *clay bird* od *pigeon* | ~nschießen [n] *c.-p. shooting, trapshooting* [2]**~techniker** m ⟨wir⟩ *soundman* [2]**~träger** m *sound reproduction medium* ≃**treu** a *hifi* (*record*) **~trickfilm** m *animated sound film* **~umfang** m *compass* **~verhältnis** n *interrelation of sounds* **~verschiebung** f *shifting of accent* **~verstärker** m ⟨wir⟩ (*sound-*) *-amplifier* [1]**~waren** f pl *pottery* [2]**~wert** m ⟨paint⟩

tonal value | ≃richtig [a] ⟨phot⟩ *true-tone* (*reproduction*); ~richtigkeit [f] ⟨phot⟩ *correct rendering of tones* | v vollendeter **~wiedergabe** f *high fidelity* [attr] [2]**~zeichen** n *note* ‖ ⟨gram⟩ *accent* [2]**t·onen** vt [h] ⟨phot⟩ *to tone* **ton·al** a (Ggs atonal) ⟨mus⟩ *tonal* **≃it·ät** f *tonality* **t·önen** **I.** vi [h] *to sound, toll, ring* ‖ tief ~d *booming*; hell ~d *sonorous* | ⟨fig⟩ *to breathe*, ⟨sl⟩ *to twaddle* **II.** vt (färben) *to tint, tone* [1]**t·önern** a **1.** *earthen, fictile* ‖ (*feet*) *of clay*; *earthenware* (*vessel*) **2.** *clayey, argillaceous* **t·onig** a *clayey, argillaceous* [2]**T·onika** f ~/-ken ⟨mus⟩ *tonic* [2]**t·onisch** a ⟨med & mus⟩ *tonic*

T·onga- ~archipel m *Tonga Archipelago* **~inseln** f pl *Tonga* (od *Friendly*) *Islands* pl

T·ongking n (N.-Indochina) *Tonquin* [Fr]

T·onka- ~baum m *tonka* **~bohne** f *t.-bean*

Tonn·age [–ʒə] f ~/~n *tonnage* ‖ Schiffe mit e–r ~ von 30000 Tonnen *ships totalling* od *aggregating 30000 tons* **T·önnchen** n *student's drinking-cap* **T·onne** f ~/~n **1.** (gr) *tun*, (kl) *cask* ‖ (Bier≃) *barrel* ‖ (Regen≃) *tub* | ⟨fig⟩ (P) *regular barrel* (*of a man*) **2.** (Seezeichen) *buoy* **3.** (Maß) (1000 kg) *ton* → Bd I, S. 1112 ‖ ⟨mar⟩ *ton* (*of shipping*) | **~n- ~band** n, **~reif** m *cask-hoop* **~fisch** m *salt cod* **~fracht** f *freight by the ton* **~gehalt** m ⟨mar⟩ *burden, tonnage, capacity* **~geld** n *tonnage* **~gewölbe** n *barrel-vault* **~macher** m *cooper* **~last** f, **~maß** n ⟨mar⟩ *tonnage* **≃weise** [adv] *by barrels*, etc

Tons·ur f ~/~en *tonsure* **≃·iert** a *tonsured*

T·önung f ~/~en *tint, tinge, tone, tonality* verschiedene ~en *varying hues* | ~semulsion [f] ⟨cosm⟩ *colo*(*u*)*r emulsion*

Top·as m –ses/–se *topaz* **~fluß** m *artificial t.*

Topf m ~(e)s/≃e *pot* ‖ (eiserner Koch≃) *sauce-pan* ‖ (irdener) *earthen vessel* ‖ (*cocoa*) *jug* ‖ (Krug) *jar* ‖ (Nacht≃) *chamber* ‖ ⟨cards etc⟩ *pool* ‖ ⟨fig⟩ jeder ~ findet s–n Deckel *every hen comes to roost* | in alle ≃e gucken *to poke one's nose into everything* ‖ in ≃e setzen *to pot* (*plants*) ‖ in einen ~ werfen ⟨fig⟩ *to lump together* **~blume** f *flower growing in a pot* **~brett** n *pot-board* ‖ *shelf for flower-pots* **~deckel** m *pot-lid* **~fabrik** f *pottery* **~flicker** m *mender of pots and pans* **~gagelstrauch** m *sweet gale* **~gucker** m ⟨fam⟩ *meddler in domestic details, man pottering about the kitchen* **~hut** m (Damen≃) *cloche* Fr **~kuchen** m *pound cake* **~lappen** m *kettle-holder* **~lecker** m *lick-platter, -trencher* **~markt** m *crockery-fair* **~pflanzen** f pl *potted plants, pot-plants* pl **~reiniger** m *steel wool*; *pad* **~schrubber** m *pot-scourer* **≃voll** m *potful* [pl –*s*] **T·öpfchen** n ~s/~ *small pot*, etc ‖ *mug* (*of beer*) ‖ (Nacht≃) *chamber* **T·opfen** m ~s/~ ⟨österr cul⟩ (= Quark) *curds* pl **T·öpfer** m ~s/~ *potter* **~arbeit** f *p.'s work, pottery* **~erde** f *p.'s clay* **~geschirr** n = –ware **~gesell** m *journeyman potter* **~handwerk** n *p.'s trade* **~kunst** f *ceramic art* **~markt** m *pot-market, -fair* **~meister** m *master-p.r* **~scheibe** f *p.r's wheel*; ⟨a.⟩ *lathe* **~ton** m *p.r's clay* **~ware** f *p.r's ware*; *p.ry, earthenware, crockery*; → *ceramics* pl **~werkstatt** f *p.r's workshop* **~zeug** n = –ware **Töpfer·ei** f ~/~en *pottery* ‖ (Werkstatt) *potter's shop*

T·opik f ~/ ⟨philos⟩ *topics* **t·opisch** a ⟨med⟩ *topical, local* **Topogr·aph** m ~en/~en *topographer* **~·ie** f *t.phy*; *geodetic service*; *General Survey* N **≃isch** a *t.phic*(*al*[*ly* adv]); ~er Dienst *field survey*

topp! *done*!, *agreed*! *all right*! ‖ ~, ich wette! *I'm on*!, *done with you*!

Topp m ~s/~e ⟨mar⟩ *top, mast-head* ‖ vor ~ u Takel *under bare poles* ‖ über die ~en geflaggt *fully dressed* (*ship*) **~flaggen** f pl (setzen *to hoist*) *masthead flags* **~mast** m *top-mast* **~reep** n *guy* **~segel** n *topsail* **≃slastig** a *top heavy* **t·oppen** vt [h] ⟨mar⟩ (Rahen) *to peak*

Tor[1] m ~en/~en *fool, simpleton*, ⟨fam⟩ *silly*

Tor[2] n ~(e)s/~e **A.** *gate* ⟨a. mar⟩: *the Golden Gate* (*of Frisco*) ‖ (Scheunen≃) *door* ‖ (Stadt≃) *gate* ‖ (Schleusen≃) *lock-, sluice-gate* ‖ ⟨fort⟩ *port* ‖ (Schloß≃) *portals* pl ‖ (Einfahrt) *gateway* ⟨a. fig⟩ ‖ ⟨hist⟩ (Zoll≃) *bar* | ⟨ftb⟩ *goal*; Abschlag, Abstoß v ~ *goal-kick* ‖ ⟨crick⟩ *base*; *wicket* ‖ (Krocket) *hoop* ‖ (Hockey) *cage* **B.** z ~ hinein (hinaus) gehn *to enter at* (*to go out of*) *the gate* ‖ vor das ~ gehen *to take a walk out-side the town* ‖ ⟨mil⟩ vor den ~en *at the gates* | ⟨ftb⟩ ein ~ m *to shoot* bzw *score a goal* ‖ das ~ bewachen *to keep goal* **~angel** f *hinge* **~ball**(**spiel** n) m *cricket* **~baum** m *bar of a gate* **~bogen** m *archway* **~fahrt** f *gateway* **~flügel** m *wing of a gate* **~geld** n *gate-money* **~graben** m *outer moat* **~halle** f ⟨arch⟩ *porch* **~hüter** m *gate-keeper, porter* **~latte** f ⟨sport⟩ *cross-bar* **~linie** f ⟨sport⟩ *goal-line, bowling-crease* **~pförtchen** n ⟨crick⟩ *wicket* **~-raum** m ⟨ftb⟩ *goal-area* **~richter** m ⟨sport⟩ *linesman at the goal* **~riegel** m *bar of a gate* **~schaltung** f ⟨comp⟩ *gate-circuit* **~schließer** m = –hüter **~schluß** m *shutting of the gates*; ⟨engl univ⟩ *the gates* ‖ noch vor ~ ⟨fig⟩ *at the eleventh hour* ‖ noch nach ~ hinein *or* ans Ziel k ⟨fam⟩ *to get in under the wire* **~schreiber** m *tollman, gate-clerk* **~schuß** m ⟨ftb⟩ *goal* **~sperre** f *gate-shutting* **~stoß** m ⟨sport⟩ *goalkick* **~turm** m ⟨Eg⟩ *pylon* **~wache** f *guard at a gate* **~wächter, ~wart** m ⟨sport⟩ *goal-, wicket-keeper*; ⟨fam⟩ *goalie* **~-wärter** = –hüter **~weg** m *gateway, archway* **≃weit** a *very wide* **~zoll** m *gate-money* ‖ *excise*

Tor·eut m ~en/~en = Bossierer, Ziseleur **~ik** f *toreutics* [a. sg konstr]

Torf m ~(e)s/~e *peat*; [Ir] *turf* ‖ (stechen *to cut*) **~asche** f *p.-ashes* pl **~boden** m *p.-soil* **~bruch** m & n *p.-bog* **~erde** f *p.y mould* **~geschmack** m *p.y flavour* (*of whisky*) **~grube** f *p.ery* **~land, ~moor** n *p.-soil, -bog, -moss* **~moos** n ⟨bot⟩ *sphagnum* **~mull** m *peat* (*dust*) **~soden** f pl *sods of p.* **~stecher** m *p.-cutter* **~stich** m *p.-cutting* **t·orfen** vt [h] *to manure with peaty mould*

T·orheit f ~/~en *folly, foolishness, silliness* | *piece of folly* ‖ ~en begehen *to do foolish ths* **t·öricht** a *foolish* (*virgins*) ‖ *absurd* ‖ *silly* [adv *sillily*] | es wäre ~ v mir z sagen *it would be foolish for me to say* .. | [adv] sich ~ benehmen *to make a fool of o.s.*; *to act like a* (*regular*) *fool* ‖ ~ reden *to talk like a f.* **≃erw·eise** [adv] *in a silly manner* **T·örin** f ~/~nen *fool*(*ish woman*), *simpleton*

t·orkeln vi [s] *to stagger, totter, reel*; ⟨sl⟩ *to barge* (*against, into*) ‖ nach Hause ~ *to roll home*

Törn m ~(e)s/~e ⟨mar⟩ *turn*

Torn·ister m ~s/~ *knapsack*, ⟨mil⟩ *kit-bag* ‖ ⟨school⟩ *satchel* ‖ (ab–) umhängen *to* (*take down*) *put on* | ~empfänger [m] *k.-b. receiver*; ~funkgerät [n] *portable* od *field radio set*; *pack*(*-type*) od *k.-b. transmitter*; ~gerät [n] *portable set*; ~sprechfunkgerät [n] ⟨Am⟩ *walkie-talkie*

Tor·onto n (kanad. Stadt)

torped·ieren vt [h] *to torpedo* ‖ ⟨fig⟩ *to wreck* (*a plan*) **Torpedo** m ~s/~s **1.** ⟨ich⟩ *electric ray* **2.** ⟨mar⟩ *torpedo* (mit Zielsucher *homing t.*) ‖ Luft≃ *aerial t.* ‖ Übungs≃ *dummyhead t.* (einschießen *to try*, schießen *to discharge*) **~blasenbahn** f *wake of a t.* **~boot** n *t.-boat* | ~zerstörer [m] *destroyer* **~flugzeug** n *t.-plane* **~kopf** m *war head* **~laufbahn** f *t.track* **~netz** n *crinoline* **~reiter** m *one-man t.* **~rohr** n *t.* od *launching tube* (schwenken *to train*) **~sicherung** f *whisker* **~sucher** m *t. finder* **~überwasserausstoßrohr** n *t. tube on deck* **~wulst** m *bulge*

Torsi·on f ~/~en *torsion, twist*(*ing*) **~saufhängung** f *t.n suspension* **~sbeanspruchung** f *t.nal stress* **~sfestigkeit** f *torsional strength* **~smoment** m *torque* **~swiderstand** m *twisting resistance*

T·orso m ~s/~s ⟨sculp⟩ *torso* ⟨a. fig⟩

Tort m ~(e)s/ *wrong, injury* || ⟨jur⟩ *tort* || jdm e–n ~ antun *to play a p a nasty trick* || e–m zum ~ *to spite a p*

T·örtchen n ~s/~ *tartlet, flan* **T·orte** f ~/~n *tart, fancy-cake* | **~n-** ~bäcker [m] *pastry-cook*; ~boden [m] *flan*; ~form [f] *cake-mould*; ~heber [m] *cake-server*; ~spritze [f] *pipe*; ~unterlage, ~spitze [f] *doily*

Tort·ur f ~/~en *torture, rack* (→ Folter) || es war mir e–e ~ *it was absolute agony for me*

t·osen vi [h & s] (Wind, Meer) *to roar, rage, rave, surge, storm* || (Kind) = toben || ~d *uproarious* (*laughter*) || *thunders of applause*

Tosk·ana n ⟨It⟩ (Landschaft) *Tuscany* **Tos-k·a-ner** m *Tuscan, native of Tuscany* **tosk·anisch** a *Tuscan*

tot a **A.** *dead* || (gehob. Spr.) *deceased, defunct* || *lifeless, inanimate* || ⟨sl⟩ *cashed-in* || ~ u begraben *dead and gone* || f ~ erklärt *legally dead* | lieber ~ als Sklave *rather death than dishonour* | ⟨fig⟩ *dead* (*place, town, load, language*; *the D. Sea*) || (öde) *desolate, dreary* || *deserted* (*streets*) || ⟨rail⟩ *disused* (*line*) || *useless* (*knowledge, burden*) || *proud* (*flesh*) || *dull, dead* (*eyes, colours*) || ⟨com⟩ *dull* (*season*) **B.** (**Ball**) ⟨ten⟩ *not up*!; ⟨ftb⟩ *out* (*of play*) || (Buchstabe) *dead, meaningless* | ⟨mach⟩ ~er **Gang** *play*; *slack*; *lost motion* || ⟨mot⟩ *dead gear* || ⟨min⟩ ~es Gebirge *exhausted mines* || ~es **Gleis** *blind track, dead-end siding*; ⟨fig⟩ aufs ~e Gl. schieben *to shelve* (*a p, a th*) || ⟨jur⟩ ~e **Hand** *mortmain*; an die ~e H. veräußern *amortize* (dazu: *amortization*) | ⟨prov⟩ ~e Hunde beißen nicht *dead men tell no tales* || (Inventar) *dead* || (Kapital) *dead, dormant* || ~e **Last** *tare* || das ≗e Meer (in Vorderasien) *the Dead Sea* || ⟨mach⟩ ~er Punkt *dead-centre, -point*; ⟨fig⟩ *deadlock, hitch* || ⟨sport⟩ ~es Rennen *dead heat* || ⟨typ⟩ (Taste) *dead* || ~er Schußwinkel(bereich) *dead area* || ~es Wasser *neap tide* || ~er **Winkel** *dead angle*, ⟨mil⟩ *dead ground* || (Zahlen) *meaningless* || ~e Zeit *dull* od *dead season* || ~e Zone ⟨wir, ball⟩ *skip zone* **C.** der (die) **Tote** *the dead* (*wo*)*man, the departed* od *deceased* || [pl] *the dead* || laß die ≗en ruhen *leave the dead in peace* || das Tote *lifeless objects* pl **Tot-** °≗·**anständig** a *fair and square, awfully sporting*; ⟨Am sl⟩ *that's bully* od *white of him* ≗|**arbeiten,** sich ~ [h] *to work o.s. to death* ≗|**bleiben** vi [s] *to be killed* (*on the spot*, ⟨mil⟩ *in action*) ≗·**ernst** a *grave as a judge* ≗**geb·oren** a *still-born* | ≗e(s) [n] *still birth*; ≗enquote [f] *st.-b. quote* ≗**gebrannt** a *deadburnt* (Gips) **~geburt** f *still birth* °≗|**gehen** vi [s] *to peg, pop, pip out*; ⟨Am a.⟩ *to cash in* ≗**geglaubt** a *supposed to be dead* ≗|**jagen** vt [h] ⟨hunt⟩ *to run down* ⟨fig⟩ *to hunt* (*a simile*) *to death* ≗**kriegen** vi [s] nicht –zukr. = unverwüstlich ≗|**lachen,** sich [h] *to laugh o.s. to death*; *to laugh one's head off, to split one's sides with l.ing* || zum **~lachen** *screaming* (*affair*); es ist z ~ *it's too funny for words, killing*(*ly*) *funny*; *it would make a donkey laugh*; *he is a riot* ≗|**laufen,** sich [h] *to exhaust o.s., to be exhausted,* ⟨sl⟩ *to peter out* ≗**liegend** a ⟨fig⟩ *dead* (*capital*) | ≗e(s) [n] ⟨min⟩ *deads* pl ≗|**machen** vt [h] *to kill* ⟨a. *fig*⟩ || (e–e S) *to hush, suppress* || ⟨sport⟩ *to put* (*a p*) *out* **~punkt** m ⟨fig⟩ *deadlock* | ~marke [f] ⟨mot⟩ *timing mark* ≗|**schämen,** sich [h] *to be thoroughly ashamed of o.s.* ≗|**schießen** vt [irr] [h]; *to shoot, kill*; *to shoot to death* || sich ~ *to blow out one's brains* || ich lasse mich ~, wenn .. *my life on it that* || es ist zum **~schießen** *it's too funny for words* **~schlag** m (vor 1943) ⟨m. m.⟩ *manslaughter*; ⟨Am⟩ *murder in the 2nd degree*; (seit 1943) → Tötung || (im Affekt *in the heat of passion*) ≗|**schlagen** vt [irr] [h] *to kill* ⟨a. fig⟩; *to waste* (*one's time, money*); *to beguile* (*the time*) || dafür laß' ich mich ~ *I'd stake my life on it* **~schläger** m *manslayer, homicide* || (Waffe) *life-preserver*, ⟨Am⟩ *blackjack* ≗|**schweigen** vt [irr] [h] *to burke, to hush up*; *to ignore* (*a p, a th*) *totally* ≗**s·icher** a *cock-sure*; *sure as death* od *a gun*; ~! *a dead certainty*! (e–e ~e S) ≗|**stechen** vt [irr] [h] *to stab to death* ≗|**stellen,** sich [h] *to feign death* ≗|**trampeln,** ≗|**treten** vt [h] *to trample, kick to death* ≗|**weinen,** sich [h] *to cry one's heart out* **~zeit** f ⟨tech etc⟩ *unproductive time, non--cutting* (etc) *t., down t.*

tot·al a *total* (*war*); *complete*; ⟨fam⟩ *all-out* || [adv] *totally, quite, altogether, utterly* || ⟨sl⟩ *plumb* (*crazy, forgotten*) **Tot·al-** [in comp] ⟨pol⟩ *totalitarian* (*state, warfare*) **~ansicht** f *general view* **~betrag** m (*sum*) *total, whole amount* **~bilanz** f *final balance* **~eindruck** m *general impression* **~finsternis** f *total eclipse* **~leistung** f ⟨tech⟩ *gross effect* **~summe** f = –betrag **~verlust** m *total* od *dead loss* **Totalis·ator** m ~s/–sat·oren *totalizer, totalizator*; *pool* **totalit·är** a ⟨pol⟩ *totalitarian* (Macht)

T·otem n ~s/~s Ind (Stammeszeichen) *totem* | ~glauben [m] *t.ism*; ~pfahl [m], ~säule [f] *t.-pole*

t·öten I. vt [h] *to kill, to put to death* || ⟨bes Am⟩ *to slay* (*his sons slain in the war*) || ⟨fam⟩ *to do for* | ⟨fig⟩ *to destroy*, ⟨Am a.⟩ *to abort* || *to kill* (*a ball*), ⟨ten⟩ (gerade übers Netz *by a drop-shot*) || (Farben, ⟨dent⟩ Nerv) *to deaden* || (das Fleisch) *to mortify* || die Zeit ~ *to kill time* | **sich** ~ ⟨a.⟩ *to lay hands on o.s., to commit suicide* **II.** ≗ n = Tötung || *the destruction* (*of moths*)

T·oten- ⟨off⟩ *funeral, dead*(*ly*) **~acker** m *churchyard* ≗**ähnlich** a *deathlike* **~amt** n *burial-service*; ⟨R. C.⟩ *mass for the dead*; ⟨mus⟩ *requiem* **~bahre** f *bier* **~baum** m Sw *coffin* **~beschwörung** f *necromancy* **~bestattung** f *burial, sepulture* **~bett** n *deathbed* ≗**blaß,** ≗**bleich** a *d.*(*ly*) od *deathly pale*; ⟨fam⟩ *cadaverous, ghastly* (*complexion, face*); *d. white* **~blässe** f *paleness of death, d.ly pallor* **~buch** n ⟨R. C.⟩ *obituary*; ⟨Eg ant⟩ *book of the dead* **~eule** f *screech-owl* **~farbe** f *death-, livid colour* **~farbig** a *livid*, ⟨fam⟩ *cadaverous* (*complexion*) **~feier** f *f.l rites, exequies* pl, *memorial celebration* **~fest** n ⟨ec⟩ *festival in commemoration of the dead* **~flagge** f ⟨mar⟩ *flag at half-mast* **~gebeine** n pl *bones of the dead* **~geläut**(e) n *knell, passing-bell* **~geleit** n *f.l procession*; jdm das ~ geben *to attend a p's f.l* **~gerippe** n *skeleton* **~geruch** m *cadaverous smell* **~gerüst** n *catafalque* **~gesang** m *f.l song, dirge* **~gespräch** m *dialogue of the dead* **~glocke** f *f.l bell, knell, passing-bell* **~gräber** m *grave-digger, sexton* || ⟨ent⟩ *burying-beetle* **~gruft** f (*f.l*) *vault* **~halle** f *morgue* **~haus** n *dead house* **~hemd** n *shroud* **~hügel** m ⟨(praehist)⟩ *barrow, tumulus* **~käfer** m *churchyard beetle* **~klage** f *lamentation for the dead*; ⟨Am⟩ *death--wail*; ⟨Lit⟩ *nenia, elegy* **~kopf** m *death's-head* || ⟨med, mil⟩ *skull and cross-bones* pl || ⟨ent⟩ *death's-head moth* **~kopfäffchen** n ⟨zoo⟩ *saimiri* **~krampf** m ⟨path⟩ *tetanus* **~kranz** m *f.l wreath* **~leuchte** f *graveyard turret*; *dead man's lantern* **~lied** n *f.l chant*; *dirge* **~liste** f *obituary, bill of mortality, list of the dead* **~mahl** n *meal at a f.l* **~marsch** m *funeral march* **~maske** f *death-mask* **~messe** f *mass for the dead*, ⟨mus⟩ *requiem* **~musik** f *f.l music* **~opfer** n *sacrifice offered for the dead* **~register** n = –liste **~reich** n *realm of the dead, Hades* **~richter** m *judge of the dead* **~schau** f *coroner's inquest* **~schauer** m *coroner* **~schein** m *death-certificate, c. of d.* **~schild** n ⟨her⟩ *hatchment* **~schlaf** m *sleep of death* || ⟨fig⟩ *death-like sleep* °≗**s·icher** a (*as*) *sure as death* → totsicher **~sonntag** m ⟨Ger⟩ *remembrance-sunday* **~stadt** f *necropolis* **~starre** f *rigidity of death* ≗**st·ill** a (*as*) *still as death* || es wurde ~ *it* (*suddenly*) *grew deadly quiet* **~st·ille** f *dead calm, dead*(*ly*) *silence* || ~ trat plötzlich ein *a sudden hush fell upon everybody* **~tanz** m ⟨arts⟩ *Dance of Death, danse* *macabre* Fr **∼uhr** f ⟨ent⟩ *death-watch* **∼urne** f *f.l* od *sepulchral urn* **∼verbrennung** f *cremation* **∼wache** f *wake* **∼wagen** m *hearse* **∼wurm** m ⟨ent⟩ *death-watch* **∼zahl** f ⟨bes mot⟩ *number of fatalities* **Tötung** f ∼/∼en *kill(ing)* ‖ (→ Totschlag, Mord) versuchte ∼ *homicidal attempt*; vorsätzliche ∼ *voluntary manslaughter*; zufällige ∼ *accidental homicide* ‖ ∼ der Leibesfrucht *prolicide* ‖ fahrlässige ∼ ⟨Ger⟩ *homicide through negligence*, ⟨engl⟩ *involuntary manslaughter*; ⟨Can⟩ *criminal negligence causing death* | ⟨fig⟩ *destruction* ‖ (des Fleisches) *mortification* | ∼sdosis [f] *lethal dose* ⟨a. at⟩

°**T·oto** n ∼s/∼s → Totalisator; *pool*, im ∼ *on the p.s* ‖ *numbergambling* | ∼spieler [m] *p. player*

Toul·on [tu'lɔ̃] n ⟨Fr⟩ (Kriegshafen)

Toul·ouse [tu'lu:z] n ⟨Fr⟩ (Stadt)

Toupet [tu'pe:] n ∼s/∼s ⟨obs⟩ *toupet, hair-piece*; (neuerdings wieder modern)

Tour [tu:r] f ∼/∼en (Umdrehung) *turn, round* ‖ ⟨mach⟩ *revolution*; auf ∼en k *to pick up*; ⟨fig⟩ (P) *to get worked up, excited* ‖ auf ∼en bringen *to speed up* ⟨a. fig⟩ | (e–s Tanzes) *figure, set* ‖ (Strick≈) *round* | (Haar≈) *front (of [false] hair)* | (Ausflug) *excursion, trip, tour*; e–e .. ∼ *to go on for an 8 hours' walk* ‖ gr Kavaliers≈ *grand tour* ‖ e–e ∼ m *to tour, to make a trip, an exc.* | ⟨com⟩ (Kundenbesuch) auf ∼ *on (business) tour* | °**auf** ∼en k *to hit one's stride*; (vor Wut) ⟨fig⟩ *to get up steam* ‖ auf ∼en bringen ⟨aero⟩ *to rev up* | **außer** der ∼ *out of one's turn* | **in** e–r ∼ *at a stretch* **Touren-** **∼fahrt** f ⟨mot⟩ *touring competition*; *touring car race* **∼schwankung** f *variation of speed* **∼wagen** m *touring car, roadster* **∼zahl** f *number of revolutions*; *rotation speed* ‖ ∼veränderung [f] *change of rotation speed* **∼zähler** m ⟨mach⟩ *revolution counter*; *speed-indicator* **Tour·ist(in** f) m ∼en/∼en *tourist*, ⟨fam⟩ *tripper* **∼enfahrkarte** f *excursion ticket* **∼enrummel** m *t. boom* **∼enverkehr** m *t. traffic* **Tourn·ee** f ∼/∼s *tour* ‖ ⟨theat [mus]⟩ *(starring-, [concert-]) tour* ‖ auf ∼ gehen *to go on a tour* **Tourn·üre** ⟨obs⟩ f ∼/∼en *good form* ‖ (Kleidung) *bustle*

Tours [tu:r] ⟨Fr⟩ (Stadt)

Trab m ∼(e)s/ *trot* ‖ im Trab *at a trot*; ⟨fig fam⟩ *on the run* ‖ ∼ reiten *to trot* ‖ (Pferd) in leichten ∼ setzen *to lift .. to an easy trot* | ⟨fig⟩ jdn auf den ∼ bringen *to make a p find his legs, to bring a p to the scratch*, ⟨übtr⟩ *to haul a p over the coals* **∼reiten** n *trotting* **∼rennen** n *trotting-race* ⟨Am⟩ *harness racing* **∼rennwagen** m › *sulky* **tr·aben** vi [h & s] *to trot* (a. P) ‖ deutsch, (leicht) ∼ *to trot assis(e)* (*enlevé*[e]) Fr ‖ (Pferd) hoch ∼ *to be a high stepper* ‖ ∼ l *to trot* [vt] **Tr·aber** m ∼s/∼ *trotter* **∼wagen** m *sulky*

Trab·ant m ∼en/∼en ⟨hist⟩ *life-guardsman* ‖ ⟨astr⟩ *satellite* | ⟨fig⟩ [mst pl] *children* ‖ ⟨pol⟩ *satellites* ‖ jds ∼ s *to be moons to a p*

Trach·ee f ∼/∼n ⟨ent⟩ *spiracle, trachea*

Tracht f ∼/∼en **A. 1.** (Last) *load, charge* ‖ (Schiffs≈) *shipment, cargo* **2.** *litter (of kittens,* etc) **3.** ⟨arch⟩ *bearing, span* **4.** ⟨agr⟩ *crop, yield* **5.** *yoke (for pails)* **6.** (Teil des Hufes, Sattels) *bar* **7.** (Kleider) *dress, costume, apparel, garb* ‖ (Kleidermode) *fashion* **8.** *(bee's) honey flow*; Sommer∼ *summer f. of h.* **B.** ∼ Prügel ⟨fam⟩ *flogging, (a) sound drubbing* od *thrashing*; e–e ∼ Pr. verdienen *to want the stick* ‖ ∼ Wasser *full supply of water (in pails)*

Tr·achten I. n ∼s/ (nach) *striving (to do; for, after)*; *endeavours* pl, *aspiration (after)* ‖ *pursuit (of)* ‖ sein ganzes ∼ war .. *he was all for (doing it), his sole object was (to do it)* **II.** ≈ vi [h] (nach) *to endeavour, strive (after, for), to aspire (to), to aim (at), to be out (for)* ‖ *to set one's head (on a th)*; danach ∼, etw sicherzustellen *to lay o.s. out for a th* ‖ *to study (to avoid a th)* ‖ (zu) *to endeavour, try (to)* ‖ jdm nach dem Leben ∼ *to attempt* od *to seek a p's life* **tr·ächtig** a *pregnant* (⟨a. fig⟩ *times*); *(big) with young* ‖ *(cow) with calf*; *(mare) in foal* ‖ ⟨min⟩ *metalliferous* **≈keit** f ∼/ *pregnancy, gestation* (a. Dauer)

Trach·yt m ∼(e)s/∼e ⟨geol⟩ *trachyte*

Trad·ent m ∼en/∼en ⟨rel⟩ *traditor* **Traditi·on** f ∼/∼en *tradition*; bewahrte, heilige ∼ *hallowed t.* ‖ Sklave der ∼ s *to be hidebound* ‖ durch ∼ gefestigt *vested (interests)* ‖ an der ∼ festhaltend *orthodox* ‖ der ∼ entsprechen *to be in the t.n* | **≈·ell** a *traditional* ‖ *vested (rights)* | adv *t.ly*; ∼ festgelegte Verhaltensweisen v Gruppen ⟨eth⟩ *(going) institutions* | **≈s-** **∼feindlich** a *unorthodox* **∼gemäß** a *according to tradition* ‖ [adv] *traditionally*

traf 1. & 3. sg pret v treffen | ≈ Sw = treffend

Traf·ik m, [österr] f ∼/∼en = Tabakladen | ∼·ant [m] [∼en/∼en] Besitzer e–s Tabakladens

Tr·afo m ∼s/∼s ⟨fam⟩ = Transformator

Trag·ant m ∼(e)s/ ⟨bot⟩ **1.** *tragacanth* ‖ *milk-vetch* **2.** *(gum) tragacanth*

Tr·ag- **∼altar** m *portable altar* **∼arm** m ⟨arch⟩ *supporting bracket* **∼bahre** f *stretcher, litter* **∼balken** m ⟨arch⟩ *girder*, ⟨a. fig⟩, *transom, summer(-tree)* **∼band** n ⟨arch⟩ *strap, brace* ‖ ⟨surg⟩ *suspender* **∼baum** m *carrying-pole* ‖ ⟨arch⟩ *bearing-bar* ‖ ⟨pap⟩ *arbor* ‖ *shaft (of a carriage)*; ⟨mil⟩ *perch* **∼bett** n *portable bed* **∼bogen** m ⟨arch⟩ *subarch* **≈fähig** a *capable of bearing* | ∼keit [f] *carrying-power, lifting capacity, capacity of holding, (maximum) load*; (Brücken≈) *safe l. carrying capacity, l. limit*; ⟨arch⟩ *supporting strength* ‖ ⟨mar⟩ *tonnage* ‖ ⟨agr⟩ *productiveness* **∼feder** f *supporting* (⟨mot⟩ *suspension-)spring* **∼figur** f *burden-bearer* **∼fläche** f ⟨aero⟩ *wing*; *airfoil* | ∼n(abwurf)behälter [m] *wing (drop)tank*; ∼nbreite [f] *w.-spread*; ∼nende [n] *w. tip*; ∼nholm [m] *spar*; **∼n-, ∼flügelboot** n *hydrofoil (ship), flying boat, naviplane* **∼gestell** n *pack frame* **∼griff** m *carrying handle* **∼himmel** m *canopy, baldachin* **∼holz, ∼joch** n (f Eimer) *yoke* **∼kleidchen** n (Baby≈) *long clothes* **∼knospe** f ⟨hort⟩ *fruit-bud* **∼konstruktion** f ⟨arch⟩ *weight-carrying structure* **∼korb** m *back-basket* **∼kraft** f ⟨arch⟩ *bearing-power* ‖ ⟨mar⟩ *tonnage, capacity* ‖ (e–s Krans) *lift(ing-power)* **∼kranz** m (f. d. Kopf) *pad* **∼lager** n *journal bearing* **∼leinen** f pl (Fallschirm) *shroud lines* pl **∼mulde** f ⟨arch⟩ *hod* **∼orgel** f *portable o.* **∼pfeiler** m ⟨arch⟩ *pillar* **∼pferd** n *sumpter-horse* **∼riemen** m *strap* ‖ ⟨mil⟩ *sling* ‖ (e r Kutsche) *main brace* **∼schrauber** m ⟨aero⟩ *gyroplane, autogyro* **∼seil** n *lift wire*; *carrying cable* **∼sessel** m *sedan(-chair)* **∼stange** f *pole* **∼stein** m ⟨arch⟩ *summer, console, corbel-head* ‖ *keystone* **∼tier** n *beast of burden, pack-animal* | ∼kolonne [f] *pack train* **∼vermögen** n *carrying capacity (of vehicles)* **∼weite** f ⟨ball⟩ *range* ‖ ⟨fig⟩ *reach, significance, magnitude, impact (of a problem)*; *import(ance)*; v gr ∼ *of considerable i.ance*; *consequence*; *moment* (nur in: *of great m.*) **∼werk** n ⟨aero⟩ *wing unit, supporting surfaces* **∼zeit** f ⟨zoo⟩ *(time of) gestation* **tr·agbar** a *portable* | (Kleidung) *wearable*, noch gut ∼ *still quite decent* | ⟨agr⟩ *productive, fertile, fruitful* | ⟨fig⟩ *tolerable, tenable, sustainable, to be endured* ‖ (Vorschlag) *appropriate* ‖ als Lehrer nicht ∼ *impossible as a teacher* | im Rahmen des **≈en** *within the limits of possibility* **≈keit** f *portability* ‖ (v Kleidung) *wearing quality*; *respectability* ‖ ⟨agr⟩ *productiveness, fertility* ‖ etc **Tr·age** f ∼/∼n *hand-barrow, litter* | ∼tasche [f] *carrier* **tr·agen** [trug/ge∼] [h] **I.** vt **A. 1.** (Bewegliches) *to carry (arms,* ⟨fig⟩ *a p's picture in one's heart)* **2.** *to bear (seed[s], news, one's lot)* ‖ *the earth bears mankind, the legs bear the table-top* **3.** *to wear (clothes, rings; a crown, beard; glasses, honours)* ‖ *to be (dressed) in (black)* **4.** (heben)

(Kran) *to lift* **5.** (stützen) *to support, uphold* **6.** (halten, fassen) *candelabra hold many candles* **7.** (befördern) *to carry (a parcel), to take (a letter) (to the post-office)* || *to convey, transport* **8.** (hervorbringen) *to bring forth; to bear, yield, produce* **9.** ⟨fig⟩ (ertragen) *to bear, suffer, endure;* leicht z ~ *tolerable, bearable* **B. Angriffe** vorwärts ~ *to carry .. forwards* || den Arm in der Binde ~ *to have one's a. in a sling* || Bedenken ~ *to have misgivings (as to); to hesitate, scruple* || das Datum vom 1. ~ *to be dated from the 1st;* ein falsches Datum ~ *to be wrongly dated* || das Elend ~ *to shoulder the sufferings* || das Haar lang ~ *to wear one's hair long* || ein **Herz** im Busen ~ *to have a kind h.* || das Herz auf der Zunge ~ *to have one's h. in one's mouth* || ein Kind (unterm Herzen) ~ *to be great with child,* ⟨sl⟩ *to be in the family way* || **(Kopf)** *to hold .. (straight), to carry .. (high)* || (Kosten) *to defray* || (Mode) gerne ~ *to favo(u)r* || (Namen) *to have* || e–e Natur an sich ~ *to partake of the nature (of ..)* || (Schall) *to carry* || (Scheitel) *to have* || die Schuld an etw ~ *to be the cause of;* wer trägt die Sch.? *who is to blame?* || Sorge ~ um *to be anxious about* || **Stiefel** krumm ~ *to wear .. down on one side* || die Verantwortung ~ *to be responsible (for)* || (Verlangen) *to have* (nach *for)* || den Verlust ~ *to pay the damage, to bear the losses* || (Zinsen) *to bring in, to yield* **C.** jdn **auf** Händen ~ *to make much of a p, to hold a p dear* | **bei** sich ~ *to carry .. on one's p* || *to carry (a stick, an el. torch)* || *I carry it about with me, I have it about me* || beim Sport z ~ *for sports wear* | **in** die Luft ~ *to bear aloft* || ⟨fig⟩ Erregung ins Volk ~ *to cause exc. among the p.;* etw in sich ~ *to bear (the stamp of genius); a good deed carries its own reward;* die Gründung trug den Keim des Verfalls in sich *the disaster could be traced from the very foundation itself* | **zur** Schau ~ *to expose, exhibit, show;* (eitel) *to sport* **II. A. sich** ~ (P) *to dress (simply), to be (neatly) dressed* || sich gut ~ (P) *to carry o.s. well* | (v Stoffen) *to wear (well, badly); this is a good wearing material, there's a great deal of wear in it;* sich dünn ~ *to grow threadbare* || (S) sich (finanziell) selbst ~ *to pull its weight; to earn its own way;* sich leicht ~ *to be easy to carry* || ⟨com⟩ sich selbst ~ *to pay its way* **B.** ⟨fig⟩ **sich mit** etw ~ *to be (pre)occupied with, to have .. on one's mind, to brood over; to toy with (a plan); to entertain (an idea); to cherish (the hope that ..); to worry o.s. with (troubled thoughts)* || man trägt sich mit dem Verdacht *it is suspected* **III.** vi *to carry loads* || schwer z ~ h *to be heavily laden* (an *with)* || **(Augen)** *to reach* || (Baum) *to bear fruit* || **(Eis)** *to bear;* nicht ~ *to be unsound* || (Geschütz) *to range;* (weit) *to carry a long way* (→ weit) || **(Land)** *to bear (tenfold)* || (Luft) ⟨aero⟩ *there is plenty of lift in the air* || (Stimme) *to carry [well]* || (T) → trächtig s || gut **~der** Baum *good bearer;* **~de** Fläche ⟨aero⟩ *supporting surface* **IV. getragen** *second hand (clothes)* || *dirty (linen)* | *solemn (frame of mind)* | (Töne) *sustained* || ge~ w *to be sustained (by moral strength)* | ⟨übtr⟩ getr. **von**: *(a government) borne on (the trust of the people)* || ⟨fig⟩ *his art, his decision was determined by* || viel getr. w *to be in wear* **V.** ≃ n *carrying,* etc || *carriage* || (Haltung) *deportment* || ⟨gyn⟩ *gestation* | *wear (out of shape with w.)* **Tr·äger** m ~s/~ (f ~in) *carrier* (a. ⟨mil⟩ & Krankheits≃); *(bacteria) agent* || (P) (Last≃) *porter; stretcher-bearer* || ⟨golf⟩ *caddie* | ⟨übtr⟩ *representative* || (Inhaber) *holder (of power, an idea); bearer (of a name, of the guilt)* | (Kleider≃ etc) *wearer* | ⟨agr⟩ *(a good) cropper* | ⟨anat⟩ *atlas* | ⟨tech⟩ *support, girder* (⟨a–n⟩ *duralumin g.)* | ⟨arch⟩ *beam girder, summer* || *bracket* || *pillar* ⟨a. fig⟩; *support* | ⟨tail⟩ *(shoulder) strap* | ⟨hunt⟩ *(stag's) neck* | ⟨at⟩ *vehicle* | ⟨übtr⟩ ~ s: *(schools are) administered* od *operated, maintained by (the municipalities);* Sw *the National Bank is responsible for determining Sw. monetary policy* **~brücke** f *girder-bridge* **~flugzeug** n *carrier(-based* od *-borne) aircraft* **~karawane** f *porter train* **~kolonne** f ⟨mil-med⟩ *stretcher party* **~lohn** m *port(er)age, carriage* **≃los** a ⟨tail⟩ *strapless* **~material** n ⟨glass⟩ *supporting material* **~rakete** f ⟨a–n⟩ *launch vehicle; carrier rocket* **~rock** m *skirt with shoulder straps* **~-schürze** f *apron* **~schwelle** f ⟨carp⟩ *bres(t) summer* **~strom** m ⟨telph⟩ *carrier current*

tr·äge a *lazy, indolent* || (faul) *slothful; shiftless* || (stumpf) *dull* || (langsam) *sluggish (stream, temper)* || (leblos) *inert* ⟨a. phys⟩ **Tr·ägheit** f ~/ *laziness, indolence, inertness, languor; remissness; sloth, sluggishness* || ⟨physiol⟩ *phlegm* || ⟨phys⟩ *inertia;* → Verdauungs≃ || .. aus s–r ~ aufrütteln *to rouse .. from torpor* **~sgesetz, (~smoment)** n *law, (moment) of inertia* **~shalbmesser** m *radius of gyration* **~snavigationssystem** n ⟨a–n⟩ *inertial navigation system* **~ssteuerung** f (Rakete) *i.l guidance*

Tr·agik f *tragedy (the t. was that ..)* || *tragicalness; tragic nature, feature, note;* innere ~ *bitter agony of spirit* | **~er** m ~s/~ *tragic poet, tragedian* **Tr·agi- ≃k·omisch** a *tragicomic* [adv *-ally*] **~kom·ödie** f ~/~n *tragicomedy* **tr·agisch** a *tragic (must)* || ⟨fig⟩ ~es Ende *sad end* | ~e Schuld *guilt of the hero of a tragedy causing the catastrophe* || ~e Verwicklung *tragedy* | ⟨fig⟩ *tragical* [adv *-ally*], *lamentable, mournful (event)* | ⟨fam⟩ alles ~ [adv] nehmen *to take ths too seriously to take too gloomy a view of ths* || nimm's nicht so ~ *don't take it so hard* (od *to heart so much)* **Trag·öde** m ~n/~n *tragic actor, tragedian;* (f –din) *tragic actress, tragedienne* **Trag·ödie** f ~/~n *tragedy* **~ndichter** m *tragic poet*

Tr·agung f ~/ zur ~ der K. verurteilt s *to have to pay the costs;* → tragen

Train [trɛŋ, trɛ̃:] m ~s/~s ⟨mil⟩ *Army Service Corps* **~kolonne** f *supply column* **~soldat** m *wagoner* **~wesen** n *army service, military transport* | **~er** m [trɛ–] ~s/~ *coach(er* ⟨Am⟩), ⟨racing⟩ *timer* **≃·ieren** vt/i [h] ⟨mst sport⟩ *to train, to coach* (zu *for)* || (Pferd) ⟨a.⟩ *to school* **~ingsanzug** m *track suit*

Traj·ekt(schiff n) m ~(e)s/~e ⟨rail⟩ *ferry*

Trak·ehner m ~s/~ *horse from the stud of Trakehnen (former E. Prussia)*

Trakt m ~(e)s/~e *tract (of land)* || *wing (of a building)* **~am·ent** n ~(e)s/~e *treatment* | (Bewirtung) *entertainment* | (Löhnung) *wages* pl, ⟨mil⟩ *pay* **~·at** m, n ~(e)s/~e (Abhandlung) *treatise* || (Vertrag) *treaty* **~·ätchen** n ~s/~ ⟨rel mst hum⟩ *tract* **≃·ieren** vt [h] *to treat* | *to entertain,* ⟨fam⟩ *to give a treat to;* (mit etw) *to stand (a drink) to .., to ply (with)* | (mit jdm) *to negotiate (with a p)* || °er hat mich ordentlich –tiert *he gave me what for,* ⟨Am⟩ *he laid into me with a vengeance* **~or** m ~s/–·oren ⟨tech⟩ *tractor* || *argrimotor* || durch ~ gezogen *t.-drawn* **~·orenkraftstoff** m *vapo(u)rizing oil* **~or·ist** m ⟨DDR⟩ *t. driver*

trall·a! *tra-la!, ho-ho!, trolly!* **tr·ällern** vt [h] *to hum, lilt (a tune)*

Tr·am- ~(bahn) f *tramway, tram-line* | ~wagen [m] *tram-car* || **Tr·amseide** f *tram*

Tr·amp- ~dampfer m *tramp* **~schiffahrt** f *t.-shipping* **Tr·ampel** m ~s/~ ⟨fam⟩, **~tier** n *lout, boor, bumpkin,* ⟨Am sl⟩ *hick* || –tier ⟨zoo⟩ *camel* **~pfad, ~weg** m *beaten path, b. track* °**tr·ampen** vi [h & s] ⟨fam⟩ *to (hitch-)hike* **tr·ampe(l)n** vi [h] *to tramp(le)* (auf *on), to clump* || mit den Füßen ~ *to stamp one's feet* || ⟨fig⟩ *to walk heavily* || °⟨cycl vulg⟩ *to push-bike* **Tr·amper** m ~s/~ *h.-h.r,* ⟨Am sl⟩ *thumber* **Trampol·in(e)** f ~/~(n) *spring-board* **~sprung** m *leap from the s.-b.*

Tran m ~(e)s/ *train(-oil), whale-oil* || *blubber* || ⟨fig hum⟩ im ~ *tipsy, fuddled, boozy, topheavy,* *tight, oiled* °**~funsel** ⟨hum⟩ (= **~lampe** f *blubber-lamp*) ‖ ⟨fig⟩ *slowcoach* (⟨a.⟩ **~suse, ~tute**) *sour-puss*; ⟨hum⟩ *flat tire* **~seife** f *soft soap* **~speck** m *blubber*; → tranig

Trance f ~/ [traːns] *trance* ‖ dazu: *to tr.*

Tranch·ee f [trɑ̃'ʃeː] ~/~n *trench* **tranch·ieren** [traŋ'ʒiːrən] vt [h] *to carve*; *to cut up* **Tranch·ier-~besteck** n (ein *a pair of*) *carvers* pl **~brett** n *trencher* **~messer** n *carving-knife* **~wagen** m ⟨hot⟩ *trolley*

Tr·äne f ~/~n **A.** *tear* (⟨a. im Käse⟩ ‖ ⟨fig⟩ *drop* **B.** sich der ~n **enthalten** *to keep o.s. dry* ‖ °u ihre ~n fließen wie's Bächlein auf der Wiesen *she works the tear-pump* ‖ sie fühlte die ~n k *a sense of t.s came to her* ‖ ihm wurde k–e ~ nachgeweint *there were no tears shed when he left* ‖ den ~n nahe s *to be on the verge of* (od *near to*) *tears* | **rollen:** *t.s trickled down her cheeks*; jdn z ~en rühren *to force tears from a p's eyes*; ~ standen ihm in den Augen *there were t.s in his eyes* ‖ treten in: *t.s welled to her eyes* ‖ ~n vergießen *to shed t.s, to weep*, ⟨fam⟩ *to cry*; ~ des Glücks v. *to cry happily*; s–e ~n unterdrücken, wegdrücken *to dash one's t.s away* **C. in** ~n *tearfully* ‖ in ~n aufgelöst *dissolved in t.s*; *in floods of t.s* ‖ sie war ganz in ~n aufgelöst *she was all t.s* ‖ in ~n ausbrechen *to fall* od *break, burst into* (*a flood of*) *t.s* ‖ in ~n zerfließen *to be bathed in t.s*; (*of eyes*) *to swim with t.s* | **unter** ~n *amid t.s*; u. ~n lächeln *to smile through t.s* | von ~ erstickte Stimme *voice choked with t.s* | **zu** ~n gerührt *moved to t.s*; *wet-eyed* **tr·änen** vi [h] *to run with tears* od *drops* ‖ (*of eyes*) *to water* ‖ ~d *watery, tearful* (*eyes*) **Tr·änen-** **~auge** n *weeping eye* **~bach** m ⟨fig⟩ *flood of tears* **≃bedeckt, ≃benetzt** a *t.-stained, moist with t.s* **~bein** n, **~drüse** f, **~fistel** f *lachrymal bone, gland, fistula* **~fluß** m *lacrimation* **~gas** n *t.-gas*; dazu *to t.-g.* **~gefäß** n *lachrymary vessel* **~kanal** m *t.-duct* **~krug** m *lachrymatory* **~krüglein** n *pitcher filled with t.s*; ⟨fig⟩ *p given to weeping* **≃leer** a *without t.s, t.less* **~quell** m ⟨poet⟩ *source of t.s* **≃reich** a *t.ful, bathed in t.s* **~sack** m *lachrymal bag* | die **~schleusen** öffnen *to turn the taps on* ⟨fig⟩ **≃-schwer** a *heavy with t.s* **~strom** m *flood of t.s* **~träufeln** n *epiphora*; *overflow of t.s* **≃umflort** a (*eyes*) *misted with t.s* **~urne** f *lachrymatory* **≃voll** a *t.ful*

tr·anig a *tasting* od *smelling of train-oil* ‖ °⟨fig⟩ *dull, slow*; *dopy*; → Tran

Trank m ~(e)s/≃e *drink, beverage* ‖ ⟨med⟩ *potion, draught*; *decoction*; *infusion* | (f Schweine) *swill* **~opfer** m *drink-offering* **~tonne** f *pig's trough* **trank** 1. & 3. sg pret v trinken **Tr·änk-~eimer** m *water-bucket* **~masse** f *impregnant* **~trog** m *watering-trough* **Tr·änke** f ~/~n *watering-place* ‖ (f Pferde) *horsepond* ‖ zur ~ führen *to water* (*cattle*) **tr·änken** vt [h] *to give a p to drink* ‖ *to still a p's thirst* ‖ (Kind) *to suckle* ‖ (Vieh, Felder) *to water* ‖ (die Erde) *to moisten, wet* ‖ ⟨cul⟩ *to macerate* | (durch~) *to steep, soak* (mit *in*); ⟨tech & fig⟩ *to impregnate* (*wood, paper*, etc. *with* ..) ‖ ⟨fig⟩ *to imbue* ‖ ⟨chem⟩ *to saturate* ‖ mit Karbol etc ~ *to carbolize*, etc **Tr·änkung** f ~/~en *stilling a p's thirst* ‖ *watering* (*cattle*) ‖ ⟨tech⟩ *impregnation* ‖ ⟨chem⟩ *saturation*

tr·ans- ⟨school⟩ ≃ f ~/~en *key* **~alp·inisch** a *transalpine* **≃atlantikhöhenflugzeug** n *stratoliner* **~atl·antisch** a *transatlantic* **Tr·ansfer** m ~(s)/ *transfer* | ~agent [m] ⟨bank⟩ *t. a.*; ~bewilligung [f] *t.* od *exchange licence* (⟨Am⟩ *–nse*) **≃·ieren** vt [h] *to tr.* **≃formati·on** [–ts–] f ~/~en *transformation* **≃form·ator** m ~s/–'oren ⟨el, wir⟩ *transformer* **≃·istor(gerät** n) m *transistor*; mit ~ ausgerüstet *t.ized* **Tr·ansit** m ~(e)s/~e *transit* **~güter** n pl *tr.-goods* pl; (unter Zollverschluß) *goods in bond* **~handel** m *tr.-trade* **~lager** n *bonded warehouse* **~verkehr** m *through traffic* ‖ *tr.-trade* **~versicherung** f *insurance in tr.* **~zoll** m *tr.-duty* **tr·ans-** **~it·iv** [–f] a *transitive* | ≃um [–vum] [n] ~s/–va *tr. verb* **~it·orisch** a *transitory* **~loz·ieren** vt [h] *to translocate, shift* **≃missi·on** f ~/~en ⟨tech⟩ *transmission*; *belt-drive* | ~sanlage [f] *gearing*; ~sapparat [m] *transmitter*; ~swelle [f] *connecting shaft* **~ozeanisch** a *Atlantic* (*cable*) **~par·ent** a *transparent* | ≃ n ~(e)s/~e (Bild) *transparency, diaphane*; ⟨bes SBZ⟩ *banner* | ~kopie [f] ⟨rep⟩ *translucent copy* **≃pirati·on** f ~/ *perspiration* **~pir·ieren** vi [h] *to perspire* **~po-n·ieren** vt/i [h] ⟨mus⟩ *to transpose* **≃p·ort** m ~(e)s/~e **1.** *transport*(*ation* ⟨Am⟩), *conveyance, carriage* ‖ *delivery*; *haulage* ‖ ⟨mar⟩ *shipment* | auf ~ befindlich *in transit* **2.** (Übertrag) (*amount*) *carried forward* | *carrying forward* | ~anforderung [f] *t.n request* N; ~arbeiter [m] *transport worker*; ~band [n] *conveyor-belt*; ~behälter [m] ⟨allg⟩ *shipping case*; *carrying container* ‖ ~dampfer [m] *transport steamer*; ≃fähig, ≃·ierbar [a] *transportable, ready* od *fit for conveyance*; ⟨med⟩ *transferable*; ~flugzeug [n] *transport* (*air*)-*plane*; *air-freighter*; ~führer [m] *train commander*; ~geschäft [n] *carrying trade* ‖ (Einzelfirma) *forwarding business* ‖ (Möbel≃) *furniture-removing business*; ~-Kapazität [f] *clearance capacity* ‖ ~leitstelle [f] *staging centre* | ~mittel [n] *means of transportation* od *carriage*; ~kosten [pl] *carriage*; *charges for transport*; *shipping-charges* pl; ~offizier [m] *t.n officer* N; ~ (v Korps u Division) *field t.n o.* N; ~planung [f] ⟨mil⟩ *routing* ‖ ~risiko [n] *transit risk* | ~schiff [n] ⟨mar⟩ *transport* (*vessel*); ~schnecke [f] ⟨tech⟩ *screw* od *worm-conveyor*; ~sperre [f] *transportation ban*; ~wesen [n] *transportation*; ~truppe [f] *T.n Corps* N; ~versicherung [f] *transit insurance*; (niedriger) ~wagen [m] *dolly* **≃p·orter** m ~s/~ ⟨mar, aero⟩ *transport* **≃porteur** [–'tøːr] m ~s/~e *transporter*; *forwarding agent*; (Möbel≃) *remover* ‖ ⟨math⟩ *protractor* **~port·ieren** vt [h] *to transport, convey*, ⟨mar⟩ *to ship*; (Möbel) *to remove* ‖ ⟨phot⟩ *to feed* vi/t (Buchführung) *to carry forward* **≃uran** n *transuranic element* **~v·aal** n (in Süd-Afrika) **~vers·al** a, **≃e** f ~/~n *transversal* [a & s] **~zend·ent, ~·al** a *transcendent*(*al*)

Trap·ez n ~es/~e ⟨math⟩ *trapezoid* ‖ ⟨gym⟩ *trapeze* **~flügel** m ⟨aero⟩ *tapered wing* **≃förmig** a *trapezoid* **~künstler** m *trapezist* **Trapezo·id** n ~(e)s/~e *trapezium*

Trapez·unt n (Kleinasien) *Trabzon, Trebizond*

Trapp m ~s/~e ⟨minr⟩ (Auswurfgestein) *trap*

trapp! **I.** [intj] *tramp*! ‖ ~, ~! *hurry up*! ‖ ⟨hors⟩ ~, ~! *clip, clip*! **II.** [adv] ~, ~ *clitter-clatter* (*down the stairs*), *clicketty-clack* (*over the road*) **III. das** ≃~ *the clatter*(*ing*) (*of hooves*)

Tr·appe[1] f ~/~n ⟨orn⟩ → *bustard*

Tr·appe[2] f ~/~n *foot-print* **tr·appeln** vi [h] *to patter, clatter, trample, trot* **tr·appen, tr·apsen** vi [h & s] *to tramp, stamp, clump, pound*

Tr·apper m ~s/~ [v ⟨engl *trap*] *trapper*

trar·a! (⟨a.⟩ trar·i-trar·a!) **I.** [intj] *tantara*! **II. das** ≃ *much ado* (*about nothing*)

†**Trasim·enischer See** m (jetzt Lago di Perugia) *Lake of Trasimeno* od *Perugia*

Traß m Trasses/Trasse ⟨min⟩ (Tuffstein; vgl It *terrazzo*) *trass* **~mörtel** m *t. mortar*

Trass·ant m ~en/~en ⟨com⟩ *drawer* **Trass·at** m ~en/~en ⟨com⟩ *drawee* **Tr·asse** f ~/~n *alignment* ‖ ⟨rail⟩ *line* ‖ ⟨tech⟩ *directrix* **Trass·ier-** **~buch** n ⟨telph⟩ *survey book* **~leine** f ⟨carp⟩ *line* **trass·ieren**[1] vi/t [h] ⟨com⟩ *to draw* (auf [acc] *on*) ‖ trassierter Wechsel [m] *draft* **trass·ieren**[2] vt ⟨surv, rail⟩ *to trace*

trat 1. & 3. sg pret v treten

°**Tr·atsch** [aː] m ~es/ *gossip*; ⟨fam⟩ *jam, jaw* | **≃en** vi [h] *to gossip*; *to drivel, jabber*; ⟨sl⟩ *to chew the rag* od *fat* **~maul** m *prattler*

Tr·atte f ~/~n ⟨com⟩ *draft* (auf *on*)

Tr·au- **~altar** m *marriage-altar* **~formel** f *m.-formula* **~handlung** f *m.-ceremony* **~rede** f *m.-sermon* **~register** n *register of m.s* **~ring** m *wedding-ring* **~schein** m *m.-certificate*; *m.-lines* ‖ *m,-licence* **~zeuge** m *witness to a m.*

Tr·aube f ~/~n *bunch of grapes* | ⟨bot⟩ *cluster* ‖ (Beere) *grape* ‖ ~n lesen, pflücken *to gather grapes* ‖ saure ~n! ⟨fig⟩ *the g.s are sour* (*said the fox, because he could not reach them*) **Tr·auben-** **~̈artig** a *g.-like*, *in clusters* **~beere** f *g.* **~blut** n *g.-juice* ‖ ⟨fig⟩ *wine* **~blüte** f *vine-blossom* **~eiche** f *sessile oak* **~̈förmig** a *g.-like* **~geländer** n *vine-trellis* **~kamm** m *g.-stalk* **~kern** m *g.-stone* **~kirsche** f *bird cherry* **~krankheit** f *vine-disease* **~kur** f *g.-cure* **~lese** f *vintage* **~most** m = –blut **~presse** f *wine-press* **~̈reich** a *abounding in g.s* **~rosinen** f pl *raisins in bunches* **~saft** m = –blut **~säure** f ⟨chem⟩ *racemic acid* **~schimmel** m ⟨bot⟩ *g.-mould*, ⟨scient⟩ *botrytis* **~süßmost** m *unfermented g. j.* **~zeit** f *vintage* **~zucker** m *starch* od *g.-sugar*, *dextrose* **tr·aubig** a *grape-like*, *clustered*

tr·auen I. vt [h] *to marry* ‖ sie sind kirchlich getraut *they had a church wedding* ‖ sich ~ l *to get married*, *to marry* **II.** vi [h] **1.** (jdm) *to trust* (*a p*); *to confide*, *believe* (*in a p*); unbedingt *to put implicit confidence in a p* ‖ e–m, e–r S nicht ~ *to distrust a p*, *a th* ‖ ich konnte m–n Augen nicht ~ *I couldn't believe my eyes* ‖ jdm nicht über den Weg ~ *not to trust a p out of one's sight* od *round the corner* | ⟨prov⟩ trau, schau, wem! *look before you leap*! ‖ dem Glück ist nicht z ~ *fortune is fickle* **2.** ~ **auf** [acc] *to trust in*; *to rely on* **III. sich** [dat] ~ [h] *to venture* (*to do*), *to dare*: (*d. he do it*?, *does he d. to do it*?; *he d. go*, *he d.s to go*) vgl getrauen

Tr·auer f ~/ **A. 1.** *mourning*, *sadness* ‖ (Schmerz) *sorrow*, *affliction*, *grief*; *regret* **2.** (Kleidung) *m.-dress* **B.** ~ an– (ab)legen *to go into* (*come out of*) *m.* (um *for*) ‖ ~ h *to be in m.* ‖ tiefe ~ *deep m.* ‖ er ist voller ~ darüber *he is very sorry about it* ‖ die ~ verscheuchen *to banish care* ‖ in ~ über .. *in m. at the death of* .. **~anzeige** f *announcement of a death* **~anzug** m *m.-suit* **~binde** f *crape* **~birke** f *weeping birch* **~botschaft** f *sad* od *mournful news* sg **~brief** m *m.-card* ‖ ⟨fig⟩ *mournful letter* **~fahne** f *black flag* **~fall** m *death* **~feier** f *funeral* (⟨C. E.⟩ *burial*) *service* **~flor** m *crape*; *sleeve-* (Fr *lapel-*)*band*; ⟨fam⟩ *weeper* **~gedicht** n *elegy* **~gefolge** n = –geleit **~geläut(e)** n *knell* **~geleit** n *funeral train* od *procession* **~gemeinde** f *companions in sorrow* **~gepränge** n *funeral pomp* **~gesang** m *dirge* **~gestalt** f *sad figure* **~gottesdienst** m = –feier **~haube** f *widow's cap* **~haus** n *house of m.* **~jahr** n *year of m.*; *the y. of her weeds*; *sad y.* **~kapelle** f *memorial chapel* **~klage** f *lamentation* **~kleid(ung** f) n *m.* ‖ in ~ *in black* ‖ ~ ablegen → ~ B. °**~kloß** m ⟨hum⟩ *duffer*; *sober-sides*; *stick-in-the-mud*; ⟨sl⟩ *creep* **~kutsche** f *m.-coach* **~mahl** n *funeral repast* **~mantel** m *m.-cloak* ‖ ⟨ent⟩ *Camberwell beauty* ‖ ⟨bot⟩ *lady's mantle* **~miene** f *sad face* **~marsch** m, **~musik** f *funeral march*, *dirge* **~nachricht**, **~post** f *sad news* sg **~papier** n *black-edged* (*note-*)*paper* **~rand** m *m. border* ‖ **~̈er** [pl] (unter den Fingernägeln) *m.-bands* ‖ du hast ~ *you're m. for the whole family*, *for the cat* **~rede** f *funeral oration* od *speech* **~schleier** m *m.-veil*, ⟨fam⟩ *weeper* **~spiel** n *tragedy* **~̈spielartig** a *tragical* **~spieldichter** m *tragic poet* **~tag** m *day of m.* **~̈voll** a *mournful*, *sad* **~weide** f ⟨bot⟩ *weeping willow* **~zeit** f *m.-time* **~zug** *funeral procession* **tr·auern** vi [h] *to mourn* (um *for*); ~ um ⟨a.⟩ *to m.* (*a p*, *a th*) ‖ *to grieve about* | (in Schwarz s) *to be in m.ing* (um *for*) | **~d** [a] *afflicted*, *grief-stricken* (*relatives*) **Tr·auernde** m [der ~, ein ~r] & f ~n/~n *mourner*

Tr·auf- **~bad** n *shower-bath* **~brett** n ⟨carp⟩ *fascia-board* **~faß** n *water-tub* **~rinne** f (*house-*)*-gutter*; ⟨arch⟩ *eaves-cornice* **~röhre** f *gutter-pipe* **~schale** f, **~teller** m (Kerzen~̈) ⟨bes ec⟩ *socket* **~stein** m *gutter*; *sink* **~wasser** n *rain-water* **Tr·aufe** f ~/~n *drip* ‖ *eaves* pl, *gutter* **tr·äufeln I.** vi/t [h & s] *to drip*, *drop*, *trickle* **II.** vi (Kerze) *to gutter* **III.** vt ⟨fig⟩ *to pour* (*balm*) (auf *on*) **tr·aufen**, **tr·äufen** vt/i [h & s] *to drop*, *drip*

tr·aulich a (behaglich) *cosy*, *snug*; *homely*; *nestling* (*hamlet*) ‖ (herzlich) *cordial*, *intimate*, *familiar* **~̈keit** f ~/ *cosiness* ‖ *familiarity*, *cordiality intimacy*, etc

Traum m ~(e)s/~̈e *dream* (.. h *to have* ..) ‖ böser ~ *nightmare* ‖ wacher ~ *day-dr.* ‖ ⟨fig⟩ *vision*, *fancy*, *imagination* ‖ der ~ m–r Jugend *the one dr. of* .. ‖ *she*, *that hat*, *this place is a dr.* | wie **im** ~ *in a dr.* ‖ im Reich der ~̈e *in dr.land* ‖ nicht einmal im ~ an etw denken *never even dream of a th* ‖ im ~ sprechen *to talk in one's sleep* ‖ er spricht im ~! *he is d.ing*! ‖ das fällt mir nicht im ~e ein! *I shouldn't dr. of it*!, ⟨sl⟩ *I'm damned if I do*! | ⟨prov⟩ ~̈e sind Schäume .. *are but shadows* ‖ ~̈ treffen selten ein .. *seldom come true* **~bild** n *vision*; böses ~ *nightmare* **~buch** n *dr.-book* **~deuter** m *dr.-reader* **~deutung** f *interpretation of dr.s* **~fabrik** f ⟨film⟩ *dr.-factory* **~gebilde**, **~gesicht** n = –bild **~gott** m *god of dr.s* (*Morpheus*) **~haus** n *dr. home* **~land** n *dr.land* **~leben** n *dr.-life* ‖ ein ~ führen *to live in a cloud* **~̈los** a *dr.less* **~mädchen** n *glamour* (⟨print⟩ *cover*) *girl* **~spiel** n *phantasmagoria* **~̈verloren** a, **~̈versunken** a *lost in dr.s* **~vorstellung** f *imagination of dr.* **~welt** f *imaginary world*, *world of dreams* **~zustand** m (hypnotischer ~) *trance* **tr·äumen I.** vt/i [h] (von) *to dream* (*of*) ‖ schwer ~ *to have heavy dr.s* ‖ wachend ~ *to have day-dr.s* ‖ du träumst wohl *you are dr.ing*; *are you all there*? **II.** vi imps [h] (jdm) *to appear in a dr.* (*to a p*) ‖ mir hat (etw Furchtbares) geträumt *I dr.t* (*I had a horrible dr.*) (daß *that*) ‖ sich [dat] nicht ~ l *not to have the least inkling of* ‖ ich hätte es mir nie ~ l *I never expected* (od *d.ed of*) *it* ‖ wobei sie sich kaum ~ l *little dr.ing* (*what* ..) ‖ laß dir was Schönes ~! *happy dreams*! träume(n Sie) süß! *golden dreams*! ‖ das soll er sich nicht ~ l *he must not think of such a th* **Tr·äumer** m ~s/~ *dr.er* ⟨a. fig⟩ ‖ ⟨fig a.⟩ *visionary* **~·ei** f ~/~en *dr.ing* | ⟨fig⟩ *day-dr.* ‖ *reverie* ⟨a. mus⟩ ‖ *musing*, *brooding*; ⟨fam⟩ *brown study* **~̈isch** a *starry-eyed* (*p*); *dreamy* (*eyes*); ~er Blick *faraway look* ‖ (zerstreut) *absent*, *abstracted*, *preoccupied* ‖ ~er Mensch *visionary* ‖ ~es Wesen *dr.iness* **tr·aumhaft** a *dr.like*

traun! [intj] ⟨obs⟩ (*surely*!, *certainly*!), *faith*!

tr·aurig a **A.** (P) *sad* (über [acc] *at*), *mournful*, *grieved*, *sorrowful*; *heavy-hearted*; *cheerless* ‖ *somber*; *dolorous* ‖ *melancholy*, *gloomy* (*state of mind*) ‖ (erbärmlich) *wretched* ‖ (schmerzlich) *distressing*, *grievous*, *lamentable*, *unfortunate*, *disheartening*; *painful* (*incidents*) ‖ (unheilvoll) *dismal* ‖ (öde) *dreary*, *bleak* **B.** (**Anblick**) *sorry*, *sad*, *deplorable* ‖ (Ausruf) *doleful* ‖ (Berühmtheit, Ereignis) *sad* ‖ (Jugend) *unhappy* ‖ ~er **Kerl** *sad kind of fellow* ‖ Ritter v der ~en Gestalt *K. of the Doleful Countenance* ‖ (Verhältnisse) *dismal* ‖ (Zeichen) *bad* ‖ (**Zeiten**) *sad* **C.** er **ist** ~ *he is dejected*, *depressed*, *grieved*, *dismal* (*about*) ‖ es ist (sehr) ~, daß *it is a pity* (*a thousand pities*) *that*; es ist ~, aber wahr *the unpleasant truth is* .. ‖ es war ~ anzusehen *it was a sad sight*, *it made one feel sad* ‖ ~ gestimmt über etw *hipped on a th* ‖ .., so ~ es **klingt**, .. (*for*), *sad to say*, (*it was so*) ‖ sehr ~ stehen ⟨fig⟩ *to be at a low ebb* ‖ ~ stimmen *to sadden* **D. das** ~̈e dabei ist *the sad part of it is* **~̈keit** f ~/ *sadness* ‖ *gloom* ‖ *wretchedness* ‖ (persönliche) *melancholy*, *depression*, *dejection*

traut a *beloved, dear* (⟨a.⟩ = traulich) | °~e f ~/ (*courage*) ‖ nicht die ~ h *not to have the guts* ⟨sl⟩ **Tr·auung** f ~/~en *marriage-ceremony*; kirchliche ~ *religious m.*; (Hochzeit) *wedding* **~stag** m *wedding-day*

Travanc·ore n (vorderind. Gebiet)

Trav·erse f ~/~n (Eisrand) ⟨mount⟩ *traverse* **t-sieren** vt/i *to traverse*

Travest·ie f ~/~n *travesty* (auf *of*) **≃ren** vt [h] *to travesty, burlesque*

Tr·eber [pl] *husks* (*of grapes*), *shells* pl ‖ (Bier-≃) *draff* sg, *brewer's grains*; *spent hops* pl od *malt*

Treck m ~(e)s/~e *trek* **~schute** f *draw-, canal--boat* **~seil** n *towing-rope, hawser* **~weg** m *t.g.-path* **tr·ecken I.** vt [h] *to draw, drag, tug* **II.** vi ⟨SAfr⟩ *to trek* **Tr·ecker** m ~s/~ ⟨mot⟩ *tractor*

Treff[1] n ~s/~(s) ⟨cards⟩ *clubs* pl **~b·ube** *kn. of clubs*; vgl *trefle* Fr (Dreiblatt, Klee)

Treff[2] m ~s/~e *blow* ‖ ⟨fig⟩ *good hit* ‖ (*spy's*) *secret rendez-vous* **~fähigkeit** f ⟨artill⟩ *effectiveness* **~genauigkeit** f ⟨mil⟩ *accuracy of fire* **~punkt** m *meeting-place, rendez-vous* ⟨hunt⟩ *meet* ‖ ⟨tact⟩ *meeting point* | ⟨ball⟩ *objective point*; mittlerer Längen≃ *range centre*; ⟨allg⟩ *mean point of impact*; theoretischer ~ *set-forward point* ‖ **≃sicher** a ⟨übtr⟩ *unerring* (Urteil[skraft]) | ≃heit [f] *accuracy of aim*; *marksmanship* ‖ ⟨med⟩ *hitting quota* **~weite** f *striking distance*

Tr·effen n ~s/~ **A. 1.** (Zus–kunft) *meeting, gathering, rally* (→ ansetzen) ‖ ⟨sport⟩ *match* **2.** *hitting* **3.** ⟨mil⟩ *action, encounter, engagement, fight* **4.** *line of battle* ⟨a. mar⟩ ‖ vorderes ~ *front line*; mittleres ~ *centre*; hinteres ~ *rearguard* **B.** ein ~ führen, liefern *to join, offer, give battle* ‖ es kam zum ~ *it came to an engagement* (bei *at*) | **ins** ~ führen ⟨fig⟩ *to urge*; *to bring forward* **tr·effen** [traf/getroffen] [h] **I.** vi *to hit, to hit the mark* ⟨a. fig⟩ ‖ nicht ~ *to miss* ⟨a. fig⟩ ‖ (nicht), [gut] getroffen! (*miss*!), *hit* [*home*]! ‖ e–e jede **Kugel** trifft ja nicht *not every bullet finds its billet* ‖ **(Schuß)** *to take effect* (⟨a. fig⟩ Witz), *to tell* (⟨a. fig⟩ Wort), *to go home* (⟨a. fig⟩ *that went home*) ‖ **(Schütze)** gut (todsicher) ~ *to be a good* (*dead*) *shot* | ~ **auf**: *to meet with, to encounter*; *to run against*; (auf den Feind) *to face in with*; durch Zufall .. *to happen on* ‖ **ins** Schwarze ~ *to make a bull's eye*, ⟨fig⟩ *to hit the mark* **II.** vt **A. 1.** *to hit, strike, beat*; (leicht) *to lick, snick* ‖ das Ziel (nicht) ~ *to hit* (*miss*) *the mark, goal*; ⟨fig⟩ **es** ~ ⟨fam⟩ *to hit it off*; es nicht ~ ⟨fig⟩ *to miss one's aim* ‖ ⟨mil-aero⟩ *to strike* | (S) *to hit, meet*; *greet, salute* (*the eye, ear*), *to burst upon* (*the ear*) | ⟨mus⟩ den Ton ~ *to hit, strike the right note* ⟨a. fig⟩ **2.** (finden) *to find* (*the th wanted*) ‖ *to strike* (*the right road*) ‖ (auf Anhieb) *to hit* (*the bridge*) *off* ‖ (den Sinn) *to seize* | ⟨paint, phot etc⟩ *to strike off* (*a p's features*) ‖ bin ich getroffen? *is it a good likeness* (*of me*)? .. *you have come out quite well* **3.** (erreichen) *the letter will not reach him in time* **4.** (jdm begegnen) *to meet with* (⟨a. übtr⟩ *with difficulties*); (zufällig) *to light* od *blunder on, to fall in with, to happen to meet*, ⟨fam⟩ *to run into* (*a p*), ⟨übtr a.⟩ *to encounter* | er hat es **mit** dem Kauf nicht schlecht getroffen *he didn't fare badly in the buying* **5.** (an|~) (P) *to find at home* ‖ wir w dort Bekannte ~ *we shall be among friends there* | *he had never struck an atmosphere like this* **B.** (zuwege bringen) **(Abkommen)** *to come to* (*terms with*) ‖ **(Entscheidung)** *to take, form* | (ins Werk setzen) (Vorbereitungen) *to make* ‖ (Vorsichtsmaßregeln, s–e **Wahl)** *to take* **C.** Sie h **es** getroffen *you've hit it* od *the mark*; *right* (*you are*)!, *exactly*!; ⟨fam⟩ *that's about the size of it* ‖ **es** glücklich ~ *to come at the right time* ‖ **es** schlecht ~ *to strike a bad patch, to come at an unfortunate time* ‖ Sie ~ **es** gut, daß *it is lucky that* **D.** ⟨**fig**⟩ **1.** (Beileidigung) *this offence strikes us all* ‖ wie v **Blitz,** Donner getroffen *thunderstruck* ‖ der Fluch soll ihn ~! *curse him*! ‖ (Licht[strahl]) *to strike* ‖ **(Los)** *to fall on* ‖ (Nachricht) *to come to* od *upon* (*a p*) ‖ die Reihe traf ihn *it was his turn* ‖ **(Schlag)** (*the blow*) *caught him* ‖ (Schicksalsschlag) *to fall upon* (*a p*) ‖ ⟨path⟩ v Schlag getroffen *struck with apoplexy* ‖ .. wird von den Strahlen .. getroffen (*the rock*) *catches the rays* (*of the setting sun*) ‖ wen trifft die Schuld? *who's to blame*? ‖ **(Unfall)** *to befall, affect* ‖ das Unglück (der Vorwurf) traf mich (ihn) *I had the misf.*, (*the blame rested upon him*) ‖ (Verordnung) *to hit, affect* (*a p*) **2. das** trifft Sie *that's meant for you, that touches, concerns you* **3.** jdn **empfindlich,** schmerzlich ~ (P) *to be hard on a p*, (S) *that had hit him hard* (od *where it hurts most*); jdn tief ~ *to wound a p cruelly*; er war zutiefst getroffen *it was a dreadful blow to him* **4.** sich getroffen **fühlen** *to feel hurt* **5.** ⟨prov⟩ wer sich getroffen fühlt, fasse sich an die Nase *let him whom the cap fits wear it* ‖ getroffene Hunde bellen *if the cap fits wear it* **III. 1. sich** ~ (P) *to for(e)gather, rally*; (mit) *to meet* [*with*], ⟨Am a.⟩ *to visit with a p* **2. es** traf sich, daß *it chanced that*; wie sich **das** trifft! *how fortunate*!, *how well that suits*!, *what a coincidence*! **3. sich** ~ (S) *to happen* ‖ **es** traf sich, daß (wir) *it so happened that* (*we happened to be there*) ‖ wie gut **es** sich trifft! *how pat this comes in*!, *how lucky*!; *it's a good th* ‖ wie **es** sich gerade trifft *as chance will have it, as it happens, as often happens* ‖ ⟨fam⟩ wie sich's trifft! *as occasions may require* **tr·effend** a ⟨fig⟩ (schlagend) *striking* ‖ *explicit* (*formulation*); *felicitous* (*expression*) ‖ (passend) *right* (*word*), *proper, appropriate* (*term*), *pertinent* (*remark*); *apt* (*reply*), *neat* (*retort*); ~es Argument *clincher*; Ihre Behauptung ist ~ *the point you make is well taken*; ~e Bemerkung ⟨Am fam⟩ *nifty* ‖ (*it is*) *to the point* od *purpose* **Tr·effer** m ~s/~ *good shot* ‖ ⟨mil⟩ *hit* (erzielen *to score*); leichter ~ *sitter* ⟨a. fig⟩; (harter Schlag) ⟨Am sl⟩ *sock* ‖ ⟨fig⟩ (*to make a*) *lucky hit*; (*that was a*) *nailer*! ‖ e–n ~ m ⟨Am⟩ *to strike oil* ‖ (Lotterie– etc ≃) *prize* ‖ ⟨Lit⟩ *bestseller* ‖ ⟨theat fam⟩ *draw* **~bild** n *target diagram* **~ergebnis** n ⟨mil⟩ *score* **~lage** f; gute ~ *good hits* pl **~quote** f ⟨med, etc⟩ *hitting quota* **tr·efflich** a *excellent, exquisite* ‖ ⟨fam⟩ ~, ~! *capital*!, *fine*! **≃keit** f *excellence, choiceness, perfection*; *patness*

Tr·eib- *drift* **~anker** m *d.-anchor, drag* od *sea a.* **~arbeit** f *embossed work* **~bake** f *floating beacon* **~beet** n *hotbed* **~eis** n *driving ice* | ~scholle [f] *ice-floe* **~fäustel** n (kl) *hammer*; (gr) *maul* **~gas** n *power* od *fuel, liquified gas* **~hammer** m *mallet*; *embossing h.* **~hauspflanze** f *hot-house plant* **~herd** m ⟨met⟩ *cupelling-furnace, refining-hearth* **~holz** n *d.-wood* ‖ (Böttcherei) *hoop driver* **~jagd** f *battue*; *organized drive* **~kraft** f *moving power, propelling force* **~ladung** f *propelling charge* **~mine** f *floating mine* **~mittel** n *propellant* ‖ (Hefe etc) *raising agent* **~netz** n *d.-net* **~öl** n *motor oil* **~prozeß** m ⟨met⟩ *cupellation, refining* **~rad** n *fly-wheel*; (Uhr≃) *pinion* **~reis** n *sprout* **~riemen** m *driving belt* **~sand** m *quicksands* pl **~satz** m *propulsive charge*; *rocket composition* **~schacht** m ⟨min⟩ *drawing pit* **~segel** n *d.-sail* **~stange** f ⟨mach⟩ *main rod, connecting rod*; ⟨weav⟩ *working beam* **~stoff** m *propellant*; *fuel* | ~ergänzung [f] *refuelling*; ~lager [n] *f. depot*; ~zusatz [m] *dopes* pl **~strahl** m ⟨turbo⟩ *driving jet* **~- u Schmierstoffe** pl *petroleum, oil, and lubrication* **~welle** f ⟨mach⟩ *main shaft* **~werk** n *driving gear* **Tr·eiben** n ~s/ *driving*, etc ‖ (geschäftiges) *activity, stir*; (lärmendes) *bustle* | (Tun) (*a p's*) *doings, dealings, goings-on* pl ‖ *ways* (*of the world*) ‖ wüstes ~ *riotous scenes* pl | *germination* ‖ *budding* (*of leaves*) ‖ ⟨met⟩ *cupellation* ‖ ⟨hunt⟩ *battue* | ⟨fig⟩ *urging* (*on N.'s u.*)

tr·eiben [trieb/getrieben] **I.** vt [h] **A. 1.** *to drive* (*cattle to pasture*) || *powder propels the bullet* || *steam runs the turbines* || *he drove her* (*gently before him*) *and propelled her* (*over the threshold*), *herding her* (*into the room*) **2.** *to put in motion* || *the water sets the mill* (*a-*)*going* **3.** (an|~) *to incite, impel, move*; *to drive, hasten, urge* (*on*) **4.** (drängen) *to urge, press*; *to rush* (*he refused to be r.ed*) | ⟨fig⟩ *to hound* (*a p*) || *to make a p hurry* **5.** (Wind) *to waft* **6.** ⟨hort⟩ *to force* (*plants*) **7.** (be~) *to carry on* (*a trade*) || *to exercise, practise* (*an art*) || *to follow* (*a profession*) || *to cultivate* (*a science*) || *to go in for* (*Latin, sports*) || *to work* (⟨fam⟩ *grind*) *at* (*Latin*) **8.** *to emboss*; getriebene Arbeit *embossing*; *embossed work* **B. getrieben w** ⟨a.⟩ *to be moved* od *actuated* (*by an impulse*) || *to be blown* (*before the gales*) || ⟨mar⟩ *to heave* (*ahead, astern*) || (Rauch) *to drift* (⟨a. fig⟩ *into war*) **C. sich** ~ **l** (*he refused*) *to be rushed* || *to drift* (*the policy of dr.*) || ⟨mar sport⟩ *to surf* **D. Aufwand** ~ *to live in great style* || (Ball) ⟨ftb⟩ *to dribble* || e–m das Blut ins Gesicht ~ *to make a p blush* || (Blüten) *to put forth* || (Eis) *the river is drifting with ice* || ⟨min⟩ **(Erz)** *to extract* || Geschäfte ~ *to do business* || (Gewerbe etc) *to carry on, practise, ply* || (Häute) *to soak* || (Herden) *to tend* || ⟨prov⟩ ein **Keil** treibt den andern *one nail drives out another* || Kindereien ~ *to do childish ths* || (Kreisel) *to whip, spin* || Kurzweil ~ *to amuse o.s.* || (Maschine) *to work* || (Metall) ⟨arts⟩ (hoch|~) *to emboss*, (tief|~) *to chase*; ⟨met⟩ *to cupel, refine* || **(Musik)** *to study, cultivate* || (Nägel) *to drive in* || (Pfähle) *to plant, sink* || Politik ~ ⟨fam⟩ *to dabble in politics*; praktische P. ~ *to adopt a practical policy* || die **Preise** ~ *to force* od ⟨fam⟩ *jack up prices*; (b. Auktion) *to bid up* || Reifen auf ein Faß ~ *to hoop a cask* || (Schößlinge) *to throw out* || **(Schweiß)** *to promote* || Sport ~ *to go in for, to engage in sports*; *to play games* || (Sprachen) *to study* || ⟨min⟩ (Stollen) *to drive* || Unfug ~ *to do mischief*, ⟨fam⟩ *to be up to m.* || **Unsinn** ~ *to play foolish tricks*; wir l k–n U. mit uns ~ *we won't stand any nonsense* || Bier treibt **(Urin)** *b. is diuretic* || sein Wesen ~ *to be full of fun, pranks, mischief* || ⟨hunt⟩ (Wild) *to beat* (*up*) **E. 1. es** treibt mich .. *I feel compelled* (*to go away*), .. z sagen *I feel I must tell you* **2. es** gemütlich ~ *to take it* od *ths easy* || es zu arg, toll, weit ~ *to carry things too far* || *you have been going it*! .. *going the pace too hard*! || so weit möchte ich **es** nicht ~ *I should not altogether wish to go so far* | ⟨prov⟩ wie man's treibt, so geht's *as you sow, so shall you reap*!, *do well and have well*! **3.** es toll ~ ⟨fam⟩ *to come it strong* || **was** treibt er? *what's his trade* || was ~ Sie da? *what are you doing* (od *up to*) *there*? **F. an**: *to drive a country to the verge of chaos* | **aufs** äußerste ~ *to carry .. to extremes* | **aus** dem Amt ~ *to drive* od *force .. out of office* || aus s–m Besitz ~ *to disposses, eject* || aus dem Lande ~ *to banish, exile* | jdn **in** jds Arme ~ *to push a p on to a p* || **in** die Enge ~ *to drive* od *press hard*, ⟨fam fig⟩ *to push* (*a p*) *into a corner*; *to bait, stalemate* || in die Flucht ~ *to put to flight*, (völlig) *to rout* || *to plunge, goad* (*into war*) || in die Höhe ~ → D. Preis | **von** e–a ~ *to separate, scatter* | **vor** sich her ~ *to hustle before one, to push in front of one*; ⟨ftb⟩ *to dribble* | **zu** etw ~ *to urge, incite* (*a p*) *to do, to bid* (*a p*) *do* || zum Äußersten ~ *to put a p to his trumps* || zur Eile ~ *to hurry*, ⟨Am⟩ *hustle* || Not treibt e–n zu manchem *needs must when the devil drives* || zur Verzweiflung ~ *to drive to despair* **II.** vi [h & s] **A. 1.** *to be carried along* || (schwimmend) *to drive, float* (*along*), (*be a*)*drift*; (mit der Flut) *to tide* **2.** (Bier) (aus dem Faß) .. *overflows the vat* || (Hefe) *ferments* || (Schiff) *heaves* (*stern-way*) || (Schnee) *drifts* || (Wolken) *send* **3.** ⟨bot⟩ *to shoot forth, to germinate, to bud* (*greenly*) || (Gras) *springs* || (Saft) *rises* || ~ l *to force* (*plants*); ein Boot ~ l *to cut adrift* **B.** ⟨mar⟩ **an** die Küste ~ *to be cast* od *washed ashore* || an den Strand ~ *to run aground* | **auf** e–n Felsen ~ *to foul a rock* | **vor** Anker ~ *to drag the a.* **tr·eibend** a *driving*, etc || *motive* (*power*) **Tr·eiber** m ~s/~ **1.** (P) *driver* ⟨a. mach⟩ || (Vieh≈) *drover* || ⟨hunt⟩ *beater*(*-up*) | (An≈) *instigator*; (*main*) *spring*; *life and soul* | Dränger ⟨com⟩ *oppressor* | Arbeiter≈ *taskmaster*, ⟨Am⟩ *hustler* **2.** (S) ⟨tech⟩ *driver, propeller, driving-wheel, -gear* **~·ei** f ~/~en **1.** *driving, urging* **2.** [mst pl] *intrigue*(*s pl*)

Tr·eidel m ~s/~ *tow-line, towing-rope* **~pfad, ~steig, ~weg** m *tow*(*ing*) *path* | **≈n I.** vt [h] *to tow* **II.** ≈ n (⟨a.⟩ | **~·ei** f) *towing* **Tr·eidler** m *tower*

Tr·ema n ~s/~s ⟨gram⟩ *diaeresis*

×**Tr·emse** f ~/~n [nordd] *cornflower*

Tremul·ant m ~en/~en (Orgel≈) *tremolo-stop* **t-l·ieren** vi [h] ⟨mus⟩ *to quaver, trill*; *to sing tr.*

Tr·endel m ~s/~ **1.** ⟨dial⟩ (Spielzeug) *top* **2.** (⟨a.⟩ Trendler) *dawdler*; → Langweiler, Trödler

tr·ennbar a *separable, divisible*; (Ehe) *dissoluble* **≈keit** f *separability*, etc **Tr·enn- ~anstalt** f ⟨telph⟩ *intermediate station* **~bühne** f *separating dam* **~isolator** m *disconnecting insulator* **~kreis** m ⟨wir⟩ *selection circuit* **~linie** f *breaching line* **~maschine** f *ripper* **~messer** n *ripping-knife* **~punkte** m pl *diaeresis* **~schacht** m ⟨min⟩ *parting shaft* **~schalter** m ⟨el⟩ *circuit* od *contact breaker*; *disconnecting switch* **≈scharf** a ⟨wir⟩ *selective* **~schärfe** f ⟨phot⟩ *selectivity*; hohe ~ (*extremely*) *precise separation* **~schicht** f ⟨telph⟩ *separator* || ⟨phot⟩ *septum* **~wand** f *wall separating*; ⟨mech⟩ *diaphragm* **tr·ennen I.** vt [h] **1.** *to separate*; *divide*; *split*; (Kämpfende, Liebende) *to part* **2.** (sondern) *to segregate*; *sunder* (*sharply -ed senses*) || *to sever* (*the head from the body*) || (eng Verbundenes) *to disjoin*; Farbe u Geruch sind nicht z ~ .. *go together* || (ablösen) *to detach* **3.** ⟨mil⟩ *to break* (*the enemy's ranks*) || (Naht) *to rip up* || ⟨telph⟩ *to disconnect*; *cut off* **4.** (Ehe) *to dissolve* || (Gatten) *to separate, divorce* | **getrennt** *separate* (*ways, packages*) || getr. leben *to be separated* || getr. w *to be drifted apart* **II. sich** [acc] ~ *to part* (*company*) || ⟨com⟩ *to dissolve partnership* || (Tanzpaar) *to break up* || (Gatten) *to separate*, ⟨jur⟩ *to be*(*come*) *divorced* || (Wege) *to branch off*; wo sich die Wege ~ *at the parting of* .. | **in**: *to sort o.s. out into* (*two parties*) | **von**: *to part with*; *to separate, secede*, (⟨fam⟩ *bolt*) *from* || *to cut o.s. adrift from* || *to drop a p* (*at his door*) || ⟨fig⟩ .. nicht .. *to stick to a p* || sich v s–r Frau ~ *to divorce one's wife* **Tr·ennung** f ~/~en *separation, severing*; *division, disunion, disjunction* || *partition, splitting* || *parting* (*of fighters, friends*) || (Abfall) *defection* || ⟨telph⟩ *disconnexion* || (Ehe≈) *divorce* || (Silben≈) *division* || ⟨wir⟩ *spacing* (*of frequences*) || ~ v Staat u Kirche *ch.-st. separation*; *schism between ch. and st.*; ⟨jur⟩ *separation* (*from bed and board*) **Tr·ennungs- ~entschädigung** f *s.n allowance* od *indemnity* **~fläche** f ⟨cryst⟩ *plane of cleavage*; zw 2 Körpern *interface* **~linie** f *dividing line*; ⟨mil⟩ *boundary* N **~partikel** f ⟨gram⟩ *disjunctive particle* **~schmerz** m *wrench* (*of parting*) **~strich** m *hyphen* **~stunde** f *parting-hour* **~wand** f *wall of partition*; ⟨mech⟩ *diaphragm* **~zeichen** n (Trema) *diaeresis* || (Divis) *hyphen*

Tr·ense f ~/~n *snaffle* || [dat] ~ anlegen *to sn.*

tr·ensen vt [h] ⟨mar⟩ *to worm* (*a rope*)

Tr·enton n (Stadt) (*N. Y., U.S.A.*)

Trep·an m ~(e)s/~e ⟨surg⟩ *trepan* **≈·ieren** vt [h] *to trepan* **~·iersäge** f *trephine*

trepp- ~·ab [adv] (*coming*) *downstairs* **~·auf** [adv] (*going*) *upstairs* || t.auf, t.ab *upstairs and dowstairs* **Tr·eppe** f ~/~n ⟨arch⟩ *staircase*, ⟨Am⟩ *stairway* || (Frei≈) (*flight of*) *steps*; (Vor≈) *door steps* || ⟨allg⟩ (*flight* od *pair of*) *stairs*; fahrbare ~ *gangway* || ⟨mar⟩ *ladder* || *to fall* *down the stairs* ‖ *to go, (throw a p) downstairs* ‖ die Spanische ∼ (in Rom) *the Spanish Steps* ‖ zwei ∼n hoch *on the second floor* ‖ e–e ∼ höher *on the next floor* | ⟨fig⟩ °die ∼ herabfallen *to have one's hair cut* ‖ die ∼ hinauffallen ⟨fig⟩ *to be kicked upstairs, to fall on one's feet* **Tr·eppen-** **∼absatz** m *landing*; oberer ∼ *stair-head* **∼anlauf** m ⟨arch⟩ *springing* **≗artig** a *staircase (pattern)* **∼baum** m = –spindel **∼fenster** n *staircase window* **∼flucht** f *flight of stairs* **∼flur** m = –absatz **≗förmig** a *laddershaped* **∼geländer** m *banisters* pl **∼giebel** m ⟨arch⟩ *corbie* od *stepped, recessed gable* **∼haus** n *well of a staircase, entrance-hall* **∼läufer** m *stair-carpet* **∼leiter** f *step ladder* **∼pfosten** m *newel-post* **∼schritt** m ⟨ski⟩ *side step* **∼spindel** f *upright, newel* **∼stufe** f *step, stair* **∼teppich** m *stair-carpet* **∼visier** n ⟨mil⟩ *graduated sight* **∼vorplatz** m *foot of stairs* **∼wange** f ⟨carp⟩ *notch-board* **≗weise** adv ∼ aufgestellt *in tiers* **∼witz** m *after-wit* ‖ ∼ der Weltgeschichte *paradox in* od *of history*

Tres·or m ∼(e)s/∼e *treasury* ‖ (Geld≗) *safe* ‖ ⟨bank⟩ *strong room*

Tr·espe f ∼/∼n ⟨bot⟩ *brome*

Tr·esse f ∼/∼n *galloon, lace* ‖ ⟨mil⟩ *stripe* | **∼n- ∼hut, ∼rock** m *laced hat, coat* **∼winkel** m ⟨mil⟩ *chevron* Fr

Tr·ester(n) [pl] *husks, grounds* pl, *rape(s)* **∼kuchen** m *grape-cake* **∼wein** m *rape* od *after-wine*

Tr·et- **∼anlasser** m ⟨mot⟩ *kick-starter* **∼butte, ∼kufe** f *treading-vat* **∼karre** f ⟨cycl vulg⟩ *push-bike* **∼lager** n ⟨cycl⟩ *pedal-bearing* **∼mine** f *anti-personnel mine* **∼mühle** f *treadmill* ⟨a. fig⟩; ⟨fig⟩ *humdrum round (of duty), daily round of toil*; ⟨fam⟩ *grind* **∼rad** n *treadwheel* **∼schalter** m *floor-switch* **∼schemel** m ⟨weav⟩ *treadle* **∼zuber** m = –butte **tr·eten** [trat/ge∼] **I.** vi [h & s] **A.** [h] **1.** *to tread, walk, step (on, into a th)*; ⟨mil⟩ kurz ∼! *half step*! **2.** ⟨cycl⟩ *to pedal, treadle* **3.** (ausschlagen) *to kick* **4. (heftig)** *to slam, stamp (on a th)* ‖ leise ∼ *to go, walk, step softly*, ⟨fig⟩ *to (be a) sneak, to be artful* ‖ (plötzlich) *to snap (on a th)* ‖ (plump) *to lumber* **B. 1.** [s] *to (take a) step* **2.** die Augen traten ihm vor Entsetzen **aus** dem Kopf *the eyes were almost starting out of his h. with horror* ‖ **beiseite** ∼ *to stand* od *step aside* ‖ daneben ∼ [a. h] *to make a false step* ‖ **dazwischen** ∼ ⟨fig⟩ *to intercede, interpose*; wenn nichts dazw. tritt *if nothing happens in the meantime* ‖ ∼ Sie **dorthin,** (hierher) *go over there, (come here)* ‖ heraus ∼ *to go out (on the balcony)* ‖ **näher** ∼ *to approach*; zu jdm *to draw nearer to a p*; ⟨fig⟩ (e–r S) *to consider* ‖ ∼ Sie näher! *walk, step in!, step this way*! ‖ jdm zu nahe ∼ *to offend a p, to hurt a p's feeling*; ohne Herrn N. zu nahe z ∼ *with all due respect, deference to Mr. N.* ‖ e–n Schritt seitwärts ∼ ⟨a.⟩ *to edge a step away* **3. an**: *to step on to, to advance toward, to go to (the window)* ‖ (P) *to step into (the light)*; (S) *to come to light (= to become known)* ‖ ⟨theat⟩ *to appear before (the footlights* Rampe) ‖ *to come to (a p's side)* ‖ an die Spitze ∼ *to take the lead (of)* ‖ ⟨gram⟩ die Endung tritt an den Stamm .. *is joined to* .. ‖ an jds Stelle ∼ *to take a p's place* | **auf**: (→ A. 1, 4) ⟨a.⟩ *to get upon, to mount* ‖ e–m auf den Fuß ∼ *to tread on a p's foot*, (bei Tisch) *to kick a p (under the table)* ‖ auf das Podium ∼ *to step on* .. ‖ nicht auf den Rasen ∼! *do not walk on the grass* ‖ auf die Seite ∼ *to step aside*, ⟨fig⟩ auf jds .. *to side with a p* ‖ der Schweiß trat ihm auf die Stirn *p. stood upon his brow* | **aus** dem Dienst, Weg ∼ *to retire from s., to stand out of the way* | **in**: (→ A. 1.) ‖ *tears came into her eyes* ‖ in Beziehung ∼ zu *to enter into relations with* ‖ *to put one's foot in (a flower-bed)* ‖ ins Dasein ∼ *to come into existence* ‖ in Dienst ∼ *to enter into s.* ‖ in den Ehestand ∼ *to get married* ‖ ins Haus (10. Jahr) ∼ *to enter the h. (one's tenth y.)* ‖ ins Leben ∼ (P) *to emerge into the world, to make one's appearance*; (S) *to come into existence* ‖ *the sun enters Leo* (den Löwen) ‖ in den Priesterstand ∼ *to take holy orders* ‖ in s–e Rechte ∼ ⟨jur⟩ *to resume one's rights* ‖ jdm in den Weg ∼ *to stand in* (od *block*) *a p's way*, ⟨fig⟩ *to oppose a p* ‖ ins [in (s)ein Zimmer] ∼ *to come into the [to enter a (gain one's)] room* | ∼ **über** *to pass, cross; to overflow (its banks)* | jdm **unter** die Augen ∼ *to appear before, to face a p*; tritt mir nicht mehr .. *never let me see your face again* | **von**: *he stood away from (the door)* ‖ von .. auf .. *he shifted from one foot to the other* | **vor**: *to appear before a p*; (Wolke) .. *passed over the sun* ‖ ⟨fig⟩ jdm vor Augen ∼ *to spring to, (to rise in) a p's mind* | **zu**: *to walk (step, go) up to a p; to move up to*; wieder zu (e–m Truppenteil) ∼ *to rejoin* .. ‖ ⟨fig⟩ *to take his side* ‖ zutage ∼ *to rise, come to the surface*, ⟨fig⟩ *to appear; to become evident* **II.** vt [h] **A.** *to tread, kick* (wiederholt *trample*) *on* ‖ ⟨physiol⟩ **(Henne)** *to tread* ‖ Pflaster ∼ *to lounge about the streets* ‖ (Rad) *to ply* ‖ ⟨fam⟩ (Schuldner) *to dun* ‖ d. Takt ∼ *to beat time with one's foot* ‖ ⟨tech⟩ *to tread(le)*; (Ton, Trauben) *to tread* ‖ **Wasser** ∼ *to tread the w.* ‖ e–n Weg ∼ (= m) *to beat* .., (gehen) *to follow a path* **B.** sich [dat] e–n Nagel **in** den Fuß ∼ *to get* od *run a nail in(to) one's f.* | ⟨fig⟩ (jds Gefühle) **mit** Füßen ∼ *to trample down*; sein Glück .. *to spurn one's fortune* | **in** den Staub, **zu** Boden ∼ *to crush under foot* ‖ (jdn) zu Tode ∼ *to trample to death* **C.** (etw) **entzwei** ∼ *to break .. by treading on* ‖ s–e Schuhe schief ∼ *to wear one's shoes down on one side* ‖ (Tiere) **tot** ∼ *to crush, kill .. by treading, stamping on* **Tr·eter** m ∼s/∼ *treader*

treu I. [a] **A.** *faithful, true (to)*; [abs] *true-blue* | (ergeben) *devoted, loyal (to)* ‖ (aufrichtig) *sincere*; (Briefschluß) Dein ∼er .. *Yours sincerely* .. ‖ (aufrecht) *upright* ‖ (zuverlässig) *trustworthy, reliable*; *trusty (sword)* ‖ *staunch (follower, friend)*; *constant (friend, patient)* ‖ *stalwart (defender)* ‖ *firm (allies)* ‖ (P) *faithful (soul)* ‖ *retentive, faithful (memory)* ‖ *close (translation)* ‖ ⟨bib, poet⟩ du ∼er Gott *Lord God of truth* **B.** ∼ **wie** Gold (P) [pred] *(as) true as steel; all wool and a yard wide* ‖ sich selbst ∼ *true to o.s.* ‖ **zu** ∼en Händen *in trust* ‖ s–n Grundsätzen ∼ *true to* .. ‖ [dat] **∼bleiben** *to stick to (a p, a party)*; s–m Versprechen, (Vorsatz) ∼ bleiben *to stand by one's pledge, (to stick to one's purpose)* ‖ s–r S ∼ bl. *to stick to one's colours* ‖ das Glück blieb ihr ∼ *her luck held* **II.** [adv] ∼ festhaltend an *in loyalty to* ‖ es mit e–m ∼ meinen *to mean well by a p* ‖ ∼ wiedergeben (übersetzen) *to render closely* ‖ (Briefschluß) Ihr ∼ ergebener .. *Yours faithfully* **Treu** f ∼/ = Treue; auf ∼ u Glauben *on trust* ‖ (bei) m–r ∼ *upon my honour; egad!* **∼bruch** m *breach of faith, disloyalty, perfidy* **≗brüchig** a *faithless, disloyal, perfidious* **∼eid** m *oath of allegiance* **≗erg·eben** a *loyal (to)* **∼gut** n *trust property* **∼hand** f ⟨jur⟩ *trust* | ∼gesellschaft [f] *trust-company* ‖ ∼schaftsgebiet [n] *trust territory* **∼händer** m *executor (of a will)*; *trustee* | ∼staat [m] *custodian country* **≗herzig** a *ingenuous, candid, simple-minded, guileless* | ∼keit [f] *i.ness, g.ness* **∼l·iebchen** n *true-love* **≗los** a *faithless, perfidious* ‖ [adv] ∼ verlassen *to desert, to throw over, to jilt* **∼losigkeit** f *faithlessness, (to[wards]) perfidy* ‖ [konkr] *treacherous deed* **Tr·eue** f ∼/ (→ Treu) *faithfulness* (a. fig: ∼ e–s Berichts; e–r Übersetzung ⟨a.⟩ *closeness*) ‖ (im Halten e–s Versprechens etc) *faith* ‖ (nur v P) *fidelity (to)*, etc (→ treu A.) ‖ punische ∼ *Punic faith* | ⟨übtr⟩ ∼ (der Wiedergabe) *fidelity* ⟨a. phys⟩ | den Eid der ∼ **ablegen** *to take the oath of allegiance, to swear all. to* ‖ die ∼ brechen *to break faith*; e–r S .. *to betray a cause* ‖ (jdm) ∼ **geloben** *to declare one's loyalty to* ‖ e–m die ∼ halten *to remain* *faithful to a p, to keep faith with a p; to be loyal to (the king)*; ⟨fam⟩ *to run straight* || sie schworen sich ~ *they plighted their troth* **~gelübde** n *vow(s) of fidelity* **~kundgebung** f *tokens* [pl] *of loyalty* **~verhältnis** n *spirit of good comeradeship* **tr·eulich** [adv] *faithfully, truly*, etc || *conscientiously*, etc || (wahrheitsgemäß) *truthfully*

Tri·ade f ~/~n ⟨Gr poet⟩ → *triad*

Tr·i·angel m ~s/~ *triangle* ⟨a. mus⟩ **triangul·ieren** vt [h] *to triangulate* || *to survey by trigonometry* **Triangul·ierung** f ~/ *triangulation*

Tri·arier m ~s/~ ⟨hist⟩ *triarian*

Tr·ias f ~/ *triad* || ⟨geol⟩ *trias* **~gebirge** n *triassic formation*; so: *t.c sea*

tribul·ieren vt [h] *to trouble, plague, vex*

Trib·un m [~(e)s & ~en/~e(n)] *tribune* **~·al** n ~(e)s/~e *tribunal* || vor dem ~ der Geschichte *at the bar of history* **~·at** n ~(e)s/~e *tribuneship*

Trib·üne f ~/~n (Redner≗) *platform* || (Zuschauer≗) *(grand) stand* **Tr·ibus** f ~/~ ⟨hist⟩ *tribe*

Trib·ut m ~(e)s/~e *tribute* ([dat] auferlegen *to impose on*) || ⟨fig⟩ *old age took* (forderte) *its toll of him, a terrible toll of life*; geforderter ~ *(terrible) toll exacted (by accidents)* **≗frei** a *exempt from t.te* **≗pflichtig** a *t.tary (to)* || ~ m *to lay .. under t.te* || sich jdn ~ halten *to hold .. to t.te*

Trich·ine f ~/~n *trichina* **~nbeschauer** m *meat inspector* **~nkrankheit** f, **Trichin·ose** f ~/ *trichinosis* **trichin·ös** a *trichinous*

Tr·ichter m ~s/~ *funnel* || (Granat≗, Vulkan≗) *crater* | ⟨tech⟩ Füll≗ *filler* || (Kaffee≗) *filter* || (bes Mühl≗) *hopper* || Schall≗ *horn*; ⟨telph⟩ *trumpet*, Sprech≗ *mouthpiece* || ⟨mot⟩ (Vergaser–) Luft≗ *choke* | ⟨hum⟩ Nürnberger ~ *royal road to learning* **~feld** n ⟨mil⟩ *shell-torn ground* od *area* **≗förmig** a *funnel-shaped* **~gewölbe** n ⟨arch⟩ *fan-vaulting* **~nische** f ⟨arch⟩ *squinch* **~öffnung** f ⟨geol⟩ *crater* **~wagen** m *hopper wagon* **tr·ichtern** vt [h] *to pour through a funnel, to decant*

Trick m & n [~s/~e & ~s] *dodge*; *stunt*; *trick* ⟨a. cards; water-ski⟩ (Figur); ⟨Am sl⟩ *(a) fast one*; *gimmick* = Stich); ⟨fam⟩ *hanky-panky*; ⟨sl⟩ *racket*, ⟨Am fam⟩ *gag* || (beim Ringen) *chip* || ⟨fig⟩ e–n ~ versuchen bei *to try a game on ..* || ⟨film⟩ figürlicher ~ *animation* || ⟨com⟩ ein ~ jagt den anderen *gimmick after g.* **~aufnahme** f ⟨rec⟩ *trick recording* **~film** m *stunt* od *trick film* od *picture*; *film* od *animated cartoon* || (gezeichneter ⟨a.⟩) *cartoon-film* | ~zeichner [m] *animator* **~kunst** f ⟨Am sl⟩ *gimmickery* **~taste** f ⟨rec⟩ *trick button* **~track** n ~s/ *backgammon*

trieb 1. & 3. sg pret v treiben **Trieb** m ~(e)s/~e **1.** (Wachstum) *growth, germinating power* **2.** (Schößling) *sprout, (young) shoot* || geiler ~ *proud branch* **3.** (Antrieb) *impulse*; (heftiger) *impetus* || (Natur≗) ⟨biol⟩ *drive*; *instinct* || (Neigung) *inclination, liking, bent* || (Hang) *propensity* || (Verlangen) *appetency, desire* || aus innerem, eigenem → Antrieb | sinnliche ~e *carnal desires* || ~ **zu** *love of (study, one's country)* **4.** (~kraft) *moving force, movement, propulsive force*; ⟨phys, artill⟩ *momentum* **~achse** f *driving shaft* **≗artig** a *instinctive* **~feder** f *(elastic) spring* || ⟨fig⟩ *motive, main-spring, guiding principle*; ⟨Am⟩ *urge* || die ~ (e–r S) s *to be at the bottom of* **~handlung** f *impulsive act* **~kasten** m *pinion box* **~kraft** f *motive power, driving power, driving force* ⟨a. fig⟩; ⟨bot⟩ *growth* || ⟨tech⟩ *propelling* (⟨fig⟩ *motive) power*; ⟨fig⟩ *drive*; *impulse* **≗mäßig** a *instinctive* **~rad** n *driving-wheel* || (Getriebe) *pinion* **~sand** m *shifting sand, quicksand, silt* **~schlag** m ⟨ten⟩ *drive* **~stange** f *connecting rod* **~stoff** m *fuel* **~wagen** m *rail-motor, -car*; *autorail*; ⟨Am rail⟩ *shuttle-car* | ~zug [m] *multiple unit train* **~welle** = –achse **~werk** n ⟨el⟩ *power plant* **~werk** n *machinery, gear*; ⟨aero⟩ *power unit*; (intermittierend) *pulse u.* || ⟨fig⟩ *clock-work* | ~gondel [f] ⟨aero⟩ *engine cowling*; ~steuerung [f] *engine controls* pl **~wurzel** f ⟨bot⟩ *large* od *main root* **tr·iebhaft** a *conative, impulsive, impetuous*; *instinctive* | [adv] ~ handeln *to act on instinct* (od *under an impulse*)

Trief- ~auge n *blear-eye, running eye* **≗äugig** a *blear(-eye)(e)d* **~nase** f *running nose* **≗näsig** a *snivelly* **≗n·aß** a *dripping wet* **tr·iefen** [troff/getroffen] & reg [h] *to trickle* || *to ooze, drip, drop, stream* (von *with*) || *to be dripping* od *wet (with sweat)* || ⟨fig⟩ *to overflow (with kindness)* | (Augen) *to run* | (durchnäßt s) *to be wet all over* || v Regen ~ *to sop with rain* **tr·iefig** a *dripping, running*, etc

Tri·ennium n ~s/–nien *triennial period*

Tri(d)·ent n *Trent* || ~·iner Konzil [n] *Council of Trent* (1545–1563)

Trier n ⟨Ger⟩ (Stadt) *Treves* [Fr]

Tri·ere f ~/~n ⟨ant mar⟩ *trireme*

°**tr·iezen** vt [h] [du triez(es)t] *to vex, bully*

trifft 3. sg pres v treffen

Trift f ~/~en *pastur(ag)e, common* || (Herde) *drove, herd* || (Weg) *cattle-track* || (Holz≗) *floating* || (Aue) *meadow* || ⟨geol⟩ *drift* || ⟨mar⟩ 1. *drift-current* 2. *wreck(age)* **~bach, ~kanal** m ⟨for⟩ *flume*; *floating channel* **~(gerechtigkeit)** f *right of pasturage* **tr·iftig**[1] a ⟨mar⟩ *adrift, drifting*

tr·iftig[2] a *weighty, valid, plausible, strong (reason)*; *cogent (proof)*; *urgent, conclusive, convincing (argument)* || aus ~en Gründen *for weighty reasons* **≗keit** f ~/~ *weightiness, validity, cogency, plausibility*

Tri- ~g·eminus m ~/ ⟨anat⟩ *trigeminal nerve* **~gl·yph** m ~(e)s/~en *triglyph* **~gon·alaspekt** m ~(e)s/~e ⟨astrol⟩ *trine* **~gonometr·ie** f ~/~n *trigonometry* **≗gonom·etrisch** a *t.metrical* **≗kl·in** a ⟨cryst⟩ *tricline* **~kol·ore** f ~/~n (Fr) *tricolour*

Trik·ot [tri'ko:] m & n ~s/~s *stockinet* || *sweater* || (Zirkus≗) *tights, fleshings* pl **~·age** [–'ta:ʒə] f ~/~n *hosiery* **~bluse** f *jersey blouse* **~hemd** n ⟨sport⟩ *singlet (in shorts and s.)* **~jacke** f *jersey* **~stoff** m *tricot*; (leichter) *stockinet* **~unterhose** f *stockinet pants* pl

Tr·iller m ~s/~ ⟨mus⟩ *shake, trill, quaver* **~pfeife** f *alarm* od *thunder whistle* **~sänger(in f)** m *warbler* **tr·illern I.** vi/t [h] *to shake, trill, quaver* || (Vögel) *to warble* **II.** vt *to adorn* od *vary with trills* || *to hum (a tune)*

Trilli- ~arde f ~/~n *thousand trillions* **~·on** f ~/~en (1 mit 18 Nullen) ⟨engl⟩ *trillion*, ⟨Am, Fr⟩ *quintillion*

Tri- ~l·ith m ~s/~en ⟨praehist⟩ *trilith(on)* **~lob·it** m ~s/~en ⟨zoo⟩ *trilobite* **~log·ie** f ~/~n → *trilogy* **~m·ester** n ~s/~ *three months term* **≗m·etrisch** a ⟨pros⟩ *trimetric(al)*

Trimm m ~s/ ⟨mar, aero⟩ *trim* **~anlage** f *t.ming system* **~klappe** f, **~ruder** n ⟨aero⟩ *t.(ming) flap* od *tab* **~lage** f *trim* **~rad** n *t.mer* **~tank** m *t.ming tank* **≗en** vt [h] *to trim* (⟨mar⟩ *the yards*) **~ungsanzeiger** m *t.-flap position indicator*

Tr·ine f ~/~n (Katharina *Kate*) ⟨fig⟩ *silly goose*

Trinit·arier m ~s/~ ⟨ec⟩ *Trinitarian* **Trinit·ät** f ~/ *Trinity* **Trinit·atis**: Sonntag ~ *Trinity Sunday* **Trin·itro- ~tolu·ol** n ~s/ *trinitrotoluene* (T.N.T.) **~zellul·ose** f ~/ *trinitrocellulose*

Trink- ~becher m *drinking-cup, mug*; ⟨mil⟩ *tin can* **~bruder** m *tippler* **~ei** n *fresh egg* **~fest** [a] er ist ~ *he's a three-bottle man* **~gefäß** n *dr.-vessel* **~gelage** n *dr.-bout, carousal* **~geld** n *gratuity*, ⟨fam⟩ *tip* || ~er annehmen *to receive gratuities* || jdm ein ~ (zu hohes) geben ⟨fam⟩ *to (over)tip a p* || wir bitten v ~ern abzusehen *we do not accept gratuities* | ~ablösung [f] *commutation of gratuities* **~geschirr** n *dr.-vessel* **~gesell-**

schaft f *wine-party*; *company of drinkers* (⟨fam⟩ *of tipplers*) **~glas** n (*wine-*)*glass*, *tumbler* **~halle** f *refreshment-stall* od *-bar* ‖ (Kur≃) *pumproom* **~halm** m (*dr.*) *straw* **~horn** n *dr.-horn* **~kur** f *water cure*; e–e ~ m *or* gebrauchen *to drink the waters* **~lied** n *dr.-song* **~napf** m (f Vögel) *fountain* **~schale** f *dr.-cup* **~spruch** m *toast* (auf *of*) (auf das Königshaus) *loyal t.* (→ Hoch 1.) **~stube** f *tap-room*; ⟨rail⟩ *refreshment-room* **~szene** f *orgy* **~wasser** n *potable* od *dr. water* **tr·inkbar** a *drinkable*, *potable* ‖ nicht ~ *undr.* ‖ ⟨hum⟩ dieser Wein ist durchaus ~ .. *isn't half bad* | ≃keit [f] ~/ *drinkableness* ‖ *matured state* (*of a wine*)
tr·inken vt/i [trank/getrunken] [h] **A. 1.** *to drink* (aus: *out of a glass*, *from the bottle*) ‖ ⟨allg, a. med⟩ *to take* ‖ ⟨fig⟩ *to imbide* (*air*, *ideas*), *to draw in* (*air*) ‖ (an der Brust) *baby is nursing* ‖ *to have* (*tea without sugar*); *he had a bottle of beer*; heimlich ~ *to soak* ‖ in kl Schlucken v etw ~: *to sip of the wine* **2.** [abs] er trinkt *he's fond of the bottle* **B.** ~ **wie** ein Loch *to drink like a fish* ‖ es wurde **viel** getrunken *there was a lot of drink flowing* ‖ **was** ~ Sie? *what do you take*, *how will you have it*?; ⟨fam⟩ *name yours*! *give it a name*!; *what's your drink* (⟨sl⟩ *poison*)? ‖ ⟨fam⟩ **e-n** ~ *to take a drop*; gern **eins** ~ *to be fond of a drop* ‖ °e–n ~ ⟨sl⟩ *to liquor* ‖ ~ Sie noch ein Glas? *have another glass* (⟨sl⟩ *peg*) ‖ (Glas) **leer** ~ *to empty* | **sich** [dat] e–n Rausch ~ *to get tipsy* (⟨fam⟩ *boozed*) | **auf** jdn *or* etw ~ *to toast*, *drink to*; *to have a drink on* (*an event*) ‖ **mit** jdm e–e Fl. ~ ⟨fam⟩ *to crack a bottle with a p* ‖ ~ Sie ein Glas Wein mit mir? *will you join me in a glass of wine*? | **sich** [acc] arm, bewußtlos ~ *to drink o.s. poor*, *insensible* ‖ sich voll ~ *to drink one's fill* | das Weinchen läßt sich ~ .. *goes down nicely* → trinkbar **Tr·inker** m ~s/~ *drinker*; ⟨fam⟩ *tippler* ‖ (Gewohnheits≃) *drunkard* ‖ ein starker ~ *an habitual drinker* **~·ei** f *habitual drinking* **~gesicht** n *grog blossoms all over the face* | s–e **~gewohnheiten** [f pl] *his drunken habits* **~heilstätte** f *inebriates' home*
Trin·om n ~s/~e ⟨math⟩ *trinomium* ≃**isch** a *trinomial* **Tr·io** n ~s/~s *trio* | m °(→ Tripper) er hat e–n Heiden≃ ⟨euph⟩ *he has a very bad cold*
Tri·ole f ~/~n ⟨mus⟩ *triplet* **Tr·ipel** m ~s/ ⟨min⟩ (versteinert *fossil*) *tripoli* **~allianz** f ⟨hist⟩ *Triple Alliance* **~takt** m ⟨mus⟩ *triple time* **Tripl·ett** n ~s/~e *triplet* **tripl·ieren** vt [h] *to treble* **Tripl·ik** f ~/~en ⟨jur⟩ *surrejoinder*
Tr·ipolis n *Tripoli* **tripolitanisch** a *Tripolitan* ˣ**tr·ippen** vt [h] [nordd] = tropfen **tr·ippeln** vi [h & s] *to trip*, *patter*; *to mince one's steps* ‖ .. getrippelt *she came tripping along* ‖ ⟨hors⟩ *to beat the dust*
Tr·ipper m ~s/~ ⟨path⟩ *gonorrhœa*, ⟨fam⟩ *clap* **Tr·iptik** n ~s/~e ⟨mot⟩ *triptyque* **Tr·iptychon** n ~s/–cha ⟨ec paint⟩ *triptych* **Trir·eme** f ~/~n ⟨ant mar⟩ *trireme*
tr·ist(e) a [Fr] *sad*, *wretched* ‖ *dismal* (*room*)
Tr·iste f ~/~n [bay, österr, Sw] *hay* od *straw heaped round a pole*
Tritt m ~(e)s/~e **A. 1.** *tread*(*ing*), *step*, *pace* ‖ (Geräusch) *footfall*, *footstep* ‖ schwere ~e *tramp* [sg] ‖ (Fuß≃) *kick* **2.** (Spur) *footprint*, *footstep* **3.** (Stufe) *step*; ⟨arch⟩ (Fenster≃) *estrade*; ⟨mount⟩ *foothold* | (Fußbank) *footstool* | *carriage--step* ‖ (Trittbrett) *foot-board* ‖ ⟨tech⟩ *treadle* ‖ ⟨cycl⟩ *pedal* | (Leiter) (ein ~ *a pair of*) *steps* pl; *step-ladder* **B. bei** jedem ~ *at every step* | **im** ~ *in step*, ⟨mil⟩ (*keep*) *time*!, **ohne** ~! *break step*! (*march*) *at ease*!; ohne ~ (marsch)! *rout* od *break step* (*march*)!, ohne ~ marschieren *to march at ease* | **in** falschem ~ *out of step* | **mit** schwerem ~ *with a heavy gait* | e–n ~ **bek** ⟨fig⟩ *to get the boots* [pl] od *hoof* ‖ e–n guten ~ **einschlagen** *to hit up a good pace* ‖ ~ fassen *to fall in step* (*with*); ~ halten *to keep pace* (*with*) ‖ e–m e–n ~ **geben** *to give a p a kick* (⟨fig⟩ .. *the sack*) ‖ e–m ~e geben *to kick a p* ‖ e–m e–n ~ in den Hintern geben *to land a foot in a p's behind* ‖ e–n sicheren ~ h *to be sure-footed* ‖ ~ halten ⟨mil⟩ *to keep pace* (mit *with*) ‖ ~ wechseln! ⟨mil⟩ *change step*, *change over* **tritt** imp & 3. sg pres v treten **Tr·itt-~anlasser** m *kick-starter* **~brett** n *carriage-step*; ⟨mot, rail⟩ *foot-board*; ⟨mot⟩ *running-board* ‖ ⟨tech⟩ *treadle* ‖ (der Orgel) *pedal* ‖ rollendes ~ ⟨sport⟩ *roll-scooter* **~harfe** f *pedal-harp* **~leiter** f (e–e ~ *a pair of*) *steps* pl, *step-ladder* **~rad** n ⟨spin⟩ *spinning-wheel with a treadle* **~siegel** n ⟨hunt⟩ *slot* **~stufe** f *carriage-step* **~wechsel** m *change of step*, *changing over*
Tri·umph m ~(e)s/~e *triumph* ⟨a. fig⟩ (feiern *to enjoy*) ‖ im ~ *t.antly* ‖ gr ~e feiern ⟨fig⟩ *to achieve great success* **~bogen** m, (**~lied** n, **~wagen** m) *t.al arch* (*song*, *car*); ⟨ec arch⟩ *rood-arch* **~geschrei** n (Graugans≃) ⟨eth⟩ *t. ceremony* **~zug** m *t.al procession*, ⟨fig⟩ *t.ant sweep* ≃**al** a *t.al* (*progress*, etc) ‖ *glorious*, *sublime* ‖ ~er Fortschritt der W. *t. of scientific development* **~ieren** vi [h] (über [acc]) *to triumph* (*over*), *to exult* (*over a p*, *at a th*); *to have the laugh of a p* ‖ *to be jubilant* ‖ zu früh ~ *to count one's chickens before they are hatched* | **~d** (*the Church*) *triumphant*; *triumphantly* (*they carry him*)
Tri·umvir m [~s & ~n/~n] *triumvir* **~·at** n ~(e)s/~e *triumvirate* **trivi·al** a *trivial*, *commonplace*, *hackneyed*, *trite* ≃**it·ät** f ~/~en *triviality*, *platitude* [mst pl]; *triteness* ‖ [pl] *trivia* pl; ⟨a.⟩ *small talk* **trizon·al** a *trizonal*
Troch·äus m ~/–äen *trochee* | dazu: *trochaic* (*lines*)
trocken a **A.** *dry* (⟨a. arts⟩ Zeichnung) ‖ ⟨agr⟩ (dürr) *arid* ‖ (Holz) ⟨a.⟩ *well-seasoned* ‖ (unfruchtbar) *barren* ‖ (prosaisch) *dry*(*-as-dust*), *dull* ‖ ganz ~ *bone-dry*, (*as*) *dry as a stick* od *bone* ‖ ⟨fig⟩ höchst ~ (*as*) *dry as dust* **B.** ⟨fig⟩ (Empfang) *cool* ‖ (Frost) *black* ‖ ~en Fußes *dry-shod* ‖ ~es Futter ⟨agr⟩ *fodder* ‖ ~es Gedeck *dinner without wine* ‖ (Humor) *dry* ‖ (Peter, Kerl) *prosy* ‖ ~er Mensch ⟨fam⟩ *stick* ‖ (Stil) *bald* ‖ (Wahrheit) *plain* ‖ ⟨com⟩ (Wechsel) *drawn on o.s.* ‖ (Wein) *dry* ‖ ~es Wetter *drought* **C.** ~ **aufbewahren** *to keep dry* ‖ kein Auge blieb ~ *no eye was dry* ‖ sein Brot ~ essen *to eat dry bread* ‖ °du bist noch nicht ~ hinter den Ohren *hang your number out to dry*, *your number's still wet*, *you're as green as grass*; ~ legen *to change* (*a baby*) → ~|legen ‖ (Wäsche) ~ schleudern *to spin-dry* ‖ hübsch ~ sitzen (sich wohlbefinden) *to be in a dry ditch*; jdn ~ sitzen l *to offer a guest no refreshment* ‖ ~ stehend (Kuh) *not in milk* ‖ ~ w ⟨a.⟩ *to dry up*; *to run dry* **D. das** ≃**e** *dry land* od *part* | ⟨mar⟩ **auf** dem ~en sitzen *to be stranded*; *to sit high and dry* ⟨a. fig⟩; ⟨fig⟩ *to be put on the rocks* | **im** ~en sitzen *to be under cover*, ⟨fig⟩ *to be* (*in security* od) *out of harm's way*, (reich s) *to be in clover* **Tr·ocken-** *dry* **~apparat** m *d.ing-apparatus*, ⟨chem⟩ *desiccator* **~aufziehverfahren** n ⟨phot⟩ *d.-mounting process* **~bagger** m *steam-navvy* **~batterie** f ⟨el⟩ *d.*(*cell*) *battery*, *d. pile* **~bewirtschaftung** f ⟨Am agr⟩ *d. farming* **~boden** m *d.ing-loft* **~dock** m *d.-dock* **~eis** n *d. ice* **~element** n ⟨el⟩ *d. cell* **~entwicklung** f ⟨phot⟩ *d. process* **~farbe** f *pencil-colour* **~farm** f *d. farming* **~fäule** f *d. rot* **~firnis** m *d.ing varnish* **~fluß** m *intermittent river* **~früchte** f pl *dried fruit* **~futter** n *fodder provender* **~fütterung** f *stall-feeding* **~gebiet** n *arid district* **~gemüse** n *dehydrated v.s* **~gestell** n *d.ing frame*; *hurdle* **~gewicht** n ⟨com⟩ *d.* od net *weight* **~haut-Reinigungsmittel** n ⟨cosm⟩ *d. skin cleaner* **~hefe** f *d. yeast* **~kammer** f *d.ing-room*; *loft* **~klebeband** n *pressure sensitive adhesive tape* **~kultur** f = –farm ≃|legen vt [h] (Kind) *to change*; (Land) *to drain*, *reclaim*, *dehumidify*; *to*

make .. d. by prohibition; tr.gelegt w *to go d.* **~legung** f *drainage* (*of soil*) **~leine** f *d.ing-line* **~malerei** f *crayon-painting* **~maschine** f *steam--chest* (*for cloth*, etc) **~maß** n *d. measure* **~milch** f *milk powder*; ~ in Wasser gelöst *reconstituted m.* | ~mixgetränk [n] *milk shake* **~mittel** n (*de*)*siccative, desiccating agent* **~obst** n *dried fruit* **~pflanze** f *xerophyte* **~platte** f ⟨phot⟩ *d. plate* **~platz** m *d.ing ground* od *yard* **~pause** f *diazo print* **~rasierer** m (S) *d.-shaver*; (P) ich bin ~ *I use a d.-sh.* **~reinigen** vt [h] *to d.-clean* (*clothes*) **~rückstand** m ⟨chem⟩ *d. residue*; *r. on evaporation* **~schlamm** m *d. sludge* **~schrank** m *d.ing cabinet* **~ständer** m *d. rack* **~stube** f *d.ing room*; *loft* **~substanz** f *d. matter* **~trommel** f *rotary drier* **~verfahren** n *d.ing-process* **~vorrichtung** f ⟨tech⟩ = Trockner **~wald** m *xerophyte forest* **~**|**wohnen** vt [h] *to be the first tenant of* (*a newly built house*) **~zonenforschung** f *arid zone research* **Tr·ockenheit** f ~/ *dryness* || (Dürre) *aridity* || (des Wetters) *drought* || ⟨fig⟩ *dulness*, ⟨a.⟩ *aridity* (*of a book*) **tr·ocknen** vt [h] *to dry* (*one's face on a towel*, etc || (lagern) *to season* || (Land) *to drain* || (Erbsen) *to parch* || (Wäsche) *to air* || ⟨bes scient⟩ *to dehydrate* **Tr·ockner** m *dryer, drier* (*hair-d.*)

Tr·oddel f ~/~n *tassel*; ⟨mil⟩ (*sword*) *knot* || (Mützen~) *tuft* | m ×→ Trottel

Tr·ödel m ~s/ *second-hand goods* [pl] od *furniture* || (Kleider) *slops* pl || (Gerümpel) *lumber, junk* || der ganze ~ ⟨fam⟩ *the whole lot* **~bude** f *s.-h. shop*; *marine store* **~frau** f *dealer in s.-h. goods* **~fritze** m (→ trödeln) *soggy type*; *slow-coach* **~geschäft** n *trade in old clothes*, etc || *o. c. shop* **~kram** m = Trödel **~laden** m ⟨sl⟩ *junk shop* **~markt** m *jumble market, rag fair* **~ware** f = Trödel **Trödel·ei** f ~/~en (Plunder) *frippery* | ⟨fig⟩ *tarrying, dawdling, loitering*; *dalliance* **tr·ödeln** vi [h] *to deal in* od *to sell s.-h. goods* | (zögern) *to dawdle, loiter*; ⟨fam⟩ *to dilly-dally* **Tr·ödler** m ~s/~ *second-hand dealer*; *old-clothes-man*: *chandler* || ⟨fig⟩ *loiterer, dawdler, slow-coach*; ⟨Am fam⟩ (*slow*)*poke* **~laden** m *junk-shop*

troff 1. & 3. sg pret v triefen

Trog m ~(e)s/~e *trough* || (Futter~) *manger* || *mason's hod* || ⟨min⟩ *cradle, hutch*; im ~ waschen *to hutch* **~muschel** f ⟨zoo⟩ *trough-shell*

trog 1. & 3. sg pret v trügen

Troglod·yt m ~en/~en *troglodyte*

†**Tr·oja** n *Troy* †**Troj·aner** m, **~in** f *Trojan, inhabitant of Troy* †**troj·anisch** a *Trojan, Troic*

Troll m ~(e)s/~e *troll, hob-goblin* **~blume** f *globe-flower* **tr·ollen** vi [s] ⟨fam⟩ *to toddle along* | **sich** ~ [h] *to toddle off, to take o.s. off* || trolle dich! *be off! hurry up!*

Tr·ombe f ~/~n ⟨meteor⟩ *water-spout*

Tr·ommel f ~/~n *drum* (rollt *beats*; rühren *to beat*) | ⟨anat⟩ *tympanum* || ⟨arch⟩ *tambour*; (Kuppel–, Säulen~) ⟨a.⟩ *drum* || ⟨min⟩ *trommel* || (*paper*) *reel* || ⟨tech⟩ *barrel*; *ironing cylinder*; *brake d., cartridge d.*; *film d.* || *coffee-roaster* | ⟨fig⟩ s–e eigene ~ rühren *to blow one's own trumpet* || f jdn die ~ rühren *to praise a p to the skies* **~bahn** f ⟨comp⟩ *track on the magnetic d.* **~baß** m *d.-bass* **~fell** n *d.-skin*; ⟨anat⟩ (*ear-*)*d.*, ⟨scient⟩ *tympanic membrane* || schreien, daß e–m das ~ platzt *to shout a p's ears off*; **~erschütternd** *ear splitting* (*noise*) **~feuer** n ⟨mil⟩ *d.* od *running fire*; *heavy bombardment* od *shelling*; ⟨Am⟩ *d.fire*; im ~ *under heavy fire* || ⟨fig⟩ *r.g fire* (*of comment*) **~kasten** m *barrel of a d.* **~klang** m *roll of d.s*; gedämpfter ~ *ruffle* **~klöppel** m = –schlegel **~schlag** m *stroke upon* od *beat of a d.*, *d.ming* || mit *or* unter (lautem) ~ *with d.s beating*, (*with a loud beating of d.s*) || bei gedämpftem ~ *with muffled d.s* **~schläger** m *d.mer* **~schlegel, ~stock** m *d.stick* **~sieb** n *revolving screen* **~speicher** m (*magnetic*) *d. store* | ~ung [f] (*m.*) *d. storage* **~sucht** f ⟨path⟩ *tympanitis, tympany* **~süchtig** a *tympanitic* **~taube** f *d.-pigeon* **~wirbel** m *d. roll, roll*(*ing*) *of d.s, rub-a-dub*; gedämpfter ~ *ruffle* **tr·ommeln I.** vt [h] *to* (*beat the*) *drum* || es trommelt *the d.s are beating* || (v Hasen) *to tap* | mit dem Finger ~ **auf** .. *to drum a finger on* ..; auf dem Klavier ~ *to strum on the p.* || wir l nicht auf uns ~ *we won't be played with* | **mit** den Fingern (Füßen) ~ *to beat the devil's tattoo*, (*to stamp one's feet*) **II.** vt [h] e–n Marsch ~ *to beat a march on the d.* || °Gott [dat] sei's ge–lt u gepfiffen! *thank goodness!* | aus dem Schlafe ~ ⟨fig⟩ *to rouse with much noise* **Tr·ommler** m ~s/~ *drummer*

Tr·ompe f ~/~n ⟨arch⟩ *squinch* **Tromp·ete** f ~/~n **1.** *trumpet* (schmettert *blares*) || in die ~ stoßen, die ~ blasen *to sound the t.* **2.** ⟨anat⟩ eustachische ~ *Eustachian tube* **3.** °(Nase) ⟨fam⟩ *honker, post-horn, nozzle* **tromp·eten** vt/i [h] *to* (*sound the*) *t.t* || es trompetet *the t.t sounds* | e–n Marsch ~ *to play a m. on the t.t* **Tromp·eten-** **~baum** m ⟨bot⟩ *snake-wood* **~bläser** m *t.ter* **~blume** f ⟨bot⟩ *salpiglossis*; rankende ~ *t.t-flower*, → –rebe **~geschmetter** n *blare, flourish* (*of t.ts*; *bray* **~narzisse** f *daffodil* **~rebe** f *t.t-vine* **~register** n = –zug **~schall** m *sound of t.ts* **~schnecke** f *marine t.t* **~signal** n *t.t-signal*; (z Aufsitzen) *boot and saddle* **~stoß** m *t.t-call, t.t-blast* **~tusch** m *flourish of t.ts* **~zug** m (der Orgel) *t.t-stop* **Tromp·eter** m ~s/~ *t.ter* **~korps** n *brass band* **~marsch** m *t.t-march* **~stückchen** n *flourish* **~tisch** m *side-table*

Tr·ope f ~/~n **1.** ⟨rhet⟩ *trope* ⟨a. ec⟩; *metaphor* **2.** ⟨geogr⟩ [nur pl] *the tropics* pl **Tr·open-** **~ausrüstung** f *tropical kit* **~fest, ~sicher** a *t.c-proof*; *tropicalized*; *resistent to tropical conditions*; ~ m *to t.calize* **~fieber** n *t.l fever* **~gegend** n *t.l country* **~helm** m *pith-helmet*, ⟨Ind⟩ *topee, topi* **~hut** m (*sola*) *topee* **~isoliert** a *insulated for t.cal service* **~koller** m *t.l frenzy* **~länder** n pl *t.cs* pl **~sonne** f *t.c sun* **~uniform** f *khaki* || in der **~welt** f *in the t.cs*

Tropf m ~(e)s/~e *ninny, noodle, simpleton, dunce*, ⟨fam⟩ *juggins* pl [sg konstr]; ⟨bes Am⟩ *numskull, gaby*, ⟨sl⟩ *goof* || alter ~ ⟨sl⟩ *old buffer* || armer ~ *poor wretch* **~bar** a *liquid* || ~-flüssiger Körper *liquid* | ~keit [f] *liquid state* **~brett** n *drainer* **~flasche** f ⟨med⟩ *drop bottle* **~glas** n *pipette* **~n·aß** a *dripping wet* **~öler** m *d.i.g oil-feeder* **~pfanne** f *d.i.g-pan* **~rinne** f *gutter* **~röhrchen** n *dropper* **~stein** m *stalactite*; (stehender) *stalagmite* **~steinartig** a *s.c.c* **~steinhöhle** f *s.c.te cave* **~trichter** m *tap funnel* **~wassergeschützt** a *drip-proof* **Tr·öpfchen** n ~s/~ **1.** *little drop* **2.** (Bier etc) *modest quencher*; (Schnaps) *spot* **tr·öpfeln I.** vt/i [h & s] *to drop, drip, dribble, trickle* (v *down from*) || *to form* (od *fall in*) *drops* | **es** tröpfelt *we are having a few drops of rain* | vt ⟨med⟩ *to dispense in drops* **II.** ~ n *drip* (*of the rain*) **tr·opfen** vi [h] *to drop, drip* (aus, v *from*) || (Kerze) *to gutter* || **es** tropft (nur) *it is spitting rain*, (⟨fam⟩ *it's only dripping*) **Tr·opfen** m ~s/~ **A.** *drop*; *blob* || ⟨cul⟩ *minim* || *taste* (*of a drink*) || *tear* || *bead* (*of sweat*) || [pl] ⟨med⟩ *d.s* || (Trunk) *modest quencher* **B.** noch e–n ~ Sherry ⟨fam⟩ *a d. more sh.* || **bitterer** ~ ⟨fig⟩ *wormwood*; ein **guter,** edler ~ *a capital wine*; e–n guten ~ schätzen *to be fond of one's d.s* || den letzten ~ Blut aus dem Volke saugen *to suck the life blood of the p.* || ⟨fam⟩ e–n ~ (Schnaps) z sich nehmen *to take a d. of sth, a spot* (*of whisky*) || e–n ~ über den Durst *a d. too much* | ⟨fig⟩ nur ein ~ auf den heißen Stein *a mere d. in the ocean* od *bucket, no more than a pebble d.ped into the sea* | ⟨prov⟩ steter ~ höhlt den Stein *constant d.ping will wear down a stone*; der ~, der .. zum Überlaufen bringt *the last straw* **~fänger** m *drip-catcher* **~förmig** a *shaped like a drop* **~messer** m *d.-meter* | (dorische) **~platte** f ⟨arch⟩ *mutule* **~weise**

dropwise | [adv] *in, by d.s, by dribblets, d. by d.* || *by sips*; ~ trinken *to sip* || ~ hineinfluten in (P) *to dribble into* **~zähler** m ⟨med⟩ *d.ping tube, d.per*

Troph·äe f ~/~n *trophy* **tr·opisch** a ⟨geogr⟩ *tropic(al)* || fast ~ *subtropical* | ⟨rhet⟩ *tropical, metaphorical*

Troß m Trosses/Trosse ⟨mil⟩ *baggage(-train)* || Gefechts~ *first line transport*; gr ~ *regimental b.*; Verpflegungs~ *supply* od *transport column* od *lines* pl || ⟨mst fig⟩ *hangers-on* || ⟨mar⟩ *fleet auxiliaries* | (Schar) *crowd, set, gang, crew* **~bube, ~knecht** m ⟨hist⟩ *b.-boy, waggoner* **~pferd** n *b.-, pack-horse* **~schiff** n *auxiliary vessel* **~wagen** m *b.-waggon, -cart*

Tr·osse f ~/~n *line, cable(t)* || ⟨mar⟩ *hawser*

Trost m ~es/ *consolation* || (~worte) *soothing words* pl || magerer, schlechter ~ *cold* od *Dutch comfort* | ~ **bereiten** *to give c.t (to)* || ~ finden in *to derive c.t in* || es gereicht mir z ~, daß *it is a relief* od *c.t to me to think that ..* || sich ~ holen ⟨hum⟩ *to have a drop of sth* || ~ schöpfen (aus) *to take c.t (from)* || e–m ~ zusprechen *to (speak words of c.t to), to console a p* | ⟨fam⟩ du bist wohl nicht (ganz) bei ~? *have you taken leave of your senses? are you a bit off (your head)* **~bedürftig** a *needing c.n,* etc **~brief** m *letter of condolence* **~bringend** a *c.ting* **~grund** m *consolatory argument* **~los** a *disconsolate, inconsolable*; *dismal, gloomy*; *drab (region* etc) || ⟨fig⟩ *wretched, deplorable, dreary, bleak* || ~e Erkenntnis *desolation of knowing* **~losigkeit** f *desolation, disconsolateness* || ⟨fig⟩ *wretchedness,* etc **~preis** m *c.n* (⟨fam⟩ *booby-)prize* **~reich** a *consolatory, c.ting, consoling* **~rennen** n *c.n race* **~wort** n *word of c.n* od *c.t* **tr·östen** vt [h] **1.** *to comfort*; *to console* (wegen, über *for)* || ~ Sie sich (damit, daß)! *take c.t!, cheer up! (console yourself with the fact that ..)!* || Gott tröste ihn! *God rest his soul!* || nicht z ~ s *to be inconsolable* (od *beyond c.t)* **2.** sich ~ *to solace o.s.* (über .. *against a th)*; er hat sich über sie (darüber) schnell getröstet *he has soon forgotten her (soon put up with it)* **Tr·öster** m ~s/~ *comforter, consoler* || ⟨ec⟩ *the Comforter, Holy Ghost* || ein schlechter ~ *a Job's c.r* | ⟨fig⟩ *old book*; *(baby's) rubber-teat*; ⟨hum⟩ *a drop of sth*; ⟨iron⟩ *rod, cane, stick* **tr·östlich** a *consolatory*; *comforting, consoling* || *pleasant, pleasing, cheering* **~keit** f ~/ *consolatoriness,* etc **Tr·östung** f ~/~en *c.n, c.t*

Trott m ~(e)s/ *trot* || ⟨fig⟩ der alte, übliche ~ *the old jog-trot* **Tr·ottel** m ~s/~ *idiot, nit(wit)* || ⟨fig⟩ *blockhead,* ⟨sl⟩ *juggins* pl [sg konstr]; ⟨Am sl⟩ *wampus* **tr·otteln** vi [s & h] *to trudge along* || *to straggle, jog, lurch* || *to loiter* **tr·otten** vi [s & h] *to trot, jog (along)* **Trottoir** [trɔ'twɑːr] n ~(e)s/ ~e *pavement, footway* || ⟨Am⟩ *side-walk*

Trotz m ~es/ *defiance* || (Störrischkeit) *refractoriness, obstinacy* || *independence (of spirit)*; *boldness* || *insolence* | **aus** ~ *out of (sheer) spite* | [dat] **zum** ~ *in spite* od *defiance, (the teeth) of* || ihnen z ~ *in their despite* | jdm ~ **bieten** *to defy, brave, beard a p*; *to fly in the teeth of a p* || *to weather (a storm)* **trotz** prep [gen & dat] *in spite (of), in the face* od *teeth (of)* || *(she was easy to carry) for all (her height)* || ~ alle(de)m *in spite of all, (for all that), all* od *just the same, all right, nevertheless*; *for all you may say*; *the fact remains that he is a great artist* || *pace N. N.* L **Tr·otz-~kopf** m *stubborn* od *pigheaded p,* (kl) *obstinate little th* **~köpfig** a *stubborn,* etc | **~keit** [f] *stubbornness,* etc **~winkel** m *pouting-corner* **tr·otzdem** **I.** [adv] *nevertheless, just* od *all the same, even so, for all that, after all, notwithstanding*; ⟨Am a.⟩ *same time* **II.** (statt: obwohl) ~ (daß) [conj] *although (he be* od *is poor), despite (his being poor)* || *for all (he was there) he ..* **tr·otzen** vi [h] **1.** (schmollen) *to sulk, mope*; *to be sulky (with a p)*; ⟨fam⟩ *to be in the sulks* **2.** (störrisch s) *to be obstinate* **3.** [dat] ~ *to defy (a p, a th)*; *to baffle (detection, all endeavours)*; *to brave (dangers)*; *to weather (the storm)* || *to breast (waves)* | *to face out (a situation)* || *to defy (scouring)* || allen Unbilden ~ *to be impervious* **4. auf** etw ~ *to boast of, to glory in, pride o.s. in a th* **tr·otzig** a *sulky*; *sullen* || (störrisch) *refractory*; *recalcitrant* || (hartnäkkig) *obstinate, headstrong, perverse* || *intrepid (valour)*; *daring (courage)* || (herausfordernd) *disdainful, defiant* || (anmaßend) *arrogant, haughty, insolent* | in ~er Laune *in an affronted mood*

Tr·ubel m ~s/~ *disturbance, racket* || *turmoil* || *excitement* || (Wirrwarr) *bustle, confusion* || (Lärm) *hubbub, row*

Tr·üb- **~äugig** a *dim-eyed* **~selig** a *sad, woeful, dismal* || (jammervoll) *lamentable, pitiful, piteous, wretched* || in ~er Stimmung *in the dumps* || (Aussehen) *woe-begone, forlorn* | **~keit** [f] *woefulness, misery, affliction, sadness* || *woe-begone appearance, forlornness* **~sinn** m *low spirits* pl, *sadness, dejection, melancholy, gloom*; ⟨fam⟩ *the mopes* pl **~sinnig** a *sad, dejected, melancholy* || *sullen, dismal*; *depressing*; *gloomy (company)* **tr·üb(e)** **I.** [a] (Wasser) *muddy, thick, troubled, turbid, mothery*; (Wein) *cloudy* || (Wetter) *cloudy, overcast*; *grey*; *gloomy* | (Glas) *dull* || (Edelstein) *clouded* || (matt) *dim, dull* || (Himmel, Licht) *wan, murky* | ~ m, w *to tarnish* | ⟨fig⟩ *dejected, sad, gloomy, downcast (state of mind), gloomy (thoughts), drab (days)*; *dismal (times)* || *sad (experience), dim (prospects)*; *unhappy (memories)* || *wan (smile)* | **im ~n** fischen *to fish in troubled waters,* ⟨sl⟩ *to do a slime* **II.** [adv] die Lampe brennt ~ .. *burns dimly* || es sah (sehr) ~ damit aus *ths looked unpleasant (desperate)* **~werden** n *opacification* **tr·üben** vt [h] (Flüssigkeit) *to trouble*; *to make thick* od *muddy*; **sich** ~ *to become turbid* ⟨a. path⟩ | (Glas) *to dim*; ⟨fig⟩ *to disturb (the atmosphere)*; *to blur, dim (perception)* || (Urteil) *to obfuscate, dull* || (Metall) *to tarnish* || (verdunkeln) *to obscure, darken* | ⟨fig⟩ *to make sad, dismal, gloomy*; *to sadden* || (Freude) *to spoil* || (Stimmung) *to sour, darken*; *to cast a cloud on, over* || (Beziehungen) *to cloud* || (Glück) *to dim* | **es trübt sich** *the sky is getting overcast,* ⟨fam⟩ *looks lowery* **Tr·übe, Tr·übheit** f ~/ *turbidness* || *dimness, dulness* || *opaqueness* || (des Wetters) *cloudiness, dul(l)ness* || ⟨fig⟩ *dreariness, gloom(iness)* **Tr·übsal** [f] ~/~e, [n] ~(e)s/~e *affliction, grief* || (Not) *distress* || (Drangsal) *tribulation*; ⟨rel⟩ *trial* | [konkr] *trouble, calamity, misery, tragedy* || ⟨fam⟩ ~ blasen *to mope,* ⟨fam⟩ *to be in the dumps,* ~ blasend *mopish* **~bläser** m *mope* **Tr·übung** f ~/~en *troubling* || (Zustand) *turbidity* || (Glas etc) *cloudiness* || *clouding*; *opacity (of a lens)* | ⟨fig⟩ *disturbance* **~smesser** m *turbidimeter*

Tr·uchseß m –sses/–sse *Lord High Steward*

Tr·udel **I.** m ~s/~ *loose, fast girl* **II.** f ~/~n [dim v Gertrud] ⟨fig⟩ *dumpy, stumpy little girl*

tr·udeln **1.** vi [s], vt [h] *to roll, trundle*; ⟨bes aero⟩ *to spin*; *to list heavily* || ⟨aero⟩ sich ~ l *to go into a spin* **2.** ~ n ⟨aero⟩ *tailspin* **tr·udelsicher** a ⟨aero⟩ *non-spinning*

Tr·üffel f ~/~n ⟨bot⟩ *truffle* **~brut** f *young tr.s* **~hund** m *tr.-dog* **~jagd** f *searching for tr.s* **~(leber)pastete** f *tr.-pie, (Strassburg pie)* **~leberwurst** f *tr.d liver sausage* **~zucht** f *cultivation of tr.s* **tr·üffeln** vt [h] *to flavour with tr.s*

trug 1. & 3. sg pret v tragen

Trug m ~(e)s/ *deceit, deception*; *sham* || *fraud, imposition* || ohne ~ *fairly* || er (sie) ist ohne ~ *he is an upright man (she is guileless, unsophisticated)* | (Sinnen~) *delusion* || → Lug **~bild, ~gebilde** n *phantom, phantasm*; *apparition* **~dolde** f ⟨bot⟩ *cyme* **~gestalt** f *phantom* **~gewebe** n *tissue of lies* **~los** a *artless, guileless, unsophisticated*

~ratte f ⟨zoo⟩ *octodon* **~schluß** m *false conclusion; fallacy* ‖ ⟨log⟩ *paralogism, sophism* **~̈voll** a *deceptive; delusive* **~werk** n *fraud, deception* ‖ (der Sinne) *delusion* **tr·ügen** vt [trog/getrogen] [h] *to deceive; delude* ‖ (*if my eyes don't deceive me*) | vi [h] *to be deceptive, deceitful* **tr·ügend, tr·ügerisch, tr·üglich** a *fallacious; deceitful, deceptive; delusive; false; illusive, illusory* ‖ ⟨log⟩ *sophistical* ‖ (Wetter) *treacherous* ‖ ~e Natur *deceitfulness* ‖ ~e Erfindung ⟨fam⟩ *a mare's nest*

Tr·uhe f ~/~n *chest, trunk*; (*clothes-*)*press*

°**Tr·ulle** f ~/~n (Dirne) *trull*

Trum m ~s/ ⟨min⟩ *leader, branch*

Trumeau [try'mo:] m *tr.*; **~spiegel** m *pier-glass*

Trumm m & n [~(e)s/~e & ~̈er] *lump; strand* (schlaffer ~ *slack st.* od *rope*); *end* ‖ ⟨weav⟩ *thrum* ‖ freies ~ *loose end* (*in lifting tackle*) ‖ ein ~ v e–m Kerl (P) *a big hulk* **~erz** n *ore in broken pieces* **~säge** f *cross-cut saw* **Tr·ümmer** [pl v Trumm] *debris, fragments* pl ‖ (v Gebäuden) *rubble; ruins* pl ‖ (v Schiffen) *wreck*(*age*) | ⟨fig⟩ **aus** den ~n erstehen *to rise from the ashes* | **in** ~ gehen *to go to pieces*; ⟨fig⟩ *to go to wreck and ruin*; in ~ legen *to lay in ruins*; in ~ schlagen *to wreck* **~̈besät** a *strewn with debris* **~beseitigung** f *removal of debris* | (verbombtes) **~feld**, **~grundstück** *bombed site* **~gestein** n ⟨geol⟩ *rubble*; ⟨scient⟩ *breccia* **~haufen** m *heap of ruins* ‖ ⟨übtr⟩ *wreck*(*age*) **~räumer** m (S) *power-blade grader* **~verwertungsanlage** f *rubble utilization plant* **~wolle** f *shoddy* **tr·ümmerhaft** a *ruinous, decayed*

Tr·umpf m ~es/~̈e ⟨cards⟩ *trump* ‖ ohne ~ ⟨bridge⟩ *no t.s*; [attr] *no-t.* ‖ ~ ausspielen *to lead t.s* ‖ was ist ~? *what are t.s*? ‖ Herz ist ~ *hearts are t.s* | ⟨fig⟩ (*fair play is*) *everything*; (*culture is the*) *note* ‖ e–n ~ daraufsetzen *to answer smartly* ‖ s–e ~̈e, (den letzten ~) ausspielen *to play one's t.-card; to use every advantage*, (*to play one's last t.*) ‖ alle ~̈e in der Hand h *to have all the t.s in hand* ‖ e–n ~ in petto h *to have an ace-in-the-hole* ‖ jdm die ~̈e aus der Hand nehmen ⟨fig⟩ *to steal a p's thunder* **~b·ube** *knave of t.s* **~farbe** f *t.(-suit)* **tr·umpfen** vt [h] *to trump* ‖ ~ auf *to pride o.s. on* ‖ *to insist on*

°**tr·ündeln** vt/i [h & s] *to trundle, roll*

Trunk m ~(e)s/~̈e **1.** (Getränk) *drink, beverage* **2.** (Schluck) *draught* (tun *to take*) ‖ (gr) *gulp* ‖ auf einen ~ *at one d.t* **3.** (Gelage) *drinkingbout* **4.** (das Trinken) *d.g*; stiller ~ *solitary d.g*; *drunkenness* ‖ dem ~ ergeben *given to d.g*; *liquorish*; ⟨scient⟩ *dipsomaniac* ‖ sich dem ~ ergeben *to take to d.g* ‖ dem ~ frönen *to be on the drink* **~̈fest** a *hard-drinking* **~sucht** f *intemperance; mania for d.g* ‖ ⟨med⟩ *inebriety, dipsomania* **~̈süchtig** a *given to d.g* **~süchtige(r)** m *drunkard* ‖ ⟨med⟩ *dipsomaniac* **tr·unken** a *drunk*(*en* [attr]) ‖ *inebriated, intoxicated* ⟨a. fig⟩ ‖ ⟨fig⟩ *elated* (von *with*); *wild, exuberant* (*with joy*) ‖ jdn ~ m *to make a p d.* (⟨a. fig⟩ *with confidence*) **~̈bold** m ~(e)s/~e *d.ard, sot* **~̈heit** f ~/ *d.enness* ‖ ⟨fig⟩ *intoxication, elation* ‖ in der ~ ⟨a.⟩ *d.en*; *in one's cups* | ⟨mot⟩ ~ am Steuer *driving while intoxicated*, ⟨sl⟩ *hooch and gas*

Trupp m [~(e)s/~s & ~e] *troop, band, gang* ‖ ⟨mil⟩ *section, detachment, picket, party*; (*small*) *patrol* | ⟨hunt⟩ = Rudel **Tr·uppe** f ~/~n *company, troupe* Fr (*of actors*) ‖ ⟨mil⟩ *troop, body*; ⟨Am a.⟩ *crowd* ‖ ~n [pl] *troops, forces* pl; ~ in Regimentsstärke *combat group* ‖ ausgehobene ~n *levy*; eigene ~ *friendly forces*; einzelne ~n *units* pl ‖ kämpfende ~ *fighting services* pl | ~(n) abschreiten *to troop the line* | er hat sich unerlaubt v d. ~ entfernt *he is absent without official leave* (⟨fam⟩ *AWOL*) | **~n-** **~akte** f *service records* pl **~ansammlung** f *troop concentration* **~arzt** m *unit medical officer* **~aushebung** f *levy, conscription* **~befehlshaber** m *commanding officer* **~betreuung** f *recreation* N; (Abteilung) *Special Service*[*s* pl] | ~soffizier [m] *welfare officer* **~bewegungen** f pl *military movements* **~dienst** m *line assignment, service with troops, field-duty* | **~̈lich** unterstellt [dat] *under the administrative control of* **~einteilung** f *task organization* **~führung** f *tactics* pl **~gattung** f *kind of troops, branch* od *arm of service*; (*soldiers of all services*) **~helferin** f *woman auxiliary* **~krankenstube** f *unit's sick room* **~körper** m *body of troops* **~nachschub** m *reinforcements* pl **~offizier** m *regimental o.*; *o. of the line* **~parade** f *parade*; (Wachparade) *trooping the colour*(*s*) **~schau** f *tattoo; military review* **~schiedsrichter** m *field umpire* **~schleier** m *veil, screen* **~schule** f *service school*, ⟨Am⟩ *academy* **~stärke** f *troop level* **~teil** m *unit; troop element* **~transporter** m ⟨mar⟩ *troop-ship, t. carrier* ‖ ⟨fam⟩ *trooper*; ⟨aero⟩ *troop carrier* **~übungsplatz** m (*permanent*) *training area* **~- u Waffengattung** f *branch of service* **~verband** m *body* | ~platz [m] *regimental aid post* **~verpflegung** f *provisioning of troops* | (zahlenmäßige) **~verminderung, ~verringerung** f *run-down* **~verschiebung** f *dislocation of troops; troop shift* **tr·uppweise** [adv] *in troops*, etc; *in flocks*

Tr·üsche f ~/~n ⟨ich⟩ *burbot*

Trut- **~hahn** m *turkey*(*-cock*) (kollert *gobbles*) ‖ rot wie ein ~ (*as*) *red as a t.-c.* **~henne** f *turkey-hen* **~hühner** n pl *turkey fowls, turkeys* pl

Trutz m ~es/ = Trotz **~bündnis** n *offensive alliance* **~lied** n *defiant song* **~waffe** f *o.e arm*

Trypanos·oma n ~s/–men ⟨bact⟩ *trypanosome*

Tsch·adsee m (Zentralafrika) *Lake Chad*

Tsch·ako m ~s/~s ⟨mil etc⟩ *shako*

Tschangsch·a n (chin. Stadt) *Changsha*

Tsch·apka f ~/~s *lancer's cap*

Tsch·apperl n ~s/~ [österr] *silly little one*

tschau! intj ⟨fam⟩ ([It] ciao) *bye-bye*

Tsch·eche, Tsch·echin f, **tsch·echisch** a *Czech*

Tsch·echerl n ~s/~n [österr] = (Kaffee-) Kneipe

Tschechoslowak·ei f, die ~ *Czechoslovakia*

Tschengt·u n (chin. Stadt) *Chengtu*

Tsch·enstochau n (poln. Stadt) *Czestochowa*

Tscherk·esse m, **–k·essin** f (Volksstamm im Kaukasus) *Circassian, Tcherkess* **tscherk·essisch** a *Circassian* **–k·essengebiet** n *Circassia*

-tscherl [–tʃəl] österr suff zur Bezeichnung bester Qualität: das ist ein Kaff·ee~! *this is some coffee*!

Tsch·ibuk m ~s/~s *chibouk*

Tsch·ik m ~s/~e (Zigarrenstummel) [österr] ⟨Am fam⟩ *snipe* | ~sammler [m] *s. shooter*

tsch·ilpen vi [h] ⟨orn⟩ *to twitter, chirp*

Tsch·ungking n (chin. Stadt) *Chungking*

°×**tschüß**! [intj] (aus adieu) *so long! tata! toodleoo*!

Ts·etsefliege f ⟨ent⟩ *tsetse*(*-fly*)

Ts·ingtau n ⟨†Ger⟩ (chin. Hafen)

T·uba f ~/–ben ⟨mus⟩ *tuba* **T·ube** f ~/~n *tube* (*with a screw cap*) ‖ °drück auf die ~! ⟨mot⟩ *step on the gas* od *on it*; ⟨fam⟩ *put your foot on the floor*; *put her along*; ⟨sl⟩ *pep her, step on the juice*; ⟨bes aero⟩ °*give her the gravy* od *gun* **Tub·erkel** f ~/~n ⟨path⟩ *tubercle* **~bazillus** m *t.-bacillus* | ~bazillen-Ausscheidung [f] *excretion of t.-bacilli*; t.-haltiger Urin *t.-b.i carried along from the urine* **~̈förmig** a *t.cular* **tuberkul·ös** a *t.cular, -lous* **Tuberkul·ose** f ~/ ⟨path⟩ *t.culosis* **Tuber·ose** f ~/~n ⟨bot⟩ *tuberose* **T·ubus** m [~/–ben & –busse] *tube* ‖ (Fernrohr) *telescope* | ~kamera [f] ⟨phot⟩ *rigid c.*

Tub·uai-Inseln f pl (in Polynesien) *Tubuai*

Tuch n ~(e)s/~̈er **A. 1.** *cloth* (bes a. Tischtuch), pl *cloths* [klɔ:ðz] **2.** ⟨com⟩ [pl] ~e *cloth*, pl *cloths* [klɔ:θs], *woollen fabric* | zwei Stücke ~ *two pieces of cloth* **3.** ⟨mar⟩ *sail*(*s* pl) **B. Bade**~̈ *bath-*

-towel || Einschlage≃ *pack-sheet* || Hals≃ *neckerchief*; *scarf, muffler* || Hand≃ *towel* || Jagdtücher [pl] *toils* pl || **Kopf**≃ (*head*)*kerchief* || Mantel≃ *wrap* || Mund≃ *napkin* || Staub≃ *duster* || Taschen≃ *handkerchief* || Umschlage≃ *wrap, kerchief* || Wickel≃ *long flannel* || Wisch≃ *rag* **C.** ⟨hist⟩ zweierlei ∼ *soldiers*, ⟨engl⟩ *red coats* pl, .. tragen *to be in the army* || auf e–n wirken wie ein rotes ∼ *to be like a red rag to a bull, to be a red rag to a p* **T·uch-** ⟨mst⟩ *cloth-* **~abfälle** m pl *cuttings* pl **~arten** f pl *c.s* ≃**artig** a *like c.* **~ballen** m *bale of c.* **~baum** m ⟨weav⟩ *c.-beam* **~bereiter** m *c.-dresser* **~fabrik** f *c.-factory, -mill* **~fabrikant** m *c.-manufacturer, c.ier* | ein roter **~fetzen** m *a piece of torn red c.* | auf, in **~fühlung** f ⟨mil⟩ *shoulder to shoulder* || ∼ halten, nehmen *to stand in closed order* **~halle** f *c.iers'* od *drapers' hall* **~handel** m *c.-trade, drapery* **~händler** m (*woollen-*)*draper, c.-merchant, c.ier* || ⟨paint⟩ (Rembrandts) ∼ *The Syndics of the D.s* **~handlung** f, **~laden** m *c.ier's* od *draper's shop* **~kratze** f *card* **~lager** n *c.-warehouse, c.-department* **~lappen** m pl *bits of c.*; *c. rags* pl **~macher** m *c.ier, c.-maker* **~machergilde** f *the C.m.s' Company* **~nadel** f *shawl-, breast-pin* **~nopper** m *napper* **~presse** f *c.-press* **~rahmen** m *c.-frame, tenter* **~rauher** m (P) *carder* **~rock** m *c.-coat* **~schere** f *c.-shears, twitchers* pl **~schermaschine** f *c.-shearing machine* **~ware** f *drapery* **~walker** m *fuller* **~weber** m *c.-weaver* | ∼ei [f] *c.-factory* **~zeichen** [n pl] auslegen ⟨aero⟩ *to spread ground signals* **T·üchelchen** n ∼s/∼ *little handkerchief* **t·uchen** a *made of cloth* **T·üchlein** n ∼s/∼ *small cloth* || (Taschentuch) *little handkerchief*

t·üchtig I. [a] **A.** *able, fit, apt, competent, qualified, efficient* || (ausgezeichnet) *excellent* || (geschickt) *skilled, clever, smart*; ⟨sl⟩ *salted* (*journalist*) || (gr) *large, big, great* || (beträchtlich) *considerable, good* || (gesund) *hearty*; *sound* (⟨a. hum⟩ *beating, price*) || (kräftig) *strong, vigorous*; *stalwart, sturdy* || *heavy* (*blow*) || (gründlich) *thorough* **B. in**: *proficient, good, clever* od *strong in* (*geometry*); *good at* | **zu**: *fit, suited, qualified for* **C. (Arbeiter)** *good* || e–e ∼e Reise etc *quite a journey, walk* || **(Reiter,** Trinker) *a hard-riding, -drinking* (*squire*) || ein ∼es Stück Arbeit *quite a job* || ∼er Schluck, Zug ⟨sl⟩ *swig* || (Schüler) *clever, smart* **II.** ⟨fam⟩ [adv] *much, largely*, etc **1.** ∼ etw **abbekommen** *to get it in the neck*; *you will get it hot*! || ∼ arbeiten an ⟨Am fam⟩ *to peg along at* || (bluten) *freely* || ∼ essen *to make a good meal*; (*they were eating*) *right enough* || ∼ **feiern** *to make a day* od *night of it* || (fluchen) *roundly*; *to go r.y to work* || sich ∼ plagen *to work with a vengeance* || es muß ∼ gescheuert w *it wants a good scrub* || **(schreien)** *lustily* || ∼ schütteln! *shake the bottle well* || (schwitzen) *profusely* || ∼ trinken *to drink deep*; → ⟨a.⟩ trinken **2.** ∼ **warm** *rather warm*, ⟨Am⟩ *good and warm* **3.** ⟨sl⟩ *like the devil, like old boots, like blazes*, ⟨Am a.⟩ *to a fare-you-well* **III. dem** ≃**en** gehört die Welt *victory always goes to the strong* || freie Bahn dem ∼! *career must be open to talents* || der ∼ste im Geschäft *the best in the business* | ≃**keit** f ∼/ *ability* || *efficiency, capacity* || *competence* || *proficiency* || (körperliche) *fitness* || (militärische) *military prowess* || ⟨aero, mar⟩ *airworthiness, seaworthiness* (*of a plane, ship*)

°**Tuck** m ∼(e)s/ = Streit, Zank | ≃-≃! [intj] *chuck, chuck*! °**T·ucke** f ∼/∼n (Weib) *vixen, snake* ⟨fig⟩

T·ücke f ∼/∼n *malice, insidiousness, malignity, spite* || *knavery, perfidy, treachery* || (Streich) *trick* (⟨a.⟩ des Schicksals); *prank* || ⟨fig⟩ *whims* pl (*of fortune*) || die ∼ des Objekts *the malice of ths* od *matter* || ohne ∼ *guileless* **t·ückisch** a *malicious, insidious, cunning, artful, spiteful* || *malignant* (*disease*) || *vicious* (*horse*)

t·uckern vi [h] ⟨mot fam⟩ *to put-put*

T·üder m ∼s/∼ [niedd] ⟨agr⟩ *tether*

Tuff(stein) m ∼(e)s/∼e ⟨min⟩ *tufa, tuff* **t·uffartig** a *tufaceous*

Tüftel·ei f ∼/∼en *hair-splitting* **t·üftelig** a *punctilious, fussy* **t·üfteln** vi [h] *to subtilize, quibble*; *to be fussy* || wir wollen nicht ∼ *never mind the fine point* | ∼ **an** [dat] *to puzzle* od *pore over*; *to quibble about, over*

°×**T·üften** f pl (= Kartoffeln) ⟨dial & vulg⟩ *taters*, ⟨fam⟩ *praties*

T·ugend f ∼/∼en *virtue* || *good quality* || es sich zur ∼ m *to make a v.* (*of doing*) || ⟨prov⟩ die ∼ hat ihren Lohn in sich selbst *v. is its own reward* **~bild** n *model* (⟨emph⟩ *paragon*) *of v.* **~bold** m ⟨mst iron⟩ *paragon of v.*; *out-and-outer in morals* **~bund** m ⟨Ger stud⟩ 1808–16 (–bündler [m] *member of the*) *League of V.* ≃**fest,** ≃**haft** a *virtuous* **~haftigkeit** f *virtuousness* **~held** m = –bold **~lehre** f *ethics, morals* pl; *moral philosophy* **~lehrer** m *moralist* **~pfad** m *path of v.* ≃**reich** a *very* od *most virtuous* **~richter** m *censor, moralist* ≃**sam** ⟨obs⟩ [a] *virtuous* **~spiegel** m *model of all the virtues* **~stolz** m *priggishness* ≃**stolz** a *priggish* **~wächter** m *Puritanical fanatic*

Tuk·an m ∼s/∼e ⟨orn⟩ → Pfefferfresser

Tularäm·ie f ∼/ ⟨vet⟩ *tularemia*; *rabbit fever*

T·ulasilber n ⟨Russ⟩ *Tula-metal*

Tulip·ane f ∼/∼n ⟨bot⟩ (Tulpe) *tulip*

Tüll m [∼(e)s/⟨com⟩ ∼e] *tulle*, ⟨engl⟩ *bobbinet* **~gardine** f *lace-curtain* **~spitzen** f pl *net-lace*

T·ülle f ∼/∼n (am Leuchter etc) *socket* || (Gießröhre) *spout, nozzle* || ⟨cul⟩ *icing-tube*

T·ulpe f ∼/∼n ⟨bot⟩ *tulip* || (Bierglas) *half pint-glass* **T·ulpen- ~baum** m *t.-tree* **~beet** n *bed of t.s* **~flor** m *blooming* od *profusion of t.s* ≃**förmig** a *t.-type* (Ventil) **~glas** n *claret-glass* **~holz** n *t.-wood* **~liebhaber, ~züchter** m *t.-fancier, -grower* **~zwiebel** f *t.-bulb*

t·ummeln vt [h] *to put in motion, to set going*; *to stir about* || (ein Pferd) *to exercise, work* | **sich** ∼ [h] *to run* od *bustle about, to romp, frisk* || (sich beeilen) *to hurry up*, ⟨fam⟩ *to make it snappy* || tummel dich! ⟨fam⟩ *look sharp*!, *buck up*!, *get a move on*! **T·ummelplatz** m *playground*, ⟨Am fam⟩ *stamping ground* || *wrestling-place* || *exercise-ground* || *riding-school* || ⟨fig⟩ *arena, lists* pl; *scene of action, battle-ground* **T·ummler** m ∼s/∼ **1.** *horse-breaker* **2.** = **T·ümmler** m ∼s/∼ (Taube) *tumbler* || (Zahnwal) *porpoise, dolphin*; → Delphin

T·ümpel m ∼s/∼ *pool*; *pond*

Tum·ult m ∼(e)s/∼e *tumult, commotion*; *turmoil*; *uproar, row* || *disturbance* || (Aufruhr) *riot* (⟨a. theat⟩ *riot* [*scenes*]) **~u·ant** m ∼en/∼en *rioter* ≃**u·arisch** a *t.tuons*; *riotous, rioting* ≃**u·ieren** vi [h] *to raise a t.t*; *to* (*cause a*) *riot* || ⟨fam⟩ *to kick up a row*

Tun n ∼s/ *doing, action* || *behaviour, conduct* || jds ∼ u Lassen *a p's doings* pl; unser ∼ u L. *our commissions and omissions*; ∼ u Leiden *activities and sufferings* || ∼ u Treiben [n] *ways and doings, goings-on* pl || ⟨prov⟩ Sagen u ∼ sind zweierlei *promising is one th and keeping one's promise is another* **tun** [tat/getan] [h] **I.** vt **A. 1.** *to do* (*he has done it*) || etw ganz gern ∼ *not to grudge doing a th* || er kann ∼ u l, was er will *he can do as he pleases* **2.** (ausführen) *to perform, effect, make* **3.** (arbeiten) nichts ∼ *to do nothing, to idle away one's time* || wir h (etw)'z ∼ *we have business* od *work on hand, we are busy* **4.** (wirken) Wasser tut es nicht *water alone will not do* **5.** (dazu|∼, bewirken) *I can do nothing in the matter* **6.** e–m etw (an)|∼ *to injure, hurt, harm* (→ B. Schaden, C. etw, nichts, viel) **7.** dazu ∼ *to add* **8.** (irgendwohin [–her] ∼) *to put* (*on, into*) [*to take* (*out of*)] **9.** (S) (ausmachen, bedeuten) *to signify, matter* (*much, little*) **10.** klug etc ∼ → IV. **B.** → **Abbitte** etc || er kann nichts Besseres ∼ *he* *cannot do (anything) better* || (e–e Bitte) *to make,* e–e B. an jdn ~ *to petition a p* || e–n (tiefen) **Blick** ~ in *to cast a glance at* (*to gain a deep insight into*) || Buße ~ *to repent* || ⟨mil⟩ Dienst ~ *to see service*; ⟨allg⟩ (e–m e–n D.) ~ *to do* || andere Dinge → C. anderes || (Eid) *to take* || Einspruch ~ *to protest* || e–n **Fall** ~ *to have a f.* || e–e Frage *to ask a q.* || e–n Gang ~ *to go on an errand*; (Gebet) *to make* || e–m Gutes ~ *to act well by a p* || e–n Knall ~ *to give a report* || sein Möglichstes ~ *to do one's best* (*to do*) || e–m Schaden ~ *to do a p harm* || ich denke e–n langen **Schlaf** z ~ *I mean to take ..* || e–n Schlag ~ *to strike a blow* || e–n Schluck, Zug ~ *to take a d.* || (Schritt) *to take* || das Seinige ~ *to do one's part* (⟨fam⟩ *bit*) || (Spruch) ⟨jur⟩ *to pronounce j., a s.* || e–n Sprung ~ *to take a l.* || → Teufel || (Wunder) *to do* **C. alles** ~ f ⟨a.⟩ *to go any lengths for* || ich habe z ~ (→ I A. 3.) *I have some work to do*; *I'm busy*; ich habe anderes z ~ *I have other business to attend to*, ⟨fam⟩ *other fish to fry* || **das** können Sie ~ oder l *or* ⟨fam⟩ ~ wie der Pfarrer Aßmann *you may do or not do it* (*just as you please*); ⟨fam⟩ *please y.s.* || warum h Sie uns das getan? *why have you done us such wrong*? || das will getan s *that wants doing* || *that requires time and care* || *it will not be amiss* (übel) *if you do that* (das) || dasselbe ~ ⟨a.⟩ *to follow suit* || **es**: *he knew what he had to do, and he did it* (es) || tu's! *do*! || .. wie N. es bei ihm tat *as N. did to him* || das tut's (genügt) *that will do* || damit ist es nicht getan *that is not all* od *enough* | [f vorangehendes Verb] wer soll singen, wenn du es nicht tutst *who is to sing if you don't* || *she wept as a child does* | er täte **gut daran** z gehen *he would be well advised to go* | **es z ~ bek mit**: *they will have trouble with* (*the police*); .. mit ihm ⟨fam⟩ *you'll have him down on you*; es z ~ h mit jdm *to have to do with a p*; er hat es mit **mir** z ~! *he's up against me*! || er hat mit den Nieren z ~ *there is sth the matter with his k.s* || sie bekam es mit den Nerven z ~ *her nerves began to go wrong* || **etwas** ~, etw z ~ h (→ A. 3.), ⟨a.⟩ *to be about sth* || e–m etw ~ (→ A. 6.) *to do a p a harm*; *he feared that she might do sth to him* || niemand wird dir etw ~ *nobody is going to hurt you* || es hat ihm k–r etw getan *nobody has done him any harm* || er hat **genug** z ~ *his work is cut out for him* || **mehr** z ~ h *to have more work to do* | **so etw** tut man (nun mal) **nicht** *it* (*simply*) *isn't done* | **nichts** ~ *to do nothing* (→ A. 3.), *to be idle, to play*; (jdm) (→ A. 6.) *to spare a p*; das tut ihm (gar) n.! ⟨fam⟩ *that won't hurt him*! *he thinks nothing of it*! | (das, es) tut [fast gar] nichts! (→ A. 9.) *it doesn't matter*; *it is of no* (od *small*) *consequence*; *don't mention it*! *never mind*! [*that's all right*!] || das tut n. z S *that does not alter ths* od *get us any further*; ⟨fam⟩ *that's neither here nor there* | das hat hier n. **zu** ~ *that is out of place here, does not belong here* || n. z ~ h *to have no work*, ⟨fam⟩ *to be at a loose end* || *if you are not doing anything you might ..* || **nichts** z ~ h **als** .. *to be for ever* (*scolding*); da **kann man n. anderes** ~ als .. *there is only one th to do and that is ..*; *there was nothing to be done other than to return* || sie h **da** n. z ~ *they have no business there* || ich kann da n. ~ *I can do nothing in the matter* || **n. z ~ h mit** *to have no part* (aber auch gar nichts *nor lot*) *in a th, to be no party to ..*; *to have no concern* od ⟨fam⟩ *truck with*; er hat mit diesem Beruf gar n. z ~ *he is not at all connected with ..*; .. **damit** .. *he's not in it*; das hat damit n. z ~ *that has no application to it*; Mitgefühl hat damit nichts z ~ *s. doesn't enter into it*; .. h **wollen** mit *to wash one's hands of, to let* od *leave .. severely alone*, (mit jdm) *to shut the door on*; ⟨fam⟩ *I will have no truck with people who ..*; *I would not touch him with a barge--pole* || n. mehr .. *to dissociate o.s. from a th*; *I have done with him*, ⟨Am⟩ *I'm through with ..* | **so** ~, **als ob** *to go through the motions of*; .. als ob man .. wäre *to pretend* (⟨vulg⟩ *lay on*) *to be*; es wurde allgemein so getan, als ob .. *there was a general pretence that ..*; ~ wir so (als ob)! *let's make on*; .. als ob nichts wäre *to ignore a th* od *the matter* | **viel** z ~ h *to have much work on hand* od *to do*, ⟨com⟩ *to have a rush of orders* || übermäßig viel z ~ h *to have a long day* || h Sie v. z ~? *are you very busy*? || es ist v. z. ~ *there is a great deal to be done* || des Guten z v. ~ *to over-shoot o.s.* od *the mark, to burn one's candle at both ends* | **was** taten Sie dann? *what did you do then*? || was soll ich tun? *what am I to do*?, .. nun weiter ~? *what else is to be done*; *how am I to proceed*? || was h Sie heute getan? *what have you done with y.s. to-day*?; was h Sie hier **zu** ~? *what business have you here*? | Probleme, mit denen wir z ~ h *p.s we are facing* || was h sie dir getan? *what have they done to you* | was tut's (→ A. 9.) *what does it matter*?, ⟨fam⟩ *what of it*? || was tut ein M. **mit** ..? *what does a girl want with education*? || was h wir eigentlich damit z ~? *where exactly do we come in*? | **irgendwie damit** z ~ h *to be somewhere in the picture of it* | ~ Sie, **was** Sie wollen! *do as you please* od *like*! ⟨fam⟩ *please y.s*!; sie kann ~ u l, w. .. *she can pl. h.s.* | mochte er ~, was er wollte *do what he might* od *would* || was er auch ~ mochte, .. *try as he would, he couldn't ..* || er weiß, was er tut *he knows, what he is about* || sehen, was sich ~ läßt *to see what can be done* || was Gott tut, das ist wohlgetan *God's works are good works* || ~ können, **wie** man will *to have it all one's own way* (*with*) **D. sich** [dat] **z ~ machen** *to busy o.s.*; an: ⟨fam⟩ *to mess about* (*a th*); mit: *to experiment, fiddle*, ⟨fam⟩ *to fuss with* (*a th*), *to nurse* (*a stick*); in: *to potter about ..*, [zwischendurch] *to put in an hour or two* (*in the garden*) | **sich** (nicht) ~ **l** *to be* (*im*)*practicable*; *that can*(*not*) od *may be done*; *what's to be done, what shall we do* (da *in the matter*)? **E. 1. ~ auf**: *to put, place on* || **aus**: *to take out of* **2.** was soll man **da**(**bei**) ~? = läßt sich ~ (→ D.) || **damit** ist es (*or* die S) getan *that settles it* **3. danach** ~ *to act up to* (*a th*) **4. darum** ist mir (sehr) z ~ *I am anxious about it, it is of* (*great*) *consequence to me*, (*I set great store by it, I attach great importance to it*) **5.** ich kann nichts **dagegen** ~ *I can't help it*; °kann man nichts dagegen (⟨vulg⟩ da nichts gegen) ~? *do you feel like that*? || **dazu** ~ (beitragen) *to contribute* (vgl. A. 7.) **6.** tu es **dorthin** *put it down there* **7. in**: *to put into*; wieder: *he returned the papers to their envelope* || in die Schule ~ *to send to sch.* || ⟨com⟩ in dem Artikel wird nichts getan *nothing is doing in this article* **8.** (es) **mit** dem Herzen z ~ h *to have trouble with one's heart* (→ C. es .. mit) || jetzt h nur wir zwei mit–e–a z ~ *now it rests with you and me* **9.** es ist **um** dein Glück z ~ *it is only for your h.*; .. ihm nur ums Geld .. *m. is all he wants, he only cares about the m.*; .. ihm um nichts z ~ als *he has no other object in view but* || es ist um mich getan *I'm done for* **10. von** sich ~ *to remove* (od *get rid of*) *a th*; *to put away*, (ausziehen) *to take off* **11.** jdm etw **zum** Possen ~ *to play a p a trick* (*by doing*) || jdm etw zu wissen ~ *to let a p know* **12.** Wasser **zum** Wein ~ *to put w. to the w.* **II. v/refl** °**sich** dicke ~ *to show off* || er tut sich mit allem leicht (schwer) *he takes ths easy* (*finds everything difficult*) || das tut sich auch so *it can be done either way* || °(wie geht's?) – Es tut sich! (..?) *So-so*! **III. v/aux** arbeiten ~ sie schon, aber .. *they do work, but ..* || essen ~ sie nicht viel *they don't eat much* || satt w ~ wir hier wirklich nicht! *they don't give us enough to eat, do they*? | ⟨poet⟩ die Augen täten (= taten) ihm sinken *his eyes fell* || ⟨hum⟩ er tät sich verlieben *he fell in love* **IV. vi** [**h**] **1.** *to act, do* || Sie täten **besser,** zu gehen *you had better go* || er tut nicht gut *he takes bad courses*

|| sich gütlich ~ *to make merry*; .. **an** *to do o.s. well on* || **klug** *or* wohl daran ~ *to act wisely* || Sie h recht getan, daß Sie .. *you did well to* (*leave*), *you did right in* (*leaving*) || ⟨prov⟩ tue recht, scheue niemand *do right and fear no one* || jdm wehe ~ *to grieve, hurt a p* || **wütend** ~ *to make a show of rage* **2.** [ell] z ~ h *to be busy* || (es) z ~ h mit *to have to do with*; *to be concerned with* (*a th*) | er hat tüchtig z ~ ⟨a.⟩ *his work is cut out for him* (um z ~ *to do*) **3. das, es tut nicht gut** *no good will come of it, that will never* od *not do* || es täte gut, wenn *it would be well if* || es tut mir leid *I am sorry, I regret* || not ~ *to be necessary* || das tut e–m wohl *that does one good* **4.** (sich [ver]stellen) (so) ~ **als ob** *or* wenn *to affect* od *pretend to* (*do*), *to pretend that* (*it is*); *he made as* (*if*) *to write* od *as if he would* .. || ⟨Am⟩ *we let on we don't know you* || ~ Sie, als ob nichts wäre *do nothing about it* (⟨dial a.⟩ nicht dergleichen ~) || ~ Sie, als ob Sie z Hause wären *make y.s.* (*y.selves*) *at home* | **betrübt** etc ~ *to assume an air of sadness*, etc || böse etc ~ *to pretend to be angry*, etc || fromm ~ *to play the saint* || geheimnisvoll ~ *to be mysterious* || **groß** ~ *to give o.s. airs* || schön ~ mit *to flirt with* || ~ Sie doch nicht **so**! *don't pretend, don't make a fuss*, ⟨fam⟩ *don't sham*! || er tut nur so *he is only pretending* || spröde ~ *to play the prude* || **vertraut** ~ *to affect intimacy*

T·unichtgut m ~s/ → Taugenichts, ⟨Am sl a.⟩ *bum* **t·unlich** a *feasible, possible, practicable* || (angemessen) *suitable, opportune, convenient* **≗keit** f ~/ *feasibility, practicableness*; (Ratsamkeit) *expediency* **t·unlichst** [adv] *if* (od *as far as*) *possible*

T·ünche f ~/~n ⟨a. fig⟩ *whitewash, whiting*; *calcimine* || (farbige) *lime-wash* || ⟨fig⟩ *varnish* **≗n** vt [h] *to l.-w., whitewash*, **~r** m ~s/~ *whitewasher*

T·undra f ~/–ren ⟨Russ⟩ (Sumpfsteppe Sibiriens) *tundra* **~moor** n *muskeg*

Tun·esien n (n.-afrik. Gebiet) *Tunesia* **T·unis** n **1.** (Stadt) *Tunis* **2.** (Gebiet) *Tunesia*

Tung·use m, **Tung·usin** f (v altaisch. Volksstamm in NO.-Asien) *Tungus, –goose, –gusian*

T·unika f ~/–ken ⟨ant⟩ *tunic*

T·unke f ~/~n *sauce, dip* || (Fleischsaft) *gravy* || (süße) *cream* | ⟨tech⟩ *dipping* **t·unken** vt/i [h] *to dip, steep*; ⟨Am a.⟩ *to dunk* | *to sop one's bread* **T·unkenschüssel** f, **T·unknäpfchen** n *sauce-dish, -boat*

T·unnel m ~s/~ *tunnel, subway* (bohren *to drive, cut*; anlegen durch: *to t.* [*a hill*]) **~arbeiter** m *t.ler* **≗artig** a *t.-like* **~bau** m *t.ling* **~ofen** m ⟨ceram⟩ *t. kiln*

Tupf m ~(e)s/~e, **T·üpfel** m & n ~s/~, **T·üpf(el)chen** n ~s/~ *tittle, spot, point*; *dot* (*on the i*) || aufs ~ genau *to a T* **t·üpfeln** vt [h] *to dot, spot, dapple*; ⟨paint⟩ *stipple* **t·üpf(e)lig** a *dotted*, etc **T·üpfel-** **~analyse** f ⟨chem⟩ *drop analysis* **~bogen** m *pattern of combined letters* **~farn** m ⟨bot⟩ *polypody* **T·üpfelung** f ~/ *mottling* **T·upfen** **I.** m ~s/~ = Tupf etc **II.** ≗ vt/i [h] **1.** *to touch lightly, to tip*; ⟨bes med⟩ *to dab* **2.** *to dot, dab* **T·upfer** m ~s/~ ⟨med⟩ *swab, tampon* || ⟨mot⟩ (Ventil≗) *tickler* | ⟨cul⟩ *dollop of* (*whipped cream*)

T·ür(e) f ~(e)/~en **A.** (Haus-, Zimmer≗) *door* ([gen] *to a house*) (→ Angel) | ⟨übtr⟩ (Haus) eine (zwei; [ein paar]) ~(n) weiter *next door* (*but one*); [*a few doors from here*] **B. Außen≗** *outer* od *front door*; ⟨engl stud⟩ *oak* (diese verschlossen [offen] halten *to* [*un*]*sport one's oak*) || blinde ~ *dead d.* || eingestemmte ~ *framed d.* || Fall≗ *trap-d.* || Flügel≗ *swing doors* pl || Gitter≗ *wired gate* || Halb≗ *hatch* || Schiebe≗ *sliding d.* || selbstschließende ~ *automatically closing d.* || Tapeten≗ *jib d.* | (Tag der) offene(n) ~ *open house*, → C. || 2-teilige ~ *Dutch d.* **C.** ⟨fig⟩ offene ~n **einrennen** *to talk to an open d., to burn daylight, to beat the air, to flog a willing horse* || die ~ öffnen (auf Klopfen, [Klingeln]) *to answer the door* [*the ring*] || ⟨fig⟩ jdm die ~ weisen *to show a p the d.* || als er die ~ hinter sich zugemacht hatte ⟨a.⟩ *when he was well inside* od *outside the d.*; er machte mir die ~ vor der Nase zu *he shut the d. in my face* **D. bei** verschlossener ~ *with the d. locked* || ⟨fig⟩ **mit** der ~ ins Haus fallen (*to blurt out*), *to spring a mine* (jdm *on a p*) | **nach** der ~ sehen: *he has been to the d.* ⟨fig⟩ *he saw to escape* | **von** ~ zu ~ gehen *to knock at d.s* || **vor** der ~ *at* od *outside the d., out of doors* || ⟨fig⟩ vor s–r eigenen ~ *at one's very doors*; .. kehren *to mind one's own business* || jdn vor die ~ setzen *to turn a p out* (*of doors*) || vor der ~ stehen (S) *to be impending* od *near at hand*; *Christmas is close*; vor der ~ stehen müssen *to have to stand on the mat* || .. **zur** ~ hereinstecken *to pop .. in at the d.* || **zwischen** ~ u → Angel *on the point of leaving*; .. stecken ⟨fig⟩ *to be in a scrape* **~abtreter** m *d.-mat* **~angel** f (*d.-*) *hinge* **~anschlag** m *doorstop* **~band** n *loop* **~beschlag** m *d.-mounting* **~bogen** m *doorway* **~drücker** m *d.-handle* **~einfassung** f *d.-frame* **~feld** n *d.-panel*; → Tympanon **~flügel** m *leaf of a d.*; *folding* **~fries** m *head casing* **~futter** n *d.-jamb* **~gerüst** n *frame for a d.*; ⟨min⟩ *gallery frame* **~gesims** n *cornice of a d.* **~glocke** f *d.-bell* **~griff** m *d.-handle, d.-knob* **~hüter** m *janitor*; *d.-keeper* **~joch** n *d.-bay* **~kette** f *d.-chain* **~-klinke** f **1.** (*d.-*)*latch* **2.** *d.-handle* **~klopfer** m *knocker* **~kontakt** m *electric alarm* | ~schalter [m] ⟨el⟩ *interrupter, -tor of d. contact* **~kratzer** m *d.-scraper* **~matte** f *d.-mat* **~öffnung** f *d.-way* **~pfosten** m *d.-post* **~platte** f *d.-plate* **~puffer** m *d.stop* **~rahmen** m *d.-frame*, ⟨Am⟩ *d.-trim* **~riegel** m *d.-bolt*; (autom.) *snap-b.* **~ritze** f *chink in a d.* **~säule** f *gate post* **~schild** n *d.-plate* **~schließer** m **1.** *d.-closer* **2.** (P) = –hüter, ⟨theat⟩ *box-keeper* **~schloß** n *lock of a d.* **~schlüssel** m *d.-key* **~-schnalle** f ⟨österr⟩ (= Türklinke) (*d.-*)*latch* **~-schwelle** f (*d.-*)*sill, threshold* **~steher, ~hüter** m ⟨jur⟩ *usher* **~sturz** m *d.-lintel* **~verkleidung** f *d.-frame, d.-case*; ⟨mot⟩ *panel* **~wand** f ⟨theat⟩ *d.-flat*

T·uras m ~/ ⟨tech⟩ *dredger drum*

T·urban m ~s/~e *turban* || ⟨Ind⟩ *puggaree*

Turb·ine f ~/~n *turbine* | **~n-** **~anlage** f *t. plant* **~antrieb** m *t.-drive* **~dampfer** m ⟨mar⟩ *t. steamer* **~flugzeug** n *jet plane*; ~ mit Propellerantrieb *prop-jet* (*plane*) **~gehäuse** n *t.-casing* **~luftstrahlmotor** m *turbo-jet engine* **~motor** m *turbo jet*; ~ mit Prop.-Antr. *propeller turbine* **~rotor** m *t.-disc* **~schaufel** f *t.-blade* **~schiff** n *t.-driven vessel* **T·urbo-** *turbo* .. ~gebläse [n] *t.-blower*; ~kompressor [m] *t.-compressor*; ~lader [m] *t.-*(*super*)*charger*

turbul·ent a *turbulent, whirling* (*motion*) || ~e Strömung *eddy flow* **Turbul·enz** f ~/ *turbulence*

Tur·in n ⟨It⟩ (Stadt) **Tur·iner(in** f**)** m *inhabitant* (od *native*) *of Turin*

T·ürke m ~n/~n *Turk* || °⟨mil⟩ e–n ~n drehen *or* vormachen *to do a bishop* | **~n-** **~bund** m ⟨bot⟩ *Turk's cap, martagon* **~krieg** m *Turkish war* **~säbel** m *scimitar* **~sitz** m (*to sit*) *tailor-fashion* **~zug** m *expedition against the Turks* **Türk·is** m –ses/–se ⟨min⟩ *turquoise* **t·ürkisch** a *Turkish* || ~er Honig *Turkish delight* || ~er Teppich *Turkey carpet* || ~er Weizen *Indian corn*; *maize*, ⟨Am⟩ *corn* || ~ Rot *Turkey-red*

Türk·ei f *Turkey* **T·urkestan** n (mittelasiat. Landschaft) **Turkm·enen** pl (türk.-tatar. Volksstamm) *Turk*(*o*)*mans* pl **Turkm·enistan** n ⟨Russ⟩ **T·urko** m (alger. Fußsoldat) *Turco, Zouave*

Turm m ~(e)s/≗e *tower* || (Kirch≗) *steeple* || (Glocken≗) *belfry* || (Burgverlies) *keep* || (Kerker) *dungeon*; ⟨übtr⟩ *jail, prison* || ⟨mil⟩ (Geschütz≗) *turret* || ⟨mar⟩ *turret*; (Kommando≗) *conning t.r* || ⟨aero⟩ *pylon*; ⟨anti-aero⟩ *tower* | ⟨chess⟩ *castle, rook* **≗artig** a *t.rlike* **~bau** m *building of a t.r* ‖ ∼ z Babel *the t.r of B.* **~drehkran** m *t.r crane* **~eule** f *screech-owl* **~fahne** f *vane* **~falke** m ⟨orn⟩ *kestrel* **~garage** f ⟨mot⟩ *autosilo* **~geschütz** n *turret-gun* **~haube** f ⟨mar⟩ *sighting hood* **~haus** n *sky-scraper* **~helm** m ⟨arch⟩ *spire* **≃hoch** a *t.ring*, ⟨fig⟩ *lofty* | *mountains high* ⟨a. fig⟩ | [adv] ∼ über *beyond* (*all praise*), .. stehen *to tower over* (*a p, a th*) ‖ jdm ∼ überlegen s *to excel a p by far* (*she is head and shoulders above him*) **~hüter** m *warder of a t.r* ‖ *jailer* **~knopf** m *pommel* **~plattform** f *platform of a tower* ‖ ⟨theat⟩ *perch*, ⟨Am⟩ *p.m for tormentor spot* **~schiff** n ⟨mar⟩ *t.t-ship* **~schwalbe** f, **~segler** m ⟨orn⟩ *swift* **~schwenkvorrichtung** f *t.t training gear* **~spitze** f *spire* **~springen** n ⟨sport, gym, swim⟩ *high diving* **~uhr** f *t.-, church-clock* **~verlies** n *dungeon* ‖ (e–r Burg) *keep* **~wärter** m *watchman on a t.r*, etc **T·ürmchen** n ∼s/∼ *turret* ‖ mit ∼ *turreted* **t·ürmen I.** vt [h] *to pile up* **II.** vi *to barge* (*against, into*) ‖ °(fliehen) ⟨sl⟩ *to cut, to* (*make a*) *bolt* (*of it*), ⟨fam⟩ *to skedaddle* ‖ ⟨mil⟩ *to leg it*; ⟨allg⟩ *to make a quick getaway* → °abhauen **III. sich** ∼ *to tower, to rise high* ‖ **getürmt** a *towered, turreted* ‖ *piled up, in heaps* **T·ürmer** m ∼s/∼ *watchman on a tower*, etc

Turmal·in m ∼(e)s/∼e ⟨min⟩ *turmaline*

T·urn- **~anstalt** f *school for gymnastics* **~fahrt** f *excursion* od *trip of gymnasts* **~fest** n *athletic sports* **~gerät** n *g.c apparaturs* **~halle** f, **~saal** m *gym*(*nasium*) ‖ ⟨Am⟩ *armory* **~hemd** n *jersey*; *gym shirt* **~hose** f *gym pants* pl **~kleidung** f *sports dress*, ⟨fam⟩ *gym outfit* **~klub** m *athletic club* **~kunst** f *g.cs* pl [a. sg konstr] **~künstler** m *gymnast* **~lehrer** m *teacher of g.cs*; ⟨engl⟩ *drill-instructor* ‖ (∼in f *teacher of callisthenics*) **~platz** m *athletic grounds* **~reck** n *horizontal bar* **~riege** f *group of gymnasts* **~schuh** m *sports* od *jumping, rubber shoe*; ⟨fam⟩ *gym-shoe*; *sneaker* ‖ *racing pump* **~spiele** n pl *athletics, athletic sports* **~stunde** f *lesson in g.cs*; ⟨engl⟩ *drill-hour* **~übung** f *g.c exercise* **~vater** m *founder of g.cs* (⟨Ger⟩ F. L. Jahn) **~verein** m *g.c* od *athletic club, turnverein* **~wart** m *leading gymnast* **~wesen** n *g.cs* pl [a. sg konstr] **T·urnen** n ∼s/ (Hallen- *indoor*) *gymnastics, athletics* pl ‖ ⟨mil, engl school⟩ *drill*; *physical training* ‖ (f Mädchen) *callisthenics* pl [mst sg konstr] ‖ Boden≃ *exercises on the floor*; Kunst≃ *acrobatic ex.s*; Schau≃ *gymnastic display* **t·urnen** vi [h] *to do gymnastics* ‖ ⟨mil, engl school⟩ *to drill* **T·urner** m ∼s/∼ *gymnast* (**~in** f *lady g.*) ‖ [oft Ger] *turner* **≃isch** a *gymnastic* (*feat*) [adv *-ally*] **Turn·ier** n ∼(e)s/∼e *tournament* ‖ ⟨hist a.⟩ *joust, tilt* **≃fähig** a *qualified to a tilt* **~helm** m *j.ing-helmet* **~lanze** f *tilting-lance* **≃mäßig** a *according to the rules of t.g* **~pferd** n *j.er* **~platz** m *tilt-yard, lists* pl **~reiter** m *t.nt rider* **~rennen** n *t.g* **~richter** m *umpire* ‖ ⟨hist⟩ *marshal of the lists* **~schranken** f pl *lists* pl **turn·ieren** vi [h] ⟨hist⟩ *to tourney, joust, tilt* **Turn·üre** f ∼/∼n **1.** [abstr] *good form* **2.** [konkr] *bustle* **T·urnus** m ∼/ *rotation* ‖ [österr] (Arbeitsschicht) *shift* | im ∼ *by turns* | sich ≃weise im Dienst ablösen *to rotate duties*

T·urteltaube f *turtle-dove* | ⟨fig⟩ ∼n [pl] *love-birds*

Tusch[1] m ∼es/∼e ⟨mus⟩ *flourish* (blasen *to sound*) ‖ ⟨Am sl a.⟩ *tiger* (*three cheers and a t.*)

Tusch[2] m ∼(e)s/∼e ⟨stud sl⟩ (*slight*) *affront provoking a duel* **tusch·ieren** vt [h] *to touch, affect* ‖ ⟨univ sl⟩ *to insult*

T·usch[3]**-** **~ätzung** f *aquatint* **~farbe** f *water-colour* **~feder** f *inking pen* **~kasten** m *paintbox* (*with water-colours*) **~manier** f ⟨arts⟩ *aquatint* **~napf** m *saucer* (*for painting*) **~pinsel** m *water-colour brush* **~zeichnung** f *Indian-ink sketch* od *wash* **T·usche** f ∼/∼n *India ink*; ⟨Am⟩ *indian ink*; lithographische ∼ *autographic writing-ink* **t·uscheln** vi [h] *to whisper* **t·uschen** vt [h] *to wash, to draw with* od *in India ink*

Tuskar·oratief n ⟨Jap mar⟩ *Tuscarora Deep*

T·ütchen n ∼s/∼ *small paper-bag* **~dreher, ~krämer** m ⟨fam⟩ *shop-keeper* **T·üte** f ∼/∼n *paper-bag* ‖ (spitze) *screw* ‖ Waffel≃ (mit Eis) *cornet* ‖ ⟨fam fig⟩ nicht in die ∼! *catch me* (*at it*); *not I*! *not a bit of it*! *you may whistle for it*! *nothing doing*!; ⟨sl⟩ *not on your nelly*!

T·ute f ∼/∼n, **Tuthorn** n (*watchman's*) *horn*

Tut·el f ∼/ ⟨jur⟩ *guardianship*

t·uten vi [h] ⟨fam⟩ *to toot*(*le*) ‖ ⟨mot⟩ *to honk* | hat v ≃ u Blasen k–e Ahnung *has no idea of anything, hasn't a clue*; *knows damn all about it*

T·utor m ∼s/–oren *tutor*, ⟨sl⟩ *coach*

°**T·utte, T·ütte** f ∼/∼n ⟨anat⟩ *nipple*

T·üttel(chen n) m ∼s/∼ *dot* ‖ ⟨fig⟩ bis aufs ∼ *to a T*; nicht ein ∼ *not a tittle* od *jot*

ˣ**Tw·iete** f ∼/∼n (*narrow*) *side lane, alley*

Twist m ∼(e)s/∼e *twist*; *waste-wool*

T·ympanon n ∼s/–na ⟨arch⟩ *tympanum*

Typ m ∼s/∼en *type* ⟨a. tech⟩ (Stellung!) Rechner ∼ 33 *type 33 calculator* ‖ ⟨fig⟩ nicht gerade mein ∼ *not exactly my line* (P) ‖ *sort*

T·ype f ∼/∼n *type, printing-type* ‖ ⟨fam⟩ *photo*; *snap*(*shot*) ‖ ⟨fam⟩ (P) *queer fish* ‖ so 'ne ∼! *quite a character*! | **~n-** **~anschlag** m ⟨typewr⟩ *impression*; eingestellte Stärke des ∼s *i. control setting* **~art** f *type face* **~hebelbeschleunigung** f *acceleration of type-bars* **~lehre** f ⟨psych⟩ *system of human types* **~prüfung** f *prototype tests* pl **~normung, ~vereinheitlichung** f *standardization* **~schild** n ⟨rec, etc⟩ *armature plate*

t·ypen vt [h] ⟨fam⟩ *to photo*(*graph*); *to snaphot*

typh·ös a ⟨path⟩ *typhoid, typhous*

T·yphus m ∼/ ⟨path⟩ Unterleibs≃ *typhoid* od *enteric fever* (ausbrechen *to break out*) ‖ Fleck≃ *typhus, camp-fever* **≃artig** a = typhös **~kranke(r)** m *patient suffering from typhus*, etc

t·ypisch a *typical* (f *of*) ‖ ∼es Beispiel *case in point* | [adv] das ist ∼ Hans *that's John all over*; das ∼ Wienerische *everything associated with Viennese* | das Typische [gen] *the typical character* (*of*) **typis·ieren** vt [h] ⟨arts⟩ *to produce as types* ‖ ⟨tech⟩ *to standardize* **T-rung** f *standardization*; *typification*

Typogr·aph m ∼en/∼en *typographer* **~·ie** f ∼/ *typography* **≃isch** a *typographic*(*al*) [adv *-ally*] **Typolog·ie** f ∼/ = Typenlehre **T·yposkript** n *typescript* **T·ypus** m ∼/–pen *type*

Tyr·ann m ∼en/∼en *tyrant, despot*; ⟨fig⟩ *tiger* ‖ ⟨ant⟩ *tyrant, king, ruler* **~·ei** f ∼/∼en *tyranny* | **~en-** **~herrschaft** f *despotism, tyranny* **~mord** m, **~mörder** m *tyrannicide* **tyr·annisch** a *tyrannical, tyrannous, despotic* **tyrannis·ieren I.** vt [h] *to tyrannize* od *domineer over*; *to oppress*; *to ride roughshod over a p* **II.** vi *to act the tyrant*

†**Tyrrh·ener** m (⟨Gr⟩ = Etrurier) *Tyrrhenian* **–nische Meer,** das *the Tyrrhenian Sea*

†**T·yrus** n (Stadt im alten Phönizien) *Tyre*

U

U, u n ~/~ *U, u* **U-Bahn** f (→ Untergrund–) *tube* **U-Boot** n *U-boat, submarine*; ~ mit Kernantrieb *nuclear s.*, ⟨fam⟩ *nuke*; mit ~ angreifen, versenken *to s.* | ~abwehr, ~bekämpfung [f] *anti-s. warfare*; ~bunker [m] *s. pen*; ~drachen [m] *explosive paravane*; ~falle [f] *decoy-vessel, Q-ship*; ~hebeschiff [n] *s. salvage vessel*; ~jagd [f] *hunting-killer operation*; ~jäger [m] *s. chaser*; ~krieg [m] *s. campaign*; uneingeschränkter ~ *unrestricted s. warfare*; ~mutterschiff [n] *s. depot ship*; ~-Raketen [pl] *submarine launched missiles*; ⟨Am⟩ *ULMS* (*underwater launched missile system*) **U-Eisen** n *channel iron* **U-Tal** n *U-shaped valley*

Übel n ~s/~ *evil* ⟨a. bib⟩; *ill* ‖ (*a necessary evil*) ‖ das kleinere ~ *a choice of evils* | (Unglück) *trouble, mischief* | (Übelstand) *grievance, abuse* | (Krankheit) *malady, disorder, complaint*; ⟨fig⟩ *canker*, altes ~ *an open sore* | es ist **vom** ~ *it is based on evil*, ⟨bib⟩ (*whatever is more*) *cometh of evil* ·**übel I.** [a] *evil*; *ill*; *bad* [compr *worse*]; (das wäre) nicht ~ *that would not be bad*, ⟨iron⟩ *a fine th, I must say*! → B. ‖ ⟨fig⟩ *black, foul* **A. (Auslegung)** *unfair* ‖ (⟨phon⟩ Aussprache) *faulty* ‖ e–m e–n üblen Dienst erweisen *to do a p an ill turn* ‖ übler Kerl etc *nasty fellow*, ⟨fam⟩ *bad egg* od *lot*; (⟨fig⟩ Kunde) *ugly* ‖ übler **Laune** [gen] *in a cross humour* ‖ jdn in üble Nachrede bringen *to slander a p* ‖ (S) *nasty* (*th, trick, fall*) ‖ (Viertel) *low* (*neighbourhood*) ‖ (Wetter) *foul*; ⟨fam⟩ *cruel*, ⟨Am⟩ *fierce* **B. kein** übler Bissen *a dainty morsel*, .. Gedanke! *I rather like the idea*, .. Mensch! *not a bad sort* | (gar) **nicht** (so) ~! *not* (*so* od *half*) *bad*!; ⟨iron⟩ *the idea*! → vor A. ‖ es gefällt mir n. ~ *I rather like it* ‖ das klingt n. ~ *that sounds* (*pretty good* od) *rather nice* ‖ n. ~ Lust dazu h *to have a good* od *great mind to do it* ‖ nehmen Sie es n. ~ ⟨a.⟩ *no offence* (→ C.) ‖ n. ~ s: *the room is not amiss*; *it will not be amiss if you do it* ‖ es wäre n. ~ *that would not be a bad plan*, .., wenn wir hier äßen *we might do worse than have lunch here* **C.** [adv] *ill, badly* [compr *worse*] ‖ ~ **angebracht** *misplaced* ‖ bei jdm ~ ank *to catch a Tartar* ‖ ~ auslegen *to misconstrue* ‖ ~ aussehen *to look ill* ‖ sich ~ befinden *to be in poor* od *bad health* ‖ ~ behandeln *to mal-, mistreat* (*a p*) | e–m ~ bek *to disagree with a p* ‖ ⟨fig⟩ es bekam mir ~ *I came off badly* ‖ es wird ihm noch ~ bek *he'll have to suffer for it yet* ‖ es ist ihm (sehr) ~ bek *he had to pay for it* (*dearly*) ‖ ~ beraten *ill-advised* ‖ v e–m ~ **denken** *to think ill of a p* ‖ ~ deuten *to misinterpret* ‖ es ist ihm ~ ergangen *he didn't prosper* ‖ **sich** ~ fühlen ⟨fam euph⟩ *to be ill*; → mir ist ~ ‖ e–m ~ mitspielen *to treat a p badly*; ⟨fig fam⟩ *to get one's knife into a p* ‖ etw (nicht) ~ **nehmen** (→ B.) *to take .. in* (*good*) *bad part*; *to take .. amiss, to take* (*mild*) *offense at a th, to blame a p for a th*; n. Sie es nicht ~! *never mind*! ‖ ~ riechen (schmecken) *to have a bad smell* (*a disagreeable taste*) ‖ **mir ist** ~ *I feel sick, queer, squeamish, unwell*; ⟨Am fam⟩ .. *like throwing up*; .. z Mute *I feel uncomfortable* ‖ er ist ~ auf dich z sprechen *you are in his bad books* ‖ **es sieht** ~ um ihn aus, es steht ~ mit ihm *he is in a bad way* ‖ es wird mir ~ dabei ⟨vulg⟩ *it gives me the sick*(*s*) | **ihm wurde** ~ *he felt* (*sick* od) *his gorge rise, he heaved* ‖ dabei kann e–m ~ w *it's enough to make one sick* ‖ jdm ~ **wollen** *to be a p's ill-wisher, to wish a p ill* **D. aus** ~ ärger w *to go from bad to worse* | ~ (um so übler) **daran** s *to be in a bad way* od *sad plight*, ⟨fam⟩ *to be badly off*; (*it will be the worse for you*) **II.** n **Übles** v e–m reden *to talk badly of a p* ‖ jdm (viel) ~ tun *to do a p* (*great*) *harm* **Übel- ~befinden** n *indisposition* **≃beleumundet** a *ill-famed, of ill fame*; *disreputable* **≃gelaunt** a *ill-humoured, -tempered* ‖ *cross* **≃gesinnt** a *evil-minded*; *malignant* ‖ jdm ~ s *to bear a p a grudge* **≃launig** a *bad-, ill-humoured*; ⟨Am fam⟩ *grouchy* | ~keit [f] *ill-humour* **≃|nehmen** vt irr [h] *to take* (*a th*) *amiss* od *in ill part, to resent, to be offended at* **≃nehmend, ≃nehmerisch** a *touchy, huffy, easily offended* **≃riechend** a *evil-smelling, smelly, malodorous*; *fetid* ‖ *foul* (*breath*) **~sein** n *nausea* **~stand** m *inconvenience, drawback* **~tat** f *misdeed, crime* **~täter** m *malefactor, evil-doer, criminal* **~tun** n *wrong-doing* **~wollen** n *ill-will, malevolence* **≃|wollen** vi irr [h]; jdm ~ *to bear a p a grudge, to wish ill to a p*; *to get one's knife into a p* **~wollend** a *malevolent, spiteful*

·**Übelkeit** f ~/~en *nausea, sickness* ‖ ~ empfinden *to feel sick* ‖ e–m ~ verursachen *to turn a p's stomach* ‖ v ~ befallen w *to suddenly feel sick* ‖ ~ erregend *nauseating* ‖ Haltung bei ~ ⟨aero⟩ *bracing position*

·**üben I.** vt/i [h] **A. 1.** *to exercise* (*limbs, faculties, a horse*) ‖ *to practise* (*the flute*; *music, running, drawing*, etc) ‖ ⟨mil⟩ *to drill, train* | **sich** ~ *to get one's hand in*, .. im Fechten etc ~ *to practise fencing*, etc, *to address o.s. to fencing* **2.** (gebrauchen) *to use, exert, to give play to* **B. Betrug** ~ *to practise* .. ‖ (Gastlichkeit) *to show* (an *to*) ‖ (Geduld) *to have* ‖ (Gerechtigkeit) *to do* (gegen *to*) ‖ (Gewalt) *to use* ‖ (Großmut) *to practise* ‖ (ein Handwerk) *to carry on, to pursue* ‖ (Kritik) *to raise* ‖ (e–e Kunst) *to cultivate* ‖ (Milde) *to show* (gegen *to*) ‖ **Nachsicht** ~ gegen *to deal leniently with* ‖ (Rache) *to take* (an *on*) ‖ (Sorgfalt) *to exercise* .. **II.** ≃ n *exercise, practice* **III. geübt** a *disciplined, practised*; *skilled, skilful, well versed* od *experimenced* (*in*); *clever* (*at*) ‖ mit ~er Hand ⟨fig a.⟩ *with a knowing hand* ‖ v uns ~e Methode *our own m.*

·**über I.** prep (wo? [dat], wohin? [acc]): e–r ~ dem/den andern *one on top of the other* | (wo?) *above, over*; *higher than*; (*above the water*) | (wohin?) (hinüber) *across* (*the river*) ‖ (*looking*) *over* (*the hedge*) **A.** [dat] **1.** (oberhalb) *above* (*our heads*) ‖ ~ uns (*the blue sky*) *overhead*; (*a bird hovers*) *over* (*the wood*) ‖ ⟨fig⟩ stehen ~ *to be superior to* (*a p, a th*) ‖ es schwebt Dunkel ~ der S *there is a mystery hanging over the affair* **2.** (jenseits v) *they live across the street* **3.** (infolge v) ~ dem Lärm etw überhören *not to hear a th on account of the noise* **4. (zeitlich & bei)** → B. 8.; *in the process of*; *during, while* **‖** ~ der **Arbeit** *at work*; *busy* ‖ ~ den Büchern sitzen *to sit* (*poring*) *over one's books* ‖ ~ dem Dichter den Menschen vergessen *to f. the man in the poet* ‖ ~ dem **Essen** *at mealtimes, during dinner*, etc ‖ ~ e–m Glase Wein *over a g. of w.* ‖ ~ dem Lesen einschlafen .. *while reading* ‖ ~ dem **Spiel** die Arbeit vergessen *to be so absorbed in playing that one forgets one's work* ‖ ~ dem Zanken *whilst quarrelling* **B.** [acc] **1. (örtlich)** (vgl. I. vor A.) ‖ (*to brush*) *over a th* | ⟨rail etc⟩ *by* (*way of*) *Hannover, via H.* | ~ das Ziel hinausschießen ⟨a. fig⟩ *to overshoot the mark* ‖ ⟨fig⟩ ~ etw hinaus *added to*; *on*; *after* **2.** (Bereich) *to rule over* (od *govern*) *a nation* **3.** (Häufung) (noch dazu) F. ~ F. *mistake upon m.* (→ d.) **4.** (höher als) *higher than* | (mehr als) *more than* (*50 girls, 20 yards, £ 10, 10 minutes*) ‖ etw ~ 10 Pfd *ten pounds odd* ‖ weit ~ .. *over and* *above* (*any cash value*) **5.** (Vorzug) das geht mir ~ alles *I put it above everything* **6.** (wegen) *on account of* ‖ traurig s ~ *to grieve over* od *about, to be sad about, to be grieved at* .. **7.** (betreffend) *with regard to*; *about*; *concerning* ‖ *to talk about* (Unbestimmtes) ‖ (*statistics*) *about* (⟨Am⟩ *on*) ‖ *Addison on Italy* ‖ *J. St. Mill, On Liberty* **|** ⟨com⟩ ein Scheck ~ 10 M *a ch. for 10 marks* **8.** (zeitlich) = nach ‖ während **||| a.** ~ **Berg** u Tal *over hill and dale* ‖ ~ den Betrag .. hinaus *in excess of the amount* ‖ ~ Bord fallen *to fall overboard* ‖ ~ e–e Brücke gehen *to cross a bridge* ‖ ~ alle Erwartung *beyond expectation* ‖ ~ **Gebühr** *more than is right* od *due* ‖ es ~s Herz bringen *to find it in one's heart to do it* ‖ (heute) ~s **Jahr** *next year*; *in a y.* (*from to-day*) ‖ ~ 20, 30, 40 Jahre alt s *to be upwards of 20, over* (⟨fam⟩ *on the shady side of*) *30*, ⟨fam⟩ (*she'll never see 30 again*); *to be past 40*; ~ die besten Jahre hinaus s *to be past one's prime* ‖ ~ ein **kleines** *after a little while* ‖ ~ solche Kleinigkeiten erhaben *above such trifles* ‖ ~ die Köpfe .. *to be promoted over the heads of the others* ‖ ~ kurz oder lang *sooner or later* ‖ ~ Land ⟨fam⟩ *'cross country* ‖ ~ die *or* alle **Maßen** *beyond all measure*; *exceedingly, incomparably*; (unmäßig) *immoderately* ‖ ~ Nacht *overnight*; ⟨prov⟩ ~ N. kommt Rat *night is the mother of counsel* ‖ (Reise) ~ See .. *across the sea* ‖ ~ die Straße gehen *to cross the st.* ‖ **Tag** → II. ‖ Sonntag oder heute ~ 8 Tage *Sunday or this day week* ‖ ~ Verdienst *beyond a p's desert* ‖ ~ s–e Verhältnisse leben *to live beyond one's means* ‖ 10 Minuten ~ die **Zeit** *10 minutes behind time*; ~ die Z. arbeiten *to work over hours*, .. ausbleiben *to stay out beyond one's time*, (of ship, mail) *to be overdue* **||| b.** jdn **ausschelten** ~ *to upbraid a p with* .. ‖ einig w ~ *to agree as to* (*terms*) ‖ ⟨aero⟩ *to fly over the town* ‖ ~ die Dörfer **gehen** *to go by the v.s* ‖ ~ die Kräfte g. *to go beyond one's strength* ‖ Zufr. geht ~ Reichtum *contentment is better than riches* ‖ das geht (mir) ~ alles (*I prefer that to e. else* [vgl B. 5.]), *that beats e.* ‖ das geht ~ das Maß des Erlaubten *that goes too far* ‖ es geht nichts ~ (Rheinwein etc) *there's nothing like* (*hock*), *there is noth. better than* (*truth*), *give me* (*the old times!*) ‖ das geht ~ m–n Horizont *that's beyond me* ‖ es ~ sich gewinnen *to bring o.s.* (*to do it*) ‖ ~ .. **hinaus** *over and above* (*the reports*); ~ etw **hinaus** s *to be past* (*vanity*) ‖ klettern ~ *to climb* (*a wall*) ‖ .. ~ alles lieben *to love .. beyond* od *above all ths* od *more than anything* ‖ ~ das Knie **reichen** *to reach below the k.* ‖ ~ H. reisen *to go by* (*way of*) od *via Hanover* ‖ **rinnen** ~ (*tears trickle*) *down* (*her cheeks*) ‖ .. setzen, stellen ~ *to place .. over* (*a p, a th*) ‖ schreiben ~ *to write* (*up*)*on* (*a matter*) ‖ reden, **sprechen** ~ *to speak about* od *of* (*a th*), .. *on* (*a subject*), *to talk* (*philology*) (vgl B. 7.) ‖ setzen, **springen** ~ *to leap over* (⟨sport⟩ *to take*) (*a fence*) ‖ Tränen vergießen ~ *to shed tears at* (*a loss*) ‖ ~ jdn viel vermögen *to have great influence over a p* ‖ **weinen** ~ *to weep over, to shed tears at* (*a loss*) ‖ die Wolke zieht ~ den Berg .. *moves over* .. **||| c.** m–e **Ansicht** ~ die S *my opinion about the matter* ‖ Aufsatz ~ *essay on* (*Milton*) ‖ Erkundigungen einziehen ~ *to inquire about* ‖ die Fahrt [der Übergang] ~ (*the*) *crossing* (*of*) *the bar*, [*the river*] ‖ **Macht** h ~ .. *to have power over* .. (vgl B. 2.) ‖ 10 Minuten ~ 9 *ten m.s past 9* ‖ Vorteil h ~ *to have advantage over* (*a p*) **||| d.** (vgl B. 3.) **Briefe** ~ **Briefe** *letter after letter* ‖ Geld ~ G. *more and more m.* ‖ ein Mal ~ das andere *over and over again* ‖ Verlust ~ V. *loss on loss* **||| e. [ell] Fluch** ~ dich! *a curse upon you!* ‖ o ~ die Eitelkeit *oh, vanity!* ‖ o ~ diesen Narren *oh, what a fool!* ‖ o ~ die Jugend *oh, youth, youth!* ‖ wehe ~ euch! *woe to you!* **II. [adv] 1. über und über** *all over, over and over, through and through, completely, thoroughly* ‖ ~ u ~ naß *wet through*; (P) ⟨a.⟩ *soaked to the skin* (⟨hum⟩ *bones*) ‖ ~ u ~ erröten *to blush up to one's ears* ‖ ~ u ~ voll *brimful* **2.** ⟨mil⟩ Gewehr ~! *slope arms!* **3.** den (ganzen) Tag ~ *during the day*, (*all day long*) ‖ die ganze Zeit ~ *all the time*, ⟨fam⟩ *all along* **4.** ⟨fam⟩ darin ist er mir ~ *in this he beats me* ‖ die S ist mir ~ *I'm tired* (⟨fam⟩ *sick*) *of it* **5.** ⟨fam⟩ (übrig) (*I have 5 marks*) *left* **|** (vor~) (*the fever is*) *gone*; (*those times are*) *past*; (*the rain is*) *over* **6.** ⟨dial⟩ (verdorben) (*the meat is*) *tainted* **·über- [in comp]** [bei vi & mst nur trennbar, wenn ~ den Hauptton trägt (z. B. ~|bleiben;) (Mantel) ~|ziehen *to slip on*] [aber: (Konto) ~z·iehen *to overdraw* ist untrennbar] **|** ~̊- *excess* (*pressure, luggage, strain, temperature*) **| [in a]**: *more than* (*zealous*); *over*(*-anxious*), *over*(*wise*); *excessively* (*nervous*); *hyper*(*critical*) **~|ackern** vt [h] [pp –ge–rt] *to plough over again*; **~·ackern** vt [h] [pp –rt] *to plough lightly* **~·all** [adv] *everywhere, whereever you go, all over* ‖ *throughout* ‖ ~ bekannt s *to be* (*known*) *all over the place* (*that*) ‖ ~ um mich her *all around me* ‖ ~ gegenwärtig *ubiquitous*, ⟨rel⟩ *omnipresent* ‖ Hans ~̊ (und Nirgends) *Paul Pry*; **~·her** [adv] *from all sides*; **~·hin** [adv] *in every direction, everywhere* **·~·altert** a *superannuated*; *over-age* (*applicant*); (*to be*) *o. a.* **·~̊angebot** n *excessive supply* **·über- ~·anstrengen** vt [h] *to overtax, -strain, -reach, -exert, o.work* (sich *o.s.*); *to push a p beyond his power* ‖ sich bei der Arbeit ~ *to work too hard*; sich nicht ~ ⟨fam⟩ *to look on* **|** –gt (Zustand) *wrought-up* (*nerves*) → –reizt; (P) *run-down, stale* **~̊·anstrengung** f *over-exertion*; *overpressure* (*of children*) ‖ ~ der Augen *eyestrain* ‖ geistige ~ *brain-fag* ‖ ohne ~ (*to row*) *within o.s.* **~·antworten** vt [h] *to deliver up, to surrender*; *to yield* (*a p*) (*to*) **~̊·antwortung** f ~/~en *delivery, surrender*, ⟨bes com⟩ *submittance* (an *to*) **·~̊anzug** m *overall*(*s* ⟨Am⟩) **~̊arbeit** f ~/ *overwork* ‖ (~̊stunden [pl]) *overtime* **~arbeiten** vt [h] *to do over again* ‖ ⟨Lit⟩ *to revise* ‖ ⟨arts⟩ *to touch up, to finish* ‖ sich ~ *to overwork* (*o.s.*) **~|arbeiten** vi [h] *to do* (.. *hours of*) *overtime* **~·arbeitet** [pp] a ⟨fig⟩ *over-wrought* **~̊·arbeitung** f ~/~en ⟨allg⟩ *finishing off* ‖ *revision*; *touching-up* ‖ (Überanstrengung) *overwork*; (*occupational*) *fatigue* **~̊ärmel** m ~s/~ *oversleeve* **~·aus** [adv] *exceedingly, extremely* ‖ ⟨fam⟩ *awfully*; *mighty* (*little*), *sadly* (*ill*); *jolly* (*good*) ‖ *nothing if not* (*courageous*) **~backen** vt [h] *to brown, gratinate* **~̊ballonreifen** m ⟨mot⟩ *giant tyre* **~̊bau** m ~(e)s *superstructure* ‖ *projecting part* **~b·auen** vt [h] *to build over* (*a plot, a story*) ‖ **sich** ~ *to ruin o.s. with building* **|** vi *to build higher* **~bedenklich** a (*over*)*scrupulous* °**~|bek** vt [h] etw ~ *to get a thrashing* **|** es ~ *to get sick of it* **~|behalten** vt [h] *to keep* (*one's cloak*) *on* ‖ (übrig beh.) *to have left, to keep over* **~̊bein** n ~(e)s/~e *node*, ⟨surg⟩ *bony excrescence* ‖ ⟨scient⟩ (Sehne) *ganglion*, (Knochen) *exostosis* **|** plötzliche **~̊belastung** ⟨el⟩ *rush of current* **~belegt** a *overcrowded* (*dwelling*) **~|belichten** vi/t [h] ⟨phot⟩ *to over-expose* **~̊belichtung** f ⟨phot⟩ *over-exposure* **~bemessen** a *oversized* **~besetzt** a *overcrowded* (*profession*); (mit Personal) *overstaffed* **~̊besetzung** [f] mit Arbeitskräften *overmanning* **~̊bett** n *coverlet, quilt* **~|beugen** vt [h] (sich) *to bend over* ‖ **sich** ~ ⟨a.⟩ *to lean over* **~bevölkert** a → –völkern **~b·ieten** irr vt [h] (jdn) (Versteigerung) *to outbid* (*a p*); *to cap* (*a p's bid*); alles ~ *to top all off*; s–e U. war nicht z ~ *his impudence was sublime* **| sich** ~ *to bid too much* ‖ ⟨fig⟩ *to surpass*; sich in Höflichkeiten ~ *to overreach o.s.* (bzw *to vie with each other*) *in civilities* ‖ im Lügen bist du nicht z ~ ⟨sl⟩ *for lying you are it*; –treffen **~b·ildet** a *overeducated, too refined* **~̊b·ildung** f ~/~en *over-refinement*

≗binde f ⟨surg⟩ *outer bandage* **~|binden** vt irr [h] *to bind upon* od *over* **~b·inden** vt [h] *to tie up* od *dress (a wound)* **~bl·ättern** vt [h] *to skip, miss (a passage)* || *to skim (a book)* **~|blättern** *to turn over the leaves (of)* **~|bleiben** vi irr [s] *to be left, to remain* || die Ü.bl·iebenen *the survivors* pl **≗bleibsel** n ~s/~ *remainder, remnant, residue, rest*; ⟨Am a.⟩ *hangover* || [pl]: *remains, leavings,* ⟨Am⟩ *leftovers* pl || ⟨biol & fig⟩ *vestige* || kümmerliche ~ [pl]: *wrecks* pl, *wreckage* **~|bl·enden** vt [h] *to blend in* [adv] **≗bl·ender** m ⟨phot⟩ *fader* **~blendvorrichtung** f *change-over* **≗blick** m ~(e)s/~e *general view, information, survey* (über *of*); *summary* || flüchtiger ~ *cursory glance,* ⟨Am⟩ *once-over* | ⟨fig⟩ (Abriß) *summary, outline, sketch* || (Beherrschung) *control* || (sich) e–n groben ~ verschaffen *or* bek über (den ~ wiedergewinnen) *to (re)orientate (o.s.) on*; *to glimpse* vt **~bl·icken** vt [h] *to overlook, survey*; (Situation) *to take in* || ⟨fig⟩ *to control*; etw besser ~ *to see more clearly in a matter* **≗bord-** ~spülen [n] *washing over board*; ~werfen [n] *jettison* **~|breiten** vt [h] *to spread over* **≗brettl** n ~s/~ *cabaret of cabarets* **~br·ingen** vt irr [h] *to take* (od *bring, carry*) (*to*), *to deliver, transmit* || (gehob Spr) *to present (a th to a p)*; persönlich ~ ⟨m. m.⟩ *to turn in in p* **≗br·inger(in** f) m ~s/~ *deliverer* || *bearer (of a letter, cheque, message),* durch ~ *per b.* | ~scheck [m] *open cheque* **≗br·ingung** f ~/ *delivery* **~br·ückbar** a *bridgeable* **~br·ücken** vt [h] *to bridge (over), to span (a river)* || ⟨fig⟩ *to bridge (the gulf)* **≗br·ückung** f ~/~en ⟨rail etc⟩ *culvert* | **~s-** *interval* [attr] (*stocks*); ~|kredit [m] *emergency credit* **~b·ürden** vt [h] *to overburden, -task, -work*; (mit Steuern) *to overtax* **≗b·ürdung** f ~/~en *overburdening*; *-work*; ⟨school⟩ *-strain, -pressure* **~chlorsauer** [–k–] a *perchloric* || ~es Salz *perchlorate* **≗dach** n *penthouse, shed, shelter* **~d·achen** vt [h] *to roof (in, over)* | –chte Anfahrt *canopy*; → –denken **~d·auern** vt [h] *to outlast*; ⟨tail⟩ *to outwear* || (Gefahren) *to survive* **≗decke** f *upper cover* || (Bett) *coverlet* **~d·ecken** vt [h] *to cover over* [adv] (*with*); ⟨arch⟩ *to vault (over)*; ⟨cul⟩ *to mask*; ⟨phot⟩ *to register* **~d·em** = überdies **~d·enken** vt irr [h] *to think* od *go over, to rethink; to reflect* od *ponder upon* || *to turn* od *revolve in one's mind* || *to reason out* || wohl überdacht *well considered* **~d·ies** adv *besides, moreover* **~dr·ehen** vt (Uhr) *to overwind* || (Gewinde) *to strip* **≗drehzahl** f *excess revolutions per minute*; ⟨aero a.⟩ *overspeed* **~dröhnen** vt [h] *to roar out above* **≗druck** m (Umdruck) *transfer* || (Briefmarken) *surcharge* || ⟨tech⟩ *over-pressure* || ⟨typ⟩ *supernumerary sheets* pl | ~anzug [m], ~kombination [f] ⟨a–n⟩ *spacesuit*; ~papier [n] *transfer-paper*; ~ventil [n] *o.-p.* od *relief, safety valve*; *pressure release (v.)* **≗druß** m –drusses/ *weariness* (an *of*) || (Übersättigung) *satiety* || (Ekel) *disgust* || zum ≗ *to satiety, to surfeit, to the point of tautology*; *ad nauseam* L **~drüssig** a [gen] *weary, tired, sick (of)*; *disgusted,* ⟨fam⟩ *fed up (with)* || jds ~ w *to grow tired of a p* **~durchschnittlich** a *above-the-average* .. | [adv] ~ begabt ⟨Am⟩ *accelerated (child)* **~·eck** [adv] *across, diagonally* || ~ liegen *to angle across (the entrance)* **≗eifer** m ~s/ *excess of zeal* **~eifrig** a *too zealous, over-officious* **~·eignen** vt [h] ⟨jur⟩ *to make over*; *to assign, convey, transfer* **≗·eignung** f ~/ ⟨jur⟩ *assignment, conveyance, transfer* | **~s-** ~klausel [f] ⟨jur⟩ *granting clause*; ~- u Eigentumsklausel *bargain and sale deed* **≗eile** f *overgreat hurry* **~·eilen** vt [h] *to precipitate, overhurry*; *to spoil by hurry* || ~ Sie nichts! *don't hurry ths! don't go doing anything in a h.* || (die Arbeit) *to scamp* || die Nacht –eilte uns *night overtook us* || **sich** ~ *to hurry too much, to be overhasty, to overshoot the mark* || ~ Sie sich nicht! *take your time!* **~·eilt** a *over-hasty, rash, heady, precipitate*; zu ~ *too previous* || ⟨fam⟩ *slapsdash (decisions)* || (voreilig) *premature* || (unbedacht) *inconsiderate* || ~e Schlüsse ziehen *to jump to quick conclusions* | [adv] ~ handeln *to do a rash th* **≗·eilung** f ~/~en *hurry, precipitation, precipitancy* || nur k–e ~! *take your time!* || z ~ neigend *over-hasty (judgment)*

über·ein [adv & sep pref] *conformably*; *in accord(ance)*; ≗k [n] ~s/~; **≗kunft** f ~/–künfte (ohne Vertrag *gentlemen's*) *agreement*; *arrangement* (treffen *to make*); eine endgültige ~ schließen *to close up ranks* || ⟨com⟩ *arrangement* || *convention* (a. stillschweigendes) || (Vergleich) *settlement* || nach gegenseitigem ~ *by mutual agreement* od *consent* || laut ~ *as arranged* **~|k** vi irr [s] *to agree* (über *on, about*); [abs] *to come to an agreement* od *understanding*; *to compromise (in a decision)* | *to be conformable (to)*; *to answer (a th)*; ~ mit jdm *to fall in with a p,* .. in etw *to join a p in a th* | –ge– s *to be in accord (with)*; sie sind –ge– *agreement was reached* **~|stimmen** vi [h] (mit) (P) *to agree (with a p* über *on)*; *be of a p's opinion (as to)* || völlig ~ mit jdm *to indentify o.s. with a p, to see eye to eye with a p* || nicht ~ (mit) *to differ* od *disagree (with)* || in e–r Frage *to split on a qu.* | (S) *to tally, square, check, coincide, harmonize (with)* || *to be in accord (with)*; *to be in line (with a th)* || *(opinions) coincide*; mit e–m Ding ~ *to chime* od *jump with a th* || fast völlig ~ mit *to tie in closely with (opinions, etc)* | ⟨gram⟩ *to agree (with another word in gender)* | ~d [a] *agreeing, conformable, consonant, corresponding* || (folgerichtig) *consistent* | [adv] *in accordance* od *of a piece with* **≗stimmung** f *accord, agreement, correspondence, concurrence, conformity, harmony (with)* || es herrscht allg. ~ *there is general agreement, it is common ground (that)* || in ~ mit *consonant with*; *in answer to*; *in concert* od *line, key, agreement, conformity, compliance, accordance, keeping with* || in ~ bringen *to adjust,* .. mit *to bring into unison with* || zeitlich in ~ bringen *to synchronize* || es herrscht allg. ~ *it is generally agreed* || nicht in ~ mit *out of accord with* || in ~ bringen *to bring into line,* ⟨phot, print⟩ *to bring into register* || ⟨com⟩ *to make (the receipts) cover (the expenses)* || in ~ s mit *to be congruous with*

überein·ander [adv] *one above* od *upon the other, over one another* || in Reihen ~ *in tier upon tier* **~|greifen** vi [h] *to overlap* **~|legen** vt [h] *to lay one upon another,* od (ths) *on top of one another* || (in Haufen) *to pile up* || (quer) *to cross* || –gelegt = **~liegend** a *superposed*; *in layers*; *overlapping*; ⟨arch⟩ *superimposed*; (Federn) ⟨orn⟩, (Schuppen) ⟨ich⟩ *imbricated* ⟨a. fig⟩ **~|schlagen** vt [h] *to fold (one's arms)*; *to cross (one's legs)*; mit –ge–en Armen *with folded arms, with one's arms folded*

·über- **~·eisen** vt *to cover with ice* **~·eist** a *frozen over* **~empf·ind-** **~lich** a *hyper-, over-sensitive*; *allergic*; ~ f Rot *red-sightedness* | ≗keit [f] *oversensitivity* **~sam** a *psychedelicate* **~entwickelt** a ⟨phot⟩ *cooked* **~erfüllung** f (des Soll) ⟨bes SBZ⟩ *overfulfilment* **~ernährung** f *hyperalimentation* **~·essen** itt [h] sich ~ *to overeat (o.s.)* || [vt] sich [dat] etw ~ *to sicken o.s. of a dish* **≗extrem** n *extreme of extremes* **~|fahren** vt irr [h] [pp –ge–] *to ferry over* | vi irr [s] *to pass over, to cross* **~f·ahren** vt irr [h] [pp ~] (jdn) *to ride* od *run, knock over a p* || etw ~ *to hit*; die weiße Linie ~ *to pass over the wh. l.* | ~ w ⟨fam⟩ *to be bowled over (by a bike)* || (Gebiet, Fluß etc) *to traverse, cross* || ⟨mot⟩ ein Haltezeichen ~ *to run a red light* || (mit der Hand etc darüberhin) *to pass (one's hand) over a th* **≗fahrgeld** n *fare, ferriage* **≗fahrt** f ~/~en ⟨allg⟩ *passage* ⟨a. mar⟩, ⟨mar⟩ e–e gute (schlechte) ~ h *to have a smooth (dreadful) crossing* (nach *to*) || während der ~

on the way across | ~schiffskarte [f] *ship ticket* || (~stelle) *ferry*; die ~kosten abarbeiten *to work one's passage* **≗fall** m ~(e)s/–fälle *assault*; *sudden attack* || *surprise* || *robbery, onslaught*, ⟨Am sl⟩ *racket* || (auf ein Land) *inroad, invasion*; ⟨mil⟩ *raid* || ⟨decor⟩ *pelmet* || (Schloß≗) *hasp*; (Wehr) *overfall, weir* | ~kommando [n] (Polizei) *flying squad*; ⟨bes Am⟩ *riot sq.*; ⟨Am fam⟩ *hold-up*; das ~ anrufen *to send a riot call*; ~nummer [f] ⟨telph⟩ *emergency number*; ~trupp [m], ~kommando [n] ⟨mil⟩ *raiding party* **~|fallen** vi irr [s] [pp –ge–] *to fall* od *topple over* **~f·allen** vt irr [h] [pp ~] *to surprise, to attack* (od *to fall upon*) *suddenly* || (Land, Bank) *to raid* || ⟨fig⟩ jdn ~ *to burst* od *butt in on a p*; ⟨Am⟩ *to gang up on*; *to hold up*; ~ (u berauben) ⟨Am sl⟩ *to hijack* || am Wege or auf dem Wege ~ w *to be waylaid* | ⟨hum⟩ *descend, to come down on a p*, mit e–m Vorschlag etc *to spring a proposal, surprise upon a p*, (zu Besuch) *to come in on a p* || (Krankheit, Dunkelheit) *to overtake* (*night overtook him*) || der Sturm (Regen) –fiel uns *we were caught in the storm* (*rain*) || Schrecken, Heimweh, (der Schlaf) überfiel mich *I was seized with terror, overcome with homesickness*, (*sleep stole upon me*) || [so]: *a fear came upon me, desolation swept down upon her* **~fällig** a *past due*; *overdue* (Rechnung), *missing* (*plane*) **~f·eilen** vt [h] ⟨fig⟩ *to touch up* **~fein** a *superfine, over-refined* || (Geschmack) *fastidious* **≗f·ettung** f *superfatting* (*of soap*) **~f·irnissen** vt [h] *to varnish over* **~fl·echten** vt irr [h] *to cover with wicker-work* || überflochten *wicker-* (*w.-bottle*) **~fl·iegen** vt irr [h] *to fly* (⟨aero a.⟩ *go*, dicht *skim*) *over* od *across* || den K. ~ *to fly the channel* || ⟨fig⟩ der Blick –gt etw *the glance sweeps* (*over*) *a th*; (ein Buch) ~ *to run one's eyes over*; (e–n Brief) *to skim*; *to glance, hurry over* .. || *her eyes* (*mind*) *went over the garden* (*circumstances*) || *a smile spread over her face* **~fl·ießen** vt irr [h] *to swamp, inundate* || –flossen *flooded* (*fields*) **~|fließen** vi irr [s] *to overflow* (*the banks*), *to flow over* || (Milch) *to run over* || (Augen) *to well* od *swim* (*with tears*) || ⟨fig⟩ *to be profuse* (*in excuses*); *to gush* (*with*) || *to brim over* (*with joy*) || z ≗ voll *brimful* **~fl·ügeln** vt [h] ⟨mil⟩ *to outflank, outwing* || ⟨fig⟩ *to surpass*; *outmatch, outstrip*; *to leave* (*a p, a th*) (*far*) *behind* **≗flurhydrant** m *pillar hydrant* **≗fluß** m –flusses/ *abundance*; *plenty*; *profusion* (reichlich *great*); *luxury* || (an Worten) *redundancy* || ⟨com⟩ (Überangebot) *glut* || etw im ~ geben *to be prodigal of a th* || ~ h an [dat] *to abound in* od *with*; .. an Geld *to be flush of m.* || sich des –sses erfreuend *affluent* (*society*) || im ~ leben *to be* od *live in clover* || im ~ vorhanden s *to abound* || zu allem ~ *to cap it all, to make matters worse* | ~gesellschaft [f] *affluent society* **~flüssig** a *redundant*; *abundant, plentiful* || (unnötig) *superfluous, uncalled-for*; *supererogatory*; *needless, useless* || ~ m ⟨a.⟩ *to obviate* **~fl·uten** vt [h] *to overflow, swamp, inundate* || *to deluge, submerge, flood* ⟨a. fig⟩ | dem **≗flutetwerden** Einhalt gebieten *to stem the tide* ⟨a. fig⟩ **~f·ordern** vt [h] *to overcharge*; *-exert, -task* (*a p, o.s.*), ⟨com⟩ *to put it on* ||–rt w ⟨fam⟩ *to pay through the nose* **≗f·orderung** f *overcharge*; *excessive demand*; (unstatthafte) *exaction* **≗form** f ⟨sculp⟩ *mantle* **≗fracht** f ~/ *overfreight, excess freight* || ⟨rail⟩ *overweight, excess luggage* **~fr·achten** vt [h] *to overfreight* | da bin ich **~fragt** (*I'm afraid I don't know*) *there you have me*! ⟨Am sl⟩ *search me*! (**~fr·emden** vt [h]), **≗fr·emdung** f ~/ ⟨demog⟩ *alienation*, ⟨com⟩ (*to*) *control by foreign capital* **~fr·ieren** vi irr [s] *to freeze over* **~fr·oren** a *frosted* (*the window is f.*) **≗fuhr** f ~/~en [österr] *ferry* **~|führen** vt [h] [pp –ge–rt] *to lead across*; *to convey* od *carry over, to transport* || ⟨mach⟩ *to shift* (*the belt*) **~f·ühren** vt [h] [pp –führt] *found guilty* (*of a charge*)] (jdn [gen]) ⟨jur⟩ *to convict* (*a p of a crime*, etc) || (überzeugen) *to convince* || (transportieren) *to transport* (*luggage, a corpse*) | ~d [a] *convincing* **≗f·ührung** f ~/ ⟨jur⟩ *conviction* || (Versendung) *conveyance, transport*(*ation*) || *transfer* (⟨a. fig⟩ *to another school*) || ⟨rail⟩ (*over*)*bridge, br. over, overhead way, crossing, viaduct*; Straßen≗ *flyover*; ⟨Am⟩ *overpass*; schienengleiche ~ *level* (⟨Am⟩ *grade*) *crossing* **≗fülle** f ~/ *superabundance, exuberance, profusion*; ⟨med⟩ *plethora* ⟨fig⟩ || ~ des Herzens *ful*(*l*)*ness of one's heart* **~|füllen** vt [h] *to pour from .. into ..* **~f·üllen** vt [h] *to overfill, cram, overcharge* || (mit Pn) *to* (*over*)*crowd, throng*; –llt ⟨rail fam⟩ *jam-packed* || (Magen) *to glut* || (den Markt) *to overstock, glut* | **sich** ~ *to surfait* **≗f·üllung** f ~/ *overfilling, repletion*; ⟨demog⟩ *overcrowding, congestion* (*of cities*) || ⟨com⟩ *glut* || (des Magens) *surfeit, glut*(*ting*) **~f·üttern** vt [h] *to overfeed*; ⟨fig⟩ *to surfeit* **≗gabe** f ~/ ⟨mil⟩ *surrender* || (auf Bedingungen) *capitulation* || z ~ auffordern *to summon* (*a garrison*) *to surrender*; geschickte Abfassung v Aufforderungen z ~ *skilful appeals to s.* || (e–s Amts) *handing over* || (Überbringung) *delivery, handing over, handover* || (Übereignung) *transfer* | ~verhandlung [f] ⟨bes mil⟩ *negotiation for s.* **≗gang** m ~(e)s/≗e *passage* (*across the Alps*) || *crossing* | *crossing* (*a bridge, river, the Alps*) (*for pedestrians*) | ⟨fig⟩ *transition, change, turn* | ⟨rail⟩ *crossing* (→ –führung) || (zum Feind) *going over* || ⟨com⟩ *sale, transfer* || ⟨mus⟩ *modulation* || ⟨paint⟩ *shades* pl; ⟨film etc⟩ *blending* || ⟨parl⟩ *passing* (*to the order of the day*) || ⟨jur⟩ (e–s Rechts) *devolution* (auf *on*) | **~s-** *change-over* [attr] || **~bestimmungen** f pl *provisional* od *temporary regulations* od *provision, arrangements* pl **~brücke** f ⟨rail⟩ *gangway between two cars* **~form** f ⟨typ⟩ *transitional* **~gebirge** n ⟨geol⟩ *transition rocks* pl **~gebührnisse** pl ⟨bes mil⟩ *separation allowance* **~kabinett** n *caretaker government* **~konus** m *junction cone* **~lagerung** f *transit storage* N **~mantel** m *interseasonal coat* **~periode, ~zeit** f *period of transition* **~punkt** m ⟨rail⟩ (*level*) *crossing* **~signal** n *road crossing signal* **~stadium** n *stage of t.n* **~stärke** f: elektronische ~ *intensity of electronic t.n* **~stecker** m ⟨el⟩ *plug adapter* **~stelle** f *crossing point* **~stil** m *t.nary style* od *period, work*; *period of t.n* **~stück** n ⟨tech⟩ *adapter, taper, reducer* **~wahrscheinlichkeit** f *t.n probability* **~zustand** m *t.nal state, temporary arrangement*

·**über- ~gar** a ⟨cul⟩ *overdone* || ⟨met⟩ *over-refined* (*copper*), *burnt* (*steel*) **≗gardine** f *lambrequin* **~g·eben** vt irr [h] *to deliver* (*up*); *to hand over* (*the command*); *to give up* || (anvertrauen) *to give away* (*the bride*); *to entrust* (*a th to a p*) || (als Erbschaft) *to hand down* (*to*) || (e–e Festung etc) *to surrender* || (ihrer Bestimmung) *to inaugurate* (*school, building*): *the Minister cut the tape and declared the road open* || (den Flammen) *to consign* (*to*) || dem Gericht ~ *to take legal proceedings* (*against a p*) || dem Verkehr ~ *to open .. for traffic* || ⟨mil⟩ (die Wache) *to turn over* .. | **sich** ~ *to surrender* || sich ~ [erbrechen] (müssen) *to turn sick, to vomit*; *was sick in the coal bin*; ⟨fam⟩ *to be ill*, ⟨Am⟩ *to throw up* **≗gebot** n *higher bid, advance* **~gebührlich** a *supererogatory* **≗g·ebung** f = –gabe **~|gehen** vi irr [s] [pp gegangen] *to pass over* (*to*) (⟨a. fig⟩ *to a subject*) || (sich wandelnd) *to change* (*into*; *to cigars*) || (allmählich) *to grad*(*u*)*ate, grade* (*into*); *to merge gradually in ..* || (gleitend) *to slide* (*into*) || (unmerklich) *to shade* (*into, to*) | **an** : *to go to, to be taken over by a p* | **auf**: *the estate passed to him* || ⟨fig⟩ (v Gedanken) *to be carried on to* || *the responsibility devolved upon him* | **in** [acc]: *to turn, merge into, to switch to, to issue in* || ⟨mus⟩ *to modulate into* || in Fäulnis ~ *to grow rotten, to* *become putrid* || in andere Hände ~ *to change hands* || in–e–a ~ *to blend; to shade off into one another; mood melts into mood* **| von** .. auf .. *to descend from father to son* **| zu** etw ~ *to proceed to, to lead up to* || zum F. ~ *to go over to the enemy* || (–treten zu) *to secede* (*to*), ⟨ec⟩ *to be converted to a religion* = *to become a convert*; ⟨allg⟩ *to change one's religion* || zur Gegenpartei ~ *to change sides*, ⟨pol a.⟩ *to rat* || z e–m andern Gegenstand ~ *to change to* .., (in Erzählungen) *to pass on to* **|** ˣ~ [n] z e–r anderen Marke *brand-switching* **|** die **Augen** gingen ihm über .. *filled with tears* || ⟨fig⟩ daß ihm die A. übergingen *to utter exhaustion* || ⟨bib⟩ wes das Herz voll ist, des geht der **Mund** über *out of the fullness of the h. the m. speaketh* **~g·ehen** vt irr [h] [pp –g·angen] (auslassen) *to skip, miss, omit, overlook* || *to drop .. out; to by-pass, pass over* od *up* [adv]; (widerrechtlich) *to leave* (*a p*) *out* (⟨fam⟩ *in the cold*), *he felt very much left out* || (unberücksichtigt l) *to pass* od *slide over in silence, to pass by*, ⟨Am⟩ *to pass* (*a p*) *up* **| sich** ~ *to overtire o.s. with walking* ˣ~**g·ehung** f ~/~en *passing over; omission* || ⟨rhet⟩ *pretermission* **~gen·au** a (in Moral) etc) *straight-laced* **~gen·ug** [adv] *more than sufficient, enough and to spare* || ⟨fig⟩ (*to know*, etc) *to satiation* **~geordnet** a *superordinate; higher* (⟨mil⟩ *formation, headquarters*); *overriding* (Erwägung) ˣ~**gepäck** n *excess luggage* **~geschäftig** a *bustling* **~geschnappt** a *crazy*; ⟨mil⟩ *gone dis*(*connected*); ⟨sl⟩ *off one's block*; total ~ *as mad as a hatter* (→ –schnappen) ˣ~**gewicht** n ~(e)s/ *overweight* || ⟨fig⟩ *preponderance, superiority* (*over*) || das ~ behaupten *to maintain one's superiority*; .. bek *to get the ascendancy*; .. gewinnen *to prevail*; .. h *to predominate* || im ~ s *to preponderate* **~|gießen** vt irr [h] [pp –gegossen] *to pour over* || (versehentlich) *to spill* **~g·ießen** [pp –g·ossen] *to pour upon, to overflow, douse, dash* (*with*) || mit Licht ~ *to bathe in light* || mit Wasser ~ *to pour w. on* || mit Zucker ~ *to candy* || ⟨fig⟩ mit Schamröte –g·ossen *blushing all over* || es –g·oß sie purpurrot *she turned crimson* || M. –goß d. E. *moonlight suffused the earth* **~g·ipsen** vt [h] *to plaster, parget* **~gl·änzen** vt [h] *to glaze*; ⟨fig⟩ *to eclipse* **~gl·asen** vt [h] *to glaze* ˣ~**gl·asung** f ~/~en *glazing* **~glücklich** a *overjoyed, radiantly happy, enraptured*; ⟨fam⟩ *as happy as happy can be* **~gnädig** a *too gracious* **~g·olden** vt [h] *to gild* ⟨a. fig⟩ ˣ~**g·oldung** f ~/~en *gilding* **~|greifen** vi [h] *to overlap*, ⟨mus⟩ *to shift* || ~ auf *or* in [acc] ⟨fig⟩ *to encroach* (*up*)*on* (*a p's rights*), *to trench on* (*a domain*) **|** (Feuer, Epidemie) *to spread to* .. ˣ~**griff** m *encroachment, inroad* (*on*); *trespass*(*ing*) **~groß** a *overlarge, royal, immense, excessive, huge, enormous*; ⟨tail⟩ *outsize* [attr] ˣ~**größe** f ⟨tail⟩ *outsize* ˣ~**guß** m ⟨cul⟩ *crust*, (Zuckerˣ~) *icing*, (Bratenˣ~) *basting* **~gut** a *good to a fault* || ⟨com⟩ *above the standard, superfine* **~|haben** vt irr [h] || (e–n Mantel etc) *to have on* || (übrig h) *to have left* || ⟨fam⟩ *to have enough of, to be tired* (⟨fam⟩ *sick*) *of* **~|halten** vt [h] ⟨for⟩ *to maintain* || [österr] jdn ~ = –vorteilen ˣ~**hälter** m ⟨for⟩ *veteran, standard*

Überh·and- **~nahme** f *rapid growth, increase, spread*(*ing*); *excess*; *rampancy* ˣ~**|nehmen** vi irr [h] *to prevail, to gain ground; to increase, grow* (*rapidly*); *to spread* (*far and wide*); (of vices) *to be rampant* || (of disease) ⟨a.⟩ *to run riot*

·**Überhang** m *curtain* || ⟨arch⟩ *projection*; ⟨tech⟩ *sally* || *overhanging rock*, etc || ⟨mot⟩ (vorderer) hinterer ~ *angle of* (*approach*) *departure* || ⟨com⟩ *back-log* **|** ~gardine [f] *pelmet* ·**über|hangen** vi irr [h] *to hang over, to overhang* || ⟨arch⟩ *to lean over; to jut forth* **|** ~d *projecting, beetling* (*brows*)

·**über- ~|hängen I.** vi [h] = –hangen **|** ~d ⟨print⟩ *kerned* (*letter*) **II.** vt [h] *to hang* (*a th*) *over, to cover* || *to put on; to sling* (*a gun*) *over one's shoulder* **~h·asten** vt [h] *to hurry* (*a th*) **~h·äufen** vt [h] (mit) *to overwhelm* (*with*) || *to ply, pelt, pepper* (*with questions*) || *to swamp* (*with a th*) || jdn mit Liebe (Schmähungen, [Spott]) ~ *to lavish one's affection on a p* (*to heap insults upon a p* [*to pour one's scorn on a p*]) || *to glut* (*the market*) || mit Arbeit –häuft *over head and ears in work*; mit zuviel .. s *to have too many irons in the fire* || –ft w mit *to get a load* (*of honours*) || *to smother with* (*kisses*) || *to be snowed under* (*with applications*) ˣ~**h·äufung** f ~/ *overwhelming* || ⟨com⟩ *glut* **~h·aupt** [adv] *in general, generally, on the whole, actually, after all; altogether* || das Beste ~ *the best of all* || ~ nicht *not* od *never at all*, ⟨Am a.⟩ *none* (*I slept none that night*) || ~ kein .. *no* .. *whatever* || ~ nicht ⟨sl⟩ *not for nuts* || [neg & in Frage] *anyway* (*what's the good of it a.*?) || (*how did it start,*) *anyway*?; *what on earth did he mean*? *what anyhow does it mean*? || taugt er ~ zu etw? *does he have any use in the world*? || .. ~ noch? *does she love me any more*? || wenn .. ~ *if .. at all, if .. really* || .., wie ja ~ (+ Inversion) .., *as indeed was her whole bearing* **~h·eben** vt irr [h] [gen] *to exempt, excuse* (*from*), *to dispense* (*of*) || der Mühe –h·oben s *to be spared the trouble* (*of*); jdn e–r M. ~ *to save a p the t.* **| sich** ~ *to* (*over-*)*strain o.s. by lifting* || (stolz s) *to presume, to be overbearing*; [gen] *to be too proud of* || ohne mich ~ z wollen *without boasting* **~h·eblich** a *arrogant; superior* (*smile, manner*); *consequential*, ⟨sl⟩ *cocky*; ~ w *or* s *to get above o.s.* **|** ˣ~keit, ˣ~h·ebung [f] ~/~en *presumption, overweening, arrogance; airs* pl; *stuckupness; superiority; hybris* Gr **~|helfen** vi irr [h] (jdm) *to help* (*a p*) *over* **~h·eizen** vt [h] *to overheat* **~h·in** [adv] *over* || ⟨fig⟩ *superficially, slightly* **~h·itzen** vt [h] *to overheat* (⟨a. fig⟩: *-ed brain*) || (Dampf) *to superheat* **~|h·obeln** vt [h] *to rough-plane* **~hoch** a *extremely high* **~h·öhen** vt [h] ⟨bes tact⟩ *to command* || ⟨arch⟩ *to surmount* || ⟨mus⟩ *to culminate; to bring to a close* **|** –ht *banked* (*curve*); ⟨arts etc⟩ *raised* ˣ~**h·öhung** f *command* || ⟨rail⟩ *superelevation* (*of the outer rail*) ˣ~**h·ol-** ~fahrbahn, ~spur [f] ⟨mot⟩ *fast*(*er*) od *acceleration lane; passing line*; ⟨engl⟩ *the outer* (⟨Ger⟩ *inner*) *lane is for overtaking*; ~verbot [n] *no passing*! *overtaking prohibited* **~|holen** [pp –ge–lt] **I.** vt [h] (jdn) *to fetch* (*a p*) *over* || hol über! *ferryman ahoy*! || ⟨mar⟩ etw ~ *to haul a th over* || die Segel ~ *to shift sails* **II.** vi [h] (⟨mar⟩ = schief liegen) *to heel* **~h·olen I.** vt [h] [pp –h·olt]; (hinter sich bringen or l; übertreffen) *to overtake, to get ahead of; to* (*out*)*distance, outrun, -pace, -walk, -ride; to ride* bzw *row down; to cast behind*; ⟨ten⟩ *to pass*; ⟨allg⟩ *to outstrip* ⟨a. fig⟩; ~de Verfolgung ⟨mil⟩ *encircling manœuvre in pursuit* || ⟨mar⟩ *to overhaul* || ⟨mot⟩ *to overtake*; nicht ~! *no passing*! links ~! *overtake on the left*!; knapp ~ *to cut in* [vi] || (ausbessern) *to overhaul; recondition, refit* **II.** ˣ~ [n] Vorsicht beim ˣ~ *overtake* od *pass with care* od *caution*; ˣ~ verboten! *do not pass, no passing*! ˣ~ nur auf linker Fahrbahn! *left lane passing only*; nur beim ˣ~ links fahren *keep right except to pass* **~h·olt** a *obsolete; outdated, out-of-date; antiquated*; [pred] *out of date* od *fashion; passé* Fr || *superseded* (Befehl) || ~ s *to be made obsolete* **|** (repariert) *reconditioned, overhauled* **~h·olung** f *overhaul* **|** ~sgleis [n] *siding* od *passing track* **~h·ören** vt [h] (jdn) *to hear* (*a p say* od *repeat his lessons*) || (etw) *to fail to catch a th, to miss, lose, not to hear; I didn't catch your last words* || (absichtlich) *not to listen to, to ignore* ˣ~**hosen** f pl *overalls* pl ˣ~**-Ich** n ~s/ *superego* **~irdisch** a *superterrestrial, celestial, aerial, supernatural, weird*; ⟨poet⟩ *supernal*, ⟨fam⟩ *heavenly, divine, unearthly* (*beauty*) **~j·agen** vt [h] *to override, overdrive* || *to overwork* (*a horse*)

∼jährig a *more than a year old* ‖ (alt) *superannuated* ‖ ⟨for⟩ *overseasoned* (Baum, Schlag) °**∼kandidelt** a *crazy* **≗karton** m *paper-board cover(ing), outer carton* **∼k·aufen, sich** ∼ *to (ruin o.s. by) buy(ing) too dear* **∼|kippen** vt/i [h & s] *to tip* od *tilt over; to upset* ‖ (P) *to overbalance* **∼k·ippt** ⟨geol⟩ *inverted (fold)* **∼kl·eben** vt [h] *to paste* od *glue, paper over* (mit *with*) **≗kleid** n *upper garment* ‖ (z Schutze) *overall(s* pl ⟨Am⟩) **∼kl·eiden** vt [h] *to cover a th over, to clothe, drape (in)* **∼kl·eistern** vt [h] *to paste over* **∼|klettern** vt/i [h & s] ‖ *to cross (the mountains)* ‖ *to climb over* **∼klug** a *overwise, would-be wise, sapient* ‖ [pred] *too clever by half* ‖ ∼er Mensch *wiseacre* **∼|kochen I.** vi [s] *to boil over* ‖ ⟨fig⟩ *to boil (with rage), to be in a towering passion* **II.** ≗ [n] ⟨eig⟩ *ebullience* **∼k·ommen** vt irr [h] *to obtain, get, receive* ‖ wir h es v unsern Vätern ∼ *it has come down to us from ..* | (v Gefühlen) (jdn) *to befall, seize* ‖ *to grow upon* ‖ Angst, (Ekel) –k·am ihn *he was seized with fear, (suddenly he felt sick; disgust obsessed him), a fear came upon him; fear took him; exasperation got the better of him; a wave of bitterness swept over him* | ∼ [pp] *overwhelmed* (v *with embarrassment)* | vi [s] [dat] (Sitten etc) *to be transmitted to*; (Geld) *to fall to* | [pp] *visited* (v *by a feeling of ..*); ∼es Gut *legacy*; ∼es Übel *evil legacy* ‖ ∼er Brauch *traditional usage* **∼kompensation** f ⟨a. psych⟩ *overcompensation* **∼konfessionell** a *non-denominational (school)* **∼|kopieren** vt [h] ⟨phot⟩ *to overprint* **∼kräftig** a *too powerful* **∼|kragen** vi [h] *to overlap* ‖ ⟨arch⟩ –gt *corbelled* **∼kr·euz** [adv] *cross-wise, across* **∼kr·itzeln** vt [h] *to scribble (all) over* **∼kr·onen** vt [h] ⟨dent⟩ *to crown* **∼kr·usten** vt [h] ⟨cul⟩ = –backen | °sich **∼k·ugeln** *to roll over, to go sprawling* **∼kultiviert** a *sophisticated* **≗kultur** f ∼/ *over-refinement, -civilization* **∼k·ünsteln** vt [h] *to overdo* **≗lack** m ⟨cosm⟩ *polishield; top coat* **∼|laden** vt irr [h] [pp –ge–] *to trans-ship, shift* **∼l·aden I.** vt [pp ∼] *to overload, overcharge, overfreight* ‖ ⟨übtr⟩ *to overcrowd (a room)* ‖ ⟨fig⟩ *to surfeit, cloy*; mit Arbeit *to overwork (a p)* | **sich** ∼, (s–n Geist) ∼ *to stuff o.s. (with)* ‖ sich [dat] den Magen ∼ *to overeat o.s.* **II.** ∼ [a] ⟨fig⟩ *(too) elaborate; overdone* ‖ *flamboyant (costume, style)* ‖ ⟨arts, Lit, mus⟩ *florid*, ⟨Lit⟩ *redundant (style)* **≗l·adung** f ∼/ *overload(ing), overcharging* ‖ (des Magens) *repletion, surfeit* ‖ ⟨el⟩ *overcharge* ‖ ⟨arts etc⟩ *floridness* ‖ ⟨fig⟩ *elaborateness* **∼l·agern** vt *to superimpose* ‖ ⟨wir⟩ *to heterodyne* **∼l·agerung(s-)** f ⟨wir⟩ *heterodyne (receiver)* | ∼sempfänger [m] ⟨a.⟩ *superhet*; ∼sfrequenz [f] *beat fr.y* **∼l·and** [adv] *'cross country* | ∼bus [m] *c.-c. bus*, ⟨Am⟩ *coach* ‖ ≗eisenbahn [f] *transcontinental railway*; ≗flug [m] *cross-country flight*; ≗reise [f] *overland route*; ≗telegraph [m] *overland t.*; ≗zentrale [f] ⟨el⟩ *super-power station, long-distance power station* **∼lang** a *overlong, too long*; ⟨tail⟩ *outsize* [attr] | ∼e [adv] ausbleiben *to stay out beyond one's time* **∼|langen** vi/t [h] *to reach over* | *to hand over* ‖ °jdm e–e ∼ *to box a p's ear* **∼l·appen** vt/i [h] *to overlap* ‖ –pte Schweißnaht ⟨tech⟩ *lap-welded seam* **≗l·appung** f ⟨comp⟩ *time sharing*; ⟨tech⟩ *lap joint* **∼l·assen** vt irr [h] *to leave; to give* od *yield up; to resign*; widerstandslos ∼ *to make no effort to resist ..* ‖ (–tragen) *to transfer* ‖ (preisgeben) *to abandon* ‖ (abtreten) *to cede* ‖ ⟨com⟩ *to sell* | jdn [etw] sich selbst (s–m Schicksal) ∼ *to leave a p to h.s. (to his fate; to let a p stew in his own juice* ⟨fam⟩), [*to let a th* (⟨sl⟩ *go hang* od) *take care of itself*] ‖ ⟨übtr⟩ den Wellen ∼ w *to be cut adrift*; das bleibt ihm ∼ *he is left to do it, that rests with him, he is at liberty to do as he pleases* ‖ jdn (etw) sich [dat] selbst ∼ *to leave a p to his own devices (to allow a th to run its course)* | es muß unserer Phantasie [dat] ∼ [pp] bleiben *we can only imagine*; ihm blieb die Entsch. ∼ *the decision fell to him*; es jdm (ganz) ∼ z tun *to give free rein to a p to do*; ∼ Sie das mir! *leave it to me!* | **sich** ∼ (dem Schmerz, Vergnügen etc) *to give o.s. up (to), to give way to*; sich s–m Genius ∼ *to abandon o.s. to his genius* ‖ *to surrender to an instinct* **≗l·assung** f ∼/∼en *leaving, yielding, relinquishment; resignation* ‖ ⟨jur⟩ *cession* **≗last** f ∼/ *overweight* ‖ ⟨fig⟩ *nuisance, trouble, burden* | ∼barkeit [f] ⟨tech⟩ *overload capacity*; ∼ventil [n] *o. valve* **∼l·asten** vt [h] *to overload* ‖ ⟨el⟩ *to overcharge* ‖ ⟨fig⟩ *to overburden* | sich ∼ ⟨fig⟩ *to overtask o.s.* **∼lastig** a *overloaded, -burdened* **∼lästig** a *troublesome, importunate* **≗lastung** f (Arbeits≗) *heavy commitments* pl **≗lauf** m *overflow* ⟨a. comp⟩ ‖ ⟨tech⟩ *spillway* | ∼adresse [f] *non-home address*; ∼leitung [f] *overboard drain*; ∼rohr [n] *overflow-pipe* **∼|laufen** vi irr [s] [pp –ge–] *to run, flow, boil over* ‖ ⟨typ⟩ *to run over* ‖ (of eyes) *to be filled with tears* ‖ ⟨mil & fig⟩ *to desert*; z Gegner ∼ *to go on the other track*; ⟨parl⟩ *to rat* | z ≗ voll *brimful* **∼l·aufen** vt irr [h] [pp ∼] *to outrun, outstrip (a p)* ‖ *to inundate (a field)* ‖ (sich verbreiten über) *to run* od *spread over* ‖ (gewaltsam niederrennen) *to overrun* ‖ (jdn belästigen) *to importune, pester, annoy (a p)* ‖ der Arzt ist ∼ .. *is regularly besieged by patients; I am rather rushed* ‖ *to invade (a house)* ‖ (flüchtig durchsehen) *to run over* | **sich** ∼ [h] *to over-run o.s.* | vt imps [h]; es **überläuft** mich kalt *my flesh creeps* ‖ *cold sweat broke over him* **≗läufer** m ∼s/∼ *deserter, transfuge, runaway* ‖ ⟨rel⟩ *renegade, proselyte* ‖ ⟨pol⟩ *turncoat; rat*, ⟨Am⟩ *flopper* | ⟨hunt, agr⟩ *squeaker* ([*wild*] *pig one year old up to two years)* **∼laut** [a & adv] *overloud*, ∼er Redner *vocal disputant; too noisy* [adv *noisily*] **∼l·eben I.** vt [h] *to outlast, survive, outline (a p, a th)* (um .. *by 10 years*); *to live out, to last (the night)* ‖ das kann ich nicht ∼ *that will be the death of me* | ⟨fig⟩ das hat **sich** *or* **ist -l·ebt** *that has had its day, that has gone out of fashion*; ⟨fam⟩ *it dates* ‖ er ist –l·ebt *he is a survival* (→ u.) **II.** ≗ [n]: Politik des gemeinsamen ∼s *co-survival* **≗l·ebende** m [der ∼, ein ∼r] & f ∼n/∼n *survivor* **∼l·ebens**-∼gr·oß [a] *larger than life, above life-size*; ≗ordnung [f] ⟨stat⟩ *life table*; ≗versicherung [f] *survivorship insurance*; ≗wahrscheinlichkeit [f] *probability of survival*; ∼ der Ledigen *p. of single s.*; ∼ Methode der ∼en *s. ratio technique*; ≗wert [m] ⟨biol⟩ *s. value* **∼l·ebt** a *disused, antiquated, out of date; (out)dated; (p who) has had his day*; ∼e Frage *dead issue* **∼|legen** vt [h] [pp –ge–gt] *to lay (a th) over (a th)* ‖ ⟨fam⟩ (jdn) ∼ *to turn up* (= *to flog*) **∼l·egen I.** vt/i [h] [pp –gt] *to overlay (with boards)* | ⟨fig⟩ [vi] *to brood, ponder, reflect* ‖ sie ∼ nicht lange *they don't think twice; they don't let the grass grow under their feet* | [vt] *to reflect upon, to consider, to think over; to turn .. over in one's mind*; ich will es mir ∼ *I'll see about it, let me see* ‖ sich [dat] (etw) anders ∼ *to change one's mind (about)*; etw immer wieder ∼ *to turn a th over and over in one's mind*; bei sich ∼ *to debate .. within o.s.*; es gründlich ∼ *to think it all out*; ∼ Sie sich [dat] das nur mal! *give one thought to the th*; sich die Folgen ∼ *to count the costs* ‖ wenn man's genau –gt *considering all ths* ‖ das will genau –gt s *that requires careful consideration* ‖ ich will es mir ∼! *I'll think it over!* | [vi] hin u her ∼ *to consider well* ‖ l Sie mich ∼! *let me see* od *think* ‖ ∼ Sie wohl! *think hard!, now be careful, mind you!* ‖ ∼ Sie mal ⟨sl⟩ *hold your horses* **II. ∼l·egen** a *lofty, superior* (Miene *air*, ⟨mil⟩ *leadership*) ‖ [dat] ∼ s *to be s. (to); to outdo, ..* (an) *to surpass a p (in); to be more than a match* od *too much* od *many for a p; to have (very much) the better of a p* ‖ *you may meet with your master* (jdn, der dir ∼ ist); ⟨sl⟩ *to have a bulge on a p*; jdm nicht ∼ s ⟨Am fam⟩ *to have* *nothing on a p* ‖ im Kampf *to outfight* | **~d** [a] *reflective, ruminative, thoughtful, deliberative, methodical* | ≗heit [f] ~/ *superiority (over)* ‖ (an Zahl) *the odds (are not so desperate)* **III.** ≗**l·egene(r)** m *top dog* **~l·egt** a *premeditated (crime)* ‖ (klug) *deliberate, prudent, considerate* | [adv] ~ handeln *to act with good judgment* | ≗heit [f] *thoughtfulness*, etc ≗**l·egung** f ~/~en *consideration, deliberation, reflection, cogitation; planning*; besondere ~en [pl] *special p.g* ‖ (urteilende) *judgment* | aus kluger ~ *diplomatically* ‖ bei näherer ~ *on second thoughts, on thinking it over* ‖ mit ~ *leisurely, leisurably*, .. verübt *premeditated, done with c.n* ‖ nach reiflicher ~ *after* od *on mature d.n*; nach (ganz) kurzer ~ *after a moment's reflection* ‖ ohne ~ *inconsiderately, on the spur of the moment* | **sich ~|lehnen** [h] *to lean over* **~|leiten** vt [h] *to lead over* od *up (to)* ‖ ⟨med⟩ *to transfuse (blood)* ‖ (Geld) *to turn over (to)* | vi [h] *to form a transition* ≗**leitung** f ~/~en *transition* ‖ ⟨med⟩ *transfusion* | ~s– *delivery (tube)* **~|lernen** vt [h] *to go over* od *learn (one's lesson) again* **~|lesen** vt irr [h] *to read* od *run (a th) over, to peruse* **~l·esen** vt (übersehen) *to skip in reading* | sich ~ *to read too much* **~l·iefern** vt [h] *to deliver; to give up* ‖ ⟨mil⟩ *to surrender* | ⟨fig⟩ (Brauch, ⟨Lit⟩) *to transmit* ‖ (jdm) *to hand down (to posterity)* ‖ –rt *traditional* ‖ –rt w ⟨a.⟩ *to come down (to)*; (nur) mündlich –rt *passed on by word of mouth* ≗**l·ieferung** f ~/~en *delivery* ‖ ⟨mil⟩ *surrender* ‖ ⟨Lit⟩ *transmission (of a text)* ‖ ⟨fig⟩ *tradition* ‖ mündliche ~ *w.-o.-m. transmission* **~|liegen** vi irr [h] ⟨mar⟩ *to heel* ‖ stark ~d *with a heavy list* | ⟨com⟩ *to lie over (time)*; ~ l *to allow (to be) on demurrage* ≗**liegetage** m pl; ≗**liegezeit** f *demurrage* **~l·isten** vt [h] *to outreach, outsmart, outwit; circumvent, dupe, defraud*, ⟨fam⟩ *pip; come it over, score off a p* ‖ ⟨sl⟩ *snooker*; geschickt *to outmanœuvre*; jdn z ~ suchen *to play tricks on a p* ≗**l·istung** f ~/~en *outwitting fraud, deception, circumvention* ≗**lochposition** f ⟨comp⟩ *additional p.* **~-l·ochung** f *overpunch* **·überm** etc ⟨fam⟩ = über dem etc **·über- ~m·achen** vt [h] (jdm) *to make over, to send, transmit, consign (to a p)* ‖ (Geld) *to remit* ‖ ⟨com⟩ die v uns übermachte Summe *our remittance* ≗**macht** f ~/ *superiority* ‖ ⟨mil⟩ *overwhelming manpower; superior numbers* pl bzw *force* od *power*; *(to fight against, to face great) odds*; der ~ weichen *to yield to s.r force* **~m·ächtig** a *predominant, superior, paramount, overwhelming* ‖ *too powerful* ≗**m·achung** f ~/~en *making over, consignment, remittance* **~|malen** vt [h] [pp –ge–lt] *to paint over* **~m·alen** vt [h] [pp –m·alt] ein Bild ~ *to paint a new picture over another, to paint out, to repaint, to touch up .., to retouch* ≗**m·alung** f ~/~en *retouch* **~mang·ansauer** a ⟨chem⟩ *permanganic*; ~es Kali *permanganate of potash* **~m·annen** vt [h] *to overcome, -power, -whelm* ≗**m·annung** f ~/ *overmatching, conquering* ≗**mantel** m ⟨sport⟩ *sweat-suit* ≗**maß** n ~es/ ⟨tail⟩ *oversize* ‖ ⟨übtr⟩ *extravagance, excess* ‖ (im Essen) *gluttony* ‖ (im Trinken) *intemperance* ‖ im ~ *(to use) in excess, (to take) to excess* ‖ im ~ ausgeben, produzieren *to overissue, -produce*; bis z ~ *to a fault* **~mäßig** a *over..; -abundant*; ~e Bevorratung ⟨com⟩ *-stocking* ‖ *immoderate, excessive* ‖ *fulsome (praise); undue (concern, costs)* ‖ ⟨fam⟩ *terrible* ‖ (Preis, Gewinn, Ehrgeiz) *exorbitant* ‖ (→ Genuß) | [adv] *excessively, beyond all bounds*, ⟨Am a.⟩ *overly* ‖ ~ arbeiten *to work too hard; (to eat) to excess*; ~ viel kaufen ⟨bes Am⟩ *to go on a spending splurge* ‖ ~ groß *enormous* | ≗keit [f] ~/ *immoderateness, excess* **~m·astet** a ⟨mar⟩ *overmasted* **~m·auern** vt [h] *to wall* od *mure up* **~mechanisiert** a *over-engined* **~m·eistern** vt [h] *to overpower* ≗**menge** f *overage* ≗**mensch** m ~en/~en *super-, overman* **~menschlich** a *super-human* **~|messen** vt irr [h] *to measure; to give overmeasure of ..*; v .. in *to fill from .. into* **~m·essen** vt [h] *to take in at a glance* **~mittelgroß** a *above middle height* **~m·itteln** vt [h] *to hand over; to deliver, transmit; to convey (to a p the thanks, etc of ..)* ≗**m·ittlung** f ~/~en *transmission, passage (of orders)*; technische ~ ⟨mil⟩ *electrical transmission* | ~sdienst [m] ⟨wir⟩ *transcription service* **~modern** a *ultra-fashionable* **~m·ögen** irr vt [h] = besiegen **~morgen** [adv] *(on) the day after tomorrow*, ⟨Am⟩ *d. a. t.-m.* **~m·üdet** a *overtired; fatigued (driver)* ≗**m·üdung** f *overfatigue* ≗**mut** m *high* od *wild spirits* ‖ (Ausgelassenheit) *sportiveness, frolicsomeness* ‖ *excessive joy* od *merriment* | (Mutwille) *wantonness* | (Anmaßung) *haughtiness, insolence, presumption, arrogance* ‖ ⟨prov⟩ ~ tut selten gut *pride goes before a fall* **~mütig** a *in high spirits, playful* ‖ (ausgelassen) *sportive, frolicsome, rollicking* | (mutwillig) *wantom* | (anmaßend) *haughty, insolent, supercilious, presumptuous, overweening* ‖ ⟨fam⟩ *uppish, cocky* **~nächst** a *the next but one* ‖ ~es Jahr *the year after next* ‖ *I shan't leave until week after next* ‖ am ~en Tage *two days later* **~n·achten** vi [h] *to pass* od *stay the night* (bei jdm *with*) ‖ ⟨sl⟩ *to doss* **~nächtig** a *exhausted by a sleepless night; haggard, fatigued, worn; weary (eyes)* ‖ ~ aussehen ⟨fam⟩ *to look seedy* ≗**n·achtung** f ~/~en *spending the night; a night's shelter; overnight accomodation* od *stay*; ~en [pl] ⟨hot⟩ *bed-nights* ≗**nahme** f ~/ *taking-over* ‖ ~ (e–s Betriebes etc) ⟨com etc⟩ *takeover* ‖ (Besitznahme) *taking possession of* ‖ (e–r Erbschaft) *coming into, acceptance* ‖ (v etw Anvertrautem) *taking charge (of)* ‖ (e–r Arbeit) *undertaking* ‖ (e–r Anleihe) *negotiation* ‖ (e–s Amtes) *entering (upon)* ‖ (P) endgültige ~ *establishment (after a satisfactory period of employment)* | ~datum [n] (e–s Betriebes etc) *vesting date*; ~kurs [m] *transfer-rate*; ~liste *consigner's list of prices; inventory* ×≗**name** m *surname, nickname* **~n·arben** vi [s] *to form a scar* **~national** a *supra-, supernational* **~natürlich** a *supernatural; unearthly* ‖ *miraculous* ‖ ~es Ereignis *miracle* **~|nehmen** vt irr [h] [pp –genommen] *to take over* ‖ ⟨cards⟩ *to overtrump* ‖ (Mantel etc) *to put on* **~n·ehmen** vt irr [h] [–nommen] *to take .. on* ‖ ⟨mar⟩ *to hoist in* ‖ *to take possession of* ‖ (jdn) ~ *to overcharge* | (Amt) *to enter upon* ‖ (Anleihe) *to negotiate* ‖ (Anvertrautes) *to take charge of* ‖ (Arbeit) *to undertake* ‖ ⟨mil⟩ (Batterien) *to take over* ‖ (Aufgabe, Befehl) *to assume* ‖ Bürgschaft ~ *to become* od *stand surety* ‖ (in Empfang nehmen) *to accept* ‖ die Führung (das Kommando) ~ *to take the lead (the command)* ‖ (Geld) *to receive* ‖ (Geschäft etc) *to take over* ‖ (Land) *to take a c. over* ‖ die Macht ~ v *to take over authority from* ‖ (Methode, Idee) *to adopt*; *(word) adopted from the French* ‖ (das Protektorat über) *to undertake .. (of)* ‖ ⟨theat⟩ (Rolle) *to take* ‖ (Pflicht, Verantwortung etc) *to take upon o.s., to assume* ‖ die Verwaltung e–r S *to take control of (a theatre)* ‖ übernimm du's *take it off my hands* | –nimm **es** bitte *take it off my hands* | **es** übernahm ihn die Angst, der Zorn *he was seized with fear, overcome with rage* | **sich** ~ *to overstrain, -reach, -task o.s.; to undertake too much; to overtax one's strength*; (im Essen) *to surfeit o.s.* ≗**n·ehmer** m ~s/~ *he who takes over* (od *upon h.s.*) ‖ (e–r Arbeit etc) *undertaker* ‖ (e–r Anleihe, Lieferung, e–s Baues) *contractor* ‖ ⟨jur⟩ (Rechtsnachfolger) *transferee* ≗**n·ehmung** f ~/~en *acceptation, undertaking* **~|ordnen** vt [h] *to place* od *set over* od *above* **~parteilich** a [pred] *above party lines*; [attr] *non-partisan* | ≗keit [f] *superiority to party politics* **~persönlich** a *more--than-personal (idealism)* ≗**pflanze** f ⟨bot⟩

epiphyte **~|pflanzen** vt [h] *to transplant* **~pfl·anzen** vt [h] *to plant* (*with*) **~p·ichen** vt [h] *to do over with pitch* **~p·inseln** vt [h] *to paint* od *daub over* || *to anoint* (*with iodine*) **~p·olstern** vt [h] *to cover with cushions, to upholster* **≗produktion** f ~/ *over-production* **~pr·üfen** vt [h] *to inspect, tally, check*: nochmals ~ *to take another, a second look at* (*a th*), (auf Schäden) *to overhaul* || .. im Geist ~ *to run a th over in one's mind* || (Lage) *to go over* (*a position*), *to take stock of* (*a situation*) || (Entscheidung) *to reconsider* || (auf Richtigkeit) *to* (*re-*)*examine* || (Übersetzung) *to revise*, dazu: *reviser* || (Kassenbücher) *to audit* | *to screen* ⟨a. fig pol⟩ **≗pr·üfung** f *overhaul, revision, examination, proving*; *audit* (→ Urteil); sicherheitsmäßige ~ (P) *security screening*, äußere ~ *visual inspection* ⟨bes aero⟩ || ⟨comp⟩ (automatische) ~ der Ein- u Ausgabe *checking of punched cards at both input and output stages* | ~smöglichkeiten [f pl] *testing facilities* ⟨a. comp⟩ **~p·urzeln,** sich ~ [h] *to tumble head over heels* **~|quellen** vi irr [s] *to bubble over* || ~ vor *to swim with* (*pleasure*) **~quellend** ⟨fig⟩ ~e Neugier *abounding curiosity* **~qu·er** [adv] *athwart, crosswise* **~qu·eren** vt [h] *to cross* (*the road*) || Grünstreifen nicht ~! ⟨mot⟩ *keep off median!* **≗qu·erung** f des A. *the Atlantic crossing* **~|ragen** vi [h] *to overhang, project* | ~d (*load*) *jutting out over the end of the vehicle* **~r·agen** vt [h] *to rise above* (*a th*), *to overtop, overlook* || ⟨fig⟩ *to surpass, excel, outstrip, eclipse* | ~d ⟨fig a.⟩ *commanding* (*power*), *transcendent* od *supreme* (*human achievement*); alles ~d *sovereign* **~r·aschen** vt [h] *to surprise, startle, overtake*; *to take aback* od *unawares* od *by surprise*; *to come upon* (*a p*) (*suddenly*) || (*death, the night*) *overtook him* || es kann bei ihm nicht ~ *it is not astonishing* od *surprising in him* || das –rascht mich an Ihnen *it's a surprise from you* || nicht –rascht s *to be unsurprised* (*by*) || der Regen –schte uns *we were caught in the rain* || –scht v *surprised at* | (besuchen) *to drop in on* | ~d [a] *surprising, astonishing, astounding*, etc; *surprise* [attr] (*attack*) → erschrecken | [adv] *amazingly, surprisingly*, etc; (*he said*) *out of a blue sky* || (unerwartet) *unexpectedly* || jdm ~ k *to come as a surprise to* .. | höchst –scht s *to jump out of one's skin* **≗r·aschung** f ~/~en *surprise* || z ihrer ~ *to her s.* || welche ~, Sie hier z sehen! *fancy seeing you here*; jdm e–e ~ bereiten *to make a p open his eyes* || e–r S die ~ nehmen *to kill the s. of a th* | ~sangriff [m] ⟨mil⟩ *sneak raid*; ~moment [n] ⟨bes mil⟩ *element of surprise*; ~stoß [m] ⟨mil⟩ *s. thrust* **~|rechnen** vt [h] *to examine* (*an account*) **~r·echnen** *to calculate, compute* **≗r·echnung** f ~/ *calculation, computation* **~r·eden** vt [h] *to persuade*; *to talk over*; *to talk* od *bring .. round* (*to one's point of view*) || sich ~ (–zeugen) [beschwatzen] l *to be prevailed upon* (*to do*), [*to be talked* (*into a th*)]; er ließ sich nicht ~ *he would not allow h.s. to be persuaded* || jdn z ~ suchen *to reason with a p* | ~d [a] *persuasive* **≗r·edung** f ~/~en *persuasion* | ~sgabe, ~skunst [f] *gift* od *power of p.n, persuasive power*; ~strick [m] *sell* **~r·eichen** vt [h] *to deliver, present*; *to hand* od *pass over* || ⟨com, etc⟩ *to submit* (*a price list*) **~r·eich(lich)** a *extremely rich, teeming* (an *with*), *super-abundant* (*in*) **≗r·eichung** [f] ~/ *delivery, presentation, handing over* **~reif** a *over-ripe* **~r·eiten** vt irr [h] *to run down* || (ein Pferd) *to founder, override* || (überholen) *to overtake* (*on horseback*) **~r·eizen** vt [h] *to over-excite* || (Nerven) *to overstrain* **~r·eizt** a *overstrung*; *overwrought, wrought-up* (*mind, nerves*) **≗r·eizung** f ~/ *over-excitement* || *overstrain* || ⟨path⟩ *brain-storm* **~r·ennen** vt irr [h] *to run down* || (Land) *to overrun* || ⟨bes⟩ den Feind ~ ⟨mil⟩ *to rush the enemy* || (überholen) *to outrun* **≗rest** m *rest, remains* pl || (⟨arith⟩ & im Buchhandel) *remainder* || (bes Tuchrest) *remnant* ⟨a. fig⟩ || ⟨chem⟩ *residue* | ~e [pl] *odds*; *debris*, ⟨Am⟩ *left-overs* (*of a meal*) || ⟨geol⟩ *detritus* || ⟨arch⟩ *ruins* || sterbliche ~e *mortal remains*; *relics* (*of a saint*) **~rheinisch** a *trans-Rhenish* **~r·ieseln** vt [h] *to irrigate* **≗r·ieselung** f ~/~en *irrigation* **≗rock** m ~(e)s/≗e *overcoat, topcoat* || (Gehrock; & ⟨mil⟩) *frock-coat* || (für Frauen) *skirt* **~r·umpeln** vt [h] *to* (*take by*) *surprise*; *to throw a p off his guard* || sich ~ l *to be taken by s., to be caught napping* (vgl –raschen) **≗r·umpelung** f ~/~en *surprise, sudden attack* **~runden** vt [h] → –h·olen **·übers** ⟨fam⟩ = über das **·über- ~s·äen** vt [h] *to sow over* || ⟨fig⟩ *to stud, dot, strew* (*with*) **~s·ät** a *bespangled* (*with stars*) **~satt** a *surfeited, glutted* (v *with*); *cram-ful*, ⟨fam⟩ *crammed* **~s·ättigen** vt [h] ⟨chem⟩ *to oversaturate* || ⟨fig⟩ *to surfeit, cloy* | sich ~ *to gormandize* **~s·ättigt** a (Dampf) *superheated* || ⟨fig⟩ (v) *tired* od *sick* (*of*) **≗s·ättigung** f ~/~en *repletion* || ⟨chem⟩ *super-, oversaturation* || ⟨fig⟩ *surfeit* **~s·äuern** vt ⟨chem⟩ *to overoxidate* || den Magen ~ *to produce heart-burn* **~schall** m *ultra-, supersonics* [a. sg konstr] | **~-** *ultra-, supersonic* (*airplane, wind tunnel, speed*); ~knall [m] ⟨aero⟩ *s.c bang* **~sch·allen** vt [h] *to outring* **~sch·arf** a *razor-sharp* **~sch·atten** vt [h] *to overshadow* || ⟨fig⟩ *to eclipse* (*moon, sun, earth*) **~sch·ätzen** vt [h] *to overrate, overestimate* || (steuerlich) *to overassess* (*a p, a house*) || jdn ~ *to have too good an opinion of a p* **≗sch·ätzung** f *over-estimate* || (Steuer) *overassessment* || ~ s–r selbst *overweening estimation of o.s.*; *conceit* **~sch·auen** vt [h] *to overlook, survey* || ⟨fig⟩ *to command a view of* (*a place*); *to take in* (*a situation*) **~|schäumen** vi [h] *to froth over*; *to bubble* (*over*) (⟨a. fig⟩ *with laughter, wrath*) | ~d [a] ⟨a.⟩ *ebullient* (*temperament*); *exuberant* (*mirth*) **≗schicht** f *extra shift, overtime* || ~en m or arbeiten *to work overtime* **~sch·icken** vt [h] = –senden **≗sch·iebung** f ⟨geol⟩ *overthrust* | ~sdecke [f] *nappe*; ~fläche [f] *thrust plane* **~|schießen** vi irr [s] [pp –geschossen] || (–neigen u fallen) *to fall forward* || (–fließen) *to overflow* || (übrigbleiben) *to be in excess* | die ~de Summe *the surplus amount*; (Saldo) *the balance* (*left*) || der ~de Ballast *the shifting ballast* **~sch·ießen** vt irr [h] [pp –schossen] *to outshoot, to beat* (*in shooting*) || *to overshoot* (*the mark*) | sich ~ ⟨sport⟩ *to come* od *go a cropper, to turn somersaults* **~|schiffen I.** vt [h] [pp –ge–fft] *to transport in a ship, to convey across the water* **II.** vi [s] *to sail across*; *to cross over* (*to* ..) **~sch·iffen** vt [h] [pp –fft] *to sail over, to cross* (*the ocean*) **~-schlächtig** a *overshot* **~schl·afen** vt [h] *etw* ~ *to consult one's pillow* | sich ~ *to oversleep o.s.* **≗schlag** m ~(e)s/≗e *computation, rough calculation* od *estimate* || ⟨el⟩ *spark-, flashover* || ⟨gym⟩ *somersault* || ⟨aero⟩ *loop*(*ing*), *roll*; (am Boden) *nosing over* || ⟨tail⟩ *facing* | ~decke [f] *rug, horse-cloth*; ~rechnung [f] *rough estimate*; ~spannung [f] *s.o., f.o. voltage*; ~weg [m] ⟨el⟩ *s.o., f.o. path* **~|schlagen** vi irr [s] [pp –ge–] *to turn, tumble, fall over, to lose one's balance* || ⟨mot, aero⟩ *to nose over, to overturn* || ⟨el⟩ (*sparks*) *flash out* od *over, across* || (Waagschale) *to drop, descend* || (Stimme) *to break* || ⟨fig⟩ in etw anderes ~ *to turn* (*suddenly*) *into sth else* | vt irr [h] (ein Tuch etc) *to put .. over* || (die Beine) *to cross* || mit –ge–nen Beinen ⟨a.⟩ *cross-legged* **~schl·agen** vt irr [h] [pp ~] *to turn* od *fall* || (–g·ehen) *to pass over, to skip, omit*; ⟨rail⟩ e–n, zwei Züge in B. ~ *to stop at B. between trains* | (kalkulieren) *to estimate roughly, to compute* | **sich** ~ *to tumble* od *roll over, to be overturned*; *to go head over heals*; ⟨mot⟩ *to lurch over* || ⟨gym⟩ *to turn a somersault* || ⟨mot⟩ *to turn over* || ⟨aero⟩ *to loop the loop* || ⟨fig⟩ (im Eifer) *to overplay, outdo o.s.* (*in*); *to tumble over o.s.* | ⟨mil⟩

~der Einsatz *employment by echelon*; in ~dem E. *by leap-frog movement*; .. vorgehen *to l.-f.* **~schl·agen** a (Wasser) *tepid, lukewarm* **~schlau** a *sophisticated* **~|schlucken** vt [h] *to swallow* **~schm·ieren** vt [h] *to besmear, rub* (*with*) **~|schnappen** vi [s] *to snap, slip, jerk over* ‖ (Stimme) *to squeak*; (mit der St.) *to sing falsetto* | °⟨fig⟩ *to go mad* (od ⟨Am sl⟩ *haywire*), *to turn crazy, to topple over the edge* ‖ –ge–ppt *dotty*, .. s *to be off one's head, to have a tile loose* **~schn·eiden** vt [h] sich ~ *to intersect* ‖ ⟨fig⟩ *to overlap* (*with*), *to cover the same ground* **≗schneidungsstelle** f *point of intersection* **~schn·eien** vt [h] *to snow over* ‖ –schn·eit *snowed-up* (*road*) **~schr·auben** vt [h] *to strain* (*a vice*) **~schr·eiben** vt irr [h] *to write over* ‖ (Auf–, Überschrift geben) *to superscribe, head*; (Brief) *to address* ‖ (·umschreiben) *to transcribe* ‖ ⟨com⟩ (bes: den Übertrag) *to carry over* ‖ jdm etw ~ *to settle a th upon a p* **≗schr·eibung** f ~/~en *transcription* **~schr·eien** vt irr [h] *to outcry, to cry down* | **sich** ~ *to cry o.s. hoarse, to overstrain one's voice* **~schr·eiten** vt irr [h] *to cross*; *to pass over*; *to go, pass, stride across* (*a th*) ‖ ⟨fig⟩ *to transgress* ‖ *to override* (*one's commission*) ‖ (Gesetz) *to infringe* ‖ e–e Grenze ~ *to pass beyond a boundary* ⟨a. fig⟩; in s–r Uneigennützigkeit die G.e der Vernunft ~ *to carry one's disinterestedness beyond the bounds of reason* ‖ (das Maß) *to exceed, to go beyond* ‖ s–e Machtbefugnisse ~ *to strain one's authority* ‖ (Einkommen) *to overspend* ‖ s–n Kredit ~ *to overdraw one's account* od *balance* ‖ (Zeit) *to overstep, overstay* | der Höhepunkt der Krise war –schritten *the crisis had reached and passed its zenith* **≗schrift** f *superscription*; *heading, headline*; (Reklame≗) *caption* ‖ *title, inscription* ‖ (Adresse) *address* **≗schuh** m *galosh* ‖ (Gummi≗) *overshoe* **~sch·uldet** a (P) *involved in debt* ‖ *encumbered* (*property*) **~sch·uldung** f *heavy indebtedness* **≗schuß** m –schusses/–schüsse *surplus, excess* ‖ *spill-over*; *overspill* (*of population*) ‖ ⟨com⟩ (*favo*[*u*]*rable*) *balance* ‖ reiner ~ *net profit* ‖ ~ abwerfen *to yield a profit* | Feuchtigkeits≗ *excess of moisture*; Wärme≗ *surplus heat* | ~chlorierung [f] ⟨chem⟩ *superchlorination* **~schüssig** a *surplus*; *exceeding*; *left over*; *odd* ‖ *abundant*; *spare* (*energy*) **~|schütten** vt [h] *to pour over*; (verschütten) *to spill* **~sch·ütten** vt (mit) *to cover*, ⟨fig⟩ (jdn) *to overwhelm* (*with*), *to heap* (*abuse*) *on a p's head, to shower .. on a p* ‖ –t w mit ⟨a.⟩ *to be snowed under with* (*applications*) **≗sch·üttung** f ~/~en *covering* ‖ *overwhelming* **≗schwang** m ~(e)s/ *superabundance, exuberance* ‖ im ~ *in the excess* (*of his loyalty*) **~|schwappen** vi/t [s & h] *to slop* (*over* od *out*) **~schw·emmen** vt [h] *to overflow, flood, submerge, deluge* ‖ *the sky was swept with light* ‖ ⟨com⟩ (den Markt) *to overstock, congest, glut* ‖ ⟨fig⟩ *to inundate*; (Land) *to overrun*; –mte Weg(-etc)-strecke ⟨a.⟩ *water splash* **≗schw·emmung** f ~/~en *inundation* ⟨a. fig⟩; *freshet*; *spate*; ⟨ent⟩ *infestation* | ~s-gebiet [n] *flood area* od *plain, basin, zone* **~-schwenglich** a *super-abundant, exuberant*; *excessive, boundless* ‖ ⟨fig⟩ *extravagant, enthusiastic, effusive, demonstrative, gushing*; *vaulting* (*imagination*), *rapturous* (*joy*); *profuse* (*thanks*, etc); *expansive* (*mood*) ‖ in ~en Worten *in lavish terms* | ~ [adv] reden *to gush* (über *about*) | ≗keit [f] ⟨fig⟩ *excess*; *effusion, ebullience*; *exuberance* ‖ (im Ausdruck) *gush*, ⟨Lit⟩ *high-flown style*; ⟨rhet⟩ *hyperbole* **~|schwenken** vi [s] ⟨fig⟩ *to apostatize* (*from .. to*) **~schwer** a *overheavy, too heavy* ‖ ⟨fig⟩ *very difficult* **≗schwung** m ~(e)s/≗e ⟨österr mil⟩ *uniform belt* **≗see** f ~/ *oversea*(*s*) ‖ nach ~ gehen *to go o.s.*; v ~ *from across the seas* | ~- [in comp] *oversea* (*bank, trade, orders*); ~dampfer [m] *ocean liner*; ~dienst [m] *Overseas Services* pl; ~gespräch [n] *talk over the long-distance telephone*; ~packung [f] *sea-proof packing*; ~(brief)papier [n] *foreign paper* **~seeisch** a *oversea* ‖ *transmarine* (*cable*) ‖ (Dampfer) *transoceanic* (*liner*) ‖ ~es Telegramm *cablegram* **~|segeln** vt [h] (·ansegeln) *to sail over, to run down, to run foul of a ship* **~s·egeln** vt (überh·olen) *to outsail, to beat* **~s·ehbar** a *visible at a glance, observable* ‖ die Folgen sind nicht ~ *the consequences are not to be foreseen* **≗s·ehen** n ~s/, **≗s·ehung** f ~/~en *oversight, mistake* ‖ (v Fehlern) *connivance* **~s·ehen** vt irr [h] **1.** = –blicken ‖ sich nicht ~ l, nicht zu ~ s = nicht übersehbar s ‖ die Straße gut ~ können *to have a clear view of the road* **2.** (auslassen) *to omit*; *to by-pass* **3.** (nicht sehen) *to overlook*; ~ w *to escape a p*('*s notice*); *to lose sight of*; leicht ~ w *easily to escape notice*; kann ~ w ⟨a.⟩ *cannot be noticed* **4.** (nicht beachten) *to take no notice of*; *to neglect, ignore, disregard* ‖ (Fehler) *to wink* od *connive at* ‖ *to blink* (*a fact*) ‖ man übersah sie, sie wurden ~ *they were taken no notice of* ‖ Kindern zu viel ~ *to overindulge children* | (sich etw noch einmal) **~|sehen** *to look once more over* (*one's lesson*) | sich ein Stück –ge– h *to be sick of seeing a piece, to have seen it too often* **~|sein** *to remain over* ‖ das ist mir ·über *I am weary* (od *sick* [*and tired*]) *of it* ‖ sie ist ihm ~ *she is above him*, .. darin *there she beats him* **~selig** a *overjoyed, most happy* **~s·enden** vt irr [h] *to send, forward, transmit* ‖ *enclosed I send you* .. ‖ (Waren) *to consign* ‖ (Geld) *to remit* | .. wird gesondert –sandt .. *separate cover* **≗s·endung** f ~/ *sending, conveyance, transmission, consignment, remittance* **~s·etzbar** a *translatable* **~|setzen** vi [s] [pp ~ge–tzt] *to leap over*; (über e–n Fluß) *to pass over* (*in a ferry*), *to* (*ferry a*)*cross* | vt [h] *to carry a p over* **~s·etzen** vt [h] [pp –s·etzt] **1.** *to translate, to turn* (*into French*) ‖ (dolmetschen) *to interpret* ‖ viel ~ *to do many translations* ‖ falsch ~ *to mistranslate* ‖ frei ~ *to give a free rendering* **2.** ⟨tech⟩ *to overcharge, overload* ‖ *to overcrowd, overstock* **≗s·etzer** m ~s/~ *translator*; (Dolmetscher) *interpreter* **≗s·etzung** f ~/~en *translation* (*from .. into ..*), *version* ‖ falsche ~ *misrendering* ‖ ⟨school⟩ (unerlaubte) ⟨sl⟩ *crib*; ⟨Am⟩ *pony, trot* | ⟨comp⟩ *conversion* | ⟨tech cycl⟩ *gear, ratio of gearing*; *transmission* ‖ gr (kl) ~ *top* (*bottom*) *gear*; doppelte ~ *two-speed gear*; ⟨mot⟩ langsame ~ *underdrive* **~s-** ~aufgabe [f] *translation*; *exercise*; ~fehler [m] *misrendering*; ~getriebe [n] ⟨mot⟩ *internal reduction gear*; ~programm [n] ⟨comp⟩ *translator*; *compiler* ‖ ~recht [n] *right of tr.*; ~verhältnis [n] ⟨tech⟩ *transmission-, speed-, gear-ratio* **≗sicht** f ~/~en *view, sight* ‖ (Fernblick) *prospect* | ⟨Lit, etc⟩ *survey* ‖ (Abriß) *summary, sketch*; *account, review* ‖ Nachrichten-≗ ⟨wir⟩ *headlines* pl ‖ ⟨scient⟩ *synopsis*; *synoptical tables* ‖ (Gabe) *mental vision* ‖ (Beherrschung) *control*; *over-all information* (über *about*) ‖ alle ~ verlieren *to loose all perspective*; die ~ v. ⟨a.⟩ *to be bogged down* (*by details*) **~(≗)sichtig(keit** f) a *long-sighted*(*ness*) **~sichtlich** a *visible at a glance*; *clear, distinct*; *easy to survey*; (*terrain*) *with good observation* ‖ (klar dargestellt) *well-digested, clearly arranged, perspicuous, lucid* (*exposition*) | ≗keit [f] *clearness*; *lucidity* (*of style*), *lucid arrangement* **≗sichts-** ~bemerkungen [f pl] *capsule comments*; ~karte [f] *outline map*; ⟨mil⟩ *general map*, ~ der Funkanlagen *radio facilities chart*; ~plan [m] *plan of site*; ~skizze [f] *general sketch*; ~tabelle [f] *synoptic table* **~|siedeln** vi [s] (nach) *to* (*re*)*move* (*to*) ‖ (auswandern) *to emigrate* (*to*) | vt [h] *to remove, transplant* **≗sied(e)lung** f ~/~en *removal* (nach *to*) ‖ *emigration* ‖ jds ~ nach .. durchsetzen *to get a p transferred to* .. **≗s·ied(e)lung** des Bodens *excessive density of population* **~s·ilbern** vt [h] *to silver over, to plate* **~s·ingen, sich ~** *to* *spoil one's voice* (od *to get a sore throat*) *by singing too much* **~sinnlich** a *supersensual* (*lover*) || *supernatural, transcendental, metaphysical* **~s·ommern** vi [h] *to* (*pass the*) *summer* | vt *to* (*keep through the*) *summer* **~|spannen** vt [h] [pp –gespannt] *to strain* od *stretch over* od *across* **~sp·annen** vt [h] (mit etw) *to cover .. over* (*with ..*) || *to span* (*with the hand*) || (z sehr spannen) *to overstrain, overstretch* || ⟨fig⟩ *to exaggerate; to stretch a point; to overdraw a th* | ⟨tech⟩ (Dampf) *to overheat* || ⟨fig⟩ *to overexcite* (*the mind*) || *to heat* (*the imagination*) **~sp·annt** a ⟨fig⟩ *eccentric, extravagant, wild* (*opinions*) || (P) ⟨a.⟩ *crazy, cracked; going it rather strong; high-flown; gushing* | ≂heit [f] ~/~en *overwrought state, exaltation of mind* || *excentricity, extravagance, exaggeration* **≂sp·annung** f ~/ *overstraining* || ⟨el⟩ *excess voltage* || ⟨fig⟩ *overexcitement* || *exaggeration* | ~sableiter [m] ⟨el⟩ *surge diverter* **·~|spielen** vt [h] [pp –ge–lt] *to play too often* **~sp·ielen** vt [h] (Gegner) ⟨ftb⟩ *to pass* || ⟨rec⟩ (Band) *to re-record* **~sp·ielt** a [pp] (übertrainiert) *overtrained* **~sp·innen** vt irr [h] *to spin over* || (mit Seide) *to gimp* || (Draht) *to cover* || (Knöpfe) *to coat* **~sp·itzung** f ⟨fig⟩ *overstatement* **~sp·onnen** a [pp] (Saite) *spun* **~|springen** vi irr [pp –gesprungen] [s] *to leap over, to jump across*; ⟨el⟩ (Funken) *to flash* od *dart over* || ⟨fig⟩ (P, Handlung) *to switch off* (*on to*) || (v Thema z Th.) *to flit; to run from one topic to another* | ⟨path⟩ (Sehne) *to start*; (Krankheit) *to shift* (*from .. to ..*) **~spr·ingen** vt [pp –spr·ungen] [h] *to leap* (*a ditch*); *to jump, leap over* od *across ..* || e–n (im Amt) ~ *to be put over the head of a p* | (überg·ehen) *to skip, omit, miss; to leave out* || das Fieber übersprang e–n Tag .. *discontinued for a day* | **sich** ~ *to hurt o.s. in jumping* **~|sprudeln** n [s & h] ⟨a. fig⟩ *to bubble* od *gush over* (⟨fig⟩ vor .. *with joy*; *to brim with confidence* || ~d *exuberant* (*joy, mirth*), *sparkling* (*wit*) **≂sprung(s)-** ⟨eth⟩ ~bewegung, ~geste [f] *displacement activity* **~staatlich** a *super-, supranational; cosmopolitical* (*institutions*) **≂stand** m ⟨tech⟩ *excess end* **≂stander** m = –hälter **~ständig** a *stale, flat; overripe* (*fruit, tree*), *overseasoned* (*wood*) **~stark** a *overstrong, too strong* **~|stechen** vi irr [pp –gestochen] [h] *to play a higher card,* (mit Trumpf) *to trump* | vt [pp –st·ochen]; (jdn) *to beat,* (mit Trumpf) *to overtrump* **~|stehen** vi irr [pp –gestanden] [h] *to stand out* od *over, to jut* (*out, forth*), *to project* || (Ziegel etc) *to overlap* **~st·ehen** vt irr [h] *to overcome, endure, surmount; to tide over* || *to pass* (*a test*) || *to survive* (*an accident*), *to get over* (*an illness*) || ⟨a. fig⟩ *to weather,* (⟨mar⟩ *to ride out*) (*a storm*) || ⟨fig⟩ die Krise ~ *to turn the corner* ⟨fig⟩ || er hat es (gut) –standen *he is at rest* [= *dead*], (*he stood it well*) **≂steig** m (über e–n Zaun) *stile*; → Zauntritt **~st·eigbar** a *surmountable; negotiable* (*obstacle*) **~|steigen** vi irr [s] [pp –gestiegen] *to step* od *climb over* || (Fluß) *to overflow* (*the banks*) || ~ auf *to shift to* **~st·eigen** vt irr [h] [pp –st·iegen] *to cross* od *scramble over ..* || *to scale, negotiate* (*a wall*) | ⟨fig⟩ *to surmount, overcome* (*difficulties*) || *to beggar* (*description* jede B.) || *to override* (*other desires*) || das –gt alles! *that beats all* od *the Dutch*! || (Bedarf) *to be in excess of* || (Begriffe, Erwartungen) *to exceed, surpass* || das –steigt m–e Fähigkeiten *that's beyond me, ..* Begriffe ⟨sl⟩ *this licks* od *hits me*; (jds Kräfte) *to get beyond a p* | sich ~ *to mount too high; to miss one's way* (bzw *overexert o.s.*) *in climbing* **~st·eigern** vt [h] *to raise* (*the price*) *immoderately* || *to outbid* (*a p*) **~st·eigert** a *ultra-* (*u.-fancifulness*) **≂st·eigung** f ~/ *surmounting,* etc **≂sterblichkeit** f *excess mortality* **≂stich** m ⟨cards⟩ *higher card* od *trump* **~st·immen** vt [h] ⟨parl etc⟩ *to outvote* || (Antrag) *to vote down* || ⟨mus⟩ *to tune too high* **~stolz** a *overproud* **~st·o-ßung** f ⟨geog⟩ *overgrazing* **~str·ahlen** vt [h] *to shine* od *irradiate upon* || (verdunkeln, & fig) *to outshine, eclipse* **~str·eckt** a [pp] *dilute* (*soup*), *doctored* (*wine*) **~|streichen** vt irr [pp –gestrichen] [h]; (Fett, Öl etc drauftun) *to spread .. over* || (Wand, Zimmer etc ~) *to paint* (*over*) **~str·eichen** vt irr [h] [pp –str·ichen) *to smear, brush, spread, wash, paint* (*with*) || mit Firnis ~ *to varnish* || mit Pech ~ *to pitch* || mit Schwarz *to blacken* **~|strömen** vi [s] [pp –geströmt] *to flow over; overflow* (*the banks*) | (vor) *to exult* (*with joy*); *to leap* (*with life*) || (v) *to be loud* od *gushing* (*in a p's praise*) **~str·ömen** vt [h] [pp –str·ömt] *to flood, overflow, overrun, submerge, inundate* **~strömend** a ⟨a.⟩ *abounding* (*stream, energy*) **≂ström(ungs)rohr** n *overflow-pipe* **~|studieren,** sich ~ [h] *to study too much, to overtax one's brains* | –studiert [a] *bookish* **~|stülpen** vt [h] *to put* od *tilt over* **≂stunde** f *extra hour* || [mst pl] ~n *overtime* (*hours*), (ohne Entgelt) *stretch-out* (*in work*) || ~n m *to work o.e* | ~nbezahlung [f] *o.e pay* **~|stürzen** vi [pp –gestürzt] [s] *to fall* od *topple over* || nach hinten ~ *to fall backwards* **~st·ürzen** vt [pp –st·ürzt] [h] *to overturn, upset* || *to hurry, precipitate, rush* | **sich** ~ [h] *to tumble topsy turvy, to tumble* (*right*) *over* || (über–e–a) *to fall over one another, to stumble upon each other's heels* || (Nachrichten etc = sich drängen) *to press one another* || *events precipitate themselves* || (sich übereilen) *to act precipitately* od *rashly*; vor Eifer *to fall over o.s.* || ~ Sie nichts (*or* sich nicht)! *take your time*!, *don't rush matters*!, *there is no hurry*! **~st·ürzt** a *heady, headlong, rash, precipitate*; ~e Eile *hurry-scurry* **~st·ürzung** f ~/~en *haste, rashness, precipitancy* || nur k–e ~! = –stürzen Sie nichts! ⟨a. fam⟩ *go it gently* **~süß** a *oversweet* **~t·äfeln** vt [h] *to wainscot* **~t·akelt** a ⟨mar⟩ *oversparred* **~t·äuben** vt [h] *to stun, deafen* **≂t·äubung** f ~/ *stunning, deafening* **~|taxieren** vt [h] *to over-estimate* **~teuer** a *too dear; exorbitant* **~t·euern** vt [h] *to charge too much for ..* || *to overcharge* (*a p*) **≂t·euerung** f ~/~en *overcharge* || *excessive raising of prices* **~t·ieft** a ⟨geog⟩ *overdeepened* (*valley*) **≂tischtuch** n *napkin, serviette* (*to cover the table-cloth* **~t·ölpeln** vt [h] *to overreach, gull, dupe, cheat*; ⟨fam⟩ *to take* (*a p*) *in, to come round* (*a p*); → –listen || ⟨sl⟩ *to noodle* || leicht z ~(d) *gullible* **~t·önen** vt [h] *to deafen, outring, mute, drown, kill; to roar out above* (*a sound*) ([oft pass] *to be -ed by*) **≂topf** m *flower-pot cover* **≂trag** ⟨com⟩ m ~(e)s/≂e ⟨com⟩ *carrying over, transfer, carry-forward; amount brought forward* od *carried over* || (Buchführung) *carried forward* od *over; brought forward* od *over* || ⟨comp⟩ *carry* | ~(s)– ~fehler [m] *copying error* **~tr·agbar** a **1.** = übersetzbar **2.** *transferable* (auf *to*) || ⟨com⟩ nicht ~ *non-negotiable* (*receipt*); (*the license*) *shall not be transferred* (*by the licensee*) | ≂keit [f] *communicability* **3.** ⟨path⟩ *catching* **~|tragen** vt irr [h] [pp –getragen] ⟨com⟩ *to carry over* od *forward* || *to enter* (*in another book, in the ledger*), *to transcribe* | (Kleid) *to wear .. over* (*another*) **~tr·agen** vt [pp ~] *to transfer, transmit, convey*; (Aufgabe) *depute; to settle* (*a th*) *on a p*; *to vest* (*title to a th*) *in a p* | ⟨surg⟩ (Gewebe) *to graft* (in *into*) || ⟨wir⟩ *to relay, transmit* | etw **auf** jdn ~ *to transfer, assign, convey a th to a p* || auf jds Namen ~ *to register in a p's name* || etw auf etw ~ *to transfer, enter to ..*; das Resultat läßt sich nicht auf unseren Fall ~ *.. cannot be applied to our case* | = übersetzen (**aus** Kurzschrift; **in** Lautschrift etc) *to transcribe* | | (jdm) (Amt) *to confer an office* (*upon*) || (e–e Arbeit) *to hand over* (auf *to*) || (Bewegung, Kraft, Nachricht, Talent, Titel) *to transmit* || (Besitz) *to make over, to cede* || (Besorgung e–r S) *to charge* od *commission* (*a p with a th*) || (Krankheit) *to transmit, communicate, convey* (auf *to*) || (Leitung) *to turn over* (an *to*) || (Macht) *to delegate* ([dat] *to*), *to vert* (*in*) || (Professur etc) *to appoint* (*a p to* ..) | **sich** ~ *to carry too heavy loads* || ⟨hort⟩ *to bear too much* (*fruit*) || (v Krankheiten) *to be contagious, catching, infectious*; (auf) *to attack* ..; *to be transmitted* (*to*) | ~e Bedeutung *figurative* (od *metaphorical*) *sense* **≃träger** m (v Bakterien) *vector* **≃tr·agung** f ~/~en *transport*; *transfer* ⟨a. comp⟩ || *cession, assignment* || *transcription* || ⟨comp⟩ *reproduction* || *transference* (auf *to*) || *handing over* || ⟨com⟩ *carrying over* || *translation* || ⟨comp⟩ *exchange* || ⟨wir⟩ *broadcast*(*ing*), *relay* || ⟨mach, phys, med⟩ *transmission* || ⟨surg⟩ *transplantation* (⟨a.⟩ v Herz u Niere) || ⟨psych⟩ *displacement* | **~s-** ~apparat [m] *transmitter*; ~befehl m ⟨comp⟩ *move statement*; ~brief [m] *deed of conveyance*; ~kanal [m] ⟨comp⟩ *channel*; ~papier [n] *transfer paper*; ~schraube [f] *transmission-screw*; ~urkunde [f] *conveyance*, ⟨bank etc⟩ *deed of transfer* **~trainieren** (sich ~) *to overtrain* (*o.s.*) **~tr·effbar** a *surpassable* **~tr·effen** vt irr [h] *to surpass, excel, exceed*; *outdo, conquer* (an, in *in*) || *to beat, overtop*; *outstrip, -match, -rank, -vie, -shine* (*a p*) || (gerade) *to go one better* (*than*) || (weit) *to eclipse, overshadow*; (°haushoch) ⟨fam⟩ *to beat a p hollow*, ⟨sl⟩ *to flog, to knock .. into a cocked hat*; sich selbst ~ *to outdo o.s.* || (v S) (Erwartungen) *to outdistance*; (an Alter) *to outdate* || (an Glanz) *to outshine* || (an Größe) *to top* || ⟨sport⟩ (nach Punkten) *to outpoint* || (im Laufen etc) *to outrun* etc || (im Bauen) *to outbuild* || an Reichweite ~ ⟨mil⟩ *to outrange* (um .. *by* ..) || (an Zahl) *to outnumber, to exceed* || ⟨tech⟩ *to outclass* || alles ~ ⟨sl⟩ *to take the cake*, ⟨Am⟩ *to beat the band* || das –trifft alles (Dagewesene) *this is beyond everything*, .. *beats all*; .. *the most astonishing th I have ever heard of* || er ist nicht z ~ *he is past-master* (⟨sl⟩ *a corker*), *there is no one who can beat* etc *him* **~|treiben** vi irr [s] *to flow over* **~tr·eiben** vt irr [h] (ein Pferd) *to founder, overdrive* | ⟨fig⟩ *to exaggerate* [a. abs]; [abs] gewaltig *to draw* od *pull the long bow* || *to overdo, overstate, overdraw, magnify* || ⟨fam⟩ *to pile it on, to come* od *pitch it strong*; *to cut it too fat* || ⟨sl⟩ *to talk through one's hat* || ⟨theat⟩ *to overact, overdo* (*a part*) || –b nicht! *draw it mild*; ohne z ~ *to d. it m.* **≃tr·eibung** f ~/~en *overdriving* || ⟨fig⟩ *exaggeration, excess, overstatement*; offensichtliche ~ ⟨rhet⟩ *hyperbole* || man kann ohne ~ sagen *it is no exaggeration to say* (*that*), *it is not too much to say*; ohne ~! *to draw it mild* || ⟨phot⟩ perspektivische ~ *exaggerated perspective* || ⟨Am com⟩ schwulstige ~ (Reklame) *blurb* **~|treten** vi irr [s] [pp –getreten] (zu) *to go, pass, step over* (*to*) || (Fluß) (austreten) *to overflow* || zu e–r andern Partei (Religion) ~ *to change sides* (*one's religion*) || ⟨rel⟩ (zu) *to convert* (*to*) || er trat zum Katholizismus ü. *he turned Roman Catholic* **~tr·eten** vi irr [h] [pp ~] sich [dat] den Fuß ~ *to sprain one's ankle* || ⟨fig⟩ *to exceed, transgress* || *to tresspass against*; *infringe, violate, contravene, break* (*a law*); *to act contrary to* (*an order*) **≃tr·eter(in** f) m *transgressor, trespasser* **≃tr·etung** f ~/~en *transgression, trespass, violation, infringement, contravention*; *breach* (*of law*) || sich e–r ~ schuldig m *to trespass, offend* || im ~sfall *in case of t.n* **~tr·ieben** a [pp v übertr·eiben] *excessive, exaggerated, disproportionate, vaulting* || *immoderate* || *exorbitant* (*price*) || *extreme* (*views*) || *extravagant* (*notions*) || übertr·iebene alte Damen *fussy old ladies* || *unreasonable* (*demands*) | es ist nicht ~ z sagen *it is no exaggeration* (od *not too much*) *to say* (*that*) || aus ~em Eifer *through excessive zeal* || in ~em Maße ⟨a.⟩ *freely* | [adv] ⟨a.⟩ *painfully* (*modern*), *hyper-* .. (*h.-critical*); ~ genau *finicky*; ~ gekleidet etc *overdressed*, etc | ~heit [f] *extravagance*; ~ streng gegen *too hard* (*up*)*on* (*a p*) **≃tritt** m *going over* (*to*) || *change* (*of religion*), *conversion* (zu *to*) **~tr·umpfen** vt [h] *to overtrump* || ⟨fig⟩ *to outvie, surpass, outdo, outwit*; *to score off* (*one's friends*) **~t·ünchen** *to whitewash* | ⟨fig⟩ *to gloss over, to varnish* || *to veil* (*the truth*) **~t·üncht** ⟨a.⟩ *sham*(*-politeness*) **~t·ürmen** vt [h] *to surmount* (*with*) **≃- u Untersetzung(sverhältnis** n) f *direct drive and reduction ratio* **≃verdichter** m ⟨mot⟩ *supercharger* **≃verdienst** m *extra profit* **≃vergrößerung** f ⟨phot⟩ *supersize blowup* **~|versichern** vt [h] *to overinsure* **~v·ölkern** vt [h] *to overpopulate* || (Wohnungen) *to overcrowd* | –rt *congested* (*district*) **≃völkerung** f *overpopulation* || *congestion of population* (od *of numbers*) **~v·oll** a *overfull, chockfull, brimful*, (Raum) *overcrowded* **~v·orteilen** vt [h] *to overreach, defraud, circumvent, cheat* || *to impose upon* || ⟨fam⟩ *to take in, to best*; ⟨Am⟩ *to sting*, ⟨sl⟩ *hornswoggle* **≃v·orteilung** f ~/~en *imposition, overreaching*; ⟨fam⟩ *take-in* **~w·achen** vt [h] *to watch over* (⟨Am a.⟩ *after*); *to superintend, supervise, overlook, police* || *to monitor* ⟨a. mil & telph⟩; (Feind) *to keep under observation*, scharf ~ *to watch narrowly* || (v Detektiv) *to shadow* || (Druck) *to see .. through the press* || **≃w·achung** f ~/ *watching over, superintendence*, (*police*) *surveillance*; *control* (*refugee c.*) || scharfe ~ *close supervision, observation* | **~s-** ~anlage [f] *monitor*(*ing device* od *equipment*); ~ausschuß m ⟨Am pol⟩ *watchdog committee* ~bestimmungen [f pl] *supervisory regulations*; ~gebiet [n] *area of control*; ~system [n]: gegenseitiges ~ (der Regierungsorgane) ⟨Am pol⟩ *system of checks and balance* **~w·achsen** vt irr [h] *overgrow* | ~ [a] [pp] *clad* (mit *in*), *overrun* (*with*) | **sich** ~ *to outgrow one's strength* **~|wallen** vi [s] *to run, simmer, boil, gush over* || ⟨fig⟩ *to be seething with passion* **~w·ältigen** vt [h] *to overcome, -whelm, -master, -power, subdue*; ⟨mil⟩ *take* (*post*); ⟨fam⟩ *floor*; *to swamp* (*a p*[*'s emotions*]) **~w·ältigend** a ⟨fig⟩ *overwhelming*; *crushing*; *imposing* (*scene*), *sweeping* (*attack*); *staggering, shattering*, ⟨fam⟩ *killing* (*effect*); *overpowering* (*elegance*) **≃w·ältiger** m ~s/~ *vanquisher, subduer* **~|walzen** vt [h] *to smooth with a roller* **≃w·asser-** ~schiff [n] *surface ship*, ~e [pl] *s. force*; (Schiffsteil) *top sides*; ~stoßrohr [n] *above water tube*; ~streitkräfte [f pl] *surface craft* od *forces* **~w·eise** a *overwise* **~w·eisen** vt irr [h] *to assign, transfer* (⟨bes a.⟩ v Konto z K.) (*to the credit of a p*), *to pass* (v *from*, auf *to*); (e–m Gericht) *to commit for trial* || (höherer Stelle zur Entscheidung) *to refer, remit* ([dat] *or* an [acc] *to*) || ⟨mil⟩ Truppen ~ *to transfer* N || ⟨parl⟩ (an e–e Kommission) *to devolve upon, to transfer to* || (e–s Verbrechens) *to convict* (*of*) || *to prove guilty* (*of*) || s–s Irrtums *to convince a p of his error* **≃w·eisung** f ~/~en *assignment* || (Besitz) *transfer* || (urkundliche) *conveyance* || (Summe) ⟨bank⟩ *remittance* || (zur Entscheidung) *reference, remitting* || ⟨parl⟩ *devolution* || telegraphische ~ *telegraphic* (bzw *cable*) *transfer* | ~s-auftrag [m] ⟨com⟩ *credit-note* **~|weißen** vt [h] *to whitewash* **~w·endlich** a *overcast* (od *whipstitch*) (*seam*) || [adv] ~ nähen *to oversew, whip* **~|werfen** vt irr [h] [pp –geworfen] *to throw over* || (Kleid) *to slip* od *cast on* || **sich ~w·erfen** [pp –w·orfen] mit jdm *to fall out, quarrel, break with a p*; *to fall foul of a p* || sich mit jdm –worfen h *to be out with a p* **≃w·erfung** f ~/ ⟨fig⟩ *quarrel* **≃wert** m ~(e)s/ *surplus* od *excess value* **~w·erten** vt [h] *to rate* (*coins*) *at more than their face value* **~wertig** a *standing* od *quoted above par*; *superior* **~wichtig** a *too heavy* || ⟨fig⟩ *most important* **~w·ickeln** vt [h] *to envelop*; *to wrap up* **≃w·ick(e)lung** f ~/~en *wrapping up* **~w·iegen** vt irr [h] *to outweigh*; *to be in excess of* | vi irr [h] *to prevail, preponderate, predominate* (*over*) | ≃ [n] ~s/

preponderance | ~d [a] *paramount, preponderant; predominant* ‖ *prevailing* ‖ (erdrückend) *overwhelming, crushing, vast* (*majority*) **~w·indbar** a *conquerable* ‖ ⟨fig⟩ *superable, surmountable* **~w·inden I.** vt irr [h] *to traverse* (*obstacles*) ‖ *to overcome, conquer, vanquish, overpower, subdue* ‖ Schwierigkeiten ~ *to turn the corner* ⟨fig⟩ ‖ ⟨fig⟩ *to surmount, override* (*obstacles*) ‖ alle ~ *to put all behind one* ‖ (Widerwillen) *to shake off* ‖ (Gefühl) *to live down* ‖ (Krankheit) *to throw off* ‖ (Triebe) *to control, conquer* ‖ (Krise) *to master* ‖ das Schlimmste e–r S ~ *to break the back* od *neck of a th* ‖ **sich** ~ *to overcome o.s., to prevail upon o.s., to bring o.s.* (*to do*) ‖ sich z ~ suchen *to make an effort over o.s.* ‖ ich konnte mich nicht ~ zu reden *I could not find it in my heart to speak* **II.** ≗ [n] ⟨mil⟩ *passage* (*of obstacles*) **≗w·inder** m ~s/~ *conqueror, vanquisher* **~w·indlich** a = –w·indbar **≗windung** f ~/ *conquest* (*of selfish instincts; of time and space*); *overcoming* ‖ *passage* (*of an obstacle*) ‖ (Anstrengung) *self-command, struggle, effort* (*it cost him a great effort to do it*) ‖ *self-restraint, -control* (*it requires great s.-r.* od *s.-c. to do it*) ‖ (Widerstreben) *reluctance* (*he did it with r.*) **~w·intern** vi [h] *to* (*pass the*) *winter* ‖ ⟨bot⟩ *to last through the w.* ‖ ⟨zoo⟩ *to hibernate* ‖ (Auto) *to winterize* **≗w·interung** f ~/ *wintering, hibernation* **~w·ölben** vt [h] ⟨arch⟩ *to vault* od *to arch over, to overarch* **~w·ölbt** a *vaulted, arched* **~w·ölken** vt [h] *to overcast* ‖ sich ~ *to grow cloudy* **~w·ölkt** a *overcast, cloudy* **~w·uchern** vt [h] *to overrun, -grow* **~w·unden** a [pp v –w·inden] (*the crisis is*) *over*; etw ~ h *to be clear of a th* ‖ ~er Standpunkt m ⟨fam⟩ *exploded idea, obsolete custom* **≗wurf** m ~s/≗e *wrap, shawl* ‖ (Kittel) *overall(s* pl ⟨Am⟩) ‖ ⟨österr⟩ (Zierdecke) *ornamental covering* | ≗mutter [f] ⟨tech⟩ *screw--cap* **≗zahl** f ~/ *majority; numerical superiority, superior number(s* pl) ‖ ⟨mil⟩ *superior forces* ‖ gr ~ *heavy odds* pl ‖ in ~ *outnumbered* **~z·ählen** vt [h] *to count .. over* **~zählig** a *redundant* (*workmen*); *supernumerary; odd* (*shillings, pence*) ‖ ~es Geld *m. left over* ‖ ~e Menge *overage* ‖ ~er Schauspieler *supernumerary*, ⟨fam⟩ *super* | ≗keit [f] ~/ *supernumerariness* **≗zahn** m ~(e)s/≗e *projecting tooth* **~z·art** a *overdelicate* **~z·eichnen** vt [h] ⟨com⟩ *to oversubscribe* | ≗ n ~s/ *o.scription* **~zeitig** a *overripe* **~zeitlich** a *supertemporal* **~z·eugen** vi/t [h] **1.** vi *to carry conviction* **2.** vt [h] [gen] *to convince, persuade* (*of*), *to satisfy* (*as to*) (*I am not satisfied that ..*) ‖ *I am firmly* (fest) *convinced; I am sure* (*he will come*) ‖ ⟨parl⟩ *to carry* (*the House*) ‖ jdn v etw ~ *to bring a th home to a p*; v Gegenteil *to disconvince a p, to persuade a p to the contrary*; v der Nutzlosigkeit e–r S *to talk a p out of a th* ‖ jdn v etw z ~ suchen *to argue with a p*; .. mit Erfolg *to argue a p into ..* | **sich** ~ *to satisfy o.s.*; durch Augenschein *to ascertain by evidence*; ~ Sie sich selbst! *see* od *look for y.s.!* ‖ *I saw it with my own eyes* ‖ sich ~ l *to be open to conviction* | ~d [a] *convincing*, (zwingend) *cogent, conclusive* ‖ *compelling, forcible* (*speaker*) ‖ ~ s *to carry conviction* | [adv] (*to describe*) *persuasively*, (*to prove*) *conclusively* **~z·eugt** a *confident* (*that*); ~er Demokrat *man of democratic conviction*, → eingefleischt ‖ seien Sie (davon) ~! *I assure you!* ‖ fest ~ s *to be quite positive, to have every confidence* (*that*) ‖ v e–r S ~ s *to be* od *feel sure of a th*, ~ s, daß .. *that*; **≗z·eugung** f ~/~en *conviction, belief, satisfaction* ‖ (Überredung) *persuasion* ‖ (Grundsätze) *principles* ‖ über etw zu k–r ehrlichen ~ k können *not to be able to assure o.s. honestly of a th* ‖ jdm die sichere ~ geben *to assure a p* ‖ es ist m–e feste ~, ich bin der festen ~ *I am* od *feel thoroughly convinced* (*that; of it*) ‖ aus ~ *by c.n* ‖ f s–e ~ einstehen *to demonstrate the courage of one's c.n* ‖ gegen s–e ~ (*to act*) *contrary to one's c.ns* ‖ nach jds bester ~ *to the best of a p's belief, to a p's best b.* ‖ v der ~ durchdrungen *imbued with the c.n* (*that*) ‖ z der ~ k, die ~ gewinnen *to come to the conclusion* od *opinion* (*that*), *to decide* (*that*) ‖ jdn v s–r ~ abbringen *to unconvince a p* | ~skraft [f] *cogency*; (*there is much force in the argument*), *persuasive* od *convincing power* od *force; persuasiveness* **~zieh-** ~hose [f] (lederne) ⟨Am⟩ *chaps* pl; ~jacke [f] mit (kurzen) Ärmeln *slip-over* **~z·iehen** vt irr [h] (⟨a.⟩ sich ~) [pp –z·ogen] *to cover, coat, overlay, -spread*, (Schiff) *sheathe* (*with*) ‖ (v Licht, Farbe) *to suffuse* (*a face*) | ein Bett ~ *to put fresh linen on* od *to sheet a bed*; ein frisch –z·ogenes B. *a bed with fr. l.* ‖ (Flugzeug) *to stall, overclimb, -zoom* ‖ (Konto) *to overdraw* (um *by*) ‖ ein Land mit Krieg ~ *to invade a country* ‖ (Sofa) *to cover* ‖ mit Fett, Gips, Tapeten, Zucker *to grease, plaster, paper, ice* ‖ ⟨cul⟩ *to mask, coat* ‖ –z·ogen *coated, caked* (*with filth*), *filmed* (*with dust*) | **es -zieht sich** (mit Wolken) *it looks lowery* **~|ziehen** vt irr [h] [pp –gezogen] *to slip, pull, put on* od *over* ‖ *to draw* od *pull to the other side* | ⟨fam⟩ jdm eins ~ *to give a p a cut* od *blow with a stick*; jdn ~ *to flog a p* | vi [s] *to move* od *pass over* ‖ (in ein neues Haus) ~ *to* (*re*)*move* (*to*) od (*to shift into ..*) **≗zieher** m ~s/~ *overcoat, great-coat* ‖ langer ~ *ulster* ‖ Sommer≗ *summer overcoat, dust--coat* | ⟨sex⟩ *johnny* **≗zieh-** ~geschwindigkeit [f] ⟨aero⟩ *stalling speed*; ~hose [f] (e–e *a pair of*) *overalls* pl; ~jacke [f] *loose j.; slip-over*; ~socken [f pl] *golf socks* **~z·innen** vt [h] *to tin over* **~z·ogen** a (Summe) ⟨bank⟩ *overdrawal* ‖ frisch ~es Bett *bed with fresh sheets* ‖ °er ist sehr v sich °~ (statt –zeugt) *he thinks a lot of h.s.* **~z·uckern** vt [h] *to sugar over* ‖ *to candy* (*fruit*) ‖ *to ice* (*cakes*) ‖ ⟨fig⟩ *to gild* (*a pill*) | ≗ [n] *candying, icing* **~zuckert** a *sugar-coated* (*pill*) ⟨a. fig⟩ **≗zug** m *case, cover(let), coat(ing)* ‖ *plating* ‖ leichter, dünner *fluff, down, film* ‖ ⟨el-met⟩ *electro-plating* ‖ ⟨min⟩ *crust* ‖ (der Zunge) *fur* ‖ gewebter, gewirkter Möbel≗ etc *tapestry*; (Bett≗) *bedtick, case* | ≗hülle [f] ⟨aero⟩ *balloon envelope*; ~papier [n] *colo(u)red paper* **~zw·erch** [adv] *across, athwart, crosswise* | [a] ⟨fam⟩ *crazy*

Ubikati·on [–ts–] f ~/ ⟨österr mil⟩ *barracks*

·üblich a *usual; customary* (*it is c. to do*); *accustomed* ‖ *conventional* ⟨a. tech, mil⟩ ‖ *routine, normal, ordinary* (*operations*) ‖ *prevailing* (*custom*) ‖ *common* (*expression*); *accepted* (*sense*); *normal* (*term*); (Redensart) *much used .., .. in general use* ‖ allg. ~ *standard*, ⟨Am a.⟩ *stated* ‖ nicht mehr ~ *out of use; obsolete* ‖ es ist ~, daß jd tut *it is customary for a p to do* ‖ wie es ~ war *as was the custom* ‖ weil es so ~ ist *as a matter of routine* | **≗keit** f ~/ *customariness*

·übrig a **1.** [pred] *left* (*over*) **2.** [attr] *remaining* ‖ *odd* (*pence*) ‖ *spare* (*cash, time*) ‖ *my other money* ‖ im ~en England *in the rest of E.* ‖ die ~en 6 *the odd six* | (überflüssig) [attr] *superfluous*; [pred] (*your remarks are*) *out of place* **3. die ~en** [pl] *the others, the rest* pl; (T) *the remainder* ‖ **das ~e** *the remnant, remainder*, ⟨scient⟩ *residue* ‖ **ein ~es** tun *to do more than necessary; to strain* od *stretch a point; to go out of one's way* (*to do; for*); *to make an exception* ‖ **~ bleiben** *or* s *to be left* (*over*), *to remain* ‖ es bleibt mir ~ z tun *it remains for me to do* ‖ *all that was left to him was .., nothing was left to him but this pearl; .. for him but to advance* ‖ es bleibt (uns) nichts anderes ~ als z w. (etc) *there is nothing for it but to wait,* (*we have no option but to utilize ..*); *there is only one th* (*for us*) *to do and this is to .., we have no choice but to ..* | unpaarig –geblieben *odd* | **~ haben** *to have left* od *remaining*

|| k–e Zeit ~ h f *to have no time to spare for ..* | ⟨fig⟩ etw ~ h f *to care for* od *about* | ⟨fig⟩ nichts ~ h f *to have no use for* (*tennis, the country*); *they do not go in much for ..*; *to have no good word for* (*this country*); *they don't think much of him*; .. f e–a *there's no love lost between them* | viel ~ h f *to have a soft place* od *sore spot in one's heart for* || ~ **lassen** *to leave, spare* || ~ s = ~ bleiben || **im übrigen** = **übrigens** [adv] *after all*; *anyway* (*what's happened to you, anyway?*) || (*as*) *for the rest* || (außerdem) *besides, moreover* || (beiläufig) *by the way, by the bye* || (indessen) *however* || (oft Satzanfang) *as a matter of fact*

·Übung f ~/~en **A.** *exercise, exercising*; *practice*; *practising* (*on the piano*) | ⟨sport fam⟩ *workout* | ⟨mil⟩ *drill(ing), discipline, training*; *manœuvres* | (Gewohnheit) *use, custom* | (~s-stück) ⟨mus⟩ *exercise, study*; ⟨school⟩ *lesson* | (*bodily*) *exercise* || (*mental*) *gymnastic* || (*daily*) *routine, experience* | ⟨univ⟩ ~en *classes* pl **B.** er hat k–e ~ mehr im F.sprechen *his French has become rusty* || ⟨prov⟩ ~ macht den Meister *practice makes perfect* **C. aus** der ~ s *to be out of practice* || außer ~ s *to be out of fashion, to have fallen into disuse* | **durch** bloße ~ ⟨a.⟩ *by rote* | **in** ~ bringen *to put in practice* || in ~ bleiben, sich in ~ erhalten *to keep in training*, ⟨fam⟩ *to keep one's hand in* || gut in ~ s *to be in form* | **~s-** ⟨oft mil⟩ *training* | e–n **~angriff** m *to simulate an attack* **~aufgabe** f *exercise* **~bälle** m pl ⟨ten⟩ *hit-up* **~beginn** m *beginning of the exercise* **~bombe** f *t.g bomb* **~buch** n (*printed*) *schoolbook* (*containing e.es*) **~flug** m ⟨aero⟩ *practice-flight* **~flugzeug** n *trainer* **~gelände** n *t.g* od *e.e, manœuvre area* **~gerät** n ⟨mil⟩ *simulator, trainer* **~geschwader** n ⟨mar⟩ *manœuvring squadron* **~gewehr** n *drill rifle* **~hang** m ⟨ski⟩ *p.ce slope* **~heft** n *e.e book* **~ladung** f ⟨mil⟩ *reduced charge* **~lager** n *t.g-camp* **~leitung** f ⟨mil⟩ *e.e directing staff* **~marsch** m ⟨mil⟩ *route-march* **~munition** f *blank ammunition* **~platz** m ⟨mil⟩ *drill-ground* **~spiel** n ⟨sport⟩ *trial-match* **~schießen** n *musketry* od *rifle* bzw *artillery* od *gunnery practice* **~stück** n *exercise*

U·ckermark f ⟨Ger⟩ *U(c)kermark*

·Ufer n ~s/~ (Fluß~̂) *bank*; Gleit~̂ (Prall~̂) *slip-off* (*undercut*) *slope of a river* || (See~̂) *shore* || (Meeres~̂) *shore, beach* || steiles Fels~̂ *bluff* || am ~, ans ~ *ashore* || an den ~n des Nils *on the banks of ..* || am ~ gelegen *by the riverside* od *seaside* **~anlieger, ~anrainer** m *frontager*; *riparian owner* **~bahn** f *railway along a river's banks* od *a seashore* **~bauten** m pl *embankment*; *sea-walls* **~bewohner** m *coast-dweller, coaster* **~bezirk** m *waterfront*; *riparian* od *coastal district* **~damm** m *quay* || (⟨Am⟩ Fluß~̂ a.) *levee* **~fliege** f *stone-fly* **~front** f, **~gelände** n *frontage of a river, riparian lands* **~geld** n *pierage* **~land** n *littoral*; (salzreiches) *salting* **~̂los** a *shoreless* | ⟨fig⟩ *endless* (*discussion*), *boundless* (*ambition*), *extravagant* (*plans*), *wild* (*schemes*), *adventurous* (*policy*) || ins ~̂lose steigen *to become too much of a good th* **~mauer** f *seawall* || *embankment* **~recht** n *riparian right* **~schnepfe** f ⟨orn⟩ (*black-tailed*) *godwit* **~schwalbe** f ⟨orn⟩ *sand-martin* **~staat** m *riparian state*

uff! [intj] *ugh*!

Uff·izien [pl] (in Florenz) *Uffizi Gallery*

°**Uffz(ier)** m ~(e)s/~e ⟨mil⟩ → Unteroffizier

·Ufo n ~s/~s („Fliegende Untertasse") *unidentified flying object*

Ug·anda n (Republik in Zentralafrika) || †⟨brit⟩ ~-Protektor·at [n] *Uganda Protectorate*

·ugrisch a *Ugrian*; → Ungarn, finnisch

uh! [intj] (staunend) *oh*! ⟨Am⟩ *gee*! || (erschreckt) *ugh*!

Uhr f ~/~en (kl) *watch*; ⟨sl⟩ *ticker* || (gr) *clock* **A.** Armband~̂ *wrist watch* || Eier~̂ *egg-timer* || elektrische ~ *quartz c., impulse driven c.* || Sand~̂ *sand-glass* || Spiel~̂ *musical box* || Stech~̂ *check-clock* || Stutz~̂ *timepiece, mantel clock* || Taschen~̂ *watch* || Taxi~̂, Turm~̂ (Wand~̂) *clock* (*hanging at the wall*) || Wasser~̂ *watermeter* || Weck~̂ *alarm clock* **B.** s–e ~ ist **abgelaufen** *his clock has run down*, ⟨fig⟩ *his sands have run out* || die ~en gehen gleich .. *synchronize*; m–e ~ geht nach/vor *my w. is slow/fast*, ⟨a.⟩ *I'm fast*; gleichgehend *synchronous* || die ~ geht gut .. *is a good goer*, .. *keeps good time* || e–e ~ stellen *to set a watch, to regulate a timepiece* (nach *by*) **C.** [nur sg] (Stunde, Zeit) *hour, time* (*of the day*) | **wieviel** ~ ist es? ⟨fam⟩ was ist die ~ *what is the time* || können Sie mir sagen, wieviel ~ es ist? *can you tell me the time*? || ⟨fam⟩ wieviel ~ h Sie? *what time do you make it*? || es ist 5 ~, halb 6 ~ *it is five o'clock, half past five* || *it was half-an-hour from twelve when ..* || v 4–1/₂5 *from 4 to half-past* **D.** wie **nach** der ~ *like clockwork* || ein Mann nach der ~ *a punctual man* || nach der ~ arbeiten *to work against time* || nach der ~ fragen *to ask the time* || nach s–r ~ sehen *to look at one's w.* || *it was 6*²⁰ (*at*), *by*, (*on*) (nach [dat]) *his w.* | **um** wieviel ~? *at what o'clock*? *at five o'clock* || der um 2 ~, 2 ~ 30 (2³⁰) abfahrende, ankommende Zug *the two o'clock*, (*two-thirty*) *train* || um 20 ~ 30 ⟨mil⟩ *at twenty thirty hours* | v 8²⁰ bis 14²⁰ *from 0820* [*ou eight hundred and twenty*] *to 1420 hours* **~armband** n *watch strap* **~band** n *w.-guard* **~deckel** m *outer case of a w.* **~feder** f *w.-spring, mainspring* **~futteral** n *w.-case* **~gehänge** n *w.-trinkets* pl **~gehäuse** n *clock-case* **~getriebe** n *pinion of a w.* **~gewicht** n *c.-weight* **~glas** n *w.-glass*, ⟨Am a.⟩ *crystal* **~glocke** f *glass shade over a c.* **~haken** m *w.-hook* **~halter** m *w.-stand* **~kapsel** f *w.-case* **~karte** f *job card* **~kasten** m *c.-case* **~kette** f *w.-chain*; Frack~̂ mit Anhänger ⟨Am⟩ *fob* **~macher** m *c.-, w.maker* || °⟨aero⟩ (schlechter Flieger) *flatspin* (od *ham*) *pilot* | ~kunst [f] *c.making* **~schlüssel** m *w.-key* **~schrank** m *c.-case* **~tasche** f *fob* **~werk** n *c.work, works* pl, *movement*; mit der Regelmäßigkeit e–s ~s *with c.w. regularity, like c.w.* | ~zünder [m] *c.-w. fuse* **~zeiger** m *hand, finger* (*of a w.* od *c.*) || den ~ zurückdrehen *to turn back the clock* ⟨a. fig⟩ || im (entgegengesetzten) Sinne des ~s (*counter-*)*clockwise* **~envergleich** m *synchronization of w.es*

·Uhu m ~s/~e ⟨orn⟩ *horn-, eagle-owl* (*hoots*)

u·k-gestellt [u'ka:–] a (unabkömmlich ..) *in reserved occupation*

·Ukas m –ses/–se *ukase*

·Ukelei m ~s/ ⟨ich⟩ *bleak*

Ukr·aine f ⟨Russ⟩ die ~ *the Ukraine* **ukr·ainisch** a *Ukrainian*

UKW- [uka'we:] (Ultra-Kurzwelle[n]) ~-Drehfunkfeuer [n] *very high frequency omnidirectional radio range* N; ~-Peilfunkstelle [f] *v. h. f. direction finding station*

Ul·an m ~en/~en ⟨mil⟩ *uhlan, lancer* **~enattacke** f *charge of a body of l.s* **~ka** [–ŋk–] f ~/~s *l.'s tunic*

Ulk m ~(e)s/~e *fun, practical joke* || ⟨fam⟩ *spree, lark* || ⟨sl⟩ *gag, wheeze* || ~ m *to skylark* || ~ treiben mit *to make fun of* **~bild** n *caricature* | **~er·ei** f ~/~en *skylarking* **·ulken** vi [h] *to play practical jokes*; *to lark, joke, fool*; *to be on the spree* **·ulkig** a *funny, droll, amusing*; sehr ~ *screaming, side-splitting* || es war recht ~ *it was great fun*

Ulm n ⟨Ger⟩ (Stadt)

·Ulme f ~/~n ⟨bot⟩ *elm*(*-tree*) | **~̂n** a (*made of*) *elm*(*-wood*) | ~nkrankheit [f] *elm disease*; ~n-splintkäfer [m] *elm bark beetle*; ~nwäldchen [n] *elm-grove*

·Ulster m ~s/~ (~mantel) *ulster*

Ultim·atum n [~s/~s & –ta] *ultimatum* (an

to) || jdm ein ~ stellen *to deliver* od *issue an u. to a p*

·**ultimo** [adv] *on the last day of the month* | ≃ m [~s/~s & –mi] ⟨com⟩ *last day* od *end of the month* || ~ Mai *end* (od *last day*) *of May* || per ~ *for the monthly settlement* **~abschluß** m *m. s.* **~geschäft** n *business done for the m. s.* **~regulierung** f *m. clearance*

·**Ultra** m ~/~ *extremist* ≃**h·och** a *ultra high (frequency)* ≃**konservativ** a *extreme conservative* | ≃**e(r)** m ⟨pol fam⟩ *stick-in-the-mud* **~kurz**~photographie [f] *ultrahigh-speed ph.y*; ~welle [f] ⟨wir⟩ → *microwave* || ~n- (UKW, → o.) ≃**liberal** a *ultra-liberal* **~linke** f *e.e left* **~mar·in** n ~(e)s/ *u.-marine* ≃**mod·ern** a *the last word* od *cry in* ≃**mont·an** a *u.montane*; ~e Partei *extreme Roman-Catholic party* **~mont·ane(r)** m *u.montanist* ≃**rotdurchlässig** a *transparent to infra-red* **~schall** m *ultrasonics* | ~bohrer [m] ⟨dent⟩ *carvitron*; ~frequenz [f] *supersonic fr.y* ≃**schallen** vi/t [h] ⟨phys⟩ *to sonicate* **~viol·ett** n *ultra violet* (⟨Am⟩ *u.v.*) | ≃es Licht ⟨theat⟩ *black light* **~vi·olglas** n *vita glass*

ulzer·ös a ⟨path⟩ *ulcerous* | ~-kavernös [a] *ulcero-cavernous*

um I. prep [acc] **A. 1.** (örtlich) *(a)round, (r.) about* **a)** die ~ ihn (her[um]) *those (a)r. him* || *I put my arm r. her* || (⟨Am⟩ *a)r. the corner* || *the wind blew ar. the walls* || *sitting r. the fire* || *the galleries r. the pit* || sich drehen ~ *to turn* od *revolve r. (a th)*; ⟨fig⟩ es dreht sich alles ~ ihn *everything depends on him* **b)** (unbestimmter) *about* || *they were seated a. a table* || *a smile played a. her lips* || *he looked a. him* (~ sich) || ~ sich schlagen *to lay a. one* || *the dead were still a. her* || er ist immer ~ sie *he is always (hanging) a. her* || .. wie mir **ums** Herz ist .. *how (sad* etc) *I feel* | ein **ums** andere Mal *over and o. (again)* **c)** (ungefähr) *about 20 yards* **2.** (zeitlich) *about what time?* || *a., near, towards 5 o'clock, the fifth hour* (Stunde), *midnight*; ⟨Am⟩ *ar. 5 o'clock*; so ~ 6° *(ring me up) about 6* || *r. about the beginning of May* | (genau) *at what time?*; *at 5 o'clock* **B.** (**Betrag,** Unterschied, Abstand) ~ e–n Kopf größer *a head taller, taller by a head* || *older by 2 years, 2 years older* || ~ ein bedeutendes besser *considerably* (od *a great deal*) *better* || ~ die Hälfte mehr *half as much again*; .. verkleinern *to lessen by one-half* || sich ~ 10 M verrechnen *to make a mistake of 10 marks, to be 10 marks out* od *wrong* | es kostet nur (⟨österr⟩ um) wenig mehr *it doesn't c. much more* | ~ **so** *or* **desto** mehr *all the more* || *her love grew the stronger* || ~ so mehr, **da** *or* **als** .. *the more so as, particularly as* od *since* || ~ so anziehender *all the more attractive* || ~ so besser (schlimmer) *all* (od *so much*) *the better (worse; worse luck!)* || ~ so mehr (so), wenn *doubly so, if* || ~ so weniger dürfen Sie es tun *so much less reason for your doing it* || ~ **wieviel** mehr ..! *how much more (is he to be envied)!* **C.** [**a)** Abwechslung, **b)** Aufeinanderfolge] e–n ~ den anderen: **a)** *alternately (with), by turns* || Jahr ~ J.; ein J. ~ das andere **a)** *every other year*; **b)** *y. by y., every y., one y. after the other* || Familie ~ F. *family after f.* **D.** (**Preis,** Lohn) *(in exchange) for* || *(to buy* od *sell) for* || *to work for money* od *wages* (Lohn) || ~ jeden Preis *at any cost* od ⟨fig⟩ *rate* || ~ ein billiges *at a moderate price* || nicht ~ alles in der Welt *not for all the w.*; ⟨sl⟩ *not for nuts* || Aug' ~ Auge *an eye for an eye* || ~ nichts (u wieder nichts) *for nothing* **E. um** e–r S, jds **willen** (*or* **wegen**) *for the sake of a p, a th; in a p's name* || ~ Gottes etc willen *for God's, Heaven's, mercy's sake!* || (was tut man nicht) ~ des [lieben] Friedens willen? *for peace's sake*; *(anything for peace [and quietness]!)* **F.** (**Ursache,** Betreff, Zweck) *for*; *because of*; *on account of*; *about* || *to like a p for his considerateness* | sich **ängstigen** ~ *to be anxious about ..* || ~ etw bitten, schreiben *to ask, write for* || e–n ~s Leben bringen *to kill a p* || es ist ~ mich geschehen *I'm done for* || (Verlust) ~ etw **k** *to lose sth*; ums Leben k *to perish* || es **ist** doch ein wundersam Ding ~ die Liebe *there is sth wonderful about* od *in love*; *surely Love is a wonderful th* || es ist e–e ernste S ~ den Tod *it is a serious th to die* || (es ist) schade ~ ihn! *what a pity he should have gone wrong!* || schade ums Geld! *it's a pity for the m. (spent)!* || es ist ihm ~ nichts anderes z tun *this is all he cares for* || es sieht schlecht ~ ihn aus *he is in a bad way* || wie **steht** es ~ die S? *what about it?*, *how are ths going on?* || wie steht es ~ ihn *how is he (getting on)?* || ~ etw **wissen** *to know about a th, to be informed of a th* **II. conj. 1.** je mehr er hat, ~ **so** (*or* ~ desto) mehr will er h *the more he has, the more he wants* || **2. um** .. **zu** .. [inf] *(in order) to (do)* || *to see if* .., *(we must find out ..)* || *to have this (one had to be rich)* || *(we stood up) to go* || *to be exact I must add ..* || *(he has not enough) to live upon* || um nur ja nicht reden z müssen *for fear of having to talk* | *(he went there) with a view to* (od *with the view of*) *studying* || *(this was his first step) towards bringing them together* || *(he said it) by way of excuse* od *by way of breaking the ice* | sie ist **zu** scheu, **um** es **zu** sagen *she is too shy to say it* **III.** [adv] **1. um sein a)** (räumlich) dieser Weg ist (weit) ~ *this is a (very) round about way* **b)** (zeitlich) *finished, expired, out, up, past, gone* || *(my) time is up* || *his time* (od *the year*) *had expired* || *the week is past* | ⟨dial⟩ es ist ~ *the full hour has struck* **2. um u um** *all round about, on* od *from all sides*; *(from) everywhere* || *entirely* || *(to turn a th) over and over* od *inside out* **3.** [ell] ~ **mit** dem Baum! *down with that tree!* | **rechts** ~! *right turn!* **IV.** ≃ [n] das ~ u Auf der S *the core of the matter* ·**um-** [in comp] **1.** (haupttonig) [sep]: ~|arbeiten, ~|drehen, ~|fallen, ~|füllen, ~|legen, ~|pflügen || ~|fassen *to reset* || ~|flechten *to plait again* [pp –ge–] **2.** (nicht haupttonig) [insep]: ~fl·iegen [pp –fl·ogen], ~g·ehen, ~sch·iffen, ~st·ehen **~|ackern** vt [h] *to plough up* || (Unkraut) *to plough down* | ⟨fig⟩ fam⟩ *to stir up, to turn over and over* **~|adressieren** vt [h] *to redirect* **~ad·um-** österr [in comp] = herum (z. B. ~ liegen) **~an·and** österr [in comp] = umher (z. B. ~ liegen) **~|ändern** vt [h] *to change, alter* || *rearrange* || *transform*; ⟨fam⟩ *revamp* || ⟨Lit⟩ *to revise* ≃**änderung** f *change*, etc **~|arbeiten** vt [h] *to recast, remodel, revamp*; *to make a th over* [adv]; (Haus) *recondition*, (Hut, Kleid) *refashion, alter*, (Schriften) *rewrite, revise*, (Boden) *to turn up* ≃**arbeitung** f ~/~en *recast, revision*, etc **~·armen** vt [h] *to clasp .. in one's arms* || *to throw one's arms round a p* || (⟨a.⟩ sich ~) *to embrace, hug*, ⟨Am sl⟩ *to neck* **~·armung** f ~/~en *embrace, hug(ging)* || ⟨sex⟩ *close hug* od *kiss* ≃**bau** m *reconstruction* (im ~ *under r.*), *rebuilding* || *alterations to a house* || *altered premises, new building* || ⟨theat⟩ *change of scene*, ⟨Am⟩ *sc. shift* || ⟨rail⟩ *repair, relaying (of a track)* || (Wieder≃) f zivile Zwecke *(re)conversion* | ~strecke [f] ⟨rail⟩ *section under repair* **~|bauen** vt [h] [pp –gebaut] *to convert*; *rebuild, reconstruct, renovate* || *to convert (a barge)* || *to make alterations in ..* || ⟨fig⟩ *to modify* **~b·auen** vt [h] [pp –b·aut] *to build in, to surround with buildings*; *to wall, hem, shut in* **~|behalten** vt irr [h] *to keep on* **~|benennen** vt irr [h] *to rename* (nach *after*); *to relabel* **~beschrieben** a ⟨math⟩ ~er Kreis *circle described about (a triangle)* ≃**besetzung** f ⟨fam⟩ *shake-up* **~|betten** vt [h] *to put into a fresh* od *another bed* **~|bezeichnen** vt [h] *to relabel* **~|biegen** vt irr [h] (⟨a.⟩ sich ~) *to bend*; *to turn up* od *down* | *to dog's-ear (the leaves of a book)* || ⟨fig⟩ *to twist (names) into a new form* || (Urteil) *to deflect* ||

(Sinn) *to wrest* **~|bilden** vt [h] *to transform, rearrange, reform, recast, remodel* ‖ (Kabinett) *to reorganize, reshuffle* **ˊ∼bildung** f ∼/ *transformation, reform(ation), recast(ing)* ‖ ⟨rail⟩ *re--forming, re-assembly (of a train)* ‖ ⟨pol⟩ *(cabinet) shuffle* **~|binden** vt irr [h] *to tie* od *wrap round* ‖ (e–e Schürze etc) *to put on* ‖ *to knot (a shawl) round one's neck* ‖ ⟨bookb⟩ *to rebind* **~|blasen** vt irr [h] *to blow down* od *over* **~bl·asen** [a] (von) *exposed (to every wind)* **ˊ∼blatt** n *binder (of a cigar)* **~|blättern** vt/i [h] *to turn over (the leaves* od *leaf* [vt]); *to leaf over (the pages)* **ˊ∼blick** m *survey, panorama* ‖ *glancing back* ‖ ⟨fig⟩ *retrospect* **~|blicken,** sich ∼ [h] *to look round* (nach *for, after*) **~bl·ühen** vt [h] *to surround with flowers*

·Umbra f ∼/ ⟨minr⟩ *umber* (dazu: *to u.*)

·um- ~|brassen vt ⟨mar⟩ *to brace about* **~br·ausen** vt [h] *to roar round* ‖ v. Stürmen (Jubel) –braust *exposed to the storms, (amid acclamations)* **~|brechen** vt irr [h] [pp –gebrochen] *to break down* od *up* ‖ (den Boden) *to break (up)* ‖ (Rand) *to double* | vi [s] *to break down* **~br·echen** vt irr [h] [pp –br·ochen] ⟨typ⟩ (zu Seiten) *to make up (into pages)* ‖ (Zeilen) *to overrun* **~|bringen** vt irr [h] *to kill, slay, murder*; ⟨fam⟩ *to make away with (a p)*; ⟨sl⟩ *to put away,* ⟨Am⟩ *to get* | sich ∼ *to kill o.s., to make away with o.s.*; lieber bringe ich mich um *I'd sooner kill m.s.* ‖ ⟨fig⟩ sich ∼ vor .. *to dance with (rage)*; *to kill o.s.* od *to die with (laughing)*; *to gush with (effusiveness)*; sich beinahe, rein ∼ (etw z tun) *to fall over backwards .. to fall over o.s.*; vor Arbeit *to run off one's legs* **ˊ∼bruch** m ⟨agr⟩ *newly broken soil* ‖ ⟨min⟩ *side-adit* ‖ ⟨typ⟩ *paging, make-up*; *making-up* ‖ ⟨pol, etc⟩ (a. geistiger) *revolution, upheaval* **ˊ∼buchung** f *cross-entry* **~d·ämmen** vt [h] *to embank* **~|decken** vt [h] *to lay the table differently* ‖ *to retile, reslate (a roof)* **~|denken** vi/t [h] *to change one's thoughts (about)* **~|deuten** vt [h] *to give a new interpretation to ..* **~|dichten** vt [h] *to recast* **ˊ∼doppeln** n ⟨comp⟩ *duplication* **~dr·ängen** vt [h] *to crowd, throng swarm, press, flock round* od *about (a p)*; *to mob (a bridal car)* **~drehbar** a *reversible* **~|drehen** vt [h] *to turn (round; end for end)* ‖ ⟨fig⟩ *to twist* ‖ ⟨mar⟩ *to reverse* ‖ e–m Hahn den Hals ∼ *to wring a cock's neck* ‖ ∼! ⟨typ⟩ *(vertatur* L) *turn type* | sich ∼ [h] *to turn* (kurz *on one's heel*; schnell *to spin*) *round, to turn one's back* (vor *on*) ‖ sich um s–e Achse ∼ *to revolve, rotate* ‖ alles dreht sich ·um [adv] *everything goes round*

Umdr·ehung f ∼/∼en *revolution* ⟨fam⟩ *rev*; ∼ in der M. (U/min) *r.s per minute (RPM)* | ⟨phys⟩ *rotation* ‖ e–e ganze ∼ m *to come full circle* | **~s-** ∼bewegung [f] *rotatory motion*; ∼geschwindigkeit [f] *velocity of revolution*; *verticity*; ∼punkt [m] *centre of rotation*; ∼zähler [m] *counter*; ∼zeit [f] *period of revolution*

·Umdruck m *reprint, transfer(-printing, process)*; *mimeograph reproduction* | ∼papier [n] *offset paper, transfer-paper*; ∼verfahren [n] *metallography* **·um- ~|drucken** vt [h] *to reprint* **ˊ∼drucker** m *duplicator* **~d·uften** vt [h] *to surround with* (od *wrap, clothe in*) *perfume* **~d·unkeln, ~d·üstern** vt [h] *to wrap* od *clothe in darkness*; *to cast a gloom over* **~|etikettieren** vt [h] *to relabel* **ˊ∼esterung** f *interesterification* **~f·ahen** ⟨obs poet⟩ = umfangen **~|fahren** [pp –ge–] vt irr [h] *to drive* od *run over (a p)*; *to run (a p) down* | vi [s] *to take a (long) way about*; *to drive a roundabout way* **~f·ahren** vt irr [h] [pp ∼] *to drive round* ‖ (die Erde) *to circumnavigate* ‖ ⟨mar⟩ *to double, round (a cape)* **ˊ∼fahrt** f *tour, round* (e–e ∼ m *to make a r.* [um *of*]) ‖ ⟨jur⟩ *circuit* (e–e ∼ halten *to go upon c.*) **ˊ∼f·ahrung** f ∼/∼en *driving round* | ∼straße [f] ⟨österr⟩ = ⟨Ger⟩ Umgehungsstraße **ˊ∼fall** m ∼(e)s/ *fall, tumble, upsetting* ‖ ⟨parl⟩ *defection, ratting* **~|fallen** vi irr [s] *to fall (down* od *over)*; *to drop (to work till one drops)*; *to have a fall*; da konnte k–r ∼ *there was no room to swing a cat (in)* ‖ (v Wagen) *to (be) upset* ‖ (v Vieh) *to die* ‖ ⟨fig⟩ *to give in*; *to go over*; (*of spies*) → zus–brechen; ⟨parl⟩ *to change sides, to rat* | ˊ∼ [n] z ˊ∼ müde *ready to drop*; *dead tired* **ˊ∼fang** m *circumference,* ⟨a. math⟩ *circuit* ‖ ⟨math⟩ *periphery* ‖ ⟨tail⟩ *width* ‖ ⟨for⟩ *girth (of a tree)* ‖ 2 m ∼ h *to be 2 m round* ‖ v gr ∼ *of large dimensions*; *spacious* | (Bereich) *domain, sphere* | (Ausdehnung) *extent, size* ‖ *sweep (of influence)* ‖ *scope (of obligations, observation)* ‖ ⟨mus⟩ *compass, range* ⟨a. fig⟩ ‖ *volume (of a voice, of traffic,* etc) ‖ körperlicher ∼ *bulk* ‖ e–n (gr) ∼ annehmen ⟨fig⟩ *to grow to (large* od *big) proportions (which)* ‖ k–n größeren ∼ h als *to bulk no larger than* ‖ e–n gr ∼ h *to cover a great extent (of territory)* | **in** vollem ∼ *completely* **~f·angen** vt irr [h] *to encircle, surround, enclose* ‖ ⟨mil⟩ *to hem in, to envelop* | ⟨fig⟩ v Gefahren ∼ [pp] *encompassed with perils* | (umarmen) *to embrace* **~fangreich** a *extensive, wide* ⟨a. fig⟩ ‖ (Buch etc) *big, voluminous, sturdy* ‖ ⟨com⟩ *volume* [attr] *(demand)*; *margin (of solvency)* ‖ sehr ∼ *immense (body)* ‖ (geräumig) *wide, spacious* ‖ ⟨fig⟩ *copious (subject), comprehensive (term, grasp)* ⟨a. Lit⟩ **ˊ∼fangs-** *peripheral, circumferential (speed)* **~|färben** vt [h] *to redye, to dye again* **~|fassen** vt [h] [pp –gefaßt] (Ring) *to remount* ‖ (Perle etc) *to reset* **~f·assen** vt [h] [pp –f·aßt] **1.** (greifend) *to span, clasp* ‖ (fest) *his hand tightened on it* **2.** (umarmen) *to clasp, embrace* **3.** (blickend) *to take in* ⟨a. fig⟩ **4.** ⟨mil⟩ *to hem in, envelop, outflank* **5.** ⟨fig⟩ (enthalten) *to contain, comprise, comprehend, include* ‖ *to involve (a group of ps)* ‖ etw auch ∼ *to extend to* ‖ *the college embraces 3 departments* ‖ *the thesis ran to 300 pages* ‖ *the word covers this and more* **~f·assend** a *(very) comprehensive (library), encyclopaedic* ‖ *extensive (inquiry, lists),* ⟨Am⟩ *extended (lists), large (preparations), blanket (approval), capacious (memory), all-* (⟨Am⟩ *a.-a)round (education), embracing (importance)* ‖ *sweeping (changes), wide-reaching (concessions), ample (precautions)* ‖ (geräumig) *wide, vast, capacious* ‖ all∼ *global*; den ganzen Staat ∼ *state-wide*; weit ∼ ⟨tech⟩ *all-over, highly integrated (operations)*; möglichst ∼ *of the broadest possible scope*; das ∼ste Angebot der Welt an .. *the world widest range of* ‖ alle Produktionszweige ∼ *integrated* (⟨ind⟩ *plant*) **ˊ∼f·assung** f ∼/∼en *encompassing, embracing* ‖ (Einfriedigung) *enclosure* ‖ ⟨mil⟩ *(single) envelopment* ‖ ⟨fort⟩ *enceinte* | ∼sangriff [m] = ∼; ∼sbewegung [f] ⟨mil tact⟩ *turning movement*; ∼smauer *enclosure-wall*; ⟨fort⟩ *mantle wall* **ˊ∼feld** n *surrounding area* **~fl·attern** vt [h] *to flutter round* | ⟨fig⟩ *to flow loosely round* ‖ ⟨fam⟩ *to dangle around (a p)* **~fl·echten** vt irr [h] *to twist about, to plait round* ‖ (Draht) *to braid* ‖ –flochtene Flasche *wicker-bottle* **~fl·iegen** vt irr [h] *to fly round* **~fl·ießen** vt irr [h] *to flow round, to surround* ‖ v Licht –flossen *in a blaze of light* ‖ v Meer –flossen *washed by the sea* **~fl·oren** vt [h] *to wind about with crape, to muffle* ‖ ⟨fig⟩ *to dim (the sight)*; umflorter Blick [m] *eyes dimmed with tears*; sich ∼: *his voice became husky with sentiment* **~fl·uten** vt [h] *to flow about* od *round, to encompass with waves* **~|formen** vt [h] *to transform, reshape, remodel, remould, recast, reword* ‖ ⟨el⟩ *to transform, convert* ‖ (Schule) *to recondition* **ˊ∼former** m ∼s/∼ ⟨el⟩ *transformer, converter, inverter* | ∼satz [m] *i. motor-generator-set* **ˊ∼formung** f ∼/∼en *transformation, remodelling, recast*; ⟨mus⟩ *transposition* ‖ ⟨el⟩ *conversion of energy* **ˊ∼frage** f ∼/∼en *inquiry (all around)*; *poll, survey*; *sampling* ‖ ∼ halten *to make inquiries (a. r.)* (bei .. *of a p*) ‖ bei weiterer ∼ *on further inquiries (a. r.)* **~fr·ieden** vt [h] *to enclose*;

to fence in ≗**fr·ied(ig)ung** f ~/~en *enclosure*; ⟨hist a.⟩ *precinct* ≗**führung** f → –leitung ~|**füllen** vt [h] *to transfuse, decant*

·Umgang m ~(e)s/≗e **A. 1.** (*going*) *round* (halten ⟨a.⟩ *to take a turn round*); *circuit* ‖ (feierlicher) *procession* (halten *to hold*) **2.** ⟨arch⟩ (*circular*) *passage, gallery* **3.** ⟨hors⟩ (Geschirr) *breeching* **4.** ⟨phys⟩ *rotation, revolution*; (e–s Rades) ⟨a.⟩ *turn* **5.** ⟨soc⟩ *acquaintance, relation, association, intercourse, commerce, dealing* (*with*) ‖ schlechter ~ *evil communications* ‖ geschlechtlicher ~ *sexual* (⟨euph⟩ *intimate*, ⟨jur⟩ [außerehelich] *criminal*) *intercourse* (*with*), *carnal knowledge* (*of*) | [koll] *circle of friends* **6.** (schonender *prudent*) *handling* (*of material*) **B.** ~ h *or* **pflegen** mit *to have i.* od *to associate* (*with a p*) ‖ k–n ~ h *to live a retired life*; .. mit *not to mix with* (*a p*); sie h k–n ~ mit–e–a *they don't visit* od *associate* ‖ schlechten, guten ~ h *to keep bad, good company* ‖ wenig ~ h *to see* od *keep little c.* ‖ jdn s–s ~s würdigen *to consort with a p* **·umgänglich** a; (nicht) ~ (*un*)*sociable*, (*un*)*companionable* ‖ *affable*, (*un*)*pleasant* ‖ ein ~er Mensch ⟨Am a.⟩ *a good mixer* ‖ ~ s ⟨a.⟩ *to be pleasant company* | ≗**keit** f ~/ *sociability, companionableness*; *affability* **·Umgangs- ~formen** f pl (*good*, verfeinert *polished*) *manners* pl, (*modes of*) *address, deportment* ‖ strenge ~ ⟨a.⟩ *etiquette* **~sprache** f *colloquial speech, usual language*; *current tongue*; die englische ~ *colloquial* od *spoken English* ‖ familiäre ~ → *slang* **~ton** m (*the proper*) *tone*

·um- ~g·arnen vt [h] *to ensnare, enmesh* ⟨a. fig⟩ **~g·aukeln** vt [h] *to hover, flutter, dance, play* (*a*)*round*; *to haunt* ~|**geben** vt irr [h] [pp –ge–] (e–n Mantel) *to help on with* **~g·eben** vt irr [h] [pp ~] *to surround, lap*; (mit Mauern) *to wall* (*in*); (mit e–m Zaun) *to fence in* ‖ *gardens gird the city*; *to ring a p with* .. ‖ *she was wreathed with smiles* ‖ *a cold night was now upon me*; .. mit e–m Dunkel ~ *to throw a cloak of mystery around* .. | ~ [pp] **von** *beset* (*with difficulties*); *ice-bound*; *landlocked* ≗**g·ebung** f ~/~en *environs, surroundings, purlieus, precincts* pl, *neighbourhood*; *ambiance*; ⟨biol⟩ *environment* ‖ s–e ~ *the people around him* ‖ nahe ~ *vicinage, vicinity*; *outskirts* pl (*of a town*) ‖ die ländliche ~ *the country round* | (Gesellschaft) *company*; *ps around one* ‖ (*of princes*) ⟨a.⟩ *attendance, entourage* | ⟨übtr⟩ *setting, background* ‖ ⟨fig⟩ *environment* | ≗sbedingt [a] *environmental*, ~slärm [m] *surrounding* od *ambient noise*; ~slicht [n] → Raum–; ~stemperatur [f] *ambient t.* ≗**gegend** f ~/ *environs* pl, *neighbourhood* ‖ (nahe) *vicinity* (v *of*) ‖ andere Häuser in der ~ *other h.s thereabouts* (so: *people from round about*) ~|**gehen** vi irr [s] [pp –gegangen] **A. 1.** *to go round, to circulate, to make a circuit* **2.** (als Geist) *to haunt the place, to walk* ‖ hier geht **es** um *this place is haunted* **3.** *to go a roundabout way* ‖ 1 Meile ~ *to go a mile out of one's way* **4.** (Rad etc) *to go* (*turn, spin*) *round* ‖ der Reihe nach ~ *to come alternately*; ⟨übtr⟩ *an infection*, etc *is about* | .. **lassen** *to take .. by turns*, e–n Brief ~ l *to let a letter circulate* **5.** (Wind) *to change, shift* **6.** ⟨fig⟩ (Gerücht) *to run, to be rife* ‖ *news goes the round* ‖ *gossip travels quietly* ‖ *stories are abroad* **7.** (*a disease*) *is about* **B. ~ mit 1.** (S) *to deal with a th*; *to handle* od *treat a th* | geschickt ~ mit etw *to be apt with a th* | ⟨übtr⟩ *to set about a th* ‖ (Plan etc) *to be about* od *thinking of*; *to turn over in one's mind*; *to intend, plan*; (Geld, sparsam) *to go easy on m.* ‖ (P behandeln) *to use*; (*not to know how*) *to manage* (*a p*) ‖ (Mordgedanken) *to meditate murder* ‖ *to contemplate* (*treachery*) ‖ damit ~ z tun *to think of doing* | (**frei**) *to take liberties with* (*a text*) ‖ (gut, schlecht) *to treat* od *use* (*a p, a th*) *well, ill* ‖ (leichtsinnig) *to play fast and loose with* (*one's father's money*) ‖ (nicht richtig) *to go the wrong way to work* ‖ (**schonend**) *to nurse* ‖ (verständig) *to humour* ‖ (vorsichtig) *to mind* **2.** (P) mit jdm ~ = Umgang h mit ‖ ⟨prov⟩ sage mir, mit wem du umgehst, und ich werde dir sagen, wer du bist *birds of a feather flock together* ‖ *to approach* (*girls*) | (**gern**) *to like a p's company* ‖ (grob) *to play horse with a p* ‖ (gut) → B. 1. ‖ (**hart**) *to treat a p harshly* ‖ (nachsichtig) *to deal leniently with a p*; (zu n.g) *to be too indulgent toward* ‖ mit ihm ist schwer –zu– *he is not easy to manage* | mit Menschen –zu– **wissen** *to know how to get on* (od *to have a* [*wonderful*] *way*) *with people* ‖ du verstehst nicht mit ihm –zu– *you can't manage him* **umg·ehen** vt irr [h] [pp –gangen] *to go round* od *about* ‖ *to take a turn round* ‖ *to take a circuitous route round* .. | den Feind ~ *to turn the enemy*(*'s flank* od *position*), *to outflank* .. | ⟨fig⟩ *to avoid, shirk, elude*; *sidestep* (*a barrier*) ‖ *to evade, to get out of* (z tun *doing*) ‖ (Gesetz) *to evade, break*, ⟨Am⟩ *to beat* ‖ *to detour* (*a question*); *to make a d. around* (*an issue*) ‖ (Pflicht) *to baulk* ‖ (Gefahr) *to obviate* ‖ *to get round* (*the regulations*), (*the r.s. are got round by subterfuges*) ‖ wenn es zu ~ ist *if I/you can help it*; man kann die Schwierigkeit ~ *there is a way around the d.* | **·~d** a *next* ‖ mit ~er P. *by return of post* ‖ ~e Antwort erbeten *kindly inform us* (*by return* od [höflicher]) .. *at your earliest convenience* | [adv] *at once*; *immediately*; e–r S ~ nachgehen *to give a matter early attention* ‖ ~ Schritte tun *to take immediate steps* ≗**g·ehung** f ~/~en *going round*; *way around* ‖ ⟨mil⟩ *flank-movement, turning the* (*enemy's*) *flank*; = –fassung | ⟨fig⟩ *shirking, avoidance, evasion, elusion*; ~ der Wahrheit *prevarication* | ~sbewegung [f] *turning movement*; ~smarsch [m] *flanking march*; ~sstraße [f] *bypass* (*road*); *orbital r.* **·umgekehrt** a (→ ·umkehren) *opposite, contrary, reverse*; ⟨Am a.⟩ *contrariwise* ‖ entsprechend ~ *reciprocal* (*mistake*) ‖ mit ~er Hand *with the back of the hand* ‖ ~e Ordnung *inversion*; in ~er O. *inversely* ‖ ~e Seite (e–r Münze) *reverse*, (e–s Tuchs) *wrong side*, ⟨fig⟩ *opposite side* ‖ im ~en Verhältnis stehen *to be in inverse proportion* (*to*); es wirkt sich ~ aus *it works the other way round* | (*he is entirely*) *changed* ‖ jetzt its's gerade ~ *now the boot is on the other leg, conditions are reversed* | [adv *or* ell] *con.., re.., inversely, vice versa* ‖ *on the other hand* ‖ ~! *just the opposite* od *reverse*! *just the other way* (*round*)!, *on the contrary*!; ~ wird ein Schuh daraus *the boot is on the other leg* od *foot*; aus Herren w Diener u ~ *slaves and masters change places* **·um-|gestalten** vt [h] *to transform, recast, metamorphose, reshape, remodel, remould, refashion* ‖ *to reorganize, reform* ‖ sich ~ *to be*(*come*) *transformed* ≗**gestaltung** f ~/~en *remodelling* etc ‖ *recast, transformation, metamorphosis*; *reform, reproportioning, reorganization* ~|**gießen** vt irr [h] *to decant*; *to pour* (*from .. into*) ‖ ⟨met⟩ *to refound, newcast* **~g·ittern** vt [h] *to surround with* (*a railing, grating*), *lattice-work* ≗**gliederung** f ⟨mil⟩ *reorganization* N ~|**graben** vt irr [h] *to cut the ground*; *to dig* od *break, turn up* **~gr·enzen** vt [h] *to set bounds to*; *to bound, encircle, enclose, border, limit* ‖ (Linie ziehen) *to circumscribe* | ⟨fig⟩ *to limit, define* ≗**gr·enzung** f ~/~en *boundary* | ⟨fig⟩ *limitation* | ~slinie [f] der Fahrzeuge *rolling stock* (⟨Am⟩ *equipment*) *clearance line* ~|**gruppieren** vt [h] *to rearrange, realign, recompose*; ⟨mil⟩ *regroup, reorganize* ‖ ⟨pol⟩ *shift, reshuffle* ≗**gruppierung** f ⟨pol⟩ *shake-up* ~|**gucken**, sich ~ [h] (zurückschauen) *to look round* ‖ (prüfend umherblicken) *to look about one* ‖ (suchend) *to look* (nach *for*) ‖ ⟨fam⟩ er wird sich schön ~ *he may whistle for it, he will be much astonished* ~|**gürten** vt [h] [pp –ge–tet] *to gird on* ‖ (Schwert) *to buckle on* **~g·ürten** vt [h] [pp –tet] *to gird up* (*one's loins*) ‖ ⟨fig⟩ *to encircle* od *gird* (*a town with besiegers*, etc) || –tet *girt* (*with one's sword*) **≗g·ürtung** f *girding* **≗guß** m *transfusion* || *recast*(*ing*) **~|haben** vt irr [h] *to have .. on, to be wrapped up in ..* **~|hacken** vt [h] *to hew down, to fell* || ⟨hort⟩ *to hoe* (*up*) **~h·alsen** vt [h] *to hug, embrace* **≗h·alsung** f ~/~en *embrace, hug*(*ging*) **≗hang** m ~(e)s/≗e *shawl* || *cape* || (*lady's*) *opera-cloak*, (*loose*) *wrap*; ⟨Ind⟩ *sari* | *curtain* **~|hängen** vt [pp –ge–gt] [h] *to hang in another place* || (anziehen) *to put on* || ⟨mil⟩ Gewehre ~! *sling arms*! || *they wrapped their coats about them* **~h·ängen** vt [pp –gt] [h] *to hang round* (mit *with*) **·Umhänge-** ~kragen [m] *cape, fur collar*; ~riemen [m] *shoulder-strap*; ~tasche [f] *case with shoulder strap* || ~tuch [n] *wrap, shawl* **~|hauen** vt irr [h] *to hew* od *cut down, to fell* || jdn ~ *to knock a p* (*out*) *cold* **~h·egen** vt [h] *to cherish*

umh·er 1. [adv] (*all*) (*a*)*round*, (*round*) *about* || *up and down, this way and that, here and there, in all directions* **2.** [in comp] → herum .. [pref, sep] **~|blicken** vi [h] *to look a.t* (*one*) **~|bummeln** vi [s] *to loaf* (od *knock*) *about*; *to stroll a.t* **~|flattern** vi [s] *to flutter a.t* **~|fuchteln** vi [h] *to saw the air, to gesticulate* **~|fühlen** vi [h] *to fumble* **~|führen** vt [h] *to take a.t* **~|gaffen** vi [h] *to stand gaping* **~|gehen** vi [s] *to walk a.t* (*in*), *to go to and fro a.t* (*the garden*) **~|irren** vi [s] *to roam a.t* **~|laufen** vi irr [s] *to ramble, wander*; (ruhelos) *to gad about* **~|liegen** vi [h] = herumliegen || *to lie littered a.t* (*the floor*) || Papier lag umher in .. *the room was littered with paper* **~|lungern** vi [s] *to lounge a.t* **~|reisen** vi [s] (in) *to travel a.t* (*England*) || in der Welt ~ ⟨fam⟩ *to knock a.t the world* **~rudern** vi [h] (wie Krebse) *to flounder around* **~|schleichen** vi [s] (in) *to prowl a.t* (*the house*) **~|schlendern** → –bummeln **~|schwärmen** vi [s] (P) *to racket about* **~|schweifen** vi [s] *to rove, to ramble*; *to roam about* || s–e Blicke ~ l *to let one's eyes wander freely* || (in) *to turn a wandering eye a.t* (*the room*) **~|staken** vi [s] (P) → –gehen, *to strut around* **~|stehen** vi irr [s] *to stand a.t* **~|streifen** (→ –schweifen) *to roam about* od *around* **~|strolchen** vi [s] (in) *to knock a.t* (*town*) **~|tappen** vi [s] *to flounder* **~|tollen** vi [s] *to romp* | sich **~|treiben** [h] *to knock a.t* **~|ziehen** vi irr [s] *to rove, wander* **~ziehend** a *roving*; *itinerant*; *strolling* (*company*)

†·Umbrer pl (altital. Volk) *Umbri* [L] pl **·Umbrien** n ⟨It⟩ (Landschaft) *Umbria* **·Umbrier** m, **·umbrisch** a *Umbrian*

umh·in [adv] ich kann nicht ~ zu (weinen etc) *I cannot help* (od *refrain from*) (*crying*, etc) || *I c.t* (*do otherwise*) *but* (*accept*) || *I c.t forbear* (*to laugh*) || wenn ich ~ kann *if I can help it*

·um- **~|hören** vi [h] sich [acc] nach etw ~ *to inquire about a th* **~h·üllen** vt [h] *to wrap up, to envelop*; *to surround*; *to cloak in* || ⟨tech⟩ *to case* **~|hüllen,** sich [dat] ein Tuch ~ *to wrap o.s. up in a shawl* **≗h·üllung** f ~/~en *envelope*; *wrapping* (*material*); *wrap*(*per*), *cover*(*ing*); pompöse ~en *wrappings and trappings* || ⟨tech⟩ *case, jacket*; (Kabel≗) *coating* **~h·üpfen** vt [h] *to hop* od *skip round* **~j·ubeln** vt [h] *to cheer* od *greet enthusiastically* **~k·ämpft** a: hart ~ *hotly contested* (*hill*) **≗kehr** f ~/ *return* || ⟨el⟩ *reversal* || e–e ~ [gen] herbeiführen *to reverse* (*a process*) || ⟨mil⟩ z ~ zwingen *to compel to reverse* | ⟨fig⟩ *conversion* || ⟨pol⟩ (*drastic*) *turn-about* | ~anstalt [f] ⟨phot⟩ *reversing station*; ≗bar [a] *convertible* || *reversible*; ~dienst [m] *reversal service*; ~entwicklung [f], ~film [m] *r.l process, r.l* (*micro*)-*film*; ~motor [m] *reversible engine*; ~punkt [m] ⟨math⟩ *cusp point*; ~schluß [m] *argumentum e contrario* L; ~spiegel [m] *redressing m.* **~|kehren A.** vt [h] *to turn* (*round* od *about*) || (das Unterste zu oberst) (⟨fam a.⟩ um- u ~) *to upset, upend, overturn, to turn upside down* od *end for end* || *to tip* (*a cart*) *over* || (Tasche, Beutel etc) *to turn .. (inside) out* || (Augenlider) *to evert* || ⟨mus, gram, math⟩ *to invert* || ⟨el⟩ *to reverse* | ⟨fig⟩ (Wort) *to turn .. tail first*; (Worte, Sinn etc) *to invert, pervert* || ⟨log⟩ *to convert* (*a proposition*) | **sich** ~ *to turn round*; *to turn over* (*in one's bed*) || da kehrt sich [acc] mir das Herz um *it makes my heart ache* **B.** vi [s] *to turn back, to return* || ⟨mot⟩ *to reverse the car* || (auf demselben Wege) *to retrace one's steps* | ⟨fig⟩ *to mend one's ways* || → umgekehrt **≗kehrung** f ~/~en *overturning* || *eversion* (*of eyelids*) || ⟨el, opt, phot⟩ *reversal* || ⟨mus, gram, math⟩ *inversion* || ⟨log⟩ *converse, conversion* | ⟨fig a.⟩ *subversion*; ~ der Beweislast *reversed onus of proof*; völlige ~ ⟨fam⟩ *topsyturvydom* (*to cause a topsyturvy*) | ~serscheinung(en [pl]) [f] *reversal phenomenon*, (*-mena* pl) **~|kippen** vt [h] *to upset, overturn*; *to cant* (*over*); *to tip .. up* | vi [s] *to tilt* od *topple over*; *to go end for end* || (of car) *to turn over, to upset* || (of ship) *to capsize* **~kl·ammern** vt [h] *to tighten upon, to clasp, embrace*; *twine* | ⟨box⟩ *to clinch* (⟨a.⟩ sich ~) | (Tischkante) *to clutch* (*the end of the table*) | ⟨fig⟩ *to cling to* **≗kl·ammerung** f ~/~en *embrace*, ⟨box⟩ *clinch* || ⟨mil⟩ = –fassung; ~sangriff [m] *pincer movement* **~|klappen** vt [h] *to turn down* | vi [s] *to drop down, to collapse* **~|kleiden** vt [h] [pp –ge–det] *to dress anew* od *again* || **sich** [acc] ~ *to change* (*one's dress* od *clothes*) **~kl·eiden** vt [h] [pp –det] *to dress, cover, clothe*; *to case* (*with stone*) || schwarz ~ *to hang* od *drape with black* || ⟨fig⟩ *to couch, veneer* **≗kleideraum** m ~s/≗e *changing-room* ⟨a. *sport*⟩ **≗kl·eidung** f ~/~en *clothing* || ⟨fig⟩ *couching* **~|knicken** vt [h] *to crack* || *to snap off* || = ~|kniffen | vi [s] *to break down* || mein Fuß ist –ge–ckt *I have sprained my foot* **~|kniffen** vt [h] *to fold down* **≗kodierung** f ⟨comp etc⟩ *conversion* **~|k** vi irr [s] *to perish* (vor .. *with fright*), *to die* (*of hunger*); vor Hunger fast ~ ⟨fam⟩ *to starve* || *to fall* (*in battle*) || → Hitze etc || *to be consumed* (*with sleep*) || vor Erregung, Spannung (fast) ~ *to be on tenterhooks* (od *on pins and needles*) || im Elend ~ ⟨a.⟩ *to die a dog's death* | (verderben) *to spoil, to go bad* || ⟨fig⟩ *to go to wreck* (*and ruin*) **~|kopieren** ⟨phot⟩ *to reprint* **~kr·änzen** vt [h] *to wreathe, crown, festoon* || *to adorn with garlands* **≗kreis** m –es/–e *circumference, circuit, compass*; *orbit* || ⟨math⟩ *periphery* || im ~ v .. *within a radius of*, .. v 10 Meilen *for ten miles round*; 10 Meilen im ~ ⟨a.⟩ *10 miles each way* **~kr·eisen** vt [h] *to circle* od *turn* (od ⟨astr⟩ *revolve, rotate*) *round* (*a th*); ⟨a–n⟩ *to orbit* || (jdn) *close in upon* **~|krempeln** vt [h] *to tuck* od *turn up* || (völlig) *to turn .. inside out* | ⟨fam⟩ **sich** ~ *to change one's entire nature* | ⟨fam⟩ das ist z ≗ *that's enough to make one die with laughter* **~kristallis·ieren** [h] sich ~ *to recrystallize* **~|laden** vt irr [h] *to reload* (*a van*) || (Güter) *to shift*, ⟨mar⟩ *tranship .. (from .. to ..)* **≗ladung** f ~/ *reloading* || *shifting* || ⟨mar⟩ *transhipment* **≗lage** f ~/~n *tax, assessment of taxes* || *contribution, levy* (v allen .. wurde e–e ~ erhoben *a l. was made on all ..*) || städtische ~ *local rates* pl || ⟨agr⟩ *conversion* (*of arable to pasture or vice versa*) **~l·agern** vt [h] *to besiege, encompass*; *to hem in* || ⟨fig⟩ *to beset, to beleaguer* **~|lagern** *to re-store* (*goods*) || sich ~ *to change one's couch*, etc

·Umlauf m ~(e)s/≗e ⟨astr⟩ *revolution* || (Blut≗) *circulation* || Geld≗ *currency* || ⟨med⟩ *onychia* || ⟨phys⟩ *gyration, rotation* || ⟨rail⟩ *turn-round* (*of wag*[*g*]*ons*) || (Schreiben) *circular* | (Geld) aus dem ~ ziehen *to immobilize* | in ~ bringen *to put into c.n*; *to give currency to* (*a th*) (Gerücht) *to spread*; (Geld) *to issue, emit*, (falsches G.) *to utter*; (Anleihe) *to float*; (Schreiben) *to circulate* || ⟨a–n⟩ *to orbit* || im ~ s *to circulate*; (Gerüchte) *to be bruited about, to be abroad* || in

∼ setzen *to circulate* (*book*, etc); *to start* (*rumor*, *satellite* **~aufzug** m *continuous lift* od ⟨Am⟩ *elevator* **~bahn** f ⟨astr⟩ *orbit* (auf der *in*); dazu: *to o.* vt/i ‖ ⟨a–n⟩ *circular path* (*around the moon*) ‖ ⟨phys⟩ (Elektron-∼) *orbit* **~bewegung** f *rotary movement* **~getriebe** n *planetary gearing* **~kapital** n *floating* od *working capital* **~mappe** f *circulation* od *float file* **~mittel** n *circulating medium*, *currency* **~motor** m ⟨aero⟩ *rotary engine*; *engine with revolving cylinders* **~geschwindigkeit** f *running speed* **~öl** n *circulating oil* **~schmierung** f *circulatory lubrication* **~schreiben** n *circular* (*letter*); (f verlorene S) *tracer* **~rad** n ⟨tech⟩ *planet gear* od *wheel* **~szeit** f ⟨astr⟩ *revolution*, *period*; ⟨rail, mar⟩ *turn-round* **~vermögen** n *liquid* od *current* (⟨Am⟩ *quick*) *assets* pl; ⟨bal⟩ *receivables* ˈ**um-**

~|laufen vt irr [h] [pp –ge–] *to run over* od *down* | vi [s] *to revolve*, *rotate* ‖ (Umweg m) *to take a roundabout way*, *to go* (.. *miles*) *out of one's way* ‖ (in Umlauf s) *to circulate* ‖ (Gerücht) *to spread*, *run* **~lˈaufen** vt irr [h] [pp ∼] *to run around* **≃laut** m ∼(e)s/∼e ⟨gram⟩ *umlaut*; *vowel mutation* (z. B. a > ä) ‖ *modified vowel* **~|lauten** vt [h] *to umlaut*; *to modify* (*a sound*) | vi [h] *to be modified* | –ge–tet *modified* (*vowels*), *mutated* (*forms*) **~|leeren** vt [h] *to empty into another container* **~legbar** a *reversible* (⟨phot⟩ *finder*) **≃lege-** ∼kalender [m] *desk diary*; ∼kragen [m] *turn-down collar* **~|legen** vt [pp –ge–gt] [h] *to lay round* od *down*, *to bend about* ‖ (Rand) *to double*; (Saum) *to tuck* ‖ (v Hagel, Wind: die Saaten ∼) *to beat down* ‖ ⟨hunt⟩ (Tier) *to lay low*; ⟨fam⟩ (jdn) *to kill*, *shoot*, ⟨sl⟩ *to pot*; ⟨Am fam⟩ *to blot out*; ⟨sex⟩ *to do* (*her*) *down* | (Kragen etc umbinden) *to put on* ‖ (Gürtel) *to gird* (*on*) ‖ ⟨med⟩ (Verband) *to apply* | (anders legen) *to place differently* ⟨a. cards⟩, *to shift* ‖ e–n Schaltschlüssel ∼ *to throw a key*; (Schienen etc) *to re-lay*; *to change the route of a track* | ⟨mar⟩ (die Segel) *to put* od *tack a ship about*, *to shift the sails*; (Schornstein) *to pull down*; (das Schiff z Reinigung) *to careen* | (Truppen) *to shift* ‖ ⟨telph⟩ *to put* (*a call*) *through* (auf zu *to*) | ⟨fig⟩ (die Kosten) *to apportion* | **sich** ∼ [h] *to lie down* ‖ (Spitze, Schneide) *to bend over* ‖ (Wind) *to veer*, *shift*, *change* ||| vi [h] ⟨mar⟩ *to tack about* **~lˈegen** vt [pp –gt] *to lay* (*a th*) *round* (mit *with*) **≃legung** f ⟨agr⟩ *re-distribution* (*of land*), → Zus– **~|leiten** vt [h] *to lead another way*, (Verkehr) *to divert*, *reroute* ‖ ⟨el⟩ *to reroute*; ⟨wir⟩ *we turn you over* (*to Berlin*) **≃leitung** f *roundabout*, ⟨mot⟩ *diversion*; *detour*, *d. road*, [abstr] *rerouting*; ⟨rail⟩ *loopway* | ∼sstraße *by-pass* **~|lenken** vt/i [h] *to turn* (*round* od *back*), *to switch* (⟨a.⟩ jdn) ‖ ⟨fig⟩ [abs] *to change one's mind* **≃lenk-** *deviating* (*prism*, *mirror*) | ∼rolle [f] ⟨tech⟩ (*guide-*)*pulley* **~|lernen** vt/i [h] *to learn anew* od *from experience*, *to unlearn* ‖ ⟨fig⟩ ganz ∼ müssen *to have to relearn one's lessons* **~|liegen** vi irr [h] *to lie on the ground* ‖ *to lie* (*a*)*round* **~liegend** a *circumjacent*, *neighbouring*; *outlying* (*villages*) ‖ ∼e Gegend *surrounding country*, *environs* pl **≃mˈantelung** f ∼/∼en ⟨tech⟩ *jacket*, *sheathing*, *casing*; *cladding* ⟨a. at⟩ **~mˈauern** vt [h] *to wall in* od *round*, *to surround with a wall* **~|modeln** vt [h] *to transform*, *refashion*, *remodel*; (gänzlich) *to put into the melting-pot* **~|montieren** vt [h] *to remount* **~|münzen** vt [h] *to recoin* **~nˈachten** vt [h] *to surround with darkness* ‖ sich ∼ [h] (geistig) *to become deranged* **~nˈachtet** a ⟨fig⟩ *deranged* (*mind*) ‖ (P) *benighted* [pred] **≃nˈachtung** f ∼/ ⟨fig⟩ *mental derangement*; *spiritual darkness*; *obfuscation* ‖ (plötzliche) *brain-storm*; → *aberration* **~nˈähen** vt [h] *to hem* ‖ (Saum) *to tuck*, *overcast* ‖ (Rand) *to fell* **~nˈebeln** vt [h] *to wrap in mist* od *fog*, *to fog* ⟨a. fig⟩ **~nˈebelt** a *befogged* ‖ ⟨fig⟩ *benumbed*; *slaphappy* **~|nehmen** vt irr [h] *to put on*, *to wrap* od *take round* **~|numerieren** vt [h] *to renumber* **~|ordnen** vt [h] *to rearrange* **≃ordnung** f ⟨rail⟩ *re-arrangement* (⟨Am⟩ *re-forming*) (*of a train*) **≃organisation** f ⟨Am⟩ *shake-up* **~orientiert** a → → neu– **~|packen** vt [h] *to repack* ([a. abs] *to r. one's trunk*) **~pˈanzern** vt [h] *to cover with* (*armour* od) *a coat of mail* **~pˈanzert** a *steel-clad* **~pfˈählen** vt [h] *to surround with pales*, *to palisade* **~|pflanzen** vt [h] [pp –ge–zt] *to transplant*, *replant*; *to prick* od *plant out* (*seedlings*) **~pflˈanzen** vt [h] [pp –zt] (mit) *to plant* (*with*) *round* (*the bed*, etc) **≃pflanzung** f ∼/ *transplantation*, *replanting* **~|pflastern** vt [h] *to repave* **~pflˈastern** vt [h] *to pave all round* (*a house*) **~|pflügen** vt [h] *to plough up* **~|polen** vt [h] ⟨el⟩ *to commutate* **~|prägen** vt [h] *to recoin* ‖ ⟨fig⟩ *alter*, *remodel*, *revamp* **≃prägung** f ∼/ *recoinage* **~|purzeln** vi [s] ⟨fam⟩ *to tumble* od *topple over* od *down* °**~|pusten** vt [h] du hättest mich ∼ können *you might have knocked me down with a feather* **~|quartieren** vt [h] & sich ∼ [h] *to remove to other quarters* ‖ *to shift* (*troops*) **~rˈahmen** vt [h] *to frame* ‖ *to form a frame round* **~rahmt** a *boxed-off* (*list*, etc) **≃rˈahmung** f ∼/∼en *frame* **~randet** a: ∼e Überschrift [f] *boxheading*, *boxhead* **~rˈändern** vt [h] *to rim*, *border*, *edge* **~rˈanken** vt [h] (mit etw) *to entwine* (*with*) | ⟨fig⟩ *to cling to* | efeuumrankt [a] *ivy-clad* **~rˈauschen** vt [h] *to roar round* ‖ –scht *surrounded* (*by roaring waves*) **~|rechnen** vt [h] (in [acc]) *to reduce* (in .. *to marks*); *to convert* (*paper money into gold*; *to an annual base*)

ˈ**Umrechnung** f ∼/ *conversion*, *reduction* | **~s-** *conversion* [attr] **~konstante** f *c. constant* **~kurs** m *rate of exchange* **~satz** m ⟨bank⟩ *rate of c.* **~tabelle** f *c.* od *reduction table*; *tables* pl *of exchange* **~wert** m *parity* ‖ z ∼ v *at p. of* **~zahl** f *c. factor*

ˈ**um-** **~rˈeisen** vt [h] *to circumnavigate*, *to travel round* (*the globe*); *to* (*make a*) *detour around* **~|reisen** vi [s] *to go out of one's way* **~|reißen** vt irr [h] [pp –gerissen] *to pull* od *break down* ‖ (v Wind) *to blow down* ‖ *to knock down* od *take* (*a pole in one's stride*) ‖ –gerissen (of trees) *come down* **~rˈeißen** vt irr [h] [pp –rˈissen] *to outline*, *thumbnail*, *sketch*; (Lage) *to summarize*, (jds Leben) *to survey* ‖ scharf, (roh) –rissen *sharply marked*; *s.y defined* (*plan*); *roughly sketched*; *clearcut* (*definition*) **~|reiten** vt irr [h] [pp –geritten] *to ride down* od *over* .. | vi irr [s] *to ride* (*a long way*, etc) *about* **~rˈeiten** vt irr [h] [pp –rˈitten] *to ride round* (*a place*) **~|rennen** vt irr [h] *to run* (.. *down* od) *over* .. **~rˈingen** vt [h] *to encircle*, *surround* ‖ (dicht) *to enclose* ‖ ⟨fig⟩ *to beset* ‖ ⟨mil a.⟩ *to hem in* **≃riß** m –sses/–sse *outline*, *contour*; *shape* | [pl] der Küste *the coast line*, (des Gesichts) *outline*; *the superficial* od *external contours* pl od *outline of a th* ‖ (hingeworfen) *rough sketch* | –sse [pl] (*she could barely make out his*) *figure* | in gr –ssen *in broad outlines*; *roughly*; in –ssen skizzieren *to block out*; in kräftigen –rissen schildern, zeichnen *to sketch in bold outlines* ‖ (Bericht) im ∼ geben *to sketch*, *skeleton*(*ize*) | ∼karte [f] *skeleton-map*; ∼linie [f] *outline*; (gegen den Himmel) *skyline*; ∼radierung [f] *line engraving*; ∼skizze [f] *thumbnail sketch*; ∼zeichnung [f] *sketch* **≃roller** m ⟨rec⟩ *rewinder* **~|rühren** vt [h] *to stir* (*up*) | (Fabrik) **~|rüsten** [h] *to retool* **ums** ⟨fam⟩ = um das

ˈ**um-** **~|sägen** vt [h] *to saw down* **~|satteln** vt [h] *to saddle afresh* | vi [h] ⟨fig⟩ *to change one's profession* od *studies* ‖ zur Philologie ∼ *to become a student of languages* ‖ ⟨pol⟩ *to change sides* **≃satz** m ∼(e)s/≃e ⟨com⟩ *turn-over* ‖ (Einnahme) *returns* pl ‖ (Verkauf) *sale*; ⟨bal⟩ *sales*; ⟨exch⟩ ohne ∼ *no business* ‖ rascher ∼ *early return* | ∼ausgleichsteuer [f] *t.-o. equalisation tax*; ∼betrag [m] ⟨exch⟩ *business done*; ∼kapital [n] *working capital*; ∼karte [f] ⟨comp⟩ *accounting detail card*; ∼kurve [f] *sales cu.*; ∼steuer [f] *turnover tax, salestax*; ~steuervergütung [f] *t. tax-refundment* **~s·äumen** vt [h] *to hem*, mit e–r Borte ~ *to purl* ‖ ⟨fig⟩ *to enclose* (mit .. *in hedges*) ‖ *the plain was seamed by* .. **~s·ausen** vt [h] *to howl around* **~|schaffen** vt [h] *to transform, remodel* **~|schalten** vt [h] ⟨el⟩ *to commute, reverse* (*the current*); *to switch* ‖ ⟨mot⟩ *to change the gear* ‖ ⟨übtr⟩ (Interesse) *to switch over* (*from* .. *to* ..) **|** ≃ [n] ⟨mot⟩ *gear changing* **≃schalter** m ⟨el⟩ *commutator*, (*change-over*) *switch*; selbsttätiger ~ ⟨el⟩ *cut-out* **≃schalt-** ~brett [n] *switchboard*; ~feststeller [m] ⟨typwr⟩ *shift-key lock*; ~hebel [m] ⟨el⟩ (*change-over*) *switch*; ~pause [f] *answer lag*; ~taste [f] ⟨typewr⟩ *shift--key* **≃schalter** m ⟨bes wir⟩ *selector* (od *change--over*) *switch*; ⟨typwr⟩ *shift key* **≃schaltung** f ⟨el⟩ *commutation* ‖ ⟨tech⟩ *change-over* **~sch·anzen** vt [h] *to entrench, circumvallate* **≃sch·anzung** f *entrenching, -ment, circumvallation* **~sch·atten** vt [h] *to shade, overshadow* **≃schau** f ~/ *look*(*ing*) *round* **|** ~ halten *to look round* (*about*); *to visit* (in *a city*); ⟨mil⟩ *to scout*; ⟨fig⟩ *to muster, review* ‖ .. nach *to look out for* **~|schauen,** sich ~ [h] *to look round* od *back*; sich ein bißchen ~ *to knock about a bit* **~|schaufeln** vt [h] *to turn* (*with a shovel*), *to stir* **~|schichten** vt [h] *to pile anew* ‖ ⟨fig⟩ *to rearrange, regroup* **~schichtig** [a & adv] *in layers* ‖ ⟨fig⟩ *in turns* **~|schießen** vt [h] *to shoot down* **|** vi [s] (of wind) *to chop* od *shift about* **~|schiffen** vt [h] [pp –ge–fft] *to tranship* **~-sch·iffen** vt [h] [pp –fft] *to sail round* od *about*; *to circumnavigate* (*the globe*) ‖ (Kap) *to double*

·Umschlag m ~(e)s/≃e (Wechsel) *sudden change* (*of the weather*), *break, turn* ‖ *reverse* (*of fortune*) ‖ ⟨com & mar⟩ *transhipment*; *re-loading*; (Brief≃) *envelope* ‖ (Paket≃) *wrapper, cover* ‖ (Buch≃) *jacket*, in ~ *wrappered* ‖ ⟨tail⟩ *cuff*; *collar*; *facing, hem*; (Hosen≃) *turn-up*; (Kleid≃) *tuck* (*to let out the tucks*) ‖ ⟨med⟩ *poultice*; (Brei≃) *cataplasm*; kalter ~ (*cold*) *compress* ‖ heißer ~ *stupe* ‖ e–n ~ m um .. *to poultice* (*a leg*) **~bogen** m *casing* **~deckel** m *cover* **~geschwindigkeit** f *rate of turn-over* **~karton** m ⟨pap⟩ *cover card* **~kragen** m *turn-down collar* **~(e)papier** n *wrapping-paper* **~hafen** m *port of transhipment* **~(e)platz** m *centre for the distribution of goods* **~punkt** m ⟨chem⟩ *endpoint* **~reaktion** f ⟨chem⟩ *reversal* **~saum** m *turned-in seam* **~stelle** f *reloading* od *reconsignment point*; *in-transit storage point*; (LKW) *truck-head*, ⟨rail⟩ *railhead* N **~etuch** n *shawl, wrap*

·um- [(in)sep] pref **~|schlagen** vi irr [s] *to upset, to fall down, to turn over*; *to go end for end* ‖ (of car) *to upset* ‖ (of ship) *to keel over, to capsize* ‖ (Bier etc) *to turn* (*sour*); ⟨chem⟩ ~ auf *to revert to* ‖ (of voice) *to crack* **|** (wechseln) *to change suddenly*, völlig ~ *to ch. course through 180 degrees* ‖ (Wetter) *to break* ‖ das Wetter schlug um *there was a break-up in the w.* ‖ (Wind) *to shift* (*to*) ‖ (Stimme) *to break* ‖ (Glück) *to veer round* ‖ (Krankheit) *to take a new turn* **|||** vt [h] (fällen) *to cut* od *knock down* **|** (um etw) *to put* od *wrap* (*round a th*) ‖ (Tuch etc) *to put on, to wrap* (*o.s.*) *up in* .. ‖ *to apply* (*wet rags*) **|** (Nagel) *to clinch*; (Saum) *to turn up* ‖ (den Kragen) *to turn down* ‖ (Ärmel) *to tuck up* ‖ (Seite) *to turn over* ‖ ⟨cards⟩ *to turn up* ‖ *to load and unload* (*goods*) **|||** ≃ n *upset*(*ting*), etc; *reversal* ‖ ⟨path⟩ *crisis* ‖ *veering* (*of the wind*) ‖ *break-up* (*in the weather*) **~schl·eichen** vt irr [h] *to sneak round* **|** vi → herum|–schleichen **~schl·eiern** vt [h] *to veil* **~schl·ießen** vt irr [h] *to enclose, surround, lap* ‖ ⟨tech⟩ *to embed* ‖ ⟨mil⟩ *to invest*; (belagern) *to besiege* ‖ mit den Armen ~ *to hug* **≃schl·ießung** f ~/ *enclosure* ‖ ⟨mil⟩ *blockade*; *investment*; *siege* **~schl·ingen** vt irr [h] [pp –schl·ungen] *to embrace, to clasp round, to cling to* ‖ e–a –schl·ungen halten *to be locked in each other's arms* **~|schlingen** vt [h] [pp –geschlungen] *to twist, wind round*; *to w. o.s.* (*a*)*round*; *to twine* ‖ sich [dat] ein Tuch ~ *to wrap a shawl round one* **≃schl·ingung** f ~/~en *embrace* **~schm·eicheln** vt [h] *to flatter* °**~|schmeißen** = ~|werfen **~|schmelzen** vt irr [h] *to melt again, to new-cast, recast* **~|schmieden** vt [h] *to forge anew* **~|schnallen** vt [h] *to buckle on* (*a sword*), *to strap* (*a belt*) **~schn·üren** vt [h] *to cord, strap*; *to tie up* **~schr·änken** vt [h] *to confine, limit*; *to fence in* ‖ ⟨fig⟩ *to restrict* **~|schreiben** vt irr [h] [pp –geschrieben] *to rewrite* ‖ (in andere Schriftart) *to transcribe, transliterate* ‖ (Besitz ~ auf jdn) *to transfer* od *convey to a p* ‖ ⟨com⟩ (Wechsel) *to endorse over* **~schr·eiben** vt irr [h] [pp –schrieben]) ⟨bes math⟩ *to circumscribe* ‖ (durch Worte) *to paraphrase* ‖ ~d *periphrastic* **≃schreibung** f *transcription* ‖ *transfer, conveyance* **≃schr·eibung** f *circumlocution*; *paraphrase*; → *periphrasis* **~schr·ieben** a → –schreiben; rücksichtsvoll (etc) ~ *discrete* (*localization*); scharf ~ *succinct* **≃schrift** f ~/~en *transcription* ‖ ⟨num⟩ *legend, inscription* **~|schulen** vt [h] *to remove from one school to another* ‖ *to retrain*, ⟨soc⟩ *rehabilitate*; ⟨bes pol⟩ *re-educate* **|** ⟨aero⟩ vi [h] *to have training* (auf .. *on a new type*) **≃schulung** f *transition training*; ⟨bes aero⟩ *con*(*version*) *course* ‖ ⟨soc⟩ *vocational rehabilitation* **|** ~swerkstätte [f] ⟨bes Am⟩ *r. center* **~|schulden** vi [h] *to convert a debt, to change the terms of debentures* **≃schuldung** f ~/ *conversion of a debt* ‖ ⟨agr⟩ *modification of the terms of agricultural loans* **~|schütteln** vt [h] *to shake up, to stir* ‖ vor Gebrauch –zu– *to be shaken before use* **~|schütten** vt [h] *to pour into another vessel* ‖ (verschütten) *to spill* ‖ (~|werfen) *to upset, overturn* **~schw·ärmen** vt [h] ⟨a. fig⟩ *to swarm* (*a*)*round* ‖ ⟨mil⟩ *to harass* ‖ ⟨fig⟩ *to enthuse about* (*a p*) ‖ von Anbetern –rmt *surrounded by a crowd of adorers* **~schw·eben** vt [h] *to hover* (*flutter, float*) *round* **≃schweife** m pl *circumlocution*; *fuss*; *talk* ‖ lange ~ m *to make a long rigmarole* (*of it*) ‖ k–e ~ m *not to mince matters* ‖ ohne ~ *without* (⟨fam⟩ *frills*) *much ado*; *point-blank* **|** [adv], *roundly*; *then and there* ‖ durch ~ ⟨a.⟩ *indirectly*; *with many roundabouts* **~schweifig** a *roundabout* **|** [adv] *round about* **~schwenken** vi [h] *to turn round* (od ⟨pol⟩ *double*); ⟨mil⟩ *to wheel about* ‖ (Wind) *to veer round* ⟨a. fig⟩ (*from* .. *to* ..) **≃schwung** m ~s/ *revolution* ‖ ⟨gym⟩ *swing* (*round the bar*) ‖ *sudden change*; *reaction*; *change--over* (*from* .. *to* ..) ‖ *revulsion* (*of feeling*) ‖ *vicissitudes* pl (*of fortune*) ‖ *veering round*; völliger *about-face*; *landslide* (*of public opinion*) ‖ ⟨Lit⟩ *reversal*; dramatischer ~ im L. *dramatic reversal in life* ‖ e–n ~ herbeiführen *to turn the tide* **~|segeln** vt [h] *to run foul of* (*a boat*) **|** vi [s] *to sail a roundabout way* **~s·egeln** vt [h] = –sch·iffen **~|sehen,** sich ~ irr [h] *to look round* od *back* ‖ (neugierig) *to peer around*; sieh dich (nicht) ~! *look round*! (⟨sl⟩ *don't rubber*!) **|** (untersuchend) *to look about one*, ⟨fam⟩ *to have a look round* ⟨a. fig⟩, ⟨fig⟩ *to get one's bearing* ‖ *to take a view* od *survey* (*of*) **| in**: *to have a look round* (*the library*); *to look about* (*the room*); *to take a turn round* (*a place, town*) ‖ (in der Welt) *to see a good bit* (*of the w.*) **| nach**: *to look back* (⟨Am⟩ *around*) *at* (*a p*) ‖ ⟨fig⟩ *to look* (*round*) *for* (*customers, a job*); *to cast about for* (*a seat, the means of doing so*); nach e–r Tätigkeit .. *as to what one can do* **|** ⟨fig⟩ (→ –|gucken); er wollte sich nach .. ~ *he went to see about some car* **| eh** man sich –sieht, im ≃ *in a twinkling, in* (*less than*) *no time*, ⟨fam⟩ *before you can say Jack Robinson* **| ohne** sich –zu– *without a moment's hesitation* ‖ er mag sich anderswo ~! *he must find sth elsewhere* ‖ der kann sich **lange** (danach) ~! *he may whistle for it*! **~seitig** [adv] *overleaf* **~setzbar** a ⟨com⟩ *convertible, negotiable* ‖ (in bares Geld) *realizable*

~|setzen I. vt [h] *to place differently; to transpose, shift* || (Reihenfolge ändern) *to permute* || ⟨hort⟩ *to transplant, repot* || ⟨typ⟩ *to reset* || ⟨mus⟩ *to transpose* (*into another key*), *to rearrange* || ⟨arts⟩ (aus e–r Kunst in die andere) *to translate* (*from .. into*) || (verwandeln) *to turn into* || ⟨com⟩ (z Geld m) *to realize* || (Kapital) *to return* || (Waren) *to sell* || Zucker wird wenig –gesetzt *there is little doing in s.* || (Geld) *to turn over, to have a turnover of* || Worte in die Tat ~ *to put into action, to realize* [*an idea*], *to suit the action to the word; to carry* od *put .. into practice* || (v Arbeitskräften) *to redeploy*; dazu *r.ment* **II.** vi [h] der Wind setzte um *the wind shifted* **≁sichgreifen** n ~s/ *spread(ing)* || *growth* || *expansion, increase, progress* **≁sicht** f ~/ *prudence, circumspection, vigilance* || (Takt) *discretion* | **≁ig** [a] *circumspect, prudent, discreet, wary, cautious* | [adv] ~ handeln *to use discretion, to act cautiously* | ~igkeit [f] = ~ **~|siedeln** vt [h] (P) *to resettle, transfer* | vi [s] *resettle*; dazu *r.ment*; *transfer* s, *displacement* **~ sinken** vi irr [s] *to sink down* (ohnmächtig *in a faint*) || *to drop down* (vor .. *with fatigue*) **~som·ehr** → um I. B. **~s·onst** [adv] *without payment, gratis, gratuitously, for nothing* || ⟨fam⟩ (*to be had*) *for the mere asking*; (*to play*) *for love*; (*to buy*) *for a mere song, for next to nothing* || (vergeblich) *in vain, vainly, to no purpose, uselessly, unavailingly* || nicht ~ *not without good reason* || *it was not for nothing that he had boasted*; er tut nichts ~ *he does nothing for n.*; das soll er nicht ~ getan h *he shall pay for it yet!* || *Mr. N. is not a Spaniard for nothing* || sich ~ ab-, bemühen *to lose one's labour; to have one's labour for one's pain* od *one's work for nothing; he tried hard to please, but got only grumbles for his pains; he worked hard but had only sore hands for his pains* || fast ~ *for the asking*; f so gut wie ~ *for a nominal fee* | ⟨prov⟩ ~ ist der Tod (und der kostet's Leben) *nothing for nothing* (*and really remarkably little for sixpence*); *no pay, no work* **~|spannen** vt [h] [pp –ge–nnt] *to change horses* || ⟨el⟩ *to transform* **~sp·annen** vt [h] [pp –nnt] *to span, encompass* || (mit) *to spread* (*sth*) *round* (*a place*) **≁spanner** m ~s/~ ⟨el⟩ *transformer* **≁speicherung** f ⟨comp⟩ *exchange* **~sp·ielen** vt [h] *to play round* || ein Lächeln –lte s–n Mund *a smile played* od *lingered about* od *flickered on his lips* || ⟨mus⟩ *to embroider* **~|spielen** vt ⟨bes film⟩ *to re-record* **~sp·innen** vt irr [h] *to spin* (*all*) *round* || (Draht) *to cover* (*cotton* [od *silk*] *covered wire*) || ⟨fig⟩ *to ensnare* °**~|sprechen**: es spricht sich ~ *it gets round* **~|springen** vt irr [s] [pp –gesprungen] (Wind) *to change suddenly; to veer* od *haul* (*round*); *the wind shifts round* (auf *to*); (wiederholt) *to chop about* | ⟨fig⟩ (mit jdm) *to deal* (*with a p*); mit jdm grob, brutal ~ *to get down on a p*; .. kurz ~ *to make short work of* || (mit etw) *to manage, handle, settle* (*a th*) || –zu– wissen mit *to know how to manage* | ~d *untrue* (Magnetnadel) **~spr·ingen** vt irr [h] [pp –sprungen] *to skip* od *leap around* || (Wind) *to go round* **≁sprung** m ⟨ski⟩ *jump turn* **~sp·ülen** vt [h] (Wellen) *to lap* od *wash round* **~|spulen** vt [h] *to rewind, respool* **≁spuler** m *r.ing device* **~spulzeit** f ⟨rec⟩ *rewind time*

·Umstand m ~(e)s/≁e **A. 1.** *circumstance, fact* || *occurrence, occasion, event, incident* || der ~, daß er tot ist (*the fact of*) *his being dead* **2.** ⟨gram⟩ *adverb*(*ial clause* od *phrase*) **3.** [pl] *circumstance*(*s* pl), ⟨fam⟩ *circs* || (*a happy evolution of c.ce; the brutality of c.ce; triumph of character over c.ce; the c.ce*(*s*) (bei .. *or*, die z. T. führten *of a death*) **4.** [pl] (Zustand, Lage) *state* (*of affairs*), *conditions* pl, *situation* **5.** [pl] (Einzelheiten) *details, particulars*; alle ≁e darlegen *to go into, to give full d.s* od *p.s* **6.** [pl] (Formen) *ceremony* (*without c.*), *formalities* **B. erschwerende** ≁e [pl] *complication* || mildernder ~ *redeeming feature*, ⟨jur⟩ *mitigating* od *alleviating c.ces* || kleinste ≁e *minutiae* || nähere ≁e *further particulars* **C.** jdm ≁e **m** *to give a p much trouble* || gr ≁e m *to cause* od *raise great difficulties* || (viel[e]) ≁e m *to be ceremonious* od *formal* || wir wollen k–e ≁e m *we want no ceremony* || k–e ≁e bitte, m Sie (unsertwegen) k–e ≁e *don't trouble y.s.*, ⟨fam⟩ *don't put y.s. out* (*on our account*), ⟨fam⟩ *go to!* || wenn's k–e ≁e macht ⟨Am fam⟩ *if it won't put you out* (*any*) || nicht viel ≁e m *to make no fuss* || nicht lange ≁e m mit *to make short work of* || ohne viel ≁e z m *without ceremony, w. much ado* **D.** es kommt **auf** die ≁e an *it all depends* (*on c.ces*) | **aus** dem ~, daß *from the c.ce of* od *that* | **in** anderen *or* gesegneten ≁en s *to be with child*, od ⟨euph⟩ *in a certain* od *delicate* od *an interesting condition* od ⟨fam⟩ *in the family way* || in guten (beschränkten) ≁en s *to be in easy circumstances, to be well-to-do, to be well* (*badly*) *off*; in erbärmlichen ≁en s *to be down at heels*; den ≁en **nach** *considering* (*he was quite well c.*) | ohne viel ≁e *unceremoniously* | **unter** ≁en *c.ces permitting; perhaps, possibly; as things go* || unter allen ≁en *in any case, at all events, anyhow, most certainly, emphatically, on all grounds; rain or shine* od *no r.* | ich will u. a. U. wissen *I am determined to know* || u. diesen U. *in these c.ces* od *conditions* || u. den (ganz) gleichen U. (*all*) *other ths being equal* | u. k–n U. *on no* (od *not on any*) *account, by no manner of means, not on all grounds* || u. solchen U. ⟨a.⟩ *as matters stand* **·u≁ehalber** [adv] *owing to circumstances* **·u≁lich** a *circumstantial, minute, detailed* (*account*) | (förmlich) *ceremonious, fussy precise* | (kompliziert) *complicated, troublesome* || das ist mir z ~ *that is far too much bother for me* | [adv] ~ erzählen *to go into details, to particularise* | **≁keit** [f] ~/ *circumstantiality, fussiness* || *formality, ceremoniousness* || *complicatedness, bother* **·Umstands- ~bestimmung** f *adverbial modification* **~brötchen** n *sandwich* **~kleid** n *maternity* od *maturity dress* **~krämer** m ⟨fam⟩ *precision; slowcoach; fuss-pot* | ~ei [f] *f.-pottery* **~satz** m *adverb*(*ial*) *clause* **~wort** n ⟨gram⟩ *adverb* || ~ ohne Endung *flat adverb* **·um- ~|stauen** vt [h] ⟨mar⟩ *to restow* **~|stechen** vt irr [pp –gestochen] [h] ⟨hort⟩ *to turn up* || (Kupferstich) *to cut* od *engrave again* **~st·echen** vt irr [pp –st·ochen] [h] *to stitch all round* **~|stecken** vt [h] [pp –ge–ckt] *to pin differently, to re-arrange* **~st·ecken** vt [h] [pp –ckt] *to stick round about* **~st·ehen** vt irr [h] *to stand round* **~stehend** a *standing around* || das ~e Bild *the p. overleaf* || *on the next* od *opposite page* || siehe ~! *see over!* || wie ~ *as stated overleaf* | die **≁en** [pl] *the bystanders* pl **≁steige-**~karte (⟨fam a.⟩ ≁steiger [m]) [f] *connection-, through-, correspondence-ticket*; ⟨Am⟩ *transfer* (*ticket*); ~ort [m] *changing point; transfer* **~|steigen** vi irr [s] ⟨rail, etc⟩ *to change* (*trains*) (nach *for Paris*) || ⟨Am⟩ *to transfer* (*to a car*) **||** ≁ [n] *change*, ⟨Am⟩ *transfer* **~stellbar** a *reversible* **~|stellen** vt [h] [pp] –ge–llt] *to place differently; to shift; transpose* ⟨a. print⟩; (Reihenfolge, & ⟨gram⟩) *to invert* || ⟨mach⟩ *to reverse* || ⟨com, num⟩ *to reduce* od *convert* (auf [acc] *to*) || (Interesse) *to switch over* || sich ~ *to change one's attitude; to revise one's life; to accommodate o.s. to new conditions, to dance to another tune*, nutzlos *to box the compass* || .. auf *to adapt o.s. to* **~st·ellen** vt [h] [pp –llt] *to surround, beset* (*with*) || *to enclose* || ⟨mil⟩ *to round up* (*a farm*) || ⟨hunt⟩ *to hold up* (*a covert*) **≁|stellung** f ~/~en *transposition*; ⟨rail⟩ → –ordnung || ⟨gram⟩ *inversion* || ⟨pol⟩ *readjustment* || ⟨com-num⟩ *conversion* (*to*) || *adaptation* (*of industry from .. to*) || ⟨biol a.⟩ *modification* || ⟨fig⟩ *change-over* (*from .. to*) || *conversion* (*to diesel working* = ⟨Am⟩ *dieselization*); so: *containerization* (dazu: *to containerize*)

|| ~ auf das metrische System *metrication*; ~ auf das Dezimalsystem *decimalisation, -zation* **~steuerbar** a *reversible* **~|steuern** vt [h] ⟨mach, el⟩ *to reverse* **≚steuerung** f ~/ *reversal* || (Vorrichtung) *reversing gear* **~|stimmen** vt [h] *to alter the tune of, to tune anew* || (jdn) *to move* od *turn a p from his purpose, to bring a p round, to change a p's mind* || sich nicht leicht ~ l *to be difficult to move* od *convert* **≚stimmungstherapie** f *irritation* od *stimulation therapy* **~|stoßen** vt irr [h] *to knock down* od *over*; *to overthrow, overturn, upset* | ⟨fig⟩ *to upset, annul, revoke, invalidate*; (Befehl) *to countermand*; (Urteil) *to reverse, quash*; (Gesetz, Brauch) *to abolish*; (Kauf) *to undo*; (Entschluß) *to unmake* **≚stoßung** f ~/ *overthrow, -turning* || *upsetting* || *annulment* || *reversal* **~str·ahlen** vt [h] *to beam* od *shine round, to enwrap in rays* **~str·icken** vt [h] [pp –ckt] *to surround with net-work* || ⟨fig⟩ *to ensnare* **~str·itten** a *disputed, controversial, open to question*; die Frage .. ist ~ *it is an o. qu.* (*whether .. or*); viel ~ *vexed* (*qu.*) || hart ~ *closely contested* (*game*) **~str·ömen** vt [h] *to stream about* || (Meer) *to wash* **~|studieren** vi [h] *to change one's studies* **~|stufen** vt [h] (Gehalt, Stellung) *to regrade* **~|stülpen** vt [h] *to turn* od *tilt over* || *to invert* || sich ~ (Schirm) *to blow inside out* **≚sturz** m ~es/ *downfall, overthrow* || (völliger) *cataclysm* || (sozialer) *subversion, revolution, upheaval*; *upset* ⟨a. fig⟩; ⟨Am⟩ *overturn* ||| ~- *subversive* (*activity, movement, tendencies*) | ~lehren [f pl] *subversive* od *revolutionary doctrines* pl; ~partei [f] *destructive* od *revolutionary party, revolutionists* pl **~|stürzen I.** vt [h] *to throw down, tip over, lay low*; *to upset, upend, overturn, -throw* **II.** vi [s] *to fall down, to tumble* || (Boot) *to capsize* || (Baum) *to come down* || (Wagen) *to upset* **≚stürzler(in** f) m ~s/~ *revolutionist* | ≚isch [a] *revolutionary, subversive* **≚stürzung** f ~/ *overthrowing, overturning* **~|taufen** vt [h] *to rechristen* ⟨a. fig⟩ || ⟨ec⟩ *to rebaptize* || ⟨fig⟩ jdn ~ *to change a p's name* **≚tausch** m ~(e)s/ *exchange* **~tauschbar** a ⟨a.⟩ *convertible* (*letters*) **~|tauschen** vt [h] *to* (*ex*)-*change, swap* (gegen *for*); e–e S ~ gegen e–e andere *to give a th up for* **~|treten** vt [h] *to tread down* **≚triebe** m pl *practices, intrigues, machinations, stratagems* pl **≚trunk** m: e–n ~ halten *to have a drink all round* **~|tun** vt irr [h] *to put on, to take about one* | sich ~ (nach) *to cast* od *look about* (*for*) || (nach e–r Stelle) *to apply* (*for a situation*) || (bei Leuten) *to make inquiries*; überall *to busy o.s. in every direction* **≚w·allung** f ~/ *circumvallation* || ⟨fort⟩ *enceinte* Fr; ⟨hist a.⟩ *precinct* **~|wälzen** vt [h] *to overturn*; *to roll round* || ⟨fig⟩ *to revolutionize* | sich ~ [h] *to roll over, to revolve* | ~d ⟨fig⟩ *revolutionary*; *uprooting* (*change*); *sweeping* (*reform*, etc); *overriding* (*factor*); *landmark* (*experiment*) || *cataclysmal* **≚wälzpumpe** f *circulating p.* **≚wälzung** f ~/~en *turning about* || ⟨fig⟩ *revolution* || *change-over* (*from .. to*) || *upheaval*; völlige ~ ⟨pol⟩ *cataclysm* **~wandelbar** a ⟨com⟩ *convertible* **~|wandeln** vt [h] [pp –ge–lt] *to change, refashion*; *to transform* (⟨a. el⟩; Strom) (in [acc] *into*), *to turn* (*a th into another th*) || ⟨Am⟩ *to make* (*a p*) *over* (*into*) || ⟨com⟩ (Aktien, Zinsfuß) *to convert* || ⟨jur⟩ (Urteil, Strafe, Rente etc) *to commute* (*into*) || er ist wie –gewandelt *he is quite altered* | sich ~ *to change*; *to be transformed*; ⟨physiol⟩ *to become assimilated* || *to turn* (*into a th*) **~w·andeln** vt [h] [pp –lt] *to walk round* **≚wandlung** f ~/~en *change, transformation* || ⟨phys a.⟩ *fusion*; ⟨biol⟩ *transmutation* || ⟨com, chem, phys⟩ *conversion* (*into*); *c. of merchant ships into warships*; ⟨comp⟩ *c. of file data*; || ⟨jur⟩ *commutation* (*to*) | **~s-** ~programm [n] ⟨comp⟩ *assembler*; ~prozeß [m] *metamorphosis*; ~temperatur [f] *equilibrium* od *critical t.* **~w·eben** vt [h] *to weave a web round* || –woben ⟨fig⟩ *adorned* (von .. *with ancient myths* = *mysterious* **~|wechseln** vt [h] *to exchange* (*for*) || (Geld, Kleider) *to change* || (Drähte) *to change over* **≚wechs(e)lung** f ~/~en *alternate use* || *changing money*; *exchange* || (v Schecks) *encashment* **≚weg** m ~(e)s/~e *roundabout way, detour*; ⟨rail⟩ *loop-way* || (in Gedanken) *digression* || es ist nur ein ~ v 3 Meilen *it is only 3 miles out of the way* | **auf** gr ~en *by long circuits* || auf ~en ⟨mil telph⟩ *by way of alternate routing*; ⟨fig⟩ *indirectly*; ⟨fig⟩ *by hints* od *indirection* || auf ~en erfahren *to hear through a side-channel* || ohne ~e *straight to the point* | e–n ~ m *to take a roundabout way, to make a detour* || ~e gebrauchen ⟨fig⟩ *to employ evasions* || jdn e–n ~ m l *to take a p out of his way* | ~schaltung [f] ⟨el, telph⟩ *alternating routing* **~|wehen** vt [h] [pp –ge–ht] *to blow down* **~w·ehen** vt [h] [pp –ht] *to blow round, to fan* **~w·eht** a *breathed upon* **≚welt** f ~/ *environment, surroundings* pl; *atmosphere*; *life around*; *ambient*; *milieu* | ~akzente, ~situationen [pl] ⟨arts⟩ *environments*; Änderung der ~bedingungen [f pl] ⟨biol⟩ *changes of e.t* | ≚bedingt [a] *conditional on the surroundings*; ~forschung [f] *ecology*; ≚gestört [a] ⟨soc⟩ *maladjusted*; ~hygiene [f] *e.tal hygiene*; ~lehre [f] *euthenics* [sg konstr]; ~wechsel [m] *change* **~|wenden** vt irr [h] *to turn round* od *about* || (in e–m Buche) *to turn over* (*a leaf*); bitte ~! *please turn over*! (*P. T. O.*) || es wendet mir das Herz um *it makes my heart ache* || mit –gewandter Hand *with the back of the hand, backhand* (*stroke*) | sich ~ *to turn* (*round*) || (Wind) *to veer* (*round*) **~w·erben** vt [h] *to court, woo* || sie ist viel –w·orben *she has many suiters* **~|werfen** vt irr [h] *to overthrow, overturn, upset, subvert*; → –stürzen || *to bowl* (*a p*) *over*; ⟨fig⟩ *to upset a p*; das wirft ihn um *that'll set him on his heels, .. knock him off his feet* || *to knock* od *tumble over* (*chairs*) || (Glas, Wagen) *to upset*; (Hürde) *to knock down* || ⟨agr⟩ (die Erde) *to turn up ..* || (Kleider) *to throw* od *fling round, over, on* || (Gewehr) *to sling about* || (Urteil) *to reverse* | vi [h] (v Wagen) *to upset* || ⟨fam com⟩ *to fail*, ⟨fam⟩ *to go smash* **~|werten** vt [h] *to revalue* **≚wertung** f ~/~en *revaluation*; *revision* (*of values*) || (Nietzsche:) *transvaluation* (*of all values*); ⟨psych⟩ (unbewußt) *sublimation* **~|wickeln** vt [h] [pp –ge–lt]; (Bindfaden etc, Papier etc um etw wickeln) *to wind* (*cord*, etc) *round* (*a th*), *to wrap* (*paper*, etc) *round* od *about* (*a th*) || (anders wickeln) *to wrap differently* **~w·ickeln** vt [h] [pp –lt] *to wind* (*with*) || (einpacken) *to wrap* (*up*) (mit *in*) **~|winden** vt [h] *to wind* od *twine around* **~w·inden** vt [h] *to encircle, swathe* (*with*); *to crown* (*a p's forhead with laurel*) **~w·ittern** vt [h] *to hover, breathe, waft round ..* **≚wohner** m pl *neighbours* pl, *p.s living around* **~w·ölken** vt [h] *to cloud, darken* ⟨a. fig⟩ | sich ~ *to become overcast* || –kt *clouded* (*moon, mind*) **~|wühlen** vt [h] *to uproot, to grub up* || ⟨fig⟩ *to ransack* **≚wurf** m → –hang **~z·äunen** vt [h] *to fence in* || (mit e–r Hecke) *to hedge in* **≚z·äunung** f ~/~en *hedge, enclosure, fence* **~|zeichnen** vt [h] *to draw afresh* || ⟨com⟩ *to re-mark* (*goods*) **~z·eichnen** vt [h] *to adorn all round with drawings* **~|ziehen** vt irr [h] [pp –gezogen] *to pull down* || (s–e Schuhe) *to put on fresh ..* || (ein Kind) *to change a child's clothes* | sich ~ *to change* (*one's* [od *into other*] *clothes*) || vi [s] *to go* od *move round about* || (in e–e andere Wohnung) *to shift* (*one's lodgings*); *to* (*re*)*move* (nach *to*), *to change one's residence, dwelling, apartments, quarters*, (b. Dienstboten) *situation* **~z·iehen** vt irr [h] [pp –zogen]; (mit etw umgeben) *to surround, to hang round with* || (sich erstrecken um) *to run round* || (einhüllen) *to cover all round* || (umr·eißen) *to draw the outlines of* || (um etw herummarschieren) *to go* od *move round about* | sich ~ (Himmel) *to*

cloud over, to become overcast **~z·ingeln** vt [h] *to surround, encompass, encircle* || ⟨mil⟩ *to hem* od *hedge in* || *to round up* | nicht **~zubringen(d)** a *unkillable*

·**Umzug** m ~(e)s/⁼e *procession* || (Wohnungswechsel) *removal, move*; ⟨Am⟩ *moving*; (v Dienstboten) *change of situation* | **~s-** **~arbeiter** m *removal-man* **~geschäft** n *furniture-removal business* **~gelder** pl *move allowance* **~gut** n *personal effects* pl, Einwanderer⁼ *immigrant's e.s* ⁼-**halber** [adv] *owing to removal* **~kosten** pl *removal expenses, cost* [sg] *of removing* | ~entschädigung [f] *removal allowance* **~tag** m, **~termin** m *day, time fixed for removal*, ⟨Am⟩ *moving-day*

·**un..** pref [in comp, s, a, adv, pres p, pp] **A. 1.** [neg] ⁼glück, ⁼tiefe a) | [a] ~echt, ~würdig, ~dichterisch || ~ähn**lich,** ~acht**sam,** ~ausspr·ech**lich,** ~auff·ind**bar** etc → verb | [adv] ~gern | [pres p] ~genügend etc → verb | [pp] ~gebildet, ~erfahren || ~bedacht, ~bed·acht; ~beobachtet, ~be·obachtet etc → verb **2.** ⟨dero⟩ ⁼mensch, ⁼tier **3.** ⟨emph⟩ ⁼geld, ⁼menge, ⁼tiefe b) **B. I.** [bei s oft]: *lack* od *want of*; ⟨a.⟩ *un..*: *unstate, unnature*, etc **II.** [bei a] **1.** *in..*: ~duldsam *intolerant* **2.** *un..*: ~stet *unstable* **3.** *not*: ~schwer *not difficult* **4.** *..less*: ~blutig *bloodless* (*victory*) **5.** *non ..*: ~starr *non-rigid* **6.** *past*: ~h·eilbar *past cure*; so: *past endurance* **7.** *without* (*wings*) **8.** *anti..*: ~kirchlich *anticlerical* **III.** [bei adv oft:] **1.** *without* + s **2.** *without being* (*asked*)

unab- [pref] un- + [pref] ab- **~·änderlich** a *unalterable* || *unchangeable, immutable* || *irrevocable* | ⁼keit [f] ~/ *unalterableness*; *irrevocability* **~d·ingbar** a *inalienable* (*right*); *irreducible* || *inevitable, unavoidable*; ~e P *free agent* **~gefertigt** a *undispatched* **~gestimmt** a *unbalanced* **~hängig** a *independent* (v *of*); ⟨eco⟩ *self-supporting, -contained*; *antarchic(al)*; *sovereign* (*individual*) || ~e P *free agent*; ~er Vertreter *free lance* | ⁼e(r) [m] ⟨pol⟩ *maverick* | [adv] ~ v–e–a *independently* ⁼-**hängigkeit** f ~/ *independence, detachment* || wirtschaftliche ~ *self-sufficiency* | ~sbewegung [f] *indep. movement*; ~serklärung [f] ⟨Am⟩ *Declaration of I.* (⟨hist Am⟩ 4. 7. 1776); ~ssinn [m] *independent spirit* **~kömmlich** a (P) *indispensable* ⟨a. mil⟩ || *required at one's post* || ich bin heute ~ *I am not at liberty to-day* | ⁼**e** [der ~, ein ~r] m ~n/~n (→ a) ⟨fam⟩ *vip* (= *very important p*) | ⁼keit [f] *indispensability* **~lässig** a *unceasing, continual, unremitting, ceaseless*; *incessant* (*toil*) || (P) *unrelenting* (*efforts, pressure*) | [adv] *without letup*; jdm ~ folgen *to dog a p* || etw ~ tun *to keep doing a th* || sich ~ bemühen *to be unrelenting in one's efforts* (*towards* ..); ~ weitergehen etc *to walk* (*to ride*) *on and on*; ~ schwätzen *to talk nineteen to a dozen* **~l·ösbar** a *undetachable* || (Hypothek) *irredeemable* || ~e Anleihe *consolidated fund* || (Rente etc) *perpetual* **~r·eißbar** a ⟨übtr⟩ (Kette) *continuous* **~s·ehbar** a *immeasurable* || *incalculable* (*effects*); *unbounded* || *not to be foreseen* || ⟨fig⟩ in ~er Ferne *out of sight, far ahead* | [adv] *immensely* **~setzbar** a *irremovable* **~sichtlich** a *unintentional* || [adv] *involuntarily* **~st·ellbar** a *that cannot be turned off* od *stopped*; *unchangeable, irremediable* **~w·eislich** a *imperative* || *urgent* || *inevitable* **~w·endbar** a *inevitable, irremediable* || *appointed by fate*; *fated*

·**un-** **~achtsam** a *inattentive*; *negligent, careless*; (zerstreut) *absent-minded* || ~ s *to be off one's guard* | ⁼keit [f] ~/ *inadvertency, inattention* || *negligence*, etc || aus ~ *through inadvertence*, etc, *inadvertently* **~ad(e)lig** a *not noble* od *titled* || ⟨übtr⟩ *ignoble* || die ⁼en *the commoners* ⟨a. pol⟩ **~ähnlich** a *unlike, dissimilar* || (P) *bearing no resemblance* ([dat] *to*) | ⁼keit [f] ~/ *unlikeness, dissimilarity, dissimilitude* **~andächtig** a *in..* od *undevout* **~anfechtbar** a *incontestable, undisputable* || *unassailable* (*argument*) || [pred] *beyond exception*

·**unange-** ([pref] un- + [pref] an- + [pp-*particle*] -ge-) **~baut** a ⟨agr⟩ *uncultivated* **~bracht** a *out of place* | *misplaced*; *inopportune*; *uncalled for* **~fochten** a *uncontested, undisputed* || (unbehelligt) *unmolested, unaffected, unswayed* (v *by*) || ~ l *to allow .. to go unchallenged*; laß mich ~! *let me alone*! **~kleidet** a *undressed, not dressed* || *in deshabille* **~kündigt** a (→ ⟨a.⟩ unangemeldet) *unheralded* **~lehnt** a ⟨tact⟩ *exposed* (*flank*) **~-meldet** a *unannounced* | [adv] *without being announced* || *without announcement* (od ⟨com⟩ *notice*) **~messen** a *incongruous, unsuitable* || (unziemlich) *improper* || (unzulänglich) *inadequate* | ⁼heit [f] *-ness* **~nehm** a *unpleasant, disagreeable* || *embarrassing* || *uncomfortable* (*awakening*) || *offensive* (*odour*) || *rude* (*beginnings*) || ~ v Geschmack *unpalatable* || ~e Lage *awkward plight* || (P) *unprepossessing*; *troublesome*; *ugly* (Kerl *customer*) || die ~e Seite *the seamy side* (*of life*) || jdm etw ⁼es sagen ⟨Am fam⟩ *to sound a sour note* | [adv] ~ berühren *to jar* od *grate upon*; ~ berührt *unpleasantly struck* || ~ empfinden *to resent* (*a th*); [neg & interr] *to mind* (*if you don't m.*; *would you m.?*) **~rührt,** **~tastet** a *untouched*

·**unan-** **~greifbar** a ⟨chem⟩ *incorrodible* **~greiflich** a *untouchable, unassailable* **~nehmbar** a *unacceptable* ⁼**nehmlichkeit** f ~/~en [mit pl] *unpleasantness*; *discomfort* || (Übelstand) *drawback, inconvenience* || [pl] *annoyances* | [ohne pl] *disagreeableness* || ~en z gewärtigen h *to be in for trouble* | sich ~en zuziehen *to get into trouble* (⟨fam⟩ *into hot water*) || jdn ~en aussetzen *to i.ce a p, to put a p to i.ce*, ⟨fam⟩ *to put a p about* **~sehnlich** a *mean-looking, plain, homely* || ⟨bot⟩ *inconspicuous* (⟨a. fig⟩ *hotel*) || *insignificant* | ⁼keit [f] ~/ *homeliness, mean appearance, plainness* || *insignificance* **~ständig** a (Betragen etc) *improper, indecent, indecorous*; *shocking*; ⟨euph⟩ *not a nice* (*song*) || es gilt als ~ *it is bad form* | (P) *ill-mannered* | [adv] *immodestly* (*dressed*) | ⁼keit [f] ~/~en *indecency, indecorum* **~stellig** a *clumsy, awkward* **~stößig** a *inoffensive, unoffending, unobjectionable, correct* | [pred] *without offence* **~t·astbar** a *intangible* || *unimpeachable* || *inviolable* || *unassailable* (*validity*); *inexpugnable* (*merits*) **~wendbar** a *inapplicable* | ⁼keit [f] ~/ *inapplicability*

·**unappetitlich** a *distasteful, unsavoury*; *unprepossessing* (*p*); ⟨emph⟩ *nasty, disgusting* ·**Unart** **1.** f ~/ [ohne pl] *bad conduct, want of good manners, ill breeding, rudeness, incivility* || (b. Kindern) *naughtiness* | [mit pl: ~en] *bad habit* || ⟨hors⟩ *vice* || *naughty* od *rude trick* **2.** m ~(e)s/~e (P) *naughty child*; *rude p*; ⟨fam⟩ *rascal, pickle*, ⟨Am⟩ *hellion* | ⁼**ig** a *ill-bred, -behaved, -mannered* || (gegen Frauen) *ungallant* | (v Kindern) *fractious, naughty* || *bad, mischievous* (*boy*) || seid nicht so ~! *behave yourselves*! **~igkeit** f ~/~en = Unart ·**un-** **~artikuliert** a ⟨gram⟩ *inarticulate* **~ästhetisch** a *offensive, coarse* || *vulgar* || *disgusting, nasty*

Una-Sancta-Bewegung f *an oecumenical movement*

·**unauf-** **~dringlich** a *undemonstrative*; (P) *unassuming, retiring, unobtrusive*, dazu: *-ness*; *quiet* (*colour*) **~fällig** a *unobtrusive, inconspicuous* | [adv] *quietly* **~findbar** a *undiscoverable unfindable* **~gefordert** a *unbidden* || *uncalled, u. for* | [adv] *spontaneously*; *of one's own accord* || etw ~ tun *to volunteer a th* **~geklärt** a *unexplained, mysterious* || (P) *unenlightened*; *unilluminated* **~geschlossen** a *unexploited* (*country*) || *reserved* (*p*) **~geschnitten** a *uncut* **~h·altsam** a *irresistible, resistless* || *unavoidable* || *unflagging* (*advance*) **~h·örlich** a *incessant, ceaseless*; *uninterrupted,* *unremitting*; *un-* od *never ending*; *continuous, constant* || *perpetual* || *endless, interminable* | [adv] *without ceasing* od *intermission* || *for ever* || ~ tun *to keep doing* **~lösbar, ~löslich** a *indissoluble*; *insoluble* ⟨a. chem, math⟩ || (Geheimnis) *inexplicable* || (Knoten, Aufgabe) *inextricable* || ⟨fig⟩ *unbreakable* (*ties*) | ~́keit [f] ~/ *indissolubility* (*of marriage*) **~merksam** a *inattentive* || *absent-minded*; *unseeing* | ~́keit [f] ~/ *inattention, inattentiveness* **~richtig** a *insincere* || *double-faced* || *deceitful* || *false* (*friend*); *disingenuous, backhanded* | [adv] (*to ring*) *hollow* | ~́keit [f] ~/ *insincerity*; *deceit* **~sch·iebbar, -lich** a *not to be postponed* od *delayed* || *urgent, pressing*

·unaus- **~bl·eiblich** a *unfailing, infallible, inevitable* || *certain* || [pred] *bound to happen* | ~́keit [f] ~/ *infallibility* **~f·ührbar** a *impracticable*, ⟨Am⟩ *impractical* || *unfeasible* || *impossible* || *unworkable* (*plan*) | ~́keit [f] ~/ *impracticability* || ⟨Am⟩ *impracticality* || etc

·unausge- ([pref] un- + [pref] aus- + [pp-*particle*] -ge-) **~arbeitet** a, **~baut** a *unfinished* **~backen** a *slack-baked* **~bildet** a ⟨mst mil⟩ *untrained* || (unfertig) *undeveloped* || ⟨bot, zoo⟩ *rudimentary* **~führt** a *unexecuted, uneffected*; ⟨arts⟩ *unfinished* **~füllt** a *not filled up* || (Formular) *blank* **~glichen** a *unbalanced*; *maladjusted* || *inequitable, iniquitous, unjust*; *unstable* || *outstanding* (*debt*) | ~́heit [f] *imbalance, unbalance*, etc **~goren** a ⟨fig⟩ *crude* || *uncultivated, rough, undeveloped*; *half-baked* (*ideas*) **~macht** a *undecided* || *open* (*question*) || *uncertain* (*matter*) || *questionable* (*gain*) **~nützt** a *unexploited* | adv ~ laufen: *the water pours over* (od *runs*) *to waste* **~setzt** a *continual, uninterrupted, unremitting, restless, constant* | [adv] *without intermission* **~sprochen** a *unsaid*; *unspoken* (*consent*) | ⟨fig⟩ *implied* || *neutral* (*colour*)

·unaus- **~l·öschlich** a *inextinguishable, ineffaceable*; *indelible* (*ink*) || *quenchless* (*thirst*) | ⟨fig⟩ *lasting* (*impression, gratitude*) || [pred] *deeply engraved* (*in one's mind*) **~r·ottbar** a *ineradicable* || ⟨zoo⟩ *not exterminable* || ⟨fig⟩ *besetting* (*weakness*) **~s·öhnlich** a *irreconcilable* **~spr·echbar** a *unpronounceable*, ⟨fam⟩ *jaw-breaking* **~spr·echlich** a *inexpressible*; *ineffable* (*grace*), *unspeakable* (*horror*) || ⟨emph⟩ die ~́en (= Hose) [f pl] *the inexpressibles, inexplicables, unmentionables, unutterables*, ⟨fam obs⟩ *ineffables* pl || [pred] *beyond words* **~st·ehlich** a *insupportable, insufferable, intolerable*; *odious* || ⟨fam⟩ *awful, horrible* (*noise*) || [pred] [dat] *I loathe* (*the very thought of it*) || || er ist ihr ~ *she can't bear the sight of him* || ⟨Am fam⟩ (*he's*) *a pain in the neck* **~t·ilgbar** a = –löschbar **~w·eichlich** a *inevitable, ineluctable, unavoidable, inescapable* | ~́keit [f] *inevitability*, etc; → *poetic justice* **~wischbar** a *ineffaceable*, → –löschlich

·un- **~́band** m ~es/ *unmanageable child*; *young Turk* || *wayward p* | ~́ig [a] *unruly, intractable, irrepressible*; *unmanageable*; *untoward* || *insensate* (*fury*); *incontinent* (*enthusiasm*) | ⟨fam⟩ ([adv]) *extreme*(*ly*), *awful*(*ly*) *tremendous*(*ly*), *immense*(*ly*), ⟨sl⟩ *wild*(*ly*) || [adv] ⟨sl⟩ *like hell* || er hat sich ~ gefreut *he was as pleased as Punch* **~barmherzig** a *uncharitable, unmerciful, merciless, pitiless* || ⟨übtr⟩ *bitter, unrelenting, relentless, remorseless, unremitting*; ⟨hum⟩ *unhumorous* | ~keit [f] ~/ *cruelty, remorselessness*, etc **~bärtig** a *beardless*

·unbe- **~absichtigt** a *unintentional*; *unwilling* **~achtet** a *unnoticed* || (absichtlich ~) *disregarded* || ~ l *to ignore, neglect* || ~ bleiben *to escape notice* **~amtet** a *noncommissioned* **~anstandet** a *not objected to*; *unopposed, unimpeached* || ~ l *to let* (*a th*) *take its course* **~·antwortet** bleiben *to go unanswered* || ~ l *not to answer* **~·antwortlich** a *unanswerable* **~·arbeitet** a *untreated*; (*subject*) *not yet treated before* || ⟨tech⟩ *unwrought, unprocessed*; *raw, crude* || *untanned* (*skins*) **~·aufsichtigt** a *unattended to, not looked after* **~b·aubar** a ⟨agr⟩ *unfit for cultivation* **~b·aut** a (Gelände) *not built on*; *vacant* (*plot*); *idle* (*land*); ⟨hort, agr⟩ *uncultivated, untilled* **~dacht(sam), ~dächtig** a *inconsiderate*; *heedless, thoughtless, indiscreet, rash*; *feckless* (in Geldsachen) | [adv] ~ handeln ⟨a.⟩ *to go it blind* **~deckt** a *uncovered, bare*(*-headed*) **~d·enklich** a (P) *unhesitating, unscrupulous* || (S) *harmless, unobjectionable* | [adv] *without hesitation* | ~́keitsbescheinigung [f] *clearance certificate* ⟨a. marzoll⟩; ~keitserklärung [f] *clearance* ⟨a. mil⟩ **~deutend** a *insignificant* || *unimportant, immaterial, inconsequential, two-by-four* || *petty, trifling, trivial* || (*s*)*light* (*error*) || ~er Mensch [m] *small fry*, ⟨Am⟩ *small potatoes* || ~e S *straw*; *molehill* (*of danger*), *inferior* (*position*) || *negligible* (*quantity*) || *minor* (*matters* = *bagatelles*) || ⟨fam⟩ [pred] *small beer, nothing to write home about, off the map* | [adv] *in a small way* **~d·ingt** a *unconditional* (*satisfaction*) || *unqualified* || (–schränkt) *unlimited, absolute* || (Gehorsam) *implicit*; in ~er Treue ergeben s *to be sturdily loyal* | [adv] *certainly, by all means* || *without fail* od *reserve* || ~ notwendig *or* verlangt (*definitely*) *required* (*subject*) || ich will sie ~ kennenlernen *I've got to know her*; so: *I do have to talk to him* ich will ~ wissen *I am determined to know* || er ist ~ dazu entschlossen ⟨Am fam⟩ *he's dead set to do it* **~eidigt** a *not sworn, unsworn* **~einflußt** a *uninfluenced, unprejudiced* **~einträchtigt** a *unimpaired*; *untainted* (*by drugs*) **~endigt** a ⟨a.⟩ *incomplete* **~fähigt** a *without talents* od *qualifications*; *incompetent, unqualified* **~fahrbar** a *impassable, impracticable* || ⟨mar⟩ *not navigable* **~fahren** a *trackless* || ~es Volk *inexperienced sailors*, ⟨fam⟩ *green hands* **~fangen** a *unprejudiced, unbiassed*; *impartial* || (offen) *frank, open, candid*; *unsophisticated, ingenuous* || *natural, unaffected*; *dispassionate*; *open* (*mind*) || (gleichmütig) *unconscious, nonchalant*, ⟨fam⟩ *easy*(*-going*) | ~heit [f] ~/ ⟨a.⟩ *ease, candour, naiveté, simplicity* **~festigt** a *unfortified* || *open* (*town*) || *unsurfaced* (*road*) **~fiedert** a *unfledged* (*bird*); *featherless* (*arrow*) **~fl·eckt** a *unpolluted, unsullied, stainless* ⟨a. fig⟩ || ⟨fig⟩ *untainted* (*virtue*); *immaculate* (*conception of the Virgin*) **~frachtet** a ⟨a.⟩ *empty* **~friedigend** a *unsatisfactory, insufficient*; *lame* (*excuse*) **~friedigt** a *unappeased* || *ungratified* (*wish*); *unsatisfied, not contented* (v *with*) || es hat mich ~ gelassen *it disappointed me* || ⟨sex⟩ ~e ältere Frau *dissatisfied matron* **~fruchtet** a *unimpregnated* **~fugt** a *unauthorized, incompetent* || ~́en ist der Eintritt verboten *no admittance except on business, authorized p.s only* || ~es Betreten (e–s Grundstücks) ⟨jur⟩ *trespassing*, .. bei Strafe verboten *trespassers will be prosecuted* || [adv] ~erweise *without authority* **~gabt** a *untalented* || ~er Kerl *duffer, dullard* **~gangen** a *unfrequented*; *untrodden* (*path*) **~geben** a *undisposed of, unsold* **~glichen** a *unliquidated* (*debts*) **~greiflich** a *incomprehensible, inconceivable*; *irrational*; *unlikely* (*mistake*) || es erscheint mir ~ *I can't see* ..; es war ~, daß niemand .. war *it was i. that nobody should be able to* | ~́keit [f] ~/ *incomprehensibility* || *mysterious affair, mystery* **~grenzbar** a *illimitable* **~grenzt** a *unbounded, boundless*; *unlimited* (*diversity*) || [adv] ⟨a.⟩ *indefinitely* **~gründet** a ⟨fig⟩ *groundless, unfounded* (*criticism*), *unsupported* (*charges*), *false* (*hope*) | der Glaube ist ~ *there is no basis for* .. **~gütert** a *landless*; *having no* (*landed*) *property* || ⟨allg⟩ *not rich*; *impecunious* **~haart** a *hairless* || ⟨bot, zoo⟩ *smooth* || *bald* (*head*) || *bare* (*place*) || ⟨scient⟩ *glabrous* **~́hagen** n ~s/ *uneasiness, qualm*; *malaise* || (*to his*) *dismay* od *discomfort* ‖ (*with an air of*) *distaste* **~haglich** a *uneasy*; *uncosy, uncomfortable, unpleasant* ‖ sich ∼ fühlen *to feel ill at ease* od ⟨fam⟩ *out of it* od *sorts* | ≗keit [f] ∼/ *discomfort*, etc **~hauen** a ⟨fig⟩ *unpolished, coarse* **~helligt** a *unmolested, undisturbed* **~herrscht** a *unrestrained, uncontrollable, uncontrolled, unruled, unbalanced* | ∼ handeln ⟨a.⟩ *to shoot the works*; ∼ laut sprechend *unable to control one's voice* | ≗heit [f] ∼/ ⟨a.⟩ *abandonment* **~herzigt** a *unnoticed, disregarded* ‖ ∼ l *to disregard* **~herzt** a *fainthearted, discouraged* **~hindert** a *unimpeded, unopposed, unshackled*; *unfettered*; *foot-loose*; *untrammeled*; *unincumbered* (*by*); ∼ durch *clear of* (*the trees*) | [adv] *freely* **~holfen** a *awkward, heavy-handed*; *clumsy* (⟨a. fig⟩ *sentence*); *uncouth* (*style*) ‖ (schwerfällig) *heavy, ungainly* ‖ (verlegen) *embarrassed* | ≗heit [f] *awkwardness, clumsiness*; *heaviness* **~·irrbar** a *determined*; *imperturbale* **~·irrt** a *unswerving*; *undaunted*; *resolute, unfaltering*; *persevering*; *dogged, steadfast*; ∼ bleiben ⟨a.⟩ *to sit tight* ‖ ∼ durch *uninfluenced, undeterred by* | [adv] ⟨a.⟩ *unerringly, calmly*; *firmly*; *steady* ‖ ∼ weitergehen *to go straight on* **~kannt** a (→ neu) *unknown* (⟨a. math⟩ *quantity* Größe; ⟨mil⟩ *unidentified*; jdm *to* .., v Ansehen *by sight*) ‖ **(mit)** *unacquainted* (*with*), *ignorant* (*of*) ‖ (Land) ⟨a.⟩ *unchartered*; ([*terra*] *incognita* L) ‖ (⟨fig⟩ Gebiet) (*land*) *beyond the rainbow*; *unfamiliar* (*ground*) ‖ (P) *obscure* ‖ die schöne ≗e *the fair stranger* | ich bin hier selbst ganz ∼ *I am quite a stranger here m.s.* ‖ er ist mir (völlig) ∼ *I don't know him* (*he is a perfect stranger to me*) ‖ das war mir ∼ *I was not aware of that* ‖ **es** wird dir nicht ∼ s, daß *you know, of course, that* ‖ es dürfte dir nicht ∼ s, daß *you cannot be ignorant of the fact that* **~kannterweise** [adv] (grüßen) .. *although I do not know him personally* ≗**kanntheit** f (*his*) *obscurity* ‖ ⟨a.⟩ = ≗**kanntschaft** f (mit) *unacquaintance, unfamiliarity* (*with*), *ignorance* (*of*) **~k·ehrbar** a *inconvertible, callous* **~kleidet** a ⟨a.⟩ *bare*; *without nothing on* **~kümmert** a *careless, nonchalant*; *happy-go-lucky*; *negligent* ‖ (um) *reckless* (*of*); *indifferent* (*as to*); *unconcerned*; (unbedacht) *heedless*; (sorglos) *insouciant* Fr ‖ ∼ um (ohne Rücksicht auf) *mindless of* ‖ ⟨fam⟩ *noncarish* (*about*) ‖ sei ganz ∼! *don't alarm y.s.* | ≗heit [f] *carelessness, airiness, recklessness*; *unconcern*(*edness*) **~laden** a *unloaded* ‖ ⟨mar⟩ *without cargo* **~lastet** a ⟨fig⟩ *carefree, unincumbered* **~lästigt** a *unmolested* **~laubt** a *leafless, bare* **~lebt** a *inanimate, lifeless*, ⟨com mst⟩ *dull* ‖ (Straße) *unfrequented* ‖ (P) *apathetic* ‖ ∼e Dinge *stocks and stones* **~leckt** a ⟨fig, fam⟩ v der Kultur ∼ *without any suspicion of culture*; *uncivilized* **~lehrbar** a *unconvincible* ‖ ∼ s *to take no advice* **~lehrt** a *uninstructed* **~lesen** a *illiterate, unlettered, unlearned* | ≗heit [f] ∼/ *illiteracy, want of reading* **~liebt** a *disliked, very little* od *not much liked* ‖ (beim Volke) *unpopular* (bei *with*; ⟨fam a.⟩ *with a p*) ‖ (S) *at a discount* | ≗heit [f] ∼/ *unpopularity* **~lüftet** a *unventilated* (*grain*); *unvented* (*toilet*) **~mannt** a ⟨mar, aero⟩ *unmanned* **~m·erkbar** a *imperceptible* **~merkt** a *unnoticed, unperceived* ‖ [adv] *without being noticed, w. detection*; das Alter kam ∼ über ihn *age creeped upon him* etc ‖ (verstohlen) *stealthily* **~mittelt** a *poor, without means, necessitous* (*students*); ⟨hum⟩ *impecunious* **~namt** a = **~-nannt** a *unnamed, anonymous* ‖ ⟨math⟩ *abstract* (*number*) ∼**nommen** a *permitted, allowed, not prohibited* ‖ es bleibt Ihnen ∼ *you are free* od *welcome* od *at liberty* (*to do*) **~nutzbar** a *unserviceable* **~nutzt** a *unused, unemployed* ‖ *dormant*; (Geld) *idle* ‖ ∼ bleiben, liegen *to lie by*; ∼ l *to pass up* (*chances*); das wird er nicht ∼ l *he will not fail to make good use of it, he will not let the opportunity slip by* **~quem** a *inconvenient, uncomfortable*; *troublesome*; *disagreeable*; *unhandy* (*arrangement*); *embarrassing* (*to*) | ≗lichkeit [f] ∼/ *inconvenience, discomfort*; gr ∼ *hardship* ‖ jdm ∼en bereiten *to put a p to trouble* **~r·echenbar** a *incalculable* (⟨a.⟩ *p*); *unpredictable* (*consequences*); *wayward* ‖ ⟨fig⟩ (P) *erratic, kittle*; *whimsical*; *unreliable* ‖ *uncertain* (*player*) ‖ *veering* (*temper*) | ≗keiten [f pl] *vagaries* **~rechnet** a *free of charge* **~rechtigt** a *unwarranted, unauthorized*; *unqualified* ‖ *unfounded, misplaced*, → unverdient | ∼erweise [adv] *without authority* **~reist** a *untravelled* **~richtigt** a *uncorrected* ‖ *unpaid* (*bill*) **~ritten** a (P) *unmounted* ‖ (Pferd) *not broken in* **~r·ücksichtigt** a *unconsidered, disregarded* ‖ ∼ l *to ignore, miss*; *to leave out of count, to make no allowance for* **~r·ufen** a *uncalled for, impertinent* ‖ *intruding, officious* | [adv] *without being asked, intrusively* | ∼! [superstitious intj] *touch wood*! **~rühmt** a ⟨a.⟩ *obscure* ≗**rührbarkeit** f *untouchability* **~rührt** a *untouched, unaffected*; *not influenced* od *altered*; ⟨übtr⟩ *innocent* (*hair* .. *of comb, face* .. *of water*) *unmoved* ‖ ⟨cul a.⟩ *untasted* ‖ *undisturbed* ‖ *virgin* (*soil*) ‖ ∼ l ⟨fig⟩ *to pass over in silence* **~schadet** prep [gen] *without prejudice* od *detriment to* ‖ *quite apart from* (*your claim*) **~schädigt** a *unhurt*, ⟨com⟩ *undamaged, in good* od *mint condition, uninjured* ‖ *unspoilt* **~schäftigt** a *unemployed, out of work* ‖ (frei) *disengaged, vacant*; *at leisure* **~scheiden** a *immodest, exacting* ‖ (anmaßend) *presumptuous, arrogant, insolent* ‖ (Preis) *unreasonable* | ≗heit [f] ∼/ *exaction*; *want of modesty* ‖ *presumption, insolence* etc **~schlagen** a (Pferd) *unshod* ‖ ⟨fig⟩ (in) *not versed, unskilled* (*in*); *unfamiliar* (*with*) **~schnitten** a (Jude) *uncircumcised* ‖ (Münze) *unclipped* ‖ (Buch) *uncut*; ∼e Seiten *conjugates* ‖ (Baum) *untrimmed, uncut* **~scholten** a *irreproachable* (*life*), *blameless* (*conduct*); *of unblemished, stainless* (od *completely good*) *character* ‖ ⟨jur⟩ er ist noch ∼ *he has an honourable record* | ≗heit [f] *integrity* **~schottert** a = –ge– **~schrankt** a ⟨rail⟩ *unguarded* **~schränkt** a *unlimited, unrestricted, unbounded* ‖ *absolute* (*monarchy*, etc) ‖ *unstinted* (*praise*, etc); ⟨com⟩ Gesellschaft mit ∼er Haftpflicht *joint-stock company* **~schr·eiblich** a *indescribable, inexpressible, past* od *beggaring, beyond* (*all*) *description* ‖ *unspeakable* (*misery*), *unutterable* (*scoundrel*); *ineffable* (*grandeur, mercy*, etc) | [adv] ⟨a.⟩ *extremely, exceedingly* **~schrieben** a (Papier) *blank* ‖ ⟨fig⟩ *undescribed* °**~schr·ien**! = –berufen! **~sch·uht** a *unshod* **~schützt** a *unprotected, unguarded* **~schwert** a *unburdened* ‖ *easy, light* (*conscience*); ∼ v Sorgen *unworried*; (P) *light-hearted* **~seelt** a *inanimate, lifeless* **~sehen** a *unseen, unexamined* ‖ etw ∼ kaufen *to buy a pig in a poke* **~setzt** a ⟨a.⟩ *vacant* (*post, chair*) **~s·iegbar, ~s·ieglich** a *invincible, undefeatable* ‖ *irresistible* ‖ *unquenchable* (*good humour*) **~soldet** a *unpaid, unsalaried* ‖ *honorary* (*post*) **~sonnen** a *thoughtless, inconsiderate*; *heedless*; *light-headed*; *headlong*; ⟨fam⟩ *giddy* ‖ *reckless, rash*; → –dacht, ⟨Am⟩ *dizzy* ‖ *indiscreet* (*words*) | ≗heit [f] *indiscretion* **~s·orgt** a *careless easy, unconcerned*; → –dacht ‖ seien Sie ∼! *make your mind easy*!, *never fear*!; *don't worry* (*about* ..)! | [adv] etw ∼ unternehmen *to go it blind* | ≗heit [f] *indiscretion* **~stallt** a *uncommissioned* ≗**stand** m ∼(e)s/ = Unbeständigkeit **~ständig** a *unsteady, unstable* (*character*) ‖ *fickle, inconstant*; *fly-away* (*p*) ‖ (Wetter) *unsettled* | ≗keit [f] ∼/∼en *inconstancy, fickleness* ‖ *unsettled state* ‖ *vacillation* (*of the female sex*) ‖ *impermanence* **~stätigt** a *unconfirmed*; *unsupported* (Meinung) **~stechlich** a *incorruptible, unbribable* | ∼ s *to be proof against bribes* | ∼keit [f] ∼/ *integrity* **~-steigbar** a *unaccessible, unscaleable* **~stellbar** a *undeliverable* ‖ (auf Briefen) *unknown*; wenn *or* falls ~ .. *in case of non-delivery, if undelivered* (*return to* ..) || ~er Brief *dead letter* || ⟨agr⟩ (*field*) *that cannot be tilled, unfit for the plough* **~stellt** a *not ordered* || ⟨agr⟩ *not cultivated, untilled* || (Brief) *undelivered* **~steuert** a *untaxed* **~stimmbar** a *indeterminable, undefinable* **~stimmt** a *uncertain, unsettled, undecided; loose* (*promise*) || (unbegrenzt) ⟨gram⟩ *indefinite* || auf ~e Zeit *for an indefinite period, indefinitely*; ⟨parl⟩ (*to adjourn*) *sine die* L | (unentschlossen) *irresolute* || (undeutlich) *vague* (*expression*) || *amorphous* (Gestalt) *casual* (*in a c. way*) || ⟨math *indeterminate* (*equation*) | ≃heit [f] ~/ *uncertainty* || *indeterminacy*, etc; *indefiniteness* || *irresolution* || *vagueness* **~straft** a ⟨jur⟩ = –bescholten || ~ bleiben *to go unpunished* **~str·eitbar** a *indisputable, incontestable; incontrovertible* (*fact*); *unquestionable* **~stritten** a *unchallenged, unquestioned* **~teiligt** a *unconcerned, dis-, uninterested* (an *in*) || (unparteiisch) *impartial, unbiassed, unprejudiced* || (gleichgültig) *indifferent* || ~ s bei *to have* od *play no part in* (*a th*); *to be no party to* (*an action*) || ≃sein [n] *detachment* | ≃e [pl] *disinterested parties, outsiders* pl **~tont** a *unaccented, unstressed* **~trächtlich** a *inconsiderable, trifling* **~tretbar** a *inaccessible* **~treten** a *untrodden* (*path*), *unbeaten* (*track*); *trackless* (*Andes*) **·unbeugsam** a *unbending, inflexible, unshakable* (*will*), *indomitable* (*pluck*) || *firm* (*mind*); *granite* (*law*); ⟨dero⟩ *stubborn* (*mind*) || (P) *obstinate, unyielding, rigid, uncompromising, undeviating* || ~ s *to keep a stiff upper lip*; ~ bleiben *not to budge*; jdn ~ m *to stiffen a p* (*he, that stiffened me*) **·unbe- ~wacht** a *unwatched* || ⟨fig⟩ *unguarded* (*moment*) **~waffnet** a *unarmed* || mit ~em Auge *with the naked eye* **~wahrt** a *unguarded* **~waldet** *unwooded* (*district*); *bare* (*mountain*) **~wältigt** a *unmanaged, unmastered* (*past*) **~wandert** a (in [dat]) *unversed, inexperienced, unstudied; unskilled* (*in*) **~weglich** a *immovable, motionless; fast* || ⟨fig⟩ *apathetic, inflexible, impassive, callous* || (Fest) *set* || *set, frozen* (*face*) || ~es Gut ⟨jur⟩ *real estate* || ~e Güter *immovables* pl || ~es Inventar *installed property* || ~ m *to immobilize* || ~ stehen *to stand motionless* od *still*, (am Fenster) *not to move* (*from* „); ~ stehen bleiben *to remain fixed on the spot* ≃**wegtheit** f *impassivity* **~wehrt** a *unarmed, defenceless* **~weibt** a *unmarried, single* || ~ bleiben, s *to stag it, to go stag* | ~heit [f] ~/ *wifeless condition; bachelorhood* **~weint** a *undeplored, unwept* (*for*) **~weisbar** a *undemonstrable, admitting no proof* **~wiesen** a *unproved* || ⟨jur⟩ *not proven* || völlig ~ s *not to have a leg* .. od *to have no leg to stand on* **~wirtschaftet** a *decontrolled* (*goods*); *unpooled* (*fuel*) **~wohnbar** a *uninhabitable*; f ~ erklären *to condemn* **~wohnt** a *uninhabited* (*district*) || *unoccupied, vacant* (*house*) || *desert* (*island*) **~wölkt** a *cloudless* **~wußt I.** a **1.** (nicht bekannt) *unknown* || das war mir ~ *I knew nothing about it* || es geschah (mir) ganz ~ *it happened quite without my knowledge* || es ist Ihnen sicher nicht ~ *you know, of course*, .. **2.** (unwillkürlich) *involuntary, mechanical, automatical* || *instinctive* **3.** (nicht wissend) [gen] *unconscious* (*of*) || sich [dat] e–r S ~ s *not to be aware* od *conscious of a th* | [adv] ⟨a.⟩ *unconsciously, unintentionally, unknowingly* **II.** das ≃e ⟨philos⟩ *the unconscious* | ≃heit [f] ~/ *unconsciousness* **~z·ahlbar** a *invaluable, beyond* (*all*) *price* || *impayable, priceless* ⟨a. fig⟩ || ⟨fam⟩ *capital* **~zahlt** a *unpaid* || (Forderung) *outstanding* | ~e Schuhe knarren *a pig bought on credit grunts all the year* **~z·ähmbar** a *uncontrollable, indomitable, unconquerable* **~zeugt** a *unwitnessed* **~zogen** a *uninhabited* (*house*) || *unstringed* (*violin*) || *unhung, uncurtained* (*window*) || *uncased* (*pillow*); *unmade* (*bed*) **~zw·eifelbar** a *indubitable* **~zw·eifelt** a *undoubted, unquestioned* **~zw·inglich** a *unconquerable, invincible* || *impregnable* (*fort*) || *indomitable* (*courage*) || *unsurmountable* (*obstacle* ⟨a. fig⟩)

·un- ~biblisch a *unscriptural* **~biegsam** a *inflexible, unbending* || *rigid, stiff* | ≃keit [f] ~/ *inflexibility* ≃**bildung** f *ignorance* ≃**bill** f ~/–bilden *injustice, injury, insult, hardship, wrongs* pl || *inclemency* (*of the weather*), *severity* (*of winter*), *vicissitudes* (*of life*), *buffets* (*of circumstances, of an air journey*), *stress* (*of the war*) **~billig** a *unfair, unjust* || *unreasonable; wrong* | ≃keit [f] ~/ *injustice, unfairness, unreasonableness* || [pl] *acts of injustice* **~blutig** a *bloodless* (*victory*), *not stained with blood* | [adv] *without shedding blood* || ⟨engl hist⟩ *glorious* (*revolution 1688*) **~botmäßig** a *unruly, insubordinate, disobedient* **~brauchbar** a *useless, of no use, unsuitable, unserviceable*; ⟨bes Am⟩ *unavailable* || *good-for-nothing* || *inefficient* || (P) *incompetent, unfit* || *unseaworthy* (*ship*) || ich bin heute ~ *I'm a wreck* .. || ~ m *to foul, spoil; disable* (*a gun*), *jam* (*a machine*) || ~ gewordenes, umzutauschendes Material ⟨bes mil⟩ *salvage* N | ≃keitserklärung [f] *condemnation* **~brechbar** a ⟨opt⟩ *irrefrangible* **~brennbar** a *unflammable* **~brüderlich** a *unbrotherly; unkind* **~bußfertig** a *impenitent* || *obdurate, hardened* (*sinner*) || [adv] (of criminals) (*to die*) *game* ≃**christ** m *non-Christian; infidel, unbeliever* **~christlich** a *unchristian* | ≃keit [f] ~/ *unchristianness*

und (abbr u.; &) [conj] *and* || Vieh, Milch ~ Butter *c. and m. and b.* || *the 19th and the 20th c.y* od *the 19th and 20th c.ies; the Oxf and Cambr colleges; the Old and New Testaments; the first and the second chapter; the 24th and* [zugleich] *last chapter* | sie sah ihn an, u die Farbe wich aus ihrem Gesicht *she .. with the c. gone from her f.*; so: *she sat with her hands folded* | (nicht) ~ **nicht,** (kein) ~ **kein** *nor* (*neither bread nor money*); ~ ich auch nicht *nor I either*; (*he didn't go*) *nor* od *neither did I* | ~ dergleichen (abbr u. dgl.) *and the like*, ⟨fam⟩ *and that* || ~ **so** fort *or* weiter (abbr usf.; usw.) *and so on* od *forth*; ⟨fam⟩ *and all* (*that* [*sort of ths*]) || ~ **wenn** *even if* | **da ~ da** *in such and such a place* || der ~ der *such a man* od *one* || durch ~ durch *thoroughly* || fort ~ fort *on and on* || für ~ für *continually* || größer ~ größer *larger and larger* || zwei ~ zwei *two and two, two at a time* || ~ **dabei** noch .. *and .. as well* || ~ dafür noch reisen! *and to travel for it too!* || ~ damit basta! *now you know!, and there's an end of it!* | [ell] ~? *well?; what then?*; **na** ~?! *so what?* || .. ~ **noch** dazu falsche .. *and false ones at that* ich ~ Angst (Geld) h? *me afraid!* (*me, and m.!*) | [co- statt subordinierend] er kam ~ holte mich ab *he came to fetch me*; so: *wait and see* || sei so gut ~ gib mir .. *will you kindly* (od *be so kind as to*) *give me* .. || da steht er ~ betet sie an .. *adoring her* | ~ **ob** *or* **wie**! *and how!* | ~ zwar schnell (*he must disappear*) – *and quickly too*

·Undank m ~(e)s/ *ingratitude* || [prov] ~ ist der Welt Lohn *ingratitude* od *that is the way of the world* | ≃**bar** a (P) (gegen) *ungrateful, unthankful* (*to*); *unappreciative* (*of*); *ingrate* || (S) *thankless* (*task*) | **~barkeit** f ~/ *ingratitude* || *thanklessness*

·un- ~datiert a *undated* **~defin·ierbar** a *undefinable, nondescript; impredictable* (*element*) || gänzlich ~ *neither fish, flesh nor fowl* **~deklin·ierbar** a *undeclinable* **~d·enkbar** a *unimaginable, inconceivable, impossible*; ⟨philos⟩ *unthinkable* || [pred] *out of the question* **~d·enklich** a; seit ~er Zeit *from time immemorial* od .. *out of mind; for ages* **~deutlich** a *indistinct* || (Bild) *hazy, blurred; shadowy* (*outlines* ⟨a. phot⟩) *dim* (*recollection*) || (Laut) *inarticulate*; ~es Sehen *dimness of vision* || ⟨fig⟩ *unintelligible, obscure, ill-defined, vague* || [adv] ~ sprechen *to gabble, mumble* || ~ aussprechen to slur | ≗keit [f] ~/ indistinctness || dimness, etc || inarticulateness || unintelligibility **~deutsch** a un-German (style), not German || contrary to German ideas, etc || (Redewendung) unidiomatic **~dicht** a not tight; leaking (kettle) || ⟨mar⟩ leaky || ~e Stelle leak | ~ s to leak; ⟨tech⟩ not to fit tight | ≗w [n] leakage **~dichterisch** a unpoetical **~dienlich** a unserviceable, unsuitable, inconvenient, inexpedient; useless **≗dienst** m (schlechter Dienst) ⟨soc⟩ disservice **~dienstfertig** a disobliging **≗ding** n chimera, impossibility, absurdity; es ist ein ~ it is absurd (z tun to do) **~diszipliniert** a undisciplined **~duldsam** a intolerant (gegen of) | ~ w gegen .. to become impatient at .. | [adv] with intolerance **~durch-** ~dacht [a] ill-considered || immature (plan), crude (method) | ~dr·inglich [a] impenetrable ⟨a. fig⟩, impervious, (f to) || = –lässig || etw ~ m to proof a th (für, gegen against) || ⟨fig⟩ inscrutable; ~forstet [a] unthinned (Wald); ~führbar [a] impracticable, unworkable | ~lässig [a] impermeable; impervious; moisture-proof; ≗lässigkeit [f] tightness; impermeability, etc ~schossen [a] ⟨typ⟩ unspaced; ~sichtig [a] opaque, not transparent | ≗sichtigkeit [f] ~/ opacity, non-transparency **~eben** a uneven, rugged, broken (ground); scraggily || rough, bumpy (road) | ⟨fig⟩ unsuitable, inconvenient | kein ~er Mensch quite a good fellow, a tractable man enough || nicht so ~ ⟨fam⟩ tolerably od rather od fairly good, not half bad, not amiss | ~bürtig [a] of inferior rank, birth, descent || ⟨fig⟩ inferior | ≗heit [f] unevenness; ruggedness; ~en [pl] uneven surface || ⟨übtr⟩ inequality || ~mäßig [a] wanting symmetry od proportion; unsymmetrical, disproportionate **~echt** a not genuine, false || ⟨sl⟩ bogus, ⟨Am⟩ phon(e)y (notes) || (nachgemacht) spurious (document), counterfeit, sham, imitation (pearls) || ~er Bruch ⟨math⟩ improper fraction || (Farben) fading, not fast || (Kind) illegitimate || (Waren) adulterated || (Zähne) artificial **~edel** a ignoble; mean, vulgar || base (metals) **~ehelich** a illegitimate (birth); natural (child) || illicite (relationship) || (Kind) f ~ erklären ⟨jur⟩ to bastardize | [adv] ~ geboren born out of wedlock **~ehr-** ~bar [a] dishonourable, disgraceful, indecent | ≗e [f] ~/ dishonour, discredit, disgrace, disrepute; e–m zur ~ gereichen, ~ m or bringen to disgrace a p, to cast od bring dishonour on a p; ~enhaft [a] = –bar | ≗igkeit [f] dishonesty | ~erbietig [a] disrespectful (silence) || (gegen Eltern etc) undutiful || ⟨rel⟩ irreverent | ~lich [a] dishonest; false, underhand; unfair, crooked; [pred] out of the straight; not straightforward; (that's) not cricket || ⟨ftb⟩ foul || [adv] ~ kämpfen ⟨box⟩ to hit below the belt ⟨a. fig⟩; ≗lichkeit [f] ~/ dishonesty, disgrace, infamy; bad faith **~eigen-** ~nützig [a] disinterested, unselfish || das ≗nützigste the least self-centered attitude | ~tlich [a] improper, figurative, not literal **~ein-** ~bringlich [a] irrecoverable, irretrievable; abandoned (claims) | ~gebunden [a] unbound | ~gedenk [a] [gen] unmindful, forgetful (of) | ~gelöst [a] unredeemed (pledge) | ~geschränkt [a] unrestrained, unlimited; unreserved; stintless (praise) || unconditional, unqualified; absolute || free (trade); ungrudging, unstinted (praise) || untrammelled (control) || ~gesehen [a] ⟨mil⟩ (area) in defilade; ~gestanden [a] unconfessed, unadmitted; ~geweiht [a] uninitiated, uninformed | ≗geweihte [pl] ⟨fam⟩ outsiders | ~heitlich [a] not uniform, diversiform, mixed | ~ig [a] disagreeing, disunited, divided || ~ w to quarrel, to fall out (with) || ~ s to disagree, to be at variance (with a p on ..) || [pred] at odds (with) || ich bin mit mir selbst noch ~ I have not quite made up my mind yet | ≗igkeit [f] ~/ disharmony, disagreement, variance, discord, disunion || division || mit jdm in ~ leben not to hit it off with a p | ~nehmbar [a] impregnable | ~s [a] = uneinig | ~sichtig [a] unreasonable | ~träglich [a] unprofitable | ~treibbar, ~ziehbar [a] bad (debts) **~elegant** a inelegant, dowdy **~emp-** ~fänglich [a] insensible, -sitive (f to); unimpressionable || (unzugänglich) impervious, irresponsive (für to) || (unempfindlich) insusceptible (of) || ~ m ⟨gyn⟩ to immunize | ~findbar [a] imperceptible | ~findlich [a] insensible (f .. to love) || (gegen) insensitive, unfeeling (to); immune (to), ~ g. Arznei drug-fast, g. Kälte ⟨bot⟩ hardy || ⟨phot⟩ slow (film) || (Kleidung, Schuhe etc) rugged, sturdy, robust || (P) (gleichgültig) (f) indifferent (to), deaf (for) || cold; apathetic, callous, hard-hearted || inured (to cold) || hardened (against blows, etc) || ~ m to benumb (limbs); ⟨med⟩ to narcotize, ⟨scient⟩ to anaesthetize; ⟨phot⟩ to desensitize | ≗keit [f] insusceptibility; immunity, etc **~·endlich** a endless || infinite ⟨a. math⟩ || ⟨fig⟩ countless (multitude); immense, boundless || [adv] ~ viel no end of, a world of (good), a power of (work) || (it will cheer him up) no end | auf ~ einstellen to focus for infinity, dazu i. adjustment || das geht ins ≗e there is no end to it; ins ≗e to infinity, ad infinitum [L] **~englisch** a un-English; not English || contrary to English ideas etc || (Redewendung) unidiomatic **·unent-** ~b·ehrlich [a] indispensable, necessary; ~er Gegenstand necessity; essential (foodstuffs) || das Buch ist mir ~ I cannot do without the book || er dünkt sich ~ ⟨a.⟩ he is a fly on the wheel | ~deckt [a] undiscovered, unspotted | ~flammbar [a] flame-proof || ~geltlich [a] gratuitous, free (entrance); ⟨com⟩ free of charge | [adv] gratis [⟨a.⟩ a] | ~haltsam [a] intemperate; incontinent (bes geschlechtlich); ≗keit [f] ~/ intemperance; incontinence | ~r·innbar [a] unescapable; ineluctable | ~schieden [a] undecided, undetermined || pending, doubtful || (Frage) open || ~es Rennen dead heat || (Schlacht, Spiel) drawn || es ist noch ~ it is still in dispute (as to whether) || ~ l to leave in suspense; to leave (a matter) at a loose end; die ~en Wähler the floating vote; ~ s to hang in the balance || [adv] ~ spielen to draw | ≗ [n] ⟨sport⟩ tie, draw(n game) (to play a draw); ≗heit [f] ~/ undecided state, doubtfulness, indecision | ~schlossen [a] irresolute, wavering, hesitating; ⟨fam⟩ shilly-shally || ~ s not to have made up one's mind (about), ⟨pol⟩ to sit on the fence, ⟨Am⟩ to straddle | ~sch·uldbar [a] inexcusable | ~wegt [a] unflinching; undeviating (industry); unswerving, unwavering; firm, ⟨hum⟩ last-ditch (imperialist); ≗e(r) [m] ⟨pol⟩ stalwart, last-ditcher die-hard; [adv] imperturbably etc || ~ borgen to go on borrowing | ~wickelt [a] undeveloped; inchoate (embryo); embryo (state) | ~wirrbar [a] inextricable | ~z·ifferbar [a] undecipherable | ~z·ündbar [a] un(in)flammable, nonignitable

·uner- **~·achtet** prep [+ gen] = –geachtet **~baulich** a unedifying, vulgar **~beten** a unsolicited; unwelcome **~b·ittlich** a inexorable; stony, relentless; implacable, unrelenting (foe) || (streng) harsh, stern || ⟨fig⟩ stubborn (facts), hard (reality) || der ~ste Feind the most remorseless enemy || ~ gegen Bitten proof against petitions | [adv] ⟨a.⟩ (to fight) tooth and nail **~br·ochen** a unbroken (seal) || intact (lock) || unentered (room) || unforced (door) **~d·enklich** a unimaginable || vor or seit ~en Zeiten from time immemorial **~fahren** a inexperienced (in) || callow (youth, girl); half-baked; verdant (youth); ⟨mil, fam⟩ raw || ~ s in etw to be an innocent about (wordly affairs) | ≗e(r) [m] ⟨fam⟩ greenhorn **~f·indlich** a undiscoverable || ⟨übtr⟩ inconceivable (reasons) || es ist mir ~ it baffles me **~f·orschlich** a inscrutable, impenetrable, unsearchable **~freulich** a unpleasant || shameful || afflicting || disagreeable ||

thankless (*task*) | viel ≃es ⟨fam⟩ *plenty of vinegar* **~füllbar** a *chimerical* ‖ *unrealizable* (*hope*) **~füllt** a *unfulfilled* etc ‖ (Gelübde) *broken* ‖ (Weissagung) *proved false* ‖ (Erwartung) *disappointed*; *frustrated* (*wish*) **~giebig** a *unproductive*; *barren* **~gr·ündlich** a *unfathomable*; *bottomless, abysmal, vast* ‖ *impenetrable, inscrutable* **~heblich** a *inconsiderable, insignificant, unimportant, unconclusive*; *irrelevant* (f *to*) ‖ *trifling, trivial* (*costs*) **~h·ört** a *unprecedented*; *unheard* od *undreamed of* ‖ (nicht gewährt) *not granted* ‖ (empörend) *shocking, intolerable, outrageous* (*scandal*); das ist ~ *that beats everything* (od ⟨Am⟩ *the band*); ganz ~ *never heard of* ‖ (Preis etc) *fabulous, exorbitant* | ⟨fam⟩ *infernal, murderous*; *egregious* (*folly*), *thundering* (*mistake*) | ~ bleiben *to find no hearing* ‖ ~ l *to turn a deaf ear to* | ~! *well!* | [adv] *incredibly* (*fine*), *disgracefully* (*rusty*), ⟨fam⟩ *ruthlessly, riotously* (*popular*) | **das** ≃e n *the outrageousness* **~kannt** a *unrecognized* ‖ [adv] ⟨a.⟩ *incognito* **~kennbar** a *unknowable* **~kenntlich** a *ungrateful* **~kl·ärlich** a *inexplicable, unaccountable* ‖ was mir ~ ist *what beats me* (*is* ..) ‖ etw ~ finden *to be puzzled to account for a th* | ~erw·eise [adv] *inexplicably* **~klimmbar** a *unscalable* **~l·äßlich** a *indispensable, irremissable*; *mandatory* ‖ ≃keit [f] *indispensability* **~laubt** a ⟨a.⟩ *forbidden*; *unlawful, illicit*; *illegal* (*abortion*); *prohibited* ‖ ~er Ausschank ⟨Am⟩ *speakeasy* ‖ ⟨mil⟩ ~e Entfernung *absence without* (*official*) *leave* (AWOL) **~ledigt** a *unsettled*; *not disposed of* ‖ *undispatched* ‖ *undischarged* (*duty*); *open* (*file*); *pending*; [pred] *in suspense* ‖ etw ~ zurückl ⟨a.⟩ *to leave a th at a loose end* **~m·eßlich** a *immeasurable, immense, incalculable* ‖ *boundless, infinite, endless* ‖ ⟨fam⟩ *enormous, huge, vast* **~m·üdlich** a *untiring, indefatigable* ‖ (Fleiß) *unflagging, unresting* ‖ *unwearied* ‖ (Arbeit) *unstinting* **~örtert** a; ~ bleiben *not to be discussed*

·unerotisch a *free from eroticism*

·uner- ~probt a *untried* etc ‖ (Erz) *unassayed* **~quicklich** a *unpleasant, unedifying* ‖ höchst ~ *annoying* **~r·eichbar** a *unattainable, inaccessible* ‖ [pred] *out of reach* **~reicht** a ⟨fig⟩ *unequalled* (an *in*), *unrivalled*; *second to none*, ⟨sport⟩ *record* (*performance*); ⟨bes Am⟩ *all-time* (*high*) ‖ ~ dastehen *to stand alone, to be the last th* (*in comfort*) **~sättlich** a *never surfeited*; *insatiable* (*zest for life*) ‖ *unappeasable* (*yearning*) ‖ *unquenchable* (*zeal*) ‖ (heißhungrig) *ravenous* ‖ (gierig) *greedy* **~schlossen** a (Land) *undeveloped*; *untapped* (*potential*, etc) **~schöpflich** a *inexhaustible* **~schöpft** a *unexhausted* **~schrocken** a *intrepid, undaunted, dauntless* ‖ *unflinching* ‖ *daring* **~sch·ütterlich** a ⟨fig⟩ *unshakeable* (*conviction*) ‖ *stolid, imperturbable, immovable*; *unflinching*; *staunch, steadfast*; *unassailable* (*argument*); ~ s in s–m Entschluß *not to budge from* .. | [adv] ~ eintreten f *to stand foursquare for* .. ‖ ≃keit [f] *imperturbability*; ⟨a.⟩ *aplomb* **~sch·üttert** a (P) *untroubled* **~schw·inglich** a ⟨fig⟩ *prohibitive, exorbitant* (*price*) ‖ *enourmous* (*costs*) ‖ [pred] jdm ~ *out of reach of a p, beyond a p's means* **~s·etzlich** a *irreplaceable* ‖ *irreparable, irrecoverable, dead* (*loss*) ‖ (*p*) *who cannot be replaced* ‖ niemand ist ~ *there are good fish in the sea as ever came out of it* ⟨prov⟩ | ≃keit [f] *irreplaceableness* **~s·innlich** a *inconceivable* **~sprießlich** a *unprofitable*; *fruitless* ‖ *unpleasant* **~st·eigbar** a *inaccessible* **~tr·äglich** a → untragbar; *intolerable, insufferable* ‖ *horrible* (*bore*); *deadly* (*monotony*) ‖ *overpowering* (*heat*) ‖ [pred] *past endurance* ‖ ~ w *to pall*; der Gedanke ist mir ~ *I can't bear to think of it*; *I can't endure his voice*; *his behavio(u)r can't be endured* **~wachsen** [–ks–] a *not grown up, under age* ‖ *immature, young* **~wähnt** a *unmentioned* (*u., what is can become as though it not were*) ‖ etw ~ l *not to mention* (od *to make no mention of*) *a th* **~wartet** a *unexpected, unanticipated, sudden, unthought-of* ‖ *surprise* (*visit*); *chance* (*corner*); ~es Erscheinen *unexpectedness*; ~er Vorfall *emergency, adventure* ‖ [adv] ⟨a.⟩ *all of a sudden* **~w·eichlich** a ⟨fig⟩ *unrelenting* **~w·eislich** a *unprovable, indemonstrable* **~w·idert** a *unanswered* ‖ (Liebe) *unrequited, unreturned* **~wiesen** a *unproved* **~wünscht** a *unwanted, not wanted*; *unwelcome*; *uncalled-for, unwished-for*; ~ Elemente *tares*; ~ s ⟨m. m.⟩ *to discourage* ‖ das kam ihm sehr ~ [adv] *it came as a great blow to him* **~zogen** a *uneducated, untutored* ‖ (ungezogen) *ill-bred*; *badly braught up*; *rude*

·un- ~etikettiert a *unlabelled* **~fachmännisch** a *unprofessional* **~fähig** a *incapable* (*of*) ‖ (außerstande) *unable* (*to do*) ‖ (ungeeignet) *unfit* (*for*) ‖ *inefficient* ‖ *feckless* (*and unpractical*) ‖ ~ z zahlen *insolvent* ‖ jdn ~ m *to disable a p* (zu *for*) | ≃keit [f] *inefficiency* **~f·ahrbar** a *impracticable, impassable* (*way*) ‖ ⟨naut⟩ *not navigable* **~fahrplanmäßig** a *unscheduled* (Zug) **~fair** ['unfɛr] a [engl] → unehrlich **·Unfall** m ~(e)s/≃e *accident*; ⟨mot a.⟩ *emergency, breakdown*; ≃e durch Fall(en) *falling a.s* ‖ er hatte e–n schweren ~, es ist ihm ein .. ~ zugestoßen *he has met with a severe a.* ‖ Helft ≃e verhüten! *Safety first!* ‖ ⟨mot, rail⟩ *accident*, ⟨rail a.⟩ *derailment* ‖ (schwerer) *wreck* **≃anziehend** a *a.-prone* **~flucht** f *leaving* od *fleeing the scene of an a.*, → *hit and run driving* **~kommando** n *traffic a. squad* **~rente** f *a. annuity* **≃sicher** a *a.-proof* **~station** f *casualty* od *emergency station, first-aid post* **~stelle** f *scene of a.* **~- u Schadenversicherung** f *accident and material damage insurance* **~verhütung** f *prevention of accidents* | ~smaßnahmen [f pl] *safety measures*; ~svorschrift [f] *regulation for the p. of a.s* **~versicherung** f *a. insurance* | ~neurose [f] (Renten–) *compensation neurosis*; ≃(s)frei [a] *a.-free* (*driving*); ~sgesellschaft [f] *a.-i. company*; ~sgesetz [n] *a.-i. bill*, ⟨engl⟩ *Workmen's Compensation Act*; ~skasse [f] *provident fund* **~zeuge** m *witness of an a.* **·un- ~f·aßbar** a *intangible* ⟨a. fig⟩; ⟨fig⟩ *irrational*; *incomprehensible, unseizable, inconceivable* ‖ das ist mir ~ *that passes my comprehension*, ⟨fam⟩ *that beats me* **~f·ehlbar** a *infallible* (*Pope, rule*) ‖ *unmistakable* (*proof*) ‖ *safe* (*medicine*) ‖ ⟨fam⟩ *dead* (*tip*); ein ~ er Blick *an unerring eye* | [adv] *without fail* ‖ er wird ~ l vb *he will not fail* od *he is sure* (*to win*) **~fein** a *indelicate, coarse* ‖ *impolite* ‖ ⟨sport⟩ *unfair* ‖ *bad* (*manners*); *vulgar* ‖ ~er Mensch ⟨sl⟩ *bounder* **~fern** [adv] *not far off, near* ‖ ~ von *or* ~ [prep] [gen & dat] *not far from* **~fertig** a *unfinished, inchoate*; *rough and ready, roughhewn* ‖ ⟨fig⟩ *immature*; *half-baked* (*p*); *crude* (*theory*) **≃flat** m ~(e)s/ **1.** *filth, dirt* ‖ ⟨fam⟩ *beastly mess* ‖ (Zoten) *smut* **2.** = **≃fläter** m ~s/~ *filthy* od *dirty-minded* od *smutty fellow* | ~·ei [f] *filth*(*iness*), *nastiness, lewdness*; *smut* **~flätig** a *gross, nasty, filthy, dirty* ‖ (zotig) *obscene, smutty*; *dowdy* | ≃keit [f] ~/~en *nastiness, filthiness* ‖ *obscenity* **≃fleiß** m ~es/ *laziness*; *want of application*; *idleness*; *indolence* | ≃ig [a] *lazy, indolent, idle* **~flektierbar** a ⟨gram⟩ *taking no inflexions* **≃fluchten** n *misalignment* (⟨a. mot⟩ *of tyres*) **~folgsam** a *disobedient, recalcitrant, wilful* ‖ *wayward* (*child*) **≃form** f *deformity*; *monster* **~förmig** a *deformed, mis-shapen, shapeless* ‖ *disproportionate* ‖ *enormous, monstrous* **~förmlich** a **1.** = –förmig **2.** *informal, free and easy* (*manners*), *off-hand* (*way*) ‖ *rude, unpolished* | ≃keit [f] *unceremoniousness* **~frankiert** a *unpaid, not prepaid* **~französisch** a vgl –deutsch **~frei** a *unfree, not free* ‖ *not freed*; *serving* | ≃e(r) [m] *bondsman, serf*; ~e Sendung ⟨com⟩ *shipment collect* | ~gebig [a] *illiberal, parsimonious, close* ‖ *mean* | ≃heit [f] (Knechtschaft) *bondage, serfdom* ‖ ⟨fig⟩ *constraint* | ~willig [a] *involun-*

tary, compulsory || *unwilling (passenger)* || ⟨physiol⟩ *reflex (action)* **~freundlich** a *unfriendly (act* ⟨a. pol⟩) || (unliebenswürdig) *unamiable, unkind, ungracious* || *harsh; surly; rude* || (übel gelaunt) *sullen, sulky* | *ungenial, unclement (weather)* || *cheerless (habitation)* || *inhospitable (land)* || *uncomplimentary (rumour)* | e–m ~ [adv] begegnen *to be rude to a p* **~freundschaftlich** a *unfriendly* **≃friede** m ~ns/ *discord, dissension, disunion* || *contention, strife, controversy* || ⟨fam⟩ *sparring, tiff* || ~ säen *to sow the seeds of discord* | ~nstifter [m] *mischief-maker;* ⟨vulg⟩ *mixer* **~friedfertig, ~friedlich** a (friedlos) *unpeaceable* || (unverträglich) *discordant, quarrelsome* **~fruchtbar** a *barren* ⟨a. fig⟩, *sterile* || *poor,* ⟨Am⟩ *bad (lands);* ⟨fig⟩ *unproductive, fruitless; feeble, effete; negative (criticism)* || ⟨com⟩ *unprofitable* | auf ~en Boden fallen *to fall upon stony ground, to make no impression* (bei jdm *upon a p)* | (zeitweilige *temporary)* ≃keit → *sterility;* ~ v Ehen ⟨demog⟩ *infertility, childlessness* | ≃machung [f] *sterilization* **≃fug** m ~(e)s/ **1.** *misdemeanour, mischief* || *offence, wrong* || ⟨fam⟩ *flim-flam* || grober ~ *malicious mischief,* ⟨jur⟩ *public nuisance; gross misdemeano(u)r* || ⟨fam⟩ *horse-play* || ~ treiben *to cause a nuisance; to be up to mischief, to play tricks* **2.** ⟨fam⟩ ~! *nonsense!* ⟨sl⟩ *rats!* || laß den ~! *stop that rot!* || und all der ~! ⟨übtr Am⟩ *and all that jazz* **~fügsam** a *unmanageable, unyielding, intractable, unruly* **~fühlbar** a *impalpable, intangible* || *imperceptible* | ≃keit [f] *imp.ness, int.bility; imp.bility* **~galant** a *discourteous (to ladies), ungentlemanly* **~gangbar** a *impassable, impracticable* || (Münze) *not current* || (Waren) *unsalable; odd (size)* || (Wort) *unusual, rare* **~gar** a ⟨cul⟩ *underdone, raw* || *undertanned (skin)*

·Ungar(in f) m, ≃**isch** a *Hungarian* | **~n** n *-ry*

·un- **~gastlich** a *inhospitable*

·unge- **~achtet 1.** [a] (verachtet) *not esteemed* od *respected; despised, contemned* **2.** [prep] [gen] *notwithstanding; regardless* od *despite of; with (all its strain it was a delightful trip)* || des ~ *in spite of* (od *for) all that* **3.** [conj] *(al)though* **~ahndet** a *unpunished* || [adv] *with impunity* **~·ahnt** a *not anticipated; unthought-of, never dreamt-of (velocity)* || (ungehofft, unerwartet) *unhoped-for, unexpected* **~bahnt** a *unbeaten (track), untrodden (path)* **~bändigt** a *untamed* (⟨a. fig⟩: *passions), unbroken (horse)* ⟨a. fig⟩, *unsubdued* **~bärdig** a *unmannered, unmannerly* || (störrisch) *refractory, unruly* **~beichtet** a *unshriven* **~bessert** a *dirt (road)* **~beten** a *unbidden (guests), uninvited, unasked* || ~er Gast *intruder,* (Schmarotzer) *sponger* || ~e Gäste ⟨sl⟩ *gate-crashers (they crashed the gate)* | [adv] *without being asked; of one's own accord* **~b·eugt** a *unbent, uncurbed* | ~heit [f] ~/ *indomitable* od *uncurbed spirit* **~bildet** a *uneducated; unlearned; uncultured; (c)rude, untutored;* ⟨fam hum⟩ *non-U (not upper class)* || nicht ~ *cultivated* || (Benehmen) *unpolished, unrefined, ill-bred* || *uncivilized, primitive, barbarous* **~blümt** a *without a pattern, plain* **~boren** a *unborn* **~bräuchlich** a *obsolete (word)* || *unusual, uncommon* || ~ w *to fall, go, pass out of use, to grow obsolete, to be obsolescent* **~braucht** a *unused, quite new; not worn* **~bräunt** a *untanned (face)* **~br·ochen** a *unbroken; virgin (soil)* || ⟨opt⟩ *unrefracted (rays)* || ⟨fig⟩ *undejected* **≃bühr** f ~/ *unseemliness, indecency, impropriety* || *injustice* || *abuse, excess* || *contempt* (vor G. *of court);* sich e–r ~ [gen] schuldig m *to be in c.;* wegen ~ z Verantwortung ziehen *to hold up for c.* || zur ~ *unfairly, unduly, to excess* | ≃end, ≃lich [a] *unbecoming, unmannerly (behaviour); unseemly (action); indecent, rude* || *unjust, unfair* | [adv] *unduly* **~bunden** a *unbound; untrammeled* || (Buch) *not bound;* (noch roh) *in sheets* || ~e Rede *prose* || ⟨phys⟩ *uncombined (heat)* | ⟨fig⟩ *free, unrestrained, unconventional* || ⟨dero⟩ *licentious, dissolute, loose* || ein ~es Leben *a Bohemian* od *free and easy life,* ⟨dero⟩ *a dissolute* od *wild life* | ≃heit [f] ~/ ⟨fig⟩ *unrestraint, freedom; license* || leichtlebige ~ *Bohemianism* || ⟨dero⟩ *licentiousness,* etc **~dämpft** a ⟨wir⟩ *continuous (wave)* **~deckt** a *uncovered* ⟨a. com⟩; ~er Scheck ⟨bes Am⟩ *rubber ch.; unrequited* (Einfuhr) || *bare (table);* der Tisch ist noch ~ *the table* od *cloth is not yet laid* || (schutzlos) *unsheltered, unprotected* || ⟨mil⟩ *without cover* || ⟨com⟩ *unsecured;* ⟨fam⟩ *rubber (check)* || (Notenumlauf) *fiduciary* **~deihlich** a *unprofitable, not thriving* || *unwholesome (food)* || *unhealthy (climate)* **~druckt** a *unprinted, not yet in print* || *unpublished* **≃duld** a *impatience* || vor ~ brennen *to burn with a desire (to do)* || ⟨fam⟩ (P) ~! *fidget!* (= *impatient child)* | ≃ig [a] ⟨a.⟩ *fidgety, peevish (child); poor (patient)* || ~ w *to grow restive* | [adv] *(to expect) anxiously* **~eignet** a *unfit, inapt, inappropriate; unsuitable, unsuited* (zu *for)* || *inopportune, bad; ill-adapted, -sorted* || [pred] *out of place;* → -günstig || ~ wie der Igel z Halstuch etc *as a square peg in a round hole* **≃fähr** n ~s/ *chance* || v u. *by chance, by accident;* er fragte v u. *he chanced to ask* || er traf sie ganz v u. *it was quite by chance that he met her, he happened to meet her* || das kam nicht v u. *it was no mere accident* **~fähr** a *approximat(iv)e, rough (estimate)* || *chance (blow)* | [adv] (→ etwa) *approximately, roughly, about, nearly,* ⟨Am⟩ *around* || *almost (a pound); (a pound) or so; just on (6 feet); sth like (two thirds); in the region of (200)* || *some (3 years ago)* || *(a month* od *on the 12th) or thereabouts;* ~ dasselbe *much the same* || er sagte ~ dasselbe wie *he spoke much to the same effect as* || .. oder ~ dasselbe *(it was fraud) or near neighbour to it* || ~ so wie *much as* || das ist es so ~ *that's about it* || nur ~ kennen *to know vaguely;* das stimmt so ~ *that's more or less correct;* ich weiß es ~ ⟨fam⟩ *I kind of know* || wo ~? *whereabouts?* **~fährdet** a *safe, out of danger, well secured* **~fährlich** a *innocuous, unrisky; harmless, mild* || *not ..:* k–e ~e Lage *not a wholesome situation* **~fällig** a (P) *disobliging, unobliging, unkind* || (S) *ungraceful, unpleasant, homely* **~färbt** a *undyed,* etc, *untouched-up* || *natural* || *raw (silk)* || ⟨fig⟩ *unvarnished (truth), ungarbled (news)* **~faßt** a *unmounted (jewel), rimless (lens)* **~federt** a *springless* **~fesselt** a ⟨fig⟩ *unrestrained, free from all restraint* **~festigt** a *unbalanced; unsettled (state)* **~fettet** a ⟨mot, etc⟩ *uncompounded* (Öl) **~fiedert** a = -befiedert **~flügelt** a *wingless, without wings* || ⟨zoo, bot⟩ *apterous* **~fragt** a *unasked* | [adv] *without being asked* **~frierbar** a *in-, uncongealable* **~frühstückt** a *without a breakfast* **~füge** a *unwieldy; clumsy, rude* **~fügig** a *recalcitrant, unyielding, unpliant, intractable* || *stubborn* **~f·üttert** a ⟨tail⟩ *not lined* || (T & ⟨hum⟩ P) *unfed* **~genständlich** a ⟨arts⟩ *abstractious* **~g·erbt** a *untanned* **~g·essen** a *uneaten* | [adv] (nüchtern) *without dinner, supperless* **~gliedert** a ⟨zoo, bot⟩ *inarticulate* || ⟨fig⟩ *unorganized* **~grüßt** a *unsaluted* **~halten** a *unkept, unfulfilled* || (unwillig) *indignant, angry* (über jdn *with a p;* über etw *at a th), displeased (with)* || ~ w *to become annoyed* **~härted** a *untempered (steel)* **~heißen** a *unbidden, unordered, spontaneous* | [adv] *voluntarily, of one's own accord* **~heizt** a *unwarmed* || (Zimmer) *without a fire* **~hemmt** a ⟨fig⟩ *unchecked, uncurbed, unrestrained; free* | [adv] *without restraint* **~heuchelt** a *unfeigned; candid* **≃heuer** n ~s/~ *monster, prodigy;* "*Frankenstein*" | ≃ [a] *huge, immense, vast, colossal, prodigious, enormous, jumbo-sized; atrocious* || *gargantuan (packet); tremendous (crush)* || *appalling (crime); fabulous, untold (wealth); egregious (folly); flagrant* | ⟨fam⟩ *whacking (blow, stick); terrific, thumping (mistake); thundering (nui-*

sance); *no end of* (*trouble, a quack*); *fiendish* (*capacity*); *desperate* (*fool*) | [adv] *terribly*, etc | ⟨fam⟩ *ruinously* ‖ *no end* (*disappointed*) ‖ .. *sth desperate* | ~ viel z tun *immensely to do* ‖ **das ~e** ⟨a.⟩ *the tragic event*; *the atrocity* (*of this war*); *the dreadful deed* | ≃lich [a] *monstrous*; *unnatural* (*crime*) | ~lichkeit [f] ~/ *monstrosity*; *enormity* ‖ *monstrous deed* ‖ ~en [pl] *atrocities* **~h·indert** [a & adv] *untrammel(l)ed, unchecked*; *without let or hindrance*; *complete* **~hobelt** ⟨fig⟩ *uncultured, unpolished, coarse, rude, rough*(*-and-ready* aber gediegen); *uncouth*; *boorish*; ~er Mensch ⟨fam⟩ *cad* **~hofft** a *unhoped-for, undreamt-of* (*luck*) **~hopft** a *without hops* **~hörig** a *undue* ‖ (unziemlich) *unseemly*; *improper* (*it would be i. in me to do*); *off-colo(u)r* (*remark*) ‖ ⟨sport⟩ *unfair, foul* | [adv] ~ anwenden *to misapply* ‖ sich ~ benehmen *to misbehave* (*o.s.*), ⟨Am⟩ *to carry on* **~horsam** **1.** [a] *disobedient* ‖ ⟨mil⟩ *insubordinate* ‖ ~ s (gegen) *to disobey*; *to play up* **2.** ≃ [m] ~s/ *disobedience* (gegen *to*) etc ‖ ⟨jur⟩ *default*; *contempt* (vor G. *of court*) ‖ ich dulde k–n ~ *I will not be disobeyed* ‖ Beweise des ~s *contumacies* pl

·ungeistlich a *unspiritual* ‖ *wordly, temporal*; *secular* ‖ *unclerical* ‖ *not becoming a clergyman*

·unge- ~kämmt a *unkempt* ‖ (Wolle) *not carded* **~klärt** a *obscure* (*situation*); [pred] *up in the air* **~kostet** a *untasted* (*meal*) **~kränkt** a *unharmed*, etc ‖ das läßt mich ~ *that does not hurt* od *disturb me* | [adv] *in peace* **~künstelt** a *artless simple* ‖ (–zwungen) *unstudied* ‖ (echt) *unaffected, unsophisticated*; *natural, genuine* **~kürzt** a *uncut*; (Ausgabe etc) *unabridged* ‖ (*to be published*) *in entirety* ‖ *unexpurgated*; *full* (*performance*) **~läufig** a ⟨fig⟩ *unfamiliar* ‖ das war mir ~ *I had not heard about it, I didn't know that* **~läutert** a *unrefined*, etc; *raw* (*spirits*)

·Ungeld n ⟨fam⟩ *no end of money*

·unge- ~leckt a *unlicked* (⟨fig⟩ Bär *cub*) **~legen** a *inconvenient, unseasonable, inopportune, untimely* (*remark*) ‖ (jdm) *embarrassing* (*to a p*) | [adv] *out of season* ‖ ~ k *to come at the wrong time* ‖ das k–t mir ~ *this comes in very awkwardly* | ≃heit [f] ~/~en *inconvenience* ‖ [konkr] *trouble* ‖ jdm gr ~en m *to put a p to much inconvenience, to give a p a great deal of trouble* **~legt** a *unlaid*, (⟨fig⟩ *unhatched*) *eggs* **~lehrig** a *indocile*; *unintelligent*; *slow* **~lehrt** a *unlearned*; *illiterate* | ≃heit [f] ~/ *illiteracy*; *want of learning, ignorance* **~lenk** a *stiff* (⟨a. fig⟩ *style*); *unhandy, angular* ‖ ⟨fig⟩ *clumsy, awkward* **~lernt** a (Arbeit[er]) *unskilled* **~locht** a ⟨comp⟩ *unpunched*; ~e Karten *rejects* **~löscht** a *unquenched* ‖ (Kalk) *unslaked* **~löst** a *unsolved*; ~ l *to leave* (*a problem*) *in the air* **≃mach** n ~(e)s/~e *discomfort, hardship, adversity, calamity, trouble* ‖ *evil, toil* ‖ *inclemency* (*of the weather*) | ~ erleiden *to undergo hardship* **~mäß** a *incongruous* ([dat] *with, to*) **~mein** a *uncommon, extraordinary* | [adv] *extremely*; *very much* ‖ *immensely, exceedingly*, ⟨fam⟩ *mighty* (*interesting*); *deeply* (*touched*); *vitally, quite* (*important*) | ⟨fam⟩ *devilish* (*funny*); ⟨fam⟩ *a whale of time, of a fine cook* ‖ ⟨Am⟩ (*it pleases me*) *no end* | ~ gr *enormous* ‖ ~ viel *plenty of* **~m·essen** a ⟨fig⟩ *unlimited, infinite* ‖ ins ≃e gehen *to come to an immense amount* **~mischt** a *unmixed* (⟨a. fig⟩ *joy*) ‖ ⟨mot⟩ *unalloyed* **~münzt** a *uncoined* ‖ ~es Gold *or* Silber [n] *bullion* **~mustert** a (v Stoffen) *plain* **~mütlich** a *uncomfortable, cheerless, dreary, dull, dismal* ‖ (P) *disagreeable, nasty, unpleasant* (~ w *to grow u. to deal with*); der ~ste Ort *the least cheerful place* **~nannt** a *unnamed, anonymous* **~nau** a *inexact, inaccurate* | [adv] ~ gehen (Uhr) *to keep* (*such*) *bad time* **~neigt** a *disinclined, not disposed* (z *to*) ‖ (jdm) *unfriendly* (*towards*)

·ungeniert [–ʒe–] a *unceremonious, free-and--easy*; → genieren

·unge- ~nießbar a *not eatable* od *drinkable*; f ~ erklären *to condemn*, dazu: *c.ation* ‖ (nicht schmackhaft) *unpalatable* ⟨a. fig⟩ ‖ ⟨fig⟩ (P) *unbearable, intolerable* | ≃keit [f] ~/ *inedibility inedibleness, unfitness for food* od *drink* **~nügend** a *insufficient*; *unsatisfactory* ‖ *inadequate*; ⟨school⟩ *bad* | [adv] ~ frankiert *short-paid* (*letter*) ‖ ⟨mar⟩ ~ bemannt *undermanned* **~nügsam** a *insatiable, greedy* ‖ *exacting* ‖ *grasping* **~nützt** a *unused* ‖ *unprofited by* ‖ (Kräfte, Material) ~ l *to leave .. wasting* **~ordnet** a *unsettled, unarranged, confused*; ⟨comp⟩ (*of cards*) *in random sequence* ‖ *dissolute* (*life*) ‖ *ill-assorted* (*knowledge*) ‖ ~e Verhältnisse [n pl] *disorder, muddle* **~pflastert** a *dirt* (*road*) **~pflegt** a *uncared-for, untended, neglected*; *scruffy* ‖ (P) *slovenly, untidy, unneat*; *dowdy, shabby, frumpish*; *unkempt* (⟨a. fig⟩ *lawn*); *unweeded* (*garden*) **~prüft** a *unexamined* ‖ *untested, untried* ‖ ⟨com⟩ *unaudited* ‖ *uncertificated* (*teacher*) **~putzt** a (P) *unadorned, simple*; *plainly dressed* ‖ *untrimmed* (*lamp*) ‖ (Schuhe) *not polished*; *uncleaned* **~rächt** a *unavenged* ‖ *unpunished* **~rade** a *not straight* ‖ *uneven* (*surface*) ‖ *odd* (*number*); ~r Achter (Hirsch) *seven-pointer* **~radwertig** a *odd-valent* **~raten** a **1.** *unsuccessful, miscarried* ‖ (Kind) *undutiful, spoilt, ill-bred* **2.** *unsolved, not guessed* **~rechnet** a *not counted* od *included* | [adv] *without including* od *taking into account* ‖ Reisekosten ~ *without reckoning the travelling expenses* **~recht** a (gegen) *unjust* (*to*), *unfair* (*on*); höchst ~ *iniquitous* **~rechtfertigt** a *unwarranted, unjustified, -fiable*; *unjust* (*enrichment*) **≃rechtigkeit** f ~/~en *injustice* ‖ *iniquity* (*of the conditions*) ‖ e–e ~ begehen *to commit an injustice* ‖ ~en beseitigen *to remedy injustice* **~regelt** a *not regulated*; *irregular* (⟨dero⟩ *disorderly*) (*life*) **~reimt** a (Vers) *unrhymed, rhymeless*; ~e Verse [pl] *blank verse* ‖ ⟨fig⟩ *absurd, preposterous*; *incongruous* ‖ ~es Zeug reden *to talk nonsense* od ⟨fam⟩ *rot* | ≃heit [f] ~/~en ⟨fig⟩ *absurdity, preposterousness, inconsistency, galimatias, incongruity* **~richtet** a ⟨tech⟩ *untrue* ‖ *non-directional* (Funkfeuer *radio beacon*) **~rinnbar** a *incoagulable*

·ungern [adv] *unwillingly, reluctantly, regretfully* ‖ ~ tun *to hate doing* od *to do* ‖ nicht ~ tun *not to grudge doing* ‖ jdm etw ~ hergeben *to begrudge a p a th* ‖ ich höre ~ *I am sorry* (⟨emph⟩ *grieved*) *to hear* ‖ ~ gesehen *unpopular* → ⟨a.⟩ gern

·unge- ~rochen = –gerächt **~rufen** a *unbidden* | [adv] *without being called* **~rügt** a *unreproved*, etc ‖ ich kann nicht ~ l *I cannot help blaming* **~rührt** a ⟨fig⟩ *impassive* (*face*) **~rupft** a ⟨fig⟩: ~ davonk *to get off unfleeced* od *scot-free* **~sagt** a *unsaid* ‖ ~ bleiben *to be omitted* ‖ ~ l *to leave unmentioned* **~salzen** a *unsalted*; *fresh* ‖ ⟨fig⟩ *insipid, dull* ‖ *stale* (*joke*) **~sattelt** a *unsaddled* | [adv] (*to ride*) *bare-backed* **~sättigt** a *unsat*(*iat*)*ed*, ⟨mst⟩ *not satisfied* **~säuert** a *unleavened* **~säumt** a **1.** ⟨tail⟩ *unseamed, seamless, unhemmed* **2.** (sofortig) *immediate, prompt* | [adv] *immediately, without delay, at once, this minute* **~schält** a → Schale; *uncleft wood* **~schehen** a *undone* ‖ ~ m *to undo* ‖ das kann man nicht ~ m *it cannot be undone* **~scheut** [adv] *without fear*; *boldly* **~-schichtlich** a *unhistorical, not based on history*; *ficticious* **≃schick** n ~es/, ~lichkeit, ~theit [f] ~/ *awkwardness, clumsiness* ‖ (des Geistes) *ineptitude* | ≃t a (S & P) *awkward, clumsy* ‖ (P) *unskilful*; ~e Hände *butterfingers*; (geistig) *stupid, inept* | ~ läßt grüßen! *how clumsy* (⟨iron⟩ *clever*) *I am* od *you are*? | [adv] etw ~ anfangen *to go the wrong way to work* ‖ ~ handhaben *to thumb* ‖ sich ~ anstellen *to make a poor hand* (bei *at*) **~schlacht** a *uncouth, unwieldy, hulking, burly, bulky* ‖ *boorish, rude* ‖ *coarse* ‖ *uncivilized* **~schlechtlich** a *asexual* ⟨a. bot⟩ ‖ *unsexed* **~schliffen** a *blunt* (*knife*) ‖ *unpolished* ‖ *uncut* (*jewel*) ‖ *rough* (*diamond*; ⟨a. fig⟩: Edelstein) ‖

⟨fig⟩ *coarse, unmannerly, rude, impolite, uncivil; boorish, rugged* (*manners*) **~schmälert** a *undimished*, etc ‖ *intact, whole* **~schmeidig** a *not pliant* od *malleable*, etc ‖ *inflexible, intractable* ‖ ⟨fig⟩ *unyielding* **~schminkt** a *unpainted; unmade-up* (*lips*, etc) ‖ ⟨fig⟩ *crude, plain* (*facts*) ‖ *unvarnished* (*truth*) ‖ *sincere, true* (*account*) **~schönt** a *brut* (*wine*) **~schoren** a *unshorn* ‖ *uncut* (*velvet*) ‖ ⟨fig⟩ *unmolested* ‖ jdn ~ l ⟨fam⟩ *to leave a p alone*; ~ davonk *to break even*; ~ zurück s *to be safely back* **~schottert** a *unmetalled* (Weg) **~schult** a *untrained, untutored, unschooled* **~geschützt** a *unprotected*, etc; ⟨tact⟩ *exposed* (*flank*) ‖ (gegen Wind etc) *exposed* (*to*) **~schwächt** a *unweakened, unimpaired* (*energy*) ‖ mit ~en Kräften (Mitteln) *vigorously* (*with undiminished means*) **~schwänzt** a *tailless*, ⟨scient⟩ *acaudal* **~schworen** a *unsworn* ‖ ich glaube es dir ~ *I take your word for it* **~sehen** a *unseen* ‖ etw ~ kaufen *to buy a pig in a poke* **~sellig** a *unsociable* ‖ *shy* ‖ *misanthropic* **~setzlich, ~setzmäßig** a *illegal, illicit* **~sichert** a ⟨bank⟩ *unsecured*; → ge– **~gesiebt** a *unpicked*, → sieben [vt] **~sittet** a *uncivilized, rude* (*hordes*) ‖ *unmannerly, ill-bred* **~sperrt** a ⟨typ⟩ *set solid* **~sprächig** a *taciturn* **≃stalt** f ~/ *deformity* **~stalt(et)** a *misshapen, ill-shaped, deformed* **~standen** a = –einge– **~stärkt** a .. ‖ *unstarched* (*collar*) **~stempelt** a *unstamped* ‖ *undefaced* (*stamp*); ~e Marken ⟨philately⟩ *mint* **~stielt** a *stalkless, stemless* **~stillt** a *unappeased* (*hunger*), *unquenched* (*thirst*), *unsatisfied* (*wish*), *unstanched* (*bleeding*), *unstilled* (*pain*) **~stört** a *undisturbed, unmolested*; ~er Besitz ⟨jur⟩ *quiet enjoyment* ‖ ~ l *to leave alone* ‖ ~ verlaufen *to go off smoothly* **~straft** a *unpunished* | [adv] *with impunity* ‖ ~ bleiben ⟨fam⟩ *to go scot-free* **≃stüm 1.** [n] ~(e)s/ *impetuosity, violence* ‖ *vehemence* (*of eloquence*), *furiousness* (*of driving*) ‖ *stress* (*of weather*) ‖ mit ~ *impetuously* **2.** ≃ [a] *impetuous, tempestuous; headlong; violent* ‖ *raging* ‖ *stormy, blustering* (*weather*); *torrential* (*force*) ‖ ⟨fig⟩ *gusty* **~sucht** a *unsought(-for)* ‖ ⟨fig⟩ *artless, unaffected, simple, natural* **~sund** a *unhealthy, sickly* ‖ *insanitary; injurious to health; noisome* (*vapo[u]r*) ‖ *insalubrious, unwholesome* (*climate, place*) ‖ ⟨fig⟩ *unnatural* ‖ *unsound* (*state of affairs*) **~süßt** a *brut* (*wine*) **~tan** a *undone* ‖ ~ l *to leave* (*undone*) **~teilt** a *undivided* ‖ (einstimmig) *unanimous* ‖ (ganz) *entire* ‖ (einfach) *simple* °**≃tier** n *monster* **~treu** a *faithless, unfaithful, perfidious, treacherous* **~trübt** a *untroubled* ⟨a. fig⟩ ‖ *cloudless; serene* (*happiness*) ‖ *unmixed* (*pleasure*) ‖ *unchallenged* (*happiness, possession, property*) **≃tüm** n ~(e)s/~e *monster, prodigy* ‖ ⟨fig⟩ *Leviathan* **~übt** a *unpractised*, etc ‖ (Arbeiter) *inexperienced* (*hands*) ‖ *raw* (*recruits*) **~walkt** a *unfulled* (Wollstoff, Loden, *cloth*) **~wandt** a *awkward, clumsy, slow* **~warnt** a *unforewarned* **~waschen** a *unwashed* ‖ *dirty* ‖ (*wool*) *in the grease* ‖ ~es Maul *insolent* (*malicious, foul, slanderous*) *tongue* ‖ ~es Zeug reden *to talk rot* **~wiegt** [adv] *without being rocked* ‖ ~ schlafen *to sleep like a top* **~wiß** a *uncertain; doubtful* ‖ *precarious, problematic(al)* ‖ *undecided* ‖ *vague* ‖ *depending on circumstances* ‖ *uncharted* (*future*) ‖ *hazardous* | nichts –sses ⟨a.⟩ *no loose ends* | aufs –sse *at random, at a venture* ‖ im –ssen *at a loose end*, im –ssen bleiben *to be left in the dark* od *air* ‖ im –ssen l *to keep .. in the dark* od *air*, ⟨Am⟩ *to keep .. guessing* ‖ sich ins –sse wagen *to take a leap in the dark* | **≃heit** [f] ~/ *uncertainty, doubt* (*-fulness*), etc ‖ e–n in ~ l *to keep a p in suspense* ‖ in schrecklicher ~ s *to be in terrible suspense*, ⟨fam⟩ *on the rack* od *on tenter-hooks*

·**Ungewitter** n ~s/~ *violent* (*thunder-*)*storm*

·**unge- ~witzigt** a *inexperienced* **≃wohnheit** f ~/ *unwontedness, want of practice; strangeness, novelty* **~wöhnlich** a *unusual, uncommon, untoward; unconventional* ‖ *singular, strange; eccentric*; ganz ~ *novel*, ‖ *unorthodox* (*conduct*) ‖ *extraordinary, exceptional, remarkable* ‖ *odd*, ⟨fam⟩ *off-beat*; ⟨Am⟩ *broken* (*sizes*) ‖ etw ≃es *sth out of the common* od *ordinary*; ein ~er Mensch *a man unlike the common lot*; nichts ≃es *no uncommon th, no out-of-the-way th* | [adv] ~ fein etc *exquisite* | ≃keit [f] *unusualness* **~wohnt** a (P) [pred] *unaccustomed* (*to*) ‖ (S) [attr] *unwonted, unusual; strange* (*bed*) | ≃heit = Ungewohnheit **~wollt** a *unwilled* **~zählt** a **1.** *uncounted* ‖ ⟨fig⟩ *unnumbered, untold* ‖ ⟨mst com⟩ *in the lump* **2.** = zahllos **~zähmt** a *untamed* ‖ ~er Falke *haggard* | ⟨fig⟩ *uncurbed* (*spirit*), *unbridled* (*passions*) **~zeichnet** a (Brief) *unsigned* ‖ (Ware) *unmarked* **≃ziefer** n ~s/~ *vermin* [pl konstr] ‖ ⟨fig a.⟩ *pests* pl ‖ v ~ geplagt *vermin-ridden* (*soldier*) ‖ voll ~ ⟨a.⟩ *verminous* | ~befall [m] *vermination, verminosis* ~vertilgung [f] (*vermin*) *disinfestation; disinsectization* **~zielt** a *wild* (*blow, shot*); *random* (*bombing*) **~ziemend** a **1.** *improper, indecent* ‖ *unbecoming* **2.** = frech **~ziert** a *unaffected* | [adv] (*to say*) *bluntly* **~zogen** a *ill-bred, -mannered; rude, uncivil; insolent* ‖ (Kind) *naughty, disobedient* | ≃heit [f] ~/~en *ill-breeding, unmannerliness, rudeness* ‖ *naughtiness* | [konkr] *rude action* ‖ (Wort) *impertinence* **~zügelt** a *unbridled; untrammel(l)ed* ‖ ⟨fig⟩ *uncontrolled, unruly, licentious* ‖ *unsorted* (*masses*) | [adv] *unrestrainedly* **~zwungen** a *unforced, un(con)-strained* ‖ ⟨fig⟩ *natural; unaffected; unstudied*; ~ s *to be at one's ease*; (*free and*) *easy* (*manners*); *easy* (*style*); *unlaboured* (*style*); *informal, casual* (*behavio(u)r, meeting*); *unceremonious, comfortable*; (P) *sociable*; ~e Unterhaltung *ease of conversation* | [adv] etw ~ tun .. *spontaneously, of one's own accord* ‖ *offhand, in the o.h. way* ‖ sich ~ geben *or* benehmen *to behave freely* | ≃heit [f] ~/ *unconstraint* ‖ *naturalness, informality; freedom; spontaneity; unconventionality; unaffectedness, ease; sociability*

·**un- ≃glaube** m ~ns/ (gegenüber Pn *or* Nachricht) *disbelief, incredulity* ‖ ⟨bes ec⟩ *unbelief, unbelieving* ‖ (heidnischer Glaube) *infidelity* **~glaubhaft** a *unauthenticated* (*documents*); *incredible; unworthy of belief* ‖ *unreliable* (*news, witness*); *untrustworthy* (*p., source*) | [pred] *beyond belief* **~gläubig** a *incredulous, disbelieving* ‖ *sceptical* ‖ *doubting* (*Thomas*); ⟨bib arts⟩ *The D. of St. Th.*; ⟨ec⟩ *unbelieving*; (heidnisch) *infidel* | [adv] jdn ~ anstarren *to stare at a p in unbelief* | ≃e(r) m ~n/~n *unbeliever* ‖ *infidel* ‖ *sceptic* **~gl·aublich** a *incredible, undreamt-of* (*velocity*); *cock-and-bull* (*story*); *extraordinary* (*ths*) ‖ ⟨fam⟩ *infernal* ‖ (Damensprache) auf so ~e Art *in such a way* | ~ s *to defy belief* | ~! *rats!; there now!* | adv (*insolent*) *beyond belief, marvellously* (*bright*) ‖; [adv] ~ gr *incredibly big*; .. ist ~ gr .. *is so big you can't believe it* ‖ ~ gut ⟨sl⟩ *thundering* (*meal*); ~ viele Fehler m *to make more errors than you could believe* **~glaubwürdig** = unglaubhaft **~gleich** a *unequal* ‖ (unähnlich) *unlike, dissimilar* ‖ *varying, wavering* ‖ (*they are*) *different from each other* ‖ *disproportionate, inconsistent* (*with*) ‖ ⟨scient⟩ *heterogeneous* ‖ (uneben) *uneven* ‖ (Zahlen) *odd* | *irregular* (*pulse*) ‖ *odd* (*socks*) ‖ *changeable, unbalanced, inconstant, inconsistent, whimsical* (*temper*) ‖ *changeable* (*weather*) ‖ ~e Räder h ⟨mot⟩ *to be out of line* ‖ ⟨com⟩ v ~er Güte *varying in quality* | adv *unequally* ‖ [vor compr] *a great deal, incomparably, much, (by) far* (*better, more beautiful*) | ~artig [a] *different, dissimilar*, ⟨scient⟩ *unhomogeneous, heterogeneous* | ≃artigkeit [f] *dissimilarity* | ~blättrig [a] *heterophyllous* | ~farbig [a] *variegated* | ~förmig [a] *not uniform, unequal; unsymmetrical; irregular* ‖ *unlike* ‖ → –artig | ≃förmigkeitsgrad [m] *degree* *of unbalance* | ≗gewicht [n] *disequilibrium*; *non-uniform* | ~mäßig [a] *disproportionate*, *unsymmetrical*, *unequal*, *irregular* || (wechselnd) *fitful*, *changeable*; ⟨mach⟩ *uneven* (*working*) | [adv] ⟨sl⟩ *very on and off* | ~namig [a] ⟨math⟩ *of different denominations* || ⟨phys el⟩ *opposite* (*poles*) | ~seitig [a] *with unequal sides* || *scalene* (*triangle*) | ~silbig [a] *imparisyllabic* | ~teilig a ⟨scient⟩ *heteromerous* **≗gleichheit** f ~/~en *inequality* || *unlikeness*, *dissimilarity* || *unevenness*, etc || (soziale) *disparity* **≗glimpf** m ~(e)s/ *harshness* || *insult*, *outrage* || *wrong*, *injury* | ≗lich [a] *ungentle*, *harsh*, *rigorous*, *insulting* || ~ behandeln *to deal harshly with*, ⟨fam⟩ *to be hard on* (*a p*) **·Unglück** n ~(e)s/ *misfortune* (*it was her m. that ..*) || (Miß-geschick) *ill luck* ⟨a. cards, etc⟩ | [pl ~sfälle] *mishap*, *piece of ill luck*; *misfortune* (*visited by grave m.s*) || (Unfall) *accident* ⟨a. rail⟩; (schwerer ~sfall) *calamity*, *disaster*; *hard lines* pl | (Leid) *adversity*, *distress* || (Elend) *misery* | Gefühl v nahendem ~ *feeling of bad to come* | ~ h *to be unlucky* (*in love*, *at cards*); *to be crossed* (*in love*); um das ~ voll z m *to make matters worse* || das ~ will es, daß *the trouble is that* || wie es das ~ will *as ill-luck will have it* | **ins** ~ geraten *to fall on adversity* od *evil days* || °sich ins ~ stürzen (heiraten) ⟨mar⟩ *to jump off the dock*, ⟨mil⟩ → Sprung || **zum** ~ *unhappily*, *unfortunately* (f *for*) || z ~ kam er *the misfortune was that he came* | ⟨prov⟩ ein ~ k–t selten allein *it never rains but it pours*; vgl Sh., Hamlet: *When sorrows come, they come not single spies, but in battalions*; *One woe doth tread upon another's heel so fast they follow* || kein ~ ohne Glück *it is an ill wind* (*that*) *blows nobody any good* ||| ≗bringend [a] *unpropitious*, *disastrous*; ≗selig [a] *luckless*, *wretched*, *unhappy*, *miserable*, *unfortunate* || (S) *disastrous*, *calamitous* || ~seligkeit [f] *lucklessness*, etc, *misery* **·unglücklich** a (innerlich ~) *unhappy* (⟨a.⟩ *marriage*); *wretched*, *miserable*, *broken-hearted*; *disconsolate*, *afflicted* || (v Glück nicht begünstigt) *unfortunate*, *unlucky*; *luckless* (*queen*) || ⟨Scot⟩ *mischancy* || *ill-starred* (*victim*) | (unheilvoll) *fatal* (*mishap*); *untoward* (*injury*); *unpropitious* (*circumstances*) || ⟨fig⟩ *awkward* (*wording*) | (verhängnisvoll) *disastrous* | ~e Liebe *thwarted love*, *disappointment in love* || ~ in der Liebe *unlucky in one's lovers* | es trifft sich ~ *it's unfortunate* || ~er Ausdruck *infelicitous expression* | [adv] ~ enden *to fail*, ⟨fam⟩ *to turn out a failure*; *to end in disaster* || ~ lieben etc *to be crossed in love*, *unlucky at cards*, etc **~erweise** adv *unfortunately*, *unluckily* || ~! *worse luck*! **·Unglücks- ~bote** m *bearer of ill news* **~botschaft** f *evil tidings*, *bad* od *fatal news* pl **~fall** m *misfortune*; (schwer) *calamity*, *disaster* || (Unfall) (*fatal*) *accident*, *casualty* || Tod durch ~ *accident death*, *d. by misadventure* **~bringer** m (P & S) *hoodoo* **~gefährte** m *companion in misfortune*, *fellow-sufferer* **~jahr** n *disastrous y.* °**~mensch** m *unfortunate p*, ⟨fam⟩ *unlucky chap* **~prophet** m *foreteller of misfortune* || ⟨fam⟩ *croaker* **~rabe, ~vogel** m *bird of ill omen*, ⟨fam⟩ *croaker* || ⟨fig & fam⟩ (= Pechvogel) *unlucky fellow* od *dog*, *poor devil*; ⟨Am⟩ *regular Jonah* **~stätte** f *scene of the accident* **~tag** m *bad*, *fatal*, *unfortunate day*; *day of misfortune*; ⟨fam⟩ *Black Monday*, *black-letter day* **·Ungnade** f ~/ *disgrace*, *disfavo(u)r* || in ~ ⟨fam⟩ *in the doghouse*, .. fallen *to fall out of favo(u)r* od *into disgrace* (*with a p*), *to become disgraced* || sich jds ~ zuziehen *to incur a p's displeasure*, ⟨fam⟩ *to get into a p's bad books*

un- ~gnädig a *ungracious*, *unkind*, *harsh* || *ill-humoured*, *cross*, *angry* || *unfavourable* (*reply*), *unpropitious* (*fate*) || wenn sie am ~sten war *at her most disapproving* || ~ s gegen *to frown upon* (*a p*) | [adv] ~ aufnehmen *to take .. amiss* **~grad(zahlig)** a *odd* **~grammatisch** a *ungrammatical* **~graziös** a *ungraceful* **~gründlich** a ⟨fig⟩ *superficial*, *inaccurate*, *inexact*, *shallow* | [adv] ⟨a.⟩ *on the surface* (*only*)

·ungültig a *invalid*, *void* (*gifts are void*) || [pred] *null* || (Fahrkarte) *not available* || (Münze) *not current* || ⟨ten⟩ ~! *let*! || ~ m, f ~ erklären *to invalidate*, *annul*, *cancel*; ⟨pol⟩ *to declare* (*an election void* || ~ w *to expire*, *to be cancelled* **≗erklärung** f *invalidation*, *nullification*; Klage auf ~ e–r Ehe *nullity suit* **≗machen** n = –erklärung **≗werden** n *extinction*, *nullification* **·Ungunst** f ~/ *disfavour*, *disaffection* || (des Wetters) *inclemency* || (der Verhältnisse) *unpropitiousness* || bei jdm in ~ stehen *to be in a p's black books* || es fiel z s–n ~en aus *it* ((⟨jur⟩ *the lawsuit*) *went against him* || das spricht z s–n ~en *that tells against him*

un- ~günstig a *unfavo(u)rable* (*news*, *development*) || *inauspicious*; *unpropitious* (*sign*) || *disadvantageous* (*bargain*) || *untimely*, *ill-timed*, *unseasonable*; *untoward* (*event*) || *adverse* (*balance*, *weather*) || *bad* (*light*) || *ill* (*tidings*) || *inopportune*, *inappropriate*, *inexpedient*; *inconvenient*, *unbefitting* | im ~sten Falle *if the worst comes to the worst* | ~er Wind *head wind* | (abgeneigt) [dat] *ill-disposed* (*towards*) | [adv] ~ beeinflussen *to prejudice* (*an issue*) **~gusti·ös** a ⟨österr⟩ = unappetitlich; → G·usto **~gut** a (nicht) f ~ nehmen *to take amiss* od *in ill* (*good*) *part* || nichts f ~! *no offence*!, *nothing personal* (*was*) *meant*!, *no harm meant*! *no ill will*! *never mind*!; nehmen Sie es nicht f ~, wenn ich .. *don't think it unkind of me if I* (*say so*) od *of me* (*to tell you ..*) **~gütig** a *unkind*, *unfriendly* | [adv] ~ aufnehmen *to take amiss* **~haltbar** a ⟨a. fig⟩ *untenable* (*fortress*, *opinion*) || *unwarrantable* (*conjecture*) || *unsustainable* (*position*, *opinion*) | *not lasting* od *durable* od *solid* | (*promises*) *that cannot be kept* **~handlich** a *unwieldy*, *unhandy*, *unmanageable* (*trunk*) **~harmonisch** a *inharmonious*; *discordant* ((⟨a. fig⟩ *roof*); *jarring* **·Unheil** n ~(e)s/ *evil*, *mischief*, *harm*, *trouble* || *ruin*, *frustration* || ~ anrichten *to do* (*make*, *cause*) *mischief* | ≗ahnend [a] *prescient of disaster* | ≗bringend [a] *fatal* (*to*) | ≗drohend [a] *ill-boding*, *ominous*; *sinister* | ≗schwanger [a] *fraught* od *big with misfortune* od *mischief* | ~stifter [m] *mischief-maker*, ⟨sl⟩ *jinx* | ≗verkündend [a] = –drohend | ≗voll [a] *fatal*, *disastrous*, *calamitous*; *unfortunate* || *destructive*, *malefic*, *malign* (*influence*) **·un- ~h·ellbar** a *incurable*; ~e Kranke [pl] *incurables* ⟨fam⟩ *goners* pl || [pred] *past remedy* od *recovery* || (S) *irreparable* || *irremediable* (*antagonism*) **~heilig** a *unholy* || *profane*, *wordly* || *impious* **~heimlich** a *weird*, *eerie*; *uncanny* (*affair*), ⟨Am fam⟩ *funny* (*business*) || *dismal*, *haunted* (*place*) || *sinister* (*look*); ein ~es Gefühl h *to feel creepy all over* | [adv] *ghastly*, *viciously*, *terribly*, ⟨sl⟩ *beastly* | ~ viel .. *lots of* (*money*), *an immense number of* (*people*) **~höflich** a *impolite*, *uncivil* || *discourteous* || *disobliging* || *disrespectful*, *rude* (*words*) | [adv] ⟨a.⟩ *in an offhand way* **≗hold(in** f) m ~(e)s/~e *monster*, *fiend*, *demon* || *sorcerer*; (*sorceress*, *hag*) || *dragon* **~hold** a *ungracious*, *unfriendly*, *unkind* || [dat] *ill-disposed* (*towards*) **≗holz** n ⟨for⟩ *undesirable tree*[*s* pl] **~hörbar** a *inaudible* || (Stimme) ~ m *to drown* **~hygienisch** a *in-*, *unsanitary*

°**·Uni** f ~/~s (~versit·ät) ⟨sl⟩ *Varsity* **un·iert** a *united* | ≗**e** m pl *members of the Union*; ⟨Ger⟩ *members of the United Protestant Church* **Uni-f·orm** f ~/~en *uniform*, *regimentals* pl || in gr [kl] ~ *in full-dress* [*undress*] (*uniform*), ⟨fam⟩ *in full fig* || nicht in ~ *in plain clothes*, ⟨mil⟩ *in mufti* | ~besatz [m] *piping*; ~kappe, –mütze [f] *dress cap* | **≗·ieren** vt [h] *to* (*render*) *uniform* || (kleiden) *to* (*put into*) *uniform* | **~it·ät** [f] ~/ *uniformity* **·Unikum** n ~s/~s & ~ka *unique* (*th*, *object*, *instance*, *copy*) | ⟨fam⟩ (P) *queer customer*

·un- ~interessant a *uninteresting* || *colourless*, *unattractive* (*p*), *incurious* (*th*), *uninspiring* (*game*);

drab, dull **~interessiert** a *uninterested* || (uneigennützig) *disinterested* | ⩪heit [f] *want of interest; disinterestedness* **~irdisch** a (wesenlos) *unsubstantial*

Uni·on f ~/~en *union* | ⩪·**istisch** a *unionist* **unis·ono** adv ⟨mus⟩ *in unison* **Unit·arier** m ~s/~ ⟨ec⟩ *Unitarian* || die Lehre der ~ *Unitarianism* **-r·ismus** m ⟨pol⟩ *unitarism* **u.-r·istisch** a ⟨pol⟩ *unitary* **univers·al** a *universal* [a. mst in ⟨tech⟩ comp] | *all-purpose* || ⩪erbe [m] *sole heir*, ⟨jur⟩ *residuary legatee*; ⩪genie [n] *all-round man*, ⟨hum⟩ *Jack of all trades*; ⩪lexikon [n] *(en)cyclop(a)edia*; ~maschine [f] *all-round m.*; ⩪mittel [n] *universal remedy, panacea*; ⩪schraubenschlüssel [m] *monkey-wrench*; ~sucher [m] ⟨phot⟩ *u.l multifocus*; ⩪werkzeug [n] *all-purpose tool*; ⩪zange [f] *(a pair of) pliers* pl **univers·ell** a *universal* **Universit·ät** f ~/~en *university* || die ~ Marburg *M. U.* || die ~ zu Berlin *B. U.* || die ~ (B.) beziehen *to go to the u. (of B.)*; ⟨engl mst⟩ *to go to college* || auf der ~ s *to keep one's terms*; ⟨engl mst⟩ *to be at college* || die ~ verlassen ⟨a.⟩ *to come, go down* || zur ~ k *to go, come up* | **~s-** ~bildung [f] *u. education*; ~dozent [m] *teacher in a u.*; ~druckerei [f] *U. Press*; ~ferien [pl] (gr *long*) *vacation*; ~freund [m] *fellow-student, college friend*; ~gericht [n] *Court of the U.*; ~jahre [n pl] *college years* pl; ~kirche [f] *u. church*; ~lehrer [m] *lecturer in a u.*; ⟨engl a.⟩ *college-tutor*, ⟨fam⟩ *don*; ~pedell [m] *beadle*, ⟨fam⟩ *bulldog*; ~professor [m] *u. professor*; ~rektor [m] *chancellor of the u.*; ~richter [m] *proctor*; ~studium [n] *u. studies* pl, *reading at college*; ~unterricht [m] *academic teaching*; ~verwaltung [f] *General Board*; ~vorlesungen [f pl] besuchen *to attend u. lectures*; ~wesen [n] *(the) -ties* pl; ~zeit [f] *undergraduate days, college years* pl **Univ·ersum** n ~s/ *universe*

Unizi·ale f ~/~n ⟨print⟩ *unicial*

·un- ~jagdbar a *not fit* od *unfit for the chase* od *hunt* **~kaufmännisch** a *unbusinesslike*

·Unke f ~/~n *(red-bellied) toad* || ⟨fam, fig⟩ (P) *croaker* || voll wie e–e ~ *drunk as a lord* **~nruf** m *croaking* ⟨a. fig⟩ | ⩪**n** vt/i [h] *to croak*

·un- ~kenntlich a *indiscernible* || (P) *not to be identified, unrecognizable*; ~ in s–n M. gehüllt *cloaked against recognition* || ~ m *to disguise*, ⟨mil⟩ *to camouflage* | ⩪keit [f] ~/ *indiscernable*, etc *condition* || *disguise* || (Entstellung) *disfigurement* || bis zur ~ *past recognition*; .. entstellt *distorted out of all resemblance to the fact* ⩪**kenntnis** f ~/ *ignorance* || *i. of the law excuses no one* (.. schützt vor Strafe nicht) od *is no excuse* || sich [acc] in völliger ~ e–r S befinden *to be quite ignorant of a th* || e–n über etw in ~ halten *to keep a p in the dark about sth* **~keusch** a *unchaste, lewd* || [adv] ~ leben *to lead a lascivious* od *an impure life* **~kindlich** a *unchildlike* || (lieblos) *unfilial* || (frühreif) *precocious; forward* **~kirchlich** a *taking no interest in church matters* || ⟨emph⟩ *anticlerical* || *secular, worldly* **~klagbar** ⟨a. jur⟩ *not actionable* **~klar** a *not clear, not evident* || *indistinct, vague, dim* | ⟨mar⟩ *unclear, foul (rope), fouled (anchor)* || ~ laufen v *to run* od *get foul of* | (trüb) *troubled, muddy* || (nebelig) *misty, hazy* | ⟨fig⟩ *unintelligible, unapparent; abstruse, dark, obscure; opaque (language)* | ⟨fam⟩ *woolly, loose (thinking), muddled, muddy (style)* || ~e Vorstellungen h über *to be vague about* || ich bin mir im ~en über [acc] *I am not quite certain about, I am hazy* (od *in two minds*) *about* || jdn im ~en l *to leave a p (in the dark* od) *wondering (whether)* | ~heit [f] *want of clearness; vagueness, obscurity, uncertainty, ambiguity*; ~en [pl] *dubiosities* **~klassifizierbar** a ⟨fig⟩ *non-descript* **~klug** a *imprudent, injudicious* || *unwise, foolish* || *thoughtless* || *impolitic* | [adv] das war ~ gehandelt *that was acting rashly* od *unwisely* || ~erweise [adv] *unwisely* | ⩪heit [f] ~/ *imprudence*, etc || [konkr] *foolish action, piece of folly* **~kollegial** a *unlike a colleague* **~kompliziert** a *uncomplicated, simple, clear, unsophisticated* **~königlich** a *unkingly* || *antiroyal* **~konventionell** a *unconventional* (⟨a. mil⟩ *warfare* [*UW*]) **~körperlich** a *disembodied(ly* adv); *incorporeal, immaterial; insubstantial* || *spiritual* ⩪**kosten** pl (allg.e ~ → Gemein–) *charges, (general) expenses, costs* pl || gegen Erstattung der ~ *with out-of-pocket expenses* || nach Abzug aller ~ *charges paid* || hohe ~ ⟨Am⟩ *a large overhead* | gerade die ~ decken *to break even* || jdm ~ m *to put a p to expense* || sich in ~ stürzen *to go to (great) expense* || die ~ tragen ⟨a.⟩ *to foot the bill* **~kräftig** a *feeble, weak* || *low, sloppy (diet)* ⩪**kraut** n ~(e)s/ ⟨bot⟩ *weed(s* pl) || (P) ⟨fig⟩ *tares of civilization*; ⟨bib⟩ *(to sow) tares (among the wheat)* || v ~ säubern *to weed* || stark v ~ bewachsen *weed-ridden* || ⟨fig⟩ (P) *never-do-well* || ⟨prov⟩ ~ verdirbt nicht *ill weeds grow apace* || ~-ex [n] *weed-killer, weedicide, herbicide* **~kriegerisch** a *unwarlike* **~kulant** a *unaccomodating* **~kultiviert** a *uncultivated* || (P) *uncultured, uncivilized, unpolished* ⩪**kultur** f ~/ *want of culture* od *civilization; barbarism* **~kündbar** a (Staatspapiere) *irredeemable* || (Rente) *perpetual* || (Hypothek) *not to be foreclosed* || (Anstellung) *secured against dismissal* ⩪**kunde** f ~/ *ignorance* **~kundig** a [gen] *ignorant (of), unacquainted (with)* || *not knowing (one's way)* || *knowing no* (od *having no knowledge of*) *(Latin)* **~künstlerisch** a *inartistic (work)* || *unartistic (p)* **~landig** a *sterile, infertile (soil, ground)* **~längst** adv *lately, of late, recently, not long ago; the other day* **~lauter** a *sordid, squalid, impure* || *ignoble, mean, self-interested (p)* || *unfair (competition)* **~leidlich** a *intolerable, unbearable* || ich finde ihn ~ *I can't bear* (⟨fam⟩ *the sight of*) *him* **~lenkbar** a ⟨aero⟩ *ungovernable* **~lenksam** a *indocile, unmanageable, intractable, unruly (p)* **~leserlich** a *illegible*; ⟨emph⟩ *undecipherable* || ~ m *to blot* **~l·eugbar** a *undeniable* || *evident* || *indisputable, incontestable* || es ist ~ *there is no denying* | [adv] *undeniably*, etc **~lieb** a *disagreeable* || es ist mir [nicht] ~ *I am sorry (that ..; to see ..; for ..)* [*I am rather glad*] | [adv] e–m nicht ~ k *not to come amiss to a p* **~liebenswürdig** a *unkind, unamiable; sullen, surly* **~liebsam** a *unpleasant, disagreeable* **~liniert** a *unruled; plain (paper)* **~logisch** a *illogical* || ⟨fam⟩ *loose (thinking)* || ~erweise *illogically* **~l·ösbar, ~l·öslich** a *indissoluble (matter)* || *insoluble (problem)* || (Geheimnis) *inexplicable* || (Knoten, Aufgabe) *inextricable* **~l·öschbar** a *unquenchable, inextinguishable* ⩪**lust** f ~/ (Verdrossenheit) *listlessness* || (Unbehagen) *uneasiness, discomfort* || (Abneigung) *aversion, dislike, disinclination* || ~ z Essen *want of appetite* || ⟨com⟩ *slackness* **~lustig** a *listless* ⟨a. com, exch⟩ || *uneasy* || *morose* || (zu) *averse, disinclined, reluctant (to)* | *displeasing* **~magnetisch** n *non-magnetic* **~manierlich** a *unmannerly, ill-mannered* | [adv] *in an unmannerly way* **~maniriert** a *natural, unaffected, ingenuous* **~männlich** a *unmanly* || *effeminate* ⩪**maß** n ~es/ *immensity, excess* || im ~ *to excess* ⩪**masse** f ~/~n *vast* od *enormous quantities* pl || *a world of (trouble), a host of (difficulties), a power of (work)*; ⟨fam⟩ *like a ton of bricks* || *shoals* od *a shower of (letters); gallons of (tea); (beef and ale) galore* [adv] || ⟨fam⟩ *loads, tons, heaps, lots, oceans* [pl] od *no end of (money)* || ⟨sl⟩ *a sight of (questions)* || ⟨Am sl⟩ *oodles, scads* **~maßgeblich** a *unauthoritative* || (bescheiden) *unpresuming, humble* || nach m–r ~en Meinung *in my poor* od *humble opinion*; s–e ~e M. äußern *to proffer one's o. for what it is worth, to speak under correction* | [adv] *without prejudice,* *with due submission* od *deference* **~mäßig** a *immoderate* (*devotion*), *excessive*, *inordinate* (*pride*) || im Trinken *intemperate* || (ausschweifend) *dissolute, licentious* | [adv] ⟨a.⟩ *to excess*; (*to drink, live*) *deeply* | ~keit [f] *intemperance* ⩪**menge** f = –masse; *loads of* (*time*); ~n [pl] davon *dozens*, ⟨Am⟩ *boodles of it* ⩪**mensch** m *monster, fiend* || *what a feelingless brute*! || ⟨hum⟩ ich bin kein ~ *I won't refuse* **~menschlich** a *inhuman* (*cruelty, condition*); *non-humanly* (*religious, moral, intellectual*) → über– || *brutal* (*cad*) || *barbarous* | *superhuman, enormous, mighty* (*strength*) | [adv] *mighty, immensely* (*pleased*) | ⩪keit [f] ~/ *inhumanity, brutality* || [konkr] *atrocity*; *fiendish act* **~m·erklich** a *imperceptible, insensible*; *unobservable* **~m·eßbar** a *immeasurable* **~methodisch** a *unmethodical, casual*; *touch-and-go* [attr] | [adv] *on a desultory basis* **~mißverständlich** a *unmistakable* (–bly adv), → eindeutig; *clear*; *quite obvious* **~m·itteilbar** a *incommunicable*; *unfit for publication* **~m·itteilsam** a *reserved*; *taciturn* **~mittelbar** a *immediate* (⟨hist⟩ *States*) || *literal* (*sense*), *direct* (*cause*) || *actual* (*possession*) || *live* (*interest*, ⟨wir⟩ *transmission*) || *close* (*air support*) || | [adv] *just* (*before his departure*), *directly* (*after* ..) || ~ darauf *i.ely afterwards*; ~ davor *on the* (*very*) *eve of it* || (*to apply*) *directly* (*to a p*) || ~ eintreten: *death must have been instantaneous* || ~ folgen *to follow hard* (*upon*) || hier ~ *right here* | ⩪keit [f] ~/ *immediateness* || ⟨fig⟩ *immediacy, directness* (*of observation*), *convincingness* (*of style*) **~modern** a *old-fashioned, unfashionable* || *frumpish, dowdy* (*lady*) || ~ w *to go out of fashion* **~m·öglich** a *impossible* (⟨a. fig⟩: *brown hat*) || fast ~ *next to impossible* || ganz ~ *quite out of the question* || ⟨fig⟩ *intolerable* (*wages*); *barbarous, hopeless* (*stairs*) || (*at such an*) *unearthly* (*hour*) | (etw) als ~ betrachten *to rule out* || es wäre nicht ~ *it might happen* || wird nicht f ~ gehalten *seems to be possible* | (durch Kritik) ~ m *to prevent, kill* || sich ~ m *to compromise o.s., to make an ass of o.s.*; .. so ~ .. *she had made h.s. so much of a nuisance that* | [ell] ~! *well, I never!, perfectly deadly*! | ⩪es leisten *to do wonderful ths* || ⩪es verlangen *to cry for the moon* || ⩪es kann man v niemand verlangen *one must not expect impossibilities* | [adv] *not possibly*; ich kann ~ zurückkehren [einsehen] *I can't possibly return, it is impossible for me to return* [*I fail to see*] || sich [acc] ~ benehmen *to behave* (*very*) *badly* .. läßt sich ~ putzen etc *the salver defies scouring, the problem defies solution* || das ist ~ z erreichen *that is impossible of attainment* | ⩪keit [f] ~/~en *impossibility* || praktische ~ *impracticability* || das ist ein Ding der ~ *it is quite impossible* **~monarchisch** a *not monarchical, contrary to m. principles* **~moralisch** a *immoral, unprincipled* **~motiviert** a *groundless, gratuitous*; *without any motive, uncalled for* **~mündig** a *minor* || [pred] *under age, not of age* || ~es Kind *young infant, babe* | ⩪e [m; der ~, ein ~r] & f ~n/~n *minor* | ⩪keit [f] ~/ *minority* || *infancy* **~musikalisch** a *unmusical* || (P) *not musical*; *tone-deaf* ⩪**mut** m ~(e)s/ *ill humour* || (Entrüstung) *displeasure, indignation, petulance* || *annoyance* **~nachahmlich** a *inimitable* **~nachbarlich** a *unneighbourly* **~nachgiebig** a *relentless* (*hostility*) || *unyielding, inflexible*; *unbending*; *obstinate*; *grim*; *stern*; *stubborn*; *uncompromising, intransigent*; *intractable*; *unalterable*; *adamant* || ~ s *to keep a stiff upper lip* | ⩪er *die-hard* | ⩪keit [f] *intransigence*, etc **~nachsichtig, ~nachsichtlich** a *unrelenting, uncharitable, relentless* || *strict, severe, hard* | [adv] *without indulgence* **~n·ahbar** a *unapproachable, inaccessible* ⟨a. fig⟩ || ⟨fig⟩ *stand-offish, distant, aloof, exclusive*; ⟨fam⟩ *not-come-at-able* | ~keit [f] ~/ *u.ness, st.-o.ness, aloofness* ⩪**natur** f ~/ *unnaturalness*; ⟨emph⟩ *monstrosity* || (Geziertheit) *affectation* **~natürlich** a (abweichend vom Naturgesetz) *non-natural* || (gegen die Natur) *unnatural*; ⟨emph⟩ *monstrous* || *constrained*; (geziert) *affected*; *she had a strained laugh that disfeatured her* **~n·ennbar** a (nicht in Worte faßbar) *inexpressible* || (mehr als Worte besagen) *unutterable, ineffable* || (anstandshalber ~) *unmentionable* **~notiert** a ⟨com⟩ *unquoted* **~nötig** a *unnecessary, needless* || *superfluous* (*word*) || *uncalled-for*, (mutwillig) *gratuitous* | (etw) ~ m *to obviate*; *to eliminate the need of* | [adv] (⟨a.⟩ ~erweise) *needlessly*, etc; *without necessity*; *for nothing* **~nütz(lich** †) a *useless, fruitless, vain, unprofitable* || ⟨hort⟩ *barren* || ⟨fam⟩ [pred] *no good* | *idle* (*talk*) || ~es Zeug *nonsense, rot*; *rubbish, trash* || ⩪es tun *to plow sand* | sich ~ m *to make o.s. obnoxious* | adv (Truppen) ~ (über)anstrengen *to fatigue* .. *unnecessarily*; ~ verschwendend *futile*; ⟨bib⟩ den Namen des Herrn ~lich führen *to take the name of God in vain*; → unausge~t **~ordentlich** a (Ort u S) *confused, untidy, disorderly* || *unkempt* (*garden*) || *rough* (*dress, appearance*) || ⟨fam⟩ *scruffy*; *messy* | (P) *disorderly, negligent, careless* || *frowzy, unkempt* (*appearance*) || (Anzug) *untidy, slovenly* (= schlampig) || mit ~em Haar *dishevelled* || (Lebenswandel) *irregular, disorderly, loose, dissolute* | ⟨mil⟩ ~e Flucht *headlong flight*; *rout* | [adv] ~ umherliegen *to lie littered about* ⩪**ordnung** f ~/ *disorder, untidiness, disarray, confusion* || ⟨mil⟩ *rout* || (im Zimmer etc) *muddle, confusion*; ⟨fam⟩ *mess* | **in** ~ bringen *to upset, unsettle*; *to* (*throw into*) *disorder*, ⟨fam⟩ *to clutter up* (*with* ..); *to play* (*the*) *mischief with* (*a th*); .. gr .. *to make a mess of a th* || (Haar) *to ruffle, derange*, ⟨Am⟩ *to muss* || ⟨mach⟩ *to throw out of gear* || in ~ ⟨tech⟩ *out of adjustment*; in ~ bringen *to derange*; *throw into a confusion*; *mess up*; in ~ k, in ~ geraten *to fall into disorder, to get out of order*; *to fall out of square*; in ~ liegen *to lie up and down* || in ~ s *to be all in a muddle*, (Stube) *in a litter*, ⟨fam⟩ .. *mess* || in ~ zurückl ⟨a.⟩ *to leave* .. *at a loose end* || sich in ~ zurückziehen *to retire tumultuously* **~organisch** a *unorganic* [adv -*ally*] **~organisiert** a *free* (*labo*[*u*]*r*); *wild*(*cat*) (*strike*) **~orthographisch** *misspelt* | [adv] ~ schreiben *to spell badly* **~paarig** a (Zahl) *odd* || (Handschuhe etc) *not even*; (einzeln) *odd*; *without a fellow* || ⟨comp⟩ *unmatched* (*card*) | [adv] ~ gefiedert ⟨bot⟩ *imparipinnate* ⩪**paarzeher** m ⟨zoo⟩ *perissodactyl* **~parlamentarisch** a *unparliamentary* **~partei-** ~isch, ~lich [a] *impartial* || (unbefangen), *detached*; *unbiassed* || *unprejudiced* (*judgment*) || *evenhanded* (*justice*) | ⩪liche [m] [der ~, ein ~r] ⟨crick, ten, etc⟩ *umpire*; ⟨ftb, box⟩ *referee* || als ~r fungieren *to u.* bzw *r.* | ⩪lichkeit [f] ~/ *impartiality*; *detachment* || *evenness of judgment, fairness* **~paß** a [pred] (→ –päßlich) *unwell*, ⟨fam⟩ *out of sorts* **~passend** a *unsuitable, inappropriate* || (unschicklich) *improper, unseemly* || *misplaced* (*remark*) || *incongruous* (*circumstances*) || nichts ⩪es *no incongruity*; etw ⩪es sagen *to say the wrong th* | [adv] *in an unbecoming* (etc) *way* **~passierbar** a *impassable, impracticable* || *unfordable* (*river*) **~päßlich** a *indisposed, ailing*, ⟨fam⟩ *seedy* || [pred] *poorly*, ⟨fam⟩ *out of sorts* | ⩪keit [f] ~/ *indisposition*, (*slight*) *ailing* **~persönlich** a *impersonal* **~pfändbare** Gegenstände *exempts* pl **~politisch** a *non-political, apolitical* || ⟨fig⟩ *impolitic* [adv -*ally*], *imprudent* **~praktisch** a *unpractical* (*p*), *unbusinesslike* || *impracticable* (*scheme*, ⟨Am a.⟩ *p*) **~produktiv** [–f] a *non-* od *unproductive* | ⩪ität [–v–] [f] *unproductiveness* **~programmäßig** a *unscheduled* **~proportioniert** [–ts] a *not well proportioned* || *disproportionate* || *out of proportion* **~pünktlich** a *unpunctual*, ⟨Am⟩ *tardy* || *irregular*, *inexact* | ~ k *to be slow in arriving* **~qualifizierbar** a *unqualifiable* **~rasiert** a *unshaven* || ~ s *to need a shave* || °~ u fern der Heimat ⟨mil⟩ *°fucked and far from home* | [adv] *without having shaved* **≗rast** f *restlessness* || *restless child* **≗rat** m ~(e)s/ *dirt, rubbish* || (Abfall) *garbage, refuse, ordure* || *excrements* pl || ⟨fig⟩ ~ merken *to smell a rat* | ~haufen [m] *rubbish-heap*; ~kasten [m] *dust-bin*; ~schnüffler [m] ⟨Am pol⟩ *muckraker*; ~schreiberling [m] *mud-slinger* **~rationell** a *wasteful* **~ratsam** a *unadvisable* || *inexpedient* **·Unrecht** n ~(e)s/ [abstr & konkr] *injustice* || (moralisch Un[ge]rechtes, Falsches) *wrong* (an, f *to*) || ⟨jur⟩ *tort* || (Schädigung) *injury*; *harm* | ein ~ **begehen** *to commit an injustice* || bei dir bekommt er nie ≗ *in your opinion he is never w.* || sein ~ eingestehen *to stand corrected* || es ist ihm ~ geschehen *he has been w.ed* || ≗ h, (**im** ~ s) *to be* (*in the*) *w., to be mistaken* (od *in* [*at*] *fault*) || jdn ins ~ setzen *to put a p in the w.* || ~ leiden *to be w.ed* || **mit,** zu ~ *wrongly, unjustly* || nicht mit, zu ~ (loben etc) *not unreasonably* || (e–m) ≗ tun *to do* (*a p*) *w., to w. a p, to injure a p* | ⟨prov⟩ besser ~ leiden, als ~ tun *better suffer ill than do ill* | ~staat [m] *law-neglecting* od *l.-ignoring state* **·unrecht** a (→ [nicht] recht) **1.** *wrong, incorrect* || (ungerecht) *unjust, unfair* || (ungeeignet) *improper, unsuitable* || jdm ~ **geben** *to decide against a p* **2.** das ist der **≗e** *that is not the man* || irgend etw ≗es *anything out of the way* || an den ≗en **k** *to come to the w. shop, to get into the w. box, to catch a Tartar* **3.** ⟨prov⟩ ~ **Gut** gedeihet nicht *ill-gotten gain never thrives* || in (die) ~e(n) Hände fallen *or* k *to be delivered to the w. address, to fall into dishonest hands* || in die ~e Kehle k *to go down the w. way* || (Worte etc) am ~en Orte *misplaced, out of the place* || ~e Seite ⟨tail⟩ *w. side* || z ~en Zeit *out of season, unseasonably, inopportune* | [adv] *w.ly* || ⟨fam⟩ ~ ank → o. 2. an den ≗en k || ~ h *to be w.* || Sie h nicht so (ganz) ~! *you are not altogether* od *far w.* od *out*! || k wir ~? *have we come at the w. time*? || ~ verstehen *to misunderstand, mistake* | **~lich** a *unjust, w.ful* || *illegal, unlawful* || *dishonest*, ⟨rel⟩ *unrighteous* | **~mäßig** a *illegal*; *unlawful* (*possession*) || *illegitimate* (*child, heir*) || *false* (*imprisonment*) || ~er Besitzer *usurper* | [adv] (⟨a.⟩ ~erweise) *unlawfully, without authority* | ≗keit [f] *unlawfulness, illegality*; *illegitimacy* **·un- ~redlich** a *dishonest, unfair* || *underhand* | ≗keit [f] ~/ *dishonesty* || [konkr] *unfair dealing* **~reell** a ⟨com⟩ *dishonest*; *unsound* || *unreliable* **~regelmäßig** a *irregular, erratic* || ~e Salven [pl] ⟨mil, bes artill⟩ *ragged volleys* pl || *abnormal, out of the common* | [adv] ~ leben *to lead an irregular life* **~reif** a *unripe, immature* ⟨a. fig⟩ || ⟨fig⟩ *crude* (*scheme*) || *raw, callow, verdant*, ⟨fam⟩ *half-baked* (*youth*) **≗reife** f ~/ *unripeness, immaturity* || ⟨fig⟩ *crudity, rawness*; *nonage* **~rein** a *unclean, dirty* || ⟨tech⟩ *recrementicious* || ⟨fig⟩ *impure* (*air, colour, whisky, mind*) || ⟨mus⟩ *inaccurate, discordant*; *false* (*note*), [pred] *out of tune* [a. adv] || *viscious* (*pronunciation*) || *foul* (*abode, coast*) || *cloudy* (*gem*) || *inelegant, bad* (*style*) || *tainted* (*atmosphere*) | **das** ≗**e** *the foul copy* || ins ≗e schreiben *to jot down* **≗reinigkeiten** f pl *contaminants* **~reinlich** a *uncleanly* ([adv] *uncleanlily*) || *dirty, filthy* | ≗keit [f] ~/ *uncleanliness* **~rentabel** a *unremunerative, not profitable* od *paying*; ⟨agr⟩ *submarginal*; Abteilung, Angestellter, Mitglied etc *deadwood* **~rettbar** a *hopelessly lost*; *irrecoverable*; *past recovery* od *saving, unsavable* | [adv] ~ verloren (S) *irretrievably lost* || (P) *in a hopeless condition*; *ruined* **~richtig** a *wrong, incorrect, erroneous* || *unjust* (*weight*, etc); (*to be*) *out* (*in one's calculations* || (→ [nicht] richtig) | [adv] (⟨a.⟩ ~erweise) *incorrectly*, etc, *by mistake* | ≗keit [f] ~/ *fallacy, incorrectness, error, erroneousness, fault*(*iness*)

~ritterlich a *unchivalrous*; *unsportsmanlike* | ≗keit [f] *u. conduct* od *action* **·Unruh** f ~/~en (Uhr≗) *balance* | ~scheibe [f] *b.-ring, cock* **·Unruhe** f ~/~n **A. 1.** (e–r P, e–s Volkes) *unrest* (*to sow u. in the population*) || (Rastlosigkeit) *restlessness*, (nervöse) *fidget*(*iness*), ⟨fam⟩ *sweat* || (Aufregung) *flutter*; *tremulous excitement* || (Besorgnis) *disquiet*(*ude*); *anxiety, uneasiness* || (Kummer) *trouble* || (Verlegenheit) *embarrassment* || (Aufregung) *excitement, agitation*; *alarm* || (Störung der öffentlichen Ruhe) *disturbance*; (Aufruhr) *riot, turmoil* ((⟨a. fig⟩ *mental t.*) **2.** (P) *fidget*(*y fellow*) **B.** jdm ~ **bereiten** *to occasion a p concern*, etc || in jds Leben ~ bringen *to muddle a p's life* || in ~ geraten ⟨fig⟩ *to take the alarm, to grow uneasy* || in [gr] ~ s *to be* (*on edge* od) *ill at ease*, [*very anxious*]; .. über *troubled about* || ~stiften *to stir up trouble* || mit (nervöser) ~ tun *to fumble*; in ~ versetzen *to disturb, perturb, alarm, upset* **~herd** m *storm-centre*, ⟨fig⟩ *trouble spot, scene of t.* **~stifter** m *mischief-, trouble-maker, agitator*; *disturber* (*of the peace*) **≗voll** a *restless, unsettled*; *full of trouble*; *troubled* **·unruhig** a *unquiet, restless*; *leisureless*; ~ w ⟨a.⟩ *to boggle* || (lärmend) *turbulent* || (aufgeregt) *excited* || (besorgt) (über [acc]) *uneasy* (*about*), *alarmed* (*at*) || (nervös) *fidgety* | (schlaflos) *broken, restless* (*night*) | *stirring, unsettled, troubled* (*days, periods, times*) || ⟨mot⟩ *irregular* (*running*); *restive* (*horse*) || *rough* (*sea*) | ~ m, w *to stir* [vt/i] || sich ~ bewegen ⟨a.⟩ *to flutter* || ⟨fig⟩ ich bin ~ *my mind is not at ease* **·unrühmlich** a *inglorious* **·unrund** a ⟨tech⟩ *untrue* (*running*) | ≗laufen [n] ⟨a.⟩ *eccentricity beat*

uns 1. pron pers ([dat & acc] v wir) *us, to us* || gib ~ *give us*; 5 v ~ *five of us* || ein Freund v ~ *a friend of ours* || alle v ~ .. *all of us* (*children*) || .. v ~ beiden (*kindest regards*) *from both of us* **2.** pron refl *ourselves* || aber: wir freuten ~ *we rejoiced* || *we looked below us* | (einander) (*to*) *each other*, (*to*) *one another* || aber: wir trafen ~ *we met* || unter ~ *between you and me, between ourselves*

·un- ~sachgemäß a *inexpert* **~sachlich** a (nicht zur S gehörig) *irrelevant, impertinent* || (voreingenommen) *partial, biassed, prejudiced* | [adv] *off the point* **~s·agbar, ~s·äglich** a *unspeakable, ineffable, unutterable* || *untold* (*damage*) || *huge, terrible* | [adv] ~ töricht ⟨a.⟩ *too silly for words*; ~ kl *extremely small* **~sanft** a *ungentle*; *rude, harsh* (*words*), *rough* (*treatment*) | [adv] ~ behandeln ⟨fam a.⟩ *to pull a p about* || ~ behandelt w ⟨a.⟩ *to be severely handled* (*by*); ~ aus Träumen gerissen w *to come down with a bump*; (*to hustle a p*) *not without force* (*into the street*) **~sauber** a *unclean*(*ly*) [adv *-ly, -lily*]; *untidy* || (Aussehen) *squalid, unkempt* | ⟨fig⟩ *impure* (*motives*) || *sharp* (*practice*) || ~e Mittel *underhand dealings* || e–e ~e S *a fishy affair* **~säuberlich** a *dirty* || e–n ~ behandeln *to treat a p roughly* **~schadhaft** a *intact, sound* **~schädlich** a *innoxious, innocuous, harmless* | ~ m (P) *to get .. out of the way*, ⟨sl⟩ *to out*; *to draw a p's teeth* || (S) *to scotch* || (Gift) *to neutralize* | ≗keit [f] *h.ness*, etc; ⟨cul⟩ *innocuity* **~scharf** a ⟨opt⟩ *poorly defined*; *blurred, fuzzy* (*picture*) **≗schärfe** f *poor definition* **~sch·ätzbar** a *inestimable, incalculable* (*sum*); *invaluable, priceless* (*possessions*) || v ~em Wert *beyond all price* | [adv] ~ wertvoll *priceless* **~scheinbar** a *insignificant, trifling, trivial* || (einfach) *plain, homely* || ein ~er, kleiner Mann *a humble little man* || *dull, dark* || *unsightly* (*house*) || *inconspicuous* (*hotel*) || *nondescript* (*young man*) || *a slip of a* (*boy*) | ≗keit [f] *plainness, homeliness* **~schicklich** a *unbecoming, indecent, improper, unseemly*; sehr ~ *outrageous* || [pred] *out of place*; es ist f ihn *or* v ihm ~ *it ill-behooves him* | ~keit [f] ⟨a.⟩ *solecism* **·Unschlitt** m ~(e)s/ *tallow, suet* || ~kerze [f] *t. candle* **·un- ~schlüssig** a *irresolute,* *uncertain, undetermined* || *doubtful* || *perplexed, puzzled* || ~ s *to hesitate, waver, shilly-shally*; *to stand suspended*; *to be in two minds* (*about*) | ~keit [f] 〈a.〉 *dubiety* **~schmackhaft** a *unpalatable, insipid*; *flat, stale, tasteless*; *savourless, flavo(u)rless* | ≗igkeit [f] *unsavo(u)riness* **~schm·elzbar** a 〈chem〉 *infusible* | ≗keit [f] *infusibility* **~schön** a *plain, ugly, homely, unlovely, unsightly, uncomely* || 〈fig〉 *unkind, unfair* || nicht ~ *not too bad* ≗**schuld** f ~/ *innocence* || *purity* (*of heart*); *chastity* || im Stande der ~ (*man*) *in the state of primitive i.nce* || in aller ~ *no harm being meant* | kl ~ (P) *i.nt* od *unsophisticated little girl* || verfolgte ~ *injured i.ence* || °~ v Lande *country cousin*; *turnip* || s–e ~ beteuern *to protest one's i.nce*, 〈jur〉 *to plead "not guilty"* || ich wasche m–e Hände in ~ *I wash my hands of it* | ~sengel [m] 〈hum〉 *i.nt little boy*, etc; ≗svoll [a] *i.nt* **~schuldig, ~schuldvoll** a (an [dat]) *innocent, guiltless* (*of*) || *guileless*; *ingenuous* || (harmlos) *harmless* (*remark*) || (rein) *pure* || ~ wie ein Kind *i.ent as a lamb* || (keusch) *chaste*; *virgin* (*man*) || f ~ erklären *to acquit* **~schwer** a [mst pred] *not difficult*; *easy* | [adv] *without difficulty*; *easily* || ~ erraten *to have no d. in guessing* **~schwesterlich** a *unsisterly* | [adv] *in an unsisterly way* ≗**segen** m ~s/ *adversity* || *disappointments* pl, *ill success* od *luck* || (Fluch) *curse* || sich z ~ auswirken *to lead to misfortune* **~selbständig** a *dependent* (*on others*) || 〈fig〉 *irresolute, unable to stand up* od *act for o.s.* **~selig** a *unfortunate, unhappy, luckless, ill-fated, wretched* (*p*) || *fatal* (*event*) || *accursed* (*propensity*) **~sentimental** a *hard-boiled* (*play*)

·unser 1. [pron pers] (gen v wir) *of us* || 〈bib〉 Vater ~ .. *Our Father* (*which art in Heaven*) || erbarme dich ~ *have mercy upon us* || wir sind ~ drei *there are three of us* **2.** [pron poss] *our* ([*own*] *method*) [pred] *ours* || diese ~e Freunde *these friends of ours* || **~er, ~e, ~es** *ours* (*is a sad story*) **~einer, ~eins** [pron] *one of us, one in our position*; (*such as*) *we, people like us, men like me*; 〈fam〉 *the likes of* (*you and*) *me* **~seits** [adv] *as for us* od *ourselves, for* od *on our part* **~sgl·eichen** [pron] *the like of us*; 〈fam〉 *our sort* **~thalben, ~twegen, (um) ~twillen** [adv] *for our sake(s), on account of us, on our behalf, for* (*the sake of*) *us* **·uns(e)rige** (der, die, das) [pron] *ours* || das ≗ *our property, share, duty* || die ≗n *our family, people, men, soldiers, party*

·un- ~seriös a *questionable, unreliable, dubious* **~sicher** a *insecure* (→ unsolide) || (gefährlich) *unsafe* || (ungewiß) *uncertain, doubtful* || *unsettled, precarious* (Leben *existence*) || *erratic* (*course*) || *weak, bad* (*memory*) || *unsteady, shaky* (*hand*) || (auf den Beinen) *shaky, groggy*, 〈sl〉 *wonky* || *floating* (*vote*) | Stadt u Land ~ m 〈a. hum〉 *to swarm in the country*; (die Gegend etc) ~ m *to haunt*, 〈fam〉 *to be all over* (*the place*); *to paint* (*the town*) *red*; *to infest* (*the roads*) || es war sehr ~, ob .. *it was touch and go whether* .. | [adv] 〈a.〉 (*to mention*) *falteringly* | ~heit [f] 〈a.〉 *dubiousness*, –sfaktor [m] *f. of uncertainty* **~sichtbar** a *invisible, imperceptible, lost to view* || *hidden* (*side of the moon*) || *obscure* (*rays*) || 〈fam〉 sich ~ m *to make o.s. scarce* || das ≗e *the invisible world* **~sichtig** a *hazy* **·Unsinn** m ~(e)s/ **A. 1.** → *nonsense* 〈a. Lit〉; *fiddle-faddle*; *absurdity*; *Rabelaisian cranks* pl || Alles ~! *Stuff and n.*! *Bosh*! *Fudge*! *Rot*! *Rubbish*! 〈sl〉 *Piffle*! *Rats*! **2.** *foolish pranks* od *tricks* **B.** barer, blühender ~ *downright n.* || das ist ja ~! *now, you are talking n.*! || es klingt wie ~ *it sounds n.* || ~ reden *to talk rubbish* || was soll der ~? *what's the idea*? || ~ treiben *to fool about*; ~ verzapfen *to talk through one's hat* | ≗ig a *nonsensical, foolish, absurd* || (toll) *mad* (*fashion*), *insane* (*proposal*); *nonsense* (*world*); *wild* (*guess*); *insensate* (Kräfte); etw ganz ~ erscheinen l *to reduce a th to absurdity* | [adv] ~ verliebt *madly in love* | **~igkeit** f ~/ *madness, insanity, foolishness* || *foolish, absurd action* ≗**lich** a *not sensual* || *Platonic* (*love*) || *spiritual, transcendental* **·Unsitte** f ~/~n *bad custom* od *habit* || (Mißbrauch) *abuse* || (Mißstand) *nuisance* **·unsittlich** a *immoral* || *licentious* || *indecent* | ≗**keit** f ~/ *immorality, indecency* || *immoral* (etc) *act* **·un- ~soldatisch** a *unsoldierlike, unmilitary* **~solid** a *not solid* || 〈com〉 *unreliable* || 〈fig〉 *loose, fast, dissipated* (*life, fellow*) || *wild-cat* (*finance* 〈a.〉 Spekulation) | adv ~e gebautes Haus etc *shaky house*, etc **~sorgfältig** a *careless*; 〈fam〉 *non-carish* **~sortiert** a *unpicked* **~sozial** a *unsocial* **~sportlich** a *unsportsmanlike* **~staatsmännisch** a *unstatesmanlike* **~ständig** a *impermanent* | [adv] *not steadily* od *permanently* || ~ Beschäftigte *casual workers*, [koll] *casual labour* **~starr** a 〈aero〉 *non-rigid* (*airship*, kl *blimp*) **~stät, ~stet** a *unsteady, discontinuous, unstaid, inconstant, fickle, unstable* (*character*); ~er Mensch *rolling stone* 〈fig〉; *unsettled* (*mind*) || *not fixed* (*abode*) || (unruhig) *restless* || (wanderlustig) *vagrant* (*life, thoughts*) || (umherschweifend) *wandering, roving, unsettled* (*life, people*) || *vacant* (*look*), *furtive* (*glance*); *mobile* (*eyes*) || ~ u flüchtig *fugitive and vagabond* (*p*) | [adv] ~ umherschweifen *to rove* (*aimlessly*) *about* **~stätig** = ~stet || ~e Größe 〈math〉 *discrete quantity* | ~keit [f] *discontinuity* etc **~statthaft** a *inadmissible* || *illicit, illegal, unlawful*; *invalid* || *forbidden* || *unsuitable* || *an impermissible question* od *happiness* **~sterblich** a *immortal*; ~er Schlager *evergreen*; *undying* (*fame*) || ~ m *to immortalize* || sich ~ [adv] blamieren *to make an ass of o.s.* | ≗keit [f] ~/ *immortality*; °über die ~ der Maikäfer nachdenken 〈fam〉 *to chew the cud, to think about breakfast* ≗**stern** m ~(e)s/ *unlucky* od *evil star* || 〈fig〉 *misfortune, disaster, ill luck, adversity, adverse fate* **~stet** = ~stät **~st·illbar** a *unappeasable, unquenchable* || (Blut) *sta(u)nchless* ≗**stimmigkeit** f ~/~en *inconsistency, discrepancy*; ~en [pl] *unpleasantness* (*between*), *grave dissensions, disagreements*; *disputes* || (Streit) 〈fam〉 *tiff* **~st·örbar** a *impertubable, fixed, impassive*, 〈jur〉 *incommutable* (*possession*) **~str·äflich** a *irreprehensible, irreprochable, blameless* || *inculpable* **~streitig** a *incontestable, unquestionable* | adv 〈a.〉 *undoubtedly, certainly, undeniably*; *beyond* od *without dispute* **~studiert** a *unstudied* (*action*) || (ungesucht) *easy, natural, unaffected* || (P) *unread, unlearned*; 〈emph〉 *uneducated, illiterate* **~s·ühnbar** a *inexpiable* || *irreconcilable* ≗**summe** f ~/~n *vast* od *immense amount* **~sündig** a *sinless* **~symmetrisch** a *unsymmetrical* **~sympathisch** a *unattractive, unpleasant*; *uncongenial*; *disagreeable* || er ist mir ~ *I don't like him* **~t·adelhaft, ~t·ad(e)lig** a *blameless, unimpeachable, irreproachable, impeccable, unobjectionable* || *faultless* || [pred] *above* od *beyond reproach* | adv 〈a.〉 *immaculately* (*dressed*) ≗**tat** f ~/~en *misdeed, crime, outrage, atrocity* **~tätig** a *inactive, idle*; *vacant*; *supine, indolent*; *idle* (*waiting*); *dormant* (*volcano*) || ~ bleiben *to lie by*, ~ dabeistehen (–sitzen) *to stand* (*sit*) *by* | [adv] *idly*, etc | ≗keit [f] 〈a.〉 *inaction, idleness, leisure*; *drift* (*the policy of d.*) **~tauglich** a (S) *unfit* (*for*); *unserviceable* | (P) *inefficient* || 〈mil〉 *unfit, disabled*; 〈fam〉 *C 3* || 〈mar〉 *unseaworthy* (*ship*) | ~ m *to disqualify, incapacitate*, 〈mil〉 *disable* || f ~ erklären *to disqualify, unfit* (*a p*), *to condemn* (*meat*) | 〈med〉 jdn f ~ erklären *to condemn* .. *medically* | die ≗en 〈mil, mar〉 *the inefficients* | ~keit [f] *unsuitableness* **~t·eilbar** a *indivisible* **~teilhaft** a [gen] *not partaking* (*of*), *having no share* (*in*)

·unten [adv] **A.** *below* 〈a. typ〉, ganz ~ *bottom*; *beneath, underneath*; (*it fell into the garden b.h*) || *at the bottom, foot, end* | (im **Haus**) *downstairs*, *on the ground-floor*; *down* (*in the parlour*) || ~ befindlich *downstair*[*s*] (*room*) | ~ **liegen** *to lie below* od *u.th*, ⟨fig⟩ *to be worsted* || siehe ~! (abbr s. u.) *see below*! **B.** ~ **an**: *down by* (*the lake*) || ~ **an**; **auf**; **in**: *at the bottom of* (*the hill, stairs*; *page*; *cask*) || ~ **auf** der Erde *here below*; *down on the ground* || **bis** ~: → oben || ~ **durch** *down through* || ⟨fam⟩ ~ durch s *to be ruined*; bei e–m .. *to be in a p's black books* || **hier** (dort) ~ *down here* (*there*) || ~ **hinaus** *out below* || ~ **im** Lande *in the valley* bzw *plain* || **nach** ~ *downwards*; (*to sink*) *aground*; (*take it*) *downstairs, below-stairs*; (*don't hold the bottle*) *upside down* || **tief** ~ *far below* (*lay the lake*) || **von** ~ an *or* auf: *right up from below* || v ~ auf dienen *to rise* od *serve from the ranks* || **weiter** ~ *further down* ·**unten- ~·an** [adv] *at the bottom, foot, end* **~benannt** a *mentioned* (*at* [*the*] *foot of the page* od) *below*; ⟨jur⟩ *as hereunder* **~her** [adv] *from below* **~hin** [adv] *downwards, down below, near the bottom* **~stehend** ≠ –benannt

·**Unter** m ~s/~ (Bube) ⟨cards⟩ *knave* **unter I.** [adv] (*gone*) *below, under* ..; [ell] die Sonne ist ~ .. *is down* od *has set* **II.** [prep] **A. 1.** (wo? [dat] u. a. [dat] *amongst other ths*; *a quarrel among children*; ~ Brüdern *between brothers* wohin? [acc]) *under*; *he is counted among the classics*; *to fall among thieves, distribute it amongst your children* | ~ Gleichartigem: *he was found among the dead* [als Toter] → zwischen, *a.g his comrades*; ~ Ungleichartigem: *to sow tares a.gst the wheat*) | ~ dem Tisch, ~ den T. *u. the table*; (*every bridge they had passed under* .., unter der ..); den Kopf ~ dem Flügel *with head under wing*; (im Buch) siehe ~ .. *look out under the head of* .. | *beneath* (*he broke down b. his load*) | *underneath* (*her kindness she had an iron hand*) | *below* (*the horizon*) || er wohnt ~ mir *he lives in the room*(*s*) *below mine* | ~ dem Tisch **hervor** *from under*(*neath*) *the t.* || *he stared from under his brows* **2.** (niedriger als) ⟨com⟩ ~ Pari *below par* | ~ Preis verkauft .. *for less than the value* | (untergeordnet) ~ dem Befehl N.s *under the command of N.* || *he is below me* (*in rank*) || .. ~ Mittelgröße *a man less than of middle height* | .. ~ **sich h** *to have 500 men at one's command*; (e–e S) *to be in charge of, to have the care of* (*a th*) || °jdn ~ sich h wollen *to want to be top-dog to a p* | ~ jdm (etw) **stehen** *to be inferior to a p* (*to be subject to the law*) **3.** (weniger als) ~ 30 Jahren *under 30, on the sunny side of 30* || *all p.s under 60* (*years of age*) || ~ 3 Wochen *in less than three weeks* || ~ oder über 50 *they are all a year or two either side of 50* || nicht ~ dem (~ 5.– DM) z h *not to be had at less* (*than 5 marks*) **4.** (zeitlich) ~ s–r Regierung *in* od *under his reign* || ~ dem heutigen Datum *under date of to-day* || ~ dem 1. dieses (Monats) *under the date of the 1st instant* || ~ dem Gebet *during prayer*(*s*) || ~ der Zeit *meanwhile, in the meantime* || ~ ·einem ⟨österr⟩ *at the same time*; → zugleich **5.** (zwischen) *among*(*st*) || ~ anderem (abbr u. a.) *among other ths* || (bei) *among* (*the Greeks*) || *amongst his papers* || ~ sich leben *to live privately*; ~ e–r **Zahl** (auswählen) .. *from among a n.* || *not one in a hundred* || 90 ~ 100 *nine out of ten* || ~ zwei ..: *of two evils choose the least* | ~ **uns** *among ourselves, in our midst* || *the tallest of us*; *not one of us* || *we had many young men among us* | (~ **zweien**) ~ uns (gesagt) *between ourselves, between you and me* (*and the gatepost*) || es bleibt ~ uns *it is between us* || **mitten** ~ *amid*(*st*), *in the midst of* **6.** (wie?) ~ dem Donner (Schutz) der Kanonen *amidst the roar of artillery* (*under the cover of guns*) || ~ dem fdl. Feuer *exposed to the enemy's fire* || *to these shouts the curtain falls* || *amidst the cheers of* .. **7.** (mit, durch) was verstehen Sie ~ ..? *what do you understand by* (*this expression*)? **B.** ~ Anwendung e–r S: *to perform an operation under an anaesthetic* || ~ der **Axt** (*forests crashing*) *to the axe* || ~ dieser Bedingung *on this cond.*; ~ jeder B. *upon any terms*; ~ der B., daß *on c. that* || ~ Bezugnahme auf [acc] *with reference to* || ~ der **Erde** *underground*; ~ die E. bringen *to bury*, ⟨fig⟩ *to be the death of* (*a p*) || ~ Glockengeläut *with bells ringing*; *the festival opened to the pealing of bells* || ~ 50 Grad nördl. Breite *in 50 degrees north latitude* (*in 50° N. L.*) || ~ der **Hand** *secretly* || etw ~ den Händen h *to have a th in hand*; *it grew beneath his hands* || ⟨mus⟩ ~ der Leitung von N. *with N. conducting* || ~ den Leuten .. (*there is a rumour*) *abroad* || ~ dem Meerespiegel *below sea-level* || ~ Menschen k *to see the world* || ~ Mittag *at noon* || ~ dem Namen *by the name of* || ~ **Null** *below zero* || ⟨bookb⟩ *in* (*the press*) || ~ die Räuber fallen *to fall among thieves* || ~ Schloß u Riegel *under lock and key* || °~ aller **Sau** *or* **Kanone** *infra dig*(*nitatem* L) || ~ Segel gehen *to put to sea* || ~ die Soldaten gehen *to enlist, to join up* || ~ dem Strich *among miscellaneous items* || ~ Tage *underground* || ~ den **Tisch** fallen ⟨fig⟩ *to be given up* od *forgotten* || ~ Tränen *with tears in one's eyes* || ~ diesen Umständen *under these circumstances, in this case* || ~ dem Vorwande *pretending, under pretence* (*that*) || ~ **Wasser** (*to swim*) *beneath the w.*; ~ W. setzen *to inundate*; ~ W. tauchen *to immerse*, (Schwimmer) *to dive* || ~ der Zahl war *in the number there was* ·**unter(e)** a *low*(*er*), *inferior* (*limit*), *under*(*neath*) .. || *minor* (*official*); *lower* (*jaw, picture, Rhine*, ⟨soc⟩ *classes*, ⟨school⟩ *forms*); *under* (*side*); *nether* (*millstone*); *lower* (*end of the table*); *bottom* (*rooms*) || ⟨school⟩ (Stufe) *junior* (*school*) | **der ~ste** [sup] *the lowest, nethermost, last*; ⟨school⟩ *the lowest boy* (*in his form*) || *bottom* (*button*); ~ste Treppenstufe *bottom-step* || das ≗ste *the lowest part*; *the foot, base* || das ~ste zu oberst kehren *to turn everything* (*upside down* od) *topsy-turvy*, ⟨fam⟩ *to upset the apple cart* || **zu** ~st *undermost, nethermost*; *at the bottom, in the lowest part* || die **≗sten** *inferiors* pl, *the refuse* (*of society*)

·**unter..** pref [bei v, s, a] **I.** [bei v]: **1.** [betont: sep] ~|schlagen: er schlug die Arme ~; so: ~|binden [–gebundenes Band; –b·undener Verkehr]; ~|breiten [–gebreitete Decke; –br·eiteter Vorschlag]; ~|drücken *to tie, spread, push under*(*neath*) **2.** [unbetont: insep] ~schl·agen: er ~schl·ug Gelder; ~sagen [pp ~sagt]: ~richten [pp ~richtet] **II. 1.** [bei s]: ≗amt *inferior office* || ≗ärmel *undersleeve* || ≗bau *substructure*, so: *subinspector* || ≗lippe *nether* (od *under-*)*lip* || ≗br·echung *interruption* || ≗dr·ückung *suppression* || ≗rhein *Lower Rhine* **2.** [bei a]: ~n·ehmend *enterprising* || ~gärig *fermented from below* || ~schlächtig *undershot* || ~w·ürfig *submissive* ·**Unter- ~abschnitt** m *subsector*; ⟨mil⟩ *subarea* N; ⟨jur typ⟩ *subsection* **~abteilung** f *subdivision*, ⟨com, etc⟩ *department, branch* **~ägypten** n *Lower Egypt*; → Oberägypten **~amt** n *inferior office* **~antrag** m *amendment* **~arm** m *forearm* **~ärmel** m *u.sleeve* **~art** f *subspecies, subvariety* **~arzt** m *assistant* od *junior surgeon* **~aufseher** m *subinspector* **~ausschuß** n *sub-committee* **~balken** m ⟨arch⟩ *lower beam, architrave* **~bau** m *substructure, foundation, basement* || (Hafen–, Flugplatz≗ etc & mil⟩ *infrastructure* || ⟨rail⟩ *groundwork*, ⟨Am⟩ *roadbed* || ⟨fig⟩ *basis* ≗|**bauen** vt [h] *to build below* ≗**b·auen** vt [h] *to u.pin, to furnish with a* (*new*) *substructure*, ⟨fig⟩ *to provide a pedestal for a th* **~baum** m (Wagen≗) *pole, shaft* **~beamte(r)** *subordinate* **~bediente(r)** m *inferior servant* **~befehlshaber** m *second in command* **~behörde** f *inferior authorities* pl **~beinkleid** n (~er [pl], ein ~ *a pair of*) *pants* || (Frauen) *drawers* pl || (ohne

Beine) ⟨Am⟩ *briefs* pl ≗**belegt** a *insufficiently* (od *u.*-)*occupied* (*house*) ≗**belichten** vt [h] ⟨phot⟩ *to under-expose* | –tet ⟨a.⟩ *undershot* ~**belichtung** f *u.-exposure* ≗**beschäftigt** a *u.worked* ≗**besetzt** a ⟨mil etc⟩ *u. staffed* ~**bett** n *u.-bedding* ≗**(be)völkert** → –völkert ~**bewertung** f *understatement* ≗**bewußt** a *subliminal* ~**bewußtsein** n ~s/ *subconsciousness* || etw im ~ h *to have a th at the back of one's mind* ≗**b·ieten** vt irr [h] *to u.bid* || (Preise) *to u.cut* || (Konkurrenz) *to u.sell* || (Rekord) *to lower* ~**b·ieter** m *price-cutter* ~**bilanz** f *deficit*; *adverse balance* ≗|**binden** vt irr [h] *to tie* (od *bind*) *u.neath* ≗**b·inden** vt irr [h] ⟨surg⟩ *to tie* od *bind up, to ligature* || ⟨fig⟩ *to stop* || *to tie up* (*traffic*); e–m die Lebensader ~ *to drain a p's life* ~**b·indung** f ⟨surg⟩ *ligature* || ⟨fig⟩ *stoppage* ~**bischof** m *suffragan* ~**blatt** n *lower leaf* || (Zigarren≗) *filler* ~**bl·eiben** n *nonperformance, discontinuation, cessation, omission* ≗**bl·eiben** vi irr [s] *to remain undone, to be left undone, not to* (*happen* od) *take place, to be discontinued* || –bt (*the allusion to* ..) *is forgone* || das muß ~ *that must be stopped* || es kann ~ *it may be dispensed with* ~**boden** m (Knopf≗) *base*; (Uhr≗) *lower plate* ~**bogen** m ⟨arch⟩ *subarch* ~**bootsmann** m *boatswain's mate* ≗**br·echen** vt irr [h] *to interrupt, intercept* || ⟨fam⟩ *to talk out of turn* || ⟨rail etc⟩ *to stop off* || (nicht fortsetzen) *to discontinue, stop* (⟨mil⟩ *firing*), ⟨mil comm⟩ *to disrupt* || *to suspend* (*one's duties*) || *to break* (*a journey, the silence*, ⟨el⟩ *the circuit*) || (in der Rede) *to cut short* || Verzeihung, wenn ich –e ⟨iron⟩ *oh, after you!* || ⟨jur⟩ –brach die Verhandlung (*the court*) *recessed* || ⟨telph⟩ –brochen w *to be cut off* | ⟨comp⟩ *to halt*; ⟨el⟩ *to switch off, to disconnect* || ⟨sport⟩ *the match was interfered with by rain* || sich ~ *to stop short* ~**br·echer** m ⟨tech; el⟩ *interrupter* || *conduct* od *circuit, magnets breaker* | ~kontakt [m] *make and break c.*; ~nocken [m] ⟨mot⟩ *ignition cam* ~**br·echung** f *interruption*, etc; *break* (*in studies*) || ⟨el, etc⟩ *disconnection*; gewaltsame Verkehrs– etc ≗ *disruption* || *intermitted* (*work*) || mit ~en *interruptedly* || ohne ~ *without intermission*, etc | ~sfunke [m] ⟨el⟩ *spark at break* ≗**br·eiten** vt [h] [pp –tet] jdm *to submit* (⟨Am fam⟩ *put up*) (*a document*) (*to a p*) || *to lay* od *place* (*proposals*) (*before a p*) ~**breitung** f (v Antrag) *submission* ≗|**bringen** vt irr [h] *to place*; *to tuck away*; *to provide a place for* || (Waren) *to dispose of* || (Geld) *to put out, to invest* || (Wechsel) *to negotiate* || (Anleihe, Kapital) *to place* || *to dispose of* (*in marriage*) || *to slip in* (*a remark*); *it is difficult to squeeze the word into the sentence* | außer Hause ~ *to put out* (*child*); (jdn im Hause etc) *to lodge*; *to install* (*at a hotel*); *to accommodate with a lodging* || ⟨fam⟩ *I shall be able to put you up* || *to stable* (*horses*) || *the museum is housed here* || (Truppe) *to lodge, billet* || jdn (in e–r Stellung) ~ *to find a situation for a p, to fix a p up, to get a p on a job* | ⟨fig⟩ (= erkennen) *I could not place him* ~**bringung** f ~/ *placing* || *disposal* (*of*) || *investment* || *accommodation*; *quarters* ~**deck** n ⟨mar⟩ *lower deck* ≗**derhand** adv *in secret, s.ly*; *under-the-counter* [attr] (Verkauf) ≗**d·es**, ≗**d·essen** [adv] *in the meantime*; *meanwhile*; *by that time* ~**drehzahl** f, –geschwindigkeit [f] ⟨bes aero⟩ *underspeed* ~**druck** m *low pressure*; *vacuum*; ⟨mot⟩ Reifen≗ *underinflation* | ~bremse [f] *v. brake*; ~dampfheizung [f] *vapo(u)r heating system*; ~förderer [m] *v. tank*; ~förderung [f] *v. feed*; ~kammer [f] ⟨aero, a–n⟩ *altitude chamber*; ~messer [m] *v. ga(u)ge*; ~steuerung [f] ⟨rail⟩ *l.-p.* (⟨Am⟩ *v.*) *control*; ~verstellung [f] *v. advance* ≗**dr·ücken** vt [h] *to suppress*; *muzzle* || (niederhalten) *to curb, check, control* || (hart behandeln) *to oppress*, ⟨fam⟩ *bully* || (Kirche) *to dragoon* || (jdn) *to override*, ⟨fam⟩ *to sit on* (*a p*) || (Seufzer) *to repress* || (Ton) *to muffle* || (Lachen) *to restrain*; er konnte ein L. nicht ~ *he could not help laughing* || (Ärger) *to smother* || (Gefühl) *to stifle*; *to swallow down* (*resentment*); s–e Gefühle ~ *to bottle up one's feelings*; *to quench* (*desire*); mit Mühe *to choke for* (*a p's absence*); *to pocket* (*one's disapproval*); *to swallow* (*a scream*) || (Aufstand) *to quash, quell, crush* ~**dr·ücker** m *oppressor* ≗**drückt** a ⟨fig⟩ *downtrodden* (*the d.*) ~**dr·ückung** f *suppression* || *curbing* || *oppression* || *repression* || *restraint* (*of trade*) | ~smaßnahmen [f pl] *repressive measures* ≗|**ducken** vt (⟨a.⟩ sich) *to duck* ·**untere** → unter(e) [a] ·**unter-** ~einander [adv] *one beneath the other* | ~e–·a [adv] *each other, one* (*with*) *another, among one another, mutually* || [in comp] (= durch–e–a) *pell-mell, confusedly* || (*to put*) *topsy-turvy*, (*to lie*) *higgledy-piggledy* || [bei Verben oft]: *inter..* (*to interconnect, intermarry, interchange*; *interrelated*); (*they are pleased*) *with themselves* || ~ abgestimmt ⟨übtr⟩ *tailored to each other* ·**Unter-** *under..* ≗**ernährt** a *-fed, -nourished* ~**ernährung** f ~/ *-feeding, malnutrition* ≗|**fahren** v(t)/i [h] & [s] *to put up* (*one's carriage*) ≗**f·ahren** vt [h] ⟨arch⟩ *to -pin*; ⟨min⟩ *to drive right under* (*a lode*) ≗**f·angen 1.** vt irr [h] ⟨arch⟩ *to -pin* **2.** sich [acc] (e–r S [gen]) *to dare, venture, presume, attempt, undertake* (*a th*) (z tun *to do*) ~**f·angen** n *bold enterprise, venture, attempt* ≗|**fassen** vt [h] *to support* || jdn ~ *to take a p's arm* || sich ~ *to walk arm in arm* ~**feldherr** m *second in command* ~**feldwebel** m *sergeant* ~**f·ertigte** m [der ~, ein ~r] *undersigned* ~**fläche** f *base* ≗|**flechten** vt [h] *to entwine* ≗**fl·echten** *to interlace, mix, mingle* (*with*) ~**führer** m *junior leader* od *officer* ~**f·ührung** f *subway*, ⟨rail a.⟩ *platform underpass*; *underground passage*, ⟨bes Am rail⟩ *underpass*; *grade separation* | ~stunnel [m] *subway*, ⟨Am⟩ *u.g. passage* ~**futter** n (*inner*) *lining* ≗**f·üttern** vt [h] *to line* ~**gang** m ⟨astr⟩ *setting* || (Fall) *fall, ruin*; ⟨com⟩ *failure* || (Vernichtung) *destruction* (z. B. v Zollgut *of bonded goods*) || ⟨pol⟩ *downfall* || (Welt≗) *end* (*of the world*) || (e–s Schiffes) *sinking, shipwreck* || (Aussterben) *extinction* | ⟨fig⟩ *fate, doom* (*to escape one's d.*) || der ~ des Abendlandes (*Spengler's*) *The Decline* od *Downfall of the West* || Venedig ist dem ~ geweiht *Venice is doomed* ≗**gärig** a (*beer*) *fermented from below* ~**gärung** f *sedimentary fermentation* ~**gattung** f *subspecies* ~**gebäude** n *substructure, under-building* ≗**g·eben** a; jdm ~ s *to be under a p's care* od *control* ~**g·ebene** [der ~, ein ~r] *subordinate, inferior* ~**gegangen** a (→ –gehen) *lost* (*ship*) ≗|**gehen** vi irr [s] ⟨astr⟩ *to go down, to set* (*the setting sun*) || (Welt) *to come to an end* || (Schiff) *to sink*; *founder, to go down* || ⟨fig⟩ *to be obliterated*; *to perish, fall*; (P) *to go to the wall*; ⟨sl⟩ *to peg out* || *to be destroyed* || (aussterben) *to become extinct* (*extinct animals*) || (Einrichtung) *to go under* || (Stimme) *to be drowned* || siegen oder ~ *sink or swim* ~**gehölz** n = –holz ≗**geordnet** a *subordinate, inferior*; *secondary* (*role, question*); *lower-level* (*position*) || v ~er Bedeutung *of secondary importance* || ~e Rolle *minor part* ~**gericht** n ⟨jur⟩ *inferior court* ≗**geschoben** [pp v ≗schieben] a (Kind) *supposititious, foisted* || (Dokument) *forged, spurious* || (Abschnitt) *interpolated* ~**geschoß** n *lower ground-floor, basement* ~**gestell** n *stand, trestle* || *under-carriage* ⟨a. aero⟩, ⟨mot⟩ *chassis* ~**gewand** n *u.garment* ~**gewicht** n *u.weight*; der Ballen hatte ~ .. *was found short in weight* ~**glas·urdekor** n *u.glaze decoration* ≗|**graben** vt irr [h] ⟨agr⟩ *to dig* od *turn in* ≗**gr·aben** vt irr [h] *to cut up by the roots, to u.cut, u.mine, sap* ⟨a. fig⟩ || ⟨fig⟩ *to subvert, destroy*; *to dig the grave of* (*one's reputation*) || [pp] *compromised* (*business*); *ruined, shattered* (*health*) ≗**grädig** a (Spiritus) *u. proof* ~**griff** m ⟨gym⟩ *u.grasp* ~**grund** m ~(e)s/ *substratum,* *subsoil* ‖ ⟨arts⟩ *ground* | ~bahn [f] *u.ground* (*railway*), (~ fahren *to travel u.g.*;), ⟨Am⟩ *subway*, (Londoner) *tube*; ~bewegung [f] ⟨pol⟩ *u.ground* ‖ ~pflug [m] *subsoil-plough* ≗**gründig** a *underground* (⟨a. fig⟩ *underground way*) **~guß** m ⟨phot⟩ *pre-coat*, *substratum* ≗|**haben** vt [h] *to wear .. u.neath*; (P) *to have worsted* ≗|**haken** vt [h] jdn ~ *to take a p's arm* ≗**halb** [adv] prep [gen] *u.neath*, *below*, *u.*; *further down than*, *beyond* (*the bridge*) **~halt** m ~(e)s/ *support* ‖ (Lebens≗) *subsistence*, *maintenance*, *sustenance*, *keep* (*to earn one's k.*) ‖ ⟨jur⟩ (~ der geschiedenen Frau) *alimony*; f jds ~ aufk *to provide for a p's keep* | ~sbeihilfe [f] *maintenance subsidy* od *grant*; ≗sberechtigt [a] ⟨jur⟩ *entitled to alimony*; ~spflicht [f] *obligation of m.*; ≗spflichtig [a] ⟨jur⟩ *obliged to pay alimony*; ~szuschuß [m] = –beihilfe ≗|**halten** vt irr [h] [pp –ge–] *to hold u.*(*neath*) **~h·alten** vt irr [h] [pp ~] *to support*, *maintain*, *keep* ‖ (Feuer etc) *to feed*, *replenish* ‖ (Gebäude) *to keep in repair* ‖ (Unternehmen) *to run* (*a canteen*, etc) ‖ (durch Reden etc) *to entertain*, *amuse* ‖ e–n Briefwechsel ~ *to keep up* od *carry on a correspondence* ‖ **sich** ~ *to make conversation*; *to converse* (mit jdm über etw *with a p on* od *about a th*), *to discourse* (über etw [*of*, *upon*] *a th*); h Sie sich gut ~? *did you have a good time*? ‖ sich ~ mit *to play at* ‖ sich gut ~ *to enjoy* od *amuse o.s.* ‖ sich mit jdm gut ~ können *to be company for a p* ‖ sich auf E. ~ *to speak in English* ≗**h·altend** a *entertaining*, *amusing*, *lively* | guter **~halter** *brilliant conversationalist* od *entertainer*; ⟨a.⟩ *he is good company* **~halts-** → –halt ≗**haltsam** a *entertaining*, *engaging*, *appealing* (*play*, *film*) **~h·altung** f ~/~en *maintenance*, *support*, *keep* ‖ (Gespräch) *conversation*, *talk*; jdn zu lebhafter ~ anregen *to strike sparks in a p's mind* ‖ ⟨arts⟩ Heilige ~ *Holy C.*, ⟨bib⟩ *Madonna enthroned with Saints* ‖ (Gegenstand der ~ *topic of c.*) ‖ (formelle) *colloquy* ‖ (lustige, zerstreuende etc) *amusement*, *entertainment* ‖ musikalische ~en *musical occasions* pl; ~ u Instandsetzung *m. and repair* ‖ e–e ~ führen *to carry on a conversation* ‖ zur ~ beitragen *to oblige* (*with a song*) | **~s-** *care-and-m.* ~blatt [n] *family magazine*; ~gabe [f] *conversational powers*; ~konzert [n] ⟨fam⟩ *pop*(*ular*); ~kosten [pl] *cost*(*s*) *of maintenance* (⟨a.⟩ f Gebäude, Wege etc); (e–r P) *keep*; ~lektüre [f] *light reading*; *novels*; ~literatur [f] *light* od *recreative*, *escape literature*; ~programm [n] ⟨telv⟩ *light pr.* ‖ ~stück [n] ⟨theat, mus⟩ *entertainment*; ~ton [m] *c.nal tone*; ≗weise [adv] *by way of c.n*, *c.nally* ≗**h·andeln** vi [h] (mit jdm) *to negotiate*, *treat*, (heimlich) *to tamper* (*with a p*) ‖ ⟨mil⟩ *to parley* **~h·ändler** m ~s/~ *negotiator*, *mediator*; (im Lohnkonflikt) *bargainer* ‖ ⟨dero⟩ *go-between* ‖ ⟨com⟩ *broker*, *agent* ‖ ⟨mil⟩ *commissioner*; *bearer of a flag of truce* **~h·andlung** f *negotiation*, *transaction* ‖ ⟨mil⟩ *parley* ‖ ~en anknüpfen *to start n.s*; in ~ treten mit *to enter into n.s*, ⟨mil⟩ *to parley with* ‖ in ~ stehen mit *to be in treaty with* (wegen [gen] *for*) | ~skunst [f] *diplomacy* ≗**h·auen** vt [h] ⟨min⟩ *to hollow out from below* ‖ °⟨fam⟩ *to sign* **~haus** n ⟨engl, pol⟩ *House of Commons*, *Lower House*, ⟨Am⟩ *House of Representatives*; ⟨Am⟩ (in einigen Staaten) *Assembly* **~hemd**(e) n *vest*, ⟨Am⟩ *u.shirt*; (Damen≗) *vest* ‖ (wollenes) *singlet* ≗**h·öhlen** vt [h] *to undermine*, → –gr·aben **~holz** n *u.wood*, *u.growth*, *copsewood* **~hose** f (eine *a pair of*) & **~hosen** f pl = –beinkleid; kurze ⟨Am⟩ *briefs* pl ≗**irdisch** a **1.** *subterranean*; *u.ground* (*railway*, *shelter*); *submerged* ‖ ~e Begräbnisstätte *catacomb* ‖ ~er Gang *subway*; *tunnel* **2.** ⟨myth⟩ *infernal* (*regions*, *gods*) **~jacke** f ~/~n *u.vest* ≗**j·ochen** vt [h] *to subjugate*, *subdue*; *enslave* **~kämmerer** m *vice-chamberlain* ≗**k·ellern** vt [h] *to provide with a cellar* **~kiefer** m ~s/~ *lower jaw* | ~wackler [m] (Bürokrat) ⟨fam⟩ *barnacle* **~klasse** f ~/~n *l. class*; pl *l. school* **~kleid** n *u.garment* ‖ (Wäschestück für Damen) *slip* ‖ pl (⟨a.⟩ ~ung [f]) *u.clothes*, *u.things* pl, *u.clothing*, *u.wear* **~koch** m *u.-cook* ‖ ⟨mar⟩ *cook's mate* **~kommen** n ~s/ *accommodation*, *lodging*(*s*), *shelter* ‖ ⟨fig⟩ *place*, *employment*, *situation* ≗|**kommen** vi irr [s] *to get a l.*, *to find a.*; ⟨fam⟩ *to put up* ‖ (Beschäftigung finden) *to find a situation* od *employment* ‖ [österr] (S) = vor– **~könig(in** f) m *viceroy* (*vicereine*) **~körper** m ~s/ *lower part of the body* ≗**kopieren** vt ⟨phot⟩ *to u.print* ≗|**kriechen** vi [s] *to creep u.* ‖ ein Plätzchen zum U. *a place where to hide*; ⟨fig⟩ *some employment*, ⟨fam⟩ *a job of sorts* ≗|**kriegen** vt [h] ⟨fam⟩ *to bear down*; *to worst*; *to get the better of* ‖ ⟨fig⟩ sich nicht ~ l *not to give in*, *to hold one's sway*; *to keep a stiff upper lip* ⟨fig⟩; da hast du mich –ge–gt *you have me there*; wir l uns nicht ~! *we'll not be beaten*! ‖ nicht –zu–(d) *unquenchable* (*good humour*) ≗**k·ühlt** a *supercooled* **~k·ühlung** f ⟨phys⟩ *u.-*, *supercooling* **~kunft** f ~/≗e **1.** ⟨mil⟩ *quarters* pl, *billet*(*s* pl); in der ~ *in unit lines* ‖ freie ~ *quarters in kind* **2.** = –kommen | ~gerät [n] ⟨mil⟩ *barrack stores* pl, *billeting equipment* | **~s-** ⟨mil⟩ *housekeeping*; ~bereich, ~raum [m] *shelter area*, *cantonment* ‖ ~hütte [f] *shelter-hut for mountaineers*; ~stärke [f] *quartering strength* **~lack** m ⟨cosm⟩ *base coat* **~lage** f *foundation* ⟨a. tail⟩; *groundwork*, *base* ⟨a. rail⟩; Straßen≗ *sub-base*, *-grade*; ⟨cosm⟩ *foundation* ‖ *bed*, *bearing*, *rest* | ⟨arts etc⟩ *foil* ‖ ⟨geol⟩ *substratum* ‖ ⟨hort⟩ (Wildling) (*parent*) *stock* ‖ ⟨tail, tech⟩ *lining* ‖ ⟨typ⟩ *wedge*, *key* | (Baby≗) *rubber* bzw *flannel square*; *pilch* ‖ wasserdichte Baby≗n [pl] *spreads* pl | (Schreib≗) *blotting-pad* ‖ (Teppich≗) *u.lay* | ⟨fig⟩ *datum*, [pl] *data* ‖ (Beleg) *voucher* ‖ (Beweis) *evidence* ‖ [pl] (Urkunden) *dossier* Fr ‖ ~n [pl] ⟨off⟩ *records*, *documents*; ⟨tech, contr⟩ *descriptive material* od *d.s*; ⟨comp⟩ *basic r.s*, lesbare ~n *written r.s* ‖ ohne ~n *unsupported* (*by d.s*) ‖ k–e ~n h *to have nothing to go upon*; als ~ f *in support of* | ~plane [f] ⟨mil⟩ *ground sheet* **~lagerungs-** *sub-audio* (*telegraphy*) **~land** n *lowland*, *low country* **~länder** m *lowlander* **~laß** m; ohne ~ *without intermission*, ⟨fam⟩ *letup*; *continually*, *incessantly* ≗**l·assen** **1.** vt/i irr [h] *to omit* (*to do* od *doing*); (*it is better*) *not to do* (*it*) ‖ (versäumen) *to fail* (*to do*), *to miss* (*doing*) ‖ (vernachlässigen) *to neglect* (*doing*) ‖ (sich enthalten) *to abstain* od *refrain from* (*doing*), *to forbear* (*doing* od *to do*) ‖ (aufhören mit etw) *to leave off*, *to stop*, *drop* (*doing*) ‖ ~ Sie das! *leave that alone*!; ⟨fam⟩ *drop that* (*noise*)!; *cut that out*! ‖ ~ Sie nicht *don't fail* (*to write*) ‖ nichts ~ *to do everything in one's power*, *to leave nothing undone* ‖ k–e Mühe ist ~ *no effort is spared* (*to do*) ‖ ich kann es nicht ~ *I can't help it* ‖ etw ganz ~ *to let a th go by default* **2.** ≗ n ⟨bes mil⟩ *inactivity* **~l·assung** f ~/ *omission*, *neglect*; *failure*; ⟨stat⟩ *under-enumeration*, *-registration* ‖ (Übersehen) *oversight* ‖ ⟨jur⟩ *default*, ~ der Anzeige *misprision* ‖ e–e ~ begehen *to do an act of omission* | **~s-** ~befehl [m] (f Dauer– *permanent*, vorläufig *temporary*) *injunction* (*authoritative order* ⟨bes jur⟩); ~fall [m] *case of ommission*, etc ‖ im ~ *in default thereof*; ~klage [f] ⟨jur⟩ *action for injunction*; ~sünde [f] *sin of omission*; ~versprechen [n] *negative covenant* **~last** f ~/ ⟨mar⟩ *ballast* **~lauf** m *lower course*; *lower reaches* od *stretches* (*of a river*) ≗|**laufen** vi irr [s] [–ge–] *to run u.* od *for shelter* ‖ (v Fehlern etc; ⟨a.⟩ mit ~ *to slip*, *run*, *creep in* (in *into*) ‖ ~ l *to edge* od *slip in* (*a word*) ≗**l·aufen** **1.** vt [h] (das feindl. Feuer) ~ *to advance within* od *pass inside the effects of* | [a] *suffused* (*with blood*) ‖ (Augen) *bloodshot* ‖ blau ~

black and blue **~läufer** m *interloper; smuggler* **~leder** n ~s/ *u.leather, sole-leather* **~́|legen** vt [h] [pp –ge–gt] *to lay* od *put u.* | [dat] frische Windeln ~ *to change (a baby's) linen*; e–r S e–e Bedeutung ~ *to assign a meaning to a th*; e–n andern Sinn ~ ⟨fig⟩ *to put another construction upon, to give another meaning to* || *to put (words to an air)* || (Melodie) mit –gelegtem Text ⟨typ⟩ *with words* **~́l·egen** vt [h] [pp –gt] (mit Kork, Gummi, Filz etc) *to underlay (with)* || (mit Stoffutter etc) *to line (with)* **~́l·egen** [pp] v –liegen **~l·egene** m [der ~, ein ~r] *under-dog* **~legscheibe** f (Einlegstück) ⟨tech⟩ *washer, shim* **~lehrer** m *junior* od *assistant master* **~leib** m *abdomen, belly* | **~s-** ~gegend [f] *abdominal region*; ~krankheit [f] *abdominal disorder*; ~typhus [m] *enteric (fever)* **~́l·iegen** vi irr [s] *to be defeated, overthrown, worsted* | [dat] *to succumb* || (e–r Last etc) *to sink under* || ⟨sport⟩ *to lose to (a team)* | [h] (dem Zoll etc) *to be subject/liable to* || das –liegt starkem Zweifel *this is open to grave doubt* || k–m Zweifel ~ *to admit of no doubt* **~lippe** f ~/ *u.lip, lower lip* **·unterm** ⟨fam⟩ = unter dem **·Unter-** **~́m·alen** vt [h] ⟨arts⟩ *to ground* **~m·alung** f ⟨mus⟩ *background* **~maß** n *minus allowance* **~́m·auern** vt [h] ⟨arch⟩ *to u.set; to u.pin* ⟨a. fig⟩ **~́|mengen** vt [h] *to mix into* od *among* **~́m·engen** vt [h] *to intermix, to mingle, to mix up (with)* **~menschentum** n *subhumanity* **~miete** f → –pacht **~mieter** m ~s/~ *subtenant; lodger*; ⟨jur⟩ *sublessee*; ⟨Am⟩ *roomer* **~́min·ieren** vt [h] *to u.mine; to sap* ⟨a. fig⟩ **~́|mischen** = untermengen **·untern** ⟨fam⟩ = unter den **·Unter-** **~nächte** f pl *Twelfthnight* **~́n·ähen** vt [h] *to line; to stitch u.neath* **~́n·ehmen** **1.** vt irr [h] *to undertake* (⟨a.⟩ *a journey*) || *to charge o.s. with; to take upon o.s., to attempt*, (Schweres) *to face* || (sich einlassen auf) *to engage in, to venture upon* || ⟨com⟩ *to contract* || *to move (against in a th)*; nichts ~! *take no action!* || zu viel ~ *to burn one's candle at both ends* **2.** **~́** n ~s/~ [abstr] ⟨a. mil⟩ *operation, action stunt*; → Unternehmung; aussichtsloses ~ *forlorn hope*; gewagtes (aussichtsloses) ~ *forlorn hopes* pl zweifelhaftes, gr Gewinn versprechendes ~ *get-rich-quick scheme*; sich in ein schwieriges ~ wagen *to tackle a problem* | ~sforschung [f] *industrial research*, → Operations–; ~sführung [f] *management*; Ingenieur als innerbetrieblicher Berater f ~ *industrial engineer* **~́n·ehmend** a *enterprising, bold, daring* || *pushing* **~n·ehmer** m *enterpriser*; ~ v Filialbetrieben *chain operator* || (vertraglicher) *contractor* || ⟨arch⟩ *builder* || (Arbeitgeber) *employer* | ~konzern [m] *syndicate, pool*; ~tum [n] ~s/ *speculators* pl || *capitalism* || *competitive trade* || freie ~wirtschaft *free enterprise economy* **~n·ehmung** f ~/~en *undertaking, enterprise, scheme, (ad)venture* || ⟨mil⟩ *operation*, ~en z Bandenbekämpfung *counterguerilla o.s* || ⟨ind, etc⟩ *plant; concern; establishment* || ⟨com⟩ [in comp oft] *agency, company* | ~sgeist [m] *initiative, (spirit of) endeavo(u)r* od *enterprise*; ⟨Am, sl⟩ *get-up, go-aheadativeness* || ohne ~ *unenterprising (man)* || ~slust [f] *enterprise*, ~́slustig [a] *enterprising, keen; adventuresome*, → aggressiv; ⟨fam⟩ *up and coming* **~norm-** *substandard* [attr] **~́normal** a *subnormal* **~offizier** m (Rangklasse) *non-commissioned* (⟨mar⟩ *petty*) *officer (N.C.O.)* || (Rekruten~́) *drill-sergeant*; dienstältester ~ *colour-sergeant*; ~ vom Dienst *Orderly Sergeant* || ~e u Mannschaften [pl] *other ranks; rank and file; enlisted men* N | ~tressen [f pl] *sergeant's stripes* pl **~́|ordnen** vt [h] *to subordinate* (sich *o.s.*) || sich ~ ⟨fam a.⟩ *to take a backseat* **~ordnung** f **1.** *subordination* (unter *to*) ⟨a. fig⟩ **2.** *inferiority* **3.** = –abteilung **4.** ⟨reth⟩ → *hypotaxis* **~pacht** f *subletting; sublease, subtenancy* **~pächter** m *subtenant* **~pfand** n *pledge, pawn* || als ~ h *to hold as security* || z ~ geben *to pledge* **~́pfändlich** a *hypothecary* **~pfarre** f *curacy* **~pfarrer** m *curate* **~́|pflügen** vt [h] *to plough down* || Samen ~ *to sow u.furrow* || ⟨fig, pol⟩ –gepflügt w *to be winnowed out* || ich laß mich nicht ~ *I'm not going to be winnowed out* **~́ph·osphorsauer** a *hypophosphoric* **~prima** f *lower sixth* **~programm** n ⟨comp⟩ *subroutine* **~́r·eden**; sich ~ [h] *to converse, confer* (mit *with*) **~r·edung** f ~/~en *conference, interview* || ⟨com⟩ *business talk* || *speech (with a prisoner* etc) **~richt** m ~(e)s/ *instruction* (Einzel~́) *tuition* || *classes (at school) (to disturb the class)* || (Unterrichtswesen) *education* || englischen ~ nehmen (bei) *to take lessons in English (of, from)* || guten ~ geben *to teach well* **~́r·ichten** vt [h] *to instruct (in), teach* || (jdn v etw) *to* (falsch *mis-*)*inform (a p of a th), to warn* → raten; *to put a p wise (to a th)*, (laufend) *to keep a p informed* od *apprised* || [abs] er –tet an e–r Schule *he teaches school* || **sich** v *or* über etw ~ *to obtain information of a th, to make o.s. acquainted with a th* || sich e–s Besseren ~ *to undeceive o.s.* || über jdn genau –tet s *to know a p exactly* | unterrichtet *well informed* (v *of*); halb –tet *in twilight ignorance*; wenn wir richtig –tet sind *for all we know*; nicht –tet s *to have no information* (über *as to*) **~́r·ichtend** a *instructive* **·Unterrichts-** **~anstalt** f *educational establishment* **~briefe** m pl *correspondence-lessons* pl **~fach** n, **~gegenstand** m *subject of instruction* **~film** m *documentary film* **~hilfsmittel** pl *teaching* od *training aids* **~methode** f *method of teaching* **~minister** m *minister of public instruction*; ⟨engl⟩ *President of the Board of Education* **~stufe** f *level* od *stage of e.* **~stunde** f *lesson* **~werk** n *school-book* **~wesen** n *public i.* **·Unter-** **~richtung** f *instruction* **~riegel** m ⟨telg⟩ *earth traverse* **~rock** m *petticoat* **·unters** ⟨fam⟩ = unter das **·Unter-** **~́s·agen** vt [h] (jdm etw) *to forbid (a p doing* od *to do a th)*, (amtlich) *to prohibit (a th [being done]* od *a p from doing a th)* || es ist untersagt (zu) *it is not allowed (to)* || die Ärzte ~ ihm das Rauchen *the doctors do not allow him to smoke* **~s·agung** f ~/~en *interdiction, prohibition* **~satz** m *support(er), basis, base* || (Teller~́) *mat* || ⟨arch⟩ *socle, pedestal* || (Topf~́) *saucer* || (Ständer) *stand* || (Bock) *trestle* || ⟨mot⟩ °fahrbarer ~ *car*; steuerbarer ~ *roll scooter* | ⟨log⟩ *minor (premise)* **~schale** f *saucer* **~schallgeschwindigkeit** f ⟨bes aero⟩ *subsonic speed* **~́sch·ätzen** vt [h] (etw) *to u.value* (⟨a.⟩ Gegner), *u.rate, u.estimate, minimize; to make too light of*; nicht ~ *to appreciate* **~schätzung** f *depreciation, u.rating, minimizing* **~́sch·eidbar** a, (nicht) ~ *(in)distinguishable, (in)discernible* (von *from*) **~́sch·eiden** vt irr [h] (wahrnehmen) *to discern* || (Verschiedenheit bemerken, feststellen) *to distinguish, to discriminate (between)* || ⟨scient⟩ *to differentiate* || (in Gruppen etc teilen) *to distinguish into* || nicht z ~ = nicht –scheidbar | **sich** wesentlich ~ *to differ (greatly); to be (very) different* (v *from*) || ich kann ihn kaum v s–m Bruder ~ *I can hardly tell him from his b.* || ich kann sie nicht ~ *I don't know which is which* **~́sch·eidend** a *distinctive* **~scheidung** f ~/~en *(contra)distinction, discrimination*, etc || ~en machend *divisive* | **~s-** ~begriff [m] ⟨log⟩ *specific difference*; ~gabe [f] *discernment* || ~merkmal [n] *distinctive* od *characteristic trait* od *feature, mark* | ~vermögen [n] *power of discrimination* || ~zeichen [n] *mark of distinction; badge* || ⟨log⟩ *criterion* || ~zoll [m] ⟨com⟩ *differential duty* **~schenkel** m *(lower part of the) leg* **~schicht** f *lower stratum*, ⟨geol⟩ *substratum* || ⟨agr⟩ *subsoil* **~́schieben** vt irr [h] *to shove* od *put under* || (an die Stelle setzen) *to substitute, interpolate* || ⟨fig⟩ (jdm) *to attribute falsely (to a p)*, (S) *to foist* (⟨a.⟩ Kind), (Kind) *to father (upon a p)* || jdm e–e Lüge ~ *to make a liar of a p* || [dat]

e–n falschen Sinn ~ *to put a wrong construction (upon)* ‖ ein Testament ~ *to forge a will* ‖ jdm ein Buch ~ *to pass off a book as a p's work* ‖ → –geschoben **~schied** m ~(e)s/~e *difference; distinction* (fein *nice*) ‖ *dissimilarity; variation, deviation*; kl ~e *niceties* pl; alle noch so gr ~e *all differences however great* ‖ ohne ~ des Ranges *without regard to rank* | das ist ein gr ~ *that makes a great* (⟨fam⟩ *all the*) *difference* ‖ es macht wenig ~ ⟨a.⟩ *it matters little* ‖ das macht k–n ~ ⟨a.⟩ *it's all the same* ‖ es ist ein ~ ob .. oder ob .. *it's one th to .. it's quite another to ..*; es ist nicht der geringste ~ zw ihnen *there is nothing to choose between them*; es ist ein gr ~ zw .. u .. *a well-read man is one th and a writer another* ‖ ein ~ wie Tag u Nacht! *they are as different as chalk and cheese* ‖ das ist eben der ~! *there is all the difference in the world* ‖ ohne ~ *indiscriminately* ‖ ohne ~ der Konfession *irrespective of creed* ‖ e–n ~ m (zw 2 Dingen) *to discriminate (between two ths)* ‖ z ~ v *unlike (most books), in contrast to* ≗**sch·ieden** a *different, diverse, distinct* ≗**schiedlich** a *different, diverse; discrete* ‖ ~e Behandlung *discrimination (against, among)* **~-schieds-** ~empfindlichkeit [f] ⟨eth⟩ *discrimination sensivity*; ≗los [a] *indiscriminate, undiscriminating* | [adv] *indiscriminately, without distinction* od *exception, promiscuously* ≗**sch·ießen** vt [h] *to undershoot* ≗**schlächtig** a ⟨tech⟩ *undershot (mill-wheel)* ≗|**schlagen** vt irr [h] [pp –ge–] *to cross (one's arms, legs)* ≗**schl·agen** vt irr [h] [pp ~] (Geld) *to embezzle* ‖ (Briefe) *to intercept* ‖ (Testament) *to suppress* **~schl·agung** f ~/~en *embezzlement*, ⟨sl⟩ *graft* ‖ *interception* ‖ *suppression; theft by conversion* **~schleif** m ~(e)s/~e *fraud, malversation, embezzlement, defalcation*, ⟨jur⟩ *peculation* **~schlupf** m *shelter, refuge*; ohne ~ *shelterless* ≗|**schlüpfen** vi [s] *to find shelter (under), to slip (underneath)* ≗**schr·eiben** vt irr [h] (–zeichnen) *to sign, subscribe* ‖ (sich einzeichnen) *to subscribe to (a loan*, etc) ‖ etw ~ *to endorse a th* ⟨a. fig⟩; ⟨fig⟩ *to approve of* ≗**schr·eiten** vt [h] *(the proceeds) fall short of (the estimate)*; nicht z ~(d) *irreducible (time)* **~schrift** f *signature* ; eigenhändige ~ *sign manual*, ⟨arts⟩ *inscription*; ⟨typ⟩ (unter Bild) *underline* ‖ (auf Listen etc) *subscription* ‖ mit s–r ~ versehen *to sign* ‖ laut eigener ~ *witness his* (etc) *hand*; ~ u Siegel ⟨jur⟩ *hand and seal* | ~enfolge [f] ⟨bes pol⟩ *alternat* | ~szeuge [m] ⟨eng jur⟩ *subscribing witness* **~schule** f ~/~n *preparatory school* **~schuß** m = Defizit **~-schwelle** f ~/~n *sill, threshold* ‖ ⟨rail⟩ *sleeper* ≗**schwellig** a ⟨fig⟩ *subt(i)le, subliminal* **~seeboot** n *submarine (boat)* → U-Boot ≗**seeisch** a *submarine* **~segel** n *lower sail* **~s·egelgehen** n *setting sail* **~seite** f ~/~n *lower side* **~sekunda** f ~/ *lower fifth* ≗|**setzen** vt [h] *to set, put, place under(neath)* ‖ *to affix (one's name)* ≗**s·etzen** vt *to support* (mit *by*) ‖ *to mix (with)* **~setzer** m ~s/~ *mat*; ⟨a–engl⟩ *small plate; saucer* ‖ (f Blumentöpfe) *stand, support* ≗**s·etzt** a *thick-set, squat*; ⟨fam⟩ *dumpy, stumpy; short-handed* (vierschrötig) *square-built* ‖ (stämmig) *stocky* **~setzung** f (Ggs Über-) *(speed) reduction* (einfache *single*); *r. unit; r. gear; reducing g.ing* ≗**s·iegeln** vt [h] *to seal; to put one's seal to* ≗|**sinken** vi irr [s] *to go down, to sink (under)* ≗**sp·ülen** vt *to wash away, to hollow out (from below)* **·unterst** a [sup] v unter(e) **·Unter-** *under* **~st·aatssekretär** m *U.-Secretary of State* **~stadt** f ~ *lower town* **~-stamm** m ⟨zoo, bot, etc⟩ *sub-phylum, subkingdom* **~stand** m *shelter* ‖ ⟨mil⟩ *dug-out*; (bombensicherer) *bomb-proof*; ständiger ~ *deliberate sh.* | ~s-los [a] ⟨österr⟩ (obdachlos) *unhoused* **~stärke** f ⟨for⟩ *diameter at butt-end* **~statthalter** m *Deputy-Governor* ‖ (in den britischen Kolonien) *lieutenant-governor* ≗|**stecken** vt *to put* od *to stick u.* ‖ *to incorporate* ≗|**stehen** vi irr [s] [pp –gestanden] (zum Schutze) *to find shelter u., to stand below* ‖ bei Regen: *we stood up* ≗**st·ehen** vi irr [h] [pp –st·anden] *to be subordinate* od *subject to, to be u. the control of* ‖ *to come u. (a department)* ‖ e–m strengen Herrn ~ *to serve u. a severe master*; .. ~ dem K. .. *are controlled at corps level* | **sich** ~ *to dare, venture; to make bold (to do)* ‖ er wird sich nicht ~ *he won't have the impudence* (⟨fam⟩ *the cheek*) *(to do it)* ‖ was ~ Sie sich? *how dare you?* –h dich (j·a nicht)! *you (just) dare!* ≗|**stellen** vt [h] [pp –ge–llt] *to place* od *put u.*; (Wagen) *to garage* ‖ sich ~ *to take shelter (u.)*; (bei Regen) *to stand up, to get out of the rain* ≗**st·ellen** vt [h] [pp–llt] (jdm) *to put u. a p's command* od *authority; to assign*, ⟨mil⟩ *attach (to)*; jdm –t s *to be subordinated to a p* | (zuschreiben) *to impute (to a p), to insinuate, suggest (that ..)* ‖ man darf ~ *we may suppose (that ..)*; jdm (etw) ~ *to attribute .. to a p* **~st·ellung** f *imputation, insinuation* ‖ ⟨mil⟩ (vorübergehende) *attachment* | ~sverhältnis [n] *command relationship*; klare ~s- u Befehlsverhältnisse *a well-defined chain of command* **~sterblichkeit** f ⟨stat, ins⟩ *light mortality* **~steuermann** m ⟨mar⟩ *second mate* ≗**str·eichen** vt irr [h] *to u.line, u.score*; doppelt –strichen *with double u.line* ‖ ⟨fig⟩ *to emphasize, stress, punctuate* **~streichung** f ⟨typewr, etc⟩ *u.sc.* | ~staste [f] *u.sc. key* **~strömung** f *u.-current* **~stufe** f *lower grade* ‖ ⟨school⟩ *lower forms* ≗**st·ützen** vt [h] *to prop (up), support* | ⟨fig⟩ *to assist, uphold, back; support* ⟨a. mil⟩, *aid; abet*; (fördern) *to sponsor* ‖ *to favour, patronize, countenance* ‖ (zustimmend sanktionieren) *to give sanction to* ‖ nicht ~ *to discountenance* ‖ ⟨mil⟩ *to reinforce*, ⟨ftb⟩ *to back up* ⟨a. fig⟩ ‖ *to sustain, second (proposals)* ‖ *to strengthen* ‖ staatlich –tzt *subsidized (theatre), state-aided (school)* **~st·ützer** m *supporter, patron*; ⟨parl⟩ *promoter (of a bill)*, ⟨Am a.⟩ *backer* **~st·ützung** f *support* ‖ *aid, assistance*; Plan f d ~ der Bundeswehr *German Army Ass. Plan* N; unmittelbare ~ durch Luftwaffe *close air support* N; mit der ~ v etw rechnen *to count on the s. of a th*; ~ u Beratung .. ⟨cyb⟩ *programming help and ass.*; z ~ [+ gen] *in s. of (a tender)* ‖ (mit Geld) *subsidy* ‖ (Almosen) *relief* ‖ *allowance* ‖ jdm ~ angedeihen l *to give* od *lend countenance to a p, to throw one's support behind a p*; ~ erhalten *to draw support* (aus *from*) | **~s-** ~anspruch [m] *claim*; Ihr ~ ist erschöpft *you have no more benefit (to your credit)* ~anstalt [f] *charitable institution*; ≗bedürftig [a] *indigent*; ≗berechtigt [a] *entitled to relief*; ~empfänger [m] *p in receipt of public ass.*; ~fonds [m] f Entwicklungsländer *development loan fund*; ~gesuch [n] *application for relief*; ~kasse [f] *charity* od *provident fund*; ~mauer [f] ⟨arch⟩ *bearing-wall*; ~punkt [m] ⟨tech⟩ *fulcrum*; ~verein [m] *friendly* od *provident society* **Unter-~such** m ~s/ Sw = ~ung ≗**s·uchen** vt [h] *to examine, investigate*, (genau) *canvass*; → prüfen ‖ *to look* od *go into (a matter); to explore (a problem)*; (Fingerabdruck) *to check* ‖ (genau) *to scrutinize; sift (to the bottom); to probe (a matter) home* ‖ (ergründen) *to inquire* od *search into* ‖ ⟨mot⟩ *to go over (a car)* ‖ (erforschen) *to explore* | ⟨chem⟩ *to analyse; test* (auf *for*) ‖ ⟨med⟩ *examine* ‖ ~ l *to have (one's eyes) seen to* ‖ *the doctor ought to see him* ‖ (mit der Sonde) ⟨surg⟩ *to probe* | ⟨mar⟩ (Tiefe) *to sound* ‖ ⟨jur⟩ *to make an inquiry into (a case)* **~s·uchung** f ~/~en (am Ort *field*) *investigation; inquiry* ‖ (eingehende) *scrutiny* ‖ e–e gründliche ~ ⟨Am⟩ *a general check-up* ‖ (Prüfung) *examination* | ⟨philos⟩ *research (on, into)*; dazu: *to r.* ‖ (Abhandlung) *treatise*, (lange) *disquisition, lucubration*; ⟨scient⟩ (Buchtitel) *observation* (über *on*) ‖ ⟨mil⟩ *inspection* ‖ ⟨jur⟩ *judicial inquiry; trial* ‖ ⟨med⟩ *examination,* (genaue) *exploration*; übliche ~ *routine physical check-up* | in ~ s *to be under ex.n* | ⟨jur–med⟩ (e–r Leiche) *inquest* | ⟨tech⟩ (gründliche) *overhaul* || ⟨chem⟩ *analysis* | **~s-** ~akten [f pl] *documents relating to a case under trial* || ⟨jur–med⟩ *proceedings at an inquest*; ~ausschuß [m] *committee of inquiry* (f *into*) || *medical* etc *board*; ~gefangene(r) *prisoner upon trial*; ~gericht [n] *court of inquiry*; ~haft [f] ⟨jur⟩ *pre-trial custody*; *imprisonment on remand*; *detention pending trial* || in ~ nehmen *to commit for trial* (wegen *on a charge of*); in ~ zurücksenden *to remand*; ~kommission [f] *rogatory com.*; methode [f] ⟨med⟩ *m. of examination*; ~probe [f] *test specimen*; ⟨med⟩ *t. sample*; ~richter [m] ⟨jur⟩ *examining magistrate* **~tagförderung** f *deep-mined output* **~taille** [–taljə] f *under-bodice* **~|tan** m ~s & ~en/~en *subject*; ⟨Am⟩ *citizen* || [pl a.] (*the king's*) *people* || ´~ a [pred] *subject* (*to*) || sich [dat] ~ m *to subdue, conquer* (*a p, a th*) | **~en-** ~eid [m] *oath of allegiance*; ~pflicht [f] *allegiance*; ~treue [f] *loyalty*; ~verstand [m] beschränkter ~ *short-sighted views of the common herd* **´~tänig** a *subject* || ⟨fig⟩ *submissive, humble* || (knechtisch) *obsequious* | ´~keit [f] ~/ *submission* || ⟨fig⟩ *obsequiousness, submissiveness, humility* | **~st** [obs a] *most humble and obedient* | [obs adv] *most obediently* **~tasse** f ~/~n *saucer* „Fliegende ~" *flying s.* (= *unidentified f.g object* ["*Ufo*"]) **´~tauchbar** a *submersible* **´~|tauchen** vt [h] *to dip, duck, immerse* | vi [s] *to dive* ⟨a. fig⟩ || *to plunge, dip, duck*; ⟨fig⟩ *to be lost* (*in the crowd*) **~|teil** m [n] *lower part, base* || ⟨sex, fam⟩ *the Netherlands, the Low Countries* **~t·eilt** a *subdivided* **~t·eilung** f *break-down* **~teller** m *saucer* **~tertia** [–ts–] f *lower fourth* **~titel** m (e–s Buches) *subhead(ing), subtitle*; ⟨typ⟩ *caption*; (mit Autor) ⟨Am⟩ *by-line* **~ton** m ⟨phys⟩ *accessory sound* **´~tr·eiben** [irr] vi/t *to u.state*, dazu: *u.st.ment*, → Litotes **´~|treten** vi irr [s] *to seek* od *take shelter* (*against the rain*), *to stand up* **´~t·unneln** vt [h] *to tunnel* **~vermieter** m *subletter* **~veterinär** m *assistant veterinary surgeon* **´~v·ölkert** a *u.populated* **´~-w·achsen** a (Fleisch) *streaky* || mit Unkraut ~ *weedy* **~wald** m *brushwood* **~wanderung** f ⟨pol⟩ *undermining*; *infiltration*; *penetration*; *subversion* **´~wärts I.** [adv] *downwards, u.neath* **II.** prep [gen] *on the lower side of* **´~w·aschen** vt irr [h] *to u.wash, u.mine* **~wäsche** f ~/ = –kleidung; *smalls*; (f Damen) ⟨a.⟩ *lingerie* Fr, ⟨fam⟩ *undies* pl **~w·asser-** ~atmungsgerät [n] *aqualung*; ~bau [m] *subaqueous works* pl; ~bombe [f] (gegen U-Boote) *depth-charge*; ⟨Am fam⟩ *can*; bombenmörser [m] ⟨fam⟩ *squid*; ~boot [n] *submarine boat* || → Horchapparat; ~forscher [m] *aquanaut*; ~forschungsprogramm [n] *man-in-the-sea-program*; ~geschwindigkeit [f] *submerged speed*; ~glocke [f] *submarine bell*; ~lab·o-r(at·orium) [n] *sea-lab(oratory)*; ~ortung [f] *subaqueous ranging*; ~ortungsgerät [n] *sonar*; ~-rohr [n] *u.water* (*torpedo*) *tube*; ~schallempfänger [m] *hydrophone*; ~-Sprengtrupp [m] *u.w. demolition team* N; ~streitkräfte [f pl] *undersea craft*

·**Unter-** **~w·alden** n (Sw Kanton) **~w·äldner(in** f) m *inhabitant of U.* **´~w·egen** [adv] Sw ~ l = unterl·assen **´~w·egs** [adv] *on the way* || ⟨aero⟩ *in flight* || ⟨mil⟩ *on the march, en route* N || immer ~ *always on the move* || ⟨fam⟩ ~ l *to leave undone* || ~ schlafen: *you can sleep your way* || ~ s nach *to be on the road to*; derweil wir ~ sind *as we go along* **´~w·eilen** adv 1. = bisweilen || 2. = unterdessen **´~w·eisen** vt irr [h] *to instruct* (*in*), *teach* (*sth*) **~w·eisung** f *instruction* (*in*), *teaching*; *tuition, training* (*in*); ⟨bes pol⟩ *indoctrination* | ~smittel [n] *tool of learning* **~welt** f *Hades, nether world, Shades* [pl] *below, lower regions* pl || (Verbrecherwelt) *u.world*, ⟨Am⟩ *gangsters* pl **´~w·erfen** vt irr [h] *to subdue, to beat* (*a p*) *into submission*; e–r Probe ~ *to submit to a test* || ⟨mil⟩ *to reduce* || (e–m Verhör etc) *to subject* || sich ~ *to submit, yield*, jdm *to knuckle under to a p*; sich den Regeln ~ *to comply with the rules* || → –w·orfen **~|w·erfung** f ~/ *conquest* (*of the Celts*); *subjection* (unter *to*) || (–würfigkeit) *submission* || (Ergebung) *resignation* (*to*) || (Ergebung in) *acquiescence* (*in*) **~werk** n ⟨el⟩ *substation* **´~w·inden** irr [h] sich ~ *to venture, dare, presume* **~wind** m *u.current of air* || ⟨tech⟩ *u.-grate draft* od *blast* **´~w·orfen** a [pp v –w·erfen]; e–r S [dat] ~ s *to be liable, addicted, subject, exposed, open to a th* **´~w·ühlen** vt [h] *to root up* || ⟨fig⟩ *to u.mine* **´~w·ürfig** a *submissive, abject, grovelling* || *servile* || (ehrerbietig) *obsequious* || den ´~en spielen *to knuckle u.* || sich [dat] e–n ~ m *to bring a p into subjection*; *to beat a p into submission* | [adv] *hat in hand* | ´~keit [f] ~/ *submission, submissiveness* || *obsequiousness* **~zahn** m *lower tooth* **´~z·eichnen** vt [h] *to sign* || *to initial* || *to subscribe* (*one's name*) || (Vertrag) *to ratify* || (Versicherungsschein) *to underwrite* **~z·eichner** m *signer* || (e–s Vertrags) *signatory* || ⟨com a.⟩ *u.writer, subscriber* **~z·eichnete** m [der ~, ein ~r] ~n/~n (*the*) *undersigned* **~z·eichnung** f *subscription, signature* || (e–s Vertrags) *ratification* **~zeug** n *u.garments, u.wear, u.clothing* **´~|ziehen** vt [h] [pp –gezogen] (Kleidung) *to put on u.neath* || *to insert* (*a lining*) || *to fix* (*a beam*) *u.neath* **´~z·iehen** vt irr [h] [pp –z·ogen] [dat] *to subject to* | **sich** + [dat] ~ *to u.take*, (*bend to*) (*a task*) || *to take* (*medical treatment*); (e–r Operation) *to u.go* || (e–r Prüfung) *to sit* (od *go in*) *for* || sich der Mühe [dat] ~ *to take the trouble to do it* **~zug** m ⟨arch⟩ *truss*

·**un-** **~tief** a *shallow, low* **´~tiefe** f **1.** *shallow place*; *flat, shoal, sands* pl, *sandbank* || voll v ~n *shoaly* **2.** (*bottomless*) *abyss* || ⟨poet⟩ *unfathomable deep* **´~tier** n *monster, beast* ⟨a. fig⟩ **~t·ilgbar** a (unauslöschlich) *inextinguishable, indelible* || (Anleihe) *irredeemable* || (Schulden) *not payable* **~tr·agbar** a ⟨übtr⟩ *intolerable*; *unbearable, unendurable*; *insupportable, unwarrantable, unmaintainable*; [pred] ⟨pol⟩ (*he is a*) *security risk*; *it is beyond endurance* **~tr·ennbar** a *inseparable* || [adv] (*to belong*) *inalienably* (*to*) **~treu** a *faithless, unfaithful* || ([dat], gegen) *perfidious, disloyal* (*to*) || *false* (*to a th*) || (e–r S) ~ w *to break* (*one's pledge*), *to desert* (*a cause*); *to forsake, abandon* (*a th*) || ⟨pol⟩ *to rat* || jdn s–r Pflicht [dat] ~ m *to turn a p from the path of duty* **´~treue** f ~/ *faithlessness, perfidy*; ⟨jur⟩ *breach of trust*; grobe ~ *felony*; || ⟨prov⟩ ~ schlägt ihren eigenen Herrn *treachery will home to the traitor* **~trinkbar** a *undrinkable* **~tröstlich** a *inconsolable, disconsolate, comfortless* | ´~keit [f] *desolation*; *inconsolableness*, etc **~trüglich** a (S) *unmistakable, sure, certain* || (P) *infallible, unerring, never failing* **~tüchtig** a *unfit* || *inefficient, useless* less (zu *for*) || (ungeeignet) *incapable* || (v Schiffen) *unseaworthy* || ~ m *to disable* **´~tugend** f *vice* (⟨a.⟩ *in a horse*), *bad habit* **~tu(n)lich** a *impracticable*, ⟨Am⟩ *impractical*; *unfeasible* || *impossible*

·**unüber-** **~brückbar** a *unbridgeable* ⟨a. fig⟩ **~hörbar** a: *one cannot fail to hear it* **~legt** a = unbedacht || ⟨a.⟩ *loose* (*talk*); *ill-considered* (*action*); *injudicious, unreflecting* (*p*); *snap judgment* **~schr·eitbar** a *insurmountable* ⟨a. fig⟩, *impassable* **~s·ehbar** a *vast, immense* || ~e Zahl *no end of* (*pictures*) **~s·etzbar** a *untranslatable* || ~keit [f] ~/ *impossibility of translating* **~sichtlich** a *badly arranged, unmethodical* || *confused* (*matters*) || *tangled* (*country*); ⟨mot⟩ *blind* (*corner*) **~st·eiglich** a *insurmountable* ⟨a. fig⟩ || ⟨fig⟩ *insuperable* **~tr·agbar** a *not transferable* od *negotiable* || ⟨jur⟩ *unassignable* **~tr·efflich, ~-tr·offen** a *unsurpassable, unequalled, unrivalled* ||

matchless || *superlative* || *supreme* || ⟨fam⟩ *top--notch* || ~ s in *to be a past-master in*; (*for lying*) *you are it* **~w·indlich** a ⟨a. fig⟩ *invincible, unconquerable* || *insurmountable, insuperable* (*difficulties*) || *impregnable* (*fort*)

·unum- ~gänglich a (*absolutely*) *indispensable, unavoidable, inevitable*; *necessary*; *imperative* | [adv] *absolutely* (*necessary*) | un·umgänglich [a] (P) *unsociable, angular* **~schränkt** a *unlimited* || ⟨pol⟩ *absolute, sovereign discretionary, full* (*power*); *autocratic* **~st·ößlich** a *irrefragable, irrefutable*; *irrebuttable*; *incontrovertible* (*fact*) || *self-evident* || *axiomatic* || (unwiderruflich) *irrevocable* || (unbestreitbar) *incontestable*; *hard* (*facts*); *established truth* **~stritten** a *undisputed*; *uncontested* **~wunden** a *frank, open, candid*; *unreserved* || *free* (*confession*) | [adv] *in plain words*; *pointblank*; *bluntly*; *without hesitation* | mit gemessener ≗**wundenheit** [f] *with measured directness*

·ununter- ~brochen a *unbroken, uninterrupted, unremitting continuous* || *incessant* || ⟨el⟩ *continuous* (*current*) | [adv] *uninterruptedly, without intermission* od *break* || ~ e–e Woche lang *for a week on end* **~richted** a *uninformed* **~sch·eidbar** a *undistinguishable* || *indiscernible* **~sucht** a *unexamined* || wir w es ~ l ob *we will not inquire whether*

·un- ~väterlich a *unfatherly* || [adv] *in an u. way*

·unver- ~·änderlich a *unchangeable, unalterable* || *immutable, stable*; *constant*; → unnachgiebig || ⟨gram⟩ *invariable* | ≗keit [f] ~/ *invariance*; ⟨a.⟩ *fastness* (*of colour*) (gegen .. *to light*) **~·ändert** a *changeless*; *the same as before* | ~ bleibende Lage *static position* od *situation* | [adv] *as before* || *no change* || ⟨med⟩ *in his/her usual* (*sc. state of health*); ~ l *to leave* (*a th*) *as it was* || ⟨st exch⟩ ~ notiert *marking time* **~antwortlich** a (P) *irresponsible* || (unentschuldbar) *inexcusable, unjustifiable* || in ~er Weise ⟨a.⟩ *unwarrantably* || [adv] sich ~ benehmen ⟨fam a.⟩ *to play the giddy goat* | ≗keit [f] ~/ *-ness*, ⟨a.⟩ *irresponsibility* **~arbeitet** a *unwrought, raw* || ⟨weav⟩ (Stoff) *not made up* || ⟨fig⟩ *crude* **~·äußerlich** a *inalienable* (*right*) || *unsaleable* || (Grundbesitz) ⟨engl⟩ *entailed* **~b·esserlich** a (P) *incorrigible, irreclaimable* || *incurable* ⟨a. fig⟩, ⟨fig⟩ *hopeless, confirmed* (*bachelor*) || *inveterate, sad* (*drunkard*) | (S) *unmendable* || (vollkommen) *faultless* || ⟨Am fam⟩ (Südstaaten) *unreconstructed* (*rebel*) **~b·indlich** a *not binding, not obligatory, not compulsory*; *noncommittal* || *free trial* (*demonstration*) || (unfreundlich) *disobliging* | [adv] *without guarantee, obligation*; *w. commitment* (*on my part*) **~blümt** a (vgl –geschminkt) *plain, frank, direct, open, undisguised* || *naked* (*truth*) | [adv] *bluntly*; *without mincing matters*; *point-blank*; ⟨Am fam⟩ (*to talk*) *turkey* || sich ~ ausdrücken *to be* (*extremely*) *outspoken* | ~heit [f] *frankness* **~b·orgen** a *unconcealed* **~br·ennbar** a *incombustible, indeflagrable* || *fire-proof* **~br·üchlich** a *inviolable* || *undeviating* (*faith*); *unswerving* (*loyalty*) || *absolute* (*secrecy*) **~bunden** a *unconnected, uncombined* (*with*) || ⟨med⟩ *not bandaged* **~bürgt** a *unwarranted* || *unvouched, u. for* || (Nchricht) *unconfirmed* **~dächtig** a *unsuspected, trustworthy* ⟨a. med⟩ **~daulich** a *indigestible* || ⟨fig⟩ *crude* **~derblich** a *incorruptible* ⟨a. fig⟩ **~derbt** a *uncorrupted, unspoilt* **~dient** a *undeserved, unmerited* || *gratuitous* || (Geld) *unearned* (⟨bal⟩ *increment*) || ~ermaßen [adv] *undeservedly* **~dorben** a = –verderbt || *untainted* (*meat*) || *fresh* (*air*) || ⟨fig⟩ *innocent, pure, unsophisticated* **~dr·ießlich** a *ungrudging* **~dr·ossen** a *indefatigable, unwearied* || *assiduous*; *painstaking* | [adv] *cheerfully, without complaining* || ~ weiterarbeiten ⟨fam⟩ *to plod, plug on* (*an at*) **~dünnt** a *undiluted, neat*; ⟨bes Am⟩ *straight* (*drink*) **~edelte** Pflanze *wildling* **~ehelicht** a *unmarried, single* || *spinster* (*lady*) || ⟨jur⟩ die ~e N. N. *N. N., spinster* **~eidigt** a *unsworn* **~·einbar** a (mit) *incompatible, incongruous, inconsistent, out of keeping* (*with*) || ~ s mit *to be at variance with* | ~keit [f] ~/ *incompatibility, irreconcilability, contrariety, variance*; *inconsistency* **~f·älscht** a *unadulterated* || *sterling* || ⟨fig⟩ *genuine, pure, undiluted* (⟨a. fig⟩ *text*) || *unsophisticated* || *dyed--in-the-wool* (*German*) | das ≗e ⟨Am⟩ *the goods* **~fänglich** a *harmless, not insidious, not captious* **~formbar** a ⟨tech⟩ *non-workable* **~froren** a (frech) *cheeky, pert, unabashed*; *brazen-faced impudent* || ⟨Am⟩ *sassy* || höchst ~ ⟨fam⟩ *cool and cucumberish*; *as cool as a cucumber* ~er Bursche ⟨fam⟩ *cool customer* od *fish* || (unerschütterlich) *imperturbable, unabashed* | [adv] *most unconcernedly* | ≗heit [f] ~/ *impudence, imperturbability, coolness*; *effrontery*; ⟨fam⟩ *cheek* || ⟨Am a.⟩ *sass* || er hatte die ~ ⟨fam⟩ *he had the cheek to* .. || e–e unglaubliche ~ besitzen ⟨sl⟩ *to have an awful lot of neck* **~g·änglich** a *imperishable* || *everlasting* || *immortal* || *perennial* || *undying* (*fame*) **~gessen** a *unforgotten* **~g·eßlich** a *never to be forgotten, ever memorable, unforgettable* || das wird mir ~ s *I shall never forget it* || mein ~er Lehrer .. *whose memory will ever live in my heart* **~gleichbar** a *incommensurable* **~gl·eichlich** a *incomparable, unparalleled, unimitable, unequal(l)ed*; *peerless* || *unrivalled, matchless* || *unique*; *not to be matched* **~golten** a *unrequited* (*crime*) || *unrewarded* **~goren** a *unfermented* **~hältnismäßig** a *disproportionate, inadequate* || *excessive* | [adv] ~ schwer bestrafen *to break a fly on a wheel* **~heiratet** a *unmarried* || *my maiden sister* **~h·offt** a *unexpected, unhoped--for* || ~e Einnahme, Erbschaft *windfall* || ⟨prov⟩ ~ kommt oft *it's always the unforeseen that occurs* | ≗e(s) n *adventure* **~h·ohlen** a *unconcealed, undisguised, open, frank*; *bare-faced* | [adv] *openly, straightforwardly, without reserve, unreserved(ly)* **~h·üllt** a *unveiled* || *naked, bare* || ⟨fig⟩ *frank* (*speech*); *unabashed* (*accent*) **~j·ährbar** a ⟨jur⟩ *imprescriptible* **~j·ährt** a *not forfeited by prescription* || *still in force* **~käuflich** a (ungeeignet z Verkauf) *unsaleable, unmarketable* || ~e Ware *dead stock* | (nicht verk.) [pred] *not for sale* **~kauft** a *unsold*; [pred] *on hand* **~k·ennbar** a *unmistakable*; *evident, obvious*; sein Einfluß ist ~ *there is no mistaking his i.* **~kittet** a *uncemented* **~kleidet** a ⟨tech⟩ *unlined* **~kl·einert** a *undiminished, unimpaired* **~k·ürzt** a *uncurtailed* || (Text) *unabridged* **~langt** a *unsolicited* || ⟨com⟩ *not ordered* **~l·etzlich** a *invulnerable* || ⟨fig⟩ *inviolable*; *imprescriptible* (*rights*); *sacred* (*oath*) | ≗keit [f] ~/ *invulnerableness* || *inviolability* **~letzt** a (P) *unhurt, uninjured* || (S) *undamaged, intact* **~l·ierbar** a *that cannot be lost*; *safe* **~loren** a *not lost*; *safe* **~l·öschlich** a *unextinguishable* **~mählt** a *unmarried* ≗**meidbarkeit** f *inevitableness* **~m·eidlich** a *inevitable* (*that .. should*), *unavoidable*; das war ~ (= mußte kommen) *that had to happen* || ⟨emph⟩ *fatal* || sich ins ≗e fügen *to accept* (od *to bow to*) *the inevitable*; ins ≗e ergeben *resigned* **~m·engt** a *unmixed, unmingled* **~merkt** a *unperceived, unnoticed* | [adv] *unawares, without being noticed* **~mietet** a *unlet, untenanted* || (Haus) *vacant* **~m·indert** a *undiminished, unabated* (*fury, interest*); *unabashed* (*interest*) **~mischt** a *unmixed* || ⟨fig⟩ *unalloyed*; *pure* (*breed*); *undiluted* (*joy*) **~m·ittelt** a *sudden, abrupt* | adv *out of the blue sky* ≗**mögen** n ~s/ (Unfähigkeit) *inability, incapacity* || (Unbefugtsein) *incompetence* || (Kraftlosigkeit, Machtlosigkeit) *impotence* (a. geschlechtl.) || (Zahlungsunfähigkeit) *insolvency* **~mögend** a; ~ etw zu tun *unable to do a th, incapable of doing a th* || (unbefugt) *incompetent* || [abs] (kraftlos) *impotent, powerless* || (zahlungsunfähig) *insolvent* || (mittellos) *penniless, without means, impecunious* **~mutet** a *unexpected, unlooked-for* | [adv] *unawares, unexpectedly, as a surprise* **~nehm·lich** a *indistinct, inaudible* **≗nunft** f ~/ *want of reason, unreasonableness, unreason, absurdity* || höhere ~ *the height of folly* **~nünftig** a *void of reason, unreasonable, insensate*; *irrational* (*creatures*) || ~e Tiere (*dumb*) *brutes* || so handelt nur ein ≗er *no p in his senses would act like that* **~packt** a *unpacked, loose,* ⟨fam⟩ *naked*; ~es Lockmittel ⟨com⟩ *gimmick* || ⟨mar-com⟩ *in bulk* **~richtet** a *unperformed* || ~er Dinge *or* S *unsuccessfully*; *without having effected one's object, with empty hands, with nothing achieved* **~r·itzt** a ⟨min⟩ *virgin, untouched* (*mountain*) **~r·ückbar** a *immovable*; dazu: *i.bility* **~r·ückt** a *fixed, unmoved, steady* **~schämt** a *shameless, impudent, brazen-faced, barefaced, audacious*; ~e Antwort *back talk* || *saucy, pert,* ⟨fam⟩ *uppish, brassy, cheeky* || *impertinent* (*fellow*!) || *unconscionable* (*price, demand*) || *barefaced* (*lie*) || ~es Gesicht *face like brass* || ~e Herausforderung *insolence, affront, insult* || Sie ≗er! ⟨fam⟩ *you have some cheek*!, → frech | ~ auftreten *to brazen it out* | ≗heit [f] ~/~en *shamelessness, impudence, effrontery, brazenness, audacity, audaciousness, back talk* || ~! *what a colossal nerve*!; (S) *a bit hot* od *thick*! || die ~ h ⟨fam⟩ *to have the nerve* od *brass* (*to do*) || s–e ~ war nicht z überbieten *his i. was colossal* || sich mit ~ durchhelfen *to brazen* (⟨fam⟩ *cheek*) *it out* **~schlossen** a *unlocked, unclosed* **~schlüsselt** a ⟨telg⟩ *plain*; mit ~er Anschrift *plaindress* **~schnitten** a *untrimmed* (*tree*) || ⟨zoo⟩ *entire*; **~schont** a *unspared* **~schuldet** a (schuldenfrei) *not in debt, unindebted* || *unencumbered* (*estate*) || (unverdient) *undeserved* || ~erm·aßen [adv] *undeservedly, innocently* **~schult** a ⟨for, hort⟩ *untransplanted* **~schwiegen** a *indiscreet* **~s·ehens** [adv] *unexpectedly, unawares, unintentionally* || *all of a sudden* || ⟨mil⟩ ~ überfallen *to surprise* **~s·ehrt** a = unverletzt **~seifbar** a *unsaponifiable* (*fat*) **~sichert** a *uninsured* **~s·iegbar** a *inexhaustible, ever-flowing, unfailing* (*source*) **~siegelt** a *unsealed* **~s·öhnlich** a *implacable, irreconcilable* | ≗keit [f] ~/ *-ness* **~söhnt** a *unreconciled* **~sorgt** a *unprovided* (*u. for*); *dependent* (*children*) || *without means* **≗stand** m ~(e)s/ *want of judgment* od *sense*; *indiscretion, ignorance* || (Torheit) *folly, stupidity* **~standen** a **1.** .. **2.** (verkannt) *misunderstood* **~ständig** a *imprudent, injudicious, unwise*; *foolish* | ≗keit [f] ~/ *folly, imprudence* **~ständlich** a *unintelligible, incomprehensible, ungraspable*; *obscure* (Vorfall); *enigmatic* || die S ist mir ganz ~ *I can't make head or tail of it* **~stellt** a *undissembled* || *undisguised* **~steuert** a *duty unpaid* || → –verzollt **~s·ucht** a *untried, unattempted* || nichts ~ l *to leave no stone unturned, to leave nothing undone* (um zu *to*) **~t·ilgbar** a *indelible, ineradicable* **~träglich** a (P) *unaccommodating, quarrelsome, unconciliating, unsociable* || (S) ⟨a. cul⟩ *incompatible* (mit *with*); ⟨med a.⟩ *intolerant* (f *to*) **~wahrt** a *unguarded* **~wandt** a **1.** *fixed, unmoved* || (Blick) *steady, steadfast*; *unblinking* (*gaze*) | [adv] *fixedly, steadily* || s–e Blicke ~ richten auf *to fix one's eyes upon* **2.** (P) *not related* || (S) *incongruous* **~wechselbar** a *unalterable* || *unmistakable* **~w·ehrt** a *unprohibited, not forbidden* || es ist Ihnen unverwehrt zu .. *you are at liberty to* .. **~w·eigerlich** a *not be refused* **~w·eilt** a (sofortig) *immediate* || (unaufhörlich) *incessant* | [adv] ⟨a.⟩ *without delay, at once* **~w·elklich** a *unfading*; *never fading* ⟨a. fig⟩; ⟨fig⟩ *for ever young* **≗wendbarkeit** f *unemployability* **~w·erflich** a *unobjectionable, unexceptionable* **~w·eslich** a *incorruptible, imputrescible* **~w·indbar** a (Verlust) *irreparable* **~w·ischbar** a *ineffaceable, indelible* **~w·undbar** a *invulnerable* (*against*) **~w·üstlich** a *indestructible*; *iron* (*health*) || (P & S) ⟨fam⟩ *scuff-proof* || (Stoff) *everlasting* || ⟨fig⟩ *unquenchable, imperturbable* | ~keit [f] *never-failing ruggedness* **~zagt** a *intrepid, undaunted, unshrinking, undismayed* | [adv] ⟨a.⟩ *resolutely* || sei ~! *never say die*! | ≗heit [f] ~/ *intrepidity, undauntedness* **~z·ehrt** a *unconsumed* **~zeichnet** a → –zerrt **~z·eihlich** a *inexcusable, unpardonable* || in ~er Weise *beyond all pardon* **~zerrt** a *undistorted* **~z·insbar, ~z·inslich** a *bearing no interest*; *non-i. b.* || *free* (*loan*) | [adv] *free of interest* **~zogen** a → –schult **~zollt** [a & adv] *duty unpaid* || (unter Zollverschluß) *in bond* **~z·üglich** a *immediate, prompt, instantaneous* || [adv] ⟨a.⟩ *instantly*; *at once, without delay, at short notice*; *on the nail*

·un- **~volkstümlich** a *unpopular* **~vollendet** a *unfinished* || (*to leave a th*) *half finished* **~vollkommen** a *imperfect* || (mangelhaft) *defective*; *short* (*delivery*) || ~ ⟨biol⟩ *inchoate* | ≗heit [f] *flaw, defect, deficiency*; *imperfection* **~vollständig** a *incomplete*; *fragment* [attr]; *sketchy* | ≗keit [f] *–ness* **~vollzählig** a *incomplete*

·unvor- **~aussehbar** a *not to be foreseen* **~bereitet** a *unprepared, unprovided*; ⟨mar⟩ *all standing* || *spontaneous* (*revolt*) || ~ auf den Tod *unready for one's death* || (Übersetzung, Rede) [a & adv] *extempore* || (*to be*) *starched and ironed before one is washed* | ~ sprechen *to talk extemporaneously, to extemporize* **~d·enklich** a *immemorial* || seit ~en Zeiten *time out of mind, from time immemorial* **~eingenommen** a *unprejudiced, unbiassed, impartial* | ~heit [f] *lack of prejudice* od *bias*; *unprejudiced attitude* **~gr·eiflich** a *unpresuming, humble* **~h·ergesehen** a *unforeseen, unlooked-for*; *unanticipated, unprovided* || (*it was*) *a bolt from the blue* | [adv] *as a surprise* **~hersagbar** a *unpredictable* **~sätzlich** a *undesigned, unintentional* || (unvorbedacht) *unpremeditated* || [adv] *unintentionally* **~schriftsmäßig** a ⟨mil⟩ *non-regulation* **~sichtig** a *incautious, imprudent*; *inconsiderate* || *careless* || ~ w *to drop one's guard* | ~erweise [adv] *from lack of caution, from carelessness, by mistake, unguardedly* **~stellbar** a *unimaginable*; *unthinkable*; es scheint mir ~ *I cannot imagine* (*that*) **~teilhaft** a *unprofitable, disadvantageous* || ~ aussehen *not to look one's best*

un- **~w·ägbar** a *imponderable*; das ≗e *the imponderable* || ≗keit [f] ~/ *imponderability*; ~en [pl] *imponderabilia* [L] **~wählbar** a *ineligible* **~wahr** a *untrue, false* || (erdichtet) *fictitious* || (P) *lying, hypocritical* **~wahrhaftig** a *unveracious, untruthful, lying* | ≗keit [f] ~/ *unveracity, want of veracity* || *untruth*(*fulness*) **≗wahrheit** f ~/~en [abstr ohne pl] *untruthfulness, mendacity* | [konkr mit pl] *untruth, falsehood*; *lie,* ⟨fam⟩ *fib* || die ~ sagen *to lie*; wissentlich .. *to tell a deliberate falsehood* **~w·ahrnehmbar** a *imperceptible* **~wahrscheinlich** a *improbable, implausible*; *unlikely* || es ist sehr ~, daß er es tut *he is most unlikely to do it* || nicht ~ *plausible* **~w·andelbar** a *immutable, unchangeable, unvarying, unalterable*; *unswerving, undeviating* (*loyalty*) || ⟨gram⟩ *indeclinable* **~wegsam** a *impassable, impracticable*; *inaccessible* **≗weib** n *virago, termagant, fury, dragon* **~weiblich** a *unwomanly* | ≗keit [f] *unwomanly character, unwomanliness* **~w·eigerlich** a (widerstandslos) *unresisting, unhesitating* || (unablehnbar) *unrefusable, undeniable* || (unvermeidbar) *inevitable*; *certain* || *unquestioning* (*obedience*) | [adv] *unhesitatingly* || *without fail* || *certainly*; *inevitably* || ~ tun müssen *to be liable to do* **~weise** a *unwise, imprudent*; *foolish* **~weit** prep [gen] *not far from* || *off* (*Fleet Street*) | [adv] *not far* (*off*) **≗wert** m *unworthiness, worthlessness* || *futility* **~wert** a [gen] *unworthy* (*of*) **≗wesen** n ~s/ *monster* || *nuisance*; *dreadful state of things*; *disorder* || sein ~ treiben *to do* (od *to be* *up to) mischief* || *to haunt* (*a place*) || dem ~ steuern *to stop excesses* || sein ~ treiben ⟨a.⟩ *to swarm in the country* **~wesentlich** a *unessential, immaterial* (für *to*) || (nebensächlich) *accidental; extrinsic* || ~e Dinge *nonessentials* pl; *unimportant ths*; es ist ~ *it does not matter* | sich ans ≗e klammern *to grasp at shadows* **≗wetter** n ~s/~ *bad* od *stormy*, (⟨mar⟩ *dirty, foul*) *weather* || (Gewitter) *thunderstorm* || (heftiger Sturm mit Regen) *tempest* || drohendes ~ *gathering storm* **~wichtig** a *unimportant, inconsequential; of no consequence, insignificant; trifling* | ~ erscheinend *apparent trivial, seemingly unimportant* (*detail*) **~widerl·egbar, -lich** a *irrefutable; incontrovertible, unanswerable* (*proof*) || [pred] *beyond dispute* **~widerlegt** a *unrefuted* **~widerr·uflich** a *irrevocable, irreversible* | [adv] (*gone*) *beyond recall* **~widerspr·echlich** a *incontestable* **~widerspr·ochen** a *uncontradicted, unprotested*; das blieb nicht ~ *that was not received without dissent*; ~ bleiben *to go unchallenged*; es blieb alles ~ *not a word was raised in protest* **~widerst·ehlich** a *irresistible, compelling* (*force*) || *overpowering* (*desire*) || (P) *tantalizing* || ⟨fam⟩ *killing* (*fashion*) | [adv] ~ drangen die F. vor *the onset of the French was irresistible*; *nothing could withstand them* | ≗keit [f] ~/ *irresistibility* **~wiederbr·inglich** a *irrecoverable, irretrievable, irreparable; past recovery* **≗wille** m ~ns/ *displeasure, indignation* || *impatience; exasperation* (*with a p*) || *animosity* || (Zorn) *anger* || jds (allgemeinen) ~n erregen *to incur a p's displeasure* (*to scandalize everybody*) **~willfährig** a *unyielding, uncomplying, disobliging* | ≗keit [f] ~/ *disobligingness, non--compliance* **~willig** a *impatient* (*answer*); (über etw [acc]) *indignant, angry* (*at*); *displeased* (*with*) | (über jdn) *displeased, angry* (*with*) || es machte ihn sehr ~ *it greatly vexed him* || (nicht wollend) *unwilling, reluctant* (*to do*) | [adv] ⟨a.⟩ *testily* **~willkommen** a *unwelcome, unbidden; untoward* (*news*) | [adv] *as an unwelcome gift*, etc **~willk·ürlich** a *involuntary* || *mechanical* || *instinctive* | [adv] ⟨a.⟩ *unintentionally, automatically; without knowing why* || man muß ~ denken *you cannot help thinking*; er tat es ~ *he did it without thinking what he was at* **~wirklich** a *unreal, fictitious; in-, unsubstantial* **~wirksam** a *ineffectual, inoperative, inefficient, inefficacious* || *null, void* || ~ m ⟨a.⟩ *to nullify, neutralize, frustrate* || ⟨fig⟩ *to kill* (*a colo(u)r*); *to cut out* (*rays*, etc); ⟨chem⟩ *to deactivate* **~wirsch** a *cross, unfriendly, nettled, peevish* || *surly, rude* **~wirtlich, -sam** a *inhospitable* || (Gegend) *desolate, dreary* || *rough* (*weather*) **~wirtschaftlich** a (S) *uneconomic, unprofitable* || (P) *uneconomical, unthrifty, wasteful* **~wissend** a *illiterate, ignorant* | *not cognizant* od *ill informed of* | [adv] *unknowingly, unwittingly, unconsciously* **≗wissende(r)** m *ignorant person* || ⟨fam⟩ *ignoramus, dunce* **≗wissenheit** f ~/ (grobe *rude*) *ignorance* (in *of*), *illiteracy* || (*to act* [aus] *from ignorance*) || in s–r ~ *he fondly* (*imagined*) **~wissenschaftlich** a *unscientific* [adv *-ally*] | ≗keit [f] ~/ *want of scientific method, unscientific ways* pl, *empiricism* **~wissentlich** [adv] = –wissend [adv] **~wohl** a *indisposed* || (*to feel*) *unwell*, ⟨fam⟩ *out of sorts*, (*to look*) *seedy* || immer ~ *always ailing* | sich ~ fühlen ⟨a.⟩ *to feel upset* **≗wohlsein** n ~s/ *indisposition* || ⟨gyn⟩ *menses* pl, *menstruation* **~wohnlich** a *uninhabitable* || *uncomfortable, cheerless* || *inhospitable* (*land*) **~wüchsig** a ⟨for⟩ *unthrifty* **≗wucht** f *unbalance* (*of a wheel, shaft*) | ~kraft [f] *out-of-balance force*; ~scheibe [f] *eccentric weight* **~würdig** a *unworthy* ([gen] *of*); *discreditable, unseemly; undignified* (*policy*) || s–r ~ *beneath him* || s–r ~ handeln *to derogate from o.s.* **≗zahl** f ~/ *vast* od *immense number* || *a world, shower, host*, ⟨fam⟩ *no end* (*of difficulties*) **~z·ählbar** a *innumerable, numberless, countless* **~z·ählig** a *countless, innumerable; untold* (*years*) || ~e Leute *a power of people* || ~e Male *over and over again*, ⟨fam⟩ *hundreds of times, ever so many times* **~z·ähmbar** a *untamable, indomitable, fierce* | ≗keit [f] ⟨a.⟩ *ferocity* **~zart** a *indelicate, rude, rough*

·Unze f ~/~n **1.** (engl = 28,35 g) *ounce* (Gold *of gold*) → Maßtabelle **2.** ⟨zoo⟩ *ounce*

·Unzeit f ~/ *unseasonable* od *wrong time* || zur ~ *untimely out of season, unseasonably, inopportunely, ill-timed* || (*vorzeitig*) *prematurely* **≗gemäß** a *untimely* [a. adv] || *inopportune* || (unmodern) *oldfashioned, unfashionable* | **≗ig** a *unseasonable, ill-timed; untimely* [a. adv] || *inopportune* || *independent* || (unreif) *immature* ⟨a. fig⟩ || (vorzeitig) *premature* (*birth*); *untimely*

·Unzen- ~perlen f pl *seed-pearls* pl **≗weise** [adv] *by ounces* → S.

·unzer- ~brechlich a *unbreakable; infractible, infrangible* **~l·egbar** a *indecomposable* || *elementary, simple* **~r·eißbar** a *untearable* **~st·örbar** a *indestructible* (≗keit [f] *-ness*) **~t·eilbar** a *indivisible* | ≗keit [f] *-ness* **~tr·ennlich** a *inseparable* || *indissoluble* (*friendship*) || *inherent* (*qualities*) || ≗e [pl] ⟨orn⟩ *love-birds* pl

·Unzeug n ~(e)s/ *rubbish, trash, junk*

Unzi·albuchstabe m *uncial letter*, → Uniziale

·un- ~ziemlich a *unseemly, unbecoming, improper, indecent* **≗zier(de)** f ~/ *disfigurement* || *stain, blemish* || e–m z ~ gereichen *to disfigure a p* **~zierlich** a *inelegant, uncomely, ungraceful* | ≗keit [f] ~/ *inelegance* **~zivilis·ierbar** a *incapable of culture* **~zivilisiert** a *uncivilized, savage, primitive* || *rude* || *barbarian* (*races*) **≗zucht** f ~/ *unchastity, lewdness* || *indecency* || ⟨fam⟩ *buggery* || *lewd and immoral practices*; mit Tieren *sodomy* | (gewerbsmäßige) *prostitution; practising vice professionally* (treiben *to practise*) || ~ treiben *to commit fornication, to lead an unchaste life*, .. mit *to bugger* (*a p*) **~züchtig** a *unchaste, lascivious, lewd, bawdy; libidinous* (*life, p*) || ~e Entkleidung *or* Entblößung *exhibitionism* || ~e Schriften *pornography* | ≗keit [f] ~/ *unchastity, obscenity* **~zufrieden** a (mit) *discontented, dissatisfied*, ⟨fam⟩ *disgruntled* (*with*) || mit s–m Los ~ s *to quarrel with one's bread and butter* || die ≗en [pl] *the discontented* (*ones*) || ⟨prov⟩ die ≗en h nie genug *a discontented mind is never satisfied* | ≗heit [f] ~/ *discontent, malcontent(edness); dissatisfaction* (über *at*) || ⟨pol⟩ *disaffection* **~zugänglich** a *inaccessible*; ⟨übtr⟩ (P & S) *unapproachable* | ⟨fig⟩ *unsusceptible* (f *of*) || *intractable* || [dat] *proof against* (*flattery*) || ⟨fig⟩ ~ f *insensible to*, ~ s f *to turn a deaf ear to* .. **~zukömmlich** a ⟨österr⟩ = unzulänglich, unzureichend **~zulänglich** a *insufficient, inadequate* || *scanty, short* (*supply*) || *inadequate* || *incompetent* (*lecture*) || *poor, slim* (*dinner*) || völlig ~e Luftdeckung *gross inadequacy of air cover* | ≗keit [f] ~/ ~en ⟨a.⟩ *futility, deficiency; inadequacy, insufficiency, inability unsatisfactoriness; incompetence* (*as a nurse*) || ~en [pl] *shortcomings* **~zulässig** a *inadmissible* **~zumutbar** a *inequitable, unfair, unjust*; (Preis) *unreasonable* | ~keit [f] *injustice; unfairness* **~zurechnungsfähig** a *irresponsible* || *unfit for reasoning* || (schwachsinnig) *weak--minded, imbecile* || ⟨jur⟩ *non compos* (*mentis*) L || ⟨fam⟩ *insane* || ~ m: *passion has blinded his judgment* **~zureichend** a = –länglich, *inadequate* ⟨mil⟩ (*forces*) || *wan* (*satisfaction*) || *sketchy* (*meal*) || *rough and ready* (*method*) | [adv] ~ versehen mit *starved for* (*raw materials*); ~ versorgt ⟨mil⟩ *poorly supplied* (*forces*) **~zusammenhängend** a *unconnected, incoherent; disjoined, disjointed; discursive, excursive* (*speech*) || *loose, scrappy* (*thinking*) || *desultory* (*remarks*), *rambling* (*speech*) || [pred] *lacking in context* | [adv] ~ reden *to ramble* **~zuständig** a *incompetent* **~zu-**

stellbar a *undeliverable* (*letter*), (Vermerk) *no such, address unknown* | ~keit [f] *non-delivery* **~zuträglich** a *disadvantageous* || *inconvenient* || (ungesund) *unwholesome, unhealthy* **~zutreffend** a *inapposite, wrong, false* || ≗es [n] *that which does not apply*; ≗es streichen! *delete* (od *cross out*) *what does not apply* **~zuverlässig** a *unreliable, untrustworthy* || *shuffling, shifty*; ⟨sl⟩ *wonky* || *uncertain* || *elusive, treacherous* (*memory*) || *inexact, inaccurate* || *unpunctual* || *doubtful* || ⟨com⟩ *shaky* (*firm*) **~zweckmäßig** a *impractical, unfeasable, unworkable*; *inexpedient, unsuitable, inappropriate*; *not to the purpose* **~zweideutig** a *unequivocal, unambiguous*; *explicit*; *simple, plain*; *self-evident* **~zw·eifelhaft** a *undoubted, indubitable*; *unquestioned, decided*; *established* (*fact*) | [adv] *doubtless, unquestionably, easily* || *that is, no doubt, true* || .. *and no mistake* | ≗igkeit [f] ~/ ⟨a.⟩ (*dead*) *certainty*

·Upas- ~baum m ⟨bot⟩ *antiar* **~saft** m *upas*

·üppig [a] **A. 1.** (reich) *opulent, abundant, luxurious* (⟨a. fig⟩: Phantasie, Gesundheit etc) || (reich blühend) *luxuriant, exuberant*; *lush* (*grass*) **2.** (sinnlich) *sensual, voluptuous* **3.** (übermütig) *presuming, arrogant* **B.** *full*(*y developed*) (*figure, bust*) || *rank* (*weeds* pl), *rich* (*pastures* pl, *repast*); *sumptuous* (*meal*) || *succulent* (*landscape*) || *lush* (*grass*) || ~es Leben *life of self-indulgence*; *luxury* | [adv] ~ leben *to live in clover, to live high* || ~ wachsen *to wanton, luxuriate*; *to grow in great profusion* | ≗keit [f] *luxuriance*

·Uppsala n (schwedische Stadt) *Up*(*p*)*sala*

Ur m ~(e)s/~e ⟨zoo⟩ *aurochs*

·Ur- [in s & a comp] *original* (*meaning*), *primary, primitive* (*notion*); *prime* (*origin*); *Proto..*; *germinal*; *pristine*; *primeval* (*forest*) || *ancestral* | (Kern ..) *out and out, thorough* | ([mit a] ⟨emph⟩: urgemütlich) *extremely* | = er.. (Urlaub, Urteil) **~abstimmung** f (in e–m Betriebe) *vote* (*of all the workers*) **~ahn** m [~(e)s & ~en/~en] *great-grandfather*; *ancestor* **~ahne** f *great-grandmother, ancestress* ≗**alt** [a] (S) *very old* od *ancient*; *old as the hills* || (P) *very aged* | *age-old* (*doctrines*) || *time-honoured* (*custom*) || er ist ~ *he's as old as Methusalah*; seit ~en Zeiten *from time immemorial*

Ur·al m ⟨Russ⟩ **1.** (Gebirge) *Ural Mountains* pl **2.** (Fluß) *Ural, Oural*

Ur·an n ~(e)s/ ⟨chem⟩ *uranium* | **~-** *uranic*; ~gehalt [m] *u.m content*; ~glimmer [m] *uranite*; ~gummi [m] *gummite*; ≗haltig [a] *uraniferous*; ~ig [a] *uranous*; ≗sauer [a] *uranic*, ≗saures Salz *uranate*

·Ur- ~anfang m *first beginning* ≗**anfänglich** a *original, primordial, primeval* ≗**aufführen** vt [h] *to play for the first time*; *to première* Fr **~aufführung** f ⟨theat, film⟩ *world première*; deutsche ~ *German pr.*, → Erst– || ⟨film⟩ *release*; *first run*

·urassen vi/t [h] ⟨österr⟩ = verschwenden

Ur·äusschlange f ⟨zoo, Eg arts⟩ *uraeus*

urb·an a *urbane, affable, polite*; dazu: *urbanity*

·urbar 1. a *arable, cultivated, under cultivation* || ~ m *to cultivate, clear, reclaim* (*from the wild*) **2.** ≗ n ~s/~e *cadastral register* ≗**machung** f ~/ (Sw ~is·ierung) *cultivation, clearance, reclamation*

·Ur- ~bedeutung f ~/ *primitive signification, original meaning* **~beginn** m = –anfang **~begriff** m ~(e)s/~e *primitive idea* od *notion* || [pl] *rudiments, elements* pl (*of a science*) **~bestandteil** m *primitive element* **~bewohner** m pl *aborigines* pl | ~- *indigenous* **~bild** n ~es/~er *prototype, original* || ⟨fig⟩ *ideal* ≗**bildlich** a *original, archetypical* || *ideal* **~bräuche** m pl *primitive* od *early customs* ≗**chig** a Sw = urwüchsig, echt **~christentum** n ~s/ *early christianity* ≗**deutsch** a *thoroughly German* ≗**eigen** a *quite original* || *innate* || (*one's*) *very own* || *most peculiar* ≗**eingesessen** a *autochthonous, aboriginal* ≗**einwohner** = –bewohner **~eltern** [pl] *first parents, ancestors* pl **~enkel** m ~s/~ *great-grandson, great-grandchild* **~enkelin** f ~/~nen *great-granddaughter* **~fassung** f *original version* **~faust** m (*Goethe's*) *original "Faustus"* **~fehde** f ~/~n ⟨hist⟩ *oath* od *promise to keep the peace*; *oath of truce* od *peace* ≗**fidel** a *very jolly* **~form** f *primitive form* **~gebirge** n *primitive mountains* od *rocks* pl **~geist** m *innate spirit* || *uncreated being*; *the Deity* ≗**gemütlich** a *extremely jolly* od *snug* ≗**germanisch** a *Teutonic* **~geschichte** f *primeval history* **~gestein** n *prim*(*a*)*eval rock, bedrock* ⟨a. fig⟩ **~großeltern** [pl] *great-grandparents* **~großmutter** f *great-grandmother* **~großvater** m *great-grandfather* **~grund** m *primary* (*first, original*) *cause* **~heber(in** f) m ~s/~ *author*(*ess* f), *artificer, founder*; *creator, originator*; *agent, mover*; (Anstifter) ~ s *to be at the bottom* (*of it*); geistiger ~ *mastermind*, g. ~ s *to m.* | ~recht [n] *copyright* (Verletzung *infringement*) | ≗rechtlich [adv]; .. geschützt *copyright* | ~schaft [f] ~/ *authorship*

·Uri n (schweiz. Kanton) **·Urner(in** f) m *inhabitant of* (*the canton of*) *Uri*

·Urian m ~s/ ; Meister ~ *His sable majesty*

Ur·ias m npr *Uriah* **~brief** m *treacherous letter*

ˣ**·urig** a = urtümlich; komisch; originell

Ur·in m ~(e)s/ *urine* || ~ l = urinieren | ~blase [f] *urine-bladder*; ~drang [m] ⟨path⟩ *micturition*; ~fluß [m] *u.-flow*; ~glas [n] *urinal*; ≗treibend [a] *diuretic* || ~untersuchung f *uroscopy*; *urinalysis* **urin·ieren** vi [h] *to make water, to urinate* **urinog·en** a *urinogenic* (*infection*)

·Ur- ~keim m *primitive germ* ≗**komisch** a *extremely funny, highly amusing*; *too funny for words* **~kraft** f ~/≗e *original* od *primitive power* od *force* || *moving principle* ≗**kräftig** a *very strong* od *powerful* || *of original force* **~kunde** f ~/~n *document, instrument*; *record*; *muniment, deed, writ* | Bürgerrechts-, Einbürgerungs-, Staatsangehörigkeits≗ *certificate of naturalization*; Gründungs≗ → *c. of incorporation*; öffentliche ~ *official d.t*; standesamtliche ~n [pl] *vital statistics* | eigenhändig geschriebene ~ *holograph* || (Freibrief) *charter* || zu ~ dessen ⟨jur⟩ *in witness whereof* | e–e ~ ausstellen *to make out* .., .. unterzeichnen *execute* .., .. vorlegen *present, produce, tender a d.t* | **~n-** ~abschreiber [m] *engrosser*; ~bewahrer [m] *keeper of the records*; ⟨engl⟩ *Master of the Rolls*; ~beweis [m] *documentary evidence* (erbringen *to furnish*); ~buch [n] *record, register*; ⟨ec⟩ *cartulary*; ~fälschung [f] *falsification of d.ts*; ⟨jur⟩ *forgery* (*of an instrument*); ~kenntnis [f] *diplomatics* pl; ~sammlung [f] *archives* pl; ~schrank [m] *safe for deeds*, etc; ~werk [n] *collection of records* **urkundlich** a *documentary, –tal* || (verbürgt) *authentic* [adv *-ally*] | [adv] (*to prove*) *by documents* || ~ belegen *to support by d.ts*; ~ belegt *documental*; ~ dessen *in witness whereof* **·Urkundsbeamte(r)** m *court clerk*

·Urlaub m ~(e)s/~e *leave* (*of absence*); *holidays* pl (bezahlt *with pay*); ⟨Am⟩ *vacation* || ⟨mil⟩ *l.* (*of a.*) (*privilege l.*; *compassionate l.*; *sick l.*) || ⟨scool⟩ *exeat* L || auf ~ *on holiday* od *leave*; .. gehen *to vacationize* || ~ nehmen *to take one's holiday*; ~ erhalten *to be granted l.* || ⟨mar⟩ (Land≗) *shore l.* || s–n ~ im Ausland verbringen *to vacation abroad* | **~er** m ~s/~ ⟨mil⟩ *leave-man* | ~schiff [n] *liberty boat*; ~zug [m] *leave-train* | **~s- ~anspruch** m *leave credit* od *entitlement*; aufgelaufene ≗e *accumulated vacation* **~gesuch** n *application for leave* (*of absence*) || sein ~ einreichen *to ask for l.* **~jahr** n ⟨Am univ⟩ *sabbatic*(*al*) *year* **~schein** m *permit* || ⟨mil⟩ *l. pass* **~überschreitung** f *absence over l.* **~verlängerung** f *prolongation of leave*

Ur- **~licht** n ∼(e)s/ *primitive light* **~mensch** m ∼en/∼en *primitive man* ‖ ⟨fig⟩ *original* | ∼enaffe [m] *primeval ape* **~meter** n *standard m.* **~mund** m *blastospore* **~mutter** f ∼/ *(our) first mother, mother of mankind*

·**Urne** f ∼/∼n *urn* ‖ Aschen≈ ⟨crem⟩ *container for ashes* **~nfeld** n *urn-field* **~nkammer** f *urn-chamber*

·**Urning** m ∼(e)s/∼e *pederast*

·**Urochs** m ∼en/∼en ⟨zoo⟩ *aurochs*

Uro- ∼genit·altuberkulose [f] *urogenital t.*; ∼gramm [n] *urogram*; Auswasch≈ *wash-out u.*; Früh≈ *rapid sequence u.*; ∼l·oge [m] ∼n/∼n *urologist*; ∼log·ie [f] ∼/ *urologist*

·**Ur-** **~pflanze** f *primitive plant* **≈plötzlich** a *sudden* | [adv] *all of a sudden* **~quell** m ∼s/ *fountain-head, original source* ‖ ⟨fig⟩ *first source, well-spring* **~sache** f ∼/∼n *cause* (*no effect without c.*); eigentliche ∼ *root c.*; letzte ∼ *ultimate c.*; unmittelbare ∼ *proximate c.* ‖ (Grund) *reason* (*to have no r. to do* ..) ‖ (Beweggrund) *motive* ‖ (Anlaß) *occasion*; Sie h k–e ∼ .. *there is no o. for you to say so*; *he has no business to* .. | **k-e** ∼! *don't mention it*! ⟨bes Am⟩ *you are welcome*!, *pray don't apologize*! ‖ wir h ∼ zu .. *there is reason to believe* ‖ wenig ∼ h z .. *to have little c. for* .. ‖ die ∼ s v *to be* od *lie at the bottom* od *root of* | **aus** was f e–r ∼? *for what reason* od *c.*?, *what for*?, *from what motive*?, *why*? | u nicht **ohne** ∼ *and well he* (etc) *might, and he was right* ‖ kl ∼n, gr Wirkungen *great events often come from little c.s* | ∼nforschung [f] *etiology* **≈sächlich** a *causal* ‖ ⟨gram⟩ *causative* **~sage** f *ancient tradition* **~satz** m *axiom* **~schleim** m ∼s/ (*primordial blob of*) *protoplasm* **~schrift** f ∼/∼en *original* (*text*) ‖ (erster Entwurf) *first draft* od *sketch* ‖ *autograph* **≈schriftlich** a *autographic* | [adv] ∼ zurückgeben *to return* (*a letter*) **~sitz** m *first domicile* **~sprache** f *primitive* od *primeval language* ‖ (e–r Übersetzung) *original l.* **~sprung** m *source* ‖ ⟨fig⟩ *origin, primal cause* ‖ (Abstammung) *extraction, origin* ‖ deutschen ∼s *of German origin* ⟨a. gram⟩ od *extraction*; *native of G.y*; ⟨com⟩ *G.-made, made in G.y* | v ∼ (an) ⟨fig⟩ *from the birth* | s–n ∼ h *or* nehmen v *or* in *to originate in, to descend* od *come from* **≈spr·ünglich** a *germinal, pristine*; *original, primitive* ‖ *primary* (*meaning*); *primal* (*joy*) | [adv] *at first, in the beginning*; (*Greek*) *in origin* ‖ ∼ aus Dld. stammend *of German origin, coming from G.y* | ≈keit [f] ∼/ *primitiveness, originality* **~sprungs-** ∼land [n] *country of origin*; *c. where goods come from*; ∼nachweis [m] *certificate of origin*; ∼zeichen [n] ⟨com⟩ *symbol of o., manufacturer's mark* **~stand** m *primitive state* **~ständ** f ∼/ ⟨poet⟩ *resurrection* **~stoff** m *primary element* od *matter, first principle* ‖ ⟨chem⟩ *element* | ∼lehre [f] *atomism* **~stromtal** n *urstromtal* (*glacial v.* od *spillway*)

·**Urteil** n ∼(e)s/∼e **A.** (Meinung) *judg(e)ment, opinion, views* (über *of*); gesundes ∼ *sanity* | ⟨philos⟩ *proposition* | ⟨jur⟩ *verdict, sentence*; (der Geschworenen) *verdict* (*the v. .. is guilty* lautet auf ..), *finding* ‖ (des Schiedsrichters, des Sachverständigen) *award* ‖ (Präzedenz≈) *precedent* ‖ vorläufiges *interlocutory j.* (b. Ehescheidung) (provisorisches) *decree nisi*, (endgültiges) *degree absolute* ‖ ∼ Salom·onis, des Paris *J. of S.*, *of P.* **B. nach** m–m ∼e *in my o.* od *j.*, *as far as I can judge* ‖ nach dem allgemeinen ∼ *in the eyes of the world* ‖ nach fachmännischem ∼ (*the book*) *decreed* (*the best edition*) **C.** ein ∼ **abgeben** *to express an o.*, sein .. *to give one's o.* ‖ ein ∼ (in der Berufungsinstanz) aufheben *to reverse a j.* (*on appeal*) ‖ sich ein ∼ bilden über ⟨a.⟩ *to size up* (*a p*) ‖ ein reifes ∼ erwerben *to cut one's wisdom teeth* ‖ ein ∼ fällen (gegen) *to pass* od *pronounce j.* od *sentence* (*upon*), *to s.* (*a p*) ‖ ein gutes ∼ h *to have j.*, *to be a good judge* ‖ sein eigenes ∼ h *to have a mind of one's own, to judge for o.s.* ‖ ∼ sprechen *to deliver j.*; ein (Todes-)∼ ausspr. über *to d.* (*a*) *sentence* (*of d.*) *on* (*a p*), *to return a v.* ‖ sich selbst das ∼ sprechen *to implicate o.s.* ‖ ein ∼ vollstrecken, –ziehen *to enforce a j.*, *to carry a* (*judicial*) *sentence into execution* **≈bildend** a *j.-forming*

·**urteilen** vi [h] *to judge* (über jdn nach s–n Taten etc *a p by his* [*her*], *deeds*, etc, (über etw [acc], von etw [dat] *of a th*) ‖ *to give one's opinion* (*on, about*) | **nach** etw [dat] z ∼ *judging by* od *from a th* ‖ nach s–n Reden z ∼ *according to him* ‖ ∼ **über** *to reason on*; darüber kann er nicht ∼ *he is no judge of such matters* ‖ wenn ich recht urteile *if I am any judge* ·**Urteiler** m ∼s/∼ *judge*

·**Urteils-** **~eröffnung** f *publication of a judgment*, etc **≈fähig** a *judicious, discriminating, competent*, (*a man*) *of judgment* **~kraft** f (*faculty of*) *j.*, *discernment*, (*Kant's critique of the*) *aesthetic faculties* pl; *reasoning* **≈los** a *undiscerning, injudicious* **~spruch** m *judgment*; *sentence*; *verdict*; *decree* (vgl Urteil) **~vermögen** n = –kraft **~vollstreckung** f *carrying out a sentence* ·**Urtel** n ∼s/∼ ⟨dial, poet⟩ = Urteil

·**Ur-** **~text** m *original* (*text*) **~tier(chen)** n *protozoon*, pl *protozoa* **≈tümlich** a *original, natural, innate, genuine* **~typus** m = –bild; Herstellung als ∼ *prototype work* ·**Urur-** **~ahn** m *great-great-grandfather* ‖ *progenitor* **≈alt** a *very, very old* ‖ (P) a *very advanced in years* **~eltern** [pl] *ancestors* pl **~großmutter** f ∼/≈er *great-great-grandmother*

·**Ur-** **~vater** m *forefather, first parent* **≈väterlich** a *ancestral* **~väterzeit** f *olden times* pl, *days of yore* **~vernunft** f *supreme* od *divine reason* **≈verwandt** a *cognate* °**~vieh** n *he-, cave-man* ⟨fig⟩ **~volk** n *primitive people*; *aborigines* pl **~wahl** f *preliminary election* **~wähler** m *primary elector* od *voter* **~wald** m *primeval* od *virgin forest* ‖ ⟨Am⟩ *backwoods* pl **~weib** n *primitive woman* ‖ *type of a w.* ‖ *ideal w.* **~welt** f ∼/ *primeval world* **≈weltlich** a *primeval, primordial* ‖ *antediluvian* (*animal*) **~wesen** n ∼s/∼ *primordial being* | *originality* **~wort** n *primitive word* **≈wüchsig** a *original, native* ⟨a. fig⟩, *racy* ‖ *rough*; ⟨hum a.⟩ *neolithic* **~zeit** f ∼/ *primeval times* od *period* | ≈lich [a] *p.l* **~zeugung** f *spontaneous generation* **~zustand** m *primordial* od *primitive state*; ⟨fig⟩ *germ* ‖ *original condition*

Urugu·ay m (südamerik. Fluß & Land)

Usance [y:'zã:s] f ∼/∼n ⟨com⟩ *usage, custom, practice* **≈mäßig** a *according to custom* | [adv] *as is customary* **usu·ell** a *usual* ·**Uso** m ⟨com⟩ (Wechselzeit) *usuance* **~wechsel** m ⟨com⟩ *bill at usance*

Usb·eken pl (türk. Volk in Usbekistan) *Uzbegs, Uzbecks* pl **Usb·ekistan** n

Usch·ebti m ∼s/∼ Eg „Antworter" *ushebti*

Usurpati·on [–ts–] f ∼/∼en *usurpation* **-p·ator** m ∼s/–t·oren *usurper* **u-pat·orisch** a *usurping* **u-p·ieren** vt [h] *to usurp*

·**Usus** m ∼/ *usage* ‖ ⟨fam⟩ das ist bei uns so ∼ *it's the fashion with us*

·**Utah** n (Staat der U.S.A.)

Utens·ilien [pl] *utensils, implements, tools* pl **~kasten** m *ditty-box* **Utilit·arier(in** f) m ∼s/∼ *utilitarian* ‖ Lehre [f] der ∼ *utilitarianism* **utilit·arisch** a *utilitarian* **Utilit·ät** f ∼/ *utility* **~sprinzip** n *utilitarian principle* **~srücksichten** f pl *considerations* pl *of utility*

Utop·ie [–i:] f ∼/∼n [–i:ən] *Utopian idea* od *scheme, chimera* **Ut·opien** [–iən] n ∼s/ → *Utopia* **ut·opisch** a, **Utop·ist(in** f) m ∼en/∼en *Utopian*

·**Utrecht** n (holl. Stadt)

Uzb·eken pl → Usbeken

·**uzen** vt [h] ⟨fam⟩ *to chaff, quiz, tease*; *to pull* (*a p's*) *leg* | ≈ n, **Uzer·ei** f ∼/∼en *teasing, mockery*; ⟨Am⟩ *ribbing*

V

V, v [fau] n ~/~ *V, v* || ⟨rail obs⟩ V (= vormittags) *a. m., in the morning* || **V-Form-Winkel** m ⟨aero⟩ *dihedral angle* || **V_1-, V_2-Geschoß** n *robot bomb 1* bzw *2*; V_1-Geschoß ⟨fam⟩ *doodlebug*; **V-Mann** ⟨mil⟩ *asset*; **V-Motor** m *V-type engine*; **V-Waffe** f ⟨Ger⟩ *V-weapon*

Vab·anquespiel n *matter of ne(ve)r or nothing*

Vadem·ekum [v–] n ~s/~s *v.-mecum, guide--book* || (Mundwasser)®

Vad·uz [v–] n (Hauptort Liechtensteins)

vag [v] a *vague* **Vagab·und** [v–] m ~en/~en *vagabond, vagrant, tramp* || ⟨dero⟩ *rapscallion*; *prowler* **≈enhaft** a *vagabond* **~entum** n *vagrancy, vagabondage* || [koll] *vagabonds* pl, etc **vagabund·ieren** [v–] vi [h] *to tramp about*, ⟨fam⟩ *to tramp it* **Vag·ant** m ~en/~en ⟨hist⟩ *travelling scholar* **v·age** a ⟨fig⟩ *shadowy* **V·agheit** f ~/~en *vagueness* **vag·ieren** vi [h & s] *to ramble, wander*

vak·ant [v–] a *vacant*; *unoccupied* **Vak·anz** f ~/~en *vacancy* ([gen] *in*) || (Ferien) *vacation* **v·akat** (L es fehlt) *wanting* || (Amt) *vacant* **V·akuum** [v–] n ~s/V·akua *vacuum* || unter ~ verschließen *to seal* od *stopper under v.* **~bremse** f *v. brake* **≈dicht** a *vacuumtight, v.sealed*; *hermetic* **≈gekühlt** a *v. annealed* **≈getrocknet** a *v.-dried* **~(m)eter** n *v. gauge* **~pfanne** f → Zuckerkoch– **~raum** m *vacuum* od *evacuated space* od *volume* **~reiniger** m, **~sauger** m *cleaner* **~röhre** f ⟨el⟩ *v. tube* || ~ mit 3 Elektroden *three-electrode valve* | ~nverstärker [m] *thermionic amplifier* **~schlauch** m *v. tubing* **~technik** f *vacuum engineering* od *technology*

Val·encia [v–] n (span. Stadt & Provinz)

Val·et [v–] n ~s/~s *valediction, farewell* || [dat] ~ sagen *to bid farewell* (*to*) **Val·eur** [va'lœr] f ~/~s ⟨paint⟩ *tonal value* **valid·ieren** [v–] **I.** vt [h] *to validate, to make valid* || ⟨com⟩ e–e Summe ~ l *to set off a sum against* **II.** vi [h] *to be valid* **Validit·ät** f ~/ *validity* **Val·uta** [v–] f ~/–ten ⟨com⟩ *value* (8.5.71); *currency* || *par* od *rate of exchange* || feste, veränderliche ~ *fixed, fluctuating standard* | Verlust aus ~differenz [f] *loss on exchange*, ~regulierung [f] *regulation of the currency* **valut·ieren** [v–] vt [h] *to value* **Valvati·on** [v–] f ~/ ⟨num⟩ *valuation*

Vallad·olid [v–] n (span. Stadt & Provinz)

Valpar·aiso [v–] n (Stadt & Provinz in Chile)

V·ampir [v–] m ~(e)s/~e ⟨zoo⟩ *vampire* ⟨a. fig⟩; ⟨fam fig⟩ *vamp*

Van Allens Strahlengürtel ⟨astr⟩ *V. A.'s Radiation Belt*

Vanc·ouver [v–] n (Stadt in Brit. Kolumbia)

Vand·ale [v–] m ~n/~n ⟨a. fig⟩ *Vandal* **v-lisch** a *Vandal*; *vandalic* **-l·ismus** m *vandalism*

Vand·iemensland [f–] n → Tasmanien

V·änersee [v–] m (Schweden) *Lake Vener, Vänern*

Vanille [va'niljə] f ~/ ⟨bot⟩ *vanilla* **~pudding** m *v. dessert* **~schote** f *v.-bean* **~stange** f *stick of v.* **~zucker** m *v. sugar*

Vareuse [va'rœz] f [Fr] ~stil [m] *sailor--blouse style*

V·aria [v–] pl [L] ~/ *sundries* pl **vari·abel** a *variable* (⟨comp⟩ Länge *length format*) **Vari·ante** f ~/~n *different reading, variant* **Variati·on** [v–] f ~/~en ⟨math⟩ *variation* || ⟨mus⟩ *variation, paraphrase* **~sbreite** f ⟨stat⟩ *range* **≈sfähig** a *variable* **~smerkmal** n ⟨biol⟩ *varietal character* **~srechnung** f ⟨math⟩ *calculus of variations* **Vari·anz** f ~/~en ⟨stat⟩ *variance* **Variet·ät** [v–] f ~/~en *variety* **Variété** [v–] n ~s/~s ⟨theat⟩ *variety*, ⟨Am a.⟩ *vaudeville* | ~akt [m], ~nummer [f] *turn*, ⟨Am⟩ *v.e act*; ~theater [n] *v. theatre, music hall*; ~vorstellung [f] *v.* (*show*) **vari·ieren** [v–] vt/i [h] *to vary* (nach Zeit u Ort *with* ..) || ⟨mus⟩ (Thema) *to compose* od *play variations* (*on an air*) || *to ring the changes on a th* **Variom·eter** n ⟨aero⟩ *statoscope*

Vas·all [v–] m ~en/~en *vassal, retainer* **Vas·allen- ~dienst** m *feudal service* **~pflicht** f *fealty* **~schaft** *vassalage* || (Gesamtheit der Vasallen) *vassalry, vassals* pl **~staat** m *tributary* (*state*), *satellite nation* **~treue** f *vassal fealty*

V·ase [v–] f ~/~n *vase*

Vasel·in [v–] n ~(e)s/, **Vasel·ine** f ~/ *vaseline, petrolatum*; *petroleum* od *universal jelly* | ~öl [n] *light liquid paraffin*

V·ater m ~s/≈ *father*; ⟨sl⟩ *governor* || ⟨ec⟩ ehrwürdiger ~ *Most Reverend F.* || ⟨fig⟩ ~ Winter *Old Man W.* || (T bes ⟨hors⟩) *sire* || Gott ~ *God the F.* || himmlischer ~ *our F. in Heaven*, ⟨R.C.⟩ *Holy F.* || unsere ≈ *our forefathers* || die ≈ der Stadt *the city-f.s* || er könnte ihr ~ s *he is old enough to be her father* || z s–n ≈n versammelt w *to be gathered to one's f.s, to join the majority* || → Wunsch || den strengen ~ herauskehren ⟨fam⟩ *to do the heavy father* || °das ist was f m–m ~ s–n Sohn ⟨mil⟩ *that's the stuff to give the troops* || bei ~ Philipp ⟨mil⟩ *limbered*; ~ u Sohn ⟨aero⟩ *target and drones* **~bild** n *f. figure* **~freuden** f pl *pleasures* pl *of fatherhood, paternal joys* **~haus** n *home*; *p.l roof* **~herz** n *p.l heart* **~-Kind-Beziehung** f *parenthood* **~land** n *native country*; ⟨Ger⟩ *fatherland* || f König u ~ *for king and country* || Heimkehr ins ~ *repatriation* | v·≈isch [a] *national* || (gesinnt) *patriotic* [adv *-ally*] | **~s-** ~freund(in [f]) [m] *patriot*; ~liebe [f] *love of one's* (*own*) *country*; ⟨a.⟩ *patriotism*; ≈liebend [a] *patriotic*; ≈los [a] *unpatriotic, unnational*; ~verteidiger [m] *defender of one's country* **~liebe** f *p.l love* **≈los** s *fatherless* **~-mord** m & **~mörder(in** f) m *parricide* | ⟨fam⟩ **-der** (Stehkragen) *high-wing collar* **≈mörderisch** a *parricidal* **~recht** n *patriarchate* **~schaft** f ~/ *fathership, fatherhood* || ⟨jur⟩ *paternity* ⟨a. fig⟩; Feststellung der unehelichen ~ *filiation* | ~sblutprobe [f] *blood test* || ~sklage [f] *affiliation case* **~sname** m *surname* **~stadt** f *native* od *home town* **~stelle** f *place of a f.* || ~ an jdm vertreten *to act a f.'s part by a p* **~tag** m (Himmelfahrt) ⟨Am⟩ *F.'s Day* (Mai/Juni-Sonntag) **~teil** n *patrimony* **≈- u mutterlos** a *without f. or mother* **~·unser** n ⟨ec⟩ *the Lord's Prayer*, ⟨R. C.⟩ (*a*) *paternoster* (.. beten *to say* ..) **V·äterchen** n ~s/~, **V·ati** m ~s/ *dad(dy)* **v·äterlich** a *fatherly* || (Besitz, Verwandtschaft) *paternal*; *ancestral* (*soil*) || ~es Erbteil *patrimony* || sein ~es Geschäft, Haus *his father's business, house* || ~er Stamm *parent stock* | [adv] *fatherly, fatherlike, like a father* **~erseits** [adv] *by* od *on the father's side* || ~ verwandt *agnate* **V·ati** [f] m ~s/~s ⟨fam⟩ *dad(dy), pa*

Vatik·an [v–] m *Vatican* **≈isch** *Vatican* (*City*)

V·ättersee [v–] m (in Süd-Schweden) *Lake Vetter*

vaz·ieren vi [s] ⟨österr⟩ *to move from place to place*

Veget- ~ab·ilien [v–] [pl] *vegetables* pl **≈ab·i·lisch** a *vegetable, vegetal* **~·arier(in** f), –arianer

---

Aussprache: Falls nicht anders (: [*v*]) angegeben, ist v = [*f*] zu sprechen.

[m] ∼s/∼ *vegetarian* ≈·**arisch** a *vegetarian* [attr s] ‖ ∼e Lebensweise *vegetarianism* ∼**ati·on** [v–] f ∼/∼en *vegetation*; grüne ∼ *verdure* | ≈slos [a] *barren* ≈**at·iv** [–f] a *vegetative* ≈**t·ieren** vi [h] *to vegetate* ‖ ⟨fig a.⟩ *to lead a bare existence, to rub along*

Vehem·enz [v–] f ∼/ *vehemence* **Veh·ikel** [v–] n ∼s/∼ *vehicle* ⟨a. pharm⟩; ⟨mst dero⟩ *rattle; trap*

V·eigelein n ∼s/∼ ⟨poet⟩ *wallflower* ‖ ⟨dial =⟩ **V·eilchen** n ∼s/∼ ⟨bot⟩ *violet* ≈**blau** a *violet; purplish-blue* ‖ ∼e Augen *eyes of a v. blue*; °⟨fig⟩ *as tight as a drum* ∼**dienstag** m *Shrove Tuesday* ∼**duft** m *scent* od *fragrance of v.s* ∼**fresser** m *lady-killer*, ⟨fam⟩ *masher* ∼**geruch** m *odour of v.s* ∼**holz** n *v.-wood* ∼**stock** m *v.-plant* ∼**strauß** m *bunch of v.s* ∼**wurzel** f ⟨bot, pharm⟩ *orrisroot*

V·eiling ['feiliŋ] n ∼s/ [holl] *Dutch auction*; → Auktion

Veits- ∼**bohne** f ⟨bot⟩ *kidney-bean, French bean* ∼**tanz** m ⟨path⟩ *St. Vitus's dance; chorea* L

V·ektor [v–] m ∼s/–·oren *vector* ≈**i·ell** a *vectorial*

Velin [ve'lɛ̃:, ve'lɛŋ] n ∼(e)s/ *vellum(-paper)*

†**V·elo** [v–] n ∼s/∼s; ∼**zip·ed** n ∼(e)s/∼e *velocipede*

Velours [və'lu:r] m ∼s/∼s *velours* ‖ ∼hut [m] *v. hat*

Veltl·in [f–] n ⟨It⟩ (oberes Addatal) *Valtelline*

V·ene [v–] f ∼/∼n ⟨anat⟩ *vein* ∼**nblut** n *veinous blood* ∼**nentzündung** f *phlebitis* ∼**nerweiterung** f *varicosity* **ven·ös** a *venous*

Ven·edig n [v–] *Venice* †**Ven·eter** pl (Volksstämme in Norditalien) *Veneti* [L] pl **Veneti·aner**

ven·erisch [v–] a ⟨path⟩ *venereal*; → Venus

Venezi·aner m [v–], **venezi·anisch** a *Venitian* | ≈er Meerbusen *Gulf of Venice*

Vent·il [v–] n ∼(e)s/∼e **A.** *valve* ‖ ⟨mus⟩ *stop, piston* ‖ ⟨fig⟩ *tap (emigration t.)* **B.** Einschleifen der ∼e *valve grinding* **C.** ·Ablaß≈ *blow-off valve*; Absperr≈ *shut-off v.*; ·Anlaß≈ *starting v.*; ·Auslaß≈ *exhaust v.*; *outlet v.*; **B**·oden–, F·uß–, Schn·arch≈ *snifting v.*; ·Einlaß≈ *inlet v.*; Drei-W·ege≈ *three-way v.*; hängendes ∼ *overhead v.*; K·ugel≈ *ball v.*; ·Öl≈ *lubricator v.*; Reduz·ier≈ *reducing v.*; R·ückschlag≈ *check v.*; S·icherheits≈ *safety-v.*; Steuer≈ *levelling v.*; Überström≈ *by-pass v.* ∼**klappe** f *flap-v.* ∼**kolben** m *v.-piston* ∼**leine** f *v.-cord*, ⟨aero⟩ *rip-cord* ∼**schaft** m *v. stem* ∼**steuerung** f *v.-gear* ∼**stößel** m ⟨bes aero-mot⟩ *v. lifter* od *tappet* ∼**stütze** f *v.-guard* ∼**teller** m *v. head* **Ventilati·on** [v–'tsio:n] f ∼/ *ventilation* ⟨a. med⟩ ‖ ∼smaschine [f] *air-m.*; ∼sklappe [f] ⟨bes theat⟩ *louvre*, ⟨Am⟩ *louver* **Ventil·ator** m ∼s/–t·oren *ventilator*, ⟨el⟩ *fan* ‖ Fenster≈ *whirligig-v.* **ventili·eren** vt [h] *to ventilate* ‖ ⟨fig⟩ *to discuss*; → diskutieren

V·enus [v–] ∼**berg** m ⟨anat⟩ *mons Veneris, hill of Venus* ‖ ⟨vulg⟩ *shooter's hill* ∼**gürtel** m *girdle of V.* ⟨a. fig⟩ ∼**haar** n ⟨bot⟩ *maiden-hair, adiantum* ∼**muschel** f ⟨zoo⟩ *venus*

ver.., ≈.. [pref] [lebend; insep] [bei v & Ableitungen (s, a)] **1.** (Versehen) ∼dr·ehen *to turn the wrong way* **2.** (Irrtum) sich ∼t·un *to be mistaken* **3.** (Erschöpfung) ∼brauen etc *to use up .. in brewing*, etc ‖ ∼t·un *to waste* **4.** (Nutzung) ∼pl·audern *to talk away (the time)* **5.** (Umräumen) ∼sch·ieben, ∼r·ücken *to shift* **6.** (Aus–, Überfüllen) ∼p·esten *to taint* ‖ ∼s·alzen *to oversalt* **7.** (Bedecken) ∼st·ecken, ∼b·ergen *to hide* ‖ ∼g·olden *to gild (over)* **6.** (Umwandlung) besser: ∼b·essern *to correct*; gering: ∼r·ingern *to lessen*; edel: ∼·edeln *to ennoble*; Gott: ∼g·öttern *to deify* **9.** (Aufhören) ∼gl·immen *to die away* ‖ (Sterben) ∼·atmen etc ‖ ∼h·ungern *to starve* **10.** (Gegenteil des Simplex) ∼l·ernen *to forget*; ∼·achten *to despise* **11.** ⟨emph⟩ ∼b·uchen *to book*; ∼k·ünden *to announce* **12.** [abgeschwächt] ∼d·ienen, ∼l·angen, ∼l·ieren, ∼z·ichten etc | **NB**: **Verbal-Flexion** → das jeweilige Simplex **ver-** °∼·**aasen** vt [h] *to waste, squander* ∼·**abfolgen** vt [h] *to deliver, remit; to hand over* ‖ (Papiere) *to pass* ‖ *to plant (a blow)*; ⟨fam⟩ e–m e–e ∼ *to land* od *administer a p a box on the ear* od *a rebuke* ‖ ∼ l *to let have* ‖ nicht ∼ l *to retain* ∼·**abreden** vt [h] (etw mit jdm) *to agree upon (a th with a p)* ‖ *to appoint (an hour)* ‖ *at the appointed time* ‖ *to fix (a th) up* ‖ sich ∼ *to arrange to meet (a p), to make an appointment* (⟨Am⟩ *a date*) *with*; ⟨Am a.⟩ *to date (a p) up* ‖ ich bin auf morgen mit ihm –det *I am to meet him to-morrow* ∼·**abredetermaßen** [adv] *as agreed upon, according to arrangement* ≈·**abredung** f ∼/∼en *agreement, arrangement* | ⟨a.⟩ *tryst, assignation* ‖ frühere ∼ *previous engagement* ‖ e–e ∼ h (treffen) *to have (make) an appointment* (⟨Am⟩ *a date*) (*with*); ⟨Am a.⟩ *to be a p's date* ‖ laut ∼ *by appointment* ‖ ∼ z .. *a luncheon engagement* ‖ ∼ mit Unbekanntem, –ter ⟨Am sex⟩ *blind date* ∼·**abreichen** vt [h] *to deliver, give* ‖ ⟨med⟩ *to dispense* ‖ ⟨fam⟩ = –abfolgen ∼·**absäumen** vt [h] *to neglect* ‖ *omit* ‖ *forget, fail (to do)* | vorsätzliche **V.mung** *wilful default* ∼·**abscheuen** vt [h] *to abhor, detest, loathe, abominate* ‖ *to hold in detestation* od *execration* ∼·**abscheuungswürdig** a *abominable, detestable, execrable, loathsome* ∼·**abschieden** vt [h] *to dismiss, discharge, discard* ‖ ⟨mil⟩ (auflösen) *to disband* ‖ (den einzelnen ∼) *to dismiss*; (Offizier) *to gazet out* ‖ *to place on the retired list* ‖ (mit Pension) *to pension off*; *to reduce to halfpay* | ⟨parl⟩ *to pass (a bill)* | **sich** ∼ *to take one's departure*; (bei jdm) *to take (one's) leave (of a p), to say good-bye (to a p)* | **-det** a ⟨mil⟩ *half-pay (colonel)* | **V.dung** f ⟨parl⟩ *passage* ∼·**achten** vt [h] *to despise, disdain to (hold in) scorn* ‖ *to look down upon* ‖ *to be contemptuous (of flattery)* ‖ *to brave (death)* ‖ nicht zu ∼ *by no means negligible*, ⟨fam⟩ *not half bad, not to be sneezed at* ∼·**achtfachen** vt [h] *to octuple* ∼·**ächtlich** a **1.** (z ver·achten[d]) *abject; despicable, contemptible*; (P) *worthless* ‖ *abject (apology)*, ⟨sl⟩ *snide (reference)*; *base, scummy*; ⟨sl⟩ *lous(e)y* ‖ ∼ m *to deride, flout*; *to run down*; *to expose .. to contempt*; das wird dich in s–n Augen ∼ m *that will make him despise you* **2.** (verachtend) *contemptuous, scornful, disdainful*; ⟨fam⟩ *sniffy* ‖ mit ∼em Lächeln abtun *to laugh to scorn* | [adv] ∼ behandeln *to treat with scorn*, etc; ⟨fam⟩ *to snort at, to snap one's finger at*; *to turn the scornful shoulder on (a th)*; *to snub (a p)*; auf jdn/etw ∼ herabschauen *to sneer at ..* | ≈keit [f] ∼/ **1.** *despicableness, contemptibleness* ‖ *contemptuousness* **2.** *scornfulness* | ∼machung [f] ∼/ *disparagement* ≈·**achtung** f ∼/ *contempt* ([gen] *for*), *disdain, scorn* ‖ mit ∼ strafen *to look down upon*; *to freeze* ‖ mit ∼ behandeln → verächtlich 2. ‖ jdm ∼ bezeigen etc *to turn one's nose up at a p* ‖ der ∼ [dat] preisgeben *to show up* ‖ unter ∼ v (Gefahr etc) *in the teeth of* | ≈svoll [a] → verächtlich 2.; ≈swürdig [a] → verächtlich 1. ∼·**ähnlichen** vt [h] (⟨a.⟩ sich ∼) *to assimilate* ∼**akkord·ieren** vt [h] *to job out* ∼·**albern** vt [h] *to make a fool of (a p), to pull (a p's) leg, to poke fun at* ∼**allgem·einern** vt [h] *to generalize* **V.rung** f ∼/∼en *generalization* ∼·**alten** vt [s] *to become* od *grow obsolete, to get out of date* od *fashion*, ⟨theat⟩ *to date* ∼·**altet** a *obsolete, old-fashioned, antiquitated; out of date; off the map* ‖ (eingewurzelt) *inveterate* ‖ *archaic (word)* ‖ ∼er Ausdruck *archaism* ‖ als ∼ kennzeichnen *to date*

Ver·anda [v–] f [∼/–den] *veranda(h)*; ⟨Am⟩ *porch*; ⟨S.-Am⟩ *gallery*

Verbal-Flexion der Verben mit der Vorsilbe **ver-** → das jeweilige Simplex

ver- ~·änderlich a *changeable, mutable; adjustable (resistor)* || ⟨gram, math, tech⟩ *variable;* ≈e [f] *variable* || *unsettled (weather)* || ⟨fig⟩ *inconstant, fickle* || das Barometer zeigt auf ~ *the glass points to change* | ≈keit [f] ~/ *changeableness, variableness, variability* || ⟨fig⟩ *fickleness* **~·ändern** vt [h] (→ ab–) *to change, alter;* (Reihenfolge) *to disturb* || (wechseln) *to vary* || ⟨theat⟩ *to shift (the scene)* || s–n Wohnsitz ~ *to move* | **sich** ~ *to vary, change, alter;* ⟨biol⟩ (plötzlich) *to sport;* (P) *to change one's place;* ⟨vulg⟩ *to get married;* er hat sich gar nicht –rt *he looks just the same* | (Wetter: .. z Schlechten) *to break* | sich vorteilhaft ~ *to change for the better, to improve, to find a better place;* sich nachteilig ~ *to deteriorate,* ⟨com⟩ *to fall off* || sein Gesicht –te sich *a change came over his face* | er sieht ganz –rt aus *he seems all different;* –rtes Aussehen *new look* ≈**·änderung** f ~/~en *change* || *variation* || (bauliche) *alteration* (an *to*) || *change (in* od *of the weather)* || *alteration (in a will)* || ⟨med⟩ *(tubercular) affections;* funktionelle ~ des .. *alteration in the function of ..;* ausgedehnte ~en *extensive destructions* | *what change has the house undergone?* || *what difference does this make to the light* || in der Färbung des B.s war k–e ~ z sehen *no new colo(u)r in the ground could be seen* | [pl] *chops and changes* | ~sliste [f] *modification list* N **~·ängstigen** vt [h] *to intimidate, terrify* | –gt ⟨a.⟩ *frightened, scared; cowed* **~·ankern** vt [h] ⟨arch⟩ *to grapple* || *to bind (a vault)* || ⟨mar, aero⟩ *to anchor, moor* || ⟨fig⟩ *to rivet* (in *in*) || *to em-, imbed (in)* **~·ankert** *rooted, engrained, grounded (in), inwrought (into)* ⟨a. fig⟩; ⟨fig⟩ *lodged (in),* in der Wissenschaft –rt *science-grounded* **V.rung** f ~/~en ⟨tech⟩ *stay(ing)* || ⟨mar, aero⟩ *anchoring bolts; mooring; anchorage* ⟨a. fig⟩ **~·anlagen** vt [h] (steuerlich) *to assess (.. z .. he was assessed 100 marks)* | –gt [a] *inclined* || künstlerisch ~ *artistically inclined, talented* || hoch ~ *highly gifted* || schlecht ~ *tainted* || ~ s f *to have a head for (politics), to be suited for ..* **V.gung** f ~/~en → vor. *assessment* || *talents* pl, *giftedness* **~·anlassen** vt [h] (jdn zu) *to induce, cause, bring, set (a p to do)* || *to lead (a p to suppose)* || *to make, bid (a p do)* || *what made you do it?* | (etw) *to occasion, cause; to bring about; to lead on* || *to arrange for (the withdrawal);* in dieser S ist noch nichts –ßt worden *no action has yet been taken in this matter;* mit der Bitte, das Erforderliche z ~ → **V.ssung** f ~/~en *occasion, inducement, cause* | **auf** m–e ~ *at my suggestion; by my orders* || auf wessen ~? *on whose initiative* || aus gegebener ~ *for a particular reason* | **ohne** jede ~ *without any provocation;* zur ~ an ⟨off⟩ *action addressee;* z weiteren ~ *for (necessary* od *appropriate) action (please), for the necessary attention* | **~ geben** z *to give rise to; to give a handle to (rumours);* jdm ~ geben z *to cause a p (to do);* es gibt k–e ~ dazu *there is no call for it* || **~ h**: *I had occasion to do it;* k–e ~ h: *to have no reason to do; there is no occasion for you to say so* || *you had no business to do that* **~·anschaulichen** vt [h] *to illustrate, to be illustrative* od *descriptive of* **V.chung** f ~/~en *illustration, demonstration* || Mittel z ~ *material for object-lessons* **~·anschlagen** vt [h] (auf [acc]) *to estimate, rate, value (at); to cast up* || ⟨arch⟩ *to make an estimate of* || z hoch ~ *to overrate* (so: *to underrate)* || im Budget ~ *to budget for (a th)* **V.gung** f ~/~en *estimate, valuation, calculation* **~·anstalten** vt [h] *to get up; to arrange, manage, organize, sponsor* || *to give (a banquet, concert); to put on, to stage (a show); to make (a noisy show of sympathy)* **V.ter(in** f) m ~s/~ *organizer, manager* || *host* **V.tung** f ~/~en *performance, arrangement (to make a.s); (a.s for to-day); management* || *display; (the Lord Mayor's day); proceedings* pl || *(musical) entertainment* || ⟨sport⟩ *event, fixture;* ⟨Am sl⟩ *shindig* | ~sprogramm [n] *program of activities* **~·antworten** vt [h] *to answer* od *account for* ([dat] *to*); ⟨Am⟩ *to stand for* || es z ~ h ⟨a.⟩ *to be responsible (for it)* || das w wir schon ~! *leave that to us!* | **sich** ~ *to defend* od *justify o.s.;* .. wegen .. bei: *to justify one's doings before (a p)* **v.tlich** a (P) (für) *responsible, answerable, accountable (for)* || die ≈en feststellen *to fix the responsibilities (for a crime)* || man kann I. nicht ~ m *India cannot be blamed (if)* || ~ m f *to make* od *hold (a p) responsible for (a th);* jdn .. *to fix the responsibility for a th on a p* || (P) f etw ~ s *to be in charge of;* vor sich selbst .. *to be r.ble to o.s.* | (S) *justifiable* | [adv] ~ zeichnen f ⟨com⟩ → per Prokura || ⟨fig⟩ *to make o.s. responsible for* | ≈ensyndrom [n] ⟨med⟩ *manager's disease* | ≈keit [f] ~/ *responsibility, answerableness* || *accountability (for a debt)* || gegenseitige ~ *solidarity* **V.tung** f ~/ (Rechtfertigung) *justification, defence, vindication* | (Verantwortlichkeit) *responsibility* || ~ f *charge of* | die ~ abschieben, –wälzen ⟨Am fam a.⟩ *to pass the buck* (auf *to*) || **auf** m–e ~! *I'll be answerable!* || auf Ihre ~! *at your risk! on your responsibility!* || auf eigene ~ *(I did it) on my own* || die ~ tragen f *to be responsible for; to accept responsibility for (the consequences); the burden is on you!* || ich lehne jede ~ ab *I wash my hands of it!* || jdn z ~ ziehen *to call a p to account;* ⟨jur⟩ *to impeach* | **~s-** ≈bewußt [a] *responsible;* ~freude zeigen *to enjoy one's responsibilities;* ≈freudig [a] *ready to take responsibility;* ~ s *to willingly accept r.y* | V.igkeit [f] *willingness to assume r.y;* ~gefühl [n] *feeling of r.y, regard for the r.ies placed on one's shoulders;* ≈los [a] *irresponsible;* ≈reich, ≈voll [a] *responsible (position)* || ~e Aufgaben auf sich nehmen *to accept r.ies* °**~·äppeln** vt [h] *to ridicule, quiz, tease; to sneer at;* ⟨Am fam⟩ *to horse; to run on (a p),* ⟨sl⟩ *to josh, to give (a p) the rash* **~·arbeiten** vt [h] ⟨tech⟩ *to manufacture; to work up* (zu *into*) || (Speisen etc & fig) *to digest* || ⟨fig⟩ *to ponder over* || (abnutzen) *to wear out* || *to consume* || weiter ~ *to process* ⟨a. ind, film, comp⟩ || ⟨met⟩ –tet *wrought* | ⟨fam⟩ e–n tüchtig ~ *to pull a p to pieces, to pick holes into a p* || zu ~de Daten ⟨comp⟩ *basic data* **~arbeiter** m (–fertiger) (v Halbzeugen) *fabricator* **V.tung** f ~/ *working up, manufacturing, manufacture, converting* || *digestion* ⟨a. tech⟩; ⟨tech⟩ *processing; finishing* ⟨a. phot⟩; ~ zu *conversion to* | ~sgüte [f] *workmanship;* | ~skosten [pl] *processing expenses;* ~stoleranz [f] *machining allowance* **~·argen** vt [h] (jdm etw) *to take (a th) amiss from (a p), to find fault with (a p for a th)* || es ist k–m z ~, wenn *nobody is to be blamed, if* || das kann Ihnen niemand ~! *no one can blame* (od *think the worse of) you for it!* **~·ärgern** vt [h] *to vex, annoy (a p);* –rt *annoyed* (über *at a th, with a p,* wegen *for a th);* [abs] *sullen* **~·ärgert** a *vexed, sullen;* ⟨fam⟩ *roily; put out;* ~ über *vexed with (a p);* .. (etw) *disgruntled (at), in anger, in disgust* || ~ s *to peeve;* .. über *to be exasperated by* **~·armen** vi [s] *to become* od *grow poor* | –mt [a] *reduced to poverty* || (ganz, völlig) *poverty-stricken* || –mtes Land *impoverished land* || ~mt und verschämt *shabby-genteel* **V.mung** f ~/ *improverishment, pauperization* **~·arzten** vt [h] *to attend (a patient)* || ⟨fig⟩ *to work (a p)* **~·aschen** vt [h] ⟨chem⟩ *to incinerate* **~·ästeln,** sich ~ [h] *to ramify* ≈**·äst(e)lung** f ~/~en *ramification* **~·atmen** vi [h] *to breathe one's last, to expire* **~·ätzen** vt [h] *to burn* | V.zung [f] *burn* **~auktionieren** vt [h] = versteigern **~·ausgaben** vt [h] *to spend, expend (on, for), to pay away (for)* |

Aussprache: Falls nicht anders (: [*v*]) angegeben, ist v = [*f*] zu sprechen.

sich ~ *to run out* (od *short*) *of money* ‖ ⟨fig⟩ *to spend o.s.*; *to burn one's candle at both ends* | V.bung [f] *expenditure* **~·auslagen** vt [h] *to disburse* ≃**·äußern** m ~s/~ *alienator* **~·äußerlich** a *alienable* **ver·äußern** vt [h] *to alienate* ‖ *to dispose of, to sell* **V.rung** f ~/~en *alienation, sale* | ~sverbot [n] *restraint of a.n*

Verb [v–] n ~s/~en; **V·erbum** n ~s/–ba *verb* ‖ ~ + Adverbium ⟨engl oft⟩ [vt + a + s]: *he smoked a pensive cigarette*; *he laid a tentative hand on her sleeve*; *he waved an indifferent hand* **Verb·al-** **~form** f *verbal form* **~injurie** f (*verbal*) *insult* **~note** f ⟨dipl⟩ *note verbal* **~substantiv** n ⟨gram⟩ *verbal noun*

ver- **~b·acken** reg & irr **I.** vt [h] *to make bread, etc of* ‖ *to use up* (*in baking*) ‖ *to bake* .. (zu *into*) **II.** vt/i [h & s] *to spoil* (*in baking*) ‖ [vi] *to be badly baked* **~b·alhornen** vt [h] *to transmogrify* (*make worse instead of better*) ‖ ⟨Lit⟩ → verschlimmbessern ≃**b·and** m ~(e)s/≃e **A.** ⟨med⟩ *dressing, bandage* | (Verein) *association*; (*workmen's*) *union*; Gewerkschafts≃ *trade-union* ‖ ⟨mil⟩ *unit, formation, squadron, group*, etc, *force* (gemischter ~ *combined arms unit*) Angriff im ~ *formation attack*; kombinierter ~ (der Alliierten 1944) *combined force*; ⟨mar⟩ *unit* (*afloat*) ‖ ⟨pol⟩ *commonwealth* (*of civilized nations*) | ⟨tech, arch⟩ *binding, bond* | ⟨com⟩ *combine* **B.** e–n ~ an–, ablegen ⟨med⟩ *to apply, remove a dressing* | ⟨mar⟩ im (geschlossenen) ~ fahren *to sail in company, in close formation* **~holz** n ⟨carp⟩ *framing-timber* **~kasten** m *surgeon's case, ambulance box* **~päckchen** n *first-aid packet* od *kit* **~platz** m ⟨med⟩ *field dispensary*; ⟨mil⟩ *dressing station*, f Schwerverwundete *serious wounds ambulatory* N | **~s-** ⟨aero⟩ *formation* [attr] (*bombing, flying, training*) ≃eigen [a] ⟨mil⟩ *organic*, ~flug auflösen *to break formation*; ~preis [m] *combine-price* **~stoff** m; ~e [pl] *bandaging material* **~stück** n ⟨carp⟩ *framing piece* **~watte** f *sterile absorbent cotton* **~zeug** n *dressing material*; *ambulance outfit*; *first-aid kit* **~b·annen** vt [h] *to banish* ⟨a. fig⟩, *to exile* ‖ ⟨fig⟩ *to dispel, dislodge* (*from one's mind*); *to cast* (*one's sorrows*) *away* (od *from one's mind*) ≃**b·annte** m [der ~, ein ~r] ~n/~n *exile, outlaw* ‖ als ~r *in exile* ≃**b·annung** f ~/~en *banishment* ‖ (Ort) *exile* (*to live in e.*) ‖ in die ~ gehen *to be exiled*, (freiwillig) *to expatriate o.s.* **~b·arg** 1. & 3. sg pret v verbergen **~barrikad·ieren** vt [h] (Straße) *to barricade*, (Zugang) *to block* ‖ sich ~ *to entrench o.s.* **~b·at** 1. & 3. sg pret v verbitten **~b·auen** vt [h] *to build up* (*a thoroughfare*) ‖ *to obstruct* (*the view of a house*) ‖ *to use up*, (Geld) *to spend in building* ‖ (verrammeln) *to barricade* ‖ (falsch bauen) *to build badly* | **sich** ~ *to ruin o.s.* bzw *to blunder in building* ‖ ⟨min⟩ (Zeche) *to pay* (*its way*) **~b·auern** vi [s] *to become countrified, to get into boorish ways* **~b·eißen** vt irr [h] (Baum) ⟨for⟩ *to nibble*; *to bourse on*; → –biß; ⟨fig⟩ *to suppress by an effort* ‖ *to stifle, swallow* (*one's anger* = *to bite one's lips*) | **sich** [dat] das Lachen ~ *to bite one's lips* ‖ ich konnte mir das L. nicht ~ *I couldn't help laughing* | **sich** ~ (in [acc]) *to lock the teeth in biting*, ⟨fig⟩ *to stick doggedly* od *obstinately* (*to a th*), *to be mad* (*after a th*) ‖ → verbissen **~b·ergen** vt irr [h] *to conceal*; *to hide* (a. Spiel); *to couch* (*a th in terms of* ..) ‖ (Diebesgut) ⟨sl⟩ *to plant* ‖ (P) *to secrete* ‖ *to bury* (*in one's heart*) ‖ *to harbo(u)r* (*thoughts*, etc) ‖ *not to show* od *to bottle up* (*one's feelings*) | **sich** ~ *to be in hiding, to hide* (vor *from*); .. hinter *to shelter behind* ..; .., h. dem .. *hesitation diguised as assurance* ‖ → verborgen gehalten w vor *to be kept from* (*a p*) ≃**b·esserer** m ~s/~ *improver* ‖ *reformer* ‖ *corrector* **~b·esserlich** a *amendable, corrigible, reformable, improvable* ‖ verbessert *revised* (*text, edition*) **~b·essern** vt [h] *to improve* ‖ (Fehler) *to correct*, (*a*)*mend* ‖ *to reform* ‖ ⟨arts⟩ *to touch up* | **sich** ~ *to improve* ‖ (i. Rede) *to correct o.s.* ‖ (i. Betragen) *to mend, reform* ‖ (i. Umständen) *to better o.s.* | **~d** [a] *corrective* **V.rung** f ~/~en *change for the better* ‖ *amelioration, amendment, improvement* ‖ ⟨artill⟩ (*precision*) *adjustment* ‖ (der Fehler) *correction*, ⟨Lit⟩ *emendation*; Maßnahmen z ~ *corrective measures* | **~s-** ~antrag [m] ⟨parl⟩ einbringen *to move an amendment*; ≃bedürftig [a] *needing improvement*; ≃fähig [a] *capable of i.* **~b·eten** [pp v verbitten] ‖ Blumen ~ *no flowers by request* ‖ Beileidsbesuche ~ *no visitors will be received* **~b·eugen,** sich ~ [h] (vor jdm) *to* (*make a*) *bow* (*to a p*) ‖ (leicht, tief) *to give a little, low bow, to make a slight inclination of one's head*; ⟨theat⟩ *to take a call* **V.gung** f ~/~en *bow*; *reverence, obeisance* ‖ (tiefe) *prostration* ‖ ⟨fig⟩ *genuflection* (*before*) ‖ jdn mit e–r ~ z s–m St. geleiten *to bow a p to his seat* ‖ ⟨mot⟩ (Brems≃) *longitudinal dip* **~b·eulen** vt *to batter* | –lt ⟨a.⟩ *dented* **~b·iegen** vt irr [h] *to bend* (*the wrong way*); *to spoil by bending*; *to twist, distort* | **sich** ~ *to twist* ‖ °(P) sich ~ .. *to go out of one's way* .. (Holz) *to warp* **V.gung** f ⟨tech⟩ *buckling* °**~b·iestern** vt [h] *to flabbergast* **~b·ieten** vt irr [h] (jdm etw) *to forbid a p* (*to do*) *a th*; ⟨off⟩ *to prohibit* (*a th*; *a p from doing a th*); ⟨jur⟩ *to outlaw* ‖ (Buch, Wettspiel) ⟨Am⟩ *to ban* ‖ *to suppress* (*a journal*); ⟨R. C.⟩ *to put* (*a book*) *on the index* ‖ nicht ~d *permissive*; → verbeten, verboten **~b·ilden** vt [h] *to distort, disfigure*; (sich) ~ *to form wrongly* ‖ ⟨fig⟩ *to pervert, vitiate* ‖ (falsch erziehen) *to educate* od *to train wrongly* od *badly* ‖ –det *sophisticated* | ⟨path⟩ *misshapen, deformed* **~b·ildlichen** vt -h] *to symbolize, typify* **~b·ildung** f ~/ *distortion, deformation, defacement* ‖ *wrong education* ‖ (Mißbildung) *deformity* **~b·illigen** vt [h] *to reduce* (od *bring down*) *the price of, to cheapen* ‖ –gt *cut-price* (*ticket*) **V.gung** f ~/~en *reduction in price* °**~b·imsen** → –dreschen **~b·inden** irr [h] **I.** vt **1.** *to tie, bind* (*up*) ‖ ⟨med⟩ *to bandage, dress* ‖ (vereinigen) *to unite, join* (mit *with*) ‖ (Getrenntes) *to connect*; ~ mit *to couple* (*a th*) *with* ‖ *to join, add* (*a th to*) ‖ *to join end to end* | (eng) *to link* (*a th*) *up* (*with*), *to marry* (*a th*) *to* .. ‖ (fest) *to dovetail* | *to attach* (*a meaning to a word*); zu e–r Masse *to concrete* ‖ jdm die Augen ~ *to blindfold a p*; sich .. *to blind o.s.* (*to a th*) ‖ dem Ochsen das Maul ~ *to muzzle the ox* | (P) *to pledge, engage, ally* ‖ *to bind* (*a p to do*) **2.** ⟨bookb⟩ *to misbind* **3.** ⟨el⟩ *to connect* (*to*), mit der Erde *to earth* **4.** ⟨telph⟩ *to put* (*a p*) *through* od *on* (wieder *back*) (mit *to*) (*please, put me on to 430*; *please, give me the station*) ‖ verbunden s (w) *to be* (*get*) *through* (*to*) ‖ sich ~ l mit *to get on to, to put a call through to* **5. zu** e–r Schleife ~ *to loop* **6.** (sich [dat]) [z Dank] ~ *to oblige*; *I am much* od *greatly* (sehr) *obliged to you* **7. verbunden** → d.; ~ mit *along with* (*this problem is the danger*), (*associated*) *with this* (*was this interest*) ‖ (S) ~ s mit *to be bound up with* (*interests*), *to have* (*advantages*), *to involve* (*dangers*); die damit ~en Umstände *the surrounding c.s.* ‖ *he was closely associated* (⟨fam⟩ *hand in glove*) *with them* ‖ ehelich ~ *joined in wedlock*; *wedded, married* **II.** vt/refl **(sich)** ~ (S) *to connect up* (*with*); **(unter-e-a)** *to interconnect*; ⟨chem⟩ *to combine* ⟨a. fig⟩, mit Quecksilber (Sauerstoff) [Wasserstoff] *to amalgamate* ⟨a. fig⟩, (*oxidize*), [*hydrogenize*] ‖ (sich) zu e–m Bunde ~ *to ally* ‖ durch Heirat verbunden *connected by m.* **III.** vrefl **sich** ~ *to unite, join* [*forces*] (*with a p z* .. *in doing*), *to combine* (*in*) ‖ *to form an alliance, to make common cause* (*with*) | ⟨pol⟩ *to confederate* |

Verbal-Flexion der Verben mit der Vorsilbe **ver-** → das jeweilige Simplex

⟨com⟩ to enter into partnership, to associate (with) | ⟨Am⟩ to affiliate (with) | (ehelich) to marry (mit .. a girl) | (eng) to link up (with) ⟨a. mil⟩ | ⟨tech⟩ (v Rädern) to mesh (with) | ⟨telph⟩ to get through to | | **sich jdm** ~ to oblige a p **~b·indend** a ⟨a.⟩ connective; ⟨log⟩ synthetical **~b·indlich** a binding, obligatory, compulsory ‖ (gefällig) obliging, attentive | ~sten Dank! ich danke ~st [adv]! my best thanks! ‖ jdm ~sten D. sagen to thank a p most sincerely | **sich ~ m** to bind od engage o.s. ‖ Sie h sich ~ gemacht you are in duty bound ‖ sich jdm ~ m to oblige a p (dadurch, daß .. by [doing]; durch with) ‖ (Schiedsspruch) für ~ erklären to declare to be binding | e–m etw ≗**es** sagen to pay a p a compliment | ≗keit [f] ~/~en **A. 1.** obligation, liability ‖ mündliche verbal promise **2.** binding force (of a treaty) **3.** (Kompliment) compliment **4.** (Zuvorkommenheit) obligingness, kindness; readiness to oblige; polite way; favour **B.** ~en [pl] ⟨bal⟩ accounts payable; payables; ~en h gegen jdn to be obliged to a p ‖ s–n ~en nachkommen to meet one's liabilities od engagements ‖ ⟨com⟩ ohne ~ without engagement, prejudice, liability ‖ mit gegenseitiger ~ mutually binding ≗**b·indung** f ~/~en **A. 1.** union ‖ (Zusammenhang) connexion, junction; es besteht k–e ~ zw .. there is no link between .. ‖ ⟨comm⟩ communication; ⟨mil⟩ liaison, rückwärtige ~(en) c.n(s), lines of c.n ‖ (Beziehung) relation(ship) **2.** (geschäftliche) (business) connexion, friend ‖ ⟨pol⟩ coalition, alliance **3.** (~ von Ideen) association ‖ combination (of word with word) ‖ (consonant-)comb. ‖ fusion (of theory and practice) ‖ innige ~ nexus (of interests); amalgamation ‖ ~ v Umständen juncture **4.** (~ v P) society, ⟨bes stud⟩ association, club; ⟨Am stud⟩ (secret) fraternal society, (Greek letter) fraternity od sorority (z. B.: ΒθΠ; ΚΣ; Φ Γ Δ) ‖ eheliche ~ matrimonial alliance, matrimony, marriage **5.** ⟨rail, mil, telgr⟩ communication ‖ ⟨telph⟩ connection (to sever the c.) ‖ ⟨wir⟩ (zw Sendern) hook-up **6.** ⟨chem⟩ ([un]stable) chemical composition od compound ‖ blending (of colours) **B.** in ~ mit in conjunction with, together with **C.** ~en **anknüpfen** to make contacts ‖ ⟨mil⟩ ~ aufnehmen to establish contact, to communicate (with) ‖ k–e ~ bekommen ⟨telph⟩ to fail to get a connection ‖ in ~ **bringen** mit (Ereignis) to link up od associate .. with, (P) to connect .. with (a crime) ‖ (jdn) to put a p in touch with ‖ e–e ~ eingehen ⟨chem⟩ to form a compound ‖ ⟨telph⟩ ~ **erhalten** to get through (mit to), h Sie ~? are you through? ‖ ~ h (verlieren) to be in (to lose) touch ‖ die ~ herstellen ⟨tech⟩ to establish a connection, .. mit to reach (a p); ⟨telph⟩ to put the call through ‖ in ~ kommen mit to get on to a p ‖ sich in ~ **setzen** mit to communicate with, to contact (od to get in touch with) (a p) ‖ in ~ stehen to be connected with (a th) ‖ to be in touch with (a p), (brieflich) to correspond with; .. mit to be related, kindred, akin to; connected, affiliated, associated, allied with; (Zimmer) to communicate, mit–e–a to intercommunicate ‖ ⟨telph⟩ die ~ trennen to switch off ‖ in ~ treten mit to take up od to liaison with; ⟨telph⟩ to get through to a p (on the telephone); (brieflich) to get into communication with; ~ (Kontakt) verlieren to lose touch ⟨a. mil⟩; alle ~en zerreißen to sever all contacts | **in ~ mit** in co-operation with **~b·indungs- ~bahn** f ⟨rail⟩ junction-line; loop line **~dame** f lady guest of a students' club **~drähte** m pl bonds **~flugzeug** n comm. airplane **~gang** m ⟨arch⟩ connecting passage; ⟨mil⟩ transversal gallery **~glied** n connecting link; ⟨comp⟩ interface **~graben** m ⟨mil⟩ communication-trench **~kabel** n trunk-cable **~klammer** f splicing clamp **~klemme** f ⟨el⟩ connector **~leute** m ⟨mil⟩ connecting files **~linie** f ⟨mil⟩ line of comm. **~mann** m ⟨pol⟩ contact-man, liaison agent **~muffe** f ⟨tech⟩ fixing sleeve **~offizier** m liaison officer **~punkt** m juncture **~schraube** f ⟨el⟩ terminal **~spähtrupp** m contact party N **~stange** f ⟨tech⟩ connecting rod **~stelle** f juncture, ⟨el⟩ joint **~stück** n ⟨arch⟩ tie **~student** m member of a student's club **~trupp** m ⟨mil⟩ contact patrol **~verhältnis** n ⟨chem⟩ combining proportion **~weg** m line od way of comm.; ~e [pl] z See sea lanes of comm. **~wort** n **1.** copula **2.** conjunction **~zeichen** n (bei Korrektur) close-up mark (⌒) **~zone** f ⟨mil⟩ communications zone (Com Z) **~b·irg** imp v verbergen ≗**b·irgung** f ⟨geol⟩ warping, bending; flexure; distortion **~b·iß** 1. & 3. sg pret v verbeißen | ≗ m ⟨for⟩ browsing (by game) **~b·issen** a [pp v verbeißen] ⟨fig⟩ suppressed ‖ (ingrimmig) crabbed, sour(ed) ‖ (hartnäckig) dogged; savage (fighting) ‖ ~ s in [acc] to stick doggedly to **~b·itten** vt irr [h]; sich [dat] etw ~ to decline (a visit), to beg to decline a th; sich etw ~ (ausbitten) to deprecate a th; .. v jdm to insist on a p not doing a th; .. künftig to insist on a th not being repeated ‖ das verbitte ich mir! I won't suffer od stand that!, none of that! ‖ I object to (such a treatment) | → verbeten **~b·ittern** vt [h] to embitter ‖ e–m das Leben ~ to e. a p's life, to worry a p's l. out; (s–e Antwort) –rte sie .. turned bitter in her mind | **sich** ~ to grow sullen od bitter ‖ **-rt** a (P) embittered; bitter, soured, exacerbated **V.rung** f ~/ exasperation, bitterness (of heart), embitterment **~bl·asen** vt [h] **1.** → ver– **2.** ⟨paint⟩ to dilute (colours); [a] vaporous (Malweise) **3.** to refine (metals) | ≗sein ⟨paint⟩ clouding **~bl·assen** vt [s] to grow od turn pale ‖ ⟨fig⟩ they all paled beside her | (Farbe) to fade ⟨a. fig⟩ ‖ ~ l to (make) dim (memory) ‖ (sterben) to pass away; ⟨fig⟩ he (it) pales into insignificance (gegen besides ..) ‖ –ßt washed-up (shirt); weakened (meaning), faded (metaphor) **~bl·ättern** vt [h] (Buch, Seite) to lose one's place, page ≗**bl·eib** m ~(e)s/ whereabouts (I don't know anything about the wh. of those papers = I don't know what has become of them) ‖ ⟨off⟩ z dortigen ~ for your retention **~bl·eiben I.** vi irr [s] to remain (⟨a.⟩ im Briefschluß) ‖ es verblieb mir nichts I had nothing left ‖ bei s–r Ansicht etc ~ to persist in od abide by one's opinion etc ‖ l wir es dabei ~ let the matter rest there; ~ wir dabei let's abide by it **II.** ≗ [n]; dabei muß es sein ~ h there matters shall rest ‖ hier ist m–s ~s nicht I cannot stay here any longer | ~d lingering (hope) **~bl·eichen** vi irr [s] **1.** to discolo(u)r; to grow od turn pale; to become od grow tawdry ‖ (Farbe) to fade ⟨a. fig⟩; nicht ~d fadeless (fabric), unfading (colour) **2.** ⟨poet⟩ des Todes ~ to pass away ‖ → verblichen **~bl·eien** vt [h] to lead ‖ to seal bzw alloy with l. | ≗bl·eiung [f] ~/ äußere (innere) lead coating (lining) **~bl·enden** vt [h] **1.** to dazzle, delude, infatuate, blind ‖ –det blind (love); dazzled (by one's good fortune) **2.** ⟨arch⟩ to face ‖ (verbergen, ⟨bes mil⟩) to screen, mask ≗**bl·endstein** m facing-stone ≗**bl·endung** f ~/ blindness, infatuation, delusion ‖ ⟨arch⟩ facing ‖ ⟨mil⟩ mask(ing) °**~bl·euen** vt [h] to thrash ⟨fam⟩ larrup, ⟨Am sl⟩ lam (a p) **~bl·ichen** a [pp v verbleichen] faded; dull; tarnished ‖ (gestorben) deceased ‖ Verblichene [der ~, ein ~r] & f [~n/~n] deceased, departed **~bl·ieb** 1. & 3. sg pret v verbleiben **~bl·ödet** a idiotic, ⟨Scot⟩ doited ‖ ⟨fam⟩ dotty, crazed **V.dung** f dottiness **~bl·üffen** vt [h] to stagger, dumbfound, startle, stun, amaze, disconcert, nonplus ‖ ⟨fam⟩ to floor, flummux, flabbergast; pose, stump | **~d** bewildering; startling (result) | **-fft** a ⟨a.⟩ bewildered, nonplussed | [pred] taken aback, thunder-

---

Aussprache: Falls nicht anders (: [v]) angegeben, ist v = [f] zu sprechen.

struck, struck dumb (vor *with*) ‖ ⟨fam⟩ *struck all of a heap*, ⟨Am⟩ *cornered* ‖ ein ∼es Gesicht m *to look blank* (od *taken aback*) | ≗heit [f], **≗bl·üffung** f ∼/ *bewilderment, amazement, perplexity* **∼bl·ühen** vi [h & s] *to cease flowering* ‖ (verwelken) *to wither, fade, to go off* (⟨a. fig⟩ *faded beauty*) ‖ °⟨fam⟩ verblühe! *be off!* ⟨Am⟩ *scram!* **∼bl·ümt** a *veiled, figurative, indirect* | [adv] etw ∼ ausdrücken *to hint at a th* **∼bl·uten** vi [s] & sich ∼ [h] *to bleed to death* ‖ ⟨fig⟩ (Land) *to drain away* ‖ die S ist –tet *the matter has died a natural death* °**∼b·ocken** vt [h] *to mismanage, blunder* **-ckt** a *obstinate, sulky* **∼b·odmen** vt [h] (ein Schiff) *to hypothecate* **∼bogen** a *crooked, bent* **∼b·ohlen** vt [h] *to plank* **∼b·ohren** vt [h] ⟨carp⟩ *to pin* | **sich** (in [acc]) *to bend o.s.* (*to*), *to be madly bent* (*on*), *to go mad* (*about*) ‖ ⟨fam⟩ *to be gone* (*on*) **∼b·ohrt** a *cranky; faddy* ‖ *obstinate, pigheaded* **∼b·ollwerken** vt [h] *to block up* **∼bomben** vt [h] ⟨aero⟩ *to stonk* **∼b·orgen** vt [h] *to lend out* **∼b·orgen** a [pp v verbergen] *concealed, hidden*; ⟨phys⟩ *latent* ‖ (heimlich) *secret* ‖ *covert* (*threat*) ‖ im ∼en *secretly, stealthily, on the sly* ‖ ∼ liegen *to be* (*in*) *hiding*; wohl ∼ liegen *to lie snugly* ‖ etw ∼ halten vor *to keep a th a secret from* | ≗heit [f] ∼/ *concealment, secrecy* ‖ (Zurückgezogenheit) *retirement, seclusion* ‖ die ∼ suchen *to retire from society* **≗b·ot** n ∼(e)s/∼e *prohibition, interdiction* (f *to*) ‖ *ban, taboo; injunction* ‖ *don't* ‖ ⟨jur⟩ *inhibition* (*of*), *law* (*against*) ‖ ein ∼ erlassen *to issue a prohibition*, lockern *to ease* ‖ ∼ e–r S [gen] *ban on a th*; *suppresion* (*of a book* etc) **∼b·ot** 1. & 3. sg pret v verbieten **∼b·oten** a [pp verbieten] *forbidden*, streng ∼ (*smoking*) *strictly prohibited!* ‖ Spucken, Rauchen ∼ *do not spit!, no smoking! don't → litter!* ‖ ∼e Ware *contraband goods* pl ‖ ∼er Eingang! *no admission* ‖ ∼er Weg! *private way!* | ⟨fam⟩ [adv] er sah einfach ∼ aus *he looked a perfect fright, his aspect was* (*so*) *forbidding* (*that*) **∼br·ach** 1. & 3. sg pret v verbrechen **∼br·acht** pp v verbringen **∼br·ämen** vt [h] *to edge, line, border, trim*; (mit Pelz) *to fur*; (mit Spitzen) *to lace* **V.mung** f ∼/∼en *border, edging, trimming* **∼br·annt** a [pp v verbrennen] (v der Sonne) *sunburnt* ‖ Politik der ∼en Erde *scorched earth policy* **≗br·auch** m ∼(e)s/ *consumption* ‖ übermäßiger ∼ *waste* | ≗en [vt] [h] *to consume, use* (*up*), *spend* ‖ (abnutzen) *to wear out* ‖ (erschöpfen) *to exhaust* ‖ (vergeuden) *to waste* | (Kraft) *to drain* ‖ (Nerven) *to fray* ‖ ⟨mot⟩ (viel Öl) *to be heavy on* (*oil*); –cht 12 l auf 100 km *does 20 miles on the gallon* | ∼er [m] ∼s/∼ *consumer* | ∼erleitung [f] ⟨el⟩ *service main*; ∼ergenossenschaft [f] *consumer's cooperative society*; ∼ernachfrage [f] *consumer demand*; –umfrage [f] *c. survey* **∼brauchs-** *expendable* ∼artikel [m] *article of consumption*, pl *commodities, consumer goods* pl; ⟨bes mil⟩ [pl] *articles in use*; ∼einschränkung [f] *containment of consumption* ; ∼güter [n pl] *consumer goods*; ∼material [n] *m. exp. supplies*; ∼menge [f] → Tageskopf≗ ∼soll [n] *nominal consumption*; ∼steuer [f] *excise*(*-duty*); ∼steuerbar [a] *excise-taxable, subject to e. tax*; ∼st.schuld [f] *debt of e. t.*; ∼wettbewerb [m] ⟨mot⟩ *economy run* **∼br·aucht** a ⟨fig⟩ *stale, vitiated* (*air*); *cast-off* (*clothes*); ⟨el⟩ *finished* (*battery*), [pred] *run down* **∼-br·ausen** vi [s] *to cease roaring* bzw *fermenting* **∼br·echen** n ∼s/∼ *crime*, ⟨jur⟩ *felony* ‖ (leichtes) *delinquency, offence* ‖ ⟨übtr⟩ *outrage* (*against*), *misfit* **∼br·echen** vt irr [h] *to commit* (*an offence*) ‖ ⟨fam⟩ *to perpetrate* (*a novel*) ‖ was h wir verbrochen? *what* (*harm*) *have we done?* **≗br·echer** m ∼s/∼; (**≗br·echerin** f ∼/∼nen) (schwerer *desperate*) *criminal*, ⟨jur⟩ *felon* ‖ (leichter) *delinquent* ‖ (*youthful*) *offender* ‖ erstmaliger *first offender* ‖ (Gewohnheits≗) *gaol-bird* ‖ (bewaffneter) *gangster* ‖ flüchtiger ∼ *fugitive from justice*; (überführter) *convict* | ⟨übtr⟩ (Pferd) *rogue* (⟨a. hum⟩ unartiges Kind) | ⟨sl⟩ *crook*, ⟨Am⟩ *tough, bad-man*, (Haupt≗) *big shot* | ∼album [n] *rogues' gallery*; ∼foto [n] *mug*, dazu: *to m.*; ∼jagd [f] *man-hunting* ∼karren [m] ⟨hist⟩ *tumbrel*; ∼kneipe [f] *tavern frequented by criminals*; ∼kolonie [f] *convict colony, penal settlement*; ∼laufbahn [f] *criminal career*; ∼physiognomie [f] *gallows look* | verbrecherisch [a] *criminal* ‖ ⟨jur⟩ *felonious* ‖ ∼er Akt ⟨a.⟩ *foul play* ‖ das ≗e *the criminality* (*of an action*) **V.tum** n *delinquency* **V.unwesen** n *gangsterism* **∼br·eiten** vt [h] *to spread, diffuse* ‖ (aussäen) *to disseminate* ‖ (Ansicht, Glauben, Mode) *to propagate*; die A. ist weit –tet *the view prevails* ‖ (Nachricht etc) *to divulge* ‖ (Gerücht) *to bandy .. about, to spread .. abroad, to circulate* ‖ (Nachricht) schnell ∼ *to flash* ‖ **sich** ∼ *to spread*, (Öl, Feuer) *to run*; (of news) ⟨a.⟩ *to get about* ‖ (ein Gerücht) ∼ *to bruit*; *to sow* (*doubts* über *about* ..); es hat sich das G. –tet *the rumo*(*u*)*r goes* ‖ sich ∼ **über** *to overrun* ‖ (über ein Thema) *to dilate, enlarge, expiate, descant upon* **∼breitet** *widely-held* (*opinion*), *common, popular* (*views, usage*), *general, over-all* (*custom*), *current* (*rumo*[*u*]*r*) ‖ über die ganze Welt ∼ *world-wide* **≗br·eiter** m ∼s/∼ *divulger, propagator* **∼br·eitern** vt [h] (sich) ∼ *to broaden, widen* **≗br·eitung** f ∼/ *spread*; *spreading* (*of education*); *circulation*; *diffusion* (*of cheap goods*) ‖ *dissemination* (*of knowledge*) ‖ *dispersal* (*of seeds*) (über .. hin *over*); *prevalence* (*of a disease*) ‖ (Werbung) *propagation* ‖ (e–s Gerüchts etc) *divulgation* ‖ (Ausdehnung) *extension* ‖ ⟨bot, zoo, etc⟩ (*geographical*) *distribution* ‖ (Mode) *vogue* ‖ (Zeitung, Reklame) *coverage, distribution* ‖ ∼ ⟨agr⟩ Fachkenntnisse *popularisation of rural economy* | ∼sbezirk [m] ⟨bot, zoo⟩ *habitat*; ∼sgebiet [n] *territory*; *range* (*of a plant*) **∼br·ennbar** a *combustible* **∼br·ennen** irr **I.** vt [h] *to burn* (*up*) ‖ (Leichen) *to cremate* ‖ (versengen) *to scorch* | **sich** [dat] die Finger ∼ *to burn one's fingers* ⟨a. fig⟩; so: *to sting one's hands* (an .. *with nettles*); ⟨fig⟩ *to make o.s. trouble with one's mouth* ‖ sich selbst ∼ *to set o.s. on fire* od *f. on o.s.*; [dazu:] Selbstverbrennung *act of self-buring* **II.** vi [s] *to be burnt* (*down*), *to be consumed by fire* ‖ (lebend) *to be burnt to death* **III. sich** ∼ [h] *to scald* od *burn o.s.* ‖ ⟨fam, sex path⟩ *to catch the disease* **≗br·ennung** f ∼/∼en *burning, combustion*; schlechte ∼ *imperfect c.* ‖ ⟨path⟩ *flash burns* ‖ (als Todesstrafe) *death by fire* ‖ (Ketzer≗) *auto-da-fé* ‖ ⟨crem⟩ *cremation* | **∼s-** ∼druck [m] (Rakete) *explosive thrust*; ∼halle [f] *crematorium*; ∼kammer [f] = –raum; ∼maschine [f]; –motor [m] (*internal*) *combustion engine, fuel consuming motor*; Fahrzeug mit ∼ *f. c. m. vehicle*; ∼ofen [m] *cremator, incinerator*; ∼prozeß [m] *process of combustion*; ∼raum [m] *combustion chamber* ‖ (f Kessel) *furnace*; ∼vorgang [m] *process of c.*; ∼wärme [f] *heat of c.* **∼br·iefen** vt [h] *to promise by writ, to confirm by documents* | **sich** ∼ *to bind o.s. by a deed*; (für e–n) *to stand security* | verbrieft *vested* od *chartered* (*rights*), –te Forderung *claim in security form*; ∼e Schulden *obligations* **∼br·ingen** vt irr [h] *to spend, pass* (*one's time*), *to squander* (*one's money*) ‖ (Zeit) müßig ∼ *to drone away*; nützlich ∼ ⟨fam⟩: *to put in* (*an hour* mit .. *doing*); *to transport, ship* (*goods*); (Vermögen, Wagen, ins Ausland) *to remove, transfer* **∼br·üdern** vt [h] *to unite closely* ‖ sich ∼ *to fraternize* (mit *with*) **V.rung** f ∼/∼en *fraternization* | ∼sfest [n] *feast of brotherhood* **∼br·ühen** vt [h] *to scald* **V.hung** f ∼/∼en *scald*

Verbal-Flexion der Verben mit der Vorsilbe **ver-** → das jeweilige Simplex

~b·uchen vt *to book, enter, register* || (Schiffsladungen) ~ *to tally* (*cargos*) **~b·uhlt** a *amorous*; *wanton* || (feil) *meretricious*

V·erbum = Verb || ~ fin·itum [n] [L] *finite verb*

ver- ~b·ummeln I. vt [h] (vertändeln) *to trifle away* || (vergessen) *to forget* || (die Zeit) *to loiter* od *idle away* **II.** vi [s] *to fall into idle ways, to go to the dogs* | **-lt** a *wasted* || (P) *loafing about*; total ~ *rakish* || ein ~es Genie s *to have wasted one's talents* **^~b·und-** *compound* (*steam-engine*, etc) | ~bremse [f] *all-wheel brake*; ~guß [m] *bi-metal*; ~karte [f] ⟨comp⟩ *dual purpose c.*; ~röhre [f] ⟨el⟩ *binode*; ~system [n] *strap-on arrangement* **~b·unden** a [pp v verbinden] *combined* (*forces*); *united*; Operation mit ~en Waffen *joint operation*; Führungsstand f ~e O. *joint op.s centre* || ~ bleiben mit *to stick to* (*a th, a p*) | falsch ~ *wrong number*; sich [acc] mit jdm eng ~ fühlen *to feel on peculiarly intimate terms with a p*; (ich bin Ihnen) sehr ~! (*I am*) *much obliged to you*! || ~ mit .. (*beauty*) *allied to* (*intelligence*), *incidental to, attendant on*; *life in P. entails great expense*; .. *that goes with* .. | **^~heit** [f] *affection*; (*old*) *association*; *union*; enge ~ mit (P) *deep attachment for* .. || in ~ Ihr N. *yours affectionately N.* | **^~sein** [n] ⟨a. fig⟩ *concreteness* (*of details*) **~b·ünden** vt [h] *to unite, ally* (*the allied armies*) || **sich** ~ [h] (mit) *to ally o.s.* (*with*) || ⟨pol⟩ *to league o.s.* (*with*) **V.dete** m [der ~, ein ~r] ~n/~n *ally, confederate* **V.dung** f ~/~en *alliance* **~b·ürgen** vt [h] *to warrant, guarantee* (*a th*; *that*); *to sponsor* | **sich** ~ *to answer, vouch* (*for*); *to give security* (*for*); *to undertake* (*I'll u. to say*) || (Bürge s) *to stand* od *go bail* (*for a p*) | –gt *assured, authentic, well-founded* | V–gtheit [f] *assurance* °**~b·uttern** vt [h] ⟨fig⟩ *to squander* **~b·üßen** vt [h] *to atone for* || die Strafe ~ *to undergo one's term of imprisonment, to complete one's sentence, to serve* (⟨fam⟩ *do*) *one's time* **~chr·omt** a *chromium-plated* **^~d·acht** m ~(e)s/ *suspicion* || k–n ~ aufk l *to repress s.* es besteht ~ gegen sie *s. is upon her* || in falschen ~ bringen *to slander* || ~ erregen *to arouse susp.* || wir h den stärksten ~ *we very strongly suspect* || im ~ h *to suspect* (*a p*, wegen *of*) || ~ hegen gegen *to entertain a s. of* (*a p*) || in ~ k *to excite s.* || ~ schöpfen *to grow suspicious* || im ~ stehen *to be suspected* (wegen *of*) | **auf** den ~ hin *on the strength of s.* || ⟨fam⟩ [abs] auf ~ *on the supposition that it is so*; *hoping that it will turn out a success* || **unter** dem ~ [gen] *on the suspicion of* (*treachery*) **~d·ächtig** a [gen] *suspected* (*of*); *suspicious*; (*observations*) *of a suspicious nature* || [pred] *suspect* || *untrustworthy*; ⟨fam⟩ *queer*; *fishy* (*sth f. about it*); ⟨sl⟩ *leery* || *doubtful, questionable* | ~ w *to fall under suspicion* || ~ m = ~en [vt] [h] *to throw* od *cast suspicion on* || jdn e–r S [gen] ~ *to impute a th to a p* || sich ~ ⟨jur⟩ *to inculpate o.s.* | **^~keit** [f] ~/ *suspiciousness* | **^~ung** [f] ~/~en (*making an*) *insinuation* (*against a p*) || *casting suspicion* (*on a p*) **~d·achts-** ~grund [m] *reason for suspicion*; ~moment [n] *suspicious fact*; ~person [f] *suspect* **~d·ammen** vt [h] *to condemn* || *doom*; *to cry out against* od *on* (*a th*) || ⟨ec⟩ *to damn* || ⟨fam⟩ ich will –mt s, wenn *I'll be damned, if* || Gott verdamm' mich! ⟨fam⟩ *curse me*!, ⟨sl⟩ *stop my vitals* || ⟨fig⟩ –mt s z (of activity) *to be fated to* (*cessation*) | ~swert = **~d·ammlich** a *condemnable* || *damnable* || *detestable* **^~d·ammnis** f ~/ *condemnation* || ⟨ec⟩ *damnation* || (ewige) *perdition*; *everlasting death* **~d·ammt** a *damned, cursed* | ~er Kerl! *damn the bloke*! || *beastly* (*stench*) || ~e Situation, Lage ⟨fam⟩ *pretty pass* | ⟨sl⟩ *blasted* (*church*) || ⟨vulg⟩ *bloody*; ⟨euphem⟩ *ruddy, blooming, blessed* | ~! *confound it*! *confounded*! *bother*! || ~ noch mal *or* °u zugenäht! *damn* od *dash* od *hang it all*!; (*I hope, wish*) *to hell*; (*he*) *damn* od *dashed well* (*would do it*)! | [adv] *infernally* (*hot*), *beastly* (*cold*) || ⟨fam⟩ *precious* (*dear, little*) = ⟨vulg⟩ *a fat lot*! || *jolly* (*green*); *immense* (*fine* schöne *woman*) || ⟨sl⟩ *a damn' sight* (*better, more*) || ~ schnell ⟨sl⟩ *p. d. q.* (= *pretty damn quick*) || °~ u zugenäht (*then they*) *damn well* (*ought to*) **^~d·ammung** f ~/~en *condemnation* || ⟨ec⟩ *damnation* | ~surteil [n] *sentence of condemnation*; **^~swürdig** = verdammlich **^~d·ampfanlage** f *evaporator plant* **~dampfbar** a *evaporable, vaporizable* **~d·ampfen I.** vi [s] *to evaporate, vaporize, volatilize* **II.** vt [h] *to evaporate* || ⟨fam⟩ (viel Tabak) *to smoke away* **V.pfung** f ~/ *evaporation, vaporization* | **~s-** *evaporative* | ~temperatur [f] *evaporation* od *–ting t.* **~d·anken** vt [h] (jdm etw) *to be indebted* (*to a p for a th*), *to owe* (*a th to a p*) || *to derive* (*one's fortune from trade*) || das –kt er [dat] *that is due to* (*his negligence*; man –kt .. (*the detection of gravity*) *is due to N.* **~d·arb** 1. & 3. sg pret v verderben **~d·attert** a ⟨fam⟩ = –dutzt **~d·auen** vt [h] *to digest* || mehr nehmen als man ~ kann *to bite off more than one can chew* || ⟨fig⟩ *to get over* (*a th*) **~d·aulich** a *digestible* || leicht (schwer) ~ (*not*) *easily digestible, easy* (*hard*) *to digest* | **^~keit** [f] ~/ *digestiveness, digestibility* **^~d·auung** f ~/ *digestion*; s–e ~ ist in Ordnung *his bowels act* od *move regularly* **^~fördernd** a *peptic, digestive* **Verd·auungs-** [in comp mst] *digestive* (*powers* pl, *remedy, organ, system*) **~beschwerden** f pl *indigestion, dyspepsia* **~drüse** f *organ of digestion* **~ferment** n *pepsin* **~kanal** m *alimentary canal* **^~los** a *dyspeptic* **~mittel** n *digestive* **~saft** m *gastric juice* **~schnaps** m *digestif* Fr **~schwäche** f *weak digestion*, ⟨med⟩ *dyspepsia* **~spaziergang** m *constitutional* **~stoff** m *pepsin* **~störung** f ⟨path⟩ *indigestion, dyspepsia* || *bilious attack* **~trägheit** f *sluggish digestion, s. bowel activity* **ver- ^~deck** n ~(e)s/~e *covering, awning* || (Wagen^~) *hood, cover, top* || ⟨mot⟩ ⟨a.⟩ *roof*, (abnehmbar) *canopy*; ohne ~ *topless*; das ~ öffnen *to lower the hood* || (mit Sitzplätzen) *top, roof* || ⟨mar⟩ *deck* (auf dem, das ~ *on deck* | ~koffer [m] ⟨mot⟩ *roof trunk*; ~leder [n] *leatherhood*; ~sitz [m] *top seat*; ⟨mar⟩ *deck-chair* **~d·ecken** vt [h] *to cover* (*tracks*); *to hide, screen* || (Aussicht) *to interrupt*, jdm *to cut off from a p* || (Gesicht) *to mask, veil* || ⟨mil & tech⟩ *to mask* || ⟨fig⟩ *to cloak, palliate, to black out* | **-ckt** *covered* (*dish*), *masked* (*battery*), *covert* (*way*, ⟨mil⟩ *action*), *blind* (*staircase*); *subversive* (*action* Kampf); ⟨bes Am mil⟩ ~er Kampf *insurgency warfare* N | [adv] *under cover*; ⟨fig⟩ *in veiled language* ×°**~d·eibelt** a = –teufelt *deuced* **~d·enken** vt irr [h] = verargen **^~d·erb** m ~(e)s/ *ruin, destruction, undoing* || *waste*; Kampf dem ~ *anti-waste campaign*; ..! *avoid waste*! **^~d·erben** n ~s/ *corruption*; *waste*; *decay* || (Untergang) *destruction, doom*; *fate, undoing*; ⟨rel⟩ *perdition* || (moralisches) *moral ruin, corruption* || (Unglück) *ruin* || in sein ~ rennen *to rush to one's ruin, to go over the edge* || e–m ~ bringen, e–m z ~ gereichen *to prove a p's ruin* || *to bring a country within an ace of destruction* (an den Rand des ~s) || (jdn) ins ~ stürzen *to ruin, undo* || Weg des ~s *road to ruin* **v.bringend** a *destructive, ruinous, fatal* || *ominous, portentous* **~d·erben** [–darb/–dorben] **I.** vt [h] *to spoil* || etw gründlich ~ (–pfuschen) *to make a mess of a th* || (moralisch) *to pervert, corrupt, debauch, deprave, debase* || (zugrunde richten) *to ruin, destroy* || ⟨Lit⟩ *to wreck* (*a play*) || jdm den Abend ~ *to spoil the e. for a p* || jdm die Freude ~ *to mar a p's joy* || jds Laune ~ *to ruffle a p's good h.*, *to put a p out of temper* || jdm an etw die Lust ~

Aussprache: Falls nicht anders (: [*v*]) angegeben, ist v = [*f*] zu sprechen.

to set a p against a th || Suppe → versalzen || viel ~ *to do much harm* || **sich** [dat] die Augen (den Magen) ~ *to ruin one's eyes* (*to get indigestion*) || **es** mit jdm (nicht) ~ *to fall out with a p, to incur a p's displeasure, to get on the wrong side of a p,* (*to keep in with a p*) || er will es mit niemandem ~ *he tries to please everybody* **II.** vi [s] (Ware) *to go bad*; *to spoil* || ⟨mar⟩ *to be damaged* || *to* (*go to*) *waste* || (Ei) *to addle* | ⟨fig⟩ *to be ruined*; *to decay, perish*; *to come to grief* | → verderbt, verdorben **≈d·erber(in** f) m ~s/~ *corrupter, spoiler, destroyer* **~d·erblich** a **1.** *fatal*; *dangerous*; *ruinous, pernicious, destructive*; *demoralizing* (alle: *to*) || [dat] ~ w *to prove fatal* etc (*to*) || ~er Einfluß ⟨a.⟩ *blight, blast* **2.** (v Waren) leicht ~ *perishable* | ≈keit [f] ~/ *destructiveness, perniciousness* | *perishableness* **≈d·erbnis** f ~/ *corruption, perversity, depravity* || (Unglück) *perdition* **~d·erbt** a *rotten*; *corrupt(ed)* || *corrupt* (*text*) || (verworfen) *depraved, demoralized, perverse, vicious*; *tainted* (*creature*); ⟨ec⟩ *unregenerate* | ≈heit [f] f ~/ *corruptness, corruption, perversion* || (Verworfenheit) *depravity* || (*worldly*) *pollution*; *wantonness* **≈d·erbung** f ~/ *corruption, depravation, perversion* **~d·eutlichen** vt [h] *to make plain* od *clear* || (durch Beispiele, Zeichnungen etc) *to illustrate* | **~d** a *illustrative* **V.chung** f *elucidation* **~d·eutschen** vt [h] *to translate into German* || ⟨fig⟩ *explain* || ⟨allg⟩ *to Germanize* **V.schung** f ~/~en *translation into German, G. version* || *Germanization* **~d·ichten** vt [h] *to condense, thicken, compress,* (Gase) *solidify*; *to augment* (*the* ⟨comm⟩ *coverage*); *to intensify,* dadurch wird die Aufklärung –tet *this int-fies the rec. effort* | **sich** ~ *to condense, thicken*; *to become solid, consolidated,* | etc; (*opposition*) *hardens* **V.ter** m ⟨tech⟩ *compressor, condenser* **V.tung** f ~/~en *condensation, concentration* || *compression, solidification* | ~s-faktor [m] *packing f.*; ~sraum [m] ⟨mot⟩ *swept volume of piston, clearance v.* (*of cylinders*); ~s-verhältnis [n] (optimales *highest useful* od *optimum*)) *compression ratio* (*HUCR*); ~szündung [f] *c.n ignition* **~d·icken** vt [h] & sich ~ *to thicken, condense* || *to boil down* || *to turn into jelly* || ⟨chem⟩ *to inspissate* | V.kungsmittel [n] *thickening agent* **~d·ienen** vt [h] (Geld) *to gain, earn* (durch *by*), *to be worth* (*£ 10 a day*) || genug ~ *to pay one's way* || gut ~ *to be doing well, to make a good living*; *to pick up a profit*; jdn (besser) zu ~ geben *to get a p into* (*better*) *money* || dabei ist nichts zu ~ *there is no money in that* || **an** [dat]: *to cash in on* (*a th*); *to make m. out of* (*a p, a th*), viel .. *to do well out of* | **durch**: *he earned much praise by it* | **womit** *or* wie hat er das –nt? *what has he done to deserve that*? | ein Vermögen ~ *to make one's fortune* | (Belohnung, Lob, Strafe etc) *to deserve, merit* || *deserving of our consideration* || h wir das um Sie –nt? *have we deserved that from you*? || etw nicht ~ *to be unworthy* (*of*) *a th* | er hat es wohl –nt ⟨Am fam⟩ *he has it coming to him* | (Aufmerksamkeit) *to claim* || es verdient bedacht z w *it is worth considering*; so: *he is worthy* (*to be considered* od) *of consideration* || mehr Glück ~ als h *to be more deserving than lucky* || e–m geben, was er –nt *to give one his deserts* | **sich** verdient m **um** *to deserve well of* || → verdient **≈diener** m in der F. *family breadwinner* **Verd·ienst 1.** m ~es/ *profit, gain*; *earnings* pl; [österr] *earned income* || mein ganzer ~ *all I make* (*by it*) **2.** n ~es/~e *merit, desert, worth* (*a man of highest w., great merit* od *deserts*); das zweifelhafte ~ *the dubious hono(u)r* (*of doing*) || ~e [pl] um *services to* (*one's country*) | **nach** ~ *deservedly* || jeder nach s–m ~ *each man to his own reward* || nach ~ behandelt w *to get one's due* || nicht ohne ~ *not undeserving* | **es** ist dein ~, daß *it is owing to you that* || **es** sich (jdm) als ~ anrechnen *to take* (*give a p*) *credit* (*for doing*), *to count it one's* (*his*) *glory* (*to do*) | **sich** [dat] ~e erwerben um *to deserve well of*; er hat sich durch sein Wissen gr ~e um das Geschäft erworben *the firm is greatly indebted to him for his knowledge* **~adel** m *title of nobility* (⟨engl⟩ *peerage*) *attained by merit* **~aristokratie** f ⟨a.⟩ *meritocracy* **~ausfall** m *broken time* **~kreuz** n, ~medaille [f] *Distinguished Service Cross* bzw. *Medal* **≈lich** a *creditable*; *deserving* **≈los** a *destitute of merit, undeserving* || ⟨com⟩ *unprofitable* **~spanne** f ⟨com⟩ *margin* **≈voll** a *deserving, distinguished*; *worthy* (*man*); (*th*) *of merit* **verd·ient** a (P) *deserving, hono(u)red* (*man*), (*man*) *of merit*; ⟨DDR⟩ ~er Aktivist *hono(u)red a.* || (S) *deserved, merited* || *well-earned* (*rest*) || *well-deserved, condign* (*punishment*) | ~ h *to deserve* (*a thrashing*); sich ~ m bei *to make a meritorious contribution to* (*a th*), dabei .. *his efforts in this direction were worthy of merit* | **~erm·aßen** [adv] *deservedly*

verdieseln vt [h] ⟨rail⟩ *to change to diesel working,* ⟨Am⟩ *to dieselize*

Verd·ikt [v–] n ~(e)s/~e ⟨jur⟩ *verdict*

ver- **≈d·ing** m ~(e)s/ **1.** *hiring out* **2.** *contract*(*ing for work*) || im ~ *by contract* || in *or* auf ~ nehmen *to contract for* | ≈en [vt irr & reg] [h] *to put out* (als Diener *to service,* bei *with*) || (vermieten) *to hire* od *let out* || (Arbeit) *to put out* (*work*) *by contract, to contract for* .. | **sich** ~ *to engage o.s.* (*to*), *to enter service* (*with*), *to hire o.s. out* || (als Matrose) *to ship* || (als Lehrling) (bei) *to bind o.s. apprentice* (*to*) | ≈lichen vt [h] *to hypostatize* | ~ung [f] ~/~en *hiring* (*out*) || *agreement, contract* **~d·irb** [imp] v verderben **~d·olmetschen** vt [h] = dolmetschen **~d·onnern** vt [h] ⟨fam⟩ *to sentence, to condemn*; zu 40.– M *to fine a p 40 marks* **-rt** a *thunderstruck* | [adv] *tremendously* (*fast,* etc); ~ viel .. *an awful lot of* (*money*) || ~ dastehen *to stand and stare* **~d·oppeln** vt [h] *to* (*re*)*double* (*one's zeal*) || *to quicken* (*one's pace*) **≈d·opp(e)lung** f ~/~en *doubling, duplication* || ~ der Versicherungssumme *double indemnity* **~d·orben** a [pp v verderben] (Ware etc) *spoiled*; *unsound* (Obst) || *polluted* (*supplies*) || *vitiated* (*air*), *addled* (*egg*), *tainted* (*meat*), *putrid* (*water*) | (P) *corrupted, depraved, debauched* || an ihm ist ein Jurist ~ *he would have made a good lawyer* || er ist z Juristen ~ *he has not the making of a l.* || dazu ist er ~ *he is not fit for it* | ≈heit [f] ~/ **1.** *spoilt state, deterioration* **2.** = Verderbtheit **~d·orren** vi/t [s/h] *to dry up, wither* **~dr·ahten** vt [h] *to wire* (*a place*) **~dr·ängen** vt [h] *to push* od *drive away, to crowd out*; ⟨jur⟩ *to oust, extrude* (*from*) || ⟨mil⟩ *to dislodge* || ⟨tech⟩ *to displace* (*water*); *to replace,* –gt w durch *to be r.d by* || ⟨fig⟩ *to supplant* (*a rival*), *to supersede* (*a craft*) || *to repress* (*instincts*) || aus s–m Besitz ~ *to dispossess* || jdn ~ bei *to cut a p out with* **-gt** ⟨a.⟩ *repressed* (*instincts*) **V.gung** f ~/ *displacement* (bes. Wasser≈) || *supplantation* || *dislodgement* || *dispossession* || ⟨psych⟩ *repression, inhibition* **~dr·eckt** a *filthy, soiled* || → dreckig **~dr·ehen** vt [h] *to twist* || (gewaltsam) *to wrench, skew* | *to put* (*a lock*) *out of order* || (Glied) *to sprain* || die Augen ~ *to screw* od *turn up* (od *roll*) *one's eyes* | ⟨fig⟩ *to misrepresent, pervert, distort* (*the meaning of*) || (dem Sinne nach) *to misinterpret*; *pervert, distort, warp, twist*; *to put a false construction* (*on*), *to give a f. colo*(*u*)*ring* (*to*) || *to wrest* (*the law to suit o.s.*) || jdm den Kopf ~ *to turn a p's head* || das Recht ~ *to pervert justice* || (Worte) *to wrest* | **-ht** a °⟨fig⟩ *dotty, cranky, odd, crochety*; ⟨bes Scot⟩ *daft,* ⟨Am sl⟩ *woozy* (*p*), [pred] *off one's chump, cracked,*

Verbal-Flexion der Verben mit der Vorsilbe **ver-** → das jeweilige Simplex

crazy; ⟨sl⟩ *balmy* | *queer* (*head*) ‖ *mad* (*plans*) **V.hung** f ~/~en *distortion*; *sprain*; *twist* ⟨a. fig⟩ ‖ ⟨fig⟩ *misrepresentation* ‖ *perversion* (*of facts*) | ~sbeanspruchung [f] ⟨mech⟩ *torsional stress*; ~sfestigkeit [f] *t.l strength*; ~skünste [f pl] *sleights and tricks* **~dr·eifachen** vt [h] (sich) *to treble*, *triple* **~dr·eschen** vt (⟨fig⟩) *to* (*give a p a good*) *trash*(*ing*), (*to give it a p hot*), (*to give a p beans*); (⟨fam⟩ *to dust a p's jacket*; ⟨sl⟩ *to lick*, ⟨Am⟩ *lam*) **~dr·ießen** vt & imps [–droß/–drossen] [h] *to vex*, *annoy*, *disgust*, *grieve*, *irk* ‖ **es** verdrießt mich *it grieves*, etc *me* ‖ er ist (es hat ihn) verdrossen, daß .. *he feels vexed at your not writing* | **sich** etwas nicht ~ l *not to shrink from a th*, *not to be discouraged by a th* ‖ sich (nichts *or*) k–e Mühe ~ l *to spare* od *grudge no pains* **~dr·ießlich** a **1.** (S) *vexatious*, *tiresome*, *annoying*, *troublesome*; *unpleasant*; *untoward* **2.** (S) *morose*, *peevish*, *ill-humoured*, *sore*; *edgy*; *testy*; *sulky*; *petulant*; *saturnine*; *gloomy*; *bilious*; *out of sorts*; *irksome*; *depressed*; überaus ~ *as cross as two sticks* ‖ (ärgerlich) (über [acc]) *vexed* od *annoyed* (*about* od *by*) | [adv] (*to look*) *glum* ‖ ~ blickend *beetle-browed* ‖ ~ stimmen *to jar upon* (*a p*) | ≈keit [f] ~/~en *troublesomeness*, etc ‖ [konkr] *bother*, *annoyance*, *vexation* (*to cause a p b.*, *a.*, *v.*) **~dr·oß** 1. & 3. sg pret v verdrießen **~dr·ossen** a [pp verdrießen] = verdrießlich 2. ‖ ⟨a.⟩ *fretful* ‖ *lazy* ‖ (unlustig) *listless*, *reluctant* | [adv] ⟨a.⟩ *with a bad grace* **~dr·ucken** vt [h] ⟨typ⟩ *to misprint* ‖ (verbrauchen) *to use up* od *spend in printing* **~dr·ücken** vt [h] **1.** *to crumple*, *crush*, *crease* **2.** ⟨fam⟩ *to devour* **3.** °**sich** ~ *to decamp*, ⟨mil⟩ *to go awol*; ⟨Am sl⟩ *to skidoo* ≈**dr·uß** m –sses/ **A. 1.** *displeasure*, *discomfort*, *vexation*, *annoyance*, *trouble*, *chagrin* **2.** [konkr] *bother*, *unpleasantness* ‖ ⟨hum⟩ e–n ~ h *to be hunch--backed* **B.** (jdm) ~ bereiten *or* m *to give trouble*, *to vex*, *annoy* ‖ mit ~ tun *to do reluctantly* (od *with a bad grace*) ‖ jdm etw z ~ tun *to do a th to spite a p* ‖ z s–m ~ *to his dismay* od *chagrin* ‖ z m–m ~ sehe ich *I am annoyed to see* **~d·uften** vi [s] *to evaporate* ‖ °⟨fam⟩ *to make o.s. scarce*; *to scuttle*, *bolt*, *decamp* | ⟨sl⟩ *to hop* od *beat it*, *to clear out*, *to buzz* od *take off*, ⟨Am⟩ *to skedaddle*, *vamoose* ‖ °–te! *hop it*! ⟨Am⟩ *scram*! *skidoo*! ‖ bei Nacht mit allem ~ ⟨fam⟩ *to shoot the moon* **~d·ummen 1.** vt [h] *to make stupid*; *to hebetate*, *stultify*, *besot* ‖ (viehisch) *to brutalize* **2.** vi [s] *to become stupid*, etc, *to get dull* **-mt** a *stupefied*, *besotted* **V.mung** f ~/ *stultification*; *brutalization* ‖ ~smethode [f] *obscurantism* **~d·umpfen** vi [s] *to grow stuffy*, ⟨mus⟩ *hollow*, ⟨fig⟩ *callous*, *blunt* **~d·ungen** pp v verdingen **~d·unkeln** vt [h] *to obscure*, *darken*, *becloud* ⟨a. fig⟩ ‖ ⟨theat⟩ *to dim* ‖ ⟨astr⟩ *to eclipse* (⟨a. fig⟩ = überstrahlen); ⟨fig⟩ *to outshine*, *blur*, *film*, *overshadow* ‖ (v Wolken u ⟨fig⟩ v Kummer etc) *to cloud* | ⟨mil⟩ [a. abs] (völlig) *to black-out* (⟨phot⟩ *a window*) ⟨a. theat⟩, teilweise ~ *to brown out* | **sich** ~ *to darken* ⟨a. fig⟩ ‖ (durch Wolken) *to cloud* (*up*, *over*) ‖ *the sky becomes overcast* ‖ ⟨fig⟩ *to pale*; *to cloud* **V.lung** f *darkening*, *obscuring* ‖ *obscuration* ‖ (geistige) *obfuscation* ‖ (des Sachverhalts) *collusion* ‖ ⟨mil⟩ *blackout* ⟨a. theat⟩ ‖ ⟨astr; fig⟩ *eclipse* | **~s-** **~gefahr** f ⟨jur⟩ *danger of collusion*; ~ verhüten *to prevent any prejudice to the course of justice* **~grenze** f ⟨mil⟩ *light line* **~lampe** f *blackout lamp* od *light* ≈**manöver** n ⟨fig⟩ *collusion* **~material** n *dark curtain material* ≈**übung** f *trial black-out* ≈**vorschriften** f pl *blacking-out instructions* pl ≈**zeit** f *blackout period* **~d·ünnen** vt [h] *to attenuate*, *thin*, ⟨cul⟩ *to thin out* ‖ (Flüssigkeiten) *to dilute*; mit Wasser *to water* ‖ (Farben) *to temper* ‖ (Gase) *to rarefy* ‖ ⟨fig⟩ *to attenuate* | **sich** ~ *to thin*, (allmählich) *to taper* (*off*) ‖ **-nnt** a *weak* (*solution*) °**~dünnisieren** vt [h] sich ~ = verduften ⟨sl⟩ **V.nung** f ~/~en *thinning*, *attenuation*, *dilution*; ohne ~ *without having to be diluted* ‖ *rarefaction* ‖ °bis zur ~ *till one gets sick of it*, *to the end of the last chapter* | ~smittel [n] *thinner*; *diluent* | (leicht) **~dunstbar** a *volatilizable* **~d·unsten** vi [s] *to evaporate*, *exhale*; *volatilize* **V.ter** m (im Zimmer) *humidifier* **V.tung** f *volatilization*; durch ~ aus d. Meer gewonnenes Salz *solar salt* | **~s** ~eis [n] *evaporation ice*; ~kälte [f] *cold due to evaporation*; ~messer [m] *psychrometer* **~d·ünsten** vt [h] ⟨chem⟩ *to evaporate*, *vaporize* **~d·ürbe** 1. & 3. p sg subj. pret v verderben

Verd·un [verˈdœ̃] n ⟨Fr⟩ (Stadt, im ersten Weltkrieg [1916] heldenhaft verteidigt)

Verd·üre [v–] ~/~n Fr (⟨bes⟩ *tapestry-*) *verdure*

ver- **~d·ursten** vi [s] *to starve*, *perish*, *die with thirst* ‖ ~d *parched* (*with thirst*) **~d·üstern** vt [h] (sich) ~ *to darken*, *dim*, *cloud* ‖ **-rt** a ⟨fig⟩ *gloomy* **~d·utzen** vt [h], –tzt m = verblüffen; –tzt *nonplus*(*s*)*ed*; *at a nonplus*; ⟨Am sl⟩ *balled-up* ‖ –tzt aussehen *to look sheepish*, *aghast*, *puzzled* ‖ –tzt s *to be taken aback* | [adv] ~ dreinschauend *agape* **≈·ebben** vi [s] *to subside*; (of wind) *to die down* od *away*; (of tumult, etc) *to spend itself* ≈**·ebnung** f *planation* | ~sfläche [f] *erosional surface* **≈·ecktes** Gehörn *buck's horns in his 2nd year* **≈·edeln** vt [h] *to ennoble*; (moralisch) *to elevate*; (zieren) *to adorn* ‖ *to process*, *finish* (*goods*) ‖ (verfeinern) *to refine* ‖ ⟨agr⟩ *to breed* (*cattle*); *to improve* (*horses*) ‖ ⟨hort⟩ *to graft*, *improve* (*trees*) ‖ ⟨fig⟩ *to cultivate*, *sublimate* | **sich** ~ *to improve* **V.dler** m ⟨m. m.⟩ *improver* ≈**·ed(e)lung** f ~/~en *improvement*, *refinement*; *processing*; *cultivation*; ⟨met⟩ *age-hardening* ‖ (Erz) *enrichment* ‖ **~s-** *finishing* (*industry*); ~sanlage [f] ⟨agr⟩ *seed cultivating plant*; ~gut [n] *goods for pr.g* ⟨a. cust⟩; ~svorgang [m] *refining process* **≈·ehelichen** vt [h] & sich ~ *to marry* ‖ sich ~ ⟨a.⟩ *to get married* ‖ Hanna R., verehelichte H. *Jane Roper*, *by marriage Mrs. Hunt* **V.chung** f ~/~en *marrying*, *marriage* **≈·ehren** vt [h] *to respect*, *honour*, *revere*, *reverence*, *venerate* ‖ (anbeten) *to worship*, ⟨fig⟩ *to admire*, *adore*; abgöttisch ~ *to cherish to the point of idolatry* | **jdm** (etw) ~ *to make a p a pr·esent of*, *to pres·ent a p with* **V.rer(in** f ~/~nen) m ~s/~ (der Gottheit) *worshipper* (⟨a. fig⟩ *Goethe w.*) ‖ (Anhänger) *partisan* ‖ (Liebhaber) *adorer*, *admirer*, *lover*; *follower*; *bean* ‖ ⟨fig⟩ (jds) ~ s *to admire* (*a poet*) ‖ ein ~ des schönen Geschlechts *a gallant lover of the sex* ‖ ⟨fig⟩ *devotee* (*of photography*) | ~post [f], ~zuschriften [f pl] *fan mail* | **v.rlich** a *estimable*, *honoured* ‖ Ihr ~es Schreiben *your kind letter*, ⟨com⟩ *your favour* **v.rt** a *honoured*, *estimable* ‖ (sehr) ~er Herr N.! (*dear*) *Sir*, *dear N.*, ~ Herr Doktor! *dear doctor*! **V.rung** f ~/~en *reverence*, *veneration* | (Anbetung) *worship* (⟨a. fig⟩: *nature-w.*); ⟨a. fig⟩ *adoration*; ⟨fig⟩ *admiration* ‖ m–e hohe ~ *my great respect* (f *for*) | ≈swürdig [a] *venerable*, *respectable*, *honourable*; *adorable* | [pred] *worthy of profound respect* **≈·eid(ig)en** vt [h] *to administer* od *tender an* od *the oath to a p*, *to put a p* (*up*)*on* (*his*) *oath* ‖ (Zeugen) *to swear* ‖ (Amtsantritt & ⟨mil⟩) *to swear in* | **-det, -digt** a *sworn* (*in*) **V.d(ig)ung** f ~/~en *swearing*(*-in*), *attestation*

Ver·ein m **1.** [abstr] *union*; *alliance* ‖ im ~ mit *in company* od *conjunction with*, *together with* **2.** (Gesellschaft) *association*, *society* ‖ (nicht-) eingetragener ~ *membership corporation* (*m.p association*) ‖ (geselliger) *club*; *sociable* ‖ ⟨fam fig⟩ ein toller (etc) ~! ⟨sl⟩ *a damned show* od *lot* ‖ ⟨tax⟩ Nonprofit-~ *nonprofit-making organization* ≈**bar** a *compatible*, *consistent* (*with*) ‖

Aussprache: Falls nicht anders (: [*v*]) angegeben, ist v = [*f*] zu sprechen.

schlecht ~ s *to consist ill* (*with*) ≈**baren** vt [h] *to agree upon* ‖ *to arrange* ‖ *to reconcile* ‖ *to stipulate* (*that*; *qualities*); *concert* ‖ (daß) *to make an agreement* (*with a p*) (*that*) ‖ sich ~ l *to be consonant, to square, blend* (*with*); etw mit .. ~ wollen *to square a th with*; schwer z ~ *hardly compatible* ≈**bart** a *concerted* (*action*) ‖ (*for pay*) *agreed upon* ‖ wir h .. ~ *we have discussed* £ 50 *per week* ~**barkeit** f ~/ *compatibility* ~**barung** f ~/~en *arrangement, agreement*; nach ~ *by a.* od *a.*; ~en treffen *to* (*come to* od) *make an a.* od *a.* (*with a p*) ‖ laut ~ *as arranged* ≈**fachen** vt [h] *to simplify*; *reduce* (Förmlichkeiten); *to ease* (*a problem*) ~**fachung** f ~/~en *simplification* ‖ wirtschaftliche ~ *rationalization* ≈**(ig)en** vt [h] *to join, unite, unify*; *fuse, merge*; *weld*; *link*; *combine, coalesce*; *synthesize* ‖ (einverleiben) *to incorporate* (*with*) ‖ ⟨com⟩ (Geschäfte, Interessen) *to consolidate* ‖ (Eigenschaften) *to combine* ‖ (versammeln) *to assemble*; (Strahlen) *to focus* ‖ (zus-passen) *to fit together* ‖ (in Einklang bringen) *to reconcile* (*with*) ‖ (Bemühungen) *to coordinate* ‖ ⟨mil⟩ (Feuer) *to concentrate* ‖ (Kräfte) *to pool* ‖ etw mit etw ~ *to add a th to a th* ‖ in sich ~ *to embody* ‖ (Stimmen) auf sich [acc] ~ ⟨pol⟩ *to gain* | **sich** ~ *to join* (*forces*), mit ⟨mil⟩ *to link up with*, (wieder *to re-*)*unite* ‖ (Flüsse, Linien etc) *to meet* ‖ (zur Verfolgung gemeinsamer Interessen) *to associate, combine* ‖ (in e–m Klub etc) *to corporate* ‖ ⟨mil⟩ *to effect a junction*, (wieder) *to rally* ‖ ⟨chem⟩ *to combine* ‖ ⟨fig a.⟩ *to conspire* ‖ sich ~ mit ⟨Am a.⟩ *to tie* od *team up with* (*a p*) ‖ sich mit–e–a ~ *to merge* ‖ sich ~ l mit *to be compatible with* | ≈**t**: mit ~en Kräften *with* (*our*, etc) *united strength* od *combined efforts, at* (*our*) *joint expense* ‖ ~es Handeln *joint* od *concerted action* ‖ eng ~ s *to be serried* | ≈**igt**: die ≈en Staaten v N.-A. *the United States of North America* [sg konstr] (abbr U.S.A.), ⟨Am a.⟩ *the Union* ≈**heitlichen** vt [h] *to unify, standardize* ~**heitlichung** f *regularization, typification, unification*, etc ‖ ~ der Handelspolitik *achievement of a uniform commercial policy* **Ver·einigung** f ~/~en *union, junction, combination* ‖ (innige) *fusion, amalgamation* ‖ *confluence* (*of rivers*) ‖ ⟨pol⟩ *coalition, alliance, confederacy* ‖ (Verein) *association*, etc ‖ (Treffen) *meeting, gathering, assembly* ‖ ⟨com a.⟩ *pool* ‖ ⟨jur⟩ ~ v 2 oder mehr Pn zu rechtswidrigem Handeln *conspiration* ~**sort** m *place of assembly*, etc; *meeting-place* ~**spunkt** m *point of union* (⟨fig⟩ *of agreement*) ‖ *rallying-point*; *juncture* ‖ ⟨mil⟩ *rendezvous* ‖ ⟨phys⟩ *focus* ~**srecht** n = Vereinsrecht **ver-** ~·**einnahmen** vt [h] *to take in* **Ver·eins-** ~**abend** m *club-night* ~**gebiet** n ⟨Ger hist⟩ *states* [pl] *belonging to the* Zollverein ~**haus** n *club-house* ~**kasse** f *society-funds* pl ~**meier** m *lover of club-life* ~**mitglied** n *member of a society* ~**recht** n *freedom of association*; *right of combination* ~**register** n *r. of membership corporations* ≈**staatlich** a *United States* [attr] ~**wesen** n *unions and associations* pl ‖ *cooperative movement* od *system* ‖ (Arbeiter≈) *unionism* **ver-** ~·**einsamen** **1.** vt [h] *to isolate* **2.** vi [s] *to become isolated, solitary, lonely* **V.samung** [f] *loneliness* ~·**eint** a → –einen | ≈e Nationen *UNO*, → Organisation | ≈**blütler** [m] ⟨bot⟩ *composite* ~·**einzeln** vt [h] (jdn) *to isolate* (*a p*) ‖ *to separate, detach* ‖ *to take* od *treat separately* ‖ *to spoil* (*a pair* od *set*) ~·**einzelt** a *sporadic, isolated* (*case*); *odd* (*number*); *stray*(*ing*) (*piece*); *scattered* (*names*), *rare* (*trees*); *desultory* (*snow flakes*, ⟨mil⟩ *fire*) | [adv] *sporadically, here and there, now and then* ‖ ~ auftretend *sporadic* ‖ ~ liegen *to be scattered* ‖ ~ Regen ⟨meteor⟩ *scattered showers* ~·**eisen** vi/t [s & h] *to freeze, congeal* ‖ ⟨aero⟩ *to ice-up* ‖ –st *ice-bound, icy* (*road*), *glazed* (*r.-surface*) ‖ ⟨geol⟩ *glaciated* **V.sung** f ~/~en *congelation* ‖ ⟨bes aero⟩ *icing*(*-up*) ‖ ⟨geol⟩ *glaciation* ‖ ⟨aero⟩ Mittel gegen ~ *de-icer* ~·**eiteln** vt [h] (Absichten) *to frustrate, foil, prevent, checkmate, thwart, baffle* ‖ (Plan) *to defeat, kill* ‖ (Hoffnung) *to disappoint, shatter* ‖ ⟨mil⟩ *to repel* ‖ e–n Plan (völlig) ~ *to disconcert a plan*; jds Pläne ~ ⟨fig⟩ *to spike a p's guns, to cook a p's goose* ‖ z ~ suchen *to discourage*; *to pour cold water on, to throw a wet blanket over* .. ≈·**eitelung** f *frustration* ~·**eitern** vi [s] *to fester, suppurate* ~·**ekeln** vt [h]; jdm etw ~ *to disgust a p with a th* ‖ *don't put me off my food*! ~·**elenden** vi [s] *to grow miserable* od *wretched, to sink into poverty and squalor* | V.dung [f] ~/ (*increasing*) *misery*; *pauperization* ~·**enden** vi [s] ⟨hunt, agr⟩ *to die, perish* ~·**enge(r)n** vt/refl [h] *to narrow* | vt *to straiten* ‖ (zus–ziehen) *to contract* ‖ –gte Fahrbahn ⟨mot⟩ *road narrows* pl | V.g(e-r)ung [f] ~/~en *narrowing, straitening* ‖ *contraction* ‖ ⟨path⟩ *stricture* ≈·**engländerung** f ~/ *Anglomania* **v.lischen** vt [h] *to anglicize* ~·**erben** vt [h] *to transfer by will*; *to leave, bequeath* ‖ ⟨fig⟩ (Krankheit, Anlage) *to transmit* (*to*) ‖ *to hand down* (*a tradition*) | **sich** ~ (erblich s) *to be hereditary* ‖ sich ~ (auf [acc]) *to devolve* (*up*)*on*; *to descend, to be handed down*; (Titel) *to transmit* (*to*) ~·**erblich** a *inheritable* ‖ *transmissible* ‖ *hereditary* ≈·**erbung** f ~/~en *leaving* ‖ (⟨biol⟩ *hereditary*) *transmission* ‖ *heredity* ‖ ⟨biol⟩ *heredity, inheritance*; ~ u Umgebung ⟨biol⟩ *nature and nurture* | ~**s-** *genetic* | ~gesetz [n], ~theorie [f] *law, theory of heredity*; ~keim [m] ⟨biol⟩ *gene*; ~lehre [f] *genetics*; ~wissenschaftler [m] *geneticist*; –ftlich [a] *genetic*(*al*) ~·**erzen** **1.** vt [h] *to mineralize* **2.** vi [s] (& sich ~) *to turn to ore* **V.zung** f *mineralization* ~·**ewigen** vt [h] (Zustand) *to perpetuate* ‖ (unsterblich m) *to immortalize, eternize* ‖ ⟨fam⟩ sich ~ *to inscribe one's name* | **-gt** a (verstorben) *deceased, departed, late*, der ≈e *the deceased* **V.gung** f *perpetuation* ≈**f·ahren** n ~s/~ *proceeding*; *method* ‖ ⟨jur⟩ *procedure* ‖ ⟨chem, tech⟩ *process*; ~, das bei der Herstellung v .. angewendet wird *techniques of production of* .. ‖ ⟨jur⟩ *action*; das ~ einleiten (einstellen) *to take* (*stop*) *proceedings* ‖ ehrliches (hinterlistiges) ~ *honest* (*underhand*) *dealing* | ≈smäßig 1. [a] *procedural* 2. [adv] *procedurally* ~sweise [f] = ~, ⟨a.⟩ *practice* ~**f·ahren** irr **1.** vi [s] *to proceed*; *to go to work* (nach .. *on a system*) ‖ ⟨jur⟩ gerichtlich (strafrechtlich) ~ **gegen** *to take legal proceedings against* (*to prosecute a p*) ‖ **mit**: *to deal with* (*a p, a th*), gemein *to play it low on* (*a p*); mit jdm gut/schlecht ~ *to treat a p well/badly* mit Strenge ~ *to act severely* ‖ schlecht ~ mit *to treat* (*a p, a th*) *badly*; vorsichtig ~ mit *to handle* (*a th*) *carefully* ‖ ⟨com⟩ mit etw **nach** Anweisung ~ *to dispose of a th according to orders* **2.** vt [h] (Geld) *to spend on vehicles* ‖ (Weg) *to spoil* ‖ ⟨fig⟩ (verpfuschen) *to mismanage, bungle, muddle, embroil* ‖ die S ⟨fam⟩ Karre ist total ~ *the whole th has been badly mismanaged* od *is in a hopeless confusion, the matter is deeply entangled*, ⟨fam⟩ *it's a regular muddle* | ⟨min⟩ e–n Gang ~ *to work a mine*; s–e Schicht ~ *to finish one's task* **3. sich** ~ *to miss* od *lose one's way* od *road* ‖ ⟨fig⟩ *to blunder grossly*, ⟨fam⟩ *to get muddled* ≈**f·ahrens-** ~anweisung [f] ⟨tech⟩ *procedure guide*; ~forschung [f] → Operations–; ~lehre [f] *methodology*; ~prüfung [f] ⟨tech⟩ *pr.e proving*; ~recht [n] *adjective law*; ~standhafter [m] ⟨jur⟩ *p* etc *accepting service*; ~technik [f] *process engineering* od *research*; *processing* (*technique*); *process technology*; ≈technisch [a] *operational* (Gesichtspunkt); ~überwachung *pr.e supervision*;

Verbal-Flexion der Verben mit der Vorsilbe **ver-** → das jeweilige Simplex

~vorschrift [f] *rule of pr.e*; ~weise [f] *method, process*; *policy* **Verf·all** m ~(e)s/ *decay*; *decadence*; *declension*; *decline* (*of physical strength*); *ruin* || *downfall* || ⟨arch⟩ *dilapidation* | (Ausartung) *degeneracy*; ~ der Kräfte etc ⟨med⟩ *collapse* || (Sitten~̊) *corruption, depravity* | (e–s Rechtes) *forfeiture* || (e–r Klage) *nonsuit* | ⟨com⟩ *expiration, maturity* || **bei** ~ *when due, at maturity* || **in** ~ geraten *to go to ruin*; *to decay*; in ~ g. l, dem ~ preisgeben *to allow to fall into decay* || im ~ s *to be on the decline, to be going down* **~buch** n *bill-book* **~datum** n *expiration date*; *day* od *date of maturity*; *due-date* **~erklärung** f *confiscation* **~frist** f *maturity* **~serscheinung** f *symptom of decline* **~tag** m *day of payment* **~zeit** f *time of payment*, → –datum || vor ~ *before due* || zur ~ *when due* || bis zur ~ *till due, until maturity* **verf·allen** vi irr [s] **1.** *to decay* || ⟨arch⟩ *to fall down*; *to get out of repair* || ⟨fig⟩ *to deteriorate, degenerate*; *to decline*; ⟨a. fig⟩ *to go to seed* || *to fall into disrepair* | durch Versäumnis, Achtlosigkeit ~ l *to let the matter slide* | e–m traurigen Schicksal ~ *to meet with a sad fate* **2.** (ablaufen; ungültig w) *to expire* (*the ticket is* od *has -d*) || ⟨com⟩ *to fall due, to expire* || (Pfand) *to become forfeited* || (Lehen, Recht) *to lapse*; wieder ~ *to relapse* **3.** [dat] jdm ~ *to devolve on a p, to fall to a p's share, to become a p's property* || e–r S ~ *to fall under the spell of a th* **4.** (körperlich) *to lose flesh, to decline in health, to waste away, to be failing* (*fast*) **5. auf** etw [acc] ~ *to fall to* (*doing*), *to take a fancy to a th* || (wieder) *to fall back upon a th* || (plötzlich) *to hit* od *to pitch* (*up*)*on a th* || auf das wäre ich nie ~ *I should never have thought of that* || **in** [acc] ~ *to run, fall, lapse into* (*a notion, gloom*) || *to break into* (*English*) || in Barbarei etc ~ *to fall barbarous* etc || in die alten Fehler ~ *to slip back into one's old ways* || in Geldstrafe ~ *to be fined* || in Hysterie ~ *to go off in hysterics* || in e–e Krankheit ~ *to fall ill* || in Nachdenken ~ *to grow pensive* || in Strafe ~ *to incur a penalty* || wieder in [acc], der Sünde [dat] ~ *to backslide* **verf·allen** a *decayed, ruinous* || *dilapidated, tumble-down* (*cottage*) || ~e Gesichtszüge [m pl] *worn* od *faded features* || ⟨com, jur⟩ *forfeited* (*pledge*) || (Hypothek) f ~ erklären *to foreclose* || am 1. April ~ *due on April 1st* (= *the first*) || *confiscated* (*estate*) || e–m Laster ~ *addicted to a vice* **ver- ~f·älschen** vt [h] *to falsify* || (Münzen) *to debase*; *to tamper* (*an account*) || ⟨Lit⟩ (e–e Stelle) *to interpolate* || (Urkunden, Handschrift) *to forge* || (Ware, Wein) *to adulterate*, ⟨fam⟩ *to doctor* **~̊f·älscher(in** f) m ~s/~ *falsifier* || *interpolator* || *forger* || *adulterator*; → vor. **~̊f·älschung** f ~/~en *falsification* || *corruption, interpolation* || *forgery* || *adulteration* | ~smittel [n] *adulterant* **~f·angen 1.** vi irr [h] (Erfolg h) *to tell* (bei *on*), *to* (*avail* od) *go down* (*with*) || nicht ~ *to be of no use*; der Trick –fängt (nicht) *the t. catches on* (*does not prove effective*); das verfängt bei mir nicht! *that cock won't fight with me*! **2. sich** ~ *to get* od *be caught* od *become entangled* || (S) *to catch, hitch, hook*; *mesh* (*in*) || (Wind) *to go down* (*into the chimney*) || ⟨fig⟩ *to betray o.s.* **~f·änglich** a *enticing* || *risky, awkward, embarrassing* || (Frage) *captious, insidious*; *loaded, tricky* || *fallacious, deceptive* (*argument*) || (Witz) ⟨Am⟩ *off-color* **~f·ärben** vt [h] *to discolour* | **sich** ~ *to lose colour, to fade* || (Gesicht) *to* (*change*) *colour, to grow pale* || (Haar, Laub) *to turn* **V.bung** f ⟨chem⟩ *discolo*(*u*)*ration* | ~smethode [f] *patch test* **~f·assen** vt [h] ⟨Lit⟩ *to compose* || *to write* (*a book*) || *to pen* (*a letter*) || ⟨jur⟩ *to draw up* **~f·asser(in** f) m ~s/~ *author, writer, composer* || *compiler, lexicographer* || ⟨jur⟩ *draftsman* || der ~ dieses Buches etc *the present author* | ~schaft [f] ~/ *authorship* **~̊f·assung** f ~/~en (→ Ab–) **1.** ⟨pol⟩ *constitution*; *polity* **2.** (Zustand) *state, condition* (*in good, bad c.*); in bester ~ ⟨fam a.⟩ *in the pink, fine as silk*; in guter ~ *in fine shape* || in trauriger ~ *in a wretched plight*, ⟨fam⟩ *in a terrible way*; du bist ja in e–r netten ~! *you are in a way*! **3.** (Gemüts~̊) *state* od *frame of mind*; *disposition* **4.** (gute Körper~̊) *trim* (*to keep o.s. in t.*); in bester ~ *as fit as a fiddle* **~̊gebend** a *constituent* **Verf·assungs- ~anhänger** m *constitutionalist* **~bruch** m *breach of the constitution* **~̊mäßig** a *constitutional* | ~keit [f] *c.lity* **~schutz** m *defence* (⟨Am⟩ *-se*) od *protection of the establishment* od *constitution* **~staat** m *constitutional state* **~̊treu** a *loyal to the c.* **~urkunde** f *charter of the C.* **~tag** m *C. Day* **~̊widrig** a *unconstitutional* **ver- ~f·aulen** vi [s] *to rot, putrefy* | –lt *rotten* (*egg, cloth, wood, rope*), *rotted* (*leaves*); *unsound* (Obst) **~f·aulenzen** vt [h] (die Zeit) *to idle away* (*one's t.*) **~f·echten** vt irr [h] *to stand up for* || *to defend, advocate* (*a cause*) || *to fight* (*a case*) || *to argue* (*a point of view*) || *to maintain* (*an opinion*) || *to assert* (*one's right*) || *to defend, champion* (*principles*), *stand up for* (*them*) || ⟨obs⟩ was verficht's? *what does it matter*? **~̊f·echter(in** f) m ~s/~ *champion, advocate, defender*; *proponent* || ⟨fig⟩ *apostle* (*of Free Trade*), *exponent* || hartnäckiger ~ e–r S [gen] *standpatter* **~f·ehlen** vt [h] *to miss* (*aims, trains, one's vocation*); etw ~ *to come short of a th*; *to miss* (*a blow*) || den Anschluß ~ ⟨rail⟩ *to miss connection* || jdn ~ *not to find a p at home* || den Weg ~ *to miss* od *lose one's way* || s–n Zweck ~ *to miss one's aim*; (S) s–e Wirkung nicht ~ *to tell, not to be lost* (*upon a p*) || nicht ~ z ..: *I shall not fail to ..* || den Zweck ~ *to fail one's* (*its*) *purpose* || ~ Sie ja nicht es z tun *be sure to* (⟨fam⟩ *and*) *do it* | **sich** ~ *to miss each other, to fail to meet* **~f·ehlt** a *unsuccessful, abortive* (*attempt*); *miscarried* (*plan*) || ~e S *or* Geschichte *failure, miss* | [pred] es ist ~ *it is unsuitable, beside the mark, a mistake* **~̊f·ehlung** f ~/~en *lapse, delinquency* || ⟨jur⟩ *failure* **~f·einden** vt [h] (jdn mit jdm) *to set* (*a p*) *against* (*another*), *to embroil* (*a p*) *with* (*another*) | **sich** ~ (mit jdm) *to make an enemy* (*of a p*), ⟨fam⟩ *to fall out* (*with a p*) | –det [a] (*bitterly*) *hostile*; *at daggers drawn* (*with*) **~f·einern** vt [h] *to refine, polish, urbanize* || *to fine down* (*features*) || ⟨fig⟩ *to subtilize* || ⟨tech⟩ *to improve, purify* ⟨a. fig⟩ | **sich** ~ *to refine, to become refined* | **-rt** ⟨a.⟩ *cultivated* (Stil) **V.rung** f *refinement, elaboration*; *polish*, etc; ⟨fig⟩ *urbanization* **~f·emen** vt [h] *to outlaw, proscribe, boycott* || *to ostracize* (in .. *from society*) **~f·ertigen** vt [h] *to make, manufacture* || ⟨mach⟩ *to construct* || ⟨pharm⟩ *to prepare, dispense* || ⟨Lit⟩ *to compose* **~f·estigen** vt [h] *to strengthen, solidify, consolidate* | sich ~ ⟨übtr⟩ *to become usual*; ein Vorurteil –gt sich *a prejudice solidifies* **V.gung** f ⟨tech⟩ *work-hardening*; *hardness increase* **~̊f·ettung** f ~/~en ⟨path⟩ *fatty degeneration* **~f·euern** vt [h] *to burn* (*fuel*) || *to fire away* (*powder*, etc) **~f·iel** 1. & 3. sg pret v verfallen **~f·ilmen** vt [h] *to* (*put on the*) *screen, to film* (*a play*) | f V.mung geeignet *filmable* **~f·ilzen** vt [h] *to felt* || (Haar) *to mat* | **sich** ~ [h] *to get entangled* od *matted* || (Haar) *to mat*, **-zt** ⟨a.⟩ *kinky* **V.zung** f *felting* || (Haar~̊) *Polish plait* **~f·instern** vt [h] *to darken, obscure* || ⟨astr⟩ *to eclipse* | **sich** ~ *to darken* ⟨a. fig⟩ || ⟨astr⟩ *to be eclipsed* **V.rung** f ~/~en *darkening* || ⟨astr⟩ *eclipse* **~f·irsten** vt [h] *to ridge* (*a roof*) **~f·itzen** vt [h] *to entangle* | **sich** ~ *to become entangled* **~fl·achen** vt *to flatten* | **sich** ~ *to become level*; *to level* (*off*) || ⟨fig⟩ *to become* od *run* od *grow shallow, trite, flat* **V.chung** f ⟨fig⟩ (*intellectual*) *decline* **~fl·ackern** vi [s] *to flicker away, to flare*

Aussprache: Falls nicht anders (: [*v*]) angegeben, ist v = [*f*] zu sprechen.

out **~fl·echten 1.** vt/refl irr [h] (sich) *to interlace, entwine, interweave* (*with*) ‖ *to plait badly* | ⟨fig⟩ **in** [acc] *to entangle* od *involve* (*o.s.*) (*in*) **2.** vt *to use up in plaiting* ‖ sich ~ in *to weave into* **V.tung** f *interlacing* | ⟨fig⟩ *complexity*; *entanglement, involving* ‖ *hook-up* (*of companies*, etc) ‖ *nexus* (*of interests*) ‖ ~ v Umständen (*strange*) *coincidence* **~fl·iegen** vi irr [s] *to fly off* od *away* ‖ (verdunsten) *to evaporate* ‖ (Öl) *to volatilize* ‖ ⟨fig⟩ *to wear off, to blow over, to vanish* ‖ (Zeit) *to pass rapidly*: *how time slips away*! | ≈ n ⟨a.⟩ *transience* | **sich** ~ *to fly too far, to lose o.s.* | **~d** *volatile* | **verflogen** *stray* (*bees*, etc) **~fl·ießen** vi irr [s] *to flow off* od *away* ‖ *to subside* ‖ (Farben) *to mix, blend* ‖ (Zeit) *to elapse, expire, pass* ‖ | ~d ⟨phot⟩ *fading* (*background*); → verflossen °**~fl·ixt** a (⟨euphem⟩ = verflucht) *damned, confounded, blooming*; *bleeding, bally* (f *bloody*) ‖ e–e ~e S *a deuce of a business* ‖ die ~en Kinder! *bother the children* ‖ ~er Kerl *devil of a fellow* | ~! *confound it*! *dash it*! *blame it*!; ⟨vulg⟩ *blow it*! ⟨Am sl⟩ *raspberries*! *razz*! ‖ ~ noch 'mal *dash it all*!; (*then they*) *damn well* (*ought to*!) | [adv] *viciously, shockingly* (*old*) ‖ *damn, dem* (*fine woman*) ‖ *dashed* (*awkward*); *ghastly* (*early*) **~fl·ocht** 1. & 3. sg pret v verflechten **~fl·ochten** a [pp verflechten] *interlacing* ‖ *bound up* (in *in*) **~fl·og** 1. & 3. sg pret v verfliegen **~fl·oß** 1. & 3. sg pret v verfließen **~fl·ossen** a (Zeit) *past* ‖ im ~en Jahre *last year, in the past year*; in ~en Jahren *in former years* ‖ der ~e Minister *the ex-Minister* **~fl·ößen** vt [h] *to transport by means of rafts* **~fl·uchen** vt [h] *to curse, damn, execrate* ‖ ⟨ec⟩ *to anathematize* **~s-wert** a *execrable* **≈fl·ucher** m ~s/~ *curser* **~fl·ucht** a *execrable*, (*ac*)*cursed* | ⟨fam⟩ *confounded, deuced* ‖ *damned* (*duty*) ‖ ⟨sl⟩ *blooming, blessed*; *bloody* (*fool*) ‖ die ~e Tür! *drat that door*! | ~! *confound it*! *damn*! ‖ o ~! *oh hell*! ‖ ~ nochmal! *dash* od *hang it all*! | [adv] *jolly* (*cold*), *dreadfully* (*mean*), *precious* (*little*), *infernally* (*angry*), *beastly* (*awkward*), *dead* (*serious*) **~fl·üchtigen 1.** vt [h] *to volatilize* **2.** vi [s] & **sich** ~ [h] *to become volatile*; *to volatilize, evaporate, melt*; (of mist) *to dissipate*; ⟨fig⟩ *to vanish into thin air* ‖ ⟨fam, fig⟩ *to scuttle, decamp* ‖ sich ~d *volatile* **V.gung** f *volatilization*; *sublimation* **≈fl·uchung** f ~/~en *malediction, execration, imprecation* ‖ ⟨ec⟩ *anathema*(*tization*) **≈fl·uß** m –usses/; nach ~ von *after the lapse* od *expiration of* **~fl·üssigen** vt/refl [h] *to liquefy* (*gas*), *fuse* (*metal*) **V.gung** f ⟨phys⟩ *liquefaction*; ⟨min⟩ *magmatism* **≈f·olg** m ~(e)s/ *continuation, progress* ‖ im ~ [gen] *in pursuance* (*of orders*) ‖ (im Verlauf) *in the course of* ‖ ⟨com⟩ im ~ unseres Schreibens *reverting to ours* | ≈bar [a] *easy to pursue* ‖ ⟨jur⟩ *suable* **~f·olgen** vt [h] (P & Weg, Ziel) *to pursue* ⟨a. mil⟩ ‖ (unablässig) *to dog, track* (*dogged by bad luck*) ‖ (unbemerkt) *to shadow* ‖ etw ~ *to keep track of a th* ⟨a. fig⟩ ‖ s–n Kurs weiter ~ *to hold on one's course* ⟨a. fig⟩; ein G. bis zu s–m Ursprung ~ *to run a rumor back to its source*; .. aufmerksam .. (beobachtend) *to watch a th* (*a course, process*) ⟨Am⟩ *with the ear to the ground* ‖ (mit Haß, Grausamkeit; mit Fragen etc belästigen) *to persecute* ‖ (Kirche) *to dragoon* | ⟨fig⟩ (v Ideen, Träumen) *to haunt* ‖ (v Dämon) *to obsess* ‖ (Laufbahn, Spur, Gegenstand) *to follow up* ‖ *to follow* (*a trade*) ‖ *to trace* (*the course of a subject*) ‖ er hat die neueste Literatur nicht mehr –gt *he fell behind the forward march of l., not kept up with the latest l.* | gerichtlich ~ *to prosecute*; infolge Entschädigung nicht ~ *to compound* | *to chase* (*a ship*) ‖ ⟨hunt⟩ *to course* | ⟨mar⟩ *to hold* (*one's course*) ‖ (S, Vorhaben) *to push on* od *forward* ..; (bis ans Ende) *to carry out* .. ‖ (Vorgang, Ziel) *to follow* ‖ (Weg) *to go*; (weiter) *to continue* ‖ (zurück) *to trace back* ⟨a. fig⟩ | –gt v .. *obsessed by* (*an idea*) ‖ e–e Liste der V.gten *a l. of the hunted men* **~f·olger(in** f) m ~s/~ *pursuer* ‖ *persecutor* **~f·olgung** f ~/~en (hitzige *hot*) *pursuit* (in der ~ *in the p.*); sich der ~ entziehen *to outrun the p.*; v Angriff z ~ übergehen *to convert the a. into a p.* ‖ *persecution* ‖ *prosecution*; *chase* | ⟨fig⟩ *pursuance* | **~s-** ~gefecht [n] *hot p.*; ~nachtjagd [f] ⟨aero⟩ *night-fighter p.*; ~geist [m], ~sucht [f] *spirit of persecution* | ~vorstellung [f]; an ~en leiden *to have a persecution complex*; ~wahn [m] ⟨path⟩ *persecution*(*al*) *mania*; *obsession*; *delusion of p.n* **≈formung** f *deformation, disfigurement*; *change* **~fr·achten** vt [h] (Waren) *to load, freight* ‖ ⟨mar⟩ *to ship* ⟨Am allg⟩ | *to transport*; v Eis –tet *ice-borne* | (bezahlen) *to pay freightage for* | *to charter* (*a ship*) ‖ *to hire out* (*a van*) | ⟨fig fam⟩ *to bundle* (*a p*) *off*; sich ~ ⟨vulg⟩ *to take o.s. off* **≈fr·achter** m ~s/~ *freighter, shipper* ‖ *charterer* **≈fr·achtung** f ~/~en *freighting, shipment* ‖ *chartering* °**~fr·anzen** v/refl; sich ~ ⟨aero⟩ *to lose one's bearings, to wander off course*, ⟨sl⟩ *to get lost* **≈fremdung** f *alienation* **~fr·essen I.** vt irr [h] ⟨fam⟩ (sein Hab u Gut) *to waste* ‖ **sich** ~ *to overeat* **II.** pp a ⟨fam⟩ *voracious* **~fr·ieren** vi [s] *to freeze* (*to death*) **~fr·ühen** vt/refl [h]; (sich) ~ *to do* (*be*) *before the time* ‖ **-ht** a *premature* (*delivery, confinement, birth*) **~f·ügbar** a *available* (*resources*); *at one's disposal* ‖ (Kapital) *uninvested* ‖ ~es Geld *cash in hand*; frei ~ *discretionary* (*income*) | ≈keit [f] melden! *advise a.bility*! **~f·ügen I.** vt [h] *to order, decree* ‖ (vorschreiben) *to prescribe* ‖ (v Gesetzen) *to provide, enact* (*that* ..) **II.** vi [h] (über [acc]) *to have at one's disposal, to be provided with* | *to dispose of* (letztwillig *by will*) | *to be in control of a th*; *to have* (*good knowledge of* ..) ‖ *to command* (*a th*; *that*); ⟨Am⟩ *to swing* (*a majority*) ‖ Sie können über mich ~ *I am at your service*; über sich (frei) ~ *to possess o.s.* (*freely*); über s–e Zeit ~ *to be master of one's time, to have one's time on one's own hands* **III. sich** ~ nach *to betake o.s. to* **≈f·ügung** f ~/~en **A.** (behördl. Erlaß) *order, decree, ordinance*; ⟨mil⟩ *regulation* N ‖ laut ~ [gen] *as directed by* ‖ (gesetzl.) *enactment* ‖ (Anweisung) *instruction, provision* ‖ letztwillige ~ *testamentary disposition*; *provision* (*of a will*) ‖ ⟨jur⟩ einstweilige ~ *injunction* **B.** zur ~ h *to have .. at hand, to have* (*a lot of time*) *on one's hands*; *to command* (*a th*) ‖ zur besonderen ~ *at disposal for special duty* ⟨a. mil⟩ ‖ zur ~ halten *to hold* (*money*) *to the order* (*of a p*); sich .. *to stand by* ‖ zur ~ stehen *to be available*, od *on hand* od ⟨fam⟩ *tap*; (P) *to be in attendance*; *to stand by*; jdm .. *to be at one's disposal*; ganz .. *to be at a p's beck and call* ‖ zur ~ stellen *to make available*, ⟨mil⟩ *to assign* (*a.ed forces*); jdm (etw) *to place .. at a p's disposal, to make a p free of, to offer a p* ..; *to give* (*one's service*) *to a p* ‖ ~en treffen *to make arrangements, to give orders* | **~s-** ~befugnis [f] *power of disposition*; ~personal [n] ⟨mil⟩ *casuals*; ~raum [m] ⟨tact⟩ *assembly* od *maintenance area*; ~recht [n] über sein Geld bek *to come into one's own m.* | technische ~truppen [pl] *service support units* **~f·uhr** 1. & 3. sg pret v verfahren **~f·ührbar** a *corruptible* ‖ (Frau) *seducible* **~f·ühren** vt [h] **1.** *to mislead, misguide, misdirect* ⟨a. fig⟩ **2.** ⟨fig⟩ *to tempt, allure* ‖ *to induce* .. (*to do*) ‖ *to corrupt* ‖ (Frau) *to debauch, seduce* ‖ (Zeugen) *to suborn* **3.** *to make* (*a fearful noise*), ⟨fam⟩ *to kick up* (*a row*) **≈f·ührer** m ~s/~ *tempter, corrupter, seducer* ⟨a. fig⟩; *ravisher* ‖ ⟨fam⟩ *Don Juan* | ~in [f] *vamp* | ≈isch [a] *seductive*; *enticing* ‖ ⟨rel⟩ *leading into temptation* | ⟨fig⟩ *tempting*; *alluring, fascinating*; *seducing*; *tantalizing* **≈f·ührung** f ~/~en *cor-*

Verbal-Flexion der Verben mit der Vorsilbe **ver-** → das jeweilige Simplex

ruption || *seduction* || *subornation* | ~skunst [f] *art of seduction* || [pl] *fascinating ways* pl; ~s-mittel [n] *means of s.* || (z Bestechen) *bribe* **~f·üllen** vt [h] **1.** *to pour from one vessel into another* **2.** *to fill into a wrong vessel* **~f·ünffachen** vt/refl [h] *to increase fivefold* **~f·üttern** vt [h] *to use up as fodder* od *provender* || *to overfeed* **~g·ab** 1. & 3. sg pret v vergeben **≈gabe** f → –geben A. 2. **~gabung** f Sw = Schenkung, Vermächtnis °**~g·affen,** sich ~ [h] (in [acc]) *to fall in love with*; *to fall for* (*a new face*); ⟨fam⟩ *to be smitten with* (*a p, a th*) || –fft in ⟨fam⟩ *st(r)uck on* **~g·ähnen** vt [h] (Zeit) *to yawn away* **~g·ällen** vt [h] *to denature embitter, sour, mar* (*a p's joy*) || jdm etw ~ *to set a p against a th* || sich das Leben ~ *to embitter one's life* | –llt ⟨chem⟩ *methylated* (*spirit*) °**~galopp·ieren,** sich ~ ⟨fam⟩ *to blunder*; *to overshoot the mark* || *to allow one's tongue to run away with one* **~g·alt** 1. & 3. sg pret v vergelten **~g·angen** a [pp vergehen] *past, gone* || ~en Mai *May last* || im ~en Jahr, ~es Jahr *last year* || ~e Zeiten [pl] *bygone days* pl || (*in days long gone by*) || laß das ≈e ruhen *let bygones be bygones*; ≈es [n] ⟨fam⟩ *has-been* | ≈heit [f] ~/ *the past, the time past*; *past times* || in der jüngsten ~ *in the recent past* || ⟨gram⟩ *past tense* || (Vorleben) *antecedents* pl || (*this book has a*) *history* || das gehört der ~ an *that's a past matter* od *a m. of the p., belongs to the p., that's over and done with*; mit der ~ brechen, sich v der ~ lösen *to cut o.s. off from the past* **~g·änglich** a *transient, transitory, passing, evanescent* || *perishable*; *temporal, mortal*; ~ s *to perish* || (Glück, Leben etc) *frail* | ≈keit [f] *transitoriness, transience, mortality*; *transiency* (*of life*) **~g·ären I.** vt [h] *to throw off* (*all impurity*) *in fermenting* **II.** vi [s & h] *to cease fermenting* **~g·asen** vt ⟨chem⟩ *to gasify* || ⟨mot⟩ *to carburet* || ⟨pol & mil⟩ *to gas* **≈g·aser** m ~s/~ ⟨mot⟩ *carburettor*; (~brand [m] *fire in the c.*) || ~ mit Saugförderung *suction c.*; ~ mit Unterdrucksteuerung *vacuum-controlled c.*; ~ mit Vorwärmung *heated c.* || am ~ tippen *to flood the c.* | ~einstellung [f] *c. setting*; ~gestänge [n] *c. linkage*; ~kraftstoff [m] *motor spirit*; ~vereisung [f] *c. freezing* od *icing*; ~vorwärmer [m] *c. heating* **-sung** f ~/ *vaporization*; ⟨fig fam⟩ bis zur ~ *till you get sick of it* **~g·aß** 1. & 3. sg pret v vergessen **~g·attern** vt [h] *to grate* || ⟨mil⟩ *to assemble .. by beat of drum* **V.rung** f ~/ ⟨mil⟩ *assembly, signal to assemble* **~g·ebbar** a *pardonable* (*sin*) → folg. **~g·eben** vt irr [h] **A. 1.** (verzeihen) *to pardon* (*a p sth*), *to forgive* (*a p* [*for*] *sth*), (*for doing*) || es soll dir ~ s *you shall be forgiven*; das ist ~ u vergessen *bygones are bygones*; die Frage mag e–m ~ s *one might be forgiven for asking the question* || *to remit, condone* (*an offence*) **2.** (gewähren) *to give away* (an *to*), *to bestow* od *confer on* || *to dispose of* || *to yield up* od *cede* (*one's rights*) || alle Abende ~ h ⟨Am fam⟩ *to be dated up* **3.** ⟨cards⟩ [a. abs] *or*: sich ~ *to misdeal*; es ist ~ *it's a misdeal* **B.** (Pfarre, Ehre etc) v jdm ~ w *to be in the gift of a p* || (of scholarship) ~ w *to be tenable* (*for 3 years*) **C.** **(Amt)** ~ an: *to bestow .. on, to appoint* (*a p*) *to ..* || (Arbeit) ⟨agr⟩ *to farm out* || ⟨com⟩ (Aufträge) *to place* (*orders*); *to give away, to let* (*the contracts for*) || s–r **Ehre** nichts ~ *to be jealous of one's h., not to compromise o.s.* || (Geld) *to pass out* (*m.* **an** *to*) || die (Hand s–r) Tochter ~ *to give one's d. in marriage* || ihre Hand ist bereits ~ *she is engaged* (*to be married*) || e–e Pfründe z ~ h *to have the patronage of a b.* || (Preise) ~ ⟨sport⟩ *to give* || sich v s–m **Recht** etw ~ *to allow one's right to be infringed* || die Stelle ist noch nicht ~ .. *is still vacant* || möge Gott mir die Sünde ~! *may God pardon my sin*! || ist der Montag auch ~? *is M. gone too*? || e–n **Tanz** ~ h *to be engaged for a d.*; ~ [pp] s *to be engaged*, ⟨Am fam⟩ *fixed up* (*for this evening*) || s–r Würde *or* **sich** etw ~ *to derogate* (*from one's dignity*); *to compromise* od *forget o.s.* **~g·ebens** [adv] *in vain, vainly* || *to no purpose, to no end*, ⟨fam⟩ (*of*) *no use* || ~ reden *to waste one's words* || es war ~ *it was of no end* od *result whatever* **~g·eblich** a *idle, fruitless, vain, futile* (Geste, Versuch); *unavailing, abortive* (effort) || *useless* (*errand*) || (unnötig) *needless* (*fear*); ~e Arbeit m *to plough sands* | adv = vergebens; sich ~ abmühen *to beat the air* od *wind, to have one's trouble for nothing* | ≈keit [f] *uselessness*, etc **≈g·ebung** f ~/ *forgiveness, pardon*(*ing*) || ⟨ec⟩ *remission* (*of offences, sins*) || (Gewährung) *bestowal, conferment* (an [acc] *on*) || *cession* (*of a right*); jdn f ~ e–s Auftrags in Aussicht nehmen *to contemplate placing an order with a p* || ⟨ec⟩ *collation* (*to a benefice*) || ⟨com⟩ *placing* (*of orders*) | (ich bitte) um ~! *excuse me!*, *pardon me*! || jdn um ~ bitten *to ask a p's forgiveness* **~g·egenständlichen** vt [h] *to objectify, objectivate, hypostatize, reify* || dazu: *reification*, etc **~gegenw·ärtigen** vt [h] *to represent*; *to bring home* (*to*) | sich [dat] etw ~ *to realize, imagine, visualize a th, to bring a th to* (*one's*) *mind*; *to wake up to a th*; sich s–e Pläne nochmals ~ *to review one's plans* **V.gung** f *realization*, geistige *visualization* **≈g·ehen** n **1.** ~s/ *disappearance* || (von der Zeit) *flight, lapse* **2.** ~s/~ *offence*, ⟨Am⟩ *offense*; *trespass, sin* || ⟨jur⟩ *misdemeanour*; *tort* **~g·ehen** irr **I.** vi [s] **1.** (Zeit) *to go by*; *to pass, run, elapse* || (inzwischen) *to intervene*; *it is bound to be some time before* (bis) || *12 months were out* || ⟨bib⟩ (Tage) *to be consumed* || e–e kurze Weile ~ l *to let it ride for a minute* **2.** (aufhören) *to cease, end* || *to work itself out*; *it will pass off by itself* || (Zorn) *to blow over* || sich etw ~ l *to give up all thoughts of a th* **3.** (verblassen) *to fade* **4.** (verschwinden) *to disappear, evanesce, vanish*; *fade*; (Schnee) *to melt away* **5.** (sich verlieren) *to abate, subside* **6.** (P, hinsiechen) *to pass away*; *to droop, perish, die* | ⟨fig⟩ **vor** [dat]: *to almost swoon away with*; *to die of* (*shame*) || (Angst) *to be in mortal dread* || (Gram) *to pine away* || (Neid) *to be eaten up with envy* || (Sehnsucht z tun, [Ungeduld]) *to be dying* (*to do*) [*with impatience*] **7.** **(mit P** [dat]**) mir** war der Appetit (Atem) vergangen *I had lost my a.* (*b.*) || (Hören u Sehen) *my sight and hearing failed me, I was stunned*; .. vor Angst .. *I was frightened out of my senses* || (Lachen) *I laughed on the wrong side of my mouth* || (Lust) *I had lost all desire for it* (dazu) || (Redeschwall) *all my ranting had dropped away from me* **II.** vt sich [dat] die Beine ~ *to stretch one's legs, to take exercise* **III.** **sich** ~ *to commit an offence, to fail in one's duty* || (bes geschlechtlich v Frauen) *to go wrong* || sich **an** jdm ~ (geschlechtlich) *to violate*, (tätlich) *to assault a p* | **gegen**: *to trespass against, to insult, injure a p* || *to offend, infringe, break, violate* (*a law*, etc) || *to fall foul of the law* **≈g·ehung** f ~/~en = Vergehen 2 **~g·eistigen** vt [h] *to spiritualize, intellectualize, etherealize* || ⟨chem⟩ *to alcoholize* || –gter (Gesichts-)Ausdruck *spiritual expression* **V.gung** f ⟨psych⟩ *sublimation* **~g·eltbar** a *requitable* **~g·elten** vt irr [h] [–gilt!] *to recompense, requite, repay, reward* || (heimzahlen) *to retaliate* || e–m e–n Dienst ~ *to remunerate a p for ..* || jdm etw ~ ⟨fam⟩ *to put it across a p* || vergelt's Gott! *God bless you for it*! || etw schlecht ~ *to return evil for good*; jdm nichts ~ *to give a p nothing in return* || **mit**: *she returned courtesy for c.*; Gleiches mit Gleichem ~ *to give tit for tat, to pay back in the same coin*; Gutes mit Bösem ~ *to render evil for good, to bite the hand that feeds one* | **~d** *retributive* **V.ter(in** f) m ~s/~ *rewarder* || (Rächer) *avenger* **V.tung** f ~/ *requital, retribu-*

Aussprache: Falls nicht anders (: [*v*]) angegeben, ist v = [*f*] zu sprechen.

tion, return; göttliche ~ *nemesis* || (Heimzahlung) *pay-off*; *retaliation, reprisal* ⟨a. mil⟩ || zur ~ *in retaliation, in return*; *as a reprisal* (Belohnung) *reward, recompense* || ~ üben *to retaliate* (an *on*), ⟨fam⟩ *to give tit for tat*; ⟨Am sl⟩ *to get back at a p* | **~s-** *retaliation* (*fire, attack, power, raid*) | ~angriff [m] *reprisal attack*; ⟨aero⟩ *spite-raid, three-star* od *Baedeker raid* | ~feuer [n] *retaliatory fire*; ⟨Ger⟩ *strafe* | ~maßregel [f] *reprisal*; ~recht [n] *right of retaliation* od *reprisal*; ~tag [m] *day of retribution* **~gem·einschaften** vt [h] *to communize* **~ges·ellschaften** vt [h] (sozialisieren) *to socialize* ||–tetes Gebiet ⟨pol⟩ *collective* || (zur Aktienges.) *to convert into a company* || **sich** ~ *to associate* (*with*) **~g·eßbar** a *soon forgotten* **~g·essen 1.** a ⟨a.⟩ *unremembered* **2.** vt [vergaß/~] [h] *to forget*; ⟨Am a.⟩ *to disremember* || (übersehen) *to overlook*; (auslassen) *to omit* || (liegen l) *to leave behind* || alles ~ ⟨a.⟩ *to become oblivious of e.* | ich **habe** es ~ *it has slipped my mind*; ~ Sie's nicht *keep it in mind*! || ich –gaß die S z erwähnen *I did not think of mentioning the matter* || das durfte man nicht ~ *it was to be remembered*; es darf nicht ~ w *it must be borne in mind*; ~ l *to unteach*; *to put .. out of m.* || ich habe s–n Namen ~ *I forget* (!) *his name* || ich habe es ganz (⟨fam⟩ total) ~ *I forgot all about it*, ⟨Am fam⟩ *I plumb forgot* | ~ Sie nicht z k! *be sure and* od *to come*! | wir ~ **darüber** .. *it makes us forget our troubles*; alles um sich ~d *lost to the world* | **sich** ~ (P) *to forget o.s.*, *to lose one's head* || (S) *to slip one's memory* | ≃heit [f] ~/ *oblivion* || (* = Vergeßlichkeit) | der ~ anheimgeben *to consign to o.*, *to put .. out of mind* || der ~ entreißen *to rescue from o.* || in ~ bringen *to wipe out* || in ~ geraten *to fall into o.*; ganz .. *to pass into complete o.*; *it passed out of people's* od *everybody's mind* **~g·eßlich** a **1.** (P) *forgetful, oblivious* **2.** (S) *soon* od *easily forgotten* **~g·eudenvt** [h] *to waste, lavish, squander, dissipate* || *to throw* (allmählich *play* od *fritter* ⟨a.⟩ Zeit) *away* (an, f *on*) || restlos ~ ⟨Am⟩ *to pour down the drain* || (Geld) *to throw away*, ⟨sl⟩ *to spill* || (Jugend) *to misspend* || (Kräfte) *to burn the candle at both ends* | **-det** w ⟨a.⟩ *to run to waste* **V.der(in** f) m ~s/~ *squanderer, spendthrift* **V.dung** f ~/~en *lavishing, waste, dissipation* **~gew·altigen** vt [h] *to commit a criminal assault* (Frau: *a rape*) *on*, *to do violence to* || (Frau) *to violate* || (Mädchen) *to ravish* | ⟨fig⟩ *to coerce, force, bully, oppress, terrorize, straitjacket* | (S) *to distort, twist*; *to assault* (*a language*) **~gew·issern** vt [h] jdn e–r S [gen] ~ *to convince* od *assure a p of a th* | **sich** [gen] ~ *to ascertain*; *to make sure* (*of*); *to satisfy o.s.* **V.rung** f ~/ *assurance* **~g·ib** imp v vergeben **~g·ießen** vt irr [h] **1.** *to shed* (*tears, blood*), *to weep* (*bitter tears*) || *to pour out* (*one's blood*) | *to spill, slop* (*milk*) **2.** ⟨tech⟩ *to fix, fasten* (*with molten lead*) | ⟨met⟩ *to spoil in casting* **3. sich** ~ *to make a mistake in pouring out* | ⟨met⟩ *to cast badly* **~g·iften** vt [h] (durch Gift töten; ⟨fig⟩ Freude etc verderben) *to poison* || ⟨fig⟩ *to embitter* (*a p's life*) || (Blut, Luft, Wasser, Boden, Waffen infizieren; ⟨fig⟩ korrumpieren) *to poison, to envenom* || ⟨fig⟩ (Gesinnungen, Handlungen, Worte) *to envenom* | **sich** ~ *to take poison* **V.ter** m ~s/~ *poisoner* **V.tung** f ~/~en *poisoning*; (durch Schlange) *venenation* **~g·ilben** vi [s] *to* (*turn*) *yellow* || **-bt** ⟨fig⟩ *moss-grown* (*doctrines*) **V.bung** f ⟨bes phot⟩ *y.ing*; *y. discoloration* **~g·ilt** imp v vergelten **~g·ing** 1. & 3. sg pret v vergehen **~g·ipsen** vt [h] *to plaster* **~g·iß** imp v vergessen | ≃meinnicht [n] ~(e)s/~e ⟨bot⟩ *forget-me-not*(*s* pl) **~g·ittern** vt [h] *to furnish with a grating* od *with trellis-work*, *to wire in*; *to grate up*; *to bar* | ≃**rt** a *latticed, trellised, barred* **V.rung** f ~/~en *grating, lattice-work* **~gl·asbar** a *vitrifiable* **~gl·asen** vt [h] & vi [s] *to glaze* (⟨a. fig⟩: *eyes*) | ([sich] in Glas verwandeln) *to vitrify* | vt *to glaze* (*a window*); –st ⟨phot⟩ *glass-bound* (Dia) **V.sung** f ~/~en *glazing* || ⟨arch⟩ *windows* pl || ⟨tech⟩ *vitrification* **Vergl·eich** m ~(e)s/~e **1.** (Vergleichung) *comparison* ⟨a. Lit⟩ | ⟨Lit⟩ *simile*, entwickelter ~ *epic* od *Homeric s.*, hinkender ~ *mixed metaphor* || ein ~, der hinkt *a leaden-footed comparison* | *collation* (*of records*) | e–n ~ anstellen *to draw a parallel* (*between*) || den ~ aushalten *to bear c.* (*with*); er kann k–n ~ aushalten mit .. *he cannot hold a candle to him* | durch ~ erledigen *to compound* vi | **im** ~ zu *in c. with*; (*as*) *compared to* od *with*; die Vorteile v X im ~ zu Y *the relative merits of X and Y* || das ist nichts im ~ z *it does not compare to*, ⟨fam⟩ *that's nothing to* || kein ~ damit! ⟨fam⟩ *not a patch on it*! | **über** allen ~ *beyond c.* | etw zum ~ heranziehen *to enter a th into c.* **2.** (gütlicher) (*private* od *amicable*) *arrangement, agreement, accomodation, adjustment* || *compromise* ⟨a. jur⟩ || *contract*, (mit Gläubigern ⟨a.⟩) *composition, accord* || e–n ~ schließen *to come to terms* pl, *an arrangement, an agreement, to make a composition* (*with*) | **~s- ~basis, ~grundlage** [f] *basis of c.n*; **~bild** [n] *reference print* **~friede** m *peace by agreement* ≃**mäßig** a *stipulated*; *agreed upon*; **~mittel** [n] *means of reconciliation*; ~probe [f] *c.n test, check sample*; ~sterbeindex [m] *c.ve mortality i.*; **~summe** f *compensation* **~termin** m *day of settlement* ~- u Schiedsordnung [f] *rules of conciliation and arbitration* **~verfahren** n *arbitration* ≃**weise** [adv] *by way of comparison* bzw *agreement* || ~ [a] Erfüllung (e–r schuldrechtl. Verpflichtung) ⟨jur⟩ *accord and satisfaction* **~zahlen** f pl *c.ve figures* **~zweck** m *purpose of comparison* **ver- ~gl·eichbar** a *comparable, paralleled* (*to*) **~gl·eichen** vt irr [h] **1.** (mit/u) *to compare* (*with*); *you can't c. poetry and politics* || *to liken* (*to*) || *to draw a parallel* (*between*) || *to collate* (*records*) || nicht zu ~, sich nicht ~ l–nd *not to be compared* (*with*), ⟨fam⟩ *not a patch on*; *nothing like* ..; es ist mit nichts z ~ *it is incomparable, it hasn't its equal, there's nothing like it* || ~ u richtigstellen *to match* **2.** ⟨fig⟩ *to adjust, settle* (*disputes*) || *to reconcile* (*parties*) | **sich** ~ mit .. *to compound with, to make up matters with* (*a p*); sich gütlich ~ *to make an amicable arrangement, to compromise*; über .. *to c.d one's liabilies* | **~d** *comparative* (*literature*) ≃**gl·eichung** f ~/~en **1.** = Vergleich 1. | **2.** *adjustment, settlement* | ~spunkt [m] *article of agrrement* || *point of comparison*; ~-stufe [f] ⟨gram⟩ *degree of comparison*; 1., 2., 3. ~ *positive, comparative, superlative degree* **~-gl·etschern** vi [s] *to turn into glaciers*; ⟨scient⟩ *to glaciate* **V.rung** f ~/~en *formation of glaciers* **~gl·ich** 1. & 3. sg pret v vergleichen **~gl·immen** vi reg & irr [s] *to cease glimmering* od *glowing*; *to go out, to die away* | ~d *dying* (*embers*) **~gl·ühen I.** vi [s] *to cease glowing* || *to cool down* | *to perish by fire* **II.** vt [h] *to spoil by heat* | ⟨tech⟩ *to fire* (*porcelain*) ≃**gn·ügen** n ~s/~ *pleasure, enjoyment, amusement*; das Leben ist kein reines ~ *l. is not beer and skittles*; [pl] (*rural*, etc) *sports* || viel ~! *have a good time*! || es machte gr ~ *it was great fun, it was* (*awfully*) *good sport*, .. mir .. *it highly delighted* od *amused me*; es ist mir ein ~ z .. *I am only too glad to* .. || jdm viel ~ m *to give a p a good time* || m Sie mir das ~ u besuchen Sie mich *give me the pleasure of a visit* || wenn's Ihnen ~ macht *if you like it* || es wird mir ein ~ s z *I shall be pleased to* || es ist gerade kein ~ ⟨fam⟩ *it's no picnic* || ~ finden an [dat] *to love* (*a th*), *to* (*take*) *delight in* || wir h viel ~ *we have great fun* | **mit** ~ *gladly*; mit größtem ~ (*very*) *willingly, with the*

Verbal-Flexion der Verben mit der Vorsilbe **ver-** → das jeweilige Simplex

greatest pleasure | **zum** ~ *for pleasure, for fun* || nur z ~ *just for the fun* od *pleasure of it* **~gn·ügen** vt [h] *to please, delight, amuse, divert* | **sich** ~ *to enjoy, disport, divert o.s.*; *to make merry*; *sich* ~ an [dat] *to take pleasure in*; sich ~ mit *to play at* **~gn·üglich** a (S) *pleasing, pleasant, amusing, delightful* | (P) [pred] *pleased* **~gn·ügt** a **1.** *merry, cheerful* | [pred] *glad*; (über [acc]) *delighted* (*at*), *pleased* (*with*) | [adv] *amusedly* **2.** (Freude erregend) *happy, merry, glad, joyous* **~gn·ügung** f ~/~en *pleasure, amusement* || (im Freien) *sport*(*s* pl), *outdoor games* || ~en nachgehen ⟨fam⟩ *to racket* (*about*) | **~s-** **~dampfer** m *cruise ship* **~fahrt** f *joy-ride* || ~ m *to j.-r.*; *to thrill-r.* (durch .. *a country*) **≃freudig** a *p.e-loving* **≃halber** [adv] *for p.e* **~kommissar** m *maître de plaisir* **~kommission** f *entertainment committee* **~ort** m *place of public amusement* od *resort* **~park** m *a.t park* **~reise** f *p.e-trip, outing, excursion* || (gr) (*grand*) *tour, cruise*; ⟨mar⟩ *cruise*, dazu: *to cr.* **~reisende(r)** m *excursionist* || *tourist* **~steuer** f *entertainment tax* **~sucht** f (*inordinate*) *love of p.e* **≃süchtig** a *hedonistic*; *p.e-mad*; *frivolous, p.e-seeking* (dazu: *p.-seeker*) **~zug** m ⟨rail⟩ *excursion-train* **Verg·olde-** **~grund** m *gilding-size* **~kunst** f *art of g.g* **~leim** m *gilder's size* **~pinsel** m *g.g-brush* **~stempel** m ⟨bookb⟩ *pallet* **ver-** **~g·olden** vt [h] *to gild* ⟨a. fig⟩; galvanisch ~ *to electro-gild* || –det *gilt* **V.der** m ~s/~ *gilder* **V.dung** f ~/~en *gilding* || nasse, trockene ~ *water-, leaf-g.g* || Feuer≃ *hot g.g* **~g·olten** pp v vergelten **~g·önnen** vt [h] *to grant, permit, allow* (*a p a th*) || jdm etw nicht ~ (miß–) *to grudge a p a th*; es war mir –nnt, z *I had the privilege* od *pleasure of* || .. nicht .. *it was not granted* od *given to me to* (*see him alive*) **~g·oß** 1. & 3. sg pret v vergießen **~g·öttern** vt [h] *to deify* || ⟨fig⟩ *to idolize, worship* **V·rung,** V.gottung f ~/~en *deification* || ⟨fig⟩ *adoration, worship, idolatry, idolization* **~gr·aben** vt irr [h] *to hide in the ground, to bury* ⟨a. fig⟩ || *to put one's forehead down in one's hands* | **sich** ~ ⟨mil⟩ *to entrench o.s.*; ⟨fig fam⟩ *to poke o.s. up*, in Arbeit *to dig in* || ⟨zoo⟩ *to burrow*; *to hole up* **V.bung** f ~/ *burying, interment* **~gr·ämen** vt [h] (Leben) *to pass .. in grief* | ⟨hunt⟩ *to scare* (*game*) | *to make* (*a p*) *sad* od *angry*; *to rub a p the wrong way* | **sich** ~ *to fret one's life out* | **-mt** a *careworn* **≃grauung** f (Wäsche≃) *greying* **~gr·eifen** vt irr [h] ⟨mus⟩ *to touch a wrong* (*note* od *string*) | sich [dat] die Hand ~ *to sprain* od *wrench one's hand* | **sich** [acc] ~ *to mistake* (*in seizing*), *to seize wrong* || ⟨mus⟩ *to touch a wrong note* | **an** [dat]: *to lay* (*violent*) *hands* (*on a p*); (mit Worten *to insult a p*) || sich an Schwächeren *or* Kleineren ~ (*an easy th*) *to find a stick to beat a dog* || (Geld, Kasse) *to embezzle* (*money*) || (Gesetz) *to infringe, violate* || (Heiligtum etc) *to profane, violate* || (S) *to steal* | sich **im** Ausdruck ~ *to express o.s. badly* | ⟨com⟩ **~griffen** (Ware) *sold out* od *exhausted* || (Buch) *out of print* || schnell ~ s: *the edition is likely to be taken up rapidly* || schnell ~e Waren [pl] *goods selling like wildfire* **~gr·eist** a *superannuated* → Greis **~gr·iff(en** pp) 1. & 3. sg pret v vergreifen **~gr·öbern** vt/refl [h] *to coarsen* **~gr·ößern** vt [h] (a. sich) *to enlarge* ⟨a. phot⟩ (in ~rtem Maßstab *on an enlarged scale*) | *to add to*; *to increase, augment* || noch ~ *to increase* (*still*) *further* | (erweitern) *to expand*; (Pupille) *to dilate* (a. sich) | ⟨opt⟩ *to magnify* ⟨a. fig⟩; stark ~d *powerful* (*glasses*); stark (schwach) ~d ⟨opt⟩ *high-* (*low-*) *-power lens* || *to swell* (*the numbers of ps*) | ⟨path⟩ (a. sich ~) *to hypertrophy* | ⟨fig⟩ *to aggrandize, exaggerate* || **sich** ~ *to increase* **V.rung** f ~/~en *enlargement* ⟨a. phot; fam: *blow-up*⟩ (als Wanddekor) *photomural*; *increase* || *thickening* (*of features* || ⟨path⟩ *hypertrophy* || ⟨opt⟩ *magnification, power* || ⟨fig⟩ *aggrandizement, exaggeration* | **~s-** ~apparat [m] ⟨phot⟩ *enlarger*; *projection printer*; ~glas [n] *magnifying-glass*; ~kraft [f] *magnifying power*; ~laterne [f] *magic lantern*; ~silbe [f] *augmentative s.*; ~spiegel [m] *concave m.*; ~stärke [f] *magnification capability*; ~verfahren [n] ⟨phot⟩ *enlarging process*; ~wort [n] *augmentative* **~großstädtern** vt/i *to urbanize*; *to become u.d* **~gr·ub** 1. & 3. sg pret v vergraben **~gr·übeln** vt [h] *to waste* (*one's time*) *in brooding* **~g·ucken,** sich ~ [h] ⟨fam⟩ = vergaffen **~g·ülden** vt [h] ⟨poet, obs⟩ = vergolden †**≃g·unst** f ~/; mit ~ *by your leave* **≃g·ünstigung** f ~/~en *privilege, concession, permission, favour*; *courtesy* || ⟨soc⟩ *benefit*, besondere ~en *fringe b.s* || ⟨com⟩ *deduction, allowance* | ~stage [m pl] *days of grace*; ~starif [m] ⟨ins, etc⟩ *preferential tariff* **≃guß(masse** f) m *grouting* **~gütbar** a *heat-treatable* (*steel*) | **≃**keit [f] *susceptibility to hardening* **~g·üten** vt [h] **1.** ⟨tech⟩ *to fine* || (Stahl) *to temper, anneal* (–tet ⟨a.⟩ *hardened and drawn*); (Erz) *to beneficiate* || –tet (a. antireflex) *coated* (*lens*) **2.** jdm etw ~ *to indemnify* od *compensate a p for a th* || *to reimburse* (*expenses*; *a p*) || (Verlust) *to make good*; *to make up for* **V·tung** f ~/~en ⟨met⟩ *age-hardening* || ⟨com, etc⟩ *indemnification, compensation, reimbursement, allowance* (*for*); besondere ~ *remuneration* || *refund* (*of* [*a loss*]) | (ärztl. etc) *fee* | ~sanspruch [m] *claim* **≃h·ack** m ~(e)s/~e = Verhau | **≃**en [vt] [h] *to hack, chop* | *to fence round .. with a* Verhau | °**≃**stücken [vt h] = besprechen B. **≃h·aft** m ~(e)s/; in ~ *under arrest* || in ~ nehmen *to arrest* || auf e–e S ~ legen *to lay an embargo on a th* | **≃**en vt [h] **1.** *to fasten with hooks* od *clasps* **2.** *to arrest, apprehend, imprison*; *to take into custody* || ~ l *to give in charge* || –tet *under arrest* || e–r S [dat] –tet *in the grip of a th* || der V.tete *the prisoner* | **~s-** ~befehl [m] *writ of arrest* || ⟨jur⟩ *capias* L || e–n ~ gegen jdn erlassen (vollziehen) *to issue a warrant for the apprehension of a p* (*to serve a writ upon a p*) **≃h·aftung** f ~/~en *arrest, imprisonment* || (bei Flucht) *capture* **~h·ageln** vi [s] *to be damaged by hail* **≃hagerung** f ⟨for⟩ *impoverishment* **~h·aken** vt [h] = verhaften 1.; sich ~ ⟨tech⟩ *to jam* **~h·alf** 1.&3. sg pret v verhelfen **~h·allen** vi [s] *to fade, die away*; *to be lost*; verhallt ⟨fig⟩ *extinct* (*fame*) || sanft ~d *lingering* **≃h·alt** m ~(e)s/~e *state of affairs* || der wahre ~ *the real facts* pl **~h·alten** a *suppressed* (*laughter*) || *suspended* (*breath*) || *smouldering, bottled, pent-up* (*anger*, etc); *guarded* (*commendation*); *chained-up* (*fury*) | (P) *reticent* | **mit** ~em Atem, Lächeln *with bated breath, suppressing a smile*; mit ~em Ausdruck (*to sing*) *with measured sweetness*; mit ~er Stimme *in a low voice, in an undertone, below one's breath* **~h·alten** irr **I.** vi [s] *to stop* **II.** vt [h] **A.** *to restrain, repress*; *to keep back*, ⟨hors⟩ *to rein* od *rope in* || *to control, master* || *to dissimulate, hide* || *to compel* **B. (Atem)** *to hold in* || *to stanch* (*blood*) || *to restrain* (*one's laughter*), *to keep* (od *restrain o.s.*) *from* (*laughing*) || **(Pferd)** *to pull*; *to rope in* || (Urin) *to retain, stop* || (Zorn) *to suppress control* **III. sich ~ A.** (P) *to act, behave* (*I don't know how to act in this case*) || *to conduct, demean, comport o.s.* | **abwartend**: *to wait for sth to turn up* || artig, brav: *to behave o.s.* || gut (mit jdm): *to get on well* (*with a p*) || passiv: *to maintain a passive attitude* || **ruhig**: *to keep quiet, to hold one's peace* od *tongue* || vorsichtig: ⟨a.⟩ *to lie low* **B.** (S) *to be* || anders: *to be different* || die S verhält sich so: *matters stand* od *ths are like this, these are the facts of the case* || wenn **es** sich so verhält *if that be the case* || umgekehrt: *to be in inverse ratio* (*to*) | es verhält sich **mit** ihm wie mit ihr

---

Aussprache: Falls nicht anders (: [*v*]) angegeben, ist v = [*f*] zu sprechen.

it is with him as it is with her | ⟨math⟩ **zu**: *to be (in proportion) to* ‖ *A is to B as X is to Y* ‖ *the length is to the breadth as 4 to 3* **~h·alten** n ~s/ **1.** (Zurückh.) *restraining, suppression (of)* **2.** (Benehmen) *behaviour, (line of) conduct; demeanour; deportment* ‖ *attitude* (gegen *toward*), feindseliges *bitterness (against)*; vornehmes ~ *bearing* ⟨a. N⟩; richtiges ~ *proper comportment* ‖ *procedure* ‖ *manner* (od *way, mode, method*) *of acting* | wie -hält es sich damit? *how about that?* | ⟨chem⟩ *reaction* (gegen *upon*) ‖ ⟨eth⟩ *behavio(u)r* | **~s-** ~forschung [f] *investigation of b.r; ethology*; ~inventar [n] *ethogram*; ~weise [f] *b.r, b.r pattern; conduct; demeanor*; ~n [pl] *b.r p.ns*; ⟨soc⟩ (v Gruppen) *institutions* **~h·ältnis** n -nisses/-nisse **A. 1.** *proportion* ‖ das richtige ~ *the due p.* | ⟨math⟩ *ratio*; ~ v .. u .. *size and price r.* ‖ gerades, quadratisches ~ *direct, duplicate r.* ‖ in k-m ~ stehen zu *to be incommensurate with* **2.** die -sse [pl] (Umstände, Lage) *circumstances* (angenehm *easy*); (umgebungbedingt) *surroundings* pl ‖ *matters* pl ‖ *condition(s* pl); *the climatic c.s* ‖ günstige -sse *facilities* (f *for*) ‖ normale -sse [acc] zeigen ⟨med⟩ *to prove normal* ‖ *state, situation* ‖ (Stellung) *position* ‖ Befehls-, Dienst-, Unterstellungs-sse ⟨mil⟩ *chain of command* ‖ (Vermögen) *means* pl **3.** (Beziehung) *relation(ship)* (zu *with*), *footing, bearing* ‖ gegenseitiges ~ *correlation* ‖ (Liebes~) *love-affair, liason* (h *to carry on*) ‖ sträfliches ~ *illicit intercourse* **4.** ⟨fam⟩ (Geliebte) *mistress*; ⟨fam⟩ *steady* **B. aus** kl -ssen *of humble birth* od *origin* | **bei** sonst gleichen -ssen *other ths being equal* | **im** ~ *comparatively* ‖ im ~ **zu** *in p. to*; *compared with, relatively to* ‖ u alles andere im ~ *and the rest accordingly* ‖ im ~ v 7 z 10 *in the p. of 7 to 10* ‖ das steht in k-m ~ z *that is out of all p. to* ‖ im selben ~ *p.ately; he became dominant to the exact p. that* (in dem) *politics became obscure* ‖ in guten (schlechten) -ssen *well (badly) off, in easy circumstances*, (⟨fam⟩ *hard up*); ⟨Am fam⟩ *on easy street* ‖ in freundschaftl. ~ mit *on friendly terms with* ‖ (nicht) im richtigen ~ stehend *(dis)p.ate, in (out of) p.* ‖ im umgekehrten ~ *in inverse ratio* | **nach** ~ der Anwesenden *in p. to ..* | **über** s-e -sse leben *to live beyond one's means*, ⟨fam⟩ *above one's weight* | **unter** diesen -ssen *under these circumstances, such being the case* | ~anteil [m] *quota, share; dividend*; ~anzeiger [m] ⟨math⟩ *exponent*; ~mäßig [a] *proportionate, proportional, relative, comparative* | [adv] *comparatively (speaking)*; *(in c. recent times)*; *by comparison, in proportion* ‖ ⟨fam⟩ *(pretty well) considering*; ~regel [f] ⟨math⟩ *rule of proportion*; ~stufe [f] *degree of p.*; ~wahl [f] ⟨m. m.⟩ *p.al representation*; ~widrig [a] *disp.ate*; ~wort [n] ⟨gram⟩ *preposition*; ~zahl [f] *p.al number; ratio* **~h·altung** f ~/ *suppression* ‖ ⟨path⟩ *retention (of urine)* ‖ *concealment* | ~sart [f] *(line of) conduct*; ~sbefehl [m] *instruction, direction*; ~smaßregel(n pl) [f] *instructions, orders* pl (jdm .. auferlegen *to enjoin lines of conduct on a p*) **~h·andeln** vt/i [h] *to discuss, transact* ‖ *to treat about ..* | ⟨jur⟩ *to try (a case)*, mündlich *to hear arguments; to plead*; -lt w ⟨a.⟩ *to be up (before a court)* | (verkaufen) *to sell* ‖ ⟨dero⟩ *to deal in; to lose in trade* | (mit jdm; wegen e-r S) *to negotiate, confer, treat (with a p; for a th); to debate (upon)* ‖ ~ Sie nicht lange mit ihm *don't argue with him* | ⟨jur⟩ gegen jdn ~ wegen [gen] *to try a p for a th* **V.dlung** f ~/~en *discussion, negotiation, transaction* ‖ ⟨parl⟩ *debate* ‖ ⟨mil⟩ *parley* ‖ ⟨jur⟩ *pleading; hearing, trial, case*; zur ~ k (Fall) *to be up for trial* ‖ pl (e-r Versammlung) *(to open) proceedings* pl ‖ Urteil ohne streitige ~ *summary judgment*; ⟨mil⟩ Vernichtungs~ → *certificate of destruction*, Verlust~ *c. of loss* | **~s-** ~apparat [m] *machinery of negotiations*; ~bericht [m], ~buch [n] ⟨jur⟩ *minute-book, minutes*; ~friede [m] *peace by negotiation*; ~führer [m] *recorder; clerk of sessions*; ⟨Am⟩ *parliamentarian*; ~partner [m] *associate in negotiation*; ~saal [m] *session-hall, -court*; ~termin [m] *day fixed for trial* | dicht **~hangen** *or* **~hängt** a *close curtained* **~h·ängen** vt [h] **1.** *to cover by hanging, to cover (over), to hang, veil* (mit *with*) **2.** *to ordain, decree* | (über [acc]) *to decree (against a p); to clamp (control on a th)*; Belagerungszustand ~ *to proclaim* od *establish martial law in a town*; (Blockade, Interdikt) *to impose (on); to impose (sanctions)* ‖ e-e (die Todes-)Strafe über jdn ~ *to inflict a penalty [up]on a p (to sentence a p to death)* **3.** (dem Pferd) die Zügel ~ *to give the reins* ‖ mit verhängtem Zügel *at full speed* **V.gung** f *imposition*, etc **~h·ängnis** n -nisses/-nisse *fate, destiny* ‖ *misfortune, mischance* ‖ ⟨rel⟩ *heavenly decree* ‖ besonderes ~ *strange fatality* ‖ schlimmes ~ *doom* ‖ z ~ w f *to be(come) fatal to* ‖ ⟨fig hum⟩ mein ~ (Braut) *my fate*; ~glaube [m], ~lehre [f] *fatalism*; ~voll [a] *omnious, portentous; ill-fated; bleak* (Warnung etc); *fatal, fateful* ‖ (unheilvoll) *disastrous* **~h·ärmen** vt (a. sich) [h] *to pine away* | -mt *care-worn, worried* **~h·armlosen** vt [h] *to minimise; to (try to) represent as harmless* od *innocent* **~h·arren** vi [h & s] *to remain (I remain yours sincerely)* | (auf [dat], bei, in [dat]) *to persist (in)* **V.rung** f ~/ *perseverance* **~h·arschen** vi [h] (Wunde) *to cicatrize, close* ‖ (Schnee) *to form a crust*; -scht *caked (snow)* **~h·ärten** vi/t [s/h] & sich ~ [h] *to harden, indurate* ⟨a. fig⟩; *his face went hard* | vt den Leib ~ *to constipate the bowels* | **-tet** a ⟨a. fig⟩ *hardened, callous, obdurate* **V.tung** f ~/~en *hardening, hardened state* | (Leib) *constipation* ‖ (Haut) *callosity* | ⟨fig⟩ *obduracy, callousness, induration* **~h·arzen 1.** vt [h] *to smear over with resin* **2.** vi/refl [s/h] *to turn to r.; to become r.ous* **V.zung** f *resinification* **~h·aspeln,** sich ~ [h] *to be caught (in)* ‖ *to tangle* ‖ ⟨fig⟩ *to get muddled* | -lt ⟨a.⟩ *fouled up* **~h·aßt** a *hated, odious; hateful; invidious* ‖ *(looks) of hatred* (jdm *to*) | es ist mir ~ *I hate* od *loathe it*, es wurde mir ~ *I came to hate it* ‖ sich ~ m bei *to make o.s. unpopular with* **~h·ätscheln** vt [h] *to coddle, cosset, pamper; to cocker up* **~hatscht** a: ~e Schuhe ⟨österr⟩ *worn-out shoes* **~h·au** m ~(e)s/~e *abat(t)is, barricade of trees, (tree* bzw *wire) entanglement* **~h·auchen 1.** vi [h] = veratmen **2.** vt [h] *to exhale* **~h·auen** vt [h] *to hew down* ‖ *to use up in cutting* ‖ *to spoil by cutting* | ⟨fam⟩ *to beat soundly; to thrash, whack, lick*; (tüchtig) *to give a p a (good) hiding, drubbing, leathering, thrashing* | ⟨fenc⟩ e-m das Gesicht ~ *to gash a p's face* ‖ ⟨mil⟩ e-m den Weg ~ *to bar a p's way* | °⟨fig⟩ (etw) *to mull*; (Ball) *to miss, muff, fluff*; (Spiel) *to spoil* | **sich** ~ *to cut badly*, ⟨fenc⟩ *to expose o.s.* ‖ ⟨fig⟩ *to blunder* **~h·eben** vt irr [h] *to lift in a wrong way* ‖ sich [dat] den Arm ~ *to sprain one's arm in lifting* | **sich** ~ *to strain, hurt, injure o.s. in lifting* °**~heddern** vt [h] *to entangle* ‖ sich ~ *to get e.d; to get o.s. tied up* ⟨a. fig⟩, (im Examen) *to make a mess of it* **~h·eeren** vt [h] *to lay waste; to harry, destroy; to devastate, ravage (with fire and sword)* | **~d** a *destructive, disastrous*; auf etw ~ wirken *to play havoc with a th* ‖ ⟨fig⟩ *devastating (headache), racking (pains)* ‖ ⟨sl⟩ *rotten* ‖ ~! ⟨sl⟩ *rot!* **V.rer** m ~s/~ *devastator, destroyer* **V.rung** f ~/~en *devastation* ‖ ~ anrichten unter *to make havoc of* ‖ *terrible havoc was caused by the storm* **~h·eften** vt [h] *to sew wrong* ‖ ⟨bookb⟩ *to misplace the sheets* ‖ ⟨surg⟩ *to sew up* ‖ *to use up in sewing* | -tet! *binding fault* **~h·ehlen** vt [h] *to conceal, hide, dissemble* ‖ sich e-e Tatsache ~ *to*

Verbal-Flexion der Verben mit der Vorsilbe **ver-** → das jeweilige Simplex

disguise a fact from o.s. **V.lung** f ~/~en *c.ment, hiding* **~h·eilen** vi [s] *to heal up* **~h·eimlichen** vt [h] (jdm etw) *to conceal* (od *to keep a th secret*) *from a p*, (schweigend) *to hush up* ‖ *to pocket* (*evidence*) | *to dissemble, disguise* | *to receive* (*stolen goods*) **~h·eiraten** vt [h] *to give .. in marriage, to wed* od *marry* (mit, an [acc] *to*); *to marry off one's daughter* | **sich** (wieder) ~ [h] *to* (*re*)*marry, to get married* (*again*) ‖ sich mit jdm ~ *to marry a p* ‖ sich unter–e–a ~ *to intermarry* ‖ sich glücklich ~ *to make a good match* | **-tet** *married* (mit *to*); ⟨Am sl⟩ *hitched, sealed* ‖ ~ s *to have a wife/husband* ‖ ⟨fam fig⟩ wir sind ja nicht ~! *we are not wedded to each other!* **V.-tetsein** n *nuptiality* **V.tung** f ~/~en *marrying, marriage* (*to*) ‖ vor s–r ~ ⟨a.⟩ *before he got married* **~h·eißen** vt irr [h] *to promise* ⟨a. bib⟩ | nichts Gutes ~d *ominous* **V.ßung** f ~/~en *promise* ‖ das Land der ~ *the Land of Promise* | ≗svoll [a] *promising, auspicious* **~h·elfen** vi irr [h] (jdm zu etw [s–m Recht]) *to help a p to a th* (a. bei Tisch), *to put* (*a p*) *in the way* (*of a th*) [*to see a p righted*] **~h·errlichen** vt [h] *to glorify, exalt, blazon; solemnify*; ⟨fam⟩ *glamo*(*u*)*rize, lionize* ‖ ⟨Lit⟩ *to celebrate*; im Lied *to sing* | **-cht** a ⟨Lit⟩ *famed* **V.cher** m *glorifier, admirer* ‖ ⟨fig⟩ *herald* **V.chung** f ~/~en *glorification* **~h·etzen** vt [h] *to instigate, incite* ‖ *to goad on* ‖ (jdn gegen) *to set* (*a p against*) **V.zung** f (aktive) *demagogy* **~h·euern** vt [h] *to hire out* ‖ (Schiff) *to freight, charter* | **sich** ~ *to sign on* **~h·exen** vt [h] *to bewitch, enchant* | **-xt** *spellbound* **~h·ielt** 1. & 3. sg pret v verhalten **~h·ieß** 1. & 3. sg pret v verheißen **~h·ilf** imp v verhelfen **~h·immeln** vt [h] *to praise up to the skies, to deify* | **-lt** s *to be in raptures* od *ecstasy* **V.lung** f *deification, adulation* | *ecstasy, rapture* **~h·indern** vt [h] *to hinder, prevent, obstruct, block* ‖ jdn an e–r S ~, daß jd tut *to prevent a p from* (⟨fam⟩ *a p*) *doing* od *a p's doing* ‖ (Blick) *to interrupt* ‖ er konnte es nicht ~ *he could not help h.s.*; → z –eiteln suchen **V.rung** f ~/~en *prevention, hindrance* ‖ [konkr] *impediment* | im ~sfalle *in case I* (*you*,etc) *should be prevented* (*from coming* etc) **~h·ing** 1. & 3. sg pret v verhängen **~h·ob** 1. & 3. sg pret v verheben †≗**h·offen** n ~s/; wider alles ~ *contrary to all expectation* **~h·offen** vi [h] ⟨hunt⟩ (of game) *to wind, scent* **~h·ohlen** [pp v verhehlen] *surreptitious, underhand; artful* **~h·öhnen** [⟨fam⟩ verhohnepiepeln ⟨Am sl⟩ *to razz*] vt [h] *to scoff* (*sneer, jeer, mock*) *at* ‖ *to deride, ridicule, jeer, flout* ‖ *to insult* (*reason*) **V.hnung** f ~/~en *derision, mockery* (*of*) **~h·ökern** vt [h] *to huckster* ≗**h·ol-** ~boje [f] *tow-buoy*; ~tau [n] *warp*(*ing line*) **~h·olen** vt [h] ⟨mar⟩ *to haul, tow, move* **~h·olzen 1.** vi [s] *to turn into wood, to lignify* **2.** vt [h] ⟨fam⟩ *to thrash, cudgel* **V.zung** f ⟨for⟩ *lignification* ≗**h·ör** n ~(e)s/~e *trial, examination*, (polizeilich) *interrogation*; ⟨jur⟩ *hearing; interrogaroty, oyer* ‖ ins ~ nehmen *to* (*cross-*)*question, to cross-examine* ‖ zum ~ ziehen *to bring* (*a p*) *up for e.n* **~h·ören** vt [h] ⟨jur⟩ *to try, interrogate* (über *on*); *to* (*cross-*) *-examine* ‖ (Zeugen) *to question* | (abhören) *to hear* (*pupils*['*lessons*]) | nicht ~ *not to lose* (*a word*) | **sich** ~ [h] *to misunderstand* °**~h·udeln** vt [h] *to spoil, botch, bungle, daub* **~h·üllen** vt [h] *to cover over, to wrap up, to veil, drape* | ⟨fig⟩ *to cloak, to black out* ‖ (die Wahrheit) *to disguise* ‖ schlecht –llt *thinly veiled* od *diguised* ⟨a. fig⟩; in –llten Worten *in veiled language* **V.llung** f ~/~en *covering, veiling; disguise, veil, cover* **~h·undertfachen** vt [h] (a. sich) *to centuple* **~h·ungern I.** vi [s] *to die of hunger, to starve* ‖ um nicht z ~ *to keep body and soul together* ‖ ~ l *to starve to death, to let die of hunger* | **-rt** aussehen *to look half-starved* od *famished* **II.** ≗ n *starvation* ‖ er kam dem ~ nahe *he sank to st.* **~h·unzen** vt [h] *to spoil, bungle, botch, boggle, daub; to make a mess* od *botch of* ‖ *to murder* (*a language*) **~h·uren** vt [h] *to spend on harlots* | **-rt** *debauched* (*p*) **~h·üten** vt [h] *to prevent* (*misfortune*), *avert* (*a calamity*), *obviate* (*danger*); *to avert* ‖ Gott verhüt's! *God forbid!*; → z –eiteln suchen | **~d** *preservative, preventive*, ⟨med⟩ *prophylactic* **V.tung** f ~/~en *prevention, protection* (v *against*); *averting*, etc | **~s-** *preventive* (*measures*); ~mittel [n] *preventive, preservative*, ⟨med⟩ *prophylactic* **~hüttbar** a *smeltable* **~h·ütten** vt [h] ⟨met⟩ *to work* (*off*), *smelt, treat* **~h·utzelt** a *shrivelled up* ‖ (P) *wizened*

verifiz·ieren [v–] vt [h] *to verify*

ver- **~·innerlichen** vt [h] *to intensify, deepen* . **-cht** a *introspective* **~·innigen** vt [h] *to intensify* ‖ *to make more intimate* | **sich** ~ *to become more i.* od *cordial* **~·irren** vi [s] sich ~ [h] *to go astray, to lose one's way*, ⟨aero⟩ .. *bearings* | **-rrt** *stray* (⟨rel⟩ *misguided*) (*sheep*), *stray* (*bullet*); ⟨fig⟩ *distempered* (*fancy*) **V.rrung** f ~/~en ⟨fig⟩ *aberration, error*; (wiederholte) *backsliding* ‖ (*youthful*) *mistake* ‖ *divagation* (*of a madman*) ‖ (moralisch, religiös) *perversion*

Ver·ismus [v–] m ~/–men ⟨arts, Lit⟩ *verism*

ver- **~j·agen** vt [h] *to drive* od *chase away, to expel* ‖ ⟨mil⟩ *to put to flight, to dislodge* ‖ ⟨fig⟩ *to dispel* **V.gung** f ⟨a.⟩ *expulsion* **~j·ährbar** a (durch Besitz) *prescriptible* **~j·ähren** vi [s] *to become void through disuse* od *by passage of time* ‖ (a. sich ~) *to grow obsolete* ‖ *to be lost by* od *to come under the statute of limitations* | **-rt** a *statute-barred, cancelled by the st. of l.* ‖ ⟨a.⟩ *out of date* ‖ *superannuated* (*claim*) ‖ *prescriptive* (*debt, right*) ‖ *stale* (*check*) ‖ ⟨com jur⟩ *barred under the State Limits* **V·rung** f ~/~en *superannuation* ‖ *prescription* bzw *negative p.*; Klage≗ *limitation* ‖ ~ geltend m *to plead l.n* ‖ Ruhen der ~ *suspension of period of limitation* | **~s-** ~frist [f] ⟨a–engl⟩ *term of l.*; ~gesetz [n] ⟨engl⟩ *statute of l.n*; ~recht [n] *statute of l.* **~j·ammern** vt [h] *to pass in wailing* **~j·ubeln** vt [h] (Zeit) *to pass in revelry* od *merry-making* ‖ (Geld) *to lavish; to make ducks and drakes of* (*one's m.*); *to play about* **~j·uden** vt/i *to Judaize* | **-det** a *Jew-ridden* | **V.dung** f ~/ *Judaization* **~j·üngen** vt [h] *to make young, to rejuvenate* ‖ ⟨fig⟩ *to renovate, regenerate* ‖ (Maßstab) *to reduce* ‖ (spitz zulaufen l) *to taper* | **sich** ~ *to grow young again, to rejuvenate* ‖ ⟨biol⟩ *to rejuvenesce, -nize*; sich ~d *juvenescent* ‖ (spitz zulaufen) *to taper* (*off*) ‖ in verjüngtem Maßstabe *on a small scale* **V.gung** f ~/~en *rejuvenescence*, etc ‖ ⟨cosm⟩ *rejuvenation* (*of the skin*) ‖ ⟨arch a.⟩ *diminution* ‖ *reduction* | **~s-** Creme [f] *Skin Relax* (*Cream*)®; ~kur [f] *rejuvenating cure*, (*monkey-*)*gland cure*; ~maßstab [m] *reduced* od *r.cing* od *small scale*; ~quell [m] *fountain of youth* °**~j·uxen** vt [h] = (Geld) verjubeln **~k·affern** vi [s] *to go native* **~k·alben** vi [h] *to calve before the time* ‖ ⟨fig⟩ *to miscarry* **~k·alken** vi [s] & sich ~ [h] *to calcify* | ~ vt [h] ⟨chem⟩ *to calcine* | **-kt** ⟨fig⟩ *hardened* (*imagination*) ‖ (P) *rusty, antiquated*, ⟨sl⟩ *gaga, soft, dotty* **V.kung** f ~/ ⟨path⟩ *calcification* ‖ ⟨chem⟩ *calcination* **~kalkul·ieren**; sich ~ *to miscalculate* **~k·am** 1. & 3. sg pret v verkommen ≗**kammerung** f ⟨pol⟩ *compartmentalization* **~k·annt** a [pp v verkennen] *misunderstood* ‖ *unappreciated* (*genius*) **~k·anten** vt [h] *to cant* (a. ⟨mil⟩ *the sights*) | –tet ⟨phot⟩ *tilted sidewise* **V.tung** f *tilt* **~k·appen** vt [h] *to disguise, mask* | **-ppt** a *disguised, secret* ‖ (*a priest*) *in disguise*; (*a writer*) *under an assumed name* **V.ppung** f ~/~en *disguise* **~k·apseln,** sich ~ [h] ⟨med⟩ *to become encysted* **~k·arsten** vi [s] *to become bare rock*; → Karst | –tet *presenting karst topography* **V.tung** f (*process creating*) *k. t.* °**~kasemat·ucken** vt [h]

Aussprache: Falls nicht anders (: [*v*]) angegeben, ist v = [*f*] zu sprechen.

⟨fam⟩ to gollop **~k·äsen** vi [s] to turn into cheese **| -st** ⟨fig⟩ deadly white **V.sung** f caseation ⟨a. path⟩ °**~k·atert** a seedy, miserable, low-spirited (after a carouse); crapulent; ⟨sl⟩ blue, green, yellow, queer about the gills **⁓k·auf** m ~(e)s/⁓e sale ‖ z ~ on s. ‖ z ~ ausstellen to put up for s. ‖ z ~ stehen to be for s. ‖ ~ nur gegen bar our terms are cash **~k·aufen** vt [h] (**an** [acc]) to sell (a. sich ~ = Käufer finden); to dispose of (to) ‖ ⟨st exch⟩ to unload; to realize (shares) ‖ zu ~ to be sold, for sale ‖ billiger ~ als to undersell (a p) ‖ mit Schaden ~ to sell at a loss **|** –ft w ⟨a.⟩ to go (cheap) **|** ⟨fig⟩ jdm etw ~ to sell a p on a th **| sich** ~ (P) to prostitute o.s.; für to give o.s. for .. ‖ (zu teuer kaufen) to make a bad bargain ‖ (S) sich gut (schwer) ~ to sell readily od well, to meet with a good sale (to be a drug in the market) ‖ sich nicht ~ to find no sale ‖ ⟨prov⟩ an guter Ware –ft man sich nie a good article is never dear **⁓k·äufer(in** f) m ~s/~ seller ‖ ⟨jur⟩ vendor ‖ (im kleinen) retailer ‖ (im Laden) shop(wo)man, sales(wo)man, (shop-girl, sales g.); shop-assistant [m & f] ‖ ⟨Am rail⟩ butcher ‖ pl sales people **|** Anstrengungen der ~ sales-force efforts **~k·äuflich** a saleable, vendible ‖ (zu verkaufen) for sale ‖ leicht (schwer) ~ easy (hard) to sell ‖ nicht ~ ⟨a.⟩ frozen ‖ schnell ~ quick selling (article) ‖ (Wechsel) negotiable **|** ⟨fig⟩ (P) venal, mercenary **|** [adv] by sale ‖ ~ überlassen to sell **Verk·aufs- ~abteilung** f ⟨ind-com⟩ sales department **~apparat, ~automat** m slot-machine, ⟨Am⟩ vending m. **~aufträge** m pl ⟨st exch⟩ selling **~bedingungen** f pl terms of sale **~buch** n sales-book **~bude** f stall, booth **~druck** m selling pressure **~feldzug** m selling campaign **~förderung** f sales promotion **~gewandtheit** f salesmanship **~kanone** f supersalesman **~kniff** m ⟨Am sl⟩ sales gimmick **~kontrolle** f sales control **~laden** m shop, ⟨Am⟩ store **~lager** n assortment **~leiter** m sales manager **~organisation** f sale organization **~plan** m selling plan **~preis** m asking price, (fester fixed) s.g-price **~räume** m pl trading premises; die 3 ~ (Amerika, Eurafrika, Australien) ⟨aero geog⟩ the three Conference Areas **~rechnung** f sales account **~recht** n right to sell **~schein** m bill of sale **~schlacht** f battle for sales **~stelle** f (Großhandel) outlet **|** energische **~technik** f high-pressure salesmanship **~tüchtigkeit** f s.p **~urkunde** f deed of sale **~wirkung** f pull **~zettel** m sales and charge slip **|** ~kontrolle [f] ⟨comp⟩ check sales slip **~ziffer** f sales figure

Verk·ehr m ~(e)s/ **A. 1.** traffic (a. Straßen⁓, einseitig unidirectional; öffentlich public transports; stark heavy t.c) ‖ ⟨allg a.⟩ come and go **|** ⟨rail, aero⟩ service **2.** (gesellig & ⟨sex⟩) intercourse (mit with), ⟨sex a.⟩ carnal knowledge (of) ‖ anregender ~ interesting friends **|** inniger ~ communion, communing (⟨a. fig⟩ with nature) ‖ ⟨jur⟩ (nach Scheidung; mit den Kindern) access (to) **3.** (Verbindung) (inter)communication; ~ mit der Öffentlichkeit public relations pl **4.** (Handel) commerce, trade (H. u ~ t. and c.) ‖ freier ~ free trade **|** ⟨st exch⟩ market (at the opening of the m.) ‖ (Geld⁓) circulation **B.** den ~ mit jdm **abbrechen** to break with a p, to drop a p's acquaintance, to send a p to Coventry ‖ den ~ aufhalten to tie up t.c ‖ ~ h or pflegen mit to associate (od have intercourse) with ‖ dem ~ übergeben to open for t.c; [pp] open to t.c **| aus** dem ~ ziehen to withdraw from service (Geld: from circulation) **|** (Ware) **im** freien ~ for concumption **| in** ~ treten mit to enter into (friendly) relations [schriftlich: correspondence] with **| mit** ~ überladen [pp] t.c congested (road) **verk·ehren I.** vt [h] to turn (the wrong way od upside down) ‖ to invert, reverse ‖ ⟨fig⟩ to pervert **|** (umwandeln) (in [acc]) to turn, change, convert (into) **| sich** ~ in to change into **II.** vi [h] (Züge, Dampfer) to run, ply; ~ l to run (bus, etc) **| an** e–m Ort ~ to frequent a place **| bei** jdm ~ to be among a p's friends **| in** der gr Welt ~ to frequent the great w. ‖ ⟨allg⟩ in: to mix, mingle in (society), (the s. with which he mixes); in guter (schlechter) Gesellschaft ~ to move in good s. (to run in bad company) **| mit** jdm: to associate [⟨Am⟩ visit] (od to have intercourse) with; to be od keep on (visiting) terms with; to mix with (people); ⟨fam mst dero⟩ to consort with a p; durch Zeichen to communicate with a p by signs ‖ (intim) to be very intimate, ⟨fam⟩ to hobnob with, to rub shoulders with a p ‖ nicht: not to have to do with ‖ wir ~ nicht mit–e–a we are not on visiting terms, we do not visit ‖ (of a girl) to walk out with ‖ intim: to carry on with a p; ⟨sex⟩ to have intercourse with, to lie with ‖ ⟨com⟩ to traffic, trade with **| unter:** to mix among (officers) **Verkehrs-** traffic **~abwicklung** f handling of t. **~ader** f thoroughfare, arterial road **~ampel** f t.-light od signal; ⟨Am fam⟩ stop-go **~amt** n → Straßen⁓; tourist information office **~andrang** m rush (of t.) **~anlagen, ~anstalten** f pl t. facilities, transport installations **~aufkommen** n auf der Strecke ⟨rail⟩ volume od density of t.c on the line **~ausmaß** n vehicular volume **~belastung** f ⟨tech⟩ onslaught of t.c; ~ e–r Straßendecke impact of t.c **~bericht** m ⟨rail⟩ t.c returns pl **~betriebe** m pl transport operators **~büro** n travel agency **~chaos** n ⟨mot⟩ havoc (on the road) **~delikt** n violation of t.c **~dichte** f density of t.c; e–r Straße number of cars frequenting a road **~dienst** m point-duty **~disziplin** f courtesy on the road; r. discipline, (good) roadsmanship **~eignung** f t.-cability **~einrichtungen** f pl arrangements for t.c **~erleichterungen** f pl (new) facilities for t.c od trade **~erziehung** f road education **|** ~swoche [f] safe t.c week **~fähigkeit** f t.c capacity of roads **~fibel** f ⟨mot⟩ illustrated highway code **~flugzeug** n air-liner, civil plane **~freiheit** f free trade **~gewicht** n (mit Ladung) ⟨mot⟩ gross vehicle weight **⁓gewöhnt** a used to t.c **~gewühl** n t.c jungle **⁓günstig** a: ~ liegen to be easily reached od accessible by car, train, etc **~gürtel** m belt, → Ring **~halle** f ⟨rail, etc⟩ concourse **~insel** f refuge island; ~ f Straßenbahn loading i. **~kavalier** m courteous driver, ⟨dero⟩ road hog **~knoten** m cross-roads **~kraftwagen** m motor-coach **~last** f carrying capacity **~leistung** f number of persons carried **~leiter** m superintendent of t.c **~leitnetz** n ⟨telph⟩ t.c control network **~licht** n t.c light **~minister** m M. of Transport **~mittel** n means [sg] of communication ‖ vehicle ‖ (Geld) currency ‖ öffentliches public conveyance **~opfer** n victim of a motorcar (etc) accident; casualty **~ordnung** f t.c regulations pl **~plan** m ⟨aero⟩ time-table **⁓politische Fragen** problems of t.c policies **~polizist, ~posten** m t.c post **~regelung** f t.c organization; flow regulation **|** ~skompanie [f] t.c control c. N **~regler** m t.c policeman; p.m. od constable on point-duty; pointsman; ⟨sl⟩ t.c- od speed-cop **⁓reich** a crowded (street) **|** Winken in **~richtung** f ⟨mot⟩ waving on t.c °**~salat** m t.c jam **~schild** n road sign **~schutzmann** m point-policeman **⁓schwach** a; ~e Zeit slack period, off-peak hours **⁓sicher** a roadworthy (car) **|** ⁓heit [f] safe t.c **⁓stark** a busy ‖ ~e Zeit rush hours pl **~stauung** f congestion of t.c, t.c block **~stern** m multiple crossing **~stockung** f jam; stoppage; off-peak hours **~störung** f interruption of t.c, block(ade ⟨Am⟩) ⟨Am a.⟩ tie-up ‖ ⟨rail⟩ break-down ‖ ~en [pl] hold-ups **~straße** f highway of t.c, main road, thoroughfare ‖ ⟨allg⟩ trade-route **~streife** f ⟨fam⟩ speed cop **~sünder** m violator of t.c, t.c sinner od offender

---

Verbal-Flexion der Verben mit der Vorsilbe **ver-** → das jeweilige Simplex

~system n; öffentliches ~ *public transit s.* **~-technik** f *t.c engineering* **~technische** Anlagen *t.c-handling system* **~teilnehmer** m *r.-user* **~-transportleistung** f *volume of goods carried* **~-truppen** f pl *army service corps* **~überwachung** f *patrolling* | ~smaßnahmen [f pl] *t.c enforcement operations*; ~sposten [m] *t.c control post* N **~-üblich** a *ordinary* (Sorgfalt *care*) **~unfall** m *t.c* od *road accident*; ~e pl *the toll (of the road)* | ~zeichen [n] *emergency t.c sign* **~unternehmen** n (öffentl. *public*) *carrier* **~unterricht** m *t.c instruction*, ⟨fam⟩ *kerb drill* **~verbot** n (f ⟨mot⟩) *no road for cars*, ⟨allg⟩ *prohibited for vehicles*; *entry p.d* (f *to*)! **~verein** m *travel-bureau* | Verletzung der **~vorschriften** f pl *violation of t.c regulations* **~wacht** f *Trans Highway Service* **~werbung** *tourist t.c propaganda* **~wesen** n *t.c* || ⟨rail⟩ *service* **~widrig** a *improper* (*driving*); (*behaviour*) *contrary to the rules of the road* | [adv] ~ über die Straße gehen *to jaywalk* **~zählung** f *t.c census* **~zeichen** n *road* od *t.c sign*

ver- ~k·ehrt a *upside down, inverted, reversed* || *inside out*; *back to front* || (falsch) *wrong* (*side*) || [pred] *amiss* | ⟨fig⟩ *perverted*; *absurd, preposterous*; *wrong-headed* (*fellow*) || Kaffee ~ *milk with a dash of coffee* || ~e Welt *the world turned topsy-turvy* || an den ~en k *to take the wrong sow by the ear, to catch a Tartar* | [adv] *perversely, wrong, awry* || etw ~ anfangen *to begin all wrong*; *to get hold of the wrong end of the stick, to put the cart before the horse* | ~ eiförmig [a] *obovate*; ~ herzförmig [a] *obcordate* | ~heit [f] ~/~en *absurdity, perversity*, etc || (Handlung) *piece of folly* **~k·ehrung** f ~/~en (*over*)*turning, inversion* || *perversion* || *misstatement* (*of facts*) || ⟨opt, phot⟩ *reversal*, → Um– **~k·eilen** vt [h] *to fasten with wedges*; *to wedge tight* | ⟨fam⟩ **1.** (verhauen) *to trash* **2.** *to sell* **V.lung** f ~/~en *wedging* **~k·ennbar** a *mistakable, easily misunderstood* **~k·ennen** vt irr [h] *to mistake* (*for another p*); *to fail to recognize* || es ist nicht z ~ *it is quite obvious*; *there is no mistaking* (*it*) || (falsch beurteilen) *to misunderstand, misjudge* || (Schwierigkeit) *to be unaware of* || (leugnen) *to deny* | –kannt *misunderstood* (*p*); *unappreciated, neglected* (*genius*) **~k·etten** vt [h] *to chain together* od *up* || ⟨fig⟩ *to concatenate*; *to link together*; *interlink* **V.ttung** f ~/~en *chaining-together* || ⟨fig⟩ *connection, linkage* (*with*); *concatenation, enchainment* (*of facts*; *with*) || *interdependency, conspiracy* ⟨fig⟩ **~k·etzern** vt [h] *to charge with* od *to accuse of heresy, to brand as a heretic* || ⟨fig⟩ *to brand*; *to calumniate* **~k·ieseln** vt [h/s] *to silicify* || –lt *silicated* **~k·irchlichen** vt *to put under clerical rule*, etc **~k·itten** vt [h] *to cement, putty* || ⟨chem⟩ *to lute* **~kl·agbar** a *suable, indictable* **~kl·agen** vt [h] *to accuse* (.. *of high treason*) || ⟨jur⟩ *to sue*, (wegen .. *for debt*); *to bring an action against* (wegen *over*) **V.gte** m [der ~, ein ~r] & f [~n/~n] *accused* || ⟨jur⟩ *defendant* **~kl·ammen** vi [s] *to get numb* **~kl·ammern** vt [h] *to cramp* **~kl·ang** 1. & 3. sg pret v verklingen **~kl·aren** vt [h] *to make sea-protest* | **V.rung** f *ship's protest* **~kl·ären** vt [h] *to glorify*; *transfigure* ⟨a. bib⟩ | ⟨fig⟩ *to illumine* | **sich** ~ *to become transfigured* od *radiant* | **-rt** a ⟨fig⟩ *delighted, happy* || (verstorben) *late* || *radiant, star*[*ry*]*eyed* (*look*) || *glorified* (*body*) || *bright* (*countenance*) || ein ~es Aussehen h *to look radiant, to beam* (*with delight*) **V.rung** f ~/ *glorification, transfiguration* || *ecstasy* **~kl·atschen** vt [h] ⟨fam⟩ **1.** (P) *to calumniate, slander, backbite, defame* **2.** (S) *to gossip* od *prattle away* **~klausul·ieren** vt [h] *to guard* od *insure by clauses, to provide against* || *to stipulate* | *to insert clauses in* | **-rt** *specially provided* (*for*) **~kl·eben** vt [h] *to paste* (*a th*) *over* od *up* || ⟨med⟩ *to plaster over* || *to gum up* || *to glue* **~kl·eiden** vt [h] *to disguise* || ⟨tech⟩ *to line, panel, case*; (täfeln) *to wainscot* || ⟨arch⟩ *to face* || ⟨min⟩ *to timber, line* || *to plank* (*a ship*) | **sich** ~ *to disguise o.s.* | **-det** ⟨a.⟩ *dressed up*, ⟨theat⟩ *made up* (als T. *as a Turk*) **V.dung** f ~/~en *disguise* || ⟨theat⟩ *make-up* || ⟨tech⟩ *covering, enclosure*; *lining, facing, casing* etc; ⟨aero, mar⟩ *fairing* | ~sblech [n] *panel* ⟨a. aero⟩ **~kl·einern** vt [h] *to diminish, lessen* || (Pläne, ⟨math⟩, etc) *to reduce*; stark –rt *small-scale* (*reproduction*); in –tem Maßstab *scaled down* | ⟨fig⟩ (herabsetzen) *to detract* od *derogate from*; *to disparage, belittle, slander* || *to chop down, whittle* (*budget*, etc) | (jds Verdienst) *to disparage* || den Wert e–r S ~ *to depreciate a th* | –rt *scaled down*; –rte Wiedergabe *reduction* **V.rung** f ~/~en *diminution*; *miniaturization* || *reduction, microcopy* ⟨a. phot⟩ || ⟨fig⟩ *belittlement*; *detraction, derogation* | **~s-** ~glas [n] *diminishing glass*; ~kopie [f] *reduction print*; ~maßstab [m] *scale* od *ratio of reduction*; ~silbe [f] ⟨gram⟩ *diminutive ending*; ~wort [n] *diminutive* **~kl·eistern** vt [h] *to glue, patch, paste up* od *together* || ⟨brew⟩ *to gelatinize* **V.rung** f *gluing-up*, etc | sich **~klemmen** *to jam* **~kl·ingen** vi irr [s] *to die away* ⟨a. fig⟩ || (Ton) *to fade away* ⟨a. fig⟩ || ⟨film⟩ ~ l *to fade out* **~kl·opfen**, ⟨fam⟩ **-ppen** vt [h] *to thrash* || °**~kn·acken** vt [h] ⟨fam⟩ **1.** = verurteilen **2.** = aufessen **~kn·acksen** ⟨fam⟩, sich (den Fuß etc) ~ *to sprain* (*one's foot*, etc) **~kn·allen I.** vt [h] *to waste* (*one's powder*) | °**sich** ~ (–lieben) in ⟨sl⟩ *to fall for* **II.** vi [s] *to explode* | °⟨fam⟩ **-llt** (–liebt) in ⟨sl⟩ *gone* od *soft on* **~kn·appen** vi [s] *to become scarce* **V.ppung** f ~/ *scarcity* (*of goods*; *of money*) °**~knautscht** a (launisch) *out of sorts, plaintive* **~kn·eifen** vt irr [h] *to pinch* | *to screw up* (*one's eyes*) | ⟨fam⟩ sich [dat] etw ~ *to deny o.s. a th* || ich konnte es mir nicht ~ *I couldn't help doing it* °**~kn·eipen** vt *to waste* (*one's money*) *in pubs* **~kn·iffen** a [pp v verkneifen] (Gesicht, Miene) *screwed up, puckered up* **~kn·ipsen** vt [h] *to use up* od *waste in making snapshots* **~kn·ittern, ~kn·üllen** vt [h] *to crumple, ruffle, crease* **~kn·öchern** vi/t [s/h] *to ossify* | vi ⟨fig⟩ *to grow callous* od *narrow-minded, to fossilize* | ⟨fig⟩ **-rt** *pedantic* (*fellow*); ~e P ⟨fam⟩ *fossil* **V.rung** f ~/~en *ossification* || ⟨fig⟩ *fossilization, fossilism* **~kn·orpeln** vi [h] & sich ~ *to turn to cartilage* **~kn·oten I.** vt [h] *to knot, tie, kink, entangle* **II.** °vi [s] *to become a cad* (Knote) **~kn·üpfen** vt [h] *to tie* od *knot* (*together*) || ⟨fig⟩ *to connect, combine*; *to attach* (*a th to a th*) || mit Kosten etc **-pft** *attended with* od *involving expense*, etc || ~ s mit *to be linked* od *bound up* or *interlocked, interwoven with* **V.pfung** f ~/~en ⟨fig⟩ *linkage, connexion, combination, nexus* || ~ v Umständen *coincidence, concurrence* || logische ~ ⟨commun⟩ (z. B.: &) *logical connective* °**~kn·urren** vt [h] = verurteilen (zu) | **sich** ~ mit *to fall out with* °**~kn·usen** vt [h]; ich kann ihn nicht ~ *I have a down on him, I hate the very sight of him* **~k·ochen I.** vt [h] *to spend in boiling, to use up in cooking* || *to boil to rags* **II.** vi [s] *to boil away* || *to be spoiled in cooking* | ⟨fig⟩ (Zorn) *to blow over* **~k·ohlen I.** vt [h] *to char, carbonize* | °⟨fig⟩ (= Kohl m mit) *to hoax*; *to pull a p's leg* **II.** vi [s] *to turn to coal, to get charred* **~k·oken** vt [h] (& sich) *to coke* **~k·ommen I.** vi irr [s] *to decay, rot*; *to go to ruin*; ⟨gard⟩ *to run to seed* | ~ l *to neglect*; *waste* || ⟨fam⟩ *to go to the bad* | (P) *to come down in the world* || *to die* (vor *of*); ⟨sl⟩ *to go to the dogs* || verkomm! ⟨österr⟩ (verdufte!) *be off!* **II.** a *decayed, gone to the bad* || (sittlich) *demoralized, depraved, debased, profligate*; *abject*; *degenerate*; *disreputable* | ~heit [f] ~/ *demoralization, depravity*; *rottenness* **~k·oppeln** vt [h] *to couple*; ⟨a–n⟩

Aussprache: Falls nicht anders (: [*v*]) angegeben, ist v = [*f*] zu sprechen.

(Kapseln) *to dock* **~k·orken** vt [h] *to cork* (*up*) **V.kung** f ⟨bot⟩ *suberifaction* °**~k·orksen** vt [h] = verpfuschen; ⟨Am fam⟩ e–e S ~ *to spill the beans* ‖ sich den Magen ~ *to upset one's st.* ‖ ⟨so:⟩ *my liver is upset* **~k·örpern** vt [h] *to embody* ‖ (als P darstellen) *to personify, personalize, incarnate, represent*; ⟨theat⟩ *to feature* **V.rung** f ~/~en *embodiment, personification*; *incarnation*; *picture* (*of health*, etc); er ist die ~ v .. *the soul of probity* **~kosten** vt [h] → abschmecken **~k·östigen** vt [h] *to board* **~kr·achen I.** vi [s] *to become bankrupt*; ⟨com Am sl⟩ *to go broke* **II. sich** ~ mit *to fall out* (od *to split*) *with* | **-cht** a *unsuccessful*, ⟨fam⟩ *broke* ‖ ~e Existenz *failure* **~kr·aften** vt [h] ⟨mil⟩ *to mechanize* ‖ *to motorize, electrify* ‖ *to introduce motor-truck service* (*between 2 places*) ‖ ⟨fig⟩ *to digest*; *afford* **~kr·amen** vt [h] *to mislay* **~kr·ampfen** vt [h] *to cramp, clench* (*with clenched fists*) ‖ sich ~ *to tighten* (*her heart tightened with fear*) | **-ft** *tight* (*cough*); *convulsed* (*face*) **V.fung** f *crampiness*, ⟨psych⟩ *frustration* **~kratzt** a *marred* **~kr·iechen**: sich ~ irr [h] *to creep into* (*a hiding-place*), *to hide, cower*; *to lie close* ‖ ⟨hunt⟩ *to kennel* (*up*), *burrow*; *to hole up* ‖ sich vor jedem ~ *to shun everybody* ‖ ⟨fig⟩ sich ~ müssen vor *to be no match for*, ⟨fam⟩ *to be not a patch on* **~kr·och** 1. & 3. sg pret v verkriechen **≁kröpfung** f *corbelling* **~kr·ümeln** vt [h] *to crumble*; *to fritter away* ‖ °**sich** ~ *to disappear, to be lost* od *mislaid* ‖ (P) *to slink away* **~kr·ümmen I.** vi [s] (& sich [h]) *to grow crooked* **II.** vt [h] *to bend, curve, deform* | **-mmt** ⟨a.⟩ *misshapen, out of shape* **~kr·üppeln I.** vt [h] *to cripple, maim* ‖ (verkümmern) *to stunt* **II.** vi [s] *to become crippled* od *stunted* | **V.lung** f *deformity* ‖ *stunted growth* **~kr·usten** vi [s] (& sich [h]) *to become incrusted* | **V.tung** f *incrustation* **~k·ühlen I.** vi [s] *to cool down, to get cold* **II.** vt [h] *to cool, chill* | **sich** ~ *to catch* (*a*) *cold* **V.lung** f ⟨österr⟩ (= Erkältung) *cold* **~k·ümmern I.** vt [h] *to stunt* ‖ *to embitter* (*a p's life*) ‖ *to spoil* (*a p's pleasure*) ‖ *to encroach upon* od *to curtail* (*a p's rights*) **II.** vi [s] *to wear away*; *to starve, languish*; *to become stunted* ‖ ⟨scient⟩ *to atrophy* ‖ (körperlich) *to fall* (*waste, pine*) *away* ‖ ~ l *to starve, stunt* | **-rt** a ⟨anat, bot⟩ *stunted*; *scrubby* (*tree*) ‖ ⟨fig⟩ *thwarted* (*senses*) | **V.rung** f ~/~en ⟨a.⟩ *embitterment, curtailment* ‖ *stunted growth* ‖ *pining-away* ‖ ⟨anat⟩ *stuntedness, atrophy* **~k·ünd(ig)en** vt [h] *to announce* ‖ *to make known* ‖ *the bell gave out the hour of 5* ‖ (öffentlich) *to proclaim, publish*; (laut) *to blazon* | *to pronounce* (*sentence*) ‖ *to preach* (*the gospel*) | (im voraus) *to foretell, presage, prophesy, herald, bode* (*it bodes nothing good*) | Schlechtes ~d *portentous, ominous* **V.(ig)er** m ~s/~ ⟨a.⟩ *harbinger* ‖ *proclaimer* ‖ *herald* ‖ *prophet* **V.igung** f ~/~en *announcement* ‖ *publication, proclamation* ‖ *prediction, prophesy* ‖ Mariä ~ ⟨ec⟩ *Annunciation, Lady-day* **~k·ünsteln** vt [h] *to over-refine* ‖ *to spoil by too much art* **~k·upfern** vt [h] *to copper* ‖ ⟨typ⟩ *to copper-face* **~k·uppeln** vt [h] *to pander, pimp, prostitute, sell* ‖ ⟨tech⟩ *to couple* **~k·ürzen** vt [h] *to* (⟨paint⟩ *fore*)*shorten* ‖ *to lessen, diminish*; *contract* ‖ (Lohn) *to reduce, cut* ‖ (beschränken) *to stint, curtail* ‖ (abkürzen) *to abridge* ‖ *to pass away* od *to beguile* (*the time*) ‖ jdn ~ *to do a p wrong* ‖ jdm (die Rationen) ~ *to cut a p short in* .., (das Leben) *to shorten* ‖ jdn um etw ~ *to stint a p in a th* ‖ (etw) um 1 Jahr ~ *to lop a y. off* (*the period of* ..) | **-zte** Arbeitszeit *short time*; *abridged* (*edition*); ⟨paint⟩ *foreshortened*, dazu: *foreshortening* | **sich** ~ *to grow shorter, to shorten* **~l·achen** vt [h] *to laugh at*; *to deride, ridicule* | ≁ n *derision, laugh* ([gen] *at*) **≁l·ad** m ~s/ Sw = –ladung **≁l·adebahnhof** m *entraining station* **~brücke** f *shipping* od *loading bridge* **~dokumente, ~papiere** n pl *sh.g documents* **~(flug)hafen** m *port of* (*aerial*) *embarkation* **~offizier** m ⟨aero, mar⟩ *loading officer* **~plan** m *e.g scheme* **~platz** m (z Landungsunternehmen) *e.g point* **~rampe** f *e.g* od *l.g platform* **~l·aden** vt irr [h] *to load* ‖ ⟨mar⟩ *to ship, freight* (lose *in bulk*) ‖ ⟨rail⟩ *to forward, consign* ‖ ⟨aero⟩ *to emplane* ‖ ⟨mil⟩ *to entrain*; *embark*; *embus*; (auf Lkw) *entruck* | **V.der** m ~s/~ *loader* ‖ *shipper*; *shipping-agent* ‖ ⟨rail⟩ *consignor* | **V.dung** f ~/~en ⟨a.⟩ *shipment* N ‖ *consignment*; nach Einheiten ⟨mil⟩ *administrative loading* N | **~s-** ~gebühren [f pl] *shipping* od *loading charges*; ~kosten [pl] *shipping expenses* pl; ~schein [m] ⟨com⟩ *bill of lading* **≁l·ag** m ~(e)s/~e *publication* (*of books*); in ~ nehmen *to undertake the p. of* | (Firma) *publishing house, publisher*(*s* pl) ‖ im ~e von, ~ .. *published by* ‖ Bier≁ *brewer's agency*, (Vertrieb) *sales office* (*of an agent*) **~l·agern** vt [h] (& sich) *to shift* ‖ ⟨fig⟩ sich ~ (Interesse) *to be switched over* (*from* .. *to*) | **V.rung** f *dislocation, displacement* ‖ ~skosten [pl] *removal expenses* **≁l·ags- ~anzeige** f *p.r's advertisement* **~artikel** m *publication* **~buchhandel** m *publishing business* **~buchhändler** m *publisher* **~buchhandlung** f *publishing house, firm of publishers* **~geschäft** n = ~buchhandel **~ort** m [gen] .. *where* .. *is published* **~recht** n *copyright*, ≁liche Ausgabe *c. edition* **~vertreter** m *book salesman* **~werk** n *publication* **~zeichen** n (*publisher's*) *imprint* **ver-~l·anden** vi [s] (of lake, etc) *to silt up* **≁-l·angen** n ~s/ (Forderung) *demand, request* | (Sehnsucht) *longing, desire*; *appetite*; (heftig) *craving*; ⟨a. fig⟩, *lust*, ⟨fig⟩ *craze* (nach *for*); (beharrlich) *insistence* (*on*); *urge* (*to do*); brennendes ~ fühlen *to be itching* (nach *for*; *to do*) | ⟨cant⟩ *yen* (*for opium*, etc) | ~ h *or* tragen nach *to crave, long, hanker*, (sinnlich) *lust for*; (*her breasts'*) *desires* pl; nach der er ~ hatte *the longed-for*; die z besitzen er ~ hatte *the lusted-after* ‖ kein ~ h ⟨a.⟩ *to have no curiosity* od *ambition* (*to do*) ‖ sein ~ stillen an *to have one's will of* (*a p*) | **auf** jds ~ *at a p's request, by a p's desire* ‖ auf ~ *by request*; ⟨com⟩ *on command*; (*payable*) *at call*; auf ~ v ⟨contr, etc⟩ (*if*) *required by* **~l·angen I.** vt [h] **A. 1.** (fordern) *to ask*; *exact*; *demand* (*satisfaction*) ‖ *to command, compel* (*attention*) ‖ *to call for* (*the bill*; ⟨a. fig⟩: *praise*) ‖ v jdm etw dringend ~ *to exact a th from a p* ‖ (laut) *to clamour*, etc *for* ‖ (klingelnd) *to ring for* ‖ stürmisch ~ nach *to shout for a p, a th* ‖ ⟨com⟩ *to charge* (*a price*); der meist ~gte (Herd) .. *mostly asked-for* **2.** (erfordern) *to require* ‖ die Logik –gt es, daß *l. dictates that* **3.** (wollen) *to will* (*if he willed it*) **4.** (wünschen, ersehnen) *to desire, want, crave* **B.** er –gt Gehorsam *he will be obeyed*; (*the situation*) *dictates* .. ‖ k–e Gunst, k–n Vorteil ~ *to ask no odds* (*from a p*) ‖ tun, was –gt w kann *to do anything in reason* ‖ mehr ~ *to ask for more* ‖ mehr kann man nicht ~ *one cannot wish for more* ‖ viel ~ *to set a high standard* ‖ was ~ Sie v mir? *what do you want of me*? ‖ was ~ Sie dafür? *how much do you charge for it*? ‖ das ist zu viel –gt *that's asking too much* ‖ das ist reichlich viel –gt! *that's a tall order*! **II.** vi [h] (**nach** [dat]) *to ask* (*for*) ‖ *to wish to see* (*a doctor*) | (sich sehnen) *to long* (*for*), *to hanker, crave* (*after*) | ~, daß *to ask that* (.. *should*) ‖ ~ es z sehen *to demand to see it*; *I want to do it* ‖ *my stomach cries for food* **III. es** –gt mich zu erfahren *I am anxious to know*; es –gt ihn darnach *he is eager for it* **~l·ängern** vt [h] (& sich) *to lengthen* | vt ⟨math⟩ *to produce* (*a line*) ‖ (Paß) *to renew* ‖ (Frist etc) *to prolong, extend, protract* ‖ (Wechsel) *to renew* ‖ (fortsetzen) *to continue*; *to spin out* | **V.rung** f ~/~en *lengthening* ‖ *prolongation, extension* ‖ *the small* (*of one's*

Verbal-Flexion der Verben mit der Vorsilbe **ver-** → das jeweilige Simplex

back) ‖ ⟨math⟩ *production* ‖ ⟨sport⟩ *extra-time* | (Vorsprung) *projection* | (Fortsatz) ⟨anat⟩ *process* ‖ *additional piece* | (Wechsel≗) *renewal, prolongation,* ⟨jur⟩ *protraction* | ~ der Lebenserwartung *increased expectation of life* | **~s-** ≗-**fähig** a ⟨com⟩ *protractile* **~kabel** n ⟨rec, etc⟩ *extension leads* pl **~punkt** m ⟨mus⟩ *dot* **~rohr** n *extension* od *elongation pipe* od *tube* **~schnur** f ⟨el⟩ *extension cord* **~spiel** n *period of extra time* **~stück** n *lengthening-piece* ‖ *allonge* (*of a bill*) **~l·angsamen I.** vt (& sich) [h] *to slow down, to decelerate, slack(en)* ‖ ⟨mot⟩ das Tempo ~ *to slow down* (auf *to*) | –mtes Tempo *slower motion* **II.** ≗ n (der [gen] Arbeits-, Produktionsleistung) *ca'canny*; ≗ *or* **V-mung** f *slowing down* (⟨a.⟩ v Neutronen) **~l·äppern** vt [h] ⟨fam⟩ *to dawdle, trifle,* (⟨fam⟩ *fribble*) *away* ‖ sich ~ *to dribble away* **~l·arven** vt [h] (& sich) *to disguise, mask* ‖ ⟨ent⟩ *to enter the larva(l) state* **~l·as** 1. & 3. sg pret v verlesen **~l·aschen** vt [h] ⟨rail⟩ *to fish* ‖ –schter Stoß *fish-plate* ≗**l·aß** m –lasses/ *reliance* ‖ ~ setzen auf *to place dependence on, to rely on* ‖ es ist kein ~ auf ihn *he is not to be relied on, there is no relying on him* **~l·assen I.** vt irr [h] **1.** (S) *to leave* (*behind*) (⟨a.⟩ Dienst, Raum) *to quit* ‖ (S) *to relinquish* | (böslich) *to abandon, forsake, desert*; *to let* (*a p*) *down*; *to run away from* | (Braut) *to jilt*; jdn ~ (im Stich l) *to throw a p over* ‖ (Ort) *to come away from* ‖ (Universität) *to go down from* ‖ (Bewegung) *to fall out of* ‖ das Haus nicht ~ *not to move from the h.*; das Z. ~ *to walk out of the room* | (räumen) *to vacate* **2.** ⟨fig⟩ (Thema) *to dismiss*; *all recollection went from him* ‖ (of feelings) *to go out of, to drop away from* ‖ s–e Kräfte ~ ihn *his strength fails him* ‖ (of thoughts) jdn nicht ~ *to haunt a p* **II. sich ~ auf** [acc] *to rely* od *depend upon* (.., daß du tust *I rely on you to do*); *to put dependence on a p*; *to build upon a th*; *to count* (⟨Am a.⟩ *bank*) *on*; *to trust* (*a p*; *one's eyes*); .. in e–r S *to entrust sth to* (*a p*) ‖ ~ Sie sich darin auf mich *stand on me for that* ‖ darauf kannst du dich ~! *you may rely on it! and no mistake!*, .., daß *you may rest assured that* ..; man kann sich nicht darauf ~ *one couldn't swear by it* ‖ sich auf sich selbst ~ *to paddle one's own canoe* **III.** [a] *forsaken, abandoned* ‖ (allein) *lonely, alone* ‖ (hilflos) (*for*)*lorn* ‖ (öde) *desolate*, (Straße) *deserted*, (Haus) *derelict*; *deserted* (*village*) | v Gott u der Welt ~ *forsaken of God and man* **IV.** ≗ n der Autobahn *leaving the motorway* ‖ böswilliges ≗ (des Ehegatten) *abandonment* | ≗heit [f] ~/ *abandonment* ‖ *forelornness* ‖ *loneliness* | ≗schaft [f] ~/ *property left*; ≗werden [n] ⟨a.⟩ *desertion* **~l·ässig, ~l·äßlich** a *reliable, dependable*; *trustworthy*; *stanch, staunch* (Anhänger, Freund etc) ‖ (S) *sure, certain*; ⟨fam⟩ *straight* (*information*); es ist nicht ~ *one couldn't swear by it* **~lastet** a ⟨mil⟩ *lorried*; *trucked* (Truppe) **~l·ästern** vt [h] *to slander, calumniate* **V.rung** f ~/~en *slander(ing), calumny* ≗**l·aub** m ~(e)s/ mit ~ *by your leave, with your permission, saving your presence* ≗**l·auf** m ~(e)s/ *lapse, expiration* | (Entwicklung) *course*; *progress* ⟨a. med u mil⟩; *process*; (*line of*) *development* ‖ weiterer ~ *sequel* ‖ Ansatz u ~ e–s Angriffs *planning and execution of offensive operations*; ~ des Gefechts *course of the battle* ‖ ⟨cosm⟩ *contours* (*of the skin*, etc) | **im** ~ v *in the course of* ‖ **nach** ~ v *after* [*the lapse of*] (*a few weeks*) ‖ e–n guten (schlimmen) ~ nehmen *to come off well*; ⟨med⟩ *to take a normal* od *good course*; (⟨a. med⟩ *to take a bad turn, to end fatally*); den üblichen ~ nehmen *to run to pattern*; (das Konzert) nahm e–n guten ~ .. *came off well* | ~kette [f] (Schmuck) *chute*, → enge K. **~l·aufen I.** vi irr [s] (Zeit) *to pass* ‖ (Frist) *to expire, elapse* | (ablaufen) (of events) *to pass* od *go* (*off*), *to turn out* .., *to take a* .. *course* | (Farben) in–e–a ~ *to shade off, to blend* ‖ (Pudding etc) *to run* ‖ (Bewegung) *to be* (*in the opposite direction*); (Straße) *to run*, schräg *to slant* | **bei** erfolgreich ~dem Angriff *when an attack is going well* **II.** vt [h] *to pass* od *spend in running* od *walking* ‖ *to digest* (*dispel, cure*) *by running* ‖ *to walk off* (*one's headache*) ‖ e–m den Weg ~ *to block a p's way, to stop a p* | **sich** ~ *to go astray, to drift away*, ⟨fig hum⟩ *to get lost* (a. S), *to lose one's way* ‖ wie h Sie sich hierher ~? *what made you come here?* | (sich zerstreuen) *to disperse, scatter, to be scattered* ‖ (Gebirge) *to slope gently* ‖ (Wasser) *to fall, subside* **III.** [a] *abandoned* (*girl*) ‖ *stray* (*cattle, dog*) ‖ ~er Kerl *vagrant* **~laust** a *lice-ridden*, ⟨mil⟩ *cooty, loppy* **~l·autbaren I.** vt [h] *to divulge, report, publish*; *to make known* **II.** vi [h] = –lauten | **V.rung** f ~/~en *transpiration*; (amtliche) *communiqué* ‖ (inoffizielle) *statement* **~l·auten** vi [h] *to transpire, to be spread about* ‖ es –tet, daß *it is reported* od *learned that* ‖ wie –tet *according to what people say, as it is rumoured* ‖ ~ l *to give to understand*; *to say, hint, intimate* (*that*) **~l·eben** vt [h] (Zeit) *to spend, pass* ‖ ⟨fam⟩ *to have* (*they had a fine time, their honeymoon at*) | **-bt** a ⟨fig⟩ *used up, played out, worn out* ‖ (altersschwach) *decrepit* **~leb·endigen** vt [h] *to vivify* **~l·edern** vt [h] ⟨tech⟩ *to* (*line with*) *leather* | ⟨fig⟩ *to give a p a good thrashing* od *licking* **~l·egbar** a *movable* **~l·egen I.** vt [h] **1. (örtlich)** *to transfer* (*the centre of gravity to* ..) ‖ *to throw all one's weight on one's left leg* ‖ *to shift*; *to move, remove* (⟨a. mil⟩ Truppen, ⟨com⟩ Geschäft), ⟨mil⟩ (Truppen, Feuer) *to transfer* N, e–e Einheit ⟨a.⟩ *to relocate* ‖ ⟨Lit⟩ (Schauplatz) *to lay, locate* (*the scene in* ..) ‖ ⟨tech⟩ (Leitung etc) *to lay*, (anders) *to relay*; (Bausteine) *to set* | (verlieren) *to mislay, misplace* ‖ sich ~ l *to transfer* (*the play will t. well to the open air*) | (den Weg etc) *to bar, block, obstruct, stop*; *to cut off* ‖ ⟨hunt⟩ (Fuchsröhren) *to put to* [adv] | (im Buchhandel) *to publish* **2. (zeitlich)** (verschieben) (auf [acc]) *to put off* (.. *to a later date*), *to postpone* (*till*) ‖ *to adjourn* (*the meeting*) ‖ ~ in .. *to project a th into the future*; etw in e–e Zeit ~ *to ascribe* .. *to a period* **3. sich** ~ auf [acc] *to apply o.s. to, to take up* (*Latin*), *to go in for* (*tennis*) **II.** [a] **1.** *stale, spoiled* od *damaged by lying* **2.** (verwirrt) *embarrassed, confused*; *disconcerted, distraught*; *abashed*; *puzzled*; *perplexed*; *uneasy, constrained*; *self-conscious* (*in the presence of one's betters*); ⟨fam⟩ *nonplussed* ‖ nach e–r ~en Pause *after a moment's hesitation* | ~ m *to baffle, embarrass, puzzle*, etc | ~ s ⟨a.⟩ *to be discomfited* (*at being seen*), *to be ill at ease* (jdm gegenüber *with a p*); .. **(um)** *to be struck for a th*; *to be at a loss* (*for an answer, a dancing partner*); *to be in urgent need* (*of*), *pressed* (od *hard up*) (*for money*); nie um e–e Aushilfe ~ s *never to be at a loss for a valid expedient* ‖ **vor**: *inarticulate with rage* | [adv] ⟨a.⟩ *awkwardly, blankly* | ≗heit [f] ~/~en *embarrassment* ‖ *awkwardness* ‖ (Schwierigkeit) *perplexity, hole, predicament, dilemma*; *difficulty* (*to help a p out of a d.*) ‖ äußerste ~ *nonplus* | e–m ~en bereiten *to give a p trouble* | sich **aus** der ~ ziehen *to extricate o.s. out of a difficulty*, etc ‖ **in** ~ s *to be at a nonplus*; *at a loss* (um *for*), *pressed* (*for time*) ‖ ⟨fam⟩ *to be in a scrape, fix* ‖ in (Geld-) ~ s *to be in financial straits*, ⟨fam⟩ *to be hard up*; .. äußerst .. *to be stuck up for* ..; *in a hell of a mess* ‖ in ~ bringen, setzen = verlegen m ⟨a.⟩ *to corner, stump*; *to stick* (*a p*) *up*; *to put a p* (*on the spot*) od *about, to make ill at ease, to put out of countenance, to cause* (*a p*) *embarrassment*, ⟨fam⟩ *to floor* od *tree* (*a p*) ‖ jdn in finanzielle ~ bringen *to straiten a p* ‖ in ~ k *to get embarassed*;

Aussprache: Falls nicht anders (: [v]) angegeben, ist v = [f] zu sprechen.

to get o.s. into a scrape; in ~ s *to be hard pressed, pinched, hard up, straitened* (*to do*) | ~sgeste [f] ⟨eth⟩ *displacement activity* ≃**l·eger** m ~s/~ *publisher* → Verlag; er hat f ihr Buch e–n ~ gefunden *he got her b. published for her* ≃**l·egung** f ~/~en *removal*; *transfer, move* ⟨a. mil⟩ | (*mis*)-*laying* | *stopping* | *putting-off, postponement* | *publishing, publication*; ⟨mech⟩ *obturation*; ⟨tech⟩ offene ~ auf Putz *exposed wiring*, etc | ~smarsch [m] ⟨mil⟩ *administrative march* **~l·eiden** vt [h] jdm etw ~ *to make a p sick of, to disgust a p with, to spoil a p's pleasure in a th* | es ist mir –det *I have taken a dislike to it*, ⟨fam⟩ *I'm sick of it* ≃**leih** m ~(e)s/~e ⟨film, etc⟩ *renting agency*; *distribution* | ~kopie [f] *release copy* od *print* **~l·eihen** vt irr [h] **A.** *to lend* (*out*) ‖ (gegen Miete) *to let* od *hire out* ‖ (auf Zins) *to put out* od *lend* (*at interest*) **B. jdm** etw ~ *to award a th to a p* ‖ (Amt) *to appoint a p to* ‖ (⟨univ⟩ Grad) *to tender* ‖ (Güter) *to grant away* ‖ (v Gott: Gesundheit, Leben, Segen) *to grant* ‖ (Hilfe) *to render* (*assistance*) ‖ (Lehnsgut) *to invest a p with* ‖ (Pfründe) *to collate* .. ‖ (Recht, Titel etc) *to confer* od *bestow on* ‖ (Stelle) *to grant* .. *to* | (**e-r S**) *to confer upon* ‖ *to bring* (*new life*) *to* .. ‖ *to lend* (*life, vehemence, interest*) *to* ‖ (Aussehen, Glanz, Farbe etc) *to impart* (*speed*, etc) ‖ dem Leben Sinn ~ *to make life mean sth* ‖ e–m Charakter Leben ~ *to bring a ch. to life* | (s–n Gefühlen etc) Ausdruck ~ *to give utterance* od *voice to* .., *to express* (*one's joy*) **C. -liehen** erhalten *to be conferred* od *awarded* (*a decoration*) | ~ w (Stipendium) *to be tenable* (auf .. *for 4 years*), .. v *to be in the gift of* | e–m ~e Gaben *talents one is endowed with* ≃**l·eiher(in** f) m ~s/~ (von Geld) *lender* ‖ (Vermieter) *jobber* ‖ (e–s Rechts etc) *bestower*, etc, ⟨jur⟩ *grantor* ‖ ⟨ec⟩ *collator, patron* | **-hung** f ~/~en *lending out* ‖ *letting out* ‖ *investiture* ‖ *endowment, bestowal* ‖ *grant*(*ing*) ‖ ⟨jur⟩ *concession*; ⟨ec⟩ *collation* ‖ (ehrende) *award* **~l·eimen** vt [h] *to glue up* **~l·eiten** vt [h] (irreführen) *to mislead, to lead on* od *astray* ‖ (veranlassen) *to induce* ‖ (verführen) *to seduce, entice* (*to*); *to inveigle, deceive* (*into*); *to delude* od *trap* (*a p*) (zu *into*, z tun *into doing*); jdn ~ z glauben *to deceive a p into thinking, to incline* od *lead a p to think*; .. z tun *to put* od *set a p up to do*; *to suborn* od *procure a p* (*to commit perjury*) *to carry a p away into doing* ‖ **sich** ~ l z *to commit o.s. to, to be betrayed* od *trapped into* ≃**l·eiter** m ~s/~ = –führer; **-tung** f ~/~en *misleading* ‖ *seduction* ‖ ~ z Meineid *subornation of perjury* **~l·ernen** vt [h] *to unlearn, forget* (das Tanzen *how to dance*); *to fall out of* (*fencing*) **~l·esen I.** vt irr [h] *to recite*; *to read* (*aloud* od *out*) | *to pass* (*the day*) *in reading* | *to misread* | (Namen) *to call over*, ⟨mil, school⟩ *to call* (*the roll*) | (Kaffee, Gemüse) *to pick* | **sich** ~ *to make a slip in reading, to read wrong* **II.** [a] *madly fond of reading* **V.sung** f ~/~en *reading, recital* ‖ (Namen≃) *roll-call* **~l·etzbar** a (S) *violable, damageable*; *frail, delicate, brittle* ‖ (verwundbar) *vulnerable* ‖ (empfindlich) (P) *touchy, susceptible* **~l·etzen** vt [h] *to wound, injure, hurt*; *to grate upon* (*ears, nerves*) | den Anstand ~ *to offend against decency* ‖ (Eid, Ehre etc) *to violate* ‖ (Gefühle) *to harrow* ‖ (Gesetz) *to break, outrage* ‖ jds Interessen ~ *to wrong a p* ‖ s–e Pflicht ~ *to fail in one's duty* ‖ *to encroach upon* (*a p's rights*) ‖ *to infringe* (*a rule*) ‖ (Sinn) *to outrage* ‖ (jds Würde) *to ruffle* | ⟨fig⟩ *to hurt a p's feelings*; *to offend, bite* | **sich** am Bein ~ *to injure one's leg* | leicht –tzt *sensitive, easily offended*, ⟨fam⟩ *touchy* | sich –tzt fühlen *to feel aggrieved*, im Innersten .. *to be pained to the depths of one's being*; –tzte Eitelkeit *wound to one's vanity* ‖ Tote u V.te *dead and injured* | **~d** a *offensive, cutting*; *wounding* (⟨a. fig⟩ ~de Redewendung *w.g phrase*) **V.zer** m *offender*; (e–s Patents) *infringer* **V.zung** f ~/~en *hurt, wound, injury*; ⟨path⟩ *lesion* (*of the brain*); ~en, denen er erlag *injuries that proved to be fatal* | ⟨fig⟩ *wrong*(*ing*) ‖ (e–s Gesetzes) *violation, infraction* ‖ *infringement* (*of a patent*) ‖ *breach* (*of priviledge, confidence, duty*); ~ der ehelichen Treue *infidelity, unfaithfulness* ‖ (Beleidigung) *offence, outrage, insult* ‖ *laceration* (*of feelings*) **~l·eugnen** vt [h] (Eigenschaft etc) *to deny* ‖ (Einfluß) *to belie* ‖ *to renounce* (*a p*); (Kind etc) *to disown, disavow*; *to ignore, cut* ‖ (Grundsätze) *to act against, to renounce* (*one's belief*) ‖ ⟨cards⟩ Farbe ~ *to revoke, not to follow suit* ‖ nicht ~ können ⟨a.⟩ *to betray* | **sich** ~ *to practise self-denial* ‖ sich ~ l (vor jdm) *to have o.s. denied, not to be at home* (*to a p*) ‖ sich nicht leicht ~ (l) *not to be easy to hide* **V.ner** m ~s/~ *abnegator, denier, disowner* **V.nung** f ~/~en *denial, disavowal* ‖ *renunciation* ‖ Petri ~ *Denial of P.* **~l·eumden** vt [h] *to calumniate, slander, traduce, defame, backbite, malign, vilify*, ⟨bes Am⟩ *frame*; jdn ~ (anschwärzen) *to blacken a p's character* **V.der(in** f) m ~s/~ *calumniator, backbiter, slanderer* **v.derisch** a *calumnious, slanderous, defamatory* **V.dung** f ~/~en *calumny, slander, libel, defamation, detraction*; *vilification, aspersion* | ~skampagne [f] *smear*; ~sklage [f] *libel suit, action for libel* **~l·ieben** [h] sich (sterblich) ~ in [acc] *to fall* (*over head and ears*) *in love with*; *to take a fancy to, to become enamoured of* ‖ ⟨sl⟩ *to fall for* ‖ sich in–e–a ~ ⟨fam⟩ *to click* ‖ sich leicht ~ *to be amourously inclined* | **-bt** a (in [acc]) *in love* (*with*); *enamoured, fond* (*of*); (närrisch) *infatuated, smitten* (*with*) ‖ [abs] *amorous*, ⟨fam⟩ *head over ears* | ⟨fam⟩ *sweet* od *gone* (*on*) | ~ s in ⟨sl⟩ *to be nuts, spoony, patty on*; wahnsinnig –bt in *madly in love with* | (jdm) ~e Augen m *to cast amorous* (⟨sl⟩ *goo-goo*) *glances at*, ⟨fam⟩ *to make sheep's eyes at, to give* (*a p*) *the glad eye* ‖ ~er Auftritt *love-scene* | **V.bte(r** m) f *lover*; *love-sick* (*youth*) *girl* | **V.btheit** f *amorousness*; *being in love*; *infatuation*; *amorous disposition* ‖ In-sich-selbst-~ *narcissism* **~l·iederlichen I.** vt [h] *to waste in* bzw *ruin by dissipation* **II.** vi [s] (P) = verkommen **~l·ief** 1. & 3. sg pret v verlaufen **~l·iegen I.** vt [h] (Zeit) *to spend* od *waste in lying* ‖ *to crease by lying on it* ‖ **sich** ~ (P) ⟨obs⟩ *to lose all activity* ‖ (S) = **II.** vi [s] *to get spoiled through lying too long* **~l·ierbar** a *easily lost* **~l·ieh(en)** 1. & 3. sg (pl) pret, (pp) v verleihen **~l·ieren I.** vt [–lor/–loren] [h] **A.** *to lose* ‖ (Blätter, Geweih, Schale, Zähne etc) *to shed*; *to cast* (*one's teeth*) ‖ Geld ~ ⟨a.⟩ *to drop m.* ‖ den Grund ~, den Boden unter den Füßen ~ *to get out of one's depth* ‖ (Gewohnheit) *to outgrow*; Kopf u Kragen ~ ⟨fig⟩ *to lose one's shirt*; die Selbstbeherrschung ~ ⟨fam⟩ *to blow up* **B.** wir h k–e 5 M. z ~ *we have not 5 minutes to spare* ‖ da ist k–e Zeit z ~ *there is no t. to be lost* **C.** ~ **an** [dat]: *to lose* (*money*) *by* (*an article*), (*a friend*) *in* (*a p*) | **an** jdn: *to lose in playing* od *dealing with a p*; *I lost £ 2 to him* ‖ **aus** den Augen ~ *to lose sight of* | **bei** jdm ~ *to sink in a p's estimation* ‖ .. war bei ihr –loren *all entreaties were lost on her* ‖ dabei (Geld) ~ *to lose .. over it* ‖ kein Wort **darüber** ~ *not to waste any words on it* ‖ ein Spiel ~ gegen ⟨Am⟩ *to lose out to* (*a p*) ‖ er –lor k–e Zeit mit s–r Antwort *he replied in no time* ‖ e–n Kampf betrügerisch ~ *to throw a fight* **II.** vi [h] *to come off as a loser* ⟨sport⟩ *to lose* (gegen *to*) ‖ das Bild hat (an Schönheit) –loren .. *has lost sth of its beauty, has fallen off* **III. sich** ~ *to be* od *get lost* | (P) *to lose one's way* ‖ ⟨fig⟩ *to lose o.s.*; *to steal away*; (Menge) *to disperse* | (S) ⟨fig⟩ *to wear off, to melt away*; *to drop out of sight*, (unmerklich) *to dwindle*; s–e Schritte –loren sich .. *receded* ‖ (Farbe) *to fade* ‖ sich in fremde

---

Verbal-Flexion der Verben mit der Vorsilbe **ver-** → das jeweilige Simplex

Gebiete ~ ⟨fig⟩ *to wander off into alien fields* ‖ sich ins Blaue ~ *to melt into blue* ‖ (Fleck) *to disappear* ‖ (Gespräch) *to drift into* (in) ‖ (Schmerz) *to subside* ‖ (Töne) *to die away* | sich **an** e–n Ort ~ *to find o.s. at a place* ‖ sich **in** Gedanken (Reden) ~ *to be lost in thought*, (*to ramble*) | → –loren **IV.** er ist am ≗ *he plays a losing game* ≗**lierer(in** f) m ~s/~ *loser* ‖ schlechter ~ ⟨Am fam⟩ *sorehead* ≗**l·ies** n –ses/–se *dungeon, keep* **~l·ies** imp v –lesen **~l·ieß** 1. & 3. sg pret v –lassen **~l·oben** vt [h] (mit) *to affiance, engage* (*to*), *to betroth* (*with*) ‖ sich ~ (mit) *to engage o.s.* (*to*), *to become engaged* (*to*) ‖ sie gelten als –bt *their names are bracketed together* ≗**l·öbnis** n –sses/–sse = –lobung ≗**l·obte(r)** m (Verlobte f) ~n/~n *betrothed, fiancé(e* f) Fr ‖ ⟨fam⟩ (*his, her*) *intended*; *young* (*wo*)*man* ‖ die ~n [pl] *the engaged couple, the betrothed* ≗**l·obung** f ~/~en *betrothal, engagement* (mit *to*) (.. abbrechen *to break off*) ‖ ~ der hl. Katharina *Mystic Marriage of S. C.* | **~s-** ~anzeige [f] (*public*) *announcement of an e.*; ~feier [f] ⟨a–engl⟩ *e. festivities* pl; ~ring [m] *e.-ring*; ~stunde [f] *trysting hour* **~l·ocken** vt [h] *to entice, allure, seduce, tempt, inveigle*; *to lead* (*a p*) *on* | **~d** a *tempting, inviting, enticing, attractive* **V.er** m ~s/~ *misleader, seducer* **V.ung** f ~/~en *allurement, enticement*; *seduction*; *temptation* **~l·odern** vi [s] *to cease burning* **~l·ogen** a *lying, mendacious* | ≗heit [f] ~/ *mendacity, untruthfulness* **~l·ohnen** vi imps [h]; es verlohnt die (*or* sich der) Mühe *it is worth* (*while* od) *the trouble*, .. nicht ⟨fam a.⟩ *it doesn't pay* ‖ es v. sich z tun *it is worth doing* **~l·or** 1. & 3. sg pret v –lieren **~l·oren** a [pp v –lieren] **A.** *lost* ‖ (hilflos) *forlorn*; (ratlos) *quite* od *all at sea* ‖ ⟨fig⟩ *done for, ruined* ‖ ~e Arbeit *labour lost* ‖ ⟨cul⟩ *poached* (*eggs*) ‖ *vain* (*hope*) ‖ (Kugel) *stray* ‖ ~e Liebesmühe *Love's Labour's Lost* ‖ *Paradise Lost* ‖ ~er Mann ⟨fam⟩ *goner* ‖ ~e Partie *losing game* ‖ das Spiel ist ~ ⟨fig⟩ *the game is up* ‖ ⟨mil⟩ ~er Haufe, Posten *forlorn hope* ‖ auf ~em Posten *in a very exposed position* ‖ *random* (*shot*) ‖ unwiederbringlich ~e S ⟨fam⟩ *goner*, [pred] *gone with the wind* ‖ ⟨bib⟩ *prodigal* (*son*) **B.** etw (das Spiel) ~ **geben** *to give a th up as lost* (*to throw the game up*, ⟨fig⟩ *to give in*) | –|**gehen** *to be* od *get lost*; (Brief) *to miscarry*; (Schiff) *to founder* ‖ –gegangen *missing* (*book*) ‖ an ihm ist ein .. –gegangen *in him a good teacher has been lost, he was cut out for an actor*, etc ‖ alle Kraft ~ h *to be quite wasted out* ‖ hier **hast** du nichts ~! *you are not wanted here!* ‖ alles ist ~ *the game is up* | ⟨prov⟩ Ehre ~, alles ~! *give a dog an ill name and hang him!* **~l·öschbar** a *extinguishable* **~l·öschen I.** vt [h] *to extinguish* ‖ (Schrift) *to efface, obliterate* **II.** vi [–losch/–loschen] [s] *to be extinguished, to go out*; *to die* (*dying fire*) ‖ ⟨fig⟩ *to become extinct* **~loschen** a *dead* (*coals*), *effaced* (*inscription*); *dead* (*traffic, light*, etc) **~l·osen** vt [h] *to dispose of by lot, to raffle for, to draw* od *cast lots for* **V.sung** f ~/~en *raffle, lottery*; ⟨com⟩ *allotment* **~l·öten** vt [h] *to solder up* **V.tung** f ~/~en *soldering* **~l·ottern I.** vt [h] *to dissipate* ‖ (Zeit) *to fritter away* **II.** vi [s] (P) *to go to the bad* ‖ (S) *to go to rack and ruin* | –rt [a] *dissipated, disreputable*; *ill spent life* **~l·udern** vi/t [s & h] = –lottern **~l·ud** 1. & 3. sg pret v –laden **~l·umpen** vi [s] *to go to rags* ‖ ⟨fig⟩ *to go to the dogs, to come down in the world* | **~pt** a *ragged* ‖ ~er Kerl *ragamuffin* ‖ → = –lottert ≗**l·ust** m ~es/~e *loss* (*sustained*); *damage* (*suffered*) ‖ *forfeiture* (*of the crown*) ‖ *disappearance* (*of a ring*) ‖ (Todesfall) *bereavement* ‖ schwere ~e *heavy tolls* ‖ ⟨cards, etc⟩ *losings* pl | ⟨mil⟩ (erlittene) ~e [pl] *casualties* pl N ‖ [dat] ~e beibringen *to inflict losses* (*on the enemy*) ‖ e–n völligen ~ bringen *to make a dead loss* ‖ ~e erleiden *to suffer losses*, gr .. *to be thrown for a big loss*, schwere ~e e. *to lose heavily*; ~ ertragen *to afford to incur a loss* ‖ die Bevölkerung hatte ~e *there were civilian casualties*; kostet ~e *costs c.s* | ⟨tech⟩ *breakage, waste* ‖ (Gas etc) *escape, leakage* ‖ ~ an Zeit *or* Lohn *broken time* | **bei** ~ von *on* od *under pain of, under penalty of losing, with forfeiture of* | **in** ~ geraten *to disappear*; *to be* od *get lost* | **mit** ~ *at a loss* od *sacrifice*; mit ~ arbeiten *to operate in the red* | **ohne** eigene ~e *without loss*; gerade noch ohne ~ abschneiden, ohne ~ durchk *to break even* | **unter** schweren ~en *with heavy losses* | sich **vor** ~en schützen *to save one's bacon* **v.bringend** a *involving* (*a*) *loss, prejudicial, detrimental*; *red-ink* (*business*); *losing* (*game*) **v.frei** a *lossfree* **V.konto** n *loss account* **V.liste** f ⟨mil⟩ *casualty list*; *casualties* pl **v.reich** a ⟨tech⟩ *wasteful* ‖ ⟨mil⟩ *involving heavy losses* **V.träger(in** f) m *loser* **V.ziffer** f *casualty figure* **~l·ustig** [pred] a; [gen] *deprived of*: jdn e–r S für ~ erklären *to declare a p to have forfeited a th* ‖ sich ~ m, ~ gehen *to lose, miss, forfeit* (*a th*) **~m·achen** vt [h] (jdm) *to bequeath, will, leave* (*to a p*) ‖ (*I was left £ 500*) ≗**m·ächtnis** n –sses/–sse **1.** *will* **2.** *settlement*; *legacy, bequest*, → Legat ‖ *to come into a legacy* ‖ ⟨fig⟩ *trust* | ~erbe [m] *legatee*; ~geber [m] *legator*; ~nehmer [m] (e–r bewegl. S) *legatee* (→ *devissee*) **~m·ahlen** vt [h] [pp ~] ⟨tech⟩ *to grind up* **V.lung** f *crushing and pulverisation* **~m·ählen** vt [h] *to give in marriage, to marry* (mit *to*) | **sich** ~ *to marry, to get married* | **~lt** a *married*, ⟨geh Spr⟩ *wedded* (*to*) ‖ die **V.lten** [pl] *the bridal couple*; Neu–lte [pl] ⟨bes Am⟩ *newlyweds* **V.lung** f ~/~en *nuptials* pl, *marriage* | ~sfeier [f] *wedding ceremony* **~m·ahnen** vt [h] *to exhort, admonish* **~maled·eien** vt [h] *to curse* **-deit** a *confounded* (*fellow*) ‖ ⟨sl⟩ *blooming* (*business*) ‖ ~! *confound it!* **V.d·eiung** f ~/~en *imprecation, malediction* **~m·annigfachen** vt [h] *to diversify, vary*, (farblich) *variegate* ‖ *to reproduce*; *multiply* **~m·anschen** vt [h] ⟨fam⟩ *to mess up* **~m·arken** vt [h] *to mark off* (*by landmarks*) **~m·aß** 1. & 3. sg pret v vermessen °**~m·asseln** vt [h] *to bungle, muddle*; ⟨fam⟩ *muff*; ⟨sl⟩ *botch* ≗**massung** f ~/ etwa: *loss of individuality and levelling of social and intellectual characteristics*, dazu: v.massen *to lose i. and be levelled as to* .. **~m·auern** vt [h] *to wall up* ‖ (einmauern) *to wall in*, (lebendig) *to immure* **~m·ehrbar** a *multipliable* **~m·ehren** vt [h] & sich ~ *to augment, multiply, increase, enlarge* (um *by*) ‖ ~ *to add to* (*a p's joy*) ‖ sich ~ ⟨bot⟩ *to propagate*, ⟨zoo⟩ *to breed* | **-rt** noch .. *and even more emphatically* .. **-rte** Auflage [f] *enlarged edition* **V.rung** f ~/~en *increase, multiplication*, etc; *addition* **~m·eidbar** a *avoidable* **~m·eiden** vt irr [h] *to avoid, side-step* (*an obstacle*) ‖ (geschickt) *to elude, evade* ‖ (ängstlich) *to shun, shirk* ‖ *to escape* (*from*) ‖ ⟨mar⟩ *to steer clear of* ⟨a. fig⟩ ‖ (Fragen, Ton) *to eschew* ‖ wenn er es ~ kann *if he can help it* ‖ sich ~ l *to be avoidable* | **-dlich** a *avoidable* **V.dung** f ~/ *avoidance, eschewal* ‖ bei ~ v *under pain of* **~m·einen** vi [h] *to suppose, presume, think, imagine, believe* **~m·eintlich** a *supposed, reputed, presumed, alleged* ‖ *pretended, would-be* [attr] ‖ (Erbe) *presumptive* (*heir pr.*) ‖ *ficticious* (*wealth*) **~m·elden** vt [h] *to mention, announce, notify* ‖ mit Respekt (→ Verlaub) z ~ *saving your presence* ‖ es ist mir –det worden *I have been informed* **~m·engen** vt [h] *to mingle, mix, blend* | ⟨fig⟩ *to confound, confuse*; ⟨fam⟩ *to mix up* ‖ in e–e S –gt *involved in* (od *mixed up with*) *an affair* **~m·enschlichen** vt [h] *to clothe with* (od *to represent under*) *a human form* ‖ *to humanize, civilize* ‖ (höhere Wesen) *to anthropomorphize*

Aussprache: Falls nicht anders (: [*v*]) angegeben, ist v = [*f*] zu sprechen.

V.chung f ~/ *humanization* **≗m·erk** m ~(e)s/~e *mark, jotting*; *note, entry*; *remark*; *memorandum* || Inhalts≗ *docket* || mit ~ versehen *to docket, to tick .. off, to indorse* | ≗en [vt] [h] *to note down, to make* od *take a note of, to record* || übel ~ *to take amiss* **~m·essen I.** vt irr [h] *to measure* || (Land) *to survey* || **sich** ~ *to measure wrong* || (sich erdreisten) ([gen] *or* z tun) *to make bold* (*to do*); *to dare, presume, venture* (*a th* od *to do*); *to boast* (*of doing* od *that one would do*) || sich z hoch *or* viel ~ *to be too self-confident* **II.** [a] *bold, daring, audacious* || (in Ansprüchen) *presumptuous, arrogant, overweening* || (frech) *impudent* | ≗heit [f] ~/ *boldness, audacity, temerity* || *presumption* || *self-confidence*, etc **≗m·esser** m ~s/~ *surveyor* | **-ssung** f ~/~en *measurement* || (v Geschützstellungen) *position area survey*(*ing*); (v Land) *s.*(*ing*) (⟨a.⟩ ~sarbeit) || ⟨a–n⟩ (Flugbahn≗) *tracking* | **~s-** ~beamte(r) [m] *surveying officer*; ~kunde [f] *geodesy*; ~punkt [m] *fixed point*; ~stab [m] *arrow*; ~station [f] ⟨a–n⟩ *tracking station*; ~unterlagen [f pl] *survey information*; ~wesen [n] *surveying* **~messingt** a *brass-plated* **~m·ied** 1. & 3. sg pret v –meiden **~m·ietbar** a *rentable* **~m·ieten** vt [h] *to let* (*out*) (⟨a.⟩ Schiff) || (Pferd, Wagen) *to job* || ⟨jur⟩ *to hire out, to lease* || Haus, Zimmer z ~ *h., r. to let, for letting*, ⟨Am⟩ *for rent* || Möbel etc z ~ *f.*, etc *on hire* | **sich** ~ = sich –dingen || (S) sich leicht ~ *to let readily* **≗m·ieter(in** f) m ~s/~ *letter*, ⟨Am⟩ *renter*, ⟨jur⟩ *lessor* || *landlord* (*landlady*) | *jobber* | (v Gegenständen) *hirer out* | **-tung** f ~/~en *letting* (*out*), etc || ⟨a.⟩ *lease* | ~sbüro [n] *house-agent's office* **~m·indern** vt [h] *to diminish, lessen* (⟨a.⟩ vi = sich ~) || *to lower* || *reduce* (an [Zahl] *in*, um *by*) || (Ausgaben) *to retrench* || (Kräfte) *to impair* || Fahrt ~ *to ease* od *slacken speed* || ⟨artill⟩ (Ladung) *to reduce* || ⟨mus⟩ (um $^1/_2$ Ton) *to flatten* | **sich** ~ *to grow less, to decrease*; *to fall back* || (Preis etc) *to go down, to fall* || (Schmerz etc) *to abate, subside* | **~rt** ⟨mus⟩ *diminished* (*third*) | **V.rung** f ~/~en *diminution, decrease*, etc || *reduction* ([gen] *in wages*, ⟨mil⟩ *in force*); ~ der Truppenstärke *rundown* | ~szeichen [n] ⟨mus⟩ *flat* || *impairment*; → Beruhigung **~m·inen I.** vt [h] *to mine*; *to lay mines in* **2.** ≗ n *mine-laying* ([gen] *in*) **~m·ischen** vt [h] *to mix* (*up*), (*inter*)*mingle* || mit Wasser *to dilute, water* || (Farben, Tees etc) *to blend* || ⟨fig⟩ *to amalgamate* || (Metalle mit–e–a) *to alloy* || (Rassen) *to interbreed, cross* | **sich** ~ *to mix, mingle, blend* (*with*) || sich leicht ~ (l) *to blend well, to go well together* | **~scht** a *mixed*, etc || (in Zeitungen) *miscellaneous* (*news*, etc) || ~e Aufsätze [m pl] *miscellany* **V.schung** f ⟨demog⟩ *miscegenation* **~m·iß** imp v vermessen **~m·issen** vt [h] *to miss* || *to weary for* (*a p*) || (beklagen) *to regret, deplore* (*the loss of*) | **-ßt** a *missing*, ⟨mil⟩ *missed in action*; als –ßt melden *to report missing* | –ßt w *to be missing* (auf .. *from the farm*); *to be* (sehr *greatly*) *missed* (*his absence is greatly felt, he leaves a great gap*) || etw ~ l *to lack*; *to be without* | die **V.ßten** pl *the ps missing*; ⟨mil⟩ *the missing* **~m·itteln I.** vt [h] *to mediate* || *to pass* (*a th*) *on* (*to a p*) || (Zusammenkunft, Aussöhnung, Kauf etc) *to effect, arrange* || (Frieden, Anleihe etc) *to negotiate* | ⟨fig⟩ *to convey* (*an idea*), *to put* (*an idea*) *across* || *to reconcile* (*conflicting notions, a contradiction*) || *to transmit* (*an art to a country*) || Arbeit ~ *to arrange for placement*; (Wissen) *to impart* (*to*) **II.** vi [h] *to mediate* || *to intervene* (bei .. *in a th, with a p*) || *to intercede, interpose* (zw *between*) **~m·ittels, -lst** prep [gen] *by* (*means* od *way of*), *through* **V.(e)lung** f ~/~en *mediation, intervention* || *arrangement* || *conciliation* || (Beilegung) *accommodation, settlement* || ⟨com⟩ *brokerage* || durch jds freundliche ~ *by a p's good offices* | *agency*; ⟨theat, film⟩ *casting directory, c.-agents* | **~s-** ~amt [n] ⟨telph⟩ *exchange*; *switching center* ⟨a. comp⟩; ~anstalt [f] *agency*; ~ausschuß [m] *good offices committee*; ~büro [n] *registry-office* (*for servants*); ~schnur [f] ⟨telph⟩ *patching cord*; ~stelle [f] *agency* || ⟨telph⟩ *exchange*; ~versuch [m] *attempt at reconciliation* || *attempted settlement*; ~vorschlag [m] *proposal for an arrangement* od *settlement* **≗m·ittler** m ~s/~ *mediator, intermediary*; *intercessor* || (S) *medium* (*through the m. of*) || ⟨fig⟩ *vehicle* (*of ideas*) | ⟨com⟩ *go-between, agent, middle-man* || ~ verbeten! *no agents*! | ~in [f] *mediatress, mediatrix* | ~vergütung [f] (*agency*) *commission* °**~m·öbeln** vt [h] **1.** *to turn into money* || *to waste* || *to sell at any price* **2.** (verdreschen) *to thrash, wallop*, ⟨Am sl⟩ *to lam* || *to scold* **~m·ochte** 1. & 3. sg pret v vermögen **~m·odern** vi [s] *to moulder away*; *to rot, decay* || längst ~rt *long dead and gone* **~m·öge** prep [gen] *by* od *in virtue of* (*our arrangement*) || *by dint of* (*work*, etc) || *on the strength of* || *in consequence of* || *according to* **≗m·ögen** n ~s/~ *faculty, power, ability* || (Reichtum) *fortune, wealth*; *means, riches* pl | bares ~ *assets* pl || bewegliches ~ *personalty* || unbewegliches ~ *real estate* | ein ~ aufhäufen *to roll up a fortune* | ~ erwerben *to make a fortune*, ⟨Am sl⟩ .. *one's pile* || ~ h *to be a man of property* od *substance* || .. im ~ h *to be worth* (*£ 5000*) || das geht über mein ~ *that is beyond my power* od *me* || sein ~ verlieren *to lose one's money*, ganzes ~ v. *to lose one's all* || v eigenen ~ lebende P *p of independent means* **~m·ögen** vt/i irr [h] *to be able* (*to do*) || *to have the power* (*to do*) || wir ~ das nicht *we cannot do it* || wir ~ nicht z verhindern *we cannot prevent* || wir w tun, was wir ~ *we will do all that lies in our power* | etw ~ *to have influence* (bei jdm *with a p*; über jdn *over a p*) || sie ~ alles bei ihrer Mutter *they can do anything with their m.* | jdn z etw ~ *to prevail upon* od *induce a p to do a th* | **es** über sich ~ *to prevail upon o.s.* od *to bring o.s.* (*to do*) | **~d** *powerful* || (reich) *wealthy, rich, well-to-do* (*farmer*) | [pred] *well off* || sehr ~ *of great substance, of large means* | die ≗en [pl] *the well-to-do* **V.s-** **~abgabe** f *capital levy, l. on c.* **~anlage** f *investment* **~aufnahme** f *valuation of property* **~aufstellung** f *statement of affairs, financial st.t* **~bestand** m *amount of p.* || *assets* pl (*of a bankrupt*), ⟨jur⟩ *estate* **~bilanz** f *balance* **~erträge** m pl *interest earned* **~lage** f *pecuniary circumstances* pl **~nachweis** m *information concerning one's financial position* **~pfleger** m *committee of the estate* (*of a lunatic*) **~prüfung** f *means test* **≗rechtlich** a *in right of one's property* || [adv] *in money matters* **~steuer** f *property tax* **~umstände** m pl, **~verhältnisse** n pl *means* pl || *assets* (*of a debtor*) || in guten ~n *in easy circumstances* **~verfügung** f in betrügerischer Absicht ⟨jur⟩ *fraudulent transfer of property* **~verwalter** m *trustee* **~vorteil** m *financial benefit* **~werte** m pl *property, estate*, etc **~m·öglich** a *well-to-do, wealthy* **~m·orschen** vi [s] *to moulder, rot* **~m·uckern** vi [s] *to grow sanctimonious* || ⟨fam⟩ *to turn saintly* od *goody-goody* **~m·ummen** vt [h] (⟨a.⟩ sich) *to mask, disguise* || der, die V.mmte *the mask* || V.mmte [pl] *masqueraders* **V.mmung** f ~/~en *disguise, masquerade* **~m·uren** vt [h] ⟨mar⟩ *to moor* **~m·uten I.** vt [h] *to suppose, conjecture*; *suspect, surmise*; *expect*; *guess*; *imagine, fancy* || dürfen wir ~? *may we presume*? || wir ~, er war es *or* daß er es war *we imagine* (od *have an idea*) *it was he* || nichts Arges ~ *to suspect no harm* || mehr als man ~ kann *more than meets the eye* || niemand –tete es (*or* etw davon) *nobody had any suspicion of such a th* || nicht ~d *unsuspecting* (*of an attack*) || nicht –tet *unsuspected*

Verbal-Flexion der Verben mit der Vorsilbe **ver-** → das jeweilige Simplex

supposition || nach m–m ≈ *in my opinion* || wider alles ≈ *contrary to all expectation* **~m·utlich** a *likely, probable, presumable* || (Erbe) *presumptive* | [adv] *probably, I suppose* **≈m·utung** f ~/~en *guess, supposition* || ~en [pl] *guess-work, conjecture* || bloße ~ *mere surmise* || aller ~ nach *to all appearances* || ~en anstellen über *to guess at* || das brachte mich auf die ~ *that gave me the idea* || darüber gibt es mancherlei ~en *it is almost anyone's guess* **~n·achlässigen** vt [h] *to neglect* (*a th, o.s.*) || *to be derelict in* (*one's duty*) || *to ignore* (*forms*) || *to bestow little care on* (*a p*) || (geringschätzig) *to slight* || ⟨jur⟩ (Grundstück) *to waste* || s–e Arbeit ~ *to slack on one's job*; etw zu lange ~ *to let ths go too long* | **-gt** a *untended* **V.gung** f ~/~en *neglect*(*ing*) || *dereliction* || *careless treatment* || ~ der Aufsichtspflicht ⟨jur⟩ *neglect of tutelage* **~n·adern** vt [h] [österr] *to denounce; inform against* **~n·ageln** vt [h] (Tür) *to nail* (*up*) || (Geschütz) *to spike* || *to prick* (*a horse*) *in shoeing* | *to stud with nails* | ⟨fig fam⟩ **-lt** [a] *blockheaded, slow-witted, dense, dull* || ich war wie –lt *I was stunned*; ein vernagelter Schädel *a closed mind* **~n·ähen** vt [h] **1.** *to sew* od *stitch up* **2.** *to use up* bzw *spend in sewing* **~n·ahm** 1. & 3. sg pret v –nehmen **~n·arben** vi [s] *to cicatrize; to heal, scar, skin* (*over*) **~n·arren**: sich ~ [h] (in [acc]) *to become foolishly fond* (*of*), *to become infatuated* (*with*), *to lose one's head over* od *heart to* ..; ⟨sl⟩ *to fall* (*for*) | **-rrt s in** *to be infatuated* od *smitten with*, ⟨fam⟩ *wrapt up in, gone* (⟨sl⟩ *nuts* od *potty*) *on* (*a p*); *to dote on* (bes *child*); *to be wild* od *faddy about* (*caviar*); in–e–a *to be crazy about one another* || ~ in *stuck on* || *she loves him with madness* **V.rrtheit** f *infatuation* **~n·aschen** vt [h] *to squander* od *spend on sweets*, etc | **-scht s** *to have a sweet tooth* **~n·ebeln** vt [h] *to befog*, ⟨mil⟩ *to smoke* **V.lung** f *smoke screening; concealment by smoke* **~n·ehmbar** = –nehmlich **~n·ehmen I.** vt irr [h] *to hear, perceive* || es war deutlich z ~ *it made itself distinctly heard* | (erfahren) *to understand, learn, hear* | ⟨jur⟩ *to examine, interrogate; to take* (*a p's*) *statements*; .. in e–r S *to put a p through a th* | **sich** ~ l *to intimate one's opinion* | **sich** mit e–m ~ *to come to an agreement with a p* **II.** ≈ [n] ~s/ *perception* || (Nachricht) *intelligence, communication* || (Verständnis) *understanding* || gutes, schlechtes ~ *good, bad terms* pl | dem ~ **nach** *according to rumour* od *report, by all accounts, from what I hear* od *gather* || gutem ~ nach ist es so *we have it on good authority that it is so* | **v.mlich** a *audible* || (deutlich) *distinct, articulate, clear; resounding* (*blow*), *loud*; s–e St. ist weit ~ *his voice carries far* | [adv] *aloud*; sich ~ aussprechen *to articulate o.s.*; *distinctively* (*American idiom*) **V.mung** f ~/~en ⟨jur⟩ *hearing, examination, trial*; mündliche *parol evidence* | ~soffizier [m] *interrogation officer* **~n·eigen**: sich ~ [h] (Herr:) *to bow*, (Dame:) *to curtsy* (vor [dat] *to*); ⟨fig⟩ *to pay tribute to* **V.gung** f ~/~en *bow, curtsy* || e–e ~ m *to* (*make a*) *b., to* (*drop a*) *c.* (*to*) **~n·einbar** a *deniable* **~n·einen** vt [h] *to* (*answer in the*) *negative* || *to gainsay, contradict* || die Frage ~, daß etw geschieht *to rule out the possibility of a th happening* || (leugnen) *to deny, disavow* || er –nte die Frage *he returned a negative, his answer* (*to the qu.*) *was in the n.* || ⟨parl⟩ die Anfrage wird –nt *the answer is in the n.* | **~d** a *negative* **V.nung** f ~/~en *negation, denial* | **~s-** ~fall [m]; im ~e *in case of an answer* (od *should the a. be*) *in the negative*; ~satz [m] *negative sentence*; ~wort [n] *negative*

verni mou n [invar] Fr ⟨engr⟩ *soft ground*

ver- ~n·ichtbar a *destructible* **~n·ichten** vt [h] ⟨a. fig⟩ *to annihilate, undo, unmake; rout* || (S) *to bring to nought* || *to nullify, annul* || *to abolish* || (ausrotten) *to extirpate, exterminate* || (zerstören) *to destroy* || (Namen) *to obliterate* || (Knospen) *to nip* ⟨a. fig⟩ | ⟨fig⟩ *to kill, slay, crush, blast, scotch, blight, overthrow; to knock* (*wipe, snuff*) *out* || *to disappoint, extinguish* (*hopes*) | (völlig) *to annihilate; nullify; to smite* (*a p*) *hip and thigh* || *to wreck* (*a p's happiness*) ⟨mil a.⟩ *to mop up* | –tet w (Plan etc) *to fall to the ground* || alles ist –tet! ⟨sl⟩ *that has torn it* | **~d** (Antwort, Niederlage) *crushing* || (Kritik) *destructive, scathing, devastating* | *annihilating* (*remark*), *killing* (*reply*), *withering* (*glance, scorn*) || e–a ~d *internecine* || *destructive* (Kritik) | [adv] ~ schlagen *to defeat* | v Regen –tet *rain-stricken* **V.ter** m ~s/~ *destroyer, annihilator*, etc **V.tung** f *destruction, annihilation, extinction*, etc || *wreckage, overthrow* || *annulment, abolition* || etw mit ~ bedrohen *to strike at the root of a th* | **~s-** ~feuer [n] ⟨mil⟩ *destructive* od *destruction fire*; ~kampf, ~krieg [m] *internecine war, war of extermination, war to the knife*; ~lager [n] *extermination camp*; ~maschine [f] (Akten≈) *shredding machine*; ~mittel [n pl] *engines of destruction*; ⟨ent⟩ *insecticides*; ~schlag [m] *knock-out blow*, ⟨box a.⟩ *smasher*; ~waffe [f] *mass-destruction weapon* **~n·ickeln** vt [h] *to* (*coat with*) *nickel* | **V.lung** f *nickel-plating* **~n·ieten** vt [h] *to clinch, rivet* | **V.tung** f ~/~en *clinching*, etc **~n·imm** imp v –nehmen || ~ mein Gebet! *hearken to my prayer*!

Verniss·age [verni'sɑ:ʒ] [eig n, mst f] ⟨paint⟩ *preview*

vern·ommen pp v vernehmen

ver- ≈n·unft f ~/ *reason* || (Urteilskraft) *judgment* || (Verstand) *understanding, intellect* || gesunde ~ *common sense* | ~ annehmen *to listen to* (od *to see*) *r.* || nimm ~ an! *be your age*! || aller ~ bar s *to have taken leave of one's senses* || das zeugt v ~ *that makes good sense* || z ~ bringen *to bring* (*a p*) *to his senses* od *to r.* || durch Zureden *to talk* (*a p*) *to r.* || (wieder) z ~ k *to come* (*back*) *to one's senses; to steady* || das geht über alle ~ *that is beyond the reach of r.* || es entspricht der ~, daß *it stands to r. that* || es ist wider die ~ *it is contrary to r.* | ≈begabt [a] *rational, r.able, sensible*; ~beweis [m] *proof founded on r.*; ~ehe [f] *marriage of convenience*; ≈gemäß [adv] *according to r., r.able, logical, commonsensical*; ~glaube [m] *rational belief, rationalism*; ~gründen [m pl dat] unzugänglich *incapable of reason*; ~heirat [f] = –ehe; ≈los [a] *irrational, senseless, unr.able*; ~losigkeit [f] ⟨a.⟩ *want of r.*; ≈mäßig [a] *r.able, r.ed; rational*; [adv] ~ erklären *to rationalize*; ~recht [n] *rational law*; ~religion [f] *natural* od *rational religion*; ~schluß [m] *r.ing, ratiocination* || ⟨log⟩ *syllogism*; ~standpunkt [m] *rationalism*; ~wahrheit [f] *truth founded on r.*(*ing*); ~wesen [n] *rational being*; ≈widrig [a] *irrational, contrary to r., illogical, unr.able* **≈nünftel·ei** f ~/~en *sophistry, subtlety, hairsplitting* **~n·ünfteln** vi [h] *to subtilize* **~n·ünftig** a *sane, sober, sound* (*idea*); (einsichtsvoll; nicht unbillig) *reasonable* || (–nunftbegabt) → o.; *level-headed* (*p*) || (–ständig) *sensible, intelligent, knowing, bright, clear-witted; alert, smart, clever; sharp-, quick-witted; astute; level-headed; commonsensical, sober-minded; prudent, wise, judicious* || *logical* || ~er Mann [m] *man of sense* || jeder ~e Mensch *every man in his proper senses* || in das ~e Alter k *to arrive at the years of discretion*, ⟨fam⟩ *to cut one's wisdom teeth* || mit jdm ein ~es Wort reden *to have a straight talk with a p* || zu ~ s z tun *to know better than to do*; dazu solltest du (schon) zu ~ s *you ought to know better* || sei ~! ⟨a.⟩ *steady on*!; *be your age*! || (z Kindern) *be good*! || ~ s *to have sense* || das ist *or* klingt (mir) sehr ~ *that makes good sense* (*to me*) |

Aussprache: Falls nicht anders (: [*v*]) angegeben, ist v – [*f*] zu sprechen.

[adv] (*to act*) *sensibly* ‖ ~ reden *to talk sense*; man kann mit ihm nicht ~ r. *there is no reasoning with him* | ~erw·eise [adv] *from a rational point of view* ‖ *rationally speaking* ‖ *as was* od *is reasonable* | ≃keit [f] ~/ *reason*, *rationality* **≃n·ünftler** m ~s/~ *subtle reasoner, hairsplitter, sophist* **~n·uten** vt [h] (falzen) *to groove* **~·öden I.** vt [h] *to devastate, to lay waste* ‖ *to depopulate* **II.** vi [s] *to become desolate, to run to waste* | **-det** ⟨a.⟩ *deserted* **V.dung** - ~/ *desolation*, etc ‖ ⟨st exch⟩ (des Verkehrs) *stagnation* (*of the market*) **~·öffentlichen** vt *to make public* ‖ *to publish* (*books*) ‖ *to promulgate* (*a law* ⟨a. mil⟩) ‖ (durch Anzeigen) *to advertise* ‖ in Fortsetzungen ~ *to serialize* **V.chung** f ~/~en *publication*, etc; in F. *serialization* | ~shonorar [n] *reproduction fee* **~·ölt** a (Zündkerze) ⟨mot⟩ *oiled up*

Ver·ona [v–] n ⟨It⟩ (Stadt)

Ver·onika [v–] f ~/ ⟨bot⟩ *speed-well* | ~tuch [n] *vernicle*

ver- ~·ordnen vt [h] *to ordain, institute*, ⟨jur⟩ *decree, enact* ‖ ⟨med⟩ *to order, prescribe* (jdm *for a p*) ‖ (einsetzen) *to appoint, nominate* (*a p* zum R. *as a judge*, etc) **V.nete(r)** m ~n/~n *delegate, commissioner* **V.nung** f ~/~en *order, institution, ordinance, regulation* ‖ ⟨jur⟩ *decree, edict* ‖ ⟨med⟩ *prescription* ‖ *appointment* | **~s-** ~blatt [n] *official gazette*; ≃gemäß, ≃mäßig [a] *according to* (*an*) *order, appointment*, etc; *by order*; *as enacted* **~östlichen** vt/i [h/s] *to easternize* **~p·achten** vt [h] *to farm* (⟨hunt⟩ *let*) *out* ‖ ⟨jur⟩ *to lease* **V.tung** f ~/~en *farming out, leasing* **≃p·ächter(in** f) m ~s/~ *lessor* **~p·acken** vt [h] *to pack* (*up*), *to put up* ‖ *to wrap up* (*in paper*, etc) | *to use in packing* | *to pack the wrong way* | °⟨fig⟩ jdn ~ *to bundle a p off* **≃p·ackung** f ~/~en (das Packen) *packaging, packing-up*; ⟨mar⟩ *stowage* ‖ (in Dosen etc) *tinning*, etc ‖ (Hülle) *packing*(*-case*), *wrapper, package* ‖ (*inner*) *lining* | **~s-** ~gewicht [n] *tare*; ~leinwand [f] *balecloth, sackcloth*; ~material [n] *wrapping* (*material*); ~technik [f] *package, packaging engineering* **~p·äppeln** vt [h] (Kind) *to pamper* **~p·assen** vt [h] *to lose by delay, to let slip* ‖ (Augenblick) *to miss* (*one's chance*) ‖ °⟨fig⟩ den Anschluß ~ *to miss the bus* ‖ *to pass up* (*a chance*) ‖ (Zug) *to miss, lose* ‖ verpaßte Gelegenheiten *might-have-beens* | (Kleid) *to fit on*; *to adjust* (*mask*, etc) ‖ °⟨fig⟩ → verabfolgen °**~patzen** vt [h] = vermasseln, ⟨Am⟩ *to flunk* ‖ –tzt [a] ⟨Am mil sl⟩ *snafu* **~p·esten** vt [h] *to infect, poison, taint*; *to foul* (*the air*) | **~d** ⟨a.⟩ *mephitic, pestilential*; (*air-*)*fouling* **V.tung** f *infection, pollution* °**~p·etzen** vt [h] *to tell tales about a p* ⟨school-sl⟩ *to peach* (*up*)*on* od *against* **~pf·afft** a *priest-ridden* **~pf·ählen** vt [h] *to palisade*; *to fence in with stakes* ‖ ⟨arch⟩ *to support on piles* **V.lung** f *paling, palisade*; ⟨fort⟩ *stockade* **~pf·änden** vt [h] *to pawn, pledge*; ⟨sl⟩ *spout*, ⟨Am⟩ *hock* | ⟨jur⟩ *mortgage* | ⟨fig⟩ sein Wort ~ *to pledge one's word, to plight one's faith* **V.der** m ~s/~ *pledger* ‖ *mortgager* **V.dung** f ~/~en *pawning, pledging* ‖ *assignment* (*of wages*) **~pf·effern** vt [h] **1.** *to overpepper* | ⟨fig⟩ *to spoil* **2.** °= (Munition) –pulvern °**~pfeifen** vt [h] *to turn a p in*; *to sell a p down the river* **~pfl·anzen** vt [h] *to transplant* (⟨a. fig⟩ nach *to*) ‖ (in Töpfe) *to pot*; (aus Töpfen) *to pot out* **V.zung** f ~/~en ⟨surg⟩ *transplantation* (⟨a.⟩ v Herz u Niere) **~pfl·egen** vt [h] (sorgen f) (Kinder etc) *to take care of* ‖ (Kranke) *to nurse* ‖ (mit Nahrung) *to feed*; *board, maintain*; sich selbst ~ *to get one's own board* ‖ (als Lieferant) *to cater for, to victual* ‖ ⟨mil⟩ *to supply with rations, to ration*; (ein Heer) *to provision* **V.gung** f ~/~en *care* ‖ ⟨jur⟩ *maintenance* ‖ *food, board* ‖ *rations* pl ‖ *victualling*, etc; [konkr] *victuals* pl; ⟨mil⟩ letzte Ausgabe warmer ~ *last meal furnished* ‖ ⟨med⟩ *diet* | **~s-** ~amt [n] *poor-law board* ⟨mil⟩ *commissariat department*; *victualling-office*; ~ausgabestelle [f] *supply issuing station*; ⟨mil⟩ *rations distributing point* N; ~empfang [m] *supply issue*; ~entschädigung [f] *allowance for board*; ~geld [n] ⟨mil⟩ *messing money*; *ration allowance*; ~kolonne [f] *supply column*; ~offizier [m] *mess*(*ing*) *officer*; °~onkel [m] ⟨mil, mar⟩ *bread-bags* [sg konstr]; ~satz [m] *ration* N; ~stärke [f] *ration strength*; ~unteroffizier [m] *catering sergeant* **~pfl·ichten** vt [h] *to bind, oblige, engage* ‖ jdn eidlich ~ *to bind a p by an oath* ‖ **zu** etw –tet *in duty bound to do* ..; (*the conditions under which*) *it is obligatory* (*on ships to engage a pilot*); ⟨contr⟩ *to be under a duty* (*to*; *to do*) ‖ z Arbeit ~ *to requisition* ‖ jdn z Dank ~ *to lay a p under an obligation* ‖ ich bin Ihnen sehr z Dank –tet *I am greatly indebted to you* ‖ z Zahlung (etc) –tet *liable to payment* (, *for service*) ‖ –tet s *to be under an obligation* (*to do*) ‖ ⟨theat⟩ f 2 M. –tet s *to be booked through to 2 months* ‖ jdm –tet s *to be bound* od *obliged to a p*; .. z Dank .. *to be* od *lie under obligation to a p* | **sich** [dat] jdn ~ *to put a p in one's debt, to make a p one's debtor, to covenant a p* (*to do*), *to oblige a p* (*by doing*) | **sich** ~ (z etw) *to bind* od *engage, pledge o.s. to* (*a th*), *to undertake* (*to do a th*), *to commit o.s.* (*to doing*); .. mit Wort .. *to give* od *pledge one's faith* ‖ sich e–r S [dat] ~ *to espouse a cause* ‖ ⟨com⟩ sich ~ *to contract* (*to do*) | **~d** a *obligatory* **V.tete(r)** m ⟨contr⟩ *covenantor* **V.tung** f ~/~en *obliging, undertaking, commitment*, etc | (Pflicht) *obligation* (gegenüber *to*), *duty*; schuldrechtl. *o.n of contract* ‖ (heilige) *trust* ‖ (übernommene) *liability, engagement*; *commitment*; ~en [pl] *bondages*; ~en der Versicherten ⟨ins⟩ *warranties* pl | e–e ~ eingehen *to enter into a contract* od *engagement, to undertake a responsibility* ‖ gegen jdn ~en h *to be* od *lie under obligation to a p* ‖ s–n ~en (nicht) nachk *to meet one's engagements* od *liabilities*, (an Geld) *to pay off* od *settle a score* (*to default*) ‖ es lag ihm die ~ ob *there was an obligation on him* (*to do*) ‖ e–e ~ übernehmen *to assume an obligation* | **aus** e–r ~ entlassen *to remove a liability from* (*a p's*) *records* **~pf·uschen** vt [h] *to bungle, muddle, botch, scamp, muff*; ⟨fam⟩ *to make a mess* (od *botch, muck, hash*) *of*; *to foul up, to fudge*; ⟨sl⟩ *to foozle* ‖ (Aufführung dramat., musikal. Werke) *to murder* | –scht [a] *botched, scamped* (*work*); die S ist –scht *the fat is in the fire* **~p·ichen** vt [h] *to pitch* ‖ –cht [a] ⟨fig⟩ [pred] = erpicht °**~p·impeln** vt [h] *to coddle, featherbed* **~pl·appern, ~pl·audern** vt [h] (die Zeit) *to prattle away* | **sich** ~ *to blab out a secret, to talk away*; ⟨fam⟩ *to let slip*; *to let the cat out of the bag* ‖ die Zeit –rt sich .. *slips by when one is chatting* **~pl·empern** vt [h] (übergießen) *to splash* ‖ ⟨fig⟩ (Zeit etc) *to spend* od *waste foolishly*; ⟨Am sl⟩ *to boondoggle* ‖ Geld ~ ⟨sl⟩ *to spill m.*; *to play about* | **sich** ~ ⟨fam⟩ *to fritter away one's time and energy on divided aims* ‖ (an e–e Frau) *to get hooked* (*by a woman of inferior social position*) **~p·öbeln** vt [h] *to hoot at* **~p·önen** vt [h] *to put a penalty on* ‖ ⟨fig⟩ *to taboo* **~p·önt** a *prohibited, taboo*(*ed*) **~pr·assen** vt [h] *to squander in luxury, to dissipate*; *to play ducks and drakes with* (*one's fortune*) **V.sser** m ~s/~ *spendthrift* **~pr·eußen** vt [h] *to Prussianize* **~proviant·ieren** vt [h] *to victual, provision*, → –pflegen **V.rung** f ~/~en *victualling* **~prozess·ieren** vt [h] *to squander in lawsuits* **~pr·ügeln** vt [h] *to thrash, lick*; ⟨sl⟩ *hide*, ⟨Am⟩ *clobber* | das ≃ der Ehefrau *wife beating* **~p·uffen I.** vi [s] ⟨chem⟩ *to detonate, explode* ‖ ⟨fig⟩ *to fizzle out* **II.** vt [h] *to waste* | **sich** ~ ⟨fig⟩ *to spend every farthing* **V.fung** f *deflagration* | **~s-**

Verbal-Flexion der Verben mit der Vorsilbe **ver-** → das jeweilige Simplex

explosive; *explosion* (*oil engine*) **~p·ulvern** vt [h] ⟨fig fam⟩ (Geld) *to fritter away* ‖ *to run through* (*a fortune*) °**~p·umpen** vt [h] *to lend* **~p·uppen**: sich ~ [h] *to pupate* °**~p·usten**: sich ~ [h] *to recover breath* ≗**p·utz** m ~es/~e *plaster, coat*(*ing*) **| v.en** vt [h] *to daub*; ⟨arch⟩ *to finish down* (*walls*), *to roughcast* | ⟨fam⟩ **1.** (Geld) *to squander* **2.** (Essen) *to polish off, to put away, to clean up* **~qu·almen I.** vi [s] *to dissolve in smoke* **II.** vt [h] *to spend on tobacco, cigars*, etc **| -mt** *filled with smoke* **~qu·asen** vt [h] nordd = –geuden **~qu·ellen** vi irr [s] *to swell up*; *to warp* (*by moisture*) ‖ → –quollen **~qu·er** [adv] = quer; es ging (mir) ~ *it went wrong* **~qu·icken** vt [h] ⟨chem⟩ *to amalgamate* ‖ ⟨fig⟩ *to mix up* (mit *with*) **V.kung** f ~/ *amalgamation* ‖ *mixing-up* **~qu·oll** 1. & 3. sg pret v verquellen **~qu·ollen** a [pp v verquellen] (Holz) *warped* ‖ (Gesicht) *bloated* **~r·amme(l)n** vt [h] *to bar*(*ricade*), *to block up* **~r·amschen** vt [h] *to job off* **~r·ann** 1. & 3. sg pret v verrinnen **~r·annt** a [pp v verrennen] ‖ ⟨fig⟩ *stubborn, extravagant*; *rampant* (*theorist*), *rabid* (*socialist*) ‖ (in [acc]) ⟨fig⟩ *stuck fast* (*in a th*) ‖ ~er Geselle *crank* ≗**r·at** m ~(e)s/ *treason, treachery* (an *to*); *betrayal* (*of*); ~ des Judas *b.l of Christ* ⟨a. arts⟩ ‖ ~ begehen an *to betray* **~r·aten I.** vt [h] **1.** (jdn) *to betray*; ⟨sl⟩ *to blow upon*, ⟨Am⟩ *sell out* **2.** (Geheimnis etc) *to divulge, betray, disclose, reveal*, ⟨sl⟩ *spill* ‖ ⟨fam⟩ *to blab* od *let out, to give away* ‖ das G. ~ ⟨fam⟩ *to let the cat out of the bag*; ⟨sl⟩ *to blow the gaff*, ⟨Am⟩ *to spill the beans* ‖ jdm ein G. ~ *to confide .. to a p, to let a p in on a secret* ‖ s–e Gesinnung etc ~ *to show one's mind* ‖ um die Absicht nicht z ~ *so as not to compromise the plan, so as to prevent the pl. from being revealed*; °die ganze Stellung ~ ⟨urspr mil⟩ *to give away the* (*whole*) *show* | kein Wort ~ *to breathe no word* ‖ nichts ~! *don't tell tales!*; er –riet s–e Angst durch Miene u Blick *he showed his fear by his face and eyes* | (Stellung) ⟨mil⟩ *to disclose*; ⟨fig fam⟩ die ganze St. ~ *to unmask one's batteries* ‖ jdm ~, daß ⟨sl⟩ *to let on to a p that* **3.** ⟨fig⟩ (hinweisen auf) *to suggest, argue, show, indicate, bespeak, denote, prove* ‖ es –rät die Meisterhand *it proclaims the hand of a master* **4. sich** ~ *to betray* od *commit, disclose o.s.*, ⟨fam⟩ *to give o.s. away* ‖ sich nicht ~ *to be noncommittal, to lie low* **II.** a; **~ u verkauft** *lost*, ⟨fam⟩ *sold, booked* (*I'm b. all right*) ≗**r·äter(in** f) m ~s/~ *traitor* (f *traitress*) (an *to*) ‖ *betrayer* (*of a secret*) ‖ ⟨pol fam⟩ *rat* ‖ an e–m z ~ w ⟨sl⟩ *to do the dirty on a p* | ~ei [f] ~/~en *treachery*; *treason*; ⟨fam⟩ *foul play*, ⟨Am sl⟩ *graft* | ≗isch [a] *treacherous*, ⟨a.⟩ *traitorous*; *faithless, disloyal, perfidious* ‖ ⟨pol⟩ *treasonable* (*action*) ‖ ⟨fig⟩ *telltale* [attr subst] (*cushion, tears*) °**~r·atzt** a *lost* → verraten II.; er ist ~ *he's a goner* **~r·auchen I.** vi [s] *to go off in smoke* ‖ (verdunsten) *to evaporate* ‖ ⟨fig⟩ *to cool down* ‖ ~ l ⟨fig⟩ *to let cool, to let pass away* (*one's rage*, etc); s–e Wut ist –cht .. *has gone dead* **II.** vt [h] *to spend on tobacco, cigars*, etc **~r·äuchern** vt [h] *to fill .. with smoke* ‖ *to burn* (*incense*) **| -rt** a *smoky* (*room*) **~r·äumen** vt [h] *to mislay, misplace* **~r·auschen** vi [s] *to rush past* od *along* ‖ (Zeit) *to pass away* ‖ ⟨fig⟩ *to die away* **~r·echnen** vt [h] *to reckon* (*up*), *charge*; *to place to account* ‖ (ausgleichen) *to settle up* **| sich** ~ *to miscalculate* (*gravely*); *to be out of one's calculation* od *reckoning* ‖ ⟨fig⟩ *to make a* (*great*) *mistake, to be* (*much*) *mistaken* od (*sadly*) *disappointed* **V.nung** f ~/~en *reckoning-up* ‖ (Fehler) *misreckoning, mistake* ‖ ⟨com⟩ *clearing, settlement, liquidation* ‖ nur zur ~ ⟨com⟩ *not-negotiable* (*cheque*) **| ~s-** *agreement* (*currency*), *clearing* (*dollars*); ~scheck [m] ⟨engl⟩ *crossed cheque* (⟨Am⟩ *check*), ⟨com⟩ *transfer ticket*; ~s [pl] ⟨Am a.⟩ *exchanges*; ~stelle [f] *clearing office*; ~vertrag [m] *clearing agreement* **~r·ecken** vi [s] (T) *to die, perish* ⟨a. fig⟩; ⟨sl⟩ *to croak* ‖ °nicht ums ≗! *not for the life of me*, ⟨sl⟩ *not by a dinged sight, I'll see you further first!*; .. nachgeben ⟨fam⟩ *to hang on by one's eyebrows* ‖ °ich will ~, wenn *I'll eat my head if* **~r·eden** vt [h] *to forswear, abjure, to take a vow against* ‖ ich will es nicht ~ *I have half a mind to do it* | sich ~ *to make a slip of the tongue* ‖ *to betray o.s.* **~r·egnen** vi [s] *to be spoilt by rain* ‖ –net [a] *rain-spoilt* (S); (*the game was*) *rained out* **~reiben** vt irr [h] *to pulverize completely* ‖ *to grind down* od *well* ‖ *to rub away* ‖ *to use up by rubbing* **~r·eichlichen** vt [h] *to put under the control of the Reich* **~r·eisen I.** vt [h] *to spend in travelling* **II.** vi [s] *to go* (*away* od) *on a journey* ‖ oft ~ *to travel about a good deal* ‖ (nach) *to set out* od *start* (*for*) ‖ er ist (geschäftlich) –st *he is away* (*on business*) ‖ wie lange ist er schon –st? *how long has he been travelling* od *away*? **~r·eißen** vt irr [h] (Kleider) *to wear out* ‖ er –riß den W. ⟨mot⟩ *the car started skidding* | (scharf kritisieren) *to pull to pieces, to chastise* (*a p*) *roundly* **~r·enken** vt [h] sich das Knie ~ *to dislocate* (⟨scient⟩ *luxate*) *one's knee*; *I got my k. dislocated* ‖ *to sprain* (*one's foot*), *to strain* (*one's back*) **V.kung** f ~/~en *dislocation, sprain*; leichte ~ *wrick* **~r·ennen** vt irr [h]; jdm den Weg ~ *to bar a p's way* **| sich** ~ *to run a wrong way*; ⟨fig⟩ *to overshoot o.s.* ‖ sich ~ in [acc] ⟨fig⟩ *to get stuck* od *involved in* od *tied up in* (*a th*) ‖ → verrannt **~r·ichten** vt [h] *to do, execute*; *fulfil*; *achieve, accomplish* ‖ s–e Andacht ~ *to perform one's devotions* ‖ schwere Arbeit ~ *to slave* ‖ s–n Dienst ~ (P) *to officiate*, (S) *to answer the purpose* ‖ → Gebet, Notdurft **V.tung** f ~/~en *doing, performance*, etc ‖ *act* (*the first a. of the day*) ‖ (der Organe) *function* ‖ (Geschäft) *business* (⟨a. fig⟩ bei dieser ~ *at this b.*) ‖ ~en [pl] *doings* pl; ~en des Alltags *daily chores* ‖ s–e ~ *what he has done, the way in which he has done it* ‖ tägliche ~en *daily routine work* ‖ gute ~ wünschen *to wish every success* **~r·ieb(en)** 1. & 3. sg pret (pp) v verreiben **~r·iechen** vi [s] *to lose its smell* **~r·iegeln** vt [h] *to bolt, bar* **V.lung** f ⟨tech⟩ (*inter*)*locking device*; *lock* | **~s-** ~kupplung [f] ⟨mot⟩ *interlocking clutch* **~r·iet** 1. & 3. sg pret v verraten **~r·ingern** vt [h] (⟨a.⟩ sich ~) *to diminish, decrease, lessen* ‖ vt *to reduce*; *to depreciate* (*the coinage*); (Tempo) *to drop* **V.rung** f ~/~en *diminution, reduction, decrease* **~r·innen** vi irr [s] *to run off* od *away* ‖ ⟨fig⟩ (Zeit) *to elapse, pass* ‖ (schnell) *to flit by, to fly* **~r·itt(en)** 1. & 3. sg pret (pp) v verreiten **~r·öcheln** vi [h] *to breathe one's last, to expire* **~r·ohen I.** vt [h] *to brutalize* **II.** vi [s] *to become brutalized, to grow brutish* **~r·onnen** pp v verrinnen **~r·osten** vi [s] *to rust* ⟨a. fig⟩ ‖ –stet [a] *rusty* **~r·otten** vi [s] *to rot* | –ttet [a] *rotten* (⟨a. fig⟩ *conditions*) ‖ ⟨fig⟩ *antiquated* (*notions*), *exploded* (*ideas*) **~r·ucht** a *villainous, wicked* (*p*) ‖ *atrocious, heinous* (*crime*) ‖ ~er Mensch *villain* ‖ ~e Tat ⟨a.⟩ *atrocity* | ≗heit [f] ~/~en *villainy, wickedness* ‖ *atrociousness* | (Tat) *atrocity* **~r·ücken** vt [h] *to displace, dislocate*, (*re*)*move* ‖ (verschieben) *to shift* | *to disarrange*, ⟨typ⟩ *to squabble* ‖ *to disturb* (*a p's plans*) ‖ (Uhrzeiger) *to put on* bzw *back* ‖ jdm den Kopf ~ *to turn a p's head* **| -ckt** a ⟨fig⟩ *insane*; *crazy, mad*; *zany* | ⟨fam⟩ *dotty, cracked, off one's chump* ‖ *hare-brained* ‖ ⟨Am sl⟩ *squirrely* (*job*) ‖ du bist wohl ~ *are you mad?* ‖ rein ~ ⟨fam⟩ *clean gone* ‖ total ~ *as mad as a hatter* ‖ wie ~ *like mad* | ~ **auf** [acc] *wild about*, ⟨Am sl⟩ *stuck on ..* ‖ ~ nach [dat] *crazy for*; *mad after, for, on* | jdn ~ m *to drive a p mad, to make a p crazy, to turn a p's head*; ⟨Am sl⟩ *to set a p nuts* ‖ °~ spielen *to feign o.s. mad* ‖ ~ w *to go out of one's mind*, ⟨sl⟩

Aussprache: Falls nicht anders (: [*v*]) angegeben, ist v = [*f*] zu sprechen.

to go off one's chump; hier kann e–r ∼ w ⟨Am fam⟩ *I'm going nuts here* ‖ °ich werd' ∼! *I'll go hopping to hell!*, ⟨euphem⟩ *blow me! I'm blowed!* ‖ es ist um ∼ z w! *it's enough to drive one mad* (od ⟨fam⟩ *dotty*) | **∸e(r)** m (∸e f) *lunatic, mad(wo)man* | ∸heit [f] ∼/∼en *insanity* ‖ *craze* ‖ *craziness* ‖ *lunacy* ‖ (Handlung) *act of madness, foolish action* **V.kung** f ∼/∼en *displacement*, ⟨a. phys⟩ *removal, derangement* **∸r·uf** m ∼(e)s/ *discredit, disparagement* ‖ in ∼ ⟨fig⟩ *under a cloud* ‖ in ∼ bringen (k) *to bring* (*get*) *into discredit*; *to discredit, disparage, decry*; *cry down*; s–n guten N. .. *to bring* od *cast a slur on one's own good name* ‖ in ∼ erklären *to declare infamous* ‖ in ∼ k *to get into bad odour* ‖ in ∼ tun *to boycott* ‖ (gesellschaftlich ächten) *to send to Coventry* **∼r·ufen I.** vt [h] *to decry, to cry down* **II.** a *ill--reputed, ill-famed, notorious, disreputable*; ⟨Am⟩ *off-color* (*place*) ‖ [pred] *in bad repute* **∼r·ühren** vt [h] (Eier) *to scramble* ‖ *to whip* **∼r·ußen** vt/i [h & s] *to soot* **∼r·utschen** vi [s] (Schlips) *to ride up*, (Last) *to shift* | –scht *crooked* (*cap*), (*your stocking seams are*) *cr.* (= *slipped to one side*), ⟨tech⟩ *off-center* ‖ die Last (ist) –tscht *the load slips* (.. *is displaced*)

Vers m –ses/–se *verse* ⟨a. bib⟩ ‖ (Zeile) *line* ‖ (Strophe) *stanza* ‖ ∼e ohne Reim *blank verse* sg ‖ in –e bringen *to put into verse*; ∼e schreiben *to write poetry* ‖ ⟨fig⟩ sich [dat] e–n ∼ auf etw m *to work out a th for o.s.*; ich kann mir k–n ∼ daraus m *I cannot make head or tail of it* **∼abschnitt** m *hemistich* **∼akzent** m *metrical accent* **∼bau** m *versification* **∼brechung** f *enjambment* **∼emacher** m *versifier* **∼eschmied, ∼künstler** m *versifier* **∼fuß** m *foot* **∼kunst** f *versification* **∼maß** m *metre*

ver- ∼s·achlichen vt [h] ⟨arts, etc⟩ *to debunk* °**∼s·acken** vi [s] *to sink* **∸s·agen** n ∼s/ *failure* ‖ *intermittence* ‖ (zeitweises) (P) *escape*; ⟨comp⟩ *bug* **∼s·agen A. I.** vt [h] *to deny, refuse* ‖ jdm etw ∼ *to withhold a th from a p* ⟨a. fig⟩; den Dienst ∼ (S) *to break down* ‖ die Beine ∼ mir den D. *my legs fail me* **II.** vi [h] *to fail, to break down*; (S) (langsam) *to fizzle out*; (P) (lächerlich) *to fall on one's face* ‖ (Gesundheit) *to give way* ‖ (Stimme) *falter, break*; *give out* ‖ (Flinte) *to miss fire* ‖ (Flinte, Motor) *to misfire*; *the machine wouldn't work* ‖ in etw ∼ *to fall short in* (*knowledge*, etc) **B. sich** [dat] etw ∼ *to deny o.s. a th, to go without a th* ‖ sich ∼ z tun *to abstain* od *refrain from doing* ‖ es sich nicht ∼: *he could not resist doing it* | –gt [pred] (verlobt, z Tanze) *engaged*; (Stelle *vacancy*) *filled up* ‖ (Ware) *disposed of* ‖ der Erfolg muß (jdm) –gt bleiben .. *s. will remain out of reach* (*of a p*); anderweitig ∼ s *to have a previous engagement* | –nd [a]; nie ∼ *unfailing* **V.ger** m ∼s/∼ ⟨mil⟩ *misfire*, ⟨sl⟩ *dud* (⟨a. fig⟩ P); (P) *failure* ⟨a. (S) tech⟩; *cropper*; (S) *malfunction, flash in the pan* **V.gung** f ∼/∼en *denial, refusal* ‖ die ∼ ihrer Hand *her previous engagement* **∼s·ah** 1. & 3. sg pret v versehen

Vers·albuchstabe m, **Vers·alie** f *capital letter* ‖ kursiv ∼n *italic capitals*

ver- ∼s·alzen vt [h] [pp –zt & ∼] *to oversalt* | ⟨fig⟩ [pp nur: ∼] *to spoil, mar* ‖ e–m die Suppe ∼ *to queer the pitch for a p*, ⟨fam⟩ *to cook a p's goose* **∼s·ammeln** vt [h] *to assemble*; ⟨mil⟩ *to rally* ‖ (einberufen) *to convene, convoke* ‖ ⟨hors⟩ *to gather* | –lt s *to be g.ed* | **sich** ∼ *to assemble, meet, g.* (*the horse g.ed himself*) ‖ ⟨ec⟩ *congregate* | **zu** s–n Vätern –lt w *to be g.ed to one's f.s* **V.mlung** f ∼/∼en **1.** *assembling*, etc **2.** [konkr] *assembly, meeting, conference*; beratende *Consultative Assembly*, öffentl. *public meeting*; ⟨aero⟩ (nach dem Start) *forming-up* ‖ (gesellige) *g.ing, party* ‖ ⟨mil⟩ *rendezvous* ‖ ⟨pol⟩ *congress* ‖ ⟨ec⟩ *congregation* ‖ ⟨scient⟩ *conference* ‖ (Zuhörer) *audience* | e–e ∼ fand statt *a meeting was held* ‖ die ∼ verlassen *to walk out of the m.* | **∼s-** ∼haus [n] *house of assembly*; *club*; *casino*; *assembly--rooms* pl; (e–r Sekte) *meeting-house*; ∼leiter [m], Leiter der V. *chairman*; (H. C.) *speaker*; ∼ort [m] *meeting-place*; ⟨mil⟩ *meeting point* N ⟨a. tact⟩; ∼raum [m] *assembly room* ‖ ⟨mil⟩ *rendezvous area*, ⟨Am⟩ *concourse* ⟨a. arch⟩; ∼recht [n] *right of* (*public*) *meeting*; ∼saal [m] *meeting-hall* ‖ ⟨engl stud⟩ *common room*; ∼verbot [n] *prohibition of assembly*; ∼zimmer [n] ⟨theat⟩ *green-room* **∸s·and** m ∼(e)s/ *dispatch, forwarding*, ⟨allg⟩ *shipping*; *posting, mailing*; (Ausfuhr) *export* ‖ N. & N., alleiniger ∼ *N. & N. sole distributors* | ∼abteilung [f] *forwarding department*; ∼anzeige [f] *forwarding advice*; ∸bereit [a] *ready for dispatch*; ∼analyse [f] *transport analysis*; ∼artikel [m] *article of export*, pl *exports*; ∼auftrag [m] ⟨allg⟩ *shipping order*; ∼behälter [m], ∼kiste [f] *shipping container*; ∼bier [n] *beer for exportation*; ∼buchhändler [m] *export bookseller*; ∸fähig [a] *fit for shipment*; ∼faß [n] *trade cask*; ∸fertig [a] *ready for dispatch*; ∼geschäft [n] *mail order business*; ∼liste [f] *mailing list*; ∼papier [n] *shipping document*; ∼station [f] *point of origin*; ∼- u Lieferzeit [f] *shipping terms* **∼s·anden** (→ Sand) vi/t [s/h] *to silt* (*up*) ‖ ⟨fig⟩ *to sink into oblivion* **V.dung** f → o.; (e–s Reservoirs) *sand filling* **∼s·andt, -s·ang, -s·ank, -s·aß** 1. & 3. sg [pret] v versenden, –singen, –sinken, –sitzen **∸s·atz** m ∼es/ **1.** ⟨min⟩ *stowing, packing, gobbing* ‖ *gob stuff* **2.** *pawning* ‖ in ∼ geben *to pawn* | ∼amt, ∼haus [n] *pawn-shop*; ∼berge [m pl] ⟨min⟩ *wastes* pl; ∼kran [m] ⟨min⟩ *shifting crane*; ∼maschine [f] ⟨min⟩ *packer*; ∼ständer [m] ⟨theat⟩ *standard flood*; ⟨Am⟩ *floodlight* (*on stand*); ∼stück [n] ⟨theat⟩ *set piece*; *cut-out* °**∼s·auen** vt [h] ⟨fam⟩ *to mess, to make a mess of*; ⟨sl⟩ *to bitch a th* (*up*) **∼s·auern** vi [s] *to become* od *turn sour* ‖ ⟨fig⟩ *to get rusty, to harden into a Philistine* **∼s·äuern** vt [h] *to* (*make* [*too*]) *sour* °**∼s·aufen I.** vt irr [h] *to squander away in drink* (⟨fam⟩ *booze*) ‖ s–n Verstand ∼ *to muddle one's brain* (*with drink*) **II.** vi [s] = ertrinken ‖ → –soffen **∼s·äumen** vt [h] (Stunde, Appell, Gelegenheit, Zug) *to miss* ‖ (Pflicht) *to neglect* ‖ (unterlassen) *to leave undone*; *to omit, forget, fail* (*to do*) **V.mnis** f ∼/–nisse; n –nisses/–nisse *failure to exploit an opportunity omission, neglect* ‖ *loss of time* ‖ ⟨jur⟩ *dereliction, delinquency*; (vorsätzlich *wilful*) *default*; (*culpable*) *negligence* | ∼liste [f] *list of the absent*; ∼urteil [n] *judg(e)ment in* od *by default* **∼sch·achern** vt [h] *to barter* od *chaffer away*; *to job off*; *to peddle* (*a th to a p*) **∼sch·affen** vt [h] *to procure, provide* ‖ jdm etw ∼ *to get* od *procure a th for a p*; *to bring* (*pleasure*) *to a p* ‖ Linderung ∼ *to give ease* od *relief*; *to give* (*satisfaction*) | **sich** [dat] etw ∼ *to get o.s., to obtain, secure a th* (*an enjoyment which money could purchase* das man sich mit Geld ∼ konnte) ‖ (Geld) *to raise* ‖ sich Gehör ∼ *to obtain a hearing* ‖ sich jds Hilfe ∼ *to enlist a p's aid* ‖ (Kenntnisse) ⟨mil⟩ *to gain* ‖ sich Recht ∼ *to obtain redress*; *to take the law into one's own hands* ‖ sich z ∼ wissen *to manage to get hold of* **∼sch·äkern** vt [h] *to dally away* **∼sch·alen**[1] vt [h] *to furnish with a shell* od *cover* | (Wände) *to board, lath, plank*; ⟨min⟩ *to timber*; → Schale **∼sch·alen**[2] vi [s] *to grow stale*; → schal **∼sch·alken** vt [h] ⟨naut⟩ *to batten down* **∼sch·allen** vi [s] **1.** [pp –llt] *to cease sounding, to die away* **2.** [pp –ollen] *to sink into oblivion, to be forgotten* **∸sch·alung** f ∼/∼en *planking*, etc; → Schale **∼sch·ämt** a *bashful, shamefaced* ‖ *timid, modest* ‖ *confused* ‖ die ∼e Armut *the respectable* od *deserving poor* pl ‖ ∼ tun *to put on a bashful*

Verbal-Flexion der Verben mit der Vorsilbe **ver-** → das jeweilige Simplex

air | ≗heit [f] ~/ *bashfulness, shamefacedness* || *timidity; modesty* || *confusion* | ≗tun [n] *prudishness, simpering* °**~sch·andeln** vt [h] *to disfigure, deface, spoil, mar; vandalize;* ⟨Lit, mus⟩ *to murder* || jdn ~ *to spoil a p's looks* | **V.lung** f ~/~en *disfiguration, -rement* **~sch·anzen** vt [h] *to entrench, fortify* || sich ~ ⟨fig⟩ *to take shelter* (hinter [dat] *behind*); *to let a p bear the brunt* od *take the blame* **V.zung** f ~/~en *entrenchment* **~sch·ärfen** vt [h] *to heighten, sharpen, intensify; to add to; to give an edge to* || (Blockade) *to tighten* || *to exacerbate* (*the situation*) || *to raise* (*a p's fines, penalty*) | -fter U-Bootkrieg *unrestricted submarine warfare* | **sich** ~ *to increase, heighten, intensify; aggravate, worsen;* die Krise -fte sich *the crisis deepened* **V.fung** f *intensification; tightening-up; aggravation; increase* (*of political tensions*) **~sch·arren** vt [h] *to cover with earth* **~sch·atten** vt [h] *to overshadow* || ⟨paint⟩ *to shade* **~sch·auen** vrefl [h] sich ~ in → -gaffen, -lieben **~sch·äumen** vt/i [h/s] *to turn into froth* | vi *to cease frothing* || *to foam away* **~sch·eiden** vi irr [s] *to expire, decease, die; to pass* (*away*), *to depart this life* || im ≗ liegen *to breathe one's last* **~schieden** *late* (*Mr. N.*) || der ≗e, die ≗e *the deceased;* [pl] die ≗en *the deceased* pl **~sch·enken** vt [h] *to make a present of, to give away* || (Getränke) *to retail* °**~sch·erbeln** vt [h] ⟨sl⟩ *to flog* **~sch·erzen** vt [h] **1.** *to trifle away* **2.** (⟨a.⟩ sich [dat]) *to forfeit, lose, alienate;* .. jds Gunst .. *to get wrong with a p* || sein Glück ~ *to spurn one's good fortune* || -zte Jugend *youth trifled away* **~sch·euchen** vt [h] *to scare* od *frighten away, to shoo up* | ⟨fig⟩ *to banish* || die Sorgen ~ *to banish care* °**~sch·euern** vt [h] = -scherbeln **~sch·icken** vt [h] *to send off; to consign, forward, dispatch, transmit* (dazu: *transmission*) | (verbannen) *to banish, exile, deport* (dazu s: *deportation*); ⟨mil⟩ (P) *to evacuate* **~sch·iebbar** a *sliding* || ~er Teil ⟨tech⟩ *rider* ≗**sch·iebe-** ~anlage [f] ⟨rail⟩ *marshalling* ⟨Am⟩ *classification yard;* ~bahnhof [m] → Rangier-; *m.g yard* N; ~lokomotive [f] *shunting l.;* ~schaltung [f] *selection system of gear shifting* **~sch·ieben** vt irr [h] **1.** *to remove, shift, displace* || ⟨rail⟩ *to shunt* || ⟨mil⟩ (Truppen) *to redeploy* || (Waren) *to sell underhand; to smuggle abroad* || (in Unordnung bringen) *to disarrange* || **sich** ~ *to get out of place, to shift,* ⟨tech⟩ *to misalign* **2.** (zeitlich) = aufschieben; -be nichts (*or* es nicht) auf morgen *do it now;* -schoben worden s ⟨parl⟩ *to lie on the table* **3.** ≗ n ⟨bes comp⟩ *adjustment, shift* **V.bung** f ~/~en *removal, shifting* || *illicit sale; smuggling* || ⟨fig⟩ *dislocation* || ⟨pol⟩ *switch* || ⟨artill⟩ Seiten≗ *deflection* **~sch·ied(en) I.** 3. sg pret (pp) v verscheiden **II.** a **1.** *different, differing, distinct* (von *from*) || *dissimilar, unlike* || *many-sided, versatile, diversified, varied, assorted* || mit ~en Frequenzen *heterogenous* | himmelweit ~ *as different as chalk from cheese* | ~ m *to diversify* | ~ s *to be unlike* (v .. *a p, a th*); wir sind nun mal ~er Meinung *let's agree to differ* || (unter wenigen) *to differ,* (unter mehreren) *to vary* **2.** ~es = manches; ≗es = *ths which differ;* ~e [pl] *several, various, divers, some, sundry, separate, of all sorts* || e-e Reihe ~er Töne *a variety of notes* || von ~ster Größe *of all sizes* || zu ~en Malen *on various occasions* | ≗e(s) *sundry matters, different ths,* ⟨com⟩ *sundries* pl || °⟨fig⟩ da hört denn doch ≗es auf! *well, that's the limit!* | ~artig [a] *of a different kind* etc, *varied, various, miscellaneous* || ⟨scient⟩ *heterogeneous* || ~e Formen *a variety of forms;* ≗artigkeit [f] *difference of nature,* etc; ⟨scient⟩ *heterogeneousness;* ~farbig [a] *variegated, variously colo(u)red* (*objects* pl); *of different colours, parti-coloured, motley; separate colo(u)red* (*keytops*) | ~erlei [a] [inv] *divers, various, sundry, several* || [abs] = Verschiedenes | ≗heit [f] ~/~en *difference* || (Mannigfaltigkeit) *diversity, variety* || *divergence* (*in the means*) | ~st [a pl] *an almost endless variety of* | ~tlich [adv] *differently* || *severally, repeatedly; several times* **~sch·ienen** vt [h] *to rim;* → Schiene **~sch·ießen** irr **I.** vt [h] *to spend in shooting* || (abschießen) *to discharge* || sein Pulver ~, die Munition ~ (⟨a.⟩ **sich** ~) *to use up one's* (od *to run out of*) *ammunition* || ⟨fig⟩ sie h ihr P. verschossen *they are worn out, they are at the end of their tether* | **sich** ~ *to overshoot o.s.* || *to miss one's aim* || ⟨fig⟩ *to blunder* || ⟨fam⟩ (verlieben) *to fall in love* (in *with, to fall for*) **II.** vi [s] (Stoffe) *to fade, to lose colour* || (Farben) *to wash out* || nicht ~d *unfading, fast* **~sch·iffbar** a *fit* od *ready to be shipped* **~sch·iffen** vt [h] *to export, to ship* (*goods*) || *to freight, lade* **V.ffer** m ~s/~ *shipper* | **-ffung** f *shipping* || *shipment* | **~s-** *shipping;* ~agent [m] *sh.g agent;* ~hafen [m] *port of shipment;* ~muster [n] *sh.g sample, s. from the bulk;* ~papiere [n pl] *sh.g documents;* ~spesen [pl] *sh.g charges* **~sch·immeln** vi [s] *to get mouldy* | **-lt** ⟨fig⟩ *antiquated, moss-grown* (*doctrines*) **~schimpf·ieren** vt [h] *to disfigure* °≗**sch·iß** m -sses/ ⟨stud sl⟩ im ~ *in the doghouse* **~schl·acken** vi [s] *to* (*turn into*) *dross* od *slag* **V.kung** f ~/ *scorification* **~schl·afen I.** vt irr [h] *to sleep through* (*an event*); *to miss* (od *lose, neglect*) *by sleeping* || (Ärger, Müdigkeit, Stunden) *to sleep away* | es, die Zeit ~, **sich** [acc] ~ *to oversleep* (*o.s.*) **II.** a *sleepy* (*eyes, place*); mit ~en Augen *sleepy-eyed; drowsy* (*hum*); *somnolent* (*years*); *indolent, slothful* (*p*) ≗**schl·ag** m ~(e)s/≗e *partition(-wall)* | (Koje) *booth, box* || *closet* || (Lattenkiste) *crate* **~schl·agen** irr **I.** vi [s] **1.** ⟨mar⟩ = ~ w **2.** *to cool, to grow lukewarm* || ~ l *to take the chill off* **II.** vt [h] *to beat* (*gold*) || (mit Latten, Nägeln etc) *to board, nail* | *to spoil by beating; to blunt* (*the tools*) | Buch, Seite ~ *to lose one's place* || (Ball) *to lose* | ⟨mar⟩ ~ w *to be driven out of one's course;* .. in *to be thrown in* (*a country*) ⟨a. fig⟩ || vom Sturme ~ *storm-tossed* | **sich** [dat] etw ~ *to miss* **III.** imps [h] **es** -schlägt nichts *it doesn't matter, it makes no difference* || was -schlägt's? ⟨fam⟩ *what's the odds?, what then?* || es -schlug ihm die Sprache *it made him inarticulate* od *speechless;* es schien ihm d. Sp. ~ z h *the words seemed to stick in his throat;* .. den Atem *it took his breath away* **IV.** a *cunning, sly, subtle, crafty, artful,* ⟨fam⟩ *deep, slick;* ~ wie ein schlauer Fuchs *canny as a badger* | (lau) *lukewarm* | ≗**heit** f ~/ *cunning, craftiness, subtleness, slyness,* ⟨fam⟩ *depth* **~schl·ammen** vi/t [s/h] *to silt* (*up*) **V.mung** f *sludge accumulation; silting* **~schl·ampen I.** vt [h] *to ruin, lose, forget* **II.** vi = verkommen **~schl·ang** 1. & 3. sg pret v verschlingen **~schl·echtern** vt [h] *to make worse; to impair, debase, deteriorate* | **sich** ~ *to deteriorate, worsen, sink; to change for the* (od *to grow*) *worse* || (Ware) *to fall off in quality;* (Wetter) *to break* **V.rung** f ~/~en *deterioration, change for the worse, worsening; debasement* **~schl·eichen I.** vi [s] (Zeit) *to crawl along* **II. sich** ~ *to slink away* **~schl·eiern** vt [h] *to veil* ⟨a. fig⟩ || ⟨mil⟩ *to screen* | ⟨fig⟩ *to wrap in mystery, to obscure; to cover up* (*one's age*); (Bilanzen) ⟨fam⟩ *to cook* || verschleierter Blick *dimness of vision* | **-rt** a *fogged* (*sun*), ⟨fig a.⟩ *sibylline;* ⟨fig⟩ *disguised* (*restrictions*) **V.rung** f ~/~en *veiling* ⟨a. fig⟩ || ⟨fig⟩ *concealment* (*of facts*) || ⟨mil⟩ *camouflage* Fr || (v Bilanzen a.) *window-dressing* | ~sverkehr [m] ⟨wir, mil⟩ *deception signal traffic* **~schl·eifen** vt [h] *to spoil in grinding* od *by dragging* | ⟨mus⟩ *to slur, blend* || *to let* (*syllables*) *run together* || ⟨gram⟩ *to slur over* **~schl·eimen** vt [h] *to fill* od *obstruct*

Aussprache: Falls nicht anders (: [*v*]) angegeben, ist v = [*f*] zu sprechen.

with mucus od *phlegm* || *to foul* (*a gun*) | **(sich)** ~ vi/(refl) [s/h] *to be filled with slime*, etc; *to get stopped up* || (Gewehr) *to foul* | **-mt** a *furred* (*tongue*) **V.mung** f ~/~en *obstruction through mucus* || *fouling* || (Zungen~́) *coating* **Verschl·eiß** m ~es/~e (*sale by*) *retail* || (Abnutzung) *attrition*, *deterioration*; *wear and tear* (⟨a. fig⟩: an: *of nerve and body*) | (hoch)~́fest [a] (*highly*) *wear-resistant*; [pred] *standing w. and t.*; ~festigkeit [f] *resistance to wear*; ~schicht [f] (e–r Straße) *wearing course*; ~teil [n] *working part* **~schl·eißen** vt/i·irr [h/s] *to wear out*, *to waste* | vt *to* (*sell by*) *retail* | ~schlissen *tattered*, *threadbare* (*clothes*); *frayed* (*shirt*); [pred] *in tatters*, *in rags* **~schl·emmen** vt [h] *to squander in eating and drinking*, *to lavish* od *dissipate*, (Zeit) *to spend in feasting* **~schl·endern** vt [h] (Zeit) *to idle* od *saunter away* **~schl·eppen** vt [h] *to mislay*, *misplace* || (heimlich) *to purloin*, *pilfer* || (P) *to deport*; ⟨pol⟩ *to displace*: –ppte P *displaced p* (*D. P.*) || (Kind) *to abduct* || (Krankheiten) *to spread*, *carry* | (in die Länge ziehen) *to delay*, *protract*, ⟨Am a.⟩ *to stall*; sie ~ alles *they're a dilatory lot* || ⟨parl⟩ *to obstruct* (*a bill*) | **sich** ~ *to suffer delay*, *to drag on* **V.ppung** f ~/~en *misplacing*, etc; (P) *displacement* || *spread*(*ing*) || *procrastination*, *delay*(*ing*) || *obstruction* || *abduction* | **~s-** ~manöver [n pl] anwenden *to put a p off with excuses*, etc; ~politik [f] *obstructionism*; ~schriftsatz [m] ⟨jur⟩ *frivolous plea* ~́**schl·euderer** m ~s/~ *spendthrift*, *squanderer*, *lavish p* **~schl·eudern** vt [h] *to fling away* || ⟨fig⟩ *to waste*, *squander*, *lavish*, *dissipate* || (Geld) *to throw .. about*, *to make ducks and drakes of ..*, ⟨sl⟩ *to blue* | ⟨com⟩ *to sell* (*under price* od) *at a loss*; (ins Ausland) *to dump* **V.rung** f ~/~en *dissipation* || *waste* || *selling under price*; *dumping* **~schlicken** vi/t [s/h] *to silt* (*up*) **V.kung** f *silting*, *siltation* **~schl·ief** 1. & 3. sg pret v –schlafen **~schl·ießbar** a *provided with a lock* od *bolt* || *lock-up* (*shop*) **~schl·ießen** vt irr [h] *to shut*, *close*, *seal* || (**mit** e–m Schlüssel) *to lock* (*up*); (mit e–m Vorhängeschloß) *to* (*secure with a*) *padlock* || (Tür) *to fasten*, **hinter** sich [dat] *to lock the door on o.s.* | **in**: *to lock up in* (*a drawer*) || in sich ~ *to keep* (*a secret*) *locked up in one's bosom* | (fest) *to bolt and bar* (*a door*), *to screw up* (*a room*) | **etw in sich** [dat] ~ *to keep a th to o.s.*; die **Augen** ~ gegen ⟨fig⟩ *to wink at*, *to turn a blind eye to* || (Brief) *to seal* || (Hafen) *to blockade* || sein **Herz** ~ gegen *to harden* (*close*) *one's heart against* (*to*), *to turn a deaf ear to* | e–m sein Herz ~ *to hide one's feelings from a p* || **jdm** etw ~ *to close a th against a p*; (*no sphere was closed to him*) | **sich** ~ (der Einsicht [dat] etc) *to close one's mind to*, *to shut one's eyes to*, *to resist* (*a th*); er konnte sich der Beweiskraft nicht ~ *he could not but see ..* || sich in sich selbst ~ *to be wrapt up in o.s.* **V.ßung** f ⟨physiol⟩ *obturation* | **~schl·ossen**: bei ihr ist alles ~ *everything is under lock and key at her house* || (P) *tight-lipped*; *uncommunicative*, *secretive*, *close*, *cag*(*e*)*y*; *taciturn*; *reserved*; ⟨fam⟩ *buttoned up* || ~e Miene [f] *poker face*; in sich selbst ~ *shut-up in o.s.* | –heit [f] *unc.veness*, *s.veness*, etc; *reserve*; *taciturnity*; ⟨sex⟩ = Unfruchtbarkeit(speriode) **~schl·immbessern** = verbalhornen **~schl·immern** vt [h] *to impair*; *make worse* || ⟨fig⟩ (Lage etc) *to aggravate* || *to deprave* || (Krankheit) *to exacerbate* | **sich** ~ *to get* (od *grow*) *worse*, *to deteriorate* | (stärkere) **V.rung** f ⟨path⟩ *increased progressivity* **~schl·ingen** vt irr [h] **1.** (verflechten) (⟨a.⟩ **sich** ~) *to twist*, *entangle*, *intertwine*, *interlace* **2.** (verschlucken) *to swallow* (⟨fam⟩ *gobble*) *up*, *devour*, *wolf*; *gulp down* || *to guttle* (*three courses*); ⟨fam⟩ *to tuck .. in* | (viel Geld) *to cost* (*a mint of m.*) || (*his illness had run away with all his m.*) || (Gedanken, Verse) *to absorb* || (Buch; mit Blicken) *to devour* || e–n mit den Augen ~ *to stare at a p openmouthed* || .. als wollte er e–n ~ .. *as if he would eat you* | (v Meer, Dunkelheit) *to engulf* || (v der Erde) *to open and swallow* **V.gung** f *entanglement*; *maze*, *intricacy*; ~en [pl] *twists and turns* ⟨a. fig⟩ **~schl·iß** 1. & 3. sg pret; **~schl·issen** pp v verschleißen **~schl·ossen** pp v → –schließen **~schl·ucken** vt [h] *to swallow* || ⟨fig⟩ *to absorb* ⟨a. chem⟩; *drink in*; *gulp down*; *suppress* || (Buchstaben) *to clip*, (H) *to drop* (*one's aches*); (Endungen) *to slur over*; (den Rest s–r Rede) *to check o.s.* | **sich** ~ *to swallow the wrong way*, *to be embarrassed* od *choked* (*by one's tea*), ich habe mich –ckt *it has gone down the wrong way* **~schl·ug** 1. & 3. sg pret v –schlagen **~schl·ummern** vt [h] *to sleep away* **~schl·ungen** a [pp v –schlingen] *tortuous* || *meandering*, *winding* (*path*) || ⟨fig⟩ *complicated*, *intricate* ~́**schl·uß** m –usses/–üsse *lock*, *catch*, (wasserdicht) *seal*; ⟨physiol⟩ *obturation* || ⟨tail, bookb⟩ *clasp* || ⟨tech⟩ (a. Geruchs~́) *trap* || (Stöpsel) *plug* || ⟨artill⟩ *breech* (*mechanism*), (Mündungs~́) *muzzle cover* || (~mittel) *fastener*, *fastening* || ⟨phot⟩ *shutter* || (Zollplombe) *seal* || (Ware) in ~ legen *to bond* || unter ~ h *to keep .. under lock and key*, (zollamtlich) *in bond* | ~einstellung [f] ⟨phot⟩ *shutter scale* bzw *setting*; ~hahn [m] *stopcock*; ~kappe [f] *screw-cap*, *safety cap*; ~lamelle [f] ⟨phot⟩ *blade*; ~laut [m] *stop*, *explosive*; ~sache [f] ⟨bes mil⟩ *serial* od *security*, *classified matter*; ~schraube [f] *screwed plug*; ~streifen [m] *label*; *sealing strip*; ~stück [n] ⟨tech⟩ *plug* || ⟨artill⟩ *breech-block*; ~zeit [f] ⟨phot⟩ *shutter speed* **~schl·üsseln** vt [h] (Text) *to encode*; ~lter T. *cryptogram*, *-graph* **V.lung** f (selbsttätige *automatic*) *coding* **~schm·achten** vi [s] *to faint away*, *to languish* || sein Leben ~ *to pine away* || vor Durst ~ *to die of thirst*, *to be parched with thirst* || vor Hitze ~ *to be suffocated with* (*the*) *heat*, *to swelter* **V.tung** f ~/ *languor*, *slow death* **~schm·ähen** vt [h] *to disdain*, *scorn* (*a th*, *to do*, *doing*); *despise* || sie ~ die Arbeit *they refuse to work* || ⟨cul⟩ *not to care for* (*a dish*); .. nicht .. *I shouldn't mind a drink* || (Verlobte [n]) *to jilt* || (Freier) *to reject* || (Liebhaber) *to reject*, *to turn down* ||–ht *despised* (*love*); *castoff*; *rejected* (*lover*); *forsaken* (*wife*), *deserted* (*girl*), *jilted* (*sweatheart*) **V.hung** f ~/ *disdain*, *scorn*, *refusal*, *rejection* ~́**schmälern** vt [h] *to narrow*, *constrict*, *diminish* **V.rung** f ⟨a.⟩ *thinning* (*of interspaces*) **~schm·ausen** vt [h] *to eat up* || *to spend on good fare* **~schm·elzen** irr **I.** vi [s] *to melt into one another* (⟨a. fig⟩ v Farben) || ⟨met⟩ *to fuse* ⟨a. fig⟩ || ⟨fig⟩ *to coalesce*; *to merge* (*with*, *into*); *to blend* (bes v Farben) **II.** vt [h] *to blend* || ⟨met⟩ *to fuse* ⟨a. fig⟩ || ⟨fig⟩ *to amalgamate*, *unite*; (Texte etc) *to contaminate* **V.zung** f ~/ ⟨fig⟩ *coalescence*, *blending*, *fusion*, *amalgamation*, *merger*; *contamination* **~schm·erzen** vt [h] *to get over* (*the loss of*), *to put up with*, *to make the best of* || wir h es nicht –zt *it is still rankling* ⟨fig⟩ || er kann es ~ *he can well afford to lose it* **~schm·ieren** vt [h] *to fill* od *stop up* (*with clay*, *lime* etc), *to smear over*, *to daub* | (Tinte) *to spill* || (Papier) *to waste in scribbling* od *daubing* || (bekritzeln) *to bescribble* | *to use up in smearing* **~schm·itzt** a *cunning*, *sly*, *crafty*, *cute*, *shifty* (*p*); *mischievous* (*smile*) | [adv] a *archly* **~schm·olz(en)** pret (pp) v –schmelzen [vi] || ⟨fig⟩ ~en s mit *to be affiliated with* **~schm·oren** **I.** vt [h] *to use up* (*butter*) *in cooking* || ⟨fig⟩ *to parch* **II.** ⟨cul⟩ *to be* (*overdone* od) *too much boiled* || ⟨fig⟩ *to be parched*, *to parch* **~schm·utzen** **I.** vt [h] *to dirty*, *foul*, *soil* **II.** vi [s] *to get dirty* **V.zung** f ⟨tech⟩ *impurities* pl → ..seitig | **~s-** ~grad [m] *degree of soiling* **~schn·appen**: sich ~ ⟨fam⟩ [h] *to blurt out the secret*, *to let the cat out of the bag*, *to give o.s.*

Verbal-Flexion der Verben mit der Vorsilbe **ver-** → das jeweilige Simplex

away, to commit o.s. **~schn·auben, ~schn·aufen 1.** vi (⟨a.⟩ sich) [h] *to stop for breath, to (get back* od) *recover one's b., to draw b.* ‖ *let's get our wind* | (Pferd) ∼ l *to wind* **2.** ≗ n (⟨a.⟩ –fer) (Rast), *breather*; ⟨mil⟩ *breezer* **~schn·eiden** vt irr [h] (verderben) *to spoil in cutting, to cut badly* | (die Flügel) *to clip, to cut (away)* ‖ (Bäume) *to prune* ‖ (T) *to castrate, geld*; (Kognak) *to blend*; (Wein) *to adulterate* **V.dung** f ∼/ (T) *castration* **~schn·eien** vi [s]; verschneit s *to be snowed up* **~schn·itt I.** 1. & 3. sg pret v verschneiden ‖ –tten [pp] *diluted (wine,* etc) ‖ (T) *gelded,* etc | ≗ne(r) [m] *eunuch*; –nes Tier *gelding* **II.** ≗ m ∼(e)s/ *blend* ‖ ⟨carp⟩ *chips* **~schn·örkeln** vt [h] *to adorn with flourishes* **~schn·upfen** vt [h] *to snuff up* ‖ *to spend on snuff* | [a. imps] (jdn) *to nettle, pique, vex, offend* | **-pft s** *to have a cold*; ⟨fig⟩ *to be offended, to feel vexed, to take offence* (über [acc] *at*); ⟨sl⟩ *to have a grouse* (über *about*) **~schn·üren** vt [h] *to (bind with) cord; to tie up; to lace* (⟨a. tail⟩ mit Litzen) **~sch·ob(en)** 1. & 3. sg pret (pp) v –schieben **~sch·oll** 3. sg pret v –schallen **~sch·ollen** a *not heard of (again), forgotten, unremembered; obscure (author)* ‖ *lost* ‖ *missing (ship)* ‖ *(ages) long past; out of date* ‖ für ∼ erklären *to declare dead* | in ≗heit [f] geraten (s) *to disappear,* etc; (P & S) *to be forgotten,* etc **≗schollenerklärung** f ⟨a.⟩ *declaration of absence* **~sch·onen** vt [h] *to spare* ‖ (jdn mit etw) *to let (a p) off (a th), to exempt* od *excuse (a p from a th), to spare (a p a th): spare me that!* | **-ont** bleiben *to be spared,* ⟨path⟩ *to remain immune* **~sch·öne(r)n** vt [h] *to embellish, beautify, adorn; to set off* ‖ **sich** ∼ *to grow handsome* od *beautiful, to improve (in looks); to prettify o.s.* | **~d** ⟨fig⟩ *face-lifting* **V.rer** m ∼s/∼ *beautifier* **V.rung** f ∼/∼en *embellishment, improvement* | ∼srat [m] ⟨hum fam⟩ *beauty-doctor*; ∼sverein [m] *society for the improvement of local amenities; amenity s.* **≗sch·onung** f ∼/ *sparing, forbearance; exemption* **~sch·ossen** a [pp v –schießen] ⟨fig⟩ (–liebt) in [acc] *smitten with, gone*; ⟨fam⟩ *sweet, stuck*; (⟨sl⟩ *mashed, spoons, nuts) on* ‖ (Farben) *faded, discoloured, rusty* | ≗heit [f] *infatuation* (in *for*) **~schr·änken** vt [h] *to interlace, interlock* ‖ (Arme) *to cross, fold* ‖ (Balken) *to joggle* ‖ (Hände) *to clasp* | –kt *(arms) folded* (auf, über *across*) **~schr·auben** vt [h] *to screw (on)* ‖ *to screw (on) the wrong way* ‖ *to overscrew* **V.bung** f *screwing; screw connection* od *coupling* **~schr·eiben** vt irr [h] **1.** (Papier), [Zeit] *to use [spend] in writing* **2.** (bestellen) *to write for; to order* **3.** (falsch schreiben) *to miswrite* od *to write incorrectly* **4. (jdm etw)** *to give (a p a th) under hand and seal* ‖ ⟨jur⟩ *to assign, transfer (.. to a p)* ‖ ⟨med⟩ *to prescribe (.. for a p)* **5. sich** ∼ *to make a slip* od *a mistake in writing* ‖ sich e–r Lehre ∼ *to subscribe* (od *to give one's allegiance) to a doctrine* ‖ sich dem Teufel ∼ *to sell one's soul to the devil* **V.bung** f ∼/∼en (Bestellung) *order* ‖ (Fehler) *slip of the pen* ‖ ⟨med⟩ *prescription* ‖ ⟨jur⟩ *bond, obligation, assignment* ‖ e–e ∼ ausstellen *to give a bond* | ∼s- ∼pflichtige Arznei *prescription drug* **~schr·eien** vt irr [h] *to decry, to cry* (⟨fam⟩ *run) down* **~schr·ien** a [pp v –schreien] *ill reputed of* ‖ ∼ als *notorious as*; ∼ s als *to have the name of (a miser)* **~schr·ieb(en)** 1. & 3. sg pret (pp) v –schreiben; e–r S ∼en s *to be given over completely to a th* **~schr·oben** a ⟨fig⟩ *eccentric* ‖ *queer, cranky, crochety, odd* ‖ *intricate* | ∼er Einfall etc, Mensch *crank*; Kerl ⟨Am sl⟩ *screwball* (⟨a.⟩ S) | ≗heit [f] ∼/∼en *eccentricity* ‖ *queerness,* etc ‖ *intricacy* **~schr·oten** vt [h] *to grind up* **~schr·otten** vt [h] *to scrap; to break up* **V.tter** m (P) *(ship-)breaker* **~schr·umpfen** vt/i [h/s] *to shrivel up; to shrink,* *wither* ≗**schublok** f → Rangier– **~sch·üchtern** vt [h] *to intimidate, scare* | **-rt** *scary* ≗**sch·ulden I.** n ∼s/ *wrong, fault* ‖ ohne mein (etc) ∼ *without any* (od *through no) f. of mine (f. on the part of ..)* ‖ das ∼ liegt an, bei ihm *the f. is with him*; dem .. kann ein ∼ nachgewiesen w *the buyer can be proved to be at f.* **II.** ≗ vt [h] **1.** (P) *to involve in debt,* (S) *to encumber (with debts)* | **sich** (weiter, mehr) ∼ *to go (further, deeper) into debt* od *the red* **2.** (etw) *to bring on, to be guilty of, to be the cause of* ‖ was habe ich –det? *what (wrong) have I done?* ‖ Sie h ihr Unglück selbst –det *you have brought your misfortune upon y.s.* **3.** (verdienen) *to incur (blame)* **~sch·uldet** a *in debt; encumbered* ‖ ⟨fig⟩ e–m ∼ s *to be indebted to a p* | ∼erm·aßen [adv] *deservedly* **V.dung** f ∼/ *offence, fault* ‖ (Verschuldetsein) *indebtedness* | ∼shaftung [f] *liability arising from negligence* **~sch·ulen** vt [h] ⟨hort⟩ *to line out* °**~sch·ütt** gehen *to go to waste*; ∼ gegangen (P) *in limbo (= prison)* ‖ (S & P) *lost* **~sch·ütten** vt [h] *to spill, slop (a liquid)* ‖ (Gräben etc) *to fill up with earth* ‖ (Ort) *to overwhelm* ‖ (versperren) *to block up* ‖ (P) *to bury* ‖ –ttet w v .. *to be buried under (an avalanche)* | ⟨fam⟩ er hat es bei ihr –tt(et) *he has got into her bad books* ‖ sich [dat] alles ∼ *to make a mess of it* °**~sch·üttgehen** vi [s] = –loren gehen → –schütt **~schw·ägern**: sich ∼ [h] *to become related by marriage, to ally o.s. by marriage (to)* | **-rt** ⟨fig⟩ *affiliated; relative by m.* | **V.rte** pl *relations by m.* **V.rung** f ∼/∼en *relationship by m.* ‖ ⟨fig⟩ *affinity* **~schw·and** 1. & 3. sg pret v –schwinden **~schw·ärmen I.** vi [h] (of bees) *to cease swarming* **II.** vt [h] (Tag, Nacht) *to pass .. in revelry*; ⟨fam⟩ *to make a day, night of it* **~schw·ärzen** vt [h] ⟨fig⟩ = anschwärzen **~schw·atzen** vt [h] (die Zeit) *to gossip away* ‖ *to forget .. in chatting* ‖ (P) *to backbite*; (S) *to blurt out* | **sich** ∼ *to betray o.s., to let the cat out of the bag* **~schw·eigen I.** vt irr [h] *to keep .. dark* od *secret; to keep silent about; to conceal, suppress* ‖ *to pass over in silence* ‖ (Wahrheit) *to hold back* ‖ e–m etw ∼ *to hide* od *keep a th from a p* ‖ → –schwiegen bleiben *to remain a secret* **II.** ≗ n ∼s/ *silence* ([gen] *about truth*) **V.gung** f ∼/ *concealment* ‖ *silence (regarding ..)* **~schw·elgen** vt [h] = verprassen **~schw·ellen** vi irr [s] *to swell (out); to close in swelling* **~schw·enden** vt [h] *to squander; waste, lavish* (auf *on*); ⟨a.⟩ *to throw (one's money) away* ‖ –det *lost (labour), useless (trouble)* **V.der** m ∼s/∼ *squanderer, spender, spendthrift, prodigal*; (Wüstling) *wastrel* | ≗isch [a] *wasteful, extravagant; unsparing* (mit *in*); ⟨geh Spr⟩ *prodigal (of)* ‖ (reich) *profuse, luxuriant* ‖ ∼ umgehen mit *to be lavish with* **V.dung** f ∼/∼en *waste(fulness); extravagance* | ≗ssucht [f] *lavishness, prodigality,* ⟨fam⟩ *squandermania* **~schw·iegen** a [pp –schweigen] (P) *secretive, close(-mouthed), reserved, discreet, reticent* (über *about*); ([wo]*man) of discretion* | (S) *suppressed; kept secret* | ⟨fig⟩ *snug (place)* | ≗heit [f] ∼/ *discretion, reserve; reticence; secrecy (under the seal of s.)* ‖ Mangel an ∼ *irreticence, -cy* **~schw·ielen** vi [s] *to callous, horny* °**~schw·iemeln** vt [h] *to waste* | **-lt** ⟨fam⟩ *seedy (look)* **~schw·immen** vi irr [s] *to dissolve* | (undeutlich w) *to become blurred, to grow hazy, to fade away* | *to merge* od *melt into one another*; (Farben) *to blend* ≗**schw·ind(e)-** ∼lafette [f] *disappearing mounting*; ∼linie [f] *vanishing line*; ∼punkt [m] ⟨paint⟩ *v.g point*; ∼scheibe [f] *v.g target* **~schw·inden** vi irr [s] *to disappear, vanish* ‖ *to fade, shade, pass (away); to go; to come to nought, to peter out; to be lost (in the night)* ‖ *(the land) grows distant* ‖ (plötzlich) *to pop out (of sight), to dive (into a shop)* ‖ (Lächeln) *to die (from)* ‖ ∼! → verdufte!, *now vanish!* | °(ausreißen) *to bolt, decamp,* ⟨fam⟩ *to make o.s. scarce* ‖ der Weg –det im Tal *the road dips into the v.* ‖ ∼ ne-

---

Aussprache: Falls nicht anders (: [*v*]) angegeben, ist v = [*f*] zu sprechen.

ben *to sink into insignificance by the side of* ‖ ~ l *to put out of the way*; (zaubernd) *to spirit away* | ~d klein *imperceptible, infinitesimal* ‖ leicht ~d *fugitive* (*colour*) | verschwunden s *to be missing* od *gone* | im ≗ s (S) *to be on the way out* **~schw·istern**: sich ~ [h] *to form a sisterly union* ‖ ⟨fig⟩ *to associate* od *unite intimately* | **-rt** a *brother and sister* | ⟨fig⟩ *closely united* ‖ *congenial* (*souls*) ‖ *sister* (*virtues*) ‖ *kindred* (*spirits*) **V.rung** f ~/ *sisterly* (od *brotherly*) *union* ‖ ⟨fig⟩ *close union* od *alliance* **~schw·itzen I.** vi [s] *to pass off as sweat* **II.** vt [h] *to spoil by perspiration* | °⟨fig⟩ *to forget*; *to lose knowledge of* (*French*); wir h .. ganz –tzt *our French has grown very rusty* **~schw·ollen** a [pp v –schwellen] *swollen* (*cheek*) **~schw·ommen** a *dissolving* (Bilder *views*); *blurred, indistinct*; *shadowy*; *hazy* (⟨a. phot⟩ *picture*), *dim, faint, vague* (*thoughts*); *turbid* (*thinking*); *ambiguous*; *muddy* (*style*) ‖ ~ m *to blur* | –heit [f] *vagueness* ⟨a. fig⟩, etc **~schworen** [pp v ≗] s–r Arbeit [dat] ~ *wedded to his job*; (*to be*) *sworn* (*to fealty*) *to* **V.ne** [der ~, ein ~r] m & f ~n/~n *conspirator, plotter*, (f *conspiratress*) **~schw·ören** vt irr [h] *to abjure, forswear* | *to curse* | das Trinken ~ *to renounce drinking* | **sich** ~ *to protest with oaths* (*to do*) ‖ (komplottieren) *to form a conspiracy*; *to plot, conspire* | sich ~ **zu** etw *to plot a th* | **V.rer(in** f) m ~s/~, **~schwor(e)ne** [der ~, ein ~r] m & f ~n/~n *conspirator, plotter*, (f *conspiratress*) **V.rung** f ~/~en *conspiracy, plot*; *cloak and dagger* [attr] | *abjuration, renunciation* **~schw·unden** a [pp a verschwinden] **~sechsfachen** vt [h] *to multiply by six*; *to sextuple* | *to increase sixfold* (⟨a.⟩ sich ~) **≗s·ehen** n ~s/~ (*clerical*) *error*; *mistake, oversight, inadvertency, slip*(*-up* ⟨Am⟩), *blunder* | *fright* (*during pregnancy*) aus ~, ≗tlich [adv] *inadvertently, by an oversight, by mistake* ‖ durch das ~ *by the lapsing* (*of*) **~s·ehen** vt irr [h] **I. 1.** *to overlook, neglect, miss, mistake* (*a th*) ‖ *to err* od *blunder in* (*a th*) **2.** *to attend to* (*a th*) ‖ das **Amt** e–s Lehrers ~ *to be* (od *act as*) *a t.* ‖ (e–n **Dienst**) *to administer, perform*; jds D. ~ *to do duty for a p, to fill his place* ‖ *to run* (*the post-office*) ‖ *to do the work of* (*a sergeant*) ‖ Geschäfte ~ *to transact business* ‖ den Gottesdienst ~ *to hold s.* ‖ (Haushalt, Hof, Küche, Stall etc) *to look after* ..; *to do* (*the cooking, housekeeping*) ‖ **(Lager)** *to tend* (*the store*); wohl ~es L. *well-assorted stock* ‖ (Pfarre [f e–n anderen]) *to take charge of* ‖ (Pflichten) *to go about* (*one's duties*) ‖ e–n Sterbenden ~ *to administer the last sacrament to a p*; sich ~ l *to receive the l. s.* **3. es bei** jdm ~ h *to be in a p's bad books, to incur a p's displeasure* ‖ wir h es **darin** ~, daß .. *we have made a mistake in coming* **4.** ~ **(mit)**: *to furnish, provide, supply, fit* (*with*) | [pp] *–ed*: mit e–r Rüstung ~ *armoured* | *to stock* (*a farm, pond*) (*with*) ‖ *to feed* (*a machine*) (*with*) ‖ mit dem Akzept (Giro) ~ *to accept, endorse* (*a bill*) ‖ wohl ~ [pp] mit .. *strong in* .. ‖ reichlich mit Geldmitteln ~ s *to have* (*plenty of money* od) *ample means* ‖ mit Hausrat ~ *to furnish* (*a house*) ‖ mit Lebensmitteln ~ *to stock* (*a place*) *with provisions, to victual* ‖ mit e–m Motor ~ [pp] *motor-equipped* ‖ e–n mit dem Nötigen ~ *to keep a p supplied with all he requires* ‖ mit Personal ~ *to staff* ‖ mit e–m Saum ~ *to hem* ‖ mit den Sterbesakramenten → 2. ‖ mit Unterschrift ~ *to sign* (*a document*), .. [pp] *bearing a signature* ‖ mit Vollmacht ~ *to invest with full power*(*s*) ‖ [pp] °⟨sex⟩ *hooked up* (mit *by*) ‖ ⟨off⟩ mit e–m Zeichen ~ *to check off* **II. sich** ~ *to make a mistake, commit an error, get it wrong, go wrong* ‖ ⟨prov⟩ ~ ist auch verspielt *a miss is as good as a mile* | (e–r S [gen]) *to expect a th* ‖ ehe ich mich dessen *or* mir's versah *before I was aware of it, before I knew it* (od *where I was*), *all of a sudden, in the twinkling of an eye* ‖ ehe man sich's versah ⟨fam⟩ *before you could* (*think* od) *say Jack Robinson* | **an** [dat]: *to be frightened* od *take fright at* ‖ **mit**: *to make provision of*; vgl I. 4. **~s·ehren** vt [h] *to wound, injure, hurt* ‖ (beschädigen) *to damage* | **-rt** ⟨mil⟩ *disabled* | **V.rten-** ~rente [f] *invalid's pay*; (*physical*) *disability benefit* od *pension*; ~wiederherstellung [f] *rehabilitation* **~s·eifbar** a ⟨chem⟩ *saponifiable* **~s·eifen** vt/i [h/s] *to saponify, to turn to soap* | vt ⟨fam⟩ *to thrash* (*a p*) **V.fung** f *saponification* **~s·eilen** vt [h] *to strand* **~s·elbständigen** vt [h] *to make independent* **~s·endbar** a *transportable* **~s·enden** vt irr [h] *to send* (*off*); *to forward, dispatch, consign* ‖ (ins Ausland) *to export*, ⟨a.⟩ *ship* ‖ es wird in Flaschen versandt *it comes* bzw *goes in bottles* **V.der** m ~s/~ *dispatcher, consignor*; *exporter* **V.dung** f ~/~en *sending, conveyance, transmission, transport, shipment* | **~s-** ~art [f] *mode of conveyance*; ≗fähig [a] *transportable*; ~güter [n pl] *goods for exportation*, etc; ~kosten [pl] *forwarding expenses, charges for carriage*; ~liste [f] *shipping-list* **~s·engen** vt [h] *to scorch, sear, burn* (⟨a.⟩ v der Sonne); *to singe* **~senkbar** a *sinkable* (*ship*); *drop-head* (*sewing machine*); *flush* (*fitting*); *stow-away* (*back-seat*); *elevator* (*orchestra pit*) **~s·enken I.** vt [h] *to sink*, ‖ (Sarg) *to lower* ‖ (Schiff) *to submerge, sink*, (selbst) *to scuttle*; wurde v s–r Mannschaft –kt (*the ship*) [*had*] *sc.d herself* ‖ –kt *flush* (*fitting*) ‖ (Bolzen) *to countersink* | **sich** ~ ⟨fig⟩ *to dive into meditations* ‖ **in** [acc]: *to become immersed in* ‖ in Gedanken –kt *absorbed in thought* **II.** ≗ [n] (v Schlamm) im Meer *dumping* (*sludge*) *at sea* **V.kung** f ~/~en *sinking* ‖ *scuttling, submersion*; ⟨sub–mar⟩ ~en [pl] *sinkings* ‖ ⟨theat⟩ *trap*(*-door*), *grave*(*-trap*), ⟨fam⟩ *slot* ‖ °⟨fig⟩ in der ~ verschwinden *to sink into insignificance, to vanish into space* ‖ innere ~ ⟨fig⟩ *inward communion* | **~s-** ⟨theat⟩ ~fläche [f] *bridge* (*in stage*), ⟨Am⟩ *st. elevator*; ~klappe [f] *trap*; ~öffnung [f] (*bridge*) *cut*, ⟨Am⟩ *st. elevator*

V·erseschmied m → Vers

ver- **~s·essen** a [pp v –sitzen] (auf [acc]) (*dead*) *bent, set* (*upon*); *mad* (*after*); *wild, crazy* (*about*); ⟨fam⟩ *ravenous* (*for*); ⟨Am sl⟩ *stuck on* ‖ sie war ~ darauf *her heart was set on it* ‖ wie ~ auf Arbeit *a demon for work* **~setzbar** a *transferable* | ≗keit [f] *t.bility* **~s·etzen I.** vt [h] **A.** (falsch) *to misplace* ‖ (anders) *to displace, shift, remove* (*displaced p* [*D P*]) ‖ (mit–e–a vertauschen) *to transpose* ⟨a. typ⟩ ‖ ⟨math⟩ *to permute* ‖ ⟨min⟩ *to pack* (*an empty space*); *to stow* **B. 1.** e–m den **Atem** ~ *to take one's breath away* ‖ (Beamte) *to place, transfer* ‖ ⟨bib⟩ (Berge) *to remove* ‖ (Betonung) *to alter* ‖ (Bischöfe) *to translate* ‖ (Hieb etc) *to give, deal*, ⟨fam⟩ e–m **eins** ~ *to deal, deliver* (⟨sl⟩ *land*) *a p a* (*heavy*) *blow*,; ⟨fam⟩ *to let one have it*; (mit dem Fuß) *to kick a p in the pants*; mit dem Holzhammer *to knock a p for the loop*; ⟨sl⟩ *to sock a p one* ‖ ⟨met⟩ *to temper, alloy* ‖ (P) ⟨a. mil⟩ *to re-assign*; *post*; ‖ (Offiziere) *to transfer* N ‖ (Pfahl) *to resite* ‖ (als **Pfand**) *to pawn, pledge*; ⟨sl⟩ *to* (*put up the*) *spout, to pop*; → –tzt ‖ (Pflanzen) *to transplant* ‖ (Rhythmus) *to transpose* ‖ **(Schüler)** *to move* (*up*), *promote* (in [*in*]*to*) ‖ (Zaun) *to resite* **2.** °⟨fig fam⟩ jdn ~ *to let .. wait, to leave .. in the lurch, to disappoint a p*, ⟨sl⟩ *to stay* (*a p*) *up* **C.** (erwidern) *to reply, rejoin, retort* **D. in** Angst ~ *to alarm, frighten, terrify* ‖ → Anklagezustand ‖ (in e–e Lage) *to put* od *land into* ‖ in üble Laune ~ *to put out* ‖ in Not ~ *to distress* ‖ in e–e Notlage ~ *to lay* (*a p*) *under a necessity* ‖ in die Notwendigkeit ~ *to reduce to the necessity* (*of doing*), *to compel* (*to*

Verbal-Flexion der Verben mit der Vorsilbe **ver-** → das jeweilige Simplex

do) ‖ → Ruhestand ‖ in Schwingung ~ *to set .. vibrating* | **(mit)** *to mix, combine, dash, adulterate, dilute*; ⟨met⟩ *to alloy (with)* ‖ (versperren) *to bar, block; dam up, obstruct (with)* | **(unter)** *to rank, enrol (among the gods)* **II. sich** ~ (S) *to change its place, to shift* ‖ (v Blähungen) *to settle*; –tzte Bl.n [pl] *flatulency* [sg] | (P) sich **in** jds Lage ~ *to put, imagine, place o.s. in another's position* ‖ ~ wir uns in .. *let us go back to (those times)* ≗**s·etz-** ~amt [n] *pawn-shop*; ~grube [f] *tan pit*; ~schiene [f] ⟨rail⟩ *switch*; ~stücke [n pl] *movable scenery* **~setzt** a ⟨tech, tail⟩ *staggered (row, seam)* ‖ –es Muster [n] ⟨tex, etc⟩ *transposed pattern* ‖ °(P) *stood up*; ~ s ⟨a.⟩ *to cool one's heels* ‖ °(verpfändet) *up the spout* od *flue* | [adv] ~ angeordnet *staggered* **V.zung** f ~/~en *misplacement; displacement*; ⟨aero⟩ *drift, deviation* | *transposition* ‖ *inversion (of words)* ‖ *permutation* | (Beamte etc) *transfer*; ⟨mil⟩ *(permanent) change of assignment* ‖ (Bischof) *translation* ‖ ~ nach *removal to Berlin* ‖ (Schule) *remove* | *transplantation* | *pawning, pledging* | *mixture, alloy, combination; dilution* (Streckung) | s–e ~ erhalten ⟨mil⟩ *to get a shift* | **~s-** ~arbeit [f] ⟨school⟩ *test-paper*; ~befehl [m] ⟨mil⟩ *order of transfer, posting order*; ~prüfung [f] *examination for promotion*; ~zeichen [n] ⟨mus⟩ *sign of transposition* **~s·euchen I.** vt [h] *to infect, taint*; ⟨at⟩ *contaminate; pollute* ‖ durch Gas ~ *to gas* ‖ von Ratten –cht *rat-infected* **II.** vi [s] *to become infected* **V.chung** f ~/~en *infection*; etc; *(radioactive) contamination*; ⟨mil⟩ *chemical and/or biological c.n* ‖ (moralische) *contagion* **~s·eufzen** vt [h] *to pass in sighing, to sigh away* **~s·icherbar** a *insurable* **V.rer** m ~s/~ *insurer* ‖ (Lebens≗) *assurer* ‖ ⟨mar⟩ *underwriter* **~s·ichern** vt [h] **1.** (gegen) *to insure* (sich *o.s.*) *(against)* (bei *in*); [abs] sich ~ (l) *to take out an insurance* ‖ er –rte sein Leben auf .. *he took out a life in.ce policy for £ 250* **2.** (beteuern) *to assert, affirm, declare, protest* ‖ (jdn e–r S *or* jdm etw) *to assure, convince (a p of a th)*: ich –re dir (*or* dich) *I assure you*; .., daß es wichtig ist *I can promise you of its importance* ‖ seien Sie –rt, daß *you may depend upon it that* **3. sich** ~ [gen] *to make sure (of), to secure (a th), to arrest (a p)* **V.rte** [der ~, ein ~r] m & f ~n/~n *policy-holder* **V.rung** f ~/~en (Eigentums≗, selbst abgeschlossen *direct) insurance (policy)* (auf *on*) (abschließen *to take out*) ‖ (Lebens≗) *assurance*; ~ auf Gegenseitigkeit *mutual benefit assurance*; auf den Erlebensfall *endowment a.ce*; ⟨Am⟩ *in.ce* ‖ → Reisewetter≗; ~ gegen alle Gefahren *all risks* (od *comprehensive) in.ce*; ~ gegen einfachen Diebstahl *larceny and theft in.ce*; ~ auf festen Zeitpunkt *fixed term in.ce*; ~ f fremde Rechnung *in.ce for account of third parties*; ~ auf fremdes Leben *assurance on the life of another*; ~ mit Karenzfrist *ass. with period of partial benefit, ass. with qualifying period for p. b.*; ~ mit (ohne) Prämienrückgewährung *in.ce with(out) return of premium* ‖ durch ~ gegen Arbeitsunfähigkeit gedeckt *or* .. –sichert *covered on disability* ‖ (Beteuerung) *assurance, assertion, profession* ‖ die ~ abgeben *to give the assurance* | e–e ~ abschließen *to effect an i.* ‖ die ~ erlischt *the policy lapses* | **~s-** ~agent [m] *i.-agent*; ~antrag [m] *proposal form*; ~betrag [m] *amount insured*; ~anstalt, ~gesellschaft [f] *i.-company*; ~fall [m] *occurrence of event insured against*; ~gericht [n] *maritime court*; ~kasse [f] auf Gegenseitigkeit, [österr] wechselseitige ~kasse *mutual in.ce fund*; ~leistung [f] *i. payments*; ~mathematik(er [m]) [f] *actuarial theory; (actuary)*; ~nehmer [m] *insurant, the insured; policy holder*; ~pflicht [f], ~zwang [m] *obligation to insure*; ~police [f] ⟨obs⟩ = –schein; ~prämie [f] *i.-premium, rate of i.* | fester ~satz *set i. rate*; ~schein [m] *i.-policy*; (vorläufiger) *binder*; ~schutz [m] *coverage*; ~techniker [m] *actuary*; ≗technisch [a] *actuarial*; ~träger [m] *i. carrier, insurer*; ~umfang [m] *scope of in.ce*; ~wesen [n] *scheme of i., i.-matters* pl **~sichtbaren** vt [h] *to make visible* **~s·ickern** vi [s] *to ooze away* **V.rung** f *percolation* **~s·ieden** vt/i [h/s] *to boil away* **~s·iegbar** a *exhaustible, liable to run dry* **~s·iegeln** vt [h] *to seal (up)* ‖ ⟨jur⟩ *to put under seal* ‖ ⟨fig⟩ *his lips were glued* **~s·iegen** vi [s] *to dry up, to be drained* od *exhausted; to peter* od *give out*; ⟨fig⟩ *to ebb; (the poetic vein) ran out* ‖ nie ~d *never-failing, inexhaustible (source)*

vers·iert [v–z–] a *versed* (in *in*)

versifiz·ieren [v–s–] vt [h] *to versify*

ver- **~s·ilbern** vt [h] *to silver, plate* ‖ galvanisch –rt *electro-plated*; –rte Waren *plate-goods* | ⟨fam, fig⟩ *to convert into money, to realize* **V.rung** f ~/~en *silvering, plating* | *realization* °**~s·impeln** vi [s] *to grow silly* od *imbecile* | **-lt** *dull, stupid, pedantic* **~s·ingen I.** vt [h] (Zeit) *to spend .. in singing* | **sich** ~ *to sing out of tune* **II.** vi [h] *to lose in a singing contest* **~s·inken I.** vi irr [s] *to sink (down); to become submerged* (*or* in e–m Abgrund *engulfed)* ‖ (Schiff) *to founder* | in den Boden ~ *to dive down to soil* | in die Erde ~ *to sink into the earth* | im Laster ~ *to plunge into vice* | –sunken in [acc] ⟨fig⟩ *absorbed, lost, wrapt in (thought)* ‖ im Laster –sunken *depraved* **II.** ≗ n *submersion* ‖ zum ~ *bottomless* **~s·innbild(lich)en** vt [h] *to symbolize, allegorize, typify* **~s·innlichen I.** vt [h] *to body forth, to materialize* ‖ *to symbolize, illustrate* ‖ *to make sensual* **II.** vi (⟨a.⟩ sich ~) *to become sensual* **V.chung** f ~/~en *symbolization*

Versi·on [v–z–] f ~/~en *version*

ver- **~s·ippt** a: ~ s *to be cousins* **~s·ittlichen** vt [h] *to civilize* **~s·itzen** vt [h] *to spoil by sitting on* ‖ (Zeit) *to pass .. sitting (idle)* ‖ *to miss by sitting idle* | **sich** ~ *to lose the use of one's limbs by sitting too much, to lead a sedentary life* | → –sessen **~skl·aven** vt [h] *to enslave*; den Karten –vt s *to be in slavery to the c.s* °**~s·offen** a [pp v –saufen] *sodden; given to boozing* ‖ *habitually drunk* [pred] ‖ *drunken* [attr] | *beery (look)* ‖ ~er Kerl *drunkard, tippler* | ≗heit [f] ~/ *drunkenness* **~s·ohlen** vt [h] *to sole* | ⟨fam⟩ (jdm das Fell *or* jdn) *to thrash (a p), to give (a p) a good hiding*; ⟨Am⟩ *to paddle* **~s·öhnen** vt [h] *to appease; reconcile* (mit jdm *to, with*; ⟨fig⟩ mit etw [dat] *to)* ‖ *to propitiate (Heaven)* | **sich** ~ *to bury the hatchet*; (mit) *to become reconciled (with)*; sich –nt h *to have made up one's difference* ‖ ⟨fig⟩ (mit) *to become reconciled, to resign o.s. (to)* | **~d** *conciliatory; redeeming (features)*; ⟨rel⟩ *expiatory* **V.ner** m ~s/~ *reconciler, propitiator, mediator, peace-maker* **~s·öhnlich** a *placable, forgiving*; ⟨rel⟩ *propitiable* ‖ *conciliatory (deed)* ‖ ~ stimmen *to conciliate* | ≗keit [f] ~/ *placableness, placability* ‖ *forgivingness* **V.nung** f ~/~en *reconciliation, reconcilement* ‖ ⟨rel⟩ *propitiation, expiation* | **~s-** ~bund [m] *covenant of grace*; ~fest [n], ~tag [m] *day of reconciliation*; (jüdisch) *Day of Atonement*; ~opfer [n] *expiatory sacrifice*; (T) *e.y victim*; ~politik [f] *peace-policy*; ~tod [m] *e.y death*; ~werk [n] *e.y work* **~s·onnen** a *lost in thought* | ~heit [f] ~/ *blue* od *brown study* **~s·orgen** vt [h] (mit) *to provide, supply (with)* ‖ mit Wasser ~ *to water* ‖ mit Lebensmitteln ~ *to purvey for (the army); to cater to ..* (vgl –sehen I. 4.) ‖ (sorgen für) *to take care of, to maintain* ‖ (Kinder) *to provide for, to settle (in life)* **V.ger** m ~s/~ *provider* ‖ *maintainer, supporter, patron* ‖ ~ der Familiengemeinschaft ⟨mst⟩ *breadwinner* ‖ ⟨fig⟩ *main-stay*

Aussprache: Falls nicht anders (: [v]) angegeben, ist v = [f] zu sprechen.

-gung f ~/~en *provision, supply for* || *support* ⟨a. mil⟩, *maintenance of* || Alters≚ *old age pension* || ⟨mil⟩ *supply, provisioning*; (–sverwaltung) *administration* N; *logistical support* (od *effort*); *logistic operations*; *logistics* [sg konstr] N || durch Seefahrzeug *naval mobile l.c s.t*; die ~ durchführen *to carry out l.cal s.t functions* | (Versorgtsein) *settlement* || (Brotstelle) *situation* || **mit**: *water* (etc) *s.y*; (mit Verpflegung) *catering* | **~s-** *s(uppl)y, s(uppl)ies, l(ogisti)c, l(ogisti)cal, c(atering)g, a(dministrati)ve* | **~amt** n *pension office* **~anlage** f *s.y installations* pl, ⟨tech⟩ *feeder* **~anspruch** m *claim to assistance* od *maintenance, benefits*; *c. to preferential status* (*of veterans*) od *to social security* od *to a pension* **~anwärter** m ⟨mil⟩ *time-expired soldier* **~anstalt** f *charitable institution*; *almshouse* **~basis** f *s.y base* **≚berechtigt** a *entitled to maintenance*, ⟨mil⟩ *time-expired* (*soldier*) **~betrieb** m *s.y factory* || *public utility plant*; ⟨mil⟩ *utility* N **~bombe** f *s.y bomb* **~ehe** f *marriage of convenience* **~einheit** f *ancillary* (⟨mil⟩ *service*) *unit* **~einrichtung** f *s.y* od *l.cal* (od *c.g*) *facility* od *installation*; öffentl. *utility* **~-Endbahnhof** m *s.y railhead* N **~engpaß** m *bottle-neck in s.ies* **~fahrzeug** n *a.ve* od *s.y vehicle*, ⟨engl mil⟩ *B v.* **~fluß** m *movement of s.ies* **~führung** f *l.cal leadership* od *command*; *l.c support management* (*LSM*) **~gebiet** n *s.y area* **~güter** n pl *items of s.y*; *s.ies* | Bereitstellung v ~n *preparation of s.ies*; Bestand an ~n *level of s.ies in hand*; Klassifizierung der ~ *Federal S.y System* **~kette** f *s.y line* **~kolonne** f *s.y train* N **~kompanie** f *service c.* | Beurteilung der **~lage** f *l.cal estimate* **~lager** n ⟨mil⟩ *s.y dump* ~leine, ~leitung f ⟨a–n⟩ *umbilical cord* **~netz** n *a.ve net*; *network of electric power connections*; ⟨tech⟩ *s.y* od *distribution system* **~offizier** m *s.y officer* **~regelung** f *a.ve order* **~schiff** n *s.y vessel* **~stab** m *a.ve command* N **~stand** m ⟨mil⟩ *level of s.y* **~station, ~stelle** f *s.y station* ⟨a. a–n⟩ **~straßen** f pl *s.y routes* (befehlen *to designate*) **~stützpunkt** m *s.y centre* **~trosse** m pl (2. –kompanie) *field trains* **~truppen** f pl *service* (*support*) *troops* od *units* **~verkehr** m *l.cal traffic* **~wege** m pl *l.c routes*; *communications*; [konkr] ⟨a.⟩ *pipelines* **~wesen** n *state provision for the deserving* **~zone** f *service district* **~zug** m *s.y train*

ver- ~sp·annen vt [h] *to stay, brace* **~sp·aren** vt [h] (auf e–e Zeit) *to defer, delay* (bis, auf *to, till*) **~sp·äten** vt [h] *to delay, retard*; jdn ~ (zu spät k l) *to make a p late* | **sich** ~ *to be late, to be behind time* || der Zug hat sich verspätet *the train is overdue* | **-tet** a *belated*; ~es Auftreten *retardation* **V.tung** f ~/~en *lateness, tardiness, coming too late*; *late arrival* || (Verzögerung) *delay* || der Zug etc hat 10 M. ~ .. *is ten minutes late* od *overdue*, ⟨bes Am⟩ *behind schedule* (⟨a.⟩ mit ~) **~sp·eisen** vt [h] *to eat up*; ⟨fam⟩ *to polish off* **~spekul·ieren** vt [h] *to lose by speculation* | **sich** ~ *to make a bad sp.*; *to ruin o.s. by sp.* **~sp·erren** vt [h] *to block up, to bar*(*ricade*), *encumber*, ⟨fam⟩ *jam* || den Zugang ~ zu .. *to clutter up access to* .. || (e–m ..) *to obstruct, intercept* (*a p's view*) **V.rrung** f ~/~en *blocking-up, barricade, obstruction* || (e–s Hafens) *blockade* || (beim Dominospiel) *closing* **~sp·ielen I.** vt [h] *to lose* (*at play*), *to play* od *gamble away* || viel ~ *to lose heavily* || (Zeit) *to pass .. in playing* **II.** vi [h] *to lose the game* || bei jdm ~ *to get into a p's bad books* | **-lt** a *playful* (*kitten*), *kittenish*; *childlike* (*joy, pleasure*); *coquettish* (*adaptation for the stage*) | [adv] ~ tun ⟨fam⟩ *to act up* | ≚heit [f] *playfulness* **~sp·illern** vi [s] ⟨bot⟩ = verkümmern **~sp·innen** vt [h] *to use up in spinning* | sich ~ *to get entangled* **~sp·otten** vt [h] *to mock* od *scoff* (*at*); *to deride, ridicule, flout* || *to jeer at* || (neckend) *to tease, chaff* || (höhnisch) *to lash a p in scornful words* **V.ttung** f ~/~en *derision, mockery, chaff*(*ing*, etc) || ~ Christi *Mocking* od *Scorning of Christ* **~spr·ach** 1. & 3. sg pret v **~spr·echen I.** vt irr [h] *to* (*give one's*) *promise* (fest *for certain*) || *to say* (*you said you would*) || jdm die Ehe ~ *to promise to marry a p*; sie sind –sprochen *they are engaged* (*to be married*) || ⟨allg⟩ ich bin f morgen schon –sprochen *I am already engaged for to-m.* || sie halten, was sie ~ *they do what they preach, they are men of their word*; mehr halten, als .. *to be better than one's word* || es (auf Treu u Glauben) ~ *to pledge one's word* (*one's honour*) || sie ~ (gr Menschen) z w *they bid fair to become* ..; den größten Erfolg (nichts) ~ *to hold the greatest promise of success* (*to be without pr.*); das Wetter –spricht gut z w or bleiben .. *promises well* | sich [dat] etw ~ *to hope for a th* || sich etw (nichts) ~ v *to expect great ths* od *much of* (⟨a.⟩ *to disbelieve in, to set no great hopes in*); zu viel ~ *to overpromise* | viel ~d *very hopeful* od *promising* (*youth*) **II. sich** ~ *to make a mistake in speaking* || ich h. mich, er h. sich –sprochen *it was a slip of the tongue* | *to become engaged* | er **ließ** sich v mir ~ *he made me promise* **III.** ≚ n ~s/~; **-chung** f ~/~en *promise* (erfüllen, halten *to keep, fulfil*; *to make good* ..) || sich durch ein ~ binden an *to take a pledge to* || e–m das ~ abnehmen *to exact a promise from a p, to make a p promise* (*to do*) || ein ~ geben *to make a promise*, (bindendes) *to give an undertaking*; sein ~ geben *to engage* od *give, pledge one's faith* || sein ~ nicht halten *to fail in one's promise*; e–m gr –ungen m *to hold out great hopes to a p* | **-chens-** ~empfänger [m] *promissee*; ~geber [m] *promisor* **~spr·eizen** vt [h] *to prop* **~spr·engen** vt [h] *to disperse, scatter* (*troops, a multitude*) || ⟨billards⟩ *to knock* (*a ball*) *off the table* | **-gt** *scattered* (*units*), *isolated* (*body of troops*) **V.gte(r)** ⟨mil⟩ *straggler* **-gten-** ~aufnahmelinie [f] *st. line* N; ~s·ammelstelle [f] *st. collecting point* **~spr·ingen**; sich [dat] den Fuß ~ *to sprain one's foot in jumping* **~spr·itzen** vt [h] *to squirt away* || (versehentlich) *to spill* || (sein Blut) *to shed* | **sich** ~ (of waves) *to dash* (*against the rocks*) **~spr·ochen** pp v versprechen || das ≚e *the thing*(*s*) *promised* | ~erm·aßen [adv] *according to promise* **~spr·ühen I.** vt [h] *to spout, spray* **II.** vi *to cease sparkling*, etc (→ sprühen) **~sp·unden** vt [h] *to bung up* **~sp·üren** vt [h] *to perceive, feel* **~st·aatlichen** vt [h] *to turn into state property* || ⟨rail, telph, etc⟩ *to take over* || (Land) *to nationalize* || (Kirchengut) *to secularize* **V.chung** f ~/ *acquisition by the state*; *nationalization*, etc **~st·äben** vt [h] ⟨arch⟩ *to chamfer, channel* **V.bung** f ⟨a.⟩ *cabling* **~st·ach** 1. & 3. sg pret v verstechen **~st·ädtern** vt [h] *to urbanize* **V.terung** f *urbanization* **~st·adtlichen** vt [h] *to municipalize* **~st·ählen** vt [h] *to steel, harden* **~st·ampfen** vt [h] *to crush, pound*

Verstand m ~(e)s/ **A. 1.** *understanding*; *intellect, intelligence*; *mental powers* pl **2.** (Auffassung) *comprehension* **3.** (Urteilskraft) *judgment, discernment* **4.** (Geist) *wit, mind* **5.** (Klugheit) *sense* **6.** *(Bedeutung) *meaning, sense* (→ D. in) **B. gesunder** ~ *common* (od *good*, ⟨emph⟩ *horse-*) *sense*; *sanity* || ein klarer ~ *a clear head* || e–n klaren ~ h *to have a good head* || kühler ~ *cool head*; mit kühlem ~ u warmem Herzen *soberly but sympathetically*; ~ u Herz (*the*) *heart and* (*the*) *soul* || scharfer ~ *sagacity*; *subtle understanding*, (*a man of*) *quick parts* || wacher ~ *alert brain* od *mind* **C.** s–n ~ gebrauchen *to use one's brains*; ⟨prov⟩ ~ **kommt** erst mit den Jahren *reason comes with years*; *one cannot put old heads on young shoulders* || ⟨fam⟩ mir steht der ~ still! *I'm at my wits' end!, it's too much for*

Verbal-Flexion der Verben mit der Vorsilbe **ver-** → das jeweilige Simplex

me! ‖ den ~ verlieren *to lose one's wits* od *reason* ‖ sein (⟨fam⟩ bißchen) ~ zus-nehmen *to collect one's thoughts*, ⟨fam⟩ *to have all one's wits about one*; .. für *to set one's wits to* .. **D.** ⟨path⟩ **bei** ~e bleiben *to retain one's mental faculties* ‖ (nicht) bei ~e s *to be in one's wits* (*out of one's mind* od *senses, not to be in one's right mind*); ⟨sl⟩ *he's not quite there*; bis z Tode bei vollem ~ *lucid until the last* | **in** jedem ~e *in every respect* | **mit** ~ (*to talk*) *sensibly* ‖ ⟨fam⟩ etw mit ~ essen *to appreciate eating sth* | **nach** m–m geringen ~e *in my humble opinion* | **ohne** ~ *without brains*; ohne klaren ~ *out of one's head* | das geht **über** m–n ~ *that passes my comprehension*, ⟨fam⟩ *that's beyond me, that passes me* | jdn **um** den ~ bringen *to drive a p out of his senses*; *to turn a p's wits* | **zu** ~ k *to arrive at years of discretion*

ver- **~st·and** 1. & 3. sg pret v verstehen **~st·anden** [pp v verstehen]; ⟨fam⟩ ~! ⟨wir⟩ *roger*!; ~? *got that*?, *do you follow*?, *do you get* od *take* (nach Befehl *mind*) *me*? | wohl ~! *let it be understood*! *and no mistake*! | mit darunter ~ *included* **≗st·andes-** **~begriff** m ⟨philos⟩ (*abstract*) *idea* **~gabe** f *gift of intellect* **~heirat** f *marriage of convenience* °**~kasten** m *brain-box* **~kräfte** f pl *intellectual powers* pl od *faculty* **≗mäßig** a *reasonable, rational, intellectual* **~mensch** m *rationalist*; *calculating* od *matter-of-fact p* **~schärfe** f *sagacity, penetration, acumen* **~schwäche** f *weak-mindedness* **~tätigkeit** f *activity of the brain*; *mentation* **~welt** f *intellectual world* **~wesen** n *intelligent being* **~st·ändig** a *intelligent*; *understanding, judicious*; *discreet*; *sensible* (*age, idea, woman*), (*man*) *of sense* ‖ (vernünftig denkend *or* gedacht) *reasonable* ‖ ~es Alter ⟨a.⟩ *age of discretion* ‖ ~ genug s .. *to have the sense* (*to do*; *to be silent*) | **≗keit** [f] *sensibleness, good sense* **~st·ändigen** vt [h] (über [acc], von) *to inform* (*of*), *to acquaint* (*with*), ⟨fam⟩ *to put .. up* (*to*) | **sich** mit jdm ~ *to come to terms* od *an understanding, arrangement, agreement with a p* (über .. *on a th*); *to arrange with a p* (*about a th*) **V.gung** f ~/~en *information* ‖ (Übereinkunft) *agreement, accommodation* | ~smittel [n] *means of making each other understand*; ⟨tech⟩ *means of communication* **~st·ändlich** a *intelligible*; *clear, distinct, perspicuous* ‖ *easy to understand, understandable* ‖ allgemein ~ *popular*; leicht ~ *plain*; schwer ~ *difficult to grasp*; *abstruse, recondite* | sich (jdm) ~ m *to put one's ideas over* (*to make o.s. understood by a p*) ‖ etw leichter ~ m *to simplify* ‖ jdm etw ~ m *to make a p understand a th*; s–n Standpunkt ~ m *to put over one's points* | **≗keit** [f] ~/ *intelligibleness, clearness, lucidity* **Verst·ändnis** n –nisses/ **1.** (für) *perception* (*of*), *insight* (*into*) ‖ (Verstehen) *apprehension, appreciation, comprehension, understanding* (f *of*) | (Einverständnis) *agreement, concord*; heimliches ~ *secret understanding* **2.** ~ erwecken *to promote u.g*; ~ h f *to appreciate*; tiefes ~ h f ⟨a.⟩ *to be deeply sensible of*; dafür hat er kein ~ *he cannot see the point* od *joke* ‖ szenisches ~ h *to understand scenic effects* ‖ e–m das ~ f e–e S eröffnen *to explain a th to a p*, .. in der Bevölkerung .. stärken *to strengthen the public's realization* (f *of*) **≗innig, ≗voll** a *understanding, sympathetic*; *intelligent* (*appreciation*) ‖ *knowing* (*glance*) ‖ *responsive, broad-minded, charitable, sympathetic* ‖ *appreciative* (*smile, words*) | [adv] ~ beobachtet *seen with an understanding eye*; e–m ~ zunicken *to give a p a knowing wink* **≗los** a *devoid* od *incapable of understanding* ‖ *unappreciative* (*of*), *irresponsive* (*to*) [adv] (*to listen*) *stupidly* **~losigkeit** f *stupidity*

ver- **~st·änkern** vt [h] *to fill with stench* (od ⟨mot⟩ *with exhaust gases*) **~st·arb** 3. sg *pret* v –sterben **~st·ärken** vt [h] *to strengthen, fortify* ‖ *to bolster* ‖ –kter Einband *reinforced binding* ‖ ⟨el⟩ (Strom) *to energize* ‖ *to sharpen out* (*an ability*); ⟨fig⟩ *to give an edge to a th* ‖ ⟨chem⟩ *to concentrate* | ⟨fig⟩ *to augment, accentuate*; *to intensify* (*an attack, a photograph, an impression*); *to swell* (*notes*); *to deepen* (*colours*), *to raise* (*the voice*) ‖ (Gefühl) *to add .. to* ‖ ⟨mil⟩ *to reinforce* ‖ ⟨wir⟩ *to amplify* ‖ (dicker m) *to enlarge* ‖ (ärger m) *to aggravate* | **sich** ~ *to grow stronger* | –kt ⟨tex⟩ *stitched* (*sateen*, etc) ‖ –kt ⟨übtr⟩ *growing* (*mechanization*) **V.ker** m ~s/~ ⟨wir⟩ *amplifier*; ~ mit Dynamiksteigerung u Gegenkopplung ⟨wir⟩ *dynasonic feedback amplifier* ‖ ⟨phot⟩ *intensifier* | ~anlage [f] *public address system*; ~anschluß [m] ⟨rec⟩ *amplifier connection*; ~maschine [f] ⟨el⟩ *amplidyne*; ~röhre [f] *amplifying valve* **V.kung** f ~/~en *strengthening*; ~ e–r Wirkung *potentiation* ‖ ⟨tex⟩ *lisle-thread* (*of stocking*); ⟨tech⟩ *struts* pl; ⟨wir, etc⟩ *gain* ‖ ⟨fig⟩ *intensifying, intensification* ‖ ⟨mil⟩ [pl] (bis z Eintreffen v *pending the arrival of*) *reinforcements* ‖ ⟨wir⟩ *amplification* | **~s-** *strengthening* (*rib*); *stiffening plate*; ~flasche [f] ⟨el⟩ *Leyden jar*; ~regelung [f] *gain control*; ~truppen [f pl] *reinforcements* pl; ~wort [n] ⟨gram⟩ *augmentative* **~st·atten** vt [h] *to permit, allow, grant* **V.ttung** f ~/~en *permission, leave* **~st·auben** vi [s] *to get covered with dust* ‖ *to fly off as dust* | –bt *dusty* ‖ ⟨fig⟩ *musty and fusty*; –bt s *to be covered with dust* ⟨a. fig⟩ **~st·äuben** vt [h] *to reduce to dust, to pulverize* **V.ber** m *spray-diffuser* **~st·auchen** vt [h] *to sprain* (sich den Fuß ~ .. *one's foot*), *wrench, dislocate* **V.chung** f ~/~en *spraining*, etc; *dislocation* **~st·auen** vt [h] *to stow* (od *tuck, pack*) *away* (*in*) **~st·echen** vt irr [h] *to stitch together, to sew up* ‖ ⟨cards⟩ (Trümpfe) *to use up* ‖ (Lanzen) *to break* **≗st·eck** n ~(e)s/~e *lurking-, hiding-place, cover*; ⟨Am a.⟩ *hide-out* ‖ ⟨mil⟩ *ambuscade* ‖ ~ spielen *to play* (*at*) *hide-and-seek* od ⟨fam⟩ *peek-a-boo* **~st·ecken** vt [h] *to hide, conceal* ‖ ⟨fig⟩ *to tuck away* | **sich** ~ *to hide* (vor *from*) ‖ sich –ckt halten *to be in hiding* od *lurking*, ⟨fam⟩ *to lie low*; ⟨Am⟩ *to hide out* (vor *from*), *to stash away* ‖ .. hinter .. *to shelter behind* .. ‖ sich hinter falschem Namen ~ *to masquerade under a f. n.* | (S) **-ckt** liegen *to be tucked away* | –ckt (entlegen) *obscure* (*village*); ⟨hunt⟩ *under cover* | ⟨fig⟩ sich vor e–m ~ müssen *to be no match for a p* **~st·eckt** a *hidden* ‖ ⟨fig⟩ *indirect, veiled* (*hints*) ‖ *covert* (*reproach*) ‖ *secretive, close* (*p*); *sly, cunning, underhand* (*p*) ‖ ~er Kerl ⟨fam⟩ *sly-boots* | **≗heit** [f] *closeness*; *cunning, slyness* **~st·ehen** vt/i irr [h] (→ –standen, erkennen, wissen) **A.** *to understand*; ⟨fam⟩ *to follow* | (erfassen) *to comprehend, grasp, catch*; *to take in*; der Sinn wurde –standen *the idea got across*; ich –he es nicht *it baffles me* | (können) *to know* (*French*, vorzüglich *thoroughly well*) ‖ ich hoffe, Sie ~ mich *and no mistake*! [nachgestellt] ‖ die Pointe ~ ⟨sl⟩ *to savvy* **B.** wir dürfen nicht **dahin** –standen w, daß *we must not be understood to imply that* .. ‖ wir können es nicht ~ *we cannot make sense of it*; wir ~ **das** (*or* die S) nicht *we cannot make it out*, ⟨fam⟩ *we don't see it, that beats us* ‖ ~ Sie (das bzw mich)? *do you u.d*? ‖ ich –he nicht, daß *I wonder that* .. ‖ **etw** ~ *to know all about a th*; ⟨fam⟩ *to know what's what*; .. genau ~ *to get to the bottom of a th*; ich –he Sie vollk *I quite u.d you*; etw klar z ~ geben *to make a th clear*; ganz falsch ~ *to get it wrong* ‖ das Geschäft am besten ~ *to be the best in* (od *to have the best knowledge of*) *the business* ‖ ich –he nicht was los *or* gemeint ist ⟨fam⟩ *I can't make it out* ‖ etw Gr. ~ *to know some Greek, to have a smattering of G.* ‖ **e-n** ~ ⟨a.⟩ *to take* od *get one* (*I don't quite get you*) ‖ ~ Sie mich ⟨fam⟩ *get*

Aussprache: Falls nicht anders (: [*v*]) angegeben, ist v = [*f*] zu sprechen.

me? ‖ s–e S ~ *to know one's job* ‖ **darunter** ~ *to imply*; **was** ~ Sie **darunter**? *what do you mean* bzw *u.d by it* ‖ ~ Sie, was er damit sagen will *do you see what he is driving at*? ‖ wie wir es ~ *as we take it* ‖ **(Worte)** *I didn't catch the last words* ‖ ~ Sie, was ich meine? *do you get me*? | ⟨prov⟩ jeder macht's, wie er's –ht *everyone according to his lights* **C. aufs** Wort ~ *to be quick of u.ding* ‖ **aus** dem Grunde ~ *to know thoroughly* ‖ e–n (etw) **falsch** *or* unrecht ~ *to misu.d a p* (*a th*, ⟨fig⟩ *to take a th in bad part*), jds Wort .. *to misconstrue a p's words* ‖ etw glänzend ~ ⟨fam⟩ *to be a good hand at a th, to have a knack of* (*doing*) *a th* ‖ ~ Sie mich **recht**! *mind you*!, *don't misu.d me*! ‖ Sie h mich nicht recht –standen ⟨Am fam⟩ *you didn't get me straight* ‖ etw schwer ~ *to find it difficult to u.d* **D.** ~ **zu tun** *to know how to do* | **zu** ~ **geben** *to give it to be understood* (, daß *that he would*); *to convey*; *to insinuate, hint, intimate* (*that*); jdm .. *to give a p to u.d, to make it clear to a p*; *to let a p realize that* .. ‖ man gab mir ausdrücklich z ~, daß *I have been expressly told that* .. ‖ dadurch soll z ~ gegeben w, daß *that is to say that* **E. sich** (= e–a) ~ *to u.d one another*, gut *to get on very well* ‖ daß wir uns richtig ~! *and no mistake*! | **(das)** –ht sich (*that is a matter*) *of course*!, *that's* (*self-*)*understood*!, *evident*; .. v selbst (⟨fam⟩ am Rande) *it stands to reason, it goes without saying* | sich ~ **auf** [acc] *to be a judge of*, *to be skilled* (od *at home*) *in*, *to* (*be in the*) *know* ‖ ich –he mich gut auf Pferde (Teppiche) *I'm pretty good with horses*, (*I know all about carpets*) ‖ sich auf s–n Vorteil ~ *to know which side one's bread is buttered* ‖ sich ~ **mit** *to have an u.ding with* (*a p*) ‖ sich ~ **zu** *to agree* od *consent to*, *to acquiesce in*; *to bring o.s. to accept* (*a theory*) ‖ sich dazu ~ *to condescend to do it* °≈**st·ehstemich** m [invar] (= Verstehst du mich) (Verstand) (*he has*) *savvy*, *gumption*; *know-how* **~st·eifen** vt [h] *to stiffen*; ⟨tech⟩ *to stout, brace, prop* | **sich** ~ (Gelenke) *to ankylose*; ⟨fig⟩ .. (auf [acc]) *to become set* (*upon*), *to stick obstinately* (*to*); *to make a point of* ‖ sie ~ sich darauf (nicht) z tun *they will* (*not*) *do* | ⟨st exch⟩ *to stiffen, harden* | **-ft** *trussed* (Rahmen) **~st·eigen** irr [h] sich ~ *to climb* (⟨fig⟩ *soar, aspire, aim*) *too high* ‖ *to lose o.s. among the precipices of a mountain* | ⟨fig⟩ *to fly high* ‖ sich ~ **zu** *to have the audacity to* ‖ sich (so weit) ~ zu *to go* od *venture so far as to*; ich –ge mich höchstens zu .. *I would not venture beyond* .., *I don't rise above* .. **V.gerer** m ~s/~ *auctioneer* **v.gern** vt [h] *to sell by* (⟨Am⟩ *at*) *auction* ‖ ~ (l) *to bring to the hammer*, *to put up for sale* **V.gerung** f ~/~en (*selling by*) *auction*; *public sale*; ~ unter allmählicher Preisherabsetzung *Dutch auction* **~st·einern** vi [s] ⟨a. fig⟩ *to petrify* (⟨a.⟩ sich ~) ‖ –rt *petrified*, *fossil*(*ized*) ‖ –rtes Holz *woodagate* ‖ wie –rt ⟨fig⟩ *dumbfounded*; *frozen to stone*; *as though turned to* (od *carved in*) *stone* **V.rung** f ~/~en [abstr & konkr] *petrifaction* | [konkr a.] *fossil* | ~skunde [f] *palæontology* **~st·ellbar** a *movable, sliding, adjustable, variable* | ≈keit [f] *mo*(*va*)*bility* ≈**st·ell-** ~bereich [m] ⟨mech⟩ *range of adjustment*; ⟨aero⟩ ~flosse [f] *adjustable stabilizer*; ~motor [m] *actuator*; ~propeller [m] *variable-pitch propeller*; ~vorrichtung [f] *shifter*; *regulating device* **~st·ellen** vt [h] **1.** (anders) *to shift* ⟨a. tech⟩; *remove, displace* ‖ (falsch) *to misplace, disarrange* ‖ (–sperren) *to block, bar, obstruct* | ⟨tech⟩ (richtig) *to adjust* **2.** (Handschrift, Stimme) *to disguise, dissemble* | **sich** ~ *to d.ble, sham, pretend, feign*; (simulieren) *to play possum*; (gegen jdn) *to act the hypocrite* (*towards a p*) ‖ sich gut ~ können *to know how to d.ble, to be a good d.bler* (⟨theat⟩ *actor*), ⟨theat⟩ *to act* od *play* (*one's part*[*s*]) *well* | **-llt** a ⟨a.⟩ *sham* (*love*, etc); ⟨tech⟩ *maladjusted*, [pred] *out of adjustment* **V.llung** f ~/~en *dissimulation*, *sham*(*ming*), *make-believe*; *hypocrisy* | ~skunst [f] *art of dissembling*; *hypocrisy* ≈**st·eppung** f ~/~en *transformation of woodland into steppe* **~st·erben** vi irr [s] *to expire, die* ‖ → –storben **~st·euern** vt [h] *to pay duty on* ‖ **-rt** senden *to send* .. *duty-paid* **V.rung** f ~/~en (*payment of*) *duty on a th, excise* **~st·ieben** vi irr [s] *to fly* (od *be blown*) *away*, *to be scattered* (*like dust*) ‖ ⟨fig⟩ *to go* (*with the wind*); → Staub **~st·ieg** 1. & 2. sg pret v –steigen | **~en** [pp] a ⟨fig⟩ *extravagant* (*idea*); *eccentric, high-flown*; *cranky* **~st·ielen** vt [h] *to helve* **~st·ieß** 1. & 3. sg pret v verstoßen **~st·immen** vt [h] ⟨mus⟩ *to put out of tune, to untune* ⟨a. fig⟩ ‖ ⟨fig⟩ *to annoy, to put a p out* (*of humour* od ⟨fam⟩ *sorts*) | **sich** ~ *to get out of tune* | **-mmt** a *out of tune* ‖ ⟨fig⟩ *annoyed* (über *at a th*, durch *with a p*, wegen *for a th*); *depressed, dejected, upset*; [pred] *out of humour*; *in a bad temper*; *cross* (über [acc] *with*), *disgruntled* (*at*) ≈**st·immtheit**; ≈**st·immung** f ~/~en ⟨fig⟩ *ill-humour, -temper* ‖ *depression*, *dejectedness* ‖ *ill feeling, bad blood* (zw *between*) ‖ (Ärger) *resentment* (über *at*) ‖ ~en [pl] *morbid moods* **~st·ob(en)** pret (pp) v –stieben **~st·ochen** pp v –stechen **~st·ocken I.** vt [h] *to harden* | **sich** ~ *to grow callous* **II.** vi [s] *to grow musty*, ⟨fig⟩ .. *callous* **-ckt** a *obdurate, obstinate, sullen, stubborn* (*p*); *hardened*, ⟨rel⟩ *unrepenting* (*sinner*); *impenitent* (*heart*) | ≈heit, **V.ckung** f ~/~en *obduracy, induration, callousness, stubbornness*; ⟨rel⟩ *impenitence* **~st·ohlen** a *surreptitious, secret, clandestine, underhand*; *stealthy, furtive* (*glance*) ‖ jdm e–n ~en Blick zuwerfen *to steal a glance* od *have a squint at a p* ‖ jds ~en Blick sehen *to see the corner of a p's eye* | **~, ~erweise** [adv] ⟨a.⟩ *by stealth*, ⟨fam⟩ *on the sly*; ~ aufblicken *to sneak a look* **~st·opfen** vt [h] (Loch) *to stop* (*up*) ‖ (–korken) *to cork up* ‖ (–spunden) *to bung up* | (Kanal etc) *to choke, obstruct, jam* | (Ritzen) *to fill up* ‖ (den Leib) *to constipate* | sich ~ *to become choked*, etc | **-pft** a ⟨path⟩ *constipated, costive*; *stopped-up* (*pipe, nose*); *congested* (*street*); ⟨tech⟩ ~ s *to need cleaning* **V.fung** f ~/~en *obstruction*; ⟨tech⟩ (e–s Rohrs) *stoppage* ‖ ⟨path⟩ *constipation, costiveness* ‖ an ~(en) leiden *to be constipated* od *costive* ‖ ~ lösend(es Mittel) *purgative, aperient* **~st·öpseln** vt [h] *to cork* **~st·orben** a [pp v –sterben] [pred] *dead* ‖ [attr] *late* (*my l. wife*) ‖ ⟨a. jur⟩ *defunct, deceased* ‖ längst ~ *dead and gone* ‖ (Zeitungsrubrik) *Deaths* pl ‖ der, die ≈e *the deceased* ‖ [pl] die ≈en *the dead*, ⟨rel⟩ *the departed*; (allzu) jung ~ *whose life was cut short too soon* **~st·ört** a *disturbed, distracted, distraught*; *upset, scared, troubled, bewildered, stricken*; *wild* (*look*) ‖ (geistig) *crazy* ‖ ~ aussehen *to look haggard* od *distracted* | ≈heit [f] ~/ *distraction* ‖ *haggardness* ≈**st·oß** m ~es/≈e *offence* (gegen *against*); *breach* (*of etiquette*), schwerer ~ ⟨Am fam⟩ *break*; *infraction* (*of the law*) ‖ *contravention*, *infringement* (*of*), *lapse* (*of good taste*); ⟨gram⟩ *solecism* ‖ (Schnitzer) *blunder, error, mistake*; *faux pas* Fr ‖ e–n ~ m gegen *to offend against*, *to violate* (*a th*) | ≈**en I.** vt irr [h] (jdn, etw) *to reject, repudiate* | (Sohn) *to disown, renounce*; *to cast off* ‖ (Frau) *to divorce* ‖ *to expel* (*from a club*) ‖ *to turn out* (*of the house*) | der, die ≈e *the outcast* **II.** vi [h] (gegen) *to transgress, infringe, violate*; *to break the most implacable* (strengst) *laws*; *to break* (*a rule*); *to act contrary* (*to*), *to offend* (*against*); (stärker) *to impinge* (*on*), *to run counter* (*to the truth*) ‖ *to commit a breach* (*of etiquette*) ‖ *not to be in keeping* (*with the metre* Versmaß) ‖ Gefahr laufen, gegen die Moral z ~ *to sail close to the wind* | gegen die Form ~d *unorthodox*

Verbal-Flexion der Verben mit der Vorsilbe **ver-** → das jeweilige Simplex

(*conduct*) **V.ßung** f ~/~en *rejection*; *repudiation* || *disownment, divorce* || *expulsion* **~str·ahlen** vt [h] ⟨at⟩ *to contaminate*: *~d area, area ~d by radioactivity* **V.lung** f *emanation*; *radioactive emission*; *contamination*; Sicherheit gegen ~ *radiological safety* N **~str·eben** vt [h] ⟨tech⟩ *to strut* **V.bung** f ~/~en *strut, brace*; *bracing* **~str·eichen** irr **I.** vi [s] (Zeit) *to elapse*; *go* od *slip by*; *pass* (*away*) || (Termin, Frist) *to expire* || (zw) *to intervene* **II.** vt [h] (Ritze etc) *to stop* od *fill up* || mit Gips *to plaster* || mit Pech *to pitch* || Mauer *to rough-cast* | *to use up .. in spreading* | *to spread* (*butter*) **~str·euen** vt [h] *to scatter, disperse* || *to* (*use for*) *litter* || (Unrat etc) *to litter* | **-eut** *erratic* (*blocks*), (*houses*) *dotted* (*on* ..), *loose* (*pieces of information*) || ~ liegen auf *to strew* (*the floor*) **~str·ich(en)** 1. & 3. sg pret (pp) v –streichen **~str·icken** vt [h] *to use* (*up*) od *spend in knitting* | ⟨fig⟩ (jdn) *to entangle, ensnare* (*a p*) | **sich** ~ *to get entangled, enmeshed, mazed* (*in*) **V.ckung** f ~/~en *ensnaring, entanglement, enmeshment* **~str·ömen** vi [s] *to surge forth* (*like a cascade*) (⟨a.⟩ sich ~) **~stud·ieren** vt [h] *to spend .. in studying* || *to ruin* (*one's health*) *by overstudy* | **-rt** *worn with study* **~st·ümmeln** vt [h] (P) *to mutilate, deform, disable* || (Glied) *to maim* || (Text) *to mangle* || (Bericht) *to garble* (⟨mil⟩ ~d [Spruch]) || ⟨rhet Lit⟩ *to curtail* **V.lung** f ~/~en *mutilation* || *curtailment* || ⟨arts⟩ *vandalism* || *corruption, perversion* (*of text, word*) **~st·ummen** vi [s] *to grow dumb* || *to become speechless* od *silent* || ⟨fam⟩ *to dry up* || (vor Erstaunen) *to be dumbfounded* od *struck dumb* | *to cease to sound* || *to dwindle into silence*, → still w; *the music died away*; plötzlich *to stop short* (*in one's speech*) || *every voice fell* | ~ m *or* l *to silence, hush, mute* | z ≃ bringen *to still* (*the clamo(u)r*; *to look* (*a p*) *into silence* **~st·ünde** 1. & 3. sg subj pret v –stehen

Vers·uch m ~(e)s/~e ⟨phys⟩ *experiment* (an *with*) || ⟨tech⟩ *test* ⟨a. fig⟩; ~ im Kleinen *pilot scheme* || ⟨fig⟩ *trial*; *attempt* (*to escape*); *effort*; *venture* || *bid* (um *for* [*recognition*]) || ⟨Lit⟩ *essay* || ⟨ftb⟩ *try* || kühner ~ *long shot* || schwacher ~ *diffident effort, feeble attempt* (*to do*); mißlungen *flash in the pan* || ~e anstellen *to make experiments* (*on*) || e–n ~ m *to make* od *embark upon*) *an attempt*; *to try*; ⟨fam⟩ *to have a go* od *shot*; bei jdm *to try it on with a p*; mit jdm, etw *to give a p, a th a trial*; *to put .. to the test*; er machte e–n bescheidenen ~ ⟨bes Am⟩ *he made a timid stab* (*at*); bei s–m 2. ~ *on his second try* || es kommt auf e–n ~ an! *we can but try*! || ein ~ kann nicht schaden *it can do no harm to try* || es lohnt den ~ ⟨fam⟩ *it's worth the shot*; ⟨so:⟩ *at the first shot* || bei mir ist jeder ~ vergeblich *no use trying it on with me* | ~ an Ort u Stelle *field* (od *in situ* L) *test* | **≃en** vt [h] **A. 1.** *to try*, *to* (*make an*) *attempt* (*to do*); *to experiment on* || mühsam ~ *to struggle* (*to smile*) || ~ etw z erlangen *to try for a th* || es ~ mit *to try* (*water*), *to have a go at* (*a th*) || ~ z tun ⟨a.⟩ *to try and do* || zu öffnen ~ *to try* (*a door*) || ~ Sie es! *have a try*! **2.** (auf die Probe stellen) *to put .. to the test* **3.** (kosten) *to taste* **4.** ⟨fig⟩ (jdn) *to tempt, allure, entice* **B. alles** ~ *to make every possible effort* (um z *in order to*) || sein Äußerstes ~ *to do one's utmost* || sein Glück, Heil ~ *to try one's chance* od *luck, to seek one's fortune* || es mal ~ ⟨Am fam⟩ *to take a stab at it* **C.** ~ **an,** bei *to try on ..* | **es** ~ **mit** *to resort to*, mit jdm *to give a p a chance* **D. sich** ~ (an) *to try one's hand, to take a turn* od *have a go* (*at*) | **auf** allen Gebieten *to try everything* | **im** Kriege *to try the chances of war*; in der Welt *to see life* od *the world* **V.er(in** f) m ~s/~ *tempter* (f * *temptress*) || *seducer* [a. f] || [m] ⟨ec⟩ *the Devil* **≃s·uchs-** [in comp] *test* (*piece*, etc), *experiment* (*plot*); *experimental* (*object, craft, station, school*) **~anlage** f ⟨tech⟩ *e.l* od *pilot plant* ⟨a. ind⟩ **~anordnung** f, **~aufbau** m *experimental arrangement* od *mounting*; *trial mounting* od *system* od *set-up* **~anstalt** f *testing shop, test plant* **~ballon** m *trial balloon* ⟨a. fig⟩; ⟨meteor⟩ *pilot b.*; ⟨fig⟩ e–n ~ steigen l *to fly a kite* **~bataillon** n *trial battalion* **~baumuster** n ⟨a. mil⟩ *trial model* **~bedingungen** f pl *conditions of tests* **~fahrt** f *test run* **~feld** n ⟨agr⟩ *e.t plot*, ⟨min⟩ *proving grounds* **~flug** m *trial flight* | ~zeug [n] *test airplane* **~kaninchen,** °**~karnickel** n *test rabbit*, ⟨fig⟩ *cat's paw* || e–n z ~ m ⟨fam⟩ *to try it on the dog*; ~ s *to be the guinea-pig* **~labor** n *laboratory stage* **~ladung** f ⟨mil⟩ *proof-charge* **~last** f *proof load* od *weight* **~modell** n *working model* **~person** f *p experimented upon*; ⟨med psych⟩ *volunteer* | (Flugzeug) als **~pilot** einfliegen *to test-pilot* **~produktion** f ⟨ind-tech⟩ *pilot production* **~schacht** m ⟨min⟩ *prospecting shaft* **~schießen** n *firing test* **~stand** m *test bay* **~stop** m ⟨at⟩ *atomic test ban*; *suspension* od *cessation of atomic tests* **~strecke** f ⟨min⟩ = –feld; ⟨mot⟩ *test track* **~tier** n *test animal* **~tigel** m *cupel* ⟨a. cul⟩ **≃weise** a *experimental*; *tentative* ⟨a. mil⟩ | [adv] *by way of trial, on trial, as an experiment, on approval, tentatively*; ~ herausbringen ⟨com⟩ *to test-market* **≃s·uchung** f ~/~en *temptation* (⟨bib⟩ *to lead into t.*; *T. of Christ*) || in ~ k *to be tempted* (*to*) || ich kann allem widerstehen, nur der ~ nicht *I can resist everything but temptation* **~s·udeln** vt [h] *to soil, besmear* || ⟨fam⟩ *to mess up* **~s·umpfen** vi [s] *to become boggy* od *marshy* od *a swamp* | ⟨fig⟩ *to stagnate, to grow rusty* od *dissolute* | ⟨fam⟩ (P) *to go to the dogs* **V.fung** f *conversion into a swamp* **~s·ündigen**: sich ~ [h] (an [dat]) *to sin, offend* (*against*) || sich an jdm ~ *to wrong a p* **V.gung** f ~/~en *sin*(*ning*), *offence* **~s·ungen** pp v –singen **~s·unken** a [pp v –sinken] ⟨fig⟩ *absorbed, steeped, wrapped* (*in*); *preoccupied* || ganz ~ in *well away in, rapt, lost in* | **≃heit** [f] ~/ ⟨a. fig⟩ *degradation* || *demoralization* || *absorption, preoccupation*; Ausdruck tiefer ~ *absorbed expression* **~s·üßen** vt [h] *to sweeten, to sugar* (*too much*) | **sich** ~ *to become sweet*(*er*) **V.ßung** f ~/ *sweetening* **~t·äfeln** vt [h] *to wainscot* **~t·agen** vt, ⟨a.⟩ sich ~ [h] ⟨parl⟩ *to adjourn* (⟨jur⟩ unbestimmt *sine die*); (bis auf weiteres) *to prorogue* || *their lordships rose* | **-gt** (*bill*) *that has fallen due, the b. was tabled* **V.gung** f ~/~en *adjournment* || *prorogation* **~t·ändeln** vt [h] *to trifle* od *laze away, to spend foolishly* **~t·anzen** vt [h] *to spend* od *waste in dancing* || *to dance off* (*one's sorrow*) **~t·at** 1. & 3. sg pret v –tun **~t·äuen** vt [h] (Boot) *to moor* **~t·aumeln** vt [h] *to spend in a whirl of gaiety* od *exuberance* **~t·auschbar** a *exchangeable, permutable* **~t·auschen** vt [h] *to exchange*, ⟨fam⟩ *swap, swop* (für, gegen, mit, um *for*) || (Plätze) *to change* || (Waren) *to barter* (*for*) || ⟨math⟩ *to permute* | (irrtümlich) *to mistake for* || ich habe m–n Hut –t *I have got the wrong hat* **V.schung** f ~/~en *exchange* || *permutation* **~t·ausendfachen** vt [h] *to increase a thousandfold* (⟨a.⟩ sich ~); *to multiply by a thousand* **~t·äuung** f ~/~en *moorings* pl **~t·eidigen** vt [h] ⟨a. jur⟩ *to defend* (*one's life*) (gegen *from*) || ⟨mst jur⟩ *to advocate* (*a cause*), *to fight* (*a case*) || etw ~ *to plead* || *to stand up for, to maintain, vindicate* (*one's right*) || *to maintain* (*a position, a proposition*) || *to support* (*truth*) || (bes abwesende P) ~ ⟨Am fam⟩ *to stick up for a p* | **sich** ~ *to defend, justify o.s.* || ⟨mil⟩ *to offer resistance* **V.ger** m ~s/~ *defender* || *supporter* (*of a proposition*) || ⟨jur⟩ *defence* (⟨Am⟩ *-se*) *council*; *advocate* ⟨a. fig⟩, ⟨crim l⟩ *defending counsel* || ⟨ftb⟩ *back*, ⟨Am⟩ *quarter-back* | **-gung** f ~/~en ⟨a. jur⟩ *defence*, ⟨Am⟩ *-se*;

Aussprache: Falls nicht anders (: [*v*]) angegeben, ist v = [*f*] zu sprechen.

advocacy || vindication || justification || maintenance || support || ⟨mil⟩ hinhaltende (offensive) ~ delaying od retrograde (active) d., vorderer Rand der ~ (VRV) ⟨tact⟩ main line of resistence; der ~ dienend defensive; sich auf die ~ beschränken to keep on the defensive || in die ~ gedrängt w to become defensive || z ~ m–r Ehre in defence of my h. | **~s- ~anlagen** f pl ⟨mil⟩ d.ive works pl, tiefgegliedert d.se in depth N **~anstalten** f pl preparations [pl] for d.se **~bezirk** m military region | ~skommando [n] (VBK) m. r. command (MRC) **~bündnis** n d.sive alliance **~́fähig** a tenable (assumption) **~kampf** m d.sive combat operations pl **~kreiskommando** n (VKK) military subregion command **~krieg** m d.sive war **~linie** f ⟨mil⟩ l. of d.se **~́los** a d.seless **~maßnahme** f pl d.sive measures, d. effort **~minister** m m. of d., ⟨engl⟩ M. for the Coordination of D.ce, ⟨Am⟩ Secretary of D.se **~mittel** n means of d. **~möglichkeit** f, **~stellung** f defensiveness **~-pakt** m d.sive alliance **~plan** m f d. Alarmfall Emergency D. Plan N. **~rede** f (speech for the) d. **~schrift** f apology; ⟨jur⟩ d.ce **~stand** m ⟨mil⟩ in ~ setzen to put .. in a state of d. **~stellung** f d.sive position **~system** n ⟨fort⟩ entrenchment, inneres ~ retrenchment **~waffe** f weapon of d. **~́weise** [adv] by way of d. **~wille** m will to resist || ⟨mil⟩ will od resolve to defend one's country **~zustand** m = –stand

ver- ~t·eien vt [h] = vertäuen **~t·eilbar** a distributable, divisible **~t·eilen** vt [h] to distribute || (aufteilen) (unter [acc]) to apportion, allot (to); (unter sich) to share, pool | (Almosen) to dispense (charity); in kl Mengen to dole out || (Arbeit) to spread (auf over [zeitlich]) || (Farben etc, Risiko) to spread || ⟨theat⟩ (Rollen) to assign || (Steuern) to assess || (Urlaub) gleichmäßig über e–n Zeitraum ~ to stagger | **unter**: to divide .. among | **sich** ~ to spread || (Geschwulst) to dissolve || sich ~ auf to be divided among **V.ler** m ~s/~ distributor, dispenser ⟨a. mil⟩; ⟨off⟩ distribution list; ⟨el⟩ d.n frame, cable terminal box **~bahnhof** m d.buting station **~draht** m ⟨telph⟩ jumper wire **~relais** n switching relay **~rohr** n manifold **~-scheibe** f ⟨telph⟩ distributor **~schrank** m d.buting switchboard **~(schlüssel)** m d.n code **~stelle** f d.buting point **~tafel** f d.butor board **V.lung** f ~/~en (Gaußsche Gaussion probability) distribution; division || dissemination, dispersion; scattering || ~ der Beute pay-off || apportionment ⟨a. paint⟩, allotment || assessment || schlechte ~ maldistribution || (verhältnismäßige) repartition || ⟨theat⟩ Rollen~́ cast of the characters || örtl. ⟨demog⟩ geographical od spatial d.n; ⟨stat⟩ structure || ⟨mil⟩ räumliche deployment; Quartier~́ quartering (of troops) | **~s-** ~kanal [m] ⟨el⟩ trough for d.n cable; ~kasten [m] d.n case; ⟨theat⟩ shoe, ⟨Am⟩ plugging box; ~plan [m] plan of d.n; ~reservoir [n] d.buting-r.; ~rohr [n] intake manifold; ~stelle [f] d.buting agency **~t·euern** vt [h] to make dearer, to raise the price of **V.rung** f ~/~en enhancing of the price; ⟨bes Am⟩ mark-up **~t·eufelt** a ⟨fam⟩ devilish [a. adv], deuced, infernal || enormous (fun) || e–e ~e Geschichte an awkward od a confounded business, a pretty fix || ~er Kerl devil of a fellow || in e–r ~en Lage between the devil and the deep sea || etw ganz ~́es (women are) the deuce and all || ~es Glück or Pech the devil's own luck | [adv] with a vengeance || like the devil || ⟨fam⟩ awfully (fine girl) || terribly (hot) || ~ hoch the deuce of (a price) || ~ schlau too clever by half || ~ schwer z verkaufen s to be the devil to get rid of **~t·iefen** vt [h] ⟨a. fig⟩ to deepen || to sink (a well) || to hollow out (a dish) || to chisel out (features) || ⟨fig⟩ to emphasize | **sich** ~ to deepen, droop; to grow deeper || to immerse (into a book) || (geistig) in [acc]: to be lost in, to be od become wrapt od absorbed in (thought); to go deep, plunge, pore into; to bury od engross o.s. in; to dig deeply (into the facts) | | **~ft** in [acc] absorbed (in), deeply engaged (in study) ganz ~ in deeply immersed in (a th) | ~́sein [n] preoccupation **V.fung** f ~/~en deepening, etc || (Loch) cavity, excavation, hole, hollow, dip; (im Boden) depression, ⟨Am a.⟩ swale || (in der Wand etc) recess || ⟨arch⟩ glyph || ⟨fig⟩ absorption **~t·ieren I.** vt [h] to brutalize, bestialize **II.** vi [s] to grow brutish | **-rt** a [pp] brutish, bestial

vertik·al [v–] a vertical; ⟨comp⟩ ~e Arbeiten miscellaneous listing; ~e statistische A. multiple-total adding-subtracting | ~́linie [f] vertical line; ~projektion [f] orthographic projection

V·ertiko [v–] n ~s/~s elegant cabinet

ver- ~t·ilgbar a exterminable, eradicable; destructible | **-gen** vt [h] to exterminate; extirpate, eradicate; to wipe out || to destroy, annihilate | ⟨cul⟩ to polish off, to make away with; ⟨sl⟩ to demolish a meal || (austrinken) ⟨a.⟩ to discuss **V.ger** m ~s/~ exterminator, destroyer **V.gung** f extirpation, extermination, destruction; (vermin) disinfestation | ~skrieg [m] war of extermination, war to the knife **~tippen** vt/refl [h] ich habe mich –ppt ⟨typwr⟩ I made a mistake; ⟨sport⟩ I backed the wrong horse °**~t·obaken** vt [h] ⟨sl⟩ to whop **~t·onen** vt [h] ⟨mus⟩ to compose, to set (to music) **~t·önen** vi [s] to die away **~t·örnen** vt [h] to twist **~tr·ackt** a ⟨fam⟩ confounded (business) || odd, queer (fellow) || strange (gestures) || ⟨sl⟩ blooming e–e ganz ~e Frage quite a perplexing question ~́**tr·ag** m ~(e)s/~́e contract (.. abschließen, m to make a c.), agreement (to come to od to make an a.) || Arbeits~́ c. of employment; Dienst~́ c. for services; Kauf~́ a. of purchase and sale; Leih~́ c. of loan for use; Liefer~́ c. for supply of goods; durch (einfache) Unterschrift beurkundeter ~ c. under hand; Werk~́ c. for material and labo(u)r || ⟨com a.⟩ settlement | ⟨pol⟩ treaty (to conclude a t.), convention, covenant || Gesellschafts~́ social compact; ~ über Nichtverbreitung v Kernwaffen → Sperr~́ || ⟨jur⟩ dinglicher ~ conveyance; (mit Formzwang) deed || ~ mit aufgeschobener Wirkung forward contract || aufgrund e–s ~es under a treaty od contract; (Verpflichtung) aus e–m ~e .. pursuant to a treaty od c. || e–n ~ brechen to break (⟨fam⟩ jump) a c. || der ~ gilt als geschlossen the c. shall be deemed to have been entered into **~tr·agen** irr **I.** vt [h] **1.** (Kleider) to wear out **2.** (wegtragen) to carry away **3.** (ertragen) to suffer, endure, tolerate, bear | (v Magen) to digest **B.** ich kann das nicht (bzw nicht viel [Bier]) ~ I can't stand that (bzw much [beer]) || wir ~ k–e Butter b. does not agree with us; ⟨fam⟩ (I like it but) it doesn't like me || (Gift) to tolerate; to carry (a lot of liquor) || (Hitze) to bear (schlecht poorly) || wir ~ k–e Seereisen we are poor sailors || (Verluste) to sustain || (Widerspruch) to stand || °ich könnte jetzt .. ~ I feel like .., he could do with (a little brightening up) **II. sich** ~ (P) to agree; to understand each other; to get on (well, ill) together, ⟨fam⟩ to hit it off well || sich weiter ~ mit to keep in with a p; sich wieder ~ to be reconciled (mit to), ⟨fam⟩ to make (it) up (with) || sich wie Hund u Katze ~ to live a cat-and-dog life || –gt euch wieder ⟨fam⟩ kiss and make up | (S) to be compatible, to square od tally with || sich nicht ~ to clash, to be incompatible with **III.** ~ [pp] v Winde windborne; gone with the w. **~tr·aglich** a contractual, stipulated by contract | [adv] ~ verpflichtet bound by contract (zu .. to do) || ~ ausgemacht (it was) in the bargain **~tr·äglich** a (P) sociable; peaceable; goodnatured; accommodating | (S) (mit) con-

---

Verbal-Flexion der Verben mit der Vorsilbe **ver-** → das jeweilige Simplex

sistent, compatible (*with*) | ∽keit [f] ∼/ *sociability* ‖ *compatibility* ∽**tr·ags-** **~artikel** m *article of agreement* **~arzt** m *contract surgeon* N **~auflösung** f (als Titel) *rights at termination* **~bestimmungen** f pl *terms* (*of c.*) **~bruch** m *breach of c.*; Klage wegen ∼s ⟨jur⟩ *assumpsit* ∽**brüchig** a *defaulting* **~hafen** m *treaty port* | gegenseitiges **~interesse** *privity of c.* **~klausel** f *covenant* (*of a deed*) ∽**mäßig** a *stipulated* (*right*) ‖ *in accordance with the agreement, agreed upon*; ∼ herstellen *to ensure that* (*the product, plant*, etc) *complies with the c.* | ∼keit [f] *conformity with the agreement* **~partei** f *party to a c.* **~partner** m *contracting party*, pl *c.g parties* **~prämie** f *premium stipulated for a contract* **~recht** n *right of concluding treaties* ‖ *right accorded by a treaty* **~schluß** m *formation of a c.* **~spieler** m (*soccer*) *parttimer* **~strafe** f *liquidated damages* pl **~urkunde** f *indenture*; *deed of c.*, mit Siegel *deed* | das **~verhältnis** [n] aufheben *to terminate the engagement* **~verletzung** f *infringement of a c.* ∽**widrig** a *contrary to c.*, etc | ∼keit [f] *contravention to a c.*, etc **~tr·ällern** vt [h] *to pass* (*time*) *in humming* ‖ *to hum away* **~tr·ank** 1. & 3. sg pret v –trinken **~tr·at** 1. & 3. sg pret v –treten ∽**tr·auen** n ∼s/ (auf, in [acc], zu) *confidence* (*in*) ‖ (erwerben *to win*, gefährden *to imperil*, täuschen *to betray a p's c.*) ‖ das ∼ fördern *to promote the trust* (*of the population*); (jdm) das ∼ entziehen *to discredit* ‖ jds ∼ genießen *to be in the c. of a p* | ∼ h auf, in, zu, sein ∼ setzen auf, (e–m) sein ∼ schenken, sein ∼ setzen auf/in *to put* (*place, have*) *c. in, to rely on, to trust* (*a p*), *to have* (*good*) *faith in*; ⟨sl⟩ *to pin one's faith on* .. ‖ kein ∼ h zu ⟨a.⟩ *to disbelieve in*; man kann zu ihm kein ∼ h *he is not to be trusted* | **im** ∼ *privately, confidentially*; .. auf *trusting to, relying on* (*his justice*); (ganz) .. sagen *to tell in* (*strict*) *c.*; jdm im strengsten ∼ sagen *to say for a p's strictly private ear*; .. gesagt *between ourselves* | **ins** ∼ ziehen *to take* od *admit into* (*one's*) *c.* | **v** ∼ getragen *upheld by c., full of c., buoyed up by c.* ∽**erweckend** a *inspiring trust* ‖ ⟨fig⟩ *promising* **vertr·auen I.** vt [h] *to confide, entrust* ‖ jdm etw ∼ *to entrust a th to a p*(*'s care*) | **sich** e–m ∼ *to unbosom o.s. to a p* **II.** vi [h] (jdm, **auf** [acc]) ∼ *to confide, trust* (*in*); *to rely* (*upon*); *to place one's confidence* (*in*) ‖ ∼ Sie mir! *trust me!* ‖ auf Gott ∼ *to put one's trust in God* ‖ zu sehr auf sich selbst ∼d *too self-confident* **Vertr·auens-** **~amt** n (*place of*) *trust* **~arzt** m *confidential medical adviser*; *public health commissioner* **~beweis** m *confidence* **~bruch** m *indiscretion* ‖ *breach* od *betrayal of trust, confidence, faith* **~frage** f; die ∼ stellen *to ask for a vote of c.* **~krise** f *crisis of* (*public*) *c.* **~mann** m *delegate*; *c.tial agent* ‖ (Quelle) *authority* ‖ ⟨school⟩ *prefect*; *class spokesman* **~person** f *c.tial p* **~pflege** f *human* od *public relations* pl **~posten** m *position of trust, responsible p.n* **~rat** m ⟨Ger⟩ *Mutual Trust Council* **~sache** f *c.tial matter*; *m.* od *question of* (*mutual*) *c.* ∽**selig** a *confiding* od *trusting blindly* | ∼keit [f] *blind c.* **~stellung** f *position of trust* ∽**voll** a *trustful, trusting* **~votum** n *vote of c.* ∽**würdig** a *trustworthy* **ver-** **~tr·auern** vt [h] *to pass .. in mourning* | **sich** ∼ *to pine away* **~tr·aulich** a (Mitteilung) *confidential*; (Brief) ∼! (streng *private and*) *c.tial* ‖ (Mitteilung) *off the record*; *inside* (*information*) ‖ (Verkehr) *intimate*; *familiar* (⟨a. fig⟩ *style*) ‖ (Sitzung) *private* | (P) *matey* | auf ∼em Fuß leben mit *to be on familiar terms with* | [adv] (Auskunft) streng ∼ behandeln *to keep strictly c.tial* ‖ sehr (recht) ∼ tun *to be very affable* (*to be rather familiar*) ‖ streng ∼ *in strict c.* | ∽keit [f] ∼/∼en *c.* | *c.tiality, privacy* | *familiarity, intimacy* ‖ *freedom* (*of his endearing epithets*) ‖ sich [dat] ∼en herausnehmen *to take liberties* od *freedom, familiarities* (gegenüber *with a p*) **~tr·äumen** vt [h] *to dream away* ‖ (Zeit) *to pass .. in dreaming* ‖ sein Glück ∼ *to miss one's chance by dreaming* | **-mt** a *dreamy, dreaming* (*p, eyes*); *stareyed, starry-eyed* (*p*) ‖ (*time*) *wasted in reveries* ‖ *sleepy* (*place*) **V.-mtheit** f ∼/ (*his*) *dreaminess*, ⟨fam⟩ *woolgathering* **~tr·aut** a *familiar*; *intimate, special, close, old* (*friend*); *common* (*sight*) | (bewandert) *conversant* (mit *with*), *at home* od *well acquainted* (*with*), *well informed* (*of*), *well versed* od *experienced* (*in*); ⟨fam⟩ *up* (*to a th*) | **sich** mit etw ∼ m *to make o.s. conversant, to familiarize o.s. with a th*; ⟨aero⟩ *to make o.s. comfortable in* (*one's seat*) ‖ sich mit dem Gedanken ∼ m *to resign o.s. to the notion* | **auf** ∼em Fuße stehen *to be on familiar terms*, ⟨fam emph⟩ *to be hand-in-glove* (*with a p*) ‖ mit jdm ∼ w *to enter upon familiarity with a p* ‖ sich in jds Gesellschaft ∼ fühlen *to feel at home with a p* ∽**tr·aute** m [der ∼, ein ∼r] & f ∼n/∼n *confidential* od *intimate friend*; *confidant*(*e* f); ⟨fam⟩ *chum* ∽**tr·autheit** f ∼/ *intimacy* ‖ *familiarity* (⟨a.⟩ mit *with*) ‖ mit: *thorough knowledge of* (*a th*) ∽**tr·eib-** **~bürste** f *softening-brush* **~pinsel** m *softener* **~tr·eiben** vt irr [h] **A.** *to drive* od *chase away*; *to expel, -trude*; *scare* ‖ (aus–e–a) *to scatter, disperse* **B.** **(Farben)** *to scumble, soften, subdue, melt, blend* ‖ (Feind) *to dislodge* ‖ (Furcht) *to sweep out* ‖ (Gedanken) *to dismiss* ‖ sich [dat] die Grillen ∼ *to dispel care and grief* ‖ (Krankheit) *to cure* ‖ (Sorge) *to dissipate* ‖ (Umrisse) *to soften* ‖ **(Waren)** *to sell, retail* ‖ (Wolken) *to disperse* ‖ sich [dat] die Zeit ∼ *to pass away* (od *beguile, kill*) *the t.*; *to amuse o.s.* ‖ (Zeitungen) *to distribute* **C.** **(jdn)** **~ aus**: *to extrude .. from*; aus e–m Besitz *to dispossess*, ⟨jur⟩ *eject, evict*, aus dem B. *to disseise, -ze*; aus dem Hause *to turn .. out*; aus dem Lande *to banish*; aus s–r Wohnung *to turn .. out of house and home* | Gewalt **mit** G. *to repel force by force* | **von**: *to turn a p out of his place, to sweep the pirates from the sea* ‖ v Haus u Hof vertrieben *evicted* (*tenant*) ∽**tr·eibung** f ∼/∼en *expulsion* ‖ *banishment* ‖ *ejection* ‖ ⟨mil⟩ *dislodgment* ‖ ⟨paint⟩ *softening*, etc ‖ ⟨com⟩ = Vertrieb ‖ Die ∼ aus d. Paradies *The Expulsion from Eden*; Die ∼ der Händler aus dem Tempel *The E. of .. from the T., Christ driving the m. from the T.* **~tr·etbar** a *capable of being substituted* ‖ *worth being advocated*; *justifiable* ‖ *tenable* (*argument*) **~tr·eten** vt irr [h] **A. 1.** *to tread* od *trample under foot* **2.** (eintreten f) *to advocate, champion* ‖ das Gegenteil ∼ *to plead to the contrary* **3.** (verantworten) *to answer for* (*a th*) **4.** (jdn) *to represent* ⟨a. jur⟩ ‖ *to act, substitute, deputize for* ‖ (f jdn auftreten) *to appear* od *plead for* (*a p*) ‖ e–n bei jdm ∼ *to intercede with a p for a p* **5.** ⟨com⟩ am stärksten ∼ [pp] *most numerous*; nicht ∼ *not to be found* (*in the market*) **B.** **(Ansicht)** *to hold, take* (*the view that ..*), *to be an exponent of*; *to expound* (*an idea*); s–e A. ∼ *to preach one's own theme*, etc; energisch *to push one's views* ‖ sich die Beine (den **Fuß**) ∼ *to stretch one's legs* (*to sprain one's ankle*) ‖ jds Interesse ∼ *to attend* od *see to a p's interest* ‖ jds S ∼ *to uphold, support* (⟨jur⟩ *plead, advocate*) *a p's cause* ‖ jds **Stelle** ∼ *to take* od *supply a p's place, to act as a p's substitute* ‖ (Wahlbezirk) *to represent*; *to sit for* ‖ jdm den **Weg** ∼ *to stop a p's passage, to stand in his way* ∽**tr·eter** m ∼s/∼ *representative* ⟨a. pol, com⟩; *delegate*; *deputy*; *proxy*; (e–r Lehre, Partei) *exponent* ‖ ⟨med⟩ *locum tenens* L ‖ (im Amte) *deputy*; gesetzlicher ∼ *statutory agent*, (der Eltern) *st.y guardian*, (e–s Kindes) *legal g.*; (ohne Vertretungsmacht) ⟨jur⟩ *volunteer* ‖ (Verfechter) *holder* (*of a view*), *advocate, champion* | ⟨com⟩ *commercial traveller* ‖ alleiniger ∼ *sole agent*; *concessionary* (*for a*

Aussprache: Falls nicht anders (: [*v*]) angegeben, ist v = [*f*] zu sprechen.

service or amusement) | ⟨fam⟩ merkwürdiger ~ *queer customer* ‖ übler ~ *bad egg* od *hat*; *politician*; ⟨fam⟩ (*he is a*) *tough proposition* | ~bezüge [pl] *agent's remunerations*; ~schaft [f] ~/~en *representative body* ≗**tr·etung** f ~/~en *representation* ‖ *replacement* ‖ *advocacy* | ⟨com⟩ *agency* | ⟨med⟩ e–e ~ h *to do a locum tenens* | in ~ *by proxy* ‖ in ~ des .. *appearing* od *acting for* ..; *Mr. X will act for me, will be my proxy* ‖ die ~ des beurlaubten N. übernimmt Herr X *Mr. X will undertake duty for Mr. N.* | (unterzeichnet) in ~ *signed for* ≗**tr·ieb** m ~(e)s/ *sale, distribution*; *retail trade* **~tr·ieben** pp ⟨paint⟩ *soft* v vertreiben | ≗**e** m [der ~, ein ~r] & f ~n/~n *expellee*; *expelled p*; *refugee*; *exile* ≗**tr·iebs-** **~gefüge** n *structure of distribution* **~gesellschaft** f *trading company* **~gestaltung** f *marketing* **~kanal** m *channel of d.n* **~kaufmann** m *agent*, ⟨Am⟩ *solicitor* **~kosten** [pl] *d.n cost(s)* **~recht** n *right of sale*, (v Büchern) *copyright* **~vorgang** m ⟨com⟩ *marketing operation*, → lahmlegen **~tr·immt** a *out of trim* **~tr·inken** vt irr [h] *to spend in drinking* ‖ *to drink* (*one's earnings*); ⟨fam⟩ *to d. up* (*the charity*) ‖ *to drown* (*one's troubles*) *in liquor* **~tr·ocknen** vi [s] *to dry up* ‖ *to be parched* ‖ ⟨agr⟩ *to wither* | **-net** *dry* (*foliage*) **~tr·ödeln** vt [h] *to trifle* (*dawdle, loiter, idle, fool, fritter*) *away* (*time, money*) | ⟨com⟩ *to hawk about* **~tr·ommeln** vt [h] *to pummel* (*a p*) **~tr·östen** vt [h] *to put off* (*with fine words*) ‖ jdn auf [acc] ~ *to put a p off till, to feed a p with hopes of* **V.tung** f ~/~en (auf [acc]) *fair words, empty promises, hopes* pl ≗**trotteltsein** n (diskretes) *bufferism* **~tr·ug** 1. & 3. sg pret v –tragen **~tr·umpfen**: sich ~ ⟨cards⟩ *to play all one's trumps* **~tr·unken** pp v –trinken **~tr·usten** vt [h] *to pool* **V.tung** f *trustification* **~t·üdern** vt/refl [h] niedd = –wirren ≗**t·uer** m ~s/~ *spendthrift* | ≗isch [a] *extravagant* **~t·un** **I.** vt irr [h] *to spend, squander* ‖ *to use up*; *to fool away* (*money, time*); *to go through* (*a fortune*); Geld ~ *to play about* ‖ er hat nichts zu ~ *he has nothing to spare* | °**sich** ~ *to make a mistake*; .. bei .. *to slip up on a th* **II.** vi [h] er hat –tan *he is done for* **~t·uschen** vt [h] *to hush* od *cover .. up*; *to suppress, conceal*; *to keep .. dark* od *secret* ‖ *to gloss .. over* **V.schung** f ~/~en *cover-up, hushing-up* | ~spolitik [f] *hushing-up system* **~·übeln** vt [h] *to take amiss, to resent* ‖ (jdm etw) *to blame a p for a th* **~·üben** vt [h] *to commit*, ⟨jur⟩ *to perpetrate* ‖ *to practise* (*acts of violence*) ‖ *to play* (*tricks*) ‖ Grausamkeiten ~ an *to use cruelty towards* **~·ulken** vt [h] *to make fun of*; (P) *to guy, kid, rag, rib* ≗**·umständung** f Sw = Umstand

ver·un- **~edeln** vt [h] *to debase, degrade* **~ehren** vt [h] *to dishonour, disgrace, disparage* ≗**ehrung** f ~/~en *dishonour, disgrace*; *affront* (*to a p's memory*) **~einigen** vt [h] *to disunite, to set at variance* | **sich** ~ *to fall out, to quarrel* **V.gung** f ~/~en *disunion, discord* **~glimpfen** vt [h] *to defame, denigrate, smear, abuse, revile*, ⟨fam⟩ *to run down* ‖ (verleumden) *to slander, calumniate, backbite* **V.fer** m ~s/~ *defamer, calumniator, detractor* **V.fung** f ~/~en *defamation, calumniation, detraction* ‖ *insult* (e–r S *to a th*) **~glücken** vi [s] (P) *to meet with an accident, to come to grief* ‖ (tödlich) *to be killed, to perish* ‖ (S) *to miscarry, fail* ‖ (Schiff) *to be lost* | | **-ckt** ⟨fig⟩ *abortive* (*attempt*) ‖ der ≗e, die ≗e *the victim*; *casualty*; (tödlich) *fatality* **~krautet** a *weedy* **~möglichen** vt [h] Sw = unmöglich m **~reinigen** vt [h] *to soil*; *to defile* ⟨a. fig⟩; ⟨fam⟩ *muck* ‖ (Wasser etc) *to contaminate, pollute* ‖ (Luft) *to infect* | ~de Stoffe *pollutants, contaminants* **V.gung** f ~/~en *soiling, defilement, pollution* ‖ *contamination* ‖ ~ (dieses Ortes ist) verboten! *commit no nuisance!* ‖ ~en [pl] ⟨tech⟩ [konkr] *impurities*; *pollutants* **~schönen** vt [h] *to uglify* ≗**sicherung** f ⟨links-radikalpol⟩ *creation of insecurity within the establishment*; *undermining of the traditional values of the e.*; *fomenting dissension in the e.* **~stalten** vt [h] *to disfigure, deface, deform*, ⟨fig⟩ *to pockmark, flaw, spoil, mar* **V.tung** f ~/~en *disfigurement*, etc ‖ ⟨a.⟩ *blot* (*on the landscape*) **~treuen** vt [h] *to embezzle* (Gelder *money*); ⟨jur⟩ *to peculate* **V.euer** m *embezzler, peculator*; *defaulter* **-euung** f ~/~en *embezzlement, fraud*; *peculation*, ⟨Am sl⟩ *graft* ‖ ~ öffentlicher Gelder *defalcation* **~zieren** vt [h] *to disfigure, spoil, mar* **ver-** **~·ursachen** vt [h] *to cause*; *give*; *occasion*; *generate*; *produce*, → hervorrufen ‖ *to call forth, bring about*; *to give rise to* ‖ *to involve* (*expense*); *to make for* (*complications*) ‖ *time has worked* od *wrought many changes* ‖ jdm Kosten (Unannehmlichkeiten) ~ *to put a p to expense* (*inconvenience*) ‖ (Krankheit) *to bring on* od *forth* ‖ (Streit) *to engender* **V.cher** m *author, originator*; *instigator* **~·urteilen** vt [h] *to condemn*; ⟨fig⟩ *deprecate*, ⟨Am⟩ *to call down* ‖ (zu e–r Strafe) *to sentence* [*to death*] ‖ zu e–r Geldstrafe v 5.– DM ~ *to fine* (*a p*) *5 marks* | ⟨fig⟩ **-lt zu** *reduced to* (*keeping*) *a diet*; z Scheitern –lt *foredoomed to failure* | **V.lte(r)** m *condemned p* **V.lung** f ~/~en *condemnation* ‖ ⟨jur⟩ *conviction* ‖ (Strafe) *sentence* ‖ (jds z Tode) (*passing a*) *death-sentence* (*upon*) **~v·ielfältigen** vt [h] *to multiply* ‖ (nachbilden) *to copy, reproduce* ‖ (Schriftstück) *to manifold, multigraph, duplicate* ‖ ⟨film⟩ (Drehbuch) *to micrograph* | **sich** ~ *to snowball* **V.ger** m ~s/~ *multiplier duplicator* ‖ *reproducer* **V.gung** f ~/~en *multiplication* ‖ *reproduction* ‖ *manifold copy* | **~s-** ~apparat [m] *duplicator, -ting machine*; ~arbeiten [f pl] *duplicating work*; ~büro [n] *duplicating service*; ~papier [n] *manifolds* pl **~v·ierfachen** vt [h] *to quadruple* | sich ~ *to multiply fourfold* **~v·ollkommnen** vt [h] *to perfect*; *to carry* (*a th*) *to perfection*; *to improve* (gegenüber *upon*) | **sich** ~ *to acquire accomplishments* **V.nung** f ~/~en *perfection, improvement*; *elaboration* | ~sfähigkeit [f] *perfectibility* **~v·ollständigen** vt [h] *to complete, integrate, supplement, complement*; *to piece out*; *to round off* (*book*) ‖ ⟨mil⟩ *to bring to the full number* ‖ ⟨com⟩ *to replenish* (*the stock*) **V.gung** f, ~/~en *completion* **~w·achen** vt [h] *to pass* (*nights*) *in watching* **~w·achsen** irr **I.** vi [s] (zus–) *to grow together* | (überwachsen, ⟨a.⟩ **sich** ~) *to become overgrown* (*with*) ‖ (Wunde) *to heal, close* | *to become deformed* **II.** vt [h]; s–e Kleider ~ *to grow out of one's clothes* ‖ Sie h Ihre Narbe ~ *your scar has quite disappeared* | **sich** ~ zu *to grow into* **III.** a [pp] *deformed, crooked, humpbacked* | *entangled* | *natural* (*ground*) | *grown together* | ⟨fig⟩ ~ mit *attached to*; *interwoven with*; *grown into* (*his own nature*) **IV.** ≗**sein** n ~s/ *concreteness* ⟨a. fig⟩ **V.sung** f ~/~en *cicatrization* ‖ *deformity* ‖ ⟨fig⟩ *attachment* **~w·ackeln** vt [h] ⟨phot⟩ *to shake* ≗**w·ahr** n ~(e)s/~e = ~ung | **v.ren** vt [h] *to take care of*; *to keep, guard* (vor [dat] *from*) ‖ *to put .. in its* (od *in a safe*) *place* ‖ (schützen) *to preserve* ‖ gut –rt *well kept, preserved, packed* ‖ sich gut ~ l *to keep well* vi ‖ trocken ~ *to keep dry* ‖ e–m etw z ~ geben *to give a th in a p's charge, to deposit it with a p*, (Geld) *to entrust m. to a p('s care)* | (sicherstellen) *to safeguard* | **sich** ~ ⟨fig⟩ *to protest, remonstrate* (gegen *against*); gegen: *to secure o.s. against*; vor [dat] *to keep o.s. from* **V.rer** m ~s/~ *keeper* ‖ *guardian* ‖ *preserver* ‖ *trustee* ‖ *depositary* **v.rlosen** **I.** vt [h] *to* (*spoil by*) *neglect* **II.** vi [s] *to be neglected, to spoil* [vi] *through neglect*; *to become delinquent* | **-st** a *neglected, uncared-for*; *ill-kept* (*garden*) ‖ (P) ⟨a.⟩ *unkempt*; *dead-end* [attr] (Kind) | **V.sung** f

---

Verbal-Flexion der Verben mit der Vorsilbe **ver-** → das jeweilige Simplex

~/~en (*injury caused by*) *neglect*; *negligence*; *negligent treatment* || *idle and disorderly indigence* **≃w·ahrung** f ~/~en *keeping*, *custody*, *guard*, *preservation* (vor [dat] *from*) || (Obhut) *charge* | in ~ geben *to deposit*, *to give into a p's charge* || etw (jdn) in ~ nehmen *to take charge of a th* (*to take a p into custody*, *to put a p in jail*) | ~ einlegen gegen ⟨fig⟩ *to* (*enter a*) *protest against* | **~s-** ~bruch [m] ⟨jur⟩ *wilful breach of duty by official custodian* || ~mittel [n] *preservative*; ⟨jur⟩ *protest*; ~ort [m] *depot* || (f Möbel) *repository*; ~vertrag [m] *deposit-contract* **~w·aisen I.** vt [h] *to orphan* **II.** vi [s] *to become an orphan* | **-st** a *orphan*(*ed*), *bereft of one's parents*, *unparented* || ⟨fig⟩ *deserted*, *destitute* **V.sung** f *orphaned state* || ⟨fig⟩ *destitution* **~w·alten** vt [h] *to manage* (f *for*), *administer* (*a school*, *hotel*, etc) || *to be* (*placed*) *in charge of* (*the shop*) || *to superintend*; *to run* (*a town*) || (führen) *to conduct*, *govern*, *rule* || schlecht ~ *to mismanage* || (ein Amt) *to hold* || die Regierung ~ *to hold the reins of government* || (ein Vermögen) *to manage*; *to look after*; (jds V.) *to act as trustee to a p's property* | **-tend** administrative | **V.ter(in** f) m ~s/~ *administrator* [f ⟨a.⟩ *administratrix*], *manager* [f ⟨a.⟩ *manageress*]; *agent* || (e-s Gutes) *steward* || (Konkurs≃) *trustee* | **V.tung** f ~/~en *administration* ⟨a. hot⟩ || *management*, *operation* || (Führung) *direction*, *charge* (*of*) || *trusteeship* || (Staatsdienst) *Civil Service*; *government* | (Behörde) *authorities* pl || *managing board* || *government*; *governing body* **≃w·altungs-** ⟨oft⟩ *administrative*, *-tration* **~abteilung** *ad.tive department* **~akademie** f *public ad.n college* **~apparat** m *organization* **~ausschuß** m *managing* (⟨Am⟩ *prudential*) *committee*; *Bench* **~beamte(r)** m *ad.tive officer*; *magistrate* **~behörde** f *government-board*, *b. of management* **~bezirk** m *ad.tive district*; ⟨engl⟩ *riding*; ⟨Am⟩ *ward* **~büro** n *paymaster's office* **~dienst** m *Civil Service* **~direktor** m *managing director* **~fach** n *ad.tive department* **~gebäude** n *business premises* pl **~jahr** n *year of ad.n* **~kosten** [pl] *ad.tive expenses* **~kreis** m = –bezirk **~macht** f (der Uno) *administering authority* **~ministerium** n *ministerial department* **~offizier** m → Zahlmeister **~organ** n *ad.tive body* ⟨a. pol⟩ **~rat** m *board of directors* od *ad.n* || (P) *director* | ~sitzung [f] *board meeting* **~recht** n *ad.tive law* **~weg** m; auf dem ~e *ad.tively* **~wesen** n *ad.n* **~zweig** m *branch of the ad.n*, *ad.tive department* **~w·amsen** vt [h] → –dreschen, –prügeln **~w·and** 1. & 3. sg pret v –winden **~w·andeln** vt [h] (in [acc]) *to change* ⟨a. theol⟩; *turn*; *convert* ⟨a. com, chem⟩; *transform*, *reduce* ⟨a. math⟩ (*into*) || ⟨met⟩ *to transmute* || ⟨myth & biol⟩ *to metamorphose* | zu **Asche** ~ *to reduce to ashes* || *he reduced chaos into order* || in Geld ~ *to realize* || in Staub ~ *to turn to dust*, *to pulverize* || (Strafe) *to commute* | **sich** ~ *to alter*; *to change*, *turn* (in, zu [*in*]*to*); *the scene shifts* (in *to*); *a th resolves itself* (*into*); (P) *to make o.s. into a graceful woman* **V.dlung** f ~/~en *transformation* ⟨a. theat⟩; ⟨theat⟩ *shifting of scenes*, offene *visible scene change*, schnelle *quick change* || *conversion* ⟨a. com⟩ || *reduction* || *change* ⟨a. chem⟩, *alteration* || *metamorphosis* || ⟨theol⟩ *transubstantiation* || *commutation* | **~s-** ~kleid [n] *three-*, *two-in-one dress* || ~künstler [m] *quick-change artist*; *ringer* | ~szene [f] *t.f.n.-scene* **~w·andt 1.** pp v –wenden || ~ stricken *to purl* **2.** [a] (mit) *related*, *allied* (*to*) ⟨a. übtr⟩ (*how are you related to her*?) | [nur pred] *akin* ⟨a. fig⟩; ⟨fig⟩ *associated* (*with*) | ⟨fig⟩ *cognate* (*words*, *ideas*); *analogous* (*idea*, ⟨biol⟩ *organ*); *kindred* (*languages*) | ~e Seelen [f pl] *twin souls*, *congenial spirits* pl || er ist mit mir ~ *he is a relative of mine* || wir sind nahe (weitläufig) ~ *we are near* (*distant*) *relatives* | **≃e** m [der ~, ein ~r] & f ~n/~n *relative*, *relation* || entfernt .. *cousin*, nächster ~r ⟨jur⟩ *next of kin* | [pl] (*my*) *kin* (*are*) || angeheiratete ~ [pl] ⟨a.⟩ *in-laws* pl **≃w·andtschaft** f ~/~en *relationship* || (Bluts≃) *consanguinity* || entfernt *cousinship* || (Heirats≃) *affinity* | [konkret] *relations*, *kinsfolk* pl || m–e nächste ~ *my immediate people* | ⟨fig⟩ *congeniality* || *connexion* (*of ideas*) || ⟨chem & fig⟩ *affinity* | zur ~ gehören *to be one of the family* | **sich** zur ~ zählen mit .. *to call cousins with* .. | **~s-** ~beziehung [f] *points* pl *of r.p*; ~grad [m] *degree of r.p*, etc, *remove*; ~verhältnis [n] (v Sprachen) *filiation* **~w·andtschaftlich** a *kinsmanlike*, *kindred* | [adv] *like kinsfolk* **≃w·andtsein** n ~s/ *relationship* **~w·anzt** a *buggy*; → Wanze **~w·arf** 1. & 3. sg pret v –werfen **~w·arnen** vt [h] *to* (*fore*)*warn* || (strafend) *to reprimand*, ⟨ftb⟩ *to caution* **V.nung** f ~/~en *warning* || *reprimand*, *caution* || gebührenpflichtige ~ *on the spot fine*, ⟨fam⟩ (*traffic*) *ticket* ⟨bes Am⟩; **~w·aschen I.** vt irr [h] *to use* (*up*) .. *in washing* || (wegwaschen) *to wash away* od *out* || ⟨arts⟩ *to blend*, *wash* **II.** [a] *washed-out*, *faded* | ⟨fig⟩ *ill-defined*, *vague*, ⟨fam⟩ *wishy-washy*; *slurred* (*speech*) **~w·ässern I.** vt [h] ⟨a. fig⟩ *to dilute*; *to water* (*down*) ⟨a. fig⟩ || ⟨fig⟩ *to enfeeble*; *to make insipid* **II.** vi [h] *to soak too long* || *to become weak* (⟨fig⟩ *insip*) | **-rt** a *dilute*, *sloppy*; *wishy-washy*; ⟨fig⟩ –rtes Kapital *watered capital*, ⟨Am⟩ *w.d stock* **V.rung** f ~/ *dilution* ⟨a. fig⟩ || ⟨fig⟩ *spinning out* **~w·eben** vt reg & irr [h] *to use* (*up*) .. *in weaving* || *to interweave* ⟨a. fig⟩ & sich ~ || ⟨fig⟩ *to intertwine* (in [acc], mit *with*) || *his life was knit up with hers* **~w·echselbar** a (*inter*)*changeable* || *easily to be mistaken* (*the one for the other*) **~w·echseln** vt [h] *to exchange* (*we exchanged hats*), *to change by mistake* || (mit) *to mistake* (*for*), *confound*, *confuse*, *mix up*, *muddle up* (*with*) || (Begriffe) *to confound* (*with*) || zum ≃ ähnlich *as like as two peas* || mir u mich ~ ⟨m. m.⟩ *to drop one h's* || Bäumchen-~-sich spielen *to play Puss-in-the-corner* (*in a wood*) **V.lung** f ~/~en *exchanging* || *confusion* (*of names*) || (Irrtum) *mistake* **~w·egen** a *adventurous*, *risky* || *audacious*, (wagemutig) *daring*, *bold*, *hardy*, *dashing* || *rash* || *determined*; (frech) *saucy*; *insolent*; *presumptuous*; (aus Verzweiflung) *desperate* | [adv] ~ auftreten *to put a bold face on it* | ≃heit [f] ~/~en *temerity*, *boldness* || *audacity* || *insolence*; *derring-do* || *rash* (etc) *action* **~w·ehen I.** vt [h] (Wolken) *to blow away* || *to scatter* || mit: *to cover* .. *with* (*snow*) || v Sturme –ht *storm-tossed* || ⟨fig⟩ v Winde –ht *gone with the wind*; –hte Hoffnungen *blighted hopes* **II.** vi [s] *to blow over* || *to scatter* [vi] || **~w·ehren** vt [h]; jdm etw ~ *to prevent* (od *keep*, *debar*) *a p from* (*doing*) *a th*, *to forbid a p to do a th* || jdm den Eintritt ~ *to deny entrance to a p* **~w·eichlichen I.** vt [h] *to coddle*, *pamper*, *emasculate*, *unman*; *to* (*render*) *effeminate* **II.** vi [s] (& sich ~ [h]) *to become* od *grow effeminate* | **-cht** (*gone*) *soft*, *flaccid*, *limp*, *weak*, *lardy-dardy* **V.chung** f ~/ *effeminacy*, *emasculation* **~w·eigern** vt [h] *to deny*, *refuse* || die Aussage ~ *to refuse to give evidence*; den Befehl ~ *to flout an order*; jdm den Gehorsam ~ *to disobey a p* || ⟨hors⟩ e–e Hürde *to refuse a hurdle*, [⟨a.⟩ abs] *to refuse* **V.rung** f ~/~en *denial*, *refusal* || ~ der Annahme *non-acceptance*; ~ der ehelichen Pflichten *repudiation* | im ~sfall *in case of refusal* **verw·eilen I.** vt [h] *to stop*, *delay* (*a p*) **II.** vi [h] am F. ~ *to continue at the window*; *to c. in a place* || (bei) *to abide*, *tarry*, *linger*, *stay* (*with*) || ⟨fam⟩ *to stop* (in *at*) || ⟨fig⟩ (bei) *to dwell*, *enlarge*, *insist* (*on*) **III.** ≃ n ~s/ *tarrying*, *abiding* || ⟨fig⟩ (bei) *dwelling* (*on*) | **V.l-** ⟨med⟩ *indwelling* (*catheter*) **~w·einen** vt [h] (Zeit) *to spend* .. *in weeping* ||

Aussprache: Falls nicht anders (: [*v*]) angegeben, ist v = [*f*] zu sprechen.

(Tränen) to shed || (Schmerz) to ease .. by weeping || sich die Augen ~ to cry one's eyes out | **-nt** a; ~e Augen h to have one's eyes red with weeping od tears, tear-stained eyes **≗w·eis** m –ses/–se **1.** ⟨Lit⟩ reference **2.** reproof, reprimand, check, rebuke; ⟨fam⟩ setdown || jdm e–n ~ erteilen to rebuke, reprimand a p, ⟨fam⟩ to rap a p's knuckles od fingers; to give a p a wigging **~w·eisen** vt irr [h] **A.** (jdn) ~ **an** (jdn, etw) [a. abs] **auf** (etw [acc]) to refer .. to || man hat mich an Sie verwiesen I have been directed to apply to you || auf: to relegate a p to (an island), to put a p in (his humble place) || (jdn) ~ to banish, exile (⟨a.⟩ des Landes or **aus** dem L.e) || **aus, von**: to expel (from school); ⟨univ⟩ to send down (from college) | jdn **von** der Bahn ~ ⟨sport⟩ to warn a p off the track | jdn **vor** ein Schwurgericht ~ to commit a p for trial at the assizes **B. jdm etw** ~ to reprimand, rebuke a p for (od because of) a th; to upbraid, reproach a p with a th || jdn **zur** Ordnung ~ to call a p to order | **V.sung** f ~/~en ⟨lit⟩ reference (to) || banishment, exile || expulsion, ⟨univ⟩ rustication || commitment, relegation | ~szeichen [n] (mark of) r.ce **~w·elken** vi [s] to wither, wilt, fade **~w·elschen** vt/i [h/s] to Frenchify **V.schung** f ~/ Frenchification **~w·eltlichen I.** vt [h] to make worldly || (Klöster) to secularize **II.** vi [s] to become worldly **~w·endbar** a available, suitable (for); (wieder re)usable; applicable (to) || ~ s als ⟨a.⟩ to be employed od utilized as || nicht ~ unsuitable | ~keit [f] applicability **~w·enden** vt [h] **A.** to turn away || ich kann kein Auge v ihr ~ I can't take my eyes off her || mit –deter or verwandter Hand with the back of the h. **B.** (gebrauchen) to employ (a p, a th); to dispose of || –det w to be in use || nützlich ~ to utilize || ungetreu ~ to misappropriate | (**auf** [acc], **f,** z) to apply .. (to), to use .. (for), to spend .. (in, on), to employ (at, in, for) || (Kapital) to invest | **auf**: (Sorgfalt) to bestow .. upon; (Zeit) to devote .. to; (die nötige Zeit) to give .. to | das M., das **bei** Herstellung v .. –det wird the materials pl of production of .. | **zu**: (e–m bes. Gebrauch) to assign to .. **C. sich** ~ to intercede, intervene, to use one's influence (f on behalf of, bei with), to speak up (for a p) **V.dung** f ~/~en utilization || application, use, employment || investment; expenditure || (für jdn) intercession (for a p) || ~ finden als to be employed etc as || (k–e) ~ h f to be able to use etc (to have no use for) (I cannot make use of it) | **zur** bes ~ (z. b. V.) (for) special duty; z ~ im Rahmen ihrer Aufträge in the furtherance of their missions | **~s-** ≗(un)fähig [a] serviceable, (un)fit for use; ~karte [f] classification card od record; ~test [m] feasability test; ~zweck [m] purpose; use; applicability **~w·erfen I.** vt irr [h] **A. 1.** to use (up) in throwing **2.** to scatter od throw about **3.** to throw into a wrong place **4.** ⟨zoo⟩ to miscarry, slink vt/i **B.** ⟨fig⟩ to reject (⟨a. parl⟩ a bill), to condemn, disallow || to throw a th over || ⟨jur⟩ to turn down, to quash | to disapprove of || to spurn, repudiate || ⟨bib⟩ to cast away | als parteiisch to challenge (a jury) || e–e Klage ~ to dismiss a case, to nonsuit the plaintiff || (Urteil) to overrule **C. sich** ~ to throw badly od wrong(ly) || ⟨cards⟩ to play a wrong card || (Holz) to warp || ⟨min⟩ to leap || ⟨geol⟩ to distort; to be dislocated **II.** ≗ n ~s/ ⟨zoo⟩ abortion, miscarrying; seuchenhaftes ~ epizootic od infectious a.n || **-flich** a objectionable, exceptionable, reprehensible || condemnable, wicked; ⟨emph⟩ abominable **V.fung** f ~/~en refusal, rejection, disapproval, condemnation || ⟨jur⟩ quashing || (Holz≗) warping || ⟨min, geol⟩ dislocation, fault, heave; ⟨min⟩ hitch; ~ in die Höhe (Tiefe) upcast (downcast) dyke | **~s-** ~spalte [f] ⟨geol⟩ fault **~w·erten** vt [h] to utilize, to turn to account || to make use of; (Abfälle etc) wieder ~ to reprocess; (zu Geld m) to realize, sell || sich gut ~ l to be most useful, ⟨com⟩ to fetch a good price **V.tung** f ~/ utilization, employment; turning to account || ~ v Abfall salvage || realization, sale || wir h k–e ~ dafür we have no use for it || unter ~ e–r S in the light od on the basis of a th | **~s-** ~anlage [f] utilizing plant **~w·esen I.** vt [h] to manage, administer || jds Amt ~ to do duty od act as substitute for a p || das Reich ~ to act as regent **II.** vi [s] to rot, putrefy, decompose, decay **V.ser** m ~s/~ administrator; vicegerent || ⟨ec⟩ locum tenens L || (Reichs≗) regent **~w·eslich** a perishable, corruptible, putrefiable | ≗keit [f] ~/ perishableness, corruptibility **V.sung** f ~/ administration, management | (Fäulnis) corruption, putrefaction, decomposition || in ~ begriffen in a state of decay **~w·etten** vt [h] to bet, stake | (verlieren) to lose by betting **~w·ettert** a weather-beaten | ⟨fig⟩ damned, confounded | → –wittert **~w·ichen** a former, past (times); last (year) °**~w·ichsen** vt [h] to squander | (prügeln) to thrash, trounce **~w·ikkeln** vt [h] (in [acc]) to (en)tangle, ⟨fig⟩ involve, implicate (in) || ⟨fig⟩ to complicate, embroil || in ein Gefecht ~ to engage | **sich** ~ to entangle o.s., to get involved od mixed (in) od ⟨fam⟩ mixed up (with); to be embroiled (in war); to let o.s. in for (difficulties) | **-lt** a involved, implicated (in) || intricate, complicated, knotty (affair), [pred] fouled up || complex (character) || ~e Dinge wheels within wheels **V.lung** f ~/~en entanglement || ⟨fig⟩ complication, implication, intricacy, complexity | (Verwirrung) confusion, tangle || plot (of a play) || twist || embroilment; imbroglio It **~w·iegen** vt irr [h] to weigh out **V.ger** m ⟨min⟩ check weighman **~w·iesen** pp v –weisen | ≗**e** m [der ~, ein ~r] & f ~n/~n exile, outlaw **~w·ildern** vi [s] to grow wild; ⟨bot⟩ to run to seed || (Felder) ~ l to leave uncultivated | ⟨fig⟩ to degenerate, to become intractable, to run to waste || (Kinder) ⟨a.⟩ to run wild || to become brutalized | **-rt** a wild, savage brutal(ized) || uncultivated || (Park) weed-grown || ⟨fig⟩ (P) intractable, unruly || (Haar) untrimmed **V.rung** f ~/ growing wild || ⟨fig⟩ running wild, demoralization, brutalization || uncultivated od untrimmed state **~w·inden** vt irr [h] (etw) to get over (a th), to overcome || ⟨tech⟩ to distort, twist, wind **V.dung** f ~/~en ⟨tech⟩ distortion || ⟨aero⟩ wing twisting | **~s-** ~klappe [f] ⟨aero⟩ aileron; ≗steif [a] torsion-resistant **~w·irken** vt [h] to forfeit, lose || (Strafe) to incur | ⟨tech⟩ to work up || to knead (dough) || to consume **~w·irklichen** vt [h] to realize, establish; effect; objectivate; actualize; to put into practice; (e–n Wunsch) (ganz) ~ to carry .. into (full) fruition | **sich** (nicht) ~ to materialize, to come true, to be realized (to prove delusive) || nicht zu ~d unrealizable | –cht w to come into operation **V.chung** f ~/~en realization || attainment (of the objectives of a treaty) ≗**w·irkung** f ~/ forfeiture **~w·irren** vt reg & irr [h] to entangle; to disarrange, rumple, ⟨bes Am fam⟩ muss (⟨a.⟩ Haar); to throw into disorder; to unsettle (opinions) || ⟨fig⟩ (S) to complicate; (e–e Frage) to mudde (an issue) || (P) to perplex, puzzle, bewilder, confuse, confound; discomfit; to embarrass (⟨a.⟩ –rrt m) || (aus der Fassung bringen) to discompose, disconcert, abash || e–n im Kopfe –rrt m to fog, daze, warp (⟨fam⟩ to muddle) a p's brain | **sich** ~ to get entangled; ⟨Am a.⟩ to run afoul (mit of); to get o.s. tied up; ⟨fig⟩ (im Reden) to be put out, ⟨fam⟩ to get muddled | **~d** a ⟨a.⟩ mazy (crowd), unsettling, awkward | **-rrt** a complicated, intricate, entangled || ⟨fig⟩ puzzled, flustered, blank || disconcerted; ganz .. out of good countenance, overwhelmed with confusion || (im Geiste) astray,

---

Verbal-Flexion der Verben mit der Vorsilbe **ver-** → das jeweilige Simplex

distracted, dazed **V.rrung** f ~/~en *entanglement* | ⟨fig⟩ *bewilderment; confusion; perplexity* ‖ *disarray, distraction, derangement* ‖ ~ anrichten *to bring about confusion* ‖ jdn in ~ bringen *to baffle a p, to put a p to confusion* ‖ in ~ geraten *to be(come) embarrassed,* etc ‖ ~ hervorrufend *upsetting,* ⟨emph⟩ *raising the Devil* ‖ (S) in höchster ~ *at sixes and sevens* **~-w·irtschaften** vt [h] *to squander away; to waste, lose, dissipate* **~w·ischbar** a *effaceable; easily wiped out* **~w·ischen** vt [h] *to wipe* od *blot out* (⟨a. fig⟩ *from the memory*) ‖ ⟨arts, etc⟩ *to obliterate;* (Zeichnung) *to blur,* (mit dem Wischer) *to stump, soften* ‖ ⟨hunt⟩ (Fährte) *to wear away, to kill* ‖ ⟨typ⟩ *to mackle* ‖ ⟨fig⟩ *to efface, obliterate, blur; to cover (one's tracks)* | **sich** ~ *to become effaced* od (Zeichnung) *blurred* ‖ ⟨fig⟩ *to vanish* **~w·ittern I.** vi [s] ⟨a. fig⟩ *to be(come) weather-worn* od *-beaten; to weather, decompose, crumble, moulder* ‖ ⟨chem⟩ *to effloresce* **II.** vt [h] *to decompose, decay* **V.rung** f ~/~en *weathering; decomposition, disintegration* ‖ ⟨chem⟩ *efflorescence* ‖ ⟨arts⟩ *defacement* ‖ ⟨geol⟩ *weathering* | **~s-** ~krume [f] *top soil;* ~kruste [f] *crust of weathered material;* ~material [n] *top soil and mantle rock;* ~schutt [m] *mantle rock* **~w·itwen** vi [s] *to become a widow(er* m) f | **-et** a *widowed* ‖ –er Vater *widower-father* ‖ die –e Königin etc *the Queen-,* etc *Dowager; the dowager Lady N.* ‖ die –e Frau N. *the widow of the late Mr. N.;* Frau M., –e N. *Mrs. Miller, the former widow Nut* **V.wung** f ~/ *widowhood* ‖ seit ihrer ~ *since she became a widow* **~w·oben** [pp v –weben]; ⟨fig⟩ *interfused, -laced, -meshed* **~w·ogen I.** pp v –wägen & –wiegen **II.** a = –wegen **~w·ogen** vi [s] (Wellen) *to abate* ‖ (Töne) *to die away* **~w·ohnen** vt [h] *to damage (rooms) by occupation* **~w·öhnen** vt [h] *to spoil, coddle, pamper, spoon-feed; to cocker (up)* ‖ (im Essen) *to make .. fastidious* ‖ ⟨fam⟩ –hnte P *molly-coddle* | **sich** ~ *to overindulge o.s., to acquire luxurious habits* **V.hntheit** f ~/, **V.hnung** f ~/ *spoiling,* etc ‖ *bad habits; fastidiousness* **~w·orfen** pp v –werfen ‖ ⟨geol⟩ *warped (rock)* | ⟨fig a.⟩ *outcast, abject; profligate, depraved* ‖ *vile, base* ‖ *abandoned (woman)* ‖ ~er Kerl *villain, profligate* | ~heit [f] ~/ *profligacy, abjection, depravity* **~w·orren** a [pp v –wirren] *intricate, tanglesome chaotic; mixed-up, fouled-up* ‖ *confused, vague, hazy, mazy;* ⟨fam⟩ *muddled (ideas),* (S) *in a mess* ‖ *muddy (thinking)* ‖ *muddle-headed (p)* | ≗heit [f] ~/ *confusion, intricacy* ‖ (geistige) *distracted* (⟨fam⟩ *muddled) state; perplexity* **~w·uchs** 1. & 3. sg pret v –wachsen **~w·undbar** a *vulnerable;* ~e Stelle *Achilles heel* ‖ ⟨fig⟩ *sentitive,* ⟨fam⟩ *touchy;* ~ Stelle *sore spot, weak point;* ~e Ziele ⟨mil⟩ *sitting ducks* ⟨fig fam⟩ | ≗keit [f] ~/ *vulnerability* **verw·unden** vt [h] *to wound, hurt, injure* ⟨a. fig⟩; *to bruise* ‖ (empfindlich) *to wound to the quick* ‖ (am Arm, Flügel) *to wing* ‖ (Boden) ~ ⟨for⟩ *to scarify* | **sich** ~ mit *to cut* od *gash o.s. with* **V.dete(r)** m (*wounded p* od *soldier*) *casualty* **V.deten-** ~abschub, –abtransport [m] *casualty* od *medical evacuation;* ~abzeichen [n] *badge for wounded soldiers,* ⟨engl⟩ *gold stripes, (five-) wound stripes;* ⟨Am⟩ *purple heart;* ~sammelstelle [f] *casualty-clearing station;* ~- u Gefallenen-Abtransport mit Flugzeug *casualties air evacuation* N **~w·unden** pp v verwinden **~w·underlich** a *strange, astonishing* ‖ wenig ~ *little wonder (that)* ‖ ~ erscheinen *to surprise,* etc **~w·undern** vt [h] *to astonish,* ⟨emph⟩ *amaze* | **sich** ~ *to wonder, to be surprised* od *a.shed* (über [acc] *at*) ‖ **es** ist nicht z ~, daß *it is no w.r that* ‖ das ist z ≗ *that is remarkable* od *a.shing* od *to be w.red at* | **-rt** [a] *wide-eyed* | [adv] *w.ringly, in amazement;* sie starrte ihn (ganz) ~ an *she gave him a stare of a.t* ‖ ich frage mich ~, wie .. *I w.r (to m.s.) how* ‖ sich ~ stellen *to feign surprise* **V.rung** f ~/ *surprise, a.shment* ‖ mit einiger/gelinder ~ *in mild a.t* ‖ ⟨emph⟩ *amazement* (in ~ setzen *to fill with a.*); viel ~ *much shaking of heads* ‖ zu s–r ~ fand er *he was astonished to find* | ~sausruf [m] *exclamation of s.e;* ≗svoll [a] *amazed* **≗w·undung** f ~/~en *wound(ing), hurt, injury* (⟨mil⟩ *due to operation of war*) ‖ tödliche ~ *mortal* od *fatal wound* ‖ nach ~ gestorben *died of wounds* **~w·unschen** a *enchanted (princess)* ‖ *haunted (house)* **~w·ünschen** vt [h] *to curse, execrate* ‖ (behexen) *to bewitch, enchant* ‖ *to rue (the day)* ‖ *to imprecate curses on (a p)* | **-scht** a *cursed, detestable,* ⟨fam⟩ *deuced* | ~! *confound it!, damn it* | [adv] *awfully,* ⟨fam⟩ *deucedly (clever)* **V.schung** f ~/~en **1.** *curse, malediction, execration* ‖ ~en ausstoßen gegen *to curse; to hurl imprecations at (a p)* **2.** *enchantment, spell* °**wurstelt** a [bes österr] *fouled-up* **~w·urzelt** a *deeply rooted* ‖ ⟨fig⟩ *engrained (in)* ‖ tief ~ *ineradicable* **~w·ürzen** vt [h] ⟨cul⟩ *to season too much* **~w·usch** 1. & 3. sg pret v –waschen **~w·üsten** vt [h] *to devastate, wreck, ravage; to lay waste;* ⟨mil⟩ *to scorch* | –tet s (Land) *to be (made) a wilderness* **V.ster** m ~s/~ *devastator, destroyer* **V.stung** f ~/~en *devastation, desolation;* ⟨mil fam⟩ *blowdown* ‖ [pl] *ravages* ‖ ~en anrichten *to cause wreak/havoc to make ravages,* .. an *to make havoc of* **~z·agen I.** vi [s] *to lose courage* od *heart, to despond* ‖ (verzweifeln) *to despair* (an [dat] *of*) ‖ nicht ~! *never say die!* **II.** ≗ n *despondency, despair* | **-gt** a *discouraged, despondent, desponding, dejected, downhearted, disheartened; poor-spirited, half-hearted* ‖ ~ m *to dishearten, discourage* ‖ ~ w = –gen | ≗heit [f] ~/ *despondency, dejectedness, dejection; faint-heartedness; despair* **~z·ählen**: sich ~ [h] *to miscount, to count wrong* **~z·ahnen** vt [h] (Rad) *to tooth, cog* ‖ ⟨carp⟩ *to indent, joggle, notch, dovetail* ‖ ⟨fig⟩ *to link together;* (mit d. Feinde) –nt *interlocked* od *engaged with ..* | **sich** ~ *to dovetail* **V.nung** f ~/~en *toothing; toothwork, (tooth-)gearing; indentation; joggling;* ⟨fig⟩ *interlocking* **~z·apfen** vt [h] **1.** *to sell (liquor) by retail* od *on draught; to dispense* ‖ –pft w *to be on tap* | °⟨fig⟩ *to concoct;* (Weisheit etc) *to give out* ‖ es wird heute nichts –pft *you'll get nothing to-day* ‖ ⟨fig⟩ frisch v Faß –pft *straight from the horse's mouth* **2.** ⟨tech⟩ *to mortise, tenon* **~z·appeln** vi [s] & sich ~ *to exhaust o.s. with struggling* od *wriggling* **~z·ärteln** vt [h] *to coddle, pamper, spoil, indulge; to featherbed* | **sich** ~ *to pamper* od *coddle o.s.* | **-lt** *effeminate, spoilt* ‖ –lte P ⟨fam⟩ *molly-coddle* **V.lung** f ~/ *coddling,* etc; *over-indulgence* ‖ (Zustand) *effeminacy* **~z·aubern** vt [h] (behexen) *to bewitch, charm; to enchant* (⟨a. verwandeln: *-ed prince*); **in:** *to turn, transform by magic into* | **-rt** *spellbound* **V.rung** f ~/~en *enchantment* **~z·äunen** vt [h] *to hedge* od *fence in* **V.nung** f *fencing-in,* etc ‖ *fence* **~z·echen** vt [h] ⟨fam⟩ *to spend in boozing* **~z·ehnfachen** vt [h] *to decuple* ‖ *to increase tenfold* (⟨a.⟩ sich ~) **~z·ehnten** vt [h] *to pay tithes of* **≗z·ehr** m ~(e)s/ *consumption of food* | **≗bar** a *consumable* | **≗en** vt [h] *to consume* ⟨a. fig⟩; *to eat (up), to dispose of;* ⟨fam⟩ *to finish off;* ⟨sl⟩ *to demolish* ‖ ⟨fig⟩ *to absorb, sap* ‖ gemütlich ~ *to discuss* | **sich** ~ ⟨fig⟩ (vor) *to be consumed* (vor .. *in anxiety*); *to burn o.s. out, to eat one's heart out, to be eaten up (by), to pine away (with)* | ⟨fig⟩ **-d** *consuming, ardent (passion); consumptive (hate)* | ⟨fig⟩ **-rt** v *eaten up with (passion)* ‖ *consumed, destroyed by (fire); smitten (by love)* ‖ *ravaged (by desire)* **V.rer** m ~s/~ *consumer* **V.rung** f ~/ *consumption* **~z·eichnen** vt [h] **1.** (⟨a.⟩ sich [acc] ~) *to draw badly* od

---

Aussprache: Falls nicht anders (: [*v*]) angegeben, ist v = [*f*] zu sprechen.

incorrectly **2.** (aufzeichnen) *to note* od *write down* | *to list, register* ‖ (amtlich) *to record* ‖ (einzeln) *to specify* ‖ e–n Erfolg z ∼ h *to have a record of achievement*; er kann ∼ *he can show a record* (*of a.t*) | **-net** *figuring* (*on*) *marked* (*on a map*); ⟨st exch⟩ *quoted* ‖ ⟨paint⟩ *distorted* **V.nis** n –nisses/–nisse *list* (*of names*, etc), ⟨mil⟩ *muster--roll* ‖ (amtliches) *register*; (Tabelle) *schedule* | ⟨mst com⟩ *specification, catalogue* ‖ ⟨com⟩ (Lieferungs≗ & ⟨cust⟩) *invoice*; (Preis≗) *list of prices* | (v Möbeln) *inventory* | (Steuer≗) *roll* | ⟨Lit⟩ *table* (*of contents*), (alphab.) *index*; *dictionary* **V.nung** f ∼/∼en **1.** *bad drawing, misdrawing, mistake* ‖ ⟨phot, etc⟩ *distortion*; (*lens*) *aberration* **2.** *noting-down* | **∼s-** ≗frei [a] ⟨opt, phot⟩ *nondistorting* (*lens*) **∼z·eigen** vt [h] Sw = anzeigen **∼z·eihen** vt irr [h] *to pardon, forgive* (e–m etw *a p a th*) ‖ *to pass over* (*a p's fault*) ‖ *to overlook* (*mistake, offence, -se*) ‖ ⟨ec⟩ *to remit* (*sins*) | (entschuldigen) *to excuse* ‖ ∼ Sie! *I beg your pardon*!, ⟨fam⟩ (*so*) *sorry*!, ⟨Am mst⟩ *excuse me*; .. 1000mal [unlogisch!] *a thousand pardons*! ‖ (nicht) z ∼ (*un*)*pardonable*, (*in*)*excusable* ‖ das soll dir –ziehen s *you shall be forgiven that* ‖ ihm ist –ziehen *he is forgiven* ‖ ∼ Sie! *you won't mind, will you*? | **sich** [dat] (etw) nicht ∼ können *not to be able to forgive o.s. for* .. | **∼d** *charitable*; ∼es Wesen *forgiving nature*; *ch.ness* **∼z·eihlich** a *pardonable* ‖ *venial* (*sin*) ‖ *excusable* | ≗keit [f] ∼/ *pardonableness*, etc ‖ *veniality* **≗z·eihung** f ∼/ *pardon, forgiveness* ‖ ⟨ec⟩ *remission* (*of sins*) ‖ (ich bitte um) ∼! *I beg your pardon*; ⟨Am⟩ *beg pardon* ‖ ⟨fam⟩ (*I'm*) *sorry*! ‖ ich bitte 1000mal um ∼! *a thousand pardons*! **∼z·erren** vt [h] *to distort, twist* ‖ den Mund ∼ *to make a wry m.* ‖ etw stark ∼ *to put a th badly out of form* | ∼de Auslegung *violent construction* ⟨fig⟩ | **sich** ∼ *to* (*become*) *distort*(*ed*) | **-rrt** *distorted, wrenched* (*face*); *drawn* (*look*); sie hatte ein –rrtes L. *she had a crooked smile*; [pred] *awry*; –rrt darstellen *to caricature, distort* **≗z·errung** f ∼/∼en *distortion* ⟨a. telph, etc⟩ ‖ (Zerrbild) *caricature* ‖ (des Gesichts) *grimace, twist* ‖ ⟨fig⟩ *warp* | ≗sfrei [a] *d.n-free* **∼z·etteln** vt [h] **1.** *to scatter, disperse* ‖ *to mislay* ‖ (vergeuden) *to waste, squander* | sich ∼ *to* (*get*) *scatter*(*ed*), etc. ‖ *to take an interest in too many ths* ‖ *to dissipate* (*forces*) ⟨a. mil⟩ **2.** *to take notes of* .. *on special slips* **V.lung** f ∼/ *waste* **≗z·icht** (⟨a.⟩ ∼leistung [f]) [m] ∼(e)s/∼e *renunciation, resignation*, ⟨jur⟩ *abandonment, release* ‖ ∼ auf Gewaltanwendung *non-violence* (*treaty*) ‖ ⟨fig⟩ *abstention* (*from*) ‖ ∼ leisten (auf [acc]) *to waive one's claim to, to disclaim* = | ≗**en** vi [h] (auf [acc]) *to renounce* (*a title*), *resign* (*a th*), *to do without* (*a th*); *to divest o.s. of* ..; ⟨fam⟩ *to pass* .. *up* ‖ *to forego* (*a pleasure, major effects*) ‖ *he could never refuse to have fun* | ⟨jur⟩ *to abandon*; *to give up* (*a claim to*); *to waive* (*a right, a claim*) ‖ auf Handlung ∼ *to dispense with action* ‖ ⟨iron⟩ ich verzichte! *thank you for nothing*! ⟨Am⟩ *I'm not taking any* ‖ auf (etw) ∼ müssen *to go without* od *to deny o.s.*; auf .. kann –tet w *can be dispensed with* | **-erklärung** f *letter of renunciation* **-politik** f *policy* od *politics of renunciation* od *resignment*; ⟨a.⟩ *appeasement* **-politiker** m *r.tion politician* **∼z·ieh(en)** 1. & 3. sg pret (pp) v verzeihen **∼z·iehen I.** vi **1.** [h] (verweilen) (P) *to delay, tarry, stay*; (sich hinziehen) (S) (⟨a.⟩ sich ∼) *to drag on* **2.** [s] (aus e–r Wohnung) *to move* (*into town*), *to remove from* .. *to* .. ‖ wenn verzogen *in case of change of address* **II.** vt [h] *to distort, twist*; *draw* ‖ (Sämlinge) *to prick* ‖ k–e Miene ∼ *not to move a muscle* ‖ den Mund (das Gesicht) [zu e–m Lächeln (Weinen)] ∼ *to draw* od *screw up one's m.* (*f.*) [*with laughter*], (*to make a little face*) [*to smile wryly, to put on a forced smile* (*to laugh on the wrong side of one's mouth*)]; .. verächtlich *to make one's face scournful* ‖ sich [dat] e–e Sehne ∼ *to strain a sinew* | ⟨min⟩ *to measure* (*a mine*) | ⟨fig⟩ (Kinder) *to spoil*; –zogen ⟨bes Am⟩ *non-frustrated* (*child*) | **sich** ∼ °(P) ⟨fam⟩ *to make o.s. scarce*; *to disappear, vanish*; *to slip away*; *to make off*; °–h dich! *be off*! *get away with you*! ‖ (im Brettspiel) *to make a wrong move* | (Dampf etc) *to dissolve* ‖ (Gesicht) *to wrinkle up*; *to work, twist*; *his lips became contorted to a faint smile* ‖ (Geschwür) *to subside* ‖ (Gewitter) *to pass over* ‖ (Holz) *to warp* ‖ (Kleid) *to hang badly, to drag* ‖ (Volksmenge, Wolken) *to disperse*; (Staubwolke) *to settle* **∼z·ieren** vt [h] *to decorate, adorn, ornament*; *to set off* ‖ ⟨tail⟩ *to trim* ‖ *to illustrate* (*a book*) ‖ –rt ⟨mus⟩ *figurate* (*counterpoint*); ⟨typ⟩ *ornamented*; *fancy* [attr]; reich ∼ [allg] *finely wrought* **V.rung** f ∼/ *decoration, adornment, ornamentation* | [konkr] *decoration* ⟨a. cul⟩, *ornament*, ⟨arch⟩ *ornamental work* ‖ ⟨mus⟩ *flourish* ‖ ⟨tail⟩ *trimmings* pl ‖ durchbrochene ∼ *fret* ‖ spiralförmige ∼ *scroll* ‖ °brich dir man k–e ∼ ab *don't be so finnicky*, ⟨sl⟩ *stop putting on the dog* **∼z·immern** vt [h] *to timber* ‖ *to line* (*a mine*), *to repair* (*a ship*) *with timber-work* **∼z·inken 1.** vt [h] *to zinc*(*ify*); *galvanize* **2.** ⟨carp⟩ *to dovetail* | **-kt** *galvanized* (*wire*) | *d.led* **V.ker** m *zinc-worker* **V.kung** f ∼/ *zinkification*; *zinc plating*; *galvanizing* **∼z·innen** vt [h] *to tin*; wieder *to retin* | **-nnt** *tinned, tin--coated* (*sheet-iron*) **V.nner** m *tinker* **V.nnung** f *tinning, tin plating, tin coating* | V.nnkolben [m] *soldering-iron* **∼z·insen** vt [h] *to pay interest on* od *for* ‖ e–e Summe zu 3% ∼ *to pay 3 per cent. on a sum* ‖ mit 3% –st *bearing 3% i.t* | **sich** zu 3% ∼ *to yield* (*pay, bear*) *an i.t of 3%* ‖ es –st sich nicht *it does not pay*, (Kapital) *lies dormant* **∼z·inslich** a *bearing* (etc) *i.t* ‖ ∼ anlegen *to put out at i.t* ‖ ∼e Papiere [n pl] *i.t-bearing securities* pl **≗z·insung** f ∼/∼en *i.t-payment* ‖ (*yielding*, etc) *i.t* **∼z·og(en)** 1. & 3. sg pret (pp) v –ziehen **∼z·ögerlich** a *dilatory* **∼z·ögern** vt [h] *to delay, retard*; *hinder*; *protract*; *procrastinate* | **sich** ∼ *to be protracted* etc, *to delay*; *to hang fire*; (–langsamen) *to decelerate* **V.rung** f ∼/∼en *delay, dalliance*; *retardation, procrastination* ‖ ⟨phys⟩ *negative acceleration* ‖ ⟨physiol⟩ *delay* (*of secretion*) | **∼s-** ∼apparat [m] *air delay gear*; ∼mine [f] *d.ed-action mine*; ∼zünder [m] ⟨mil⟩ *delay-action fuze*; ∼zündung [f] ⟨mot⟩ *late ignition*; Bombe mit ∼ *d.ed-a.n bomb* **∼z·ollbar** a *subject to duty, dutiable, excisable* **∼z·ollen** vt [h] *to pay duty on*; *to take out of bond* ‖ ⟨mar⟩ *to clear* ‖ h Sie etw zu ∼ *have you anything to declare*? | **-llt** a *duty-paid* **V.llung** f ∼/∼en *payment of duty* ‖ ⟨mar⟩ *clearance* **∼z·otteln** vt [h] *to disarrange* **∼z·ucken** vi [s] *to cease throbbing, to die* **∼z·ücken** vt [h] *to ecstasize, enrapture* | **-ckt** a *ecstatic, rapt* (*up, away*) ‖ *in raptures*; *rapturous* | [adv] *ecstatically* **V.cktheit, V.ckung** f *ecstasy, rapture*; *trance*; *transport*; *ravishment* | in ∼ geraten über *to go into raptures over a th*; in ∼ setzen *to entrance*; Gesicht –ckt verziehen *to make a grimace of ecstasy* **∼z·uckern** vt [h] *to sugar* ‖ (Früchte) *to candy* ‖ (Kuchen) *to ice* ‖ ⟨chem, brew⟩ *to saccharify* **≗z·ug** m ∼(e)s/ **1.** ohne ∼ *without delay, at once* ‖ Gefahr im ∼ *impending danger*; es ist Gefahr im ∼ *there is no time to be lost, there is danger ahead* ‖ es duldet k–n ∼ *it must not be delayed* ‖ ⟨jur⟩ im ∼ s *to* (*be in*) *default*; → Schuldner **2.** (P) *spoilt child* **3.** ⟨min⟩ *lining* **4.** ⟨met⟩ *distortion* **5.** ⟨carp, etc⟩ *warpage* | **∼s-** ∼aktien [f pl] *deferred shares*; ∼kosten [pl] ⟨mar⟩ *demurrage*; ∼tage [m pl] *days of grace*; ∼zeit [f] ⟨artill⟩ *dead time*; ∼zinsen [m pl] *interest on arrears, past due i.*; *accrued i.*; ∼zün-

---

Verbal-Flexion der Verben mit der Vorsilbe **ver-** → das jeweilige Simplex

der [m] *delayed fuse* **~z·upfen** vt [h] *to ravel out* (*lint*) °**~zw·atzeln** vi [s] = **~zw·eifeln I.** vi [s] *to* (*be in*) *despair* ‖ ~ an [dat] *to despair* (*of*) ‖ es ist zum ~ *it is enough to drive one mad* ‖ nicht ~! *bear up! never say die!* | **-lt** [a] *in despair; despairing* ‖ *desperate* (*struggle*); ⟨fam⟩ *dreadful* (*business*) ‖ [pred] (*matters are*) *past hope*; er war ganz –lt *his heart sank* ‖ ~e Hoffnung hegen *to hope against hope* ‖ e–e ~e S *a matter of neck or nothing* | [adv] *in a desperate way*, ⟨fam⟩ *terribly, dreadfully* (*dull, difficult*); ⟨vulg⟩ *something* (*impatient*); e–n –lten Schritt tun *to do sth desperate* | [adv] sich ~ bemühen *to go to desperate lengths*; (*to fight*) *like a cornered rat* **II.** es ist z ~ *it makes your heart sink* **V.lung** f ~/ (helle *blank*) *despair* ‖ aus reiner ~ *from sheer desperation, in sheer despair* (*over*) ‖ in heller ~ *with desperation*; in tiefster/höchster ~ *in abject despair* ‖ in ~ geraten *to* (*fall into*) *despair* ‖ (s–e Eltern) zur ~ bringen *to exasperate, to render desperate, to drive to despair* (*to be the d. of one's parents*) ‖ sich der ~ hingeben *to yield to d.* | **~s-** ~kampf [m] *desperate fight*; ~mut [m] *courage of despair*; ~voll [a] *desperate* **~zw·eigen** vt [h] ⟨el⟩ *to derive* | **sich** [h] *to ramify* ⟨a. fig⟩; *to branch out* | **-gt** *branched*; ⟨bot⟩ *ramous* ‖ ⟨fig⟩ *many-threaded* **V.gung** f ~/~en *ramification*; ⟨comp⟩ *branch* | **~s-** ~leitung [f] *branching line*; ~punkt [m] *b.g point* **~zw·ergen** vi [s] *to become dwarfed* od *stunted* **~zw·icken** vt [h] *to prune* (*vines*) ‖ ⟨tech⟩ *to rivet* | **-ckt** a ⟨fig⟩ *complicated, intricate, odd* ‖ *crabbed* (*phraseology*) ‖ (seltsam) *queer* ‖ *awkward* (*business*) ‖ ~e Lage [f] *quandary*; *imbroglio* It **V.theit** f *intricacy* [pl *-cies*]

V·esper [f–] f ~/~n *evening*(*-time*) ‖ ⟨ec⟩ *vespers* pl ‖ ⟨hist⟩ (*Sicilian*) *Vespers* **~bild** n *Our Lady of Pity* od *Sorrows, Virgin of the Seven S.s*; *Mater Dolorosa* L **~brot** n (*afternoon*) *tea* ‖ *supper* **~glocke** f *e.g-bell* **~predigt** f *a.n sermon* **~zeit** f *a.n, e.g-time*; ⟨poet⟩ *eventide* ‖ ⟨ec⟩ *vesper-hour* **v·espern** [f–] vi [h] *to take afternoon tea* od *supper*

Vest·alin [v–] f ~/~nen *Vestal* (*virgin*)

V·este [f–] f ~/~n ⟨obs⟩ = Feste

Vestib·ül [v–] n ~s/~e *vestibule*

Ves·uv [veˈzuːf] m (*Mount*) *Vesuvius*

Veter·an [v–] m ~en/~en *veteran* (*soldier*) ‖ alter ~ *old campaigner* od *warhorse*

Veterin·är [v–] m ~(e)s/~e *veterinary surgeon*; *veterinarian*; ⟨fam abbr⟩ *vet* **~offizier** m *officer in the Royal Army Veterinary Corps*

V·eto [v–] n ~s/~s *veto* ‖ ein ~ ausüben *to wield a v.*; ein ~ einlegen gegen *to v.*; *to put a v. upon*

V·ettel [f–] f ~/~n *old hag, slut, harridan*

Vetter m ~s/~ (*male* od *man* od *boy*) *cousin* ‖ ~n [pl] (*first*) *cousins*; ~n zweiten Grades *second* od *kissing cousins* | ~**lich** a *cousin-like* **v·ettern** vt [h] *to treat as a cousin* ‖ sich ~ *to call each other cousin* ~**gunst** f *nepotism* ~**reise** f; e–e ~ m *to visit one's relations* ~**wirtschaft** f *nepotism*; *protectionism*; *patronage system* | ~**schaft** f ~/ *relationship* ‖ [koll] *cousins* pl

Vettur·in [v–] m ~s/~e *vetturino* [It]

Vex·ier- [v–] **~becher** m *conjuring-cup* **~bild** n *picture-puzzle* ("*find the ..*") **~dose** f *magic box* **~schloß** n *puzzle-lock* **~spiegel** m *distorting mirror* **~spiel** n *puzzle-game* **~stück** n *puzzle* ‖ *trick* **vex·ieren** [v–] vt [h] *to quiz, puzzle* ‖ *to tease*

Vez·ier [veˈziːr] m ~(e)s/~e *vizier*

Viad·ukt [v–] m ~(e)s/~e *viaduct*

Vi·atikum [v–] n [~s/–ka & –ken] **1.** (Reisepfennig) *viaticum* **2.** ⟨rel⟩ *extreme unction*

Aussprache: Falls nicht anders (: [*v*]) angegeben, ist v = [*f*] zu sprechen.

Vibrati·on [v–ts–] f ~/~en *vibration* | **~s-** ~massage [f] *vibro-massage*; ~rinne [f] ⟨separator⟩ *v.n channel*; ~sieb [n] *v.n screen* **vibr·ieren** [v–] vi [h] *to vibrate* ‖ ~d ⟨a.⟩ *vibratory*; *tremulous* (*voice*)

vice versa [ˈviːtsə v–] *vice versa* L **V·ice ..** [f–] = Vize– **Vicomte** [viˈkɔ̃t] m ~s/~s ⟨engl⟩ *Viscount*

Victoria- → Viktoria-

vidim·ieren [v–] vt [h] *to visa, legalize*

Vieh [ˈfiː] n ~(e)s/°Viecher (unvernünftiges Tier) *beast, brute*, ⟨a. fig⟩; Menschen u ~ *men and beasts* | (in Herden) *cattle* [stets pl] ‖ ⟨agr & mil⟩ *live stock* ‖ 5 Stück ~ *5 head of cattle* ‖ z ~ m *to brutalize* **~ausstellung** f *cattle show* **~besitzer** m *owner of c.*, ⟨Am⟩ *cattleman* **~bestand** m *live stock* **~bremse** f ⟨ent⟩ *gad-fly* **~dieb** m *c. stealer*; ⟨Am⟩ *rustler* **~diebstahl** m *c. stealing* ~**d·umm** a *brutish* **~futter** n *stock* od *cattle feed, animal food*; *fodder, provender, forage* **~halter** m *keeper of c.*; *stock farmer, stockman* **~haltung** f *keeping of c.* **~handel** m *c.-trade* **~händler** m *c.-dealer* **~hirt(in** f) m *herds*(*wo*)*man* **~hof** m *c.-yard* **~knecht** m *farmer's man* **~krankheit** f *c. disease* **~magd** f *maid for tending c., dairymaid* **~markt** m *c.-market* ~**mäßig** = viehisch **~mast** f *fattening of c.* ‖ (Futter) *mast* **~mäster** m *c.-fattener* **~pacht** f *lease of c.* **~salz** n *salt for c.* **~schaden** m *loss of c.* ‖ *damage done by c.* **~schwemme** f *watering-place for c., horsepond* **~seuche** f *rinderpest, c.-plague* **~sperre** f *prohibition to import c.* **~stall** m *c.-shed, cowhouse* **~stamm** m *breed of c.* **~stand** m *stock of c., live stock* **~sterben** n *c.-plague* **~steuer** f *c.-tax* **~stück** n ⟨arts⟩ *c.-piece* **~tränke** f = ~schwemme **~treiber** m *drover* **~trieb** m, **~trift** f *pasture-ground* **~wagen** m *c.-truck* ‖ ⟨rail⟩ *c.-van* **~weg** m *pasture* **~weide** f *pasture, pasturage* **~weider** m ⟨Am⟩ *rancher* **~wirtschaft** f = ~zucht; [konkr] *c.-farm*, ⟨Am⟩ *ranch* **~zeug** n *animals* pl **~zoll** m *c.-duty, duty on livestock* **~zucht** f *livestock raising*; *stock-farming, c.-breeding* **~züchter** m *stock farmer, c. breeder* **v·iehisch** [ˈfiː(h)iʃ] a *beastly, brutal, bestial*

viel a & adv [compr: mehr, sup: meist] **A.** *much* ‖ ~e [pl] *many* ‖ ~es, das er schrieb *much that he wrote* ‖ nicht ~es, aber ~ *not many ths but much*; *non multa, sed multum* L | ~ **erleben** *to see a great deal* ‖ es fehlt ~ (daran), daß *much is wanting* (*to*); *it is far from true that* ‖ es hätte nicht ~ gefehlt, so hätte ich *a little more and I would have* ‖ ⟨iron⟩ wer **fragt** ~ danach? *who cares?*; ich frage ~ danach! *what's that to me?*, *I don't care a straw!* ‖ wer ~ fragt, kriegt ~ Antwort *ask no questions and you'll be told no lies* ‖ ~ gelesen h *to be widely read* ‖ ~e sagen *many* (*people*) *say* ‖ und das will ~ sagen *which is saying a good deal* | wenn es (sehr) ~ **ist** *at the most* ‖ es ist nicht ~ damit los *it's not much of* (*a place*, etc) ‖ wo ~ ist, kommt mehr dazu *money breads m.* ‖ ~ wagen *to take risks of considerable magnitude* **B. in ~em** *in many respects* ‖ **mit ~em** nicht einverstanden *not agreeing with a great many ths* ‖ **um ~es** *by far* (*easier*), *ever so much* (*better*) **C.** ~ **besser** *much better* ‖ *I looked much the more foolish* ‖ ~ eher (*they would*) *far rather* (*believe*) ‖ ~ lieber ⟨fam⟩ *a sight sooner* ‖ ~ mehr als *much* (od *a great deal*) *more than* **D.** ~ **Ärger** *no end of trouble* ‖ sehr ~e Dinge *a hundred ths* ‖ durch ~en Fleiß *by dint of great industry* ‖ sehr ~ **Geld** *a mint* (od *a great deal*) *of m.* ‖ das ~e Geld *the amount of m.* ‖ trotz s–s ~en Geldes *with all his m., in spite of all his riches* ‖ s–e ~en Geschäfte *his numerous affairs* ‖ die ~en **Male** *the number of times* ‖ so ~e Male wie nötig *as often as required* ‖ (sehr) ~e Menschen *a* (*very*) *large number of people* ‖ die ~en Menschen, welche *the great number of persons who* ‖ ~(e) tausend (..) *many thousands* (*of*) ‖

enorm ~ Zeit ⟨fam⟩ *a whale of time* **E.** ein **bißchen** ~, ein wenig ~, etw ~ *rather too much* || ebenso *or* gleich ~ (*just*) *as much* || **gar** ~ *a great deal* || gleich ~ h *to have the same* (*amount*) || möglichst ~ aus sich m *to make the best of o.s.* || nicht ~ *not much, hardly any* || recht *or* **sehr** ~(e) *very much* ([⟨a.⟩ *a great*] *many*), *plenty of, a great deal* [⟨fam⟩ *a power* od *sight*] *of, a world* (*she did a w. for him*) || sehr ~ halten v ⟨fam⟩ *to think the world of* || ich verstehe nicht gerade sehr ~ v *I don't know the first th about* (*cooking*) || **so** ~ *as much* || so ~ wie *as good as* || → so || noch einmal so ~ *as much again* || → unendlich || **wie~** er auch gelernt h mag *however great may be his learning* || wie~(e) Kinder er auch h mag *however many children he may have* || ziemlich ~(e) *pretty much, a good deal* [*of*], (*a good many*; *quite a few*) || **v·iele** [abs] *many people*; e–r v ~n *one among many*; das ist **zu** ~ ⟨a.⟩ *that is going too far* || zu ~ des Guten *too much of a good thing* **F.** ~ **zu** gut *far too good* || ~ zu ~e *many too many* || es ist ~ z tun, *there is much work to do* || zu ~ zu tun h mit *to be too busy with* **~ährig** a *many-eared*, ⟨scient⟩ *polystachyous* **~armig** a *m.-armed* **≗arten** f pl *manifold forms* **~artig** a *multifarious, various, manifold* **~äugig** a *many-eyed* **~bändig** a *of m. volumes* **~bedeutend** a *significant* || *having m. significations* **~beschäftigt** a *very busy* || ~er Arzt, Advokat *doctor, lawyer* (*in large practice* od) *much sought after* **~besprochen** a *much talked of* **~bestaunt** a *very noticeable*; *the subject of admiring glances*, etc **~besucht** a *greatly frequented* **~besungen** a *oft celebrated* **~betreten** a *well-beaten* (*path*) **≗decker** m ⟨aero⟩ *multiplane* **~deutig** a *having many meanings, ambiguous*; (zweideutig) *equivocal* | ≗keit [f] *ambiguity* **≗eck** n ⟨geom⟩ *polygon* **~eckig** a *polygonal* **≗ehe** f *polygamy* **~ehig** a *polygamous* **~erfahren** a *much experienced* **≗esser** m *glutton* | ~ei [f] *gluttony* **~fach, ~fältig** a *manifold, multifarious*; ein –facher M. *manytimes a millionaire* **~fach** [adv] *frequently, often*; .. w ~ zitiert *his utterances are widely quoted* | das ≗e *the multiple*; um ein ≗es *many times*; ≗umschalter [m] ⟨telph⟩ *multiple switch* **~fältig** a 1. = –fach; 2. abundant | ≗keit [f], **≗falt** f *manifoldness, multifariousness, multiplicity, variety, diversity* **~farbig** a *many-coloured, variegated* | ≗keit [f] *variegation, variety of colours* **≗flach** n *polyhedron* **~flächig** a *polyhedrous* **≗fraß** m *glutton, stodger* || ⟨zoo⟩ *glutton*; *wolverine, -rene* **~fräßig** a *gluttonous* **≗fuß** m *multipede, polypod* **~füßig** a *polypod, having many feet* **~gattig** a ⟨bot⟩ *polyandric* **~geliebt** a *dearly* (od *well-*)*beloved* **~genannt** a *often mentioned* || (berühmt) *famous* **~gepriesen** a *much boasted* (*of*), *much vaunted* **~geprüft** a *much tried* **~gereist** a *travelled* **~gerühmt** a *much praised* **~geschäftig** a *much occupied* || ~er Mensch ⟨iron⟩ *busybody* | ~keit [f] *over-, hyperactivity* **~geschmäht** a *much abused* **~geschossig** a *multifloored, many-storeyed* **~gestaltig** a *polymorphic, -morphous, multiform*; *protean* || ⟨fig⟩ *complex, multifarious*; *serrate*(*d*) (*roof*) **~gliedrig** a *with* (od *composed of*) *many members* || ⟨zoo⟩ *many-jointed* || ⟨math⟩ *polynomial*; ~e Größe *polynome* **≗götterei** f *polytheism* **~gradig** a *of many degrees* **~griffelig** a ⟨bot⟩ *polystylous* **~händig** a *many-handed* **≗herrschaft** f *polyarchy* **~hufig** a *multungulate* **~jährig** a (*friendship*) *of many years' standing, very old* (*friend*), *of many years, many years old, many years'* (*experience*) **~köpfig** a *manyheaded* || ⟨fig⟩ *large* (*crowd*) **≗liebchen** n 1. ⟨eig⟩ *darling* 2. ⟨fig⟩ *philippina, philopena* || guten Morgen ~! *bon jour, ph.*! || ein ~ essen *to eat a ph.* **~mal** adv *many times, frequently* **~malig** a *often repeated* **~mals** = –mal || ich danke Ihnen ~ *many thanks*, (*thank you*) *so much* || entschuldigen Sie ~ (falsch statt: ich bitte Sie ~ um Entschuldigung) *a thousand pardons* **≗männer·ei** f *polyandry* **~männig** a ⟨bot⟩ *polyandrous* **~m·ehr** [adv] *rather*; es ist nicht so sehr wissenschaftlich als ~ impressionistisch *it is not so much sc. but rather impr.* **~motorig** a ⟨aero⟩ *multi-engined* **~namig** a *polyonymous* **~polig** a ⟨el⟩ *multipolar* **≗radantrieb** m ⟨mot⟩ *multiple-wheel drive* **≗rederei** f *logomania, overtalkativeness* **~reihig** a *in many rows*, ⟨scient⟩ *multiserial* **~sagend** a (*highly, most*) *significant, telling*; *suggestive, expressive*; *comprehensive*; *full of meaning*; *descriptive* (*name*) **~saitig** a *many-stringed* **~samig** a ⟨bot⟩ *polyspermous* **~säulig** a *many-columned, polystyle* **~schichtig** a *laminated*; ⟨soc⟩ *the many strata* od *levels of* **≗schreiber** m *prolific writer*; *penny-a-liner, writer of pot-boilers*; ⟨dero⟩ *scribbler* | ~ei [f] *prolificalness, quill-driving*; (*endless*) *scribbling* **~seitig** a ⟨geom⟩ *multilateral*; ~er Körper *polyhedron* | ⟨fig⟩ *extensive* (*knowledge*) || *complex* (*sentence* ⟨gram⟩); *extended* (*facilities*); (*food*) *of a good variety* || (P) *of varied talents, versatile, many-sided*; ~ gebildet *versatile, cultivated, all-round* | ≗keit [f] *manifoldness*; *many-sidedness, versatility* ⟨a. tech⟩; *broad culture* **~silbig** a *polysyllabic*; ~es Wort *polysyllable* | ≗keit [f] *polysyllabism* **~sprachig** a *many-languaged*; *in many languages, of many tongues*; *polyglot* (*bible*) **~stimmig** a *of many voices, many-voiced* || ⟨mus⟩ *polyphonic* || ~er Gesang [m] *partsinging* | ≗keit [f] *polyphony* **~stufenrakete** f *multi-stage rocket* **≗tätigkeit** f *many-sided activity* **~t·ausendmal** adv *a thousand times* **~teilig** a ⟨bot⟩ *multipartite*; ⟨math⟩ *multinominal* **≗tuer** m *busybody* | ~ei [f] *fussiness, officiousness* **~umfassend** a *extensive, vast, comprehensive* **~umstritten** a *much discussed, vexed* (*question*) **~umworben** a *much wooed*; *eagerly competed for* **~verheißend** a *very promising* od *of great promise, hopeful* **~vermögend** a *powerful, influential* **~versprechend** a *promising, auspicious*; *rich in promise*; ~e P ⟨fam⟩ *comer*; *up and coming* [attr] **≗weiber·ei** f *polygamy* (dazu: *-mist*) **~weibig** a ⟨bot⟩ *polygynous* **~wink(e)lig** a ⟨geom⟩ *many-angled, polygonal* **≗wissen** n *extensive knowledge*; *great learning* | ≗d [a] *learned* **≗wisser** m *man of great learning*; ⟨hum⟩ *pundit*; ⟨dero⟩ *smatterer, walking dictionary, sciolist* | ≗·ei [f] ⟨dero⟩ *smattering of many ths, sciolism* **≗zahl** f *multitude*; *great number* (*of*); *scores* (*of*) | ~werksmaschine [f] ⟨comp⟩ *multiple-total machine* **~züngig** a *many-tongued*; ⟨fig⟩ = –sprachig **~zweck-** *multiple-purpose* (*house*)

v·ielerlei a *of many kinds, different, various, multifarious* || *many* (*are the dangers*) || [abs] *a lot* od *a variety of things* || ~ u nichts Wertvolles *odds and ends* || aus ~ Gründen *for many ths* | ~ zugleich vorhaben *to have many irons in the fire* **V·ielheit** f ~/ *multitude, great quantity* || *plurality* || *multiplicity* **viell·eicht** adv *perhaps, possibly*; ⟨bes Am⟩ *maybe* (*a little darker m.*; *he had been told m. that*; *the fault is m. his, I'll m. get used to it*) | *perchance, peradventure* | ~! *I wonder*! | ⟨oft iron⟩ (*is your name B.*) *by any chance* | Sie h ~ recht *you may be right*; ⟨so:⟩ *effects which I may be possessed of* || er hätte es ~ nicht getan *he mightn't have done it* || wenn es ~ regnen sollte *should it happen to rain*; ⟨so:⟩ *should he chance to come* || ~ erzählen Sie mir *suppose you tell me* | ~ bringen Sie ihn doch herein *you had better show him in* || ~ wäre es doch besser *not that it mightn't be better* | ⟨hum fam⟩ das war ~ 'ne Kolonne! *they were a nice lot*!; das w·ar ~ in Ordnung! *that was a bit of all right*!

Verbal-Flexion der Verben mit der Vorsilbe **ver-** → das jeweilige Simplex

Vier f ~/~en *number* od *figure four* || ⟨cards⟩ *four* **vier** a (⟨fam⟩ [abs] ⟨a.⟩ ~e) *four*; → acht **A.** je ~ u ~ *by fours* || ~undzwanzig *twenty-four*, * *four-and-tw.* || wir sind unser ~ → zu ~en | alle ≈e v sich strecken *to lie sprawling*, ⟨fig⟩ *to expire* || ~e lang (= mit 4 Pferden) fahren *to drive four-in-hand* **B.** die „~ Buchstaben" (Pop·o) *the btm* (= bottom) || ⟨her⟩ in ~ Felder teilen *to quarter* || ~ Wochen *a month* **C. auf** allen ≈en (*to go*) *on all-fours* || in s–n ~ Pfählen *at home* || **um** halb ~ *at half past three* || **unter** ~ → Augen || wir sind **zu** ≈en *we are 4, there are 4 of us* || ⟨ten⟩ zu ≈en *fourhanded* (*game*) || zu ≈en abmarschieren! *form fours*! || ⟨bot⟩ zu je ~en vorhanden *quaternary* **Vier-** ≈**beinig** a *four--legged* **~blatt** n ⟨bot⟩ *quadrifolium*; *four-leaved trefoil* || ⟨arch⟩ = –paß || ⟨carp⟩ *quarter* || ⟨fig⟩ *quartette* (*of friends*) || ⟨cards Ger⟩ *hand* bzw *sequence of four* (*cards*) ≈**blätt(e)rig** a ⟨bot⟩ *four--leaved* || ⟨scient⟩ *tetrapetalous* (*flower*) **~bund** m *quadruple alliance* **~decker** m ⟨aero⟩ *quadruplane* **~draht** m ⟨tail⟩ *linsey-woolsey* **~eck** n *quadrangle*, *quadrilateral* [s] || *square* ⟨a. mil⟩ || rechtwinkliges ~ *rectangle, oblong* || verschobenes ~ *rhomb* ≈**eckig** a *quadrangular, square* || ~ m *to square* || ~er (Hals-)Ausschnitt m ⟨tail⟩ *square neckline* ≈**fach,** ≈**fältig** a *fourfold* [a. adv], *quadruple* **~f·arbendruck** m *four-colour printing* **~f·elderwirtschaft** f ⟨agr⟩ *four-course system* **~flach** n *tetrahedron* ≈**flächig** a *tetrahedral* **~fürst** m *tetrarch* | ~entum [n] *tetrarchy, tetrarchate* ≈**füßig** a *four-footed, quadruped* || ~er Vers *tetrameter* || ~es Tier [n] = **~füß(l)er** m *quadruped* ≈**gängig** a *quadruple-threaded* (*screw*) **~gespann** n *four-in-hand, carriage-and-four*; ⟨hist⟩ *quadriga* ≈**gestrichen** a *four-tailed* (*note*); ~es F *F in altissimo* **~gleisig** a *with 4 rails* ≈**gliedrig** a *four-membered*; ⟨cryst⟩ *tetragonal*; ⟨math⟩ *quadrinomial*; ⟨Am mil⟩ *square* (*division*) **~händer** m *quadrumane* [pl *-na*] ≈**händig** a *quadrumanous* || ⟨mus⟩ *four-handed* (*piece*) || ~ spielen *to play duets* od *with 4 hands* **~heber** m ⟨pros⟩ *tetrameter* **~herrscher** m *tetrach* **~herrschaft** f *tetrarchy* ≈**hundert** [a] *four hundred* **~h·undertstel** n *four-hundredth* **~j·ahresplan** m *four-year plan* ≈**jährig** a *four years old, quadrennial* || *four-year-old* (*child*) ≈**jährlich** [a] *every 4 years*, *quadrennial* **~kant** n *square* | ~eisen [n] *square iron*; ~knopf [m] ⟨tech⟩ *sq. head*; ~scheibe [f] *sq. washer*; ~schraube [f] *sq. h. bolt* ≈**kantig** [a] *square, four-cornered* **~kursfunkfeuer** n *radio range* **~l·ande** n pl (Landschaft bei Hamburg) ≈**lappig** a *quadrilobated, four-lobed* **~mächte-** *quadripartite* (Besatzung) ≈**mal** [adv] *four times* ≈**malig** [a] *four times repeated* ≈**männig** a ⟨bot⟩ *tetrandrous* ≈**monatig** a *of four months' duration* ≈**motorig** a *four-engined*; ~er Bomber *flying fortress* **~paß** m ⟨arch⟩ *quatrefoil* **~pfünder** m ⟨artill⟩ *four-pounder* ≈**pfündig** a *weighing four pounds* **~plätzer** m ~s/~ Sw = –sitzer **~rad** n *quadricycle* | ~antriebwagen [m] ⟨mot⟩ *four-wheel drive tractor*; ⟨fam⟩ *four-by--four*; *quad*; ~bremse [f] ⟨mot⟩ *f.-w. brake* ≈**räd(e)rig** a *f.-w.ed* || ~er Wagen *f.-w.er* **~r·öhrenapparat** m ⟨wir⟩ *f.-valve set* ≈**rud(e)rig** a ⟨mar⟩ *f.-oared* || ~es Schiff [n] ⟨hist⟩ *quadrireme* ≈**saitig** a *f.-stringed* || ⟨hist⟩ ~e Leier *tetrachord* ≈**samig** a *tetraspermous* ≈**schrötig** a *square--built, robust, thick-set*; *compact-looking*; ⟨fam⟩ *strapping* || ~er Kerl, ~es Frauenzimmer ⟨fam⟩ *strapper* ≈**seitig** a ⟨geom⟩ *quadrilateral, f.-sided* ≈**silbig** a ⟨gram⟩ *quadrisyllabic, of four syllables* || ⟨scient⟩ *tetrasyllabic* || ~es Wort [n] *quadrisyllable* **~sitzer** m ⟨bes mot⟩ *f.-seater* ≈**sitzig** a *with f. seats* **~spänner** m *f.-in-hand, carriage and f.* ≈**spännig** a *drawn by f. horses* || ~ fahren *to drive* (*in a carriage and f.* od) *f.-in-hand* ≈**spitzig** a *f.-cusped* ≈**spurig** a *f.-lane* (Autobahn) ≈**stellig** a *f.-figure* ≈**stimmig** a ⟨mus⟩ *in f. parts* || ~es Stück *quartette, f.-part song* ≈**stöckig** a *f. stories high, five-storeyed* (*house*) → Stock ≈**stündig** a *of f. hours' duration* || ⟨univ⟩ (*lecture*) *given 4 times a week* ≈**stündlich** a *once every 4 hours* ≈**tägig** a *every four days* || ⟨med⟩ (Dauer) *of four days' duration*; *quartan* (*fever*) **~takt-** ~motor [m] *f.-cycle* od *f.-stroke motor* od *engine*; ~system [n] *f.-st. cycle* **~teil** = Viertel ≈**teilen** vt [h] *to divide into f. parts* || (bes Verbrecher) *to quarter* ≈**teilig** a ⟨bot⟩ *quadripartite* || ⟨her⟩ *quartered* || ⟨math⟩ *quadrinomial* **~teilung** f *quatering* **~unds·echzig-** ~erformat [n] ⟨typ⟩ *sixtyfour-mo* (abbr *64mo*); ~stel [n] *sixty-fourth* (*part*) || ~note [f] *hemidemi-semiquaver*, ⟨Am⟩ 1/64 *note* **~v·ierteltakt** m ⟨mus⟩ *common time* **~w·aldstätter See** m *Lake of Lucerne* ≈**weibig** a ⟨bot⟩ *tetragynous* **~weghahn** m ⟨tech⟩ *f. way cock* **~wertig** a ⟨chem⟩ ~ s *to have 4 bonds* ≈**wink(e)lig** a ⟨geom⟩ *quadrangular* **~zahl** f *quaternary number* ≈**zählig** a ⟨bot⟩ *quaternary* ≈**zehig** a *f.-toed* ≈**zehn** a *fourteen* || ~ Tage *a fortnight*; ⟨Am⟩ *two weeks* || alle ~ Tage *every f.t* || heute in ~ Tagen *this day f.* || heute vor ~ Tagen *a f. ago* || ~ Uhr *2 o'clock p. m.* ≈**zehnte** a *fourteenth* || Ludwig XIV. (= der V.e) *Louis XIV* (= *the F.th*) || Datum → dritte **~zehnjährige(r)** m *fourteen-year-old* [pl .. *-olds*] ≈**zehntägig** a *fortnightly*; *fortnight's* (*holiday*) ≈**zeilig** a *of four lines* || ~e Strophe *quatrain* ≈**zinkig** a *with four points* | **v·ieren** vt [h] *to quarter* **V·ierer** m ~s/~ = Vier || *wine of the year* (19)04 || (Ruderboot) *four* [pl ~s] || *soldier of the fourth regiment* || ⟨a.⟩ **~spiel** ⟨golf⟩ *foursome*; ⟨cards⟩ *quadrille* **~zug** m *four-in-hand* **v·iererlei** a (vgl dreierlei) **V·ierling** m ~/~e; [pl] *quadruplets, four children* (etc) *at a birth* || [sg] ⟨anti-aero⟩ *pompom* | **~s-** *quadruple*; ~-MG [n] *qu. machine gun*; ~turm [m] ⟨mar⟩ *qu. turret* **viert** adv; wir sind zu ~ *we are 4, there are 4 of us* **v·ierte** a *fourth* || Heinrich IV. (= der Vierte) *H. IV* (= *the F.*) || ~s Kapitel *f. ch., ch. the f.* || der ~ (den, am ~n) Mai (*on*) *the f. of May, May the f.*; (im Brief) *May 4th*, ⟨oft⟩ *4 May* **v·iertehalb** a *three and a half* **V·iertel** **I.** n ~s/~ *fourth* (*part*) || (von Maßen; ~dollar, Mond≈, ⟨cul⟩ [v T]) *quarter* || (Stadt≈) *ward*, *q.r, district*; Fabrik–, Geschäfts–, Wohn≈ *industrial, trading, housing estate* || das ärmere (Stadt-) ~ ⟨a.⟩ *the seamy side* | (~stunde) *q.r of an hour* || akademisches ~ ⟨univ Ger⟩ *15 minutes grace* || ein ~ (auf) fünf *a q.r past four* || drei ~ fünf *a q.r to five* || um ~ vor eins *at a q.r to* (⟨Am⟩ *of*) *one* || es ist noch kein ~ *it is not the q.r yet* || es hat ~ geschlagen *it has struck the* (*first*) *q.r* | erstes [letztes] ~ (des Mondes) *prime, first q.r* [*wane*] (*of the moon*) || der Mond ist im vorletzten ~ *the m. is gibbous* | ich war 3/4 im Schlaf *I was three parts asleep* || mit e–m ~ der Verluste *with one q.r the losses* **II.** [a] e–e ≈ Elle *one* od *a q.r of a yard* **~bogen** m *q.r of a sheet* **~drehung** f *q.r turn* **~faß** n *q.r-cask*, etc, (Butter) *firkin* **~hundert** n *twenty-five* **~jahr** n *q.r*; *three months* | ~(es)-ziffer [f] *q.rly rate*; ~h·undert [n] *q.r of a century*; v≈ig [a] *of three months*; *q.rly*; v≈lich [a] [adv] *q.rly, by the q.r, every three months*; ~schrift [f] *q.rly* (*review*, etc); ~gehalt [n] *q.r's salary*; ~geld [n] *q.rly allowance* od *pay* **~kreis** m ⟨geom⟩ *quadrant* **~m·eile** f *q.r of a mile* **~morgen** m *rood* (= 10,117 Ar) **~n·ote** f ⟨mus⟩ *crotched*, ⟨Am⟩ 1/4 note **~p·ause** f ⟨mus⟩ *crotchet--rest*; ⟨Am⟩ 1/4 *rest* **~pf·und** n *q.r of a pound* ≈**pf·ündig** a *weighing a q.r of a p.* **~schwenkung** f *q.r-wheel* **~stab** m ⟨arch, etc⟩ *q.r-round* **~st·unde** f *q.r of an hour*('*s walk* od *drive*); ⟨Am fam⟩ *q.r h.*; e–e ganze ~ *for the whole q.r of an h.*; in 5 ~n

---

Aussprache: Falls nicht anders (: [*v*]) angegeben, ist v = [*f*] zu sprechen.

in one h. and a q.r **~st·ündchen** n (Schlaf) °er hält sein ~ *he takes an easy* **⁓st·ündig** a *of a q.r of an h.* **⁓st·ündlich** [adv] *every q.r of an h.* **~takt** m *f.th of a bar* **~ton** m ⟨mus⟩ *q.r-tone, f.th* **~t·onne** f *q.r of a ton* **~triolen** f pl ⟨mus⟩ *crotchet triplets* **~wendung** f ⟨mil⟩ *q.r-wheel* **~z·entner** m *q.r of a hundredweight* **v·iertens** [adv] *fourthly, in the fourth place* **V·ierung** f ~/~en **1.** *squaring* || *quadrature (of the circle)* **2.** ⟨ec arch⟩ *intersection, crossing* | **~s-** ~turm [m] *lantern-tower*; ~kuppel [f] *central cupola* **V·ierzeiler** m ~s/~ → *quatrain*; → *quartet* **v·ierzig** a *forty* || etwa ~ Jahre alt *fortyish*; über ~ .. *on the wrong* od *shady side of forty* || → dreißig || bald ~ .. *getting on toward forty* | ~jährig [a] *forty years old*; **~tägig** [a] *lasting forty days*; ~e Fastenzeit *Lent* **V.ger(in** f) m ~s/~ *man* (f *woman*) *of forty* || → Vierer || in den **V.gern** (Zeit & Alter) *in the forties* pl **v·ierzigste** a *fortieth* || ⁓l, ~ns vgl Viertel etc | **40-Stundenwoche** f *forty-hour week*

V·ietn·am [vi:et–] n (in Hinterindien) *Viet Nam*; → Annam **Vietnam·ese** m –n/–n *Vietnamese*

vif [vi:f] a *lively, brisk*; *bright*

vigil·ant [v–] a *watchful, vigilant* || *up and coming* **Vig·ilie** [v–] f ~/~n **1.** ⟨ec⟩ *vigil, eve* || ~n [pl] *vigils* pl **2.** ⟨ant⟩ *watch*

Vignette [vin'jetə] f ~/~n ⟨typ, phot⟩ *vignette*; ⟨typ a.⟩ *(printer's) flower*; *ornament*

Vigognewolle [vi'gɔnjə–] f ⟨com⟩ *vicugna*

Vik·ar m [v–] ~(e)s/~e *curate* || *substitute* od *locum tenens (of a prelate)* | **~i·at** n ~(e)s/~e *curacy* || *temporary employment* od *office* | **⁓i·ieren** vi [h] *to act as a curate* od *vicariously*

V·iktor-V·iktor! ⟨aero⟩ (Verstanden!) *Roger*!

Vikt·oria [v–] f **1.** ~ rufen *to shout victory* || ~ schießen *to fire salute for victory* **2.** (Wagen) *victoria* | v.·anisch [a] *Victorian* | ~fälle [m pl] (des Sambesi) *Victoria Falls*; ~land [n] (am Südpol) *Victorialand*; ~see [m] (in S.-Afrika) *Lake Victoria*

Viktu·alien [v–] n [pl] *victuals, provisions* || ~händler [m] *provision-dealer, purveyor*; ~laden [m] *grocery store*; ~markt [m] *foodstuff market* (z. B. in München)

V·illa f [v–] ~/–llen *villa, country-house* || (halb) freistehende ~ *(semi-)detached v.* **Villegiat·ur** [v–] f ~/ *stay in the c.*; *ruralizing* **V·illen-** [v–] **~kolonie** f *garden-city* **~viertel** n *residential district*

Vindikati·onsklage [v–] f *action of detinue*; *replevin* **-diz·ieren** vt [h] *to vindicate, claim*

Vi·ola f [v–] ~/–len ⟨mus⟩ *viola* || ⟨hist⟩ *viol* **-le** f ~/~n ⟨bot⟩ *violet* **v.lett I.** a *violet* || (dunkel-)~ *purple* **II.** ⁓ n *violet (colour)* **~blau** a *violet blue* | ⁓farbband [n] ⟨typewr⟩ *purple ribbon*; ~stichig [a] *purplish-blue*

Viol·in- **~bogen** m *(violin-)bow*, ⟨fam⟩ *fiddle-stick* **~kasten** m *v.-case* **~saite** f *v.-* (⟨fam⟩ *fiddle-)string* **~schlüssel** m ⟨mus⟩ *treble-clef* **~schule** f *v.-exercises*; *v.-method* **~spiel** n *playing (on) the v.* **~spieler** m = Violinist **~steg** m *bridge of a v.* **~stimme** f *v.-part* **~virtuose** m, **-sin** f *famous v.ist, masterly performer on the v.* **Viol·ine** [v–] f ~/~n *violin* || die erste ~ spielen *to play the first v.*, ⟨fig⟩ *to play first fiddle* **Violin·ist(in** f) m ~en/~en *v.ist, v.-player* **Violonc·ell(o)** [–tʃ–] n ~s/~e *(violon)cello* | **~·ist** m *cellist*

V·iper [v–] f ~/~n ⟨zoo⟩ *viper, adder*

Virg·inien n (Staat der U.S.A.) *Virginia* **–nische Inseln** f pl (Westindien) *Virgin Islands* pl

Vir·ilstimme [v–] f *single* od *individual vote*

Virologe m –n/–n *virologist*

virtu·ell [v–] a *virtual* **virtu·os** [v–] a *masterly* | [adv] (⟨a.⟩ –senhaft) *in a masterly way* | ⁓, ⁓e m –sen/–sen *virtuoso*, ⟨mst⟩ *great artist* od *master* | **-sentum** n ~s/, **-sit·ät** f ~/ ⟨mst⟩ *mastery, ease, facility, virtuosity*; *artistic perfection*

virul·ent [v–] a ⟨med⟩ *virulent* **V·irus** n ~/–ren (abgeschwächtes *attenuated*) *virus* | ~-forscher [m] *virologist*; ~-Gegen⁓-Methode *or* -Therapie [f] *virus interference*; ~krankheit [f] *v. disease*; ~krieg [m] *v. warfare*; ~kunde [f] *virology*

V·isa n [v–] ~s/~ *visa* °**Vis·age** [vi'za:ʒə] f ~/~n *phiz (a rum ph. = physiognomy)* || ⟨dero sl⟩ *mug*; ⟨Am sl⟩ *map*; *snoot* **Visav·is** [viza'vi:] n ~[–s]/~[–s] *p (sitting* od *living) opposite* **Vis·ier** [v–] n ~(e)s/~e (Helm–, Lese⁓ etc) *visor* || ⟨fig⟩ mit offenem ~ *fearlessly* | (am Gewehr) *aim, (back-)sight* | ⟨opt⟩ *sight* **~ebene** f *plane of direction* **~einrichtung** f *sight(ing device)* **~fernrohr** n *rifle telescope* **~kimme** f *notch of sight* **~klappe** f ⟨mil⟩ *leaf* **~kontrolleinrichtung** f *bore sighting telescope* **~korn** n *aim* **~lineal** n *dioptric rule* **~linie** f *line of sight* || ⟨mar⟩ *bearing* **~loch** n *pin-hole* **~maß** n *gauge* **~scheibe** f ⟨surv⟩ *sliding-vane* **~schieber** m *sight slide* **~stab** m ⟨surv⟩ *rangingpole* || ⟨tech⟩ *gauging-rod* **~stellung** f *adjustment of sight* **~weite** f *sighting range* **~winkel** m *angle of dispart* bzw *of elevation* | **⁓en I.** vt [h] *to aim*; sorgfältig ~ *to take a careful sight* || (Gefäße) *to gauge* || ⟨tech⟩ *to adjust* || (Pässe) *to visa, visé* **II.** vi [h] *to (take) aim* (nach *at*) **V.rer** m ~s/~ *gauger* **V.rung** f ~/ *gauging* || *visaing* **Visi·on** [v–] f ~/~en *vision* | **~·är** m ~s/~e; **⁓·är** a *visionary* [s & a] **Visitati·on** f ~/~en *inspection* || (Durchsuchung) *search, inquiry* | ~srecht [n] *right of search* **Visit·ator** m ~s/–·oren *searcher* || (Zoll⁓) *excise-officer* **Vis·ite** f ~/~n *visit* || kurze ~ *flying visit* || e–e ~ m *to pay a visit* **Vis·iten-** **~karte** f *(visiting-*, ⟨Am⟩ *calling) card* (abgeben *to send in*; hinterlassen *to leave*) ⟨a. fig aero⟩ (Bomben) | ~ntäschchen [n] *card-case* **Visit·ier-** ~eisen [n] ⟨artill⟩ *searcher*; (Zoll⁓) *excise-officer's probe*; ~ronde [f] ⟨mil⟩ *counter--round* | **⁓en** vt [h] *to search* || (besichtigen) *to inspect* **V·ista** f It: a ⁓ *at sight* | ~wechsel [m] *sight-bill* **visu·ell** a *visual* **V·isum** n [~s/–sa & ~s] *visé, visa* || mit ~ versehen *to visé*

visk·os [v–] a *viscous* | **⁓e** f ~/ *viscose (fibre, silk, rayon)*

vit·al [v–] a *vital*; ~e Malerei *action painting* **⁓it·ät** f ~/ *vitality* | **~s-** ~index [m] *vital index* **Vitam·in** n ~s/~e *vitamin(e)*; mit ~en anreichern *to vitaminize* | ~gehalt [m] *v. content*; ⁓haltig [a] *fortified, vitaminized*; ~mangelkrankheit [f] *avitaminosis*; ⁓reich [a] *vitaminized (milk), enriched (bread)*

Vitr·ine [v–] f ~/~n *glass show-case, -window* **Vitri·ol** m & n ~s/~e ⟨chem⟩ *vitriol, copperas* | ~äther [m] *v.(ic) ether*; ~erz [n] *v.ic ore*; ~öl [n] *oil of v.*; ~säure [f] *v.ic acid*; ~siederei [f] *v.-works* pl [a. sg konstr]

v·ivat! [v–v] *long live* ..!, ⟨fam⟩ *three cheers for* ..!, .. *for ever* | ⁓ [n] *cheer* || e–m ein ⁓ bringen *to cheer a p* | **⁓s-** °~nase [f] ⟨dial ['fifat]⟩ ⟨hum⟩ *celestial* **v·ivipar** [vivi–] a *viviparous* | **⁓·ie** f ~/ *viviparity* **Vivisekti·on** [vivi–] f ~/~en *vivisection*

V·ize- [f–] **~admiral** m *vice-admiral* **~f·eldwebel** m *vice-sergeant-major* **~kanzler** m *vice--chancellor* **~könig** m *viceroy* || (für Irland) *Lord Lieutenant* **~königin** f *vicereine* **~königs-** *vice-regal* | **~s-** ~würde [f] *viceroyalty* **~konsul** m *viceconsul* **~präsident** m *vice-president, deputy--chairman* **~statthalter** m *deputy-governor* **~wirt** n *landlord's agent*

Vizin·al- [v–] **~bahn** f ⟨rail⟩ *branch-line* **~straße** f *parish-road*

Vitzlip·utzli m ~s/ [Aztec] ⟨nursery⟩ *bog(e)y*

V·iztum m ~s/ [f–] ⟨ec⟩ *vidame*

Vl·ame [f–] m → Flame

Verbal-Flexion der Verben mit der Vorsilbe **ver-** → das jeweilige Simplex

Vlies [f–] n –es/–e *fleece* | ~stoffe ⟨tex⟩ *nonwovens*

Vl·issingen [f–] n (holl. Hafenstadt) *Flushing*

V·ogel m ~s/⁓̈ **A.** *bird* ‖ (Falke) *falcon* ‖ (Huhn) *fowl* [pl ~*s*] ‖ die Vögel unter dem Himmel *the fowl of the air* | ~ Bülow *golden oriole*, ~ Strauß *ostrich* | männl. ~ *cock* (*bird*); weibl. ~ *hen bird* | (Zielscheibe) *popinjay* **B.** ⟨fig⟩ durchtriebener ~ *sly bird* ‖ **loser,** lockerer ~ *wag*; *sad dog* ‖ lustiger ~ *jolly dog* ‖ gerupfter ~ *one who has been fleeced* ‖ müder ~ ⟨aero sl fig⟩ *lame duck* **C.** ⟨fig⟩ den ~ **abschießen** *to ring the bell*; *to bring home the bacon* ‖ der ~ ist ausgeflogen *the bird has* od *is flown* ‖ beringen *to band* ‖ friß, ~, oder stirb *do* (od *root hog*) *or die* ‖ °e–n ~ h ⟨sl⟩ *to be plumb crazy*, *to have bats in the belfry* od *a bee in one's bonnet* (*about sth*); ⟨Am sl⟩ *to have a cuckoo* ‖ die Vögel, die früh singen, holt die Katze *don't sing till you are out of the wood*; (v Kindern) *early ripe, early rotten* ‖ wie der ~, so das Ei *a wild goose never laid a tame egg* ‖ jeder ~ singt, wie ihm der Schnabel gewachsen *every bird is known by its note* ‖ nur ein schlechter ~ beschmutzt sein eigen Nest *it is an ill bird that fouls its own nest* | **~-** *bird*; *fowling* **~art** f *species of b.* **~bauer** n *b.-cage*; (gr) *aviary* **~beerbaum** m *mountain-ash*; *rowan* **~beere** f *rowan-berry* **~beize** f *hawking* **~beobachter** m *b.-watcher, b.er* | –tung [f] *b.-watching* **~deuter** m *augur* **~dreck** m *b.-droppings* pl **~dünger** m *guano* **~dunst** m *small-shot* **~fang** m *b.-catching, f.g* **~fänger** m *b.-catcher, fowler* **~flinte** f *f.g-piece* **~flöte** f *b.-call* **~flug** m *flight of b.s*; *flyway* **⁓̈frei** a *outlawed, proscribed* ‖ f ~ erklären *to outlaw* ‖ ~ s *to be an outlaw* ‖ ⟨fig⟩ *fair game* **~futter** n *b.-food* ‖ (Samen) *b.-seed* **~garn** n *b.-net* **~gesang** m *song* od *singing of b.s* **~geschrei** n *cry of b.s* **~gezwitscher** n *twittering of b.s* **~händler** m *b.-seller, -fancier* **~haus** n *aviary* **~hecke** f *breeding-cage, aviary* **~herd** m *f.g-floor* **~käfig** m *b.-cage* **~kenner** m *ornithologist* **~kirsche** f *wild* od *b.-cherry* **~klaue** f *b.'s claw* **~knöterich** m *knot-grass* **~koje** f *b. sanctuary* **~kraut** n ⟨bot⟩ *chickweed* **~kunde** f *ornithology* **⁓̈kundig** a *ornithological* **⁓̈leicht** a (*as*) *light as a feather* **~leim** m *b.-lime* **~liebhaber** m *b.-fancier* **~miere** f = –kraut **~mist** m *b.-dung, guano* **~näpfchen** n *seed-box, food-box* **~nest** n *b.'s nest* ⟨a. bot⟩ ‖ [pl] *b.s' nests* **~nesterausnehmen** n *b.'s nesting* **~netz** n *b.-net* **~perspektive** f *b.'s eye view* ‖ Berlin aus der ~ *a b.'s eye view of B.* ‖ aus der ~ entworfener Plan *b.'s-eye sketch* **~pfeife** f *b.-call* **~schau** f = –perspektive **~schauer** m *augur* **~scheuche** f *scare-crow*; ⟨fig⟩ *frump, guy, gorgon* **~schießen** n *shooting at a popinjay* **~schrot** m & n *small-shot* **~schutzgebiet** n = –koje **~spinne** f *b.-(catching) spider* **~stange** f *perch* **~stellen** n *b.-catching* | ⁓̈ vi [h] *to go b.-c.* **~steller** m *b.-catcher, fowler* **~straußpolitik** f → Strauß **~strich** m *passage of b.s* **~wahrsager(ei** f) m *augur(y)* **~warte** f *ornithological station* **~weibchen** n *hen-bird* ‖ (gr) *female* (*b.*) **~weide** f 1. *aviary* 2. = –beize **~welt** f *feathered world* **~wicke** f ⟨bot⟩ *b.s' tares* **~wild** n *feathered game* **~züchter** m *b.-fancier* **~zug** m *migration of b.s of passage* | **⁓̈chen** n ~s/~ *little b.* ‖ ich hab' ein ~ singen hören *a little b. told me* °**v·ögeln** [f–] vt/i [h] ⟨vulg⟩ *to shag, do, jiggle, bounce* | vi (v Mann) *to have bit of jam* **V·ogler** m ~s/~ *fowler*

Vog·esen [v–] pl (⟨a.⟩ Wasgau → d.) *Vosges*

Vogt [f–] m ~(e)s/⁓̈e *overseer* ‖ (Statthalter) *governor*; Sw ⟨a.⟩ = Vormund ‖ ⟨agr⟩ *steward* ‖ (Amtmann) *bailiff, warden* | **~·ei** f ~/~en *prefecture, bailiwick*; *office* (bzw *residence, jurisdiction*) *of a bailiff*, etc **~land** [f–] n *the Saxon Vo(i)gtland*

Vok·abel [v–] f ~/~n *vocable*, ⟨mst⟩ *word* **~buch** n *vocabulary, word-book* **-bul·ar(ium)** [v–] n ~s/–re *vocabulary* **Vok·al** [v–] **I.** m ~(e)s/~e *vowel* ‖ gutturaler (palataler) ~ *back* (*front*) *vowel* **II.** ⁓̈ a *vocal* **~·anlaut** m *initial vowel* **~·auslaut** m *final v.* **~·inlaut** m *intermediate v.* **~musik** f *vocal music* **~schwund** m *falling-off of vowels* **vok·alisch** a *vocalic* | **-is·ieren** **I.** vt *to vocalize* **II.** vi ⟨mus⟩ *to sol-fa* **V.·ismus** m *vocalism, vowel-system* **Vokat·iv** [v–f] m ~(e)s/~e [–və] ⟨gram⟩ *vocative* | **~us** m ~/–ve ⟨fam⟩ *loose fish, sly dog*

V·oland m [f–] ~(e)s/ Junker ~ (Teufel) *the cloven hoof*

Vol·ant [vo'lã] m ~s/~s **1.** ⟨tail⟩ *flounce* **2.** ⟨mot⟩ *steering-wheel* | ~besatz [m] *frillery*; ~schaltung [f] ⟨mot⟩ *st.g-column control*

volens-nolens [v–] L *whether (s)he willed it or not*

Volk n [f–] ~(e)s/⁓̈er **A.** *people* [pl konstr] ‖ (Nation) *nation* | (Kriegs⁓̈) *men, troops* pl; *soldiery* ‖ (Schiffs⁓̈) *crew* | viel ~s *a great multitude of people* | gemeines ~ *common people*; *lower classes*; *rabble, mob, populace* | die breite Masse des ~es *the masses, multitude, million* | die Entscheidung des ~es einholen ⟨parl⟩ *to go to the country* ‖ **aus** dem ~e hervorgegangen *popular*; **beim** ~ (nicht) beliebt (*un*)*popular* ‖ **ins** ~ bringen *to popularize* **B.** ⟨fig⟩ *race* | kl ~ (= Kinder) *little folks* pl, *small-fry* **C.** (T) *troop, herd* | (v Vögeln) *covey, flight*; *skein* (*of wild fowl*) | ⟨hunt⟩ zwei ~ *or* Völker Rebhühner *two coveys of partridges* | *bevy* (*of quails*), *flock* (*of sparrows*) | *swarm* bzw *colony* (*of bees*) **v·olk-** **~arm** a *thinly peopled* **~leer** a *deserted* **~reich** a *populous* **V·ölkchen** n *tribe, clan* ‖ *set* (*of people*) ‖ mein ~ *my little ones* ‖ ein lustig ~ *a merry party* **V·ölker-** **~ball** m ⟨Ger⟩ *kind of ball-game* **~beschreibung** f *ethnography* **~bund** m *League of Nations* | **~s-** ~rat [m] *League Council*; ~statut [n] *Covenant of the L. of N.* **~friede(n)** m *universal peace* **~frühling** m *revival of a nation* (⟨Ger⟩ 1848) **~gemeinschaft** f *community of nations* **~gemisch-** *multinational* (*empire*) **~gewimmel** n *welter of nations* **~krieg** m *international war* **~kunde,** **~lehre** f *ethnology* **~psychologie** f *ethnopsychology* **~recht** n *law of nations*, *international* od *public law*; *jus gentium* L, Delikte geg d. ~ (v Einzelperson) *delicta juris g.* **⁓̈rechtlich** a *international*, *relating to the law of nations* **~schlacht** f *the Battle of Leipsic* (1813) **~stamm** m *race* **~straße** f *highway of nations* **~verkehr** m *international intercourse* **~wanderung** f *migration of* (*the*) *nations, the Barbarian Invasions* pl **V·ölkerschaft** f ~/~en *tribe*; *people*; *nation* **v·ölkisch** a *national*, *popular* ‖ *racial* ‖ *ethnic*(*al*) ‖ ~er Egozentrismus *ethnocentrism* **v·olklich** a *ethnic*(*al*) **V·olks-** **~aberglaube** m *popular superstition* **~abstimmung** f *plebiscite* (*to hold a p.*) **~angelegenheit** f *national affair* **~anwalt** m *people's advocate* od *tribune* **~armee** f: Nationale ~ (NVA) *East German Army* **~aufklärung** f *public enlightenment* **~auflauf** m *crowd*; ⟨jur⟩ *unlawful assembly* **~aufruhr** m *riot* **~aufstand** m *popular rising* **~aufwiegler** m *demagogue, agitator* **~ausdruck** m *popular* od *common expression* **~ausgabe** f *popular* od *omnibus edition* **~ausrottung** f *genocide* **~ballade** f *folk-ballad* **~begehren** n *demand for a plebiscite*; *initiative* **~beschluß** m *plebiscite* **~bewegung** f *popular commotion* od *rising* **~bewußtsein** n *national feeling* **~bibliothek** f *free* od *public library* **~bildung** f *public* od *national instruction*; *education of the masses* **~blatt** n *pop. newspaper* **~brauch** m *national usage*, ⟨Am⟩ *folkway* **~buch** n *book for the people, pop. b., chap-b.* **~charakter** m *national ch.* **~demokratie** f *people's d.* **~deutscher** m *German of foreign citizenship*; *ethnical G.*

Aussprache: Falls nicht anders (: [*v*]) angegeben, ist v = [*f*] zu sprechen.

⟨a.⟩ a **~dichter** m *people's poet, pop.* od *nat. poet* **~dichtung** f *pop.* od *nat. poetry* **~drama** n *folk play* **≃eigen** a ⟨SBZ⟩ *nat.ly owned*; ~er Betrieb *n.o. firm*; *People's Enterprise* | ~tum [n] *n.(ly owned) property* **~empfänger** m ⟨wir⟩ *people's set* **~empfinden** n *instincts of a people*; gesundes ~ *sound public concept* **~entscheid** m *plebiscite, referendum* **~erhebung** f *insurrection, popular rising* **~etymologie** f *pop. et.* **~feind** m *enemy of the people* **~fest** n *pop.* od *public festival* **≃fremd** a *alien to the people* od *race*; *not native*; *foreign* **~freund** m *friend of the people, patriot* **≃freundlich** a *popular* **~front** f ⟨anti-nazi⟩ *pop. front* **~führer** m ⟨dero⟩ *demagogue* **~gasmaske** f *general civilian respirator* **~geist** m *public spirit* od *mind* **~gemeinschaft** f [konkr] *the community* || [abstr] *national unity* **~genosse** m *fellow citizen*; *brother* **~gerichtshof** m ⟨Ger⟩ *the People's Court* **~glaube** m *pop. belief*; ⟨rel⟩ *nat. creed* **~gruppe** f *ethnic group* **~gunst** f *popularity (of the million)* || nach der ~ streben *to play to the gallery* **~gut** n ⟨SBZ⟩ *nat.ly owned farm* **~haufe** m *mob, crowd,* (die große Masse) *populace* **~heer** n *nat. army* **~heim** n (städtisch) *community centre* **~herrschaft** f *democracy* **~hochschule** f *University Extension*; *adult education department* **~hymne** f *national anthem* **~justiz** f *lynch* od *mob law* **~kalender** m *almanac for the million* **~kammer** f ⟨SBZ⟩ *People's Chamber* **~kommissar** m *commissar* **~körper** m *nation* **~krieg** m *nat. war* **~küche** f *public soup-kitchen* **~kunde** f *folk-lore* **~kundler** m *student of f.-l.* **~kunst** f *folk art* **~leben** n *social life of the people* **~lied** n *pop. song, folk-song* **~mann** m *pop. man* **~märchen** n *pop. tale* **≃mäßig** a *popular* **~meinung** f *public opinion* od *feeling* **~melodie** f *pop. air* **~menge** f *multitude, crowd* **~mord** m *genocide* **~mund**; im ~e *popularly* **≃nah** a *popular* **~opfer** n *nat. sacrifice* **~partei** f *people's party* **~polizei** f (VP) *people's police* **~polizist** m (Vopo) *people's policeman* **~recht** n *right of the people* **~redner** m *people's orator, pop. speaker*; (Agitator) *mob* (⟨Am⟩ *stump*) *orator* **~regierung** f *democracy* **~republik** f *people's rep.* (*of Albania*) **~sage** f *nat. legend, folk-tale* **~schädling** m *wrongdoer against the people* **~schicht** f *social stratum, class of population* **~schlag** m *race of people* **~schrift** f *book for the people* **~schriftsteller** m *pop. writer* **~schul-** ~bildung [f] *primary education*; ~lehrer [m] *associate teacher* **~schule** f *elementary* od *primary school* || staatliche ~ *provided school* || ⟨Am⟩ *public* od *grade(d) school* **~schulwesen** n *primary education* **~schwund** m *decline of birthrate* **~seele** f *inner mind of a nation* **~sitte** f *national custom* **~souveränität** f *s. of the people* **~sprache** f *vernacular* od *vulgar tongue* od *speech*; *vernacular*; *demotic language* **≃sprachlich** a ⟨a. fam⟩ *non-U(pper Class)* **~staat** m *republic* **~stamm** m *tribe, race* **~stimme** f *voice of the people* **~stimmung** f *public feeling* od *disposition* **~sturm** m *people in arms* **~tanz** m *folk-dance* **~tracht** f *national costume* od *dress* **~trauertag** m *day of nat. mourning* **~tribun** m *tribune of the people* **≃tümelnd** a *folksy* **≃tümlich** a: ~e Gebräuche etc *folklore* **~überlieferung** f *pop. tradition* od *legend* **~unterhaltung** f *pop. entertainment* **≃verbunden** a *social*; [pred] *closely bound up with one's nation* || ⟨Am fam⟩ *grass-roots* (*movement*) **~verführer** m *demagogue, rabble-rouser* **~vermögen** n *nat. property* **~versammlung** f *pop. assembly, public meeting* **~vertreter** m *representative of the people, deputy* **~vertretung** f *parliamentary representation*; *r.n of the people* || [koll] *representatives* pl **~wagen** m ⟨mot⟩ *people's car* **~wald** m *nat.(ly owned) forest* **~weise** f ⟨mus⟩ *pop. air* **~wirt(schaftler)** m *political economist* **~wirtschaft** f (praktische) *pol. economics* pl **~wirtschaft(s-lehre)** f *pol. economy* **~wohlfahrt** f *nat. welfare*; *nat. social service*; ⟨engl⟩ Minister f ~ *M. of Health* **~zahl** f (*number of the*) *population* **~zählung** f *census* (halten *to take*) **~zeitung** f *people's paper* **V·olkstum** n ~(e)s/ *nationality* || *national individuality* bzw *heritage* od *characteristics* pl **v·olkstümlich** a *national* || (beliebt) *popular* | **≃keit** f ~/ *nationality* || *popularity* || *national trait* || *popular saying*

Verbal-Flexion der Verben mit der Vorsilbe **ver-** → das jeweilige Simplex

voll a **A. 1.** *full*, (*filled*) || des Lobes ~ *f. of praise*; ~ des süßen Weines ⟨fam⟩ *glorious* || ~e U. *maximum assistance* | ~ v → A. 5. **2.** ⟨oft⟩ **~er** [+ s ohne art] *f.* (*of joy, hope, cunning*) | ~(er) Papier liegen *to be littered with p.* **3.** [pred] der Mond ist ~ *we have f. m.*, ⟨a.⟩ *the m. is* (*at the*) *f.* || *the theatre was crowded* **4.** (Räume) *f.* (*of people*), *crammed* (*f.*), *packed*; (über)~ (*over*)*crowded* **5.** ⟨fig⟩ ~ **mit** *or* **von** *laced, loaded, charged,* °*crammed with*; *pregnant, replete, fraught, big, rife with* (*incident, significance,* etc); *thick with* (*leaves, snow,* etc); *well stocked with* (*goods*); z Überlaufen ~ mit/v *brimming with* || ~ s v *to abound with* || (P) *compact of* (*superstition*); *his position is c. with difficulties*; *to be a mass of* (*bruises*); (*atmosphere*) *surcharged with* (*violence*); ⟨emph⟩ *chock-f. of* (*disappointments*) **6. ganz** ~ (Glas etc) *brimful, brimming*; g. ~ s *to brim* || *f.* od *filled to capacity*; es war °dick(e) *or* gestopft ~ *it was cram-f.* || (P) g. ~ s v jdm *to be wrapped up in a p* **7.** ⟨tech⟩ *solid* (*shaft* Welle) **8.** (P) (beleibt) *plump, buxom, corpulent, stout* | (Körperformen) *well filled out, round(ed)* || ~ im Gesicht *f. in the face* **9.** (vollständig) *whole, complete, entire* **10.** (satt) *f.* (*of meat and drink*), *replete*, ⟨fam⟩ *crammed* | (betrunken) [pred] *drunk*; ⟨sl⟩ *glorious, tanked, pickled, plastered, ripe*, ⟨Am⟩ *soused* [pred]; °~ wie e-e Strandhaubitze *drunk as blazes*; °sich [acc] ~ laufen l *to swill o.s. drunk* → D. **B. [attr]** ~e **Anzahl,** ~e Besetzung ⟨a.⟩ *complement* || in ~er Arbeit *f.y occupied, in the midst of work* || (Geldbörse) *well-filled* || aus ~er Brust *at the top of one's voice, heartily* || (Bus etc) ~ (besetzt) *f. up* (*inside*)! || (Busen) *ample, f.* || um ein ~es Drittel herabsetzen *to reduce by fully one third* || in ~em **Ernst** *in dead* od *good e.* || ~e Fahrt *f.-power run* || in ~em Galopp *f. gallop* || vor ~en Häusern spielen ⟨theat⟩ *to play to packed houses* || aus ~em Herzen *from the bottom of one's heart* || ein ~es **Jahr** *a whole y.*; ~e 30 J.(e alt) *quite 30 years* (*old*); ⟨so⟩: *quite ten y.s ago* || ein ~es Jahrhundert (*it is*) *f.y a c. since* || mit ~er Kraft *with full force, with might and main*, ⟨mar⟩ ~e K. voraus! *f. speed ahead*! || in ~em **Maße** *f.y, to the f.* || (Mond) *f.* (vgl A. 3.) || *my just right*; *with perfect r.*; er sagte mit ~em Recht *he was quite right in saying* || im ~en Sinn des Wortes *in the f.est s. of the w.* || unter dem ~en Stand *below establishment* || (Stimme) *f., fruity, round* || (Summe) *entire* || 3 ~e Tage *three clear days* || in ~em Trab *at f. trot* || (Wahrheit) *the f., whole, plain tr.* || (Wein) *fruity* **C. [nach s]** ein **Arm** ~ Holz etc *an armful of wood, a bagful of gold, a glass(ful) of wine* || den Kopf ~(er) Gedanken h *to be f. of thoughts* od *ideas* **D. [a & adv]** für ~ **annehmen** *to accept* (*coins*) *as current* || (P) f ~ ansehen *to treat as a responsible being* || ~ beladen mit *loaded up* (⟨Am⟩ *down*) *with* || ~ beschäftigt *whole-time* [attr] || ~ **besetzt** *packed to the doors*; (Bus, Hotel) (*we are*) *f. up* || ~ bezahlen *to pay in f.* || ~ bezahlte Stelle *f.-time job* || ~ eingezahlt *f.y paid up* || ~ dasein ⟨fam⟩ *to be* (*very much*) *all there* || ~ elektrisch *all e.* || (sich) ~ entfalten *to develop f.y*; ~ –tet *f.-blown*, ⟨so⟩: *f.-grown*; ~ zur E.tung k *to reach f. development* || ~ erfaßbar *f.y understandable* od *comprehensible* ||

sich ~ (fr)essen *to eat one's fill*, ⟨emph⟩ *to gorge o.s. to repletion* || noch nicht für ~ **gelten** *not to be considered grown up yet* || e–r S ~ gerecht w *to do full justice to a th* || ~ gießen, schenken, packen *to fill (up)* || °sich ~ laufen l *to drink one's fill*, → A. || °⟨fig⟩ die Hosen ~ h *to be in a blue funk* || ~ liegen v *to be high with (papers)* || ~m *to fill (up)* || *to make up (the sum)* || die Hosen ~ m *to mess one's breeches* || (vervollständigen) *to complete* || um das Unglück ~ z m *to make matters still worse, to crown it all* || ⟨fam⟩ e–n ~ m *to make a p drunk* || sich ~ m *to mess o.s. (up)* || die Lunge ~ **nehmen** *to fill one's lungs deeply*; nicht f ~ z nehmen (P) *hardly to be taken seriously* || °sich ~ saufen *to drink one's fill* || e–m den Buckel ~ schlagen *to give a p a sound hiding* || °sich den Bauch ~ schlagen *to gorge o.s.* || → E. || die Seite ~ schmieren *to scribble all over the page* || e–m die Ohren ~ schreien *to deafen a p with shouting* || ~ s v *to be f. of* od *filled with* || e–n ~|spritzen *to splash a p all over* || **~|stopfen** *to stuff, cram*; sich (mit Essen) ~ *to stuff (o.s.)* || über etw ~ verfügen *to have f.* od *complete disposal of a th* || ~ w *to become filled (with)*, ⟨fig⟩ *to get drunk (on)* | **~ u ganz** (verstehen) .. *perfectly well*; jdm ~ (u ganz) zustimmen *to agree f.y* od *entirely with a p* **E.** **[als s]**: die Uhr schlägt ~ .. *strikes the (f.) hour* || 10 Minuten nach ~ *10 m.s after the hour* || aus dem ~en schöpfen *to have plenty, to spend out of f. pockets, to draw freely from one's store of wealth, ideas,* etc; *to draw from the ful(l)ness of one's wealth of* .., .. *from one's complete resources*; .. wirtschaften *not to stint o.s.* || im ~en leben *to live in abundance, to be in clover* **V·oll-** **[betont**; bei *verb* **sep**; → u. **Voll-]** **≃ährig** *f.-eared* **~aktie** f *paid-up share* **≃amtlich** a *f.-time (lecturer)* **≃·auf** [adv] *in abundance, abundantly, plentifully, plenty of, plenty (to do)* || er hat ~ *he is very well-to-do* || (gänzlich) *to the f.* **~ausschlag** m (e–s Zeigers) *full-scale deflection* **~aussteuerung** f ⟨wir⟩ *f. modulation* **~automatisch** a *f.-scale* od *f.ly* (od *all-*) *automatic*; nicht ~ *manually assisted, operations done by hand* **≃automatisiert** a *automated (production)* **≃backig** a *f.-cheeked*; *chubby (child)* **~bad** n *complete bath, plunge(-b.), lie-down b.* **~bahn** f ⟨rail⟩ *trunk-* od *main line* **~bart** m *beard* **~belastung** f *f. load* **≃berechtigt** a *f.y qualifed* **≃beschäftigt** a *f.-time (worker)* **~beschäftigung** f *f. employment*; (des einzelnen) *whole-time job* **~besitz** m *f. possession* **~bier** n *entire (beer)* **~bild** n *f.-length picture* **≃blumig** a *f.-flavo(u)red (wine)* **~blut** n, (**~blüter** m) *blooded horse*; *thoroughbred (horse)* || ⟨hors⟩ ~ = Araber [m] *pure-strain Arab* | ~pferde [n pl] *bloodstock* (⟨a.⟩ ~ [koll]) **≃blütig** a *f.-blooded* ⟨a. fig⟩, *sanguineous* || ⟨path⟩ *plethoric* [adv *-ally*] || ⟨hors⟩ *thoroughbred* | ≃keit [f] *f.-bloodedness, repletion* || ⟨scient⟩ *plethory* **~blutpferd** n *f. blood, thoroughbred* **~blutstute** f *blood-mare* **≃brüstig** a *f.-breasted* **~bürger** m *burgess, f. citizen* **≃bürtig** a *born of the same parents, whole-blood*; *f. (brother)* | ≃keit [f] *descent of the same parents* **≃busig** a *f.-bosomed, curvaceous* **~dampf** m *f. steam*, ⟨fig⟩ *energy* || mit ~ voraus *f. speed ahead* **≃elastisch** a *all-stretch (stocking)* **≃elektrisch** a *all-electric (kitchen)* **≃ends** [adv] *quite, altogether, entirely, wholly* || (völlig) *completely* || (obendrein) *besides, moreover, furthermore* **≃entfalteter** Charakter *rounded personality* **~erbe** m *unrestricted heir* **≃fett** *rich* (Käse) **≃|füllen** etc vt *to fill (up)* → voll D. **~gas** n ⟨mot⟩ *f. throttle* [⟨a.⟩ adverbiell]; ~ geben *to give f. thr.*; ⟨aero⟩ *to go through the gate*; gib ~! *gun her!* || mit ~ *with open thr., with engine f. out* || *she opened out to f. speed* **~gefühl** n *(full) consciousness* || im ~ s–r Würde *f.y conscious of* .. **~gehalt** m *f. value*; *good alloy* | ≃ig [a] *standard (coin)* **≃gelaufen** a *waterlogged (boat)* **~genuß** m *f. enjoyment* **≃gepackt** a: *packed f.* (mit *of*) **≃gepfropft, ≃gestopft** a *crammed (full)* || der Raum war ~ .. *was packed* od *crowded*; ⟨rail⟩ *jam-packed*; ~ v ⟨a.⟩ *chock-a-block with* **~geschoß** n *solid shell* °**≃gesoffen** a *tanked (up)* **≃gesogen** a ⟨fig⟩ *waterlogged (with studies)* **≃gültig** a *of f. value*; [attr] *sterling* || ⟨fig⟩ *unexceptionable* || *conclusive (evidence)* **~gummi** n [a. m] *solid rubber* | ~reifen [m] ⟨mot⟩ *solid tire* **~hering** m *f. herring* **~holz** n ⟨for⟩ *log* | ≃ig [a] *full-boled* **≃hufig** a ⟨hors⟩ *hoof-bound* **~idiot** m *blank idiot* **≃inhaltlich** a *complete* | [adv] *to its (their) f. extent, all around* **≃jährig** a *of age* || ≃e(r m) f *adult* | ~keit [f] *f. age*; *majority* || die ~ erlangen *to come of age* | ~s- ~erklärung [f] *emancipation, declaration of majority* **~jude** m *a jew by his father and by his mother* **~ketten-** *f.y-tacked (vehicle)* **~klang** m *f. chord* **≃klingend** a *resonant* **≃kommen** a [⟨a. –·–] *full*; *perfect* || ⟨fam⟩ *regular, all out* || (~ ausgebildet) *accomplished, out-and-out* || (–·endet) *consummate* || (gründlich) *thorough, all-round* || (unbedingt) *absolute* || ⟨sl⟩ *blithering (idiot)* || *utter (desolation)* || ~ m *to perfect, accomplish* | [adv] *wholly, completely*; ⟨Am⟩ *plumb (crazy, forgotten)* || das ändert die S ~ *that makes all the difference* || e–n ~ in Anspruch nehmen *to absorb a p('s mind)*; ~ ruhig stellen (S) *to put .. at complete rest* | das ≃ste *the last word (in)* | ~heit [f] *perfection* || *accomplishment*; *polish*; auf ~ bedacht *perfectionist* [attr] *(plan)* **~kornbrot** n *whole-meal, -grain bread* **≃körnig** a *f.-grained* **~kraft** f *f. vigour* || in der ~ der Jahre *in the prime* od *flush of life* **≃kräftig** a *vigorous* **~kugel** f ⟨artill⟩ *round shot* **≃|laufen** vi [s] *to be filled to overflowing*, (of boat) *to get waterlogged*; → voll A. & D.; ~ u sinken ⟨mar⟩ *to founder* **≃lautend** a *sonorous* **≃leibig** a *corpulent, stout* | ~keit [f] *corpulence, stoutness* **≃|machen** vt [h] *to fill (up)* || ⟨fig⟩ *to complete* || (beschmutzen) *to dirty* **~macht** f *f.* (⟨Am⟩ *mandatory*) *power(s* pl) || ⟨com⟩ *(form of) proxy* || ⟨jur⟩ *power* .., (Urkunde) *letter* od *warrant of attorney*; außer-(inner)halb der ~ *ultra (intra) vires* L; unbeschränkte ~ *discretionary powers* || jdm ~ erteilen *to empower* od *authorize a p, to give a p blank cheque* od *carte blanche* Fr || ohne ~ *without authority*, s–e ~ überschreiten *to exceed one's au.* | ~-geber [m] ⟨jur⟩ *mandator, constituent*; ~haber, ~träger [m] *mandatory* || ⟨com⟩ *proxy*; ~widerruf [m] *revocation of p. of att.* **≃mast** adv & auf ~ *(the standard) (flying) at the mast-head* od *-end* **~matrose** m *able-bodied seaman* (abbr *A. B.*) **~mensch** m *complete personality* **~milch** f *rich* od *whole, unskimmed milk* | ~pulver [n] *powdered* od *dried wh. m.* **~mond** m *f. moon*; es ist heute ~ *there is a f. m. tonight*; → voll A. | ~gesicht [n] *pudding face*; *moon-shaped face* ⟨a. med⟩ **≃mundig** a (Wein) *f.-bodied* **~munition** f (MG) *ball ammunition* **≃|packen** vt [h] etc → voll D. *to fill (up)* **≃|pfropfen** vt [h] *to stuff f.*; (Raum wie mit Heringen) (P) *to sardine* || mit Kenntnissen ~ *to cram* || sich ~ *to gorge o.s.* **~plastik** f ⟨arts⟩ *detached statuary* **≃|pumpen** vt [h] *to pump up* **~rad** n *solid wheel* **~reif** a ⟨fig⟩ *full-blown (woman)* **~reifen** m ⟨cycl⟩ *solid tire* | jdm den Laden **~|rotzen** ⟨aero mil sl⟩ *to paste away at* **≃saftig** a ⟨hort⟩ *f. of sap*; ⟨cul⟩ *juicy, succulant*; ⟨med⟩ *replete* | ~keit [f] *abundance of sap, succulence*; *repletion* **≃|schenken** vt [h] etc → voll D. **~schiff** n *f.-rigged ship* **≃|schlagen** vi [s] ⟨mar⟩ *to be swamped* || → voll D. **≃schlank** a *pleasantly plump*; *fuller (figure)* **~sicht-** ~kanzel [f] ⟨aero⟩ *clear vision* od *f.-view cockpit*; ~rückfenster [n] ⟨mot⟩ *wrap-*

Aussprache: Falls nicht anders (: [v]) angegeben, ist v = [f] zu sprechen.

-around rear glass; ∼scheibe [f] f.-width (⟨Am⟩ panorama) wind-screen; ∼verglasung [f] wr.-ar. windshield **∼sitzung** f = –versammlung **≗spurig** a, **∼spur** f ⟨rail⟩ broad-ga(u)ge | ∼weite [f] standard g. **≗ständig** a complete, entire, f. || sweeping (reform, measures); utter (defeat); total (eclipse); vgl voll D. || ∼e Adresse add. in full | [adv] entirely, quite, wholly, altogether; ⟨fam⟩ down to the ground || (P) ∼ im unklaren all abroad, utterly at sea || ∼ weg clean gone | ≗keit [f] a complement | ∼s- ∼appell [m] ⟨mil⟩ show-down inspection; ∼prüfung [f] ⟨comp⟩ parity check **≗stimmig** a ⟨mus⟩ full-voiced, -toned | ≗keit [f] f. tone, complete harmony ≗|**stopfen** vt [h] to cram, clutter; to stuff (f.) || zum Platzen ∼ to stuff to bursting point || → vollstr·eck- ·**∼str·etch-** [in comp] ⟨tex⟩ fully elasticated **≗synthetische** Fasern synthetics pl **∼-tastatur-** Kontrolltastfeld [n] ⟨comp⟩ f. keyboard features pl **≗tönend** a ringing, rich (voice); sounding, sonorous, stereophonic; ⟨rhet⟩ (Satz) well-rounded **∼treffer** m ⟨artill⟩ direct hit **∼verlust** m total loss **∼versammlung** f plenary od general meeting od assembly **∼versicherung** f full value i. **≗wangig** a = –backig **∼waise** f orphan **≗wertig** a perfect; of good value od high quality; f. || (v Münzen) sterling || ⟨biol⟩ complete (Eiweiß) || ⟨fam⟩ f.-blown, f.-fledged (Mitglied) **≗wichtig** a of f. weight; ⟨fig⟩ momentous, weighty | ∼keit [f] f. weight || ⟨fig⟩ weightiness **≗wüchsig** a f.-grown **≗zählig** a complete; [pred] (P) everyone (of them); ∼e Versammlung f. assembly, ⟨parl⟩ f. house || ∼ m to complete, ⟨mil⟩ to put up to establishment | ∼keit [f] completeness **∼ziegel** m solid brick

Voll- [**unbetont**; bei verb **insep**, → o. **V·oll-**] **≗br·acht** pp v –bringen || nach ∼er Tat when the deed was done || ⟨bib⟩ es ist ∼ it is finished **≗br·ingen** vt irr [h] to accomplish, achieve || (ausführen) to execute; (Pflicht) to perform; (Verbrechen) to perpetrate **∼br·inger** m ∼s/∼ achiever, etc **∼br·ingung** f ∼/ achievement, accomplishment || performance, perpetration **≗·enden** vt [h] to finish, complete; (Buch) to round off; nur wenigen ist es gegeben, das Werk, welches sie begonnen h, auch z ∼ it is given to few to attempt a work and to achieve it || ⟨fig⟩ to accomplish; ⟨bib⟩ (Lukas 13, 32) to perfect **∼·ender** m ∼s/∼ finisher, etc **≗·endet** a ⟨fig⟩ ⟨arts etc⟩ elaborate || perfect, finished, fine (gentleman); complete (fool) || consummate (organizer) || accomplished (fact) || die früh ≗e the girl who died so young; thorough (rogue) || ⟨bib⟩ perfected **∼·endung** f ∼/∼en accomplishment ⟨a. fig⟩ || ⟨fig⟩ perfection ⟨a. bib⟩ || finishing, termination || (Schliff) finish ⟨a. arts⟩ || (fertig) completion || nach ∼ dieses having done this **≗f·ühren** vt [h] to execute, accomplish || → ·ausführen **∼k·ommen** → v·ollk **vollstr·eck-** **∼bar** a admitting of execution | ≗keit [f] ∼/ ⟨jur⟩ possibility of carrying out (a sentence); ∼e Forderung judgment debt | **∼en** vt [h] to carry out, to execute | **∼end** a executive **≗er(in** f) m executor (f executrix); ∼ e–s Todesurteils executioner **≗ung** f execution; Abwendung der ∼ stay of e.n | ∼s- ∼beamte(r) [m] e.n officer; ∼befehl [m] writ of e.n; ([provisionally] enforceable Zahlungsbefehl); ∼schutz [m] exemption from judicial e.n

Voll- [unbetont] **≗z·iehen** vt irr [h] to execute, to carry out || (Trauung, Operation) to perform || sich ∼ to happen, pass || ∼d [a] executive || ∼de Gewalt the executive **∼z·ieher(in** f) m executor (f executrix) **∼z·iehung** f execution || consummation (of marriage) | **∼s-** ∼befehl [m] warrant; ∼gewalt [f] executive (power) **≗z·og** 1. & 3. sg pret v ∼ziehen **≗z·ogen** a comsummated (marriage) **∼z·ug** m ∼(e)s/ = ∼z·iehung; in ∼ e–r S in fulfilment of a th

V·öller m ∼s/∼ glutton **Völler·ei** f ∼/∼en gluttony, high-living, selfindulgence || crapulence **V·ollheit** f ∼/ fulness, plenitude, completeness **v·öllig** a entire, whole, full; blank, absolute (Enttäuschung); blank (silence); total (silence, darkness, blindness, abstinence) || utter, stark (nonsense) || positive, downright (atheist) | (Kleid) ample, amply wide enough | [adv] completely, absolutely, entirely, quite, fully, altogether || stark (naked, mad) || (dirty) all over || wide (awake) || dead (drunk, level, sure) || clean, ⟨bes Am⟩ plumb (forgotten)

Volont·är [vɔlɔ̃:'tɛr] m ∼s/∼e volunteer || ⟨com⟩ unsalaried (training) clerk; improver; trainee

†**V·olsker** [f–] m, **∼in** f (altital. Volk in Latium) Volsci [L] pl †**v·olskisch** a Volscian

V·olt [v–] n ∼s/∼e ⟨el⟩ volt **≗·aisch** a voltaic

V·ol|te [v–] f ∼/∼n ⟨fenc & hors⟩ volt | **-tigeur** [vɔlti'ʒø:r] m ∼s/∼e vaulter || ⟨mil⟩ voltigeur, light-infantry soldier **v.g·ieren** [vɔlti'ʒi:rən] vi [h] to vault

Volubilit·ät [v–] f ∼/ volubility **Vol·umen** n [∼s/∼ & –mina] volume, bulk | ∼gewicht [n] weight by v.; ≗mäßig [a] by (od in terms of) v.; ∼prozent [n] percent. (by) v.; ∼steigerung [f] v.trical increase; ∼unterschied [m] disparity in v. **v.min·ös** a voluminous, massive || (Pappe) high-bulking

vom = von dem **Vombl·attspielen** n ⟨mus⟩ playing at (first) sight

vom·ieren [v–] vi [h] to vomit **Vomit·iv** [v–f] n ∼(e)s/∼e emetic

von prep [dat] **A.** (Urheberschaft, Ursprung) by || ∼ jdm getötet w to be killed by a p || ∼ Natur by nature; ∼ Beruf by trade od profession || .. ∼ Geburt (a German) by birth; by birth (an Irishman) || v Hand manually || das Stück ist ∼ Ibsen the piece is by I. || ∼ Gottes Gnaden by the grace of God || a child of od by his first wife | ∼ selbst of itself; of one's own accord, spontaneously **B.** (Trennung, Herkunft) (to come) from Berlin || ∼ B. kommende Züge down trains || three steps from me || a merchant of B. = a Berlin merchant || ∼ weitem from afar || ∼ neuem anew || ∼ allen Seiten from every side, on all sides | ∼ goldenen Tellern essen to eat off gold plate | Ihr Brief vom 6. d. M. your l. of the 6th inst. | (Adelsprädikat) Herr ∼ N. Herr von od de N.; Herr Baron ∼ N. Baron N.; das ≗ ⟨Ger⟩ the mark of nobility **C.** [= gen] the master of the house, the Duke of York || the situation of Hull || the siege of Lille || portraits of him (ihn darstellend) | (Besitz) a book, friend of his, of mine, of Will's | [gen partitivus]: one of you || essen Sie ∼ diesem Brot have some of this br. | (= unter) in (ten in a hundred) || (11) out of (12); ⟨so:⟩ one out of many | das Schlimmste ∼ allem the worst of it all **D.** (= ∼ seiten) this letter of my father's || it was right of you || (it is the most abominable th höchst abscheulich) of you || (it was kindly meant) on his part || (to receive kindness) at a p's hands || das war ein dummer Streich ∼ ihm that was a silly th of him to do || v mir aus ist alles in Ordnung it's all right with me **E.** (Eigenschaft) a man of character, of small stature; he is small of st. || an angel of a girl, a fool of a husband; ein Muster ∼ Abgeordneter [dat f], A.tem [dat m] the paragon of representatives || an affair of importance | a woman of 50 years; ⟨so:⟩ a child two years old (∼ 2 J.), a two-year-old ch. **F.** (Stoff) to build of wood || .. ∼ Holz a wooden pole | (Gesprächsstoff) (to speak) of, about || (a speech) [up]on, concerning, respecting .. || .., ∼ dem ich

---

Verbal-Flexion der Verben mit der Vorsilbe **ver-** → das jeweilige Simplex

spreche (*the book*) *of* od *about which I am speaking* od *which I am speaking about* (od *of*) || *of what/whom are you speaking?*; *what/whom are you speaking about?* **G.** vom Original **abschreiben** *to copy from the o.* || *born of honest parents* || *one can't dine off sixpence* || ~ e–m gehen *to leave a p* || ich **hörte** es ~ ihr *I heard* od *have it from her, I was told by her* || leben ~ .. *to live on* (*air, one's income*), *by* (*one's trade*) || ~ der Arbeit ruhen *to rest from work* || ~ Glück **sagen** *to thank one's stars* || sich ~ s–r Frau scheiden l *to divorce one's wife* || vom Tisch wegnehmen *to take away from the table* || was **wollen** Sie ~ mir? *what do you want from* (*of, with*) *me?* **H.** ~ jetzt *or* nun (heute etc) **ab** *or* **an** *from now, henceforth*; (*from this day forward, from that time onward*) || ~ den Hüften **abwärts** *from his hips down* || ~ **außen** *from without*; (*he locked the door*) *on the outside* | ~ .. **bis** *from Paris to Berlin* || *from 3 to* od *till 4* (*o'clock*) || ~ oben bis unten *from top to bottom* | ~ **da** *or* dort *from there*; (*from*) *thence*; *when the wind was that way* (~ dort kam) || ~ .. **herab** *from* (*the pulpit*) || ~ hinnen *hence* || ~ hinten *from behind, from the back* || ~ **innen** *from* od *on the inside* || ~ **oben** *from above* || ~ oben herab *from on high* || ~ Rechts **wegen** *by right(s)* || ~ wo (aus *or* her)? *from where*; *whence* || ~ Fall zu Fall *as the case arises* || ~ Ufer zu U. *cross-river* (*traffic*) || ~ Zeit **zu** Z. *from time to time* **~ein·ander** [adv] = aus–e–a || ~ gehen *to part, separate* || ~ abhängen *to interdepend* **~n·öten** a *necessary, needful* || ~ h *to want, to stand in need of* || ~ s *to be needful* od *necessary* **~statten** [adv]; ~ gehen *to progress, proceed*; *to come* od *pass off* || gut ~ gehen *to go* (*on*) *well*; *to prosper*; *to be a success* **~w·annen** [adv] *whence* **~w·egen** prep = wegen || ⟨fam⟩ ja, ~! *you may whistle for it!, don't expect me to do that!, not I!*

V·opo(s pl) = Volkspolizist(en pl)

vor I. prep (wo? [dat], wohin? [acc]) **A. 1.** **(räumlich)** *in front of, before, opposite* (*the house*) | *in front of* (*the fire*) || (*he drove them*) *in front of him* | e–e kl Strecke ~ ihm *a little ahead of him*; *ahead of me I saw ..*; *the bus stops just ahead of ..*; *he ran ahead of us*; *his car is far ahead of us*; *a mile ahead of us* | *she stood before him* || *we had the sea before us* || *before the king all the people are equal* | ~ **Augen** h ⟨fig⟩ *to intend* || ~ jds sehenden Augen *before a p's very eye* || e–m (sich) e–e Kugel ~ den Kopf schießen *to lodge a ball in a p's head* (*to blow one's brains out*) || Schritt ~ S. *step by step* || ~ das **Tor** gehen *to go out of the gate* || ~ dem Tore *outside the gate* || ⟨fig⟩ ~ der Tür s *to be impending* || ~ der Tür warten .. *at the door* || e–n ~ die Tür setzen *to turn a p out* || ~ dem Zeitwort stehen *to precede the verb* | das Haus ~ **sich** h *to face the house, to be faced by the h.* | ⟨fig⟩ sich ~ e–m Dilemma sehen *to see o.s. confronted with a d.* || ~ dem Ruin, Untergang stehen *to be on the verge of ruin, to be faced with ruin* **2.** **(in Gegenwart v)** *in full view of* (*the enemy*) || *in the eyes of* (*God*), *in the presence of* (*God, the enemy, a miracle*) || *to find o.s. in the royal presence*; *he escorted him to the presence of the king* || *in front of, in the hearing of* (*the court*) **3.** (Vorzug) *in preference to*; *before* || ~ allen Dingen, ~ allem *above all, first of all*; .. sind ~ allem *priority* (*objectives*) || sich auszeichnen ~ .. *to distinguish o.s. above ..* || (etw) erhalten ~ .. *to obtain .. in preference to ..* || (P) ~ jdm den Vorrang h *to take precedence of a p* **4.** (Trennung) Geheimnisse h ~ .. *to keep secrets from ..* || k–e Ruhe h ~ .. *never to have a moment's peace with ..* || fliehen ~ *to flee from* || sich hüten ~ *to beware of* || schützen ~ *to protect from* od *against* || geschützt ~ *sheltered from* (*the rain*) || sicher ~ *safe* od *secure from* || sich ~ der Welt verbergen *to hide o.s. from the w.* || sein Herz verschließen ~ *to shut one's h. to* od *against* **5.** **(Gefühl)** Furcht h ~, sich fürchten ~ *to be afraid of, to fear* || e–e Abneigung ~ *an aversion for* od *to* **6.** **(Ursache)** *on account of*; *with*; *through* || *for* (*fear, joy*); *with* (*rage*) || *because of* (*the rain*) || (*to perish, tremble*) *with* (*cold, fear*) || (*weak*) *with* (*hunger*); (*to die*) *of* (*hunger*) || (*to cry*) *with* (*joy*) || (*stiff*) *with* (*cold*), (*black*) *with* (*rain*) || (*could not see ..*) *for* (*clouds*) **7.** · ~ **sich** gehen (S) *to take place, to pass off* || (P) ~ sich hin murmeln etc *to mutter* (*trill*) *to o.s.* || etw (im Geiste) ~ sich h *to see a th*; (*a noble aim*) *in view*; .. Zukunft .. *he is bound to go far* || ~ **sich selbst** *in one's own eyes* **B.** **(zeitlich) 1.** **(Zeitpunkt)** *before* (*sunrise*) || *earlier than* (*you*) || *antecedent to, previous to, prior to* (*the attack*); die N. ~ dem Start ⟨a-n⟩ *the pre-launch night* || ⟨Am a.⟩ *back of* || da s ~ .. *to exist before ..*; *to be there* ([*an hour*] *ahead of* od) *before ..* || (*the light reaches us ahead of the sound*) || ~ dem 1. 4. *prior to April 1st* || 14 Tage ~ dem 12. 7. *within a fortnight of July 12th* || der Tag ~ dem Fest *the day before* (od *the eve of*) *the festival* | **bis** ~ kurzem *until a short time ago* || (*he was a few months*) *of* (*his death*) | ~ **4 Uhr** ⟨a.⟩ *this side of 4 o'clock*; kurz .. *just on 4 o'clock* || 10 Min. ~ 4 = *10 minutes to* (⟨Am⟩ *of, till*) *4* || ich kann nicht ~ 6 k *I shall not be able to come till 6*; *in advance of publication* (~ [der] V.) || ~ der **Zeit** *before the time, too early, prematurely*; (*an hour*) *ahead of time*; (*payment*) *in advance* || ~ Zeiten *formerly* || ~ langen *or* alten Zeiten *in ancient times, in times of old* | ~ **sich** h: *we have a busy day ahead of us* || er hat noch .. ~ sich *his regency has 3 years more to run* || es noch ~ sich h *to have still to do it* | **nicht** ~ *not till* (*2 o'clock*) || *not until* (*the 18th century*) | (*he wasn't expected back*) *for some hours* **2.** **(Zeitdauer)** heute ~ 8 Tagen *a week ago* od *since* || ~ einigen Tagen *the other day* || ~ einigen Jahren ⟨a.⟩ *a few years back* || ~ Tausenden von Jahren *thousands of years ago*, ⟨Am⟩ *way back thousands of years* | (im Vergangenheitsbericht) *a few weeks back* od *before* **II.** das **Vor** u Nach *the before and after* **III.** [adv] ~! (*step*) *forward!*, (*skirmishers*) *advance!*, (*Germans*) *to the front!* | nach wie ~ *now/then as before*

V·or- [in comp mit s] (Ggs Hinter-) *front* (*garden*) || (Ggs Nach-) *pre-*(*adamite*) || *preliminary* (*round, inquiry*) **v·or-** [in comp] **I.** [mit a]: ~adamitisch *preadamic* || ~christlich *pre-Christian* || ~sintflutlich *antediluvian* **II.** [mit verb] (immer trennbar) **1.** → vor I. A. 1. **2.** → ~|bedingen **3.** → vor I. A. 2. & ~|lesen | (belehrend) → ~|zeichnen 1. **4.** → ~|herrschen *to predominate* **vor·ab** [adv] **1.** = im voraus; ~ erforderlich *prerequisite* | ≗druck [m] *pre-print* **2.** (vornehmlich) *especially*; *above all* **V·or- ~abend** m *evening before* || *eve* **≗adamitisch** a → vor- I. ≗|**ahnen** vt [h] *to have a presentiment* od *foreboding of* || ~d *prophetic* **~ahnung** f ⟨a.⟩ *anticipation, premonition*; böse ~ ⟨a.⟩ *misgiving, apprehension* **~alarm** m *fore-warning, blue alarm* **~alpen** pl *Lower Alps*

vor·an [adv] *before, in front, ahead, first* || ~! ~! *go ahead!, go on!* **~|eilen, ~|fliegen, ~|laufen** vi [s] *to hurry* od *hasten on before, to go* od *run in front* ([dat] *of*) **~|gehen** vi [s] *to go* od *walk before, to lead the way, to precede* (jdm *a p*) || *to go on ahead* | ⟨fig⟩ *to* (*take the*) *lead* || (nach Rang, Tüchtigkeit) *to precede* (jdm *a p*; e–r S [dat] *a th*); *to take precedence* (*of*) | s–e Mutter ging ihm v. *he was preceded by his m.* || mit gutem Beispiel ~ *to set* (*a p*) *a good example* **~|kommen** vi [s] *to* (*make*) *progress, to go ahead*; gut ~ *to make headway* od *good time* || ⟨übtr⟩ *to do well* || mit jdm (gut) ~ ⟨fig⟩ *to make headway with a p*

Aussprache: Falls nicht anders (: [v]) angegeben, ist v = [f] zu sprechen.

|| jdm im Tod ~ *to predecease* (*die before*) *a p* **~|machen** vi [h] *to hasten* || mach ~! *hurry up*! ⟨fam⟩ *look sharp*!

V·or- (→ vor) **~ankündigen** vt [h] *to announce in advance* **V.gung** f *advance notice*, ⟨film⟩ *preview* **~anmeldung** f ⟨telph⟩ *personal call* **~anschlag** m (*previous*) *estimate, rough calculation* (aufstellen *to formulate*) || Kosten~ *forecast* || ⟨parl⟩ *budget* || (⟨so:⟩ *Navy estimates*)

vor·an- **~|schreiten** vi [s] *to stride ahead, to make progress* || ~d *progressive* **~|stellen** vt [h] *to place in front* (od *ahead*) (*of*); (etw e–r S [dat]) ~ *to give .. precedence to* **~|stürmen** vi [s] *to rush forward* od *ahead* **~|treiben** vt [h] *to urge on*; *to carry ahead* od *forward*; ⟨fig⟩ *to push* (*a th*) *through*

V·or- **~anstalten** f pl *preparatory measures* pl **~anstrich** m *primer coat* **~anzeige** f ~/~n *warning*; *previous notice, prospectus* || ⟨film⟩ *preview* **~arbeit** f *preparatory work* || ~en [pl] *preliminary works* od *studies* pl, *spade-work* **~|arbeiten** vt/i [h] (etw) *to prepare* (*a th*) || e–m ~ *to work in advance of a p*; *to show a p the way to work*; ⟨fig⟩ *to pave the way for a p* || wir h –ge–tet *we have done work in advance* | **sich** ~ *to forge ahead* ⟨a. mil⟩ **~arbeiter** m *foreman*; *overseer*; *leading hand*; *charge-hand*; ⟨fam⟩ *gaffer, ganger*; *young boss*; *butty* **~ärmel** m *false sleeve* **vor·auf** [adv] *before, in front*

V·orarlberg n (österr. Landschaft)

vor·aus [adv] **(örtlich)** *before, foremost, in front, in advance, on ahead*; ⟨mar⟩ *ahead*! || (jdm) ~ s *to have the advantage over, .. the edge on* (*a p*) | **(zeitlich)** *beforehand, in advance* | ~ vor *ahead of* || [dat] *ahead of* (*one's time*) || 8 Punkte ~ s *to be up 8 points* || (Briefschluß) im ~ bestens dankend *thanking you in advance*; im ~ notwendig *prerequisite*; im ~ schätzen *to forecast* || (nicht) im ~ bestellt (*un*)*reserved* || .. 1 Jahr im ~ .. (*to arrange a th*) *a y. ahead* | ⟨fig⟩ nichts vor jdm ~ h *to have nothing on a p* || etw jdm ~ h *to have an advantage* od *a pull over a p* | als ~ [n] *by way of preferential benefit* | [in comp] *forward*; (*in*) *advance*; *beforehand* **~abteilung** f ⟨mil⟩ *spearhead* **~angriff** m *probing attack* **~|bedenken** vt [h] *to think of* od *over b.d* **~bedeutend** a *auguring* **~|bedingen** vt [h] *to stipulate in a.e* || sich etw ~ *to reserve .. to o.s.* **~berechnung** f ⟨demog, stat⟩ *projection* **~bestellen** vt [h] *to order* (*bespeak, book*) *in a.e*; *to reserve* **~bestellung** f *order given b.d*, ⟨theat⟩ (*a.e*) *booking* **~bestimmung** f → Vorbestimmung **~bezahlt** a *a.ed* (Fracht) **~bezahlung** f *payment in a.e* **~|datieren** vt [h] *to foredate* **~|denken** *to think ahead* | ~de Persönlichkeit *p.y who can th. a.d* **~|eilen** vi [s] [dat] *to run ahead* (*of*) || ⟨fig⟩ [dat] *to be ahead* (*of*), *to outrun* (*one's age*) **~|empfinden** vt [h] [pp –empfunden] *to have a presentiment* **~|gehen** vi irr [s] *to go before* || (jdm) *to walk in front of, to precede* (*a p*); nur ein wenig ~ *to move only a little in front of*; .., damit der andere nachkommt *to go ahead of a p* || ihm gingen .. v. *he was preceded by* || ⟨typ⟩ *to preface* (*a report*) || im ~den *above* **~gesetzt,** daß *provided that*; *if only* **~|haben** vt irr [h]; etw ~ vor jdm *to have an advantage* od *edge over a p*; nichts .. ⟨a.⟩ *to have nothing on a p* **~meldung** f *initial report* **~|nehmen** vt irr [h] *to anticipate* **~nutzen** m *preferential benefit* **~|reiten** vi [s] *to go ahead* **~|sagen** vt [h] *to predict, forecast, foretell,, prophesy* **~sagung** f *prediction, prophecy* **~|schauend** a *in a.e* od *anticipation* (*of*); *contemplated* (*employment*); *pre-planned* **~|schicken** vt [h] *to send* (*in advance* od) *on* || ⟨fig⟩ *to mention before, to premise*; etw e–r S [dat] ~ *to precede a th by a th* | dies –ge–ckt .. *this being premised ..* **~|schreiten** vi [s] jdm ~ *to go ahead of a p* **~|sehen** vt irr [h] *to foresee, anticipate*; *to see* (*a th*) *coming*; *to augure* (*the worst*) || ~d *prescient* (*of*) **~|sein** vi [s] *to be ahead* ([dat] *of*); dazu: *one-upmanship* **~|senden** vt [h] *to send on* (*a trunk*) **~|setzen** vt [h] ⟨fig⟩ *to assume, presume,* (*pre*)*suppose*; *postulate*; *to take for granted* || stillschweigend ~ *to take .. tacitly for granted*; *to understand, imply, to make assumption* (*that*); *the devil implies God*; → | –ge–tzt **~setzung** f *assumption,* (*pre*)*supposition*; *condition* (f *of*); notwendige ~ *qualification* (*of*), (*material*) *prerequisite* (*to*) || –setzungen [pl] ⟨contr, etc⟩ *conditional clauses* || unter der ~ *on the a.n* od *understanding* (*that*) | **~s-** ~los [a] *unconditioned* **~sicht** f *forecast, prescience*; *foresight, prudence, forethought* || in der ~, daß *in anticipation of ..* || aller ~ nach *in all probability* **~sichtlich** a *prospective, probable, presumptive*; ~er Nachfolger *heir-apparent*; *expected, estimated* (*time of arrival*) (ETA); *tentative* (*start time*) | [adv] *probably, presumably*; ~ in Dienst *expected to be in service* **~truppe** f *a.ed detachment* od *unit* pl; (mit Funk) *pathfinder* N **~|verkündigen** vt [h] *to prophesy* **~|werfen** vt [h] *to order out* (*troops*) **~|wissen** vt irr [h] *to foreknow, anticipate* || er wußte (es) alles voraus *he knew all this would happen* **~zahlung** f *prepayment*

Vor- **~band** m ⟨met⟩ (Muster auf Packung, Schublade) *specimen* **~bau** m *front-structure, -building* | *projecting part of a building, portico* || ⟨com⟩ *front* || °⟨fig⟩ (Bauch) *bay-, bow-window* | ~stempel [m] ⟨arch⟩ *provisional pit prop* **~|bauen** vi ⟨fig⟩ [dat] *to prevent, obviate*; *to provide for the future, to take precautions* (*against*) | vt [h] ~ (vorspringend bauen) *to build out* **~bedacht** m ~(e)s/ *forethought, premeditation* || mit ~ ⟨a.⟩ *on purpose*; *deliberately*; ⟨jur⟩ *with malice prepense*; ohne ~ *unintentionally* **~bedacht** a *studied*; *premeditated* (*crime*) **~bedeuten** vt [h] [pp –tet] *to forebode, presage, portend* **~bedeutung** f ~/~en *foretoken, foreboding, portent, omen, prognostic* || gute ~ *good augury* || v übler ~ *inauspicious*; *foreboding evil* **~bedingung** f *precondition*; *preliminary condition*; ⟨jur⟩ *condition precedent*; erste ~ *prerequisite* (f *to*) || notwendige ~ *qualification* (f *of*) **~befehl** m *warning order* **~begriff** m *preliminary notion* **~behalt** m ~(e)s/~e (still *mental*) *reservation* ⟨a. jur⟩; *reserve* (*with all r.*); dinglich gesicherter ~ *restrictive covenant* | mit ~ [gen] *with reservation* (*as to*); mit allem ~ hinnehmen! *you must take it for what it's worth* || mit *or* unter ~ (*with the reservation* od) *provided that, reserving* | mit ~ aussagen *to understate* || unter ~ aller Rechte *all rights reserved* || mit ~ m–r Rechte *without prejudice to my rights* || ohne ~ *unconditionally* || ⟨com⟩ mit dem üblichen ~ *with the usual proviso* **~|behalten** vt irr [h] *to reserve* || sich [dat] ~ *to reserve* (*to o.s.*) || jdm ~ bleiben *to be left* od *reserved for* od *to a p*; *the decision is incumbent* (⟨fam⟩ *is up*) *to him* || f mil. Zwecke ~ *reserved* (*route*) **~behaltlich** prep [gen] *subject to*; *with the reservation* (*that*); *with r.n* (*as to*) || ~ anderweitiger Anordnungen *unless otherwise directed* **~behaltlos** a *unreserved, unconditional* **~halts-** ~gut [n] ⟨jur⟩ *separate estate*; ~klausel [f] *saving clause*; ~preis [m] *reserve-price* **~behandlung** f *primary* od *preliminary treatment*; *preparatory t.t, pret.t*; *preconditioning* ⟨tech & med⟩

vorb·ei [adv] **1. (örtlich)** *along, past, by* (*Pen rushed by Blanche* an .. ~) **2. (zeitlich)** *past, over, finished, gone*; die Krise ist ~ *the crisis has passed* ⟨a. fig⟩ || *the time is past* || *it is past ten o'clock* (10 Uhr ~) || es ist f immer ~ *it is gone for ever ..*; ein f allemal ~ *past and done with* || s–e Tage sind ~ *he* (*has*) *had his time* || es ist ~ mit ihm *he is done for* || 3 Schuß ~! *mis-*

Verbal-Flexion der Verben mit der Vorsilbe **ver-** → das jeweilige Simplex

sed three times | ⟨prov⟩ ~ ist ~ *bygones are bygones* **~|benehmen** vi [h]; sich ~ *to disgrace o.s.* **~|eilen** vi [s] (an [dat]) *to hurry past* (*a p*); *to brush, speed* (etc) *by* **~|fahren, ~|gehen, ~|kommen** (→ u.) *vi irr* [s] (an [dat]) *to pass* (*by*) (*a p*); *to drive, sail*, etc *past* (*a th*) || geh' ~! *pass!* **~fliegend** a *passing* (Ziel) | °**~|fegen, ~|flitzen** vi [s] *to whizz* od *shoot, sweep by* **~flug** m ⟨a–n⟩ *fly-by*; dazu: *to f. by* (*a p*); *to flash* od *brush past* **~|führen** vt [h] *to lead past* || *the road led along the garden* || wenn irgend dein Weg –rt *any time you are passing* **~|gehen** → o. || ⟨fig⟩ (an e–r Tatsache) ~ *to overlook, to fail to see* ..; (Gelegenheit) ~ l *to slip* || im ≈ *in passing*, ⟨fig⟩ *by the way* **≈gehende** [pl] *passers-by* | unbemerkt **~|gelangen** vi [s] *to get by* **~|gelingen** vi [s] °es ist ihm –gelungen *he has failed* **~geschossen**! *wide of the mark!* **~|kommen** → o. || wenn Sie ~ *any time you are passing* || *our agent will come round* || ich kam gerade v. *I was passing this way* || bei jdm ~ *to look a p up* || an (jdm) ~ *to get around* (*another car*) **~|können** *vi irr* [h] *to be able to pass* **~|laufen** vi irr [s] *to run past* **~|lassen** vt irr [h] *to let pass, to let go by* **≈marsch** m *pass in review*; *march past* (an jdm *a p*) || den ~ der Truppen abnehmen *to take the salute of the troops* **~|müssen** vi [h] *to be obliged to pass* (an [dat] *by*) **~|reden** vi [h]; an–e–a ~ *to be* od *talk at cross-purposes* (*with*) || an etw ~ *to fight shy of a th*; *to miss the point* **~|schicken** vt [h] (Boten) *to send along* **~|schießen** vi **1.** [h] *to miss the mark, to shoot to one side* **2.** [s] *to shoot past* **~|schlagen** vi [h] *to miss in striking* **~|tragen** vt irr [h] *to carry past* **~|ziehen** vi irr [s] *to march past* || (langsam) *to drag by*

V·or- *preliminary* (*p.l.y*), *preparatory* (*p.p.y*) **≈|bekommen** vi [h] *to have* (*a pinafore*) *put on* || ⟨sport⟩ *to be given .. points* || °etw hinten ~ *to get a thrashing* **≈belastet** a *compromised*; *having a previous record* **~bemerkung** f *prefatory* od *p.l.y note*; *introduction*; ⟨jur⟩ *preamble* **≈benannt** a *aforesaid* **≈|beraten** vt irr [h] *to discuss in advance* **~beratung** f *p.l.y discussion* **≈berechtigt** a *major* (*road*) **≈|bereiten** vt [h] *to prepare*, ⟨Am a.⟩ *to fit* (*a p for his work*) || *to make* (*a p*) *disposed* (f *for*) || *to provide, prepare* (*a th*); *to warn* (*a p*) *of a th*; sich ~ (auf, zu) *to prepare* (*o.s.*) *for*; *to get ready* (*for*); *to study to enter a profession*; ⟨sport⟩ *to train* (*for*) || ~d *p.p.y* || nicht –tete Arbeit ⟨school⟩ *unseen* **V.tung** f ~/~en *preparation*(*s*), *training*, etc || ~en treffen *to make arrangements* || ungenügende ~ *unpreparedness* || in ~ *under way* | **~s-** ~arbeiten [f pl] ⟨comp⟩ *clerical operations*; ~feuer [n] ⟨artill⟩ *preparation fire*; ~handlung [f] ⟨jur⟩ *act preparative to a crime*; ~maßregel [f] *p.l.y measure*; ~raum [m] ⟨mil⟩ (f Einsatzbesprechung etc) *staging area* N; ~schule [f] *p.p.y school* || *training-college* (*for teachers*, etc) **~berg** m *spur of a mountain*, ⟨Am⟩ *foot-hill* **~bericht** m *p.l.y report* || *introduction, preface* || (z e–m Gesetz) *preamble* **≈beruflich** a *prevocational* (*training*) **≈besagt** ⟨obs⟩ a *aforesaid* | ~ermaßen [adv] *as previously stated* **~bescheid** *p.l.y decree* **~besichtigung** f *private view* **~besitzer** m *previous possessor* **~besprechung** f *p.l.y discussion* bzw *review* **≈|bestellen** vt [h] *to make reservation of* **V.lung** f *booking*, ⟨Am⟩ *reservation* (*of seats*) || ⟨Lit⟩ *subscription* **≈|bestimmen** vt [h] *to predetermine* **~bestimmung** f *predestination, predetermination* **≈bestraft** a *previously convicted*; darf nicht ~ s *must have no police records* **≈|beten** vt [h] (jdm etw) *to recite, repeat, rehearse* (*a prayer* etc *to a p*) | vi [h] *to lead in prayer* || (bei Tisch) *to say grace* **~beter** m ~s/~ *precentor* **≈|beugen** vi [h] ⟨fig⟩ [dat] *to prevent, obviate, preclude* || sich ~ *to bend* od *lean forward* || ~d *preventive* || ⟨scient⟩ *prophylactic* **V.gung** f ~/~en ⟨fig⟩ *prevention*, ⟨med⟩ *prophylaxis* | **~s-** ~maßregel [f], ~mittel [n] *preventive measure*; *preservative*; ⟨med⟩ *prophylactic* (*against*) **~bilanz** f *trial balance* **V·orbild** n ~(e)s/~er *pattern* ⟨a. Lit⟩; *paragon, model, standard* || (Beispiel) *example* (*a bad e. to Henry* f H.); durch ~ u B. *by precedent and ex.* || (Urbild) *prototype* || (Tat) als ~ hinstellen *to hold up as one's model* .. | **≈en** vt [h] *to train*, ⟨Am a.⟩ *to fit* | **≈lich** a *model* [attr]; *exemplary, representative* (f *of*); *typical* (f *for*) || *model* (*how m. of you!, a m. boy*) || ~ s f *to be the model of* || ~ w *to become a byword* (wegen *for*) | ~keit [f] *exemplariness* | **~ung** f ~/ *preparatory training*; *qualification* (*for*) || allgemeine ~ *general education* (*required for* ..) **V·or- ≈|binden** vt irr [h] *to tie on* (*an apron*), *to put on* || *to show how to tie* || *to put .. at the beginning* ([dat] *of a book*) || °sich [dat] e–n ~ *to haul a p over the coals* **~blase** f ⟨path⟩ *fore-bladder* **≈|blasen** vt irr [h]; jdm etw ~ *to play a th* (*on the horn*, etc) *to a p* **~blatt** n ⟨bot⟩ *bract* **~block** m ⟨met⟩ *cogged ingot* **~bogen** m ⟨typ⟩ *introductory matter* **≈|bohren** vt/i [h] *to open with an auger* od *a gimlet* **~börse** f ~/ *morning exchange* **≈börslich** a (*noted*) *before* (*the official*) *hours* **~bote** m ⟨a. fig⟩ *herald, harbinger, forerunner, precursor* || ⟨fig & path⟩ *symptom* **~bram-** ~brasse [f] *fore-topgallant brace*; ~rahe [f] *f.-t. yard*; ~stenge [f] *f.-t. mast* **≈|brechen** vi irr [s] *to sally forth* **≈|bringen** vt irr [h] *to bring forward* (*out, up*); *to produce, proffer*; e–e gute Idee ~ *to come up with* ..; *to tender* (*a request, apologies*, etc); (unerwartet) *to spring* (*charges against* ..) || (anführen) *to allege, quote, adduce, urge, to put forth* od *forward* | **(Anliegen)** *to set forth* || (Ansicht) *to utter, advance, state* || (Beweis) *to bring forward* (*e.*) || (Einwand) *to interpose* || (Entschuldigung) *to offer, make* (*an apology*), *to advance* (*an excuse*); etw als E. ~ *to plead* .. || (Klage) *to make* (*a complaint*), ⟨jur⟩ *to prefer* (*a charge*) || (Plan) *to propose* || (kein Wort) *to say, utter* | **(behauptend)** *to maintain, assert* || (immer dasselbe) *to trot out*; (in neuer Fassung) *to ring the changes on* ..; mit Nachdruck ~ *to weigh in* (*an argument*) || (z Beweise) *to argue* (*that* ..) **≈|buchstabieren** vt [h] (jdm) *to spell out* (*a word to a p*) **~bühne** f ⟨theat⟩ *apron-stage, forestage*, ⟨Am⟩ *apron*; ~ l., r. *downstage l., r.* | **~n-** ~beleuchtung [f] *front of house* (*F.O.H.*) *lighting*, ⟨Am⟩ *auditorium beam* **~burg** f *outer works of a castle* **≈christlich** a *pre-Christian* **~dach** n *pent-house*; ⟨ec arch⟩ *canopy* **≈|datieren** vt [h] *to antedate* **≈d·em** [adv] *formerly, once*

V·order- [in comp oft] *front*(-) (*axle, door, garden, seat, view, wall*); *fore*(*arm, ..leg*); *fore*(*house, ..part*); *forward* (*combat zone*) **~asien** n *Hither* od *Anterior Asia* **~blatt** n (Schuh≈) *vamp* || ⟨cul⟩ = **~bug** m *shoulder* (*of mutton*), *fore-quarter* **~bühne** f ⟨theat⟩ *proscenium* **~deck** n ⟨mar⟩ *fore-deck*, ⟨hist⟩ *forecastle, fo'c'sle* **~eisen** n ⟨hors⟩ *front shoe* **~ende** n *fore-end*; *front end* **~front** f ⟨arch⟩ *front* **~gaumen** m *hard palate* **~gebäude** n ⟨arch⟩ *front*(*al*) *building* **~gestell** n *fore-carriage* **~giebel** m ⟨arch⟩ *front gable* **~glied** n ⟨mil⟩ *front-rank* || ⟨zoo⟩ *front limb* || ⟨math, log⟩ *antecedent* **~grund** m *foreground* || (sehr) im ~ stehen *to stand* (*well*) *to the fore*, ⟨fig⟩ *to be prominent*; im ~ aller Überlegungen (*is*) *a primary consideration* || im ~ stehen (P) *to be in the spotlight*; muß im ~ stehen (*must*) *receive priority in all planning and actions*; *at the focal point of all considerations is* ..; (*one's own mission must*) *remain paramount* || jdn in den ~ stellen *to show a p off*; etw .. *to put in the foreground*, ⟨fig⟩ *to bring* (*to the front* od) *into prominence, to throw into relief*; ⟨Am fam⟩ *to play up* || sich in den ~ schieben ⟨fig⟩ *to put o.s. forward* ||

Aussprache: Falls nicht anders (: [*v*]) angegeben, ist v = [*f*] zu sprechen.

in den ~ rücken [vi], treten *to come to the front*, (Frage) *to crop up* ~̲**gründig** a *apparent*; *superficial*; *literal*; *very* od *most important*; *prominent* (Aufgabe) ~**hand** f ⟨anat⟩ *fore-part of the hand*, ⟨scient⟩ *metacarpus* || ⟨hors⟩ *fore-hand* || ⟨cards⟩ *lead(er)* ~**hang** m *forward slope* ~**haupt** n *fore-part of the head*, ⟨scient⟩ *sinciput* || *forehead* ~**hausbewohner** m *frontager* ~**indien** n *Hither India, Hindustan* ~**instanz** f ⟨jur⟩ *court below* ~**kante** f der Tragfläche ⟨aero⟩ *leading edge* ~**kastell** n ⟨mar hist⟩ *forecastle, fo'c'sle* ~**lader** m *muzzle-loader* ~**lastig** [a] = vorlastig ~**lauf** m ⟨hunt⟩ *foreleg* ~**leder** n *front part* (*of a shoe*) ⟨mot, rail⟩ *headlight* ~**loge** f ⟨theat⟩ *front box* ~**luke** f ⟨mar⟩ *fore-hatchway* ~**mann** m *front-rank man*; *man in front*; *file-leader*; ⟨mil⟩ ~! *cover off*! || ⟨mar⟩ *ship next ahead* || ⟨com⟩ *previous endorser* || ⟨cards⟩ *leader*; *elder hand* | ~ halten *to keep in file* od *line* || ~ nehmen *to get covered* | ⟨fig⟩ jdn auf ~ bringen *to make a p toe the line*; ⟨pol⟩ *to drill*; e–n ~ h *to have one man ahead of one* ~**mast** m *foremast* ~**plattform** f ⟨rail⟩ *front platform* ~**pferd** n *leader* ~**rad** n *front wheel* | ~antrieb [m] *f.* (*w.-*)*drive* ~**raum** m ⟨mar⟩ *forehold* ~**reihe** f *frontrow* od *rank* ~**rhein** m *Fore-Rhine* ~**satz** m ⟨log⟩ *major, premise, antecedent* || ⟨gram⟩ *protasis* ~**schiff** n *bow* ~**segel** n *foresail* ~**seite** f ⟨arch⟩ *front, face* || ⟨num⟩ *obverse* || ⟨typ⟩ *recto*; (Buch~̲) *odd page* || an der ~ ⟨bes Am⟩ *out front* ~**steven** m *stem* ~**stube** f *front-room* ~**teil** m *forepart*; *front end* || ⟨tail⟩ e–s Kleidungsstücks *front of a garment* || ⟨mar⟩ *prow* || ⟨aero⟩ *nose* || °⟨sex⟩ (*her*) *front attic* od *door, garden, parlour*, ⟨hum⟩ (*her*) *Antipodes* ~**treffen** n ⟨mil⟩ *first line*; *van(guard)* ~**türe** f *front-door* ~**viertel** n ⟨cul⟩ *fore-quarter* ~**wagen** m ⟨artill⟩ *fore-carriage* ~**wand** f *face* (*of a mountain*) ~**zahn** m *front-tooth* ~**zeug** n ⟨hors⟩ *breast-plate* ~**zimmer** n = –stube ~**zwiesel** m *pommel*

v·ordere a *front* (*rank*), *fore(-part)*, *anterior*, *foremost*; → Vorderwand || ~ Kampfzone [f] *forward combat zone* (*FCZ*) **vorderhand** [adv] *for the present* od *moment*, *for the time being* **v·orderste** a *foremost*, *first* || ~r Graben *fire-trench* || ~ Front *firing line* || in der ~n Reihe *in the forefront*

V·or- ~**dienstzeit** f ([*non-*]*reckonable*) *periods of previous service* ~̲|**dränge(l)n**: (sich) ~ [h] *to press* od *push forward* | ⟨fig⟩ *to put o.s. forward*, *to push o.s.*; (rücksichtslos) ⟨Am sl⟩ *to horn in* | sich ~d *obtrusive, pushing* ~̲|**dringen** | vi irr [s] *to advance, to push* (*forward, ahead* od) *one's way* || ⟨fig⟩ *to get down* (*to*) || nach N. ~ *to press north* || ~ bis zu *to penetrate to* | ⟨mil⟩ *to gain ground* **2.** ~̲ [n] der Atomenergie *nuclear development* ~̲**dringlich** a *pushing* || (vorlaut) *forward, pert* || (zudringlich) *intruding* || (wichtig) *urgent*; ~st *first*; *most important* ~**druck** m (*wine of the*) *first pressure* || ⟨typ⟩ *first impression* || (Formular) (*printed*) *form* ~̲|**drucken** vt [h] ⟨typ⟩ *to prefix* (*in print*) ~̲|**dudeln** vt [h] e–m etw ~ *to sing* (etc) .. *in a humdrum tone to a p* ~**ebbe** f *beginning of the ebb-tide* ~̲**ehelich** a *antenuptial*; *pre-nuptial*, *-marital* (*conception*) ~**eil-** ~winkel [m] ⟨telv⟩ *angle of advance* ~̲|**eilen** vi [s] *to hasten forward*; *to hurry on before* || e–m ~ *to outrun, precede a p* || e–r S [dat] *to anticipate* ~̲**eilig** a (*over*)*hasty, forward, rash, precipitate*; *premature*; *ill-considered*; *premature* (*answer*); *snap* (*judgment*) || ~ s in s–r Annahme *to count one's chickens before they are hatched* | [adv] *hastily* etc; ~ anfangen ⟨fam⟩ *to jump the gun*; ~ handeln ⟨Am a.⟩ *to go off half-cocked* | V.keit [f] *hastiness, forwardness, rashness, precipitation*, *overhaste* ~̲**einander** [adv] *in front of each other* || Anordnung ~ *tandem arrangement* ~**einflugzeichen** n ⟨aero⟩ *outer beacon* od *marker* (*OM*) ~̲**eingenommen** a *biassed, prejudiced* (für *in favour of*, gegen *against*) | V.heit [f] *prepossession prejudice, bias*; zu ~ führen *to lead to pre-judgment* ~**eltern** [pl] *ancestors, forefathers* pl ~̲|**empfinden** vt irr [h] *to foresee, anticipate*; *to have a presentiment of* ~̲|**enthalten** vt irr [h] (jdm etw) *to keep .. back, to withold* od *conceal* (*a th from a p*); ⟨Am fam⟩ *to hold out* (*money*) *on a p* || ⟨jur⟩ *to detain* || das V.e ⟨jur⟩ *the detinue* **V.tung** f *withholding, detention* ~**entscheidung** f *preliminary decision* || ⟨jur⟩ *precedent* ~̲**entwässert** a *previously dewatered* (Gips) ~**ernte** f *first harvest* ~̲**·erst** [adv] *first of all, before all, firstly* || *for the present, for the time being* ~̲**erwähnt** a *before-* od *afore-mentioned, aforesaid* ~̲|**erzählen** vt [h] *to relate* (*a th to a p*) ~**erzeugnis** n (z. B. Gewebe) *semi-finished goods* pl ~̲|**essen 1.** vt [h] *to eat* (*sth*) *in presence of* (*a p*) || *to eat beforehand* || das ist –gegessenes Brot *that is counting your chickens before they are hatched* **2.** ~̲ [n] ⟨cul⟩ *entrée*; Sw = Ragout ~**fabel** f ⟨Lit⟩ *antecedents of a plot* ~̲|**fabeln** vt [h] e–m etw ~ *to tell a p tales about a th* ~**fabrizierung** f → –fertigung ~**fahr** m ~en/~en *ancestor*; ~ in gerader Linie *lineal a.*; ⟨fig⟩ (*legend is history*) *many times removed* (der G.) ~̲|**fahren** vi irr [s] *to draw up* || (bei jdm) *to drive up* (*to a p's house*) || (den Wagen) ~ l *to order* || ~ mit .. *to draw up* (*the bays*) *in front of the door* ~**fahr(rech)t** (n) f ⟨mot⟩ *right-of-way*; V.t beachten! *major road ahead*! *yield right of way*!; dem anderen die V.t l *to give way* (*to traffic*) **V.t-** ~straße [f] *major road*; ~zeichen [n] *sign of priority* ~**fall** m *occurrence, incident* || (Unfall) *accident* || (Fall) *case*; (Begebenheit) *event* | ⟨path⟩ *prolapsus* || (e–r Uhr) *detent* ~̲|**fallen** vi irr [s] **1.** *to fall forward*, ⟨path⟩ *to prolapse* **2.** *to happen, occur*; *to come to pass* || was ist ~gefallen? *what has happened*? ~̲|**fechten** vt [h] (e–m) ~ *to show* (*a p*) *how to fence* ~**fechter** m *fencing-master* || ⟨fig⟩ *champion* ~**feier** f ~/~n **1.** *preliminary celebration* **2.** –fest ~**feile** f *bastard file* ~**feld** n ⟨mil⟩ *forefield*; ⟨aero⟩ (Hallen~̲) *apron* ~**fenster** n *outside window* ~**fertigung** f *prefabrication* ~**fest** n ~es/~e *eve, vigil* ~̲|**finden** vt irr [h] *to find, to meet with* || *to light upon* | sich ~ *to appear, to be found, to be met with* ~**flügel** m ⟨aero⟩ *slat* ~̲|**flunkern** vt [h]; jdm etw ~ *to swindle a p with* (*a story*, etc); *to tell a p fibs* ~**flut** f *coming-in tide* ~̲|**fordern** vt [h] *to summon, cite* ~**forderung** f *summons* sg ~**frage** f *preliminary* (⟨parl⟩ *previous*) *question* ~̲|**fragen** vi [h] (bei jdm) *to call on a p to inquire* ~**freude** f *anticipated joy* od *pleasure* ~̲|**frischen** vt [h] ⟨met⟩ *to refine* ~**frucht** f *green* od *foregoing crop* ~**frühling** m *early spring* ~̲|**fühlen** vt [h] *to anticipate*; vi [h] ⟨mil⟩ *to seek the contact* | ~d *tentative* ~**führ-** ~apparat [m] ⟨film⟩ (*cine-*)*-projector*; ~dame [f] *mannequin*; ~dauer [f] ⟨film⟩ *running time* (⟨a.⟩ –zeit); ~raum [m] ⟨film⟩ *projection booth* ~̲**führen 1.** vt [h] *to bring forward*; *to produce* ⟨a. jur⟩ || ⟨theat⟩ *to present* (*a play*); (jdm etw) *to put* (*a th before a p*), *to submit* (*a th to a p*) || *to show* (*trained animals*) || *to demonstrate* || (Kleider) *to parade* || (Pferd) *to lead* od *trot out* (⟨a. fig⟩ *one's wines*) || (Verbrecher) *to lead out, to make appear in court* **2.** ~̲ [n] (der Angriffstruppen) *approach march* ~**führer** m *demonstrator* || ⟨film⟩ *operator*; *projectionist* ~**führung** f *bringing forward*; *production* || *submission* || *demonstration* || ⟨film⟩ *show(ing)*; *view* || *demonstration* || *exhibition* || *display* || ⟨telv⟩ (öffentlich) *public show(ing)* | ~**s-** ~befehl [m] ⟨jur⟩ *warrant to appear*, (*writ of*) *habeas corpus*; ~modell [n] *d.n model*; ~saal [m] *showroom* ~**gabe** f ~/~n ⟨sport, etc⟩

Verbal-Flexion der Verben mit der Vorsilbe **ver-** → das jeweilige Simplex

points od *odds* pl (given), *handicap start*; ⟨racing⟩ *head st.* || ohne ~ ⟨a.⟩ *from the scratch* || Spieler ohne ~ *scratch player* || e–e ~ erhalten *to take odds* | ~rennen, ~spiel [n] *handicap* **~gang** m ~(e)s/≈e *occurrence, event* || [pl] ⟨a.⟩ *practices, goings-on* pl || ⟨theat⟩ *act* || (Hergang) *process, operation, proceedings* pl; ⟨comp etc⟩ *transaction*; *t. movement* || (Vorzug) *priority* || (Präzedenzfall) *precedent* || → –tritt || ~ liegt hier nicht vor *this office has no record of ..* **~gänger** m *predecessor* **≈gängig** a *previous* || *preliminary* **~garten** m *front g.* **≈|gaukeln** vt [h] jdm etw ~ *to conjure up* (*a th*) *before a p*; *to deceive, humbug*, (z Spaß *to hoax*) *a p* || –gegaukelt *plausibly told* **≈|geben** vt irr [h] ⟨sport, etc⟩ *to give* (sich [dat] ~ l *to take*) *odds* od *points, handicap* (*to a p*) || *to give a start* (*of 10 yards*) | ⟨comp⟩ *to preset* | (behaupten) Uneigennutz ~ *to assume disinterestedness*; *to pretend* od *allege, affect* (*to be*); [abs] *to play possum*; (als Entschuldigung) *to plead* || ⟨sl⟩ *to let* od *lay on* (*to do*) | ≈ n *pretence, pretext* || *plea* || *allegation* **~gebirge** n *foothills* || ⟨mar⟩ *promontory, cape, head*(*land*) || steiles ~ *bluff* **≈geblich** a *ostensible, pretended* || *sham* (*illness*) || *supposed* (*heir*) || *would-be* (*poet*) **≈gebrannt** a *pre-burnt* (*stone*) **≈geburtlich** a *pre-natal* **≈gedacht** = –erwähnt **≈gedruckte** Karte ⟨geog⟩ *map blank* **≈gefaßt** a *preconceived* (*notion*) || ~e Meinung *preconception, prejudice* **~gefecht** n *preliminary skirmish* **≈gefertigt** a *prefab*(*ricated*) (Haus) **~gefühl** n *presentiment, foreboding* (*of*); ⟨fam⟩ *hunch* (*that ..*) || (banges) *misgiving*(*s* pl) | mit **≈gehaltener** Pistole *at the point of a p.* **≈|gehen I.** vi irr [s] **1.** *to advance* (*against*) || ⟨mil⟩ *to push forward, to march* (auf *on*); z Angriff ~ *to launch an attack*; ~ gegen *to move against* (in *in*); energisch *to take a strong* (*firm*) *line toward* (*with*); [abs] ⟨fam⟩ *to make the dust fly* || *to move on* (*inflation*) || vorsichtig ~ [abs] *to feel one's way* **2.** (vorausgehen) *to go first*; *to lead* (*the way*) **3.** e–m ~ *to precede*, ⟨fig⟩ *outstrip a p*; *to have precedence of a p* || ⟨fig⟩ *to have the preference, to have* od *take the precedence* ([dat] *of*) | Arbeit geht vor *business first*; dies geht allem anderen vor *this takes precedence over all other ths* || e–m als Muster ~ *to serve a p as model* **4.** (Uhr) *to be* (*5 minutes*) *fast*; *to gain* **5.** ⟨arch⟩ = vorragen **6.** (verfahren) *to proceed* (⟨a. jur⟩ *against*) || energisch ~ *to take a strong line* || methodisch ~ *to proceed with method* || gerichtlich ~ = einschreiten 2. || in e–r S ~ *to move in a matter* || behutsam ~ *to go warily*; geschickt ~ *to operate with skill*; sachte ~ mit *to proceed gently with*; scharf ~ *to act severely*, → Maßnahmen; unklug ~ *to play one's cards badly* **II.** v/imps (**sich ereignen**) = vorfallen 2 || *what has happened*? || *what is going on here*? *what's the matter*? = ⟨fam⟩ *what's up*? || während dies –ging ⟨a.⟩ *in the meanwhile* || es geht etw v. *sth is in the wind* || ich weiß nicht, was in mir (ihm) vorging *I don't know what I felt* (*.. what was in his mind*) || wann ging dieser Wandel in mir vor? *when did this change come to me*? **III.** ≈ n **1.** *advance* || *march forward*; im ~ s *to push forward*; ~ über eigene Truppen hinaus *passage* N **2.** *precedence* **3.** (*mode of*) *procedure* || (Verfahren) *proceeding*(*s* pl): gemeinsames ~ *concerted* od *common, joint action* || ⟨mil⟩ *combined movement* **≈|geigen** vt [h] (jdm etw) *to play* (*a th*) *on the violin* (*before* od *to a p*) **~geiger** m *leader* **≈gelagert** a *put up in front of*; ⟨mil⟩ *distant* (Warnkette) **~gelände** n *outlying lands* || ⟨mil⟩ *ground in front of a position* || *foreground* **~gelege** n *gearing, countershaft* **~gemach** n *anteroom* **≈gemeldet, ≈genannt** a *before-mentioned* **~genuß** m *anticipated enjoyment* || *foretaste* (*of pleasure*) **~gepackt** a *packaged* (*food*) **~gericht** n *entrée*; pikantes ~ *appetizer* **≈gerückt** a *advanced* (*age*), ⟨a.⟩ ~es Alter *decline of life*; in ~em A. *advanced in years*; ~ in Jahren *well along in years*; *late* (*hour*) **~gesang** m *introductory song* **~geschichte** f ~/~n (e–r S) *past* od *previous history* || *prehistoric times* || (e–r P) *antecedents* pl; *background*; ⟨med⟩ *case history* **≈geschichtlich** a *prehistoric* **~geschmack** m *foretaste* **≈geschoben** a [pp v –schieben]; ~e P *man of straw* || ~er Posten ⟨mil⟩ *advanced post*; *forward* (*observer*; *defence position* N), *advanced* (*position*); ⟨mount⟩ *a.d* (*base*) || zu weit ~ *too far forward* **≈geschrieben** a *compulsory, obligatory* (jdm *on a p*) || *regulation-*(*uniform*), (*holidays*) *of obligation*; ⟨univ⟩ *statuable* (*age*); ⟨jur⟩ *mandatory*; innerhalb der ~en Frist *within the prescribed period* **≈geschritten** a [pp v –schreiten] ⟨fig⟩ *advanced*; weit ~ *far a.d* (*disease*) **≈gesehen** a *proposed* (*production*); nicht ~ *unprovided for*, im Programm *unscheduled* || das ist ~ *that is in the arrangement*; wie ~ *as arranged*; ~ für (P & S) *intended, designed for* **~gesetzte(r)** m *superior, chief*, ⟨Am⟩ *boss*; ⟨mil⟩ *senior* (*officer*) | ~n-verhältnis [n] *authority* **~gespinst** n *slub*(*bing*), *roving* **≈gestern** [adv] (*on*) *the day before yesterday*, ⟨Am⟩ *d. b. y.* || ~ abend *on the evening before last* **≈gestrig** a *of the day before yesterday* **≈gestülpt** a *protruded* **≈getäuscht** a *make-belief* [attr] **≈gezeichnet** ⟨mus⟩ was ist ~? *what is the key* od *signature*?; ~ u zugeschnitten *dried and cut* (*plan*) **≈gezogen** (→ –ziehen) *forward control* (⟨mot⟩ Fahrersitz) **~giebel** m *front-gable* **~glacis** n *avant-glacis* **≈|glänzen** vi *to shine forth* || e–m ~ *to be a brilliant example to a p* **~graben** m *avant-fosse* **≈|greifen** vi irr [h] **1.** *to stretch out* (mit .. *one's hand*) **2.** ⟨fig⟩ [dat] *to anticipate, forestall* (*a p* || *a th* ⟨a.⟩ mit) || *to prejudge* (*a question*) || [abs]: *we are advancing matters* || *to encroach* (in .. *on a p's rights*) || ~d *anticipatory* **~grund** m *foreground* **≈|haben I.** vt irr [h] **1.** (jdm) *to have before* (*a p*) **2.** (Schürze) *to have .. on, to wear ..* **3.** (jdn vornehmen) *to examine, question* (*a p*), *to take* (*a p*) *to task* || *to scold, rebuke, reprimand* (*a p*) **4.** (beabsichtigen) *to intend, meditate, purpose, project* (*a th*; *to do*) || etw ~ ⟨fam⟩ *to have sth up one's sleeve, to be up to sth* || *I propose to leave the party*; *I don't propose to do it* || *to have a matter in contemplation* || (ernstlich ~) *I have a great mind to do it* || Böses ~ *to have evil designs, to be plotting some mischief* || → vielerlei || was h sie vor? *what are they after*? || was anderes ~ *to be otherwise engaged*; besseres ~ *to have other fish to fry* || was h Sie heute vor? *what are your plans for to-day*? || h Sie .. etw vor? *are you doing anything to-night*? || mit jdm etw ~ *to have plans for a p* || was h Sie **mit** ihm vor? *what do you intend to do with him*? || etw (Großes) mit jdm ~ *to have designs upon* (*to have great schemes with regard to*) *a p* || er hat **es** gut mit dir vor *he means well* (*by you*) **5.** (beschäftigt s mit) *to be busy with* || *I have an inquiry on hand* **II.** ≈ [n] *intent*(*ion*), *design, purpose, plan, project, scheme* (*he had to abandon his scheme*) **~hafen** m *out*(*er*)*port* **~halle** f *vestibule,* (*entrance-*)*hall* || ⟨ec, etc⟩ *porch, portico* (⟨a.⟩ Säulenhalle) || ⟨theath, parl⟩ *lobby* || (Hotel≈) *lounge* || ⟨fig⟩ *rudiments* (*of a science*) **~halt** m ~(e)s/~e **1.** *remonstrance* || *reproach* || (ernst) (⟨a.⟩ ~ung) *expostulation* || jdm ~e m über [acc] *to remonstrate with a p* (*up*)*on a th* **2.** ⟨mus⟩ *suspension* **3.** ⟨mil⟩ *aiming-off, allowance* | **≈en** irr sep [h] **I.** vt ⟨artill, etc⟩ *to allow* (f *for*) || jdm etw ~ *to hold a th before a p* || ⟨fig⟩ *to remonstrate* od *expostulate with a p on the subject of, to reproach, upbraid a p with a th* || .. wird ihm vorgehalten *his low birth is being*

Aussprache: Falls nicht anders (: [v]) angegeben, ist v = [f] zu sprechen.

cast into his teeth | sich [dat] etw ~ *to bear a th in mind* **II.** vi *to last*; ⟨cul⟩ *to be substantial*; ⟨tail⟩ *to wear well* | **~e-** ~punkt [m] *set-forward point* (⟨a.⟩ theoretisch); *future position (of target)*; ~winkel [m] ⟨artill⟩ *deflection angle*; *angle of lead*; ⟨aero-mil⟩ *dropping angle* | **~ung** f ~/~en = Vorhalt I. **~hand** f ⟨cards⟩ *lead, elder hand* ‖ die ~ h, in der ~ s *to have the lead* ‖ ⟨com⟩ *to have the refusal (of a bargain)* ‖ ⟨hors⟩ *forehand* ‖ ⟨ten⟩ ~-*fore-hand (stroke)* ‖ anderen die ~ l ⟨fig fam⟩ *to take a backseat* **≗h·anden** a *at hand*; *present, ready*; wirklich ~ *real (risk)* ‖ (Lebendes) *existing* ‖ (Lebloses) *extant (his e. dramas)* ‖ ⟨com⟩ [pred] *on hand*; *in stock*; *available* [a. attr]; noch ~ *remnant*; nur beschränkt ~ s *to be in short* od *limited supply* ‖ (bestehend) *extant, existing* ‖ ~ s *to exist*; *to be met with*; *to be at hand* ‖ nicht ~ s *to be non-existent* ‖ reichlich ~ s *to abound, to be abundant* ‖ noch ~ s *to remain, subsist* ‖ es ist nichts mehr davon ~ *there is no more of it*, ⟨com⟩ *we are out of it* **≗sein** n *existence, presence* ‖ Nicht≗ *absence* **~hang** m ~(e)s/≗e *curtain* (⟨a. theat⟩; eiserner *fire* od *safety c.*; ⟨pol⟩ *iron c.*, Bambus≗ *bamboo c.*); ⟨Am a.⟩ *shade*; ⟨theat⟩ Akt≗ *act* (⟨Am⟩ *close-in) drop*; Fall≗ *drop c.*; Raff≗ *traverse* od *tableau c.* (⟨fam⟩ *tabs*), ⟨Am⟩ *traveler*, Saal~ *house c.*; ⟨bib⟩ *veil* ‖ [pl] *hangings* pl ‖ durch ~ abschließen *to curtain off* ‖ ⟨theat⟩ der ~ geht aus (fällt) *the c. rises (drops)* | ~kabinett [n] *c. set*, ⟨Am⟩ *drapery setting*; ~ring [m] *c.-ring*; ~schnur [f] *drawstring*; ~stab [m], ~stange [f] *c.-rod*; ~zugstange [f] ⟨theat⟩ *track* **≗|hangen** *⟨poet⟩ vi irr [h] *to hang before* ‖ *to jut out* **≗|hängen** vt [h] *to hang* od *put before* | vi [h] = vorhangen **~hängeschloß** n *padlock* **~haupt** (Brücken≗) n *forestarling* **~haus** n *entrance-hall, vestibule* **~haut** f ⟨anat⟩ *foreskin, prepuce*; mit (halb)zurückgezogener ~ *(half-)fully uncapped* ‖ Verengung der ~ *phimosis* **~hemd(chen)** n *shirt-front*, ⟨fam⟩ *dicky* ‖ (f Frauen) *chemisette*

vorh·er [adv] *before, previously, beforehand* ‖ (im voraus) *in advance* ‖ lange (kurz) ~ *long (a short time) before*; *a few days previously* ‖ am Abend ~ *(on) the previous evening, the night before* | [in comp oft] = vor(aus)- **~|bedenken** vt irr [h] *to premeditate*; *to consider beforehand* **~|bestimmen** vt [h] *to arrange beforehand, to predetermine* ‖ ⟨rel⟩ *to predestin(at)e* **≗bestimmung** f *predetermination*; *predestination* ⟨a. rel⟩ **≗dasein** n *preexistence* **~|gehen** vi irr [s] [dat] *to go before, to precede* ‖ ~d [a] *foregoing, previous, preceding* ‖ ~d *previous* (Befehl); allem ~d *antecedent* ‖ am ~den A. etc *(on) the evening before, on the previous day* ‖ auf: *in the foregoing pages* ‖ aus dem ~en folgt *it follows from what has already been said* ‖ im ~den ist .. *it has been previously mentioned* ‖ in der ~den W. *the week before* **~|sagen** vt [h] = vor·aussagen ‖ v·orher|sagen *to say previously* **≗sage, ≗sagung** f *prediction, prophecy* **~sehbar** a *foreseeable* **~|sehen** vt irr [h] *to foresee, forecast* ‖ es war -zu- *it could be expected* **~|verkündigen** vt [h] *to foretell, predict* **≗verkündigung** f *prediction* **~|wissen** vt irr [h] *to foreknow*

V·or- **~herbst** m *early autumn* **≗h·erig** a *preceding, previous* ‖ *former, last* ‖ (Zahlung) *(made in) advance* **~herrschaft** f *hegemony, supremacy, ascendency* ‖ die ~ h *to predominate* (über *over*) ‖ → **≗|herrschen** vi [h] *to prevail, predominate*; *to be uppermost* od *rampant* | ~d [a] *predominant, prevalent* **≗|h·eucheln** vt [h]; e-m (etw) ~ *to pretend (fidelity) to a p*; *to feign (friendship) for a p* **≗|heulen** vt [h] (jdm etw) *to whine (to a p about a th)* **~himmel** m *first heaven* **≗h·in** [adv] *before*; *some time ago, a little while ago* ‖ *quite recently, just now* **≗hinein** [adv]: im ~ *in advance* **~hof** m *front yard, outer court*; *entry, vestibule* ‖ ⟨ec⟩ *parvis* ‖ ⟨anat⟩ Herz≗ *auricle*; Ohr≗ *vestibule* **~hol-** ~einrichtung [f] (⟨a.⟩ ~er [m]) ⟨artill⟩ *recuperator*; ~feder [f] *r. spring* **≗|holen** vt [h] *to bring out, produce* ‖ ⟨mar⟩ *to haul .. home* **~hölle** f *limbo* **≗|hören** vt; man hört .. vor *(her voice) is heard above* (unter) *all the others* **~hut** f *right of first pasturage* ‖ ⟨mil⟩ *van(guard)* **≗ig** a *former, preceding, previous* ‖ (letztvergangen) *last (week*, etc) ‖ im ~ *above* **~instanz** f ⟨jur⟩ *lower court* **~jahr** n *preceding year, last y.* **≗jährig** a *last year's* **≗|jammern** vt/i [h] (jdm [etw]) *to whine (to a p [about a th])* **~kammer** f *anteroom* ‖ Herz≗ *auricle* ‖ ⟨tech⟩ *precombustion chamber*, ⟨mot a.⟩ *antechamber* **≗|kämpfen** vi [h] *to fight before* (e-m *a p*); *to fight in the front rank* ‖ *to set an example to the other combatants* | sich ~ ⟨mil⟩ *to gain ground* **~kämpfer(in** f) m ⟨fig⟩ *champion, pioneer, partisan* **≗|kauen** vt [h] *to chew (for a child)* ‖ ⟨fig⟩ *to repeat* od *explain over and over* **≗|kaufen** vt [h] *to forestall* **~kaufsrecht** n *(right of) pre-emption*; *first right of purchase*; (bedingtes *first right of*); *refusal* (auf *of*); ein ~ ausüben *to pre-empt* **≗|kehren** vt [h] *to sweep forth* **~kehr(ung** f ~/~en) f ~/: ~ treffen *to take preventive measures*; .. *precautions*; *steps*; *to make preparations, provision, arrangements*; .. für *to provide for*; .. z tun ⟨Am⟩ *to fix on a th to do*; .. gegen .. *to meet (trouble) halfway* **~keim** m ⟨bot⟩ *prothallium* **~kenntnis** f *preliminary* bzw *previous knowledge* (v *of*) ‖ -nisse [pl] *elements, rudiments* pl ‖ er hat gute -nisse in [dat] *he is well grounded in the elements of ..* **~kette** f (Berg-) *lower chain* ‖ (Ausläufer) *spur* **~kirche** f *porch* **≗klassisch** a *pre-classic(al)* **≗|klimpern** vt [h]; jdm etw ~ *to strum a tune to a p* **≗|klingen** vi irr [h] *to sound in one's ear* ‖ *to sound louder than the rest*, ⟨fig⟩ *to predominate* ‖ *to sound beforehand* **≗klinisch** a ⟨med⟩ *preparatory* (⟨sl⟩ *preppie*) *(terms)* **≗kochen** vt [h] *to precook* **~kommando** n ⟨mil⟩ *advanced party* **≗|kommen I.** vi irr [s] **A. 1.** *to come to the front* ‖ ⟨com⟩ (Wechsel) *to be presented* **2.** jdm etw ~ *to pledge a p* **3.** = zu~ **4.** (zugelassen w) *to be admitted* **5.** (zu Besuch) *to call* (bei jdm *on*), *to look in (on a p)* **6.** (zur Verhandlung) *to be proposed, to be brought forward* ‖ ⟨jur⟩ *to be tried* **7.** (geschehen) *to occur, happen*; *to take place* **8.** (sich finden) *to be found, to be met with*; häufig ~ *to swarm*; selten ~ *to be of rare occurrence* ‖ ⟨bot, zoo⟩ *to range* (in *in*) häufig: *this bird is common* (in *to*); ‖ ⟨Lit. a.⟩ *to come* (bei .. *in Goethe*) **9.** (erscheinen) *to seem, appear* **B.** das -mt in den besten Familien vor *such ths happen in the best-regulated family*; der größte Schwindler, der mir je -ge- ist .. *whom I ever came across*; so -mt er mir vor *that's the impression he makes on me*; er -mt mir unmenschlich vor *I don't feel him to be human* ‖ **es** -mt **mir** (selbst so) vor *it seems to me (I feel that way myself)*; so etw ist mir noch nicht -ge- *I never met with such a th before*; *it is unprecedented*; ⟨fam⟩ *well, I never!* ‖ das -mt mir sonderbar vor *that strikes me as peculiar, I think it rather strange* ‖ es -mt mir vor, als ob *I have an idea that* | **sich** [dat] ~ *to picture o.s.* (*in*); sich verlassen ~ *to feel lost*; sich ~ als *to imagine o.s. (a modern Dürer)* ‖ sich sehr gescheit ~ *to feel rather clever* ‖ sich wichtig ~ *to fancy o.s.* ‖ wie k Sie mir vor? *I do not understand you!, what is the matter with you?*; *what do you mean by it?, what's the idea?* **sich** weit älter ~, als man ist *to feel o.s. much older than one's age*; sich sehr läppisch ~ *to feel very foolish* | sich ~, als flöge man *to think of o.s. flying* | wenig **-d:** bei -der Gelegenheit *when occasion offers*; *should the case arise*; schlechthin überall

---

Verbal-Flexion der Verben mit der Vorsilbe **ver-** → das jeweilige Simplex

~d *of world-wide occurrence* **II.** ~̽ n ⟨min⟩ *occurrence, presence; deposit;* (*oil*) *reservoir* || ⟨bot⟩ *habitat* || ⟨com⟩ (v Wechseln) bei ~ *on presentation* **~kommnis** n –nisses/–nisse *contingency, event, occurrence, incident* **~korrektur** f *first proof* **~kost** f *hors-d'œuvre*(*s* pl) ~̽|**kosten** vt [h] *to essay, foretaste* ~̽|**kragen** vi [h] ⟨arch⟩ *to jut out; to project* ~̽|**kriechen** vi [s] *to creep forward* **~kriegs-** [in comp] *pre-war* [attr] || .. seit der ~zeit *he knew him from before the war* ~̽**kühlen** vt [h] *to precool*; dazu: ~*er* ~̽|**laden** vt irr [h] ⟨jur⟩ *to summon, cite* || (bei Strafe) *to subpœna* **~lader** *summoner* **~ladung** ⟨jur⟩ *citation* || *summons, writ; subpœna* **~lage** f *text, copy; original* ⟨a. rep⟩ || ⟨Lit⟩ gemeinsame ~ *common source* || (Muster) *pattern* | *drawing-copy* | (Destillier~̽) *receiver*; ⟨chem⟩ *recipient* | *bedside carpet* | ⟨tech⟩ *eking-piece,* (Watte~̽) *wad* | ⟨med⟩ *maternity* od *obstretical pad* (*OB pad*) | ⟨artill⟩ *flash reducer* | ⟨parl⟩ *bill* (einbringen *to submit*) | [abstr] *submission* (*of a record*); *production* (*of a certificate*) | ~blatt [n] *pattern* ~̽|**lagern** vi [s], sich ~ [dat] *to extend in front of* ~̽|**lallen** vt [h] *to lisp* od *stammer to* **~land** n *foreland, cape* ~̽|**langen** vt [h] *to take out, to draw forth* ~̽**längst** [adv] *long ago, long since* ~̽|**lassen** vt irr [h] (voran l) *to let pass before, to give the precedence to, to allow* (*a p*) *to come forward* || ⟨sport⟩ *to allow* (*a p*) *to get the start of one* bzw *to pass one* || (zulassen) *to show into a p's presence, to admit* **~lassung** f *access, admittance, admission* **~last** f ⟨tech⟩ *initial load* ~̽**lastig** a ⟨mar⟩ *down by the head* || ⟨aero⟩ *nose-heavy* **~lauf** m ⟨tech⟩ (e–s Kolbens) *forward stroke*; ⟨sport⟩ *start; heat*; ⟨ftb⟩ *charge* || (Branntweinbrennerei) *first runnings* pl | ⟨phot⟩ *leader*; ⟨film⟩ *l. strip* | ~band [n] mit Einsatzfeldern ⟨film⟩ *synchronizing l.* ~̽|**laufen** vi irr [s] *to run before* || [dat] (überholend) *to outrun, overtake* || ⟨ftb⟩ *to charge* **~läufer** m *forerunner, precursor; antecedent*; ⟨med⟩ *symptom* ~̽**läufig** a *provisional, preliminary, temporary*; (*reports*) *so far available* || *first, initial; tentative* (*appointment, finding* || *result* ⟨a. mil⟩) | [adv] *provisionally; for the present, for the time being; temporarily*; ~ nicht *not so far* ~̽**laut** a *pert, forward; flippant* || ~es Wesen [n] *pertness* || ⟨hunt⟩ *giving tongue too soon* **~**|**leben** n ~s/ *former life* || *antecedents* pl; *past* (*a girl with a p.*) **V·orlege-** **~besteck** n (ein *a pair of*) *carvers* pl **~blatt** n *drawing-copy* **~bracke** f *swingle tree* **~gabel** f *carving-fork* **~kelle** f *fish-slice* **~löffel** m *soup-ladle; gravy-spoon* **~messer** n *carving-knife* **~pferd** n *additional horse* **~schloß** n *padlock* **~welle** f *intermediate shaft* **Vor-** ~̽|**legen** vt [h] **1.** (etw) *to push forward* **2.** (jdm) *to lay* od *place, put before* (*a p*) || *to put on* (*a padlock*) || *to put* (*fresh horses*) *to* .. || *to present* (*a bill* ⟨com & parl⟩) || *to expose* (*goods for sale*) || (zur Ansicht) *to display, exhibit* (e–m *before a p*) **3.** (vorschlagen) *to submit, propose* || (vorbringen) *to produce* || (zur Prüfung) *to submit a th to a p*; wieder *to resubmit, re-present* **4.** jdm etw (bei Tische) ~ *to help a p to a dish* || .. noch einmal .. *to give a p a second helping* | *to give* (*the cattle hay*) **5. sich** ~ *to lean forward* **~leger** m ~s/~ Bett~̽ etc *rug* **~legung** f ~/~en *putting-before* || *submission* || *presentation,* etc **~legierung** f *master alloy* ~̽|**lehnen,** sich ~ [h] *to lean forward; to sit f.d* (*in the chair*) ~̽|**leiern** vt [h]; jdm etw ~ *to play a th monotonously to a p* || *to din sth into a p's ears* || immer dasselbe ~ ⟨fig⟩ *to be always harping on the same string* **~leistung** f *advance commitment* ~̽**lesbar** a *fit to be read aloud* **~lese** f *early vintage* ~̽|**lesen** vt irr [h] **1.** *to read aloud* || jdm etw ~ *to read a th to a p* || sich [dat] ~ l *to be read to*; wir l uns Sh. ~ *we have Sh. read aloud to us* **2.** [abs] *to gather the first ripe grapes* **~leser** m *reader, reciter, elocutionist* || (Vortragender) *lecturer* **~lesung** f *lecture*; öffentliche ~ *open l.* || ~en halten *to give* (*a course of*) *l.s*; .. über [acc] *to l. on* || ~en hören *to attend l.s* || ~en belegen *to join a class* **~lesungs-** [in comp] *lecture-* (*fee, list*) ~̽**letzt** a *last .. but one* || ⟨gram⟩ *penultimate* || ~e Silbe *penult*(*imate*) || im ~en Jahr *the year before last* ~̽|**leuchten** vi [h] [dat] *to carry a light before, to shine before* || (überglänzen) *to outshine* || ⟨fig⟩ *to set a good example to* ~̽**l·ieb**|**nehmen** (für–) vi [h] (mit) *to be satisfied, to content o.s.; to be content, to put up* (*with*); [abs] *to take pot-luck* **~liebe** f ~/ *predilection, preference, partiality, liking* (h *to have*) (f *for*); *bias* (f *toward*); launenhafte ~ *fancy* (*for*) || e–e ~ h f ⟨a.⟩ *to be* (*very*) *partial to, to be prepossessed in favour of* || e–e entschiedene ~ *a decided liking* || mit ~ *for, by preference; for choice*; mit Vor-Liebe heiraten ⟨sex-hum⟩ *to sit down to dinner before grace is said*; sie heiraten mit „Vor-Liebe" ⟨sex-hum⟩ *they sat down to dinner before grace was said* **~**|**liegen** vi irr [h] *to lie before* || dem P. *to be up before parliament* || ⟨com⟩ [dat] (Brief) *to have come to hand* || so wie es –gt *as it is* | ⟨fig⟩ *to present itself, to be under consideration* || hier liegt D. vor *this is a case of theft* || hier muß ein Irrtum ~ *there must be some m. here* || heute liegt nichts vor *there is nothing to be discussed* (etc) *to-day*; ⟨fam⟩ *nothing doing to-day* || ~ zw .. u *to range from .. to ..* | **~d** a ⟨fig⟩ (*matter*) *in hand*; (*case*) *in question; present* (*volume*) || (*reports*) *to hand,* (*news*) *at h.,* (*matter*) *in h.* ~̽|**lügen** vt irr [h] (jdm etw) *to tell a lie* (*to a p*), *to lie* (*about a th to a p*) **vorm** ⟨fam⟩ = vor dem **V·or-** ~̽|**machen** vt [h] (Brett etc) *to put on* od *before* || *to put* (*an apron*) *on* | jdm etw ~ *to show a p how a th is done* | ⟨fig⟩ **(sich** [dat]**)** *to pretend to a p* (*to o.s.*) (*that*); *to impose upon, to fool* (⟨sl⟩ *kid*) *a p*; der Welt (sich) etw ~ *to be masquerading* (*to delude o.s.*); er versuchte **sich** –zu– *he tried to make h.s. believe*; sich nichts ~ *to have no illusions* (*about*); sich nichts ~ l *not to stand any nonsense* **~macht** f *leading power* || *hegemony* (⟨a.⟩ -stellung) **~magen** m *omasum* ~̽|**malen** vt [h] *to show* (*a p*) *how to paint* | ⟨fig⟩ *to describe, paint* ([dat] *to*) ~̽**malig** a, ~̽**mals** [adv] = ehemalig, –mals **~mann** m *foreman, captain* || ⟨cards⟩ *elder hand* || (Spiel) *first player* || (b. Rudern) *stroke* || ⟨com⟩ = Vordermann **~marsch** m ⟨mil⟩ *advance* (auf *on*); ⟨fig⟩ *onward march* | ~straße [f] *road* od *route of approach* **~mars-** ~segel [n] ⟨mar⟩ *fore-topsail*; ~fall [n] *f.-t. halyard* **~märz** m (~̽lich [a]) *period before* ([a] *previous to*) *the March* (*revolution of 1848* ⟨hist⟩); ([a] ⟨fig fam⟩ *antediluvian*) **~mast** m ⟨mar⟩ *foremast* **~mauer** f *outer wall* **~merk-** ~buch [n] *memorandum-book*; ~gebühr [f] *registration-fee*; ~liste [f] *waiting list* ~̽|**merken** vt [h] *to put* od *note .. down; to book* od *reserve* (f *for*) || ⟨com⟩ *to make a note of; to enter* (*a p for a job*), *to mark down* (*for* ..) ~̽|**messen** vt irr [h] (jdm) *to measure before a p* ~̽**militärisch** a *para-, premilitary* **~mittag** m *forenoon, morning* || am ~ *in the m.* || gestern ~̽ *yesterday m.* | ~̽**s** [adv] *in the m.* | **~s-** ~besuch [m] *m. call*; ~gottesdienst [m] *m. service*; ~stunde [f] *m. hour* bzw *lesson*; ~wache [f] *forenoon watch* ~̽**mittägig** a *morning* [attr s] **~mitternacht** f *the time before midnight* **~mund** m ~(e)s/~e & ~̽er *guardian, trustee* **~mundschaft** f ~/~en *guardianship; tutelage* (⟨a. fig⟩; *over*) || unter ~ stellen *to place under the care of a guardian* | ~̽**lich** a *belonging* od *relating to a guardian*(*'s duties*), *tutelar*(*y*) | **~s-** ~behörde [f], ~gericht [n] *guardian court, Court of Chancery*; ~gelder [n pl] *trust-money*;

Aussprache: Falls nicht anders (: [*v*]) angegeben, ist v = [*f*] zu sprechen.

~ordnung [f] *order in Ch.*; ~rechnung [f] *account rendered of t.-m.*; ~wesen [n] (*matters* pl *relating to*) *guardianship* ≈|**müssen** vi [h] *to be obliged to* (*come forth* od) *advance, appear* (⟨theat⟩ *before the curtain*)

vorn = vorne | ⟨fam⟩ = vor den | **~·an** [adv] *in front* || (*to sit*) *in the front row*

V·or- ~nahme f ~/ *taking* (*a th*) *in hand* **~name** m *Christian*, ⟨bes Am⟩ *first, middle* (⟨Am a.⟩ *given*) *name*

v·orn(e) 1. a *before*; *in front* | ganz ~ *right in the fr.* || weiter ~ *further forward* | ~ im Buch *at the beginning of the b.* || ~ eintreten *to enter by the fr. door* || ~ s *to be on in fr.* | ~ u hinten *before and behind*; ⟨mar⟩ *fore and aft*; ⟨fig⟩ *here, there, and everywhere*; .. alles dran ⟨sex⟩ *obviously the right number* (*e.g. 37–24–36*); ⟨Am⟩ *it's what's up front that counts* | **nach** ~ *to the front* ⟨a. fig⟩; ⟨theat⟩ *downstage*; .. fallen *to fall forward* || mit dem hinteren Ende nach ~ (S) *end on* || (nach) ~ hinaus (*to live*) *in the front*; *front* (*room*); (*room*) *facing the street* || nach ~ zeigen *to point ahead* || der Drang nach ~ *the forward impetus* | **von** ~ *from before* || (P) *full-face* || (von neuem) *from the beginning*; *over again*; *anew, afresh*, ⟨mus⟩ *da capo* || v ~ anfangen *to begin at the beginning, to start from the scratch*; wieder .. *to begin all over again, to start all afresh, to make a new start* || v ~ bis hinten ⟨mar⟩ *from stem to stern* || ich sah ihn v ~ *I saw his face* **II. das** ≈ u Hinten *both front and back* **~her·ein** [adv]: v ~ *from the first*; *straight away*; *offhand*; sich v ~ übersehen l: *situations can seldom be fully anticipated* **~h·in** [adv] *to the front* **~hinein** [adv] *in by the front* **~·über** [adv] *head foremost* || (*to bend one's head*) *forward* **~w·eg** [adv] *from the first* || *to begin with*

V·or- ≈nehm a **A. (P)** *of noble birth, of* (*superior*) *rank, of quality*; *aristocratic*; *eminent, prominent, grand*; *sophisticated*; (⟨fam⟩ *good and*) *lofty*; ⟨fam⟩ *swell* || ⟨vulg⟩ *genteel* | (*man*) *of distinction*; *distinguished* (*company*) || *gentleman* (*farmer*) || *grand* (*people*) || *high* (*life*); *select* (*society*) || *aristocratic* (*air, bearing, house*) || *great, grand, refined* (*house*) || *distinguished* (*air, appearance*); ~er Stil *style*; | ~e Gesinnung *high mind* || ~e Welt *polite* od *great world, the w. of fashion*; *high life*; *the Society* || ⟨vulg⟩ *the quality* || ein ~es Wesen annehmen *to assume an air of superiority* || den ≈en spielen *to play the fine gentleman*; ⟨fam⟩ *to do the swell* **B. (S)** *elegant, stylish* || *fashionable*; *polite* (*club*) || *exclusive* (*models, store*) || *high-class* (*shop. journal*); die ~ste Sorge *the number one concern* **C.** die ≈en *people of rank* (od *of quality*) || ~ u gering, ≈e u G–e *both high and low* **D.** [adv] ~ geformt *nobly-shaped* || ~ gekleidet *elegantly dressed* || ~ tun *to put on fine* od *great airs, to give o.s. airs*; *to be a snob*; ⟨fam⟩ *to swell it* || ~ tuend *snobbish* **E. ~st** [sup] *principal, chief*; *first* (⟨a. bib⟩: *commandment*); *best* (*houses*) || *crowning* (*quality* [*of leadership*]) || die ≈sten *the first* od *foremost people*; *the leading people* (e–r Stadt *in a t.*) ≈|**nehmen** vt irr [h] **A.** *to take before one* || (Schürze) *to put on* .. | ⟨fig⟩ *to take up* (*a p, a th*) || *to undertake*; *to take in hand* || *to make* (*changes*) || wieder ~ *to resume* || –genommen w (S) *to come on* **B.** (→ A. ⟨fig⟩) (jdn) ~ *to reprimand, rebuke*; *to call .. to account*, ⟨fam⟩ *to haul .. over the coals*; (strafend) *to take .. to task* || jdn tüchtig ~ *to put a p through his paces* (*I'll give him a talking-to*) **C. sich** [dat] ~ *to resolve on*; *to promise o.s.*; *to propose* (*a th*); .. ernstlich *to give/put one's mind to* (*a th*); *to make up one's mind* (*to do*) || *to propose .. to o.s.* || *to intend, purpose, design* (*doing*); *to intend* (*firmly*) (*to do*) **V·ornehm- ~heit** f ~/ *distinction, rank*; *grandeur* || *exclusiveness, refinement* || *elevation* (*of character*) || gesuchte ~ *gentility* ≈**lich** [adv] *chiefly, principally, especially, particularly, largely* **~tuer·ei** f ~/ *pretence of social superiority*; *snobbery*; → vornehm D.

V·or- ≈|neigen: sich ~ [h] *to bend forward* || (grüßend) [leicht] *to* (*give a* [*slight*]) *bow* **~ort** m ~(e)s/~e *suburb* || (e–s Vereins etc) *administrative centre* | **~(s)-** *suburban* ~bahn [f] *district railway*; *s.n line*, ⟨bes Am⟩ *commuter train*; ~bewohner [m] *s.nite*; ~gesellschaft [f] *suburbia*; ~verkehr [m] *s.n traffic*; ~zug [m] ⟨rail⟩ *s.n train* ≈|**pfeifen** vt irr [h]; jdm etw ~ *to whistle sth to a p* **~platz** m (*fore-*)*court* || (Treppenabsatz) *landing* || (in der Wohnung) *hall*(*way* ⟨Am⟩); ⟨Am a.⟩ *stoop* ≈|**plaudern** vt [h] (jdm) *to prattle* (*to a p*) (*about*) **~pommern** n *Hither Pomerania* **~posten** m ⟨mil⟩ *outpost*; *outlying picket*; [pl] *contact unit* || ~ ausstellen *to throw out pickets* || auf ~ *on o.t duty* | ~boot [n] *patrol boat*; ~flotille [f] *naval p.l units* pl; ~gefecht [n] *o.t skirmish*; ~kette [f] *line of o.ts*; *stationary screen*; ~linie [f] *o.t line* N; ~stellung [f] *o.t position*; ~tätigkeit [f] *o.t action* ≈|**predigen** vt [h] (jdm) *to preach* (*to a p*) (*about*) || ⟨übtr⟩ *to hold forth* (*to a p*), *to sermonize*; jdm etw dauernd ~ *to din a th into a p('s ears)* **~prallen** vi [s] *to forge ahead*; *to f. in front* ≈|**prellen 1.** vi [s] *to surge* od *push ahead*; *to take the lead* || ~ vor *to go ahead of* **2.** ≈ [n] *excessive advance* ≈|**prüfen** vt [h] *to examine beforehand* **~prüfung** f ~/~en *preliminary* od *previous examination* ≈**pumpen** vt [h] *to prime* ⟨a. mot⟩ ≈|**ragen** vi [h] *to project, protrude* || ⟨arch⟩ *to jut out* **~rang** m *precedence* (*of*), *superiority, pre-eminence* (*over*), (⟨rail⟩ *train*) *priority* || ohne ~ ⟨telg⟩ *routine* [attr] || den ~ einnehmen vor *to be higher on the list than* || dem Wichtigsten den ~ geben *to put first ths first* || den ~ h (vor [dat]) *to rank before* (od *to have* od *take precedence of*) (*a p*); ~ h.d *priority* [attr] || jdm den ~ l *to give precedence to a p*, ⟨mot⟩ *to give way* (*to pedestrians*); [dat] ~ geben vor .. *to accord priority to .. over ..* | **mit** ~ *on a p.y basis* | ~stellung [f] *superiority*; ~zug [m] *p.y train, t. having p.y* **~rat** m *stor*(*ag*)*e, stock, provision, supply* (an *of*) || sich e–n ~ anlegen an *to lay in store of sth* || ~ auf Lager *stock on hand* || in ~ halten *to keep in stock* || mit ~ überhäuft *overstocked*; bis ~ verbraucht *until exhausted* ⟨a. mil⟩ | ⟨prov⟩ ~ nimmer schad't *store is no sore* ≈**rätig** a *ready* (*articles*); [pred] *in stock, on hand* || nicht mehr ~ h *to be* (od *to have run*) *out of ..* || nicht ~ *out of stock* || ~ bei .. *to be had of ..* **~rats-** ~achse [f] *spare axle-tree*; ~anzeiger [m] *quantity gauge*; *contents indicator*; ~behälter [m] ⟨mil⟩ *magazine*; ~bunker [m] *storage bin*; ~haltung [f] *maintenance of stocks and supplies*; ~haus [n] *store*(*-house*), *magazine*; ~kammer [f] *store-room*; ⟨fig⟩ *still-room*; ⟨cul⟩ *larder*; ~kauf [m] *stock-piling purchase*; ~schrank [m] *pantry, safe*; ~tank [m] *storage tank* ~verzeichnis [n] *inventory*; ~wagen [m] ⟨mil⟩ *store-wagon* **~raum** m *hall*(*way* ⟨Am⟩) ≈|**rechnen** vt [h] (jdm) *to count out* od *to reckon up* (*to a p*) || das kann ich ihnen leicht ~ *I can easily show you that* **~recht** n *prerogative, privilege*; ⟨a.⟩ *freedom*; (f Fußgänger) *right-of-way* || ~ h auf *to have the first call on* || (älteres Recht) *priority* ≈|**recken** vt [h] *to stretch forward* || den Hals ~ *to crane* (*one's neck*) **~rede** f *prefatory remark*; (Gesetzes-≈) *preamble* || ⟨Lit⟩ *preface* || mit e–r ~ versehen *to preface* || ⟨fig⟩ sich nicht lange mit der ~ aufhalten *to waste no time on preliminaries*; ohne lange ~ *without ceremony* ≈|**reden** vi/t [h]; jdm etw ~ *to humbug a p with, to tell a p tales about*

Verbal-Flexion der Verben mit der Vorsilbe **ver-** → das jeweilige Simplex

a th | sich [dat] ~ l *to be taken in* **~redner** m *the gentleman who spoke last; previous speaker* || ⟨parl, etc⟩ mein geehrter ~ *the honourable member (gentleman) who spoke last* **~reiber** m ⟨tech⟩ *catch*; (am Fenster) *turnbuckle* **≃reif** a *premature* || *precocious (child)* **~reigen** m *opening of a ball* || den ~ h *to lead the dance* **≃|reißen** vt [h] *to make a first sketch of* || *to trace* **≃|reiten** vi irr [s] [dat] *to ride before; to overtake; to show a p how to ride* | vt [h] ein Pferd ~ *to put a horse through its paces* || ⟨fig⟩ jdm etw ~ *to parade a th before a p* **~reiter** m ~s/~ *outrider* || *postilion* **≃|rennen** vi irr [s] *to run before* || (jdm) *to outrun (a p)* **≃|richten** vt [h] *to prepare, to fit up* || (Stoffe) *to dress* **~richtung** f; ~en [pl] *preparations, arrangements* pl (zu *for*) || (Apparat) *contrivance, appliance, apparatus; attachment*; (⟨a.⟩ *selfacting*) *mechanism*; kl ~ *gadget* || e–e sinnreiche ~ *an ingenious device* (zu *for*) **≃romanisch** a ⟨a–engl⟩ *preromanesque* **~romantik** f *Preromanticism* || ~er [m] *Precursor of R.* **≃|rücken I.** vt [h] *to move* od *put forward, to advance* || (Uhr) *to put on* || jdm etw ~ *to reproach* od *upbraid a p with a th* **II.** vi [s] *to advance, to (go a)head, to push on*; (langsam) *to edge up* (zu *to*) || die Arbeit rückt vor .. *is progressing* || ⟨mil⟩ ~ l *to push forward (troops)* || in vorgerücktem Alter (–ter Stunde) *at an advanced age (at a late hour)* **III.** ≃ n *advance, progress* **≃|rufen** vt irr [h] *to call forth* od *up*; ⟨jur⟩ *to summon* **~runde** f ⟨sport⟩ *preliminary round* **~saal** m *entrance-hall, entry, ante-room* od *-chamber* **≃|sagen** vt [h] *to rehearse, recite (a th to a p)* || *to tell (a p a th) (many pretty ths)* || du sagst mir das nur so vor *you are only saying so* | (flüsternd) *to whisper (a th to a p)* || [abs] *to prompt (a p)* **~sammellinse** f *field lens* **~sänger** m ⟨ec⟩ *precentor; leader of a choir* **~satz** m *purpose, design, intent(ion)* || *wilful act* || fester ~ *determination; specific intent* || böser ~ *evil* od *criminal intent*, ⟨jur⟩ *(malus) dolus* || mit ~ *deliberately, intentionally, on purpose*; mit ~ lügen *to tell a deliberate lie* || e–n ~ fassen *to take* od *form a resolution* || den ~ h *to design, intend* | ~blatt [n] ⟨bookb⟩ *prefixed folio; front-, end-paper*; ~linse [f] *supplementary* od *front lens*; ⟨theat⟩ *spotting attachment*; ~papier [n] *fancy paper, fly-leaf p., end p.* **≃sätzlich** a *intentional, deliberate* | [adv] *on purpose, purposely*; ~ beschädigen ⟨a.⟩ *to sabotage (a car)* || ⟨jur⟩ *with malice prepense* **≃schalten** [vt h] ⟨tech⟩ *to superpose* **~schaltwiderstand** m ⟨el⟩ *switch resistance* **~schanze** f *redoubt* **~schau** f *preview* ⟨a. film & com⟩, ⟨film⟩ *trailer* **~schein** m: z ~ bringen *to bring forward* od *to light, to produce, to put forward* | z ~ k *to come to light, to make one's appearance, to turn up; to appear*; wieder .. *to reappear*; mit etw .. *to come out with a th* **~schicht** f ⟨geol⟩ *first layer* **≃|schicken** vt [h] *to send forward* od *to the front* ⟨a. mil⟩ || *to send in advance* || (Boten) *to send round* (bei *to*) || *to let a p bear the brunt* **≃|schieben** vt irr [h] *to shove* od *push before* bzw *forward* od *on* || ⟨mil⟩ *to throw out (pickets, etc), to dispatch (patrols)* || ⟨mil-tact⟩ die Front ~ *to advance the line* | ⟨fig⟩ *to interpose, plead (as an excuse), pretend*; jdn ~ *to let a p bear the brunt* || den Riegel ~ *to shoot* od *slip the bolt*; [dat] e–n R. ~ ⟨fig⟩ *to prevent, obviate* **~schieber** m *slide-bolt* **≃|schießen** vt irr [h] (e–m) *to shoot in presence of; to show .. how to shoot*; sich [acc] (im Wechsel v Feuer u Bewegung) ~ *to push vigorously forward (alternately employing fire and movement)* || (Geld) *to advance, lend, supply, find* || (Riegel) *to shoot* | vi [s] *to swoop forward, to dart forth* **~schiff** n *fore-body, bow, prow; forecastle* **~schlag** m *proposal, proposition*; ⟨parl⟩ *motion* || ~ zur Güte *friendly* (⟨hum⟩ *excellent*) *p.l* od *suggestion* || (Anerbieten) *offer* | ⟨mus⟩ *grace-note* || ⟨phon⟩ *initial weak element*; durch ~ e–s „e" *by prefixing an "e"* || ⟨pros⟩ *anacrusis* | ⟨typ⟩ *blank space (on the first page)* || ⟨bookb⟩ *templet* | e–n ~ annehmen *to agree to a p.l* || auf jds ~ *on the p.l of a p* || in ~ bringen *to propose*, ⟨parl⟩ *move* || (jdm) e–n ~ m *to make (a p) a p.l* || andere ≃e m *to propose alternatives* | **~-** ~hammer [m] *forehammer*; ≃(s)fähig [a] *presentable, proposable*; ~sliste [f] *list of persons proposed for ..*; ~snote [f] = Vorschlag ⟨mus⟩; ~silbe [f] ⟨pros⟩ *anacrusis* **≃|schlagen I.** vt irr [h] *to strike forward* bzw *in advance* || (jdm) den Takt ~ *to beat time (to a p)* | (jdm etw) ~ *to propose, suggest*, ⟨Am a.⟩ *propound (a th to a p; doing, to do* = daß ich tue; *his* [⟨fam⟩ *him*] *doing*); ⟨a.⟩ *to request (to do; that; a p to do)*; er schlug ihnen vor, mit ihm zu gehen *he suggested they should go with him* | (jdn) *to propose (a p for an office); to nominate (a p for an election)*; ⟨ec⟩ *to present (a p to a living)*; der Vorgeschlagene *the nominee* bzw *presentee* | (empfehlen) *to recommend* || (anbieten) *to offer (to do)* | ⟨gram⟩ *to prefix (a syllable*, etc) | ⟨com⟩ *to overcharge one's customers* || auf e–e Ware 2 Mark ~ *to ask 2 marks more for sth than one expects to get for it*, ⟨fam⟩ *to clap 2 marks on the price of ..* **II.** vi [s] *to fall* bzw *rush (headlong) forward* | [h] *to have the first stroke*; ⟨ftb⟩ *to knock on* **~schliff** m *coarse surfacing* **~schlußrunde** f ⟨sport⟩ *semi-final* **~schmack** m ~(e)s/ *foretaste* **≃|schmecken** vi [h] *to predominate* **≃schmeicheln** vt [h] [dat] *to flatter (a p)* **~schneide-** ~brett [n] *trencher*; ~messer [m] *carving-knife* **≃|schneiden** vt irr [h] (bei Tische) *to carve* || ⟨fig⟩ *to make (grimaces* od *faces at a p)* **~schneider** m ~s/~ *carver* **≃schnell** a = –eilig **≃schnellen** vi [s] (of snake) z Biß ~ *to strike* **≃|schreiben** vt irr [h] (jdm etw) *to set a copy of a th to a p* || (anordnen) *to prescribe, order* || wir l uns nichts ~ *we will not be dictated to* || Sie h mir nichts –zu– *I am not under your orders* || v der Natur –geschrieben *(rules) laid down (for us) by n.* **≃|schreien** vt [h] e–m (etw) ~ *to yell, din, bawl into a p's ears* **≃|schreiten** vi irr [s] *to step forward* || *to proceed (to an attack)* | (weitergehen) *to march on* || *to advance* ⟨a. fig⟩: *advanced (students, state)* || jdm ~ *to outstep* bzw *precede a p* **~schrift** f *(writing-)copy, copy-head* | ⟨med⟩ *prescription, recipe* || ⟨ec, etc⟩ *rule*; (genau) nach ~ arbeiten, ⟨off⟩ Dienst nach ~ (→ Bummelstreik) *to work to rule* || (Anweisung) *direction, instruction* || (Dienst≃) *regularion(s pl)* ⟨a. mil⟩ N; v der ~ abweichen *to waive* N || (Befehl) *order, command* | jdm ~en m *to prescribe for a p, to dictate to a p*; du hast mir k–e ~en z m *you can't police me* || nach ~ *according to regulations; as directed* od *prescribed* | ~enbuch [n] *book of instructions*, ⟨school⟩ *copybook* | **~s-** ≃mäßig [a & adv] *according to regulations, regulation* [attr s] *(r. uniform, r. size); in due form; (as) prescribed*, etc; *proper, correct (position); authorized (abbreviation)*; ~schild [n] *mandatory sign*; ≃widrig [a & adv] *contrary to regulations* **~schub** m ⟨sport, etc⟩ *first throw* || den ~ h *to throw first* | ⟨comp⟩ *carriage* | ⟨fig⟩ *aid, assistance, countenance, support* || [dat] ~ leisten *to favour, countenance, assist, help, encourage; to lend one's countenance to; to aid and abet (a p); to pander to (a th)* → unterstützen | ~getriebe [n] *feed gear*; ~schaltung [f] *f. control*; ~wagen [m] *travel(l)er* **~schuh** m *forepart, front; upper leather; vamp* **≃|schuhen** vi [h] (Stiefel) *to vamp (up)* **~schule** f *preparatory school*, ⟨Am⟩ *grades* pl || ⟨fig⟩ *elementary course, introduction*; (Buchtitel) *Primer* **~schuß** m *first shot* || den ~ h *to shoot first* | ⟨fig⟩ *cash-advance, payment in advance,*

Aussprache: Falls nicht anders (: [*v*]) angegeben, ist v = [*f*] zu sprechen.

money advanced ‖ (Darlehn) *loan* ‖ ⟨jur⟩ (auf Sachwalterhonorar) *retaining fee* | ~ bewilligen *to grant an advance* ‖ ~ leisten *to advance money* ‖ um 100 Mark im ~ s *to be 100 marks in advance* | °⟨sex⟩ sie nahmen ~ auf die Seligkeit *they sat down to dinner before grace was said* | ~kasse [f] *loan fund*; ~verein [m] *loan society*; ~́weise [adv] *as an advance*; *by way of a loan*; ~zahlung [f] *payment in advance*; ~zinsen [m pl] *advance interest* sg ~́|**schütten** vt [h] *to erect* (*dikes*) | [dat] *to pour out* (*before*) ‖ Futter ~ *to give food* (*to*) ~́|**schützen** vt [h] *to use .. as a pretext*; *to pretend* (Krankheit *to be ill*); Krankheit ~ ⟨mil⟩ *to malinger* ‖ *to plead* (*ignorance, a headache*, etc [*as an excuse*]) ‖ nur k–e Müdigkeit –ge–tzt! *don't tell me you are* (*too*) *tired*! **~schützung** f (*hollow*) *pretence, pretext, plea*(*ding*) **~schwarm** m (of bees) *first swarm* ~́|**schwatzen** vt [h]; jdm etw ~ *to prattle about a th to a p* ~́|**schweben** vi [h] ⟨fig⟩ (jdm) *to be present in* od *to one's mind* ‖ mir schwebte etw anderes vor *I had sth else in my mind* ‖ es schwebt mir (nur noch) dunkel vor *I have* (*only*) *a dim recollection* (od *notion*) *of it* ~́|**schwindeln** (⟨fam a.⟩ ~́|**schwefeln**) vt [h]; jdm etw ~ *to humbug a p with* od *about sth, to tell a p a pack of lies* **~segel** n *foresail* ~́|**segeln** vi [s] *to sail before* bzw *in advance* ‖ [dat] *to outsail* ~́|**sehen** vt irr [h] (voraussehen) *to foresee* ‖ (im voraus erwägen) *to consider* (*beforehand*); *to provide* od *stipulate for* bzw *that* ‖ im Gesetz nicht –ge– *not provided for by law* ‖ im Budget ~ *to budget for* ‖ (e–n Angriff) *to* (*lay down* od) *make provisions for ..* ‖ *to schedule* (*a p for a lecture*) ‖ es war –ge–, daß *provision was made that* | ~ **für** (P & S): *to design*(*ate*), *intend for ..* | **sich** ~ *to take* od *have a care*; *to take heed* od *care* ‖ *to look* (od *watch*) *out*; ⟨a.⟩ *to walk on one's toes* ⟨fig⟩ ‖ –ge–! *look out*! *take care*! ⟨Am sl⟩ *cheeze it*! ‖ sich **mit** etw ~ *to lay in a stock* (od *store*) *of sth, to provide o.s. with a th* ‖ sich ~ **vor** *to be on one's guard against* **~sehung** f *providence* ‖ die göttliche ~ (*Divine*) *Providence* ‖ v der ~ ausersehen *predestined* (*place*) ~́|**sein** vi irr [s] *to be in advance* (*of ..*) ‖ e–m ~ *to be before a p* ‖ ⟨fam⟩ was ist jetzt vor? *what's on now*? ⟨a. jur⟩; ⟨jur⟩ vor gewesen s *to have already been tried* ‖ da sei Gott vor! *God forbid*! **~semester** n *propaedeutic term* **~setz-** ~blatt [n] ⟨bookb⟩ *blank leaf*; ~fenster [n] *outside* (*double*) *window*; ~gitter [n] *grating*; ~laden [m] *shutter*; ~papier [n] = Vorsatzpapier; ~stück [n] ⟨theat⟩ *shifting scene*; ~zeichen [n] ⟨mus⟩ *signature* (♯ = *sharp*, ♭ = *flat*) ~́|**setzen** vt [h] *to put forward* ‖ ⟨chess⟩ e–e Figur ~ *to cover a man* ‖ ⟨cards⟩ hoch ~ *to cut a high card* | [dat] *to set, put, place before ..*; *to place at the head of ..* | ⟨cul⟩ *to serve* (*food to a p*) was darf ich Ihnen ~? *may I offer you any*(*thing* od) *refreshments*? ‖ vorgesetzt (→ d.) bek *to be served* (*a lunch*) ‖ das kann man k–m ~ *this is not fit for the table* | ⟨mus⟩ e–r Note ein ♭ ~ *to mark a note with a flat* ‖ ⟨gram⟩ e–m Worte Silben ~ *to prefix s.s to a w.* | jdn e–m Amte ~ *to appoint a p to an office* | ⟨fig⟩ [dat] ~ *to set .. over ..*, *to prefer .. to* | **sich** [dat] ~ (vornehmen) *to intend*; *to resolve upon*; *to determine* (*to do*) ‖ ich habe es mir fest –gesetzt *I have thoroughly made up my mind to* (*do*) *it* **~setzer** m *screen*; *fender* ‖ *outside window-blind* ‖ ⟨met⟩ *gate-shutter*

V·orsicht f [~/pl ~smaßregeln] (Voraussicht) *foresight* ‖ (Behutsamkeit) *prudence, caution* ‖ (Umsicht) *circumspection, precaution*; der ~ halber *as a pr.* ‖ ~! (auf Kisten) *with care*!; (Ausruf) *look out*!, *take care*! ‖ ~ Stufe! *watch your step*! ‖ ~ (Gefahr)! *keep off*! | mit viel ~ zu Werke gehen *to act very cautiously* od *prudently* ‖ mit einiger ~ hinnehmen *to discount*; *to take a th with a grain of salt* ‖ ohne ~ tun *to drop one's guard* (*doing*) ‖ jdn zur ~ mahnen *to give a p a warning message*; z ~ mahnend *cautionary* (Angabe) | ~ ist die Mutter der Weisheit (*or* ⟨fam⟩ Porzellankiste) *caution is the m. of wisdom* ‖ ~ ist besser als Nachsicht (*an ounce of*) *prevention is better than* (*a pound of*) *cure* ‖ alle ~ außer acht l *to throw one's cap over the windmill* | ~́**ig** a *cautious, careful* ‖ *prudent*; *wise*; *wide-a-awake*; *circumspect, discreet*; *wary* (*man*) ‖ *guarded* (*words, statement*) ‖ *safe* (*driver*) ‖ *conservative* (*estimate*) ‖ sei ~ *be on your guard*! ‖ ~! *steady*! ‖ ~ s mit *to be careful of ..* ‖ ~en Gebrauch m v *to use .. with discretion* | [adv] sehr ~ handeln ⟨a.⟩ *to use every precaution* ‖ ~ vorgehen *to proceed with caution, to go slow, to feel one's way* ⟨a. fig⟩ ‖ ~ aushorchen *to feel one's way through* ‖ ~ abgießen *to decant* ‖ ~ spielen *to play for safety* ⟨a. fig⟩ | **~s-** ~́halber [adv] *by way of precaution, in order to be on the safe side*; er hat ~ das Tor .. *he has taken the precaution to look ..*; ~maßregel [f] *precaution*(*ary measure*) ‖ ~n [pl] treffen *or* ergreifen *to take precautions*; ~zeichen [n] *signal* "*Caution*", ⟨mot⟩ "*Slow*!" **~signal** n ⟨rail⟩ *distant* od *warning signal* **~silbe** f ⟨gram⟩ *prefix* ~́|**singen** vt irr [h]; jdm etw ~ *to sing a th to a p* | [vi] *to audition* (⟨a.⟩ ~ l), *to be ~ed* ‖ ⟨theat⟩ dem Direktor ~ *to have an audition with the manager* | vi *to lead the choir* **~singer** = –sänger ~́**sintflutlich** = –sündflutlich **~sitz** m *chair* ‖ den ~ h *or* führen *to be in the chair, to preside* (bei *at, over*) ‖ den ~ übernehmen *to take the chair* **~sitzende** m [der ~, ein ~r] & f ~n/~n *chairman* [⟨a.⟩ f], (*lady*) *president* ⟨Am a. com⟩ ‖ mit .. als ~m *with .. in the chair* **~sommer** m *early summer* **~sorge** f *care, precaution* ‖ *provision for the future* ~ treffen *or* tragen *to provide f. the f.* = ~́|**sorgen** vi [h] *to take precautions*; .., daß *to take care that ..* ‖ ~ f *to provide for*; f alles ~ *to p. for all eventualities* ‖ vorgesorgt ist halb getan *well begun is half done, a stitch in time saves nine* ~́**sorglich** [a] *provident, thoughtful* | [adv] *as a precaution*; *in advance* **~spann** m ~(e)s/~e *relay*; (*extra*) *team of horses*; *additional horses* pl (leisten *to supply*) ‖ ⟨rail⟩ *helper engine*; *double heading*; Zug mit ~ *d.-headed train* ‖ ⟨film⟩ *leader*; *credits* pl ‖ ⟨wir⟩ *signature tune* ‖ ⟨rep⟩ *title strip* ‖ ⟨typ⟩ *label* | ~́en [vt sep h] *to put additional horses to* | ~band [n] ⟨rec⟩ *leader tape*; ~bremse [f] *servo brake*; ~dienst [m]; ~e leisten ⟨fig⟩ *to help, to assist*; ~leistung [f] *impressment of carriages*; ~maschine [f] ⟨rail⟩ *additional engine*; ~pferd [n] *relay-horse* **~spannung** f ⟨tech, el⟩ *pre-load*; *grid potential*; *initial stress*; *bias* **~speise** f *entrée*; *appetizer*; *hors d'œuvre*(*s* pl) ~́|**spiegeln** vt [h] (jdm) *to pretend* (*to a p*); *to affect* od *delude a p by a fine show* ‖ (etw) *to show a p a th in a brilliant light, to dazzle a p's eyes with a th* ‖ –ge–lte Hoffnungen *false hopes* **~spiegelung** f *affectation*; *illusion, sham, pretence* (⟨Am⟩ *-se*); ⟨fam⟩ *putting on* ‖ unter ~ falscher Tatsachen ⟨fam⟩ *by window-dressing* ⟨fig⟩; ⟨jur⟩ *by misrepresentation of facts, under false pretences* pl **~spiel** n ⟨theat *introductory piece*; ⟨fam⟩ *curtain-raiser* ‖ ⟨mus⟩ *prelude, overture* ‖ (Orgel~́) *voluntary* | ⟨fig fam⟩ *window-dressing for what is to come* ~́|**spielen** vt [h] (jdm etw) *to play a th to, to make music for* (*a p*); *to audition* (⟨a.⟩ ~ l), *to be ~ed* ~́|**spinnen** vt [h] *to rove* **~spinn-** ~krempel [m] *rover*; ~maschine [f] *roving-frame, slubber* ~́|**sprechen** vi irr [h] (bei jdm) *to call* (*on a p, at an office*) ‖ *to drop* od *look in* (*at the bank*) ‖ *to pay a p a flying visit* | [vt] jdm etw ~ *to tell a p what to say*; *to teach a p how to pronounce* (*a word*) ~́|**sprengen**

Aussprache: Falls nicht anders (: [*v*]) angegeben, ist v = [*f*] zu sprechen.

vi [s] *to gallop* (*in advance* bzw) *forward* ≃|**springen** vi irr [s] *to leap forward* ‖ (S) *to jut* od *stick out*; *to protrude, project* ‖ (drohend) *to beetle* | ~d *projecting, salient*; ~des Fenster *bay-window*; *jutting* (*chin*); ⟨mil⟩ ~de Linie *salient, bulge* **~sprung** m *projection, prominence*; *salient part* ‖ ⟨arch⟩ *moulding* ‖ (Fels≃) *ledge, brow* ‖ (Gebirgs≃) *spur* | ⟨übtr⟩ ~ v 6 Stimmen *six vote margin* | (Zeit≃) (vor [dat]) (*time*) *lead, advantage* (*of, over*), (gr *long*) *start* (*of*) (gewinnen *to get* od *have*) ‖ ⟨sport⟩ *lead*; jdm e–n ~ abgewinnen *to to gain on a p*; e–n ~ erhalten *to get a good start*; mit knappem ~ besiegen ⟨fam⟩ *to nose out*; (an) ~ verlieren *to blow one's l.* **~spuk** m *omen, portent* ‖ *ghostly warning* ≃|**spuken** vi [h] *to appear as an omen*, etc; *to cast its shadow before* **~stadt** f *suburb*(*ia*) | ~ring [m] *suburbia*; ~theater [a] *second-rate theatre* **~städter** m *resident in a s.*; *suburban*(*ite* ⟨Am⟩) ≃**städtisch** a *suburban* **~stagsegel** n *fore-staysail* **~stand** m [koll] *directory*; *board of directors* od *management* ⟨bes bank⟩; *managing* od *executive committee* ‖ (P) *director, head, principal* | **~s-** ~mitglied [n] *director*; *member of a managing committee*; *delegate* (*of the Oxf. Univ. Press*); ~sitzung [f] *board meeting*; ~tisch [m] *high table*; ~wahl [f] *election of the directors*, etc ≃|**stechen** vi irr [h] ⟨fig⟩ (a. Farbe) *to predominate* | ~d [a] *outstanding* **~stecher** m ⟨tech⟩ *punch, piercer* **~steck-** ~ärmel [m] *oversleeve*; ~blume [f] *buttonhole*; ~lätzchen [n] *bib*; ~lünse [f] ⟨tech⟩ *linch-pin*; ~nadel [f] *breast-pin*; ~nagel [m] *pin, peg, forelock*; ~scheibe [f] (*take-up*) *washer*; ~schleife [f] *jabot* Fr; ~stift [m] (Uhr≃) *stud*; ~wagen [m] ⟨comp⟩ *carriage* ≃|**stecken** vt [h] *to stick* (od *fasten on*) *before* ‖ *to stick out*; *to poke* od *put out* (*one's head*) ‖ er hat sich e–e Perle –ge–kt *he wears a pearl in his tie* | *to mark out beforehand* ‖ sich [dat] ein Ziel ~ *to aim at sth* ‖ das –ge–kte Ziel erreichen *to obtain one's object* ‖ ≃ [n] das ~ der Formulare ⟨comp⟩ *aligning forms* **~stecker** m *pawl, plug, peg,* (*linch-*)*pin, bolt* ≃|**stehen** vi irr [h & s] **1.** *to project, protrude*; *to stick out*; *to overhang*; ~ aus *to poke from* **2.** *to stand* (*come, rank*) *before*; → ~d **3.** ⟨hunt⟩ (*hounds*) *point* od *set* **4.** (e–r S, P) *to look after, to be in charge of* ‖ *to manage* (*the house*) = *to keep* (*house*) ‖ *to hold* (*an office*) ‖ *to represent* (*a firm*) ‖ (e–r Anstalt etc) *to administer, head, govern, direct, manage* ≃**stehend** a (Seite) *last, above, preceding* ‖ das V.e *the above remarks* ‖ im V.en *above, hereinbefore* ‖ (Auftrag) *foregoing* **~steher(in** f) m *director, manager*, (f *directress, manageress*), *head, chief* ‖ ⟨school⟩ *head master* (f *h. mistress*) ‖ ~ (e–r Gemeinde [gen]), Gemeinde≃ [m] *headman* ‖ (Gefängnis≃, Museums≃) *warden* ‖ (Büro≃) *managing clerk* | ~amt [n] *office of a director*, etc; *management*; ~drüse [f] ⟨anat⟩ *prostate* **~stehhund** m *pointer*, ⟨a.⟩ *gun dog*; (langhaarig) *setter*, (rauhaarig) *griffon* Fr ≃**stellbar** a *presentable* ‖ (denkbar) (nicht) ~ (*un*)*imaginable*, (*un*)*thinkable*, (*in*)*conceivable* | ≃keit [f] *imaginableness* ≃|**stellen** vt [h] **1.** (Fuß) *to put forward* ‖ (Uhr) *to set ahead* od *forward* (um 5 M. *5 minutes*) **2.** *to put* od *place before* (od *in front of* ⟨a.⟩ schützend) **3.** (bedeuten) *to signify, mean*; *to stand for* .. | (darstellen) *to represent*; ⟨theat⟩ *to play* (*a part*); *to personate, act* (*a character*) | sie stellt **etw** vor *her appearance is striking* | etw ~ wollen (das man nicht ist) *to give o.s. airs, to pose* (*to set up for what one is not*) | wenig ~ *to be insignificant* od *of no consequence* | was **soll** das ~ *what is that? this plot is intended to be a garden* ‖ wen soll das (Bild) ~? *for whom is that portrait meant?* **4.** (**sich**) jdm ~ *to introduce* (geh Spr *present*) (*o.s.*) *to a p* ‖ darf ich [mich] ~: .. *may I present* .., (*I want you to*) *meet* .., *this is* .. [*allow me* od *I beg to introduce m.s. to you*] ‖ sich im Büro ~ *to report to a p's office* ‖ ⟨parl⟩ sich ~ (Regierung) *to meet* ‖ sich jdm ~ l *to get* (*o.s.*) *introduced* (bei Hofe: *presented*) *to a p* ‖ l Sie sich m–r Frau ~ *come and be introduced to* .. **5.** jdm etw ~ *to* (*point out* od) *represent a th to a p* ‖ *to remonstrate with a p about sth* ‖ (eindringlich) *to urge a th upon a p* **6. sich** [dat] ~ *to figure, imagine, fancy* (*i.* od *f. my joy!*); man kann sich ~, daß .. *the matter could conceivably lead to* ..; ich kann es mir nicht ~ *I can't bring m.s. to believe it*; .. als .. *I can't see him as soldier*; .., daß *I can't see m.s. getting a rich man* ‖ (als wirklich) *to realize* ‖ *to visualize* (*that, what*) ‖ *to envisage* (*the situation*) ‖ *to think* (*I can't th. how*) ‖ ich kann mir (nichts Besseres etc) ~ *I can conceive* (*no better*); (*it is hard*) *to conceive of* (*a solution*) ‖ stellen Sie sich das einmal vor! *just think of it!* ‖ sich .. ~ **als**: *one always thinks of him as a German* ‖ man kann sich ~, **daß** so etw vorkommt *one can imagine such a th happening* ‖ sich ~ **wie** .. *to imagine a p writing* ≃**stellig** a: ~w *to complain* ‖ ~ w bei *to visit*; *to apply to*; *to make representations to* ⟨a. pol⟩; *to send in a petition to*; *to take up the matter with the authorities* **~stellung** f ~/~en **1.** *presentation*; *introduction* (→ vor. 4.) **2.** ⟨theat⟩ (→ Aufführung) *performance*; ~ mit 1. Besetzung *star-p.* ‖ heute k–e ~! *the theatre will be closed to-day!* **3.** (Gedanke) *idea* (*there is an i. prevalent that*) ‖ (*to see a p in one's*) *mind* ‖ *conception* (*that is my c. of it*) ‖ (eingebildete) *fancy* ‖ falsche ~ *misconception*; falsche ~en h v *to be wrong about* ‖ *notion* (*I have not the least n. of it*) ‖ das übertrifft alle ~ *it is simply inconceivable* | ⟨philos⟩ *ideation* ‖ ⟨psych⟩ *presentation*; *mind-picture* | lebendige ~ *realization* **4.** (Tadel) *remonstrance, expostulation* ‖ dringende ~en *urgencies* ‖ ⟨pol⟩ ~en [pl] *intercession* (bei *with*) ‖ jdm ~en m (wegen) *to remonstrate with a p* (*on*) | **~s-** ~gabe [f] *imagination*; ~gruppe [f] ⟨psych⟩ *complex*; ~kraft [f] *imaginative power*; mit ~ begabt *gifted with imagination*; ~leben [n] *outlook* (*of a people*); ~vermögen [n] *imaginative faculty*; *imagination*; ≃weise [f] *way of putting* (od *looking at*) *ths* **~stenge** f ~/~n ⟨mar⟩ *fore-topmast* **~steven** m ⟨mar⟩ *stem* **~stich** m ⟨tail⟩ *running stitch* ≃|**stopfen** vt [h] *to put before* (*a hole*) **~stoß** m ⟨tech⟩ *projection* ‖ *eking-piece* ‖ ⟨chem⟩ *adapter* ‖ ⟨mil tail⟩ *piping, edging, braid*; mit ~ *piped* (*vest*) | ⟨mil⟩ (*sudden*) *advance* ⟨a. fig, pol⟩, *push, dash, thrust, raid* ‖ ⟨sport⟩ *rush*; e–n ~ m *to rush*, ⟨mil⟩ *to make a dash*, etc | **~-** ~papier [n] *intermediate sheet* ≃|**stoßen** vt irr [h] *to push forward* od *out* od *up* ‖ (Saum) *to edge* | vi [s] ⟨bes mil⟩ *to advance suddenly, to push forward, to forge ahead* ‖ (Boot etc) *to nose* (*into*) ‖ (vorragen) *to project, protrude* **~strafe** f *previous conviction* | **~n-** ~verzeichnis [n] *criminal record* ≃|**strecken** vt [h] *to stretch forward* ‖ (Hals) *to crane* ‖ (Kopf) *to put .. forward*, halb *to poke* ‖ (Zunge) *to put out* .. | (Geld) *to advance, lend* ≃|**streuen** vt [h] *to strew* (etc) *before* ‖ *to throw .. to* (*the cattle*) ≃|**stricken** vt [h] *to knit .. on to*; *to refoot* (*stockings*) **~stube** f *anteroom* **~stück** n *piece in front*; ⟨theat fam⟩ *curtain-raiser* **~studie** f *preliminary study* ‖ ~n m z *to read up* (*a subject*) **~stufe** f *preceding stage, pre-* od *fore-stage* ‖ *first step* ‖ *beginning* ‖ (Einleitung, Vorschule) *elementary course*; *primer* ‖ als ~ f *preparatory to*; ~ zu *preliminary to* ≃|**stürzen** vi [s] *to rush forward* ≃|**suchen** vt [h] *to search* ⟨fam⟩ *rummage out* (*of* ..) ≃**sündflutlich** a *antediluvian* ⟨a. fig⟩ **~synchronisation** [f] ⟨film⟩ *pre-dubbing* **~tag** m;

Aussprache: Falls nicht anders (: [*v*]) angegeben, ist v = [*f*] zu sprechen.

am ~e *the day before*; in den ~en *in the previous days* ⁓|**tanzen** vi [h] *to lead (off) the dance* **~tänzer(in** f) m *leader of a dance* ⁓|**täuschen** vt [h] *to pretend, fake, sham, feign, simulate*; ⟨tact⟩ *demonstrate* (dazu: *demonstration*) || Wahnsinn ~ *to feign o.s. mad* || sich [dat] ~ *to delude o.s.* (*that* ..) **~teig** m Sw = Hefestück **~teil** m ~(e)s/~e **A.** *advantage* ⟨a. ten⟩ || *benefit, profit, interest, gain, emolument* || s–e ~e *his assets* pl || ~ des Windes *weather-gauge* || Vor- u Nachteile *boone and bane* **B.** e–m den ~ ab|gewinnen *to get the better of, to gain on*; *to get the wind of a p* || zu jds ~ ausschlagen *to redound to a p's ad.* || ~e [pl] ⟨a.⟩ *facilities*; worin bestehen die ~e? *what are the ad.s*? || (e–m) ~ bringen *to be of ad.* od *ad.ous*; *to yield p., to bring water to the mill,* (*to profit* od *benefit a p*) || jeder ~ **gilt** *all's fair in love and war* || es hat nur ~e *it is all to the good* || den ~ h *to have the inside track* ⟨fig⟩ || ~ h durch *to benefit by*; die M. hat den ~, daß *the ad. of this method lies in* ..; den ~ vor jdm h *to have the pull of a p*; s–n ~ herausschlagen *or* h–zuwissen *to play one's cards well* || jeden ~ mitnehmen! *all is grist to our mill* || der ~ ist auf s–r Seite *the odds are on his s.* || jdm (unerlaubte) ~e verschaffen *to weight the scales in favo(u)r of a p* || ~ ziehen aus *to turn .. to account*; .. aus allem .. *all is fish that comes to his net* **C. auf** den eigenen ~ bedacht *self-seeking*; *sharp* || auf s–n ~ sehen *to have an eye* (*to the main chance* od) *on one's own interest, to look to one's own i., to know on which side one's bread is buttered, to take care of number one*; nicht .. *to be disinterested* || er weiß **aus** allem (s–n) ~ zu ziehen *all is grist that comes to his mill* || (jeder) **für** s–n ~ .. *for his own hand* || **im** ~ s *to have the ad.*; .. gegen *to have the pull* (⟨sl⟩ *a bulge*) *on* (*a p*); nicht .. ⟨Am⟩ *to have nothing on a p* || **mit** ~ (verkaufen) .. *at a profit* || es kann nicht von ~ s *there can be no good* (*in doing*) || **zu** Ihrem ~ *to your ad., in your i.* || e–m z ~ gereichen *to turn out to a p's ad.,* ⟨fam⟩ *to turn up trumps*; .. dir .. *the ad.s will be yours* ⁓**teilhaft** a *advantageous, profitable, lucrative* (f *to*) || *favourable* (*opportunity*) || *expedient* (*solution*) || *vantage* (*ground, point*) || f den Verbraucher ~e .. *consumer benefit sales* | das ⁓este *the most profitable th to do* (*would be*) | [adv] ⟨a.⟩ *with advantage*; aufs ~este *to the best ad., most ad.ously*; ⟨com⟩ *at the best price* ⁓**tonig** a ⟨gram⟩ *pretonic* **~trab** m ⟨mil⟩ *van(guard)* **~trag** m ~(e)s/⁓e **A. 1.** (Stil des ~ens) *delivery* ⟨a. theat, mus⟩; *elocution, diction* **2.** (e–s Gedichts etc) *recitation, rendering* || ⟨mus⟩ *execution, recital* **3.** (Bericht) *report* || ⟨wir⟩ *talk* || *discourse* (über *on*) **4.** (Vorlesung) *lecture* **5.** ⟨com⟩ (⟨a.⟩ ~ auf neue Rechnung) *balance carried forward* **B.** e–n schönen ~ h *to have a fine delivery* || den ~ h *to speak* || beim König ~ h *to be in personal attendance on the k.* | ~ **halten** (→ 3.) *to make a report* | ⁓e halten (→ 4.) *to deliver* od *give lectures, to lecture* (vor *to*, über *on*) | ⁓|**tragen** vt irr [h] *to carry forward* (⟨a. com⟩: Saldo) || ⟨mil⟩ den A. ~ *to carry the attack* (*into the depth*) | (berichten) *to* (*make a*) *report on* (jdm *to a p*) || (Gedicht etc) *to recite* || ⟨mus⟩ *to play, perform, recite, execute*; (Lied) *to sing* || (Predigt etc) *to deliver* .. (über *on*) || (Meinung) *to express* || e–e Bitte ~ *to make a request* || (Gedanken) *to state* **V.ende(r** m) & f *performer, executant, lecturer* || ~r Rat *councillor* (*who makes reports*) **V.ge-** ~kreuz [n] ⟨ec⟩ *processional cross* **V.gs-** ~art [f] → A. 1.; ~bezeichnung [f] ⟨mus⟩ *markings* pl *for performance*; ~kunst [f] *elocution*; ~künstler(in) *reciter, elocutionist*; ~reise [f] *lecture tour*; ⟨pol⟩ *speaking t.* || *lecturing-trip*; ~weise [f] → A. 1. ⁓**tr·efflich** a *excellent, admirable, splendid*; *rare*; *choice* (*food*) || *famous* (*story*) || *capital* (*fellow*) || ~! *well done!, very good!* | adv *to perfection* || (*to play*) *beautifully* | ⁓keit [f] ~/ *excellence* ⁓|**treiben** vt [h] *to drive on* bzw *before* || ⟨min⟩ (Stollen) *to drive*; *to push forward* ⁓|**treten** vi irr [s] *to step* od *come forward* || ~! ⟨mil⟩ *fall out*! || mit etw nicht ~ wollen *to hold back with a th* || (vorragen) *to project, protrude* **~trieb** m *propulsion* ⁓|**trinken** vt [h] *to drink first,* (e–m) *to drink before* (*a p*), *to drink a p's health* **~tritt** m *precedence* || den ~ h vor *to take precedence of* || jdm den ~ l *to give precedence to a p* || unter ~ [gen] *preceded by* | **~s-** ~recht [n] *right of priority* **~trupp** m ⟨mil⟩ *advance party* **~truppen** f pl *advanced troops* **~tuch** n *neckerchief worn in front* || (f Kinder) *bib* || ˣ*apron* ⁓|**tun** vt irr [h] *to put on* || *to do beforehand* || *to show how to do* || es e–m ~ *to surpass a p in doing* || –getan u nachbedacht hat manchem großes Leid gebracht *look before you leap* **~türe** f *outer door* || ⟨engl univ⟩ *oak* ⁓|**turnen** vi [h] *to lead* (*at gymnastic exercises*) **~turner** m ~s/~ *leader* (*at g. e.*) ⁓|**üben** vt [h] *to exercise previously*

vor·über adv *by, past, along* || (zu Ende) *over*; *gone by*; *finished* || (*before the night was*) *through* || ihr Ärger war ~ *she was past her anger* || ~ s: *when the first rush had passed*; *school is out*; *his fame had faded*; *the rain is over* **~|fliegen** (etc) vi [s] *to fly* (etc) *past* **~|gehen** vi irr [s] *to pass by* || (zeitlich) *to pass* (*away*) || ⟨fig⟩ *to blow over* | an e–m ~ *to pass by a p* (*she passed me by*; *she passed by her brother*); ⟨fig⟩ *to ignore a p* || ⟨übtr⟩ .. spurlos –gegangen s (*age doesn't seem*) *to have had no* (*any*) *effect on her* || ~ l *to miss* (*a chance*) || im ⁓ *in passing,* ⟨fig⟩ *by the way* **~gehend** a *passing* || ⟨fig⟩ *transient, transitory, temporal, temporary* || *impermanent*; *ephemeral*; *evanescent*; *momentary*; *fleeting*; *for the* (*time being* od) *moment* || schnell ~ *short-lived* (*success*) || sich ~ an e–m Ort aufhalten *to make a short stay at a place* || die ⁓en [m & f pl] *the passers-by* pl **~|können** vi [h] *to be able to pass* **~|stieben** vi [s] *to blow past* **~|ziehen** vi [s] *to march past* || ~de Gewitter [pl] *passing storms*

V·or- ~übung f *previous exercise, preliminary practice* **~- u** Rücklaufhebel m *forward-reverse lever* | etw ⁓- **u** rückwärts kennen *to know a th frontwards and backwards* **~untersuchung** f ⟨jur⟩ *preliminary inquiry* od *trial* (bei der ~ *at the* ..)

V·orurteil n *prejudice* || *prepossession, bias* || voller ~e *prejudiced* || ~e gegen sich h, ~en unterworfen s *to lie under some p.es* || sich v ~en frei|machen *to get the better of one's prejudices* || in jdm ~e wecken *to prejudice a p* | **~s-** ⁓frei, ⁓los [a] *impartial, objective, unprejudiced, unbiassed*; ~losigkeit [f] *open-mindedness, detachment, impartiality*; ⁓voll [a] (*much*) *prejudiced, biassed*

V·or- ~vater m *progenitor, ancestor* **~verdichter** m ⟨mot⟩ *supercharger* **~vergangenheit** f ⟨gram⟩ *pluperfect* **~verhandlungen** f pl *preliminaries* pl; ⟨jur⟩ *pleadings* pl **~verhör** n *pre-examination* **~verkauf** m ⟨com⟩ *advance sale* | ⟨theat⟩ *booking in advance* || im ~ besorgen *to book* || im ~ zu h *bookable* | **~s-** ~kasse [f] ⟨theat etc⟩ *booking office* ⁓|**verlegen** vt [h] *to antedate*; (Termin) *to bring forward* (um *by* [*2 weeks*]); (Zeitplan) *to move up* || um 1 St. ~ *to put forward* (*by*) *an hour* | ⟨artill⟩ *to lift* (*the fire*) **~verstärker** m *input* (od *pre-*)*amplifier* **~versuch** m *pilot experiment*; *preliminary test* **~vertrag** m ⟨jur⟩ *contract of agreement*; *binder* **~vordern** m pl *ancestors* pl ⁓**vorgestern** adv *three days ago* ⁓**vorig** a *last .. but one, the* (*week*) *before last* ⁓**vorletzt** a *last .. but two* || ⟨gram⟩ *antepenultimate* **~wachs** n *bee-glue* **~wache** f *advanced guard*

Verbal-Flexion der Verben mit der Vorsilbe **ver-** → das jeweilige Simplex

≈|**wagen**: sich ∼ [h] *to venture forth*; sich [acc] zu weit –ge–gt h *to find o.s. out on a limb* (Rand) ≈|**wägen** = –wiegen 2. ∼**wahl** f *preliminary election*; *nomination*; ⟨Am⟩ *straw-vote*; *primary* ‖ ⟨telph⟩ *pre-selection* ∼**wähl-** ∼nummer [f] *call-prefix*; (*area*) *code* (*I dial the c. 4 and then the number*) ∼**wähler** m ⟨telph⟩ *pre-selector* ∼**wald** m [bes bay] ⟨geog⟩ *forest foothills* ≈|**-walten** vt [h] *to prevail, predominate* ∼**walz-** ∼werk [n] *reducing rollers* pl ∼**walze** f ⟨met⟩ *billet roll* ≈|**walzen** vt [h] *to rough down* ∼**wand** m *pretence, pretext, plea*; *excuse*; ⟨sl⟩ *stall* ‖ ein ∼ ist bald gefunden *any stick to beat a dog* ‖ unter dem ∼e, daß *under pretence* od *show of*; *on the plea*, etc *of* od *that* ≈|**wärmen** vt [h] *to preheat* ∼**warnung** f *early warning* ⟨a. mil⟩; ⟨aero⟩ *alert signal* ∼**wegweiser** m ⟨mot⟩ *advance* (*direction*) *sign* (→ ⟨a.⟩ vorw·eg)

v·orwärts [adv & sep pref] *forward, on, along* ‖ ∼! *go ahead*!, (*come, move*) *on*!; *start*!, *go on*! *go* (⟨fam⟩ *it*)! ‖ Stoß nach ∼ *lunge forward* **A.** sich ∼ bewegen *to move forward, to advance*; ∼ eilen *to hurry on*; ∼ fahren *to face the engine*; ∼ gehen *to proceed*; es will damit nicht ∼|gehen (→ u.) *it doesn't get on*; jdm ∼ helfen *to help a p along* | ∼ k *to get on, to make headway*, ⟨fig⟩ *to make one's way, to do well* | langsam kommt man auch ∼ *slow and sure wins the race* ‖ ∼ streben *to push ahead*; ∼ strebend *pushing* **B.** sich ∼|**arbeiten** etc → vorarbeiten etc ≈**beuge** f ⟨gym⟩ *bending forward* ≈**bewegung** f *onward movement* | sich ∼|**bringen** *to push o.s. on in the world* ∼|**drängen** *to to press forward*; *to forge ahead* ≈**gang** m ⟨mot⟩ *forward gear* od *speed* ∼|**gehen** ⟨fig⟩ *to improve* ∼|**kommen** *to advance, progress*; (in der Welt) ∼|k *to get on in the w.* ‖ mit jdm ∼ ⟨fig⟩ *to make headway with a p* ∼|**schreiten** = –gehen; die Zeit –tet v. *time marches on* ∼**sitz** m *forward-facing seat* ≈**streben** n *push* ∼|**tragen** vt [h] (fördern) *to advance* (*war*, etc) ∼|**treiben** vt *to propel, to urge on* ‖ ⟨fig⟩ *to spur*; *to go ahead with* ≈**turbine** f *ahead-turbine*; → ⟨a.⟩ A. ‖ **NB.** Verben ⟨eig⟩ 2 Wörter; ⟨übtr⟩ 1 Wort

vorw·eg [adv & sep pref] (→ ⟨a.⟩ Vor-) *before*(*hand*), *from before* ‖ *before the time* ‖ ∼ genießen *to anticipate enjoyment* ‖ mit der Zunge ∼ s *to have a loose tongue* ≈**nahme** f *anticipation* ∼|**nehmen** vt *to anticipate*

V·or- ≈**weihnachtlich** a *pre-Yule* ≈|**weinen** = ∼jammern ≈|**weisen** vt irr [h] *to show, produce, exhibit* ∼**welt** f *prehistoric world* ‖ *former ages* pl ‖ *forefathers* pl ≈**weltlich** a *primeval*; *fossil* ≈|**werfen** vt irr [h] *to throw forward* bzw *before*; [dat] *to throw* (*food*) (*to*) | ⟨fig⟩ jdm etw ∼ *to upbraid* od *charge, reproach a p with a th, to taunt a p with doing*; ⟨fam⟩ *to cast a th in a p's teeth* ‖ es wird ihm Habgier –geworfen *he is taxed with avarice* ‖ sie h e–a nichts –zu– *there are six of one, and half a dozen of the other* ‖ ich habe mir nichts –zu– *I have nothing to reproach myself with* ∼**werk** n *by-farm* ‖ ⟨fort⟩ *outwork* ‖ ∼e [pl] *advanced forts* ≈|**wiegen** 1. vi irr [h] *to predominate, prevail* **2.** vt = e–m ∼ *to weigh out .. before* od *to a p* ‖ ∼d [a] *preponderant, prevalent* | [adv] *for the most part* ∼|**wimmern,** ∼|**winseln** → vorjammern ∼**wind** m *head-wind* ∼**winter** m *early winter* ∼**wissen** n *foreknowledge*; (*previous*) *knowledge*; *prescience* ‖ mit m–m ∼ *with my* (*full*) *knowledge and consent* ‖ ohne mein ∼ *unknown to me* ‖ ohne ∼ der Eltern *without their* (etc) *parents knowing of it* ∼**witz** m (Neugier) *curiosity, inquisitiveness* ‖ ⟨fam⟩ (P) kl ∼! *Paul Pry*! | (Keckheit) *forwardness, pertness* | (Neigung zur Einmischung) *meddlesomeness* ‖ was d–s Amts nicht ist, da laß d–n ∼ *mind your own business* ≈**witzig** a *inquisitive, prying* ‖ *forward, pert* ‖ *meddlesome* ∼**wort 1.** n ∼(e)s/∼e *preface*; *prefatory note*; *advertisement to the reader* **2.** n ∼(e)s/≈er ⟨gram⟩ *preposition*

V·orwurf m **A.** *reproach*; *charge, accusation*; *allegation* ‖ (Tadel) *blame* | (Gegenstand) *subject, theme, study*; ⟨arts⟩ *motif*; etw z ∼ nehmen *to take a th as text* **B.** den ∼ der Feigheit gegen jdn erheben *to reproach a p with cowardice* ‖ es gereicht ihm z ∼ *it casts a slur upon him* ‖ jdm ≈e m *to blame a p* (*for*), *to reproach a p* (*with*) ‖ sich ≈e m *to reprove o.s.* (über *about*) ‖ jdm etw z ∼ m *to throw a th into a p's teeth* ‖ es wird ihm z ∼ gemacht, daß er es tat *he is blamed for having done it* ≈**sfrei** a *free from blame*, etc; *blameless, irreproachable* ≈**svoll** a *reproachful, upbraiding, rebuking* | adv ⟨a.⟩ *reprovingly, accusingly*

V·or- ≈|**zählen** vt [h]; (jdm etw) *to count out* .. od *enumerate .. to* od *before* ∼**zählung** f ∼/∼en *enumeration* ∼**zahn** m *buck-tooth* ≈|**zaubern** vt [h] (e–m etw) ⟨fig⟩ *to delude a p with a th* ∼**zeichen** n *omen, token, symptom* ‖ ⟨math⟩ *sign* ‖ ⟨mus⟩ *signature*; [pl a.] *flats and sharps*; (Versetzungszeichen) *accidental* ≈|**zeichnen** vt [h] **1.** e–m etw ∼ *to show a p how to draw a th* **2.** *to draw before* **3.** ⟨fig⟩ *to sketch*; *to trace out* **4.** (vorschreiben) [dat] *to indicate, mark, prescribe*; *to point out* (*to*); (Stickerei) *to draw the pattern* (zu *for*) **5.** ⟨mus⟩ *to put the sign of the clef* ‖ was ist –ge–net? *what is the* (*key-*)*signature*?; es ist ein Kreuz –ge–net *there is a sharp in the key* ∼**zeichnung** f (Vorlage) *drawing-copy, model, design, pattern* ‖ ⟨mus⟩ *signature* ‖ ⟨fig⟩ *prescription, indication* ≈**zeigen** vt [h] *to show* (⟨a.⟩ *tickets*), (Paß) *to produce, exhibit* ‖ ⟨rail⟩ Fahrkarten ∼! *tickets, please*! ‖ ⟨com⟩ (Wechsel) *to present* ∼**zeiger** m *bearer, presenter* ‖ ∼ dieses *the bearer of this* (*letter*) od *of the present* ∼**zeigung** f ∼/ *producing, exhibition* ‖ ⟨com⟩ bei ∼ *on presentation* ∼**zeit** f *remote antiquity, olden times* pl ‖ graue ∼ *days of yore*; aus/zu grauer ∼ *from/at some dark age* ≈**z·eiten** adv *formerly*; *many years ago*; *in former times* ≈**zeitig** a *early, untimely* (*death*), *premature* (*birth*) ‖ *unscheduled* ‖ *precocious, anticipated* ‖ ∼e Exmatrikulation, ∼es Aufgeben der Schulausbildung *dropout* | [adv] (*to tie down forces*) *prematurely*; etw ∼ beenden *to abort a th*; ∼ veröffentlichen ⟨journ⟩ *to jump the gun* | ≈keit [f] der Geburt *prematurity* ≈**zeitlich** a *ancient* ∼**zerkleinerung** f ⟨mill⟩ *preliminary crushing* ≈|**ziehen I.** vt irr [h] **1.** *to draw* (*in front of*) **2.** *to draw forth, to pull forward* ‖ ⟨mil⟩ *to put .. further to the front*; *to move* (*groups*) *forward* **3.** ⟨fig⟩ [dat] *to prefer .. (to ..), to give preference* (*to*), *to like .. better than ..* ‖ ich ziehe vor zu bleiben *I would rather stay, I prefer to stay* ‖ [+ acc + dat] *I'd rather have fruit than ices* ‖ –zu– *preferable* **II.** vi [s] ⟨mil⟩ *to march before* ‖ *to advance* ‖ *to move to the front* ∼**zimmer** n *ante-room, ante-chamber* ∼**zug** m **1.** ⟨rail⟩ *relief* (*train*); ⟨mil rail⟩ *pilot train* **2.** *preference* (*above, to*) ‖ (Überlegenheit) *superiority* ‖ (Vorrecht) *privilege, prerogative* ‖ (Vorteil) *advantage*; ≈e [pl] ⟨a.⟩ *excellent points*; *highlights* ⟨a. com⟩ ‖ (Tugend) *virtue* ⟨a. fig⟩, *grace* ‖ (Vorzüglichkeit) *merit*, ⟨emph⟩ *excellence* ‖ *asset* (*openness is a great a.*) ‖ den ∼ geben (vor [dat]) *to give the preference* (*over*) ‖ den ∼ h vor *to have the advantage over, to be preferred to* ‖ wir h den ∼ *we are privileged* (*to do*) **3.** (P) ⟨school⟩ *nevvy* ≈**z·üglich** a *superior, excellent, remarkable, exquisite, choice, first-class* | *dainty* (*dish*) ‖ *delicious* (*pastry*) ‖ *principal* (*part*) ‖ *picked* (⟨sl⟩ *crack*) (*regiment*) ‖ auf ∼en Beziehungen mit *on capital terms with* (*a p*) | [adv] *particularly, especially* | ≈keit [f] ∼/ *superiority, excellence* ‖ *superior quality*; *choiceness* **Vorzugs-** ⟨oft⟩ *preferential* ∼**aktie** f ⟨bank⟩ *priority* od *preference-*

Aussprache: Falls nicht anders (: [v]) angegeben, ist v = [f] zu sprechen.

(〈Am〉 *preferred*) *share*; ~en [pl] 〈Am〉 *p.d stock* **~behandlung** f *p.l treatment* **~druck** m *artist's proof* **~gläubiger** m *preferred creditor* **~-Kundeneintragung** f 〈com〉 *docket* **~liste** f *priority list* **~milch** f *certified* od *designated milk* **~preis** m 〈com〉 *exceptional* od *special price* **~tarif** m *p.l tariff* **´~weise** adv *especially, p.lly*; *for choice* **~zoll** m *p.l duty* od *tariff*

V·orzündung f *advanced ignition, pre-ignition*; 〈mot〉 *spark advance*

vot·ieren [v–] vt/i [h] *to vote* || die ´~den *the voters* pl

Vot·iv- [v–f] *votive* (*church, picture, tablet*)

V·otum [v–] n [~s/–ten & –ta] *vote, suffrage*

vulg·är [v–] a *vulgar* | ´~sprache [f] *demotic l.*

Vulg·ata [v–] f ~/ 〈ec〉 *Vulgate* **v·ulgo** [v–] L adv = gemeinhin

Vulk·an [v–] m ~(e)s/~e *volcano* (*tätig burning*) **´~isch** a *volcanic* [adv *-ally*] **~asbest** m *vulcan-asbestos* **~fiber** f *vulcanized fibre* | ~koffer [m] *vulcan fibre trunk* **~glas** n *tempered glass* **~kraterrand** m *lip, rim of the crater of a v.* **~schlot** m *vent* **Vulkanis·eur** m ~s/~e (P) *vulcanist* **Vulkanis·ier-** **~anstalt** f *vulcanization works* pl [a. sg konstr] **~apparat** m *vulcanizer* | **´~en** vt [h] *to vulcanize*, 〈Am mot〉 *to recap*

W

W, w [n] ~/~ *W, w* || °W. C.! [ve:'tse:] (〈hum, abbr〉 f *W. C.* = „wohl kaum") *not much! not* (〈sl〉 *bloody*) *likely*!

W·aadt(land n) f (schweiz. Kanton) (*Pays de*) *Vaud, country of Vaud,* (*Canton of*) *Vaud* **W·aadtländer** m, **~in** f *Vaudois, inhabitant of* (*the country of*) *Vaud* **w·aadtländisch** a *Vaudois, of* (*the country of*) *Vaud*

W·aage f ~/~n **A. 1.** *balance*; (e–e ~ *a pair of*) *scales*, 〈Am a.〉 *a scales* | Brief´~ *letterbalance*; (Brücken´~, Tafel´~) *weighing-machine*; (f Wagen) *weigh-bridge*; (Eier´~) *egg-weigher*; (Feder´~) *spring balance*; Lkw-~ *truck scale*; Personen´~ *weigher*; (Laufgewichts–, Schnell´~) *steelyard*; (Wasser´~) *level*; (Zeiger´~) *dial balance*; *indicator weighing-machine* **2.** *weigh-house* **3.** 〈astr〉 *Libra* (*the sun enters Libra*) **4.** 〈gym〉 *horizontal stand* **B.** [dat] die ~ halten *to counterbalance*; in der ~ halten *to hold in equilibrium*; das Zünglein an der ~ s *to tip the balance*; schwer in die ~ fallen → Waagschale **~balken** m *scalebeam* **~geld** n *weighing-fee* **~haus** n *weigh-house*; *public scales* **~meister** m *public weigher* **´~recht** a *horizontal, level* || ~e Fläche *level* | ´~e [f] *h.l line* **~zunge** f *needle of a balance* **W·aagschale** f *scale* (*of a balance*) || [pl] *scales* || die ~ sinken m *to turn the balance* || 〈fig〉 schwer in die ~ fallen gegenüber .. *to weigh heavily against*; gewichtiger in die ~ fallen als *to outweigh* (*a th*); die ~ schlägt aus *the scale has tipped* (nach .. *the other side*); die ~ neigt sich zu jds Gunsten *the balance is weighted on a p's side* **W·aagenschneide** f *balance blade*

Waal f (Mündungsarm des Rheins) *Waal*

w·abbelig a *flabby, wobbling* (P) 〈fam〉 *groggy*

W·abe f ~/~n *honey-comb* | **~n-** ´~artig [a] *alveolar*; **~honig** m *honey in the comb* **~kühler** m *h.-c. radiator* **~verwitterung** f *h.c. weathering* **~zelle** f *honey-cell*

W·aberlohe f ~/ *flickering flames* pl

wach a *awake* (*to lie awake*); *wakeful* (*state*) || völlig ~, mit ~en Sinnen *wide awake* || ~er Traum [m] *day-dream* || ~ u munter *alive, brisk* || 〈übtr & fig〉 *lively, unsleeping, tireless* || mit sehr ~em Aug' u Ohr *very alive in e. and e.* || ~ w *to wake up, to stir,* 〈fig〉 *to quicken* **W·ach-** **~aufzug** m 〈mil〉 *guard-parade* od *-mounting* **~bett** n *nurse's bed, camp-bed* **~boot** n *patrol vessel* **~buch** n (*book of*) *guard reports*; *g. b.* **~dauer** f *tour of g.-duty* **~dienst** m 〈mil〉 *guard-* (〈mar〉 *watch-*)*duty* **~einteilung** f 〈mar〉 *w. allocation* **~frau** f *nurse* **´~frei** a *off duty* (〈mar〉 *watch*) **´~habend** a *on duty* | ~er [m] *guard commander*; ~er Offizier 〈mar〉 *officer of the watch* od *deck* **´~|halten** vt [h] 〈fig〉 *to cultivate* (*a feeling*) || das wird mich die ganze Nacht ~ *I shall have to sit up with this all n.* **~hund** m *g. dog* **~mann** m = Schutzmann | ~schaft [f] *g. detail* **~offizier** m 〈mar〉 *watchkeeper* **´~rufen** vt irr [h] *to wake* || 〈fig〉 *to call forth, to* (*a*)*rouse, waken* || *to bring back* (*memory of* an); in jdm .. ~ *to stir a p to m.ries of* **~schiff** n *g.-ship*; (Küsten´~) *weather ship* **~sein** n *wakefulness* **~vergehen** n *neglect of duty while on g.* **~vorschrift** f *g. regulations* pl **~welle** f *stand-by frequency* **~zeiten** f pl *g. d. hours* **W·ache** f ~/~n *guard*, 〈mar〉 *watch* || Brücken– etc-´~ 〈mil〉 *target-force* || (Gebäude) *police-station*; 〈mil〉 *guard-room* || (P) *sentinel, sentry*; [koll] (*men on*) *guard* | die ~ h, auf ~ s, ~ °schieben *to be on guard* od *duty*; (auf) ~ stehen *to stand sentry* 〈mar〉 *watch* || Aufziehen der ~ *mounting the g.* || auf ~ ziehen *to mount g.* || von ~ abziehen *to be relieved* || ~ 'raus! *turn out, g.*! || die ~ ablösen *to relieve g.* || 〈med〉 die ~ übernehmen *to take charge* || 〈fig〉 ~ halten *to watch, to keep a good lookout, to be on the l.* (*for*) **w·achen I.** vi [h] *to be awake* || (über [acc]) *to watch* (*over*), *to care* (*for*); eifersüchtig über s–e Frau ~ *to keep tabs on ..* || bei jdm ~ *to sit up with a p,* 〈med〉 *to nurse* (*a p*) **II.** ´~ n 〈a.〉 *wakefulness* **w·achsam** [xz] a *watchful,* 〈emph〉 *vigilant, alert, on one's guard* || ein ~es Auge h auf *to keep a sharp eye on ..* || ~ s über *to* (*keep*) *watch over* || (Hund) ~ s *keep good watch* | **´~keit** f ~/ *watchfulness, vigilance*; *alertness*; unablässige ~ *watch and ward*; → Wacht

Wach·older m ~s/~ 〈bot〉 *juniper* **~beere** f *j.-berry* **~drossel** f 〈orn〉 *fieldfare* **~branntwein, ~geist** m *gin* **~harz** n *gumjuniper* **~strauch** m *juniper-tree*

Wachs [ks] n ~es/~e *wax* || mit ~ bestreichen, putzen *to wax* **~abdruck** m *impression in wax* **´~artig** a *waxy* **~ausschmelzverfahren** n 〈met〉 *lost wax process* **~bild** n *wax-figure, waxen image* **~bildner·ei** f *modelling in wax* || *w.-work* **´~bleich** a *pale as death* **~bleiche** f *place for bleaching wax* **~blume** f *wax-flower* || 〈bot〉 (Hoya *hoya*) *wax plant, waxflower*; 〈mst〉 *honeywort* **~bohne** f *butter* od 〈Am〉 *wax bean* **~bohner** m *floor-polisher* **~fackel** f *wax-torch* **~farbe** f *wax-colour* | **~n-** ~malerei [f] *encaustic* **´~farbig** a *wax-coloured* **~figur** f = –bild **~figurenkabinett** n *waxworks* pl **´~gelb** = –farbig **~händler** m *wax-chandler* **~haut** f 〈orn〉 *cere* **~kerzchen** n = –streichholz **~kerze** f *wax-candle, taper* **~leinwand** f *oil-cloth* **~licht** n *wax-candle* **~malerei** f *encaustic painting* **~maske** f *wax-mask* **~modell** n *wax model* od *mould* **~papier** n *waxed* od *paraffin* od *wax-coated paper* **~perle** f *wax pearl* **~pflaster** n *cerate, wax-plaster* | auf ~-platten aufnehmen 〈Am wir〉 *to wax* **~pomade** f *wax-pomatum* **~puppe** f *wax-doll* **~salbe** f *cerate* **~schablone** f → Batik **~scheibe** f *cake of wax* **~sonde** f 〈surg〉 *bougie* **~stock** m *wax-taper* **~streichholz** n (*wax-*)*vesta* **~tafel** f *wax-tablet* **~taf(fet)t** m *oiled silk* **~tuch** n *oil-cloth, American* *leather* | ~fabrik [f] *o.-c. manufactory* ≗**weich** a *soft like wax* || ~es Ei *medium boiled egg* ~**zieher** m *wax-chandler* ~**zündholz** n *(wax-)vesta* **w·achsen,** ≗ [ks] vt [h] *to wax* **w·ächsern** a *waxen, ([made] of) wax*

w·achsen [ks] vi irr [s] **A.** *to grow* (⟨a. fig⟩ an W. *in wisdom*) || ⟨bot a.⟩ *to come up*; (Obst ⟨a.⟩) *to wax*; ihr ~ schon Flügel ⟨hum⟩ *she's sprouting wings* | ⟨fig⟩ *to spring up*; *to thrive*; *to (be on the) increase* (⟨a.⟩ Mond, ⟨a.⟩ *to be waxing*) || (Wasser) *to rise* || (fortschreiten) *to advance* || sich [dat] e–n Bart ~ l *to grow* (⟨Am⟩ *to raise*) *a b.* || ⟨fig⟩ (mit sich) ~ l: *the story accreted emotion* **B. krumm** u schief ~ *to grow crooked* || z schnell ~ *to outgrow o.s.* || üppig ~ *to wanton* **C. aus** den Kleidern ~ *to outgrow one's clothes* || **in** die Breite ~ *to grow broad, to extend* || in die Höhe ~ *to grow tall, to shoot up* || ins Holz (Kraut) ~ *to run to wood (leaf)* || **über** → Kopf || es wuchs unter s–n Händen .. *upon his h.s* **D. sich** fest|~ *to take root* **E.** ≗ n *growing, growth, increase, accretion, augmentation* || ⟨chem⟩ *crystallization* || *rising (of water)* || *expansion, development (of trade)* **F. gewachsen:** *solid* (Fels) | Sie sind aber g.! *how you have grown!* || er muß sehr g. s *he must have done a great deal of growing* || gut g. *well-made* || krumm g. *of crooked growth* || ·e–r S (jdm) [nicht] g. s *to be [un]equal to a th (to be a [no] match for a p)* → gewachsen

W·achstum n ~s/ *growth*; *germinating power* || ⟨fig⟩ *increase* || ⟨bot⟩ *vegetation*, üppiges ~ *rank* od *wanton growth*, eigenes ~! (Wein) *home produce!* | übermäßiges ~ *overgrowth* || im ~ hindern *to stunt* || → Ausweitung | ≗fördernd [a] *vegetative* | ~**s-** ~schwierigkeiten [pl] ⟨fig⟩ *teething troubles* **W·achsweh** n *growing pains* pl

Wacht f ~/~en *guard*; ⟨mar⟩ *watch* || die ~ am Rhein *the W. on the Rhine* || auf der ~ s *to be on the alert* ~**bett** n *camp-bed* ~**boot** n *g.-boat* ~**dienst** m *g.-(⟨mar⟩ w.-)duty* ~**feuer** n *w.-fire* ~**habende(r)** m *commander on g.* ~**haus** n *g.house* ~**lokal** n *g. room* ~**mannschaft** f *guard* ~**mantel** m *sentry's w.coat* ~**meister** m ⟨mil⟩ *cavalry sergeant* ~**parade** f ⟨mil⟩ *g.-mounting* ~**posten** m *sentry, post, guard, picket*; ⟨mar⟩ *look-out* ~**schiff** n *g.-ship* ~**stube** f *g. room* ~**turm** m *w.-tower* | → Wach-

W·ächte [ɑ] f ~/~n *snow-drift, cornice*

W·achtel f ~/~n ⟨orn⟩ *quail (the q. calls* = ruft, schlägt) || °sich zur ~ m *to make an exhibition of o.s.* ~**fang** m *q.-catching* ~**garn** n *q.-net* ~**hund** m (= -**hündchen**) *(king Charles') spaniel* ~**könig** m ⟨orn⟩ *landrail*; *corncrake* ~**pfeife** f *bird-call, q.-call* ~**ruf,** ~**schlag** m *call of a q.* ~**strich** m *passage of q.s* ~**weizen** m *cow-wheat*

W·ächter m ~s/~ *watchman*; *keeper* || ⟨mar⟩ *look-out man* || ⟨fig⟩ *guardian* (über *over*) || (London-Tower≗) *beefeater* ~**geld** n *watchman's fee* ~**häuschen** n *watchman's hut*, ⟨rail⟩ *watch-box* ~**lied** n *aubade* ~**ruf** m *watchman's call*

W·acke f ~/~n ⟨geol⟩ *rock-stone, wacke*

w·ack(e)lig a *tottering* || *doddering (old man)* *shaky* (⟨a.⟩ *health*) || (S) *unsteady* || (Haus) *ramshackle, crazy* || (Zahn) *loose* || (Möbel) *rickety* || (Wagen) *jolting* | ⟨fig sl⟩ *dicky (business)* || auf ~en Füßen *in a shaky condition* **w·ackel-** ≗kontakt [m] ⟨el⟩ *loose contact* od *connection*; ~köpfig a *with a shaky head* ≗peter [m] = Flammeri

w·ackeln vi **1.** [h] *to totter, shake* || mit dem Kopf ~ *to shake* od *wag one's head* || ⟨aero⟩ (mit den Flügeln) ~ *to rock wings* **2.** [s] (watscheln) *to totter, waddle (along)*

w·acker a *gallant, brave, valiant* | [adv] *well* || sich ~ halten *to acquit o.s. bravely* od *like a Trojan*; *to come out well* | ~! *bravo!*

W·ade f ~/~n *calf (of the leg)* [pl *calves*] | ~**n-** *sural* ~**bein** n ⟨anat⟩ *splint-bone, fibula* ~**krampf** m *cramp in the calf* ~**stecher** m ⟨ent⟩ *stable fly* ~**strümpfe** m pl *golf-hose* || *calf length socks* pl

W·affe f ~/~n *weapon (of defence, attack)*; *arm* ([mst pl] *in arms*) || ~n [pl] Christi *Instruments of Passion* || ⟨hunt⟩ (→ Gewehr B.) *(boar's) tushes* || Volk in ~n *armed nation* | (~ngattung) *arm* | blanke ~ *side-arm*; *cold steel*; mit der blanken Waffe *by bayonet charges* || leichte Infanterie≗n, Kleinkaliber≗n [pl] *small arms*; Stangen≗ ⟨hist⟩ *shafted weapon*; Wurf≗ *missile w.* || e–e ~ beherrschen *to master a w.* || sich mit der ~ befreien *to shoot one's way out* || zu den ~n eilen *to fly to arms*, .. greifen *to take up arms* || ~n tragen *to carry arms* || die ~n niederlegen, strecken *to lay down one's arms* || die ~n wegwerfen *to abandon one's arms* || unter den ~n s *to be up in arms, to stand to arms* || ⟨fig⟩ jdn mit s–n eigenen ~n schlagen *to beat a p at his own game, to play with a p at his own weapons*

W·affel f ~/~n → Wabe *waffle, wafer*; (gr) *gofer* || gefüllte ~ *slider* ~**eisen** n *waffle-iron*

W·affen- ~**amt** n *ordnance department* ~**arbeit** f *war* ~**art** f *type of weapon* ~**ausbildung** f *w.s training* ~**beistand** m *armed assistance* ~**beute** f *booty in arms* ~**bruder** m *brother in arms, comrade*; *br. officer*; ⟨hum⟩ *brother blade* ~**brüderschaft** f *the bonds between brothers-in-arms* ~**depot** n *arsenal* ~**dienst** m *military service* ~**ehre** f *glory of arms* | gemeinsames Programm f ~**entwicklung** f *Mutual Weapons Development Program* N ~**fabrik** f *arms-factory* ≗**fähig** a *able to bear arms* ~**fett** n *rifle oil* ~**gang** m *passage at arms* ~**gattung** f *arm*; *branch* N *(of service)* ~**gefährte** m *companion-in-arms* ~**geklirr** m *clash* od *clang of arms* ~**getöse** n *din of arms* ~**gewalt** f: mit ~ *with arms, by force of arms* ~**glück** n *fortune of war*; das ~ versuchen *to appeal to arms* ~**handwerk** n *profession of arms* ~**hemd** n *coat of mail* ~**herold** m *king-at-arms* ~**kammer** f *armo(u)ry* ~**lager** n *arsenal* ≗**los** a *unarmed, defenceless* ~**losigkeit** f ⟨pol⟩ *non-violent resistance* ~**meister(·ei** f) m *armo(u)rer (armo(u)ry; ordnance shop)* ~**offizier** m *o. officer* ~**platz** m *place of arms* ~**probe** f *trial of arms* ~**prüfgelände** n *ordnance* od *proving ground* ~**prüfung** f *o. proving* ~**rock** m *tunic*, ⟨hist⟩ = –hemd ~**ruf** m *call to arms* ~**ruhe** f *suspension of hostilities, cease-fire* | ~**-** *trucial* ~**ruhm** m *military glory* ~**schau** f *review* ~**schein** m *gun-licence, -se*; *fire-arm certificate* ~**schmied(e** f) m *armourer('s workshop)* ~**schmuck** m *trophy* || *warlike accoutrement*; im vollen ~ *in full armour*, ⟨fam fig⟩ *in full war-paint* ~**schmuggel** m *gun-running* ~**sperre** f *arms embargo* ~**-SS** f ⟨nazi⟩ *armed SS* ~**st·illstand** m *armistice, cease-fire, truce (with)* ~**streckung** f *capitulation* ~**tanz** m *war-dance*; ⟨fig⟩ *war, battle* ~**tat** f *warlike deed, feat of arms* ~**tragen** verboten! *it is forbidden to carry arms* ≗**tragend** a *armigerous, bearing arms* ~**träger** m ⟨mil⟩ *armed man*; ⟨hist⟩ *armour-bearer, esquire* ~**übung** f *military exercise* ~**unteroffizier** m *ordnance NCO* ~**verbot** n *ban on weapons* ~**wache** f *knight's watch by his armour* ≗**weise** [adv] *according to the arm* ~**wirkung** f *effect of arms* || die ~ früh z vollen Geltung bringen *to bring the full effectiveness of weapons to bear early* ~**zimmer** n ⟨hunt⟩ *gun-room*

w·affnen vt [h] *to arm* || mit gewaffneter Hand *arms in hand* || sich gegen etw ~ *to guard against a th* || sich mit Geduld ~ *to possess one's soul in patience*

w·ägbar a *ponderable* †**W·ag(e)** .. → Waage

W·ag(e)- (→ wagen) ~**hals** m *dare-devil*; *foolhardy person* ≗**halsig** a *rash, adventuresome* || e–e ~e S unternehmen *to enter upon a daring enterprise* ~**halsigkeit** f *daring, dare-devilry*; angeborene ~ *essential liking for thin ice* ~**mut** m *daring; enterprise; derring-do; dash* **~mutig** a *daring; enterprising; bold; dauntless; dashing; adventurous* **~stück** n *dangerous venture; bold attempt*

W·ägelchen n ~s/~ *little carriage*; → Wagen

w·agen I. vt [h] **A.** *to dare* || *to risk (everything)* || *to stake (one's life)* || ⟨fam⟩ *to chance a th* || *to hazard (a remark)* || *to venture (an opinion)*; zu viel ~ *to v. too far*; *to v. on (another glass)* || (versuchen) *to attempt* **B. es** ~: ich wag's *I'll risk it* || er hat's gewagt *he has taken the risk* || es ~ *to take the plunge* || ⟨fam⟩ es noch einmal ~ ⟨sl⟩ *to try it on again* || wir ~ es nicht *we dare not do it* || wenn Sie es ~! *here, you!* || es mit e–m ~ *to try a fall* (od *to cross swords*) *with a p* **C.** wir ~ **zu** sagen *we make bold to say* || soviel ~ wir zu behaupten *we'd go as far as to say* || ~ etw z tun *to risk doing a th* || sie ~ nicht es z tun *they are afraid* (od *have not the heart* od *courage*) *to do it, they dare not do it* **D.** frisch gewagt! *take your chance!* || ⟨prov⟩ wer nicht wagt, der nicht gewinnt *nothing venture, nothing have* || frisch gewagt ist halb gewonnen *well begun is half done*; *none but the brave deserve the fair*; *faint heart never won fair lady* **E. sich** ~ *to venture* (an *upon*, aus *out of*, in *into*) || sich unter die Leute ~ *to v. into society* || sich nicht vor die Tür ~ *not to v. out of doors* **F. gewagt** a *venturesome, risky, hazardous* || *daring (deed)*; *bold (enterprise)*; → S. **II.** ≃ n ~s/ in kühnem ~ *by taking a bold risk*

w·ägen vt [h] = wiegen vt *to weigh, balance* || *to poise (a sword in one's hand)*; *to heft a th (for weight)* || *to consider (one's words)* || ⟨prov⟩ erst wäg's dann wag's *look before you leap*

W·agen m ~s/~ **A.** ⟨allg⟩ *carriage* ⟨a. comp, typwr etc⟩ || *vehicle, conveyance* | ⟨astr⟩ der gr. ~ *Charles's Wain* || ⟨el⟩ *car* || ⟨mot⟩ *car*, offener *roadster*; ~ der Mittelklasse *compact car* || ⟨rail⟩ *carriage, coach*, ⟨Am⟩ *car*; ~ 2. Klasse *second-class c.* **B. Acker~** *cart*, ⟨poet⟩ *wain* || Aussichts≃ *sight-seeing car* || Beschickungs≃ *charging hopper* || *beer cart* od *van* || (Droschke) *cab* || Einkaufs≃ (in Selbstbedienungsladen) *push-cart* || Erz≃ *ore wag(g)on* || Feldbahn≃ *truck* || Fracht≃ *wag(g)on, cart* | ⟨rail⟩ Gepäck≃ *luggage-van*, ⟨Am⟩ *baggage-car*; Güter≃ *goods--van*, ⟨Am⟩ *freight car* | Hand≃ *barrow* || Holländer≃ *three-wheeled truck* || → Kinder≃ || Kranken≃ *ambulance* | Kutsch≃ *carriage, coach*; 2-rädriger ~ *sulk, trap, gig*, ⟨hist⟩ *hansom*; ⟨Am⟩ *buggy*, (gedeckt) *cariole* | Last≃, Fracht≃ *lorry*, ⟨mot⟩ *truck* || *milk cart* || Leih≃ *courtesy car* || Möbel≃ *van* || Prunk≃ *state coach, gala chariot* || *Pullman-car* || Roll≃ = Last≃; *lorry, dray* || Rungen≃ *platform truck* || *saloon-carriage* || Schlauch≃ *hose-reel* || *spindle--carriage* || Sport≃ *go-cart* || Stuben≃ *wheeled cradle* || Vieh≃ *van*; *horse-box*; ⟨Am⟩ *box-car* || Wohn-, Zirkus≃ *caravan* **C.** °e–m **an** den ~ fahren ⟨Am⟩ *to put one over on a p* || **durch** *or* mit ~ *by* od *per van* || e–n **im** ~ mitnehmen *to give a p a lift* || ich will mal nach dem ~ sehen ⟨euph⟩ (= austreten) *I'll just post a letter* || **unter** den ~ k *to be worsted* || ein ~ voll *a vanful, a wagon-load* **D. ~abteil** n ⟨rail⟩ *compartment* **~achse** f *axle-tree* **~antrieb** m ⟨comp-el⟩ *machine operation* **~bauer** m = –macher **~breite** f ⟨comp etc⟩ *carriage length* **~brücke** f *floating-, roll--bridge* **~burg** f *barricade of waggons*; ⟨S.Afr.⟩ *laager* **~decke** f *cover*; *awning*; *tilt* **~deichsel** f *coach-pole, shaft (of a cart)* **~fähre** f *carriage ferry* **~feder** f *road spring* **~führer** m *driver* **~gabel** f (Einspänner≃) *shafts* pl **~geleise** n *cart-rut* **~geschirr** n *harness* **~gestell** n *frame*; ⟨mot⟩ *chassis* **~halle** f *garage* **~heber** m ⟨mot⟩ *(lifting-)jack*; fahrbarer ~ *troll(e)y jack* | ~-bühne [f] *electric jack*; ~stange [f] *jack-handle* **~kasten** m *body* **~kette** f *trigger* **~klappe** f ⟨mot⟩ (hintere) *tail-board* **~klasse** f ⟨rail⟩ *class*; Fahrkarte erster Kl. *first-cl. ticket* **~kolonne** f *supply park*; ⟨mot Am⟩ *autocade, motorcade* **~korb** m *hamper* **~ladung** f *carload, cargo* **~lautsprecher** m *in-car speaker* **~leiter** f *w.-ladder, cart-rack* **~lenker** m ⟨hist⟩ *charioteer* **~löser** m ⟨typewr⟩ *carriage-release lever* **~macher** m *cartwright, coach-maker* **~material** n ⟨rail⟩ *rolling stock* **~meister** m ⟨rail⟩ *w.-master* || ⟨hot⟩ *doorman* **~park** m *car lot*; *fleet of cars*; ⟨rail⟩ *rolling stock*; ⟨mil⟩ *park* **~pferd** n *carr.-horse* **~pflege** f ⟨mot⟩ *servicing*; *maintenance (of a car)* **~plane** f *awning, hood* **~rad** n *carr.-wheel* **~remise** f *coach-house, shed for carr.s* **~rennen** n *chariot--race* **~rücklauftaste** f ⟨comp⟩ *carriage return key* **~runge** f *pin bar* **~schlag** m *carr.-door* **~schmied** m *coach-builder* **~schmiere** f *cart--grease* **~schuppen** m = –remise **~spur** f = –geleise **~tritt** m *carr.-step* **~umläufe** m pl ⟨min, rail⟩ *roundabouts* **~verkehr** m *wheeled* od *vehicular traffic* **~vor-** u Rücklauf [m] ⟨comp⟩ *forward and return carriage movement* **~wechsel** m *change of carr.s* **~winde** f *draw-beam, screw-jack*

W·äger m ~s/~ *weigher*

w·aggeln vi [h] ⟨golf⟩ *to waggle*

Waggon [–ˈgɔŋ] m ~s/~s ⟨rail⟩ *carriage*, ⟨Am⟩ *car* || (f Güter) *van*; (offener) *truck* **~ladung** f *carload* **~-** u Lokbau m ⟨rail⟩ *rolling stock manufacturing* **≃weise** [adv] *by the wagon-load*

W·agner m = Wagenmacher

Wagneri·aner m ~s/~ ⟨mus⟩ *Wagnerian*

W·agnis n –isses/–isse *venture, risk(y undertaking), hazard(ous enterprise)* || ein ~ auf sich nehmen *to take the plunge* **W·agstück** n = Wagestück; → wagen

W·ägungsfaktor m ⟨stat⟩ *weight*

Wahl f ~/~en **A. 1.** *choice* || *choosing (of a p for ..)* **2.** ⟨parl, etc⟩ *election* (z *to*) *(the e. went republican* .. fiel r. aus); (geheime ~ durch Kugeln *or* Zettel *secret) ballot* **3.** (freie Entscheidung) *option (if I had the o.*; *to leave a th at a p's o.)* **4.** (Auslese) *selection* || (zw 2 Dingen) *alternative* **B. direkte** ~en *ele. by direct suffrage* || engere *or* Stich≃ *second* od *final ballot* || entscheidende ~ *runoff ele.* || freie ~ ⟨a.⟩ *refusal* || geheime ~ *secret ballot* || örtliche ~ ⟨Am⟩ *primary* **C. auf** ~ begründet *elective* || auf ~en bezüglich *electoral* | **aus** freier ~ *of one's own choice* | **in** engerer ~ *on the short list* (dazu: *shortlisted [candidate]*) | **nach** ~ ⟨com⟩ *at (your) choice*; ⟨tech a.⟩ *special* | **vor** die ~ stellen *to let a p choose* | **zur** ~ vorschlagen *to put .. up for election*; *to nominate .. as candidate*; zur engeren ~ stehen *to be on the short list* **D.** da fällt mir die ~ schwer *I find it hard to choose, it's Hobson's choice* || die ~ h *to have one's choice* || k–e ~ h *to have no alternative* od *option* (als *but*) || wir h k–e ~ *it's a case of Hobson's choice* || jdm die ~ l *to let a p take his ch., to leave a th to a p* || e–e ~ treffen *to make a ch.*; nach getroffener ~ *having selected*, etc || die ~ selbst treffen *to make one's own selection* || e–e ~ veranstalten *to call an ele.* | ⟨prov⟩ wer die ~ hat, hat die Qual *the less ch., the greater comfort*; *the larger the choice the greater the puzzle*; *embarras de richesse!* Fr **~agitation** f *electioneering* **~akt** m *poll* **~akten** f pl *election--returns* pl; ⟨Am⟩ *tally sheet* **~amt** n *elective office* **~aufruf** m *election-address, manifests* **~beeinflussung** f *electoral corruption* **≃berechtigt** a [act] *entitled to vote*; [pass] *eligible* || Anzahl der W.en *voting strength* **~bericht** m *return* **~bestechung** f *corrupt practices* pl **~beteiligung** f *turn-out* **~bewegung** f *election-campaign* **~bezirk** m *constituency*, ⟨Am⟩ *district*, (in der Stadt) *ward*; ⟨Am fam a.⟩ *beat* || sich um s–n ~ kümmern *to nurse one's c.*, ⟨Am⟩ *to look after one's fences* **~bühne** f ⟨parl⟩ *hustings* **~ergebnis** n *result of an election; poll; e. returns* pl **~fach** n *optional subject;* ⟨Am⟩ *elective* **≃fähig** a (zu) **1.** = –berechtigt **2.** [pass] *eligible* (zu *for*) **~fähigkeit** f *elective franchise* ‖ [pass] *eligibility* **~feldzug** m *canvass,* ⟨Am⟩ *campaign* **~fonds** m *c.-fund,* ⟨Am⟩ *barrel* **≃frei** a *optional,* ⟨Am⟩ *elective* ‖ welche Fächer sind ~? *what options are allowed?* **~gang** m *ballot* (*at the third b.*) **~geometrie** treiben *to gerrymander* **~gesetz** n *election-law* **~handlung** f = –akt **~heimat** f *country of one's choice* od *of adoption* **~kampf** m *election contest* od *campaign* **~kommissar** m = –leiter **~könig(reich** n) m *elective king(dom)* **~körper** m *constituent* od *elective body* **~kreis** m = –bezirk **~kugel** f *ballot* **~leiter** m *returning officer* **~liste** f *electoral list; register of electors;* (Kandidaten ⟨Am⟩) *ticket, slate* ‖ auf der ~ stehen *to be up for election* **~lokal** n *election-room, polling station;* ⟨Am a.⟩ *ward-room* **≃los** a *indiscriminate, promiscuous* (*human* u *sexual relations*) ‖ [adv] *–ly; at random* **~mache** f *boom* **~macher** m *vote manipulator;* ⟨Am fam⟩ *ward heeler* **~mann** m *delegate, constituent;* ⟨Am⟩ *elector* | zwei(erlei) **~möglichkeiten** [f] h *to have two options* **~modus** m, **~ordnung** f *mode of election* **~periode** f *Parliament* (*the 22nd P*) **~programm** n *platform; election manifesto,* ⟨Am⟩ *ticket* **~propaganda** treiben *to electioneer* **~protest** m *petition* **~protokoll** n = –akten **~prüfer** m *scrutineer* **~prüfung** f *scrutiny* **~recht** n *right to vote, franchise* ‖ [pass] *eligibility* ‖ allgemeines ~ *universal suffrage* ‖ das ~ erhalten *to be enfranchised* **~rede** f *electioneering address* ‖ ~n halten *to electioneer;* ⟨Am fam⟩ *to stump* **~redner** m ⟨Am fam⟩ *stump-orator;* als ~ umherziehen *to stump the country* **~reform** f *electoral reform* **~reich** n *elective empire,* bzw *kingdom* **~schalter** m ⟨el⟩ *selector switch* **~schiebung** f *ballot-rigging* **~spruch** m *device, motto* **~stimme** f *vote, suffrage* **~tag** m *day of election, election-day* **~tasten** f pl ⟨comp⟩ *selection* **~umtriebe** m pl *electioneering practices* pl **≃unfähig** a *ineligible* **~urne** f *ballot-box, polls* pl (*at the p., to go to the p.*) **~ventilgerät** n *selection valve unit* **~versammlung** f *electoral assembly,* ⟨Am⟩ *caucus* **≃verwandt** a *congenial;* (Seelen) *kindred* (*spirits*) **~verwandtschaft** f ⟨chem⟩ *elective affinity* ‖ ⟨fig⟩ *congeniality* **~vorschlag** m *party-ticket* **≃weise** a ⟨comp⟩ *random* [attr]; ~r Weg *alternative route* **~werber** m *campaigner* **~zelle** f *polling-booth* **~zettel** m *ballot-, voting-paper* **~zimmer** n = –lokal; (Papstwahl) *conclave* **w·ählbar** a *eligible* **≃keit** f ~/ *eligibility* **w·ählen** vt/i [h] **A.** *to choose* (*one's residence*) ‖ ~ Sie! *take your choice* ‖ (auslesen) *to select;* sorgfältig *to hand-pick* ‖ *to pick* (*one's words carefully*) ‖ zw 2 Dingen ~ müssen ⟨mst⟩ *you can't have it both ways* ‖ ⟨telph⟩ *to dial* ‖ ⟨parl⟩ *to elect;* gewählt w *to get in* **B. gut ~** *to make a good choice* ‖ liberal ~ *to go Liberal* ‖ weise ~: *there was wisdom in his choice of her* ‖ e–e Liste ~ *to vote a ticket* ‖ s–n Verteidiger selbst ~ *to reserve one's defence* **C. ins** P. ~ *to return to parliament* ‖ sie ~ ihn **zum** Führer *they choose him for their leader;* so: *they chose for king someone who ..* ‖ zum König ~ *to elect .. (as) king* ‖ zum Professor ~ *to elect .. to a chair* ‖ zum Vorsitzenden ~ *to vote .. into the chair* **D. gewählt** a *refined* (*language*); *select* (*society*) **W·ähler(in** f) m ~s/~ *elector* (f *electress*), *voter; constituent* ‖ parteiloser ~ ⟨Am⟩ *floater* ‖ ⟨el⟩ *selector* ⟨a. comp⟩ | ~besuch [m] *canvassing;* ⟨telph⟩ ~scheibe [f] *selector dial; finger plate;* ~vermittlung [f] *dial service* **≃risch** a ⟨cul⟩ *fastidious, dainty; picky:* er ist im Essen sehr ~ *he's a picky eater* ‖ *nice, finical* ‖ *particular* (*in one's choice*) ‖ *exclusive* ‖ ⟨fam⟩ *choosey; finicky* **~schaft** f ~/ **1.** *body of voters; electorate;* ⟨parl⟩ *constituency* **2.** [abstr] *franchise*

W·ahn m ~(e)s/ *false* od *erroneous opinion* od *idea* ‖ *illusion, delusion* ‖ *madness, folly* ‖ in dem ~e stehen *to fancy; to labour under the delusion* **~begriff** m *false notion, erroneous conception* **~bild** n, **~gebilde** n *phantom, phantasm; chimera* **~glaube** m *erroneous belief;* (Aberglaube) *superstition* **~hoffnung** f *vain hope* **≃kantig** a ⟨for⟩ *waney* (*tree*); *dull-edged* (*wood*) **~sinn** m *madness; insanity* ‖ ⟨fig⟩ (*poetic*) *frenzy* ‖ das war reiner, völliger, heller ~ *it was sheer* od *staring, pure madness* (*to have done it*) ‖ dichterischer ~ *poetic* (→) *madness;* religiöser ~ *religious mania; theomania* ‖ stiller ~ *melancholy* ‖ tobender ~ *raving madness* ‖ jdn z ~ treiben ⟨sl⟩ *to drive a p to crackers* **≃sinnig** a *insane, mad* ‖ ⟨fig⟩ *frantic* ‖ ⟨fam⟩ (P) *cracked; splitting* (*headache*) ‖ (vor Furcht) *mad* od *wild* (*with fear*) ‖ ~ m *to drive mad* ‖ ~ w *to go mad* ‖ es ist rein z ~ w *it's enough to drive one mad* | adv *frantically* ‖ (wie) ~ lieben *to be madly in love* (*with a p*), *to love to distraction* ‖ ⟨fam⟩ *awfully* (*excited*) ‖ (wie) ~ (*he ran*) *like mad* **~sinnige(r** m) & f *insane p; madman, madwoman* **~witz** m *insanity, madness* **≃witzig** a *mad* **w·ähnen I.** vt [h] *to fancy, imagine; think, believe; presume, suppose* **II.** ≃ n *imagining, fancy(ing), delusion, illusion*

w·ahr a **A. 1.** *true* [adv *truly*] ‖ es ist ~, er hatte *true he had;* .. in bezug auf *it is true of ..* **2.** (P) *truthful, sincere* ‖ *accurate* (*report*) **3.** (echt) *real, genuine* **4.** (eigentlich) *proper* **5.** ⟨emph⟩ *right-down* (*shame*) ‖ nur zu ~ *right enough* **B. nicht** ~? *don't you think so?, isn't it?, eh?* ‖ *do(n't) you know?* ‖ (*take it down,*) *will you?* ‖ (*he is well,*) *isn't he?;* (*he is not well,*) *is he?* ‖ (*one can't suspect him,*) *can one?* **C.** [+ subst] *true* (*friend*) ‖ sein ~es **Gesicht** zeigen *to show the cloven hoof* ‖ es ist ein Glück *it is really most fortunate* ‖ *rational* (*horizon*) ‖ der ~e Jakob *the real Simon Pure,* ⟨sl⟩ *the real McCoy* ‖ *true* (*love*) ‖ ⟨a.⟩ *but* (*a fool*) ‖ ~e **Natur** (e–r S) *reality ..;* das ist nicht s–e wahre N. *that's not like him* ‖ (Null) *a mere cipher* ‖ *a good straight novelist* ‖ im ~en **Sinne** des Wortes *literally; a literal hail of questions, a true tumour* ‖ *downright nonsense* ‖ es ist kein ~es Wort daran *there's not a word of truth in it* **D.** was ~ ist, muß ~ **bleiben** *upon my word* ‖ (Behauptung) als ~ erweisen *to substantiate* (*a claim*); sich als ~ erweisen *to be verified* ‖ nicht **~haben** wollen *to disavow;* er will es nicht ~h *he will not admit it; he does not want to know it* ‖ f ~ halten *to believe in* (*a th*) ‖ ~ m *to fulfil; to live up to* (*one's threats*); *to make good* (*one's word*); *to prove the truth of* (*the saying* Sprichwort) ‖ als ~ nachweisen *to verify* ‖ ~ **reden** *to speak true* od *the truth* ‖ ~ w *to come true, to be realized* **E.** ~ u ~haftig! *really and truly* ‖ **so** ~ mir Gott helfe! *by Heaven!,* od *so help me God!* ‖ so ~ ich lebe! .. ich hier sitze/stehe! *as sure as I live* (*by bread*); so ~ Gott lebt *as true as there is God above!* °schon bald nicht mehr ~! (*it's*) *frozen!* **F. Das ≃e** *truth;* .. daran *the fact of the matter;* .. daran ist *the truth of it is* ‖ es war **etw ≃es** an .. *there was sth* (od *some truth*) *in* (*what he said*) ‖ es muß schon etw ≃es daran s! *no smoke without fire!*

w·ahren vt [h] (schützen) *to guard; to watch over* ‖ den Anstand ~ *to preserve decency* ‖ *to unhold* (*one's interests*) ‖ *to safeguard* (*rights*) ‖ sein/das Prestige ~ *to save one's face* ‖ den Schein ~ *to keep up* od *save appearances* pl ‖ *to maintain* (*one's dignity*) ‖ ~ Sie Ihre Zunge! *take care what you say!* | **sich** ~ *to take care* (*of*), *to be on one's guard* (*against*) ‖ → bewahren

w·ähren vi [h] *to last, to continue* ‖ ewig ~ *never to die* ‖ ewig ~d *eternal, everlasting* ‖ es währte nicht lange, so .. *it was not long before* (*he came*) ‖ es mag noch lange ~ bis *or* ehe .. *it may be a long while before* (*he comes*) ‖ ⟨prov⟩

was lange währt, wird endlich gut *good work takes time*

w·ährend I. prep [gen] *during* od *in* (*the night, the reign of* ..) || *for* (*a year*) || *pending* (*the inquiry*) || *I have not seen him this holiday* **II.** conj *while, whilst* || .. *as* (*he passed*) || *while* (*I was*) *in camp I* .. || [⟨engl⟩ *with* + *part* etc] .. *with the army reeling* ..; (*sitting in silence*) *with the house quiet around her* || ~ ich dies gerade schreibe *at the moment of my writing this* | [bei Ggs] (*I* ..) *whereas* (*he* ..) | **~d·essen** (*in the*) *meanwhile*; *by that time*

W·ahrer m ~s/~ *guardian* (*of peace*)

w·ahrhaft a *true* || (aufrichtig) *veracious, truthful* || (beim) wahrh·aften Gott! *by God that is above*! | adv *fairly* (*terrible*) || *really* (*grand*) **-h·aftig** a *genuine, real* | adv *truly, really, in truth, in all conscience* | *I declare* (*I don't know*) || (*upon*) *my word*! || *by Jove*! || *yes indeed*! || da hat er ~ .. *if he hasn't* .. || ⟨iron⟩ (*he would give you relief*) *all right*! || Ja ~! *Isn't it*? || Nein, ~ nicht! *Oh, dear me, no*! | ~? *do you mean it*? *you don't say so*!; ~! *you bet*! | ≗keit [f] *veracity, truthfulness* **W·ahrheit** f ~/~en *truth*; *the th which is* || ~en [pl] *verities* pl; ungeschminkte, unverblümte ~en *home truths* | in ~ *in t.* || der ~ gemäß *truly* | das ist die volle ~ *that's the whole t.*; *it is God's t.* || ⟨jur⟩ die reine ~ *the whole t. and nothing but the t.*; *I want the straight of it from you* || die ~ **beugen** *to bend the t.* || es mit der ~ nicht allzu genau nehmen *to stretch the t.* || v der ~ durchdrungen *utterly convinced of the t.* || die ~ finden *to find the t.*; .. zu spät .. *to get wise to a th after the event* || die ~ gestehen ⟨fam⟩ *to come across* || die ~ sagen (sprechen) *to tell* (*speak*) *the t.* || er sagt die ~ *there is t. in what he says* || man hat ihm die volle ~ gesagt *he has been told the plain t.* || um die ~ z sagen *to tell the t.* || jdm (gehörig) die ~ sagen *to tell a p* (*some home-t.s* od) *what's what, to give a p a piece of one's mind* || er will die ganze ~ wissen *he wants to get to the bottom of it all* | **~(s)- ~beweis** m; den ~ antreten *to prove the truth of one's statement* ≗**gemäß,** ≗**getreu** a *true, truthful*; *faithful* (*rendering*) | adv *truly, with perfect truth, in accordance with truth* **~liebe** f *love of truth, veracity* ≗**liebend** a *truth-loving*; *truthful, veracious* **~sucher** m *inquirer after truth*; *t.-seaker* **~treue** f ⟨arts⟩ *truth to nature* **w·ahrlich** adv *truly, in truth* || *to be sure*!, *indeed*! || (*most*) *certainly*! || (*you can't*) *very well* (*pretend* ..); ⟨so:⟩ *now*!

w·ahr- (→ wahren) **~nehmbar** a; (nicht ~ *im*)*perceptible*, (*not*) *noticeable*; *apprehensible* || (*in*)*visible* || kaum ~ *inconspicuous* || f. d. Geruch nicht ~ *indistinguishable to smell* | ≗keit [f] ~/ *perceptibility* **~|nehmen** vt irr [h] *to perceive, observe* || ⟨physiol⟩ *to discern, descry*; mit den Sinnen -genommen *sensed* (*evidence*) || (sorgen f) *to look after, to take care of, to attend to* || die Gelegenheit ~ *to take* od *seize* (od *make use of*) *the opportunity* || ⟨univ⟩ e–e Professur ~ *to occupy a chair* | ⟨philos⟩ das Wahrgenommene *the percept* | äußere Reize ~d *extroceptive* ≗**-nehmung** f ~/~en *perception, observation*; genaue ~ *appreciation* || (Sorge f) *looking* (*after*), *care* (*of*) || mit der ~ der Geschäfte beauftragt *acting*; → stellvertretend | ~svermögen [n] *perceptive faculty, power of observation*; ~szeit [f] *perception* od *recognition time*

W·ahrsage- ~kunst f *fortune-telling, divination* | ≗**n** vi [h] *to tell fortunes*; *to foretell, prophesy* || sich [dat] ~ l *to have one's fortune told* **~r(in** f) m ~s/~ *fortune-teller, soothsayer*; *prophet* (*-ess* f) || ⟨ant⟩ *augur*; *haruspex* **~r·ei** f ~/~en *fortune-telling* ≗**risch** a *divinatory, prophetic* [adv *prophetically*] **W.sagung** f ~/~en *fortune-telling* **w·ahrsch·einlich** a *likely, probable* [adv *-bly*]; *estimate* (*time of arrival*); sehr ~ *quite likely* || *the most probable solution* || die Geschichte ist nicht sehr ~ *it is not a very likely story* || es ist sehr (nicht) ~, daß er kommt *he is most* (*not*) *likely to come, there is every* (*no*) *chance of his coming* || es ist mehr als ~ *it's a better than even chance* | [adv] es wird ~ bald regnen *it's likely to rain soon* || *it is odds* (*that*); *the odds* od *chances are* (*that*) || sehr ~ *as likely as not* (→ höchst~) ≗**keit** f ~/~en *verisimilitude*; *likelihood*; *probability* (⟨a. stat, demog⟩ empirische ~); (*logical*) *p.y*; (*inductive*) *p.y* || e–e 4mal größere ~ f sich h *to stand a 4 times greater chance* (*of* ..) || er hat die ~ auf s–r Seite *the chances are on his side* || aller ~ nach *in all probability, very probably* | **-keits-** *experience* [attr] ~rechnung [f] ⟨math⟩ *calculation of probabilities, probability calculus*; ~theorie [f] ⟨a.⟩ *probabilities* **W·ahr- ~spruch** m ⟨jur⟩ *verdict, finding* **~traum** m *prophetic dream* **~zeichen** n ~s/~ (*land*)*mark* || ⟨fig⟩ *token, sign, emblem*; *omen symptom*

W·ahrung f ~/ *maintenance* || (Schutz) *protection*; *maintaining* (*justice*); *safeguarding* (*of military information* Geheimnisse); unter ~ der Grundsätze *provided that nobody infringes the principles*

W·ährung f ~/~en *standard*; *currency* (*in German c.*) || von echter ~ *of sterling quality* || ~en [pl] ⟨bank⟩ *moneys*, ⟨Am⟩ *monies* | **~s-** ~ausschuß [m] *Monetary Committee*; ~beschränkungen [f pl] *monetary restraints*; ~einheit [f] *m.y unit*; Internat. ~fonds [m] *International M.y Fund*; ~gebiet [n] ⟨com⟩ *currency area*; ~gewinn [m] *profit on exchange*; ~reform [f] *c. reform*; ~risiko [n] *exchange risk*

Waid m ~(e)s/ ⟨bot⟩ *woad* || mit ~ färben *to woad* **~asche** f *woad-ashes* pl ≗**blau** a *woaded blue* **~färber** m *woad-dyer* (**~mann** m etc = Weid- etc)

W·aise f ~/~n *orphan* || ~ w *to be orphaned*; e–e ~ durch .. *orphaned* (*of one's mother*) *at birth* **W·aisen-** *orphan* **~geld** n *money belonging to o.s* **~haus** n *o.-asylum, o.age* **~kind** n *o.-child* **~knabe** m *o. boy* || ⟨fig⟩ *novice, tiro*; ein ~ gegen ihn *not a patch on him* **~mutter** f (Oberin) *matron of an o.-asylum* **~rente** f ⟨ins⟩ *orphan's annuity* **~stand** m *o.age* **~vater** m (Direktor) *director of an o.-asylum*

Wal etc ⟨zoo⟩ = [fälschlich] Walfisch ⟨zoo⟩ *whale* || Barten≗ *wh.bone wh.*; Finn≗ *rorqual*; Pott≗ *sperm wh.*; Zahn≗ *toothed wh.*; →-fisch- | **~rat** m & n *spermaceti* **~roß** n *walrus*

Walach·ei f (in Rumänien) *Walachia*

W·ald [valt] m ~(e)s/≗er *wood*(*land*); (gr) *forest*; (kl) *grove* || in ≗ern lebend *sylvan* || er sieht den ~ vor lauter Bäumen nicht *he misses the wood for trees* | ⟨prov⟩ wie man in den ~ ruft, so schallt's heraus *as the question, so the answer* | ⟨fig⟩ *forest* (*of chimneys, masts*) || ~ v Haaren *thick head of hair* | ⟨fam⟩ nicht für'n ~ voller Affen *not for nuts* **~abhang** m *hanger* **~ameise** f *red ant* **~arbeiter** m *lumberman*, ⟨Am⟩ *logger* ≗**arm** a *destitute of f.s*; *sparsely w.ed* **~artig** a *sylvan* **~aufnahme** f ⟨phot a.⟩ *sylvan shot* **~aufseher** m *ranger* ≗**·aus** adv *out of the f.* **~bach** m *f.-brook* **~bahn** f (Holzweg) *log-line* **~bau** m *f.-culture* **~baum** m *f.-tree* **~bauschule** f *school of f.ry* ≗**bedeckt** a *wellw.ed* **~beere** f = Heidelbeere ≗**bekränzt** a *adorned with f.s* **~bewohner** m *inhabitant of a f.* **~biene** f ⟨ent⟩ *wild bee* **~birne** f *wild pear* **~blume** f *w. flower* **~boden** m *floor of the f.* **~brand** m *f. fire* **~dickicht** n *bush* ≗**·ein** adv *into the f.* **~einsamkeit** f *sylvan solitude*; (Ort) *w.land retreat* **~erdbeere** f *wild* od *Alpine strawberry* **~esel** m *wild ass* **~eule** f ⟨orn⟩ *wood-owl* **~farn** m *wood-fern* **~flachs** m ⟨bot⟩ *flax-weed* **~frevel** m *mischief done in a f.* **~gebiet** n *wooded area*; *woodland* **~gebirge** n *w.y mountains* pl **~geflügel** n *w.-birds* pl **~gegend** f *w.land* **~gehege** n *park, preserve* **~geist** m *w.-goblin, sylvan spirit*; *faun, satyr* **~gelände** n = -gebiet **~genossenschaft**

f *f.ry association* **~gerechtigkeit** f *rights* pl *over a f.* **~glöcklein** n ⟨bot⟩ *blue-bell* **~gott** m *sylvan god* **~göttin** f *w.-nymph* **~gründe** m pl *depths of the f.* **~hang** m *hanger* **~honig** m *wild honey* **~horn** n *French horn*, ⟨poet⟩ *bugle* **~hornist** m *bugler* **~huhn** n *grouse* **~hüter** m *(f.-)keeper, ranger* **~kampf** m; in ~en *in f.fighting* **~kantig** a = wahn– **~kapelle** f *chapel in a f.* ‖ °(mit Anspielung auf *W. C.*) *chapel of ease* **~kauz** m *screech--owl* **~kirsche** f *wild cherry* **~landschaft** f *w.land scenery* **~lauf** m *cross-country race* **~läufer** m *ranger* **~lerche** f *w.-lark* **~leute** [pl] *w.men, f.-folk* pl **~lilie** f ⟨bot⟩ *w.-lily* **~mann** m *f.er*; *inhabitant of a f.* ‖ *dog's name* **~maus** f *longtailed field-mouse* **~meister** m ⟨bot⟩ *w.ruff* **~mensch** m *wild man, satyr* **~nymphe** f *w.-nymph, dryad* **~ordnung** f *f.-laws* **~parzelle** f *strip of f. land*; ⟨bes Am⟩ *wood-lot* **~pflege** f *f.ry* **~planierraupe** f ⟨tech⟩ *tree-dozer* **~plateau** n *w.ed plateau* **~rand** m *edge (of a w.)* **~rebe** f ⟨bot⟩ *clematis*; aufrechte ~ *erect traveller's joy* **~recht** n *f. laws* pl ‖ *privileges* pl *of the owner of a f.* **~reich** a *abundant in f.s, w.y* **~reiter** m *mounted ranger* **~reichtum** m *abundance of f.s* **~revier** n *preserve* **~säge** f *cross--cut saw* **~sänger** m *f.-songster* **~schaden** m *damage done in a f.* **~schnepfe** f *w.cock* **~schrat** m *w.-goblin* **~schule** f *open-air school* **~schwamm** m ⟨bot⟩ *(tree-)fungus* **~streu** f *f. litter* **~strom** m *w.-torrent* **~stück** n *grove*, ⟨Am⟩ *w.lot* **~taube** f ⟨orn⟩ *w.-pigeon* **~teufel** m *satyr* ‖ ⟨zoo⟩ *mandrill* **~- u Wiesen-Spielart** f *garden* od *common variety* **~versicherung** f *insurance on growing timber* **~verwüstung** f *f. devastation* **~vogel** m *w.-bird* **~weg** m *w.-path* **~wiese** f *(f.-)glade* **~wirtschaft** f *management of w.s, w.culture, f.ry* **~wolle** f *pine--needle wool* **~ziest** m ⟨bot⟩ *hedge-nettle* **W·äldchen** n ~s/~ *grove, shrubbery*; ⟨Am⟩ *w.lot* **W·aldes- ~dunkel** n *f.-gloom* **~grün** n *verdure of the w.s* **~kühle** f *coolness of the f.* **~saum** m *fringe of a f.*; am ~ entlang gehen *to skirt the f.* **~stille** f *stillness of the f.* **w·aldig** a *wooded, woody* **W·aldung** f ~/~en *woods, forests* pl; *woodland*

Wald·aigebirge n, **Wald·aihöhen** f pl **Wald·aiplateau** n ⟨Russ⟩ *Valdai Hills* pl

Wald·enser m *Waldensian*

W·äldersee n *Lake of the Woods*

Wales [weilz] n ⟨Engl⟩ *Wales*

W·alfisch m ⟨zoo⟩ [fälschlich f Wal] *whale* ‖ pl ⟨scient allg⟩ *cetacea*; ⟨eig⟩ *balaenidae* **~bai** f (W.-Küste-Hafen S. Afrikas) *Walvis Bay* **~barte** f *wh.-bone* **~fang** m *wh.-fishery, wh.-fishing, wh.--catching* ‖ auf ~ gehen *to go whaling* **~fänger** m (P & S) *wh.r* **~fleisch** n ⟨fam⟩ *sea-pork* **~flotte** f *whaling fleet* **~fett** n, **~speck** m *blubber* **~tran** m *train-oil*, ⟨Am⟩ *speck*

w·älgern vt [h] ⟨bak⟩ *to roll down* **W·älgholz** n *rolling-pin*

Walh·alla f ~/ *Valhalla*; → –küre, –statt ‖ *Valhalla-memorial near Regensburg upon the Danube*

W·alk- ~faß n *fulling-tub* **~mühle** f *f.g-mill* **~müller** m *fuller* **~trog** m *f.g-trough* **~werk** n = ~mühle **~wolle** f *felted wool* **W·alke** f ~/~n *fulling* ‖ *fullery* ‖ (Maschine) *f.g-machine* **w·alken** vt [h] ⟨tech⟩ *to full* ‖ ⟨fig fam⟩ *to thrash* **W·alker** m ~s/~ *fuller* **~erde** f *fuller's earth* **~ton** m *f.g-clay* **Walker·ei** f ~/~en (Fabrik) *f.g-mill* ‖ [abstr ohne pl] *f.g*

Walk·üre (⟨a.⟩ ′–..) f ~/~n *valkyr(ie), valkkyria*; → –halla

Wall m ~(e)s/~e ⟨fort⟩ *rampart* | (Erd~) *mound (of earth), dam, bank, dike* | ⟨mar⟩ *coast, shore* **~absatz** m ⟨fort⟩ *berme* **~anker** m *shore--anchor* **~gang** m *terrepleine* Fr **~graben** m *moat* **~meister-** ⟨mil⟩ ~gruppe [f] *demolition engineer group*; ~trupp [m] *d. e. team* **~moräne** f *morainic ridge* **~riff** n *barrier reef* **~schild** m ⟨fort⟩ *ravelin* **~wurz** f ⟨bot⟩ → *comfrey*

Wall- [→ wallen²] **~fahrer** m *pilgrim* **~fahrt** f *p.age* | **~s-** ~kirche [f] *P. church*; ~ort [m] *place of p.age*

W·allach m ~s/~e *gelding* ‖ °⟨fig sex⟩ *mule*

w·allen¹ vi [h] *to boil up, to bubble* ‖ (gelinde) *to simmer* ‖ (Meer) *to roll* | ⟨fig⟩ *to be in motion*; (Blut) *to boil*; (Haar) *to wave, float*; (Fahne) *to float, flutter*; (Gewand) *to flow*; (Rauch) *to curl* **w·ällen** vt [h] *to (let) boil* od *simmer*

w·allen² vi [s] *to wander, to go on a pilgrimage*

W·aller m ~s/~ *wanderer, pilgrim* ‖ → Wels

w·allfahr(t)en vi [s] *to go on a pilgrimage*

W·allis n **1.** ⟨Sw⟩ (Kanton) *Valais* **2.** ⟨Engl⟩ *Wales* **Wal(l)·ieser(in f)** m **1.** *Valaisan*; *inhabitant of Valais* **2.** *Welsh(wo)man*; *inhabitant of Wales*; ⟨hist⟩ *Cymbrian, Cambro-Briton*

Wall·one m ~n/~n, **wall·onisch** a *Walloon*

W·allung f ~/~en *ebullition*; *surge (of the sea)* | ⟨fig⟩ *effervescence, agitation, excitement, flutter* | in ~ bringen *to excite*; *to make (a p's blood) boil*; (Land) *to convulse* ‖ sein Blut (Puls) ist in ~ .. *is up (is high)* ‖ in ~ geraten *to fly into a passion*

W·alm m ~(e)s/~e ⟨arch⟩ *hip* **~dach** n *hip--roof* | **~en** vt [h] *to slope (a roof)*

W·alnuß f *walnut* ‖ ~baum [m] *walnut-tree*

Walp·urgisnacht f *W.-night, witches' sabbath*

W·alstatt f ~/~en *battlefield*, → Walhalla, –küre

W·alten n ~s/ *rule, government* ‖ das ~ der Vorsehung *the hand of Providence* **w·alten** vi [h] **A.** *to rule, govern, sway* ‖ seines Amtes ~ *to do one's duty* ‖ das walte Gott! *God grant it!, amen!* **B. im** Hause ~ *to manage* bzw *rule the house* ‖ ~ **über** *to attend to*; *to manage* **C.** ~ **lassen** *to dispense (justice), to show (mercy)* ‖ e–n ~ l *to let a p do as he pleases* ‖ Gott ~ l *to leave everything to God*; laßt Gott nur f euch ~ *make God your agent* ‖ ⟨rel⟩ s–e Gnade ~ l über: *God bestows his mercy on ..* ‖ Milde ~ l gegenüber .. *to extend clemency to ..* **W·alter** m ~s/~ = Verwalter

W·altiere n/pl *cetacea* pl → Walfisch, Wal

W·alz- ~blech n *rolled plate* **~blei** n *sheet-lead* **~bruder** m *tramp* **~draht** m *wire rod* **~eisen** n *rolled (sheet) iron* **~splitter** m pl *slivers* pl **~werk** n *rolling-mill* **W·alze** f ~/~n *cylinder* ⟨a. math⟩ ‖ ⟨agr, hort, typ, etc⟩ *roller* ‖ ⟨typewr⟩ *platen* (dazu: *p. detent* –nlöser, *p. knob*) ‖ ⟨tech⟩ *drum, barrel* (a. f Orchestrion etc) | Bürsten~ *brush roll* ‖ Dampf~ *steam-roller*; wie e–e ~ rollen über *to steam-roll over* ‖ Glas~ *gl. cyl.* ‖ Gummi~ *rubber roller* ‖ Kalander~ *calender bowl* ‖ Messer~ *cyl. cutter* ‖ Straßen~ *planing roller* | ⟨fig, fam⟩ (Wanderschaft) auf der ~ *on the tramp* **w·alzen 1.** vt [h] *to roll* ‖ (Teig) *to roll out* ‖ (Blei) *to mill* ‖ (Eisen) *to roll* ‖ ⟨agr, hort⟩ *to roll* **2.** vi [h] *to (dance a) waltz* | [s] ⟨fam⟩ *to tramp* **W·alzen** n ⟨tech⟩ *extrusion* **~brecher** m (Gr– *giant*) *roll crusher* **~bürste** f *revolving-brush* **~druck** m *cylinder printing* **~förmig** a *cylindrical* **~formpresse** f *roller press*; *type pelletizer* **~gestell** n ⟨typ⟩ *roller frame* **~kessel** m *cylindrical boiler* **~lager** n ⟨tech⟩ *roller bearing* **~mange** f ⟨weav⟩ *calender* **~presse** f *rolling-press* **~trockner** m *rotary drier* **W·alzer** m ~s/~ *waltz* ‖ ~ tanzen *to w.* (mit jdm *a p*)

W·älz- ~lager [n] ⟨mill⟩ *roller bearing*; ⟨aero-mot⟩ *anti-friction bearing* **W·älzer** m ~s/~ ⟨fam⟩ (Buch) *tome* **w·älzen** vt [h] *to roll* od *turn about* ‖ ⟨fam⟩ (Bücher) *to thumb* ‖ ⟨fig⟩ dauernd denselben G. (in sich) ~ *to keep chewing the same thought* ‖ die Schuld auf jdn ~ *to lay the blame on a p*; .. v sich ~ *to exculpate o.s. (from)* | **sich** ~ *to wallow, welter*; sich auf dem Boden ~ *to roll on the ground* ‖ (Menschenmenge) *to pour along* ‖ (Wale) *they hunched themselves (out)* ‖ (Wellen) *to wash (over)* ‖ (Wasser) *to dash*; (vor Lachen) *to be convulsed with laughter* ‖ sich in s–m Blute ~ *to be bathed in b.* ‖ sich im Gelde ~

to be rolling (*in m.*) || sich schlaflos im Bett ~ *to toss from side to side* || es war z ≃ (Lachen) *it was* (*a scream* od) *screaming*

W·amme f ~/~n (*of cattle*) *dewlap* || *belly* (*of skins*) | ⟨fig fam⟩ (Bauch) *paunch* || (Backen≃) *gills* pl; er hat die ~ voll *he's fishy about the gills* **Wams** n –es/≃er *jacket* || ⟨hist⟩ *doublet, jerkin* **w·amsen** vt [h] ⟨fam⟩ *to thrash*

Wand f ~/≃e *wall* || (Berg–, Fels≃) *side* .., *wall*, "*Wand*" || ⟨theat⟩ *flat* (schmal *narrow*), ⟨Am⟩ *jog*; zurückspringende ~ (*scenic*) *return* || ⟨film⟩ *screen* (a. weiße ~) || (Gefäß≃) *side* .. || Graben≃ *escarp* ⟨a. mil⟩ || (Magen≃) *coat, lining* || Scheide≃ *partition* || Seelen≃ *bore surface* || Seiten≃ (des Hufes) *side-wall* || spanische ~ *folding screen* || ⟨tech⟩ (Wange) *cheek* || (Wagen≃) *panel* | ≃e h → Ohren || leeren ≃en predigen *to talk to empty chairs* | **an** dieser ~ *on this w.* || ⟨fig⟩ an die ~ drängen, drücken *to send, push to the w.* ⟨a. fig⟩; .. gedrückt w *to go to the w.* || alle anderen an die W. spielen *to steal the show* || an die ~ stellen *to have a p against the w.* = *to shoot* || in s–n 4 ≃en ⟨fig⟩ *under one's roof--tree* || °z An-den-≃en-Hochgehen! *that's the limit*! **~arm** m *bracket* ⟨a. theat⟩ **~bank** f *bench placed against the w.* **~bekleidung** f *wainscot*(*ing*); untere ~ *dado* **~bespannung** f *w. covering* **~bewurf** m *plaster* **~brett** n *shelf, bracket* **~dose** f ⟨el⟩ *w.-box* **≃fest** a *fixed to the w.* **~fliese, ~kachel** f *w.-tile* **~gemälde** n *mural* (*painting*); *fresco* **~kalender** m *sheet-almanac* **~karte** f *w.--map* **~leuchter** m *bracket, sconce* **~malerei** f *mural painting* **~pfeiler** m ⟨arch⟩ *w.-pier, pilaster* **~putz** m *plaster*(*ing*) **~schirm** m *folding-, draught--screen* **~schrank** m *w.-chest* **~spiegel** m *pier-glass* **~stärke** f *thickness* (*of a pipe*, etc) **~stecker** m *w. plug* **~tafel** f *blackboard* **~täfelung** f *wainscot*(*ing*) **~teller** m *decorative plate* **~teppich** m *hangings* pl, *tapestry* **~uhr** f (*hanging*) *hall-clock* **~verkleidung** f *wainscot*(*ing*) **~vertiefung** f *niche*

W·andel m ~s/ **1.** *mutation, change* || ~ schaffen in *to bring about a ch. in* || es ist ein ~ mit ihm vorgegangen *a* (*great*) *change has come over him* || im ~ der Zeiten *during time's changes* **2.** (Lebenswandel) *behaviour, conduct, course of life* **3.** Handel u ~ *trade and traffic* **~altar** m *polyptych* **~anleihe** f *conversion loan* **~bahn** f (*covered*) *walk* **~bild** n *phantom* **~dekoration** f ⟨theat⟩ *shifting scenery* **~gang** m, **~halle** f ⟨parl⟩ *lobby* (dazu: *to l.* = in der ~ besprechen); ⟨theat⟩ *foyer* **~gänger** m ⟨pol⟩ *lobbyist* **≃los** a *unalterable, immutable, changeless* **~stern** m ⟨astr⟩ *planet* **w·andelbar** a *changeable, mutable, variable, inconstant, fickle* || *fragile* | ≃keit [f] ~/ *changeableness, inconstancy, impermanence, fickleness* **w·andeln 1.** vi [s] *to walk, travel, wander* || ⟨bib⟩ den Weg der Gerechtigkeit ~ *to walk in the ways of righteousness* **2.** vt [h] (sich) ~ *to change* || sich ~ in [acc] *to turn into*

W·ander- ⟨oft⟩ *itinerant, travel*(*l*)*ing* **~ameise** f *visiting-ant* **~arbeiter** m pl ⟨bes Am⟩ *transient labor* **~ausstellung** f *touring exhibition* (dazu: *to tour*) **~block** m ⟨geol⟩ *erratic block* **~buch** n *road-book for t.g journeymen* **~bühne** f *t.g theatre*; *road company* od *show* **~bursche, ~gesell(e)** m *t.g journeyman* **~drossel** f ⟨Am⟩ *robin* **~düne** f *shifting dune* **~falk(e)** m *peregrine* (*falcon*) **~geschütz** n ⟨artill⟩ *roving gun* **~gewerbe** n *hawking*; *i.t trade* | ~treibender [m] *i.t merchant*, ⟨Am⟩ *i.t vendor* **~händler** m = Hausierer **~heuschrecke** f *migratory locust* **~jahr** n *year of t.g* || ~e [pl] ⟨fig⟩ *years* pl *of travel* **~laden** m *mobile shop* **~leben** n *vagrant life* **~lehrer** m *i.t lecturer* **~lied** n *wanderlied* **~lust** f *passion for t.g, desire to see the world*; *wanderlust* **≃lustig** a *fond of t.g*; ~ s *to have an itching foot* **~niere** f *floating* od *movable kidney* **~pokal** m ⟨sport⟩ *challenge cup* **~prediger** m *i.t preacher*; *evangelist* **~preis** m *challenge cup*; *t.g trophy* **~ratte** f *sewer rat*; *brown* od *Norway rat* **~rost** m ⟨tech⟩ *moving* od *t.g grate* **~stab** m *t.g-staff* || den ~ ergreifen *to set out* (*on one's travels*) **~taube** f *passenger--pigeon* **~trieb** m *wandering impulse* **~truppe** f ⟨theat⟩ *strolling* od *touring company* **~versammlung** f *i.t congregation* **~vogel** m *bird of passage* || ⟨fig⟩ *hiker, wandervogel*; ⟨engl⟩ *boy-scout* | ~bewegung [f] ⟨Ger⟩ *youth movement* **~volk** n *nomadic tribe* **~wege** m [pl] *hiking trails* **~zeit** f = –jahre **~zirkus** m *t.g circus* ⟨a. fig mil⟩ (fliegende Division etc) **W·and(e)rer** m ~s/~ *wanderer, traveller*; *tourist*; *hiker*; *pilgrim* **w·andern** vi [s] *to wander, stroll, travel* (*on foot*), *hike, tramp* || *to go* (*one's way*; .. *to prison*); dahin ~ *to walk along*; weit ~ *to range* | ⟨übtr⟩ (Hitzewelle) *to travel* || (S) *to go* (*to the pawnshop*) | [abs] (Vögel) *to migrate*; (Dünen) *to move, to be shifting* | ~ **durch** *to range* (*the woods, over rough country*); durch die Straßen ~ *to w. about the streets* | den Blick ~ l über .. *to run one's eyes over* .. | **sich** müde ~ *to tire o.s. with walking* | **~d** *strolling* (*players*); *nomadic* (*tribe*); *itinerant* (*singer*); ⟨phys⟩ *moving* (Feld) **W·anderschaft** f ~/ *travels, wanderings* pl, *travelling* || auf der ~ *on a tour*, ⟨fam⟩ *on the tramp* || auf die ~ gehen *to go abroad, to go on one's travels, to take to the road* **W·andersmann** m *traveller* (*on foot*); ⟨geh Spr⟩ *wayfarer* **W·and(e)rung** f ~/~en *wandering*(*s* pl); *migration*, Erfassen des ~ssaldos *measurement of m.* | *excursion*, (*walking-*) *tour*; *trip, outing, ramble, rambling, tramp, jaunt* (*to take a j.* = *to make a trip, tour, an excursion*)

· **W·andlung** f ~/~en *change* (innere *of heart*); *transformation* || e–e gewaltige ~ *a sea-change* ⟨fig⟩ || ⟨theol⟩ *transubstantiation*; (Teil der Messe) *consecration* | e–e ~ vollzieht sich *a ch. takes place* | ~en [pl] ⟨a.⟩ *vicissitudes* **≃sfähig** a *versatile* (*mind*) || (dazu: *versatility*) **w·andte** 1. & 3. sg pret v wenden **W·andung** f ~/~en ⟨arch⟩ *body*; → Laibung

W·ange f ~/~n **1.** ⟨mst poet⟩ *cheek* || Scham rötete ihre ~n *she blushed for shame* **2.** ⟨tech⟩ *cheek* (*of a vice, press*, etc) **3.** ⟨arch⟩ (Treppen≃) *string-board*; Abschluß–, End–, Gestühl–, Stirn-≃ *bench end* | **~n-** **~bein** n ⟨anat⟩ *cheek-bone* **~grübchen** n *dimple in the cheek* **~rot** n ⟨cosm⟩ *cream rouge* **~tisch** m *trestle table* **..wangig** a: rot~ *rosy-cheeked*

Wank: nur in: ohne ~ *without hesitation* od *wavering* **W·ankel-** **~mut** m *fickleness, inconstancy, instability*; *tergiversation* **≃mütig** a *fickle, inconstant, mutable, variable, wavering*; *mutable*; *unsettled* (*mind*); ~ s ⟨a.⟩ *to be capricious, flighty*; *to blow hot and cold*, ⟨Am fam⟩ *to straddle* **~mütigkeit** f = –mut **w·anken** vi [h & s] *to shake, totter, stagger* || (*his knees began*) *to sag* | ⟨fig⟩ *to be irresolute, to waver, flinch* || nicht ~d *unswerving* || nicht ~ u nicht weichen *to be as firm as a rock* || ins ≃ bringen *to unsettle, shake*; die S in ≃ br. *to rock the boat* ⟨fig⟩ || ins ≃ geraten *to reel* || ~d w *to falter* (*in one's decision*)

wann I. [adv] *when* || dann u ~ *now and then*; *now and again* || *sometimes* || immer ~ *when ever* || seit ~ ist das so? *how long* od *since what time has it been so*? || bis wann? *till when*?, *by what time*? *how soon*? || ich weiß nicht ~ ⟨a.⟩ *any time* **II.** [conj] ich weiß, ~ er kommt .. *at what time he will come* || es sei, ~ es wolle *whatever time it may be* || ~ immer .. *any time* (*an issue arises*) **III. (von) ~en** (*from*) *whence*

W·anne f ~/~n **1.** *tub* || (Bade≃) *bathtub, bath* **2.** ⟨aero⟩ *cockpit* **3.** (Schwinge) (*winnow*[*ing*]-) *fan* **4.** ⟨geog⟩ *basin* **5.** Panzer≃ *hull* | **≃n** vt [h] *to winnow* | **~n-** ~bad [n] *tub-bath*, ⟨fam⟩ *tubbing*

W·annsee m (gr Badesee bei Berlin)

W·ansee m (in Kleinasien) *Lake* (*of*) *Van*

Wanst m ~es/≃e ⟨fam⟩ *belly, paunch*

Want f ~/~en [⟨mar⟩ mst pl] *shrould* (anziehen *to tauten*) || gr ~en *main shrouds* || jdn an die ~en binden *to seize a p up* **~klampe** f *shroud-cleat* **~tau** n *shroud*

W·anze f ~/~n (⟨Am⟩ *bed-*) *bug*, ⟨Am a.⟩ *chinch* || °⟨fig a–n⟩ (Mondfähre, –landegerät) *bug*, → Spinne | **~n- ~kraut** n ⟨bot⟩ *bugwort* **~nest** n ⟨fig⟩ *nasty place infested by vermin* **~same** m ⟨bot⟩ *tickseed* **~stich** m *bug-bite* **~tod** m = –kraut **w·anzig** a *buggy*

Wap·iti(hirsch) m *wapiti* (*American elk*)

W·appen n ~s/~ (*coat of*) *arms* (führen *to bear*) || (⟨typ⟩ & Siegel) *crest* || mit ~ schmücken *to emblazon* || in sein ~ aufnehmen *to quater in one's shield* || ein ~ deuten *to blazon* | ~ oder Schrift? *heads or tails*? **~amt** n *Herald's office* **~ausleger** m *herald* **~auslegung** f *h.ry, blazonry* **~bild** n *h.ic figure*; *charge* **~buch** n *armorial* **~decke** f *pavilion* **~erklärung** = –auslegung **~feld** n *field*, (Viertel) *quarter* **~figur** f = –bild **~halter** m *supporter* **~herold** m *h.-* od *king-at-arms* **~könig** m *King of Arms* **~kunde, ~kunst** f *h.ry, blazonry* **~kundige(r)** m *person skilled in h.ry* **~maler** m *blazoner* **~mantel** m *mantling* **~scheibe** f *h.ic glass* **~schild** n (*e*)*scutcheon* **~schmuck** m *emblazonry* **~spruch** m *motto, device* **~tier** n *h.ic animal*, ⟨Ind⟩ *totem* **w·appnen** vt [h] *to arm* | sich ~ f *to gird o.s. for* .. | ⟨poet⟩ der Gewappnete *the man-at-arms* [pl *men-at-arms*]

war 1. & 3. sg pret v sein

†**War·äger** m pl *Varangians* pl

War·an m ~s/~e ⟨zoo⟩ *monitor*

warb 1. & 3. sg pret v werben

ward 1. & 3. sg pret v werden ⟨mst poet⟩

Ward·ein m ~(e)s/~e *warden* (*of the mint*)

W·are f ~/~n *article, commodity* || ~n [pl] *goods* [pl] *ware*(*s* pl), *merchandise* [nur sg] || ⟨com a.⟩ *line* (*they are very good line*) || baumwollene (wollene, seidene) ~n [pl] *cotton* (*woollen, silk*) *goods* od *fabrics* pl || ganz u halb fertige ~n *finished and semi-finished products* || irdene ~n [pl] *crockery* [sg] || kurze ~ *small wares*, ⟨met⟩ *hardware* || sofort lieferbare ~ *spots* pl || verbotene ~ *contraband goods* || ⟨com⟩ beste deutsche ~ *best German make* || ⟨com⟩ ausgesuchte ~ *choice quality* od *description*; unverkäufliche ~ *drug in the market* || ~n im Durchgangsverkehr *goods in transit* | ~ aufkaufen *to corner the market* || Bezahlung in ~ *truck*(*-system*); ~n beziehen v/bei *to get one's supplies from* | ⟨fig⟩ das ist teure ~ *that's a luxury* || ⟨prov⟩ gute ~ lobt sich selbst *good wine needs no bush* | **~n- ~absatz** m *sale of goods* **~abschluß** m *contract in goods* **~absender** m *consigner, shipper* **~adr·eßzettel** m *label, docket* **~ausfuhr** f *exportation* (*of goods*) | gesamter **~austausch** m *exchange of all goods* **~ballen** m *bale of goods* **~beschlagnahme** f *arrest of goods* **~bestand** m *stock on hand* od *in trade*, ⟨engl bal⟩ *stock* **~best·ellbuch** n *order book*; *b. of commission* **~bezieher** m *importer* **~börse** f *produce-exchange* **~einfuhr** f *importation of merchandise* **~·einsender** m *consigner* **~empf·änger** m *consignee* **~haus** n *store*(*s* pl); *department store* **~hausdieb** m *shop-thief* **~kenntnis** f *knowledge of commercial articles* || er hat gute ~ *he is well acquainted with the articles* **~konto** n *goods-account* **~kunde** f = –kenntnis; (Buchtitel) *commercial dictionary* **~lager** n *warehouse* || (Vorrat) *stock, assortment* **~lieferant** m *contractor* **~liste** f *list of goods*; e–e lange ~ *a wide range of articles* **~makler** m *broker* **~marke** f *brand* **~markt** m *produce-market* **~muster** n *commercial sample* **~niederlage** f *warehouse* **~paß** m ⟨mar⟩ *navicert* **~probe** f *sample, pattern* || *inspection of goods* **~prüfung** f ⟨com⟩ *quality control* **~rechnung** f *invoice* **~sendung** f *consignment of goods* **~stempel** m *trade-mark* **~steuer** f *duty, excise* **~tausch** m *barter* **~verkauf** m *sale of goods* **~verk·aufsbuch** n *book of sales* **~verkehrswert** m *trade value* **~versender** m *transmitter of goods* **~verzeichnis** n *list of goods*; *inventory* || (Faktur) *invoice* **~vorrat** m *stock on hand* **~zeichen** n *trade-mark*; *brand* | ~schutz [m] *t.-m. registration* **~zettel** m *docket, mark* **~zoll** m *duty payable on goods*

warf 1. & 3. sg pret v werfen

warm a **A.** *warm*; *hot* | ⟨fig⟩ *w.* (*colo*(*u*)*r*, etc) || ⟨hunt & übtr⟩ *hot* (*scent*) | ~! (Suchspiel) *warm*! mir ist ~ *I am w.* || weder ~ noch kalt ⟨fig⟩ *neither fish nor flesh* | *affectionate* (*respect*) || *open-armed* (*reception*) || *snug* (*corner*) || *effusive* (*words*); mit ~en Worten ⟨a.⟩ *warmly* || ~e Luftschicht *stratum of w. air* || ~er Luftstrom *w. air current* **B.** sich ~ **arbeiten** *to get w.* od *heated with work* || ⟨cul⟩ ~ auftragen *to serve up hot* || ~ baden *to take w. baths* || sich ~ einpacken *to bundle up*; *to snuggle* || den Hals ~ halten *to keep the throat well wrapped up* || möchten Sie etw ≈es essen *would you like* (*sth w. to eat* od) *a hot meal*? || °etw ≈es in'n Leib °⟨sex⟩ *hot milk*; *hot pudding for supper* | (**sich**) ~ halten *to keep* (*o.s.*) *w.* || sich [dat] jdn ~ halten *to keep a p in good humour, to keep in a p's good books* || ⟨mot, etc⟩ sich ~ **laufen**, ~ laufen l *to run hot* | ~ m *to heat*; e–m ~ m *to make it w. for a p*; e–m den Kopf ~ m *to worry one* | die Sonne scheint ~ .. *is hot* || ~ sitzen *to sit in a w. place*, ⟨fig⟩ *to be warm* od *in clover* || ~ stellen *to put to warm*, ⟨cul⟩ *in the oven* | ~ w ⟨fig⟩ *to warm up* (an, bei, f, mit *to*), *to grow enthusiastic* (*about*) od *excited* od *passionate* (*over*); (Herz) *to soften*; mit jdm ~ w.: *to take to a p* **C.** ≈**e** [n]: er sitzt im ~n ⟨fig⟩ → warm s. **W·arm- ~aufziehen** n ⟨tech⟩ *shrinking-on* **~bad** n *warm* od *hot bath* || *thermal springs* pl **~behandlung** f ⟨tech⟩ *heat treatment* **~bier** n *hot* od *mulled ale*, ⟨fam⟩ mit „Schuß" (Schnaps) *hot flannel* od *tiger* **~blüter** m *warm-blooded animal* ≈**brüchig** a *brittle when red-hot* **~brunnen** m *hot wells* pl **~grube** f ⟨tech⟩ *soaking pit* **~halter** m *plate-warmer*; *tea-cosy* **~haus** n *hot-house* ≈**herzig** a *warm*(*-hearted*), (*a man*) *of heart*; *out-going* (*child*) | ~keit [f] *warmth of heart* **~laufen** n *overheating* (*of a bearing*) **~luft-** ~heizung [f] *heating with hot-air pipes*; ~strom [m] ⟨meteor⟩ *thermal current* **~w·asser-** ~heizung [f] *hot-water heating*; ~kessel [m] *boiler*; ~spender [m] *geyser* ['gi:zə]; ~versorgung [f] *hot-water supply* **W·ärm-** *warming* **~flasche, ~kruke** f *hot-water bottle* **~ofen** m *stove* **~pfanne** f *w.g-pan*, ⟨Am⟩ *chafing-dish* **~stein** m *w.g-stone* **~stube** f *warmed room* (*for the poor*) **~teller** m *heater, w.g-plate* **W·ärme** f ~/ ⟨a. fig⟩ *warmth*; ⟨fig⟩ *glow* (*in one's heart*; *of colo*(*u*)*r, excitement*) || *heartiness* || ⟨phys, physiol⟩ *heat* || gebundene (freie) ~ *latent* (*radiant*) *h.* || 5 Grad ~ *5 degrees of h.*; aufnehmen *to absorb*, abführen *remove, abstract*; ~erzeugend *calorific* | **auf** ~ ansprechend *thermophile* || **mit** ~ ⟨fig⟩ *with great warmth* || [in comp] *heat, warmth, calorific* **~abfuhr** f *heat dissipation* **~abgabe** f *h. emission*; ⟨phys⟩ *liberation of h.*; *dissipation of h., thermal dissipation* **~ableitung** f *dissipation of h.* **~abstrahlung** f *h. radiation* **~apparat** m *stove* **~auf-** ~nahme [f] *h. absorption*; ~wind [m] *thermal upcurrent* **~aus-** ~beute [f] *th.l efficiency*; ~dehnung [f] *th.l expansion*; ~gleich [m] *h.* od *thermal balance* ~nutzung [f] *utilization of h.*; ~strahlung [f] ⟨phys⟩ *h. emission* **~behandlung** f *h.* od *th.l treatment* ≈**beständig** a *high-temperature* [attr] (*cellophane*) **~beständigkeit** f *resistance to h.* **~bestrahlungsbehandlung** f *radiant h. therapy* **~deformation** f ⟨tech⟩ *th.l buckling* **~dehnungsmesser** m *dilatometer* **~durchsatz** m *rate of h. transfer* **~einheit** f *unit of h.*, ⟨phys⟩ *caloric unit* **~elektrizität** f *thermo-electricity* ≈**erzeugend** a *c.c* [adv

-ally] **~erzeugung** f *production of h.* || ⟨physiol⟩ *thermogenesis* **~gewöhnung** f *h. conditioning* **~grad** m *temperature*; hoher ~ *high t.* **~haltung** f *h. retention* **~haushalt** m *h. economy* **~isoliert** a *h. insulated* **~kapazität** f *c.c capacity*; spezifische ~ *specific th.l c.* **~kopie** f ⟨rep⟩ *thermic copy* **~kraft** f *th.l power* | ~anlage [f] *th.l p. installation*; ~lehre [f] *therm(odynam)ics* [sg konstr]; *theory of h.*; ~maschine [f] (*internal*) *combustion engine*; ~motor [m] *h. engine*; ~werk [n] *th.l power station* **~leitend** a *h.-conducting* **~leiter** m *conductor* **~leit-** ~barkeit, ~fähigkeit [f] *th.l conductivity*; ~faktor [m] *coefficient of th.l c.* **~messer** m *thermometer* **~messung** f *calorimetry* **~nutzung** f *utilization of h.* **~quelle** f *source of h.* **~regler** m ⟨tech⟩ *thermostat*; ⟨el a.⟩ *damper* **~rückgewinnungsanlage** f *h. recovery plant* **~schild** m ⟨a–n⟩ *h. shield* **~schutz** m ⟨tech⟩ *insulation against loss of h.*; *h. protection* | ~m·antel [m] *heater shield*; *heat-insulating jacket* | ~material n [n] *h. preserving material*; ~speicherungsmasse [f] *h. retaining mass* **~spektrum** n *th.l sp.* **~stau** m *localization of h.* **~stoff** m *caloric* **~strahl** m *ray of h.* || k–e ~en durchlassend *athermanous* **~strahler** m *radiator* **~strahlung** f *radiant h.* **~stromdichte** f *h. flow vector* **~über-** ~gang [m] *h. transfer*; ~schuß [m] *surplus h.*; ~tragungsgleichung [f] ⟨at⟩ *h. flow equation* **~umlaufkühlung** f ⟨mot⟩ *natural circulation water cooling* **~wirkungsgrad** m *h. efficiency* **~wirtschaft** f *h. economy* **~zeiger** m *thermoscope* **~zufuhr** f *h. input*; *supply of h.*; → wärmen

w·ärmen vt [h] *to warm, to heat* || sich ~ *to w. o.s.* || sich [dat] die Füße ~ *to w. one's feet* **W·ärmung** f ~/ *warming*

W·arn- **~boje** f *fairway buoy* **~dienst** m *warning duty* **~eidechse** f ⟨zoo⟩ *monitor* **~farbe** f ⟨biol⟩ *w.g coloration* **~flagge** f *danger flag* **~gerät** n ⟨at⟩ → *monitor* **~glocke** f *signal bell* **~kette** f ⟨mil⟩ (P) *w.g line* **~kreuz** n *traffic sign* (*at level crossing*) **~lampe** f *warning* od *pilot lamp*; *tell-tale l.* **~leuchte** f ⟨mot, aero⟩ *indicator lamp* **~ruf** m *warning cry* | akustisches **~signal** *audible alarm* od *signal* **~schild** n *caution plate*; *w.g sign* (⟨a. mot⟩ beim Überholen) **~streik** m *token strike* **~tafel** f *danger notice*

w·arnen vt [h] *to warn* (vor *of a th*, *against a p*); *to caution* (*against*) (davor z tun *not to do, against doing*) || vor Taschendieben wird gewarnt! *beware of pickpockets* || jdn rechtzeitig ~ *to give a p a fair warning* || sich (nicht) ~ l *to take* [*a p's*] (*to heed no*) *warning* | [vi] vor e–r Katastrophe ~ *to cry havoc* | **~der** Ton ⟨fig⟩ *cautionary note*; .. mit ~der Gebärde .. *she* (*laid a*) *warning* (*finger on her lips*) **W·arner** m ~s/~ *warner, admonisher* || ⟨zoo⟩ (Eidechse) *monitor* **W·arnung** f ~/~en *warning, caution, admonition* || l Sie sich das zur ~ dienen *let that be a w. to you*; als ~ dienend *admonitory* || ~ z tun *a warning against doing* | **~s-** **~anzeige** f *public warning* **~laterne** f *danger-light* **~schuß** m *summoning gun*; *w.g shot* **~signal** n *danger-signal* || *warning siren* || *alert* || *beacon* **~streik** m *token strike* **~tafel** f *notice-board*

W·arp [m & n] ~(e)s/~e ⟨mar & weav⟩ *warp* **~anker** m *kedge* **~leine** f *warp* **w·arpen** vt [h] ⟨mar⟩ *to tow, kedge* || sich durch ~ bewegen *to k.*

W·arschau n *Warsaw* **~er(in)** *Varsovian*

W·art m ~(e)s/~e *warden* || ⟨aero⟩ *ground engineer*; *g.-mechanic maintenance man* | ~burgfest [n] ⟨pol⟩ (1817, 1848) **W·arte** f ~/~n *watch-tower, belfry, look-out* | ⟨fig⟩ *point of view* || v hoher ~ aus *from a high level* **~flughöhe** f ⟨aero⟩ *holding altitude* **~frau** f = Wärterin **~frist, ~zeit** f ⟨ins⟩ *benefit* od *qualifying period* **~geld** n *fee for attendance*; *waiting(-list) salary*; *tide-over allowance*; ⟨mil⟩ *half-pay* || auf ~ setzen *to put on h.-p.* || (Liegegeld) *demurrage* **~raum** m ⟨aero⟩ *holding area* **~saal** m ⟨rail⟩, **~zimmer** n *waiting-room* **~stand** m *inactive status* || in den ~ versetzen *to place on the waiting list* **~stelle** ⟨mot racing⟩ *pit* **~zeit** f *time of waiting* ⟨a. mar⟩, *wait*; *grace* || ⟨com⟩ *demurrage* **w·arten** **I.** vt [h] [acc, *gen] *to wait upon, look after, nurse, tend* (*a p*) || *to mind* (*children*), *groom* (*horses*); ⟨tech⟩ *to service* | [gen:] s–s Amtes ~ *to attend to one's duties* || schlechte Nachrichten ~ s–r *there is bad news in store for him* || s–r ~ schlechte Zeiten *he is up against bad times* **II.** vi [h] **A.** *to wait*; *to be in expectancy* od *on the look-out* || *the car was in attendance* || (bleiben) *to stay* | ⟨fam⟩ ~ Sie mal! *just a moment*!, *wait a minute*!, *let me see*! || (drohend) na warte! *let me catch you*!, *you will catch it*! **B.** ~ **auf** [acc] *to wait for* || *what are you waiting here for*? || *without pausing for a reply* || auf e–e G. ~ *to bide one's opportunity, to look for an o.* || die Arbeit –tet auf ihn *his work is cut out for him* || ⟨rel⟩ auf ein Z. ~ *to be looking for a sign* | auf **sich** ~ l *to keep* (*a p*) *waiting* || (*the criticism*) *won't be long in coming* || (der Regen) wird nicht (mehr) lange auf sich ~ l .. *won't hold off long* | **mit** dem Tee etc (auf jdn) ~ *to wait tea*, etc (*for a p*) || ~ Sie mit der Heirat noch 1 Jahr *postpone the ma.e for another year, wait ano. y. before marrying* **C.** ~ **bis** jd tut *to wait for a p to do* || *wait until I come*!, .., bis es ihm paßt! *wait his convenience*! || darauf ~, daß *they waited for the weather to break*; *the work is still waiting to be done* **D.** auf Antwort **brauchte** man nicht z ~ *there was no a.* || er **kann** ~! *let him wait*! || da kannst du lange ~ *or* ~ bis du schwarz wirst! ⟨iron⟩ *you'll* (*have to*) *wait a long time for it*; *you may wait till doomsday* or *till the cows come home*!; *you may whistle for it*!; *I'll teach you*! || jdn ~ l *to keep a p waiting* || lange auf sich ~ l *to be long* od *late in* (od *a-*)*coming*; (S) ⟨a.⟩ *to hang fire*; immer: *he is never in time* || wir h ~ **gelernt** *we can play a w.g game* || endlos ~ müssen *to be kept w.g for a long time*, ⟨fam⟩ *to cool one's heels* **III.** ~ n; des ~s müde *tired*, ⟨fam⟩ *sick of w.g* || Zeit des ~s *wait* (*during the w.*) | sich [acc] aufs ~ verlegen *to play a w.g game*

W·ärter m ~s/~, (**~in** f ~/~nen) *keeper, attendant* [a. f] || (Kranken~) (*male*) *nurse* || (Gefängnis~) *warder* || (Wächter) *custodian, watchman* **~häuschen** n ⟨rail⟩ *signal-man's box*

W·artung f ~/~en *attendance*; *upkeep* || *care*; *service, -cing* || ⟨tech, mach⟩ *maintenance*; ~ bei der Truppe *organizational m.ce* || etc → warten || gute ~ h *to be well looked after* | **~s-** ~frei [a] *requiring no m.ce*; ~personal [n] *m.ce* od *servicing personal*; ~werkstatt [f] *m.ce shop*

..wärts [adv-suff] .. *ward* (*homeward*) [L *verto*]

war·um adv *why, wherefore, what .. for* (*what did he do that for*?) || *for what reason*?, *on what account*? | ~ bin ich nicht tot! *I wish I were dead* | der Grund, ~ er's tat *the reason for his doing it* | ~ denn? *why so*?; ~ denn das? *what for*?; ~ nicht? *why not*?, .. *just as well*!; ~ auch nicht? *and why not, indeed*?; ~ nicht gar! *certainly not*! *you don't say so*!; ~ geht man dann überhaupt erst hin *why go there at all*?; ~ kommt er eigentlich überhaupt her? ⟨fam⟩ *what's the strength of his coming here*?

Warwickshire ['wɔrikʃə] n ⟨engl⟩ (Grafschaft)

W·arze f ~/~n *wart* ⟨a. ent⟩ || ⟨bot⟩ *tubercle* || ⟨tech⟩ *stud* | (Brust~) *nipple*, ⟨zoo⟩ *teat, dug* | **~n-** ~artig [a] *warty*; ~förmig [a] *papillary*; ~fortsatz [m] ⟨anat⟩ *mastoid*; ~hof [m] ⟨anat⟩ *halo*; ~hütchen [n] *nipple-cap*; ~kürbis [m] *squash-gourd*; ~melone [f] *cantaloup*; ~ring [m] = –hof; ~schwein [n] *wart-hog*; ~schweißung [f] *projection welding*; ~stäubling [m] ⟨bot⟩ *puff-ball* **w·arzig** a *warty, full of warts*

was I. pron interr 1. [als Subjekt *or* Objekt] *what* (*what's that*?, *what did you say*?) | ⟨vulg⟩

~? *what (is it)*? ⟨sl⟩ *how much*? (statt: wie bitte? *I beg your pardon*!) | ~ bek Sie (z Kunden) *what can I show you*?, (z Kellner) *how much is it*?, (z Kutscher) *what's your fare*?, (z Verkäufer) ⟨a.⟩ ~ macht das? *how much does it cost*? || ~ beliebt? *what is your pleasure*? || ~ hilft's *what's the good of it*? || ~ ist dir? *what's the matter with you*?, *what's wrong*? || ~ ist die Uhr *what's the time*? || ~ ist sein Vater (v Beruf)? *what is his father* || ~ tun? *what am I to do*? || ~ mag er verdienen *I wonder how much he earns* || ~ weiter? *is that all*? || oder ~ (sonst [noch])? ⟨fam⟩ *or sth* || u z ~ das alles? *what's the big idea*? **2.** (Ausruf) ach ~! *pshaw*!, *tut*!; ⟨fam⟩ *nuts*! || .. u ~ nicht alles! ⟨fam⟩ .. *and what not*! || ~ wir nicht alles gesehen h *what have we not seen*! || ~ sie tanzt! *how well she dances* || ~ sie lachen kann! *what a one she is for laughing*! || ~ h wir gelacht! *how we laughed* || ~ Sie nicht sagen! *you don't say so*! || u ~ sonst noch alles *and all*; *and what not* **3.** ~ **für** Bücher? *what books*? || ~ f ein ..? *what sort of (man is he*?), *what wine* od *book (is that*?) | (Ausruf) ~ f ein (Pech etc)! *what a (misfortune, lovely day)*; *oh, what fun* od *nonsense* || ~ f ein Mädel (Regen)! ⟨fam⟩ *some girl (rain)*! || .., und ~ f eine! (*there is a new situation) with a vengeance* || ~ das f ein lästiger Mensch ist! *what a bore that man is*! || ⟨bes dero⟩ *he saw what he had for a father* **II. pron rel 1.** das zeigt, ~ das f ein Kerl ist .. *what sort of fellow he is* (→ I. 3.) **2.** [ohne Beziehungswort = das, was] *what* (dafür ⟨a.⟩ *that which*) || *what cannot be cured must be endured* (→ ändern) || *never put off till to-morrow what you can do to-day* (→ verschieben) || ~ mich betrifft *as for me* || ~ ich dir sage! *I assure you* || ~ noch mehr ist .. *and what is more* .. **3.** [mit Bezug auf **sup**: *the first, last, only* od neutrales pron: *all, everything, nothing*, etc] *that*: *the worst that could happen*; *all (that) I can do*; *there is nothing that we need be afraid for* **4.** [mit Bezug auf ganzen Satz] *which*: *he won the game which none of us had expected* **5.** [verallgemeinernd] ~ **auch** (immer), ~ **nur** .. *what(so)ever* || ~ er auch sagt *whatever he may say*; *no matter what he says*; ich lief ~ ich nur konnte *I ran as fast as I could* || koste es, ~ es wolle *let it cost what it may* **III.** ⟨fam⟩ **pron indef** (= etwas) ~ Neues *sth* od *anything new* || das ist ~ andres *that's quite another th* || ⟨iron⟩ das ist auch schon ~ (Rechtes)! *that's nothing*! ⟨iron⟩ *a fat lot*! || so ~ gibt's!, so ~ lebt nicht! *fancy*! *such a th has never been seen* (od *heard of*); ⟨fam⟩ *well, I never*! || ich will dir ~ sagen *I'll tell you what* || schäm' dich ~! *shame on you* || hat sich ~! *not I*!, *not he*! || da mach ~! *nothing doing*! || so sicher wie nur ~! *as sure as eggs are eggs* || das ist so ~ f ihn *that's nuts for him* **IV.** ⟨fam⟩ (= **warum**) ~ weinst du? *what are you crying about* || ~ rennt ihr so? *why are you running*? **V.** ⟨fam⟩ [nach Frage, Vermutung = **nicht wahr**?] *don't you think so*? || (*that's all the same to you,*) *eh*? *what*? *isn't it*?

Wasch- *cleaning, wash(ing)* **~anleitung, ~anweisung** f *washing instructions* **~anstalt** f *laundry* **~apparat** m = –maschine, ⟨chem⟩ *purifier* **~automat** m (öffentl.) *laundromat* **~bank** f *w.g-bench* **~bär** m ⟨zoo⟩ *rac(c)oon* **~becken** n *w.(ing)-, hand-basin*; ⟨Am⟩ *w.bowl* **~benzin** n *cleaner's naphtha* **~beständigkeit** f *w.g fastness* **~blau** n *w.g-blue* **~bleuel** m *w.g-beetle* **~bock** m *w.g-horse* **~brett** n *w.g-board* **~bühne** f ⟨min⟩ *buddling-dish* **~bürste** f *c.g brush* **~bütte** f *w.-tub* **~dauer** f = –zeit **≈echt** a *w.able (material)*; *fast to w.g*; *dyed in the wool* ⟨a. ftg⟩; *fast (colour)*; *fast to wash* || ⟨fam & fig⟩ *real, genuine, thorough, straight*; *through and through* [pred] || ein ~er Kerl *a true blue* | ~ s *to wash well* | **≈**heit [f] *w.g resistance* **~erz** n *buddled ore* **~faß** n = –bütte **~flasche** f *wash bottle* **~frau** f = Wäscherin || ⟨fam⟩ das kannst du d–r ~ erzählen *tell that to the (horse) marines*; *that cock won't fight*! **~gelegenheit** f *lavatory* **~geschirr** n *w.g-utensils* pl; (f Waschtisch) *toilet-set* **~gold** n *w.-gold* **~handschuh** m (Lederhandschuh) *w.-leather glove* || ⟨cosm⟩ *glove-face cloth* **~haus** n *w.-house, laundry* **~kessel** m *laundry boiler, copper* **~kleid** n *w.able dress* **~korb** m *clothes-basket* **~kraft** f *detergent power*; *detergency* **~küche** f = –haus, ⟨fig⟩ *foggy weather* **~lappen** m *face-cloth*; *dish-cloth*; ⟨Am⟩ *w.-cloth, -rag*; ⟨fig⟩ *milksop*; *lame duck*; ⟨fam⟩ *softie* **~lauge** f *lye* **~leder** n *w.-leather*; *shammy* [a. attr = **≈ledern** a: *sh. (gloves)*] **~leine** f *clothes-line* **~magd** f *laundry-maid* **~maschine** f *laundry* od *w.g-machine*; *washer* | **≈**nfest [a] *m.e w.able* **~mittel** n *lotion*; *detergent* **~napf** m *w.-basin* **~pritsche** f *w.g-boat* **~pulver** n *w.g powder*; *detergent* **~raum** m ⟨rail, etc⟩ *lavatory*; ⟨euphem⟩ *powderroom* **~samt** m *w.g velvet* **~schüssel** f = –becken **~seife** f *plain soap (for w.g)* **~tag** m *w.(ing)-day* **~ständer** m, **~tisch** m, **~toilette** f *w.(ing)-stand* || (modern) *basin fixture* **~trog** m *w.g-trough*; ⟨min⟩ *standing-buddle*, (f Gold) *cradle* **~wanne** f *w.(ing)-tub* **~wasser** n *water for w.g* || *dish-water*; ⟨fig⟩ *slops* pl || ⟨pharm⟩ *lotion* **~weib** n *w.er-woman* ⟨a. fig⟩; ⟨fig⟩ *chatterbox* **~wirkung** f *detergent action*; *detergency* **~zeit** f *w.g time* **~zettel** m *w.(ing)-bill* od *-list* || ⟨fig⟩ *publisher's note*; *blurb* **~zuber** m = –faß **~zwang** m ⟨psych⟩ *mysophobia*

w·aschbar a *washable* **W·äsche** f ~/~n **A. 1.** *washing (free board and w.)* || gr ~ *great* od *family wash* | ⟨min⟩ *buddling*, (Gold**≈**) *w.g* **2.** (Zeug) *linen (for* od *from the wash)*; *(clean, dirty* od *soiled) linen*; *laundry* || *(under-)linen* || (Damen**≈**) *lingerie* **3.** (Ort) *wash-house* | ⟨min⟩ *dressing floor*; (f Gold) *place for w.g* **B.** frische ~ anziehen, die ~ wechseln *to change* || ~ aufhängen *to air laundry* || in die ~ geben *or* tun *to get* od *have washed* || heute h wir (gr) ~ *this is w.g-day* || in der ~ s *to be in the wash* || jds schmutzige ~ waschen ⟨fig⟩ *to do a p's dirty work* || ~ zeichnen *to mark linen* **~beutel** m *soiled-linen bag* **~fabrik** f *linen-drapery* **~geschäft** n *under-linen business*; *lingerie shop* **~gestell** n *clothes-horse* **~kammer** f *linen closet* **~klammer** f *clothes-peg* **~korb** m *clothes-basket* **~leine** f *clothes-line* **~mangel, ~rolle** f *mangle* **~pfahl** m *clothes-post* **~schleuder** f *hydro-extractor, spin-drier*, ⟨fam⟩ *whizzer* **~schrank** m *linen press* **~stoff** m (feiner) ⟨Am⟩ *broad-cloth* **~zeichen** n *laundry mark* **~zeichenfarbe** f *(indelible) marking ink* **w·aschen** vt/i [wusch/ge~] [h] *to wash, launder*; wir ~ heute *this is washing-day* || sie ~ sich [dat] das Gesicht *they are w.g their faces* || ⟨fig⟩ sich [dat] die Gurgel ~ *to wet one's whistle* | ⟨fig⟩ *to chatter* || jdn rein|~ *to white-wash a p* | ⟨min⟩ *to buddle*, (Gold) *to wash* | ⟨mot⟩ (Wagen) *to wash down* | ⟨tech⟩ (wässern) *to dulcify* | **sich** ~ *to wash (o.s.)*, ⟨fam⟩ *to have a wash*; um mich z ~ *for a wash* || ~ **lassen** *to get* od *have washed* || außer dem Hause ~ l *to put out one's w.g* || (Zeug) **sich** ~ l *to wash (well)* || °das hat sich ge~ *that's capital* **W·äscher** m ~s/~ *washer* (f ~in *wash(er)woman*; feinere: *w.-lady, laundress*) **~lohn** m *charge for w.g* **W·aschung** f ~/~en *washing* (a. Gold**≈**); gründliche ~ *washdown*; ⟨min⟩ *buddling* || ⟨med⟩ *lotion* || ⟨rel⟩ *ablution* || ⟨chem⟩ *bath*

W·asen m ~s/~ **1.** *sod, turf*; *lawn* **2.** *faggot-bundle* **3.** *steam* **~meister** m *knacker*

W·asgau, W·asgenwald, der *the Vosges (Mts)*

W·ashington ['wɔʃiŋtən] n

W·asser n ~s/~ & **≈** [die ~ des Himmels; Ab**≈**, Duft**≈**, Mineral**≈**] **A. 1.** *water* **2.** ⟨geogr⟩

piece of w.; das gr ~ (Atlantik) *the big ditch* **3.** *tears* || *sweat* || *urine* **4.** (Duft≈) *perfume* || Kölnisches ~ *eau-de-Cologne* **5.** (v Diamanten etc) *lustre* **B. fließendes** kaltes u warmes ~ *hot and cold running w.*; geweihtes ~ *holy w.*; hartes, weiches ~ *hard, soft w.* || salziges, süßes ~ *salt, fresh w.* || Leitungs≈ *tap-w.* || Verfahren mit schwerem ~ *heavy w. system* || Trink≈ *drinking w.* || stehendes ~ *pool*; *stagnant w.* || totes ~ *backwater* || ⟨fig⟩ stille ~ sind tief *still w.s run deep* || .. wie ~ (*he speaks French*) *fluently*; wie ~ auf der Regenhaut ⟨fig⟩ *like w. off a duck's back* | ein schönes ~ h (Diamant) *to be of a fine w.*; (Seide) *to be finely watered* **C.** jdm das ~ **abgraben** *to cut the ground from under a p's feet* || ⟨obs⟩ sein ~ abschlagen = ~ l || das ~ abschrecken *to add hot w. to cold* || ~ braucht nicht (daran)! (z Grog) *naked*! *due north*! ⟨sl⟩ *neaters*! || ~ einnehmen ⟨mar, rail⟩ *to water* || bis dahin fließt noch viel ~ ins Meer etc *much w. will drift under the bridges before that, there's many a slip between the cup and the lip* || viel/wenig ~ führen *to carry much/little w.*, kein .. *to be dry* || (T, Pflanzen) ~ geben *to water* || das ~ **hat** k–e Balken *the sea is not planked over* || das ~ kocht *the kettle is boiling* || ~ l *to make* od *pass w.* || das Bade≈ laufen l *to turn on taps* || das ~ läuft e–m dabei im Munde zus *it makes one's m. water* || das ~ lief ihm v Leibe herunter *he was in a bath of perspiration* || er reicht ihm nicht das ~ *he is not fit to hold a candle to him, he is no patch on him* || ~ mit e–m Sieb schöpfen *to beat the air* || das ist ~ auf s–e Mühle *that's grist to his mill* || voll ~ stehend (Augen) *brimming with tears*, (Schiff) *water--logged* || ~ ins Meer tragen *to carry coals to Newcastle* || ~ treten *to tread w.* || ~ ziehen (Stiefel) *to let in w.*; ⟨mar⟩ *to leak* **D. am** ~ arbeitend etc *w.-side* [attr]; **ans** ~ gebaut h *to be given to crying*; ⟨vulg⟩ *to be leaky* | wie **aus** dem ~ gezogen (vor Hitze) ⟨fam⟩ *in a stew* | **bei** ~ u Brot sitzen *to be put on b. and w.* | **im** ~ lebend (wachsend) *aquatic, hydrophilous*; ins ~ fallen ⟨fig⟩ = z ~ w *to fall* (*to the ground* od) *through, to come to nothing*; ins ~ gehen *to drown o.s.* || e–n Schlag ins ~ tun *to beat the air* (*to fail*) | **mit** ~ verbinden ⟨chem⟩ *to hydrate*; mit ~ verdünnen *to water* | **über** ~ fahren (U-Boot) *to run on the surface*; über das gr ~ fahren *to cross the ocean*; über ~ halten *to nurse*; *to keep .. going* || sich über ~ halten *to keep one's head above w.* ⟨a. fig⟩; ⟨fig⟩ *to keep one's end up*; *to rub along*; mit Mühe .. *to have difficulty in making both ends meet* | **unter** ~ halten *to hold .. under* || unter ~ setzen *to flood, submerge*, ⟨emph⟩ *inundate* | **von** ~ umgeben *w.-bound*; v ~ durchtränkt *drenched with w.* || v reinstem ~ *of the first w.* ⟨a. fig⟩, ⟨pol⟩ *fine-crusted* | **zu** ~ u z Lande *by sea and l.*; *naval and military* || z ~ m *to frustrate*; *to bring to naught*; (Pläne) *to upset a p's* (od *the*) *apple-cart* || z ~ reisen *to go by w.* || z ~ w *to turn into w.*; ⟨fig⟩ *to miscarry*; *to end in smoke*; *to go phut* **~abfluß** m *outlet for w.* | ~hahn [m] *w.--discharge vent, w.-drain tap*; ~leiste [f] ⟨arch⟩ *w. table* **~ablaß** m *drainage*; *draining* **~ablauf** m *gutter, spout* | ~rinne [f] *drip-nose* **≈abstoßend** a *w.-repellent* **~abzug** m *drain, culvert* | ~sgraben [m] *catch pit* **~ader** f *vein of w.* || ⟨anat⟩ *lymphatic vessel* **~ampfer** m *w.-dock* **~amsel** f *w. ouzel*; *dipper* **≈arm** a *waterless, arid* **~armatur** f *w.-fittings* pl **~armut** f *want of w.* || gr ~ *w.-famine* **~aufbereitungs-** | ~anlage [f] *w. handling plant* **~aufnahme** f *w. absorption* | ~vermögen [n] *w. absorbing capacity* **~bad** n *w.-bath* ⟨a. chem⟩; ⟨cul⟩ *bain-marie* Fr **~ball(spiel** n) m *w.-polo* **~bau** m f *w. processing w.-works, hydraulics* pl | ~kunst [f] *hydraulic architecture*; ~meister [m] *hydrotechnologist* **~becken** n *basin*; ⟨hort a.⟩ *sheet of w.* **~bedarf** m *w. requirement* **~behälter** m *reservoir, w.-tank, cistern* || ⟨rail⟩ *w.-house*; (im Tender) *tank* || ⟨cul⟩ *boiler* || ⟨mach⟩ *well* **~beschreibung** f *hydrography* **≈bindend** a *hydraulic*; *w. absorbent* **~blase** f *bubble*; ⟨path⟩ *pustule* **~blattern** f pl *w.-pox* **≈blau** a *marine blue*; *pale blue, bluish* (*eyes*) **~blei** n ⟨min⟩ *molybden* **~blume** f *aquatic flower* **~bombe** f ⟨mar⟩ *depth bomb* od *charge* | ~nwerfer [m] *Y-gun* (*anti--submarine mortar with 2 barrels*) **~brei** m *hasty--pudding, paste, pap* **~brett** n (aus Kunststoff) ⟨mot⟩ *jet board* **~bruch** m ⟨path⟩ *hydrocele* **~damm** m *dam, dike* **~dampf** m *steam* || gespannter ~ ⟨phys⟩ *steam under pressure* **≈dicht** a ⟨tail, etc⟩ *w.proof* (*paint*) || ~er Mantel *mackintosh* || ⟨mar, etc⟩ *w.-tight* (*cover*) **~doktor** m *quack* **~dosten** m ⟨bot⟩ *hemp-agrimony* **~druck** m *hydrostatic pressure* | ~lehre [f] *hydrodynamics*; ~mine [f] *oyster mine*; ~zündung [f] *hydrostatic ignition* **~dunst** m *w.y vapour* **~durchfluß** m *passage of w.* **≈durchlässig** a *permeable* **≈echt** a *w. resisting* **~effekt** m ⟨theat⟩ *sea effect* **~eimer** m *w.-pail, bucket* **~einbruch** m *inrush of w.* **~einlaß** m *w. inlet pipe* **~einziehungsgebiet** n *intake area* **~entgasung** f *w. degassing* **~enthärtung** f *w. softening* **~entölung** f *oil separation from w.* **~epidemie** f *w.-borne epidemic* **~eppich** m ⟨bot⟩ *w.-parsley* **~erhitzer** m ⟨engl⟩ *geyser* **~fahrt** f *boating, excursion by w.*; *row, sail* **~fahrzeug** n *w.craft* (⟨a.⟩ ~e), *vessel* **~fall** m (*w.-*)*fall*, (gr) *cataract*, (künstlicher) *cascade* || wie ein ~ reden *to talk in torrents*; *to talk nineteen to the dozen* **~farbe** f *w.-colour*; *wash* (*in wash*) **~farn** m ⟨bot⟩ *quill-wort* **~faß** n *w.-cask, w.-tub* **~fenchel** m ⟨bot⟩ *bladder-wort* **≈fest** a *indelible* (*ink*) **~filtersack** m *w. sterilizing apron* od *bag* **~fläche** f *sheet of w.*; (Oberfläche) *surface of the w.* || nutzbare ~ *useful area of w. surface* **~flasche** f *w.-bottle* **~fliege** f ⟨ent⟩ *w.-fly* **~floh** m *w. flea* **~flora** f *aquatic vegetation* od *flora* **~flugzeug** n *seaplane, hydroplane* | ~hafen [m] *s.p. base, seadrome* **~flut** f *flood, inundation* **~förderung** f *raising of w.* **~fracht** f *w.-carriage*; *w.age* **≈frei** a *free from w.* || ⟨chem⟩ *anhydrous*; *absolute* (*alcohol*) **~freund** m *lover of aquatic sports* **~front** f *w.-front*, ⟨übtr⟩ *seaside* **≈führend** a ⟨min⟩ *w.-bearing* (Schicht) **~führung** f ⟨geog⟩ *discharge, run-off* **~furche** f *w.-furrow* **~gang** m *aqueduct, canal*; *drain* || ⟨mar⟩ *w.-way* **~gebläse** n ⟨met⟩ *hydrostatic blast* **~gefäß** n *w.-tub* **~gefahr** f *danger of inundations* **~geflügel** n *w.-fowl* **~gehalt** m *moisture* od *w. content*; *percentage of w.* || ~ im Dampf *primage*; zulässiger ~ *w. tolerance* **~geist** m *w.-sprite, nixie* **~geld** n (Abgabe) *w.-rate* **~gerechtigkeit** f = –recht [n] **~geschwulst** f *œdema* **~gesetzgebung** f *legislation relating to rivers*, etc **~gewächs** n *aquatic plant* **~glanz** m ⟨weav⟩ *moire* **~glas** n *tumbler* || ⟨chem⟩ *w.-glass*; *sodium silicate*; *soluble glass* || Sturm im ~ *st. in a tea-cup* **≈gleich** a *level, horizontal* **~graben** m *ditch* || ⟨agr⟩ *drain* || ⟨fort⟩ *moat* **~grube** f *cistern* **~gurke** f *pickled cucumber* **~guß** m *downpour* || *sink* **~hahn** m *w,-tap*, ⟨bes Am⟩ (*w.-*)*faucet*; ⟨tech⟩ *cock* (andrehen *to turn on*) **≈haltig** a *containing w.*; ⟨chem⟩ *hydrated* **~haltung** f ⟨min⟩ *draining, drainage* | **~s-** ~maschine [f] *pumping engine*; ~schacht [m] *engine pit* **≈hart** a *air-dried* (*pottery*) **~haushalt** m *w. economy* ⟨a. geog⟩ | *river regimen* || ⟨biol⟩ *w. balance* **~hebemaschine** f *hydraulic engine* **~heilanstalt** f *hydropathic* (*establishment*) **~heilkunde** f *hydropathy* **~heilkünstler** m *hydropathist* **~heizung** f *hot-w. heating* **≈h·ell** a *as clear as w.* **~höhe** f *w.-line* **~holder** m ⟨bot⟩ *guelder rose* **~hose** f ⟨meteor⟩ *waterspout* **~huhn** n *coot* **~hülle** f ⟨meteor⟩ *hydrosphere* **~hund** m *w.-spaniel* **~jagd** f *shooting of aquatic birds* **~jungfer** f *naiad* || ⟨ent⟩ *dragon-fly* || ~n werfen *to play* (*at*) *ducks* *and drakes* **~käfer** m *w.-beetle* **~kanne** f *w.-pitcher, w.-jug*; ⟨com⟩ *ewer* **~kante** f *seaside* **~karte** f *hydrographic chart* **~kasten** m *w.-reservoir; w.-drum; w.-tank* **~kessel** m *kettle* ‖ (gr) *copper* ‖ ⟨mach⟩ *boiler* **~kissen** n ⟨med⟩ *w.-cushion* **~kitt** m *hydraulic cement* **~̊klar** a *liquid* (*eyes*) **~klee** m ⟨bot⟩ *marsh-trefoil* **~klosett** n *w.-closet* (*W. C.*) **~kopf** m ⟨path⟩ *hydrocephalus* ‖ *p with* (*w. on the brain* od) *h.s* **~korso** m *regatta* **~kraft** f *w.-power* | ~lehre [f] *hydrodynamics*; ~motor [m] *hydromotor*; ~strom [m] *hydro-electric power*; ~werk [n] *h.-e. p. station* **~kreislauf** m *w. loop* od *cycle* **~kresse** f ⟨bot⟩ *w. cresses* pl **~krug** m *w.-jug* **~kühler** m ⟨mot⟩ *radiator* **~kühlung** f *w. cooling* **~kultur** f ⟨bot⟩ *hydroponics* [a. sg konstr] **~kunde** f *hydrology* **~kunst** f *fountain, waterwork*; ⟨tech⟩ *w.-work*; ⟨mach⟩ *hydraulic engine* **~kur** f *w.-cure, hydropathic treatment* **~lache** f *pool* **~l·andflugzeug** n *amphibian* **~landung** f = Wasserung **~lauch** m ⟨bot⟩ *w.-garlic* **~lauf** m *w.-course* **~läufer** m ⟨ent⟩ *w.-strider, w.-skipper* ‖ ⟨orn⟩ *sand piper* **~̊leer** a *dry* **~leitung** f *aqueduct* ‖ *w.-pipe* | (im Hause) *w.-supply, w.-service* ‖ e–e ~ legen *to have the w. laid on* | (Hauptrohr) *main* ‖ (Nebenrohr) *service-pipe* **~lilie** f = Schwertlilie ‖ (Seerose) *w.-lily*; (königliche) *Victoria regia* **~linie** f ⟨mar⟩ *w.-line* ‖ ⟨com⟩ *load-line* ‖ *high-w. mark* **~linsen** f pl ⟨bot⟩ *duck-weed* **~̊los** a *w.-less* **~̊löslich** a *water soluble*, ⟨scient⟩ *hydrosoluble* **~losung** f ⟨min⟩ *drainage* | **~s-** ~stollen [m] *deep adit* **~mangel** m *w.-shortage; want* od *scarcity of w.* **~mann** m ⟨myth⟩ = –geist ‖ ⟨astr⟩ *W.-carrier, Aquarius* **~mantel** m ⟨tech⟩ *w.-jacket* **~marke** f (*high-*) *w.-mark* **~maschine** f *hydraulic engine* **~masse** f *body* bzw *flow of w.*; ~n [pl] *w.s* **~meister** m *w. inspector* **~melone** f *w.-melon* **~menge** f *quantity* bzw *plenty of w.* **~messer** m *hydrometer, water-gauge* **~milbe** f *w.-mite, w.-tick* **~molch** m *newt*; (mexik.) *ax·olotl* **~mühle** f *w.-mill* ~**nehmen** n ⟨mar⟩ *watering* **~nix**(e f) m *nixie* (f a. *naiad, w.-nymph, mermaid*) **~not** f *scarcity of w., drought*; (gr) *w.-famine; drought* (vgl –snot) **~nymphe** f = –nixe **~opal** m ⟨min⟩ *aqueous opal* **~orgel** f *hydraulic* od *w.-organ* **~partie** f = –fahrt **~perle** f *imitation pearl* **~pest** f (kanadische) *w.-weed* **~pfahl** m *pile in the w.* **~pfeffer** m ⟨bot⟩ *w.-pepper, smartweed* **~pfeife** f *narghile, hooka(h)* **~pflanze** f *aquatic plant* **~pforte** f ⟨mar⟩ *limber* **~pfuhl** m, **~pfütze** f *pool* **~platz** m *w.ing-place* **~pocken** f pl *chicken-pox* sg **~probe** f (Gottesgericht) *W.-ordeal* **~pumpe** f *w.-pump* **~quelle** f *spring of fresh w.* **~rabe** m ⟨orn⟩ *cormorant* **~rad** n *w.-wheel* **~ralle** f ⟨orn⟩ *w.-rail* | Achtung **~rast**! f *beware of the w.-splash*! **~ratte** f *w.-rat* ‖ ⟨fig⟩ *w.-* od *sea-dog*; ⟨mar⟩ *old salt* **~̊recht** a *level* **~recht** n *w. right* **~̊reich** a *abounding in lakes*, etc ~**reich** n *watery kingdom* **~reis** n ⟨hort⟩ *w.-shoot, w.-sprout* **~reise** f *journey by w., voyage* **~riese** f ⟨for⟩ *flume* **~rinne** f *w.-channel, spillway*; ⟨arch⟩ *gutter* **~rohr** n, **~röhre** f *w.-pipe* **~rose** f *water-lily*; weiße ~ *nenuphar* **~röste** f *w.-retting* (*of flax*) **~rübe** f *turnip* | vermehrte **~rückresorption** ⟨path⟩ *increased reabsorption of w.* **~rutschbahn** f (*w.-*) *shoot* **~sammelgebiet** n *w. catchment area* **~̊satt** a *w. logged* (Holz), ⟨tech⟩ *w.-saturated* **~säugetier** n *aquatic mammal* **~säule** f *column of w.* ‖ ⟨at⟩ *w. plume* | **~n-** ~druck [m] *hydraulic head*; ~maschine [f] *w.-pressure engine* **~schacht** m ⟨min⟩ *draining-shaft* **~schaden** m *damage by w., damage caused by inundation* **~schale** f *pan of w.* **~schatz** m ⟨geog⟩ *w. resources* **~schaufel** f *w.-scoop* ‖ *float* (*on a w.-wheel*) **~scheide** f *w.-shed*; ⟨Am⟩ *divide* **~schenkel** m ⟨arch⟩ *weather-board* **~scheu** f *dread of water*; ⟨sl⟩ *water-funk*; ⟨path⟩ *hydrophobia* **~̊scheu** a *afraid of water*, er ist ~ *he's a w.-funk* ‖ ⟨path⟩ *hydrophobic*

~schi m (–ski) *w. ski* ‖ ~ fahren *od* laufen *to w.-ski* **~-Schienen-** *w.-rail* (Transport) N **~schierling** m ⟨bot⟩ *w.-hemlock* **~schiff** n (im Herd) *boiler* **~schildkröte** f *turtle, sea-tortoise* **~schlange** f *w.-snake*; ⟨myth, astr⟩ *Hydra* **~schlauch** m *w.-hose* ‖ ⟨bot⟩ *bladder-wort* **~schloß** n *moated castle* **~schlund** m *abyss of w.* **~schöpfanlage** f *w.-scooping plant* **~schöpfrad** n *wheel for drawing up w.* **~schraube** f *hydraulic screw* **~schutzpolizei** f *river police* **~schwärmer** m *w.-rocket* **~schwein** n *w.-hog* **~schwere** f *specific gravity of w.* **~seite** f *w.side* **~semmel** f *plain roll* **~skorpion** m ⟨ent⟩ *w. scorpion* **~speier** m *gargoyle* **~spiegel** m *w.-level; surface of the w.* | *expanse of w.* **~sport** m *aquatics* pl | ~fest [n] *swimming gala*; ~leistung [f] *w.-craft* **~spritze** f *w.-engine; squirt* **~spülung** f *flush, flushing, waterflush* **~stag** m ⟨mar⟩ *bob-stay* **~stand** m *w.-level* ‖ höchster ~ *high w.* | ~glas [n] *w.-glass*; ~messer [m], ~szeiger [m] *w.-gauge*; ~zeichen [n] *w.-mark* °**~ständer** m °⟨sex⟩ *morning pride* **~station** f ⟨rail⟩ *w.ing station* **~staub** m *spray* **~stein** m (*boiler*) *scale* | ~ansatz [m] *scale formation, incrustation* **~stelle** f *w.ing-place; w.supply point* **~stiefel** m pl *jack-boots, waders* pl **~stoff** m ⟨chem⟩ *hydrogen*; normaler ⟨chem⟩ *protium* ‖ mit ~ verbinden *to hydrogenate* | ~blondine [f] *peroxide* od *platinum blonde*; ~bombe [f] *hydrogen* (od *H-*) *bomb*; ~gas [n] *h.n gas*; ~̊haltig [a] *hydric*; ~peroxid [n] *h.n peroxide*; ~verbindung [f] *hydride* **~stollen** m *w.-conduit* **~strahl** m *jet of w.* | ~ableiter [m] *spray arrester*; ~pumpe [f] *w. j. air pump* **~straße** f *w.-way* **~strecke** f *expanse of w.*; (e–s Flusses) *reach* **~streifen** m (im Brot etc) *watery streak* **~strudel** m *whirlpool* **~sucher** m *w.-diviner* **~sucht** f ⟨path⟩ *dropsy* **~̊süchtig** a *dropsical* **~suppe** f *w.-gruel*, ⟨fam⟩ *slops* pl **~taufe** f *baptism* od *christening with w.* **~tiefe** f *depth of w.* **~tier** n *aquatic animal* **~tonne** f *w.-cask*; ⟨mar⟩ *buoy* **~tor** n *flood-gate* **~tracht** f ⟨mar⟩ (*ship's*) *draught of w.* **~träger** m *w.-carrier* **~tragesack** m *canvas w. bucket* **~transport** m *conveyance by w.* **~̊treibend** a ⟨med⟩ *diuretic* **~trense** f *w.ing-bit* **~triebwerk** n ⟨min⟩ *hydraulic machine* **~trog** m *w.-trough* **~tropfen** m *drop of w.* **~tümpel** m *pool of w.* **~turm** m *w.-tower* **~uhr** f *w.-meter*; ⟨hist⟩ *w.-clock, clepsydra* **~umlauf** m *w. circulation* **~umschlag** m ⟨med⟩ *wet compress* **~velo** n *pedalo* **~verdrängung** f ⟨mar⟩ *displacement* ‖ ⟨fig⟩ (P) ⟨fam⟩ *avoirdupois*; wonnige ~ ⟨sex⟩ *outstanding projections* (34–22–34) **~vergoldung** f *w.-gilding* **~verschluß** m *trap*; *w. seal* **~verschmutzung, ~verunreinigung** f *w. pollution* **~versorgung** f *w.-supply* **~vogel** m *aquatic bird*; *w.fowl* [mst koll als pl] **~vorrat** m *supply of w.*; (auf Kamelen) *w.-carriage* **~waage** f *level*; ⟨phys⟩ *hydrostatic balance* **~wägung** f *levelling* **~weg** m *w.-way*; *channel* ‖ auf dem ~ *by w.* **~wegerich** m ⟨bot⟩ *w.-plantain* **~wehr** n *wear* **~weide** f ⟨bot⟩ *w.-willow, osier* **~wellen** f pl ⟨cosm⟩ *w. waves* **~welt** f *aquatic world* **~werfer** m *w.-cannon, w.-gun* **~werk**(**e** pl) n *w.-works* pl **~wirbel** m *whirlpool, eddy* **~woge** f *large wave, billow* **~wüste** f ⟨mst poet⟩ *endless ocean* (*seen as a desert*) **~zeichen** n *w.-mark* **~zement** m *hydraulic c.* **~̊ziehend** a *hygroscopic* **~zins** m *w.-rate* **~zoll** m *w.-toll, w.age* **~zuber** m *w.-tub* **W·ässerchen** n ~s/~ *brooklet* ‖ ⟨fig⟩ er sieht aus, als ob er kein ~ trüben könnte *he looks as if butter wouldn't melt in his mouth* **w·ässerig** a ⟨cul⟩ *sloppy; watery* (*beverage*); *aqueous* (*solution*), *diluted*; ~e Substanz [f] *liquid* ‖ ⟨fig⟩ *washy* (*stuff*), *liquid* bzw *rheumy* (*eyes*); *insipid* (*style*), *flat* (*joke*) ‖ jdm den Mund ~ m *to make a p's mouth water* (nach *for*) | ~̊keit [f] ~/ *wateri(sh)ness*; (v Getränk) *weakness* ‖ ⟨fig⟩

insipidity, flatness **w·assern** vi [h] ⟨aero⟩ *to surface; to alight on water* **w·ässern I.** vt [h] *to water (wine), irrigate (land, wound)* || ⟨tech⟩ *to dulcify*; ⟨phot⟩ *to wash; to soak, steep (skins)*; (einweichen) *to macerate*; (Stoffe) *to water, tabby* **II.** vi [h] (Augen, Mund) *to water* || (im Wasser liegen) *to soak* **W·assersnot** f *distress caused by flood, high flood* (vgl Wassernot) **W·asserung** f ~/~en *alighting (of seaplanes)*; ⟨a–n⟩ *splash-down* **W·ässerung** f ~/~en *watering, irrigation* **w·äßrig, ≗keit** = wässerig, ≗keit

Wat f ~/~en ⟨obs & poet⟩ *cloth(ing), garment*

w·aten vi [h & s] *to wade (in, through)* || (durch Schneeschlamm) ⟨sl⟩ *to mush*

×**W·aterkant** f ~/ = Wasserkante

W·atsche(n m) f [bay, österr] → Ohrfeige

w·atscheln vi [h & s] *to waddle, shamble, toddle (along)* | **-lig** *waddling*, etc

Watt n ~s/~ ⟨el⟩ *watt (400 watts)* **~messer** m *w.-meter* **~leistung, ~stärke** f *w.age* **~stunde** f *w.-hour* (Wh)

Watt n ~(e)s/~en; *tidal mud-flats* pl *(between coast and island)* **~enfischerei** f *shoalfishing* **~enmeer** n *shallows* pl

W·atte f ~/~n *wadding*, ⟨bes med⟩ *cotton wool* || ⟨fig⟩ in ~ gewickelt *nursed in cotton* **~bausch** m *wad of cotton*; ⟨surg⟩ *tampon, pad* || (Tupfer f Abstriche) *swab* **~nmacher** m *manufacturer of wadding* **~nrock** m *wadded coat*, etc **watt·ieren** vt [h] *to wad, pad, quilt* **W.rung** f *wadding*, etc

W·atvogel m *wading bird* || pl *waders*

Wau m ~(e)s/~e ⟨bot⟩ *weld; dyer's weed*

W·auwau m ~s/~s ⟨Kindersprache⟩ (Hund) *bow-wow* || ⟨fig⟩ *bogy, bugbear* | ≗ [intj] *bow-wow*

w·ebbar a *textile* **Web- ~art** f *mode of weaving; fabric, texture* **~blatt** n *reed* **~fehler** m *flaw (in the cloth)* **~geschirr** n *harness* **~industrie** f *weaving i.* **~kante** f → ~e- **~maschine** f *power-loom* **~schule** f *weavers' school* **~stoff** m *woven material, textile fabric, tissue*; pl *textiles* (⟨a.⟩ = –waren [f pl]) **~stuhl** m *loom* **W·ebe** f ~/~n *web, weft; piece of linen* **~kante** f *selvage* **~leine** f ⟨mar⟩ *ratlin(e)* [mst im pl] **w·eben I.** vt/i [reg &] irr [h] *to weave* ⟨a. fig⟩; ⟨fig⟩ *to intertwine* || *to work (tapestry)* || damastartig ~ *to damask* || was die Parzen ~ *what's woven by the Fates* | vi (sich regen) *to move, stir* || leben u ~ *to be full of life* od *activity* || **an** ihr lebt u webt alles *she's full of life* || leben u ~ **in** *to be absorbed in*: ⟨bib⟩ *in Him we live and move (and have our being)* | **~d** ⟨zoo⟩ *telarian* **II.** ≗ n *weaving* || ihr Leben u ~ *her whole life and thought* **W·eber(in** f ~/~nen) m ~s/~ *weaver* **~arbeit** f *weaver's work; weaving* || *web, tissue* **~baum** m *weaver's beam, yarn-beam* **~blatt** n ⟨tech⟩ *w.'s reed* **~distel** f *teasel* **~einschlag** m *weft, woof* **~gesell(e)** m *journeyman-w.* **~handwerk** n *w.'s trade* **~kamm** m = –blatt **~karde** f *teasel* **~knecht** m = –gesell || ⟨ent⟩ *harvester, harvest-spider*, ⟨Am⟩ *h.tman*; ⟨fam⟩ *daddy-long-legs* **~knoten** m *w.'s knot* **~lade** f *batten* **~meister** m *master w.* **~schiffchen** n *shuttle* **~schlichte** f *w.'s starch* **~spule** f *bobbin, spool* **~tritt** m *treadle* **~vogel** m *w.-bird* **~zettel** m *warp* **Weber·ei** f ~/~en **1.** *weaving; weaver's trade* **2.** *texture* **3.** *tissue* **4.** (Fabrik) *weaving-mill*

W·echsel m ~s/~ **1.** *change, changing* || ⟨pol⟩ *change-over* Regierungs≗ || ständiger ~ *chops and changings* | (Glücks≗) *vicissitude* **2.** (regelm. ~) *turn, alternation* || (Saat≗) *rotation (of crops)* || *phases* pl *(of the moon)* || *succession (of seasons)* | (Ablaut) grammatischer ~ *grammatical change* || ⟨biochem⟩ *turnover* (der roten Blutkörperchen in 90 Tagen) || in regelm. ~ sich ablösende Fronteinheiten *rotation combat units*; → vorschießen **3.** (Tausch) *exchange* (a. *of [wedding]-rings*), ⟨box⟩ *of blows* || *interchange* || (v Geld a.) *change* || *relay (of horses)* **4.** (des Wildes) *path, runway; haunt* **5.** ⟨com⟩ *bill (of exchange)*; ⟨sl⟩ *paper* || ~ auf Sicht *bill payable at sight* || (Auslands≗ = Devise) *foreign bill* || gezogener *or* trassierter ~ *draft* (auf 3 M.e Ziel *at 3 months*) || eigener *or* trockener ~ *note of hand, promissory note* || kurz(fristig)er ~ *short bill* || langer ~ *long dated bill* || offener ~ *letter of credit (L./C.)*; *blank cheque* | e–n ~ ausstellen *or* ziehen auf *to draw on (a p* über .. *for £ 80)*; e–n ~ einlösen *to answer* od *honour a bill (of exchange)*, .. f jdn *to accept a bill for the h. of a p*; e–n ~ honorieren *to meet a bill* **6.** ⟨stud⟩ (Monatsgeld) *allowance* **7.** ⟨tech⟩ *joint(-pipe)* **8.** ⟨carp⟩ *trimmer* **~achse** f ⟨rec⟩ *changer spindle* **~agent** m *bill-broker* **~agio** n *premium on exchange*; (Geschäft) *exch.* **~akzept** n *acceptance (of a bill)* **~allonge** [–a'lõʒə] f *rider* **~arbitrage** f *(bill-)arbitrage, arbitration of exch.* **≗armig** a *with alternate arms* **~arrest** m *confinement for non-acceptance of a bill* **~bad** n *alternating* od *contrast bath, hot-and-cold b.* **~balg** m *changeling* || (ungezogenes Kind) *urchin* **~bank** f *discount-house* **~begriff** m (–bewegung [f]) *correlative; reciprocal notion, (r. movement)* **~beziehung** f *correlation, interrelation, mutual relation* || in enge ~ bringen mit *to correlate highly with* || in ~ stehen(d) *to correlate* [mit, z *with, to*] *(correlative)* **~brief** m *bill (of exch.)* **~bürge** m *bail* od *surety of a bill* **~bürgschaft** f *guarantee of .., surety for a bill* **~chor** m ⟨mus⟩ *antiphony* **~courtage** f = –provision **~devise** f *par of exchange* **~diskont** m *bill-discount* **≗fähig** a *able (entitled, authorized) to draw bills* | ~keit [f] *right to draw and endorse bills* **~fälle** m pl *variations; vicissitudes* pl *(of life)* || in den ~n des Kampfes *under the varying conditions of operations* **~fälschung** f *forgery of bills* **~farbe** f *changeable colo(u)r* **≗farbig** a *iridescent* **~feuer** n ⟨aero⟩ *alternating light (in colo(u)r)* **~fieber** n ⟨med⟩ *intermittent fever* **~folge** f *rotation* **~forderung** f *claim based on a bill*, pl *bills* od *notes receivable* **~frist** f *usance; days* pl *of grace* **~geber** m *drawer* **~gebrauch** m *usance* **~gebühr** f *discount* **~geld** n *bank-money* || (Aufgeld) *agio* || (Kleingeld) *small coin, change*; (in der Ladenkasse) *till-money* || zu wenig ~ herausgeben *to short-change* **~gesang** m *alternate song; responsive singing* **~geschäft** n *exch.-, banking-business* | *discounting transaction* | (Ort) *bill-broker's business* **~gespräch** n = –rede **~getriebe** n *change-over speed-gear* **~gläubiger** m = –inhaber **~händler** m *bill-discounter, -broker* **~handlung** f = –geschäft **~heirat** f *intermarriage* **~inhaber** m *holder of a bill* **~jahre** n pl *climacteric, menopause* **~klage** f *action arising out of a bill* **~konto** n *bill-account* **~kontor** n *exch.-office* **~kopierbuch** n *bill copy-book* **~kredit** m *paper-credit* **~kurs** m *rate of exch.* | ~berechner [m] *arbitragist*; ~berechnung [f] *arbitration of exch.* **~lager** n ⟨tech⟩ *double thrust bearing* **~makler** m *bill-broker* **≗mäßig** a *according to bill-regulations* **~nehmer** m *taker of a bill, payee* **~ordnung** f *exch.-regulations* pl **~platten-Speicher** m ⟨comp⟩ *data record file* | ~-Steuerung [f] *d. r. f. control* **~protest** m *protest* **~provision** f *bill-brokerage; change* **~prozeß** m = –klage **~punkt** m (Flak≗) *mid-point* **~rad** n *loose gear* **~rahmen** m *passe-partout* **~rechnung** f *bill-account* **~recht** n *legislation concerning bills of exch.* **~rede** f *dialogue* **~reime** m pl *alternate rhymes* pl **~reiter(·ei** f) m ⟨com⟩ *bill-jobber (b.-jobbing; cross-acceptance*; ⟨sl⟩ *kite-flying)* || (~ treiben ⟨sl⟩ *to fly kites)* **~richter** m ⟨el⟩ *vibrat(ion)or, inverse rectifier* **~schalter** m ⟨el⟩ *two-way switch* **~schritt** m *change of step(s* pl) **~schuld** f *debt (on a bill)*, pl *bills payable* **≗seitig** a *reciprocal, mutual* || ~e Beziehung *interrelation* (zw *of*) | ≗keit [f] *reciprocity* **~sendung** f *remittance* **~spiel** n *interplay (of forces)* **≗ständig** a ⟨bot⟩ *alternate*

~stellung f ⟨artill⟩ *alternating emplacement* **~stempel** m *bill-stamp* **~strom** m ⟨el⟩ *alternating current* (*A. C.*) | ~generator [m] *alternator*; ~maschine [f] *alternator* **~stube** f *exch.-office* **~unterricht** m (f geburtenstarke Jahrgänge) ⟨school⟩ *shift-work* **~verhältnis** n *reciprocal relation*; im ~ stehen *to have a reciprocal relationship* **~verkehr** m *alternating communication*; ⟨com⟩ *circulation of bills* **≗voll** a *varie(gate)d*; *checkered*; *eventful*; *changeful* ‖ ~e Kämpfe *battles which swayed to and fro* | ~ gestalten *to diversify* **~vorgang** m ⟨rec⟩ *changer cycle* **≗weise** adv *reciprocally*, *mutually* ‖ (abwechselnd) *by turns*, *alternately* **~winkel** m ⟨geom⟩ *alternate angle* **~wirkung** f *interplay*; *reciprocal effect*; *interrelationship*; ⟨biol⟩ *antagonism* ‖ unter–e–a. in ~ stehen *to be correlated to each other* **~wirtschaft** f ⟨agr⟩ *rotation farming* od *of crops* **~wucher** m *usurious discounting* **~zahl** f ⟨el⟩ *frequency* **~zustand** m *reciprocity* **W·echseln** n ~s/ (*ex*)*changing* ‖ ewiges ~ (*constant*) *chopping and changing* ‖ ich habe nicht genug Kleingeld zum ~ *I am short of change* **w·echseln I.** vt [h] (ändern) *to change*, *shift* (a. Wohnung) ‖ *he changes his views as easily as his shirt*, Ansicht, Partei ~ *to turn one's coat* | (Worte, Blicke, Briefe, Schüsse, etc austauschen) *to exchange* | (etw durch etw ersetzen) *to substitute* | (abwechseln mit) *to vary* | (umschichtig ~) *to alternate* | die Farbe ~ *to change colo(u)r*, ⟨cards⟩ .. *suit* ‖ (Geld) *to change*; ⟨a.⟩ *to give* (*a p*) *change for a £* ‖ die Kleider (die Schuhe) ~ *to change one's clothes* (⟨fam⟩ *one's feet*) ‖ den Besitzer ~ *to change hands* od *masters* ‖ die Plätze ~ *to change places* (*with*) (⟨fig⟩ = die Rollen ~) ‖ Tritt ~ *to change step* (od *foot* od *feet*) ‖ ⟨mil⟩ die Front ~ *to change front* ⟨a. fig⟩ ‖ ⟨fig⟩ s–n Standpunkt ~ *to shift one's ground* ‖ Worte ~ mit *to bandy words with ..* ‖ ⟨a.⟩: *to have* (*a few words with ..*) (→ o.) ‖ die Zähne ~ *to get new teeth* **II.** vi [h] (sich ändern) *to change*, *shift* ‖ (Wind) *to veer round* (*from .. to*) ‖ ewig ~ *to be for ever chopping and changing* | (abwechseln) *to alternate* | (veränderlich s) *to vary* (*from .. to*) | ⟨hunt⟩ *to pass* ‖ ⟨min⟩ die Wetter ~ *there is a good current of air* | **~d** ⟨a.⟩ *non-constitant* (*terrain*) **W·echsler** m ~s/~ *money-changer* | ~laden [m] *m.-ch.'s shop*

Weck m ~(e)s/~e ⟨cul⟩ *roll* (⟨a.⟩: **~e** f ~/~n

W·eckapparat m ⟨Ger®⟩ *preserving apparatus*

W·eck- ~schwelle [f] ⟨mot⟩ *jiggle-bar*; uhr [f] → Wecker **w·ecken I.** vt [h] *to wake* (*up*), *to waken*, *to awake*(*n*), *to call*, ⟨engl a.⟩ *to knock up* ‖ ⟨fig⟩ *to wake* (*up*), *to rouse* ‖ ⟨telph⟩ vt/i *to ring* (*a p up*) ‖ hat es geweckt? *was there a ring*? ‖ (Gedanken) *to inspire* ‖ (Gefühl) *to stir*; jds Eigenwillen ~ *to excite a p's wilfulness*; (Interesse) *to stimulate* ‖ jds Mut wieder ~ *to put new c. into a p* **II.** ≗ n ⟨mil⟩ *rouse*, *reveille*, *the first post* **W·ecker** m ~s/~ *awakener*, *waker* ‖ (Uhr) *alarum-clock*, ⟨Am⟩ *alarm c.* ‖ ⟨telph⟩ *alarm--bell* ‖ ⟨tech, el⟩ *generator* | ⟨fig⟩ ~ der Lebensgeister *eye opener* | °(P) jdm auf den ~ fallen *to throw a p into a tizzy*; (S) das fällt mir auf den ~ ⟨sl⟩ *that gets my goat* **~batterie** f ⟨el⟩ *ringing-b.* **~knopf** m ⟨el⟩ *bell-push* **~vorrichtung** f *alarm--apparatus*

W·eda m ~s/~s & –den ⟨Ind⟩ (heilige Schrift) *Veda*

W·edel m ~s/~ *brush*, *whisk* ‖ (Staub≗) *duster* ‖ (Fächer) *fan* ‖ ⟨hunt⟩ *brush*; (Rotwild≗) *single* ‖ ⟨bot⟩ *frond*; [pl koll] *frondage*; mit ~n besetzt etc *frondose* **~bürste** f *whisk*; *sprinkling--brush* **w·edeln** vt/i [h] *to fan* ‖ mit dem Schwanze, ⟨hors⟩ Schweife ~ *to wag the tail* (*the horse whisks with his tail*), (*the dog wags his t.*); ⟨fig⟩ *to fawn* (vor *upon*), *cringe*, *crawl* (*before*) | ⟨ski⟩ *to wedel*

w·eder [conj]; ~ .., noch (*or* *weder) .. *neither .. nor ..* (*neither he nor she has* [!] *done it*) | (nach Negation) *either .. or ..*: *it wasn't either he or she*; *without either youth or health* | *I neither saw him or wrote to him*

°×**weeß Kn·eppchen**! *by Jing*(*o*)

Weg [ve:k] m ~(e)s/~e **A.** *way*, *path* ‖ in der Mitte des ~es *midway* [adv] ‖ *lane* (⟨a.⟩ Hecken≗) ‖ (Abschneide≗) *cut* ‖ (Reise≗) *route* ‖ (Landstraße) *road* ‖ (Gang) *walk*, (kl) *turn*; (Besorgung) *errand* ‖ (Durchgang) *passage* ⟨a. anat⟩ ‖ ~ hinab *descent* ‖ ~ unter etw *subway* | ⟨anat⟩ *tract* (*seminal and urinary t.s*) | ⟨comp⟩ *trunk* | ⟨fig⟩ (Art, Methode) *manner*, *means*; *approach* (zu *to*) ‖ (Handlungsweise) *course* ‖ *path* (*of peace*) ‖ *line* (*of least resistance*) ‖ *approach* (*to a p's heart*) ‖ *avenue* (*to fame*, *of wealth*) ‖ *journey* (*through life*) ‖ *trend* (*in the direction of* [zu] *stream-lined bodies*) **B. enger** ~ *alley*(*way* ⟨Am⟩), ⟨fig⟩ *bottle-neck* (*of liberty*) ‖ gedeckter ~ *masked road*, ⟨fort⟩ *covert-way* ‖ der gerade ~ ist der beste *honesty is the best policy* ‖ ein langer, weiter ~ *a long distance* ‖ kein leichter ~ *no royal road* (*to success*) ‖ der einzig mögliche ~ ⟨a.⟩ *the only possible tack* ‖ mühseliger ~ *trudge* ‖ der nächste ~ *the nearest way* bzw *route*, *the shortest cut* ‖ steiniger ~ *rocky way* ⟨a. fig⟩ ‖ Verbotener ~! *No thoroughfare*!, *Private*! ‖ vernünftiger ~ ⟨a.⟩ *logic* **C. [im gen]** (vgl ..wegs) e–e Meile ~s *the distance of a m.* ‖ ein tüchtiges Stück ~s *a good distance* ‖ e–e Stunde ~s *an hour's drive*, etc | s–s ~es (s–r ~e) gehn *to go* (*on*) *one's way*, ⟨Scot⟩ *to gang one's gait* ‖ geh d–r ~e! *be off*!, *go about your business*! ‖ desselben ~es mit e–m gehen *to come a p's way*, *to go the same way as a p* ‖ e–n s–r ~e gehen l *to let a p be* od *alone* ‖ des ~es k *to come walking along*, (zufällig) *to happen along* | woher (wohin) des ~s? *where do you come from* (*where are you going*)? **D.** sich [selbst] e–n ~ **bahnen** *to fight* (*plough*, *push*, *thrust*, *weave*) *one's way*, [⟨fig⟩ *to strike out for o.s.*, *to carve out a career for o.s.* ‖ jdm den ~ bereiten ⟨fig⟩ *to blaze the trail for a p* ‖ ~e besorgen *to run* (od *go on*) *errands* | den ~ **ebnen** *to clear the way* ‖ e–n Weg einschlagen *to take a route* od *turning*, ⟨fig⟩ *to take a line*, *to adopt a course*, (falschen a.) *to mistake the way*, (neuen) ⟨fig a.⟩ *to make a new departure*, (eigenen) ⟨fig a.⟩ *to strike out a line of one's own* | ~e **finden** *to arrange* (*to do*) ‖ ⟨prov⟩ alle ~e führen nach Rom *there are many roads to R.* | ~e **gehen** = ~e besorgen ‖ den selben ~ g. mit → C. ‖ sie g. jeder s–n ~ *they go their several ways* ‖ e–n so weiten ~ g., um z .. *to come all this way to ..*; s–n ~ allein g. ⟨fig⟩ *to plow a lonely furrow*; den kürzesten ~ g. *to take the shortest cut* ‖ völlig neue ~e g. ⟨tech⟩ (of device) *to take entirely new forms* ‖ *he trod once again all the paths which* ‖ s–n eigenen ~ g. ⟨fig⟩ *to strike out for o.s.*, *to follow the bent of one's own mind*, ⟨fam⟩ *to cut the painter* ‖ ⟨bib⟩ *to go the way of all flesh* ⟨a. übtr sex⟩ | denselben ~ **h** *to be bound in the same direction*, (*their ways lay together*), .. wie jd *to go a p's way* ‖ wir h noch e–n kl ~ vor uns *we have still a little way to go*; .. weiten .. nach *we are still a long way from ..* ‖ nur den einen (gangbaren) ~ l als .. *to leave no other way to turn than* ⟨a. fig⟩ ‖ ⟨fig⟩ es hat (damit) gute ~e *there is no danger*, *there is no hurry for that*, ⟨iron⟩ *we shall not see it in a hurry* ‖ ~e u Stege **kennen** *to know all the ins and outs* ‖ jds ~ kreuzen *to cross a p's path* ‖ s–n ~ nehmen *to pick one's way* (*through ..*) | s–n ~ **suchen** *to pick one's way* (*carefully*); sich s–n (Lebens-)~ selbst suchen *to map out a career for o.s.* ‖ jdm den ~ weisen *or* zeigen *to show a p the way*, *to direct* od *guide a p*; ⟨fig⟩ *this points the way to the later phase*; jdm den richtigen ~ w. ⟨fig⟩ *to put a p right* ‖ e–n s–e ~e weisen *to*

send a p about his business || neue ~ weisen *to take the lead* || s–n ruhigen ~ weitergehen *to go on one's own way quietly* || denselben ~ zurückgehen *to retrace one's steps*; jdn den alten ~ zurückführen ⟨fig⟩ *to start a p back on his way* **E. am ~e** *by the roadside* | **auf dem ~e** *on the way, approaching, at hand* || (*to go shopping*) *on the way*; (*to visit friends*) *on one's way to* ..; .. zu .. *on the road to* ..; (*he was shot*) *while on his way to* ..; (*he escaped*) *by the route to*; (*to stray*) *by the way*; (*to go back*) *by the same way* || auf dem geraden ~ bleiben ⟨fig⟩ *to keep straight* || auf dem richtigen ~ s *to be on the beam*; auf dem ~e s nach ⟨a.⟩ *to be on the move to*; .. z Erfolg s *to be in a fair way* ..; über *via* (*Hamburg*), *by way of* (*the Strand*) || .. zu (*to be*) *in the way* (*to get, to become*) || auf dem ~ z ihr *on his* od *the way to her house* || *on his road to becoming an officer* | auf dem besten ~e *getting on*; *on the* (*high*)*road* (z .. *to success*). *well on the way* (*to*), *in a fair way* (*to*) || auf dipl. ~e *through diplomatic channels* || auf direktem ~ *by the direct road* || auf dem ganzen ~e *all the way* || die S ist auf gutem ~e *the matter is fairly progressing* || auf gütlichem ~e *amicably* || e–m auf halbem ~e entgegenkommen *to meet a p halfway* ⟨a. fig⟩ || ⟨chem⟩ auf nassem ~e *by moist process* || auf den rechten ~ bringen *to put in the right way* || auf offiziellem (zugelassenem) ~e *through official* (*authorized*) *channels* || auf dem schnellsten ~e (melden) .. *by the most expeditious means*; auf dem vorgeschriebenen ~e *through the prescribed channels* | auf dem ~e der Besserung *mending, on the mending hand, on the improve*, a. d. ~e d. Erfahrung *experimentally*, a. d. ~e d. Güte *amicably* | Glück **auf den** ~! *good luck*! | auf den ~ bringen *to despatch, send*, ⟨fig⟩ *introduce, start*; .. gebracht w v *to get a fair start from* || wird sofort .. gebracht *is being dispatched at once* || jdm etw auf den ~ geben *to give a p sth to take with him* || sich auf den ~ m *to start*; *to start* od *go* (*to set out*) *on one's way, to set off*, ⟨fam⟩ *to be getting along*, .. nach *to set out for* (*the town*) || auf d. rechten ~ zurückführen *to correct a p* | **aus dem ~e gehen** *to stand aside, to get out of the way*; jdm (weit) .. *to make way for, to get out of a p's way*, ⟨fig⟩ *to withdraw from a p, to give a p the go-by* (*to give a p a wide berth*) || (e–r S) *to walk* od *get away from* (*a danger*); *to side-step* (*a question*); (vermeiden) *to avoid* (*a p*), *shun, dodge, shirk, blink* (*a th*) || das liegt **aus** *or* **außer m-m ~e** *that is out of my way*, ⟨fig⟩ .. *not in my line, I know nothing of that* || → räumen | gut **bei ~e s** *to be in good health* | **im** ~e Rechtens *by law* || im ~e e–r Verordnung *by way of a regulation* | jdm **in den ~ k** (P) *to fall in with a p, to get in a p's way*; (S) *everything that came his way* || e–m in den ~ laufen (P) *to run into a p*('*s arms*); (S) *to occur to, befall, thwart a p* || e–m etw in den ~ legen *to oppose a p*, (Hindernisse) *to put difficulties into a p's way, to thwart a p*('*s plans*), (nichts) *to give a p no let or hindrance* || in die ~e leiten *to start, initiate, effect, prepare*; *to bring about, arrange for, set afoot, see to*; e–n Plan in die ~e leiten *to launch a plan* | im ~e s *or* stehen *to be in the way*; [dat] *to be* od *stand in the way of, to oppose, impede*; ⟨ftb⟩ *obstruct*; (e–r Ehe) *to vitiate* || nichts steht dem im ~e, daß sie tun *nothing prevents them from doing* || was steht [dat] im ~e? *what's wrong with* (*a game*)? || sich selbst im ~e stehen *to stand in one's own light, to act against one's own interest*; vor allem .. *to be one's own first obstacle* || sich jdm in den ~ stellen, jdm in den ~ treten *to put obstacles in a p's path*; *to oppose, cross, thwart a p* | jdm **über den** ~ laufen *to come across a p* || ich traue ihm nicht über den ~ *I do not trust him out of sight* | jdn **vom ~e** abführen *to lead a p out of the way* || vom (rechten) ~e abk *to lose one's way*, ⟨fig⟩ *to stray from the right path* || von wegen → wegen || **zu** ~e → zuwege ||
weg [vek, veç] adv **A.** *away*; *gone* (*the charm is g.*), *lost* | [ell] sie sind ~(gegangen) *they are gone*; wir w 2 St. ~ s *we shall be 2 hours*; ganz ~ s = → außer B. 3. sich s || wir wollen ~ *let's be off*! || ~ wie der Blitz *off like a shot* **B. hinter-**e–a ~ *one after another, in rapid succession* | **in** einem ~ *without stopping*, ⟨fam⟩ *at one go* || 6 Monate in e–m ~ *6 consecutive months* | **über** etw (hin)~ s *to be beyond, have passed a th* | ~ **von** London, ⟨univ⟩ Oxford *down* || weit ~ v *far away* od *back from* || °da ist das Ende v ~ *it's coming it too strong* **C.** ⟨fig⟩ (P) ganz *or* rein ~ *quite beside o.s.* (über *about*, vor *with* [*joy*]), *smitten* (*with love*) **D.** [intj] ~! *away with you*!; *be off* (da *there*) || frei ~! ⟨mil, gym⟩ *forward, march*! || frisch ~! *smartly*! *look alive*! || Hände ~! *hands off*! || Kopf ~! *look out for your head*! | ~ damit! *take it away*! || ~ **mit** .. *away with* ..; *spare* (*your compliments*)! || ~ mit dem! *nothing of that*! || ~ mit dir, Satan! *avaunt, s.*! | ⟨fam⟩ ~ mit Schaden *I sell it at a loss* | ~ davon! *keep off*! || **W·eg-** [ve:k] **~abkürzung** f *short cut*, ⟨Am⟩ *cut-off* **≗bahnend, ≗bereitend** a *pathbreaking* **~bereiter** m *pioneer*; *forerunner*; *initiator*; *trailblazer* || er war der ~ f Ibsen *he prepared the way for I.* **~genosse** m *fellow--traveller, travelling companion* **~gerechtigkeit** f *right of way* **≗lahm** a: ~ *or* ~müde s to be *marched-out* **~leitung** f Sw = Anweisung **~markierung** f *trail mark* **~scheide** f *cross-way* **~schnecke** f ⟨zoo⟩ *slug* **~strecke** f *stretch of road*; schlechte ⟨mot⟩ *bad surface* **~stunde** f *an hour's walk* **~übergang** m *crossing* | ~s-Läutewerk [n] *level-crossing bell*, ⟨Am⟩ *road-crossing b.* **~wart** m ⟨bot⟩ *chicory, succory* **≗weisend** a *leading* ⟨a. fig⟩; *heuristic* (*method*); *index* (*case*) **~weiser** m *finger-post, signpost*; ⟨Am⟩ *sign-, finger--board* || (Vor-)~ ⟨mot⟩ (*advance*) *direction board* od *sign*; ⟨bes mot⟩ *indicator board*; *route confirmation sign* || (P) *guide*; ⟨fig⟩ *pioneer* || (Buch) *guide-book, vademecum* | ⟨fig⟩ *heuristic principle* || *gradus* (*a g. to geography*) || *cue, hint, index* **~zehrung** f *food for the journey*; → Wege
weg [adv] (P) *gone* (v *on*); (*the sound is*) *out*
..weg [veç, vek] [adv suff] flott~ *boldly*; schlecht~ *plainly, simply*
w·eg.. [vek, veç] pref [betont, bei Verben immer trennbar] → weg ⟨mst⟩ *away, off* **w·eg-** (vgl fort-) **~|arbeiten** vt [h] *to work off* || etw ~ *to go through with* .. **~|ätzen** vt [h] *to corrode, cauterize* **~|begeben**: sich ~ irr [h] *to go away*; *to leave, withdraw* **~|beißen** vt irr [h] *to cut* (*a p*) *out*; → beißen **~|bek** vt irr [h] *to get away* || dabei etw ~ *to be the loser by it* || (lernen) *to get the knack of* || ⟨fam⟩ e–e ~ *to get a blow* **~|berufen** vt [h] *to call away* **~|beten** vt [h] *to get rid of by praying* **~|blasen** vt irr [h] *to blow away* || wie –ge– ⟨fig⟩ *without leaving a trace*, (Kopfschmerzen) *quite gone* **~|bleiben** vi irr [s] (P) *to stay away* || bleiben Sie davon weg! *keep off*! *don't meddle with it*! || bleiben Sie ja nicht weg! *be sure to come*! || er blieb nicht lange ~ *he was not long in coming back* | ⟨fig⟩ *to faint away* | (S) *to be omitted*; (Buchstabe etc) *to drop out* **~|blicken** vi [h] *to look away*; *to look another way*; ~ v *to take one's eye off* od *from* **~|brechen** vt irr [h] *to break off* **~|brennen** vt irr [h] *to burn away* | vi [s] *to burn down, to be burnt down* **~|bringen** vt irr [h] (P & S) *to take away* || er ist nicht –zu– ⟨fam⟩ *he sticks like glue* || *to remove*; (Flecken) *to take out* °**~|bugsieren** vt [h] *to pinch*; *to lead, shove* (*a p out of a crowd, out of a room*) **~|denken** vt irr [h] *to outthink, to imagine as not being there* || sich ~ *to fancy o.s. away* **~|disputieren** vt [h] *to argue away* **~|drängen** vt [h] *to push* od *edge away* || (P) ⟨fig⟩ *to cut out* **~|dürfen** vi irr [h]

to be permitted to go || darf ich weg? *may I leave?*

W·ege- **~amt** n *road-office* **~aufseher** m *surveyor of roads* **~bau** m *road-making* | ~meister [m] *constructor of roads* **~besserung** f *repair of the roads* **~biegung,** **~krümmung** f *bend (in a road)* **~dorn** m ⟨bot⟩ *buckthorn* **~enge** f *defile* **~geld** n *toll; pedage* | ~einnehmer [m] *toll-collector* **~kehre** f *serpentine* **~kreuzung** f *cross-roads* **~lagerer** m *way-layer, highwayman* **~̂lagern** vi [h] *to waylay travellers* || das ~̂ *highway robbery* **~meister** m = –aufseher **~messer** m ⟨tech⟩ *odometer* **~recht** n *highway regulations* | *right of passage* || *easement* **~̂reich** a *well-roaded (country)* **~säule** f *milestone* **~tritt** m ⟨bot⟩ *knot-grass* **~zoll** m = –geld; → ⟨a.⟩ Weg–

w·eg|eilen vi [s] *to hasten away* || ⟨fig⟩ ~ über *to hurry over, touch on, to skim (a th)* || → u.

w·egen prep [gen; ˣ& vulg dat] *on account (of), because (of), by reason (of)* | (infolge) *owing (to)* | (ˣ's isch nich' wege d·em, s'isch wege s·ellem *that*) | (um .. willen) *for the sake of, for* | (betreffs) *on behalf of; with regard to* | v Amts ~ *ex officio* L || v Polizei ~ *by order of the p.* || v Rechts ~ *by right* | ⟨fam⟩ v ~! *nothing doing!* | ~ m–r (⟨dial⟩ mir) = meinetwegen

W·egerich m ~(e)s/~e ⟨bot⟩ *plantain* || (Spitz~̂) *rib-grass*

w·eg- **~|essen** vt irr [h] *to eat up (greedily* od *quickly)* | ⟨fam⟩ jdn ~ *to give a p a farewell-dinner* **~|fahren** irr vt [h] *to carry away* | vi [s] *to drive away; to start, sail, depart* | ~ über *to drive over*; mit der Hand .. *to pass one's hand over ..* **~̂fall** m *omission; abolition, suppression* || (Aufhören) *cessation* || in ~ bringen *to abolish, suppress* || in ~ k = –fallen ⟨fig⟩ **~|fallen** vi irr [s] *to fall away* || *(the comma must) go* || (aufhören) *to cease* | ⟨fig⟩ (ausgelassen w) *to be omitted, dropped* || (abgeschafft w) *to be abolished, suppressed*; (Bestimmung) *to become void* || (ausfallen) *not to take place* **~|fangen** vt irr [h] *to snatch away, to intercept* **~|faulen** vi [s] *to rot away* od *off* **~|fegen** vt/i [h/s] *to sweep/hurry away* **~|feilen** vt [h] *to file off* **~|fischen** vt [h] ⟨fig⟩ *to snatch away* ([dat] *from*) **~|fliegen** vi irr [s] *to fly away* || ~ über .. *to fly over* **~|fressen** vt irr [h] *to eat off* od *away* **~|führen** vt [h] *to lead* od *carry away* **~|gabeln** vt [h] = –fischen **~̂gang** m *going away, departure* || beim ~ (aus) *on leaving (on going out of)* **~|geben** vt irr [h] *to give .. away*; ⟨com⟩ *to sell* || *to send .. away (to school, etc)* **~|gehen** vi irr [s] *to go away* od *off; to leave, depart* || eilig ~ *to hurry away* || e–n ~ heißen *to bid a p be gone* || über etw ~ *to pass over* od *ignore a th* | v/imps es geht weg *we are leaving* **~|gewöhnen** vt [h] e–n ~ v *to wean a p from* **~|gießen** vt irr [h] *to pour away* **~|haben** vt irr [h] *to have got* od *received (one's share)* || sie möchten .. ~ *they want to get rid of ..* | ⟨fig⟩ *to understand*, ⟨fam⟩ *to twig* || Sie h es weg *you have hit it* || etw schnell ~ *to be quick in seeing through a th* | e–n ~ ⟨fam⟩ *to be tipsy; to have bats in the belfry* || eins ~ *to catch a box on the ear* **~|halten** vt irr [h] *to keep off* od *away; to turn away* **~|hängen** vt irr [h] *to hang away* od *elsewhere* **~|haschen** vt [h] *to snatch away* **~|hauen** vt irr [h] *to cut off* od *away* **~|heben** vt irr [h] *to lift away* || hebe dich weg v mir! *begone!; avaunt, (satan)!* **~|helfen** vi irr [h] e–m ~ *to help a p to escape, to aid a p in his flight* **~|holen** vt [h] *to fetch away* **~|hüpfen** vi [s] *to hop away, to skip off* **~|huschen** vi [s] *to flit away* || ⟨fig⟩ über etw ~ *to skip over a th* **~|jagen** vt [h] *to drive away, to expel* (aus *from*); *to turn (a p) out* | vi [s] *to gallop off* **~|kapern** vt [h] *to capture (a ship)* || ⟨fig⟩ *to snatch away* **~|kaufen** vt [h] *to buy up* **~|kehren** vt [h] *to sweep away* || das Gesicht ~ *to turn one's face away* **~|kommen** vi irr [s] → fortk- || *to get away, to leave; to be moved* || mach' daß du –k.st! *begone!* ⟨fam⟩ wir m, daß wir ~ *we are off* | (abhanden k) *to be lost* || der Schlüssel ist (mir) –ge– .. *is missing (I have mislaid* od *lost ..)* || glücklich dabei ~ *to get away with it* || gut (schlecht) ~ *to come off well (badly)* (bei *over*); schlecht ~ *to get the thin end of the stick*; am besten dabei ~ *to have the best of it*; am schlimmsten ~ *to have* od *get the worst of it* || ~ über *to get over (a difficulty, etc) (I hope we shall tide over the d.)* **~|können** vi irr [h] *to be able to go* od *get away* || ich kann (wgen des Geschäfts) nicht weg *I cannot leave home (I am detained in business)* **~|kriegen** vt [h] ⟨fam⟩ = –bek **~|lassen** vt irr [h] = fort- **~̂lassung** f ~/~en *omission* **~|laufen** vi [s] *to run off* **~|lecken** vt [h] *to lick off* **~|legen** vt [h] *to put away, to lay aside* **~|leihen** vt [h] *to lend out* **~|leiten** vt [h] *to conduct to another place* || ⟨fig⟩ *to turn aside* **~|leugnen** vt [h] *to deny flatly* **~|loben** vt [h] *(to get rid of [an unpleasant p] by recommending him for another office), to kick (a p) upstairs* **~|löschen** vt [h] *to blot out, to efface* **~|machen** vt [h] *to take away, to remove* || (Flecken) *to take out* || ⟨fam⟩ → fortm 1. | sich ~ *to decamp, to get off; ..* v *to clear out from* **~|marschieren** vi [s] *to march away* od *off* **~|mögen** vi [h] *to like to leave* **~|müssen** vi irr [h] (P) *to be obliged to go* || ich muß weg *I must be off* || ⟨fig⟩ *to have to die* | (S) das muß weg *that must be removed*; der Baum muß weg *that tree must come down* **~̂nahme** f ~/ *taking (away)* || (Beschlagnahme) *seizure, confiscation* || (Festung, Schiff) *capture* **~|nehmen** vt irr [h] *to take* od *snatch away* (jdm *from a p*), *to deprive* od *strip a p of (a th), to strip (a th) from a p* || (Geschirr) *to collect, remove* || (Hand) *to take off* || *to withdraw (from school)* || ⟨mot⟩ (Gas) *to throttle down*, (Zündung) *to switch off (the engine)* || (Flecken) *to take out* || (beschlagnahmen) *to seize (upon)* || (Zeit, Raum) *to take up, to occupy* || (erobern) *to capture* | ~̂ n *removal* **~|packen** vt [h] *to pack away* || sich ~ ⟨fam⟩ *to take o.s. off, to pack off; ..* v *to clear out from* **~|praktizieren** vt [h] ⟨fam⟩ *to shuffle* od *spirit away* **~|prügeln** vt [h] *to drive off with cudgels* **~|putzen** vt [h] *to remove by cleaning* | ⟨fam⟩ (wegschießen) (jdn) *to bowl over*, ⟨Am⟩ *to rub out*; (aufessen) *to finish*; ⟨fam⟩ *to tuck in*; ⟨sl⟩ *to put out of sight, to polish off*; (stehlen) *to abstract* **~|radieren** vt [h] *to erase* **~|raffen** vt [h] *to snatch away* || *to carry off (by disease)* **~|rauben** vt [h] *to steal* || (Vieh) *to lift* **~|räumen** vt [h] *to clear .. away, to remove* (a. Hindernisse); ⟨min⟩ *to stow* **~̂reise** f *departure* **~|reisen** vi [s] *to depart, leave; to start (on a journey)* **~|reißen** vt irr [h] = fortr. || (Häuser) *to pull down*; (vom Sturm) *to carry off*; (P) alles mit sich ~ *to carry all before one* **~|reiten** vi irr [s] = fortr. **~|rennen** vi irr [s] = fortr. **~|rollen** vt [h] & vi [s] = fortr. **~|rücken** vt [h] = fortr. | vi [s] *to draw off, to edge away, to withdraw* **~|rudern** vi [s] *to row away* | *to row away; to push off* (⟨a.⟩ vt [h] Boot) **~|rufen** vt irr [h] = fortrufen **~|sacken** vi [s] = absacken **~|sägen** vt [h] *to saw off* **~|schaben** vt [h] *to shave* od *scrape off* **~|schaffen** vt [h] → fortsch. || (⟨a.⟩ Hindernisse); *to clear .. away, to get rid of, to dispose of ..* || ⟨arith⟩ *to eliminate* **~̂schaffung** f *removal, riddance; elimination* **~|scharren** vt [h] *to rake away* **~|schenken** vt [h] *to give away* **~|scheren** vt irr [h] *to clip* || (Bart) *to shave off* | ⟨fam⟩ sich ~ *to take o.s. off, to be* od *toddle off* **~|scherzen** vt [h] *to joke away, to laugh off* **~|scheuchen** vt [h] *to frighten* od *scare away* **~|schicken** vt [h] = fort- **~|schieben** vt irr [h] *to shove away, to remove* **~|schießen** irr vt [h] *to shoot away, to kill (off) by shooting*, ⟨fam⟩ *to bowl over* | vi [s] *to dart* od *shoot off* **~|schlagen** vt irr [h] = fort- **~|schleichen**: (sich) ~ irr [h]

= fort- **~|schleifen** vt irr [h] *to grind off* od *away* **~|schleppen** vt [h] = fort- **~|schleudern** vt [h] → fort- 1. **~|schließen** vt [h] = fort- °**~|-schmeißen** vt irr [h] *to throw* .. *away*; ⟨fam⟩ *to chuck* .. *up* **~|schmelzen** irr vi [s] *to melt away* | vt [h] *to melt off* **~|schnappen** vt [h] *to snatch away* ([dat] *from*); *to take* (*the bread*) *out of a p's mouth* **~|schneiden** vt irr [h] *to cut away*; *to retrench* || ⟨hort⟩ *to lop off* || ⟨surg⟩ *to amputate*; (heraus-) *to excise* **~|schnellen** vt [h] *to fling away* **~|schreiten** vi [s] über .. *to stride across* .. **~|schütten** vt [h] = fort- **~|schwemmen** vt [h] *to wash* od *sweep away* **~|segeln** vi [s] *to sail away*; ~ nach .. *to set sail for* .. **~|sehen** vi irr [h] *to look away* od *the other way* || ⟨fig⟩ über etw [acc] ~ *to shut one's eyes to a th* || ⟨fig⟩ über jdn ~ *to cut a p dead* **~|sehnen**: sich ~ [h] *to wish o.s. away, to long to get away* **~|sein** vi irr [s] *to be gone, to be away* || (nicht zu finden) *to be lost* || °er war ganz weg v ihr *he was real gone on her* || über etw [acc] ~ ⟨fig⟩ *to be above* (*minding*) *a th* **~|senden** vt irr [h] *to send away* **~|sengen** vt [h] *to singe* (*off*) **~|setzen** vt [h] *to put away* || ⟨fig⟩ sich über etw [acc] (andere) ~ *to be above a th, to disregard a th* (*to think o.s. superior to other people*) | vi [s] (über [acc]) *to jump* (*over*), *to clear* (*a th*) **~|sollen** vi [h] = fortmüssen **~|sprengen** vt [h] & vi [s] = fort- **~|spülen** vt [h] *to wash away* || (Ufer) *to encroach upon* **~|stechen** vt [h] *to remove with sth pointed* || *to carry off* (*the ring in tilting*) **~|stecken** vt [h] *to put away* || (ver–) *to hide* **~|stehlen** vt irr [h] & sich ~ → fort– **~|stellen** vt [h] = fort– **~|sterben** vi irr [s] *to die away* od *off* **~|stoßen** vt irr [h] = fort– **~|streichen** vt irr [h] *to rub away, to erase* || *to take off* (*a number*, etc) || *to smooth away* (⟨a.⟩ Haare) **~|strömen** vi [s] *to stream off, to flow away* **~|stürmen, ~|stürzen** vi [s] = fort- **~|tragen** vt irr [h] = fort- 1. **~|treiben** irr vt [h] *to drive away* | vi [s] *to drift away* **~|treten** vi irr [s] *to step aside* || ⟨mil⟩ *to break the ranks*; –(ge)–! *fall out*! *dismiss*! | ~ l ⟨mil⟩ *to dismiss* **~|tun** vt irr [h] *to put away* od *aside, to remove*; *to put in a safe place* || *to discard, junk* || tu die Hände weg! *hands off*! **~|wagen** v/refl = fortw. **~|wälzen** vt [h] = fortw. **~|wandern** vi [s] = fortw. **~|waschen** vt irr [h] *to wash away* **~|wehen** vt [h] *to blow away* od *off* **~|weisen** vt irr [h] = fortw. **~|wenden** vt reg & irr [h] (sich) ~ *to turn away* od *off* od *aside* || (das Gesicht) *to avert* **~|werfen** vt irr [h] *to chuck away*; *to throw away* (a. Geld) || ⟨cards⟩ *to throw out* || (als unbrauchbar) *to reject* | sich ~ *to abase, degrade, lower o.s.* || sich ~ an *to throw o.s. away upon* (*a p*) **~|werfend** a *disparaging, disdainful, deprecating, supercilious* **~werfpackung** f *lost container pack* **~werfwindel** f *disposable napkin* **~|wischen** vt [h] *to wipe away* || °e–n ~ *to have a drink* **~|wollen** vi irr [h] *to want to go* || nicht ~ *to refuse to go* **~|wünschen** vt [h] *to wish away* **~|zaubern** vt [h] *to spirit away* || wie weggezaubert *dissolved in thin air* **~|zerren** vt [h] *to tear* od *drag away* **~|ziehen** irr vt [h] → fort- || *to draw* od *pull away*; ⟨theat⟩ *to fly* | vi [s] *to march away* || (den Wohnsitz wechseln) *to* (*re*)*move, leave* || ⟨orn⟩ *to migrate* **≈zug** m *removal, departure,* (*e*)*migration*

Weh n ~(e)s/ *pain* || (seelisch) *grief, pang, woe* || *misfortune* || *cry of woe*; mit ~ u Ach *with groans and lamentations* **w·eh(e) I.** [intj] *woe*!, *alas*! || au ~! *oh, oh*! ~ mir! *woe is me* || ~ ihm *woe betide him*!; *woe to him* (*if he* ..) || ~ u ach schreien *to lament* **II.** [a] **1.** [attr] *painful* (*impressions*) || *sore* (*anger*; *finger*, etc) || *sorrowful* (*feeling*) **2.** [pred *or* adv] mir **ist** ~ ums Herz *or* zumute *my heart aches, I am sick at heart* || es ist mir ~ danach *I long for it* | [dat] ~ **tun** *to cause pain to* (*a p*); *to ail* || (seelisch) *to pain, hurt, offend, distress*; .. unbewußt .. *to give a p unwitting pain* || der Kopf (die Schulter) tut mir ~ *my h. aches* (*my sh. hurts* [*me*]) || es tat ihm ~ *he smarted* (*inwardly*) || tat es ~? *did it hurt*? || .. tut mir an den Ohren ~ *that grates upon my ears* || das tut mir in der Seele ~ *that cuts* od *grieves me to the heart*; *it gives me a pain in my heart* || es tut mir ~ z sehen *it pains me to see* || ⟨fig⟩ ihm tut kein Zahn mehr ~ *his troubles are at an end* | **sich** [dat] ~ tun *to hurt o.s.* || ich tat mir dabei an den Augen ~ *I hurt my eyes with it* || ohne sich selbst –zu– *without any hurt to o.s.* **Weh- -dag** m ~s/~e [niedd] = Schmerz; Unglück; Krankheit **~frau** f *midwife* **~gefühl** n *feeling of grief* od *sadness* **~gesang** m *plaintive song* **~geschrei** n *woeful cries, screams of pain, wailings* pl **~klage** f *lament*(*ation*), *wailing* **≈klagen** vi [h] (über [acc]) *to lament* (*for, over*), *to wail* (*over*); *to sing sorrow* **≈leidig** a *sorry for o.s., plaintive, lackadaisical*; ⟨fam⟩ *ouchy, snivelling*; ~ tun *to snivel* **~mut** f (*tender*) *sadness,* (*pensive, tender*) *melancholy*; *woefulness*; *ache in one's heart*; nachdenkliche ~ *wistfulness*; in ~ aufgelöst *suffused with tender m.* **≈mütig** a *sad*; *melancholy*; *doleful*; *wistful* **~mutter** f *midwife* **~tag** m [obd] = –dag **~w·ehchen** n ~s/~ ⟨fam⟩ *little pain*; *sore place*; ⟨fig⟩ *trouble, complaint* **W·ehe** f ~/~n; [oft pl]: *throes* pl (*of childbirth*), *labour-pains*; lange in ~n liegen *to be long in labour* od *travail*

W·ehe f ~/~n (Sand≈, Schnee≈) *drift of* .. | **≈n I.** vi [h] (Wind, Staub etc) *to blow*; *to waft* ⟨a. poet⟩; *to breeze* || (flattern) *to fly, flutter, stream, wave*; ~ l *to fly* (*a flag*) || es weht ein starker Wind (kein Lüftchen) *there is a strong wind* (*not a breath stirring*) **II.** vt [h] *to blow along, to drift* | **~n-** ~mittel [n] *ecbolic, oxytoric*

Wehr n ~(e)s/~e *dam*; (Wasser≈) *weir* | ~bau [m] *dam*; ~baum [m] *barrier*; ~damm [m] *mole*; ~kante [f] *w. crest* **Wehr** f ~/~en *defence, resistance* | (Waffe) *weapon*; schimmernde ~ *shining armour* || ⟨zoo⟩ *tusk* | ⟨fort⟩ *bulwark* | *body of armed men* | sich zur ~ setzen *to offer resistance, to show fight, to get on one's hind legs* ⟨fig⟩; .. kräftig .. *to make a fight of it*; ..laut .. *to cry remonstrance*; (v Wild) *to stand* od *turn at bay* ⟨a. fig⟩ || mit ~ u Waffen *fully armed* **~anstalten** f pl *preparations for defence* **~auftrag** m *defence* (⟨Am⟩ –se) *order* **~beauftragte(r)** m *deputy in military affairs* **~bereichskommando** n (WBK) *military district c.*; *HQ, M. D.* .. **~bereitschaft** f *preparedness* **~bezirk** m *military district* **~bez·irkskommando** n *recruiting office*; *Enlistment* (⟨Am⟩ *Selective*) *Command* **~dienst** m *service with the armed forces*; *colour* od *military s.* | ~beschädigung [f] *disability incurred in line of duty*; ~entlassene(r) [m] ⟨Am⟩ *separatee*; ~entlassung [f] *civilianization*; ≈untauglich [a] *unfit* (*for active* od *mil. s.*); ⟨rel⟩ ~verweigerer [m], Gegner des ~es *conscientious objector*; ⟨fam⟩ *conchy*; aktiver ~ *active duty* **~ers·atz-** ~amt [n] *recruiting office*; ~verwaltung [f] *r.g administration*; **~zentrale** f *Enlistment* (⟨Am⟩ *State Selective*) *Service Headquarters* pl **~ertüchtigung** f *physical culture,* (*pre-*)*mil. training* **≈fähig** a *able-bodied, fit*; *capable of bearing arms* || → –haft | ~keit [f] *ability to bear arms* **~gang** m ⟨hist⟩ *wall passage* **~geist** m *spirit* **~gehänge, ~gehenk** n *shoulder--belt,* (*sword-*)*belt* **~gesetz** n *national defence law, Army Act* **~gestell** n *gun-rack* **≈haft** a = –fähig || ⟨a.⟩ *valiant, armipotent* **~hoheit** f *armament* od *mil. sovereignty* **~kirche** f *fortified church* **~kraft** f *military power, fighting strength* | ~zersetzung [f] *undermining the willingness to serve and the discipline of the Forces* **~kreis** m *district of an army corps* **≈los** a *unarmed, defenceless* || ⟨fig⟩ *weak, unprotected* || ~ m *to disarm* **~losigkeit** f *defencelessness* **~macht** f (*mil.* od *armed*) *forces* pl **~machtbericht** m *bulletin* Fr **~machtteil** m *service* **~mann** m *warrior*; *militiaman* **~minister** m *Minister for Home Defence* **~nummer** f *service number* N **~ordnung** f *army statute*; *conscription regulations* **~paß** m *service and conduct book* **~pflicht** f *obligation to serve in the army* ‖ allgemeine (*universal*) *compulsory* (*military*) *service*; (*universal*) *conscription*; *universal service system* **≗-pflichtig** a *liable to military service* | (einberufener) ≗e(r) [m] *national service man*; *inductee* **≗politisch** a *politico-strategic* **~sold** m *soldier's* od (*war*) *service pay*; ⟨mar⟩ *wages* pl **~sport** m *mil. sports* pl **~stamm-** ~nummer [f] *personal number*; ~rolle [f] *service* od *personnel roster* **~stand** m *mil. profession* ‖ *mil. classes* pl; *the military*, *the army* **~steuer** f *mil. tax*, ⟨Ger⟩ *defence* (⟨Am⟩ *-se*)*-tax* **~überwachung** f *counter-espionage* **~-übung** f *refresher course* **≗unwürdig** a *unworthy to bear arms* **~verein** m *national defence league* **~verfassung** f *mil. organization* **~verhältnis** n *service status* **~vorlage** f ⟨parl⟩ *Army Bill* **~wesen** n *mil. matters* pl **~wille** m *morale*; *moral armament* **~wirtschaft** f *defence economics* **≗wirtschaftlich** a *military* **~wissenschaft** f *mil. science* | ~ler [m] *soldier scientist* **~zahn** m ⟨zoo⟩ *tusk*

w·ehren I. vi [h] [dat] *to restrain*, *obviate*, *prevent*, *check* (*she checks the boys*) ‖ *to curb* (*a th*) ‖ *to repel* (*an attack*) ‖ dem Feuer ~ *to arrest the spread of the fire* | e–m etw ~ *to stop* od *keep a p from doing a th*, *to forbid a p to do a th* ‖ wer will es ~? *who prevents it*? **II. sich** ~ (gegen) *to defend o.s.*, *to fence*; *to fight back*; *to offer resistance* (*against*); *to resist*; *to set one's mind against*; sich tüchtig ~ *to make a good defence* ‖ sich gegen e–n Gedanken ~ *to demur to an idea* ‖ sich mit Händen u Füßen ~ *to fight tooth and nail* | sich s–r Haut, s–s Lebens ~ *to fight for one's life*

Weib n ~(e)s/~er **1.** *woman* (ganz ~ *all w.*); ⟨cont⟩ *female*; ⟨sl⟩ *tart*, ⟨Am⟩ *jane* ‖ die ~er *womankind* ‖ altes ~ *harridan* ‖ böses ~ *vixen*; *shrew* ‖ schönes ~ ⟨a.⟩ *lovely creature* ‖ ein Dragoner v e–m ~e *a grenadier of a w.* **2.** (Ehefrau) *wife* ‖ zum ~e geben *to give .. in marriage* ‖ zum ~e nehmen *to take for a wife*; *to marry* [vt] **W·eibchen** n ~s/~ *little woman* od *wife*; *wifie*; ⟨zoo⟩ *female*, *she*; ⟨orn⟩ *hen* **W·eiber- ~arbeit** f *women's work* **~art** f *women's ways* pl **~einfluß** m *petticoat influence* **~feind** m *woman-hater*, *misogynist* **~feindschaft** f *enmity between women* ×**~gedöns**, **~gehabe**, **~getue** n *women's fuss* **~geklatsch**, **~geschwätz** n *women's gossip* **~gunst** f *favour of women* ‖ ⟨prov⟩ ~ ist wie Aprilwetter *women are as fickle as April-weather* **~haß** m *hatred of women*; *misogyny* **~hasser** m = –feind **~haus** n *harem* ‖ *brothel* **~held** m *lady-killer*, *ladies' man*, *carpetknight*; ⟨sl⟩ *wolf* **~herrschaft** f *petticoat-government* **~knecht** m = –held **~krieg** m *women's war* **~laune** f *feminine whim* **~leh(e)n** n *female fief* **~liebe** f **1.** *love for women* **2.** *woman's love* **~list** f *women's wile*(*s* pl) od *artfulness* **~narr** m *amorous fellow who runs after every petticoat* **~raub** m *rape*, *abduction* **~regiment** n = –herrschaft **~rock** m *petticoat* **~sache** f *women's concern* **≗scheu** a *afraid of women* **~schläue** f *womancraft* **~sommer** m = Alt≗ **~staat** m *women's finery* **~stamm** m *female line* **≗toll** a *mad after women* **~tracht** f *female apparel* **~volk** n ⟨fam⟩ *womenfolk* **~zwinger** m *harem*

w·eiberhaft a *womanlike* ‖ ⟨dero a.⟩ **weibisch** a *womanish*, *effeminate* ‖ ~er Mann ⟨sl⟩ *nan-boy*, *Nancy* (*boy*)

W·eibesschönheit f *female beauty* **..weibig** a ⟨bot⟩ drei~ *having three pistils* **w·eiblich** a *womanly* ‖ *feminine* ⟨a. gram, pros⟩ | *wifely* (*fidelity*) | ⟨bot, zoo⟩ *female* | ~e Arbeitskräfte *woman-power* ‖ ~e Gäste *women guests* ‖ ~es Getue, ~e Geschäftigkeit *frou-frou* ⟨fig⟩ ‖ ~e Linie *spindle side* ‖ ~es Mitglied des Stabes ⟨hum⟩ *distaff staffer* ‖ ~es Stimmrecht *women's vote*, dessen Anhänger *woman suffragist* ‖ das ewig W.e *the Eternal Woman* ‖ viel W.es *much that is feminine* od *womanly* | **≗keit** f [abstr] *femininity*; *womanliness*; *womanhood*; ⟨a.⟩ *feminality* ‖ *feminine charm*, *reserve*, *weakness*, etc ‖ [koll] *women* pl, *womankind* ‖ die holde ~ *the fair sex* **Weibs- ~bild** n ⟨fam⟩ *female* ‖ ⟨hum *or* cont⟩ *baggage*, *wench*, *hussy* ‖ liederliches ~ *slut* **~leute** pl *females* pl **~person** f, **~stück** n *female*; ⟨Am sl⟩ *twist*, *skirt* **~volk** n *womankind*, *women* pl °**W·eibsen** n ~s/~ = Weibsbild ‖ ⟨hum⟩ [pl] *womenfolk*

†**W·eibel** m ~s/ → Amts–, Gerichtsdiener | ~stab [m] *mace*

weich a **A.** *soft* (⟨a.⟩ *hair*, *iron*, *water*) ‖ sich ~ anfühlend *s. to the touch* ‖ *soft*(*-boiled*) (*eggs*) **B.** *silky* (*hair*) ‖ (Flausch, Haar) *fluffy* ‖ *mellow* (*fruits*) ‖ *slack* (*dough*) ‖ *woolly* (*air*) ‖ *velvety* (*wine*) | ⟨mus⟩ *soft*, *sweet*, *melodious* (*tune*); ~e Tonart *minor key*; ⟨paint⟩ *melted*, *blended* (Farben) **C.** (geschmeidig) *supple* ‖ (glatt) *smooth* ‖ (Flugzeug im Ruder) *sloppy* **D.** ⟨fig⟩ *soft*, *tender*, *gentle*, *sympathetic*, *sensitive*, ⟨bib⟩ *faint* (*heart*) ‖ (Gemütsart) *gentle* (*disposition*) ‖ *lyrical* ‖ (schwach) *weak*, *effeminate* **E.** Fleisch ~ kochen *to boil meat until tender* | ~ m *to tenderize* (*meat*); *to soften* (a. Stahl); ⟨fig⟩ *to move* | ~ w *to soften* (⟨a. fig⟩ Herz), ⟨fig⟩ *to be moved* od *touched*; *to relent* (gegen *towards*) ‖ es wird mir ~ ums Herz *my heart is melting* ‖ ⟨fam⟩ nur nicht ~ w! *keep a stiff upper-lip*!; das machte ihn ~ in den Knien ⟨fam⟩ *that gave him the jitters* **≗blei** n *soft lead* **≗bottich** m, **≗faß** n *steeping-tub*, *-vat* **≗fresser** m *insect-eating bird* **~geglüht** a ⟨met⟩ *annealed* **~gekocht**, **~gesotten** a *soft-boiled* **~gestimmt** a *in a gentle mood* **≗grad** m ⟨brew⟩ *steep* [attr]; *ripeness* **≗grundverfahren** n ⟨engr⟩ *soft ground*; *verni mon* Fr **~herzig** a *tender-hearted*, *soft* | ≗keit [f] *t.-h.ness*, *softness*; *emotionalism* **≗holz** n *softwood* **≗käse** m *cream-cheese* **≗kübel** m = –faß **~lande-** ~fahrzeug, ~flugzeug [n] *softlander* **≗löten** n *soft soldering* **≗macher** m ⟨chem⟩ *softener*; (Kunststoff≗) *plasticizer* **~-mäulig** a ⟨hors⟩ *tender-mouthed* **~mütig** = –herzig **≗porzellan** n *frit-porcelain* **~schalig** a *soft-shelled* ‖ *soft-skinned* (*fruits*) **≗strahler** m ⟨phot⟩ *flood lamp* **≗tier** n *mollusc* **≗wasser** n *water for soaking* **≗zeichner** m ⟨phot⟩ *Duto lens*

W·eiche[1] f ~/~n ⟨poet⟩ *softness* ‖ ⟨bes brew⟩ *steep* ‖ ⟨anat⟩ *side*, *flank*; pl *groin* | ~ngegend [f] *groin*; *inguinal region* **w·eichen**[1] vt/i [h & s] *to soften*, *soak* | vt *to steep*

W·eichbild n *precincts*, *outskirts* (*of a town*)

W·eiche[2] f ~/~n ⟨rail⟩ *switch*, *siding*, *shunt* ‖ die ~n (um)stellen *to shift* (*reverse*) *the points*

weichen[2] **I.** vi [wich/gewichen] [s] *to give* od *make way* ([dat] *to*), *to lose ground* (a. v der Stelle ~), *to yield* ⟨a. fig⟩; nicht e–n Zoll ~ *not to give an inch of ground*; sein Blick wich nicht e–e Sekunde v .. *his eyes never left* (*the window*); ⟨fig⟩ *to give in* ‖ (Boden) *to sink in* | ⟨mil⟩ *to retreat* | ⟨st ex⟩ (Kurse) *to go down*, *to drop* ‖ ~de Preise *sinking*, *falling pr.* | **aus**: *the colour had fled his face*; *his rage had gone out of his voice* ‖ aus dem Wege ~ *to make room* | **von**: *the fragile quality had gone from his chin* ‖ *the irritation melted from her face* ‖ *all his vaunting had dropped away from him* ‖ v jdm ~ *to forsake*, *abandon a p* ‖ jdm nicht v der Seite ~ *not to budge from a p's side*, *to stick to a p* ‖ nicht v der Stelle ~ *not to budge* (⟨fig⟩ *bate*) *an inch* ‖ k–n Fingerbreit v Gottes Wegen ~ *never to forsake the path of virtue* ‖ v der Küste ~ *to make for the offing* **II.** ≗ n: z ~ bringen *to make* (*a p*) *yield*, *to drive* (*the enemy*) *back* ‖ ⟨st ex⟩ (Kurse) ins ~ k, im

~ s *to be falling off* od *receding* **W·eichen-**[2] **~bock** m *switch-box* **~laterne** f *point indicator lamp* **~schiene** f *siding-rail* **~sicherung** f *point locking* **~signal** n *switch-signal* **~stell-** ~er [m] *switchman, pointsman*; ~ung [f] *shifting* bzw *position of the points*; ~vorrichtung [f] *point-setting device*; ~stellwerk [n] *switch-stand* **~wechsel** m *change of line*

W·eichheit f ~/ *softness*; *smoothness*; *mellowness* || (Schwäche) *weakness* || (Zartheit) *tenderness* (a. Fleisch), ⟨fig a.⟩ *gentleness* **w·eichlich** a (*somewhat* od *too*) *soft*, *tender* | ⟨fig⟩ *weak*, *effeminate*; *milky* || *insipid*, *tame* (*style*) || (Gefühlsweise etc) *sloppy* || nichts ≗es ⟨fam⟩ *nothing sissy* (*about him*) | [adv] ~ aufgezogen *delicately brought up* | ≗keit f ~/ *softness*, *tenderness* | ⟨fig⟩ *weakness*, *effeminacy*; *milkiness* || *sloppiness* **W·eichling** m ~(e)s/~e *molly-coddle*, *milksop* | *voluptuary* || ⟨sl⟩ *pansy*, *nan-boy*, *Nancy* (*boy*), *sissy*

W·eichsel, die (Fluß) *the Vistula* †**W·eichselkorridor** m → Polnischer Korridor

W·eichsel f ~/~n ⟨bot⟩ *sour cherry*, *mahaleb* **~kirschbaum** m *mahaleb-tree* **~kirsche** f = ~ **~rohr** n *cherry-stick tube* **~zopf** m ⟨med⟩ *elflock*, *Polish plait*, ⟨scient⟩ *plica polonica*

Weid- ⟨hunt⟩ **~genosse, ~geselle** m *fellow-huntsman* ≗**gerecht** a *skilled*, *trained* **~geschrei** n *hunting-cry* **~mann** m *sportsman*, *huntsman* ≗**männisch** a *sportsmanlike* **~mannschaft** f *sportsmanship* **~mannsh·eil!** *good sport!*; *good hunting* ⟨a. fig⟩ **~mannssprache** f *hunters' slang* **~messer** n *hanger* **~recht** n *huntsmen's law* **~sack** m *game-bag* **~spruch** m *huntsman's salute* **~werk** n *chase*, *hunting*; ⟨obs⟩ *venery* || das edle ~ *the noble sport of hunting* || niederes ~ *small game* **~wort** n *hunting-term* ≗**wund** a *wounded in the bowels* || ~ schießen *to tailor*; (*a poor t.ing shot* [Ggs *a clean kill*]); → weidlich **W·eide**[1] f ~/~n (Vieh≗) *pasture*(*-ground*) (*to drive .. to pasture*) | ⟨fig⟩ (Augen≗) *delight*, *feast* **~grund** m, **~land** n, **~platz** m *pasture-ground*, *grazing* (*land*); ⟨Am⟩ *range* **~recht** n *right of pasture* **~vieh** n *grazing cattle* **~wirtschaft** f *pasture-farming* **w·eiden I.** vt vt [h] (Vieh) *to* (*lead .. to*) *pasture*; *to feed*; *to turn .. out to grass* || s–e Augen *or* Blicke an [dat] ~ *to feast one's eyes on* || **sich** ~ an *to revel in*, (boshaft) *to gloat over* od (*up*)*on* **II.** vi [h] *to pasture*, *graze*, *brouse*, *feed* ≗**lassen** n ⟨agr jur⟩ *agistment*

W·eide[2] f ~/~n ⟨bot⟩ → *willow* | **~n- ~bach** m *brook fringed with w.s* **~band** n *w.-band*, *withe* **~baum** m *w.*(*-tree*) **~bitter** n ⟨chem⟩ *salicin*(*e*) **~blatt** n *w.-leaf* **~bohrer** m ⟨ent⟩ *goat-moth* **~busch** m *w.-bush*, *osier-bush* **~erde** f *w.-mould* **~geflecht** n *wickerwork* **~gebüsch, ~gehölz** n *w.-plot* **~gerte** f = –rute **~holz** n *w.-wood* **~kätzchen** n *w.-catkin* **~korb** m *wicker-*, *osier-basket* **~laub** n *w.-leaves* pl **~raupe** f *w.-caterpillar* **~röschen** n ⟨bot⟩ *w.-herb*, *salicaria* **~rute** f *w.-twig*, *withe*, *osier*, *switch* **~werder** m *w.-culture* **~wespe** f ⟨ent⟩ *w.-sawfly* **W·eiderich** m ~(e)s/~e ⟨bot⟩ *w.-herb*, *bayw.*, *loosestrife*

w·eidlich adv (→ Weid-) *greatly*, *thoroughly*, *with a vengeance*

W·eife f ~/~n ⟨spin⟩ *reel* ≗**n** vt [h] *to r.*, *wind*

w·eigern: sich ~ [h] *to refuse*, *decline* (*to do*) || sich ~ anzunehmen ⟨a.⟩ *to shrink from acceptance*; er –rt sich zu gehen *he won't leave* | (e–m) etw ~ = verweigern **W·eigerung** f ~/~en *refusal* **~sfall** m; im ~e *in case of refusal* (⟨com⟩ *of non-acceptance*)

W·eih(e) m ~en/~en; **W·eihe** f ~/~n ⟨orn⟩ *kite* || ~n [pl] → *harrier*

W·eih- ~altar m *holy* od *consecrated altar* **~becken** n (*holy-water*) *font* **~bild** n *sacred image*, *votive picture* **~bischof** m *suffragan* (*bishop*) **~brunnen** m = –becken **~gebetbuch** n *benedictional* **~gelübde** n (*ordination*) *vow* **~gesang** m *hymn* **~gabe** f, **~geschenk** n *offering*, *oblation* **~kessel** m = –becken **~nacht** → d. **~rauch** m (*frank*)*incense* || ⟨fig⟩ *incense*, *flattery*; e–m ~ streuen *to flatter a p* (⟨a.⟩ e–m ≗**räuchern**) **~rauchfaß** n *incense-boat*, *censer* **~tafel** f *votive tablet* **~wasser** n *holy water* | ~becken [n], ~kessel [m] = –becken | ~schwinger [m] (P) *thurifer* **~wedel** m *aspergil*(*lum*); *holy-water sprinkler* **W·eihe** f ~/~n *consecration* (*of a bishop*, *of colours*) || (Priester≗) *ordination*; die ~ empfangen (erteilen) *to take* (*bestow*) *holy orders* || (Freimaurer≗) *initiation* | (Einweihung) *inauguration* || (e–r Kirche) *dedication* | ⟨fig⟩ *inspiration*, *sacred fire* **~frühling** m *consecrated spring* **~krone** f *votive crown* ≗**los** a *profane* **~rede** f *solemn speech* **~stunden** f pl *solemn hours* pl ≗**voll** a *solemn* **w·eihen** vt [h] (Bischof, Fahne) *to consecrate* || (Kirche) *to dedicate* || (Freimaurer) *to initiate* || (Priester) *to ordain*; geweiht w *to take holy orders* | ⟨fig⟩ *to dedicate*, *devote* || *to fill with sacred fire* | **geweiht** *sacred*, etc (*to God*) || *doomed* (*to death*, *destruction*, etc)

W·eiher m ~s/~ (*fish-*)*pond*

W·eihnacht(en pl) f *Christmas* (abbr *Xmas*) || ⟨fam⟩ ihr (etc) ~ = ~sgeschenk | **~s- ~abend** m *Christmas Eve* **~baum** m *Chr.-tree* || °⟨aero⟩ *flares* pl **~bescherung** f (*distribution of*) *Chr. presents* pl **~feier** f *celebration of Chr.* **~feiertag** m *Chr.-day* **~fest** n *Chr. festival* || das ~ *Christmas* **~gans** f *Chr. goose* (vgl. *Chr. turkey*) **~geschenk** n *Chr. present*, (an Postboten etc) *Chr.-box* **~karte** f *Chr. card* **~kind** n *the child Jesus* **~lied** n *Chr.-carol* **~mann** m *Santa Claus*; *Father Chr.* ⟨a. fig⟩ || den ~ spielen *to play F. Chr.* **~markt** m *Chr.-fair* **~messe** f *Chr.-matins* pl **~sänger** m pl *waits* pl **~spiel** n *nativity play* **~stollen** m *Chr. cake* **~tag** m *Chr. Day*; zweiter ~ *Boxing Day* **~zeit** f *Chr.-time*, *Yule-tide*

weil [conj] **1.** *because*; *since*, *as* || .., ~ sie krank war *because she was ill*, *owing to* (od *because of*) *her illness* || .., ~ ich weine (*don't think the worse* [schlecht] *of me*) *for these tears* | [bei gleichem Subjekt] *she* .. (*because of her*) *being ill* || [bei ungl. Subj.] *he* .. *because of her being ill* | nicht ~ ⟨a.⟩ *not that* || ~ nun einmal *considering that* || ~ dem nun so ist *this being the case* **2.** ⟨poet⟩ (= während) *while*, *whilst*, *as long as* (*strike the iron while it is hot*) **w·eiland I.** adv *sometime*, *formerly*, *once* **II.** a *late*, *deceased*, *defunct* **W·eilchen** n ~s/~ (*wait a*) *little while*, ⟨fam⟩ *bit* || nachdem er ein ~ gegangen war *after walking for a brief space* **W·eile** f ~/ **A. 1.** *while*, *short* (*space of*) *time* **2.** (Muße) *leisure* **B.** e–e (kl) ~ (*for*) *a* (*little*) *while*; (Zeitperiode) *a spell* (*just for a sp.*) || nach e–r ~ *presently* || über e–e kl ~ *before long* || e–e ganze, gute, geraume ~ (*for*) *a good while*, (*for*) *quite a long time* || damit hat es gute ~ *there is no hurry* (*about it*), (⟨Am⟩ *it's still a long way off*) || lange ~ → Lange≗ || nächtlicher ~ [= gen] *at night-time*, *during the night* **C.** ⟨prov⟩ eile mit ~ *more haste, less speed*; *they stumble that run fast* (Shak R. & J. II. 3.) || gut Ding will ~ h *haste makes waste*; *nothing is done in a hurry* **w·eilen** vi [h] *to stay*, *be*, *dwell* || (Augen) *to rest* || (säumen) *to tarry*, *linger* || ⟨geh Spr⟩ ~ bei .. *to live among* ..; wo mag er jetzt wohl ~? *I wonder where he is now*; → ver~

W·eiler m ~s/~ *hamlet* || vgl Fr *village*

W·eimutskiefer f *Weymouth pine*

Wein m ~(e)s/~e *wine* || ~, Weib u. Gesang *wine and woman and song* || edler ~ → Spitzen≗; offener ~, Ausschank≗, Pokal≗, Schoppen≗ *w. in a carafe* od *by the glass*; *w. from the wood*; voller ~ *full-bodied w.* || ~e [pl] *wines* || (Trauben) *grapes* || beim ~ *over his cups* || ⟨bot⟩ *vine* || ⟨bot⟩ wilder ~ *Virginia creeper* | ~ bauen *to grow wine* || ~ keltern *to press grapes* pl || ~

lesen *to vintage* || ~ trinken *to take w.* | ⟨fig⟩ jdm reinen ~ einschenken *to tell a p the plain truth*; *to make a clean breast of it* **≈arm** a *producing* (*but*) *little w.*, *poor in w.* **~art** f *sort of w.* **≈artig** a *vinous* **~bau** m *vine-culture*, *cultivation of vines*, *w.-growing*, *viti-culture* **~bauer** m *w.-grower* **~becher** m *w.-cup*, (gr) *goblet* **~beere** f *grape* **~beerkern** m *gr.-stone* **~bereitungslehre** f (*o*)*enology* **≈bekränzt** *vine-clad* **~berg** m (bestimmter *named*) *vineyard*, → Wingert | ~schnecke [f] *edible snail* **≈bewachsen** a *overgrown with vines* **~birne** f *w.-pear* **~blatt** n *v.-leaf* | ~laus [f] ⟨ent⟩ *phylloxera* **~blume** f *bouquet of w.* **~blüte** f *v.-blossom* || (Jahreszeit) *blossoming-time of the vine* **~bohrer** m ⟨ent⟩ *v.-borer* **~brand** m *brandy* | ~verschnitt [m] *adulterated b.* **~bütte** f *w.-coop*, *w.-tub*; *grape-hod* **~creme** f *w. cream*, *w. jelly*; *tipsy cake* **~drossel** f ⟨orn⟩ *redwing* **~ernte** f *vintage* **~essig** m *w.-vinegar* **~farbe** f *colour of w.* **≈farben** a *w.-coloured* **~faß** n *w.-cask*; ⟨fig hum⟩ (P) *w.-bibber* **~flasche** f *w.-bottle* **~fleck** m *w.-spot* **~garten** m *vineyard* **~gärtner** m *v.-dresser*, *w.-grower* **~gärung** f *fermentation of w.*, ⟨chem⟩ *vinous f.* **~gegend** f *w.-* (*growing*) *district* **~gehalt** m *vinosity* **~geist** m *spirits of wine*, *alcohol* | ~haltig [a] *alcoholic*; ~messer [m] *alcoholometer*; ~thermometer [n] *spirit-th.* **~gelage** n *w.-party* **~gelände** n *vine-clad hills* pl **~geländer** n *trellis for vines* **~geruch** m *flavour of w.* **~geschmack** m *vinous* od *winy taste* **~glas** n *wine-glass* **~gott** m *god of w.*, *Bacchus* **≈grün** a *v.-leaf green* **~gut** n *named vineyard* **≈haltig** a *vinous* **~handel** m *w.-trade* **~händler** m *w.-merchant*, *vintner* **~handlung** f (gr) *w.-business*; (kl) *w.-*(*merchant's*) *shop* **~hauer** m [österr] = Winzer **~haus** n *w.-tavern* **~heber** m *siphon for drawing w.* **~hefe** f *dregs* od *lees* pl *of w.* **~jahr** n *vintage*, *w.-year* **~kaltschale** f *cold w.-soup* **~kanne** f *tankard*, *w.-can* **~karaffe** f *decanter* **~karte** f *w.-list*, *price-list of w.s* **~kauf** m *purchase of w.* **~keller** m *w.-cellar*, *w.-vault*(*s* pl) || (Ausschank) *w.-tavern*, (spanischer) *bodega* **~kelter** f *w.-press* **~kenner** m *good judge* (od *connoisseur*) *of w.s* **~kern** m *grape-stone* **~kneipe** f *w.-tavern* **~koster** m *w.-taster* **~krug** m *w.-pot*, *tankard* **~kufe** f *w.-tub* **~küfer** m *w.-cooper* **~kühler** m *ice-pail* **~lage** f *position of a vineyard* **~lager** n *stock of w.* || (Keller) *w.-vaults* pl **~land** n *w.-growing country*, (*France is the greatest*) *w.-producer* (*in the world*) **~laub** n *v.-leaves* pl **~laube** f *v.-arbour* **~laubstab** m *thyrsus* **~laune** f; in ~ *in one's cups*; in bester ~ ⟨fam⟩ *glorious* **~lese** f *vintage* || ~ halten *to gather in the vintage* **~leser(in** f) m *vintager* **~lied** n *w.-song* **~markt** m *w.-market* **~meister** m *steward of vineyards* || *head cellarer* od *butler* **~messer** m *w.-gauge* || [n] *pruning-knife* **~met** m *vinous hydromel* **~monat** m *w.-month*, *October* **~most** m *must* **~nase** f *red nose* **~niederlage** f *w.-store* **~palme** f *toddy-palm* **~panscher(·ei** f) m *adulterator* (*adulteration*) *of w.* **~pfahl** m *v.-prop* **~presse** f *w.-press* **~probe** f *sample of w.* || *tasting of w.* | ~schale [f] *w.-taster* **~prüfer** m *w.-t.* **~pudding** m *w.-pudding* **~ranke** f *v.-branch*, *tendril* **~raupe** f *v.-fretter* **~rausch** m *intoxication occasioned by w.* **~raute** f *rue*; *herb of grace* **~rebe** f *v.-branch*, *shoot of a vine* || *vine* | ~nart [f] *v.-plant* **≈reich** a *abounding in w.* od *vines*, *viny* **~reisende(r)** m *traveller for a w.-firm* **≈rot** a *ruby* **~salon** m *tavern*; ⟨Am obs⟩ *saloon* **≈sauer** a *vinous*, *winy*; ⟨chem⟩ *tartaric* **≈säuerlich** a *somewhat winy* **~säufer** m *w.-bibber* **~säure** f *tartaric acid* **~schank** m *retail of w.* | ~recht [n] *w.-license* **~schaum** m ⟨cul⟩ *sabayon* Fr **~schenk** m *tavern-keeper*, *vintner* **~schenke** f *w.-house* od *-shop* **~schlauch** m *w.-skin*; ⟨fig⟩ (P) *w.-bibber* **~schmierer** m = –panscher **~schöne** f *gelatine for fining w.s* **~schröter** m *w.-porter* **~schuld** f *debt for w.* **≈selig** a *exhilarated with w.*, *tipsy*, *in one's cups*, ⟨fam⟩ *glorious*; ~e Freundschaft *drunken fr.* **~sorte** f *brand of w.* || ~n [pl] *wines* **~spalier** n *trellis for vines* **~stein** m ⟨chem⟩ *tartar* || gereinigter ~ *cream of tartar* | ≈artig [a] *tartareous*; ~rahm [m] *cream of tartar*; ~säure [f] *tartaric acid*; ≈saure(s) Salz [n] *tartrate* **~steuer** f *w.-duty* **~stock** m (⟨Am⟩ *grape*)*vine* **~stube** f *w.-room*, *w.-shop*, *w.-lodge* **~suppe** f *w.-soup*, *caudle* **~traube** f *bunch of grapes*; grüne (blaue) ~ *white* (*black*) *grape* **~trauben** pl (Obst) *grapes* | ~kur [f] *grape-cure* **~treber** pl, **~trester** pl *husks of w.* **~trinker** m *w.-drinker* **≈trunken** a *drunk with w.*; ⟨vulg⟩ *winy* **≈umrankt** a *vine-clad* **~-und Sp·eisewirt** m *restaurant-keeper licensed to sell w.* **~verfälscher** = –panscher **~waage** f *w.-gauge* **~wachs** m *growth of w.* || guten ~ h *to produce good* od *much w.* **~wetter** n *weather favourable for the vines* **~wirt** m *vintner* **~wirtschaft** f = –haus **~zeichen** n *tavern-sign* **~zieher** m (Heber) *siphon* **~zierl** m ~s/~[n] ×[bay, österr] = Winzer **~zoll** m *duty on w.*; *tunnage* **~zwang** m *obligation to take wine with one's meal*

w·einen I. vi [h] (über [acc]) *to weep* (*for*), *to cry*, *to shed tears* (*about*, *at*); ⟨fam⟩ *to blubber* || um e–n ~ *to bewail a p* || still vor sich hin ~ *to shed silent tears*, *to cry to o.s.* || sie fühlte, daß sie ~ mußte *a sense of tears came to her* **II.** vt [h] (Tränen) *to shed* (*tears*) || **sich** in den Schlaf (zu Tode) ~ *to cry o.s. to sleep* (*to death*) || sich [dat] die Augen aus dem Kopfe ~ *to cry one's heart* od *eyes out*, *to cry fit to break one's heart* **III.** ≈ n; es ist z ≈ *it makes one feel inclined to weep*; e–n z ~ bringen *to move a p to tears* **Weiner·ei** f ~/ *whining*, ⟨fam⟩ *blubbering* **w·einerlich** a *inclined to weep*; *whining* | *tearful* (*nature*), ⟨fam⟩ *teary* || *whimpering*, *whining* (*tone*) || ~es Schauspiel *domestic drama* || ~es Lustspiel *comédie larmoyante* | mir ist *or* wird ~ *I feel inclined to weep* **W·einkrampf** m *fit of weeping*; *crying-fit*; *convulsive sobbing*; *hysterics* pl

weis- [in comp] → ~machen etc **w·eise** a *wise* || → vernünftig || (klug) *prudent*, ⟨fam⟩ *knowing* || 9mal ~ ⟨mst iron⟩ *sapient*; *too clever by half* || ~ Frau *midwife*; *fortune-teller* | **der** ≈ *the wise man* (*the 7 wise men of Greece*); *the sage*, *philosopher* || die drei ≈n aus dem Morgenlande *the three Magi* || Stein der ≈n *philosopher's stone* **W·eise** m [der ~, ein ~r] ~n/~n → weise [a]

Weise f ~/~n **A.** *mode*, *manner*, *way* || *method*, *style* || (Gewohnheit) *habit*, *custom* || ⟨mus⟩ *tune*, *air*, *melody*; Text u ~ *words and music* || ⟨gram⟩ *mood* **B. auf** [acc], **in** [dat] .. ~: (diese) *in this way*, *like this*; (dieselbe) ⟨a.⟩ *alike*; (e–e oder andere) (*in*) *one way or another*; (jede) *in every way*, *in any case*; *in thousand and one ways*; (k–e) *in no way*, *not in any way*, *by no means*; (welche?) ⟨a.⟩ *how?* | jeder nach s–r ~ *each one after his own fashion* **C. auf, in** + [a] + ~ *or* [in comp]: oft durch [adv]: auf glückliche ~, **glücklicher**≈ *fortunately*, *happily* (⟨so:⟩ unverantwortlich: *unwarrantably*, gleich: *likewise*) (so: *cruelly*, *tragically*, etc) || zufälliger≈ *accidentally*, *by accident*; in ähnlicher, gleicher ~ ⟨a.⟩ *in like manner*; in gewisser ~ *in a way* | eimer≈ *in bucketfuls*; kolonnen≈ *in columns*; ruck≈ *by jerks*; scherz≈ *in fun*, *for fun*; stufen≈ *by degrees*, *by stages*; stunden≈ *by the hour* || in höchst ungleicher ~ *in the most unequal degree*(*s* pl) | auf irgendeine ~, auf diese oder jene ~ *somehow or other*, *by hook or by crook* || auf anständige ~ *by fair means* **..weise** → vor. C.; suff z Bildg v [a & adv] z Bezeichnung der Art u Weise, in der etw geschieht: z B phasen~ *phase-by-phase* **W·eisel** m ~s/~ *queen-bee* **w·eisen I.** vt [wies/gewiesen] [h] **A.** *to point out*, *to show*; ⟨fig⟩ *to sign-post* (*the road to defeat*) | ⟨fig⟩ e–m die Tür (die Wege) ~ *to show a p the door* (*to bid a p begone*) || e–m die Zähne ~ *to defy a p* || er will sich nicht ~ l *he* *won't listen to reason* **B.** jdn ~ **an** [acc] *to refer a p to* || man wies mich an Sie *I was referred to you* || der Uhrzeiger wies **auf** 8 *the hand pointed to 8* || mit dem Finger ~ auf *to point out* (*a th*), *to point* (*one's fingers*) *at* (*a p*) | **aus**: *to expel from*) (*school, the town*), *to order .. out of* (*the room*) || aus dem Lande ~ *to banish, exile* | ⟨mil⟩ **ins** Quartier ~ *to billet* | **nach**: *to direct a p to*; *the word points us to ..* | **von**: *to order .. off* (*the premises*); *to direct off* (*the road*) || v der Hand ~, v sich ~ *to repudiate, refuse, reject*; *scout* (*proposal, notion*); (e–n Gedanken) *to put behind one*; etw .. weit .. *to deprecate* (*a th*, z tun *doing*), *to scorn* (*to do*), *to snub* (*an idea*) | **zu**: *to motion* (*a p*) *to* (*a seat*) **II.** [refl] das wird **sich** bald ~ *we shall soon see* **W·eiser** m ~s/~ (der Uhr) *hand* || (Weg≗) *signpost* || (* P) *indicator, guide*

W·eisheit f ~/~en (→ weise) *wisdom* || (Klugheit) *prudence* || der ~ letzter Schluß *the last resort* || mit s–r ~ am Ende *at his wits' end*; da bin ich mit m–r ~ am E. ⟨a.⟩ *you've got me there* || er tut, als hätte er die ~ mit Löffeln gegessen *he is a wiseacre, he is!* | **~s-** **~dünkel** m *priggishness*; *intellectual conceit* **~krämer** m *wiseacre* **~lehre** f *philosophy* **~zahn** m *wisdom-tooth* (bek *to cut*) **w·eislich** adv *wisely, prudently* **w·eis|machen** vt [h]; jdm etw ~ *to tell a p stories*; *to make a p believe a th* || ⟨bes Am⟩ *to put a th over on a p* || m Sie das andern weis! *tell that to the horse-marines!* || wir l uns das v dir nicht ~! *don't pull that stuff on us!* || l Sie sich nichts ~! *don't be taken in!* || er wollte mir ~, daß *he would have me believe that ..*

Weiß n ~es/ *white* (*colour*), *whiteness* || ~ auflegen ⟨cosm⟩ *to put on white paint* || in ~ gekleidet *in white* **weiß** a **A.** *white*; aus ~ u blauer Seide/aus blau u ~er S. *of white and blue silk* || ⟨her⟩ *argent* || (sauber) *clean* (*linen*) || (unbeschrieben) *blank* (*to leave bl.*) || (Haar ⟨a.⟩) *hoary*; das Weiße Meer ⟨Russ⟩ (Bucht) *the White Sea*; ~e Kohle ⟨fig⟩ *water-power* || ~er Rabe ⟨fig⟩ *white crow* || ~e Stelle ⟨typ⟩ (unbedruckte Stelle) *white* || ⟨ec⟩ *Low* (*Sunday*) || ~e Ware *linen* **B.** ~ gerben *to taw* || ~ kleiden *to dress in white* || ~ m *to whiten, blanch, bleach* || ~ nähen *to do plain sewing* || ~ sieden *to blanch* || sich ~ brennen *or* waschen *to exculpate* od *whitewash o.s.* **C.** e–e ≗e mit Schuß *a glass of Berlin-beer with a dash of raspberry-vinegar*; → Weißbier **Weiß-** **~anstreichen** n *painting white*; (Tünchen) *whitewashing* **≗armig** a *wh.-armed* **~bäcker** m *fancy baker* **~bart** m (*man with a*) *wh. beard* **≗bärtig** a *wh.-bearded* **~bier** n *pale* (*Berlin*) *ale* **~binder** m **1.** *cooper* **2.** *whitewasher* **≗blau** a *pale blue* **~blech** n *tin-plate*; ~ f Konservendosen *hot-dipped t.-p.*; ~ erster Güte *primes* | ~waren [f pl] *tinware* **~bleiche** f *cotton-bleaching* **~bleierz** n *white lead-ore* **≗bluten** vt [h] *to bleed .. wh.*; bis z ≗ *to the dead finish* **~blütigkeit** f *leucemia* **~brot** n *white bread* **~brötchen** n *roll* **~buch** n ⟨Ger pol⟩ *Wh. Book* **~buche** f ⟨bot⟩ *hornbeam* **≗busig** a *wh.-bosomed* **~dorn** m ⟨bot⟩ *hawthorn* **~fichte** f ⟨bot⟩ *spruce-fir* **~fisch** m *bleak*; *dace*; *whiting* || (Gattung) ~e [pl] *whitebait* ⟨a. cul⟩ **≗fleckig** a *white-speckled* **~fluß** m ⟨path⟩ *leucorrhœa* **~fuchs** m **1.** *silver fox* **2.** *light sorrel horse* **≗gar** a ⟨tech⟩ *tawed* **≗gekleidet** a *dressed in wh.* **≗gelb** a *wh.-yellow, pale y.* **~gerber** m *tawer* **≗glühend** a *wh.-hot, incandescent* **~glühhitze** f *wh. heat* ⟨a. fig⟩; *incandescence* **~gold** n *platinum* **~güldenerz, ~güldigerz** n *wh. silver-ore* **≗haarig** a *wh.-haired* **~huhn** n ⟨orn⟩ *wh. grouse* **~kehlchen** n ⟨orn⟩ *wheatear* **~kohl** m, **~kraut** n (*wh.*) *cabbage*, → Kohl **~kopf** m (*p with a*) *wh. head* **~kreuz** n ⟨mil⟩ *tear gas* **~mehl** n *fine flour* **~metall** n *wh. metal, queen's m., Babbitt-m.*; mit ~ausguß *babbitted* **~näherei** f *plain* (*needle*)*work* **~näherin** f *plain seamstress* **~pappel** f ⟨bot⟩ *wh. poplar* **~pinseläffchen** n ⟨zoo⟩ *squirrel-monkey* **~russe** m *Byelorussian* **≗scheckig** a *wh.-speckled* **≗seiden** a (*of*) *wh. silk* **~sieder** m *blancher* **~sudkessel** m *blanching-boiler* **~stein** m *granulite* **~tanne** f ⟨bot⟩ *fir* **~wal** m *wh. whale* **~waren** f pl *linen goods* pl, *linen drapery* | ~geschäft [n] *linen-drapery shop*; ~händler [m] *draper* **~wein** m *wh. wine* **~wurst** f *wh. sausage* (*filled with calves' brains, spleen and veal*) **~zeug** n *linen* **W·eiße 1.** [f] ~/ *whiteness, white* | [~/~] e–e ~ *a glass of pale* (*Berlin*) *ale*; *a glass of pale* (*Munich*) *wheaten beer*; → weiß, Weißbier **2.** [n] ~n/ *the white* (*of the eye, of the egg*) || (in der Scheibe) *bull's eye* **3.** m [der ~, ein ~r] & f ~n/~n *white* (*man*), *Causasian* || [pl] die ~n *the white races*; *the whites* (*and the negroes*) **w·eißen I.** vt [h] *to whiten* || (übertünchen) *to whitewash* **II.** ≗ n ~s/ *whitening* **w·eißlich** a *whitish, whit(e)y* || ~ wd *albescent* **W·eißling** m ~(e)s/~e ⟨ent⟩ (*cabbage*) → *white butterfly* || ⟨bot⟩ *agaric*

w·eissagen [insep] vt [h] (→ wissen) *to prophesy, foretell, predict* || jdm Gutes ~ *to prophesy well of a p* | **~d** *prophetic* **W.ger(in** f) m ~s/~ *prophet* (f *prophetess*), *soothsayer* **W.gung** f ~/~en *prophecy, divination*

W·eistum n ~(e)s/≗er ⟨obs Ger jur⟩ *precedent* || *record* od *statement concerning* (*local*) *legal customs*

W·eisung f ~/~en *order, direction, instruction* || ~en u Zeichen v Polizeibeamten *directions and signals given by policemen* || nach ~en des Truppenführers *according to the guidance furnished by the commander*

weit I. [a] **A.** → weiter **1.** (entfernt) *distant, far, remote, far* (od *a long way*) *off*; (*a mile*) *off* **2.** (ausgedehnt) *spacious, ample, extensive* | (breit) *broad, wide*; *large*; *vast* **B.** ~er **Blick** *commanding view*, ⟨fig⟩ *far-sightedness* || in ~em Felde liegen *to be far from settled* || in ~er Ferne *in the far distance* || (Gebiet) *extensive* || (Gewissen) *elastic*, ein ~es G. h *to have no scruples* || ⟨fig⟩ (Herz) *large* || **(Kleid)** *wide, full* || (Meere) ⟨a.⟩ *broad* || (Reise) *long* || im ~esten Sinne (*education*) *in the broadest sense*; *in the most comprehensive* od *generous sense* || ~este Strecke, die .. *that was the farthest she went* || ein 20 cm ~er Topf *a pot 7 inches wide* || (Umweg) *long way about, very circuitous route* (m *to go*) || (Weg) *long* || (Welt) *wide*; in die ~e W. ziehen *to go out into the world* || (die Zeit) ist nicht mehr ~ .. *is drawing near* **II.** [adv] **A.** (*a*)*far, far off* || ⟨fig⟩ *widely, much, greatly*; .. nicht ~ .. (*it is*) *no far cry* (*to the Manchester standpoint*) || ~ u breit *far and wide* od *near* || .. e–n Spalt ~ .. *the door opened a crack* **B.** ~ **abgesetzt** *established far out* || ~ aus-e-a-stehende Augen *widely set eyes* || ~ ausgeschnitten *low* (*-necked*) || ~ **entfernt** *far-away* (*object*); [pred] ⟨Am a.⟩ *way back* || ..! *far from it!*; .. v .. (*to be*) *wide of* od *remote from* (*the truth*); .. z s: *he is the last remove from a pedant*; .. z h: ⟨Am⟩ *the King does not begin to have the President's power* || ~ **mehr** *vastly more* || ~est **möglich**: *the widest possible interpretation* || ~ offen *wide open* **C.** ⟨emph⟩ [bei compr & sup] *far* (*greater distance*) || ~ besser, größer *much* (od *a great deal*) *better, larger*; ⟨sl⟩ *a long sight better*, etc || ~ eher *far rather*; ~ lieber *far sooner* || es ist mir ~ lieber *I greatly prefer* (*it*) || ~ tiefer ⟨Am fig⟩ *it's way below any question of just yes or no* **D.** ~ **davon** ist gut vorm Schuß *prudence is the better part of valour* | (da) ~ draußen *away out there*; ⟨Am⟩ *way out* | ~ drüben ⟨Am⟩ *way over* | v ~ **her** *from afar, from a long way off*; er ist (v) ~ hergek *he has come a long way* || er (das) ist nicht ~ her *he comes from near by* (*that's of little value, that's not much*); es ist nicht ~ her mit ihm *he doesn't count* | ~ **hin** *far off, to a great distance, widely*; sich ~hin erstrecken *to stretch out* | ~ **hinaus** gehen *to go far afield* | ~ **hinter** uns ⟨Am⟩ *way back* (*along the road*) | ~ links *away to the left* || (es) ~ **nach** Hause h *to be a long way from home* | **so** ~(!) *thus far*(!), *up to this point*; (*you may be right*) *so far* || es ist so ~! ⟨a.⟩ *this is it*!; es war noch nicht so ~ *the moment was not yet ripe* || .. so ~, daß er .. (*he did it*) *to the extent of* (*doing*), (*his anger went*) *to the point of his refusing* || er ist so~ genesen *he has sufficiently recovered* (, daß *to do*; ⟨fam⟩ [abs]) || so~ ich mich entsinne (ich zurückdenken kann) *as far* (*back*) *as I can remember* || so~ Sie zustimmen *as far as you approve of it* || **(in)so~** *in so far as* | ~ **über** *well over* (*60*), *long after* (*4 o'clock*) | ~ **unten** ⟨Am⟩ *away down* | ein Zoll ~ **von** der Decke *an inch from* .. | ~ **weg** *well away*, ⟨fig⟩ *absentminded* || .., **wie** ~ *the extent to which* || → inwie~ || ~ zurückliegend *way back* (*in 1681*) || am ~esten **zurück** *the farthest back* **E.** ~ aufmachen *to open .. wide* || es ~ **bringen** *to get on*; er wird es nie sehr ~ br. *he will never amount to very much* || e–n so ~ br., daß er *to drive a p so far as to* (*do*) || so ~ **gehen** z tun *to go so far as to do*; *to venture* (*to assert*), *to go to the length of doing*; nicht .. *to stop short of doing* || zu ~ g. *to overstep one's bounds, to overshoot the mark, to overreach o.s., to overdo it, to overplay one's hand*; .. in s–n Behauptungen *to overstate one's case*; zu ~g. ⟨fam⟩ *to cut it too fat*; in der Richtung zu ~ g. ⟨fig⟩ *to err on the side of* .. || das geht zu ~ *that is going too far* || wir h es noch ~ bis *we are still a good distance from* (vgl D. nach) || ⟨typ⟩ den Satz ~ halten *to drive out the matter* | ~ **kommen** *to get far*, recht ~ gek s in *to be well on the way in* | es ist (so) ~ gek *ths have come to a pretty* (*to such a*) *pass*; (*to show the pass to which ths have come* .. mit ihm .. *with him*; *he is far gone*; .. so ~ .. *he has come to that*) | ~ **sein** *to be far advanced* || sind Sie so ~? *are you ready*? || wie ~ sind Sie? *how far are you*?, .. damit? *how far have you advanced with it*? || ⟨fig⟩ so ~ sind wir noch nicht *it has not come to that yet*; wir wollen warten, bis es so ~ ist *let's wait till it is time*; *wait and see*! || Tränen sind mir nicht ~ *I am near crying* || es ist nicht mehr ~ *it is but a little way* (*from here*) | ~ u breit **suchen** u schlechter dabei fahren (*you could*) *go far and do worse* | es zu ~ **treiben** *to go too far* | e–n ~ **übertreffen.** e–m ~ überlegen s *to excel a p by far* | ~ verbreiten *to spread wide* | ~ **werden** (Herz) *to expand* || e–n Vergleich zu ~ ziehen *to run a parallel too far* || wie ~ schien diese Zeit zurückzuliegen! *how long ago that time seemed*! **III. bei ~em** etc → Weite [n] **IV.** → weiter **w·eit-** **~·ab** adv *far away, a long way from here* **~atmig** a *expansive*; *spacious* **~·aus** adv *by far, a long way, far and away* (*the best*) **~·ausgedehnt** a *extensive, wide* **~·ausgreifenden** Schrittes *in a lengthened pace* **~bek·annt** a *well-* (od *widely*) *known* **~bew·undert** a *much admired* **≗blick** m *far-sightedness* (*of mind*), *foresight* **~blickend** a ⟨fig⟩ *far-sighted* **~entl·egen** a *far-off* (*farm*) **~gehend** a ⟨fig⟩ *sweeping, vast, far-reaching* || [sup] –estgehend (⟨vulg⟩ –gehendst) *extreme* **~ger·eist** a *travelled* **~gespannt** a ⟨fig⟩ *extensive, comprehensive* **≗gespräch** n ⟨post off⟩ *out-of-town call*; *trunk-call*; ⟨Am⟩ *long-distance call* (⟨allg⟩ Fern-) **~greifend** a *extensive*; *wide-ranging* (*trade*) **≗halsflasche** f *wide-mouthed, w.-neck bottle* **~h·er** adv → weit II. D. **~h·ergeholt** a *far-fetched* **~herzig** a ⟨fig⟩ *broad-minded, large-hearted* (*p*), *enlarged* (*ideas*) **~h·in** adv → weit II. D. **~läufig** a *ample, large, wide, extensive, spacious*, ⟨emph⟩ *vast* | *distant*; (zerstreut) *scattered*, (Dorf) *straggling*; [adv] *far from each other* | (umständlich) *detailed, elaborate* || (Verwandtschaft) *distant* || (~schweifig) [adv] *at great length*; *in a round-about way* || die S ist sehr ~ *it is a very complicated matter* || sich ~ auslassen über *to expatiate upon* | **≗**keit [f] *vast extent*; *amplitude, largeness*; (e–s Dorfes) *straggling character* || *elaborateness*, = –schweifigkeit || ~ der Verwandtschaft *remoteness* || ~en [pl] *intricacies, difficulties* pl || (Formalitäten) *formalities* pl **~maschig** a *with wide meshes* **~mäulig** a *wide-mouthed* **~m·öglichst** → weit II. B. **~räumig** = geräumig; ⟨a.⟩ *widely dispersed*; *extensive* (*effects*) **~reichend** a *far-reaching, rangy* **~schichtig** a *with layers wide apart*; ⟨fig⟩ *large, ample*; ⟨emph⟩ *vast* **≗schlag** m ⟨golf⟩ *drive* **≗schuß** m *over* **~schweifig** a *prolix, diffuse, circuitous, circumlocutory, verbose, rambling* | [adv] ~ reden *to talk capiously*; → –läufig | **≗**keit [f] *prolixity, diffuseness*; *circumlocution*; *verbosity* **~sichtig** a *long-sighted*; ⟨fig⟩ *far-s.d*; ~ s ⟨pol⟩ *to take a long view* | [adv] ~ planen *to see ths in a large way* | **≗**keit [f] *l.-s.dness*; (im Alter) *presbyopia* || ⟨fig⟩ *f.-s.dness* **≗sprung** m *long* od *broad jump* **~spurig** a ⟨rail⟩ *broad-gauged* **~tragend** a *of a long range*; *long-range* (*gun*) || ⟨fig⟩ *portentous, far-reaching* **~umf·assend** a *comprehensive, extensive* **~verbreitet** a *wide-* (od *widely*) *spread, widely held, prevalent* (*opinion*) | adv *all abroad* **~verzweigt** a *wide-branching* | ~ **vorstehend** a *jutting* (*far*) *out, salient* **≗winkel** m ⟨phot⟩ *panorama-lens* | ~-Beobachtungsposten [m] *wide-angle look-out-post* ⟨a. a–n⟩; ~objektiv [n] (extremes *ultra*)*w.-a. lens* | extremer **≗**winkler (180°) ⟨phot⟩ *fish-eye lens* **W·eite I.** [f] ~/~n *wideness, largeness, width* || ⟨math, astr⟩ *amplitude* || (Schiffs≗) *breadth of beam* || (Raumgehalt) *capacity* || (Kleid≗) *fulness* || ~ der Landschaft *openness of the landscape* || (Durchmesser) *diameter*, lichte ~ *inner* od *inside diameter* od *width*; *clearance*; *clear span* || (Bohrung) *bore* || (Handschuh≗ etc) *size*; welche ~ h Sie? *what size do you take*? || (Entfernung) *distance* || (Schuß≗) *range* || (Ferne) in die ~ ziehen *to go on a far journey* | ⟨fig⟩ *extent, expanse, reach*; ⟨emph⟩ *vastness*; *breadth* (*of vision* od *outlook*); die ~ ihres Könnens *the versatility of their abilities* **II.** [n] ~n/; des ~n u Breiten erzählen *to relate at length* || das ~ suchen *to decamp, abscond, to make off, to take to one's heels* || ⟨fam⟩ *to hook it*, ⟨Am⟩ *to beat it* || **bei ≗m** [adv] (*by*) *far, far and away, easily, much, by long* od *all odds* (*better, the best*); *a great deal* (*better*) | bei ≗m nicht *not by a* (*great deal* od) *long way* ⟨fam⟩ *sight* od *chalk*; *far from* (*complete*); .. bei ≗m nicht denselben Preis wie (*they are not paying*) *anything like the price that* || bei ≗m nicht so gut *not nearly so good, nothing like as good* (*as*) | ganz **im ≗n** *quite uncertain* || das geht ins ~e *that's beyond all bounds* | **ins** ~ schauen *to look at space* | **von ≗m** *from afar*; *a long way off* **w·eiten** vt & sich ~ [h] *to widen, expand, enlarge*; (Handschuh) *to stretch* **w·eiter** a & adv; adv [österr] ⟨a.⟩ ~s **A. 1.** *wider*, etc; *more distant*; *remoter*; *farther*; *further* ⟨bes fig⟩ || etw ~ *a little farther on* (*is* ..); (Kleid) *a thought looser* || in der ~en Umgebung v .. *in the general vicinity of* .. || (*two rooms*) *along* || wir konnten nicht ~ sehen als bis .. *we could not see beyond the next street corner* **2. ~ entfernt** *more distant, farther off* || ~ links *more* od *away to the left* || ~ nördlich (*we turned*) *more north* || 30 m ~ vorwärts *30 m. ahead* || am ≗esten zurück *hindmost* **3.** (Fortsetzung) (nur) ~! *go on*! *keep going*! *proceed*! || *come now*! || *don't mind me*! || es regnet ~ *it keeps raining*, ⟨fam⟩ *the rain keeps up* || h Sie ~ **etw** z sagen? *have you anything further to say*? || immer ~ *on and on* || ~ hat es k–n Zweck *that is all it is good for, it serves no other purpose* || **.. nicht** ~ *no longer* || nicht ~! *stop*!, *no more of this*! || Ausreden dulde ich nicht ~ *I won't allow any further excuses* || ~ **nichts** *nothing more* od *else*; *just that*; *not a word more* (*could he utter*) ‖ nichts ~ davon! *not another word about it*! ‖ ~ nichts als .. *just* .. ‖ ~ h wir nichts z sagen *we have nothing to add* ‖ das hat ~ nichts z sagen *that's of no consequence* ‖ wenn's ~ nichts ist *if that is all* ‖ ~ niemand *or* n. ~ *nobody else* ‖ **und** ~? *and then*? ‖ und so ~ (abbr usw.) *and so forth* od *on*, *et cetera* (abbr: etc, & c) ‖ **was** ~? *what more* od *else*? ‖ was ist da ~ (dabei)? *what does that matter*?, *what of that*? ‖ was ist das ~? *that's not much*! ‖ **wer** ~? *who else*? **B.** ohne ~en **Aufschub** *without further delay* ‖ *three more* (*books*) ‖ *a further* (*example*) ‖ ~e Entwicklung → Weiter– ‖ in immer ~er **Ferne** *distance beyond distance* ‖ (Forderungen) *further* ‖ nach ~en 100 Jahren *in another 100 years* ‖ (Kind etc) *additional* ‖ in ~en **Kreisen** (vgl A. 1.) *widely* ‖ *another* (*8 miles*, *member*) ‖ (Schwierigkeit) *additional*, *new* ‖ ohne ~e Umstände *without much ado*; *unceremoniously*, → ohne weiteres ‖ e–e ~e Wohltat *another of the benefits* **C.** → a. weiter- ‖ etw ~ **tun** *to go on* od *continue doing* ‖ *do not leave off smoking*! ‖ wenn er uns ~ stört ⟨a.⟩ *if he annoys us any more* | ~ **ausführen** *to amplify* (*a story*) ‖ ~ bringen *to take forward*; *to help on*; *to further*, *advance*, *promote*; (Schüler) *to get on* ‖ (P, S) ~ empfehlen *to recommend to others* ‖ .., erklärte er ~ .. *he went on to explain* ‖ ~ führen *to carry on*, *to continue* ‖ ~ **gehen** als *to walk further than*, ⟨fig⟩ *to go beyond* (*a p*) ‖ e–m ~ helfen *to help a p along* ‖ **hör'** ~! *listen to* (od *hear*) *what follows* ‖ komm' ~! *come along*! ‖ → ~kommen ‖ nicht ~ **können** *to be unable to proceed*; *to be stuck*; ⟨rail⟩ *to stop short*; ⟨fig⟩ *to be up against a brick wall*; vor Müdigkeit .. *to be too tired to get along*; (im Sprechen) *to break down* ‖ **lies** ~! *go on* (*reading*)! ‖ m Sie ~ → A. 3. ‖ ich muß ~ *I must be getting along* ‖ ~ schweigen (sprechen) *he continued silent* (*speaking*) ‖ ~ tragen als *to outrange* (*a gun*) ‖ sich ~ wagen *to venture on* ‖ ich will ~ *I'll be getting along* **D.** [in comp] pref [betont, bei Verben stets trennbar] **E.** → Weitere [n] W·eiter- → a. Fort- ~́|**arbeiten** vi [h] *to carry on*; *to persist* (an *with*) ~́|**befördern** vt [h] *to send on*; (S, P) *to tran*(*s*)*ship* (*by Train Ferry Service*) **~bestand** m, **~bestehen** n *continued* od *further existence* ~́|**bilden** vt [h] *to improve*, *develop*; sich ~ *to continue one's studies*, *to further* od *develop one's abilities* | das wird ihn **~|bringen** *that will carry him to greater lengths* ~́|**drehen** vt [h] ⟨phot⟩ (Film) *to advance* ~́|**eilen** vi [s] *to run along* ~́**empfehlen** vt [h] (P, S) *to recommend to others* **~entwicklung** f (*further*) *development*; *future trends in the d.* ‖ ⟨path⟩ *progression* ~́|**erzählen** vt [h] (Gerücht) *to retail* ([dat] *to*) ~́|**fahren** vi irr [s] *to drive on*; ~! *go ahead*! **~fahrt** f *continuation of a journey* ~́|**führen** vt [h] *to carry on*; *to keep .. up to date*; (Leitung) *to extend* **~führung** f *continuation* ‖ (v Gleisen etc) *extension* **~gabe** f ⟨mil⟩ *dissemination* (*of orders*); ~ auf dem Dienstweg *routing through channels* ~́|**geben** vt irr [h] *to pass on* (an *to*): *your letter has been passed to me for attention* ‖ *to pass* (*a signal*) ‖ ⟨wir⟩ *to transmit*; ⟨telph, telg a.⟩ *to retell* ‖ bitte ~! *please pass on*! ‖ ⟨ftb⟩ (Ball) *to pass* ‖ v Mund zu M. ~ *to relay* (*message*, etc) ~́|**gehen** vi irr [s] *to walk* od *pass*, *go on* ‖ ~! *move on*!, *keep moving*! ‖ ⟨fig⟩ ~ z *to proceed to*, *to pass on to* ‖ ich will ~ *I'll be getting along* (nach *to*) ‖ ⟨übtr⟩ (fortfahren) (⟨a.⟩ v S) *to go on*, *to continue* (⟨a.⟩ auf e–m Wege *along a road*); wie soll es mit uns ~? *how are we to go on*? | der Kampf geht ~ *the struggle is still in progress* | jdm ~́|**helfen** *to help a p along* ‖ sich [dat] selbst ~ ⟨fam⟩ *to fend for o.s.* ~́**hin** adv *further* ‖ (zeitlich) *for the future*; ~ m *to continue to make* ‖ ~ vorwiegend trocken ⟨meteor⟩ *continuing mainly dry* ~́|**kommen** vi irr [s] *to advance*, *progress*; *to get on* ‖ m Sie, daß Sie ~ *off with you*! ~́|**können** vi irr [h] → weiter C. ~́|**leben** vi [h] *to linger on* ~́|**leiten** vt [h] *to pass on* bzw *along* (auf e–m Wege *a path*); ⟨phys⟩ *to transmit* ~́|**machen**! *go*/*carry on*! *continue*! ‖ ‖ mutig ~ *to keep it* (od *one's end*) *up* ‖ nur so ~ *to keep the pot boiling*; → fortfahren **~marsch** m vgl –fahrt **~reise** f = –fahrt ~́**reisen** vi [s] *to continue one's journey* ~́|**rücken** vi [s] (P) *to move up* ~́|**sagen** *to retell*, *repeat*; ~! *pass the word along*! ‖ nicht ~! *keep it a secret* **~|schlafen** vi [h] *to sleep on* adv; (nach Erwachen) *to go back to sleep* ~́|**schreiten** vi [s] *to move on*, (Tag) *to wear on* °~́|**schuften** vi [h] ⟨fam⟩ *to peg on* ~́|**senden** vt [h] *to forward* **~|tippeln** vi [s] ⟨mil⟩ *to knock along* ~́|**tragen** vt [h] = forttr. ‖ (Gerücht) *to bandy about* ~́|**treiben** vt [h] *to drive on* ‖ ⟨übtr⟩ *to keep up* (*music*, etc) **~|verarbeiten** vt [h] *to process* ‖ (*p.ed goods*) **~|verkaufen** vt [h] *to scalp* (*tickets*) **~|verpflichten** vt [h] (sich) ~ *to reenlist*; → kapitulieren **~|wachsen** vi [s] *to continue to grow* ~́|**wandern**, ~́|**ziehen** vi [s] *to continue one's march* | nicht mehr **~|wollen** vi [h] *to hang back* od *off* °~́|**wursteln** vi [h] *to muddle on* **W·eitere(s)** n ~n/ *rest* ‖ (nähere Angaben) *further details* pl; (*he will tell you*) *anything further* ‖ das ~ morgen *the rest to-morrow* ‖ das ~ wird sich finden *for the rest*, *we shall see* ‖ des ~n belehren *to give further information* | **bis auf** ~́**s** *until* od *pending further notice* od *orders*; *for the present*; *temporarily* | **ohne** ~́**s** ([österr] ohneweiteres) *without* (*much ado*, *further ceremony* od) *doubt*; *simply*, *implicitly*, *automatically*, *immediately*, *unhesitatingly*; *out of hand*, *straight away* ‖ das leuchtet ohne ~́s ein *it is easily understood*; etw ohne ~́s glauben *to believe a th blindly*; ohne ~́s verstehen *to grasp readily* ‖ (etw) ohne ~́s zugeben *to admit .. freely* **W·eiterung** f ~/~en *difficulty* ‖ (*it may lead to*) *complications* pl **weith·er** [insep] adv *from afar* [aber sep] → weit II. D. **W·eitung** f ~/ *widening*, *expansion*; *broadening* ⟨a. fig⟩

W·eizen m ~s/ *wheat*; ⟨engl a.⟩ *corn* ‖ türkischer ~ *maize*, *Indian corn* ‖ ⟨fig⟩ sein ~ blüht *he is in luck's way* od *in clover*; (*the film-industry*) *prospers* od *is flourishing* **~ähre** f *wheat-ear* **~älchen** n *wh. nematode* **~backschrot** m & n *wh. whole meal* **~bau** m *wh.-growing* **~bier** n *wh.en beer* **~boden** m *soil adapted for wh.-growing* **~brand** m *collarbags* pl **~brot** n *wh.en bread* **~ernte** f *wh.-harvest* **~feld** n *wh.-field* **~flocken** f pl *wh.ies* **~graupen** f pl *wh.-groats* pl **~grieß** m *grits* pl *of wh.* ‖ (Grießmehl) *semolina* **~keimöl** n *wh. germ oil* **~kleber** m *gluten* **~kleie** f *wh.-bran*, ⟨a.⟩ *offal* **~korn** n *grain of wh.* **~malz** n *wh.-malt* **~mehl** n *wh.en flour* **~schrot** n & m *bruised* od *shredded wh.* **~stroh** n *wh.*(*en*) *straw* **~vollkornbrot** n *whole wh. bread*

welch [inv vor: unbest. Art.; attr a; im Ausruf] ‖ ⟨sonst⟩: **~er, ~e, ~es I.** [interr] **1.** [a] **A.** (unter mehreren) *which* ([*wo*]*man*, *book*)? ‖ ~es Ding *which of the th.s*? **B.** (Art) ~er Mann (Erfolg)! *what a man* (*success*)! ‖ ~ Glück! *what* (*a*) *luck*! ⟨so⟩ ~ schöner Tag/~er schöne Tag! **2.** [pron] **A.** (→ 1.) (..) ~́er? *Which one*? ‖ ~es sind ..? *which are his sons*? ‖ ~er v beiden? *which of the two*? | [indir] .., ~es die einzelnen Stücke waren? .. *which piece was which*?; (*that shows*) *what* (*direction* [in ~er R.] *the wind blows*) | (gleich) ~er **auch** immer der Grund s mag *regardless of the cause*(*s*) **B.** (→ 1.) *what* (*is your name*)?; (*I didn't know*) *what* (*other name to give it*); (Freunde?) was für ~e? *what kind of friends*? **II.** [rel] **1.** [pron] (P) *who* ([acc] *whom*) (⟨a.⟩: *a thrush who hopped*); (S, a. Kind) *which*; (S & P [außer bei Eigennamen u beschränkten Begriffen wie *father*, etc]) *that* (*the man that* [od *who*]) ‖ die Aussicht, ~e herrlich war .. *which was a* *magnificent one* | [gen sg m & n] **dessen,** [f] **deren,** [gen pl] **deren** (P) *whose* (*son*); (S) (*the house*[*s*]) *of which* (*the roof*[*s*]) od (*the roof*[*s*]) *of which* | [als acc fällt *whom, which* ⟨fam⟩ oft aus]: *the man I mean was tall*; ⟨Am a. [nom]⟩: *there are two belong to us* | ⟨vulg⟩ (*who is that*) *as* (*Mr. N. is with*) | **derjenige,** ~er *he who*; diejenigen, ~e *those who, such as* | **k–r,** ~er **nicht** wüßte *no one but knows* **2.** [a] 100 M, ~e Summe .. *5 pounds, which* (*sum*) *I enclose* || .., ~ **letzterer** (*a doctor and a lawyer*) *the latter of whom* **III.** [indef pron] *some* || ~e .., ~e .. *some .., some ..* || (*have you*) *any*? – (*Yes, we have*) *some* **IV. ~er auch (immer)** *who*(*so*)*ever*; *which*(*so*)*ever* (*of them*); *what*(*so*)*ever* (*his age may be*) vgl ~erlei **w·elcher- ~gest·alt** adv *in what manner, by what means, how*; *in consequence of which* **~l·ei** a *of what kind* od *whatever* (*his reasons may be*); *what kind of* (*reasons he may have*) **~w·eise** adv *in what way*

Welf m & n ~(e)s/~e ⟨hunt⟩ *whelp, cub* **w·elfen** vi [h] *to cub* **W·elfe** m ~n/~n *Guelph* | **~n- ~fonds** m *Guelphic Fund* **~geschlecht** n *race of the Guelphs* **~partei** f *Guelph Party*

welk a *withered, faded* || (schlaff) *flabby* || (Gesicht) *shrivelled*; (runzlig) *wrinkled* || ~ w, ~ m *to fade, wither* | **~en** vi [s] *to wither, fade, decay* **≗heit** f ~/ *withered state, withering, flabbiness, decay* **≗krankheit** f *wilt disease*

Well- ~baum m *shaft* || *windlass* || (e–s Mühlrads) *axle-tree* || (e–r Glocke) *beam* **~blech** n *corrugated iron* od *plate* | ~baracke [f] *Nissen* od *Dallas hut* **~fleisch** n *boiled pork* **~holz** n *rolling pin* **~hornschnecke** f *whelk* **~pappe** f *corrugated cardboard* **~rad** n *arbor-wheel* **~zapfen** m *pivot*; → Welle 1. & 3.

W·elle f ~/~n **A. 1.** *wave* (⟨a. fig⟩ & Haar≗) || (Gefühls≗) *thrill* || (Woge) *billow* || (kl) *ripple* || (Sturz≗) *breaker* | Bug≗ *bow-wash* || Boden≗, Gelände≗ *undulation of ground*; *rideau* Fr || Licht≗ *ray-wave* || Luft≗ *wind w.* | ⟨wir⟩ lange ~ *long w.length* **2.** (Reisigbündel) *faggot* **3.** ⟨tech⟩ *axletree, shaft* || Flügel≗ *wind-sh.* || Haupt≗ *king sh.* || Hinterachs≗ ⟨mot⟩ *rear axle sh.* || Seil≗ *rope windlass* || Nocken≗, Steuer≗ *camshaft* || Steuerungs≗ *distributing sh.* || Treib≗ *cardan axle* || Verteiler≗ *timer sh.* || Vorlege≗ *countershaft* **4.** ⟨gym⟩ *turn round the horizontal bar*; e–e ~ m *to revolve round the h. b.* **5.** ⟨mil⟩ (Angriffs≗) *echelon* **6.** ⟨com⟩ (*buying/selling*) *splurge* **B. durchgehende** Stahl≗ *steel sh. throughout the mill* || gekröpfte ~ *crank-shaft* || ([un]gedämpfte) ~ [*continuous*] (*damped*) *wave* || stehende ~ ⟨tech⟩ *vertical sh.*, ⟨phys⟩ *stationary w.* **C.** sein Grab in den ~n finden *to find a watery grave* || die ~n gehen hoch *the w.s are running high, there is a heavy swell* || ~n reiten *to surf* || ~n schlagen *to rise in w.s, to undulate* || v den ~n hin- u hergeschleudert *w.-tossed* **w·ellen** vi/t [h] *to boil* || (Haar) *to wave* (a. = sich ~) || (Blech) *to corrugate* || (Papier) *to rib* | vt (Haar) *to wave* || ⟨cul⟩ *to let boil* | gewellt *wavy* (*hair*) **W·ellen- ~anzeiger** m ⟨wir⟩ *detector* **~bad** n *sea-bath*; *bath with artificial w.s* **~baum** m ⟨tech⟩ *shaft*; *axle-tree* **~bereich** m ⟨wir⟩ *w.-range* **~berg** m *elevation of a w.* **~bewegung** f *undulating motion, undulation*; (der Erdoberfläche) *pulsation* **~brecher** m *breakwater* **~effekt** m ⟨theat⟩ *w. effect* **~erzeuger** m *oscillator* **~filter** m ⟨wir⟩ *w. filter* **≗förmig** a *waving, in w.s, undulating*; *rolling* (*country*) **~gang** m *sweep, swell* **~gekräusel** n *rippling* **~kamm** m *crest of a w.*; schaumiger ~ *white-cap, white horse* **~kupplung** f *shaft coupling* **~lager** n *shaft bearing* **~länge** f *w.length* || ⟨wir⟩ die ~ einstellen *to turn in*, auf dieselbe ~ abstimmen *to syntonize* **~leitung** f *driving shaft* **~linie** f *waving line*; *winding curve*; ⟨typ⟩ *waved rule* **~mechanik** f ⟨phys, wir⟩ *w. mechanics* **~messer** m ⟨wir⟩ *wavemeter* **~reiten** n *surf*(*-rid*)*ing* **~reitereffekt** m *aquaplaning* **~rosse** n pl *skipper's daughters* **~schlag** m *beating,* (*wash, dashing*) *of the waves*; kurzer ~ *choppy sea* || (Brandung) *surf* **~schwingung** f *undulation* **~sittich** m *budgerigar* **~tal** n *trough* **~theorie** f ⟨phys⟩ *undulatory theory* **~transmission** f *shafting* **~verbindungsmuffe** f *sleeve coupling* **~ziffer** f *standing w. ratio* N

W·eller- ~arbeit f (**~decke** f) *work consisting* (*ceiling formed*) *of loam and straw* **~mauer, ~wand** f *loam-, mud-wall* **w·ellern** vt/i [h] *to wall up with mud, to make mud walls*

W·ellington [w–] n (Hptst. v Neuseeland)

W·elpe m ~n/~n *whelp*; *cub*; *puppy*

w·ellig a *wavy* (⟨a.⟩ Haar); *undulating* || *rolling* (*country, plain*) || ~ m *to wave* | ~keit [f] ⟨a.⟩ *ripple*

Wels m ~es/~e ⟨ich⟩ *sheat-fish, wels*

welsch a *Italian*; *French* || (walisisch) *Welsh* || (fremdländisch) *foreign* || ~er Hahn *turkey* || ~e Nuß [f] *walnut* **≗kohl** m, **≗kraut** n *Savoy--cabbage* **≗korn** n *maize, Indian corn* **≗land** n *Italy*; *France* **≗tir·ol** n *Italian Tirol* **≗tum** n ~s/ *foreign* (etc) *manners*, etc **w·elschen** vi [h] *to speak with a French* (etc) *accent* || *to jabber, gibber*

Welt f ~/~en **A.** *world* (⟨a. fig⟩ *the musical w., art w.*) || (~all) *universe* || ⟨fig⟩ die ~ der Banken ⟨a.⟩ *the banking interest*; die ~ des Films ⟨Am⟩ *moviedom* || e–e ~ f sich *a. w. of one's own* | (die Leute) *people* pl **B.** (⟨fam⟩ Gott u) **alle** ~ *everybody*; *each and everyone*; *all the w.* (⟨fam⟩ *and his wife*); alle ~ kennen *to be in with people*; alle ~! *good heavens* || die elegante ~ *the smart set*; die feine *or* gr, vornehme ~ *society*; *the quality*; *the polite* od *great w.*; *the beau-monde*; ⟨Am sl⟩ *tophats* || die ganze ~ *the whole w.* || die gelehrte ~ *the world* od *republic of letters* || die junge ~ *youth* **C.** der ~ **entsagen** *to forsake the w.* || ⟨fig⟩ ~ h *to be wellbred* || die ~ aus den Angeln heben *to shake the w. to its foundations*; *to unhinge the w.* (⟨fig⟩ *the old order*); ein Mann, der die ~ erschüttert *a w.-shaker*; die ~ in Aufruhr versetzen *to set the Thames on fire* || lehr' mich die ~ kennen! *teach your grandmother to suck eggs*! || da ist die ~ mit Brettern vernagelt *that's beyond the wit of man* || Lauf → D. in || der ~ zugewandt (P) ⟨fig⟩ *extrovert* || das Licht der ~ erblicken = **D. auf** die ~ k *to be born*; wenn wir nochmal auf die ~ k *if we had our time over again* || auf der ~ *in the w.* || auf der ganzen ~ *all the w. over, all over the w.*, .. Beachtung finden *to attract w.-wide notice* || das geht mich auf der ~ nichts an *I have no earthly concern in it* || nichts auf der ~ *no earthly consideration* (*shall induce me ..*) || (er tut) nichts auf der ~ *absolutely nothing* | **aus** der ~ schaffen *to do away with* (*a p*), *to cover* (*a th*) *up* (*by doing*), *to settle* (*a matter*); wir sind ja nicht aus der ~ (leicht z finden) *we're not out of the w.* || aus aller ~ *from all parts of the w.* || sich **durch** die ~ schlagen *to make one's way in the w.* | **für** die ~ nicht, nicht um alles **in** der ~ *not for the w., not for the life of me* (*him*, etc) || um alles **in** der ~ *by all means*; *for goodness' sake*; → u.: um; was, warum ..? *what, why on earth*; wie .. ? *how in the name of wonder* (*did that happen*)? || so geht's in der ~, das ist der Lauf der ~ *that's the way of the w., so the w. wags, such is life* || sich in die ~ schicken *to accommodate o.s. to the times* od *to circumstances* || in die ~ setzen (Kinder) *to beget*; ⟨fig⟩ *to start* || ein Märchen in die ~ setzen *to spark a myth* || in der **ganzen** ~ *throughout the w.*; *all over the w.*; *the w. over*; *in all parts of the w.* || in der g. ~ herumgek s *to have been all over the w.* || in die ~ treten (als Debutante) *to come out* | e–e Reise **um** die ~ m *to go round the w.*;

→ o.: in, für; nicht um alles in der ~ *not for the w.; the last th in the w.; he would die rather than do it* | .. **von** der ~ (*the best man*) *going, living, alive, under heaven* || ein M. v ~ *a man of the w.* | **zur** ~ bringen *to give birth to*; ⟨fig⟩ *to bring forth, to produce, breed* **W·elt-** [in comp] *of* bzw *over* (etc) *the world; world* (*war*); *worldly* (*vanity*); *international* (*union*); *universal* (*literature*); *cosmic* (*period*); *cosmo*(*graphy*); *globe* (*-trotter*) ≗·**abgeschieden** a *secluded, lonely* ≗·**abgewandt** a *detached from the w.*; *unworldly* (*thoughts*) ~**achse** f *axis of the earth* ~**all** n *universe* ~**alter** n *age, era; cosmic period, p. in history* ~**angeln** f pl *poles of the w.* ≗**anschaulich** a *ideological* ~**anschauung** f *philosophy of life, outlook* (*on life*), *view of life; weltanschauung; ideology; creed* ~**auge** n *Providence* ~**ausstellung** f *i.l* od *u.l, w. exhibition*, (⟨a.⟩ *Paris*) *W.'s Fair* ~**ball** m *globe* ~**bau** m *universe; c.c system* ~**begebenheit** f *w.* od *historical event* ~**beglücker** m *starry-eyed idealist, w. benefactor* ⟨iron⟩ ~**beherrscher** m *ruler of the w.* ≗**bekannt** a, ≗**berühmt** a *w.-renowned* od *-famous* (*figure*), *known all over the w.* | ~heit [f] (*p of*) *w.-wide fame* ~**beschreiber** m *cosmographer* | nichts ~**bewegendes,** ~**erschütterndes** ⟨fam⟩ *no great shakes* ~**bild** n *w.-picture* ~**bildung** f *cosmogony* | *good breeding* ~**blatt** n *paper of a w.-wide circulation* ~**brand** m *u.l conflagration* ~**bummler** m *globe-trotter* ~**bund** m *i.l union* ~**bürger** m *cosmopolite*; ⟨fam⟩ ein kl ~ ist angek *a little stranger has arrived* | ≗lich [a] *cosmopolitan* ~**dame** f *woman of the w.*; (*fashionable*) *lady* ~**diener** m *worldling* ~**ehre** f *worldly honour* ~**eislehre** f *glacial cosmogony* ~**ende** n *end of the world* | ~glaube [m] *adventism* ≗**entrückt** a *solitary; secluded, remote* (P & S) ~**entstehungslehre** f *cosmogony* ~**ereignis** n *event of i.l importance* ≗**erfahren** a *experienced in the ways of the w.* od *in w.ly affairs; w.ly-wise, sophisticated* ~**erlöser** m *redeemer* ~**eroberung** f *w. conquest* ≗**erschütternd** a *w.-shaking*; → –bewegendes ~**firma** f *firm of w.-wide reputation* ~**flotten** f pl *i.l* od *w.'s merchant fleets* ~**flucht** f *escapism* ≗**fremd** a *unworldly*; ~ w *to be lost to the w.* ~**friede(n)** m *u.l peace* ~**gebäude** n *c.c system* ~**gegend** f *region of the w.* || die vier ~en *the cardinal points* ~**geist** m *spirit of the universe*; ⟨rel⟩ *w.ly spirit* | ~liche(r) [m] *secular priest* ~**geltung** f *prestige* ~**gericht** n *Day of Judgment, Doomsday* ~**geschehen** n *w.-affairs* pl ~**geschichte** f *u.l history*; da hört doch die ~ auf! *well, I never!* | w.tlich [a] *historical; most important* (*event*) ~**getümmel** n *bustle of w.ly affairs, fret and fever of life* ≗**gewandt** a = –erfahren ~**gürtel** m *zone of the globe* ~**handel** m *world's trade* od *commerce, i.l trade* ~**händel** pl *w.ly affairs* pl ~**haus** n = –firma ~**heiland** m *Saviour of the w.* ~**herrschaft** f *w.-dominion* ~**herrscher** m *ruler of the w.* ~**hilfssprache** f *i.l auxiliary* od *artificial language* ≗**historisch** a *w.-historic* ~**jugendfestspiele** n pl ⟨SBZ⟩ *W. Youth Festival* ~**karte** f *map of the w.* ~**kenntnis** f *knowledge of the w., w.ly wisdom*; (k–e) ~ h *to be* (*un*)*acquainted with the ways of the w.* ~**kind** n *child of this w.*; *w.ling; earthly man* ≗**klug** a *politic, worldly-wise, prudent*; ~ s *to know all the answers* | ~heit [f] *w.ly wisdom, sophistication* ~**körper** m *heavenly body; globe* ~**kreis** m *universe, world* ~**krieg** m *w. war* || (1914–18) *Great War* || der erste, zweite ~ *W.W. I, II*; zw den ~en (gelegen) *inter-war* [attr] ~**kugel** f *globe* || ⟨herald, etc⟩ *orb* (*of sovereignty*) ~**kunde** f *cosmology* ≗**kundig** a *notorious* || = –erfahren ~**lage** f *i.l position* ~**lauf** m *course of the w.*; das ist der ~ *such is life, that is the way of the w.* ~**lehre** f *cosmology* ~**leute** pl *w.lings* pl ~**literatur** f *u.l literature* ~**lust** f *w.ly pleasure* ~**macht** f *w.-power* | ~politik [f] *imperialism* ~**mann** m *man of the w.* ≗**männisch** a *well-bred, gentlemanly* ~**markt** m *w.'s market, i.l trade*, (Handelszentrum) *emporium* | ~bedingungen [f pl]: Preise zu ~ *prices obtained on the w. m., w.-m. p.s* (⟨a.⟩ ~preise) ~**meer** n *ocean, main*; die ~e [pl] *the seven seas* ~**meister(in** f) m *champion of the w.* ~**meisterschaft** f *w.'s championship*; Kampf um die ~ *w. series* ~**mensch** m *worldling* ≗**müde** a *w.-weary* ~**öffentlichkeit** f *the w. at large* ~**ordnung** f *system of the w., scheme of the universe* || die jetzige ~ *the w. as it is to-day* || die sittliche ~ *the eternal ethical laws* ~**police** f ⟨ins⟩ *world-wide policy* ~**politik** f *global policy* ~**p·ostverein** m (*U.l*) *Postal Union* ~**priester** m *secular priest* ~**rätsel** n *enigma of the w.* ~**raum** m (→ Raum) (*interstellar* od *outer*) *space*; ~ außerhalb der Milchstraße *metagalaxy* | ~behörde [f] ⟨Am⟩ *Sp. Agency*; ~fahrer [m] *astronaut; sp. travel(l)er* od *rider*; ~fahrt [f] *sp. travel; astronautics* [⟨a.⟩ sg konstr]; ~flug [m] *sp. flight* || ~flughafen [m] *cosmodrome* ~forschung [f] (*outer-*)*sp. research*; ~karte [f] *sp. map*; ~medizin [f] *space medicine*; ~navigation [f] *astronavigation*; ~rakentenfahrt [f] *interplanetary* (*rocket*) *travel*; ~schiff [n] *sp. ship*; –führer [m] *skipper*; ~spaziergang [m] *extra-vehicular activity* [*EVA*]; bemannte ~station [f] *manned orbiting* od *orbital laboratory*; ~strahlen [m pl] *c.c rays*; ~technik [f] *celestial mechanics* ~**reich** n *empire; u.l e.* || *world* || ~- *Imperial* (*affairs*) ~**reise** f *global trip; round-the-w.-tour* od *voyage; journey round the w.*; ⟨mar⟩ *w.'s cruise* || e–e ~ m *to go round the w.* | ~nde(r) [m] *globetrotter* ~**rekord** m *w. record*; ⟨aero⟩ *air speed r.* ~**rolle** f *globalism* ~**ruf** m *w.-wide renown* od *reputation* ≗**scheu** a *solitary, recluse* ~**schmerz** m *w.-weariness, sentimental pessimism; weltschmerz; nostalgia; Wertherism* ~**schmerzler(in** f) m *pessimist* ~**schöpfer** m *Creator* ~**seele** f *soul of the universe* ~**sicherheits-** *world security* (*charta, council,* etc) ~**sinn** m *w.ly disposition* ~**spartag** m *w. savings day* (31. Okt.) ~**sprache** f *universal* (bzw *w.-wide*) *language* ~**stadt** f *metropolis, great city* ≗**städtisch** a *metropolitan* ~**stellung** f *great position in the w.* ~**strich** m *part of the w., clime* ~**system** n *astronomical system* ~**teil** m *part of the world, continent* ~**telegraphenverein** m *i.l telegraphic union* ~**treffen** n der Pfadfinder *Jamboree* ≗**umfassend** a *w.-wide; global; ecumenical* ~**umsegler** m *circumnavigator* (*of the globe*) ≗**umspannend** a *w.-embracing, u.l, global, w.-wide* ~**untergang** m = –ende ~·**uraufführung** f ⟨theat, film⟩ *w. premiere*, → Ur- ~**verachtung** f *cynicism* ~**verbesserer** m *social reformer*, ⟨iron⟩ *do-gooder; critic*, ⟨dero⟩ *faultfinder* ~**verkehr** m *i.l traffic* ~**weise(r)** m *philosopher*; den –sen spielen *to pundit* ~**weisheit** f *philosophy* ≗**weit** a *w.-wide* ~**wende** f *turning point in w.'s history* ~**wirtschaft** f *w. economy; global* od *i.l, w. economics; w. trade and industry* | ~**s-** ~konferenz [f] *i.l economic c.*; ~krise [f] *the w.'s economic crisis; the Great Depression*; ~lehre [f] *economic theory* ~**wunder** n *wonder of the w.* ~**zeit** f *Greenwich time* | ~uhr [f] *u.l time clock*

W·eltergewicht n ⟨box⟩ *welterweight* (nicht über 133 Pfd, ⟨engl⟩ *147 lbs*)

w·eltlich a *mundane; worldly* ⟨a. rel⟩ || ⟨ec⟩ *temporal* (*power*), *secular* (*state*) || ~ gesinnt *w.ly-minded* || *material* (Güter) || ~ m (geistliche Güter) *to secularize* || am ≗en hängen *to be fond of the ths of this w.* | ≗**keit** f ~/ *w.liness* || *secular state* || *civil power* || ~en [pl] *temporal rights* **W·eltling** m ~(e)s/~e = Weltkind

wem pron ([dat] v wer) *to whom* || mit ~ .. *who(m) one is dealing with* || von ~ *of whom, by whom*; ⟨fam⟩ *do you know who that is by?* ≗**fall** m *dative* **wen** pron ([acc] v wer) *whom* || ~ auch *whom(so)ever* || .., wen er zum Vater hatte

⟨bes dero⟩ *he saw what he had for a father*; → was für ~**fall** m *accusative*

W·ende m, **W·endin** f *Wend* †**w·endisch** a *of the Wends, Wendic, Wendish*

W·ende f ~/~n *turn(ing[-point])* ‖ (Biegung) *bend* ‖ ⟨skating⟩ *turn* ‖ ⟨gym⟩ *front vault* ‖ ⟨mar⟩ *tack* ‖ ⟨fig⟩ *change* ‖ an der ~ des Jhs *at the turn of the century* **~gleis** n (mit 3 Weichen) *Y-track* **~hals** m ⟨orn⟩ *wryneck*; *rubberneck* ⟨a. fig⟩ **~kreis** m ⟨geog⟩ *tropic* ‖ ~ des Krebses (Steinbocks) *Tropic of Cancer* (*Capricorn*) ‖ zw den –sen liegend *intertropical* | ⟨mot⟩ *turning circle* **~marke** f ⟨aero⟩ *t.g-point*, *pylon* **~pflug** m *swivel plough* **~punkt** m *t.g-point* (bedeuten *to mark*); ⟨fig⟩ *landmark* (*in history*, *in a p's career*) (*crucial*) *juncture*, *crisis*; *epoch* (*in history*) ‖ ⟨astr⟩ *solstitial p.* ‖ ⟨geom⟩ *p. of inflexion* ‖ wir stehen an e–m wichtigen ~ *we are at the parting of ways* **~turm** m ⟨aero⟩ *pylon* ~- (u Querlagen-) Zeiger ⟨aero⟩ *turn and bank indicator* **W·endeltreppe** f (*flight of*) *winding stairs* pl; e–e eiserne ~ *a circular iron staircase* | ⟨zoo⟩ (Schnekke) *wentle-trap* **w·enden** reg & [wandte/gewandt] [h] **I.** vt **A.** *to turn* (*about*) ‖ ⟨aero⟩ *to yaw* ‖ ⟨tail⟩ *to turn* ‖ ⟨fig⟩ *to twist* (*a th to one's own purpose*) ‖ ⟨fam⟩ etw auf sich [acc] ~ *to spend some money on o.s.* **B.** (**Acker**) *to plough* ‖ (Arbeit, Geld) ~ an [acc] *to spend on* ‖ die Augen ~ auf *to cast one's eyes on ..* ‖ kein Auge ~ v *not to take one's eyes off* (*a p*) ‖ (Heu) *to turn over* ‖ (den Kopf) ⟨a.⟩ *to screw* ‖ s–e Kräfte ~ auf *to devote one's strength to* (*a th*) ‖ gewendeter Rock *coat that has been turned* ‖ jdm den Rücken ~ ⟨fig⟩ *to turn one's back upon a p* ‖ man kann die S drehen u ~ wie man will *you can look at the matter from whatever angle you like* ‖ (Schiff) *to veer .. round, to put .. about* ‖ (Seite) *to turn over*; (bitte) ~! (*please*) *turn over*! (abbr b. w. *P.T.O.*), ⟨Am⟩ *over*! ‖ (Sinn) *to change, alter* ‖ (Wagen) ~ nach *to head .. for* **II. sich** ~ *to turn* (*round*), *bend* ‖ ⟨fig⟩ *to undergo a change, to be on the turn*; .. um 180° *to change course through 180 degrees* | **an**: *to approach* (*a p*); *to get in touch with* (*a p*); *to turn to* (*a p* um *for*), *to address o.s. to*, (fragend) *to apply to*, (bittend) *to appeal to*, (um Schutz etc) *to have recourse to, to repair to* (*a p*); (um Rat) *to consult* (*a p*) ‖ .. mit .. *to put* (*the matter*) *to* (*a p*) | **auf**: (Gespräch) *to turn upon* | **gegen**: *to turn on* od *against* (*a p*); *to set one's face against*, ⟨Am⟩ *to sit down hard on* (*a th*) ‖ alles –det sich gegen mich *I find matters going against me* | sich **hin-** u her|~ ⟨fig⟩ *to hedge, dodge, shilly-shally* | **nach:** *to make for* ‖ sich (Marsch) nach Osten ~ *to strike eastward* | **von:** *to turn away from* | sich **zum** Guten ~ (P) *to turn over a new leaf*, (S) *to take a good turn* ‖ sich zur Linken ~ *to turn to the left* ‖ sich wieder zu etw ~ *to revert* od *return to* **III.** vi *to turn* ‖ ⟨mar⟩ *to veer round, to tack* ‖ ⟨sport⟩ (scharf) *to double* ‖ mit ~der Post *by return* (*of mail*) **IV.** ~ n; ⟨mar⟩ klar zum ~! Ree! *ready about*! *hee-o*! **W·ender** m ~s/~ ⟨cul⟩ *turnspit* ‖ ⟨el⟩ *commutator* ‖ ⟨agr⟩ *hay tedder* **w·endig** a *flexible*; ⟨mot⟩ *steered easily, e.y manageable*; ⟨aero⟩ *sensitive*; ⟨hors⟩ *light in hand* ‖ (P) *elastic*, ⟨fig⟩ *adroit*; *adaptable, resourceful*; *flexible* (*mind*) | ~**keit** f *manœuvrability* ⟨a. aero⟩; ⟨mot a.⟩ *cornering ability* | ⟨fig⟩ *versatility* (*of mind*), *flexibility* (*of decision*) **W·endung** f ~/~en **A.** *turn*(*ing*) ‖ *twist* ‖ ⟨mil a.⟩ *facing* ‖ ~en m *to wheel round* ‖ ⟨fenc⟩ *volt*; (der Hand) *guard* ‖ ⟨hors⟩ halbe ~ *caracole, demi-volt* ‖ ⟨mar⟩ *tack*(*ing*), (taktische) *turn together* ‖ ⟨med⟩ *crisis* ‖ ⟨Lit⟩ *catastrophe* | (Rede~) *phrase, idiom, locution* ‖ stehende ~ *stock phrase*; *tag* ‖ stereotype ~ *cliché* Fr ‖ ⟨mus⟩ *inflection* | ⟨fig⟩ *turn, change* ‖ ~ zum Guten (Schlechten) *ch. to* od *turn for the better* (*worse*), (*un*)*favourable t.* ‖ bei dieser ~ der Dinge *at this juncture* ‖ e–e ~ zum Liederlichen *a ribald t.* **B.** e–r S e–e andere ~ geben *to give a th a new t.* ‖ e–e ~ (zu jds Gunsten) herbeiführen *to t. the scale* ‖ e–e andere ~ nehmen *to take a new t.* ‖ es muß e–e ~ nehmen *it must have a t.*

W·enersee m → Vänersee

w·enig I. a & adv **A.** *little* ([compr] *less*, [sup] *least*) ‖ ⟨iron⟩ herzlich ~ ⟨sl⟩ *a fat lot* ‖ ⟨prov⟩ ~ aber gut *little and good* **B. ein** ~ *a little* ‖ *somewhat, a little, a trifle, lightly* (*better*); *a mite* (*worried*), *the least bit* (*uneasy*); *a thought* (*monotonous, too thin*); *just* (*too heavy*) ‖ ⟨Am a.⟩ *some* (*it had warmed up some*) ‖ ⟨fam⟩ *sort of* (*I am sort of hurt*) **C.** nach ~en **Augenblicken** *a moment or two later* ‖ ein ~ v .. *a bit of* (*both*) ‖ ein ~ **Geld,** Wasser *a little m., w.* ‖ mein ~es Geld *the little m. I have* ‖ ~ **Gutes,** Hoffnung *little good, hope*; s–e ~e Hoffnung auf Erfolg *or* E. z h *the* od *what small hope he has* (od *had*) *of succeeding* ‖ die ~en **Male,** daß *the few times that* od *when* ‖ ~e gute Menschen *few good people* ‖ in nur ~en Minuten *in a matter of minutes* ‖ die ~en Polizisten *the few police* ‖ nur ~e Schritte *but a few steps* ‖ diese ~en Treuen *these faithful few* ‖ mit ein ~ Ungeduld *with a touch of impatience* ‖ mit ~en Worten *in a few words* **D.** .. ~ entwickelt (*trade was still*) *on a small scale* ‖ es **fehlte** ~ u er wäre ertrunken *he was nearly drowned* ‖ ~ geachtet *held in light esteem* ‖ er sprach (nur) ein ~ Englisch *he had little E.* ‖ nur sehr ~ wissen v *not to know more than a very little of ..* ‖ ihm ist ~ z trauen *he is not much to be trusted* | **nicht** ~ .. *rather* (*conceited*), *not a little* (*surprised*), ⟨fam⟩ *half* (*afraid*) **E. so** ~ *so little, such a small quantity* ‖ er ist so ~ dumm, daß er vielmehr .. *he is so far from being an ass, he is rather ..*; er ist so ~ mitteilsam *his is so uncommunicative* (*that ..*) ‖ so ~ auch *however little* ‖ ebenso ~ wie *no more than, as little as* ‖ 5 Mark **zu** ~ *five marks short*; wir h eh schon zu ~ N. *we are short enough of food already* [aber: du weißt zu~, ein Zu~ an Fleiß) **II.** subst **A.** (einige) ~e *few* (*people*) (*think so*) ‖ die ~en *the few* (*persons*, etc), (welche *who*) ‖ **einige** ~e *some few, a few* ‖ einige ~e Begünstigte *a favo*(*u*)*red few* ‖ nicht ~e *not a few* ‖ nicht ~e mehr *a good many more* ‖ so ~e auch *however few* **B. das** ~e, was .. *the* od *what little* (*he knew*) ‖ dieses ~e *this small amount*, etc ‖ mein ~es *the little I have* | **um** ein ~es besser *a trifle better* ‖ ⟨prov⟩ viele ~ m ein Viel *many a little makes a muckle* od *mickle* **w·eniger** a *less*; [pl] *fewer* ‖ immer ~ *l. and l.*; *f. and f.* ‖ 8 ~ 4 (ist 4) *8 minus 4* (*leaves* od *is 4*), *4 from 8 ..* | ~ bedeutend *lesser* | **desto** *or* um so ~ *all the less* (*should he do it*), .. als .. *all the less as* od *since* (*it is not true*) ‖ **nicht** ~ als *no less than*; .. 50 *no*(*t*) *fewer than 50, as many as 50*; (*that costs*) *no less than ..* ‖ nichts ~ als *anything but* (*rich*), *nothing less than* (*murder*) | ~ w *to diminish, to* (*be on the*) *decrease* **W·enigkeit** f **1.** ~/ *smallness, littleness* ‖ *fewness*; *small number* od *quantity* **2.** ~/~en *trifle* ‖ m–e ~ *my humble* od *little* od *poor self*; *your humble servant*; ⟨iron⟩ (m. m.) *Number One*; ⟨fam⟩ *Yours truly*; ⟨sl⟩ *this child*; Leute wie m–e ~ *the likes of me* **w·enigste** a *least*: *the least damage*; *the fewest people* ‖ die ~n *the smallest number* ‖ das ist das ~ste! *that is the least of it*!; .., was Sie tun können *that is the least you can do* | **am** ~n *least of all*; ich hatte ihn am ~n (v allen) erwartet *he was the last* (*of all*) *I had expected to come* | **zum** ~n *at least* ‖ nicht zum ~ *not least* (*of all*), *last but not least, chiefly* (*because*) **w·enigstens** adv *at* (*the*) *least* ‖ (*she'll have a hundred thousand*) *if she's a penny* ‖ er ist ~ 50 Jahre alt *he's 50 if he's a day*

wenn I. [conj] **1.** (wann) *when* (*wh. he arrives, wh. the Cabinet meet, they will discuss it*) | (so bald, [lange] als) *as soon*, [*long*] *as*; (so oft als) *whenever* 2. A. (bedingend) *if, in case* || (vorausgesetzt, daß) *provided* (*that*) || (einräumend) *granted* (*that*) | ∼ es *or* dem so ist *if it's like that* || *if I move it hurts* || *if you are in time* .. || °∼ m–e Großmutter Räder hätte, wär sie'n Omnibus *if my aunt had been a man she'd have been my uncle* || ich will Max heißen, wenn .. *I'll be hanged if* .., *sink me dead if* .. | *with* (*w. mother in that mood* ∼ M. .. ist); ∼ das klar ist/war *with that settled* | *that* (*it is her own fault that nobody likes her*) | .., wenn ich .. (*I shall be pleased*) *to learn* || .., wenn sie .. (*it is false*) *for them to argue* | .., wenn **man** .. (*it is not good*) *to eat too much*; *to hear him speak* (*one would think that* ..); *warming a liquid* (*makes it move*); *on being heated* ..; *when heated* .. | ∼ es k–e Mühe macht! (*I think I'll* od) *may I trouble you for it* | ∼ er vor ihr stirbt, .. *if he should die before her* .. || ∼ ich die W. sagen **soll** (*if I am*) *to tell the truth* || ∼ es wahr s sollte *if it should be true* | ∼ ich du **wäre,** .. *if I were you* .. || *if I knew* (wüßte, würde ich) *I should tell you*; *if I had known* (gew. hätte, hätte ich) *I should have told you* || *had Mr. N. been present he would have wondered why* .. || ∼ ich das **täte** .. *if I were to do it* (*they'd nab me*) || [⟨bay, österr⟩ Metathese] des ∼ mai Oide seng dat! (= ∼ das m–e Alte sehen täte! = sähe) **B. allemal** ∼ *whenever* | **als** ∼ *as if, as though* (*he did it on purpose*); (*he turned as though to go back*); es ist, als ∼ er .. *one would think that he did it on purpose*; *it was for him like passing out of a dream*; ⟨Am⟩: *he looked like he didn't know better* || als ∼ er sagen wollte *as though to say* || nicht als ∼ .. wäre *not as if it were not true* | ∼ **anders** *if* .. *at all, provided that* | ∼ **auch** (*al-*)*though*; *even if*; *granted* (*that*); *if*: *beautiful if a reproduction*; (*with a cheerless sunshine*) *certainly*; *while* (*regretting it, he realized* ..) || *small though my resources are*; *king though he be* (ist) || ∼ er auch .., so .. *ignorant as he was of women, he was not so blind that* || ∼ auch! *what's that*! || ∼ auch noch so kl *no matter how small, sm. though it be, be it ever so small* | ∼ er sie **auch nur** anlachte *if he so much as smiled at her* | **außer** ∼ *unless* | ∼ .. **bloß** .. *if only it were done*!; (*I shudder*) *only to think of it* | ∼ **doch** *if only* || ∼ es doch schon Zeit wäre *I do wish it were time* || ∼ es doch einmal dazu kommt *since it will happen any way*; ⟨so:⟩ *since we must die some time* | ∼ **einmal,** ∼ **erst** (*when, if*) *once* | ∼ **gleich** = ∼ auch | ∼ **immer, jedesmal** ∼ *any time, whenever* (*you are passing*) | ∼ **nicht** *unless*; *failing this*; *but that* || ∼ .. nicht wäre *if it were not* od *were it not for* (*him*), *but for* (*him*) (*I should be in time*) || ∼ sie nicht mit den N. z tun hätte *but for her nerves* (*she* ..) || ∼ nicht .., so doch *if not* .. *yet* od *then* || ∼ nicht d·och *unless* (*it be true*) | ∼ **nichts** dazw kommt *unless sth unforeseen should happen* | und ∼ es **noch** so spät ist *though it be ever so late* | ∼ **nur** vgl ∼ anders, ∼ bloß; *if only* (*it is warm enough*); *so long as* (*it is cheap*) || ∼ er nur dich hat, der *with only you to* (*help him*) || ∼ ich nur daran denke, .. *the mere thought of it* (*makes me shudder*) || .., ∼ du sie nur fragtest (*she would have you*) *for the asking* || ∼ nur im geringsten *though* (*it be*) *ever so little* | **schon** ∼ man daran denkt *only to think of it* .. || ∼ schon vgl ∼ auch || ∼ er schon recht hat *though he may be right* | °na ∼ schon! *well let it be!, even so*! || ∼ schon, denn schon *if at all then thoroughly, as well be hanged for a sheep as a lamb*; ⟨Am sl⟩ *let's go the whole hog* | **selbst** ∼ *even if* (*that be so*), *even if* (*I could*), *granted* (*that*) .. | **und** ∼ du dich auf den Kopf stellst! *whatever you may say*! || **wie** ∼ = als ∼ | ∼ .. **zu** erwarten (ist) *if* .. *is imminent* **II.** ⩪ n; wer das ⩪ u das Aber erdacht (hat aus Häckerling Gold schon gemacht), ∼ das Wörtchen ∼ nicht wär' (wär' mein Vater Millionär) *if ifs and ans were pots and pans* || ohne ⩪ u Aber (*unreservedly*), *without any ifs and ans* **wenn- ∼gl·eich, ∼schon** [conj] → ∼ I. 2. B.

W·enzel m ∼s/∼ ⟨cards⟩ *knave*, ⟨fam⟩ *jack*

wer [pron] [wes, wessen/wem/wen] **1.** [interr (dir & indir) *who*? (*who is there*?) || ⩪ ist's? '*Who is Who*?' || ∼ ist der Täter? *who*('*s*) *done it*? | (aus beschränkter Anzahl) *which*? (*wh. of you*?) | ∼ bist du, der du ..? *who are you that* || ⟨fam⟩ ∼ ist denn alles da? *who are all the people who are present*? || ⟨mil⟩ ∼ da? *who goes there* || ∼ anders *or* sonst? *who else*? **2.** [rel] *who*; *he who* od *that* (*opens the book will find*) || ∼ will, der kann *where there is a will there is a way* || k–e Ahnung h, ∼ jd ist *not to know a p from Adam* **3.** [indef] ⟨fam⟩ ist ∼ da? *anybody in*? || ist da ∼? *is there anybody*? || da ist ∼ *there is somebody* (*wants to see you*) || ∼ auch (immer) *who*(*so*)*ever* (*it may be*); *anybody who* od *that* | (wünschend) ∼ das könnte! *if one could only do it* | ⩪**fall** m *nominative*

Wer- ∼geld n *wergild* **∼wolf** m *werwolf*

W·erbe f ∼/∼n *ad*(*vertisement*) | **∼-** *advertising, publicity* [attr] **∼abteilung** f *a.g department* **∼ankündigung** f ⟨telv, etc⟩ *commercial announcement* **∼antwortkarte** f *a.g reply-card* **∼beilage** f (in der Packung) *package insert* **∼berater** m *a.g agent* **∼brief** m *p.y letter* **∼büro** n *p.y* od *a.g office*; ⟨mil⟩ *recruiting office* **∼dekorationskosten** pl *display expenditure* **∼druck-** ∼sache [f] *a.g printed matter*; ∼schrift [f] *prospectus* **∼durchsage** f ⟨wir, telv⟩ *commercial*; ⟨Am⟩ eingestreute ∼ *spot announcement* **∼ethik** f *a.g ethics* **∼fachmann** m *a.g specialist*, ⟨Am⟩ *adman* **∼feldzug** m *a.g* od *publicity campaign, battle for sales*; ⟨Am fam⟩ *drive* **∼fernsehen** n *commissioned television* od *TV* | Kurzfilm im ∼ *c.d film* **∼film** m *a.g film* **∼fläche** f *a.g space* **∼funk** m *wireless a.g*; *commercial broadcasting* **∼geld** n ⟨mil⟩ *bounty*; ⟨engl⟩ *King's shilling* **∼gesellschaft** f *a.g agency* **∼graphik** f *commercial art* **∼graphiker** m *a.g artist* **∼kosten** pl ⟨com⟩ *a.g expenses* **∼kraft** f *attraction* **∼leiter** m *p.y manager* **∼liste** f ⟨mil⟩ *roll, list of recruits* **∼mätzchen** n *gimmick* **∼mittel** n *a.g medium* **∼nummer** f *complimentary copy* **∼offizier** m *recruiting-officer* **∼plakat** n *a.g poster* **∼rummel** m ⟨sl⟩ *ballyhoo* **∼schrift** f *prospectus* **∼sendungen** f pl ⟨wir⟩ *commercials* **∼tätigkeit** f *propaganda* **∼text** m *blurb* **∼texter** m *sloganeer* **∼träger** m *means of a.g* **∼treibender** m *advertiser* **∼trommel** f ⟨mil⟩ die ∼ rühren *to beat up for recruits*; ⟨com⟩ → werben **∼wesen** n *publicity*; → Reklame- | zu **∼zwecken** in Auftrag gegeben *sponsored* (Programm) **w·erben I.** [warb/geworben] [h] **1.** [vi] (um) *to apply* (*for*) || (um ein Mädchen) *to sue, court, woo* (*a girl*); *to propose* (*to a g.*), (f e–n anderen) *to ask a g. in marriage for* .. || ⟨com, etc⟩ ∼ f *to make propaganda for*, ⟨Am⟩ *to publicize* (*a th*) **2.** [vt] e–n f etw ∼ *to win a p over to a th* || (Soldaten) *to recruit, enlist, raise*; (durch Gewalt) *to press* || Kunden ∼ *to tout*, ⟨Am⟩ *to drum* || ⟨pol⟩ *to canvas, solicit* (*votes*); ⟨Am⟩ *to climb aboard the bandwagon* || ∼des Kapital *capital bearing interest* **II.** ⩪ n; *the wooing* (um *of*) **W·erber** m ∼s/∼ *suitor* || ⟨mil⟩ *recruiting-officer, recruiter*; ⟨hist⟩ *crimp* || ⟨com, pol⟩ *canvasser* || ⟨com⟩ *business getter* **W·erbung** f ∼/∼en ⟨com⟩ *acquisition* (*of new business*), *canvassing*; *publicity, promotion*, ⟨wir, telv⟩ *commercial recruiting* || (um ein Mädchen) *courtship, suit*; *courting, wooing* (*of*) || (Stimmen⩪) *canvass* | **∼s-** ∼kniff, ∼trick [m] (*sales*) *gimmick*; ∼kosten [pl] **1.** = Werbekosten **2.** (v der Steuer abziehbare ∼) *maintenance charges, working expenses*, (EStG) *business allowance*

W·erda(rufen) n *sentinel's call* od *challange*

W·erde n ~/ *the Creator's fiat* **~gang** m *evolution, history* ‖ (P) *background* ‖ ⟨scient⟩ *genesis* **~zeit** f *time of growth, period of development* **w·erden I.** vi [s] [wurde, ⟨poet⟩ ward/geworden, ⟨poet⟩ & [aux] (→ II. 2.) worden] **A.** *to become, be, get* ‖ (allmählich) *to grow* ‖ (plötzlich) *to turn* ‖ (endlich) *to turn out, prove* (*a failure*) ‖ (entstehen) *to arise, to come into existence, to spring to life* **B.** nun, wird's bald?! *hurry up*!, *look alive*! ‖ wann wird Friede? *when shall we have peace*? ‖ ⟨poet⟩ heute muß die Glocke ~ .. *must be cast* ‖ es werde Licht! u es ward L. *let there be l.*! *and there was l.* ‖ ⟨fam⟩ die S **wird**! *the matter is getting on, the affair will come off* ‖ alle Tage, die Gott ~ läßt *every d. which G. gives* (*us*) ‖ was mag nur ~? *what is going to happen*? ‖ was nicht ist, kann noch ~ *we never know what may happen* (⟨a.⟩ man weiß ..) **C. anders** ~ *to change, turn* ‖ gut, schlecht ~ ⟨phot⟩ *to come off well, badly* ‖ ⟨fam⟩ (die Kranken) ~ wieder .. *begin to mend* **D. adlig** ~ *to be ennobled* ‖ bekannt ~ (S) *to get abroad*; (P) mit e–m .. *to make a p's acquaintance* ‖ dunkel ~ *to dim* ‖ geringer ~ *to diminish* ‖ gesund ~ *to recover* ‖ hell ~ *to get light* ‖ katholisch ~ *to turn Roman Catholic* ‖ länger ~ ⟨a.⟩ *to lengthen* ‖ lebendig ~ *to come alive* | (langsam) *to grow* (*stout, wise, scarce, obsolete, old, angry, longer, worse*); ⟨a.⟩ *to wax* (*fat, old, merry, angry*) | (plötzlich) *to fall* (*ill, silent, due*; *into weakness* schwach); *to run* (*mad*); *to turn* (*sour, mouldy*) ‖ (schließlich) *to become* (*blind, aware*); *to go* (*white, green*, etc; *domestic*); *to turn out to be* (*green*, etc); *to go the colour of* (*ashes*, etc) **E. (Arzt,** etc) *to become* (*a doctor*), *to b.* (*ruler*) ‖ Abstinenzler ~ *to go teetotal* ‖ Christ ~ *to become a Christian* ‖ Hauptmann ~ *to be promoted to c.* ‖ Kaufmann ~ *to go into business* ‖→ Landstreicher ‖ Offizier ~ *to go into the army, to obtain one's commission* ‖ *to come to be* (*a good cyclist*) ‖ *to rise to be* (*chairman*) | ⟨sport⟩ (*it takes 4 years*) *to make* (*a good ski-er*) | **was** will er ~? *what is he going to be*?; was soll ich ~? *what shall I be*? | *Mr. N. has now turned actor* | (nachdem er) Herr geworden *become master* **F. [dat]** euch soll Recht ~ *justice shall be done to you* ‖ und was wird mir dafür? *and where do I come in*? ‖ was wird ihm zum Lohne? *what will he receive as* (*a*) *reward*? | **mir wird angst u bange** *I begin to feel afraid* ‖ .. wieder besser *I* (*begin to*) *feel better* ‖ wie wird mir?, mir wird ganz schwach *I feel faint* ‖ es wird mir *or* mir wird übel *I feel sick* ⟨fam⟩ *queer* ‖ e–m (zu eigen, zuteil) ~ *to fall to a p's share* | **[dat ethicus]** ihm wurde der D. krank *the servant went ill on him*; ⟨so:⟩ *the egg went bad on the cook* **G. aus** ihm (dir) wird nie etw (⟨fam⟩ nichts) ~ *he will never get on in life* (*nothing will ever be made of you*) ‖ aus Herren ~ Diener u umgekehrt *slaves and masters change places* ‖ aus Wochen wurden Monate *the weeks passed into months* ‖ was ist aus ihm geworden? *what has become of him*?; *what has happened to him*?; .., was aus uns gew ist (*we now see*) *what we are* ‖ aus der Heirat wurde nichts *it did not come to a m.* ‖ was kann daraus ~? *what will be the consequence*? ‖ daraus wird nichts! *that won't do*!, (*it's*) *out of the question* | wie wird es **mit** .. *what about* (*your visit*)?, *what is happening to* (*our trade*)? | **(zu)** etw ~ *to turn* (*in*)*to* (*steam*) ‖ zum Gelächter ~ (P) *to become a laughing-stock* ‖ du kannst dir denken, wie mir zumute wurde .. *how I felt* ‖ z nichts ~ *to come to nothing* ‖ z Staub ~ *to fall to d.* ‖ z Stein ~ ⟨a.⟩ *to be petrified* ‖ z Wasser ~ (Eis) *to melt*, ⟨fig⟩ *to come to nothing, nought* **H. es** muß anders ~ *ths must change* ‖ es **wird** dunkel *it is getting dark, the night gathers*; .. jetzt früh .. *the days are growing short* ‖ es wird hell (kalt) *day is breaking* (*it is getting cold*) ‖ es ist Mode geworden *it has become the fashion*, (daß .. *to do*) ‖ es wird Nacht *night is setting in* ‖ es wird Zeit, daß wir aufbrechen *it is time for us to start* **II.** v/aux **1. [future** *or* **conditional]** *I shall* (*come*), *you will* (*come*); *shall you* (*come*)?; *we shall* (od *we are going to*) *drive* (fahren) ‖ *nobody is going to do it* ‖ es wird regnen *it's going to rain* ‖ er wird dir bekannt s *he must be known to you* ‖ wir ~ morgen abreisen *we are leaving tomorrow*; ⟨so:⟩ *she is never coming back* | *I will* (*tell him*) ‖ ich werd' euch (k)! *you shall get it*! | ich würde es getan h, wenn *I would have done it if* | sie ~ anwesend s *they are to be present* ‖ wie wird die Ernte (~)? *how will the h. turn out*? ‖ es wird schon ~! *all will come right* | [= **pres**] wer wird denn da gleich weinen? *who would cry about spilt milk*? ‖ das wird nicht wahr s (= es wird sich zeigen, daß es nicht w. ist) *that's hardly true* ‖ er wird doch nicht ernstlich krank s *I hope he isn't really ill* ‖ wo werde ich nur m–e Brille h? *where can I have put* .. **2. [pass] [pp worden]** wir ~ (geliebt, gemalt) *we are* (*loved, being painted*) ‖ ich bin gemalt worden *I have been painted*; *they were beaten* ‖ geweckt ~ *to get woken up* | [⟨engl⟩ oft vi]: getrennt ~ *to divide*, ⟨so:⟩ *to drift*, etc | erwogen ~ *to be under examination* | **mir** wurde die Uhr gestohlen *I had my w. stolen*; ⟨so:⟩ *the house had its walls painted, you have your tea brought to you, he had his arm amputated* | **es** ist uns gesagt worden *we have been told* ‖ es wurde viel gelacht *there was a good deal of laughing* **III.** ≁ n *growing, growth, becoming* ‖ *formation* ‖ *origin, birth, rise*, ⟨scient⟩ *genesis* ‖ *development, evolution* ‖ **im** ≁ *nascent, in embryo*; (*great ths are*) *preparing*; (*a crisis was*) *in the making* **w·erdend** a *nascent, incipient* ‖ *up-and-coming* (*generation*); *developing* (*genius*) ‖ ⟨scient⟩ *embryonic*

W·erder m ~s/~ (Flußinsel) *ait, eyot*

w·erfen vt [warf/geworfen] [h] **A.** *to throw* [⟨a.⟩ vi; nach *at*] (⟨a. mil⟩ .. *troops into a town*) ‖ *to sling*, ⟨fam⟩ *to chuck* (.. *over the banister*), *to dump* (.. *to the floor*) ‖ *to pelt*, ⟨sl⟩ *sock* (*stones*, etc nach *at*) ‖ ⟨artill⟩ *to project* | (drehend) *to spin* (*plates*) ‖ (leicht) *to flip, flick* (*ashes*; auf *on to*) ‖ (ruckartig) *to jerk* ‖ (schleudernd) *to fling, hurl* ‖ (schnell) *to rush* (*troop into* ..) ‖ (schwingend) *to sling* | ⟨fig⟩ (Anker; Auge, Blick; Licht, Schatten; Los; Lot) *to cast* | (jdn) *to thrust* (*a p into a chair*) ‖ *to trip* (*a p*) (⟨a. film⟩ *in mob scenes*) er warf ihn ⟨gym, etc⟩ *he grassed him* (→ ⟨a.⟩ Boden I. A. 2., 5. b) | [pass:] *he was swept out of his saddle, he was tumbled from his seat* ‖ hin- u hergeworfen w *to be jounced* od *tossed* **B.** (→ ⟨a.⟩ A. ⟨fig⟩) **(Ball)** *to throw*, ⟨fam⟩ *pitch* ⟨a. crick⟩ ‖ (Blasen) *to blow, form* ‖ Bomben ~ *to bomb, to drop bombs* ‖ Falten ~ *to wrinkle* ‖ (den Feind) *to put* .. *to flight, to dislodge* (aus *from*) ‖ (im Turnier s–n Gegner) *to unhorse* ‖ **Junge** ~ *to bring forth young*; *to throw, produce* .. (→ C.) ‖ (den Kopf) *to jerk* (*one's h. from side to side*) ‖ e–m ein **Loch** in den Kopf ~ *to break a p's h.* (*with a stone*) ‖ das Los ~ *to cast lots* (über *for*) ‖ (das Lot) *to cast, heave* ‖ Schatten ~ *to cast a shadow*, (kühlenden) *to give shade* ‖ das **Spiel** ~ *to throw down the cards* ‖ (Steine) ⟨fam⟩ *to shy*, ⟨sl⟩ *to bung* (nach *at*) ‖ (Strahlen) *to dart forth* ‖ (Wasserstrahl) *to play* **C.** [abs] **1.** (vgl B. Junge ~) *to drop*, (Raubtiere) *to cub*; *to whelp* (⟨a.⟩ Hunde); (kalben) *to calve*; (fohlen) *to foal*; (ferkeln) *to farrow, litter* **2.** (würfeln) *to* (*have the* [*first*]) *throw*; *to make* (*five*) | ~ **nach** *to have a fling at* **D.** e–m Steine **an** den Kopf ~ *to throw stones at a p's h.* ‖ ein Auge (den Blick) ~ **auf** *to cast* od *glance an eye at* .., *to squint at* ‖ aufs Papier ~ *to jot down* ‖ e–n Verdacht ~ auf *to suspect* (*a p*) ‖ aufs Krankenlager ~ *to make* (*a p*) *ill*; → E. | e–n **aus** dem Hause ~ *to turn a p out of doors* || **durch-e-a** ~ *to jumble up* || **in** Brand ~ *to set .. on fire* || ins G. ~ *to put, throw, cast .. into prison* || Truppen in e–e Stadt ~ *to garrison a t.* || alles in einen Topf ~ *to treat all ths alike* || **mit** etw ~ nach *to throw a th at ..* || mit Beleidigungen (englischen Brocken) [Versprechungen] um sich ~ *to insult people all round* (*to spice one's discourse with English tags*), [*to be lavish of promises*], (→ Geld B. 2.) | Steine ~ **nach** *to throw*, etc *stones at ..* (→ C.) || über den Haufen ~ *to upset, overthrow* | **um, über**: *to throw a cloak over one's shoulders* || **unter-e-a** ~ *to jumble up* | **von**: *her words startled me out of my seat* || v sich ~ *to throw*, etc .. *from one* od *away*, (Mantel) *to whip off ..* | e–m etw **vor** die Füße ~ *to throw*, etc *a th at a p* | **zu**: → Boden I. A. 2. b. **E. sich** ~ (S) *to buckle*; (v Holz) *to warp*, sich nicht ~d *warp-proof*; (v Wasser) *to flutter* || sich müde ~ *to tire o.s. with throwing*, etc | sich ~ **auf** *to rush at, to hurl o.s. on, to seize upon* (*a p*), ⟨fig⟩ *to apply o.s. to* (*a th, one's studies*); eilig .. *to rush, plunge into* (*studies*); sich wieder ~ auf *to fall back upon* (*a matter*) || sich aufs Straßenpflaster ~ *to fling o.s. to the street* || sich aufs Pferd ~ *to leap into the saddle* | **in:** *to get into* (*one's clothes*), in die Brust ~ *to bridle* (*up*), *strut, swagger*; *to give o.s. airs* || sich in die Kleider ~ *to fling one's clothes on* || sich ins Zeug ~ *to put one's shoulder to the wheel* | sich jdm **zu** Füßen ~ *to throw o.s. at a p's feet, to prostrate o.s. before a p* **W·erfer** m ~s/~ ⟨sport⟩ (P) *pitcher* || ⟨mil⟩ (S) *projector*

Werft m ~(e)s/~e ⟨weav⟩ *warp* | ~enzähler [m] *reader*

Werft f ~/~en *dockyard, shipyard, wharf* **~arbeiter** m *docker*, ⟨Am⟩ *roustabout* **~aufseher, ~besitzer** m *wharfinger* **~division** f ⟨mar engl⟩ *technical division* **~geld** n *wharfage* **~halle** f ⟨aero⟩ *repair hangar* **~kommandant** m *admiral* od *captain superintendent* **~pr·obefahrt** f *preliminary trial*

Werg n ~(e)s/ *tow* || (gezupftes [geteertes]) [*black*] *oakum* (zupfen *to pick*)

W·erk n ~(e)s/~e **A.** (Arbeit) *work* || (Tat) *act, action, deed* || (Ergebnis) *workmanship* || (Leistung) *performance, feat, achievement* || (Erzeugnis) *production*; *work* (⟨a. Lit⟩: *a w. by D., the works of D., D.'s works*), (⟨a. ec⟩ *works of charity*) || ⟨mus⟩ *opus* | (Fabrik) *works* pl [sg, konstr], (*manu*)*factory, mill* || ⟨tech⟩ *mechanism*; (Maschine, Uhr) *works* pl || ⟨fort⟩ *works* pl | ⟨comp⟩ 2–19 ~e *from 2 to 19 totals* **B.** das ist sein ~ *that is* (*of*) *his doing* od *way* **C. am** ~ s *to be at it*; *to perform* (*they p. with great delight*) | **ans** ~! *to work!*, *now for it!* || ans ~ gehen, sich ans ~ m *to set to work*; frisch .. *not to let the grass grow under one's feet* | **im** ~ s *to be on foot, to be doing* || ins ~ setzen *to set on foot, to put in practice*; *to execute, perform*; *to bring about* | **zu** ~e gehen *to go to work*; *to proceed* (*with caution*); *to set about it*; vorsichtig z ~e gehen ⟨a.⟩ *to play safe, to feel one's way* **~angehörige(r)** m *employee* **~bahn** f ⟨rail⟩ *industrial track*; *private siding* **~bank** f *work-table, shop-board* **~blei** n *crude lead* **~bücherei** f *works' library* **~bund** m *arts and crafts society* **~druckpapier** n *book printing paper* **~führer** m *foreman* **~halle** f *factory shop* **~haus** n *workhouse* **≃heilig** a *hypocritical* **~heiligkeit** f *hypocrisy* **~hof** m *stone-, timber-yard* **~holz** n *timber* **~kunstschule** f *design school* **~leistungsgewerbe** n *service sector* **~leute** pl *workmen, hands* pl **~mannsarbeit** f (*fine piece of*) *workmanship* **~meister** m *foreman, superintendant*, ⟨Am⟩ *overseer, boss* **~meisterin** f *forewoman* **~nummer** f *factory serial number* **~platz** m = –hof **~probe** f ⟨met⟩ *specimen of the cast* **~prüfung** f *shop test* **~satz** m ⟨typ⟩ *book-work* **≃schaffend** a *working* **~schar** f *labour group* || ⟨Ger⟩ *Choral* od *Dramatic Society* **~schüler** m *half-timer* **~schutz** m *industrial police*; ⟨mil⟩ *i.l plant protection* **~seide** f *floss silk* **~spionage** f *i.l espionage* **~statt, ~stätte, ~stelle** f (*work*)*shop* || ⟨rail⟩ (*harness-*, ⟨Am⟩ *railroad-*)*shop* || ⟨arts⟩ *studio* **~statt-** ~flug [m] *test flight*; ~montage [f] *shop assembly*; ~schiff [n] *repair ship*; ~zeichnung [f] *manufacturer's drawing* **~stein** m *freestone* **~stoff** m *synthetic material*; *plastic*(*s* pl); (*ceramic*, etc) *material*; *ceramics* | ~ermüdung [f] *fatigue of material*; ~wissenschaft [f] *materials science* **~stube** f *working-room* **~stück** n ⟨tech⟩ *workpiece* **~student** m *halftimer*; ⟨Ger⟩ *student who works his way* **~stuhl** m ⟨weav⟩ *loom* **~tag** m (Alltag) *workday, weekday*; *working day* (a. Zeitmaß) **~tag-** *workday* (*clothes*) **≃tags** adv *on week-days* **≃tätig** a *working* || (praktisch) *operative, practical* **~tisch** *bench*, → –bank **~unterricht** m *manual instruction*; ⟨Swedish⟩ *sloid, sloyd* **~vertrag** m *labour contract* **~vorschrift** f *working specification* **~wohnung** f *cottage* **~zeitung** f *house organ* **~zeug** n *tool, implement* || ⟨physiol⟩ *organ*; °⟨sex⟩ *gear* || ⟨fig⟩ *instrument*; (P) *stooge, tool, puppet*; *cat's paw* (*to be used as c.'s p.s by a p*) | ~e [pl] *tooling*; mit Hilfe v ~n arbeiten *to work with machine tools, to machinetool* | ~ausstattung [f] ⟨mot⟩ *tool-kit*; ~kasten [m] *tool-box*; ~maschine [f] *machine tool* | ~n- –bau [m] *m.-t. industry*; –bauer [m] *m.-t. builder*; –einrichter [m] *machine tool setter* | ~schlitten [m] *t. carrier*; ~schlosser [m] *toolmaker*; ~schuppen [m] *implement shed*; ~tasche [f] *tool-bag* || ⟨cycl⟩ *tool-case wallet* **W·erkel** n österr → Leierkasten **~tag** m = Werktag

W·ermut m ~(e)s/ ⟨bot⟩ *wormwood* || (Wein) *vermouth, absinth*; italienischer ~ *it* ⟨fam⟩ || ⟨fig⟩ *gall* **~baum** m *tree-wormwood* **~becher** m *cup of bitterness* (leeren *to drain*)

Werst f ~/~e ⟨Russ⟩ *verst* (1,067 km)

Wert m ~(e)s/~e **A. 1.** (wirklicher, innerer) *worth* (*of a man*) **2.** (äußerer, schwankender) *value* (f *to*) (a. ⟨math:⟩ *v, of the unknown quantity*); v bleibendem ~ *of lasting value*; effektiver ~ (S) *root mean square value*; tatsächlicher ~ *effective value* || f $^1/_3$ des ~es *for one third its v.* | ⟨comp⟩ *information* **3.** (Preis) *rate, price* **4.** (~schätzung) *appreciation* **5.** (Münz≃) *standard* **6.** (Vorzug) *merit* (*of a p*), *virtue* (*of a play, gun*); *asset* (*the only a.*) **7.** ⟨com⟩ ~ heute *v. from to-day*; *v. 8.5.68*; ~ 1. Mai *due May 1st* || der ~ in Faktura *v. as per invoice* || ~ in mir selbst *v. in m.s.* | ~e [pl] ⟨bank⟩ *securities, funds, shares* pl, *stock* || belgische ~e *Belgian stocks*; chemische ~e *chemicals*; Montan- etc ≃e *mines*, etc **8.** ⟨tech⟩ ~e *figures, data*; (Höhe etc) *level* **B.** ⟨math⟩ fester ~ *fixed quantity* || geistige ~e *spiritual values* || geschätzter ~ *valuation* || größter ~ *maximum value* **C.** e–r S ~ **beilegen** *to value*, ⟨Am⟩ *feature a th*; gr (geringen) *to set great* (*little*) *store by a th* || (e–r S [dat] k–n ~ beimessen *to devaluate* || ⟨com⟩ ~ erhalten *value received* || jds wahren ~ erkennen *to appreciate a p at his true value* | k–n ~ h *to be good for nothing*, .. für *to be of no use to* || das hat k–n ~ *that is no good* || es hat alles k–n ~ *it is all to no purpose* | gr ~ **legen** auf *to stand on* (*a th*); *to attach great importance to, to set great value on* || ich lege ~ darauf festzustellen, daß *I want to make it quite clear that* || (gr) ~ darauf legen, daß *to lay* (*great*) *stress on* (*a p being present*), .. z tun *to be desirous of doing, to make it a point* od *to be anxious to do it* || wenn Sie ~ darauf legen .. *if you care* (*to see it*) || **liegen** in: *its virtue lies on* || vollen ~ ziehen aus *to get full value out of* **D. an** ~ verlieren, verloren h *to be deprecated* | **im** ~e v *to the value of* od *valued at* (*£ 50*) || im ~e sinken *to depreciate, recede* || im ~e steigen *to* *increase in value* | **von** ~ s *to matter* || v geringem ~ *of small value* || v gleichem ~e *equivalent* (*to*)

wert a **1.** [+ acc des Maßes] **A.** (P & S) s–e 100 Mark ~ *worth .. marks* || Geld ~ *worth some m.*, ⟨fig, fam⟩ (*that's*) *rich*! || die S ist nicht die Mühe ~ *the game is not worth the candle* || das Lesen ~; ~, daß man es liest; ~ gelesen z w *worth reading, worthy to be read*; *readable* || ~ veröffentlicht z w *newsworthy* **B. es** ~ s *to be worth it, to deserve it* || **etw** ~ s *to be worth one's salt* | **nicht** ~ beachtet z w *beneath notice* | **nichts** ~ *worthless, good for nothing*, ⟨sl⟩ *pretty good rot* | **viel** (wenig) ~ *worth much* (*little*) (mir *to me*) || das ist viel ~ *that is a great th*, .. nicht .. ⟨sl⟩ *not up to much*, .. f mich .. *of little use to me* || das ist schon was *or* viel ~ *that's a great point gained* || e–r ist so viel ~ wie der andere *one is as good as the other*; ebensoviel ~ wie *equivalent to* || weniger ~ *less valuable* **2.** [+ gen] *worth* (*a th*) || des Hörens, der Beachtung, Mühe ~ *worth hearing, notice, while* od *the trouble* || nicht der Rede ~ *not worth speaking of, nothing to speak of, not worth mentioning*; ..! *don't mention it*! **3.** (würdig) [gen] ~ s *to be worthy of, to deserve* (*a th*) || des in ihn gesetzten Vertrauens ~ *worthy of the confidence you may place in him* **4.** (teuer) ⟨fig⟩ *dear* || (geehrt) *honoured*; *esteemed* (*letter*); *valued* (*order*) || Ihre ~e Familie *your f.* || wie ist Ihr ~er Name? *may I ask your name* || Ihr ~es Schreiben vom 12. ds Mts *yours of the 12th inst.* | **jdn ~ m** *to endear a p* (jdm *to a p*) **~|achten** vt *to esteem, respect* **≈angabe** f *declaration of v., declared v.* **≈ansatz** m *valuation* **≈ausgleich** m ⟨com⟩ *clearing* **≈begriffe** m pl *values* **≈berichtigung** f ⟨bal⟩ *adjustment* **~beständig** a *of fixed* od *stable value*; *stable* (*currency*) **≈bestimmung** f *valuation, appraisement* **≈brief** m *insured letter*, ⟨Am⟩ *money-letter* **≈erhöhung** f *raising the value* **≈ermittlung** f *official valuation* **≈ersatz** m *equivalent, compensation* **≈gegenstand** m *article of value* **~geschätzt** a *esteemed* **~|halten** vt irr [h] (bes S) *to value, appreciate*; (bes P) *to honour, esteem* **≈herabsetzung** f *depreciation* **~los** a *worthless*; ⟨sl⟩ *not worth a dam* || ~ s (P) *to have no merit at all* || (gering) *trumpery* (*furniture, arguments*); (*building of*) *paltry* (*houses*); ⟨sl⟩ *dud* || (nutzlos) *useless, futile, nugatory* || ~ m *to stale*; ~ w ⟨fig⟩ *to go to seed* **≈messer** m *standard*; *criterion, ga(u)ge, yardstick* **≈minderung** f *depreciation* **≈paket** n *registered parcel, parcel with value declared* **≈papiere** n pl *securities*; *stocks and bonds*; ⟨bes bal⟩ *investments* pl; nichtfestverzinsliche ~ *equities* **≈sache** f *valuable* (*thing*) **~|schätzen** vt [h] *to esteem, appreciate, value, prize, cherish, treasure* **≈schätzung** f *appreciation*; *esteem, estimation, regard* (*for*) || ~ h f .. *to be appreciative for* (*a p, a th*) **≈schrift** f Sw = –papier **≈sendung** f *article of value remitted* || (Geld) *remittance* **≈steigerung** f *increase in value* **≈stellung** f → ~ A. 7. **≈urteil** n *value-judgment*; antikausales ~ *antipathy towards causal explanation* **~voll** a *of great value, valuable, precious*; ⟨Am a.⟩ *worth-while* (*friend*); künstlerisch u politisch ~ *artistically meritorious and politically constructive* **≈zeichen** n *stamp* | ~geber [m] *automatic st. dispenser* **≈zuwachs** m *increment* (*value*) | ~steuer [f] *increment value* (⟨Am⟩ *betterment*) *tax*; → werten etc

w·erten vt [h] *to value, appraise* || ⟨med⟩ *to call* (*positive*) || hoch ge–tet w *to take high rank*

W·ertigkeit f ~/ ⟨chem⟩ *valency, atomicity*

W·ertung f ~/~en *valuation*

wes [gen v wer] *whose* || ~ Geistes Kind *what kind of a p* || ~ Brot ich ess', des Lied ich sing' *whose bread I eat, his opinion I hold* || → Herz E. 2. a. **≈fall** m *genitive* **~h·alb, ~w·egen** adv & conj *wherefore, why*; *therefore, so*

W·esen n ~s/~ **1.** (Geschöpf) *being*; (*living*) *thing* od *soul*; ⟨fam⟩ *body* || kl ~ *mite* **2.** (S) *nature, character*(*istic*), *quality, property, make-up, disposition, tendency*; (das wahre Sein) *essence*; *gist, core, kernel, pith* || das gehört z ~ der S *that's the very essence of the th* || das innerste ~ ⟨fam⟩ *the ins and outs* (*of a th*) **3.** (Dasein) *existence* **4.** ⟨philos⟩ *entity* **5.** (Veranlagung) *character, nature, disposition*; unfreundliches ~ *unkindness* || (Eigenschaft) *virtue*; dem ~ nach *virtual* (*ruler*), [adv] *virtually* || (Zustand) *condition* **6.** (Benehmen) *conduct, demeanor*; *way*(*s*), *manner*(*s* pl) || *the ways* (*of war*) || [⟨engl⟩ a + *-ness*] (z. B. *snappishness*) || eigentliches ~ *quiddity*; finsteres ~ *grimness*; fühlende ~n ~ [pl] *sentients*; gezwungenes (vornehmes) ~ *affected* (*superior*) *air*; stolzes ~ *airs* pl **7.** (Art des Seins) *mode of existence* **8.** (Aufhebens) *noise, ado*; kein ~ m aus *to make no account of*; viel ~s m (v) *to make much ado* od *a fuss* (*about*) || sein ~ (an e–m Orte) treiben *to haunt a place* **9.** (Organisation) *establisment, body, concern* || *department* || das Gemeine ~ *the Commonwealth* **10.** [in comp] z. B.: Bank- u Finanz≈ *banking and finance*; Finanz≈ *financial affairs, matters, concerns* pl; *finances* || Bank≈ *banks* (od *banking*) *in general* || Minen≈ *mining* || Kriegs≈ *military art* | **~s- ~ähnlichkeit** f *homoiousie* **~änderung** f *change in character* **~einheit** f *identity*; ⟨theol⟩ *consubstantiality* **~lehre** f *ontology* **≈los** a *unsubstantial, unreal, shadowy* **~losigkeit** f *unreality* **~verschiedenheit** f beider *disparity between their two natures* **~zug** m *characteristic feature, essential trait*; *vein* | eigene nationale **~züge** m pl *a separate national identity* **w·esenhaft** a *real* || *organic*; *intrinsic* || ⟨philos⟩ *substantial*

W·esenheit f ~/ *essence, nature* || *substance* || (Wirklichkeit) *reality*; *substantiality* **w·esentlich** a *essential, substantial, material* (*to*) || *intrinsic, fundamental*; *inherent* || *highly important* | *appreciable* (*difference*); *specific* (*distinction*); *material* (*modification*); *positive* (*advantage*); *integral* (*part of* ..); (*to a*) *substantial* (*degree*) || ⟨med⟩ *essential* (*clinical characteristic*) | ~er Bestandteil *constituent* || als ~ betrachten *to make a point of* || Übereinstimmung in den ~sten Punkten *substantial agreement* | in ~en Dingen *in essentials* || ~e Eigenschaft *essence* || ~er Inhalt *meat, substance* (*of a book*) || in nicht ~em Maße *not to any appreciable extent* || die ~sten Punkte, Umstände *the main essentials, the elements* | [adv] ~, im ~en *chiefly, virtually, practically*, etc; *in the main, in substance*; (*to differ*) *materially* || (*he is*) *much* (*younger than she*) || ~ beitragen zu *to contribute materially to* | das ≈e *the vital point, the essential part*; das ≈e außer acht l *to grasp at shadows and let the substance go*; das ≈e e–r S berühren *or* treffen *to strike the keynote* || (⟨engl⟩ *the game's*) *the thing*! | **≈keit** f ~/ *essentiality, reality* | ~/~en *essential matter* od *th*

W·eser f ⟨Ger⟩ (Fluß) **~bergland** n *Weser Hills* **~m·ünde** n (Stadt)

weshalb etc → wes

Wes·ir m ~s/~e *vizier* **~·at** n ~s/~e *viziership*

W·espe f ~/~n ⟨ent⟩ *wasp* | **~n- ≈ähnlich** a *wasp-like* **~bussard** m ⟨orn⟩ *honey-buzzard* **~königin** f *queen wasp* **~nest** n *wasps' nest* || in ein ~ stechen *to stir a w.s' nest*, ⟨fig⟩ *to bring a hornets' nest about one's ears, to get o.s. into a scrape* **~stich** m *sting of a wasp* **~taille** f *wasp-waist*

w·essen [gen v wer u was] **1.** [interr] *whose* || ~ Hut ist dies? *whose is that hat*? || ~ ist er angeklagt? *what is he charged with*? **2.** [relat] .., ~ er angeklagt ist .. (*which*) *he is charged with*

W·est m ~(e)s/~e *west* || *west wind* || ~ gegen Süd *west by south* || ⟨poet⟩ *Occident* **~afrikanische Mulde** ⟨mar⟩ *South-Eastern Atlantic Basin* **~alpen** pl *Western Alps* **~australien** n (westl.

Staat des australischen Bundes) *Western Australia* **~(er)gotland** n (Teil v Schweden) *West Gothland, Westergötland* **~deutschland** *West(ern) Germany* **~ende** n *the West End* **~erland** n ⟨Ger⟩ Badeort auf der Insel Sylt **~ermannland** n (schwed. Provinz) *Vestermanland* **~europäisch** a *Western European* (*Community, Union*) ‖ ~e Zeit *Greenwich Mean Time* N **~f·ale** m, **~f·alin** f ⟨Ger⟩ *Westphalian* **~f·alen** n *Westphalia* **≃f·älisch** a *Westphalian, of Westphalia* **~gebiete** n pl *Western territories* pl **†~g·ote** m, **~g·otin** f *Visigoth*, ⟨a.⟩ *Western Goth* **~g·otisch** a *Visigothic* **~grenze** f *western boundary* **~·indien** n (die Inselwelt der Antillen) *West India, the West Indies* pl **≃·indisch** a *West Indian* **~·indienfahrer** m ⟨mar⟩ *West-Indiaman* **~küste** f *west(ern) coast* **~mächte** f pl *Western Powers* pl **~nordw·est** m *West-North-West* **~-Ost**-Handel [m] *East-West trade*; ~-~-Verhandlungen [f pl] *E.-W. negotiations* **†~preuße** m, **~preußin** f ⟨Ger⟩ *West Prussian* **~preußen** n *West(ern) Prussia* | äußerste **~spitze** *westernmost tip* (*of an island*) **≃römisch** a *Western, Occidental* (*Empire*) **~seite** f *west(ern) side* **~-Virg·inien** n (Staat der U.S.A.) *West Virginia* **~wall** m ⟨mil⟩ *Siegfried Line* **≃wärts** adv *westward* **~wind** m *west(erly) wind* **~zone** f *Western zone*

W·estchen n ~s/~ ⟨tail com⟩ *baby vest*

W·este f ~/~n *waistcoat*, ⟨tail & Am⟩ *vest* ‖ (Uniform≃) *coatee* ‖ ⟨fam⟩ feste auf die ~! *let him have it!* ‖ e–m auf die ~ geben *to dust a p's coat for him* ‖ ⟨fig⟩ e–e reine ~ *a clean slate*; k–e reine ~ h *to have a blot on one's escutcheon*; °sich [dat] die ~ bekleckern ⟨fam⟩ *to blot one's copy-book* ‖ sich s–e weiße ~ bewahren ⟨Am fam⟩ *to keep one's nose clean* **~ntasche** f *w.-pocket* ‖ kennen wie s–e ~ *to know the ins and outs of* (*it*), *to know the highways and byways of* (*it*); in der ~ z tragen *vest-pocket* [attr] | **~n**-~kreuzer [m] *pocket battleship*

W·esten m ~s/ = West; → Norden ‖ (e–r Stadt) *the West End*, ⟨Am⟩ *Side* ‖ gegen *or* nach ~ *westward* ‖ im ~ nichts Neues *all quiet on the Western Front* ‖ sich nach ~ neigend *westering* (*sun*) **w·estlerisch** a *western* (*thought*) **w·estlich** a *western, westerly* ‖ die ~en Staaten ⟨Am⟩ *the West* ‖ ~e Sitten etc annehmen *to westernize o.s.* ‖ [adv] ~ (von) *westward* (*of*) ‖ ~st *westernmost*

w·eswegen adv = weshalb; → wes

wett adv *equal, even* ‖ ~ m *to compensate for* (*a th*); *to recover* (*one's losses*), *to make up for* ‖ ~ s *to be quits* **Wett-** **~annahme** f *betting office* od *pool* **~bewerb** m *competition*; ⟨Am school⟩ *exhibition* ‖ ~ bis aufs Blut *cut-throat c.* ‖ ehrlicher, unlauterer ~ *fair, unfair c.* ‖ starker, scharfer ~ *keen c.* ‖ wilder ~ *rat race*; zunehmender ~ *tightening c.* | auf ~ eingestellt *competitive* | außer ~ *above class* | in ~ treten *to enter into c.* (*with*) **~bewerber** m *rival, competitor* **~bewerbs-** *competing* | ~fähigkeit [f] *ability to compete*; ~freudigkeit, -neigung [f] *competitiveness* –**bewerb(ung)sgeist** m *competitive sense* **~-büro** n = –annahme **~eifer** m *emulation, rivalry* **≃eifern** vi [h] (mit) *to emulate* (*a p*); *vie, compete* (*with*) (an *in*); *to try to outdo* (*a p*) ‖ ~d *emulous*; mit–e–a ~d *falling over one another* ⟨fig fam⟩ **~einsatz** m *stake* **~fahrt** f *race* **~fliegen** n *air race* **~gesang** m *singing-match* **~kampf** m *contest, match, competition* (→ hart) ‖ sportliche –kämpfe [pl] *competitive sports* **~kämpfer(in** f) m *agonist*; *competitor* (f *competitress*) **~kurs** m *odds* [sg konstr] **~lauf** m *running-match* ‖ (Kurzstrecken≃) *sprint* **≃laufen** vi irr [s] *to run a race* **≃|machen** → wett **~preis** m *stake* **~rennen** n (*horse-*)*race*; ⟨fig⟩ *race* **~rudern** n (⟨mar a.⟩ –pullen [n]) *boat-race*; am ~ teilnehmen *to row the race* **~rüsten** n *arms race* **~schwindler** m *welsher* **~segeln** n *regatta* **~spiel** n, **~streit** m (*test*) *match, contest* ‖ jdn z ~ herausfordern *to challenge a p* **~turnen** n *gymnastic match* **~zettel** m *betting slip* **W·ette** f ~/~n *bet* (⟨a.⟩ ~gegenstand: *this team is a good b.*) ‖ was gilt die ~? *what's the betting* (*he is back*)?; *what will you bet?, name your wager!* ‖ die ~ gilt! *done* ‖ e–e (ungleiche) ~ eingehen *to make* od *take a bet* (*to lay* [*heavy*] *odds*); ich gehe jede ~ ein *I'll bet you anything* (*you want*); *I'll go bail*; e–e ~ m *to lay a wager* | **in** e–r ~ *for wager* ‖ **um** die ~ *in rivalry*; .. laufen *to race each other* (mit jdm: *I'll walk you* [*ten miles*]); .. kriechen *to vie in cringing* ‖ etw mit jdm um die ~ tun *to try to outdo a p in doing* .. **w·etten** vt/i *to bet* (mit *with*, auf *on*, um etw *a th*) ‖ ⟨hors⟩ *to play the races* | ich wette (mit Ihnen) (um) was Sie wollen! *I bet you the wealth of Dives against the widow's mite* od *all Lombard street against an orange*, (daß wir h *we have*)! | ⟨fam⟩ ~-**daß**?! *what's the betting?*, ⟨Am fam⟩ *put up or shut up!* ‖ ich wette, daß .. *I'll lay* (*he won't come*) ‖ ich wette, daß du es nicht kannst *I defy you to do it* ‖ ich wette (m–n Kopf) **darauf**! *I'll bet it is so* (*I will stake my life on it*)! .. kannst du jede ~ eingehn *you bet your life!* | 10 **gegen** 1 ~, daß .. *to lay ten to one that* .. ‖ man kann 100 gegen 1 ~, daß ⟨fam⟩ *it is 100 to 1 that* | **auf** ein Pferd ~ *to back a horse* ‖ ich wette auf Kopf (Schrift) *I guess heads* (*tails*) | **so** h wir nicht gewettet *that's not what we agreed upon* | **im** ≃ verlieren [vt] *to bet away* **W·etter** m ~s/~ *better, backer*

W·etter n ~s/~ *weather* ‖ (Unwetter) (*thunder-*) *storm, tempest*; ⟨fig⟩ *row* ‖ schlechtes ~ *bad weather* ‖ schönes ~ *fine w.* ‖ es ist schönes ~ *the w. is fine, it is a fine day* ‖ das schönste ~ h *to have the best possible w.* ‖ das ~ blieb den ganzen Tag schön, .. hielt sich .. *the w. held up all day* ‖ ein ~ braut sich zus ⟨a fig⟩ *stormclouds are gathering* ‖ schönes ~ w *to turn out fine* ‖ trübes ~ *dull w.* ‖ wie ist das ~? was ist für ~? *how is the w.?* ‖ bei jedem ~ *in all w.s*, (*in*) *rain or shine* ‖ infolge widrigen ~s *under stress of w.* ‖ durch schlechtes ~ festgehalten *weather-bound* | alle ~! *confound it!, hang it all!, gosh!* | ⟨min⟩ *air, intake, ventilation*; [pl] matte ~ *oppressed air*; schlagende ~ *fire-damp* | **~ablauf** m *course* **~ansage** f = –bericht **~beobachtung** f *meteorological observation* | ~sballon [m] *shroud balloon, b. sonde* **~beratung, ~besprechung** f ⟨aero⟩ *weather briefing* **~bericht** m *w. forecast* od *report* **~dach** n *penthouse, eaves* pl **~damm** m ⟨min⟩ *ventilation dam* **~dienst** m *meteorological* od *w. service* | ~assistent [m] *m.l a.* **~fahne** f, **~fähnchen** n *w.cock, vane* ‖ ‖ ⟨fig⟩ *turncoat, time-server* **~fahrt** f ⟨min⟩ *air-shaft* **≃fest** a *w.-proof, -tight* (→ –hart); ~ m *to w.ize* °**~frosch** m *meteorologist*, °*rainmaker*; ⟨mil⟩ *the Met*(*eorological Officer*) **~führung** f ⟨min⟩ *ventilation* **~galle** f ⟨mar⟩ *w.-gall* **~geschehen** n *w. events* od *processes* **~glas** n *w.-glass, barometer* **~gott** m *Jupiter Pluvius* L **~hahn** m = –fahne **≃hart** a = –fest; (P) *w.-beaten* (*crew*) **~häuschen** n *w.-box* **~karte** f *w.-chart* °**~kerl** m *devil of a fellow* **~kleidung** f *w. wear* **~kunde** f *meteorology* **~kurve** f *w. graph* **~lage** f *state of the w., atmospheric* od *w. conditions* **~leitung** f ⟨min⟩ *air-hole* **~leuchten** n *sheet* od *heat lightning* **≃leuchten** vi [imps] [h] *to lighten* **~loch** n *quarter from which rain and storms come* °**~mädel** n *devil of a girl* **~männchen** n *figure in a toy-hygrometer* **~maschine** f ⟨min⟩ *ventilator* **~meldung** f *w.-report* **~prognose** f *w.-forecast* **~prophet** m *w.-p.* **~rakete** f *meteorological rocket* **~satellit** m *w. satellite* **~schacht** m ⟨min⟩ *air-shaft* **~schaden** m *damage done by the w.* **~scheide** f *m.l divide* od *limit* **~schenkel** m ⟨arch⟩ *w.-board* **~schiff** n *w. ship* **~schirm** m *shed* **~schlag** m *clap of thunder* **~see**

m, Vätter See [m] (in Schweden) *Lake Vetter* **~-seite** f *w.-side* || ⟨mar⟩ *w.-board* **~spinne** f ⟨artill⟩ *wind-component indicator* **~stein** m *belemnite* **~strahl** m = Blitzstrahl **~strecke** f ⟨min⟩ *air--gallery*; *wind way* **~sturz** m *rapid fall of temperature* || *break* **~tür(e)** f ⟨min⟩ *air-*, *trap-door* **~trommel** f = –maschine **~umschlag** m *snap* **~versicherung** f (Reise≗) ⟨ins⟩ *rain-check* **~verhältnisse** n pl *atmospheric contitions* **~versorgung** f = Wetterung **~vorhersage** f (langfristige *long--distance*) *w.-forecast* | ~karte [f] *prognostic chart* **~wart(e** f) m *meteorological* (*observatory*) *observer*; (*w. bureau*) || ⟨min⟩ *fireman* **~wechsel** m *change of w.* || ⟨min⟩ *current of air* **≗wendisch** a *versatile*, *changeable*, *fickle*, *capricious*; ~er Mensch *w.cock* || ~ s ⟨a.⟩ *to blow hot and cold*; *to play fast and loose* **~winkel** m *storm-point* **~wolke** f *thunder-cloud* **~zeichen** n *w.-symbol* (*on maps*) || *sign of bad w.* **w·ettern 1.** vi imps [h] *to thunder and lighten* **2.** vi ⟨fig⟩ *to curse*, *swear*, *storm*; *to thunder*, *fulminate* (*against*) **W·etterung** f ~/ ⟨min⟩ *ventilation*

Wetz- ~stahl m *steel* ⟨a. cul⟩ **~stein** m *whetstone*, *scythe-stone*, *oilstone*, *hone* **w·etzen 1.** vt [h] (schärfen) *to whet*, .. *sharpen* ⟨a. fig⟩ **2.** vi [h] *to scrape* (an etw *a th*) || *to brush* (*against*) | °(rennen) *to breeze* (*along*), *to hare*, *scamper*, *tear*

W·eymouthskiefer f *Weymouth* od *white pine*

whigg·istisch a ⟨pol⟩ *Whig* (*party*)

Wh·ipcord m –s/–s ⟨tex⟩ *whipcord*; → Cord

Wh·isky-Soda [m] *whisky-soda*, ⟨Am fam⟩ *highball*; ~-Punsch [m] *wh. toddy*

wich 1. & 3. sg pret v weichen

W·ichs [–ks] m ~es/ *gala*; sich in ~ werfen ⟨mil, stud⟩ *to dag up*; *to deck o.s. out*; in vollem ~ *in full fig*, *in f. war paint* **~bürste** f *b.g-brush* **~glanz** m *polish* **~lappen** m *rubbing-cloth* **~zeug** n *b.g-ths* | **~e** f ~/~n *blacking*; *polish* || °⟨fam⟩ ~ kriegen *or* bek *to get a good thrashing* **w·ichsen** vt [h] (Faden) *to wax* || (Boden) *to polish* || (Stiefel) *to black*, *shine* | °vi [h] ⟨sex⟩ *to toss* od *jerk off*, *to w(h)ank* | °gewichst *decked out*, *looking smart* **W·ichser** m ~s/~ *boot-black*; ⟨Am⟩ *shoe--shine boy*

Wicht m ~(e)s/~e *wight* || armer ~ *poor fellow* od *wretch* || elender ~ *tick* || kl ~ ⟨fam⟩ *little chap*; *urchin*; *chit* **~elmännchen** n *imp*; *little goblin*

W·ichte f ~/~n = spezifisches Gewicht **w·ichtig** a ⟨eig⟩ *weighty* | ⟨fig⟩ *important*; *salient*; *meaningful*; *serious*; *material*; *essential* (⟨a. telph⟩: *e. call*); *high* (*affairs*); *of* (*great*) *importance* od *moment*; ⟨Am sl⟩ *big-time* [attr] | ⟨mil⟩ taktisch ~ *vital* (Gelände *area*, *terrain*, *ground*); ~er Platz *strategic point* | ~ f *relevant to* | ~er Faktor *asset*, ~ste Bedingung *prime c.* | ~ tun, sich ~ m *to give o.s. airs*, *to put o.s. forward*, *to put on airs* | ist es ~, daß ..? *is it a point* (*to do it just now*)? | **~ere** Dinge z tun h ⟨fam⟩ *to have other fish to fry* | die **~sten** Akten *the papers that matter most* | **das ≗e** (*here's*) *the point* || etw ≗es *sth important*; das ≗ste *the first th* **≗macher, ≗tuer** m *pompous p*, *busybody*; *fuss-pot*; *squirt* || (Beamter) *Jack in office*, *panjandrum* **≗tuer·ei** f ~/ *pomposity*; *pretentiousness*; *self-importance*; *show-off*; *squirtism* **~tuerisch** a *self-important* **W·ichtigkeit** f ~/ *importance* (*nature is of overruling i.*); gr ~ *impact*; ~ f *relevance to* || ohne ~ *of no importance* od *consequence* (S v gr ~ *matter of great cons.*)

W·icke f ~/~n ⟨bot⟩ *vetch* || (kl) *early v.* || Garten≗ *sweet-pea* || gemeine ~ *tare* || °in die ~n gehen *to decamp*; *to go to the dogs* | **~n-**~futter [n] *oats and v.es* pl; ~stroh [n] *v.-straw*

W·ickel m ~s/~ *roller*, *roll* || ⟨bot⟩ *cincinnus* || Zigarren≗ *filler* || Haar≗ (*hair-*)*curler* || ⟨med⟩ *pack* || ⟨fam⟩ e–n beim ~ (= Haar) packen *to collar a p* **~band** n *swaddling-band* **~bär** m *honey-bear*, *kinkajou* **~blatt** n (der Zigarre) *wrapper* **~gamasche** f *puttee* **~kind** n *baby* **~kittel** m, **~schürze** f ⟨com⟩ *wrapover apron* **~kommode** f *baby's chest of drawers* (*to swathe it on*) **~maschine** f ⟨spin⟩ *winder* **~pappe** f *draper's board* **~presser** (f Zigarren) *box prizer* **~puppe** f *baby doll* **~ranke** f ⟨bot⟩ *tendril* **~rock** m (f Damen) ⟨mod com⟩ *wrapover skirt* **~schwanz** m ⟨zoo⟩ *prehensile tail* **~tuch** n *wrapper* || *baby's napkin* **~watte** f *carded cotton*; *nonabsorbent cotton* **~zeug** n *baby-clothes* **w·ikkeln** vt [h] *to roll*, *wind*, *coil* (um *round*) || (Wolle) *to wind* || (Kind) *to swathe*, *swaddle*, ⟨mst⟩ *to change*; ⟨fig⟩ °schief ge–lt = 1. im Irrtum 2. schlecht gelaunt || (Haar) *to put .. in curlers* || sich Locken ~ *to curl up one's hair* || (Zigarren) *to make* | **auf**: *to wind on* (*a spool*) | **aus-e-a~** *to unroll*, *untwist*, *undo* || sich aus der S ~ *to get out of the scrape* || etw **in** etw ~ *to wrap a th up in sth*; ⟨fig fam⟩ in Watte ~ *to wrap in cottonwool* | **um**: *to twist* od *wrap* (*a scarf*) *round* (*one's neck*) || ⟨fig⟩ e–n um den Finger ~ *to turn a p round one's little f.* | **zu**: *to roll into* (*a ball*) **W·ickler** m ~s/~ ⟨ent⟩ *leaf-roller*, *tortrix* L || Trauben≗ *grap codling moth* **W·icklung** f ~/~en ⟨el⟩ *winding*

W·idder m ~s/~ ⟨zoo & tech⟩ *ram*, *tup* || ⟨mil-hist⟩ *battering-ram* || ⟨astr⟩ *Aries* **~kopf** m *ram's head* **~schwärmer** m (a. **-chen** n) ⟨ent⟩ *burnet-fly*

w·ider I. prep [acc] *against*; *contrary to* || für u ~ *pro and con* || ~ Willen *reluctantly*; *in spite of o.s.* **II.** [adv] hin u ~ *to and fro* || *now and then*

W·ider-, w·ider- pref **1.** [s & a] = gegen **2.** [verbs, mst insep] (Entgegnung, Entgegenstreben) → wider|hallen [betont, sep] [pp –gehallt]; widerrufen [unbetont, insep] [pp ~] **W·ider- ~beklagte(r)** m *cross-defendant* **≗bellig** a *cantankerous* **≗borstig** a ⟨fig⟩ *cross-grained*, *recalcitrant*, *obstinate* | ≗keit [f] *truculence* **~christ** m *antichrist* **≗f·ahren** vi irr [s] (jdm) *to happen* (*to a p*), *to befall* (*a p*); was –fuhr ihm? *what was his fate*? || mir ist viel Gutes v ihm ~ *I have received great kindness at his hands* || jdm Gerechtigkeit ~ l *to give a p his due*, *to do a p justice* **≗haarig** a ⟨fig⟩ *fractious*, *refractory*, *cross-grained*; ~ w ⟨Am sl⟩ *to get one's back up* **~haken** m *barbed hook*, *barb* || mit ~ *barbed* **~hall** m *report*; *echo* ⟨a. fig⟩ || ⟨fig⟩ *response* || ⟨mus⟩ *resonance* || ~ finden *to strike a response*, .. bei *to appeal to* **≗ hallen** vi [h] *to* (*re-*)*echo* ⟨a. fig⟩, *to ring*, *resound* (v *with*) **~halt** m *support*, *prop* **≗haltig** a *resisting* || ⟨cul⟩ *substantial* **~klage** f *cross--complaint*, *counterplea*; *counterclaim*, ~erheben *to c.* **~kläger** m *defendant alleging c.* **~lager** n ⟨arch⟩ *counter-fort*, *spur*, *abutment* **≗l·egbar** a (nicht) ~ (*ir*)*refutable*, (*ir*)*rebuttable* **≗l·egen** vt [h] *to refute*, *disprove*; *to explode* (*a claim*); (Beweis) *to knock down*; *to give the lie to* (*one's own words*) || durch sein Verhalten ~ *to live down* || (jdn) *to prove* (*a p*) *wrong* **≗l·eglich** a = –legbar **~legung** f *refutation*; *rebuttal* **≗natürlich** a = unnatürlich || ⟨a.⟩ *monstrous* **~part** m *opposition* || (P) *opponent*, *adversary* || [dat] ~ halten *to oppose* **~prall** m *rebound* **≗r·aten** vt irr [h] (jdm etw) *to advise* (*a p against a th*), *to dissuade* (*a p from a th*) **≗rechtlich** a *unjust*, *illegal*, *unlawful*; *false* (*imprisonment*) || (unbillig) *unfair* | [adv] ~ betreten *to trespass* (*up*)*on* | [adv] *usurpingly* || **sich** [dat] ~ aneignen *to usurp* || ~ verwenden *to misapply* **~rede** f *contradiction*, *objection*; (freche) *back-talk* || ohne ~ ⟨a.⟩ *unquestionably* || ~n h *to answer back* **~rist** m *withers* pl; an ~druck leidend ⟨hors⟩ *nappy* **~ruf** m *revocation*, *recantation*, *disavowal* || ⟨jur⟩ *disclaimer* || (e–s Angebots, Befehls) *cancellation* || (e–r Behauptung) *withdrawal*, *retraction* || bis auf ~ *until recalled*, etc; ⟨com⟩

unless countermanded **≃r·ufen** vt irr [h] *to recant, retract, revoke, cancel* ‖ *to unsay, withdraw* (*words*); *to eat* od *swallow* (*one's words*) ‖ *to repeal* (*a law*) ‖ (Wunsch) *to unwish* ‖ (Versprechen) *to repudiate* ‖ ⟨jur⟩ *to quash* (*a sentence*) **≃r·uflich** a *revocable* **~r·ufung** f = –ruf **~sacher(in** f) m *adversary, antagonist, opponent* ‖ ⟨rel⟩ der ~ *Satan* **~schein** m *reflection* **≃s·etzen**: sich ~ [h] [dat] *to resist, oppose* ‖ (dem Gesetz) *to disobey* ‖ (e–r Meinung) *to fight against* ‖ (e–r S) *to object to*; *to stand up against* (*a p, a th*); *to set o.s.* od *one's face against a th* ‖ (v Sn) *to defy*; *to be recalcitrant to* **≃s·etzlich** a *refractory* ‖ (im Dienst) *insubordinate* **|** ≃keit [f] *refractoriness; insubordination* **~sinn** m *nonsense, absurdity; paradox* **≃sinnig** a *nonsensical, absurd; preposterous, inconsistent, paradoxical; contrary to common sense* **|** ≃keit [f] *absurdity, incongruity* **≃spenstig** a *refractory, recalcitrant* (*to*), *wilful, headstrong, rebellious, obstinate, stubborn* ‖ *unruly, unmanageable, froward* (*child*) ‖ *restive, fractious* (*horse*) ‖ *intractable* (*material*) **|** die ≃e *the shrew* **|** ≃keit [f] *unruliness, refractoriness, obstinacy* ≃|**spiegeln** vt [h] *to reflect*; ⟨fig⟩ *to mirror*; *to flash back* ‖ sich ~ *to be reflected* (in [dat] *by*) **~spiegelung** f ⟨opt⟩ *reflex* **~spiel** n *contrary, counterplay, counterpart* **≃spr·echen** vi irr [h] [abs] *to argue* ‖ [dat] *to contradict, gainsay* ‖ (e–m Vorschlage) *to oppose* ‖ (e–r Behauptung) *to deny, contest* ‖ dem wurde allgemein –sprochen *this raised general opposition* ‖ ⟨fig⟩ *to be in contradiction to* ‖ sich [dat] ~ *to contradict o.s., to differ from o.s., to be at variance with o.s.* ‖ (S) *to be inconsistent* od *contradictory*; (dem Gefühl) *to be repugnant to* **≃spr·echend** a *contradictory, discordant; conflicting; inconsistent* (*results*) ‖ bei sich so ~en Ansichten *with such a clashing of opinions* **~spruch** m *contradiction*; (innerer *c. in terms*); *discrepancy* ‖ (gegen e–n Vorschlag) *opposition* ‖ sich in ~ setzen z etw *to fly in the face of* ‖ ⟨fig⟩ ~ zw *inconsistency between* ‖ im ~ stehen mit *to be* (*in contradiction* od) *repugnant to, inconsistent* od *at variance with*; *to conflict with* (*a th*), *defying* (*a pattern* Vorbild) ‖ ~ erheben gegen *to object* ‖ ~ herausfordernd *provocative* **~-sprucħs-** ~geist [m] *contradictoriness*; ≃los [a] *consistent* ‖ [adv] *without objection* od *opposition*; ≃voll [a] *incongruous, inconsistent*; (in sich selbst *self-*)*contradictory; conflicting, discrepant* **~stand** m *resistance* ⟨a. el⟩ (entschlossenen ~ leisten *to offer stout r.*), *opposition*; heftigen ~ l. gegen *to set one's face* od *o.s. against* .. **|** [dat] (P & S) ~ bieten, entgegensetzen, l. *to oppose; to put up r. to*; k–n ~ l. *to lie down, to take it lying down* ‖ feindlichen ~ brechen *to overcome enemy r.* **|** passiver ~ *civil disobedience* ‖ der ~ bricht zus *r. is crumbling* **| auf** (eisernen) ~ stoßen *to be up against opposition* (*to bite on granite*) ‖ auf heftigen ~ stoßen *to meet with* (od *to face*) *stiff opposition* **|** (Hindernis) *drag* ⟨a. a–n⟩ **~stands-** ~bewegung [f] *underground* od *subversive movement*; Mitglied der ~ *patriot*; ≃-fähig [a] *of a great resisting power; strong; heavy-duty* (*wire*) ‖ (gegen) *refractory, resistent* (*to*) ‖ ⟨tech⟩ *tenacious, enduring*; ~fähigkeit, ~kraft [f] *power of resistance* ‖ ⟨bot, zoo⟩ *hardiness* ‖ innere ~ *inner power of r.*; ~linie [f] *defence line*; ≃los [a] *unresisting*; ~losigkeit [f] ⟨links-radikal mil-pol⟩ *unarmed resistance, non--violent r.*; ~messer [m] *ohm-meter, megger*; ~moment [n] *momentum of r.* **≃stehen** vi [h] irr [dat] *to resist, withstand, oppose* ‖ beharrlich ~ *to stand out, to*; *to set one's face against* ‖ der Versuchung (nicht) ~ [können] *to withstand* (*to yield to*) *t.* ‖ *I can resist everything but temptation* (O. Wilde) ‖ nicht z ~ *irresistible* **|** (jdm zuwider s) *to excite* (*a p's*) *disgust, to be repugnant* (*to a p*), ⟨cul⟩ *to disagree* (*with a p*), *to be distasteful* (*to a p*); *to make* (*a p*) *heave* **≃st·ehlich** a *resistible* **~str·eben** n *opposition, resistance, reluctance; antagonism* ‖ mit ~ *reluctantly* [adv] ‖ ohne ~ *unresistingly, readily, with a good grace* **≃str·eben** vi [h] [dat] *to go, strive, struggle* (*against*), *to be opposed* (*to*), *to resist* ‖ (jdm zuwider s) *to be repugnant* (*to a p*), *to go against* (*one's*) *stomach* ‖ es -t mir z tun *I am reluctant to do* **|** ~d *grudging; warring* (*influences*) ‖ [adv] *reluctantly, with reluctance* **~streit** m *contradiction, opposition* ‖ ⟨fig⟩ *clash, variance; conflict* (*of opinions*) **≃str·eiten** vi irr [h] [dat] *to clash with, to militate against, to be contrary to* ‖ ~d *opposing, conflicting, antagonistic; warring* (*qualities*) **≃wärtig** a *unpleasant, disagreeable, objectionable; loathsome repulsive, revolting, obnoxious, outrageous, offensive* ‖ *untoward* (*incident*), *annoying*, ⟨sl⟩ *beastly, rotten* ‖ *distaseful, hateful, disgusting* (*affair*) ‖ ⟨Am⟩ *mean* (*job, weather*) **|** (P) ⟨a.⟩ *hateful, odious* **|** ~keit [f] [abstr] *unpleasantness, repulsiveness* ‖ *hatefulness, odiousness* **|** ⟨fig⟩ *eyesore* **|** [konkr] *untoward incident* ‖ ⟨fam⟩ *tiresome affair; bother, nuisance* ‖ ~en [pl] *adversities* pl, *the fret and fume* (*of life*), *the horrors* (*of a bachelor's life*) **~wille** m (gegen) *reluctance, repulsion; repugnance* (*against*); *shrinking* (*from*); *aversion* (*to*); *dislike*, (Ekel) *disgust* (*for*) ‖ mit ~n *reluctantly, with a bad grace, with a certain distaste, in spite of o.s.* ‖ ~ empfinden ⟨a.⟩ *to revolt* (über *at*, gegen *against*) **≃willig** a *reluctant, unwilling; grudging* **|** [adv] ⟨a.⟩ *in disgust* ‖ ~ tun *to shrink from doing* **~worte** n pl; ~ h *or* m *to answer* od *talk back* (*to*), *to give back-chat* **w·iderlich** a *disgusting, nauseous; sickly* (*smell*) ‖ ⟨fig⟩ *disagreeable, revolting, repulsive, repugnant, rancid* ‖ ~er Kerl ⟨fam⟩ *shag-nasty; loathsome* (*row*), *hateful* (*night*), *fulsome* (*flattery*), ⟨sl⟩ *beastly* (*noise*), *poisonous* (*heat*) ‖ .. ist mir ~ *flattery is my abhorrence* **|** adv ⟨a.⟩ *sickly* (*sweet*) **| ≃keit** f ~/ *loathsomeness, fulsomeness, nastiness* **w·idern** vi [h] das –rt mir, es –rt mir davor *it makes me feel sick, I loathe it*; → an|~

w·idmen vt [h] (zueignen) *to dedicate, inscribe* (*a poem to a p*) ‖ (hingeben) *to devote* (*one's time, a few words* [*to*]); reichlich viel .. *to lavish* (*time and trouble on a th*) **| sich** ~ [dat] *to devote, abandon o.s.* (*to*), *to go in* (*for*), *to take up* (*a cause*); *to give o.s. up to, to take to, to address o.s. to* (*a th*); *to give one's service to* (*a p*); *to give o.s. over to* (*a passion*); .. e–m Berufe *to follow a profession* ‖ gewidmet s: *room V is given to* (*foreign painting*) **W·idmung** f ~/~en *dedication* **| ~s** ~exemplar [n] *presentation copy*

w·idrig a (→ wider) *contrary; adverse* (*wind, circumstances*), *untoward* (*event*); *inimical* ‖ widriger Wind ⟨bes mar sailing⟩ *foul wind* (abstoßend) *repulsive, nauseous* **~enfalls** [adv] *failing this; in default of this* od ⟨jur⟩ *whereof; which failing, f. wh.; otherwise, else* **≃keit** f ~/~en *contrariety, adverseness; adversity; untowardness* ‖ (das Abstoßende) *repulsiveness* ‖ (ungünstiger Umstand) *adversity*

wie I. adv & conj **| 1. | [interr] A.** *how?, in what way* od *degree?, like what?* **|** ~ beliebt, ~ bitte? *I beg your pardon?; Sir?, Madam?*; ⟨fam⟩ *what* (→ was) (*did you say*)? ‖ (*you didn't touch it?*), *did you?* **|** ~ denn sonst? *how else?, of course!* ‖ .., ~ .. wohl ..? *I wonder how* .. **B. ~ alt** .. *how old* (*is he*)? ‖ ~ hoch ist .. *what is the height of* ‖ **~ lange** (sind Sie schon hier) waren Sie dort? *how long* (*have you been here*) *did you stay there?* ‖ ~ spät ist es? *what's the time?* ‖ ~ stark war der Besuch? *how many people were there* od *present?* **C.** ~ **gefällt** es Ihnen in P. *how do you like Paris?* ‖ → gehen ‖ ~ heißt's gleich? *what do you call it?* ‖ **~ kam's**? ⟨Am⟩ *how come?*,

~ kam es, daß ..? *how was it that* ..? || ~ macht der Hund? *what does the dog say*? (wauwau) || ~ meinen *or* sagten Sie? = ~ bitte? → A. || ~ ist *or* **steht** es mit Zucker? *have you any s.?, do you want some s.*? ⟨fam⟩ *what about s.*? || ~ wäre es mit e–r Tasse Tee? ⟨a.⟩ *what's wrong with* ..? || ~ **(wäre** es), **wenn** wir .. *what if we* .., *how would it do for us* (*to say so*); ~ wär's, wenn Sie mich anriefen? *how about ringing* (⟨Am⟩ *calling*) *me up*? || ~ wär's, wenn du das ließest?! *supposing you were to stop that* || ~, **wenn** er doch käme *how if he were to come after all*? || ~ aber, wenn er krank wäre? *but suppose he is ill* | **[indirekt]** (ich weiß nicht), wie ich handeln soll .. *how to act* || weißt du, wie er's meint? .. *what he means by it*? || er zeigte ihr, ~ sie z halten waren *he showed her the way to hold them*; ⟨so:⟩ *you should have heard the way he talked to me* (~ er .. sprach); *I have tried your way* (~ du es machst) | (= daß) er sagte, ~ sehr er es bedauerte *he told us how sorry he felt for it* | **2.** | **(Ausruf) A.** ~! .. *what*! (*did he really do it*) || ..? – **Und** ~! ..? ⟨fam⟩ *Rather*! *and how*! *with a vengeance*!; ⟨Am⟩ *in a big way*!; ⟨sl⟩ *not half*! *my hat*! *with knobs on*! || ~ der Deibel! *like anything*! *like a shot*! *like a house on fire*! **B.** ~ **mancher** *how many a one* || ~ viele .. *what a number* (⟨fam⟩ *lot*) *of* .. **C.** ~ **glücklich** .. *how happy* (*we were*)! || ~ leicht man sich täuschen läßt! *how easily one is deceived*! [eingeschoben] wir h es ihm, ~ oft, gesagt *we told him so many times* || ~ sehr h wir uns geirrt! *how greatly we were mistaken*! **D.** ~ sie's m! *at the rate they are going* (*it*) || ~ siehst du aus! *how ill* (etc) *you look*!, *you do look a sight*! || .., wie es regnet! ⟨Am⟩ *listen to it rain* | **3.** | **(in Vergleichen) A.** (= ähnlich) *like* (*mad, a madman, many others*) || ⟨so:⟩ *to sleep like a top*; *he cried like a child*; *he looked like a king*; *to act like a gentleman*; *men like Mr. N.*; .. ~ e–e Trophäe .. *trophy fashion* .. || *attacks like these*; *stillness like the grave* || (*you have them all,*) *so to speak* (*on a string*) **B.** (= gleich) *as* (*above*; *previously mentioned*; *follows*) || (so) weiß ~ .. (*as*) *white as snow* || ⟨so:⟩ *the boy was treated as a man*, .. *ought to be treated as a boy*; *a radiance as of holiness*; *he was not as other boys*; *she hated him as indeed did all the servants* || ein (solcher) Mann ~ er *a man like him, such a man as he* || es war hier alles ~ früher ⟨a.⟩ *nothing was changed here* || .. ~ gewöhnlich (*work goes on*) *the same as usual* || ~ vom Donner gerührt *thunderstruck* || [so schnell ~/als möglich; († & ⟨poet⟩ **als)** ~: Du bist so elend nicht, als wie du glaubst. – Und bin ich denn so elend wie ich scheine? Goethe, Tasso V. 5. (aber nur:) er ist ebenso gr ~ ich] || *as* (*with rare china you could see through it*) | ~ sich's gehört *as is proper* || ~ gesagt *as I told you before* | ~ man mir sagte *as* (od *from what*) *I have been told* || ~ ich sehe, ist es so *I see it is so* || ~ die Dinge jetzt stehen *as matters now stand* || ⟨so:⟩ ~ ich war *just as I stood* od *was* || ~ es verabredet war *as had been arranged* | .., ~ du dir denken kannst, ..., *as you may imagine*, .. || .., *as it is called*, .. | **[nach a]** gewissenhaft ~ er ist, wird er *conscientious as he is* .. || (in dem Maße ~) *he loves wine as he hates beer* **C.** [irreal] ~ betrunken *as if* od *though he were drunk* **D.** [nach compr] (statt [besser] als) **E.** ~ **auch** *as also* (*did the others*) || alle Theater ~ auch alle Museen .. *all theatres* (*are closed*), *as are* od *and so are all museums* | (einräumend) ~ sehr auch (immer) *how(so)ever* || ~ sehr er auch zu bemitleiden ist *much as he is to be pitied* || ~ schwer es mir auch fällt *however much it may cost me*; ⟨so:⟩ *however different they are*; *however much Rome may hate Moscow* || ~ schlau sie auch war *crafty as she was* || ~ dem auch sei *be that as it may* || .. ~ **nur** einer (*he can dance*) *with any one*; (*he did his work*) *with unprecedented speed* || **so** .. **wie** ..; **wie** .., **so** .. → so || [sowohl] die Kunst ~ das Gewerbe hat/haben .. || ~ sie, so nahm auch er *like her he took* || so leicht ~ e–e Feder (*as*) *light as a feather* || wie .. so .. *just as the story, so the play* || so ~ er ist *such as he is* || er liebte e–n Garten (eben)so sehr ~ sie *he loved a g. as much as she did* || eins ist so gut ~ das andre ⟨fam a.⟩ *it's much of a muchness* || ~ gesagt, so getan *no sooner said than done* | ⟨prov⟩ ~ der Herr, so's Gescherr *like master, like man* || ~ du mir, so ich dir! *tit for tat*; ~ man sich bettet so schläft man, ~ man's treibt, so geht's *as you make your bed, so you must lie*; ~ gewonnen so zerronnen *soon come, soon gone* | **und** ~ sie **alle** *or* **nur** heißen mögen *whatever their names may be* (vgl 2.) || ~ **wenn** *as if, as though* || viele ~ **z. B.** Herr N. *many people like Mr. N., for instance* | **4.** | **(zeitlich)** (= als) *as, when, while, as soon as* || ~ ich so vorbei kam (*just*) *as I was passing by* || ~ ich das sah, .. *on seeing that, I went away* || ich sah, ~ er .. gebracht wurde *I watched him taken to the hospital* **II. das** ~ ~/~; das ~ u Warum *the why and the wherefore* || auf das ~ kommt's an *it all depends on how it is done* od *said*

W·iebel m ~s/~ ⟨ent⟩ *weevil*

W·iede f ~/~n *withe*; *willow twig*

W·iedehopf m ~(e)s/~e ⟨orn⟩ *hoopoe, hoopoo*

w·ieder 1. [adv] *again, anew, afresh* || ~ 2 Monate ohne Nachricht *another two months* .. || immer ~, ~ u ~ *over and over again, time after time*; *continually* | (zurück) *back*; *in return* | ~ erstarkt *or* gekräftigt s *to be reinvigorated*; ~ gesund w *to recover* || ~ geltend m *to reassert* || ~ gut m *to make up for*; ⟨sport⟩ (Niederlage) *to come back* || °ich hau mich ~ hin ⟨sl⟩ *I shall cut back to bed* || ~ lebendig m *to revive* || ~ neu m *to restore* | da sah man's ~ *there it was* || da bin ich ~ *here I am again* || als ich ~ im Hotel war, tat ich .. *once back* .. *I* .. || niemand hörte ~ etw v ihm *nobody heard any more of him* | sich ~ setzen *to reseat o.s.* || (etw) ~ auf den Tisch stellen *to return* .. *to the t.* || ~ in Dienst stellen *to recommission* || e–m ~ etw z Gefallen tun *to return a p's favours* || e–n ~ grüßen *to return a p's bow* || ~ v vorn (anfangen) *all over again* || (Speisen) ~ v sich geben *to up* .. *again* **2.** [in comp] [mit Verben (betont *or* unbetont) immer trennbar] ~|beginnen: ich begann ~/~begonnen || ~|·ab|drucken: ich drucke ~ ·ab / ~ ·abgedruckt **W·ieder-** ~·**abdruck** m ⟨typ⟩ *reimpression, reprint* ~|·**ab**|**drucken** ⟨typ⟩ *to reprint* ~|·**ab**|**geben** *to return* ~|·**ab**|**hauen** vi [h & s] ⟨sl⟩ *to beat it back* ~|·**ab**|**sagen** *to countermand* ~|·**ab**|**schreiben** *to recopy* ~|·**ab**|**schließen** *to re-lock* ~|·**ab**|**treten** *to retrocede* ~·**abtretung** f *retrocession* (an *to*) ~|·**an**|**fangen** vt/i [h] *to begin anew, to recommence* || (Schule) *to reopen* ~|·**an**|**gehen** vi irr [s] *to begin anew* || (Schule) *to reopen* ~·**ankauf** m *come-back* ~|·**an**|**knüpfen** vt ⟨fig⟩ *to renew* | ⟨comp⟩ ein Programm (v e–m Stützpunkt aus) ~|·**an**|**laufen** l *to back up a pr.* ~|·**an**|**legen** vt (Geld) *to reinvest* ~·**anpassung** f ⟨soc⟩ *rehabilitation* ~|·**an**|**schließen** vt/refl (sich) ~ *to rejoin* ~|·**an**|**stellen** vt [h] *to reappoint, reinstal* ~|·**an**|**treten** vt [h] (Reise) *to resume* ~|·**an**|**wachsen** vi [s] *to grow afresh* ~|·**an**|**wenden** *to reapply* ~|·**an**|**zünden** vt [h] *to rekindle* ~·**aufbau** m *reconstruction*; ⟨pol & com⟩ *recovery* | ~bank [f] *Reconstruction Loan Corporation*; Europ. ~programm [n] *European Recovery Program* (*ERP*) ~|·**auf**|**bauen** vt [h] *to rebuild* ~|·**auf**|**blühen** vi [s] *to blossom again* | ~ n ⟨fig⟩ *revival* (*of art*) ~|·**auf**|**bringen** vt *to revive* ~|·**auf**|**erwecken** vt [h] *to resuscitate* ~|·**auf**|**fin-**

den vt [h] *to recover* **~·aufflammen** n ⟨path⟩ *recrudescence* **~·aufführung** f ⟨theat⟩ *revival*; ⟨film⟩ *rerun*, (e–s alten Films) *to re-release* **≃·auffüllbar** a *replenishable* **≃|·auf|greifen** vt [h] (Frage) *to reopen*; (Gedanken) *to revive* **≃|·auf|holen** vt [h] (eigene Verluste) *to recover* **≃|·auf|kommen** vi irr [s] *to recover one's health* || (Mode) *to come into fashion again* **~·aufleben** n *resurrection*, ⟨fig⟩ *revival*, *renascence*; ⟨path⟩ *recrudescence* **≃|·auf|leben** vi [s] *to revive* **≃|·auf|-legen** vt [h] (Hörer) *to replace*; (Buch) *to reissue*; **|** (Trockenmilch etc) **≃|·auf|lösen** [h] *to reconstitute* **~·aufnahme** f *resumption* ⟨theat⟩ *revival*; ⟨film⟩ *retake* **≃|·auf|nehmen** vt irr [h] *to take up again, to resume*; (Debatte) *to renew*; (Frage) *to reopen* || jdn ~ *to take a p back*; ⟨ec⟩ *to reconcile* || ⟨comp⟩ *to rerun* **≃|·auf|richten** vt [h] *to raise again, to set up again* || sich ~ *to right o.s.* **~·aufrichtung** f *re-erection* **≃|·auf|rühren** vt [h] ⟨fig⟩ (Frage) *to reopen* **~·aufrüstung** f *re--armament* **≃|·auf|stehen** vi irr [s] *to rise again* **~·aufstieg** m ⟨fig⟩ *resurgence* **~·auftauchen** n *reemergence*; ⟨pol⟩ *comeback* **~·auftreten** n ⟨theat⟩ *comeback*, (dazu: *to make a c.*) || ⟨path⟩ *recurrence* **≃|·auf|treten** vi [s] *to reappear*; ⟨path⟩ *to recur* ⟨a. fig⟩; ~d *recurrent* **~·aufteilung** f *repartition* **≃|·aus|liefern** vt [h] ⟨mil⟩ (Gefangene) *to return* **~beginn** m *reopening* **≃|beginnen** vt [h] (Arbeit) *to resume* **≃|bekommen** vt irr [h] *to recover, retrieve*; *to get back* **≃|beleben** vt [h] *to revive, reanimate*, durch künstl. Atmung *to resuscitate* **~belebung** f *reanimation*, ⟨fig⟩ *revival* || ⟨med⟩ *resuscitation* **| ~s-** ~mittel [n] *restorative*; ~versuch [m] *revival attempt*; durch künstl. Atmung *resuscitation efforts* pl || an jdm ~e anstellen *to attempt to resuscitate a p* **~beschaffungspreis** m *replacement price* **≃|besetzen** vt [h] (Land) *to reoccupy*; (Gehege) *to restock*; e–n Lehrstuhl ~ *to fill a vacant chair* **≃|bezahlen** vt [h] *to repay, reimburse* **~bezahlung** f *reimbursement* **≃|bringen** vt irr [h] *to bring back*; *to restore, return* **≃bringlich** a *retrievable, restorable* **~bringung** f *restoration* **≃|·ein|bringen** vt irr [h] *to retrieve* (*a loss*) **≃|·ein|bürgern** vt [h] *to repatriate* **≃|·ein|führen** vt [h] *to reintroduce*, ⟨fig⟩ *to re-establish* **|** berufliche **~·eingliederung** f *vocational rehabilitation* **≃|·ein|lösen** vt [h] *to redeem, to take out of pawn* **≃|·ein|nehmen** vt irr [h] *to recapture*; (Platz) *to resume* **≃|·ein|richten** vt [h] *to re-establish, reorganize* **~·einrichtung** f ⟨med⟩ *reduction* (*of a fracture*) **≃|·ein|rücken** vt [h] *to reinsert* **≃|·ein|schiffen** [h] *to re-embark* **~·einschiffung** f *re-embarkation* **≃|·ein|schlafen** vi [s] ⟨fig⟩ die S ist –einge– *the matter has been dropped* od *shelved* **≃|·ein|setzen** vt [h] *to replace, restore* || (jdn) *to reinstate, reinstal* (*a p in office*, etc); *to reestablish* (*a p in his rights*); (Herrscher) *to restore .. to the throne* || ⟨jur⟩ *to rehabilitate*; .. in jds Gunst *to re-establish .. in a p's favo(u)r* **|** vi [h] (of fever) *to recur* **~·einsetzung** f *restoration*, etc; ⟨ins⟩ *reinstatement* **≃|·ein|stellen** vt [h] (zuvor entlassene) P ~ *to take a p on again*; ⟨mil⟩ *to call out again* || sich ~ *to return, reappear* **~·einstellung** f *restoration* **≃|·ein|treten** vi [s] (P) *to re-enter*, ⟨mil⟩ *re-enlist* || (Ereignis) *to recur* **~·eintritt** (v Ereignissen) *recurrence*; ⟨comp⟩ *link*; ⟨a–n⟩ *reentry* **| ~s-** ~korridor [m] in die Erdatmosphäre ⟨a–n⟩ *reentry corridor* **≃|erhalten** vt irr [h] *to recover, retrieve* **~erhaltung** f *recovery* **≃|erholen**: sich ~ [h] (v Krankheiten) *to recover* **~er·innerung** f *remembrance, recollection* **≃|erkennen** vt irr [h] *to recognize* (*again*) || sie waren nicht –zu– *we hardly knew them again* || nicht –zu– *unrecognizable, past recognition*, (Buch) *out of all knowledge* **~erkennung** f *recognition* **≃|erlangen** vt [h] *to recover* || den Thron ~ *to be restored to ..* **~erlangung** f *recovery*; ~ des → Selbstbewußtseins, Selbstvertrauens *regaining of one's self-assurance*; *s.-reass.* **≃|ernennen** vt [h] *to reappoint* || –ernannt w ⟨Am⟩ *to succeed o.s.* **≃|erobern** vt [h] *to reconquer* **~|erreichen** vt [h] *to regain* **≃|erscheinen** vi [s] *to reappear* || (Buch) ~ l *to republish* **≃|ersetzen, ≃|erstatten** vt [h] *to restore, to make up for* || (Auslagen) *to refund, reimburse* **~erstattung** f *restitution* || (Auslagen) *r.dment, r.ement* **≃|erw·achen** vi [s] ⟨fig⟩ = –aufleben **≃|erzählen** vt [h] *to tell again, to repeat* **≃|fangen** vt ⟨a.⟩ *to recapture* || (Flugzeug) *to flatten out* **≃|finden** vt irr [h] *to find again* || (Verlorenes) *to recover* || *to regain* (*one's composure*) **≃|fl·ottmachen** vt [h] *to refloat* **≃|fordern** vt [h] *to ask back* **~gabe** f *restitution, return* || ⟨fig⟩ *rendering, representation, reproduction*; (Übersetzung) *translation*; (e–r Rolle) *interpretation*; ⟨mus⟩ *rendition*; ⟨rec⟩ *playback*; ⟨radar⟩ *display* || ⟨a.⟩ Life-~ ⟨wir, a-n-comm⟩ *readout* **|** ⟨rec⟩ ~gerät [n] *reproducer*; ~knopf [m] *playback button*; hohe ~treue *high fidelity* **≃|gebären** vt irr [h] ⟨fig⟩ *to regenerate* || –geboren w *to be born again* **≃|geben** vt irr [h] *to give back*; *to return*; e–m s–e Ehre etc ~ *to restore a p's h.*, etc || ⟨fig⟩ *to render, reproduce*; (Rolle) *to interpret*; (Tatsachen) *to put forward*; .. genau .. *to give* (*a p's exact words*); *I shall give the impression he made on me*; ⟨rec⟩ *to play back* || (Gefühl) *to reflect* **≃geboren** a *regenerate* **~geburt** f *rebirth*; ⟨theol⟩ *regeneration* **≃|genesen** vi irr [s] *to recover* (*one's health*) **~genesung** f *recovery* **~|gestellen** vt [h] ⟨cust⟩ *to re-present* **≃|gewinnen** vt irr [h] *to regain, retrieve* || e–e Schlacht ~ *to retrieve the day* || Stellung, Ruhm etc ~ ⟨fam⟩ *to stage a comeback* || nicht –zu-(d) *irretrievable* **≃|grüßen** vt [h] *to return a bow*, ⟨mil⟩ *salute* (*to*) **≃|g·ut|-machen** vt [h] (Fehler) *to make good*; (Verlust) *to recoup, repair*; (Schande) *to live down* || *to redress, expiate* (*wrong*); *to atone for* (*a th*) || nicht –zu-(d) *irretrievable* (*disaster*) **~g·utmachung** f *reparation, atonement, restitution* (*R. Court*) **≃|g·ut|werden** vi [s] *to heal again* || ⟨fig⟩ (e–a) *to become friends again* **≃|haben** vt irr [h] *to have back* **≃|her·aus|geben** vt [h] *to give up*; (Buch) *to reissue* **~herrichten** n (v Gut) *reclamation* **≃h·erstellbar** a *reparable* **≃|h·er|stellen** vt [h] *to reestablish, reconstruct* ⟨a. fig⟩; *restore, renovate* || s–e Ehre ~ *to clear o.s.* || (Rechte) *to reinstate* || (Gleichgewicht) *to redress* || (Kranke) *to cure*; –ge–t s *to have recovered* **~h·ersteller** m *restorer* **~h·erstellung** *restoration* || (e–s Kranken) *recovery*; ⟨med⟩ (*physical*) *restoration, rehabilitation*; ~ der Arbeits-, Dienstfähigkeit *ph.l reconditioning* **| ~s-** ~fähigkeit [f] ⟨med⟩ *reparative power*; ~mittel [n] *restorative*; ~zeichen [n] ⟨mus⟩ *natural* **≃h·olen** insep vt [h] [pp –h·olt] *to repeat, reiterate, renew*; *to say* (*over*) *again*; *to sum up* || *to go over* (*one's lesson*) || (Angriff) *to resume* || Bekanntes ~ *to go over old ground again* || ⟨comp⟩ *to rerun*; ⟨rec⟩ *to replay* || jds Worte ~ *to echo a p* **| sich** ~ (P) *to repeat o.s., to say the same th over and over again* || (S) *to be of frequent occurrence* || es läßt sich nicht ~ *it does not bear repeating* **|** sich ~d *iterative, repetitious, repetitive* **|** oft **-lt** *continual*; → erneut **|** adv *repeatedly* || [~ + s oft durch pl]: ~es Bitten *entreaties* **|** ~lt w ⟨wir, telv⟩ *to be returning to the air again* **≃|holen** sep vt [h] [pp –geholt] *to bring* od *fetch back* **|** z **-h·olten** Malen = **≃h·olentlich** adv *repeatedly, again and again, on more than one occasion* **~h·olung** f *repetition* (⟨a. bib⟩ End≃: Psalm 115, 9ff., 118, 2ff.) || es sind ~en [pl] *they are repetitions* || *recurrence* || ⟨mus⟩ (nach Beifall) *encore* Fr || ⟨film⟩ *cut-back*; (e–r Aufnahme) *retake*; ⟨rhet⟩ (durch Definition) *systrophe* (*Macbeth* II, 2. 34ff.) **| ~s-** ~aufnahme [f] ⟨film⟩ *retake*; im ~fall *should it occur again*; ~impfung [f] *revaccination*; ~kurse [m pl] *refresher courses*; ~prüfung [f] ⟨Am fam⟩ *make-ups* pl; ~spiel [n] *re-play* (⟨so:⟩ *re-row*, etc); ~taste [f] ⟨rec⟩ *back-space control*; ~zeichen [n] ⟨mus⟩ *repeat* **~hören** n; auf ~! ⟨telph⟩ *so long*!, ⟨wir⟩ *good night, everybody*! **~inbesitznahme** f (S.recht) *re-entry* **~inkraftsetzung** f ⟨ins⟩ *reinstatement of cover* **~inkrafttreten** n ⟨jur⟩ *revival* **≈|inst·andsetzen** vt [h] *to recondition* **≈|käuen** vi/t [h] *to ruminate*; *to chew the cud* ⟨a. fig⟩; ⟨fig⟩ *to go back over* (*the old ground*); *to repeat .. over and over again, to harp on* (*it*) **~käuer** m *ruminant*; ⟨fig⟩ *p who keeps telling the same stories* | ~mägen: → Pansen, Netz-, Blätter-, Labmagen **~kauf** m *repurchase*; *redemption* **≈käuflich** a *redeemable* **~kaufsrecht** n *right of redemption* **~kehr** f *return* ⟨a. arch⟩ || (v Ereignissen) *recurrence*, (regelmäßige) *periodical occurrence* || 25jährige ~ *25th anniversary* **≈|kehren** vi [s] *to return* || *to recur* ⟨a. math⟩ || (*seasons*) *come round* | **~d** *recurrent* **≈|klingen** vi irr [h] *to reverberate* **≈|kommen** vi irr [s] *to return* | [aber:] ≈ k *to come again* °**≈|kriegen** vt [h] *to get back again* **~kunft** f *coming back, return* || ⟨theol⟩ *second advent* (*of the Lord*) **≈|machen** vt [h] *to make* od *do again* || *to repair* **~nahme** f *taking back* || ⟨mil & mar⟩ *recapture* **≈|nehmen** vt irr [h] *to take back* || ⟨mil & mar⟩ *to retake, recapture* **≈|rufen** vt [h] *to call back*; → wider– **≈|sagen** vt [h] *to tell again, to repeat* **~|sammeln** vt [h] *to reassemble* || ⟨mil⟩ *to rally* (*troops*) **≈|schaffen** vt [h] *to restore* **≈|schenken** vt [h] *to give in return* **≈|schicken** vt [h] *to send back* **≈|schimpfen** vt/i [h] *to return an insult* **~schlag** m *return-stroke* **≈|schlagen** vt irr [h] *to strike*, etc .. *back* **~sehen** n *meeting again*; ~ mit ⟨theat m. m.⟩ (*her*) *comeback* || auf ~! (*I hope to*) *see you again*!, *good-bye* (*for the present*)!, ⟨fam⟩ *so long*! *see you tomorrow*! ⟨Am fam⟩ *I'll be seeing you* || °~ macht Freude ⟨fam⟩ *it's got a back to it* **≈|sehen** vt & sich ~ irr [h] *to see* od *meet again* **≈|senden** vt irr [h] *to send again* **~solv·enzerklärung** f ⟨com⟩ *whitewash* **≈|suchen** vt [h] *to seek* (*again*) **~taufe** f *rebaptism* **≈|taufen** vt [h] *to rebaptize* **~täufer** m *anabaptist* **~|treffen** vt [h] *to rejoin* (*a p*) **≈|tun** vt irr [h] *to do in return* || *to do again, to repeat* || daß du (mir) das nicht –st! *don't* (*let me see you*) *do that again* || ich will's nicht ~ *I will never do so any more* **~·übernahme** f *resumption* (*of the command*) **≈um** adv *again, anew, afresh* || *in return* || (*those*) *in their turn* || *on the other hand* **≈|·um|kehren** vi [s] *to turn back, to retrace one's steps* **≈|vereinigen** vt [h] *to reunite* || sich ~ mit *to rejoin ..* **~vereinigung** f *reunion*; *reunification* (*of Germany*) **~verf·ilmung** f *retake* **≈|vergelten** = vergelten **≈|verheiraten** vt & sich ~ [h] *to remarry* **~verheiratung** f *remarriage* **~verkauf** m *resale* || (im kleinen) *retail* | **~s-** ~wert [m] *value on resale, trade-in v.* **≈|verkaufen** vt [h] *to sell again, to retail* **~verkäufer** m *retailer* **~verschlimmerung** f ⟨path⟩ *recrudescence* **~versöhnung** f *reconciliation* **~verwendbar** a *reutilizable, reusable* (*container*, ⟨a. a–n⟩ Rakete, Stufe); *for repeated use* **~verwendung** f (benutzten Materials) *salvage*; *reuse* | (zur) **~vorlage!** [f] *to be resubmitted*! | ~mappe [f] *suspense file* **~wahl** f *re-election* **≈|z·u|lassen** vt [h] *to readmit* **~z·ulassung** f *readmission* **~z·unahme** f *fresh increase* **≈|z·u|stellen** vt [h] *to return* **~z·ustellung** f *return* **≈|z·u|teilen** vt [h] *to reallot*

W·iege f ~/~n *cradle* ⟨a. artill⟩ || ⟨fig⟩ v der ~ bis zur Bahre *from birth to death, from the womb to the tomb* || das ist ihr nicht an der ~ gesungen worden *one could not have foretold her that at her birth* **~messer** n *chopping-knife* **~stempel** m *stamp of the weight* **~vorrichtung** f *weighing device* **w·iegen 1.** vt reg [h] *to rock .. (in a cradle)* || *to dance .. (in one's arms)* || *to dandle .. (on one's knees)* | (zerkleinern) ⟨cul⟩ *to chop* | **sich** ~ *to sway* (*to and fro*); ⟨Am⟩ *to teeter* || sich auf s–m Sitz ~ *to roll about on one's seat* || sich ~ in [acc] *to lull o.s. in*(*to*); .. in dem Glauben ~, daß *to hug the idea* (*of ..*) | ~der Gang *lilting gait* **2.** vt/i [wog/gewogen] [h] *to weigh* || (v Waagen) ungenau ~ *to be fast* bzw *slow* || schwerer ~ als ⟨fig⟩ *to outweigh* (*a matter*); ob .. als .. *whether .. will have more serious consequences than ..* || weniger ~ als *to be lighter than* | (Jockei & sich) vor/nach dem Rennen ~ *to weigh out*/*in* || er wiegt .. *he weighs* (*12 stone*) | **gewiegt** ⟨fig⟩ *clever, smart* || ~ in *well versed in* **W·iegen-** **~druck** m *cradle-book*; *incunabulum* **~fest** n *birthday* **~kind** n *infant in the cradle* **~korb** m *bassinet, cot, basket-cradle* **~lafette** f *cradle mounting* od *carriage* **~lied** n *lullaby*

w·iehern I. vi [h] *to whinny*, ⟨mst⟩ *neigh* | ⟨fig⟩ *to shout, howl*; (lachend) *to guffaw* || ~des Gelächter *guffaw, horse-laugh* **II.** ≈ n *neigh*

Wiek f ~/~en [niedd] (kl Bucht) *creek*

W·iem(en) m ~s/~ [niedd] = Latte(ngerüst) || ⟨orn⟩ *roost*

Wien n *Vienna* **~er(in f)** m *inhabitant of Vienna, Viennese* || die ~ pl *the Viennese* **~er Wald, ~wald** m (Gebirge im Westen v Wien) *Wienerwald* **≈erisch** a *of Vienna, Viennese*

W·iener- **~schn·itzel** n *veal cutlet* **~w·ürstchen** n *Wiener*, ⟨Am fam⟩ *wienie* | **≈n** vt/i [h] ⟨mil sl⟩ *to bullshit*

wies 1. & 3. sg pret v weisen

W·iesbaden n ⟨Ger⟩ (Stadt)

W·iesbaum m *binder, hay-pole* **W·iese** f ~/~n *meadow* (auf *in*) || ⟨poet⟩ *mead* || leicht abfallende ~ *slow-droping meadow*

W·iesel n ~s/~ ⟨zoo⟩ *weasel*; gr ~ *stoat* || Freizeit≈ ⟨sport & Spiel⟩ *scate-boards* pl

W·iesen- **~ampfer** m ⟨bot⟩ *sorrel* **~bau** m *cultivation of meadows* **~bauer** m *meadower* **~blume** f *meadow-flower* **~champignon** m *field mushroom* **~egge** f *chain*(*-link*) *harrow* **~erz** n ⟨min⟩ *m.-ore* **~fläche** f *stretch of m.* **~gras** n *m.-grass* **~grund** m *m.-ground* | sanfter **~hang** m *slow-dropping meadow* **~kerbel** m *cow-parsley* **~knarre** f ⟨orn⟩ *corn-crake* **~knopf** m ⟨bot⟩ *great burnet* **~knöterich** m ⟨bot⟩ *bistort, adder's-wort* **~kresse** f ⟨bot⟩ *m.-cress* **~kümmel** m ⟨bot⟩ *caraway* **~lerche** f ⟨orn⟩ *m.-pipit* **~pfad** m *path across the m.s* **~plan** m *lawn* **~ralle** f = –knarre **~salbei** m *m.-sage* **~sch·aumkraut** n ⟨bot⟩ *lady's smock, cuckoo-flower* **~tal** n *green valley* **~wachs** m *grass-crop* **~w·ucherblume** f *ox-eye daisy*

wies·o? *how is that*, **how so*? *how do you mean*? || ~ wußten Sie davon? *how is it* (⟨Am fam⟩ *how come*) (*that*) *you knew of it*? **wiev·iel** (in Frage u Ausruf) *how much* || ~ *or* wie viele Kinder *how many children* || um ~ mehr ..! *how much more* (*should it be so*)! || ~ **auch** *however much* || **~mal**? *how many times*? **wiev·ielte** a *which* (*of a number*) || der ~ ist (*or* den ~ten h wir) heute? *what date is it to-day*? *what day of the month is it*? || zum ~n Male? *how many times*? **wiew·eit** → in~, ob **wiew·ohl** [conj] (*al*)*though*

W·iking(er) m *Viking* || ~erschiff [n] *Viking ship*

Wild n ~(e)s/ ⟨hunt⟩ *game* [sg & pl konstr] (Groß≈ *big g.*; Hoch≈ *large g.*, ⟨cul⟩ *big g., venison* || Klein≈ *small g.*; ⟨cul⟩ *game*) || (Stück) ~ *head of g.* || (Reh) *deer* | **wild I.** a **A.** *wild* ⟨a. bot⟩ || (unzivilisiert) *savage, barbarous* || (ungebildet) *uncultured, unpolished* || (ungestüm, grimmig) *fierce* || (ungezähmt) *feral* || (v Gemüt) (P) *truculent*; *ferocious* (*beast*), *unruly* (*child*), *brutal* (*fellow*) || (zornig) *angry, furious*; ~ wie ein angeschossener Eber *hog-wild* || ⟨fig⟩ *rampant, extravagant* (*theorist*); *rabid* (*militarist*);

unlicensed (*bookmaker*) ‖ *rude* (*chaos, passion, scenery*) ‖ (lärmend) *raucous* (Gelage) ‖ ⟨phys⟩ *spurious* (Strahlung) | ⟨fam⟩ ∼ auf *crazy about* ‖ → planlos **B.** ∼er **Anschlag** *fly posting* ‖ (Boden) *virgin* ‖ (Ehe) *unlawful*; in ∼er Ehe leben ⟨fam⟩ *to live tally* ‖ in ∼er Eile *in a whirl* ‖ ⟨path⟩ (Fleisch) *proud* ‖ ∼e **Flucht** *headlong fl.*; ⟨mil⟩ *rout* ‖ ∼ Gebirgslandschaft *the wilds* ‖ (Geflügel) *wild* ‖ (Gegend) *wild, rugged* ‖ ∼es Gestein *dead rock* ‖ *dishevelled, unkempt* (*hair*) ‖ ∼e **Jagd** *wild ch.*, ⟨fig⟩ *hectic hunting*; *uproar* ‖ *wild, disorderly, dissolute* (*life*) ‖ ∼es Mädchen *tomboy* ‖ ⟨fig⟩ ∼er Mann *bogey* ‖ (Pferd) *intractable* ‖ ∼e Spekulationen [pl] *wildcat finance* ‖ *wild, lightning* (*strike*) ‖ (Volk) *savage, truculent* ‖ ⟨phys⟩ (*of rays & radiation*) *spurious* **C.** ∼ **aufwachsen** (P) *to run wild* ‖ ∼ blicken *to have a wild look* ‖ ∼ drauflosreiten *to ride for a fall*, ∼ drauflosschießen *to shoot wild* ‖ ∼ m (P) *to enrage, exasperate*; (T) *to frighten, to make shy* ‖ ∼ wachsen(d) *to grow wild* (*selfsown*) ‖ alles lag ∼ umher *ths were lying about in a most disorderly state* ‖ ∼ w *to run amok, to fly into a passion*; (Pferd) *to get out of hand*; ⟨m. m.⟩ *to turn beat* **D.** nicht **so** ∼! *don't be so noisy!, come, come!* ‖ **wie** ∼ ⟨sl⟩ *like old boots*; ∼ wie ein angeschossener Eber *hog-wild* **II.** ≈**e** m [der ∼, ein ∼r] & f ∼n/∼n *a savage* | ⟨fig⟩ ⟨soc⟩ (Arbeiter) *free rider*; *candidate for a final examination who has not attended the school* ‖ ⟨univ⟩ *student belonging to no club*, ⟨stud sl⟩ *tosher*, → Fink; ⟨Am⟩ *barb* ‖ ⟨parl⟩ *free lance*; *below the gangway* ‖ ⟨arts⟩ die „∼en" *the fauves* Fr, *the fauvist movement* (1905ff.) ‖ **das** ≈**e** *the wildness* (*of* ..) **∼acker** m *preserve in a park* **∼bach** m *mountain stream*; *torrent* | ∼verbau [m] *t. control work* **∼bad** n *thermal springs*; *watering place* **∼bahn** f *hunting-ground* ‖ (*lane through a*) *preserve* **∼bann** m (*exclusive*) *hunting-right* ‖ (Gehege) *preserve* **∼braten** m *roast game* od *venison* **∼bret** n *game, venison* (→ Wild) ‖ ∼keule [f] *haunch of v.* **∼dieb** m *poacher* **∼dieber·ei** f *poaching* **∼esel** m *onager* **∼fährte** f (–wechsel [m]) *game path, game trail* **∼fang** m (Mädchen) *romp, tomboy, hoyden* ‖ (Junge) *madcap, pickle, harum-scarum* **∼-forst** m *forest-preserve* ≈**fr·emd** a *quite strange* ‖ er ist uns ∼ *he is an utter stranger to us* ‖ ∼e Leute *perfect strangers* **∼garten** m = –park **∼geflügel** n *wildfowl*; *game birds* **∼geruch** m *smell of game* ‖ ∼ h *to be high*; den ∼ annehmen l *to hang* (*game*) **∼geschmack** m *gamy flavo(u)r* ≈**geworden** a *running wild* **∼grube** f *pitfall* **∼hackfleisch** n *salmi* (*ragout of game*) **∼händler** m *dealer in game* **∼heuer** m *one who mows grass on mountain--ridges* **∼hühner** n pl *wild fowl* **∼hüter** m *game--keeper* **∼kalb** n *fawn*; *hind calf* **∼katze** f *wildcat, catamount* **∼leder** n, ≈**ledern** a *deerskin, buckskin* ‖ (Handschuh) *doe-skin* ‖ (Schuhe) *fawn-skin* | ∼lederimitation [f] ⟨tex com⟩ *velveteen* **∼-meister** m *ranger* **∼obst** n *wild-grown fruit* **∼park** m *preserve(s), park* **∼pret** = –bret **∼recht** n *quarry* ≈**reich** a *abounding in game* **∼reservat** n *reservation*; *wildlife refuge*; *National Bison*, etc *range* **∼rind** n *wild ox* ≈**romantisch** a *wild* (*scenery*) **∼ruf** m *call* **∼schaden** m *damage done by game* **∼schonung** f *game-preservation* **∼schur** f *bearskin, furred cloak* **∼schütz(e)** m *poacher* **∼schutzgebiet** n, **-park** m = ∼reservat **∼schwein** n *wild boar, sow* | ∼jagd [f] *pigsticking* **∼spur** f *track* **∼stand** m *lair of deer* ‖ (Bestand) *stock of deer* **∼verbiß** m *browsing by game* ≈**wachsend** a (*growing*) *wild*; *self-sown*; *spontaneous* **∼wasser** n *torrent* **∼wechsel** m *game path*, ⟨mot⟩ *deer pass!* **∼w·est-** ∼film [m] ⟨Am sl⟩ *horse opera*; *Western*; *blood'n' thunder epic*; ∼schau [f] ⟨Am⟩ *rodeo*; ∼reiter [m] *dead fall* **∼zaun** m *park-paling* **∼zustand** m ⟨bot⟩ *spontaneity* **W·ilde** m [der ∼, ein ∼r] & f ∼n/∼n → wild II. **w·ildenzen** vi [h] *to taste gamy* **W·ilderer** m ∼s/∼ *poacher* **Wilder·ei** f ∼/ (Fisch≈ *fish*) *poaching* **w·ildern** vi [h] *to poach* ‖ ⟨bot⟩ *to become wild* **W·ildheit** f ∼/ (vgl wild) *wildness* ‖ *savageness* ‖ *fierceness* ‖ *ferocity* ‖ *anger* ‖ *ruggedness* | ∼en [pl] *atrocities* **W·ildling** m ∼(e)s/∼e ⟨bot⟩ *wildling, wild stock* od *tree* ‖ ⟨fig⟩ (P) *ruffian, barbarian* **W·ildnis** f ∼/–isse *wilderness, desert, wilds* pl ‖ ⟨fig⟩ *chaos*

W·ilhelm [npr] ‖ °falscher ∼ *false* (*postiche* Fr) *tress of hair* ‖ °dicker ∼ (P) *swell*; den dicken ∼ markieren *or* spielen *to come the heavy*

W·ille(n) m ∼ns/ **A.** *will*; *strength of mind* ‖ ⟨philos⟩ *volition*; *intention* ‖ (Verlangen) *mind, wish, pleasure, inclination* ‖ (Absicht) *design, purpose* ‖ ∼ zur Macht *will to power* **B. böser** ∼ *ill-will*; *malice, malignity* ‖ .. eigener ∼ (*it was your*) *own wish* ‖ k–n eigenen ∼n h *to have no will of one's own* ‖ (*free*) *will*, ⟨philos a.⟩ *agency* ‖ (*good*) *intention*; guter ∼ *willingness*; den guten ∼n zeigend *token* [attr] (Einfuhr) ‖ (*last*) *wishes* pl; *will* (*and testament*) **C.** s–n ∼ **durchsetzen, h** *to get, have one's way, to carry one's point*; .. bei jdm *to work one's will upon a p* ‖ er setzte s–n ∼n durch *his will prevailed* ‖ guten (besten) ∼ns s *to be* (*very*) *willing* ‖ den guten ∼n (f die Tat) gelten l *to take the will for the deed* ‖ Ihr ∼ soll geschehen *you shall be obeyed* ‖ e–m s–n ∼n l *to let a p have his own way* ‖ wenn es Ihr ∼ ist *if you wish it* ‖ e–m s–n ∼n *or* jds ∼n tun *to do as a p wishes, to humour a p* ‖ sich G.s ∼n fügen *to submit to the w. of God* ‖ dem Feind den ∼n z Behauptung entgegensetzen *to confront the e.y with one's determination to protect o.s.* **D. aus** freiem ∼n *voluntarily*; *willingly* [adv] ‖ aus eigenem ∼n *on one's own volition, of one's own accord* | **beim** (*or* mit dem) besten ∼n *for the life of me, despite one's best intentions*; *try as one* (*I, he*) *will*; *as much as I should like to* ‖ *really* (*I r. couldn't tell you*); (*I don't know*) *at all* | **gegen** s–n ∼n *against one's will, despite of o.s.* ‖ *unwillingly, reluctantly* | **mit** ∼n *on purpose, purposely, intentionally, designedly* ‖ mit jds Wissen u ∼n *with a p's knowledge and consent* | **nach** ∼n *as one pleases* ‖ nach jds ∼n *in accordance with a p's wishes* ‖ es ging mir nach ∼n *I had my wish* ‖ wenn es nach m–m ∼n ginge *if I could have my way* ‖ jdn nach s–m ∼n tanzen l *to have one's way with a p* | **ohne** m–n ∼n *without my consent* | **um** [gen] ≈n *for* (*the sake of*) ‖ um Gottes ≈ *for God's sake* ‖ wider ∼n *reluctantly, unwillingly* | jdm **zu** ∼n s *to comply with a p's wishes, to be willing to please a p* ‖ sie war ihm zu ∼n *she gave him his will of her, she gave herself up to him* **w·illen** → Wille D. um .. ∼ **W·illen-** ≈**los** a *without a will of one's own*; *drifting* **∼losigkeit** f *want of will, weakness* (*of purpose*); ⟨scient⟩ *aboulia* **w·illens** a; ∼ s *to be willing, to intend, to have a mind* ‖ nicht ∼ *lo(a)th* (*to do*) **W·illens-** **∼akt** m *act of volition* **∼änderung** f *change of mind* **∼anstrengung** f *effort of will* **∼äußerung** f *expression of one's will* **∼bestimmung** f *testamentary disposition*; *will* **∼bildung** f *forming* od *training of mind* od *will-power*; *mind training* **∼entschluß** m *volition* **∼erklärung** f *declaration of intent(ion)*, ⟨jur⟩ *declaratory act* **∼freiheit** f *free will, freedom of* (*the*) *will* **∼kraft** f *strength of mind, will-power, strong will* ‖ (*power of*) *volition* **∼lähmung** f ⟨scient⟩ *aboulia* ≈**mäßig** a *volitional* **∼meinung** f *will, pleasure* ≈**schwach** a *weak-minded* **∼schwäche** f ⟨a.⟩ *velleity*; ⟨scient⟩ *aboulia* ≈**stark** a *strong-minded* (*p*); *strong--willed* (*leadership*) **∼stärke** f *strength of will* od *purpose* **w·illentlich** [adv] = mit Willen

willf·ahren vi [h] [dat] *to comply with, to accede to* (*a p's request*); *to humour* (*a p*); *to gratify* (*a p, a p's wishes*) ‖ s–m Antrag ist (ge)willfahrt worden *his petition has been granted* **w·illfährig** a *compliant, willing*; *complaisant,* *obliging* || ⟨dero⟩ *obsequious* | **×~keit** f ~/ *compliance, readiness, complaisance* || ⟨dero⟩ *obsequiousness* **W·illfahrung** f ~/~en *compliance* (*with*); *gratification, grant* (*of*) **w·illig** a *willing* (*servant*), (⟨bib⟩ *the spirit is w.*) || *ready* (*purchasers*) || *tractable* (*child*) || *gentle* (*horse*) || *ungrudging* (*labour*) || sich ~ finden l z *to show o.s. willing to* || mit ~em Herzen = ~ [adv] *willingly* || °~es Mädchen ⟨sex⟩ *easy mark* od ⟨vulg⟩ *meat* || [compr] ~er ⟨st exch⟩ (Geld) *easier* **..willig** [in comp]: Auswanderungs-~e(r) *prospective emigrant* **w·illigen** vi [h] = ein|willigen **W·illigkeit** f ~/ *willingness, readiness* **W·illkomm(en** n) m ~s/ *welcome, salutation*; herzlicher ~ ⟨fam⟩ *glad hand* **~empfang** bereiten *to unroll the red carpet* **~-Höft** n (in Hamburg) *welcome point* **~(s)gruß** m *welcome* **~(s)becher, ~(s)trunk** m *cup of w.*; *loving cup* **~(s)worte** n pl *words of w.* **willk·ommen** a & adv *welcome* ⟨a. fig⟩; ⟨fig⟩ *pleasant, pleasing, grateful, gratifying* || ~! *welcome* (auf, in *to*)! || ⟨fig a.⟩ *agreeable, acceptable* | (herzlich) ~ heißen *to* (*bid a p a hearty*) *w.e*; *to make a p w.e*; *they always made one w.e* (*to one's home*), *to give a p a glad hand* || seien Sie (mir, uns) ~! *happy to see you*! || das ist mir sehr ~ *that comes most opportunely* || jdm ein ×~ bereiten *to give a p a welcome*; ⟨cul⟩ *to make a p very welcome to a meal* **W·illkür** f ~/ *arbitrariness* || (Belieben) *discretion* (*I leave that to your d.*) || *arbitrary power* bzw *action* || der ~ jds ausgeliefert *put to a p's mercy* | nach ~ *at* (*your*) *pleasure*; *ad libitum*; ⟨fam⟩ *to the top of one's bent* **~herrschaft** f *despotism, tyranny* **~verfahren** n *arbitrary proceeding* **w·illkürlich** a *arbitrary, despotic* || *absolute* (*power*); *high-handed* (*treatment*); ⟨tech⟩ *manual* (*control*) | [adv] ~ verteilen *to randomize* | **×~keit** f ~/~en *arbitrariness* || [konkr] *arbitrary act, caprice*

W·ilna n ⟨Litauisch-Russ⟩ (Stadt) *Vilna*

w·immeln vi [h] (von) *to swarm, crawl*, ⟨fig⟩ *to be full* (*of*), *to teem, abound* (*with*) || ge–lt k *to come in crowds* || (Käse) *to be alive* (*with maggots*) || v Personen ~ *to be alive with persons*

w·immen vi [h] Sw = Trauben lesen ×**W·immer** m = 1. Weinlese 2. Winzer

W·immer(l n [bay-österr]) m ~s/~ = Knorren, Warze (*pustale, blister*)

W·immerholz n *fiddle with a twangy sound*

w·immerig a *wavy-grained, –fibred* (Holz)

w·immern vi [h] *to whimper, snivel*; *moan, whine* (über *about*)

W·impel m ~s/~ *pennon, pennant, streamer* || ~fall [n] *pennant-halyard*; ~stock [m] *pennant-staff*

W·imper f ~/~n *eyelash* || mit den ~n klimpern *to flutter the e.shes* || ohne mit der ~ zu zucken *without* (*batting an e.sh* od) *winching*; *unwinking*; *with unblinking eyes* | ⟨zoo, bot⟩ ~n [pl] *cilia* || mit ~n *ciliate*(*d*) (a. gewimpert) **×~artig** a *ciliary* **~automatik** f ⟨cosm⟩ *automatic mascara* **~nformer** m *e.sh former* **×~förmig** a *ciliform* **~kiemen** f pl *ciliated gills* **~tierchen** n pl *Ciliata* pl [L] **~ntusche** f (haltfeste *fixia*) *mascara*; *eye make-up, eye-black* **w·impern** vi [h] *to wink* | gewimpert *ciliate*(*d*)

W·imperg m ~(e)s/~e ⟨arch⟩ *canopy*; *gable*

Wind m ~(e)s/~e **A. 1.** *wind, breeze* || wie der ~ *like a shot* | ⟨met⟩ *hot blast* **2.** ⟨med⟩ (Blähung) *wind, flatulence, flatus* **3.** ⟨hunt⟩ (Witterung) *scent*; v Fuchs ~ bek *to wind the fox* **4.** ⟨fig⟩ ~! *wind*!, *humbug*! *bosh*! *gas*! || (*he is talking nothing but*) *hot air* **B.** **(un)beständiger** (*choppy*), *steady*, (un)günstiger (*ill*), *fair*, halber *side*, scharfer *piercing*, starker ~ *high w.* || sanfter *gentle*, steifer ~ *stiff breeze* || stürmischer ~ *storm* || ~ v vorn *head-w.* **C.** ⟨fig⟩ ~ **bek v** *to get wind of* || es geht, weht ein starker ~ *there is a gale blowing, it is blowing hard* || ⟨mar⟩ guten ~ h *to run before the w.* || was f ~ h wir? *where is the w. from*? || den ~ im Rücken h *to have the w. astern* || woher kommt der ~? *in what quarter is the w.*? .. v Norden *the w. is in the north* | e–n ~ l *to break w.* || ~ m ⟨fig⟩ *to boast, brag*; (faseln) *to gas*; °**mach** nicht so viel ~! *give it a rest*! || ~ in die Segel nehmen *to catch the w. in the sails* || jdm den ~ aus den Segeln nehmen *to take the w. out of a p's sails, to steal a p's thunder*; e–r S .. *to blanket a th* || das ist ~ in s–e Segel *that is grist to his mill* || wehen → C. gehen; sich den ~ um die Nase w. l *to see the world* | ⟨prov⟩ wer ~ sät, wird Sturm ernten *he that sows the w. will reap the whirlwind* **D.** näher **an** den ~ drehen [vi], (Schiff) an den ~ bringen *to luff* vi/t || an den ~ gehen *to haul* (*upon*) *the w.* | (dicht) **beim** ~e (*to sail*) *on the w., close-hauled* || bei ~ u Wetter *in storm and rain* | **gegen** den ~ *into the w., upwind* [adv]; .. fliegen ⟨orn⟩ *to breast the w.*; .. segeln *to sail in the w.'s eye* od *into the wind* | still im ~e liegen *to lie hove-to* | **in** den ~ reden *to preach to the w.s*; .. schlagen *to disregard, to make light of, to set at naught*; *to fling* (*caution*) *into the w., to cast* od *throw .. to the winds* || in alle ~e tragen *to spread .. abroad*, .. zerstreuen *to scatter to the four w.s of heaven* | **mit** dem ~e (*to fly*) *down the w.* || ⟨mar⟩ mit halbem ~e *with a beam-w., on a tack* || mit dem ~e segeln *to sail with the w.* ⟨a. fig⟩; → u. vor | **nach** → Mantel | **über** den ~ k *to gain the w.* | **unter** dem ~ *under the lee, leeward* | **vom** ~ abhalten *to pay off* || vom ~e abk *to fall to leeward* || vom ~e gepeitscht, umtobt, zerzaust *w.-swept* || vom ~ getragen *wind-borne* (*pollen, seeds*) || vom ~e verweht *gone with the w.* | mit vollem *or* **vor** dem ~e segeln *to run before the w.* **~berücksichtigung** f *w. allowance* **~beutel** m (Gebäck) *cream-puff* || ⟨fig⟩ (P) (Schwätzer) *w.-bag, -jammer* || *boaster, humbug* || *rattle-brain, -pate* **~beutel·ei** f *humbug, swaggering* **~blattern** f pl ⟨path⟩ *chicken-pox* **~bluse** f *anorak* **~bohne** f *runner* **~bruch** m *w.-breakage, w.fall*, ⟨Am⟩ *slash* **~büchse** f *air-gun* **~drehung** f *change of the w.* **~druck** m *w. pressure* **×~durchweht** a *breezy* **~ei** n *w.-egg, addled egg* **~einfluß** m ⟨artill⟩ *w.age* **~eisen** n ⟨ec arch⟩ *w.ow-bar* **~fahne** f *weather-cock, vane* **~fall** m *w.fall* | ~-holz [n] *w.falls* **~fang** m ⟨min⟩ *airtrap*; ⟨tech⟩ *ventilator*; ⟨arch⟩ *porch* **~flaute** f = Flaute **~flügel** m ⟨mot⟩ *fan blade* **~form** f ⟨met⟩ *tuyère* **×~frei** a *sheltered* **~geschwindigkeit** f *w. velocity* **~geschwulst** f ⟨med⟩ *emphysema* **~hafer** m *wild oats* pl **~harfe** f *Aeolian harp* **~hauch** m *waft* od *breath of w.* **~hose** f *w.-spout, tornado, whirlwind*; ⟨Am⟩ *twister* **~hund** m *greyhound* || ⟨fig fam⟩ (P) *happy-go-lucky*; *sad dog* ⟨a. = –beutel⟩ **~instrument** n *w.-instrument* **~jacke** f *w.-jacket, w.-cheater, field-, trench-jacket* **~kanal** m ⟨aero⟩ *w. tunnel* **~kappe** f *cowl* (*of a chimney*) **~kasten** m (Orgel×~) = –lade **~kessel** m ⟨mach⟩ *air chamber* **~klappe** f *air-valve* **~kolik** f ⟨path⟩ *flatulent* od *w.-colic* **~lade** f (Orgel×~) *sound-board, w.-chest* **~lehre** f *anemology* **~licht** n *candle protected by a globe*; ⟨hist⟩ *link, torch* **~loch** n ⟨met⟩ *vent-hole* **~lotte** f ⟨min⟩ *air-channel* **~macher** m ⟨fig⟩ = –beutel ⟨fig⟩ **~maschine** f ⟨theat⟩ *w. machine* **~messer** m *w.-gauge, anemometer* **~mühle** f *w.mill*; holländ. ⟨a.⟩ *smock-mill* || ⟨fig⟩ gegen ~n kämpfen *to fight w.mills*; *to beat the air* od *wind*; *to flog a dead horse, to bite/gnaw a file* | **~n-** ~flügel [m] *wing* od *sail of a w.mill*; ~flugzeug [n] *autogiro* **~müller** m *miller* **~ofen** m *vent-furnace* **~pocken** f pl = –blattern **~rad** n ⟨tech⟩ *fan-blower, ventilator*; *water-pump w.mill*; ⟨aero⟩ *fan* **~reep** n ⟨mar⟩ *top-rope* **~richtung** f *direction of the w.* **~riemen** m ⟨mot⟩ *fan belt* **~rohr** n *air-pipe* **~röhre** f (der Orgel) *w.-pipe* **~röschen** n ⟨bot⟩ *anemone*

~rose f *compass-card* || ⟨bot⟩ *anemone* || nach allen Richtungen der ~ *in all directions* **~sack** m ⟨aero⟩ *w.-sleeve*, ⟨Am⟩ *w.-sock*; ⟨meteor⟩ *w. cone* **~schacht** m ⟨min⟩ *air-shaft* **~schaden** m *damage done by the w.* **~schatten** m *lee* (*side*); im ~ *out of the w.* **≗schief** a *warped, bent* || ~ w *to warp* **~schirm** m *w.-screen*; ⟨arch⟩ *pentice* **≗schnell** a (*as*) *quick as lightning* **≗schnittig** a *streamlined* **~schutz** m *w.break* | ~scheibe [f] ⟨mot⟩, (*w.-*)*screen*, ⟨aero⟩ *w.-shield* || –nenteiser [m] *w.-sh. de-icer*; –nklebezettel [m] *car sticker* **~seite** f *w.ward* od *w.y side* || ⟨mar⟩ *weather gauge* **~sichter** m ⟨tech⟩ (*fine*) *air separator* **~spiel** n (dog) *whippet* **~stärke** f *velocity of the w.* || ~ 8 *w. force 8* | ~tabelle [f] ⟨engl⟩ *Beaufort scale* **≗still** a *calm, breathless* **~stille** f *lack of w.*; (*dead*) *calm* || in e–e ~ geraten *to be becalmed* **~stoß** m *gust* od *rush of w.*; (leicht, plötzlich) *puff of breeze* || heftiger ~ *squall* | ~frisur [f] *w.-swept hairdo, upsweep* **~streichholz** n *fusee* **~strich** m *point of the compass*; *rhumb* **~tunnel** m *w. channel* **≗wärts** adv *w.ward, upwind* [adv] **~wehe** f *snow-drift* **~wurf** m ⟨for⟩ *blowdown* **≗zerzaust** a *w.-swept* **~ziffer** f ⟨artill⟩ *w. reference number* **~zug** m *draught of air*

W·inde f ~/~n **1.** ⟨tech⟩ *windlass, winch* ⟨a. mar, aero⟩; (Garnwinde) *reel* || Hebe≗ *lifting jack*; ⟨mot⟩ *jack* || Lade≗ ⟨mar⟩ *loading hoist* || liegende ~ *whim* || (Speicher≗) *hoist* || stehende ~ *capstave* **2.** ⟨bot⟩ *bindweed* **~kraft** f *hoisting power* **~maschine** f ⟨spin⟩ *winding machine* **~welle** f *winding shaft* (*of a mill*) **W·indel** f ~/~n *napkin, diaper*, ⟨fam⟩ *nappy*; ⟨a.⟩ *swaddling--clothes* pl ⟨a. fig⟩; ⟨Am a.⟩ *swaddle* || °als du noch in die ~n machtest, machte ich schon Krieg *I was cutting barbed wire, while you were cutting your teeth* **~band** n *swathing-band* **~bohrer** m *centre-bit* **~geruch** m ⟨fam⟩ *smell of nappies* **~hös|chen** n (aus Kunststoff) *plastic pants* pl **~kind** n *baby* **~schnur** f = –band **≗w·eich** a ⟨fig⟩ *limp* || ~ schlagen ⟨sl⟩ *to beat to a jelly* od *mummy, pulp*; *to beat hollow* od *into next week*, ⟨Am sl⟩ *to knock the tar* od *stuffing out of* (*a p*) **w·inden** vt [wand/gewunden] [h] *to wind, twist* || (Zwirn etc) *to reel*; von der Weife (ab)~ *to unreel* || (Wäsche) *to wring* || e–n Kranz ~ *to make* od *bind a wreath* || (in die Höhe) *to hoist* | jdm etw **aus** den Händen ~ *to wrest a th out of a p's hands*; **um** sich: *to wrap a th about one* | **sich** ~ *to wind* (um *round*); (Fluß) *to meander*; (wie ein Wurm) *to wriggle* ⟨a. fig⟩; ⟨fig⟩ .. *like an eel*; (Tau) *to coil* (um *round*) || (P) *to squirm* || ⟨bot⟩ *to twine* || sich ~ durch .. *to squeeze* (⟨mot⟩ *thread*) *one's way through* ..; (wie ein Wurm) *to worm* || ⟨fig⟩ *to squirm* || (in, vor Schmerzen) *to writhe* (*with pain*) | sich **~d** *winding, twisty* (*road*) || *sinuous* (*valley*) | **gewunden** a *tortuous, winding* (*path*) **W·inden- ≗artig** a ⟨bot⟩ *convolvulaceous* **~schwärmer** m ⟨ent⟩ *convolvulus hawk-moth* **W·indung** f ~/~en *winding, turn, convolution* || ⟨bot, anat⟩ *torsion* || ⟨zoo⟩ *coil* || (e–s Flusses, Weges) *bend, sinuosity, turn* (*in sharp turns*) || (e–s Taues) *coil* || (e–r Schraube) *worm* || (e–r Muschel, Spirale) *whorl*

W·indeseile f; mit ~ *at lightning speed*, (*at*) *full pelt*; sich mit ~ verbreiten (Gerücht etc) *to spread like wildfire* **w·indig** a *windy*; *breezy* || es ist ~ *it is windy, there is a wind* | ⟨fig⟩ (P) *empty, shallow, giddy* || (S) *shaky, doubtful* | **≗keit** f ~/ *windiness* || ⟨fig⟩ *shallowness* **W·indsbraut** f ⟨poet⟩ *gale, hurricane*; *whirlwind* (*personified*) **W·indsorknoten** m (des Schlipses) *spiv--knot*

×**W·ingert** m ~s/~e *vineyard*; → Weinberg

Wink m ~(e)s/~e *sign* || (mit den Augen) *wink, twinkling*, (m. d. Hand) *beckoning, wave*, (m. d. Kopf) *nod* (mit *of*) || ⟨fig⟩ *hint*; zarter ~ *inkling*; *gentle reminder*; ~ mit dem Zaunpfahl *broad hint* | (*wink, nod, hint*: geben *to give*; verstehen, befolgen *to take*) || ⟨Am fam a.⟩ *pointer* || er versteht selbst den ~ mit d. Z. nicht *a nod is as good as a wink to a blind horse* | auf jds ~ *at a p's sign, at a gesture from* ..; .. warten *to be at a p's beck and call* || e–m e–n guten ~ geben ⟨fam⟩ *to give a p the straight tip* **~flagge** f *signal flag* **~zeichen** n *sign*; ~ [pl] geben *to wigwag* vi

W·inkel m ~s/~ **A. 1.** *angle* (bilden *to make*, messen *to take*) (abgestumpfter ⟨arch⟩ *cut-off*, brechender ⟨opt⟩ *refracting*, einspringender *re-entering*, rechter *right*, spitzer *acute*, stumpfer *obtuse*, toter ~ ⟨fort etc⟩ *shielded* od *dead a.*) **2.** (Ecke) *corner* (⟨fig⟩ entlegen *remote*) **3.** = ~eisen, ~maß, Zeichendreieck **4.** ⟨fig⟩ (*quiet*) *nook*, (*snug*) *corner* || die tiefsten ~ *the deepest recesses* (*of the heart*) **B. auf** den ~ prüfen, **in** den ~ bringen *to square* || im ~ v *at an angle of* (*45°* → Gehrung) || im rechten ~ *at a right angle, squarely*; .. stehend *square*; .. anbringen *to square* || im ~ abbiegen *to angle*; im ~ anbringen *to adjust .. to angle*; im ~ stehend z *at a.s with* || im toten ~ liegendes Gelände *dead ground* || in allen ~n u Ecken *in every nook and corner* **~advokat** m ⟨fam⟩ *hock attorney*; *pettifogger*; ⟨bes Am sl⟩ *shyster* **~band** n ⟨tech⟩ *angle* **~beschleunigung** f *angular acceleration* **~blatt** n *small local paper* **~bogen** m ⟨math⟩ *arc of an a.* **~börse** f ⟨fam⟩ *bucket-shop* **~dach** n *square roof* **~druckerei** f *obscure* bzw *secret press* || *clandestine printing* **~ehe** f *hedge-marriage* **~endmaß** n *a. block* **~eisen** n *a. bar* || *iron rule* || *L-, T-iron* **≗förmig** a *angular* **~fräser** m *a.r milling-cutter* **~funktion** f ⟨math⟩ *circular f.* **~gasse** f *back-lane* **~haken** m ⟨typ⟩ *composing-stick* **~hebel** m *bent lever* **~hobel** m *a.-plane* **~klammer** f *cramp-iron* **~lineal** n *set-square* **~makler** m *outside broker* **~maß** n *rule, square* **~messer** m *protractor*; *goniometer* **~messung** f *goniometry* **~naht** f ⟨anat⟩ *lambdoid suture* **~neigung** f *angular tilt* **~öffnung** f ⟨phot⟩ *a.r aperture* **~-Planierungspflug** m *a.dozer* **~poet** m *poetaster* **~presse** f *obscure press* **~räumpflug** m *a.dozer* **≗recht** a *square, rectangular* || [adv] *at right a.s* **~rohr** n = Kniestück **~scheibe** f *astrolabe* **~schenke** f *hedge ale-house, low tavern* **~schreiber(ling)** m *obscure writer* **~schule** f *hedge-school* **~spiegel** m *optical square* **~spiel** n *puss-in-the-corner* **~stahl** m *a. steel* **≗ständig** a ⟨bot⟩ *axillary* **~stoß** m *a. joint* **~treppe** f *backstairs* pl **≗treu** a *conformal* **~treue** f *isogonality* **~zug** m *evasion, trick, shift* || –züge m *to shuffle, prevaricate, dodge*; ⟨Am fam⟩ *to pull strings* || etw durch .. erreichen ⟨engl sl⟩ *to scrounge* **w·ink(e)lig** a *angular* || ⟨tech⟩ *bent* (*at right angles*) || *winding* (*street*) | [in comp] *-angled* **W·inken** n ~s/ *nodding, beckoning* || *wink* || ⟨mil⟩ *flag-wagging* || ~ in Verkehrsrichtung ⟨mot⟩ *waving on traffic* **winken** vi [h] **1.** ([abs] *or* **jdm**) *to make a sign, to nod* od *sign* (*to a p*); *to signal, flag*(*wag*) ⟨a. mar, mil⟩ (*to a p*) || **mit** den Armen ~ *to throw one's arms about*; mit den Augen *to wink one's eyes* (*at a p*); m. d. Hand *to beckon* (*a p*); m. d. Taschentuch *to wave one's h.* (*to a p*); ⟨fam⟩ m. d. Zaunpfahl etc *to give a broad hint*; man braucht (ihm) nicht gleich mit dem Z. z ~ *a nod is as good as a wink* || er braucht nur z ~ *his very nod is obeyed* **2. jdm** ~ näherzuk *to wave a p nearer, to beckon* (od *motion for*) *a p to come up* || das Glück winkt mir *some good fortune is in store for me*; vgl *an advantage is in prospect for him* **3.** [vt] **jdn** beiseite (heran) ~ *to beckon a p aside* (*to come up*) || (e–m) **etw** ~ *to enjoin .. by signs* || e–m Stillschweigen ~ *to make signs to a p to be silent* **W·inker** m ~s/~ *flagman* || ⟨mot⟩ *direction indicator*; Pendel≗ *semafore-type indicator* | ~flagge [f] *Morse flag*; ~krabbe [f] *calling crab* **w·inkern** vi/t [h] ⟨mar⟩ = winken **Wink-**

~gerät n *semaphore* **~spruch** m *flag-wagging message*

W·innipeg [w–] n (⟨Can⟩ Stadt) **~see** m *Lake W.*

W·insel- **~affe** m ⟨zoo⟩ *weeper, capuchin* **~stimme** f *whining* od *moaning voice* °**Winsel·ei** f ~/ = Gewimmer **W·inseler** m *whining p,* ⟨fam⟩ *sniveller* **w·inselig** a *whining; puling,* ⟨fam⟩ *snivelling (child)* **w·inseln** vi [h] *to whimper, whine, wail* ‖ (Kind) *to pule,* ⟨fam⟩ *snivel* ‖ e–m die Ohren voll|~ *to deafen a p with one's complaints*

W·inter m ~s/~ *winter;* Herr ~ *Jack Frost* ‖ f den ~ vorbereiten *to w.ize* ‖ im ~, ≗s, des ~s *in w.* ‖ im ~ 1916/17 *in the w. of ..* ‖ mitten im (tiefsten, strengsten) ~ *in the depth of w.* ‖ den ~ verbringen *to pass the w.;* ⟨zoo⟩ *to hibernate* ‖ der ~ zog sich (sehr) lange hin *or* zog sich in die Länge *the winter wore on very long* **~abend** m; e–s ~s *on a w.-evening* **~apfel** m *w.-apple* **~arbeit** f *w.-work* **~aufenthalt** m *w. abode* ‖ (Ort) *w. resort* **~bestellung** f *w. fallowing* **~fahrplan** m *w. time-table* **~feld** n *field sown with w. corn* **~feldzug** m *w. campaign* **~fenster** n *outer window* **≗fest** a: ~e Pflanze *hardy annual;* ~ m *to make weatherproof, to winterize* **~frische** f *w. resort* **~frucht** f *w. corn* **~garten** m *w. garden* ‖ (Gewächshaus) *conservatory* **~gerste** f *w. barley* **~getreide** n *w. corn* **~gewächs** n *perennial plant* **~grün** n ⟨bot⟩ *w.-green* ‖ *periwinkle* **~haar** n ⟨zoo⟩ *w.-coat* **~hafen** m *w. harbourage* **~halbjahr** n *w. half-year* **~handschuhe** m pl *furred gloves* pl **≗hart** a *hardy (plant)* **~haus** n *w.-house* ‖ ⟨hort⟩ *hothouse* **~hilfe** f, ⟨Ger⟩ **~hilfswerk** n *W. Relief Fund* **~kälte** f *w. cold* **~kleid** n *w.-dress* ‖ ⟨zoo⟩ *w.-coat;* ⟨orn⟩ *w.-plumage* **~kleidung** f *w. clothing* **~kohl** m = Grünkohl *kale* **~könig** m ⟨hist⟩ *king for one w.* ‖ ⟨orn⟩ = Zaunkönig **~korn** n *w. corn* **~kresse** f ⟨bot⟩ *w. cress* **~kurort** m *w. (health) resort* **~lager** n = –quartier **~landschaft** f *w. landscape, w. scenery* **~mantel** m *w. overcoat* **~märchen** n *w.'s tale; Twelfth-Night (Shak)* **≗mäßig** a *wintry* **~nacht** f *w. night* **~obst** n *w. fruit* **~quartier** n *w. quarters* pl **~rock** m *greatcoat* **~rose** f ⟨bot⟩ *Christmas rose* **~ruhe** f ⟨biol⟩ *w. rest period* **~saat** f *(sowing of) w. corn* **~schlaf** m *hibernation* ⟨a. fig⟩, ⟨fig⟩ *dormancy;* künstl. ~ *hypothermia* ‖ den ~ halten *to hibernate* ⟨a. fig⟩, ⟨fig⟩ *to lie dormant;* sich z ~ begeben *to den up* **~schlußverkauf** m ⟨com-ad, etc⟩ *winter sale* **~seite** f *north(ern) side* **~semester** n *w. term;* ⟨engl⟩ *Hilary term* **~sonne** f *w. sun* | **~n-**~wende [f] *w. solstice* **~sport** m *w. sports* pl | **~-**~platz [m] *w. sport centre* **~sturm** m *w. storm* **~tag** m *w. day* ‖ e–s ~s, an e–m ~ *one winter's day* **~überzieher** m = –mantel **~vergnügen** n *amusement for the w.* **~weizen** m *w. wheat* **~wetter** n *wintry weather* **~zeit** f *winter time* ‖ zur ~ *in w. t.* **w·interlich** a *wintry* | adv *as in winter* **w·intern** **1.** vi imps [h] *to grow winter, to get wintry* **2.** vt [h] *to (keep through the) winter* **w·inters** [adv] = des Winters

W·inzer m ~s/~ **1.** *vine-dresser, v.-grower* **2.** (Traubenleser) *vintager* [⟨a.⟩ f] **~fest** n *vintage* **~messer** n *vine-knife*

w·inzig a (→ wenig) *weeny; tiny (little boy, man); diminutive (stature); puny (child)* ‖ *wee (little bit); minute (particle); trifling (sum);* → unbedeutend

W·ipfel m ~s/~ *top (of a tree)* **w·ipfeln** **1.** vt [h] *to lop (trees)* **2.** vi [h] & sich ~ *to tower, to rise aloft* °**W·ippchen** n ~s/~ ⟨fam⟩ jdm ~ vormachen *to tell a p fibs* ‖ mach' mir k–e ~! *none of your tricks!* **W·ippe** f ~/~n **1.** *balance* ‖ (für Kinder) *seesaw* ‖ ⟨hist⟩ = Wippgalgen **2.** ⟨tech⟩ (e–r Brücke) *bascule* **3.** ⟨gym⟩ *balancing* **4.** *whip* **5.** ⟨telph⟩ *tumbler(-switch)* **6.** (Nadlerei) *header* **7.** ⟨fig⟩ auf der ~ *on the point of falling* **8.** ⟨theat⟩ *trampolin,* ⟨Am⟩ *safety net* **w·ippen** **1.** vt [h] *to balance, rock, seesaw, teeter* ‖ sich ~ *to play seesaw* **2.** vi [h] mit: *to rock;* ⟨orn⟩ *to flirt* od *wag its tail; to flap the wings* **Wipper·ei** f ~/ *money-clipping* **Wipp-** **~brücke** f *bascule* **~galgen** m *strappado* **~sterz** m ⟨orn⟩ *wagtail*

wir pers pron [1. pl] *we;* (⟨fam⟩ *us)* ‖ ~ alle *all of us* ~ (alle) *5 the 5 of us* ‖ ~ beide *both of us* ‖ ~ selbst *we ourselves* | ~ Armen *we poor ones* ‖ ~ Deutsche(n) *we Germans* | ~ h *we have, ours is* ‖ ~ sind es *it is we* | ~, die ~ nichts h *we who have nothing* | ⟨fam⟩ ~ sind ein Esel, Paul *you are an ass, P.* ‖ (als Toast) ~ sind ~! *our noble selves!*

wirb imp v werben; → ~st, ~t

W·irbel m ~s/~ **A. 1.** (~bewegung) *whirl* ‖ (im Wasser) *eddy;* (gr) *whirlpool, vortex, maelstrom* ‖ (des Rauchs) *wreath, eddy* ‖ (Luft≗) *whirlwind, blast* ‖ *flurry (of dust)* | ⟨fig⟩ *giddiness, whirl (of traffic, of passion); turmoil; ferment; unrest; commotion; turbulence;* kl ~ ⟨fig⟩ *little excitement; whirligig (of time)* **2.** ⟨anat⟩ (Haar≗) *crown (of the head),* ⟨scient⟩ *vertex* | (Rücken≗) *vertebra,* zum ~ gehörig *vertebral* **3.** ⟨mus⟩ *warbling (of birds)* ‖ *roll, hurry (of a drum)* **4.** ⟨tech⟩ *swivel, lever* ‖ (e–r Drehbank) *collar* ‖ (Fenster≗) *button, bolt* ‖ (Geigen- etc ≗) *peg* ‖ (e–s Spinnrads) *sheave* | ⟨aero-dyn⟩ *burble* **B.** sich im ~ drehen *to whirl round* ‖ e–n ~ schlagen (Trommel) *to sound a roll;* ⟨orn⟩ *to warble, trill* | vom ~ bis zur Sohle *from top to toe* **~bein** n, ~knochen [m] ⟨anat⟩ *vertebra* **~bildung** f ⟨aero⟩ *formation of vortices; turbulence* **~block** m ⟨mar⟩ *swivel-block* **~dost** m ⟨bot⟩ *basil-weed* **≗förmig** a *spindle-shaped;* ⟨bot⟩ *verticillate* **~gelenk** n ⟨tech⟩ *swivel-joint;* ⟨anat⟩ *vertebral articulation* **~haken** m ⟨tech⟩ *swivel-hook* **~kammer** f *turbulence* od *whirl chamber* **~kasten** m (der Geige etc) *peg-box* **~kopf** m ⟨fig⟩ *rattle-pate* **≗los** a ⟨zoo⟩ *invertebrate;* –lose Tiere *invertebrates* pl **~säule** f *vertebral column; spine* **~strom** m ⟨el⟩ *eddy current* **~sturm** m *cyclone, tornado* **~sucht** f ⟨path⟩ *vertigo* **~tanz** m *whirl* **~tier** n *vertebrate* **~wert** m *vorticity potential* **~wind** m *whirlwind;* wie ein ~ hineinstürmen (in) ⟨sl⟩ *to blow in;* **w·irb(e)lig** a *whirling, vertiginous* ‖ ⟨fig⟩ *giddy* **w·irbeln** **1.** vi [h & s] *to whirl, spin;* (Schnee) *to drift,* (Wasser) *to eddy;* (Nebel) *to swirl* | [h] mir wirbelt der Kopf, es w. mir im K. *my head swims* od *turns, reels* | *thoughts were dancing in his head* | an, auf e–n Platz ~ ⟨sl⟩ *to blow into a place* | ~d zuk auf *to spin up to* **2.** vi/t [h] (Lerche etc) *to warble (a song)* ‖ (trommeln) *to sound a roll* ‖ jdn rundum ~ *to send a p spinning* **W.lung** f ~/ *turbulence*

wirbst, wirbt 2., 3. sg pres v werben

wird/wirft 3. sg pres ~ werden/werfen

Wirk- (→ wirken) **~bank** f *(baker's) kneading-board* **~eisen, ~messer** n *(farrier's) paring-knife* **~maschine** f *stocking-frame* **~material** n *active m.* **~meister** m *master weaver* **~stoff** m ⟨biol⟩ *active material;* ⟨tech⟩ *agent* | natürlicher ~komplex ⟨cosm⟩ *bio-energizer* **~strom** m ⟨el⟩ *active current* **~stuhl** m *(tapestry-)loom* **~tisch** = –bank **~ware** f *woven* od *knitted goods* pl ‖ (Strumpfwaren) *hosiery* sg **~widerstand** m *effective resistance* **W·irken** **I.** n ~s/ *activity* **II.** ≗ vt/i [h] **1.** vt *to work (wonders), to produce, effect* ‖ giftig ~ *to have a poisonous effect* (auf *on*) ‖ gut ~ auf *to influence .. for good;* Gutes ~ *to do good* ‖ nachhaltig ~ *to produce a lasting effect* od *impression* ‖ (Salz) *to boil* ‖ (Teig) *to knead* ‖ (den Huf) *to pare* **2.** vi **A.** *to be at work, to operate* (auf *on*); *to have effect* ⟨a. med⟩ ‖ (v Worten) *to tell (to go home)* ‖ das –kte *the shot told* ‖ das –kt sehr *that goes a long way* (bei *with*) ‖ nicht ~ *to be of no effect* **B. an**: *to teach at (a school)* | **auf**: *to act* od *bear on, to have an effect* od *influence upon;* (nachteilig) *to tell (up)on (a p's health),* (auf

Augen, Haut etc) *to affect* || die Reize der Landschaft ~ auf ihn *the scenery exerts all its fascination on him* || *it gives me the effect of* .. (wie) | **bei**: *nothing makes any impression on him, nothing has any effect with him*; *these excuses do not go down with me* || (*this ought*) *to cure him* | **dahin** ~, daß .. *to see that sth be done* | **durch**: *to work by*; durch sein Beispiel anspornend ~ *to lend encouragement by one's example* | **gegen**: *to militate against* | **gegen**-e–a ~ *to counteract each other* **w·irkend** a *acting*, etc; *active*; *efficacious*; *telling* || stark ~ *drastic*; *highly effective* **W·irker** m ~s/~ *weaver* || (Teig≚) *kneader* || → wirken II. 1. **w·irklich A.** [a] *real, actual* (*focus*) || (echt) *true* (*character*); *genuine* (*gold, indignation*) | ~er Bestand ⟨mil⟩ *effective force*(*s* pl) od *strength* || *real* (*debt, profit*) || *substantial* (*gain*) || *visible* (*supply*) || *positive* (*fact*) || ~er Vorfall *matter of fact* || im ~en Sinne *in the immediate sense* || (Titel) *acting* (*privy councillor*) **B.** [adv] *really, actually, positively, truly*, ⟨Am a.⟩ *honest*; *a real complete gentleman* | *just too* (*lovely*); *quite* (*delightful*) | (*that was the car*) *all right* || (*you can't*) *very well* (*pretend* ..) || das ist ~ nicht zum Lachen *it's no joke, it isn't* || (*that is sth*) *now* || *I'm sure* (*I don't know*); ich weiß ~ nicht, ob .. *I am not quite sure whether* .. || (*very kind of you*) *to be sure* | ~? *is that so*?, (*are you*) *sure*? (a.: ~ nicht); *is* (*was*) *it*?, *is* (*was*) *he*?; *do you mean it*? || ⟨oft iron⟩ *indeed*! *i.*? || (*are you*) *sure* (*you don't want to go*)? | ~! (*in*) *fact*! *I mean it*! | | [oft durch betontes *to do*]: *we did find it difficult* || [oft durch die *progressive form*]: *when it was being proposed* .. | ≚**keit** f **1.** ~/ *reality*; *real life* od *existence* || *actuality* (*events of a.*), *truth* | sich auf den Boden der ~ stellen *to start from reality* || ~ w *to materialize, to come true, to be brought to pass, to come, soar* etc *into life* || ~ w l *to turn* (*dreams*) *into reality, to give form to* (*a hope*) | **in** ~ *in reality, in* (*point of*) *fact, in practice*; *really* || in die ~ umsetzen, zur ~ m *to realize, materialize* | **mit** der ~ übereinstimmend *veridical* **2.** ~/~en *actual fact, positive case* | ≚**keits-** ~**form** f *indicative* ≚**fremd** a *unrealistic*; ⟨psych⟩ *dereistic* ≚**nah** a *realistic*; *objective* (*mind*); *extensional* (Ansicht), auf e–r ≚eren Ebene *on more e.l levels*; ~e Darstellung [f] *realism* ~**sinn** m *realism, common sense*, ⟨fam⟩ *horse sense* ≚**treu**, ≚**wahr** a *veracious* **w·irksam** a *efficacious*; *effective* ⟨a. mil⟩; *efficient* (*p*) || *active* (*principle*) || *effectual* (*measures*) || *dynamic* (*energy*) | (eindrucksvoll) *telling, impressive* || *cogent* (*form*) | ⟨med⟩ *operative, efficacious* (bei *in*); äußerst ~ *energetic*; *powerful, sovereign* (*remedy*), *heroic* (*drug*); (e–e Droge etc) ~ m *to actualize* (*a drug, a plan*); ~ gegen *good for* | noch ~s *to be still at work*; voll ~ bleiben *to remain in full force and effect*; am ~sten *best* (*can b. be done*) | ≚**keit** f ~/ *efficacy, efficiency* || *impressiveness* (*of a play*) || *activity* (*of a p*) || (Kraft) *virtue* || ⟨chem⟩ *strength* | außer ~ setzen ⟨tech⟩ *to throw out of gear*, ⟨jur⟩ *to suspend* (*a law*) || in ~ s *to be at work*, ⟨jur⟩ .. *in force* || in ~ treten ⟨jur⟩ *to come into operation, to take effect* **W·irkung** f ~/~en (Bewirktes) *effect* || (Tätigkeit) *agency, operation*; *action* ⟨a. tech⟩ (~ h auf *to act upon*) || heilende ~ *curative properties* pl || (Ergebnis) *result* (⟨mil⟩ *with good results*); geringere ~ *reduced r.s*, größere ~ *r.s of greater magnitude* || (Folge) *consequence* || ⟨el⟩ *action of a current* || *appeal* (*of a play*); *reaction to a film* || *virtue*, (getane) *execution* (*of guns*) (h *to do great e.*) | die ~ abschwächen *to dilute the effectiveness*; (e–e) ~ (aus)üben auf [acc] *to act* od *tell upon*, (Eindruck m) *to affect, impress* || ~ h, s–e ~ tun *to take effect, to work*; .. **auf** ⟨a.⟩ *to have bearing on*; ~ auf Menschen ⟨a. at⟩ *personnel effects* | der ~ [gen] berauben *to take the edge off* (*an argument*) | k–e ~ h, ohne ~ bleiben *to produce no effect, to fall flat, to hang fire, to prove ineffectual*; *to cut no ice*; .. **bei** jdm *not to go down with, to be wasted* od *lost on a p* || s–e ~ tun *to make play*; .. tun l *to let* (*the lesson*) *sink in* || s–e ~ nicht verfehlen *to strike home* || e–r S [dat] ~ verleihen *to give effect to a th*; *to put teeth into* (*neutrality*) || | **in** ~ treten (Gesetz) *to come into force* | **mit** ~ v *with effect from* | .. **zu** einheitlicher ~ bringen *to shape* .. *into a unified effort* | ⟨prov⟩ k–e ~ ohne Ursache *no smoke without* (*a*) *fire* | ~**s-** ~**art** f *mode of action*, etc ~**bereich** m –kreis; *radius of effect*; ⟨ad⟩ *coverage* (⟨bes Am a.⟩ e–s Gesetzes) || ⟨mil⟩ *effective range* ~**grad** m ⟨tech⟩ *efficiency* ~**kraft** f *efficacy, virtue* ~**kreis** m *orbit*; *sphere* (*of activity*), *extent of action*; *province, domain*; *purview of authority* ≚**los** a *ineffectual, inefficacious, inefficient* ~**losigkeit** f *inefficacy* ~**radius** m (R_w [ABC]) *damage radius* ~**schießen** n *firing for effect* ~**stätte** f *place of work* ~**vermögen** n *potentiality* ≚**voll** a *efficacious, effective, efficient* (*drug*); *operative*; *energetic* || ⟨theat⟩ = (nachhaltig) wirkend → d.

wirr a *tangled, confused*; *disjointed*; *light-headed*; *in a tangle* || (Haar) *wild, dishevelled* || ~es Durch–e–a *chaos, confusion*; *jumble* (*of words*) || *huddled* (*heap*) || *mazy* (*crowd*) || *loose* (*talk, thinking*) || ~ im Kopf *muddle-headed* | [adv] (*to dream*) *wildly* || ~ durch–e–a *at sixes and sevens*, ⟨fam⟩ *higgledy-piggledy* || mir ist ganz ~ im Kopfe *my head goes round* **Wirr-** ~**garn** n *tangled yarn* ~**kopf** m *giddy-head, scatter-brain*; ⟨Am sl⟩ *screwball* ≚**köpfig** a *confused*, ⟨fam⟩ *muddle-headed* ~**seide** f *tangled silk* ~**stroh** n *short straw* ~**sal** n, ~**warr** m *confusion*; *welter* (*of creeds, policies*, etc); ⟨fam⟩ *muddle, mess, jumble, junket*; *snarl, topsy-turvydom*; *imbroglio* It; (Lärm) *hurly-burly, hubbub*, ⟨fam⟩ *shindy* || in ~ bringen *to throw into confusion*; → Verwirrung **W·irre** f ~/~n *tangle, confusion*; ⟨fig⟩ *chaos*; *labyrinth* || ~n [pl] *troubles, disorders, agitations* pl || (Verwicklungen) *complications* pl **W·irrnis** f ~/–isse; **W·irrsal** n ~(e)s/~e *confusion, disorder*; *chaos*; irdisches ~ *mortal coil*

W·irsing m *savoy* (*cabbage*) || ⟨fig⟩ (Kopf) → Birne

wirst 2. sg pres v werden

W·irtel m ~s/~ ⟨spin, bot⟩ *whorl*; ⟨arch⟩ *annulet*

w·irten vi [h] Sw *to keep an inn* etc **Wirt(in** f) m ~(e)s/~e **A. 1.** (Gastgeber) *entertainer*; *host*(*ess* f) ⟨a. biol⟩ **2.** (Gast≚) *inn-, bar-, hotel-keeper*; *landlord* (⟨a.⟩ = Haus≚, Zimmer≚) ([f] *innkeeper's wife*; *landlady*); ⟨hum⟩ *mine host* (der ~ zur Traube *m. h. of the grapes*) **3.** (Haushälter) *economist, manager* (*a good, bad m.*) **B.** den ~ m *to do the honours* || die Rechnung ohne den ~ m *to reckon without one's host*; auf R. des ~s (*drinks* etc) *on the house* **w·irtlich** a **1.** *hospitable* || *habitable* **2.** *economical, thrifty* | ≚**keit** f **1.** *hospitality* || *habitable state* **2.** *economy, thrift* **Wirts-** ~**haus** n *inn*; *public house*; ⟨Am⟩ *saloon*; ⟨fam⟩ *pub* || an e–e Brauerei gebundenes ~ *tied house* | ewig im ~ sitzen *to be for ever at the pub* ~**hausleben** n *life in restaurants and hotels* ~**(haus)tisch** m *ordinary* ~**junge** m *pot-boy* ~**leute** pl *landlord and landlady*; *host and hostess* ~**stube** f *common room, bar-parlour* **W·irtschaft** f ~/~en **A. 1.** (Hauswesen) *household, establishment*; ⟨agr⟩ *farm* **2.** (Haushalten) *management of a household, housekeeping*; (ländliche) *farming, husbandry*; (e–s Gemeinwesens) *economy*; *economic system* od *conditions* **3.** (Handel u Gütererzeugung) *trade, industry, business*; *commercial life* | Energie- u Wärme≚ *power engineering and heat economy* **4.** (Gastwirtschaft) *inn, public house, restaurant, refreshment-room, bar*(*-room*) ||

(Kneipe) *ale-house* **5.** (Treiben) *doings* pl **B.** ~! *house, ho*! ‖ diese ~ *this sort of th* ‖ freie ~ *private enterprise* ‖ die ganze ~ *the whole show* ‖ ⟨fam⟩ polnische ~ *topsy-turvydom* ‖ e–e schöne ~! *a nice mess*! *a pretty business*! *fine doings*! *a nice kettle of fish*! ‖ e–e tolle ~ *a mad proceeding* | [dat] die ~ **führen** *to keep house* (*for*) ‖ viel ~ m *to be fussy* ‖ was ist das f e–e ~? *what's going on here*? ‖ (sich auf) die ~ gut verstehen *to be a good house-keeper* | ≃**en** vi [h] *to keep house* ‖ *to manage a farm*, etc ‖ (mit) *to administer* (*property*) ‖ gut ~ *to manage well, to economize* ‖ schlecht ~ *to mismanage* ‖ sparsam ~ *to be thrifty* | ⟨fig⟩ (herumwühlen) *to rummage*; *to mess about* ‖ arg, toll ~ *to make a great hubbub, to make sad havoc* (mit *of*) | ~**er(in** f) m ~s/~ *housekeeper* (bei *to*); *manager*; ⟨agr⟩ *steward* | ~**ler** m ~s/~ *economist* | ≃**lich** a **1.** (die Wirtschaft betreffend) *economic, of economy*; *agricultural*; *industrial* ‖ vom ~en Standpunkt *e.cally* (*speaking*) **2.** (sparsam) *e.cal, thrifty* ‖ ~ gestalten *to rationalize* ‖ [adv] *with e.y* **3.** (rentabel) *e.cal*; *profitable*; in ~ster Weise *in the most efficient manner* | [adv] ~ gut gestellt *prosperous* | ≃**keit** f ~/ *e.y, thrift*; *e.c performance* od *efficiency* ‖ *price ratio*; ⟨mot⟩ *consumption-to-mileage ratio* ‖ *e.y of operation* ‖ ⟨ad⟩ größte ~! *biggest money saver*! ‖ (Ertragsfähigkeit) *remunerativeness, profitableness* ‖ auf ~ bedacht *e.y-minded* ‖ mit weitestgehender ~ *most e.cally* **W·irtschafts-** ~**abkommen** n *e.c* od *trade agreement* ~**ablauf** m *e.c cycle* ~**abteilung** f *trade-section* ‖ *industry branch* ~**amt** n *distribution office* ~**ankurbelung** f *e.c recovery*; *promotion of trade*; (staatlich) ⟨fig⟩ *pump priming* ~**anstieg** m *e.c upswing* ~**ausschuß** m *e.c committee* ~**ausweitung** f *e.c expansion* ~**beamte(r)** m *manager of a farm*; *steward* ~**bedarf** m *household requirements* pl ~**beihilfe** f *subsidy, grant* ~**beilage** f = –teil ~**belebung** f *uptrend* ~**berater** m *e.c adviser*; *business consultant* ~**bereich** m (*e.c*) *sector* ~**betrieb** m *management of a household* (*a farm, an inn, a commercial* od *industrial undertaking*) ~**bezirk** m *industrial district* ~**block** m *e.c block* ~**blockade** f *e.c blockade* ~**buch** n *housekeeping book* ~**demographie** f *e.c d.* ~**depression** f *business d.* ~**einheit** f *e.c unit* ~**entwicklung** f *commercial* od *e.c development* od *growth* ~**expansion** f *e.c growth* ~**fortschritt** m *e.c progress* ~**fragen** f pl *e.c problems* ~**friede** m *industrial peace* ~**führer** m *captain of industry, industrialist* ~**führung** f *management* ~**gebäude** n *farm-buildings* pl ‖ *steward's house* ~**gebiet** n *e.c field*; ⟨geog⟩ *e.c region* od *district* ~**geld** n *housekeeping money* ~**geographie** f *e.c geography* ~**gerät** n *household-utensils* pl ~**gruppe** f *corporation trust* ~**güter** n pl *e.c goods*; *resources* ~**hilfe** f *e.c assistance* od *aid* (f *to* [*Turkey*] ‖ *co-operative association* ~**interessen** n pl *business interests* ~**inspektor** m *steward* ~**jahr** n *financial year* ~**kammer** f *Chamber of Commerce* ~**kampf** m *trade competition* ~**kenntnis** f *trade knowledge* ~**konferenz** f *trade c.* ~**kontrolle** f *industrial control*; *dirigism* ~**konzern** m *business group* ~**körper** m *e.c unity* ‖ *self-help organization* ~**krieg** m *e.c warfare* ~**krise** f ~**krisis** f *e.c crisis* ~**kunst** f *husbandry* ~**lage** f *e.c situation*; *condition of the market* ~**leben** n *e.c life* ~**lehre** f *economics* ~**lenkung** f *control of e.y*; ⟨pol⟩ *controlism* ~**macht** f *e.c power* ~**ministerium** n *Ministry of E.cs*, ⟨Am⟩ *Department of Commerce* ~**normen** f pl *trade standards* ~**ordnung** f *e.c system* ~**planung** f *e.c planning* ~**politik** f *e.c policy*; *e.cs* sg/pl ≃**politisch** a *politico-economical*; [adv] *with regard to e.c policy* ~**potential** n *e.c p.* (im Kriege *for war*) ~**programm** n *trade p.* ~**prüfer** m *chartered accountant*, ⟨Am⟩ *certified public a.* ~**quellen** f pl *resources* ~**rat** m *e.c and social council* ~**räume** m pl *service rooms*; *domestic* od *back regions*; *offices*; *outhouses* | (allg) ~**rückgang** m *recession* ~**sabotage** f *e.c s.* ~**sachverständige(r)** m *e.c expert* ~**schürze** f *overall* ~**struktur** f *business structure* ~**system** n *e.c s.*; *economies* (*the totalitarian e.ies of U.S.S.R. and its satellites* ~**teil** m (Zeitung) *business supplement* ~**verband** m *trade* od *business association* ~**verhandlungen** f pl *trade negotiations* ~**verkehr** m *e.c relations* ~**vertrag** m *commercial treaty* ~**vorteile** m pl *trade advantages* ~**wesen** n *e.c life* ~**wissenschaft** f *e.cs* [a. sg konstr] | ~ler [m] *economist* ~**wunder** n ⟨Ger⟩ (nach 1945) *German e.c miracle* ~**zentrum** n *commercial centre* ~**zus-schluß** m *e.c merger* ~**zwecke** m pl *commercial purposes* ~**zweig** m *branch of trade* bzw *of industry*

Wisch m ~es/~e *clout* ‖ *whisk* (*of grass*); (Stroh≃) *wisp of straw* ‖ (Papier) *scrap of paper* ‖ (Schimpfblatt) *rag* ‖ *trashy writing* (od *print, copy*) ~**baumwolle** f *cotton waste* ~**gold** n *gold leaf* ~**gummi** m ⟨bes mot⟩ *squeegee* ~**lappen** m *wiping clout* ‖ (f Geschirr) *dish-cloth* ‖ (Staubtuch) *duster* ‖ (f Fußböden) *mop* | (Gewehr-) ~**strick** m *pull-through* ~**tuch** n *wiper, wiping-cloth*; *duster* ‖ *dish-cloth* ‖ (Feudel) *swab*; *house-flannel* °~**wasch** m *tittle-tattle, chit-chat* **w·ischen 1.** vt [h] *to wipe, mop, sponge* ‖ sich die Augen ~ *to wipe one's eyes* ‖ mit dem Arm ~ über *to wipe one's arm across* (*the face*) | ⟨fam⟩ e–m e–e ~ *to give a p a box on the ear* ‖ ⟨fam⟩ e–m eins ~ *to play a p a trick* **2.** ⟨fam⟩ vi [s] *to slip away* ‖ vorbei ~ *to flit by* **W·ischer** m ~s/~ *wiper, rag, rubber* ‖ ⟨artill⟩ *sponge*; (Rohrwischer) *cleaning-rod* | ⟨arts⟩ *stump* (dazu: *to stump*) ‖ ⟨film⟩ *wipe* | ⟨fam fig⟩ (Rüge, Schelte) *wigging* (*to get a good w.*); (Schlag) ⟨sl⟩ *wipe*

W·isent m ~s/~e ⟨zoo⟩ (*European*) *bison*

W·ismut m & n ~(e)s/ ⟨chem⟩ *bismuth* ≃**en** vt [h] *to solder with b.* ~**chlorid** n *chloride of b.* ~**oxid,** ~**oxyd** n *b. oxide*

w·ispern vt/i [h] *to whisper*

Wiß- ~**begier(de)** f ~/ *craving for knowledge* ‖ (Neugier) *curiosity* ≃**begierig** a *desirous of knowledge, eager to learn* ‖ (neugierig) *curious, inquisitive* **W·issen** n ~s/ **A. 1.** *knowledge* ‖ ~ um ⟨a.⟩ *awareness of* **2.** (Kenntnisse) *knowledge, learning* **B.** oberflächliches ~ ⟨a.⟩ *smattering* ‖ praktisches ~ ⟨tech⟩ *know-how* ‖ tiefes ~ *erudition*; er besitzt tiefes ~ *he is an allround scholar* ‖ mit s–m ~ ist's nicht weit her *his learning is not great* (od ⟨fam⟩ *not up to much*) ‖ ~ **um** etw *consciousness of a th*; ~ **um** die Dinge *intuition* **C.** m–s ~s ist er .. *he is .., as far as I know* | **mit** (eigenem) ~ u Willen *intentionally, on purpose*; mit jds ~ u W. *with a p's knowledge and consent* | **nach** bestem ~ (u Ge≃) *to the best of one's kn.* | **ohne** mein ~ *without my kn., unknown to me* ‖ sie tun es ohne ihr [pl] ~ *they do it unknowing(ly)* | **wider** besseres ~ (u Ge≃) *against one's better judgment* **w·issen** vt/i [wußte/gewußt] [h] **A.** *to know* (*of*); *to be aware* od *informed of*; *to have knowledge of* ‖ *to understand* **B.** das mag der Himmel, **Gott** ~! weiß Gott! weiß der H.! *Heaven knows*! *God knows,* (*I don't*); G. weiß, wo .. *G. only knows where* ‖ .. weiß Gott nicht! (Beteuerung) ..: (*she couldn't*) *for goodness gracious* (*tell why*) | **wer** weiß? *search me*! *who knows*? *how should I know*? *it beats me*! | ⟨fam⟩ was weiß **ich**? *how can I know*? ‖ (wo ist er?) °Weiß ich's? ⟨sl⟩ *search me*! ‖ –, weißt du, – ⟨oft⟩ *don't you know* | ⟨prov⟩ **was ich** nicht weiß, macht mich nicht heiß *what the eye does not see the heart does not grieve over*; *I don't worry about it, I won't hear of it*! *what I don't see doesn't exist*! (Galsworthy) **C. nicht ein** noch aus ~ *not to know which way to turn*, ⟨fam⟩ *to have a wolf by the ears* ‖ **genau** ~, daß *to be positive that*; (etw) g. ~ *to be thoroughly acquaint-*

ed with | **nicht** ~ *to be ignorant of* || *I don't know* (⟨fam⟩ *dunno*); *I had no idea* (*you were here*); *I can't see* (*what's to become of you*) | **man** weiß **nicht** .., man **kann nicht** ~ .. *there's no telling* (*what may happen*) | **nicht daß** ich wüßte! *I don't know about that!*; *not to my knowledge*; *not that I know* (od *am aware*) *of*; *not as far as I know* || als wenn ich das nicht wüßte! *don't I know it!* || ~ Sie es **sicher**? *are you sure* (*of it*)? || (nicht) **soviel** ich weiß (*not*) *to my knowledge*; *for aught I know*, *for all I can tell*; *I understand* (*that*) | **wie** Sie ~ *as you know*, *as you are aware*; (*he is ill*) *you know* | **woher** ~ Sie das? *where did you hear that?*, *who has told you so?* || **wohl** ~ *to know full well* (*that*); (etw) .. *to be cognizant of*, *to know inside out*; wir ~ sehr wohl, daß *we are fully aware that* .. || sie wußten wohl, was sie taten, als sie *they had their wits about them when they* **D.** → **Bescheid**, Dank || wir ~ **es** *we know* || nun ~ Sie's! *so there!* || daß Sie's nur ~! *and no mistake!* || sie ~ **es** nicht besser *they know no better* || ohne **es** z ~ *unknowing(ly)* || **es** aus guter Quelle ~ *to have it on good authority* || wir ~ es v ihm *we know it from him* || **von etw** ~ *to be in on a th* | wir ~ **ihn** in Sicherheit *we know him* (*to be*) *safe* | **nichts** ~ v ⟨a.⟩ *to be quite in the dark about* ..; rein gar nichts ~ *not to know a th*; nichts ~ wollen v *not to recognize* (*a th*); er weiß v nichts *he's ignorant*, .. *a know-nothing*, *an ignoramus*; *he doesn't know what's what* (od ⟨sl⟩ *beans about it*); ⟨Am⟩ *he knows from nothing* || ich weiß nichts mehr z sagen *I'm past my Latin* || nichts mehr v sich selbst ~ *to have lost consciousness* | **sich** [dat] k–n **Rat** ~ *not to know what to do*; wir ~ uns k–n besseren Freund *we know of no better fr.* || ich weiß nicht **was** *something or other* || ⟨fam⟩ ~ Sie was? .. *I'll tell you what* (*,we'll drive*); *do you know* (*it is very funny but*) || ich würde, ich weiß nicht was, geben *I would give the world* (*to know*) **E.** sie ~ ihn **zu bereden** ~ *they will arrange to talk him over*; zu berichten ~ *to report*; z entfliehen ~ *to contrive to escape* || z leben ~ *to know how to live* || → nehmen D. || sie ~ z reden *they can talk* **F.** das **möchte** ich gerne ~ [⟨a.⟩ abs] *I wonder!*; ich möchte gerne ~, **ob** ⟨fam a.⟩ *I wonder if* || wir ~ nicht, **wann** *we don't remember the time when* || ~, **was** man tut *to know what one is about*; nicht mehr ~, **was** man tun soll *not to know what to do* || sie ~ nicht, was sie wollen *they don't know their own minds* || wer weiß **w·ie** *like anything*, .. *you wouldn't believe* | .. **wer w·eiß wie** *like anything*; (es war), wer weiß wie glatt ⟨vulg⟩ .. *so slippery you wouldn't believe* [abs]; .. wer weiß wie spät *ever so much o'clock at night*; und wer weiß, was sonst noch (alles) *and what not* || ⟨fam⟩ als wäre er, wer weiß was *as if he were ever so grand a p* | ich weiß, **wo** Barthel den Most holt *I know what's o'clock tolerably well*; ⟨so:⟩ *he knows his onions* od *a th or two* od *on which side his bread is buttered* || weiß Gott *or* **wer weiß woher** *from no one knows where* || man weiß nie, **woran** man ist *you never know* (*where you are*) **F. an** allem etw z tadeln ~ *to find fault with everything* | **auf, gegen** e–n etw ~ .. *against* .. | **über**: *about* | **um, von** etw ~: *of* || mit um e–e S ~ *to be privy to a th* || von k–r Sorge ~ *to know no care* **G. zu** ~ **bek** *to come to hear of* || man **kann** nie ~ *there is no knowing*, .. (bei Männern) *you never can tell* (*with men*) | **e-n ~ l**, e–m **zu ~ tun** *to acquaint a p with*; *to let a p be aware of*; *to let a p know*; *to send a p word*; *to tell a p* || l Sie's die Leute ~! *put out the word!* || wenn Sie es durchaus ~ **wollen** *if you must be told* || er will alles besser ~ *he thinks he knows everyth. better* || andere wollen ~, daß *others have it that* .. || man will ~, daß *it is rumoured that* || etw getan ~ wollen *to want to see a th done*, *to wish a th to be done* || er wollte nichts ~ v *he wished to have nothing to do with* .., *he would have none of* (*Mr. N.*); *he would not* (*look at* od) *hear of* od *discuss* (*cars*) || er will nichts davon ~ *he does not want to hear of it* **w·issend** a *knowing* || ~ um *cognizant of* **W·issens- ~drang, ~durst** m *thirst* od *craving for knowledge* **≗durstig** a *eager for k.e k.e-thirsty* **~gebiet** n *branch of k.e*; ~e [pl] ⟨a.⟩ *sectors of learning*; andere ~e überblicken *to perceive other areas of k.e* **~trieb** m = –drang **≗wert, ≗würdig** a *worth knowing*, *remarkable*, *interesting* **~würdigkeit** f *th worth k.g*, *remarkable fact* **~zweig** m *branch of k.e* **W·issenschaft** f ~/~en **A.** *science* (bes Natur≗) || *learning* | (Gelehrsamkeit) *scholarship* (*a great loss to* ~); *erudition* | (Kenntnis) *knowledge* | (Kunde) *intelligence*, *notice* **B.** Christliche ~ ⟨rel⟩ *Christian Science* || die klassische ~ *humanities* pl || die exakten ~en *the exact sciences* || philologisch-historische ~en *arts* pl || die schönen ~en *polite learning*, *the belles lettres* Fr | **~ler** m *man of science* od *learning*; (*true*) *scholar*; Abwanderung v ~n *brain drain* | **≗lich** a *scientific* [adv *sc.ally*] || ~e Bildung *scientific attainments* pl, .. h *to be a scholar* | [adv] ~ gebildet *learned*, *scholarly* | **≗**keit [f] *scientific nature*, *method*, etc **w·issentlich** a *knowing* || *deliberate*; ⟨dero⟩ *wilful* | [adv] ⟨a.⟩ (*I did it*) *on purpose* || ⟨jur⟩ *scienter* L

W·itfrau f ~/~en *widow*; → Witwe

w·ittern vt [h] (→ Wetter) *to scent*, *nose*, *smell* ⟨a. fig⟩ || ~ nach *to smell* od *nose about for* (*a th*) | ⟨fig⟩ *to get wind* (od *an inkling*) *of* (*a th*) || (Verrat) *to suspect* || ⟨fam⟩ Unrat ~ *to smell a rat* **W.rung** f ~/~en *weather*; *state of the atmosphere* (⟨min⟩ *of the air*) | ⟨hunt⟩ (Sinn & Fährte) *scent* || (Köder) *scented bait* | feine ~ ⟨fig⟩ *delicate intuition*; bei günstiger ~ *weather permitting* || bei jeder ~ *in all weather* | v scharfer ~ *quick-scented* | v etw ~ bek *to get scent* od *wind of a th* | **~s- ~anzeichen** n *sign of the coming weather* **~bericht** m *w. report* **≗beständig** a *w.-proof* (Kleidung) **~einflüsse** m pl *influence of the w.*; gegen ~ widerstandsfähig m *to w.ize*, *to w.proof* **~kunde, ~lehre** f *meteorology* **~lage** f (österr ⟨a.⟩ Witters–) = –verhältnisse **~kundige(r)** m *meteorologist* **~verhältnisse** n pl *atmospheric* od *meteorological conditions*, ⟨fam⟩ *atmospherics* pl **~vermögen** n ⟨hunt⟩ *scent* pl **~wechsel** m ⟨meteor⟩ *change in the w.*

†**W·it(t)ib** f ~/~e *widow* **W·ittum** n ~(e)s/~e & ≗er *jointure*, *dower*, *dowry* **W·itwe** f ~/~n (abbr Wwe) *widow* (*his w. mother*) || (v Stande) *dowager* (z. B. *Queen d.*; *d. duchess*) | **~n- ~blume** f *field scabious* **~gedinge** n *dower* **~gehalt, ~geld** n *widow's pension*; *jointure* **~jahr** n *w.'s year*, *year of mourning* **~kasse** f *w.s' fund* **~schleier** m *w.'s veil* **~sitz** m *w.'s residence* **~schaft** f, **~stand** m *w.hood* **~trauer** f (Kleidung) *w.'s weeds* **~verbrennung** f *suttee* **~vogel** m *whida*(*-bird*) **W·itwer** m ~s/~ *widower* **~stand** m *w.hood*

Witz m ~es/~e **1.** (Geist) *wit*(*tiness*), *brains* pl, *sense* | beißender, scharfer ~ *caustic*, *biting wit* || v raschem ~ *quick-witted*; v schlagfertigem ~ *good at repartee*, *having a ready wit* || weder ~ noch Verstand *neither rhyme nor reason* || sie h ~ *they are witty* **2.** (Einfall) *joke*, *witticism*, *witty remark*; (Wortspiel) *pun* || (Scherz) *pleasantry*, *practical joke* || (Spaß) *jest* || ⟨stud sl⟩ *merriment*, ⟨fam⟩ *lark* || ⟨theat⟩ *gag* | alter ~ *stale*, *standing joke*, ⟨fam⟩ *old chestnut*; beißender ~ *sarcasm*; *salt*; derber ~ *crude joke*; fauler ~ *bad* od *poor sort of joke*; guter, *capital*, schlechter *bad*, frecher ~ ⟨sl⟩ *smart crack*; harmloser ~ *mild jest*; schmutziger ~ ⟨sl⟩ *dirty crack*; stehender ~ *standing joke*; ein ~ der immer einschlägt *a never-failing joke* | ~e m *or* reißen *to crack jokes*, .. über jdn *to be witty about a p* **3.** ⟨fig⟩ das ist ein großartiger ~ *that's a good 'un* || das ist ja der ~ *that's the fun of it*, *that's where the fun comes in*; *that's where it lies* || das ist der ganze ~ *that's all*; ⟨Am⟩

that's the gag (Trick) **~blatt** n *comic (paper)* **~bold** m *wit(ty fellow)*; *punster* || (zu Streichen aufgelegt) *wag* **~ecke** f *comic column* **≚los** a *without wit, not funny*; ⟨fig⟩ *dull, stale*; *silly* **≚reich** a *witty* **≚sprühend** a *of sparkling wit* **~wort** n *sally, witticism* **W·itzelei** f **1.** ~/ *joking, punning* **2.** ~/~en *witticism, pun* || (Am a.) *wisecrack* || *poor sort of joke* **w·itzeln** vi [h] *to quib*; *to affect wit* || (über [acc]) *to joke (at), to poke fun (at)* **w·itzig** a *witty*; (mst S) *funny* || (erfinderisch, sinnreich) *ingenious* || ~e Antwort *smart reply*; ~e Bemerkung *sally*; ~er Einfall *bright idea, brilliant remark*; ~e Entgegnung *clever repartee*; er ist ein ~er Kopf *he is quite a wit* || was ist daran ~? *where does the joke come in*? **w·itzigen** vt [h] *to teach wit* od *a lesson*; *to make wiser* || gewitzigt w *to learn a lesson* **W·itzigkeit** f ~/ *wittiness* **W·itzling** m ~(e)s/~e *wag* || *poor joker* od *punster*

Wladiwost·ok n ⟨Russ⟩ *Vladivostok*

wo I. [adv] **A.** **(örtlich)** **1.** [interr] *where?, in what place?* || *(I know) where (he lives)* || ~ denn nur (in aller Welt)? *where on earth?* || ~ h Sie das her? *where did you get it?* || → woher, wohin || von ~ kommst du? *where do you come from?* **2.** [rel] *(it is here) where* od *that (he lives)*; *(the house) in which (he lives)*; *where there (is a will there is a way)* || *(there is no town) that (I have not been to)* || v ~ *(a place) whence (I could see her house)* **3.** [indef] (irgendwo) *somewhere* || ~ auch, ~ immer, ~ nur *wherever* **B.** **(zeitlich)** [rel] zu e–r Zeit, ~ [besser: da *or* als] *at a time when* || jetzt, ~ die Preise so hoch sind *(I can't live on my wages) with prices what they are*; heutzutage, ~ es Dienstmädchen nicht mehr gibt .. *with maids a th of the past (the woman is doing the harder job)* **C.** (= wie) [ell] ~ werd ich! *do you think I'm a fool?* || ach ~! *I wouldn't dream of it!, not I!, not at all!, no such th!* **II.** [conj] (= wenn) *if* || ~ nicht *if not, unless (if I'm not* od *unless I am mistaken)* || ~ möglich *if possible* **III.** ≚ n; auf das ≚ kommt's an *it all depends on the locality* od *on where it is to be* **wo·anders** [adv] *somewhere else, elsewhere*

wob 1. & 3. sg pret v weben

wob·ei [adv] **1.** [rel] *whereby, by which, at which, in (connection with) which*; *in which case* || ~ mir einfällt, daß *which reminds me that* || ~ es blieb *and there the matter rested* **2.** [interr] *at* od *near what place?*; *near where?*; *where (did I stop)?*

W·oche f ~/~n *week* || noch diese ~ ⟨fam⟩ *inside of a w.* || zweimal die ~ *twice a w.* || in e–r ~ *in a w., a w. hence* || ~ f ~ *w. by w., w. after w.* || heute in/vor drei ~n *to-day three w.s* || v ~ z ~ *w. in, w. out* || ich habe die ~ *it is my w.* || stille ~ *Passion W.* || ⟨com⟩ weiße ~ *white sale* | ⟨fig⟩ in die ~n k *to be brought to bed*, mit e–m Sohn .. *to be delivered of ..*, zu früh .. *to have a miscarriage* || in den ~n liegen *or* s *to be confined, to be lying in* | **~n-** **~arbeitsplan** m *w.ly work schedule* **~ausgabe** f *w.ly edition* **~bericht** m *w.ly report*; (in Zeitschriften *w. by w.*; ⟨film, telv⟩ *newsreel* **~besuch** m *visit to a woman lying-in* **~bett** n *childbed, lying-in (period)*; *puerperism* || ins ~ k *to be confined* || im ~ dahingerafft w *to die in childbed* | ~psychose [f] *puerperal psychosis* **~binde** f ⟨med⟩ *maternity* od *obstetrical pad* **~blatt** n *w.ly (paper)* **~einnahme** f *receipts during a w.* **~end(e)** n *w.-end* || das ~ verbringen *to w.-e.* **~endler** m *w.-ender* **~fieber** n *puerperal fever* **~geld** n *w.ly allowance* || = –lohn **~hilfe** f *maternity relief* od *grant*; ⟨ins, soc⟩ *m. benefit* **~karte** f ⟨rail etc⟩ *weekly season-ticket* **~kind** n *new-born child (baby during the first six w.s after its birth* ⟨a. med⟩) **~kleid** n *every-day dress* **≚lang** [adv] *for w.s* pl **~lohn** m *w.ly wages* pl od *pay* **~löhner** m *labourer paid by the w.* **~markt** m *w.ly market* **~pflege** f *post-natal care* **~pflegerin** f *monthly nurse* **~predigt** f *w.-day sermon* **~rechnung** f *w.ly bill* **~schau** f ⟨film⟩ *news(reel)* | ~-Kameramann *n.l cameraman* **~schrift** f *w.ly paper* **~stube** f *lying-in room* **~tag** m *w.day*; *day of the w.*, **≚tags** [adv] *on w.days* pl **~übersicht** f *w.ly review* || ⟨fig cul⟩ gedrängte ≚ ⟨sl⟩ *resurrection-pie* **≚weise** [adv] *by the w.*; *a w.*; *w.ly* **~zettel** m *bill for the w.* ⟨a. theat⟩ **w·öchentlich** a *weekly* | [adv] *weekly, by the week, every week* || zweimal ~ *twice a week* **W·öchnerin** f ~/~nen *woman in childbed* | **~nen-** ~heim [n] *maternity* od *lying-in hospital*; ~station [f] *m. ward*

W·ocken m ~s/~ *distaff*

W·odka m ~s/ ⟨Russ⟩ *vodka*

wo- **~d·urch** [adv] **1.** [rel] *whereby*; *by* od *through which* **2.** [interr] *by* od *through what?*, *by what means?* **~f·ern** [conj] *if*; *provided that* || ~ nicht *if not*; *unless*; *except if* **~f·ür** [adv] **1.** *for what? what for? wherefore?* || ~ ist das gut? *what is that good for?* || ~ halten Sie mich *what do you take me for?* **2.** [rel] *for which ..*, ~ wir Ihnen bestens danken *and thank you for same* || etwas, ~ wir k–e Zeit h *sth (that) we have no time for* || ~ es auch dienen mag *whatever it may be meant for* **~g·egen I.** [adv] **1.** *against what?* **2.** [rel] *against which*; *in exchange* od *return for which* | = wofür **II.** [conj] *while, whereas*, → –her etc

wog 1. & 3. sg pret v wägen & wiegen

W·oge f ~/~n (→ bewegen) *billow, wave* || ⟨fig⟩ *(s)well (of sympathy)*; *thrill (of feelings)* **w·ogen I.** vi [h] (See, Menschenmenge, Gefühle) *to surge* || das Meer wogt *the sea is rough, there is a swell on* || (Baum, Kornfeld) *to wave* || (hin u her) *to fluctuate, sway* || (schwellend) *to heave* (a. Busen, Menschenmenge) || (Rauch) *to billow* || ⟨fig⟩ *to boil* || (Gefühle) ⟨a.⟩ *to (s)well* | ~der Gang *undulating walk* **II.** ≚ [n] *surging, rolling, undulation (of waves)*; *heave (of the sea)*; *heaving (of her bosom, of the crowd)*; *billowing (of the smoke)* **≚drang, ≚prall, ≚schwall** m *rushing, dashing, surging of waves* **~weise** adv *in waves* **w·ogig** a *wavy, billowy, surging* || *rough (sea)*

woh·er [adv] **1.** *from what place? from where?, where .. from?* | ⟨fig⟩ *how, why?* || ~ wissen Sie das? *how do you know that?* **2.** [rel] *from which* || ~ auch .. *wherever (he may come from)* **woh·in** [adv] **1.** *where (.. to)? where are you going (to)?* || ⟨gram⟩ *whither?* **2.** [rel] der Ort, ~ ich ziehe *the place (where) I am moving to* || einerlei ~ *no matter to what place, to whatever place*; ~ auch .. *wherever (he may go)* **3.** [indef] *somewhere*, ⟨Am⟩ *(take me) some place (where ..)* || °ich muß ~ (= aufs Klosett) *I go to see Mrs. Jones, I must go to see a man about a dog* **~·ab** [adv] *down where?* || [rel] *down which* **~·aus** [adv] *which way? in what direction?* || ~ soll das noch führen? *where will that end?* **~g·egen** [conj] *whereas, while, whilst* **woh·inter** [adv] **1.** *behind what?* **2.** [rel] *behind which*

Wohl n ~(e)s/ *welfare, well-being, prosperity* || leibliches ~ *physical well-being* || (Gesundheit) *health* || das gemeine ~ *the general welfare, the public good, the common weal, the good of the commonwealth* | (auf) Ihr ~! *your health!*; ⟨fam⟩ *here's to you! here's how!* ⟨Am⟩ *here's looking at you!* | **auf** jds ~ trinken *to drink a p's health, to raise one's glass to a p* | **um** das öffentl. ~ besorgt *public spirited* | **zu** jds ~ *for the benefit of a p*; etw z ~e der Allgemeinheit gestalten *to turn a th to the public good* | das ~ u Wehe *the weal and ill* od *woe*; dein ~ u W. *your interest (is nearest to my heart)* **wohl I.** pred a & adv [~er *or* besser/am ~sten *or* besten] **1.** **[betont]** **A.** (gesund) *well, fit* || ~ **aussehen** *to look well* | sich ~ **fühlen** (vgl ~ s) *to be quite all right, .. äußerst .. to be in the pink* *of condition*, .. bei jdm *to feel at home with a p*, .. in .. *to hug* (*one's misfortune*) || sich nicht ~ fühlen ⟨a.⟩ *to be feeling rather off*, ⟨fam⟩ *to be out of sorts*; ⟨fig⟩ *to feel ill at ease* (*in society*) || (⟨a.⟩ sich in s–r Haut nicht recht ~ f., ⟨Am sl⟩ *not to feel so bobbish*) || ich fühle mich am ~sten, wenn ich allein bin *I am happiest when alone* | jdn wieder ~ m *to restore a p* || ~ s *to be well, to* (*be in* od) *enjoy good health* || den Toten ist ~ *the dead are happy* || es **war** ihm ~ z Mute *he was in good spirits* || wieder ~ w *to recover* **B.** [adv] ~ **bekomm's**! *may you enjoy it*!, ⟨iron⟩ *much good may it do you*! || ~ berechnet *well calculated* || das h wir uns ~ gedacht *we thought as much* || ich glaube ~ ⟨a. iron⟩ *I daresay* || **leben** Sie ~! *farewell*!, *good-bye* || er hätte es ~ m können *he might very well have done it* || sich ~ in Acht nehmen *to be very careful* || **schlaf** ~! *sleep well* || wünsche (Ihnen) ~ z schlafen *I wish you a good night*(*'s rest*) || ich sehe wohl *I see clearly* || sich's ~ s l *enjoy o.s.* || es **tut** mir ~, wenn *I feel happy when* || das tut ~! *it does you good*! || Sie tun ~ daran zu [+ vb] *you do well to* .. || sehr ~ wissen *to know all right* od *full well*; *to be fully aware* (*that*) **C.** [ell] ~! *well then*!; ⟨mar⟩ *aye, aye, Sir*! || **ja** ~! *certainly, to be sure, of course* || ~ **oder** übel *willy-nilly, whether one likes it or not*; *for better for worse*; *perforce* || **so** ~ → so **D.** ~ **dem**, der *happy he who* || ~ mir! *happy for me*! || ~ ihm, daß er entkam *lucky he to have escaped* **2.** [**unbetont**] **A.** (leicht) *easily* || ~ 4 Wochen *about a month* || ~ zehnmal *at least ten times* | (gewiß) *doubtless, indeed* || (*this is your sister*) *I presume* || ~ nicht *hardly* **B.** Sie **irren** sich ~ *I fear you are mistaken* || ich kann es ~ selbst nicht *very likely I* .. || es **kann** *or* mag ~ s, das könnte ~ s *that may* (*well*) *be so*, ⟨fam⟩ *most likely*; → sagen || was kommt ~ jetzt? *what next, I wonder*?, *I w. what will come next* || es ist (sehr) ~ möglich, daß *quite possibly* (*there is a good possibility that* ..) || siehst du ~! *do you see now* (*that* ..) || das wird ~ stimmen *I daresay it's true* || das **ist** ~ alles *I think* (⟨Am⟩ *guess, reckon*) *that's all* || das ist ~ der Doktor *that'll be the d.* || er wird es ~ gesehen h *I presume he has seen it* || er wird uns ~ (nicht) kennen *I* (*don't*) *suppose he will know us* || er war ~ größer *he would be taller* || ich **möchte** ~ wissen *I should like to know*; *I wonder* || ⟨poet⟩ ~ über den Rhein (*right*) *across the Rh.* **C.** [interr] sind Sie ~ Herr N.? *you'll be Mr. N., sir*? || waren wir ~ auch so?, **ob** wir ~ auch so waren? *were we like that, I wonder*? *I wonder whether* .. || (*where did it come from*) *do you suppose*? || (*what other reasons*) *do you think* (*there can have been*?) | ×(das war doch so!) ~? [vgl?] .. *wasn't it*? **D.** ~ .., **aber** *indeed .. but*; *it is true .. but* || (nicht 50) aber ~ 40 .. *but perhaps 40* || .. **doch** ~ .. (*this is*) *as I think you will agree* (*self-evident*) || ~ **kaum**: *he had hardly time to do it I should think* **II.** [conj] **ob** er wohl .. (= obwohl er) *although he* (*was late*) **w·ohl- ~achtbar** a *respectable, esteemed* || **~·an**! [adv] *well*!, *come*!, *now then*!, *all right*! **~·angebracht** a *w.-timed, seasonable* **~anständig** a = anständig **~·auf**! *well*! *cheer up*! || [a]; ~ sein *to be w.* od *in good health* **≃bedacht** m; mit ~ = –bedacht [adv] **~bedacht** a *w.-considered, deliberate* | [adv] *considerately, deliberately, on purpose*; → –durch- **~bedächtig** a *considerate, deliberate* **≃befinden** n *good health*; (*bodily*) *well-being* **~befugt** a *quite competent, w. qualified, justly entitled* **~begabt** a *highly gifted* **~begründet** a *legitimate*; *valid* (*absenteeism, argument*) **≃behagen** n *ease, comfort* || wahres ~ *gusto, zest* **~behalten** a *safe* (*and sound*); recht ~ heimk *to arrive home in fairly good shape* **~bekannt** a *w.-known* || ⟨dero⟩ *notorious* **~beleibt** a = beleibt, ⟨a.⟩ *portly* **~beschaffen** a *in good condition* **~besetzt** a *w.-filled, -stored* **~bestallt** a *duly installed* **~bestanden** a *w.-stocked with trees* || (Examen) *passed with honours* **~betagt** a *stricken in years* **~bewandert** a *w.-skilled* **~durchdacht** a *w. planned*; *w.-thought-out*; *mature*; *set* (*speech*) **~·edel** a ⟨obs⟩ *high and noble* **~·ehrwürdig** a *reverend* **~erfahren** a *experienced, w.skilled, expert* **≃ergehen** n *welfare, well-being, prosperity*; ⟨fam⟩ *easy street*; → –befinden **~erhalten** a *in good condition, well-preserved* **~erprobt** *w.-tried--out* **~erwogen** a *w.-considered* **~erworben** a *duly acquired* **~erzogen** a *w.-bred, w.-brought-up, w.-behaved* | ≃heit [f] *good breeding* **≃fahrt** f *welfare, prosperity* || soziale ~ *w.e-work* || öffentliche ~ *public w.e activities* pl; Leute die der ö.n ~ z Last fallen *men of relief* | **~s-** ~amt [n] *W.e* od *Relief Office*; ≃ausschuß [m] (*public w.e* od) *vigilance committee*; ≃pflege [f] *w.e-work* od *-services*; *social service*; ~pflegerin [f] *social worker*; ~staat [m] *w.e state*; ≃staatlich [a] *welfarist* [attr]; ~staatspraktiken [pl], –wesen [n] *welfarism*; ~verein [m] *provident society* **~feil** a *cheap*; ~ wie Brombeeren *plenty as* .. | [adv] *at a low price* || ~ ist nicht billig *a good bargain is a pick-purse* || ~ davonk *to get off easily* **≃feilheit** f *cheapness* **~geartet** a *w.--mannered, -behaved* **~gebaut** a *w.-built* || (P) *w.-shaped, w.-knit* **~gebildet** a *w.-formed, -made* **~geboren** a *w.-born* || (Anrede ⟨obs⟩) Ew. ≃ *Sir* || (auf Briefen ⟨obs⟩) *Esquire*; Sr. ≃ Herrn N. N. *N. N. Esq.* (abbr f *Esquire*) (ohne *Mr.*!) **≃gefallen** n *pleasure* (*at your p.*), *delight, satisfaction* || (Beifall) *approval* || sein ~ h, finden an [dat] *to take delight in, to form a liking for*, ⟨bib⟩ *my beloved Son in whom I am w.- pleased* || sich in ~ auflösen ⟨fam⟩ *to end satisfactorily, to pass off happily*; ⟨iron⟩ *to end in smoke* **~gefällig** a *pleasant, agreeable* || Gott [dat] ~ *w. pleasing to G.* || (etw) ~ [adv] (aufnehmen) .. *graciously, with pleasure*; .. betrachten *to regard a th with satisfaction* || (selbstgefällig) *complacent* | ≃keit [f] *pleasantness* || *complacency* **~geformt** → –gestalt **~gefügt** a *w.-integrated* (*whole*) **≃gefühl** n *pleasant feeling*; *ease* **~|gehen** vi imps irr [s]; es geht ihm wohl *he is doing w.* **~gel·itten** a *popular* **~gem·eint** a *w.-meant*; *friendly* (*advice*) **~gemerkt** [adv] [vorgestellt] *mind*! [nachgestellt]; aber: *mind you, I hardly know him*; *let it be noted, nota bene* L **~gemut** a *cheerful, merry, light-hearted*; ⟨sl⟩ *cocky* **~genährt** a *w.-fed, corpulent, plump* **~geneigt** a *w.-inclined* ([dat] *towards*) || *affectionate, kind* **~geordnet** a *w.--ordered, -disposed, -arranged* **~gepflegt** a *w.--kept* **~geraten** a *w.-performed* || *w.-bred, good* (*child*) **≃geruch** m = Duft **≃geschmack** m *agreeable taste, pleasant flavour* **~gesetzt** a *w.-worded* (*speech*), *w.-chosen* (*words*) **~gesinnt** a *w.--disposed, friendly*; jdm ~ s *to wish w. to a p* **~ges·ittet** a *w.-mannered* **≃gestalt** f *fine shape* od *figure*; *shapeliness* **~gestalt(et)** a *w.-shaped, -turned*; *handsome, shapely* **~getroffen** a *striking, speaking* (*portrait*) **~gewogen** a *w.-affected, kind, benevolent* **≃gezogenheit** f *good manners* pl, *good breeding* **~habend** a *wealthy, well-to-do*; *leisured* (*classes*); ~es Aussehen *air of substance*; [pred] *w.-off* **≃habenheit** f *opulence, affluence, wealth*; *easy circumstances* pl **~kalkuliert** a *calculated* (*risk*) **≃klang** m *euphony* ⟨Lit⟩; *harmony*; *music* (*in a p's ears*) **~klingend** a *sweet--sounding, melodious, dulcet, harmonious* **≃laut** m = –klang **≃leben** n *life of ease* od *pleasure*; *high living* || (Üppigkeit) *self-indulgence, luxury* || *feasting* **~löblich** a *worshipful* **~meinend** a *w.--meaning, w.-intentioned*; *friendly* **~riechend** a *sweet-scented, fragrant* **~schmeckend** a *savoury, flavo(u)rsome, toothsome, relishing*; *tasty, palatable* **≃sein** n *welfare, good health* || Ihr ~! *your health*! **≃stand** m *comfort, prosperity, welfare*;

wealth; affluence, opulence | **~s-** ~gebiet [n] *boom area*; ~gesellschaft [f] *affluent society* **≈tat** f *benefit, kindness, good action* ‖ e–m ~en erweisen *to confer benefits upon a p* | ⟨fig⟩ *blessing, treat, mercy*; das ist e–e wahre ~! *that is a comfort* od *relief*! **≈täter(in** f) m *benefactor* (f *benefactress*) **~tätig** a *beneficent* (*effect*); *charitable* ‖ (S) *salutary* | ≈keit [f] *beneficence; charitableness, charity* | **~s-** –basar [m] *ch.y bazaar*; –gabe [f] *eleemosynary gift*; –kollekte [f] *ch.y ballot*; –verein [m] *charitable society*; –vorstellung [f] *ch.y performance; benefit* **~tuend** a *beneficent; soothing, pleasant; comforting, genial* (*warmth*); *grateful* (*sleep*) **~|tun** vi irr [h] [dat] *to do good* (*to*), *to benefit* ‖ (jdm angenehm s) *to be pleasing* od *give pleasure to* ‖ das tut e–m wohl! *it does you good!, it's good for you* | ≈ trägt Zinsen *giving much to the poor, doth increase a man's store* **~überl·egt** a *w.-considered, deliberate; judicious; studied; set* (*speech*); *calculated* (*risk*) **~unterrichtet** a *w.-informed* **~verdient** a *just, w.-deserved*; (*a man*) *of great merit; w.-earned* (*rest*) | ~erm·aßen [adv] *deservedly* **≈verhalten** n *good conduct* **~verleih** m ⟨bot⟩ *arnica* **~vers·ehen** a; ~ mit den Sterbesakramenten *fortified by the rites of the Church*; ~ mit Geld *w.-heeled* **~verstanden** a; ~! *and no mistake! mark my words!*, ⟨fam⟩ *you know* **~w·eise** a *most wise* **~w·eislich** adv *wisely; cunningly* ‖ ich verhielt mich ~ still *I was careful to keep quiet* **~w·issend** a *w.-knowing* **≈wollen** n *goodwill; benevolent regard, benevolence* ‖ *grace* ‖ (Gunst) *favour, patronage* **~|wollen** vi irr [h] (jdm) *to wish* (*a p*) *w., to be* (*a p's*) *w.-wisher* | ~d [a] *benevolent, kind; sympathetic* (*consideration*) **w·ohlig** a *comfortable; easeful* (*feeling*); *delightful* (*calm*) ‖ (P) *happy*

W·ohn- *dwelling; resident* (*population*) **~bezirk** m *r.tial section*, ⟨Am⟩ *neighborhood* **~block** m *block of flats* **~dichte** f ⟨soc⟩ *residential* od *housing density*; ⟨demog⟩ *crowding index, degree of c.g* **~fläche** f ⟨demog⟩ *surface area* **~gebiet** n ⟨bot, zoo⟩ *habitat* **~gegend** f *urbane* od *built-up area* **~gelegenheit** f *accommodation* **~gebäude, ~haus** n *dwelling-, manor-house* ‖ (gr Miethaus) *mansion* | –häuser [pl] *residential houses* **~hausbau** m *domestic architecture* **~heim** n ⟨stud⟩ *hostel; hall of residence*; ⟨Am⟩ *dormitory* **~küche** f *kitchen-parlo(u)r* **~lage** f: in bester, ruhiger ~ ⟨m. m.⟩ *living in privacy and comfort* **~möglichkeiten** f pl *living accommodations* **~ort** m (*place of*) *residence, d.g-place; home* ‖ ⟨zoo⟩ *habitat* **~raum** m *living-room*; ≈e [pl] *l.g quarters* **~recht** n *right to reside; privilege of residence; title* **~schlafzimmer** n *bed-sitting room*, ⟨Am⟩ *bedsitter* **~sitz** m *place of residence; domicile, abode* ‖ (*country-*)*seat*; fester ~ *settled address*; P ohne festen ~ *p of no fixed abode*; ⟨a.⟩ *vagrant*; Geburts≈ *natural d.*; gesetzlicher ~ *d. by operation of law*; ~ kraft Abstammung *d. of origin*; Wahl≈ *d. of choice* ‖ s–n ~ im Ausland h *to be d.d abroad*; s–n ~ aufschlagen *to take up one's r.e* ‖ sie liebt Berlin als ~ *she likes B. to live in* ‖ s–n ~ nehmen *to settle down* **~stätte** f *abode, residence* **~straße** f *r.tial street* **~stube** f *sitting-room* **~verhältnisse** n pl *housing conditions* **~viertel** n *r.tial area* od *district, section, quarters* pl; (neues) *housing estate*; ruhiges ~ *quiet r.tial area* **~vorort** m ⟨Am⟩ *dormitory suburb* **~wagen** m *caravan* | ~anhänger [m] (*c.*) *trailer* **~zelt** n *living tent* **~zimmer** n *sitting room, parlo(u)r* **w·ohnen** vi [h] *to live*, ⟨geh. Spr.⟩ *to dwell, reside* (*in a place, at a hotel*) ‖ (als Mieter) *to lodge* ⟨a. orn⟩; ⟨Am⟩ *to room* (bei *with*) ‖ bei jdm ~ ⟨a.⟩ *to live at a p's, to stay with a p* ‖ umsonst ~ *to have free quarters* ‖ ⟨univ⟩ *to room* (*in private houses*) ‖ wo ~ Sie? *where do you live?* ‖ so wahr wie ein Gott im Himmel wohnt *as true as there is a G. in H.* | hier wohnt **sich's** billig *this is an inexpensive place to live in* **w·ohnhaft** a *living; dwelling, residing* ‖ ⟨jur⟩ *domiciled* ‖ ~ s *to reside* ‖ Herr N, ~ Hohe Str. 45 *Mr. N. of 45 High Street* **w·ohnlich** a *comfortable, cosy, snug* | ≈keit [f] *livability, habitability; cosiness* **W·ohnung** f ~/~en *dwelling, lodging, habitation; place* (*at his p.*) ‖ 3-Zimmer-~ *three room apartment* ‖ ⟨jur⟩ *domicile* ‖ (Wohnräume mit Zubehör) *dwelling* (⟨off⟩ *accommodation*) *unit; rooms* ⟨a. univ⟩, *lodgings, apartments* pl; ⟨jur⟩ *chambers* (*to take ch.s*) ‖ (Etagen≈) *flat* (*at his f.*) ‖ ~ in 2 Stockwerken ⟨Am⟩ *duplex apartment* ‖ die ~ liegt im 2. Stock *the flat is on the second floor* | **~s-** **~anschluß** m ⟨telph⟩ *subscriber's residence station* **~anzeiger** m *directory* **~bau** m *housing construction*; sozialer ~ *h.g project* | ~kunst [f] *domestic architecture*; ~projekt [n] *h.g development plan*; ~verband [m] *h.g association* | der ~bewirtschaftung unterliegend *subject to rent control* **~einrichtung** f *funiture* **~entschädigung** f = –geld **~frage** f *housing question* | Ministerium f ~n u Kommunalverwaltung *Ministry of H.g and Local Government* **~geld** n *lodging allowance*; ⟨bes mil⟩ *a.e for quarters and rent* | ~zuschuß [m] *residential* od *rental a.e* **~mangel** m, **~not** f *h.g problem, house shortage* **~nachweis** m *accommodation registry* **~politik** f *h.g policy* **~suche** f *house-hunting* **~vermieter(in** f) m *lodging-house keeper* **~wechsel** m *change of address*

W·oilach m ~s/~e *horse-rug, saddle blanket*

Woiw·od(e) m ~en/~en *voivode*

W·ölbe- **~dach** n *vaulted roof* **~höhe** f *elevation of an arch* **~stein** m *archstone*, letzter ~ *keystone* **w·ölben** vt [h] *to vault, arch* (⟨a.⟩ = sich ~) ‖ *to barrel* (*a road*) ‖ mit gewölbter Brust *deep-chested* ‖ gewölbter Gang *arched passage*, g.r Keller *vault* **W·ölbung** f ~/~en *vault(ing)* | (gewölbte Form) *curvature* ‖ Gaumen≈ *roof of the mouth*; Stirn≈ *dome* (*of forehead*) ‖ ⟨arch⟩ *intrados* bzw *extrados* (*of an arch*) ‖ konvexe ~ *camber* ‖ (Fahrbahn≈) *crossfall* ‖ ⟨übtr⟩ *dome* | **~s-** ~frei [a] *non-buckled*

Wolf m ~(e)s/≈e **A. 1.** *wolf* ‖ hungrig wie ein ~ *as hungry as a hunter* **2.** ⟨med⟩ *wolf, excoriation, chafe, gall*; sich e n ~ holen *to get sore*, ⟨fam⟩ *to lose leather* (*in walking, riding*) **3.** ⟨spin⟩ *willow* ‖ ⟨met⟩ *devil* ‖ (Stein≈) ⟨mech⟩ *lewis* **B.** ⟨fig⟩ ~ im Schafpelz *wolf in sheep's clothing, snake in the grass* ‖ ~ u Schäfchen (Spiel) *fox and geese* ‖ wenn man den ~ nennt, kommt er gerennt; der ~ in der Fabel *talk of an angel and you see his wings* ‖ mit den ≈en heulen *to follow the cry* od *multitude*; .. muß man h. *do at Rome as Rome does!* **w·olfen** vt [h] ⟨spin⟩ *to willow* **w·ölfen** vi/t [h] (⟨a.⟩ of dog) *to whelp* **W·ölfin** f ~/~nen *she-wolf* **w·ölfisch** a *wolfish* **W·olfram** n ~s/ ⟨min⟩ *wolfram, tungsten; arsenical iron-ore* **≈haltig** a *tungsteniferous* **~lampe** f *tungsten lamp* **≈sauer** a *wolframic* **~säure** f *tungstic acid* **W·olfs-** **~angel** f *wolf-trap* **~art** f *species of w.* ‖ *w.'s nature* **~balg** m *w.'s skin* **~barsch** m ⟨ich⟩ *bass* **~brut** f *pack of young wolves* **~eisen** n, **~falle** f *w.-trap* **~fang** m *w.'s tooth* **~fell** n *w.'s hide* od *skin* **~gebiß** n ⟨hors⟩ *sharp bit* **~gesicht** n *w.ish face* **~gestalt** f *lupine shape* **~grube** f *w.-trap*; ⟨mil⟩ *pitfall* **~hetze** f *w.-baiting* **~hund** m *Alsatian* **~hunger** m *ravenous appetite* **~jagd** f *w.-chase* **~jäger** m *w.er* **~kirsche** f *belladonna* **~klaue** f *w.'s claw* **~magen** m ⟨fig⟩ *ravenous appetite* **~milch** f ⟨bot⟩ → *spurge*, → Springwurz **~pelz** m *w.'s skin* **~rachen** m ⟨anat⟩ *split palate* **~schlucht** f *wolves' glen* **~sucht** f ⟨path⟩ *lycanthropy* **~zahn** m ⟨hors⟩ *w.-tooth*

W·olga, die (russ. Strom) *the Volga*

Wolh·ynien n ⟨Russ⟩ (Landschaft) *Volhynia*

W·ölkchen n ~s/~ *cloudlet* ‖ ⟨fig⟩ *film*;

⟨path⟩ *nebula* **W·olke** f ~/~n *cloud* ‖ mit ~n bedeckt *c.ed*; Flug über den ~n *over-the-top flight* ‖ aus allen ~ fallen ⟨fig⟩ *to come back to earth*; wie a. d. ~n f. ⟨fig⟩ *to come down with a bump*; ich war wie aus den ~n gefallen *I was thunderstruck, .. utterly dumbfounded*; *you could have knocked me down with a feather* ‖ sich [acc] in den ~n fühlen *to feel high as a kite* ‖ sich in die ~n verlieren *to be apt to be in the c.s* ‖ ~n ziehen auf *c.s are gathering* | ⟨fig⟩ *swarm* ‖ *flaw, film*; ⟨path⟩ *nebula* **w·ölken** vt/i [h] *to cloud* ‖ sich ~ *to become overcast* **W·olken-** **~achat** m *c.ed agate* **≃·an** adv *up to the c.s* **~apparat** m ⟨theat⟩ *c. machine*, ⟨Am⟩ *c. projector* **~bruch** m *violent downpour c.-burst*; *rainstorm*; der reinste ~! *some rain*! | **≃**artig [a] *torrential* **~decke** f *cover of c.s*; geschlossene ~ *continuous c.*, ⟨meteor⟩ *overcast* N; die ~ durchstoßen *to come down through the o.* **~echo** n ⟨radar⟩ *c. return* **~fahne** f *c. banner, b. c.s* **~fetzen** m pl *scattered clouds* **~himmel** m *c.y sky, c.iness* **~höhe** f ⟨aero, mil⟩ *ceiling* N **~kratzer** m *skyscraper* **~k·uckucksheim** n *never-never land, c.land, Utopia* **~landschaft** f *sky-scape* **≃los** a *c.less, serence, clear* | **≃**igkeit [f] ⟨meteor⟩ *unlimited ceiling* **~lücke** f *break in the c.y sky* **~massen** f pl *masses of c.s* **~sammler** m *c.-gathering Jove* **~scheinwerfer** m *ceiling light projector* **~schieber** m ⟨theat⟩ *scene-shifter* **~sofitten** f pl ⟨theat⟩ *sky-pieces* pl **~untergrenze** f *ceiling* **~wand** f *bank of c.s* **~zug** m *drift of the c.s* **w·olkig** a *cloudy, clouded* ⟨a. fig⟩ ‖ ⟨fig⟩ *filmy*; (*gem*) *with a flaw, full of flaws*

W·oll- **~abgang** m *wool-waste* **~arbeit** f *w.-work* **~arbeiter(in** f) m *w.-dresser* **≃artig** a *w.ly* **~baum** m ⟨bot⟩ *Kapok-tree, silk-cotton tree* **~bedeckung** f *pile* **~bezeichnungsgrundsätze** pl *w. description terms* **~brecher** m ⟨spin⟩ *devilling-machine* **~decke** f *w.len rug* ‖ (Bettdecke) *blanket* **~entstäuber** m *w.-duster* **~färber·ei** f *w.-dyeing* **~fett** n *w.-oil, lanolin, yolk* **~garn** n *w.len yarn*; *worsted* **~gras** n ⟨bot⟩ *cotton-grass* **~grossist** m *w.-stapler* **~haar** n *w. hair* **~hadernsortierer** m *w. rag sorter* **~handel** m *w.-trade* **~händler** m *dealer in w.*; *stapler* **~handlung** f *w.-business* **~handschuh** m *worsted gl.* **~hemd** n *w.len shirt, guernsey* **~industrie** f *w.len industry* **~jacke** f *jersey, guernsey* **~kamm** m *carding-comb* **~kämmer** m *w.-carder* **~kratze** f *w.-card* **~kraut** n ⟨bot⟩ *mullein* **~krempel** f *w.-card* **~markt** m *w.-market* **~maus** f *chinchilla* **~molton** m *treble-milled flannel* **~musselin** m *muslin-de-laine* **~mütze** f ⟨mar⟩ *watch-cap* **~plüsch** m *worsted shag* **~produzent** m *w.-grower* **~reiniger** m (P & S) *w.-picker* **~reißer** m *w.-carder* **~rips** m *Russell cord* **~sachen** f pl *woollies* **~sack** m *bag of w.* ‖ ⟨engl parl⟩ *w.-sack* **~sam(me)t** m *plush, velveteen* **~schere** f *w.-shears* pl **~schur** f *sheep-shearing* **~schweber** m ⟨ent⟩ *bee-fly* **~sortierer** m *w.-picker* **~spinner** m *w.-spinner* **~spinnerei** f *w.-spinning*; (Fabrik) *w.-mill, w.-spinning factory* **~spinnerin** f *w.-spinstress* **~staub** m *w.-dust velvet-powder*; ⟨pap⟩ *w.-flocks* pl **~stickerei** f *crewel-work* **~stoffe** m pl *w.len stuff(s* pl), *w.lens* pl **~waren** f pl *w.len goods, w.lens* pl | ~händler [m] *w.len-draper* **~wäsche(rei)** f *w.-washing*; *w.len underwear* (*w. scouring plant*) **~weber** m *w.len-(stuff) weaver* **~weste** f *w.len jacket, pullover*; *cardigan* **~züchter** m *w.-breeder* **~zupfen** n *w.-picking* **~zupfer** m *w.-picker* **W·olle** f ~/~n *wool* ‖ ⟨bot⟩ *down, cotton* ‖ ⟨zoo⟩ *pelage*; ⟨hunt⟩ *hair, down* ‖ langschürige ~ *long-stapled w.* ‖ ungewaschene ~ *w. in grease* ‖ ~ z Stricken *knitting w.* ‖ in der ~ gefärbt *dyed in grain*; ⟨fig⟩ *genuine, double-dyed* | ⟨fam⟩ in der ~ sitzen *to be in clover*, ⟨fam⟩ *to sit pretty*, ⟨Am sl⟩ *to be in the dough* ‖ ⟨fam⟩ ~ l müssen *to get fleeced*; jdn in die ~ bringen *to get a rise out of a p* **w·ollen** a *woollen*, (⟨Am a.⟩ *woolen*); *made of wool* ‖ (Strümpfe) *worsted* | ganz *or* rein ~ *all--woollen* | **≃**e [pl] *woollies*; [comp] → u.

W·ollen n ~s/ *will(ingness)*; *aspiration, inclination* ‖ ⟨philos⟩ *volition* ‖ (Absicht) *purpose, intention* ‖ das ~ f die Tat nehmen *to take the will for the deed* **w·ollen I.** vt/i [ich will/wollte/gewollt] [h] **A.** [pres] *I, he, you, they will* (Kurzform *'ll*); *thou wilt* ⟨archa⟩; [pret & cond] *I, he, we, you, they would* (Kurzform *'d*); *thou wouldst* ⟨archa⟩; [andere Formen nicht im Gebrauch] **B. Umschreibungen 1. (Wunsch**, Verlangen) *to want* (*they w. war*), *to wish* (*I w. to read it*), *desire, like*; *to demand, request*; *to care* (*should you care to go*?) ‖ du hast gar nichts z ~! *beggars can't be choosers*! mach, **was** du willst *have it your own way* **2. (Absicht)** *to mean, intend* (*they i. to specialize*; *I meant to do it*); *to have a mind* (*to do*) ‖ er wollte schon gehen *he was all ready to go* ‖ *he expects to leave tomorrow*; → G. **3. (Entschluß)** *to be resolved, determined* ‖ sie will durchaus, daß wir abreisen *she insists on our leaving* **4. (Bereitwilligkeit)** *to be willing, to choose* (*if he chose, he could be* ..); *to care* (*he knows more than he cares to say*) **5. (im Begriff s)** *to be going*, od *about* (*to do*), *to be on the point* (*of doing*) ‖ ich wollte gerade darauf k *I was just coming to it* **6. lieber** ~ *to prefer* ‖ ich will (wollte) lieber *I would rather* (*go*) **7. [dat]** → übel, wohl **C. Gott** will es *G. wills it*; so G. will *please G.* ‖ **ich** will es *I wish it* (*to be done*) ‖ er wollte es *he would have it* ‖ ich will, **daß** es geschieht *I will have it done* ‖ ~, daß jd tut *to want a p to do* ‖ wir ~ gehen *let's go, let's get going* ‖ ~ wir gehen? *shall we go*? ‖ ich will es (**nicht**) tun *I will* (*will not* od *won't*) *do it*; er will es nicht einmal versuchen ⟨Am⟩ *he does not even begin to try* ‖ wir ~ denn doch mal sehen! *I should like to see that done*! ‖ was ~ Sie damit sagen? *what do you mean to say by it*? ‖ m Sie, was Sie ~! *do your worst*! ‖ wenn Sie ~! *if you please*! | ~ **mit**: *what does a girl want with education*? | was ~ Sie **von** mir? *what do you want of me* | **wollte** Gott! *would to G.*!; das wolle G. nicht! *G. forbid* ‖ f Auskunft wolle man sich wenden an *for particulars apply to* | (P & S) **nicht** ~ *to refuse* (*to do*) (*the trunk refused to move* → G.) ‖ nicht gern ~: *he did not care to be reminded* ‖ .. will **nicht mehr** ⟨fam⟩ .. *has packed up* | nicht ~, daß: *she would not have him think that* ‖ er wollte nicht gesehen w *he did not want to be seen* ‖ mag er ~ oder nicht *whether he likes it or not, willy-nilly* | ⟨prov⟩ was du nichts willst, daß man dir tu', das füg' auch k–m andern z *do as you would be done by* ‖ ⟨fam⟩ wer nicht will, hat schon! *go without it then*! ⟨m. m.⟩ *it's your own look-out*! *take it or leave it*! *if you don't want it you may lump it*! **D. 1. (angeblich)** k–r will's gewesen s *everybody asserts it wasn't he* (⟨fam⟩ *him*) ‖ ich will nichts gesagt, gesehen h *never mind what I said* (*I'll pretend not to have seen it*) ‖ er will es selbst gesehen h *he insists on having seen it himself* **2.** ich will mich gerne geirrt h (**hoffend**) *I wish I may be mistaken*, (**einräumend**) *I admit I was wrong* **3. (pleonastisch)** das will ich wohl glauben *I willingly believe it* ‖ ich will nicht hoffen, daß er *I hope he* (*will not do it*) ‖ ich will nur hoffen, daß *I do hope that* .. ‖ das will ich meinen! *I should just think so*! ‖ wollte es e–r finden *if anyone were to find it* ‖ sie wollte umsinken *she was about to faint* **E. [ell]** ich will euch! *you'll get it* ‖ sie wollte ihn nicht (h) *she refused him* ‖ was ~ Sie dafür (h)? *how much is it*? ‖ mit → C.; was willst du damit? *what do you want it for*? | (**Bewegung**) (→ ⟨a.⟩ C.) es will mir nicht **aus** dem Sinn *I can't forget it* ‖ der Kork will nicht heraus .. *won't come off* ‖ wo ~ Sie **hin**? *where are you going* (*to*)? ‖ hoch hinaus ~ *to have high-*

-flying ideas || wo will das hinaus? *what's to become of it?* || das will mir nicht **in** den Kopf hinein *that's beyond me* || wir ~ **nach** Hause *we want to go home*; *they were bound for London* || z wem ~ Sie? *who is it you want to go to?*; *whom do you want to see?* || *I was on the point of seeing you* || e–m z Leibe ~ *to attack a p* **F. (im Nebensatz) .., wann** ich will *at my own liking* || wissen, **was** man will *to know one's mind* || ich sehe, was Sie ~ *I see your point* || denken Sie, was Sie ~ *you are welcome to your own opinion* || .., **wie** du willst *as you choose*; (*call it*) *what you will*; (*do it all*) *your own way* || wie gern ich auch wollte *however much I should like it* || (er konnte,) wenn er wollte .. *if he would* od *chose* || **wenn** sie auch nicht wollte, **ohne** es z ~ *in spite of herself, unintentionally* || wenn man so will, .. *if that's the way you want to look at it* **G. (S) die Pflanze** will viel Wasser (h) .. *requires* .. || das will getan s *it takes a bit of doing*, → H. 1; *it wants cleaning, it wants a brush* || das will Zeit h *it demands t.* || gut Ding will Weile (h) *things done well cannot be done quickly* || das Holz will nicht brennen .. *won't burn* || → C., nicht || nichts wollte gehen, wie sie wollte *nothing would go her way* (vgl F.) | **(pleonastisch) das** will was (nichts) heißen, sagen *that is saying a good deal*; *that is sth* (*nothing*) || **es** will damit nicht vorangehen *the matter is not progressing* || es will Nacht w *night is coming on* || geschehe, was da wolle *happen what may* || es sei, wo es wolle *wherever it may be* || **(es)** sei dem, wie ihm wolle *be this as it may* || mir will scheinen *it seems to me* || vgl ⟨a.⟩: **H. 1.** (= **müssen**; [neg] = **dürfen**) das will überlegt s *that has to be considered first* || das will getan s *it's got to be done*, → G. || so ein Irrtum will rechtzeitig erkannt w .. *must* .. || das will nicht übereilt s *ths must not be hurried* **2.** (= **können**) das wollte dir wohl gefallen *I daresay you would like it* || ich wollte es im Dunkeln finden *I could* .. || was wollte ich m? *what was I to do? what could I do?* **3.** (= **sollen**) das will nichts heißen *that doesn't mean a th* || das will nicht viel sagen *that doesn't mean very much* || damit will gesagt s, daß .. *that implies that* .. **4.** (= **m**) dann ist nichts z ~ *then it can't be helped* || damit ist nichts z ~ *it's good for nothing* || da ist nichts mehr z ~ *there is nothing you could do about it* **5.** (= **w**) wir ~ sehen *we'll see* || ich will .. *I'm going to speak quite frankly* || was ~ wir tun? *what shall we do?* **I. [nach inf** = gewollt] er hat nicht hören ~ *he would not listen to reason* || wir h nur Spaß m ~ *we were only joking* || er hat es nicht tun ~ *he did not intend to do it* **II. gewollt** *intended, desired*; *studied, intentional, deliberate*; *voulu* Fr

W·ollen- *worsted, woollen* **~atlas** m *w.d satin* **~band** n *w.d binding* **~fabrik** f *w.n-cloth factory* **~garn** n etc = Wollgarn etc **~stoffe** m pl *w.ns* pl **~weber** = Wollweber **~zeug** n *w.n-cloth* **w·ollig** a *woolly* || *downy, fleecy* || *wool-* bzw *cotton-bearing, laniferous*

W·ollust f ~/≃e *voluptuousness, lust*; *sensual pleasure*; (*the breasts'*) *desire* || (wüste ~) *lasciviousness* || höchste ~ ⟨sex⟩ *orgasm* | der ~ ergeben *given to debauchery* **w·ollüstig** a *voluptuous, sensual, hot* || *lascivious* || *salacious* **W·ollüstling** m ~s/~e *sensualist*; *voluptuary*; *libertine* || (Wüstling) *debauchee*

W·ombat m ~(e)s/~e (Beuteltier) *wombat*

wo- ~m·it adv *with* od *by what?* (*what are you occupied with?* = *how do you spend your time*) | [rel] *with* od *by which, where-with* (*a th I am not satisfied with*; *by which I do not mean to say* ..) || ⟨com⟩ *which* (*settles our account*) **~m·öglich** adv *if possible*; *possibly, perhaps*; (*it'll make it worse*) *if anything* **~n·ach** adv *after what?* || *what* (*is he asking*) *for?* | [rel] *after which, whereupon* || (zufolge) *according to which*

W·onne f ~/~n *delight, pleasure, bliss, rapture* in ~ schwimmend *enraptured* || in ~ u Weh *in joy and sorrow* || ⟨fam⟩ mit ~ *lovingly* **≃bebend** a *quivering with delight* **~gefühl** n *rapturous feeling, feeling of delight*; *thrills* pl °**~kloß** m *delightful baby and plump as a partridge* **~leben** n *delightful life* **≃leer, ≃los** a *joyless* **~monat, ~mond** m *month of delight* od *of May* **~schauer** m *thrill of delight, shiver of pleasure* **~taumel** m *rapture, ecstasy* **≃trunken** a *enraptured, in raptures* **≃voll** a *delicious* **w·onnig(lich)** a *delightful, blissful, delicious*

wor- [-r = Gleitlaut] **~·an** adv **1.** *by what* (*which*)?, *at what* (*which*)?; **whereby* || ~ denkst du? *what are you thinking of?* || ~ erkennt man es? *what does one know it by?* **2.** [rel] *at which*; **whereat, whereby* || ich weiß nicht, ~ ich bin (mit ihm) *I do not know how I stand* (*with him*) || man weiß, ~ man ist *you know where you are* **3.** [indef] (= an irgend etw) (*you must have been thinking*) *of sth* **~·auf** adv (*up*)*on what?* | [rel] *on which, whereupon* || (zeitlich) *whereupon, after which* **~·aus** adv *where from?*; *out of* (od *from*) *what?* | [rel] *from which*; *out of which*; *whence* ⟨obs⟩

Worcestersoße f ['wustə–] (Würze) *Worcester sauce* (nach Worcester [n] Stadt in England)

w·orden (= ge~) pp [mst pass] v werden || er ist überfahren ~ *he was* (*he has been*) *run over*

wor- ~·ein adv *where?* || ~ mischen Sie sich? *what are you meddling with?* | [rel] *into which* (vgl in [acc]) **~·in** adv *in what?* || ~ bestehen ..? *what are* (*the advantages*)? | [rel] *in which*; **wherein* (vgl in [dat])

W·orf- ~schaufel [f] *fan*; ~tenne [f] *fanning-floor* | **≃eln** vt [h] *to winnow, fan*

Worms n ⟨Ger⟩ (Stadt am Rhein)

Wort n [~(e)s/(einzelne) ≃er ⟨so⟩ ≃erbuch (zus–hängende) ~e] ⟨so⟩ Trost≃e **A. 1.** *word* (*the ~ Whig means* ..) ⟨a. comp⟩ || einige ~e des Beileids *a w. of condolence* **2.** (Ausdruck) *term, expression* **3.** (Ausspruch) *saying*; jds ~e ⟨Am⟩ *the say-so of a p* **4.** ⟨mus⟩ die ~e *the words* pl **5.** ⟨bib⟩ das ~ *the W.* || Gottes ~ *the W. of G.* **6.** *solution* (*of the enigma*) **B. abgewogene,** abgezirkelte ~e *carefully chosen w.s*; s–e ~e abmessen, abwägen *to choose one's w.s, to speak with deliberation* || ein **anderes** ~ f *a synonym for* || **mit** anderen ~en *that is to say* || mit ausdrücklichen ~en *in express terms* || mit dürren ~en *dryly, explicitly* || dein ~ in **Ehren** (, aber ..) *with due deference to you* (*I can hardly believe it*) || falsches ~ ⟨gram⟩ *misnomer* || geflügelte ~e *familiar quotations* || genug der ~e! *enough has been said*; *say no more!* || grobe ~e gebrauchen *to let fly* || ⟨prov⟩ ein **gutes** ~ findet e–n guten Ort *a kind w. is never lost* || harte ~e schaden nicht .. *break no bones* || **kein** ~ mehr! *not another w.!*; k. ~ darüber! *keep it dark*; ⟨prov⟩ k. ~ ist auch ein ~ *silence is consent*; k. ~ Englisch können *to know no w. of E.* || **leere** ~e *idle w.s* || das letzte ~ ⟨a.⟩ *ultimatum*, .. über *the last w. of* || mein letztes ~! *that's flat!* || ⟨fig⟩ das letzte ~ (→ ⟨a.⟩ C. haben) || ⟨com⟩ *the last w.* (liegt bei ihm *lies with him*); *the last w.* (in Hüten *in hats*), ⟨Am fam⟩ *it* || ein ~ **mit** 5 Buchstaben *a five-letter w.* || neues ~ *neologism* || sämtliche ≃er (e–r Sprache) *the whole vocabulary* || (gegen etw) scharfe ~e führen *to give the edge of one's tongue* (*to* ..), ⟨fam⟩ *to speak daggers* || schlüpfriges ~ *four-letter w.* || unverständliche ~e reden *to gibber* || mit jdm ein vernünftiges ~ r. *to converse intelligently with a p* || es ist kein **wahres** ~ daran *there isn't a w. of truth in it* || ein ~ z rechten Zeit *a w. spoken in season* **C.** jdm das ~ **abschneiden** *to cut a p short* (*by saying*) || (jdm) das ~ abtreten *to allow another p to speak* || ein ~ anbringen *to put in a w.* || ~e ausstoßen *to* *cast out w.s* || sein ~ **brechen** *to break one's w.* || ein ~ einfließen l = .. anbringen || e–m das ~ entziehen ⟨parl⟩ *to stop a p* (*speaking*), *to rule a p out of order* || das ~ **ergreifen** *to* (*begin to*) *speak*, ⟨parl⟩ *to take the floor, to address the House* || ⟨parl⟩ das ~ erhalten *to catch the Speaker's eye, to get* od *have the floor*; jdm .. erteilen *to call on a p* (*to speak*) || ein ~ fallen l v *to drop a hint of* || k–e ~e finden *to be speechless* || den ~en die Tat folgen l *to suit the action to one's w.s* || das ~ **führen** *to be spokesman*, ⟨fig a.⟩ das gr. ~ f *to engross* od *monopolize the conversation, to lay down the law, to swagger* || er führte allein das ~ *all the talking was on his side* || sein ~ **geben** *to give* od *pledge, pass one's w.*; jdm gute ~e g. *to give a p fair w.s, to speak a p fair* || ein ~ gab das andere *one w. led to another* || es gibt k–e ~e f .. (*his self-sacrifice*) *is beyond w.s* || das ~ h ⟨fam⟩ *to have one's say*; ⟨parl⟩ *to have the ear of the House* || das ~ **hat** Herr N. *Mr. N. will speak to you now* || Sie h das ~ ⟨fam⟩ *the floor is yours* || das letzte ~ h: *the last w. must lie with the members* || °haste ~e!? *did you ever? well, I never!* || er wollte es nicht ~ h *he refused to admit it* || (nicht) ~ **halten** *to keep* (*break*) *one's w.* (e–m *to a p*), ⟨fam⟩ *to make good one's w.*; er hält sein ~ *he's as good as his w.* || man kann sein eigen ~ nicht hören *you can't hear your own voice* || (nicht) viel ~e m *to babble, rant*; *to speak pompously*; (*not to argue*) || sie m nicht viel ~e *they are* (*wo*)*men of few w.s* || ohne viel ~e m z brauchen *for the asking* || um nicht viel ~e z m *to cut a long story short* || [dat] das ~ **reden** *to speak in favour of, to advocate*; einige ~e r. mit *to have a w. with*; ein ~ mit sich r. l *to listen to reason* || das ~ an e–n richten *to address a p* || ohne ein ~ z **sagen** *without a w.* || sein ~ ist ihm heilig *his w. is his bond* || das ist/war ein ~! *now you are shouting!* || .. ohne ein ~ z sprechen: (*we ate*) *a wordless meal*, → D. || das letzte ~ sprechen *to say ..*; vor (Neid) konnte er kein ~ sprechen *he was inarticulate with ..* || e–m das ~ im Munde verdrehen *to misinterpret a p's w.s* || (s–n Gedanken) ~e verleihen *to clothe .. in w.s* || kein ~ verlieren über .. *to waste no w. about ..*; um kein ~ z v. *to save breath*; ohne darüber ein ~ z v. *tacitly* || ~e wechseln mit .. *to bandy w.s with ..* || jdm ein ~ widmen *to give a w. to a p* || s–e ~e widerrufen *to eat one's w.s* **D. am** ~e klebend *literal* (*translation*) | **auf** ein ~! *can I have a w. with you?* || auf mein ~! *upon my w.!* || auf Grund s–r eigenen ~e .. (*to stand condemned*) *out of one's own mouth* || auf sein ~ hin *on the strength of his remarks* || aufs ~ (*to obey, believe*) *implicitly* | **bei** diesen ~en *at these w.s* (*she left*), *talking thus* (*they came*) || e–n beim ~ nehmen *to take a p at his w.*; ⟨Am⟩ *I'll take you up at* od *on that* | ~ f ~ *w. for w., literally* | .., **in** ~en (zehn Mark) *in W.s ..*; .. *say ..* || in die ~e ausbrechen: *to burst out* || etw in ~en ausdrücken *to phrase a th* || e–m ins ~ fallen *to interrupt a p*; *to cut a p short*; *to break in on a p*, ⟨fam⟩ *to snap a p up* || s–e Gedanken in ~en ausdrücken *to express one's thoughts*; in freien ~en ausgedrückt *loosely w.ed* || in ~e fassen *to put .. into w.s*; etw in andere ~e f. *to make a th read differently*; in einfache ~e gefaßt *simply worded* || in kurzen (wenigen) ~en zus–fassen *to put .. in a nutshell* || etw gut in ~e kleiden *to phrase a th well* || Geläufigkeit im E. in ~ u Schrift *fluency in spoken and written English* || in ~ u Tat *by w. and deed, in profession and practice* | **mit**: *in* || mit anderen ~en *put in another way*; mit 1 ~ *in a w.*; mit 3 ~en *in a nutshell* || mit bewegten ~en schildern *to describe vividly*; etw mit k–m ~ erwähnen *not to say a w. about a th* || mit wenigen ~en ⟨a.⟩ *briefly* || mit den ~en schließen *to wind up by saying* || mit ~en spielen *to quibble, pun* (vgl B.) || (**nach** den ~en,) die zw uns gefallen sind .. *that have passed between us* || dem ~e nach verstehen *to take literally* | **ohne**: → C.; sie trennten sich ohne böse ~e *they parted without quarreling* | **ums** ~ bitten *to ask permission to speak*; ⟨parl⟩ *to try to catch the Speaker's eye* | ein Mann **v** ~ .. *of his w.* | **zu** ~e k *to get a hearing*; kaum/nicht .. *hardly get a w. in edgewise*; mehr .. ⟨fig⟩ *to become more articulate* || jdn z ~ k l *to let a p talk*, niemanden .. *to engross the conversation* || z s–m ~e stehen *to be as good as one's w., to be a man of his w.* || sich zum ~ melden *to* (*try to*) *catch the chairman's eye* **Wort-** **~ableitung** f *etymology* **~akzent** m *natural accent, word-stress* **~·ähnlichkeit** f *synonymy* **~anfang** m *beginning of a w.* **≃arm** a *poor in w.s* **~armut** f *paucity of w.s*; *poverty of language* **~art** f ⟨gram⟩ *part of speech* **~aufwand** m *profusion of w.s* **~·auslaut** m *final sound of a w.* **~bedeutung** f *lexical meaning* | **~s-** ~lehre [f] *semantics* pl **~beugung** f *inflection* **~bildung** f *formation of w.s* | **~s-** ~lehre [f] *morphology* **≃brüchig** a *faithless*; *false to one's w.*; *disloyal* || ~ w *to break one's w.* | ≃e(r) [m] *break-promise*; ≃keit [f] *faithlessness, perfidiousness*; (e–s Liebhabers) *breach of promise* **~endung** f *termination of a w.* **~entsprechung** f (Übersetzung) *verbal equivalent* **~entstellung** f *malaprop*(*ism*) **~erklärung** f *definition* **~fechter** m *stickler* | ~·ei [f] *haggling about w.s* **~forscher** m *etymologist* **~forschung** f *etymology* **~fügung** f *construction* || (Lehre v der ~) *syntax* **~führer(in** f) m *speaker*; (nur [m]) *spokesman* || *foreman* (*of a jury*) || ⟨dipl⟩ *doyen* ⟨a. übtr⟩ **~fülle** f *abundance of words, wordiness, verbosity* | falscher **~gebrauch** *misnomer* **~gebühr** f ⟨telg⟩ *w. rate* **~gedächtnis** n *verbal memory* **~gefecht** n *debate, dispute*; *controversy*; heftiges ~ *the cut and thrust of dialogue* **~geklingel** n *jingle of words* **~geplänkel** n *banter* **~gepränge** n *bombast* **~gesäusel** n *slobberings* pl **~gestammel** n *glossolalia* **≃getreu** a *literal, faithful*; *close* (*translation*); *verbatim* L [a. adv] **≃gewandt** a *glib of tongue* | ~heit [f] *verbal nimbleness, wordmanship*; ⟨fam⟩ *gift of the gab* **≃gläubig** a *orthodox* **~gut** n *words, vocabulary* (*of a language*) **≃habend** a *being spokesman* (→ das ~ h) **~held** m *swaggerer, windbag* **≃karg** a *tight-lipped, inarticulate, short-spoken, short* od *sparing of w.s*; *taciturn, laconic*; (*man*) *of few w.s* **~klangbild** n *acoustic image* **~klasse** f ⟨gram⟩ → –art **~klauber(in** f) m *hair-splitter, quibbler* **~klauber·ei** f *hair-splitting*; *mincing w.s* **~kram** m *verbiage* **~krämer** m *phrase-monger* | ~·ei [f] *verbalism* **~kritik** f *verbal criticism* **~kunde** f *lexicology*; *etymology* **~kundige(r)** m *etymologist* **~kunst** f *style* | ≃el·ei [f] *affectation of style, affected language* **~laut** m *reading, wording*; *text*; *the exact terms* (*of a declaration*); ⟨bes jur⟩ *tenor*; im ~ *verbatim* (*repetition*); nach dem ~ ⟨contr⟩ *by the terms* || folgenden ~ h *to run as follows* **≃los** a *speechless* || adv *without a word* **~macher** m *idle* od *big talker* | ~·ei [f] *i.* od *b. talk* **~maler·ei** f *w.-painting* **~mangel** m = –armut **~meldung** f → sich z W. melden || nach ~ des Herrn N. ⟨parl⟩ *after Mr. N. had addressed the meeting*; es lagen k–e ~en (mehr) vor *there was nobody* (*any more*) *who had asked leave to speak* **~neubildung** f *neologism* **~phantom** n *phantom w.* (*e.g. slug-horn* > *sloggorne* > *slogan*) **~rätsel** n *enigma*; *lopogriph* **~register** n *index* **≃reich** a (v Sprachen) *rich* (*in w.s*) || (weitschweifig) *wordy, verbose, prolix, voluble* | ~tum [m] *richness, wealth of words*; *abundance in w.s*; *w.age* || *wordiness, verbosity* **~salat** m *w. salad* **~schatz** m *vocabulary* **~schwall** m *torrent* od *stream, spate of w.s*; *verbiage*; *verbosity*; *fustian, bombast*; *tirade*, ⟨fam⟩ *fireworks* pl **~sinn** m *literal sense* **~spiel** n → *pun, quibble*; *play upon* *w.s*; → *paragram* **~spieler(in** f) m *punster* **~stamm** m *stem of a w.* **~stellung** f *order of w.s* **~streit** m *dispute*; *controversy*; *argument*; ⟨fam⟩ *squabble* ‖ mit (jdm) e–n ~ h *to parry w.s with ..* **~tarif** m ⟨telg⟩ *w. rate* **~träger** m ⟨phys⟩ *w.-token* **~teilung,** -trennung [f] ⟨gram⟩ *division of a word* **~treue** f *literal reading* **~ungeheuer** n *monstrous w.* **~verdreher** m *equivocator*; *prevaricator*; *windjammer* **~verdrehung** f *quibbling, distortion of* (*one's*) *w.s*; *equivocation* **~vergeßlichkeit** f *verbal amnesia* **~verkürzung** f *syncope* **~versetzung** f *transposition of w.s*; ⟨gram⟩ *inversion* **~verstand** m *literal sense* od *meaning* **~verstümmelung** f ⟨telg⟩ *clipping* **~vertauschung** f → *heterophemy* **~verwechslung** f *confusion of terms* **~wechsel** m *discussion* ‖ (Streit) *dispute, altercation* ‖ erregter ~ *high w.s*; *heated passage of arms* ‖ e–n ~ h mit .. *to have* (*high*) *w.s with ..* ‖ in e–n heftigen ~ geraten *to come to high w.s* **~witz** m *pun* **≗w·örtlich** a *w.-for-w.* (*translation*) **~zähler** m *w. counter* **~zus-setzung** f *parasynthesis* **~zus-ziehung** f *portmanteau w.* (*e.g. brunch*) **~zw-raum** m *space between w.s* **W·örtchen** n ~s/~ *little word*; ⟨gram⟩ *particle* ‖ ein ~ mit|reden ⟨fam⟩ *to put in one's two cents worth*; ein ~ –zu- h *to have a vote in the matter*; mit jdm ein ernstes ~ reden *to give a p a lick with the rough side of the tongue* **W·örter-** ~buch [n] **1.** *dictionary* **2.** = Glossar; ~verzeichnis [n] *list of words, vocabulary* **w·örtlich** a *verbal, literal* ‖ ~e Beleidigung *verbal insult* | adv *word for word, verbatim* L; *literally* (*to take a th too l.y*) | **≗keit** f *literalness, faithfulness*; *literal character*

wor- (→ –·an) **~·über** adv **1.** *over* (od *about, of, at, upon*) *what*? ‖ *what were they talking about*?; *what are you laughing at*?; *what are you complaining of*? **2.** [rel] *over* (od *about, at, upon*) *which* ‖ *whereat, whereof*, etc ‖ .., ~ ich mich ärgerte *at which I was angry* ‖ das ist es, ~ ich mich so wunderte *that's what astonished me so* **~·um** [adv] **1.** *about* od *for what*? ‖ ~ dreht es sich? *what is it about*? **2.** [rel] *about* od *for which* **~·unter** [adv] **1.** *under* od *among what*? **2.** [rel] *under* od *among which* **wos·elbst** [adv] *where* **wov·on** [adv] **1.** *of* od *about what*? **2.** [rel] *of which* **wov·or** [adv] **1.** *before* od *of what*? **2.** [rel] *before* od *of which* **woz·u** [adv] **1.** *to* od *for what* ‖ (warum?) *why*? ‖ ~ das? *what is that for*?, *what's the use*? ‖ *what have we come here for*? **2.** [rel] *to which* **3.** [indef] (irgend ~) *for sth* (*or other*)

Wotj·aken pl (finnische Völkerschaft in O.-Rußland) *Votiaks*

Wrack n [~(e)s/~e & ~s] *wreck* (⟨a. fig⟩: *old w.*) ‖ verlassenes ~ *derelict* **~boje** f *w.-buoy* **~gut** n *w.ed goods* pl, *w.age*; *flotsam, jetsam* **~teile** n pl *derelicts* pl **wrack** a *cast off*; *waste, worthless* ‖ ~ w *to be wrecked*

wr·icken, wriggen vi/t [h] *to scull*

wr·ingen [wrang/gewrungen] vt [h] *to wring* **Wr·ingmaschine** f *wringing-machine, wringer*

Wr·uke f ~/~n *Swedish turnip, swede*

W·ucher m ~s/ *usury* ‖ (mit Waren) *profiteering* ‖ ~ treiben *to practise usury* ‖ *to profiteer* ‖ ⟨fig⟩ mit ~ vergelten *to repay with interest* **~blume** f ⟨bot⟩ *ox-eye daisy* **~gesetz** n *law against usury* od *profiteering* **~gewinn** m *excess profit* **~handel** m *usurious trade* **~miete** f *rack-rent* **~pflanze** f *rank weed* **~preis** m *cut-throat price* **~system** n *system of usury*, ⟨Am⟩ *juice racket* **~zinsen** m pl *usurious* (*rate of*) *interest* **Wucher·ei** f ~/~en *usury*, ⟨Am⟩ *juice racket* **W·ucherer** m ~s/~ *usurer*; ⟨fam⟩ *shaver*, ⟨Am⟩ *loan-shark, juice racketeer* **w·ucherhaft, w·ucherisch** a *usurious* **w·uchern I.** vi [h] **1.** *to practise usury*; (mit Waren) *to profiteer* **2.** ⟨biol⟩ *to proliferate* ‖ ⟨bot⟩ *to grow exuberantly, to luxuriate*; üppig ~ *to pullulate, to run up* od *wild* ‖ ⟨path⟩ *to form proud flesh* ‖ ⟨fig⟩ *to be rampant*; *to give a good return* **3.** ⟨fig⟩ sein Geld ~ l *to put out .. at usurious interest* ‖ mit s–m Pfunde ~ *to make the most of one's opportunities* **II.** ≗ n *usury* ‖ *rank growth* **W.rung** f ~/~en *usury* ‖ ⟨bot⟩ *exuberance, vegetation, rank growth* ‖ ⟨path⟩ *excrescense*; *proud flesh* ‖ ⟨biol⟩ *proliferation*

Wuchs [–ks] m ~es/≗e *growth, development* | (Leibesgestalt) *stature, shape*; ⟨fam⟩ *build, make* ‖ *height, size* ‖ v edlem ~ *finely shaped*; *well-made* **wuchs** [–ks] 1. & 3. sg pret v wachsen

Wucht f ~/ *weight, burden* ‖ (Gewalt) *force*; ⟨mil⟩ *heat*; Angriffs≗ *impact*; *volume* (*of fire*) ⟨mech, fig⟩ *energy, momentum* ‖ der ganzen ~ e–r S ausgesetzt s *to bear the brunt of a th* ⟨a. mil⟩ ‖ an ~ gewinnen *to gather momentum* ‖ mit aller *or* voller ~ rennen gegen *to run full tilt, to cannon against* ‖ mit aller ~ ⟨Am⟩ *in a big way* °**~brumme** f ⟨teens⟩ *A-bomb*, (*girl with*) *oomph*, (*she's got oomph*) **w·uchten 1.** vi [h] *to weigh* od *press heavily* **2.** vt [h] *to raise by lever, to force* od *prize* (*up, open, out*) **wuchtig** a *weighty, ponderous* ‖ *swinging* (*blow*) | ⟨fig⟩ *terrific*; *hulking* (Figur) | adv ⟨a.⟩ *hard* (*to hit hard*)

Wühl- **~arbeit** f ⟨fig⟩ *insidious agitation, subversive activity* **~maus** f *vole* **~tisch** m ⟨com⟩ *rummage table* **w·ühlen I.** vi *to dig* ‖ ~ in *to rake* (*a th*), *to rummage in* ‖ ⟨zoo⟩ *to burrow*; (v Schweinen) *to grub up* ⟨a. fig⟩, *to root* ‖ (v Wasser) *to wash* od *excavate holes, to undermine the ground*; ⟨fig⟩ *to roll about* od *wallow* (*in money*) ‖ sich [dat] im Haar ~ *to run one's hands through one's hair* | ⟨fig⟩ *to agitate*; gegen jdn ⟨fam⟩ *to frame a p* ‖ ⟨pol⟩ *to be on the stump* | (S) ~ in *to tear at* (*a p's heart*), *to gnaw at* (*a p vitals*) ‖ in e–r Wunde ~ *to open an old sore* ‖ in s–n eigenen Eingeweiden ~ *to rage against o.s.* **II. sich** ~ *to flounder* (*through*), *to burrow* (*into*) | **~d** a ⟨fig⟩ *splitting* (*headache*), *violent* **W·ühler** m ~s/~ ⟨fig⟩ *agitator, demagogue, stump-orator* | **~·ei** f ~/~en *agitation* ‖ ⟨pol⟩ *demagogism, stump-oratory* ‖ kl ~en ⟨fam⟩ *little digs* | **≗isch** a *agitative, inflammatory, incendiary, revolutionary*

W·u(h)ne f ~/~n *ice-hole*

Wulst m ~(e)s/≗e; f ~/≗e *swelling, bulge* | ⟨anat⟩ *torus* | (Polster) *pad*; (Kopftragepolster) *roll, ring* | ⟨tail⟩ *dress improver, bustle* | (Bausch) *puff* | (Haar≗) *chignon* | ⟨tech⟩ *bulb* | ⟨arch⟩ *roundel*; (Kapitell≗) *cushion pad, coussinet*; (Basis≗) *torus* ‖ ⟨mar⟩ U-Boot≗ *blister* | ⟨fig⟩ *halo* (*of gossip*) **~eisen** n *bulb iron* | **≗en I.** vt [h] *to puff up*; *to form into a pad* | sich ~ & **II.** vi [s] *to* (*form a*) *puff, to swell* | **≗ig** a *puffed up, padded, stuffed* ‖ ~e Lippen *thick* (⟨fam⟩ *blubber-*)*lips* pl ‖ ⟨anat, zoo, bot⟩ *torous, torose*

W·umm m ~(e)s/~e *whump* | **≗ern** vi [h] *to boom*; °es –rt ⟨mil⟩ *there is the droning hum of cannon*

wund a (offen) *sore*; ⟨fig⟩ *stricken* (*heart*) ‖ (verwundet) *wounded* | ~ laufen [vt] *to make* (*one's feet*) *sore with walking* ‖ sich ~ liegen *to get bed-sore* ‖ ~ reiben *to gall* ‖ sich ~ reiten *to gall one's skin in riding* ‖ sich ~ reiben (= ~ w) *to chafe* | ~e Stelle *sore* ‖ ⟨fig⟩ ~er Punkt *heel of Achilles*; *tender* od *sore spot*, mein ~er P. *my foible*; e–n ~n P. berühren *to skate over thin ice*; jdn an s–r ~en Stelle treffen *to catch* od *touch a p on the raw* **Wund-** **~arzneikunst** f *surgery* **~arzt** m *surgeon* **≗ärztlich** a *surgical* **~balsam** m *balm for wounds, vulnerary balsam* **~behandlung** f *treatment of a w.*; keimfreie ~ → Asepsis **~fieber** n *w.-fever* **≗gedrückt**, **≗gelaufen** a *chafed* **~klee** m ⟨bot⟩ *anthyllis* **~mal** *scar, cicatrice*; ~(e pl) ⟨rel⟩ *stigma*(*ta*); (*the five w.s of our Lord, the Five Wells of Pity*) **~mittel** n *vulnerary* **~pflaster** n *woundplaster* **~pulver** n *styptic powder* **~rose** f ⟨path⟩ *erysipelas* Gr **~salbe** f *salve, ointment for wounds*

W·unde f ~/~n *wound* (an *in*) (offen *raw w., open sore*); *hurt* || (Tritt≃) ⟨ftb⟩ *hack* || (Schnitt≃) *cut* || klaffende ~ *gash* || leichte (schwere) ~ *slight* (*severe*) *injury* || [dat] e–e ~ schlagen *to injure* ⟨a. fig⟩ || ⟨fig⟩ alte ~en aufreißen *to rake up old sores* || aus 1000 ~n blutend *battered and exsanguine* || v ~n bedeckt *seamed with w.s*

W·under n ~s/~ **A. 1.** *wonder, marvel* **2.** (Übernatürliches) *miracle*; *the miraculous* (*it borders on the m.*) **3.** *wonderful th, sth wonderful* || (P & S) *prodigy, phenomenon* **4.** (Erstaunliches) *marvel*(*lous event*) || (*he is a literary*) *portent*; *portent* (*of technics*) **5.** (Unübertreffliches) *paragon* (*of beauty*), *prodigy* (*of valour*) **B.** o ~! *how wonderful* || es gibt doch noch ~! *wonders will never cease* || wie durch ein ~ *miraculously* || ~s halber *for curiosity's sake* | **ist** es ein ~, daß ..? *is it any w. that* ..? || es ist ein ~, daß .. *the w. is* (*that*) ..; kein ~, daß *no w. that, it is not w.ful that* **C.** sein blaues ~ **erleben** *to get the shock of one's life* (*we'll, they'll give him the time of his life*), .. an, bei, mit *to be amazed at* || er hat mir ~ erzählt über .. *he gave me a song and dance about* .. | es **nimmt** mich ≃ *I wonder, I am surprised* || es kann nicht ≃|nehmen, daß .. *it is small w. that* .. || ~ schreien *to cry marvel upon marvel* || ~ **tun,** verrichten, wirken *to work miracles*, ⟨fig⟩ *to do w.s* (*for a p*), ⟨übtr⟩ *to wring water from a flint* || *to perform prodigies* (*of valour*) **D. was** ~?! *what w.* (*that* ..) || was ~, wenn *it is not to be wondered at if* | ~ **was** *God knows what*; *a world* (*she did a world for him*) || ich dachte ≃, was es wäre *I couldn't think what it was, I expected sth w.ful* || er denkt ≃, was er tut (ist) *he thinks that he is doing sth extraordinary,* (*he thinks no small beer of h.s.*) || sich ≃ was einbilden auf .. *to pride o.s. ever so much on* .. || ≃ was halten v *to think the world of* | ≃ **wie** artig *w.fully good* **E.** [**in comp**] *wonder*(*ful*[*ly*]), *wondrous, miraculous, admirable* ≃**alt** a *w.lly old* **~bau** m *a.e structure* **~bild** n ⟨ec⟩ *m.s image* **~blume** f ⟨bot⟩ *marvel of Peru* **~ding** n *w.s th, prodigy, marvel* **~doktor** m *quack* **~geschichte** f *legend*; *marvellous story* || ⟨ec⟩ *history of miracles* **~geschöpf** n *w.l creature, prodigy* **~glaube** m *belief in miracles* **~hand** f *w.r-working hand* ≃**herrlich** a *a.e, glorious* ≃**h·old** a *w.lly sweet* **~horn** n *magic horn* ≃**h·übsch** a *exceedingly nice* od *handsome* **~kerze** f *sparkler* **~kind** n *infant* od *boy prodigy* **~knäuel** m *surprise packet* **~kraft** f *magic* od *m.s power* || s–e ~ ausüben auf *to work one's w.r upon* **~kur** f *m.s cure* **~lampe** f *magic lantern* **~land** n *wonderland, Fairyland* ≃**l·ieblich** a *extremely lovely* **~mann** m *miracle-worker* || *w.l man* **~mär** f *marvellous tale*; *legend* ≃**mild** a *w.lly gentle* ≃**sch·ön** a *w.lly fine, exceedingly beautiful*; *lovely*; *w.s fair* | [adv] *capitally* ≃**s·elten** a *extremely rare* **~spiegel, ~stab** m *magic mirror, m. wand* **~tat** f *miraculous deed* || *wonderful deed* **~täter** m *worker of miracles* ≃**tätig** a *performing miracles, m.s*; *w.-working* (Kur) **~tätigkeit** f *m.s virtue* || *miracle-working* **~tier** n *monster* || ⟨fig⟩ *prodigy* || ⟨fam⟩ *big gun*; *lion* ≃**voll** a *w.l, m.s* || *perfect* (*day*) **~welt** f *world of w.rs* **~werk** n *miracle* **~zeichen** n *m.s sign*; *portent* **w·underbar** a **A.** *wonderful, marvellous* (*that she should care for me*) || ⟨geh. Spr.⟩ *wondrous* || *supernatural, miraculous* || (zauberhaft) *magic*(*al*) || (erstaunlich) *astounding, amazing, surprising* || (ungewöhnlich) *extraordinary, remarkable* || (sonderbar) *strange, singular, odd* **B.** ~e Errungenschaften *portents* || ein ~er Kerl *a perfect marvel* || auf ~e Weise *miraculously* || das ≃e an *what is so marvellous in* **~erw·eise** [adv] *miraculously, mysteriously*; *strange to say* | ≃**keit** f **1.** *wonderfulness* **2.** [pl] ~en *wonders*; *strange ths* **w·underlich** a *strange, odd* || *queer, peculiar, curious, quaint* || ⟨fam⟩ *funny, rum* | (launisch) *whimsical, crotchety, wayward*; *fastidious*; *difficult to please* | ~e Einfälle *vag·aries* || ~er Heiliger, Kauz *original*; *queer fish* | [adv] es ist ihm ~ ergangen *he has met with strange adventures* | ≃**keit** f ~/~en *strangeness, oddness* || *eccentricity*; *comicality* || *whimsicalness, peevishness* || ~en [pl] *oddities* **w·undern I.** vt [h] *to surprise* || das –rt mich *that astonishes me* || es –rt mich (sehr, daß) *I wonder at it, I am surprised,* (*amazed that* ..) || es soll mich doch ~, ob .., es –rt mich, ob .. *I wonder whether* .. || das –rte mich gerade *that is exactly what I was wondering* || das soll mich ~! *I wonder*! || es würde mich nicht ~ *I shouldn't wonder* **II. sich** ~ (über [acc]) *to wonder* (*at*), *to be surprised* (*at*); *to be surprised* (sehr *amazed*) *to learn*, etc || ich würde mich nicht ~, wenn *I should not be surprised if* || man –rt sich *or* muß sich ~, daß .. *the wonder is that* ..; [neg] *it was no wonder* (*to hear*) *that* .. **w·undersam** a = wunderbar

Wunsch m ~es/≃e **A.** *wish*, (stärker) *desire* (nach *for*) || (Streben) *aspiration* | (Gegenstand des ~es) *th wished for* || ein Wagen war schon lange mein ~ *I have long wished for a car, a car has been my wish for a long time* | ≃e [pl] ⟨mus⟩ *request numbers* || ⟨com⟩ wird Ihren ≃en voll u ganz gerecht w! *Best Buy*! || der ~ war der Vater des Gedankens, das war nur ein frommer ~ *that was just* od *wistful thinking* **B.** jds ~e [dat] willfahren *to grant a p's request* || wenn du nur den ~ aussprichst *if you say the word*; *just for the liking* || *the wish was* (*the*) *father to the thought* (des Gedankens) || *your wish is a command to me* (ist mir B.) **C. auf** ~ ⟨com⟩ *if desired, on application, by request* || auf jds ~ *at a p's request* od *desire* | **gegen** m–n ~ *against my wish* | **mit** den besten ≃en (zum Fest etc) *with best wishes* (*season's greetings*) (*wishing you the compliments of the season*) (*with best wishes for your husband's recovery*) | **nach** ~ *as desired*; *to one's heart's desire* || es geht ihm alles nach ~ *everything works out according to his wishes* od *seems to be going his way* || sich nach jds ≃en richten (*or* [dat] fügen) *to attend to* od *comply with a p's w.es* **~bild** n *ideal* **~form** f *optative form* **~gedanke** m *wish*(*ful*) *thinking* ≃**gemäß** a *in accordance with your desire* **~hütlein** n *wishing-cap* **~konzert** n *request program* **~küche** f *dream kitchen* **~traum** m *wish-dream*, ⟨Am fam⟩ *pipe-dream* ≃**weise** [adv] *by way of a wish* **~zettel** m *list of wishes* (*for one's birthday*, etc); *letter to Santa Claus* **W·ünschelrute** f *magic wand, divining-rod* || (f Wasser) *dowser's rod*; mit der ~ gehen *to dowse* | **~n-** ~gänger [m] *water diviner* **w·ünschen** vt/i [h] **A.** *to wish* || (ersehnen) *to desire*; *to long for* | sich [dat] etw ~ *to wish for a th* || wir ~ uns *we should like to have, we wish we had* || (sehnlichst) ⟨fam⟩ *to be spoiling for* ..; man könnte sich nichts Besseres ~ *you could ask for nothing better* | es läßt **zu** ~ übrig *it is not quite what one could wish*; was viel z ~ ü. l. *leaving much-to-be-desired*; sein Glück l. nichts z ~ ü. *he had his full share of luck* || es läßt nichts zu ~ übrig *it leaves nothing to be desired* | **wie** Sie ~! *as you please*, ⟨fig iron fam⟩ *help y.s.*! **B.** wir ~ Ihnen gute **Besserung** *we trust you may soon be better* || ich wünsche **es** (Ihnen) v ganzem Herzen *I wish it* (*for you*) *with all my heart* || wenn er es wünschte *if he so wished* || wie man es sich nicht besser ~ könnte *just what could be wished* || ~ Sie sonst noch etw? *is there anything else you'd like*? (⟨com⟩ *will there be* od *can I show you*) *anything else*?, ⟨iron⟩ *a. e.*? || jdm **Glück** ~ *to wish a p joy*, .. zu *to congratulate a p upon* || wenn sie mich ~ *if they want me* || sich an jds Stelle ~ *to wish o.s. in a p's place* || jdm guten Tag ~ *to give a p a good day* || e–n Wechsel ~ *to wish for a change* | **was** ~ Sie (v mir)? *what can I do for you*?; .. (zu trinken) ⟨fam⟩ *what is yours*? | **sich** [dat] etw ~ *to want a th* (*for o.s.*) **C.** ~, **daß** .. *to* *want* (*a th to be done*) || ich wünschte, ich wäre tot *I wish I were d.* || beinahe *or* fast ∼, es z tun *to have half a mind to do it* || wir ∼ **nicht** .. z w *we don't choose to be dodged about*, .., daß er .. *we should not like him to know it* | das v ihnen ge–te Buch *the b. they wanted* **∼swert** a *desirable*

wupp! *whisk*! *bang*! *there goes*!, ⟨fam⟩ *in two shakes*! °**W·uppdich** m ∼/∼; mit e–m ∼, im ∼ ⟨fam⟩ *in a jiffy*

W·upper f ⟨Ger⟩ (Nebenfluß des Rheins) **∼tal** n (†Elberfeld & Barmen) ⟨Ger⟩ (Stadt)

w·ürbe 1. & 3. sg pret conj v werben

w·urde/(∼̈) 1. & 3. sg pret (conj) v werden

W·ürde f ∼/∼n **A.** *dignity, honour* || (Hoheit) *noble air* od *bearing* || *elevation* (*of style*) | (Amt) *office* || (*university-*)*degree* || → Amt | *intrinsic value, merit, virtue* **B.** s–r ∼ etw vergeben *to compromise one's dignity* || ∼n sind Bürden *the more worship the more cost* | auf ∼ halten *to stand on one's dignity* || unter m–r ∼ *beneath me*, ⟨fam⟩ *infra dig*(*nitatem*) || f unter s–r ∼ halten ⟨a.⟩ *to disdain* (*doing, to do*) || unter aller ∼ *beneath contempt* || zu den höchsten ∼n gelangen *to attain the highest honours* **∼̈los** a *undignified* **∼̈voll** a *dignified*; *of noble bearing*; *grave, portly*; *statuesque* **W·ürdenträger** m *dignitary, notable* || hoher ∼ *magnifico* **w·ürdig** a [gen] *worthy* (*of*) || (vornehm) *dignified* || (verdient) *deserving* (*of*) || [abs] *respectable, estimable* || er ist dessen nicht ∼ *he does not deserve it* || e–r besseren S ∼ *worthy of a better cause* | **∼en** vt [h] (schätzen) *to appreciate, value*; *to pay* (*a* od *one's*) *tribute to* (*a th, a p*) || z ∼ wissen *to attach the right value to* (*a th*), *to appreciate* (*fully*), *to savour* || jdn e–r S (Antwort) ∼ *to deign to give a p a th, to consider a p worthy of a th* (*to condescend to give a reply to to a p*) || e–r eingehenden Beschreibung ∼ *to describe minutely* || ich würdigte ihn keines Blicks *I never so much as looked at him* | **∼d** *appreciative* | **∼keit** f ∼/ *worthiness* || (Verdienst) *merit* || (würdige Erscheinung) *dignified appearance* **W.gung** f ∼/∼en *appreciation*; *estimation* || *valuation*

Wurf m ∼(e)s/∼̈e **A.** *throw, cast* (⟨a.⟩ Ball–, Würfel–, Netz∼̈) | ⟨zoo⟩ *litter, brood*; (Kaninchen) *nest*, (Katzen) *kindle* ⟨dial⟩ || ⟨mech⟩ *projection* || ⟨arts⟩ *sketch*; der erste ∼ *the first outline* || ⟨tail, etc⟩ *fall* (*of a drapery*) **B.** den ersten ∼ h *to throw first* || e–n ∼ tun *to throw*, ⟨fam⟩ *shy* || e–n glücklichen ∼ tun *to make a hit* | ⟨fig⟩ alles auf einen ∼ setzen *to put all one's eggs in one basket* || jdm in den ∼ k *to come in a p's way*, ⟨fam⟩ *to run against a p* | ⟨poet⟩ wem der gr ∼ gelungen .. *he that had the great fortune* **∼angel** f *fishing-line* **∼anker** m ⟨mar⟩ *kedge*(*-anchor*) **∼bahn** f ⟨aero⟩ *bomb trajectory path* **∼bewegung** f *projectile motion* **∼blei** n (*sounding-*)*lead* **∼bild** n *projection* **∼erde** f *earth thrown up* **∼feuer** n ⟨mil⟩ *trench-mortar fire* **∼geschoß** n *projectile, missile* **∼gestell** n ⟨mil⟩ *frame for firing rockets* **∼gewehr** n ⟨mar⟩ *line throwing gun* **∼haken** m ⟨mar⟩ *grappling-hook* **∼höhe** f *hight of projection* **∼holz** n ⟨Eg hunt ant⟩ *throwing stick* **∼keule** f *missile club* **∼ladung** f *thrown charge* **∼leine** f ⟨mar⟩ *stream-cable* **∼linie** f *line of projection, projectile curve* **∼maschine** f *catapult* || (f Tontauben) *trap* || ⟨agr⟩ *winnowing-machine* **∼mine** f *thrown explosive* **∼netz** n *casting-net, drag-net* **∼parabel** f *bomb trajectory* **∼riemen** m ⟨hunt⟩ *leash* **∼ring** m = –scheibe **∼schaufel** f *winnowing-shovel* **∼scheibe** f *discus, quoit* **∼sendung** f *postal mailing* **∼spieß** m *javelin, dart* **∼taube** f *clay pigeon* | **∼n-** ∼schießen [n] *skeet shooting* **∼waffe** f *missile* **∼weite** f *stone's throw*; ⟨artill⟩ *range* **W·ürfel** m ∼s/∼ ⟨geom⟩ *cube* || ⟨arch⟩ *dado* || (Spiel∼̈) *die* [pl *dice*] (falsch *loaded*); ∼ (*or* mit ∼n) spielen *to* (*play at*) *dice*; ⟨Am fam⟩ *to roll the bones* || die ∼ sind gefallen *the die is cast* || ⟨cul⟩ ∼ schneiden *to dice* **∼becher** m *dice-box* **∼brett** n *draught-board* **∼bude** f *dice-playing booth* **∼erz** n *cube ore* **∼fall** m *fall of the dice*; *number thrown* **∼̈förmig** a *cubic*(*al*), *cubiform* **∼kapitell** n ⟨arch⟩ *cubiform capital* **∼kohle** f *screened* od *small coal*; *nuts* pl **∼muster** n *checkered pattern, checker*(*s* pl), *checks* pl **∼spiel** n *game of dice* || *dice-playing* **∼spieler** m *dicer* **∼zucker** m *lump* od *tablet, cube-sugar* **w·ürf(e)lig** a *cubic*(*al*) || (v Stoffen) *chequered* || ⟨arch⟩ *tessellated* **W·ürfeln I.** n ∼s/ *dicing* **II.** ∼̈ vi [h] (um) *to play at dice* (*for*) || (einmalig) *to cast, throw* **W·ürfler** m ∼s/∼ *dice-player, dicer*

W·ürg- **∼engel** m *destroying angel* **∼falke** m *lanner* **∼halskette** f *choker*; → Verlauf∼̈ **∼knebel** m ⟨tech⟩ *packing-stick* **∼leine, ∼schnur** f ⟨tech⟩ *choker* **∼schwert** n, **∼stahl** m *exterminating sword, sword of destruction* **W·ürge-** **∼band** n ⟨arch⟩ *clip* **∼birne** f *choke-pear* **∼bohrung** f *choke-bore* (⟨a.⟩ Flinte mit ∼) **∼mal** n *strangulation mark* **∼verbindung** f ⟨telph⟩ *American twist joint* **w·ürgen I.** vi [h] *to choke* || (beim Erbrechen) *to retch* || (beim Essen) *to gulp* || der Bissen würgt ihm *or* er würgt (sich) an dem B. *the morsel has stuck in his throat* || ⟨fig⟩ er wird daran z ∼ h *he will find it a tough morsel*; an e–r Arbeit ∼ *to sweat over a task* **II.** vt [h] *to seize by the throat* || *to strangle, throttle*; *to choke* ⟨a. tech & fig⟩ | **es** –gte sie (in der Kehle) *her throat felt thick* od *choked up* **III.** ∼̈ n ein ∼ im Hals *a choky feeling, a choke in the throat*; ⟨fam⟩ mit (Hängen u) ∼̈ *by the skin of one's teeth, with the greatest difficulty* **W·ürger** m ∼s/∼ *strangler*; *cut-throat* || ⟨orn⟩ → *shrike, butcher-bird* || °(hoher Kragen, enge Halskette) *choker* **∼̈isch** a ⟨fig⟩ *destructive, murderous* **W·ürgung** f ⟨tech⟩ *choke*

W·urm m ∼(e)s/∼̈er *worm* (⟨a. fig⟩ P) || ⟨poet⟩ *reptile*; *dragon* (⟨a. fig⟩: *the d. of dissatisfaction*) | (im Obst etc) *maggot* | (am Finger) *whitlow* || ⟨vet⟩ *farcy* | ⟨fig⟩ (Kind) (*tiny*) *tot, dot, chit*; (*poor*) *mite*; ⟨Am⟩ *tad* || ⟨dero⟩ (*ungrateful*) *wretch* | sich wie ein ∼ krümmen ⟨fig⟩ *to cringe and creep* || voller ∼̈er *wormy* || v ∼̈ern zerfressen *w.-eaten* || jdm die ∼̈er aus der Nase ziehen ⟨fig⟩ *to pump a p* || ⟨fig⟩ e–n ∼ h *to have a bee in one's bonnet* || das war der Kopf des ∼es *that was the critical point* **∼̈abtreibend** a = –treibend **∼̈ähnlich, ∼̈artig** a *w.-like, vermicular* **∼doktor** m *quack* **∼farn** m ⟨bot⟩ *shield-fern* **∼fieber** n *w.-fever* **∼̈förmig** a *w.-shaped, vermiform* **∼fortsatz** m ⟨anat⟩ *appendix* **∼fraß** m *damage done by w.s* || *w.-hole* **∼̈fräßig** a *w.-eaten* **∼̈krank** a *suffering from w.s* **∼krankheit** f *w.s* pl, *helminthiasis* **∼mehl** n *w.-dust* **∼mittel** n *vermifuge* **∼pillen** f pl *w.-pills* pl **∼pulver** n *w.-powder* **∼same(n)** m *w.-seed* **∼stich** m *w.-hole* **∼̈stichig** a *w.y, w.-eaten*; *rotten, unsound* (*timber*) || ⟨fig⟩ *corrupt* | ∼keit [f] *w.iness*; *w.-eaten state* || ⟨fig⟩ *corruptness* **∼̈treibend** a *de-worming, vermifugal, helminthic* || ∼es Mittel [n] *vermifuge, helminthic* **W·ürmchen** n ∼s/∼ *little worm* || ⟨fig⟩ *little mite* **w·urmen** vt/i [h] *to fret, vex* || es wurmt mich *it vexes* od *annoys me*, ⟨fam⟩ *it riles me*; *it rankles* [vi] | (P) = wurmisieren | es wurmt mir im Magen ⟨fam⟩ *I have the gripes* **W·ürmer-** **∼̈erzeugend** a ⟨scient⟩ *vermiparous* **∼fressend** a ⟨scient⟩ *vermivorous* **∼lehre** f *vermeology* **w·urmig** a *wormy, full of worms* || (Mehl) *weevily*; (Obst) *worm-eaten* || (P) ⟨fig⟩ *vexed*, ⟨fam⟩ *maggoty* **wurmis·ieren** vi [h] *to brood, worry* (über *over*)

°**Wurscht** = Wurst **wurschtig** = wurstig **Wurst** f ∼/∼̈e *sausage*; Blut∼̈ *blood pudding* || ⟨bes Am⟩ *knackwurst, mettw., bratw., beerw.*, Jagd∼̈ *yachtw.*, Zervelat∼̈ *saveloy*; heiße ∼ mit Semmel ⟨Am sl⟩ *hot dog* || ⟨arch⟩ *roll, pad* || ⟨fig⟩ (Fesselballon) *s.e*, ⟨mil sl⟩ *the maiden's prayer* | ⟨fig⟩ es ist mir (ganz) ∼ (⟨a.⟩ ∼̈eg·al, ∼̈epiepe) ⟨fam⟩ *I don't care a pin, rap,* (*brass*) *farthing,* *damn, hoot* || ~ wider ~ *tit for tat*; *dog eats dog*; *I take my change out of it* || jetzt geht's um die ~ *everything is at stake now* || mit der ~ nach der Speckseite werfen *to throw a sprat to catch a herring* od *whale* **~gift** n *s.e-poison* **~händler** m *pork-butcher* **~horn** n *s.e-filler* **~kessel** m °im ~ sitzen *to be in a nice scrape* **~lippe** f *blubber-lip* **~maul** n *blubber-lips* pl **~kraut** n *marjoram, savory* **~reiter** m *parasite* **~speiler** m *skewer* **~suppe** f *pudding-broth* **~vergiftung** f *s.e-poisoning*, ⟨scient⟩ *botulism* **~wagen** m ⟨hist-artill⟩ *ammunition-waggon* **~zipfel** m *s.e-end* **W·ürstchen** n ~s/~ *small s.e* || heißes ~ ⟨Am sl⟩ *hot-dog* || (P) ⟨fig⟩ armes ~ *small fry* **w·ursteln** vi [h] *to make s.es* || ⟨fig fam⟩ weiter ~ *to rub on* od *along, to muddle through* || es wird weiter ge–lt *we go on in the old jog-trot way* **W·ursteltheater** n *Punch and Judy show* **w·urstig** a **1.** = wulstig **2.** °⟨fig & fam⟩ *non-carish, devil-may-care*; ~er Mensch ⟨bes Am⟩ *hipster* **≃keit** f ~/ *d.-m.-c. attitude*; *callousness*, ⟨fam⟩ *non-carishness* || völlige ~ zur Schau tragen *to play it cool* || auf dem Standpunkte der ~ stehen *to be quite non-carish*

W·urt(e) f ~/~e(n) *mound in a flood-endagered area* | ~ensiedlung [f] *farmstead on such a mound*

W·ürttemberg n *Würt(t)emberg* od *Wurtemberg* **≃isch** a *of Würt(t)emberg*, bisw. *Wurtembergian*

W·ürzburg n ⟨Ger⟩ (Stadt am Main)

Wurz f ⟨obs⟩ ~/~en *root, herb* **Würz- ~brühe** f *court-bouillon* **~fleisch** n *spiced meat* **~geruch** m *aromatic flavour* **~geschmack** m *a.c taste* **~kräuter** n pl *a.c herbs* **≃los** a *not spiced* || ⟨fig⟩ *flat, insipid* **~pfanne** f ⟨brew⟩ *wort kettle*; *copper* **~stoff** m *spice, seasoning* **~tunke** f *condiment*, indische ~ *chutney* **~wein** m *spiced wine* **~zusatz** m *zest* **W·ürze** f ~/~n *condiment, seasoning, spice, flavour*; *zest* || *spicy* od *hot taste* || ⟨fig⟩ *piquancy* || ⟨brew⟩ *wort* || ~ des Lebens *salt of life* **W·urzel** f ~/~n ⟨a. math, anat, gram⟩ *root* || ⟨anat⟩ (des Haares) *bulb*; ~ des Fußes *tarsus* || ⟨agr, cul⟩ *carrot* || ⟨fig⟩ *basis* | ⟨math⟩ zweite, dritte, vierte ~ *square, cubic, biquadratic root*; die ~ ziehen (aus) *to extract the root* (*of*) | ~ fassen, ~ schlagen *to take* od *strike root* || mit der ~ ausreißen *to root up*, ⟨fig⟩ *to eradicate* || ⟨fig⟩ die ~ des Übels s *to be* od *lie at the root of the trouble* od *evil*; bei der ~ fassen *to take .. by the throat*; ein Übel an der ~ f. *to strike at the r. of an evil* **~ausläufer** m, **~ausschlag** m = ~schößling **~auszieher** m ⟨med dent⟩ *stump-forceps* **~ballen** m *conglomerate of r.s* pl **~behandlung** f ⟨dent⟩ *r.-treatment* **≃betont** a ⟨phon⟩ *rhizotonic* **~bildung** f *radication* **~buchstabe** m *radical letter* **≃echt** a *ungrafted* **~exponent** m *index* **~faser** f *r.-fibre, r.let* **~filz** m ⟨for⟩ *matting of r.* **~fleisch** n ⟨cul⟩ *boiled meat with carrots*, etc **~fressend** a ⟨zoo⟩ *rhizophagous* **~füßler** m ⟨zoo⟩ *rhizopod*(*a* pl) **~gemüse** n (*dish of*) *carrots* pl **~gewächse** n pl *r. crops* **~größe** f ⟨math⟩ *radical quantity* **~haar** n *r.-hair* **~haube** f *r.-cap* **~haut** f ⟨dent⟩ *periodontum* | ~entzündung [f] *periodontitis* **~heber** m ⟨dent⟩ *elevator* **~keim** m *radicle* **~knolle** f *bulb, tuber* **~knöllchen** n *r.-tubercle* **~knoten** m *r.-nodule knot of a r.* **~münder** m ⟨zoo⟩ *rhizostome* **~schöpfung** f ⟨gram⟩ *r. creation* **~schößling** m = –sproß **~silbe** f *radical syllable* **~sproß** m *sucker, runner* **≃sprossend** a *sending out runners* **~stand** m ⟨bot⟩ *radication* **≃ständig** a *radical* **~stock** m *root-stock*, ⟨zoo⟩ *rhizome* || *rhizocaul* **~werk** n ⟨bot⟩ *roots* pl **~wort** n *radical word, stem* **~zeichen** n ⟨math⟩ *radical sign* ($\sqrt{\ }$) **W·ürzelchen** n ~s/~ *radicle* **w·urzelhaft** a *basic* || ⟨gram⟩ *radical* **w·urz(e)lig** a *rooty* **w·urzeln** vi [h] *to be rooted* ⟨a. fig⟩; ⟨fig⟩ *to be grounded* (*in*) || *to take* od *strike root* || fest gewurzelt *firmly* od *deep-rooted* **w·ürzen** vt [h] *to season, flavour, spice* || *to perfume, scent* || ⟨fig⟩ *to season, to make spicy, to spice*; *to pepper* (*a speech*) || scharf gewürzt *highly seasoned, hot, devil(l)ed*; *spicy* ⟨a. fig⟩, ⟨fig⟩ *piquant* || ~der Zug *flavouring* **w·ürzig** a *spicy* || (duftig) *fragrant* || ⟨fig⟩ *juicy, piquant, fruity* || das ≃e *the spiciness* (*of a dish*) **W·ürzung** f ~/~en *seasoning*

wusch 1. & 3. sg pret **w·üsche** conj v waschen

w·uschelig a *straggly, wispy, untidy* (*hair*) **W·uschelkopf** m *tousled hair*; du ~! *you're well-thatched* || ⟨fig⟩ *scatter-brained p*

w·useln vi [h] *to crawl about, to swarm* **w·uselig** a *swarming, crawling*

w·ußte 1. & 3. sg pret **w·üßte** conj v wissen

Wust [u:] m ~es/~e *confused mass, chaos* || *mop* (*of hair*) || *trash, rubbish* || gelehrter ~ *learned lumber* **wüst** a (Ort) *waste, desert, des·erted* || ⟨agr⟩ *uncultivated* || ⟨mil⟩ ~ legen *to lay waste* | (liederlich) *wild, riotous, dissolute* (*life*) || (roh) *brutal, rude* || (im Kopf) *confused* || *deafening* (*noise*) || ⟨dial⟩ *ugly, wicked, vile* | ~ u leer *waste*, (⟨bib⟩ *without form*) *and void* **W·üste** f ~/~n *desert, wilderness* (*Kalahari D., Libyan D.*), Fels≃ *rock d.*; Lehm≃ *loamy d.* || Sprache der ~ *desert l.* || ⟨bib⟩ Prediger in der ~ *voice crying in the wilderness* || in die ~ gehen ⟨a. fig⟩ *to go into the w.*; in d. ~ geschickt w ⟨Am sl⟩ *to get the gate* **w·üsten** vi [h] *to live wildly* || mit dem Gelde ~ *to waste one's m.* || mit s–r Gesundheit ~ *to play the devil with ..* **W·üsten- ~bewohner, ~sohn** m *inhabitant of the desert* **~schiff** n ⟨fig⟩ *ship of the desert* (= *camel*) **~steppe** f *semi-d.* **Wüsten·ei** f ~/~en = Wüste **W·üstheit** f ~/ *wilderness* || *dissoluteness* || *brutality* || *wickedness* **W·üstling** m ~(e)s/~e *wastrel*; *libertine, debauchee, rake, Lothario, Lovelace*; *roué* Fr **W·üstung** f ~/~en *deserted village*; *abandoned house* od *settlement*

Wut f ~/ (→ Zorn) **1.** *rage, fury, infuriation*; *violent anger*; *fit of bad temper*; *madness* (über *at*) || ⟨path⟩ *mania* || ⟨vet⟩ *rabies* || s–e ~ auslassen (an [dat]) *to vent one's rage* (*on*) || in ~ bringen *to infuriate, enrage*; (⟨fam⟩ *that makes me wild*) || in ~ bringen *to incense*; ⟨Am⟩ *don't get him mad*! | in ~ geraten *to fly into a passion, to lose one's temper, to take fire*; leicht .. *to get burned up easily* || in ~ s *to rage* (über *at*) || sich in .. steigern *to lash o.s. into a fury* || °wenn ich e–e ~ im Bauch habe *when my dander is up* || v ~ erfüllt s *to see red* || ~ schnauben *to breathe fury* || ich könnte die ~ kriegen *or* mich packt die ~, wenn ich bedenke *it makes me mad to think* || ich koche vor ~ *I'm boiling with rage*; wenn mich die ~ packt *when I get into a rage* || vor ~ platzen *or* schäumen *to be boiling* od *foaming with rage, to fret and fume*; ⟨Am⟩ *to burn up* || jdn in ~ versetzen *to put a p in a fury* **2.** ⟨fig⟩ *mania, passion, craze* (z tun *for doing*) **~anfall, ~ausbruch** m *fit of passion* od *rage*; ⟨sl⟩ *wax*; ⟨Am fam⟩ *conniption* **≃entbrannt** a *furious infuriated, enraged, wrathful, incensed*; *wild with anger* od *rage* **~geschrei** n *yell of rage* **≃schnaubend** a *foaming with rage, raging with fury, in a towering passion* **≃verzerrt** a (*face*) *wild with anger* **w·üten I.** vi [h] *to rage, fume, storm* | ⟨fig⟩ (P, Pest, Meer, Sturm) *to rage*; (Krieg) *to make* (*terrible*) *ravages* **II.** ≃ n *fury* **w·ütend** a *furious* (auf, über *with*); ⟨Am⟩ *mad* (*at*, vor *with*); wie ein angeschossener Eber *boiling with rage*, ⟨Am⟩ *mad as hops* || *enraged* (über *at*) || *irritable, rabid* (*dog*) || *ravenous* (*appetite*) || das ~e Heer *the Wild Huntsman* || mit ~em Grinsen *grinning with rage* || ~ m *to enrage, madden, incense, infuriate* || ~ s *to fume* (über *over*); ⟨sl⟩ *to be waxy* || sich ~ stellen *to make a show of rage* || ~ w = in Wut geraten, ⟨a.⟩ *to get one's temper up, to lose one's t.* (über jdn *with a p*) **W·üterich** m ~(e)s/~e *tartar, barbarian, tyrant* **w·ütig** a = wütend

wutsch! = wupp! | **~en** vi [s] *to hurry*

Wy·oming [wai'oumiŋ] n (Staat der U.S.A.)

X

X, x n ~/~ *X, x* || ⟨fig sl⟩ *umpteen* || Herr X *Mr. what's his name* || jdm ein X für ein U vormachen *to hoodwink a p, to pull the wool over a p's ears*; ⟨sl⟩ *to do a p in the eye*; er läßt sich [dat] kein .. *one can't put anything over on him* || sich ein X für ein U m l *to be easily taken in* **X- ~-Achse,** –Koordinate f ⟨math⟩ *abscissa* **~beine** n pl *knock-, in knees* pl **≗beinig** a *knock-kneed* **≗beliebig** a *any*; *random* || nur ein ~er R. *only another reporter* **~-Chromosom** n → *x-chromosome* **≗-fach** a *hundred-fold* **≗förmig** a *decussate* °**≗mal** [adv] (*over and over again, ever so many times, time and again*); *thousands of times*; *time and again*; ⟨sl⟩ *umpteen times*, **~strahlen** m pl *X-rays* pl **~-Zeit** ⟨mil⟩ *zero hour*, ⟨Am⟩ *H-hour* N; zur ~ *at the h. of z.*

Xanth·ippe f ~/~n *Xanthippe* ⟨a. fig⟩; ⟨fig⟩ *termagant*, ⟨Am⟩ *battle-axe*

X·enie f ~/~n *epigram* | **~n- ~dichter** m *epigrammatist* **~streit** m *controversy raised by the epigrams of Goethe and Schiller*

X·ereswein ['çe:res–] m *sherry*

Xerograph·ie f ⟨el–phot⟩ *xerography*

·xte a; ⟨math⟩ ~ Potenz *xth power* || ⟨fam⟩ zum ~n Male *for the hundredth* od *dozenth* od *nth* od ⟨sl⟩ *umpteenth time*

Xylogr·aph m ~en/~en *xylographer* | **~·ie** f ~/ *xylography, wood-engraving* | **≗isch** a *xylographic(al)* **Xyl·ol** n ~s/ ⟨chem⟩ *xylene, xylol(e)* **Xyloph·on** n ~s/~e ⟨mus⟩ *xylophone*

Y

Y, y n ~/~ *Y, y* **Y-Achse, Y-Koordinate** f ⟨math⟩ *Y-axis, Y-coordinate* **Y (- Eule** f) n ⟨ent⟩ *Y-moth* **Y-Strebe** f ⟨aero⟩ *Y-strut*

Yack m ~s/~s ⟨zoo⟩ *yak*

Yale-Schüssel m *yale(-type) key*

Y·amswurzel f ⟨bot⟩ *yam*

Y·ankee ['jɛŋki:] m ~s/~s *Yankee*; ([a. attr]: *Y. enterprise*) **~tum** n ~(e)s/ *Yankeedom*

Y·atagan [j–] m ~s/~s *yataghan*

Y·ellowstone-Nation·alpark ['jeloustoun-] m *Y. National Park* (*Wyo., U.S.A.*)

Y·erkumstrauch [j–] m ⟨bot⟩ *mudar*

Y·ogaphilosophie [j–] f *yogism*

York [jɔ:k] n *York* (engl. Stadt)

Youngstown ['jʌŋstaun] n (Stadt) (*O., U.S.A.*)

·Ypern [i:] n (belg. Stadt) *Ypres*

·Ypsilon n ~s/~; ein Straßen≗ *a Y-road* **~eule** f = Y-Eule **~knorpel** m *Y-cartilage*

·Ysop ['i:zɔp] m ~(e)s ⟨bot⟩ *hyssop* | ~nelke [f] *h.-leaved pink*

·Ytter- ['ytər] **~erde** f ⟨chem⟩ *yttria* **≗haltig** a *yttrious*

Yucat·án, Y·ukatan n (mexikanische Halbinsel & Stadt) *Yucatan*

Y·ucca ['juka:] f ~/~ ⟨bot⟩ *yucca*

Y·ukon m (Fluß in Kanada & Alaska)

Z

Z, z n ~/~ *Z, z*; → v A bis Z | Z-Draht m ⟨tex⟩ *z-twist*

Z·abern n (Stadt im Elsaß) *Saverne* [Fr] **~er St·eige** od **St·iege** f *col de Saverne*

Z·ack m ~s/ ⟨mil sl⟩ *drill* **zack-b·um** [intj] ⟨artill⟩ *ker-bang* **Z·äckchen** n ~s/~ *denticle* || *small prong* || (Spitzen≗) *purl* || ⟨tail & pap⟩ *pinking* **Z·acke** f ~/~n; **Z·acken** m ~s/~ *indent(ation)* || (Säge–, Kamm≗) *tooth* || (Eisengitter≗, Oszillogramm≗) *spike* || (Gabel≗ etc) *prong* || (Mauer≗) *crenel* || (Rad≗) *cog* || ⟨bot⟩ *crenature* || (Felsen≗) *jag* || (Geweih≗) *tine, point* || (Kristall≗) *point* || (Eis≗) *icicle* || (~n [pl], am Kleid) *scallops* pl || ⟨fig⟩ e–m e–e ~ aus der Krone brechen *to tarnish a p's glory, to take away from a p's g.* || °e–n ~n h = beschwipst s **Z·ackelwolle** f *refuse* (*of*) *wool* **z·ackeln** vi [h/s] ⟨hors⟩ → zuckeln **z·acken** vt [h] *to tooth, indent, point* || (Stoff auszacken) *to scallop* | **sich** ~ *to be indented*, etc **Z·acken- ~blatt** n *indented leaf* **~borte** f *purl* **~fels** m *crag* **≗förmig** a *notched, jagged* **~haupt** n *craggy* (*mountain-*)*peak* **~kreuz** n *Maltese cross* **~linie** f *zigzag line* **~schnitt** m *indentation* **~schote** f ⟨bot⟩ *sweet silique* **~walze** f *dented roller* **z·ackig** a *pronged, toothed, indented* || (Felsen) *jagged* || ⟨bes anat, zoo, bot⟩ *serrated*; (Blätter etc) *crenate(d)* || (Verzierung) *pinked*, ⟨tail⟩ *scalloped* | ⟨fig fam⟩ *smart* || e–e ~e Ehrenbezeugung m ⟨mil sl⟩ *to whip up a smart one* (immer *smart ones*) | .. **zackig** a suff 5– *five-point(ed)* (*star*)

×**Z·agel** m ~s/~ *tail* || *plait* || °⟨sex⟩ *cock, tail*

zag a = ~haft **z·agen I.** vi [h] *to lack* (*in*) *courage, to be in fear, to be faint-hearted* || *to hesitate* || *to quail* **II.** ≗ n *lack of courage*; *fear* || → Zittern **z·aghaft** a *faint-hearted, timorous* || (schüchtern) *shy, timid* || (unentschlossen) *wavering, irresolute* || ~e P ⟨Am⟩ *milquetoast* || ~ m *to intimidate* | **≗igkeit** f ~/ *f.-h.ness, timidity, shyness, i.ness, wavering*

Z·agreb (→ Agram) *Zagreb*

zäh(e*) a *tough* (*meat*), *tenacious* ⟨a. fig⟩ || (sehnig) *sinewy, wiry* (*p*) || (P) *enduring, dogged* || ⟨met⟩ *ductile* || (klebrig) *clammy, ropy, viscous, sticky* || ein ~es Leben h *to be tough*; *to be tenacious of life, to die hard*; ~ s wie e–e Katze *to have a cat's nine lives* | [adv] *stubbornly, doggedly* (*defended*) **~flüssig** a *viscid, viscous* | ≗keit [f] *consistence* (*of a liquid*); *viscidity, viscosity* **Zähe,** ⟨met⟩ *malleability* **Zäh(igk)eit** f ~/ *toughness* || *stickiness viscosity, ropiness* || ⟨phys⟩ *holdfastness* || ⟨fig⟩ *tenacity, doggedness, enduringness* | **~s-** ~grad [m] (nach CGS-System) (*centi*)*poise*

Zahl f ~/~en *number*; (0–9) *digit* || ⟨tech⟩ *rate* (*of revolutions*) || (Ziffer) *figure, cipher* | ⟨demog⟩ bereinigte, berichtigte ~ *corrected, revised rate*; *sex* od *masculinity ratio* || ganze ~ *integer* ⟨a. comp⟩ || gr ~ *shoal(s* pl), .. Reiter ⟨hunt, etc⟩ *large field* || e–e gr ~ Leute *n.s* pl || die größere (kleinere) ~ *the majority* (*minority*) || ohne ~ *in a thousand and one ways* | ~en eintasten *to index amount keys* || (beim Zählen) die ~ vergessen *to lose count* || um die ~ vollzumachen *to make up the n.* | **an** ~ *numerically* (*superior*); an ~ (ums doppelte) übertreffen *to* *outnumber* (*two to one*); 5 an der ~ *numbering 5*, 600 .. *600 strong* || ohne ~ = ≗los **~adverb** n (z. B. 5mal) *numeral adverb* **~buchstabe** m *Roman numeral* | **~n-** ~schrift [f] → *chronogram* **~größe** f *numerical quantity* **≗los** a *numberless*, *innumerable*, *countless*; ⟨fig⟩ *a thousand and one* (*apologies*, *stories*, etc) **~losigkeit** f *n.lessness* **≗reich** a *numerous* || [adv] *in great quantities*, *in force* **~wort** n *numeral* **~zeichen** n *figure*, *cipher* **Zahl-** [v zahlen] **~amt** n = –stelle **~brett** n ⟨com⟩ *money-tray* **≗fähig** a *solvent* **~karte** f (Postscheck) ⟨Ger⟩ *paying-in slip*; durch ~ *by postal money-order* **~kellner** m *head waiter*, *cashier* **~meister** m ⟨mil⟩ *paymaster* ⟨a. fig⟩, ⟨Am⟩ *US Property and Disbursing Officer* || ⟨mar⟩ *purser* = °**~mops** m ⟨mil sl⟩ *bakshee king* **~pfennig** m *counter* **~stelle** f *pay-office*; *finance disbursing section* N **~tag** m *pay-*, *quarter-day* || heute ist ~ ⟨Am sl⟩ *the eagle screams today* **~tisch** m *counter* **Zähl-** **~apparat** m *counter* **~blatt** n *schedule*; ⟨demog⟩ u Standesamts≗ *transcript*(*ion*), *draft entry* **~brett** n *counting-board* **~fehler** m *mistake in the counts* **~kandidat** m *test-candidate* **~karte** f *census-paper* || *scoring-card* **~maschine** f *tabulating-*, *numbering-machine*; *punched card m.* **~register** n ⟨comp⟩ *tally r.* | (Geiger-)**~rohr** n *Geiger counter* **~strich** m *tally* **~vorrichtung** f ⟨mach⟩ *counter* || (f Pn) *turnstile* **~werk** n *clockwork*; *register*; (*drum-type*) *counter*; *timing element* || *counting mechanism* || ⟨comp⟩ ~ der Tabelliermaschine *tabulator counter* **~zettel** = –karte **z·ahlbar** a *payable* (an .. *to order*); ~ bei Auftragserteilung *to be paid with* (*the*) *order*, ~ bei Lieferung *cash on delivery* (*c. o. d.*) || ~ w *to fall due* | ≗keit [f] *solvency* **z·ählbar** a *computable* **z·ahlen** vt/i [h] *to pay* (jeden vernünftigen Betrag *anything in reason*); ⟨fam⟩ *to fork* od *shell out* (*costs*); *to come across*; *how much will it send me back?* || (bitte) ~ Sie an der Kasse .. *pay at the cash desk* || den vollen Betrag ~ *to pay in full* || ~! *the bill, please!* ⟨Am⟩ *waiter, check please!* || den Schaden ~ wir *the damage is on us* || die Rechnung ist pünktlich bezahlt worden .. *has been duly hono*(*u*)*red* || etw f jdn ~ *to treat a p to a th* || z ~ s *to be owing* || (nicht) imstande z ~ (*in*)*solvent* | z ~de Summe *amount payable* || nicht ≗der *defaulter* || ~des Mitglied *dues-payer* **z·ählen I.** vt/i [h] ⟨a. fig⟩ *to count* || ⟨ten, etc⟩ *to score* || ⟨parl⟩ *to tell* (*the votes*) || (Volk, Heer) *to take the census of* || (Geld) *to count down* || Stimmen ~ ⟨fam⟩ *to count noses* | (sich belaufen auf) *to number* (*a thousand men*) || s–e Tage sind gezählt .. *numbered*, Augenblicke .. *his sands are running out* | etw **nicht** ~ *to discount* | er zählt nicht *he does not count* | **an** den Fingern ~ *to count on one's fingers* (bis 30 *to 30*) || ⟨a–n⟩ *to count down* | (**auf** [acc]) *to count* (*on*) || das zählt f mich *that scores for me* || zähle 3 **zu** 4 *add 3 to 4* | er kann nicht bis 3 ~ *he can't say boo* || er sieht aus, als ob er nicht bis 3 ~ könnte *he looks as if butter would not melt in his mouth* || ehe man 3 ~ konnte *before you could say Jack Robinson* | nicht viel ~ *to be of no particular consequence* | **~ zu** *to class with* (*the reptiles*); sich ~ zu *to count o.s. in* (*selected company*) | **gezählte** P ⟨demog⟩ *informant*, *respondent* **II.** ≗ n; nach ~! ⟨mil⟩ *by numbers* **Z·ahlen-** **~angabe** f *figures* pl; ~n [pl] *numerical data* **~aufbereitungs-, -eingabeproblem** [n] ⟨comp⟩ *input pr.* **~bruch** m *numerical fraction* **~darstellung** f ⟨comp⟩ *notation* **~eingabe** f *data input* **~folge** f *n.l order*, *series* **~größe** f *n.l quantity* **~lehre** f *arithmetic* **~lotterie** f *lottery by numbers*, *lotto* **≗mäßig** a *numerical*; ~e Angaben *n.l data*; ~er Unterschied *disparity of number* || [adv] *in n.l figures*; ~ stark/weit überlegen *very superior in number*; ~ in der Minorität s *to be the minority in numbers* [dat] ~ überlegen s *to outnumber*; bei ~ überlegenem Feind *outclassed by enemy strength* **~mensch** m ⟨fig⟩ *man of figures*, *matter-of-fact man* **~ordnung** f = –folge **~rechnung** f *arithmetic* **~reihe** f *series of numbers*, *n.l progression* **~-scheibe** f *scale dial* **~schloß** n *secret lock* **~schlüssel** m *coding scheme* **~sinn** m *head for figures* **~system** n *a.cal system*; dezimales ~ *decimal number system* **~tabelle** f *statistical table* **~tafel** f *synopsis* **~theorie** f *theory of numbers* **~verarbeitung** f *processing* | **~s-** ~maschine [f] ⟨comp⟩ *data processing machine* **~verhältnis** n *n.l proportion* **~verteiler** m ⟨comp⟩ *emitter* **~wert** m *n.l value* **Z·ahler** m ~s/~ *payer* || ein schlechter ~ *one who pays badly* od *who is slow in his payments* **Z·ähler** m ~s/~ *counter* ⟨a. comp⟩ || ⟨parl⟩ *teller* || ⟨math⟩ *numerator* || (Strom-, Gas≗, ⟨mot⟩) *meter* || ⟨demog, stat⟩ (P) *interviewer*; *field worker* | ~ablesung [f], ~stand [m] *meter reading*; ~eichung [f] *test of a meter*; Befehls≗-Register [n] ⟨comp⟩ *address counter*; ~schaltuhr f ⟨tech⟩ *meter change-over clock*, *m. time switch* **Z·ahlung** f ~/~en [abstr & konkr] *payment* || *settlement*, *clearance* (*of a debt*) || gestaffelte ~ *p.t spread*; gestundete ~ *deferred p.t*; sofortige ~ *spot cash*; ~ sofort nach Erhalt der W. *p.t on receipt of goods*; ~ bei Erhalt der Ware *p.t* (od *to be payed*) *on delivery*; ~ in Raten → Raten≗; ⟨ins⟩ *p.t over a period* | die ~en einstellen *to stop p.t* || ~ erhalten [pp] *paid*, *received* || ~ fordern *to claim p.t* || ~ leisten *to pay*, *to make p.t* || e–e ~ v £ 50 in bar verlangen *to want £ 50 cash* | ⟨jur⟩ **an** ~s Statt *in lieu of p.t* | **in** ~ nehmen *to accept* .. (*as p.t*), *to take* .. *in part exchange*; (Ihr Gebrauchtwagen) wird in ~ genommen ⟨ad⟩ *allowance for* .. **Z·ählung** f ~/~en *counting* || (Berechnung) *computation* (nach roher ~ *at a rough c.*) || *enumeration* || (Volks≗) *census* || ~ der Stimmzettel *scrutiny of the ballot-box* || falsche ~ *miscount* | **~s-** ~vorgang [m] *enumeration* **Z·ahlungs-** **~anspruch** m *demand for p.t*(*s*) **~anweisung** f *order* || *draft*, *cheque* || *post-office order*; telegraphische ~ *telegraphic money-order* **~aufforderung** f *request* od *application for p.t*; ⟨ins⟩ *notice* **~aufschub** m *postponement* od *delay of p.t* || ~ gewähren *to extend the term of p.t*, *to grant a respite* **~auftrag** m ⟨com⟩ *order to pay*, ⟨bank⟩ *banker's order* **~ausgleich** m; Bank f internat. ~ *Bank for International Settlement* (*B.I.S.*) **~bedingungen** f pl *terms* pl **~befehl** m *writ of execution*; *request* (*by the* Amtsgericht) *to alleged debtor to pay debt*; *order to pay* **~bilanz** f *balance of p.t*; (aktive [passive]) [*un*]*favorable b. o. p.ts* **~einstellung** f *stoppage* od *suspension of p.t* **~-Ein- u -ausgänge** m pl *receipt and p.ts* **~empfänger** m *payee* **~erleichterungen** f pl *facilities for p.t*, *easy to purchase terms* **≗fähig** a *solvent*, ⟨Am a.⟩ *sound* | ~keit [f] *solvency* **~frist** f *date of p.t* **~mittel** n *means* od *instrument of p.t*; gesetzliches ~ *legal tender*; als ges. ~ gelten *to be receivable* **~modus** m *p.t plan* **~rückstand** m *failure* (*to pay*) **~schein** m *acquittance*, *receipt* **~sperre** f *stop p.t* **~termin** m *time of p.t* **≗unfähig** a *insolvent*, ⟨sl⟩ *knocked out* || sich ~ erklären *to file one's petition* | ≗keit [f] *insolvency*, → Konkurs **~verbindlichkeit** f *liability to pay* **~verkehr** m *p.ts* pl, *clearing* (*system*) **~verweigerung** f *refusal of p.t* **~verzug** m *delay in p.t*, *deferred p.t*; in ~ geratene Partei ⟨jur⟩ *defaulting party* **~weise** f *manner of p.t* **~wert** m *money value* **~zeit** f *expiration*, *maturity* **~zertifikat** n *scrip money*

zahm a *tame*(*d*), *domestic*(*ated*) || ⟨fig⟩ *gentle*, *tractable*, *manageable*; *mild* || ~ m *to tame* **≗bar** a *tamable* | ≗keit [f] *tamability* **z·ähmen** vt [h] *to tame* ⟨a. fig⟩, *domesticate* || (ein Pferd) *to break in* || ⟨fig⟩ (Ungeduld, etc) *to curb*, *subdue*;

(Leidenschaft) *to control, master, check, restrain* || **sich** ~ *to restrain, check, control o.s.* **Z·ähmer** m ~s/~ *tamer* **Z·ahmheit** f ~/ *tameness* ⟨a. fig⟩ **Z·ähmung** f ~/ *taming, domestication* || der Widerspenstigen ~ *Taming of the Shrew*

Zahn m ~(e)s~̈e **A.** *tooth*; falsche ~̈e *false* (⟨Am⟩ *store*) *teeth*, retinierte ~̈e *impacted teeth* || (Wolfs~̈, Hunde~̈, Gift~̈) *fang* || (Eber~̈, Stoß~̈) *tusk* || (Rad~̈ etc) *cog*, ⟨cycl⟩ *tooth* || (Säge–, Kamm~̈) *tooth* || der ~ der Zeit *the ravages* pl *of time* **B.** die ~̈e auf–e–a–beißen *to clench one's teeth* || sich die ~̈e **ausbeißen** *to bite a file*, .. an etw .. ⟨fig⟩ *to get one's teeth into a th* || ~̈e bek *to cut one's teeth* || jdm die ~̈e einschlagen *to break a p's teeth* || gute ~̈e h *to have a good set of teeth* || die ~̈e weisen *or* zeigen *to show one's teeth* od *claws* || die ~̈e fletschen *to bare one's teeth*, °(lachen) ⟨vulg⟩ *to flash* od *sport one's ivory* || die ~̈e zus–beißen *to set one's teeth*, ⟨fig⟩ *to keep a stiff upper lip* **C.** ⟨fig⟩ bis **an** die ~̈e bewaffnet *armed to the teeth* | jdm **auf** den ~ fühlen *to sound a p, to feel a p's pulse* (= *to test his knowledge*) | °e–n ~ drauf h *to go the pace* | °„~" ⟨vulg fig⟩ (Mädel) *bit of hair*; ⟨teens⟩ steiler ~ *smasher, smashing line* **~arzt** m *dental surgeon*, (*surgeon*) *dentist* **~̈ärztlich** a *dental(-hospital)*; ~e Behandlung *dentist's attendance* **~auschlag** m *tooth-rash* **~ausziehen** n = –ziehen **~balken** m ⟨carp⟩ *indented built beam* **~bein** n *dentine* **~bildung** f *dentition* **~bogen** m *toothed segment* **~brecher** m *tooth-drawer* **~breite** f ⟨tech⟩ *face width* **~buchstabe** m *dental* (*letter*) **~bürste** f *toothbrush* **~durchbruch** m *dentition* **~ersatz(stück** n) m *dental prothesis* **~fäule** f ⟨path⟩ *caries* **~feile** f *raspatory* || (Uhr~̈) *equalling file* **~fieber** n ⟨path⟩ *teething fever* **~film** m ⟨med⟩ *dental film* **~fistel** f ⟨path⟩ *abscess* (*tooth*) **~fleisch** n *gum*(*s* pl); ⟨med⟩ *gingiva* | ~entzündung [f] *gengivitis* | ~tasche [f] *gingival trough* od *crevice* **~formel** f ⟨zoo⟩ *dentition*; *dental formula* **~̈förmig** a *dentate, toothed* **~fräser** m *cutter of gear wheels* **~füllung** f *filling* **~geschwür** n ⟨path⟩ *tooth abscess* **~heilkunde** f *dentistry* **~höhle** f *alveole, socket* **~klammer** f *dental brace* °**~klempner** m ⟨hum⟩ *ivory carpenter*; *gum-puncher*, ⟨mil sl⟩ *fang-farrier* **~klinik** f *dental hospital* **~kranz** m ⟨tech⟩ (*traversing*) *rack* || *spur-gear* || *toothed rim* **~kreis** m *pitch circle of teeth* **~krone** f *crown of a tooth* **~künstler** m *dentist* **~laut** m *dental* (*sound*) **~leiste** f *saw-teeth* pl **~lilie** f ⟨bot⟩ *dog's-tooth violet* **~l·ippenlaut** m *labiodental* (*sound*) **~̈los** a *toothless*; ⟨ent⟩ *edentate* **~lücke** f *gap in the teeth* **~lücker** m pl ⟨zoo⟩ *edentals*, ⟨scient⟩ *edentata* **~̈lückig** a *gap-toothed* **~meißel** m *dentist's scraper*; ⟨arts⟩ *ripping chisel* **~mittel** n *remedy for toothache* **~nerv** m *nerve of a tooth* **~operation** f *dental operation* **~ordnung** f *dentition* **~pasta** f *tooth-paste* **~pflege** f *care of one's teeth* **~pulver** n *tooth-powder* **~putzmittel** n *dentifrice* **~rad** n *toothed wheel, rack-, cog-wheel*; kl ~ *pinion* | ~antrieb [m] *cog-wheel drive*; *transmission gear*; ~bahn [f] *rack-railway*; ~getriebe [n] *toothed gearing*; (kl) *pinion*(*-gear*); mit ~ *geared*; ~ mit Zwischenrad *intermediate wheel gear*; ~̈los [a] *toothless* (Antrieb); ~nabe [f] *gear hub* **~reihe** f *set of teeth* **~reinigungsmittel** n *dentifrice* **~reißen** n *toothache* **~schmelz** m *enamel of a tooth* **~schmerzen** m pl *toothache*; ~ h *to have a t.* **~schmerztropfen** m pl *odontalgic drops* pl **~spange** f *dental brace* **~stange** f ⟨rail⟩ *cog rail* || ⟨mach⟩ (*toothed-bar* od *spur-*)*rack* | **~n-** ~getriebe [n] *rack and pinion*; ~säge [f] *rack saw* **~stein** m *tartar*; ⟨arch⟩ *toothing stone*; ~ansatz [m] *tartar deposit*; ~entfernung [f] *scaling* **~stift** m *peg* (*for fastening an artificial tooth*) **~stocher** m *tooth-pick* **~stumpf** m *stump* **~technik** f *dentistry* **~techniker** m *dental mechanic*; *dentist* **~trieb-** ~einstellung [f] *rack and pinion adjustment*; ~welle [f] *gear shaft* **~übersetzung** f *gearing* **~wal** m ⟨zoo⟩ *toothed whale* **~wasser** n *tooth-wash* **~wechsel** m *second dentition* **~weh** n = –schmerzen **~werk** n ⟨mach⟩ *rack work* || (Uhr~̈) *clockwork* **~wurm** m *caries* **~wurzel** f (*tooth*)*root* **~zange** f *pelican* **~ziehen** n *tooth pulling* od *extraction* **Z·ähnchen** n ~s/~ *little tooth* || (e–r Muschel) *dentile* || ⟨tech⟩ *dentile* **Z·ähne-** **~fletschen** n *show*(*ing*) *one's teeth*; ⟨fig fam⟩ *sporting one's ivory* **~klappern** n *chattering of teeth* **~knirschen** n *gnashing of* (*one's*) *teeth* **z·ähne(l)n** vt [h] *to indent* || (Stein) *to pick* **Z.lung** f *indentation* **z·ahnen I.** vt [h] *to tooth, notch, indent* || ⟨carp⟩ *to dent* **II.** vi [h] *to teethe, to cut one's teeth*

Z·ähre ⟨poet⟩ f ~/~n *tear* → Träne

Zain m ~(e)s/~e ⟨met⟩ *bar, ingot* || ⟨hunt, vulg⟩ *pizzle* | ~eisen [n] *rod-iron* **~form** f *ingot mold* **~hammer** m *slitting-h.r* **~silber** n *bar-* od *ingot-silver* **z·ainen** vt [h] ⟨met⟩ *to make into bars* od *ingots* **Z·ainer** m ~s/~ *master smith*

Z·amperl n ~s/~ ⟨bay fam⟩ *any dog* | *mongrel*, ⟨Am sl⟩ *mutt*

..zän [Gr suff] ⟨geol⟩ (= neu) *..cene*: P·aleo~ = unterstes; ·Eo~ = mittleres; ·Oli~ = oberstes Alt-Tertiär | ·Mio~ = unteres; Pl·io~ = oberes Jung-Tertiär | Pl·eisto~ = unteres Quartär (= ⟨obs⟩ Diluvium); Holo~ = oberes Quartär (einschließlich Gegenwart (= ⟨obs⟩ Alluvium)

Z·ander m ~s/~ ⟨ich⟩ *pikeperch, perchpike*

Z·ange f ~/~n (eine *a pair of*) *tongs* pl; (*fire-, pipe-, sugar-, crucible-tongs*) || (kl) *pincers* pl (⟨a.⟩ Falz~̈) || Draht~̈, Zeiger~̈ (des Uhrm.s) *pliers* || Klupp~̈ *tweezers* || Loch~̈, Ösen~̈, Knips~̈ *punch* || Kneif~̈ *cutting nippers* || Schnecken~̈ *snail-tongs* || Zucker~̈ *sugar-tongs* || ⟨surg⟩ (*a pair of*) *forceps* sg & (pl) || ⟨zoo⟩ *forcipated claw* || ⟨ent⟩ *palp* | ich möcht' ihn nicht mit der ~ anfassen *I wouldn't touch him with a barge-pole* | **~n-** ~angriff [m] *double envelopment*; ~bewegung [f] ⟨mil⟩ *pincers movement*; ~geburt [f] ⟨surg⟩ *delivery by means of the forceps*; ~schanze [f] ⟨fort⟩ *tenail*; ~schraubstock [m] *jaw-vice* **Z·ängelchen** n ~s/~ (ein ~ *a pair of*) *pincers, tweezers, nippers* pl

Zank m ~(e)s/ *quarrel, wrangle, altercation* || (kl) ⟨sl⟩ *tiff* (*of lovers*) || (lärmender) *row, squabbles* pl, *brawl* || ~ u Streit *bickering and biting*, immer .. h *to be for ever squabbling* od *nagging* || mit e–m ~ suchen *to pick a q.l with a p* **~apfel** m ⟨fig⟩ *apple of discord, bone of contention* **~drache** m ⟨fig⟩ *shrew, vixen, virago* **~sucht** f *love of q.lling, q.lsomeness* **~̈süchtig** a *q.lsome* **~teufel** m = –drache; ⟨a.⟩ *wrangler, brawler* °**~tippe** f ~/~n ⟨hum⟩ = Xanthippe **z·anken I.** vi [h] *to quarrel, bicker, wrangle* || sich ~ (mit) *to fall out, to* (*have a*) *q.l, to dispute, bicker, to have* (*high*) *words* (*with*) (um nichts, um des Kaisers Bart *about trifles*) **II.** ~̈ n *bickering*, etc **Z·änker(in** f) m ~s/~ *q.lsome p, bickerer, squabbler*; (nur f: *scold, shrew, termagant*) | **~·ei** f ~/~en *bickering, q.l*(*ling*); *altercation, contention*; (kl) *tiff*; → Zank **z·ankhaft, z·änkisch** a *q.lsome, cantankerous*

Z·anzibar n → Sansibar

Z·apf m ~(e)s/~e → Ausschank || *hydrant* **~bier** n *beer from the tap* **~hahn** m *tap, bib-cock*; ⟨bes Am⟩ *faucet* **~kellner** m *tapster* **~rohr** n *tapping pipe* **~säule** f (*petrol-*)*pump*; ~ mit Preisanzeige *computor p.* **~stelle** f ⟨mot⟩ *filling station*, ⟨Am⟩ *point of draw* **Z·äpfchen** n ~s/~ *little peg* || ⟨anat⟩ *uvula* || [in comp] ⟨gram, anat⟩ *uvular* [a] || ⟨med⟩ (Darm~̈) *suppository* **Z·apfen** m ~s/~ *pin, peg, plug* || (Faß~̈) *bung, spigot* || (Well~̈) *journal* || *tang* (*of a knife*, etc) || (Dreh~̈) *pivot*; ⟨rail⟩ *truck center pin*; (am Geschützrohr) trunnion; Kipp≃ tipping trunnion || Lager≃ journal || (liegender) gudgeon; (stehender) pivot || ⟨carp, etc⟩ tenon | ⟨bot⟩ cone | ⟨anat⟩ uvula; (Aug≃) → Stäbchen | (Zapfhahn) tap; ⟨fig⟩ ein voller ~ a drunkard | °⟨fig⟩ über den ~ wichsen ⟨mil sl⟩ to smash a pass → ~streich **z·apfen** vt [h] to tap (beer, a dropsical patient) **Z·apfen-** **~baum** m conifer **~bier** n tap-droppings pl **~bohrer** m tap-borer; (des Uhrm.s) pivot-drill **≃gelagert** a trunnion-supported **~lager** n socket, rest; (e–r Tür) pan || ⟨mach⟩ bearing || ⟨artill⟩ bed || (e–r Maschine) pillow-block **~loch** n ⟨carp⟩ mortise, (f Zapfhahn) tap-hole **~streich** m ⟨mil⟩ tattoo, retreat; last post; (Signal) taps pl || (gr) torchlight tattoo || den ~ schlagen to beat a tattoo **≃tragend** a ⟨bot⟩ coniferous **~verschluß** m pin-hinge ⟨a. theat⟩ ˣ**~zieher** m → Kork- °**zappenduster** a: jetzt ist ~ (= aus) it's a wash-out **Z·apfer** m ~s/~ tapster, barman || (rubber- etc) tapper

Z·appel- ~mann [m] jointed doll, jumping-jack; °~fritze, ~philipp [m] fidget, ⟨Am a.⟩ jitterbug **z·app(e)lig** a fidgety, ⟨bes Am⟩ jittery; er wird dabei ganz ~ it gives him the fidgets | ~keit [f] (vor Aufregung) dither, ⟨Am sl⟩ jitter(s) **z·appeln** vi [h] to sprawl; to struggle (with hands and feet) (struggling eel) || (Baby) to kick || (Fisch) to jigger || (im Wasser) to flounder || (vor Ungeduld) to fidget | ~ l (Fisch) to play; ⟨fig⟩ to have (a p) on the string; to keep (a p) on the rack

Z·ar m ~en/~en czar, tsar | ~entum [n] tsardom; ~ewitsch [m] ~/~ tsarevitch; ~in [f] ~/~nen czarina, tsarina; ≃isch [a] czarish, tsarish

Z·arge f ~/~n border, edge || (Rahmen) frame, case || (Geigen≃) side

zart a tender (meat, conscience, heart) || delicate (child, skin, lips, health, complexion, flower) || frail (health), fragile (constitution) | thin, slender, slim, fine, nice | soft (skin) || pale, subdued (colour) || mellow (tone) | ⟨fig⟩ gentle (hint, sex) | [adv] ~ besaitet sensitive; thin-skinned **~fühlend** a tender of feeling, delicate, sensitive, thin-skinned, tender-hearted **≃gefühl** n tenderness od delicacy of feeling, tact (f of), sensitiveness **~gr·ün** a pale green **≃puder** m ⟨cosm⟩ blush-on **≃ried** n ⟨bot⟩ club-rush **≃sinn** m delicacy **~sinnig** a delicate **Z·ärte, Z·artheit** f ~/~en tenderness, delicacy || fragility || softness || ⟨fig⟩ gentleness **z·ärtlich** a tender, soft, delicate || sweet (nature, disposition) || (verliebt) amorous, fond || (liebevoll) affectionate | = zart | [adv] (to love) fondly, dearly || ~ tun to bill and coo, to make great display of affection | **≃keit** f ~/ tenderness, softness, delicacy; (demonstration of) affection; endearment || amorousness, fondness | ~/~en pl caresses, sweet words pl | **~s-** ~bezeigungen [f pl] terms of endearment **Z·ärtling** m ~(e)s/~e molly-coddle, milksop

Z·ase(l, ~r) f ~/~n ⟨bot⟩ catkin **Z·aser** f ~/~n fibre, filament | **≃ig** a fibrous, filamentous **z·asern** vt [h] to untwine || sich ~ [h] to fray out

Z·aspel f ~/~n skein, 20 ~n 20 skeins

°**Z·aster** m ~s/ (= Geld) ⟨sl⟩ dibs pl, tin, putty, dust, ⟨Am⟩ jack, sugar; spondulic(k)s pl; ⟨vulg⟩ lolly

Zäs·ur f ~/~en ⟨pros⟩; (klingende, stumpfe) ~ (feminine, masculine) cæsura || ⟨übtr⟩ break

Z·auber m ~s/ **A.** spell, charm; magic effect || lure (of a language) || (~ei) enchantment || (Ver≃ung, ~formel) incantation || °(Buden≃) booby trap **B.** ⟨fam fig⟩ fauler ~ ⟨fam⟩ humbug; ⟨Am⟩ monkey business; phoneyness || der ganze ~ all the (blessed) lot **C.** e–n ~ ausbreiten über to throw a spell (⟨Scot⟩ glamour) over || den ~ brechen to break the spell od charm **D.** wie durch ~ as if by magic || vom ~ gebannt spellbound **~apparat** m juggler's apparatus **~bann** m spell **~becher** m magic cup **~bild** n m.c image || enchanting creature **~blick** m fascinating look **~brunnen** m m.c fountain **~buch** n conjuring-book **~flöte** f m.c flute **~formel** f spell, m.c formula, charm **~garten** m e.ed garden **~geschichte** f fairy-tale **~hasel** f witch-hazel **~kasten** m conjuring-box **~kraft** f m.c power, witchcraft || ⟨übtr⟩ wizardry (of words) || ein Name v gr ~ a name to conjure with || ≃e [pl] m.c properties **≃kräftig** a m.c(al); talismanic **≃kundig** a weird **~kunst** f m.c (art), witchcraft, wizardry; in der ~ bewandert wise **~künste** f, **~kunststücke** n pl conjuring-tricks pl **~künstler** m conjurer, m.cian, juggler, illusionist **~land** n e.ed land; fairyland **~laterne** f m.c lantern **~lehrling** m m.cian's apprentice **~märchen** n fairy-tale **~mittel** n m.c agency, charm **~posse** f; **~reich** n fairy-comedy, -realm **~ring** m m.c ring **~rute** f = –stab **~schlaf** m; **~schloß** n e.ed sleep, castle **~segen** m spell, charm **~spiegel** m m.c mirror; show-glass **~spruch** m incantation, spell, charm **~stab** m m.c wand **~stück** n conjuring-trick **~trank** m m.c potion, elixir; (Liebestrank) philtre **~wald** m e.ed forest **~welt** f m.c world **~werk** n witchcraft, spell **~wesen** n [abstr] magic, sorcery || (P) bewitching creature **~wort** n m.c word || ~e [pl] spell sg **Zauber·ei** f ~/~en (böse black) magic; witchcraft sorcery,; wizardry ⟨fig⟩ charms pl, fascination, enchantment | (Taschenspielerei) conjuring, juggling, sleight-of-hand **Z·auberer** m ~s/~ magician, sorcerer, wizard || (Taschenspieler) conjurer, juggler, illusionist || ⟨fig⟩ charming p **z·auberhaft, z·auberisch** a magic(al), enchanting ⟨a. fig⟩ | ⟨fig⟩ fascinating, charming, bewitching; marvellous | [adv] ~ wirken to have a m.c effect **Z·auberin** f ~/~nen sorceress, witch || ⟨fig⟩ enchantress, charmer **z·aubern** vi [h] to practise magic || vt [h] to produce .. by m.c, to charm .. (up bzw down one's sleeve), to conjure .. (out of a p's pocket) || e–n jung ~ to make a p young by m.c

Zauder·ei f ~/~en hesitation || delay, tarrying, slackness **Z·auderer** m ~s/~ irresolute od dilatory p || loiterer, lingerer, tarrier || procrastinator; temporizer || ⟨ant⟩ (Fabius) Cunctator **z·audern I.** vi [h] to linger, falter, delay; to hang off || (schwankend) to waver, hesitate (z tun doing) || (abwartend) to temporize; to shilly-shally | ~d faltering (⟨a. fig⟩ f.g step) **II.** ≃ n lingering, etc || hesitation || temporization || dilatoriness (mit over a th)

Zaum m ~(e)s/≃e ⟨hors⟩ bridle, rein || im ~e halten to control ⟨a. fig⟩; to keep .. well in hand; s–e Zunge .. to have control over one's lips || ⟨fig⟩ jdn .. to keep a p straight; (Begierden) to restrain, curb, bridle; (Zunge) to (keep .. in) check | ~geld [n] purchaser's tip to the groom; ≃los [a] ⟨fig⟩ unbridled; ≃recht [a] accustomed to the bridle; ~zeug [n] head-gear (of harness), bridle **z·äumen** vt [h] to bridle, to put the bit on .. | (bändigen) to curb, bridle | ⟨bib⟩ = zähmen

Zaun m ~(e)s/≃e hedge, fence; geflochtener ~ wicker fence; lebendiger ~ quickset hedge; versteckter Park≃ ha-ha; sunk fence || mit e–m ~ umgeben to fence od hedge in | ⟨fig⟩ etw v ~e brechen to drag a th in by the head and shoulders, (Streit) to pick (a quarrel); to start an argument (with a p) || das ist nicht hinter jedem ~e z finden ⟨fam⟩ you can't pick it off hedges || hinterm ~e sterben to die in a ditch **~buche** f horn-beam **~gast** m intruding looker-on, intruder **~könig** m ⟨orn⟩ wren **~pfahl** m pale || e–m mit dem ~ winken ⟨fig⟩ to drop a hint as heavy as flat irons (= to give one a broad hint) **~rebe** f ⟨bot⟩ Virginia creeper **~recht** n right of making a hedge **~rübe** f ⟨bot⟩ bryony **~tritt** m (Übersteig) stile **~winde** f ⟨bot⟩ bindweed

z·ausen vt [h] (⟨a.⟩ sich ~) to pull (each other) about, to tug (at); (Haar) to tousle, ⟨fam⟩ to wool

°**Zebed·äus** [n pr] °⟨sex⟩ John od Sir Thomas

Z·ebra n ~s/~s *zebra* | **~streifen** m ⟨traffic⟩ *z. crossing*; mit ~ *striped like a z.*

Zech- **~bruder** m *tippler, toper,* ⟨fam⟩ *boozer* ‖ *boon companion* **≈frei** a *scot-free* (*to go s.-f.*) ‖ e–n ~ halten *to treat a p* **~genosse, ~kumpan** m *pot-, boon-companion* ‖ = –bruder **~gelage** n *drinking-bout, carouse,* ⟨sl⟩ *tear* **~gesellschaft** f *drinking-company* **~preller** m *welsher* (dazu: *to welsh*) | ~·ei [f] *welshing* (*decamping without paying one's score*) **~stein** m ⟨min⟩ *Permian limestone* | ~formation [f] ⟨geol⟩ *P.n formation*
Z·eche f ~/~n **1.** (Wirtshausrechnung) *bill, score, reckoning* ‖ die (ganze) ~ bezahlen *to pay the bill, to stand treat*; ⟨fig⟩ *to pay the piper, to suffer the consequences*; was macht die ~? ⟨fam fig⟩ *what's the damage*?; um die ~ spielen *to stradde* **2.** *banquet,* ⟨fam⟩ *booze* **3.** (Bergwerk) *mine* **4.** *mining company* **5.** (Innung) *corporation, guild* **z·echen** vi [h] *to drink, banquet,* ⟨fam⟩ *tipple, tope, booze* **Z·echen-** ~besitzer [m] *mine-owner*; ~koks [m] *foundry-coke*; ~preis [m] *pit-head price* **Z·echer** m ~s/~ *toper, tippler* ‖ edler ~ *worthy child of beer* | **~·ei** f ~/~en *carouse, spree* (*on the s.*)

Zech·ine f ~/~n *sequin* ‖ °das wird etliche ~n kosten *that will cost a pretty pot of money*

Zeck n ~s/ (Laufspiel) *tag* **Z·ecke** f ~/~n ⟨ent⟩ *tick* **z·ecke(r)n** vt/i [h] *to tag* ‖ *to tease* **Zecker·ei** f *teasing*

Zed·ent m ~en/~en ⟨com⟩ *endorser* ‖ ⟨jur⟩ *ceder, assignor* **zed·ierbar** a *transferable* **zed·ieren** vt [h] ⟨jur⟩ *to cede, transfer*

Z·eder f ~/~n ⟨bot⟩ *cedar* **~kiefer** = Zirbel **~tanne** f *cedrela* **≈nholz** n *cedar-wood*

Z·edrachbaum m *China Tree*

Z·eh(e f ~/~n) m ~s/~en *toe* ‖ ⟨zoo⟩ *digit* ‖ gr (kl) ~ *big* (*little*) *toe* ‖ auf den ~n *atiptoe*; .. gehen *to* (*walk on*) *tiptoe* | **~en-** **≈frei** a *peep--toe(d)* (Schuh), ~e Schuhe *toe-peepers* **~gänger** m ⟨zoo⟩ *digitigrade* **~spitze** f *tiptoe* ‖ auf den ~n *on t.*; sich auf die ~n stellen *to get on t.* **..zehig** a *toed* (*three-toed*)

Z·ehlendorf n (Stadtteil v Groß-Berlin)

Z·eh(e)nt n ~(e)s/~e *decade* **Z·ehn I.** f ~/~en (*number*) *ten* ‖ ⟨cards⟩ *ten* (*-spot* ⟨Am⟩) **II.** ≈, ⟨fam a.⟩ ~e [abs] [a] *ten* ‖ Zeitraum v ~ Jahren *decennium, decade* ‖ alle ~ Jahre *decennially, every ten years* ‖ halb ~ (Uhr) *half past nine* ‖ ⟨bot⟩ mit ~ Staubfäden *decandrian* | ⟨fam⟩ zu ~en = zu ~t **≈blättrig** a *decaphyllous* **~c·ent-stück** n ⟨Am⟩ *dime* **~eck** n *decagon* **≈eckig** a *decagonal* **~ender** m *stag of ten* (*antlers*) **≈fach, ≈fältig** a & adv *tenfold* ‖ das ≈e *ten times the amount,* etc **~fingersystem** n ⟨typewr⟩ *touch system* **~flach** n, ≈ner [m] *decahedron* **~füßer** m ⟨zoo⟩ *decapod*(*a* pl) **≈jährig** a *ten years old, of ten years*; *ten-year-old* (*child*) **≈jährlich** [a] *decennial,* [adv] *every ten years* **~kampf** m ⟨sport⟩ → *decathlon* **≈mal** adv *ten times* **≈malig** adv *ten times repeated* **≈männig** a ⟨bot⟩ *decandrian* **~m·arkschein** m *bank-note of 10 marks* **~pf·ennigstück** n *ten-pfennig piece* **~pfünder** m *ten-pounder* **≈pfündig** a *of ten pounds* **~pf·und-note** f *ten-pound note,* ⟨fam⟩ *tenner* **≈silbig** a *decasyllabic* **≈stündig** a *of ten hours* **≈tägig** a *lasting ten days* **≈tausend** a *ten thousand* ‖ die oberen Z. [pl] *the upper ten* od ⟨bes Am⟩ *crust*; ⟨Am⟩ *the Four Hundred* pl ‖ Z.e *tens of thousands* (*of*) **≈teilig** a *of* od *in ten parts* **≈weibig** a ⟨bot⟩ *decagynian* **Z·ehner** m ~s/~ **1.** *number* (*of*) *ten* ‖ ~ u Einer *tens and units* **2.** = Zehnpfennigstück **3.** ⟨cards⟩ (*the*) *ten*(*-spot* ⟨Am⟩) **4.** *wine of the year 1910* **5.** *soldier of the tenth regiment* **6.** **in** den ~n stehen *to be in one's teens* **≈lei** a *of ten different sorts* **~logarithmen** pl *common logarithms* **~potenz** f ⟨math⟩ *power* od *factor of ten* · **~reihe** f *column of tens* **Z·ehnt-** **~ablösung** f *commutation of tithes* **~acker** m *field under tithe* **≈frei** a *free from tithe* **~herr** m *tithe-owner* **~land** n *land subject to tithe* **≈pflichtig** a *tithable* **~recht** n *right to levy tithe* **~schaft** f ⟨hist⟩ *tithing* **Z·ehnte I.** m ~n/~n *tithe*; den ~n entrichten *to pay t.* (an *to,* v *on*) ‖ mit dem ~n belegen *to tithe* **II.** ~([r] m) f: der ~ *the tenth* ‖ nicht der ~ *not one out of ten* **III.** ≈ [a] (*the*) *tenth* ‖ der ~ Mai *May the tenth* (*May10th*), *the tenth of May* ‖ ~s Kapitel *chapter the tenth, chapter X* | **~n-** ~scheune [f] *tithe barn* **Z·ehntel** n [Sw m] ~s/~ *tenth* (*part*) ‖ fünf ~ *five-tenths* **z·ehnten** vt [h] (besteuern) *to tithe* ‖ ⟨mil⟩ *to decimate* **z·ehntens** adv *tenthly* (*10thly*)

Zehr- **~fieber** n ⟨path⟩ *hectic fever* **≈frei** a *with free board* **~geld** n, **~pfennig** m *board-expenses* pl, *travelling-money* **~vorrat** m *provisions* pl **~wurz** f ⟨bot⟩ = Aronstab ‖ (ägyptische) *taro* **z·ehren I.** vi [h] **A.** **1.** *to eat and drink* **2.** [abs] *to make thin*; *to give an appetite* **3.** [h & s] (P) *to lose flesh, to grow thin*; (S) *to shrink* **B.** ~ **an** *to live on* (*a th*) ⟨a. fig⟩ ‖ an e–m Schinken ~ *to eat off* od *at a ham* ‖ ⟨fig⟩ (v Kummer etc) (an der Gesundheit etc) *to gnaw at, to prey upon, to undermine, consume, to waste* (*away*) | **auf** anderer (Leute) Kosten ~, **aus** fremdem Beutel ~ *to feed* od *live at another's expense* | **von** s–n Zinsen ~ *to live on one's interest* ‖ v der Erinnerung ~ *to enjoy the recollection* (*of*), *to feast on memories of the past* **II.** ***sich** ~: die Sorgen ~ sich tief in sein Herz *grief is eating into his heart* **z·ehrend** a ⟨path⟩ *consumptive*; *hectic* (*fever*) **Z·ehrung** f ~/~en **1.** (Mundvorrat) *provisions* pl | ⟨ec⟩ letzte ~ *viaticum* **2.** ⟨obs⟩ (= Zeche) *score* **3.** (Unterhalt) *living* ‖ freie ~ h *to have free board* **4.** (Schwinden) (S) *waste, shrinkage*; ⟨path⟩ *consumption* | **~s-** **~kosten** pl *expenses for food, board-expenses* (f Dienstboten) *b.-wages* pl **~steuer** f *duty on articles of food*

Z·eichen n ~s/~ **A.** **1.** *sign* (⟨a. math, mus, astr⟩; ⟨ec⟩: *s. of the cross*) ‖ (verabredetes) *signal* (*alarm-s.*); ⟨wir⟩ *signature-tune* ⟨a. Zeit-≈⟩ ‖ ⟨aero⟩ *beacon* ‖ ⟨typ⟩ *signature*; *symbol* ⟨a. phon⟩ ‖ (Bezug) Ihr ~ *your serial* ‖ (Diktat-≈) *reference* ‖ ⟨mus⟩ (Vor≈) (*key*) *signature* ‖ ⟨comp⟩ *figure*; *pattern*; *character* | ~ [pl] v *or* der [gen] *signals given by* (*policemen*) **2.** *sign* (*of an inn*) ‖ ⟨mar⟩ *beacon* | (Ab≈) *badge,* [pl a.] *insignia* ‖ (Kenn≈) *mark*; (Stempel) *stamp*; (eingebranntes) *brand* (⟨a.⟩ Waren≈) ‖ (Wäsche-≈) *initials* pl **3.** ⟨übtr⟩ (An≈) *indication, token,* ⟨path⟩ (subjektiv) *symptom,* ⟨med⟩ (objektiv) *sign,* sicheres ~ *safe index* [pl *indices*] (auf *to*) ‖ (Vor≈) *omen* ‖ (Beweis) *proof, testimony* **B.** **1.** ~ u Wunder *signs and wonders* ⟨a. bib⟩; es geschehen noch ~ u W. *wonders will never cease* ‖ ~ geben *to* (*give* od *make a*) *sign, to signal* ‖ das ~ geben ⟨a.⟩ *to give the word,* .. z Angriff *to give the sign for the a.,* .. z Halten *to signal the halt, to wave down* (*a car*); ⟨theat⟩ .. z Heben des Vorhangs *to ring up the c.,* .. z Start *to drop the flag* ‖ ich nehme das als gutes ~ *I deem it a happy omen, that augurs well* **2.** welches ~s sind Sie? *what is your trade*? ich bin m–s ~s Schn. *I am a tailor by trade* **3.** **auf** ein ~ v *at a sign from* | **auf** ein ~ warten *to be looking for a sign* | **im** ~ [gen] *in the days of* (*technics*), *under the banner of* (*freedom*); ⟨astr⟩ *in* (*Cancer*) ‖ im ~ des Todes *death-stricken* (*winter*); wir stehen im ~ des Handels *the signature of our time is commerce* | **in** dem ~ [† gen] stehend *marked by* ⟨a. theat⟩ | etw **mit** e–m ~ versehen *to print on* od *in a th* | **unter** e–m glücklichen ~ (*born*) *under a lucky star* | **zum** ~ [gen] *in token of*; z ~, daß *as a proof that* **~abfühlung** f ⟨comp⟩ *mark sensing* **~adressierung** f ⟨comp⟩ *character addressing* **~block** m *drawing-block* **~brett** n *d.-board* **~buch** n *d.-book* **~deuter** m *soothsayer*; *augur* **~deuter·ei** f *astrology* **~dreieck** n *square triangle* **~ereignis** n

⟨commun⟩ *sign-event* **~erklärung** f ⟨typ⟩ *key* (*of the signs*) **~feder** f *d.-pen* **~film** m *trick-film, -picture, animated cartoon* **~garn** n *marking-yarn* **~geber** m ⟨telg⟩ *communicator* || ⟨hot⟩ *teleseme* || ⟨mot⟩ *direction indicator* **~heft** n *d.-book* **~kreide** f *d.-chalk* **~kunst** f *art of d.* **~lochen** n ⟨comp⟩ *mark sensing* **~locher** m *m.-s. reproducer* **~lehrer, ~meister** m *art-* od *d.-master* **~papier** n *d.-paper*; rauhes *scraper-board* **~pult** n *d.-desk, -stage* **~saal** m *studio*; ⟨tech⟩ *d.-office* **~schule** f *art school* **~setzung** f ⟨gram⟩ *punctuation* **~sprache** f *language of signs* **~stereometer** n ⟨tech⟩ *tracing st.* **~stift** m *d.-pencil*, (bunt) *crayon* **~stunde** f *d.-lesson* **~talent** n *talent for d.* **~telegraph** m *semaphore* **~tinte** f (f Wäsche) *marking-ink* **~tisch** m *d.-stage* **~träger** m ⟨comm⟩ *sign-token* **~trickfilm** m *animated* od *cartoon film* **~tuch** n *canvas for marking* **~unterricht** m *d.-lessons* pl **~vorlage** f *d.-copy* | 10 **~/Zoll** ⟨comp⟩ (*at*) *10 characters to inch* **z·eichnen I.** vt/i [h] **1.** *to draw, delineate* ⟨a. fig⟩ (nach .. *from life, models*, v der Seite *in profile*); *to trace* (*figure,* [*out*]*line*) | (flüchtig) *to outline, sketch* || nicht gut ~ *not to be much of a hand at drawing* || verkürzt ~ *to foreshorten* **2.** (Muster, Entwürfe) *to design* || ⟨geogr⟩ Karten ~ *to map*, ⟨surv⟩ *to plot* (auf *on*) **3.** (mit Zeichen versehen) *to mark*; (Vieh) *to brand*; schön ge–net *beautifully marked* (*dog*, etc); ⟨fig⟩ (P) ge–net *marked*; *a face seamed with worry* **4.** (e–e Schrift, s–n Namen unterschreiben) *to sign* || ich zeichne hochachtungsvoll ⟨com⟩ *I am, Yours faithfully* || ⟨fig⟩ verantwortlich ~ f *to be responsible for* **5.** e–e Summe ~ *to subscribe* (f *to*, auf e–e Anleihe *to a loan*; Aktien *for shares*; z e–m Denkmal etc *towards the erection of a m.*) **6.** ⟨hunt⟩ der Hund –net die Fährte .. *draws on the sc.* || das Reh –net .. *shows marks of being hit* **II.** ≗ n; ~ aus freier Hand *free hand drawing* **Z·eichner(in** f) m ~s/~ *draughts*(*wo*)*man, designer* || *subscriber* (*to a loan*) **Zeichner·ei** f ~/ *bad* od *poor drawing* **z·eichnerisch** a: ~e Darstellung *graph* **Z·eichnung** f ~/~en *drawing*; *sketch*; *design* || erläuternde ~ *diagram, graph* || (f ein Fresko) *cartoon* || (auf Knochen) *engraving* || ⟨phot⟩ ~ in den Schatten *shadow details* pl || ⟨fig⟩ *delineation* || (Kennzeichen) *mark* || (Summe) *subscription* || (Unter≗) *signature* || e–e Anleihe zur ~ auflegen *to issue a loan*; (v Aktien) *application* | **~s-** ~berechtigung [f] *a. right*; ~formular [n] *a. form*; ~jahr [n] ⟨ins⟩ *y. of acceptance*; ~preis [m] *price of issue*

Z·eidel- **~bär** m *common bear*; (P) *grumpy old man* **~meister** m *beemaster* **Z·eid(e)ler** m ~s/~ *bee-keeper*

Z·eige- ~finger [m] *forefinger, first f., index*; ~geschäft [n] ⟨theat, sex⟩ *showbusiness*; ~lust [f] ⟨sex⟩ (Exhibitionismus) *exhibitionism*; ~stock [m] *pointer* **z·eigen I.** vt/i [h] **A. 1.** (**sich**) ~ *to show* (*o.s.*) || (deuten auf) *to point* (*at, to, out*); *to indicate* || (z Schau stellen) *to exhibit* ⟨a. path⟩; *to display* || ⟨theat, film⟩ *to present* | (Thermometer) 5 **Grad** ~ *to stand at 5°* || die Uhr –gte 4 *the watch/clock said 4* || sie ~ ihm die Tanzschritte *they put him through the steps* || ~ Sie mir s–n Brief *let me see his l.* || jdm den **Weg** ~ *to show, tell, point a p the way, to direct a p* (nach *to*) || was mir gezeigt wurde *what I have been shown*; *he was shown* (*all the rooms*) || → erklären, erläutern **2.** ⟨fig⟩ (klar m) *to point out* || (darlegen) *to unfold* || (am Objekt, durch Experiment etc) *to demonstrate*; *to be demonstrative* || der Krieg hat deutlich gezeigt, daß .. *has made it plain that* .. || (beweisen) *to prove, evidence*; *to give evidence of* || (an den Tag legen) *to display, manifest* || (aufweisen) *to present* | ⟨a.⟩ *to register* (*enthusiam*), *to display* (*astonishment*), *to evince* (*interest*) || jetzt heißt es ~, was e–r kann *that'll make us or break us* **3.** jdn ~ **als** *to show a p to be* **B. 1. sich** ~ *to appear, show*; *emerge*; *issue* (*forth*); *to come in sight*; *to make one's appearance*; *to come to light, to turn out* od *up*; *to become apparent, evident, manifest*; *to come forward, to crop up* ⟨fig fam⟩ *to show the flag* || *to be seen* (mit *in a p's company*) || (Charakter) *to peep out* || wahre Künstler ~ sich in .. *the proof of an artist is in* .. | **das** wird sich ~ *that remains to be seen* **2.** sich **als** (etw) ~ *to prove o.s.* (*to be*) ..; .. gegen jdn *to come* (*the Baronet's son*) *over a p* **3.** sich **mutig** ~ *to show pluck* || sich richtig ~ *to show what one can do*, .. *what* (*a th*) *is good for* || sich im wahren Lichte ~ *to expose o.s.* (od *to come out*) *in one's true colours* **4.** sich ~ (vgl sich sehen l) **können** || sich ~ wollen (= protzen) *to show off* **5. es zeigt sich, daß** *we see* od *it appears that* || jetzt zeigt sich's *now it becomes evident* (daß *that*) || es zeigte sich, daß er .. ist/war *he turned out to be* || das wird sich ~! *we shall see*! **C.** [als vi]: ~ **auf** *to indicate* (*a p, a chair*), .. mit dem Finger *to point the finger at*; (Uhr): *the clock marked six, the hand of the clock pointed to six* | **in** derselben Richtung ~ *to point the same way* | **nach**: (Nordnadel) *to point to the north* | jdm deutlich ~, **daß** *to make it clear to a p that* || (S) ~, daß er ist *to prove him to be* | **wie** Figur 9 zeigt *as shown in fig. 9*; → erklären, erläutern **II.** ≗ n *showing*, etc || *indication, exhibition, display, presentation* **Z·eiger** m ~s/~ (Uhr) *hand* (gr *long*, kl *short*) || (Waage, Barometer etc) *pointer* || ⟨tech⟩ *indicator*; *index* ⟨a. math.⟩ **~ausschlag** m *deviation of the pointer*; *printer deflection, meter deflection* **~barometer** n *wheel-barometer* **~blatt** n, **~platte** f *dial* **~rad** n *dial-wheel* **~schwankung** f *pointer fluctuation*; *needle flutter* **~stellung** f *pointer setting* **~telegraph** m *dial-telegraph* **~uhr** f *clock which does not strike* **~visier** n *quadrant sight* **~waage** f *bent-lever balance* **~werk** n (Uhr) *hour train* **z·eihen** vt [zieh/geziehen] [h]; jdn e–r S [gen] ~ *to impute a th to a p* || *to accuse a p of* od *tax* od *charge a p with a th* || jdn e–r Lüge ~ *to give a p the lie*

Z·eile f ~/~n **1.** *line*; im Brief: *these few lines*; *I wrote him a few lines* || auf fixe ~ ⟨comp⟩ *snap-on* [attr] || in die nächste ~ übergehend *run-on* (*line*) || zw den ~n *interlinear* || zw den ~n e–r Rede lesen *to read a speech between the lines* || ⟨typ⟩ ~ halten *to keep to the line* || jede ~ e–s Buches lesen *to read a b. from cover to cover* || der Schreiber dieser ~n *the present writer* **2.** *row* (*of houses*) || *range* (*of ths*) || *lane* (*of persons*) || ⟨hort⟩ in ~n *in rows* | **~n-** **~abstand** m *line spacing*; mit doppeltem ~ (*to type*) *in double sp.g* **~breite** f, **~maß** n ⟨typ⟩ *measure* **~drucker** m ⟨comp⟩ *line printer* **~durchschuß** m ⟨typ⟩ *reglet* **~einsteller** m ⟨typewr⟩ *interliner*; dreifacher ~ *three position line spacer* **~einstellung** f ⟨comp⟩ (*variable*) *line adjuster* **~fräsen** n *straight milling* **~gießmaschine** f *line-casting machine* **~satz** m ⟨typ⟩ *slug* **~schreiber** m *penny-a-liner* **~setz- u -gießmaschine** f *linotype* **~schaltung** f ⟨comp⟩ *form spacing*; dreifache ~ *three different line-sp.g* **~schinderei** f *penny-a-lining* | 625 **~standard** m ⟨telv⟩ *625-line standard* **~stellhebel** m *adjustable spacing lever* **~vorschub** m ⟨comp⟩ *line spacing* **~wahl** f ⟨comp⟩ *automatic pre-determined sp.g of each line of print* ≗**weise** adv *by the line, line for line* **~zittern** n ⟨telv⟩ *bounce* **..zeilig** a; vier~ *four-lined*

Z·eisig m ~(e)s/~e ⟨orn⟩ *siskin, greenfinch* || ⟨fig⟩ lockerer ~ *loose fish, sad dog* ≗**grün** a *canary-green*

Zeit f ~/~en **A. 1.** *time* ⟨a. mus⟩ || (⟨Am⟩ v 15 z 15°: *Eastern, Central, Mountain, Pacific time*) || Echt≗ *real-t.* ⟨a. comp⟩; Einheits≗ *legal t.*; Ortsstern≗ *local sidereal t.*; fahrplanmäßige ~ *scheduled t.*; mittlere ~ v G. *Greenwich M-T.* **2.** (~abschnitt) *period* ⟨a. med⟩, *time*, *epoch, age; term* || *days* pl (*the fashion of those d.; his London d.*) **3.** (~punkt) ihre ~ *her time* (*of delivery*) || *date* (*up to d., to fix a d., at an early d.*) **4.** ⟨gram⟩ (*past, present, future*) *tense* **B. [im nom]** die ~, bis ein Befehl durchdringt *the t. required for an order to get down through channels* || die ~ enteilte *or* floh nur so *time sped* || **als** die ~ **erfüllet war** *in the fullness of time* || d. ~ erlaubt es nicht, fliegt *t. forbids, flies* || als d. ~ kam, daß sie .. *when the t. came for her to* (*return*) || d. ~ wird e–m lang *t. hangs heavily on one's hands* || s–e ~ läuft ab *his sands are running out* || d. ~ wird's lehren *t. will show* || **es ist** ~, ..! *t., Gentlemen, please*! || was ist die ~, welche ~ ist es *what's the t.* (auf Ihrer Uhr? *by your watch*)? || es ist jetzt (nicht) d. ~ f Kirschen *cherries are in* (*out of*) *season* || d. ~ ist um *t. is up* || es muß einige ~ vergehen, bis .. *it is bound to be some t. before* .. || d. ~ ist vorbei, da *or* als er .. *t. has gone by* od *was when he* .. **C. [adverb a]** (→ ⟨a.⟩ D.): **1. [im gen]**: jeder ≃ (aber: zu jeder ~) *any t.* s–r ~ **a)** (*he was* ..) *in his day* od *time*; die K. unserer ~ *contemporary art* **b)** *at one t., at the t.* **c)** (futurisch) *in due t., at a suitable moment* **2. [im acc]**: **a)** .. erst e–e (kurze) ~ *he had known her a very short t.* || e–e lange ~ *a long while* **b)** die (ganze) ~ her *or* über *during the whole t. ever since, all the while, all along* || e–e kurze ~-lang *for a little while* || lange ~ vorher *long before this* **c)** ≃ s–s Lebens *during every day of his life,* (*his*) *lifetime, all his lifetime*; *for the rest of his life* **D. aller ~en** *of all time*; *all-t.* (*record*) | seit ältesten ~en *from the earliest t.s* | noch einige ~ *some t. longer*; (*to wait*) *a little longer* | in der ersten ~ *during the first weeks*, etc, *in the beginning*, .. nach *immediately after* | seit **ewigen** ~en *from t. immemorial* | vor ewigen ~en ⟨fam⟩ *donkey's years ago* | in der folgenden ~ *in the following years*, etc | **freie** ~ *leisure*; (*spare*) *t.*; ⟨a.⟩ *odd moments* | in früher ~ *at an early period* od *date* || v den frühesten ~en an *from the earliest ages* || die ganze ~ *all the time,* ⟨Am⟩ *all along* || → gegeben, geraum, gesamt | vor **grauen** ~en *in days of yore* || es ist ~, daß ich *it is high t. for me* (*to go* od *that I should go*) | die **gute** alte ~ *the piping times of yore*; *the good old t.s* od *days* | harte ~en *hardships* | herrliche ~en h *to have a good t.* | es ist höchste ~ *it is high t.* (, daß du es tust *you did it*; *that I should go, for me to go*) | bei den jetzigen ~en *as t.s go* || in kommenden ~en *in the days to come* | **kurze** ~ ⟨a.⟩ *spell, flash, snatch*; f kz ~ ⟨fam⟩ *for a minute*; in [so] kzr ~ (*with*)*in a short t.,* [*at such short notice*], in kürzester ~ *in no t.*; nach kzr ~ *presently* | e–e **lange** ~ *for a long t., a dog's age,* sehr .. *donkey's years* || l. ~ hinter–e–a *for long at a t.*; noch l. ~ *for years to come* | seit **langer** ~ *for ages* || vor langer ~ *a long t. ago, a long way back* || die längste ~ ihres L.s *the greater part of her life* || in der letzten ~ *lately, of late* (*years*) | ach du **liebe** *or* m–e ~! *oh dear!, well, I never*! | .. der neusten ~ *latter-day* (*biographers*) | z rechten ~ *in* (*due*) *t., in season,* gerade .. *in the nick of t.* | schlechte ~en ⟨a.⟩ *a rainy day* | die schönste ~ verpassen *to miss the best t.* | schwere ~ *hard t.s* || vor *or* seit undenklichen ~en *t. out of mind* | verkehrsschwache (-starke) ~ *slack* (*busy*) *hours* | noch **viel** ~! *heaps of t.!*; (ein) wenig ~ (*a*) *little t.* | wahre ~ *solar* od *apparent t.* | wertvolle ~ (*waste of*) *t. otherwise valuable than that of drowsy bureaucrats* **E.** es ist *or* wäre **an der** ~ *t. has come, it is* (*about*) *time* (*to act*) (, daß ich ginge *for me to go* od *that I should go*) | das ist nicht mehr an der ~ *the right t. for that is now past* || wieviel ist es an der ~? *what's the t.*? || früh an der ~ *early* || (es ist) zw 4 u $^1/_2$5 an d. ~ *between 4 and half-past*; ⟨so⟩: *from 2 to h.-p.* | ⟨com⟩ **auf** ~ *on trust, term, credit, account* || auf ewige ~en *for ever and ever* || bis auf diese ~ *up to now* || auf unbestimmte ~ verschoben *postponed indefinitely* || noch auf *or* f einige ~ *for a little longer* | .. **aus** der ~ vor dem K. *this dates from before the war* | **außer** der ~ *untimely, out of season* || → beizeiten | **bei** diesen ~en *nowadays, as t.s go* od *are* | **durch** die ~ geheiligt *t.-honoured* | **hinter** der ~ zurück *behind the age* | **in** absehbarer ~ *in the foreseeable future*; in der (Zw.-)~ *in the meantime*; schon in d. ~ [+ gen] *as early as the t. of* ..; in der ~ e–s Monats, v 8 Tagen *within a m., a week*; in letzter ~ *of late*; in unserer ~ *nowadays, in this age* || in jener ~ *at the* od *that t.* || in der ~ der Kreuzzüge *at the t. of the c.* || in e–r ~ v Null-Komma-nichts *in* (*next to*) *no t.* || wir leben in e–r ~ der Unruhe *ours is an age of u.* || sich in die ~ schicken *to comply with the t.s, to temporize* | **mit** der ~ *in* (*the course of*) *t., in process of t.*; *with t., as t. goes on, in the end* (od *long run*); mit genügend ~ (z Verfügung) *given t.* || mit der ~ (nicht) mitgehen *to keep pace with the t.s,* (*to be out of time and step*) | **nach** einiger (geraumer) ~ *after a* od *some t.* (*after a considerable interval*); nach e–r ~ v 20 M. *after 20 minutes' t.*; er hielt schon nach kurzer ~ an *he wasn't long in stopping, he soon stopped*; nach ~ entwickeln ⟨phot⟩ *to develop t.* | **seit** der ~ *since that t.*; (bis heute) *ever since* || seit einiger ~ *for some t. past* || seit langer *or* längerer ~ *for a long t.,* ⟨emph⟩ *for ages* | **über** [acc]: (*it is now* [= schon] *a week*) *past the t.*; *beyond one's t.* || sich über e–e lange ~ erstreckend *secular* | **um** welche ~? *at what t.*?, *when*?; um diese ~ des J.s *about this t. of year*; morgen um diese ~ *this t. to-morrow*; um die ~ der Ernte *about harvest-t.* | **von** ~ z ~ *from t. to t.*; *t. and again*; (*every*) *now and then, occasionally, at intervals*; *by fits* (*and starts*); *at one t. or another*; (*to make*) *periodical* (*visits*); **vor** der ~ *before the t.* | → vorzeiten || **vor** einiger (kurzer) ~ *some* (od *a short*) *t. ago*; vor langer ~ ⟨a.⟩ *long ago*; vor noch nicht l. ~ ⟨a.⟩ *not so long back* | **während** der ~ *during that t., in the meantime*; während der (ganzen) ~ (*all*) *the while*; .., daß *whilst* | **zu** ~en *sometimes, at t.s, now and then* || zu allen ~en, z jeder ~ *at any t., in and out of season, always* || z der ~, als *or* da .. (*at the t.*) *when* (*I was born*) || z e–r ~, deren sich einige erinnern *within the memory of some people* || z gegebener ~ *at one time or other* || noch z gehöriger ~ *in proper t.* || z gleicher ~ *at the same t., simultaneously* || *in normal t.s* || z m–r ~ *in my t.* od *day* || alles z s–r ~ *all in good t.*; alles wird z s–r ~ erledigt w *all will be done in t.*; z allen (Jahres)~en *in and out of season* || z ungelegener ~ *at the wrong t.* | **bis z** dieser ~ *by that t.* | **zur** ~ *at present, for the time being*; genau .. *punctually to t.* || zur rechten ~ k *to come in well*; noch eben zur ~ k *to cut it fine*; zur gegebenen ~ (dann) *at the t.* || zur ~ [gen] *in the t.* od *days of* || (noch) z ~ k *to be* (*just* od *still*) *in* (⟨Am⟩ *on*) (*good*) *t.* || gerade z (rechten) ~ *in the nick of time* (z Essen *for dinner*), *opportunely*; er hustet immer z unrechten ~ *he times his coughs ill* **F.** die ~ **abstoppen** *to time* || die ~ f etw aufbringen *to spare the t. for a th* || ⟨fam⟩ e–e ~ ausmachen *to make a date* || die ~ sehr knapp bemessen *to cut it fine* || lange ~ brauchen z tun *to be a long t. doing*; *that house would take some* (*t.*) *selling* || schlechte ~en erleben *to come on bad t.s*; .. durchmachen ⟨a.⟩ *to have a thin t.* || es **fehlt** ihm d. ~ dafür, dazu *he has not* (*he hasn't got*) *t. for it* || d. ~ des Abgangs (v Befehlen) festhalten *to record the t. of dispatch* || e–e ~ festsetzen *to fix* od *appoint a t.,* .. f .. *to time* (*a journey*) || dazu ~ finden *to get round to it* || es gab ~en *there were occasions* || ~ gewinnen *to gain t.*; ~ z gew. suchen *to play for t.* || ~ gönnen = ~ 1 || (k–e) ~ h *to have* (*no*) *t.* || wir h noch ~ genug *we have plenty of t.* | das **hat** ~ *there is* (*plenty of*) *t. for that* || damit hat es gute ~ *there is no hurry about that, that can wait, that matter will keep*; *no rush*! || es hat ~ bis morgen *it need not be* (*done*) *until to-m.*; alles hat s–e ~ *there is a t. for everything* || es hat ~ (dauert noch lange), bis *it will be some t. before* || welche ~ h Sie *what t. do you* (*make it* [auf Ihrer Uhr *by your watch*] od) *have*? | jdm ~ l *to give a p t.* (*to do*) || sich [dat] ~ l *or* **nehmen** *to take one's t., to make small haste,* ⟨Am⟩ *to take one's good old time*; .. mit etw *to be long about a th*; sich 5 M. ~ l *to give o.s. 5 minutes' grace* || man muß sich zu allem ~ l *everything requires t.* || sich k–e ~ l ⟨a.⟩ *not to loiter*; sich ~ lassend *foot-dragging* || er hat die längste ~ gelebt *his race is run* || sich mehr ~ nehmen *to allow o.s. more t.* || ihre ~ war oft anderweitig in Anspruch genommen *there were many other claims on her t.* || ich will Ihre ~ nicht länger i. A. n. *I won't take up any more of y. t.* | die ~ schlug halb *the clock struck the half-hour* || die ~ steht nicht still *t. keeps going by* | dem Herrgott die ~ **stehlen,** s–e ~ vergeuden *to idle one's t. away, to dawdle* || wie die ~en stehen *as t.s go* || die ~ (schreitet fort *or*) vergeht *t. is getting on* || k–e ~ verlieren ⟨a.⟩ *not to take chances* || sich [dat] die ~ vertreiben *to pass the t.* || °die ~ vertrödeln, verplempern *to dawdle, dally, quiddle,* ⟨Am⟩ *to boon, doggle*; wir h k–e ~ z verlieren .. *no t. to waste* || sich die ~ verkürzen *to while away the time* || d. ~ aufs beste verwenden *to redeem the t.* **G.** ⟨**prov**⟩ **andre** ~en, andre Sitten *other t.s bring other manners* || ⟨bib⟩ ein jegliches **hat** s–e ~ *to everything there is a season* || ~ **ist** Geld *t. is m.* || ~ gewonnen, alles gew. *t. is everything* || **kommt** ~, k–t Rat *we will cross the bridge when we come to it*; *don't cross the river before you get to it, all in good t., t. heals all ths, never trouble tr. till tr. tr.s you*; *t. to decide, t. to decide*! || jedes Ding währt s–e ~ *there is an end to everything* | spare **in** der ~, so hast du in der Not *waste not, want not* | **mit** der ~ kommt man auch weit *many a little makes a mickle* || sich mit der ~ abfinden *to comply with the t.s* || mit der ~ pflückt man Rosen *all things come to him who waits* || alles **zu** s–r ~ *there is a t. for everything* || *it wouldn't have been possible at any other time* || wer nicht k–t z rechten ~, der muß essen, was übrig bleibt *last come, last served* **Zeit- ~abschnitt** m *epoch, period* **~abstand** m *interval*; in kurzen ~en ⟨a.⟩ *every little while* **~alter** n *age*; *millennium* (des Glücks); in jenem ~ *in those days* || neues ~ *new era* **~angabe** f *date* || ⟨wir⟩ *time-signal* || ohne ~ *without date, undated* **~ansage** f ⟨wir⟩ *timing* **~arbeiter** m *temporary worker* **~aufnahme** f ⟨phot⟩ *time-exposure* **~aufwand** m *sacrifice* od *loss, expenditure of t.* **~auslösung** f ⟨tech⟩ *t.-limit release* **~ball** m *t.-ball* **~basis** f ⟨radar⟩ *t.-base* **~bedingt** a *dependent on prevailing circumstances*; (außer Kraft) *lasting* od *meant only for a t.*; *not valid any longer* **~bedürfnis** n *needs of the t.* **~begebenheit** f *event* **~begrenzt** a ⟨eth, biol⟩ *specific* (*appetite*) **~behelf** m *temporary expedient* **~beschreibung** f *chronography* **~beständig** a *impervious to t.* **~bestimmung** f *fixing of the t., chronology, observation for t.*; ⟨jur⟩ *limitation of t.* **~bezogen** a ⟨comp⟩ *real-t.* [attr] **~bogen** m ⟨astr⟩ *arc of t.* **~bombe** f *t.-bomb,* ⟨fam⟩ *sleeping b., sleeper* **~buch** n *chronicle*; *annals* pl **~dauer** f *space of t., period; term* **~dehner** m *high-speed motion picture* **~differenz** f ⟨astr⟩ *difference of t.* **~droschke** f *cab hired by the hour* **~einheit** f ⟨phys⟩ *unit*(*y* ⟨theat⟩) *of t.*; *t. unit* ⟨a. med⟩ **~einstellung** f *t. adjustment* **~einteilung** f *division of t.* **~enthoben** a *t.less* **~ereignis** n *event* **~ersparend** a *t.-saving* **~ersparnis** f *saving* od *economy of t.* **~fern** a *ancient* **~folge** f *chronological order* || ⟨gram⟩ (mst ~enfolge) *sequence* od *concord of tenses* **~form** f ⟨gram⟩ *tense* **~forscher** m *chronologist* **~fracht** f ⟨mar⟩ *t.-charter* **~frage** f *topic of the day* || *question of t.* | (Arbeit), ein rechter **~fraß** m *loss of t.* **~freiwillige(r)** m *irregular* **~funk** m *topic*(*al talk*) **~geber** m ⟨comp⟩ *timing pulse generator*; *clock* **~geist** m *spirit of the age*; *zeitgeist* **~gemäß** a *timely, seasonable, opportune*; *down to date* || (modern) *up-to-date* (*apparatus*) **~genosse** m, **-ssin** f *contemporary* **~genössisch** a *c.y, contemporaneous, coeval* **~geschäft** n ⟨com⟩ *option business, t.-bargain* **~geschichte** f *contemporary history* **~geschichtlich** a *contemporary*; *period* (*dress*), *chronicle* (*play*) || [adv] *in its period* **~geschmack** m *prevailing taste* **~gewinn** m *gain* od *economy of t.* **~gleichung** f *equation of t.* **~glied** n *t.* od *timing element* **~grenze** f *t. limit* **~gruppe** f *t. group* N **~hafen** m *tidal harbour* **~karte** f ⟨rail⟩ *season-,* ⟨Am⟩ *commutation-ticket* || mit ~ fahren ⟨Am⟩ *to commute* | ~nbenutzer [m] *commuter, seasonal ticket holder* **~kauf** m *t.-bargain* **~konstante** f *t. constant* **~kontrolle** f (bis z Start) *count-down* ⟨a. a–n⟩ **~kundig** a *versed in chronology* **~kürzend** a *entertaining, amusing* **~lage** f *juncture* **~lang** f *spell* (*did a sp. of carpentering*) || e–e ~ *for a while, for some* (od *a period of*) *t.*; nur e–e ~ *only for a t.* | die **~länge** prüfen ⟨film⟩ *to time the script* **~lauf** m *course of t.* od *events* **~läuf(t)e** m pl *conjunctures* pl **~l·ebens** adv *for life*; → Zeit C. 2. c) **~lehen** n *temporary fief* **~linie** f *t. vector* **~lohn** m ⟨comp⟩ *daywork* **~los** a *ageless, dateless* **~lose** f ⟨bot⟩ = Herbst~ **~losigkeit** f *t.lessness* **~lupe** f *t.-retarder, -lense* | **~n-** ~aufnahme [f] *slow-motion picture*; im ~tempo [n] *in slow motion* **~mangel** m *want of t.* **~maß** n *measure of t.* || ⟨gram, pros⟩ *quantity* || ⟨mus⟩ *time, measure* **~messer** m *chronometer, timer*; ⟨mus⟩ *metronome* **~messung** f *timing*; *chronometry* **~nehmer** m ⟨sport⟩ *timekeeper, timer* **~ordnung** f *chronological order* **~pacht** f *lease for a certain t.* **~plan** m *schedule* N, *timetable* | ⟨soc⟩ *time-budget* | ~ung [f] *scheduling* ⟨a. comp⟩ **~punkt** m *point, moment, date* || günstiger ~ *opportunity* || ⟨hist⟩ *epoch* || z frühest möglichem ~ *at earliest practicable date* || ~ des Abtransports ⟨mil⟩ *shipping date* N; ~ der Einsatzfähigkeit, der Abfahrbereitschaft *readiness date* N; ~ des Eintreffens *t. of arrival*; bis z dem gesetzlich vorgeschriebenen ~ *within period limited by statute*; ~ des Inkrafttretens *date of entry into force, d. of application* **~quant** m (sehr kl ~abschnitt) ⟨commun, comp⟩ *epoch* **~raffer** m ⟨film⟩ *time accelerator, quick-motion apparatus* | ~aufnahme [f] *q.-m. picture* **~raubend** a *taking* (*up*) *much t., t.-consuming*; *wearisome* **~raum** m *space* (*of t.*), *period*; *t. interval*; ~ v 4 Jahren *a four-y. term* || übersehbare ~e [pl] *foreseeable periods*; in geologischen ~en gesehen *in geological terms* **~rechnung** f *chronology* || christliche ~ *Christian era* || Verstoß gegen die ~ *anachronism* **~reihe** f ⟨stat⟩ *t. series* **~relais** n, **~schalter** m ⟨el⟩ *t.-lag relay* **~rente** f *annuity* **~schrift** f *journal, periodical, magazine*; *review*; ~ aus Glanz-, Kunstdruckpapier *glossy m.* | **~en-** ~lesesaal [m] *periodical room*; ~schau [f] *digest*; ~schönheit [f] (Bild) *pin-up girl*; ~ständer [m] *m. rack* **~signal(kugel f)** n ⟨mar⟩ *t.-ball* **~sinn** m *t.-sense* **~spanne** f *t.-span*; ~ zw Ursache u Wirkung *t.-lag* **~strömung** f *tide of events*; *tendency of the period* **~tafel** f *chronological table* **~umstände** m pl, **~verhältnisse** n pl *times, circumstances* pl, *conjunctures* pl || bei den heutigen ~n *as times go*; *in the present state of affairs* **~verkürzung** f *t.-shortening*; (unterhaltend) *entertaining* **~vergeudung, ~verschwendung** f *waste of t.*; *dalliance* **~verlust** m *loss of t.* || ohne ~ *without delay, immediately*; kein ~ *no t. lost* **~verpflichtete(r)** m *temporary* **~verschiebung** f → Sommerzeit **~verschluß** m ⟨bes el⟩ *t. locking*; ⟨phot⟩ *t. shutter* **~vertreib** m *pastime, amusement* || z ~ *for am., to pass the t.*; sie tut es nur z ~ *it's just a passtime with her* **≗vertr·eibend** a *amusing, entertaining* **~verzögerung** f *t. delay, t. lag*; *t. element* **~-Weg-Diagramm** n *t.-travel diagram* **≗weilig** a *temporary*; nicht ganztägig *part-time* | adv ~ anwesende P ⟨stat⟩ *transient visitor*; ~ ausschließen *to suspend* (*a p*); ~ aussetzend *intermittent, periodic*; ~ einstellen *to suspend* (*hostilities*) | ~keit [f] *impermanence, -cy* **≗weise** adv (v Z. z Z.) *from t. to t., occasionally* || (f e–e gew. Z.) *for a t.* **~wende** f *turn of t.*; *new epoch* od *era* || vor (der) ~ *B. C.*; nach (der) ~ *A. D.* **~wort** n ⟨gram⟩ *verb* **~zähler** m ⟨tech⟩ *hour meter* **~zeichen** n ⟨wir⟩ *t.-signal, tuning signal*; ~ synchronisieren ⟨aero⟩ *to pip in* **~zünder** m (*variable*) *t.-fuse*, ⟨fam⟩ *sleeper* **z·eitig** a & adv *early* | ~ anfangen, aufbrechen *to get an early start*; (reif) *mature* ⟨a. med⟩ [nur attr] | [adv] (*to come*) *in good* od *due time* || (immer) ~ heimkommen *to keep early hours* **z·eitigen** vt [h] & vi [s] *to ripen*; *to mature* (⟨a. fig⟩: *plans*) | *to breed, occasion*; ⟨med⟩ *to bring to a head* || (Resultate) *to compass*; ⟨allg⟩ *to bring on*; *to work to* (*opposite ends*); *to give rise to* (*new works*) **Z·eitigung** f ~/ *maturation, seasoning*

z·eitlich a *temporal, temporary, worldly, earthly* || (zeitig) *early, timely* || das ≗e segnen *to depart this life* | [adv] ~ das erste *the first in date* || ~ abstimmen *to synchronise*; ~ einstellen *to time*; ~ festgelegt *periodic* || ~ feststellen *to time* || ~ nahestehend *close* (*in point of* od) *as to time* || ~ planen *to schedule* N

Z·eitung f ~/~en **1.** (*news*)*paper, journal* || (amtliche) *gazette* || → Schandblatt || (Teil) *sheet*; mit Trauerrand *black-bordered paper* | e–e ~ halten *to take in a paper*; f e–e ~ arbeiten *to newspaper*; was die ~ schreibt, was in der ~ steht *what's in the p.* || in die ~ setzen *to insert, advertise* **2.** (Nachricht) *news, tidings* pl || e–e angenehme ~ *a pleasant piece of intelligence* | **~s-** **~abonnement** n (**~abonnent** m) *subscription* (*subscriber*) *to a p.* **~anzeige** f *advertisement* **~artikel** m *n.r article, press-notice*; ⟨fam⟩ *item*, ⟨Am⟩ *story* **~ausgabe** f *issue of a paper* **~aushang** m *wall-n.r* **~ausschnitt** m (*press*) *cutting* od *clipping* (aus *from*) | ~dienst [m] *cl.g bureau*, ⟨Am⟩ *presscutting agency* **~beilage** f *supplement to a n.r* **~berichterstatter** m *n.r correspondent, reporter* **~blatt** n *single number* (*of a n.r*) **~deutsch** n *journalese* **~druck** m *n.r work* | ~papier [n] *newsprint* **~ente** f *canard, hoax* **~expedition** f *n.r office* **~frau** f *woman carrying about n.rs* **~händler** m *news-agent*, ⟨Am⟩ *news-dealer* **~inserat** n *advertisement* **~jargon** m *journalese* **~junge** m *n.r-boy* **~katalog** m *press-guide* **~kiosk** m *news-stall* od *-stand* **~mache** f *puff* **~mann** m (Reporter, Redakteur) *newspaperman* **~nachricht** f *n.r report* **~notiz** f *item* **~papier** n (f Druck) *newsprint*, (altes) *old newspaper* **~redakteur** m *editor of a n.r* **~reklame** f *n.r advertising* **~schreiber(in** f) m *journalist* **~setzer** m *news compositor* **~sprache** f *journalese* **~stil** m *journalese* **~träger(in** f), **~verkäufer(in** f) m *news-vendor* **~verleger** m *newsman*, ⟨Am⟩ *publisher* **~wesen** n *journalism, press*

Zelebr·ant m ~en/~en *officiating priest* **z.rieren** vt [h] *to celebrate* ([high] *mass*) **Z.rität** f ⟨obs⟩ ~/~en *celebrity* || (P) *p of note*; *celebrity*; ⟨fam⟩ *lion*

Zell- **~bruder** m *hermit* **~gewebe** n *cellular tissue* **~glas** n *cellophane* **~horn** n *celluloid* **~kern** m (⟨biol⟩ *cell*) *nucleus* **~kolonie** f *group of cells* **~stoff** m *cellulose*; (*chemical wood*) *pulp* | ~kocher [m] *c.e digester* **~wolle** f (Viskosefaser) *viscose staple fibre* **~woll-** ~trikot [m & n] *rayon staple fibre tricot* **Z·elle** f ~/~n *cell* ⟨a. ent, bot, anat, el⟩; ⟨el a.⟩ *element* || Gummi≗ (für Geisteskranke) *padded cell* || lichtelektrische ~ *photo-(electric) c.* || ⟨commun⟩ *quantum c.* || (*bathing-*) *cabin*; *foot-, arm-bath* || ⟨telph⟩ *cabinet* || (Wahl≗) *polling-box* || ⟨anat-dent⟩ *socket, alveolus* | **~n-** **≗artig** a *honeycomb type* [attr] **~bau** m *c. structure* **~bildung** f *cell-formation*, ⟨pol⟩ *formation of small groups* **~faser** f *cellular fibre* **≗förmig** a *cellular*; (raumsparend) *honeycombed* | ~keit [f] *cellularity* **~gefängnis** n *prison with solitary cells* **~gewebe** n = Zellgewebe **~kühler** m *c. radiator* **~lehre** f *cytology* **~rad** n *bucket-wheel* **~schmelz** m *cloisonné* (*enamel*); *cell enamel* od *work* **~teilung** = Furchung **~verglasung** f *colo*(*u*)*red glass passes* **z·ellig** a *cellular, cellulous* **Zelloph·an-**(Klebe-)Band [n] *cellotape*, ~(papier) [n] ~s/ *cellophane* **zellul·ar** a *cellular* (*pathology*) **Zellul·oid** [tseluˈlɔit] n ~(e)s/ *celluloid, xylonite*; *cellulose nitrate* **Zellul·ose** f ~/ ⟨chem⟩ *cellulose* | ~lack [m] *c. finish* od *lacquer*

Zel·ot(in f ~/~nen) m ~en/~en *zealot, fanatic* | **~entum** n *fanaticism* | **≗isch** a *fanatic*(*al*)

Zelt n ~(e)s/~e *tent* || (gr) *pavilion* || (Ausstellungs≗) *marquee* || (Indianer≗) *wigwam* || ⟨mar⟩ *awning* || ⟨bib⟩ *tabernacle* || → Zirkus || ~e aufschlagen (abbrechen) *to pitch* (*strike*) *tents* || in ~en *under canvas* **~ausrüstung** f *tent-equipment*; *t.age* **~bahn** f *t.-square*, (*tar*)*paulin*; ⟨mil⟩ *canvas* **~baracken** f pl *t.-barracks* **~bau** m *t.-pitching* **~bett** n *canopy-bed* **~bude** f *t.-booth* **~dach** n *awning* || *t.-roof* **~decke** f *awning, marquee* **~haus** n *pavilion* **~hering** m *t.-peg* **~lager** n *t.-camp* || im ~ *under canvas* **~leben** n *wigwam way of life* **~leine** f *t.-rope* **~leinwand** f, **~tuch** n *t.-cloth* **~pflock** m *t.-peg* **~platz** m *camp site* od *ground* **~stadt** f (Zirkus) *t.ed circus* **~stange** f *t.-pole* **~tür** f *t.-flap* **~wagen** m *wagon with an awning*; *baggage-wagon* **z·elten** vi [h] *to tent*; *to camp* (*out*) | ≗ n *camping*

Z·elter m ~s/~ *ambler, ambling horse* || ⟨archa, poet⟩ *palfrey* | ~gang [m] *amble, ambling-pace*

Zem·ent m (& n) ~(e)s/~e *cement* (abbinden *to set*) (*slow/quick setting c.*) | ~brühe [f] *slurry*; ~fabrik [f] *c.-works* pl [a. sg konstr]; ~kupfer [n] *precipitated copper*; ~ofen [m] *c.ing-furnace*; ~putz [m] *plaster of c.*; ~stahl [m] *converted* od *blister steel*; ~tiegel [m] *c.-crucible* | **≗·ieren** vt [h] *to cement* || ⟨met⟩ *to convert, precipitate* | **~·ierer** m ~s/~ *cementer* | **~·ierung** f ~/~en *cementation* || ⟨met⟩ *converting*

†**Z·endvolk** n (die alten Perser) *the Zends* pl

Zen·it(h) m (& n) ~(e)s/ *zenith* || im ~ *at the z.* ⟨a. fig⟩ || ⟨fig⟩ (Gipfel) den ~ erreichen *to reach the z.* | ~abstand [m] *z.-distance*

Zenot·aph(ion, -ium n ~s/~ien) n ~s/~e *cenotaph*

zens·ieren vt [h] *to review, criticize* || (scharf) *to censure* || (amtlich) *to censor* || *to license* (*books*) || ⟨school⟩ *to mark, certificate, report* **Z·ensor** m ~s/Zens·oren *censor, reviewer* | ~amt [n] *censorship* **Zens·ur** f ~/~en *censure* || *censorship* (*to impose c. on a th*) || *Board of Censors* || (Zeitungs≗) *censorship* || ⟨school⟩ *grade*; (Zeugnis) *certificate, marks* pl; (Tertialzeugnis) *report*; (Note) (*good, bad*) *mark* || der ~ unterworfen *censurable* **Z·ensus** m ~/ *census* (vornehmen *to take*)

Zent·aur m ~en/~en *centaur* ⟨a. astr⟩ | ~enkampf [m] *centauromachy*

Zent f ~/~en ⟨hist⟩ (Gau) *hundred* | *criminal jurisdiction* | ~ding, ~gericht [n] *hundred-court*; ~graf [m] *criminal judge* **~en·arfeier** f ⟨obs⟩ *centenary* **≗esim·al** a *centesimal* | ≗einteilung [f] *c.l division*, (f Thermometer) *centigrade scale*; ≗waage [f] *c.l balance* **Zenti-**

~f·olie f ~/~n ⟨bot⟩ *cabbage-rose* **~gramm** n *centigram* **~meter** n *centimeter* | ~maß [n] *tape-measure*; ~wellen- *centimetric* (*radar*) **Zent·il** n ~(e)s/~e ⟨stat⟩ *percentile* **Z·entner** m ~s/~ *hundredweight* (abbr *cwt*) **~gewicht** n *hundredweight* **~last** f ⟨fig⟩ *heavy burden* od *weight* (*off one's mind/heart*) **≗schwer** a ⟨fig⟩ *excessively heavy* || es lag mir ~ auf der Seele *it weighed heavily on my mind* **≗weise** a & adv *by the hundredweight*

zentr·al a *central* (*authorities, power, control, committee, bank, government, railway*) **≗abschnitt** m *waist line sector* **≗amt** n f Feindnachrichten *Central Intelligence Agency* **≗bau** m *c. block, rotunda* **≗behörde** f *c. authority* **≗einheit** f ⟨comp⟩ (*c.*) *processor* **≗heizung** f *central heating* | **~s-** ~anlage [f] *c. h.g system*; ~kessel [m] *c. h.g boiler* **≗kartei** f *master file* **≗komitee** n ⟨DDR⟩ *c. committee* (*ZK*) **≗n·ervensystem** n *c. nervous system* **~nerv·ös** a *of the c. n. s.* **≗punkt** m *centre* **≗r·ichtanlage** f ⟨mar-artill⟩ *firing director* **≗schärfe** f ⟨photo⟩ *c. definition* **≗schlachthof** m *town abattoir* **≗schmierung** f ⟨aero-mot⟩ *centralized lubrication* **≗sekundenzeiger** m *centre seconds hand* **≗speicher** m ⟨comp⟩ *core memory* **≗stelle** f *centre*, ⟨a–n⟩ *tracking center*; ⟨com etc⟩ *main office* **≗steuerung** f ⟨rail⟩ *centralized control* (*of signals*) **~symmetrisch** a *centrosymmetric* **≗uhrenanlage** f *electrical time-distribution system* **≗verschluß** m ⟨phot⟩ *inter-, between-lens shutter* **~wert** m ⟨stat⟩ *median* **Zentr·ale** f ~/~n ⟨com, telph⟩ *head-office* || ⟨el⟩ *central station* || || ⟨mar⟩ *control station* || ⟨mach⟩ *c.l power plant* || ⟨wir⟩ *c.l radio station* || ⟨math⟩ *line joining two centres* **Zentralisati·on** [–ts–] f ~/~en *centralization* **z-sieren** vt [h] *to centralize* **Zentri- ≗fug·al** a *centrifugal* | ≗kraft [f] *tangential force*; ≗maschine [f] **~f·uge** *centrifuge*; *separator* **≗fug·ieren** vt [h] *to centrifugate* **≗pet·al** a *centripetal* **~winkel** m *angle at the centre* **Zentr·ier- ~ansatz** m *spigot* **~blende** f ⟨phot⟩ *centering diaphragm* **~fläche** f ⟨phot⟩ *c.g surface* **~glas** n *c.g lens* **~maschine** f ⟨opt⟩ *centre-lathe* **~wulst** f ⟨artill⟩ *c.g band* **~zapfen** m ⟨tech⟩ *spigot*; durch ~ befestigt [a] *s.t-mounted* **zentr·ieren** vt [h] *to centre*, ⟨Am⟩ *center* **Z·entrum** n n ~s/–tren ⟨a. parl⟩ *centre*, ⟨Am⟩ *center* || ⟨com⟩ *emporium* || ⟨fig⟩ *navel*; *headquarters* pl || ins ~ treffen *to hit the bull's eye*; ⟨fam⟩ *to make a bull* || v ~ aus geleitet etc *centrally-controlled* **~bohrer** m ⟨tech⟩ *centre-bit* **~spartei** f *centre party*

Zent- [ts–] **~umvir·at** [–v–] n ⟨ant⟩ *centumvirate* **~uri·atkomitien** [–tsiən] pl *centuriate comitia* pl **~·urie** f ~/~n *century*

Z·ephalo.. *cephalo..* **~p·ode** m ~n/~n *c.pod*

Z·ephir, -yr m ~s/~e (⟨poet⟩ = milder Wind & ⟨com⟩ Stoff) *zephyr* **~garn** n, **~schal** m *zephyr* **~krepp** m *light crape* **~wolle** f *Berlin wool*

Z·epter n (& m) ~s/~ *sceptre* || (Amtsstab ⟨parl, univ⟩) *mace* || das ~ führen *to wield the sceptre* **~träger** m *monarch* || *mace-bearer*

zer-, **≗-** prefix, insep = *dis-* (*dismember*), *over-* (*overpress*); *asunder, away, to pieces*; *to spoil* od *destroy by* od *with* || [bei v/relf] *to extinction* od *death* **~·arbeiten** vt [h] ⟨a.⟩ *to crush* || sich ~ *to work* (⟨fam⟩ *fag*) *o.s. to death* **~b·eißen** vt irr [h] *to bite* (*to pieces*) || *to crack* (*nuts*) || *to crunch* (*bones*) **~b·eizen** vt [h] *to destroy with caustics* **~b·ersten** vi irr [s] *to burst* od *split asunder* **~beulen** → ein- **~b·issen** pp v –beißen **~bl·asen** vt irr [h] *to blow away* od *apart* **~blättern** vt [h] *to strip of leaves* || sich ~ *to exfoliate* **~bl·euen** vt [h] *to beat soundly, to thrash* **~b·orsten** pp v –bersten **~br·echen** irr vt [h] & vi [s] *to break, snap, shatter, smash* (*to pieces*) | vt (Glied, Knochen) *to fracture* | ⟨fig⟩ jdn innerlich ~ *to break a p up* | **sich** [dat] den Kopf ~ ⟨fig⟩ *to rack one's brains* (über *about*) || sich das Kreuz ~ *to break one's back* | [vi] *to go to pieces* || *to get broken* || *many marriages break up* | **~ an** *to fail owing to, to collapse* od *break on* **~br·echlich** a *fragile, brittle* || „~!" "*with care!*" | ≗keit [f] ~/ *fragility, brittleness* **≗br·echung** f ~/ *breaking, fracturing* **~br·ochen** pp v –brechen **~br·öckeln** vt [h] & vi [s] *to crumble* [vt]; (Brot) *to crumb* | vi *to fritter away* **~dr·ücken** vt [h] *to crush, squash, bruise* || = zerknittern || ⟨fig⟩ *to wink away* (*a tear*)

Zere·alien pl *cereals, bread-stuffs* pl || ⟨ant⟩ (Feste) *cerealia* pl L

Zerem- ~on·ie f ~/~n *ceremony, form*(*ality*) **≗oni·ell** I. n ~(e)s/~e *ceremonial, etiquette* II. ≗ a *ceremonious, formal*; *precise, punctilious*, ⟨fam⟩ *fussy* **~·onienmeister** m *Master of the Ceremonies* (*M. C.* ⟨fam⟩ [*em si:*]) **≗oni·ös** a = zeremoniell a || äußerst ~ s *to stand upon ceremonies*

Zerev·is [–v–] n ~/~ 1. *beer* 2. *student's* (*brimless*) *gala cap* | auf ~! *upon my honour!*

zer- ~f·ahren 1. vt irr [h] *to ruin* (*by driving over*) 2. vi [s] *to burst asunder* 3. [pp a.] *rutted, rutty* (*way*) || ⟨fig⟩ *inconsistent* || (P) *absent-minded, thoughtless*; *distraught, scatter-brained*; *flighty, giddy*; ~er Kerl *or* Mensch *harum-scarum* | ≗heit [f] ~/~en *inconsistency, desultoriness* || (P) *absent-mindedness, flightiness, thoughtlessness, giddiness* **≗f·all** m ~(e)s *decomposition*; *ruin, decay* || ⟨chem⟩ *degradation* || ⟨at⟩ *desintegration, decay* || ⟨fig⟩ *decadence* | ⟨at⟩ ~geschwindigkeit [f] *rate of decay*; ~produkt [n] *decomposition product* **~f·allen** 1. vi irr [s] *to fall to bits* od *pieces* od *into ruin* || *to collapse* || in Stücke ~ *to crumble to pieces* || völlig ~ *to go to rack and ruin* || (in so u so viel Teile ~) *to fall* od *divide into*; ⟨übtr⟩ *to fall under* (.. *heads*) || (verwittern) *to decay* || ⟨chem⟩ *to disaggregate*; ⟨pharm⟩ *to disintegrate* | ⟨fig⟩ (S) *to fail*; *the Empire broke up* | (P) *to fall out* (mit jdm *with a p*) || mit jdm ~ s *to be at variance* od *outs with a p* 2. vt [h] sich [dat] das Knie ~ *to hurt one's knee by a fall* 3. [pp a.] *wrecked, in ruins*; *dilapidated* (*house*); mit: *at odds with* (*the whole world*) **≗f·aserer** m ⟨pap⟩ *shredder, pulper* **~f·asern** vt [h] *to unravel*; ⟨fig⟩ *to analyse* | vt/i (Wollstoff) *to fuzz* **~f·eilen** vt [h] *to file down/through* **~f·etzen** vt [h] *to tear* od *hack to* od *in pieces* || *to shred* | ⟨fig⟩ *to riddle, maul* (*a theory*); *to mangle, mutilate*; ⟨hunt⟩ *to tailor* (*hare, bird*) **~f·etzt** *slashed* (*face*); *tattered* (*clothes*), [pred] *in tatters* || ~ aussehen *to look tattered and torn* **Z.zung** f *di*(*laceration*) **~fl·attern** vi [s] *to flutter away*; im Winde ~ *to be cast to the winds* **~fl·eddert** a *battered* (*book*) **~fl·eischen** vt [h] *to lacerate, mangle*, ⟨zoo⟩ *maul*; *to tear to pieces* || e–a ~d *internecine* (*war*) **~fließbar** a *deliquescent* | ≗keit [f] *–scence* **~fl·ießen** vi irr [s] *to dissolve, melt* || (Farben) *to run* || ⟨chem⟩ *to deliquesce* (dazu: *d.nce*) || ⟨fig⟩ *to diffuse out* (in *into*) || in Tränen ~ *to be dissolved in tears* | ~d *diffluent* **~fr·essen** 1. vt irr [h] *to eat away, to gnaw* || (ätzen) *to corrode* ⟨a. fig⟩ | v Rost (Wurm) ~ [pp] *rust-*, (*worm-*) *eaten*; (am Rande) *erose* | ⟨path⟩ *to canker* || ~d ⟨a.⟩ *corrosive* 2. a *fretted* 3. ≗ n ⟨tech⟩ *corrosion* **~f·urchen** vt [h] *to make deep furrows* od *wrinkles in* **~g·ehen** vi irr [s] *to dissolve*; *to melt* (*away*) || ⟨chem⟩ *to deliquesce* || (Nebel) *to disperse* || in nichts ~ *to dwindle to nothing* **≗gl·iederer** m ~s/~ *dissector, anatomist* || ⟨fig⟩ *analyst* **~gl·iedern** vt [h] (ein Land etc) *to dismember* || ⟨anat⟩ *to dissect* || ⟨gram⟩ *to parse* || ⟨fig⟩ *to analyse* || ~d *analytic* (*mind*) **≗gl·iederung** f ~/~en *dismemberment* || *dissection*; (lebender Tiere) *vivisection* || *analysis* || *breakdown* (v Zahlen) **~h·acken** vt [h] *to hack* (*to pieces*) ||

(Fleisch klein ~) to mince **⁓h·acker** m ⟨el⟩ vibrator; chopper; make-and-break (circuit) **~-hackt** slashed (face); ~es Eisen, Blei slugs pl **~h·auen** vt irr [h] to cut to pieces od asunder ‖ to chop up (a sheep) ‖ to cut (the Gordian knot) **~k·auen** vt [h] to chew, masticate (well) **~kl·ei-nern** vt [h] to comminute, crush; to reduce to small pieces, to break; ⟨cul⟩ to shred ‖ (Holz) to chop up ‖ ⟨min⟩ to break up, crush, pulverize (ore) **Z-rung** f ⟨tech⟩ crushing, reducing, etc **| ~s-** ~maschine [f] c.g (and grinding) machine **~kl·opfen** vt [h] to beat, knock, pound to pieces; (Schotter) to mash od break down (ballast) **~kl·üftet** a cleft; broken (country); ravined (pla-teau) ‖ riven, fissured **⁓kl·üftung** f cleft, cleavage; fissure **~kn·acken** vt [h] to break by cracking, to crack (nuts) ‖ to crunch (a bone) **⁓knall** m explosion **~kn·icken** vt [h] to break, crush **~kn·irscht** a contrite **⁓kn·irschung** f ~/ con-trition; remorse; repentance **~kn·ittern, ~kn·ül-len, ~kn·utschen** vt [h] to (c)rumple, crease, ruffle **~k·ochen** vt/i [h/s] to cook to rags **~kr·a-chen** vi [s] to burst with a noise **~kr·atzen** vt [h] to scratch ‖ to spoil with scratches ‖ to mar | sich **~kr·iegen** to have a row **~kr·ümeln** vt/i [h/s] to crumble; to crumb [nur vt] **~l·assen** vt irr [h] (Fett) to melt (-ed butter, → molten) ‖ to dissolve **~l·aufen 1.** vi [h] = –fl·ießen **2.** sich [dat] die Schuhe ~ to run down one's shoes **~l·egbar** a divisible ⟨a. math⟩ ‖ (Modell etc) detachable ‖ (f Transport) portable; ⟨tech⟩ constructed to dias-semble **~l·egen** vt [h] to take to pieces; to disjoin, disintegrate, undo ‖ dissect, anatomize; knock down ‖ to dissolve, decompose ‖ ⟨cul⟩ to cut up; (Braten) to carve ‖ ⟨tech⟩ to disassemble; to take apart; (Waffe, Wagen) ⟨a.⟩ to strip ‖ in zwei Teile ~ to divide in two ‖ ⟨mech⟩ to resolve (forces) ‖ ⟨geom⟩ to reduce (to triangles) ‖ ⟨math⟩ to factorize ‖ ⟨anat⟩ to dissect ‖ ⟨chem & fig⟩ to analyse; to crack (oil) ‖ (weißes Licht) in s–e farbigen Bestandteile ~ to disperse .. into its components of different wavelengths **⁓l·egung** f → –gliederung ⟨a.⟩ stripping (of an engine); division; splitting (of trains); ⟨chem⟩ breaking--off; ~ e–r S in ihre Bestandteile disassembly, taking-down; fractionation **| ~s-** ~wärme [f] heat of decomposition **~l·esen 1.** vt [h] (Buch) to read to pieces, to dog's-ear **2.** a well-thumbed; battered (book) **~l·umpt** a ragged, tattered ‖ [pred] in rags; ~er Kerl ragamuffin, tatter-demalion **~m·ahlen** vt [h] to grind, powder, pulverize, triturate **~m·almen** vt [h] to crush, bruise, crunch, bray ‖ = –mahlen ‖ ⟨mil⟩ ~d brisant **~m·artern** vt [h] to torment; torture (to death) ‖ sich das Gehirn ~ to rack one's brains **~m·ürben** vt/i [h] to wear (out od down), to crush ‖ den Feind ~ to grind the enemy ⟨bes mil⟩ ‖ (Nerven) to fray ‖ to prey on | ~d ⟨a.⟩ grinding ⟨a. fig⟩ **~m·ürbt** [pp, a] ⟨fig⟩ broken down ‖ torn (by) ‖ ⟨fig⟩ hag-ridden; jaded (nerves); ~ s to be all to pieces **⁓m·ürbungskrieg** m war of attrition **~n·agen** vt [h] to gnaw down ‖ (ätzen) to corrode ‖ ⟨fig⟩ to erode

zern- ~·ieren vt [h] ⟨mil⟩ to invest, blockade, besiege **Z.rung** f ~/~en ⟨mil⟩ i.tment, b.e, siege

zer- ~pfl·ücken vt [h] to pluck to pieces ‖ ⟨fig⟩ to slash, dissect, riddle; (bekritteln) to pick holes in(to) a th; jdn ~ to cut a p verbally to ribbons **~pl·atzen** vi [s] to burst (to pieces od) asunder ‖ to explode ‖ (Blase) to break ‖ (Glas) to crack; (bulb) to shatter ‖ ⟨fig fam⟩ (P & S) to bust up; to go phut **~qu·etschen** vt [h] to crush, bruise, (s)quash, jam; to mash (potatoes) ‖ (T) to swat **~r·aufen** vt [h] to dishevel ‖ to tear (a p's hair)

Z·err- ~bild n ~(e)s/~er distorted image; cartoon; caricature, ⟨fam⟩ take-off ‖ ⟨fig⟩ distor-tion **~linse** f ⟨phot⟩ distorting lense **~sichtigkeit** f astigmatism ⟨a. fig⟩ **~spiegel** m d.g mirror; > zerren

zer- ~r·eiben vt irr [h] to grind od rub to powder; to grind down; to bray, crumble, pul-verize, pound; triturate; ⟨chem, pharm⟩ to levigate

Zerr·eiß- ⁓bar a lacerable **~bolzen** m breaker bolt **~festigkeit** f tearing od tensile strength **~grenze** f ⟨tech⟩ break point **~maschine** f tension testing machine **~probe** f tensile test; [konkr] tension od tensile test specimen **~punkt** m ⟨a.⟩ snapping point ⟨a. fig⟩ **~stab** m test bar **~versuch** m ⟨tech⟩ tear test **~wolf** m (S) (f Akten etc) paper shredder

zer- ~r·eißen irr **1.** vt [h] to tear (up), to rend ⟨a. fig⟩, split, disrupt ‖ to break (a thread, a p's heart, one's chains) ‖ (Blüte) to mangle ‖ (viel Kleider) to wear out ‖ (Land) to distract, rend; (zerstückeln) to dismember ‖ (v wilden Tieren) to lacerate ‖ ⟨path⟩ to rupture ‖ e–m das Ohr ~ ⟨fig⟩ to grate upon a p's ear ‖ ich ließe mich eher in Stücke ~ I would rather be torn to pieces ‖ sich ~ ⟨fig⟩ to dart to and fro; sich f jdn ~ l to go through fire and water for a p **2.** vi [s] to tear, snap ⟨a. fig⟩; to be torn; to burst asunder ‖ (Faden) to break ‖ (Kleider) to wear out **Z-ßung** f ~/ rending, tearing ‖ dismemberment ‖ laceration | ~/~en ⟨path⟩ rupture

z·erren vt [h] to pull, tug (an [dat] at, bei by) ‖ to drag (in den Kot through the mud; to make a th lousy ⟨sl⟩) ‖ e–m die Kleider v Leibe ~ to tear .. off a p ‖ (Sehne) to strain ‖ (P) sich or e–a ~ to scuffle; → Zerr-

zer- ~r·innen vi irr [s] to dissolve, to melt away ‖ ⟨fig⟩ to vanish, dissolve, evanesce ‖ in nichts ~ to dwindle od fade away; to fall in a heap **~r·issen** a torn ‖ (zerlumpt) out at elbows od heels ‖ (innerlich) (P) distracted; disrupted (nation) | ~heit [f] ~/ torn condition ‖ (Zer-lumptheit) raggedness ‖ ⟨fig⟩ distraction, disrup-tion **~r·ühren** vt [h] to stir (to a pulp) ‖ to beat up (eggs) **~r·upfen** = –pflücken **~r·ütten** vt [h] to ruin ‖ (e–e Einrichtung) to disarrange, to disorganize ‖ (Gesundheit, Nerven, Finanzen) to shatter, disorder, disrupt, upset ‖ (den Geist) to derange, unhinge **~r·üttet** a (P) distraught; dis-tracted, unsettled ‖ (Gesundheit) broken, worn--out, ruined ‖ (Nerven, Finanzen) shattered ‖ in ~en Verhältnissen financially ruined ‖ ⟨fig⟩ ~ s to be all to pieces **⁓r·üttung** f ~/~en disorder; disruption; disorganization ‖ (des Geistes) de-rangement, distraction **~s·ägen** vt [h] to saw (to pieces od) through, up **~sch·ellen 1.** vt [h] to dash, smash **2.** vi [s] to be smashed; ⟨aero⟩ to crash ‖ (Schiff) to be wrecked, to split **~sch·ießen** vt irr [h] to shoot to pieces, to batter, to riddle with shot **~sch·inden** vt [h] irr to bruise; –schunden bruised **~schl·agen 1.** vt irr [h] to knock od smash to pieces, to break ‖ (P) ⟨fam⟩ to knock into a cocked hat ‖ (Angriff) to break up, (Truppe) to scatter, smash, neutralize; (Entwicklung) to cut across ‖ to explode (a myth, view) | **sich** ~ ⟨fig⟩ to be broken off, to come to nothing ‖ (Hoffnung) to be disappointed **2.** a beat (hand, knee) ‖ beaten down (by hail) ‖ (P) bruised; ⟨fig⟩ knocked out, cut up ‖ ich bin wie an allen Gliedern ~ I'm a rag, I feel knocked up **~schl·eißen** vi irr [s] to wear off **~schl·itzen** vt [h] to slit od rip up **~schm·eißen** vt irr [h] to dash to pieces, to smash **~schm·elzen** vt reg [h] & vi irr [s] to melt, dissolve | **~d** ⟨a.⟩ deliquescent **~schm·ettern 1.** vt [h] to dash to pieces; to crush, smash, shatter ‖ mit –rtem Leibe with every bone broken **2.** vi [s] to get shattered od smashed, ⟨fam⟩ to go to smithereens **~schn·eiden** vt irr [h] to cut up (in parts); to cut to pieces od through ‖ to slit (paper, film) ‖ in kl Stücke to shred ⟨a. cul⟩; (Fleisch) to mince, (bei Tisch) to carve ‖ ⟨fig⟩ e–m das Herz ~ to break a p's h.

~schn·itten a ⟨fig⟩ *intersected* (*country*) **~schr·ammen** vt [h] *to bruise* **~schr·oten** vt [h] *to rough-grind, bruise* **~s·etzen** vt [h] ⟨a.⟩ sich ~ *to decompose, disintegrate, dissolve*; sich ~ (moral.) *to dry rot* || ⟨chem⟩ *to disaggregate* | ⟨fig⟩ *to poison* | ~d *dissolvent, corrosive*; ⟨pol⟩ *seditious*; *fractionary* (*work*) **≗s·etzung** f ~/~en *decomposition, dissolution*; *disintegration* ⟨a. pol⟩; ⟨mil⟩ *subversion*; ⟨at⟩ *damage* || (moral.) *putrefaction*; *dry rot* || ⟨pol⟩ *sedition* | **~s-** ~prozeß, ~vorgang [m] *process of d., d., d.* **~sp·alten** vt [h] *to cleave, s(p)lit, rive* **~sp·alten** a [pp] *cleft, s(p)lit, riven* **~spl·ittern** vt [h] & vi [s] *to break into shivers*; *to split, shiver, splinter*; ([s–e] Truppen) *to disperse, scatter* | vi ⟨artill⟩ *to burst* | **sich** ~, s–e Kräfte ~ *to fritter away one's powers*; ⟨tact⟩ *to dissipate* **~spl·ittert** ⟨surg⟩ *splintered, comminuted* || ⟨parl⟩ *disunited*; *scattered* (*votes*) **≗spl·itterung** f *splitting*, etc; ⟨tech⟩ *fragmentation* || ⟨mil⟩ *dispersal*; ⟨tact⟩ (Kampfkraft≗) *dissipation* || ⟨parl⟩ *disunion, cleavage, disruption* **~spr·engen** vt [h] *to burst* (*into pieces*), *to blow up, to explode* | (Ansammlung) *to disperse*; ⟨mil⟩ *to rout*; ⟨mar⟩ *to scatter* **~spr·ingen** vi irr [s] *to fly to pieces* od *asunder* || *to snap, burst, explode* || (Saite) *to break* || (Holz) *to split* || (Glas) *to crack*; (of a bulb) *to shatter* || der Kopf will mir ~ *my h. is splitting* **~st·ampfen** vt [h] *to crush* ⟨a. mil⟩ || ⟨tech⟩ *to bray, pound, pulverize, pestle* **~st·äuben 1.** vt [h] *to reduce to dust, to pulverize* || (Parfüm etc) *to spray* || ⟨phot⟩ *to vaporize* | ⟨fig⟩ *to disperse, scatter* **2.** vi [s] *to fall to dust* **≗st·äuber** m ~s/~ *pulverizer* || (Flüssigkeits≗) *spray(er)*; *fuel nozzle* || ⟨cosm⟩ *scent spray, atomizer* || ⟨med⟩ *atomizer, vaporizer* || ⟨tech⟩ (Farb≗) *air brush* **~st·äubung** f *pulverization*, ⟨phys⟩ *atomization*, ⟨tech⟩ *scattering*, etc | **~s-** ~anlage [f] *sprays* pl; ~düse [f] *spraying nozzle*; ~scheibe [f] ⟨tech⟩ *spinning disc atomizer*; ~trocknung [f] *spray-drying* **~st·echen** vt irr [h] *to prick* od *sting* (*all over*); *to spoil by pricking*, etc || v Flöhen –stochen *flea-bitten* **~st·ieben** vi irr [s] *to scatter, disperse* (⟨a.⟩ P); *to vanish* | –stoben *scattered* **~st·örbar** a *destructible* | ~keit [f] ~/ *destructibility* **~st·ören** vt [h] *to destroy* ⟨a. mil⟩; (Geleise) *to tear up* || (Hoffnungen) *to blight, frustrate, dash, gut* || (Betrieb) *to disorganize* || (Blüten) *to nip* || (Glück) *to blast* | ⟨fig⟩ (Bild) *to shatter* | (vernichten) *to mar, undo, overthrow, ruin* || (verwüsten) *to devastate, ravage* | **~d** *destructive*; ⟨fig⟩ *subversive* (*views*) | **-rt** *ruined, broken* (*health*) **≗st·örer(in** f) m ~s/~ *destroyer* ⟨a. mar⟩; ⟨mar⟩ kl ~ *frigate* || ⟨aero⟩ *destroyer-plane, fighter* || ⟨fig⟩ *subverter* **~st·örerisch** a *destructive, vandal(ic)* **≗st·örung** f ~/~en *destruction, frustration*; *ruin, overthrow*; *demolition, wrecking* || gr ~en *great devastation, ravages* pl; ⟨path⟩ selbst bei ausgedehnten ~en *even if the organ has been destroyed to a great extent* | *fall* (*of Carthage*) | **~s-** ~angriff [m] ⟨aero⟩ *hit-and-run raid*; ~arbeiten f pl *demolitions*; ~feuer [n] *destructive fire*; ≗frei [a] *non-destructive*; ~geist [m] *spirit of destruction*; *subversive spirit*; ~kraft [f] *destructiveness*; ~krieg [m] *war of destruction*; ~trieb [m] *destructiveness*; *instinct of destruction*; ~wut [f] *vandalism* **~st·oßen** vt irr [h] *to bruise* || (im Mörser) *to crush, pound, bray*; ⟨bes Am⟩ *mull* | **sich** ~ (P) *to hurt o.s.*; (S) *to break* | sich **~-streiten** [h] mit *to get wrong with* (*a p*) || sich –stritten h mit *to be at odds with* .. **~str·euen** vt [h] *to scatter, disperse* || (Bedenken) *to dispel, dissipate, allay* || (Sorge) *to drive away* | **sich** ~ *to disperse, scatter*; (*of gas, smoke*) *to drift away* || (belustigen) *to amuse, divert o.s.*; *to seek diversion*; *to sport* || sich ~ l *to allow o.s. to be diverted* **~str·eut** a *scattered, dispersed* || *detached* (*farms*) || *loose* (*papers*) || *sparse* (*population*) || *diffuse*, ⟨opt⟩ *spread* (*light*) | in alle Winde ~ *scattered to the four winds* | ⟨fig⟩ *absent-minded, preoccupied*; *abstracted* (*gaze*); ⟨fam⟩ *wool-gathering* (*p*) || *rambling* (*thoughts*) || ~er Kopf, Geist, Sinn *wandering mind* || ~ w *to forget o.s.*; ~ s *to be lost in thought* | [adv] ~ (antworten) *abstractedly* | ≗heit [f] ~/ *absent-mindedness, abstractedness*; ⟨fam⟩ *wool-gathering* **≗str·euung** f ~/~en **1.** *dispersion* **2.** (Unterhaltung) *amusement, diversion* || sich ~ m *to amuse o.s.* **3.** = Zerstreutheit | **~s-** ~linse [f] ⟨opt⟩ *dispersive* od *negative, divergent, diverging lens*; ~literatur [f] *escape literature*; ~sucht [f] *dissipation*; ≗süchtig [a] *pleasure-hunting* **~st·ükke(l)n** vt [h] *to cut into pieces*; *to mangle* || (Land, Körper) *to dismember* || (Güter) ⟨agr⟩ *to parcel out, to partition* || (Text) *to dissect* **≗st·ück(e)lung** f ~/~en *dismemberment*; *spalliation*; *morcellation*; *morcellement* || ⟨fig⟩ *disintegration* (*of a p's works*) **~t·anzen** vt [h] *to wear out in dancing* **~t·eilbar** a *divisible* **~t·eilen** vt [h] **1.** (⟨a.⟩ sich ~) *to divide, separate*; *split* || (S) (zerstreuen) *to disperse* **2.** ⟨math, med⟩ *to resolve* || ⟨phys⟩ *to decompose* || ⟨fig⟩ *to analyse* **≗t·eilung** f ~/~en *division, separation* || *decomposition* || *analysis* || *resolution*

Zertifik·at n ~(e)s/~e *certificate* ⟨a. mar⟩, *warrant* || ein ~ ausstellen über *to certify*

zer- ~tr·ampeln vt [h] *to trample* (*under foot* od) *down* **~tr·ennen** = trennen **~tr·eten** vt irr [h] = –trampeln; *to stamp out, to crush* **~tr·ümmern I.** vt [h] *to break up*; *to smash, demolish, destroy, wreck* || ⟨at⟩ *to split* **II.** vi [s] *to break* **Z-rung** f ~/~en *destruction, demolition* || ⟨fig⟩ *wreckage* | **~s-** ~ladung [f] ⟨tech⟩ *breaching charge*

Zervel·atwurst f *saveloy*; *German sausage*

zer- ~w·erfen vt [h] *to smash* | sich mit jdm ~ *to quarrel* od *break with a p* **~w·ühlen** vt [h] *to root up* || *to rummage in* || *to dishevel* (*hair*) **≗w·ürfnis** n ~ses/~se *discord, disunion, difference, dissension, dispute, quarrel* **~würgen** vt [h] *to foul* (*a screw*) **~z·ausen** vt [h] *to dishevel, tousle, ruffle, rumple* || (Kleider) *to disarrange* || (jdn) *to pull about* **≗zaust** a *rumpled, touseled* (*hair*) ⟨a.⟩ *unkempt, untidy, shaggy* || v Winde ~ ⟨a.⟩ *wind-slashed, blast-beruffled* **~z·upfen** vt [h] *to pick to pieces*, etc

Zessi·on f ~/~en *assignment, cession, transfer* || *abandonment* (*of claims*) | **~·ar** m ~s/~e *cessionary, assignee, transferee* | **~s- ~akte** f *deed of transfer*

Z·eter n ~s/; ~ (u Mordio) schreien *to cry murder, to raise a hue and cry*; ⟨fam⟩ *to kick up a hullabaloo* || ~! *death*! *murder*! | ~geschrei, ~m·ordio [n] *outcry*; *cry of murder*; *yells* pl | **≗n** vi [h] *to brawl, to kick up a shindy* | *to storm* | (jammern) *to wail, lament* (über *about*)

Z·ettel[1] m ~s/~ ⟨weav⟩ *warp* **~baum** m *warp-beam* **~ende** n *fag-end* **~kötzer** m *warp-cop*

Z·ettel[2] m ~s/~ *ticket*; *slip of paper* || (*voting-*) *paper* || (Etikette) *label* (anbringen *to affix*) || (beschriebener) *note* || (Plakat) *placard, poster, bill* || ⟨theat⟩ *play-bill* || (Beleg) *voucher* **~ankleber** m *bill-sticker, -poster* **~ankleben verboten**! *stick no bills*! **~bank** f ⟨com⟩ *bank of issue* **~fahrkarte** f ⟨rail⟩ *leaflet ticket* **~kasten** m *pigeon-hole, card-index box, filing cabinet* **~katalog** m *card index* **~träger(in** f) m *bill distributor* **~wahl** f *ballot(ing)* **~wirtschaft** f *untidy note-slips*

zeuch! **zeuchst, zeucht** ⟨obs⟩ = zieh(e)! ziehst, zieht

Zeug n ~(e)s/~e **1.** *stuff* (Diebesgut & a. ⟨pap⟩); *matter* **2.** ⟨weav⟩ *material, fabric*; (Tuch) *cloth* || gewürfeltes ~ *checks*, seidenes ~ *silks* **3.** (Gerät) *utensils, appliances, implements, tools* pl || *pots and pans*; *crockery* || *dough*; *baking*

powder || ⟨hors⟩ *harness, trappings* pl || ⟨hunt, etc⟩ *equipment, nets* pl; *fishing-tackle* || ⟨mil hist⟩ *arms, ordnance* || ⟨mar⟩ *tackle* || ⟨pap⟩ *pulp* || ⟨met⟩ *ore; cast metal* || *type-metal* || gehendes ~ *machinery* **4.** ⟨fig dero⟩ ~(s) *things*, ⟨fam⟩ *concerns* pl || dummes ~ *foolishness*; kindisches ~ ⟨Am⟩ *kid stuff* **|** (Geschwätz) *nonsense; stuff* (*and nonsense*); das ganze ~ hat k–n Sinn *the whole th makes no sense* || tolles ~ treiben *to carry on mad pranks* || wertloses ~ *trash, trumpery* **5.** er **hat** (nicht) das ~ dazu *he's got what it takes, he is cut out for it* (*it is not in him*) || das ~ zum guten Soldaten *the nature of soldiers* || er hat das ~ z .. *he has the stuff for* (*an actor*) *in him, he has the makings of* ..; (P, die) das ~ zu e–m Star (hat) *star material*, ein Mann, der das ~ zum Pr. hat *a man of presidential timber* || jdm **am** ~ flicken *to pick holes in a p* **| ins** ~ gehen, sich ins ~ legen ⟨fig⟩ *to push along*; (⟨Am sl⟩ *to go jazz*); *to put one's back into it, to put one's shoulder to the wheel* od *one's hand to the plough* ⟨fig⟩; *to draw the bow up to the ear*; ⟨sport⟩ *to extend o.s.* || .. bei etw .. *to get one's teeth into a job* **| was** das ~ hält *as much as possible*, ⟨fam⟩ *with a vengeance* **~amt** n *ordnance department* **~baum** m ⟨weav⟩ *cloth-beam* **~bütte** f ⟨pap⟩ *pulp-vat* **~druck** m *printing stuff* || *cloth printing* **~drucker** m *calico-printer* **~druckerei** f *fabric print works* [sg konstr] **~fabrik** f *cloth-factory* **~handel** m *drapery-trade* **~haus** n *arsenal* **|** °~munie [f] (alter Offizier) ⟨mil sl⟩ *d'ugout* **~kammer** f *tool-room* || ⟨mil⟩ *armoury* **~kasten** m *linen-chest*, ⟨pap⟩ *stuff-chest* **~kiste** f ⟨typ⟩ *hell-box* **~meister** m *master of the ordnance* **~schmied** m *artillery-, tool-smith, edge-tool maker* **~schuhe** m pl *cloth* od *prunella shoes* pl **~ware** f *textiles* pl **~wäsche** f *scrub and wash clothes* **~weber, ~wirker** m *weaver of textile goods* **Z·euge** m ~n/~n *witness, deponent* || vor ~n *in the presence of w.es*; ~ der Gegenpartei *adverse w.* || ⟨rel⟩ *Jehovah's w.es* **|** (nur) tote ~n schweigen *dead men tell no tales* || z ~n aufrufen *to call to w.* (*to a th*) || jdn als ~n anrufen ⟨jur⟩ *to call a p into evidence*; als ~ aussagen *to w.*; z ~n nehmen *to take to w.* || ~ s *to be a w.* (*of a th*), *to be present* (*at a th*) || e–n ~n stellen *to produce evidence* **z·eugen I.** vt [h] *to engender*; (Kind) *to father* || ⟨demog⟩ *to reproduce; to beget* ([dat] *on a woman*) || ⟨zoo⟩ *to bring forth* || (Hengst) *to sire* ⟨a. übtr⟩; *to s. 90 children* || ⟨fig⟩ *to generate, breed, produce, to give being to* || die ≃den *the parents* pl **II.** vi [h] *to witness, to give evidence* **|** ~ **für** (gegen) *to testify* od *to bear evidence to* (*against*) **|** ~ **von** *to show, prove; to be evidence* od *proof of* **Z·eugen-~aussage** f *statement, deposition* (*of a witness*), *evidence, testimony* **~bank** f *w.-box*, ⟨Am⟩ *w.--chair* **~beweis** m *evidence* **~eid** m *oath of a w.* **≃eidliche** Vernehmung *examination of a sworn w.* **~gebühr** f *w.'s fee* **~stand** m *w.-box* **~verhör** n, **~vernehmung** f *hearing of w.es* **Z·eugin** f ~/~nen (*female*) *witness* **Z·eugnis** n ~ses/~se **1.** (Zeugenaussage) *statement, deposition, testimony, evidence* || beredtes ~ *eloquent testimony* (f *to*) || ~ ablegen (P) *to bear evidence, to attest* (*to a th*); (S) *to give proof* (*of*); .. f etw *to attest to a th* || ⟨bib⟩ falsch ~ reden *to bear false witness* (*against one's neighbour*) || zum ~ dessen *in w. whereof* || z ~ m–e Unterschrift *w. my hand* **2.** (Bescheinigung) *testimonial; certificate* ⟨a. med⟩ (ausstellen *to give*); Ehefähigkeits≃ *nubility c.*; Führungs≃ → *c. of good conduct*; Lufttüchtigkeits≃ *c. of airworthiness* || (Schule) *report, school-certificate, record-card*; schlechtes ~ *bad marks*; ~ der mittleren Reife ⟨m. m.⟩ *c. of general education* || jdm ein gutes ~ ausstellen *to give a p a good character* **~ablegung** f *deposition* **~brief** m *testimonial* **~verweigerung** f (**~zwang** m) *refusal* (*obligation*) *to give evidence*

Z·eugung f ~/~en *procreation, generation, begetting, breeding*; ⟨demog⟩ *reproduction* **| ~s- ~akt** m *progenitive act* **≃fähig** a *capable of generation; procreative* **|** ≃keit [f] *generative capability*; Periode der ~ ⟨bes demog⟩ *reproductive* od *childbearing period* **~kraft** f *generative power* **~organe** n pl *genital organs* **~schritte** m pl ⟨biol⟩ *filial relation* **~trieb** m *procreative instinct* **≃unfähig** a *impotent* **|** ~keit [f] f *impotency*

Z·ibbe f ~/~n *ewe(-lamb)* || *doe-rabbit*; → *Zippe*

Zib·ebe f ~/~n *Damask raisin*

Zib·et m ~(e)s/ *civet* **|** ~baum [m] ⟨bot⟩ *durian*; ~katze [f] ⟨zoo⟩ *civet-cat*

Zib·orium n ~s/–ien ⟨ec⟩ *pyx, pyxis*

Zich·orie f ~/~n *chicory, succory*; [attr] *ch. coffee*

Z·icke f ~/~n **1.** = Ziege; ⟨fig⟩ (ekelhafte Frau) *lemon* **2.** ⟨fig fam⟩ ~n m *to kick over the traces* || mach k–e ~n *don't be funny* **| ~n-** °~draht [m] ⟨teens⟩ *creep; lemon; spoil-sport; men seldom make passes at girls who wear glasses* **z·ickeln** vi [h] *to kid* **Z·icklein** n ~s/~ *kid* **z·icke-z·acke,** ~, hoi-hoi-hoi! ⟨ftb⟩ *rah! rah! rah!* **Z·ickzack** m ~(e)s/~e *zigzag* || **im** ~ *zigzag*; (im) ~ fahren, fliegen *to z.*, laufen *to* (*run*) *z.*, (Hase) *to double*, reiten *to caracole*, segeln *to tack about* **~bergstraße** f *switbacks* pl **~fahrdraht** m ⟨rail⟩ *stagger* (*of contact wire*) **≃förmig** a *zigzag* || ~ (an)ordnen *to stagger* **~-kurs** m ⟨mar⟩ *traverse* || ~ fahren = im Zickzack fahren **~profil** n ⟨mot⟩ (Reifen≃) *z. tread* **~rüsche** f ⟨tex⟩ *rick-rack braid*

Z·ider m ~s/ *cider* **~apfel** m *eleot* **~essig** m *cider-vinegar*

×**Z·ieche** f ~/~n *tick*

Z·iefer n ~s/~ [swd] *poultry*; → Unge≃, Ge≃

Z·iege f ~/~n (*she-*)*goat* || ⟨fig⟩ → Zicke **| ~n- ~bart** m ⟨bot⟩ (Pilz) *goat's beard* || (v Menschen) *French beard*, ⟨fam⟩ *goatee* **≃bärtig** a *goateed* **~bock** m *he-g.*; ⟨fam⟩ *billy-g.* || ⟨fig⟩ (Schneider) *snip* **~fell** n *g.skin* °**~futter** n ⟨cul⟩ *rabbit food* od *meat* **~haar** n *g.'s hair* **~hainer** m *knotty stick* (*as cut at* –hain *near* Jena) **~hirt** m *g.herd* **~käse** m *g.-cheese* **~leder** n *kid*; schwedisches ~ *suede* **~melker** m ⟨orn⟩ *g.sucker* **~milch** f *g.'s milk* **~peter** m ⟨med⟩ *mumps* pl **Z·ieger** m ~s/~ [bayr] = Quark(käse) *curds* pl

Z·iegel m ~s/~ (Dach≃) *tile* || (Mauer≃) *brick* || Luft≃ *air-b.* || ~ streichen *to mould t.s* || mit ~n decken *to t.* **~arbeit** f *b.work* **~bau** m *b. building* **~brenner** m *t.maker, t.r, b.-maker* **|** ~ei [f] = Ziegelei **~brocken** m *b. rubble* **~dach** n *t.d roof* **~decker** m *b.-layer, t.r* **~erde** f *b.-clay* **~form** f *t.-mould* **~mauer** f *b.-wall* **~mehl** n *b.-dust* **~ofen** m *t.-, b.-kiln* **~r·ohbau** m *rough b.-work* **≃rot** a *b.-red* **~stein** m *b.*, roher ~ *loam b.* **~streicher** m = –brenner **~werk** n *b.-work* **Ziegel·ei** f ~/~en *t. kiln, b.-yard, -kiln, -works* pl

zieh 1. & 3. sg pret v ziehen **Zieh-** (→ a. Zug-) **~arm** m *crank, handle* **~band** n ⟨tech⟩ *iron cramp, band, hoop* **~bank** f (Büchsenmacherei) *rifling-bench, -machine* || (Drahtzieherei) *wire--drawing bench* **~brücke** f *drawbridge* **~brunnen** m *draw-well*; ⟨Eg⟩ *shādūf* **~eisen** n *wire-drawing plate* **~fenster** n *sash-window* **~garn** n ⟨hunt⟩ *draw-net* **~geld** n *charges* pl *for nursing* **~harmonika** f *accordion, concertina* **|** ~wirkung [f] ⟨mot etc⟩ (e–r Kolonne) *harmonica effect* **~hund** m *cart-dog* **~kartei** f ⟨comp⟩ *pulling* od *tub file* **~kind** n *foster-child* **~klimmen** n *climbing with the aid of one's hands only* **~kloben** m ⟨tech⟩ *pulley* **~knoten** m *bowknot, slipknot* **~kraft** f *traction power*; ⟨fig⟩ = Zugkraft **~leine** f *draw--line, towing-rope* **~maschine** f *wire-drawing machine* **~mutter** f *foster-mother* **~pflaster** n *blister, vesicatory* **~säge** f *jack-saw* **~schacht** m ⟨min⟩ *working-shaft* **~seil** n *towing-rope* **~stange** f *rifling-rod* ‖ *pump gear, (well) sweep* **~tag** m *moving day* **~vater** m *foster-father* **~weg** m *towing-path* **~werk** n *engine for hauling* ‖ *wire--drawing shop* **~zange** f *pliers, nippers*; ⟨med⟩ *forceps* **z·iehen** [zog/gezogen] **I.** vt [h] **A. 1.** *to draw* (*a carriage, a card, water, the sword, lots, a blank*, etc) (*he drew the child to him heartily*) ‖ *to pull* (*one's hat over one's eyes, a glove on one's hand, a man in a rickshaw*); *to give* (*a th*) *a* (*strong*) *pull* **2.** ⟨chess, etc⟩ *to move* **B.** (gleitend) *she slid the letter from the envelope* ‖ (heftig, schleppend) *to drag* (*a p with one, the coat closely round one, a p into the court*) ‖ ⟨fam⟩ *to tug* ‖ (schnell) *to whip* (*out of*) **|** stramm|–, fest|~ *to tighten* **C. groß** ~ *to bring up, to rear* (*a child*) ‖ *to grow, cultivate* (*plants*); *to raise* (*plants from layers*, ⟨a.⟩ Gemüse) ‖ *to rear* (*trees*) ‖ *to rear, breed* (*cattle*) **D.** (die **Bilanz**) *to make up, to strike* ‖ ⟨med⟩ (Blasen) *to raise* ‖ (Boote) *to tow, haul* ‖ **(Draht)** *to draw*; ⟨telg⟩ *to stretch*; °Draht ~ *to decamp*, → ab|hauen ‖ (Flachs) *to pull*; durch die Hechel *to hackle* ‖ (Fratzen) *to make* ‖ ⟨agr⟩ (Furchen) *to make* ‖ (Geld) *to draw* (*m. from a bank*) ‖ viel Geld ~ aus *to make a great deal of m. by* ‖ (Gesichter) *to make, pull*; das G. in Falten ~ *to frown* ‖ (Gewehrläufe etc) *to rifle*; gezogenes Rohr *rifled barrel* ‖ (Gewinn) ~ aus, v *to derive .. from* ‖ Glocke → Schelle ~ ‖ (e–n Graben) *to dig*, ⟨mil a.⟩ *to throw up* ‖ (Haar) *his hair was trained back* ‖ (den Hut) *to take off*, vor jdm *to raise .. to a p* ‖ Kerzen → Lichte ~ ‖ (Korken) ~ aus *to take .. out of* ‖ ich muß die Konsequenzen daraus ~ *I must take the c.s of it* ‖ (Kreis) *to describe* ‖ den kürzeren ~ *to get the worst of it, to come off the loser* (*badly*) ‖ (Lasten hoch|~) *to haul* ‖ e–e Lehre ~ aus *to take a lesson from* (*it*) ‖ **(Lichte)** *to dip*; gezogene Lichte *dip candles* ‖ (Linien) *to draw* ‖ (Mauern) *to build* ‖ ein schiefes Maul ~ *to put on a wry face* ‖ ⟨met⟩ *to draw out* ‖ Narben ~ *to grain leather* ‖ (e–e Niete) → A. 1. ‖ (Nutzen) → Gewinn ~ ‖ (Obst) *to train* (*wall-trees*, etc) ‖ (die Schelle) *to pull, ring* ‖ **(Schiff)** *to tow* ‖ (Schleppnetze) *to drag* ‖ (Schlüsse) *to draw* (aus *from*) ‖ (Schnur) *to lace* (*through*) ‖ (Schrauben) *to extract* ‖ (die Senkrechte) *to draw, drop, erect* ‖ (e–n Strich) *to draw*, am Rande *to run a line down the page*; ⟨fig⟩ unter *to draw the line at* (*a th*) ‖ (Vergleiche) *to make, draw* (zw *between*) ‖ (Vorteil) → Gewinn ~ ‖ (Wagen) *to draw*; leicht z ~ *of easy draught* ‖ **(Wasser)** → A. 1.; *the sun sucks up w.*; *the ship leaks*; *the shoes let in w.* ‖ (e–n Wechsel) *to draw* ‖ (Worte) *to drawl* ‖ (Zähne) *to extract* ‖ (Zäune etc) *to erect, build* **E. an**: *to clasp a p to one's breast*; *to drag a p by the arm, to pluck a p by the sleeve, to pull a p's hair* ‖ ans Land ~ ⟨mar⟩ *to haul .. ashore* ‖ ⟨fig⟩ ans Licht ~ *to bring .. to light* ‖ an demselben Seil ~ *to play the same game* ‖ an sich ~ *to attract, collect, absorb, monopolize*; (P) *to win over to one's side* **| auf** Draht ~ *to file*, auf Fäden ~ *to thread*, auf Flaschen ~ *to bottle* ‖ auf s–e Seite ~ = an sich ~ (P) ‖ ⟨com⟩ auf jdn ~ *to draw a bill on a p* ‖ auf sich ~ *to attract* (alle[r] Augen *universal attention*) ‖ etw auf sich ~ *to call down on o.s.*, die Augen der Öffentlichkeit .. *to catch, attract the public eye* ‖ das fdl. Feuer *to draw the enemy's fire* ‖ Saiten auf e–e Geige ~ *to string a v.* **| aus**: *he pulled a pipe, tore whipped a knife out of* od *from his pocket*; vgl B.; *to take the cork out of a bottle* ‖ Geld, Gewinn → D. ‖ aus allem Vorteil ~ *to turn everything to account* ‖ aus–e–a ~ *to pull asunder*, (Gummi) *to draw out* ‖ sich [dat] aus etw e–e Lehre ~ *to take a th to heart* ‖ wie aus dem Wasser gezogen *drenched* **| durch**: *to pass a lace through an eyelet* ‖ *to drag .. through the mud* ⟨a. fig⟩ **|** jdn **hinein**|~ *to involve a p* (*in a th*) **| in** (vgl durch) ‖ in Betracht, Erwägung ~ *to take .. into consideration* ‖ ins Geheimnis ~ *to take .. into the s.* ‖ in die Höhe ~ *to pull up, to hoist* ‖ (ein Volk) in den Krieg ~ *to plunge .. into war* ‖ mit in den Krieg gezogen w *to drift into war* ‖ ins Lächerliche ~ *to ridicule* ‖ in die Länge ~ *to protract, prolong* ‖ in sich ~ *to imbibe* ‖ e–n ins Unglück ~ *to involve a p in m.*, ⟨fam⟩ *to drag a p in* ‖ in Verdacht ~ *to suspect* ‖ ins Vertrauen ~ *to take .. into confidence* ‖ in Zweifel ~ *to question, doubt* **| nach** sich ~ ⟨fig⟩ *to bring about*; *to cause, entail, involve*; *to have* (*serious consequences*) **| über**: *to put on one dress over another*; *to pull one's hat over one's eyes*; *to draw a veil over, to stretch a wire across a th* ‖ e–m das Fell über die Ohren ~ *to fleece a p* **| unter**: *she tucked her hind legs under her* **| von**: (→ Leder) ‖ *to tear the mask from a p's face* = *to unmask a p* ‖ (Vorteil) → ~ aus **|** (e–n) **vor** Bericht ~ *to summon .. before a court of law* **| zu** Boden ~ *to pull down* ‖ → Feld ‖ sich [dat] etw zu Gemüte ~ *to take a th to heart* ‖ zu Rate ~ *to consult* ‖ jdn zur Strafe ~ *to punish a p* ‖ jdn zur Tafel ~ *to invite a p to dinner* **II. sich** ~ *to extend* (a. Gebirge) ‖ (Stoff) *to stretch* (a. sich ~ l) ‖ (Linie) *to run* **| durch**: *to pass through*; *to run through* (*a book*); *one spirit threads the whole* ‖ *she was drawing a comb through her hair* **| in**: *to penetrate* bzw *soak into* ‖ sich in die Länge ~ *to drag on* **| nach**: (*the socks*) *take the shape of* (*the foot*) ‖ (P) *to move to a place* ‖ sich (**zu** Fäden) ~ *to go to threads, to be ropy* **III.** vi **A.** [h] ⟨chess, etc⟩ *to move* ‖ ⟨stud sl⟩ *to drink* ‖ ~, wer gibt ⟨cards⟩ *to draw for deal* ‖ (Gewicht) *to turn the scale* ‖ (Ofen, Tee, Zigarre) *to draw* ‖ (Schraubenzieher) *to bite* ‖ (= Käufer, Besucher anlocken) *to draw customers, a large audience*; *to be* od *prove a success* ‖ (= Gewicht h) *to weigh* ⟨fig⟩ (bei *with*); ⟨fam⟩ *these excuses don't go down with me* **|** nicht ~ ⟨mot⟩ *to be slipping*; ⟨fig⟩ *this ad has no pull* **| ~ lassen** ⟨cul⟩ *to macerate*; (bei 100°) *to simmer*; (unter 100°) *to coddle*; *to let the coffee draw* (*thorougly*) **| | es zieht** hier *there's a draught here* ‖ es zieht mir im Knie *I have pains in ..* **| | ~ an** [dat] *to pull* od *tug at*; ‖ *to wrench at* (*a chain*) ‖ *to drag* (*a cart*) ‖ ⟨mar⟩ *to haul at* (*the ropes*) ‖ *to puff at* (*a cigar*) **| mit**: ⟨chess⟩ *to move* (*the queen*) **| von**: → Leder **B.** [s] **1.** *to advance* (*slowly*), *to migrate* **2.** (marschieren) *to move on*; *to march, go, draw* (*toward*) **|** gezogen k *to come along* ‖ laß mich ~! *let me go!* **3. durch**: *to pass through* **| hinter** jdm her ~ *to trail* od *troop after a p* **| in**: *we all trooped into the dining-room* ‖ in die Fremde ~ *to go abroad* ‖ in den Kampf ~ *to march to battle* ‖ in den Krieg ~ *to go to* (*the*) *war* **|** der Herbst zog ins Land *autumn was upon the land* **| (mit** Wagen) *to trek* ‖ **nach**: (Gewitter etc) *to pass over to* ‖ in Schwärmen ~ nach *to swarm to* ‖ nach Hause ~ *to make for home* ‖ nach Süden ~ ⟨orn⟩ *to be bound for the south* ‖ übers Meer ~ *to cross the sea* **4. (Wohnung wechseln)** *to move, quit* ‖ aufs Land ~ *to remove to the c.* ‖ in: *to move into* (*a house*), *to go to live in* (*the town*) ‖ in ein anderes Zimmer ~ *to change one's room* ‖ v Ort z Ort ~ *to move about* ‖ zu jdm ~ *to take lodgings with a p* **5. (v. Dienstboten)** *to go out of service* **IV.** ≈ n (→ I. A. 1.) *drawing*, etc; *pull, tug* ‖ ⟨tech⟩ *extension* ‖ ⟨rail, etc⟩ *traction* **|** (→ I. A. 2. & III. A. mit) ⟨chess, etc⟩ *to move* **|** (→ I. C.) *cultivation, rearing*, etc **|** (→ III. A. Ofen, Zigarre) *draught* ‖ (Tee) *infusion* ‖ ⟨path⟩ *pains* ‖ (Anziehung) *attraction*; *attractiveness* ⟨a. theat⟩ **|** (→ III. B.) *march, migration*, ⟨orn a.⟩ *passage* **|** (→ III. B. 4.) *removal* **z·iehend** a ⟨path⟩ *griping* (*pain*) **Zieher·ei** f ~/~en ⟨met⟩ *drawing plant* **Z·iehung** f ~/~en *drawing* (*of lots, in a lottery*) **| ~s-** ~liste [f] *lottery-list*; ~tag [m] *drawing-day*

Ziel n ~(e)s/~e **A.** *aim* (*his aim is*) || (Scheibe) *butt, target* || ⟨mil⟩ *objective* (begrenzt *limited*) (⟨a.⟩ Angiffs≗), *march o., o. area*; ⟨aero a.⟩ *target* || ⟨sport⟩ *winning-post* || (Reise≗) (*place of*) *destination* | (Grenze) *limit, boundary*; (Schranke) *bounds* pl || (Zeitpunkt) *term* | ⟨fig⟩ *end* (*of one's life*), (*the highest ends*); *purpose*; (*final*) *objective*; *scope*; *view* (*with a v. to* ..), *goal* || ⟨pol a.⟩ *object* | **höhere** ~e *major objectives*; weitgesteckte ~e *distant o.s* **B.** ein bestimmtes ~ **abstecken** *to stake out a specific o.* || ein ~ ansprechen *to designate a target* || das ~ aufsitzen l ⟨mil⟩ *to put the foresight below the object aimed at* || ein ~ bekämpfen *to engage* od *attack a target* || sein ~ unbeirrt im Auge behalten *to keep one's objective firmly in mind* || ein ~ **erreichen** *to attain an end, reach a goal, obtain an objective*; das ~ erreichen ⟨Am fam a.⟩ *to make the grade*; das gesteckte ~ err. *to achieve the assigned* (*desired*) *o.* ⟨a. mil⟩ || sein ~ err. *to carry one's point, achieve one's object* || ⟨aero⟩ ein ~ fliegen *to reach one's destination* || jdn s–n ~n geneigt m *to bend a p to one's own interests* || halten → Maß || nur ein ~ kennend *of single purpose, singleminded* | [dat] ein ~ **setzen** *to set bounds, limits to*; *to put a stop to*; *to make an end of* || wir h uns vor allem das ~ gesetzt *our principal aim is* (*to do*) || sich ein (zu) hohes ~ setzen *or* stecken *to aim at s.th great,* (*to aim to high*) || das ~ treffen *to hit the mark* || das ~ überschreiten *to exceed the limits* || das ~ verfehlen *to miss the mark* ⟨a. fig⟩ || sein ~ verfolgen *to pursue one's point* **C. am** ~ s–r Wünsche s *to have attained* (*the object of*) *one's desires* || er war endlich am ~ *he had finally arrived* ⟨a. fig⟩ | **an** kein ~ gelangen *to get nowhere, not to get anywhere* | **ans** ~ gelangen *to reach one's goal,* ⟨Am a.⟩ *to get there, to win out*; ⟨sport⟩ *to get home* || vgl das ~ erreichen | **auf** ~ ⟨com⟩ *on credit* od *terms*; auf kurzes (3 Monate) ~ *at short* (*3 months'*) *date* || nur auf ein ~ gerichtet ⟨fig⟩ *single-minded* || auf dieses ~ hinarbeiten *to work with this aim in mind* || stracks aufs ~ losgehen *to drive straight to the point*; ⟨fig⟩ *to be single--minded* od *-hearted in one's aim* | **durchs** ~ gehen ⟨sport⟩ *to breast the tape, to cross the finishing line*; gleichzeitig .. ⟨racing⟩ *to come in neck and neck* | **ohne** ~ *aimless* | **übers** ~ hinaus *past one's mark*, .. schießen *to overshoot the mark* | weit **vom** ~ ⟨fig⟩ *quite beside the mark* | kurz **vorm** ~ geschlagen w ⟨sport⟩ *to be beaten on the post* | nicht **zum** ~ führen *to fail, miscarry* || ein Weg, der schnell z ~e führt ⟨fig⟩ *a quick way* **~abschnitt** m *section of fire* **~anflug** m *approach flight* ⟨a. mil⟩ **~ansprache** f *designation of a target* **~ansteuerung** f ⟨aero⟩ *homing* **~auffassung** f *t. acquisition*; *detection* ⟨a. radar⟩ **~aufnahme** f ⟨sport-phot⟩ *photofinish* **~auswanderung** f *target displacement* **~band** n ⟨sport⟩ *tape* **~beleuchter** m ⟨aero⟩ *path-finder* **~beobachtung** f ⟨mil⟩ *firing control* **≗bewußt** a *purposeful*; *steady, stable, single-minded*; *methodical* **~echo** n ⟨radar⟩ *pip* **~einweisungsposten** m *target director post* N **~erfassung, ~erkundung** f *target spotting* **~fernrohr** n *telescopic sight* **~findung** f ⟨aero⟩ *homing* **~flagge** f ⟨sport⟩ *chequered flag* **~flug** m *homing* | ~zeug [n] *target and drone* **~gebiet** [n] f zus–gefaßtes Feuer *concentration area* **~gerade** f ⟨racing⟩ *home stretch* **~gerät** n *optical sight*, ⟨mil⟩ *gunsight*; ⟨röntgen⟩ *spot film device* **≗gerichtet** a *subject-minded*; ⟨scient⟩ *teleological*, nicht ~ *dysteleological* **~geviert-tafel** f *target designation grill* **~karte** f ⟨artill⟩ *target map* **~kennzeichnungsrakete** f (f Bomben) *ground marker* **~landung** f ⟨aero⟩ *precision* od *accuracy, spot landing*; Anflug z ~ *p.n approach* **~linie** f *line of sight*, ⟨sport⟩ *finishing line* **≗los** a *aimless, purposeless*; *haphazard, random* [attr]; *erratic* || ~er Mensch *drifter* | ≗igkeit [f] *purposelessness* **~markierung** f *target indicator* | Schlag in **~nähe** f ⟨golf, etc⟩ *approach shot* **~ortung** f *target location* **~peilung** f ⟨aero⟩ *destination bearing*, ⟨fam⟩ *homing* **~pfosten** m *goal post* **~photographie** f *race-finish recording*, → –aufnahme **~punkt** m *goal*; *bull's eye, white* (*in a target*) **~rakete** f *target rocket* **~richter** m ⟨sport⟩ *judge* (*proper*) | Beobachtung in **~richtung** f ⟨mil⟩ *axial spotting* **~scheibe** f *butt, target* (⟨a. fig⟩; [gen] *for*) || ~ des Spottes *laughing-stock, fair game* **~schiff** n *target-ship* | ~schießen [n] ⟨fam⟩ *throw-off practice* **~setzung** f *aim, outlook, purport, purpose* **≗sicher** a *sure of one's aim*; *steady* ⟨a. fig⟩; ⟨fig⟩ *purposeful* | ≗heit [f] *accuracy of aim* **~kizze** f *target sketch* **~spiegel** m *aiming corrector* **~sprache** f (beim Übersetzen) *target language* **~stachel** m *foresight*; ⟨phot a.⟩ *peep sight* **≗strebig** a *purposive, resolute* | [adv] (*to work*, etc) *with a set purpose* | ~keit [f] ⟨a.⟩ *singleness* od *tenacity of purpose* od *mind*; ⟨bes eth⟩ *directiveness* **≗suchend** a *homing* (*weapon*) **~übungen** f pl *aiming drill* **~unterlage** f *datum* (pl *data*) ⟨a. aero⟩ **~vorrichtung** f *aiming gear*, ⟨aero a.⟩ *bomb sight*; (*rocket*) *launching rack* **~zuweisung** f *indication of targets*

z·ielen vi [h] (auf [acc], nach [dat]) *to aim, point* (*at*) ⟨a. fig⟩, *to take aim* (*at*); (mit ..) *to aim* (⟨artill⟩ *train*) *the gun* (*at*) || ⟨fig⟩ *to allude, tend, refer* (*to*); *to drive* (*at*) **Z·ieler** m ~s/~ *marker*

z·iemen vi & sich ~ [h] (für) *to become* (*to*) || es –mt sich f jdn *it behoves* (*to*) *a p* || das ziemt sich nicht! *that won't do*! || es ziemt sich nicht, daß du *it is not becoming for you to* .. **z·iemlich** [a] (passend) *fit, suitable, becoming* || (beträchtlich) *moderate, tolerable, middling, fair* | e–e ~e Anzahl *a good* od *fair number* || e–e ~e Menge *quite a few* || mit ~er Sicherheit *as likely as not* || ein ~es Stück *a considerable piece*, .. entfernt *a good way off* || e–e ~e Überraschung *somewhat of a s.* | [adv] *reasonably*; *pretty* (*often*); *tolerably* (*well*); (*natural*) *enough*; *rather*, ⟨fam⟩ *it hurts quite a bit*; *it took q. a long time*; *q. a b. late* || ~ umständlich ⟨bes Am⟩ *kind of awkward* (f *for*) | so ~ **alles** ⟨a.⟩ *anything after a fashion* || so ~ dasselbe *very nearly* (⟨fam⟩ *pretty much*) *the same th*; °.. in Grün ⟨fam⟩ *much of a muchness* || .. ist so ~ am Ende (*my patience*) *has just about come to an end*; so ~ ganz .. *pretty much* (*according to his fancy*) || ~ gr *siz(e)able* || ~ gleich groß s ⟨fam⟩ *to be much of a height* || ~ gut *pretty good*; *fair* || ~ **lang** etc; .. wo sie ~ lange verweilte *where she continued for a considerable time*; *we waited rather a long time*; *the best part of* (*10 miles*) || etw ~ Schweres *a tidy weight* || ~ sicher (*I*) *half* (*expected*) || ⟨fig⟩ ~ stark *more than a hint of* (*Irish accent*) || ~ **viel** *a good deal* (*of*) || ~ viele *a good many* || so ~ von m–m Alter *about my age* || ~ weit *a rather long way* (*off*) || ⟨Am⟩ *kind of* (*tattered*) || ⟨fig⟩ ~ weit entfernt v *a pretty far cry from* (*what is meant*)

Z·iemer m ~s/~ **1.** (Fleisch) *hind-quarter*; ⟨cul⟩ *haunch* **2.** *penis, pizzle, yard*; *whip*

z·iepen I. vt [h] **1.** (P) *to pull by the hair* **2.** (S) *to pinch* **II.** vi ⟨orn⟩ (piepen) *to cheep*

Zier f ~/~en = Zierde **~äffchen** n (Frau) = –puppe **~affe, ~bengel** m *fop, coxcomb, dude*; ⟨fam⟩ *swell, masher* **~beet** n ⟨hort⟩ *ornamental bed* **~drahtgeflecht** n (*gold/silver*) *filigree* **~druck** m *decorative printing* **~garten** m *flower-, pleasure--garden*, ⟨Am⟩ *dooryard* **~gärtner** m *ornamental gardener* **~gewächs** n, **~pflanze** f *ornamental plant* **~giebel** m ⟨arch⟩ *gablet, pediment* **~knopf** m ⟨bes tail⟩ *ornamental button* **~leiste** f ⟨typ⟩ *border*; *flourish, vignette* || ⟨carp⟩ *moulding* **~puppe** f (Frau) *affected* od *dressy little minx*; *dudine* **~rahmen(schild** n) m *scroll* **~rippe** f ⟨arch⟩ *surface-rib* **~schrift** f *fancy letters* pl **~schürze** f *fancy apron* **~stich** m ⟨tex, embr⟩ *ornamental stitch* **~stück** n ⟨typ⟩ *fancy-type* **~taschentuch** n *display handkerchief* **~werk** n *fancy-work* **Z·ierat** m ~(e)s/~e *ornament, finery, decoration* || (Tand) *baubles* pl || (Schnörkel) *flourish* || ⟨fig⟩ *honour* ([gen] *or* f *to*) **Z·ierde** f ~/~n *ornament* ⟨a. fig⟩; *decoration, embellishment* || ⟨fig⟩ *credit, honour* ([gen] *or* f *to*) **z·ieren** vt [h] *to adorn, decorate, grace, garnish; to be an ornament to, to embellish; to set off* | **sich** ~ *to behave affectedly, to give o.s. airs, to strike an attitude; to refuse from sheer affectation; to stand on ceremony* || (Frau) *to be coy, prim, prudish, affected, dainty* || sich (nicht) ~ *to put on* (*no*) *frills* || ~ Sie sich nicht! *don't be fussy!, come on!* | geziert reden *to mince one's words* **Ziererei** f ~/~en *affectation,* (*putting on*) *airs and graces* **z·ierlich** a *elegant, graceful, dainty, polite* || (hübsch) *pretty, neat, nice* | **~keit** f ~/ *grace* (*-fulness*), *elegance, daintiness* || *neatness*

Z·iesel m ~s/~, ~maus [f] *ground-squirrel*

Ziest m ~es/~e ⟨bot⟩ *hedge-nettle*

Z·iffer f ~/~n **1.** *figure* (⟨a. typ⟩ & der Uhr), *numeral* || römische ~n *Roman numbers* || Zahl v 4 ~n *n. of four digits* ⟨a. comp⟩ || (Kenn~) *key* (*number*) **2.** (Schriftzeichen) *cipher* (*to write in c.*[*s*]) **3.** ⟨jur typ⟩ *figure, subsection*; ⟨contr⟩ *item* || ⟨ad⟩ *box number* || ⟨demog⟩ (*divorce*, etc) *rate* **~blatt** n *dial*(*-plate*), *clock-face* || ⟨fig⟩ (= Gesicht) ⟨sl⟩ *dial* **~brief** m *letter in cipher* **~kasten** m ⟨typ⟩ *figure-case* **~(n)mäßig** a *statistical* || [adv] ⟨a.⟩ *by figures* **~(n)rechner** m *digital computer* **~rechnung** f *ciphering* **~schrift** f *code* **~(n)taste** f *amount key* **~telegramm** n *code-telegram*

..zig 1. [suff in 20–29 etc] || **2.** [abs] ⟨fam⟩ ~ andere *tens of others* || zig-mal → x-mal; *umpteen times* || '~ andere *tens of others* | **~er** [suff z. B.] Zwanziger *soldier of the twentieth regiment* || *wine of 1920*, etc || in den 20er Jahren *in the twenties* || ein Fünfziger *a fifty-pfennig piece; a man of about fifty years* (*of age*) || ein hoher Fünfziger *a man of nearly sixty years* | **~st** z. B. zwanzigst *twentieth* | **~stel** z. B. Zwanzigstel n *twentieth* (*part*) | **~stens** [adv] *in the twentieth* (*20th*) *place*

Zigar·ette f ~/~n *cigarette*; ⟨sl⟩ *fag* (→ Stäbchen, Spreizen) || sich e–e ~ drehen *to make a c.* | **~n-** ~asche [f] abschnippen *to flick the ash from a c.* **~schachtel** f, **~päckchen** n (*a crumpled*) *c. packet* **~spitze** f *c.-holder* **~stummel** m *fag-end*; ⟨bes Am⟩ *butt* **~tabak** m *tobacco for c.s* **~töter** m *extinguisher*

Zig·arre f ~/~n *cigar*, ⟨fam⟩ *weed* (leicht *light*, schwer *heavy*; rauchen *to smoke*; wickeln *to roll*; → ziehen III. A.) || ewig e–e ~ im Mund h *to be for ever puffing at a c.* || die ~n h k–e Luft .. *don't draw* || °steck dir 'ne ~ ins Gesicht ⟨vulg⟩ *shove that in your face* || ⟨fig⟩ ⟨mil sl⟩ *raspberry*; °e–m e–e (kalte) ~ verpassen *to give a p snuff; to haul a p over the coals,* (*to rebuke a p*); er bekam e–e ~ ⟨mil sl⟩ *he came a gutser* | **~n-** **~abschneider** m *c.-cutter* **~behälter** m *humidor* **~deckblatt** n *wrapper* **~einlage** f *filling* **~etui** n *c.-case* **~füllblätter** n pl *filler leaves* **~geschäft** n *tobacconist's* **~händler** m *tobacconist* °**~kippe** f ⟨sl⟩ *old soldier* **~kiste** f *c.-box* **~macher** m *c.-twister* **~spitze** f *c.-tip* || (Mundstück) *c.-holder* **~stummel** m *butt*(*-end*) *of a c.* **~tasche** f *c.-case*

Zig·euner m ~s/~ *gipsy*; ⟨Lit⟩ *Romany* **~bande** f *gang of gipsies* **~bursche** m *g.y lad* **~leben** n *g.y life*; ⟨fig⟩ *roving life* **~mädchen** n *g.y girl* **~musik** f *tzigane music* **~sprache** f *Romany, g.y-language* **~volk** n *gipsies* pl, *g.y tribe* **~wagen** m *g.y* (*cara*)*van* **Zig·eunerin** f ~/~nen *g.y-woman, -girl*

Zik·ade f ~/~n ⟨ent⟩ *cicada*

Zille f ~/~n (*small*) *barge*

Z·illertal n (österr.) **~er Alpen** *Zillertal Alps*

z·ilpen vi [h] ⟨orn⟩ *to twitter*; → schilpen

Z·imbel f ~/~n ⟨mus⟩ *cymbal*

Z·imbern pl *Cimbri* **z·imbrisch** a *Cimbrian* (*peninsula*); ~e Halbinsel [f] → Jütland

Zim·ier n ~(e)s/~e *crest of arms*

Z·immer n ~s/~ **1.** *room, apartment* (mieten *to take*; wir hatten uns ~ gemietet *we were in rooms* [*by the sea*]; im Hotel nehmen *to engage*); ~ [pl] mit voller Pension ⟨ad⟩ *rooms and board*; ~ mit Bad *room with a bath*; ~ u Frühstück ⟨hot⟩ *bed and b.t* || Wohnung mit 4 ~n *four-roomed flat* || (un)möblierte ~ (*un*)*furnished rooms* pl || ~ mit 2 Betten *two-bedded room* || ~ nach vorn (hinten) *front* (*back*) *room* **2.** ⟨arch⟩ *timber* | ⟨com⟩ *bale of forty skins* **~antenne** f *indoor aerial* **~arbeit,** **~axt** f *carpenter's work, c.'s axe* **~bekleidung** f *wainscotting* **~büchse** f *saloon rifle* **~decke** f *ceiling* **~dekoration** f *upholstery*; ⟨theat⟩ *chamber* (⟨Am⟩ *interior*) *set* **~einrichtung** f *furnishing* || (Möbel) *furniture* **~flöße** f *floating of timber* **~flucht** f *suite apartments* **~fräulein** n ⟨bay⟩ (Untermieterin) *female lodger* **~genosse** m *room-mate*; ⟨fam⟩ *chum* **~geselle** m *journeyman-carpenter* **~gymnastik** f *indoor gymnastics* pl **~handwerk** n *carpenter's trade, carpentry* **~herr** m *lodger*; ⟨Am⟩ *roomer* **~hof** m *timber-yard* **~holz** n *timber* **~kamerad** = –genosse **~kellner** m *floor-, bedroom-waiter* | auf **~lautstärke** stellen ⟨wir⟩ *to tune down* **~luft** f *close air* **~mädchen** n *housemaid, chambermaid* **~mann** m [pl –leute] *carpenter* || ⟨fig⟩ e–m zeigen, wo der ~ das Loch gelassen hat *to show a p th door: there's the door the carpenter made! to tell a p where to get off* **~meister** m *master-carpenter* **~nummernanzeiger** m *annunciator* **~orgel** f *harmonium* **~pflanze** f *house* od *indoor plant* | e–e (geschickte) Hand für ~n *a green thumb* **~polier** m *carpenter foreman* **~reihe** f *suite of apartments* **~schmuck** m *interior ornament* **~spiel** n, **~sport** m *parlour-game* **~temperatur** f *room temperature*; normale ~ *standard room t.* (*30° C*) **~verband** m ⟨arch⟩ *construction of frame work* **~vermieter(in** f) m *lodging-house keeper* **~verteiler** m (im Hotel) ⟨bes Am⟩ *room clerk* **~warm** a (of wine) *at room temperature* **~werk(statt** f) n *carpenter's work-*(*shop*) **z·immern** vt [h] *to carpenter, cut, construct, make* || ⟨fig⟩ *to frame* **Z·immerung** f ~/ *carpentering* || ⟨min⟩ *timberwork; timbering*

Z·im(me)t m ~(e)s/~e *cinnamon* || ⟨fig sl⟩ ~! *stuff* (*and nonsense*)! || der ganze ~ *the whole caboodle* || was für'n ~! *what trash!* **~apfel** m *sweet-sop* **~baum** m *c.n-tree* **~blüte** f *c.n-flower* **~braun** a *c.n-brown* **~farbe** f *c.n-colour* **~farbig** a *c.n-coloured* **~näglein** n = –blüte **~öl** n *c.n-oil* **~rinde** f *c.n*(*-bark*) **~stange** f *stick of c.n* **~wasser** n *c.n-water*

z·imperlich a *affected, simpering, prim, nimini-pimini, finicking, maudlin,* ⟨Am⟩ *finicky* || (prüde) *prudish, fastidious, squeamish* || ~ tun *to put on a prim appearance, to simper* | **~keit** f ~/ *affectation, primness* || *fastidiousness, prudery* **Z·imperliese** f *prude* || *prim, prudish, simpering girl*

Z·indel m ~s/ **~taft** m *light taffeta*

Z·ink m & n ~(e)s/ *zinc* || ⟨min, com⟩ *spelter* || mit ~ belegen *to zinc* || chromsaures ~ *z. chromate* || schwefelsaures ~ *sulphate of z.* **~asche** f *z.-dross* **~ätzung** f *zincography* **~beschlag** m *z. sheathing* **~blech** n *z. plate; galvanized sheet* **~blende** f ⟨min⟩ *sphalerite* **~blumen** f pl ⟨chem⟩ *flowers* pl *of z.* **~dach** n *z.*(*-covered*) *roof* **~einlage** f; mit ~ *z.-lined* **~eisenerz** n *franklinite* **~erz** n *z.-ore* **~glaserz** n *z.-glance* **~haltig** a *z.iferous* **~hütte** f *z.works* [sg konstr] **~(platten)druck** m *anastatic printing, z.ography* **~salbe** f *z.-ointment* **~sarg** m *z. coffin* **~spat** m *calamine*; *z. spar* **~vitriol** n *white vitriol*

~walzwerk n *z. rolling mill* **~wanne** f *z. bath* **~wasser** n *z. lotion* **~weiß** n ⟨chem⟩ *z.* od *Chinese white*

Z·inke f ~/~n; **Z·inken** m ~s/~ (Gabel≗) *tine, prong* || (Kamm≗) *tooth* || ⟨carp⟩ *dovetail; tenon* || (*beggar's*, etc) *mark* || ⟨mus⟩ *cornet*, ⟨hist⟩ *clarion* || ⟨fig fam⟩ (Nase) *proboscis*, ⟨sl⟩ *boko* **Z·inken- ~bläser** m *cornet-player* (⟨a.⟩ Zinken·ist [m]) **~horn** n *cornet* **~register** n, **~zug** m (e–r Orgel) *cornet-register* **-z·inkig** [in comp] *pronged* (*four-p. fork*)

Z·inn n ~(e)s/ *tin* || (Hausgerät) *pewter* **~ader** f ⟨min⟩ *tin-lode* **~asche** f *tin-ashes* pl, *putty* **~bergwerk** n *tin-mine, stannary* **~blättchen** n *tinfoil* **~blech** n *tin-plate* **~block** m *bar of tin* **≗ern** a *made of pewter*; *p.* od *tin* [attr] **~erz** n *tin-ore* **~farbe** f *vermillion* **~folie** f *tinfoil, leaf-tin* **~geschirr** n *pewter* **~gießer** m *tin-founder, pewterer* | ~arbeit [f] *tinware*; ~ei [f] *pewterer's workshop* **~grube** f *tin-mine* **≗haltig** a *stanniferous* **~kies** m *tin-pyrites* sg **~kraut** n *horsetail* **~legierung** f *tin alloy* **~löffel** m *pewter spoon* **~lot** n *soft solder* **~·ober** m ~s/ *cinnabar*; ⟨chem⟩ *vermilion* | ⟨fig fam⟩ (Zauber) *mess, trash, rubbish; nonsense* || der ganze ~ *all the* (*blessed*) *lot*; (Budenzauber) *booby trap* | ~rot [n], ≗rot [a] *vermilion* **~oxid** n *stannic oxide* **~salz** n *tin salt* **~säure** f *stannic acid* **~schmelzer** m *blower* **~soldat** m *tin soldier* **~stufe** f *lump of tin-ore* **~teller** m *pewter-plate* **~waren** f pl *tinware, pewter* **~wäsche** f ⟨min⟩ *tin buddle*

Z·inne f ~/~n ⟨arch⟩ *pinnacle* || ⟨mil fort⟩ *battlement* [mst im pl] || mit ~n *b.ted*

Z·innie [–iə] f ~/~n ⟨bot⟩ *zinnia*

Zins m ~es/~en *interest* || (Miete) *rent* || (Tribut) *tribute* || → Zinsen pl **~abschnitt** m *coupon* **~acker** m *rent-field* **≗bar** a *tributary* **~bauer** m *copyholder* **~brief** m *copyhold-deed* **≗bringend** a *bearing interest*; ~ anlegen *to put out at i.t* **~buch** n *rental, rent-roll* **~forderungen** f pl ⟨bal⟩ *i.t receivables* **≗frei** a & adv *rent-free*; ⟨com⟩ *free of i.t* || ~es Gut *freehold* | ~heit [f] *exemption from paying rent* **~fuß** m = –satz **~groschen** m *tribute-money* **~gut** n *leasehold* **~hahn** m *duty-fowl* || rot wie ein ~ (*as*) *red as a turkey-cock* **~herabsetzung** f *reduction of i.t* **~herr** m *lord of the manor* **~kupon** m *coupon* **~last** f; drückende ~ *heavy i.t rates* **~lehen** n *fee-farm* **~leiste** f *talon* **≗los** a *non-i.t-bearing* (*notes*) **≗pflichtig** a *subject to rent*; ⟨hist⟩ *tributary* **~rechnung** f *i.t-account* **~satz** m *rate of i.t* **~schein** m (*i.t*) *coupon* || (f Aktien) *dividend warrant* | ~bogen [m] *c. sheet* **~tabelle** f *table of i.t* **~tag** m *rent-day, quarter-day* **~termin** m *i.t-due date* **≗weise** [adv] *as rent, as i.t* **~zahlen** f pl ⟨com⟩ *red numbers* pl **Z·insen** [pl] *interest* || ~ bringen *to bear, yield i.* || entstehende ~ *accruing i.* || || die ~ laufen von *the i. is payable from* || auf ~ leihen *to put out at i.* || 3% ~ tragen *to bear i. at the rate of three per cent.* || k–e ~ tragend *non-i.-bearing* (*notes*), (*capital*, etc) *lying dormant* || ⟨fig⟩ mit ~ zurückzahlen *to return with usury* **z·insen** vi [h] *to yield interest* od *rent* || *to pay rent* od *tribute* **Z·insen- ~berechnung** f *interest-account* **≗tragend** a *bearing interest* **Z·inseszins** m (auf *at*) *compound interest*

Zion·ismus m ~/ *Zionism* **Z·ions- ~brüder** m pl *Sionites* **~schwestern** f pl *sisters of Zion* **~wächter** m *guard of Z.*; ⟨iron⟩ *fanatic divine; zealot*

Z·ipfel m ~s/~ *tip, edge, point* || (e–s Tuches) *corner* || (am Rock) *lappet* || ⟨fig⟩ e–e S beim rechten ~ anfassen *to tackle a th in th right fashion* || etw bei allen vier ~n anfassen *to go cautiously to work* **~mütze** f *night-cap*; ⟨com⟩ *stocking cap* **≗sinnig** a; das macht mich ~ *that makes me crazy* **zipfelig** a *having tips*, etc; ⟨bot⟩ *laciniform*

Zip·olle f ~/~n *onion*; → Zwiebel

Z·ippe f ~/~n = Zibbe || °⟨fig vulg⟩ (Frau) *heifer*

°**Z·ipperlein** n ~s/ *gout*; → Gicht

Z·irbel f ~/~n, **~kiefer** f ⟨bot⟩ *cembra-pine* **~drüse** f ⟨anat⟩ *pineal gland* **~nuß** f *cedar-nut*

z·irka [adv] *about, nearly*

Zirk·assien n *Circassia* **-ier** m *Circassian*

Z·irkel m ~s/~ (Kreis) *circle*; teuflischer ~ *vicious c.* || ⟨poet⟩ der goldene ~ *the crown* || (Instrument) (ein *a pair of*) *compasses* pl; ~ mit Stellbogen *quadrant compass* || ⟨fig⟩ mit dem ~ abgemessen *done by rule and compass* | ⟨fig⟩ (*social*) *circle, society, company* **~beweis** m = –schluß **~bogen** m *arc* **≗förmig** a *circular* **~kasten** m *geometry set* **~linie** f *c.r line* **≗rund** a *c.r* **~schluß** m ⟨log⟩ *vicious circle* **~schmied** m *maker of compasses* **~schnur** f *carpenter's line* **~spitze, ~weite** f *point, span of the compasses* **z·irkeln** vt [h] = abzirkeln **Zirkul·ar** n ~(e)s/~e, ~schreiben [n] *circular* || (Brief) *c. letter*; ~erlaß [m] *order issued in form of a c.* **Zirkulati·on** [–ts–] f ~/~en *circulation* | **~s-** ~pumpe [f] *circulating-pump* **zirkul·ieren** vi [h] *to circulate* || (*of blood, bus*) *to run* || ~ l ⟨fig⟩ *to send* od *pass round* || (Gerüchte) *to spread about*; unter Leuten ~ *to go the round of people* **Zirkumfl·ex** m ~es/~e ⟨gram⟩ *circumflex*; mit e–m ~ versehen *to* (*mark with a*) *c.* **Z·irkus** m [~/–usse & –ken] *circus* ⟨a. ant & fig⟩; ⟨fig⟩ der reinste ~ *as good as a play* | ~klown [m] *clown*, ⟨Am⟩ *white face*; ~reiter(in [f]) [m] *circus-rider*; ~zelt [n] *c.-tent*, ⟨Am⟩ *big top*

Z·irpe f = Zikade | **≗n I.** vi [h] ⟨ent, orn⟩ *to chirp*, ⟨ent⟩ *stridulate*, ⟨orn a.⟩ *squeak* || ~d ⟨ent⟩ *stridulant* **II.** ≗ n *chirping, stridulation*

Z·irrus m ~/~, **~wolke** f *cirrus* (*cloud*)

Z·irze f ~/~n (→ Kirke) ⟨fig⟩ *man-trap*

zirz·ensisch a ⟨ant⟩ *circensian* (*games*)

zisal·pin(isch) a *cisalpine*

Z·isch m ~es/~e *hiss* **≗-b·um** ⟨artill⟩ *whizz-bang* **~el·ei** f ~/~en *whispering* **~hahn** m ⟨tech⟩ *compression-tap* **~laut** m *hissing sound*; ⟨gram⟩ *sibilant* **z·ischeln I.** vi [h] & vt [h] *to whisper* **II.** ≗ n *whisper*(*ing*) **z·ischen I.** vi [h & s] *to hiss, fizz*; ⟨cul⟩ *to frizz*(*le*) || (schwirren) *to whiz*(*z*) || (Kessel) *to sing* || ⟨fam⟩ das zischt, wenn man so 'nen Brand hat *nothing like that beer, when the coppers are hot*, ⟨Am⟩ *that hits the spot* || ⟨sl⟩ einen ~ *to take a drop, to cool one's coppers, to wet one's clay*; gehen wir e–n ~! *come and wash your neck*! | ~d heiß *piping hot* **II.** ≗ n *hisses* pl

Ziseleur [–'lø:r] m ~s/~e (*en*)*chaser* **Zisel·ier-** ~arbeit [f] *chased work*; ~kunst [f] *chaser's art, chasing* **zisel·ieren** vt [h] *to* (*en*)*chase*

Zisso·ide f ~/~n ⟨math⟩ *cissoid*

Z·iste f ~/~n ⟨praeh⟩ *cist* **Zist·erne** f ~/~n *cistern*, (*rain-water*) *tank* | **~n-** ~flugzeug [n] *chemical spraying plane*; ~wagen [m] *tank car*

Zisterzi·enser m ~s/~ *Cistercian* (*monk*)

Z·ist(us)röschen n ⟨bot⟩ → *cistus, rock-rose*

Zitad·elle f ~/~n *citadel* || ⟨fig⟩ *stronghold*

Zit·at n ~(e)s/~e *quotation, reference* || abgedroschenes ~ *tag* || falsches ~ *misquotation*; Ende e–s ~s *end quote* || das ~ beenden *to unquote* | **~en-** ~schatz [m] (*book of*) *Familiar Q.ns* **~i·on** f f [–'tsio:n] ~/~en ⟨jur⟩ *citation, summons* **zit·ieren I.** vt [h] ⟨jur⟩ *to summon* || (Geister) *to call* od *conjure up*; *to raise* || (e–e Stelle) *to cite*; *to quote* (*from an author*) || *to give* (*page and line*) || jdn in bezug auf etw ~ *to quote a p on a matter* || ich –re, v mir –rt *my quotes*! || als Beispiel ~ *to instance* || falsch ~ *to misquote*; genau, wörtlich ~ *to speak by the book* **II.** ≗ *summons* || *conjuration* || *quotation, citation*

Z·ither f ~/~n *zither* || ⟨ant⟩ *cithara, lyre* || ~ spielen, die ~ schlagen *to play the zither* | ~spieler(in [f]) [m] *zither-player* | ~ring [m] *plectrum*

Zitron·at n ~(e)s/~e *candied* (*lemon*) *peel*; ⟨cul⟩ *citronella* | ~-Zitrone *citron* **Zitr·one** f ~/~n *lemon* | **~n- ~baum** m *l.-tree* **~falter** m ⟨ent⟩ *brimstone-butterfly* **≃farben, ≃gelb** a *l.-coloured* **~gras** n ⟨bot⟩ *citronella* L **~kringel** m, **~spirale** f *twist of l. peel* **~limonade** f *l.ade*, *l.-squash* **~melisse** f *l.-balm* **~presse** f *l.-squeezers* pl **~saft** m *l.-juice* **~säure** f *citric acid* **~schale** f *l.-peel*; ⟨cul⟩ *zest of l.*; *a strip of l. rind on the top* | **~n-** ~spritzer [m] *twist of l. p.* od *r.* **~scheibe** f *slice of l.* **~stecher** m *l.-scoop* **~strauch** m *l. verbena* **~wasser** n *l.ade* **~zeisig** m ⟨orn⟩ *citril finch* **Z·itrus-** ~früchte [f pl] *citrus fruit* sg; ~gewächs [n] *citrus*

Z·itter- **~aal** m *electric eel* **~anfall** m *fit of shivering* **~gras** n *quaking-grass* **~laut** m ⟨phon⟩ *trill* **~nadel** f *aigrette* **~pappel** f ⟨bot⟩ *aspen*(*-tree*) **~roche(n)** m ⟨ich⟩ *electric ray* **~signal** n (f Fernlenk-Raketen) *dither* **~spiel** n *spillikins* pl **~stimme** f *trembling voice* **~wels** m ⟨ich⟩ *thunder-fish, electric catfish* **z·itterig** a *trembling, shaking, tremulous*, ⟨fam⟩ *doddering, doddery* **Z·ittern** n ~s/ *trembling, shivering* **z·ittern I.** vi [h] (P) *to tremble, quake, quiver* (**vor** .. (→ u.) *with fear, excitement*; *before a p*, vor dem Tode *for fear of death*); *his heart fluttered with fear*; *to shake*; ~u beben *to tr. and sh.* (⟨a.⟩ vor Schwäche) | **mir** ~ alle Glieder *I am shaking in every limb* | **am** ganzen Leibe ~ *to tremble all over*, ⟨fam⟩ *to be all of a tremble* od *in a shiver* || **um** jdn ~ *to be in fear for a p* || ~ **wie** Espenlaub *to shake like a leaf* || ~d ⟨a.⟩ *atremble, aquiver* | **vor** Kälte ~ *to shiver with cold* || (vor Unruhe) *to flutter, flurry* (→ o.) | (Erde) *to quail, quake* || (Licht) *to waver, quiver* || (schwingend) *to vibrate, oscillate* || (Stimme) *to shake, quaver, falter* **II. mit** ≃ u Zagen *trembling with fear*; ⟨fam⟩ *shaking in one's shoes*

Z·itwer m ~s/ ⟨bot⟩ *zedoary* **~same(n)** m *worm-seed* **~wurzel** f *zedoary*

Z·itz m ~es/~e [Ind = bunt] **~kattun** m *chintz, printed calico* **~kleid** n *printed dress*

Z·itze f ~/~n *nipple* || ⟨dero & zoo⟩ *dug, teat* | **≃n-** ~förmig [a] *nipple-shaped, mammiform*

Ziv·il [-v-] n ~s/ (Zivilpersonen) *civilians* pl || in ~ *in private* od *plain clothes*, ⟨mil a.⟩ *in mufti*, ⟨fam⟩ *in civvies* || Polizist in ~ *plain-clothes man* **ziv·il** [-v-] a *civil* ⟨a. jur⟩ || *reasonable* od *moderate* (*price*) || ~er Bevölkerungsschutz *C. Defence* **Ziv·il-** [in comp mst] *civil* .. **~anwärter** m *p having a claim to a government appointment* **~anzug** m *plain clothes* pl, ⟨mil⟩ *mufti*, ⟨fam⟩ *civvies* pl **~beamte(r)** m *c. servant* | durch **~behörden** [f pl] geregelt/bearbeitet *in hands of c. authorities* **≃berufliche** Fachkenntnisse *c.ian occupational speciality* **~bevölkerung** f *c.*(*ian*) *population* **~courage** f *courage of one's convictions* od *opinions* **~dienst** m *c. service* **~ehe** f *c. marriage*; obligatorische (fakultative) ~ *m. which must* (*may*) *be entered into either before a clergyman or an officer, registrar or magistrate* **~fliegen** n *c. flying*, *c. aviation* **~flugzeugführerschein** m *c. pilot's licence* **~gericht** n *c. court* **~gesetzbuch** n [Sw] (ZGB) *code of c. law* **~ingenieur** m *c. engineer* **~kleidung** f *c.ian dress* || in ~ → Z. **~kourage** f → -courage | im **~leben** ⟨mil a.⟩ *on the outside* **~liste** f *c. list* **~person** f *civilian* **~prozeß** m *c. law-suit* od *procedure* | ~ordnung [f] (ZPO) ⟨m. m.⟩ *C. Practice Act, Code of C. Law* **~recht** n *c. law* **≃rechtlich** a ⟨jur⟩ *civil* || jdn ~ verfolgen *to bring a c. suit against a p* **~stand** m *legal status* (*of a p*) | (Bürgerstand) *the middle classes* pl | **~standesamt** n Sw = Standes- **≃versorgungsberechtigt** a *having a claim to a government appointment* **~verteidigung** f *c. defence* N, *c. emergency planning* N **~verwaltung** f *c. service* **Zivilisati·on** [-ts-] f ~/ *civilization, culture* | **~s-** ~bestrebungen [f pl] *civilizing efforts* pl **Z.is·ator** n ~s/-sat·oren *civilizer* **z.isat·orisch** a *civilizing* **z.is·ierbar** a *amenable to civilization*; *civilizable* **z.is·ieren** vt [h] *to civilize* || ⟨fig⟩ *to polish* **Zivil·ist** m ~en/~en **1.** *civilian*, ⟨Am⟩ *citizen* ⟨dero⟩ *cit* **2.** ⟨jur⟩ *civil jurist*; *expert in* (*German or Roman*) *private* (*substantive*) *law* **ziv·iliter** [-v-] adv ⟨jur⟩ *by civil process*; *in the civil court*

Zn·üni m & n ~s/ Sw (Gabelfrühstück) *lunch*

Z·obel m ~s/~ ⟨zoo⟩ *sable* **~fell** n *s.-skin* **~pelz** m *s.-fur* || (Mantel) *s.-cloak* || (Wollstoff) *zibel(l)ine* **~tier** n = Zobel **~verbrämung** f *s.-trimming* **≃weich** a ⟨cosm⟩ *sable*

z·ockeln vi [s] *to toddle* (*along*); → za-, zuckeln

Zodiak·allicht n *zodiacal light* **Zod·iakus** m ~/ ⟨astr⟩ (Tierkreis) *zodiac*

Z·ofe f ~/~n *personal maid*, ⟨hum⟩ *Abigail*

zog 1. & 3. sg pret v ziehen **Z·ögerer** m ~s/~ = Zauderer **z·ögern I.** vi [h] *to delay, pause, tarry, linger, loiter*; *to hang back* || (schwanken) *to hesitate, defer*; *to shilly-shally* || (weichen) *to draw back* || nicht ~ (mit, z tun) *to lose no time* (*in, in doing*), ⟨sl⟩ *to make no bones* (*about, of*; *to do*) || es läßt e-n ~ *it gives one pause to think* | ~d *dilatory, halting*; ⟨a.⟩ *tentative* **II.** ≃ n (⟨a.⟩ **Zögerung** f) *dilatoriness* (mit *over*) || ohne ~ *unhesitatingly*; *unquestioningly*; *without delay* od *hesitation* || nach langem ~ *after a good deal of hesitation*; nach einigem ~ *after a hesitation* **Z·ögling** m ~(e)s/~e *pupil, scholar*; *boarding-school student*; *pupil under the care of a private tutor*; *ward* (*under a p's care*); → Fürsorge≃

Zölest·in m ~s/ ⟨minr⟩ *celestine*

Zölib·at m & n ~(e)s/ *celibacy* || ⟨hum⟩ *single blessedness*

Z·oll[1] m ~(e)s/~e (Maß) *inch*, ⟨astr⟩ *digit* || zwei ~ dick *two-inch* (*plank*) || ~ für ~ *inch by inch*; (*a gentleman*) *to his fingertips* || ⟨fig⟩ *step by step*; sich ~ f ~ nähern, fortbewegen *to inch* **≃breit** a *one inch wide* || e-e nur ~dicke Mauer ⟨a.⟩ *but an inch or two of wall* **~maß** n *inch-measure* **~stock** m (*folding*) *inch-* od *foot-rule*

Z·oll[2] m ~(e)s/≃e **1.** (Abgabe) *custom*(*s*), *duty* || Einfuhr≃ *tariff* || (Brückenzoll etc) *toll* || ⟨fig⟩ *tribute* || aus dem ~ nehmen *to clear* (*goods*); mit ~ belegen *to tariff* **2.** = -amt **~abfertigung** f *clearance* **~abgabe** f (*c.-*)*duty*, *c.s* **~amt** n *c.-house*, *-office* **≃amtlich** a; ~e Mitwirkung *cooperation of the c.s office* || *for c.s purposes* || ~e Untersuchung *examination by revenue-officers* | [adv] ~ abgefertigt *c.s cleared* **~angabe, ~anmeldung** f *c.s entry* od *declaration*; *bill of entry* **~ansatz** m, **~anschlag** m *tariff-rate* **~aufschlag** m *additional duty* **~aufseher** m *surveyor of the c.s* || ⟨mar⟩ *tide-waiter* **~(behandlungs)bahnhof** m *c.s station, st. with c.s facilities* **~beamte(r)** m *c.-house revenue-officer* **~beförderung** f *c.s transport* **~befreiung** f *exemption of c.s duties* **~behörde** f *c.s* od *c.-h. authorities* pl **~beschau** m *c.s examination*; ⟨Am⟩ *c.s check* **~beschränkung** f *c.s restrictions* pl **~bestimmung** f *c.s regulation* **~bewachung** f *c.s guard* **~buße** f *c.s fine* **~deklaration** f = -angabe **~einnehmer** m *collector of c.s* **~fahrzeug** n ⟨mar⟩ *revenue-cutter* **~formalitäten, ~förmlichkeiten** f pl *c.-h. formalities*, *c.s processing* **≃frei** a *duty-free, free of c.s*; ⟨com⟩ *duty paid* || ~er Verkehr *free trade* || Gedanken sind ~ *thought is free* | ≃heit [f] *exemption from duty* **~gebiet** n *c.s territory* **~gebühr** f *duty, c.s*, ⟨rail⟩ *c. charges* **~geleitschein** m *permit* **~gesetz** n *c.s law* **~grenze** f *c.s-frontier* **~gut** n *c.able goods* pl; *g.s under* (od *subject to*) *c.s control* **~haus** n *c.-house* **~hinterzieher** m (Z.hung [f]) *defrauder* (*defraudation*) *of c.s* **~inhaltsangabe, -erklärung** f f ⟨post⟩ *c.s declaration* **~inspektor** m *c.s-officer* **~krieg** m *tariff war* **~mauer** f *wall of protectionism* **~niederlage** f *bonded warehouse* **~oberinspektor** m *chief inspector of c.s* **~ordnung** f *c.-h. regulations* pl **~papiere** n pl *clearance papers, c.s documents* **≃pflichtig** a *liable to duty,* ⟨Am⟩ *dutiable* **~politik** f *c.s policy* **~quittung** f *docket* **~raumverschluß** m *c.s bond* **~recht** n *c.s legislation* **~revision** f *c.s examination,* ⟨rail⟩ *examination of passenger's luggage* || Befreiung v der ~ ⟨Am⟩ *the courtesies of the port* **~satz** m *rate of duties, tariff rate* **~schein** m *permit, clearance(-bill)* **~scherereien** f pl *bother at the c.-h.* **~schiff** n *revenue cutter* **~schranke** f *c.-barrier* **~schreiber** m *c.-h. clerk* **~schuld(ner** m) f *c.s debt(or)* **~speicher** m = –niederlage **~spesen** pl *c.-h. charges* pl **~station, ~stelle** f ⟨rail⟩ *c.s-station* **~system** n *c.-h. system* **~tarif** m *tariff* | auf **~treue** verpflichtet *bound to c.s loyalty* | Allg. **~- u Handelsabkommen** n *General Agreement on Tariffs and Trade (GATT)* (Genf seit 1948) **~verband, ~verein** m *c.s-union*; ⟨Ger⟩ *Zollverein* **~veredelung** f *processing under c.s control* | **~s-** ~verkehr [m] *c.s p.g trade* **~verfahren** n *c.s processing* **~vergehen** n *c.s offence* **~vergünstigung** f *sufferance* **~vergütung** f *reimbursement of c.s duties* **~vermerkschein** m *c.s document* **~verschluß** m *bond* || unter ~ *in b., bonded* **~verwaltung** f *c.s administration* **~vormerk** m *c.s bond* | **~-** ~verfahren [n] *c.s recording procedure*; ~verkehr [m] *c.s recorded trade* **~vorschriften** f pl *c.s regulations* **~wächter** m ⟨mar⟩ *tide-waiter* **~wesen** n *customs* pl, *c.s procedure; tariff system* **z·ollbar** a *liable to duty* od *custom,* ⟨Am⟩ *dutiable* **z·ollen** vt [h] **1.** *to pay duty on* **2.** *to pay, give* || [dat] Achtung ~ *to respect* || [dat] Beifall ~ *to appland* || e–m Dank ~ *to express one's gratitude to a p* **Z·öllner** m ~s/~ *collector of customs* || ⟨bib⟩ *publican*

..zöller n, **..zollig, ..zöllig** a; z. B. drei~ *of three inches, three-inch (plank)*

Z·one f ~/~n *zone (the frigid, temperate, torrid ~)*; die kalten ~n ⟨a.⟩ *the frozen zones* || (Landstreifen) *belt (the fever, cotton b.)* || ⟨pol⟩ die ~ = ⟨SBZ⟩, ⟨DDR⟩ || ⟨min⟩ *horizon* || ⟨comp⟩ fehlerhafte ~ *field of error* | **~n-** ~fehler [m] ⟨opt⟩ *zonal aberration*; ~grenze [f] *z.l border*; ⟨Ger⟩ *interzonal b.*; ~kapazität [f] *field capacities* (ausfüllen *to fill*); ~schmelzverfahren [n] *zone melting*; ~tarif [m] ⟨rail⟩ *zone tariff*

°**Zoo** m [tso:] ~s/~s = Zoologischer Garten **Zoo-** [tso:ɔ–] ~latr·ie [f] ~/~n [–i:ən] (Tierkult) *zoolatry*; ~l·ith [m] ~en/~en ⟨geol⟩ *zoolite* ~l·og(e) [m] ~en/~en *zoologist*; ~log·ie [f] ~/~n *zoology*; ≃l·ogisch [a] *zoological*; ~er Garten *zoological gardens* pl; ⟨fam⟩ *Zoo*; ~e Handlung [f] *pet shop*; ~n·ose [f] *zoonosis* (v T > P übertragen); ~tom·ie [f] ~/ *zootomy*

Z·opf m ~(e)s/≃e **1.** *plait of hair; tress* || *(long tresses)* || Zöpfe tragen *to plait one's hair* | (der Männer) *pigtail* || in Zöpfe flechten *to plait* || e–m e–n ~ drehen ⟨fig⟩ *to play a p a trick* || ⟨fig⟩ alter ~ *old-fashioned man* od *habit; pedantry*; ⟨mil⟩ *pipe-clay*; ⟨pol, etc⟩ *red tape* **2.** ⟨for, arch⟩ *tree-top* **3.** *plaited bun* **~holz** n *top branches of a tree* **~mensch** m *pedant, red-tapist* **~muster** n ⟨tex, embr, etc⟩ *cable-stich pattern* **~perücke** f *tie-wig* **~stil** m *rococo,* ⟨fig⟩ *pedantic style* **~zeit** f *age of pigtails* **z·opfig** a ⟨fig⟩ *pedantic* || ⟨mil⟩ *pipe-clay,* ⟨pol, etc⟩ *red-tape (system)*

Z·ores m ~/ [hebr] m Sie k–n ~! *don't fuss!*

Z·orn m ~(e)s/ *wrath, anger, indignation*; ~ der Gerechtigkeit, des Gerechten *righteous wrath*; heller ~ *fury* || ⟨poet⟩ *ire* | in ~ ausbrechen *to flare out (against)* || s–n ~ auslassen (an [dat]) *to vent one's anger (on); to take it out on a p; to pour out the vial of wrath* (→ Schale) *upon a p* || jds ~ besänftigen ⟨fam⟩ *to smooth a p's ruffled feathers* || s–n ~ dämpfen *to subdue one's anger* || in ~ geraten *to get angry, to fly into a passion*; ⟨Am fam⟩ *to blow one's top*; sich in ~ hineinsteigern *to whip o.s. into anger* || im ~ *in hot blood* || als sich sein ~ legte *when he cooled down*; sein ~ wird bald verraucht s *his anger will soon have spent itself* || bleich, rot vor ~ *livid, red with rage* od *anger*; vor ~ erröten *to flush angrily* || zu ~ geneigt *irascible* || zum ~ reizen *to make angry, to provoke, to rouse a p's anger* || ⟨sl⟩ *to get a p's back* (od *monkey*) *up* **~ader** f *frontal vein* **~anfall, ~ausbruch** m *fit of anger*; ⟨fam⟩ *wax* **~(es)blick** m *angry look* **≃funkelnd** a *(eyes) blazing (with fury)* **≃glühend** a *boiling with rage, ablaze with anger* **≃mütig** a *irascible, choleric* | ~keit [f] *irascibility* **~röte** f *flush of anger* **~rute** f *rod of God's wrath* **≃wütig** a *raging, furious* **z·ornig** a *wrathful; angry, irate,* ⟨Am⟩ *mad* (auf, über *at,* vor *with*), *hasty (words)* || ⟨fam⟩ *in a temper* || ~ w *to get angry*

°**Z·osse** m ~n/~n (Pferd) *nag, dobbin*

Z·ote f ~/~n *ribald joke; smutty* od *dirty story*; ⟨sl⟩ *dirty crack* || *obscenity* || ⟨fam⟩ ~n reißen *to talk smut,* ⟨Am sl⟩ *to pull some raw stuff* **z·otenhaft, z·otig** a *loose, ribald, smutty, obscene* || ~ w = Zoten reißen **Z·otenreißer** m ~s/~ *obscene talker*

Z·otte f ~/~n ⟨anat⟩ *villus* L [pl *villi*] **~nhaut** f *chorion* **Z·otte(l)** f ~/~n *(matted) tuft* || ~n [pl] *matted hair* **Zottel·ei** f ~/ *toddling (along)* **Z·ottelkopf** m *shaggy head* **z·otteln** vi [s] = watscheln *to toddle* od *shuffle along* **z·ott(el)ig** a *shaggy, matted, scraggly* || ⟨anat⟩ *villous* || ⟨bot⟩ *downy*

Z·ötus m ~/–ten ⟨school⟩ *section of a form* || Zöten *parallel forms* pl

zu I. prep [dat] (zum = zu dem, zur = zu der) **A. 1. (wohin?)** ⟨mst⟩ *to* || ~ jdm gehen *to go to (see) a p* || ~r Schule gehen *to go to school* || er setzte sich ~ mir (ihr) *he came (went) and sat down by me (her)* || er bestellte, bat ihn ~ sich *he ordered, asked him round (to his place)* || ~r Bühne gehen *to go on the stage* || *(at the entrance) to the house* (~ dem H.) || *(from house) to house* (~ H.) | [ell] ~r S! *(come) to the point!* | (Richtung) *towards* | → **bis** I. A. ~ **2. (hinzufügend)** *in addition to; with* || *(to pour wine) on* od *into a th*; *(to add wine) to a th* || .. ~ allem anderen *(this worry) on top of all the others* || *to eat bread with one's meat* (~m Fl.) **3. (wo?)** ~ Hause *at home, in* || ~ Wasser *at sea* (vgl 5. & B.) || ~m Fenster hinaussehen (herausblicken) *to look out of (at) the w.,* ⟨Am a.⟩ *.. out the w.* || *to fly out at the w.*; *to ride in* bzw *out at the gate* | (Großstadt) ~ B. *in Berlin* || (Kleinstadt) *at Marburg*; (Aufenthaltsort des Sprechenden) *in Marburg* || *(the university) of M.* **4. (wann?)** *at (noon, midnight)* (vgl B.); *at (the same day, hour, time)* || *(from day) to day* (~ T.) **5. (wie?)** ~ D. *in German* || ~ F. *on foot,* ~ Pf. *on horseback,* ~ Rade *by bicycle,* ~ Schiff *by ship,* ~ Wasser *by sea* (→ B.) | mir ist nicht ~m Lachen *I don't feel in a laughing mood* || ~m Sterben *enough to kill a p* || ~m Teil (abbr z. T.) *partly* | (= aufs) ~m besten *for the best, in the best way* **6.** (= **als**) *(she had a hero) for a father* (~m V.) || er hat sie ~m Weibe *she is his wife*; er hat e–n Engel ~m W. *he has an angel of a w.* **7. (Zweck)** ~r A. *for* (od *by way of*) *a change* || → gebrauchen || *he came for the inquest* (~r Leichenschau) || Tuch ~ e–m Rock .. *for ..* || ~ allem entschlossen *ready to go all lengths* **8.** [= gen obj] Liebe ~ Gott *love of God* || aus Liebe ~ dir *from affection for you* **9.** ~m **Preise** v *at a price of* || ~ 5 Mark das Stück *at 5 marks each* **10. (Verhältnis)** wie 5 ~ 1 *as 5 to 1* **11. (Zahl)** ~ 1. b *in reference to 1. b* || ~ dreien or dritt *three in number, we (you) three, three of us* || ~ vieren or viert spielen *to play with three (people)* || ~m ersten *to begin with* || ~m ersten!, zweiten! und dritten (letzten) *going!, going!, gone!* || ~ guter Letzt *finally, to finish up with* ||

~ Tausenden *by thousands* || ~ zweien *two and two, in couples, by twos*; ~ zweit *two of them*, etc **B.** ~ **Abend** etc essen *to dine*, etc; *to have dinner*, etc || ~ Anfang *in* od *at* bzw *for the beginning* || → Beispiel || ~ Berg fahren *to go to* od *up the mountains*, .. *up-stream* || .. ihm ~m Bilde (*God created man*) *in his own image* || → Boden || ~ ebner **Erde** wohnen *to live on the ground floor* || ~ m–m Erstaunen *to my a.* || ~ m–r gr Freude (*I saw*) *with great pleasure* || e–n ~m Freunde h *to have a p for a fr.* (→ A. 6.) || e–n ~ **Gaste** bitten *to invite a p* (*to dinner, to stay*) || dir ~ Gefallen *to please you* (→ A. 7.) || ~r Hälfte *by half, half of it* || ⟨mus⟩ ~ 4 Händen *arranged for 4 hands* || ~ jds rechten Hand sitzen .. *on* od *at* .. || ~ Händen (abbr z. H.) des Herrn N. *into the hands of Mr. N.*; (*for the*) *attention of Mr. N.* (→ Hand, zu) || ~ **Hause** *at home, in* || e–m ~ Liebe, aus Liebe ~ e–m *out of love for a p* || → Lohn || ~m ersten Male *for the first time* || ~ **Nacht** *at n., by n.*; ~ N. essen *to sup, to have supper* || ~r Not *if need be* || ~ Ihrem Nutzen *for your benefit* || → Paar || mir ~m Schaden *to my detriment* || e–m ~r Seite sitzen .. *at* .. || ~r Stadt gehn *to go to t.* || ~ **Tal** fahren *to go down the hills*, .. *down-stream* || ~ Tisch gehen (führen) *to go* (*take* .. *in*) *to dinner* || ~m Tore hinaus *out at the gate* || Wasser ~m Trinken *drinking-water* || ~r Tür hinaus *out by the d.* || ~ jds Unterhaltung *for a p's entertainment* || ~ s–r Verteidigung *in his defence* || Geld ~m Verspielen (*to have no*) *m. to lose* || ~ **Wasser** *at sea, by sea* (→ A. 3, 5.); ~ W. u ~ Lande *by sea and land* **C. 1.** ~m Fürsten **erheben** *to raise* .. *to the rank of a prince* || ~m General ernannt w *to be made general* || ~m Schauspieler geboren *a born actor* || das **machte** mich ~ s–m Gegner *that made me his adversary* || ~m Narren w *to grow foolish* || ~ Staub w *to turn to dust* || ~m Verräter w *to become a t.* **2.** (**Hinsicht**) ~ etw beglückwünschen *to congratulate* .. *upon a th* || ~ etw lachen *to l. at a th* || Lust ~ e–r S h *to have a liking for a th* || ~ etw schweigen *to be silent respecting to* (od *to take no notice of*) *a th* || ~ .. (wird gemeldet *report*[*ing*]) *in compliance with* .. || ⟨scient⟩ (in Titeln) zur Glaziologie .. *Aspects of the G.* (*of Iceland*) **3.** [**vor inf**] (→ **gebrauchen**) || es ist ~ h *it is to be had* || es ist *or* steht ~ hoffen *it is to be hoped, it may be hoped for* || ich erinnere mich, es gesehen ~ h (dort gewesen ~ s) *I remember seeing it* (*having been there*) || der Brief ist ~ **schreiben** .. *must be written* || ganz davon ~ schweigen, daß *not to mention that* .. || es ist schwer ~ sagen *it is hard to say* || wir h ~ tun *we have to work* || was ist ~ **tun**? *what is to be done*? || .., nicht weil .. befohlen hatte, es ~ tun (*so he wrote the letter*), *not because his father had told him to* || es ist ~ unterscheiden *a distinction must be made* || ~ verkaufen *to be sold, for sale* || ~ vermieten *to let* | ich komme Sie ab~holen .. *to fetch you* | [**nach prep**] **anstatt** selbst ~ gehen (nach~denken) *instead of going* (*thinking*) *o.s.* || **ohne** es ~ wissen (wollen) *without knowing it*, (*unintentionally*) || **um** ihn ~ ärgern (*in order*) *to tease him* **4.** [**vor pres p**] e–e nicht ~ ertragende Hitze *an unendurable heat* || ein nach~ahmendes Beispiel *an e. worthy of imitation* || ein wohl ~ überlegender Schritt *a step requiring careful consideration* || ein ~ verbessernder Fehler *an error* (*to be corrected* od) *requiring correction* || das ~ verkaufende Haus *the h.* (*which is*) *to be sold* **II. adv 1.** [**vor a & adv**] *too* (*big, small, discrete*) [wie *very* nie bei Verben!] || ~ freigebig s ⟨a.⟩ *to err on the side of generosity* || ~ groß ⟨a.⟩ *excessive* || ein (gar) ~ pedantischer Mann *much too pedantic a man* || ~ sehr, ~ viel *too much* (*exaggerated*) || ~ sehr Kind *too much of a child* || ~ vorsichtig *over-cautious* || ~ stark *or* weit + Verb *over*..: ~ stark betonen *to overstress*; ~ weit gehen *to overreach o.s.* | **all~**, gar ~, nur ~ *far* od *all too* (*familiar*); *rather* od *much too* (*small*) **2.** (= **verschlossen**) *closed, shut*; (*the brakes are*) *on* **3.** (**Richtung**) nach N. ~ *to*(*wards*) *the north* || nach der Stadt ~ *in the direction of the t.* || die S. neigte sich dem W. ~ *the sun wore on due west* **4.** [**bei Verben**] (immerzu): er lief ~ .. *on and on, he kept on running* || *for ever* (*the wind is for ever blowing*) **5.** → **ab** u ~ **6.** Glück ~! *good luck*! **III.** [**sep pref**] (→ ~m etc) || geh' ~ *go* od *get on*! || schlag ~! *strike*! || schieß ~! *fire away* | [ell] ~! *forwards*!, *on*! (⟨a.⟩ immer ~!) || → zu- **Z·u-, z·u-** pref [bei Verben, Adjektiven & Substantiven] [immer betont; bei Verben trennbar] **1.** (Verschließung) z. B. z·u|machen, z·u|scharren, z·u|schließen **2.** (Hinzufügung) z. B. Z·ubehör, z·u|bekommen l., z·ubenannt, Z·ubuße, Z·ukost, Z·uwachs **3.** (Richtung) z. B. auf e–n z·u|k, e–m z·u|trinken **4.** (Beteiligung) z. B. z·u|hören, z·u|sehen **5.** (Zuerteilung) z. B. e–m etw z·u|k l, z·u|teilen **6.** (Fortfahren, Beschleunigung) z. B. z·u|essen 2; z·u|fahren l. **z·u|ackern I.** vt [h] *to cover* (od *fill*) *up by ploughing* **II.** vi [h] *to plough on* **zu·aller-** **~erst** adv *first of all* **~letzt** adv *last of all*; *at the very end* **z·u|arbeiten I.** vi [h] *to work on* **II.** vt [h] *to join on to*

Zu·ave [ts–və] m ~n/~n *zouave*

z·u- **~|ballern** vt *to shut with a bang, to bang to* **~|bauen** vt [h] *to wall* od *build up* od *in*; *to block up* (*a view*) **~|behalten** vt [h] *to keep shut* (bzw *buttoned up*) **≗behör** n ~(e)s/ *belongings, trimmings, accessories, appurtenances, fittings*; ⟨Am⟩ *fixings*, (Installation) *furnishings* (ohne ~ *bare, plain*) pl || ⟨tech⟩ *fixture*; *mountings* pl; *tools and machinery* || ⟨agr⟩ *premises, buildings* || (Vorhänge etc) *soft furnishings* || ⟨cul⟩ *dressing*; *trimmings* pl || Arbeit u ~ *work and materials*; (*six-roomed flat with all*) *conveniences* pl | **~-** ~industrie [f] *accessories industry*; ~teil [m] *attachment, part* **~|beißen** vi irr [h] *to bite* od *snap at a th* || ⟨fig⟩ *to jump at an offer* || ⟨fam⟩ tüchtig ~ *to eat away with a good appetite*, ⟨sl⟩ *to pack away one's grub* **~|bekommen** vt irr [h] **1.** *to get in addition* **2.** *to succeed in closing* od *fastening* || nicht ~ *to be unable to close*, etc **~benamt, ~benannt** a *surnamed*

Z·uber m ~s/~ (Zweihenkelbottich) *tub*

z·u- **~|bereiten** vt [h] *to prepare, adjust, fit* || (Pelze, Speisen) *to dress* || (Speisen) *to cook, do*; ⟨chem⟩ *to make up* (*a solution*) **≗bereitung** f ~/~en *preparation* || *dressing* || *cooking* **≗b·ettegehen** n; beim ~ *on going to bed* (⟨fam⟩ *to roost*) **~|biegen** vt irr [h] *to close by bending* **~|billigen** vt [h] *to allow, grant, concede* **≗billigung** f *concession* **~|binden** vt irr [h] *to tie* od *bind up, to lace* || jdm die Augen ~ *to blindfold a p* **≗biß** m (*a glass of wine with*) *sth to eat* **~|blasen I.** vt irr [h] **1.** → zu- 1. **2.** ⟨fig⟩ jdm etw ~ *to suggest* od *prompt a th to a p* **II.** vi → zu- 6. **≗bläser** m ~s/~ *prompter* **~|bleiben** vi irr [s] *to remain shut*, etc **~|blinken** vi [h] **1.** e–m ~ *to shine in a p's eyes* **2.** = **~|blinzeln** vi [h]; jdm ~ *to* (*tip* .. *a*) *wink* (⟨fam⟩ *to cock one's eye*) *at a p* **~|bringen** vt irr [h] (jdm) *to bring* (*to a p*) || *to throw* (*business*) *a p's way* || (Klatsch etc) *to report* || e–m e–n Trunk ~ *to pledge a p* || die Zeit ~ *to pass* od *spend one's time* (mit Spielen *playing*) (mit etw *at a th*) || das Zugebrachte *the dowry* || zugebrachte Kinder *children by a former marriage* **≗bringer** m ⟨typ, num⟩ *layer-on*; ⟨tech⟩ *feeder* || (im Weltraumverkehr) ⟨a–n⟩ *space shuttle* | ~bahn, ~linie [f] ⟨rail⟩ *feed*(*er*)*-line*; ~bus [m] (P) ⟨aero⟩ *airport bus*; ~feder [f] *magazine spring* (*of a rifle*); ~flugzeug [n] *feeder machine*; *shuttle plane*; ~straße [f] *tributary* od *slip road*; ~(zug) [m] ⟨rail⟩ *shuttle-train* **~|brocken** → zu- 2. || ⟨fig, fam⟩ etw –zu– h *to have sth to live* *upon, to have an income of one's own* ×≗**brot** n ⟨fig⟩ *extra earnings* pl ≗**buße** f ∼/∼n *contribution* ⟨a. min⟩ ∼|**büßen** vt [h] *to contribute, to supply* | (verlieren) *to spend, lose* (⟨a.⟩ °zu|buttern)

Zucht f ∼/ **A. 1.** (Aufzucht) *rearing, breeding* || (v Bienen, Seidenraupen, Bakterien) *culture*, (v Austern, Fischen ⟨a.⟩) *farm*; (v Pflanzen) *cultivation, growing* **2.** (Rasse) *breed, race* **3.** [konkr] *brood, young stock* **4.** (Kinder≗) *education* **5.** (Mannes≗) *discipline, moral(e)* || scharfe ∼ *biting discipline*; strenge ∼ *deep d.* **6.** (gesittetes Benehmen) *decency, modesty, manners, propriety* **7.** ⟨dero⟩ was ist das f e–e (tolle) ∼! *what a mad way of acting!, this is Bedlam let loose!* **B.** in ∼ u Ehren, **in allen Züchten** *with due propriety, courteously, most respectably* **C.** k–e ∼ **annehmen** *to be utterly intractable*; der ∼ entwachsen s *to have outgrown the rod, to be beyond control*; nicht an ∼ u Ordnung gewöhnt *undisciplined*; in ∼ halten *to keep in hand* od *under discipline*; jdn zur ∼ anhalten *to discipline a p* (zu übergr ∼ u Ordnung –ge– *overdisciplined*); z ∼ halten *to keep for breeding*; unter jds ∼ stehen *to be under a p's care*; sich der ∼ unterwerfen *to submit to discipline* ∼**biene** f *queen-bee* ≗**bildend** a *disciplinary* ∼**buch** n *stud-book* ∼**bulle** m *breeder* od *seed bull* ∼**eber** m *stud-boar* ∼**esel** m *stallion (ass)* ≗**fähig** a *capable of reproducing the race* || *yielding to discipline* ≗**gewohnt** a *disciplined* ∼**haus** n *house of correction* || z (10 Jahren) ∼ verurteilt *condemned to imprisonment with (to ten years) hard labour* || lebenslängliches ∼ *penal servitude for life* || im ∼ sitzen *to be imprisoned with hard labour*, ⟨sl⟩ *to do a stretch, to pick oakum* || mit e–m Bein im ∼ stehen *to have one foot in gaol* ∼**häusler(in f)** m *convict* || ⟨sl⟩ *jail-bird*; lebenslängliche(r) ∼(in) *prisoner under life sentence*, ⟨sl⟩ *lifer* ∼**hengst** m *stud-horse, stallion* ∼**huhn** n *brood-hen* ∼**kuh** f *breeder cow* ≗**los** a *undisciplined* ⟨a. mil⟩ || *loose, dissolute (life)* ∼**losigkeit** f *want of discipline, demoralization* ∼**meister** m *task-master* || *disciplinarian* ⟨bes mil, school⟩; ⟨mil⟩ *martinet* ∼**mittel** n *corrective*; *disciplinary measures* pl ∼**ochse** f *bull* ∼**perle** f *cultured* od *seed pearl* ∼**pferd** n *stud-horse* ∼**rute** f *rod of correction* || ⟨fig⟩ *scourge* ∼**sau** f *brood-sow* ∼**schaf** n *ewe (for breeding)* ∼**schule** f *school of discipline* ∼**stallung** f ⟨orn, cul⟩ *battery* ∼**stier** m = –bulle ∼**stute** f *brood-mare* ∼**vieh** n *brood cattle, cattle for breeding* || gutes ∼ *good breeders* pl ∼**wahl** f (natürliche *natural*) *selection (and selective recombination), s.e breeding* **z·üchten** vt [h] (T) *to breed, rear* || ⟨a.⟩ *to raise (cattle), to keep (bees)* || ⟨hort, agr⟩ *to cultivate, grow* || ⟨bact⟩ *to culture* **Z·üchter(in f)** m ∼s/∼ *breeder*; *raiser (of cattle)* || ⟨hort, agr⟩ *nurseryman* [nur m]; *grower, cultivator (of)* || (v Bienen) *keeper* **Züchter·ei** f ∼/∼en *stock-farm* || ⟨hort, agr⟩ *nursery* **z·üchtig** a (sittsam) *modest, coy, demure* || *decorous (behavio[u]r)* || (keusch) *chaste* || (achtbar) *respectable* | ∼**en** vt [h] *to correct, punish* || (körperlich) *to chastise, lash, flog* || mit Worten ∼ *to scold, reprove, censure* || sein Fleisch ∼ *to mortify one's flesh* | ≗**keit** f ∼/ *modesty, demureness, coyness* || *chastity* || *decency, respectability* | ≗**ung** f ∼/∼en *correction, punishment, chastisement* || körperliche ∼ *flogging*; *corporal punishment* **Z·üchtung** f ∼/∼en *breeding* || ⟨hort, agr⟩ *cultivation, growing* || ⟨bact⟩ *culture*

Z·uck I. m ∼(e)s/∼e *jerk, twitch* || (mit der Schulter) *shrug* || (Nu) *trice (in a t.)* **II.** ≗ [intj] *crack!, bang!* | ∼fuß [m] ⟨vet⟩ = Hahnentritt; ∼krampf [m] *clonic spasm* **z·uckeln** vi [s] *to jog, toddle (along)*; *to trip* ⟨a. hors⟩ **Z·ucken** n ∼s/ *palpitation, convulsion*; nervöses ∼ *start* **z·ucken I.** vi [h] (zitternd) *to quiver* || (einmalig) *to jerk* || (krampfhaft) *to twitch* || (schmerzlich) *to wince* || (Blitz) *to flash* || (Gesicht) *to work* || (Herz) *to palpitate, throb* || (Licht) *to flicker* || das zuckte ihm durch alle Glieder *it sent a thrill all through him* || ∼de Bewegung *jerk* || er zuckte hoch *he jerked up* || → Wimper **II.** vt [h] *to draw, jerk, tug* || die Achseln (mit den A.n) ∼ *to shrug one's shoulders* **z·ücken** vt [h]; den Degen ∼ *to draw the sword (upon a p)* || den Dolch gegen jdn ∼ *to point one's dagger at a p* **Z·uckung** f ∼/∼en *convulsion* || *quiver*; *palpitation* || *thrill* || ∼en bek *to be seized with c.ns* || in ∼en liegen vor *to be throbbing with*

Z·ucker m ∼s/ *sugar* (roh *raw*, gestoßen *granulated*, → Puder≗); Hut≗ *loaf of s.*; Läuter≗ *syrup*; Staub≗ *icing-s.*; Streu≗ *castor s.*; ∼ in Stücken *lump-s.*; ein Stück ∼ *a lump of s.*; Vanille≗ *vanilla-s.*; ∼ in Würfeln *cube-s.* | ∼ sieden *to bake* od *refine s.* || in etw ∼ tun *to s.* od *sweeten a th* || in ∼ einmachen *to candy* || (Stärke) in ∼ verwandeln *to saccharify* || z ∼ w *to turn to s.* || nicht aus ∼ s *to be neither s. nor salt* ∼**ahorn** m ⟨bot⟩ *su.-maple* ∼**apfel** m ⟨bot⟩ *sweet-sop* ∼**arten** f pl *sugars* pl ∼**bäcker** m *confectioner* | ∼ei [f] *confectioner's shop* ∼**backwerk** n *confectionery* || *pastry* ∼**bau** m *cultivation of the su.-cane* ∼**birne** f *su.-pear* ∼**brezel** f *sweet cracknel* ∼**brot** n *su.-bread* || *pastry, cake*; ⟨fig⟩ ∼ u Peitsche *a carrot and stick policy*; *st. and c.* ∼**büchse,** ∼**dose** f *su.-basin, -bowl* ∼**erbse** f *green* od *su.-pea* || (Bonbon) *comfit, sweet, su.-plum* ∼**fabrik** f *su. factory* od *works* pl ∼**faden** m (schwach/stark *soft/hard*) *thread* ∼**flug** m *(soft/hard) ball* ∼**früchte** f pl *candied fruit* [sg] ∼**gärung** f *saccharine fermentation* ∼**gast** m ⟨ent⟩ *su.-mite* ∼**guß** m *(su.) icing, frosting*; mit ∼ *with su.-coating* ≗**haltig** a *sacchariferous, saccharated* ∼**handel** m *su.-trade* ∼**hut** m *su.-loaf* ∼**kalk** m ⟨chem⟩ *su.-lime* ∼**kand** m; brauner ∼ *caramel* || –kand(is) [m] *su.-candy* ∼**kochapparat** m *vacuum pan* ≗**krank** a, ≗e(r) [m], ≗e [f] *diabetic* ∼**krankheit** f *diabetes* ∼**mandel** f *su.ed almond*; (gebrannte) *burnt a.* ∼**mäulchen** n *sweet tooth* ∼**mehl** n *powdered su.* ∼**melone** f *sweet melon* ∼**messer 1.** m *saccharometer* **2.** n *su.-cleaver* ∼**palme** f *arenga* ∼**pflanzung** f *su.-plantation* ∼**plätzchen** n *lozenge, comfit, drop*; ⟨bes fig⟩ *su. plum* ∼**portionierer** m *su. dispenser* ∼**puppe** f ⟨fig⟩ *darling, peach*; ⟨Am⟩ [bes als Anrede] *honey!, sugar!* ∼**raffinerie** f *su.-refinery* ∼**-rohr** n *su.-cane* ∼**rübe** f (weiße) *sweet turnip*; (rote) *su.-beet* | ∼**n**- ∼schnitzel [n] *su.-b. chip* ∼**ruhr** f ⟨path⟩ *diabetes* ∼**sachen** f pl = –waren ∼**säure** f (Glukozuckersäure) ⟨chem⟩ *saccharic acid* ∼**schale** f *su.-basin* ∼**sieder** m *su.-boiler, -refiner* ∼**siederei** f *su.-refinery, -works* pl ∼**sirup** m *molasses* pl [sg konstr], *treacle* ∼**stange** f, ∼**stengel** m *su.stick*; ⟨Am⟩ *lollipop*, ⟨fam a.⟩ "*lolly*" ∼**streuer** m *su.-dredger, -castor* ≗**s·üß** a *as sweet as su., su.ed* ∼**tüte** f *screw of su.-plums* ∼**verbindungen** f pl ⟨chem⟩ *saccharates* ∼**waren** f pl, ∼**werk** n *sweetmeat, confectionery*; *sweets, comfits* pl, ⟨Am⟩ *candy* ∼**wasser** n *su.ed water* ∼**watte** f ⟨cul bes Am⟩ *candy floss* ∼**werk** n ⟨fig⟩ *mealymouthed ths*; → o. ∼**wurzel** f *skirret* ∼**zange** f (eine *a pair of*) *su.-tongs* ∼**zwieback** m *sweet biscuit* **z·uckerig** a *sugary* ×**Z·uckerl** n ∼s/∼ = Bonbon **z·uckern** vt [h] *to sugar, sweeten*

z·u- ∼|**d·ämmen** vt [h] **1.** *to dam up* **2.** (Schlagloch) *to stop up* ∼|**decken** vt [h] *to cover* || (jdn) fest ∼ *to tuck .. up* || ⟨hort⟩ *to dress (with straw, etc)* || ⟨fig⟩ *to cloak, conceal* || **sich** ∼ *to cover o.s. (up)*; → ein– ∼**d·em** adv *besides, moreover* ∼|**denken** vt irr [h] **1.** (jdm etw) *to destine, design, intend (a th for a p)* (z Geschenk *as a pr.*) **2.** = hinzu|denken ∼|**diktieren** vt [h] [dat] *to inflict* od *impose (a penalty) on, to sentence a p to (a pen.)* ≗**drang** m ∼(e)s/ *inrush (of visitors)* || *rush* (zu .. *on a bank, to a place*); *crowd (pressing toward)*

~|drängen & sich ~ [h] *to press forward* || (zu) *to intrude* (*on*), *crowd* (*to*) **~|drehen** vt [h] *to shut off* || (Hahn) *to turn off* || jdm den Rücken ~ *to turn one's back upon a p* **~dringlich** a *importunate, officious, obtrusive*; ⟨fam⟩ *pushing* || ~e Bitten *importunities* | ≈keit [f] ~/~en *importunity* [*-ties* pl]; *officiousness, obtrusiveness* **~|drücken** vt [h] *to close by pressure, to shut* || ein Auge ~ *to stretch a point*, (bei) ⟨fig⟩ *to connive, wink* (*at*), die A.n ~ vor ⟨fig⟩ *to shut the eyes to ..* **~·eigen**; sich etw ~ m: → machen I. 10. b. **~|eignen** vt [h] (ein Buch) *to dedicate, inscribe*; (zuschreiben) *to attribute, ascribe* || sich [dat] ~ *to seize, to appropriate* (*to o.s.*); *to take possession* (*of a th*) || (widerrechtlich) *to usurp, assume* ≈**eignung** f ~/~en *appropriation* || *dedication*; *dedicatory poem* || *usurpation* **~|eilen** vi [s] (auf [acc]) *to hasten up* (*to*), *to run, rush, hurry* (*towards*) || s–m Verderben ~ *to hasten to one's ruin* **~ein·ander** adv *to each other* || (*their*) *mutual* (*location*) || ~ in Beziehung stehen *to be correlated with one another*; Bez. ~ *interrelation* **~|erkennen** vt irr [h] *to acknowledge*; *to decree* | e–m (etw) ~ *to confer* (*a dignity, an honour*) *on a p*; *to give* (*the preference*) *to a p*; *to award a p* (*a prize*); *to condemn a p to* (*a punishment*); *to admit a p's* (*right to do sth*) ≈**erkennung** f ~/ *acknowledgement, award, adjudication*, etc | **~s-** ~urteil [n] *adjudicative sentence* **~·erst** adv (als erste[r], –s) **A.** *first* (*of all*) || *in the first place* || (vor allem) *before everything else* | (anfänglich) *at first*; *initially* || (gleich) ~ *at the* (*very*) *beginning* || (erstens) *firstly* | *for the first time* | (erstlich) *in the first instance* || die alte Frage, was kam ~, .. *the old priority question* (*hen or egg*) **B.** der ~ Ank.de, Angek.e *the first comer* || ~ am Platz *first on the spot* || ~ einmal: .. = .., *to begin with* || (jdn) ~ grüßen *to hail* || ~ tun wir .. *we begin by doing* .. || er sprach ~ *he was the first to speak* || wer schoß ~? *who started shooting*? || wer ~ kommt, mahlt ~ *first come, first served* **~|erteilen** vt [h]; e–m etw ~ *to confer, bestow a th on a p* || *to allot, assign, award, apportion a th to a p* **~|essen** vt [h] **1.** *to eat* (*bread*) *with one's* (*meat*) **2.** ⟨fam⟩ iß zu! *peg away*! **~|fächeln** vt [h]; jdm Kühlung ~ *to fan a p* **~|fahren** vi irr [s] **1.** *to drive* od *go on* || *to drive at a brisk pace* **2.** ([dat] *or* auf [acc]) *to drive towards* (*the farm*); ⟨mar⟩ *to make for* (*land*) || (auf) *to rush upon*, ⟨fig⟩ *to rush* od *fly at* (*a p*) || blind auf etw ~ *to rush headlong upon a th* **3.** (Tür) *to slam* ≈**fahrt** f *approach* (⟨a.⟩ = | **~(s)-** ~kreuz [n] (Autobahn≈) ⟨mot⟩ *interchange*; ~straße, versenkte ~ *areaway* || *access road* ⟨mot⟩ *slip road*; örtliche *local service road*) || ⟨arch⟩ *drive* ≈**fall** m **A.** *chance, accident, coincidence, hazard*; (*subject to the whims of*) *fortune* || ⟨stat⟩ *chance occurrence* || durch (reinen) ~ *by* (*a mere*) *chance* od *accident*, (*quite*) *accidentally*; d. ~ oder Absicht *by accident or design* **B.** glücklicher ~ *fluke*; *lucky chance* od *hit*; *stroke of luck*; (un)glücklicher ~ *lucky* (*bad*) *break*; ein reiner ~ *quite an accident*, ⟨fam⟩ *a mere toss-up* (⟨a.⟩ = e–e S des ~s) || widriger ~ *mischance, misfortune, piece* od *stroke of ill-luck* **C.** es hängt v ~ ab, ob *it is a matter of chance whether* || es dem (Spiel des) ~(s) überlassen *to leave it to* (*the turn of*) *chance*; *to hazard* (*a th*); sich auf den ~ verlassen ⟨a.⟩ *to trust to the chapter of accidents* || der ~ wollte es, daß .. *as it happened* (*there were 4 rooms*); *it chanced that* .. | **~s-** *accidental*; ⟨fam⟩ *fluky*; ~artig [a] = zufällig; ~bekanntschaft [f] *casual acquaintance*; ~erscheinung [f] *accident*; ≈mäßig anordnen *to randomize*; ~probe [f] *contingency sample* ⟨a. a–n⟩ (Mond≈); ~prozeß [m] *random process*, ~spiel [n] = Hasardspiel || welch tolles ~! *what a desperate chance to take*!; ~stichprobe [f] *probability sample*; ~treffer [m] ⟨fam⟩ *pot-shot*, ⟨mil⟩ *chance hit*; ~zahl [f] *random number*; ~zugriff [m] ⟨comp⟩ *random access* **~|fallen** vi irr [s] **1.** *to shut of itself* || (Tür) *to fall shut*; heftig ~ *to slam* || die Augen fallen mir zu *I cannot keep my eyes open* **2.** e–m ~ *to fall to a p's share* od *lot*; *to pass to, to have the hono(u)r of*; (S, Erbschaft) *to go* od *come to a p* || .. fiel [dat] zu *the .. accrued to the hospital* || (Arbeit, Aufgabe) *to devolve upon a p* || die Schuld fällt ihm zu *the blame rests with* od *accrues to him* **3.** ~ auf *to fall towards*; *to rush upon* ≈**fällig** [a] *accidental, contingent*; *casual* (Blick, Bekanntschaft etc); *fortuitous* (*coincidence*); *chance, random* [attr] (*fluctuations*) || ein ~er Kunde etc *a chance customer, a coincidence* || ~es Ereignis *contingency*; ~es Geschehen ⟨stat⟩ *chance occurrence* | (unwesentlich) *unessential, adventitious* || [adv] (⟨a.⟩ ~erweise) *by chance, by* (*blind*) *hazard, incidentally*; ~ oder absichtlich *by accident or design* od *intent* || (gelegentlich) *occasionally, casually* || er war ~ da *he happened to be there*; er hatte es ~ gerade getan *as it happened he had just done it* | ~keit [f] ~/~en *accidentalness* || [mst im pl] *casualties, contingencies, hazards* | ~s- –probe [f] *contingency sample*, → Zufalls– **~|fassen** vi [h] **1.** *to clutch, seize, catch* (*a th*) **2.** *to lend a hand* **~|fertigen** vt [h] *to forward, dispatch, send* **~|flicken** vt [h] *to patch up, darn, mend* **~|fliegen** vi irr [s] (Tür) *to slam, bang* || ⟨fig⟩ [dat] *hearts went out to her*; *knowledge comes easily to him* | (auf [acc]) *to fly* (*to, towards*) | vt (Flugzeug) *to zero in* **~|fließen** vi irr [s] [dat] *to flow* (*to, towards*) || dem Meere ~ *to flow into the sea* || ⟨fig⟩ jdm ~ *to redound, accrue to a p*; (Gedanken) *to come* (*readily*) *to a p* || *money had come to him largely* || (*the profits*) *go to* (*a charitable fund*) || ein Gewinn fließt ihm zu aus .. *he derives a profit from* || die Worte fließen ihm nur so zu *he has a great flow of language* | [dat] ~ l ⟨fig⟩ *to bestow on* ≈**flucht** f ~/ *refuge, shelter* || ⟨fig⟩ letzte ~ *last resource* || jdm ~ gewähren *to afford a p refuge* || s–e ~ nehmen zu *to have recourse to, to* (*have*) *resort to, take refuge with, to fall back upon* (*a th*), *to turn to* (*a p, a th*), .. zu den Waffen *to appeal to arms* || ~ suchen ⟨hist⟩ *to seek sanctuary* | **~s-** ~haus [n] *house of refuge*, ⟨hist⟩ *sanctuary*; ~hafen, ~platz, ~ort [m], ~stätte [f] *place of refuge*; *retreat, haven*; *shelter*; *asylum*; ⟨bes hunt⟩ *covert* ≈**fluß** m –usses/≈sse *flowing in, inflow* || *influx, inrush* (*of tourists*) || *flow* (*of blood to the head*) || ⟨tech⟩ *feeder* || ⟨com⟩ *supply* (*of goods*) || (Nebenfluß) *tributary* | ~rohr [n] *supply-, feeding-, inlet-pipe*; *feeder* **~|flüstern** vt [h] (jdm etw) *to whisper* (⟨fig⟩ *insinuate*) (*a th to a p*); ⟨theat⟩ *to prompt* (*a p*) **Z.rung** f ~/~en *whisper* || *insinuation* **~f·olge** prep [gen & dat] *in consequence* (*of*); *according, owing* (*to*) || [dat] *pursuant to* od *in pursuance of* (*the law*) **~fr·ieden** a [pred] *content* (*with*), ⟨Am a.⟩ *proud*; [a. attr] (nicht) ~ (*dis*)*contented*, (*dis*)*satisfied*, (*dis*)*pleased* (*with*) | sich ~ geben (mit) *to content o.s., to rest* od *be content* od *satisfied* (*with*), *to acquiesce* (*in*); *to settle for* (*e.g. a loss*); mit weniger *to settle with less* | ~ l *to leave undisturbed* od *alone* | ~ s mit: (*and hope you will*) *find they are* (*in every way*) *satisfactory*; mit allem .. *to put up with anything* | ich bin **es** ~, ich gebe mich ~ *all right*! | ⟨prov⟩ der ≈e hat immer genug *contentment is better than riches* | ~heit [f] ~/ *content*(*ment*), *contentedness, satisfaction*; zu m–r vollen ~ *very satisfactory*; er führte sich zu m–r größten ~ *he gave great s.n while with me* | ~|stellen [vt h]; e–n ~ *to content, satisfy a p*; *to gratify a p's wishes*; ~stellend [a] *satisfactory* (*answer*), *satisfying* (*meal*) **~|frieren** vi irr [s] *to freeze up* od *over* **~|fügen** vt [h] *to add* || jdm ~ *to cause a p* (*sorrow*), *to do a p* (*an injury*) || jdm Böses ~ *to inflict pain* (*heavy losses*) (*up*)*on a p* || v *or* mit eigner Hand zugefügt *self-*

-inflicted (*wound*) ⁓**fuhr** f ~/~en *importation, supply* (*of goods*) ‖ (Waren) *imports*; *supplies* pl (⟨a. mil⟩: *to cut off the enemy's s.*) ‖ (Lebensmittel) *provisions* pl ‖ ⟨tech⟩ (Kohlen⁓ etc) *feed* | ~stutzen [m] ⟨aero, mot⟩ (*air*) *adapter* ~|**führen** vt [h] *to bring, convey* ([dat] *to*) ‖ *to introduce* (*friends, customers*) ‖ *to waft over* (*scents, sounds*) | ⟨tech, mach, comp⟩ *to feed*; ⟨comp⟩ (Karten) *to load into a hopper*; (Waren) *to supply, import* ‖ (Lebensmittel) *to provision* (*an army*) | jdm e–e Braut ~ *to procure a wife for a p* ‖ jdn der gerechten Bestrafung ~ *to punish a p as he deserves* ‖ jdn s–m Untergange ~ *to cause a p's ruin* | ~d *afferent* (⟨anat⟩ *vessels*, ⟨bot⟩ *ducts*) ⁓**führer** m ⟨tech⟩ *feeder* ⟨a. mil⟩ | ~kreuz [n] (Autobahn⁓) ⟨mot⟩ *interchange* ⁓**führung** f ⟨tech⟩ *feed, supply* | ~**s**- ~anlage [f] *conveying system*; ~raum [m] ⟨crem⟩ *committal room*; ~schlauch [m] *supply tube* ~|**füllen** vt [h] (e–n Graben) *to fill up* ‖ (Wasser) *to add*

Zug m ~(e)s/⁓e **A.** (das **Ziehen**) **1.** *drawing, pull*(*ing*) (⟨a.⟩ beim Rudern); *tug*(*ging*); *stretch*(*ing*) | (mit dem Zügel) *jerk* (⟨a.⟩ Ruck) | ⟨übtr⟩ in groben ⁓en (*describe*) *in broad outline* **2.** (v Zugtieren) *draught* **3.** ⟨mech⟩ *traction, stretching, stress*, (Spannung) *tension*; → ~kraft, Schub **4.** (Fisch⁓) *haul* **5.** (e–s Heeres) *march*(*ing*), *progress, expedition* ‖ → C. ‖ (Feld⁓) *campaign*; *expedition* ‖ s–n ~ nehmen durch *to pass through* **6.** ⟨orn⟩ *migration, flight, passage* **7.** (Luft⁓) *draught* (⟨Am⟩ *draft*), *current of air* ‖ leiser ~ *light air*; *whiff* ‖ (künstlicher) *ventilation* ‖ (im Ofen) *flue*; (im Hochofen) *blast* | die Öfen, Zigarren h k–n ~ .. *do not draw* (*well*) **8.** (beim Rauchen) *whiff* (*to take* [tun] *a few w.s* od *a long, smooth pull at a pipe*) **9.** (beim Trinken) *draught*, ⟨Am⟩ *draft* (*to take* [tun] *a d.* [⟨fam⟩ *pull, gulp, swig*] [aus *at*]) ‖ kl ~ *sip*; kl (gr) Züge tun *to sip* (*quaff*) ‖ e–n guten ~ h *to drink like a fish* ‖ e–n tiefen ~ tun *to drink deep*(*ly*) *of a cup* | **auf** e–n ~ (austrinken) .. *at one draught*, ⟨fam⟩ *go, gulp* | **in** langen Zügen trinken *to take deep d.s* ‖ so richtig im ~e *just nicely* (*drunk*) ‖ ⟨fig⟩ in vollen ⁓en *thoroughly, luxuriously* (s–e Freiheit) .. genießen *to enjoy .. to the full* **10.** ~ nach Westen *westward rush* **11.** (der Wolken) *course*, ⟨a.⟩ *procession* **12.** in den letzten Zügen liegen *to be dying, at one's last gasp* **B.** ⟨chess, etc⟩ *move* ‖ wer ist am ~? *whose m. is it?* ‖ Weiß ist am ~e *white to play* **C.** (**Bewegung**) *drift* (*of clouds*); ⟨fig⟩ ~ in etw bringen *to start .., to set .. going* ‖ es ist kein ~ im Geschäft (in der S) *trade is dull*, (*there's no go in the show*) | **auf** dem ~e *on the march* ‖ auf einen ~; **in, mit** einem ~e *in one breath, at one stretch, stroke* (⟨fam⟩ *go*); *uninterruptedly*; ⟨fam⟩ *straight off*; .. trinken → A. 9. ‖ wir h ihn auf dem ~e *we can't stand him* | **aus** dem ~e k *to get out of practice* | ~ **für** ~ *one by one*; *step by step*; → sofort | **im** ~e ⟨fig⟩ *in train*; (*the work is*) *in hand*, (P) ⟨fig⟩ *to be in full swing*, ⟨Am fam⟩ *to be going strong* ‖ im (besten) *or* so recht im ~e s *to be in full swing, progress, activity, motion, play*, ⟨fig⟩ *to be quite in the vein* ‖ im ~e [gen] *in accordance, compliance with*; *in consequence* od *the course of* | **in** ~ bringen *to start, to set going*; ⟨fig⟩ *to bring into fashion* ‖ in einem ~ *in a single sweep*, .. schlafen .. *without waking* (→ C. auf) | ~ **um** ~ *bit by bit*; *without delay*; ⟨com⟩ *for cash, cash down, c. on delivery*; Erfüllung ~ um ~ *contemporaneous* od *simultaneous performance*; *both parties handing .. over at the same time* **D.** ⟨fig⟩ (**Neigung**) *bent, inclination, disposition*; *bias*; *impulse*; *instinct* ‖ ~ **nach** *desire for* (*automation*, etc) ‖ dem ~e des Herzens folgen *to obey the inner voice* ‖ der ~ des Herzens ist des Schicksals Stimme *one's character is one's fate* ‖ ~ der Zeit *trend* od *sign of the time*(*s*); das ist ein ~ unserer Z. *that is characteristic of our times* ‖ etw ohne rechten ~ tun .. *half-heartedly* ‖ der ~ **zu** etw *the interest in a th* ‖ (Anwandlung) *impulse, bent, whim*; (Einfall) *idea, brainwave* **E.** (**Strich, Linie**) **1.** *stroke, dash, flourish* (*of the pen*) ‖ in gr Zügen schildern *to sketch* ‖ in kräftigen (kurzen) Zügen *in bold outlines* (*in a few strokes*); (Umrisse) *lineaments*; (Schnörkel) *flourish* **2.** (Gesichts⁓e) *features* (⟨a. paint⟩, etc); grobe ⁓e *homeliness* (mit g.n ⁓en *coarse-faced*); ohne bestimmte ⁓e *featureless* ‖ mit scharfen Zügen *sharp-featured* (*man*) ‖ ein ehrlicher ~ im Gesicht *an honest expression of countenance* **3.** (Charakter⁓) *trait, touch, characteristic, ch. tr.*; *note in* od *feature of a p's character* ‖ *the point* (*of a story*) ‖ ein melancholischer ~ *a strain* od *streak of m.* **4.** (Anflug, Spur) *suggestion, suspicion, shade, tinge, vein* **F.** (**Kette, Reihe, Schar**) **1.** (P) *file, column*; ⟨mil⟩ → u. ‖ (Arbeiter) *gang* ‖ (Gefolge) *retinue, train* ‖ (Fest⁓) *procession* (dazu: *to pr. a town* = durch ..) ‖ (Um⁓) *procession*, ⟨pol⟩ *demonstration, manifestation* | ⟨mil⟩ *platoon, troop, section*; ⟨artill⟩ *train, section*; (Reiter) *troop*; ⟨mus⟩ *band* | *coffle* (*of slaves*) ‖ ~ v Trägern *safari* **2.** ⟨zoo⟩ *herd, flock, troop, pack* | ⟨orn⟩ *flight, flock, bevy* | ⟨ich⟩ *shoal* | (Gespann) *team* **3.** (v Bergen) *range* ‖ (v Häusern) *row* **4.** (v Wagen) *file, line* | ⟨**rail**⟩ *train* ‖ D-~ *corridor-t.*; Güter⁓ *goods-t.*; Pn⁓ *passenger-t.*; Schnell⁓ *fast* od *express t., express* ‖ ⟨fig⟩ ganze ⁓e voll *trainloads* (*of*) | abgehender (ank–der) ~, ~ v (nach) London etc *down-* (*up-*) *t.* ‖ (außer)planmäßig (*un*)*scheduled*, (⟨Am⟩ *wildcat*) durchgehender (*or* FD-)~ *through* od *non-stop, direct t.* ‖ fahrplanmäßig *regular*, gemischt *mixed*, verspätet *delayed*, ~ z Überfahrtschiff *boat t.*, zus–gestellter ~ *multiple unit t.*, zuschlagpflichtig *limited*; *extra fare t.* ‖ (der ~) hat Verspätung .. *is late* od *overdue* | ablassen *to start* ‖ abfahren (ank) sollend *due out* (*in*) ‖ e–n ~ abfertigen *to dispatch a t.* ‖ den ~ erreichen (versäumen) *to catch* (*miss*) *one's t.* ‖ den ~ verlassen *to detrain* ‖ ⁓e zus–stellen *to marshal t.s* | **im** ~ ..: *to read in, to lunch on, to be in* (Am *on board*) *the t.*; in den ~ (ein)steigen *to enter* od *board the t., to get* (*on*) *the t.* | **mit**: *by the 7.15* (*t.*); *by the 5 o'clock t.*; *I come on the t.* od *by t. every day*; mit dem ~ abfahren *to leave by t.*, mit dem ~ fahren nach *to take t. to* ‖ der O. ist **zu** allen Zügen an der Bahn *the bus meets all t.s*; jdn zum ~ begleiten *to see a p off* ‖ → Geleit⁓, Leichen⁓, Fest⁓, Um⁓ **G.** ⟨**tech**⟩ (Flaschen⁓) *pulley* ‖ (im Gewehrlauf) *rifle, groove*; [pl a.] *rifling*; ohne Züge *unrifled* ‖ (Gummi⁓) *side-elastic* ‖ (Hebezeug) *hoist*; ⟨theat⟩ ⁓e *flys*, ⟨Am⟩ *flies*, mechanischer ~ *tracker line*, (⟨Am⟩ *wire*) ‖ (Kleider⁓) *drawing-string* ‖ (Klingel⁓) (*bell-*)*pull* ‖ (e–s Meilers) *air hole, funnel* ‖ (Orgel⁓) *register, stop*(*-knob*) ‖ (Pumpen⁓) *piston* ‖ (Saiten⁓) *set* ‖ (Stiefel⁓) *elastic side-spring* ‖ (Tür⁓) *contrivance to open a gate*, etc *from within* ‖ (Ösen⁓) *hoist with suspension eyes* | ⟨surv⟩ (über Tage) *survey line on surface*, .. unter Tage *draft underground* ~**abfahrt(-ankunft-)tafel** f *train departure* (*arrival*) *indicator* ~**abfertigung** f *t. dispatch* (*service*) ~**abteil** n *compartment* ~**ameise** f (etc: ⟨zoo, ent⟩) *migratory ant*, etc ~**angel** f *night-line, trimmer* ~**anker** m ⟨arch⟩ *tension anchor, tie rod, iron tie* ~**ankündiger** m *train announcer* ~**artikel** m ⟨com⟩ *popular article*; ⟨fam⟩ *draw, flat-catcher* ~**balken** m ⟨carp⟩ *anchor tie beam* ~**band** n *draw-string*; ⟨parachute⟩ *shock cord* ~**beanspruchung**, ~**belastung** f *tensile load* od *stress* ~**begleitpersonal** n *train-staff*, ⟨Am⟩ *t. crew* ~**bereich** m ⟨mil⟩ *platoon sector* ~**bildung** ⟨rail⟩ *forming of trains, making-up of a t.* | ~**s**- ~gleis [n] *classification track* ~**bolzen** m *set bolt* ~**breite** f ⟨mil⟩ *front of a platoon*, etc ~**brücke** f *draw-* (*bascule-*) *bridge* ~**dichte** f *interval between*

2 tr.s; tr. succession; block system **~dienst** m *tr. service* | ~leiter [m] *tr. dispatcher* **~druckverhältnis** n *ratio of tension and thrust* **~elastizität** f *e.y of extension* **~ende** n ⟨rail⟩ *rear of tr.* **~entgleisung** f *derailment;* ⟨Am⟩ *tr. wreck* **~exerzieren** n *drilling in files,* etc **~fähre** f ⟨rail⟩ *ferry--bridge* **~fänger** m *draught excluder* **~feder** f ⟨tech⟩ *draw* (od *tension, traction* [Uhr *barrel*]) *spring* **~festigkeit** f ⟨met⟩ *tensile strength* **~fisch** m *m. fish* **~flugzeug** n *tractor airplane* **~folge** f → –dichte **~förderung** f (⟨el⟩ *electric*) *traction* | **~s-** ~ausrüstung [f] ⟨el⟩ (*automatic*) *traction equipment;* ~leistung [f] *traction output* (*of an heat engine*) **≗frei** a *non-draught,* ⟨Am⟩ *non-draft* **~führer** m ⟨mil⟩ *platoon* (etc) *commander;* ⟨rail⟩ (*chief*) *guard,* ⟨Am⟩ *conductor* **~funk** m *train radio telephony* **~gardine** f *draw--curtain* **~garn** n *drag-net* **~gespräch** n ⟨telph⟩ *tr.-call* **~graben** m *drainage ditch* **~griff** m *handle* **~gurt** m *trace* **~haken** m *tug-iron, pole-hook;* ⟨rail, mot⟩ *draw hook;* U-förmig *clevis* **~heuschrecke** f *m. locust* **~kanal** m (Ofen) *flue* **~kette** f ⟨rail⟩ *coupling-chain* **~kilometer** m ⟨rail⟩ *tr. k.* **~klappe** f *damper* **~knopf** m *pulling knob* **~knoten** m *running knot* **~kolonne** f ⟨mil⟩ *column of platoons* **~kraft** f *tractive* od *tensile power* ‖ ⟨fig⟩ *attractiveness* ‖ ⟨ad⟩ *attention value; appeal* ‖ ⟨theat⟩ *drawing power;* ~ h *to go with a swing, to be a draw* ‖ ⟨el⟩ *traction,* ~ am Radumfang *t.n effort,* ~ bei Stundenleistung *hourly tractive effort* | ~wagen [m] *tractor; prime mover* **≗kräftig** a *attractive* **~lampe** f *rise-and-fall pendant; air lamp* **~laufmelder** (S) = –schreiber **~leine** f *towing-, drag-line;* ~n [pl] ⟨theat⟩ *set of lines,* ⟨Am⟩ *pull up* **~leistung** f *tractive output;* (T) *draught efficiency* **~linie** f = –weg **~loch** n *air-, draught-hole* **~luft** f *draught of air* | ~schraube [f] *tractor-type propeller* **~maschine** f *tractor* ‖ durch ~ gezogen *t.r-drawn* **~material** n ⟨rail⟩ *rolling stock* **~messer** m *tension dynamometer* **~mittel** n *attraction* **~netz** n = –garn **~ochse** m *draught-ox* **~ofen** m *blast-furnace* **~pause** f → –dichte **~personal** n ⟨rail⟩ → –begleit– **~pferd** n *harness-, draught-horse,* ⟨Am⟩ *drafter* **~pflaster** n ⟨med⟩ *blister* **~richtung** f → Fahrt–; ⟨tech⟩ *trajectory motion* **~riemen** m *pulling strap;* ⟨hors⟩ *trace, draught* **~rolle** f *pulley* **~schalter** m ⟨el⟩ *pull-switch* **~scheibe** f ⟨mil⟩ *vanishing target* **~schieber** m *chimney damper* **~schnur** f *string* **~schraube** f ⟨aero⟩ *tractor* **~schreiber** m *tr. describer* **~seil** n *tension rope, draw-line;* ⟨tech⟩ *hauling cable;* ⟨mar⟩ *hawser* **~sicherung** f ⟨rail⟩ *tr.-protection* **~spannung** f *tensile stress* | die **~spitze** ist Deutschlands höchster Berg **~stange** f ⟨tech⟩ *draw-beam; cylinder bolt;* ⟨theat⟩ *fly-bar* **~star** m ⟨theat⟩ *drawing card* **~stiefel** m pl *elastic-sided boots* pl, ⟨Am⟩ *congress boots* **~straße** f ⟨zoo⟩ *route of migration;* ⟨orn⟩ = –weg **~streife** f *tr. patrol* **~stück** n ⟨film⟩ *extra feature;* ⟨theat⟩ *piece that draws,* ⟨fam⟩ *hit, draw;* ⟨sl⟩ *pipper* **~tau** n *drag-rope* **~telephon** n *t. on the tr.* **~tiere** n pl *draught-animals* **~überwachung** f (zentrale *centralized*) *traffic control C.T.C.* **~unfall** m *tr. accident* **~verband** m ⟨surg⟩ *extension apparatus* **~verkehr** m *tr.* od *rail traffic; running of tr.s* **~verspätung** f *tr. delay* **~versuch** m *tensile test* **~vieh** n *draught-cattle* **~vogel** m *bird of passage* **~vorrichtung** f *draw-gear;* ⟨theat⟩ (*scenic*) *flying equipment;* ⟨mot⟩ *traction gear* **~wagen** m *camion* **~weg** m ⟨orn⟩ *flyline, flyway* **≗weise** adv *in* od *by troops, platoons,* etc; *in flocks;* ⟨mil⟩ *in platoons,* etc **~wind** m *draught of air* **~winde** f *windlass* **~zünder** m *pull igniter* od *ignitor* **~zus-stellung** f *tr. formation*

z·u- **≗gabe** f ~/~n *addition, extra, adjunct* ‖ (z Gewicht) *make-weight, surplus;* ⟨Am fam⟩ *throw-in* ‖ ⟨theat, mus, etc⟩ *encore* ‖ als ~ *into the bargain* **≗gang** m **1.** *access* (*to the sea*); *approach* (*to*) ‖ (Weg) *avenue* ‖ (Eingang) *entrance, entry* ‖ (Tor) *gate*(*way*) ‖ ⟨comp⟩ → –griff ‖ ~ h (zu) *to have access* (*to*) ‖ sich selbst ~ verschaffen *to let o.s. in* **2.** *arrival*(*s* pl), *supply* (an *in*) **3.** *increase* ⟨a. mil⟩ ‖ ⟨mil⟩ *reinforcement* **4.** ⟨com⟩ ~ u Abgang *profit and loss;* ⟨mil⟩ ≗e u Ab≗e *admission and disposition* ⟨a. med⟩ | ≗e k *to get on* (mit *with*) | **~s-** ~jahr [n] ⟨ins⟩ *y. of acceptance;* ~karte [f] ⟨comp com⟩ *receipt card;* ~stollen [m] *access* (⟨Am⟩ *entrance*) *gallery* **~gänglich** a *accessible* (für *to,* ⟨a. fig⟩) ‖ leicht ~ *easy of access* ‖ ~ f *open to* ‖ (benutzbar) *available* | (P) *of easy access; affable; responsive* (*to*); schwer ~e Stelle *hard-to-get-at place* | ~ m *to render accessible,* ⟨fig⟩ allgemein ~ m *to throw open* (*to the public*) ‖ jdm ~ m *to bring* (*a book*) *within reach of a p* ‖ mehr als was den Augen ~ ist *more than meets the eye* | (P) ein leicht ~er Mann *a man of open approach;* nicht ~ f *proof against* (*bribes*) ‖ *come-at-able* ‖ ~es Mädchen ⟨sl⟩ *bit of jam; being free of her lips, free of her hips;* → frech (aber ~) | ≗keit [f] ~/ *accessibility* ‖ *affability* **~|geben** vt irr [h] (hinzugeben) *to add* ‖ ⟨cards⟩ *to follow suit* ‖ ⟨com⟩ *to throw in; to give into the bargain* | (erlauben) *to allow, grant* ‖ *to concede* ‖ wir w es nicht ~! *we won't have it!* | (bekennen) *to confess, acknowledge* (*that*); etw (offen) ~ *to own* (*up*) *to a th;* sein Unrecht ~ *to stand corrected* | (anerkennen) *to admit* (*a th,* sein Unrecht *being in the wrong,* getan z h *doing*) ‖ ich gebe gern z, daß *I don't mind telling you that ..* ‖ man muß ~, daß .. *the Major must be allowed to have had great merit* | → **-ge-** ~**gedacht** a *destined, intended, meant* ([dat] *for*) **~gefroren** pp v ~frieren **~gegeben** a *granting, -ted; admitting, -ted, given* (*that*) ‖ *grant* (*its monotony there remains ..*)!; *true* (*she sings well*) ‖ dies ~ *this allowed for* ‖ ~! *I concede the point* **~g·egen** pred a (bei) *present* (*at*) ‖ ~ s bei ⟨a.⟩ *to assist at, to attend* **~geh-** ~frau *charwoman,* ⟨Am⟩ *clearing woman* **~|gehen** vi irr [s] **1.** *to go on, to walk faster* ‖ gut ~ *to walk a good pace* ‖ geh(t) zu! *get along!, move on!* **2.** ⟨fam⟩ (sich schließen) *to close, shut, lock* **3.** (geschehen) *to happen* ‖ wie geht (ging) es zu, daß? *how is* (*came*) *it that ..?* ‖ ⟨Am fam/vulg⟩ *how come?* [⟨a.⟩ abs] ‖ so geht es zu in der Welt *that is the way of the world, such is life* ‖ es geht merkwürdig zu in der Welt (im Reiche der Sprache) *this is a queer w., the ths that happen!* (*curious ths happen in the realm of l.*) ‖ so geht es im Kriege eben zu *war is war* ‖ es müßte mit dem Teufel ~, wenn *the devil must be in it if ..* (→ Ding) **4.** (vor sich gehen) *to proceed* **5.** (in e–e Spitze etc ~) *to end* (*in a point,* etc) **6.** jdm ~ (zugesandt w) *to reach a p, to come to a p's hand* | jdm ~ l *to forward to a p; to convey* (*an admonition*) *to a p* **7.** ~ **auf** [acc] *to move, advance, walk* (od *to direct one's steps*) *towards; to go, step, walk up to; to be getting on for; to head* od *make for* ‖ er geht auf (die) 80 zu *he's going on 80* ⟨fam⟩ | er ging **über** den Flur der Tür zu *he crossed the hall to the door* **~|gehören** vi [h] [dat] *to belong, appertain* (*to*) ‖ es gehört e–e gr Frechheit zu so etw *it is a sign of ..* ‖ ⟨cul⟩ es gehört .. zu ..: *.. should be served, eaten,* etc *with ..* **~gehörig** a **1.** (zu) *appertaining, belonging* (*to*); *appropriate* (*to, for*) ‖ *requisite* (*furniture*); (*envelopes*) *to match;* nicht ~ ⟨a.⟩ *unassigned;* ohne ~e Karte ⟨comp⟩ *with no corresponding c.* **2.** *proper, becoming* | ≗keit [f] ~/ (zu) *belonging* (*to*) ‖ (Mitgliedschaft) *membership* (*of*) ‖ Gefühl der ~ *sense of kinship* **~gekehrt** a ⟨phot⟩ *facing* (*the lens*) **~geknöpft** a ⟨fam⟩ *buttoned-up* ⟨a. fig⟩, *remote, reserved* ‖ (geizig) *costive*

Z·ügel m ~s/~ *rein,* ⟨a.⟩ *ribbon* ‖ ⟨orn⟩ *lore* ‖ (Zaumzeug) *bridle* (*to lead by* [am] *the b.*); [dat] die ~ geben *to give liberty to a mount* | **am**

~ halten *to rein in* ⟨a. fig⟩; ⟨hors⟩ geht gut am ~ *is going well up to his b.* | **im** ~ halten ⟨fam⟩ *to hold in* || [dat] **in** die ~ fallen *to seize .. by the b.* | ⟨fig⟩ *curb, restraint; reins* (*of government*) | im ~ halten *to control; to keep in check* || e–r S ~ anlegen *to put the brake on a th* || die ~ anziehen *to draw rein* ⟨a. fig⟩; .. fester .. *to take a shorter grip on the lines* || [dat] den ~ fahren, schießen l *to let go the reins, to give* (*a horse*) *his head* od *the rein*(*s* pl), ⟨fig⟩ *to let a p* (*have his fling* od) *do as he likes* | **mit** verhängtem ~ *at full gallop* **~hand** f *bridle-, near* (= *left*) *hand* **~los** a *unbridled* (⟨a. fig⟩: *tyranny*); ⟨fig⟩ *intemperate, wild, rampant, uncurbed, unchecked* || *outrageous* (*behavio*[*u*]*r*); *riotous* (*living*) || ~ w *to get out of hand* || ⟨fig⟩ *inordinate* (*pride*); *unrestrained* (*passion*); *unruly, dissolute* (*p*) || (toll) *frenetic*(*al*), ⟨a.⟩ *phr..* **~losigkeit** f ⟨fig⟩ *licentiousness, dissoluteness* || *looseness* (*of morals*) || *disorderly doings* || *extravagance* **~ring** m *terret* **~schieber** m *bridle-slide*

z·ugelassen a *allowed* || ⟨aero⟩ *airworthy* || amtlich ~ *authorized; certified* (*midwife*)

z·ügeln (→ Zügel) vt [h] ⟨a. fig⟩ *to rein* (*in*), *bridle, curb* || ⟨fig⟩ *to govern* (*the conversation*) *sharply* || sich ~ *to check* od *contain, restrain, control o.s.*

z·u- **~gemüse** n *vegetables, greens,* ⟨fam⟩ *trimmings* pl **~genannt** a *surnamed* **~geneigt** a = zugetan **~geordnet** = beigeordnet **~gereist** a: er ist ~ *he is not a native* **~geritten** a *broken-in* (*horse*) || nicht ~ *unbroken, unbacked* **~geschnitten** (→ –schneiden) || ⟨tail⟩ sehr schlecht ~ *very ill-cut* || ⟨übtr⟩ *cut out, tailored* (f *for*) **~|gesellen** vt & sich ~ [h] [dat] *to associate* (*with*) **~gespitzt** a *pointed, tapering* || ⟨phot⟩ *spaced, trimmed* (*end of a film*) || ⟨bot⟩ *acuminate* || ⟨tech⟩ konisch ~ *coned, conical* || ⟨fig⟩ *acute*; epigrammatisch ~ *turned into an epigram* **~gestandenermaßen** adv *admittedly* **~geständnis** n *admission* || *concession* || [pl] ~se m *to make c.s* **~|gesteh(e)n** vt irr [h] *to admit* || (Fehler) *to own, confess* || (e–m etw) *to grant, concede* **~getan** a *affectionate*; [dat] *attached, devoted* (*to*); mit Leib u Seele ~ *passionately addicted* (*to a p*) || e–m ~ s *to be fond of, to feel kindly to, to have a great affection for a p* **~gewandt** a ⟨eco⟩ (*Britain is*) *committed* (*to Europe*) **~|gießen** vt irr [h] *to pour on/into* || *to stop up* (*holes*)

z·ugig a *windy* (*plane*), *draughty* (*room*), *bleak* (*hill*) **z·ügig** a = schwungvoll | ⟨adv⟩ *in a fluid motion*; ⟨mot⟩ (*to overtake*) *smartly,* (*to change gears*) *smoothly* | ~keit [f] des Verkehrs *easy flow of traffic*

z·u- **~gl·eich** adv *at once* || *at the same time* (mit mir *as I*) || ~ auch .. = .. *as well, .. alike* || ~ mit *together with* || .. u ~ .. = *both .. and ..* || alle ~ *jointly, together, in a body* || mehrere *or* zu viele Dinge ~ tun ⟨a.⟩ *to burn the candle at both ends* **~|greifen** vi irr [h] **1.** *to stretch out one's hand* (*to take a th*), *to make a grab* || (v Anker) *to bite* | ⟨fig fam⟩ mit allen fünf Fingern ~ (nach) *to jump at a th* || er braucht nur –zu– *he may have it for the mere asking* || leicht ~ *to be light-fingered* **2.** (bei Tische) *to help o.s.*; ⟨fam⟩ *to fall to*; tüchtig ~ *to tuck* (⟨Am⟩ *pitch*) *in, to take one's teeth to ..* || ⟨a.⟩ kräftig ~ *to play at food vigorously* **3.** (Hand anlegen) *to bear* od *lend a hand* | ~d ⟨a.⟩ *unhesitating* **~griff** m *grip, clutch*(*es* pl) || ⟨comp⟩ (direkter *direct*, serialer *serial*, wahlfreier, beliebiger *random*) *access* [⟨a.⟩ attr]; kein ~ *access inoperable* | **~s-** ~zeit [f] (zum Speicher) *access time*; ~zeitfrei [a] *zero-access* (*storage*)

zugr·unde adv (→ Grund I. B. 2. 7) | (völlig) **~|gehen** ⟨fig⟩ *to go to* (*rack and*) *ruin*; *to perish, to come to grief,* ⟨fam⟩ *to go to pot* | ~ n *ruin*(*ation*) **~|legen** vt [h] *to take as basis*; *to presuppose* **Z.gung** f: mit *or* unter ~ v *taking as a basis* (*to work on*) | e–r S **~|liegen** vi [h] *to be at the bottom of a th*; ⟨fig⟩ *to underlie a th, to form the basis of a th* **~|richten** vt [h] *to ruin, destroy, wreck*; *to lay low*; ⟨fam⟩ *to undo*; *to do for* .. (*I'm done for*) || jdn ~ ⟨a.⟩ *to break a p* **Z.tung** f *destruction*

z·u- **~|gucken** vi [h] ⟨fam⟩ *to look on* **~g·unsten** prep [gen] *in favour of*; *for the benefit of* || ~ jds handeln ⟨a.⟩ *to play a p's game*; es läßt sich viel (nur wenig) ~ des N. N. sagen *a good* (*a bad, weak*) *case can* (*only*) *be made out for him* **~g·ute** adv; jdm etw ~ halten (anrechnen) *to account to a p for a th* || (verzeihen) *to pardon a p a th* || [dat] ~ k *to be for the benefit of*; .. kam ihm ~ *he enjoyed the b. of*; *allowance was made for* (*his youth*); jdm etw ~ k l *to give a p the benefit of a th* || e–m etw ~ tun *to treat a p to a th* | sich (etw) ~ tun *to enjoy a th*; sich auf etw ~ tun (= stolz s) *to pique, pride, plume o.s. on a th, to be very proud of a th, to take* (*much*) *credit for a th*; *to make it a boast to do, to make a b. of ..* **~guterl·etzt** (= z g. L.) adv *in the end, last but not least* **~|haben** vt irr [h] *to have shut* || den Rock ~ *to have one's coat buttoned up* **~|haken** vt [h] *to hook up, to clasp* || (Tür) *to hasp* **~|halten I.** vt irr [h] *to keep closed, to stop* || die Hand ~ *to clench one's fist* || sich [dat] die Nase, Ohren *to hold one's nose, to stop* od *cover one's ears* **II. sich** ~ *to bestir o.s.* **III.** vi [h] ~ auf [acc] *to make for* **~hälter** m ~s/~ *procurer, souteneur* Fr; ⟨sl⟩ *bully, pimp* | ~·ei [f] *trading in prostitution*; (schwere *aggravated*) *procuration*; ⟨fam⟩ *pandering*; ~in [f] *procuress*; ⟨Am sl⟩ *auntie* **~haltung** f ⟨tech⟩ *tumbler* **~hämmern** n → –nageln || ⟨mill⟩ *impact action of the grinding balls* **~h·anden** [adv] *at hand*; *ready* || *in* od *to hand* || → zu Händen **~|hängen** vt irr [h] *to hang* od *cover with a curtain* (etc) **~|hauen** irr **I.** vt [h] *to shape by hewing, to rough-hew* **II.** vi [h] *to strike* || auf: *to deal out blows to* (*a p*) **~h·auf** [adv] ⟨poet⟩ *together* **~h·ause** n ~/ *home* (*she has no h.*) || *at-h.* (*it is her at-h. today* = *she will be at h. today*) **~|hefteln** vi [h] *to clasp* **~|heften** vt [h] *to stitch* (⟨übtr⟩ *patch*) *up* **~|heilen** vt [h] & vi [s] *to heal up, to close* **~h·ilfenahme** f ~/; mit *or* unter ~ v *with the aid of* || *by* (*having*) *recourse to* **~h·interst** [adv] *at the very end* **~h·öchst** a *highest of all* | adv *at the very top* **~|horchen** vi [h] = –hören || heimlich ~ *to eavesdrop* **~|hören** vi [h] [dat] *to listen* (*to*), *to attend* (*to*); angespannt ~ *to listen with all one's ears*; genau ~ *to listen closely* || ohne –zu– *listlessly* **~hörer** m *hearer, auditor* || guter ~ *good listener* || die ~ [pl] *the audience* [pl konstr] || der Professor hat viele ~ *the p.'s lectures are well attended* | ~schaft [f] ~/ *audience* [pl konstr] || aufmerksame ~ *eagerly listening assembly* [pl konstr] **~·innerst** adv *innermost* || *in my* (etc) *heart of hearts* **~|jagen I.** vi [s] ([dat], auf [acc]) *to chase, gallop, rush* (*towards*) || jag' zu! *gallop on*!; ⟨mot⟩ *speed on*!, ⟨fam⟩ *go it*! **II.** vt [dat] *to drive* (*game*) *towards a p* **~|jauchzen, ~|jubeln I.** vi [h] (jdm) *to hail, acclaim, cheer* (*a p*) || ⟨bes Am sl⟩ *to root for* (*a p*) || e–m Beifall ~ *to applaud a p with loud acclamations* **II.** ~ n *cheers* pl **~|kaufen** vt [h] *to buy in addition* **~|kehren** vt [h] [dat] *to turn* (*to*) || jdm das Gesicht ~ *to face a p*, das G. jdm –ge–rt *with the face towards a p*; jdm den Rücken ~ *to turn one's back upon a p* || sich jdm ~ *to turn to a p* **~|keilen** vt [h] *to wedge up* **~|ketten** vt [h] *to chain up* **~|kitten** vt [h] *to cement* **~|klappen** vt [h] & vi [s] *to bang, slam* (⟨fam⟩ *to*); || (Buch) *to close* (*with a snap*) || (*the teeth*) *snap to* **~|klatschen** vi [h] (jdm) *to clap one's hands* (*to a p*), *to applaud* (*a p*) **~|kleben** vt [h] *to glue* od *paste up* **~|kleistern** vt [h] *to paste up* **~|klinken** vt [h] *to latch up* **~|kneifen** vt [h] (die Augen) *to shut* **~|knöpfen** vt [h] *to button up* || der Rock läßt sich nicht ~ .. *does not button* || → zugeknöpft **~|knüpfen** vt [h] *to tie* (*up*) **~|kommen** vi irr [s] **A.** auf e–n ~ *to come up to, to approach a p* **B.** e–m ~ **1.** *to come to a p('s hands), to reach a p; to fall to a p's lot* od *share*; (rechtmäßig) *to inhere in* (*a p*) || e~m ~ l *to let a p have .., to pass .. on to a p; to send* od *forward .. to a p*; (freundlichst) *to favo(u)r a p with* (*answer, attention,* etc) || (verschaffen) *to put a p in the way of a th* **2.** (anheimfallen) *to fall to a p's share* **3.** (angehören) *to belong to* **4.** (gebühren) *to be due to* || das k–t mir nicht zu *I have no right to it* || die mir ~de Pflicht *the duty I was called upon to fulfil* || jedem was ihm z–t *to everyone his due* **5.** (geziemen) *to become, befit* (*a p*) || es k–t dir nicht zu, das zu sagen *it is not for you to say that* || .., wie es e–m G. z–t *he acted in a gentlemanly manner* ×°**~|können** vi [h] da kann ich nichts zu *it isn't my fault* **~|korken** vt [h] *to cork* (*up*) **≗kost** f ~/ *trimmings, vegetables, preserves* pl; ⟨Am⟩ *side dish(es* pl) **~|kratzen** vt [h] *to cover* od *fill up by scratching* °**~|kriegen** vt [h] = zu bekommen **≗kunft** f ~/ *future*; *time to come* || ⟨gram⟩ *f. tense* || (Aussichten) *prospects* pl || der Mann der ~ *the coming man* || in ~ *in f., for the f.; afterwards, hereafter, henceforth; by and by; later; from here* od *now on* || der Blick in die ~ *the forward look*; in die ~ blickend *forward looking* || e–e gr ~ (vor sich) h *to have a* (*great*) *f.* (*he will go* od *is going far*) **| ~s-** ~aussichten [f pl] *prospects ahead*; ≗freudig [a] *optimistic*; ~hellsichtigkeit [f] *precognitive telepathy*; ~möglichkeiten [f pl] *prospects*; ~musik [f] *Wagnerian music* || ⟨fig⟩ *dreams* pl *of the future, castles in Spain*; ~pläne [m pl] *plans for the f.*; ≗reich [a] *very promising*; ~roman [m] *novel of the f., science n., technical fiction n.*; ~strategie [f] *forward s.y* **~künftig** a *future* || *intending* (*lawyer*) || (voraussichtlich) *prospective* (*son-in-law*); *he's by way of being my s.-in-l.* || die ~e Frau N. *Mrs. N. that is to be* || ⟨fam⟩ s–e ≗e, (ihr ≗er) *his* (*her*) *intended; his bride-to-be* od *br.-elect* **|** [adv] *in future* **~|lächeln** vi [h] [dat] *to smile* (*at*); [matt] *to give* (*a p*) *a* [*shadow of a*] *smile* || e–m Beifall ~ *to smile approval at a p* **≗ladung** f ⟨aero⟩ *disposable load* **≗lage** f ~/~n *addition* || (Zuschuß) *increase* (*of salary*), *rise*; *extra pay* || *benefit*; *allowance* (*family a.* Kinder-≗); ⟨mil⟩ Sold u ~n *pay and a.* || ⟨com⟩ *makeweight* || e–m ~ geben *to raise a p's pay* **~l·ande** [adv] bei uns ~ *in my native country* **~|langen I.** vt [h] [dat] *to hand .. to* **II.** vi [h] (bei Tisch) → zu|greifen || langen Sie noch einmal zu *have another helping* || (ausreichen) *to suffice, to be sufficient* || das wird ~ ⟨fam⟩ *that will do* **~länglich** a *sufficient, adequate* **≗laß** [m] f jedermann *open house* **~|lassen** vt irr [h] **1.** *to leave shut*, etc **2.** (einlassen) *to let in, to admit*; als Student ~ *to enter a p* (*as a student*); als Barrister –ge– w *to be called* (⟨Am⟩ *admitted*) *to the bar* || (Hengst) *to let cover* || ⟨tech⟩ *to turn on* (*steam*) **3.** (erlauben) *to allow* (a. v Mitteln), *permit, suffer* || *to accept* (*an excuse*) || ⟨film⟩ *to release* || ⟨Lit⟩ *to license* || es ~ *to consent* || es nicht ~: *she wouldn't hear of it, she objected to it*; wir l (es) nicht zu, daß es besprochen wird *we wouldn't have it discussed* || ~, daß *to suffer, yield* [+ acc + inf; ⟨a.⟩ ell]: *why did I ever suffer him* (*to be*) *away from me?* **| ~d** *permissive* **4.** *to admit of, to be susceptible of* (*doubts, an explanation*) **~lässig** a *safe* od *admissible* (*load*); ~e Bügeltemperatur *safe ironing temperature*; *permissible* (*derivation*) || *allowable, granted* || ~e Abweichung ⟨tech⟩ *tolerance*; ~er Wassergehalt *water t.*; *t. limit*; *allowance* **|** das ist nicht ~ *that is not allowed*; ⟨jur⟩ (*the appeal*) *does not lie* **| ≗keit** [f] *permissibility* **≗lassung** f ~/~en *admission* || *permission* || *approval* || ⟨Lit & off⟩ *licence*, ⟨Am⟩ *-se*; auf Grund e–r ~ *under a l.*; ~ z Studium *access to studies* **| ~s-** ~bescheinigung [f] ⟨aero⟩ *certificate of airworthiness*; ~fähigkeit [f] *acceptability*; ~gesuch [n] *application for admission* (*to an examination*); ~karte [f] *admission ticket*; ~marke [f] *voucher*; ~nummer [f] ⟨bes mot⟩ *registration* od *licence*, ⟨Am⟩ *-se n.* ~prüfung [f] *entrance-examination*; *acceptance test*; ⟨aero⟩ *certification test*; ~schein [m] *ticket of admission*; ⟨off⟩ *licence*, ⟨Am⟩ *-se*; ~zeichen [n] *registration mark* **≗lauf** m ~(e)s/ ⟨mach⟩ *inlet* || ⟨found⟩ *runner* **|** (P) *rush, crowd, concourse* || (v Kunden) *run* **|** ~ h *to be much sought after, to be "all the go"* od *in vogue*; (v Ärzten) *to have a good practice*; (v Predigern, [Professoren]) *to draw large congregations* [*audiences*]; ⟨theat⟩ *to draw full houses, to have a long run*; ⟨com⟩ *to have a large custom* **|** ~rinne [f] ⟨mach⟩ *feeding chute* **~|laufen I.** vi irr [s] **1.** *to run on* od *faster* **2.** (jdm) *to crowd* od *flock to* || –ge–er Hund *stray dog* (*having found a new home*) **3.** (auf jdn) *to run up to* **4.** spitz ~ *to end in a point, to taper* → zugespitzt **II.** ≗ n Ab- u ~ *running to and fro* **≗legemesser** n *clasp-knife* **~|legen I.** vt [h] **1.** *to cover up ..* (*with ..*) || (Messer) *to shut* **2.** *to add ..* (*for service*) || ⟨artill⟩ *to increase the range* || ⟨com⟩ noch etw ~ *to give a little more* **3.** jdm 10 Mark ~ *to raise a p's pay by 10 marks* **|** sich [dat] etw ~ *to secure* od *acquire a th, to provide o.s. with a th*; ⟨fam⟩ *to get* (*a new hat*), *to buy* (*a car*) **II.** ⟨fam⟩ vi [h] *to put on flesh* **~l·eide** [adv] jdm etw ~ tun *to hurt a p*; was h wir ihm ~ getan? *what harm have we done him?* **~|leimen** vt [h] *to glue* od *paste up, to cement* **~|leiten** vt [h] (einlassen) *to let in* || [dat] *to conduct .. to; to bring .. before*; ⟨telph⟩ *to put* (*calls*) *through to* **≗leitung** f ~/~en *conducting* **|** *supply line; feed-, inlet-pipe* || ⟨el⟩ (Stromleiter) *lead; lead-in wire* || [in comp] → Zufluß- **~|lernen** vt [h] *to go on learning* || man lernt immer zu *live and learn* **~l·etzt** [adv] *at last, lastly, finally*; nicht ~ *last but not least* || (als letzte[r], ~s) *last* || (*for*) *the last time* || ~ k *to be the last* (*to come*), *to come last, to bring up the rear* || (*when I was here*) *last* || wann h Sie ihn ~ gesehen? *when did you see him last*, ⟨a.⟩ *the last she had seen of him was getting into the car* || ~ kam er doch noch *he came after all* **~l·iebe** [adv] jdm ~ (*in order*) *to oblige* od *please a p* || (*do it*) *for my sake; for the love* od *sake of me*; jdm (gern) etw ~ tun *to do a p a good turn* **~|lispeln** vt [h] = –flüstern **~|löten** vt [h] *to solder up*

z·ullen vi [h] *to suck* **z·ulpen** vi [h] (*of water*) *to splash*; (*of brooklet*) *to babble*

Z·ulu m, **~frau** f *Zulu, Zulu woman*

zum = zu dem

z·u- ~|machen I. vt [h] *to shut, close* (⟨a.⟩ Fenster[läden], Tür) || (Brief) *to close* || (Deckel) *to put down* || (Kleidungsstück) *to button up* || (Schirm) *to put down* || (Öffnung) *to stop* (*up*) || fest ~ *to fasten* (*a door*) || ⟨com⟩ den Laden ~ *to shut up shop; to do up*, –ge–cht w *it does up* (*with zip-fastener*) **II.** vi [h] mach zu! (*make haste!*), *be quick!, hurry up!, look sharp!*, ⟨fam⟩ *buck up!* **~m·al** [adv] *especially, particularly* || ~ da .. *all the more since* **~|mauern** vt [h] *to wall up* **~m·eist** [adv] *for the most part, mostly* **≗meß-** ~düse [f] *dosing nozzle*; ~pumpe [f] *proportioning pump* **~|messen** vt irr [h] *to measure out*; (Strafe) *to mete out* || jdm etw ~ *to apportion a th to a p* || (sehr sparsam) *to dole out*; (Essen) *to keep a p at short rations* ⟨bes mil, mar⟩ || –ge– *allotted* (*part, share, portion*) **~m·indest** adv = mindestens **~m·ute** [adv] → Mut || mir ist schlecht (sonderbar) ~ *I feel out of sorts* (*it gave me an odd feeling*) **~|muten** vt [h]; jdm etw ~ *to expect sth of a p* od *a p to do sth, to suggest a th to a p* || er mutet mir viel zu *he demands a great deal from me* || jdm zuviel ~ *to expect too much of a p, to overtask, overwork a p* || sich [dat] viel ~ *not to spare o.s.* || sich zuviel ~ *to attempt too much,* *to bite off more than one can chew* **≃mutung** f ~/~en *unreasonable demand* od *expectation, suggestion* || e–e starke ~ *too much to expect*; ⟨fam⟩ *large* od *tall order* (→ stark) || was f e–e ~! *what a th to ask for*! **~n·ächst I.** [adv] *first, initially; above all*; was wir ~ tun müssen *the first th we have to do* || ~ einmal .. *to begin with* .., *in the first place*; (*we haven't time*) *for one th* od *to begin with* **II.** prep [dat] *next to* **~|nageln** vt [h] *to nail up* || (Deckel) *to nail down* || (die Luken) *to batten down* .. **~|nähen** vt [h] *to sew up* **≃nahme** f ~/~n *increase, growth, rise* || *improvement, progress* || ⟨tex, etc⟩ *widening* **≃name** m ~ns/~n *family name* || (Beiname) *surname*

Z·ünd- ~anlage f *ignition system, i.n unit* **~apparat** m *igniting-* od *priming-apparatus* || ⟨mot⟩ *magneto* **~beschleuniger** m ⟨mot⟩ *cetane booster* **~draht** m *primer* **~drehzahl** f ⟨mot⟩ *firing speed* **~einstellung** f ⟨mot⟩ *ignition setting timing of i.n* **~elektrode** f *triggering* od *starting e.*, ⟨Am⟩ *st.g anode* **~faden** m *i.n* (*wire primer* od) *filament* **≃fähig** a *inflammable*; *explosive* (*mixture*) | **≃keit** [f] *sensitivity* (v Munition) **≃fertig** a *primed* **~folge** f ⟨mot⟩ *firing* od *i.n order* **~freudigkeit** f *i.n quality* **~funke(n)** m ⟨mot⟩ *spark* **~geschirr** n *i.n wiring* **~geschwindigkeit** f *rate of flame proportion* **~glocke** f *cap-chamber* **~hölzchen** n *match* || schwedisches ~ *safety match* **~hütchen** n *percussion cap*; *amorce* | ~pistole [f] *cap pistol* **~kabel** n *high tension wire*; (f Beleuchtung) *spare cable* **~kammer** f *i.n chamber* **~kanal** m *i.n tube, flash-hole* **~kapsel** f *detonator* **~kerze** f ⟨mot⟩ (*spark*[*ing*]-)*plug*; (verrußt *sooted up*) **~kraut** n ⟨tech, hist⟩ *prime*; ~ auflegen *to prime* (*a gun*) **~ladung** f *i.g charge*; *amorce*; *exploder* **~leine** f *slow-match* **~loch** n ⟨min⟩ *touch-hole* ⟨a. °sex⟩ || ⟨artill⟩ *vent* **~magnet** m *magneto* **~nadel** f *percussion pin* | ~gewehr [n] *needle-gun, p.n-cap musket* **~papier** n, **~patrone** f *priming cartridge* **~pfanne** f *touch-pan* **~plättchen** n *amorce*; *fire loaf* **~potential** n *striking p.l* **~pulver** n *p.g-powder* **~satz** m *detonator*; *explosive train*; der Kartusche *i.g primer* **~punkteinstellung** f *i.n timing* **~rohr** n ⟨aero⟩ *flame tube* **~schalter** m ⟨mot⟩ *i.n switch* **~schlüssel** m ⟨mot⟩ *i.n key* **~schnur** f (*quick-*)*match*; *fuse* **~schraube** f (Munitions≃) *threaded primer* **~schwamm** m *tinder* **~spannung** f *i.n voltage* **~stoff** m ⟨a. fig⟩ *inflammable matter* **~vorrichtung** f → –faden **~warenfabrik** f *match-factory* **~versager** m *misfire* **~verstellung** f *octane selection* **~verzögerung** f ⟨phot–Blitz⟩ *delay of flash, firing delay* **~willigkeit** f *i.n quality* (*of* ⟨mot⟩ *fuel*) **~zeitpunkt** m *i.g timing* **z·ünden I.** vi [h] *to catch fire*; *to kindle, ignite* || ⟨mot⟩ *to spark*; nicht ~ ⟨a.⟩ *to miss* od *hang fire* ⟨a. fig⟩ **II.** vt [mst abs] *to cause a conflagration* ⟨a. fig⟩ || der Blitz zündete .. *set a house*, etc *on fire, inflamed, kindled* .. || ~d *inflammatory* || ⟨fig⟩ *stirring, inciting, thrilling* **Z·under** m ~s/ *tinder, touchwood* || ⟨met⟩ (*hammer*) *scale* || brennen wie ~ .. *like* (*old*) *blazes* || ⟨artill sl⟩ *big* od *heavy stuff*; *dirt*; ⟨fig⟩ es setzt gleich ~! *wait, you'll get it*! **Z·ünder** m ~s/~ *lighter, igniter, exploder* || ⟨el⟩ *striker* || ⟨artill, min⟩ *fuse* (stellen *to set*); ⟨hist⟩ *primer* || Aufschlag≃ *contact fuse* || Doppel≃ *double-action f.* || empfindlicher ~ *momentary f.* || Zeit≃, Brenn≃ *time f.* **~brennlänge** = –stellung **~einsteller** m (P) *f. setting operator* **~laufzeit** f *f. range* od *time* **~st·ellmaschine** f *f.-setter* **~stellring** m *f. setting ring* **~st·ellschlüssel** m *f. key* **~stellung** f *f. setting* **Z·ündung** f ~/~en ⟨tech⟩ *ignition* ⟨a. a–n⟩ || ⟨mil, etc⟩ *priming* || ⟨mot⟩ *sparking, firing* (→ Fehl–, Früh–, Spät≃) Glüh≃ *surface i.n*; Kerzen≃ *electric* od *spark i.n* || = Zündapparat || ~ ausschalten *to cut out the ignition* || ~ einregulieren ⟨mot⟩ *to adjust the timing of the spark* || ~ einschalten *to switch on the magneto* | **~s-~hebel** [m] ⟨mot⟩ *spark lever*; ~störung [f] ⟨bes mot⟩ *i.n trouble*; ⟨a–n⟩ ~- u Brennshluß-signal [n] *i.n and brennschluss-signal*

z·u- ~|nehmen I. vi irr [h] **A.** *to increase*; *to grow* (*larger*, etc), *to augment* || (Flut, etc) *to rise, swell* || (Übel) *to grow* od *get worse* || (Fortschritte m) *to improve, progress* || *to be on the increase* || (dicker w) *to fill out*; *to put on flesh* od *weight*; *to get stouter* || (Tage) *to get longer* || (Bewegung, Vorgang) *to accelerate* || ~ u abnehmen *to wax and wane* | ~ **an**: *to increase, wax, gain in* (*volume, size, power, number*); *to pick up* (*speed*) || *to advance in* (*years*) || an Kräften ~ *to grow stronger* || der W. nimmt an Stärke zu *the wind stiffens* | **im** Wert ~ *to improve in value* **B.** (beim Stricken etc) *to increase the number of stitches* **C. ~d** *crescent, waxing* (*moon*) || *increasing* (Drall) || *mounting* (*evidence*) || *accelerated* (*velocity*) || *progressive* (*twist*) | **bei** ~der Dunkelheit *at dusk* || bei ~den Jahren *with advancing years, as one grows older* **II.** vt [h] (Maschen) *to increase* **III.** ≃ n = Zunahme || der Mond ist im ≃ .. *is increasing, waxing* **~|neigen** vi [h] & sich ~ [dat] *to incline to-*(*ward*[*s*]) || sich dem Ende ~ *to draw to an end* od *close* **Z.gung** f ~/~en *inclination*; *affection* (z, f *for*), *bias* (*towards*), *goodwill* (*to*[*wards*]), *partiality* (*to*), *sympathy* (*with*) || es besteht k–e ~ zw ihnen *there is no love lost between them*; jds ~ erschleichen *to wind o.s.* od *one's way into a p's affection* || ~ fassen zu jdm, v ~ z jdm ergriffen w *to take* od *form a liking* od *fancy to, to grow fond of a p*

Z·unft f ~/≃e *company, guild, corporation* || ⟨fig⟩ *brotherhood* || ⟨dero⟩ *clique, set, band, tribe* **~brief** m *bill of incorporation*; *charter* **~buch** n *g.-book* **~geist** m *party* od *corporative spirit*; *esprit de corps* [Fr] || *sectarianism, exclusiveness, caste feeling* **≃gemäß** [a & adv] *according to the statutes of a guild* || ⟨fig⟩ *professional*[*ly* adv], ⟨fam⟩ *shoppy* [a] **~genosse** m *member of a g., freeman* || *one of the same trade* od *craft* **~kleidung** f *g. costume*(*s*) **≃mäßig** [a & adv] = z.gemäß **~(ober)meister** m (*prime*) *warden* **~recht** n *rights* pl *of a c.n* **~verwandte(r)** m = –genosse **~zwang** m *obligation to join a g.* **z·ünftig** a *belonging to a g.*; *corporate* || *competent* | ⟨fig⟩ = zunftgemäß, geziemend; ⟨fam⟩ *genuine, prime*, ⟨sl⟩ *crack* | ~ w *to be received into a g.* **Z·ünftler** m ~s/~ *guildsman*

Z·unge f ~/~n **A. 1.** *tongue* ⟨a. fig⟩ **2.** (e–r Schnalle) *catch* **3.** ⟨tech⟩ (e–r Waage etc) *t.* || ⟨rail⟩ *switch-t.* **4.** (am Blasinstrument) *mouthpiece, reed* **5.** ⟨poet & bibl⟩ (Sprache) *t., language* (*to speak in foreign* [⟨bib⟩ *with other*] *t.s*) **7.** ⟨ich⟩ *sole* **B. belegte** ~ *furred t.* || e–e böse, lose, scharfe ~ h .. *a wicked, loose, caustic, sharp t.*; böse ~n lästern *t.s wag* || e–e feine ~ h .. *a delicate palate* || e–e sehr geläufige ~ h *to have the gift of the gab* || e–e schwere ~ *an impediment in one's speech* **C.** ⟨fam⟩ ich **beiße** mir lieber die ~ ab, als daß ich's sage *I'll be hanged if* .. || s–e ~ geht mit ihm durch *his t. runs away with him* || die ~ war ihm gebunden *or* gelähmt *he was t.-tied* || die ~ herausstrecken, -bläken *to put one's t. out* (jdm *at a p*) || die ~ im Zaume halten *to bridle one's t.* | sich [dat] die ~ verbrennen ⟨fig⟩ *to put one's foot in it* || sich die ~ aus dem Halse reden *to talk one's head off* | °sich die ~ baden *to moist one's clay* **D.** (*to have a bitter taste*) **auf**: *in one's mouth* || es schwebt mir auf der ~ *I have it on the tip of my t.* || auf die ~ k ⟨fig⟩ *to spring to a p's lips*; zurückhalten, was e–m auf der ~ liegt *to bite one's t.* od *lips* || das Herz auf der ~ h *to wear one's h. on one's sleeve* || er biß sich auf die ~ (um nicht z lachen) *he had his t. in his cheek* **Z·üngelchen** n ~s/~ *tonguelet* **z·üngeln** vi [h] *to play* *with the tongue* ‖ (Flamme) *to lick* ‖ (Schlange) *to hiss* ‖ **~d** ⟨a.⟩ *lambent* (*flames*) **Z·ungen-** **~ader** f *lingual vein* °**~bad** n (Trunk) *mouth-wash, gargle* **~band** n *ligament of the t.* **~becken** n ⟨geol⟩ *terminal basin* (*of glacial erosion*) **~bein** n *t.-bone* **≗blütig** a ⟨bot⟩ *ligulate*(*d*) **~brecher** m (Wort) *t.-twister,* ⟨sl⟩ *jaw-breaker* | **≗**isch [a] *crack-jaw* (*word*) **~buchstabe** m *lingual letter* **~drescher** m *babbler* **~entzündung** f ⟨path⟩ *glossitis* **~fehler** m ⟨path⟩ *defect in one's speech* ‖ (Irrtum) *slip of the t.* **≗fertig** a *voluble* | **≗**keit [f] *glibness, volubility*; *gift of the t.* od ⟨fam⟩ *gab* **≗förmig** a *t.-shaped* **≗frei** a ⟨hors⟩ *cannon-*(*bit*) **~gebiß** n ⟨hors⟩ *t.-bit* **~geschwür** n *ulcer on the t.* **~held** m *braggart*; er ist ein ~ ⟨a.⟩ *he is a tongue--valiant p* **~krebs** m ⟨path⟩ *cancer on* od *of the t.* **~kuß** m *French kiss, t. kissing* **~lage** f ⟨phon⟩ *t.-position* **~laut** m *lingual* (*sound*) **~löffel** m ⟨med⟩ *t.-depressor* **~pfeife** f ⟨mus⟩ *reed-pipe* **~-R** n *trilled r* **~register** n ⟨mus⟩ *flute-stop* **~relais** n ⟨tech⟩ *vibrating reed relay* **~schlag** m *flap* ‖ e–n ~ h *to stammer* ‖ e–n guten ~ h *to have the t. well hung* **~schnitt** m ⟨surg⟩ *glossotomy* **~see** m ⟨geol⟩ *finger lake* **~spitze** f *tip of the t.* | ~n–R [n] *trilled r* **~stück** n ⟨cul⟩ *blade* **~sünde** f → Lüge, Verleumdung, Lästerung **~vorfall** m ⟨path⟩ *glossocele* **~wärzchen** n *papilla of the t.* **~wurst** f *t.-sausage* **~wurzel** f *base of the t.* **Z·ünglein** n = Züngelchen ‖ das ~ der Waage *the decisive weight* (*in the balance of powers*); .. zugunsten jds ausschlagen l *to allow the balance to be tipped* ..

z·u- **~n·ichte** [adv] ~ m *to annihilate, ruin, blight, blast, undo, destroy* ‖ (Plan, Absicht etc) *to frustrate*; *undo*; *nullify*; *checkmate*; *to foil* (*a purpose*); *to knock the bottom out of* (*a plan*) ‖ *to shatter, crush* (*hopes, designs*) ‖ (Versuche a.) *to condemn* ‖ ~ w *to be nullified, to come to nothing* od *to a deadend street* **~|nicken I.** vi [h] (jdm) *to nod* (*to a p*) **II.** vt e–m Beifall ~ *to nod approbation to a p* **~n·utze** [adv] ~ m *to turn to account, to utilize* | sich [dat] etw ~ m *to profit by, to avail o.s. of*; *to take advantage of a th*; *to play* od *practise on* (*a p's weakness*); *to seize* ⟨fig⟩; *to work on* (*a p's fears*); s–e Zeit .. *to take what time is there* **~·oberst** [adv] *uppermost* **~|ordnen** vt [h] = bei|ordnen ‖ –ge–net *allied, confederate* (*states*) **Z.ner** m ⟨comp⟩ *translater, interpreter* **Z.nung** f *discrimination* ⟨a. comp⟩; automatische ~ *automatic association* | **~s-** ⟨comp⟩ ~programm [n] = Z.ner; ~zähler [m] *allocation counter* **~|packen I.** vi [h] = zu|greifen **II.** vt *to pack* **III.** kühnes **≗** *bold initiative*

zup·aß [adv] ~ k *to come in the nick of time*

Z·upf- **~geigenhanserl** n *guitar-player* **~instrument** n ⟨mus⟩ *plucked i.t* **~leinwand** f *lint* **~nadel** f ⟨histology⟩ *tracer* **~seide** f *silk ravellings* pl **~wolle** f *wool-pickings* pl **z·upfen** vt/i [h] *to pull, tug, pluck* (an [dat] *at*) | (Werg Wolle) *to pick* ‖ Scharpie ~ *to make lint* ‖ (Saite) *to pluck, plunk* | jdn am Ärmel ~ *to pull a p by the sleeve* ‖ zupf dich an d–r eignen Nase! *mind your own business*!

z·u- **~|pflastern** vt [h] *to pave* (*up*) ‖ ⟨med⟩ *to plaster up* **~|pflöcken** vt [h] *to peg* od *plug up* **~|pflügen** vt [h] *to plough up* **~|pfropfen** vt [h] *to bung* od *cork up* **~|prosten** vi [h]; e–m ~ *to raise one's glass to a p*

zur = zu der **≗**m·achtkommen [n] *advent to power*; **≗**ruhesetzung [f] *pensioning off*; **≗**schaustellung [f] *exhibition*; *display*; *affectation, ostentation*; *show-off*; *flaunt*

z·u- **≗r·atehalten** n ~s/ *husbanding* **~|raten** vi irr [h] (jdm) *to advise a p to* (*do*) *a th*; *to persuade a p to do a th* od *into a th* ‖ ich will da weder zu- noch abraten *I will not advise you either for or against it* **~|raunen** vt [h] (jdm) *to whisper* (*into a p's ear*), *to suggest* (*to a p*) **~|rechnen** vt [h] **1.** (jdm etw) *to put* (*a th*) *down to* (*a p's*) *account* ‖ (zeihen) *to impute, attribute*; (zuschreiben) *to ascribe* (*a th to a p*) **2.** (hinzu|rechnen) *to include, add*; ~ zu *to count* od *number, reckon* .. *among, to class* .. *with* **Z.nung** f ~/~en *imputation, attribution*; *addition* ‖ mit ~ aller Kosten *including all charges* | **≗s-** ~fähig [a] *of sane mind, accountable, responsible*; (nicht) ~ (§ 51 StGB) (*non-*)*certifiable*; ~fähigkeit [f] ⟨mst⟩ *sound judgement* ‖ ⟨a.⟩ *accountability,* ⟨jur⟩ *capacity of criminal responsibility*; ~unfähigkeit [f] ⟨pop, jur⟩ *insanity*

zur·echt [adv & sep pref] (*a*)*right, in* (*due, good*) *order*; *to rights* ‖ *in the right place* ‖ *as it should be* **~|bringen** vt irr [h] *to set* od *put to rights* ‖ *to arrange, adjust* ‖ = zuwege|bringen **~|doktorn** vt [h] *to cook* **~|finden** vi [irr] [h]; (sich) ~ *to find one's way* (*about*) ‖ ⟨fig⟩ *to see one's way* (*in a th*) **~|frisieren** vt = frisieren ⟨fig⟩ = ⟨dero⟩ *to fudge* (*a th*) **~|hämmern** vt [h] *to hammer into shape* **~|helfen** vi [irr] [h] jdm ~ *to come to a p's help, to help a p out of a difficulty* **~|kombinieren** vt [h] *to put this and that* (od *two and two*) *together* **~|kommen** vi irr [s] *to arrive in time*; noch gerade *or* noch eben ~ *to cut it fine* ‖ ⟨fig⟩ *to get on, to manage* ‖ (mit) *to get on well* (*with*), *to manage* (*a th*); gut ~ *to fare* od *do well* ‖ es wird alles ~ *all will come all right* ‖ mit etw nicht ~ *to make a mess of a th* **~|legen** vt [h] *to lay out* .. (*in order*); *to set right, to arrange* ‖ sich [dat] etw ~ (erklären) *to explain a th to o.s., to figure* od *make a th out* **~|machen** vt [h] *to prepare arrange*; *to get* od *make ready* ‖ (Bett) *to make up,* ⟨Am⟩ *to fix* ‖ *a divan made up as a bed* ‖ (Garten, Kleid, Paket) *to do up* ‖ (Haus) *to fix* od *trim up* ‖ (Kleid, Lampe) *to trim* ‖ (Salat) *to dress* ‖ (Zimmer) *to tidy up* | (für best. Zweck) *to adapt* (*to* od *for*) ‖ ⟨dero⟩ = frisieren ⟨fig⟩ | sich ~ *to get ready*; ⟨cosm⟩ *to get* od *make* (*o.s.*) *up* ⟨a. theat⟩ **~|rücken, ~|setzen, ~|stellen** [h] *to* (*re*)*adjust*; *to set* od *put right, straight, in the right place* ‖ jdm den Kopf z.rücken, z.setzen *to bring a p to his* (*her*) *senses*; ⟨sl⟩ *to tick a p off* **~|schneiden** vt [h] *to trim* **~|stauchen** vt (jdn) *to settle a p's business for him* **~|stutzen** vt [h] *to prune* ‖ *to lick* (*a p*) *into shape* ‖ *to slant* (*speech, letter, news*) **~|weisen** vt irr [h] (jdn) *to show* (*a p*) *the way* ‖ ⟨fig⟩ *set* (*a p*) *right*; *to put a p in his place*; *to advise, correct, rebuke* (*a p*) ‖ (gehörig) *to talk to a p like a Dutch uncle* ‖ (tadelnd) *to reprove, chide, rate* (heftig *a p soundly*), *to snub,* ⟨Am⟩ *score* (*a p*); ⟨fam⟩ *to pull* .. *up* (wegen *for a th*) **≗weisung** f *instruction* ‖ (Tadel) *reprimand*; *rebuke*; ⟨bes Am fam⟩ *one in the eye* **~|ziehen** irr, **~|zupfen** vt [h] *to give the final touches to* (*one's tie*); → zur

z·u- **~|reden I.** vi [h] (jdm) *to encourage, advise, urge, persuade* (*a p* [*to do*]) ‖ *to speak words of comfort* (*to a p*) ‖ jdm gut ~ *to coax a p* (*to do*) ‖ er läßt sich nicht ~ *he does not listen to anyone, he will not be talked over* **II.** **≗** n *encouragement, advice, persuasion* ‖ *exhortation, admonition* ‖ auf ~ s–r Freunde *at the urgent request of* .. ‖ ⟨prov⟩ **≗** hilft *a little persuasion prevails* **~|reichen 1.** vt [h] *to reach, pass*; *to hand* (*over*) **2.** vi [h] & ~d s *to suffice*; *to be enough* od *sufficient* ‖ es reicht nicht zu ⟨a.⟩ *it won't do* **~|reisen** vi [s] *to travel to*(*ward*) (*a place*); *to arrive* ‖ Zugereiste *new-comers* **~|reiten** irr **1.** vt [h] *to break in* (*a horse*) (→ zugeritten), mit weicher Hand *to gentle* **2.** vi [s] *to ride on* od *fast* ‖ [dat], auf [acc] *to ride up to* **≗reiter** m *rough-rider, horse-breaker* **~|rennen** vi irr [s] *to run on* ‖ ~ auf [acc] *to run towards* **≗richt(e)-** ~axt [f] *squaring axe* ‖ ~bank [f] ⟨met⟩ *dressing-bench* ‖ ~bogen [m] ⟨typ⟩ *register-sheet* ‖ ~hammer [m] (*paver's*) *dressing--h.* ‖ ~maschine [f] *dr.-m.* ‖ ~messer [n] *dr.-kn.,* ⟨typ⟩ *overlay-kn.* ‖ ~zimmer [n] *finishing-room*

~|richten vt [h] **1.** *to prepare (the food); to leaven (the dough), to truss (a goose,* etc) **2.** ⟨tech⟩ *to dress* (a. Leder, Tuch) || (Holz, Steine) *to hew, cut;* (Holz) ⟨Am a.⟩ *to lumber* || ⟨typ⟩ *to make (the form) ready* || *to finish (a cloth)* || *to shake (the silk)* **3. arg,** böse, übel etc ~ *to damage, injure; to use badly;* ⟨bes Am⟩ *to work (a th) hard* || (P) *to maul, batter; to knock .. about,* ⟨sport fam⟩ *to punish* || (s–e Kleider) *to mess up* od *soil ..* || wie h·ast du dich zugerichtet! *you have made a pretty mess of y.s.* **≗richtung** f ~/~en *preparation* || ⟨tech⟩ *dressing,* etc || ⟨cosm⟩ *make-up* || ⟨typ⟩ *make-ready* **~|riegeln** vt [h] *to bolt (up);* → zur

Z·ürich n (⟨Sw⟩ Kanton & Stadt) *Zurich, Zürich* **Z·ür(i)cher(in** f) m *inhabitant of Z.* | ~ See [m] *Lake of Zurich*

z·ürnen I. vi [h] *to be angry* (jdm, auf jdn, mit jdm *with a p;* über, wegen *at, about)* **II.** ≗ n *anger, wrath;* → zur

z·u|rosten vi [s] *to become* od *get covered* od *stopped with rust;* → zur

z·urren vt [h] ⟨mar⟩ *to seize; to lash up; to make fast;* → zur

zur·ück I. [adv & sep pref] **1.** (wieder, heraus) *back* || (rückwärts) *backward(s)* || (hinten) *behind(hand), in the rear* || (im Rückstand) *in arrears;* ~ s *to be remiss (in)* || einige M.e ~ *a few months back* **2.** ~! *back there!, stand back!;* ⟨mil⟩ *as you were!* **3.** er ist ~ *he has returned* **4.** ⟨sport⟩ 4 Punkte ~ s *to be four down* **5.** (Ggs fortgeschritten) ~ s *to be behind (with one's work); to be backward (in French);* (Obst) *to be late* **II.** ≗ n; es gab kein ~ *there was no retracting* **~|arbeiten** vi [h] *to work backward;* ⟨mach⟩ *to be reversed* **~|beben** vi [s] *to start back* || (vor [dat]) *to shrink, recoil (from)* **~|befördern** vt [h] (im Rang) *to demote* **~|begeben** irr [h] sich ~ *to go back, to return* **~|begehren 1.** vt [h] *to demand back* **2.** vi [h] *to desire to return* **~|behalten** vt irr [h] *to retain, reserve* || *to detain, to keep back;* ⟨bes Am⟩ *to hold out (a th from a p)* **≗behaltungsrecht** n *right of detention,* ⟨jur⟩ *lien* [Fr]; das ~ geltend m auf *to lay a lien on* **~|bek** vt irr [h] *to get back* **~|berufen** vt irr [h] *to call back;* (absetzen) *to recall* **Z.fung** f *recall* | sich **~|bewegen** [h] *to back (away)* **~|bezahlen** vt [h] *to pay back, to repay, reimburse, refund* **~|beziehen** vrefl *to refer back* || ⟨gram⟩ *to be reflexive* **≗beziehung** f *reference* **~bezüglich** a ⟨gram⟩ *reflexive* **~|biegen I.** vt [h] & sich ~ *to bend back* || z.gebogen ⟨zoo, bot⟩ *recurvous* **II.** ≗ n *reclination* | sich **~|bilden** [h] ⟨biol⟩ *to regress* **~|bleiben I.** vi irr [s] *to fall (stay, remain, linger, lag) behind* || *to fall back* || *to stay at home* || *to be left behind* || ⟨racing⟩ *to be out-distanced* || ⟨sport⟩ nicht hinter jdm ~ ⟨a.⟩ *to challenge a p pretty closely* || (S) *to run behind* || (Uhr) *to lose; to be slow* (gegen *compared with*) || (Obst) *to be late* || ⟨fig⟩ *to be behind the times* || → Eindruck || (Ergebnis: ~ hinter) *to come* (od *be falling) short of expectations* || ⟨school⟩ ~ müssen *to be kept in* || (überleben) *to survive* | **~d** ⟨a.⟩ *residual;* (im Wuchs) ~der Baum ⟨for⟩ *laggard;* geistig z.geblieben *subnormal; mentally deficient* || geistig Z.ne(r) *retardate* **II.** ≗ n (z. B. *cultural) lag;* ≗ im Lesen *reading backwardness* **~|blenden** vt [h] ⟨film⟩ *to pull back (to)* **~|blicken** vi [h] *to look back* (auf [acc]: *to 30 years)* || ~d *retrospective* **~|bringen** vt irr [h] *to bring back; to return, replace* || z Gehorsam ~ *to reduce to o.* || z Leben ~ *to recall to l.* || ⟨fig⟩ e–n ~ *to reduce a p, to bring a p low* **~|bürsten** vt [h] *to brush back (one's hair)* **~|datieren** vt [h] *to date back, to antedate* **~|denken** vi irr [h] *to think back (to), to reflect on the past* || (an [acc]) *to recall to memory* **~|drängen** vt [h] *to drive (push, press, shove) back* || ⟨mil⟩ *to force back, to repel* || ⟨sport⟩ er wurde an den 3. Platz –ge–gt *he was beaten into ..* || ⟨fig⟩ *to repress, restrain (tears, feelings); (sheer privation) relegated (all else) to the background* **~|dürfen** vi irr [h] *to be allowed* od *permitted to return* **~|eilen** *to hasten* od *hurry back* **~|erbitten** vt irr [h] *to ask back* **~|erhalten** vt irr [h] = –|bek **~|erinnern** vt [h] = erinnern || soweit ich mich ~ kann *as far as my memory serves me* **~|erlangen** vt [h] *to recover* **~|erobern** vt [h] *to reconquer, recover* **~|erstatten** vt [h] *to restore, refund; to pay back;* (Gebiet) *to return* **≗erstattung** f *restitution* **~|fahren** irr **1.** vt [h] *to drive,* etc *back* || ⟨comp⟩ *to backspace* || ⟨phot⟩ (Kamera) *to dolly* od *track out* **2.** vi [s] *to drive,* etc *back* || *to return* (über: *via Paris, by France*) || (erschreckt) *to start back;* ~ über *to start at; to shy away, to recoil* (vor, v *from*) | **~d** ⟨bes mil⟩ *(vehicles) when driving to the rear* **≗fahrt** f *return(ing)* **~|fallen** vi irr [s] *to fall back* (⟨a. fig⟩: *into an error*) || ⟨jur⟩ an [acc]: *to revert to* | ⟨fig⟩ auf [acc]: (Schande) *to redound upon* || in [acc]: *to relapse into (silence, a vice;* ⟨a. path⟩), ⟨biol⟩ *to revert to (a type)* **~|fließen I.** vi irr [s] *to flow back* || ⟨mar⟩ *to ebb, recede* || ⟨fig⟩ *(good deeds) come home* (*to* auf *the benefactor*) **II.** ≗ n *reflux* **~|fluten I.** vi [s] *to ebb* || ⟨mil⟩ *to roll* od *sweep back* **II.** ≗ n *ebb* **~|fordern** vt [h] *to ask, demand back* || (Eigentum) *to reclaim* **≗forderung** f *reclamation* **~führbar** a *reducible (to), traceable (to)* **~|führen** vt [h] *to lead* (od *take* ⟨a. fig⟩) *back (to); to reconduct, reconvey* || ⟨fig⟩ auf [acc]: *to reduce to (its true value)* || (auf Ursachen etc) *to attribute to, to trace back to* || –zu– auf *due* od *traceable to; stemming from* **≗führung** f ⟨fig⟩ (Herabsetzung) *reduction* || ⟨log⟩ *reduction* (auf: *to the impossible* = reductio ad absurdum [L]) || ⟨math⟩ ~ auf das Dezimalsystem *decimalization* **≗gabe** f *giving back; restitution, return(ing)* **~|geben** vt irr [h] *to give* od *hand back; to return, restore* || ⟨school⟩ (Hefte) *to give out* || Hieb, Beleidigung ~ *to make a retort* **~gedämmt, ~gedrängt** a ⟨fig⟩ *pent-up (rage,* etc) **~gehalten** a ~e Wut *chained-up fury* **~|gehen** vi irr [s] *to go, turn, get back (to); to return* || ⟨mil⟩ *to retreat, to give way* || (–bleiben) *to fall back* || ~ l ⟨com⟩ *to send back, to return* || ~ auf *to search for (the cause);* auf die Quelle e–r S ~ *to retrace a th to its source* | (zeitlich) (S) *to date* od *go back* (auf, bis z *to*) | (schlechter w) *to deteriorate, to fall off* od *away, to be getting worse* | (sich vermindern) *to diminish* ⟨a. path⟩, ⟨path a.⟩ *to go down* || (Bewegung) *to slow down* || (Anzahl, Preis) *to recede, decline; to give way* || (Flut) *to ebb* || (Unternehmen, ⟨com⟩) *to go down, to come to grief* | (zunichte w) (Geschäft) *to fall to the ground,* ⟨fam⟩ *to be off* || (Verhandlungen, Verlöbnis) *to be broken off* | **~d** *retrogressive* || weit ~d *long descended (tradition)* **~|gelangen** vi [s] *to get back (to)* **~|gewinnen** vt irr [h] *to recover* || ⟨tech⟩ *to reclaim* || s–e Ehre etc ~ *to redeem one's hono(u)r,* etc **~gezogen** a [pp v z.ziehen] *retired, solitary (life)* | [adv] *(to live) privately* | ≗heit [f] *retirement, seclusion; privacy* **~|greifen** vi [h] ⟨fig⟩ *to begin* od *go farther back* || ~ auf *to revert to, to go* od *hark back to; to fall back upon (symbols)* || ⟨film⟩ *to cut back* **~|haben** vt [h] *to have back* || er möchte sein Wort ~ *he would like to recall his words* **~|hallen** vi [h] *to resound, to echo* **~|halten I.** vt irr [h] **1.** (sich) ~ *to hold* od *keep back* **2.** jdn ~ *to stop a p; to hold a p back* (v *from*) || ⟨racing⟩ sein Pferd ~ *to pull* | ⟨übtr⟩ *to delay, detain a p, to make a p stop* || *to keep (a schoolboy) in* || jdn etw z tun *to keep, restrain, prevent a p from doing* || ich konnte nicht k, ich wurde durch K. –gehalten *illness prevented me from coming* || im Wachstum ~ *to stunt* **3.** etw ~: *to hold (one's breath)* || *to suppress (cries)* || *to conceal (a design)* || *to repress, check, stay,* ⟨fam⟩ *pocket (one's feelings)*

|| *to contain* (*one's laughter, eagerness*) || *to bottle up* (*one's feelings*) || *to reserve, suspend* (*one's indignation, judgment, opinion*), [⟨a.⟩ vi] ~ mit .. || *to restrain* (*tears*) **4. sich** ~ (→ 1.) *to contain, restrain, check,* (bescheiden) *efface o.s.*; *to lie low* || ⟨fam⟩ *to hold off, to hold* od *stay one's hand* || sich ~ v *to pause before*; *to abstain* od *forbear from* || sich ~ z tun *to refrain from doing* **II.** vi **1.** *to be reserved, to keep aloof* **2.** ⟨com⟩ *customers are holding back* **3.** ~ mit *to withhold, conceal*; ⟨fam⟩ *to bottle up* (*a th*) || mit s–r Meinung ~ = s–e M. ~ (→ I. 3.) || mit e–r Erklärung hält man z. *comment is being reserved* || mit der Sprache ~ *to speak with the tongue in cheek* || nicht ~ mit *to be unsparing in* (*help*), .. *ungrudging in* (*praise*) || mit s–r Ansicht nicht ~ *to make no bones about one's view* **4. ~d** [pp & a] ⟨fig⟩ (P) *reserved, cautious, guarded, discreet, remote, distant*; *undemonstrative*; *retentive*; *shy*; *aloof*; *temperate*; *standoffish*; *unobtrusive*; *unostentatious*; *retiring, restrained*; *abstinent* | ⟨fam⟩ *offish* || (in Worten) *inarticulate, reticent, uncommunicative,* ⟨fam⟩ *mealy-mouthed* || *coy, demure* (*girl*); ~e Haltung *noncommittal attitude*; ~es Wesen *reservedness* | ~d s *to pause*; ⟨a.⟩ *to keep o.s. to o.s.* || ~d w ⟨a.⟩ *to dry up* **≗haltung** f **1.** ⟨eig⟩ *retention* ⟨a. med⟩, *detention* **2.** ⟨fig⟩ *restraint*; *reserve, aloofness* || *reticence* || *cautiousness, discretion* || *coyness,* etc || bescheidene ~ *self-effacement* | sich [dat] ~ auferlegen *to be reserved, to hold off* || aus s–r ~ heraustreten *to burst out of one's shell* || Mangel an ~ *irreticence, -cy* | **~s-** ~kraft [f] *retentiveness*; ≗recht [n] ⟨jur⟩ *lien* || das ~ auf etw geltend m *to lay a lien on* **~|holen** vt [h] *to fetch back* **~|jagen 1.** vt [h] *to drive back* **2.** vi [s] *to rush* od *gallop back* **~|kaufen** vt [h] *to buy back*; *to redeem*; (bei Auktion) *to buy in* **~|kehren** vi [s] **1.** *to return* (nach *to*); zu Fuß ~ nach *to walk back to*; nach Marburg –ge–rt *back in M.*; er ist –ge–rt *he has come back* od *in*; (S) in sich selbst ~d *turning upon itself* **2.** = ~|k **3.** (*of countries*) *to re-enter* (z R. *the Reich*) **4.** ⟨fig⟩ *to revert, return* (auf *to*) **~klappbar** a *swing-back* [attr] **~|kneifen** vt [h] die Lider ~ *to narrow one's eyes* **~|kommen** vi irr [s] *to come* od *get back* (*to*) || (gesellschaftlich sinken) *to come down in the world, to lose caste*; sehr –ge– *greatly reduced* || (auf [acc]) *to revert, return* (*to*), *to fall back* (*upon a th*); .. immer wieder *to ring the changes* od *to harp on a th*; auf Erlittenes .. *to nurse one's grievances* || jdm ins Gedächtnis ~ *to recur to a p's mind* || v Feld ~ *to come in from* .. || v e–r Ansicht ~ *to give up an opinion* **~|können** vi irr [h] *to be able to return*; nicht mehr ~ ⟨a.⟩ *to find o.s. out on a limb* **≗kunft** f *return* **~|kurbeln** vt [h] *to turn back(wards)* **~|lassen** vt irr [h] *to leave behind* || (e–n Eindruck) bei jdm ~ .. *on a p* || (verlassen) *to abandon* || Nachricht ~ *to leave word* (*that*) || jdn hinter sich ~ *to outdistance, outdo, outstrip,* etc *a p* || in jdm die Überzeugung ~ *to leave a p with the c.* **~|laufen** vi irr [s] *to run* (Wasser *to flow*) *back* || ⟨astr⟩ *to retrograde* **~|legen** vt [h] *to to replace* (*a th in the box*) || *to put aside, to shelve* || (Geld etc) *to lay aside* od *up, to put by*; (Geld a.) *to save* (*they never saved a bean* = e–n Pfennig), .. für *to lay up .. against* || (Jahr, Klasse etc erleben) *to accomplish, complete*; das 30. Jahr –ge–gt h *to have reached the age of thirty* || ⟨sport⟩ (Strecke) *to negotiate, lap*; ⟨mil⟩ *to travel* || den Weg ~ *to go* od *cover the distance* (–ge–gte Wegstrecke *covered distance*); .. mit dem Rade (etc) *to cycle* (etc) *the d.*; .. z Fuß ⟨a.⟩ *to do .. on foot* **~|lehnen** vt & sich ~ [h] *to lean* (sich behaglich *to snuggle*) *back* || im Sessel –ge–hnt *lounging easily in one's chair* **~|leiten** vt [h] *to lead back* **~|leuchten** vi [h] **1.** *to be reflected* **2.** e–m ~ *to light a p back* **~|liefern** vt [h] *to return*

~|liegen vi [h] das liegt lange z. *that happened long ago*; ~d *earlier* (*report*); lang *or* weit ~d *remote* (*age, time*) **~|marschieren** vi [s] *to march back* **~|melden** vt [h] *to reply* || sich ~ *to report one's return,* sich vom Urlaub ~ *to report after a leave* od *furlough* **~|mögen** vi irr [h] *to wish o.s. back, to wish to return* **~|müssen** vi irr [h] *to be obliged to return* || das Leergut muß z. *the empties* pl *have to be returned* || der Wagen muß ein bißchen z. *the car must be moved back a bit* **≗nahme** f *taking back* || *withdrawal* (*of words, troops*) || *retracing, retractation,* ⟨Am⟩ *retraction* (*of a promise*) || *revocation* (*of an edict*) || ~ e–r S verweigern *to refuse to take a th back* **~|nehmen** vt irr [h] *to take back, to withdraw, unsay* (*one's words*); *to swallow* (*one's word*); sein Wort ~ *to go back from one's w.* || s–e Worte ~ müssen *to have to eat one's words* || *to revoke, reverse, repeal, recall, rescind, cancel* (*an order,* etc) || *to withdraw* (*an offer*) || (Behauptung) *to retract* || *to go back* (*the same way*) | –genommen ⟨arch⟩ *recessed* **~|nötigen** vt *to force to return* od *retreat* **≗prall** m *repercussion* **~|prallen** vi [s] (vor [dat]) *to rebound, resile, recoil* (*from*) || *to start back* (vor .. *with fright*) || (Licht) *to be reflected* **≗pumpen** n ⟨tech⟩ *recirculation* **~|rechnen** vt/i [h] *to count back* || (in die Vergangenheit) *to reckon backward(s)* || (leere Flaschen etc anrechnen) *to allow for* **~|reichen** vi [h] *to go back* || mein Gedächtnis reicht z. bis z .. *carries me back to* || (Ereignis) *to date back* (*to*) **~|reisen** vi [s] *to travel back, to return* **~|reiten** vi irr [s] *to ride back* || *to return on horseback* **~|rudern** vt [h] & vi [s] *to row back* || (rückwärts r.) *to back-water* **~|rufen** vt irr [h] *to call back* || ⟨fig⟩ in [acc]: *to recall .. to* (*life, to a p's mind*) || ins Gedächtnis ~ *to recall* **~|sagen** vt [h]; ~ l *to send back word* (*that*) **~|schallen** vt [h & s] *to resound, re-echo* **~|schaudern** vi [s] (vor [dat]) *to recoil, to start back* (*from*) **~|schauen** → –|sehen **~|scheuchen** vt [h] *to scare away, to drive back* **~|scheuen** vi [h] (vor [dat]) *to shrink* (*back*) (vor *from*); *to wince, shy* (*at*), *flinch* (*from*) **~|schicken** vt [h] (P) *to turn back* || (S) *to send back, to return* **~|schieben** vt [h] *to shove back*; (Wagen) *to back* || ⟨fig⟩ e–n (im Amt) ~ *to pass over a p* || ⟨jur⟩ (Beweisgrund) *to retort* **~|schlagen I.** irr **1.** vt [h] *to beat* (*knock, strike, fight*) *back* od *off*; (Angriff, Feind) *to repel* || (Ball) *to return*; (Decke) *to throw off* || (Haar) *to smooth back* || –ge–nes Laken *turned-back sheet* || (Mantel) *to* (*throw*) *open* || –ge–er Wagen *open carriage* **2.** vi [s] *to fall back(wards)*; ⟨biol⟩ *to revert* (*to*) || ⟨com⟩ (Preis) *to fall, decline* || ⟨path⟩ ~ auf *to attack* (*the heart,* etc) | [h] auf jdn kräftig ~ *to give a p a Roland for an Oliver* **II.** ≗ n *back-firing* (*of flames*) **~|schließen** vi [h] *to reason a posteriori* L **~|schnellen 1.** vt [h] *to fling back* **2.** vi [s] *to rebound, recoil* **~|schrauben** vt [h] ⟨fig⟩ s–e Ansprüche ~ *to cut down one's demands*; → (Ansprüche) –stecken **~|schrecken 1.** vt [h] *to deter* (*from*), *to frighten* od *scare away, to startle* **2.** vi [s] (vor [dat]) *to start* od *shrink back, to recoil, flinch* (*from*) || ~ z tun *to stop at doing* || vor nichts ~ *to stick at nothing* **~|schreiben** vt/i irr [h] *to write back* || ⟨mil⟩ *to put on the list of reserves* **~|schreiten** vi irr [s] *to go* (*step, stride, stalk*) *back* || (rückwärts) *to walk backwards* **~|schweifen** vi [s] (of thoughts) *to go back* (auf *to*) **~|sehen** vi irr [h] *to look back* || ~ auf .. *to reflect on, to review* (*the past*) **~|sehnen** [h] sich ~ *to long to return, to wish o.s. back* || nach: *to have a longing for* (*home*), *to regret* (*the country*) **~|sein** vi irr [s] *to be back, to have returned* || ⟨school⟩ *to be backward* (*in Greek*) || (hinter der Zeit) ~ *to be behind the times* || (in s–m Fach) *not to be up to date* (*in* ..) **~|senden** vt irr [h] *to send back, to return* **~|setzen 1.** vt [h] *to put* (*set, push*) *back, to set aside, to put back in the old place*;

⟨comp⟩ *to reset* || (Zug) ⟨rail⟩ *to back-up* | sich ~ *to sit back* || ⟨fig⟩ (P) *to disregard, neglect* || (Preise) *to reduce* || (Waren) *to cast off* (*as waste*) || etw f jdn ~ *to put sth by for a p*; Z.ge–zte(r) ⟨soc⟩ *underdog* **2.** vi [s] (über) *to jump back across* (*a wall*) **3.** ⟨mot⟩ vi/t [h] (den Wagen) (⟨a.⟩ [abs]) ~ → –stoßen ≗**setzung** f ⟨fig⟩ *discrimination*; *disregard* (*shown to*), *neglect* (*of*), *slight* (*put upon* ..) ~|**sickern** vi [s] *to drain back* ~|**sinken** vi irr [s] *to fall back* || ⟨fig⟩ (in [acc]) *to relapse* (*into*) ~|**sollen** vi [h] *to be bound to return, to be ordered back* || er soll z. *he is to come back* ~|**spiegeln** vt [h] *to reflect* ~|**springen** vi irr [s] *to jump* (⟨fam⟩: *to run*) *back* || *to start back, to recoil* || ⟨phys⟩ *to rebound* || ⟨arch⟩ *to recede* || ~d ⟨a.⟩ *resilient*, ⟨fort⟩ *reentering* (*angle*) || ⟨fig⟩ (in Gedanken) ~ auf *to switch back to* ~|**stecken** vt [h] *to put back* || ⟨fig⟩ s–e Ansprüche ~ *to come down a peg or two* ~|**steh(e)n** vi irr [h & s] *to stand back* (v *from*) || (gegen [acc], hinter [dat]) *to be inferior* (*to*), *to be outstripped* (*by*) || ~d *receding* (*forehead*, ⟨a. ach⟩) || ~ müssen *to have to wait*; *to be left behind* (*in the struggle*) ~|**stellen** vt [h] *to put back* (a. Uhr) || *to replace* || *to set aside* (f *for*) || (als unabkömmlich, Reserve) *to reserve* ⟨a. mil⟩ || (Angelegenheit) *to adjourn, postpone, stop*; *to put off*; *to defer* (*major objectives*); ⟨parl⟩ *to lay on the table* || (P) *to suspend from military service* || s–e Meinung hinter die jds ~ *to yield precedence to a p's opinion* || ⟨bal⟩ *to provide for reserve* ≗**stellung** f ⟨bal⟩ *reserve* || ⟨mil⟩ *deferment*; dauernde ~ ⟨mil⟩ *total rejection* ~|**stoßen** vt irr [h] *to push back* || ⟨fig⟩ *to repel*; (anwidernd) *to repulse* || ⟨mot⟩ vt/i [h] *to back up, to reverse* ~|**strahlen** **1.** vt [h] *to reflect* **2.** vi [h] *to reflect, to be r.ed* ≗**strahlung** f *reflexion*; *reverberation* ~|**streichen** irr **1.** vt [h] *to smooth back*; *she pulled her hair back to a large low bun* **2.** vi [s] ⟨orn⟩ *to fly back* ~|**streifen** vt [h] *to turn up* (*one's sleeves*) ~|**tasten**; sich ~ *to grope one's way back* ~|**transportieren** vt [h] *to carry back* ~|**träumen**; sich ~ in etw *to be carried back to a th in a dream* ~**treiben** vt irr [h] *to drive* od *thrust back*; *to repel* ⟨a. mil⟩ || (Schweiß) *to send .. inwards* || z.getrieben w (v Strom) *to be pulled back* ≗**treibung** f *repulse* ~|**treten** vi irr [s] **1.** *to stand back* || e–n Schritt ~ *to take a step back*; vor jdm ~ *to make way for a p* || ⟨mil⟩ *to fall back* (*into the ranks*) || ⟨fig⟩ (von) *to withdraw, recede*, ⟨com⟩ *to cry off* (*from*) || ⟨sport⟩ (v Kampf) *to stand down* || v Amt ~ *to resign one's office*; ⟨bes Am⟩ *to send in one's papers* || -- l *to put in the background*, (Gefühle) *to override* **2.** (Stirn) *to recede* **3.** (Wasser) *to subside*; (Fluß in sein Bett) *to retire* (*within* ..) **4.** ⟨paint⟩ (a. perspektivisch) *to recede* **5.** ⟨path⟩ *to be checked* ~|**übersetzen** vt [h] *to retranslate* ~|**verfolgen** vt [h] (Weg) *to retrace* ~|**verlangen** **1.** vt = –fordern **2.** vi = sich –sehnen ~|**verlegen** vt [h] (P & S) *to transfer back*; ⟨mil⟩ *to withdraw* ~|**versetzen** vt [h] *to restore* (*to former place* od *condition*) || *to put back into a lower class* || ⟨mil⟩ *to degrade* || sich ~ (in [acc]) *to think back* (*to*), *to take, cast, turn one's mind* od *thoughts back* (*to*) || –tzt w *to be carried back* (*to*) ~|**verwandeln** vt [h] *to restore* (*to the former state*) ~|**verweisen** vt irr [h] (P) *to send .. back* (auf [acc] *to*) || ⟨jur⟩ (Fall) *to remit*; ⟨parl⟩ *to refer back* (an [acc] *to*) ~|**weichen** **I.** vi irr [s] *to recede* ⟨a. arch⟩ || *to retire, withdraw*; ⟨mil⟩ *to fall back* || (nachgeben) *to yield*; *to give in* || vor e–r S ~ *to shrink back from* .. || *to quail* (vor F. *with fear*) || *to wince, shy* (*at*), *flinch* (*from*) **II.** ≗ n *retreat, receding*, etc || ⟨mar⟩ *ebb* ~|**weisen** vt irr [h] *to send back* od *away* || ⟨fig⟩ *to overrule*; *refuse*; *to warn off* || (Angriffe) *to repel* || (Beschuldigungen) *to refuse to allow, to cast back*; (als Lüge) *to ram .. down a p's throat* || (Geschenke) *to decline* || (Schuld) *to rebut* || (Vorschlag) *to reject*, ⟨bes Am⟩ *to pass up*, ⟨Am⟩ *to throw down*; *to overrule* (*objections*); (verächtlich) *to scout* (*proposal, notion*) || ~ auf (⟨gram⟩ & auf e–e Buchstelle) *to refer to* | der Z.ge–wiesene *the reject* ≗**weisung** f ⟨fig⟩ *refusal, rejection, rebuttal* ~|**wenden** vt [h] & sich ~ *to turn back* ~|**werfen** vt irr [h] *to throw back* (auf *to*) ⟨a. mil⟩; ⟨mil a.⟩ *to repulse* || (e–n Blick) *to throw .. backwards* || (den Kopf) *to toss up*; *to jerk* (*the shoulders*) *back* || ⟨phys⟩ *to reflect* (dazu: *reflexion*) || (Verleumdung) *to retort* (auf *on*) || ins Elend ~ *to cast back into misery* || –geworfen ⟨Am fam⟩ (P) *thrown for a loss*, war/erschien .. ⟨biol⟩ *had suddenly thrown back atavistically* ~|**wirken** vi [h] (auf [acc]) *to react* (*upon*) ~|**wollen** vi irr [h] [ell] *to want to return* ~|**wünschen** vt [h] (P) *to wish for the return of*; (S) [sich dat] *to wish .. back, to regret* (*a th*) ~|**zahlen** vt [h] *to pay back, to repay* ⟨beide a. fig⟩, *to refund*; *to return* (*with interest*) ~|**zählen** vt [h] *to count back*(*wards*) ≗**zahlung** f *repayment* ~|**ziehen** irr **I.** vt [h] *to retire*; *to draw* od *drag back*; (Truppen) *to pull back* || ⟨chess⟩ *to retreat* || Anklage ~ *to nolle-pros* [pret *-sed*] || *to recall* (*a book*, etc) || ⟨fig⟩ *to withdraw, cancel, countermand* || (Geld) *to recover* | **sich** ~ *to retire, withdraw* || *to fall back* || ⟨mil⟩ *to retreat*; (eiligst) *to beat a hasty retreat* || auf [acc]: *to fall back upon* || auf sich selbst *to become wrapt up in o.s.*, *to retreat into o.s.* || aus: *to retire from* ⟨a. mil⟩ || nach: *to back towards* (*the door*) || von: *to quit* (*the stage*, etc); *to drop out of* (*a th*); (v e–r Freundschaft) *to fall away from, to let lapse, to give up* (*a f.p*) **II.** vi [s] *to go back again*; *to move back* (*to a place*) || ⟨zoo⟩ *to return* ≗**zieher** m ⟨billards⟩ *screw* || °⟨fig⟩ e–n ~ m *to draw in one's horns* ≗**ziehung** f *drawing back* || ⟨mil⟩ *retreat* || *revocation* (*of orders*) || *withdrawal* (*of money, of a promise*); ⟨jur⟩ (e–r Klage) *discontinuation* | (→ z–ziehen [vi]) *return*

z·u- ~|**rücken** vi [s] *to make room* ≗**ruf** m *call* || (Beifalls≗) *acclamation* (⟨a. parl⟩: durch ~ *by a.*); *cheer*(*ing*) ~|**rufen** vt/i irr [h] *to call*, [laut] *shout* (*to*) || e–m Beifall ~ *to acclaim* od *cheer a p* ~|**rüsten** vt [h] *to prepare* || (Schiffe) *to fit* (⟨fam⟩ *rig*) *out, to equip* ≗**rüstung** f *preparation* (~en treffen *to make p.s*) || *fitting out, equipment*; (Aus–) ⟨mach, etc⟩ *attachment*

zurz·eit [adv] *for the time being, at present*

z·u- ≗**sage** f ~/~n *promise, word* || (Einwilligung) *assent* ~|**sagen** **I.** vt [h] *to promise* || e–m (etw) auf den Kopf ~ *to say .. to a p's face* **II.** vi [h] *to answer in the affirmative*; (auf Einladung) *to promise* od *agree to come* od *to be present*; *to accept* | **jdm** ~ *to agree with a p* || (gefallen) *to suit, please, meet a p*; *to appeal to a p* || (behagen) *to be congenial to a p* | ~d ⟨a.⟩ *pleasing, acceptable* || (Antwort) *affirmative*

zus·ammen **I.** adv **A.** **1.** *together, jointly* (mit *with*), *in common* **2.** (zeitlich) *at the same time* **B.** ~ **mit** *along with, in company with* || sie [pl] ~ mit M. *she and Mary .. between them*; so: *between the family and the guests 20 people sat down to dinner* || ~ in: (*he saw her and him*) *sharing* (*a boat*) | **alle** ~ *one and all*, (P a.) *all .. in a body* | alles ~ *all in all*; (*I bought it*) *lock, stock, and barrel*; ⟨fam⟩ *the whole lot* | (etw) ~ **bilden** *to combine to form* || das macht ~ 100 Mark *it makes a total of* .. || wir (sie) zahlen ~ *we* (*they*) *pay it between us* (*them*) **II.** ~, ≗ pref [mit Verben sep mst *together*] °~|**addieren** vt [h] *to sum up* ≗**arbeit** f *teamwork, co-operation* (in ~ mit *with the co-op. of*); ⟨mil a.⟩ *combined operation*(*s*); auf unmittelbare ~ angewiesen ⟨z. B. artill⟩ *assigned for direct support* N, *co-operating* (*unit*) N ~|**arbeiten** **I.** vt/i [h] *to work together* || vi *to co-operate, to act in concert*; ⟨com a.⟩ *to stand in* (*with*); mit: *to liaison with*, (heimlich) *to conspire* *with*; gut ~ ⟨fam⟩ *to pull well together* | vt (Geld) *to earn* || (etw) *to stick together* || ⟨fig⟩ (e–n) *to maltreat* **II.** ≃ [n] der Verwaltungen *administrative co-operation* **~|backen** vi irr [s] *to stick together to cake* ⟨a. chem⟩ **~|ballen I.** vt & sich ~ [h] *to form into a ball*; *to mass tog.*; *to conglomerate* || die Fäuste ~ *to clench one's fists*; –geballt *caked (soil)*, ⟨bot⟩ *conglobate(d)* **II.** ≃ n, **Z.llung** f ⟨phys⟩ *conglobation, clumping*, durch ~ entstanden ⟨min⟩ *syngenetic* || ⟨übtr⟩ (v Momenten etc) *build(ing)-up, gathering, collecting, bunching--up*; ~en [pl] *bunching, congestions* **≃bau** m ⟨tech⟩ *build-up*, → Montage | ~zeichnung [f] *erection drawing* **~|bauen** vt [h] *to assemble, fit, rig* **~|beißen**: die Zähne ~ *to set one's teeth* **~|bek** *to succeed in joining* || (Geld) *to scrap tog.* **~|berufen** *to convoke, call, summon, convene* **≃berufung** f *convocation, convening* **~|bestehen** *to co-exist* || *to be consistent* od *compatible (with)* **~|betteln** vt [h] *to collect by begging* **~|binden** *to bind* od *tie tog.* || ⟨mar⟩ *to lash* **~|bitten** vt *to invite tog.* **~|blasen** vt *to summon by trumpets* || (Glas) *to blow tog.* || (Kartenhaus) *to blow down* **~|borgen** vt *to raise by borrowing* **~|brauen** *to brew*; *to concoct*; *to cook .. up* ⟨a. fig⟩ || es braut sich etw zus *a storm is brewing* ⟨a. fig⟩, ⟨fig⟩ *mischief is b.g* **~|brechen** vi irr [s] *to break down, to crack up*; *to collapse (under)* (⟨a. fig⟩ & v Pn); (v Pn a.) *to succumb (to)*; völlig ~ *to go to pieces* (a. v Pn) || ⟨fig sl⟩ *to go phut* od *to pot*, ⟨Am⟩ *to crack* ⟨a. mil⟩ || ⟨fig fam⟩ *to crumple up* (unter .. *at a threat* | **das** ≃ = –bruch || erschöpft zum ≃ *exhausted to dropping-point* **~|bringen** *to bring* od *get tog.*, *to amass* || (sammeln) *to collect* (⟨a. fig⟩: *one's thoughts*), *to assemble* ⟨a. mil⟩, *to rally (troops)* || (Geld) *to raise* || (Pn) *to introduce*; wieder ~ *to reconcile* || (Vieh) ⟨Am⟩ *to round up* || ⟨übtr⟩ (versehentlich) *to couple (a name with that of another p)* **-gebracht** *joint (property)* || ~e Kinder *halfbrothers and -sisters* pl || ~ w mit *to be thrown with* **≃bruch** m *breakdown* (der G. *in health*), *collapse* (⟨a. fig⟩ infolge v Arbeitsüberlastung) || ⟨übtr⟩ *failure*; ⟨fam⟩ *smash*; ⟨eco⟩ *ruin* || (e–s Waschmittels *lather*) *collapse* **~|drängen** vt [h] *to press tog.*, *to compress*; *squeeze* || *to crowd, serry* (⟨a.⟩ sich ~) || (kürzen) *to abridge, condense* || (Truppen) *to mass* || –ge–gt ⟨fig⟩ *terse, concise (style)*, *reduced* (auf .. *to 6 pages*) **~|drehen** & sich ~ *to twist tog.* **~drückbar** a *compressible* | ≃keit [f] *compressibility* **~|drücken** *to compress*; *to serry* (⟨a.⟩ sich ~) **≃drückung** f *compression* **~|eilen** vi [s] *to gather quickly* **~ fahren** irr **I.** vi [s] **1.** *to travel*, etc *tog.* **2.** (2 Züge) *to collide* || (Pn) *to have an encounter* **3.** ⟨fig⟩ *to shrink, recoil, (give a sudden) start* **II.** ⟨fam⟩ vt [h] *to smash (a car)* **≃fall** m *collapse* **~|fallen** *to fall to pieces*; *to collapse* (⟨a.⟩ P) || in sich selbst ~ (–stürzen) *to fall in on itself* || (P) *to fall away* || ⟨opt⟩ *to assemble in one focus* || ⟨phon⟩ *to level (under)* | (⟨math⟩ & zeitlich) *to coincide*, (zeitlich) *to be contemporary (with)* || (kollidieren) *to clash (with)* || ⟨phys⟩ *to synchronize (with)* | ~d *coincident* | **das** ≃ (zeitlich) *coincidence, synchronization* **~ falten** *to fold up* || (Segel) *to furl* **~|fassen** vt [h] *to gather up* || ⟨fig⟩ *to comprise, include, embrace* || als Ganzes ~ *to treat as a whole* || (s–e Gedanken) *to collect* || (Kräfte) *to concert, concentrate* || kurz ~ *to compress, condense, summarize*; noch einmal ~ *to recapitulate* || ~d *summary (table)* || um es kurz –zu– *to sum up* || kurz –gefaßt *concise, summary* || ~ unter *to subsume under* || (Worte) *to condense (into)*, *to reduce (to)* || –gefaßt ⟨mil⟩ *collective, concentric, -trated (fire)*, *combined (attack)* **≃fassung** f *concentration* || ⟨Lit⟩ *synopsis, digest, compendium, summary, condensation, epitome* || ~ v Feindnachrichten *intelligence summary* N || ⟨rhet⟩ *peroration, conspectus* **~|finden** vi & sich ~ *to meet, gather* || ⟨fig⟩ *to make friends* **~|flechten** *to plait tog.* **~|flicken** ⟨a. fig⟩ *to patch* od *piece up* **~|fließen** *to flow tog.*, *to meet* || ⟨tech, paint, met⟩ *to fuse* ⟨a. *fig*⟩ **≃fluß** m *confluence, junction* || *concourse* || ⟨tech etc⟩ *fusion* **~ frieren** vi irr [s] *to freeze tog.*, *to congeal* || *to shrink in freezing* **~ fügen** vt [h] *to join, unite* (⟨a.⟩ sich ~) || *to coapt* || ⟨gram⟩ *to construe* || ⟨tech⟩ *to fit* od *put tog.*; ⟨carp a.⟩ *to assemble, dovetail, mortize* || ⟨tail⟩ *to sew tog.* || ⟨phot⟩ Bilder (z Panorama) *to match up* **≃fügung** f *joining, (con)junction*, ⟨gram⟩ *construction* **~|führen** *to bring tog.* **~|geben** *to join in wedlock, to marry* **~|gehen** *to go tog.* || ~ mit *to troop with* || ⟨fig⟩ *to agree well, to match* | *to shrink*; *to melt down* || (sich schließen) *to close* **~|gehören** *to belong to one another* || (S) *to form a pair, to be fellows* **~gehörig** a *belonging to one another* **≃gehörigkeit** f (S) *homogeneousness* || (P) *solidarity, fellow feeling* (⟨a.⟩ ~sgefühl) **~genommen** a *combined*; *all told* || ~ mit *taken along with* **≃gepferchtsein** n *crowding* ⟨a. eth⟩ **~gepreßt** a *tight (lips)* **~|geraten** [s] *to collide* || (P) *to fall out* **~gesetzt** a *compound* ⟨a. gram, mus⟩ || ⟨math, bot⟩ *composite* || (aus) *composed, consisting (of)* || aus lauter Stolz ~ *brimful of pride* || ⟨fig⟩ *complex* (⟨a. gram⟩: Satz), *complicated* **~gestoppelt** a ⟨fig⟩ *scrappy* **~gewürfelt** a *mixed (company)*, *motley (crew* ⟨a. fig⟩) || ⟨sport⟩ ~e Mannschaft *scratch crew* bzw *team* || (S) *scrappy* **≃halt** m *consistence, coherence* || ⟨phys, fig⟩ *cohesion* (in Not u Gefahr *in time of stress and danger*) || *bonds, ties* pl || ⟨fig⟩ *union, understanding, concord*, ⟨Am⟩ *togetherness* **~|halten** **1.** vt a) beisammenhalten, b) gemeinschaftlich halten) *to hold* od *keep .. tog.* (→ Zeitung) || (sein Geld) *to take good care of* || (Papiere) *to clip tog.* | (vergleichend) *to collate, confront, compare (with)* || wenn wir .. ~ *in comparing ..* **2.** vi *to hold tog.*; *to stick, cohere* || (P) *to hang, stick, pull tog.*; ⟨fig⟩ *to assist one another* || (Empire) *to keep tog.* **≃hang** m (→ Verbindung) ⟨phys⟩ *cohesion* || ⟨fig⟩ (wirklich, gedacht) *connection*; k–n ~ h mit *not to be connected with* || gedanklicher ~ *coherence of ideas*; *c.e (of operations)* ⟨a. mil⟩ || (Mangel an [logischem]) ~ *(in)coherence*; des inneren ~s entbehren *not to hang tog.*; (e–r Erzählung) mehr ~ geben *to make .. more coherent* || (Beziehung) *relation*; (fortlaufend) *continuity* || *association (of ideas)*; *contingency (of events)* || (e–r Textstelle) *context (in c.)* || sich den ~ e–r S erklären *to make out the history of a th* | **aus** dem ~ reißen *to detach, separate, divorce (words) from their context* || aus dem ~ k *to lose the thread* | **im** ~ mit *in connection with*; im ~ hiermit *in this c.*; etw in ~ bringen mit *to connect a th with*; an das Alter im ~ mit gesichertem Lebensabend denken *to think of old age in terms of security*; sie denkt nicht im ~ *her thoughts are disconnected* || im ~ s (v Zuhörer) *to follow* || in ~ setzen *to associate (ideas)* || im ~ stehen mit *to be connected, to connect with*; *to have reference to* || im ~ stehend mit *(the point) in connection with* | **ohne** ~ *incoherent*; ohne ~ mit *unconnected with, independent of*; ohne ~ miteinander *mutually irrelevant* **~|hangen** (⟨a. ≃⟩) vi [h] *to hang tog.* od *side by side* || ⟨phys⟩ *to cohere* || ⟨fig⟩ *to be connected* od *continuous* || sagen Sie, wie hing das zus? *tell me all about it* od *how it all came about*; andere Dinge hingen damit zus *other ths went with it* **~|hängen 1.** vi = –hangen **2.** vt *to hang tog.* || ⟨fig⟩ *to connect* **~hangend, ~hängend** a *connected, coherent* || *continuous* || unter–e–a ~ *interrelated, interdependent* **~hanglos** a *disconnected, disjointed, incoherent*; *unrelated (actions)*; *desultory (remark)*; *loose, rambling* | adv *(to talk) with incoherence* | ≃igkeit [f] *disjointedness* **~|hauen** *to cut up* ⟨a. mil⟩ || ⟨fam⟩ *to thrash soundly*; ⟨sport⟩ *to hammer badly* || ⟨Am sl⟩ (töten) *to* *lay down* ~|**häufen** vt [h] *to heap* od *pile up, to accumulate* || (Geld) *to amass* ≃**häufung** f *piling up, accumulation* ~|**heften** *to stitch* bzw *join tog.* ~|**hausen** vi [h] *to hive*; *to herd tog.*; ⟨fam⟩ *to pig it* (*with*) ~|**heilen** vt/i [h/s] *to heal up, to close* ~|**hetzen** vt [h] *to set by the ears* ~|**holen** *to bring tog.*; *to collect*; (Leute) *to beat up* ~|**kauern**: sich ~ *to cower* od *squat* (*down*); *to huddle*; *to hunch up* ~|**kaufen** *to buy up* (vgl aufkaufen) ~|**kette(l)n** vt [h] *to chain* (⟨fig⟩ *link*) *tog.* ~|**kitten** vt [h] *to cement* ~|**klammern** vt [h] *to fasten* od *join with cramp-irons*; (Papiere) *to fasten with clips* ≃**klang** m *accord, unison, harmony* ~**klappbar** a *folding* (⟨mot⟩ top) *collapsible* ~|**klappen 1.** vt *to fold up*; *to close* (*a fan*), *to shut* (*a knife*) || die Hacken ~ *to click one's heels* **2.** vi [s] (Zähne) *to chatter* || (P) *to sink* od *break down* (vor .. *with* ..); *to have a* (*nervous*) *break-down*; recht zus.geklappt s *to look quite a wreck* ~|**klauben** vt [h] *to scrape tog.*, ⟨Lit⟩ *to compile* || *to gather up* (*ths*) ~|**kleben** vt/i [h] *to stick* od *fasten tog.* | (Melodie) ~|**klimpern** vt/i [h] *to pick out* | *to strum*, ⟨Am⟩ *bang on the piano* ~|**klingen** vi [h] *to harmonize* || ~ l *to chime* || mit den Gläsern ~ *to touch glasses* ~|**kneten** vt [h] *to knead* ~|**knüllen** vt [h] *to wad* (*up*) ~|**kommen** vi [s] *to come* od *get tog.* || *to meet, assemble* || (Kongress) *to convene* || mit jdm scharf ~ *to have high words* (od *to quarrel*) *with a p* ~|**können** vi [h] [ell] *to be able to meet* || ⟨fam⟩ es ~ *to hit it off* ~|**koppeln** vt [h] *to couple* (*tog.*) ~|**krachen** vi [s] *to* (*fall, break, come down with a*) *crash*; ⟨fig⟩ über jdm ~ *to crash about a p's ears* ~|**krampfen** vt *to wring* (*one's hands*) ~|**kratzen** vt [h] *to scratch tog.* od *up* ⟨a. fig⟩; –ge–zt ⟨fam⟩ *scratch* ~|**kriechen** irr vi [s] *to creep tog.* || *to crouch down* ≃**kunft** f ~/≃e ⟨allg⟩ *meeting, gathering, assembly*; (z Beratung) *conference* || (v 2 Pn) *interview* || (verabredete) *appointment*; e–e ~ mit jdm verabreden *to arrange to see* od *meet a p* || ⟨com⟩ (*round table*) *conference* || (gemütliche) *forgathering*, ⟨Am⟩ *sociable* || (zwanglose, gesellige) (*social*) *get-tog.*; pl *g.-tog.s* || ⟨astr⟩ *conjunction* ~**kuppeln** vt [h] *to fasten tog.* °~|**läppern**: sich ~ *to mount up by small sums* ~|**lassen** *to leave tog.* || (zus.k l) *to allow to meet* ≃**lauf** m *concourse* || (Auflauf) *riot, mob* ~|**laufen** vi irr [s] *to flock* od *crowd tog.* || *to raise a riot* || ⟨math⟩ (wieder) *to* (*re*)*converge* || (Farben) *to run tog., to blend* || (einschrumpfen) *to shrink* (*up*) || (Milch) *to curdle* | auf *or* in e–m Punkt ~ *to meet in a p.* || mit den Köpfen ~ *to knock their heads tog.* | ~**d** *convergent* ~|**läuten 1.** vt *to assemble by ringing the bells* **2.** vi .. ~ l *to set* (*all the bells*) *ringing* ~|**leben I.** vi [h] *to live tog.* || (geschlechtlich) *to cohabit* || mit e–m ~ *to live with a p* **II.** ≃ n *living tog., companionship* || *married* bzw *social life*; ihr ~ *their life tog.* || *cohabitation* || ⟨biol⟩ *symbiosis* || ⟨pol⟩ *mutual relationships* || bloßes ~ *coexistence* ~**legbar** a *folding, collapsible*; ⟨phot⟩ *extension* (*tripod*) ~**leg-** ~(geduld)spiel [n] *jig-saw puzzle* ~|**legen** vt [h] *to put tog.* || *to heap up* || (falten) *to fold up* || *to fold* (*one's arms*) || *to tuck* (*one's legs*) || *to shut* (*a penknife*) || ⟨com⟩ (Geschäfte) *to merge, unite* || *to consolidate* (*shares*) || (Geld) *to club* (*up*); *to pool* (*resources*) || *to amalgamate* (*farms*, ⟨ind⟩ *plants*) || –ge–gt w mit ⟨a.⟩ *to be located tog. with* | sich ~ *to lie tog.* ≃**legung** f *pooling*; ⟨agr⟩ *re-distribution* (*of land*), *concentration* (*of scattered holdings*) || (v Kapital, Aktien) *reduction, consolidation* || *merger, fusion*; ⟨jur⟩ *consolidation* (*of corporations*) ~|**leihen** vt [h]: sich [dat] .. ~ *to collect .. by borrowing* ~|**lesen** vt irr [h] *to collect, glean, compile*; (rasch) *to scramble* ~|**liegen** vi [h] *to lie tog.* || ⟨mil⟩ *to be quartered tog.* ~|**löten** *to solder* (*up* od *tog.*) °~|**machen** vt *to put tog.* ~|**nähen** vt *to sew up* od *tog.* ~|**nehmen** vt irr [h] *to take tog.* od *collectively* || *to gather up* (*one's cloak*) || *to pick up* (*the cards*) || *to rein in* (*a horse*) || *to collect* (*one's thoughts*) || *to husband* (*one's strength*) || alles zus–genommen *all ths considered, all in all, on the whole, all told* || alle anderen zus–gen. *all the rest taken tog.*; zus–gen. mit *taken in conjunction with* | **sich** ~ *to collect o.s.*; *to take heart* od *courage*; *to pull o.s. tog.* || *to control one's feelings*; *to shake one's wits tog.*; *to exert* od *brace o.s.*; *to tax one's energies*; (fest) *to keep a tight hold on one's nerves* || ⟨fam⟩ *to keep a stiff upper-lip* || nimm dich zus *be y.s* od *a man*!; .., oder ..! *be careful* (od *look out*) *or* ..! || (= s–e Kräfte) *to gather up one's strength, to make a great effort, to use* (od *summon up*) *all one's strength* || (aufmerksam) *to pay close attention* || (vorsichtig) *to take great care* || (im Benehmen) *to be on one's best behaviour*; aber, aber, mein Lieber, nimm dich doch zus! *now then, don't be sloppy, dear*! ⟨Am fam⟩ *snap out of it*! ~|**ordnen** *to arrange tog., to classify* ~|**packen** vt [h] *to pack* od *bundle up* ~|**passen 1.** vt [h] *to adjust, assort*; *to fit* (*tog.*) || ⟨tail⟩ *to match* **2.** vi [h] (P) *to agree, harmonize* || (Schuhe) *to be pairs* || gut ~ *to square* (mit *with*); *to be* (*well matched* od) *a good match* (od *made for each other*) || schlecht ~ *to be ill-assorted* || *mismatched pair of shoes* ~|**pferchen** vt [h] *to pen up, to fold* (⟨fig⟩ *crowd* ⟨a. eth⟩) *tog.* ≃**prall** m *collision, clash* (*with*); *impact* (*on*) ⟨a. fig⟩ ~|**prallen** vi [s] *to clash, bump* (*against*) ~|**pressen** vt [h] *to press* od *squeeze tog.*; *to wad up* || die Zähne ~ *to set one's teeth*; *it clutches my heart*; sie –ßte ihre Lippen zus *her lip tightened* ~|**quetschen** vt [h] *to squeeze* ~|**raffen** vt [h] *to scrape tog., to snatch up, to collect quickly* od *eagerly*; ⟨sl⟩ *to hog* || (Kleider) *to tuck up* | **sich** ~ *to take heart, to pick up spirit, to pluck up courage, to get o.s. in gear, to pull* od *gather o.s. tog.*; ⟨Am⟩ *to take a brace* °~|**rattern** vi [s] ⟨sl⟩ *to flop down* ~|**rechnen** vt [h] *to sum* od *figure, cast up, to total* || alles –ge–net *including everything*, ⟨fig⟩ *taking everyth. into account* ~|**reimen** vt [h] ⟨fig⟩ *to piece tog.*; *to make out, to get at the bottom of* || es sich [dat] ~ *to put two and two tog.* || ich kann mir das nicht ~ *I can't make sense* (od *head or tail*) *of it* || sich ~ *to agree, tally* ~|**reißen** vt [h] *to pull down* | **sich** ~ *to brace o.s.*; *to pull o.s. tog.*; *to buck up*; *to get o.s. in gear*; *to nerve o.s.* ~|**reiten** vt [h] *to overwork* (*a horse*) ~|**rennen** vi [s] *to run against one another* || ⟨fig⟩ *to fall out* (*with*) ~|**rollen** vt [h] *to roll, curl, coil up*; eng –gerollt *close-furled* ~|**rotten,** sich [h] *to flock, troop, band tog.*; *to mob* || (z Aufruhr) *to plot, conspire, riot* ≃**rottung** f *trooping-, banding-tog.* || (Volksauflauf) *mob, riot* ~|**rücken 1.** vt [h] *to move* od *put tog.* || (Stühle) *to put .. closer* **2.** vi [s] *to draw closer tog., to close* (⟨fam⟩ *squeeze*) *up*; ~! *close up, there*! || ⟨mil⟩ nach rechts ~ *to move to the right* ~|**rufen** vt irr [h] *to call tog., to convoke, convene* || ⟨pol⟩ *to call, summon* (auf d. 2. Mai *for May 2nd* ≃**rufung** f *convocation, calling-tog.* ~|**sacken** vi [s] *to sink down* ~|**schalten** vt [h] ⟨el⟩ *to interconnect* ~|**scharen** vt [h] & sich ~ *to form troops*, etc; *to flock* od *mass tog.* ~|**scharren** vt [h] *to scrape* od *rake tog.*; *to roll up* (*profit*) ≃**schau** f *synopsis* ~|**schau(d)ern** vi [s] *to shudder* (*with horror*) ~|**schichten** vt [h] *to heap* od *pile up* ~|**schicken** vt [h] *to send tog.* | sich ~ *to agree tog., to get on comfortably* ~**schiebbar** a *sliding* (od *telescopic, extension*) (*tripod*) ~|**schieben** vt irr [h] *to shove* od *push tog.*; *to telescope* (⟨a.⟩ sich ~) ~|**schießen** vt irr [h] *to shoot to pieces* || ⟨artill⟩ *to batter down* || Geld ~ ⟨fig⟩ *to club m. tog.*; *to get up a subscription for a p* || –geschossenes Geld *m. made up by contributions*, (bei Wetten) *sweepstake* ~|**schlagen** irr **1.** vt [h] *to beat* od *strike tog.* || *to click* (*one's heels*) || *to clap* (*one's hands*); die Hände über dem Kopf ~ *to throw up one's hands in* *astonishment* || (zus–setzen) *to join* || ⟨typ⟩ *to gather* || (Bett) *to put up* || (Decke etc) *to fold up* || (Mantel) *to wrap .. around one* | ⟨fig⟩ (Kosten) *to lump*; ⟨agr⟩ (Güter) *to unite* | (zerschlagen) *to beat to pieces* od *down* || ⟨mil⟩ (Feind) *to smash up* **2.** vi [s] *to clash* || (über [acc]) *to close over* **~|schließen** irr **1.** vt [h] *to link tog.* || ⟨fig⟩ *to unite, join* | **sich** ~ *to get tog.*; *to team up*; *to join hands*; *to close one's ranks* || ⟨Am⟩ *to bunch (up)* || sich ~ gegen *to line up against* || sich ~ mit *to hook up with*; *to align (o.s.) with* || sich ~ um *to close round* | sich zu e–m Verein ~ *to club*, z e–r Arbeitsgemeinschaft *to team up* || sich zu e–r Kolonne ~ *to form up to a c.* **2.** vi [h] *to shut* od *fit well* **≃schließung** f, **≃schluß** m *union, bond, alliance*; *combination, integration* | *tight fit* | (Interessen, Geschäfte) *consolidation* | ~ der Völker *union among the peoples* | ~ zu e–r Arbeitsgemeinschaft *organization into a study group* | ~bewegung [f] *endeavours to achieve federation* **~|schmelzen 1.** vt reg [h] *to melt, dissolve, fuse* **2.** vi irr [s] *to melt* (⟨fig⟩ *fall*) *away* (z *to*), *to dissolve* || ⟨fig⟩ *to dwindle* **~|schmieden** vt [h] ⟨fig⟩ *to construct (an epic)* **~|schmiegen**: sich ~ *to fit well* || (P) *to snuggle o.s. up* **~|schmieren** vt [h] *to compile carelessly*; Artikel ~ ⟨sl⟩ *to sling ink* **~|schnorren** vt [h] ⟨sl⟩ *to scrounge*, etw v jdm ~ *to bum a th off a p* **~|schnüren** vt [h] *to lace up* || (Paket) *to cord up*; *to fasten tog.* || ⟨fig⟩ es schnürt mir das Herz, (die Kehle) zus *it wrings my heart (it makes me choke)* **~|schrecken** vi [s] irr [pp –o–] *to startle* **~|schreiben** vt irr [h] || (Buch) *to compile* || *to write in one word* || was er alles –bt! *what a scribbler!* || sich [dat] ein Vermögen ~ *to make a fortune by one's pen* **~|schrumpfen,** ⟨fam⟩ **~|schrumpeln** vi [s] *to shrink up, to shrivel, dwarf* || (Haut) *to wrinkle* || ⟨fig⟩ *to dwindle away, to run short* °**~|schustern** vt [h] = zus–flicken **~|schütteln** vt [h] *to shake up well* **~|schweißen** vt [h] *to weld tog.* (z *into*) ⟨a. fig⟩ **≃sein** n *being tog.* || *meeting* **~|sein** vi [s] ~ mit *to associate, to be in contact with*; oft/viel mit jdm ~ *to see much* (od *quite a lot*) *of a p* **~|setzen** vt [h] *to put tog.* (⟨a.⟩ Pn) || die Gewehre ~ *to pile arms* | ⟨fig⟩ *to compose* || ⟨math, chem⟩ *to combine* || ⟨cul, med⟩ *to compound*; –ge–zt ⟨opt⟩ *compound (lens)* | **sich** ~ (P) *to sit tog.* || sich ~ aus *to consist* (od *be made up*) *of* || → –gesetzt **≃setzspiel** n *jig-saw puzzle* **≃setzung** f *composition* (⟨a. übtr⟩ *of a Cabinet*), *make-up (of society)* || *combination* || ⟨mach⟩ *construction* || ⟨gram⟩ *compound* **~|sinken** vi irr [s] (P) *to sink down* || *to fold* || *to collapse* (⟨a.⟩ Haus), in sich ~ *to sink small*; in sich –gesunken *huddled* **~|spannen** vt [h] *to yoke* (mit *to*) **~|sparen** vt [h] *to save up, to economize* **≃spiel** n ⟨theat⟩ *collective acting, acting in unison* || *concerted effort(s)* || ⟨sport⟩ *team-play*; ⟨ftb⟩ *combination*; im ~ mit *partnered by* || ⟨fig⟩ *interplay (of forces)* **~|spielen** vi [h] ⟨a.⟩ *to be partners* || ~ mit *to partner (a p)* **~|sprechen** vt irr [h] *to unite in marriage* **~|stecken 1.** vt [h] *to put* od *clip tog.* **2.** vi [h] ewig ~ *to be always tog.* **~|stehen** vi irr [h] *to stand* od *be tog.* || ⟨fig⟩ *to side with one another*, ⟨fam⟩ *to stick tog.* || gut ~ *to be on good terms (with)* **~|stellen** vt [h] *to put* od *place tog.* || (Arznei, Liste, Mannschaft etc) *to make up* || (Farben) passend ~ *to pair* || (Zug) ⟨rail⟩ *to assemble* || Wahlergebnisse ~ *to count the votes* || ⟨theat⟩ *to assemble (the cast)* || (Fahrräder) *to stack* || (Zahlen) *to collect up* | (vereinigen) *to combine* || ⟨mach⟩ *to mount* || (Material z e–m Buch) *to compile*; Beweismaterial ~ ⟨jur⟩ *to build up a case* | (ordnen) *to group, classify*; (3 Gläser) *to fit up*; schlecht –ge–lt *ill-assorted* | (vergleichen) *to compare* || ⟨comp⟩ *to assemble* **≃stellung** f *putting tog., juxtaposition* || ⟨Am⟩ *check-up* || *combination* || *compilation* || *classification* || *comparison* || *assembly (of apparatuses)* || ungewöhnliche ~ *extraordinary assortment* || ⟨comp tech⟩ ~ v Stammanlagen *setting up (card and tape) files* **~|steuern** vt [h] *to contribute, to club tog.* **~|stimmen** vi [h] *to accord, concur, agree, harmonize, tally*; *to be in harmony (with)* || nicht ~ *to disagree, jar* **≃stimmung** f *harmony, agreement, concurrence* **~|stoppeln** vt [h] *to pick* bzw *piece tog.* || *to patch up* || *to compile carelessly* **≃stoppelung** f *patch-work* **≃stoß** m *clash(ing), shock, bump* || (v Fahrzeugen) *collision, crash*; ⟨rail a.⟩ *impact*; ⟨Am⟩ *crack-up, smash-up* || ⟨mil⟩ *encounter, clash* | ⟨fig⟩ *clash (with the police)*; *clashing (of opinions)*; *conflict* || (~ zweier Landkarten) *joining edge* **~|stoßen** irr **1.** vt [h] *to knock* od *dash tog.* || *to touch, clink (glasses* die Gl., mit den Gl.n) || *to crush, pound* || *to upset* || ⟨tail⟩ *to join* **2.** vi irr [s] *to clash, to come into collision, to collide (with)* ⟨a. fig⟩; ⟨billiards⟩ *to kiss* || ~ mit *to cannon, strike against*; ⟨mil⟩ *to encounter (the enemy)*; *to join forces with* || ⟨fig⟩ *to fall foul of (a p)* | ⟨fig⟩ [h] (an–e–a–liegen) *to border upon* (od *to adjoin*) *each other* || ~d *adjoining, adjacent, contiguous* **~|streichen** vt [h] *to amass (money)* || ⟨Lit, theat⟩ *to cut down* **~|strömen** vi [s] *to flow tog.* (dazu: *conflux, confluence*) || (P) *to flock* od *crowd tog.* (dazu: *concourse, crowd*) **~|stücke(l)n** vt [h] *to piece tog., to patch up* **≃sturz** m *downfall, crash* **~|stürzen** vi [s] *to give way, to tumble down, to collapse* ⟨a. fig⟩ **~|suchen** vt [h] *to gather* od *pick up*; *to collect* ⟨a. fig⟩ **~|tragen** vt irr [h] *to get tog., to collect*; auf e–n Haufen ~ *to heap tog.* || ⟨fig⟩ *to compile* || ≃n *collection, compilation* **≃treffen** n *meeting* (→ –kunft) || ⟨übtr⟩ *blending, joining, merging*; (Übereinstimmung) *concurrence*; (v Umständen) *coincidence* ⟨a. med⟩; *juncture*; ⟨jur⟩ *joinder* (mehrerer Delikte) || (feindliches) *encounter* **~|treffen** vi irr [s] (P) *to meet* | ~ mit *to fall in with* || (feindlich) *to (have an) encounter* || (Umstände) *to coincide* || (mitwirkend) *to combine, co-operate* (z .. *in doing*) || (störend) *to interfere (with)* | (übereinstimmend) *to come up to, to correspond to*; *to answer (a p's expectations)* || ⟨mar⟩ ~ mit *to rendezvous with (a tanker)* **~|treiben** vt irr [h] *to drive* od *sweep tog.* || ⟨hunt⟩ *to beat up*, ⟨Am⟩ (Vieh) *to round up* **~|treten** vi irr [s] *to unite, combine, join* || (sich versammeln) *to meet*; ⟨parl⟩ *to assemble* **≃tritt** m *meeting* **~|trommeln** vt *to drum up*; ⟨übtr⟩ *to bring tog.*; (eilends) *to scare up (voters, etc)* **~|tun** vt irr [h] *to put* od *throw tog.* || –getan w *to be joined* (a. ehelich) | **sich** ~ *to associate, combine, consort, unite (with)* || *to join*; ⟨com⟩ *to join partnership*, ⟨Am⟩ *to go tog.*; sich gegen (jdn) ~ ⟨Am⟩ *to gang up on ..*; .. in e–e Gruppe *to herd tog.*; .. mit jdm ⟨a.⟩ *to conspire with a p* **~|wachsen** vi irr [s] *to grow tog.*; *to coalesce* ⟨a. fig⟩; [österr] = an–e–a–geraten || –ge– ⟨scient⟩ *anchylosed*, ⟨bot⟩ *accrete* | ≃ n *coalescence* || *accretion* **~|wehen** vt [h] *to blow tog.* || –ge–ht *drifted (snow)* **~|werfen** vt irr [h] *to throw tog.* || *to make into a heap* || (Gelder, Kräfte) *to pool* || ~ mit *to lump with* ⟨a. fig⟩ | = niederwerfen | = verwechseln **~|wickeln** vt [h] *to wrap* od *roll up* **~|wirken** vi [h] *to co-operate* | ~d *co-operative, concurrent* | ≃n n *interaction*; *united efforts* pl, *concerted action*; (P) *co-operation (in c. with)*; planvolles ~ *organized teamwork*; ⟨mil⟩ enges ~ *close t.w.* || (of events) *concurrence* **~|wohnen** vi [h] ⟨sl⟩ *to dig tog.*; (eingepfercht) *to pig it* **~|würfeln** vt [h] *to jumble up* || → –ge–lt **~|zählen** vt [h] *to add, sum, total* (⟨fam⟩ *tot*) *up*, ⟨Am a.⟩ *to foot up* **~ziehbar** a *contracti(b)le* **~|ziehen** irr **1.** vt [h] *to draw tog., to gather* ⟨a. tail⟩ || *to tighten* | = –|zählen | (verengern) *to contract* (⟨a.⟩ *one's brows*) || *to pucker up (one's mouth)* || *to purse (one's lips* || ⟨Lit⟩ *to contract, abridge* | (versammeln) *to assemble, gather* || (Truppen) *to concentrate, mass* | **sich** ∼ *to shrink up* || *to screw o.s. up* || (Augen) *to narrow* || (Geschwür) *to draw to a head* || (Gewitter) *to gather* || (Herz) *to tighten* || (Magen) *to contract* || (Truppen) *to assemble, gather* || (steif w) *to set* **2.** vi [s] *to take lodgings tog., to share rooms* (*with*) **∼ziehend** a ⟨phys⟩ *contractive* || ⟨med⟩ *astringent* (⟨a.⟩ ∼es Mittel) **∸ziehung** f *contraction* ⟨a. gram⟩, ⟨gram⟩ *contracted form* || ⟨med⟩ *astriction*; (krampfartige) *convulsion*; (des Herzens) *systole* || ⟨mil⟩ *concentration* **∼|zucken** vi [s] *to jerk, wince, flinch*; *to give a start* (bei *at*)

zus·amt I. [prep] *together with* **II.** [adv] *all tog.*

Z·usatz m ∼es/∼̈e *additive, addition* bzw *addendum* | (Ergänzung) *supplement* | (Beimischung) *admixture*; unechter ∼ *adulterant*; (kl) *dash* (*a d. of brandy*); (zu Metallen) *alloy*; ⟨found⟩ *addition* | (Anmerkung) *appended note* | (Nachschrift) *postscript* || (zu e–m Gesetz) *rider* || (zu e–m Testament) *codicil* || [in comp] *additional, accessory, auxiliary, booster, complementary, supplementary* **∼anode** f *s.y anode* **∼antrag** m ⟨parl⟩ *amendment* (*to move an a.*) **∼artikel** m ⟨jur⟩ *rider*; *extra clause*; ⟨parl⟩ *amendment* **∼batterie** f ⟨el⟩ *b.r battery* **∼belastung** f *a.l load* **∼blitz** m ⟨phot⟩ *b.r flash* **∼brenner** m ⟨tech⟩ *pilot burner* **∼budget** n *s.y estimates* pl **∼dividende** f ⟨ins⟩ *s.y bonus* **∼dynamo** m *b.r* **∼einrichtung** f *au.y device*; *optional* (od *special-purpose*) *feature* **∼feder** f ⟨tech⟩ *helper spring* **∼gerät** n *accessories, fittings* pl; *au.y equipment* **∼klausel** f *a.l clause* **∼ladung** f ⟨mil⟩ *booster charge* **∼licht** n *b.r light* **∼maschine** f ⟨rail⟩ (*positive*) *b.r* **∼meldung** f *c.y* (*technical*, etc) *report* N **∼metall** n *alloy* **∼mittel** n *additive* **∼patent** n *patent of addition* **∼speicher** m *backing store* **∼spritze** f ⟨med⟩ *booster shot* **∼steuer** f *a.l tax* **∼sucher** m ⟨phot⟩ *ac.y viewfinder* **∼tanks** m pl ⟨aero⟩ *wing tips* **∼transformator** m *b.r* (⟨Am⟩ *step-up*) *transformer* **∼versicherung** f *s.y insurance* **∼werbung** f *ac.y advertising* **∼wicklung** f *au.y winding* **z·usätzlich** a *additional*; *supplementary*; ⟨mil⟩ *c.y* (*report*) N; ∼e Arbeit *extra work*; ∼e Kosten [pl] etc *extra costs* pl; ⟨tech⟩ ⟨a.⟩ *optional*; ∼es Produkt ⟨chem⟩ *adduct*; ⟨tex⟩ *extra* (*backing*)

z·u- ∼sch·anden [adv]; sich ∼ arbeiten *to work o.s. to death*; ∼ gehen *to go to ruin*, ⟨fam⟩ *to go to the dogs* || ∼ hauen *to knock to pieces*, ⟨fam⟩ *to beat into a pulp* || ∼ m *to mar, disgrace, destroy, ruin*; (Absichten) *to frustrate, thwart*; (Hoffnungen) *to destroy, defeat* || (ein Pferd) ∼ reiten *to founder*; *to ride* (*a horse*) *down* || ∼ w *to come to nought, to be brought into disgrace, to be dashed to the ground* °**∼|schanzen** vt [h]; jdm etw ∼ *to put a p in the way of a th*; *to throw* (*business*) *in a p's way* || ⟨sport⟩ dem Gegner den Sieg ∼ *to throw* **∼|schärfen** vt [h] *to point, sharpen* (*a tool*), *to whet* (*a blade*) || ⟨carp⟩ *to feather off*; –ge–fte Kante *bevel* **∼|scharren** vt [h] *to fill up* **∼|schauen** vi [h] *to look on* (e–r S [dat] *at a th*); (abwartend) *to sit on the fence* || jdm *to watch* (*a p*; bei etw *doing a th*) **∸schauer(in** f) m ∼s/∼ *spectator, looker-on*, (unbeteiligter) *onlooker* (bei *at*); (zufälliger) *bystander, stander-by* || [pl] (*the*) *audience*, (*the*) *public* | ∼hausschalttafel [f] ⟨theat⟩ *house* (⟨Am⟩ *h. switch*)*board*; ∼raum [m] ⟨theat⟩ *auditorium, house*; ∼schaft [f] (*the*) *audience* ⟨a. theat⟩; ∼tribüne [f] *public gallery, spectators' stand* **∼|schaufeln** vt [h] *to shovel up* **∼|schicken** vt [h] [dat] *to send*, (Geld) *remit*, (Waren) *consign* (*to*) **∼|schieben** vt irr [h] *to close* || den Riegel ∼ *to shoot the bolt* || jdm etw ∼ *to push a th towards a p*; *to give .. secretly* || jdm den Eid ∼ *to put a p upon his* (*her*) *oath, to administer* (od *tender*) *an oath to a p* || jdm ein Kind ∼ *to father a child on a p* || jdm die Schuld ∼ *to lay the blame at a p's door* od *on a p* || jdm die Verantwortung ∼ *to shift the r.y to a p*; e–e unangenehme Aufgabe ∼ ⟨fam⟩ *to pass the buck to a p*; (z Last legen) *to put a th upon a p* **∼|schießen** irr **1.** vt [h] ⟨fig⟩ *to add, contribute* || (Blicke) *to dart* ([dat] *at*) **2.** vi [h] *to fire* (*away*) (auf [acc] *at* | [s] ⟨fig⟩ (auf [acc]) *to rush up* (*to*), *to rush* (*upon*) **∸schlag** m ∼(e)s/∼̈e (Zusatz) *addition* ⟨a. found⟩ || ⟨met⟩ *flux*, ∼kalkstein [m] *calcareous flux* | (bei der Auktion) *knocking down, acceptance of a bid* || (bei Ausschreibungen) *award of the contract* || (gerichtlicher) *adjudication* | ⟨rail⟩ *excess fare*; *extra ticket, supplement* (*payable*) || (Preis∸) *extra charge, surcharge*; f Tanzen wird ein ∼ erhoben *dancing is an extra* || (Fracht∸) *primage* || (Teuerungs∸) *booms* pl || (Steuer∸) *surtax, supertax, surcharge* | ⟨ins⟩ ∼̈e erhöhen *to increase premium by addition of loading* || (bei Ausschreibungen) den ∼ erteilen, geben (erhalten) *to award* (*obtain*) *the contract* || (Lohn– etc ∸) *additions* pl; *extra allowance* | [in comp] ∼-*additional* (⟨ins⟩ *premium*); ∼preis [m] (at auction) *contract price* **∼|schlagen** irr **1.** vt [h] (Augen) *to close* || (Ball) *to drive ..* (*towards a p*) || (Buch) *to shut* || (Tür) *to bang, slam* (a. –ge– w) | (gerichtlich) *to adjudicate* || (bei Auktion) *to knock down* (jdm *to a p*) || (bei Ausschreibungen) *to give the contract* || (hinzurechnen) *to add to* || (Summe) *to put on* (*to*) | ⟨met⟩ *to add as a flux* **2.** vi [h] *to strike* (*hard*); *to lay it on* || auf e–n ∼ *to hit a p* | [s] (sich schließen) *to shut suddenly*; *the door crashed into place*; vgl ∼ 1. (Tür) **∸schläger** m (Schmied) *striker, hammerman* **∸schlag(s)-∼(fahr)karte** [f] ⟨rail⟩ *extra* od *additional ticket*; ∼gebühr [f] *surcharge, additional fee* || ⟨rail⟩ *excess fare*; ∸pflichtig [a] *liable to additional payment*; ∼porto [n] *excess postage*; ∼prämie [f] *extra premium*; ∼steuer [f] *surtax*; ∼taxe [f] = –gebühr **∼|schleppen** vt [h] *to carry* (*to*), (e–m etw) *to get .. for a p in secret* **∼|schließen** vt irr [h] *to* (*pad*)*lock*; *to shut up, to close* **∼|schmeißen** vt irr [h] ⟨fam⟩ (e–e Tür) *to bang, slam* || (jdm etw) *to chuck* (*a th to a p*) **∼|schmelzen 1.** vt reg [h] *to close by melting, to solder up* || (luftdicht) *to seal hermetically* **2.** vi irr [s] *to close up by fusion* **∼|schmieren** vt [h] *to smear up* od *over* **∼|schnallen** vt [h] *to buckle* || (mit Riemen) *to strap up* **∼|schnappen 1.** vi [h] (mit den Zähnen) *to snap* (nach *at*) || [s] (einschnappen) *to snap to*; *to close, click* **2.** vt *to close with a snap*, ⟨Am⟩ *she snapped her bag shut* **∼|schneiden** vt irr [h] (Holz etc) *to cut up, to dress, scantle* || ⟨tail⟩ *to cut out* || ⟨film⟩ *to trim* (*ready-trimmed f.*) || ⟨phot⟩ (Abzüge) *to cut to size* | ⟨fig⟩ (etw) auf etw ∼ *to tailor* (od *cut and fashion*) *.. to suit* od *fit some need* || e–m etw (knapp) ∼ *to keep a p on short allowance, to keep a p short of a th* || ⟨fig⟩ auf jdn zugeschnittene Rolle ⟨theat⟩ *part written for a p* **∸schneider(in** f) m ∼s/∼ ⟨tail⟩ *cutter-out* **∼·ei** f ⟨tail⟩ *cutting-out room* || *cutting-out*; ⟨dero⟩ *bad cut* || ⟨carp⟩ *squaring* **∸schneidetisch** m *cutting-out table* **∼|schneien** vi [s] *to get snowed up* **∸schnitt** m ⟨tail⟩ *cut* || ⟨phot⟩ *cropping* (*of prints*) ⟨fig⟩ *arrangements* pl; *style, fashion, turn* || in .. ∼ *on a grand scale, in a great style* **∼|schnüren** vt [h] *to lace up* || (Paket) *to cord up* || jdm die Kehle ∼ *to strangle a p* || ⟨fig⟩ es schnürte mir die Kehle [das Herz] zu, mir war .. wie –ge–rt *my throat closed up* od *was tight, I felt* (⟨fam⟩ *a lump in my throat* od) *choked*, [*it wrung my very heart*] **∼|schrauben** vt [h] *to screw up* od (Deckel) *down*; weiter, fester ∼ ⟨fig⟩ *to give the screw another turn* **∼|schreiben** irr **1.** vt [h] *to add* (*a few lines*) | (jdm etw) *to write, dedicate, assign* (*to ..*) || *to place* (*a sum*) *to a p's credit* || ⟨fig⟩ (Tat, etc) *to impute, attribute, ascribe* (*a th to a p*); (Gutes) *to* (*ac*)*credit a p with a th, to accredit a th to a p* || (Schlechtes fälschlich) *to get the boot on the wrong foot* || das ist ihm –zu– *it is due to him, he is to blame for it* || er hat es sich selbst –zu– *he has h.s. to thank* od *to* *blame for it* || [dat] –zu– s: (*rattlesnakes*) *amount for* (*sth like* 2/3 *of all snakebite cases in the U.S.*) || etw e–r S ~ *to put* od *set a th down to a th* **2.** vi [h] ([jdm] schriftlich zusagen) *to accept the* [od *a p's*] *invitation* **≈schreibung** f *ascription*, etc **~|schreien** vt/i irr [h] (jdm) *to call* (*shout, cry*) *out* (*a th to a p*) **~|schreiten** vi irr [s] (auf [acc]) *to walk* (*stride, step*) *up to* od *toward* | munter *or* tüchtig ~ *to step out well, to walk briskly*, ⟨fam⟩ *to put one's best leg forward* || rascher ~ *to quicken one's pace* **≈schrift** f ~/~en *letter* || amtliche ~ *official communication* || (Widmung) *dedication* **~schriftlich** adv *by letter* **~sch·ulden** adv; sich [dat] etw ~ k l *to make o.s. guilty of a th*; *to commit* (*a new violation*); *to get on the wrong side of the law*; .. e–e Feigheit .. *to show the white feather* **≈schuß** m –sses/≈sse *extra allowance* (gewähren *to make*); *additional payment* || *subsidy* || (staatl.) *government grant* || ohne ~ ausk *to pay one's way* | ~betrieb [m] *undertaking that requires a subsidy*; ~bogen [m] ⟨typ⟩ *extra sheet*; ~steuer [f] *additional tax* od *duty* °**~|schustern** vt [h] = **1.** (etw) –setzen **2.** (jdm etw) –k l **~|schütten** vt [h] (hinzu|tun) *to add* || (auf|füllen) *to fill* (*up*) **~|schwellen** vi [s] (*the lids*) *swell shut* **~|schwören** vt irr [h] (jdm etw) *to swear* (*a th to a p*) **≈|sehen** n ~s/ *looking-on, the part of an onlooker* || bei näherem ~ *on closer examination, on nearer view* || das ~ h *to be left out in the cold, to get nothing for one's pains* **~|sehen** vi irr [h] *to look on* (*at*), *to be a spectator* || *to witness* || e–r S [dat] ~ *to watch a th* || e–m beim Spielen ~, ~, wie e–r spielt *to watch a p playing* | (zögernd) ich kann nicht länger ~ *I cannot wait* (od *stand it*) *any longer* | (Sorge tragen) *to take care* (*that*) || er mag ~, wo er .. findet *he can go and find* ..; du magst ~, wo du bleibst, da mußt du selbst ~ *look to y.s.*, ⟨fig⟩ *that's your own look-out* || sieh zu, daß .. *see to it that* ..; (sich in acht nehmend) *be on your guard that*; .., daß .. nicht .. *take care lest* (*you fall*) **~sehends** [adv] *visibly, obviously*; *rapidly* **~|sein** vi [s] *to be shut* od *closed* **~|senden** vt irr [h] = zuschicken **~|setzen 1.** vt [h] *to add, admix* || ⟨cul⟩ *to set on the fire* || ⟨met⟩ *to alloy with* | (verlieren) *to lose, sacrifice*; ~ bei *to be a loser by* ..; er hat nicht viel –zu– *he has not much to lose*; [ell] man kann dabei nur ~ *it is a losing concern*, ⟨Am⟩ *you'll be in the red* | (versperren) *to block, bar* || (Domino) *to close the game* | (hin~) e–n Wagen ~ ⟨rail⟩ *to couple another wag(g)on*; dazu: *addition of a car* **2.** vi [h] (jdm) *to press, attack, nag, urge*, ⟨fam⟩ *kick a p* (*to do*) || jdm hart ~ *to press a p hard*; ⟨fam⟩ *to put a p to it*; ⟨sl⟩ *to run a p ragged*; *he was hard put to* (→ jdn drängen); *he was sharply beset* (*by*); .. wegen e–r S *to worry a p about a th* || ⟨sport⟩ *to punish a p* | e–m mit Bitten ~ *to importune a p, to be urgent with a p* | *to ply a p* (*with questions*) || *pester a p* (*with empty talk*) || e–m aufs äußerste ~ *to corner a p* **~|sichern** vt [h] (jdm etw) *to assure* (*a p of a th*) (*good quarters are a.d*); *to promise* (*a p a th*) **≈sicherung** f *assurance*; *warrant*; *promise*; *pledge* || unter ~ [gen] *promising him*, etc (*a th*) **~|siegeln** vt [h] *to seal* (*up*) **≈speise** f *trimmings* pl **~|sperren** vt [h] *to block od bar* (*up*); *to shut, close, fasten* || ×[abs] (pleite gehen) ⟨bes Am⟩ *to fall by the wayside* **~|spielen** vt [h] jdm ~ ⟨theat, ftb⟩ *to feed a p*; jdm (etw) ~ *to play* (*a th*) *into a p's hands* || ⟨fig⟩ *to pass a th to a p on the sly* || ⟨ftb⟩ *to pass* (*the ball*) *to a p* | ≈ n ⟨ftb⟩ *pass* **~|spitzen** vt [h] *to* (*sharpen* [⟨fig⟩ *bring*] *to a*) *point* || (Nadeln, ⟨arch⟩ Bogen) *to point* || (Übel) *to sharpen* | **sich** ~ *to taper* (*off*) || ⟨fig⟩ *to come to a head* || sich ~d ⟨fig⟩ *climactic*; → –ge–zt **≈spitzung** f *taper ratio* **≈sprache** f = Zuspruch **~|sprechen** irr **1.** vi [h] (jdm) *to address, accost, exhort, comfort* (*a p*); jdm freundlich ~ *to speak kindly to a p*; jdm gut ~ *to speak a p fair* || dem Wein, der Flasche ~ *to drink copiously*; ⟨fam⟩ *to punish* (*the claret*) || (e–r Speise [dat]) *to eat heartily of*, ⟨fam⟩ *to punish* **2.** vt [h] (jdm) *to award, adjudge, adjudicate* (*a th to a p*) || (Telegramme) *to announce* || (bei Auktion) *to knock a th down to a p* | jdm Mut ~ *to cheer a p up, to encourage a p* || jdm Trost ~ *to console, comfort a p* | **e–r S** zu sehr ~ *to overindulge in a th* **~|springen** vi irr [s] [dat] *or* auf [acc] *to leap on, to rush at* od *upon* || ⟨fig⟩ *to help* || (einschnappen) *to snap to* **≈spruch** m (Ermahnung) *exhortation* || (Trost≈) *consolation, comforting* || (Mut≈) *encouragement* || (v Kunden) *run* (*of customers*) || viel ~ h (v Geschäften) *to have a good custom*; ⟨hot, etc⟩ *to be much frequented* **~|spünden** vt [h] *to bung up* **≈stand** m *condition, state*, ⟨Am a.⟩ *shape* || *frame* (*of mind*) || *position, situation*; *lot* || ≈e [pl] *state of affairs*; nette ≈e! *what a mess!* || ≈e kriegen *to have a fit*; das ist z ≈e kriegen *that gives you the creeps* || in gutem ~ *in good order, state* (in g.n ~ bringen *to condition*); ⟨arch⟩ *in good repair*; ⟨mar⟩ *in sailing trim*; (Boden) ⟨agr⟩ *in good heart*, ⟨so:⟩ in schlechtem ~ *out of heart* || (P) *in good fettle*; ein trauriger ~ *a sorry plight, a sad state of affairs*; in hoffnungslosem ~ *in a desperate pass* od *plight*; im ~ der Trunkenheit *in a drunken fit* | **~s-** ~änderung [f] *change of state*; ~beschreibung [f] ⟨logist⟩ *state-description*; ~größe [f] ⟨tech m. m.⟩ *variable state* **~st·ande** [adv]; ~ bringen *to manage, achieve, accomplish, contrive*; *to bring about*; *to set afoot* || (Gesetz) *to pass* || *to mediate* (*agreement, peace*, etc); *to effect* (*deal, sale*); (glücklich) ⟨fam⟩ *to make .. good*; (durch List) *to wangle*; (durch Verhandlungen) *to negotiate* || ~ k *to come about* od *off* || (Plan) *to materialize* || (stattfinden) *to take place* || nicht ~ k *to fail*; *to come to grief* || das Gesetz k–t nicht ~ *the bill will not pass* | ≈bringen [n] *accomplishment, achievement, realization*; ≈kommen [n] *realization, taking place* || das ~ des Festes ist gesichert (zweifelhaft) *the festival is sure to take place*, (*it is doubtful whether there will be a f.*) **~ständig** a *responsible*; *appertaining, belonging, due* (*to a p*) || ~ s f: *control(l)er X is spokesman for this deparment, while c. Y reports for* ..; ⟨med⟩ *to be doctor in charge of* (*a case*) ⟨jur⟩ *to have cognizance of*, (sachlich) *to have jurisdiction ratione materiae* L; dafür ist er nicht ~ *this is not within his j.* ⟨a. fig⟩; .. in diesem Fall .. ⟨fam⟩ *it is not our business* || ~e Behörde *appropriate authority*; die ~e Stelle *the proper quarter* || (Richter) *competent* || v ~er Seite hören *to be informed by experts* || [österr, Sw] (P) ~ nach: *right of domicile at*: .. | ≈keit [f] ~/ *competence* (*for*); *quality of having sufficient knowledge, judgement, skill, strength*; (*area/sphere of*) *responsibility*; mangelnde ~ ⟨jur⟩ *lack of jurisdiction*; es entzieht sich m–r ~ *it lies outside my scope* || **~s-** ~bereich [m] ⟨jur⟩ *jurisdiction*; innerstaatlich *domestic j.*; zum ausschließlichen ~ e–s Staates gehörig *within the d. j. of a state*; ≈halber [adv] *as/for it is competent to you to decide*; (*your letter has been passed to me*) *for attention*

z·uständlich a *neuter, not active*

zust·atten [adv]; jdm ~ k *to be useful* od *of use to a p*; *to come in handy to a p*; gut: *to stand a p in good stead, to come to a p opportunely* **~|stechen** irr [h] **1.** vi (auf [acc]) *to thrust, stab* (*at*) **2.** vt *to stitch up* **~|stecken** vt [h] *to pin* (*up*) || (jdm etw) *to convey* (*a th*) *secretly* (*to a p*); *to slip a th into a p's hands*, ⟨fig⟩ *to pour a th into a p's ears*, (Indiz) *to plant .. on a p* **~|stehen** vi irr [h] (rechtlich gebühren) *to be due to* || es steht ihm zu *he is entitled to it* || die Entscheidung steht ihm (nicht) zu *he has* (*no*) *right to decide, it is* (*not*) *for him to decide* || es steht uns nicht zu .. *it is no business of ours* .. || der Regierung stehen bes.e

Befugnisse zu *the g. is invested with special powers* **~|steigen** vi [s] ⟨rail⟩ *to join* (od *get on*) *a train* (ist) noch jd –gestiegen? *any more fares, please?* **~stellbar** a *ready for delivery* **~stellgebühr** f ⟨post⟩ *delivery charges* pl **~|stellen** vt [h] *to block* (*up*), *obstruct* | *to deliver, to hand over* || ⟨jur⟩ *to serve* (*a writ, document on a p*) **≗stellung** f ~/~en **1.** (*furnace*) *lining* **2.** *delivery* (durch Eilboten) *express*; (⟨Am⟩ *special d.*) || ⟨jur⟩ *service*; öffentliche .. *by publication* | **~s-** ~bevollmächtigt [a] (*p*) *authorized to accept s.*; ~gebühr [f] *carrier's charges* pl; ⟨Am⟩ *delivery fee*; ⟨jur⟩ *fee for serving writs*; ~urkunde [f] ⟨jur⟩ *writ of summons* **~|steuern** **1.** vt [h] *to contribute* (*to*) **2.** vi [s] ([dat] *or* auf [acc]) *to steer* od *make* (*for*); ⟨fig⟩ *to move toward* || *to drift towards* (*war*) || ⟨fig⟩ *to aim* (*at*) **~|stimmen** vi [h] *to agree* ([dat] *to a th, with a p*), *to consent, subscribe* (*to a th*) || *to fall in with* (*a plan*) || *to applaud* (*a decision*) || *to accept a th* || jdm ~ *to fall in with a p* || nicht ~ *to disagree* (*with*) | ~d *affirmative,* [adv] *approvingly* || ~d antworten *to answer in the affirmative*; ~d nicken *to nod assent*; *to nod one's head in agreement* **≗stimmung** f ~/~en *assent, consent, agreement* || nach erhaltener ~ *c. having been obtained*; unter ~ v *with the c. of* || stillschweigende ~ *tacit approval* || (allgemeine) ~ finden *to meet with approbation,* (*to carry the general consent*) **~|stopfen** vt [h] *to stop up* || *to close* (*one's ears*) || (flicken) *to darn, mend* **~|stöpseln** vt [h] *to stopper, cork* **~|stoßen** irr **1.** vt [h] *to push .. to*; (Tür) *to bang, slam* **2.** vi [s] (jdm) *to happen, occur, come* (*to a p*), *to befall* (*a p*) || ihm ist etw –ge– *he has met with an accident* || falls mir etw ~ sollte *in case anything should happen to me* | [h] *to strike*; (mit dem Schwerte) *to lunge* || kräftig ~ *to give a hard push* **~|streben** vi [h] [dat] (P) *to strive for*; *to aim at*; *to press forward to* || s–m Ziele ~ *to endeavour to attain one's object*, demselben Z. ~ ⟨fig⟩ *to work towards the same goal* | (S) *to tend toward* **~|streichen** irr vt [h] *to stop up, to smear over* **~|stricken** vt [h] *to close, finish* **≗strom** m *flow* || *flux* || (P) *influx, crowding* || ~ v Menschen ⟨a.⟩ *affluence of persons* **~|strömen** vi [s] [dat] *to stream, flow* (*to*) || ⟨fig⟩ (P) *to flock* (*to*) || *to crowd in* (*upon*) **~|stülpen** vt [h] *to cover over* **~|stürmen** vi [s] (auf [acc]) *to storm* (*on*), *to rush in* (*upon*), *to rush, dash* (*at a p*) **~|stürzen** vi [s] (auf [acc]) *to fall, rush,* (*upon*); *to hurry up* (*to a p*) **~|stutzen** vt [h] *to dock* (*a tail*); *trim* (*a hat*) || *to lop* (*trees*) || ⟨fig⟩ (→ frisieren) *to fit up, to adapt* (*for*) || (P) *to drill, train* (z *for*); ⟨fam⟩ *to lick .. into shape* || (verfeinern) *to polish* **~t·age** [adv] ~ bringen, ~ fördern *to bring to light* || ⟨min⟩ *to extract* || ⟨fig⟩ *to unbury*; ~ liegen *to be evident*; ⟨min⟩ *to show on the surface* | ~ k *or* treten ⟨fig⟩ *to come to light, to become apparent, clear, manifest, obvious*; *to reveal* od *manifest itself*; *to be manifested* || ⟨min⟩ *to crop out* (⟨a.⟩ ~ streichen) **~|tappen** vi [h & s] (unsicher gehen) *to grope one's way* || (ungeschickt handhaben) *to fumble*; *to seize awkwardly* || ⟨fig⟩ *to act without discretion*; *to blunder* (*about*) **≗tat** f ~/~en [mst pl] ⟨tail⟩ *lining and trimming*(*s* pl) || ⟨tech⟩ *raw material*; *ornamentals* || ⟨arts⟩ *addition* || ⟨cul⟩ *ingredients* pl, *garnishing, condiment* **~t·eil** [adv]; e–m ~ w *to fall to a p's share* || *to receive* (*hono*[*u*]*r, sympathy*) || (Erbschaft) *to come to* | jdm etw ~ w l *to allot* od *grant a p a th*; *to mete out* (*a treatment*) *to a p*; (Aufmerksamkeit) *to give* ..; (Blick) *to treat a p to* ..; (Willkommen) *to meet a p* **~|teilen** vt [h] [dat] *to apportion, assign* || (austeilen) *to distribute* || jdm etw ~ ⟨a.⟩ *to share out a th to a p* || ⟨jur⟩ *to adjudge, adjudicate* || (durch das Los; amtlich) *to allot* (⟨a. com⟩: Aktien, Dividende etc) || ⟨mil⟩ (P) [acc] *to attach* (*a p* als *as .. to a p*) || *to bestow* (*a title on a p*) || –ge–lte Einheit ⟨mil⟩ *complement* N; –ge–lt w = zuteil w || e–m etw reichlich ~ *to lavish a th on a p* **Z.ler** m *allocator* **Z.lung** f *assignment*; *allotment* (*of stock*); *adjudication*; *allocation*; ⟨mil⟩ (P) *attachment* || (Verhältnis≗) *approportion* || ⟨a.⟩ *allowance, rationing,* ⟨Am⟩ *issue* || ⟨mil⟩ bestimmte ~ *detail* | mit ~sbeschränkung ⟨logist⟩ *allocable* (*item*) **~t·iefst** [adv] *deeply, fundamentally* **~|traben** vi [s] (auf [acc]) *to trot* (*towards*) || *to trot on* (*at a brisk pace*) **~|tragen** vt irr [h] *to carry* (*to*) (⟨a. fig⟩: *tales*) || (Gerüchte) *to report* || *to waft* (*a smell*, etc) || **sich** ~ *to happen, occur*; *come to pass, c. about* || sollte es sich ~, daß er es täte *if he should happen to do it* || → sich begeben 2. **≗träger** m *tale-bearer, informer, tell-tale* **≗träger·ei** f ~/~en *tale-bearing, informing* **~träglich** a *advantageous, useful* ([dat]; für *to*); *conducive* (*for*) || der Gesundheit ~ *salubrious* (*climate*), *wholesome* (*food*) || jdm (nicht) ~ s *to* (*dis-*) *agree with a p*; mehr als ihm ~ ist *more than is good for him* | ≗keit [f] ~/ *usefulness*; *advantageousness* || *salubrity, wholesomeness* **~|trauen** **I.** vt; jdm etw ~ *to trust a p for a th, to give a p credit for a th, to credit a p with a th, to imagine a p capable of a th, not to put it past a p* || ich trau ihm das schon zu *I wouldn't put it past him* || jdm (nicht) viel ~ *to have a* (*no*) *high opinion of a p* || ihm wenig Gelehrsamkeit ~ *never to suspect he has so much learning* | **sich** ~, etw z tun *to feel confident to do* (*of doing*) *a th* **II.** ≗ n ~s/ (zu) *confidence* (*in*) || e–m unbedingtes ~ schenken, unb. ~ z jdm h *to trust a p implicitly, to put implicit confidence in a p* | z.–erweckend [a] *inspiring confidence*; z.svoll [a] *full of c.*; → vertraulich; z.swert [a] *trustworthy* **~traulich** a *confiding*; *not at all shy* || adv ⟨a.⟩ *without reserve* | ≗keit [f] ~/ *confidingness* **~|treffen** vi irr **1.** [s] *to happen* **2.** [h] *to prove right, to come true* || (Beweis) *to be conclusive* | es trifft alles zu *it all turns out to be true* || .. nicht immer *it does not always follow* | ~ auf *to hold good for, apply to, be* (*in keeping with* od) *true of*; *to answer* (*a description*) | **~d** = treffend: *relevent* (*report*); *pat* (*slogan*); *apposite* (*remark*); ~d s *to be to the point* || nicht ≗des ist z streichen *delete* (od *cross out*) *what does not apply* | ~ denfalls [adv] *eventually, if this should be the case* **~|treiben** irr **1.** vt [h] [dat] *to drive* (*to*[*wards*]) || Kunden ~ ⟨fam⟩ *to tout* (*for customers*) || = antreiben **2.** vi [s] auf [acc] *to drift* od *to be carried, driven, borne towards* **≗treiber** m *tout* **~|treten** irr **1.** vi [s] [abs] ([näher] herantreten) *to draw near* || (auf [acc]) *to step* (*up*) (*to*[*wards*]) *to talk over* (*to a p*) || (helfend etc) *to intervene* || näher ~ *to come* od *step nearer* (*to*) | = hinzutreten | [h] *to go on treading*; ⟨cycl⟩ *to pedal away* **2.** vt [h] *to trample over*; *to stop up .. by treading* **~|trinken** vi irr [h] (jdm) *to drink* (*to a p*), *to raise one's glass to a p, to drink a p's health* || *he nodded to P. and drank off his wine* **≗tritt** m (zu) *access* (*to*); *admission* (⟨a. theat⟩; *to court*) || ⟨arch⟩ *entrée* | ~ bek *to be admitted* (bei Hofe *at court*) || überall ~ h *to be welcome everywhere* || bei e–m freien ~ h *to have free access to a p's house, to have the freedom* (⟨fam⟩ *run*) *of* (*the castle*) || kein ~! ~ verboten! *private*! ⟨Am⟩ *no entry*! || e–m ~ verschaffen *to procure a p a free pass*; jdm den ~verwehren *to draw the bolt*(*s*) *against a p* **≗tun** n ~s/: ohne sein ~ *without his agency, help, aid, assistance, interference*; *without his having* (*had*) *a hand in the matter*; *no thanks to him* || nicht ohne sein ~ *thanks to him* (od *his help*), *had it not been for him* .. **~|tun** vt irr [h] *to close, shut* || wir h die ganze N. kein Auge zugetan *we have not slept a wink all night* | **sich** ~ *to insinuate* od *attach o.s.* || sich e–m ~ *to curry favour with* a p || → zugetan **~tu(n)lich** a (dienstfertig) *obliging*, *complaisant*; ⟨dero⟩ *officious, insinuating* || (gewinnend) *engaging* || = anschmiegsam | ∼̊keit [f] ∼/ *complaisance*; *officiousness* || *insinuating* od *engaging manners* pl **∼·ungunsten** adv [gen] → zum Nachteil **∼verlässig** a (S) *infallible* || (Nachricht) *reliable, certain, authentic* || (P) *trust(worth)y, reliable*; *staunch* (*follower*), *trusted* (*man*); *sure, dependable, tried*; sehr ∼ *solid*; ⟨pol⟩ *blue, true, t. b.* || er ist nicht ∼ *he is not to be trusted* || ⟨com⟩ *safe, sound* || v ∼er Seite erfahren, daß *to have it on good authority that* | ∼̊keit [f] ∼/ *certainty* || *reliability, trustworthiness* **∼̊versicht** f ∼/ *confidence* (auf *in*); *assurance* || *trust* (zu G. *in God*) || *hope* (*that*) || mit ∼ *confidently* || ∼ ausstrahlen *to exude c.e*; dies gibt ∼ *this lends trust* || wir heg(t)en die feste ∼, daß *we fully trust* (*we confidently expected*) *that*; neue ∼ h. f *to assemble new courage toward* || wir setzen unsere ganze ∼ in ihn *we entirely rely on him* | ∼̊lich [a] (P) *confident*; *optimistic, sanguine* | ∼e Reden *assurances*; *unshaken, secure* (*hope*) || mit höchst ∼er Miene *with an air of great assurance* | [adv] ich hoffe ∼ *I do hope* | ∼lichkeit [f] ∼/ *confidence* || (hoffende) *hopefulness* || (gezeigte) *assurance* **∼v·iel I.** [adv] (→ viel): ∼(e) *too much* (*many*) || eins ∼ *one too many* || mehr als ∼ *more than enough* || viel ∼ (*by*) *far too much* || nicht ∼ u nicht zu wenig *without waste or want* || des Guten ∼ *too much of a good th*, .. tun *to go too far* || was ∼ ist, ist ∼ *more than enough is too much* **II.** ∼ n *excess* **∼v·or I.** [adv] (= vorher) *before, first, formerly* || (*two years*) *previously* || allem ∼ *above all* || kurz ∼ *shortly before* || so klug wir ∼ *none the wiser* **II.** das ∼̊ u Hernach *the before and after* **III.** [pref] [vor Verb sep] z. B. ∼|erwägen *to consider beforehand* **∼v·orderst** [adv] *in the front rank* **∼v·örderst** [adv] *first of all, first and foremost, before all, to begin with* **∼v·or|kommen** vi irr [s] [dat] *to be before* (od *in front of*) *a p*; *to anticipate a p, a th*; *to forestall a p*; *to get the start of* (⟨Am fam⟩ *jump on*) *a p, to steal a march upon a p*; *to anticipate the other's moves* | (vorbeugen) *to prevent, obviate, forestall* | **∼d** a (P) *obliging, complaisant* || *kind, civil, courteous* | [adv] jdn ∼d behandeln *to make much of a p*; aufs ∼dste *in a most obliging*, etc *way*; *most obligingly* | ∼̊heit [f] ∼/∼en *obligingness, complaisance, civility, politeness, courtesy* **∼v·or|tun** vt irr [h]; es jdm ∼ *to outdo, outshine, excel, surpass a p* (in [dat] *in*) || es e–m zuv·orzutun suchen *to vie with a p* ×**∼̊waage** f [bay, österr] (Knochen etc) *makeweight* **∼̊wachs** m –ses/ *increase* (an *in*, gegenüber *on*); *increment, accretion* (an *of*) || *augmentation* (*of glory*) || *expansion, accessions* (*of territory*) || ⟨com⟩ *growth*, potentieller ∼ *growth potential* || e–n Anzug auf ∼ m *to make a suit so as to allow for growing* || auf ∼ berechnet *allowing for expansion*; ⟨tail⟩ *cut full and long for a p to fit* || ⟨fig⟩ *addition to the family* (= *babies*) || sie erwartet ∼ ⟨fam⟩ *she's expecting* || → Ausweitung | natürliche ∼rate ⟨stat⟩ *crude rate of natural increase*; ∼steuer [f] *increment-tax* **∼|wachsen** vi irr [s] *to get overgrown*; ⟨med⟩ *to heal up* || ⟨fig⟩ (jdm) *to accrue* (*to a p*) | ⟨agr⟩ ihm wächst alles zu *the earth* (etc) *supplies him with everything*; es ist ihm viel Jungvieh –ge– *his live stock has greatly increased* **∼|wägen** vt irr [h] *to weigh out* || ⟨fig⟩ *to dispense* | *to add in weighing* **∼̊wahl** f *co-option* **∼|wählen** vt [h] *to co-opt* **∼|wälzen** vt [h] [dat] *to roll* (*to* [-*wards*]) || ⟨fig⟩ jdm die Schuld ∼ *to lay the blame upon a p* | *to block up* (*with rocks*, etc) **∼|wandern** vi [s] *to wander to*(*ward*) || *to immigrate* || Zugewanderte [pl] *immigrants* **Z.rung** f *immigration* | **∼s-** ∼überschuß [m] *net i.n* **∼|warten** vi [h] *to wait* (*patiently*) || ∼d ⟨a.⟩ *expectant* || ∼de Haltung ⟨pol⟩ *watchful waiting*; .. einnehmen *to play a waiting game* **∼w·ege** [adv], ∼|bringen vt irr [h] *to bring about, to bring to pass, to accomplish* || *to effect, work, cause* || etw ∼ bringen *to contrive* od *manage a th*; er brachte es ∼ z tun *he managed to do it* || richtig ∼ gehen *to go the right way* (*to do*) || (mit etw) ∼ k *to complete, finish* || gut ∼ s *to be quite well, to be as fit as a fiddle* **∼|wehen** vt [h] [dat] *to waft* od *blow* (*to*[*ward*]) || (mit Schnee, Sand etc) *to block up* od *choke* (*with* ..) || e–m Luft ∼ *to fan a p* **∼w·eilen** [adv] *sometimes, at times, now and then, occasionally* **∼|weisen** vt irr [h] *to assign* (⟨a. wir⟩ Frequenz); *apportion, allocate* ⟨a. st. exch⟩; *allot* (*his a.ted portion*) || *to send, recommend* (*customers to a p*) || *to assign* (*a work to a century*) || mir wurde e–e Aufgabe zugewiesen *I was assigned a task* || zugewiesene Bestände *allotted supplies* **Z.sung** f ∼/∼en *assignment*; aus Reingewinn *transfer from profits*; ∼ v Arbeit *work a.t* **∼|wenden** vt reg & irr [h] *to turn* ([dat] *towards*) || jdm etw ∼ *to put a p in the way of a th, to let a p have a th*; (letztwillig) *to will, bequeath, devise* || jdm das Gesicht (den Rücken) ∼ *to face* [*round at*] *a p*, (*to turn one's back on a p*) || e–a –ge–det s *to be face to face* || sein größtes Augenmerk e–r S ∼ *to pay* od *turn one's chief attention to a th* || e–m s–e Aufmerksamkeit (Liebe) ∼ *to bestow one's attention* (*affection*) *upon a p* || ihm wandten sich alle Herzen zu *he won every heart* | **sich** [wieder] ∼ [dat] *to* [*re*]*turn* (*to*), *to apply o.s.* (*to*) || sich der Politik ∼ *to enter politics*; *his attention shifted* od *he shifted his a. to other matters* || (*public opinion*) *sways to his side* **Z.dung** f *grant*; ∼en [pl] *monetary award, financial support*; *subsidies*; reichliche ∼en *lavish endowments* **∼w·enig** [adv] *too little*; ∼ erhobene Gebühr *undercharge*; aber: du weißt auch z·u → w·enig | **∼w·enigst** adv = mindestens, zumindest **∼|werfen** vt irr [h] (jdm etw) *to throw, toss* (*a th to a p*), *to give* (*a p a look*), *to cast, shoot, flash* (*glances at a p*) || e–m verliebte Blicke ∼ *to make* (⟨fam⟩ *sheep's*) *eyes at a p*; ⟨sl⟩ *to give a p the glad eye* | (Tür) *to slam, bang* | (Grube etc) *to fill up* | ⟨cards⟩ *to throw down, to play* (*a card*) **∼w·ider I.** [prep] [dat] *contrary to, adversely to*; *opposed to* (*reason*); *against* (*fortune was a. us*) || [dat] ∼ s ⟨a.⟩ *to conflict* od *clash with* (*one's duty*) **II.** [pred] a (⟨dial⟩ a. [attr]) *offensive, distasteful, repugnant, repulsive, odious* || °ein ∼er Kerl *a loathsome fellow* | e–m etw ∼ m *to disgust a p with a th* || jdm ∼ s ⟨a.⟩ *to revolt a p* || es ist mir ∼ *I'm sick of it*; .. höchst ∼ .. *it is my pet abomination* || er ist mir (in den Tod) ∼ *I hate* (*the very sight of*) *him*, (*I loathe him*) || ich hoffe, es wird Ihnen nicht ∼ s *I hope you will have no objection* || e–m ∼ w *to pall on a p* **III.** ∼|handeln [vi h] [dat] *to act contrary to* od *in defiance of*; *to go against* (*a p, a th*) || (e–r Vorschrift) *to go against* (*the rules*); *to contravene, violate*; *disobey* | Z.nde(r) *offender*; ∼̊handlung [f] *contravention, breach, infringement* (gegen *of*); ∼|laufen [vi s] *to run contrary* od *counter to* (*the law*) | **sich** [dat] selbst ∼ *to defeat one's own purpose* | –nd → zuwider I. °**∼̊wurzen** m [österr] *grumpy* (*old*) *fellow*, (*he's*) *a pain in the neck* **∼|winken 1.** vi [h] (jdm) *to nod, wave, beckon* (*to*), *to throw a p a wave of one's hand* **2.** jdm ein L. ∼ *to wave farewell to a p* **∼|wölben** vt [h] *to vault over* **∼̊wuchs** m = Zuwachs **∼|zahlen** vt [h] *to pay extra* || wir mußten 5 Mark ∼ *we had to pay an additional 5 marks* **∼|zählen** vt [h] *to add* (*to*), *to include* || (jdm etw) *to count out* (*a th to a p*) **∼z·eiten** [adv] *at times* (→ bisweilen), **∼|ziehen** irr **1.** vt [h] *to draw .. to*(*wards*) || (Knoten) *to tighten* || (Tür) *to pull .. to* || (Vorhang) *to draw* | (jdn zu etw) *to invite* (*a p*) *to join* (*a th*) | (Beirat) *to take counsel's advice*; (Arzt) *to call in, to consult* || zur Tafel ∼ *to command to dinner* | **sich** [dat] etw ∼ *to bring a th upon o.s.*; *to incur* (*blame, a p's enmity*), *to draw* od *bring .. down upon o.s.* || *to* expose o.s. to (criticism); to catch, contract (a disease) || to lay o.s. open to (suspicion) || to earn (a p's hatred) || to involve o.s. in (altercations) || sich Unannehmlichkeiten ∼ wegen .. ⟨fam⟩ to get into hot water for .. | **sich** [acc] ∼ (Knoten etc) to tighten **2.** vi [s] (in ein Haus) to move in || (in ein Land etc) to immigrate || (v Dienstboten) to go to a new place || er ist zugezogen he has come to settle down here **≗ziehung** f ∼/ (Herbeiruf) calling in (a p) || (Befragen e–s Sachverständigen) consultation (of) || (Hilfe) aid, assistance, help | ⟨com⟩ unter ∼ Ihrer Spesen including your expenses **≗zucht** f ⟨agr⟩ fresh stock **≗zug** m additional population; immigration || arrival || sich gegen ∼ sperren ⟨Am fam⟩ to be sewed up || ⟨mil⟩ reinforcements pl | ⟨abstr⟩ = Heranziehung | **∼s-** ∼genehmigung [f] permit of residence; ∼ort [m] place of destination od arrival **≗zügler** m new-comer; immigrant || ⟨mil⟩ volunteer **∼züglich** prep [gen] inclusive of; plus, with **∼|zwängen** vt [h] to close with an effort || (Tür) to force to **∼|zwinkern** vi [h] jdm ∼ to give a p a (little) wink

×°**Zw·acke** f ∼/∼n (Y-Schleuder) ⟨sl⟩ tweaker | **≗n** vt [h] to pinch || ⟨fig⟩ (ärgern) to tease; to nag at; (quälen) torment; (rupfen) to fleece

zwang 1. & 3. sg pret v zwingen **Zw·ang** m ∼(e)s/ compulsion || (innerer) check, constraint; (unwiderstehlicher) necessity || (gesetzlicher) coercion (by c.) || (Gewalt) force, violence || ⟨jur⟩ duress(e) (under d.) || unter dem ∼ der Gewalt ⟨a.⟩ at the point of sword; jdn unter ∼ ausliefern an to yield a p to || (Druck) pressure ⟨a. path⟩ || ⟨fig⟩ want of ease, stiffness || aus ∼ on compulsion || [dat] ∼ antun to twist (the meaning of a passage); s–r Freude k–n ∼ antun to allow reins to one's joy; ∼ ausüben auf ⟨fig⟩ to put pressure on | **sich** [dat] ∼ antun to check od restrain o.s. || tue d–n Gefühlen k–n ∼ an don't curb your feelings, ⟨fig⟩ you needn't stand on ceremony; sich k–n ∼ auferlegen ⟨a.⟩ to let o.s. go || ein ∼ s f to be compulsory (⟨Am⟩ mandatory) on | ∼anwendung [f] ⟨a.⟩ armtwisting ⟨a. fig⟩; ≗hufig [a] ⟨hors⟩ hoof-bound; ≗los [a] unconstrained || ⟨fig⟩ without ceremony, informal, unceremonial, unceremonious, free and easy; ⟨a.⟩ off dignity [attr] || offhand (manner); unconventional (manners) || unceremonial, informal (meeting) → Beisammensein || informal (party) || Zeitschrift in ∼en Heften occasional review || ∼ w gegenüber to unbend toward(s) || [adv] freely; in a family way; sich ∼ bewegen to be at ease in the world; (to speak) without any constraint || ∼losigkeit [f] ease, informality, unconventionality, unceremoniousness, unconstraint, freedom **zw·ängen** vt [h] (in [acc], durch) to press, wedge, force (into, through) || ⟨fig⟩ to do violence to (the law) || [abs] to pinch (my shoes p.) **Zw·angs-** ⟨mst⟩ f.d = forced, c. = compulsory **∼anleihe** f f.d loan **∼arbeit** f c. labour, (im Zuchthause) hard labo(u)r **∼arbeiter** m convict; p sentenced to f.d l.; prisoner under f.d l. sentence; pr. on f.d l. **∼aushebung** f c. levy; conscription, ⟨Am⟩ draft **∼ausverkauf** m c. sale | (nicht) **≗bewirtschaftet** (non) rent-controlled (house) **∼bewirtschaftung** f control **∼beitreibung** f f. collection of taxes **∼dienst** m c. service **∼einquartierung** f c. requisitioning of rooms || ⟨mil⟩ c. quartering, c. billeting **∼enteignung** f f.d expropriation **∼ernährung** f forcible feeding **∼erziehungsanstalt** f reformatory **∼förderung** f ⟨tech⟩ pump feed **∼gesetz** n coercive law **∼gestellung** f arrest **∼haftpflichtversicherung** f common law obligatory third party insurance **∼herrschaft** f rule of force; dictatorship **∼handlung** f compulsive od imperious act **∼innung** f obligatory guild **∼jacke** f strait-jacket; dazu: to straitjacket ⟨fig⟩ **∼kurs** m ⟨com⟩ f.d currency **∼lage** f constrained position || ⟨fig⟩ strait, exigency, -ce; Hobson's choice; → Not– || in e–r ∼ in straits **≗läufig** a (→ unvermeidlich) cogent, obligatory, necessary | [adv] needs; of necessity; es mußte ihn ∼ beeinflussen it could not fail to .. | ∼keit [f] cogency **∼maßnahmen** f pl ⟨pol⟩ sanctions **∼maßregel** f coercive measure (anwenden to adopt) || ∼n ergreifen ⟨a.⟩ to use force; ⟨Am⟩ (gegen Verbrecher) ⟨fam⟩ to thirddegree **∼methoden** f pl procrustean m.s pl **∼mittel** n means of coercion; force; ⟨jur⟩ distress-warrant **∼paß** m c. passport prescribing the route to be followed **∼pflicht** f c. duty **∼recht** n right of coercion, ⟨agr-jur⟩ banality **∼schiene** f check-rail **∼sparen** n c. saving **∼umsiedler** m displaced p (D. P.) **∼verfahren** n coercive measures pl **∼vergleich** m c. settlement, composition after bankruptcy **∼verkauf** m f.d sale **∼verschickung** f deportation **≗verschickt** a displaced (p) **∼versteigerung** f f.d od c. sale od auction; sale under execution **∼verwalter** m sequestrator **∼verwaltung** f c. administration; sequestration || in ∼ geben to sequestrate | **∼s-** ∼verfügung [f] ⟨jur⟩ receiving order **∼vollstreckung** f distraint, ⟨jur⟩ execution, distress || ∼ bewirkt durch Pfändung ex. levied by seizure; ∼ e–s dinglich gesicherten Anspruchs ⟨jur⟩ foreclosure; ∼ vornehmen to levy ex. (on property); vorläufige Einstellung der ∼ arrest | **∼s-** ∼klage [f] auf Grund e–s dingl. ges. Anspr. foreclosure action **∼vorstellung** f insane delusion; hallucination; monomania L **∼wanderung** f f.d migration **≗weise** [adv] compulsorily, by compulsion, by (main) force **∼wirtschaft** f Government od State (price-)control || Aufhebung der ∼ decontrol || die ∼ aufheben to decontrol

zw·anzig I. a (→ dreißig) twenty; a score (of) || sie ist noch k–e ∼ (Jahre alt) she is still in her teens || ⟨Ger⟩ ∼ Uhr 8 o'clock p. m. **II.** ≗ f number twenty || zu ≗en by scores, by groups of 20 || sie ist über die ≗ hinaus .. out of her teens, turned 20 | ≗eck [n] ⟨geom⟩ polygon having 20 sides; ∼fach, ∼fältig [a] twenty-fold; ∼jährig [a] of twenty years; ∼pfündig [a] weighing twenty pounds **Z.ger(in** f) ∼s/∼ **1.** (wo)man of twenty **2.** the figure 20 **3.** ⟨num⟩ twenty-pfennig piece **4.** wine of the year '20 **5.** soldier of the 20th regiment **6.** in den ∼n s to be between twenty and thirty, to be out of one's teens || in den - er Jahren des vorigen Jhs in the twenties of last c.; die goldenen ∼ (1920 ff.) the roaring twenties **∼erl·ei** a of twenty (different) kinds || auf ∼ Art in twenty ways **∼ste** a twentieth || den or am 20. Mai (on) the tw. of May, May the tw. (schreib: May 20th; 20 May; 20. 5. 1970) **≗stel** n ∼s/∼ tw.th part || neun ∼ ($^9/_{20}$) nine tw.ths **∼stens** [adv] in the tw.th place

zwar [conj] indeed (grey i., but still ..); to be sure; (it is) true,;, I admit,;, certainly; admittedly; indeed || er kam ∼, aber ⟨a.⟩ he did come, but; (al)though he came, (still) ..; (he is a poor teacher) as such, but (a brilliant scholar) | **u** ∼ namely [mst unübersetzt]; and that (one); and, what is more; and .. too || u ∼ einschließlich ⟨com⟩ this is to include || u ∼ so sehr so much so

zw·atzelig a [sd] = zappelig | **-ln** = zappeln; unruhig s

Zw·eck m ∼(e)s/∼e **A. 1.** ⟨eig, obs⟩ peg || butt; ; → ∼e [f] **2.** ⟨fig⟩ aim, end, object, purpose, goal || intention, design || ∼ u Ziel davon ist the sum and substance of it is **B.** zwei ∼en **dienen** to serve two purposes || jds ∼en dienstbar subservient to a p's ends || ich sehe den ∼ nicht ein I don't see the point || denselben ∼ erfüllen to answer the same purpose || s–e ∼ erreichen (verfehlen) to get od attain (miss) one's aim, to carry one's point; to achieve one's object; (S) ⟨sl⟩ to do the trick || was hat es f e–n ∼ or welchen ∼ hat das (alles)? what is it (all) for?; .., daß wir streiten? what's the good of (our) arguing? || es hatte kaum

∼, es zu tun *there was no point in doing it* ‖ es hat k–n ∼ *it is useless* (z tun *to do*) ‖ das wird wenig ∼ h *that won't do any good* ‖ Reden hat k–n ∼ *talking is no use*; es hat k–n ∼ zu reden *it is (of) no use talking* od *to talk* ‖ sonst hat es weiter k–n ∼ *and that's all (it's meant for)* ‖ der ∼ heiligt die Mittel *the end justifies the means* ‖ denselben ∼ verfolgen *to pursue the same object*; eigennützige ∼e v. ⟨fam⟩ *to have an axe to grind* **C. für** e–n bestimmten ∼ *for a set purpose* | **mit** dem ∼ .. *with a view (to do it)* | (nur) **zu** diesem ∼ *for this purpose* od *end* (⟨jur⟩ *ad hoc* [attr]) (Vereinbarung) ‖ zu aufrührerischen ∼en einberufene Versammlung *seditious meeting*; zu welchem ∼? ⟨a.⟩ *to what intent* od *end*? ‖ zum ∼ [gen] *for the purpose of, by way of, with a view to* **~bestimmt** a (*fund*, etc) *assigned to definite purpose*; *earmarked* **≃betont** a *purposeful, purposive* **≃-dienlich, ≃entsprechend** a *expedient, serviceable, useful, suitable, relevant, efficacious, politic*; *to the purpose, answering its purpose* ‖ e–r S ∼ s *to be pertinent to a th* **~dienlichkeit** f *expediency* **≃entfremdet** a (*a th, money*) *put to use which it was not intended* **~essen** n *public* od *charity dinner* **~gebunden** a *bound to a specific purpose*; *appropriated* **~gerecht** a *functional* **~lehre** f ⟨philos⟩ *teleology* **≃los** a *aimless, purposeless* ‖ (nutzlos) *useless, futile* ‖ es ist ∼ *it's no go(od)* (daß wir .. *opposing him*); volk ∼, daß .. (*it's*) *not a bit of good* (*my trying*) | **≃igkeit** [f] *futility, purposelessness* **~lügen** f pl *expedient lying* **≃mäßig** a *answering the purpose, expedient, suitable, proper, practical, fit*; ∼ s *to serve a useful function*; → günstig | ∼keit [f] *expediency, fitness*, etc **~meldung** f *report put out that is aimed at achieving a certain, desired effect* **~neurose** f *purpose neurosis* **~optimismus** m *optimism of set purpose, pseudo-o.m* **~pessimismus** m *p.m for a purpose* **~verband** m (*local*) *administrative union*; ⟨bes pol⟩ *pressure group* **~voll** a *functional, suitable, practical, purposeful* **≃widrig** a *inexpedient, unsuitable* **Zw·ecke** f ∼/∼n *tack*, (*wooden*) *peg* ‖ (großköpfiger Sohlennagel) *hobnail* ‖ (Reiß≃) *drawing-pin*, ⟨Am⟩ *thumb-tack* **zw·ecken** vt [h] *to tack, peg* **zwecks** prep [gen] *for the purpose of*; *for* (*approval*); *by way of* (*illustration*); ∼ Prüfung der Richtigkeit *to ensure accururacy*

zween [–e:n] ⟨obs⟩ a [nur m] = zwei ‖ ⟨bib⟩ niemand kann ∼ Herren dienen *no man can serve two masters* **Zwei** f ∼/ (*the number*) *two* ‖ ⟨cards, dice⟩ (*the*) *deuce* **zw·ei** a *two* [mst inv], [abs a.] **~e** [abs & + s *or* a ohne art]: es gehören immer ∼ dazu *it takes two to make a bargain* | [gen] **~er,** [abs: dat] **~en** ‖ ein, ∼ .. funkelten *a star or two was twinkling* ‖ ∼(e) m ein Paar *two is company* ‖ durch ∼er Zeugen Mund *by the m. of two w.s* ‖ wir h es ∼en gesagt *we told it two persons* | alle ∼ *both*; alle ∼ Wochen *every two weeks, every second week* | **aus** ∼en bestehend *binary* | **in** ∼ Ausfertigungen *with a duplicate* | **mit** ∼en fahren *to drive a coach and pair*; mit ∼ Rotoren *twin-rotored*; mit ∼ Ebenen versehen [pp] *double-deck* (*street*) | **~ über**–e–a angeordnete Betten *double-decker* ‖ ∼ u ∼, zu ∼en *or* ∼t *by* od *in twos, in pairs, two and* od *by two* ‖ zu ∼en hinter–e–a *in double file* ‖ zu ∼en antreten *to double up*; zu ∼en fahren ⟨cycl⟩ *to ride double*; zu ∼en stehend *in double rows*, ⟨bot⟩ *double* ‖ das Spiel läßt sich zu ∼en spielen *two can play at that game* ‖ ⟨prov⟩ ∼ m ein Paar *or* ∼e sitzen enge, drei sind ein Gedränge *two's company, three's none* **≃achser** m ∼s/∼ *two-axle vehicle, four-wheeler* **~achsig** a *with two axes* **~adrig** a ⟨el⟩ *twin* (*cable*) **≃akter** m ⟨theat⟩ *two-act piece* **~armig** a *two-armed*; ⟨tech⟩ *with two branches* **~äugig** a ⟨phot⟩ *twin lens* (*camera*) **~bändig** a *two-volume, in two volumes* **~bahnig** a (Tuch) *of two breadths* **~basisch** a ⟨chem⟩ *dibasic* **≃bein** n *bipod* **~beinig** a *two-legged* **~bettig** a *with two beds*; *double-bedded* | **≃bett-** ∼zimmer [n] ⟨hot⟩ *double room with one bed/two beds*; ⟨path⟩ *semi-private room* **~blätt(e)rig** a ⟨bot⟩ *two-leaved, diphyllous, bipetalous* **~blütig** a *biflorate* **~brüderig, ~bündelig** a *diadelphian* **≃bund** m *dual alliance* **≃decker** m ⟨aero⟩ *biplane* **~deutig** a *ambiguous, equivocal* ‖ ⟨fig⟩ *doubtful, suspicious* ‖ (Witz) ⟨Am fam⟩ *off-color, weasel* (*words*) ‖ e–e ∼e Haltung einnehmen ⟨fam⟩ *to straddle*; ∼es Spiel *duplicity* | [adv] ∼ reden *to equivocate*, ⟨fam⟩ *to make one boot serve for either leg* | **≃keit** [f] *ambiguity, equivocation*; *duplicity of character* **~dimensional** a: ∼er Film ⟨fam⟩ *flattie* **~drahtsystem** n *two-wire system* **≃drittelmehrheit** f ⟨parl⟩ *majority of two-thirds* **~ehig** a ⟨bot⟩ *digamous* **~eiig** a ⟨biol⟩ *dizygotic*; *binovular* (*twins*) **~fach, ~fältig** a *twofold*; ∼fache Norm *double standard* | [adv] ∼fach gelagert *with two bearings* | ∼fachsucher [m] ⟨phot⟩ *two-position viewfinder* **~fädig** a ⟨tex, tail, etc⟩ *twin-thread* [attr] **~familienhaus** n *two-family* od *duplex home* **~farbendruck** m *duotone* **~farbig** ([österr] ≃) a *two-colo(u)red, dichromatic* ‖ *bicolo(u)red* (*impression*); *two-tone* (*car*) **≃f·elderwirtschaft** f *two field system* **~flügelig** a *two-winged* ‖ ⟨bot, ent⟩ *dipterous* ‖ ∼e Tür *folding-door* **≃flügler** m pl ⟨ent⟩ *dipterans, diptera* **≃frontenkrieg** m *war in two fronts* **~füßig** a *two-footed, biped(al)* **~gängig** a *double-threaded* (*screw*) **≃gesang** m *duet* **~geschlechtig** a *of double sex, bisexual, hermaphrodite, androgynous* **≃gespann** n *two-horse team* ‖ *carriage and pair* ‖ ein ∼ führen *to drive a pair* **~gestrichen** a ⟨mus⟩ *of the fourth octave* ‖ *twice-accented* ‖ ∼e Note *semiquaver* **~geteilt** a *bipartite* **~gipflig** a (Akzent) *intermittent* **~gleisig** a *double-tracked*; (*double-line* [attr]) ‖ ∼e Bahn *double line* **~gliedrig** a *having two members* ‖ ⟨zoo⟩ *biarticulate* ‖ ⟨math⟩ *binomial* ‖ ⟨mil⟩ *in two ranks* **≃händer** m *two-handed sword* ‖ ⟨zoo⟩ *bimanous animal* **~händig** a *two-handed* ‖ ⟨mus⟩ *for two hands* **≃herrschaft** f *dyarchy* **~höck(e)rig** a *two-humped* **≃holmbauart** f ⟨aero⟩ *two-spar type* **≃hufer** m *cloven-footed animal* **~hundert** a *two hundred* | ≃jahrfeier [f] *bicentenary*, ⟨Am⟩ *bicentennial*; ∼jährig [a] *lasting 200 years* ‖ *bicentennial* (*anniversary*) **~jährig** a *two years old*; *two-year-old* (*child*) ‖ ⟨bot⟩ *biennial* **~jährlich** a *occurring every 2 years, biennial* **≃kammersystem** n ⟨parl⟩ *two-chamber system* **≃kampf** m *single combat, duel* ‖ jdn z ∼ fordern *to challenge a p* **~keimblätt(e)rig** a ⟨bot⟩ *dicotyledonous* **≃kindersystem** n *principle of limiting the number of children to not more than two* **~klappig** a *two-valved* ‖ ⟨bot⟩ *bivalvular* **~köpfig** a *two-headed* **≃leitersystem** n ⟨el⟩ *two-conductor system* **≃linsenobjektiv** n ⟨opt⟩ *doublet* **~lippig** a *bilabiate* ⟨a. bot⟩ **~lötig** a *weighing an ounce* **~mal** adv *twice* ‖ ∼ im Jahr (Monat) *twice a year* (*month*); *biannual* (*bimonthly*) ‖ ⟨ten⟩ ∼ auf! *second bounce*! ‖ ∼ so alt wie er *twice his age* ‖ ∼ so viel *twice as much* ‖ er wird sich das nicht ∼ sagen l *he will need no second telling*, ⟨fam⟩ *he will jump at it* **~malig** a *done twice, twice repeated* **≃-Mann-** ∼säge [f] *two-man saw*; *double-handed cross-cut saw*; ∼-U-Boot [n] *midget submarine* **≃männig** a ⟨bot⟩ *diandrian* **≃markstück** n *two-mark piece* **≃master** m ⟨mar⟩ *two-master* ‖ ⟨fig⟩ *cocked hat* **~mastig** a ⟨mar⟩ *two-masted* **~monatig** a *of* od *lasting two months*; *two-months'* (*leave*) **~monatlich** a *recurring every two months* **~motorig** a *bimotored, two-motor, twin-engined* **~paarig** a *forming two pairs* ‖ ∼ gefiedert ⟨bot⟩ *bijugate* **~pasch** m *double-two* **≃pfünder** m ⟨artill⟩ *two-pounder* **~pfundig** a *weighing two pounds* **~polig** a *bipolar*; ⟨el⟩ *two-way* (*socket*) **≃rad** n *bicycle, machine* ‖ ⟨fam⟩

bike ‖ (Renner) racer ‖ (Tourenrad) roadster **~räd(e)rig** a two-wheeled ‖ ~er Wagen ⟨a.⟩ two-wheeler, cart, hansom, trap **~reihig** a double--rowed ‖ (Rock) double-breasted **≃röhrenempfänger** m ⟨wir⟩ two-valve receiver **≃ruderer** m ⟨ant⟩ bireme **~rud(e)rig** a two-oared ‖ with two tiers of rowers **~samenlappig** a ⟨bot⟩ dicotyledonous **~schalig** a bivalvous ‖ ~e Muschel bivalve **~schattig** a amphiscian **~schläf(e)rig** a; ~es Bett double bed **~schneidig** a double-, two-edged ⟨a. fig⟩ ‖ ⟨fig⟩ dangerous for both parts; es ist ~ it cuts both ways ⟨a. fig⟩ **~schürig** a shorn twice a year ‖ (Wolle) of the second shearing **~seitig** a two-sided, bilateral ‖ (Anzug, Stoff: auf beiden Seiten z tragen) reversible ‖ ~e Anzeige double page spread **~silbig** a dissyllabic ‖ ~es Wort [n] dissyllable **≃sitzer** m ⟨mot⟩ two-seater; sports car, ⟨Am⟩ roadster ‖ ⟨cycl⟩ tandem **~sitzig** a double-seated **~spaltig** a ⟨bot⟩ bifid ‖ ⟨typ⟩ in two columns **≃spänner** m carriage and pair **~spännig** a drawn by two horses ‖ [adv] ~ fahren to drive (in) a carriage and pair; °⟨fig⟩ (= verheiratet s) to run in double harness, ⟨vulg⟩ to do the double act **≃spitz** m two-cornered, -horned hat **~spitzig** a two-pointed **~sprachig** a in two languages, bilingual | ≃keit [f] bilingualism; two-language pattern (of a country) **~spurig** = –gleisig **≃stärkenbrille** f bifocals pl **~stellig** a; ~e Zahl double figure **~stimmig** a ⟨mus⟩ for two voices ‖ ~er Gesang duet ‖ ~es Lied two-part song **~stöckig** a two-storey [südd] three-st. (house); double-deck (bus) **~stoffsystem** n binary s. **~strahlig** [a] twin-jet **≃strom-** ~land [n] Mesopotamia ‖ ~triebwerk [n] ⟨aero⟩ double-flow engine **~stufig** a two-stage (rocket) ‖ ~e Reaktion [f] double stage reaction **~stündig** a of od lasting two hours; **~stündlich** a & adv every two hours **~tägig** a lasting two days; two days' (debate) ‖ (Alter) two days old **≃takt-** ~betrieb [m] petroil operation; ~gemisch [n] gasoline-oil mixture, ~motor [m] two-stroke, -cycle engine; ~schmierung [f] petroil (lubrication) **~tausend** a two thousand **~teilig** a (Anzug etc) two-piece; (Kleid) midriff, deux pièces Fr ‖ ~es Ensemble [n] (Damenmode) separates pl ‖ ⟨bot⟩ bipartite **~teilung** f bipartition ‖ ⟨math⟩ bisection ‖ (Gabelung) bifurcation ‖ ⟨pol⟩ dichotomy **~unddreißig-** ≃er(format) [n] ⟨typ⟩ thirty-twomo (abbr 32mo); ≃stelnote [f] demisemiquaver **~undzwanzig** a twenty-two, *two--and-twenty ‖ ⟨Ger⟩ ~ Uhr 10 o'clock p. m. ‖ er ist ~ he is 22 (years of age) **≃viertelpause** f minim rest **≃vierteltakt** m ⟨mus⟩ two-four time **≃wegschaltung** f ⟨el⟩ double-way connection **≃weiberei** f bigamy **~weibig** a ⟨bot⟩ having two pistils **~wertig** a ⟨chem⟩ divalent ‖ ~es Element dyad **~zackig** a two-pronged **≃zahl** f ⟨gram⟩ dual ‖ ⟨philos⟩ duad ‖ ⟨chem⟩ dyad **≃zahn** m ⟨bot⟩ bur-marigold **~zeilig** a of two lines ‖ ~es Gedicht [n] distich, couplet ‖ ⟨bot⟩ two-rowed (barley) **~zeitig** a having two periods ‖ ⟨bot⟩ dichronous ‖ ~e Silbe doubtful syllable **≃zimmerwohnung** f flatlet **~zöllig** a of two inches **~züngig** a two--tongued ‖ ⟨fig⟩ double-tongued **≃zweckreaktor** m ⟨at⟩ dual-purpose reactor **≃zylinderboxermotor** m flat-twin-engine

Zw·eier m ~s/~ **1.** the figure two **2.** two-pfennig piece **3.** soldier of the 2nd regiment **4.** (Boot) pair-oar **≃lei** a two sorts (etc) of; of two (different) sorts ‖ wir sind nun mal ~ Ansicht let's agree to differ; auf ~ Art in two (d.) ways ‖ ⟨fam⟩ ~ Tuch the military; ⟨engl⟩ the redcoats ‖ das ist ~ those are two d. ths ‖ .. u .. sind ~ it is one th to seek a man, and another to find him; promising is one th and keeping one's promise is another | ~schritt [m] ⟨comp⟩ binary digit

Zw·eifel m ~s/~ doubt | disbelief (an in) ‖ scruple ‖ hesitation ‖ uncertainty | nicht der leiseste ~ not a shadow of d. ‖ ~ an sich selbst self-d.(s) | **ohne** (allen) ~ without (any) d.; no d.; d.less; easily; (most) certainly ‖ über allen ~ erhaben beyond all d. | ~ äußern über to cast some d. on .., to voice one's d.s that ..; ~ beheben to resolve d.s; jdm den ~ benehmen to remove a p's d.s ‖ es besteht einiger ~ there is some question (über about); darüber bestand kein ~ .. (she was dead,) and no mistake; there could be no d. that .. ‖ s–e ~ z Ausdruck bringen to speak one's d.s ‖ ~ ficht ihn an some d. has got hold of him ‖ ~ hegen to harbo(u)r a d.; gar k–n ~ h or hegen, daß not to feel the least d. but that ‖ jdm k–n ~ l to leave no room for d., to leave a p in no d. ‖ jeden ~ überwinden to conquer all d.s ‖ es unterliegt k–m ~ there is no d. (about it) ‖ ~ verbreiten to sow d.s | **außer** (allen) ~ stellen to put beyond (a) d. | **im** ~ s to be in two minds (über [acc] about) | etw **in** ~ stellen to cast a d. on a th to throw a th into d.s; in ~ ziehen to (call in) question; to query | **von** (nagendem) ~ befallen pp assailed od beset by (gnawing) d.s **≃haft** a doubtful, dubious ⟨a. fig⟩; ⟨fig⟩ backhanded, obscure ‖ left-handed (compliment); equivocal (position); shady (business) ‖ ~e Gestalten shabby bucks and dusky dandies | etw ~ l to leave a th in suspense ‖ etw ~ m to cast doubts upon a th ‖ ~ s, ob man etw tun oder l soll to be wavering about doing a th ‖ es war sehr ~, ob .. it was touch and go whether (he would escape) **≃los** a doubtless, questionless | [adv] to be sure, to a certainty; without (beyond; out of) [all] question **~mut** m indecision, irresolution **≃mütig** a irresolute **~sucht** f scepticism **≃süchtig** a sceptical questionable ‖ precarious ‖ uncertain ‖ suspicious **zw·eifeln** vi [h] to doubt (an [dat] a p, a th); ich –fle! ⟨a.⟩ I wonder! ‖ to have one's doubts about (a th) ‖ an jds Aufkommen ~ to despair of a p's life ‖ wir ~, ob es passend ist we doubt whether it is proper ‖ wir ~ nicht daran! we have no doubt of it!, we don't question it ‖ wir ~ nicht (daran), daß .. we do not doubt but that he will come ‖ wir –ten nicht, daß er k würde we had no doubt but that he would come **Zw·eifels- ~fall** m; im ~e in case of doubt; if in d.; .. die günstige Auslegung gelten l [⟨jur⟩ in dubio pro reo] to give a p the benefit of the d. **≃ohne** adv doubtless, without doubt, undoubtedly, .., and no mistake! **Zw·eifler(in f)** m ~s/~ doubter, sceptic | **≃isch** a sceptic

Zw·eig m ~(e)s/~e (gr) bough; branch ⟨a. fig⟩ ‖ (kl) twig, sprig, spray ‖ ⟨fig a.⟩ department, section; scion; line; ⟨ins a.⟩ type (in den einzelnen ~en by t.) ‖ ⟨fig⟩ er wird nie auf e–n grünen ~ k he will never get on **~abteilung** f section **~anstalt** f branch **~bahn** f ⟨rail⟩ branch-line **~fluglinie** f feeder line **~gesellschaft** f branch of a company **~geschäft** n, **~niederlassung** f branch(-establishment) | **~s-** ~unternehmen [n] chain of stores, (Filialgeschäfte) ch. st.s **~leitung** f ⟨telph⟩ sub-main **~linie** f ⟨rail⟩ spur line | mit **~mustern** versehen to sprig **~organisation** f ⟨Am⟩ affiliate **~programm** n ⟨comp⟩ subroutine **~station** f ⟨rail⟩ junction **~stelle** f agency; ⟨bank etc⟩ branch; ⟨telph⟩ branch exchange **~strom** m ⟨el⟩ derived current **~verein** m branch society; chapter **~verkaufstelle** f ⟨Am⟩ chain store **~werk** n ⟨bot⟩ boughs pl **zw·eigen** vi/t & sich ~ [h] to bifurcate

zw·eit adv: z ~ by twos; z ~ schlafen to sleep double od together ‖ sie sind z ~ they are two, there are two of them **~älteste(r)** a second; (v zweien) younger **~beste(r)** a second-best **≃frisur** f (f Männer u Frauen) (Perücke) wig **~größte(r)** a second (city) **~jüngste(r)** the next to the youngest, the y.st but one **~klassig** a second-class, -rate; inferior; common; [pred] below standard **≃kopie** f ⟨phot⟩ reprint **~letzte(r)** a last but one; ⟨gram⟩ penultimate **≃mädchen** n second maid **~nächste(r)** a next but one ‖ am ~n Tage the *next day but one* **~rangig** a = –klassig, ⟨Am fam⟩ *one-horse* **zw·eite** a *second* ‖ *junior* (*clerk*) ‖ ~ Ausfertigung *duplicate* ‖ der ~ Band *volume two* ‖ ein ~r Cicero *another C.* ‖ ~s Ich *other self*; *alter ego* L ‖ sein ~s Ich *his double* ‖ der ~ des Monats *the second*; am *or* den 2. Mai (*on*) *the second of May*, *May the second* (schreibe: *May 2(nd)*, ⟨a.⟩ *2 May*) ‖ ~es Programm ⟨comp⟩ *alternate program*; jeder ~, den .. *every other p one meets* ‖ Heinrich II. (sprich: der Z.) *Henry II* (sprich: *the S.*) | aus ~r Hand *second-hand* ‖ zum ~n = **~ns** adv *secondly*, *in the second place*; (*for one th*) .. *for another th*

zw·erch adv *across*, *crosswise* **≈axt** f ⟨hist⟩ *twibill* **≈fell** n ⟨anat⟩ *diaphragm*, *midriff* ‖ jdm das ~ erschüttern ⟨fig⟩ *to make a p's sides split with laughing* | ~entzündung [f] *diaphragmatitis*; ≈erschütternd [a] *side-splitting*; ~erschütterung [f] *fit of laughter* **≈rippe** f (Rind) *fore rib*

Zwerg(in f) m ~(e)s/~e *dwarf*, *pygmy* ‖ ⟨fig⟩ *diminutive p*; ⟨fam⟩ *dot*, *midget*, *mite*; [nur m] *manikin*; *gnome* (*of a man*) **≈artig** a *dwarfish*, *of diminutive size*, *pygmy*, *pygmean* **~baum** m *dwarf-tree* **~bildung** f *d.ishness* **~fledermaus** f *pipistrel(le)* **~fürstentum** n *pocket(-edition) principality* **~gewicht** n ⟨sport⟩ *bantam* (*weight*) **~glühlampe** f ⟨el⟩ *miniature* (⟨Am⟩ *peanut*) *bulb* **~huhn** n ⟨orn⟩ *bantam* **~kamera** f ⟨phot⟩ *midget camera* **~kastanie** f *d. chestnut-tree* **~kiefer** f *d.-pine* **~maus** f *harvest-m.* **~mensch** m ⟨myth⟩ *pygmy* **~mispel** f ⟨bot⟩ *bastard medlar* **~obst** n *d.-fruit* **~ochse** m *runt* **~orangen** f pl ⟨Chin⟩ *cumquats* (*in syrup*) **~rohrdommel** f *little bittern* **~säger** m ⟨orn⟩ *smew* **~scharbe** f ⟨orn⟩ *pygmy cormorant* **~staat** m *puppet state* **~trappe** f ⟨orn⟩ *lesser bustard* **~volk** n *d. tribe* **~wuchs** m *stunted growth* **≈wüchsig** a *d.ish*; *stunted in growth* **zwerg(en)haft** a *dwarfish*

Zwetsch(g)e f ~/~n ⟨bot⟩ (*kind of*) *plum* ‖ (gedörrte) *prune* | **~n-** ~kuchen [m] *open plum-tart*; ~mus [n] *plum-preserve*

Zw·ickau n (†Stadt in Schlesien)

Zw·ick m ~(e)s/~e **1.** *pinch*, *nip* **2.** *whip-lash* ‖ *cut*, *smack* **3.** = Zwecke **~bohrer** m *gimlet* **~mühle** f *double-mill* ‖ (beim Spiel) *cross-ruff* ‖ ⟨whist⟩ *seesaw*; e–e ~ m *to see-saw* | ⟨fig⟩ e–e ~ h *to have two strings to one's bow* ‖ jdn in der ~ h *to have got a p into the corner* ‖ in e–r ~ sitzen *to be in a fix* od *on the horns of a dilemma* **~zange** f (e–e ~ *a pair of*) *pincers* pl; (kl) *tweezers* pl **Zw·icke** f ~/~n = Zwecke **Zwickel** m ~s/~ (im Strumpf) *clock* ‖ ⟨tail⟩ *godet*, *gusset*; (am Segel) *gore* ‖ ⟨mach⟩ *gusset* ‖ ⟨arch⟩ (Eck–, Hänge–, Kuppel≈) *spandrel*; *pendentive* **~bart** m *imperial* **~feld** n ⟨arch⟩ *panache* Fr

zw·icken vt [h] *to pinch*, *twitch*, *tweak*; *to nip* (a. v der Kälte) ‖ (den Bart) *to trim*, *clip* ‖ ⟨fig⟩ e–n ~ (u zwacken) *to torment a p* ‖ es zwickt mich im Leibe ⟨fam⟩ *I have the gripes* **Zw·icker** m ~s/~ (Kneifer) (ein *a pair of*) *eye-glasses*, ⟨fam⟩ *nose-nippers* pl; *pince-nez* Fr

Zw·ieback m ~(e)s/~ *zwieback*; *rusk*, *cracker*

Zw·iebel f ~/~n (Blumen≈) *bulb* | (Speise≈) *onion* ‖ (kl) *shallot*; Perl–, Silber≈n *pickled onions* | ⟨fam fig⟩ (Uhr) *potato*, *turnip* **≈artig** a *bulbous* **~beet** n *onion-bed* **~fische** pl ⟨typ⟩ (*printers'*) *pies* pl **≈förmig** a *bulbiform*, ⟨anat⟩ *bulbus* L **~geruch** m *smell of onions* **~gewächs** n *bulbous plant* **~kartoffeln** f pl *lyonnaise potatoes* **~(kuppel)** f ⟨arch⟩ *bulb* **~muster** n (Meißner Porzellan) *onion pattern* **~ring** m ⟨cul⟩ *onion ring* **~schale** f *onion-peel* **zw·iebeln** **1.** vi [h] *to smell* od *taste of onions* **2.** vt [h] *to rub with onions* ‖ ⟨fig fam⟩ jdn ~ *to treat a p harshly*; *to harass*, *torment*, *bully a p*; *to ride roughshod over a p*

zw·ie- **~brachen** vt [h] *to twifallow* **~fach**, **~fältig** a *double*, *twofold* **~gesichtig** a *ambivalent* | ~keit [f] *ambivalence* **≈gespräch** n *dialogue*, *duologue*, *colloquy* ‖ (*confidential*) *chat* **≈licht** n *twilight* (⟨a.⟩ *of the stars*) ‖ im ~ *at t.*; *in the dusk* | **≈ig** [a] *twilight* ⟨a. fig⟩; ⟨fig⟩ *shadowy*, *dubious*, *sinister* **≈metall** n *bi-metal* **≈natur** f *double nature* **Zw·iesel** **1.** f ~/~n *forked branch*; ⟨for⟩ *fork* **2.** m ~s/~ (am Sattel) *saddle bow*; (Vorder≈) *pommel*; (Hinter≈) *cantle* | **≈ig** a *bifurcated* **zw·ie-** **≈spalt** m *disunion*, *dissension*; *difference*, *conflict*, *discord* ‖ ⟨log⟩ *discrepancy* ‖ ⟨rel⟩ *schism* ‖ ~ der Pflichten *devided allegiancies* ‖ in ~ geraten *to fall out* (*with*) **~spältig** a *disunited*, *discordant*; *unbalanced*, *split* (*man*) | ≈keit [f] *irreconcilability* **≈sprache** f *dialogue* ‖ ~ halten *to hold a parley*, *to have an interview*; *to commune* (*with God*); *to have* od *hold communion* (*with one's own desires*) **≈tracht** f *discord* ‖ ~ erregend *divisive*; ~ säen *to sow the seeds of d.*, *to make mischief* (zw *among*; *to set .. by the ears*); → Streit | **in** ~ mit *out of time with* ⟨mus fig⟩ | ~ zw F. stiften *to set friends at variance* **~trächtig** a = –spältig **≈trachtstifter** m *mischief-maker*

°**Zw·ille** f ~/~n *slingshot*, ⟨fam⟩ *tweaker*

Zw·il(li)ch m ~(e)s/~e *tick(ing)* | **≈en** a *of ticking* **~kittel** m *blouse made of coarse linen* od *cotton* **Zw·illing** m ~(e)s/~e *twin* | ~e [pl] ⟨astr⟩ *Gemini* pl ‖ eineiige (zweieiige) ~e (*non*)*identical* od *monozygotic*, *uniovular* (*binovular*, *bizygotic*, *unlike*) *twins* | *doublebarrelled gun* | **~s-** *twin* .. **~achse** f ⟨cryst⟩ *t.ning-axis* **~antrieb** m *t. drive* **~bildung** f *t.ning*; *congemination* **~bruder** m *t. brother* **~einblick** m ⟨phot⟩ *t. oculars* pl **~energie** f *t. energy* **~geburt** f *birth of t.s*; *t. birth* ‖ er stammte aus e–r ~ *he had been born a twin* **~geschütz** n *two-barrelled gun* **~geschwister** pl *t.s* pl **~gestirn** n *Gemini* pl **~kristall** m *t. crystal*; *macle* **~leiter** m *t.* od *double conductor* **~maschine** f *t.-cylinder engine* **~-MG** n *t. machine gun* **~objektiv** n ⟨phot⟩ *t. lenses* pl **~paar** n *pair of t.s* **~reifen** m pl *t. tires* pl **~triebwerk** n *t. engine*

Zw·ing- **~burg** f (*oppressor's*) *castle*, *keep*, *citadel* **~herr** m *despot*, *tyrant*, *oppressor* **~herrschaft** f *despotism*, *tyranny* **~schraube** ⟨carp⟩ *ferrule-screw* **~-Uri** n *Fortress of Uri* **Zw·inge** f ~/~n (Stock≈) *ferrule*; (Schirm≈) *tip* | ⟨tech⟩ (Klammer) *clamp*, *holdfast* ‖ (Schraubstock) *vice* ‖ (Uhr≈) *collet* ‖ (Griff≈) *handle collar*

zw·ingen vt [zwang/gezwungen] [h] **A. 1.** (mit Gewalt) *to do violence to* ‖ (zu) *to reduce*, *constrain*, *oblige*, *compel* (*to* [*do*]) (*poverty constrained him to mix with* ..); jdn ~ etw z tun ⟨a.⟩ *to make a p do a th*; *to reduce* (*a p to submission*) ‖ jdn ~, übereilt z handeln *to force a p's hand* ‖ jdn z Frieden ~ *to force a p to make peace* ‖ (Stadt) z Übergabe ~ *to reduce* (durch Hunger *starve*) .. *into surrender* | *to force*, *coerce* (*into doing*) **2.** (S) *to call for* (*drastic measures*) **3.** (be~) *to vanquish*, *conquer*, *overcome*, *subdue*, *master* ⟨a. fig⟩ **4.** in (etw) hinein ~ *to drive* od *force into* ‖ jdn in Fesseln ~ *to cast a p into chains* **B. sich** ~ *to restrain one's feelings* ‖ ich muß mich ~ *it costs me an effort* (z tun *to do*) ‖ das läßt sich nicht ~ *it cannot be done by force* ‖ er läßt sich nicht ~ *he won't yield to force*; *he won't be driven* (*into*, *to do*) | sich ~ zu *to constrain* od *force o.s. to* ‖ sich z Lächeln ~ *to force* od *affect a smile* ‖ sie zwang sich, es z tun *she made herself do it* **C. gezwungen** s, sich g. sehen *to see o.s. obliged* (⟨emph⟩ *compelled*) (*to do*), *to be under the necessity* (*of doing*) ‖ durch die Umstände g. *under stress of circumstances* | [adv] g. lachen *to laugh on the wrong side of the mouth* ‖ freiwillig oder g. *whether he* (etc) *willed it or not* **zw·ingend** a *coercive* (*measure*) ‖ ⟨fig⟩ *cogent* (*reason*); *compelling*, *stringent* (*argument*); *imperative*; *conclusive* (*proof*); *urgent* (*circumstances*) ‖ ~e Kraft *cogency*, *validity* **Zw·inger** m ~s/~ **1.** *con-*

strainer **2.** (Bären≃) *bear-pit* || (Hunde≃) *kennel* || (Gefängnis) *prison-yard* || ⟨fort⟩ *barbican*; (Turm) *keep, dungeon, donjon* [Fr]

zw·inkern vi [h] *to blink, twinkle, wink*

zw·irbeln vt [h] *to twirl*

Zw·irn m ∼(e)s/∼e (Faden) *thread* || ⟨spin⟩ *twine; twisted yarn* || Meister ∼ *Master Snip* | ⟨fig⟩ *notions, ideas* pl || ∼ im Kopfe h *to be no fool* **~band** n *tape* **~fabrikation** f *th.d-making* **~(s)faden** m *th.d* **~glätter** m ⟨mach⟩ *th.d-finisher* **~handschuh** m *th.d-glove* **~kästchen** n *work-box* **~knäuel** n *ball of th.d* **~maschine** f *twisting-machine* **~mühle** f ⟨spin⟩ *twisting-mill, doubler* **~rolle** f = –knäuel **~seide** f *thrown* od *twisted silk* **~spitze** f *th.d-lace* **~strumpf** m *th.d-stocking* **~wickel** m *th.d-paper* **~winde** f *th.d-reel* **zw·irnen** a *of linen thread* **zw·irnen 1.** vt [h] *to twist* (*wool*, etc), *twine* (*thread*), *throw* (*silk*) **2.** vi [h] (of cats) *to purr* **zw·ischen I.** prep [dat & acc] **1.** *between* || ∼ heute u morgen *b.n this* (*day*) *and to-morrow*; ∼ G. u W. *b.n the*(!) *garden and meadow* **2.** ⟨geh Spr⟩ *betwixt*; *'twixt* (*heaven and earth*); ∼ Lipp' u Kelches Rand schwebt der finstern Mächte Hand *there's many a slip 'twixt the cup and the lip* **3.** ∼ 40 u 50 *from 40 to 50*; *40 odd* **4.** *inter* .., *inter-..*: ∼ den Kolonien *intercolonial*; so: *intero-ceanic, international, intercostal*; *intercollege* **5.** ([mitten] unter, drin) *among*(*st*): [dat]: *choose amongst these*!; *there are peas amongst the beans*; [acc]: *to sow peas/tares among the beans/wheat*; → unter || aber: *he was found* (lebend) *amidst the dead* **II.** [adv] = dazwischen **III.** [in comp oft] *intervening* (*time*; *country* ≃gelände) || *intermediate* (*trade, state*) || *provisional* (*result*) || ⟨jur⟩ *interlocutory* (*decision*) || ⟨com⟩ *interim* (*balance*) **Zw·ischen-** ⟨oft⟩ *intermediate* **~achse** f *countershaft* **~akt** m ⟨theat⟩ *entr'acte* Fr, *pause between the acts* | ∼musik [f] *intermission*; ∼vorhang [m] *act drop* **~anflug** m *i.e approach* **~artikel** m (e–r Zeitung) *padding* **~bahnhof** m *i.e station* **~balken** m ⟨arch⟩ *mid-beam* **~begebenheit** f *episode* **~bemerkung** f *incidental remark*; *digression*; *interruption* **~bericht** m *progress report* **~bescheid** m *provisional reply* **≃bezirklich** a *intersectional* **~blatt** n *interleaf* **~deck** n ⟨mar⟩ *steerage* (*to travel st.*); *between-decks* pl || ⟨milmar⟩ *tween-deck* | **~s-** ∼passagier [m] *steerage-passenger* **~ding** n *intermediate*; *cross*(*-breed*) **~(dr)ein** adv *in between* **≃dr·ein, ~·ein** adv *in between, meanwhile* **≃durch** adv *through*; *in the midst* || (zeitlich) *between whiles, at intervals, occasionally, in between* **~ergebnis** n ⟨sport⟩ *provisional result*; ⟨comp⟩ ∼e [pl] *results of a prior calculation* (*temporarily stored*) **~fabel** f *episode* **~fall** m *incident* ⟨a. mil⟩; plötzlicher ∼ *sudden blow, bolt from the blue* || es kam zu –fällen *some unforeseen* od *troublesome events took place*; ohne ∼ ank *to arrive safely* **~farbe** f *half-tint* **~fassung** f ⟨el⟩ *adapter* **~-feld** n ⟨mil⟩ *intervening ground* **~flächen-** ⟨tech⟩ *interfacial* (*tension*) **~flügel** m ⟨aero⟩ *flap* **~-frage** f *question thrown in*; *i.e qu.* **~gang** m, **~gericht** n ⟨cul⟩ *extra dish, entremet, entrée* Fr, *side-dish*; gesalzenes ∼ ⟨cul⟩ *savoury* **~gas** n ⟨mot⟩ ∼ geben *to double-declutch* **~gebäude** n ⟨arch⟩ *i.e wing* **≃gelagert** a *interstratified* **~gelände** n ⟨mil⟩ → –feld **~gesang** m *inserted song* **~geschoß** n ⟨arch⟩ *i.e story*; *entresol* Fr || mit –ssen *split-lever* (*building*) **~gitteratom** n *interstitial atom* **~glied** n *link* || ⟨tech⟩ *hickey* (*to secure a fixture to an outlet*) **~hafen** m *trading port* **~halt** m *i.e stop* **~handel** m → vor. III.; ⟨a.⟩ *carrying trade* **~händler** m *intermediary*, ⟨fam⟩ *jobber* || ⟨com⟩ *middleman*; *commission-agent* **~handlung** f *episode* **≃h·er** adv *meanwhile* **≃h·in** adv *in between* **≃inne** adv *between the two* **~kiefer** m ⟨anat⟩ *intermaxillary* (*bone*) **~kläger** m *interpleader* **≃konfessionell** a *interdenominational* **~kopie** f *i.e* (*copy* od *master*) **~kühler** m *intercooler* **~lage** f *interposition* **~lagenpapier** n *interleaving paper* **~landeplatz** m *i.e landing field* **~landung** f ⟨aero⟩ *i.e landing*; *touch-down*; *stop*(*-over* ⟨Am⟩) || ohne ∼ *non-stop* (*flight*) | **~s-** ∼flughafen [m] *staging post*; ∼punkt [m] *i.e point*; ∼raum [m] *staging area* N **~lauf** m ⟨racing⟩ *heat* **≃liegend** a *i.e*; *intervening* (*country*) **~linie** f *i.e line* **~lösung** f *solution* (*in-between* od) *for the time being* **~mahlzeit** f *light collation* **~mauer** f *partition-wall* **≃menschlich** a *interhuman* **~original** n → –kopie **~pause** f *interval* || ⟨school⟩ *recreation-time* **~pfeiler** m ⟨arch⟩ *pier*; *i.e pillar* **≃planetarisch** a *interplanetary* **~platz** m ⟨com⟩ *staple down* **~prüfung** f *i.e examination* **~rang** m ⟨theat⟩ *mezzanine* **~raum** m *interval, inter*(*mediate*) *space*, (Lücke) *interstice, gap* || (Entfernung) *distance* || ⟨typ⟩ *spacing* || ⟨mar⟩ *berth* || (Zeit≃) *period of time interval* (*at long i.s*) || in –räumen stattfindend *intermittent, periodical*; .. v 25 Jahren *at quarter-century intervals* | ∼taste [f] ⟨typewr⟩ *spacebar* **~rede** f *interruption* **~redner** m *interlocutor* **~regierung** f, **~reich** n *interregnum* **~relais** n ⟨el⟩ *supplementary relay* **~rippe** f ⟨cul⟩ *sirloin steak* **~ruf** m *loud interruption* **~satz** m *parenthesis* **~schalter** m ⟨el⟩ *adapter* **~schaltung** f ⟨tech⟩ *inserting*; ⟨el⟩ *interposition* **~schein** m *script* **~schicht** f *i.e layer, interlayer* **~sender** m ⟨wir⟩ *relay transmitter* **~soll** n *interim level* (*of supply*) **~speise** f = –gericht **~spiel** n ⟨mus⟩ *intermezzo* ⟨a. fig⟩, *interlude* || (e–r Fuge) *episode* **≃staatlich** a *international*; ⟨Am⟩ *interstate*; ∼e Autobahn ⟨Am⟩ *freeway* **~station** f *intermediate station*, ⟨Am⟩ *way-station* **~stecker** m ⟨el, wir⟩ *adapter*; *attachment plug* **~stellung** f *intermediate position* **~stock** m = –geschoß **~streifen** m *insertion* **~streit** m ⟨jur⟩ *intervention* **~strich** m ⟨mar⟩ *intercardinal point* **~stromland** n *interfluve*; *Mesopotamia* **~stück** n *insertion*; ⟨tech⟩ *intermediate* od *transition, connecting piece*; *spacer*; ⟨el, wir⟩ *adapter* **~stunde** f (*the*) *hour between*; *i.e hour*; *interval*; ⟨school⟩ *recreation-, play-time* **~summe** f ⟨comp⟩ *subtotal* **~titel** m *sub-title* **~träger(in** f) m *talebearer, telltale, go-between* **~träger·ei** f *tale-bearing, -telling* **~umstand** m *incident* **~urteil** n ⟨jur⟩ *interlocutory decree* **~verkauf** m *sale through a middleman*; ∼ vorbehalten *if unsold* **~verkehr** m *intercommunication* **~verteiler** m ⟨off⟩ *i.e distribution frame* **≃völkisch** a *international* **~vorfall** m = –fall **~vorhang** m ⟨theat⟩ *drop-scene*; *act drop* **~wall** m ⟨fort⟩ *curtain* **~wand** f ⟨arch⟩ = –mauer; ⟨biol, mech⟩ *diaphragm* **~welle** f ⟨tech⟩ *countershaft* **~wert** m *i.e value* **~wirt** m ⟨biol⟩ *i.e. host* **~zeile** f *i.e line* **≃zeilig** a *interlinear* **~zeit** f *interval, interim* || in der ∼ *meanwhile*; (*in the*) *meantime*; *in between*; *between times*; *during the interval* **~ziellinie** f ⟨tact⟩ *phase line* **~zünder** m ⟨aero⟩ *booster*

Zwist m ∼es/∼e *dissension, discord, disagreement*; *difference, dispute, quarrel, bickering, variance*; *feud* || in ∼ geraten *to begin to quarrel* (über *about*) || *it was as if a battle had been joined* **zw·istig** a (P) *discordant*; *at variance* [nur pred] || (S) *questionable, disputed* | **≃keit** f ∼/∼en = Zwist

zw·itschern I. vi [h] *to chirp, twitter*, ⟨Am a.⟩ *to chipper, chirk* || (Lerche) *to warble* **II.** ≃ n *chirp*(*ing*), etc

Zw·itter m ∼s/∼ (→ zwei) ⟨bot⟩ *hybrid*, ⟨zoo⟩ *cross* (*-breed*), *mongrel, bastard* || ⟨physiol⟩ *hermaphrodite* **~bildung** f *hermaphroditism* **~blüte** f, **≃blütig** a *hermaphrodite* **≃haft, ≃ig** a *bisexual, hybrid, mongrel* **~i·on** n *dual ion* **~wesen** n [abstr] *hybrid nature* || [konkr] = Zwitter **~wort** n *hybrid* (*word*)

zwo a **1.** ⟨obs [f]⟩ = zwei **2.** ⟨telph⟩ = zwei

zwölf I. a *twelve* (vgl zwei) || um ∼ Uhr (mittags)

at noon; (nachts) *at midnight*; ⟨fig⟩ 5 Minuten vor ∼ → (im letzten) Moment || etwa ∼ *about a dozen* (*bottles*) || die ∼ Nächte *the 12 nights between Christmas and Twelfthnight* **II.** ⩪ f (*the number*) *twelve* **Zw·ölf-** **∼eck** n *dodecagon* **⩪eckig** a *dodecagonal* **∼ender** m (*stag with twelve antlers*) ⟨hunt⟩ *royal* || ⟨fam⟩ *N.C.O. who has served 12 years* **⩪fach** *a twelve-fold* **∼f·ingerdarm** m *duodenum* || Entzündung des ∼s *duodenitis* || Geschwür am ∼ *duodenal ulcer* **∼flach** n ⟨geom⟩ *dodecahedron* **⩪flächig** a *dodecahedral* **⩪jährig** a *12 years old, of 12 years* | ⩪e(r) *girl* (*boy*) *of 12* **⩪lötig** a *weighing six ounces* **⩪mal** adv *twelve times* **⩪männig** a ⟨bot⟩ *dodecandrian* **∼pfünder** m *twelve-pounder* **⩪pfündig** a *weighing 12 pounds* **⩪seitig** a *twelve-sided* **⩪stündig** a *of 12 hours* **⩪stündlich** a *occurring every 12 hours* **⩪tägig** a *lasting 12 days* **⩪teilig** a *consisting of 12 parts, duodecimal* **zwölferl·ei** a *of twelve different sorts* **zw·ölfte** a *twelfth* (vgl zweite) || in ∼r Stunde ⟨fig⟩ → zwölf | **die ⩪n** = 12 Nächte **Zw·ölftel** n ∼s/∼ *twelfth part* **∼form** f ⟨typ⟩ *twelves* pl **∼format** n *duodecimo* (abbr *12 mo*) **zw·ölftens** adv *twelfthly*

Zy·an m ∼(e)s/ ⟨chem⟩ *cyanogen* | ∼äther [m] *cyanic ether*; ∼eisen [n] *cyanide of iron*; ∼kali(um) [n] *cyanide of potassium*; ⩪sauer [a] *cyanic*; ∼säure [f] *cyanic acid*; ∼verbindung [f] *cyanide*; ∼wasserstoffsäure [f] (Blausäure) *hydrocyanic acid* **Zy·ane** f ∼/∼n ⟨bot⟩ *corn-flower* **Zyan·id** n ∼(e)s/ *cyanide* **zy·anig** a *cyanous*

Zykl·aden pl (griechische Inselgruppe) *Cyclades*

z·yklisch a *cyclic*(*al*) **Zykl·on** m ∼(e)s/∼e *cyclone* | ∼feuerung [f] *c. firing* **Zykl·one** f ∼/∼n ⟨meteor⟩ *depression* **Zykl·op** m ∼en/∼en *Cyclop*(*s*); pl *Cyclops, Cyclôpses, Cyclopes* | **⩪isch** a *Cyclopean* **zykloth·ym** a ⟨psych⟩ *cyclothymic* (Habitus *personality*) **Z·yklus** m ∼/–len → *cycle* ⟨Lit⟩ || (v Vorlesungen) *course*

Zyl·inder m ∼s/∼ **I.** *cylinder* (aussetzen *to cut out*) || ⟨tech⟩ *drum, barrel* || (Lampen⩪) *chimney, lamp-glass* || (Meß⩪) *measuring-glass* || (Brems⩪) ⟨mil⟩ *recoil buffer* || (Hut) *silk hat, top-hat*; ⟨sl⟩ *stove-pipe hat, tile* || im ∼ *top-hatted* (*men*) || || den ∼ (= Abschied) bek *or* sich e–n ∼ kaufen (müssen) ⟨mil fam⟩ *to be given a bowler hat*; *to take felt* **II.** [in comp mst] *cylinder* (*six-c. car*), *cylindrical* (*boiler*) **∼deckel** m *c.-cover, c.al lid* **⩪förmig** a *cylindric*(*al*) **∼gebläse** n *blowing-engine* **∼hemmung** f ⟨tech⟩ *c.-escapement* **∼hut** m vgl I. **∼inhalt** m *c.-displacement* **∼mantel** m *c.-jacket* **∼rose** f ⟨zoo⟩ *sea-anemone* **∼schreibtisch** m *drop-cabinet* **∼stift** m *c.al pin* **∼uhr** f *horizontal watch* **zyl·indrisch** a *cylindrical*

Z·yma n ∼s/∼ta Gr (Gärstoff) *zyme*

Z·yniker m ∼s/∼ ⟨hist⟩ *Cynic* || ⟨fig⟩ *cynic* **z·ynisch** a *cynic, cynical* || [adv] *cynically* **Zyn·ismus** m ∼/–men *cynical philosophy* || ⟨fig⟩ *cynicism, cynicalness*

Z·yper- ∼gras [n] ⟨bot⟩ *Cyperus*; ∼katze [f] *Cyprian cat*; ∼wein [m] *Cyprus wine*; ∼wurz(el) [f] ⟨bot⟩ *galingale* **Z·ypern** n (Mittelmeerinsel) *Cyprus* **Zypr·esse** f ∼/∼n ⟨bot⟩ *cypress* | **∼n-** ∼hain [m] *c.-grove*; ∼holz [n] *c.-wood*; ∼nuß [f] *c.-cone* **Zypri·ote** m ∼n/∼n *Cypriote*

Z·yste f ∼/∼n ⟨path⟩ *cyst* | **∼n-** [in comp] *cysti*

I. EIGENNAMEN
I. PROPER NAMES

Personennamen, Vornamen & Familiennamen

Zweistämmige Namen, die als solche noch deutlich zu erkennen sind, sind durch einen Strich gekennzeichnet: z. B. Adal|bert
Die englische Aussprache der Namen steht in Band I

A

Abder·it Bew. der thrakischen Stadt Abdera, Schildbürger der Antike *Gothamite*; Wielands „Die Abderiten"

·Abraham m *Abraham* [urspr. *Abram*], [dim] *Abe*

Ach·äer m *Achaean*

Ach·illes m *Achilles*

·Achim m → Joachim

·Ada f *Ada, Adah*

·Adal|bert m *Ethelbert*

·Adam m *Adam*; ⟨schott⟩ *Edie*

·Ade|bar (Storch „Glücksbringer, Kinderbringer")

Adelaide (Fr); „~" Lied v. Beethoven; → Adelheid

·Adel|bert m → Adalbert

Ad·ele f *Adela*; Zofe in Strauß' Operette „Die Fledermaus" **·Adel|gund** f **·Adel|heid** f *Adelaide, Adelina, Adeline*, [dim] *Addy*

Adel·ine f *Adelina, Adeline*, [dim] *Addy*

·Adel|traut *f* **·Adel|ung** m

Aden|auer, Konrad (1876–1967), Bundeskanzler 1949–1963

†**·Adolar** m → *Eury·anthe*

·Ad|olf, ·Adolph m *Adolph(us)*, [dim] *Dolph(us)*

Ad·onis m ⟨myth⟩ *Adonis*

·Adri·an m **Adri·enne** f *Adriana*

·Afra f

·Agatha, Ag·athe f [Gr] *Agatha*; Agathe: Gestalt in K. M. v Webers Oper „Der Freischütz"

Äg·idius m *Ægidius*: ⟨fam⟩ *Giles*

·Agnes f *Agnes*; ⟨fam⟩ *Ness, Aggie*

Agr·ippa m (röm. Feldherr, 63–12 v. Chr.) *Agrippa* **Agrip·p·ina** f (seine Tochter)

Ah·asver m (der „ewige Jude") *Ahasuerus*

·Ala|rich m (westgot. König, 370–410 n. Chr.) *Alaric(k)*

·Alba m (span. Feldherr u Staatsmann, 1507–1582) *Alba, Alva*; → Egmont

·Alban m *Alban*

·Albe|rich m ⟨myth⟩ Gestalt der Nibelungensage u in R. Wagners „Ring des Nibelungen" *Alberic(k), Aubrey*

·Al|bert m *Albert* **Al|bert·ine** f *Albertina, Alberta* **Alb·ertus M·agnus** m (Albert, Gf v Bollstädt, 1207 bis 1280)

Albig·enser pl (nach der s.-franz. Stadt ‚Albi' *Albigensians*; → Wörterbuch

·Albin m **·Al|brecht** m *Albert*

·Alex m ([dim] v Alexander) *Aleck (Alick), Ellick, Sander, Sandy, Sawnie* **Alex·ander** m **Alex·andra** f *Alexandra*

Alexandr·ine f *Alexandrina*, [dim] *Alley* **Al·exei** [*-ei*] m **Al·exia, Al·exie** f *Alexia, Alice*, [dim] *Ally, Allie, Elsie, Alison*

Al·exis, Willibald (Pseudonym e–s dt. Romanschriftstellers, 1798–1871, „Die Hosen des Herrn v Bredow") **Al·exi(u)s** m *Alexis*

·Alfons m *Alphonso, Alfonso*

·Alf·red m *Alfred*, [dim] *Alf*

Al·ice f *Alice, Alicia*, [dim] *Alison* (frz. Verkleinerungsform, bes in Schottl. üblich), *Alie, Ailie, Ailcy, Ailsie, Elsie, Alley*

Alk·este, Alk·estis f ⟨myth⟩ *Alcestis*

Alkib·iades m (athen. Staatsmann, 450–404) *Alcibiades*

Alkm·ene f ⟨myth⟩, Gemahlin des Amph·itryon

·Alkuin m *Alcuin, Alcwin*

·Alma f *Alma*

Almav·iva, Graf ~, Gestalt in Mozarts „Figaros Hochzeit"

·Al|mut(h) f

·Alois, Alo·ysius m *Aloysius*

·Al|win m *Alwin, Alvin*

Al|w·ine f *Alvina, Albina*

Amad·eus m

Am·alia, Am·alie f *Amelia*

Am·anda f *Amanda, Amabel*, [dim] *Mandy*

Ambr·osius m *Ambrosius, Ambrose*, [dim] *Nam(by)*

Am·elia → Amalia; „~ od ein Maskenball", Oper v G. Verdi

·Amelungen Nachkommen des ostgot. Königs Amala, bes Dietrich v Bern und s–e Gefolgsleute

Amen|h·otep ([Eg myth] = Amon [ist] gnädig), ⟨Gr⟩ *Amenophis*

Amf·ortas, König ~, Gestalt in R. Wagners „Parsifal"

·Amor m ⟨myth⟩ *Cupid(o)*; *(God of) Love*; *boy God*; *bow--boy*

Ampère m (frz. Mathematiker u Physiker, 1775–1836)

Amph·itryon m ⟨myth⟩ *Amphitryon*, Gemahl der Alkmene; Lustspiel v Kleist nach Molière

·Amrei (Kurzform v Annemarie) *Mary Ann*

·Amund|sen, Roald, norweg. Südpolentdecker: 1911

An·akreon m (griech. Lyriker um 520 v. Chr.) *Anacreon*; s–e Nachahmer, Anakre·ontiker, 18. Jh.: Gleim, Hagedorn

Anast·asia, Anast·asie f *Anastasia*, [dim] *Austace*

Anast·asius m *Anastasius*

·Ander|sen m (dän. Dichter, 1805–1875)

Andr·eas m *Andrew*, [dim] *Andy*

Andr·omache f (Gattin Hektors) *Andromache*

Andr·omeda f ⟨myth⟩ *Andromeda*

Än·eas m *Æneas, Enaeas*

·Angela f *Angela* **Ang·elika** f *Angelica* **Angel·ina** f Angelina

An·ita f

·Anna f *Anna, Anne, Ann*; „~" ländliches Liebesgedicht v. G. Hauptmann; Gestalt in Mozarts Oper „Don Juan"

·Ännchen f *Annie, Nan, Nanny, Nancy, Nina*; „~ v Tharau", Volkslied v S. Dach

·Anneli f **·Anneliese** f

·Annemarie f *Anna Maria*

Ann·ette f **·Anni** f (Koseform v Anna) *Ann*

·Anno m

Ann·unzio, d' m (ital. Dichter u Politiker, 1863–1938)

Ansch·ar(ius) m *Anscarius*

·Ans|elm m *Ansel(m)*

Ans|g·ar(ius) m → Anscharius

Ant·igone f ⟨myth⟩ *Antigone*

Ant·iochus m (syr. Könige) *Antiochus*

·Anton m *Ant(h)ony, Tony*, †*Antöyn*

Ant·onia, Ant·onie f *Antonia, Antonina, Antoinette*, [dim] *Net(ty)*; Antonia wie Olympia

Anton·inus m **Ant·onius** m

·Äolus m ⟨myth⟩ *Æolus*

Aphrod·ite f ⟨myth⟩

Ap·oll, Ap·ollo m ⟨myth⟩ *Apollo*; Apoll·inisch [a] (nach Nietzsche) *Apollonian*

Apoll·onia f *Apollonia*

Apoll·onius m *Apollonius*

Appi·anus m (im 2. Jh. n. Chr.) *Appianus*

·Appius Cl·audius Caecus (etwa 312 v. Chr.), baute die Appische Straße, *Via Appia, the Appian Way*, von Rom nach Capua

Arab·ella f *Arabella*; „~" Oper v. Richard Strauß nach H.v. Hofmannsthal

·Archi(m)|bald m *Archibald*, [dim] *Archy*

Archim·edes m (griech. Mathematiker u Physiker, 287 bis 212) *Archimedes*; Archim·edisch [a] *Archimedean (screw)*

·Ares m ⟨Gr myth⟩ *Ares*; (bei den Römern) *Mars*

Ari·adne f ⟨myth⟩ *Ariadne*; „~ auf Naxos" Oper v. Richard Strauss nach H. v. Hofmannsthal

Ari·aner m (→ Wörterbuch) Anhänger der Lehre des Arius

Ar·ion m (sagenhafter griech. Dichter u Musiker) *Arion*

Ari·ost m (ital. Dichter, 1474–1533) *Ariosto*

Ariov·ist m (Suevenführer, 1. Jh. v. Chr.) *Ariovistus*

Arist·ophanes m (griech. Lustspieldichter, geb. 445 v. Chr.) *Aristophanes*

Arist·oteles m (griech. Philosoph, geb. 384 v Chr.) *Aristotle, Aristoteles* || Aristot·elisch [a], Aristot·eliker [m] *Aristotelian*

Ari·us (in Alexandria 336 †), lehrte Wesensähnlichkeit Christi mit Gott, entgegen Athanasius, Lehre von der Wesensgleichheit (Homousie)

·Arm|gard f

Ar|m·in(ius) m (Befreier Deutschlands von den Römern, 17 v. Chr.–19 n. Chr.) *Arminius* → Irmin; ⟨→ a.⟩ Her|mann [jedoch hiermit nicht sprachverwandt]

·Arnim m; Bett·ina v. ~, geb. Brentano, Goethes Brieffreundin (1785–1859)

·Arno m

·Arn|old m *Arnold*

·Arn|ulf

Artax·erxes m (pers. Könige) *Artaxerxes*

·Arthur, ·Artur m *Arthur*

·Artus m → Arthur; ~gedicht [n] *poem on the Arthurian legend*; ~ritter [m] *Knight of the Round Table*

·Äschylus m (griech. Tragiker, 525–456 v. Chr.)

Äskul·ap m ⟨myth⟩ *Æsculapius, Esculapius*

Äs·op m (sagenhafter griech. Fabeldichter) *Æsop(us)*

·Asta f

Ast·arte (phönizische Göttin) *As(h)taroth*

Athan·asia f **Athan·asius** m *Athanasius*; → Arius

Ath·ene f ⟨Gr. myth⟩ *Athena, Athene*; (bei den Römern) *Minerva*

·Attila m (Hunnenfürst, gest. 453 n. Chr.) *Attila*

·August m *Augustus*, [dim] *Gustus, Guss* **Aug·usta, Aug·uste** f *Augusta*; → Gustchen **·Augustin, August·inus** m *Augustin(us), Austin* **August·ina, August·ine** [f] *Augustina* **Aug·ustus** m *Augustus* (Mehrer [des Reichs])

Aur·elia, Aur·elie f *Aurelia*

Aur·el(ius) m *Aurelius*

Av·aren pl (ural-altaischer Stamm) *Avars*

Av·erroës m (arab. Philosoph u Arzt, 1126–1198) *Averr(h)oës*

·Axel m

B

Baal m ⟨hebr myth⟩ *Baal*

B·äbchen [n] (weibl. Vn.) → **Bab·ettchen** n (weibl. Vn.), [dim v. Barbara], Bab·ette f *Babbit(t)y, Babby, Bab*

B·acchus m ⟨myth⟩ *Bacchus*

Bach m; Joh. Seb. ~ (dt. Komponist, 1685–1750); Ph. Em. ~ (dt. Komponist, 1714–1788)

B·aedeker (dt. Buchhändlerfamilie)

Bajuv·are m (= Bayer → S. 151 *Bavarian*

B·alder m ⟨myth⟩ → Baldr

Baldr m ⟨german myth⟩

B·ald|rich m

B·ald|uin m *Baldwin*; *Bodwine*

B·aldur m ⟨myth⟩ → Baldr

B·althasar m ⟨bib⟩ *Balthazar*

Balzac m, Honoré de (fr. Schriftsteller, 1799–1850)

B·arbara f *Barbara*; → *Bäbchen*

Barbar·ossa m *Barbarossa*; (Kaiser Friedrich I., 1155–1190)

B·ärbel(chen n) f (weibl. Vn.) *Barbara, Barb, Bab*; ← *Bäbchen*

B·arlach, Ernst, dt. Bildschnitzer (1870–1938)

B·arnabas m *Barnaby*

B·arr|ing (Fn.); „Die ~s", Roman v. W. v. Simpson

B·art|hold m → Berthold

B·arthel m *Bat*

B·artholf m *Bardolph*

Bartholom·äus m *Bartholomew*

Bartók, Béla, ungar. Komponist (1881–1945)

Bas·il(ius) m [Gr.] *Basil(ius)*

B·astian ⟨fam⟩ m *Sebastian*

Bat|h·ildis f

B·athseba ['batzeba] f *Bathsheba*

Baudelaire m (fr. Dichter, 1821–1867)

Be·ata, Be·ate f *Beata*

Beatr·ice, Be·atrix f *Beatrice, Beatrix*, [dim] *Bettrice*

B·echtel m → Bert|hold

B·eda m (engl. Kirchenhistoriker, 674–735) *Bede*, "*the venerable Bede*"

B·eethoven m (dt. Komponist, 1770–1827)

B·ehrens m → Bern|hard

Behr|ing

B·elisar m (Feldherr Justinians, 505–565) *Belisarius*

B·ella f *Mabel, Bella, Bell*

Bels·azar, Bels·azer m (letzter König v. Babylon) *Belshazzar*

B·endrix m

B·enedikt m *Benedict*, ⟨fam⟩ *Benedick*, [dim] *Bennett*

Bened·ikta f *Benedicta*

B·enjamin m *Benjamin*, [dim] *Ben(ny)*

B·enno ([dim] v. Bern|hard) m *Beno(ni)*

Benz, Karl (dt. Erfinder; 1886: Vergasermotor [Benzin])

×**B·eppi** (österr.) **1.** m (Koseform f Joseph) *Joe* **2.** f (Koseform f Josephine) *Joe, Pheny*

B·erchta f → Bertha

B·ercht|old m → Bert|hold

B·eren|gar m

Beren·ice, Beren·ika f *Berenice*

B·er|lich|ingen, Götz v. [m] → Götz

B·erlioz, Hector (fr. Komponist, 1803–1869)

Bern, Dietrich v. ~ *Theodoric of Verona*

B·ern|auer, Agnes (Drama v. F. Hebbel)

B·ern|hard m *Bernard*, ⟨Ir⟩ *Barney*

Bern|·ini m (ital. Architekt u. Bildhauer, 1598–1680)

B·ern|ward m

B·err|ing m (Familienname)

B·erta, B·ertha f *Bertha*

B·ertchen n (m. Vn., [dim] v. Bertram, Herbert, Hubert etc) *Bertie, Berty*

B·erthel m → Barthel

B·ert|hold, B·ertold m

B·ert|ram m *Bertram*, [dim] *Berty*

B·essemer, H. (engl. Erfinder; 1855: ~-Birne z. Stahlerzeugung)

B·etti, B·etty f ([dim] v. Elisabeth) *Bess(y), Bet, Betsey, Betty* **Bett·ina** f; **B·etty** f, → Arnim

Bi·anca, Bi·anka f (It) *Bianca, Blanche*

B·ileam m ⟨bib⟩ *Balaam*

B·ismarck (Fürst) m (dt. Staatsmann, 1815–1898) (*Prince*) *Bismarck*

Bizet, Georges (fr. Komponist, 1838–1875)

Bj·örn|son (norweg. Dichter, 1832–1910)

Blake, William (⟨engl⟩ Dichter u. Maler, 1757–1827)

Bl·anca, Bl·anka f *Blanch(e)*

Bl·anchefleur (Fr) → Bianca

Bl·asius m *Blase*; *Blaise* (Fr)

Bl·ücher m (preuß. Generalfeldmarschall, 1742–1819)

Boccaccio m (ital. Dichter, 1313–1375) *Boccaccio, Boccace*

B·öcklin m (schweiz. Maler, 1827–1901)

Bod|mer m **B·odo** m

Bo·ethius m (röm. Staatsmann, 480–525) *Boethius, Boece* (Verfasser der *Consolatio Philosophiae*, die *Chaucer* ins Englische übersetzte. Das Werk enthält eine mittelalterliche Lösung der Fragen „Willensfreiheit des Menschen" bei „Allwissenheit Gottes")

Boileau [bwa'lo] m (fr. Dichter, 1636–1711)

B·oleslas, B·oleslaus, B·oleslaw m *Boleslas*

Bonap·arte m → Napoleon

Bonavent·ura, St. ·[m]

Bonif·acius, Bonif·atius, Bonif·az m *Boniface*

Borch|ert, [gen] **Borchers** → Burg|hart

Borgh·ese (röm. Adelsgeschlecht) *Borghese*

Borgia (spanisches, nach Italien übergesiedeltes Adelsgeschlecht)

Bor·is m

Borrom·äus m

B·otho m → Bodo

Bosch, Carl (dt. Erfinder; 1909: Stickstoffgewinnung aus der Luft)

Bottic·elli, Sandro m (ital. Maler, 1447–1510)

Bourbon [bur'bɔ̃], der Bourbone [-bonə] m *Bourbon*

Br·ahe, Tycho (dän. Astronom, 1546–1601)

Br·ahma n (später m) *Brahma, Brama*

Brahms m (dt. Komponist, 1833–1897)

Bram·ante m (ital. Architekt u. Maler, 1444–1514) *Bramante*

Braun, Wernher Frhr. v. (dt.-amerik. Raketenkonstrukteur, *1912)

Brecht, Bert(hold) (dt. Dramatiker, 1898–1956)

Brehm, Alfred (dt. Zoologe, 1829–1884)

Brent·ano, Clemens (dt. Dichter, 1778–1842)

Brig·itta, Brig·itte f *Bridget, Brigit, Bride, Biddy* **Br·ita** ⟨norw.⟩ weibl. Vorname

Britten, Benjamin (engl. Komponist, *1913)

Brock|haus dt. Verlegerfamilie

Bruch, Max (dt. Komponist, 1838–1920)

Br·uckner, Anton (österr. Komponist, 1824–1896)

Brueghel ['brœyγəl] Pieter ~ d. Ä. (Bauern~) (holländ. Maler, um 1525–1569)

Br·unhild, Br·ünhild, Brunh·ilde f *Brunehild(e)*; **Brünh·ilde,** Gestalt in R. Wagners Musikdrama „Siegfried"

Br·uno m *Bruno*

B·udden|brooks (Fn), Roman v. Th. Mann

B·uddha m *Buddha*

Buonap·arte m → Bonaparte

B·urk|hard m; **B·urck|hardt,** Jacob (schweizer. Kultur- u. Kunsthistoriker, 1818–1897)

Burne-J·ones, Sir Edward (engl. Maler, 1833–1898)

Busch, Wilhelm ~ (humorist. dt. Dichter u. Zeichner, 1832–1908)

Bus·oni, Feruccio (ital. Klaviervirtuose u. Komponist, 1866–1924)

Buxteh·ude (dt. Komponist, 1637–1707)

C

Cäc·ilia, Cäc·ilie f *Caecilia, Cecilia, Cecily, Cicily, Sisely, Cicely*; [dim] *Ciss(y), Cis, Sis*; die heilige (od. Sankt, St.) ~ *Saint Cecilia*

C·alderón m (span. Dichter, 1600-1681) *Calderon*

Calv·in m (schweizer. Reformator, 1509–1564) *Calvin*

Capul·et(ti) pl *the Capulets* (Familie in Shakespeares „Romeo u. Julia")

C·arlos ⟨span, portug⟩ → Karl

C·armen f ⟨span⟩

C·arol m ⟨rumän⟩ → Karl

C·arolsfeld, Schnorr v. (Wiener Maler, 1795–1872)

Cart·esius m → Descartes

Casan·ova m (Abenteurer, 1725–1798)

C·äsar, Cajus Julius ~ m (röm. Feldherr u. Staatsmann, 100–44 v. Chr.) *Caius Julius Caesar*

Cec·ilie f → Cäc·ilie

C·eres f ⟨myth⟩ *Ceres*

Cerv·antes m (span. Schriftsteller, 1547–1616)

Céz·anne [se'zan], Paul (fr. Maler, 1839–1906)

Chag·all, Marc (⟨russ-frz⟩ Maler u. Graphiker [in Paris], *1887)

Chamisso, Adalbert v. ~ (dt. Dichter, 1781–1838)

Charles I. von England 1600 (1625)–1649; ~ II. v. Engld. 1630 (1660)–1685

Charl·otte f *Charlotte*; → Lotte

Char·ybdis f ⟨ant myth⟩ → Skylla S. 1121, Charybdis S. 276

Chefren, Pharao ⟨Eg ant⟩ *Khafre*

Cheops, Pharao ⟨Eg ant⟩ *Khufu*

Ch·ilde|rich m *Childeric*

Chilpe|rich m *Chilperic*

Chl·od|wig [kl-] m

Chnum (Eg rel) *Khnum*

Chodowiecki [kɔdɔvi'etski] m (dt. Kupferstecher u. Maler, 1726–1801)

Chopin [ʃɔ'pɛ̃] m (poln.-fr. Komponist, 1810–1849)

Chr·iem|hild [kr-] f → Kriemhild

Chr·ista f **Chr·istel 1.** ([dim] v. Christian) [m] *Kit, Christie* **2.** [dim] Christiane, Christine [f] *Chrissie, Chrissy, Xina* **Christ·offel, Christ·öffel, Christ·ophil** m *Kester, Kit* **Chr·istoph** [kr-] m *Christopher* **Chr·istus** m (*Jesus*) *Christ*

Chrys·ost·omus m *Chrysostom*

C·icero m (röm. Staatsmann, Redner u. Schriftsteller, 106–43 v. Chr.) *Cicero*

C·illi, C·illy [ts-] f ([dim] v. Cäcilie) *Ciss(y), Cis, Sis*

Claudel [klo'del], Paul (fr. Dichter, 1868–1955)

Cl·audia [kl-] f → Klaudia

Cl·audius m → Klaudius; Matthias ~ (dt. Dichter, 1740–1815)

Clav·igo m Titelheld in Goethes Trauerspiel

Cölest·in [ts-] m *Celestin(e)*

Cölest·ine f *Celestine*

Col·onna [k-] (röm. Adelsfamilie)

Col·umbus → Kolumbus

C·on|rad m → Kon|rad

C·onstable, John (engl. Maler, 1776–1837)

Const·antius m → Konstantius

Cook, James ['dʒeimz 'kuk], engl. Entdecker von Australien u. Neuseeland: 1768 ff.

Cooper ['ku:pə], Samuel (engl. Maler, 1609–1672)

Corbusier, Le ['lə kɔrby'zie:] (fr. Architekt, 1887–1965)

Cor·inth, Lovis ['lɔvis kɔ'rint] (dt. Maler, 1858–1925)

Corneille m (fr. Dramatiker, 1606–1684)

Corn·elia, Corn·elie f *Cornelia*

Corn·elius m *Cornelius*

Corot, Camille [ka'mil ko'rɔ] (fr. Maler, 1796–1875)

Corr·egio m (ital. Maler, 1494–1534) *Corregio*

C·ortez, Fernando (Eroberer Mexikos 1517, 1485–1547)

C·osima f | **C·osimo** m

Cr·anach (deutsche Maler [pl])

Cresc·entia f; **Cresc·entius** m → Kr. **Cr·escenz** m & f → Kreszenz

Cromwell, Oliver ['ɔlivə 'krɔmwel], Protektor der engl. Republik 1599–1658)

Curie [ky'ri:], Marie (poln.-fr. Chemikerin, entdeckte radioaktive Elemente, 1867–1934)

C·ybele [ts-] f ⟨myth⟩ *Cybele*

Cypri·anus m

Cyr·ill m *Cyril* → Kyrill

C·yrus m *Cyrus*

D

D·ädalus m ⟨myth⟩ *Daedalus, Dedalus*

D·ag|mar f

D·ago|bert m *Dagobert*

Daguerre [da'gɛ:r], Louis (fr. Erfinder: 1837 ⟨phot⟩ ~otyp·ie)

Daimler, Gott|lieb (dt. Erfinder: 1885 Vergasermotor [Benzin])

D·aniel m *Daniel,* [dim] *Dan, Danny,* ⟨schott⟩ *Dann(ie)*

D·ank|mar m

D·ank|wart, -rd m

d'Annunzio → Annunzio

D·ante Alighieri (ital. Dichter, 1265–1321) *Dante*

d'Arc, Jeanne f → Johanna

Dar·ius (pers. Könige)

Darwin, Charles [tʃɑ:lz 'dɑ:win] (engl. Biologe, 1809–1882)

Daumier [do:m'je:], Honoré (fr. Maler u. Karikaturist, 1810–1879)

D·avid m *David,* [dim] *Davy*

Dawes [dɔ:z] m (amerik. Politiker, 1865–1951)

Debussy, Claude (fr. Komponist, 1862–1918)

D·egen|hard, D·ein|hart m

D·emeter f ⟨myth⟩ *Demeter*

Dem·etrios, Dem·etrius m; „~" Dramenfragment v. Schiller, Drama v. F. Hebbel

Dem·osthenes m (griech. Redner, 383–322 v. Chr.)

Deod·at(us) m *Deodate*

Descartes, René (fr. Philosoph, 1596–1650) *Descartes, Cartesius*

D·essauer m; der alte ~ (General Friedrichs des Gr.) *Leopold I., Prince of Anhalt-Dessau* (1676–1747)

D·et|lef, D·et|lev m

Di·ana f ⟨myth⟩ *Diana*

Diaz, Bartholomeo (portug. Seefahrer), Entdecker des Kaps der Guten Hoffnung
Dider·ot m (fr. Schriftsteller, 1713–1784) *Diderot*
D·ido f (sagenhafte Gründerin Karthagos) *Dido*
Diesel, Rudolf (dt. Erfinder: 1892 ~motor)
D·iet|bert m *Cuthbert* **D·ieter, D·iet|her** m **D·iet|leib** m → Det|lef **Diet|l·inde** f **D·iet|mar** m **D·iet|rich** m **1.** (als Vorname) *Derrick* **2.** ⟨hist⟩ *Theodoric(h)*, ~ v. Bern *Theodoric of Verona*
D·ike f ⟨myth⟩ *Dice*
Dim·itri m ⟨russ⟩ *Dimitri, Demetrius*
Di·ogenes m (griech. Philosoph, 404–323 v. Chr.) *Diogenes*
Diokleti·an(us) m (röm. Kaiser, 245–313 n. Chr.) *Diocletian(us)*
Dion·ys, Dion·ysios, Dion·ysius m *Dionys(ius), Dennis*; **Dion·yschen** n *Den(n)is*; **Dion·ysia** f *Dionysia*, auch *Denisot* Fr; **Di·onysos, Dion·ysos** m ⟨myth⟩ *Dionysus, Bacchus*
Dirk m
Dobson, William (engl. Maler, 1610–1646)
Dol·ores f
D·ominik m; **Dom·inika** f *Dominica*; **Dom·inikus** m *Dominic*; der heilige (od. Sankt) ~ *Saint Dominic* od. *Domingo de Gusman*
Domiti·an(us) m (röm. Kaiser, 51–96 n. Chr.) *Dominitianus*
D·onar m ⟨myth⟩ *Thor*
Don·atus m *Donatus*
Don Juan m ⟨span⟩ → Juan
Don Quich·otte, Don Quix·ote → Quichotte
D·ora f ([dim] v. Dorothea, Theodora) *Dora*; **D·orchen** n (weibl. Vn., [dim] v. Dora) *Doll, Dot, Dolly*
D·oris 1. ⟨myth⟩ *Doris* **2.** (Vorname) *Dorinda*
D·orle n (weibl. Vn.)
Doroth·ea f *Dorothea, Dorothy*; → Hermann
× **D·örte** f ([dim] v. Dorothea)
Dostoj·ewski m (russ. Schriftsteller, 1821–1881); *Dostoevsky*
Drais [drɛ], Karl v. (dt. Erfinder: 1813 ~ine [drɛ'zi:nə] Laufmaschine, Fahrrad)
Droste-Hülshoff, Annette v. (dt. Dichterin, 1797–1848)
Dsch·ingis Chan m (mongol. Eroberer, 1155–1227) *Tenghis* (od *Genghis*) *Khan*
D·ürer (dt. Maler u. Graphiker) (1471 bis 1528)
D·ürten f ([dim] v. Dorothea)
Dvořák, Anton (tschech. Komponist, 1841–1904)
Dyck [*daik*] m; van ~ (niederl. Maler, 1599–1641)

E

·Ebba f; **·Ebbo** m
·Eb|el(ing) m → Eber|hard
·Eber|hard m *Everard*; ~ der Greiner *E. the Quareller*; ~ der Rauschebart *E. the Rushbeard* (*Count of Würt(t)emberg*, †1392)
Eber|hard·ine f *Everardine*
·Eb|ert m → Eber|hard; Friedrich Ebert (Reichskanzler, sodann Reichspräsident der Weimarer Republik [1871–1925])
·Echnaton ⟨Eg ant⟩ (= Amenophis IV.) *Akhenaton*
·Eck|ard, ·Eck|art m → Ekke|hard; **·Eck|bert** m; **·Eck(e)hard, ·Eck(e)hart, Ekke|hart, Eckart** m; der getreue ~: Gefolgsmann Dietrichs v. Bern; ⟨a.⟩ wohlgesinnter Berggeist
·Ecker|mann (Goethes Sekretär, 1792–1854)
·Ede, ·Edi m ([dim] v. Eduard, Edmund) *Ned, Teddy, Ed(dy)*
·Edel|gard, ·Edel|trud f
·Ed|gar m *Edgar*
·Edith, Ed·itha f *Edith(a)*
·Ed|mund m *Edmund*, [dim] *Ed, Ned(dy), Mun*
Ed|m·unda f *Edmunda*
·Ed|uard m *Edward*, [dim] *Ed(dy), Ned(dy), Ted(dy)*
·Ed|win m *Edwin*
·Eg|bert m *Egbert*
Eg·idius m → Ägidius
·Egin|hard m *Eginhard*
·Egmont m Vorkämpfer der Freiheit Flanderns (1522–68) Titelheld v. Goethes Drama
·Egon m
·Eichen|dorff, Joseph von (dt. Dichter, 1788–1857)
Ein|hard m → Egin|hard
·Ein|stein, Albert (dt. Physiker, (1879–1955)
·Eitel m
Elag·abal m ⟨myth⟩
El·ektra f ⟨myth⟩ *Electra*; „~" Oper v. Rich. Strauss nach H. v. Hofmannsthal
Eleon·ore f *Leonora, Eleanor(a), El(l)inor*
Elfr·iede f
·Elga, 6 Szenen v. G. Hauptmann
El·ia(s) m *Elias, Elijah*
El·isa, El·ise f *Eliza*; **El·isabeth** f *Elisabeth, Elizabeth*, [dim] *Bess(y), Bet(ty), Betsy, Elsie, Liz(zy), Lizzie, Lisabel, Libby*; E. I. von England (1533–1603) E. II. v. England (seit 1952)
Eg·idius m → Ägidius
·Elke f
·Ella, ·Ellen, ·Elli, ·Elly f ([dim] v. Helena, Leonore) *Ella, Ellen, Elly, Lelly, Ellenor, Ellinor*
Elm·ira f
·Elsa, ·Else f ([dim] v. Elisabeth) *Ailsie, Alice*; Elsa von Brabant, Gestalt in R. Wagners „Lohengrin"; **·Elsabe** f; **·Elsbeth** f *Elspeth, Elspith*; abgeleitete Formen: *Elspet, Elspa, Eppie, Eps*; **·Elschen** n (weibl. Vn., [dim] v. Elisabeth) *Elise*, ⟨schott⟩ *Elsie*
Elv·ira, Elv·ire f *Elvira*
Em·anuel m → Emmanuel; „Der Narr in Christo ~ Quint" Roman v. G. Hauptmann
·Emil m *Emilius, Emelius*
Em·ilia, Em·ilie f *Emilia, Emily*; „~ Galotti" Drama v. Lessing
·Emma f *Emma*; [dim] *Em (-mie)*
Emm·anuel m *Emmanuel*
Em(m)el·ine f *Em(m)eline*
Emmerich m *Em(m)ery, Emory, Emmerick, Merick*
·Emmi f *Emmie, Emmy*
·Enak m ⟨bib⟩ *Anak*
·Engel|bert m; ~ Humperdinck → Hänsel; **·Engel|brecht** m; **·Engel|hard** m
Epamin·ondas m (theban. Feldherr u. Staatsmann, 4. Jh. v. Chr.)
Epik·ur m (griech. Philosoph, 341–270 v. Chr.) *Epicurus*; → S. 414
Er·asmus 1. von Rotterdam (Humanist, 1467 od. 69–1536) **2.** männl. Vn. *Erasmus*
·Erd|mann m; **Erd|m·ute** f
·Er|hard m
·Erich m *Eric*; **·Erika** f
·Erman|rich m (König der Ostgoten, gest. 375 n. Chr.)
·Ermelind (in der Tierfabel Gemahlin Reineckes) *Vixen*
·Ermin m → Irmin
·Erna f; **Ernest·ine** f *Ernestine*; **Ernst** m *Ernest*; Max ~ (surrealist. dt. Maler, *1891)
·Eros m ⟨myth⟩ *Eros, Cupid, Amor, Love, the god of love*
·Er|win m; ~ von Steinbach (dt. Baumeister † 1318), entwarf Westfassade, gilt mit seinen Söhnen als Erbauer des Straßburger Münsters
Esmer·alda f; Gestalt in V. Hugos „Notre Dame de Paris"
·Esra m *Ezra*
·Este (ital. Dynastie)
·Esther f ⟨bib⟩ *Esther, Hester*
·Ethel|mar(us) m *Elmar*
·Ethel|ried m *Audrey*
·Etzel m → Attila
·Eugen, Eug·enius m *Eugene, Eugenius*; Prinz **Eugen,** der edle Ritter der Türkenkriege (1663–1736); **Eug·enie** f *Eugenie, Eugenia*
Eukl·id m (griech. Mathematiker um 300 v. Chr.) *Euclid*
·Eulen|spiegel, Till m (Gestalt der dt. Volkssage)
Euph·emia f
Eur·ipides m (griech. Tragiker, 5. Jh. v. Chr.) *Euripides*
Eury·anthe, Oper v. K. M. v. Weber
Euryd·ike → Orpheus
Eu·sebius m *Eusebius*
Eust·achius, Eust·asius m *Eustace*; → Stachus
·Eva [*v* & *f*] f *Eve, Eva*; **·Evchen** n (weibl. Vn., [dim] v. Eva) *Evy*; **Evel·ine** f
E|wald m
Eyck [aik], Jan van (flandrischer Maler, um 1390–1441)
Ez·echiel m ⟨bib⟩ *Ezekiel*

F

F·abian m *Fabian*
F·anni, F·anny f *Fanny, Fannikin*
Faust m *Faustus* (Fn.) & Gestalt des Volksbuches (1587), u. der Dramen *Marlowes*, Lessings u. Goethes u. des Puppenspiels → Margarete, Gretchen
Felici·an m *Felician*; **Fel·icitas, Fel·izitas** f *Felicity*; **F·elix** m *Felix*
F·enriswolf ⟨myth⟩ *wolf Fenris*
F·eodor m ⟨russ⟩ *Feodor, Fedor* → Theodor; **Feod·osia** f ⟨russ⟩ *Feodosia* → Theodosia
F·erdinand m *Ferdinand, Fernand*; **Ferdin·ande, Ferdinand·ine** *Fernandine*
Feuer|bach, Anselm (dt. Maler, 1829–1880)
F·ichte m (dt. Philosoph, 1762–1814)
Fid·elio (Gestalt in Beethovens *Fidelio*); → Leonore
Fid·elis m *Fidelis*
F·iekchen n (weibl. Vn.) [dim] v. Sophie *Sophy*
Figaros Hochzeit Oper v. Mozart nach Beaumarchais' Lustspiel „*Le mariage de Figaro*"
Filchner, Wilhelm (dt. Entdecker; Osttibet: 1903; Zentralasien-Expedition: 1926ff.)
Fl·ora f *Flora*
Flaubert m (fr. Dichter, 1821 bis 1880)
Fl·orens, Flor·entius m *Florence*; **Flor·entia, Florent·ine** f *Florence*, [dim] *Florry, Florrie*
Fl·orestan (Gestalt aus Beethovens *Fidelio*)
Fl·orian m *Florian*; „~ Geyer" Drama v. G. Hauptmann
Font·ane (dt.-hugenottischer Dichter u. Schriftsteller, 1819 bis 98)
Fortun·at m *Fortunatus*
Frank m → Franz
Frank|lin, Benjamin (amerikanischer Staatsmann)
Franz m *Francis, Frank*
Fr·änzchen n **1.** ([dim] v. Franziska) *Fanny, Fannikin* **2.** ([dim] v. Franz) *Francie, Frank*; **Franz·iska** f *Frances, Fanny*; Zofe in Lessings „Minna v. Barnhelm"; **Franz·iskus** m **1.** → Franz **2.** ~ v. Assisi, *Francis of Assisi*; *St. Francis*
Franz Joseph I. (österr. Kaiser u. König, 1830–1916)
Fr·eia f → Freyja; **Freir** m → Freyr; **Fr·eyja, Freya** f ⟨myth⟩ *Freya*; **Freyr** m ⟨myth⟩ *Frey*; **Fr·icka** f Freyja
Freud, Sigmund (österr.-jüd. Nervenarzt, → Psychoanalyse)
Fr·idolin, Fr·iedolin m
Fr·ida, Fr·ieda f *Frederica*
Fried m → Friedel
Fr·ied|bert, Fr·iede|bert m
Fr·iedchen n **1.** ([dim] v. Friederike, Frida) *Freddy* **2.** ([dim] v. Gottfried) *Jeff(ie), little Geoffrey*; **Friede|g·und(e)** f; **Fr·iedel 1.** m ([dim] v. Friedrich) *Fred (-dy)* **2.** f → Friedchen 1.; **Fr·iede|mann** m; ~ Bach (dt. Komponist) J. S. ~s Sohn; **Fr·iede|rich** m → Friedrich; **Friede|r·ike** f *Frederica*; ~ Brion: Goethes Freundin in Sesenheim bei Straßburg; **Fr·ied|land,** Herzog v. ~, der ~er *Wallenstein, Duke of Friedland*; **Fr·ied|rich** m *Frederick, Frederic*; Kaiser ~ I. (Barbarossa = Rotbart, 1122–1190); ~ II., d. Gr., König v. Preußen (1712–1786); Caspar David ~ (dt. Maler, 1774–1840)
Fr·igga f
Fr·ithjof m
Fritz m ([dim] v. Friedrich) *Fred, Freddy*; der alte ~ (Friedrich II. v. Preußen) *Old Fred, Frederick the Great*
Fr·itzchen n **1.** ([dim] v. Fritz) *Freddy* **2.** ([dim] v. Friederike) *Freddie*
Fr·omm|hold m
F·ürchte|gott m
Furt|wängler, Wilhelm (dt. ⟨mus⟩ Dirigent, 1886–1954)
Füssli, J. H. (schweizer. Maler, 1741–1825)

G

G·äa f ⟨myth⟩ *Gaea, Ge, the (goddess) Earth*
Gabels|berger, F. X. (dt. Erfinder: 1834 Stenographie)
G·abriel m *Gabriel*, [dim] *Gabe, Gaby*; **Gabri·ele** f, ([dim] G·aby) *Gabriella*
Gains|borough ['geinzbrɔ], Thomas (⟨engl⟩ Maler, 1727 bis 1788)
Gal·en(us) m (röm. Arzt im 2. Jh. n. Chr.) *Galenus*
Galil·ei m (ital. Physiker u. Astronom, 1564–1642)
G·ama, Vasco da, m (portug. Entdecker, 1469–1524)
Gambr·inus (sagenhafter Erfinder des [bayrischen!] Biers) *Gambrinus*
Gari|b·aldi m (ital. Freiheitsheld, 1807–1882) *Garibaldi*
Gauguin [go:'gɛ̃], Paul (fr. Maler, 1848–1903)
Gauß m (dt. Mathematiker u. Physiker, 1777–1855)
G·autama, G·otama; Buddha
G·eb|hard m
Geibel, Emanuel (dt. Dichter, 1815–1884)
Genov·efa, Genov·eva f *Genevieve*; „~" Drama v. F. Hebbel
G·eorg, Ge·org m *George* **~ine** f *Georgina, Georgiana*
Gerald·ine f *Geraldine*
G·er|bert m *Gerbert*
Gerd, Gert m ([dim] v. Gerhard) *Gerry*; **G·erda** f; **G·erhart** m *Gerard, Gerald*; **G·erhild** f; **G·eri|cke, G·er|ke** m
G·er|not (König Gunthers Bruder) → Gunther; **G·ero**; **G·er|old** m *Gerald*; **Gert** m → Gerd; **G·erti** f ([dim] v. Gertrud u. Koseform v. Gert) *Gerty*; **G·er|traud, G·er|trud, Gertr·ude** f *Gertrude*
Ger|v·asius m *Gervas(e), Jarvis, Jarvy*
Ger|v·inus, G·er|win m
Gide [ʒi:d], André (fr. Dichter, 1869–1951)
G·iere|mund (in der Tierfabel Gemahlin des Wolfs) *Erswin*
Gieseking, Walter (dt. Pianist, 1895–1956)
G·il|bert m *Gilbert*
G·is|bert; **G·isela** f (⟨fam⟩ Gila) *Gisela*; **G·isel|bert** m; **G·isel|her** m; ⟨Lit⟩ König Gunthers Bruder, → Gunther; **Gisl·inde** f
Giuli·etta [dʒuli'eta], Gestalt in Offenbachs Oper „Hoffmanns Erzählungen" nach E. Th. A. Hoffmann
Gleim (⟨Lit⟩ Anakreontiker) → Anakreon, Hagedorn
Gluck, Christoph W., Ritter von (dt. Opernkomponist, 1714 bis 87)
Gn·eisen|au m (preuß. Generalfeldmarschall, 1760–1831)
G·ödel; **G·od|win** m
G·oethe, Johann Wolfgang m (dt. Dichter, 1749–1832) *John Wolfgang Goethe*
Gogh [gɔx], Vincent van (holländ. Maler, 1853–1890)
Gogol, Nikolai (⟨russ⟩ Schriftsteller, 1809–1852)
Görg, G·örge m ([dim] v. Georg) *George*
Gorki, Maxim (⟨russ⟩ Schriftsteller, 1868–1936)
G·ott|fried m *Godfrey, Geoffrey, Geffry, Jeffrey*; ~ v. Straßburg, mhd. Dichter; → Keller
G·ott|hard m *God(d)ard*; **–|helf** m; **–|hold** m *Theophilus* **–|lieb** m *Theophilus* **–|sched,** J. Chr. (dt. Dichter, 1700–1766) **–|wald** m **–|win** m *Godwin*
Götz m *Gœtz* (= *Godfrey*); ~ v. Berlichingen mit der eisernen Hand *Gœtz of Berlichingen, Gœtz of the Iron Hand* (Drama v. Goethe)
G·oya, Francisco de (span. Maler, 1746–1828)
Gr·acchen ['graxən] die ~: Tiberius u. Gajus Gracchus (römische Volkstribunen) *the Gracchi*
Gr·atia f *Grace*
Gr·eco, El („der Grieche") Maler in Spanien (1541–1614)
Gr·egor, Greg·or m *Gregory*; → S. 609
Gr·etchen n (weibl. Vn., [dim] v. Grete) *Margaret, Margary, Margery, Marjorie, Margie, Maggie, Maggy, Mag, Madge, Madgy, Meg*; * *Mer, Peggy, Peg, Padge, Gritty*; ⟨Lit⟩ weibl. Hauptgestalt in Goethes „Faust" → Margarete; **Gr·ete** f ([dim] v. Margarete) *Margaret, Margary, Mar-*

gery, *Marjorie*; **Gr·etel** n → Gretchen

Grieg, Edvard (norweg. Komponist, 1843–1907)

Gr·illparzer m (österr. Dichter, 1791–1872

Grimm (Jakob G. 1785 bis 1863, Wilhelm G. 1786–1859, Germanisten); die Gebrüder ~ *the brothers Grimm*

Gris·eldis f *Griselda*, „Griselda" Drama v. G. Hauptmann; **Gris|h·ilde** f *Grissel*

Gr·öfaz („größter Feldherr aller Zeiten") Adolf Hitler

Gr·üne|wald, Matthias dt. Maler namens Mathis Gothardt(?), wirkte 1503–1529

G·ud|run f *Gudrun*

G·udula f

Gu·ido m *Guy*, *Guido*; ~ Reni (ital. Maler, 1575–1642) *Guido Reni*

G·um|precht m; **G·und|olf** m; **G·undula** f; **G·unt|her, G·ünter, G·ünt|her** m *Gunther*; Gunther: König im Nibelungenlied; **G·unt|ram** m

G·ussy f ([dim] v. Auguste) *Gussy*, *Gussie*

G·u|stav m *Gustavus*; ~ Adolf (König v. Schweden, 1594–1632) *Gustavus Adolfus*

G·ustchen n, **G·uste, G·ustel** f, **G·ustelchen** n ([dim] v. Auguste) *Gus(sie)*, *Gussy*

G·uten|berg m (Johann Gensfleisch, Erfinder des Buchdrucks, 1400–1467)

H

H·abs|burg, das Haus *the Hapsburg* (od. *Habsburg*) *dynasty*, *the Hapsburgs* pl; **H·absburger** m, **~in** f *one of the Hapsburg family* od. *dynasty*

H·adrian m *Hadrian(us)*, *Adrian*

†**H·ad|wig** → Hed|wig

Haeckel, Ernst (dt. Zoologe, 1834–1919)

H·age|dorn (⟨Lit⟩ Anakreontiker); **H·age|mann** m; **H·agen** m

Hahn, Otto (dt. Chemiker, Uranforscher, 1879–1968)

Hals, Frans (holländ. Maler, um 1580–1666)

H·ändel m (dt. Komponist, 1685–1759) *Handel*

H·anna, H·anne f ([dim] v. Johanna) *Joan*, *Jane*; *Hannah*, *Ann*, *Anne*; **H·annchen** n (weibl. Vn., [dim] v. Hanna) *Jenny*, *Jennet*; ˣ**H·annele** n (weibl. Vn. [dim] v. Hanna) → vor.; „~s Himmelfahrt" v. G. Hauptmann; **H·annes** m → Hans; **H·anni** f ([dim] v. Johanna); **Hans** m *Jack*, *John*, *Johnny* → S. 636; „~ Heiling" (Sohn der Erdgeisterkönigin) Oper v. Marschner; **H·änschen** n *Johnny*, *Jack*, *Jack(e)y*, *Jockey*; **H·änsel** [m & n] [dim v. Hans]; „~ u. Gretel" Oper v. Engelbert Humperdinck

H·ar|ald m *Harold* (vgl. Herold)

H·arden|berg 1. Karl August v. ~ (preuß. Staatsmann 1750 bis 1822) **2.** Friedrich v. ~ → Novalis

H·arro m

H·arry m ⟨engl⟩ *Harry* (Koseform v. Henry)

H·art|mann m; ~ v. Aue mhd. Dichter; → Heinrich; **H·art|mut** m; **H·art|wig** m

H·aupt|mann, Gerhart [m] (dt. Dichter, 1862–1946)

Haydn m (österr. Komponist, 1732–1809) *Haydn*

H·ebbel m (dt. Dichter, 1813 bis 1863)

Heckel, Erich (dt. Maler u. Graphiker, 1883–1970)

H·eda, H·ede f

H·edin m (schwed. Asienforscher, 1865–1952

H·ed|wig f *Hedwig*, *Edwiga*, *Edniga*

H·egel m (dt. Philosoph, 1770 bis 1831) *Hegel*

Heid|egger, Martin (dt. Philosoph, * 1883)

H·eiko | H·eimo m

H·eine, Heinrich ~ (dt. Dichter, 1797–1856); **H·einer** m → **H·ein|rich** m *Henry*, *Harry*; ~ I. v. England (1068–1135) *Henry the First*, *Henry Beauclerk*; ~ der Finkler (876–936) *Henry the Fowler*; ~ der Löwe (1129 bis 1195); „Der arme ~", Idylle v. H. v. Aue, Drama v. G. Hauptmann; „Der grüne ~" Roman v. G. Keller; **Heinz** m ([dim] v. Heinrich) *Harry*, *Hal*

Hel·ene f *Helena*; „Die fromme ~" v. Wilh. Busch

H·elga f, **H·el|gard** f.

H·elios m ⟨myth⟩ *Helios*, *the Sungod*, *at a later time identified with Phœbus* (*Apollo*)

H·ella f

H·elma f

H·elm|olt m, [gen]: **He·lm|holtz** m

Helm|trud f

H·el|mut(h) m *Helmut(h)*

Helo·ise f *Heloisa*

H·en|lein, Peter (dt. Erfinder: 1510 Taschenuhr)

ˣ**Henner** m → Heiner; **Hen|n|ing** m → Heiner; (in der Tierfabel: der Hahn *Chanticleer*)

Henny f ⟨engl⟩ ([dim] v. *Henrietta*) *Henny*

H·enoch m *Enoch*

Henri·ette, †**Henr·ike** f *Henrietta*, *Harriet*, *Henriet*, *Harriot*, *Henny*

H·en|rik m → Heinrich

H·enschel, „Fuhrmann ~" Drama v. G. Hauptmann

H·era, Here f ⟨myth⟩ *Hera*, *Here*, *Juno*; **H·erakles** m ⟨myth⟩ (= Herkules) *Heracles*, *Hercules*; **Herakl·it** m (griech. Philosoph, um 500 v. Chr.) *Heraclitus*

H·er|bert, H·eri|bert m *Herbert*, *Heribert*

H·erder, J. G., m (dt. Schriftsteller, 1744–1803)

H·erkules m ⟨myth⟩ *Hercules*, *Heracles*, auch *Alcides*

H·er|mann m *Herman(n)*; ~ der Cherusker *Arminius* → d.; Hermann, Gestalt in Goethes Dichtung „~ u. Dorothea"; → ⟨a.⟩ Thusnelda

H·ermes m ⟨Gr myth⟩ *Hermes*, bei den Römern *Mercury*

Herm·ine f *Hermina*

Hermi·one f *Hermione*

H·ero f (sagenhafte Priesterin) *Hero*

Her·odes (jüd. Könige) *Herod*; ~ Agrippa *Herod Agrippa*; „~ u. Mariamne" Drama v. F. Hebbel; **Her·odias** f (Enkel Herodes' des Großen) *Herodias*

Herod·ot m (griech. Geschichtsschreiber, geb. um 500, gest. 424 v. Chr.) *Herodotus*

H·e|rold m

H·erta, H·ertha f *Hertha*

Hertz, Heinrich (dt. Physiker, 1857–1894)

H·er|ward m, **H·er|wig** m

Hes·ekiel [-iəl] ⟨bib⟩ *Ezekiel* → Ezechiel

Hesi·od, Hesi·odus m (griech. Dichter, 8. Jh. v. Chr.) *Hesiod*

Hesse, Hermann (dt. Dichter, 1877–1962)

Hier·onymus m *Hieronymus*, *Jerome*

ˣ**H·iesel** [ˈhiəzl] (süddeutsch [dim] v. Matthias) *Mat*

Hil·arius m *Hilary*

H·ilde, H·ilde|gard f *Hilda*, *Hildegarde*; **H·ilde|brand** m; **H·ilde|burg** f; **Hilde|g·unde** f

H·illiard, Nicholas (engl. Maler, um 1547–1619)

H·il|mar m

H·il|trud f

H·indemith (dt. Komponist, 1895–1963) → Mathis der Maler

H·inden|burg m (Paul v. Benecken|dorff u. v. Hindenburg, dt. Gen.-Feldmarschall; Reichspräsident, 1847–1934) *Hindenburg*

H·in|rich m niederd. → Hein|rich

H·iob m ⟨bib⟩ *Job*

Hipp·okrates m (Arzt, 460 bis 377 v. Chr.) *Hippocrates*

H·iskia m ⟨bib⟩ *Hezekiah*

H·itler, Adolf; ⟨nazi⟩ (1889 bis 1945) → Gröfaz

Hj·al|mar m

H·öder, H·ödur m ⟨myth⟩ *Höder*

H·odler, Ferdinand (schweizer. Maler, 1853–1918)

H·ofer m (Andreas ~, Tiroler Freiheitskämpfer, 1767 bis 1810)

Hoffmann, E. Th. A. ~, deutscher Dichter; „~s Erzählungen" Oper v. J. Offenbach

H·of|manns|thal, Hugo v. (österr. Dichter, 1874–1929)

H·ogarth [ˈhóːgɑːθ], William (engl. Maler, 1697–1764)

Hohen|st·aufen, Haus *House of Hohenstaufen* od. *of Suabia* (*Swabia*), *Suabian* (*Swabian*) *dynasty*; die ~ pl *the House of Hohenstaufen*

Hohen|z·ollern, die [pl] *the House of Hohenzollern*

H·olbein (Hans d. Ä. 1460 bis 1524, Hans d. J. 1497–1543, deutsche Maler)

H·ölderlin m (dt. Dichter, 1770–1843)

Hom·er m (griech. Dichter, 9. Jh. v. Chr.) *Homer*

Hon|egger, Arthur (schweizer. Komponist, 1892–1955)

Hor·az m (röm. Dichter, 65 bis 8 v. Chr.) *Horace*

Horst m

Hos·eas m ⟨bib⟩ *Hosea*

Hrab·anus Maurus m (dt. Theolog, 780–856)

H·ubert, Hub·ertus m *Hubert*

H·udson, Henry; Entdecker v. ~fluß u. -bay 1609f.

H·ugo m *Hugh*, †*Hugo*; Victor ~ [y'go:] (fr. Dichter, 1802 bis 1882)

H·ulda f *Hulda(h)*; (Hexe); °*sweetheart*

H·um|bert m *Humbert*

H·um|boldt (Alexander v. ~, 1769–1859, Naturforscher u. Geograph; Wilhelm v. ~, 1767 bis 1835, Gelehrter u. Staatsmann) *Humboldt*

H·um|fried m *Humphrey*, ⟨fam⟩ *Nump*

H·umperdinck → Hänsel

Hüon von Bordeaux Gestalt in K. M. v. Webers „Oberon"

Hus, Huß m (Johann ~, böhm. Reformator, 1369–1415) *Huss*

H·utten (Humanist, 1488 bis 1523) *Hutten*

H·uyghens m (holländ. Mathematiker, Physiker u. Astronom, 1629–1695) *Huyg(h)ens*

Hyazinth m

I

Ibsen (norweg. Dichter, 1828 bis 1906)

·Ida f *Ida*

Ign·atius, ·Ignaz m *Ignatius, Inigo*

·Ilsabe f; **·Ilse** f *Alice, Ailsie, Elsie*, [dim] *Lizzie*; **·Ilsebill** f

·Imma f

Imm·anuel m *Manuel*, → Emmanuel

·Immo m

·Ines f *Inez*

·Inge, ·Ingeborg, ·Ingeburg f

·Ingo m, **·Ingo|mar** m, **·Ing|-raban** m

Ingres, J. A. D. [ɛ̃gr] (fr. Maler; 1780–1867)

·Ingrid f

Innoz·entia f

Inoz·entius, ·Innozenz m *Innocent*

Iphig·enia, Iphig·enie f *Iphigenia*; „Iphig·enie" Drama v. Goethe

Ir·ene f [Gr] („Frieden") *Irene*

·Irma f; **·Irm|gard** f; **·Irm|hild** f; **·Irmin** m ⟨myth⟩; **·Irm|traut, -d** f

·Isa f

·Isaak m *Isaac*, [dim] *Niky*

Isab·ella f *Isabella, Isabel*

Isab·ellchen n (weibl. Vn. [dim] v. Isabella) *Bella, Bell, Tibbie, Tibby, Ib, Nib*

Is·aias m → Jesaias

Isch·ariot m ⟨bib⟩ *Iscariot*

·Isebel f *Jezebel*

·Ise|grim m (Wolf der Tierfabel) *Isegrim*; ⟨fig⟩ (P) *bear*

·Isidor m *Isidore, -rus*; **·Isis** f ⟨myth⟩ *Isis*

·Ismael [-ael] m *Ishmael*

Is·old, Is·olde f *Isolde*; → Tristan

·Ivo m

·Iwan (eigentl. Iw·an, Johann) ⟨russ⟩ *Ivan*

J

Jahn (dt. „Turnvater", 1778 bis 1852)

J·ahve m ⟨hebr⟩ *Jah(veh)*

J·akob m **1.** (Vorname) *James* **2.** (jüd. Patriarch) *Jacob*

Jak·oba f *Jaqueline, Jamesina*; **J·aköbchen** n (m. Vn., [dim] v. Jakob) *little) Jim, Jem, Jimmy, Jemmy*; **Jakob·inchen** n (weibl. Vn., [dim] v. Jakobine) *Jaquet*; **Jakob·ine** f *Jaqueline, Jemima*

Jan m ⟨holl⟩ → Johann

J·anus m ⟨myth⟩ *Janus*

J·aspers, Karl (dt. Philosoph, 1883–1969)

Jawl·ensky, A. v. (⟨russ⟩ Maler, 1864–1941)

Jeh·ova m ⟨hebr⟩ *Jehovah* (*Jah, Jahveh*), *the Eternal*

J·enny f *Jenny*; „Frau ~ Treibel" Roman v. Theodor Fontane

Jerem·ias m **1.** (Vorname) *Jeremias, Jeremy*; [dim] *Jerry* **2.** (Prophet) *Jeremiah*; **Jer·obeam** m ⟨bib⟩ *Jeroboam*; **Jes·aias** m ⟨bib⟩ *Isaiah*, auch *Isias, Esaias, Esay*

J·ettchen n, **J·ette** f [dim] v. Henriette) *Harriet, Har(r)iot, Henrietta, Henny, Hetty, Etta, Netta, Etty, Tiny*

J·oachim 1. (Vorname) *Joachim* **2.** ⟨bib⟩ *Jehoiachin*

Jobst m *Jocelyn*

J·ochen m → Joachim

Jod·oka f *Joyce*

Jod·okus m *Jodocus, Jocelyn*

J·ohann m *John*; **Joh·anna, Joh·anne** f *Johanna, Joan, Jane*; ~ v. Arc *Joan of Arc, Jeanne d'Arc*; die Päpstin ~ *Pope Joan*; **Joh·annes** m *Joannes, John*; der Evangelist ~ *St. John the Evangelist*; ~ der Täufer *St. John the Baptist*

J·onas m ⟨bib⟩ → *Jonah*

J·onathan m (⟨bib⟩ & Vorname *Jonathan*

Jörg m ([dim] v. Georg) *Georgie, George*; **Jörn** m → Jörg

J·osaphat m *Jehoshaphat*

J·osef, J·oseph m *Joseph*; Kaiser ~ ⟨mst⟩ *Joseph II of Austria*; **Jos·efa, Jos·epha, Joseph·ine** f *Josepha, Josephine*; [dim] *Pheny*; **J·osepfchen** n (m. Vn., [dim] v. Joseph) *Joe, Joey*

Jos·ias m ⟨bib⟩ *Josiah*

Jost m *Yost*

J·osua m ⟨bib⟩ *Joshua*

Ju·an [xu'an] m ⟨span⟩ (= Johann), Don ~ *Don Juan* Oper v. Mozart

J·udas m ⟨bib⟩ *Judas*

J·udith f ⟨bib⟩ *Judith*, [dim] *Ju(dy)*; „~" (Drama v. F. Hebbel)

J·ulchen n (weibl. Vn., [dim] v. Julia) *Juliet, July, Gill, Gillet, Jill, Jillet*; **J·ulia, J·ulie** f *Julia, Juliet, July*; Romeo u. ~ *Romeo and Juliet*; **Juli·an, J·ulian** m *Julian, Gill, Jill*; **Juli·ane** f *Juliana, Gillian, Gill, Jillian, Jill*; **J·ulius** m *Julius, Jule, Giles*

J·uno f ⟨myth⟩ *Juno*

J·upiter m ⟨myth⟩ *Jupiter, Jove*, ⟨→ a.⟩ Zeus

J·ür(ge)n m → Jörg

Jupp ⟨rheinisch⟩ Koseform f. Joseph

Just m *Jocelyn*; Gestalt in Lessings „Minna v. Barnhelm"

Justini·an (byzantin. Kaiser) *Justinian, Justinianus*

Just·inus m *Justin, Jocelyn*

J·ustus m *Justus, Justin, Jocelyn*

J·utta f *Jutta*; *Joan, Janet*

Juven·al m (röm. Dichter, etwa 60–140 n. Chr.) *Juvenal*

K

K·admus m ⟨Gr myth⟩ *Cadmus*

K·afka, Franz (böhm.-österr. Schriftsteller, 1883–1924)

K·ain m ⟨bib⟩ *Cain*

K·aiphas m ⟨bib⟩ *Caiphas*

Kall·iope f (Muse) *Calliope*

Kalv·in m → Calvin

Kand·insky, Wassily (⟨russ⟩ Maler, 1866–1944)

Kant, Immanuel (dt. Philosoph, 1724–1804)

Kan·ut m *Canute, Cnut*

K·apetinger m (Angehöriger der 3. fränk. Dynastie) *Capetian*

Karin f

Karl m *Charles*; ~ der Dicke (Kahle, Kühne) *Charles the Fat* (*Bald, Bold*); ~ der Große *Charlemagne* (800–814); **K·arla** f; **K·arlchen** n (m. Vn., [dim] v. Karl) *Charley, Charlie*; **Karl·ine** f → Karoline; **K·arlos,** Don ~, Infant v. Spanien, Drama v. Schiller; **K·arola** f → Karla; **Karol·inchen** n (weibl. Vn., [dim] v. Karoline) *Carie, Cary, Carrie, Carry, Caddie, Caddy*; **Karol·ine** f *Caroline*; **K·arolinger** m (Angehöriger des fränk. Geschlechts) *Caroling(ian)*, *Karling*; **K·arolus** m *Charles*

K·asimir m ⟨poln⟩ *Casimir*

K·aspar, K·asper m *Jasper*; K·asperle → S. 661

Kathar·ina, Kathar·ine f *Catherina, Katherine, Catherine*; ~ II. v. Rußland (1729 bis 1796) *Catherine the Second*; **K·äthchen** n, **K·äthe** f (⟨dim⟩ v. Katharina) *Cate, Katie*; *Katey, Katty, Kitty*; „Käthchen v. Heilbronn" Drama v. Kleist; → Kasperle S. 661; **K·athie** f → Käthchen; **K·athrein, K·athrin** f, → vor

Katil·ina (röm. Verschwörer) *Catiline*

Kat·inka f ⟨poln⟩ *Catinka* ⟨Ir⟩, *Kathleen, Cathlin*

K·eller, Gottfried ~, schweiz. Dichter, → Martin, Heinrich

K·epler m (dt. Astronom, 1571–1630) *Kepler*

K·ersting, Fr. G. (dt. Maler, 1785–1847)

K·ierkegaard [-go:rd] m (dän. Theologe u. Philosoph, 1813 bis 1855)

K·ilian m *Kilian*

Kirchner, E. L. (dt. Maler u. Graphiker, 1880–1938)

Kl·ara f, **Kl·ärchen** n, **Kl·äre** f *Cilara, Clare*; Klärchen: Gestalt in Goethes „Egmont"; **Klar·issa, Klar·isse** f *Clarissa*

Kl·audia f; **Kl·audius** m; **Klaud·ine** f

Klaus m ([dim] v. Nikolaus) *Nick, Nicholas*

Kl·aus|chen, Kl·äus|chen n (m. Vn. [dim] v. Klaus) *little Nicholas, Nick*

Klee, Paul (dt. Maler, 1879 bis 1940)

Kleist, Heinrich v. ~ (dt. Dramatiker, 1777–1811)

Kl·eisthenes m (athenischer Staatsmann, 6. Jh. v. Chr.)

Kl·emens m *Clement*; **Klement·ine** f *Clementine*; **Klement·inchen** n (weibl. Vn., [dim] v. Klementine) *little Clementine, Clemmy*

Kle·opatra f (ägypt. Königin, 66–33 v. Chr.) *Cleopatra*

Kl·ingsor Gestalt in R. Wagners „Parsifal"

Kl·io f (Muse) *Clio*

Kl·op|stock, F. G. (dt. Dichter, 1724–1803)

Klor·inde f *Clorinda*

Klot|h·ilde f

Knut m *Cnut, Canute*

×**K·öbes** m ⟨rheinisch⟩ → Jakob

Koch, J. A. (Tiroler Maler, 1768–1839); **Koch,** Robert (dt. Bakteriologe [Milzbrand, Tuberkulose etc.] 1843 bis 1910)

K·ohl|haas, „Michael ~" Erzählung v. H. v. Kleist

K·okoschka, Oskar (österr. Maler, *1886)

K·olbe, Georg (dt. Bildhauer, 1877–1947)

Kol·umbus, Christoph, m (Entdecker Amerikas: 1492 u. 1498) *Columbus*

Konf·ucius, Konf·uzius m (chines. Philosoph, 551–478 v. Chr.) **Konf·utse** m *Confucius*

K·on|rad m *Conrad*; **K·on|radin** m *Conradin*

Konst·antia f *Constance*; **K·onstantin** (Römische Kaiser) *Constantine*; **Konst·antius** m; **Konst·anze** f *Constance*; [dim] *Connie, Conny*

Kop·ernikus, N. m (Begründer der neueren Astronomie, 1473–1543) *Copernicus*

K·ora f

Kord·elia f *C.*; **K·ordula** f

Korn·elia f *C.*; **Korn·elius** m

K·otzebue 1. August v. ~ (dt. Schriftsteller, 1761–1819) **2.** Otto v. ~ (1787–1846; Entdecker von 399 Südseeinseln: 1815 ff)

Kraft m

Kresz·entia f *Crescentia* **-tius** m *Crescens, Crescentius*; **Kr·eszenz** m & f → Kresz·entius, Kresz·entia

Kr·iem|hild, Kriem|h·ilde f *Kriemhild, Chriemhild*; Gestalt der Nibelungensage: ~s Rache, ⟨a.⟩ Drama v. F. Hebbel

×**Kr·ischan** m → Christian

Kr·ischna m (ind. Gott) *Krishna*

Krisp·in m

Kr·onos m ⟨myth⟩ *Kronos, Saturnus*

Kr·ösus m ⟨ant myth⟩ *Crœsus*

K·undry Gestalt in R. Wagners „Parsifal"

K·uni|bert m; **Kuni|g·unde** f *Cunegund*; **K·uno** m; **Kunz** m ([dim] v. Konrad) *Conrad*

K·upido m ⟨myth⟩ *Cupid*

K·urfürst, der Große ~ (Markgraf von Brandenburg, 1620–1688)

Kurt (m Kurzform [dim] v. Konrad) *Conrad*

Kyr·ill m → a. Cyrill(us)

L

L·adislaus, L·adislaw m *Ladisla(u)s*

L·agerlöf, Selma (schwed. Dichterin, 1858–1940)

L·am|bert(us), L·am|pert, L·am|precht, |b- m *Lambert*

Landseer, Sir Edwin (⟨engl⟩ Maler u. Bildhauer, 1802 bis 1873)

L·anzelot m *Lancelot, Lance*

La·okoon m (sagenhafter trojanischer Apollonpriester) *Laocoon*

La·otse m (chines. Philosoph, geb. 604 v. Chr.)

Lapl·ace, Pierre Simon Marquis de ~ (fr. Physiker, Mathematiker u. Astronom, 1749 bis 1827)

Lät·itia f *Letitia, Lettice, Letty*

L·aura f *Laura*

Laur·entius m *Lawrence, Laurence*; [dim] *Laury, Laurie*

L·awrence ['lɔrəns] **1.** D. H. (⟨engl⟩ Erzähler, 1885–1930) **2.** Sir Thomas ~ (⟨engl⟩ Maler, 1769–1830)

L·azar(us) m *Lazarus*

Lazedem·onier m pl *Lacedæmonians*

L·ea f ⟨ant myth⟩ *Leah*

Le·ander m

L·eb|recht m

Leibl, Wilhelm (dt. Maler, 1844–1900)

L·eibniz, G. W. v., m (dt. Philosoph, 1646–1716)

L·ely, Peter (⟨engl⟩ Maler, 1618–1680)

L·ena f ([dim] v. Magdalene, Helene) *Nellie*

L·enau, Nicolaus ~ (österr. Dichter, 1802–1850)

L·enchen n, **L·ene, L·eni** f **1.** [dim] v. Helene) *Helen, Hely, Nel, Nelly* **2.** [dim] v. Magdalene) *Maud(lin)*

Len·ore f; Titelgestalt e-s Gedichts v. Gottfried August Bürger; → Leonore

×**Lenz** m (südd. v. Lorenz)

L·eo m *Leo*; **Leon|·ardo** m ⟨It⟩ → Leonhard; ~ da Vinci ['vintʃi] (ital. Maler, 1452 bis 1519); **L·eon|hard** m *Leonhard, Len, Lenny*; **Le·onidas** m (König v. Sparta); **Leon·ie L·eonie** f; **Leon·ora, Leon·ore** f *Leonora, Eleanor, Ellen, Nellie, Nora*; Leonore, genannt Fidelio, Gestalt in Beethovens „*Fidelio*"; Leonorenouvertüre v. L. v. Beethoven; **Leont·ine** f

L·eo|pold m *Leopold* → Leut|hold; **Leo|pold·ine** f *Leopoldina*

L·essing, G. E., m (dt. Dichter, 1729–1781)

L·eut|hold m **L·eut|wein** m

L·evin, L·ewin m

Leyhausen, Paul, deutscher Verhaltensforscher, *1916

Li f ([dim] Elisabeth) *Lizzie*

L·iddy f ([dim] v. Lydia) *Lyddy, Liddy, Lyd*

L·ieber|mann, Max (dt. Maler, 1847–1935)

L·ien|hard m *Leonard*

L·ies|chen n (weibl. Vn., [dim] v. Liese) *Lizzy*, ⟨schott⟩ *Lizzie*; *Liz, Liza, Libby*; *Bets(e)y, Betty, Bet, Bess, Bessy*; **L·iese** f ([dim] v. Elisabeth) *Liz, Lizz, Lizzy, Betsy*; **L·ieselotte** f; **L·ili, L·illi, L·ily** f (Kurzform v. Elise) *Lizzie, Lilian, Lil(y)*

L·ilian f *Lilian*

L·ilien|thal, Otto (dt. Erfinder: 1891 Flugzeug)

L·ina, L·ine f ([dim] v. Karoline) *Lina, Carrie*; **L·inchen** n (weibl. Vn., [dim] v. Lina) *Linny, Carry, Carrie*

L·inda f

L·isabeth f, **L·isbeth** f (Elisabeth) *Bets(e)y, Betty*; **Lisch** f

L·isa f *Liza, Lizabel*, ⟨→ a.⟩ Liese; **L·ise** f → Liese; **Lis·ette** f *Bess, Lizzie*

Liszt, Franz v. ~ (ungar. Pianist u. Komponist der „neu-

deutschen Schule", 1811–1886)
Living|stone, David; (⟨engl⟩ Forschungsreisender, Afrikaforscher: 1858f.)
L·ivius m, Titus (röm. Geschichtsschreiber, 59 v. Chr.–17 n. Chr.) *Livius, Livy*
L·izzi f *Lizziy*, ⟨schott⟩ *Lizzie*
L·ohen|grin m → Lot|har & Fr *Garin*; Gestalt der Gralssage, ⟨a. bei⟩ R. Wagner
ˣ**Loisl** m (oberd.) → Alois
L·oki m ⟨myth⟩
L·ola f [dim] v. Charlotte od. Dolores; → Montez
Loll·arden pl *Lollards* || ~-tum [n] *Lollardism*
L·olo f ([dim] v. Lotte) *Lottie*
L·oni f [dim v. Apollonia]
Lope de Vega → Vega
L·orchen n (weibl. Vn.) **1.** ([dim] v. Eleonore) *Nel, Nelly, Nora(h)* **2.** ([dim] v. Laura) *Larry, Lowry*, ⟨fam bes Ir⟩ *Larry*; **L·ore** f (verkürzt aus Leonore) *Nora*, → ⟨a.⟩ Lorchen; **Lore|l·ei, L·ore|lei,** die f *the Lorelei, the Lurlei, the Lurline*
L·orenz m *Lawrence, Laurence*; [dim] *Laury, Lowry*; Konrad ~ (österr. Verhaltensforscher: „Das sogenannte Böse" = "*On Aggression*"; *1903)
L·ortzing, Gust. Albert (dt. Operndichter u. -komponist, 1801–1851)
L·ot|har m *Lothario*
L·ottchen n, **L·otte** f *Lotty*, ⟨schott.⟩ *Lottie*; bisw. *Charley*
L·otte f; Gestalt in Goethes Roman „Werthers Leiden"
Louis m [Fr] *Lewis, Louis*
Lou·ise f → Luise
L·u f Koseform v. **L·ucia** f *Lucie*; **L·ucie, L·ucy, L·uzie** f *Luce*
L·ucifer, L·uzifer m *Lucifer*
Luc·ilie f *Lucilia*
Luc·inde, Luz·inde f *Lucinde*
L·ucius m *Lucius*
L·ude|wig m ⟨fam⟩ → Ludwig, Louis; **Ludm·illa** f; **L·ud|olf** m *Ludolph(us)*; **Ludo|w·ika, Ludo|w·ike** f *Louise, Louisa*, ⟨fam⟩ *Lou, Looey*; **L·ud|wig** m *Louis, Lewis, Ludovic*; ~ der Bayer *Lewis of Bavaria*; **Lud|wi·ga** f *Louisa*; **Lu·is|chen** n (weibl. Vn., [dim] v. Luise) *Lou, Louy, Louie*; **Lu·ise** f *Louise, Louisa*; **L·uit|pold** m *Luitpold*
L·ukas m *Luke, Lucas*; der Evangelist ~, St. ~ *St. Luke the Evangelist*, [dim] *Luky*
Lukr·etia f *Lucretia*
L·ulu; „~" Trilogie von Frank Wedekind
L·una f ⟨myth⟩ *Luna*
Lut·etia f *Lutetia*
L·uther m (dt. Reformator, 1483–1546) *Luther*; als Vn. *Martin ~ King*
Lutz m ⟨fam⟩ → Lud|wig
L·uzie f, *Lucy*; → Lucia
L·ydia f *Lydia*, [dim] *Lyd, Lyddy, Liddy, Luddy*
Lyk·urg, Lyk·urgus m (spartan. Gesetzgeber, 9. Jh. v. Chr.) *Lycurgus*

M

Macchiav·elli m (ital. Staatsmann u. Geschichtsschreiber, 1469–1527) *Machiavel(li)*
M·acke, August (dt. Maler, 1887–1914)
M·agda f *Maddy, Maddie*
Magdal·ena, Magdal·ene f *Magdalene, Magdalen, Madeline, Maudlin*
Magelhaens, Magalhães m (port.-span. Seefahrer, 1811 bis 1882) *Magellan*
M·agnus m (der Große)
M·ahler, Gustav ~ (österr. Komponist, 1860–1911)
Maill·ol [ma'jɔl], Aristide (fr. Bildhauer, 1861–1944)
M·akart, Hans (österr. Maler, 1840–1884)
M·alchen n (weibl. Vn., [dim] v. Amalie) *Amelia*
M·ahomed m → Mohammed
Male·achi m ⟨bib⟩ *Malachi*
M·alte m
Malw·ine f
Manet [ma'nɛ], Edouard [ed'wɑː] (fr. Maler, 1832–1883)
M·an|fred m *Manfred*
M·angold m
Mann, Thomas (dt. Romanschriftsteller, 1875–1955)
M·anuel m
Manz·oni m (ital. Dichter, 1785–1873)
Marc, Franz (dt. Maler, 1880 bis 1916)
Marc·oni m (Erfinder der drahtlosen Telegraphie: 1897
Marées, Hans v. (dt. Maler, 1837–1887)
M·arfa f ⟨russ⟩ → Martha
M·arga f; **Margar·eta, Margar·ete** f *Margaret*, [dim] *Margary, Margery*; „Margar·ete" Oper von Gounod → Gretchen, → Faust; **Margher·ita** f ⟨It⟩; **M·argot, M·argret** f ([dim] v. Margarete)
Mar·ia f (bei Katholiken a. Vn. v. Männern) *Mary, Maria*, →Marie, Mariechen; die heilige Jungfrau ~ *the Holy* (od. *Blessed*) *Virgin, the Virgin Mary, the Madonna*; „~ Magdalene" Drama v. F. Hebbel, „~ Stuart" Drama v. Schiller
Mari|·annchen n (weibl. Vn., [dim] v. Marianne) ⟨schott⟩ *Menie*; **Mari|·anne** f *Marianne, Mary Ann*; **Mar·ie,** ˣ**M·arie** f → Maria; die blutige ~ (Königin v. England, 1516–1558) *Bloody Mary*; **Mar·eichen** n (weibl. Vn., [dim] v. Marie) *little Mary, Poll(y), Moll(y), May*; **Mari·etta** f ⟨It⟩ → Maria; **M·arion** f [Fr]
M·arke, König ~, Gestalt in R. Wagners „Tristan und Isolde"
M·ark|olf m *Marculf*
M·arkus m *Marc, Mark, Marcus*; Evangelist ~ *St. Mark*
M·ark|wart, M·arquart m
Mars m **1.** ⟨röm myth⟩ *Mars* **2.** ⟨gr⟩ *Ares*
ˣ**M·ärten** (Martin)
M·artha f *Martha*; [dim] *Patty*; „~ oder der Markt von Richmond" Oper von Fr. Frhr. v. Flotow; → Nancy
M·artin m *Martin*; ~ Luther, dtsch. Reformator; „~ Salander" Roman v. Gottfried Keller
Marx, Karl ([eig. jüd. Mardochai) Begründer des Marxismus, 1818–1883)
M·arzell m; **Marzell·in** m; **Marzell·ine** f; **M·ascha** f ⟨russ⟩
Math·ilde f *Mat(h)ilda*; [dim] *Tilly, Malkin, Maddy, Matty, Patty, Maud*
M·athis; „~ der Maler" Oper v. Paul Hindemith; → Grünewalds Isenheimer Altar
Mat·isse, Henri (fr. Maler, 1869–1954)
Matth·äus m *Matthew*; der Evangelist ~ *St. M.*; **Matth·ias** m *Matthias, Matthew*; **Matz** m (⟨fam⟩ f Matthias) *Mat, Matty*
Maupass·ant, Guy de (fr. Schriftsteller, 1850–1893)
Max m ([dim] v. Maximilian) *Max*; „~ u. Moritz" v. Wilhelm Busch; **Maxim·ilian** m *Maximilian*
M·echthild(e) f → Mathilde
Medic·eer [ts], **M·edici** [-tʃi] (florent. Geschlecht), der ~ *Medicean, prince of the house of (the) Medici*; Mediceische Venus *Venus of Medici*
Med·usa f ⟨myth⟩ *Medusa*, ⟨a.⟩ Gorgon
M·ef|fert m (magin-frid)
M·egin|hard, M·ein|hard m, **M·ein|rad** m → Mef|fert
M·eister, „Wilhelm ~" Roman v. Goethe
Mel·anchthon, Mel·anthon m (deutsch. Reformator, 1497 bis 1560) *Melanchthon*
Mel·ania, Melan·ie, M·elanie f *Melania*
M·elcher, M·elchior m *M.*
Mel·itta f
Melus·ine ⟨myth⟩ Meerfee (Fr), dann dt. Volksbuch des 15. Jh.
M·endel, Gregor (österr. Entdecker der ~schen Vererbungsgesetze, 1822–1884)
M·endels|sohn jüd. **1.** Moses ~ (1729–86), Philosoph; **2.** Felix ~-Bartholdy (1809–47), dt. Komponist
M·enzel, Adolph v. (dt. Maler, 1815–1905)
Meph·isto, Mephist·opheles m (der Teufel in Goethes „Faust") *Mephistopheles*
Merc·edes [ts] f
Merk·ur, Merk·urius m ⟨myth⟩ *Mercury*
M·erow|inger (ältestes fränk. Königsgeschlecht) der ~ *Merowingian*; pl *the Merowingians*

×**M·erten** → Märten

Messal·ina f *Messalina*

Mess·ias m *Messiah*

M·eta f *Peggy*; → Margareta

Meth·usalem, Meth·usalah m ⟨bib⟩ *Methuselah, Methusalah*

M·etternich, Klemens Fürst v. ~ (österr. Staatsmann, 1773 bis 1859)

M·eyer, Conrad Ferdinand (schweizer. Dichter, 1825 bis 1898)

M·icha m ⟨bib⟩ *Micah*; **M·ichael** m *Michael*; der Erzengel ~ *St. Michael*; *the Taxiarch*; „~ Kramer“ Drama v. G. Hauptmann; **M·ichel** m ([dim] v. Michael) *Mick, Mike*; **Michel·angelo** m (ital. Bildhauer u. Maler, 1475–1564) *Mich(a)el Angelo* (*Buonarotti*), *Michelangelo*

M·ieze f, **M·iezerl** n ([dim] v. Maria) *May, Polly*

Mignon [minjɔ̃] (Fr) Gestalt in Goethes Roman „Wilhelm Meister“; „~“ Oper v. A. Thomas

M·ilda f

M·illais, Sir John E. (⟨engl⟩ Maler, 1829–1896)

M·illi, M·illy f ([dim] v. Emilie, Ludmilla, Maria etc.) *Milly*

M·imi ([dim] v. Emilie) *Millie*

M·inchen n (weibl. Vn., [dim] v. Minna) *Min(n)a, Minnie*

M·ine f → Minchen

Min·erva f (= Athene → d.) ⟨myth⟩ *Minerva*

M·inna f ([dim] v. Wilhelmine etc.) *Min(n)a, Minnie*; „~ v. Barnhelm“ Lustspiel v. Lessing

Minot·aur(us) m ⟨myth⟩ *Minotaur*

Mir·ó, Joan (span. Surrealist, *1893)

×**M·itzi** f südd. v. Maria → d.

M·ohammed m (Stifter des Islams, 570–632) *Mohammed*

Moli·ère m (fr. Dramatiker, 1622–1673)

M·oltke, H. Graf v. ~ (Generalstabschef, 1800–91)

M·omme m

M·ona L·isa Gemälde von Leonardo da Vinci; Oper von Max v. Schillings

Mon·et [mɔ'nɛ], Claude [klo:d] (fr. Maler, 1840–1926)

M·onika f *Monica*

M·ontez, Lola (Tänzerin, 1818–1861)

Montez·uma m (Herrscher des Aztekenreichs, um 1480–1520)

Montgolfi·er [mɔ̃gɔl'fie:]; Brüder ~ (fr. Erfinder: 1782 Luftballon)

M·örike, Eduard (dt. Dichter, 1804–1875)

M·oritz m *Maurice*; → Max

M·orpheus m ⟨Gr myth⟩ (Sohn des Schlafes, Gott der Träume); → Morphium

M·orse [mɔ:s], Samuel (⟨Am⟩ Erfinder: 1840 ~alphabet)

M·oses m ⟨bib⟩ *Moses*

M·ozart m (österr. Komponist, 1756–1791) *Mozart*

Munch [muŋk], Edvard (norweg. Maler, 1863–1944)

M·ünch|hausen, K. F. Hieronymus v. ~, der „Lügenbaron“ 1720–97

Mur·illo [iljo] m (span. Maler, 1618–1682)

M·urner im Tierepos der Kater

M·usil, Robert (österr. Schriftsteller, 1880–1942)

Muss·orgski, Modest (⟨russ⟩ Komponist, 1839–1881)

Mustafa Kemal Atatürk

Myker·inos ⟨Eg⟩ Pharao *Men|kau|re*

N

N·achti|gal, Gustav (dt. Afrikareisender, 1834–1885): Togo

N·ancy ['nænsi] Vertraute der Lady Harriet Durham in Flotows Oper „Martha“

Nandl n, **N·annchen** n, **N·annerl** n, **Nann·ettchen** n, **Nann·ette** f ([dim] v. Anna) *Nancy*

N·anni, N·anny f → ·Ännchen

N·an|sen, Frithjof (norw. Polarforscher, 1861–1930)

N·ante m ⟨fam⟩ Ferdinand

Nap·oleon m (Kaiser der Franzosen, 1769–1821)

Nat·alie f *Natalie, Natalia*

N·athan m *Nathaniel*, ⟨dim⟩ *Nat*; „~ der Weise“ Drama v. Lessing

Nath·anael m *Nathaniel*

N·eit|hard m

N·elly f ⟨engl⟩ *Nelly*

N·epomuk, Johann v (Schutzpatron Böhmens, geb. um 1340, gest. 1393) *John of Nepomuk*

Nept·un m ⟨myth⟩ *Neptune*

N·ero m (röm. Kaiser, 37 bis 68 n. Chr.) *Nero*

N·ettchen n, **N·ette, N·etti** f ([dim] v. Anna) *Nan*

N·ew|ton, Sir I. (⟨engl⟩ Physiker u. Mathematiker, 1643 bis 1727)

N·ibelungen (sagenhaftes Geschlecht), die ~ [pl] *the Nibelungs, the Nibelungers, the Nibelungen*; „Der Ring des ~“ Trilogie v. Musikdramen v. R. Wagner

N·ickel m ([dim] v. Nikolaus) *Nick*

Nicol·ai, Otto ~ (dt. Komponist, 1810–1849)

N·ietzsche (dt. Philosoph, 1844–1900) → Neid|hard

N·ike f ⟨myth⟩ *Nike*

N·ikisch, Arthur (ungar. ⟨mus⟩ Dirigent, 1855–1922)

N·iklas, N·ikolas m *Nick, Nicholas*

Niko|d·emus m ⟨bib⟩ *Nicodemus*; **N·ikolaus** m *Nicholas*; der heilige ~ *St. Nicholas*, (Weihnachtsmann) *Santa Claus*

Nils m [gen]

N·ina f | **N·inon** [ɔ̃] f [Fr]

N·oah m ⟨bib⟩ *Noah*

N·obel (König ~, der Löwe im Tierepos) *Noble*

Nob·el [no'bel] m; schwed. Chemiker, Erf. 1867 Dynamit

N·olte m ([dim] v. Arnold)

N·ora f ([dim] v. Eleonore, Leonora) *Nora*

N·or|bert m; **N·or|trud** f

N·ot|burg, Not|b·urga f

Nov·alis (Dichtername des dt. Romantikers Friedrich v. Harden|berg, 1772–1801)

O

Ob·adja m ⟨bib⟩ *Obadiah*

·Oberon, Elfenkönig, Gestalt der altfrz. Dichtung, später bei Shakespeare (Sommernachtstraum), Wieland, Weber

O·da f

·Odin m ⟨myth⟩ *Odin*

·Ödipus m (griech. Sagengestalt) *Œdipus*

Od·ysseus m (griech. Sagengestalt) *Odysseus, Ulysses*

·Offenbach, Jacques (dt.-frz. Komponist, in Paris, 1819 bis 1880)

·Olaf, ·Olav m *Olaf, Alaff*

·Olga f ⟨russ⟩

·Oliver m *Oliver*, ⟨fam⟩ *Noll*

Ol·ivia f *Olivia, Olive*

Ol·ympia Gestalt in Offenbachs Oper „Hoffmanns Erzählungen“ nach E. Th. A. Hoffmann

Oph·elia f [Gr]

Or·est(es) m ⟨Gr myth⟩ *Orestes*

Orff, Carl (dt. Komponist, *1895)

Or·igenes m (Neuplatoniker, 185–254) *Origen*

Orl·ando m [It] *Roland*

·Orpheus m ⟨myth⟩ *Orpheus*; „~ und Euryd·ike“ Oper von Chr. W. Gluck

·Ort|lieb, ·Ort|mann m; **·Ortrud** f [-t|t-], Gestalt der Lohengrinsage; **·Ort|win** m

Os·iris m ⟨myth⟩ *Osiris*

·Os|kar m *Oscar*

·Os|wald m, **·Os|win** m

·Ota|kar m → Ottokar; **·Ot|fried** m, **·Ot|mar** m; **Ott·ilie** f *Ottilia* **·Otto** m *Otto, Otho*, → Ot|fried; **·Otto** d. Gr. (936 bis 973), Kaiser → Karl d. Gr.; **Otto,** N. A. (dt. Erfinder: 1877 Viertaktmotor); **·Otto|kar** m *Ottocar*; **·Otto|mar** m;

·Overbeck, Fr. (dt. Maler, 1789–1869)

Ov·id m (röm. Dichter, 43 v. Chr. – 17 n. Chr.) *Ovid, Ovidius*

P

Pacher, Michael; österr. Maler u. Bildschnitzer (?–?1498)

Pagan·ini m (ital. Geigenvirtuose, 1782–1840)

Palestr·ina ital. Komponist (1525–1594), Hauptgestalt in Pfitzners Oper

Pankr·atius, Pankr·az m ⟨ec⟩; der heilige ~ *St. Pancras*

P·ansa → Sancho Pansa
Parac·elsus m (Arzt, 1493 bis 1541) *Paracelsus*
P·aris m ⟨myth⟩ *Paris*
P·arzival m **1.** (Artussage) *Perceval, Percival(le)* **2.** (der Held des Wagnerschen Musikdramas) *Parcival, Parsifal*; → Amfortas, Klingsor, Kundry
Pasteur [pas'tœ], Louis; fr. Chemiker, Biologe u. Mediziner (1822–1895)
Patr·icius m *Patrick*
Paul m *Paul*; **P·aula** f *Paula*; **P·aulchen** n **1.** ([dim] v. Paul) *little Paul* **2.** ([dim] v. Paula) *little Paula*; **Paul·ine** f *Paulina, Pauline*; **P·aulus** m *Paulus, Paul*; der Apostel ~ *Paul the Apostle of the Gentiles*, ⟨a.⟩ *St. Paul*
Penthesil·ea, Amazonenkönigin; Trauerspiel v. Kleist
×**P·eperl** m; ×**Pepi, P·eppi** m & f ([dim] v. Joseph ⟨oberd.⟩ & Josephine) *Joe, Joey*
P·erikles m (griech. Staatsmann, 493–429 v. Chr.) *Pericles*
Pestal·ozzi, Joh. Hch. (schweizer. Erzieher u. Sozialreformer, 1746–1827)
P·eter m; ~ v. Amiens *Peter of Amiens, Peter the Hermit*; Sankt ~ *St. Peter*; **P·eterchen** n (m. Vn. [dim] v. Peter) *little Peter, Peterkin*
P·etöfi m (ungar. Dichter, 1823–1849)
Petr·arca m (ital. Dichter, 1304–1374) *Petrarch, Petrarca*
P·etrus m *Peter*; der heilige ~ *Saint Peter*; ~ Lombardus *Peter Lombard*
Pf·itzner, Hans ~ (dtsch. Komponist, 1869–1949)
Ph·aeton m ⟨myth⟩ *-thon*
Ph·arao m *Pharaoh* (⟨eig⟩ Haus des Großen)
Ph·ilibert m *Phil(i)bert*; **Phil·ine** f; Gestalt in Goethes Roman „Wilhelm Meister" u. in A. Thomas, Oper „Mignon"; **Ph·ilipp** m *Philip*, ⟨fam⟩ *Phil*; **Philipp·ine** f **1.** (als engl. Name) *Philippa* **2.** (als Wiedergabe des deutschen Namens) *Philippine*; **Philom·ela** f *Philomela*
Ph·öbe f *Phœbe*
Ph·öbus m ⟨myth⟩ *Phoebus*
P·ia f; → Pius
Pil·atus m ⟨bib⟩ Pontius ~ *Pontius Pilate*
P·indar m (griech. Lyriker, 522- wahrscheinlich 448 v. Chr.)
P·ippa f ⟨It⟩; Hauptgestalt in R. Brownings Gedicht „~ *Passes*", „Und ~ tanzt!" Drama v. G. Hauptmann
Pipp·in m *Pepin, Pipin*; ~ der Kleine o. Kurze *P. the Short*
P·ius m
Pizarro, Francisco (1531 span. Eroberer Perus)
Planck, Max (dt. theoret. Physiker, 1858–1947)
Pl·ato m (griech. Philosoph, 429–347 v. Chr.) *Plato*
Pl·inius (römische Schriftsteller), ~ der Ältere (23–79 n. Chr.) *Pliny the Elder*; ~ der Jüngere (geb. 61 od. 62, gest. um 113 n. Chr.) *the younger Pliny, Pliny the Younger*
Plut·arch m (griech. Biograph u. Moralist) *Plutarch*
P·oldchen n; ×**Polderl** n, **P·oldi** m & f [südd. dim] v. Leopold(ine)
P·olo, Marco (bedeutendster mittelalterl. Reisender [Venetianer] im Fernen Osten, 1254 bis 1323)
Polyh·ymnia f (Muse)
Pomp·ejus m (röm. Staatsmann, 106–48 v. Chr.) *Pompey*
P·ontius m *Pontius*
P·osa, Marquis ~, Gestalt in Schillers „Don Carlos"
Pos·eidon m ⟨Gr myth⟩
Prax·edis f [griech.]
Prezi·osa f Oper von Weber
Pr·iamus m *Priam*
Prok·ofjew, Sergei (⟨russ⟩ Komponist, 1891–1953)
Pr·okop, Prok·opius m *Procopius*
Prokr·ustes m ⟨myth⟩ *Procrustes*
Prom·etheus m ⟨myth⟩ | prometh·eisch [a] *Promethean (skill, punishment)*
Pr·osper m
Pro·teus m (⟨Gr myth⟩ weissagender Meergreis der tausend Gestalten) | prot·eisch [a] *Protean*
Proust [pru:st], Marcel (fr. Schriftsteller, 1871–1922)
Prud·entia f *Prudence*
Ps·yche ['psyçə] f ⟨Gr myth⟩ „Seele"; → Psychologie
Ptolem·äus m *Ptolemy*
Pucc·ini [put'ʃi:ni], Giacomo [dʒa'ko:mo] (ital. Komponist, 1858–1924)
Pulch·eria f
P·uschkin Alexander S. (russ. Dichter, 1799–1837)
P·ylades ⟨myth⟩ Freund Orests
Pyth·agoras m (griech. Philosoph, 6. Jh. v. Chr.)

Q

Quichotte, [ki'ʃɔt], **Quixote** [ki'xo:tə], **Don Quixote** (Ritterroman v. Cervantes)

R

R·aabe (dt. Romanschriftsteller, 1831–1910)
Rabel·ais m (fr. Satiriker, 1483–1553) *Rabelais*
R·achel f → Rahel
Rac·ine J. B., m (fr. Tragiker, 1639–1699)
R·adolf m
R·afael m → Raphael; **Raffa·ello** Santi (ital. Maler, 1483 bis 1520)
R·ahel f ⟨bib⟩ *Rachel*
R·aiffeisenbank f *Raiffeisen Agricultural Credit Bank*
R·ai|mar m → Rei(n)|mar
R·ai|mund, R·ay|mund m *Raymond, Raymund*
R·ain|er m
Ralf m *Ralph*
R·and|olf m *Randolph*
R·aphael m *Raphael*
R·asmus m
R·ausche|bart m → Eberhard
Raut·endelein, Gestalt in Hauptmanns Märchendrama „Die versunkene Glocke"
Rav·el, Maurice [mo:'ris] (fr. Komponist, 1875–1937)
Reb·ekka f *Rebecca, Rebekah*, ⟨fam⟩ *Bec(ca), Beck, Bex*, (Koseform) *Becky*
R·eger, Max ~ (dt. Komponist, 1873–1916)
Reg·ina, Reg·ine f *Regina*
R·egin|ald m
R·egula f
Reh·abeam m *Rehoboam*
R·ei(n)|mar m → Raimar
R·ei|mund m
R·eineke m *Re(y)nard* (der Fuchs in der Tierfabel) vgl. Reinhart, Reinhartswald; „~ Fuchs" Tierepos v. Goethe
R·ein|(w)ald, R·ein|er m *Reginald*; **R·ein|hard, R·einhart** m *Reynard*; → Reineke; **Rein|-h·ilde** f; **R·ein|hold** m *Reginald, Reynold*; **R·ein|mar** m → Rai|-mar
Reis, Philipp (dt. Erfinder: 1861 Telephon)
R·em|brandt m (holländ. Maler, 1606–1669) *Rembrandt* → Rein|-
Ren·ata, Ren·ate f *Renata*
Renoir [rən'wa:], Auguste (fr. Maler, 1841–1919)
R·eserl n, **R·esi** f ([dim] v. Therese) *Terry, Tracy, Tess*
R·euter, Fritz (niederdt. Dichter, 1810–1874)
Reynolds ['renldz], J. (⟨engl⟩ Maler, 1723–1792)
R·ezia Gestalt in K. M. v. Webers Oper „Oberon"
Ric·arda f
R·ich|ard m *Richard*, ⟨fam⟩ *Dick, Dicky*, [dim] *Richy*; ~ Löwenherz (engl. König, 1157 bis 1199) *Richard Cœur de Lion* od. *the Lion-hearted*; **Rich|·arda**
R·ichter, Ludwig (dt. Maler, 1803–1884)
R·i(e)kchen n, **R·i(e)ke** f [dim] v. Friederike → d. *Freddy*
R·iemen|schneider, Til|man (dt. Holzschnitzer, um 1460 bis 1531)
Ri·enzi (päpstlicher Notar) Oper von Rich. Wagner
R·ilke, Rainer Maria (österr. Dichter, 1875–1926)
Rin·aldo m ⟨It⟩
R·ita f
R·o|bert m *Robert*, [dim] *Robin*, ⟨fam⟩ *Bob, Bobbie, *Rob*; → Rode|-
Robespi·erre m (fr. Revolutionär, 1758–1794)
R·ochus m
R·ode|rich m *Roderic(k)*, [dim] *Rory, Rody*
Rode|wald m

Rodin [rɔ'dɛ̃], Auguste [o:gyst] (fr. Bildhauer, 1840–1917)

R·o|ger m *Roger, Rodger, Hodge,* → Rüdi|ger

R·o|land (bei Uhland ⟨a.⟩ Rol·and) m **1.** (als Vorname) *Rowland, Orlando* **2.** ⟨hist⟩ *Roland*

Rolf m (→ Rud|olf); [gen] **Rolfs**

R·omeo m → Julia

R·omulus m (sagenhafter Gründer Roms), Gott *Quirinus*

R·öntgen m (dt. Physiker, 1845–1923): 1895 ∼strahlen

R·osa f *Rosa, Rose*; **Ros·alie** *Rosalie, Rosalia* f; **Rosa|l·inde** f *Rosalind, Rosaline*; **Rosa|m·unde** f *Rosamond*; **R·ös|chen** n (weibl. Vn. [dim] v. Rosa) *Rosy, Rosie*; **R·ose,** „∼ Bernd", Drama v. G. Hauptmann; **R·ose|marie** f; **Ros|w·itha** f

Ross·etti, Dante G. (⟨engl⟩ Maler, 1828–1882)

R·ot|bart m → *Barba|rossa*

R·other m

Rousse·au m (fr. Dichter, 1670–1741)

R·uben m ⟨bib⟩ *Reuben*; **∼s** m [gen] (niederl. Maler, 1577 bis 1640)

R·übe|zahl m (Berggeist im Riesengebirge) *Old Nip, Sprite of the Mountains* [-zahl = Zagel *tail*]

R·üdi|ger m *Roger, Hodge*

R·ud|olf, [latinisiert] R·udolph [m] *Rudolph, *Ralph*; **R·udolph** v. Habsburg, Kaiser (1273–1291); → Karl d. Gr.; ˣ**R·uodi** ([dim] v. Rudolf) *Ralph*

R·unge, Ph. O. (dt. Maler, 1777–1810)

R·u|pert m → **R·u|precht** m *Rupert, Robert*; Knecht ∼ *Santa Claus*

Ruth f *Ruth,* [dim] *Ruthy*

Rutz m (⟨fam⟩ f Rudolf) *Rudie, Rudolph*

R·yse m → Riese³, S. 1022

S

Sab·ine f (Vn.) *Sabine* (Familienname)

Sach·arja m ⟨bib⟩ *Zachariah*

Sachs, Hans (dt. Dichter u. Meistersinger, 1494–1576)

Salman·assar m *Shalmaneser*; **S·amiel** m *Zamiel*

S·alome [-e:] Tochter der Herodias; Oper v. Rich. Strauss nach Oscar Wilde; **S·alomo(n)** m ⟨bib⟩ *Solomon,* [dim] *Sol*; das Hohe Lied Salom·onis *the Song of S.*; der Prediger S.is *Ecclesiastes*; Sprüche S.is *Proverbs* (*of S.*)

S·amuel m *Samuel,* [dim] *Sam, Sammy*

S·ancho P·ansa Begleiter des Don Quixote → d.

S·anherib m (v. Assyrien, 705–681 v. Chr.) *Sennacherib*

S·appho [-pfo] f (griech. Dichterin um 600 v. Chr.)

S·ara(h) f ⟨bib⟩ *Sara(h)*; **S·ara(h)chen** n (weibl. Vn., [dim] v. Sara) *Sal, Sally*

Sardanap·al (sagenhafter letzter König v. Assyrien, um 650 v. Chr.) *Sardanapalus*

S·arto m (ital. Maler, 1486 bis 1531)

S·ascha f ⟨russ⟩

S·auer|bruch, F. (dt. Chirurg, 1875–1951)

S·avigny ['saviɲi], F. K. v. (dt. Jurist, 1779–1861)

Sch·arn|horst m (preuß. General, 1755–1813)

Sch·elling, F. W. J. v. (dt. Philosoph, 1775–1854)

Sch·iller, Fr. (dt. Dichter, 1759–1805) *Schiller*; vgl. folg.

Sch·ilt|er m [scild-her]

Sch·iwa m (ind. Gott) *Siva, Shiva*

Schl·egel, A.W. v. (dt. Dichter, Übersetzer, Literarhistoriker, Orientalist, 1767–1845)

Schl·emmer, Oskar (dt. Maler, 1888–1943)

Schl·ieffen, Alfred Graf v. (preuß. Gen.-Feldmarschall, 1833–1913)

Schl·iemann, Heinrich (dt. Altertumsforscher, 1822–1890)

Schl·üter, Andreas (dt. Bildhauer u. Architekt, 1664–1714)

Schmu(h)l m Judenname); vgl. *Fagin* in „Oliver Twist" v. Ch. Dickens

Sch·önberg, Arnold (dt. Komponist, 1874–1951)

Sch·open|hauer m (dt. Philosoph, 1787–1860)

Schr·ammel, Johann u. Josef; Wiener Musikerbrüderpaar (um 1850 – um 1895); ∼musik (2 Geigen, Gitarre, Ziehharmonika)

Sch·u|bert m (österr. Komponist, 1797–1828)

Sch·u|mann, Robert (dt. Komponist, 1810–1856)

Schütz, Heinrich ∼(dt. Komponist, 1585–1672)

Schw·eitzer, Albert (Elsässer, ev. Theologe, Arzt u. Musiker, Missionsarzt im Gabun; 1875–1965)

Schwind, Moritz (Wiener Maler 1804–1871)

Sc·ipio (röm. patriz. Familie)

Seb·adja m ⟨bib⟩ *Zebadiah*

S·ebald m

Seb·astian m

S·ei|fert, S·ei|fried m → Sieg|-fried

S·elma f; ∼ Lagerlöf, schwedische Erzählerin (Gösta Berling usw.)

Sem m ⟨bib⟩ (Sohn Noahs) *Shem*

S·eneca m (röm. Philosoph, gest. 65 n. Chr.)

S·ene|felder, Alois (dt. Erfinder: 1826 Lithographie)

S·enta f; Gestalt in R. Wagners „Fliegender Holländer"

ˣ**Sepp** m → Joseph *Joe*

S·ergius m

Serv·atius, Serv·az m ⟨ec⟩ der heilige ∼ *Saint Servatius*

Seur·at, Georges (fr. Maler, 1859–1891)

Shakespeare-Forscher *Shakespearian student*

Shaw, George Bernhard (⟨fam⟩ G. B. S.); engl.-irischer Dichter (1856–1950)

Sib·elius, Jean (finn. Komponist, 1865–1957)

Sib·ylle f *Sibylla, Sibyl*

Sid·onie f

S·ie|bert m →; **Sieg|bert** m; **S·ieg|fried** m; ⟨Lit⟩ Held des Nibelungenliedes; „∼s Tod" Drama v. Hebbel; „∼" Musikdrama v. R. Wagner; **Sieg|l·inde** f; **S·ieg|mar** m; **S·ieg|mund, S·igis|mund** m *Sigismond*; **S·ieg|ward** m; **S·ievers** m [gen] → Sie|bert; **S·igis|bert** m; **S·ig|rid** f

Silv·ester m *Silvester, Sylvester*; **S·ilvia** f *Silvia*

S·imon, S·imeon m *Simon,* [dim] *Sim, Simmy*

S·imson m ⟨bib⟩ *Samson*

S·irach, m Jesus ∼ *Ecclesiasticus*

S·ixtus m; Sixt·inisch [a] *Sistine*

Sk·ylla → Szylla

ˣ**Sneew·ittchen** n → Schneewittchen S. 1080

S·okrates m (griech. Philosoph, 470–399 v. Chr.); Sokr·atisch [a] *Socratic*

S·olon m (athen. Gesetzgeber, geb. um 640, gest. 560 v. Chr.)

Soph·ia, Soph·ie f *Sophia, Sophy*; **S·ophokles** m (griech. Tragiker, 496–406 v. Chr.)

Spin·oza, Baruch de (jüd.-holländ. Philosoph, 1632–1677) *Spinoza*

Sp·itz|weg, Carl (dt. Maler, 1808–1885)

Stachus → Eustachius

St·anislaus m *Stanislas, Stanislaus*

St·aufer m (Kaiser aus dem Hause Hohenstaufen) *Stauffer* || ∼zeit [f] *the Hohenstauffen period* (1138–1254)

St·efan, St·effen, St·ephan m *Stephen, Steve*; **St·efani, Steph·anie, St·ephanie** f *Stephana, Stephanie*

Stein, Karl Reichsfreiherr vom und zum ∼ (preußischer Staatsmann; 1757–1831) |

Stein|bach → ⟨a.⟩ Er|win (Erbauer des Straßburger Münsters)

St·ella f; Titelheldin in Goethes Trauerspiel

Stephen|son ['sti:vnsn], George (engl. Erfinder: 1825 Lokomotive)

St·ifter, Adalbert (österr. Schriftsteller, 1805–1868)

St·ine f ([dim] v. Christine) *Chris(sie)*; **St·offel** m (⟨fam⟩ f. Christoph) *Christopher, Kit*

Storm, Theodor (dt. Dichter, 1817–1888)

Stoß, Veit (dt. Bildhauer, um 1445 – um 1533)

Strauß, Joh. (Vater 1804 bis 1849; Sohn 1825 bis 1899) Wiener Komponisten

Strauss, Richard (dt. Komponist, 1864–1949)

Straw·insky, Igor F. (⟨russ⟩ Komponist, 1882–1971)

Str·ese|mann, Gustav (dt. Staatsmann, 1878–1929)

Strind|berg, August (schwed. Dichter, 1849–1912)

Stubbs, George (⟨engl⟩ Maler, 1724–1806)

Sul·eika f *Zuleikah*

Sus·anna, Sus·anne f [hebr] *Susan(na)*; Kammermädchen der Gräfin Almaviva in Mozarts Oper „Figaros Hochzeit"; **S·uschen** n, **S·use** f ([dim v. Susanna) *Susy*

Sylv·ester m → Silvester

S·ylvia f *Sylvia*

Sz·ylla f ⟨myth⟩ *Scylla*; → Skylla S. 1121, Charybdis S. 276

T

Tag·ore m (ind. Dichter u. Philosoph, 1861–1941)

Talleyrand [talɛrɑ̃] (franz. Diplomat, 1754–1838)

T·amerlan m *Tamburlaine*; „~" Oper von Händel; → Timur

T·ankred m ⟨normann⟩ *Tancred*

T·annhäuser Minnesänger; Oper v. Rich. Wagner

T·assilo m

T·asso, Torquato ~ (ital. Dichter, 1544–1595); Drama v. Goethe

Tatj·ana f ⟨russ⟩

T·elemann (dt. Komponist, 1681 1767)

Tell, Wilhelm m (sagenhafhafter schweiz. Freiheitsheld); Drama v. Schiller

T·ell|heim Major v. ~, Gestalt in Lessings „Minna v. Barnhelm"

T·elramund Gestalt in R. Wagners „Lohengrin"

Ter·entius, Ter·enz m (röm. Lustspieldichter, 195–159 v. Chr.) *Terentius, Terence*

Thadd·äus m *Thaddeus*, [dim] *Thady*

Th·ales m (griech. Philosoph, geb. um 640 v. Chr.)

Th·ea f [dim] v. Theodora

Th·ekla f *Thecla*; Gestalt in Schillers „Wallenstein"

Th·emis f ⟨myth⟩ *Themis, (goddess of) Justice*; **Them·istokles** m (athen. Staatsmann, 525–460 v. Chr.)

Th·eo|bald m; **The·ode|rich, The·odo|rich** m *Theodoric*; **Th·eodor** m *Theodore*; **Theod·ora** f *Theodora*; **Theokr·it** m (griech. Dichter, 3. Jh. v. Chr.) *Theocritus*; **Th·eophil** m; **Theophr·ast** m (griech. Philosoph, Schüler v. Plato u. Aristoteles; *um 372 v. Chr.) *Theophrastus*

Ther·es|chen n (weibl. Vn., [dim] v. Therese) *Terry, Tracy, Tess*; **Ther·ese, Ther·es(i)a** f *Theresa*

Th·ilde f → Tilde

Th·oma (dt. Maler, 1839 bis 1924); **Th·omas** m *Thomas*, ⟨dim⟩ *Tom, Tommy*; Sankt ~ v. Aquino *Thomas of Aquino, (St. Thomas) Aquinas*; ~ Morus *Sir Thomas More*; → ~ Mann; **Thom·asie** f *Thomasine*

Thor m ⟨myth⟩ *Thor*

Th·ora f

Thor|vald|sen, B. (dän. Bildhauer, 1768–1844)

Thr·aso (Bramarbas e-r Terenzschen Komödie) *Thraso*; Thras·onisch [a] *Thrasonic*

Thusn·elda f; Gemahlin Hermanns des Cheruskers, ⟨a.⟩ in Kleists Drama

Tieck, Ludwig (dt. Dichter, 1773–1853)

T·ilde f ([dim] v. Mathilde) *Til, Tilly, Tilda*

Till m → Eulenspiegel, → Diet|rich

T·illa f ([dim] v. Mathilde) *Tilly*

Tilly, Johann v. (Kaiserl. General; 1559–1632)

T·il|mann m; **T·ilo** m

Tim·otheus m *Timothy*

T·imur-Leng, der lahme [m] (asiatischer Eroberer, 1336 bis 1405) *Tamburlaine, Tamerlane, Tim(o)ur-Bey, Tim(o)ur-Leng*

T·inbergen, N., niederl. Verhaltensforscher in Oxford (*1907)

T·inchen n, **T·ine** f ([dim] v. Christine, Ernestine, Klementine etc) *Tina, Teenie, Tiny*; (v. Christine meist) *Chrissie*; → Stine

Tintor·etto m (ital. Maler, 1518–1594)

Tirpitz, Alfred v. (Großadmiral; 1849–1930)

T·isch|bein, J. H. W. (dt. Maler, 1751–1829)

Tit·ania f. Gestalt in K. M. v. Webers „Oberon"

T·itus m

T·izian, Tizi·an m (ital. Maler, 1480–1576) *Titian*

Tob·ias m *Tobias*, ⟨fam⟩ *Toby*

T·öffel → Stoffel

T·olstoi, Leo N., Graf (⟨russ⟩ Schriftsteller, 1828 bis 1910)

T·oni m & f ([dim] v. Anton & Antonia) *Tony*; **T·onio** (= Anton); „~ Kröger", Erzählung v. Thomas Mann; ×**T·önnies** m [gen] ⟨niederd.⟩ → Anton; ×**T·ünnes** m [gen] ⟨rheinisch⟩

Tr·au|gott m

Tr·autchen n, **Tr·auto** f ([dim] v. Ger|traud, Ger|trud)

Tr·inchen n, **Tr·ine** f ([dim] v. Katharina) *Kate, Katie, Kitty*; → S. 1204

Tr·istan m *Tristram*; „~ u. Isolde" Musikdrama v. R. Wagner

Tr·übner, Wilh. (dt. Maler, 1851–1917)

Tr·udchen n, **Tr·ude** f ([dim] v. Ger|trud) etwa *Gerty, Gertie, Trudy, Gatty*; **Tr·udel** f → Tr·udchen

Tschaik·owskij, Peter I. (⟨russ⟩ Komponist, 1840–1893)

T·ullius m *Tully*

Turg·enjew, Iwan (russ. Schriftsteller, 1818–1883) *Turgenev*

T·urner, J. M. W. (⟨engl⟩ Maler, 1775–1851)

U

·Uhde (dt. Maler 1848 bis 1911) (vgl. ahd. uodal); **·Udo** m; → Ul|rich; **·Uh|land** (dt. Dichter 1787 bis 1862) (vgl. ahd. uodal) **·Uli** m ⟨schweiz.⟩; **·Ul|rich** m *Ulric(h)*, vgl. Uh|land; **Ul|r·ike** f *Ulrica*

Und·ine f ⟨myth⟩ Wasserjungfrau; Oper v. Lortzing

Ur·ania f (Muse) *Urania*

·Urban m *Urban*

·Urian → S. 1257

Ur·ias m ⟨bib⟩ *Uriah*; → S. 1257

·Ursel f ([dim] v. Ursula) *Ursly, Ursy*; **·Ursula** f *Ursula*; **Ursul·inerin** [f] *Ursuline nun*

·Ute f; (⟨Lit⟩ Kriemhilds Mutter im Nibelungenlied)

Utz m [dim] → Ulrich

V

V·aland, [f-] m Junker ~ → Urian S. 1257

V·alentin [v-] m *Valentine, Val*; **Valent·ine** [v-] f *Valentine*

Valer·ie [v-] f [Fr]

Val·eska [v-] f *Valesca*

Vega, Lope de [v-] (span. Dramatiker, 1562–1635)

Veit [f-] m ([dim] v. Vitus) *Guy, Vitus*; Sankt ~ *St. Vitus*; → Urian S. 1257; Bruder ~ ⟨hum⟩ *Brother Blade (lansquenet of the 16th c.)*

Vel·azquez [veˈlaskes] m (span. Maler, 1599–1660)

×**V·elten** [f-] m ⟨alemann.⟩ ← Valentin

V·enus [v-] f ⟨myth⟩ *Venus*; → S. 1260

V·era [v-] f [russ]

V·erdi [v-] m (ital. Komponist, 1813–1901)

Ver·ena [v-] f

Verg·il(ius), Publius Virgilius Maro m (röm. Dichter, 70–19 v Chr) *Virgil, Vergil, P. V. M.*

Ver·onika [v-] f *Veronica*

V·iktor m *Victor*; **Vikt·oria** [v-] f **1.** (als Vorname) *Victoria*, [dim] *Vick, Vicky* **2.** ⟨myth⟩ *Victoria, Victory*

Vinc·entia, Vinz·entia f [v-]

V·incenz, V·inzenz [v-] m *Vincent*; ~ v. Paul *St. Vincent de Paul*

Vi·ola [v-] f *Viola*

V·irchow [v-], Rudolf (dt. Arzt, 1821–1902)

Virg·inie [v-] f *Virginia*
V·oland, [f-] m Junker ~ → Urian S. 1257
V·olk|hard [f-] m; **V·olk|mar** [f-] m
V·ol|rad [f-] m
V·olta [v-] m (ital. Physiker, 1745–1827) *Volta*
Volt·aire m [v-] (fr. Schriftsteller, 1694–1778) *Voltaire*
V·orwärts, Marschall ~ *Field-Marshal Blucher*
×**Vr·eneli, Vr·eni** [v-] f ⟨oberd. [dim]⟩; ×**Vr·oneli, Vr·oni** [v-] f ⟨oberd. [dim]⟩ v. → Veronika

W

W·ackerlos m (kl. Hund der Tierfabel) *Go-at-him*
W·agner; Gestalt in Goethes „Faust"
W·agner, Richard m (dt. Komponist, 1813–1883)
W·al|burg f → Walpurga
W·alde|mar m *Waldemar, Valdemar*
Wald|müller, F. G. (Wiener Maler, 1793–1865)
W·allen|stein m (Kaiserl. Feldherr im 30jährigen Kriege) *Wallenstein*; Drama v. Schiller
W·alli, ×**W·ältli** ([dim] v. Walter) *Walt, Wally*
Wal|p·urga, Wal|p·urgis f *Walpurge, Walpurgis*
W·alt|er, W·alt|her m *Walter* **~chen** ([dim] v. Walter) *little Walter, Wat, Watty, Wally*
W·al|traud f
W·anda f [poln]
×**Wastl** m ⟨oberd⟩ → Sebastian
Watt, James (⟨engl⟩ Erfinder: 1765 Dampfmaschine)
Watteau, Antoine [ɑ̃'twan va'to:] (fr. Maler, 1684–1721)
Watts, George F. (⟨engl⟩ Maler, 1817–1904)
W·eber m, Carl Maria v. ~ (dt. Komponist, 1786–1826)
W·ede|kind [→ Witte|kind] (Fn.), Frank ~ (dt. Dichter 1864–1918)
W·elfen pl, ~geschlecht, ~haus [n] (dt. Dynastengeschlecht) *house of the Guelphs, Guelph dynasty*
W·endelin m
W·enzel m ([dim] v. Wenzeslaus), **W·enzeslaus** m *Wen(t)zel, Wenceslas*
W·era f [russ]
W·erfel, Franz (böhm.-österr. Schriftsteller, 1890–1945)
W·erner m *Werner*
W·erther m (Held des Romans v. Goethe) *Werther*
Wh·istler, J. A. M. (⟨engl⟩ Maler, 1834–1903)
W·idu|kind m → Witte|kind (vgl. ⟨engl⟩ *wood*)
W·ie|land, Chr. M. (dt. Dichter, 1733–1813); ~ der Schmied ⟨myth⟩ *Wayland Smith*
W·iklif m *Wyclif*; Wiklif·it m *Wycliffite*; → Wyclif
W·ild|hagen m
W·il|fried m *Wilfrid, Wilfred*
W·il|helm m *William*; ~ der Eroberer *William the Conqueror*; ~ v. Oranien *William of Orange*; → Tell; **Wilhelm I.** deutscher Kaiser (1871–1888) u. König von Preußen (1858/61 bis 1888); **Wilhelm II.** dt. K. u. K. v. Pr. (1888–1918, †1941);
Wil|helm·ina, Wil|helm·ine f *Wilhelmina, Williamina*
W·illem, W·illi m ([dim] v. Wilhelm) *Will(y), Willie,* ⟨fam⟩ *Bill(y)*
W·illi|bald m *Wilibaldus*
W·ilma f ([dim] v. Wilhelmina) *Wilmett, Wilmot*
W·ilson, Richard (⟨engl⟩ Maler, 1714–1782)
W·il|trud f
W·in|fried m *Winfred, Winfrid, Winfrith*
Win|fr·iede f *Winifred,* [dim] *Winny, Winnie*
W·ini|fred f ⟨engl⟩ → Win|friede
W·inkel|mann, J. J. (Begründer der neueren archäologischen Wissenschaft, 1717 bis 1768)
W·ischnu m (ind. Gott) *Vishnu*
W·it|old m
W·itte|kind m (Herzog der alten Sachsen, 8. Jh. n. Chr.) *Wittekind, Widukind*
W·ittels|bach (dt. Fürstengeschlecht, ein ~er [m] *a member of the Wittelsbach family* od. *dynasty*
Wlad·imir, Wl·adimir m [russ] *Vladimir, Wladimir*
Wl·adislaus, Wl·adislaw m [poln + böhm] *Vladislas, Wladislaw*
W·odan, W·ode m ⟨myth⟩ *Wodan, Woden, Odin*
W·olde|mar m → Walde|mar
Wolf, W·olf|art, W·olf|ert m → Wolf|ram; **Wolf,** Hugo (österr Komponist, 1860 bis 1903)
W·olf|gang m
Wolf|ram m *Wolfram*
W·otan m → Wodan
Woyzeck Gestalt (Soldat) in Büchners gleichnamig. Drama
Wurm m; Intrigant in Schillers Trauerspiel „Kabale u. Liebe": → Kabale
W·yclif m (engl. Reformator, geb. um 1320, gest. 1384) *Wyclif(fe)*

X

Xanth·ippe f *Xantippe* → S. 1377
X·aver, Xav·er m *Xavier*
X·enia f (Gr)

Y

Yv·onne f [Fr]

Z

Zachar·ia, Zachar·ias m ⟨bes bib⟩ *Zachariah, Zechariah, Zachary,* [dim] *Zach, Zechy*
Zach·äus m ⟨bes bib⟩, ⟨fam⟩
Z·aches m *Zacch(a)eus*
Zarath·ustra m → Zoroaster
Zäz·ilie f → Cäcilie
Z·ebaoth m ⟨bib⟩ der Herr ~ *the Lord of Sabaoth* od. *Hosts*
Zebed·äus m *Zebedee*; → S. 1380
Zenz, Z·enzi f [dim] v. Vincentia, Kreszenz, Innozentia
Zeph·anja ⟨bib⟩ *Zephaniah*
Z·eppelin m (Erbauer der Zeppeline, 1838–1917)
Zerbin·etta Gestalt in R. Strauss' Oper „Ariadne auf Naxos"
Zeus m ⟨myth⟩ *Zeus,* bei den Römern *Jupiter*; beim ~! *by Jove*! ⟨fam⟩ *by jingo*!
Z·illi f → Cilli
Z·ita f
Z·oe f (Gr)
Zol·a m (fr. Romanschriftsteller, 1840–1902)
Zölest·in m
Z·oller m → Hohenzollern
Zoro·aster m (Prophet, 900 v. Chr.) *Zoroaster*
Zweig, Arnold dt. Schriftsteller (1887–1968)
Zweig, Stefan (österr. Schriftsteller, 1881–1942)
Zw·ingli m (schweiz. Reformator, 1484–1531) *Zwingli*
Zyr·illus m *Cyril*

4. Unterschiede zwischen englischer und deutscher (kontinentaler) Ausdrucksweise und Bezeichnungsweise

In Großbritannien und in den Vereinigten Staaten wird statt des Kommas der Dezimalpunkt (*decimal point*) benutzt; Beispiel: 3,58 (deutsch) = 3.58 oder 3·58 (englisch). In den USA wird aber manchmal bei Zahlen unter 1 die Null ausgelassen, z. B. 0.25 = .25.

Im Englischen muß man das Zeichen × zwischen Faktoren setzen, die durch Ziffern dargestellt werden, z. B. $4 \times 9 = 36$.

Das Abtrennen der Ziffern durch Kommata in Dreiergruppen ist in der englischen Literatur noch weit verbreitet (z. B. 2,835,000); die im Deutschen übliche Schreibweise wird empfohlen (z. B. 2 835 000).

Die *billion* in Amerika gleicht einer Milliarde in Europa einschl. Großbritannien (*milliard* = 10^9); eine amerikanische *trillion* gleicht einer europäischen Billion (10^{12}), usw.

Das Zeichen ÷ oder ⊥ bezeichnet Teilung, z. B. $2 \div 8 = 0.25$.

Das Zeichen α oder ∝ bezeichnet Proportionalität.

Benennung mathematischer Zeichen

0	0 (Ausspr.: ou); nought; zero
+	plus sign; positive sign
−	minus sign; negative sign; subtraction sign
±	plus-or-minus sign
×	multiplication sign
÷	division sign
=	equality sign
≠	non-equality sign
—	fraction bar (Bruchstrich)
/	solidus; slant
:	colon; ratio sign; division sign
: :	double colon; as (in ratios)*
.	decimal point
,	comma
′	dash; prime
-	hyphen
≡	identity sign
∼	tilde
√	root sign; radical sign
| |	modulus bars
( )	round brackets; parentheses
(	bracket open
)	bracket close
[ ]	square brackets
{ }	braces
#	number; No; item
%	infinity sign
≅	congruence sign

Sprechweise mathematischer Ausdrücke

1 – 9	one to nine; one through nine
$^1/_2$	a (one) half
$^3/_4$	three quarters; three fourths
$^{25}/_{58}$	twenty-five fifty-eights; twenty five over fifty eight
$10\frac{1}{5}$	ten and one fifth
0.2	0 (ou) point two; zero point two; nought point two
.5	point five
1.0026	one point zero zero two six
$a = b$	a equals b; a is equal to b
$a + b$	a plus b
$a - b$	a minus b
$a \pm b$	a plus or minus b
$a\,b$; $a \times b$	a times b; a multiplied by b
$a \div b$	a divided by b
$\frac{a}{b}$	a over b; a divided by b
$\frac{ab}{c + d}$	a times b over c plus d
a/b	a solidus b; a slant b
a : b	a is to b
a : b :: c : d	a is to b as c is to d
$a \propto b$	a is proportional to b; Vorzugszeichen $a \sim b$
$a \sim b$	a is asymptotically equal to b; Vorzugszeichen $a \simeq b$
$a \approx b$	a is nearly equal to b, a is approximately equal to b
$a \equiv b$	a is identically equal to b
$a \not\equiv b$	a is not identical with b
$\therefore a = b$	therefore a equals b
$\because a = b$	because a equals b

* Im Englischen: a : b :: c : d; im Deutschen: a : b = c : d

II. ABKÜRZUNGEN & KONTRAKTIONEN
II. ABBREVIATIONS & CONTRACTIONS

(GERMAN AND INTERNATIONAL)

Abbreviations and Contractions

I. Abkürzungen von Städtenamen

Städtenamen werden besonders in Briefen oft willkürlich abgekürzt, z. B.: Mbg = Marburg, Marienburg usw.; D'dorf = Düsseldorf; W'baden = Wiesbaden; Hmbg = Hamburg; ⟨bes typ⟩ Lg, Lpz = Leipzig; ⟨bes typ⟩ Bln = Berlin usw.

Offizielle Abkürzungen

1. im Postscheckverkehr:

Bln W = Berlin-West
Dtmd = Dortmund
Esn = Essen
Ffm = Frankfurt (Main)
Frb = Freiburg (Breisgau)
Hmb = Hamburg
Han = Hannover
Klrh = Karlsruhe (Baden)
Kln = Köln
Lshfn = Ludwigshafen (Rhein)
Mchn = München
Nbg = Nürnberg
Rtlng = Reutlingen
Stgt = Stuttgart

2. im Eisenbahnverkehr:

Au = Augsburg
Bln = Berlin
†Bsl = Breslau
Dre = Dresden
Erf = Erfurt
Esn = Essen
Ffm = Frankfurt (Main)
Hl = Halle
Hmb = Hamburg
Han = Hannover
Kar = Karlsruhe
Ks = Kassel
Köl = Köln
†Kbg = Königsberg (Pr)
Mz = Mainz
Mü = München
Mst = Münster
Nür = Nürnberg
†Op = Oppeln
Re = Regensburg
Sbr = Saarbrücken
Sch = Schwerin
†Stn = Stettin
Stg = Stuttgart
Wt = Wuppertal

II. Abkürzungen in Eisenbahn-Kursbüchern

F = Fernschnellzug *Express Through Train*
FT = Fernschnelltriebwagen *Express Through Diesel Car*
D = Schnellzug *Express Train*
DT = Schnelltriebwagen *Express Diesel Car*
E = Eilzug *Expedited Train*
ET = Eiltriebwagen *Expedited Diesel Car*
S = Städteschnellverkehrszug *Fast City Train* (*metropolitan*), (*no extra charges*)
ST = Städteschnellverkehrstriebwagen *Fast City Diesel Train* (*no extra charges*)
STo = Städteschnellverkehrs-Schienenomnibus *Fast City Rail Bus* (*no extra charges*)
N = Nahschnellverkehrszug *Fast Local Train* (*no extra charges*)
NT = Nahschnellverkehrs-Triebwagen *Fast Local Diesel Train* (*no extra charges*)
NTo = Nahschnellverkehrs-Schienenomnibus *Fast Local Rail Bus* (*no extra charges*)
T = Triebwagen *Diesel Car* (*no extra charges*)
TEE = Trans-Europ-Expreß, Genaueres → Abkürzungsverzeichnis S. 1468
To = Schienenomnibus *Rail Bus* (*no extra charges*)
oG = ohne Gepäck- u. Fahrradbeförderung *no luggage and bicycles conveyed*
† = verkehrt an Sonntagen und allgemeinen Feiertagen *Train is operated on Sundays and legal holidays only* (*New Year, Good Friday, Easter-Monday, Labour-Day* [*May 1st*], *Ascension-Day, Whit-Monday, Repentance Day, Christmas-Day, and Boxing-Day*)
⚒ = verkehrt nur werktags *Train is operated on Week days only*
So, (Mo, Di, Mi, Do, Fr, Sa) = *Train is operated on Sundays* (*Mondays, Tuesdays, Wednesdays, Thursdays, Fridays, Saturdays*) *only*

III. Abkürzungen der deutschen studentischen Verbindungen und Verbände etc.

ADC Allgemeiner Delegierten (od Deputierten) Convent
ADW Allgemeiner Deutscher Waffenring
AGA Arbeitsgemeinschaft Andernach
AHSC Alt-Herren Senioren Convent; → KSCV, WSC
Asta [m] Allgemeiner Studenten-Ausschuß
ATB Akademischer Turn-Bund
ATV Akademischer Turn-Verein
CC Coburger Convent
CC Corps Convent; → KSCV, WSC
CDA Convent Deutscher Akademiker-Verbände
CDK Convent Deutscher Korporations-Verbände
CV Cartell-Verband katholischer deutscher Studenten-Verbindungen; → KV

DB	Deutsche Burschenschaft
DL	Deutsche Landsmannschaft
DTB	Deutscher Turnerbund
HKSCV	Hoher Kösener Senioren Convents-Verband
KDSE	Katholische Deutsche Studenten-Einigung
KSCV	Kösener Senioren Convents-Verband
KV	Kartell-Verband katholischer deutscher Studenten-Vereine; → CV
MR	Miltenberger Ring
RSC	Rudolstädter Senioren-Convent
SB	Schwarzburg-Bund
SV	Sondershäuser Verband deutscher Sänger-Verbindungen
UV	Verband der wissenschaftlichen katholischen Studenten-Verbände Unitas
VAB	Verein Alter Burschenschaften
VAC	Verband Alter Corpsstudenten
VAW	Verband Alter Wingolfiten
VDB	Verband Deutscher Burschen
VVDST	Verband der Vereine Deutscher Studenten
WB	Wingolfsbund
WSC	Weinheimer Senioren-Convent

IV. Zeichen

Chemische Abkürzungen → S. 1501–1503; Abkürzungen der deutschen studentischen Verbindungen und Verbände → S. 1441

³ **1953** ⟨typ⟩ 3. Auflage 1953
° Grad, Altgrad; ′ Altminute; ″ Altsekunde → u. Mathematische Zeichen
′ ⟨engl⟩ *foot, feet*; ″ ⟨engl⟩ *inch, inches* → Maße S. 1485

Astronomische Zeichen

1. Das Sonnensystem

☉	Sonne
☿	Merkur
♀	Venus
♁	Erde
●	Neumond; → Mond S. 897
☽	zunehmender Mond, erstes Viertel
○	Vollmond; → Mond S. 897
☾	abnehmender Mond, letztes Viertel
♂	Mars
♃	Jupiter
♄	Saturn
⛢	Uranus
♆	Neptun
♇	Pluto

2. Der Tierkreis (Zodiakus)

♈	Widder, *Aries*
♉	Stier, *Taurus*
♊	Zwillinge, *the Twins*
♋	Krebs, *Cancer*
♌	Löwe, *Leo*
♍	Jungfrau, *Virgo*
♎	Waage, *Libra*
♏	Skorpion, *Scorpio*
♐	Schütze, *Sagittarius*
♑	Steinbock, *Capricorn*
♒	Wassermann, *Aquarius*
♓	Fische, *Pisces*

3. Mathematische Zeichen (nach DIN 1350)

+	plus *plus* ‖ positiv *positive* ‖ (nach Zahlen) und einiges mehr *approximately, with some figures omitted at the end*; z. B. π = 3,141592+
—	minus *minus* ‖ negativ *negative* ‖ (nach Zahlen) und einiges weniger
±, , ∓,	plus minus, *plus or minus* ‖ ungefähr *approximately*
× od. ·	mal *times*; *multiplied by*
: od. /	geteilt durch *divided by*
=	gleich *equals*; *is equal to*
≈	nahezu gleich, rund, etwa
≅	kongruent *is congruent to*
∼	ähnlich, proportional
<	kleiner als *is less than*
>	größer als *is greater than*
∞	unendlich *infinity*
‖	parallel
⊥	rechtwinklig zu *is perpendicular to*
√	Wurzel aus *indicating the square root of*, z. B. √81 = 9
⌀	Durchmesser *diameter*
∢	Winkel *angle*
/	je (z. B. t/m = Tonne je Meter; m/s = Meter je Sekunde)
%	vom Hundert, Prozent
‰	vom Tausend, Promille
…	bis (z. B. 12⋯15 = 12 bis 15, beide Zahlen eingeschlossen)
12…(15	= 12 bis 15 [ohne 15]
12)…15	= 12 bis 15 [ohne 12]
AB	Strecke *AB*
$\widehat{AB}$	*arc AB* Bogen *AB*
°	Grad, Altgrad *degree(s)*
′	Bogen-Minute z. B. 45° 30′
″	Bogen-Sekunde, z. B. 45° 30′ 15″

Abkürzungen & Kontraktionen

Nationalitätsangaben entsprechen den internationalen Kraftfahrzeugkennzeichen.
Chemische Abkürzungen & ⟨stud⟩ Verbindungen und Verbände → besondere Listen

A

A 1. Ampere **2.** auf Uhren: *Avancer* (Fr) schneller gehen **3.** ⟨num⟩ die erste Prägestätte e-s Landes, z. B. Berlin **4.** (Austria) Österreich ⟨a. mot⟩ **5.** ⟨chem, biol⟩ Adenin (e-e der 4 Nukleotid-Basen), → C, G, T; (in unterschiedlicher Reihenfolge am Säurefaden der DNS aufgereiht)
A. Amt, amtierend || ⟨engl⟩ *acre*; → S. 1489
Å (Maßeinheit) Ångström
a. 1. an, am: a. O. an der Oder **2.** außer → a. D.
a Ar (100 m^2)
a. *anno* (L) im Jahre
A 1 Straße 1. Ordnung
AA ⟨pol⟩ Auswärtiges Amt: z. B. AA-Staatssekretär
A. A. Auswärtiges Amt
A. A. *American Airlines*
A. A. *Automobile Association* (England)
aa auf Rezepten (Gr) *ana*, zu gleichen Teilen, in gleicher Menge
a. A. anderer Ansicht
AAA *Agricultural Adjustment Administration*
A.A.A. *American Automobile Association* Amerikanischer Automobil-Club
A.A.A.S. 1. *American Academy of Arts and Sciences* **2.** *American Association for the Advancement of Science*
A.A.C. *antiaircraft Command*
AACP *Anglo-American Council on Productivity* Anglo-amerikanischer Produktivitäts-Rat
°**a. A. d. W.** ⟨mil sl⟩ °am Arsch der Welt (auf vorgeschobenem Posten ⟨a. übtr⟩)
A.A.F. *Auxiliary Airforce*
AAM [pl AAMs] ⟨biol. eth⟩ angeborener auslösender Mechanismus (angeborenes auslösendes Schema *innate releasing mechanism*)
a. a. O. am angeführten Ort, d. h. in e–m schon genannten Abschnitt oder Buch
A.A.Q.M.G. *Acting Assistant Quartermaster General*
a. a. r. ⟨ins⟩ *against all risks*
AATA *The Anglo-American Tourist Service Association*
ab in lat. Redeweisen: von; *ab ovo* vom Ei (Anfang) an
A. B. *Aktiebolaget* Aktiengesellschaft (Schwed.)
Abb. Abbildung
ABC *Allied Banking Commission* Alliierte Banken-Kommission des HICOM, Frankfurt
ABC *American Broadcasting Company, New York* Amerikanische Rundfunkgesellschaft
ABC-Code ⟨engl⟩ der führende Schlüssel für Kurzwörter im Telegrammverkehr
ABC-Krieg **A**tom-, **B**akterien-, **C**hemischer Krieg; in Schwerpunkten der **ABC**-Abwehr *in significant CBR aspects*
ABC-Staaten die südamerikanischen Staaten **A**rgentinien, **B**rasilien, **C**hile
abds. abends
Abg. Abgeordneter
ABGB Allg. Bürgerliches Gesetzbuch für Österreich
Abh. Abhandlung
Abk. Abkürzung
A. B. M. *anti-ballistic missile* (*system*)
Abs. 1. Absatz **2.** Absender
Abt. Abteilung
Abschn. Abschnitt
ac. ⟨engl⟩ *acre*; → S. 1489
a. c. 1. *anni currentis* (L) des laufenden Jahres **2.** (auch a/c) *a conto* (It) auf Rechnung, als Abschlagzahlung
A. C. Allgemeiner Convent
ACA *Allied Commission for Austria* Alliierte Kommission für Österreich, Wien
ACAG *Allied Control Authority for Germany* Alliierter Kontrollrat, Berlin
Acc. *accepi* (ich habe angenommen)
ACE *Allied Command Europe*
Ach·ema f Allgemeine Chemie Ausstellung
a. Chr. (n.) (L) *ante Christum* (*natum*) vor Christus, vor Christi Geburt
ACI *Automobile Club d'Italia*
A. C. of S. *Assistant Chief of Staff*
ACR *Allied Commission on Reparations* Alliierte Reparations-Kommission → IARA
A/cs pay. *accounts payable*
A/cs rec. *accounts receivable*
ACTH ⟨med⟩ *adreno-corticotropic hormone* Adr·enoc·orticotrop·in [n]
ACWW *Associated Country Women of the World, Union Mondiale des Femmes Rurales* Welt-Union der Landfrauen, London
a. D. 1. außer Dienst **2.** an der Donau
A. D. *Anno Domini* (L) im Jahre des Herrn
ADAC Allgemeiner Deutscher Automobilclub
A. D. B. Allgemeiner Deutscher Burschenbund
A-D-C, A.D.C. *aide-de-camp*
ADCA, Adca Allg. Deutsche Credit-Anstalt
a. d. D. auf dem Dienstwege
ADF Aktion Demokratischer Fortschritt
ADGE ⟨Am mil⟩ *Air Defense Ground Environment(-System)*
Adgo Allg. Dt. Gebührenordnung
A. D. H. G. B. Allgemeines Deutsches Handelsgesetzbuch
ADIG ⟨bank⟩ Allg. Dt. Investment Gesellschaft mbH
ADIROPA ⟨bank⟩ Allg. Dt. Investment der Europa-Fonds
Adjt. (*Gen.*) *Adjutant* (*General*)
Adm. Admiral
ADN Allgemeiner Deutscher Nachrichtendienst (DDR), Berlin
ADP ⟨chem⟩ Adenosindiphosphat [n]
ADP *automatic data processing* automatische Datenverarbeitung
Adr. Adresse
ADSp. Allg. Dt. Spediteurbedingungen
adv. *Adverb*(*ium*) (L) Umstandswort
ad val. (*L ad valorem*) *according to value*
AE → AU
a. E. (nach Ortsnamen) an der Elbe
AEC *Atomic Energy Commission* (→ *S. C.*), *Commission de l'Energie Atomique* Atom-Energie-Kommission des Sicherheitsrates der UN
AEC *US-Atomic Energy Commission, Washington* Atom-Energie-Kommission des „Nationalen Verteidigungsrates" (NSC) der USA
AEG 1. Allgemeine Elektricitäts-Gesellschaft **2.** Allgemeines Eisenbahn-Gesetz
AEROFLOT Zivile Luftfahrtgesellschaft der UdSSR
AF *Air France, Compagnie Nationale Air France S. A.* Französische Nationale Luftfahrtgesellschaft, Paris
A.F. *Admiral of the Fleet*
AfA ⟨Ger tax⟩ Absetzung für Abnutzung
Afa **A**rbeitsgemeinschaft **f**reier **A**ngestelltenverbände
AFB amtliches Fernsprechbuch

AFL *American Federation of Labor* USA-Gewerkschaftsorganisation
AFN *American Forces Network* Amerikanischer Wehrmachtsender
AFP *Agence France-Presse*
AFREA *Association Française pour les Relations Economiques avec l'Allemagne* Französische Vereinigung für wirtschaftliche Beziehungen mit Deutschen, Paris, Frankfurt
A.F.T.R.A. *American Federation of Television and Radio Artists*
AG Aargau (Schweizer Kanton)
a. G. 1. als Gast (einer Bühne) **2.** auf Gegenseitigkeit (Versicherung)
A. G., A.-G. Aktiengesellschaft
AGer Amtsgericht
Agfa Aktiengesellschaft für Anilinfabrikation
Agm. Arbeitsgemeinschaft
AGmbH Aktiengesellschaft mit beschränkter Haftung
A.G.O. *Adjutant General's Office*
Agt. Agent || *agent*; *agreement*
A. H. (Mehrzahl: **A. H. A. H.**) (Alte Herren)
A. H. S. C. Alt-Herren Senioren-Convent
Ah Amperestunde
A.H.C. *Army Hospital Corps*
ahd. althochdeutsch
a. i. *ad interim* (L) *meanwhile*
A. I. *artificinal insemination*
AI Inner-Rhoden (Schweizer Kanton, Teil von Appenzell)
A. I. A. C. R. *Association Internationale des Automobile Clubs Reconnus*
AIBM [Fr] *Association Internationale des Bibliothèques Musicales*
AIH *Association Internationale de l'Hôtellerie* Internationaler Hotelverband, Paris
AIPS *Association Internationale de la Presse Sportive* Internationaler Sportpresse-Verband, Brüssel
AIT *Alliance Internationale de Tourisme* Internationaler Touring-Verband, Genf; → DTC
AIU *Association Internationale des Universités* Internationaler Hochschul-Verband, Paris
A. J. O. J. *April, July, October, January*
AK 1. Armeekorps **2.** ⟨stud⟩ Aktionskomitee
A.-K. Aktienkapital
°**Aki** n [pl ~s] Aktualitätenkino [n]
Akad. Akademie
Akkumula ein Investmentfonds der DWS
Ak·üdo Akademisches **Ü**bersetzungs- und **Do**lmetscher-Büro Berlin, Leipzig
A. L. *American Legion*
Al Albanien ⟨a. mot⟩
Ala. Alabama (USA)
Alas. Alaska
A. L. I. *Aviolinee Italiane S. A.* (Ital. Luftverkehrslinien A. G.) Mailand
allg. allgemein
Alu Arbeitslosenunterstützung
Am. Amtmann
AM ⟨el etc⟩ Amplitudenmodulation; → FM
a. m. *ante meridiem* (L) vormittags
A. M. *Artium* (*liberalium*) *Magister* (L) Magister der (freien) Künste
a. M. bei Ortsangaben: am Main
AMBlFin Amtliches Mitteilungsblatt der Verwaltung der Finanzen des Vereinigten Wirtschaftsgebiets
A.M.I.C.E. *Associate Member of the Institute of Civil Engineering*
Amp. ältere Abkürzung für *Ampère*
AMP ⟨chem⟩ Adenosinmonophosphat [n]
Amst. Amsterdam
Amtsh. Amtshauptmannschaft
anat. anatomisch
anger. angereichert
Anh. 1. Anhang **2.** ⟨hist⟩ Anhalt (Land)
Anl. Anlage
Anm. Anmerkung
anorg. anorganisch
A. N. St. Amtliche Nachrichtenstelle, Wien
Anst. Anstalt
Anthol. Anthologie
Anw. Anwalt
AO ⟨hist⟩ (Reichs-)Abgabeordnung
ao., a. o. ⟨univ⟩ außerordentlicher (Professor)
a. O. 1. an der Oder **2.** Kürzung von a. a. O.
A./O. April/Oktober (Fälligkeit von Zinsen)
AOG. ⟨nazi⟩ Gesetz zur Ordnung der nationalen Arbeit v. 20. Jan. 1934
A. O. K. 1. Armee-Oberkommando **2.** Allgemeine Ortskrankenkasse
AP *Associated Press* (*of America*) US-Nachrichten-Agentur, New York
Ap. Apostel, *Apostle*
a. p., a. pr. *anni praesentis* (L) „gegenwärtigen Jahres", oder *anni praeteriti* „vergangenen Jahres"
APA Austria Presse-Agentur, Wien
A.P.C. *Army Pay Corps*
a. p. c. *anno post Christum* (*natum*), im Jahre nach Christus (*or* nach Christi Geburt)
A.P.D. *Army Pay Department*
API *Art Posters International*
A.P.O. *Army Post Office*
APO Außerparlamentarische Opposition
app *Agence France-Presse*
approb. ⟨med⟩ approbiert
Apr. April
a. p. R. c. *anno post Romam conditam* (L), im Jahre nach der Gründung Roms (753 v. Chr.)
APS Arbeitsgemeinschaft politischer Studentenverbände
APT *automatic picture transmission*
Apt(s). *apartment*(*s* pl)
APTU *African Postal and Telecommunications Union*
AQL *Average Quality Level* mittlere Güte
A. Q. M. (G.) *Assistant Quartermaster* (*General*)
AR ⟨astron⟩ *Ascensio recta*, gerade Aufsteigung
AR Aufsichtsrat
AR Außer-Rhoden (Schweizer Kanton, Teil von Appenzell)
A. R. 1. Artillerie-Regiment **2.** *Army Regulations*
Ar. (vor Postleitzahl) Arkansas
Arb. Arbeits-
A. R. B. E. D. Vereinigte Hüttenwerke Burbach-Eich-Düdelingen (*Aciéries Réunies de Burbach-Eich-Dudelange*)
ArbG Arbeitsgericht
arc *arcus* (lat. Bogen)
ARCHID ⟨num⟩ *Archidux* Erzherzog
ARD Arbeitsgemeinschaft der öffentlich-rechtlichen Rundfunkanstalten der BRD
Arge ⟨tech⟩ Arbeitsgemeinschaft
a. Rh. bei Ortsnamen: am Rhein
Ark. Arkansas
A R M 1. [Fr] *Alliance Réformée Mondiale* Reformierter Weltbund, Genf **2.** *Aviation Radioman*
ARO *Asian, Relations Organization, New Delhi* Organisation für asiatische Beziehungen
Arr. *Arrondissement* (Fr)
Art. 1. Artikel **2.** Artillerie
AS. *Anglo-Saxon*
a. S. auf Sicht (Wechsel)
a. S. (Ort) an der Saale
ASA *American Standards Association*
ASCAP *American Society of Composers, Authors and Publishers*
A.S.C.E. *American Society of Civil Engineers*
ASK Arbeitsgruppe für Sozial- und Konsumforschung
a. Sp. (Ort) an der Spree
ASPAC *Asian Pacific Council*

ASPCA *American Society for the Prevention of Cruelty to Animals*

ASROC *Anti-Submarine Rocket*

Ass. 1. Assessor **2.** *Association* Vereinigung

A. S. S. C. *Air Service Signal Corps*

ASSR Autonome Sozialistische Sowjetrepublik

Asst. Assistent(in)

ASt Ausgleichsteuer [f]

a. St. alten Stils (Julianischer Kalender)

Asta m [invar] Allg. Studenten-Ausschuß m

ASV Akademischer Segler-Verband

AT *antitank* (Panzerabwehr-)

A/T ⟨com⟩ *American Terms*

at technische Atmosphäre; → S. 1497

A. T. Altes Testament

ATA *Atlantic Treaty Association*

ata(bs) svw. at, vom absoluten Vakuum aus gemessen

ATEGE® Allgemeine Transportgesellschaft, München

Atm. ⟨phys⟩ Atmosphäre; → at

ATP ⟨chem⟩ Adenosintriphosphat [n]

ATS *Agence Télégraphique Suisse, Bern* Schweizer Depeschenagentur, Bern

ATS *Applications Technology Satellite*

Att. Attaché [m]

Att(en). *attention*

Atty. (Gen.) *Attorney* (*General*)

atü Überdruckatmosphäre

A. U. astronomische Einheit *astronomic unit* $1{,}495658 \times 10^{17}$ m $\cong 10^{6}$ A. U.

AUA *Austrian Airlines* Österr. Luftverkehrs-AG

a. u. (c.) *anno urbis* (*conditae*), im Jahre (nach der Gründung) der Stadt (Rom), auch für *ab urbe condita* (753 v. Chr.)

AUD ⟨parl⟩ Aktions-Union Deutschland

Aufs. Aufsatz

Aug. Aug·ust (Monat)

AUMA Ausstellungs- u. Messe-Ausschuß der Deutschen Wirtschaft e. V.

AUS *Australia* ⟨a. mot⟩

a. u. s. *actum ut supra* wie oben verzeichnet

AusfFördG Gesetz über steuerliche Maßnahmen zur Förderung der Ausfuhr

Aussch. Ausschuß

aut. autonom

Av. ⟨engl⟩ *Avenue*

a. v. arbeitsverwendungsfähig

A. V. Angestelltenversicherung

AVBl., AV-Blatt Armee-Verordnungsblatt

AvD Automobilclub von Deutschland

avdp. *Avoirdupois* s. S. 1490

Ave[.] *Avenue*

AVG. Angestelltenversicherungsgesetz

avg. *average*

AVN Angehörige(r) der Vereinten Nationen

Avus Auto-Versuchs- und Übungs-Straße bei Berlin

a. W. (Ort) an der Weser

A.W.L. *absent with leave*

A.W.O.L. *absent without leave*

AWOP *All Weather Operation*

Az. Aufschlagzünder

B

B 1. Betrieb **2.** Belgien ⟨a. mot⟩

B, B. 1. ⟨a.⟩ **b** auf Kurszetteln: Brief (Ggs G Geld) **2.** bei röm. Namen: *Balbus* und *Brutus* **3.** ⟨chem⟩ Bor **4.** bei Aräometerangaben: *Baumé* **5.** Bund **6.** ⟨engl⟩ *Bachelor*

b ⟨meteor⟩ *Bar*; → bar; → S. 1497

b bezahlt **b.** bei

B 1 (usw) Bundesstraße 1 (usw)

BA Berg(bau)amt [n]

BAB Bundes-Autobahn [f]

BadGVBl ⟨hist⟩ Badisches Gesetz- u Verordnungsblatt

BAH Bundesamt für das Heimatwesen (Berlin)

BAM 1. Bundesaußenminister **2.** Bundesanstalt für Materialprüfung (Berlin-Dahlem)

BAOR *British Army of Rhine* Britische Rheinarmee, Bad Oeynhausen

bar ⟨meteor⟩ *Bar*; → b

barr. *barrister*

Bar(t). ⟨engl⟩ *Baronet*

BASF Badische Anilin- & Sodafabrik A.G.

BAT *Bundes-Angestellten-Tarifordnung*

Batl. Bataillon

Bay. Bayern (Obb. = Oberbayern)

BB 1. Betriebsberater **2.** ⟨hum⟩ Brigitte Bardot

Bb. Bundesbahn

b. B. (auf Kurszetteln =) bez. B.

Bbl. Börsenblatt für den deutschen Buchhandel

B. C. Burschen-Convent

BBC 1. *British Broadcasting Corporation* Britische Rundfunk-Gesellschaft, London **2.** Brown, Boveri & Cie

B. c., b. c. *basso continuo* It ⟨mus⟩

B.C.M. *British Consular Mail*

Bd./bd. Boulevard

Bd., Bde. Band, Bände

BDA Bundesvereinigung der Deutschen Arbeitgeberverbände, Köln; → ILO

B.D.A. Bund Deutscher Architekten

BdÄ Bundesministerium des Äußeren

BdF 1. Bund der Frontsoldaten **2.** Bundesminister der Finanzen

BDI Bundesverband der dt. Industrie, Köln

BdI Bundesministerium des Inneren

BdI Bundesverband der Industrie

BDL Bank Deutscher Länder

BDM ⟨nazi⟩ Bund Deutscher Mädel

BDN Bundes-Nachrichten-Dienst; → BND

BdSt Bund deutscher Studenten

BdU Bund der Unabhängigen

BDÜ Bundesverband der Dolmetscher und Übersetzer

BE Bern (⟨a.⟩ Schweizer Kanton)

B/E ⟨shipping⟩ *bill of entry*; ⟨bank⟩ *bill of exchange*

Bé Abk. für die Grade der *Baumé*-Skala

BEA *British European Airways*, Britisch-Europäische Luftfahrtgesellschaft, London

bed. bedeutend

bedw. bedingungsweise

Beig. Beigeordnete(r)

Beiw. Beiwort

BEJ Bund Europäischer Jugend, Paris

Bek. Bekanntmachung

BELGA *Agence Télégraphique Belge* Belgische Nachrichtenagentur, Brüssel

BENELUX Wirtschafts-Union zwischen Belgien-Niederlande-Luxemburg, Brüssel

Ber. Beratend(e[r])

bes. besonders

Bess. Bessemer

betr. betreffs, betreffend, betrifft

BewG Bewertungsgesetz

BEV Bergische Elektrizität-Versorgung

Bev. 1. Bevölkerung **2.** Bevollmächtigt(e[r])

Bez. 1. Bezirk **2.** Bezeichnung

bez. 1. bezüglich **2.** (im Kurszettel) bezahlt

BezA Bezirksamt

bez. B. (im Kurszettel): bezahlt(er) Brief

bez. G. (im Kurszettel): bezahlt(es) Geld

BezGer Bezirksgericht

Bf ⟨tax etc⟩ Berufungsführer

B/f ⟨account⟩ *brought forward*

BfG Bank für Gemeinwirtschaft

BFH Bundesfinanzhof

BFN *British Forces Network* Britischer Wehrmachtsender

BG Bulgarien ⟨a. mot⟩

BG. Bundesgebiet [n]

Bg ⟨cart⟩ Berg

B/G ⟨cust⟩ *bonded goods*
BGB Bürgerliches Gesetzbuch (für das Deutsche Reich v. 18. 8. 1896)
BGBl Bundesgesetzblatt (⟨a.⟩ f. Österreich)
BGD Bayerischer Gmoandepp [m] (Gemeinde-) → Depp *Bavarian village fool*
BGG Bonner Grundgesetz
BGH Bundesgerichtshof
Bgm. Bürgermeister
BGS Bundesgrenzschutz
Bgw. Bergwerk
BH Büstenhalter [m] *bra*; BH-los *No-Bra*(-Welle)
Bhf. Bahnhof
BHE Bund der Heimatvertriebenen und Entrechteten
bhp(-hr) *brake horsepower*(*-hour*[*s*])
B. I. *British India*
BIDAC *Biddings and Acceptances Committee* Unterkomitee zur Regelung von Angebot und Nachfrage, Genf; → ECE
BIG ⟨a–n⟩ *Biological Isolation Garment*
BIGA ⟨Sw⟩ Bundesamt f Industrie, Gewerbe u Arbeit
BIS *Bank for International Settlements, Banque des Règlements Internationaux* Bank für internationalen Zahlungsausgleich, Basel; → BRI, BIZ
BIT [Fr] *Bureau International du Travail*, Genf
BIZ, B. I. Z. Bank für internationalen Zahlungsausgleich, Basel
Bk. Bank
BL Basel Land (Schweizer Kanton)
Bl. Blatt
B. L. *Bachelor of Laws*
B/L att. *bill of lading attached*
Bln. Berlin
BLVD ⟨Am⟩ *Boulevard*
BLZ Bankleitzahl [f]
B. M. *Baccalaureus Medicinae* | *Bachelor of Music*
B/M, B. of M. *bill of material*
b. m. *brevi manu* (L) kurzer Hand
BMA Bundesminister f. Arbeit u. Sozialordnung
BM A.G. Beton- u Monierbau A.G.
BMBR Bundesminister f. Angelegenheiten des Bundesrates u. der Länder
BMC British Motor Corporation
BMF Bundesminister der Finanzen
BMFa Bundesminister f. Familie u. Jugend
BMG Bundesminister f. gesamtdeutsche Fragen
BMGes Bundesminister f. Gesundheitswesen
BMI Bundesminister des Inneren
BMJ Bundesminister der Justiz
B.M.J. *British Medical Journal*
BML Bundesminister f. Ernährung, Landwirtschaft u. Forsten
BMP Bundesminister f. Post- u. Fernmeldewesen
BMS Bundesminister f. Sonderaufgaben
BMSchatz Bundesschatzminister
Bmstr. Baumeister
BMV Bundesminister f. Verkehr
BMVt Bundesminister f. Vertriebene, Flüchtlinge u. Kriegsgeschädigte
BMVtg Bundesminister f. Verteidigung
BMW Bayrische Motorenwerke A.-G. München; ein BMW ⟨mot⟩ = ein Wagen der BMW
BMWF Bundesminister f. wissenschaftliche Forschung
BMWi Bundesminister f. Wirtschaft
BMWo Bundesminister f. Wohnungsbau
BMZ Bundesminister f. wirtschaftliche Zusammenarbeit
B.N. *bank note*
BND Bundes-Nachrichtendienst [m] (Spionageabwehrorgan)
B⁰ Brutto (It) roh
BO Strab Straßenbahn-Bau- u Betriebsordnung
BOAC *British Overseas Airways Corporation* Britische Übersee-Luftfahrtgesellschaft
Bob *Bobsleigh*
Bol. *Bolivia*
B.O.T. *Board of Trade*
bot. botanisch
Botsch. Botschaft(er)
Boy Scout *International Conference of the Boy Scout Movement, London* Internationale Konferenz der Boy Scout Bewegung
bP (im Kurszettel) bezahlt(es) Papier
BP 1. Bayernpartei **2.** beschleunigter Personenzug **3.** Benzin u Petroleum (⟨eig⟩ British Petrol)
b.p., bp *boiling point*
BPA Bundespresse- u. Informationsamt
BPG Bundespost-Gewerkschaft [f]
B.Q. (L *bene quiescat*) *May he rest well*, Ruhe sanft
BR 1. Bundesrat **2.** Bayerischer Rundfunk [m]
Br Bremen
Br. Bruder; ⟨geog⟩ Breite; 58° nördl(icher) Br. *Latitude 58 North*
br. (**Br.**) broschiert **br.** brutto ⟨It⟩, roh
BRD Bundesrepublik Deutschland
†**Brdb.** Provinz Brandenburg
BRI *Banque des Règlements Internationaux*, Bank für internat. Zahlungsausgleich, Basel
Briefw. Briefwechsel [m]
Brit. Mus. *British Museum*
br. m. *brevi manu*; → b. m.
brosch. broschiert, geheftet
Brsg. Breisgau [m]
BRT., Br.-Reg.-T., B. R. T. Bruttoregistertonnen
Brschw. Braunschweig
BS Basel Stadt (Schweizer Kanton)
B/S ⟨com⟩ *bill of sale* od *store*
b. & s. *brandy and soda water*
BSchG Binnenschiffahrtsgesetz
BSHG Bundes-Sozial-Hilfe-Gesetz
BSI British Standards Institute
BStBl Bundes-Steuerblatt
B.T. *Board of Trade*
BT Bundestag
BTA *British Travel Association*
BTB Branchentelephonbuch
B.T.C. *British Transport Commission*
Btl. Bataillon [n]
bto., B^tto brutto; → br.
Btr. Betreff
BTU *British Trade Union* Britischer Gewerkschaftsbund, London; → TUC
BTU mean *British Thermal Unit mean*
Bu. Burgenland
bu. ⟨Engl & Am⟩ *bushel* → S. 0000
BUP *British United Press, London* (Tochtergesellschaft von UP)
Butab **B**und der **t**echn. **A**ngestellten u. **B**eamten
B. V. Bierverruf; °⟨stud⟩ Bierverschiß; im B. V. [etwa:] *under a cloud*
B. V. (⟨a.⟩ **b. v.**) **1.** (L *Beata Virgo*) *Blessed Virgin* gebenedeite Jungfrau (Maria) **2.** (L *bene vale*!) *farewell*!
BVG 1. Bundesversorgungsgesetz v. 1950 **2.** Bundesverfassungsgericht ⟨a.⟩ BVerfG **3.** Berliner Verkehrsgesellschaft
BVW Bund versorgungsberechtigter Wehrmachtangehöriger
BW Baden-Württemberg
BWR ⟨at⟩ *Boiling Water Reactor*
bz. (im Kurszettel) bezahlt; → bez. B.
bzw. beziehungsweise *respectively*

C

C 1. röm. Zahlzeichen *Centum* = 100 **2.** auf röm. Inschriften Abk. f. *Cäsar*, *Gajus* (*Cajus*),

Cassius, Calendae, Censor, Centuria, Civitas, Consul usw. **3.** Elektrizitätsmenge *Coulomb*; → S. 1495 **4.** Celsius **5.** ⟨chem⟩ Kohlenstoff (*carbonium* L); → S. 1501 **6.** *Cent, Centime* **7.** † = c 3. **8.** ⟨biol⟩ Cytosin (eine der 4 Nukleotid-Basen), → A, G, T
c 1. Zenti = ($^1/_{100}$ irgendeiner Maßeinheit). **2.** *celeritas* (L), Geschwindigkeit **3.** Curie [n] (internationale Einheit des radioaktiven Zerfalls **4.** Karat **5.** Neuminute
c. ⟨engl⟩ *Carat*; → S. 1490, 1493
CA *Canada*
ca. *circa* L = ungefähr
c. a. ⟨mus⟩ It *coll'arco* mit dem Bogen
CAB *Consumers Advisory Board*
Cal. *California* (USA) Kalifornien
cal Grammkalorie
Cand. *Candidatus* || *cand. phil.* || *cand. rer. pol.* || *cand. jur.* || *cand. med.* || *cand. min.* || *cand. theol.* || *cand. rer. nat.*
C.A.P. *Civil Air Patrol*
cap. 1. *capitulum* (L) Kapitel *chapter* **2.** *capacity*
Car. Caritas
CARE *Corporation for American Remittances to Europe* Verein für amerikanische Liebesgabensendungen nach Europa, New York, (seit 1945) (Care-Pakete!)
Caritas *International Conference of Catholic Charities* Internationale Caritas-Konferenz, Rom, Genf, New York
CAT ⟨aero⟩ *Clear Air Turbulence*
c. b. It *col basso* mit dem Basse
C.B.D. *cash before delivery*
CBI *Confederation of British Industry*
cbm Kubikmeter (m^3)
CBS *Columbia Broadcasting System* Columbia Rundfunkgesellschaft, Columbia (USA)
CC 1. ⟨stud⟩ Coburger Convent **2.** Fr *Corps Consulaire* ⟨a. mot⟩
C. C. Chargierten-Convent; Corpsburschen-C.; Corps Convent
cc Neuseekunde; vgl. c 5.
CCC *Commodity Credit Corporation*
CCCG *Combined Coal Control Group* Vereinigte Kohlen-Kontroll-Gruppe, Essen; → DIDEG
CCCISM *Conseil pour la Coordination des Congrès Internationaux des Sciences Médicales, Council for the Co-ordination of International Congresses of Medical Sciences* (*CCIMS*), Paris
CCFA *Commandement en Chef Français en Allemagne* Französisches Oberkommando in Deutschland, Baden-Baden; → FFA
CCI *Chambre de Commerce International* Internationale Handelskammer, Paris; → IHK
CCIR Fr *Comité Consultatif International des Radiocommunications*, Genf
CCITT Fr *Comité Consultatif International Téléphonique et Télégraphique*, Genf
CCJO *Consultative Council of Jewish Organizations* Jüdischer Konsultativ-Rat, New York
ccm Kubikzentimeter (cm^3)
CCMS *Committee on the Challenges* (Aufgaben, Fragen) *of Modern Society*
CCP *Committee on Comodity Problems*
CCR *Commission Centrale pour la Navigation du Rhin* Rheinschiffahrts-Kommission
C.C.U.S. *Chambers of Commerce of the United States*
CD Fr *Corps Diplomatique* ⟨a. mot⟩
C.D. *Civil Defence*
cd Candela (Lichttechnische Einheit); → S. 1495
c. d. *colla destra* (It) mit der rechten Hand
CDA Convent Deutscher Akademikerverbände
CDH Centralvereinigung Deutscher Handelsvertreter- und Handelsmakler-Verbände
CDK Convent Deutscher Korporations-Verbände
cdm Kubikdezimeter (dm^3)
CDU Christlich-Demokratische Union ⟨parl⟩
C.E. *Civil Engineering*
CE *Council of Europe*, Fr *Conseil de l'Europe* Europa-Rat [m]
CEA *Conféderation Européenne de l'Agriculture* Verband der Europäischen Landwirtschaft, Brugg, Schweiz
CEA ⟨Am⟩ *Council of Economic Advisers*
CEC Fr *Centre Européen de la Culture*, Genf
CED *Communauté Eurpéenne de la Défense*; → EVG
C.E.M. ⟨biol⟩ *central excitational mechanism* (Beach), → Z.E.M.
Cen. Am. *Central America* Mittelamerika
CENTO, Cento *Central Treaty Organization*
CEPT ⟨philatelic⟩ *Conférence Européenne des Postes et des Télécommunications* = *Conference of European Postal and Telecommunications Administrations*
CERN Fr *Conseil Européen pour la Recherche Nucléaire*, ⟨engl⟩ *European Organization for Nuclear Research*
c. & f. *cost and freight*
c. f. *cantus firmus*; **cf., cfr.** *confer* (L) vergleiche
CFIE *Conseil des Fédérations Industrielles d'Europe* Rat der Europäischen Industrie, Paris → REI, BDI
cg Zentigramm
CGS-System Zentimeter-Gramm-Sekunden-S.
C. H. *Confoederatio Helvetica* (L) Schweizerische Eidgenossenschaft als Postleitzahl z. B. CH-8031 = Zürich
C.H. 1. *Clearing House* **2.** *Courthouse* **3.** *Customhouse*
Charb. Fr *Charbonnage* [m] Zeche [f]
Chem. Chemiker | **chem.** chemisch
Chr. Christus
chron. chronisch
CI ⟨tech, med, etc⟩ *colo(u)r index*
C/I *certificate of insurance*
CIA *Conseil International d'Alimentation* Welternährungsrat; → WFC
CIA *Central Intelligence Agency, Washington* Zentrale der geheimen Nachrichtendienste
CIAA *Confédération Internationale des Associations d'Artistes, International Confederation of Artistes Associations* (*ICAA*) Internationale Vereinigung der Kunstschaffenden, Brussel (seit 1935)
CIC *Counter Intelligence Corps* amerikanischer Abwehrdienst
CIC *Confédération Internationale des Cadres, Paris* Internationale Vereinigung der leitenden Angestellten ⟨bes. min, chem⟩; → ULA
C.I.D. *Criminal Investigation Department*
CIE *Congrès International des Editeurs* Internationaler Kongreß der Buchverleger, Genf
CIE *Centre International de l'Enfance, International Children's Centre* (→ ICC) Internationales Kinderhilfswerk, Paris
Cie. *Compagnie* (Fr), Handelsgesellschaft
CIEG *Conseil International des Employeurs du Commerce, International Council of Commerce Employers* Internationaler Handels-Rat Kopenhagen; → ICCE, Sekretariat Paris'
cif ⟨engl⟩ *cost, insurance, freight* → Bd. I.
c.i.f. & c. *cost, insurance freight & commission*
CIIA *Commission Internationale des Industries Agricoles, International Commission of Agricultural Industries* Internationaler Ausschuß für landwirtschaftliche Industrie, Paris
CIM *Conseil International de la Musique, International Music Council* (*IMC*) Internationaler Rat für Musik, Paris
CIME Fr *Comité Intergouvernemental pour les Migrations Européennes*, Genf
C.-in-C. (Med.'s) *Commander-in-Chief* (*Mediterranean's* [*Flagship*])
CIO *Comité International Olympique, Internation-*

al Olympic Committee (*IOC*) Internationales Olympisches Komitee (IOK), Lausanne
CIO *Congress of Industrial Organizations* USA-Gewerkschaftsorganisation
CIOS *Comité International de l'Organisation Scientifique*, Internationales Komitee für wissenschaftliche Betriebsführung, Genf
CIPC *Commission Internationale de Police Criminelle, International Criminal Police Commission* (*ICPC*) Internationale Kriminalpolizei-Kommission (Interpol) Paris
CIRFS Fr *Comité International de la Rayonne et des Fibres Synthétiques*; *International Rayon and Synthetic Fibres Committee* Internationale Chemiefaservereinigung
CISAC *Confédération Internationale des Sociétés d'Auteurs et Compositeurs* Internationaler Autoren- und Komponisten-Verband, Paris
CIT *Comité International des Transports par Chemin de Fer* Internationales Komitee für Eisenbahntransporte, Bern
CIT [tʃit] It *Compania Italiana Turismo* Italienisches Reisebüro [n]
CITI *Confédération Internationale des Travailleurs Intellectuels, International Confederation of Professional and Intellectual Workers* Internationaler Bund der Geistesarbeiter, Paris
Ck ⟨stud⟩ Conkneipant
cl Zentiliter
CLG ⟨Am–Ger etc⟩ *Civilian Labor Group*
cm Zentimeter
cm² Quadratzentimeter
cm³ Kubikzentimeter
C. M. ⟨engl⟩ *corresponding member* korrespondierendes Mitglied
C + M + B in Beschwörungsformeln: Kaspar, Melchior, Balthasar
CMEA *Council for Mutual Economic Aid* (*Comecon*)
cmm Kubikmillimeter, Raummillimeter
CMP *Conseil Mondial de la Paix*, *World Peace Council* (*WPC*) Weltfriedens-Rat (WFR), Prag
cm/sec, cm · sec¹ Zentimeter in der Sekunde
cn. *consolidated* (*bonds*)
c/o ⟨engl⟩ *care of* per Adresse, abzugeben bei
Co. in Firmennamen: Kompanie (*Compagnie*)
C.O.D. 1. *Concise Oxford Dictionary* **2.** *cash* od *collect on delivery*
Cod. *Codex*
Col. Colorado
Col. Sec. ⟨engl⟩ *Colonial Secretariat*
COMECON *Council for Mutual Economic Aid* Rat für gegenseitige Wirtschaftshilfe, Moskau
Cominform *Information Bureau of Communist Parties and Workers'* Kommunistisches Informationsbüro, Bukarest (Kominform)
COMISCO *Committee of the International Socialist Conference, Comité International Socialiste Consultatif* Komitee für internationale sozialistische Konferenzen, London
Comp. → Co.
COMSAT *Communication Satellite Corporation*
Conn. Connecticut (USA)
Cons. Consul
copr. *copyright*
CORE *Congress of Racial Equality*
Corv·ina *Bibliotheca Corviniana*
cos Kosinus
cosec Kosekans
COSPAR *Committee On Space Research*
cot, cotg Kotangens
cp. *compare*, vergleiche
c. p. (It) *colla parte* mit der Hauptstimme
C. P. A. *certified public accountant*
C.P.F. ⟨engl⟩ *Colonial Police Force*
c. q. (⟨engl⟩ *come quick*) zwischenstaatlicher funktelegraphischer Anruf: „An alle."
c. r. (Fr) *accusé reception* (Postwesen) mit funkentelegraphischer Empfangsanzeige
CR ⟨stud⟩ Corpsrezipient
cr. *currentis* (L), des laufenden Monats (Jahres)
Cralog-Organization ⟨Am⟩ ein Zus-schluß von rund 20 gr. Wohlfahrtsverbänden
CS Tschechoslowakei ⟨a. mot⟩
c. s. (It) *colla sinistra* mit der linken Hand
CSG *Combined Steel Group* Vereinigte Stahl-Kontroll-Gruppe, Düsseldorf
CSIT *Comité Sportif International du Travail International Workers Sport Association* (*IWSA*) Internationaler Arbeitersport-Verband, Beyne-Heusay, Belgien
ČSSR *Československá socialistická republika* Tschechoslowakische Sozialistische Republik
CSU Christlich-Soziale Union ⟨parl⟩
C. T. ⟨engl⟩ *cable transfer* Geldüberweisung durch Kabel
c. t. *cum tempore* (: 20ʰ c. t. = 20 Uhr 15)
ctg Kotangens
Ctr. Zentner
CTR Chemisch-Technische Reichsanstalt
cts *Centimes*
cu. ft. ⟨engl⟩ *cubic foot* (ft³); → S. 1489
cu. in. ⟨engl⟩ *cubic inch* (in³); → S. 1489
cu. yd. ⟨engl⟩ *cubic yard* (yd³); → S. 1489
cum Div cum (= mit) Dividende *cum d(iv)*.
cum int. *with interest* mit Zinsen
C. V. Cartell-Verband
C. V. J. M. Christlicher Verein junger Männer
CVP Christliche Volkspartei ⟨parl⟩
c.w.o. *cash with order*
Cwt ⟨engl⟩ (Gewicht) *Centweight, Hundredweight* (l = *long*; sh = *short*); → 1490

D

D 1. ⟨com⟩ Debet **2.** ⟨mus⟩ Dominante **3.** ⟨num⟩ Prägestätte München **4.** röm. Zahlzeichen für 500 **5.** D(-Zug) ⟨rail⟩ Schnellzug mit Durchgangswagen, zuschlagpflichtig **6.** ⟨telg⟩ dringend **7.** ⟨phys⟩ Dichte (spezifisches Gewicht) **8.** Deutschland (Bundesrepublik) ⟨a. mot⟩
D. *Doctor theologiae*; → Dr
d 1. Dezi- (L), $^1/_{10}$ einer Maßeinheit **2.** (L *denarius*) ⟨engl⟩ *Penny*, in der Form ₰ Abk. f. Pfennig **3.** ⟨typ⟩ *del(eatur)* zu tilgen **4.** (L.dies- ⟨astr⟩ mittlerer Sonnentag **5.** → del.
d* ⟨astr⟩ Sterntag
da *Deka-* (Schweiz, Fr, Belgien, Österreich) (das Zehnfache e–r Maßeinheit); → dk
d/a *days after acceptance*
D. A. in röm. Inschriften: *Divus Augustus*
d. Ä. der Ältere
DAB Deutsches Arzneibuch
DAB, dab Dortmunder Aktienbier
DAF ⟨nazi⟩ Deutsche Arbeitsfront
D. A. G. Deutsche Adelsgenossenschaft
DAG Deutsche Angestellten-Gewerkschaft
D. A. I., DAI. Deutsches Auslandsinstitut
DARUF Deutscher Auslandsdienst f. Rundfunk u. Fernsehen
DAS Deutscher Automobilschutz (Allg. Rechtsschutz-Versicherungs AG)
dass. dasselbe
DAT Deutsch-Atlantische Telegraphengesellschaft
dat. *datum, dato*
D. A. V. Deutscher Alpenverein
D. A. Z. (hum [dats]) Deutsche Allgemeine Zeitung
DB ⟨stud⟩ Deutsche Burschenschaft
db Dezibel (Einheit der relativen Lautstärke)
DB(B) Deutsche Bundesbahn ⟨rail⟩
D-Banken Darmstädter u Nationalb., Deutsche B. (u Diskonto-Gesellschaft), Dresdner B.
DBB Deutscher Beamtenbund

°**d. b. d. (d. h. k. P.)!** ⟨teens⟩ doof bleibt doof (da helfen keine Pillen)!

DBG. Deutsches Bürgerliches Gesetzbuch

D. C. *District of Columbia* (USA); z. B. [Stadt] *Washington* (*D.C.*)

DC *Diners Club* (internationaler, exklusiver Klub für Reisen etc ohne Bargeld)

D.C. ⟨engl⟩ *District Commissioner*

dc Deka; → dk

d. c. ⟨mus⟩ *da capo* von Anfang an

dcm Dekameter

DCZ ⟨stud⟩ Deutsche Corpszeitung

D. D. A. C. Der Deutsche Automobil-Club

DDO Deutsche Dienstorganisation; → GSO

Dép. (Fr) Département

DDr. *Doctores*; → Dr.

DDR Deutsche Demokratische Republik ⟨parl⟩ (offiz. Name der Ostzone)

DDSG ⟨österr⟩ Donaudampfschiffahrtsgesellschaft

DDT ⟨chem⟩ Dichlor-Diphenyl-Trichloräthan (Pflanzenschutzmittel gegen Insekten; gefährdet Menschen)

DEA ⟨engl⟩ *Department of Economic Affairs*

Debeg Deutsche Betriebsgesellschaft f drahtlose Telegraphie

Debeka Deutsche Beamtenkrankenversicherung

DED Deutscher Entwicklungsdienst

DEFRA Deutsche Vereinigung zur Förderung der Wirtschaftsbeziehungen mit Frankreich, Frankfurt; → AFREA

Degussa Deutsche Gold- u Silberscheideanstalt

DEHOGA Deutscher Hotel- und Gaststättenverband, Bad Godesberg

deld. *delivered*

DER **D**eutsches **R**eisebüro

Dekl. Deklination; **dekl.** dekliniert

Del. 1. Delegierte(r) **2.** Delaware (USA)

del. 1. ⟨typ⟩ *deleatur* (auf Korrekturbogen) „es werde gestrichen" (Zeichen ₰) **2.** ⟨arts⟩ *delineavit* (auf Kunstblättern) „hat es gezeichnet"

dely. *delivery*

Demag-A.-G. Deutsche Maschinenfabrik A.-G. in Duisburg

ders. derselbe

des. designiert, vorgesehen

destn. *destination*

Desy **D**eutsches **E**lektronen **S**ynchrotron

DEU Deutsche Europa-Union, Frankfurt

Deut. *Deuteronomium* (5. Buch Mosis)

Dez. 1. Dezember **2.** Dezernat **3.** Dezernent

DFG Deutsche Forschungsgemeinschaft

DFU Deutsche Friedensunion

DFVLR Deutsche Forschungs- und Versuchsanstalt für Luft- und Raumfahrt e.V.

DG Deutsche Gildenschaft

D. G. *Dei gratia* (L) von Gottes Gnaden

DGB Deutscher Gewerkschafts-Bund

dg Dezigramm

D-Geschoß Geschoß des französisch. Inf.-Gewehrs von 8 mm Kaliber

dgl. dergleichen

d. Gr. der Große

d. h. das heißt

D. H. H. Diplominhaber der Handelshochschule

D. H. V. 1. Deutschnationaler Handlungsgehilfenverband **2.** Deutscher Hugenotten-Verein, Friedrichsdorf im Taunus

d. i. das ist

DIDEG *Decartelization and Industrial Deconcentration Group* Gruppe für Dekartellierung und Dekonzentration der HICOM, Frankfurt

DIHT Dt. Industrie- und Handelstag, Bonn

dim. ⟨mus⟩ *diminuendo* (It)

DIN, Din **D**as **i**st **N**orm, ursprünglich Abk. f. **D**eutsche **I**ndustrie **N**ormen *German Industrial Standards*; DIN/A 4-Bogen ⟨m. m.⟩ *foolscap paper*

Dinta **D**eutsches **I**nstitut für (1933–1945 nationalsozialistische) **t**echnische **A**rbeitsschulung

Diöz. Diözes·an

Dipl.- Diplom; Dipl.-Hl. (-Handelslehrer), Dipl.-Ing. (-Ingenieur); Dipl.-Kfm. (-Kaufmann); Dipl.-Ldw. (-Landwirt); Dipl.-Volksw. (-Volkswirt) **Dipl. rer. pol.** *Diplomatus rerum politicarum*

Dir. 1. Dir·ektor **2.** Direkt·orium [n]

Dirig. Dirigent

Diss. Dissertation

Distr. Distrikt

Div. Division || Dividende

DIVO-Institut für Wirtschaftsforschung, Sozialforschung u. Angewandte Mathematik GmbH

D. J. Deutsches Jungvolk

d. J. 1. der Jüngere **2.** dieses Jahres

DJD Deutsche Jungdemokraten

D. J. H. Deutsche Jugendherberge

D. j. u. *Doctor juris utriusque*, Doktor beider Rechte; ⟨engl⟩ LLD

DJV Deutscher Journalisten-Verband e. V.

DK Dänemark ⟨a. mot⟩

dk *Deka* ⟨engl⟩ (Gr), das Zehnfache einer Maßeinheit; → da

DKBL Deutsche Kohlenbergbau-Leitung; → CCCG, DIDEG

dKg dekakilogramm, Dekagramm

DKP Deutsche Kommunistische Partei

DKV Deutscher Kunststudenten-Verband

DKV Deutscher Kohlenverkauf; → DKBL

DKW Deutsche Kraftwagen-Werke; ein Wagen der Auto-Union, ⟨fam⟩ „Das Kleine Wunder"

d. L. 1. der Landwehr, z. B. Hauptmann d. L. **2.** des Landtags

dl Deziliter

DLG Deutsche Landwirtschafts-Genossenschaft

D.L.O. *Dead Letter Office*

D. L. R. G. Dt. Lebens-Rettungs-Gesellschaft

D. L. V. Deutscher Luftsportverband

DM Deutsche Mark

dm Dezimeter

dm^2 Flächendezimeter, neben qdm

dm^3 Raumdezimeter, neben cdm

d. m. (It) *destra manu* mit d. rechten Hand

DMBG Dt.e-Mark-Bilanzgesetz [n]

DME-Gerät [n] ⟨N⟩ *distance measuring equipment* Funk-Entfernungsmeßgerät

DMSO Dimethylsulfoxid (Lösungsmittel für Kunststoffe u synthetische Fasern)

DMV Deutscher Motorsport-Verband, Hamburg; → FIM

D/N *debit note*

DNA 1. Deutscher Normen-Ausschuß, Berlin **2.** ⟨bio-chem⟩ *de(s)oxyribonucleic acid* (Erbmaterial [n])

DNB Deutsches Nachrichtenbüro

DNS ⟨bio-chem⟩ Desoxyribonukleinsäure (elementare Lebensträger [bestehen aus Zuckermolekülen, die durch phosphorhaltige Zwischenglieder zu Ketten aneinander gereiht sind; sie hat besondere Funktionen bei der Vererbung]); (→ Zelle, Zellkern, Chromosom, Gen) | DNS-Fäden in e–m einzelnen Zellkern, DNS-Knäuel (besteht aus DNS-Fäden) | (die DNS erzeugt e–e Überträgersubstanz, die RNS) DNS-Kette; DNS-Moleküle (die Bauelemente sind 4 Basen: → Adenin [A], Cytosin [C], Guanin [G], Thymin [T]: A-T-Sprosse, G-C-Sprosse)

DNSAP Deutsche Nationalsozialistische Arbeiterpartei; → NSDAP

D. N. V. P. Deutschnationale Volkspartei

D_2O ⟨chem⟩ Schweres Wasser

do. dito, (It) *detto, ditto* (das Gesagte) das Gleiche

d. O. der Obige

D.Ö.A.V. Deutscher und Österreichischer Alpen-Verein
DOB ⟨com⟩ Damenoberbekleidung *women's outer wear*
D. O. B. Deutscher Offizierbund
DOG Deutsche Olympische Gesellschaft
DÖV Die öffentliche Verwaltung
Doz. Dozent
DP 1. ⟨parl⟩ Deutsche Partei **2.** ⟨comp⟩ *data processing*
d.p. ⟨shipping⟩ *direct port*
dpa Deutsche Presseagentur (Westdeutschland; vgl. ADN)
DPG Deutsche Physikalische Gesellschaft
dptr. ⟨opt⟩ Dioptrie
Dr. Doktor; Dr. theol. (*Doctor theologiae*): Doktor der Theologie; Dr. rer. agr. (*rerum agrarium*) Doktor der Bodenkultur; Dr. cult. (*culturae*) Doktor der Kulturwissenschaften; Dr. e. h. (ehrenhalber) Ehrendoktor; Dr. h. c. (*honoris causa*) Ehrendoktor; Dr.-Ing. Doktor der Ingenieurwissenschaften; Dr. jur. (*juris*) Doktor der Rechte; Dr. jur. utr. (*juris utriusque*) Doktor beider Rechte; Dr. jur et rer. pol. (*juris et rerum politicarum*) Doktor der Rechts- und Staatswissenschaften; Dr. med. (*medicinae*) Doktor der Medizin; Dr. med. dent. (*medicinae dentariae*) Doktor der Zahnheilkunde; Dr. med. vet. (*medicinae veterinariae*) Doktor der Tierheilkunde; Dr. rer. mont. (*rerum montensium*) Doktor der Bergbauwissenschaften; Dr. oec. publ. (*oeconomiae publicae*) Doktor der Staatswissenschaften; Dr. phil. (*philosophiae*) Doktor der Philosophie; Dr. phil. nat. (*philosophiae naturalis*) Doktor der Naturwissenschaften; Dr. rer. nat. (*rerum naturalium*) Doktor der Naturwissenschaften; Dr. rer. oec. (*rerum oeconomicarum*) Doktor der Wirtschaftswissenschaften; Dr. rer. pol. (*rerum politicarum*) Doktor der Staatswissenschaften; Dr. rer. tech. (*rerum technicarum*) Doktor der technischen Wissenschaften; Dr. sc. naturalis (*scientiae naturalis*) Doktor der Naturwissenschaften – Dr. des. (*designatus*) Doktor zwischen Prüfung und Aushändigung der Urkunde; †Doktoren, die sich habilitiert hatten, fügten habil. hinzu, z. B. Dr. phil. habil. = habilitatus
d. R. 1. der Reserve; z. B. Hauptmann d. R. **2.** in Österreich: des Ruhestands
DRAnz. Deutscher Reichsanzeiger
dr. av. ⟨engl⟩ *dram* (*avoirdupois*); → Bd I, S. 1112
DREB Deutscher Rat der Europa-Bewegung; → Europa-Bewegung
dr. fl. ⟨engl⟩ *drachm, dram* (*fluid*); → Bd I, S. 1111
D. R. G. Deutsches Reichsgesetz
D. R. G. M. Deutsches Reichsgebrauchsmuster
D. R. K. Deutsches Rotes Kreuz
DRL Deutscher Reichsbund für Leibesübungen
D.R.P. 1. Deutsches Reichspatent **2.** †Deutsche Reichspost
DRT ⟨med⟩ Dynamisch Rhythmische Therapie
dr. t. ⟨engl⟩ *drachm, dram* (*troy*); → Bd I, S. 1112
DS ⟨stud⟩ Deutsche Sängerschaft
D. S. *Dental Surgeon*, Zahnarzt
D.S. (It *dal segno*) ⟨mus⟩ wiederhole vom Zeichen ab
d/s *days after sight*
d. s. ⟨mus⟩ *dal segno* vom Zeichen an
DSB *Drug Supervisory Body* Internationale Rauschgiftkontrolle
DSB *Drug Supervisory Board*
DSG Deutsche Schlafwagen-Gesellschaft ⟨rail⟩
D.S.I.R. *Department of Scientific and Industrial Research*
DStR Deutsche Steuerrundschau [f]
DSW Deutsches Sozialwerk
dt., Dt. deutsch
D. T. ⟨stud⟩ Deutsche Turnerschaft
DTC Deutscher Touring-Club, München
dtv Deutscher Taschenbuch-Verlag
d. U. der Unterzeichnete
d. u. ⟨mil⟩ dauernd (dienst)untauglich *C 3*
D.U.B. Dortmunder Union Brauerei; D.U. Bier
DUD Deutscher Uniondienst (CDU-Nachrichtenorgan)
DUD Deutschland-Union-Dienst (Presse)
DUF Deutsche Union der Filmschaffenden; → DGB
DurchfVO Durchführungsverordnung
DV 1. Durchführungsverordnung [f] **2.** ⟨comp⟩ Datenverarbeitung [f]; → Schneider, Taschenbuch der *DV*
DVWG Deutsche Verkehrswissenschaftliche Gesellschaft
D. W. B. Deutscher Werk-Bund
DWD Deutscher Wetterdienst
DWS Deutsche Gesellschaft f. Wertpapiersparen
dwt. ⟨engl⟩ *Pennyweight*; → Bd I, S. 1112
dyn Dyn (im CGS-System) ≡ $cm\ g\ s^{-2}$
dz Doppelzentner (200 Pfund = 100 kg)
DZB ⟨med⟩ Diagnostisches Zentrum Berlin
DZF Deutsche Zentrale für Fremdenverkehr
Dzg. Danzig
D-Zug ⟨rail⟩ Durchgangszug → D

E

E. 1. ⟨phys⟩ Elektrizitätsmenge **2.** ⟨num⟩ Prägestätte Dresden-Freiberg **3.** ⟨rail⟩ Eilzug **4.** ⟨stat⟩ Einwohner **5.** Ost **6.** (Express) Schnellstraße [f] *express street* **7.** *España* (Spanien) ⟨a. mot⟩
'e (niederd.): hei (= er), seggt'e = sagt er
e. eingetragen
EAES *European Atomic Energy Society*
EAG Europäische Atomgemeinschaft (Brüssel) *Euratom*
ebd. ebenda
EBR ⟨at⟩ *Experimental Breeder Reactor*
EC Erdölchemie [f]
e.c. L *exempli causa*; *for the sake of example* beispielshalber
ECA *Economic Commission for Africa, Addis Abeba* Wirtschaftskommission für Afrika
ECAC *European Civil Aviation Commission*
ECAFE *Economic Commission for Asia and the Far East, Bangkok* Wirtschaftskommission für Asien und den Fernen Osten
ECE *Economic Commission for Europe*, Genf *Commission Economique pour l'Europe* (*CEE*) Wirtschafts-Kommission für Europa des Wirtschafts- und Sozialrates der UN (→ ECOSOC)
E.C.E. Evangelisch-Christliche Einheit
ECLA *Economic Commission for Latin America* Wirtschafts-Kommission für Latein-Amerika des Wirtschafts- und Sozialrates der UN (→ ECOSOC), Santiago de Chile
ECM ⟨mil⟩ *Electronic Counter Measures* Elektronische Gegenmaßnahmen
ECO *European Coal Organization*, Genf, Europäische Kohlenorganisation des ECE
ECOA *Economic Cooperation Act of 1948* Gründungsgesetz für das ERP (→ dort)
ECOSOC *The Economic and Social Council, New York* Der Wirtschafts- und Sozialrat der UN
ECSC *European Coal and Steel Community* Europäische Gemeinschaft für Kohle und Stahl (EGKS) (Montanunion)
ECU Europäische Clearing (= Zahlungs)-Union
Ed. Editio (Ausgabe e–s Buches)
ed. *edidit* er hat herausgegeben; ⟨engl⟩ *edited*; *edition*; *editor*(*s* pl)
EDC *European Defence Community*; → EVG

edd. *ediderunt* haben herausgegeben
Edek·a Einkaufsgenossenschaft deutscher Kolonialwarenhändler *or* Kaufleute
EDP *electronic data processing* elektronische Datenverarbeitung
EDV [pl ~s] elektronische Datenverarbeitungsanlage[n pl]
E.E.C. *European Economic Community* Europäische Wirtschaftsgemeinschaft (EWG)
E. E., E. e. auf Abrechnungen: *Errors excepted* Irrtum vorbehalten; meist: E. & O. E. *Errors & omissions excepted*
E.E. & M.P. *Envoy Extraordinary and Minister Plenipotentiary*
EES ⟨Am⟩ *European Exchange System*
E.F. *Expeditionary Forces*
EF Einspruchsführer ⟨bes tax⟩
EFC *European Forestry Commission*
EFG Entscheidungen der Finanzgerichte
EFP Europäische Föderalistische Partei Deutschlands
EFTA *European Free Trade Association* Europäische Freihandelsgemeinschaft
e. G. eingetragene Genossenschaft
EG Einführungsgesetz
EGBGB Einführungsgesetz zum BGB
EGKS Europäische Gemeinschaft f. Kohle u. Stahl (Montanunion) Luxemburg
e. G. m. b. H. eingetragene Genossenschaft mit beschränkter Haftpflicht
EGmuH Eingetragene Genossenschaft mit unbeschränkter Haftpflicht
EH Einzelhandel
e. h. ehrenhalber; → Dr.
Ehape Einheitspreis-Geschäft, *one-price shop*
e.h.p. *effective* od *electric horsepower*
EIB *European Investment Bank* Europäische Investitionsbank
eig. eigentlich
Einl. Einleitung
Einw. Einwohner
Eir *Eire* (Republik) Irland ⟨a. mot⟩
E. K. Eisernes Kreuz; E. K. I. (II.) Eisernes Kreuz erster (zweiter) Klasse
EKD Evangelische Kirche Deutschlands, Rat der Ev. K. in D.
EKG Elektrokardiogramm
EKU Evangelische Kirche der Union
EKZ Einkaufzentrale
el ⟨Am⟩ *Elevated railroad*
ELDO *European Launcher Development Organisation* Europäische Organisation für die Entwicklung u den Bau von Raumfahrzeugträgern
ELEC *European Ligue for Economic Cooperation* Europäische Liga für wirtschaftliche Zusammenarbeit, Brüssel; → LECE
E-Lok ⟨rail⟩ elektrische Lokomotive
E. long. *east longitude* östl. Länge
ELT Brieftelegramm (Inland und Europa); → LT
Em ⟨chem⟩ *Emanation*
EM 1. Ehrenmitglied **2.** *Express Motorway* Autobahn
emb. *embargo*
EMBO *European Molecular Biology Organization* Europäische Organisation für Molekularbiologie
EMD ⟨Sw⟩ Eidgenössisches Militärdepartement
emE elektromagnetische Einheit
em(er). *emeritus* im Ruhestand
EMK elektromotorische Kraft
EMNID GmbH & Co-Institute für Marktforschung, Verbrauchsforschung, Werbeforschung, Marktpsychologie, Meinungsforschung
EMNID-Institut für industrielle Markt- u. Werbeforschung
ENEA *European Nuclear Energy Agency*, Paris
Entsch. Entscheidung
Enc., Enz. Enzyklopädie
e. o. *ex officio* (L), von Amts wegen *by virtue of his office*
e.o.d. *every other day* jeden zweiten Tag
EP 1. Europa Partei (Deutschlands) **2.** *Europress*
EPD ⟨Sw⟩ Eidgenössisches Politisches Departement
EPE Europäisches Parlament, Luxemburg
Epigr. Epigramm
e.p.t. *excess profits tax*
EPU *European Payment Union, Paris, Union Européenne de Paiement* (*UEP*) Europäische Clearing (= Zahlungs)-Union (ECU)
equ, equiv Aequivalent
ER Ergänzungsrichtlinien [f pl]
ER Europarat, Straßburg
ERA *electronic reading apparatus*
ErbSt Erbschaftssteuer
erg. ergänze
erg Erg; metrische Energie-Einheit im MKS-System: J = (Joule) 10^{-7}; im CGS-System: 1
ErgG Ergänzungsgesetz [n]
ERP *European Recovery Program* Europa-Hilfe-Programm der USA (Marshall-Plan)
ESDAC *European Space Data Center* Europäisches Weltraumdatenzentrum, Darmstadt
esE elektrostatische Einheit
ESLAB *European Space Research Laboratory*, Europäisches Raumforschungslaboratorium, Noordwijk (Holland)
ESO *European Space Organization*
Esq. ⟨engl⟩ *Esquire* (nach dem Namen, ohne *Mr.* davor)
ESRANGE *European Sounding-Rocket Launching Range*, Europäische Raketenabschußbasis, Kiruna (Schweden)
ESRIN *European Space Research Institute*, Europäisches Raumfahrtforschungsinstitut, Frascati (Italien)
ESRO *European Space Research Organization* Europäische Organisation für die Erforschung des Weltraums
ESSA *Environmental Science Service Administration*
ESt Einkommensteuer
EStDV Einkommensteuer-Durchführungsverordnung (v 1948)
ESTEC *European Space and Technology Centre* (⟨Am⟩ *Center*) Europäisches Raumfahrtforschungs- u. Technik-Zentrum, Noordwijk (Holland)
EStG Einkommensteuergesetz [n]
ESU *The English Speaking Union*
E.T. *English Translation*
etc. *et cetera* [L] und so weiter
ETH Eidgenössische Technische Hochschule (Zürich)
Ets Fr *Etablissement* Niederlassung
EUCO Europäische Cooperation
EUCOM *European Command, Heidelberg* US-Oberkommando für Europa
EUF *European Union of Federalists*; → Europa-Union
Eul·an [n] (Initialwort) [Gr] *eu-* = gut + [L] *lana* = Wolle
EURATOM, Euratom n *European Atomic Energy Community*, → EAG
EUROFIMA *European Company for the Financing of Railway Rolling Stock* Europäische Gesellschaft für die Finanzierung von Eisenbahnmaterial
Europa-Bewegung *Mouvement Européen*, Brüssel (*ME*), *European Movement*, Internationales Komitee der Bewegungen für ein freies vereintes Europa
Europa-Union *European Union of Federalists, Union Européenne des Fédéralistes, Paris*
Eurovision *European Television*
eV Elektronenvolt

E. V., e. V. (in das Vereinsregister) eingetragener Verein
E. v. ⟨com⟩ Eingang (Empfang) vorbehalten
Ev. 1. Evangelium **2.** Evangelisch
ev. 1. eventuell **2.** evangelisch
EVED (Sw) Eidgenössisches Verkehrs- und Energiewirtschafts-Departement
EVG Europäische Verteidigungsgemeinschaft [f]
evgl. evangelisch
ev.-luth. evangelisch-lutherisch
ev.-ref. evangelisch-reformiert
evtl. eventuell
Ew. 1. Einwohner **2.** alte Schreibung u. Abk. für Euer: Ew. Gnaden
EWG Europäische Wirtschaftsgemeinschaft [f] Brüssel
ex Div ex (= ohne) Dividende
exc., excud. *excudit*, auf Kupferstichen hinter dem Namen des Verlegers: hat (es) gedruckt; sind Stecher und Verleger eine Person: hat (es) verfertigt
Exchange *Exchange Telegraph, London* Internationale Presse-Agentur
Ex-Im Bank US-Export-Import-Bank, Washington
exc., exkl. *exklusive* (L) ausgenommen
EXPO 70 *Exposition 1970* Weltausstellung 1970
Ez. ⟨gram⟩ Einzahl
EZ eineiige Zwillinge

F

F 1. Farad **2.** ⟨num⟩ Prägeort Stuttgart **3.** Fahrenheit (= Grad F) **4.** ⟨chem⟩ Fluor **5.** *faster* ⟨engl⟩, geschwinder (auf Uhren) **6.** vgl. f (*focus*) **7.** Fernsprechanschluß **8.** ⟨bes mil & mot⟩ Frankreich **9.** ⟨engl⟩ *fellow* Mitglied
f (F) ⟨phys⟩ *focus* (L) Brennweite; ⟨phot⟩ auch relative Öffnung
f. folgende (Seite)
f *forte* (It) stark
Fa. Firma
FA Finanzamt
f.a. ⟨shipping⟩ *free alongside*
f.a.a. ⟨ins⟩ *free of all average*
FAA *Foreign Assistance Act* US-Auslandshilfe-Gesetz von 1948 (→ ERP), Gesetz zur Förderung des Weltfriedens und der allgemeinen Wohlfahrt
F.A.A. ⟨Am⟩ *Federal Aviation Agency*
Fabr. Fabrik(en, -ation)
f. & d. ⟨shipping⟩ *freight and demurrage*
FAG *Formations Auxiliaires du Génie* Pionierhilfsdienst
FAI *Fédération Aéronautique Internationale* Internationale Aero-Vereinigung, Paris
Fak. ⟨univ⟩ Fakult·ät [f]
FAMO *Formations Auxiliaires de Main d'Oeuvres* Arbeitshilfsdienst
FANAK Fachnormenausschuß Akustik
FAO *Food and Agricultural Organization, Rome* Welt-Ernährungs- und Landwirtschafts-Organisation des Wirtschafts- und Sozialrates (ECOSOC) der UN; → WFC
FAQ *fair average quality* gute Durchschnittsqualität
fas. *Free alongside ship*
F.A.Z. (hum [fats]) Frankfurter Allgemeine Zeitung
FBI *Federal Bureau of Investigation, Washington* ⟨Am⟩ Bundeskriminalamt, Bundespolizei
FC Fußball-Club [m]
F&D *Food and Drug* (*Administration* Kontrollbehörde f.) Lebens- & Arzneimittel
FD(-Zug) Fern-D-Zug, Fernschnellzug
FDC *food, drug and cosmetic*
FDGB Freier Deutscher Gewerkschaftsbund Ostzone
°**f. d. H.** °friß die Hälfte
FDIC ⟨Am⟩ *Federal Deposit Insurance Company*
FDIF *Fédération Démocratique Internationale des Femmes, Women's International Democratic Federation* (*WIDF*) Internationaler Demokratischer Frauenbund, Berlin
FDJ Freie Deutsche Jugend
fdk Freie Demokratische Korrespondenz
FDP Freie Demokratische Partei
FDt Schnelltriebwagen der Reichsbahn oder Bundesbahn
FDP Freie Demokratische Partei ⟨parl⟩
Febr. Februar
FEC *Far Eastern Commission* Fernost-Kommission, Washington
fec. ⟨arts⟩ *fecit* (L) hat es gemacht
FEI *Fédération Equestre Internationale* Internationaler Reiterverband, Brüssel
Feka Fernkampfartillerie
ff 1. fein fein, sehr fein; aus dem FF [adv] *astonishingly well*; ⟨hum⟩ [statt: vV] viel Vergnügen **2.** folgende (Seiten, Jahre) **3.** ⟨mus⟩ *fortissimo* (It), sehr laut
FFA *Forces Françaises en Allemagne* (früher TOA = *Troupes d'Occupation Allemande*)
FFD(-Zug) besonders schneller Fern-D-Zug [m]
FFFF Turnerwahlspruch: frisch, fromm, fröhlich, frei
Ffm., Fftm. Frankfurt am Main
FG 1. Feststellungsgesetz [n] **2.** Finanzgericht [n]
FG(er.) Finanzgericht
FGG Gesetz über die Angelegenheiten der freiwilligen Gerichtsbarkeit
FGPräs. Finanzgerichtspräsident
F. h. z. Familie hält (für die Gäste) zurück! *family hold back*!
FIA *Fédération Internationale de l'Automobile* Internationaler Automobilverband, Paris
FIAB *Fédération Internationale des Associations de Bibliothécaires, International Federation of Library Associations* (*IFLA*) Internationaler Buchhändler-Verband, Genf
FIANI *Fédération Internationale d'Associations Nationales d'Ingénieurs* Internationaler Bund nationaler Ingenieur-Verbände
FIAPF *Fédération Internationale des Associations de Producteurs de Films, International Federation of Film Producers Associations* Internationaler Verband der Filmproduzenten, Paris
FIAT ⟨It⟩ *Fabbrica Italiana Automobili Torino*
FIBA *Fédération Internationale de Basketball Amateur* Internationaler Amateur-Basket-Ballverband, Bern
FIBT *Fédération Internationale de Bobsleigh et Tobogganing, International Bobsleigh and Tobogganing Federation* Internationaler Bobverband, Paris
FIC *Fédération Internationale de Canoe, International Canoeing Federation* (*ICF*) Internationaler Kanuverband, Stockholm
f.i.c. *freight, insurance, carriage*
FIE *Fédération Internationale d'Escrime, International Fencing Federation* Internationaler Fechtsportverband, Paris
FIEJ *Fédération Internationale des Editeurs de Journaux et Publications, International Federation of Newspapers Proprietors and Editors* Internationaler Zeitungsverlegerverband, Paris; in Bundesrepublik: Gesamtverband der deutschen Zeitungsverleger, Bonn, Bielefeld
FIFA *Fédération Internationale de Football Association, Football Association International Federation* Internationaler Fußballverband, Zürich
FIG *Fédération Internationale de Gymnastique, International Gymnastic Federation* (*IGF*) Internationaler Turnverband, Genf
FIHB *Fédération Internationale de Hand-Ball,*

International Handball Federation Internationaler Handballverband, Stockholm

FIHT *Fédération Internationale de Hockey sur Terre, International Lawn Hockey Federation* (*IHF*) Internationaler Hockeyverband, Genf

Fil. Filiale

FILA *Fédération Internationale de Lutte Amateur, International Amateur Wrestling Federation* Internationaler Amateur-Ringerverband, Paris

FILT *Fédération Internationale de Lawn Tennis, International Lawn Tennis Federation* Internationaler Lawn-Tennis-Verband, Paris

FIM *Fédération Internationale Motocycliste, International Motorcycle Federation* (*IMF*) Internationaler Motorradverband, Hawkhurst, Kent, England

Fin. Finanz [f] **Fin.-A.** Finanzamt [n]

FIP *Fédération Internationale de Philatélie* Internationaler Philatelisten-Bund, Lausanne

FIS *Fédération Internationale de Ski* Internationaler Skiverband, Stockholm

FIS, Fis *Fédération Internationale de Ski* Internationaler Ski-Verband

FIT *Fédération Internationale des Traducteurs, International Federation of Translators*

f.i.t. *free in truck*

f.i.w. *free in wag(g)on*

FKK Freikörper-Kultur *nudism*

fl. *Floren, Florin* = Florentiner Gulden

Fla. Florida (USA)

Flak **Fliegerabwehrkanone**

Fleurop-Interflora Zürich u. Detroit (USA) Welt-Blumenhandels-Gemeinschaft

FM ⟨el etc⟩ Frequenzmodulation [f], → AM

F. M. 1. Feldmarschall **2.** ⟨stud⟩ Fuchsmajor

fm Festmeter

FMANU *Fédération Mondiale des Associations pour les Nations Unies, World Federation of United Nations Associations* (*WFUNA*) Weltbund der UN-Vereinigungen, Genf, New York, Paris

FMBI Amtsblatt des Bayerischen Staatsministeriums der Finanzen

FMJD *Fédération Mondiale de la Jeunesse Démocratique, World Federation of Democratic Youth* (*WFDY*) Demokratischer Weltjugendbund, Paris

FMJFC *Fédération Mondiale des Jeunesses Féminines Catholiques, Gent*; → UILFC

FML. Feldmarschalleutnant

Fn. Familienname

FNA Fachnormenausschuß; → FANAK

F. O. Felddienstordnung

fob ⟨engl⟩ **f**ree **o**n **b**oard (Lieferung frei Schiff)

FOB-*system: Fractional Orbital Bombardment System*

fol., Fol. 1. Folio, Blatt, Seite **2.** L *folia* (Blätter)

Fortran ⟨comp⟩ *Formula Translating System* Fortran Programmiersprache

f.o.t. *free on truck*

F·oto n ~s/~s → Photographie, vgl Bild

f.o.w. *free on wag(g)on*

fp *forte piano* (It), stark, dann unmittelbar leise

f.p.a.A.c. ⟨ins⟩ *free of particular average American conditions*

FPflVO Fürsorgepflichtverordnung

FPÖ Freiheitliche Partei Österreichs

f. p.s. *foot-pound-second* (*system*)

FR Freiburg (Schweizer Kanton)

fr *franco* (ital.), frei

F. R. *Fridericus rex* (König, lat.), Friedrich II. v. Preußen

Fr., fr. *Franc* & Franken

Fr Französisch

Fra (It) *frater* Bruder (nur vor Mönchsnamen)

Frc. Franc

Freist. Freistaat

Frfr. Freifrau: Carita Frfr. von Friesen

Frh. Freiherr: Hanscarl Frh. von Friesen

Fr·isko ⟨Am⟩ San Franzisko

Frl. (nur auf Formularen!) Fräulein

frz. französisch

FS Fernschreiber

FSK ⟨film⟩ Freiwillige Selbstkontrolle

F.S.P. ⟨engl⟩ *Field Service* (od *Security*) *Police*

FSU Frei-Soziale Union

Ft. Fort [n] (Festung)

ft. ⟨engl⟩ *foot, feet*

ft. lb. ⟨engl⟩ *foot-pound*

FU Freie Universität (Berlin-West)

FUACE *Fédération Universelle des Associations Chrétiennes d'Etudiants, World's Student Christian Federation* (*WSCF*) Christlicher Welt-Studentenbund, Genf

FUEV Föderalistische Union Europäischer Volksgruppen, *Rolighed* (*Rungsted Kyst*), Dänemark

FüAkademie Führungsakademie der Bundeswehr, Hamburg

F + F ⟨arts⟩ Form + Farbe (der Kunstgewerbeschule Zürich)

FVG Finanzverwaltungsgesetz [n]

Fw. Fremdwort

FZM. frühere österr. Abk. für Feldzeugmeister

G

G 1. (im Kurszettel ⟨a.⟩ g) Geld **2.** Giga- → S. 1492 **3.** Gauss ⟨geo-phys⟩ CGS-Einheit der magnetischen Feldstärke **4.** Gericht **5.** Gesetz **6.** Geheimer (z. B. Rat) **7.** ⟨chem, biol⟩ Guanin (e–e der 4 Nukleotid-Basen); → A, C, T

g 1. Gramm **2.** Groschen **3.** Neugrad *grade*

γ (Gr) Gamma *or* Mikrogramm (im CGS-System 10^{-6})

G., ..g. Gasse [f]

GA (Zeitung) General-Anzeiger

GA ⟨Am, pol⟩ *General Assembly, New York*

G/A (*con.*) ⟨ins⟩ *general average* (*contribution*)

Ga. Georgia (USA)

Gal Galilei (metrische Beschleunigungseinheit)

gal. ⟨engl⟩ *gallon*

GAL Gesellschaft für Angewandte Linguistik

G.A.T. *Greenwich apparent time*

g-atom Grammatom

g-equiv Grammaequivalent

GATT *General Agreement on Tariffs and Trade* Allgemeines Zoll- u. Handelsabkommen

Gatt., Gattg. Gattung

GB 1. Gesamtdeutscher Block ⟨parl⟩ **2.** *Great Britain* Großbritannien ⟨a. mot⟩

GB. Gesetzbuch

GBl. Gesetzblatt

GBO. Grundbuchordnung

GC Genfer Konvention

GCA ⟨aero⟩ *Ground-Controlled Approach* Radar-Blindlande-(System) **GCC** *Ground Control Centre, -ter* **GCI**-Verfahren n ⟨mil⟩ *gr. c.l interception* **GCL** *gr. c.lled landing*

G.C.T. *Greenwich civil time*

GDL Gemeinschaft Deutscher Lehrerverbände

GDP 1. Gesamtdeutsche Partei **2.** Gewerkschaft der Polizei

GE Genf, Fr *Genève* (Schweizer Kanton)

geb. 1. geboren **2.** gebunden

Gebr. Gebrüder

GebrMustG (GMG) Gesetz betr. den Schutz von Gebrauchsmustern

g. e. d. (in Protokollen) (Antrag) geht einstimmig durch

GEDAG Gesamtverband Deutscher Angestellten-Gewerkschaften

gedr. gedruckt

gef(l). gefälligst

gegr. gegründet

geh. 1. geheftet **2.** geheim
Gel Gelatine
GEM *ground effect machine*
Gem. Gemeinde
gen. genannt
Gen. 1. General **2.** Genesis (1. Buch Mosis)
Gen. G. Gesetz betr. die Erwerbs- und Wirtschaftsgenossenschaften
Gen. Kdo. General-Kommando
Genst. ⟨mil⟩ Generalstab
Ger. Gericht
germ. germanisch
Ges. 1. Gesellschaft **2.** Gesetz
ges. gesehen
Gesamtmetall Gesamtverband metallindustrieller Arbeitgeber
Ges.-Ausg. Gesamtausgabe
Gesch. Geschäft [n]
GeschmMustG (GMG; Geschmacksmustergesetz) Gesetz betreffend das Urheberrecht an Mustern und Modellen
ges. gesch. gesetzlich geschützt
Gesobau Gesellschaft für Sozialen Wohnungsbau
Gestapo ⟨nazi⟩ **Ge**heime **Sta**ats**po**lizei
ges. W. gesammelte Werke
GewSt Gewerbesteuer [f]
GVP Gesamtdeutsche Volkspartei ⟨parl⟩
Gew. 1. Gewicht **2.** Gewerkschaft [f]
Gew. St. Gewerbesteuer
GewO. Gewerbeordnung
Gewobag Gemeinnützige **Wo**hnungs**ba**u **A.G.**
gez. gezeichnet, eigenhändig unterschrieben
GF. Geschäftsführer, –rung
GFCM *General Fisheries Council for the Mediterranean*
G.F.M. General-Feldmarschall
GFR *German Federal Republic*; → BRD
Gfsch. Grafschaft
G. G. Grundgesetz [n]
ggfl. gegebenenfalls [adv]
Ggs. Gegensatz [m]
GH. Großhandel [m]
Ghzgt. Großherzogtum
gi. ⟨engl⟩ *gill*
Gk. Gewerbekammer
G. K. 1. Generalkommando **2.** ⟨cul-com⟩ Güteklasse [f] (→ H. K. [A, B, C, D])
g. Kdos [ge: ka'dɔs] ⟨mil⟩ geheime Kommandosache
GKG Gerichtskostengesetz
GKs. Generalkonsul
Gld. (Gled.) Ganzlederband
Gln. (Glein.) Ganzleinenband
GM Goldmark
G.m.b.H., GmbH Gesellschaft mit beschränkter Haftung; ⟨hum⟩ „gehste mit biste hin" *if you take part in it you are done for*
GmbHG Gesetz betr. die Gesellschaften mit beschränkter Haftung
GMC *General Motors Corporation*
GMD Generalmusikdirektor [m]
GMG → o. GebrMustG & GeschmMustG
G.M.T. *Greenwich mean time*
gn(s) ⟨engl⟩ *guinea(s)* = 21 Schilling
GO → GBO
Gouv. Gouverneur, Gouvernement
GPD Gesamtdeutsche Partei ⟨parl⟩
G. P. U. *Gossudarstwennoje politítscheskoje uprawlenije* ⟨russ⟩ staatliche politische Verwaltung (Geheimdienst)
GR Griechenland ⟨a. mot⟩
Gr 1. Griechisch **2.** Gruppe
Gr. Groß-, *Great*, *Grand*
gr. *grain* (engl. Gewicht) **gr. wt** *grain weight*
grad. Gradient
Gr B ⟨bes mil⟩ Großbritannien
Gr. H. Q. Großes Hauptquartier
Grm. Grenzmark
Gr(Erw)St Grund(erwerb)steuer
GRU Geheimdienst der Sowjet-Armee und Rüstung; → KGB
Gruga Gr. Ruhrländische Gartenbau-Ausstellung
GS Gesetzsammlung
Gs. Gesandte(r), –dtschaft
gs. *guineas*
GSO *German Service Organisation* Deutsche Dienstorganisation (DDO) hervorgegangen aus dem früheren GCLO (*German Civilian Labour Office*) Militärischer Hilfsdienst
GST ⟨DDR⟩ Gesellschaft für Sport und Technik
Gstb. Generalstab
GUVU Gesellschaft für Ursachenforschung bei Verkehrsunfällen
GV Generalversammlung
GV, Gv. ⟨teens⟩ Geschlechtsverkehr
g. v. ⟨mil⟩ garnisonverwendungsfähig
GVE ⟨DDR⟩ Großvieheinheiten [f pl]
GVG Gerichtsverfassungsgesetz
GVBl Gesetz- u. Verordnungsblatt [n]
GYA *German Youth Activities*; Deutsches Jugendhilfswerk der USA; **GYC** *German Youth Center* Deutsches Jugendhaus der USA

H

H 1. Härte **2.** (Hungaria) Ungarn ⟨a. mot⟩ **3.** Handel(s) **4.** *Hydrogenium* (= Wasserstoff); H-Bombe [f]
h 1. *hora* (L) (Stunde) z. B. 8^{h} 30 **2.** mittlere Sonnenstunde **3.** hekto (Gr.), das Hundertfache einer Maßeinheit, z. B. hg = 100 g
h. a. *hujus anni* (L) dieses Jahres
ha Hektar (100 Ar)
Hbg. Hamburg
habil. habilitatus (zu Vorlesungen berechtigt)
Hag (Kaffee-)**H**andels-**A**ktien-**G**esellschaft
HAKA ⟨com⟩ Herren- u. Knaben-Oberkleidung [f] *men's and boys' outerwear*
HAN ⟨post⟩ (auf Briefmarkenbogen) Hausauftrags-Nr.
Han. Provinz Hannover
Handb. (Hb.) Handbuch
Hanomag Hannoversche Maschinenbau-A.-G.
Hapag Hamburg-Amerika-Linie, Hamburg-Amerikanische **P**aketfahrt-**A**ktien-**G**esellschaft
HAPAG Hamburg-Amerika Paketfahrt A.G.
HB, eine Haus Bergmann-Zigarette [f]
Hb. Handbuch
Hbf. Hauptbahnhof
Hbg. Hamburg
h. c. *honoris causa* (L) ehrenhalber; → Dr.
HCRFA *Haut Commissariat de la République Française en Allemagne*, Bad Godesberg, Bad Neuenahr, Mainz; → HICOM
hd. hochdeutsch **Hdw** Handwörterbuch
Hdw. d. St. Hdw. der Staatswissenschaften
h. e. *hoc est* das heißt
hebr. hebräisch
H.E.D. ⟨med⟩ Hauteinheitsdosis
Hess. Hessen (⟨Ger⟩ Land)
HF Hochfrequenz
Hf. Hfr. Hfz. Halbfranzband
hfl holländischer Gulden
hg. herausgegeben
hg Hektogramm
HGA Hypotheken-Gewinnabgabe [f]
HGB Handelsgesetzbuch v. 10. 5. 1897
HGF. Hauptgeschäftsführer, –rung
hg. v. herausgegeben von
H. H. Handelshochschule
HICOM *Allied High Commission* Alliierte Hohe Kommission
HJ ⟨nazi⟩ Hitlerjugend
HK 1. Handelskammer **2.** Hefnerkerze, Einheit der Lichtstärke

H.K. ⟨cul-com⟩ Handelsklasse [f] (→ Güteklasse [A B C D])
H. K. S. C. V. ⟨stud⟩ Hoher Kösener Senioren Convents-Verband
hl. Hektoliter
Hl. Halbleinenband
Hl., hl. Heiliger; heilig
Hld., Hln. Halblederband, Halbleinenband
HMAS *His/Her Majesty's Australian Ship*
H.M.P. (L *hoc monumentum posuit*) ließ dieses .. errichten
HMV *His Master's Voice*® Die Stimme seines Herrn (Schallplattenmarke)
HO (staatliche) Handelsorganisation in der DDR (HO-Kostüm)
HOG ⟨a–n⟩ Hermann Oberth Gesellschaft (deutsche Raumfahrtgesellschaft)
Holl. Holland *Holland*
HP ⟨a.⟩ **h. p.** ⟨engl⟩ *horse-power* Pferdestärke
HP hr. ⟨engl⟩ *horse-power hour* → PS, S. 1495
Hpg(t). Halbpergamentband
hp.-hr. *horsepower-hour(s)*
hp. n. *horsepower nominal*
Hpst. Hauptstadt
Hptm. Hauptmann
Hptw. Hauptwort
HR Hessischer Rundfunk [m] (Frankfurt/M)
H. R. I. P. *hic requiescit in pace* (L) hier ruht in Frieden
Hrsg. Herausgeber
Hs. Handschrift
Hss. 1. Hessen **2.** Handschriften
HssN Provinz Hessen-Nassau
HTS Hochschulring Tübinger Studenten
Hts. *Heights*
h.v., HV *high voltage*
HV Heeresverwaltung
HVA Hauptverwaltung Aufklärung (Geheimdienst)
HVBl. Heeresverordnungsblatt
HW Handwerk [n]
Hwb. Handwörterbuch
HWY ⟨Am⟩ *Highway*
hyg. hygienisch
Hyp. Hypotheken
Hz Hertz (Frequenz)
HZA Hauptzollamt [n]

I

I 1. röm. Zahlzeichen 1 **2.** *Italia* (Italien) ⟨a. mot⟩
I. Insel(n) || (bei Daten) Januar (z. B. 23. I. 1899)
I. (L *Imperator*) Kaiser
Ia Eins-A
Ia Iowa (USA)
i. A. im Auftrag
i. a. im allgemeinen
IAA Internationales Arbeits-Amt, Genf; → ILO
IAAF *International Amateur Athletic Federation* Internationaler Amateur Athletik-Verband, London
IAAP *International Association of Applied Psychology*
IACCP *Inter-American Council of Commerce and Production* Inter-Amerikanischer Rat für Handel und Industrie
IADB *Inter-American Defence Board*
IAEA *International Atomic Energy Agency*, Wien
IAEO Internationale Atomenergie Organisation [f] *International Atomic Energy Organization*
i. A. u. f. R. im Auftrag und für Rechnung
i. allg. im allgemeinen
IAO Internationale Arbeitsorganisation, Genf
IAR *International Authority for the Ruhr* Internationale Ruhrbehörde, Düsseldorf
IARA *Interallied Reparation Agency* Interalliierte Reparations-Agentur, Brüssel
IARU *International Amateur Radio Union* Internationale Radio-Amateur-Union
IASC *International Association of Seed Crushers* Internationaler Ölmühlenverband [m]
IASH *International Association for Scientific Hydrology*
IASP *International Association for Social Progress*
IATA *International Air Transport Association* Internationaler Luftverkehrsverband, Montreal, London
IAW *International Alliance of Women, Equal Rights—Equal Responsabilities* Internationaler Frauen-Bund, Gleiches Recht — Gleiche Verantwortung, Stockholm
ib., ibd. *ibidem* (L) ebenda
IBCG Internationaler Bund christlicher Gewerkschaften, Utrecht; → ICCTU
IBE *International Bureau of Education*
IBFG Internationaler Bund freier Gewerkschaften, Brüssel; → ICFTU
IBM Internationale Büro-Maschinen
IBO *International Broadcasting Organization* Internationaler Rundfunk-Verband, Prag; → OIRT
IBR(A)D *International Bank for Reconstruction and Development* „Weltbank" (*World Bank*)
ICA *International Co-Operative Alliance, Alliance Coopérative Internationale* (*ACI*) Internationaler Genossenschaftsbund, London (IGB)
ICAA *International Confederation of Artistes Associations* Internationale Vereinigung der Kunstschaffenden, Brüssel
ICAO *International Civil Aviation Organization* Internat. Zivilluftfahrt-Organisation des Wirtschafts- u. Sozialrates (ECOSOC) der UN
ICBMUS **I***nter***c***ontinental* **B***allistic* **M***issile* **US**
ICC *International Children's Centre* Internationales Kinderhilfswerk, Paris
ICCE *International Council of Commerce Employers* Internat. Handels-Rat, Kopenhagen
ICCTU *International Confederation of Christian Trade Unions, Confédération Internationale des Syndicats Chrétiens* (*CISC*) Internat. Bund christlicher Gewerkschaften, Utrecht
IEC *International Electrotechnical Commission*
ICEM *Intergovernmental Committee for European Migration*
ICF *International Canoeing Federation* Internationaler Kanuverband, Stockholm
ICFTU *International Confederation of Free Trade Unions* Internationaler Bund freier Gewerkschaften (IBFG), Brüssel
ICI *Imperial Chemical Industries Ltd.* (ICI-Faser)
ICJ *International Court of Justice*, Den Haag Internationaler Gerichtshof der UN
I.C.N. (L *in Christi nomine*) im Namen Christi
ICRC *International Committee of the Red Cross*
ICRP *International Commission on Radiological Protection*
ICS *International Chamber of Shipping* Internationale Schiffahrts-Kammer, London
ICSM *International Comittee of Scientific Management* Internationales Komitee für wissenschaftliche Betriebsführung, Genf
ICSU *International Council of Scientific Unions* Internat. Rat der Wissenschaft, Cambridge
ICT *International Computers and Tabulators Ltd.*
ICW *International Council of Women* Internationaler Frauenrat, Zürich
Id. Idaho (USA)
id. *idem* (L) der-, die-, dasselbe
i. D. inklusive Dividende
IDA *International Development Association* Internationale Vereinigung für Entwicklung
IDB *Inter-American Development Bank*
IdC ⟨stud⟩ Inhaber der Corpsschleife
idg. indogermanisch

I. E. ⟨med⟩ Internat. Einheit (Penicillin); 1 I.E. = 0,6 γ des reinen kristallisierten Natriumsalzes = etwa 1 O.E. (Oxford-Einheit)

i. e. *id est* (L), das ist, heißt

i. e. R. im einstweiligen Ruhestand

i. f. (L *ipse fecit*) er machte es selbst

i. Fa. in Firma

IFAK Institut für Absatzforschung (Ketels)

IFALPA *International Federation of Air Line Pilots Association*

IFC *International Finance Corporation, Washington (D.C.)*

IFIP *International Federation for Information Processing*

IFLA *International Federation of Library Associations* Internationaler Buchhändler-Verband, Genf

IFRB *International Frequency Registration Board* Komitee zur Regelung der Frequenzen im Radio- und Funkverkehr, Genf; → ITU

I.F.S. *Irish Free State*

IFUW *International Federation of University Women*

i. G. ⟨mil⟩ im Generalstab | **i. g.** im ganzen

I. G. **1.** Interessengemeinschaft **2.** Industriegewerkschaft [f] (Bergbau etc)

IGA Internationale Gartenbau-Ausstellung [f]

IGB Internat. Genossenschaftsbund, London

IGCC *Intergovernmental Copyright Commission*

IGF *International Gymnastic Federation* Internationaler Turnverband, Genf; → FIG

IG-Farben ⟨fam⟩ Interessengemeinschaft der deutschen Farbenindustrie A.G.

ign. (L *ignotus*) unbekannt

I. H. Ihrer Hochwohlgeboren [dat]

i. H. im Hause

IHB *International Hydrographic Bureau*

IHF *International Hospital Federation*

IHF *International Lawn Hockey Federation* Internationaler Hockeyverband, Genf

IHK **1.** Industrie- u. Handelskammer **2.** Internationale Handelskammer, Paris; → CCI

IHS Jesus (aus dessen drei ersten Buchstaben in griechischer Schrift: IHΣ; willkürlich gedeutet als *Jesus Hominum Salvator* od *Jesus, Heiland, Seligmacher*; *in hoc signo (vinces)*

I, II, III, IIII röm. Zahlzeichen 1, 2, 3, 4

IIA *International Information Administration* Internationales Informations-Amt der USA

IIS *Institut International de Statistique, International Statistical Institute (ISI)* Internationales Institut für Statistik, Den Haag

IIT *International Investment-Trust*

IIT *International Telephone & Telegraph (Corporation)*

IIT *Institut International du Théâtre, International Theatre Institute* Internationales Theater-Institut, Paris

i. J. im Jahre

ikm Institut für Konsumgüter-Marktforschung, Mainz

I-Kommission (Schwangerschafts-)Interruptionskommission

Ill. Illinois (USA)

i. L. in Liquidation

ILA *International Law Association, London* Internationaler Rechtswahrer-Verband

ILCOP *International Liaison Committee of Organization for Peace* Internationales Verbindungs-Komitee der Friedensorganisationen

ILM Internationale Liga für Menschenrechte, New York; → ILRM

ILO *International Labor Organisation, Organisation Internationale du Travail (OIT)* Internationale Arbeitsorganisation (IAO), Genf

ILO *International Labor Office, Bureau International du Travail (BIT)* Internationales Arbeits-Amt, Genf (IAA)

I.L.P. *Independent Labo(u)r Party*

ILRM *International League for Rights of Man* Internationale Liga für Menschenrechte, New York (ILM)

I. M. Ihre Majestät

IMA Informationsgemeinschaft für Meinungspflege u Aufklärung e. V., Hannover

IMB Internationaler Metallarbeiterbund *International Metalworkers' Federation*

IMC *International Music Council* Internationaler Rat für Musik, Paris

IMC *International Material Conference* Internationale Rohstoffkonferenz, Washington

Imc Intensitätsmillicurie; → c 3. = Curie [n]

Imch Intensitätsmillicuriestunde. → vor.

IMCO *Inter-Governmental Maritime Consultative Organization* Zwischenstaatliche beratende Organisation für Seeschiffahrt, New York

IMF *International Metalworkers' Federation* Internationaler Metallarbeiterbund; → IMB

IMF *International Motorcycle Federation* Internationaler Motorradverband, Hawkhurst, Kent, England; → FIM

IMF *International Monetary Fund, Washington (D.C.)* Internationaler Währungsfonds (IWF)

IMNOS Interministerieller Ausschuß für Notstandsgebietsfragen (der BRD)

Imp *Imperium* Kaiserreich oder *Imperator* Kaiser

imp. (L) **1.** *imprimatur* druckfertig **2.** *impressit* hat es gedruckt

IMT *International Military Tribunal* Internationaler Militärgerichtshof, Nürnberg (nach dem 2. Weltkrieg)

IMZ Internationales Musikzentrum, Wien

In. Insel(n)

in. ⟨engl⟩ *inch, inches*

I.N.C. (L *in nomine Christi*) im Namen Christi

inc. ⟨engl⟩ *incorporated* mit den Rechten einer juristischen Person versehen (Zusatz bei Aktiengesellschaften)

incl. *inclusive*, einschließlich

incog. (It *incognito*)

Incoterms *International Commercial Terms* Internationale Handelsregeln

I. N. D. *In nomine Dei* (od *Domini*) im Namen Gottes (*or* des Herrn)

Ind. **1.** Indiana (USA) **2.** Industrie

ind. indisch

Indanthr·en (**Ind**igo + **Anthr**azen

Ind. Oz. Indischer Ozean

Inf. Infanterie

INFAS **I**nstitut **f**ür **a**ngewandte **S**ozialwissenschaft

infra dig. (L *infra dignitatem*) unter aller Würde

INFRATEST-Marktforschung, Wirtschaftsforschung, Motivforschung, Sozialforschung GmbH & Co. KG

Ing. Ingenieur; ⟨mil⟩ [nachgestellt] z. B. Hauptmann (Ing.); *(officer) of the engineer corps*

I. N. J. *In nomine Jesu*, im Namen Jesu

inkl. inklusive → incl.

in-lb *inch-pound(s)*

in loc. cit. (L) *in loco citato, in the place cited*, am angegebenen Ort

INPRO Institut für Investitions- u. Produktionsgüter-Marktforschung

Inrenta ein Investmentfonds der DWS

I. N. R. I. Kreuzesinschrift: *Jesus Nazarenus Rex Judaeorum* (L) Jesus von Nazareth, König der Juden

I.N.S. bis 1958: *International News Service*, → UPI

Ins. Insel(n)

Insp. Inspektor

Inst. Institut

Int. ⟨med⟩ Internist

INTELSAT *International Telecommunications Satellite Consortium*

Int(ern). International
Interpol *International Police* Internationale Kriminalpolizei-Kommission, Paris
Intervest ein Investmentfonds der DWS
inv. ⟨arts⟩ *invenit*, er hat [es] erfunden (unter Kupferstichen, Holzschnitten)
Investa ein Investmentfonds der DWS
IOC *Intergovernmental Oceanographic Commission*
IOC *International Olympic Committee* Internationales Olympisches Komitee, Lausanne
IOE *International Organization of Employers* Internationaler Arbeitgeberverband, Brüssel; → OIE
IOJ *International Organization of Journalists* Internationaler Journalistenverband, Prag
IOK Internationales Olympisches Komitee, Lausanne
IOS *Investors Overseas Service*
IP *Interpress*
i. p. *in perpetuum* (L)
IPA 1. *international phonetic alphabet* **2.** *International Phonetic Association*
i.p.a. ⟨ins⟩ *including particular average*
IPI Internationales Presse-Institut, Zürich *International Press Institute*
IPMC *International Police Motor Corporation*
IPPF *International Planned Parenthood Federation*
IPRA *International Peace Research Association*
i.p.s., ips *inch(es per second)*
IPU *Inter-Parliamentarv Union*
IQ Intelligenz-Quotient (60–70 Holzfäller, Bergleute, Hafenarbeiter || 80–90 Friseure, Mechaniker, Busfahrer, Verkehrspolizist, Landwirt, Angestellte || 90–100 Sekretärin, Kleinhändler, Krankenschwestern, Buchhalter, Sportlehrer, Installateure || 110–120 Lehrer, Ärzte, Juristen, Bankbeamte, Unternehmer, Dipl.-Ing. || 120+ Forscher, Erfinder, Statistiker, Universitätsprofessoren von Rang || Goethe 200
IR *Imperator Rex* (od *Imperatrix Regina*) (L) Kaiser(in) u. König(in)
IRK Internationales Rotes Kreuz
i. R. im Ruhestand
IRO *International Refugee Organization, Organisation Internationale pour les Réfugiés*, Genf
IRRA *Industrial Relations Research Association*
IRTC *International Road Transport Committee* Internationaler Straßentransport-Ausschuß
IRU *International Road Transport Union* Internationale Straßenverkehrs-Union, Genf
IS Island ⟨a. mot⟩
i. S. im Sinne
IS *Intelligence Service* Britischer bzw. U.S.-Geheimdienst
ISC *International Student Council, London*
ISF *International Shipping Federation Ltd.* Internationaler Verband der Schiffseigentümer, London
ISI → IIS
I.S.M. *Jesus Salvator Mundi*
ISO *International Organization for Standardization* Internationaler Normen-Ausschuß, Genf
ISR *International Society of Radiology*
ISSC *International Social Science Council*
ISU *International Skating Union* Internationaler Eislaufverband, Davos
IT ⟨aero⟩ *inclusive tour* (Flug)
It Italienisch
it. *item* (L) ebenso, ferner
ITA *Independent Television Authority*
ITF *International Transport Workers' Federation* Internationaler Transportarbeiterverband, London
ITI *International Theatre Institute* Internationales Theater-Institut, Paris; → IIT
ITI *International Thrift Institute* Internationales Sparkassen-Institut, Amsterdam
ITO *International Trade Organization* Internationale Handels-Organisation, Genf
ITS *International Trade Secretariats Coordinating Committee* Koordinations-Komitee der Internationalen Gewerkschafts-Sekretariate, London
ITT ⟨brew, etc⟩ *Indicator Time Test*
ITU *International Telecommunication Union* Internationale Fernmelde-Union, Genf, Komitee zur Regelung der Frequenzen im Radio- und Funkverkehr
ITV *Indipendent Television*
I.- u. H. K. Industrie- und Handelskammer
IV röm. Zahlzeichen 4
IUA *International Union of Advertising* Internationale Reklame-Union, Paris; → UIP
IUCW *International Union for Child Welfare* Internat. Union für Kinderschutz, Genf
IUCWL *International Union of Catholic Women's Leagues* Internationale Union katholischer Frauenvereinigungen, Utrecht; → UILFC
IUOTO *International Union of Official Travel Organizations* Internationale Union der amtlichen Reise-Organisationen, Genf; → UIOOT
IUPAC *International Union of Pure and Applied Chemistry*, Internationale Union für Reine und Angewandte Chemie
IUS *International Union of Students* Internationale Studenten-Union, Prag; → UIE
IUSY *International Union of Socialist Youth* Internationale Sozialistische Jugend-Union, Kopenhagen
i. V. in Vertretung, in Vollmacht
I. v. Irrtum vorbehalten
IVA Internationale Verkehrsausstellung [f]
IWC *International Wheat Council* Internationaler Weizen-Rat, London
IWF 1. Internationaler Währungsfonds **2.** ⟨SBZ⟩ Institut für wirtschaftswissenschaftliche Forschung (Spionage-Organisation)
IWSA *International Workers' Sport Association* Internationaler Arbeitersport-Verband, Beyne-Heusay, Belgien
IX röm. Zahlzeichen 9
IYHF *International Youth Hostel Federation*, Kopenhagen (Internationaler Jugendherbergsverband)
IYRU *International Yacht Racing Union* Internationaler Seglerverband, London

J

J 1. Jahr **2.** ⟨chem⟩ Jod **3.** ⟨phys⟩ Zeichen für die Arbeitseinheit *Joule*; → S. 1495
JA *Jewish Agency for Palestine* Palästina-Bewegung, Jerusalem, New York (1929–1948)
Jahrb. (Jb.) Jahrbuch
Jahrh. Jahrhundert
Jam. Jamaica
Jan. Januar
Jb. Jahrbuch [n]
J. C. Jesus Christus, Julius Caesar
jct. *junction*
J. D. *juris doctor* (L) Doktor der Rechte
JEF *Jeunesses Européennes Fédéralistes* Bund Europäischer Jugend (BEJ), Paris
JETRO *Japan Export Trade Promotion Organization*
Jg. Jahrgang
JGG Jugendgerichtsgesetz vom 16. 2. 1923
Jh. Jahrhundert
J/J ⟨com⟩ Januar-Juli (Zinstermine)
J.-N. Journalnummer

JOC *Jeunesse Ouvrière Chrétienne, Young Christian Workers* (*YCW*), Brüssel, Christliche Arbeiterjugend
Journ. Journal
JPD Juristischer Presse-Dienst
jr., jun. *junior* (L) der Jüngere
J. U. D. *juris utriusque doctor* (L) Doktor beider Rechte; ⟨engl⟩ LLD
Jur. Jurist; **jur.** juristisch
J·uso(s [pl]) ⟨Ger pol⟩ Jungsozialist(en)
Just. Just·iz.., Justiti·ar
j. w. d. [sprich: jot we 'de:] ˣjanz = ganz weit draußen (besonders in Berlin)
j. & w.o. ⟨ins⟩ *jettison and washing overboard*
JZ Juristenzeitung [f]

K

K 1. ⟨chem⟩ Kalium; → S. 1501 **2.** Karat → S. 1490, 1493
K. 1. *Kelvin* **2.** *King* **3.** *Knight*
k 1. (metrisches) Karat **2.** Kilo-, das Tausendfache einer Maßeinheit
K., -k. ⟨mst cart⟩ Kogel, -kogel; Kopf, -kopf
kA Kiloampere
Ka. Kammer ⟨pol⟩
K. a. A. (**KAG**) Kommanditgesellschaft auf Aktien
Kal Kilogrammkalorie
kal, cal (Gramm)-Kalorie
Kä. Kärnten
Kan. Kansas (USA)
kais. kaiserlich
Kap. Kapitel
kart. kartoniert
kath. katholisch
KAV Katholischer Akademikerverband
Kc. (⟨a.⟩ kHz) *Kilocycle* (Kilohertz)
Kčs tschechoslowakische Krone
kcal große Kalorie (Kilogrammkalorie)
K. d. F. NS-Gemeinschaft „Kraft durch Freude"
KdT ⟨DDR⟩ Kammer der Technik
K. d. W. Kaufhaus des Westens, Berlin
KELAG Kärtner Elektrizitäts-AG (Klagenfurt)
kelt. keltisch
Kfm. Kaufmann
Kfz Kraftfahrzeug (Kfz-Händler etc)
kg Kilogramm (⟨a.⟩ kp) kilopond (Kilogrammgewicht) CGS-Aequivalent dyn = 9,80665 × 10^5
kg-atom Kilogrammatom
kg$_p$ (⟨a.⟩ kp) Kilopond
K. G. Kommanditgesellschaft
Kg. König
KGA Kredit-Gewinnabgabe [f]
KGB *Komitet gossudarstwennoj bezopasnosti* Geheimdienst der Sowjet-Armee (betr Politik, Wirtschaft, Wissenschaft, Technik); → GRU
KG(er). Kammergericht
KGK Kürschners Deutscher Gelehrtenkalender (Walter de Gruyter & Co, Berlin 30)
kgl. königlich
kgm Kilogrammeter, **kg-m** *kilogram-meter*(*s*)
kg/qcm Kilogramm (je) Quadratzentimeter
Kgr. Königreich
kg/s *kilogram*(*s*) *per second*
kHz Kilo-Hertz *kilocycle*
Ki. Kirche [f] ⟨a. cart⟩
k. I. kein Interesse!
Kino n ⟨fam⟩ = Kinematograph [m]
K. K., *k. k. kaiserlich-königlich → k. u. k.
Kl. 1. Klasse **2.** Klein-
kl. *kiloliter*(*s*)
km Kilometer
km^2 Quadratkilometer
km^3 Kubikkilometer
km/h Stundenkilometer
kmol Kilomol (Molekular- bzw. Atomgewicht des betrachteten Stoffes) × kg
KMK Kultusministerkonferenz [f]
Kn ⟨mar⟩ Knoten
knif °kommt nicht in Frage! *nothing doing*!
KO. Konkursordnung
k. o. ⟨engl box⟩ *knock out*; ich bin ganz k. o. = erschöpft
Kol. Kolonie
Kom. Komitat
Kominform Kommunistisches Informationsbüro, Bukarest; → Cominform
Komintern Kommunistische Internationale
komm. kommissarisch
Komm. Ber. Kommissions-Bericht
Komn. Kommunal..
Koms. Kommissar, ⁓isch
Komt. Komitee
Komz. Kommerzien..
Kons. Konsistorial
konz. ⟨chem, med⟩ konzentriert
Kp Kochpunkt, Siedepunkt
Kp. ⟨mil⟩ Kompanie [f]
kp (⟨a. kg⟩*) Kilopond (Kilogrammgewicht)
KPD Kommunistische Partei Deutschlands; KPDler, KPDist = Angehöriger der KPD
KPÖ Kommunistische Partei Österreichs
Kpt. Kapitän
Kptlt. Kapitänleutnant
Kr. 1. Krone (Münze) **2.** ⟨pol geogr⟩ Kreis
kr. Kreuzer (Münze)
Kr·ad n ⁓es/⁓er = Kraftrad
Kr·adschütze Kraftfahrradschütze
Kreish. Kreishauptmannschaft
Krim. Kriminal..
Ks. Konsul(at, –arisch)
k. S. kurze Sicht (Wechsel mit Laufzeit bis zu 14 Tagen)
Ksch. Kammerschauspieler(in)
KSCV ⟨stud⟩ Kösener Senioren Convents-Verband
KStG Körperschaftssteuergesetz [n]
Kt. Kanton
KTK ⟨hist⟩ Kampftruppenkommandeur [m]
k.t.l. (Gr *kai ta loip·a*) usw., *etc.*
Ktn. Kärnten (Österreich)
k. u. ⟨hist⟩ königlich ungarisch
k. u. k. kaiserlich und königlich d. h. das ganze Doppelreich Österreich-Ungarn betreffend (bis 1918)
KunstUG Gesetz betr. das Urheberrecht an Werken d. bild. Künste und der Photographie
Kurat. Kurator(ium)
KUVG ⟨Sw⟩ Kranken- u. Unfallversicherung [f]
KV, K.-V. ⟨mus⟩ Köchelverzeichnis (zu Mozarts Werken) ⟨engl⟩ [abbr] *k.*
k. v. ⟨mil⟩ kriegsverwendungsfähig; °k v. und alles Gute! *up you go with the best of luck*!
K. V. Kartell-Verband
kV Kilovolt
kVA Kilovoltampere
KVA Kraftverkehrsamt
kval Kilogrammaequivalent
KVK Kriegsverdienstkreuz; ⟨hum⟩ Kippen von Kameraden *old bumpers* (*O. B.*)
KVÖ Konservative Volkspartei Österreich
KVSt Kapitalverkehrssteuer
kW Kilowatt
kWh (auch kWst) Kilowattstunde
kw-hr, kwhr *kilowatt-hour*(*s*)
Ky Kentucky (USA)
K·yborg kybernetischer Organismus (Maschine mit menschlichem Gehirn)

L

L 1. Lucius **2.** *Lex* (Gesetz) **3.** *Liber* (Buch) **4.** röm. Zahlzeichen für 50 **5.** *Licentiatus*, Lizentiat **6.** Lederband **7.** ⟨rail⟩ Luxuszug **8.**

⟨com⟩ (It) Lira **9.** Latein **10.** ⟨geog⟩ Länge **11.** ⟨Am⟩ *Elevated railroad, Chicago*; → el **12.** Luxemburg ⟨a. mot⟩ **13.** Leiter(in) **14.** Leitung

£ engl. Pfund (L *libra*); **£** s d (Pfund, Schilling, Pence [= Dinare] °Moneten = Geld schreib: **£** 6.11.5 oder **£** 6-12-5 (seit 15.2.1971 im Dezimalsystem), → L. St.

L/ mit dahinter stehender Zahl gibt die Länge des Geschützrohres in Rohrweiten an, z. B. hat bei der 15-cm-Kanone L/50 das Rohr eine Länge 50 × 15 = 750 cm

l 1. Liter **2.** ⟨chem⟩ vor den Namen chemischer Körper: linksdrehend **3.** *lumen* (Lichtmaß)

La. (in der Lichttechnik) Lambert

L-Antenne Antenne mit seitlicher Niederführung

La. Louisiana (USA)

LAFTA *Latin American Free Trade Association*

LAG Landesarbeitsgericht [n]

L. A. G. Lastenausgleichsgesetz [n]

LAKAM Landeskonferenz des akademischen Mittelbaus

L. A. M. *Liberalium artium magister* Meister der freien Künste

LASER *Light Amplification by Stimulated Emission of Radiation*; → S. 821

LAT *local apparant time* scheinbare Ortszeit (SOZ)

lat. lateinisch

Latein. Union Lateinamerikanische Union

Lb., lb. „*libra*" (L) ⟨engl⟩ *pound weight* Pfund(gewicht)

lb. ap. ⟨engl⟩ *pound* (*apothecary*)

lb. av. ⟨engl⟩ *pound* (*avoirdupois*)

lb. t. ⟨engl⟩ *pound* (*troy*)

l. B. laut Blatt

Lbck. Lübeck

L. C. ⟨stud⟩ Landsmannschafter-Convent

L/C *letter of credit* (pl *Ls/C*)

l. c. *loco citato* am angegebenen Ort

LCL ⟨Am rail⟩ *less-than-carload freight*

LCWIO *Liaison Committee of Women's International Organisations* Verbindungs-Komitee der internat. Frauenorganisation, London

l. & d. *loss and damage*

Ld. Lederband

Ldgem. Landgemeinde

Ld., Ltd. ⟨engl⟩ *Limited*

LdGer. Landgericht

Ldkr. Landkreis

LDP Liberaldemokratische Partei (Ostzone)

L. d. R. Leutnant der Reserve

Ld(s..). Land(es..)

Ldsch. Landschafts..

ldw. landwirtschaftlich

LECE *Ligue Européenne de Coopération Economique*, *European Ligue for Economic Cooperation* (*ELEC*) Europäische Liga für wirtschaftliche Zusammenarbeit, Brüssel

LEFA Lebensmittel-Fachausstellung [f]

Leg. Legations..

L-Eisen Winkeleisen

LEM *Lunar Exploration Modul* Mondsonde; → LM

L.E.S. *Life Extension Society* Gesellschaft zur Verlängerung des Lebens

Lex. Lexikon | **lexicog.** *lexicography*, *–pher*

lfd. laufend

lfd. m laufendes Meter

lfd. Nr. laufende Nummer

LF(in)A Landesfinanzamt

LfW Liga für Weltregierung, Köln (im WMWFG)

LG(er.) Landgericht

l. H. ⟨mus⟩ linke Hand

L. H. Landwirtschaftl. Hochschule

L.H.D. *litterarum humaniorum doctor*, *Doctor of Humanities* Dr. phil.

l-hr. *lumen-hour*(*s*)

Lic., Lic. theol. Lizentiat

Lief. Lieferung

LIFPL *Ligue Internationale de Femmes pour la Paix et la Liberté*, *Women's Internat. League for Peace and Freedom* (*WILPF*) Internat. Frauen-Liga für Fr. und Freiheit, Genf

LIHG *Ligue Internationale de Hockey sur Glace*, *International Ice Hockey Federation* Internationaler Eishockeyverband, Edmonton, Canada; Dietikon, Schweiz

Linn. *Linnaeus*

lino. *linotype*

L.I.P. *Life Insurance Policy*

LIT ⟨DDR⟩ Kader des illegalen Literaturverteiler-Apparates

Lit. 1. *Litera* Bezeichnung der Ausgabeserie auf Banknoten und Wertpapieren **2.** Literatur; LitUG = LUG

LKA Landeskriminalamt

LKW, Lkw Lastkraftwagen (Lastauto)

LL Luftlande-

L.L. *Late Latin* Spätlatein, *Low Latin* Vulgärlatein

LM ⟨a–n⟩ *Lunar Module*

lm (in der Lichttechnik) Lumen; **lmh** Lumenstunde; **lms** Lumensekunde; → S. 1495

°**lma**[2] ⟨hum⟩ °leck mich am Arsch

LMT *local mean time*; → MOZ

Ln. ⟨bookb⟩ Leinenband

L.N. *League of Nations* Völkerbund

ln ⟨math⟩ natürlicher Logarithmus

load. & dischg. *loading and discharging*

loc. cit. *loco citato*; am angegebenen Ort

log Logarithmus

Lok f ∼/∼s ⟨fam⟩ Lokomotive

L.O.X., LOX *liquid oxygen explosive*

LP ⟨rail⟩ Läutepunkt [m]

Lp. Lippe (Land)

LPG ⟨DDR⟩ Landwirtschaftliche Produktions-Genossenschaft

lpw *lumen*(*s*) *per watt*

L. S. (bei Wechseln) lange Sicht

L. S. *loco sigilli* (L) an Stelle des Siegels

LS/CLG ⟨Am Ger etc⟩ *Labor Service/Civilian Labor Group*

LSCO *Labor Service Companies* Deutsche Hilfsdienstkompanien; → EUCOM

LSD 1. Lysergsäurediäthylamid [n] *lysergic acid diethylamide* (Rauschgift mit Amphetamine, Haschisch oder Alkohol, e–e „Jet- oder Raketen-Droge", an der man qualvoll stirbt); LSD-Händler *LSD-dealer*; LSD-Reise *LSD-trip* ein LSD-Trip schluckt man, man geht auf e–n LSD-Trip || LSD_{25} Lysergid [n] **2.** → **£**

L.s.d. (L *librae*, *solidi*, *denarii*) ⟨engl⟩ *pounds*, *shillings*, *pence*

LSt Lohnsteuer [f]; LStR ∼-Richtlinien [f pl]

L. St., Lst., Lstr., meist **£**: Pfund Sterling

lt. laut

LT *lettre télégramme* (Fr) Brieftelegramm (im außereuropäischen Vorschriftenbereich)

Lt. 1. Liter; → l **2.** Leutnant

l.t. *long ton*

Ltd. *Limited* (*liability company*)

LThK Lexikon für Theologie und Kirche

Ltq. *Livre turque*, das türkische Pfund

LTU Lufttransportunternehmen [n]

LU Luzern (Schweizer Kanton)

LUG (LitUG), Gesetz betr. das Urheberrecht an Werken der Literatur und Tonkunst vom 19. 6. 1901 und 22. 5. 1910

luth. lutherisch

LVA Landesversicherungsanstalt [f]

LVG Preuß. Landesverwaltungsgesetz

Lw Lehnwort

l/w *lumen*(*s*) *per watt*

LWF *Lutherian World Federation* Lutherischer Weltbund, Genf
Lw(sch). Landwirt(schafts..)
LX Telegramm mit Ausfertigung auf Schmuckblatt
lx (in der Lichttechnik) Lux; **lxs** Luxsekunde
ly. Lichtjahr *light-year*
Lyz. Lyzeum
LZ Zeppelin-Luftschiff
L. Z. Luxuszug
L.-Z. Lazarettzug
L-Zug Luxuszug

M

M 1. röm. Zahlzeichen für 1000 (= Mille) **2.** bei Feuerwaffen: Modell, z. B. M 98 = Modell 98 **3.** Mega- = das Millionenfache **4.** ⟨el⟩ Maxwell **5.** Mark **6.** *Marcus* **7.** (Fr) *Monsieur* **8.** ⟨engl.⟩ *Master* **8.** ⟨engl⟩ *Motorway 1, 4 etc* (seit 1959) Autobahn [f]
M. Mitglied [n]
m. 1. männlich **2.** mit
m 1. Minute **2.** Meter, m^2 Quadratmeter, m^3 Kubikmeter. mm Millimeter. μ [*my*:] der griech. Buchstabe für m: $^1/_{1000}$ mm = 1 Mikron. mμ $^1/_{1\,000\,000}$ mm = 1 Millimikron
m hochgestellt: Minute z. B. 8^m
μ [my] (Gr Buchstabe) → am Ende der M-Liste
MA., M. A. Mittelalter
m. A. im Wechselprotest: mangels Annahme
mA. *milliangstrom(s)*
ma. *milliampere(s)*
M. A. 1. Mitglied der Akademie **2.** ⟨engl⟩ *Master of Arts*
mA Milliampere ($^1/_{1000}$ Ampere)
MAC *maximum allowable concentration*; → MAK
Maced. *Macedonia(n)* Makedonien (-nier)
MAD Militärischer Abschirmdienst (der Bundeswehr)
Mag. Magistrat [m]
mag. *magnitude*
Maj. Maj·or
MAK maximal zulässige Konzentration; → MAC
M. A. N. Maschinenfabrik Augsburg-Nürnberg
m. A. n. meiner Ansicht nach
Mar. *March*
marc. ⟨mus⟩ *marcato* betont
mas., masc. *masculine* männlich
MASER *Microwave amplification by stimulated emission of radiation*; → S. 871
math. mathematisch
m. a. W. mit anderen Worten *in other words*
°**M·axi(-)** ⟨tail fam⟩ ganz lang; **Mixi(-)** „knieumspielend"; **Midi(-)** halblang; **Mini(-)** ganz kurz (Rock, Mantel)
mb ⟨meteor⟩ Millibar
M.B.A. *Master of Business Administration*
MBFR ⟨mil pol⟩ *Mutual Balance Force Reduction* gegenseitige (beiderseitige, mehrseitige, allseitige) relative Abrüstung
Mc *Mac* Sohn des
mc Millicurie; → c 3. Curie
Mch. *March* März
Mckb. Mecklenburg
Mc/s ⟨telv⟩ *megacycles per second*
Md. Maryland (USA)
M. D. *medicinae doctor* (L) Doktor der Medizin
m. d. ⟨mus⟩ (It) *mano destra* rechte Hand
m/d *month(s) after date*
MDAP *Mutual Defense Assistance Program* (der USA) Programm der gegenseitigen Verteidigungshilfe (MSA, OEEC, NATO)
M. d. B. Mitglied des Bundestages
MDE Minderung der Erwerbsfähigkeit
M. d. F. G. b. Mit der Führung der Geschäfte beauftragt
M. d. L. Mitglied des Landtages
m. d. L. b. mit der Leitung beauftragt
M. d. R. Mitglied des Reichstags
MdS. Mitglied des Senats
m. d. W. d. G. b. mit der Wahrnehmung der Geschäfte beauftragt
ME ⟨Kern-phys⟩ Masseeinheit
ME Fr *Mouvement Européen* Europa-Bewegung, Brüssel
Me. Maine (USA)
M. E. Mache-Einheit (Radioaktivität)
m. E. meines Erachtens
MEA Mietseinigungsamt
Med. Medizinal
MEEC *Middle East Economic Commission* Wirtschafts-Kommission für den Mittleren Orient
Mem. *mémoires* (Fr) Denkschriften, Erinnerungen
MER Mitteleuropäisches Reisebüro
Messrs *Messieurs* (Herren), bes. bei Firmen mit Eigennamen in Briefaufschriften gebraucht
MEZ mitteleuropäische Zeit (⟨rail⟩ gilt auch f Großbritannien, Norwegen, Polen, Portugal)
MF ⟨wir, telv⟩ *medium frequency* Mittelwelle [f]
mf ⟨mus⟩ *mezzoforte* (It) halblaut
m.f. ⟨pap⟩ *machine finish*
mfr. *manufacturer*
mg Milligramm
MG Maschinengewehr, l. MG leichtes MG, s. MG schweres MG
mGal Milligal (Beschleunigung); → Gal
M. G. K. Maschinengewehrkompanie
Mg. ph. *Magister pharmaciae*, Titel der Apotheker in Österreich
Mgr *Monseigneur*; **Mgr.** Magister
mgr. *manager*
mhd mittelhochdeutsch
MHG magneto-hydraulischer Generator
M. Hon. *Most Honorable*
M.H.S. *Massachusetts Historical Society*
M.I.5 ⟨engl⟩ *Military Intelligence*; (*which deals with matters of State security*)
mi. ⟨engl⟩ *mile* (*statute*)
Miag Mühlenbau und Industrie A.-G., Braunschweig
Mich. Michigan (USA)
M·idi(-) → Maxi(-)
MIF *Miners' International Federation* Internationaler Bergarbeiterverband, London
Mij. *Maatschappij* (niederländ.), Gesellschaft
M·iko m ~s/~s ⟨hum⟩ Minderwertigkeitskomplex *inferiority complex*
mikr. mikroskopisch
Mil. Militär
Mill. Million, Millionen
MilStGB Militärstrafgesetzbuch
min. 1. Zeitminute **2.** mittlere Sonnenminute **3.** ⟨engl⟩ *minim*
Min. Minister, Ministerium
MinBlFin Ministerialblatt des Bundesministers der Finanzen
M·ini(-) → Maxi(-)
Minn. Minnesota (USA)
Mio Million(en)
M.I.P. *marine insurance policy*
MIRV ⟨mil⟩ *Multiple Independently Targetable Reentry Vehicle* N (Flugkörper mit Mehrfach-Sprengkörpern)
Mitr·opa Mitteleuropäische Schlaf- und Speisewagen-A.-G.
Mitt. Mitteilungen
mitteld. mitteldeutsch
Mixi(-) → Maxi(-)
mkg, m-kg *meter-kilogram(s)*
mkp Meter-Kilopond
MKS-System Meter-Kilogramm-Sekunden-S.
ml Milliliter

mlat. mittellateinisch
Mld. Milliarde
MLF Multilaterale (Nato-)Atomstreitmacht (. . *Force*)
Mlle. Fr *Mademoiselle* Fräulein
m. m. *mutatis mutandis* (L) nach Änderung des zu Ändernden, d. h. nach Berücksichtigung der (beiderseitigen) besonderen Merkmale
mm Millimeter; mμ Millimikron; mm^2 Flächenmillimeter; mm^3 Raummillimeter
MM 1. Matthäus Müller (Sekt) **2.** Mustermesse
MM. Fr *Messieurs*
Mme. Fr *Madame* Frau; gnädige Frau
MMM *Mouvement Mondial des Mères, World Movement of Mothers* (*WMM*), Paris
mmol Millimol; → mol
mmWS Millimeter Wassersäule
mμ Millimikron
M.N.A.S. *Member of the National Academy of Sciences*
mnd. mittelniederdeutsch
Mo. Missouri (USA)
mod. ⟨mus⟩ *moderato* mäßig, *moderate*
M·ofa n ∼s/∼s ⟨fam⟩ Motorfahrrad [n]
MOL *Military Orbiting Laboratory*
mol Mol (Einheit des Molekulargewichtes)
Mont. Montana
Montan-Union *European-Coal and Steel Community* Gemeinschaft für Kohle und Stahl
M·oped n ∼s/∼s „Motorisiertes Pedal"-Fahrrad [n]
M.O.U.S.E., Mouse M*inimum* **O***rbital* **U***nmanned* **S***atellite of the* **E***arth*
MOZ Mittlere Ortszeit *local mean time* (LMT)
M.P. *Mounted Police* Berittene Polizei
mp *mezzopiano* (It), halbleise
m. p. *manu propria* (L) eigenhändig
M.P.C. *Member of Parliament, Canada*
m.p.g., mpg *mile(s) per gallon* ⟨mot⟩
m.p.h., mph *mile(s) per hour* ⟨mot⟩
Mr, Mr. ⟨engl⟩ *Mister*; pl → Messrs
MR. Ministerialrat
Mrd. Milliarde, Milliarden
MRA *Moral Re-Armement, London* Moralische Aufrüstung (Caux-Bewegung)
Mrs, Mrs. vor Familiennamen ⟨engl⟩ *Mistress*
M+S ⟨mot⟩ Matsch- u. Schnee(-Reifen) *mud and snow* (*tire*)
M.S. *Master of Science*
M.S., M/S *motor ship*
m/sec. Meter je Sekunde
m. s., m. sin. ⟨mus⟩ *mano sinistra*, linke Hand
MS., Ms., Mskr. Manuskript, pl MSS.
MSA *Mutual Security Agency, Washington* Amerik. Verwaltung f. Gemeinsame Sicherheit
MSB *Military Security Board, Koblenz* Militärisches Sicherheitsamt der HICOM
MSEUE *Mouvement Socialiste pour les Etats-Unis d'Europe, Socialist Movement for the United States of Europe* (*SMUSE*) Sozialist. Bewegung für die V. St. von Europa, Paris
Msgr. (Fr) *Monseigneur* od (It) *Monsignore*
m. s. l. *mean sea level*
MStG. Militärstrafgesetzbuch
Mstr. Meister
m. T. ⟨exch⟩ mit Talon (Erneuerungsschein)
M.T. *mean time*; ⟨Am⟩ *Mountain time*
Mt. *mount* (Engl), *mont* (Fr), Berg
mt Metertonne; ⟨engl⟩ M.T.
MTA Medizinisch-technische Assistentin [f]
Mte. *monte* (It, Span, Portug) Berg
M. U. Dr. *medicinae universalis doctor* (L), Doktor der gesamten Medizin
Mus. Museum
MV ⟨arch⟩ Märkisches Viertel [n] (Berlin); von der Gesobau (→ d.) erstellt; MV-Planer etc
mV Millivolt
m. V. ⟨artill⟩ mit Verzögerung
m. v. *mezza voce* (It) mit halber Stimme
MVBl, MVBlatt Marine Verordnungsblatt
MW Mittelwasserstand
M. W. Minenwerfer
m. W. meines Wissens
m. w. machen wir
MWD ⟨russ⟩ Spionage-(Abwehr-)Organisation
MWO Meteorologische Weltorganisation, Lausanne; → WMO, OMM
MwSt Mehrwertsteuer [f]
Mz. Mehrzahl
μ 1. Mikron **2.** Mikro-
μb ⟨meteor⟩ Mikrobar
μc Mikrocurie; → c 3. Curie
μg Mikrogramm (⟨a.⟩ γ Gamma)
μμ Mikro-Mikron

N

N 1. Norden **2.** ⟨chem⟩ *nitrogenium* Stickstoff **3.** Newton (im CGS-System) 10^5 dyn **4.** ⟨engl⟩ Normallösung **5.** *Norge* (Norwegen) ⟨a. mot⟩ **6.** noch nicht bekannt **7.** im Wörterbuch = NATO
n 1. Neutrum **2.** netto (It) rein **3.** Nano- (Maßvorsilbe); → S. 1492 **4.** ⟨pharm, med⟩ Doseneinheit
N. Notar
N. A. Neue Ausgabe
NAC *North Atlantic Council* Nordatlantikrat
Nachf. Nachfolger
NAG Nationale Automobil-Gesellschaft A.-G.
NAM *National Association of Manufacturers*, Nationalverband der amerik. Industrie
NAPOLA [f] ⟨nazi⟩ Natonalpolitische Erziehungsanstalt
NASA ⟨Am⟩ *National Aeronautics and Space Administration* Weltraumbehörde
Nat.Ök. Nationalökonomie
NATO *North Atlantic Treaty Organization* Nordatlantik Pakt-Organisation, London, Brüssel, Washington (Atlantik-Pakt; Verteidigungsgemeinschaft)
Nat.Vers. Nationalversammlung
Naturf. Naturforscher
n. Ausg. neue Ausgabe
N. B., NB *nota bene* (L) merke wohl
n. B., n. Br. nördliche Breite
NBC *National Broadcasting Corporation* Nationale Rundfunkgesellschaft der USA
NBER ⟨Am⟩ *National Bureau of Economic Research*
NBS *National Bureau of Standards, Washington, D.C. 25*
Nby. Niederbayern
N. C. Nordkarolina
n. Chr. nach Christus
n. Chr. G. nach Christi Geburt
NCL *National Council of Labour, London* Nationaler Arbeiter-Rat Großbritanniens
ND (Feind-)Nachrichtendienst [m]
Nd. Nieder-
N. D. Nord Dakota (USA)
nd., ndd. niederdeutsch
NDP Nationaldemokratische Partei (DDR)
NDPÖ Nationaldemokratische Partei Österreich
NDR Norddeutscher Rundfunk (Hamburg und Hannover)
Nds. Niedersachsen
NE Neuenburg (Schweizer Kanton)
NE- Nichteisen- *non-ferrous* (*metal*)
Ne Nummer englisch; → Nf
NEB *New English Bible*
Neb. Nebraska (USA)
nem. con. L *nemine contradicente* wobei niemand Widerspruch erhob

nem. diss. L *nemine dissentiente* wobei niemand anderer Meinung war
NE-Metalle Nichteisenmetalle
Nep ⟨russ⟩ *Nowaja Ekonomitscheskaja Politika* (Neue ökonomische Politik)
Neth. *Netherlands* Niederlande [pl]
Neur. ⟨med⟩ Neurologe
Nev. Nevada (USA)
NF 1. Niederfrequenz **2.** ⟨DDR⟩ Nationale Front
N. F. Neue Folge
Nf Nummer französisch *French yarn count*
NFE *National Committee Free Europe, New York* National-Komitee für ein freies Europa
N. H. 1. Normalhöhenpunkt **2.** Neu-Hampshire (USA)
nhd. neuhochdeutsch
Ni ⟨chem⟩ Nickel
niederd. niederdeutsch
N. I. R. A., Nira ⟨Am⟩ *National Industrial Recovery Act* Gesetz zum Wiederaufbau der nationalen Industrie
Nirosta nichtrostender Stahl
N. J. Neu-Jersey (USA)
n. J. nächsten Jahres
NK Normalkerze = Hefnerkerze
NL Niederlande ⟨a. mot⟩
N.L. *New Latin*
NLA ⟨parl⟩ Nationalliberale Aktion
nlat. neulateinisch
N. M. Neu-Mexiko (USA)
Nm Nummer metrisch *metric yarn count*
n. M. 1. nächsten Monats **2.** nach Muster
n. mi. ⟨engl⟩ *mile* (*nautical*) Seemeile
N. N. (*nomen nescio* den Namen weiß ich nicht) irgend jemand; ⟨sport⟩ (ungenannter Spieler) *A. N. other* (= *another*); *S. O. else* (= *some one else*)
NN bei Höhenangaben: Normalnull; (500 m) über NN über dem Meeresspiegel
nn. *netto netto*, frei von jeglichen Abzügen
NNO Nordnordost
NNW Nordnordwest
NO Nordost
no. *netto* (It) rein
No., N° Numero (mst. Nr.)
N.-Ö. (Nö.) Niederösterreich
NOB Notopfer Berlin [n]
NOK Nationale Olympische Komitees [pl], → CIO
nordd. norddeutsch
nördl. nördlich
Nov. November
np. ⟨mar⟩ *neap* (*tides*)
NPD Nationaldemokratische Partei Deutschlands
Nr., N^{r}. Nummer
NRW Nordrhein-Westfalen
NRT. Netto-Registertonne
NS *Nuclear Ship*
N. S. nach Sicht (auf Wechseln)
NS. Nachschrift; **NS** Nationalsozialischisch
NSBO NS-Betriebszellen-Organisation
NSBDT. NS-Bund Deutscher Technik
NSC *National Security Council, Washington* Nationaler Verteidigungs-Rat der USA
NSchl. Niederschlesien
NSDAP ⟨nazi⟩ Nationalsozialistische Deutsche Arbeiterpartei
NSDMB NS-Deutscher Marine-Bund
NSD-Dozentenbund NS-Deutscher Dozentenbund
NSDStB NS-Deutscher Studentenbund
NSD-Studentenbund → NSDStB.
NSFK Nationalsozialistisches Fliegerkorps
NSKK Nationalsozialistisches Kraftfahrkorps
NSKOV Nationalsozialistische Kriegsopferversorgung
NSLB Nationalsozialistischer Lehrerbund
NSRB Nationalsozialistischer Rechtswahrerbund
n. St. neuen Stils, die Zeitrechnung nach dem Gregorianischen Kalender
NSU Vereinigte Fahrzeugwerke A.-G., Neckarsulm
NSV Nationalsozialistische Volkswohlfahrt
N. T. Neues Testament
nto *netto* (It) rein
NTS ⟨russ⟩ Emigranten-Organisation: „Nationaler Verband der Solidaristen"
num. No.
N-U-R Neckermann (Kaufhaus) u Reisen (führendes deutsches Flugreise-Unternehmen)
NV Notverordnung
NVA ⟨SBZ⟩ Nationale Volksarmee [f]
NVH Notverband vertriebener Hochschullehrer
NV-Vertrag Nicht-Verbreitungs-Vertrag (Atomsperrvertrag)
NW Nordwest, Nordwesten
NW Nidwalden (Schweizer Kanton, Teil Unterwaldens)
NWDR Nordwestdeutscher Rundfunk (Hamburg) ⟨wir⟩
nx (lichttechnische Einheit) Nox; → lx
N. Y. Newyork
N.Y.T. *New York Times* (Zeitung)
N.Z.Z. Neue Zürcher Zeitung

O

O 1. Osten **2.** ⟨chem⟩ *Oxygenium* (L) Sauerstoff → S. 1501 **3.** im Wechselrecht: Order (auch O/)
O/ Order (bei Wechseln)
O. 1. Ordnung **2.** Ober.. **3.** Ohio (USA)
o. oder
Ω ⟨el⟩ Ohm
OAE Organisation für afrikanische Einheit
OAS *Organization of American States* Organisation der amerikanischen Staaten, Washington
OAU *Organization for African Unity*
ÖAV Österreichischer Alpen-Verein [m]
OB Oberbürgermeister
o.B. ⟨med⟩ ohne (krankhaften) Befund
Obb. Oberbayern
Ob. d. H. Oberbefehlshaber des Heeres (bis 1945)
Ob. d. L. Oberbefehlshaber der Luftwaffe (bis 1945)
Ob. d. M. Oberbefehlshaber der Marine (bis 1945)
oberd., obd. oberdeutsch
Ober-Ost Oberbefehlshaber Ost
ObLG(er). Oberstes Landesgericht
OblR. Obligationenrecht (Schweiz)
Obm. Obmann
·Obus, der Oberleitungsomnibus
Oblt. Oberleutnant
Obstlt. Oberstleutnant
OB-West Oberbefehlshaber West
Oby. Oberbayern
O. Cap. *Ordinis Capucinorum* (L) (Mitglied) des Kapuzinerordens
O. Carm. *Ordinis Carmelitarum* (L) (Mitglied) des Karmeliterordens
OCAS *Organization of Central American States*
O. Cist. *Ordinis Cisterciensium* (L) (Mitglied) des Zisterzienserordens
O/D ⟨bank⟩ *overdraft* überzogen
od. oder
o. D(b). ohne Dividende(nbogen, -schein)
ODS Ostpolitischer Deutscher Studentenbund e.V.
OE *Old English*
O. E. Oxford-Einheit (Penicillin-Einheit); → I. E.
O.E.C.D. *Organization for Economic Cooperation and Development* Organisation für wirtschaftliche Zusammenarbeit u. Entwicklung

OECE *Organisation Européenne de Coopération Economique* Europäischer Wirtschafts-Rat; → OEEC
O.E.D., OED *Oxford English Dictionary*
OEEC *Organization for European Economic Cooperation, Paris, Organisation Européenne de Coopération Economique* (*OECE*) Europäischer Wirtschafts-Rat
OEO ⟨Am⟩ *Office of Economic Opportunity*
OEZ. osteuropäische Zeit (gilt nur noch für Bulgarien, Finnland, Griechenland, Rumänien u die Türkei; für Italien nur im Sommer)
OFD Oberfinanzdirektion
off(ic). offizinell (als Heilmittel gebraucht)
Offb. Offenbarung
Offz.-Heim Offizierheim [n]
OFH Oberster Finanzgerichtshof
O. F. M. *Ordinis Fratrum Minorum* (L) (Mitglied) des Minoritenordens (Franziskaner)
OFPräs. Oberfinanzpräsident
Ofr. Oberfranken
OG Organisation Gehlen 1945–1953, Vorgängerin des BND
OGPU vereinh. staatl. polit. Verwaltung in Rußland, Fortsetzung der Tscheka
OHG Offene Handelsgesellschaft
OHG. *Old High German*
O. H. L. Oberste Heeresleitung (bis 1918)
OIC *Office Central des Transports Internationaux par Chemin de Fer, Central Office for International Transport by Rail* Zentralbüro für internat. Eisenbahn-Transporte (ZBIE), Bern
OIE *Organisation Internationale des Employeurs, International Organization of Employers* (*IOE*) Internationaler Arbeitgeberverband, Brüssel
OIJ *Organisation Internationale des Journalistes International Organization of Journalists* (*IOJ*) Internationaler Journalistenverband, Prag
OIR *Organisation Internationale pour les Réfugiés* Internationale Flüchtlings-Organisations, Genf; → IRO
OIRT *Organisation Internationale de Radiodiffusion et Télévision*, Prag
o. J. ohne Jahr (Angabe des Erscheinungsjahres eines Buches) *n. d.* (= *no date*) ⟨a. fig⟩ (Frau) unbestimmten Alters
OK, O.K, o.k. *okay = correct* in Ordnung
OKC ⟨stud⟩ Ordentlicher Kösener Congress
OKiR. Oberkirchenrat
ÖKISTA Österreichisches Komitee für Internationalen Studentenaustausch
Okla. Oklahoma (USA)
Okt. Oktober
OKW Oberkommando der Wehrmacht (bis 1945)
ö. L. östliche(r) Länge
Oldb. Oldenburg
OLG(er) Oberlandesgericht
OLG. *Old Low German*
O. M. C. *Ordinis Minorum Conventualium* (L) (Mitglied) des Minoritenordens
O. M. Cap. *Ordinis Minorum Capucinorum* (L) (Mitglied) der Kapuziner-Minoriten
OMGUS *Office of Military Government United States*, Vorgänger von HICOG
ONA *Overseas News Agency, New York* amerikanische Nachrichtenagentur
ONO Ostnordost
O.N.R. ⟨Am⟩ *Office of Naval Research*
ONU Fr *Organisation des Nations Unies*; → UNO
o. O. 1. ohne Angabe des Erscheinungsortes **2.** ohne Obligo (Verpflichtung, Gewähr)
O.-Ö. (Oö.) Oberösterreich
o. ö. Prof. ordentlicher öffentlicher Professor
OP Operation(ssaal); OP-Schwester
Op., op. (L) *opus* Werk
o. P. ordentlicher Professor, Ordinarius
O.P., O.Pr. *Ordinis Praedicatorum* (L) (Mitglied) des Predigerordens
OPD Oberpostdirektion
Opf. Oberpfalz
OPr. (Ostpr.) Ostpreußen
OPräs. Oberpräsident
o. Prof. ordentlicher Professor, Ordinarius
o.r. *owner's risk* (*transportation*)
ÖRA Öffentliche Rechtsauskunft [f]; ÖRA-Stelle (bes in Hamburg, Berlin, Lübeck, Wilhelmshaven)
o.r.b. *owner's risk of breakage* (*transportation*)
o.r.d. *owner's risk of damage* (*transportation*)
Ord. Ordinarius; Ordnung
Ore. Oregon (USA)
ORF Österreichischer Rundfunk
org. organisch
Orgesch ⟨hist⟩ Organisation Escherich
ORNL *Oak Ridge National Laboratory* (*USA*)
ORO ⟨Am⟩ *Operations Research Office*
O.-S. Oberschlesien
O. S. A. *Ordinis Sancti Augustini* (L) (Mitglied) des Augustinerordens **O. S. B.** *Ordinis Sancti Benedicti* (L) **O. S. F.** *Ordinis Sancti Francisci*
·Osram ⟨el⟩ (Glühbirne etc) (**Osmium** + **Wolfram**
OSS ⟨Am⟩ *Office of Strategic Services* (Amerikanischer Nachrichtendienst)
Ostpr. (OPr.) Ostpreußen
OTA *Organisation Mondiale du Tourisme et de l'Automobile* Welt-Touring und Automobil-Organisation, London
OTAN [Fr] *Organisation du Traité de l'Atlantique Nord* = NATO
OTC ⟨Am⟩ *Organization for Trade Cooperation*
OTS *Office of Technical Service, Washington* Technischer (deutscher, europäischer und überseeischer) Auskunftsdienst
ÖTV Öffentliche Dienste, Transport u. Verkehr
OVA Oberversicherungsamt
OVG(er.) Oberverwaltungsgericht
ÖVP Österreichische Volkspartei
OW Obwalden (Schweizer Kanton, Teil von Unterwalden)
OWK Ost-West-Kurier (Zeitung)
ÖWR Österreichische Wasserrettung
oz. ⟨engl⟩ *ounce* Unze (Gewicht)
oz. ap. ⟨engl⟩ *ounce* (*apothecary*)
oz. av. ⟨engl⟩ *ounce* (*avoirdupois*)
oz. fl. ⟨engl⟩ *ounce* (*fluid*)
oz. t. ⟨engl⟩ *ounce* (*troy*)

P

P. 1. Pastor **2.** Pater **3.** Professor **4.** Post
P 1. (in österr. u. Frankfurter Kurszetteln) Papier (svw. Brief) **2.** Poise (im CGS-System) = Dyn × Sekunde pro Quadratzentimeter **3.** ⟨mot⟩ Parkplatz **4.** Portugal ⟨a. mot⟩ **5.** Primär- (⟨seismology⟩ primäre Wellen); → S. **000**
p 1. *pagina* (L) Seite **2.** auf Wechseln: protestiert **3.** *piano* (It) leise **4.** Pond (Gewicht-Einheit) **5.** Pico- (Maßvorsilbe); → S. 0000
PA Postanschrift [f]
p. A. per Adresse
p. a. *per annum* (L) fürs Jahr
Pa. 1. Pennsylvanien (USA) **2.** ⟨span⟩ Peseta
pa. *prima* (It) erstklassig
PAA *Pan-American World Airways Inc. Ltd.*
PAC *Pan-American Congress*
Pac(if.). *Pacific*
PachtSchO. Pachtschutzordnung (Reichs-PSchO.; Preuß. PSchO.)
p. Adr. per Adresse; ⟨engl⟩ c/o
pag. *pagina* (L) Seite
Pak Panzerabwehrkanone
Pak. *Pakistan*

PANAM *Pan-American World Airways Inc. Ltd.*
Par. Paragraph
Parl. Parlament
Pars·ec, Pars·ek Parall·ax-Sek·unde (1 ~ ist die Entfernung, aus der die mittlere große Halbachse der Erdbahn unter dem Winkel 1″ gesehen wird). 10 ~ (⟨astr⟩ Einheitsentfernung) = 32,57 Lichtjahre (ly.)
PASB *Pan-American Sanitary Bureau*
PatG Patentgesetz
path. pathologisch
PAU *Pan American Union*
Pazif. ⟨engl⟩ *Pacific* Stiller Ozean
p. c. 1. *pour cent* (Fr), *per cent.* (Engl), *pro centum* (L) Prozent **2.** *pour condoler* (Fr) um Beileid zu sagen
p. Chr. (n) *post Christum (natum)* (L) nach Christus (nach Christi Geburt)
PCM *Puls-Code-Modulation* Pulskodemodulation
PCOB *Permanent Central Opium Board* Überwachungsausschuß für Opium
P. D. Postdampfer
Pd. D. *Doctor of Pedagogy*
Ped. ⟨mus⟩ *pedale* (It) Pedal
Pemex *Petroleos Mexicanos* Regierungsbehörde f. die verstaatlichten Petroleumquellen, gleichzeitig als Touristenpropagandamission unter Wahrung der Aufgaben des Automobilklubs in anderen Ländern
PEN *International PEN-Club, London* (PEN = *P*oets, *E*ssayists, *N*ovellists) Internationale Vereinigung führender Schriftsteller
Perg. Pergament
Pers. Persönlich
Pers·il n **Per**borat + **Sil**ikat
PersStG (PStG) Gesetz über die Beurkundung des Personenstandes u. die Eheschließung v. 6. 2. 1875
PF Postfach [n]; → P.O.B.
p. f. *pour féliciter* (Fr) um Glück zu wünschen
Pf. 1. Pfennig **2.** Pfalz
Pfr Pfarrer
P.F.S.A. Fr *pour faire ses adieux* u.A.z.n.
Pfte. Pianoforte, Klavier
p. f. v. *pour faire visite* (Fr) um Besuch z m
Pg. 1. ⟨nazi⟩ Parteigenosse (eingeschriebenes Mitglied der NSDAP) **2.** = PatG
PGO ⟨Ger⟩ Peinliche Gerichtsordnung (1538)
PH Pädagogische Hochschule: PH-Student
ph Phot (Verhältnis des abgestrahlten Lichtstromes zur Größe der Fläche)
ph. *phone, telephone*
phil. philosophisch, (Dr.) der Philosophie
Phon Phon (Lautstärke; akustische Maßeinheit)
phys. physisch, physikalisch, physiologisch
p. & i. ⟨ins⟩ *protection and indemnity*
PICMME *Provisional Intergovernmental Committee for the Movement of Migrants from Europe* Provisorisches zwischenstaatliches Auswanderungs-Komitee für Auswanderer aus Europa; → IRO
pinx. ⟨arts⟩ *pinxit* (L) . . hat [es] gemalt
pizz. ⟨mus⟩ *pizzicato* (It) gezupft
pk. ⟨engl⟩ *peck* (Maß); → S. 1489
pt. ⟨engl⟩ *pint* (Maß); → S. 1489
PKW, Pkw Personenkraftwagen = Auto, Wagen
PKWY ⟨Am⟩ *Parkway* (*Cross County* ~)
PL Polen ⟨a. mot⟩
Pl., pl. Plural | **Pl., .. pl.** Platz
P. & L. *profit and loss* Gewinn u. Verlust
PLZ Postleitzahl *Code*
p. m. 1. *post meridiem*, nachmittags **2.** *pro mille* auf das Tausend **3.** *pro memoria* zum Andenken **4.** *post mortem* nach dem Tode
pmkd. *postmarked* gestempelt
Pneu [*pnø*] Pneumatik
p.n.g. L *persona non grata* unbeliebte Person
P. O. 1. *Professor ordinarius* (L) **2.** *Post Office*
po. ⟨mus⟩ *piano* (It) leise
PO politische Organisation
P.O.B. ⟨engl⟩ *Post Office Box* (Postfach)
p.o.c. ⟨shipping⟩ *port of call* Anlegehafen
P.O.D. *pay on delivery* Zahlung bei Empfang
Pol. Polizei
Pom. Pommern
Pont. Max. L *Pontifex maximus* ⟨ant⟩ Oberster Priester, ⟨R. C.⟩ eine Titulatur des Papstes
PoWi Politik und Wirtschaft
Pp. Pappband
pp ⟨mus⟩ *pianissimo* (It) sehr leise
pp. *perge perge* (L) (fahre fort!), als Nachschrift in Aufzählungen: und so weiter
pp. *postpaid* (: *postage paid*)
p. p., p. pa. *per procura* (It)
p. p. *praeter propter* (L) ungefähr
PP. *Patres* (L) (Plural von Pater)
P. P. (P. p., p. p.) *praemissis praemittendis* (L) unter Vorausschickung des Vorauszuschickenden (Anrede, Titel usw.)
p. p. c. (Fr) *pour prendre congé* „um Abschied zu nehmen“ (auf Besuchskarten)
PPI ⟨radar⟩ *plan position indicator* ⟨a–n⟩ Sternschreiber
ppm *parts per million* Teile pro Million; z. B. 6,44 ppm DDT-Gehalt
ppp ⟨mus⟩ *piano pianissimo* (It) ganz leise
PR *Public Relations*
Pr. Pr Preußen [z. B. Königsberg (Pr)]
Pr. Prüfer
Präl. Prälat
Präs. Präsident; Präsidium [n]
Preugo ⟨med⟩ Preußische Gebührenordnung [f]
Pr·eußag Preußische Bergwerks- u. Hütten A.-G.
Priv. Privat
p.r.n. L *pro re nata* gegebenenfalls
Prof. Professor
Progr. Programm
prot. protestantisch
Prov. Provinz
Proz. Prozent
pr. pa. (It) *per procura*
PrSa. Provinz Sachsen
PS Pferdestärke → HP; **PSh** Pferdestärkenstunde → S. 1489 Leistungsmaße
P. S. *Postcriptum* (L) Nachschrift
PSchG → Postscheckgesetz
Pseud. Pseudonym
PSF. Postschließfach [n]
PSK Politisch-Soziale Korrespondenz
PSK ⟨mil⟩ Psychologische Kampfführung [f]
PStG → PersStG
psych. psychisch (seelisch)
psychol. psychologisch
Pt. *point* (Engl) Punkt, Spitze
P. T. 1. *pleno titulo* (L) mit vollem Titel **2.** *praemissis titulis* (L) mit vorausgeschickten Titeln
pt/destin ⟨shipping⟩ *port of destination*
pt/disch ⟨shipping⟩ *port of discharge*
P.T.O. *please turn over* bitte wenden
PTR Physikalisch-Technische Reichsanstalt
PTT (Fr, Sw) Post-, Telegraphen- u. Telephonverwaltung [f]
PVC Polyvinylchlorid
PVG Personalvertretungsgesetz
PVP ⟨chem, brew⟩ Polyvin·ylpyrrolid·on n
Pvt. *Private* (*soldier*)
pvt. *private*
PW *Prisoner of War* Kriegsgefangene(r)
PWR ⟨at⟩ *Pressure Water Reactor* Druckwasserreaktor [m]
pwt. *pennyweight*
P.X *Post Exchange*
PZ Personenzug
Pz Panzer

Q

q. (in Maßbezeichnungen:) Quadrat: qcm Quadratzentimeter, qdm Quadratdezimeter, qkm Quadratkilometer, qm Quadratmeter, qmm Quadratmillimeter
q. ⟨engl⟩ *quintal* (*metric*) 100 od 112 lb.
q.d.a. *quantity discount agreement* Mengennachlaß-Abkommen
q. e. d. *quod erat demonstrandum* was nachzuweisen war
q. l. L *quantum libet* nach Belieben
QS, Q.-S. Quecksilbersäule
qt. ⟨engl⟩ *quart* (Maßeinheit); → q.t. in Band I.
qto. *quarto* Quartformat
q. v. (L) **1.** *quod videas* siehe dieses **2.** *quantum vis* so viel du willst

R

R 1. auf röm. Inschriften: *Roma*, *Romanus*, *rex*, *regius*, *regnum* u. a. **2.** auf Rezepten: *Recipe* (L) (nimm) **3.** ⟨math⟩ rechter Winkel **4.** bei Temperaturangaben: *Réaumur* **5.** auf Uhren: (Fr) *Retard* (Verzögerung) oder *retarder* (verlangsamen) **6.** ⟨mus⟩ rechte Hand **7.** Post: *Recommandé* (Einschreiben) **8.** ⟨exch⟩ reportiert **9.** Rat (Titel) **10.** ⟨mot⟩ Raststätte **11.** Richtlinien **12.** Reich [n] **13.** Rumänien ⟨a. mot⟩
r 1. Radius, Halbmesser **2.** Röntgen [n] (internationale Dosiseinheit für Röntgen- u. Gammastrahlen)
R. 1. *river* ⟨engl⟩, **2.** *rio* ⟨span⟩, Fluß **3.** *royal* ⟨engl fr⟩ königlich
r. rund (etwa)
RA Rechtsanwalt
rad Radiant *radian*
RAD ⟨nazi⟩ Reichsarbeitsdienst
RADIAC *Radio-Detection, Identification and Computation*
R.A.F., RAF *Royal Air Force*
RAM Reichsarbeitsministerium
RAND ⟨Am⟩ *Research and Development*
RAO Rechtsanwaltsordnung v. 1. 7. 1878 u 7. 3. 1927; Reichsabgabeordnung
RArbG Reichsarbeitsgericht
RB Radio Bremen [n]
R. & I. L *Regina et Imperatrix*; *Rex et Imperator*
Rb 1. ⟨chem⟩ Rubidium → S. 1501 **2.** Reichsbank
RBB. ⟨hist⟩ Reichsbesoldungsblatt
RBD Reichsbahndirektion
RBesBl ⟨hist⟩ Reichs-Besoldungs-Blatt
Rbl Rubel
RBO Reichsbetriebsordnung
RCA *Radio Corporation of America, New York*
R.C.C., R.C.Ch. *Roman Catholic Church*
RCDS Ring Christlich-Demokratischer Studenten
Rd. ⟨engl⟩ *Road*
rd. 1. rund (etwa) **2.** ⟨engl⟩ *rod* (Maß) → S. 1488
r.d. ⟨shipping⟩ *running days*
RDB. Reichsbund der Deutschen Beamten
RdF ⟨hist⟩ Reichsminister der Finanzen
RDK. Reichsbund der Kinderreichen Deutschlands zum Schutze der Familie
RDO. Reichsverband Deutscher Offiziere
RDP. Reichsverband der Deutschen Presse
Ref. Referent, –rendar
ref. ⟨ec⟩ reformiert
Refa Reichsausschuß für Arbeitszeitermittlung (heute *Verband für Arbeitsstudien REFA e. V.*)
Reg. L *Regina* Königin
Reg. Register; Regierung
Reg.-Bez. Regierungsbezirk
RegBl ⟨hist⟩ Regierungsblatt für Württemberg-Hohenzollern
RegDir Regierungsdirektor
Reg.-Präs. Regierungspräsident
Reg.-T. Registertonne
REI Rat der Europäischen Industrie, Paris; → CFIE
rep. ⟨exch⟩ repartiert
Rep. 1. *repetatur* (L) soll wiederholt werden **2.** Republik
resp. respektive, beziehungsweise
Reuter *Reuters Ltd., London* größte englische Nachrichten-Agentur
Rev. *Reverend* ⟨engl⟩, svw. „Hochwürden"
revs. per min. *revolutions per minute*
RF relative Feuchtigkeit [f]
RF *République Française*
rf., rfz ⟨mus⟩ *rinforzando* (It) stärker werdend
r.f. *radio frequency*
R.F.D. *rural free delivery*
RFH Reichsfinanzhof; Entscheidung des RFH
RFM Reichsfinanzministerium
RG(er.) ⟨hist⟩ Reichsgericht
RGBl. ⟨hist⟩ Reichsgesetzblatt
RGes. ⟨hist⟩ Reichsgesetz
R. G. G. Religion in Geschichte u Gegenwart
RGM Reichsgebrauchsmuster
RGSt Entscheidungen des RG in Strafsachen
Rgt. Regiment
RGW Rat für gegenseitige Wirtschaftshilfe, → Comecon
RGZ Entscheidungen des RG in Zivilsachen
RH Rechnungshof des Deutschen Reiches
R. H. ⟨engl⟩ *Royal Highness*
Rheinpreußen Rheinpreußen A.G. für Bergbau u Chemie
RHG (RHeimstG) Reichsheimstättengesetz
R. I. Rhode Island (kleinster Staat der USA, zwischen Massachusetts, Connecticut u dem Atlantik)
Ri. Richter
R.I. L *Regina Imperatrix*; *Rex Imperator*
RI *Rotary International*
RIAS Rundfunk im amerikanischen Sektor, Berlin
RIM Radiotechnisches Institut in Moskau
R. I. P. *requiescat in pace* (L) er, sie ruhe in Frieden
ritard. *ritardando* (It) langsamer werdend
RJM Reichsjustizministerium
RJWG Reichsgesetz für Jugendwohlfahrt
R. K. Rotes Kreuz
RKG. Reichsknappschaftsgesetz
RKTL. Reichskuratorium für Technik in der Landwirtschaft
RKW Reichskuratorium für Wirtschaftlichkeit
RKW Rationalisierungs-Kuratorium der deutschen Wirtschaft → OEEC
RLFM Reichsluftfahrtministerium
RM Reichsmark
rm Raummeter
RM(in)Bl ⟨hist⟩ Reichsministerialblatt
RMdI Reichsminister des Innern
Rn ⟨chem⟩ Radon *Radon*
R.N. *Royal Navy*
RNA *Ribonuclear Acid* (Verjüngungsmittel „Die Pille für den Lebensabend")
RNG Reichsnaturschutzgesetz (1935)
RNS ⟨bio-chem⟩ Ribonukleinsäure [f]
Robeco ⟨bank⟩ Rotterdam Beleggingskonsortium
Rok Reykjavik
röm. römisch
RONND ⟨russ⟩ eine radikal rechts gerichtete Emigrantenorganisation
Rotary *Rotary International* Club internationaler Verständigung und Hilfsbereitschaft der Rotarier untereinander (ohne religiöse, politische, weltanschauliche Bindung); Evanston (Illinois) USA, Zürich

Rororo Rowohlts Rotations-Roman
Rp. auf Rezepten: *Recipe* (L) nimm; ursprünglich ⟨astr⟩ ♃ (Zeichen des Jupiter)
RP (Kennzeichen für Kraftwagen der Deutschen) Reichspost
R. P. *réponse payée* (Fr) ⟨telg⟩ Antwort bezahlt bis zu 10 Wörtern zu je 15 Buchstaben)
RPA Reichspatentamt
RPD ⟨telg⟩ dringende Antwort bezahlt
RPf Rheinland-Pfalz
Rpf ⟨hist⟩ Reichspfennig **RPFG** Reichspostfinanzgesetz **RPM** Reichspostministerium **RPZ** Reichspostzentralamt
r.p.m. *revolutions per minute* Umdrehungen/Minute
R.P.O. *Railway Post Office*
RR., R. R. Regierungsrat
RSFSR *Rossijskaja Sozialistitscheskaja Federatiwnaja Sowetskaja Respublika* Russische Sozialistische Föderative Sowjet-Republik
Rsp. (Rechtspr.) Rechtsprechung
RStBl. ⟨hist⟩ Reichssteuerblatt
R.S.V.P. Fr *Répondez s'il vous plaît* Antwort erbeten
R.S.W.C. *right side up with care* Oben, Bitte nicht stürzen
R. T. Registertonne
Rt. ⟨engl⟩ *Right* vor Titeln z. B. → folg.
Rt. Hon. *Right Honourable*
RV ⟨hist⟩ Verfassung des Deutschen Reiches **RVA** Reichsversicherungs-Amt **RVG** Reichsversorgungsgesetz **RVM** Reichsverkehrsministerium **RVO** Reichsversicherungsordnung v. 19. 7. 1911/15. 12. 1924/16. 12. 1927
RVR ⟨aero⟩ *Runway Visual Range* Pistensichtweite
Rw Wirkungsradius
r. & w. *rail and water* auf dem Land- & Seewege
RWE Rheinisch-Westfälische Elektrizitäts A. G.
RWeM ⟨hist⟩ Reichswehrministerium **RWiM** Reichswirtschaftsministerium **RZA** Reichsbahn-Zentralamt

S

Words beginning with S or Sch and not given under S should be looked for under C, K, Z
s. sächlich; siehe
s Sekunde; mittlere Sonnensekunde
S. 1. Seite **2.** *San* (it., span.); *São* (port.) Sankt
S 1. Süden **2.** Sonntag **3.** Schilling **4.** ⟨mus⟩ *Segno* (It) Zeichen **5.** ⟨mus⟩ Subdominante **6.** ⟨chem⟩ Schwefel (*Sulphur*) **7.** ⟨engl⟩ *slower* langsamer (auf Uhren) **8.** *sanctus, sacer* (L) heilig **9. S-Bahn,** Stadtbahn **10.** Schweden ⟨a. mot⟩ **11. S-Wellen** ⟨seismology⟩ Sekundär-Wellen; → P.
$ Dollar, portug. Escudo, Peso u. a.; → S. 1499–1500
s* Sternsekunde
SA ⟨nazi⟩ Sturm-Abteilung; die ~ *Brownshirts*; ein ~-Mann *a storm trooper* || ~-Gruppe [f] *Storm Troop Division*
S. A. Sonderabdruck
S.A. *Société Anonyme* Aktiengesellschaft
s. a. bei bibliograph. Angaben: *sine anno* ohne Jahreszahl; → o. J.; siehe auch
Sa. Sachsen
Sa. 1. Summe **2.** ⟨span⟩ *Sierra* Gebirgskette
SAA *South African Airways*
SAC Schweizer Alpenklub
S.A.F.E., SAFE *Selected American Funds Enterprise*
SAG Starkstromanlagen-Gemeinschaft GmbH
SAL Städteplanung, Architektur, Landschaftsplanung
SALT *Strategic Arms' Limitation Talks*
San. Sanitäts..
Sanskr. Sanskrit
s. ap. ⟨engl⟩ *scruple* (*avoirdupois*); → S. 1490
S.A.R. *South African Republic*
Sar. *Sardinia*
SBB Schweizer Bundesbahn
s. B., s. Br. südliche Breite
⟨**SBZ**⟩ einst Sowjetisch Besetzte Zone, jetzt → DDR
S. C. ⟨stud⟩ Senioren-Convent
S.C. ⟨Am⟩ *South-Carolina*
s. & c. *shipper and carrier*
sc. 1. *scilicet* (L) nämlich **2.** ⟨arts⟩ *sculpsit* .. hat es gestochen
s.c. ⟨ins⟩ *salvage charges*
SC *The World Security Council, New York* Der Welt-Sicherheits-Rat der UN
Schrf. Schriftführer | **Schrl.** Schriftleiter
scil L *scilicet* nämlich
SCOOP *Scientific Computation of Optimum Programs*
SCPE *Sécrétariat Catholique pour les Problèmes Européens*
ScheckG., Sch.G(es). Scheckgesetz
SchlHlst. Schleswig-Holstein
Sch·upo, der Schutzpolizist, die Schutzpolizei
Schwb. Schwaben
SchwBeschGes Gesetz über die Beschäftigung Schwerbeschädigter
SD ⟨nazi⟩ Sicherheitsdienst [m]
S. D. Süd-Dakota (USA)
s. d. siehe dies, siehe dort
SDA Schweizer Depeschenagentur, Bern, halbamtlich
SDF *Self-Defence* (⟨Am⟩ *-se*) *Force*
S. d. N. Fr *Société des Nations*
SDR Süddeutscher Rundfunk (Stuttgart)
SDS Sozialistischer Deutscher Studentenbund
SDStB Sozialistischer Deutscher Studentenbund
s. e. *salvo errore* (L) Irrtum vorbehalten
S. E. Seine(r) Exzellenz, Eminenz
SEATO *South-East Asia Treaty Organization*
SEC Fr *Société Européenne de Culture,* Europäische Kulturgesellschaft, Venedig
sec Sekunde (Zeit)
SED Sozialistische Einheitspartei Deutschlands (Ostzone) ⟨parl⟩
SEdC *Société Européenne de Culture* Europäische Kulturgesellschaft, Venedig
SeeA Seeamt
S. E.. ed O. (S. E. O.) *salvo errori ed omissioni* (It) Irrtümer und Auslassungen vorbehalten
SeemO Seemannsordnung
SeestrO. Seestraßenordnung
SeewStrO Seewasserstraßenordnung
sek Sekunde (Zeit)
Sekr. Sekretär
Sen. Senat
sen. *senior* (L) der ältere
Sept. September
SEW ⟨parl⟩ Sozialistische Einheitspartei Westberlin (Westberliner Kommunisten)
SF *Suomi* = Finnland ⟨a. mot⟩
SF. Schließfach [n]
sf. ⟨mus⟩ *sforzato* stark betont
SFB ⟨telv⟩ Sender Freies Berlin (Charlottenburg)
SFL ⟨artill⟩ Selbstfahrlafette
SG St. Gallen (Schweizer Kanton)
sg. ⟨gram⟩ Singular (Einzahl)
SH 1. Schleswig-Holstein **2.** Schaffhausen (Schweizer Kanton)
Sh. *Shakespeare*
SHA Soforthilfeabgabe
SHAPE *Supreme Headquarter of the Allied Powers in Europe* Ober-Kommando der Alliierten Streitkräfte in Europa
SHB Sozialdemokratischer Hochschulbund
SHG/SHS Soforthilfe-Gesetz/-Sonderausgabe
SHS (*Kr·aljevina*) *S·rba, H·rvata i Slovenaca* Königreich der Serben, Kroaten und Slo-

wenen (früher amtlicher Name von Jugoslawien)
s.h.v. L *sub hoc verbo* unter diesem Wort
SI *System International* (seit 1960)
SIA Schweizerischer Ingenieur- u. Architekten Verein
Sic. It *Sicilia* Sizilien *Sicilian, Sicily*
SID *Society for International Development*
sid Sport-Informations-Dienst
sin ⟨math⟩ Sinus
sing. ⟨gram⟩ Singular (Einzahl)
S·ipo, der **Si**cherheits**po**lizist, die Sicherheitspolizei
SIS ⟨engl⟩ *Secret Intelligence Service*
S. J. *Societas Jesu* (L) Gesellschaft Jesu, Jesuitenorden
S.J.D. *scientiae juridicae doctor, Doctor of Juridical Science*
SKK Sowjetische Kontroll-Kommission
sm Seemeile
S. M. Seine(r) Majestät
SMA Sowjetische Militär-Administration
S.M.I. Fr *Sa Majesté Impériale* Seine/Ihre Kaiserliche Majestät
S.M.M. L *Sancta Mater Maria* Heilige Mutter Gottes
S. M. S. Seiner Majestät Schiff
SM-Stahl Siemens-Martin-Stahl
SMUSE *Socialist Movement for the United States of Europe*, Paris; → MSEUE
SMV Schülermitverwaltung [f]
S/N *shipping note*
SNAP *System for Nuclear Auxiliary Power*
SNB Sowjetisches Nachrichten-Büro, Berlin
SNCB *Société Nationale des Chemins de Fer Belges*
SNCF *Société Nationale des Chemins de Fer Français*
s. o. siehe oben
SO Südost, Südosten
SO Solothurn (Schweizer Kanton)
soc. *société* (Fr), *society* (Engl), *società* (It), *sociedad* (Span), Gesellschaft
SOG Schweizerische Offiziersgesellschaft
sog. sogenannt
SOS 1. ⟨wir⟩ Seenotsignal, gedeutet als: *save our souls* Rettet unsere Seelen **2.** allgemein: Hilferuf in höchster Not
SowRep. Sowjetrepublik
SOZ scheinbare Ortszeit *local apparent time* (LAT)
soz. sozialistisch
Sp. Spalte
SP 1. Siedepunkt **2.** Schützenpanzerwagen
s. p. L *sine prole* ohne Nachkommen
SPD, S. P. D. Sozialdemokratische Partei Deutschlands
spez. Gew. spezifisches Gewicht
SPÖ Sozialdemokratische, seit 1939 Sozialistische Partei Österreichs
S. P. Q. R. S*enatus* **P***opulusque* **R***omanus* Senat u. Volk von Rom
s. p. s. L *sine prole superstite* ohne lebenden Nachkommen
Sq. ⟨engl⟩ *Square*
sq. ft. ⟨engl⟩ *square foot* (ft.^{2})
sq. in. ⟨engl⟩ *square inch* (in.^{2})
sq. mi. ⟨engl⟩ *square mile* (mi.^{2})
sq. rd. ⟨engl⟩ *square rod* (rd.^{2})
sqq. L *sequentes* die Folgenden
sq. yd. ⟨engl⟩ *square yard* (yd.^{2})
SR Saarländischer Rundfunk
Sr. Seiner, z. B. Sr. Exzellenz
SRG Schweizerische Rundfunkgesellschaft
S. R. E. *Sancta Romana Ecclesia* Heilige Römische Kirche
S. R. I. L Sacrum Romanum Imperium Heiliges Römisches Reich
SRP Sozialistische Reichspartei
SS ⟨nazi⟩ Schutz-Staffel der NSDAP. *Blackshirts (body guard)*
SS ⟨It⟩ *Strada Statale* Staatsstraße: SS 7 (vgl via Appia: Rom–Terracina–Capua–Benevent–Brindisi)
SS. L *Sancti* die Heiligen
S/S Segelschiff
S. S. 1. *steamship* (engl) Dampfer **2.** *Sua Sanctitas* (L) Seine Heiligkeit
S & H Siemens & Halske
SSD Staatssicherheitsdienst (Ostzone)
SSO Südsüdost
SSS ⟨bes golf⟩ *standard scratch score* ⟨mst⟩ = Einheit → d. (72[–74] Schläge)
SSSR S*ojus* **S***ozialistitscheskich* **S***owetskich* **R***espublik*, Sowjetunion; → UdSSR
SST *Supersonic Transport* Überschallschnelles Verkehrsflugzeug
SSV Schweizerischer Schriftstellerverein
SSV ⟨com⟩ Sommer-Schluß-Verkauf
SSW Südsüdwest
SSW 1. Südschleswigsche Wählervereinigung (prodänisch) **2.** Siemens-Schuckert-Werke
st Stunde
st! L *stet* bitte stehen lassen!
St 1. Sankt, *Saint* (Heiliger) **2.** Steiermark **3.** Stadt .. **4.** Stabs.. **5.** ⟨engl⟩ *Street*
s. t. *sine tempore* (L), ohne akademische Viertelstunde, pünktlich
st. ..stelle
Sta. Staats.
Sta. *Santa* (It, span, port), Sankta (Heilige)
stacc. *staccato* (It) (Töne) scharf getrennt
STAN ⟨mil⟩ Stärke- u. Ausrüstungsnachweis [m]
StAnpG Steueranpassungsgesetz
StBlH Steuerblatt Hamburg
Ste *Sainte* (Fr), Sankta (Heilige)
St. G. Stille Gesellschaft
StGB Strafgesetzbuch
StKl Steuerklasse [f]
Sto. *Santo* (It, span, port) Sankt (Heiliger)
StPO Strafprozeßordnung
StPS. Steuerpferdekräfte
Str., ..str Straße, ..straße
Stu. Studien..
stud. *studiosus* (L) Student, Studierender z. B. stud. phil. → Dr. phil. etc.
Stuka 1. Sturzkampfflieger **2.** Sturzkampfflugzeug
StuZBl Steuer- u Zollblatt [n]
STV Stahl-Treuhänder-Vereinigung; → CSG
Stv. Stellvertreter(in)
StVO Straßenverkehrs-Ordnung [f]
StVZO Straßenverkehrs-Zulassungs-Ordnung [f]
SU ⟨bes mil⟩ Sowjet-Union, Union der Sozialistischen Sowjetrepubliken ⟨a. mot⟩
s. u. siehe unten
südd. süddeutsch
S+M Schnee- u. Matsch(-Reifen)
Sup. Superintendent
SUVA Schweizerische Unfall-Versicherungsanstalt [f]
SV ⟨stud⟩ Sondershäuser Verband
S. V. L *Sancta Virgo* Heilige Jungfrau, L *Sanctitas Vestra* Eure Heiligkeit
s. v. 1. *sub voce* (L) unter dem Stichwort **2.** *salva venia* (L) mit Verlaub
SVI Studentenverband Deutscher Ingenieurschulen e. V.
S.V.P. Fr *s'il vous plaît* wenn's gefällig ist; bitte
svw. soviel wie
SW Südwest
SWB Schweizerischer Werkbund
SWF Südwestfunk (Baden-Baden)
SWFD ⟨telph⟩ Selbstwählferndienst
Swissair *Swiss Air Transport Co. Ltd.* Schweizerische Luftverkehrsgesellschaft, Zürich

SWO = SeewStrO
s. w. u. siehe weiter unten
Synd. Syndikus
SZ 1. Schnellzug **2.** Süddeutsche Zeitung **3.** Schwyz (Schweizer Kanton)

T

T 1. in röm. Inschriften, Handschriften, auf Münzen usw.: Tertius, Titulus, Titus, Tribunus **2.** bei Bücherzitaten: *Tomus* (Band) **3.** Tara **4.** ⟨mus⟩ **a.** Tonika **b.** Tenor **c.** (auch t.) Tempo (**T. Io** = *Tempo primo* erstes Zeitmaß) **5.** *taxe* (Fr) Nachgebühr **6.** Tera- (Maßvorsilbe); → S. 1492 **7.** ⟨mot⟩ Tankstelle [f] **8.** (⟨a.⟩ Tel.) Telefon **9.** (Apo-)Terror **10.** ⟨chem biol⟩ Thymin (e–e der 4 Nukleotid-Basen); → A, C, G
t 1. Tonne (Gewicht) **2.** Temperatur
T. 1. Telefon [n] **2.** Testament [n]
TA Telegrammadresse [f]
Ta. Tara
TAA *Technical Assistance Administration*, Paris
TAB *Technical Assistance Board, New York*
TAC *Technical Assistance Committee*, Paris
Tak Tankabwehrkanone (mst: Pak)
tal. qual. L *talis qualis/tales quales* wie es kommt/sie kommen; im Durchschnitt
tan, tang Tangens
TAP *Technical Assistance Programm* der UN (: UNTAP) Programm für technische Hilfeleistung
TASS *Telègráfnoje agenstvo Sowjétskowo Sojúsa* Staatliche sowjetische Nachrichten-Agentur, Moskau. Sowjetisches Nachrichten-Büro, Berlin (SNB)
t. b. Tuberkel-Bazillus
Tb, Tbc Tuberkulose **TB** *tuberculosis*
TC *The Trusteeship Council, New York* Der Treuhänder-Rat der UN
TEAM 1. *Top European Advertising Media* **2.** Terminologie-Erfassungs- u. Auswertungsmethode
TEE ⟨rail⟩ Trans-Europ-Express: „Saphir" (Frankfurt–Ostende); „Rhein-Main" (Frankfurt–Amsterdam); „Mediolanum" (München–Mailand); „Helvetia" (Hamburg–Zürich); „Ruhr-Paris" (Dortmund-Paris); „Parsifal" (Hamburg–Paris); „L'Arbalète" Fr („Die Armbrust") (Paris–Zürich); „Lemano" (L) & „Cisalpin" (C) (Mailand–Paris); „Edelweiß" (Amsterdam–Zürich); „Le Mont-Cenis" (Lyon–Mailand); „Ligure" (Marseille–Mailand); „Gottardo" (G) & „Ticino" (T) (Zürich–Mailand); „Ile-de-France" (I) & „Etoile-du-Nord" (E) & „Oiseau-Bleu" (O) (Amsterdam–Paris); sämtlich und zurück
Teleran *Television Radar Navigation-System* (Flugsicherung durch Fernsehübertragung)
Telex Fernschreiber [m]
Temp. Temperatur
ten. ⟨mus⟩ *tenuto* (It) gehalten
Tenn. Tenessee (USA)
Terr. Territorium
Test. Testament; → T.
TEX, tex (Garnnumerierungssystem-Einheit) Gewicht einer Garnlänge von 1000 m (Kilotex, millitex)
Tex. Texas (USA)
Tfg. Tiefgang
TG Thurgau (Schweizer Kanton)
tg Tangens
TGL ⟨DDR⟩ Technische Normen, Gütevorschriften u. Lieferungsbedingungen
T. H. Technische Hochschule [f]
theol. theologisch
Thr. Thüringen
TI Tessin, (It) *Ticino* (Schweizer Kanton)
Ti. Tirol
T.I.R. *Transports Internationaux Routiers* Fr
Tit. Titel
Tl. Teil, **Tle.** Teile
t. l. ⟨ins⟩; *total loss* Gesamtverlust
T.M. *trade-mark*
TME Tausendstel-Massen-Einheit
t-mot teilweise motorisiert
TN Technische Nothilfe
tn. l. ⟨engl⟩ *ton* (*long*)
tn. sh. ⟨engl⟩ *ton* (*short*)
TNT Trinitrotolu·ol
TO Tagesordnung [f]
TOA Tarif-Ordnung für Angestellte jetzt BAT
Tom. *Tomus* (L) Band
TOA → FFA
Torr Torricelli (Druck von 1 mm Quecksilbersäule) im CGS-System s. S. 1497)
Tot. (Toto) Totalisator
Tour·opa Touristenorganisation für Europa
TR Türkei ⟨a. mot⟩
tr ⟨mus⟩ Triller
Tr·afo m ⟨el⟩ Transformator
transp. *transportation*
TRIFCO *Tripartite I. G. Farben Control Office* Dreizonen-I. G. Farben Kontroll-Büro, Frankfurt; → DIDEG
TSA *The Salvation Army* Heilsarmee, London
Tscheka ⟨russ⟩ *Tschreswytschainaja kommissija* Außerordentliche Kommission (zur Bekämpfung der Gegenrevolution, Spekulation und der Amtsverbrechen)
T. & S. *Trust and Savings* (*Bank*)
T. S. F. *télégraphie sans fil* (Fr) drahtlose Telegraphie
TTR Telegraphentechnisches Reichsamt
TUC *Trade Union Congress* Kongreß der BTU
TÜV ⟨mot⟩ Technischer Überwachungs-Verein
TVP *Textured Vegetable Protein* geformtes pflanzliches Eiweiß (aus Sojamehl)
TV-Verbände m pl ⟨mil⟩ Territoriale Verteidigungsverbände *territorial defense units* N
TWA *Trans World Airlines, New York*
T.W.I.M.C. *To whom it may concern* Wen es betrifft
TWL Technisch-wissenschaftliche Lehrmittelzentrale
TYR ⟨num-hist⟩ Tirol
TZ Teuerungszuschlag

U

U 1. Unterseeboot **2.** Uran **3.** Untergrundbahn [f]
U. 1. Unter.. **2.** *ultimo* (It.), am letzten
u. und
ü. über
u. A. unter Anzeige
u. a. 1. und andere **2.** unter anderem
u. ä. und ähnliche
u. a. m. und andere mehr
U.A.R. *United Arab Republic*
UASt Umsatzausgleichsteuer
UATI *Union des Associations Techniques Internationales* Union internationaler technischer Verbände, Paris
u. A. w. g. (auf Einladungen:) um Antwort wird gebeten
u. A. z. n. um Abschied zu nehmen
U(-Bahn) Untergrundbahn [f]
U-Boot Unterseeboot
UCI *Union Cycliste Internationale* Internationaler Radsportverband, Paris
u. dgl (m.) und dergleichen (mehr)
u. d. M. unter dem Meeresspiegel
ü. d. M., ü. M. über dem Meeresspiegel
UdSSR Union der Soz. Sowjet-Republiken
u. d. T. unter dem Titel

u. E. unseres Erachtens
UEA *Universala Esperanto-Asosio* Esperanto-Weltliga, Genf
UEF *Union Européenne des Fédéralistes, European Union of Federalists*, Union Europäischer Föderation, Paris; → EUF
UER *Union Européenne de Radiodiffusion, European Broadcasting Union*, Genf
Ufa Universum-Film A.-G.
UFI *Union des Foires Internationales* Internationaler Messe-Verband, Paris
Ufo unbekanntes Flugobjekt
U-förmiges (Gletscher-)Tal
Ufr. Unterfranken
UI *Union Interparlementaire*, Genf
UIAA *Union Internationale des Associations d'Alpinisme*, Genf
UIC *International Union of Railways*
UIE *Union Internationale des Etudiants, International Union of Students* (*IUS*) Internationale Studenten-Union, Prag
UILFC *Union Internationale des Ligues Féminines Catholiques, International Union of Catholic Women's Leagues, Utrecht* (*IUCWL*)
UIM *Union Internationale Motonautique, Union Internationale Motorboating*, Brüssel
UIOOT *Union Internationale des Organismes Officiels de Tourisme, International Union of Official Travel Organizations* (*IUOTO*), Genf
UIP *Union Internationale de la Publicité, International Union of Advertising* (*IUA*) Internationale Reklame-Union, Paris; in Bundesrepublik: Zentralausschuß der Werbewirtschaft, Bonn (ZAW)
UIPE *Union Internationale de Protection de l'Enfance, International Union for Child Welfare* (*IUCW*) Internationale Union für Kinderschutz, Genf
UIPM *Union Internationale du Pentathlon Moderne* Internationaler Verband für modernen Fünfkampf, Stockholm
UIT *Union Internationale de Tir, International Shooting Union* Internationaler Schießsportverband, Stockholm
u. k. ⟨mil⟩ (unabkömmlich); ~-gestellt *reserved* || ~-gestellte(r) [m] ⟨Am⟩ *vip* (= *very important person*)
UK *United Kingdom* Großbritannien
UKAEA *United Kingdom Atomic Energy Authority*
Ukr. S. S. R. Ukrainische Sozialistische Sowjet-Republik
UKW Ultra-Kurzwellen; **UKW**-Sender, -Station *very high frequency station* (*VHF*)
ULA Union der leitenden Angestellten, Essen
U. L. F. Unsere Liebe Frau
Ult., ult. *Ultimo, ultimo* (It) am letzten (des Monats, Jahres)
ü. M. über dem Meeresspiegel
U/min Umdrehung/Minute = r. p. m.
UN *United Nations* [sg konstr]
Unabh. Unabhängige(r)
unbes. unbesetzt
UNCTAD *United Nations Conference on Trade and Development* Welthandels- u. Entwicklungskonferenz der Vereinten Nationen
UNDP *United Nations Development Program*
UNEF *United Nations Emergency Force* UN-Streitmacht
UNESCO *United Nations Educational, Scientific, and Cultural Organization*
UNHCR *UN High Commission for Refugees*, Genf
UNICEF (*UN*) *International Children's Emergency Fund, New York* Welt-Kinder-Hilfsfonds od –werk der UN
UNIPEDE *International Union of Producers and Distributers of Electrical Energy*
UNIPPA *International Union of Pure and Applied Physics*
Univ. Universität
UnlWG (UWG) Gesetz gegen den unlauteren Wettbewerb
UN(O) *The United Nations* [sg konstr] (*Organization*) Die Vereinten Nationen, New York
u. ö. und öfter
U.P., UP *United Press Associations*
U.P.I. *United Press International* (seit 1958)
U.p.M. Umdrehungen pro Minute
U.P.U. *Union postale universelle* (Fr) Weltpostverein, Bern
UR Uri (Schweizer Kanton)
u. R. unter Rückerbittung; urschriftlich Rückgabe
urspr. ursprünglich
U. R. S. S. (Fr) (zugleich ⟨post-off⟩ Abkürzung), Union der Soz. Sowjet-Republiken
USA = U. S. A.
USA *United States Army*
U. S. (A.) *United States* (*of America*) [sg konstr]
USAEC *US Atomic Energy Commission*
USAF *United States Air Force*
·**Uschla** ⟨pol⟩ **U**ntersuchungs- u. **Schl**ichtungs**a**usschuß
usf. und so fort
USFET *United States Forces European Theater* US-Streitkräfte, Europäischer Kriegsschauplatz
U.S.G.S. **1.** *United States Geodetic Survey* **2.** *United States Geological Survey*
USIS *US-Information Service, New York*
USN *United States Navy*
USS *United States Ship*
U. S. S. R. **1.** Union der Soz. Sowjet-Republiken **2.** Ukrainische Soz. Sowjet.-Rep.
USt Umsatzsteuer; **UStG** Umsatzsteuergesetz
usw ⟨wir⟩ *ultra short wave*
usw. und so weiter; ~ usf. *and all that*
u. t. **1.** unterer Totpunkt **2.** unter Tage **3.** unmodulierte Telegrafie
ü. t. über Tage
ut sup. L *ut supra* wie oben
u. U. unter Umständen
u. ü. V. unter üblichem Vorbehalt, Vorbehalt bei Gutschriftsanzeigen über Schecks und Wechsel
UV- Ultraviolett-(Filter, -Strahlung)
u. v. a. und viele(s) andere
UW *unconventional warfare*
u. W. unseres Wissens
uwe Unterwasser-Electric® (~-Wasserkanone®; *Jet-Stream®*)
UWG = UnlWG (s. o.)
UWL Unterwasserlabor [n]
ux. L *uxor* Ehefrau
u. zw. und zwar

V

V **1.** römische Zahl 5 **2.** ⟨chem⟩ Vanadium **3.** Volt **4.** Volumen (L) Band
v **1.** Volumen (L) Inhalt **2.** *velocitas* (L) Geschwindigkeit
V. Vize, Vortragende(r)
v. **1.** *vide* siehe **2.** *verte* wende **3.** von
VA. Versicherungsamt
VA **1.** Voltampere **2.** Vermögensabgabe
Va. *Virginia* Virginien (USA)
VAC Verband Alter Corpsstudenten
val Grammäquivalent
val. Valuta
VAR Vereinigte Arabische Republik
VAW Vereinigte Aluminium-Werke AG
Vbd. Verband
V. C. Vertreter-Convent
v. Chr. vor Christus, **v. Chr. Geb.** vor Christi Geburt

VD *Vaud* (Waadt, Schweizer Kanton)
V. D. A. Volksbund für das Deutschtum im Ausland
VDE Verband Deutscher Elektrotechniker
VDI Verband Deutscher Ingenieure
VdK Verband der Kriegsbeschädigten u. Kriegshinterbliebenen
VDS Verband Deutscher Studentenschaften
V. D. St. Verein Deutscher Studenten
V.E. Fr *Votre Eminence* Eure Eminenz
VEAB ⟨DDR⟩ Volkseigener Erfassungs- und Aufkaufbetrieb
VEB ⟨DDR⟩ Volkseigener Betrieb
VEBA Vereinigte Elektrizitäts- u. Bergwesen A.G.
VELK Vereinigte Evangelisch-Lutherische Kirche Deutschlands; → LWF
Venez. Venezuela
Ver. Vereinigte; **verb.** verbessert
Verbdg. Verbindung(en)
verd. ⟨chem, med⟩ verdünnt
Ver. Dt. Met. Vereinigte Deutsche Metallwerke A. G.
Verf. 1. Verfassung **2.** Verfasser
Verh. Verhandlungen
Verk. Verkehr
Verl.G. Gesetz über das Verlagsrecht v. 19. 6. 1901
verm. vermehrt; **VermSt** → VSt
Ver. St. Vereinigte Staaten, bes. von Nordamerika (USA)
Verw. Verwalter, -tung
Verw.-Bez. Verwaltungsbezirk
Vet. Veterinär
Vfg. v. Verfügung vom
VfK ⟨SBZ⟩ Verwaltung für Koordinierung (⟨mil⟩ Nachrichtendienst der Volksarmee)
V-förmiges (Flußtal)
VGH Verwaltungsgerichtshof
vgl. vergleiche
v. Gr. von Greenwich bei Angabe der geograph. Länge eines Ortes
v. g. u. (in Protokollen) vorgelesen, genehmigt, unterschrieben
v. H. vom Hundert; Prozent
VIAG, V·iag Vereinigte Industrie-Unternehmungen A.-G.
vid. *videatur* man sehe nach
viell. vielleicht; **v. J.** vorigen Jahres
Vis(c) *Viscount, Viscountess*
Vkz Verlagskennziffer [f]
v. M. vorigen Monats
V-Mann Vertrauensmann [m]
Vn. Vorname
VO. v. Verordnung vom
VOA *Voice of America* Stimme Amerikas
VOBl Verordnungsblatt für Berlin
VOFu Vollzugsordnung für den Funkdienst (UIT)
vol. Volumen (L) **a)** Inhalt **b)** Band
Vopo Volkspolizei, Volkspolizist (Ostzone)
VOR *Very High Frequency Omnidirectional Radio Range System*
Vors. Vorsitzender, Vorsitzer
Vorst. Vorstand, Vorsteher
vox pop. L *populi* Stimme des Volks
VP Volkspartei
VS *Valais* (Wallis, Schweizer Kanton)
vs. L *versus* gegen
v. s. L *vide supra* siehe oben
VSOP (auf Weinbrandetiketten) *very superior old pale*
VSt Vermögensteuer; **VStG** ∼-Gesetz [n]
V. St. A. Vereinigte Staaten von Nordamerika
V/STOL *Vertical Short Takeoff and Landing* ⟨a. a-n⟩
Vt. Vermont (USA)
v. T. (vT) vom Tausend
VTOL-Flugzeug, **V.T.O.L.**-*plane* (*vertical take-off and landing*, Senkrechtstarter)
Vtr. Vertreter(in) | **vtrw.** vertretungsweise
v. u. von unten
v. v. L *vice versa* umgekehrt
VVG Gesetz über den Versicherungs-Vertrag
VVN Vereinigung der Verfolgten des Naziregimes
(V)VSOP (*25–40 years old*) *very special* (*12–17 years old*) *old pale* (*brandy*)
VW Volkswagen(werk); **VW AG** Volkswerk AG
Vw. Volkswirt
VWD Vereinigte Wirtschaftsdienste, Frankfurt
VZ ⟨tax⟩ Veranlagungszeitraum

W

W 1. West(en) **2.** ⟨chem⟩ Wolfram **3.** Watt **4.** Wirklicher . . .
w. 1. weiblich **2.** wenden
WAAS *World Academy of Art and Science*
WAC *Women's Auxiliary Corps* Wehrmacht-Frauen-Hilfs-Korps der US
WAPOR *World Association for Public Opinion Research* Weltvereinigung für Meinungsforschung, Washington
wahrsch. wahrscheinlich
WaR. Wassermannsche Reaktion
WarenZG (WbzG) Gesetz zum Schutze der Warenbezeichnungen
Wash. Washington (Staat USA); → D.C.
WATA *World Association of Travel Agencies*
WAY *World Assembly of Youth*, Welt-Jugend-Parlament, Brüssel
WAZ Westdeutsche Allgemeine Zeitung
WB 1. ⟨stud⟩ Wingolfbund **2.** *westbound* mit Ziel nach W
Wb 1. Wörterbuch **2.** ⟨el⟩ Weber (absolutes Maßsystem m-s-V-A); → m, s, V, A
WBFBl Amtsblatt des Finanzministeriums Württemberg-Baden
WbzG → WarenZG
W. C. *water closet* (engl) Klosett m. Wasserspülung
W.C. *War Cabinet*
WCC *World Council of Churches* Weltkirchenrat, Genf (Oekumenischer Rat der Kirchen)
W.C.T.U. *Women's Christian Temperance Union*
WDR Westdeutscher Rundfunk (Köln)
WE Wärmeeinheit
Wehrkr. Wehrkreis
WEU Westeuropäische Union, London
WEZ. Westeuropäische Zeit
WFMH *World Federation for Mental Health*
WFStab Wehrmachtführungsstab
WFC *World Food Council* Welternährungsrat
WFCYWG *World Federation of Catholic Young Women and Girls*, Gent; → UILFC
WFR Weltfriedens-Rat, Prag; → CMP, WPC
WFSW *World Federation of Scientific Workers* Weltbund der Wissenschaftler, London
WFTU *World Federation of Trade Unions* Weltgewerkschafts-Bund, Prag (WGB)
WFUNA *World Federation of United Nations Associations* Weltbund der UN-Vereinigungen, Genf, New York, Paris; → FMANU
WG Wehrgesetz
WGB Weltgewerkschafts-Bund, Prag; → IBFG, WFTU
wh., whr. *watt-hour(s)*
WHO *World Health Organization* Weltgesundheits-Organisation der UN, Genf
WHW. Winterhilfswerk des deutschen Volkes
WI Wehrpolitische Information
W.I. *West Indian*; *West Indies*
Wi. Wirtschaft ⟨a. cart⟩
WiGBl Gesetzblatt der Verwaltung des Vereinten Wirtschaftsgebietes

Witch ⟨Am⟩ *Women's International Terrorist Conspiracy from Hell* Internationale Terrorverschwörung der Frauen aus der Hölle (gegen Ausbeutung der Frau als Sexobjekt, Bruthenne, Hausdienerin u. billige Arbeitskraft)
willk. willkürlich
WILPF *Women's International League for Peace and Freedom* Internationale Frauen-Liga für Frieden und Freiheit, Genf; → LIFPL
w.i.m.c. *whom it may concern*
Wis. Wisconsin (USA)
Wiss. Wissenschaft
WJC *World Jewish Congress* Jüdischer Weltkongreß, New York
WJSC ⟨stud⟩ Wernigeroder Jagdkorporationen-Senioren-Convent
WK ⟨stud⟩ Wartburg Kartell [n]
w. L. westliche(r) Länge
WLU *World Liberal Union* Liberale Weltunion, London
WMA *World Medical Association* Welt-Mediziner-Verband, New York
WMF Württembergische Metallwaren-Fabrik
WMM *World Movement of Mothers* Welt-Mütter-Bewegung, Paris; → MMM
WMO *World Meteorological Organization* Meteorologische Weltorganisation, Lausanne (Weltwetterdienst)
WMWFG *World Movement for World Federal Government* Weltbewegung für Weltregierung, Amsterdam
WNW Westnordwest
WO Wechselordnung
Woiw. Woiwodschaft
WOMAN *World Organization of Mothers of All Nations*
WP Warschauer Pakt ⟨a. mil⟩
WPC *World Peace Council* Weltfriedens-Rat, Prag; → CMP
WPC *World Power Conference* Weltkraftkonferenz, London
WPV Weltpostverein
w.r. ⟨ins⟩ *war risk*
WRA. Wirtschafts- und Rechnungsamt
WRI *War Resisters' International* Internationale der Kriegsgegner und Kriegsdienstverweigerer, Enfield Middlesex, England
W.R.K. ⟨univ⟩ Westdeutsche Rektorenkonferenz
w.r.o. ⟨ins⟩ *war risk only*
WS, W. S. Wassersäule
WSC ⟨stud⟩ Weinheimer Senioren Convent
WSCF *World's Student Christian Federation* Christlicher Welt-Studentenbund, Genf; → FUACE
WSSR Weißrussische Soz. Sowjet-Republik
Wstf. Westfalen
WSV ⟨com⟩ Winter-Schluß-Verkauf
WSW Westsüdwest
wt ⟨engl⟩ *weight*
Wtb. Württemberg
WTB Wolffs Telegraphen Büro
WUS *World University Service* Welt-Hochschul-Dienst, Genf
W. Va. West-Virginien
WVF *World Veterans Federation*
WVG Wehrmachtversorgungsgesetz
WWF *World Wildlife Fund* Weltnaturfonds
WWI Wirtschaftswissenschaftliches Institut
WWW *World Weather Watch*
WYMCA *World Alliance of Young Men's Christian Associations*, Genf
WYWCA *World Young Women's Christian Association*, Genf

X

X 1. *Christ* **2.** röm. Zahlzeichen 10
x ⟨math⟩ **1.** die erste Unbekannte **2.** Abszisse *abscissa*
XE X- od Siegbahnsche Einheit (Röntgenspektroskopische Einheit) *X-unit*
Xmas ⟨fam⟩ *Christmas* Weihnachten
XP 1. Zeichen für den Namen „Christus“ (griech. Buchstaben X = Ch; P = R) **2.** *exprès payé* (Fr) Bote bezahlt

Y

y ⟨math⟩ **1.** die zweite Unbekannte **2.** Ordinate *ordinate*
YCW *Young Christian Workers*, Brüssel, Christliche Arbeiterjugend; → JOC
yd. ⟨engl⟩ *yard* Elle
Y. H. A. *Youth Hostel Association*
YMCA *Young Men's Christian Association* Christliche Vereine junger Männer, Genf (CVJM)
YMHA *Young Men's Hebrew Association*
yr. *year* Jahr
Yu Jugoslawien ⟨a. mot⟩
YWCA *Young Women's Christian Association* Christliche Vereine junger Mädchen, Genf

Z

Z Zeppelinluftschiff z. B. Z 127
z ⟨math⟩ die dritte Unbekannte
Z. Zeitschrift
ZA Zentralausschuß [m]
ZAW Zentralausschuß der Werbewirtschaft, Bonn
z. B. zum Beispiel
ZBIE Zentralbüro für internationale Eisenbahn-Transporte, Bern; → OIC
Zbl. Zentralblatt
z. b. V. zur besonderen Verwendung
z. D. zur Disposition
z. d. A. zu den Akten
ZDF ⟨telv⟩ Zweites Deutsches Fernsehen
ZDH Zentralverband des deutschen Handwerks, Bonn
z. E. zum Exempel
Z. E. M. ⟨biol⟩ Zentralregelnder Mechanismus
Zf. Zinsfuß
ZG Zug (Schweizer Kanton)
Z.G. *Zoological Garden*
ZGB Schweizer Zivilgesetzbuch
ZH Zürich (Schweizer Kanton u. Stadt)
z. H. zu Händen
Ziff. ⟨off⟩ Ziffer [f]
ZOB ⟨rail⟩ Zubringeromnibus-Bahnhof
zool. zoologisch
ZPO Zivilprozeßordnung
z. S. zur See; **z. T.** zum Teil
Ztg. Zeitung
Ztr. Zentner
z. tr. H. zu treuen Händen
Ztschr. Zeitschrift; **zul.** zuletzt
Ztw. ⟨mst nazi⟩ Zeitwende (= Christi Geburt)
ZustG Gesetz über die Zuständigkeit d. Verwaltungsgerichtsbehörden
ZVG Gesetz über Zwangsversteigerung und Zwangsverwaltung
z. Wv. zur Wiederverwendung
z. Z. zur Zeit

III. Nationale Kraftfahrzeug-Kennzeichen
National Identification Plates ⟨mot⟩

A	Österreich (Austria)
ADN	Aden
AL	Albanien
AND	Andorra
AUS	Australia
B	Belgique
BA	Burma
BDS	Barbados
BG	Bulgaria
BH	Brit.-Honduras
BR	Brazil
BRG	Brit.-Guayana
C	Cuba
CC	Consular Corps, Corps Consulaire
CD	Corps Diplomatique
CDN	Canada
CH	Schweiz (Confoederatio Helvetica)
CL	Ceylon
CO	Columbia
CS	Československá socialistická republika
CY	Cyprus
D	Deutschland
DK	Danmark
E	España
EAK	Kenya
EAT	Tansania
EAU	Uganda
EIR	Eire (Ireland)
EQ	Ecuador
ET	Egypt
F	République Française
FL	Fürstentum Liechtenstein
FM	Fédération malaise
G	Guatemala
GB	Great Britain and Northern Ireland
GBA	Alderney
GBG	Guernsey
GBJ	Jersey
GBM	Isle of Man
GBY	Malta
GBZ	Gibraltar
GR	Grèce (Greece)
H	Hungaria
I	Italia
IL	Israel
IND	Indische Union
IR	Iran
IRQ	Irak
IS	Island
KWT	Kuwait
L	Luxembourg
M	Palestina
MA	Maroc
MC	Principauté de Monaco
MEX	Mexico
N	Norge (Norway)
NB	North Borneo
NF	Newfoundland
NL	Nederland (Holland)
NZ	New Zealand
P	Republica Portuguesa
PA	Panama
PAK	Pakistan
PE	República del Perú
PL	Rzeczpospolita Polska
PY	República del Paraguay
R	România
RA	República Argentina
RC	Republic of China
RCH	República de Chile
RI	Indonesien
RNR	Northern Rhodesia
RNY	Nyassaland
RSM	Repubblica de San Marino
S	Sverige (Sweden)
SCV	Stato della Città del Vaticano
SF	Suomi (Finland)
SNB	Brit.-Northern Borneo
SU	Sowjet-Union
SWA	South-West Africa
TC	Cameroon
TN	Tunisie
TR	Türkiye Cümhuriyeti
U	Uruguay
USA	United States of America
VN	Viet-Nam
YU	Yugoslavia
ZA	The Union of South Africa (holl.: Zuid Africa)

Kilometres/miles (Faustregel; ungenau)

Multiply	kilometres	by 6	and	divide	by	10.
Divide	miles	by 6	and	multiply	by	10

Geschwindigkeiten **Speeds**

miles/h	10	20	30	40	50	60	70	80	90	100
km/h	16,09	32,18	48,27	64,36	80,45	96,54	112,63	128,72	144,81	160,90

IV. Die der IATA angeschlossenen Luftfahrtgesellschaften nach dem Stand vom 7. Oktober 1970

IATA Membership as at 7th October 1970 (→ Abkürzungsverzeichnis)

ACTIVE MEMBERS (91)

* Aber Lingus Teoranta (Dublin)
* Aerolineas Argentinas (Buenos Aires)
Aerolineas Peruanas S.A. (Lima)
* Aeronaves de Mexico S.A. (Mexico City)
* Aerovias Nacionales de Colombia S.A. (AVIANCA) (Bogota)
* Air Afrique (Abidjan)
* Air Algérie (Algiers)
* Air Canada (Montreal)
* Air Ceylon (Colombo)
Air Congo (Kinshasa)
* Air France (Paris)
Air Guinée (Conakry)
* Air-India (Bombay)
* Air Malawi, Limited (Blantyre)
Air Mali (Bamako)
* Air New Zealand (Auckland)
* Air-Siam Air Company Limited (Bangkok)
* Air Vietnam (Saigon)
* ALIA – The Royal Jordanian Airlines (Amman)
* ALITALIA – Linee Aeree Italiane (Roma)
* American Airlines Inc. (New York)
* Austrian Airlines (Vienna)
* Braniff International Airways (Dallas)
* British European Airways (London)
* British Overseas Airways Corp. (London)
* British United Airways Ltd. (London)
**British West Indian Airways (Trinidad)
* CP Air (Vancouver)
* Československé aerolinie (Prague)
* China Airlines Ltd. (Taipei)
Compañía Mexicana de Aviacion S.A. (Mexico)
Compañía Ecuatoriana de Aviacion S.A. (Quito)
* Servicos Aéreos Cruzeiro do Sul S.A. (Rio de Janeiro)
* Cyprus Airways Limited (Nicosia)
**Delta Air Lines Inc. (Atlanta)
* Deutsche Lufthansa AG (Köln)
* Direcção de Exploração dos Transportes Aéreos „DETA“ (Lourenço Marques)
Direcção de Exploração dos Transportes Aéreos „DTA“ (Luanda)
* East African Airways Corp. (Nairobi)
* Eastern Air Lines Inc. (New York)
* El Al Israel Airlines (Tel Aviv)
* Empresa Consolidada Cubana Aviacion (Havana)
* Ethiopian Air Lines S.C. (Addis Ababa)
* FINNAIR Oy (Helsinki)
* Flugfelag Islands H.F. (Reykjavik)
**Flying Tiger Line Inc. (Los Angeles)
* P.N. Garuda Indonesian Airways (Djakarta)
Ghana Airways Corporation (Accra)
* IBERIA, Líneas Aéreas de España (Madrid)
* Indian Airlines (New Delhi)
* Iraqi Airways (Baghdad)
* Japan Air Lines Co. Ltd. (Tokyo)
* Jugoslovenski Aerotransport (JAT) (Belgrade)
* KLM Royal Dutch Airlines (Amsterdam)
* Kuwait Airways Corporation (Kuwait)
* Libyan Arab Airlines (Benghazi)
* Línea Aerea del Cobre Ltda. (Santiago)
Línea Aérea Nacional (LANCHILE) (Santiago)
The Malta Airlines (Sliema)
* Middle East Airlines Airliban (Beirut)
**Mohawk Airlines Inc. (Utica, N.Y.)
**National Airlines (Miami)
* Northwest Airlines Inc. (St. Paul)
* Olympic Airways S.A. (Athens)
* Pakistan International Airlines Corp. (Karachi)
* Pan American World Airways Inc. (New York)
* Philippine Air Lines Inc. (Manila)
Polish Airlines „LOT“ (Warsaw)
* Qantas Airways Limited (Sydney)
* SABENA, Société Anonyme Belge d'Exploitation de la Navigation Aérienne (Brussels)
* Saudi Arabian Airlines Corp. (Jeddah)
* Scandinavian Airlines System (Stockholm)
* Seaboard World Airlines Inc. (New York)
* South African Airways (Johannesburg)
* Sudan Airways (Khartoum)
* Swiss Air Transport Co. Ltd. (Zurich)
Syrian Arab Airlines (Damascus)
* Trans-Mediterranean Airways SAL (Beirut)
* Transportes Aéreos Portugueses (TAP) (Lisbon)
* Trans World Airlines Inc. (New York)
Tunis Air (Tunis)
* Turk Hava Yollari (Istanbul)
* Union de Transports Aériens (UTA) (Paris)
* United Air Lines (Chicago)
United Arab Airlines (Cairo)
* VARIG S.A. (Vição Aérea Rio-Grandense) (Porto Alegre)
* Venezolana Internacional de Aviacion S.A. (VIASA) (Caracas)
* WAAC (Nigeria) Limited (Lagos)
* Zambia Airways Corporation (Lusaka)

ASSOCIATE MEMBERS (14)

* Ansett Airlines of Australia (Melbourne)
Ansett Airlines of Papua New Guinea (Lae)
Chicago Helicopter Airways Inc. (Chicago)
Commercial Airways (Pty) Ltd. (Johannesburg)
**Continental Air Lines Inc. (Los Angeles)
East-West Airlines Ltd. (Tamworth, N.S.W.)
Eastern Provincial Airways (1963) Ltd. (Gander)
**New York Airways Inc. (New York)
* New Zealand National Airways Corp. (Wellington)
* Quebecair Inc. (Dorval)
Suidwes Lugdiens (Eiendoms) Beperk (Windhoek, S.W. Africa)
Territory Airlines Pty. Ltd. (Goroka)
* Trans Australia Airlines (Melbourne)
Viação Aérea São Paulo S.A. (VASP) (São Paulo)

---

* Member of IATA Clearing House ** Clears via Airlines Clearing House

V. Luftverkehrsgesellschaften in Frankfurt am Main

Airlines-Verzeichnis und ihre Abkürzungen

Aer Lingus	EL
Aerolíneas Argentinas	AR
Aerolíneas Peruanas	EP
Air Algérie	AH
Air Bahama	IW
Air Canada	AC
Air France	AF
Air India	AI
Air New Zealand	TE
Alitalia	AZ
American Airlines	AA
American Flyers Airline	FF
ARIANA Afghan Airlines	FG
ATLANTIS AG	NO
Austrian Airlines	OS
Avianca	AV
Avio Genex	JJ
British European Airways	BE
British Overseas Airways Corporation	BA
British United Airways	BR
Bulgarische Luftlinien, Balkan	LZ
Canadian Pacific Airlines	CP
Capitol Airways	CL
Cathay Pacific Airways	CX
Československé aerolinie	OK
Condor Flugdienst GmbH	DF
Cyprus Airways	CY
Deutsche Lufthansa	LH
East African Airways	EC
Eastern Air Lines	EA
EL-AL Israel Airlines	LY
Ethiopian Airlines	ET
Finnair	AY
GARUDA Indonesian Airways	GA
Germanair	DV
Iberia	IB
Icelandair Flugfelag Islands	FI
Interregional Fluggesellschaft	IP
Iran National Air Lines	IR
Iraqi Airways	IA
Japan Air Lines	JL
Jugoslovenski Aerotransport	JU
Königlich Niederländische Luftverkehrsgesellschaft	KL
Kuwait Airways	KU
Loftleidir Icelandic Airlines	LL
Lufttransport Unternehmen	LT
Luxair	LG
Malaysia-Singapore Airlines	ML
Malev Ungarische Luftverkehrsgesellschaft	MA
Middle East Airlines	ME
National Airlines	NA
Nigerian Airways	WT
Northwest Orient	NW
Olympic Airways	OA
Overseas National Airways	OV
Pakistan International Airlines	PK
Pan American World Airways	PA
Philippine Air Lines	PR
Polnische Fluglinien LOT	LO
Qantas, Australiens Übersee Fluglinie	QF
Royal Air Maroc	AT
Royal Jordanian Airlines	RJ
Sabena	SN
Saturn-Airways	KS
Saudi Arabian Airlines	SV
Scandinavian Airlines System	SK
Seaboard World Airlines	SB
Società Aerea Mediterranea	MQ
South African Airways	SA
Swissair	SR
TAROM	RO
Thai International	TG
Trans Mediterranean Airways	TL
Trans International Airlines	TV
Transportes Aereos Portugueses	TP
Trans World Airlines	TW
Tunis Air	TU
Turkish Airlines	TK
Union de Transports Aériens	UT
United Airlines	UA
United Arab Airlines	MS
Varig Airlines	RG
VIASA Venezuelan International Airways S. A.	VA
World Airways	WO

Airlines-Verzeichnis nach ihren Abkürzungen

AA	American Airlines
AC	Air Canada
AF	Air France
AH	Air Algérie
Al	Air India
AR	Aerolines Argentinas
AT	Royal Air Maroc
AV	Avianca
AY	Finnair
AZ	Alitalia
BA	BOAC
BE	British European Airways
BR	British United Airways
CL	Capitol Airways
CP	Canadian Pacific Airlines
CX	Cathay Pacific Airways
CY	Cyprus Airways
DF	Condor Flugdienst GmbH (CFG)
DV	Germanair Bedarfsluftfahrtges. mbH
EA	Eastern Air Lines
EC	East African Airways
EL	Aer Lingus
EP	Aerolíneas Peruanas
ET	Ethiopian Airlines
FF	American Flyers Airline
FG	ARIANA Afghan Airlines
FI	Icelandair Flugfelag Islands
GA	GARUDA Indonesian Airways
IA	Iraqi Airways
IB	Iberia
IP	Interregional Fluggesellschaft
IR	Iran National Air Lines Corp.
IW	Air Bahama
JJ	Avio Genex
JL	Japan Air Lines
JU	Jugoslovenski Aerotransport
KL	Königlich Niederländische Luftverkehrsgesellschaft
KU	Kuwait Airways
KS	Saturn Airways
LG	Luxair
LH	Deutsche Lufthansa
LL	Loftleidir Icelandic Airlines
LO	Polnische Fluglinien LOT
LT	LTU Lufttransport Unternehmen
LY	EL-AL Israel Airlines
LZ	Bulgarische Luftlinien Balkan
MA	Malev Ungar. Fluggesellschaft
ME	Middle East Airlines
ML	Malaysia-Singapore Airlines
MS	United Arab Airlines
MQ	Società Aerea Mediterranea
NA	National Airlines
NO	Atlantis AG
NW	Northwest Orient
OA	Olympic Airways
OK	Československé aerolinie
OS	Austrian Airlines
OV	Overseas National Airways
PA	Pan American World Airways
PK	Pakistan International Airlines
PR	Philippine Air Lines
QF	Qantas, Australiens Übersee Fluglinie
	Intercity Air Service
RG	Varig Airlines
RJ	Royal Jordanian Airlines
RO	TAROM
SA	South African Airways
SB	Seaboard World Airlines
SK	Scandinavian Airlines System
SN	Sabena
SR	Swissair
SV	Saudi Arabian Airlines
TE	Air New Zealand
TG	Thai International
TK	Turkish Airlines
TL	Trans Mediterranean Airways
TP	Transportes Aereos Portugueses
TU	Tunis Air
TV	Trans International Airlines
TW	Trans World Airlines
UA	United Airlines
UT	Union de Transports Aériens
VA	VIASA
WO	World Airways
WT	Nigerian Airways

VI. Die Staaten Afrikas

Land	Staatsform oder sonstiger Status	Unabhängigkeitsdatum
Nordafrika		
Ägypten siehe Vereinigte Arabische Republik		
Algerien	Republik	3. 7. 1962
Libyen	Republik	24. 12. 1951
Marokko	Königreich	2. 3. 1956
Tunesien	Republik	15. 6. 1956
Westafrika		
Dahomey	Republik	1. 8. 1960
Elfenbeinküste	Republik	7. 8. 1960
Gambia	Republik	18. 2. 1965
Ghana	Republik	6. 3. 1957
Guinea	Republik	28. 9. 1958
Kanarische Inseln	spanische Provinz	—
Kapverdische Inseln	portugiesische Überseeprovinz	—
Liberia	Republik	26. 7. 1847
Mali	Republik	22. 9. 1960
Mauretanien	Republik	28. 11. 1960
Niger	Republik	3. 8. 1960
Nigeria	Republik	1. 10. 1960
Obervolta	Republik	5. 8. 1960
Portugiesisch Guinea	portugiesische Überseeprovinz	—
Senegal	Republik	4. 4. 1960
Sierra Leone	Republik	27. 4. 1960
Spanisch Westafrika	spanische Provinz	—
Togo	Republik	27. 4. 1960
Zentralafrika		
Angola	portugiesische Überseeprovinz	—
Äquatorial-Guinea	Republik	12. 10. 1968
Gabun	Republik	17. 8. 1960
Kamerun	Republik	1. 1. 1960
Kongo-Brazzaville	Republik	15. 8. 1960
Kongo-Kinshasa	Republik	20. 6. 1960
São Tomé et Principe	portugiesische Überseeprovinz	—
St. Helena	Britische Kronkolonie	—
Tschad	Republik	11. 8. 1960
Zentralafrikanische Republik	Republik	17. 8. 1960
Südafrika		
Botswana	Republik	30. 9. 1966
Lesotho	Königreich	4. 10. 1966
Malawi	Republik	6. 7. 1964
Moçambique	portugiesische Überseeprovinz	—
Rhodesien	Republik	11. 11. 1965 (umstritten)
Sambia	Republik	24. 10. 1964
Südafrika	Republik	12. 6. 1934
Südwestafrika	Mandatsgebiet des Völkerbunds, Status umstritten	
Swasiland	Königreich	6. 9. 1968
Ostafrika		
Burundi	Republik	1. 7. 1962
Kenya	Republik	12. 12. 1963
Komoren	französisches Überseeterritorium	—
Madagaskar	Republik	26. 6. 1960
Mauritius	Republik	—
Réunion	französisches Überseedepartement	—
Rwanda	Republik	1. 7. 1962
Sansibar siehe Tansania		
Seychellen	seit 1903 britische Kronkolonie, Autonomie seit 1968	
Tanganyika siehe Tansania		
Tansania	Republik	9. 12. 1961
Uganda	Republik	9. 10. 1962

Land	Staatsform oder sonstiger Status	Unabhängigkeitsdatum
Nordafrika		
Äthiopien	Kaiserreich	7. Jahrhundert
Französisches Territorium der Afars und Issas	französisches Überseeterritorium	—
Sokotra	seit 1967 zur Volksrepublik Südjemen	
Somalia	Republik	1. 7. 1960
Sudan	Republik	1. 1. 1956
Vereinigte Arabische Republik	Republik	

VII. Amerikanische Zeitzonen

E.S.T.	Eastern Standard Time
E.D.T.	Eastern Daylight Time
C.S.T.	Central Standard Time
C.D.T.	Central Daylight Time
M.S.T.	Mountain Standard Time
M.D.T.	Mountain Daylight Time
P.S.T.	Pacific Standard Time
P.D.T.	Pacific Daylight Time

Anm.: The clock is advanced one hour in the Spring so that one may enjoy longer Daylight hours till September. (→ p. 1494).

VIII. Buchstabieralphabete

Buchstabier-Alphabet im Fernsprechverkehr · Phonetik Alphabets

	Deutsch	*Englisch*	*Amerikanisch*	*International*	*International* ⟨aero⟩	*NATO*
A	Anton	Andrew	Abel ['eibəl]	Amsterdam	Alfa	Alfa
Ä	Ärger					
B	Berta	Benjamin	Baker	Baltimore	Bravo	Bravo
C	Cäsar	Charlie	Charlie	Casablanca	Coca	Charlie
Ch	Charlotte					
D	Dora	David	Dog	Dänemark	Delta	Delta
E	Emil	Edward	Easy	Edison	Echo	Echo
F	Friedrich	Frederick	Fox	Florida	Foxtrot	Foxtrot
G	Gustav	George	George	Gallipoli	Golf	Golf
H	Heinrich	Harry	How	Havanna	Hotel	Hotel
I	Ida	Isaac	Item	Italia	India	India
J	Julius	Jack	Jig	Jerusalem	Juliet	Juliet
K	Kaufmann	King	King	Kilogramm	Kilo	Kilo
L	Ludwig	Lucy	Love	Liverpool	Lima	Lima
M	Martha	Mary	Mike	Madagaskar	Metro	Mike
N	Nordpol	Nellie	Nan	New York	Nectar	November
O	Otto	Oliver	Oboe ['oubou]	Oslo	Oscar	Oscar
Ö	Ökonom					
P	Paula	Peter	Peter	Paris	Papa	Papa
Q	Quelle	Queenie	Queen	Quebec	Quebec	Quebec
R	Richard	Robert	Roger	Roma	Romeo	Romeo
S	Samuel	Sugar	Sugar	Santiago	Sierra	Sierra
Sch	Schule					
T	Theodor	Tommy	Tare	Tripoli	Tango	Tango
U	Ulrich	Uncle	Uncle	Uppsala	Union	Uniform
Ü	Übermut					
V	Viktor	Victor	Victor	Valencia	Victor	Victor
W	Wilhelm	William	William	Washington	Whiskey	Whiskey
X	Xanthippe	Xmas	X [eks]	Xanthippe	Extra	X-Ray
Y	Ypsilon	Yellow	Yoke	Yokohama	Yankee	Yankee
Z	Zeppelin	Zebra	Zebra	Zürich	Zulu	Zulu

IX. Frakturbuchstaben

Das deutsche Alphabet in Fraktur- und Antiquabuchstaben

𝔄	A	𝔞	a ⟨Ger⟩[ɑː];	⟨engl⟩ [ei]
𝔄̈	Ä	𝔞̈	ä ⟨Ger⟩[æ(ː)];	⟨engl⟩ [ɑː Umlaut]
𝔅	B	𝔟	b ⟨Ger⟩[beː];	⟨engl⟩ [biː]
ℭ	C	𝔠	c ⟨Ger⟩[tseː];	⟨engl⟩ [siː]
ℭ𝔥	Ch	𝔠𝔥	ch ⟨Ger⟩[tseː haː];	⟨engl⟩ [siː eitʃ]
		𝔠𝔨	ck ⟨Ger⟩[tseː kaː];	⟨engl⟩ [siː kei]
𝔇	D	𝔡	d ⟨Ger⟩[deː];	⟨engl⟩ [diː]
𝔈	E	𝔢	e ⟨Ger⟩[eː];	⟨engl⟩ [iː]
𝔉	F	𝔣	f ⟨Ger⟩[efː];	⟨engl⟩ [ef]
𝔊	G	𝔤	g ⟨Ger⟩[geː];	⟨engl⟩ [dʒiː]
ℌ	H	𝔥	h ⟨Ger⟩[haː];	⟨engl⟩ [eitʃ]
ℑ	I	𝔦	i ⟨Ger⟩[iː];	⟨engl⟩ [ai]
𝔍	J	𝔧	j ⟨Ger⟩[jɔt];	⟨engl⟩ [dʒei]
𝔎	K	𝔨	k ⟨Ger⟩[kaː];	⟨engl⟩ [kei]
𝔏	L	𝔩	l ⟨Ger⟩[el];	⟨engl⟩ [el]
𝔐	M	𝔪	m ⟨Ger⟩[em];	⟨engl⟩ [em]
𝔑	N	𝔫	n ⟨Ger⟩[en];	⟨engl⟩ [en]
𝔒	O	𝔬	o ⟨Ger⟩[oː];	⟨engl⟩ [ou], ⟨Am⟩ [o] [o-Umlaut]
𝔒̈	Ö	𝔬̈		
𝔓	P	𝔭	p ⟨Ger⟩[peː];	⟨engl⟩ [piː]
𝔔	Q	𝔮	q ⟨Ger⟩[kuː];	⟨engl⟩ [kjuː]
ℜ	R	𝔯	r ⟨Ger⟩[er];	⟨engl⟩ [ɑː]
𝔖	S	ſ 𝔰	s ⟨Ger⟩[es];	⟨engl⟩ [es]
			⟨Ger⟩ (langes) [es];	⟨engl⟩
			⟨Ger⟩ Schluß - [es];	⟨engl⟩ [es]
		ß 𝔰𝔰	ß ⟨Ger⟩[es tset];	⟨engl⟩ –
𝔗	T	𝔱	t ⟨Ger⟩[teː];	⟨engl⟩ [tiː]
𝔘	U	𝔲	u ⟨Ger⟩[uː];	⟨engl⟩ [juː]
𝔘̈	Ü	𝔲̈	ü ⟨Ger⟩[yː];	⟨engl⟩ –
𝔙	V	𝔳	v ⟨Ger⟩[fau];	⟨engl⟩ [viː]
𝔚	W	𝔴	w ⟨Ger⟩[veː];	⟨engl⟩ [ˈdʌbl juː]
𝔛	X	𝔵	x ⟨Ger⟩[iks];	⟨engl⟩ [eks]
𝔜	Y	𝔶	y ⟨Ger⟩[ˈypsilon];	⟨engl⟩ [wai]
ℨ	Z	𝔷	z ⟨Ger⟩[tset];	⟨engl⟩ zed]

Bemerkungen: 1. Gruß [uː] Grüße (vgl grüßen [yː]); Kuß [u] Küsse (vgl küssen [y])
2. Im Deutschen werden die Buchstaben nicht flektiert: man schreibt Haar mit 2 a; Bacchus mit 2 c; Ebbe mit 2 b
Man sagt: der Punkt des i (*or* auf dem i)

X. Musik – Music

Noten- und Pausenzeichen und ihre Benennung

Die Noten und Pausenzeichen sind international die gleichen. Die Benennung im deutschen wie im englischen Text des Wörterbuchs wurden an Ort und Stelle genannt (z. B. **ganze Note** *semibreve* usw.) Die amerikanischen Bezeichnungen entsprechen den deutschen (z. B. $^1/_8$ = $^1/_8$ *one eighth* usw.)

Zeichen und Erklärungen

Leger lines
Hilfslinien:
(5 Linien):
Notensystem
Hilfslinien:
Leger lines

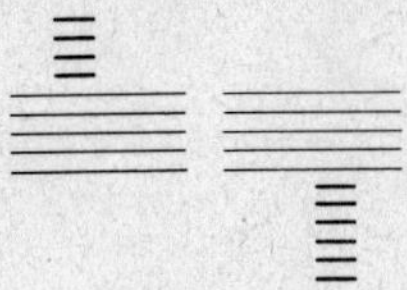

Taktstrich
bar-line

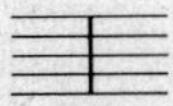

Staff
(5 Lines)

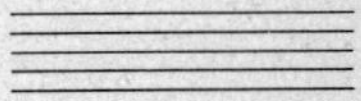

Violinschlüssel
treble clef

Baßschlüssel
bass clef

Noten und Pausen Notes and Rests

	ganze	halbe	Viertel-	Achtel-	$^1/_{16}$	$^1/_{32}$	Note
⟨engl⟩	*semibreve*	*minim*	*crotchet*	*quaver*	*semiquaver*	*demisemiquaver*	
⟨Am⟩	*whole*	*half*	*quarter*	*eighth*	$^1/_{16}$	$^1/_{32}$	*note*

Versetzungszeichen Signs of transposition

Erhöhungszeichen:

♯ = $^1/_2$ Ton, × = 2 Halbtöne

sharp double sharp

Erniedrigungszeichen:

♭ = $^1/_2$ Ton, = 2 Halbtöne

flat double flat

Auflösungszeichen: ♮
Natural

Wiederholungszeichen ||: . . . :||
Repeat

XI. MASSE (Maße) MEASURES

Maße (M), Gewichte (G), Währungen (W)
Measures (M), Weights (G), Currencies (W)

Abassi	G	Palästina
acre	M	Großbritannien, U.S.A.
Anna	W	Indien, Pakistan
Arschin	M	†Afghanistan, Rußland
Balboa	W	Panama
Ballen	G	(Baumwolle)
Bani	W	Rumänien
Baht (*Thical*)	W	Thailand
barrel	M	Gr.-Brit., U.S.A. (Petroleum)
†*Batzen*	W	Schweiz
Belga	W	Belgien, Luxemburg
Bolivar	W	Venezuela
Boliviano	W	Bolivien
bushel	M	Gr.-Brit., U.S.A. (Getreide)
Cent	W	†China, †Estland, Kanada, †Litauen, Malaia, Niederlande, U.S.A.
cental	G	Liverpool (Weizen)
Centavostos	W	Argentinien, Bolivien, Chile, Ecuador, Guatemala, Kolumbien, Mexiko, Nicaragua, Peru, Philippinen, Portugal
Centesimi	W	Italien
Centesimos	W	Panama, Paraguay, Uruguay
Centime	W	Belgien, Frankreich, Lettland, Luxemburg
Centimos	W	Spanien
cent weight	G	Großbritannien
chin	G	China
Ching	M	China
Cordoba	W	Nicaragua
Chittak	G	Indien
Cruzeiro	W	Brasilien
Deßjatine	M	Rußland, ca. 1 Hektar
Dimes	W	China
Dinar	W	Irak, Iran, Jugoslawien,
Dira Macmari	M	Ägypten [†Persien
Dollar → *Silberdollar*	W	Kanada, Malaia, U.S.A.
Draa	M	Arabien
Drachme	W	Griechenland
Dunam	M	Palästina
Escudo	W	Portugal
Färsakh	M	Persien
Feddan	M	Ägypten
Filler	W	Ungarn
Fils	W	Irak
Finmark	W	Finnland
foot	M	Gr.-Brit., U.S.A.
Forint	W	Ungarn
franc	W	Belgien, Frankreich, Schweiz, Luxemburg
Funt	G	Rußland
gallon	M	Gr.-Brit., U.S.A. (a. Petroleum)
Girsch	W	Abessinien
Goldrubel	W	Rußland
grain	G	(Edelmetalle) → S. 1490
Groschen	W	Österreich, Polen, Deutschland; → S. 612
Grosz(*y* pl)	W	Polen
Gulden	W	Niederlande, †Danzig
Guz	M	Indien
Heller	W	Tschechoslowakei
inch	M	Gr.-Brit., N.-Amerika, Indien

Joch	M	Österreich
Ka	G	Afghanistan
Kantar	G	†Abessinien, Äthiopien
Kint	M	†Abessinien, Äthiopien
Kopeke	W	Rußland
†*Kreuzer*	W	Deutschland, Österreich
Krone	W	Dänemark, †Estland, Island, Norwegen, Schweden, Tschechoslowakei
Kurusch	W	Türkei
Lat	W	†Lettland
Lepta	W	Griechenland
Leu	W	Rumänien
Lew	W	Bulgarien
Li	M	China
libre	G	Welthandel
Lira	W	Italien
Litas	W	†Litauen
Madda	M	Abessinien
Man	G	Afghanistan
Maria Theresia-Taler	W	Abessinien, Afrika
Mark	W	Deutschland; → Finmark
Meile	M	→ S. 879 & 1488–1489
Mil	W	Palästina
mile	M	Gr.-Brit., Amerika
Millièmes	W	Israel, Libyen
Milreis	W	Brasilien
Mils	W	Palästina
Miskal	G	Palästina
Morgen	M	→ S. 898
Öre	W	Dänemark, Norwegen, Schweden
ounce	G	Gr.-Brit. (Edelmetalle)
Para	W	Jugoslawien, Türkei
Pengö†	W	Ungarn, → Forint
Penni	W	Finnland
pence [pl.] v *penny*	W	Großbritannien
penny weight	G	Gr.-Brit. (Edelmetalle)
Peseta	W	Spanien
Peso	W	Argentinien, Chile, Kolumbien, Mexiko, Paraguay, Philippinen, Uruguay
Pfennig	W	Deutschland, †Danzig
Pfund	W	Ägypten, Israel, Palästina, Türkei, Peru; → *pound*
Piaster	W	Ägypten, Türkei
Picul	G	China
pound	G	Gr.-Brit., U.S.A.
pound sterling	W	Großbritannien
Pud	G	Rußland
Quabdah	M	Ägypten
quart	G	Gr.-Brit., U.S.A.
quarter	M	Gr.-Brit., U.S.A. (Getreide)
Quetzal	W	Guatemala
Rappen	W	Schweiz
Reis	W	Brasilien
Rial	W	Iran, †Persien
Rin	W	Japan
Rottel	G	Persien, †Abessinien, Äthi-
Rottoli	G	Arabien [opien
Rubel	W	Rußland
Rupie	W	Indien, Pakistan
Saschen	M	†Rußland
Satang	W	Thailand
Schekel	W	Israel
Schilling	W	Gr.-Brit., Österreich

Sen	W	Japan
Ser	G	Indien
Sheng	M	China
Silberdollar	W	China
Sol	W	Peru
Stotinki	W	Bulgarien
Sucre	W	Ecuador
Tael	W	China
Talari	W	Abessinien
†*Taler*	W	Deutschland
Tan (*Picul*)	G	China
Timan	M	Arabien
ton (*tong*)	G	Großbritannien
ton (*short*)	G	U.S.A.
Tonne	G	Deutschland usw.
Troy ounce	G	(Edelmetalle)
Troy pound	G	(Edelmetalle)
Tscherek	M	Persien
Tscherwone(*t*)*z*	W	Rußland
Tschetwert	M	Rußland
Wedro	M	Rußland
Werschok	M	Rußland
Werst	M	Rußland
yard	M	Gr.-Brit., U.S.A.
Yen	W	Japan
Zar	M	Persien
Zloty	W	Polen

Anglo-Amerikanische Maße · Anglo-American Measures

Längenmaße · Linear Measure

			abgerundetes metrisches Maß approx. metric equivalent ⟨Engl & Am⟩		
1	inch		= 25,40	mm	
12	inches	= 1 foot	= 30,48	cm	
3	feet	= 1 yard [Einheit]	= 91,44	cm	
5½	yards	= 1 pole, rod, perch	= 5,029 2	m	
4	poles, etc.	= 1 chain ⟨engl⟩	= 20,116 8	m	
10	chains = 40 rods	= 1 furlong = 220 yards	= 201,168	m	
8	furlongs = 5280 feet	= 1 statute mile = 1760 yards	= 1,609 35	km	[meile
6080.2	feet	= 1 nautical mile	= 1,853	km	= 1 Admirals-
3	statute miles	= 1 land league	= 4,828	km	

Exaktwissenschaftliche Tabelle

Brit. & US-Einheiten

Name		Abkürzung	MKS-Äquivalent m	CGS-Äquivalent cm	andere Äquivalente
Mil	⟨Brit⟩		$2{,}539\,998 \times 10^{-5}$	$2{,}539\,998 \times 10^{-3}$	0,001 inch
	⟨USA⟩		$2{,}540\,005 \times 10^{-5}$	$2{,}540\,005 \times 10^{-3}$	
Inch	⟨Brit⟩	in.	$2{,}539\,998 \times 10^{-2}$	2,539 998	$^1/_{12}$ foot; $^1/_{36}$ yard
	⟨USA⟩		$2{,}540\,005 \times 10^{-2}$	2,540 005	
Foot	⟨Brit⟩	ft.	$3{,}047\,997 \times 10^{-1}$	$3{,}047\,997 \times 10$	12 inches; $^1/_3$ yard
	⟨USA⟩		$3{,}048\,006 \times 10^{-1}$	$3{,}048\,006 \times 10$	
Yard	⟨Brit⟩	yd.	$9{,}143\,992 \times 10^{-1}$	$9{,}143\,992 \times 10$	36 inches; 3 feet
	⟨USA⟩		$9{,}144\,018 \times 10^{-1}$	$9{,}144\,018 \times 10$	
Rod	⟨Brit⟩	rd.	5,029 19	$5{,}029\,19 \times 10^{2}$	198 inches; 5,5 yards
	⟨USA⟩		5,029 210	$5{,}029\,210 \times 10^{2}$	
Mile (statute)	⟨Brit⟩	mi.	$1{,}609\,341 \times 10^{3}$	$1{,}609\,341 \times 10^{5}$	Landmeile; 5280 feet; 1760 yards; 320 rods; 8 furlongs;
	⟨USA⟩		$1{,}609\,347 \times 10^{3}$	$1{,}609\,347 \times 10^{5}$	$1{,}69 \times 10^{-13}$ Lichtjahr
Mile (nautical)	⟨Brit⟩	n. mi.	$1{,}853\,181 \times 10^{3}$	$1{,}853\,181 \times 10^{5}$	Seemeile; Länge einer Kreismitte des Erd-
	⟨USA⟩		$1{,}853\,29 \times 10^{3}$	$1{,}853\,29 \times 10^{5}$	äquators

Nach: Wissenschaftliche Tabellen 1953 der J. R. Geigy A.-G., Basel.

Mariners' Measure

6 feet = 2 yards	= 1 fathom	=	1,8288 m
1000 fathoms (approx.)	= 1 nautical mile	=	1,853 km
3 nautical miles	= 1 marine league	=	5,559 km

⟨Am⟩ Surveyors' Measure

7.92 inches	=	1 link	=	20,1168 cm
100 links	=	1 chain	=	20,1168 m
80 chains	=	1 mile	=	1609,344 m
10 square chains	=	1 acre	=	40,468 Ar

Flächenmaße · Square Measure

	1 square inch	=	100 square line	=	6,452 cm^2
(12 × 12 =)	144 square inches	=	1 square foot	=	9,29 dm^2
	9 square feet	=	1 square yard	=	0,836 m^2
	$30\frac{1}{4}$ square yards	=	1 square pole (⟨Am⟩ rod)	=	25,293 m^2
⟨Brit⟩	10 square poles	=	1 perch	=	252,928 m^2
⟨Brit⟩	40 square poles	=	1 rood	=	1011,712 m^2
⟨USA⟩	160 square rods	=	1 acre	=	40,468 Ar
⟨Brit⟩	4 roods	=	1 acre	=	40,468 Ar
	640 acres	=	1 square mile	=	259,00 Hektar
				=	2,590 km^2

Raummaße · Cubic Measure

1 cubic inch	=	1000 cubic lines	=	16,39 cm^3
1728 cubic inches	=	1 cubic foot	=	28,32 dm^3
27 cubic feet	=	1 cubic yard	=	764,533 dm^3
5 cubic feet	=	1 barrel bulk shipping		
40 cubic feet	=	1 ton shipping		
	=	1 load hard timber		
50 cubic feet	=	1 load foreign fir		

Für Flüssigkeiten · Liquid Measure

⟨Brit⟩	1	minim	=	0.0592 milliliter		=	59,2 µl
⟨USA⟩						=	61,61 µl
⟨Brit⟩	1	fluid dram	=	60 minims		=	3,552 ml (*Milliliter*)
⟨USA⟩		fluidram	=	60 minims		=	3,697 ml
⟨Brit⟩	1	fluid ounce	=	8 fluid drams		=	28,47 ml
⟨USA⟩			=	8 fluid drams		=	29,57 ml
⟨Brit⟩	20	fluid ounces	=	1 pint		=	569,4 ml
⟨USA⟩	16	fluid ounces	=	1 pint		=	473,12 ml
⟨Brit⟩	4	gills	=	1 pint	⟨mst⟩	=	0,5682 l (*Liter*)
	2	pints	=	1 quart		=	1,1364 l
	4	quarts	=	1 gallon		=	4,5459 l
				(1 brit. *Gallone* = 277,4 cubic inches)			
⟨USA⟩	4	quarts	=	1 gallon		=	3,785 l
				(1 USA -*Gallone* = 231 cubic inches)			
⟨Brit⟩	2	gallons	=	1 peck		=	9,092 l
⟨Brit⟩	4	pecks	=	1 bushel		=	36,368 l
⟨Brit⟩	8	bushels	=	1 quarter		=	2,909 hl (*Hektoliter*)
⟨USA⟩	$31\frac{1}{2}$	gallons	=	1 barrel		=	1,43198 hl
⟨USA⟩	2	barrels	=	1 hogshead		=	2,86396 hl

Für Trockenstoffe · Dry Measure

⟨Brit⟩	1 pint (abbr. pt.)	=	4 gills		=	568,3 ml
⟨USA⟩					=	473,2 ml
⟨USA⟩	1 quart (abbr. qt.)	=	2 pints		=	0,9464 l
⟨Brit⟩	1 gallon (abbr. gal.)	=	$^1/_{64}$ quarter	= 4 quarts	=	4,546 l
⟨USA⟩					=	4,41 l
⟨Brit⟩	1 peck (abbr. pk.)	=	$^1/_{32}$ qt.	= 2 gallons	=	9,092 l
⟨USA⟩					=	8,810 l
⟨Brit⟩	1 bushel (abbr. bu.)	=	4 pk.		=	36,37 l
⟨USA⟩					=	35,24 l
⟨Brit⟩	1 barrel	=	36 gal.		=	1,637 hl
⟨USA⟩					=	1,192 hl
⟨Brit⟩	1 quarter	=	8 bu.		=	2,909 hl
⟨USA⟩					=	2,421 hl
⟨Brit⟩	1 load	=	5 quarters			
⟨Brit⟩	1 chaldron	=	36 bushels			

⟨Am⟩ Wood Measure

16 cubic feet	=	1 cord foot
8 cord feet	=	1 cord

⟨Brit⟩ Yarn Measure (Cotton)

120 yards	= 1 skein	=	109,73 m
7 skeins	= 1 hank	=	768,09 m
18 hanks	= 1 spindle	=	1382,57 m

⟨Brit⟩ Yarn Measure (Linen)

300 yards	= 1 cut	=	274,32 m
2 cuts	= 1 heer	=	548,64 m
6 heers	= 1 hank	=	3291,84 m
4 hanks	= 1 spindle	=	13,16736 km

Gewichte · Weights*

Apothecaries' Weight · Medizinalgewichte

⟨Brit⟩	1 grain (abbr. gr.) ⟨a. USA⟩	= 20 mites	=	64,80 mg	
	1 scruple ⟨a. USA⟩	= 20 gr.	=	1,296 g	
	1 dram (abbr. dm.) ⟨a.	= $^1/_{256}$ lb.	=	1,772 g	
	USA⟩	= 3 scruples	=	3,888 g	
	1 drachm ⟨a. USA⟩	= 16 dm.	=	28,35 g	vgl. ↓
	1 ounce (abbr. oz.) ⟨a. USA⟩	= 8 drachms	=	31,10 g	vgl. ↓
		= 16 oz.	=	453,6 g	
	1 pound avoirdupois (lb.)	= 12 oz.	=	373,24 g	
⟨USA⟩					

Avoirdupois Weight · Handelsgewichte

⟨Brit⟩	1 ounce (abbr. oz.)	= 16 drams	=	28,35 g	vgl. ↑
		= 437$^1/_2$ grains Troy			
⟨USA⟩			=	31,10 g	vgl. ↑
⟨Brit⟩	1 pound (abbr. lb. av.)	= 16 ounces (oz.)	=	453,6 g	
⟨Brit⟩	1 stone	= 14 pounds	=	6,350 kg	
⟨Brit⟩	1 quarter	= 28 pounds	=	12,70 kg	
⟨USA⟩		= 25 pounds	=	11,34 kg	
⟨Brit & USA⟩	1 hundredweight cental (abbr. cwt. sh.)	= 100 pounds	=	45,36 kg	
⟨Brit⟩	1 hundredweight long	= 4 quarters			
		= 112 pounds	=	50,80 kg	
⟨Brit & USA⟩	1 short ton (abbr. tn. sh.)	= 2000 pounds	=	907,2 kg	
⟨Brit⟩	1 long ton (abbr. tn. l.)	= 2240 pounds	=	1016,064 kg	

⟨Engl⟩ Wool Weight

14	pounds	= 1 stone	=	6,3504 kg
2	stones	= 1 tod	=	12,7008 kg
6$^1/_2$	tods	= 1 wey	=	82,5552 kg
2	weys	= 1 sack	=	165,1104 kg
12	sacks	= 1 last		(= 29 cwt)

In außerenglischen Märkten ist der pack von 240 pounds gebräuchlich (: soviel pence je Gewichtpound, soviel £ je pack).

Troy Weight

1 grain	= 64,798 918 *Milligramm*
24 grains	= 1 pennyweight
20 pennyweights	= 1 ounce (*Unze*)
12 ounces	= 1 pound

Perlen und Edelsteine werden nach Karat (1 g) (= 4 grains = 3,2 Troy grains) gewogen. Die Troy Unze entspricht 150 Diamond Carats., vgl. S. 1493, Juwelen-Gewichte.

Gediegenes Gold nennt man 24-karätig; bei Legierungen mit einem Teil Zusatz nennt man es in England 23-karätig usf.

⟨Ger⟩ Der Feingehalt des Goldes wird in Deutschland durch Stempelung gekennzeichnet (Punzierungsgesetz), er wird nach Tausendsteln angegeben. Gleichzeitig gibt es noch die alte Rechnung nach Karat:

	1000 Teile Feingold	=	24 Karat
†für Münzen	900 „ „	=	22 „
für Zahnersatz . . .	750 „ „	=	18 „
für Schmuck . . .	585 „ „	=	14 „
	333 „ „	=	8 „

* Anm.: Dezimalstellen werden im Deutschen durch Komma, im Englischen durch Punkt abgetrennt, die alleinstehende 0 vor dem Punkt wird im Englischen weggelassen, also 0,5 (lies: null Komma 5) ⟨engl⟩ .5 (lies: point five).

Übersicht über die angelsächsischen Maßsysteme

(Seite 23 der Wissenschaftlichen Tabellen 1953 der J. R. Geigy A.G.)
Mit freundlicher Genehmigung der J. R. Geigy A.G. Basel

Lengths

Inches (in.)	Feet (ft.)	Yards (yd.)	Rods (rd.)	Miles (mi.)	Metric equivalent *
1	0,083333$(^1/_{12})$	0,027778$(^1/_{36})$	0,00505051$(^1/_{198})$	0,0000157828	2,54001 centimeters
12	1	0,333333$(^1/_3)$	0,0606061	0,000189394	0,304801 meter
36	3	1	0,181818	0,000568182	0,914402 meter
198	16,5	5,5	1	0,003125	5,029210 meters
63 360	5 280	1 760	320	1	1,60935 kilometers

Area

Square inches (sq. in.)	Square feet (sq. ft.)	Square yards (sq. yd.)	Square rods (sq. rd.)	Acres (A.)	Square miles (sq. mi.)	Metric equivalent *
1	0,0069444$(^1/_{144})$	0,0007716$(^1/_{1296})$	....	....	....	6,451626 square centimeters
144	1	0,1111$(^1/_9)$	0,0036731	$2,29568 \times 10^{-5}$	$3,58701 \times 10^{-8}$	0,092903 square meter
1296	9	1	0,03305785	$2,06612 \times 10^{-4}$	$3,22831 \times 10^{-7}$	0,8361307 square meter
39204	272,25	30,25	1	0,00625$(^1/_{16})$	$9,765625 \times 10^{-6}$	25,29295 square meters
627264	43 560	4 840	160	1	0,0015625	40,46873 square decameters
$4,0154 \times 10^9$	27 878 400	3 097 600	102 400	640	1	2,589998 square kilometers

Volume

Cubic inches (cu. in.)	Cubic feet (cu. ft.)	Cubic yards (cu. yd.)	Metric equivalent *
1	0,000578704$(^1/_{1728})$	$2,143347 \times 10^{-5}$	16,3872 cubic centimeters
1 728	1	0,0370370$(^1/_{27})$	0,0283170 cubic meter
46 656	27	1	0,764559 cubic meter

Capacity — Liquid Measure

Gills (gi.)	Pints (pt.)	Quarts (qt.)	Gallons (gal.)	Cubic inches (cu. in.)	Metric equivalent *
1	0,25$(^1/_4)$	0,125$(^1/_8)$	0,03125$(^1/_{32})$	7,21875	118,292 milliliters
4	1	0,5$(^1/_2)$	0,125$(^1/_8)$	28,875	0,473167 liter
8	2	1	0,25$(^1/_4)$	57,749	0,946333 liter
32	8	4	1	231	3,785332 liters

Apothecaries' Fluid Measure

Minims min. or ♍	Fluid drams** fl. dr. or ʒ fl.	Fluid ounces fl. oz. or ℥ fl.	Pints (pt.)	Metric equivalent *
1	0,016667$(^1/_{60})$	0,0020833$(^1/_{480})$	0,00013021	0,0616102 milliliter
60	1	0,125$(^1/_8)$	0,0078125	3,69661 milliliters
480	8	1	0,0625$(^1/_{16})$	29,5729 milliliters
7 680	128	16	1	0,473167 liter

Dry Measure

Pints (pt.)	Quarts (qt.)	Pecks (pk.)	Bushels (bu.)	Cubic inches (cu. in.)	Metric equivalent *
1	0,5$(^1/_2)$	0,0625$(^1/_{16})$	0,015625$(^1/_{64})$	33,6003	0,550599 liter
2	1	0,125$(^1/_8)$	0,03125$(^1/_{32})$	67,2006	1,101198 liters
16	8	1	0,25$(^1/_4)$	537,605	8,80958 liters
64	32	4	1	2 150,42	35,2383 liters

Mass — Avoirdupois/Commercial

Grains (gr.)	Drams (dr. av.)	Ounces (oz. av.)	Pounds (lb. av.)	Tons (short) (tn. sh.)	Metric equivalent *
1	0,03657143	0,0022857	0,00014286$(^1/_{7000})$	....	0,064798918 gram
27,34375	1	0,0625$(^1/_{16})$	0,00390625$(^1/_{256})$	....	1,771845 grams
437,5	16	1	0,0625$(^1/_{16})$	0,00003125	28,349527 grams
7 000	256	16	1	0,0005	453,5924 grams
....	572 000	32 000	2000	1	907,18486 kilograms

Mass — Troy Weight

Grains (gr.)	Pennyweights (dwt.)	Ounces (oz. t.)	Pounds (lb. t.)	Metric equivalent *
1	0,041667$(^1/_{24})$	0,0020833$(^1/_{480})$	0,0001736111$(^1/_{5760})$	64,798918 milligrams
24	1	0,05$(^1/_{20})$	0,0041667$(^1/_{240})$	1,555174 grams
480	20	1	0,083333$(^1/_{12})$	31,103481 grams
5 760	240	12	1	373,24177 grams

Mass — Apothecaries' Weight

Grains (gr.)	Scruples (℈ or s. ap.)	Drams (Brit.: Drachms) (ʒ or dr. ap.)	Ounces (℥ or oz. ap.)	Pounds (lb. ap.)	Metric equivalent *
1	0,05$(^1/_{20})$	0,016667$(^1/_{60})$	0,0020833$(^1/_{480})$	0,0001736111$(^1/_{5760})$	64,798918 milligrams
20	1	0,333333$(^1/_3)$	0,041667$(^1/_{24})$	0,0034722$(^1/_{288})$	1,2959784 grams
60	3	1	0,125$(^1/_8)$	0,0104167$(^1/_{96})$	3,8879351 grams
480	24	8	1	0,083333$(^1/_{12})$	31,103481 grams
5 760	288	96	12	1	373,24177 grams

Medical Prescription Notation

1 dram (drachm) .. ʒ i, or ʒ j.
1½ drams .. ʒ iss.
2 » .. ʒ ii, or ʒ ij.
3 » .. ʒ iii, or ʒ iij.
3½ » .. ʒ iiss.
1 gallon .. Ci, or Cj.

½ grain .. gr. ss.
1 » .. gr. i, or gr. j.
1½ grains .. gr. iss.
2 » .. gr. ii, or gr. ij.
2½ » .. gr. iiss.
4 » .. gr. iv.
8 » .. gr. viii, or gr. viij.

½ ounce .. ℥ ss.
1 » .. ℥ i, or ℥ j.
1½ ounces .. ℥ iss.
½ pint .. Oss.
1 » .. Oi, or Oj.
½ scruple .. ℈ ss.
1 » .. ℈ i, or ℈ j.
1½ scruples .. ℈ iss.
2 » .. ℈ ii, or ℈ ij.

* Bezieht sich nur auf die US-Einheiten. ** Brit.: Fluid drachms.

Gewichte und Maße nach dem Dezimalsystem

Weights and Measures, Decimal System

Prefixes · Vorsilben

(nach DIN 1301) zur Bezeichnung der Vielfachen und der Bruchteile (Zehnerpotenzen)

T =	Tera..	= 10^{12}	d =	Dezi..	= 10^{-1}
G =	Giga..	= 10^{9}	c =	Zenti..	= 10^{-2}
M =	Mega..	= 10^{6}	m =	Milli..	= 10^{-3}
k =	Kilo..	= 10^{3}	µ =	Mikro..	= 10^{-6}
h =	Hekto..	= 10^{2}	n =	Nano..	= 10^{-9}
da =	Deka..	= 10^{1}	p =	Piko..	= 10^{-12}

Metrische Längenmaße · Metric Linear Measure

Reduced to **English** Measures

1 km	(Kilometer)	= 10 hm	= 1000 m	= 1093.6143 yards	→ yard
1 m	(Meter) [Einheit] (etwa der 40millionste Teil des Äquators)	= $^1/_{10}$ Dm	= 100 cm	= 3.280 843 feet	→ foot
1 dm	(Dezimeter)	= $^1/_{10}$ m	= 10 cm	= 3.937 011 inches	
1 cm	(Zentimeter)	= $^1/_{10}$ dm	= 10 mm	= 0.393 701 inch	→ inch
1 mm	(Millimeter)	= $^1/_{10}$ cm	= 1000 µ	= 0.039 370 inch	
1 µm	(Mikrometer) oder µ [sprich my:] (Mikron)	= $^1/_{1000}$ mm	= 1000 nm		
1 nm	(Nanometer) oder mµ (Millimikron)	= $^1/_{1000}$ µ	= 10 Å		
1 Å	(Ångström)	= 10^{-7} mm	= 10^{-10} m		

1 geographische Meile = $^1/_{15}$ Äquatorgrad	= 7,420 km
1 Seemeile = $^1/_{60}$ Meridiangrad	= 1,852 km
1 Admiralsmeile = 1 nautical mile	= 1,853 km
1 Lichtjahr (abbr. ly. = light-year)	= $9{,}463 \cdot 10^{12}$ km
1 Parsek	= 32,57 ly.
1 X-Einheit (festgelegt durch den Wert der Gitterkonstanten des Kalkspats d_{18^0} = 3029,45 X)	= $9{,}98 \cdot 10^{-2}$ Å

Metrische Flächenmaße · Metric Square Measure

Reduced to **English** Measures

1 cm²	(Quadratzentimeter)	= 100 mm² = 10^8 µm²	= 0.15 500	square inch
1 dm²	(Quadratdezimeter)	= 100 cm²		
1 m²	(Quadratmeter)	= 100 dm²	= 1.1960	square yard
1 a	(Ar)	= 100 m².	= 119.60	square yards
1 ha	(Hektar)	= 100 a	= 2.4711	acres
1 km²	(Quadratkilometer)	= 100 ha	= 247.11	acres

Metrische Raummaße · Metric Cubic Measure

Reduced to **English** Measures

1 km³	(Kubikkilometer)	= 1000 hm³	= 10^9 m³	
1 m³	(Kubikmeter)	= 1000 dm³	= 10^6 cm³	= 1.307 954 cubic yards
1 dm³	(Kubikdezimeter)	= $^1/_{1000}$ m³	= 10^3 cm³	
1 cm³	(Kubikzentimeter)	= $^1/_{1000}$ dm³	= 10^3 mm³	= 0.0610 cubic inch
1 mm³	(Kubikmillimeter)	= $^1/_{1000}$ cm³	= 10^9 µm³	

⟨for⟩ 1 Festmeter = *1 cbm of stacked wood without interspaces*
⟨for⟩ 1 Raummeter = *1cbm of wood with interspaces = .7 to .8 cbm of piled wood = ca .45 cbm of trunk timber*

Metrische Hohlmaße · Metric Measure of Capacity

				Reduced to **English** Measures	
1 kl (Kiloliter)	= 1000 l	. . . .	=	3.4375	quarters
1 hl (Hektoliter)	= 100 l	= 100,0027 dm^3	=	22.00	gallons *oder*
				2.75	bushels
1 Dl (Dekaliter)	= 10 l	. . . .	=	2.200	gallons
1 l (Liter) [Einheit] → Fußnote	= 1000 ml	= 1,000 027 dm^3	=	1.75980	pints
1 ml (Milliliter)	= 1000 µl	= 1,000 027 cm^3			

N. B.! Das dm^3 ist die Einheit des Raumes und ist der Inhalt eines Würfels von der Kantenlänge 1 dm; 1 dm^3 Wasser wiegt unter Normalbedingungen 0,999 973 kg.

1 kg Wasser nimmt unter gleichen Bedingungen einen Raum von 1,000 027 dm^3 oder genau 1 Liter ein. Man sollte daher immer zwischen Liter und Kubikdezimeter usw. unterscheiden.

Metrische Gewichte · Metric Weights

					Reduced to **English** Measures	
1 t	(Tonne)	= 10 dz (Doppelzentner)	= 1000 kg	=	.984 2	ton
1 dz	(Doppelzentner)		= 100 kg	=	220.46	lbs. avoir.
1 Ztr.	(Zentner)		= 50 kg	=	110.23	lbs. avoir
1 kg	(Kilogramm) [Einheit]	= 2 Pfund	= 1000 g	=	2.204 622	lbs. avoir.
1 g	(Gramm) → Fußnote	= $^1/_{10}$ Dg	= 1000 mg	=	15.432 3564	grains troy
					.0352 7	oz.
					.002.204	lb.
1 mg	(Milligramm)	= $^1/_{1000}$ g	= 1000 µg, γ	=	.015 432	grain
1 c	(metrisches Karat)	= 0,9751 internat. Karat	= 200 mg			

N. B.! Gramm, dem Namen nach die Gewichtseinheit des metrischen Systems, ist das Gewicht von 1 cm^3 (Kubikzentimeter) destillierten Wassers bei + 4° Celsius, also im Zustand seiner größten Kondensierung.

1 gramme is the weight of 1 cubic centimetre of distilled water in its state of maximum density, i. e. of 4° Celsius or Centigrade (= 39½° Fahrenheit).

Juwelen-Gewichte

1 österr. Karat	= 206,1 mg	1 franz. Karat	= 205,5 mg
1 holländ. Karat	= 205,89 mg	1 engl. Karat	= 205,3 mg
1 preuß. Karat	= 205,54 mg	vgl. S. 1490 *Troy Weight*	

Perlengewichte

1 Karat (= rund 1 g) = *4 grains*; vgl. Bd. I S. 1112 Troy Weight

Papierformate des Deutschen Normenausschusses

Diese stimmen überein mit den Normen folgender Länder:

Belgien	Japan	Rußland
China	Norwegen	Schweden, Schweiz
Finnland	Polen	Tschechoslowakei
Holland	Rumänien	Ungarn

Kurzzeichen	Größe in mm	Kurzzeichen	Größe in mm
4 A 0	1682 × 2378	A 5	148 × 210
2 A 0	1189 × 1682	A 6	105 × 148
A 0	841 × 1189	A 7	74 × 105
A 1	594 × 821	A 8	52 × 74
A 2	420 × 594	A 9	37 × 52
A 3	297 × 420	A 10	26 × 37
A 4	210 × 297		

DIN A 4 ist die Einheitsgröße für Briefbogen. DIN A 6 ist die internationale Postkartengröße.

Zeit-Tafel · Time

7.00 MEZ (Mitteleuropäische Zeit)	= 6.00 WEZ (Westeuropäische Zeit)
	= 7.00 WESZ (Westeuropäische Sommerzeit)
	= 8.00 OEZ (Osteuropäische Zeit)
	= 9.00 MOSKZ (Moskauer Zeit)
7.00 Eastern Time	= 6.00 Central time
	= 5.00 Mountain time
	= 4.00 Pacific time

Anm.: 1 Stunde Unterschied entspricht jeweils 15 Längengraden.

Im Deutschen werden die Minuten von den Stunden durch einen Punkt getrennt, im Englischen jedoch nicht ⟨a. Am⟩: 20.17 = *2017*; 7.15 = *0715*.

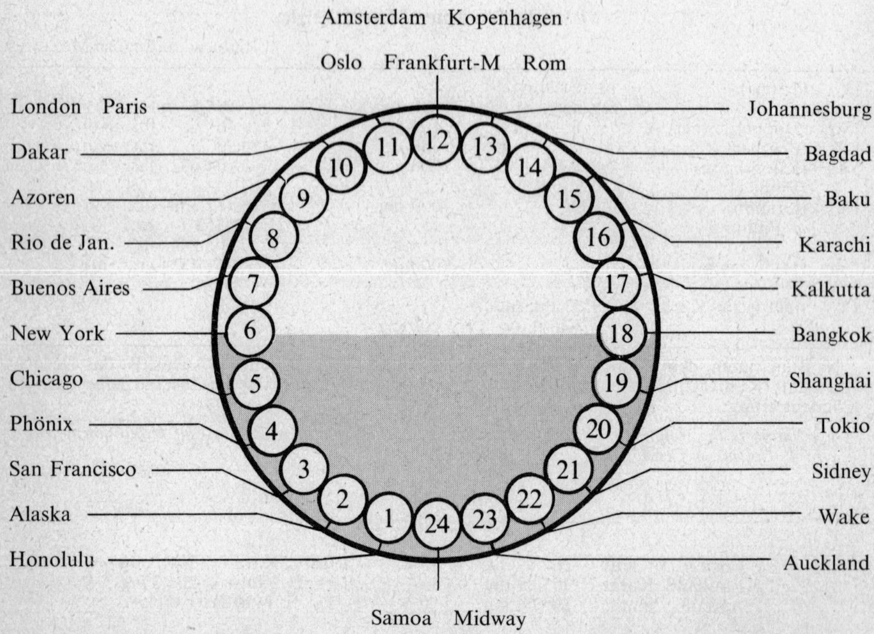

Weltzeituhr

nach
Telefonbau & Normalzeit G.m.b.H.
Frankfurt a. M.

Diese Weltzeituhr gibt die **annähernde Sonnenzeit** für die betreffenden Orte an.

Aber mit Rücksicht auf Eisenbahn- etc Fahrpläne ist für ganz **Mittel- u. Westeuropa** die **MEZ** (fast ausschließlich, → unten: England, Norwegen, Portugal) eingeführt worden.

MEZ gilt heute in Belgien, Dänemark, Deutschland, Frankreich, Italien, Jugoslawien, Luxemburg, Niederlande, Österreich, Schweden, Schweiz, Spanien, Tschechoslowakei, Ungarn; außerdem in England (als WESZ = BST), in Norwegen ab 16. November, in Portugal (als WESZ).

→ S. 1481, Amerikanische Zeitzonen.

OEZ gilt heute in Bulgarien, Finnland, Griechenland, Norwegen bis 15. November, Polen, Rumänien, Türkei.

MOSKZ gilt in der UdSSR.

Die engl. Normalzeit (im Winter) ist um 1 Stunde hinter der MEZ zurück: 12° MEZ = 11° engl. Normalzeit.

Die **engl. Sommerzeit** (summer time) von April bis Oktober entspricht der MEZ.

Die Umstellungen erfolgten bisher meist sonntags um 2° nachts. 1962 begann sie bereits am 31. März und endete am 28. Oktober. Die Umstellungen sollen in Zukunft für eine Reihe von Jahren im voraus gesetzlich geregelt werden.

Physikalische Maße · Physical Measures

Lichtmaße (teilweise veraltet)

Hefnerkerze (HK) seit 1942 Neukerze seit 1948 Candela	= Lichtstärke, mit der die unter Normalbedingungen brennende Hefner-Lampe in waagerechter Richtung leuchtet.
Lumen (lm)	= Lichtstrom. 1 lm wird erhalten, wenn die Lichtquelle die Lichtstärke 1 HK gleichmäßig in die Einheit des Raumwinkels strahlt. (lm = cd·sr)
Lux (lx)	= Einheit der Beleuchtungsstärke. 1 lx = Beleuchtungsstärke, die eine Lichtquelle von 1 HK bei senkrechtem Lichteinfall auf einer weißen Fläche in 1 m Entfernung hervorruft, bzw. wenn Lichtstrom von 1 lm auf eine Fläche von 1 m^2 eingestrahlt wird. (lx = lm/m^2)

Elektrische und magnetische Maße (teilweise veraltet)

Volt (V)	= Einheit der elektrischen Spannung (*U*). 1 V erzeugt in einem Leiter von 1 Ohm Widerstand den Strom von 1 Ampere.
Ampere (A)	= Einheit der elektrischen Stromstärke *i*. 1 A = Stromstärke, die aus einer Silbernitratlösung in 1 sec 1,118 mg Silber abscheidet.
Watt (W)	= Einheit der elektrischen Leistung. 1 W = 1 Volt × 1 Ampere = 10^7 erg/sec.
Ohm (Ω)	= Einheit des elektrischen Widerstandes *R*. 1 Ω = Widerstand einer Quecksilbersäule von 1 qmm Querschnitt, 106,3 cm Länge und 14,452 g Masse bei 0° C.
Coulomb (C)	= Einheit der Elektrizitätsmenge. 1 C = technische Einheit der Elektrizitätsmenge, die bei einer Stromstärke von 1 Ampere in 1 sec durch den Querschnitt des Leiters fließt.
Farad (F)	= Einheit für die Kapazität *C* eines elektrischen Leiters. 1 F = Kapazität eines Leiters, der bei einer Spannung von 1 V 1 Cl aufnimmt = 1 Coulomb/Volt.
Joule (J)	= Einheit der elektrischen Arbeit. 1 J = Arbeit, die geleistet wird, wenn während 1 sec 1 A in 1 Ω fließt (Wattsekunde).
Henry (H)	= Einheit der Induktivität *L*. 1 H = Induktivität, in der eine Änderung des Stromes um 1 A je sec eine elektromotorische Kraft von 1 V induziert.
Frequenz (Hertz, Hz)	= Periodenzahl je sec.

Arbeitsmaße

Arbeit	mkg	PSh	kWh	kcal
1 mkg	1	$3{,}7 \cdot 10^{-6}$	$2{,}72 \cdot 10^{-6}$	$2{,}34 \cdot 10^{-3}$
1 PSh	$0{,}27 \cdot 10^{6}$	1	0,736	632
1 kWh	$0{,}367 \cdot 10^{6}$	1,36	1	860
1 kcal	426,9	$1{,}58 \cdot 10^{-3}$	$1{,}16 \cdot 10^{-3}$	1

Leistungsmaße

Leistung	mgk/s	PS	kW	kcal/s
1 mkg/s	1	0,013	$9{,}81 \cdot 10^{-3}$	$2{,}34 \cdot 10^{-3}$
1 PS	75	1	0,736	0,176
1 kW	102	1,36	1	0,239
1 kcal/s	426,9	5,69	4,19	1

Thermometer

0° Celsius or Centigrade 0° Réaumur	Schmelzpunkt des Eises temperature of melting ice	= 32° Fahrenheit
100° Celsius 80° Réaumur	Siedepunkt des Wassers temperature of boiling water	= 212° Fahrenheit

Zur Umrechnung dienen folgende Formeln:
To convert from one scale to the other:

Umrechnung in	° Celsius	° Fahrenheit
Grad Fahrenheit	x° F = $^5/_9$ (x — 32)° C	
Grad Celsius Centigrade		x° C = $^9/_5$ x + 32° F

Comparison of Centigrade and Fahrenheit Thermometer Scales
Vergleichstabelle für Celsius und Fahrenheit

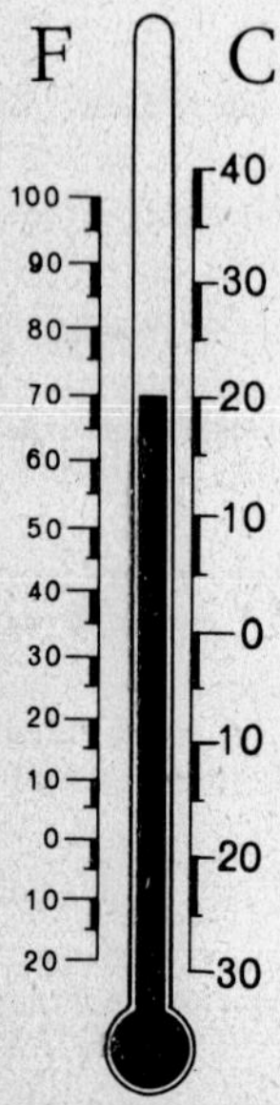

C.	F.	C.	F.	C.	F.
35°	95°	165°	329°	295°	563°
30°	86°	160°	320°	290°	554°
25°	77°	155°	311°	285°	545°
20°	68°	150°	302°	280°	536°
15°	59°	145°	293°	275°	527°
10°	50°	140°	284°	270°	518°
+ 5°	41°	135°	275°	265°	509°
± 0°	32°	130°	266°	260°	500°
— 5°	23°	125°	257°	255°	491°
— 10°	14°	120°	248°	250°	482°
— 15°	+ 5°	115°	239°	245°	473°
— 20°	— 4°	110°	230°	240°	464°
— 25°	— 13°	105°	221°	235°	455°
— 30°	— 22°	100°	212°	230°	446°
— 35°	— 31°	95°	203°	225°	437°
— 40°	— 40°	90°	194°	220°	428°
— 45°	— 49°	85°	185°	215°	419°
— 50°	— 58°	80°	176°	210°	410°
— 55°	— 67°	75°	167°	205°	401°
— 60°	— 76°	70°	158°	200°	392°
— 65°	— 85°	65°	149°	195°	383°
— 70°	— 94°	60°	140°	190°	374°
— 75°	— 103°	55°	131°	185°	365°
— 80°	— 112°	50°	122°	180°	356°
— 85°	— 121°	45°	113°	175°	347°
— 90°	— 130°	40°	104°	170°	338°

Barometer

Table of the Corresponding Heights of the Barometer in Millimetres & Inches

Barometerstand-Vergleichstabelle

mm	in.	mm	in.	mm	in.
738	29.055	757	29.803	776	30.552
737	29.016	756	29.764	775	30.512
736	28.976	755	29.724	774	30.473
735	28.937	754	29.685	773	30.433
734	28.898	753	29.645	772	30.394
733	28.858	752	29.606	771	30.355
732	28.819	751	29.567	770	30.315
731	28.780	750	29.528	769	30.276
730	28.740	749	29.488	768	30.236
729	28.701	748	29.449	767	30.197
728	28.662	747	29.410	766	30.158
727	28.622	746	29.370	765	30.118
726	28.583	745	29.331	764	30.079
725	28.543	744	29.292	763	30.039
724	28.504	743	29.252	762	30.000
723	28.465	742	29.213	761	29.961
722	28.425	741	29.174	760	29.922
721	28.386	740	29.134	759	29.882
720	28.347	739	29.095	758	29.843

Druck · Pressure

1. Anglo-Amerikanische Einheiten

1 long ton per square foot	(ltn/sq ft)	$= 8.044 \times 10^2$ Torr	$= 1{,}094$	at
1 long ton per square inch	(ltn/sq in)	$= 1.157 \times 10^4$ Torr	$= 157{,}5$	at
1 pound per square foot	(lb/sq ft)	$= .3591$ Torr	$= 4{,}882 \times 10^{-4}$	at
1 pound per square inch	(lb/sq in)	$= 51.71$ Torr	$= 7{,}031 \times 10^{-2}$	at

2. Metrische Einheiten

1 Atmosphäre	⟨phys⟩ atm	$= 760$ Torr	$= 1{,}033$	at
1 Atmosphäre	⟨tech⟩ at	$= 735{,}6$ Torr	$= 0{,}9678$	atm
1 Torr	(= 1 mm QS/cm²)		$= 1{,}316 \times 10^{-3}$	atm
1 Bar	(= 10^6 dyn/cm²) b	$= 750{,}06$ Torr	$= 0{,}9870$	atm
1 Millibar	(= 10^3 dyn/cm²) mb	$= 0{,}7501$ Torr	$= 1{,}020 \times 10^{-3}$	at
1 mm Wassersäule = WS/cm²		$= 7{,}356 \times 10^{-2}$ Torr	$= 9{,}678 \times 10^{-3}$	atm

3. Umrechnung von Druckeinheiten

1 bar = 10^3 Millibar = 10^6 Mikrobar = 10^5 Newton/m²
1 at = 1 kp/cm² = 10^4 kp/m²

	bar	atm	Torr	at
1 bar =	1	0,986923	750,062	1,019716
1 atm =	1,013250	1	760	1,033227
1 Torr =	$1{,}333224 \cdot 10^{-2}$	$1{,}315789 \cdot 10^{-3}$	1	$1{,}359510 \cdot 10^{-3}$
1 at =	$9{,}80665 \cdot 10^{-1}$	0,967841	735,559	1
1 mm WS =	$9{,}80638 \cdot 10^{-5}$	$0{,}967814 \cdot 10^{-4}$	$0{,}735539 \cdot 10^{-1}$	$0{,}999972 \cdot 10^{-4}$
1 lb. wt. ft^{-2} =	$4{,}788025 \cdot 10^{-4}$	$4{,}725413 \cdot 10^{-4}$	$3{,}591314 \cdot 10^{-1}$	$4{,}882427 \cdot 10^{-4}$
1 lb. wt. in^{-2} =	$0{,}689476 \cdot 10^{-1}$	$0{,}680460 \cdot 10^{-1}$	$0{,}517149 \cdot 10^{2}$	$0{,}703069 \cdot 10^{-1}$
1 sh. tn. wt. in^{-2} =	$1{,}378951 \cdot 10^{2}$	$1{,}360920 \cdot 10^{2}$	$1{,}034298 \cdot 10^{5}$	$1{,}406139 \cdot 10^{2}$

	mm WS	lb. wt. ft.$^{-2}$	lb. wt. in^{-2}	sh. tn. wt. in^{-2}
1 bar =	$1{,}019745 \cdot 10^{4}$	$2{,}088544 \cdot 10^{3}$	$1{,}450378 \cdot 10$	$0{,}7255189 \cdot 10^{-2}$
1 atm =	$1{,}033257 \cdot 10^{4}$	$2{,}116217 \cdot 10^{3}$	$1{,}469595 \cdot 10$	$0{,}734789 \cdot 10^{-2}$
1 Torr =	$1{,}359548 \cdot 10$	2,784496	$1{,}933678 \cdot 10^{-2}$	$0{,}966839 \cdot 10^{-5}$
1 at =	$1{,}000028 \cdot 10^{4}$	$2{,}048162 \cdot 10^{3}$	$1{,}422335 \cdot 10$	$0{,}711167 \cdot 10^{-2}$
1 mm WS =	1	$2{,}048104 \cdot 10^{-1}$	$1{,}422295 \cdot 10^{-3}$	$0{,}711147 \cdot 10^{-6}$
1 lb. wt. ft^{-2} =	4,882564	1	$0{,}694444 \cdot 10^{-2}$	$3{,}472222 \cdot 10^{-6}$
1 lb. wt. in^{-2} =	$0{,}703089 \cdot 10^{3}$	144	1	$5 \cdot 10^{-4}$
1 sh. tn. wt. in^{-2} =	$1{,}406178 \cdot 10^{6}$	$288 \cdot 10^{3}$	2000	1

Tabelle von Shillings und Pence

ausgedrückt in Dezimalstellen von einem Pfund Sterling

Am 15. Februar 1971 ist in England das Dezimalsystem eingeführt worden.

Shillings Pence	Dezimal vom Pfund	Shillings Pence	Dezimal vom Pfund	Shillings Pence	Dezimal vom Pfund	Shillings Pence	Dezimal vom Pfund
		5/ 0	.25000	**10/ 0**	.50000	**15/ 0**	.75000
0/ 1	.00417	**5/ 1**	.25417	**10/ 1**	.50417	**15/ 1**	.75417
0/ 2	.00833	**5/ 2**	.25833	**10/ 2**	.50833	**15/ 2**	.75833
0/ 3	.01250	**5/ 3**	.26250	**10/ 3**	.51250	**15/ 3**	.76250
0/ 4	.01667	**5/ 4**	.26667	**10/ 4**	.51667	**15/ 4**	.76667
0/ 5	.02083	**5/ 5**	.27083	**10/ 5**	.52083	**15/ 5**	.77083
0/ 6	.02500	**5/ 6**	.27500	**10/ 6**	.52500	**15/ 6**	.77500
0/ 7	.02917	**5/ 7**	.27917	**10/ 7**	.52917	**15/ 7**	.77917
0/ 8	.03333	**5/ 8**	.28333	**10/ 8**	.53333	**15/ 8**	.78333
0/ 9	.03750	**5/ 9**	.28750	**10/ 9**	.53750	**15/ 9**	.78750
0/10	.04167	**5/10**	.29167	**10/10**	.54167	**15/10**	.79167
0/11	.04583	**5/11**	.29583	**10/11**	.54583	**15/11**	.79583
1/ 0	.05000	**6/ 0**	.30000	**11/ 0**	.55000	**16/ 0**	.80000
1/ 1	.05417	**6/ 1**	.30417	**11/ 1**	.55417	**16/ 1**	.80417
1/ 2	.05833	**6/ 2**	.30833	**11/ 2**	.55833	**16/ 2**	.80833
1/ 3	.06250	**6/ 3**	.31250	**11/ 3**	.56250	**16/ 3**	.81250
1/ 4	.06667	**6/ 4**	.31667	**11/ 4**	.56667	**16/ 4**	.81667
1/ 5	.07083	**6/ 5**	.32083	**11/ 5**	.57083	**16/ 5**	.82083
1/ 6	.07500	**6/ 6**	.32500	**11/ 6**	.57500	**16/ 6**	.82500
1/ 7	.07917	**6/ 7**	.32917	**11/ 7**	.57917	**16/ 7**	.82917
1/ 8	.08333	**6/ 8**	.33333	**11/ 8**	.58333	**16/ 8**	.83333
1/ 9	.08750	**6/ 9**	.33750	**11/ 9**	.58750	**16/ 9**	.83750
1/10	.09167	**6/10**	.34167	**11/10**	.59167	**16/10**	.84167
1/11	.09583	**6/11**	.34583	**11/11**	.59583	**16/11**	.84583
2/ 0	.10000	**7/ 0**	.35000	**12/ 0**	.60000	**17/ 0**	.85000
2/ 1	.10417	**7/ 1**	.35417	**12/ 1**	.60417	**17/ 1**	.85417
2/ 2	.10833	**7/ 2**	.35833	**12/ 2**	.60833	**17/ 2**	.85833
2/ 3	.11250	**7/ 3**	.36250	**12/ 3**	.61250	**17/ 3**	.86250
2/ 4	.11667	**7/ 4**	.36667	**12/ 4**	.61667	**17/ 4**	.86667
2/ 5	.12083	**7/ 5**	.37083	**12/ 5**	.62083	**17/ 5**	.87083
2/ 6	.12500	**7/ 6**	.37500	**12/ 6**	.62500	**17/ 6**	.87500
2/ 7	.12917	**7/ 7**	.37917	**12/ 7**	.62917	**17/ 7**	.87917
2/ 8	.13333	**7/ 8**	.38333	**12/ 8**	.63333	**17/ 8**	.88333
2/ 9	.13750	**7/ 9**	.38750	**12/ 9**	.63750	**17/ 9**	.88750
2/10	.14167	**7/10**	.39167	**12/10**	.64167	**17/10**	.89167
2/11	.14583	**7/11**	.39583	**12/11**	.64583	**17/11**	.89583
3/ 0	.15000	**8/ 0**	.40000	**13/ 0**	.65000	**18/ 0**	.90000
3/ 1	.15417	**8/ 1**	.40417	**13/ 1**	.65417	**18/ 1**	.90417
3/ 2	.15833	**8/ 2**	.40833	**13/ 2**	.65833	**18/ 2**	.90833
3/ 3	.16250	**8/ 3**	.41250	**13/ 3**	.66250	**18/ 3**	.91250
3/ 4	.16667	**8/ 4**	.41667	**13/ 4**	.66667	**18/ 4**	.91667
3/ 5	.17083	**8/ 5**	.42083	**13/ 5**	.67083	**18/ 5**	.92083
3/ 6	.17500	**8/ 6**	.42500	**13/ 6**	.67500	**18/ 6**	.92500
3/ 7	.17917	**8/ 7**	.42917	**13/ 7**	.67917	**18/ 7**	.92917
3/ 8	.18333	**8/ 8**	.43333	**13/ 8**	.68333	**18/ 8**	.93333
3/ 9	.18750	**8/ 9**	.43750	**13/ 9**	.68750	**18/ 9**	.93750
3/10	.19167	**8/10**	.44167	**13/10**	.69167	**18/10**	.94167
3/11	.19583	**8/11**	.44583	**13/11**	.69583	**18/11**	.94583
4/ 0	.20000	**9/ 0**	.45000	**14/ 0**	.70000	**19/ 0**	.95000
4/ 1	.20417	**9/ 1**	.45417	**14/ 1**	.70417	**19/ 1**	.95417
4/ 2	.20833	**9/ 2**	.45833	**14/ 2**	.70833	**19/ 2**	.95833
4/ 3	.21250	**9/ 3**	.46250	**14/ 3**	.71250	**19/ 3**	.96250
4/ 4	.21667	**9/ 4**	.46667	**14/ 4**	.71667	**19/ 4**	.96667
4/ 5	.22083	**9/ 5**	.47083	**14/ 5**	.72083	**19/ 5**	.97083
4/ 6	.22500	**9/ 6**	.47500	**14/ 6**	.72500	**19/ 6**	.97500
4/ 7	.22917	**9/ 7**	.47917	**14/ 7**	.72917	**19/ 7**	.97917
4/ 8	.23333	**9/ 8**	.48333	**14/ 8**	.73333	**19/ 8**	.98333
4/ 9	.23750	**9/ 9**	.48750	**14/ 9**	.73750	**19/ 9**	.98750
4/10	.24167	**9/10**	.49167	**14/10**	.74167	**19/10**	.99167
4/11	.24583	**9/11**	.49583	**14/11**	.74583	**19/11**	.99583

Die Währungen der Welt

Land	Währung	
Äthiopien	äthiop. $	100 Cents
Afar+Issas Geb., Frz.	Djibouti-Franc	100 Centimes
Afghanistan	Afghani	100 Puls
Albanien	Lek	100 Qindarka
Algerien	alg. Dinar	100 Centimes
Angola	Escudo	100 Centavos
Argentinien	arg. Peso	100 Centavos
Australien	austral. $	100 Cents
Bahama-Inseln	Bahama-$	100 Cents
Bahrain-Inseln	Bahrain-Dinar	1000 Fils
Barbados	Ostkarib. $	100 Cents
Belgien	belg. Franc	100 Centimes
Bermuda-Inseln	*bisher* Bermuda-£	
	jetzt Bermuda-$	cents
Bolivien	boliv. Peso	100 Centavos
Botsuana	Rand	100 Cents
Brasilien	Neuer Cruzeiro	100 Centavos
Brunei	Brunei-$	100 Cents
Bulgarien	Lew	100 Stótinki
Burma	Kyat	100 Pyas
Burundi	Burundi-Franc	100 Centimes
Canada	can. $	100 Cents
Ceylon	Ceylon-Rupie	100 Cents
Chile	chil. Escudo	100 Centésimos
China (Volksrep.)	Renminbi/Yuan	10 Jiao/ 100 Fen
Columbien	col. Peso	100 Centavos
Costa Rica	Colón	100 Céntimos
Cuba	cub. Peso	100 Centavos
Curaçao	Ndl. Ant. Gulden	100 Cents
Cypern	Cypern-£	1000 Mils
Dänemark	dän. Krone	100 Öre
Dahomey	Franc CFA	100 Centimes
Deutschland (BRD)	D-Mark	100 Pfennig
Dominikan. Rep.	domin. Peso	100 Centavos
Dubai	Qat. Dub.-Riyal	100 Dirhams
Ecuador	Sucre	100 Centavos
Elfenbeinküste	Franc CFA	100 Centimes
El Salvador	Colón	100 Centavos
Falkland-Inseln	Falkland-£	20 sh/240 d
Fidschi-Inseln	Fidschi-$	100 Cents
Finnland	finn. Mark	100 Penni
Frankreich	franz. Franc	100 Centimes
Gabun	Franc CFA	100 Centimes
Gambia	Gambia-£	20 sh/240 d
Ghana	Neuer Cedi	100 neue Pesewas
Gibraltar	*bisher* £stg	20 sh/240 d
	jetzt £stg	100 p
Griechenland	Drachme	100 Lepta
Großbritannien	*bisher* £stg	20 sh/240 d
	jetzt £stg	100 p
Guadeloupe	Franc	100 Centimes
Guatemala	Quetzal	100 Centavos
Guayana, Frz.	Franc	100 Centimes
Guinea	Guinea-Franc	100 Centimes
Guinea Ecuatorial	Guinea-Peseta	100 Céntimos
	Peseta	100 Céntimos
Guinea (portug.)	Escudo	100 Centavos
Guyana	Guyana-$	100 Cents
Haiti	Gourde	100 Centimes
Honduras	Lempira	100 Centavos
Honduras, Brit.	Brit. Hond.-$	100 Cents
Hongkong	Hongkong-$	100 Cents
Indien	ind. Rupie	100 Paise
Indonesien	Rupiah	100 Sen
Irak	irak. Dinar	1000 Fils
Iran (Persien)	Rial	100 Dinars

Land	Währung	
Irland (Eire)	*bisher* £stg	20 sh/240 d
	jetzt £stg	100 p
Island	isländ. Krone	100 Aurar
Israel	*bisher* Schekel	Agorot
	jetzt Israel-£	100 Agorot
Italien	Lira	100 Centesimi
Jamaika	Jamaica-$	100 Cents
	Jamaica-£	20 sh/240 d
Japan	Yen	100 Sen
Jemen	Jemen-Rial	40 Bogschas
Jordanien	Jordan-Dinar	1000 Fils
Jugoslawien	Dinar	100 Para
Kambodscha	Riel	100 Sen
Kamerun	Franc CFA	100 Centimes
Kanarische Inseln	Peseta	100 Céntimos
Kapverdische Inseln	Escudo	100 Centavos
Kenia	Kenia Shilling	100 Cents
Kongo (Brazzaville)	Franc CFA	100 Centimes
Kongo (Kinshasa)	Zaire	100 Makuta
Korea Nord	Won	100 Cheun
Korea Süd	Won	100 Chon
Kuwait	Kuwait-Dinar	10 Dirham/ 1000 Fils
Laos	Kip	100 At
Lesotho	Maluti	100 Licente
Libanon	liban. £	100 Piastres
Liberia	Liberia-$	100 Cents
Libyen	Libyen-£	1000 Millièmes
Liechtenstein	schweiz. Franken	100 Rappen
Luxemburg	lux. Franc	100 Centimes
Macau	Pataca	100 Avos
Madagaskar	Franc Malgache	100 Centimes
Malawi	Malawi-£	20 sh/240 d
Malaysia	Malaysian-$	100 Cents
Mali	Mali-Franc	100 Centimes
Malta	Malta-£	20 sh/240 d
Marokko	Dirham	100 Francs
Martinique	Franc	100 Centimes
Maskat u. Oman/ Trucial States, Arabischer Golf	Rial Saidi (R.S.)	1000 Baiza
Mauretanien	Franc CFA	100 Centimes
Mauritius	Maurit.-Rupie	100 Cents
Mexico	mex. Peso	100 Centavos
Moçambique	Escudo	100 Centavos
Monaco	franz. Franc	100 Centimes
Mongol. Volksrep.	Tugrik	100 Mongo
Nepal	nepales. Rupie	100 Paisa
Neu-Guinea, Austral.	austral. $	100 Cents
Neu-Kaledonien	Franc CFP	100 Centimes
Neuseeland	neuseel. $	100 Cents
Nicaragua	Córdoba	100 Centavos
Niederlande	holl. Gulden	100 Cents
Niger	Franc CFA	100 Centimes
Nigeria	Nigeria-£	20 sh/240 d
Norwegen	norw. Krone	100 Öre
Obervolta	Franc CFA	100 Centimes
Österreich	Schilling	100 Groschen
Ozeanien, Französ.	Franc CFP	100 Centimes
Pakistan	pakist. Rupie	100 Paisa
Panama	Balboa	100 Centésimos
Paraguay	Guarani	100 Céntimos
Peru	Sol	100 Centavos
Philippinen	phil. Peso	100 Centavos
Polen	Zloty	100 Groszy
Portugal	Escudo	100 Centavos
Puerto Rico	US-Dollar	100 Cents
Réunion	Franc CFA	100 Centimes

Land	Währung	
Rhodesien	*bisher* Rhodes. £	20 sh/240 d
	jetzt Rhodes. $	100 Cents
Rumänien	Leu	100 Baňi
Rwanda	Rwanda-Franc	100 Centimes
Sambia	Kwacha	100 Ngwee
Saudi-Arabien	Riyal	20 Qirsh
Schweden	schwed. Krone	100 Öre
Schweiz	schweiz. Franken	100 Rappen
Senegal	Franc CFA	100 Centimes
Seychellen	Seychell. Rupie	100 Cents
Sierra Leone	Leone	100 Cents
Singapur	Singapur-$	100 Cents
Somalia	Somali Shilling	100 Centesimi
Sowjetunion, UdSSR	Rubel	100 Kopeken
Spanien	Peseta	100 Céntimos
Sudan	sudan. £	100 Piastres/
		1000 Mill.
Südafrika, Rep.	Rand	100 Cents
Südjemen, Volksrep.	Südjem. Dinar	1000 Fils
Südwestafrika	Rand	100 Cents
Surinam	Surinam-Gulden	100 Cents
Swasiland/Ngwana	Rand	100 Cents
Syrien, Arab. Rep.	syr. £	100 Piastres

Land	Währung	
Taiwan, Formosa	New Taiw.-$	100 Cents
Tansania	Tans. Shilling	100 Cents
Thailand	Baht (Tical)	100 Stangs
Togo	Franc CFA	100 Centimes
Tonga	Pa'anga	100 Seniti
Trinidad u. Tobago	Trinid. u. Tob.-$	100 Cents
Tschad	Franc CFA	100 Centimes
Tschechoslowakei	tschechosl. Kr.	100 haléřů
Türkei	türk. £	100 Kurus
		(Piastres)
Tunesien	tun. Dinar	1000 Francs
		(Millimes)
Uganda	Uganda Shilling	100 Cents
Ungarn	Forint	100 Filler
Uruguay	urug. Peso	100 Centésimos
Venezuela	Bolívar	100 Céntimos
V. A. R. Ägypten	ägypt. £	100 Piastres/
		1000 Mill.
Ver. Staat. v. Amerika	US-Dollar	100 Cents
Vietnam Nord	Dong	
Vietnam Süd	Piastre (Dong)	100 Centimes
Zentralafr. Rep.	Franc CFA	100 Centimes

Mit freundlicher Genehmigung der Deutschen Bank AG

Die chemische Elemente
The Chemical Elements

I. Die chemischen Elemente in alphabetischer Anordnung

Name		Symbol	Ordnungszahl
Actinium	actinium	Ac	89
Aluminium	aluminium ⟨Am⟩ aluminum	Al	13
Americium	americium	Am	95
Antimon	antimony	Sb	51
Argentum	silver	Ag	47
Argon	argon	Ar	18
Arsen(icum)	arsenic	As	33
Astatin (Astaton)	astatine	At	85
Aurum	gold	Au	79
Barium	barium	Ba	56
Berkelium	berkelium	Bk	97
Beryllium	beryllium	Be	4
(*Wismut*)	bismuth	Bi	83
Blei	lead	Pb	82
Bor(on)	boron	B	5
Brom(um)	bromine	Br	35
Cadmium	cadmium	Cd	48
Caesium	caesium	Cs	55
Calcium	calcium	Ca	20
Californium	californium	Cf	98
Carboneum	carbon	C	6
(*Cassiopeium*)	lutetium	(Cp) *Lu*	71
Cer(ium)	cerium	Ce	58
Chlor(um)	chlorine	Cl	17
Chrom(ium)	chromium	Cr	24
Cobaltum	cobalt	Co	27
(*Niob Nb*)	columbium	Cb	41
(*Kupfer*)	copper	Cu	29
Curium	curium	Cm	96
Dysprosium	dysprosium	Dy	66
Eisen	iron	Fe	26
Erbium	erbium	Er	68
Europium	europium	Eu	63
Ferrum	iron	Fe	26
Fluor(um)	fluorine	F	9
(*Francium*)		Fr	87
Gadolinium	gadolinium	Gd	64
Gallium	gallium	Ga	31
Germanium	germanium	Ge	32
(*Beryllium*)	glucinum	Gl	4
Gold	gold	Au	79
Hafnium	hafnium	Hf	72
Helium	helium	He	2
Holmium	holmium	Ho	67
Hydrogenium	hydrogen	H	1
(*Hydrargyrum*)	mercury	Hg	80
Illinium → Promethium	illinium	Il	61
Indium	indium	In	49
(*Jod J*)	iodine	I	53
Iridium	iridium	Ir	77
(*Eisen, Ferrum*)	iron	Fe	26
Jod	(iodine I)	J	53
Kadmium	cadmium	Cd	48
Kalium	potassium	K	19
Kalzium	calcium	Ca	20
Kobalt	cobalt(um)	Co	27
Kohlenstoff	carbon	C	6
Krypton	krypton	Kr	36
Kupfer	copper	Cu	29
Lanthan(um)	lanthanum	La	57
(*Blei*)	lead	Pb	82
Lithium	lithium	Li	3
Lutetium	lutetium	Lu	71
Magnesium	magnesium	Mg	12
Mangan(ium)	manganese	Mn	25
(*Quecksilber*)	mercury	Hg	80
Molybdän	molybdenum	Mo	42
Natrium	sodium	Na	11
Neodym(ium)	neodymium	Nd	60
Neon	neon	Ne	10
Neptunium	neptunium	Np	93
(*Neutron*)	neutron	Nn	0
Nickel	nickel	Ni	28
Niob(ium)	columbium	Nb *Cb*	41
Nitrogenium	nitrogen	N	7
Osmium	osmium	Os	76
Oxygenium	oxygen	O	8
Palladium	palladium	Pd	46
Phosphor	phosphorus	P	15
Platin(um)	platinum	Pt	78
(*Plumbum*)	lead	Pb	82
Plutonium	plutonium	Pu	94
Polonium	polonium	Po	84
(*Kalium*)	potassium	K	19
Praseodym(ium)	praseodymium	Pr	59
Promethium → Illinium	promethium	Pm	61
Protactinium		Pa	91
Quecksilber	mercury	Hg	80
Radium	radium	Ra	88
Radon (*Radium-Eman.*)	radon	Rn	86
Rhenium	rhenium	Re	75
Rhodium	rhodium	Rh	45
Rubidium	rubidium	Rb	37
Ruthen(ium)	ruthenium	Ru	44
Samarium	samarium	Sm	62
Sauerstoff	oxygen	O	8
Scandium	scandium	Sc	21
Schwefel	sulphur	S	16
Selen(ium)	selenium	Se	34
Silber	silver	Ag	47
Silicium	silicon	Si	14
(*Natrium*)	sodium	Na	11
Stannum, Zinn	tin	Sn	50
Stickstoff	nitrogen	N	7
Stibium	antimony	Sb	51
Strontium	strontium	Sr	38
(*Schwefel*)	sulphur	S	16
Tantal(um)	tantalum	Ta	73
Technetium	technetium	Tc	43
Tellur(ium)	tellurium	Te	52

Name		Symbol	Ordnungs-zahl	Name		Symbol	Ordnungs-zahl
Terbium	terbium	Tb	65	*Xenon*	xenon	Xe, X	54
Thallium	thallium	Tl	81				
Thorium	thorium	Th	90	*Ytterbium*	ytterbium	Yb	70
Thulium	thulium	Tm	69	*Yttrium*	yttrium	Y, Yt	39
(*Zinn*)	tin	Sn	50				
Titan(*ium*)	titanium	Ti	22	*Zer*	cerium	Ce	58
(*Wolfram*)	tungsten	W	74				
				Zink	zinc	Zn	30
Uran(*ium*)	uranium	U	92	*Zinn*	tin	Sn	50
				Zirkonium	zirconium	Zr	40
Vanadin, Vanadium	vanadium	V	23				
Wasserstoff	hydrogen	H	1				
Wolfram	tungsten	W	74				
Wismut	bismuth	Bi	83				

Die Transurane 93 Neptunium Np; 94 Plutonium Pu; 95 Americium Am; 96 Curium Cm; 97 Berkelium Bk; 98 Californium Cf.; 99 Einsteinium; 100 Fermium Fm; 101 Mendelevium Md; 102 Nobelium No; 103 Lawrencium Lw.

II. Die chemischen Elemente nach den Ordnungszahlen ihrer Atomgewichte (1953) geordnet

Uneingeklammerte Namen nach Festlegung durch die Internationale Union für Chemie in Amsterdam 1949

atomic no. *Ordnungszahl*	symbol *Zeichen*	*Lateinischer Name*	*Deutscher Name*	*Englischer Name*	atomic weight *Atomgewicht*
0	Nn	*Neutron*		neutron	—
1	H	*Hydrogenium*	*Wasserstoff*	hydrogen	1,0080
2	He	*Helium*		helium	4,003
3	Li	*Lithium*		lithium	6,940
4	Be	*Beryllium*		beryllium	9,02
5	B	*Boron*	*Bor*	boron	10,82
6	C	*Carboneum*	*Kohlenstoff*	carbon	12,010
7	N	*Nitrogenium*	*Stickstoff*	nitrogen	14,008
8	O	*Oxygenium*	*Sauerstoff*	oxygen	16,000
9	F	*Fluorum*	*Fluor*	fluorine	19,000
10	Ne	*Neon*		neon	20,183
11	Na	*Natrium*		sodium	22,997
12	Mg	*Magnesium*		magnesium	24,32
13	Al	*Aluminium*		aluminium 〈Am〉 aluminum	26,97
14	Si	*Silicium*		silicon	28,06
15	P	*Phosphorus*	*Phosphor*	phosphorus	30,975
16	S	*Sulfur*	*Schwefel*	sulphur	32,06
17	Cl	*Chlorum*	*Chlor*	chlorine	35,457
18	Ar, (*A*)	*Argon*		argon	39,948
19	K	*Kalium*		potassium	39,102
20	Ca	*Calcium*		calcium	40,08
21	Sc	*Scandium*		scandium	45,10
22	Ti	*Titanium*	*Titan*	titanium	47,90
23	V	*Vanadium*	*Vanadin*	vanadium	50,95
24	Cr	*Chromium*	*Chrom*	chromium	52,01
25	Mn	*Manganium*	*Mangan*	manganese	54,93
26	Fe	*Ferrum*	*Eisen*	iron	55,85
27	Co	*Cobaltum*	*Kobalt*	cobalt	58,94
28	Ni	*Niccolum*	*Nickel*	nickel	58,69
29	Cu	*Cuprum*	*Kupfer*	copper	63,57
30	Zn	*Zincum*	*Zink.*	zinc	65,38
31	Ga	*Gallium*		gallium	69,72
32	Ge	*Germanium*		germanium	72,60
33	As	*Arsenicum*	*Arsen*	arsenic	74,91
34	Se	*Selenium*	*Selen*	selenium	78,96
35	Br	*Bromum*	*Brom*	bromine	79,716
36	Kr	*Krypton*		krypton	83,7
37	Rb	*Rubidium*		rubidium	85,48
38	Sr	*Strontium*		strontium	87,63
39	Y, (*Yt*)	*Yttrium*		yttrium	88,92
40	Zr	*Zirkonium*		zirconium	91,22
41	Nb, (*Cb*)	*Niobium*	*Niob*	columbium	92,91
42	Mo	*Molybdaenum*	*Molybdän*	molybdenum	95,95

atomic no. *Ordnungszahl*	symbol *Zeichen*	*Lateinischer Name*	*Deutscher Name*	*Englischer Name*	atomic weight *Atomgewicht*
43	Tc	*Technetium*		technetium	—
44	Ru	*Ruthenium*	*Ruthenium*	ruthenium	101,7
45	Rh	*Rhodium*		rhodium	102,91
46	Pd	*Palladium*		palladium	106,7
47	Ag	*Argentum*	*Silber*	silver	107,880
48	Cd	*Cadmium*	*Kadmium*	cadmium	112,41
49	In	*Indium*		indium	114,76
50	Sn	*Stannum*	*Zinn*	tin	118,70
51	Sb	*Stibium*	*Antimon*	antimony	121,76
52	Te	*Tellurium*	*Tellur*	tellurium	127,61
53	J, *I*	*Jodum*	*Jod*	iodine	126,92
54	X	*Xenon*		xenon	131,3
55	Cs	*Caesium*		caesium	132,91
56	Ba	*Barium*		barium	137,36
57	La	*Lanthanum*	*Lanthan*	lanthanum	138,92
58	Ce	*Cerium*	*Zer, Cer*	cerium	140,13
59	Pr	*Praseodymium*	*Praseodym*	praseodymium	140,92
60	Nd	*Neodymium*	*Neodym*	neodymium	144,27
61	Pm (Il)	*Promethium (Illinium)*		promethium	—
62	Sm, (*Sa*)	*Samarium*		samarium	150,43
63	Eu	*Europium*		europium	152,0
64	Gd	*Gadolinium*		gadolinium	156,9
65	Tb	*Terbium*		terbium	159,2
66	Dy	*Dysprosium*		dysprosium	162,46
67	Ho	*Holmium*		holmium	164,94
68	Er	*Erbium*		erbium	167,2
69	Tm	*Thulium*		thulium	169,4
70	Yb	*Ytterbium*		ytterbium	173,04
71	Lu (Cp)	*Lutetium (Cassiopeium)*		lutetium	174,99
72	Hf	*Hafnium*		hafnium	178,6
73	Ta	*Tantalum*	*Tantal*	tantalum	180,88
74	W	*Wolfram*	*Wolfram*	tungsten	183,92
75	Re	*Rhenium*		rhenium	186,31
76	Os	*Osmium*		osmium	190,2
77	Ir	*Iridium*		iridium	193,1
78	Pt	*Platinum*	*Platin*	platinum	195,23
79	Au	*Aurum*	*Gold*	gold	197,2
80	Hg	*Hydrargyrum*	*Quecksilber*	mercury	200,61
81	Tl	*Thallium*		thallium	204,39
82	Pb	*Plumbum*	*Blei*	lead	207,21
83	Bi	*Bismutum*	*Wismut*	bismuth	209,00
84	Po	*Polonium*		polonium	—
85	At	*Astaton*		astatine	—
86	Rn	*Radon*		radon	222
87	Fr	*Francium*		francium	—
88	Ra	*Radium*		radium	226,05
89	Ac	*Actinium*		actinium	—
90	Th	*Thorium*		thorium	232,12
91	Pa	*Protactinium*		protactinium	231
92	U	*Uranium*	*Uran*	uranium	238,01
93	Np	*Neptunium*		neptunium	—
94	Pu	*Plutonium*		plutonium	—
95	Am	*Americium*		americium	—
96	Cm	*Curium*		curium	—
97	Bk	*Berkelium*		berkelium	—
98	Cf	*Californium*		californium	—

99–103 → Tabelle I auf Seite 1502

Mindest-Alkoholgehalt der Getränke
Alcoholic Strength of Drinks

Whisky	43 %	Moselwein	12,1%
Cognac, Rum, Arrak, Branntweine	38,0%	Pfalzwein	11,6%
Korn, Kümmel	32,0%	Rheinwein	11,5%
Obstliköre, Punschessenz	30,0%	Französischer Rotwein	9,6%
Kaffee-, Kakaolikör	25,0%	Champagner, Sekt	9,2%
Eierlikör	20,0%	Bockbier	4,7%
Portwein	16,4%	Pilsener Bier	3,6%
		Lagerbier	3,0%

Maße von Kleidungsstücken

Comparative Sizes

1. Ladies

Blouses

USA & Engl.	32	34	36	38	40	42
Continent	38	40	42	44	46	48

Sweaters, jumpers and cardigans

USA & Engl.	34	36	38	40	42	44
Continent	40	42	44	46	48	50

Gloves

In the USA, England and on the Continent ladies' gloves are sold in quarter sizes from $6^1/_4$ to $7^1/_2$

Dresses, coats, tailormade costumes & skirts

Junior sizes							
USA			9	11	13	15	17
England		9	11	13	15	17	
Continent		34	36	38	40	42	44
Young ladies sizes							
USA	10	12	14	16	18	20	
England	10	12	14	16	18	20	22
Continent	36	38	40	42	44	46	48
Ladies sizes							
USA			36	38	40	42	44
England		34	36	38	40	42	44
Continent		42	44	46	48	50	52

Shoes

USA	$4^1/_2$–5	$5^1/_2$–6	$6^1/_2$–7	$7^1/_2$–8
England	$3^1/_2$	$4^1/_2$	$5^1/_2$	$6^1/_2$
Continent	36–37	37–38	38–39	39–40
USA		$8^1/_2$–9	$9^1/_2$–10	
England		$7^1/_2$	$8^1/_2$	9
Continent		40–41	41–42	43

Stockings

USA & Engl.	$8^1/_2$	9	$9^1/_2$	10	$10^1/_2$	11
Continent	$8^1/_2$	9	$9^1/_2$	10	$10^1/_2$	11

2. Gentlemen

Coats, overcoats & pajamas

USA & Engl.	34	36	38	40	42	44	46	48
Continent	44	46	48	50	52	54	56	58

Shirts

USA & Engl.	14	$14^1/_2$	15	$15^1/_2$	$15^3/_4$	16	$16^1/_2$	17	$17^1/_2$	18
Continent	36	37	38	39	40	41	42	43	44	45

Underwear

USA	sm	med		lg	ex lg	
England	34	36	38	40	42	44
Continent	5	6	7	8	9	10

Gloves

In the USA, England on the Continent men's gloves are sold in quarter sizes from $7^1/_4$–9

Sweaters

USA	sm	med		lg	ex lg	
England	34	36	38	40	42	44
Continent	44	46	48	50	52	54

Shoes and Socks

USA & Engl.	5	$5^1/_2$	$6^1/_2$	7
Continent				
shoes	38–39	39–40	40–41	
stockings	$9^1/_2$	10	10–$10^1/_2$	

USA & Engl.	$7^1/_2$	$8^1/_2$	9	$9^1/_2$	10
Continent					
shoes	41–42		42–43	43–44	
stockings	$10^1/_2$–11		11	$11^1/_2$	

USA & Engl.	$10^1/_2$	11	$11^1/_2$	12
Continent				
shoes	44–45		45–46	
stockings	12		12–$12^1/_2$	

Hats

USA	$6^5/_8$	$6^3/_4$	$6^7/_8$	7	$7^1/_8$
	$7^1/_4$	$7^3/_8$	$7^1/_2$	$7^5/_8$	$7^3/_4$
England	$6^1/_2$	$6^5/_8$	$6^3/_4$	$6^7/_8$	7
	$7^1/_8$	$7^1/_4$	$7^3/_8$	$7^1/_2$	$7^5/_8$
Continent	53	54	55	56	57
	58	59	60	61	62

XII. DEUTSCHE GRAMMATIK
GERMAN GRAMMAR

Deutsche Deklination & Konjugation

A. Declension

I. The Article

1. Definite Article

	nominative	genitive	dative	accusative
sg m	der (Mann)	des (Mann[e]s)	dem (Mann[e])	den (Mann)
sg f	die (Frau)	der (Frau)	der (Frau)	die (Frau)
sg n	das (Kind)	des (Kind[e]s)	dem (Kind[e])	das (Kind)
pl m, f, n	die	der	den	die
	(Männer)	(Mäner)	(Männern)	(Männer) → II. *II*. 1.
	(Frauen)	(Frauen)	(Frauen)	(Frauen) → III. 3.
	(Kinder)	(Kinder)	(Kindern)	(Kinder) → II. *I*. 1.

2. Indefinite Article

sg m	ein (Mann)	eines (Mann[e]s)	einem (Mann[e])	einen (Mann)
sg f	eine (Frau)	einer (Frau)	einer (Frau)	eine (Frau)
sg n	ein (Kind)	eines (Kind[e]s)	einem (Kind[e])	ein (Kind)

II. The Strong Declension of Nouns (*m*, *f*, *n*)

has -(e)s *in gen sg* || no -n* *in nom pl*
(**cf*. III. *Weak Declension on page 1508*)

I. Without Umlaut

	sg nom		gen	dat	acc	pl nom	gen	dat	acc
1.	Kind	*n*	~(e)s	~(e)	~	~er	~er	~ern	~er
cf. *II*. 1.	Reis	*n*	~es	~(e)	~	~er	~er	~ern	~er
2.	Jahr	*n*	~(e)s	~(e)	~	~e	~e	~en	~e
	Not·ar	*m*	~(e)s	~(e)	~	~e	~e	~en	~e
	Aal	*m*	~(e)s	~(e)	~	~e	~e	~en	~e
	Preis	*m*	~es	~(e)	~	~e	~e	~en	~e
	Knie [*i*:]	*n*	~s	~	~	~ [-*i*:ə]	~ [-*i*:ə]	~ n[-*i*:ən]	~ [-*i*:ə]
3.	K·ater	*m*	~s	~	~	~	~	~n	~
	F·ischer	*m*	~s	~	~	~	~	~n	~
	W·ürfel	*m*	~s	~	~	~	~	~n	~
cf.	Gef·üge	*n*	~s	~	~	~	~	~n	~
II. 5.	R·ädchen	*n*	~s	~	~	~	~	~	~
4.	Bed·ürfnis	*n*	-isses	-is(se)	~	-isse	-isse	-issen	-isse
	Bram·arbas	*m*	~	~	~	-asse	-asse	-assen	-asse
5.	K·enntnis	*f*	~	~	~	-isse	-isse	-issen	-isse
	Tr·übsal	*f*	~	~	~	~e	~e	~en	~e

II. With Umlaut

	sg nom		gen	dat	acc	pl nom	gen	dat	acc
1.	Mann	*m*	~(e)s	~(e)	~	~̈er	~̈er	~̈ern	~̈er
	Rand	*m*	~(e)s	~(e)	~	~̈er	~̈er	~̈ern	~̈er
cf.	Haus	*n*	~es	~(e)	~	~̈er	~̈er	~̈ern	~̈er
I. 1.	Faß	*n*	-sses	~&-sse	~	Fässer	Fässer	Fässern	Fässer
	Dorf	*n*	~(e)s	~(e)	~	~̈er	~̈er	~̈ern	~̈er
	Wort	*n*	~(e)s	~(e)	~	~̈er & ~e	~̈er & ~e	~̈ern & ~en	~̈er & ~e
	Gut	*n*	~(e)s	~(e)	~	~̈er	~̈er	~̈ern	~̈er
2.	D·enkmal	*n*	~s	~	~	~̈er & ~e	~̈er & ~e	~̈ern & ~en	~̈er & ~e
3.	Draht	*m*	~(e)s	~(e)	~	~̈e	~̈e	~̈en	~̈e
	Schwanz	*m*	~(e)s	~(e)	~	~̈e	~̈e	~̈en	~̈e
	Raum	*m*	~(e)s	~(e)	~	~̈e	~̈e	~̈en	~̈e
	Spaß [*a*:]	*m*	~(e)s	~(e)	~	~̈e	~̈e	~̈en	~̈e
	Baß [*a*]	*m*	Basses	Basse & Baß	~	Bässe	Bässe	Bässen	Bässe
	Saal	*m*	~(e)s	~(e)	~	Säle	Säle	Sälen	Säle
	Hof	*m*	~(e)s	~(e)	~	~̈e	~̈e	~̈en	~̈en
	Hut	*m*	~(e)s	~(e)	~	~̈e	~̈e	~̈en	~̈e
	Fuß [*u*:]	*m*	~es	~(e)	~	~̈e	~̈e	~̈en	~̈e
	Kuß [*u*]	*m*	Kusses	Kusse & Kuß	~	Küsse	Küsse	Küssen	Küsse

	sg nom		gen	dat	acc	pl nom	gen	dat	acc
4.	Alt·ar	*m*	~s	~	~	~̈e & ~e	~̈e & ~e	~̈en & ~en	~̈e & ~e
	Gener·al	*m*	~s	~	~	~̈e & ~e	~̈e & ~e	~̈en & ~en	~̈e & ~e
	B·ischof	*m*	~s	~	~	~̈e	~̈e	~̈en	~̈e
5.	V·ater	*m*	~s	~	~	~̈	~̈	~̈n	~̈
	Gr·aben	*m*	~s	~	~	~̈	~̈	~̈	~̈
	(Kr·agen)	*m*	~s	~	~	~(& ×~̈)	~(& ×~̈)	~(& ×~̈)	~(& ×~̈)
	(W·agen)	*m*	~s	~	~	~(& ×~̈)	~(& ×~̈)	~(& ×~̈)	~(& ×~̈)
	·Ofen	*m*	~s	~	~	~ ~̈	~̈	~̈	~̈
6. cf. II. 5.	M·utter	*f*	~	~	~	~̈	~̈	~̈n	~̈
7.	Wand	*f*	~	~	~	~̈e	~̈e	~̈en	~̈e
cf.	Bank	*f*	~	~	~	~̈e	~̈e	~̈en	~̈e
II. 3.	Gans	*f*	~	~	~	~̈e	~̈e	~̈en	~̈e
	Nuß	*f*	~	~	~	Nüsse	Nüsse	Nüssen	Nüsse

III. The Weak Declension of Nouns (*m*, *f*, *n*)

(*cf.* II. *Strong Declension on page 1507*)

has **-n, -en** *in gen sg m & f* ‖ *has* **-(e)n, -nen** *in pl*

is ***invariable*** *in sg f* ‖ *has* ***no*** *Umlaut*

	sg nom		gen	dat	acc	pl nom	gen	dat	acc
1.	Herr	*m*	~n	~n	~n	~en	~en	~en	~en
	B·ayer	*m*	~n	~n	~n	~n	~n	~n	~n
	Kn·abe	*m*	~n	~n	~n	~n	~n	~n	~n
	Dr·ache	*m*	~n	~n	~n	~n	~n	~n	~n
2.	Mensch	*m*	~en	~en	~en	~en	~en	~en	~en
	Bär	*m*	~en	~(en)	~(en)	~en	~en	~en	~en
	Ochs	*m*	~en	~en	~en	~en	~en	~en	~en
	Sekund·ant	*m*	~en	~en	~en	~en	~en	~en	~en
	Mon·arch	*m*	~en	~en	~en	~en	~en	~en	~en
3.	Frau	*f*	~	~	~	~en	~en	~en	~en
4.	Fr·eiheit	*f*	~	~	~	~en	~en	~en	~en
	S·eligkeit	*f*	~	~	~	~en	~en	~en	~en
[abstr]	B·ürgschaft	*f*	~	~	~	~en	~en	~en	~en
	Sch·onung	*f*	~	~	~	~en	~en	~en	~en
	Gef·ahr	*f*	~	~	~	~en	~en	~en	~en
	Geb·urt	*f*	~	~	~	~en	~en	~en	~en
	Tat	*f*	~	~	~	~en	~en	~en	~en
	Profess·ur	*f*	~	~	~	~en	~en	~en	~en
	Invent·ur	*f*	~	~	~	~en	~en	~en	~en
5.	W·abe	*f*	~	~	~	~n	~n	~n	~n
	N·abe	*f*	~	~	~	~n	~n	~n	~n
	K·ette	*f*	~	~	~	~n	~n	~n	~n
	Tr·eppe	*f*	~	~	~	~n	~n	~n	~n
6.	L·eiter	*f*	~	~	~	~n	~n	~n	~n
	K·achel	*f*	~	~	~	~n	~n	~n	~n
	Tr·ommel	*f*	~	~	~	~n	~n	~n	~n
	F·ackel	*f*	~	~	~	~n	~n	~n	~n
	Sch·achtel	*f*	~	~	~	~n	~n	~n	~n
7.	B·ärin	*f*	~	~	~	~nen	~nen	~nen	~nen
	L·ehrerin	*f*	~	~	~	~nen	~nen	~nen	~nen

IV. The Mixed Declension (*m*, *n*)

			sg: strong			*pl: weak*			
	nom		*gen*	*dat*	*acc*	*nom*	*gen*	*dat*	*acc*
1.	·Auge	*n*	~s	~	~	~n	~n	~n	~n
	St·achel *m*	*m*	~s	~	~	~n	~n	~n	~n
2.	Schmerz	*m*	~es	~(e)	~	~en	~en	~en	~en
	Hemd	*n*	~(e)s	~(e)	~	~en	~en	~en	~en
3.	Dorn	*m*	~(e)s	~(e)	~	⟨bot⟩ ~en	~en	~en	~en
						[obs] (~̈er)	(~̈er)	(~̈ern)	(~̈er)
						⟨tech⟩ ~e	~e	~en	~e
	Sporn [ɔ]	*m*	~(e)s	~(e)	~	Sp·oren[o:]	Sp·oren	Sp·oren	Sp·oren
	sg: strong					***pl: strong or weak***			
4.	Mast	*m*	~es	~(e)	~	~e & ~en	~e & ~en	~en	~e & ~en
	sg: strong or weak					***pl: weak***			
5.	Pfau	*m*	~s & ~en	~ & ~en	~ & ~en	~en	~en	~en	~en
	Ahn	*m*	~s & ~en	~ & ~en	~ & ~en	~en	~en	~en	~en
	B·auer	*m*	~s & ~n	~ & ~n	~ & ~n	~n	~n	~n	~n
	sg: irregular					***pl: weak***			
6.	N·ame	*m*	~ns	~n	~n	~n	~n	~n	~n
	S·ame(n)	*m*	~ns	~n	~n	~n	~n	~n	~n
	Herz	*n*	~ens	~en	~	~en	~en	~en	~en

V. Plural with -s (*mostly foreign words*; *cf.* VI.)

	sg *nom*		*gen*	*dat*	*acc*	***pl*** *nom*	*gen*	*dat*	*acc*
1.	***Words with final consonant***								
	Trupp	*m*	~s	~	~	~s	~s	~s	~s
	Lord	*m*	~s	~	~	~s	~s	~s	~s
	Schah	*m*	~s	~	~	~s	~s	~s	~s
	Detail	*n*	~s	~	~	~s	~s	~s	~s
	Depot	*n*	~s	~	~	~s	~s	~s	~s
	Trottoir	*n*	~s	~	~	~s & ~e	~s & ~e	~s & ~en	~s & ~e
	Restaurant	*n*	~s	~	~	~s	~s	~s	~s
	Relief	*n*	~s	~	~	~s	~s	~s	~s
	Tschib·uk	*m*	~s	~	~	~s	~s	~s	~s
	Relais	*n*	~ [-*s*]	~	~	~ [-*s*]	~ [-*s*]	~ [-*s*]	~ [-*s*]
	Visavis	*n*	~ [-*s*]	~	~	~ [-*s*]	~ [-*s*]	~ [-*s*]	~ [-*s*]
	Rendezvous	*n*	~ [-*s*]	~	~	~ [-*s*]	~ [-*s*]	~ [-*s*]	~ [-*s*]
	Corps, Korps [kor:]	*n*	~ [-*s*]	~	~	~ [-*s*]	~ [-*s*]	~ [-*s*]	~ [-*s*]
	Brigg	*f*	~	~	~	~s	~s	~s	~s
2.	***Words with final vowel***								
	K·omma	*n*	~s	~	~	~s & ~ta	~s & ~ta	~s & ~ta	~s & → VI
	Z·ebra	*n*	~s	~	~	~s	~s	~s	~s
	Gen·ie [-*i*:]	*n*	~s	~	~	~s	~s	~s	~s
	K·uli	*m*	~s	~	~	~s	~s	~s	~s
	Ag·uti	*m* & *n*	~s	~	~	~s	~s	~s	~s
	K·olibri	*m*	~s	~	~	~s	~s	~s	~s
	M·aki	*m*	~s	~	~	~s	~s	~s	~s
	·Eskimo	*m*	~s	~	~	~s	~s	~s	~s
	·Auto	*n*	~s	~	~	~s	~s	~s	~s
	·Gnu	*n*	~s	~	~	~s	~s	~s	~s
	·Uhu	*m*	~s	~	~	~s	~s	~s	~s
	P·ony	*n*	~s	~	~	~s	~s	~s	~s →VI
	K·obra	*f*	~	~	~	~s	~s	~s	~s
	D·onna	*f*	~	~	~	~s	~s	~s	~s
	L·ady	*f*	~	~	~	~s	~s	~s	~

VI. Foreign Words (cf. V. 1.)

	sg nom		gen	dat	acc	pl nom	gen	dat	acc
1.	K·ultus	m	~	~	~	-te	-te	-ten	-te
	Plur·alis	m	~	~	~	-le	-le	-len	-le
						with change of accent:			
	Di·akonus	m	~	~	~	} Diak·one	-·one	-·onen	-·one
	(Diak·on)	m	(~s)	(~)	(~)				
2.	Gl·obus	m	~	~	~	-ben	-ben	-ben	-ben
	K·ubus	m	~	~	~	~ & -ben	~ & -ben	~ & -ben	~ & -ben
	·Epos	n	~	~	~	-pen	-pen	-pen	-pen
	T·uba	f	~	~	~	-ben	-ben	-ben	-ben
	T·undra	f	~	~	~	-ren	-ren	-ren	-ren
	F·irma	f	~	~	~	-men	-men	-men	-men
	·Album	n	~s	~	~	-ben	-ben	-ben	-ben
	St·udium	n	~s	~	~	-ien	-ien	-ien	-ien
	Koll·e-g(ium)	n	~s	~	~	-ien	-ien	-ien	-ien
	K·onto	n	~s	~	~	-ten	-ten	-ten	-ten
	Dr·ama	n	~s	~	~	-men	-men	-men	-men
cf.	{ D·ogma	n	~s	~	~	~ta & -men	~ta & -men	~ta & -men	~ta & -men
II. 2.	{ Th·ema	n	~s	~	~	~ta & -men	~ta & -men	~ta & -men	~ta & -men
	Id·ee [-*e*:]	f	~	~	~	~n [-*e*:*ən*]	~n [-*e*:*ən*]	~n [-*e*:*ən*]	~n [-*e*:*ən*]
	Kate-gor·ie[-*i*:]	f	~	~	~	~n [-*i*:*ən*]	~n [-*i*:*ən*]	~n [-*i*:*ən*]	~n [-*i*:*ən*]
	Harmo-n·ie [-*i*:]	f	~	~	~	~n- [*i*:*ən*]	~n [-*i*:*ən*]	~n [-*i*:*ən*]	~n [-*i*:*ən*]
	Bacchan·al	n	~s	~	~	~ien	~ien	~ien	~ien
	Materi·al	n	~s	~	~	~ien	~ien	~ien	~ien
	Konz·il	n	~s	~	~	~ien	~ien	~ien	~ien
						with change of accent:			
	·Autor	m	~s	~	~	Aut·oren	-·oren	-·oren	-·oren
	Prof·essor	m	~s	~	~	Pro-fess·oren	-·oren	-·oren	-·oren
	H·eros	m	~	~	~	Her·oen	-·oen	-·oen	-·oen
	·Atlas	m	~	~	~	Atl·anten	-·anten	-·anten	-·anten
	·Agens	n	~	~	~	Ag·enzien	-·enzien	-·enzien	-·enzien
	Ingr·e-diens	n	~	~	~	Ingre-di·enzien	-·enzien	-·enzien	-·enzien

VII. Foreign and Learned Plural-Endings

	sg nom		gen	dat	acc	pl nom	gen	dat	acc
1. [L]	M·askuli-num	n	~s	~	~	-na	-na	-na	-na
	N·eutrum	n	~s	~	~	-ra	-ra	-ra	-ra
	V·isum	n	~s	~	~	-sa	-sa	-sa	-sa
	Vi·atikum	n	~s	~	~	-ka	-ka	-ka	-ka
	Jus	n	~	~	~	J·ura	-ra	-ra	-ra
	Pron·omen	n	~s	~	~	-mina	-mina	-mina	-mina
	Vol·umen	n	~s	~	~	-mina	-mina	-mina	-mina
	S·yndikus	m	~	~	~	S·yndizi	-zi	-zi	-zi
	Musikus	m	~	~	~	M·usizi	-zi	-zi	-zi
						with change of accent:			
	Dep·onens	n	~	~	~	Depo-n·entia	-tia	-tia	-tia
2.	Th·ema	n	~s	~	~	~ta	~ta	~ta	~ta
cf.	D·ogma	n	~s	~	~	~ta	~ta	~ta	~ta
VI. 2., V. 2	K·omma	n	~s	~	~	~ta	~ta	~ta	~ta
3.	P·orto	n	~s	~	~	-ti	-ti	-ti	-ti
[It]	K·ollo	n	~s	~	~	-li	-li	-li	-li
							in Austria:		
[E]	P·ony	n	~s	~	~	(~s &)-nies	(~s &) -ies	(~s &) -ies	(~s &) -ies
	L·ady	f	~	~	~	(~s &)-dies	(~s &) -ies	(~s &) -ies	(~s &) -ies

VIII. Compound Nouns

	sg	*nom*		*gen*	*dat*	*acc*	*pl*	*nom*	*gen*	*dat*	*acc*
1.	(der)	Tausendsassa	*m*	~s	~	~		~s	~s	~s	~s
	(ein)	,,									
	(der)	Nimmersatt	*m*	~s	~	~		~e	~e	~en	~e
	(ein)	,,									
	(der)	Taugenichts	*m*	~	~	~		~e	~e	~en	~e
	(ein)	,,									
	(der)	Prahlhans	*m*	~en	~	~		~̈e	~̈e	~̈en	~̈e
	(ein)	,,					*only the second part is inflected*				
2. Adj. & Subst.	**(der)**	Hohe|priester	*m*	~n|~s	~n|~	~n|~	(die)	~n|~	~n|~	~n|~n	~n|~
	(ein)	~r|~		,,	,,	,,	(zwei)	~e|~	,,	,,	~e|~
	(das)	Hohe|lied	*n*	~n|~s	~n|~(e)	~|~	(die)	~n|~er	~n|~er	~n|~ern	~n|~er
	(ein)	~s|~		,,	,,	~s|~	(zwei)	~|~er	,,	,,	~|~er
	(die)	Lange|weile	*f*	~n|~	~n|~	~|~		—	—	—	—
					aus ~r|~		*both parts are inflected*				
3. Adj. & Adj.	(der)	Einjährig|freiwillige	*m*	~|~n	~|~n	~|~n	(die)	~|~n	~|~n	~|~n	~|~n
	([k]ein)	~|~r		,,	,,	,,	(zwei)	~|~	~|~n	~|~n	~|~n
							(keine)	~|~n	~|~n	~|~n	~|~n
		~|~r **vor**!						~|~ **vor**!			
							only the second part is inflected				

IX. Proper Names

NB. with *the article the singulars are* **not** *inflected*

NB. *the plurals are always inflected*

	sg nom		*gen*	*dat*	*acc*	*pl*	*nom*	*gen*	*dat*	*acc*
1.	H·einrich	*m*	~s	~	~		~e	~e	~en	~e
	Alex·ander	*m*	~s	~	~		~	~	~n	~
2.	·Otto	*m*	~s	~	~		~s	~s	~s	~s
						⟨hist⟩	Ott·onen	~	~	~
	P·aula	*f*	~s	~	~		~s	~s	~s	~s
	Mar·ie [-*i*:]	*f*	~(**n**)s [-*i*:(*ən*)*s*]	~	~		~n [-*i*:*ən*]	~n	~n	~n
	Soph·ie [-*i*:]	*f*	~(**n**)s [-*i*:(*ən*)*s*]	~	~		~n [-*i*:*ən*]	~n	~n	~n
3.	Fritz	*m*	~**ens**	~	~		~e	~e	~en	~e
	Franz	*m*	~**ens**	~	~		~e	~e	~en	~e
	Max	*m*	~**ens**	~	~		~e	~e	~en	~e
	Hans	*m*	{~**ens**, ~'}	~	~		~e	~e	~en	~e
4.	El·isabeth	*f*	~(**en**)s	~	~		~en	~en	~en	~en
5. (*m*)	M·äxchen	*n*	~s	~	~		~	~	~	~
(*f*)	Mar·iechen	*n*	~s	~	~		~	~	~	~
6.	Jesus Christus		**-su -ti**	**-su -to**	**-sum -tum**	(*without the article*)				
7.	Fr·iedrich H·ebbel	*m*	**F. H.s**	F. H.	F. H.	*only the surname is declined*				
	Ric·arda Huch	*f*	**R. H.s**	R. H.	R. H.					
	Otto **von** B·ülow	*m*	**O. v. B.s**	O. v. B.	O. v. B.					
8.	Hartmann **von** Aue	*m*	**H. v. A.s**	H. v. A.	H. v. A.	*though here* **von** *signifies but the place of origin*				
9.	Kaiser Otto I.		K. **O.s** I.	K. O. I.	K. O. I.	*only the name is inflected*				
	(*with the article*:) **des**		**K.s** O. I.	**dem** K. O. I.	**den** K. O. I.	*only the title is inflected**				
read:	(K. O.) der Erste		.. des ~n	.. dem ~n	.. den ~n					
	König Friedrich II.		K. **F.s** II.	K. F. II.	K. F. II.	*only the name is inflected*				
	(*with the article*:) **des**		**K.s** F. II.	dem K. F. II.	.. den K. F. II.	*only the title is inflected**				
read:	(K. F.) der Zweite		.. des ~n	.. dem ~n	.. den ~n					
	(K. F.) der Große		.. des ~n	.. dem ~n	.. den ~n					

* **NB.** Herr *is always inflected*: der Sohn des (Herrn) Amtrichters Neumann; Herrn richter Neumanns Sohn. *Say*: des Doktor Martin Luther: Doktor *has become part of th*

X. Adjectives before Nouns

1. *after the definite article* **der, die, das**

		m	*f*	*n*
sg	*nom*	**der gute Mann**	**die schöne Frau**	**das brave Kind**
	gen	des ~n ~es	der ~n ~	des ~n ~es
	dat	dem ~n ~(e)	der ~n ~	dem ~n ~(e)
	acc	den ~n ~	die ~ ~	das ~ ~
pl	*nom*	die ~n ~̈er	die ~n ~en	die ~n ~er
	gen	der ~n ~̈er	der ~n ~en	der ~n ~er
	dat	den ~n ~̈ern	den ~n ~en	den ~n ~ern
	acc	die ~n ~̈er	die ~n ~en	die ~n ~er

2. *after the indefinite article* **ein** *and its negation* **kein**
(*or a possessive pronoun* **mein, dein, sein, ihr, unser, etc.**)

		m	*f*	*n*
sg	*nom*	**(k)ein** ~r ~	**(m)eine** ~ ~	**(s)ein** ~s ~
	gen	~es ~n ~es	~r ~n ~	~es ~n ~es
	dat	~em ~n ~(e)	~r ~n ~	~em ~n ~(e)
	acc	~en ~n ~	~ ~ ~	~ ~s ~

in the plural after **alle, sämtliche, beide, keine** (*or a possessive pronoun*)

pl	*nom*	**alle**[1] ~n ~̈er	**beide** ~n ~en	**meine** ~n ~er
	gen	~r ~n ~̈er	~r ~n ~en	~r ~n ~er
	dat	~n ~n ~̈ern	~n ~n ~en	~n ~n ~ern
	acc	~ ~n ~̈er	~ ~n ~en	~ ~n ~er

[1] *For*: andere, viele etc. → 3.

3. *withont any article*

sg	*nom*	**guter, alter Wein**[1]	**gute Hoffnung**	**sächliches Geschlecht**[1]
	gen	-en, -en[2] ~es	~r ~	-chen ~(e)s
	dat	-em, -em ~(e)	~r ~[1]	**-chem** ~(e)[2]
	acc	-en, -en ~	~ ~	-ches ~
		[1] ich alter Mann [2] guten & gutes Mut(e)s	[1] du gute Frau; aus tiefer Seele	[1] welch [*invar*] gutes Herz! [2] von ganzem Herzen!
pl	*nom*	gute, alte Weine	schöne Frauen	alte Geschlechter
	gen	~r, ~r ~	~r ~	~r ~
	dat	~n, ~n ~n	~n ~	~n ~n
	acc	~, ~ ~[1, 2]	~ ~	~ ~

[1] *Thus*: andere, einige, einzelne, gewisse, manche, etc., zwei, viele **arme** Männer; *gen*: vieler, etc. armer & armen Männer. *For* alle, beide, meine, etc. → 2.

[2] *Both adjectives are inflected alike if, like here, they have the same relation to the noun*: mit frische**m**, frohe**m** Mut. | *But*: in schlechte**m** bauliche**n** Zustand (der b.e Z. ist schlecht); mit große**m** sprachliche**n** Verständnis (das V. ist nicht etwa groß und sprachlich); nach stattgefundene**m** fruchtlose**n** Pfändungsversuch (der Pf. hat zwar stattgefunden, war aber fruchtlos); bei eigene**m** schuldlose**n** Autounfall; vor herrliche**m** landschaftliche**n** Hintergrund (*different relations!*).

1. Personal Pronoun

		sg *nom*	*gen*	*dat*	*acc*	pl *nom*	*gen*	*dat*	*acc*
1st person	(*m, f, n*)	ich	meiner	mir	mich	wir	unser	uns	uns
	reflexive	—	„	„	„	—	„	„	„
2nd person	(*m, f, n*)	du	deiner	dir	dich	ihr	euer	euch	euch
	reflexive	—	„	„	„	—	„	„	„
in letters		Du	Deiner	Dir	Dich	Ihr	Euer	Euch	Euch
	reflexive	— „	„	„	„	—	„	„	„
more polite		Sie	Ihrer	Ihnen	Sie	Sie	Ihrer	Ihnen	Sie
	reflexive	—	„	„	„	—	„	„	„
obs & dial		Ihr	Euer	Euch	Euch	Ihr	Euer	Euch	Euch
	reflexive	—	„	„	„	—	„	„	„
3rd person	(*m*)	er	seiner	ihm	ihn				
	reflexive	—	„	sich	sich				
	(*f*)	sie	ihrer	ihr	sie	sie	ihrer	ihnen	sie
	reflexive	—	„	sich	sich	—	„	sich	sich
	(*n*)	es	seiner	ihm	es				
	reflexible	—	„	sich	sich				

2. Possessive Pronoun

When there is **one possessor**		**sg** *(thing possessed)* *nom*	*gen*	*dat*	*acc*	**pl** *(things possessed)* *nom*	*gen*	*dat*	*acc*
1st person *(m, f, n possessor)*	*m*	**mein**	~es	~em	~en				
	f	~e	~er	~er	~e	~e	~er	~en	~e
	n	~	~es	~em	~				
2nd person *(m, f, n possessor)*	*m*	**dein**	~es	~em	~en				
	f	~e	~er	~er	~e	~e	~er	~en	~e
	n	~	~es	~em	~				
3rd person *m possessor*	*m*	**sein**	~es	~em	~en				
	f	~e	~er	~er	~e	~e	~er	~en	~e
	n	~	~es	~em	~				
3rd person *f possessor*	*m*	**ihr**	~es	~em	~en				
	f	~e	~er	~er	~e	~e	~er	~en	~e
	n	~	~es	~em	~				
3rd person *n possessor*	*m*	**sein**	~es	~em	~en				
	f	~e	~er	~er	~e	~e	~er	~en	~e
	n	~	~es	~em	~				
When there are **several possessors**									
1st person *(m, f, n possessors)*	*m*	**unser**	uns(e)res	uns(e)rem	un(e)ren				
	f	uns(e)re	uns(e)rer	uns(e)rer	uns(e)re	uns(e)re	-rer	-ren	-re
	n	unser	un(se)res	uns(e)rem	unser				
2nd person *(m, f, n possessors)*	*m*	**euer**	eures	eurem	euren				
	f	eure	eurer	eurer	eure	eure	~r	~n	~
	n	euer	eures	eurem	euer				
3rd person *(m, f, n possessors)*	*m*	**ihr**	~es	~em	~en				
	f	~e	~er	~er	~e	~e	~er	~en	~e
	n	~	~es	~em	~				

If used without a noun, instead of **mein**, *etc.*, **unser**, *etc.*, *we say* **meiner**, *etc.*, **unsrer**, *etc.*
(for declension → 3.)
If used substantively we say **der mein(ig)e (Mein(ig)e)**, *etc.*, **der unsre (Unsre)**, *etc.*
(for declension → p. 1332 der **gute** Mann)

3. Demonstrative Pronoun

sg		*m*	*f*	*n*		**pl** *m, f, n*
a)	*nom*	dieser	diese	die(se)s	[1]	diese
	gen	dieses	dieser	dieses		dieser
	dat	diesem	dieser	diesem		diesen
	acc	diesen	diese	die(se)s		diese
b)	*nom*	der	die	das		die
	gen	des(sen)	deren	des(sen)		deren
	dat	dem	der	dem		denen
	acc	den	die	das		die
c)	*nom*	**derselbe**	**dieselbe**	**dasselbe**	[2] [3]	**dieselben**
	gen	**desselben**	**derselben**	**desselben**		**derselben**
	dat	**demselben**	**derselben**	**demselben**		**denselben**
	acc	**denselben**	**dieselbe**	**dasselbe**		**dieselben**

[1] **jener, solcher, jeder** *are declined like* dieser.
[2] **derartig** *is declined like* derselbe *but for the first syllable, which is invariable.*
[3] **derjenige** *is declined like* derselbe.

4. Relative Pronoun

⟨mst⟩ **der, die, das;** *pl* **die** *which is declined like the demonstrative pronoun* der → 3. b)
⟨* & obs⟩ **welcher, welche, welches;** *pl* **welche** *which is declined like* dieser → 3. a)

5. Interrogative Pronoun

1. Substantival

	nom	*gen*	*dat*	*ac*
m & f	wer	wes(sen)	wem	we
n	was	„	was	wa

2. Adjectival

m welcher (Mann), *f* welche (Frau), *n* welches (Kind)?
declined like the demonstrative pronoun dieser → 3.

List of German Strong or Irregular Verbs

(For compounds see the simple verbs)

Infinitive	*Present Indic.* *2nd p*	*3rd p*	*Imperf.Indic.*	*Imperf.Subj.*	*Imperative* *sg*	*pl*	*Past. Part.*
·an|fechten	fichtst an	ficht an	focht an	föchte an	ficht an	fechtet an	angefochten
·aus|löschen [vi/t] → erlöschen, verlöschen		(das Licht) lischt aus	losch aus	lösche aus	lisch aus	löscht aus	passiv: -geloschen aktiv: -gelöscht
backen [vt]	bäckst	bäckt	(buk) & backte	(büke) & backte	backe	backt	gebacken
(backen [vi]) (*to clot: weak*)	(backst)	(backt)	(backte)	(backte)	(backe)	(backt)	(gebacken)
bef·ehlen	befiehlst du	befiehlt er	befahl er	beföhle er	befiehl	befehlt	befohlen
befleißen, sich ~	befleiß(es)t dich	befleißt sich	befliß sich	beflisse sich	befleiß(e) dich	befleißt euch	beflissen
beg·innen	beginnst	beginnt	begann	begönne (begänne)	beginn(e)	beginnt	begonnen
b·eißen	beiß(es)t	beißt	biß	bisse	beiß(e)	beißt	gebissen
b·ergen	birgst	birgt	barg	bürge (bärge)	birg	bergt	geborgen
b·ersten	birst berstest	birst berstet	barst	bärste & börste	birst berste	berstet	geborsten
betr·ügen	betrügst	betrügt	betrog	betröge	betrüg(e)	betrügt	betrogen
bew·egen 1. (*to induce a p to do s.th*)	bewegst	bewegt	bewog	bewöge	beweg(e)	bewegt	bewogen
2. *to move* ⟨a. fig⟩	bewegst	bewegt	bewegte	bewegte	beweg(e)	bewegt	bewegt
b·iegen	biegst	biegt	bog	böge	bieg(e)	biegt	gebogen
b·ieten	biet(e)st (*beutst)	bietet (*beut)	bot	böte	biet(e) (*beut)	bietet	geboten
b·inden	bindest	bindet	band	bände	bind(e)	bindet	gebunden
b·itten	bittest	bittet	bat	bäte	bitte	bittet	gebeten
bl·asen	bläst	bläst	blies	bliese	blas, blase	blast	geblasen
bl·eiben	bleibst	bleibt	blieb	bliebe	bleib(e)	bleibt	geblieben
br·aten	brätst	brät	briet	briete	brat(e)	bratet	gebraten
br·echen	brichst	bricht	brach	bräche	brich	brecht	gebrochen
br·ennen	brennst	brennt	brannte	brennte	brenne	brennt	gebrannt
br·ingen	bringst	bringt	brachte	brächte	bring(e)	bringt	gebracht
d·enken	denkst	denkt	dachte	dächte	denk(e)	denkt	gedacht
d·ingen	dingst	dingt	dang & dingte	dänge & dingte	ding(e)	dingt	gedungen & gedingt
dr·eschen	drischest	drischt	drosch	drösche	drisch	drescht	gedroschen
dr·ingen	dringst	dringt	drang	dränge	dring(e)	dringt	gedrungen
d·ünken	du dünkst dich	er dünkt sich; es ~ (deucht) mich; mich dünkt	dünkte (deuchte)	dünkte (deuchte)	dünke (dich)	dünkt (euch)	mich hat gedünkt (gedeucht)
d·ürfen sg	darfst	darf	durfte	dürfte	—	—	gedurft, ich habe es nicht tun dürfen
pl	dürft	dürfen					
empf·angen	empfängst	empfängt	empfing	empfinge	empfang(e)	empfangt	empfangen
empf·ehlen	empfiehlst	empfiehlt	empfahl	empföhle	empfiehl	empfehlt	empfohlen
empf·inden	empfindest	empfindet	empfand	empfände	empfind(e)		empfunden
erbl·eichen	erbleichst	erbleicht	erblich & erbleichte	erbliche & erbleichte	erbleich(e)	erbleicht	erblichen (gestorben), erbleicht
erl·öschen (*to become extinguished*)	erlisch(e)st	erlischt	erlosch	erlösche	erlisch	erlöscht	erloschen
rschr·ecken [vi]; (*weak* …chen [vt] = … *frighten*)	erschrickst ⟨fam a. refl⟩: -e-	erschrickt -e-	erschrak -eckte	erschräke -eckte	erschrick -eck(e)	erschreckt -eckt	erschrocken -eckt
…·ägen	erwägst	erwägt	erwog	erwöge	erwäg(e)	erwägt	erwogen
…en	ißt	ißt	aß	äße	iß	eßt	gegessen
…ren	fährst	fährt	fuhr	führe	fahr(e)	fahrt	gefahren
…e	fällst	fällt	fiel	fiele	fall(e)	fallt	gefallen
…g	fängst	fängt	fing	finge	fang(e)	fangt	gefangen

Infinitive	*Present Indic.*		*Imperf.Indic.*	*Imperf.Subj.*	*Imperative*		*Past. Part.*
	2nd p	*3rd p*			*sg*	*pl*	
f·echten	fichtst	ficht	focht	föchte	ficht	fechtet	gefochten
f·inden	findest	findet	fand	fände	find(e)	findet	gefunden
fl·echten	flichtst	flicht	flocht	flöchte	flicht	flechtet	geflochten
fl·iegen	fliegst (*fleugst)	fliegt (*fleugt)	flog	flöge	flieg (*fleug)	fliegt	geflogen
fl·iehen	flieh(e)st (*fleuchst)	flieht (*fleucht)	floh	flöhe	flieh (*fleuch)	flieh(e)t	geflohen
fl·ießen	flie(e)st (*fleußt)	fließt	floß	flösse	fließ(e) (*fleuß)	fließet	geflossen
fr·agen	fragst (×frägst)	fragt (×frägt)	fragte (×frug)	fragte (×früge)	frag(e)	fragt	gefragt
fr·essen	frißt	frißt	fraß	fräße	friß	freßt	gefressen
fr·ieren	frierst	friert	fror	fröre	frier(e)	friert	gefroren
g·ären ⟨fig⟩ *weak*	gärst	gärt	gor & gärte	göre & gärte	gär(e)	gär(e)t	gegoren, & gegärt
geb·ären	gebierst	gebiert	gebar	gebäre	gebier (*gebäre)	gebärt	geboren
g·eben	gibst	gibt	gab	gäbe	gib	gebt	gegeben
ged·eihen	gedeihst	gedeiht	gedieh	gediehe	gedeih(e)	gedeiht	gediehen
g·ehen	gehst	geht	ging	ginge	geh(e)	geht	gegangen
gel·ingen[*imps*]	(es) gelingt (mir)		gelang	gelänge	geling(e)	gelingt	gelungen
g·elten	giltst	gilt	galt	gälte & gölte	gilt	geltet	gegolten
gen·esen	genes(es)t	genest	genas	genäse	genese	genest	genesen
gen·ießen	genieß(es)t	genießt	genoß	genösse	genieß(e)	genießt	genossen
ger·aten	gerätst	gerät	geriet	geriete	gerat(e)	geratet	geraten
gesch·ehen [*imps*]		geschieht (*geschicht)	geschah	geschähe			geschehen
gew·innen	gewinnst	gewinnt	gewann	gewänne & gewönne	gewinn(e)	gewinnt	gewonnen
g·ießen	gieß(es)t (*geuß(es)t	gießt *geußt)	goß	gösse	gieß(e)	gießt	gegossen
gl·eichen	gleichst	gleicht	glich	gliche	gleich(e)	gleicht	geglichen
gl·eißen	gleiß(es)t	gleißt	gleißte (*gliß)	gleißte (*glisse)	gleiß(e)	gleißt	gegleißt & geglissen
gl·eiten	gleit(e)st	gleitet	glitt	glitte	gleit(e)	gleitet	geglitten
gl·immen	glimmst	glimmt	glomm & glimmte	glömme & glimmte	glimm(e)	glimmt	geglommen & geglimmt
gr·aben	gräbst	gräbt	grub	grübe	grab(e)	grabt	gegraben
gr·eifen	greifst	greift	griff	griffe	greif(e)	greift	gegriffen
h·aben, ich habe; pl	du hast ihr habt	er hat	hatte (*hätte)	hätte	hab(e)	habt	gehabt
h·alten	hältst	hält	hielt	hielte	halt(e)	haltet	gehalten
h·angen [vi]	hängst	hängt	hing	hinge	hang(e)		gehangen
(h·ängen [vt])	(hängst)	(hängt)	(hängte)	(hängte)	(hänge)	(hängt)	(gehängt)
h·auen	haust	haut	hieb/haute	hiebe	hau(e)	haut	gehauen
h·eben	hebst	hebt	hob	höbe	heb(e)	hebt	gehoben
h·eißen	heiß(es)t	heißt	hieß	hieße	heiß(e)	heißt	geheißen
h·elfen	hilfst	hilft	half	hülfe	hilf	helft	geholfen
k·ennen	kennst	kennt	kannte	kenn(e)te	kenne	kennt	gekannt
k·iesen (→ küren)	kiesest & kiest	kiest	kor	köre	kies(e)	kiest	gekoren
kl·immen	klimmst	klimmt	klomm	klömme	klimm(e)	klimmt	geklommen
kl·ingen	klingst	klingt	klang	klänge	kling(e)	klingt	geklungen
kn·eifen	kneifst	kneift	kniff	kniffe	kneif(e)	kneift	gekniffen
k·ommen	kommst	kommt	kam	käme	komm(e)	kommt	gekommen
k·önnen ich kann; wir können	kannst ihr könnt	kann	konnte	könnte	könne	könnt	gekonnt, ich habe es nicht tun können
kr·eischen	krei-sch(e)st	kreischt	kreischte& krisch	kreischte & krische	kreisch(e)	kreischt	gekrischen & gekreischt
kr·iechen	kriechst (*kreuchst)	kriecht (-eucht)	kroch	kröche	kriech(e) (*kreuch)	kriecht	gekrochen
k·üren (→ kiesen)	kürst	kürt	kürte (kor)	kür(e)te (köre)	kür(e)	kürt	gekoren
l·aden (= aufladen)	lädst	lädt	lud	lüde	lad(e)	ladet	geladen
l·aden (= ein-laden)	ladest (*lädst)	ladet (*lädt)	lud (*ladete)	lüde (*ladete)	lad(e)	ladet	geladen
l·assen	läßt & lässest	läßt	ließ	ließe	laß	laßt	gelassen; ich habe es blei-ben lassen
l·aufen	läufst	läuft	lief	liefe	lauf(e)	lauft	gelaufen
l·eiden	leid(e)st	leidet	litt	litte	leide	leidet	gelitten

Infinitive	*Present Indic.* 2nd p	3rd p	*Imperf.Indic.*	*Imperf.Subj.*	*Imperative* sg	pl	*Past Part.*
leihen	leihst	leiht	lieh	liehe	leihe	leiht	geliehen
l·esen	liest	liest	las	läse	lies	lest	gelesen
l·iegen	liegst	liegt	lag	läge	lieg(e)	liegt	gelegen
löschen [vi] (*to be extinguished*)	lisch(e)st	lischt	losch	lösche	lisch	löscht	geloschen
→ [vt] erlöschen	lösch(e)st	löscht	löschte	löschte	lösche	lösch(e)t	gelöscht
l·ügen	lügst	lügt	log	löge	lüg(e)	lügt	gelogen
mahlen	mahl(e)st	mahlt	mahlte	mahlte	mahle	mahl(e)t	gemahlen
m·eiden	meidest	meidet	mied	miede	meid(e)	meidet	gemieden
m·elken	melkst	melkt	melkte (molk)	melkte (mölke)	melk(e)	melkt	gemelkt & gemolken (: frisch gemolkene Milch)
m·essen	mißt (*missest)	mißt	maß	mäße	miß	meßt	gemessen
mißl·ingen [*imps*]		(es) mißlingt (mir)	mißlang	mißlänge	mißling(e)	mißlingt	mißlungen
m·ögen, ich mag; wir mögen	magst	mag	mochte	möchte	—	—	gemocht; ich hätte es tun mögen
m·üssen ich muß; wir müssen	mußt ihr müßt	muß sie müssen	mußte	müßte	—	—	gemußt; ich hätte es tun müssen
n·ehmen	nimmst	nimmt	nahm	nähme	nimm	nehmt	genommen
n·ennen	nennst	nennt	nannte	nennte	nenn(e)	nennt	genannt
pf·eifen	pfeifst	pfeift	pfiff	pfiffe	pfeif(e)	pfeift	gepfiffen
pfl·egen	pflegst	pflegt	pflegte (*pflog & *pflag)	pflegte (*pflöge)	pfleg(e)	pflegt	gepflegt (*gepflogen)
pr·eisen	preis(es)t	preist	pries	priese	preis(e)	preis(e)t	gepriesen
que·llen ([vt] *is weak*)	quillst	quillt	quoll	quölle	quill	quellt	gequollen
r·aten	rätst	rät	riet	riete	rat(e)	ratet	geraten
r·eiben	reibst	reibt	rieb	riebe	reib(e)	reibt	gerieben
r·eißen	reiß(es)t	reißt	riß	risse	reiß(e)	reißt	gerissen
r·eiten	reit(e)st	reitet	ritt	ritte	reit(e)	reitet	geritten
r·ennen	rennst	rennt	rannte	rennte	renn(e)	rennt	gerannt
r·iechen	riechst	riecht	roch	röche	riech(e)	riecht	gerochen
r·ingen	ringst	ringt	rang	ränge	ring(e)	ringt	gerungen
r·innen	rinnst	rinnt	rann	ränne	rinn(e)	rinnt	geronnen
r·ufen	rufst	ruft	rief	riefe	ruf(e)	ruft	gerufen
s·äen	säst	sät	säte	säte	säe	sät	gesät
s·alzen	salz(es)t	salzt	salzte	salzte	salz(e)	salzt	gesalzen; (gesalzene Preise)
s·aufen	säufst	säuft	soff	söffe	sauf(e)	sauft	gesoffen
s·augen	saugst	saugt	sog	söge	saug(e)	saugt	gesogen
schaffen 1.) (*to create*),	schaffst	schafft	schuf	schüfe	schaff(e)	schafft	geschaffen
2.) (*to do, be busy*) *weak*	(schaffst)	(schafft)	schaffte	(schaffte)	(schaff(e))	(schafft)	(geschafft)
schallen	schallst	schallt	schallte & scholl	schallte & schölle	schall(e)	schallt	geschallt (*geschollen)
sch·eiden	scheidest	scheidet	schied	schiede	scheid(e)	scheidet	geschieden
sch·einen	scheinst	scheint	schien	schiene	schein(e)	scheint	geschienen
sch·eißen	scheiß(es)t	scheißt	schiß	schisse	scheiß(e)	scheißt	geschissen
sch·elten	schiltst	schilt	schalt	schölte	schilt	scheltet	gescholten
sch·eren	scherst & schierst	schert & schiert	schor	schöre	schier & scher(e)	schert	geschoren
sch·ieben	schiebst	schiebt	schob	schöbe	schieb(e)	schiebt	geschoben
sch·ießen	schieß(es)t	schießt	schoß	schösse	schieß(e)	schießt	geschossen
sch·inden	schindest	schindet	schund	schünde	schind(e)	schindet	geschunden
schl·afen	schläfst	schläft	schlief	schliefe	schlaf(e)	schlaft	geschlafen
schl·agen	schlägst	schlägt	schlug	schlüge	schlag(e)	schlagt	geschlagen
schl·eichen	schleichst	schleicht	schlich	schliche	schleich(e)	schleicht	geschlichen
schl·eifen 1. (*to grind*)	schleifst	schleift	schliff	schliffe	schleif(e)	schleift	geschliffen
2. (*to drag, dismantle*) *weak*	(schleifst)	(schleift)	(schleifte)	(schleifte)	(schleife)	(schleift)	(geschleift)
schl·eißen	schleiß(es)t	schleißt	schliß	schlisse	schleiß(e)	schleißt	geschlissen
schl·iefen	schliefst	schlieft	schloff	schlöffe	schlief(e)	schlieft	geschloffen
schl·ießen	schließ(es)t *schleuß(es)t	schließt *schleußt	schloß	schlösse	schließ(e) (*schleuß)	schließt	geschlossen

Infinitive	*Present Indic.*		*Imperf.Indic.*	*Imperf.Subj.*	*Imperative*		*Past Part.*
	2nd p	*3rd p*			*sg*	*pl*	
schl·ingen	schlingst	schlingt	schlang	schlänge	schling(e)	schlingt	geschlungen
schm·eißen	schmeiß(es)t	schmeißt	schmiß	schmisse	schmeiß(e)	schmeißt	geschmissen
schm·elzen [vi]	schmilz(es)t	schmilzt	schmolz	schmölze	schmilz	schmelz(e)t	geschmolzen
schn·auben	schnaubst	schnaubt	schnaubte ⟨*fig*⟩ schnob	schnaubte ⟨*fig*⟩ schnöbe	schnaub(e)	schraubt	geschnaubt ⟨*fig*⟩ geschnoben
schn·eiden	schneid(e)st	schneidet	schnitt	schnitte	schneid(e)	schneidet	geschnitten
schr·auben	schraubst	schraubt	schraubte (schrob)	schraubte (schröbe)	schraub(e)	schraubt	geschraubt& (geschroben)
schr·ecken [vi]	schrickst	schrickt	schrak	schräke	schrick	schreckt	geschrocken
schr·eiben	schreibst	schreibt	schrieb	schriebe	schreib(e)	schreibt	geschrieben
schr·eien	schreist	schreit	schrie	schriee	schrei(e)	schreit	geschrie(e)n
schr·eiten	schreit(e)st	schreitet	schritt	schritte	schreit(e)	schreitet	geschritten
schr·inden	schrind(e)st	schrindet	schrund	schründe	schrind(e)	schrindet	geschrunden
schw·ären [*imps*]		(es) schwärt (*schwiert)	schwor	schwöre	schwier schwär(e)	schwär(e)t	geschworen
schw·eigen	schweigst	schweigt	schwieg	schwiege	schweig(e)	schweigt	geschwiegen
schw·ellen	schwillst	schwillt	schwoll	schwölle	schwill	schwellt	geschwollen
schw·immen	schwimmst	schwimmt	schwamm	schwömme (×schwämme)	schwimm(e)	schwimm(e)t	geschwommen
schw·inden	schwindest	schwindet	schwand	schwände	schwind(e)	schwindet	geschwunden
schw·ingen	schwingst	schwingt	schwang	schwänge	schwing(e)	schwing(e)t	geschwungen
schw·ören	schwörst	schwört	schwur & schwor	schwüre	schwör(e)	schwör(e)t	geschworen
s·ehen	siehst	sieht	sah	sähe	sieh(e)	seh(e)t	gesehen
s·ein, ich bin; wir sind	du bist ihr seid	er ist sie sind	war	wäre	sei	seid	gewesen
s·enden	sendest	sendet	sandte & sendete	sendete	send(e)	sendet	gesandt & gesendet
s·ieden	siedest	siedet	sott & siedete	sötte & siedete	sied(e)	siedet	gesotten
s·ingen	singst	singt	sang	sänge	sing(e)	sing(e)t	gesungen
sinken	sinkst	sinkt	sank	sänke	sink(e)	sink(e)t	gesunken
s·innen	sinnst	sinnt	sann	sänne & sönne	sinn(e)	sinn(e)t	gesonnen
s·itzen	sitzest & sitzt	sitzt	saß	säße	sitz(e)	sitz(e)t	gesessen
s·ollen ich soll; wir sollen	du sollst	er soll	sollte	sollte	—	—	gesollt, ich hätte es nicht tun sollen
sp·alten	spalt(e)st	spaltet	spaltete	spaltete	spalt(e)	spaltet	gespalten & gespaltet
sp·eien	speist	speit	spie	spiee	spei(e)	spei(e)t	gespie(e)n (*gespeit)
sp·innen	spinn(e)st	spinnt	spann	spönne (×spänne)	spinn(e)	spinn(e)t	gesponnen
spl·eißen	spleißest & spleißt	spleißt	spliß & spleißte	splisse & spleißte	spleiß(e)	spleißt	gesplissen
spr·echen	sprichst	spricht	sprach	spräche	sprich	sprecht	gesprochen
spr·ießen	sprieß(es)t	sprießt	sproß	sprösse	sprieß(e)	sprießt	gesprossen
spr·ingen	springst	springt	sprang	spränge	spring(e)	spring(e)t	gesprungen
st·echen	stichst	sticht	stach	stäche	stich	stecht	gestochen
st·ecken (*to be in a place*)	steckst (*stickst)	steckt (*stickt)	steckte & stak	steckte & stäke	steck(e)	steckt	gesteckt
st·ehen	stehst	steht	stand (*stund)	stände & stünde	steh(e)	steh(e)t	gestanden
st·ehlen	stiehlst	stiehlt	stahl	stöhle & stähle	stiehl	stehlt	gestohlen
st·eigen	steigst	steigt	stieg	stiege	steig(e)	steig(e)t	gestiegen
st·erben	stirbst	stirbt	starb	stürbe	stirb	sterbt	gestorben
st·ieben	stiebst	stiebt	stob	stöbe	stieb(e)	stieb(e)t	gestoben
st·inken	stinkst	stinkt	stank	stänke	stink(e)	stink(e)t	gestunken
st·oßen	stöß(e)st	stößt	stieß	stieße	stoß(e)	stoßt	gestoßen
str·eichen	streichst	streicht	strich	striche	streich(e)	streicht	gestrichen

Infinitive	*Present Indic.* *2nd p*	*3rd p*	*Imperf. Indic.*	*Imperf. Subj.*	*Imperative* *sg*	*pl*	*Past Part.*
str·eiten	streitest	streitet	stritt	stritte	streit(e)	streitet	gestritten
tr·agen	trägst	trägt	trug	trüge	trag(e)	tragt	getragen
tr·effen	triffst	trifft	traf	träfe	triff	trefft	getroffen
tr·eiben	treibst	treibt	trieb	triebe	treib(e)	treib(e)t	getrieben
tr·eten	trittst	tritt	trat	träte	tritt	tretet	getreten
tr·iefen	triefst (*träufst)	trieft (*träuft)	troff (×triefte)	tröffe (×triefte)	trief(e) (*träuf)	trief(e)t	getrieft (*getroffen)
tr·inken	trinkst	trinkt	trank	tränke	trink(e)	trink(e)t	getrunken
tr·ügen	trügst	trügt	trog	tröge	trüg(e)	trüg(e)t	getrogen
t·un ich tue wir tun	du tust ihr tut	er tut sie tun	tat (er, es *tät); wir & sie taten (*täten)	täte	tu(e)	tu(e)t	getan
verd·erben	verdirbst	verdirbt	verdarb	verdürbe	verdirb	verderbt	verdorben
verdr·ießen	verdrie-ßest & verdrießt	ver-drießt	verdroß	verdrösse	ver-drieß(e)	ver-drieß(e)t	verdrossen
verg·essen	vergißt & vergissest	vergißt	vergaß	vergäße	vergiß	vergeßt	vergessen
verh·ehlen	verhehlst	verhehlt	verhehlte	verhehlte	verhehle	verhehlt	verhehlt & verhohlen
verl·ieren	verlierst	verliert	verlor	verlöre	verlier(e)	verliert	verloren
verl·öschen [vi]		(das Feuer) verlischt	verlosch	verlösche	verlisch	ver-löscht	verloschen
versch·allen	verschallst	ver-schallt	verscholl	verschölle	verschalle	ver-schall(e)t	verschollen
verw·irren	verwirrst	verwirrt	verwirrte	verwirrte	verwirr(e)	ver-wirr(e)t	verwirrt & verworren
w·achsen (*to grow*)	wächst	wächst	wuchs	wüchse	wachs, wachse	wachst	gewachsen
w·ägen	wägst	wägt	wog & wägte	wöge & wägte	wäg(e)	wäg(e)t	gewogen & gewägt
w·aschen	wäsch(e)st	wäscht	wusch	wüsche	(wasch(e)	wascht	gewaschen
w·eben	webst	webt	webte, ⟨bes poet⟩ wob	webte, ⟨bes poet⟩ wöbe	web(e)	web(e)t	gewebt, ⟨bes poet⟩ gewoben
w·eichen	weichst	weicht	wich	wiche	weich(e)	weich(e)t	gewichen
w·eisen	weisest & weist	weist	wies	wiese	weis, weise	weis(e)t	gewiesen
w·enden	wendest	wendet	wandte & wendete	wendete	wend(e)	wendet	gewandt & gewendet
w·erben	wirbst	wirbt	warb	würbe	wirb	werbt	geworben
w·erden	wirst	wird	wurde (*ward)	würde	werde	werdet	geworden; er ist versetzt worden
w·erfen	wirfst	wirft	warf	würfe	wirf	werf(e)t	geworfen
w·iegen [vi] (2. vt *to rock*: *weak*)	wiegst (wiegst)	wiegt (wiegt)	wog (wiegte)	wöge (wiegte)	wieg(e) (wiege)	(wiegt)	gewogen gewiegt
w·inden [vt]	windest	windet	wand	wände	wind(e)	windet	gewunden
w·issen; ich weiß; wir wissen	du weißt ihr wißt	er weiß	wußte	wüßte	wisse	wißt & wisset	gewußt
w·ollen; ich will; wir wollen	du willst ihr wollt	er will	wollte	wollte	wolle	wollt	gewollt; ich habe es tun wollen
z·eihen	zeihst	zeiht	zieh	ziehe	zeih(e)	zeih(e)t	geziehen
z·iehen	ziehst (*zeuchst)	zieht (*zeucht)	zog	zöge	zieh(e) (*zeuch)	zieh(e)t	gezogen
zw·ingen	zwingst	zwingt	zwang	zwänge	zwing(e)	zwing(e)t	gezwungen

XIII. ENGLISCHE GRAMMATIK
ENGLISH GRAMMAR

Konjugation

der starken und der unregelmäßigen schwachen

englischen Zeitwörter

Inf & 1. sg prs	Imperfect	Past Participle
abide	abode	abode
—; I am	was	been; → be
arise	arose	arisen
awake	awoke	awoke, awaked
be → am	was	been
bear	bore	borne *getragen* born *geboren*
beat	beat	beaten
become	became	become
beget	begot	begotten
begin	began	begun
bend	bent	bent; [a] (on) bended (knees)
bereave	bereft, bereaved	bereft, bereaved
beseech	besought, *beseeched	besought, *beseeched
bestride	bestrode	bestridden
bet	bet	bet
bid	bade, †bid	bidden, *bid
bide	bode, bided	bided
bind	bound	bound; [a] bounden (duty)
bite	bit	bitten
bleed	bled	bled
blow	blew	blown; ⟨sl⟩ blowed
break	broke	broken
breed	bred	bred
bring	brought	brought
build	built	built
burn	burned, burnt	burned, burnt
burst	burst	burst
buy	bought	bought
—; I can	could	—
cast	cast	cast
catch	caught	caught
chide	chid	chidden, *chid
choose	chose	chosen
cleave *spalten*	cleft	cleft; [a] cloven (hoof)
cleave *kleben*	cleaved, *clave	cleaved
cling	clung	clung
clothe	clothed, †clad	clothed, †clad
come	came	come
cost	cost	cost
creep	crept	crept
crow	crowed, crew	crowed
cut	cut	cut
dare	dared, *durst	dared
deal	dealt	dealt
dig	dug, *digged	dug, *digged
do	did	done
draw	drew	drawn
dream	dreamt, dreamed	dreamt, dreamed
drink	drank	drunk; [a] drunken (man)
drive	drove	driven
dwell	dwelt	dwelt
eat	ate, eat	eaten
fall	fell	fallen
feed	fed	fed
feel	felt	felt

Inf & 1. sg prs	Imperfect	Past Participle
fight	fought	fought
find	found	found
flee	fled	fled
fling	flung	flung
fly	flew	flown
forbear	forbore	forborne
forbid	forbade, forbad	forbidden
forget	forgot	forgotten
forgive	forgave	forgiven
forsake	forsook	forsaken
freeze	froze	frozen
get	got	got; [a] (ill-)gotten (money)
give	gave	given
go	went	gone
grind	ground	ground
grow	grew	grown
hang *hängen, hangen*	hung	hung
(hang *henken*	hanged	hanged)
have	had	had
hear	heard	heard
hide	hid	hidden, *hid
hit	hit	hit
hold	held	held
hurt	hurt	hurt
keep	kept	kept
kneel	knelt, *kneeled	knelt, *kneeled
knit	knitted, knit	knitted, knit; [a] (well-)knit (plot)
know	knew	known
lade	laded	laded, laden
lay	laid	laid
lead	led	led
lean	leant, leaned	leant, leaned
leap	leapt, leaped	leapt, leaped
learn	learnt, learned	learnt, learned
leave	left	left
lend	lent	lent
let	let	let
lie *liegen*	lay	lain
light	lighted, lit	lighted, lit
lose	lost	lost
make	made	made
—; I may	might	—
mean	meant	meant
meet	met	met
melt	melted	melted; [a] molte (iron)
mow	mowed	mowed, n
—; I must	—	—
pay	paid	paid
pen *einschließen*	penned, pent	penned, p
(pen *schreiben*	penned	penned)
put	put	put
quit	quitted, quit	quitted, q
—	quoth ⟨obs⟩	—
read	read	read
rend	rent	rent
rid	rid	rid
ride	rode	ridden
ring	rang, †rung	rung

Inf & 1. sg prs	Imperfect	Past Participle
rise	rose	risen
rive	rived	riven, rived
run	ran	run
saw	sawed	sawn, *sawed
say	said	said
see	saw	seen
seek	sought	sought
sell	sold	sold
send	sent	sent
set	set	set
sew (→ sow)	sewed	sewed, sewn
shake	shook	shaken
[v/aux] I shall	should	—
shape	shaped	shaped, *shapen
shear	sheared, *shore	sheared; [a] shorn (sheep)
shed	shed	shed
shew (→ show)	shewed	shewn
shine	shone	shone
shoe	shod	shod
shoot	shot	shot
show (→ shew)	showed	shown, showed
shred	shred	shred
shrink	shrank, shrunk	shrunk, [a] shrunken
shut	shut	shut
sing	sang, *sung	sung
sink	sank, *sunk	sunk, [a] sunken (cheeks)
sit	sat	sat
slay	slew	slain
sleep	slept	slept
slide	slid	slid
sling	slung	slung
slink	slunk	slunk
slit	slit	slit
smell	smelt, smelled	smelt, smelled
smite	smote	smitten
sow (→ sew)	sowed	sown, sowed
speak	spoke	spoken
speed	sped, speeded	sped, speeded
spell	spelt, spelled	spelt, spelled
spend	spent	spent
spill	spilt, spilled	spilt, spilled
spin	spun	spun
spit (*spucken*)	spat, *spit	spit
split	split	split
spoil	∼ed & spoilt	∼ed & spoilt
spread	spread	spread
spring	sprang, *sprung	sprung
stand	stood	stood
stave	staved, stove	staved, stove
steal	stole	stolen
stick	stuck	stuck
sting	stung, *stang	stung
stink	stank, stunk	stunk
strew	strewed	strewed, [a] strewn
stride	strode	stridden
strike	struck	struck; [a] stricken (in years)
string	strung	strung
strive	strove	striven
strow	strowed	strown, strowed
swear	swore	sworn
sweep	swept	swept
swell	swelled	swollen, swelled
swim	swam	swum
swing	swung	swung
take	took	taken
teach	taught	taught
tear	tore	torn
tell	told	told
think	thought	thought
thrive	throve, thrived	thriven, thrived
throw	threw	thrown
thrust	thrust	thrust
tread	trod	trodden
wake	woke, waked	woke, waked
wear	wore	worn
weave	wove	woven; [a] (well-)wove (paper)
weep	wept	wept
wet	wetted, wet	wetted, wet
—; I will	would	—
win	won	won
wind	wound	wound
work	worked, wrought	worked, wrought
wring	wrung	wrung
write	wrote	written

Vom Englischen abweichende amerikanische Schreibweise

1.⟨Engl⟩	theatre	⟨Am⟩	theater
	metre		meter
(**aber**:	barometer, etc		barometer, etc.)
2.⟨Engl⟩	arbour	⟨Am⟩	arbor
	colour		color
	favour		favor
	flavour		flavor
	harbour		harbor
	odour, etc.		odor, etc.
3.⟨Engl⟩	defence	⟨Am⟩	defense
	licence, -se (*Erlaubnis*)		license
	vice (*Schraubstock*)		vise
(**aber**:	device		device)
	sceptic		skeptic
4.⟨Engl⟩	connexion, -ection	⟨Am⟩	connection
	flexion, -ection		flection, etc.
5.⟨Engl⟩	tyre, -i- (*Radreifen*)	⟨Am⟩	tire
	calliper		caliper
	plough		plow
	dram, etc.		drachm, etc.
6.⟨Engl⟩	encyclopaedia, -edia	⟨Am⟩	encyclopedia
	haemorrhage, hem-		hemorrhage
	oesophagus		esophagus
	asafoetida		asafetida

(**aber**: ⟨Engl & Am⟩ aeon, aegis, aesthete, aerial, etc. Aeschylus, Oedipus, etc.)

7.⟨Engl⟩	em-, en- (*Vorsilben*)	⟨mst⟩	im-, in-
8.⟨Engl⟩	re-edit	⟨Am⟩	reëdit
	re-echo		reëcho
	re-edify		reëdify

9a) **Im Englischen wie im Amerikanischen** *wird in Ableitungen von* **einsilbigen** *Wörtern der* **Endkonsonant verdoppelt**, *wenn er auf einen einzigen Vokal folgt*:
⟨Engl & Am⟩
bag: baggage
beg: begging, beggar
swim: swimming, swimmer
(*u-Konsonant*):
squat: squatting, squatter
Dagegen: ⟨Engl⟩ wool: woollen
⟨Am⟩ woolen

b) *in Ableitungen von* **mehrsilbigen** *Wörtern nur, wenn die ursprüngliche Endsilbe den Akzent behält*: ⟨Engl & Am⟩
occur: occ·urred, occ·urring, occ·urrence
begin: beg·inner, beg·inning
beget: beg·etter, beg·etting
refer: ref·erring, **aber**: r·eference
defer: def·erring, **aber**: d·eference

c) **Ausnahmen** *bilden die Endkonsonanten* h & x, *die nicht verdoppelt werden*

10. *Im* **Englischen, nicht aber im Amerikanischen,** *wird das auf einen einzigen Vokal folgende* **-l immer verdoppelt**, *auch wenn die Endsilbe des Grundworts nicht betont ist*:

⟨Engl⟩	⟨Am⟩
tr·avel: ~led, ~ler, ~ling;	~ed, ~er, ~ing
r·ival: ~led, ~ling;	~ed, ~ing

Ausnahmen: ⟨Engl & Am⟩
parallel: ~ed, ~ism
Substantive & Adjektive auf -l *verdoppeln dieses nicht bei Bildungen auf –ism, –ist & –ish*:
social: ~ism, ~ist
devil: ~ish

11. *Während im* **Englischen End-ll** *bei Hinzutreten eines dritten Konsonanten* **vereinfacht** *wird, bleibt es im* **Amerikanischen** *meist* **erhalten**:
skill: ⟨Engl⟩ skilful ⟨Am a.⟩ skillful
install: instalment installment

12. *Die Auslassung des stummen* **-e-** *in Mittelsilben*: -edg(e)-, -idg(e)-: judgment *ist im Englischen im Vordringen, im* **Amerikanischen die Regel.**

13. *Die amerikanische Silbentrennung ist in England trotz gegenteiliger Bestrebungen im Vordringen, weshalb sie auch in diesem Wörterbuch angewandt worden ist.*

Amerikanische Aussprache[1]

I. Gliederung in drei Gruppen

Hinsichtlich der Aussprache gliedern sich die Vereinigten Staaten in drei Hauptgebiete: den äußersten **NO**, *den* **SO** *und den* **W**.

1. *Im* **NO** *kommt die Sprache dem Standard-Englisch am nächsten, steht der eigentlichen amerikanischen Aussprache also am fernsten.*

2. *Der* **SO** *weist neben Besonderheiten in Sprachrhythmus und Intonation einige Eigentümlichkeiten auf, z. B.:*

   ⟨engl⟩ [au] > [æu], *z. B. in* cow [kæu]
   Vokale > *Diphthongen*
   inlautendes [i] > [ə] *z. B. in* elevator [ˈeləveitə]

   Das Hinüberziehen des End-r zu vokalischem Anlaut des nächsten Wortes wird vernachlässigt:
   far and away [fɑː ənd əˈwei]

3. *Der* **W** *zeigt die vom Englischen am weitesten abweichenden Eigentümlichkeiten; er stellt mit fast zwei Dritteln der Gesamtbevölkerung die weitaus größte der drei Sprachgruppen dar. Das hier gesprochene Amerikanisch im engeren Sinne ist im Begriff, die beiden anderen Typen mehr und mehr zu verdrängen.*

II. Gemeinsame Eigentümlichkeiten *der drei Sprachgruppen sind:*

1. [æ](⟨engl⟩ [a:]) *ist aus dem älteren Englisch erhalten:*
   half [hæ:f]; last [læ:st]
   [ɔ] *wird fast zu* [a], *z. B. in:*
   not [nat]; lot [lat]
   [ʌ] *vor r* > ə, *z. B. in:*
   hurry [ˈhəri]; courage [ˈkəridʒ]
   wh *wird in betontem Anlaut (wie in N.-England) aspiriert:*
   which [hwitʃ]; white [hwait].
2. **Monophthongierung** *der englischen Diphthonge tritt besonders vor stimmlosen Konsonanten ein:*
   soap (⟨engl⟩ [soup]) ⟨Am⟩ [so:p]
   coat [ko:t]
   smoke [smo:k]
   cape (⟨engl⟩ [keip]) ⟨Am⟩ [ke:p]
   date [de:t]
   cake [ke:k]
3. **End-r** *wird im Amerikanischen ausgesprochen:*
   four (⟨engl⟩ [fɔ:]) ⟨Am⟩ [fɔ:r]
   door [do:r]
4. **Schwund des j-Vorschlages** *besonders vor Dentalen:*
   student (⟨engl⟩ [ˈstju:-]) ⟨Am⟩ [ˈstu:dənt]
   due [du:]
   new [nu:]
5. **Saloppe Aussprache**, *z. B. in:*
   little (⟨engl⟩ [litl]) ⟨Am⟩ [lidl, lil]
   twenty (⟨engl⟩ [ˈtwenti]) [ˈtweni]
   agile (⟨engl⟩ [ˈædʒail]) [ˈædʒəl]

[1]→ Lebende Sprachen 1958, 2–3 S. 49.

NOTIZEN

NOTIZEN